Table of Contents

Preface

The Thirty-Seventh Edition of *Who's Who in America* marks an important step forward in the history of the "Big Red Book." In its seventy-four years of publication, this standard reference resource for contemporary biographical information has become an institution known and relied upon by students, scholars, writers, and researchers throughout America and indeed, throughout the world.

This degree of acceptance has been taken by the Publisher, Marquis Who's Who, as a trust that imposes the obligation to strive, continuously, for improvement and enhancement of the usefulness and comprehensiveness of this work. Throughout its history, *Who's Who in America* has grown in size, paralleling the growth in extent and complexity of the society it serves. The Thirty-Seventh Edition comprises the largest total of biographical entries ever published in *Who's Who in America*—approximately 80,000. Included are increased numbers of representatives of professions heretofore covered only minimally, especially among the popular arts. As a concomitant result of this effort, greater numbers of young people appear in these pages than have ever appeared before. In addition, there appear more women and more minority-group Americans of all description.

The increased number of sketches published has necessitated expanding the book to a two-volume set. Each volume has been completely redesigned, employing a new format and new type style selected for improved readability.

Despite these appearances of change, however, in one respect, the book remains much the same as it was when first published by Albert Nelson Marquis in 1899. It was then that Mr. Marquis stated the selection principle that guided his effort in producing the First Edition and that has remained the guiding principle through the subsequent years of publishing *Who's Who in America.* Mr. Marquis said ". . . (we) shall endeavor to list those individuals who are of current reference inquiry because of meritorious achievement."

In the Thirty-Seventh Edition, as in the First Edition, names selection has been based on one characteristic: reference value. Thus, individuals become eligible for listing by virtue of positions achieved through election or appointment to office and by distinguished achievement in meritorious careers. Once these individuals have been identified, data about them are collected in two ways: the vast majority of the biographees furnish information by means of biographical data forms; should a prominent citizen fail to furnish his own data, however, Marquis staff members may choose to compile the information through independent research.

The persons sketched in this book include leading executives and officials in government, business, education, religion, the press, civic affairs, fine arts, law, and other fields. This edition also includes leading names in professional and collegiate athletics, top figures in contemporary art and musical styles, and persons responsible for the latest developments in science. All in all, it attempts to present a balanced picture of achievement in American society. In order to accomplish this, the Editors of *Who's Who in America* must be alert to developments in all fields of endeavor: Who is doing what? Who is winning honors and recognition? Who is propounding new theories? Who is excelling? As a result of this keen sense of awareness of what is going on, we are confident that the Thirty-Seventh Edition represents a faithful, composite biographical portrait of our time.

We feel it is important to state explicitly, that in the editorial evaluation that resulted in the selection of the names in this directory, an individual's desire to be listed was not sufficient reason for inclusion. Rather, it was the individual's demonstrated merit alone that determined inclusion. Similarly, wealth or social position was not a criterion. Indeed, many of the biographees are engaged in fields marked far more by service than by monetary reward.

Marquis Who's Who, Inc., will continue to strive to present the essential details of the lives of achievers and doers of the past as well as the present. The 1972-73 Edition marks only the latest of our efforts toward that end. Respect for our great heritage and an ever-alert awareness of the needs of today's reference users will continue to guide us in all our endeavors.

Who's Who in America®

37th edition
1972-1973
Volume 1

MARQUIS
Who's Who
Marquis Who's Who, Inc.
200 East Ohio Street
Chicago, Illinois 60611 U.S.A.

Library of Congress Catalog Card No. 4-16934
ISBN 0-8379-0137-5

Board of Advisors

The following distinguished individuals have made themselves available for review and comment during the course of compilation and publication of this Thirty-Seventh Edition of *Who's Who in America.* In no way, however, are they responsible for the selection of names published in this edition, nor do they bear any responsibility for the accuracy or comprehensiveness of the biographical data or any other material contained herein.

Mrs. Helen P. Bain
PRESIDENT, NATIONAL EDUCATION ASSOCIATION

Mr. Bill Baldwin
NATIONAL PRESIDENT, AMERICAN FEDERATION OF TELEVISION AND RADIO ARTISTS

Mr. Richard H. Blacklidge
PUBLISHER, THE KOKOMO (INDIANA) TRIBUNE

Mr. Arna Bontemps
CURATOR, JAMES WELDON JOHNSON COLLECTION, YALE UNIVERSITY LIBRARY

Edward W. Brooke
UNITED STATES SENATOR, MASSACHUSETTS

Dr. Roscoe C. Brown, Jr.
DIRECTOR, INSTITUTE OF AFRO-AMERICAN AFFAIRS, NEW YORK UNIVERSITY

John H. Buchanan, Jr.
UNITED STATES REPRESENTATIVE, ALABAMA

Mr. William Budington
EXECUTIVE DIRECTOR AND LIBRARIAN, THE JOHN CRERAR LIBRARY

Mr. Edwin Castagna
DIRECTOR, ENOCH PRATT FREE LIBRARY, BALTIMORE, MARYLAND

Dr. James E. Cheek
PRESIDENT, HOWARD UNIVERSITY

Dr. Kenneth B. Clarke
PRESIDENT (1971), AMERICAN PSYCHOLOGICAL ASSOCIATION

Dr. David H. Clift
EXECUTIVE DIRECTOR, AMERICAN LIBRARY ASSOCIATION

Mr. R. B. Colwell
PRESIDENT, UNITED STATES LAWN TENNIS ASSOCIATION

Mr. Richard W. Couper
PRESIDENT, THE NEW YORK PUBLIC LIBRARY

Reverend W. A. Criswell
PRESIDENT (1968-70), SOUTHERN BAPTIST CONVENTION

Miss Jean Dalrymple
EXECUTIVE DIRECTOR, AMERICAN NATIONAL THEATRE AND ACADEMY

Dr. Robert L. D. Davidson
PRESIDENT, WESTMINSTER COLLEGE, FULTON, MISSOURI

Mr. Hal C. Davis
PRESIDENT, AMERICAN FEDERATION OF MUSICIANS OF THE UNITED STATES AND CANADA

Mr. Robert O. Dougan
LIBRARIAN, HENRY E. HUNTINGTON LIBRARY AND ART GALLERY

The Honorable Daniel J. Evans
GOVERNOR OF WASHINGTON

Dr. Merle Fainsod
DIRECTOR, HARVARD UNIVERSITY LIBRARIES

Dr. William C. Friday
PRESIDENT, UNIVERSITY OF NORTH CAROLINA

The Honorable John J. Gilligan
GOVERNOR OF OHIO

Rabbi Roland B. Gittlesohn
PRESIDENT (1969-71), CENTRAL CONFERENCE OF AMERICAN RABBIS

Mr. W. P. Gullander
PRESIDENT, NATIONAL ASSOCIATION OF MANUFACTURERS

Dr. Philip Handler
PRESIDENT, NATIONAL ACADEMY OF SCIENCES

Mr. James L. Hayes
PRESIDENT, AMERICAN MANAGEMENT ASSOCIATION

Mr. John Hightower
DIRECTOR (1970-71), THE MUSEUM OF MODERN ART

The Honorable Linwood Holton
GOVERNOR OF VIRGINIA

Mr. Roy Innis
NATIONAL DIRECTOR, CONGRESS OF RACIAL EQUALITY

Mr. William J. Kuhfuss
PRESIDENT, AMERICAN FARM BUREAU FEDERATION

Dr. Alex Ladenson
CHIEF LIBRARIAN, THE CHICAGO PUBLIC LIBRARY

Dr. Robert E. Lane
PRESIDENT (1970-71), AMERICAN POLITICAL SCIENCE ASSOCIATION

Mr. Jacob Lawrence
ARTIST

Dr. C. Eric Lincoln
EDUCATOR

Reverend Robert J. Marshall
PRESIDENT, LUTHERAN CHURCH IN AMERICA

Dr. Benjamin E. Mays
EDUCATOR

Mr. Arthur McZier
ASSISTANT ADMINISTRATOR FOR MINORITY ENTERPRISE, SMALL BUSINESS ADMINISTRATION

Dr. Malcolm C. Moos
PRESIDENT, UNIVERSITY OF MINNESOTA

Dr. Samuel M. Nabrit
EXECUTIVE DIRECTOR, THE SOUTHERN FELLOWSHIP FUND

Board of Advisors continued

Mr. Alfred C. Neal
PRESIDENT, COMMITTEE FOR ECONOMIC DEVELOPMENT

Mr. Newbold Noyes
EDITOR, THE WASHINGTON STAR

The Honorable Richard B. Ogilvie
GOVERNOR OF ILLINOIS

Mr. Frederick O'Neal
PRESIDENT, ACTORS EQUITY ASSOCIATION

Dr. Monrad G. Paulsen
DEAN, SCHOOL OF LAW, UNIVERSITY OF VIRGINIA

The Honorable William Proxmire
UNITED STATES SENATOR, WISCONSIN

Dr. Mina Rees
PRESIDENT, GRADUATE DIVISION OF THE CITY UNIVERSITY OF NEW YORK

Dr. William Sewell
PRESIDENT (1971), AMERICAN SOCIOLOGICAL ASSOCIATION

Margaret Chase Smith
UNITED STATES SENATOR, MAINE

Dr. Michael I. Sovern
DEAN, SCHOOL OF LAW, COLUMBIA UNIVERSITY

Dr. Joseph R. Strayer
PRESIDENT (1971), AMERICAN HISTORICAL ASSOCIATION

Mr. J. Donald Thomas
EXECUTIVE SECRETARY, ASSOCIATION OF COLLEGE AND RESEARCH LIBRARIES

Mr. Lawrence W. Towner
DIRECTOR AND LIBRARIAN, THE NEWBERRY LIBRARY

Mr. Abraham S. Venable
DIRECTOR (1970-71), OFFICE OF MINORITY BUSINESS ENTERPRISE, UNITED STATES DEPARTMENT OF COMMERCE

Dr. Frederick H. Wagman
DIRECTOR, UNIVERSITY LIBRARY, THE UNIVERSITY OF MICHIGAN

Mr. Vincent T. Wasilewski
PRESIDENT, NATIONAL ASSOCIATION OF BROADCASTERS

Mr. Jerome Weidman
PRESIDENT (1969), AUTHORS LEAGUE AMERICA

Mr. Charles H. Wesley
EXECUTIVE DIRECTOR, THE ASSOCIATION FOR THE STUDY OF NEGRO LIFE AND HISTORY, INC.

Citations for Significant Contribution to Society

To be admitted to the pages of *Who's Who in America* is an honor accorded to only a select group of persons. Nevertheless, for many years the Editors have realized that within our society there are those individuals who merit exceptional recognition for outstanding achievement. Therefore, Marquis Who's Who initiated such recognition in the 33rd Edition with the award of Citations for Significant Contribution to Society. Now, for the fifth time, the Editors are privileged to continue this practice. In selecting the persons so honored, the Editors went beyond the recipients' degree of renown and attempted to weigh their unique achievements—not only over the latest two-year period, but over their entire careers.

Rudolf Bing
The British impresario was born in Vienna in 1903, and by the time he was twenty-years-old had become the director of his own concert and opera agency. Bing's dynamic approach to classical music and opera made him world famous before he assumed the directorship of the Darmstadt Theatre and Charlottenburg Municipal Opera in Berlin (1927-33). The masterful and tasteful Bing, who has always insisted upon "purity" of performance, served as the general manager of the Glyndbourne Opera Company in England until 1950 when he assumed the directorship of the Metropolitan Opera House in New York. In that capacity, Bing has consistently maintained the highest quality of artistic performance, achieving respect and admiration from maestros, from performers, and from an appreciative public at large.

Hugo Lafayette Black
Associate Justice Hugo L. Black was, for decades until his death in 1971, the recognized leader of the liberal and activist wing of the Supreme Court. Black's long and distinguished career as a senator and court justice was highlighted by his successful battling for union rights, the establishment of the Tennessee Valley Authority, and the passing of the 40-hour week and fair labor standards acts. Described as a "Jeffersonian and old-fashioned agrarian radical," Black stood as a champion and unswerving defender of the Bill of Rights. There were no qualifications in his statement: "I am for the First Amendment from the first word to the last. I believe it means what it says: Government shall not abridge freedom of the press or speech; it shall let anybody talk in this country."

Kingman Brewster, Jr.
Former Harvard law professor, Kingman Brewster, Jr. became the seventeenth president of Yale University on October 12, 1963 and immediately began to fight for the rights of students, not only on his campus but throughout the United States. Brewster believes in "a faculty that teaches students" rather than one devoted to research. Ignoring the controversy arising from his viewpoints, this much respected teacher-debater-author has consistently maintained a progressive approach to educational administration while defending the right of students to express their political views and while attacking racial discrimination in American education.

Ralph Johnson Bunche
Born in Detroit in 1904, Ralph Bunche, the grandson of a slave, became one of America's and the world's great administrators and leaders. After studies at Harvard, Capetown, and the London School of Economics, Bunche became assistant professor of political science at Howard University in Washington in 1928. A government advisor on African policy and an expert on trust territories during World War II, Bunche later drafted important sections of the United Nations charter. He was named as director of the U.N. Trusteeship department in 1947; three years later, his compassionate mediations in Palestine resulted in a cease-fire and earned for him the Nobel Peace Prize. At his death in 1971, he was a respected citizen of the world.

Pablo Casals
Born in a small village near Barcelona in 1879, Pablo Casals, as a boy prodigy of thirteen, transformed the techniques of the neglected cello from the stiff and the cumbersome to the free-flowing and experimental, employing revolutionary methods that were to astound the musical world. Alone, he discovered and presented Bach's all-but-forgotten "Six Suites for Violincello Solo," achieving for this masterpiece its proper recognition. A disciplined and inventive musical genius, Casals, through his performances, has elevated the cello to the esteemed rank of the violin. Master Violinist Isaac Stern said of Casal's playing: "Honesty to the limit, has been his lifelong motto, both as man and musician." Pablo Casals has brought classical music to new dimensions of musicianship while fighting for universal justice and peace. His talent and his burning social conscience are twin virtues compounded in one monumental legend.

Aaron Copland
A native of Brooklyn, New York, Aaron Copland, perhaps more than any other American composer, was responsible for the development of what is termed the New Music. After studying with Nadia Boulanger in Paris, Copland returned to the United States in 1924 to create true and lasting musical Americana with such celebrated works as *Billy the Kid, Rodeo,* and *Appalachian Spring.* Copland's bittersweet scores were natural outgrowths of the work of Mussorgsky, Debussy, Schönberg, Stravinsky, Bartók, and Hindemith. And he, in turn, always in the vanguard of musical composition, represents a vast and overwhelming influence on the broad and brilliant panorama of twentieth century music.

John W. Gardner
A psychologist of national renown, John W. Gardner immediately began to improve educational grants-in-aid to worthy students after being appointed the ninth president of the Carnegie Corporation, in 1955. Gardner has always stressed quality in education and insisted that the problems of colleges in America can be dealt with "if we care enough about accomplishing it. And we had better care." One of the most respected educationists in the country, Gardner adroitly points out that, "Higher education is not only shaped by the society in which it exists, but in turn it shapes society."

Richard Charles Gerstenberg
Richard Charles Gerstenberg, chairman of the board of General Motors, became a prime mover in the rehabilitation of strife-torn Detroit, Michigan. As a member of the board of trustees and vice chairman of New Detroit, Inc., and a member of the board of Detroit Renaissance, Gerstenberg worked tirelessly to rebuild the city of Detroit after devastating riots in the late 1960s. His vast civic responsibilities also extend to his energetic and fruitful drives to obtain funds from corporations for worthy Negro students seeking scholarships. In his capacity as a director of the United Negro College Fund, Inc., and as chairman of the fund's national corporation committee, Richard Charles Gerstenberg has elevated the role of the American businessman to a new and striking level of social consciousness.

Citations continued

Theodore M. Hesburgh
President of one of the largest and oldest (1843) Catholic Universities in the United States, Father Theodore Hesburgh has guided the destinies of Notre Dame since 1952. Through his expert administrative offices, Father Hesburgh has brought about a complete revitalization of the university. One of his first acts as president was to introduce a new liberal arts curriculum to his school, the first major curriculum change at Notre Dame in thirty years. This much honored religious and educational leader has also served his country well by giving of his time, wisdom, and energies as a member of the Civil Rights Commission and numerous other boards, commissions, and study groups. Father Hesburgh, a quiet, introspective man, has said: "There is reason for new hope in the very fact that all of us, Protestants, Catholics, Jews, have recognized needed strength in working together as God-loving and God-fearing Americans, standing united against those who deny God."

Mrs. Coretta Scott King
The wife of the late civil rights leader, Dr. Martin Luther King, Jr., had for her beginnings adversity and hardship. As a child, Coretta King picked cotton to further her education, earned a scholarship to Antioch College, and upon graduation, refined her considerable talents as a singer and teacher. She married Martin Luther King, Jr. in 1953 and became the Nobel Prize Winner's most ardent and faithful supporter. During Dr. King's lifetime, Coretta walked beside him in marches, fullfilled speaking engagements he was unable to attend, and worked tirelessly for the cause of civil rights. Upon her husband's death, Mrs. King assumed many of his responsibilities and became, herself, one of the most important and influencial civil rights leaders in America.

Thurgood Marshall
Known for years as America's outstanding civil rights attorney, Thurgood Marshall was one of the most aggressive and successful leaders in that field, becoming the chief legal counsel for the NAACP in 1938. Marshall's mother was a teacher in a segregated school and his father a country club steward; Marshall worked as a grocery clerk, dining car waiter, and baker to fund his education. After receiving his degree, magna cum laude, from Howard University in 1933, Marshall began to attack segregation in the schools and won many precedent-setting cases. Marshall's achievements earned for him world recognition as a leader in the fight against bigotry and intolerance, and his efforts culminated in his appointment to the Supreme Court where he faithfully continues to champion the cause of justice for all people.

Ralph Nader
Lawyer, author, and consumer advocate, Ralph Nader can take credit for the enactment of the National Traffic and Motor Vehicle Safety Act of 1966 after his one-man crusade aimed at improving car design as a means toward achieving greater auto safety. In addition, Nader has worked relentlessly to eliminate health hazards in mining, to improve the safety standards of natural gas pipelines, to upgrade the living conditions of American Indians, and to expose the gruesome conditions existing in meat processing plants. The American public's indebtedness to this untiring crusader is immeasurable.

Walter Philip Reuther
The stormy career of Walter P. Reuther, which continued so until the day of his death in 1970, contributed mightily to the betterment of the laboring men and women. Born into a union-leadership family, Reuther went to work at fifteen in a steel plant as a tool and diemaker apprentice; he was fired shortly thereafter when he attempted to organize a union to fight Sunday and holiday work. In 1927, he went to Detroit where he worked in automotive plants, organizing employees and demanding improvements in working conditions and salaries. By 1935, Reuther became the recognized union leader of auto workers and through his efforts, improvements in wages, hours, and pensions were achieved. Through the years, Walter Reuther, a courageous, impartial and dedicated leader, became a great force seeking and obtaining justice for the working men and women of America.

Harry S. Truman
As 32nd President of the United States, Harry S. Truman led America out of war and into a troubled peace during a time when strength and compassion were vital to a crippled world struggling toward survival. Years ago, pundits proclaimed Truman to be one of our weakest Presidents, but his actions and the events of his day have proved him to be one of our finest. The "Truman Doctrine" of 1947 enabled Communist-threatened nations to remain free and led to Truman's European Recovery Program, which, more than any other single act, delivered a continent from starvation, poverty, and economic ruin. In the light of present struggles, we can now turn back to Truman's courageous stands on civil rights with the sure knowledge that here was one President who lived up to FDR's credo: "The Presidency is a moral office."

Standards of Admission

The foremost consideration in determining who will be admitted to the pages of *Who's Who in America* is the extent of an individual's reference interest. Such reference interest is judged on either of two factors: (1) the position of responsibility held or (2) the level of significant achievement attained in a career of meritorious activity. Admissions based on the factor of position include the following:

- All members of the U.S. Congress.
- All members of the President's Cabinet.
- All federal judges.
- All governors of states, island possessions, and territories.
- All state attorneys general.
- Judges of state and territorial courts of highest appelate jurisdiction.
- U.S. ambassadors and ministers plenipotentiary.
- Ambassadors and ministers accredited to the United States.
- Consuls general or consuls at important posts abroad.
- Heads of the major universities and colleges.
- Officers on active duty beginning with the rank of major general in the Army, Air Force, and Marine Corps; and with rear admiral in the Navy.
- Heads of leading philanthropic, educational, and scientific societies.
- Selected members of the national Academy of Sciences, the National Academy of Design, the American Academy of Arts and Letters, and the National Institute of Arts and Letters.
- Chief ecclesiastics of the principal religious denominations.
- Principal officers of national and international businesses capitalized at or above a certain figure, or of the highest commercial "rating."
- Chiefs and heads of state of all nations of the world.
- Others chosen because of incumbency, authorship, or membership.

Admissions based on individual achievement must be decided by a judicious process of evaluating qualitative factors. To be selected on this basis, a person must have accomplished some conspicuous achievement—something that distinguishes him from the vast majority of his contemporaries.

Key to Information in this Directory

❶ **WELLINGTON, Stanley Robinson,** ❷ advt. agy. exec.; ❸ b. Cleve., Feb. 22, 1921; ❹ s. Walter and Louise (Robinson) W., ❺ B.A., Ohio State U., 1943; ❻ m. Anita Howland, Aug. 3, 1943; ❼ children—Mary Ellen, Susan Louise. ❽ Account exec. Clarke, Latham & Pease, Cleve., 1947-53, account supr., 1953-55; sr. v.p. marketing services Bowman & Crowell, Cleve., 1955-57, pres., 1957—. ❾ Lectr. advt. Cleve. Coll. Liberal Arts, 1956-60. ❿ Active Boy Scouts Am. ⓫ Mem. Cleve. Dist. Park Bd., 1963-65. ⓬ Trustee Wrightwood Jr. Coll. ⓭ Served to maj. AUS, 1943-46; PTO. ⓮ Named Man of Year, Cleve. Assn. Indsl. Advertisers, 1965. ⓯ Mem. Am. Assn. Advt. Agys., Am. Marketing Assn. ⓰ Republican. ⓱ Methodist. ⓲ Mason. ⓳ Club: Shady Knoll Country (Cleve.). ⓴ Contbr. articles profl. publs. ㉑ Home: 220 Bluff Hills Rd., Cleveland, OH. 44123 ㉒ Office: 11 Main St., Cleveland, OH. 44102

Key

❶ Name
❷ Position
❸ Vital statistics
❹ Parents
❺ Education
❻ Marital status
❼ Children
❽ Career
❾ Career related activities
❿ Civic activities
⓫ Political activities
⓬ Non-professional directorships
⓭ Military record
⓮ Decorations and awards
⓯ Professional and other memberships
⓰ Political affiliation
⓱ Religion
⓲ Lodges
⓳ Clubs
⓴ Writings
㉑ Home address
㉒ Office address

The biographical listings in *Who's Who in America* are arranged in alphabetical order according to the first letter of the last name of of the biographee. Each sketch is presented in a uniform order as in the sample sketch above. The many abbreviations used in the sketches are explained in the Table of Abbreviations.

If the sketch you are looking for does not appear in the alphabetical listing of biographical entries, be sure to check the Latest Listings section in Volume 2.

Table of Abbreviations

The following abbreviations and symbols are frequently used in this Directory

*Following a sketch indicates it was office researched:

A.A., Associates in Arts.
A.A.A., Agricultural Adjustment Administration; Anti-Aircraft Artillery.
A.A.A.S., American Association for the Advancement of Science.
AAC, Army Air Corps.
A. and M., Agricultural and Mechanical.
AAF, Army Air Force.
A.A.H.P.E.R., American Association for Health, Physical Education, and Recreation.
A.A.O.N.M.S., Ancient Arabic Order of the Nobles of the Mystic Shrine.
A.A.S.R., Ancient Accepted Scottish Rite (Masonic).
AAUP, American Association of University Professors.
AAUW, American Association of University Women.
A.B., Bachelor of Arts.
ABC, American Broadcasting Company.
A.B.C.F.M., American Board of Commissioners for Foreign Missions (Congregational).
AC, Air Corps.
acad., academy; academic.
acctg., accounting.
ACDA, Arms Control and Disarmament Agency.
A.C.L. R.R., Atlantic Coast Line R.R.
ACLU, American Civil Liberties Union.
A.C.P., American College of Physicians.
A.C.S., American College of Surgeons.
a.d.c., aide-de-camp.
adj., adjutant; adjunct.
adm., admiral, administrative.
adminstr., administrator.
adminstrn., administration.
adminstrv., administrative.
adv., advocate; advisory.
advt., advertising.
A.E., Agricultural Engineer.
A.E. and P., Ambassador Extraordinary and Plenipotentiary.
AEC, Atomic Energy Commission.
AEF, American Expenditionary Forces.
aero., aeronautical, aeronautic.
AFB, Air Force Base.
A.F.D., Doctor of Fine Arts.
A.F. and A.M., Ancient Free and Accepted Masons.
AFL (or A.F. of L), American Federation of Labor.
agr., agriculture.
agrl., agricultural.
agt., agent.
agy., agency.
A.I.A., American Institute of Architects.
AID, Agency for International Development.
A.I.M., American Institute of Management.
AK, Alaska.
AL., Alabama.
A.L.A., American Library Association.
alt., alternate.
Alta., Alberta.
Am., American; America.
A.M., Master of Arts.
A.M.A., American Medical Association.
Am. Inst. E.E., American Institute of Electrical Engineers.
Am. Soc. C.E., American Society of Civil Engineers.
Am. Soc. M.E., American Society of Mechanical Engineers.
ann., annual.
ANTA, American National Theatre and Academy.
A.P., Associated Press.
apptd., appointed.
apt., apartment.
AR, Arkansas.
A.R.C., American Red Cross.
archeol., archeological.
archtl., architectural.
Arts. D., Doctor of Arts.
arty., artillery.
AS, Air Service.
ASF, Air Service Force.
assn., association.
asso., associate; associated.
asst., assistant.
astron., astronomical.
astrophys., astrophysical.
ATSC, Air Technical Service Command.
atty., attorney.
AUS, Army of the United States.
Aux., Auxiliary.
Av., Avenue.
AZ, Arizona.

b., born.
B., Bachelor.
B.A., Bachelor of Arts.
B.Agr., Bachelor of Agriculture.
Balt., Baltimore.
Bapt., Baptist.
B. Arch., Bachelor of Architecture.
B.A.S., Bachelor of Agricultural Science.
Batn., Battalion.
B.B.A., Bachelor of Business Administration.
BBC, British Broadcasting Corp.
B.C., British Columbia.
B.C.E., Bachelor of Civil Engineering.
B.Chir., Bachelor of Surgery.
B.C.L., Bachelor of Civil Law.
B.C.S., Bachelor of Commercial Science.
bd., board.
B.D., Bachelor of Divinity.
B.E., Bachelor of Education.
B.E.E., Bachelor of Electrical Engineering.
B.F.A., Bachelor of Fine Arts.
bibllog., bibliographical.
biog., biographical.
biol., biological.
B.J., Bachelor of Journalism.
Bklyn., Brooklyn.
B.L., Bachelor of Letters.
bldg., building.
B.L.S., Bachelor of Library Science.
Blvd., Boulevard.
Bn., Battalion.
bot., botanical.
B.P.E., Bachelor of Physical Education.
B.P.O.E., Benevolent and Protective Order of Elks.
br., branch.
B.R.E., Bachelor of Religious Education.
brig.gen., brigadier general.
Brit., British; Britannica.
Bro., Brother.
B.S., Bachelor of Science.
B.S.A., Bachelor of Agricultural Science.
B.S.D., Bachelor of Didactic Science.
B.S.T., Bachelor of Sacred Theology.
B.Th., Bachelor of Theology.
bull., bulletin.
bur., bureau.
bus., business.
B.W.I., British West Indies.

CA, California.
C.Am., Central America.
CAA, Civil Aeronautics Administrn.
CAB, Civil Aeronautics Board.
Can., Canada.
CAP, Civil Air Patrol
capt., captain.
CARE, Cooperative American Relief Everywhere.
Cath., Catholic.
cav., cavalry.
CBI, China, Burma, India Theatre of Operations.
CBS, Columbia Broadcasting System.
CCC, Commodity Credit Corporation.
CD, Civil Defense
C.E., Civil Engineer, Corps of Engineers.
CEF, Canadian Expeditionary Force.
CENTO, Central Treaty Organization.
CERN, European Organization of Nuclear Research.
ch., church.
Ch.D., Doctor of Chemistry.
chem., chemical.
Chem.E., Chemical Engineer.
Chgo., Chicago.
Chirurg., Chirurgical.
chmn., chairman.
chpt., chapter.
CIA, Central Intelligence Agency.
CIC, Counter Intelligence Corps.
Cin., Cincinnati.
CIO, Congress of Industrial Organizations.
Cleve., Cleveland.
climatol., Climatological.
clin., clinical.
clk., clerk.
C.L.U., Chartered Life Underwriter.
C.M., Master in Surgery.
cnsl., counsel.
CO, Colorado.
Co., Company, County.
C. of C., Chamber of Commerce.
C.O.F., Catholic Order of Foresters.
col., colonel.
coll., college.
com., committee.
comd., commanded.
comdg., commanding.
comdr., commander.
comdt., commandant.
commd., commissioned.
comml., commercial.
commn., commission.
commr., commissioner.
condr., conductor.
conf., conference.
Congl., Congregational; Congressional.
Conglist., Congregationalist.
cons., consulting, consultant.
consol., consolidated.
constl., constitutional.
constn., constitution.
constrn., construction.
cont., controller, comptroller.
contbd., contributed.
contbg., contributing.
contbn., contribution.
contbr., contributor.
conv., convention.
coop. (or **co-op**), cooperative.
CORE, Congress of Racial Equality.
corp., corporation, corporate.
corpl., corporal.
corr., correspondent; corresponding; correspondence.
C.P.A., Certified Public Accountant.
C.P.C.U., Chartered Property and Casualty Underwriter.
C.P.H., Certificate of Public Health.
cpl., corporal.
C.S.B., Bachelor of Christian Science.
CSC, Civil Service Commn.

C.S.D., Doctor of Christian Science.
ct., court.
CT, Connecticut.
CWS, Chemical Warfare Service.
C.Z., Canal Zone.

d., daughter.
D., Doctor.
D.Agr., Daughter of Agriculture.
D.A.R., Daughters of the American Revolution.
dau., daughter.
D.A.V., Disabled American Veterans.
DC., District of Columbia.
D.C.L., Doctor of Civil Law.
D.C.S., Doctor of Commercial Science.
D.D., Doctor of Divinity.
D.D.S., Doctor of Dental Surgery.
DE, Delaware.
dec., deceased.
Def., Defense.
del., delegate.
Dem., Democratic; Democrat.
D.Eng., Doctor of Engineering.
dep., deputy.
dept., department.
dermatol., dermatological.
desc., descendant.
devel., development.
D.F.C., Distinguished Flying Cross.
dir., director.
disch., discharged.
dist., district.
distbg., distributing.
distbn., distribution.
distbr., distributor.
div., division; divinity; divorce proceedings.
D.Litt., Doctor of Literature.
D.M.D., Doctor of Medical Dentistry.
D.M.S., Doctor of Medical Science.
D.O., Doctor of Osteopathy.
DPA, Defense Production Administration.
D.P.H., Diploma in Public Health.
Dr., Doctor, Drive.
D.R., Daughters of the Revolution.
D.R.E., Doctor of Religious Education.
Dr.P.H., Doctor of Public Health; Doctor of Public Hygiene.
D.Sc., Doctor of Science.
D.S.C., Distinguished Service Cross.
D.S.M., Distinguished Service Medal.
D.S.T., Doctor of Sacred Theology.
D.T.M., Doctor of Tropical Medicine.
D.V.M., Doctor of Veterinary Medicine.
D.V.S., Doctor of Veterinary Surgery.

E., East.
E. and P., Extraordinary and Plenipotentiary.
ECA, Economic Cooperation Administration.
ecol., ecological.
econ., economic.
ECOSOC, Economic and Social Council (of the UN).
ed., educated.
E.D., Doctor of Engineering.
Ed.B., Bachelor of Education.
Ed.D., Doctor of Education.
edit., edition.
Ed.M., Master of Education.
edn., education.
ednl., educational.
E.E., Electrical Engineer.
E.E. and M.P., Envoy Extraordinary and Minister Plenipotentiary.
elec., electrical.
electrochem., electrochemical.
electrophys., electrophysical.
E.M., Engineer of Mines.
ency., encyclopedia.
Eng., England.
engr., engineer.
engring., engineering.
entomol., entomological.
ESSA, Environmental Sci. Services Administrn.
ethnol., ethnological.
ETO, European Theater of Operations.
eval., evaluation.
exam., examination; examing.
exec., executive.
exhbn., exhibition.
expdn., expedition.
expn., exposition.
expt., experiment.
exptl., experimental.

F.A., Field Artillery.
FAA, Federal Aviation Agency.
FAO, Food and Agriculture Organization (of the UN).
FBI, Federal Bureau of Investigation.
FCA, Farm Credit Administration.
FCC, Federal Communications Commission.
FCDA, Federal Civil Defense Administration.
FDA, Food and Drug Administration.
FDIA, Federal Deposit Insurance Administration.
FDIC, Federal Deposit Ins. Corp.
fdr., founder.
F.E., Forest Engineer.
Fed., Federal.
Fedn., Federation.
Fgn., Foreign.
FHA, Federal Housing Administration.
fin., finance, financial.
FL, Florida.
FMC, Federal Maritime Commn.
FOA, Foreign Operations Administration.
Found., Foundation.
FPC, Federal Power Commn.
FRS, Federal Reserve System.
FSA, Federal Security Agency.
Ft., Fort.
FTC, Federal Trade Commission; Federal Tariff Commission.

G.-1 (or other number), Division of General Staff.
GA, Georgia.
GAO, General Accounting Office.
gastroent., gastroenterological.
GATT, General Agreement on Tariffs and Trade.
gen., general.
geneal., genealogical.
geod., geodetic.
geog., geographical; geographic.
geol., geological.
geophys., geophysical.
G.H.Q., General Headquarters.
gov., governor.
govt., government.
govtl., governmental.
GPO, Government Printing Office.
grad., graduated; graduate.
GSA, General Services Administration.
Gt., Great.
GU, Guam.
gynecol., gynecological.

HEW, Department Health, Education and Welfare.
Hdqrs., Headquarters.
H.H.D., Doctor of Humanities.
HHFA, Housing and Home Finance Agency.
HI, Hawaii.
H.M., Master of Humanics.
hist., historical.
HOLC, Home Owners Loan Corporation.
homeo., homeopathic.
hon., honorary; honorable.
Ho. of Dels., House of Delegates.
Ho. of Reps., House of Representatives.
hort., horticultural.
hosp., hospital.
HUD, Dept. Housing and Urban Development.
Hwy., Highway.
hydrog., hydrographic.

IA, Iowa.
IAEA, International Atomic Energy Agency.
IBM, International Business Machines Corp.
IBRD, International Bank for Reconstruction and Development.
ICA, International Cooperation Administration.
ICC, Interstate Commerce Commn.
ID, Idaho.
I.E.E.E., Institute of Electrical and Electronics Engineers.
IFC, International Finance Corp.
IGY, International Geophysical Year.
IL, Illinois.
ILO, International Labor Orgn.
IMF, International Monetary Fund.
IN, Indiana.
Inc., Incorporated.
ind., independent.
Indpls., Indianapolis.
indsl., industrial.
inf., infantry.
info., information.
ins., insurance.
insp., inspector.
inst., institute.
instl., institutional.
instn., institution.
instr., instructor.
instrn., instruction.
internat., international.
intro., introduction.
I.O.O.F., Independent Order of Odd Fellows.
I.R.E., Institute of Radio Engineers.
IRS, Internal Revenue Service

JAG, Judge Advocate General.
J.C.B., Juris Canonici Bachelor.
J.C.L., Juris Canonici Lector.
J.D., Doctor of Jurisprudence.
j.g., junior grade.
jour., journal.
jr., junior.
J.S.D., Doctor of Juristic Science.
jud., judicial.
J.U.D., Juris Utriusque Doctor: Doctor of Both (Canon and Civil) Laws.

K.C., Knight of Columbus.
K.P., Knight of Pythias.
KS, Kansas.
K.T., Knight Templar.
KY, Kentucky.

LA, Louisiana.
lab., laboratory.
lang., language.
laryngol., laryngological.
lectr., lecturer.
legis., legislation, legislative.
L.H.D., Doctor of Humane Letters.
L.I., Long Island.
lieut., lieutenant.
lit. literary; literature.
Litt.B., Bachelor of Letters.

TABLE OF ABBREVIATIONS

Litt.D., Doctor of Letters.
LL.B., Bachelor of Laws.
LL.D., Doctor of Laws.
LL.M., Master of Laws.
L.O.M., Loyal Order of Moose.
L.S., Library Science.
lt., lieutenant.
Ltd., Limited.
Luth., Lutheran.

m., marriage ceremony.
M., Master.
M.A., Master of Arts.
MA, Massachusetts.
mag., magazine.
M.Agr., Master of Agriculture.
maj., major.
Man., Manitoba.
M.Arch., Master in Architecture.
math., mathematical.
M.B., Bachelor of Medicine.
M.B.A., Master of Business Administration.
MBS, Mutual Broadcasting System.
M.C., Medical Corps.
M.C.E., Master of Civil Engineering.
mcpl., municipal.
M.C.S., Master of Commercial Science.
mcht., merchant.
M.D., Doctor of medicine.
MD, Maryland.
M.Dip., Master in Diplomacy.
mdse., merchandise.
M.D.V., Doctor of Veterinary Medicine.
M.E., Mechanical Engineer.
ME, Maine.
mech., mechanical.
M.E. Ch., Methodist Episcopal Church.
M.Ed., Master of Education.
med., medical.
Med. O.R.C., Medical Officers' Reserve Corps.
Med. R.C., Medical Reserve Corps.
M.E.E., Master of Electrical Engineering.
mem., member.
Meml., Memorial.
merc., mercantile.
met., metropolitan.
metall., metallurgical.
Met.E., Metallurgical Engineer.
meteorol., meteorological.
Meth., Methodist.
metrol., metrological.
M.F., Master of Forestry.
M.F.A., Master of Fine Arts
mfg., manufacturing.
mfr., manufacturer.
mgmt., management.
mgr., manager.
M.H.A., Master of Hospital Administration.
M.I., Military Intelligence.
MI, Michigan.
micros., microscopical.
mil., military.
Milw., Milwaukee.
mineral., mineralogical.
mktg., marketing.
M.L., Master of Laws.
M.L.D., Magister Legnum Diplomatic.
M.Litt., Master of Literature.
Mlle., Mademoiselle.
M.L.S., Master of Library Science.
Mme., Madame.
M.M.E., Master of Mechanical Engineering.
M.M.S., Member Marquis Society.
MN, Minnesota.
mng., managing.
MO, Missouri.
Moblzn., Mobilization.
M.P., Member of Parliament.
M.P.E., Master of Physical Education.
M.P.H., Master of Public Health.
M.P.L., Master of Patent Law.
Mpls., Minneapolis.
M.S., Master of Science.
MS, Mississippi.
M.Sc., Master of Science.
M.S.F., Master of Science of Forestry.
M.S.W., Master of Social Work.
MT, Montana.
Mt., Mount.
MTO, Mediterranean Theater of Operations.
mus., museum; musical.
Mus.B., Bachelor of Music.
Mus.D., Doctor of Music.
Mus.M., Master of Music.
Mut., Mutual.
M.W.A., Modern Woodmen of America.
mycol., mycological.

N., North.
N.A.A.C.P., National Association for the Advancement of Colored People.
NACA, National Advisory Committee for Aeronautics.
N.A.D., National Academy of Design.
N.Am., North America.
N.A.M., National Association of Manufacturers.
NARS, National Archives and Record Service.
NASA, National Aeronautics and Space Administration.
nat., national.
NATO, North Atlantic Treaty Organization.
NATOUSA, North African Theater of Operations. U.S. Army.
nav., navigation.
N.B., New Brunswick.
NBC, National Broadcasting Company.
NC, North Carolina.
ND, North Dakota.
NDRC, National Defense Research Committee.
NE, Nebraska.
N.E., Northeast.
N.E.A., National Education Association.
neurol., neurological.
New Eng., New England.
N.G., National Guard.
NH, New Hampshire.
NIH, National Institutes of Health.
NIMH, National Institutes of Mental Health.
NJ, New Jersey.
NLRB, National Labor Relations Board.
NM, New Mexico
No., Northern.
NPA, National Production Authority.
nr., near.
NRA, National Recovery Administration.
NRC, National Research Council.
N.S., Nova Scotia.
NSC, National Security Council.
NSF, National Science Foundation.
NSRB, National Security Resources Board.
NV, Nevada.
N.W., Northwest.
NY, New York.
N.Y.C., New York City.

OAS, Organization of American States.
obs., observatory.
obstet., obstetrical.
OCDM, Office of Civil and Defense Mobilization.
ODM, Office of Defense Mobilization.
OECD, Organization European Cooperation and Development.
OEEC, Organization European Economic Cooperation.
OEO, Office of Economic Opportunity.
O.E.S., Order of the Eastern Star.
ofcl., official.
ofcr., officer.
OH, Ohio.
OK, Oklahoma.
Ont., Ontario.
OPA, Office of Price Administration.
oper., operations.
ophthal., ophthalmological.
OPM, Office of Production Management.
OPS, Office of Price Stabilization.
ops., operations.
O.Q.M.G., Office of Quartermaster General.
OR, Oregon.
O.R.C., Officers' Reserve Corps.
orch., orchestra.
orgn., organization.
ornithol., ornithological.
OSRD, Office of Scientific Research and Development.
OSS, Office of Strategic Services.
osteo., osteopathic.
otol., otological.
otolaryn., otolaryngological.
OWI, Office of War Information.

PA, Pennsylvania.
paleontol., paleontological.
path., pathological.
Pd.D., Doctor of Pedagogy.
P.E.I., Prince Edward Island.
P.E.N., Poets, Playwrites, Editors, Essayists and Novelists (Internat. Assn.).
penol., penological.
pers., personnel.
pfc., private first class.
PHA, Public Housing Administration.
pharm., pharmaceutical.
Pharm.D., Doctor of Pharmacy.
Pharm.M., Master of Pharmacy.
Ph.B., Bachelor of Philosophy.
Ph.D., Doctor of Philosophy.
Phila., Philadelphia.
philol., philological.
philos., philosophical.
photog., photographic.
phys., physical.
physiol., physiological.
P.I., Philippine Islands.
Pitts., Pittsburgh.
pkg., packaging.
Pkwy., Parkway.
Pl., Place.
plan., planning.
P.O., Post Office.
polit., political.
poly., polytechnic; polytechnical.
p.r., public relations.
PR, Puerto Rico.
prd., product.
prep., preparatory.
pres., president.
Presbyn., Presbyterian.
presdl., presidential.
prin., principal.
proc., proceedings.
prod., produced (play production).
prodn., production.
prof., professor.
profl., professional.
prog., progressive.
prop., proprietor, owner.
propr., proprietor.

TABLE OF ABBREVIATIONS

pros. atty., prosecuting attorney.
pro tem, pro tempore (for the time being).
psychiat., psychiatric.
psychol., psychological.
P.T.A., Parent-Teacher Association.
ptnr., partner.
PTO, Pacific Theater of Operations.
pub., public; publisher; publishing; published.
publ., publication.
pur., purchases, purchasing.
pvt., private.
PWA, Public Works Administration.

q.m., quartermaster.
Q.M.C., Quartermaster Corps.
Q.M.O.R.C., Quartermaster Officers' Reserve Corps.
quar., quarterly.
Que., Quebec (province).

radiol., radiological.
RAF, Royal Air Force.
R.A.M., Royal Arch Mason.
R.C., Roman Catholic; Reserve Corps.
RCA, Radio Corporation of America.
RCAF, Royal Canadian Air Force.
Rd., Road.
R.D., Rural Delivery.
R&D, Reaearch and Development.
R.E., Reformed Episcop
r.e., real estate.
REA, Rural Electrification Administration.
rec., recording.
ref., reformed.
reg., regional.
regt., regiment.
regtl., regimental.
rehab., rehabilitation.
rel., relations.
Rep., Republican.
rep., representative.
Res., Reserve.
ret., retired.
rev., review, revised.
RFC, Reconstruction Finance Corp.
R.F.D., Rural Free Delivery.
rhinol., rhinological.
RI, Rhode Island.
R.N., Registered Nurse.
röntgenol., röntgenological.
R.O.T.C., Reserve Officers' Training Corps.
R.R., Railroad.
rsch., research.
Ry., Railway.

s., son.
S., South.
SAC, Strategic Air Command.
SALT, Strategic Arms Limitation Talks.
S.Am., South America.
san., sanitary.
S.A.R., Sons of the Am. Revolution.
Sask., Saskatchewan.
Sat. Eve. Post, Saturday Evening Post.
savs., savings.
S.B., Bachelor of Science.
SBA, Small Business Administration.
SC, South Carolina.
SCAP, Supreme Command Allies Pacific.
Sc.B., Bachelor of Science.
Sc.D., Doctor of Science.
S.C.D., Doctor of Commercial Science.
sch., school.
sci., science; scientific.
SCLC, So. Christian Leadership Conference.
S.C.V., Sons of Confederate Veterans.
SD, South Dakota.
S.E., Southeast.
SEATO, Southeast Asia Treaty Organization.
SEC, Securities and Exchange Commn.
sec., secretary.
sect., section.
seismol., seismological.
sem., seminary.
ser., service(s).
sgt. (or **sergt.**), Sergeant.
SHAEF, Supreme Headquarters, Allied Expeditionary Forces.
SHAPE, Supreme Headquarters Allied Powers in Europe.
S.I., Staten Island.
S.J., Society of Jesus (Jesuit).
S.J.D., Doctor Juristic Science.
S.M., Master of Science.
So., Southern.
soc., society.
sociol., sociological.
SOS, Services of Supply.
S.P.Co., Southern Pacific Co.
spl., special.
splty., specialty.
Sq., Square.
sr., senior.
S.R., Sons of the Revolution.
S.S., Steamship.
SSS, Selective Service System.
St., Saint; Street.
sta., station.
statis., statistical.
stats., statistics.
S.T.B., Bachelor of Sacred Theology.
Stbizn., Stabilization.
S.T.D., Doctor of Sacred Theology.
St.L.-S.F., R.R., St. Louis-San Francisco Ry. Co.
sub., subsidiary.
supr., supervisor.
supt., superintendent.
surg., surgical.
S.W., Southwest.

T.A.P.P.I., Technical Association Pulp and Paper Industry.
Tb (or **TB**), Tuberculosis.
tchr., teacher.
tech., technical; technology.
technol., technological.
Tel.&Tel., Telephone and Telegraph.
temp., temporary.
Ter., Territory.
T.H., Territory of Hawaii.
Th.D., Doctor of Theology.
Th.M., Master of Theology.
TN, Tennessee.
tng., training.
topog., topographical.
traf., traffic.
trans., transactions; transferred.
transl., translation.
transp., transportation.
treas., treasurer.
TV, Television.
TVA, Tennessee Valley Authority.
Twp., Township.
TX, Texas.
Ty., Territory.
typog., typographical.

U., University.
UAR, United Arab Republic.
U.A.W., International Union United Automobile, Aircraft, and Agricultural Implement Workers of America-AFL-CIO.
U.B., United Brethern in Christ.
U.D.C., United Daughters of the Confederacy.
U.K., United Kingdom.
UN, United Nations.
UNESCO, United Nations Educational, Scientific and Cultural Organization.
UNICEF, United Nations International Childrens Emergency Fund.
univ., university.
UNRRA, United Nations Relief and Rehabilitation Administration.
U.P.I., United Press International.
urol., urological.
U.S., United States.
U.S.A., United States of America.
USAAF, United States Army Air Force.
USAC, United States Air Corps.
USAF, United States Air Force.
USCG, United States Coast Guard.
USCGR, U.S. Coast Guard Reserve.
USES, United States Employment Service.
USIA, United States Information Agency.
USIS, United States Information Service.
USMC, United States Marine Corps.
USMCR, U.S. Marine Corps Reserve.
USMHS, United States Marine Hospital Service.
USN, United States Navy.
U.S.N.G., United States National Guard.
USNR, United States Naval Reserve.
U.S.O., United Service Organizations.
USOM, United States Operations Mission.
USPHS, United States Public Health Service.
U.S.S., United States Ship.
USSR, Union of Soviet Socialist Republics.
U.S.V., United States Volunteers.
UT, Utah.

Va, Veterans Administration.
VA, Virginia.
vet., veteran; veterinary.
V.F.W., Veterans of Foreign Wars.
VI, Virgin Islands.
vice pres., vice president.
vis., visting.
VISTA, Volunteers in Service to Am.
vocat., vocational.
vol., volunteer; volume.
v.p., vice president.
vs., versus.
VT, Vermont.

W., West.
WA, Washington.
WAC, Women's Army Corps.
Wash., Washington (state).
WAVES, Womens Reserve, U.S. Naval Reserve.
W.C.T.U., Women's Christian Temperance Union.
WHO, World Health Organization (of the UN).
WI, Wisconsin.
W.I., West Indies.
WPA, Works Progress Administration.
WPB, War Production Board.
WSB, Wage Stabilization Board.
WV, West Virginia.
WY, Wyoming.

YMCA, Young Men's Christian Assn.
YMHA, Young Men's Hebrew Assn.
YM and YWHA, Young Men's and Young Women's Hebrew Assn.
YWCA, Young Women's Christian Assn.
Y.T., Yukon Territory.

zool., zoological.

Alphabetical Practices

Names are arranged alphabetically according to the surnames, and under identical surnames according to the first given name. If both surname and first given name are identical, names are arranged alphabetically according to the second given name. Where full names are identical, they are arranged in order of age—those of the elder being put first.

Surnames, beginning with De. Des. Du. etc., however capitalized or spaced, are recorded with the prefix preceding the surname and arranged alphabetically, under the letter D.

Surnames beginning with Mac are arranged alphabetically under M. This likewise holds for names beginning with Mc; that is, all names beginning Mc will be found in alphabetical order after those beginning Mac.

Surnames beginning with Saint or St. all appear after names that would begin Sains, and such surnames are arranged according to the second part of the name, e.g., St. Clair would come before Saint Dennis.

Surnames beginning with prefix Van are arranged alphabetically under letter V.

Surnames containing the prefix Von or von are usually arranged alphabetically under letter V; any exceptions are noted by cross references (Von Kleinsmid, Rufus Bernhard; see Kleinsmid, Rufus Bernhard von).

Compound hyphenated surnames are arranged according to the first member of the compound.

Compound unhyphenated surnames common in Spanish are not rearranged but are treated as hypenated names.

Since Chinese names have the family name first, they are so arranged, but without comma between family name and given name (as Lin Yutang).

Parentheses used in connection with a name indicate which part of the full name is usually deleted in common usage. Hence Abbott, W(illiam) Lewis indicates that the usual form of the given name is W. Lewis. In alphabetizing this type, the parentheses are not considered. However if the name is recorded Abbott, (William) Lewis, signifying that the entire name William is not commonly used, the alphabetizing would be arranged as though the name were Abbott, Lewis.

Who's Who in America®

AABYE, EDWIN GARFIELD, former electric utility exec.; b. Chgo., Mar. 31, 1904; s. Carl Johan and Elise (Mortensen) A.; B.S., Northwestern U., 1926; m. Genevieve Constance Young, May 23, 1931; children—Nancy (Mrs. G. Boyce Batey), Dianne (Mrs. John T. Black). With Pub. Service Co. Ind., 1938-69, treas., 1945-69, sec., 1950-69, ret., 1969. Mem. Am. Soc. Corp. Sec., Beta Alpha Psi. Methodist. Home: 6017 North Dearborn Street Indianapolis IN 46220 Office: 1000 East Main Street Plainfield IN 46188

AACH, HERBERT, painter; b. Cologne, Germany, Mar. 24, 1923; s. Leo and Frieda (Schloss) A.; came to U.S., 1938, naturalized, 1942; student Cologne Acad. Art, 1936-37, Pratt Inst., 1940-41, Stanford, 1942-43, Escuela de Pintura y Escultura, Mexico, 1948-50, Bklyn. Mus. Art Sch., 1946-48, 50-51; m. Doris Schein, Jan. 23, 1929; children—Christopher Jeffry, John Dennis. Tech. dir. Sargent Art Material Co., Inc., Hazleton, Pa., 1954-64; tchr. Bklyn. Mus. Art Sch., 1947-48, 50-51, Kingsbridge Community Center, 1951-53, Hazleton Art League, 1954-64, Queens Coll., 1965—, Scarsdale (N.Y.) Studio, 1965—, Pratt Inst., 1965—; exhibited one-man shows including Creative Gallery, 1952, 54, Stroudsburg Gallery, 1957, Art Direction Gallery, 1958, Evergart Mus., 1959, Landry Gallery, 1961, Pa. State U., 1962, Jacques Seligmann Gallery, 1964, 66, Hazelton Art League, 1964, Fischbach Gallery, 1966, Howard Wise Gallery, 1967; numerous group shows, 1948-. Mem. standing com. artists materials U.S. Govt., 1962, then mem. standard practices com. Served with AUS, World War II. Recipient 1st prize Creative Gallery, 1951; Hazelton Art League Annual, 1956, 63; Roberson Meml. Center Annual, 1959, numerous others. Mem. Intersoc. Color Council, Coll. Art Assn., Nat. Art Edn. Assn., Eastern Art Edn. Assn. Author articles in field. Contbg. editor Color Engring., 1962-, Arts mag., 1966-. Home: 523 East 14th Street New York City, NY 10009. Studio: 404 East 14th Street New York City NY 10009

AAGAARD, GEORGE NELSON, med. sch. dean; b. Mpls., Aug. 16, 1913; s. George N. and Lucy T. (Nelson) A.; B.S., U. Minn., 1934, B.M., 1936, M.D., 1937; m. Lorna D. Docken, Aug. 26, 1939; children—Diane Louise, George Nelson, Richard Nelson, David Nelson, Steven Nelson. Intern, Mpls. Gen. Hosp., 1936-37; successively fellow, instr., asst. prof. internal medicine U. Minn. Med. Sch., 1941-47, asso. prof., dir. continuation med. edn., 1948-51; prof. medicine, dean Southwestern Med. Sch., U. Tex., 1952-54; dean U. Washington Sch. Medicine, 1954-64, prof. medicine, 1954—, head div. clin. pharmacology, 1964—. Mem. Nat. Adv. Council for Health Research Facilities USPHS; mem. nat. adv. heart council NIH; mem. spl. med. adv. group VA, 1970—; chmn. bd. trustees Network for Continuing Edn. Mem. Am. Heart Assn. (trustee), Assn. Am. Med. Colls. (pres. 1960-61, A.M.A. (dir., chmn. com. continuing profl. edn. programs), Alpha Omega Alpha, Pharm. Mfrs. Assn. Found. (mem. sci. adv. com. 1967—), Am. Soc. Clin. Pharmacology and Therapeutics (dir. 1971—), N.Y. Acad. Scis., A.A.A.S., Washington, King County med. socs. Home: 3810 49th Avenue N E Seattle WA 98105

AALTO, HUGO ALVAR HENRIK, architect; b. Kuortane, Finland, Feb. 3, 1898; s. Johan Henrik and Sally Mathilda (Hackstedt) A.; grad. architect Tech. U. Melsinki, Finland, 1921, hon. Dr., 1949; Dr. (hon.), Princeton, 1947, Norges Teknische Hojskole, Trondheim, 1960, Eidgennössiche Technische Hochschule, Zurich, 1963, Columbia, 1964, Technische Hochshule, Wien, 1965; m. Aino Marsic, 1925 (dec. 1949); children—Hamilkar, Johanna Alanen; m. 2d, Elissa Makiniemi, Nov. 1952. Propr. archtl. offices, Jyvaskyla, Turku, Helsinki, 1923—; prof. architecture Mass. Inst. Tech., 1946-48; exhibited at N.Y.C., Paris, Zurich, Milan, Stockholm, Oslo, Copenhagen, Berlin, Hamburg, others. Decorated chevalier Legion of Honor (France); Prins Eugèn Medalj (Sweden); Royal Gold medal of Architecture (Eng.); Kommendorskorset at Danneborgen (Denmark); medaglia d'oro della Citta di Firenze; grande officiale al merito della Republica Italiana; Grand Cross of Lion (Finland); recipient Jefferson medal, 1967; others. Hon. fellow A.I.A. (Gold medal 1963); hon. mem. Am. Acad. Arts and Letters, Nat. Inst. Arts and Letters, Royal Coll. Arts London, Assn. Finnish Architects, Am. Acad. Arts and Scis., Orden pour Le Merite für Wissenschaften und Künste. Home: Iihitie 20 Helsinki Finland Office: Tillimäki 20 Helsinki 33 Finland

AARON, ABRAHAM HIGHAM, physician; b. Buffalo, May 23, 1889; s. Aaron and Elizabeth (Wark) A.; M.D., U. Buffalo, 1912. Intern Buffalo Gen. Hosp., 1912-18, now attending physician; practice of medicine, specializing gastroenterology, 1918—; prof. clin. medicine U. Buffalo, 1932-56, dir. postgrad. and continuation studies, 1934-52, emeritus prof. clin. medicine, 1956; cons. physician Buffalo Gen. Hosp. Chmn. N.Y. adv. com. Nat. Adv. Com. SSS for Med., Dental and Allied Specialists; pres. Buffalo and Erie County Tb and Health Assn. Recipient Julius Friedenwold medal for outstanding achievement in gastroenterology, 1958; citations U. Buffalo, Am. Gastroent. Assn., 1960. Diplomate Am. Bd. Internal Medicine. Fellow A.C.P.; mem. A.M.A., Am. Gastroent. Assn. (pres. 1944-45). Editor of Gastroenterology, now emeritus. Home: 64 Tudor Place Buffalo NY 14222 Office: 50 High Street Buffalo NY 14203

AARON, BENJAMIN, educator, arbitrator, govt. ofcl.; b. Chgo., Sept. 2, 1915; s. Henry Jacob and Rose (Weinstein) A.; A.B., U. Mich., 1937; LL.B., Harvard, 1940; grad. study U. Chgo., 1940-41; m. Eleanor Opsahl, May 24, 1941; children—Judith, Louise. With Nat. War Labor Bd., 1942-45; mem. labor adv. com. to Supreme Comdr. Allied Powers, Tokyo, Japan, 1946; research asso. Inst. Indsl. Relations, lectr. labor law, dept. econs. U. Cal. at Los Angeles, 1946-51, asso. dir., 1957-60, dir. 1960—, prof. law, 1960—: Faculty mem. Salzburg (Austria) Seminar in Am. Studies, 1958, 67; arbitrator labor-mgmt. disputes, 1946—; pub. mem. WSB, Washington, 1951-52; mem. Statutory Arbitration Bd. in R.R. Dispute; chmn. Cal. Farm Labor Panel, 1965-66; mem. Nat. Commn. on Tech., Automation and Economic Progress, 1965-66; pub. mem. Adv. Council on Employee Welfare and Pension Benefit Plans, 1966-68. Fellow Center for Advanced Study in Behavioral Sciences, 1966-67; named First Southwestern Legal Found. Research Fellows' Distinguished Scholar in Residence, 1971; first Howard W. Wissner Meml. Lectr., Tulane U., 1971. Mem. Nat. Acad. Arbitrators (pres. 1962, bd. govs.), Am. Bar Assn., Indsl. Relations Research Assn. (exec. bd. 1965-68, pres.-elect 1970—), Am. Arbitration Assn., Am. Assn. U. Profs., Internat. Soc. Labor Law and Sociol. Legislation (chmn. U.S. nat. com., internat. exec. com.). Author: Legal Status of Employee Benefit Rights Under Private Pension Plans, 1961. Editor: The Employment Relation and The Law, 1957; Labor Courts and Grievance Settlement in Western Europe, 1970. Home: 316 18th Street Santa Monica CA 90402 Office: U Cal at Los Angeles Los Angeles CA 90024

AARON, CHARLES, lawyer; b. N.Y. C. Dec. 28, 1890; s. Abraham S. and Fannie (Kerner) A.; LL.B., John Marshall Law Sch., 1911; m. Geraldine S. Weisfeldt, Feb. 2, 1964. Admitted to Ill. bar, 1912, since practiced in Chgo.; sr. mem. firm Aaron, Aaron, Schimberg & Hess and predecessor firms , 1922—; dir. Drovers Nat. Bank, Agar Packing Co., Mangood Corp., other corps. Bd. dirs., past pres. U.S.O., Chgo., Jewish Fedn. Chgo., Nat. Jewish Welfare Bd., Jewish Community Centers of Chgo.; former dir., mem. exec. com. Chgo. chpt. A.R.C.; fellow Brandeis U.; mem. citizens bd. U. Chgo., also mem. vis. com. Law Sch.; mem. Northwestern U. Assos. Recipient Distinguished Alumnus award John Marshall Law Sch., Julius Rosenwald gold medal Jewish Fedn. Chgo. Mem. Am., Ill., Chgo. (bd. mgrs. 1927-29) bar assns., Assn. Bar City of N.Y. Clubs: Commercial, Mid-Day, Standard, Lake Shore Country, Northmoor Country, Tavern. Home: 1300 Lake Shore Drive Chicago IL 60610 Office: 38 South Dearborn Street Chicago IL 60603

AARON, DANIEL, educator, author; b. Chgo., Aug. 4, 1912; s. Henry J. and Rose (Weinstein) A.; A.B., U. Mich., 1933; Ph.D., Harvard, 1943; Doctor of Letters (hon.) Union College, 1967; m. Janet Summers, Aug. 25, 1937; children—Jonathan, James Summers, Paul Gaston. Asst., U. Mich., 1935-36; instr. Harvard, 1936-39; mem. faculty Smith Coll., 1939—, prof. English, 1958—, Mary Augusta Jordon prof., 1961—, dir. Am. studies, 1948—; vis. prof. Bennington Coll., 1950-51, U. Helsinki (Finland), 1951-52, U. Warsaw (Poland), 1962-63, Mass. Inst. Tech., fall 1965, Harvard, 1971—; Fulbright prof. U. Sussex (Eng.), 1968-69; summer lectr. Salzburg Seminar Am. Studies, 1949—, dir., 1956—. Guggenheim fellow, 1948; fellow Center Advanced Study Behavioral Scis., 1958-59. Author: Men of Good Hope, 1952; Writers on the Left, 1961; (with W. Miller and R. Hofstadter) The United States: The History of the Republic, 1957. Editor: (with Alfred Kazin) R.W. Emerson: A Modern Anthology, 1959; Paul E. More's Shelbourne Essays in American Literature, 1963; (with Robert Bendiner) The Strenuous Decade: A Social and Intellectual Record of the 1930's, 1970. Home: 58 Paradise Road Northampton MA 01060

AARON, ELY MAYER, lawyer; b. Chgo., Apr. 29, 1896; s. Abraham B. and Fannie (Charness) A.; student U. Chgo. 1914-15; LL.B., Northwestern U., 1918; m. Helen E. Strauss, Aug. 14, 1928; chiildren—Elizabeth (Mrs. Auerbach), William Henry. Admitted to Ill. bar, 1919, since practiced in Chgo.; mem. Aaron, Aaron, Schimberg & Hess, and predecessor firms, of counsel, 1970. Mem. Chgo. (Mayor's) Commn. on Human Relations, 1947-60, chmn., 1960-66; past chmn. Mayor's Com. New Residents; chmn. Chgo. chpt. Am. Jewish Com., 1946-52, now hon. chmn.; past nat. v.p., mem. exec. and adminstrv. bds. Nat. Am. Jewish Com., now hon. trustee; pres. Jewish Vocational Service and Employment Center, Chgo., 1941-46, life dir.; bd. dirs. Leadership Council Met. Chgo.; mem. exec. bd. Chgo. Com. on Urban Opportunity. Served with U.S. Army, World War I. Fellow Am. Bar Found.; mem. Am., Ill. State, Chgo. bar assns. Clubs: City, Mid-Day, Standard (Chgo.); Lake Shore Country (Glencoe, Ill.); Harmonie (N.Y.). Home: 900 N Michigan Av Chicago IL 60611 also Duck Harbor Rd Wellfleet MA Office: One First Nat Plaza Chicago IL 60603

AARON, HENRY, right fielder for Atlanta Braves Profl. Baseball Team; b. Mobile, Ala., Feb. 5, 1934; m. Barbara Lucas, Oct. 6, 1953. Address: care Atlanta Stadium Atlanta GA 30312*

AARONS, STUART HARRY, corp. exec., lawyer; b. Yonkers, N.Y., Sept. 15, 1910; s. Martin S. and Lillian (Geller) A.; B.A. cum laude, City Coll. N.Y., 1929; LL.B. cum laude, Harvard, 1932; m. Florence Josephson, Feb. 26, 1950; children—Barry M., Philip J. Admitted to N.Y. bar, 1933; house counsel Warner Bros. Pictures, N.Y.C., 1932-53; house counsel, v.p. Stanley Warner Theatres, Inc., N.Y.C., 1953-67; sec. Glen Alden Corp., N.Y.C., 1968—; sec. ILC Industries, Inc. Vice pres., bd. dirs. Riverdale Jewish Center. Served to 1st lt., inf., AUS, 1943-46. Decorated Bronze Star medal, Army Commendation medal, Mil. medal Republic Philippines. Mem. Am. Bar Assn., Assn. Bar City N.Y., Am. Soc. Corporate Secs., Phi Beta Kappa. Club: Harvard (N.Y.C.). Home: 4525 Henry Hudson Pkwy New York City NY 10471 Office: 888 7th Av New York City NY 10019

ABADIE, LLOYD JOSEPH, banker, b. New Orleans, Sept. 2, 1929; s. Charles F. and Elsie (Karl) A.; B.C.S., Loyola U. of South, New Orleans, 1961; m. Almaree Angell, Apr. 30, 1955; children—Brenda, Elaine, Gwen, Charlene. With Whitney Nat. Bank, New Orleans, 1946—, asst. cashier, 1959-62, cashier, 1963—; sec.-treas. Whitney Holding Corp. Served with AUS, 1951-53. Mem. New Orleans C. of C., Greater New Orleans, Jefferson Parish young mens bus. clubs, Bond Club New Orleans, Am. Inst. Banking, Am. Legion. Roman Catholic. Home: 309 Jade Av Metairie LA 70003 Office: 228 Saint Charles Av New Orleans LA 70130

ABARE, PATRICK IVAN, banker; b. Pontiac, Mich., Nov. 18, 1921; s. Patrick Henry Joseph and Blythe (Honey) A.; student Oberlin Coll., 1940-42; grad. Pacific Coast Banking Sch., U. Wash., 1961-63; m. Alva Helen Eulert, Nov. 13, 1943; children—Michael R., Patrice G. Note teller Pontiac State Bank (Mich.), 1946-49; utility clk. Tulare County Nat. Bank, Visalia, Cal., 1949; distbr. Verno's Gingerale, Kern County, Cal., 1949-50; asst. cashier Kern County Bank, Oildale, Cal., 1950-52; with Crocker-Citizens Nat. Bank, 1952—, asst. v.p., mgr., Porterville and Oildale, Cal., 1958-65, v.p., mgr., Stockton, Cal., 1965-68, capital office, Sacramento, 1968-69, Sacramento main office, 1969—. Mem. Sacramento Clearing House, 1969—, pres., 1971—. Active Boy Scouts Am.; gen. chmn. Sacramento area United Crusade, 1970. Bd. dirs. Sacramento Camellia Festival, 1968—, finance chmn., 1970, vice chmn., 1969; bd. dirs. Sacramento Met. Y.M.C.A., 1968—, treas., 1969—, exec. com., 1969—, finance chmn., 1969—; bd. dirs. Golden Empire Regional Comprehensive Health Council, San Juan Mercy Hosp. Founds., Salvation Army. Served with AUS, 1942-46. Mem. Cal. Bankers Assn. (dir. 1968—, 2d v.p. 1970-71), Sacramento C. of C. (vice chmn. indsl. com. 1970). Republican. Rotarian (pres. elect N. Bakersfield 1965-66, internat. information chmn. Sacramento 1971—), Kiwanian (pres. Oildale 1954). Home: 173 Gifford Way Sacramento CA 95825 Office: 400 Capitol Mall Sacramento CA 95814

ABBADESSA, JOHN PETER, govt. ofcl.; b. Fort Dix, N.J., Nov. 14, 1920; s. Salvatore and Elvira (Oddo) A.; B.S. cum laude in Bus. Adminstrn., Am. U., 1942; M.B.A., Wharton Sch. U. Pa., 1947; grad. Advanced Mgmt. Program. Harvard, 1961; children—Jimmy (dec.), Judy, Joan. With Gen. Accounting Office, Washington, 1947-62, dep. dir. civil accounting and auditing div., 1960-62; controller AEC, 1962-. Treas. University Hills (Md.) Civic Assn., 1954; pres. Woodward High Sch. P.T.A., Rockville, Md., 1971—. Served to capt. USMCR, 1942-46. Recipient Meritorious Service award Gen. Accounting Office, 1958; Arthur S. Flemming award U.S. Jr. C. of C., 1959; Ann. Author award Fed. Govt. Accountants Assn., 1966; Distinguished Service award U.S. AEC, 1967; The Presdl. Mgmt. Improvement certificate, 1970. C.P.A., N.C. Mem. Fed. Govt. Accountants Assn. (Nat. Distinguished Leadership award 1963, v.p. 1962), Am. Inst. C.P.A.'s, Am. U. Alumni Assn. (bd. dirs. 1961-62), Omicron Delta Kappa, Pi Delta Upsilon, Pi Gamma Mu, Alpha Sigma Phi. Catholic. Home: 6900 Old Gate Lane Rockville MD 20852 Office: Atomic Energy Commn Washington DC 20545

ABBADO, CLAUDIO, conductor; b. 1933; ed. Conservatorio G. Verdi, Milan, Mus. Acad., Vienna. Permanent condr. La Scala Orch., 1968—; prin. condr. Vienna Philharmonic Orch., 1971—; guest condr. prin. orchs. in Europe and U.S.; condr. Vienna Festival, 1961—, Salzburg Festival, 1965—, Edinburgh Festival, 1966—, Prague Spring, 1966—, Luzern Festival, 1966—, Holland Festival, 1967—, Venice Festival, 1967—. Recipient Sergei Koussewitzky prize Berkshire Music Festival, 1958, Dimitri Mitropoulos prize, 1963, Philips prize, Salzburg, 1965, Diapason prize, 1966, 67, Grand Prix du Disque, 1967, 70, Deutscher Schalplatten-Preis, 1968. Address: Via Speronari 8 20123 Milan Italy

ABBE, GEORGE BANCROFT, author; b. Somers, Conn., Jan. 28, 1911; s. Harry Allen Grant and Aida (Kittredge) A.; student Cushing Acad., 1928; B.A., U. N.H., 1933; M.A., U. Ia., 1938; m. Barbara Rossiter, Sept. 22, 1934. Tchr. lit., writing Mt. Holyoke Coll., Yale, Columbia, U. Ia., U. Me., U. Pitts., Wayne U., Springfield Coll., U. N.H.; staff writers confs. U. N.H., Ida. State Coll., Corpus Christi (Tex.) Fine Arts Colony, Wooster (Ohio) Coll., Western Mass., State of Me., Cape Cod, others; co-dir. New Eng. Writers Conf., Suffield (Conn.) Acad. Editorial bd. Book Club for Poetry; adv. editor Poetry Public; faculty Tchrs. Coll. Conn., New Britain, 1955-57; asst. prof. English, Russell Sage Coll. 1958-64, asso. prof. English, 1964-67, resident author, 1958-67; prof. humanities, writer-in-residence State U. Coll., Plattsburgh, N.Y.; dir. Champlain Writers Conf. Recipient Shelley Meml. award, 1956. Mem. Poetry Soc. Am. Author: Voices in the Square, 1938; Dreamer's Clay, 1940; Wait for These Things, 1940; Letter Home, 1945; Mr. Quill's Crusade, 1948; The Wide Plains Roar, 1954; Bird in the Mulberry, 1954; Poetry, the Great Therapy, 1956; The Incandescent Beast, 1957; The Winter House, 1957; One More Puritan, 1960; (play) The Adomatic Man, 1960; The Collected Poems of George Abbe, 1935-61, 1961; Stephen Vincent Benet on Writing, 1964; You and Contemporary Poetry: An Aid-to-Appreciation, 1964; The Larks, 1965; The Non-conformist, 1966; The Funeral, 1967; (play) Shatter the Day, 1968; Yonderville, 1969; Dreams and Dissent; New Poems; 1961-70, 1971. Editor: Hill Wind, 1935. Contbr. short stories and poems to books, mags., lit. publs. Recording artist Folkways Corp. (poems). Two hour recording of poems Library of Congress. Home: Box 655 R D 3 Plattsburgh NY 12901

ABBEN, PEER, architect; b. Copenhagen, Denmark, Sept. 8, 1916; s. George Valdemar and Ingeborg (Holm) A.; certificate for skilled bricklayer, Copenhagen Guild and Trade Union, 1937; bldg. constrn. and engring. student Coll. Tech. Soc. Copenhagen, 1935-38; highest archtl. degrees, Royal Acad. Fine Arts, Copenhagen, 1943; m. Pia Vilma Jørgensen, May 10, 1943 (div. 1962) children—Pia Lee, Mei Yin. Came to U.S., 1963. Prin. own. archtl. firm, Denmark, 1948, Tanganyika (now Tanzania), E.Africa, 1949-52, Kenya, E.Africa, 1952-63; self-employed architect, Honolulu, 1964—. Indstr. architecture Royal Coll., Nairobi, 1962, 63, U. Hawaii, 1967, 68; cons. architect Oceanic Properties, Inc. planning dept., Honolulu, 1968, 69. Recipient Neuhausenske reward in architecture, 1944-45, Queen Alexandra of Eng. reward, 1946. Hielmstjerne-Rosencroneske Found. grantee, 1947. Registered profl. architect, Tanzania, Kenya, Hawaii, Wash. Fellow Acad. Assn. Danish Architects, Fedn. Danish Architects; mem. Fine Arts Soc. Denmark, A.I.A. (corporate mem.), Honolulu Acad. Arts. Club: Adventurers (Honolulu). Prin. archtl. works in E. Africa include residences, farm houses, comml. offices and bank bldgs., med. tng. center, dormitories, hosp., chs., various pub. bldgs., schs. including Arya Girls' Sch., Nairobi (Gold medal in Architecture 1957); in Honolulu, prin. works include condominium apts., townhouses, garden houses and residences. Address: 1520 Ward Av Honolulu HI 96822

ABBERLEY, JOHN J., lawyer; b. Bklyn., Dec. 16, 1916; s. Lester Stokes and Mary Abigail (Lyon) A.; A.B., Williams Coll., 1939; LL.B., U. Va., 1942; children—Lester Stokes II, Georgine M., Frederick C. Admitted to Va. bar, 1942, N.Y. bar, 1946, since practiced N.Y.C.; mem. Abberley, Kooiman, Marcellino, Clay, 1946—. Spl. asst. to dir. Office Econ. Affairs, Paris, FOA, 1953-54. Dir. Netherland-Am. Found. Trustee, Suffield (Conn.) Acad. Served as lt., USNR, 1942-46; ETO. Mem. Internat. Law Assn. (sec., treas. Am. br.), Am. Bar Assn., Assn. Bar City N.Y., Delta Kappa Epsilon, Phi Delta Phi. Episcopalian (vestryman). Home: New York City NY Office: 521 Fifth Av New York City NY 10017

ABBETT, ROBERT WILLIAM, cons. engr.; b. Jamesport, Mo., Dec. 23, 1902; s. Phillip Allen and Virginia Carter (Brown) A.; B.S., U. Mo., Rolla, 1927, C.E., 1933; M.S., Yale, 1932; Sc.D. (hon.), Gettysburg Coll., 1953; m. Ruth Virginia Bloomer, Oct. 1953; 1 son, Robert William. Surveyor, designer, engr. constrn. rys., municipal projects, bridges, bldgs. for various pvt., govt. agys., 1923-29; instr. dept. civil engring. Yale, 1929-33; asso. prof. civil engring. Union Coll., Schenectady, 1933-38; asso. Parsons, Klapp, Brinckerhoff & Douglas, also Waddell & Hardesty, cons. engrs., N.Y.C., 1938-40; asst. prof. civil engring. Columbia, 1940-41; partner Tippetts Abbett McCarthy Stratton, engrs. and architects, N.Y.C., 1945—. Cons. engr. U.S., fgn. rys., hwys., bridges, port devel., harbor works, U.S. and fgn. mineral devel. projects. Served from lt. to comdr. C.E., USNR, 1941-45. Mem. Am. Soc. C.E., Am. Inst. Cons. Engrs., Sigma Xi. Clubs: Yale, Engineers, Army and Navy, Explorers, University. Author: Engineering Contracts and Specifications, 4th edit., 1963

Editor in chief Am. Civil Engring. Practice. Contbr. articles to profl. mags. Home: Sutton Pl S New York City NY 10022 Office: 345 Park Av New York City NY 10022

ABBEY, RICHARD SARGENT, retired air force officer; b. N.Y.C., Apr. 3, 1916; s. Evers and Idamay (Sargent) A.; student U. Ala., 1935; B.S., U.S. Mil. Acad., 1940; M.A., Georgetown U., 1950; grad. Nat. War Coll., 1956; m. Eleanor Katherine Quirk, June 15, 1940; children—George Evers, Steven Quirk, William Sargent, Mary Ann Elizabeth. Commn. 2d lt. U.S. Army, 1940, advanced through grades to maj. gen. USAF, 1961; grad. flying sch., 1941; various assignments in U.S., 1941-44; comdr. 49th Bomb Squadron, Italy, 1944; dep. group comdr. 2d Bomb Group, 15th Air Force, 1944-45; staff officer, later exec. officer plans and operations div. War Dept. Gen. Staff, 1945-48; air force mem. Joint Strategic Plans Group, Joint Chiefs Staff, 1950-52; chief air force sect. MAAG, The Hague, Netherlands, 1952-55; dir. planning and programming Nat. War Coll., 1956-58; chief air policy div., dep. dir. policy, dep. plans Hdqrs. USAF, 1958, asst. dep. dir. policy, dir. plans, 1958-59; dep. comdr. 3575th Pilot Tng. Wing, Vance AFB, Okla., 1959-60; comdr. 3525th Pilot Tng. Wing, Williams AFB, Ariz., 1960-62; dir. plans and policy, Hdqrs. NORAD and CONAD, Ent AFB, Colo., 1963-65; dep. chief staff U.S. Mil. Assistance Command, Vietnam, 1965-66; asst. chief staff res. forces USAF, 1966-67; dir. NORAD, Combat Operations Center, 1967-69; commdr. 24 NORAD/CONAD region Malmstrom AFB, Mont., 1969-71; retired, 1971. Decorated Legion of Merit, D.F.C., Air medal with 2 oak leaf clusters; Croix de Guerre with palm (France). Home: 1735 Belle Haven Rd Alexandria VA 22307

ABBITT, WATKINS MOORMAN, congressman; b. Appomattox, Va., May 21, 1908; s. George Francis and Otway C. (Moorman) A.; LL.B., U. Richmond, 1931, LL.D., 1965; m. Corinne Hancock, Mar. 20, 1937; children—Anne Culvin (Mrs. William S. Kerr), Watkins Moorman, Corinne Hancock. Admitted to Va. bar, 1930, practiced in Appomattox County, 1931—; commonwealth's atty. for Appomattox Co., 1932-48; dir. Farmers Nat. Bank of Appomattox; mem. 80th to 91st U.S. Congresses from 4th Va. Dist.; mem. agr. com. Ho. of Reps. Del. state Dem. convs., 1932—; chmn. county Dem. Com., 1937—; Dem. elector, 1944; mem. Va. State Constnl. Conv., 1945; chmn. Appomattox chpt. A.R.C.; chmn. Appomattox War Bond Drive, 1942-43. Mem. 5th Jud. Circuit Ct., Va. bar assns., Am. Forestry Assn. (awards com. 1951-53, Council of State Bar (rep. 5th jud. circuit Va.), Delta Theta Phi, Omicron Delta Kappa. Democrat. Baptist. Clubs: Ruritan (pres. 1940-41), Lions (pres. 1942-43). Home: Appomattox VA 24522 Office: House Office Building Washington DC 20515

ABBOT, CHARLES GREELEY, astrophysicist; b. Wilton, N.H., May 31, 1872; s. Harris and Caroline Ann (Greeley) A.; S.B., Mass. Inst. Tech., 1894, S.M., 1895; D.Sc., Melbourne U., 1914, Case Sch. Applied Science, 1931, George Washington U., 1937; LL.D., U. Toronto, 1933; m. Lillian E. Moore, Oct. 13, 1897; m. 2d, Virginia A. Johnston, June 9, 1954. Asst., Smithsonian Astrophys. Obs., 1895, aid, acting in 1896-1906, 1896- acting dir., 1907, dir., 1907-44; Asst. sec. Smithsonian Instn., 1918-28, sec., 1928-1944; research assoc., 1944—; home sec. Nat. Acad. Sciences, 1918-23. Draper medallist of Nat. Acad. Sciences; Rumford medallist Am. Acad. Arts and Scis. Fellow A.A.A.S.; mem. Astron. and Astrophys. Soc. Am., Philos. Soc. (Washington), Washington Acad. Sciences, Nat. Acad. Sciences, Soc. Astron. de France, Soc. Astron. Mexico, Acad. Modena, Deutsche Meteorol. Gesellschaft; hon. mem. Royal Meteorol. Soc.; asso. mem. Royal Astron. Soc. of Great Britain. Home: 4409 Beechwood Road Hyattsville MD 20782 Office: Smithsonian Institution Washington DC 20560

ABBOT, JAMES LLOYD, Jr., naval officer; b. Mobile, June 26, 1918; s. James Lloyd and Helen (Taylor) A.; B.S. in Elec. Engring., U.S. Naval Acad., 1939; M.S. in Bus. Adminstrn., Geo. Washington U., 1964; m. Marjorie Grubbs, June 21, 1941; children—James Lloyd III, Charles Stevenson, Mary Neville. Commd. ensign U.S. Navy, 1939, designated naval aviator, 1941, advanced through grades to rear adm., 1966; comdg. officer Scouting Squadron 66, 1943-44, Fighter Squadron 42, 1946-48, Utility Squadron 4, 1951-52, seaplane tender U.S.S. Valcour, 1960-61, attack aircraft carrier U.S.S. Intrepid, 1961-62; dir. naval warfare analyses Office Chief Naval Operations, 1966- 67; comdr. U.S. Naval Support Force, Antarctica, 1967-69, Carrier Div. 16, 1969-70; inspr. gen. Atlantic Fleet, 1970—. Decorated Legion of Merit, Air medal, Navy Commedation medal. Episcopalian. Clubs: N.Y. Yacht; Army-Navy Country (Arlington). Author articles. Home: 2638 S Lynn St Arlington VA 22202 Office: Inspr Gen Atlantic Fleet Norfolk VA 23511

ABBOT, WILLIAM WRIGHT, educator; b. Louisville, Ga., May 20, 1922; s. William Wright and Lillian (Carswell) A.; student Davidson (N.C.) Coll., 1939-41; A.B., U. Ga., 1943; M.A., Duke, 1949, Ph.D., 1953; m. Eleanor Pearre, Mar. 31, 1958; children—William Wright, John Pearre. Tchr., Louisville Acad., 1946-47, McCallie Sch., 1951-52; from asst. prof. to prof. history Coll. William and Mary, 1953-58, 59-66; asso. prof. Northwestern U., 1958-59, Rice U., 1961-63; James Madison prof. history U. Va., 1966- . Served to lt. USNR, 1943-46. Mem. Phi Beta Kappa. Author: The Royal Governors of Georgia, 1754-1775, 1957. Editor Jour. So. History, 1961- 63; book rev. editor William and Mary Quar., 1955-61, editor, 1963-66. Home: 804 Rugby Road Charlottesville VA 22903

ABBOTT, CHARLES CORTEZ, univ. dean; b. Lawrence, Kan., Oct. 30, 1906; s. Wilbur Cortez and Margaret Ellen (Smith) A.; A.B., Harvard, 1928; A.M., 1930, Ph.D., 1933; m. Louise Slocum, 1934; children—Margaret Ellen, Louise Austin, Charles C., William S., Preston H. Instr. econs. Harvard, 1931-37, asst. prof. bus. econ. Grad. Sch. Bus. Adminstrn., 1937-40, asso. prof., 1940-46, prof., 1946-54; dean Grad. Sch. Bus. Adminstrn., U. Va., Charlottesville, 1954—; with War Shipping Adminstrn., 1942-43. Dir. Indsl. Relations Counselors, Inc., Keystone Custodian Funds, Inc., Miller and Rhoads, Chesapeake Corp. of Va. Mem. adv. council Indsl. Coll. Armed Forces. Mem. Am. Finance Assn., Am. Econ. Assn., Phi Beta Kappa Assos. Clubs: Harvard (N.Y.C.); Cosmos (Washington); Farmington (Charlottesville); Union (Boston). Author: The New York Bond Market, 1920-30, 1937; Financing Business During the Transition, 1946; Management of the Federal Debt, 1946. Editor: Basic Financial Research: Needs and Prospects, 1966. Contbr. articles profl. jours. Home: Pavilion VI East Lawn Charlottesville VA 22903

ABBOTT, CHARLES HOMER, bus. exec.; b. Houston, Tex., Dec. 29, 1909; s. Charles Howard and Lela (Hunt) A.; student U. Neb., 1928-29; A.B., Yale, 1932; LL.B., St. Lawrence U., 1938; m. Jane Millikin, Apr. 5, 1940; children—Edwin Hunt, John Millikin, Betsy, Fred Hardy. Employed sales dept. U.S. Indsl. Alcohol Co., N.Y.C., 1932-33, Nat. Distillers Products Corp., 1933-42; O.P.A. field operations officer Fuel Rationing div., 1942-43; asst. to adminstr. in charge of price bds. O.P.A., 1946-47; sp. sales rep. Gt. Lakes Steel Corp., 1947-49; Southeastern mgr. Gen. Plywood Corp., 1949-51, gen. sales mgr., 1951-52, v.p., 1952-55; sales mgr. panel and door div. Atlas Plywood Corp., gen. mgr., 1956-58; v.p. marketing Stylon Corp., Milford, Mass., 1958-62, dir., 1959-63; asst. to the pres. Samson Cordage Works, Boston, 1962-63, dir., 1962—, pres., 1963—; pres. Can. Ropes, Ltd., 1969—. Mem. exec. com. Cordage Inst. Served to lt. USN, 1943-46. Mem. Phi Delta Theta, Phi Delta Phi. Club: Yale (N.Y.C.). Home: 156 Ridgeway Rd Weston MA 02193 Office: 470 Atlantic Av Boston MA 02210

ABBOTT, CLYDE MATTHEWS, lawyer; b. Athol, S.D., July 27, 1895; s. Amos S. and Mary E. (Matthews) A.; legal edn. Ohio State U., 1923; LL.D., Salmon P. Chase Coll., 1963; m. Marguerite V. Ballinger, Feb. 16, 1926. Tchr. pub. schs., So. Ohio, 1914-17; admitted to Ohio bar, 1923, since practiced in Cin.; mem. firm Paxton & Seasongood, 1927-. Appeal agt. local SSS, World War II. Bd. regents Salmon P. Chase Coll., Cin., chmn., 1965-67; fellow of Pierpont Morgan Library, N.Y.C. Served with U.S. Army, 1918-19; AEF in France. Mem. Am., Ohio, Cin. bar assns., Cin. Art Museum Assn., Cin. Hist. Soc., Order of Coif, Acacia, Phi Delta Phi. Republican. Presbyn. Mason (32). Clubs: Queen City, Cin. Country, Travel (dir. 1952-61) (Cin.). Author: (with Robert P. Goldman) Anderson's Ohio Corporation Desk Book, rev. edits., 1956-66. Contbr. legal publs. Home: 3618 Grandin Rd Cincinnati OH 45226 Office: Central Trust Tower Cincinnati OH 45202

ABBOTT, DONALD PUTNAM, educator, marine biologist; b. Chgo., Oct. 14, 1920; s. Donald Putnam and Marion (Dummer) A.; B.A., U. Hawaii, 1941; M.A., U. Cal. at Berkeley, 1948, Ph.D., 1950; m. Isabella Aiona, Mar. 3, 1943; 1 dau., Ann Kaiue. Mem. faculty Stanford, 1950—, prof. biology, 1963—; asst. dir. Hopkins Marine Sta., Stanford, 1962-66, asso. dir., 1966—. Mem. Pacific Sci. Bd. Ifaluk Atoll Expdn., 1953, Hawaii-Philippines Sulu Sea Expdn., 1957, Galapagos Internat. Sci. Project, 1964; chief scientist TE VEGA Cruise 5, Indian Ocean, 1964, TE VEGA Cruise 18, Eastern Tropical Pacific, 1968, PROTEUS cruise 22, B.C., 1970; invertebrates adv. com. Smithsonian Oceanographic Sorting Center. Served with AUS, 1943-46. Fellow A.A.A.S., Cal. Acad. Scis.; mem. So. Cal. Acad. Scis., Am. Soc. Zoologists, Ecol. Soc. Am., Soc. Study Evolution, Soc. Systematic Zoology, Western Soc. Naturalists. Democrat. Author: (with others) Intertidal Invertebrates of the Central California Coast, 1954; (with M. Bates) Coral Island, 1958. Editorial bd. Evolution, The Veliger, Micronesica. Home: 210 Asilomar Blvd Pacific Grove CA 93950

ABBOTT, DOUGLAS CHARLES, judge; b. Lennoxville, Que., Can., May 28, 1899; s. Lewis Duff and Mary Jane (Pearce) A.; student Bishop's Coll., Lennoxville, Que., 1916, D.C.L. (hon.); LL.B., McGill Univ., Montreal, 1921, LL.D. (hon.); student Roman law. Dijon Univ. (France), 1921-22; m. Mary Winifred Chisholm, September 22, 1925; children—Elisabeth, Anthony, Lewis. Joined law firm of Fleet, Phelan, Robertson and Abbott, Montreal, Que., Can., 1922; elected to House of Commons, 1940; appt. parliamentary asst. to minister of finance, 1943-45; parliamentary asst. to minister of nat. def., 1945; minister nat. def. for naval services, 1945; minister nat. def., Aug. 1945, minister finance, 1946-54; justice Supreme Ct. Can., 1954-. Served with 7th (McGill) Siege Battery, 1916-18, R.A.F., 1918. Liberal. Mem. Ch. of England. Clubs: University of Montreal, Royal Montreal Golf, Royal Montreal Curling, Rideau of Ottawa. Home: 124 Springfield Road Ottawa 2, Canada. Office: Supreme Court Building Ottawa Ontario Canada

ABBOTT, DOUGLAS EUGENE, educator; b. Glendale, Cal., Apr. 20, 1934; s. Richard Edward and Eva (Pogue) A.; B.M.E., Stanford U., 1956, M.M.E., 1957, Ph.D., 1961; m. Doris Bernice Newmark, Dec. 16, 1956; children—Sandra Lee, Jodi Frances, Shari Evalinis, Traci Bernice. Asst. head fluid mechanics sect. Vidya div. Itek Corp., Palo Alto, Cal., 1960-64; lectr. Stanford U., 1963-64; asso. prof. Purdue U., 1964-69, prof., 1969—; staff cons. Midwest Applied Sci. Corp., Lafayette, Ind., 1964—, energy controls div. Bendix Corp., South Bend, Ind., 1967—, Westinghouse Research and Devel. Center, Pitts., 1970—. Mem. Am. Inst. Aeronautics and Astronautics, Am. Soc. Mech. Engrs., Am. Soc. Engring. Edn., Am. Phys. Soc., A.A.A.S., Pi Tau Sigma. Home: 736 Essex St West Lafayette IN 47906 Office: Sch Mech Engring Purdue U Lafayette IN 47907

ABBOTT, FRANK CURTIS, educator; b. Newtonville, Mass., Dec. 12, 1920; s. Clark Daniel and Erma (Richardson) A.; B.A., Cornell U., 1942, M.P.A., 1949; Ph.D., Harvard, 1956; m. Lois Ann Bergen. Dec. 20, 1948; children—Curtis, Jane, Jane, Paul, Kenneth, Alison. Adminstrv. asst. to Fed. Pub. Housing Authority, 1943; adminstrv. asst. to provost, also to pres. Cornell U., 1946-49; staff asso. Am. Council Edn., 1951- 58; asst. dean univ. Bucknell U., 1958-61; acad. v.p. U. Mont., 1961-65, dean Grad. Sch., 1961-64; exec. dir. Colo. Commn. Higher Edn., 1965—. Served to lt. (s.g.) USNR, 1943-46. Mem. Am. Polit. Science Assn., Assn. for Higher Education (exec. com. 1964-67). Author: The Cambridge City Manager, 1951; Government Policy and Higher Education, 1958. Editor: Faculty-Administration Relations, 1958. Home: 1776 Garland Street Lakewood CO 80215 Office: State Services Building Denver CO 80203

ABBOTT, GARDNER, banking exec.; b. Chicago Heights, Ill., Aug. 29, 1911; s. Homer and Frances M. (Gardner) A.; Ph.B., U. Chgo., 1933; LL.B., Chgo.- Kent Coll. Law, 1936; m. Marion L. Wombacher, Feb. 12, 1944; children— Katherine Frances, Mary Elizabeth. Admitted to Ill. bar, 1936; with Tractor Supply Co., Chgo., 1939-68, v.p. 1956-62, treas. 1958-60, pres., 1962-64, chmn., 1964-68, merged into TSC Industries, 1968, chmn., 1968-69; v.p. LaSalle Nat. Bank, Chgo., 1969—. Served to capt. AUS, 1941-46; ETO Mem. Chgo. Bar Assn., Delta Tau Delta, Phi Delta Phi. Episcopalian. Home: 1324 Dartmouth Road Flossmoor IL 60422 Office: 4747 North Ravenswood Avenue Chicago IL 60640

ABBOTT, GEORGE, playwright, producer; b. Forestville, N.Y., June 25, 1887; s. George Burwell and May (McLaury) A.; A.B., U. Rochester, 1911; student Harvard, 1912; m. Ednah Levis, July 9, 1914 (dec. 1930); 1 dau., Judith Ann; m. 2d, Mary Sinclair, Apr. 1946. Became an actor, 1913; writer, dir. plays and films, 1919; co-author and dir. plays including The Fall Guy; Love 'Em and Leave 'Em; Broadway; Coquette; Four Walls; Three Men on a Horse; On Your Toes; The Boys From Syracuse; Best Foot Forward; Where's Charley?; A Tree Grows in Brooklyn; The Pajama Game; Damn Yankees; New Girl in Town; dir. Chicago, Boy Meets Girl; Brother Rat; Room Service; What a Life; Primrose Path; Too Many Girls; Pal Joey; Kiss and Tell; On The Town; Billion Dollar Baby; High Button Shoes; Call Me Madam; Wonderful Town; Never Too Late; A Funny Thing Happened on the Way to the Forum; Take Her, She's Mine; Flora, The Red Menace, Fade Out-Fade In; also dir. of motion pictures including Pajama Game, Damn Yankees. Co-recipient Pulitzer Prize for Fiorello, 1960; N.Y. Drama Critics Circle award, 1960; Tony award, 1963. Clubs: Coffee House, Dutch Treat (N.Y.C.); Indian Creek (Fla.) Country; Merriewold (N.Y.C.). Office: One Rockefeller Plaza New York City NY 10020

ABBOTT, GEORGE ALONZO, former cons. chemist and toxicologist; b. Alma, Ill., July 7, 1874; s. John Baughman and Harriet, (Stuart) A.; B.S., De Pauw U., 1895, A.M. pro merito, 1896; Ph.D., Mass. Inst. Tech., 1908; LL.D., U. N.D., 1951; Sc.D. (hon.), N.D. State Coll., 1962; m. Ruth Ware, June 15, 1910; children—Marian Ware (Mrs. Russell Huxsol), Stuart Ware. Instr. chemistry Evansville (Ind.) High Sch., 1896-99, Duluth, Minn., 1899-1900, Indianapolis, 1900- 09; asst. prof. and chemist, expt. sta., State Coll., Fargo, N.D., 1909- 10; prof. chemistry, head dept., N.D., 1910-47, prof. chemistry 1948—; exchange lectr. U. Manitoba, 1912; guest prof. City Coll., N.Y. City, 1940. Spl. water cons. Nat. Resources Bd., 1937, consultant 1910—; expert toxicologist and court witness in coroners' cases and murder trials. State del. 8th Internat. Congress Applied Chemistry, 1912. Fellow Am. Inst. Chemists, Ind. Acad. Sci.; mem. Am. Assn. Univ. Profs., Am. Chem. Soc. (mem. senate on chem. edn.; charter mem. and 1st chmn. Red River Valley sect. 1948), N.D. Acad. Sci. (charter mem.; sec. since 1910), S.D. Acad. Sci. (acad. lecturer); Polytechnic Soc. (charter mem. and a founder), Phi Beta Kappa (charter member N.D. Alpha chapter; elected chapter pres. 3 times), Sigma Xi (past pres. chapter), Delta Kappa Epsilon. Methodist. Mason. Clubs: Kiwanis Internat. (gov. Minn.-Dakotas dist. 1940; key man and charter mem. local club; dist. trustee 1921-28; lt. gov. 1929. dist. gov. Minn.- Dak. Dist. 1930, Golden Anniv. Serv. award Kiwanis Internat.), Fortnightly Franklin. Contbg. editor Jour. Chem. Edn. 1924-40. Author: The First Fifty Years-a History of North Dakota Academy of Science, 1958; also bulls. and articles. Chemistry bldg. named Abbott Hall, U. N.D., in his honor. Home: 505 Hamline Street Grand Forks ND 58201

ABBOTT, JO, former banker; b. Hillsboro, Tex., Oct. 12, 1905; s. James Sturgis and Nan (Sitton) A.; grad. Am. Inst. Banking; m. Nina Sebert, Aug. 31, 1933. With San Bernardino Valley Bank (Cal.), 1922-23, Security First Nat. Bank, Los Angeles, 1924-28, Consol. Nat. Bank, Tucson, 1935; with Valley Nat. Bank, Phoenix, 1935-70, former sr. v.p. charge installment loans, also mem. exec. com., trust policy com., ret., 1970. Served to lt. col. USAAF, World War II; PTO. Mem. Am. Bankers Assn., Phoenix C. of C. (past dir.), Am. Legion, Desert Caballeres (dir.), Verde Vaguantros. Mason (Shriner). Club: Phoenix Country. Author manuals, articles. Home: 7350 Clearwater Parkway Scottsdale, AZ 85251. Office: Valley Nat Bank Phoenix AZ 85001

ABBOTT, LAWRENCE, author, economist; b. Cornwall, N.Y., July 9, 1902; s. Ernest Hamlin and May Louise (Kleberg) A.; ed. Storm King Sch., 1909-19; A.B. cum laude, honors in music, Harvard U., 1924; A.M., Columbia U., 1945, Ph.D., 1951; m. Ann Sands Tatham, October 22, 1932; children—Vaughan, Sarah Tatham, Pauline Sands (Mrs. Kenneth E. McMurtry); m. 2d, Marie Bohrn Lambert, Dec. 9, 1966. Advt. writer, publicity writer and mgr. country inn, 1924-33; contbr. to The Outlook mag. including a monthly music rev. column, "Rolls and Discs," 1925-28; mem. writing staff program dept. Nat. Broadcasting Co., 1934-42; contbg. editor Time (mag.), 1942-43; mem. faculty Hotchkiss Sch., 1943-47; instr. econs. Columbia U., 1947-51; asso. prof. econs. Mt. Holyoke Coll., 1951- 53; asso. prof. econs. Union Coll., 1953-56, prof., 1956-68, prof. emeritus, 1968—, chmn. dept. econs., 1962-66. Fulbright lectr. Pierce Coll., Athens, Greece, 1966- 67. Mem. Am. Econ. Assn., Am. Assn. U. Profs., Royal Econ. Soc. Clubs: Century. Author books: NBC Music Appreciation Hour, Student's Workbooks and Teacher's Guide, 1936-41; Approach to Music, 1940; Listener's Book on Harmony, 1941; Quality and Competition, 1955; Economics and the Modern World, 1960, rev. 1967; (song) The Ghost of John McCrae, 1928. Home: R D 2 High Street Coventry CT 06238

ABBOTT, LORETTA, dancer; d. Alfred Bruce and Agatha (Alexander Abbott); B.S., M.S. Soloist with dance companies of Paul Sanasardo, 1966, Donald McKayle, 1969, Louis Johnson, 1969; mem. Alvin Ailey Am. Dance Theatre, 1967; singer-dancer in Hallelujah Baby, 1968, Peer Gynt, 1969, La Strada, 1969, Purlie, 1970; appearance on Swedish TV spl. Rie Daiglia, 1967; guest artist Harkness Ballet, also with Robert de Cormier Chorale; guest instr. master classes Hofstra U., Nyack (N.Y.) Acad. Classical Ballet. Address: 33 Mt Morris Park W New York NY 10027

ABBOTT, LYNN DEFORREST, Jr., educator, biochemist; b. Ithaca, N.Y., Nov. 23, 1913; s. Lynn D. and Olive (Ruth) A.; B.S., Wayne State U., 1936, M.S., 1937; Ph.D., U. Mich., 1940; m. Hester May Easton, Aug. 24, 1940; children—Lynn DeForrest III, James Easton, William Lewis. Mem. faculty Med. Coll. Va., 1940—, prof. biochemistry, 1956—, chmn. dept., 1962—. Served with USNR, 1943-46. Recipient Distinguished Service award Va. sect. Am. Chem. Soc., 1970. Fellow A.A.A.S.; mem. Am. Chem. Soc. (chmn. Va. sect. 1950-51), Am. Soc. Biol. Chemists, Soc. Exptl. Biology and Medicine, Am. Inst. Nutrition, Am. Soc. Clin. Nutrition, Va. Acad. Sci. (J. Shelton Horsley Research award 1954). Contbr. profl. jours. Editor Va. Jour. Sci., 1968—. Home: 607 Horsepen Road Richmond, VA 23229.

ABBOTT, PAUL, publishing exec.; b. N.Y.C., 1898; s. Henry H. and Florence (Call) A.; grad. Yale, 1920; m. Virginia Loney. Dir., mem. finance com. McGraw- Hill, Inc.; dir. Flintkote Co., Newton Falls Paper Mill, Inc. Bd. dirs. Madison Sq. Boys Club, Am. Field Service. Decorated Legion of Merit, Bronze Star. Republican. Home: Box G Southampton NY 11968 Office: One Wall Street New York City NY 10005

ABBOTT, PHILIP, actor; b. Lincoln, Neb., Mar. 20, 1924; s. John Merriam and Helen Abbott (Boggs) Alexander; student Pasadena Playhouse, 1942, Fordham U., 1950-51; m. Jane DuFrayne, Apr. 29, 1950; children—Denise, David, Nelson. Broadway debut in Harvest of Years, 1948, other Broadway plays include Detective Story, 1950, Springtime Folly, 1951, The Square Root of Wonderful, 1957, Two For The Seesaw, 1958; appeared in motion pictures The Bachelor Party, 1957, The Invisible Boy, 1957, The Miracle of the White Stallions, 1962, Those Calloways, 1963, Sweet Bird of Youth, 1961, The Spiral Road, 1961; host-narrator TV series The House on High St., 1959-60; co-star TV series FBI, 1965—; adopted and directed for stage Robert Frost; Promises To Keep, 1965, The Web and the Rock, 1968; co-founder Theatre West, Inc., 1962, Theatre West/Club Theatre, 1969, chmn. bd., 1962-65, 67-68, 70; pres. Nelson Co. Hon. sheriff, Tarzana, Cal., 1970—. Bd. govs. Spastic Childrens Found., Los Angeles. Served with USAAF, 1943-45. Decorated D.F.C., Air medal with three oak leaf clusters. Mem. Actors Equity Assn., Screen Actors Guild, Dirs. Guild Am., A.F.T.R.A., Cinema Circulus. Home: 5400 Shirley Av Tarzana CA 91356 Office: Warner Bros QM Prodns 4000 Warner Blvd Burbank CA

ABBOTT, RANDY SAMUEL, filmmaker; b. N.Y.C., Aug. 24, 1938; s. Samuel and Gladys (Martin) A.; certificate Germain Sch. Photography, 1968, N.Y. Inst. Photography, 1960; m. Leandra Hennemann, Dec. 20, 1969; children by previous marriage—Salina Evelyne, Randy Malik. Free lance photographer, 1961-67; staff photographer Ridge Hill Center, Yonkers, N.Y., 1967-68; dir. film workshop Studio Mus. Harlem, N.Y.C., 1968-70; pres. Black Horizon Films, Inc., N.Y.C., 1969—; script and commentary writer Zambia Information Services, Lusaka, 1971—; lectr. film; organizer film festivals various colls. Served with USAF, 1956-60. Mem. Met. Area Film Instrs. Assn. Editor, dir.; San Nukas, 1969; Naturally 68, 1968; Nation Time, 1970; Bembe, 1970. Address: 100 W 92d St New York City NY 10025

ABBOTT, ROY TWINING, Jr., mgmt. co. exec.; b. Bklyn., Jan. 19, 1931; s. Roy T. and Mary I. (Bright) A.; B.A., Dartmouth, 1952, M.B.A., Amos Tuck Sch., 1953; student N.Y.U. Grad. Sch. Bus., 1953-54; m. Leigh Hinsie, Apr. 17, 1954; children—Roy T. III, Ann,

Kenneth VanHorn, William Hinsie. With Chase Manhattan Bank, 1953-66, v.p., dist. exec. charge Southwest area, 1964-66; sr. v.p. investments Gulf & Western Industries, Inc., N.Y.C., 1966-67, sr. v.p. finance, 1967—, also dir.; dir. The Bohack Corp., Brown Co., S & P Counselors Fund, Inc., Assos. Corp. N.Am.; adviser Advanced Mgmt. Research, Inc. Treas. Dartmouth Class of 1956. Trustee Pingry Sch., Elizabeth, N.J. Mem. Financial Execs. Assn., Amos Tuck Sch. Alumni Assn., Delta Upsilon. Clubs: Racquet (Short Hills); Rock Spring Country (W. Orange, N.J.). Home: 343 Long Hill Drive Short Hills NJ 07078 Office: 1 Gulf & Western Plaza New York City NY 10023

ABBOTT, WILLIAM HARVEY, mfg. co. exec.; b. Chgo., Mar. 29, 1904; s. Arthur S. and Louise (Ohlendorf) A.; B.S., U. Chgo., 1926, J.D., 1928; m. Harriet Walker, Dec. 22, 1942; 1 son, William Harvey. Admitted to Ill. bar, 1928, D.C. bar, 1935, Minn. bar, 1942; with firm Dyrenforth, Lee, Chritton & Wiles, Chgo., 1928-34; asst. solicitor Petroleum Conservation Bd., Dept. Interior, 1935; mem. firm Carpenter, Abbott & Coulter, Chgo., 1936-41, Carpenter, Abbott Coulter & Kinney, St. Paul, 1946-64; gen. counsel, v.p. legal affairs Minn. Mining and Mfg. Co., St. Paul, 1965-70, also dir.; dir. Eastern Heights State Bank, St. Paul. Pres. bd. trustees Wm. Mitchell Coll. Law, St. Paul. Served to lt. comdr. USNR, 1942-45. Mem. Com. Econ. Devel. (trustee). Clubs: Minnesota (St. Paul); White Bear (Minn.) Yacht (bd. dirs. 1963-66). Home: Peninsula Point Dellwood White Bear Lake MN 55110 Office: 3M Center St Paul MN 55102

'ABD-AL'AZIZ IBN-'ABD-AL-FAISAL IBN'-SU'UD, III KING OF SAUDI-ARABIA; see Saud III, ibn', ibn' Abd-al, 'Aziz ibn' Abd-al Faisal.

ABDULGANI, ROESLAN, Indonesian politician and diplomat; b. 1914; student Tchrs. Tng. Coll. in Surabaja (dismissed from sch. for membership in nat. movements); m.; 5 children. Active youth movements against Japanese occupation; editor Bakti, East Java, 1945; head East Java Information Service at outbreak nat. revolution; sec.-gen. Ministry Information before and during 1947; leader Indonesia delegation to confer with Dutch on Termination of Netherlands Mil. Mission in Indonesia, 1953; sec. gen. Ministry Fgn. Affairs, 1954, Asian African Conf. in Bandung, 1955; minister for fgn. affairs, 1956-57, leader Indonesian delegations to Suez Conf. in London, 1956, chmn. Indonesia delegation UN Gen. Assembly N.Y.C., 1956; vice chmn., sec.- gen. Dewan Nat. Council, 1957; vice chmn. Supreme Adv. Council, 1959-62, coordinator minister, minister information, 1963-65, dep. minister polit. instns., 1966, v.p. 24th Gen. Assembly UN, 1969—; now A. E. & P., permanent rep. Indonesia to UN Mem. Constituent Assembly. Mem. Indonesian Nationalist Party. Author numerous publications. Home: 45 East 66th St New York City NY 10021 Office: 305 E 45th St New York City NY 10017

ABE, GEORGE YOSHIMICHI, hosp. adminstr.; b. Los Angeles, Nov. 6, 1915; s. Chushiro and Saki (Shishido) A.; A.B., U. Cal. at Los Angeles, 1937; M.D., U. Cin., 1942; m. Yoshi Watanabe, July 5, 1941; children—Patricia M., Alice E., Robert Y. Intern, Wayne County Gen. Hosp., Eloise, Mich., 1942-43; resident pathology Cin. Gen. Hosp., 1943-44; resident psychiatry Longview State Hosp., Cin., 1946-48; staff Met. State Hosp., Norwalk, Cal., 1948- -, supt., med. dir., 1961—; asst. clin. prof. psychiatry U. Cal. at Los Angeles, 1961—. Dir. Commerce Pacific, Inc. Chmn. circle K com. Cerritos Coll., Norwalk, 1964. Served to capt. M.C., AUS, 1944-46. Diplomate Am. Bd. Psychiatry and Neurology. Fellow Am. Psychiat. Assn.; mem. Norwalk C. of C. Kiwanian. Home: 10357 Lesterford Av Downey CA 90241 Office: 11400 South Norwalk Blvd Norwalk CA 90650

ABEGG, EUGENE, banker; b. Blakesburg, Ia., Oct. 10, 1897; s. Walter and Katherine (Smith) A.; ed. pub. schs.; m. Florence McCaig, June 7, 1922; 1 dau., Margery (Mrs. Russell Finch). Clk., Ottumwa Nat. Bank (Ia.), 1916; clk., then cashier Kenwood Nat. Bank, Chgo., 1917-29; v.p. Hyde Park Kenwood Nat. Bank, Chgo., 1929-31; pres. S. Side Trust & Savs. Bank, Chgo., 1931-32; cashier Ill. Nat. Bank & Trust Co., Rockford, 1932-35, pres., 1935-68, chmn., 1968—; dir. Consol. Paper Co., Wisconsin Rapids, Wis., Central Ill. Electric & Gas Co. div. Commonwealth Edison Co, Woodward Governor Co., Rockford Newspapers, Inc., Charles V. Weise Co., Eclipse Fuel Engring. Co., Roper Industries, Inc. Trustee Rockford Meml. Hosp. Elk, Mason (Shriner). Clubs: Rockford Country; Mid-Day, Chicago Athletic (Chgo.); University. Home: 2203 Clinton Pl Rockford IL 61103 Office: 230 S Main St Rockford IL 61101

ABEGG, MARTIN G., univ. pres.; b. Alliance, Neb., Oct. 3, 1925; s. Frank and Mary Anna (Newberry) A.; B.S. in Gen. Engring., Bradley U., 1947; M.S. in Civil Engring., U. Colo., 1951; Ph.D. in Civil Engring., Rensselaer Poly. Inst., 1960; m. Barbara Louise Chamberlain, June 29, 1946; children—Martin Gerald, Thad William, Robert Miles. Instr. engring. Bradley U., 1947- 50, asst. prof., 1950-55, asso. prof., 1955-60, prof., 1960—, head dept. civil engring., 1960-63, dean Coll. Engring. and Tech., 1963-70, pres., 1971—. Engring. aide Ill. Div. Hwys., Dixon, 1946, civil engr., Peoria, Ill., 1948; park dist. engr., Peoria, 1953-55; cons. engr. Norman Porter & Assos., N.Y.C., 1956-57, 59. Served to lt. (j.g.) USNR, 1943-46. Recipient Putnam award Bradley U., 1961. Registered profl. engr., Ill.; registered land surveyor, Ill. Mem. Am. Soc. C.E., Am. Soc. Engring. Edn., Ill., Nat. socs. profl. engr., Am. Inst. Steel Constrn., Sigma Xi, Sigma Tau, Phi Kappa Phi, Omicron Delta Kappa, Lambda Chi Alpha, Tau Beta Pi, Chi Epsilon. Rotarian (pres. 1971—). Home: 208 Wolf Road Peoria IL 61614

ABEGG, ROLAND, educator; b. Perth Amboy, N.J., Dec. 14, 1914; s. Fritz and Ella (Fetz) A.; B.A., U. Mich., 1936; M.S., La. State U., 1939, Ph.D., 1948; m. Ellen-Lucia Smith, Apr. 14, 1938; children—Lucia (Mrs. George M. Butler), Katherine (Mrs. Earl E. Wright), Sidney Forsyth. Supt., La. State U. Quail Farm, 1937-42, mem. staff dept. zoology, summer 1943; analyst Cities Service Co., Lake Charles, La., 1943-45, Esso Standard Oil Co., Baton Rouge, 1945-46; fellow Sr. Indsl. Research, La. State U., 1946-48; asso. prof. biology Northwestern State Coll., Natchitoches, La., 1948-50; prof. biology Southeastern La. Coll., Hammond, 1950-59; prof. zoology, head dept. La. Tech U., Ruston, 1959—. Mem. La. Acad. Sci. (sec.-treas. 1952-57, pres. 1958), La. Heart Assn. (vice chmn. bd. 1957-59, v.p. 1970-71), Assn. Southeastern Biologists, Am. Soc. Zoologists, Sigma Xi, Phi Sigma, Tri-Beta. Home: 406 Pinewood Lane Ruston LA 71270

ABEL, BRENT MAXWELL, lawyer; b. Washington, May 6, 1916; s. Charles and Susan Alice (Maxwell) A.; grad. Phillips Exeter Acad., 1933; A.B., Harvard, 1937, LL.B., 1940; m. Georgiana R. Powell, May 17, 1941; children—Brent Maxwell, Molly D. Admitted to N.Y. bar, 1940, Cal. bar, 1946; asso. Cravath, Swaine & Moore, N.Y.C., 1940-41; assoc. firm McCutchen, Doyle, Brown & Enersen, and predecessor, San Francisco, 1946—, partner 1954—; vis. lectr. law U. Cal., 1955-60. Dir. Am. Express Capital Fund, other Am. Express mut. funds. Bd. dirs. San Francisco chpt. Am. Cancer Soc., 1957-63, pres., 1959-60; trustee Anna Head Sch., Oakland, Cal., Phillips Exeter Acad. Served with USNR, 1941-46; Capt. Res. Decorated Navy Cross, Navy Unit commendation ribbon. Mem. Phillips Exeter Acad. Gen. Alumni Assn. (pres. 1964-66), Bar Assn. San Francisco (pres. 1964), Am. Bar Assn., State Bar Cal., Harvard Law Sch. Assn. No. Cal. (pres. 1961), San Francisco Legal Aid Soc. (pres. 1967-68), Asso. Harvard Alumni (1st v.p. 1970-71). Clubs: Pacific Union, Berkeley Tennis (pres. 1955); Harvard (N.Y.C.); Bohemian. Home: 34 Alvarado Rd Berkeley CA 94705 Office: 601 California St San Francisco CA 94108

ABEL, CLARENCE, Jr.; lawyer; b. Indpls., Dec. 12, 1928; s. Clarence and Celeste G. (Stevens) A.; B.B.A., U. Toledo, 1950, J.D., 1958; m. Marilyn Sue Warner, Mar. 24, 1951; children—Brian Dwight, Julie Beth. Life underwriter Equitable Life of Ia., 1950-51; salary payroll adminstr., asst. credit mgr., auditor, asst. to treas. DeVilbiss Co., 1951-61; admitted to Ohio bar, 1959, since practiced in Toledo; asso. Conn. Krause & Bowman, 1961; co- founder, gen. partner Bowman, Abel, Raitz & Cox and predecessor firms, 1962—; gen. counsel for Toledo Home Fed. Savs. & Loan Assn.; rep. Kuhlman Builders Supply, Glanzman Lumber Co., Huebner Devel. Co., Aetna Life & Casualty Co., R.L. Kauffmann, Inc., USF & G. Pres. McKinley P.T.A., 1965-67. Mem. Republican Workshops, 1962-64, Lucas County Rep. Club, also Ohio Rep. Finance Com., 1963-65. Served with USMCR, 1950. Mem. Am. Judicature Soc., Am., Ohio, Lucas County, Toledo (com. chmn.) bar assns., Toledo Law Assn., Comml. Law League, Toledo Mus. Art, Toledo YMCA. U. Toledo Alumni Assn., Sigma Alpha Epsilon, Delta Theta Phi. Mem. United Ch. Christ (deacon moderator). Mason. Club: University of Toledo Tower. Home: 2825 Merrimac Blvd Toledo OH 43606 Office: Toledo Legal Bldg 416 N Erie St Toledo OH 43624

ABEL, DEFOREST WILLIAMS, ins. exec.; b. Franklin, Tenn., July 19, 1890; s. Frank Asbury and Julia Ann (Mott) A.; LL.B., Cornell U., 1915; m. Grace Isabel Marshall, July 2, 1926; children—DeForest Williams, Jr., Judith Marshall. Clk. law office, Ithaca, N.Y., 1915-16; admitted to N.Y. bar, 1918; in home office and spl. agt. N.E. Gen. Accident Fire & Life Assurance Corp., Phila., 1919-20; solicitor and br. prodn. mgr. Am. Mut. Liability Ins. Co., Boston, 1920-25; with Automobile Mut. Ins. Co. of Am. and Factory Mut. Liability Ins. Co. of Am. (operate as unit), Providence, 1925—, sec., asst. treas., 1933-39, dir., 1934—, v.p., sec., 1939-40, pres., 1940-68, chmn. bd., chief exec. officer, 1968—; sec., asst. treas. and dir. Amica Credit Corp., Providence, 1936-40, pres., 1940-68, dir., 1940—; dir. Providence Bldg. Co., Amica Life Ins. Co., Amica Underwriters, Inc.; hon. dir. R.I. Hosp. Trust Co., R.I.H.T. Corp. Served in Q.M.C., U.S. Army, 1917-18. Republican. Conglist. Mason. Clubs: Rotary, Squantum, University, Turk's Head, Agawam Hunt. Home: 17 Brentonwood Av Barrington RI 02806 Office: Ten Weybosset Street Providence RI 02904

ABEL, DEFOREST WILLIAMS, Jr., ins. co. exec.; b. Providence, Apr. 14, 1929; s. DeForest Williams and Grace Isabel (Marshall) A.; student Nichols Coll., Dudley, Mass., 1948- 49, U. Miami (Fla.), 1949-51; m. Virginia Mae Ebeling, Jan. 30, 1954; children—DeForest Williams III, Diane Christine, Wendy Lee, Richard Ellsworth, Virginia Caroline. With Automobile Mut. Ins. Co. Am. and Factory Mut. Liability Ins. Co. Am., 1951—, dir., 1965—, pres., 1968—, pres., chief exec. officer, 1971—; v.p., asst. treas., dir. Amica Credit Corp.; v.p., dir. Amica Life Ins. Co.; v.p., asst. treas., dir. Amica Underwriters, Inc.; pres., dir. Providence Bldg. Co.; corporator Old Stone Bank, Providence; dir. R.I. Hosp. Trust Nat. Bank, R.I. H.T. Corp. Mem. corporation Providence Lying-In Hosp.; bd. dirs. R.I. Jr. Achievement, also bd. dirs., mem. exec. com. Nat. Jr. Achievement; v.p., dir. Lyra Brown Nickerson Settlement House. Director, Greater Providence Chamber of Commerce. Served with USAF, 1951. Mem. Sigma Phi Upsilon. Republican. Conglist. Mason, Rotarian. Clubs: Squantum Assn., R.I. Country (Barrington); University, Turks Head, British Empire (Providence). Home: 314 Rumstick Rd Barrington RI 02806 Office: 10 Weybosset St Providence RI 02904

ABEL, ELIE, reporter, broadcaster; b. Montreal, Que., Can., Oct. 17, 1920; s. Jacob and Rose (Savetsky) A.; B.A., McGill U., 1941; M.S. in Journalism, Columbia, 1942; m. Corinne Adelaide Prevost, Jan. 28, 1946; children—Mark, Suzanne. Reporter, Windsor (Ont.) Star, 1941; asst. city editor Montreal Gazette, 1945-46; fgn. corr. N. Am. Newspaper Alliance, Berlin, Germany, 1946-47; UN corr. Overseas News Agy., 1947-49; Washington, also fgn. corr. N.Y. Times, 1949-59; Washington bur. chief Detroit News, 1959-61; with NBC, 1961-69, chief London bur., 1965-67, diplomatic corr. NBC News, Washington, 1967-69; dean Grad. Sch. Journalism, Columbia, N.Y.C., 1969—, Recipient George Foster Peabody award for outstanding radio news, 1968; Overseas Press Club Award for best interpretation of fgn. news, 1969. Mem. Sigma Delta Chi. Clubs: Century (N.Y.C.); Garrick (London). Author: The Missile Crisis, 1966; (with Marvin Kalb) Roots of Involvement, The U.S. in Asia 1784-1971, 1971. Address: Columbia U New York City NY 10027

ABEL, FREDERICK PAUL, educator; b. Glendive, Mont., Aug. 7, 1921; s. Albert G. and Harriet I. (Thompson) A.; B.S., Winona State Coll., 1943; M.A., U. Minn., 1948, Ph.D., 1960; m. Carrol E. DeWald, June 16, 1946; children—Richard, Douglas, Brian, Kathryn, David, Kristine. Asst. prin., tchr. math. and social studies, Mahtomedi, Minn., 1947-48; high sch. prin., tchr. social studies, Henning, Minn., 1948-50; prin., instr., gen. edn. U. Minn. U. High Sch., 1950-56; prin. East High Sch., Aurora, Ill., 1957-63; prof. edn., dean Sch. Edn., Western Ill. U., Macomb, 1963-70, prof. ednl. adminstrn., 1970—. Mem. curriculum cons. Sch. Dist. 131, Aurora E., 1957—; spl. cons. Adv. Council Edn. Gifted Children, 1963-68; chmn. Mayor Aurora Commn. Youth, 1962-63; mem. edn. com. Quad Cities Grad. Studies Center, 1968-71, chmn., 1970-71. Bd. dirs., chmn. budget com. Aurora Area United Community Services, 1960-63; bd. dirs. West Central Ill. Econ. Opportunity Corp.; trustee Wesley Found. Aurora. Served with USNR, World War II: ETO, PTO. Mem. Nat., Ill. (chmn. curriculum com. 1961-63) assns. secondary sch. prins., Nat. Soc. Study Edn., Nat. (life), Ill. edn. assns., Am., Ill. assns. sch. adminstrs., North Central Assn. Colls. and Secondary Schs. (dist. dir.), Phi Delta Kappa, Kappa Delta Pi, Purple Key. Methodist (ch. trustee, ofcl. bd.). Kiwanian, Rotarian. Home: Rural Route 1 Macomb IL 61455

ABEL, I. W., labor union ofcl.; b. Magnolia, O., Aug. 11, 1908; s. John and Mary (Jones) A.; grad. Canton (O.) Actual Bus. Coll.; m. Bernice Joseph, June 27, 1930; children—Karen, Linda. With Am. Sheet & Tin Plate Co. (now subsidiary U.S. Steel Corp.), Canton, O., 1925-33; staff United Steelworkers Am., 1937—, dir. Canton-Massillon, 1942—, sec.- treas. nat. orgn., 1953-65, pres. nat. orgn., 1965—. Mem. War Manpower Commn., War Labor Bd., World War II. Home: 3216 Apache Rd Pittsburgh PA 15241 Office: Commonwealth Bldg Pittsburgh PA 15222

ABEL, IRVING PHILLIP, watch mfg. co. exec.; b. N.Y.C., Oct. 27, 1909; s. Phillip and Rosina (Coen) A.; student N.Y.U., 1928-30; m. Elsie Tannenbaum, Dec. 27, 1936; children—Martin, Joan, Laura. Sales rep. Longines-Wittnauer Watch Co., N.Y.C., 1936-50, nat. sales mgr., 1950-52, v.p., 1952-54, sr. v.p., 1954-62, pres., 1962-, also dir. Asso. mem. Merchants Council, N.Y.U. Sch. Retailing. Home: 2295 South Ocean Blvd Palm Beach, FL 33480. Office: 580 Fifth Avenue New York City NY 10036

ABEL, LIONEL, critic, playwright; b. N.Y.C., Nov. 28, 1910; s. Alter and Anna (Schwartz) Abelson; student St. Johns U., 1926-28, U. N.C., 1928-29; m. Sherry Goldman, Aug. 7, 1939 (div.); 1 dau., Merry (dec. 1964); m. 2d, Gloria Becker, Sept. 3, 1970. Vis. prof. drama Columbia, 1961, Rutgers U., 1964, State U. N.Y. at Buffalo, 1965, 67; vis. prof. aesthetics Pratt Inst., 1962; prof. English, state U. N.Y., Buffalo, 1970—. Guggenheim fellow, 1958-59; Rockefeller Found. grantee, 1966. Recipient Longview award Longview Found., 1960; Nat. Inst. Arts and Letters award, 1964. Author: (critical works) Metatheatre, 1963, Italian edit., 1965, Moderns on Tragedy, 1967; (produced plays) The Death of Odysseus, 1953, Absalom (two awards best Off-Broadway prodn. 1956), 1956, The Pretender, 1960, The Wives, 1965; (translations) Some Poems of Rimbaud, 1939, Camille Pissarro, Letters to his Son Lucien, 1943, Rewald's Georges Seurat, 1943, Apollinaire's The Cubist Painters, 1944, Jean-Paul Sartre's Three Plays, 1949, Seuphor's Piet Mondrian, 1956, Ghelderode's Escurial in Modern Theatre V, 1957, Racine's Andromaque in Genius of the French Theatre, 1961; also articles. Address: English Dept State U NY Buffalo NY 14222

ABEL, MILES LEROY, corp. exec.; b. Burlington, Ia., Mar. 7, 1909; s. Lewis George and Anna Merle (Wright) A.; student Burlington Coll., 1925-27; m. Mildred Vena Karrer, Nov. 29, 1931. With Chittenden & Eastman Co., Burlington, Ia., 1928-30; local mgr. Mid Continent Petroleum Co., Freeport, Ill., 1931; credit mgr. Braun Bros. Oil Co., Chgo., 1932-36; mgr. Lunoil div. H. N. Lund Coal Co., Chgo., 1937-38; mgr. retail sales, fuel oil and equipment div. Consumers Co., Chgo., 1939-41, 1945-46; supt. constrn. U.S. Naval Air Base, Ottumwa, Ia., 1942-43; exec. v.p. Alumicast Corp., Chgo., 1946-53, Bates Expanded Steel Corp., East Chicago, 1946-51, Christiansen Corp., Chgo., 1946-57, Magnesium Co. Am., East Chicago, 1946-57; dir. Indsl. Smelting Corporation, Chicago Heights, Ill., 1947-57; exec. v.p., gen. mgr. Peerless of America, Inc., Chicago, 1957-58; v.p., works mgr. Kritzer Radiant Coils, Inc., Batavia., Ill., 1958-60; pres., treas. Aluminum Mills, Inc., Lincolnshire, Ill., 1961—. Chmn. bd. Irving Park YMCA, Chgo. Trustee, bldg. commr. Village of Lincolnshire (Ill.). Mem. Def. Orientation Conf. Assn., Washington. Served with aviation engrs. U.S. Army, 1943-45. Profl. engr., Ill. Member Ind. Soc. Chgo. Presbyn. Elk. Clubs: Thorngate Country (Deerfield, Ill.); Lions (past pres.). Home: 31 Essex Lane Lincolnshire Deerfield IL 60015 Office: 200 Schelter Road Lincolnshire IL 60069

ABEL, REUBEN, educator; b. N.Y.C., Nov. 25, 1911; s. Louis and Dora (Friedsell) A.; A.B., Columbia U., 1929; J.D., N.Y. U., 1934; M.Social Sci., New Sch., 1941, Ph.D., 1952; m. Marion Buchman, July 30, 1937; children—Richard L., Elizabeth F. Dept. store buyer, 1929-44, 46-48; faculty, New Sch. for Social Research, N.Y.C., 1950—, adj. prof. philosophy Grad. Faculty, 1967—, chmn. humanities div., 1965—. Regional unit chief OPA, 1944-46; pres., treas. Atlas Bedspread Co., Inc., N.Y.C., 1948-61. Chmn., Conf. on Methods in Philosophy and Scis., 1966-68, sec.-treas., 1950-53. Mem. Am. Philos. Assn., Am. Assn. U. Profs., Philosophy of Sci. Assn., Internat. Assn. for Philosophy of Law and Social Philosophy, Am. Soc. for Aesthetics. Author: The Pragmatic Humanism of F.C.S. Schiller, 1955; also articles, revs. encys. Editor: Humanistic Pragmatism, 1966. Home: 17 Monroe Av Larchmont NY 10538 Office: 66 W 12th St New York City NY 10011

ABEL, SIDNEY GERALD, hockey mgr., coach; b. Melville, Sask., Can., Feb. 22, 1918; m. Gloria Morandy, Aug. 21, 1943; children—Gerald, Linda. Former profl. hockey player Detroit Red Wings, now coach, gen. mgr. Recipient Hart trophy 1949. Home: 17626 Corneee Road Southfield MI 48075 Office: 5920 Grand River Av Detroit MI 48208

ABEL, THEODORE, educator; b. Lodz, Poland, Nov. 24, 1896; s. Theodore and Jadwiga (Lorenz) A.; M.A., Columbia, 1925, Ph.D., 1939; m. Theodora Mead, Nov. 9, 1923; children—Peter, Caroline, Zita. Asst. prof. U. Ill., 1925-29; faculty Columbia, 1929-51, prof., 1950-51; prof. Hunter Coll., N.Y.C., 1951-67, prof. emeritus, 1967—, chmn. dept. sociology and anthropology, 1950-67. Served in Polish Army, 1918-21. Mem. Eastern Sociol. Soc. (pres. 1956-57). Author: Systematic Sociology in Germany, 1929; Why Hitler Came Into Power, 1938; The Nazi Movement, 1966; The Foundation of Sociological Theory, 1970. Home: 4200 Sunningdale Av NE Albuquerque NM 87110

ABEL, WALTER CHARLES, actor; b. St. Paul, June 6, 1898; s. Richard Michael and Christine (Becker) A.; Student Am. Acad. Dramatic Arts, N.Y.C., 1916-18; U. Wis., 1923; m. Marietta Bitter, Sept. 24, 1926; children—Jonathan, Michael. Debut in N.Y.C. in Forbidden, 1919, has since appeared in numerous plays including Back to Methuselah, 1921, S. S. Glencairn, 1924, Mourning Becomes Electra, 1931, When Ladies Meet, 1932, Merrily We Roll Along, 1934, The Wingless Victory, 1938, The Pleasure of His Company, 1957, The Ninety Mistress, 1967, first film appearance The Three Musketeers. 1934, has since appeared in 80 films including Arise My Love, 1942, Hold Back the Dawn, 1943, Fury, 1943, Mr. Skeffington, 1944, Skylark, 1944, 13 Rue Madleine, 1944, The Fabulous Joe, 1944, Kiss and Tell, 1945; numerous radio and TV appearances. Mem. council Screen Actors Guild, 1937-47; bd. dirs. Actors Equity, 1932-34, 58-67; pres. ANTA, 1966-67; v.p. Am. Nat. Theatre and Acad., 1969—. Club: Players (N.Y.C.). Address: 167 East 71st Street New York City, NY 10021.

ABEL, WILLARD EDWARD, hotel exec.; b. Vancouver, Wash., Aug. 10, 1906; s. Charlie Edward and Julia (Wilson) A.; A.A., Centralia Jr. Coll., 1927; m. Hazel Belle Shoemaker, Nov. 1, 1930; 1 son, David. With Western Internat. Hotels Co., 1925—, successively room clk., asst. mgr., mgr., 1930-53, v.p., 1953-62, sr. v.p., 1963—; pres., gen. mgr. Hotel Sir Francis Drake, San Francisco, 1947-59; exec. v.p. St. Francis Hotel Corp., 1959-61, pres., 1961—, also dir.; pres. Internat. Western Hotels Ltd., 1965—; v.p. Western Internat. Mgmt. Co., Hoteles Biltmore de Guatemala; sr. v.p., dir. Western Internat. Hotels Co.; dir. Cal. Casualty Indemnity Exchange, Western Internat. Hotels de Mexico. Served in AUS, 1941-46, lt. col. Q.M. Mem. Am. Hotel and Motel Assn. (pres. 1965; pres., dir. ednl. inst.), Cal. Hotel Assn. (past pres., dir.), San Francisco C. of C. (dir.). Club: Presidio Golf. Home: 1659 16th Avenue San Francisco CA 94122 also 615 Tilton Road Sebastopol CA 95472 Office: Saint Francis Hotel San Francisco CA 94102

ABEL, WILLIAM EDWIN, banker; b. Phila., Aug. 15, 1916; s. William T. and Laura (Miller) A.; student Am. Inst. Banking, Phila., 1936-41, Northwestern U., 1955, Rutgers U., 1949-51, U. Pa., 1946-48; m. Cynthia S. Lynch, Jan. 1, 1944; children—William H., Alan J., Gary B., Lesley J. With Provident Co., Phila., 1935-48, First Nat. Bank, Media, Pa., 1948-51; trust officer Barclay Westmoreland Trust Co., Greensburg, Pa., 1951-53, v.p., trust officer, 1953-57; v.p., trust officer Trust Co. Morris County, Morristown, 1957-60; with So. Ariz. Bank & Trust Co., Tucson, 1960—, v.p., trust officer, 1962, v.p., sr. trust officer, 1963-67, sr. v.p., sr. trust officer, 1967—, also head trust dept. Founder, exec. dir. Trust Tng. Sch., Pa. Bankers Assn., 1957. Campaign chmn. Greater Greensburg Community Chest, 1956, pres., 1957; pres. United Fund Central Westmoreland County, 1956-57; treas. Morris County Jr. Mus., 1959-60; chmn. Morristown Dist. council Boy Scouts Am., 1960; mem. So. Ariz. Estate Planning

Council, 1960-68, U. Ariz. Found. Trustee Amphitheatre Sch. Dist. Mem. So. Ariz. Life Underwriters Assn., So. Ariz. Gen. Agts. and Mgrs. Assn., Am. (trust legislative council), Ariz. (com. chmn.) bankers assns., Western Bancorp., Ariz. (exec. com.), Corporate (pres.) fiduciaries assns. Home: 1656 E Kleindale St Tucson AZ 85719 Office: 150 N Stone Av Tucson AZ 85701

ABELE, HOMER E., judge; b. Wellston, O., Nov.21 1916 s. Oscar and Margaret (Burke) A.; LL.B., Ohio State U. Coll. Law, 1953, J. D., 1970; m. Addie Riggs, 1938; children—Terrell Ann, Peter Burke, Andy. With Anchor Hocking Glass Corp., Lancaster, O., then Austin Powder Co., McArthur, O., to 1941; patrolman Ohio State Hwy. Patrol, Van Wert, 1941-43, 46; admitted to Ohio bar, 1954; solicitor, McArthur, O.; Vinton County rep. Ohio Gen. Assembly, 1949-52; asst. to campaign mgr. Sen. Robert A. Taft, Republican Nat. Conv., Chgo., 1952; legislative counsel Spl. Transp. Com., 1953-57; del. Rep. Nat. Conv., San Francisco, 1956; Rep. nominee for Congress, 10th Ohio Dist., 1958; mem. 88th U.S. Congress from 10th Dist. Ohio; judge 4th dist. Ohio Ct. of Appeals, 1967—. Dept. judge advocate Am. Legion Ohio, 1970—; chmn. ct. sect. Am. Legion Buckeye Boy's State, 1969—. Program chmn. McArthur Devel. Assn.; Vinton County trustee Southeastern Ohio Regional Council. Served with USAAF, 1943-46. Mem. Am. Legion (exec. officer to past state comdr.), Vinton County Bar Assn. Club: McArthur Lions (past pres.). Home: McArthur OH 45651 Office: 4th Appellate Dist McArthur OH 45651

ABELES, JAMES DAVID exec.; b. N.Y.C., Mar. 24, 1916; s. James A. and Williemene H. (Kirtland) A.; student Stevens Inst. Tech., 1935-36, Mass. Inst. Tech., 1936-37; m. Elizabeth Brunet, Aug. 24, 1940; children—James B. and Elizabeth K. (twins). Tool and die apprentice Electrolux Co., 1934-35; erecting engr. U.S. Fire Protection Co., 1937-38; sales engr. Thomas F. Mason Co., 1938-39; time study engr. Waterbury Button Co., 1939-40; with Purolator, Inc., Rahway, N.J., 1940—, dir., 1954—, pres., 1955-70, chmn. exec. com., 1970—, chmn. Am. Courier Corp.; dir. Purolator Products (Can.), Ltd., Interpace Corp., Sperry & Hutchinson Co., Fidelity Union Trust Co., Fidelity Union Bancorp. Bd. dirs. Jr. Achievement of Union County; trustee Morristown (N.J.) Meml. Hosp. Mem. N.A.M., Jockey Hollow Fish and Game Protective Assn., Soc. Automotive Engrs., Chi Phi. Clubs: Somerset Hills Country (Bernardsville, N.J.); Canadian, Anglers, Economic (N.Y.C.); Detroit Athletic. Home: Corey Lane Mendham NJ 07945 Office: 970 New Brunswick Av Rahway NJ 07065

ABELES, JOSEPH CHARLES, chem. co. exec.; b. N.Y.C., Jan. 6, 1915; s. Charles and Lucy (Koerner) A.; B.S., N.Y.U., 1935; m. Sophia Weiner, Jan. 25, 1940; children—Lucille S., Nancy Jo (dec.), Barbara A. Indsl. engr. Parker- Kalon, N.Y.C., 1935-36; chem. sales agt. Fasey & Bestoff, N.Y.C., 1936- 53; v.p. sales, treas. Kawecki Chem. Co., N.Y.C., 1953-59, pres., 1958- 69; chmn. bd., chief exec. officer Kawecki Berylco Industries, Inc. (merger Kawecki Chem. Co. and The Beryllium Corp., 1968), N.Y.C., 1968—; dir. Materials Research Corp., Orangeburg, N.Y., Hexagon Labs. Co., N.Y.C. Mem. Am. Chem. Soc., Am. Soc. Metals, Engrs. Club, Chemists Club N.Y.C. Club: Elmwood Country (Westchester, N.Y.). Home: 1055 Bedford Rd Pleasantville NY 10570 Office: 220 E 42d St New York City NY 10017

ABELES, JULIAN THEODORE, lawyer; b. Little Rock, Ark., Dec. 25, 1892; s. Samuel Milton and Sarah (Alexander) A.; prep. edn. U. Ark.; LL.B., N.Y.U., 1915; m. Rose Lieberman, Feb. 14, 1917. Admitted N.Y. bar, 1916, since practiced in N.Y.C.; specialist in motion picture, music, copyright and unfair competition law since 1918; counsel for motion picture, music pub. interests; chmn. bd., general counsel Nat. Assn. Orch. Dirs., 1927-36; now general counsel Nat. Music Publishers' Assn., Inc., also for Harry Fox as agt. and trustee for music pubs. in licensing and enforcement of rights to their musical works. Mem. panel of cons. Librarian of Congress on gen. revision of Copyright Law. Mem. N.Y. State C. of C., Ark. Soc., Copyright Soc. U.S.A. (trustee). Club: Lotos. Contbr. of Ozark mountain stories to various pubs. Home: 3 E 71st St New York City NY 10021 Office: 745 Fifth Av New York City NY 10022

ABELES, ROBERT HEINZ, educator, biochemist; b. Vienna, Austria, Jan. 14, 1926; came to U.S., 1939, naturalized, 1944; s. Ernest and Carolyn (Schwartz) A.; M.S., U. Chgo., 1950; Ph.D., U. Colo., 1955; m. Barbara Anne Mincher, Sept. 20, 1948; children—Lisa Joy, Steven Leon. Postdoctoral fellow Harvard, 1955-57; asst. prof. chemistry Ohio State U., 1957-60; asso. prof. biochemistry U. Mich., 1960-64; prof. biochemistry Brandeis U., Waltham, Mass., 1964—. Mem. Am. Chem. Soc., Am. Soc. Biol. Chemists. A.A.A.S. Served with AUS, 1944-46. Editorial bd. Jour. Biol. Chemistry, 1968—. Research in mechanism of action of enzymes and co-enzymes. Home: 415 Ward Street Newton Centre, MA 02159. Office: Brandeis Univ Waltham MA 02154

ABELL, FREDERIC RUSSELL, banker; b. Lebanon, Conn., Aug. 30, 1906; s. Fred M. and Gertrude E. (Lillie) A.; student Morse Coll., 1925-26; m. Esther C. Isleib, April 23, 1932 (dec. Nov. 1967); children—Philip W., Paul L., Cynthia M.; m. 2d, Elizabeth B. Brainard, July 19, 1969. Employed with Conn. Bank and Trust Co., Hartford, 1926—, head investment div., 1950-58, sr. v.p., head trust dept., 1958-66, exec. v.p., 1964-66, vice chmn., dir., chief loaning officer comml. dept., 1966—; dir. Sage-Allen & Co., State-Dime Savs. Bank, Hartford Courant Co., Spencer Turbine Co., Hartford. Hon. trustee Loomis Sch. Club: Hartford. Home: 7 Uplands Drive West Hartford CT 06107 Office: 1 Constitution Plaza Hartford CT 06115

ABELL, GEORGE OGDEN, educator, astronomer; b. Los Angeles, Mar. 1, 1927; s. Theodore Curtis and Annamarie (Ogden) A.; B.S., Cal. Inst. Tech., 1951, M.S., 1952, Ph.D., 1956; m. Lois Everson, June 16, 1951; children—Anthony Alan, Jonathan Edward. Observer, Nat. Geog. Soc.-Palomar Obs. Sky Survey, 1953-56; lectr. Griffith Obs., 1953-60; mem. faculty U. Cal. at Los Angeles, 1956—, prof. astronomy, 1967—, chmn. dept., 1968—. Guest, Max-Planck- Institut für Physik und Astrophysik, Munich, Germany, 1965-66; guest investigator Mt. Wilson and Palomar Obs., 1958—; cons. Space Tech Labs., 1958-59, Jet Propulsion Lab., 1962-66, Douglas Aircraft, 1964-66; vis. prof. Am. Astron. Soc., 1962—. Mem. Internat. Astron. Union, Am. Astron. Soc. (Com. chmn., councelor 1969—), Astron. Soc. Pacific (dir., pres. 1968-70), A.A.A.S., Sigma Xi. Author: Exploration of the Universe, 2d edit., 1969. Contbr. numerous articles to profl. jours. Discovered numerous star clusters, planetary nebulae, clusters of galaxies, three comets; investigated distbn. of rich clusters of galaxies, properties of 86 old planetary nebulae, origin of planetary nebulae. Mailing Address Only: Office: Dept Astronomy U Cal Los Angeles CA 90024

ABELL, PAUL IRVING, educator; b. Pelham, Mass., July 24, 1923; s. Max F. and Virginia (Bennett) A.; B.S., U. N.H., 1948; Ph.D., U. Wis., 1951; m. Phyllis Killam, July 1, 1950 (div.); 1 dau., Susan E. Instr., U. R.I., Kingston, 1951-64, prof. chemistry, 1964—; Fulbright lectr., Egypt, 1965-66. Mem. research expdns. in paleontology of Omo River and Lake Rudolf regions of E. Africa sponsored by Nat. Geog. Soc., 1966-71. Served with AUS, 1943-46. Recipient Petroleum Research Fund Internat. Research grants U. Wales, 1961-62, U. Bristol, 1969-70. Mem. Am. Chem. Soc., Chem. Soc. London, Faraday Soc., Sigma Xi, Phi Kappa Phi. Mailing Address: Home: Wolf Rock Rd Kingston RI 02881

ABELL, THOMAS HENRY, lawyer; b. Wharton, Tex., May 7, 1909; s. Thomas James and Lyda (Horton) A.; student Tex. A. and M. Coll., 1926-27; LL.B., Tex. U., 1933; m. Frances Norris Wright, June 24, 1934; children—Madeleine (Mrs. Robert C. C. Wither), Alex G., Tom J. Admitted to Tex. bar, 1934, U.S. Supreme Ct., 1937; practice in Wharton, 1933—; county atty. Wharton County, 1937-40, county judge, 1943-46. Dir. Houston Lighting & Power Co. Bd. dirs. Tex. Mid-Coastal Water Devel. Assn., Palacois, Tex.; trustee Wharton Sch. Dist., 1949-58. Trustee Runnells Fund, Bay City, Tex; bd. dirs. Gulf Coast Med. Found., Wharton. Mem. Am. Simmental Assn. (trustee), Sigma Nu. Episcopalian. Home: 314 North Resident St Wharton TX 77488 Office: Box 746 Wharton TX 77488

ABELL, THORNTON MONTAIGNE, architect; b. Haven, Mich., Sept. 4, 1906; s. Charles Emery a. Cora Ida (Webb) A.; student U. Mich., 1924, U. Cal. at Berkeley, 1927; B.Arch., U. So. Cal. 1931; m. Alma Florence Hatch, Aug. 6, 1927; 1 son, Jared; 1 stepson, David. Designer, Clare C. Hosmer, Sarasota, Fla., 1925-26, Joseph J. Kucera, Pasadena, Cal., 1926, Marsh, Smith & Powell, Los Angeles, 1930-42; asso. Sumner Spaulding, Los Angeles, 1942-43, Adrian Wilson, Los Angeles, 1943-44; pvt. archtl. practice, Los Angeles, 1944—. Interior design instr. Chouinard Art Inst., 1950-52; vis. critic U. So. Cal. Sch. Architecture, 1953-61, 63-65. Charter mem. Archtl. Guild, U. So. Cal. Fellow A.I.A. (treas. So. Cal. chpt. 1958, dir. 1963-65, sec. Cal. council 1959, dir. 1958-63); mem. Am. Arbitration Assn. (arbitrator 1961—). Office: 654 South Saltair Av Los Angeles CA 90049 469 Upper Mesa Road Santa Monica CA 90402

ABELL, WILLIAM H., ins. co. exec.; b. Louisville, June 25, 1910; s. Irvin and Carrie (Harting) A.; grad. Phillips Acad., Andover, Mass., 1928; A.B., Yale, 1932; LL.B. cum laude, Harvard, 1935; m. Abby Ballard Stewart, Nov. 4, 1939; children—Abby (Mrs. Robert F. Lusky), Sally Rogers. Admitted to Ky. bar, 1935; with firm Bruce & Bullitt, Louisville, 1935-38, Cary & Abell, 1938-42, Ogden, Galphin & Abell, 1946-48; pres., chief exec. officer Commonwealth Life Ins. Co., Louisville, 1958-68, chmn. bd., chief exec. officer, 1968—; dir. Citizens Fidelity Bank & Trust Co., Capital Holding Corp., Brown Forman Distillers Corp., Reliance Universal. Chmn. Ky. Council on Higher Pub. Edn., 1966-70. Trustee Speed Mus. Served with USAAF, 1942-45. Mem. Ky., Louisville chambers commerce. Clubs: River Valley, Louisville Country, Pendennis, Wynn Stay (Louisville). Home: Mockingbird Valley Rd Louisville KY 40207 Office: Commonwealth Bldg Louisville KY 40201

ABELOFF, ABRAM JOSEPH, surgeon; b. N.Y.C., Mar. 19, 1900; s. Samuel and Rebecca Esther (Rogow) A.; A.B., Columbia, 1922, M.D., 1926; m. Gertrude Theresa Kopsch, May 15, 1953; 1 son, Tobias Samuel. Sub-surg. intern Presbyn. Hosp., N.Y.C., 1926-27; intern Lenox Hill Hosp., 1927-29; research asst. Inst. Pathology U. Freiburg (German), 1929, surg. service Frankfurt U. (Germany), U. Vienna (Austria), 1930; adj. surgeon Beth Israel Hosp., 1930-37; asso. surgeon Neurol. Hosp., N.Y.C., 1930-33; asst. adj. surgeon Lenox Hill Hosp., 1930-36, attending surgeon clinic, 1930-36, chief surgeon, 1936-42, adj. attending, 1936-46, asso. surgeon, 1946-54, attending surgeon, 1954-65, cons. surgeon, 1965—; surgeon Lexington School for the Deaf; asso. clin. prof. surgery N.Y.U. Mem. adminstrn. com., chmn. med. adv. bd. Am. Jewish Joint Distbn. Com.; adv. bd. Paul Baerwald Sch. Social Work, Paris. Pres., trustee Physicians Home; trustee Columbia, 1959-65. Served to col. M.C., AUS, 1942-46. Decorated Legion of Merit. Recipient of the Distinguished Service medal Columbia U. Alumni Fedn., 1963; Distinctive Achievement award Stuyvesant High Sch., 1965; Alumni Silver medal, Coll. Phys. & Surg.; 1969. Diplomate Am. Bd. Surgery. Fellow A.C.S., Brazilian Coll. Surgeons; mem. N.Y. Acad. Medicine, N.Y. Surg. Soc., A.M.A., N.Y. State and County med. socs., Am. Bibliog. Soc. (trustee), Assn. Alumni Coll. Phys. and Surg. Columbia U. (pres. 1956-57). Clubs: Columbia University, Grolier (N.Y.C.) Contbr. articles profl. publs. Home: 70 East 77th Street New York City NY 10021 Office: 50 Park Av New York City NY 10021

ABELOW, ROBERT, lawyer; b. N.Y.C., Dec. 29, 1902; s. Joshua and Ida S. (Krieger) A.; LL.B., St. Lawrence U., 1923; m. Miriam Steinbrink, June 1, 1931; 1 son, William J. Admitted to N.Y. bar, 1924; prin. mediation officer, asst. exec. sec. Nat. War Labor Bd., Washington, 1942; exec. dir., gen. counsel N.Y. Regional War Labor Bd., 1943; partner Weil, Gotshal & Manges, N.Y.C., 1944—. Writer, lectr. labor topics. Trustee Jewish Hosp., Bklyn. Mem. Am., N.Y. bar assns., N.Y. County Lawyers Assn., Am. Arbitration Assn., Commerce and Industry Assn. (dir., chmn. indsl. relations com.). Club: Inwood (L.I.) Country. Home: 315 E 69th St New York City NY 10021 Office: 67 Fifth Av New York City NY 10022

ABELS, JULES, author; b. Taunton, Mass., June 19, 1913; s. Bernard and Anna (Sachs) A.; B.A., Coll. City N.Y., 1934; LL.B., Columbia, 1937; M.B.A., Harvard, 1941. Econ. analyst Research Inst. Am., 1941-51, exec. editor, 1948-51; bus. trends editor Newsweek mag., 1951-53; chief economist Small Bus. Administrn., 1953-60. Littauer fellow Harvard, 1940-41. Mem. Phi Beta Kappa. Author: The Welfare State, 1951; The Truman Scandals, 1956; Out of the Jaws of Victory, 1959; The Rockefeller Billions, 1965; The Parnell Tragedy, 1966; The Degeneration of Our Presidential Election, 1968; In the Time of Silent Cal., 1969; Man on Fire: John Brown and the Cause of Liberty, 1971. Address: 1650 Harvard Street NW Washington DC 20009

ABELSON, HAROLD HERBERT, educator; b. N.Y.C., Sept. 25, 1904; s. Max and Jennie (Bernstein) A.; student Townsend Harris Hall, 1917-20; B.E., City College N.Y., 1924; A.M., Columbia, 1925, Ph.D., 1927; m. Lucie Bernard, Aug. 24, 1926; children—Jane Frances, Robert Bernard. Tutor Dept. edn. City Coll., N.Y. 1924-28, instr., 1928-35, asst. prof., 1935-42, asso. prof., 1942-48, prof., 1948—, dean Sch. Edn., 1952-66, acting dean tchr. edn. City Univ., 1966-67, prof. div. tchr. edn., 1967—, dir. ednl. clinic City Coll., 1941-52; prof. U. Colo. summer 1938, Cornell summer 1949-50, Hunter Coll. summer 1952-58; vis. lectr. New Sch. Social Research, 1948-60, Lehman Coll., 1967—; expert cons. adj. gen. office War Dept., summer 1944. President Interstate Tchr. Edn. Conf., 1962. Registered psychologist New York State, 1957—. Recipient Townsend Harris medal City Coll. Alumni Assn., 1962. Fellow American Psychol. Assn., A.A.A.S.; mem. Am. Assn. U. Profs., Am. Edn. Research Assn., Eastern, N.Y. State psychol. assns., City Coll., Columbia Grad. alumni assns., New York Acad. Pub. Edn., Phi Beta Kappa, Kappa Delta Pi. Author: Art of Educational Research; also articles. Home: 495 Odell Av Yonkers NY 10703 Office: 33 West 42d St New York City NY 10036

ABELSON, LESTER SIDNEY, distilling co. exec.; b. Niagara Falls, N.Y., Dec. 18, 1902; s. Jacob and Celia (Kantrowitch) A.; J.D., U. Chgo., 1925; m. Hope Altman, Jan. 15, 1933; children—Stuart R., Katherine A. Admitted to Ill. bar, 1925; practice in Chgo., 1926-28; with Barton Brands, Inc., Chgo., 1944—, pres., 1962—; chmn. Barton Distilling (Can.) Ltd.; pres. Barton Internat. Corp., Ky. Distbg. Co., Inc., Barton Distillers Import Corp.; v.p. Barton Western Distilling Co.; dir. Scottish Am. Distilleries, Ltd., Ho. of Stuart Bonding Co., Ltd., Barton Distillers (Europe) S.A., Alpine Trading Co. Ltd., Peter Prime Bonding Co., Ltd., D. G. Thomas Ltd., Littlemill Distillery Co., Ltd., Bowling Bonding Co., Ltd. Clubs: Standard (Chgo.); Briarwood Country (Deerfield, Ill.). Home: 1040 Lake Shore Drive Chicago IL 60611 Office: Barton Distilling Co 200 South Michigan Avenue Chicago IL 60604

ABELSON, PHILIP HAUGE, physical chemist; b. Tacoma, Wash., Apr. 27, 1913; s. Ole Andrew and Ellen (Hauge) A.; B.S., Wash. State Coll., 1933. M.S., 1935; Ph.D., U. Cal., 1939; D.Sc., Yale, 1964, So. Meth. U., 1969; L.H.D., U. Puget Sound, 1968; m. Neva Martin, Dec. 30, 1936; 1 dau., Ellen Hauge. Asst. physicist Carnegie Inst. of Washington, 1939-41; asso. physicist, Naval Research Lab., Washington, D.C., 1941-42, physicist, 1942-44, sr. physicist, 1944-45, principal physicist, 1945; civilian in charge, Naval Research Lab. branch, Navy Yard, Phila., 1944-45; chmn. Biophysics Sect., Dept. Terrestrial Magnetism, Carnegie Instn., 1953-71, pres. of instn., 1971—. Chmn. Washington, 1946-53, dir. Geophys. Lab., Carnegie Instn., 1953-. Chmn. pres. of instn., 1971. Chmn. com. on radiation cataracts NRC, 1949-57; sub-com. on shock, 1950-53; mem. AEC Plowshare Adv. Com., 1959-63, Gen. Advisory Com., 1960-63, mem. bd. sci. counselors Nat. Inst. Arthritis and Metabolic Diseases, 1960-63; cons. NASA, 1960-63; mem. phys. biology tng. grants com. NIH, 1958-60; mem. Nat. Acad. Scis., 1959—. Recipient Distinguished Civilian Service Medal; annual award phys. science Washington Acad. Sci., 1950; Distinguished Alumnus award Wash. State U., 1962; Hillebrand award Chem. Soc. Washington, 1962; Modern Medicine award, 1967. Fellow Am. Phys. Soc., Geol. Soc. Am., Mineral. Soc. Am., Geol. Soc. Washington, Am. Acad. Arts and Scis.; mem. Am. Nuclear Soc., Seismol. Soc. Am., Brit. Biochem. Soc., Brit. Mineral. Soc., Am. Chem. Soc., Soc. Am. Bacteriologists, Am. Geophys. Union (v.p. 1971), Am. Assn. Petroleum Geologists, Geochemical Soc., Washington Acad. Scis., Biophysical Soc., Philos. Soc. Washington, Phi Beta Kappa, Sigma Xi. Club: Cosmos (bd. mgmt. 1969-71, v.p. 1971) (Washington). Contbr. science lit. in field. Mem. adv. bd. Jour. Nat. Cancer Inst., 1947-52; mem. Nat. Insts. Health Biophysics and Biophysical Chemistry Study Sect., 1956-59. Editor-Researches in Geochemistry, 1959, Vol. 2, 1967. Co-editor Jour. of Geophys. Research, 1959-65. Editor: Science, 1962—. Home: 220 Locust Street Philadelphia, PA 19106. Office: 1530 P St NW Washington DC 20005

ABELSON, RAZIEL ALTER, educator; b. N.Y.C., June 24, 1921; s. Alter and Anna (Schwartz) A.; student Bklyn. Coll., 1938-40; M.A., U. Chgo., 1950; Ph.D., N.Y.U., 1957; m. Ulrike Koenigsfeld, Aug. 24, 1947; 1 son, Gabriel. Instr. philosophy Hunter Coll., N.Y.C., 1950-52; prof. philosophy N.Y.U., 1953—; vis. prof. Columbia, 1962, U. Hawaii, 1965, State U.N.Y. at Buffalo, 1967, U. Cal. at San Diego, 1970; vis. scholar Inst. Advanced Studies Behavioral Scis., Stanford, 1965. Served with U.S. Maritime Service, 1941-46. Am. Council Learned Socs. research grantee, 1968. Mem. Am. Assn. U. Profs., Am. Philos. Assn. Author: Ethics and Metaethics, 1963. Contbr. articles profl. jours. Home: 80 LaSalle St New York City NY 10027

ABELSON, RICHARD D., corp. exec: b. 1925; B.S. in Mech. Engring., Purdue U., 1945; M.B.A., U. Chgo., 1954; married. With Maremont Corp., 1945—, pres., chief exec. officer, 1969—, also dir. Address: 168 N Michigan Av Chicago IL 60601

ABELSON, ROBERT PAUL, educator; b. N.Y.C., Sept. 12, 1928; s. Miles Arthur and Margaret (Coble) A.; B.S., Mass. Inst. Tech., 1948, M.S., 1950; Ph.D., Princeton, 1953; m. Willa Donwoodie, June 11, 1955; children—John, William. Psychometric fellow Princeton, 1950-52; mem. faculty Yale, 1952—, prof. 1963—. Dir. Simulmatics Corp., 1961-67. Mem. panel sociology and social psychology NSF, 1962-64. Fellow Center Advanced Study Behavioral Scis. Fellow Am. Psychol. Assn., Am. Statis. Assn. Co-author: Candidates, Issues and Strategies, 1965; Theories of Cognitive Consistency, 1968. Home: 333 Cedar St New Haven CT 06511

ABELY, JOSEPH FRANCIS, Jr., food co. exec.; b. Boston, Jan. 22, 1929; s. Joseph Francis and Nora G. (Coffey) A.; B.S. in Bus. Adminstrn. cum laude, Boston Coll., 1950; M.B.A., Harvard, 1952, J.D., 1956; m. Brenda Conlon, Aug. 24, 1957; children—James Christopher, Karen. With W.R. Grace & Co., 1956-63, gen. mgr. equipment div. Cryovac, 1962-63; with Gen. Foods, Inc., 1963—, asst. controller, 1966-67, controller, 1967-69, v.p., 1969—, instnl. food service pres., 1970-71, v.p. finance, chief financial officer, 1971—; dir. Fore River Motors, Inc., Quincey, Mass.; lectr. bus. adminstrn. Boston Coll., 1954-55. Trustee, treas. Gen. Foods Fund, 1968—. Served to 2d lt. USAF, 1943-53. Mem. Culinary Inst. Am. (gov.), Internat. Foodservice Mfrs. Assn. (dir.). Clubs: Nutmet Curling (sec., gov.), Woodway Country (finance com.) (Darien, Conn.). Home: 3 Roland Dr Darien CT 06820 Office: 250 North Street White Plains NY 10625

ABERCROMBIE, ALEXANDER VAUGHAN, III, clergyman; b. Bridgeport, Conn., Dec. 27, 1912; s. Alexander Vaughan, Jr. and Mary Helen (Wilkinson) A.; A.B., Marietta (O.) Coll., 1937; student Harvard Div. Sch., 1946; m. Charlotte Osborne Manning, Oct. 17, 1937; children—Lois Ann (Mrs. James O. Street), Paul Manning, David Manning, Lucia Rae. Ordained to ministry Conglist. Ch.; pastor in Marietta, O., also Middleboro and Woburn, Mass., 1933-43, Providence and Taunton, Mass., 1943-48; personnel dir. Rock Mfg. Co., Stoughton, Mass., 1948-49; pastor in W. Warwick, R.I., 1949-56, Tacoma, 1956-64; pastor Congl. Christian Ch., East Orange, N.J., 1969—; exec. sec. Nat. Assn. Congl. Christian Ch. of U.S., 1964-69, chmn. commn. ministry, 1961-63. Bd. dirs. and coms. R.I. Congl. Conf., 1945, R.I. Council Chs., 1946, Wash. Congl. Conf., 1959; mem. New Eng. Bd. Pastoral Supply, 1952-55; mem. exec. com. Com. for Continuation of Congl. Christian Chs. U.S., 1949-65, recording sec., 1955. Mem. Am. Inter- profl. Inst., Internat. Platform Assn. Club: Wis. Harvard. Author: How to Gather and Order a Congregational Christian Church, 1966; Handbook for Presiding Officers, 1971. Home: 233 Prospect St East Orange NJ 07017 Office: 26 South Harrison Street East Orange NJ 07018

ABERCROMBIE, GURTH IRVING, univ. dean; b. Boston, Feb. 12, 1910; s. Frank S. and Emily (Pikerel) A.; B.S., Boston U., 1933. Accountant, Mass. Gas Co., 1933-36; dept. head New Eng. office B.F. Goodrich Co., 1936-41; treas. P.E. Dutelle & Co., Inc., 1941-51; v.p., treas. Addison Assos., Inc., 1948-50; asst. mgr. New Eng. office J.E. Porter Corp., 1951; bus. mgr. Save the Children Fedn., Inc., 1951-54; dir. placemen: Northeastern U. Sch. Bus., 1954-57, asso. dean adult and continuing edn., 1961-67, asst. dean grad. div. Sch. Bus., 1957-59, asso. dean Sch. Bus., 1959-61; dean Sch. Continuing Profl. Studies Pratt Inst., Bklyn., 1967—. Lectr. mgmt. and edn. Trustee Perry Coll., Boston, Mass. Mem. Adult Edn. Council N.Y.C., N.E.A., Am. Acad. Mgmt., Assn. U. Evening Colls. (editor newsletter, mem. exec. bd. 1962-68, parliamentarian 1969—), A.H.E., Am. Mgmt. Assn., Am. Acad. Polit. and Social Sci., Sigma Epsilon Rho. Episcopalian. Author: Selection and Training of Faculty, 1960; Teaching and Learning Problems of Adults, 1961; Primer for Management, 1962. Editor Proc. Northeastern U. Fed. and State Tax Forums. Home: 215 Willoughby Av Brooklyn NY 11205

ABERNATHY, FREDERICK HENRY, educator; b. Denver, June 19, 1930; s. Henry James and Irene (Lehman) A.; B.S., Newark Coll. Engring., 1951; M.S., Harvard U., 1954, Ph.D., 1958; m. Anna Maria Herbert, June 18, 1961; children—Sarah Louise, Marian Irene, Pauline Margherita. Fellowship student Oak Ridge Sch. Reactor Tech., Tenn., 1951-52; devel. engr. Aircraft Nuclear Propulsion Project, Oak Ridge Nat. Lab., 1952-53; asst. prof. engring. Harvard, 1959-63, asso. prof., 1963-68, asso. dean engring. and applied physics, 1967-69, Gordon McKay prof., 1968—, master South House, Radcliffe Coll., 1969-71. Mem. Nat. Com. for Fluid Mechanics Films, 1966—, chmn. 1969—; cons. Oak Ridge Lab. Inst. Def. Analysis, also Oak Ridge Lab. Dept. Transp. Mem. Am. Acad. Arts and Scis., Am. Soc. Mech. Engrs., Sigma Xi, Tau Beta Pi, Omicron Delta Kappa, Pi Tau Sigma. Home: 45 Islington Rd Auburndale MA 02166 Office: Pierce Hall Harvard U Cambridge MA 02138

ABERNATHY, JACK HARVEY, petroleum industry exec.; b. Shawnee, Okla., June 10, 1911; s. George Carl and Carrie (Howell) A.; B.S. in Petroleum Engring., U. Okla., 1933; m. Mary Ann Staig, May 13, 1932; children-Jack Harvey. Carrilee (Mrs. George L. Mothershed). Engr., Sinclair Refining Co., 1933-34; petroleum engr. Sunray DX Oil Co., 1935-41; chief engr. Oklahoma City Wilcox Pool Engring. Assn., 1942; gen. prodn. supt. Sunray DX Oil Co., Tulsa, 1943- 45; v.p. Big Chief Drilling Co., Oklahoma City, 1946-57, pres., 1958—; pres. Post Oak Oil Co., Oklahoma City, 1966—; dir. Shaft Drillers, Inc., Mercurio Mexicano, S.A. de C.V. Mexico City, Liberty Nat. Bank & Trust Co., Oklahoma City Southwestern Bank & Trust Co., Oklahoma City. Chmn. Gov. Okla. Council Petroleum Devel., 1964-68, Okla.. Bd. Registration Prof. Engrs., 1953-58, Nat. Petroleum Council, 1968-70, Pres. Frontiers of Sci. Found. Okla., 1968-70, bd. dirs., 1964; bd. dirs. Okla. U. Research Inst., 1958—; trustee U. Okla. Found., 1960—, midwest Research Inst., 1964—. Recipient Distinguished Alumnus award Okla. U. Coll. Engring., 1963. Fellow A.A.A.S.; mem. Am. Petroleum Inst. (certificate of appreciation 1956; bd. dirs. 1964—), Oklahoma City bd. dirs. 1953—, U.S. (bd. dirs. 1957-63) chambers commerce, Okla. Ind. Petroleum Assn. (bd. dirs. 1960—), Mid-Continent Oil and Gas Assn. (Pres. 1964-67), Ind. Petroleum Assn. Am. (bd. dirs. 1959—), Am. Assn. Oilwell Drilling Contractors (pres. 1956-57, bd. dirs. 1948—), Am. Inst. Mining and Metall. Engrs., Am. Soc. Oceanography, Pi Epsilon Tau, Beta Gamma Sigma, Sigma Tau, Tau, Beta Pi, Kappa Sigma. Presbyn. Home: 1141 N W 63d St Oklahoma City OK 73114 Office: PO Box 14837 Oklahoma City OK 73114

ABERNATHY, KENNETH BROOKS, mfg. co. exec.; b. Missoula, Mont., Aug. 30, 1918; s. Austin Irwin and Evelyn (Thompson) A.; B.S., Northwestern U., 1941; postgrad. Harvard Bus. Sch., 1967; m. Susan Koskinen, Mar. 7, 1942; children—Lynn (Mrs. Kenneth H. Stokoe), Gail, Kenneth Brooks. With Gen. Electric Co., 1941-62; with Brunswick Corp., 1962—; treas., 1966-69, pres. internat. div. 1968-69, Kiekhaefer Mercury div., 1969—, v.p. corp., 1969—; dir. Brunsbowl Pty., Ltd., Mascot, N.S.W., Australia, Brunswick de Argentina, S.A.I.C., Buenos Aires, Argentina, Brunswick Corp. (U.K.), Ltd., Sunbury-on-Thames, Middlesex, Eng., Brunswick Internat. (Australia) Ptj, Ltd., Dandenong, Victoria, Australia, Brunswick Nederland N.V., Breda, Netherlands, Companhia Brunswick do Brazil, S.A., Rio de Janerio, Internat. Mercury Outboards Ltd., Fond du Lac, Wis., Kiekhaefer Mercury of Con., Ltd., York County, Ont., Mercury Outboards Europe, Verviers, Belgium, Nat. Exchange Bank, Fond du Lac, Wis. Mem. Am. Mgmt. Assn., Assn. Commerce Fond duLac, Nat. Indsl. Control Council. Rotarian. Clubs: Executives, Harvard Business School (Chgo.); South Hills (Fond du Lac, Wis.); Sunset Ridge (Winnetka, Ill.). Home: 1909 Golf-Vu Dr Fond du Lac WI 54935 Office: 1939 Pioneer Rd Fond du Lac WI 54935

ABERNATHY, MAURINE HOWARD, lawyer; b. Pecan Gap, Tex., Aug. 20, 1905; d. Carey Hilton and Stella Lucy (Carmical) Howard; A.A., Central Coll. Women, Lexington, Mo., 1927; LL.B., U. Tulsa, 1938; m. Walter Smith Abernathy, Feb. 24, 1950. Admitted to D.C. bar, 1948, since practiced privately in Washington; former legal adviser Nat. League Am. Pen Women. Dir. N.E.A. Mut. Fund. Named Profl. Woman of Year, State Fedn. Bus. and Profl. Women, 1967. Mem. Bus. and Profl. Women's Club D.C. (past pres.), Nat. Assn. Women Lawyers (pres. 1959-60), Am. Bar Assn., Bar Assn. D.C., Nat. League Am. Pen Women (pres. Capital br. 1968-70, D.C. 1966-68), Panhellenic Assn. (past pres.), Phi Delta Delta, Zeta Tau Alpha. Mem. Woman's National Party. Toastmistress (named Nat. Toastmistress Month Feb. 1960). Home: The Broadmoor 3601 Connecticut Av NW Washington DC 20006

ABERNATHY, RALPH DAVID, clergyman; b. Linden, Ala., Mar. 11, 1926; s. W.L. and Louivery (Bell) A.; B.S., Ala. State Coll., 1950; M.A. in Sociology, Atlanta U., 1951; LL.D., Allen U., S.C., 1960; m. Juanita Odessa Jones, Aug. 31, 1952; children—Juandalynn Ralpheda, Donzaleigh Avis, Ralph David III. Personnel counselor, instr. social sci. Ala. State Coll., 1951; ordained to ministry Bapt. Ch., 1948; pastor First Bapt. Ch., Montgomery, Ala., 1951-61, West Hunter St. Bapt. Ch., Atlanta, 1961—. Organizer, Montgomery Improvement Assn., 1955; initiator bus. boycott, Montgomery, 1955; home and ch. dynamited, 1957; an organizer 1957, since financial sec.-treas. So. Christian Leadership Conf., v.p at large, then pres. 1965—. Mem. Atlanta Ministers Union; organizer, chmn. Operation Breadbasket, Atlanta; mem. adv. com. Congress Racial Equality. Active local A.R.C., Am. Cancer Soc., YMCA. Bd. dirs. Indsl. Areas Found., Chgo. Mem. N.A.A.C.P., Kappa Alpha Psi, Phi Delta Kappa. Mason (32). Home: 76 Cerro St SW Atlanta GA 30314 Office: 334 Auburn Av NE Atlanta GA 30303 also 775 Hunter St NW Atlanta GA 30314

ABERNATHY, TAYLOR S., banker. Chmn., dir. First Nat. Bank of Kansas City; treas., dir. Central Coal & Coke Co.; dir. Employers Reinsurance Co., Vendo Co., Army Nat. Bank, Ft. Leavenworth, Kan., Kansas City Title Ins. Co. Home: 1223 West 56th St Kansas City MO 64113 Office: 14 West 10th St Kansas City MO 64105

ABERNATHY, TOM LUTHER, steamship co. exec.; b. El Campo, Tex., Sept. 19, 1908; s. Baird and Courtney (Robertson) A.; grad. Corpus Christi (Tex.) High Sch., 1928; m. Lou Ellen Wallace, Mar. 5, 1933; 1 son, Tommy Wallace. With Lykes Bros. Steamship Co., Inc., 1928—, treas., 1965—. Club: Propeller (New Orleans). Home: 73 Driftwood Blvd Kenner LA 70062 Office: 1770 Tchoupitoulas St New Orleans LA 70150

ABERNETHY, BRADFORD SHERMAN, clergyman, educator; b. Berwyn, Ill., Apr. 19, 1909; s. William S. and Jane (Reckard) A.; A.B., Haverford Coll., 1930; B.D., Colgate-Rochester Div. Sch., 1933; postgrad. Edinburgh and Oxford, 1933, 34; m. Mary Jean Beaven, Sept. 5, 1933; children—David Beaven, William Beaven, Barbara Ann. Ordained to ministry Bapt. Ch., 1933; pastor First Ch., Columbia, Mo., 1935-41; staff Fed. Council Chs. of Christ in Am., N.Y.C., 1941-45, co-sec. Commn. on Just and Durable Peace, 1941-43, sec. Commn. on Ch. and Minority Peoples, 1943-45; chaplain, Hill prof. Bible, ethics Rutgers U., New Brunswick, N.J., 1945—. Dir. European seminar program Am. Friends Service Com., Geneva, Switzerland, 1953-55, West African Seminar Program, Togo, 1965. Mem. Nat. Assn. Coll and U. Chaplains (pres. 1949-50), World Student Service Fund (exec. com.). European Summer study tour leader, 1946, 47, 50. Home: 16 College Av New Brunswick NJ 08901

ABERNETHY, CECIL EMORY, educator; b. Charleston, S.C., Apr. 8, 1908; s. William H. and Annie Pierce (Rast) A.; A.B., Birmingham-Southern Coll., 1930; M.A., U. N.C., 1935; Ph.D., Vanderbilt U., 1940; m. Janice Johns, Aug. 24, 1940; 1 dau., Ann Tarver. Instr., English, West End High Sch., Birmingham, Ala., 1931-35, U. Ala., 1937-38, Birmingham.-So. Coll., 1939-41, asst. prof., 1941-44. asso. prof., 1944-47, prof., 1947—, Mary Collett Munger prof. English, 1970—, dean, 1958-64, 68-70, acad. v.p., 1964-68. Mem. Modern Lang. Assn., So. Assn. Colls. and Schs. (exec. com. 1969—), South Atlantic Modern Lang. Assn., Phi Beta Kappa. Presbyn. Author: Mr. Pepys of Seething Lane, 1957. Editor: (with Garland Greever), Civil War Prose, Centennial Edit. of Works of Sidney Lanier, Vol. 5, 1945. Home: 167 Glenview Drive Birmingham AL 35213

ABERNETHY, ROBERT GORDON, journalist; b. Geneva, Switzerland, Nov. 5, 1927; s. Robert William and Lois (Jones) A.; grad. Hill Sch., Pottstown, Pa., 1945; A.B., Princeton, 1950, M.P.A., 1952; m. Jean Clarke Montgomery, Apr. 30, 1955; 1 dau., Jane Montgomery. Corr., NBC, Washington, 1953-55, 58-66, London, 1955-58, Los Angeles, 1966—; sci. editor NBC News, 1965-66; writer, narrator Update, weekly news report for young people, 1961-63. Served with AUS, 1946-48. Mem. Nat. Assn. Sci. Writers. Conglist. Author: Introduction to Tomorrow, 1966. Office: 3000 West Alameda Av Burbank CA 91503

ABERNETHY, THOMAS GERSTLE, congressman; b. Eupora, Miss., May 16, 1903; s. Thomas Franklin and Minnie Agnes (Jinkins) A.; student U. Ala., 1920-23; LL.B., Cumberland U., 1924; spl. student U. Miss. Law Sch., 1924-25; m. Alice Margaret Lamb, July 5, 1936; children—Margaret Gail (Mrs. Arthur Warren Doty), Thomas Gerstle, Alice Kay (Mrs. James L. Martin). Admitted Miss. bar, 1925, practiced in Eupora, Miss., 1925-29, Okolona, Miss., 1929—. Mayor, Eupora, 1927-29; elected dist. atty. 3d Jud. Dist. Miss., 1935, re-elected, 1939; mem. 76th to 82d Congresses, 4th Miss. Dist., 83d-92d congresses 1st Miss. Dist. Dir. Northeast Miss. Council. Mem. Okolona C. of C. (pres.), Miss., Chickasaw County bar assns., Lambda Chi Alpha, Alpha Kappa Psi (hon.). Democrat. Methodist. Mason (Shriner). Club: Okolona Exchange. Home: Okolona MS 38860

ABERSFELLER, HEINZ ANDREW, govt. ofcl.; b. Frankfurt am Main, Germany, Apr. 23, 1920; s. Frank and Anna (Friedel) A.; came to U.S., 1922, naturalized, 1941; student U. Md., Am. U., also LaSalle Extension U.; m. Margaret Sturdivant, Feb. 1, 1942; 1 dau., Gretchen Anne (Mrs. Ronald E. Schmidt). With the U.S. Govt., 1944; asst. post quartermaster Heidelberg (Germany) Mil. Post., 1947-49; chief supply and logistics Office Q.M.G., Heidelberg, 1949-52, dep. asst. quartermaster gen. clothing and textile material, Washington, 1952-57; regional dir. fed. supply service Gen. Services Adminstrn., Washington, 1957-61, regional adminstr. region 10, Seattle, 1961-62, region 3, Washington, 1962-64, commr. fed. supply service, 1964—; dir. gen. services Corp. for Pub. Broadcasting, 1971—. Chmn., Pres.'s Com. Blind Made Products. Recipient Meritorious Service medal (2) Dept. Army, Gen. Services Adminstrn.; Distinguished Service award, Gen. Service Adminstrn. Exceptional Service award Gen. Service Adminstrn. Mem. Def. Supply Assn. (nat. v.p. 1967-70, gov.), Armed Forces Mgmt. Assn. (gov.). K.C., Elk. Home: 1600 S Eads St Alexandria VA 22202 Office: 888 16th St Washington DC 20006

ABERT, DONALD BYRON, newspaper exec.; b. Milw., Apr. 14, 1907; s. Byron H. and Lorraine K. (Haas) A.; B.S., U. Wis., 1928; m. Barbara Anne Grant, Aug. 1, 1936; children—Judith (Mrs. David G. Meissner), Barbara (Mrs. J. Michael Tooman), Grant. With Journal Company, publishers of the Milw. Journal and the Sentinel and operators broadcast stas. WTMJ, WTMJ-TV, WTMJ-FM, Milw., 1928—, v.p., 1952-60, exec. v.p., gen. mgr., 1960-68, pres., pub., 1968—, also dir.; pres. Matex, Inc.; treas., director Audit Bur. Circulations. Bd. dirs. United Community Services Milw., 1966-70; pres. Milw. council Boy Scouts Am., 1954-55; bd. dirs. Greater Milw. Com.; bd. dirs. Hosp. Area Planning Com., 1964-70; mem. bd. corp. Boys Club; trustee Harry J. Grant Scholarship Found.; trustee Milw.-Downer Sem., 1946-58, pres., 1948-52; bd. dirs. Milw. Symphony Orch., pres., 1968-70; trustee Milw. Art Center, Marquette U. Recipient Silver Beaver award Boy Scouts Am. Mem. Am. Newspaper Pubs. Assn. (trustee found.), Milw. Assn. Commerce, Phi Gamma Delta. Clubs: Milwaukee Country, University, Town, Rotary, Press, Milwaukee (Milw.). Home: 5370 North Lake Drive Milwaukee WI 93217 Office: 333 West State Street Milwaukee WI 53203

ABESS, LEONARD LEROY, banker; b. Providence, Mar. 28, 1904; s. Kalman and Ann (Feiner) A.; C.P.A., N.Y.U., 1925; m. Bertha Marshall Ungar, Mar. 25, 1936; children-Linda, Marcella, Leonard. Pvt. practice accounting, Miami, Fla., 1925-54; chmn. bd. City Nat. Bank, Miami Beach, 1946—, City Nat. Bank Miami, 1948—; dir. Maule Industries, Inc., Ryder System, Inc. Past pres. Dade County Community Chest, Mt. Sinai Hosp., Miami. Trustee U. Miami; bd. dirs. Miami Heart Inst. C.P.A., Fla. Mem. Orange Bowl Com., Fla. Inst. C.P.A.'s, Fla. Bd. Accountancy (past chmn.). Home: 5255 Collins Av Miami Beach FL 33140 Office: City Nat Bank of Miami Miami FL 33130

ABHAU, WILLIAM CONRAD, operations analyst, ret. naval officer; b. Baltimore County, Md., Apr. 5, 1912; s. William Conrad and Gertrude (Lewis) B.S., U.S. Naval Acad., 1935; M.S., Naval Postgrad. Sch., 1956; grad. Naval War Coll., 1957; m. Harriet Elliot Sanders, Oct. 17, 1942; children—Elliot, Marcy. Commd. USN, advanced through grades to rear adm., 1964; gunnery officer USS New Jersey, World War II; asso. with Navy Research and Devel. effort since 1945, with specialization in weapon control systems, evaluation of weapons systems effectiveness, and anti-submarine warfare devices; comdr. U.S.S. E. A. Greene, 1947-48, Escort Squadron 16, 1953-54, U.S.S. Waccamaw, 1957-58, U.S.S. Helena, 1961-63, Cruiser-Destroyer Flotilla Four, 1965, Manned Spacecraft Recovery Force, Atlantic, 1966-67, Anti-Submarine Warfare Systems Project, Washington, 1967-70, retired, 1970; research staff Inst. for Def. Analyses, 1970—. Cons. to com. on undersea warfare Nat. Acad. Scis. Decorated Legion of Merit, Bronze Star medal. Mem. Operations Research Soc. Am. Club: Annapolis Yacht. Home: 201 Scott Circle Annapolis, MD 21401. Office: 400 Army-Navy Dr Arlington VA 22202

ABIAN, ALEXANDER, educator; b. Tabriz, Iran, Jan. 1, 1925; s. Moushegh and Rimma (Yaralian) A.; B.S., U. Tehran, 1946; M.S., U. Chgo., 1954; Ph.D., U. Cin., 1956; m. Thelma Vartanian, Apr. 12, 1958; children—Rimma, Elizabeth, Andrew. Instr. math. U. Tenn., 1956-57; instr. Queens Coll., 1957-59; asst. prof. U. Pa., 1959-62; asso. prof. Ohio State U., 1962-67; prof. Ia. State U., 1967—; Fulbright scholar, 1952. Mem. Am. Math. Soc. Author: The Theory of Sets and Transfinite Arithmetic 1965; Linear Associative Algebras, 1971. Research, articles math. jours. Home: 2610 Kellogg Av Ames IA 50010

ABKOWITZ, MARTIN AARON, educator; b. Revere, Mass., Sept. 19, 1918; s. Max and Annie (Weise) A.; S.B. in Naval Architecture, Mass. Inst. Tech., 1940; A.M. in Physics, Harvard, 1949, Ph.D. in Physics, 1953; m. Davette Eisenstein, Mar. 9, 1947; children—Janis Lynne, Mark David, Suzanne Jill. Naval architect David Taylor Model Basin, 1940-42, physicist, 1946-49; faculty Mass. Inst. Tech., 1949—, prof. naval architecture, 1959—. Cons. engr., 1949—; Fulbright lectr. Denmark, 1962-63. Served to capt. AUS, 1942-46. Mem. Soc. Naval Architects and Marine Engrs., Sigma Xi. Home: 28 Peacock Farm Road Lexington MA 02173 Office: Mass Inst Technology Cambridge MA 02139

ABLON, RALPH E., holding co. exec.; student Ohio State U., 1939. With Luria Bros. & Co., 1939-62, exec. v.p., 1948-55, pres., 1955-62, pres. Ogden Corp., N.Y.C., parent orgn., 1962-71, now chmn. Served with USNR, World War II. Home: 778 Park Av New York City NY 10021 Office: 161 E 42d St New York City NY 10017

ABRAHAM, JOHN MILTON, ednl. films exec.; b. Watson, Ill., Jan. 30, 1904; s. Arthur L. and Edyth (Gladson) A.; B.S., U. Chgo., 1925; m. Esther Kelso, June 22, 1929; children—Bonnie Jean Le May, John K. Financial controller Balaban & Katz Corp., Chgo., 1929-44; with Coronet Instnl. Films div. Esquire, Inc., Chgo., 1944—, gen. mgr., 1945-68, v.p., 1948-64, sr. v.p., 1964—; pres. edn. group, Esquire, Inc., 1968—, also dir.; 1968—; dir. Jack C. Coffee Co. Fellow Royal Soc. Arts Eng.; mem. Sigma Alpha Epsilon. Clubs: Executives, Interfraternity (Chgo.). Home: 1331 Braeburn Road Flossmoor IL 60422 Office: 65 East S Water Street Chicago IL 60601

ABRAHAM, WILLARD, educator; b. Chgo., May 18, 1916; s. Edward and Sadie (Weiss) A.; B.S., Ill. Inst. Tech., 1940; M.Ed., Chgo. Tchrs. Coll., 1942; Ph.D., Northwestern U., 1950; m. June 13, 1948; children—Edward, Andrew, Amy, Rebecca. With Postal Telegraph Co., Chgo., 1935-39. Roosevelt U., Chgo., 1946-53; mem. faculty dept. edn., Ariz. State U., Tempe, 1953—, now prof. Cons. numerous orgns., including N.Y. Times Newspaper, Pres.'s Com. on Mental Retardation, Day Care Centers Am., Inc., AVCO Corp., and others. Asso. editor Exceptional Children mag. Bd. dirs. Phoenix Country Day Sch., Served with AUS, 1942-46. Recipient Faculty Achievement award Ariz. State U., 1965. Mem. Council Exceptional Children, Am. Assn. U. Profs., Phi Delta Kappa. Author: Your Post-War Career, 1945; Get the Job, 1946; A Guide for the Study of Exceptional Children, 1956; A Look at Reading, 1957; Barbara-A Prologue, 1958; Common Sense about Gifted Chidren, 1958; The Slow Learner, 1964; A Time for Teaching, 1964; A Study of the Devereaux Found., 1970. Editor: The Preparation of B(ur.) (of) I(ndian) A(ffairs) Teacher and Dormitory Aides, 1968. Contbr. profl. jours. Home: 6402 E Chapparral Rd Scottsdale AZ 85253 Office: Coll Edn Ariz State Univ Tempe AZ 85281

ABRAHAM, WILLIAM HAMILTON, educator; b. Englewood, N.J., May 20, 1929; s. Leonard G. and Ruth (Thrasher) A.; B.Ch.E., Cornell U., 1952; Ph.D., Purdue U., 1957; m. Roberta Taylor Grannis, June 27, 1953; children—Katharine Gail, David William, Jonathan Paul, Molly Susan, Sarah Louise. Chem. engr. Proctor & Gamble, summer 1952; chem. engr. E. I. duPont, Wilmington, Del., 1957-62; asst. prof. chem. engring. Ia. State U., 1962-63, asso. prof., 1963-67, prof., 1967—; indsl. cons.; cons., vis. prof. U. Philippines, 1967-69. Served to lt. USAF, 1952-54. Mem. Am. Inst. Chem. Engrs., A.A.A.S., Sigma Xi, Tau Beta Pi. Presbyn. Home: 126 Broadmoor Circle Ames IA 50010

ABRAHAMS, ROBERT DAVID, lawyer, author; b. Phila., Sept. 24, 1905; s. William and Anne (David) A.; LL.B., Dickinson Sch. Law, 1925; m. Florence Kohn, Nov. 21, 1929; children—Richard Irving, Roger David, Marjorie. Admitted to Pa. bar, 1925; sec. to commr. gen. to Europe for Sesqui-Centennial Expn., 1925; asst. city solicitor, 1927-32; editor Independent (weekly), 1932; consul at Phila. for Dominican Republic, 1931-62; asst. chief counsel Legal Aid Soc. Phila., 1933-50, chief counsel, 1950—; mem. Abrahams & Loewenstein. Faculty law Temple U.; exec. dir. Community Legal Service, 1966-67. Bd. dirs. Pa. Prison Soc., pres., 1968—; bd. dirs., trustee Dickinson Sch. Law. Pres., Community Health Center, 1945-52, Jewish Family Service, 1951-54; mem. expert com. on Low Cost Legal Service, Am. Bar Survey of Legal Profession. Decorated Order of Duarte, 1945, Order of Christopher Columbus, 1957 (Dominican Republic). Mem. Nat. Legal Aid Assn. (v.p. 1957, Reginald Heber Smith award 1962), Internat., Am., Pa., Phila. (chmn. com. on pub. service 1961-62, com. censors 1962-65) bar assns., Tau Epsilon Rho. Democrat. Jewish religion. Mason. Clubs: Philmont Country, Philadelphia Consular. Author: Come Forward (verse), 1928; New Tavern Tales (fiction), 1930; (with M.J. Meyer) Handbook of Pennsylvania Collection Practice, 1931; The Pot Bellied Gods (verse), 1932; Death After Lunch (novel), 1941; Death in 1-2-3 (novel), 1942; Three Dozen (verse), 1945; Mr. Benjamin's Sword, 1948; Room for a Son (novel), 1951; The Commodore (novel), 1954; The Uncommon Soldier (novel), 1958; Sound of Bow Bells (novel), 1962; Humphrey's Ride (novel), 1964; The Bonus of Redonda, 1967. Contbr. verse, prose to Sat.Eve.Post, Esquire, Story, other mags.; contbr. to law jours. Founder, Phila. Neighborhood Law Office Plan, 1st successful legal service plan for persons in middle income group, 1939. Home: 8204 Cedar Road Elkins Park Philadelphia PA 19117 also Morning Star Fig Tree Nevis West Indies Office: Land Title Bldg Philadelphia PA 19110

ABRAHAMSEN, DAVID, psychiatrist, psychoanalyst, author: b. Trondheim, Norway, June 23, 1903; s. Salomon and Marie (Fischer) A.; M.D., Royal Frederick U., Oslo, Norway, 1929; postgrad. Tavistock Clinic and Nat. Hosp., London, Eng., London Sch. Econs., 1936-37; M.D., U. State N.Y., 1943; m. Lova Katz, May 5, 1932; children—Inger (Mrs. Robert Karr McCabe), Anne-Marie (Mrs. William J. Foltz). Came to U.S., 1940, naturalized, 1946. Dist. pub. health officer, pvt. practice medicine, Norway, 1929-31; intern Royal Norwegian Clinics Oslo U., 1931-32; resident, asst. physician neurology and psychiatry Psychiat. Clinic, Oslo, 1932-36; dir., supr. Children's Home, Oslo, 1934-36; psychiatrist Dept. Justice, Oslo, 1938-40, St. Elizabeths Hosp., Washington, 1940-41, Ill. State Penitentiary, 1941-42; research asso. psychiatry Menninger Clinic, Southard Sch., Topeka, 1942-43; psychiatrist Bellevue Hosp., 1943-44; research asso. dept. psychiatry Columbia, 1944-53; research dir. child guidance and mental hygiene, 1950-53; dir. research, treatment behavior disorders in children Psychiat. Inst., N.Y.C., 1944-48; dir. sci. research Dept. Mental Hygiene, State N.Y. 1948-52, cons., 1955—; vis. prof. grad. faculty polit. and social sci. New Sch. for Social Research, 1959-61. Organizer, dir. Psychiat. Forum, Inc., 1946—; mem. bd. Home Adv. Council, Home Term Ct., N.Y.C., 1953—; mem. bd., adv. bd. Mus. Therapy Orgn., 1954—; mem. N.Y. Gov's Com to Propose New Legislation on Definition Legal Insanity, 1957—. Bd. overseers Lemberg Center for Study of Violence, Brandeis U. Served with Norwegian Army, 1940. Diplomate Am. Bd. Psychiatry and Neurology. Fellow A.M.A., Am. Psychiat. Assn., N.Y. Acad. Medicine; mem. Norwegian Med. Assn., N.Y. County Med. Soc., Am. Soc. Criminology, N.Y. Soc. Clin. Psychiatry, Am. Psychopath. Assn., Author's League, P.E.N. Author: Crime and the Human Mind, 1944; Men, Mind and Power, 1945; The Mind and Death of a Genius, 1946; Report on Study of 102 Sex Offenders at Sing Sing Prison as Submitted to Governor Thomas E. Dewey, 1950;

Who Are the Guilty?-A Study of Education and Crime, 1952; The Road to Emotional Maturity, 1958; The Psychology of Crime, 1960; The Emotional Care of Your Child, 1969; Our Violent Society, 1970; also numerous reports. Contbr. articles to sci., med. jours. Address: 1035 Fifth Av New York City NY 10028

ABRAHAMSON, ALBERT, educator; b. Portland, Me., Nov. 4, 1905; s. Lazarus A. and Rosa (Robinson) A.; A.B., Bowdoin Coll., 1926; M.A., Columbia, 1927. Mem. faculty Bowdoin Coll., 1928—, instr. to asso. prof., 1928-1947, prof., 1947—, chmn. dept. econs., 1956-61, dean faculty, 1969-70. Economist, Cabinet Commn. on Price Policy, Washington, 1934-35; WPA adminstr., Me., 1935-37; exec. dir. Jewish Occupational Council, N.Y.C., 1939-40; exec. dir. Nat. Refugee Service, N.Y.C., 1941-43; asst. dir. War Refugee Bd., Washington, 1944-45; spl. asst. to Sec. Labor, 1945-46; spl. cons. to chmn. NSRB, 1950; cons. President's Materials Policy Commn., 1951; economist United Jewish Appeal, 1955; mem. panel mediators, Me., 1957-63, Econ. Adv. Bd. Me., 1959-63; chmn. Me. adv. commn. U.S. Commn. on Civil Rights, 1958-60; cons. Nat. Manpower Commn., N.Y.C., 1955-62; sr. staff asso. NSF, 1964-65, cons., 1965-70. Bd. dirs. Am. Cancer Soc., 1954-55. Served with AUS, World War II. Mem. Am. Econ. Assn., Indsl. Relations Research Assn., Phi Beta Kappa, Zeta Psi. Jewish religion. Contbr. articles jours. Home: 234 Maine St Brunswick ME 04011 Office: Post Office Box 157 Brunswick ME 04011

ABRAHAMSON, BRUCE ARNOLD, architect; b. Chgo., July 21, 1925; s. Clifford Austin and Adena (Thorson) A.; B.Arch., U. Minn., 1949; M.Arch., Harvard, 1951; m. Betty L. Davis, Nov. 26, 1949; children—Sue, Lisa, Ann. Designer Thorshov & Cerny, Architects, Mpls., 1947-50; Rotch traveling scholar, Europe, 1951- 52; project designer Skidmore, Owings & Merrill, Chgo., 1952-54; partner firm Hammel, Green & Abrahamson, Inc., Mpls. and St. Paul, 1954—; asst. prof. Sch. Arch. U. Minn. Served with USNR, 1943-45. Recipient Gargoyle prize U. Minn.; Honor awards Minn. Soc. Architects; Design award Progressive Arch. Mag. Mem. A.I.A. (past pres. St. Paul chpt.), U. Minn. Inst. Tech. Alumni Assn. (past pres.). Home: 7205 Shannon Drive Minneapolis MN 55424 Office: 2675 University Av St Paul MN 55114

ABRAHAMSON, EDWIN WILLIAM, educator; b. Medina, N.Y., Jan. 6, 1922; s. Edwin W. and Doris (Reeves) A.; B.A., U. Buffalo, 1944; M.A., Columbia, 1948; Ph.D., Syracuse U., 1952; m. Corinne Manghi, June 19, 1948; children—Carla Maria, Kirsten. Research chemist Manhattan Project, 1944-46; instr. chemistry Colgate U., 1948-50; research asso. Mass. Inst. Tech., 1952-53; asst. prof. Syracuse U. Coll. Forestry, 1955-59; asso. prof. chemistry Case Inst. Tech., 1959-66; prof. chemistry Case Western Res. U., 1967—; vis. prof. Cambridge U., 1964-65, Yale, spring 1970. Mem. Nat. Research Council; mem. Internat. Com. for Eye Research. Mem. Am. Chem. Soc., Am. Inst. Chemists, Am. Phys. Soc., Am. Inst. Biol. Chemists, Sigma Xi. Research chemistry of vision, spectroscopic basis of photochemistry, photosynthesis. Hon. editor Photochemistry and Photobiology, 1970. Home: 3051 Scarborough Rd Cleveland Heights OH 44118 Office: Case Western Reserve Univ Cleveland OH 44106

ABRAHAMSON, ELMER ELLSWORTH, lawyer; b. Chgo., Oct. 15, 1902; s. Martin and Jennie (Johnson) A.; student Lewis Inst., pvt. prep. schs.; LL.B., John Marshall Law Sch., 1926; LL.D., Luther Coll., Ia., 1955; m. Erna C. Hansen, Oct. 10, 1936; children—Elmer Ellsworth, Warren E. Admitted to Ill. bar, 1927, since practiced in Chgo.; dir. Blue Cross Plan, Chgo., Luth. Ch. Prodns., Inc., N.Y. Mem. hosp. licensing bd., Ill.; bd. govs. Luth. Inst. Human Ecology; chmn. Chgo. Hosp. Council, 1952-55, now dir.; mem. Fed. Ct. Commn. Race Relations in Hosps. Chmn. trustees Am. Luth. Ch.; trustee, sec., counsel Norwegian Am. Hosp., Chgo. Mem. Am., Ill., Chgo. bar assns., Norwegian-Am., Ill. (life, pres.) hist. socs., Am. Scandinavian Found., Chgo. Hist. Soc. (life), Civil War Round Table. Republican. Lutheran. Clubs: Swedish, Law (life), Nordic Law (past pres.). Home: 3808 North Kildare Av Chicago IL 60641 Office: 120 S LaSalle St Chicago IL 60603

ABRAHAMSON, SHIRLEY SCHLANGER, (Mrs. Seymour Abrahamson), lawyer; b. N.Y.C., Dec. 17, 1933; d. Leo and Ceil (Sauerteig) Schlanger; A.B., N.Y.U., 1953; J.D., Ind. U., 1956; S.J.D., U. Wis., 1962; m. Seymour Abrahamson, Aug. 26, 1953; 1 son, Daniel Nathan. Asst. dir. Legislative Drafting Research Fund, Columbia U. Law Sch., 1957-60; admitted to Wis. bar, 1962, since practiced in Madison; mem. firm Lafollette, Sinykin, Anderson & Abrahamson, 1962—; prof. U. Wis. Sch. Law, 1966—. Mem. Mayor's Adv. Com., Madison, 1968-70; mem. Gov.'s Study Com. on Jud. Orgn., 1970—. Bd. dirs. League Women Voters, Madison, 1963-65, Union council Wis. Union, U. Wis., 1970-71; bd. dirs. Wis. Civil Liberties Union, 1968—, chmn. Capital Area chpt., 1969. Mem. Am., Wis., Dane County bar assns., Order of Coif, Phi Beta Kappa. Editor: Constitutions of the United States (National and State) 2 vols., 1962. Home: 2012 Waunona Way Madison WI 53713 Office: 110 E Main St Madison WI 53703

ABRAHAMSON, W. VINCENT, former pharm. co. exec.; b. Hinckley, Minn., June 15, 1915; s. Walfred August and Clara (Reed) A.; B.A., Gustavus Adolphus Coll., 1939; m. Pauline Pratt, Oct. 18, 1942; children—Mrs. Charles Eaton, Mrs. Joseph Elmer. With Ortho Pharm. Corp., Raritan, N.J., 1940-71, exec. v.p., 1963-64, pres., 1964-71; dir. Johnson & Johnson. Bd. dirs. Nat. Pharm. Council; trustee Somerset (N.J.) Hosp. Mem. Westfield (N.J.) Bd. Health Mem. Somerset County Republican Finance Com. Served with USAAF, 1942-45. Presbyn. Club: Plainfield (N.J.) Country.

ABRAM, DAVID EDWIN, banker; b. Beacon, Ia., Feb. 13, 1912; s. David John and Ann (Lloyd) A.; B.C.S., Drake U., 1934; m. Marguerite Hartley, on March 2d, 1935; children—Barbara Ann (Mrs. William Marksbery), Theodore David, Catherine Lynn (Mrs. John Crowley). Owner, Finance & Retail Lumber Co., Olympia, Wash., 1938-40; employee C.I.T. Corp., Memphis, 1934-38, 1940-42, Kaizer Ship-bldg. Corp., Portland, Ore., 1942-44; v.p. U.S. Nat. Bank of Ore., 1944, sr. v.p., 1962-68, exec. v.p., 1968—. Mem. lenders adv. com. FHA Title 1, 1955-60; former faculty Pacific Coast Sch. Banking, Seattle. Campaign chmn. United Good Neighbors Appeal, 1961, 1st v.p., 1962, 63, pres., 1963-64; past Ore. chmn. Nat. Fund for Med. Edn. Life trustee Lewis & Clark Coll.; bd. dirs. Emanuel Luth. Hosp. Mem. Ore. Hist. Soc. (dir.), Am. Bankers Assn. (installment credit commn. 1953-54), Portland Symphony Soc. (bd. dirs. 1955, 60-64), Portland C. of C. (chmn. bd. 1966-67), Alpha Tau Omega. Presbyn. (trustee). Clubs: University (Portland, Ore.); Arlington. Home: 4310 S W Fairview Circus Portland OR 97221 Office: U S Nat Bank 6th and Stark Portland OR 97204

ABRAM, MORRIS BERTHOLD, lawyer, former univ. pres.; b. Fitzgerald, Ga., June 19, 1918; s. Sam and Irene (Cohen) A.; A.B. summa cum laude, U. Ga., 1938; J.D., U. Chgo., 1940; B.A. (Rhodes scholar), Oxford U., 1948, M.A., 1953; m. Jane Maguire, Dec. 23, 1943; children—Ruth, Ann, Morris Berthold, Jonathan Adam, Joshua Anthony. Partner, Paul, Weiss, Rifkind, Wharton & Garrison, N.Y.C., 1962-68; pres. Brandeis Univ., Waltham, Mass., 1968-70; partner law firm Paul, Weiss, Goldberg, Rifkind, Wharton & Garrison, N.Y.C., 1970—. Pros. staff Internat. Mil. Tribunal, Nurnberg, Germany, 1946; asst. to dir. Com. for Marshall Plan, 1948; regional counsel WSB; gen. counsel Peace Corps, 1961; mem. subcom. on prevention of discrimination and protection of minorities UN, 1963-65; U.S. rep. UN Commn. Human Rights, 1965-68; mem. exec. com. President's Nat. Com. Community Relations, 1964-68; pres. Family Serv. Soc. of Fulton, DeKalb, Cobb counties, 1957-59; chmn. Atlanta Citizens Crime Com., 1958-60; nat. pres. Am. Jewish Com., 1963-68. Bd. dirs. 20th Century Fund; pres. Field Found., 1965—; bd. dirs. Morehouse Coll., Inst. Internat. Edn., Council Fgn. Relations; trustee Weizmann Inst. Sci., 1966—; chmn. United Negro Coll. Fund, 1970—; mem. Nat. Adv. Council Econ. Opportunity, 1967-68. Served to maj. USAAF, 1941-45. Decorated Legion of Merit, 1946. Fellow (hon.) Pembroke Coll., Oxford U. Mem. Lawyers Club Atlanta, N.Y. State, Am., Ga., Atlanta bar assns., Assn. Bar City N.Y., Phi Beta Kappa, Omicron Delta Kappa, Phi Kappa Phi. Co-author: How to Stop Violence in Your Community, 1950. Home: The Dakota 1W 72d St New York City NY 10023 Office: 345 Park Av New York City NY 10022

ABRAMOVITZ, MAX, architect; b. Chgo., May 23, 1908; s. Benjamin and Sophia (Maimon) A.; B.S., U. Ill., 1929; M.S., Columbia, 1931; grad. study Ecole des Beaux Arts, 1932-34; D.F.A. (hon.), U. Pitts., 1961, U. Ill., 1970; m. Anne Marie Causey, Sept. 4, 1937 (div.); children—Michael John, Katherine Paul (Mrs. John E. Coleman); m. 2d, Anita Zeltner Brooks, Feb. 29, 1964. Partner firm Harrison, Fouilhoux & Abramovitz, architects, 1940, Harrison & Abramovitz, N.Y.C., 1945—; asso. prof. Yale Sch. Fine Arts, 1939-42; dep. dir. UN Hdqrs. Planning Office, 1947-52. Cons. Brandeis U., U. Pitts. Trustee Mt. Sinai Hosp., N.Y.C. Served with C.E., AUS, 1942-45; col., 1950-52; spl. asst. to asst. sec. air force, Mar. 1952-July 1952. Recipient Legion of Merit; fellow Brandeis U., 1963; Achievement award U. Ill. Alumni Assn., 1963. Fellow A.I.A.; mem. Am. Soc. C.E., Regional Plan Assn. (chmn. bd. 1966-68, dir. 1968—), Archtl. League N.Y., N.Y. Bldg. Congress (gov. 1957-64). Club: Century Assn. (N.Y.C.). Prin. works include U.S. Embassy Bldg., Rio de Janeiro, Columbia U. Law Sch. and Library, Hilles Library of Radcliffe Coll. U. Ia. Art Mus., Philharmonic Hallat Lincoln Center, U.S. Steel Bldg., Pitts. Assembly Hall and Krannert Center Performing Arts, U. Ill.-Urbana, 3 chapels Brandeis U., La Banque Rothschild, Paris, France. Home: 431 E 85th St New York City NY 10022 Office: 630 Fifth Av New York City NY 10020

ABRAMOVITZ, MOSES, economist, educator; b. Bklyn., Jan. 1, 1912; s. Nathan and Betty (Goldenberg) A.; A.B., Harvard, 1932; Ph.D., Columbia, 1939; m. Carrie Glasser, June 23, 1937; 1 son, Joel Nathan. Instr. Harvard, 1936-38; mem. research staff Nat. Bur. Econ. Research, 1938-69; lectr. Columbia, 1940-42, 46-48; prof. econs. Stanford, 1948—, exec. head dept. econs., 1963-65. Vis. prof. U. Pa., 1955; prin. Economist WPB, 1942, OSS, 1943-44; econ. adviser to U.S. rep. on Allied Commn. on Reparations, 1945-46, to Sec.-gen. Orgn. for Econ. Coop. and Devel., 1962-63; vis. fellow All Souls Coll., Oxford, Eng., 1968. Served as lt. AUS, 1944-45. Fellow Am. Acad. Arts and Sciences; mem. Am. Econ. Assn., Am. Econ. History Ass., Am. Statis. Assn., Phi Beta Kappa. Author: Price Theory for a Changing Economy, 1939; Inventories and Business Cycles, 1950; (with Vera Eliasberg) The Growth of Public Employment in Great Britain, 1957. Editor; Capital Formation and Economic Growth, 1955. Home: 543 West Crescent Drive Palo Alto CA 94301 Office: Stanford University Stanford CA 94305

ABRAMOWICZ, ALFRED L., Cath. aux. bishop Archdiocese Chgo. Address: 211 E Chicago Av Chicago IL 60611 *

ABRAMOWITZ, MORTON I Fgn. service officer; b. Lakewood, N.J., Jan. 20, 1933; s. Mendel and Dora (Smith) A.; B.A., Stanford; M.A., Harvard, 1955; m. Sheppie Glass, Sept. 13, 1959; children-Michael, Rachel. Joined U.S. Fgn. Service, 1960; 3rd sec., vice consul, Tapei, Formosa, 1960-62; with Fgn. Area and Lan. Tng. Center, Taichung, Taiwan, 1962-63; consul, Polit. officer, Hong Kong, 1963-66; assigned Bur. Econ. Affairs, 1966-68; Sr. Inter dept. Group, 1968-69; spl. asst. under-sec. state, 1969—. Served with AUS, 1957. Mem. Phi Beta Kappa. Author articles aspects Taiwan's econ. growth Home: 5026 Klingle St N W Washington DC 20008 Office: Dept State Washington DC 20520

ABRAMS, AL, sports editor Pitts. Post-Gazette. Address: 50 Blvd of Allies Pittsburgh PA 15222 *

ABRAMS, BERNARD BRADSON, engr., ret. army officer; b. Cedar Rapids, Ia., Apr. 19, 1913; s. Harry and Selma (Petkere) A.; B.S., The Citadel, 1935; C.E., 1940; LL.B., Blackstone Coll. Law, 1948; student Ill. Inst. Tech., 1930-31, George Washington U. Law Sch., 1942-44, Loyola U., Chgo., 1936, Robertson Bus. Coll., Dallas, 1949, various army schs.; m. Jacque Rose Line, Nov. 17, 1950; children—Elizabeth Jerome, Bradson Renard; 1 stepson, Charles Kent Line. Comdt. Ga. Mil. Acad., College Park, Aug.-Dec. 1935; acct. comdt. Gulf Coast Mil. Acad., Gulfport, Miss., Jan.-June 1936; city engr., Terrell, Tex., 1937-39; head dept. engring. Tex. Mil. Coll., Terrell, 1936-38, comdt. and prof. mil. sci. and tactics, 1938-42, pres., 1946, sec. bd. trustees, 1947—, pres. emeritus, 1949. Commd. 2d lt. Corps. Engrs., U.S. Army Res., 1935, advanced through grades to col. Ordnance Corps, 1951; active duty ETO and MTO, World War II; comdr. res. orgns., 1947-49; duty with Tex. N.G., 1949-51; mem. Army Uniform Bd., 1953; exec. officer army div. N.G. Bur., U.S. Army, Washington, 1954-55, comdg. officer Tokorozawa Ordnance Depot and Fuchu Shops, 1955-56, commanding officer United States Army Logistical Depot, Japan, 1957-58; comdg. officer Rossford Ordnance Depot, 1958-60; chief repair parts br. Army Ordnance, 1960-62; chief depot operations div. Army Materiel Command, Washington, 1962-63; chmn. Army Packaging Bd., 1963-64; comdg. officer Savanna Army Depot, comdt. Army Ammunition Sch., Savanna Ill., 1964-67; chmn. Armed Services Explosives Safety Bd., Dept. Def., Washington, 1967-70; dir. phys. plant Longwood Coll., Farmville, Va., 1970—. Pres. Westmore P.T.A., Fairfax, Va., 1962-63; mem. exec. bd. Highland Community Coll., Freeport, Ill., 1966-67. Decorated Nat. Def. Service medal with oak leaf cluster, Army Commendation Ribbon with 2 oak leaf clusters, European-Africa-Middle East campaign, Am. Theater and World War II Victory medal, Armed Forces Res. medal, Legion of Merit with 2 oak leaf clusters. Registered profl. engr., Tex., D.C., S.C., Ohio, Ill., Md., Va. Mem. Packaging Inst., Am. Inst. Indsl. Engrs. (chmn. exec. com. of mgmt. div., dir., Assn. U.S. Army, Nat. Rifle Assn., Am. Inst. Mining and Metall. Engrs., Nat. Soc. Profl. Engrs., Am. Soc. Safety Engrs., Scabbard and Blade, Phi Theta Kappa, Delta Theta Phi, Tau Beta Pi. Methodist. Club: Austin, Ft. McNair Officers, Rotary, Wedgewood Country. Author: Evolution of Accuracy and Range, 1944. Contbr. numerous articles to ednl., tech. and mil. jours. Home: Rt 1 Box 146 Burkeville VA 23922 Office: Longwood Coll Farmville VA 23901

ABRAMS, CREIGHTON WILLIAMS, army officer; b. Springfield, Mass., Sept. 15, 1914; s. Creighton W. and Nellie (Randall) A.; B.S., U.S. Mil. Acad., 1936; grad. Command and Gen. Staff Coll., 1949, Army War Coll., 1953; m. Julia Harvey, Aug. 3O, 1936; children—Noel (Mrs. William J. Bradley), Creighton Williams, John Nelson, Jeanne Rejane, Elizabeth Harvey, Robert Bruce. Commd. 2d lt. U.S. Army, 1936, advanced through grades to gen. 1964; troop officer 1st Cav. Div., 1936; assigned 1st Armored Div., 194O; successively regtl. adj., regtl. exec. officer, battalion comdr., combat command comdr. 4th Armored Div., 1941-45; assigned War Dept. Gen. 1945-46; dir. tactics Armored Sch., 1946-48; comdr. 63d Tank Battalion, Europe, 1949- 53; chief staff I Corps, Korea, 1953, X Corps, Korea, 1954, IX Corps, Korea, 1954; chief staff Armored Center, 1955-56; dep. asst. chief staff res. components Dept. Army Gen. Staff, 1956-59; asst. div. comdr. 3d Armored Div., 1959-60; dep. chief staff operations Hdgrs. U.S. Army Europe, 1960; div. comdr. 3d Armored Div., 1960-62; asst. dep. chief staff mil. operations for civil affairs Dept. Army, 1962—; dir. operations Office Dept. Chief Staff Mil. Operations, 1962; asst. dep. chief staff mil. operations and requirements and programs Dept. Army, 1962-63, dep. asst. chief staff force devel., 1963; comdg. gen. V Corps, 1963-64; vice chief staff, 1964-67; dep. comdr. U.S. Mil. Assistance Command, Vietnam, 1967-68; comdg. gen. U.S. forces Vietnam, 1968—. Decorated D.S.C. with oak leaf cluster, D.S.M. with 3 oak leaf clusters, Silver Star with Oak leaf; Legion of Merit with oak leaf, Bronze Star with V device; Chevalier Legion Honor, Croix de Guerre (France); Distinguished Service Order (Great Britian); Ulchi Distinguished Service medal with gold star, Order Nat. Security Merit 2d class (Korea); knight grand cross 1st class Most Noble Order Crown Thailand. Address: COMUSMACV hdqrs USMACV APO San Francisco, CA 96222

ABRAMS, DAVID N., mfr.; b. Pitts., Aug. 17, 1929; s. Harry and Bess (Young) A.; B.S., U. Pitts., 1952; postgrad. U. Mich., 1954; m. Marjorie G. Peresman, May 3, 1953; children—Ellen Sue, Beth Lynn. Project engr. Koppers Co., Pitts., 1953; mgr. comml. marketing United Aircraft Corp., East Hartford, Conn., 1953-65; with Pioneer Systems, Inc., Manchester, Conn., 1965—, pres., dir., 1969—; dir. Parachute Industries S. Africa, Pioneer Aerodyne (Israel). Corporator Manchester Meml. Hosp. Mem. Manchester C. of C. (dir.). Home: 21 Hollister Dr West Hartford CT 06117 Office: Pioneer Industrial Park Manchester CT 06040

ABRAMS, EARL BERNARD, editor; b. N.Y.C., Feb. 18, 1911; s. Harry H. and Ethel (Shapiro) A.; student U. Va., 193O-32, N.J. Tchrs. Coll., Montclair, 1935; m. Helen Ruth Lesser, June 22, 1941; children—Susan Laurie (Mrs. Daniel A. Hall). Alice Deborah (Mrs. Alan Rose). With Bergen Evening Record, Hackensack, N.J., 1934-36, Asso. Press, Newark, 1936-37, Washington Post, 1937-40; editor Televison Digest, Washington, 1945-51; asso. editor Broadcasting mag., Washington, 1951-58, sr. editor, 1958—. Dir. adult edn. program, Fair Lawn, N.J., 1935-36; tech. information specialist Office Chief Signal Officer, AUS, 1941-45. Mem. Congl. Periodical Galleries (exec. committee), White House Corr. Assn., I.E.E.E. (assoc.), Alpha Epsilon Pi. Club: National Press (Washington). Home: 3518 N Utah St Arlington VA 22207 Office: 1735 DeSales St Washington DC 20036

ABRAMS, EUGENE BERNARD, orgn. exec.; b. Trenton, N.J., Oct. 10, 1919; s. Herman and Sarah (Hirschson) A.; student U. So. Cal., 1946-47, U. Paris (France), 1947- 48; B.A., U. Md., 1956; m. Monique Leiba, Apr. 28, 1950; nique Segal, Jacqueline Segal. Join-d U.S. Fgn. Service, 1948; assigned Embassy, Paris, 1948-51, ECA mission to France, 1951-52, ECA office spl. rep., Paris, 1952-58; with Office African Affairs, ICA, Washington 1958- 61; dep. dir. AID mission to Guinea, Conakry, 1961-63; AID affairs officer Abidjan, Ivory Coast, 1963-65; chief tech. assistance policies div. OECD, Paris, 1965-67, head econ. devel. div., 1967-68; dir. tech. assistance Orgn. for Rehab. Through Tng., 1968—. Served to 2d lt., USAAF, 1939-45. Mem. Soc. Internat. Devel. (vice chmn. Swiss chpt.), Internat. Council Voluntary Agys. (chmn. econ. and social devel. commn.). Home: 6 Chemin Haute Belotte 1222 Vesenaz, Switzerland. Office: ORT 1 Rue de VArembé Geneva Switzerland

ABRAMS, GEORGE JOSEPH, mgmt. and marketing exec.; b. Hoboken, N.J., Feb. 14, 1918; s. Leo and May (Hipp) A.; B.S. magna cum laude, N.Y. U., 1947, M.B.A., 1949; m. Mary Della Sablom, Nov. 15, 1941; 1 dau., Adele Lois. Staff writer Evening Transcript, Orange, N.J., 1934- 36; asst. to advt. dir. Nat. Biscuit Co., N.Y.C., 1936-41; product advt. mgr. Whitehall Pharmacal Co., N.Y.C., 1941-46; dir. market research Eversharp, Inc., N.Y.C., 1946-47; v.p. sales and advt. Block Drug Co., Jersey City, 1947-55; v.p. in charge advt. Revlon, Inc., N.Y.C., 1955- 59; pres., chief exec. officer cosmetics and toiletries div. Warner- Lambert Pharm. Co., 1959-60; v.p. corporate devel. J.B. Williams Corp. 1960-62; pres. Maradel Products, Inc., N.Y.C., 1962-65; sr. v.p. high marketing exec. William Esty Co., 1965-67; exec. v.p. Reach, McClinton & Co., 1967-69; pres. Cole Fischer Rogow, N.Y.C., 1969-71, George J. Abrams & Assos., N.Y.C., 1971—. Lectr. advt. mgmt. N.Y. U. Grad Sch. Bus. Adminstrn., 1951-54; mem. adv. bd. Printers' Ink, N.Y.C. Trustee East Orange (N.J.) Gen. Hosp. Served as lt. (j.g.) USNR, 1942-45. Named Outstanding Young Advt. Man of Year, Assn. Advt. Men and Women N.Y., 1954, Man of Year, Bklyn. Philharmonia, 1970; recipient achievement award Advt. Club of Washington, 1958; Free Enterprise Assn. award, 1964. Mem. Advt. Club N.J. (gov. 1955), Assn. Nat. Advertisers (Industry's Man of Year award 1970, chmn. drug and toiletry group, chmn. radio-TV com., chmn. advt. mgmt., newspaper cons.), Beta Gamma Sigma, Alpha Delta Sigma (award for advt. mgmt. 1958), Alpha Phi Sigma. Club: Pinnacle (N.Y.C.); Curzon (London). Contbr. articles to trade mags., Ency. Americana. Home: Claridge House Verona NJ 07044 Office: 110 E 59th St New York City NY 10022

ABRAMS, HARRY NATHAN, publisher; b. London, Eng., Dec. 8, 1904; s. Morris and Millie Abrahams; student N.Y.U., N.A.D., Art Students League of N.Y.; m. Nina Bolotoff, Mar. 5, 1932; children—Michael David, Robert Elihu. Art dir., prodn. mgr. Schwab & Beatty Advt. Agy., 1928-36; art dir., prodn. mgr. Book-of-the-Month Club, Inc., 1936-47, dir., 1947-50; pres. Harry N. Abrams, Inc., art book publs., N.Y.C., 1950—. Home: 33 E 70th St New York City NY 10021 Office: 110 E 59th St New York City NY 10022

ABRAMS, HERBERT KERMAN, physician, educator; b. Chgo., 1913; M.S., U. Ill., 1940; M.P.H., Johns Hopkins, 1947. Intern, Cook County Hosp., Chgo., 1940-41; chief Bur. of Adult Health, Cal. Health Dept., 1947-52; dir. Chgo. Union Health Service, 1953-66; dir. dept. community medicine Mt. Sinai Hosp., Chgo., 1966-68; prof., head dept. community medicine U. Ariz., Tucson, 1968—. Served with USPHS. Mem. A.M.A., Am. Pub. Health Assn., Internat. Med. Assn. Office: Dept Community Medicine Sch of Medicine U Ariz Tucson AZ 85721*

ABRAMS, HERBERT LEROY, radiologist, educator; b. N.Y.C., Aug. 16, 1920; s. Morris and Freda (Sugarman) A.; B.A., Cornell U., 1941; M.D., State U. Medicine, N.Y., 1946; m. Marilyn Spitz, Mar. 23, 1943; children—Nancy (Mrs. Harlan Jacobson), John. Intern L.I. Coll. Hosp., 1946-47; resident internal medicine Montefiore Hosp., Bronx, N.Y., 1947-48; resident radiology Stanford Univ. Hosp., 1948-51; practice medicine, specializing in radiology, Stanford, Cal., 1951-67; faculty Sch. Medicine Stanford, 1951-67, dir. div. diagnostic roentgenology, 1961-67, prof. radiology, 1962-67; Philip H. Cook prof. radiology, chmn. dept. radiology Harvard, 1967—; radiologist-in-chief Peter Bent Brigham Hosp., Boston, 1967—.

Radiation study sect. NIH, 1962-66; cons. survey renovascular hypertension Nat. Heart Inst.; cons. to hosps., profl. socs.; lectr., vis. faculty numerous univs., profl. socs. Nat. Cancer Inst. fellow, 1950; Spl. Research fellow Nat. Heart Inst., 1960; Malcolm Rogers Meml. lectr. Wis. Heart Assn., 1963; David M. Gould Meml. lectr. Johns Hopkins, 1964. Diplomate Am. Bd. Radiology. Mem. Assn. U. Radiologists, Am. Coll. Radiology, A.A.A.S., Am. Assn. Cancer Research, Soc. Chmn. Acad. Radiology Depts. (pres. 1970-71), A.M.A. Author: (with H.S. Kaplan) Angiocardiographic Interpretation in Congenital Heart Disease, 1956; (with others) Congenital Heart Disease, 1965. Editor: Angiography, 1971; Investigative Radiology. Contbr. articles profl. jours. Home: 294 Buckminster Rd Brookline MA 02146 Office: Harvard Med Sch Boston MA 02115

ABRAMS, IRWIN, educator; b. San Francisco, Feb. 24, 1914; s. J. Lewis and Belle (Newman) A.; A.B. with great distinction, Stanford, 1934; A.M., Harvard, 1935, Ph.D., 1938; m. Freda Webster Morrill, June 30, 1939; children—David Morrill, Carol Webster (Mrs. C. Peter Lundin), James Lawrence. Instr. history Stanford, 1938-43; personnel officer, dir. fgn. service tng. Am. Friends Service Com., 1943-46, dir. Quaker Overseas Work Camps, 1946-47; mem. faculty Antioch Coll., 1947—, prof. history, 1951—, chmn., dept., 1949-60, 64-66. Specialist, State Dept. exchange program, Germany, 1953; chmn. internat. student seminars Am. Friends Service Com., Europe, summers 1956, 57,64; ednl. dir. shipboard programs Council Student Travel, summers 1956-64: Fulbright lectr. U. Cologne (Germany), 1961; dir. Yugoslav seminar Great Lakes Colls. Assn., summers 1965-67, 69-70; adv. council grad. fellowship program Danforth Found., 1969—; cons. on internat. edn. U.S., Office Edn.; bd. dirs. Council Internat. Ednl. Exchange; co-ordinator internat. programs Great Lakes Coll. Assn., 1967—. Sheldon Traveling fellow Harvard, 1936-37. Mem. Am. Hist. Assn., Internat. Studies Assn., Am. Assn. Advancement Slavic Studies, Soc. of Religion in Higher Edn. (postdoctoral fellow 1951), Phi Beta Kappa. Mem. Soc. of Friends. Author (with others) History of World Civilization, 1957; Study Abroad, 1960; (with others) Journey Through a Wall: A Quaker Mission to Divided Germany, 1964; (with David Arnold) The American College and International Education, 1967. Bd. editors Antioch Rev., 1955-71. Home: 913 Xenia Av Yellow Springs OH 45387

ABRAMS, MANUEL, fgn. service officer; b. Phila., Jan. 18, 1919; s. Morris and Bessie (Monas) A.; B.S., Coll. City N.Y., 1939; student Am. U., 1941-44; m. Sylvia D. Shapiro, Aug. 6, 1940; children—Mona, Gabrielle. Clk., Dept. Commerce, War Dept., 1940-41; statistician, economist WPB, 1941-46; financial analyst UNRRA, 1946; program requirements analyst Nat. Housing Agy., 1946-47; internat. economist Dept. Commerce, 1947-50; with Dept. State, 1950—, fgn. service officer, 1959—; asst. chief finance and program div. ECA, Frankfurt and Bonn, Germany, 1950-55, dir. econ. div. U.S. Mission to Regional Orgn., Paris, France, 1955-58; asst. chief econ. development div. Dept. State, 1959, officer in charge European Econ. Orgn. Affairs 1960-62; econ. counselor Am. Embassy, The Hague, 1962-66, assigned Fgn. Service Inst., 1966-67; minister counselor econ., comml. affairs Rome, 1967-69; dep chief U.S. Mission to European NATO, 1957-58; adviser U.S. delegation OECD, 1960. Mem. Phi Beta Kappa. 436 Blvd Lambermont Brussels Office: USEC Brussels Belgium

ABRAMS, MEYER HOWARD, educator; b. Long Branch, N.J., July 23, 1912; s. Joseph and Sarah (Shanes) A.; A.B., Harvard, 1934, M.A., 1937, Ph.D., 1940; student (Henry fellow), Cambridge (Eng.) U., 1934-35; m. Ruth Gaynes, Sept. 1, 1937; children—Jane, Judith. Instr. Harvard, 1938-42, research asso. psycho-acoustic lab., 1942-45; asst. prof. English, Cornell U. Ithaca, N.Y., 1945-47, asso. prof., 1947-53, prof., 1953-60, Frederic J. Whiton prof. English, 1960—; adv. editor W.W. Norton & Co., Inc., 1961—; bd. editors various Cornell publs. Fulbright lectr. Royal U. Malta, Cambridge U., 1953; Roache lectr. U. Ind., 1963; Alexander lectr. U. Toronto, 1964. Rockefeller fellow, 1946, Ford fellow, 1952, Guggenheim fellow, 1958, 60-61; fellow Center for Advanced Study in the Behavioral Scis., Stanford U., 1967-68. Recipient Christian Gauss prize Phi Beta Kappa, 1954. Mem. Am. Assn. U. Profs., Modern Lang. Assn. (exec. council 1961-64), Am. Acad. Arts and Scis., Phi Beta Kappa, Sigma Xi. Club: Century Association (N.Y.C.). Author: The Milk of Paradise, 1934, 2d edit., 1970; publs. on mil. communications, 1942-45; The Mirror and the Lamp: Romantic Theory and the Critical Tradition, 1953; A Glossary of Literary Terms, 1957, rev. edit., 1970; Natural Supernaturalism: Tradition and Revolution in Romantic Literature, 1971. Editor: The Poetry of Pope, 1954; Literature and Belief., 1958; The Romantic Poets: Modern Essays in Criticism, 1960; The Norton Anthology of English Literature, 1962; rev. 1968. Home: 512 Highland Rd Ithaca NY 14850

ABRAMS, MILTON CHARLES, librarian, educator; b. Logan, Utah, Nov. 22, 1918; s. George and Nettie (Schenk) A.; B.A. in Polit. Sci., Utah State U., 1948, M.A., 1952; Ph.D., U. Utah, 1963; m. Lois Allred, Mar. 13, 1956; children by previous marriage—Douglas, Kathleen, Sharon. High sch. prin., Ida., 1946-47, tchr.-librarian, 1948-49; asso. librarian Utah State U., 1949- 55, univ. librarian, 1956-65, asso. prof. library sci., 1957—, asso. prof. polit. sci., 1964-65, prof. polit. sci., 1966—. Mem. Utah Democratic Central Com., 1965—; sec. Cache County Dem. party, 1965—, chmn., 1966-69. Served with AUS, 1942-46, 51-52. Recipient Robins Achievement award Utah State U., 1965. Mem. Mountain Plains (pres. 1959), Utah (pres. 1958) library assns., Utah Hist. Soc. (trustee). Mem. Ch. of Jesus Christ of Latter-day Saints (missionary 1939-41). Author essay. Home: 505 E Park View Circle Smithfield UT 84335

ABRAMS, MONROE ROBERT, audio-visual co. exec.; b. N.Y.C., Apr. 3, 1926; s. David and Jayne (Rein) A.; B.S. in Civil Engring., Antioch Coll., 1950; postgrad. Coll. City N.Y., 1950-51; m. Helen Peirez, Oct. 16, 1949; children—Ronald, Douglas, Jayne. Chemist Best Foods, Bayonne, N.J., 1950; salesman Penn Life Ins. Co., N.Y.C., 1951; with sales dept. Viewlex Inc., N.Y.C., 1951-60, officer, dir., 1960-70, exec. v.p., 1970—; dir. Sonic Recording Co., Monarch Record Pressing Co., Globe Albums & Prodns. Inc., Buddah Record Co., Bell Sound Studies, Andrew-Nunnary Paper & Envelope Co., Am. Record Pressing Co., Allentown Record Co. Trustee Louis A. Peirez Found. Served with USAAF, 1944-46; PTO. Mem. Nat. Audiovisual Assos., Nat. Cath. Edn. Asso., Asso. Ednl. and Communications Tech., N.Y. State Ednl. Communications Council, Robert E. Lee Assos. Washington and Lee U., Union Am. Hebrew Congregations. Democrat. Home: 5 Woods Lane Roslyn NY 11576 Office: 1 Broadway Av Holbrook NY 11741

ABRAMS, NORMAN, legal educator; b. Chgo., July 7, 1933; s. Harry A. and Gertrude (Dick) A.; A.B., U. Chgo., 1952, J.D., 1955. Admitted to Ill. bar, 1956; asso.- in-law Columbia Law Sch., 1955-57; research asso. Harvard Law Sch., 1957- 59; sec. Harvard-Brandeis Coop. Research for Israel's Legal Devel., 1957- 58, dir., 1959; mem. faculty U. Cal. at Los Angeles Law Sch., 1959-, prof. law, 1964—; vis. prof. Hebrew U., 1969-70, Bar Ilan U., 1970-71; spl. asst. to U.S. atty. gen., also prof.-in- residence, criminal div. dept. Justice, 1966-67. Reporter for So. Cal. indigent accused persons study Am. Bar Found., 1963; cons. Gov. Cal. Commn. Los Angeles Riots, 1965, Pres.'s. Commn. Law Enforcement and Adminstrn. Justice, 1966, Nat. Commn. on Reform of Fed. Criminal Laws, 1967—; spl. hearing officer conscientious objector cases U.S. Dept. Justice, 1967-68. Mem. law and justice task force Greater Los Angeles Urban Coalition. Mem. Am. Bar Assn. (membership chmn. Cal. sect. Criminal law 1964, vice chmn. com. on research sect. Criminal law 1968), Phi Deta Kappa. Office: 405 Hilgard Av Los Angeles CA 90024

ABRAMS, RICHARD, biochemist, educator; b. Chgo., Sept. 19, 1917; s. David and Matilda (Hornstein) A.; B.S., U. Chgo., 1938, Ph.D., 1941; m. Thelma E. Peterson, Oct. 31, 1947; children-Peter Arnold, Erika Karen, Kersti Elida, Lauren Jan. Staff, U. Chgo., 1941-46, group leader Manhattan Project, 1942-46, asst. prof. Inst. Radiobiology and Biophysics, 1947- 51; fellow Donner Found., Karolinska Inst., Stockholm, Sweden, 1946-47; asso. dir. Research Inst., Montefiore Hosp., Pitts., 1951-58, dir., 1958- 65; mem. faculty dept. biochemistry and nutrition U. Pitts. Grad. Sch. Pub. Health, 1959—, prof., head dept., 1965-70, prof., chmn. dept. biochemistry Faculty Arts & Scis., 1970—. Cons. neurochemistry VA Labs., Pitts., 1958-64; mem. com. on Leukemia and cancer Health Research and Service Found., 1964—; study sect. mem. NIH, 1966—. Fellow A.A.A.S.; mem. Am. Soc. Biol. Chemists, Am. Chem. Soc., Biochem. Soc. (London, Eng.), N.Y. Acad. Scis. Contbr. articles profl. jours. Home: 5315 Westminster Rd Pittsburgh PA 15232

ABRAMS, RICHARD, jazz musician, composer; m. Peggy Abrams; children—Richard, Richarda. Founder, Chgo.'s new jazz movement; leader Exptl. Band; founder, pres. Am. Assn. for Advancement Creative Musicians; influenced devel. Lester Bowie, Joseph Jarman, Roscoe Mitchell, others; rec. artist for Delmark Records. Address: 6828 S Evans Av Chicago IL 60637

ABRAMS, TALBERT, photogrammetrist, instrument mfr., sci. cons. and explorer; b. Tekonsha, Mich., Aug 17, 1895; s. William Blodgett and Sarah Elizabeth (Bruner), A.; student U.S. Naval Aero. Sch., Pensacola, Fla., 1917; D.Sc. (hon.), Mich. Coll. Mining and Tech., 1952; Eng. D. (hon.), Mich. State U., 1961; m. Leota Fry, Jan. 15, 1923. Transport pilot U.S. Air Mail Service, 1920, Mich. Aero. Service Corp., 1921; v.p. Mich. Airways, 1922; pres. Abrams Aerial Survey Corp., 1923- 58, chmn. bd. dirs.; 1958—; pres. Abrams Aircraft Corp., 1936-44, Abrams Instrument Corp. (merged with Curtiss-Wright Corp. 1961), 1937-61, Airlandia, Inc., 1954—, Aerial Explorers Corp., 1961—; chmn. bd. Abrams Aerial Survey Corp.; sci. cons. Curtiss- Wright Corp.; dir. Photogrammetry, Inc., Washington Apts., Inc., Lansing, Bank Lansing; founder Abrams Research & Test Center, Mich., 1955; mapped Isle Royale, 1929, large areas for U.S. Govt., 1917—, P.R., 1935-37, Dominican Republic, W.I., 1940-41, Cuba, 1935-44, Liberian Survey Firestone Plantations Co.; Mem. U.S. Navy-NSF Operation Deep Freeze, 1963-67; numerous aerial surveys fgn. countries; del. sev. internat. congresses; served in civilian capacity for USMC. U.S. Army, USAF, USN. Pres. Talbert & Leota Abrams Found., 1960—. Served with aviation sect. USMC, 1917-19. Recipient Civilian Service award U.S. Army; Order Arctic Realm, USAF Alaska; Hon. Centennial award Mich. State U., 1955; Community Service award City of Lansing, Mich., 1962; Order of Magellan, Circumnavigators Club, 1963; apptd. indsl. ambassador State Mich., 1958. Fellow Am. Geog. Soc.; mem. N.A.M. (nuclear energy com.), Am. Soc. C.E., (hon.), Am. Soc. Photogrammetry (pres. 1951, hon. life mem. 1962), Mich. Soc. Engrs. (hon.), Mich. Soc. Profl. Engrs. (hon.), Australian Inst. Cartographers, Quiet Birdmen, Am. Legion, Vets. of Fgn. Wars, First Marine Aviation Force Vets. Assn., Last Man Pioneer Air Mail Club, Chi Epsilon (hon.). Mason. Clubs: Rotary, Explorers, Wings (New York City, N.Y.); Lansing (Michigan) Country. Author: The Essentials of Aerial Surveys and Photo Interpretation (used as textbook, U.S.M.C., Army and Navy). Donor Talbert Abrams award, Am. Soc. Photogrammetry 1944- 75; donor Talbert and Leota Abrams Planetarium to Mich. State U., 1961, Meridian-Base Line Surveyors Park to State of Mich., 1967; loaned Stratoplane Explorer to Nat. Air Mus., Smithsonian Instn., Washington. Inventor Abrams Contour Finder, 1929, Abrams Stratoplane Explorer, 1938, 16 mm. gun camera, radar cameras, Army steroscopes, intervalometers, photogrammetric computers. Flights around the World, 1948, 58, 59, 61, 63, 66; visited 96 countries since World War II, South Pole, 1964, 66. Transport pilot. Home: 1310 Cambridge Rd Lansing MI 48910 Office: 124 Larch St Lansing MI 48910

ABRAMSON, ARNOLD ERNEST, publisher; b. N.Y.C., Oct. 12, 1914; s. Henry and Libbie (Tunick) A.; student pub. schs.; m. Doris T. Waters, Nov. 25, 1935; children—Peter, Laurie. With circulation dept. Macfadden Publs., Inc., N.Y.C. and Trenton, N.J., 1935-37, traveling supr. Midwest states, 1937-39; circulation mgr. Farrell Pub. Corp., 1939-41, gen. mgr., v.p., 1941-50; organized Universal Pub. & Distbg. Corp., N.Y.C., 1947, pres., chmn. bd., 1947—; chmn. Universal-Tandem Pub. Co., Ltd., London, pub. Ski mag., Ski Bus. mag., Golf mag., Ski Area Mgmt. mag., Golfdom mag., Family Handyman mag., Home Garden mag., others; pub. Award House Books, Award Books, Vocational Guidance Manuals, Rumapo House. Served to capt., inf., N.Y. N.G., 1942-47. Mem. Golf Writer's Assn., Ski Writer's Assn. Clubs: Dellwood Golf; Lake Isle Golf; Sun Valley Ski; Overseas Press; Yacht. Home: Laurel Hill Dr Pleasantville NY 10570 also Wilmington VT 05363 Office: 235 W 45th St New York City NY 10017 also 670 White Plains Rd East Chester NY 10583

ABRAMSON, ARTHUR SEYMOUR, educator; b. Jersey City, Jan. 26, 1925; s. Seymour and Vallie (Olshan) A.; B.A., Yeshiva U., 1949; M.A., Columbia, 1950, Ph.D., 1960; m. Ruby Melamed, June 22, 1952; children—Joseph Benjamin, David Nathan. Mem. research staff Haskins Labs., New Haven, 1959—, acting head of speech research, 1964-65; asso. prof. speech Queens Coll., City U. N.Y., 1963-64, prof., 1965-67; prof., head, dept. linguistics U. Conn., 1967—. Served with AUS, 1943-46. Fulbright grantee, Thailand, 1953-55. Mem. Acoustical Soc. Am., A.A.A.S., Internat. Phonetic Assn., Internat. Soc. Phonetic Scis., Internat. Linguistic Assn., Modern Lang. Assn. Am., Linguistic Soc. Am., Siam Soc., Asia Soc. Author: The Vowels and Tones of Standard Thai: Acoustical Measurements and Experiments, 1962, also articles; asso. editor Vol. 12 Current Trends in Linguistics. Home: Rural Route 2 Storrs CT 06268

ABRAMSON, ARTHUR SIMON, educator, physician; b. Montreal, Que., Can., June 4, 1912; s. Jacob J. and Dora (Rosenthal) A.; B.S., McGill U., 1933, M.D., 1937; m. Ruth Mary Rumsey, Aug. 1, 1956; 1 son, Daniel Rumsey. Came to U.S., 1937, naturalized, 1942. Intern Newark Beth Israel Hosp., 1938-39; resident Royal Victoria Hosp., Montreal, Que., Can., 1939-40, Montefiore Hosp., N.Y.C., 1940-41, Hosp. Joint Diseases, N.Y.C., 1941-42, Bronx VA Hosp., 1946-48; practice medicine, specializing in phys. medicine and rehab., N.Y.C., 1948—; chief phys. medicine and rehab. service Bronx VA Hosp., 1950-55; clin. prof. phys. medicine and rehab. N.Y. Med. Coll., 1950-55; prof., chmn. dept. rehab. medicine Albert Einstein Coll. Medicine, 1955—. Cons. Kingsbrook Med. Center, Misericordia, Beth Abraham, VA hosps., Montrose, Bronx, and East Orange. Mem. Gov. Rockefeller's Council Rehab. Adminstrn., 1961-65; mem. Nat. Commn. Edn. Phys. Medicine and Rehab.; mem. med. expert com. Am. Rehab. Found. Served to maj. AUS, 1942-46. Named N.Y.C. Disabled Man of Year, 1948; recipient President's trophy Handicapped Man of Year, 1956. Diplomate Am. Bd. Phys. Medicine and Rehab. (vice chmn.). Fellow N.Y. Acad. Medicine, Acad. Phys. Medicine and Rehab. (pres. 1971—), A.C.P.; mem. N.Y. Acad. Scis., A.M.A., Am. Congress Rehab. Medicine (recipient Gold Key award 1966), Am. Rheumatism Assn. Contbr. articles profl. jours. Home: Hawthorne Way Hartsdale NY 10530 Office: Albert Einstein Coll Medicine Morris Park Av Bronx NY 10461

ABRAMSON, DAVID IRVIN, physician, educator; b. N.Y.C., Oct. 14, 1905; s. Aaron and Anna (Oschrin) A.; student Coll. City N.Y., 1922-23, Columbia, 1923-24; M.D., L.I. Coll. Medicine, 1929; m. Louise Felson, Aug. 17, 1940; children—Julie Syril, Marian Beth. Intern, Bushwick Hosp., Bklyn., 1929-30; pvt. practice peripheral vascular disease, Chgo., 1946—; instr. physiology L.I. Coll. Medicine, 1930-36; dir. cardiovascular research May Inst. Med. Research, Cin., 1938-42; asst. prof. medicine U. Ill., 1946-54, asso. prof. 1954-55, prof. dept. medicine, head dept. phys. medicine and rehab., 1955—; cons. Hines and West Side VA Hosp.; attending physician Michael Reese, Mt. Sinai hosps., Chgo., 1954—. Served to maj., M.C., AUS, 1942-46. Diplomate Am. Bd. Internal Medicine, sub-specialty cardiovascular disease. Fellow A.C.P., Am. Heart Assn.; mem. Am. Physiol. Soc., Soc. Exptl. Biology and Medicine, Central Soc. Clin. Research, Am. Soc. Clin. Investigation, Chgo. Med. Soc., Chgo. Soc. Internal Medicine, Am. Congress Rehab. Medicine, Sigma Xi. Author: Vascular Responses in Extremities of Main in Health and Disease, 1944; Diagnosis and Treatment of Peripheral Vascular Disorders, 1956; Circulation in the Extremities, 1967. Editor: Blood Vessels and Lymphatics, 1962. Contbr. articles med. jours. Home: 916 N Oak Park Av Oak Park IL 60302 Office: 8 S Michigan Av Chicago IL 60603

ABRAMSON, HAROLD ALEXANDER, physician, research psychiatrist, educator; b. N.Y.C., Nov. 27, 1899; s. F. Samuel and M. Rose (Richard) A.; A.B., Columbia, 1920; M.D., 1923; m. Barbara H. Smith, June 26, 1933 (div.); children—Alexandra Howland, Harold Alexander, Barbara Howland, Howland Wilson; m. 2d Virginia T. Wildman, 1955. Asst. inorganic chemistry, Columbia, 1918-20; interne Mt. Sinai Hosp., New York City, 1923-25; research fellow, University Coll., London, 1925-26; engaged in practice medicine since 1925; nat. research council fellow, Kaiser-Wilhelm Inst. for Phys. Chemistry and Electrochemistry, Berlin, 1926-27; instr. in medicine, Johns Hopkins U., 1928-29; instr. in biochemical sciences, Harvard U., 1929-31; asso. in bacteriology and immunology, Cornell U., 1934-35; asst. prof. of physiology Columbia U., 1935-59; former chief allergy clinic Mt. Sinai Hospital, N.Y. City; research psychiatrist. The Biological Lab., Long Island, N.Y., 1952-61; dir. psychiatric research S. Oaks Psychiatric Hosp., Amityville, N.Y.; cons. research psychiatry State Hosp., Central Islip, N.Y., 1956—; cons. Community Hosp., Glen Cove, N.Y., 1958—; former cons. Department of Army. Vice president Asthmatic Childrens Foundation; trustee Biological Lab., Cold Spring Harbor, Long Island, N.Y., 1947-61. Initiated 1942, and directed penicillin aerosol therapy of lungs for Tech. Division, Chem. Warfare Service, World War II; asst. chief and chief, Defense Material: former lt. col. Medical Corps Res. Decorated Legion of Merit. Fellow Am. Psychiatric Assn., N.Y. Acad. Medicine, American College of Allergists, A.A.A.S., N.Y. Acad. Science, Am. Acad. Allergists, Am. Coll. of Chest Physicians; mem. Am. Physiol. Soc., Am. Soc. Biol. Chemists, N.Y. County Medical Society, Society for Experimental Biology and Medicine, also Alpha Omega Alpha, Epsilon Chi. Author books including: Somatic and Psychiatric Treatment of Asthma, 1952; Electrokinetic Phenomena, 1934; Electrophoresis of Proteins, 1942; The Patient Speaks, 1956; Psychological Problems in Father-Son Relationship, 1969. Editor: Problems of Consciousness, 5 vols., 1951-53; Dimensional Analysis for Students of Medicine; Annals of Allergy, Psychiatry. Editor: Neuropharmacology, (5 vols.); The Use of LSD in Psychotherapy and Alcoholism, 1967; Clinical Applications of the Ultrasonic Nebulizer, 1968. Editor-in-chief Jour. Asthma Research. Contbr. tech., sci. jours. Home: Cold Spring Harbor NY 11724 Office: 133 E 58 St New York City NY 10022

ABRAMSON, MORRIE KAPLAN, electronics co. exec.; b. Houston, Dec. 28, 1934; s. Albert and Pearl (Kaplan) A.; B.B.A., U. Tex., 1954; postgrad. U. Houston, 1956; m. Rolaine Segal, July 1, 1962; children—Karen Hope, Beth Ellen. With Sterling Electronics, Inc., Houston, 1954—, v.p., sec., 1961-68, exec. v.p., dir., 1968—; pres., dir. Kann-Ellert Electronics, Balt., 1970—, Meridian Electronics, Richmond, Va., 1970—. Mem. Houston C. of C., Nat. Electronic Distributors Assn., Phi Sigma Delta. Jewish religion. Club: Westwood Country. Home: 5622 Jackwood St Houston TX 77035 Office: 4201 Southwest Freeway Houston TX 77027

ABRAVANEL, MAURICE, musical dir.; b. Salonica, Greece, Jan. 6, 1903, s. Edouard and Rachel (Bitty) A.; ed. Gymnasium, Lausanne, Switzerland, 1917-19, U. of Lausanne, 1919-21, U. of Zurich, 1921-22; LL.D., U. Utah; m. Lucy Carasso, 1947. Came to the U.S., 1936. Began as orchestra condr., 1924; has conducted orchestras at Lausanne (Switzerland), Neustrelitz, Zwickau, Altenburg, Kassel, Berlin State Opera (Germany), Paris Symphonic, Paris Nat. Opera (France), London (Eng.); Rome, Italy; Melbourne, Sydney, Australia; New York Met. Opera; N.Y.C. Orchestra; also Boston, Phila., Washington, Pitts., Cleve.; condr. Chgo. Opera Co., 1940; musical dir. Lady in the Dark, One Touch of Venus, Seven Lively Arts, The Firebrand, Street Scene, 1946-47, Regina, 1949—; mus dir. Sydney Orchl. Soc., 1946; condr. Utah Symphony Orchestra, 1947—; now prof. U. Utah; mus dir. Acad. of the West, Santa Barbara, Cal. Guest condr. Berlin Philharmonic, Munich. Recipient Antoinette Perry award, 1950; Kilenyi Mahler medal, 1965; Ditson Condr.'s award, 1971. Hon. mem. Internat. Gustav Mahler Soc., Am. Symphony Orch. League (v.p.), Nat. Council on the Arts. Home: 1235 E 7th South Salt Lake City UT 84102

ABRECHT, PAUL ROBERT, theologion; b. Cin., Dec. 9, 1917; s. Rudy and Elsie (Ehlman) A.; B.A. in Econs., U. Cal. at Berkeley, 1944; B.D. in Christian Studies, Union Theol. Sem., 1949; m. Audrey Alice Baxter, July 19, 1941; children—Gary, Rudy, Stephen, Susan. Teaching asst. econs. U. Cal. at Berkeley, 1940- 44; lectr. applied Christian ethics Union Theol. Sem., 1947-49; exec. sec. div. studies, dept. ch. and soc. World Council Chs., Geneva, Switzerland, 1949—; organizing sec. World Conf. Ch. and Soc., 1966. Mem. Soc. Religion Higher Edn., Phi Beta Kappa. Author: The Churches in Rapid Social Change, 1961. Home: 4 rue du Mont-Blanc Geneva Switzerland Office: 150 route de Ferney Geneva Switzerland

ABRONS, HERBERT LEHMAN, corp. counsel; b. Rutland, Vt., May 4, 1912; s. Louis W. and Anne (Schroeder) A.; B.A., Yale, 1934, LL.B., 1937; m. Mary Anne Goldwater, July 8, 1937 (div. 1966); children—Henry, Alix, Anne; m. 2d, Geraldine Ballard Leavy, Dec. 5, 1969. Admitted to the N.Y. bar, 1937; practiced with firms Proskauer, Rose & Paskus, also Hess, Mela & Popkin, N.Y.C., 1937-42; spl. asst. to atty. gen. U.S., antitrust and criminal divs. Dept. Justice, 1942-43, Office Atty. Gen. and Antitrust Div., 1946-47; counsel GAF Corp., N.Y.C., 1947—, sec., 1968—; dir. Barbizon Plaza Hotel, N.Y.C. Bd. dirs. Henry Street Settlement, United Neighborhood Houses. Served to lt. (s.g.) USNR, 1943-46, Mem. Am.

Bar Assn., Bar Assn. City N.Y. Club: Yale (N.Y.C.). Home: 215 E 68th St New York City NY 10021 Office: 140 W 51st St New York City NY 10020

ABSHIRE, DAVID MANKER, govt. ofcl.; b. Chattanooga, Apr. 11, 1926; s. James Ernest and Phyllis (Patten) A.; grad. Baylor Sch., 1944; student U. Chattanooga, 1945; B.S., U. S. Mil. Acad., 1951; Ph.D. Georgetown U., 1959; m. Carolyn Lamar Sample, Sept. 7, 1957; children—Lupton Patten, Anna Lammar, Mary Lee Sample, Phyllis Anderson. Comd. 2nd lt. U.S. Army, 1951, advanced through grades to capt. 1956; co. comd., Korea, 1952-53; resigned, 1956; dir. research House Republican Policy Com., 1958-60; dir. spl. projects Am. Enterprise Inst., Washington, 1961-62; exec. dir. Center Strategic and Internat. Studies, Georgetown U., 1962-70; asst. sec. state for congl. relations, 1970—. Mem. Alexandria (Va.) Library Co. Asst. Rep. Platform Com., 1960, 64, 68. Served with AUS, 1945-46, Decorated Bronze Star with oak leaf cluster, with V for valor, V commendation ribbon with metal pendant. Mem. Fgn. Policy Assn., Am. Acad. Polit. and Social Scis., Inst. Strategic Studies, Gold Key Soc., Phi Alpha Theta. Republican. Episcopalian (vestryman 1965-70). Clubs: Chevy Chase, Internat., Army and Navy (Washington); Metropolitan (N.Y.C.). Author: (with others) Detente, 1965; The South Rejects a Prophet: the Life of Senator D. M. Key, 1967. Editor: National Security, 1963; Portuguese Africa, 1969. Home: 311 S St Asaph St Alexandria VA 22314 Office: Department of State Washington DC 20520

ABST, RAYMOND CHRISTIAN, architect; b. Salem, Ore., Apr. 26, 1923; s. Raymond Christian and Irene (Frye) A.; B.S. in Structures, U. Ore., 1949, B.Arch., 1950; m. Shirley Marguerite Webb, Sept. 1, 1946: children—Carolynn Irene (Mrs. Marcus Naranjo), Terrill Luis. Asso. architect John W. Bomberger, Modesto, Cal., 1950-58; partner firm Bomberger & Abst, Modesto, 1958-61; propr. Raymond C. Abst & Assos., Modesto, 1961—. Bd. dirs. Valley Builders Exchange, 1966-68, Stanislaus YMCA. 1964—. Mem. A.I.A. (dir., treas. Sierra Valley chpt.). Conglist. Clubs: Torch, Rotary. Prin. works include Grace Davis High Sch., Modesto Jr. Coll. Student Center and Coll. Adminstrv. Center, Riverbank High Sch., Stanislaus County YMCA, Columbia Jr. Coll. Home: 221 El Rio Modesto, CA 95351. Office: 1012 McHenry Av Modesto CA 95350

ABT, ARTHUR FREDERICK, pediatrician; b. Chicago, Ill., Sept. 7, 1898; s. Isaac A. and Lina (Rosenberg) A.; B.S., U. of Chicago, 1918; M.D., Johns Hopkins, 1923; m. Alice Mitau, Mar. 25, 1928; children—Lina Abt Steele, Arthur. Resident house officer Johns Hopkins Hosp., 1923-24; resident phys. Sarah Morris Hosp. for Children, Chicago, 1924-25; asso. prof. of pediatrics Northwestern U. Med. Sch., 1926-53; attending pediatrician Chgo. Lying- In Hosp., 1925-31, Chgo. Maternity Center, Sarah Morris Children's Hosp., 1930-53; pediatrician Northwestern U. Med. Sch. Polio Aid Team, and mem. Joint Maternal Welfare Com., Cook Co., Ill., 1948-53; dir. radioisotope unit V.A. Hosp., Durham, N.C., also professor of pediatrics, school of medicine Duke University, 1953; past chief radioisotope service VA, Martinsburg, W.Va.; attending physician Gen. Med. Clinic, Johns Hopkins Hosp., Balt., 1969. Served as lt. comdr. U.S.N.R., 1940-45, naval liaison officer OSRD. Com. on Med. Research; chem. warfare officer, Hdqrs. 9th and 12th Naval Dists.; chem. warfare officer, 1943-44, overseas; on staff Adm. William Halsey, comdr. So. Pacific, 1944; med. officer on staff Adm. George Fort, comdr. Task Force 32, Pilau invasion; in charge evacuation of all (wounded) casualties; capt. U.S.N.R. ret. Cons. in pediatrics, U.S. Naval Hosp., Great Lakes, Ill., 1946-52. Diplomate Am. Bd. Pediatrics. Fellow A.C.P.; mem. A.M.A., Soc. Pediatric Research, Am. Pediatric Soc., Am. Acad. Pediatrics, Soc. for Pediatric Research, Soc. for Exptl. Biology and Medicine, Chicago Pediatric Soc. (past pres.), Inst. of Medicine of Chgo., Am. Soc. Clin. Nutrition, Am. Inst. Nutrition, Pan Am. Med. Soc., Sigma Xi. Co-author: Year Book of Pediatrics, 1927- 47. Author: Abt-Garrison History of Pediatrics, 1965. Contbr. chpts. pediatric subjects for De Lee's Obstetrics for Nurses, Collier's Ency., Brennemann's System of Pediatrics, A.M.A. Symposium Vitamins, Tb. and Other Communicable Diseases (editor J. Arthur Myers), others; also articles on clin. and exptl. aspects pediatrics and nutrition. Address: 1101 St Paul St Baltimore MD 21202

ABUDO, LUIS A., banker; b. San Juan, P.R., Nov. 17, 1936; s. A. and Lillian (Marin) A.; B.A., U. Tampa; m. Aderlin Bravo, Nov. 23, 1960; children—Luis A., Maria F. Sales and promotion mgr. Am. Plastics, Inc., 1960-61; with Banco Popular de P.R., 1961—, asst. v.p., 1965-68, 2d v.p., supr. Western dist., 1968, v.p., chief exec. officer, N.Y.C., 1968—, also chmn. N.Y. adv. bd.; dir., chmn. exec. com. Pan Am. Nat. Bank of N.J. Commr. State of N.Y. Off-Track Pari-Mutuel Betting Commn. Mem. Pan Am. C. of C. of N.Y. (pres.), C. of C. of P.R. (dir.), N.Y. Bankers Assn., Robert Morris Assos., Inc. Roman Catholic. Clubs: Rotary (Bronx); Governors, 500, Rockefeller Luncheon, Hemisphere (N.Y.C.). Home: 1010 Fifth Av New York City NY 10022 Office: 20 W 48th St New York City NY 10036

ABU SHADI, MOHAMMED MAHMOUD, banker; b. Fayoum, U.A.R., Aug. 15, 1913; s. Mohmoud Kamel and Saddika (Hashad) Abu S.; B.Commerce, Cairo U., 1934; asso. Chartered Inst. Patent Agts., London, Eng., 1946; postgrad. Am. U.; m. Colleen Althea Bennett, Nov. 8, 1947; children—Farida (Mrs. Farouk El Tawila), Sonya, Farid, Karim. Chmn. Social Ins. Orgn., also chmn., mng. dir. Cairo Ins. Co., 1956-57; sub gov. Nat. Bank Egypt, 1955-60, mng. dir., 1961-67, chmn., mng. dir., 1967-70; chmn. Union de Banques Arabes et Francaise, Paris, 1970—. Decorated El Gamhoureya Order II, 1955, Order Merit I (Al Estihhak), 1971. Mem. Societe d'Economie Politique de Statistique et de Legislation d'Egypte, U.A.R. Club Commerce. Author: The Art of Central Banking and its Application in Egypt, 1952; Central Banking in Egypt, 1952. Home: 20 Dr Halim Abu Seif Heliopolis Cairo United Arab Republic Office: UBAF 4 Rue Ancelle 92 Neuilly sur Seine France

ABY, HULETTE FUQUA, investment exec., lawyer; b. Tulsa, Nov. 11, 1907; s. Hulette F. and Cora Mae (Hansel) A.; student U. Okla., 1926-29; LL.B., U. Tulsa, 1933; m. Jane Heverly Halpine, July 31, 1936 (div. Feb. 1966); children—Brian H., Anne H., Stephen H.; m. 2d, V. Edwina O'Fiel, Dec. 1966. Admitted to Okla. bar, 1933; pvt. practice, Tulsa, 1933-37; asst. gen. counsel Deep Rock Oil Corp., 1937-47: gen. counsel Midstates Oil Corp., 1947-58; spl. master Supreme Ct. Okla., 1952; with Tenn. Gas Transmission Co., 1958- 66, gen. atty., 1961-66; gen. atty. Tenneco Oil Co., 1963-66; v.p., gen. counsel Jayell, Inc., Houston, 1966-68; investment exec., Dallas, 1968—. Served to maj. AUS, 1942-45. Mem. Am., Okla., Fed. Power bar assns., Sigma Alpha Epsilon. Democrat. Home: 11330-B Park Central Pl Dallas TX 75230 Office: 9995 Monroe Dr Dallas TX 75220

ABZUG, BELLA SAVITSKY, (Mrs. Maurice M. Abzug), congresswoman; b. N.Y.C., July 24, 1920; d. Emanuel and Esther Savitzky; B.A., Hunter Coll., 1942; LL.B., Columbia, 1945; m. Maurice M. Abzug, June 4, 1944; children—Eve Gail, Isobel Jo. Admitted to N.Y. bar, 1947; pvt. practice, N.Y.C., 1944-70; legislative dir. Women's Strike for Peace, 1961-70; mem. 92d Congress 19th Dist. N.Y. Mem. Women's Strike for Peace, Nat. Urban League, Women's Prison Assn., Members of Congress for Peace Through Law, Democratic Study Group, Nat. Lawyers Guild, Hadassah, Am. Civil Liberties Union, UN Assn. U.S. Mem. B'nai B'rith. Home: 37 Bank St New York City NY 10014 Office: Longworth Office Bldg Washington DC 20515

ACCETTURA, GUY, communications co. exec.; b. Ceglie del Campo, Italy, Feb. 23, 1919; s. Vito L. and Maria (Roppo) A.; came to U.S., 1928; student Ill. Inst. Tech., 1936-38; B.S. cum laude in Commerce, De Paul U., 1948; m. Mabel G. Blindell, May 11, 1946; children—Raymond V., Paul G., Carl J., Janet Rosalie, Linda Margaret. With Western Electric Co., 1936-66, dir. orgn. planning, 1964-65, v.p., 1965-66; v.p., gen mgr. Bell Telephone Labs., Murray Hill, N.J., 1966-69; v.p. mfg. Western Electric Company, Newark, 1969—; dir. Sandia Corp. 1966-69, Teletype Corp., 1969—. Mem. Columbus Water Planning Commn., 1963-64. Bd. dirs. YM/YWCA of Newark and Vicinity; trustee, exec. com. N.J. Symphony Orch.; trustee, exec. com., sec. N.J. Symphony Hall; trustee Western Electric Fund, 1971—. Served with AUS, 1942-46; ETO. Decorated Bronze Star medal. Mem. Nat. Assn. Accountants, Columbus C. of C. (dir. 1963-64), Pi Gamma Mu. Rotarian. Home: 467 Carlton Rd Wyckoff NJ 07481 Office: Western Electric Co 520 Broad St Newark NJ 07102

ACE, GOODMAN, writer; b. Kansas City, Mo., Jan. 15, 1899; m. Jane Sherwood, 1928. Cub reporter Kansas City Jour.-Post, later became movie and play reviewer; writer Easy Aces, radio show, 1928-45; chief writer Danny Kaye program; supr. comedy programs CBS, 1946, charge devel. new radio programs; writer Tallulah Bankhead's radio program Big Show, 1950-52; permanent guest radio show Jane Ace, Disc Jockey, 1951-52; head writer for Milton Berle, 1952-55, also TV columnist Saturday Rev.; head writer Perry Como show, 1955-59; producer, writer variety shows, five CBS spectaculars; creator CBS Open House, 1960. Address: Ritz Tower Hotel 47th St and Park Av New York City NY 10022

ACHENBACH, GERALD HOPE, food chain exec.; b. Deer Lodge, Mont., June 9, 1910; s. H.F. and Martha Jane (Wood) A.; A.B., U. Wash., 1934; m. Sara Dean Jones, Dec. 25, 1945; children—Charles Henry II, Gerald Hope, Mary Dean, Ann Towers, John Wood. Partner A. Vere Shaw & Co, investment counsel N.Y.C. 1937-42; pres. Piggly Wiggly So., Inc., Vidalia, Ga., 1942—. Ga. Sales Co., Vidalia, 1943—, Green Realty Co., Vidalis, 1953—; dir. Seaboard Coastline Industries, Citizens & So. Nat. Bank, Whiteway, Inc. Chmn. investment com., bd. dirs. Columbia Theol. Sem.; chmn. trustees Paul Anderson Youth Home. Mem. Nat. Assn. Food Chains (chmn. bd. 1958-59, exec. com. 1952—, bd. dirs.), Supermarket Inst. (past pres.), pres. Assn. Nat. Piggly Wiggly Assn., Southeastern Chain Store Council. Nat. Assn. Food Research, Vadalia C. of C., Am. Mgmt. Assn. (bd. dirs.). Republican. Presbyn. Clubs: Union League (N.Y.C.); Oglethorne (Savannah. Ga.); Capital City (Atlanta); Vidalia Country; Augusta Nat. Golf, Pinnacle (Augusta); Royal and Ancient Golf (St. Andrews. Scotland); Pine Valley (N.J.) Golf. Home: Rocky Creek Farm Vidalia GA 30474 Office: 100 Brinson Rd Vidalia GA 30474

ACHENBAUM, ALVIN ALLEN, advt. exec.; b. N.Y.C., Dec. 11, 1925; s. Benjamin and Dora (Dworin) A.; B.S., U. Cal. at Los Angeles, 1950; M.S., Columbia, 1951; m. Barbara Ann Greenwald, June 24, 1951; children—Jonathan Peter, Lisa Jane, Martha Beth. Mgr. market research McCann-Erickson, N.Y.C., 1951-57; exec. v.p., sec., dir. Grey Advt., Inc., N.Y.C., 1957—. Mem. Citizens Adv. Com. of Irvington, 1970—. Served with USAAF, 1944-46. Mem. Market Research Council N.Y., Copy Research Council N.Y., Am. Marketing Assn., Am. Econ. Assn., Am. Standards Assn., Inst. Polit. and Opinion Research, Beta Gamma Sigma. Home: 34 Mallard Rd Irvington NY 10533 Office: 777 3d Av New York City NY 10017

ACHESON, DAVID CAMPION, lawyer, communications exec.; b. Washington, Nov. 4, 1921; s. Dean G. and Alice (Stanley) A.; B.A., Yale, 1942; LL.B., Harvard U., 1948; m. Patricia Castles, May 1, 1943; children—Eleanor Dean, David Campion, Peter Wesley. Admitted to D.C. bar, U.S. Supreme Ct. bar; with Office Gen. Counsel, AEC, 1948-49; with firm Covington & Burling, Washington, 1949-61, mem. firm, 1958-61; U.S. atty. for D.C., 1961-65; spl. asst. to sec. treasury, 1965-67; v.p., gen. counsel Communications Satellite Corp., 1967—. Mem. Democratic Central Con. D.C., 1960-61. Democrat. Episcopalian. Clubs: Metropolitan, Yale. (Washington); Century Assn. (N.Y.C.). Home: 3103 Garfield St NW Washington DC 20008 also South Yarmouth MA 02664 Office: 950 L'Enfant Plaza SW Washington DC 20024

ACHESON, ROY MALCOLM, educator, epidemiologist; b. Belfast, Ireland, Aug. 18, 1921; s. Malcolm King and Dorothy (Rennoldson) A.; B.A., Trinity Coll., Dublin, Ireland, 1945, M.A., 1949, Sc.D., 1962; B.A., U. Oxford (Eng.), 1948, M.A., 1951, B.M., B.Ch., 1951, D.M., 1954; M.A. (hon.), Yale, 1964; m. Fiona Marigo O'Brien, Mar. 16, 1950; children—Malcolm O'Brien, Vincent Rennoldson, Marigo Fiona. Came to U.S., 1962, naturalized, 1968. Intern, then resident internal medicine Radcliffe Infirmary, Oxford, 1951-55; lectr. social medicine U. Dublin (Ireland), 1955-59; reader social and preventive medicine U. London (Eng.), 1959-62; mem. faculty Yale Sch. Medicine, 1962—, prof. epidemiology, 1964—; fellow Jonathan Edward Coll., 1966—. Mem. expert com. health statistics WHO, 1966; cons., tech. adviser epidemiology and med. edn. Pan-Am. Health Orgn. in Peru, Venezuela and P.R., 1964—; cons. med. edn. AID, E. Pakistan, 1963; cons. epidemiology NIH, 1963—; mem. nat. adv. com. thrombosis Nat. Heart Inst., 1968-70; mem. epidemiology study sect. Nat. Inst. Gen. Med. Scis., 1970—. Served with Brit. Army, 1940-45. Rockefeller traveling fellow medicine, 1955-56; Commonwealth Fund traveling fellow, 1968-69; fellow Trinity Coll., Dublin, 1957-59. Mem. Am. Heart Assn. (fellow epidemiological council, council cerebrovascular disease), Internat. Epidemiological Assn. (council 1964—, gen. sec. 1964-68, ednl. sec. 1968—). Contbr. profl. jours. Editor: Comparability in International Epidemiology, 1965. Office: 60 College St New Haven CT 06510

ACHESON, WILLIAM GEORGE HAWKINS, communications co. exec.; b. Pitts., Feb. 25, 1910; s. Marcus W. and Margaret H. (Hawkins) A.; B.A., Williams Coll., 1931; LL.B., Harvard, 1934; m. Daryl Marsh, Sept. 21, 1939 (dec. June, 1965); 1 dau., Daryl. Admitted to N.Y. State bar, 1936; asso. Alexander & Green, N.Y.C., 1934-43; treas. Quimby Pump Co., Inc., Newark, 1943-45; Mgmt., Assn. U. Evening Colls. (editor newsletter, 57, sec., 1957—; also sec. dir. subsidiary cos. Mem. Chi Psi. Republican. Home: 24 E 39th St New York City, NY 10016. Office: Western Union Telegraph Co 60 Hudson St New York City, NY 10013.

ACHILLES, THEODORE CARTER, former govt. ofcl.; b. Rochester, N.Y., Dec. 29, 1905; s. Henry Lawrence and Gertrude (Strong) A.; A.B., Stanford U., 1925; student Yale, 1926-28; m. Marian Field, June 4, 1933; children—Marian (Mrs. Walter B. Smith II), Theodore Carter, Daphne Stephen. Newspaper work in Cal. and Japan, 1928-31; vice-consul, Havana, 1932, Rome, 1933; assigned to Dept. State, 1935; sec. Am. embassy, London, 1939; chargé d'affaires ad interim near govts. of Poland, Belgium, Netherlands and Norway 1940-41; Dept. of State, Washington, 1941, asst. chief. div. of Brit. Commonwealth Affairs, 1944, chief, 1944; 1st sec. Am. embassy, London, 1945, Brussels, Belgium, 1946; dir. Western European Affairs, 1947; U.S. vice dep. North Atlantic Council, London, 1950; minister, Paris, 1952; Am. ambassador to Peru, 1956-60; counselor Dept. State, Washington, 1960, spl. asst. to sec. of state, dir. Operations Center, 1961-62; cons. NASA, 1963-68 dir. Eastman Kodak Company, Atlantic Council U.S., Fed. Union. Mem. U.S. delegation to ILO Conf., 1941, UN conf. on Food and Agr., 1943, UN Conf. on Internat. Orgn., San Francisco, 1945; Council Fgn. Ministers, London, 1945; first session U.N. Assembly, London, 1946, 2d session, N.Y., 1947; Paris Conf., 1946; North Atlantic Pact Negotiations, 1948-49, NATO, 1950-52, 60, CENTO, SEATO and Colombo Plan Confs., 1960. Mem. Beta Theta Pi. Clubs. Metropolitan. Chevy Chase (Washington); Yale, Brook (N.Y.C.). Editor Atlantic Community Quart., 1963—. Home: 2855 Woodland Dr NW Washington DC 20008

ACHINSTEIN, ASHER, economist; b. N.Y.C., Dec. 6, 1900; s. Hyman and Fanny (Horowitz) A.; B.S., Coll. City N.Y., 1922; M.A., Columbia, 1924, Ph.D., 1927; m. Betty Comras, Aug. 27; 1931 (dec. Oct. 1964); 1 son, Peter; m. 2d, Martha Lantner, Apr. 3, 1966. Tchr. econs. Eastern Dist. High Sch., Bklyn., 1924-26; sr. investigator econ. research Personnel Classification Bd., Washington, 1928-29; mem. research staff Nat. Indsl. Conf. Bd., N.Y.C., 1929-30; asst. dir. N.Y. State Housing Bd., 1930-36; asst. dir. research U.S. Housing Authority, 1938-40; lectr. econs. Columbia, 1940-42; chief constrn. and planning sect. WPB, Washington, 1941-45; prof. Biarritz (France) Am. U., 1945-46; sr. specialist Legislative Reference Service, Library Congress, Washington, 1949-70; economist Council Econ. Advisers, 1953-55, U.S. Senate Banking and Currency Commn., 1955-58. Social Sci. Research Council fellow, 1927-28; Rockefeller Found. grantee U.S. housing study, 1933-34. Mem. Am. Econ. Assn. Author: Buying Power of Labor and Post War Cycles, 1927; Introduction to Business Cycles, 1950; Institutional Investors and the Stock Market, 1956; Federal Reserve Policy and Economic Stability, 1958; Congress and American Housing, 1968; Inflation and Interest Rates, 1970. Contbr. to American Economic History, 1961. Home: 8504 Meadowlark Lane Bethesda MD 20034

ACHKAR, MAROF, diplomat of Guinea; b. Coyah, Guinea, July 5, 1930; s. Moustapha and Damae (Camara) A.; ed. Breguet Engring. Sch., Paris, France, 1953; m. Rosemonde Montanary, Nov. 3, 1956; children—Lorna, Fode, Marof, Souleymane. Dir., Ballets Africains, also journalist- reporter Information Services Guinea, 1957-59; attache permanent mission Guinea to UN, 1959-60, 2d sec., 1960-61, 1st sec., 1961-62, minister-counsellor, 1962-63, ambassador, 1963-64, ambassador, permanent rep., 1964-69; chmn. UN spl. com. on policies of apartheid Govt. Republic S. Africa, 1964. Vice pres. spl. com. tys. under Portuguese adminstrn. UN, 1962, pres. ad. interim spl. on-the-spot investigation com. in Africa, 1962, pres. trusteeship and non self-governing tys. com. 18th session, 1963, pres. spl. com. apartheid, 1964, chmn. Guinean delegation to 21st session. Mem. Soc. des Auteurs et Compositeurs Francais. Address: Ministry Fgn Affairs Conakry Guinea

ACHORN, ROBERT COMEY, newspaper editor; b. Westboro, Mass., Mar. 31, 1922; s. Edward Welt and Mabel (Comey) A.; A.B., Brown U., 1943; m. Jean Mary Berlo, Sept. 23, 1950; children—Nancy Louise (Mrs. Eric Engberg), Susan Jean, Edward Christopher, Judith Joyce, Carole Lee. Reporter, Worcester (Mass.) Telegram, 1946-53; editorial writer Evening Gazette, Worcester, 1953-60, mng. editor, 1964-67; editor editorial pages Worcester Telegram & Gazette, 1964-67, asso. editor, 1967-70, editor, 1970—. Served with USNR, 1943-46. Mem. U.P.I. New Eng. Newspaper Editors of Mass. (Pres. 1969), Am., New Eng. (pres. 1968) socs. newspaper editors, New England Asso. Press News Exec. Assn. (Pres. 1971—), Phi Beta Kappa, Sigma Delta Chi. Club: Worcester. Home: 46 Upton Rd Westboro MA 01581 Office: 20 Franklin St Worcester MA 01601

ACKELL, EDMUND FERRIS, dental educator; b. Danbury, Conn., Nov. 29, 1925; s. Ferris M. and Barbara (Elias) A.; B.S., Holy Cross Coll., 1949; D.M.D., Tufts Coll. 1953; M.D., Western Res. U., 1962. Mem. faculty Western Res. U., 1957-66, asso. dean Sch. Dentistry, chief dental service, 1960-66, chmn. dept. oral surgery, 1962-66, asst. prof. oral pathology, 1960-66; dean Coll. Dentistry, U. Fla., 1966-69, prof. surgery, 1966—, provost J. Hillis Miller Health Center, 1969—. Served to lt. USNR, 1943-46. Diplomate Am. Bd. Oral Surgery. Fellow Am. Coll. Dentists; mem. Am. Dental Assn., A.M.A., Fla. Dental Soc., Am. Pub. Health Assn., Omicron Kappa Upsilon, Alpha Omega Alpha. Home: 4501 NW 13th Av Gainesville FL 32601

ACKEN, ALBERT HOWELL, c. of c. exec.; b. Portage, Pa., Aug. 22, 1897; s. Paul and Luella (Ake) A.; student Southeastern U., Washington, 1920-22; m. Laura L. Williamson, Aug. 17, 1940; children—John Y., Claire M. (Mrs. Milburn E. Noble), Marion R. (Mrs. Frank A. Pedrick). Asst. dir. traffic Mediterranean div. U.S. Shipping Bd., 1919-25; self-employed in real estate and constrn., 1925-34; with N.J. C. of C., 1934—, exec. v.p., 1960—. Pres., Council State Chambers of Commerce, 1966-67, also mem. exec. com. Chmn. bd. Yorkwood Savs. & Loan Assn., Mapelwood, N.J. Vice pres. Water Resources Assn. Del. River Basin; adv. bd. N.J. Alliance Businessmen; bd. dirs. N.J. Council Econ. Edn., Americans Competitive Enterprise System; mem. N.J. Vehicle Air Pollution Control Study Commn., 1964, Commn. Study N.J. Laws Effecting Indsl. Devel., 1957; sec. N.J. Citizens Representative Legislature, 1965-67; vice chmn. North N.J. for Met. N.Y.-N.J. Indsl. Dispersion Com., World War II. Trustee N.J. Symphony; regional dir. Nat. Conf. Christians and Jews. Served with USN, 1917-18. Recipient Humanitarian award N.J. Arthritis Found., 1969. Mem. N.J. Agr. Soc., Advt. Club N.J. (sec.), Pa. Soc. N.J., Navy League, Delta Sigma Pi. (hon. Beta Omicron chpt). Clubs: Essex, Down Town (Newark); Capitol Hill (Washington). Home: 160 Heywood Av Orange, NJ 07050. Office: 54 Park Pl Newark NJ 07102

ACKER, CHARLES EDWARD, airline exec.; b. Dallas, Apr. 7, 1929; s. Edward Morgan and Lois Jane (McCallum) A.; student N. Tex. State U., 1945-46; B.A., So. Meth. U., 1950; m. Norma Higginbotham, Sept. 5, 1952; children—Richard Morgan, Mitchell Taylor, Nell. Vice pres. Lionel D. Edie & Co., Inc., 1958- 64; v.p. finance Gt. Am. Corp., Dallas, 1964—, also dir.; sr. v.p. planning and adminstrn. Braniff Internat., 1965—, also dir., exec. v.p. Braniff Airways, Inc., 1967-70, pres., chmn. operating officer, 1970—; dir. Am.-Amicable Life Ins. Co., Franklin Life Ins. Co., Gulf Life Ins. Co., Higginbotham Corp. Mem. All Sports Assn. Dallas, Dallas Good Neighbor Council. Mem. Dallas Assn. Investment Analysts, Dallas C. of C., Newcomen Soc. N.Am., Alpha Tau Omega. Episcopalian. Clubs: Terpsichorean; Idlewild; Dallas Country; Brook Hollow Golf; Petroleum; Preston Trail Golf; Imperial. Home: 6023 St Andrew St Dallas TX 65205 Office: PO Box 35001 Dallas TX 75235

ACKER, CHARLES R., corp. exec.; b. 1912; B.S., Columbia; married, With CIT Corp., 1934-42, Machinery Bldrs. Inc., 1942-45; treas. Fischbach and Moore Inc., 1945—, also dir.

ACKER, DUANE CALVIN, univ. dean; b. Atlantic, Ia., Mar. 13, 1931; s. Clayton and Ruth (Kimball) A.; B.S., Ia. State U., 1952, M.S., 1953; Ph.D., Okla. State U., 1957; m. Shirley Hansen, Mar. 23, 1952; children—Diane Jean, LuAnn Fay. Instr. animal husbandry Okla. State U., 1953-55; mem. faculty Ia. State U., 1955-62, asso. prof.

animal sci., asso. prof. charge farm operation curriculum, 1958-62; asso. dean agr., dir. resident instrn. Kan. State U., Manhattan, 1962-66; dean agr. and biol. scis., dir. agrl. expt. sta. S.D. State Univ., Brookings, since 1966—. Cons. Schering Corp., 1959-60; curriculum planning cons. Argentina, AID, 1961, mem. U.S. team for rev. Marshall plan aid to W. Germany, 1967; co-chmn. USOA exptl. sta. task force on quality of the environment, 1967-68; del. to OECD conf. higher edn. agr., Paris 1970; Named Prof. of Year, Ia. State U. Agr., 1959; recipient Tall Corn award for academic advising IA. State U., 1962. Mem. Am. Soc. Animal Sci., Internat. Platform Assn., A.A.A.S., Farm House Frat., Nat. Assn. State Univs. and Land-Grant Colls. (chmn. div. agr. 1970—), Sigma XI, Alpha Zeta, Gamma Sigma Delta, Phi Kappa Phi. Methodist. Mason, Rotarian. Author: Animal Science and Industry, 1963-71. Home: N Medary Av Brookings SD 57006

ACKERLY, SAMUEL SPAFFORD, physician; b. Bklyn, May 20, 1895; s. George Briggs and Nancy Spafford (Brown) A.; A.B., Wesleyan U., 1921; M.D., Yale, 1925; m. Carita Clark, Oct. 17, 1925; children—William Clark, Carita Jane, Nancy Lavinia, Elizabeth Spafford. Intern at N.Y. Hosp., 1926; postgrad. London and Vienna, 1927; clin. dir. Worcester State Hosp., 1928-30; asst. prof., research asso. Yale Inst. of Human Relations, 1930-32; dir. Louisville (Ky.) Mental Hygiene Clinic, 1932-62; prof. psychiatry U. Louisville, 1932-63, Distinguished prof. psychiatry, 1963—, chmn. dept., 1947-63, psychiatrist-in-residence, 1963—; chief service Norton Psychiat. Clinic, 1949-63. Trustee Louisville Pub. Library, 1950-60; chmn. adv. com. Juvenile Ct. of Jefferson County, 1950-58; mem. adv. com. on delinquency program Louisville Pub. Schs., 1971—. Served with inf. U.S. Army, 1917-20. Mem. med. adv. board SSS, 1941-45; chmn. Gov.'s adv. council State Dept. Mental Health, 1950-60. Recipient John S. Guggenheim research fellowship, 1959. Bd. dirs. Am. Bd. Psychiatry and Neurology, 1945-49. Fellow A.C.P., Am. Orthopsychiat. Assn. (pres. 1947), Am. Psychiat. Assn. (council 1952, v.p. 1959), Coll. Am. Psychiatrists, mem. Am. Acad. Child Psychiatry (council 1959-61), Am. Acad. Psychoanalysis (sci. asso.), Am. Acad. Neurology, So. Med. Assn. (chmn. neurol. and psych. sect. 1937-38), Ky. Psychiat. Assn. (pres. 1939), Louisville Art Center Assn. (bd. dirs.), Chi Psi, Nu Sigma Nu, Phi Sigma Phi, Alpha Omega Alpha (hon.). Democrat. Presbyn. Mem. editorial bd. Am. Jour. Psychiatry, 1944-63, Psychiatry Digest, 1963-65. Home: 407 Mockingbird Valley Rd Louisville KY 40207

ACKERMAN, CARL ROBERT, physician; b. N.Y.C., Jan. 29, 1906; s. Robert Ludwig and Ida (Fischer) A.; B.A., Columbia, 1927, M.D., 1930. Practice of medicine, Bronx, N.Y., 1933-60; attending surgeon, Union Hosp. Bronx; past dir. surgery St. Francis Hosp., Bronx.; dir. United Med. Service, Inc. of N.Y.C. (Blue Shield Plan N.Y.C., 1959—), 1954—, now chmn. bd.; former chmn. bd. Nat. Assn. Blue Shield Plans. Mem. adv. com. to med. dir. Dept. Social Welfare, N.Y.C.; former co-chmn. medicare carrier adv. com. U.S. Dept. Health Edn. and Welfare. Fellow A.C.S.: mem. Nat. Assn. Blue Shield Plans (past chmn. bd.), A.M.A., Bronx Med. Soc., Med. Soc. State N.Y., Morrisania City Hosp. Alumni Assn. (past pres), Columbia Coll. Alumni Assn., Columbia U. Coll. Phys. and Surg. Alumni Assn., Bronx Surg. Soc., Assn. Blue Shield Plans N.Y. State. Home: Ridge Rd Glen Cove NY 11542 Office: United Med Service Inc 2 Park Av New York City NY 10017

ACKERMAN, EDWARD AUGUSTUS, instn. exec.; b. Post Falls, Ida., Dec. 5, 1911; s. August and Augusta (Anderson) A.; A.B., Harvard, 1934, A.M., 1936, Ph.D., 1939; m. Adrienne Desjardins, Sept. 24, 1949; children—Helen, Francis, Julia, Justin, Elizabeth. Instr., Harvard, 1940-43, asst. prof., 1943-48; prof. geography U. Chgo., 1948-55; dir. water resources program Resources for Future, Inc., 1954-58; dep. exec. officer Carnegie Inst. Washington, 1958-60, exec. officer, 1960—. Asst. chief Europe- Africa div., chief geog. reports sect. OSS, 1941-43; tech. adv. nat. resources sect. G.H.Q., SCAP, Tokyo, Japan, 1946-48; regional analyst Hoover Commn., 1948; mem. Pres.'s Water Resources Policy Commn., 1950-51; chief natural resources and pub. works br. U.S. Bur. Budget, 1951-52; asst. gen. mgr. TVA, 1952-54; chmn. ad hoc com. on geography Nat. Acad. Scis.-NRC, 1963-64; cons. to various depts. fed. govt., also Congl. coms. Trustee Washington Center Met. Studies, chmn. bd. trustees, 1964-69; bd. dirs. Analytic Services, Inc., Center for Environment and Man, Planning Found. Am., Geomet, Inc., Envirometrics, Inc. Member Assn. Am. Geographers, Phi Beta Kappa, Sigma Xi. Club: Cosmos (Wash.). Author: New England's Fishing Industry, 1941; (with J.R. Whitaker) American Resources, 1951; (with collaborators), Ten Rivers in America's Future, 1950; Japan's Natural Resources, 1953; (with G. O. G. Löf) Technology in American Water Development, 1959. Home: 3000 39th St NW Washington DC 20016 Office: 1530 P St Washington DC 20005

ACKERMAN, EUGENE, educator; b. Bklyn., July 8, 1920; s. Saul Benton and Dorothy (Salwen) A.; B.A., Swarthmore Coll., 1941; Sc.M., Brown U., 1943; Ph.D., U. Wis., 1949; postgrad. U. Pa., 1949-51, fellow 1957-58; m. Dorothy Hopkirk, June 5, 1943; children—Francis H., Emmanuel T., Amy R. Instr., Brown U., 1943; from asst. prof. to prof. biophysics Pa. State U., 1951-60; mem. faculty U. Minn. Mayo Grad. Sch. Medicine, 1960-67, prof. biophysics, 1965—; staff cons. biophysics Mayo Found. and Mayo Clinic, 1960-67; Hill Family Found. prof. biomed. computing, prof. biometry also computer scis. U. Minn., Mpls., 1967—, dir. div. health computer science dept. lab. medicine, 1969—; dir. computer facility Mayo Found., 1964-65. Cons. bioacoustics USAF, 1957- 62; mem. epidemiology and biometry tng. com. NIH, 1963-67, spl. study sect. ultrasonic applications, 1965-67, spl. study sect. lab. med. scis., 1967-68, computer and biomath. sci. study sect., 1968—. Research grantee Am. Cancer Soc., 1953-56, NSF, 1958-64, NIH, 1954—. Mem. A.A.A.S., Biophys. Soc., Am. Physiol. Soc., N.Y., Minn. acads. sci., Assn. Computing Machinery, Soc. Social Responsibility Sci., I.E.E.E., Phi Beta Kappa, Sigma Xi, Gamma Alpha. Author: Biophysical Science, 1962; also articles, tech. reports, chpts. in books. Mem. Soc. of Friends. Home: 4015 W 44th St Edina MN 55424 Office: Box 511 Mayo Meml Bldg U Minn Minneapolis MN 55455

ACKERMAN, HARRY S., advt., broadcasting exec.; b. Albany, N.Y., Nov. 17, 1912; s. Harold and Ann (Flannery) A.; A.B., Dartmouth, 1935; m. Elinor Donahue, Apr. 21, 1961; children—Brian, Peter, James, Christopher; children by previous marriage—Susan, Stephen. Free-lance writer and actor, 1935-36, radio dir., 1936-42; radio dir. Young & Rubicam, N.Y.C., 1936-42, radio prodn. head, 1942-45, v.p. charge radio programs, 1945; exec. producer CBS, N.Y.C., 1948, dir. network programs, Hollywood, Cal., 1948, v.p., dir. TV and radio, 1949-51, v.p. charge TV, 1951-55; exec. dir. spl. prodns. CBS-TV, 1956-57; pres. Ticonderoga Prodns., ind. producer TV, 1957-58; v.p. charge prodn. Screen Gems Pictures Corp., 1958—, now v.p., exec. producer Screen Gems div. Columbia Pictures Industries, Inc. Spl. radio cons. U.S. Treasury, 1944- 46. Bd. dirs. TV Acad. Found.; trustee Motion Picture Relief Fund. Mem. Acad. TV Arts and Scis. (past pres. Los Angeles), Manuscripts Soc. (charter), Am. Arbitration Assn. Club: Dartmouth Southern Cal. (trustee). Home: 3477 Valley Rd Sherman Oaks CA 91413 Office: 1334 N Beachwood Dr Hollywood CA 90028

ACKERMAN, JAMES NILS, lawyer; b. Pleasant Dale, Neb., Mar. 16, 1912; s. Albert Ferdinand and Irma Marie (Berlet) A.; A.B., Neb. Wesleyan U., 1933; LL.B., Harvard, 1938; m. Jean Caroline Doty, Aug. 8, 1939; children—Thomas Richard, Mary Alice (Mrs. Philip E. Lundblad). Admitted to Neb. bar, 1938; practice of law Davis & Stubbs, 1938-41, Davis, Stubbs & Ackerman, 1941-42, Peterson & Devoe, 1947-48, Peterson, Devoe & Ackerman, 1948-52, Peterson & Ackerman, Lincoln, Neb., 1952—; with F.B.I., 1942-47; asst. gen. counsel Bankers Life Ins. Co. Neb., 1947-55, gen. counsel, 1955—, v.p., 1960—, trustee, 1957—. Dir. Farmers Mut. Ins. Co., Gateway Bank. Dir. Lincoln Community Chest, 1965-68, Lincoln Community Council, 1950-65, Lancaster County Child Guidance Clinic, 1946-54, Lincoln Symphony Orch. Assn., 1965—. Chmn. Lancaster County Rep. Party, 1950; del. Rep. county and state convs.; mem. Pres.'s Adv. Com. for J.F. Kennedy Center for Performing Arts, 1970—. Gov. Neb. Wesleyan U., 1964—. Mem. Am., Neb., Lincoln (pres. 1957) bar assns., Assn. Life Ins. Counsel (pres. 1969-70), Am. Life Conv. (chmn. legal sect. 1960), Neb. Ins. Fedn. (pres. 1970-71), Lincoln C. of C. (dir.). Presbyn. Mason (Shriner, Jester). Clubs: Lincoln Country, Nebraska, University (pres. 1957-58) (Lincoln). Home: 6415 A St Lincoln NB 65810 Office: Cotner and O Sts Lincoln NB 68501

ACKERMAN, JAMES SLOSS, educator; b. San Francisco, Nov. 8, 1919; s. Lloyd S. and Louise (Sloss) A.; A.B., Yale, 1941; M.A., N.Y. U., 1947, Ph.D., 1952; L.H.D., Kenyon College, 1961; m. Mildred Rosenbaum, Apr. 11, 1947; children—Anne, Anthony, Sarah. Part-time instr. Yale, 1946-48; research fellow Am. Acad. in Rome, 1949-52; asst. prof. then prof. U. Cal., 1952-60; editor in chief Art Bull., 1956-60, prof. fine arts Harvard, 1960—, chmn. dept. fine arts, 1963-68; Slade prof. fine art, fellow King's Coll., Cambridge U., 1969-70. Vis. fellow Council Humanities, Princeton, 1960-61; fellow Am. Council Learned Socs., 1964-65; pres. Univ. Film Study Center, 1967-68, treas., 1970—. Trustee Am. Acad. in Rome. Recipient medal for service in art edn. Nat. Gallery Art, 1966; Centennial citation U. Cal., 1968. Fellow Am. Acad. Arts and Scis.; mem. Soc. Archtl. Historians, Coll. Art Assn., Renaissance Soc. Am. Author: The Cortile del Belvedere, 1954; The Architecture of Michelangelo, 1961 (winner Alice D. Hitchcock award Soc. Archtl. Historians 1961, also Charles R. Morey award 1963); (with Rhys Carpenter) Art and Archaeology, 1963; Palladio, 1966; Palladio's Villas, 1967. Editorial bd. L'Arte, 1966—. Contbr. 17th Century Sci. and the Arts, 1961. Home: 12 Coolidge Hill Rd Cambridge MA 02138 Office: Fogg Museum Harvard U Cambridge MA 02138

ACKERMAN, JOSEPH, agrl. economist; b. Morton, Ill., July 20, 1904; s. John C. and Elizabeth (Welk) A.; B.S., U. Ill., 1929, M.S., 1930, Ph.D., 1938; social sci. research fellow. in agrl. econs. Harvard, 1931-32; LL.D. (hon.), Elmhurst Coll., 1966; m. Elizabeth Jane Engstrand, Aug. 30, 1930; children—Elizabeth Ann, John Welk, Sara Jane, Allan J. Farm mgr. Citizens Nat. Bk., Decatur, Ill., 1930, 31; farm mgr., rural appraiser Decatur Farm Mgmt., Inc., 1933-34; extension work in farm mgmt. U. Ill., summer 1931, 32-33, 34-39, Farm Found., Chgo., land tenure specialist, 1939-41, asst. dir., 1941-42, asso. mng. dir., 1942-55; mng. dir., 1955—. Sec.-treas. Internat. Assn. Agr. Economists. Mem. at large Nat. council Boy Scouts Am. Fellow A.A.A.S., Am. Agrl. Econ. Assn. (pres. 1954-55); mem. Am. Country Life Assn. (pres. 1946-48), Am. Soc. Farm Mgrs. and Rural Appraisers (sec.- treas. 1939-44), Nat. Sch. Bds. Assn. (pres. 1966-67), Ill. Assn. Sch. Bds. (pres. 1958-60). Phi Eta Sigma, Alpha Zeta, Gamma Sigma Delta, Phi Delta Gamma, Farm House (nat. pres. 1948-52), Sigma Xi (asso.). Author: (with others) Town and Country Churches and Family Farming, 1956; agrl. reports, bulls. Editor: Farm and Rural Life After the War, 1944; (with others) Family Farm Policy, 1947, Agrarian Reform and Moral Responsibility, 1949. Home: 399 Poplar Av Elmhurst IL 60126 Office: Farm Found 600 S Michigan Av Chicago IL 60605

ACKERMAN, LENNIS CAMPBELL, ship bldg. exec; b. Los Angeles, July 28, 1917; s. Lennis Howard and Ethel (Campbell) A.; A.B., U. Cal. at Los Angeles, 1940; m. Barbara Bohlken, July 27, 1941; children—Nancy (Mrs. Michael H. Burnaugh), Janet (Mrs. Herbert Wilfert), John, Barbara, George. With Texaco, Los Angeles, 1940-43, Schenley Distillers, San Francisco, 1945-48; merchandiser Richfield Oil Corp., San Francisco, 1949-52; sales rep. Walter Mfg. Co., 1952-56, marketing adminstr., 1956-58, v.p., gen. mgr. Canadian subsidiary Galt Metal Industries, 1958-63, v.p. internat. operations parent company, 1963-65, v.p. marketing, 1965, pres., 1966-68; pres., chief exec. officer Newport News Shipbldg. and Dry Dock Co., 1969—, also dir., pres. subsidiary Nuclear Service and Constrn. Co., 1969—; sr. v.p. Tenneco, Inc.; dir. Walker Mfg. Co., J.I. Case Co., Deep Sea Ventures, 1st and Merchants Corp., 1st and Merchants Nat. Bank. Mem. shipbldg. adv. com. Naval Ship Systems Command; sec Va. Port Authority, 1971—. Mem. nat. corps. com. United Negro Coll. Fund; chmn. Sch. Bus. Adminstrn. Sponsors, Inc., Coll. William and Mary, 1970—. Mem. Va. adv. bd. Radio Free Europe Fund. Served with USAAF, 1943-45. Mem. Soc. Naval Architects and Marine Engrs., Va. Mfrs. Assn. (indsl. devel. com.), Propeller Club U.S., Am. Bur. Shipping, Soc. Naval Engrs., Navy League U.S. (Hampton Rds. council), Alpha Sigma Phi. Office: 4101 Washington Av Newport News VA 23607

ACKERMAN, LOUIS LEROY, printing co. exec.; b. Seymour, Ind., Sept. 2, 1916; s. Louis A. and Lora (Kindred) A.; grad. Seymour Bus. Coll.; m. Josephine Kruse, Apr. 24, 1938; children—Janet (Mrs. Fred H. Kaiser), Roger Louis, David Lee, Sally Jo. Purchasing agt. Arvin Industries, Inc., Columbus, Ind., 1936-50; asst. dir. purchasing Capehart div. Internat. Tel.&Tel. Corp., 1950-53; dir. purchasing Warwick Mfg. Co., Chgo, 1953-56; v.p. Columbia div. CBS, 1956-57; v.p. R.R. Donnelley & Sons Co., Chgo., 1957- -. Mem. Elmhurst (Ill.) Planning Commn.; pres. Elmhurst P.T.A., Elmhurst Youth Center, Bd. Edn. Dist. 88, Dupage County, Ill. Mem. Purchasing Agts. Assn. Chgo., Nat. Purchasing Agts. Assn., Ill. C. of C., Chgo. Assn. Commerce and Industry. Republican. Lutheran. Home: 405 Arlington Av Elmhurst IL 60126 Office: 2223 Martin Luther King Dr Chicago IL 60616

ACKERMAN, MARTIN SOL, lawyer, corp. exec.; b. Rochester, N.Y., Mar. 19, 1932; s. Louis and Rebecca (Ressel) A.; B.A., Syracuse U., 1953; J.D., Rutgers U., 1968; m. Frances Shapiro, July 4, 1954; children—Debra Sue, Richard Scott Victoria Lynn. Admitted to N.Y. bar, 1956; law sec. to judge, Elizabeth N.J., 1956-57; practice in N.Y.C., 1957—; mem. firm Rubin & Rubin, 1957-61, Cooper, Ostrin, DeVarco & Ackerman, 1962-71; pres., chmn. bd. Perfect Photo, Inc., Phila., 1962—, United Whelan Corp., N.Y.C., 1965—, Hudson Nat., Inc., N.Y.C., 1966—; chmn. bd. Equality Plastics, Inc., N.Y.C., 1965—, Studer's Photos, Inc., Tex., 1966—; chmn. bd. dirs. Hudson Nat., Inc., 1965-66; chmn. bd., pres. Perfect Film & Chem. Corp., Manhasset, N.Y., 1962—; pres. Curtis Pub. Co., 1968-69, now dir. Lectr., Am. Mgmt. Assn., Master Photo Dealers and Finishers Assn. Mem. corp. adv. bd. Syracuse U. Mem. Am., N.Y. bar assns., Phi Delta Phi, Kappa Nu. Clubs: Engineers Country (Roslyn, N.Y.). Author: Beyond the Kodak, 1964; also book rev., chpt. in book. Home: 175 Peach Dr East Hills Long Island NY 11576 Office: 58 Park Av New York City NY 10016

ACKERMAN, MAX, accountant; b. N.Y.C., Sept. 10, 1903; s. Alter and Betty (Green) A.; student Coll. City N.Y., 1922-25; LL.B., N.Y. Law Sch., 1929; m. Rose S. Steinberg, May 27, 1934; 1 dau., Ellen May. Associated with Alfred R. Bachrach & Co., C.P.A., 1925-41, partner, 1941-53; treas. Nat. Container Corp. and its subsidiaries, 1953-56, following merger with Owens Ill. Glass Co., controller Nat. Container Corp. and Mill and Bag divs. Owens Ill. Glass Co., 1956-58; partner Ackerman & Ackerman, C.P.A.'s, N.Y.C., 1958-68; partner Ackerman, Turken & Co., C.P.A.'s, N.Y.C., 1968-70. C.P.A., N.Y. Mem. N.Y. State Soc. C.P.A.'s, Am. Inst. C.P.A.'s, Nat. Asen. Accountants, Financial Execs. Inst. Address: 37 W 72d St New York City NY 10017

ACKERMAN, ORA RAY, hosp. supt.; b. Mapleton, Minn., Jan. 13, 1931; s. Ora R. and Minnie T. (Quam) A.; B.S. with distinction, U. Minn., 1953, M.Ed., 1955; certificate dir. recreation Ind. U., 1961, Ed.D., 1963; certificate recreation techniques in rehab. N.Y. U., 1966; grad. exec. devel. program, Ind. U., 1968; m. Barbara Singley, Mar. 25, 1951; children—Bruce, David, Cindy. Mental health coordinator in Cal., Md. and Ind., 1953-63; dir. edn. and activity therapy Ind. Dept. Mental Health, 1963-66; supt. Ft. Wayne (Ind.) State Hosp. and Tng. Center, 1966—. Vis. prof. psychology Ind. U., Purdue-Ft. Wayne campus, 1967—. Mem. adv. council title IV-A, Ind. State Library, 1968—; mem. gov.'s tech. planning com. for devel. plans for Correction Center, 1970—; mem. Ind. Mental Health-Mental Retardation Commn., 1970—. Mem. Nat. Recreation Assn. (dist. adv. com. 1965-68), Nat. Therapeutic Recreation Soc. (div. 1966-69), Am. Soc. Mental Hosp. Bus. Adminstrs., Am. Soc. Mental Deficiency, Am. Recreation Soc., Ind. Park and Recreation Assn. Methodist (chmn. bd. 1967, mem. commn. social concerns 1958-69). Kiwanian. Contbr. profl. jours. Office: 801 E State Blvd Fort Wayne IN 46805

ACKERMAN, RICHARD HENRY, bishop; b. Pitts., Aug. 30, 1903; s. John and Josephine (Richard) A.; B.A., Duquesne U., 1923, Litt.D., 1961; student St. Mary's Sem., Norwalk, Conn., U. Fribourg (Switzerland), U. Mich.; LL.D., Niagara U., 1953. Ordained priest Roman Cath. Ch., 1926; prof. philosophy, 1930-35, prin. high sch., 1935-40; nat. dir. Pontifical Assn. of Holy Childhood, internat. papal mission- aid soc. for benefit underprivileged children, 1940-56, pres. bd., v.p. superior council, Paris, France; consecrated titular bishop of Lares, aux. bishop of San Diego, 1956; vicar gen. Diocese of San Diego; bishop Covington, Ky., 1960—. Decorated Pro Ecclesiae et Pontifice, 1947, K.C. (4). Clubs: New York Athletic; Pittsburgh Athletic. Editor: The Paraclete, 1928-30; Annals of Holy Childhood, 1940-56. Address: 1140 Madison Av Covington KY 41011

ACKERMAN, ROBERT WILLIAM, educator; b. Swanton, O., Feb. 1, 1910; s. George R. and Zula (Stine) A.; A.B., U. Mich., 1931, M.A., 1933, Ph.D., 1938; m. Gretchen Paulus, Sept. 1, 1962; children-George William, Elinor Lawrence. Faculty, Wash. State Coll., 1938-41, Ill. Inst. Tech., 1941-42; mem. faculty Stanford, 1946—, prof. English philology, 1969—. Served to capt. USAAF, 1942-46. Mem. Internat. Arthurian Soc. (pres. Am. br.), Mediaeval Acad. Am. Author: Syre Gawene and Earl of CarelyLe: An Edition, 1947; An Index of the Arthurian Names in Middle English, 1952; Ywain the Knight of the Lion (translated with Frederick W. Locke), 1957; Backgrounds of Medieval English Literature, 1966. Home: 425 Lemon St Menlo Park CA 94025 Office: Dept English Stanford U Stanford CA 94305

ACKERMAN, THERON LENNIS, mgmt. cons.; b. Belle Fourche, S.D., Aug. 20, 1905; s. Theodore Lennis and Dena Serafia (Berglund-Anderson) A.; B.S. in Indsl. Engring., Mont. State U., 1928; m. Edith Catherine Reid, July 22, 1930; children—Donald Reid, Janet Elaine (Mrs. Eugene Leighton Lawler), Anne Brooks (Mrs. William Bryan). Employed various positions accounting dept. Mountain States Tel. & Tel. Co., Denver, 1928-56, comptroller, 1956—, v.p., comptroller, 1960-65, v.p. planning, 1965-70; v.p. Alter, Ackerman & Assos., Denver, 1970—; dir. Security Nat. Bank. Past pres. Downtown Denver Improvement Assn.; dir. Downtown Denver Master Plan Com.; devel. bd. U. Denver; trustee Colo. Med. Service. Mem. Nat. Assn. Accountants (past pres.), Financial Execs. Inst. (past pres. Rocky Mountain chpt.), Denver C. of C. (past pres., hon. dir.), Scabbard and Blade, Sigma Alpha Epsilon. Mason. Clubs: Denver, Country (Denver, Colorado). Home: 35 Sedgwick Dr Englewood, CO 80110. Office: 820 16th St Denver CO 80202

ACKERMAN, WESLEY ARDMORE, chem. co. exec.; b. Elizabeth, N.J., Apr. 29, 1921; s. Harry and Maude (Peterson) A.; student U. Ariz., 1939-42; M.B.A., Harvard, 1943; m. Jacqueline R. Henning, Sept. 11, 1948; 1 son, Michael D. With U.S. Borax & Chem. Corp. and predecessors, Los Angeles, 1947—, sec., 1957—. Served with AUS, 1943-46. Home: 26119 Basswood Av Palos Verdes Peninsula, CA 90274. Office: 3075 Wilshire Blvd Los Angeles CA 90005

ACKERMAN, WILLIAM COOPER, ednl. and cultural affairs cons.; b. Mt. Vernon, O., May 15, 1908; s. William Asa and Mildred (Cooper) A.; A.B. cum laude, Princeton, 1931; m. Margaret Green, June 3, 1933; children—Thomas Cooper, Constance Ackerman Hutchinson. Mem. editorial staff Cleve. Plain Dealer, 1932-36; mem. adminstr., staff Princeton, 1936-40; dir. reference dept. CBS, 1940-57, exec. dir. CBS Found., Inc., 1954-61, dir. spl. projects CBS News, 1957-61; spl. asst. Bur. Ednl. and Cultural Affairs, Dept. of State, 1961-62, 65-68, dep. pub. information and reports, 1962-65, dir. pub. information and reports, 1968-70, cons., 1970; staff Washington Internat. Center for Spl. Research Projects, 1971—. Exec. sec. Pres.'s Materials Policy Commn., Washington, 1951-52. Trustee, Merc. Library Assn., 1951-61, pres. 1959-60. Mem. Nat. Indsl. Conf. Bd. (council of execs. on co. contbns. 1955-61). Presbyn. (trustee). Club: Saint Albans Tennis. Home: 5501 Kirkwood Dr Westwood Washington DC 20016

ACKERMANN, ROBERT JOHN, educator; b. Sandusky, O., Mar. 5, 1933; s. Robert William and Anna Marie (Langkammerer) A.; A.B., Capital U., 1954; M.A., Ohio U., 1957; Ph.D., Mich. State U., 1960; m. Inge Margaret Gutheil, Aug. 26, 1956; children—Robert Frederick, Carl Bruce, Ilse Marie. Instr. philosophy Wash. State U., 1960; asst. prof. U. Pa., 1961; asso. prof. Washington U., St. Louis, 1963-68; prof. U. Mass. at Amherst, 1968—. Fulbright lectr., Exeter, Eng., 1964-65; Guggenheim fellow, 1968-69. Author: Theories of Knowledge, 1964; Non-deductive Inference, 1966; Introduction to Many-Valued Logics, 1967; Modern Deductive Logic, 1970; Philosophy of Science, 1970. Contbr. profl. jours. Home: 45 Applewood Lane Amherst MA 01002

ACKERMANN, WILLIAM CARL, state ofcl., educator; b. Sheboygan, Wis., Oct. 7, 1913; s. William H. and Frances E. (Shermer) A.; student Lawrence Coll., 1930-32; B.S. in C.E. with honors, U. Wis., 1935; D.Sc., Northwestern U., 1970, So. Ill. U., 1971; m. Margaret A. Koepsell, May 6, 1942; children—William C., Nancy A., Arthur J. Constrn. engr. Kimberly-Clark Corp., 1935; hydraulic engr. water control planning dept. TVA, 1935-54; head watershed hydrology sect. U.S. Dept. Agr., 1954-56; chief Ill. Water Survey, 1956—; also prof. civil engring. U. Ill.; adviser office sci. and tech. Exec. Office Pres., Washington 1963-64. Mem. com. physics research and devel., 1947-48; basin com. Fed. Inter-Agy. on Rivers, 1948-56, chmn. sedimentation com., 1955-56; mem. President's Water

Resources Policy Commn., 1950; prosdl. adv. com. Water Resources Policy, 1955. Recipient Distinguished Service citation U. Wis., 1964; Lincoln Acad. medal, 1967. Mem. Nat. Acad. Engring., Am. Geophys. Union (pres. 1966-68), NRC, Internat. Assn. Sci. Hydrology (v.p. 1967-71, pres. 1971), Ill. Acad. Sci., Am. Soc. C.E. (Collingwood award 1944, chmn. hydraulics div. 1966-67, dir. 1971—), Am. Water Works Assn., Soil Conservation Soc. Am., Sigma Xi, Chi Epsilon, Tau Beta Pi. Presbyn. (deacon 1950-53, elder 1962-65). Home: 701 Hamilton Dr Champaign IL 61820 Office: Box 232 Urbana IL 61801

ACKERT, PAUL HERMAN, educator; b. Warren, Pa., Nov. 15, 1912; s. William Edward and Ida (Kaebnick) A.; A.B., Albright Coll., 1941; B.D., United Theol. Sem., 1944; M.Ed., U. Pitts., 1950, Ph.D., 1957; m. Jeanne Helen Yoder, Aug. 18, 1962; children-Daniel Paul, Matthew Joel. Ordained to ministry Methodist Ch., 1944; minister United Meth. Chs., Bklyn., 1941-45, Valencia, Pa., 1945-47, Pitts., 1947-54; prof. Otterbein Coll., Westerville, O., 1954—. Mem. East-West Philosophers Conf., 1959, Congress Philosophy in Mexico City, 1963, Asian Study Conf., 1966. Mem. Am. Philos. Assn., Am. Assn. U. Profs. Author: The Religious Philosophy of Schleiermacher, 1957. Home: 174 Hiawatha Av Westerville OH 43081

ACKLES, DAVID THOMAS, songwriter; b. Rock Island, Ill., Feb. 20, 1937; s. Thomas H. and Queenie (Rolfe) A.; student U. Edinburgh, Scotland, 1957; B.A., U. So. Cal., 1959. Gardener, car salesman, detective, accountant, wrecker, bar pianist, choreographer, playground dir., 1959-66; asst. stage mgr. Sacramento Music Theatre and Music Theatre U.S.A. in S.Am., 1966; artist- composer Elektra Records, 1967—; child actor Columbia Pictures, 1947- 50. Presbyn. Composer score for Children On Their Birthdays, presented on NBC, 1964. Recorded albums of own songs Road to Cairo, 1968; Subway to the Country, 1969. Home: 2916 N Beachwood Dr Los Angeles CA 90028

ACKLEY, HUGH GARDNER, educator, former U.S. ambassador; b. Indpls., June 30, 1915; s. Hugh M. and Margaret (McKenzie) A.; A.B. Western Mich. U., 1936, LL.D., 1964. A.M., U. Mich., 1937, Ph.D., 1940; Doctor of Laws. Kalamazoo Coll., 1967; m. Bonnie A. Lowry, Sept. 18, 1937; children—David A., Donald G. Instr. econs. Ohio State U., 1939-40, U. Mich., 1940-41; with OPA, Washington, 1941-43, 1944-46, OSS, 1943-44; asst. prof. U. Mich., 1946-47, asso. prof., 1947-52, prof., 1952-68, chmn. dept., 1955-61, Henry Carter Adams Univ. prof. polit. econs., 1969—. Asst. dir. OPS, Washington, 1951-52; mem. President's Council Econ. Advisers, 1962-68, chmn., 1964-68; U.S. ambassador to Italy, 1968-69. Vis. prof. U. Cal. at Los Angeles, summer 1950; cons. Econ. Stblzn. Agy., Washington, 1950, Baker, Weeks and Co., Inc., N.Y.C., 1969—. Mem. Dem. Policy Council, 1969—, chmn. econ. affairs com., 1969—. Bd. dirs. Soc. Sci. Research Council, 1959-62. Fulbright scholar, 1956-57; Ford Found. Faculty research fellow, 1961-62; decorated cavaliere del Gran Croce (Italy), 1969; recipient Distinguished Alumnus award Western Mich. U., 1970. Fellow Am. Acad. Arts and Scis., Mich. Soc. Fellows (sr. fellow 1970—); mem. Am. Econ. Assn. (v.p. 1963), Econometric Soc., Am. Assn. U. Profs. (pres. U. Mich. Chpt. 1954-55), Mich. Acad. Sci., Arts and Letters, Kappa Delta Pi, Tau Kappa Alpha, Phi Kappa Phi. Author: Macroeconomic Theory, 1961. Contbr. articles profl. jours., revs. Bd. editors Am. Econ. Rev., 1953-56. Address: 907 Berkshire Rd Ann Arbor MI 48104

ACREE, EDWARD, advt. exec.; b. Jacksonville, Fla., Feb. 19, 1925; s. Joseph C. and Ethel (Brooks) A.; B.S., U. Fla., 1947; m. Angel Faulkner, Dec. 22, 1946; children—Toni Marie, Edward Scott, Jon Michael, James Christian, Patricia Dawn. Trainee advt. dept. Colonial Stores, Inc., Norfolk, Va., 1947-48, asst. div. advt. mgr., 1948-49, div. advt. mgr., 1949-55, asst. gen. advt. mgr., 1955; account exec. Cargill & Wilson, Inc., Richmond, Va., 1955-57, v.p., 1957-58, prin., 1958-61, head agy. office, Charlotte, N.C., 1961-63, sr. v.p., 1963-66; exec. v.p. Cargill, Wilson & Acree, Inc., Charlotte, 1966-68, pres., 1968—; pres. elect Affiliated Advt. Agys. Internat.; sec. Bunker Hill Packing Corp., dir. Hardware Mut. Ins. Co. of Carolinas, White Point, Me. Mem. Charlotte Citizens Com. for Pub. TV. 1968-69. Bd. dirs. Boys Town N.C. Served with USNR, 1942-45. Mem. Am. Assn. Advt. Agys. (past chmn. bd. govs. S.E. council), Hampton Rds. Sales Execs. Club (past pres.), Advt. Club Charlotte (dir.), Advt. Fedn. Am. (past gov. 3d dist.), Beta Gamma Sigma. Club: Charlotte City. Home: 6300 Burlwood Rd Charlotte NC 28211 Office: 700 Kenilworth Av Charlotte NC 28204

ACREE, JOHN THOMAS, Jr., ins. co. exec.; b. St. Louis, Aug. 5, 1909; s. John T. and Birdie Murphy (Stewart) A.; B.A. magna cum laude, Oklahoma City U., 1930; m. Margaret Deupree, Sept. 16, 1930 (dec. Dec. 1968); children—John Thomas III, Laura Diana (Mrs. C.C. Hager), Edwin L.; m. 2d, Mary M. Turner, Jan. 24, 1970. With Lincoln Income Life Ins. Co., Louisville, 1923—, sec.-treas., 1940-46, exec. v.p., 1946-49, pres., 1949-69, chmn. bd., 1962—, chief exec. officer, 1969—. Pres. Old Ky. Home council Boy Scouts Am., 1957-60; chmn. region 4, 1969-72, mem. nat. exec. bd., 1969—. Chmn. bd. trustees Lexington Theol. Sem.; trustee Am. Humanics Found., Ky. Ind. Coll. Found.; bd. dirs. Goodwill Industries Ky., Kosair Crippled Childrens Hosp. Mem. Ky. C. of C. (pres. 1970-71), Alpha Phi Omega (hon.). Home: 9103 Lexington Lane Louisville KY 40222 Office: Box 1173 Louisville KY 40201

ACREE, VERNON DARRELL, govt. ofcl.; b. Washington, June 25, 1919; s. Vernon D. and Elizabeth (Penny) A.; student U. Minn., 1945; m. Doris E. Wight, Apr. 3, 1938; children—Vernon Darrell III, Allan L., Jean (Mrs. Michael B. Winters), Mary Elizabeth. Dir. Internal Security div. Internal Revenue Service, Washington, 1954-59, asst. commnr. inspection service, 1959—. Served with AUS, World War II. Mem. Assn. Fed. Investigators (nat. pres. 1964-65). Home: 8943 Colesbury Pl Fairfax VA 22030 Office: 1111 Constitution Av NW Washington DC 20224

ACRIVOS, ANDREAS, educator; b. Athens, Greece, June 13, 1928; s. Athanase and Anna (Besi) A.; B. Chem. Engring., Syracuse U., 1950; M.S., U. Minn., 1951, Ph.D., 1954; m. Juana Vivo, Sept. 1, 1956. Came to U.S., 1947, naturalized, 1962. Mem. faculty U. Cal. at Berkeley, 1954-62, asso. prof., 1959-62; prof. chem. engring. Stanford, 1962—. Mem. Am. Chem. Soc., Am. Phys. Soc., Am. Inst. Chem. Engrs. Home: 788 Cedro Way Stanford, CA 94305.

ACTON, DAVID, lawyer; b. Phila., Feb. 13, 1933; s. Kenneth Davis and Mary (Musselman) A.; grad. Episcopal Acad., 1951; A.B., Yale, 1955; J.D., U. Pa., 1960; m. Barbara Ann Sullivan, June 18, 1955; children—Lauren Doane, Paul Bodine. Asso. Krusen, Evans & Byrne, Phila., 1960-63; asst. sec., asst. gen. counsel Leeds & Northrup Co., Phila., 1963-65, sec., gen. counsel, North Wales, Pa., 1965—; dir. Chilton Co. Dir. Fellowship House, Phila., 1967—. Served as lt. (j.g.), USNR, 1955-57. Mem. Am., Pa., Phila. bar assns., Colonial Soc. Pa., Mensa, Am. Soc. Corporate Secs. (v.p. Middle Atlantic regional group). Clubs: Union League, Philadelphia Country, Yale (Phila.). Home: 765 Newtown Rd Villanova PA 19085 Office: Sumneytown Pike North Wales PA 19454

ACUFF, ROY CLAXTON, entertainer; b. Maynardville, Tenn., Sept. 15, 1903; s. Neill and Ida (Carr) A.; ed. pub. schs., Knoxville, Tenn.; m. Mildred Louise Douglas, Dec. 25, 1936; 1 son, Roy Neil. Mem. Grand Ole Opry radio program, 1938- -; played with bands in motion pictures during 1940s; recording artist; co-owner Acuff-Rose Publs., also Hickory Records; yearly tours for U.S.O., 1949—. Nominee for gov. Tenn., 1948. Named to Country Music Hall of Fame. Address: 2510 Franklin Rd Nashville TN 37204

ADAIR, CHARLES ROBERT, Jr., lawyer; b. Narrows, Va., Sept. 29, 1914; s. Charles Robert and Margaret (Davis) A.; B.S., U. Ala., 1942, LL.B., 1948, J.D., 1969; m. Lillian Adele Duffee, Sept. 19, 1942. Admitted to Ala. bar, 1948, since practiced in Dadeville; solicitor Tallapoosa County, 1955—; vice chmn. Ala. Securities Commn., 1969—. Vice pres., dir. Dadeville Industries, Inc. D & D Concrete Co., Inc.; dir. Bank of Dadeville. Chm. Dadeville One Drive, 1960; chmn. Horseshoe Bend Regional Library, 1960-65. Served as officer USAAF, World War II. Mem. Am. Judicature Soc., Am., Ala., Tallapoosa County, 5th Circuit (pres.) bar assns., Farrah Law Soc., V.F.W., Am. Legion, Air Force Assn., Scabbard and Blade, Omicron Delta Kappa, Delta Tau Delta, Phi Alpha Delta. Democrat. Presbyn. Mason, Kiwanian. Clubs: The Club, Relay House, Downtown, Willow Point Golf and Country, Quarterback (past capt.). Home: Duffee's Hill Dadeville AL 36853 Office: Courthouse Dadeville AL 36853

ADAIR, CHARLES WALLACE, Jr., U.S. ambassador; b. Xenia, O., Jan. 26, 1914; s. Charles Wallace and Sarah Torrence (Goulard) A.; A.B., U. Wis., 1935; postgrad. Am. Inst. Banking, 1937-38, George Washington U., 1938-39, Princeton, 1947-48; m. Caroline Lee Marshall, Nov. 28, 1947; children—Marshall Porter, Caroline, Sarah. Trainee, credit investigator Chase Nat. Bank, N.Y.C., 1935-36, 37-38, Panama City, 1936-37; sect. mgr. Woodward & Lothrop, Washington, 1938-40; fgn. service officer U.S. Dept. State, 1940—, vice consul, Nogales, Mexico. 1940-41, Mexico City, 1941, Bombay, India, 1942-46, 1st sec. embassy, consul, Rio de Janeiro, 1948-51; detailed to fgn. service sch. Dept. State, 1941, India desk officer, 1946-47; detailed spl. econ. study Princeton, 1947-48; detailed Nat. War Coll., Washington, 1951-52; NATO adviser Bur. European Affairs, 1952-54; counselor embassy for econ. affairs, Brussels; dep. dir. U.S. Operation Mission, Brussels; U.S. commr. Tripartite Commn. for Restitution of Monetary Gold, 1954-56; chief Trade Agreements Div., 1956-58; dir. Office Internat. Financial and Devel. Affairs, Dept. State, 1958-59; dep. asst. sec. state for econ. affairs, 1959-61; dep. sec. gen. Orgn. Econ. Coop. and Devel., Paris, France, 1961-63; minister-counselor dep. chief mission Am. embassy, Buenos Aires, Argentina, 1963-65; U.S. ambassador to Panama, 1965-69, to Uruguay, 1969—. Chmn., Colombo Plans Ofcls. Meeting, Seattle, 1958. Mem. Phi Gamma Delta. Episcopalian. Clubs: University (Washington); Royal Bombay (India) Yacht. Address: Am embassy Montevideo Uruguay

ADAIR, CHARLES WATKINS, mfg. co. exec.; b. Dora, Ala., July 20, 1923; s. William Fred and Esther (Watkins) A.; Accounting certificate U. Ala., 1952; postgrad. LaSalle U., 1953, Harvard Advanced Mgmt. Program, 1969; m. Martha Edd Chisenhall, Mar. 21, 1947; children—Charles Edward, Marcia Diane, William Gregg. With U.S. Steel Co., Fairfield, Ala., 1941-43, 48; with U.S. Pipe & Foundry, Bessemer, Ala., 1946-47; retail salesman Home Appliance Co., Bessemer, 1947-48; with Woodward Iron Co. (Ala.), 1948—, controller, 1962-66, v.p. finance, controller, 1966—. Bd. dirs. Bessemer YMCA. Served with USAAF, 1943-46. Decorated Air medal. Mem. Financial Execs. Inst. (chpt. pres.), Nat. Assn. Accountants (chpt. pres.), Am. Accounting Assn., Am. Foundrymen's Soc., Am. Ordnance Assn., Birmingham Area C. of C., Relay House Birmingham. Presbyn. (elder). Mason. Clubs: Woodward Golf and Country (past pres.), Club (Birmingham). Home: 2133 Viking Circle Birmingham AL 35216 Office: Woodward AL 35819

ADAIR, CHESTER COLE, lawyer; b. Seattle, July 5, 1907; s. George Henry and Estella (Cole) A.; J.D., U. Wash., 1932; m. Alberta Marie Schram, Dec. 20, 1934; 1 dau., Janet (Mrs. Richard S. Eichler). Admitted to Wash. bar, 1932, since practiced in Seattle; partner Adair, Kasperson, Hennessey & Bowden; pros. atty. Island County, 1934-42. Dir. Nagy Enterprises, Farwest Garments Inc. Commr., Mercer Island Sewer District; mem. Seattle Harbor Adv. Commn., 1961- 63. Del. Wash. Republican convs., 1936, 38, 40, 42. Served to lt. comdr. USNR, 1942-44. Mem. Am., Wash., Seattle-King County (trustee 1955—, pres. 1962-63) bar assns., Delta Chi, Phi Delta Phi. Rotarian (charter pres. Oak Harbor club 1936-38). Club: Seattle Yacht (trustee, treas. 1956-61, commodore 1967-68). Home: 8830 SE 54th St Mercer Island WA 98040 Office: 1103 Norton Bldg Seattle WA 98104

ADAIR, EDWIN ROSS, diplomat; b. Albion, Ind., Dec. 14, 1907; s. Edwin L. and Alice (Prickett) A.; A.B., Hillsdale (Mich.) Coll., 1928; LL.B., George Washington U., 1933; LL.D., Ind. Inst. Tech.; m. Marian E. Wood, July 21, 1934; children—Caroline Ann (Mrs. David A. Dimmers), Stephen Wood. Admitted to Ind. bar, 1933, since practiced Ft. Wayne; mem. 82d to 91st U.S. Congresses 4th Ind. Dist.; U.S. ambassador to Ethiopia, 1971—. Bd. dirs. Parkview Meml. Hosp.; trustee Hillsdale Coll. Served in AUS, 1941-45. Mem. Am., Ind. State, Fort Wayne bar assns., V.F.W., Am. Legion, Interparliamentary Union (v.p. Am. group), Delta Sigma Phi (past nat. pres.). Mason (33, Shriner), Elk, Moose. Home: 1145 W Foster Pkwy Fort Wayne IN 46806 Office: Ft Wayne Nat Bank Bldg Fort Wayne IN 46802

ADAIR, JAMES EDWARD, educator; b. Atlanta, Jan. 15, 1938; s. Frank and Ruth (Price) A.; student Morehouse Coll., 1955-58; B.S., Fort Valley State Coll., 1962; m. Marjorie Patricia Spellen, Dec. 22, 1965; children—Andrea Denice, Tonja Michelle. Instr. art Barber-Scotia Coll., Concord, N.C., 1964-66; tchr. art Parks Jr. High Sch., Atlanta, 1967-69; lectr. art Morris Brown Coll., Atlanta, 1970—; dir. Adair's Art Gallery, Altanta, 1963-64. Served with USNR, 1963. Recipient 1st place award Annual Negro Exhibition, Atlanta, 1969. Methodist. One man shows include Miles Coll., Birmingham, Ala., 1962, Fine Arts Gallery, Atlanta, 1964, 68, and others; executed murals Ft. Valley State Coll. (Ga.), 1962, Ga. Tchrs. Edn. Assn. bldg., Atlanta, 1957. Home: 2169 Bollingbrook Dr SW Atlanta GA 30311

ADAIR, JOHN DOUGLAS, tool mfr.; b. Ardmore, Pa., May 24, 1920; s. Herbert J., Sr., and Margaret (Douglas) A.; student Dartmouth, 1938-39, George Washington U., 1940; m. Barbara Whitaker, July 23, 1940; children—John Douglas, Richard Herbert. Chief estimator Kieckhefer Container Corp., Camden, N.J., 1939-41; insp. N.Y. Shipbldg. Corp., N.Y.C., 1941-42; exec. asst. Kent-Moore Corp., Warren, Mich., 1946-47, pres., dir., 1947—; dir. Higbie Mfg. Corp., Douglas & Lomason Co., Vlasic Foods, Inc., City Bank & Trust Co. (Jackson, Mich.), Robinair Mfg. Corp., Pyles Industries, Inc., Maynard Mfg. Co., Am. Gage & Mfg. Co., Standard Forge Co., Standard Composite Die Co., Kent-Moore, Ltd. (Eng.), Kent-Moore Internat. (Switzerland). Chmn. bd. dirs. Kidney Found. Mich., 1956—; dir. Nat. Kidney Found., 1956—; v.p., dir. Mich. United Fund, 1964—. Trustee Village of Grosse Pointe Shores, Mich., 1952-55. Trustee Kent-Moore Found., 1954—; dir. Goodwill Industries of Mich., 1951-64. Served from pvt. to 1st lt., AUS, 1943-46. Mem. Soc. Automotive Engrs. Clubs: Country, Detroit Athletic (Detroit); Bloomfield Hills (Mich.) Country; Pine Valley Golf (Clementon, N.J.); Seminole Golf (N. Palm Beach, Fla.); Royal and Ancient Golf of St. Andrews (Scotland), Recess, The Hundred. Home: 22 Stratton Pl Grosse Pointe Shores MI 48236 Office: 28635 Mound Rd Warren MI 48092

ADAIR, ROBERT KEMP, physicist, educator; b. Ft. Wayne, Ind., Aug. 14, 1924; s. Robert Cleland and Margaret (Weigman) A.; Ph.B., U. Wis., 1947, Ph.D., 1951; m. Eleanor Reed, June 21, 1952; children—Douglas McVeigh, Margaret Guthrie, James Cleland. Instr., U. Wis., 1950-53; physicist Brookhaven Nat. Lab., 1953-58; mem. faculty Yale, 1958—, prof. physics, 1961—, chmn. dept., 1967-70. Served with inf. AUS, 1943-46. Guggenheim fellow, 1954; Ford Found. fellow, 1962-63; Sloane Found. fellow, 1962-63. Fellow Am. Phys. Soc. Author: (with Earle C. Fowler) Strange Particles, 1963. Asso. editor Phys. Rev., 1963-66. Home: 88 Killdeer Rd Hamden CT 06514 Office: JW Gibbs Lab Yale Univ New Haven CT 06520

ADAM CLAUS, educator, cellist; b. Sumatra, Indonesia, Nov. 5, 1917; s. Tassilo M. and Johanna (Musch) A.; ed. Austria, Germany, Holland and U.S.; came to U.S., 1931, naturalized, 1935; Philharmonic scholarship with Joseph Emonts, 1935-38; scholar with E. Feuermann, 1938-40; orch. tng. with Nat. Orch. Assn., 1935-50; m. Eleanor Randolph Bentz, Sept. 28, 1940; 1 dau., Elizabeth Johanna. Asst. 1st cellist Mpls. Symphony, 1940-43; 1st cellist sta. WOR, N.Y.C., 1946-48; cellist, organizer New Music String Quartet, 1948- 54; mem. Juilliard String Quartet, also mem. faculty Juilliard Sch. Music, 1955—; artist in residence Library of Congress, 1962-65, Colby Coll. Summer Sch., 1963; a founder Violoncello Soc., 1956; com. mem. Feuermann Meml. of Violoncello Soc.; rep. U.S. as composer I.S.C.M. at Salzburg 30 Year Festival, 1951; numerous tours U.S. and abroad, 1950—. Chmn. reviewing com. Fulbright grants for music, 1961—. Bd. dirs. Young Audiences, Aspen Music Assn. Mem. League Composers (hon.), Phi Mu Alpha. Composer Piano Sonata, 1950; String Trio, 1968; Song Cycle, Herbstgesängë, 1969. Home: 31 W 12th St New York City, NY 10011.

ADAM, JOHN, Jr., ins. co. exec.; b. Braintree, Mass., Dec. 14, 1914; s. John and Harriet E. (Hubley) A.; A.B., Oberlin Coll., 1937; m. Ruth E. Maddock, Dec. 27, 1945. Underwriter Glens Falls Ins. Co., 1938-39, mgr. inland marine dept., 1939-40; with Central Mut. Ins. Co., 1940-60, v.p., 1957-60; v.p. Worcester Mut. Ins. Co., 1960, pres., 1960—; sr. v.p. State Mut. Life Assurance Co. Am., Worcester, 1968—; pres., dir. Guarantee Mut. Assurance Co. Am.; dir. Hanover Ins. Cos., Citizens Mut. Ins. Co., Beacon Mut. Indemnity Co., Am. Select Risk Ins. Co., Am. Variable Annuity Life Assurance Co. Mem. Mass. Bd. Higher Edn. Bd. dirs. Harry J. Loman Found., Arts Council Worcester; asso. trustee Holy Cross Coll.; trustee Sch. Ins. Mem. Worcester C. of C. (past pres., dir.), C.P.C.U. Soc. (pres. 1967, dir.), Boston Sales Execs. Club (past pres.). Author: More Sales for You, 1949; also articles. Home: 180 Farm Rd Marlboro MA 01752 Office: 440 Lincoln St Worcester MA 01605

ADAM, MALCOLM, former ins. exec.; b. Phila., Feb. 21, 1895; s. James and Elizabeth (Evans) A.; LL.B., Temple U., 1920; m. Margaret E. Redheffer, June 12, 1928; children—Adrienne E. (Mrs. Sharples), Margaret E. (Mrs. Halaby). With Penn Mutal Life Ins. Co. of Phila. in various capacities, 1911-69, v.p. in charge operations, 1937-49, pres., 1949-61, chmn. bd., 1961-62, chmn. exec. com. 1962-69, now dir.; admitted to Pa. bar, 1920; lecturer, later prof. of ins. law Temple U., Phila., 1921-27; former dir. The Fidelity Bank, Phila. Formerly regional v.p. Navy League of the U.S., 4th Naval Dist., World War II. Former dir. Life Ins. Assn. Am.; past mem. Nat. Indsl. Conf. Board, St. Andrew's Soc. Republican. Presbyn. Clubs: Merion Cricket. A founder, former editor and pres. Home Office Life Underwriters Assn. Home: Glenview Rd Bryn Mawr PA 19010 Office: 530 Walnut St Philadelphia PA 19106

ADAM, ROBERT BORTHWICK, dept. store exec.; b. Buffalo, July 4, 1918; s. Robert Borthwick and Lena (Stevens) A.; grad. Phillips Andover Acad., 1937; student Yale, 1939; m. Ann D. Wende, Aug. 20, 1941; children—Wende, Ann, Trudy, Robin. Pres. Adam, Meldrum & Anderson Co., Buffalo, 1943—; dir. Mfrs. & Traders Trust Co., N.Y. State Electric & Gas Corp., Niagara Share Corp.; trustee Erie Co. Savs. Bank. Vice chmn. Buffalo chpt. A.R.C.; v.p. Greater Buffalo Devel. Found. Served from pvt. to cpl., AUS, 1943-45. Mem. Buffalo Conv. and Tourist Bur. (past pres.), Buffalo Better Bus. Bureau (past pres.), Buffalo C. of C. (dir.) Retail Mchts. Assn. (past pres.). Episcopalian. Home: 45 Penhurst Park Buffalo NY 14222 Office: 389 Main St Buffalo NY 14222

ADAMEC, CHARLES JOSEPH ret. educator; b. N.Y.C., June 7, 1895; s. Vincent and Antoinette (Skokan) A.; B.A., Yale, 1917, Ph.D., 1921; m. Edith Beatrice Teal, June 19, 1926. Asst. prof. classical langs. Alfred (N.Y.) U., 1921-23, prof., 1923-25; asst. prof. classics Knox Coll., 1925-29, prof. 1929-60; chmn. dept. classics, 1929-36, 46-60, admissions ofcr. 1928-34, dean freshmen, 1930-36, dean, 1936-46, civilian instr. math. A.A.F. Tech. Tng. Comd., 1943-46; study and travel in Italy, 1949-50, Greece and Mediterranean Area, 1956-57. Served in U.S. Army, 1917-18. Mem. Am. Philol. Assn., Linguistic Soc. Am., Classical Assn. Middle West and South, Ill. Classical Conf., Scabbard and Blade, Phi Beta Kappa, Phi Sigma Kappa. Conglist. Home: Calzada Obrero Mundial 155-402 Colonia del Valle Mexico 12 D F Mexico

ADAMS, ALFRED HUGH, coll. pres.; b. Punta Gorda, Fla., Mar. 8, 1928; s. Alfred and Irene (Gatewood) A.; B.S., Fla. State U., 1950, M.S., 1956, Ed.D., 1962; m. Joyce Morgan, Nov. 10, 1954; children—Joy, Al, Paul. Asst. dir. housing, instr. edn. Fla. State U., 1958-62, asst. dean men, asst. prof edn., 1962-64; supt. pub. instrn., Charlotte County, Fla., 1965-68; pres. Broward Community Coll., Ft. Lauderdale, Fla., 1968—; founder, pres. Educator's Investment Corp. Fla., 1966. Vice chmn. Gov. Fla. Commn. Quality Edn., 1968-70; mem. Gov.'s Adv. Com. Edn., 1966-70; mem. regional council Southeastern Edn. Corp., 1966-69. Trustee S. Fla. Edn. Center, Pub. Service TV; vice chmn. United Fund, 1971; bd. dirs. local A.R.C., 1971. Served to comdr. USNR, 1945-46. 52-55. Decorated knight Internat. Constantinian Order, 1971. Mem. Fla. Tchr. Edn. Adv. Council, Fla. Edn. Council Ethics Com. Sch. Adminstrs., Am. Assn. Sch. Adminstrs., Profl. Practices Commn., Fla. Assn. Colls. and Univs. (bd. dirs.), Fla. Inter-agy. Law Enforcement Planning Council, Omicron Delta Kappa. Kiwanian. Club: Metropolitan Dinner (bd. dirs.) Fort Lauderdale. Home: 105 N Victoria Park Fort Lauderdale FL 33301

ADAMS, ALVLN PHILIP, airline cons.; b. Brand Junction, Colo., Dec. 29, 1905; s. Orson and Letty (Low) A.; grad. Phillips Exeter Acad., 1923; Ph.B., Yale, 1927; m. Elizabeth Miller, May 29, 1929 (div. 1946); children—Nathan, Edith Low, Alvin; m. 2d, Shirley Ward, June 30, 1951; 1 dau., Helen Ward. Aviation editor Wall St. Jour., N.Y.C., 1927-29; v.p. Aero Industries, Inc., 1929-34, Nat. Aviation Corp., 1930-34; pres. Western Air Express Corp., Los Angeles, 1934-40; pres. Seaboard Airways, Inc., N.Y.C., 1940- 43; v.p. Fairchild Engine & Airplane Corp., N.Y.C., 1942-45; owner Alvin P. Adams & Assos., Los Angeles, 1944; ret. v.p. Pan Am. Airways, N.Y.C. Bd. dirs., mem. exec. com. Nat. Football Found.;

exec. com. Internat. Center, N.Y.C.; trustee Nat. Art Mus. of Sport. Mem. Far East- Am. Council (dir.). Clubs: Sky (pres.), Yale (council) (N.Y.C.); St. Andrews Golf. Episcopalian. Office: 447 E 57th St New York City NY 10017

ADAMS, ANDREW JOSEPH, army officer; b. Rose Hill, Ala., Aug. 29, 1909; s. Alfred E. and Eunice (Clements) A.; B.S., U.S. Mil. Acad., 1931; grad. Inf. Sch., 1938, Command and Gen. Staff Coll., 1942, Air Command and Gen. Staff Sch., 1946, Indsl. Coll. Armed Forces, 1953; m. DeLellis Frances Shramek, Oct. 25, 1934; children—Carol (Mrs. David Reynolds), Andrew Joseph, Elizabeth. Commd. 2d lt. U.S. Army, 1931, advanced through grades to maj. gen., 1956; chief staff, combat comdr. 7th Armored Div., ETO, 1944-45; instr. Air Command Staff Coll., 1946-49; adviser Peruvian Army, 1950-52; chief mgmt. div. Office Comptroller, U.S. Army, 1953; comdr. 23d Inf. Regt., also sr. adviser to comdg. gen. 2d Republic of Korea Army, 1954- 55; dir. personnel, also dir. supply operations Office Dep. Chief Staff for Logistics, Dept. Army, 1955-59; dep. chief staff for logistics Hdqts. U.S. Army, Europe, 1959-61; dep. comdg. gen. 7th U.S. Army, also comdg. gen. 7th U.S. Support Command and Mobile Land Force, Allied Forces Europe, 1961-62; comdg. gen. XIX U.S. Army Corps, 1962-63; dep. chief staff logistics Hdqrs. U.S. Army Pacific, 1963-66, U.S. Continental Army Command, 1966-67; chief exec. and sec. Am. Battle Monuments Commn., Washington, 1967—; dir. Fort Rucker Nat. Bank. Director Army Stock Fund, 1957-59, U.S. Army Pacific Stock Fund, 1963- 66, U.S. Army CONARC Stock Fund, 1966; chmn. bd. dirs. Pacific Army-Air Force Exchange System, 1964-66. Decorated D.S.M., Silver Star, Legion of Merit with oak leaf cluster, Bronze Star, Army Commendation medal with oak leaf cluster; Legion of Honor, Croix de Guerre with palm (France); Ulchi medal with gold star (Korea); Mil. Order Ayachucho (Peru). Home: 3412 Chiswick Ct Silver Spring MD 20906 Office: Am Battle Monuments Commn Washington DC 20315

ADAMS, ANSEL, photographer; b. San Francisco, Feb. 20, 1902; s. Charles Hitchcock and Olive (Bray) A.; student piano, also spl. studies lit. and scis.; Dr. Fine Arts (hon.), U. Cal. at Berkeley, 1961; Dr. Humanities (hon.) Occidental Coll., 1967; m. Virginia Best, Jan. 2, 1929; children—Michael, Anne (Mrs. Charles Mayhew). Piano performer and tchr., 1920-30; engaged as profl. photographer, 1932—; dir. photography dept. Art Center Sch., Los Angeles, 1939-42, Golden Gate Internat. Exposition, San Francisco, 1940; vice chmn. dept. photography Museum Modern Art, 1940-42; dir. photography dept. Cal. Sch. Fine Arts, San Francisco, 1946-49; dir. Ansel Adams Yosemite Photographic Workshop, 1955—; faculty Idyllwild (Cal.) Arts Found. (photography), 1958, 59, 60. Exhbns. include one man show, An American Place, N.Y.C., also exhibits prin. cities of world, retrospective exhibit De Young Meml. Mus., San Francisco, 1963. Trustee Found. for Environmental Design. Guggenheim fellow, 1946-47, 48- 49, 59-61,; Chubb fellow Yale, 1970. Recipient Muir award Sierra Club; 1963; Conservation Service award U.S. Dept. Interior, 1968; Progress medal Photographic Soc. Am., 1969. Fellow Royal Photo Soc. (London, Eng.); Photographers Soc. Am., Am. Acad. Arts and Scis.; mem. Trustees for Conservation (pres. 1956-57). Clubs: Sierra of California (dir. 1936—); Old Capitol (Monterey, Cal.). Author 5 portfolios of original prints, 15 books latest including (with Nancy Newhall) This is the American Earth, The Eloquent Light; Death Valley; Yosemite Valley, 1960, This We Inherit, America's Parklands; Basic Photo Series, 5 vols.; Manual, Polaroid Land Professional Photography. Home: Route 1 Box 181 Carmel CA 93921

ADAMS, APOLLONIA FISCHER OLSON, former USPHS officer, cons.; b. N.Y.C., Oct. 26, 1908; d. Peter and Lona (Roschkot) Fischer; R.N., Colis Huntington Meml. Sch. Nursing, 1931; B.S., U. Cal., 1940; M.A., Columbia Tchrs. Coll., 1946; m. Raymond W. Olson, Dec. 31, 1933; m. 2d, Edward Everett Adams. School nurse, Seattle, 1931-33; pub. health nurse, Oakland, Cal., 1940-45; chief nurse Ore. Health Dept., 1951-54; dept. chief, div. nursing resources USPHS, 1955-57, chief, 1957-61, spl. asst. to the chief Div. Nursing, 1961- 63, program dir. Career Devel. for Nurses USPHS, 1963-66, chief nurse for cancer control, 1966-67; free-lance cons. and tchr., 1967—. Ad hoc cons. AID, WHO; dir., organizer 2d Internat. Congress for Nurses, WHO, Peru, 1949; spl. cons. 1st Internat. Conf. on Survey Methodology, Brazilian Ministry of Health, Brazilian Nat. Nursing Assn., 1958. Hon. mem. Peruvian Nurses' Assn. Author: Design for Statewide Nursing Surveys, 1956; How to Study the Nursing Service of an Outpatient Department, 1957. Address: Stratford Hills Apts Chapel Hill NC 27514

ADAMS, ARTHUR HARVEY, marine corps officer; b. Jasper, Minn., Apr. 16, 1915; s. Arthur Harvey and Millie (Davison) A.; B.B.A., U. Minn., 1938; m. Kathleen L. Watson, Nov. 29, 1939; children—Frederick A., Kathleen (Mrs. Joseph A. Baczko, Jr.), Melissa J., Judith A. Enlisted in USMCR, 1936, apptd. marine aviation cadet, 1938, designated naval aviator and commd. 2d lt. USMC, 1939, advanced through ranks to maj. gen., 1967; aviator World War II, PTO; grad. Navy Test Pilot Tng. Sch., Patuxent River, Md., 1950; stationed Korea, 1952-53; staff officer Hdqrs. U.D.S. European Command, Paris, France, 1959-62; dir. information Hdqrs., USMC, Washington, 1963- 66; comdg. gen. 4th Air Wing, 196668, 3d Marine Air Wing, 196869; sr. mem. UN Command Mil. Armistice Commn., Seoul and Panmunjom, Korea, 1969-70; dep. comdg. gen. Fleet Marine Force, Pacific, 1970—. Decorated Legion of Merit, D.F.C. with four oak leaf clusters, Bronze Star with combat V and gold star, Air medal with fourteen oak leaf clusters, meritorious Service medal; Order of Nat. Security Merit 3d class. Hdqrs FMF PAC FPO San Francisco CA 96610

ADAMS, ARTHUR MERRIHEW, clergyman, sem. dean; b. Phila., Sept. 28, 1908; s. Alexander Mackie and Laura (Dickey) A.; A.B., U. Pa., 1931; Th.B., Princeton Theol. Sem., 1934; D.D., Beaver Coll., 1951; m. Margaret Baker, Oct. 23, 1934; children—Robert Merrihew, Janet Dickinson (Mrs. Henry Dana Fearon III). Ordained to ministry Presbyn. Ch., 1934; pastor Glading Presbyn. Ch., Phila., 1934-44, pastor First Presbyn. Ch., Albany, N.Y., 1945-50; Central Presbyn. Ch., Rochester, N.Y., 1950-62; prof. practical theology Princeton (N.J.) Theol. Sem., 1962—, dean sem., 1967—, trustee, 1955-62. Bd. dirs. Presbyn. Ministers Fund, 1952—; mem. United Presbyn. Council on Theol. Edn., 1957-62, 65—; vis. prof. Pacific Sch. Religion, summer 1966. Sec. Albany chpt. A.R.C., 1947-50, bd. dirs. Rochester chpt., 1959-62; mem. County Commn. Human Relations, Monroe County, N.Y., 1959-62; trustee Princeton United Fund. Mem. Acad. Religion and Mental Health, Soc. for Continuing Edn. of Ministers Assn. Club: Nassau. Author: Pastoral Administration, 1964. Editor: Administration In The Church, 1970. Home: 58 Mercer St Princeton NJ 08540

ADAMS, ARTHUR STANTON, educator; b. Winchester, Mass., July 1, 1896; s. Charles Stanton Grace Estelle (Newhall) A.; grad. U.S. Naval Acad., 1918; A.M., U. of Calif., 1926; Sc.D., Colo. Sch. Mines (fellow in metallurgy, 1926-27, 1927; recipient numerous hon. degrees, 1944—, latest being D.H.L., Akron U., 1959, Sc.D., U. Pa., 1961, LL.D., Denison U., 1958, Middlebury Coll., 1960, Clark U., 1961, Occidental Coll., 1962, U. Colo., 1962, U. of Cal., 1964, Evansville Coll., 1964, University Arkansas, 1965, Fla. State U., 1965; m. Dorothy Anderson, Nov. 21, 1918 (dec.); 1 son, John Stanton; m. 2d, Irene H. Smith, Apr. 14, 1956(dec.). Teacher, Denver high schs., 1922-23; asst. prin. The Pitts Sch., Denver, 1923-25; instr. in metallurgy Colo. Sch. of Mines, 1927-28, asst. prof., 1928-30, asso. prof. mechanics, 1930-32, prof. mechanics, 1932-40, asst. to pres., 1938- 40, asst. dean engring. Cornell U., 1940-42, dir. Engring. Sci. Management War Tng. Program, 1940-42, provost, 1946-48; pres. U. of N.H., 1948-51; pres. Am. Council on Edn., 1951-61; pres. Salzburg Seminar in Am. Studies, 1961-65; cons. to pres. U. N.H., 1965-68; cons. to New Eng. Center for Continuing Edn., 1968—. Alderman, City of Golden, Colo., 1937-39; pres. bd. of control State Industrial School for Boys, Golden, Colo., 1937-38; chmn. Res. Forces Policy Bd., 1953-55. Trustee Brookings Instn. Served with USN, 1913-21, lt., captain, 1941-45. Awarded the Legion of Merit, 1945. Recipient of the Distinguished Service award Monticello Coll., 1960. Fellow A.A.A.S.; mem. Am. Soc. of Engring. Edn., Am. Assn. of Sch. Adminstrs., Colo.- Wyo. Acad. Sci. (past pres.), Am. Assn. University Professors, Tau Beta Pi, Sigma Xi, Phi Kappa Phi, Sigma Nu, Kappa Delta Pi (laureate). Democrat. Episcopalian. Club: Cosmos (Washington, D.C.) Author: The Development of Physical Thought (with Leonard B. Loeb), 1933; Fundamentals of Thermodynamics (with George D. Hilding), 1945. Home: Cedar Point Rd Durham NH 03824

ADAMS, BEATRICE, advt. exec.; b. Belleville, Ill., Apr. 11, 1902; d. William and Viola (Cobb) A.; student extension courses Washington U., 1929—33. Advt. writer Stix Baer & Fuller, 1934; fashion editor St. Louis Star-Times, 1935; advt. writer Gardner Advt. Co., St. Louis, 1936-44, v.p., 1944-45, exec. v.p., mem. exec. com., 1945-56, dir. 1946-56, creative dir. radio-TV, 1956-58, v.p. and creative supr., 1958-67. Named Advt. Woman of Year, 1950; recognized as one of 25 outstanding women in U.S., Boston, 1951; Founders' Day citation Washington University, 1960. Mem. Advt. Fedn. Am. (past v.p.), Theta Sigma Phi, Gamma Alpha Chi. Clubs: Zonta, Women's Advertising (past pres.). Address: 530 North and South Rd University City MO 63130 Office: 915 Olive St St. Louisl, MO

ADAMS, BENJAMIN CHINN, lawyer; b. Grenada, Miss., Dec. 8, 1918; s. Benjamin Chinn and Addie (Young) A.; B.A., U. Miss., 1939, LL.B. (asso. editor Law Jour.), 1941; m. Tempe Darrow Swoope Kyser, Nov. 22, 1947; children—Tempe Kyser, Marilyn Young, Benjamin Chinn V. Admitted to Miss. bar, 1941, Tenn. bar, 1946; practice in Memphis, 1946—; partner firm Heiskell, Donelson, Adams, Williams & Wall, and predecessor, 1952—; tchr. U. Tenn., U. Southwestern at Memphis, Memphis State U. Bd. dirs. Shelby United Neighbors, 1964-66, Children's Christmas Fund, 1964—; bd. dirs., exec. com., atty. Met. YMCA, 1960—, Hosp. Crippled Adults, Memphis, 1959—. Served to lt. USNR, 1942-46; PTO. Mem. Am., Tenn., Memphis and Shelby County (bd. dirs. 1962-64) bar assns., Miss. State Bar, Am. Judicature Soc., Phi Delta Theta (chpt. pres. 1940), Phi Delta Phi. Mem. exec. com. Memphis and Shelby County Episcopal Planning Commn., 1965-68. Rotarian (bd. dirs. 1958-59,64-65). Clubs: Memphis Country (bd. dirs. 1963-66, atty. 1964-66, sec.-treas. 1965-66), Rivermont (founding mem., sec. mem. 1st bd. dirs.) (Memphis). Home: 469 Goodwyn St Memphis TN 38111 Office: First Nat Bank Bldg Memphis TN 38103

ADAMS, BENJAMIN CULLEN, Jr., gas co. exec.; b. Lincoln, Neb., Jan. 8, 1913; s. Benjamin C. and Rachel (Nicholson) A.; student U. Mo., 1931-33; B.S., U. Okla., 1936; m. Elizabeth Scarritt, Oct. 1, 1938; children—Elizabeth (Mrs. Hugh Madden), Benjamin, Patricia. Asst. to gen. supt. Okla. Natural Gas Co., 1936-42; chief gas. sect. Petroleum Adminstrn. for War, 1942-44; asst. to pres. Cities Service Gas Co., 1944-48; v.p. Trunkline Gas Supply Co., 1948-50, Tex. Gas Transmission Corp., 1950-55; v.p. marketing and dir. The Gas Service Co., Kansas City, Mo., 1955—. Mem. Tau Beta Pi, Sigma Tau, Sigma Alpha Epsilon. Clubs: University, Kansas City Country, The River (Kansas City). Home: 1230 W 58th St Kansas City MO 64113 Office: 700 Scarritt Bldg Kansas City MO 64142

ADAMS, BERNARD SCHRODER, coll. pres.; b. Lancaster, Pa., July 20, 1928; s. Martin Ray and Charlotte (Schroder) A.; B.A., Princeton, 1950; M.A., Yale, 1951; Ph.D., U. Pitts., 1964; LL.D. (hon.), Lawrence U., 1967; m. Natalie Virginia Stout, June 2, 1951; children—Deborah Rowland, David Schroder. Asst. dir. admissions, instr. English, Princeton, 1953-57; dir. admissions and student aid U. Pitts., 1957-60, spl. asst. to chancellor, 1960-64; dean students, lectr. English, Oberlin (O.) Coll., 1964-66; pres. Ripon (Wis.) Coll., 1966—; dir. Wis. Power & Light Co., 1970—. Bd. dirs. Asso. Colls. Midwest, 1966—, v.p., 1971—; bd. dirs. Council Protestant Colls. and Univs., 1967-70, sec., 1968-69. Served to 1st lt. USAF, 1951-53. Woodrow Wilson fellow, 1951. Mem. Nat. Assn. Student Personnel Adminstrs., Assn. Am. Coll., Modern Lang. Assn., Wis. Assn. Ind. Colls. and Univs. (dir. 1966—, pres. 1969-71), Wis. Assn. Higher Edn. (dir. 1967—), Council Coll. Pres., Assn. Governing Bds. Omicron Delta Kappa. Author articles. Home: 1 Merriman Lane Ripon WI 54971

ADAMS, BROCKMAN, congressman; b. Atlanta, Jan. 13, 1927; s. Charles Leslie and Vera Eleanor (Beemer) A.; B.A., U. Wash., 1949; LL.B., Harvard, 1952.; m. Mary Elizabeth Scott, Aug. 16, 1952; children—Scott Leslie, Lewis Dean, Katherine Elizabeth, Aleen. Admitted to Wash. bar 1952; partner Little, LeSourd, Palmer, Scott & Slemmons, then LeSourd, Patten & Adams, Seattle, 1952-61; U.S. atty. Western Dist. Wash., 1961-64; instr. Am. Inst. Banking, 1954-60; member 89th to 92d Congresses, 7th Dist. Wash. Nominee for pros. atty. King County, Wash., 1958; Western Wash. chmn. Kennedy for Pres. campaign, 1960. Pres. Neighborhood House, Seattle; trustee U. Wash. Alumni Assn., Civic Unity Com. Seattle. Served with USNR, 1944-46. Mem. Am., Fed., Wash., Seattle-King County bar assns., Puget Sound Assn. (pres. 1962-63), Phi Beta Kappa. Democrat. Episcopalian. Home: 1415 42d Av E Seattle WA 98102 Office: House Office Bldg Washington DC 20515

ADAMS, BURKE DOWLING, airlines cons.; b. Omaha, Neb., July 28, 1901; s. Frank Louis and May (Dowling) A.; C.E., Cornell U., 1924; m. Sarah Elizabeth Hinman, Apr. 24, 1936; children—Elizabeth Burke, Michael Dowling. With Cunard Line, 1924-26; writer, set designer Universal Pictures Corp., 1926-28; asst. sales and advt. mgr. Ryan Aircraft Corp. then Detroit Aircraft Corp., 1928-32; v.p. Brewster Aero. Corp., 1933-34; asst. sales and advt. mgr. Wright Aero. Corp., 1934-38; pres. Burke Dowling Adams, Inc., Advt., subsidiary Batten, Barton, Durstine & Osborn, Inc., Atlanta, 1939-70; v.p., dir. Batten, Barton, Durstine and Osborn, Inc., N.Y.C., 1964-70, ret., 1970; cons. Delta Airlines, Inc., 1970—. Recipient Medaille Honneur et Merite for assistance in development of tourism, Haiti. Named hon. consul Kingdom Sweden. Decorated Royal Order of Vasa (Sweden), 1970. Mem. Civil War Round Table. Club: Commerce (Atlanta). Address: 4000 Randall Mill Rd NW Atlanta GA 30327

ADAMS, CALVIN CHARLES, banker; b. Lubbock, Tex., May 12, 1925; s. Claude Edward and Nona Arabell (Griggs) A.; student Harvard, 1944-45; student exec. edn. program U. Cal. at Berkeley Grad. Sch. Bus., 1961; m. Phyllis Jeanne Wormley, July 3, 1946; children—Cynthia, Roger. With First Nat. Bank, Lubbock, Tex., 1939-42; with Bank Am., San Francisco, 1946—, positions in domestic and internat. operations, 1948-62, overseas assignments include Bangkok, Thailand, Singapore, head loan adminstrn. No. Cal. brs., 1967-70, sr. v.p., adminstrv. officer finance in charge internat. loan, fgn. exchange and money operations, 1970—. Mem. San Francisco Adv. Council Small Bus., 1969-70. Served with USNR, 1942-46. Mem. San Francisco C. of C. Club: Bankers (San Francisco). Home: 24 Crescent Dr Palo Alto CA 94301 Office: Bank Am Center San Francisco CA 94120

ADAMS, CHARLES FRANCIS, business executive; b. Boston, May 2, 1910; s. Charles F. and Frances (Lovering) A.; student St. Mark's Sch., Southboro, Mass., 1922-28; A.B., Harvard, 1932; D.B.A., Suffolk U., 1953, Northeastern U., 1959; LL.D., Bates College, 1960; m. Margaret Stockton, June 16, 1934; children—Abigail (Mrs. James C. Manny), Alison (Mrs. Alison Robinson), Timothy. Asso. with Jackson & Curtis, investment bankers, Boston, 1934-37, partner, 1937-42, merged to form Paine, Webber, Jackson & Curtis, partner, 1942-47; exec. vice pres. Raytheon Co., Waltham, Mass., 1947-48, pres., 1948-60, 62-64, chmn. bd., 1960-62, 64—, dir.; dir. Gillette Co., Bath Iron Works Corp., Liberty Mut. Ins. Co., First National Bank of Boston, Equitable Life Mortgage & Realty Investors, Pan American World Airways. Pres. Mass. Bay United Fund. Trustee Woods Hole Oceanographic Inst., Indsl. Sch. Crippled Children of Boston, Childrens Hosp. Med. Center. Served on active duty USNR, 1940-46; comd. vessels Atlantic and Pacific Theatres; released to inactive duty as comdr. Fellow Am. Acad. Arts and Scis.; mem. Nat. Security Indsl. Assn. Clubs: Somerset, Brook, Eastern Yacht, New York, Yacht, Cruising of America. Home: Dedham St Dover MA 02030 Office: Raytheon Co Lexington MA 02173

ADAMS, CHARLES FRANCIS, advt. exec.; b. Detroit, Sept. 26, 1927; s. James R. and Bertha C. (DeChant) A.; B.A., U. Mich., 1948; postgrad. U. Cal. at Berkeley, 1949; m. Helen R. Harrell, Nov. 12, 1949; children—Charles Francis, Amy Ann, James Randolph, Patricia Duncan. With MacManus, John and Adams, Inc. now MacManus, John & Adams div. D'Arcy-MacManus-Intermarco, Inc., Bloomfield Hills, Mich., 1949—, v.p., 1955, asst. to pres., 1956-58, exec. v.p., 1958-67, pres., 1967—, exec. v.p. parent co., also dir., 1970—; v.p., dir. Wajim Corp., Detroit, 1957-65, pres., 1965—; partner Hockey Club of Pitts. Mem. exec. com. Oakland Univ. Mem. Am. Assn. Advt. Agys. (past dir.), Advt. Fedn. Am. (past dir.), Nat. Outdoor Advt. Bur. (past dir.), Theta Chi, Alpha Delta Sigma (hon.). Republican. Roman Catholic. Clubs: Detroit Athletic, Bloomfield Hills Country, Bloomfield Open Hunt; Recess (Detroit); Otsego Ski. Author: Common Sense In Advertising, 1965. Home: 6139 Dakota Circle Birmingham MI 48010 Office: MacManus John and Adams Bloomfield Hills MI 48013

ADAMS, CHARLES JAIRUS, lawyer; b. Randolph, Vt., Feb. 17, 1917; s. Charles B. and Jeanette E. (Metzger) A.; B.S. in Elec. Engring., Norwich U., 1939; LL.B., Boston U., 1951; m. Mary E. Tobey, July 5, 1942; children—Mary Jean, Carol Ann. Student engr. Gen. Electric Co., also New Eng. Power Co., 1939-41; plant supt. Demeritt Co., Waterbury, Vt., 1946-48; admitted to Vt. bar, 1951; pvt. practice, Montpelier, 1951-56; partner firm Meaker & Adams, Waterbury, 1956-70; partner firm Adams & Meaker, 1970—; atty. gen. Vt., 1962-63. Bd. trustees Village Waterbury, 1956-57, pres., 1958; moderator Town Waterbury, 1961. Mem. Waterbury Pub. Library Assn., 1961—. Served with AUS, 1941-46. Mem. Am., Vt. (treas. 1951-55), Washington County (pres. 1966-67) bar assns., Am. Judicature Soc., Am. Legion, Norwich U. Gen. Alumni Assn. (pres. 1960-61). Republican. Conglist. Mason (Shriner), Rotarian. Home: 11 Swasey Ct Waterbury VT 05676 Office: 14 S Main St Waterbury VT 05676

ADAMS, CLARKE, paper co. exec.; b. Noblesville, Ind., May 28, 1910; s. Henry Joseph and Sara Ina (Roberts) A.; B.S. in Bus., U. Kan., 1935; m. Dorothea Watson, May 29, 1936; children—Jane Elizabeth (Mrs. Larry K. Hercules), Clarke. Treas., Champion Papers Inc., Hamilton, O., 1961—. Bd. dirs. Community Home, Hamilton. C.P.A., Kan. Mem. Am. Inst. C.P.A.'s, Hamilton Assn. Trade and Industry, Delta Upsilon. Home: 755 Elmwood Rd Hamilton OH 45013 Office: US Plywood Champion Papers Inc Knightsbridge Hamilton OH 45013

ADAMS, CLINTON, painter, educator; b. Glendale, Cal., Dec. 11, 1918; s. Merritt Cooley and Effie (Mackenzie) A.; Ed.B., U. Cal. at Los Angeles, 1940, M.A., 1942; m. Mary Elizabeth Atchison, Jan. 9, 1943; 1 son, Michael Gerald. Represented in collections Bklyn. Mus., Art. Inst. Chgo., Pasadena Art. Mus., Grunwald Graphics Art Found., Mus. Modern Art, Los Angeles County Art Museum, and others; instr. art U. Cal. at Los Angeles, Cal., 1946- 48, asst. prof., 1948-54; prof. art, head dept. U. Ky., also dir. Art Gallery, 1954-57; prof. art, head dept. U. Fla., 1957-61; dean Coll. Fine Arts, U. N.M., Albuquerque, 1961—, dir. Tamarind Inst., 1970—; asso. dir. Tamarind Lithography Workshop, Los Angeles, 1960-61, program cons., 1961-70. Mem. Coll. Art Assn. (program chmn. 1963) Nat. Council Fine Arts Deans (chmn. 1965-67). Author: (with Garo Antreasian) The Tamarind Book of Lithography: Arts and Techniques, 1970. Home: 1917 Morningside Dr NE Albuquerque NM 87110

ADAMS, CYRUS HALL III, former retail store exec.; b. Chgo., 24, 1909; s. Cyrus Hall and (Shumway) A.; student The Hill Sch., Pottstown, Pa., 1925-27; A.B., Princeton, 1931; m. Harriet Haynes, Aug. 14, 1936; children—Cyrus Hall, Mary Frances. With Carson Pirie Scott & Co., Chgo., 1932-68, controller, 1954-63, asst. sec., 1961-68, asst. to pres., 1963-64, v. p. civic affairs, 1965-68. Mem. Chgo. Bd. Edn. Treas. Chgo. Hist. Soc.; bd. dirs. Better Govt. Assn.; trustee Hill sch. Mem. Chgo. Assn. Commerce and Industry. Home: 1350 Lake Shore Dr Chicago IL 60610

ADAMS, DANIEL PUTNAM, retired banker; b. Buffalo, May 6, 1908; s. Roger Cook and Jeannette (Keating) A.; B.S., Sheffield Sci. Sch., Yale, 1929; m. Adelaide Barkley Koop, Nov. 14, 1935; children—Nancy Jackson (Mrs. Robert N. Downey), Marjorie Putnam. With Marine Midland Grace Trust Co. N.Y., and predecessor, 1930- 70, sr. v.p., 1964-70; dir. Potter Instrument Co., Inc., Plainview, N.Y. Mem. Robert Morris Assos. (life). Club: Wilton (Conn.) Riding. Home: Old Huckleberry Rd Wilton CT 06897

ADAMS, DAVID CHARLES, broadcasting exec.; b. Buffalo, 1913; s. Joseph and Matilda (Berkman) A.; A.B. summa cum laude, U. Buffalo, 1934, LL.B., 1937; m. May M. Grelick, Nov. 24, 1940 (dec. Jan. 1970); children—Donald J., Jonathan J. (dec.); m. 2d, Ilyana Y. Lanin, June 16, 1971. Admitted to N.Y. bar, 1937; practiced with Jules C. Randal, Buffalo, 1937-41; atty. FCC, 1941-43, 45-47, asst. to gen. counsel FCC, 1946; with NBC, N.Y.C., 1947—, asst. gen. counsel, 1947-48, v.p., gen. atty. RCA Communications, Inc., 1948-49, asst. to exec. v.p. NBC, 1949-52, v.p., 1953-56, exec. v.p. corporate relations, 1956-59, sr. exec. v.p., 1959-68, exec. v.p., 1969-72, chmn. bd., 1972—. Mem. U.S. Delegation Internat. Telecommunications Confs., 1947. Served from pvt. to cpl. A.A.A., AUS, 1943-45, 2d lt. M.I. Service 1945. Democrat. Home: 142 Old Post Rd N Croton-on-Hudson NY 10520 Office: 30 Rockefeller Plaza New York City NY 10020

ADAMS, DENVEL DALE, assn. exec.; b. Clarkton, Mo., Aug. 15, 1921; s. Omer Franklin and Corrinne (Ligon) A.; student Am. U., 1945; m. Lois E. Green, Sept. 1944 (div. Feb. 1953); children—Bruce D., Joyce Rita; m. 2d Delores Helen Sadler, Feb. 7, 1953; children—Kyle Jo, Kim Louise. With Disabled Am. Veterans, Cin., 1945—, nat. service officer, 1945-60, nat. dir. claims, 1960-62, nat. adj. 1962—. Served with AUS, 1938-44. Mem. Am. Legion, V.F.W. Mem. The Cin. Club, Inc. Home: 2233 Peppermint Lane Cincinnati, OH 45238. Office: 3725 Alexandria Pike Cold Spring KY 41076

ADAMS, DON, actor; b. N.Y.C.; student Terry Art Inst., N.Y.C.; m. Dorothy Adams; 1 dau., Stacey Noel. Formerly comml. artist; author comedy material. appeared small clubs as comedian; appeared on Arthur Godfrey's TV show, also Garry Moore's show and Steve Allen's show; regular mem. Perry Como TV show; appeared as Byron Glick on The Bill Dana Show; now starring as Maxwell Smart in Get Smart. Served with USMCR, World War II. Recipient Emmy award (2). Address: care CBS-TV 51 W 52d St New York City NY 10019

ADAMS, DONALD CROXTON, office equipment mfr.; b. Cleve., May 26, 1914; s. Walter S. and Mabel (Croxton) A.; B.A., Yale, 1935; m. Nancy Jane Downer, Aug. 18, 1938; children—Peter Webster, David Huntington. Trainee, asst. export mgr. Addressograph-Multigraph Corp., Cleve., 1935-43, asst. sec., 1943-45, export mgr., 1945-55, treas., 1955-59, v.p., treas., 1965-68, adminstrv. pres.-treasury, 1968-70, v.p. corporate services, 1970—, exec. asst. to pres., 1971—; dir. Hill-Acme Co. Trustee Lake View Cemetery Assn., 1955—, Ohio Council Econ. Edn. Mem. Newcomen Soc. N.Am., Cleve. Council World Affairs, Cleve. C. of C., Beta Theta Pi. Clubs: Union, Mayfield Country. Home: 2886 Kingsley Rd Shaker Heights OH 44122 Office: 1200 Babbitt Rd Cleveland OH 44132

ADAMS, EARL CLINTON, lawyer; b. San Jose, Cal., May 12, 1892; s. John F. and Alice (Sinclair) A.; A.B., Stanford, 1916, J.D., 1920; postgrad. Harvard Law Sch., 1916-17; m. Ilse Downey, Oct. 14, 1922; children—Nancy Camilla (Mrs. Jaquelin Smith Holliday II), Robert Pierce. Admitted to Cal. bar, 1920; practiced in Los Angeles, 1924—; sr. partner firm Adams, Duque & Hazeltine, 1946—; asst. commr. corps. State of Cal., 1923- 26; dir. Los Angeles Steel Casting Co., Hoffman Electronics Corp., Los Angeles By-Products Co. Exec. com. Los Angeles chpt. Nat. Found. Served from pvt. to 2d lt., 107th F.A., 28th Div. and 346th F.A., 91st Div., U.S. Army, World War I. Mem. Am., Los Angeles bar assns., State Bar Cal., Phi Delta Phi, Delta Tau Delta. Clubs: Stock Exchange, University, California, Los Angeles. Home: 1386 Orlando Rd San Marino CA 91108 Office: Pacific Mutual Bldg 523 W 6th St Los Angeles CA 90014

ADAMS, EDIE, actress, TV entertainer; b. Kingston, Pa., Apr. 16, 1929; d. Sheldon A. and Ada (Adams) Enke; student Julliard Sch. Music, 1945-50, Columbia Sch. Dramatic Arts, 1949-50; m. Ernie Kovacs, Sept. 12, 1955 (dec.), foster children—Betty and Kippie; m. 2d, Marty Mills, 1964. Played in Wonderful Town, 1952-53 (Donaldson award best debut actress, best supporting actress), Lil Abner, 1956-57 (Antoinette Perry award best featured actress); actress series TV variety shows ABC; appeared stage show, Las Vegas; co-star film It's a Mad Mad Mad Mad World, Call Me Bwana, 1963. Recipient Comml. Spokeswoman of Year award. Address: Henri Bollinger 3633 Crownridge Dr Sherman Oaks CA 91403

ADAMS, EDMUND MILLER, investment banker; b. Pasadena, Cal., Jan. 10, 1925; s. Walter Sidney and Adeline (Miller) A.; A.B. cum laude, Princeton, 1948; m. Florence children—Pamela Bissell, Lucia Miller. Security analyst, bond dept. Prudential Ins. Co. Am., 1948-50; with firm Crowell, Weedon & Co., Los Angeles, 1950—, partner, 1960—; dir., The Congress Co., Santa Ana, Cal., Virco Mfg. Corp. Los Angeles Bd. dirs., v.p. Midland Sch. Corp., Los Olivos, Calif. Served 1st lt., Navigator, USAAF, 1943-45; Italy. Decorated Air medal with 3 clusters. Mem. Los Angeles Soc. Financial Analysts (bd. govs. 1958-61, treas. 1958-59, v.p. 1960), Bond Club Los Angeles (past pres.), Stock Exchange Club Los Angeles, Investment Bankers Assn. Am. (exec. com. Cal. 1964-67). Home: 1485 Normandy Dr Pasadena, CA 91105. Office: One Wilshire Bldg Los Angeles CA 90017

ADAMS, EDWARD, Jr., banker; b. Yonkers, N.Y., Nov. 4, 1904; s. Edward and Annie Louise (Jones) A.; A.B., Rutgers U., 1927; m. Charlotte Robbins, June 3, 1944. Vice pres. Grace Nat. Bank of N.Y., 1929-42; sr. v.p. Nat. Bank of Detroit, 1945-60; chmn., dir. Nat. Bank & Trust Co. of Ann Arbor, Mich., 1960—; dir. Hoover Ball & Bearing Co., Ann Arbor, Besser Co., Alpina. Trustee Besser Found., Jesse Besser Fund. Inc., Alpena, Mich.; trustee, chmn. Washtenaw Community Coll. Served from capt. to lt. col., fiscal div., AUS, 1942-45. Home: 2111 Belmont Rd Ann Arbor MI 48104 Office: 125 S Main St Ann Arbor MI 48108

ADAMS, EDWARD ALBERT, design educator; b. Tucson, Aug. 3, 1898; s. Ruel J. and Florence (Powell) A.; student U. Ariz., 1917-18, Chgo. Art Inst., 1920-21, Chgo. Acad. Fine Arts, 1919; m. Marjorie Franklin, Mar. 29, 1922; 1 dau., Marjorie Daw; m. 2d, Virginia Legakes, Dec. 24, 1950. Founder, pres. Art Center Sch., Los Angeles, 1930—, also trustee. Leader team design educators to counsel on design for export problems Japanese industries, 1957. Served to 1st lt. U.S. Army, World War I. Mem. Soc. Typog. Arts., Am. Inst. Graphic Arts (past v.p.). Author: The Future of Japanese Design, 1957. Home: 2331 Cove Av Los Angeles CA 90039 Office: Art Center Coll 5353 W 3d St Los Angeles CA 90005

ADAMS, EDWARD JAMES, govt. ofcl.; b. Los Angeles, Oct. 31, 1916; s. Edward James and Nelle (Platt) A.; B.A., U. Mich., 1938, J.D., 1941; m. Kathryn Porter Johnson, June 28, 1941; children—Linda (Mrs. Russell H. Bronstein), Douglas J., Brian R. Admitted to Ohio bar, 1941, D.C. bar, 1950; gen. atty. Treasury Dept., 1946-50; with Nat. Gallery Art, 1950—, adminstr., 1965-71, sec., gen. counsel, 1971—. Hon. trustee Greater Washington Ednl. TV Assn. Served with USCGR, 1942-46; ETO, PTO. Decorated Bronze Star medal Navy Commendation medal. Mem. Fed. Bar Assn. Club: Nat. Lawyers (Washington). Home: 12809 Spring Dr Rockville MD 20850 Office: Nat Gallery Art Washington DC 20565

ADAMS, EDWARD RICHMOND, lawyer; b. Galesburg, Ill., July 7, 1892; s. Edward Quincy and Helen Louise (Gay) A.; student Knox Coll.; A.B., Harvard, 1914, LL.B., 1917; m. Frances Ruth Cummings, June 14, 1924; children—Edward Quincy, Frances Suzanne (Mrs. H. Charles Becker). Admitted to Ill. bar, 1918, also U.S. U.S. Supreme Ct. bar; practice law, Chgo., 1919—; mem. firm Gorham, Adams, White & DeYoung. Dir. John R. Thompson Co., Drovers Nat. Bank, J.R. Short Milling Co. Served as 1st lt. U.S. Army, World War I. Fellow Am. Coll. Trial Lawyers; mem. Am., Ill., Chgo. bar assns., Bar Assn. 7th Fed. Circuit, Am. Judicature Soc., Soc. Trial Lawyers Chgo. Clubs: Law, Legal, University, Mid-Day (Chgo.); Indian Hill (Winnetka, Ill.); Naples (Fla.) Yacht. Home: 200 Woodley Rd Winnetka IL 60093 Office: 1 N LaSalle St Chicago IL 60602

ADAMS, EDWARD THOMAS, photographer; b. New Kensington, Pa., June 12, 1933; s. Edward I. and Adelaide (Suprano) A.; grad. New Kensington High Sch., 1951; m. Anna Fedorchak, Aug. 27, 1955; children—Susan Ann, Edward II, Amy Marie. Staff photographer New Kensington Daily Dispatch, 1950-58, Battle Creek (Mich.) Enquirer & News, 1958, Phila. Eve. Bull., 1958-62, A.P., 1962—; lectr. in field, 1959—. Served with USMCR, 1951-54. Recipient Pulitzer prize in photography, 1969; Grand prize World Press Photography, 1969; named 3d place World Photo Reporter 1969; 2d place World Photo Reporter, 1970; recipient Sigma Delta Chi award, 1969, Overseas Press Club Am. award, 1969, George Polk Meml. award, 1969, Nat. Press Photographer award, 1969; 1st place A.P. Mng. Editors, 1968; named Photographer of Year, N.Y. Press Photographers, 1966, 67, Middle Atlantic States, 1958, 59; Phila. Art Dirs. award, 1961; others. Home: 143 Linwood Av Bogota NJ 07603 Office: 50 Rockefeller Plaza New York City NY 10020

ADAMS, EDWIN E., banker; b. Santa Cruz, Cal., Sept. 1, 1902; student pub. schs. Washington; m. Marie McElhaney, June 2, 1934; children—Nancy Sue (Mrs. Adrian G. Robertson), Janet Lee (Mrs. Eric G. Mausser). Joined Bank of Cal., 1919, asst. mgr. Seattle br., 1936-44, asst. sec., asst. cashier, San Francisco, 1944-45, v.p., 1945-46, v.p., mgr. Seattle br., 1946-50, exec. v.p. dir., San Francisco, 1950-56, pres., dir. 1956-62, vice chmn., dir. , 1962- 63, chmn., 1963-64; pres. First Participating Fund, Boston, 1964-67; chmn. bd. Tappan-Adams & Co., 1964-67; dir. Fund Am. Cos., Fireman's Fund Life Ins. Co., Fireman's Fund Ins. Co., Allied Properties Pacific Far East Line, Inc. Clubs: Family Pacific Union, Stock Exchange, San Francisco Golf; Burlingame Country (Hillsborough, Cal.). Home: 424 El Centro Rd Hillsborough CA 94010

ADAMS, EDWIN MELVILLE, govt. ofcl.; b. Gridley, Ill., Sept. 28, 1914; s. Edwin Melville and Crystal (Montgomery) A.; A.B., U. Ill., 1936, LL.B., 1939; postgrad. The Hague Acad. Internat. Law, summer 1951. Admitted to Ill. bar, 1939; atty. State Farm Ins. Cos., Bloomington, Ill., 1939-42; officer charge Brazil area, World Trade intelligence div., State Dept., Washington, 1942-43, negotiator German external assets agreements with neutral countries, 1946-48; successively assigned by State Dept. to London, Paris, Bern and Frankfort as U.S. negotiator at internat. econ. confs., 1948-50; econ. attache Am. embassy, The Hague, 1950-52; charge Italian econ. affairs State Dept., 1952-55; dep. chief mut. def. affairs, 2d sec., Am. embassy, Rome, Italy, 1955-58, chief mut. def. affairs, 1st sec., 1958-61; officer in charge econ. affairs for N. Africa, Dept. of state, 1961-64, career mgmt. officer, 1964-65; spl. asst. to the dep. under sec. state, 1965-67; asso. dean Fgn. Service Inst., 1967- 68; cons. Dept. State, 1968—. U.S. del. Conference of African States on Devel. of Edn. in africa, 1961. Served to lt. (j.g.) USNR, 1943-46; PTO. Mem. Internat Platform Assn., Phi Delta Phi, Phi Kappa Sigma. Espicopalian. Mason. Club: University (Washington). Home: 1200 N Nash St Arlington VA 22209 Office: Dept State Washington DC 20525

ADAMS, ELBERT SHERMAN, banker, economist; b. Norwalk, Conn., July 17, 1910; s. Spencer Sherman and Leila (Potter) A.; B.A., Amherst Coll., 1931; M.B.A., Harvard, 1933; Ph.D., N.Y.U., 1948; m.. Alice Hudson Lang, Aug. 24, 1940; children-Nancy Joan, Cynthia Linn, Priscilla Jane. Asst. v.p. Hanover (N.Y.) Bank, 1933-49; asst. vice chancellor, lectr. finance N.Y.U., 1949- 52; dep. mgr. Am. Bankers Assn., dir. Stonier Grad. Sch. Banking, Rutgers U., 1953-60; sr. v.p. 1st Nat. City Bank, N.Y.C., 1960-69; sr. v.p., economist Fidelity Bank, Phila., 1969—. Served as lt. USNR, 1943- 46. Mem. Am. Econ. Assn.,' Am. Finance Assn. Contbr. articles profl. jours. Home: Palmers Mill Rd Media PA 19063 Office: Broad and Walnut Sts Philadelphia PA 19109

ADAMS, ELIE MAYNARD, educator; b. Clarkton, Va., Dec. 29, 1919; s. Wade Hampton and Bessie (Calloway) A.; B.A., U. Richmond, 1941, M.A., 1944; B.D., Colgate-Rochester Div. Sch., 1944; M.A. (Colgate-Rochester grad. scholar 1944-45, Ayer fellow from Colgate-Rochester 1945-47, James H. Woods fellow 1944-46), Harvard, 1947, Ph.D., 1948; m. Phyllis Margaret Stevenson, Dec. 22, 1942; children—Steven Maynard, Jill Elaine. Asst. prof. philosophy Ohio U., 1947-48; asst. prof. U. N.C., 1948-53, asso. prof., 1953-58, prof., 1958-71, Kenan prof., 1971—, chmn. dept. philosophy, 1960-65; vis. prof. U. So. Cal., 1966, State U. N.Y., 1971. Recipient Thomas Jefferson award, 1971, Outstanding Educator of America award , 1971. Mem. Mind Assn., Am. Philos. Assn. (mem. exec. com. Eastern div. 1961-64, chmn. program com. 1965), N.C. Philos. Soc.. (past pres.), So. Soc. Philosophy and Psychology (exec. council 1963-66, pres. 1968-69). Author: The Fundamentals of General Logic, 1954; Logic Problems, 1954; The Language of Value (with others), 1957; Ethical Naturalism and the Modern World View, 1960; articles in philos. jours. Editor: Categorical Analysis: Selected Essays of Everett W. Hall on Philosophy, Value, Knowledge and Mind, 1964; Commonsense Realism, 1966. Home: 813 Old Mill Rd Chapel Hill NC 27515

ADAMS, ELIJAH, educator, biochemist; b. Buffalo, Jan. 14, 1918; s. Joseph and Matilda (Berkman) A.; B.A., Johns Hopkins, 1938; M.D., U. Rochester, 1942; m. Blanche Macoff, June 27, 1943; children—Margaret, Janet, Joseph, James. Intern, Strong Meml. Hosp., Rochester, N.Y., 1942-43; asst. pathology Yale U. Sch. Medicine, 1946-47, USPHS fellow in biochemistry, 1947-48; asst. resident medicine New Haven Hosp., 1948-49; Am. Cancer Soc. fellow physiol. chemistry U. Cal. at Los Angeles, 1949-50; vis. investigator Lab. Hereditary and Metabolic Disorders, U. Utah, 1950-52; surgeon USPHS, biochem. research Nat. Insts. Health, Bethesda, Md., 1952-55; asso. prof. pharmacology N.Y.U. Sch. Medicine, 1955-58; prof., dir. dept. pharmacology St. Louis U. Sch. Medicine, 1958-63; prof., head dept. biochemistry U. md. Sch. Medicine, Balt., 1963—. Served to capt., M.C., AUS, 1943-46. Mem. A.A.A.S., Am. Chem. Soc., Am. Soc. Biol. Chemists, Am. Soc. Pharmacology and Exptl. Therapeutics, Phi Beta Kappa, Sigma Xi, Alpha Omega Alpha. Home: 2405 Ken Oak Rd Balt. MD 21209.

ADAMS, ERMA LEE, educator; b. Durham, N.C.; d. John Silas and Flora (Bennett) Adams; A.B., Duke, 1945, M.A., 1959; Ph.D., U. N.C., 1967. Accountant, Duke U. Med. Center, Durham, 1945-49, accountant, adminstrv. asst., tchr., 1950- 57; staff accountant R.L. Steele & Co., C.P.A.'s, Raleigh, N.C., 1949- 50; asst. prof. adminstrn. Antioch Coll., Yellow Springs, O., 1957-59, asso. prof., 1959-67, chmn. dept. adminstrn., chmn. social sci. area, 1966-69, prof., chmn. dept. adminstrn., 1967—; pvt. practice pub. accounting and mgmt. cons., 1950—. Mem. audit com. Yellow Springs Credit Union, 1958-60; mem. Bd. Tax Appeals, Yellow Springs, 1968—; adviser UNICEN, West Dayton, O., 1968—. C.P.A., N.C., Ohio. Mem. Am. Inst. C.P.A.'s, Ohio, N.C., Am. Woman's socs. C.P.A.'s, Am. Assn. U. Profs., Beta Gamma Sigma. Republican. Home: 2195 Rockdell Dr Fairborn OH 45324 Office: Antioch Coll Yellow Springs OH 45387

ADAMS, EUGENE HALE, banker; b. Denver, Jan. 13, 1912; s. Clarence H. and Eugenia (McFarlane) A.; A.B., Yale, 1934; m. Eddina Eugenia Newby, September 15, 1937; children—Devon H. (Mrs. Peter David Bowes), Eugene H., Alan B. With the Internat. Trust Co., 1934-58, asst. trust officer, 1939-44, trust officer, 1944-51, pres., 1951-58, dir., 1944-58; bank consol. with First Nat. Bank of Denver, 1958; exec. v.p., dir., mem. exec. com. First Nat. Bank of Denver, 1958-59, pres., 1959—; exec. com., dir. Denver Tramway Corp., Ideal Basic Industries; dir., vice chmn. bd., mem. exec. com. First Nat. Bancorp.; dir. CF & I Steel Corp. Clubs: Denver, Denver Country, 26 (Denver). Home: 1201 Williams St Denver Co 80218 Office: 17th and Welton Sts Denver CO 80202

ADAMS, EUGENE TAYLOR, educator; b. Millersburg, Pa., Feb. 26, 1906; s. John Furman and Elizabeth (Taylor) A.; A.B. Susquehanna U., 1926, Litt.D., 1952; Ph.D., Yale, 1934; m. Esther Fowler, Apr. 30, 1943; children—Stephen F., James T., Ann Elizabeth. Tchr. English and Am. lit. Sandy Twp. High Sch., DuBois, Pa., 1926-28; mem. faculty Colgate U. 1931—, prof. philosophy 1945—, dir. div. philosophy and religion, 1947—, acting dean faculty, 1950-51, dir. univ. studies, dean faculty, 1950-51, dir. univ. studies, dean faculty; vis. prof. Biarritz Am. U., France, 1945-46. Served as lt. USNR, 1942-46. Mem. Am. Philos. Assn., Phi Beta Kappa, Alpha Tau Omega. Author: Experience, Reason and Faith (with others), 1939; The American Idea (with others), 1942. Home: 88 Hamilton St Hamilton NY 13346

ADAMS, EVA BERTRAND, mgmt. cons.; b. Wonder, Nev.; d. Verner Lauer and Cora (Varble) Adams; B.A., U. Nev.; M.A., Columbia, 1937; LL.B., Washington Coll. Law, 1948; LL.M., George Washington U., 1950; LL.D., U. Portland, 1966, U. Nevada, 1967; J.D., Am. U., 1969. Tchr. Las Vegas High Sch.; asst. dean Women, instr. English, U. Nev., 1937-40; administrv. asst. to Sen. Pat McCarran, 1940- 54, Sen. Ernest Brown, 1954, Sen. Alan Bible, 1954-61; admitted to Nev. and D.C. bars, 1950; dir. Bur. of Mint, Washington, 1961-69; mgmt. cons., 1969—; dir. Teletrip Co., Medallic Art, Nat. Bank of Washoe. Mem. Commn. on White House Fellows, 1970—. Mem. Washoe and St. Mary's Hosp. Guild. Trustee Graham-Eckes Sch., Palm Beach, Fla. Mem. Am., Fed., Nev., D.C. bar assns., Nat. Exec. Secs. Assn. (hon.), Am. Newspaper Women, Am. Women in Radio and TV, Reno C. of C., Senate Secs. Assn. (pres. 1943-44), Bus. and Profl. Women Assn., Cap and Scroll, Kappa Alpha Theta, Phi Kappa Phi, Kappa Delta Pi. Clubs: Am. Newspaper Women's, Soroptomist, 1925 F Street, National Aviation. Home: 701 Skyline Blvd Reno NV 89502 Office: 1700 Pennsylvania Av NW Washington DC 20006

ADAMS, EVERETT MERLE, sociologist, educator; b. Spencer, Ia., Dec. 27, 1920; s. Everett Merle and Irma (Beatty) A.; A.B., Doane Coll., 1942; M.A., Harvard, 1950, Ph.D., 1963; m. Jeanne Viola Clare, June 2, 1943; children—Clare, Douglas, Samuel. Instr. sociology Syracuse U., 1950-57; asst. prof. U. N.D., 1957-58; asst. prof. to prof. sociology U. Colo., 1958—, chmn. dept., 1966-70. Dir. Responsive Environments Found., Hamden, Conn., 1967—. Served with USAAF, 1942-46. Mem. Am. Sociol. Assn. Home: 907 12th St Boulder CO 80302

ADAMS, FANEUIL, lawyer; b. Concord, Mass., May 11, 1898; s. Edward Brinley and Rebecca (Ames) A.; grad. Middlesex Sch., 1915; A.B., Harvard, 1919, LL.B., 1922; m. Rose A. Bradley, Oct. 14, 1922 (dec. July 1923); m. 2d, Susanne C. Root, June 25, 1925; children—Faneuil, B. Dunkin. Admitted to Mass. bar, 1922; since practiced in Boston; partner Hill & Barlow; trustee Cambridge Savs. Bank. Mem. bd. 17 SSS, Cambridge; Planning Bd. Duxbury, Mass. Served as aspirant French Army, World War I. Mem. Am., Mass., Boston (council) bar assns., Cambridge Center Adult Edn. (past pres.), Duxbury Rural and Hist. Soc. Clubs: Union (Boston); Duxbury Yacht. Author: (with Hall) Massachusetts Law of Landlord and Tenant; The A.I.A. Contract Documents and the Law. Home: Marshall St South Duxbury MA 02374 Office: 225 Franklin St Boston MA 02110

ADAMS, FORREST HOOD, physician, educator; b. Mpls., Sept. 20, 1919; s. Edward Forrest and Helen Lea (Anderson) A.; B.A., U. Minn., 1941, M.B., 1943, M.D., 1944, M.S., 1946; m. Ruth Mary Pickhardt, Sept. 3, 1943 (div. Apr. 1968); children—Judd, Scott, Mark, Gregg, Eric, Brent, Kurt, Lynn; m. 2d, Joan Bloch Kaplan, Apr. 28, 1969; step-children—Karen, John. Intern, U. Minn. Hosp., 1943-44, fellow, 1944-46, NRC fellow pediatrics, 1948-49; instr., then asst. prof. pediatrics U. Minn. Sch. Medicine, 1948-49; asst. dir. crippled children's program, heart sect., St. Paul, 1949-50; asso. physician charge pediatrics Mpls. Gen. Hosp., 1949-50, chief pediatrics, 1950-52; physician charge Sister Elizabeth Kenny Inst., Mpls., 1949-50; dir. pediatric heart clinic U. Hosp., U. Minn., 1951-52; faculty U. Cal. at Los Angeles Med. Sch., 1952—, prof. pediatrics, 1958—, vice chmn. dept., 1962-64, head div. pediatric cardiology, 1958—. Cons. cardiology Cal. Bd. Pub. Health, 1963—; div. health exam. statistics Nat. Center Health Statistics, Office Surgeon Gen., 1965—. Trustee Am. Coll. Cardiology. Diplomate Am. Bd. Pediatrics (pres. sub- splty. bd. pediatric cardiology 1967-69). Mem. Am. Coll. Cardiology (v.p. 1968-69), Soc. Pediatric Research, Am. Acad. Pediatrics (chmn. com. residency fellowships 1961-63), Western Soc. Clin. Research, Western Soc. Pediatric Research (past pres.), Am., Southwestern pediatric socs., Am., Los Angeles County (past chmn. ad hoc com. radiation hazards) heart assns., Western Assn. Physicians, Sigma Xi. Author: (with Arthur J. Moss) Problems of Blood Pressure in Childhood, 1962; Heart Disease in Infants, Children and Adolescents; also articles. Mem. editorial bd. Am. Jour. Cardiology, 1966—. Home: 938 4th St Santa Monica CA 90403 Office: U Cal Med Sch Los Angeles CA 90024

ADAMS, FRANK THOMPSON, Jr., univ. dean; b. Cannonsburg, Pa., Jan. 10, 1915; s. Frank Thompson Blanche (Morrow) A.; A.B., U. Pitts., 1937, Litt M., 1941; Ed.D., U. Fla., 1955; m. Alice Weise, Feb. 14, 1942; 1 dau., Nancy Viers. With Gulf Oil Co., 1937-38, Chas. E. Hires Co., 1938-39; tchr. Bridgeville (Pa.) High Sch., 1939-41, Coraopolis (Pa.) High Sch., 1941-42; head dept. extension edn. for bus., extension div. U. Fla., 1946-58, asst. dean mem. univ., 1958-60, dean men, 1960—. bd. dirs. United Fund Gainesville. Served to lt. col. USAAF, World War II; lt. col. Res. Recipient William F. Mosher award Soc. Personnel Adminstrn., 1954. Mem. So. Deans Assn., Nat. Secs. Assn. (hon.), U. Fla. Alumni Assn. (dir.), Delta Sigma Phi (pres. alumni control bd. Beta Zeta chpt.), Phi Delta Kappa, Kappa Delta Pi. Presbyn. (deacon). Home: 2237 NW 11th Av Gainesville FL 32601

ADAMS, FREDERICK BALDWIN, Jr., former library exec.; b. Greenwich, Conn., Mar. 28, 1910; s. Frederick Balwin and Ellen Walters (Delano) A.; grad. St. Paul's Sch., 1928; A.B., Yale, 1932; Litt.D., Hofstra Coll., 1959; Williams Coll., 1966; A.F.D., Union Coll., 1959; L.H.D., N.Y. U., 1966; m. Ruth Potter; children—Gillian, Anne; m. 2d, Betty Abbott, June 14, 1941; children—Judith, Lauren; m. 3d, Marie-Louise de Croy Slater. Various positions Air Reduction Co. Inc., N.Y.C., 1933-48; dir. Pierpont Morgan Library, N.Y.C., 1948-69; trustee Carnegie Corp. Bd. govs. Yale U. Press, pres., 1959-71. Mem. Walpole Soc., Am. Acad. Arts and Scis., Am. Antiquarian Soc., N.Y. Hist. Soc. (pres. 1963-71.), Art Mus. Dirs. Assn., Am. Philos. Soc., Bibliog. Soc. Am. (pres. 1960-62). Clubs: Grolier (pres. 1947-51); Century; Odd Volumes; Roxburghe; Athenaeum. Contbr. books, periodicals. Home: Chateau de Villard 1814 La Tour de Peilz Switzerland

ADAMS, FREEMAN HORNIBROOK, hosp. adminstr., psychiatrist; b. Washta. Ia., Oct. 22, 1911; s. Hicks Lewis and Anna Marie (Jensen) A.; B.S., State U. Ia., 1934, M.D., 1936; m. Margaret Loretta Burke, Apr. 20, 1938; children—Kay Elizabeth (Mrs. Edd Johnson), Margaret Ann (Mrs. Donald Hoffman), Janet Marie, Linda Claire, Victoria Jean. Intern City Hosp., Akron, 1936-37; resident

Summit County Hosp., Monroe Falls, O., 1937-38; psychiatrist Ariz. State Hosp., Phoenix, 1939-41; mem. staff Stockton (Cal.) State Hosp., 1936—, asst. supt., 1952-53, supt., med. dir., 1953—. Served to lt. col., M.C., AUS, 1941-46. Fellow Am. Psychiat. Assn.; mem. Am., Cal. med. assns., San Joaquin County Med. Soc., Central Cal. Psychiat. Assn., No. Cal. Mental Health Soc. Home: 521 E Acacia St Stockton CA 95202. Office: 510 E Magnolia St Stockton CA 95202

ADAMS, GEORGE RODGERS, journalist; b. Mexico, Mo., Jan. 26, 1937; s. George P. and Louise (Innes) A.; B.A., Central Methodist Coll., Fayette, Mo., 1959; M.S. in Journalism, Columbia, 1960; m. Ruth Lenore Windsor, Aug. 14, 1965; children—Laura Lee, David Windsor. With Mpls. Star, 1960—, city editor, 1969—. Served with AUS, 1960-61. United Methodist. Home: 3905 Washburn Av S Minneapolis MN 55410 Office: 425 Portland Av Minneapolis MN 55415

ADAMS, GEORGE WORTHINGTON, educator; b. Jacksonville, Ill., Nov. 22, 1905; s. Albyn Lincoln and Minna (Worthington) A.; A.B., Illinois Coll., Jacksonville, 1927; A.M., Harvard, 1928, Ph.D., 1946; m. Mabel Rogers, Dec. 29, 1927; 1 dau., Pamela (Mrs. Charles Javis Meyers). Instructor in English and history, Massachusetts Institute Tech., 1928-30; asst. in history, Harvard U. and Radcliffe Coll., 1930-33; asso. prof. history and social scis., MacMurray Coll. for Women, Jacksonville, 1933-37, and dir. summer session, 1937; asso. prof. and head dept. of history Lake Forest (Ill.) Coll., 1937-42; dir. training, div. 8, Met. Chicago, Office Civillian Defense, 1942; asst. counsellor for veterans, Harvard, 1945-46, sec. Grad. Sch. of Arts and Sciences, also mem. faculty, 1946-49, dean of spl. students and dir. Univ. Extension, 1946-49; dir. Summer Sch. of Arts and Sciences and of Edn., 1947-49; dean of the coll. and prof. history, Colo. Coll., 1949, dir. summer session, 1950; European dir. Salzburg Seminar in Am. Studies, 1954-58; prof. history So. Ill. U., 1958-61, 62—, chmn. dept., 1958-61, 62-68; acad. v.p., prof. history U. Alaska, 1961-62. Mem. adv. council to the U.S. Civil War Centennial Cammission, 1958—; editorial bd. Ulysses S. Grant Council. Mem. board Jackson County Public Health Council. Served as naval communications officer, USN, overseas, Hawaii and Okinawa; disch. rank of lt. comdr., 1945. Recipient distinguished pub. service award Illinois College, 1959; Huntington Library Research award, 1967. Hon life mem. Austro-Am. Society. Mem. Am., Miss. Valley hist. assns., Am. Assn. U. Profs., Nat. Assn. Deans and Dir. of Summer Session (sec. 1948-49). Author: Doctors in Blue: The Medical History of the Union Army in the Civil War, 1953. Home: 904 Taylor Dr Carbondale IL 62901

ADAMS, HARLEN MARTIN, educator; b. Provo, Utah, Mar. 15, 1904; s. Walter and Violet (Martin) A.; A.B., Brigham Young U., 1925; A.M., Harvard, 1928; student Princeton, 1931-33; Ed.D., Stanford, 1938; m. Lois Carman, Dec. 26, 1938; children—Harlene (Mrs. George Beattie), Gordon M., Martin D. High sch. tchr., Provo, 1924-26, Ogden, Utah, 1928-31, Princeton, N.J., 1932-35; asst. Brigham Young U., 1924-25; instr. in speech and English, Menlo (Cal.) Jr. Coll., 1935-39; acting instr. English edn. Stanford, 1936-39, asst. prof. speech, drama and edn., 1943-46; asso. prof. speech Chico State Coll., 1939-40, prof. speech, 1940-43, dean Sch. Arts and Scis., 1946-47, dean Sch. Edn., 1947-50, exec. dean, 1950- 67, prof. speech, drama and English, 1967—. Mem. Nat. Council Tchrs. English (pres. 1953), Speech Communication Assn., United Presbyn. Men (area v.p. nat. council 1957-60), Phi Kappa Phi, Phi Delta Kappa, Kappa Delta Pi. Presbyn. (moderator Sacramento presbytery 1954, mem. synod gen. council 1952-55, 64-71, nat. council theol. edn. 1959-65, commr. Gen. Assembly 1961, vice moderator Synod 1965). Rotarian. Author: Speech Guide, 1940; Junior College Library Program, 1940; co-author: Language Arts and Skills, 1961; Speak Up!, 1964. Contbr. articles profl. jours. Home: 797 Filbert Av Chico CA 95926

ADAMS, HAROLD PLANK govt. ofcl.; b. Wilmore, Ky., Dec. 18, 1912; s. Eleazer Tarrant and Evangeline (Plank) A.; B.S., U. Ky., 1934, Ed.D., 1949; M.A., Columbia, 1939; m. Sara Kinney, Aug. 8, 1956. Tchr., supr., adminstr. Fayette County (Ky.) Schs., 1934-41; tng. specialist U.S. War Dept. and Ford Motor Co., 1942-43; registration officer VA, 1946; asso. prof. edn. U. Ky., 1949-56; dep. chief edn. div. U.S. Operations Mission to Thailand, Dept. State, AID, 1956-60, chief edn. div. U.S. AID Mission to Paraguay, 1960-63, dep. chief edn. div. Bur. for Africa, Washington, 1963-66, chief edn. div. AID Mission to Uganda, 1966-70, dep. asst. dir. for edn. U.S. Operations Mission to Thailand, 1970—. Chmn. gen. com. Nat. Study Secondary Sch. Evaluation, 1953-56; guest prof. Sch. Edn., U. N.C., 1955; cons. on tchr. edn. Govt. of Somalia, E.Africa, 1968. Served with AUS, World War II; MTO, ETO. Decorated Bronze Star medal with three oak leaf clusters. Mem. So. Assn. Colls. and Schs. (chmn. Ky. com. 1953-56), Assn. for Supervision and Curriculum Devel. (pres. Ky. chpt. 1955), Am. Assn. U. Profs., Am. Edn. Research Assn., N.E.A., Ky. Edn. Assn., Nat. Assn. Secondary Sch. Prins., Am. Assn. Sch. Adminstrs., Sigma Pi Sigma, Phi Delta Kappa, Kappa Delta Pi. Clubs: Kenwood Golf and Country (Washington); Westwood Country (Vienna, Va.); Royal Bangkok Sports; Asuncion (Paraguay) Golf. Co-author: Basic Principles of Supervision, 1953; Basic Principles of Student Teaching, 1956. Editor and co-author: Bull. of Bur. Sch. Service, U. Ky., 1949-54. Home: 34 Soi 23 Bangkok Thailand Office: USOM/Edn Am Embassy Bangkok Thailand

ADAMS, HAZARD SIMEON, univ. dean; b. Cleve., Feb. 15, 1926; s. Robert Simeon and Mary (Thurness) A.; A.B., Princeton, 1948; M.A., U. Wash., 1949, Ph.D., 1953; m. Diana White, Sept. 17, 1949; children—Charles Simeon, Perry White. Instr. English, Cornell U., 1952-56; asst. prof. U. Tex., 1956-59; vis. asso. prof. Washington U., St. Louis, 1959; from asso. prof. to prof. Mich. State U., 1959-64; prof. U. Cal. at Irvine, 1964—, chmn. English dept., 1964-69, dean Sch. Humanities, 1970—; mem. editorial bd. Epoch, 1954-56, Tex. Studies Lit. and Lang., 1957-68, Studies in Romanticism, 1966—. Served to 1st lt. USMCR, 1943-45, 51. Mem. Modern Lang. Assn., Philos. Assn. Pacific Coast, Am. Soc. Aesthetics. Author: Blake and Yeats: The Contrary Vision, 2d edit., 1969; The Contexts of Poetry, 1963; William Blake: A Reading of the Shorter Poems, 1963; Poetry: An Introductory Anthology, 1968; The Horses of Instruction, 1968; Fiction as Process, 1968; The Interests of Criticism, 1969; The Truth About Dragons, 1971; Critical Theory Since Plato, 1971. Home: 1121 Oxford Lane Newport Beach CA 92660 Office: Sch of Humanities Univ of Cal Irvine CA 92664

ADAMS, HOMER MAT, mfg. co. exec.; b. Galesburg, Ill., Jan. 14, 1911; s. Homer Mat and and Ethel A. (Allen) A.; student U. Ill., 1929-32; LL.B., Lincoln Coll. Law, Springfield, Ill., 1938; m. Catherine Weber, Oct. 21, 1932; children—Homer Mat III, John Weber. Hearing officer, chief investigation, retailers occupation tax div. Ill. Dept. Finance, 1933- 37, asst. dir. dept., 1937-41, acting dir., 1940-41; admitted to Ill. bar, 1941; practice in Springfield, 1941-42; pres. Liberian Roberts Corp., N.Y.C. and Robertsville, Liberia, 1946-49; with Johnson & Johnson, New Brunswick, N.J., 1950—, spl. asst. to chmn. bd. dirs., dir. pub. relations, 1961-66, dir. pub. affairs, 1967—. Chairman Middlesex County Sewerage Authority, 1961—; mem. N.J. Mediation Bd., 1954-63; commr. conservation and econ. devel. N.J., 1961- 63; alternate commnr. rep. N.J., Delaware River Basin Commn., 1961-; commr. N.J. State Open Space Commn., 1969—; alternate chmn. Gov.'s Econ. Evaluation Com. for Intercontinental Jetport for N.J., 1967-70; member N.J. com., bd. dirs. Regional Plan Assn. Nat. pres. Young Democrats Am., 1939-41; mem. Dem. Nat. Finance Com., 1960-61, N.J. delegate-at-large, 1964; sec. N.J. delegation Dem. Nat. Conv., 1960, N.J. del., 1968. Trustee U. Ill., 1937-43; bd. govs. Rutgers U., 1963-65; bd. dirs. Middlesex Gen. Hosp., 1956—, Water Research Found., 1961—. Served with AUS, 1942-45; ETO. Decorated Medal of Freedom, 1945. Mem. Tumas Hon. Frat., N.J. Alliance Businessmen (dep. chmn. 1968-69), Alpha Delta Phi. Clubs: Overseas Press, Press, Players (N.Y.C.). Author articles. Home: 3 Longview Rd Edison, NJ 08817. Office: Johnson & Johnson New Brunswick NJ 08903

ADAMS, JACK ASHTON, educator; b. Davenport, Ia., Aug. 3, 1922; s. Alonzo Theodore and Florence Emma (Gromoll) A.; B.A., U. Ia., 1948, M.A., 1950, Ph.D., 1951; m. Marjorie Ruth McGuire, Aug. 12, 1946; children—Samuel Ashton, Sarah Lee. Research psychologist USAF Personnel and Tng. Research Center, 1951-57; prof. psychology U. Ill., 1957—. Served with inf., AUS, 1943-45; ETO. Decorated Bronze Star Medal. Fulbright research scholar, Netherlands, 1963-64. Fellow Am. Psychol. Assn., Human Factors Soc.; mem. Psychonomic Soc. Author: Human Memory, 1967. Home: 11 Shuman Circle Urbana IL 61801

ADAMS, JAMES CARLTON, ins. co. exec.; b. Spring Valley, Wis., Sept. 13, 1921; s. Elmer James and Gertrude (Anderson) A.; student Whitewater (Wis.) State Tchrs. Coll., 1939-41; B.A., U. Wis., 1946; m. Magil Evon Olson, Dec. 21, 1946; children—Kay, Jane, David. With Nat. Guardian Life Ins. Co., Madison, Wis., 1948-54, Continental Assurance Co., Chgo., 1954-66; 2d v.p., asst. treas. Washington Nat. Ins. Co., Evanston, Ill., 1967-70, treas., 1970—; pres., dir. WNC Devel. Co. Served with AUS, 1943-45. Fellow Life Office Mgmt. Assn.; mem. Am. Inst. Real Estate Appraisers. Republican. Methodist. Mason (K.T., Shriner). Home: 1405 Canterbury Lane Glenview IL 60025 Office: 1630 Chicago Av Evanston IL 60201

ADAMS, JAMES FAIRCHILD, bus. exec.; b. N.Y.C., Nov. 9, 1892; s. William Crittenden and Grace Fairchild (James) A.; B.S., Princeton, 1915; LL.D., Union Coll., 1959; m. Katharine Place, Nov. 9, 1916; children—Grace Joy (Mrs. Joe Jones), Catherine Curtis (Mrs. C. Paul Mailloux), Jean Place (Mrs. John Ballard Blake), James Crittenden. Apprentice of the Aluminum co. of Am., New Kensington, Pa., 1915-17 research engr., Manning abrasive co., now Norton Co., Troy, N.Y., 1919-22; gen. mgr. John A. Manning Paper Co., Inc. now Manning 1922-38, mem. bd. dirs. 1923-69, v.p. gen. mgr., 1930- 38, pres. and gen. mgr., 1938-58, chmn. bd. dirs., 1958-69; pres. Internat. Purchasing Co., Boston, 1943-63, v.p., 1963-69; dir. Eberhard Faber, Incorporated. Served as 1st lt., C.W.S., U.S. Army, 1917-18. Pres. board trustees Albany (N.Y.) Med. Coll., 1953-64, v.p., 1964-67; trustee Dudley Observatory, Albany, gov. Union U., 1939- 49, 53-64; trustee Vassar Coll., Poughkeepsi, N.Y., 1939-47; Mem. Newcomen Soc. Eng. (Am. br.), Am. Legion. Clubs: Schuyler Meadows (Loudonville, N.Y.); Century Association (N.Y.C.). Home: 20 Lake Shore Office: care Manning Paper Co Box 328 Troy NY 12181

ADAMS, JAMES LUTHER, theologian; b. Ritzville, Wash., Nov. 12, 1901; s. James Carey and Lella May (Barnett) A.; A.B., U. Minn., 1924; S.T.B., Harvard, 1927; A.M., 1930; Ph.D., U. Chgo., 1945; D.D., Meadville Theol. School, Chicago, 1958; Th.D., Marburg U. (Germany), 1960; m. Margaret Ann Young, September 21, 1927; children—Margaret Eloise, Elaine Young, Barbara Jane. Ordained to ministry of Unitarian Church, Sept. 1927; minister, Second Ch., Salem, Mass., 1927-32; instr. English dept., Boston U., 1929-32; minister, 1st Unitarian Soc., Wellesley Hills. Mass., 1933-35; studied in Germany and France, 1927, 1935-36; prof. psychology and philosophy of religion, Meadville Theol. Sch., Chicago, 1936—; prof. theology, Federated Theol. Faculty, U. Chicago, 1943-46; Caleb Brewster Hackley prof. religious ethics, 1946-56; prof. Christian Ethics. Harvard Divinity Sch., Harvard, 1956-68; Distinguished prof. Christian ethics Andover Newton Theol. Sch., Newton Centre, Mass., 1969—; Hibbert lectr. Eng., 1962-63; guest prof. Marburg U., Germany, 1963. Fulbright research scholar, Germany, 1962-63. Bd. dirs. Civil Liberties Union Mass., Ams. for Dem. Action Mass., Found. for the Arts, Religion and Culture. Fellow Am. Acad. Arts and Scis. (chmn. com. internat. orgns.), Soc. Sci. Study Religion (pres. 1957-59); mem. Am. Soc. Christian Ethics (pres. 1968-69), Am. Theol. Soc. (sec. 1938-40), Am. Sociol. Soc., Société Europeènne de Culture (Venice), Center for Vol. Soc., Assn. for Vol. Action Scholars. Unitarian. Author: The Changing Reputation of Human Nature, 1943; Taking Time Seriously, 1957; translation and introductory essay, Paul Tillich, The Protestant Era, 1948; Introduction, Outlines of Church History (R. Sohm), 1959; (with others) Irving Babbitt: Man and Teacher 1941; New Perspectives on Peace, 1944; Together We Advance, 1946; Voices of Liberalism II, 1947; Religious Orientation, 1950; Religion in the State University, 1950; The Theology of Paul Tillich, 1952; Authority and Freedom, 1952; The Meaning of Love, 1953; Taking Time Seriously, 1957; Religion and Culture, 1959; Man's Faith and Freedom; The Theological Influence of Jacobus Arminius, 1962; Paul Tillich's Philosophy of Culture, Science, and Religion, 1965; Festschrift, 1966; Marx and the Western Word, 1967; Interpreters of Luther, 1968; Political and Legal Obligation, 1970; Religion of The Republic, 1971; Festschrift for Erich Fromm, In the Name of Life, 1971; book chpts. Editor: Phoenix Series on theology and philosophy of religion and social ethics; series of volumes on sociology of politics and religion; editor Christian Register, 1932; Philosophy of Culture, Science and Religion (Paul Tillich), 1965 editor, translator (Paul Tillich) What is Religion?, 1969, Political Expectation, 1971; co-editor, contbr. Pastoral Care in the Liberal Churches, 1968. Editor and contbr. to Journal of Liberal Religion, 1939-43; asso. editor and contbr. to Faith and Freedom, 1950- 1958; co-editor and contbr. Jour. of Religion 1951-56. Translator: The Dogma of Christ (Erich Fromm), 1963. Address: Harvard Divinity Sch Cambridge MA 02138

ADAMS, JAMES S., investment banker; b. Brazil, Ind., Aug. 22, 1897; s. Orley Edwin and Mary (Nees) Adams; M.L., Ind. U., also LL.D., 1959; m. Marvelle Warne, March 12, 1927 (dec.); 1 son, Peter Warne; m. 2d, Elizabeth Graham, Nov. 12, 1965. With George L. Dyer Co., New York and Chgo., 1925-28; v.p., asst. to pres. of Johns Manville Corp., New York, 1928-34; v.p. and gen. mgr. Benton & Bowles, Inc.. 1934-40; exec. v.p. Colgate, Palmolive Peet Co., Jersey City, N.J., 1940-41; pres. Standard Brands Inc., N.Y. 1942-48; gen. partner Lazard Freres & Co., 1948—; dir. Carter Wallace, Inc. Dir. Am. Cancer Soc., dir., pres. Research to Prevent Blindness Inc. U. Found. Div. chief, spl. cons. to chmn. WPB, World War II. Served as lt., pilot, A.C., U.S. Army, World War I. Decorated Medal for Merit World War II. Mem. Phi Kappa Psi, Tau Kappa Alpha. Republican. Clubs: India House, Links (N.Y.C.). Home: 9 Pecksland Rd Greenwich CT 06833 Office: 44 Wall St New York City NY 10005

ADAMS, JAMES TROY, mining co. exec.; b. El Dorado, Ark., Jan. 2, 1921; s. Garrett Lester and Eunice (Reynolds) A.; B.S., La. State U., 1943; m. Lou Ella Williams, Oct. 24, 1943; children—James Troy, George Howard, Eunice Anne. Cost accountant Aluminum Ore Co., Bauxite, Ark., 1943-44; with Freeport Sulphur Co., 1946—, analysis and planning mgr., 1961-67, adminstrv. mgr., 1967-69, controller, N.Y.C., 1969—. Bd. dirs. St. James Parish (La.) Community Action, 1968. Served to 1st lt. AUS, 1944-46. C.P.A., La. Mem. La. Soc. C.P.A.'s, Financial Execs. Inst., Am. Mining Congress (accounting asso.), Fertilizer Inst. (controllers com.), Beta Alpha Psi, Beta Gamma Sigma, Phi Kappa Phi. Home: 62 Old Driftway Wilton CT 06897 Office: 161 E 42d St New York City NY 10017

ADAMS, JOEY, comedian, author; b. N.Y.C., Jan. 6, 1911; s. Nathan and Ida (Chonin) Abramowitz; student Coll. City N.Y., 1931; Dr. Comedy (hon.), Coll. City N.Y., 1952, Columbia, 1950, N.Y.U., 1959; special honorary degree Long Island University; Dr. of Letters, Chung-Aug U., Korea; Ph.D., Fu-Jen U., Taipei, Taiwan; m. Cindy Heller, February 14, 1952. Nightclub and vaudeville entertainer throughout U.S., 1930—; motion pictures include Ringside, 1945, Singing in the Dark (also producer), 1956; theatrical appearances include The Gazebo, 1959, Guys and Dolls, 1960; radio-TV programs include Sez Who, 1958, Person to Person, 1959, Joey Adams Show, 1956-58, Gags to Riches, 1958, also guest appearances; also radio show for WEVD Syndicate; recordings for Coral Records, MGM, Roulette Records; State Dept. rep. to entertain soldiers around world, 1958. Dir. Central State Bank. Dep. commr. N.Y.C. Youth Bd., chmn. entertainment com. for youth, 1959—; del. Allied Entertainment Unions, 1959—; bd. dirs. Theatre Authority, 1959—; chmn. spl. events com. March of Dimes, 1955; pres. Am. Guild Variety Artists, 1959—, pres. retirement found., chmn. youth fund; pres. Actors Youth Fund, Sr. Citizens of Am. Fund; personal rep. of Pres. U.S. as entertainer to Asia, Africa, 1961. Named Man of Year, March of Dimes, 1958, City of Hope, 1959, N.Y.C. Police Dept., 1960; recipient Humanitarian awards Yiddish Theatrical Alliance, 1960, Am. Cancer Soc., 1952, Crusade for Freedom, 1956; Pope's Medal, 1971; honored by Israeli Govt. for work in United Jewish Appeal and Israel Bond drives, 1952; also numerous citations; Am. Guild Variety Artists created Joey Awards for talent in variety field, 1960. Mem. Screen Actors Guild, A.F.T.R.A., Actors Equity Assn. Author: From Gags to Riches (entire proceeds given to Damon Runyon Cancer Fund), 1946; The Curtain Never Falls, 1949; Strictly For Laughs, 1955; Joey Adams Joke Book, 1952; Joke Dictionary, 1961; Round the World Joke Book, 1964; Cindy and I, 1957; It Takes One to Know One, 1959; On the Road for Uncle Sam, 1963; L.B.J.'s Texas Laughs, 1964; The Borscht Belt; Ency. of Humor; Son of Encyclopedia of Humor, 1971; Laugh Your Calories Away, 1971; Childrens Joke Book, 1971; also mysteries. Motion picture: Don't Worry We'll Think of A Title. Home: 1050 Fifth Av New York City NY 10028 Office: 160 W 46th St New York City NY 10036

ADAMS, JOHN ALLAN STEWART, educator, geochemist; b. Independence, Mo., Nov. 1, 1926; s. George Carroll and Eva (Stewart) A.; Ph.B., U. Chgo., 1946, B.S., 1948, M.S., 1949, Ph.D., 1951; m. Anne Donchin, Apr. 8, 1949; children—Joanne Athena, John Allan Stewart, David Donchin, Christopher Barth. Project asso., lectr. geochemistry U. Wis., 1951-54; mem. faculty Rice U., 1954—, 1954—, prof. geology, 1960—, chmn. dept., 1965—; Am. exec. editor Geochimica et Cosmochimica Acta, 1960-66. Served with USNR, 1945-46. NSF sr. postdoctoral fellow, 1960. Fellow Geol. Soc. Am., Sigma Xi; mem. Geochem. Soc., Am. Chem. Soc., Am. Assn. Petroleum Geologists (Distinguished lectr. 1955), Mineral. Soc. Author: (with John J.W. Rogers) Fundamentals of Geology, 1966. Editor: (with W.M. Lowder) The Natural Radiation Environment, 1964. Research in geochemistry, geochronology, revised geol. time scale, new methods of exploring for nuclear fuels, environmental geology, lunar chemistry radioactivity. Home: 2365 Bolsover St Houston TX 77005

ADAMS, JOHN BERRY, univ. dean; b. Millville, N.J., Apr. 8, 1920; s. William Payne and Edith(Berry) A.; A.B., U. Cal. at Berkeley, 1953; M.S., U. Wis., 1954, Ph.D., 1957; m. Polly-Betts Goslin, Oct. 11, 1947; children—Mark David, Jane Elizabeth. European sales mgr. Wheaton Glass Co., Millville, N.J., 1946-49; broker Harris Realty, Wildwood, N.J. 1949-51; asst. prof. Mich. State U., 1957-58; reporter, copy editor Wis. State Jour., 1955-58; mem. faculty U. N.C., 1958—, prof. journalism, 1964—, dean School of Journalism, 1969—; cons., lectr. in field. Served to capt. USAAF, 1942- 46; lt. col. Res. Mem. Assn. Edn. Journalism (exec. com. 1968-70), Am. Council Edn. Journalism, Internat. Assn. Mass Communication Research (exec. com. 1966—), Phi Beta Kappa. Phi Kappa Phi. Contbr. profl. jours. Mem. editorial bd. Internat. Communication Bull., 1967—. Home: 1 Chatham Lane Estes Hills Chapel Hill NC 27514

ADAMS, JOHN CLINTON, educator; b. Phila., May 30, 1909; s. Clinton Baltzell and Julia Frances (Cascaden) A.; A.B., U. Pa., 1931; M.A., Duke, 1933, Ph.D., 1936; M.A. (hon.), Dartmouth, 1947; m. Melanie Parke Updegraff; 1 dau., Melanie Clinton. Postdoctoral fellow Social Sci. Research Found., 1936-37; instr. history Princeton, 1937-41; asst. prof. Dartmouth, 1941-47, prof., 1947—. Served as maj. AUS, 1942-46; ETO. Decorated Bronze Star medal. Mem. Phi Beta Kappa. Author: Flight in Winter: The Serbian Retreat. 1915, 1942. Translator: (Pavlov) Leningrad: The Blockade, 1965. Home: Lyme NH 08768

ADAMS, JOHN EDWIN, neurol. surgeon, educator; b. Berkeley, Cal., Apr. 18, 1914; s. George and Mary (Woodle) A.; A.B., U. Cal. at Berkeley, 1933; M.D., Harvard, 1939; m. Sally Patterson, Aug. 24, 1935; children—Susan (Mrs. Stuart R. Engs), Abligail (Mrs. Leon G. Campbell, Jr.), Henry P. Intern Peter Bent Brigham Hosp., also Children's Hosp., Boston, 1939-40; resident neurology U. Cal. Hosp., San Francisco, 1946-49; mem. faculty U. Cal. Med. Sch., San Francisco, 1946—, prof. neuro-surgery, 1955-68, Guggenheim prof. surgery, 1968—, chmn. dept., 1955—. Served to comdr., M.C., USNR, 1941-46. Decorated Letter of Citation. Mem. Neurol. Soc. Am., Am. Assn. Neurol. Surgeons, Soc. Univ. Surgeons, A.C.S. Home: 18 Langden Ct Piedmont, CA 94611. Office: Univ California Hosp San Francisco CA 94122

ADAMS, JOHN FRANKLIN, economist, educator; b. Tacoma, June 1, 1919; s. Eugene Franklin and Daisy Mabel (Danielson) A.; B.A., Linfield Coll., 1940; M.A., Coll. Puget Sound, 1942; Ph.D. (fellow Huebner, Harrison founds.), U. Pa., 1949; m. D. Louise Williams, Oct. 7, 1944; children—John Franklin, Wiliam Robert. Began career as a teaching fellow Coll. Puget Sound, Tacoma, 1940-42; fiscal analyst U.S. Bur. Budget, 1943-45; instr. Sch. Bus. and Pub. Adminstrn., Temple U., 1946-48, asst. prof., 1948-51, asso. prof., 1951-55, prof. econs., 1955-71, dir. Bur. Econ. and Bus. Research, 1949-62, on leave 1957-58, asst. v.p. charge research, 1959-66, asst. v.p. for financial affairs, asst. treas., 1966-71; prof. ins., dir. Center for Ins. Research, dir. ins. and fringe benefit programs Ga. State U., 1971—; lectr. Wharton Graduate School, U. Pa., 1955-59. Mem. employer accounts review bd. Pa. Bur. Employment Security, 1955-57, exec. dir., 1957-58. Del. div. on aging Phila. Health and Welfare Council. Pub. mem. bur. employment security Dept. Labor and Industry, Pa. Adv. Council, 1951-57; all industry exams. com. Commonwealth Pa. Ins. Commn., 1958-63. Fellow Gerontol. Soc.; mem. Greater Phila.-Del.-S. Jersey Research Councils; mem. econ. studies adv. com. Pa. Planning Bd., 1962; chmn. population sub-com. Phila. area com. White House Conf. on Aging, 1960-61. Bd. govs. Ins. Hall Fame, Internat. Ins. Seminar, 1966—. Mem. Nat. Assn. Coll. and Univ. Bus. Officers, Am. Econ. Assn., Am. Risk and Ins. Assn. (chmn. research com. 1958-65, v.p. 1964-65, pres. 1965-66), Nat. Council U. Research Adminstrs. (sec.-treas. 1963-67, v.p. 1969-71, pres. 1971-73), Phila. C. of C. (asso. chmn. manpower task force; mem. nat. commn. econ.

security), Nat. Council Adminstrv. Research Nat. Commn. Insurance Terminology (mem., editor social ins. com.), Am. Finance Assn., Am. Acad. Polit. and Social Sci. Co-author: An Introduction to Modern Economics, 1951. Gen. editor, contbr. unemployment compensation systems studies in Pa., Minnesota, N.D., Ga., Wyo.; economic resources and devels. studies S.E. Pa. and Eastwick, Pa. Editor: Proc. Joint Conferences on Problems of Making a Living while Growing Old, 1952, 53, 54, also Econs. and Bus. Bull., Experience Rating In Unemployment Compensation to Pa., 1959, Temple U. Bur. Econ. and Bus. Research; editor, contbr. monographs, univ. publs., tech. jours., govtl. pubs.; project dir., editor Older Worker Study, Phila. area, 5 vols., 1958. Home: 4253 Abingdon Dr Stone Mountain GA 30083

ADAMS, JOHN GIBBONS, lawyer; b. Ashland, Ky., Mar. 23, 1912; s. Samuel Morton and Helen (Gibbons) A.; LL.B., U. of South Dakota, 1935; LL.M., George Washington U.; m. Margaret Paxton Williams, June 11, 1946; 1 dau., Rebecca. Agt. S.D. Dept. of Justice, 1935; owner-operator Adams Oil Co., Wholesale, Sioux Falls, S.D., 1936-41; dir. young Rep. div. Rep. Nat. Com., 1946; clk. Com. Armed Services, U.S. Senate, 1947- 48; asst. gen. counsel Dept. of Def., 1949-51, dep. gen. counsel, also dir. Legislative div., 1952-53; counselor, also gen. counsel Dept. of Army, 1953-56; cons. on orgn. and mgmt. U.S. AEC, 1957-58; asso. dir. (legal and planning), bur. air operations Civil Aeros. Bd., 1959-60, dir. bur. of enforcement, 1961-65; mem. Civil Aeronautics Bd., 1965-71, counsel Leva, Hawes, Symington, Martin & Oppenheimer, Washington, 1971—. Adj. prof. law Georgetown U., 1967—; lectr. law Am. U., 1970. Vice chmn. of Young Rep. Nat. Fedn., 1941. Served from lt. to maj., AUS, 1942-45; col. Inf. Res. Decorated Bronze Star Medal. Mem. State Bar of South Dakota, Bar Association Dist. of Columbia, Sigma Alpha Epsilon. Republican. Episcopalian. Clubs: Internat., Army Navy (Washington). Home: 3415 34th Pl NW Washington DC 20016 Office: 815 Connecticut Av NW Washington DC 20006

ADAMS, JOHN HOWARD, lawyer; b. Maywood, Ill., Oct. 5, 1910; s. Edward R. and Clara (Trick) A.; B.A., U. Mich., 1933; LL.B., Chgo. Kent Coll. Law. 1938; m. Christina Joan Plumb, Oct. 2, 1948. Admitted to Ill. bar. 1939; atty. Celotex Corp., 1947—, asst. sec., 1964-65. sec. 1965—. Mem. Kappa Sigma, Phi Delta Phi. Club: Palma Ceia Country (Tampa). Home: 5112 Longfellow St Tampa FL 33609 Office: 1500 N Dale Mabry Hwy Tampa FL 33607

ADAMS, JOHN MILTON, physician, educator; b. Mpls., June 7, 1905; s. Paul and Olive (Marshall) A.; B.S. cum laude, Princeton, 1929; M.D., Columbia, 1933; Ph.D., U. Minn., 1943; m. Carolyn Frances Gaston, Mar. 24, 1934; children—John Milton, Herbert G., William M. Intern pediatrics New Hosp., 1933-34; intern surgery U. Minn., 1934-35, asst. prof. pediatrics, 1941-46, asso. prof., 1946-49; practice pediatrics Nicollet Clinic, Mpls., 1937-43; prof. pediatrics, U. Cal. Sch. Medicine, Los Angeles, 1950—, chmn. 1950-64. Diplomate Am. Bd. Pediatrics (dir.)1960-66), Nat. Board of Medical Examiners. Mem. Soc. Medicine (sec.), Pediatric Research Soc. (v.p.), Am. Pediatric Soc., Am. Soc. Clin. Investigation, Am. Acad. Pediatrics, Am. Phys. Art Assn., Soc. for History of Medicine, Western Soc. Pediatric Research pres. 1959—), Sigma Xi, Nu Sigma Nu, Alpha Omega Alpha. Author: Newer Virus Diseases, 1960; Viruses and Colds, 1967. Contbr. to Brennemann's Practice of Pediatrics (4 volumes) sci. articles nat. jours. Home: 415 24th St Santa Monica, CA 90402. Office: Med Center U Cal Los Angeles CA 90024

ADAMS, JOHN QUINCY, ins. co. exec.; b. Dover, Mass., Dec. 24, 1922; s. Arthur and Margery (Lee) A.; student St. Paul's Sch., 1941; A.B., Harvard, 1945; m. Nancy Motley, Feb. 1, 1947; children—Nancy Barton, John Quincy, Margery Lee, Benjamin Crowninshield. With John Hancock Mut. Ins. Co., 1947—, 2d v.p., 1961-65, v.p., 1965-68, sr. v.p., 1968—; dir. Fiduciary Trust Co., Federal St. Capitol Corp., Zurn John Hancock Growth Fund, John Hancock Advisers, Inc., John Hancock com. Thompson Acad., Boston, 1963—; trustee New Eng. Med. Center Hosp., Boston, 1965—, also trustee St. Wilsondale Rd Dover, MA 02023. Office: 200 Berkeley St Boston MA 02116

ADAMS, JOHN R., educator; b. Cin., July 22, 1900; s. Thomas and Margaret (Morse) A.; A.B., U. Mich., 1920, M.A., 1922; Ph.D., U. So. Cal., 1940; m. Jane Ford, June 26, 1923. Instr. rhetoric U. Mich., 1920-25; asso. in English U. Wash., 1925-28; with San Diego State Coll., 1928-, prof. English, 1940, chmn. div. langs. and lit., 1946-56, chmn. div. of humanities, 1956-68, coll. archivist, 1968—; vis. prof. summers, Alabama Poly Inst., 1925, U. So. Cal., 1940, San Francisco State Coll., 1948. Mem. Modern Lang. Assn., Am. Dialect Soc., Nat. Council Tchrs of English, Am. Assn. U. Profs., Philol. Assn. Pacific Coast, San Diego County Hist. Soc., Phi Beta Kappa. Club: University (San Diego). Author: Harriet Beecher Stowe, 1963; Books and Authors of San Diego, 1966. Office: San Diego State College San Diego CA 92115

ADAMS, JOHN WESLEY, Jr., fgn. service officer; b. Fond du Lac, Wis., Nov. 2, 1913; s. John Wesley and Mary Elizabeth (Biehn) A.; B.S., Northwestern U., 1935, M.A., 1937; m. Frances Elizabeth McStay, July 8, 1939; children—Thomas McStay, Daniel James, Katharine Odell. With U.S. Dept. State, 1941—; econ. analyst, Quito, Ecuador, 1943; tech. adviser U.S. delegation San Francisco Conf., 1945; occasional adviser U.S. rep. to UN Security Council, 1946-48; mem. U.S. delegation Inter-Am. Conf., Rio de Janeiro, 1947; adviser U.S. rep. on UN Commn. for India and Pakistan, Kashmir Commn., 1948; fgn. service officer, 1949—; 2d sec., Cairo, 1950- 52, New Delhi, 1952-55; with Am. embassy, London, Eng., 1955-59, 1st sec., 1956; Dept. State, 1959—, officer-in-charge econ. affairs Office S. Asian Affairs, 1960-63, counselor embassy, dep. chief mission, Baghdad, Iraq, 1963-66, Amman, Jordan, 1966-67, consul gen., Lahore, Pakistan, 1967-70; diplomat-in-residence U. Me. 1970-71, Dept. State officer external research, 1971—. Mem. U.S. delegations Colombo Plan confs., 1961, 62. Mem. Phi Beta Kappa. Address: care Dept State Washington DC 20521

ADAMS, JOHN WILLARD, Jr., advt. exec.; b. Brightwaters, L.I., N.Y., Mar. 27, 1921; s. John Willard and Helen (Korth) A.; student Yale, 1938-40; m. Jean-Marie McDermott, June 14, 1947; children—John III, James, Jill, Jan. Account exec. L.E. McGivena Advt., Inc., N.Y.C., 1946-47; asst. advt. mgr. Dictaphone Corp., N.Y.C., 1947-48; with Albert Frank-Guenther Law, Inc., N.Y.C., 1948—, vice chmn., 1970—. Served with USNR, 1940-45. Decorated D.F.C. Mem. Am. Arbitration Assn., Nat. Conf. Christians and Jews. Roman Catholic. Home: 25 Oak Av Larchmont NY 10538 Office: 61 Broadway New York City NY 10006

ADAMS, JOSEPH ELKAN, automotive mfr.; b. Cleve., Feb. 26, 1913; s. Samuel A. and Dorothy (Berkson) A.; B.S., Carnegie Inst. Tech., 1934; m. Eleanore Ture, Aug. 30, 1940; children—Stephen Eric, Gail M. Asst. to pres. Garland Co., Cleve., 1934-38; gen. mgr. Internat. Molded Plastics, 1938-41; dir. material control White Motor Corp. (formerly known as White Motor Co., Cleve., 1945-50, dir. purchasing and planning, 1950-55, gen. mgr. mfg., 1955, v.p. 1956-59, exec. v.p., 1959—; dir. Welcome Broadcasting Co. Spl. asst. for prodn. to v.p. operations WPB, Washington, 1941-44. Dir. Forest City Hosp.; trustee Cleve. Playhouse. Mem. Soc. Automotive Engrs., Mus. Arts Assn. Cleve. (trustee; exec. com.). Pi Tau Sigma (v.p.), Pi Delta Epsilon, Beta Sigma Rho Clubs: Mid-Day, Cleveland City, Commerce, Oakwood, Clevelander, Republic, Sharon. Home: 3031 Manchester Rd Shaker Heights OH 44122. Office: White Motor Corp 100 Erieview Plaza Cleveland OH 44114

ADAMS, JOSEPH PETER, lawyer; cons.; b. Seattle, Nov. 15, 1907; s. Joseph and Selma Margaret (Peterson) A.; A.B., U. Wash., 1928, LL.B., 1932; grad. naval aviator U.S. Naval Air Sta., Pensacola, Fla., 1930; m. Margaret B. Adams, Jan. 13, 1940; 1 dau., Janis Margaret. Admitted to Wash. bar, 1932, D.C. bar, 1953; practiced Seattle, 1932-40; dir. aeros. State Wash., 1946-49; mem. CAB, 1951-56, vice chmn., 1955-56; aviation cons. Senate interstate and fgn. commerce com. Mem. NACA, 1952-56; now exec. dir., gen. counsel Assn. Local Transport Airlines, Washington. Mem. Nat. Capital Democratic Club. Served as capt. USMCR. Decorated Legion of Merit. Mem. Am., Fed., D.C. bar assns., Nat. Pilots Assn., USMC Res. Officers Assn. (life), Marine Corps League, Nat. Aero Assn., Legion of Honor of Order of DeMolay, Sigma Alpha Epsilon, Phi Delta Phi. Democrat. Clubs: Cosmos, Aero (pres. 1962 Washington); National Aviation (award for achievement 1970), Wings (N.Y.C.); Army-Navy. Home: 2367 King Pl Washington DC 20007 Office: Wyatt Bldg Washington DC 20005

ADAMS, K. S., football exec. Pres., Houston Oilers Profl. Football Team. Address: PO Box 1516 Houston TX 77001*

ADAMS, KENNETH HOWARD, educator; b. Elgin, Ill., July 7, 1906; s. Howard William and Ora Alice (Wright) A.; B.S., U. Chgo., 1928, Ph.D., 1932; m. Ruth G. Norman, Aug. 24, 1934 (dec. Sept. 1965); 1 dau., Patricia (Mrs. Alan L. Black); m. 2d, Colma Benedict Cooper, Aug. 2, 1967. Instr. chemistry U. Chgo., 1932-39; asso. prof. Harris Tchrs. Coll., St. Louis, 1939-43; faculty St. Louis U., 1943—, asso. prof. chemistry, 1946-55, prof., 1955—. Mem. Am. Chem. Soc., Am. Assn. U. Profs., Sigma Xi, Phi Beta Kappa. Episcopalian. Home: 6635 Pershing Av St Louis MO 63130 Office: PO Box 8089 St Louis MO 63156

ADAMS, KENNETH STANLEY, ret. oil co. exec.; b. Horton, Kan., Aug. 31, 1899; s. John Valentine and Louella (Stanley) A.; grad. Kansas City (Kan.) High Sch., 1917; student U. of Kan., 1917-20; LL.D., Drury Coll., 1955, Okla. Baptist U., 1959; m. 2d, Dorothy Glynn Stephens, Nov. 4, 1946; children—Mary Louise Hoy, Kenneth Stanley, Stephen Stanley, Kenneth Glenn, Gary C., Stephanie, Lisa A. Warehouse clerk Phillips Petroleum Co. 1920-22; asst. operations mgr. prodn. dept., 1922-26, asst. to clerk, accounting div., 1926, asst. sec. 1927, asst. sec., asst. treas., 1928-32, asst. to pres., 1932-35 dir. and mem. exec. com. since 1935, treas., asst. to pres., 1935-38, exec. v.p., 1938, pres. 1938-51, chmn. bd., 1951-68, chmn. emeritus, 1968—, also mem. of the finance com.; dir. Okla. Cement Co. Served in O.T.S., Camp Zachary Taylor Louisville, Ky., Sept.-Dec. 1918; chmn. Dist. No. 2 Prodn. Com. under Petroleum Adminstrn. for War. Mem. Am. Petroleum Inst., Mid-Continent Oil and Gas Assn., Independent Petroleum Assn., Sigma Chi. Democrat. Presbyn. Mason (33, K.T., Shriner, Jester). Clubs: Hillcrest Country (Bartlesville, Okla.); Cherokee (Afton, Okla.). Home: P O Drawer A Bartlesville, OK 74003. Office: Profl Bldg Bartlesville OK 74003

ADAMS, LANE WEBSTER, assn. exec.; b. Logan, Utah, July 3, 1915; s. Orval W. and Luella (Nebeker) A.; student U. Utah, 1931-33, Grad. Sch. Banking Rutgers U., 1938-40; m. Elaine Evans, Sept. 1, 1937; children—Victoria, Anthony L. Banker, Salt Lake City, 1936-49; v.p., mem. exec. com. Zions First Nat. Bank, Salt Lake City, 1949-59; dir. Talcott Nat. Corp., Carte Blanche Corp. Bd. dirs. Am. Cancer Soc., 1948-59, treas., 1953-59, exec. v.p., 1959—. Mem. Nat. Adv. Cancer Council, 1957-58, Nat. Adv. Allergy and Infectious Diseases Council, 1966-68; state dir. SSS Mo. Bd. regents Grad. Sch. Banking Rutgers U. Clubs: Alta (Salt Lake City); Apawamis (Rye, N.Y.); Metropolitan (N.Y.C.). Home: 51 Mill Rd New Canaan CT 06840 Office: 2 Pennsylvania Plaza New York City NY 10017

ADAMS, LAWRENCE BERNARD, Jr., adj. gen. Mo.; b. Sikeston, Mo., Apr. 8, 1915; s. Laurence Bernard and Mary Beatrice (O'Connell) A.; A.B., S.E. Mo. State Tchrs. Coll., 1940; grad. basic course Inf. Sch., 1942, advanced course, 1943, cannon officers course, 1944; grad. Adj. Gen. Sch., 1947; m. Cathryn Webb Clack, Mar. 17, 1942; children—Vicki, Patrick, James, John, Cathryn Jean. Enlisted in Mo. N.G., 1932, served, 1932- 36, 37-39, 39-40; enlisted in U.S. Army, 1936, served until 1937; served from 2d lt. to maj. U.S. Army, 1940-46; with Mo. N.G., 1946-48, 49-50; dep. dir. Mo. SSS, 1948-49, 50-65, dir., 1965-69; adj. gen. Mo. with rank maj. gen., 1965—. Decorated Bronze Star medal, Combat Inf. badge. Mem. U.S., Mo. nat. guard assns. V.F.W., Am. Legion, Air Force Assn., Assn. U.S. Army. Rotarian. Home: 1431 Green Berry Rd Jefferson City MO 65101 Office: State Office Bldg Jefferson City MO 65101 also 411 Madison St Jefferson City MO 65101

ADAMS, LEE, lyricist; b. Mansfield, O., Aug. 14, 1924; s. Leopold and Florence (Ellis) A.; B.A., Ohio State U., 1949: M.Sc. in Journalism. Columbia, 1950; m. Rita Relch, July 21, 1957; 1 dau. Formerly editor and writer articles for Pageant. This Week, also local radio programs; contbr. material to Shoestring Revue, 1955, additional lyrics to The Littlest Revue, 1956. sketches to Shoestring '57, 1956, sketches to Kaleidoscope, 1957, lyrics for Bye Bye Birdie, 1960 All American, 1962; films include Bye Bye Birdie, 1963. Served with AUS, 1943-46; ETO. Recipient Antoinette Perry award, 1961. Mem. A.S.C.A.P., A.G.A.C., Dramatists Guild. Address: 40 E 89th St New York City NY 10028 *

ADAMS, LEONARD C., educator; b. Saluda, S.C., Nov. 7, 1921; s. James P. and Amelia Ann (Minnick) A.; B.S. in Elec. Engring., Clemson Coll., 1943; M.S. in Elec. Engring., Okla. State U., 1950; Ph.D. in Elec. Engring. and Physics, U. Fla., 1953; m. Rachel Adams, June 18, 1945; children—James P., Richard C., Ann S. From instr. to prof. elec. engring. Clemson Coll., 1946-58, dir. Engring. Expt. Sta., 1959-61; exptl. reactor physicist Savannah River Lab., 1958-59; now prof. elec. engring., head dept. La. State U. Pres. bd. dirs. Oak Hills Place Assn. Served to 1st lt., Signal Corps, AUS, 1943-46. Registered profl. engr., La., S.C. Mem. Am. Soc. Engring. Edn., I.E.E.E. (chmn. Baton Rouge sect.), Baton Rouge Council Engring. and Sci. Socs. (pres. 1965-66), Sigma Xi, Tau Beta Pi, Phi Kappa Phi, Eta Kappa Nu. Home: 12123 N Lakeview Dr Baton Rouge LA 70810.

ADAMS, LEONARD PALMER, educator, economist; b. Angelica, N.Y., Oct. 8, 1906; s. Frederick James and Ida (Palmer) A.; A.B., Alfred U., 1928; A.M., Cornell, 1930, Ph.D., 1935; m. Evelyn Hamilton, June 22, 1940 (div. Nov. 1967); children—Leonard Palmer, Samuel Hamilton; m. Elizabeth Selkirk Amberg, Nov. 9, 1967; stepchildren—Charles S. Amberg, and Elizabeth Jane White Began as grad. asst. and instr. in economics, Cornell, 1928-34; instr. in economics, Colgate U., 1934-35; research asso., Central Statis. Bd., Washington, 1935; economist, Social Science Research Council, 1935-36; asso. economist, div. of placement and unemployment ins., N.Y. State Dept. of Labor, 1936-42; prin. economist, U.S. Employment Service for N.Y., 1942-43; chief, div. of reports and analysis, War Manpower Commn., Region II, N.Y. City, 1946-47; dir. of research and publs., N.Y. State Sch. of Indsl. and Labor Relations, Cornell U., 1947-67, prof. indsl. and labor relations emeritus, 1967—; cons. manpower problems, since 1967—; Upjohn grantee to study economic conditions U.S., 1962; Ford Foundation grantee, New Delhi, India, 1962- 63. Member American Economic Assn., Indsl. Relations Research Assn., Am. Assn. U. Profs., Phi Beta Kappa. Author: Agricultural Depression and Farm Relief in England, 1813-1852, 1932; Wartime Manpower Mobilzation, A Study of Experience in the Buffalo Niagara Area, 1951; The Public Commuting Patterns of Industrial Workers, 1955; Workers and Industrial Change, 1957; articles, book revs. on manpower and indsl. relations. Home: 13 La Grange Rd Delmar, NY 12054.

ADAMS, LEONIE, poet, educator; b. Bklyn., Dec. 9, 1899; d. Charles Frederick and Henrietta (Rozler) Adams; A.B., Barnard Coll., 1922; D.Litt., N.J. Coll. for Women, 1950; m. William E. Troy, June 3, 1933 (dec. 1961). Guggenheim fellow, 1928-30; instr. writing, poetry N.Y. U., 1930- 32, Sarah Lawrence Coll., 1933-34, Bennington Coll., 1935-37, 42-44; lectr. English, N.J. Coll. for Women, 1945-48. Columbia, 1947-68; vis. prof., poet in residence U. Wash., 1968-69. Fulbright lectr., France, 1955-56; cons. in poetry Library of Congress, 1948-49, fellow in Am. letters, 1949-55. Mem. staff Breadloaf Writers Conf., 1956-58. Recipient Harriet Monroe award, Shelley Meml. award, 1954, Bollingen. prize in poetry, 1955; Brandeis medal for poetic achievement, 1969. Academy Am. Poets fellow, 1959; Nat. Council on Arts grantee, 1966-67. Mem. Nat. Inst. arts and Letters (award 1949, sec. 1959- 61). Club: P.E.N. Author: Those Not Elect, 1925; High Falcon, 1929; Poems, A Selection 1954. Editor: Lyrics of Francois Villon, 1932. Home: New Milford CT 06776

ADAMS, LEWIS GREENLEAF, architect; b. Lenox, Mass., Nov. 23, 1897; s. William and Alice C. (Greenleaf) A.; B.A., Yale, 1920; diplme Ecole des Beaux Arts, Paris, 1926; m. Emeline W. Kellog, July 23, 1921; children—Richard G., Lois K. (Mrs. Charles P. Rockwood). Asso., Delano & Aldrich, architects, N.Y.C., 1920-22, 27-29; partner Adams & Prentice, architects, 1929-41, Adams & Woodbridge, 1945—; works include All Saints Chapel, Princeton, N.J., Adirondack Mus., Blue Mountain Lake, N.Y. freshman doem and infirmary Hamilton Coll., Clinton, N.Y., Episcopal Ch. Center, N.Y.C. Served as ensign USNR, 1918-20, as comdr. USNR, 1942-45. Mem. A.I.A., Nat. Sculpture Soc. (hon.), Groupe Americain des Architects diplomes par le Gouvernement, Century Assn., Archtl. League N.Y. (pres. 1954-55). Home: 544 E 86th St New York City NY 10016 Office: 215 E 37th St New York City NY 10028

ADAMS, MAC CARTER, business exec.; b. Gretna, Va., Jan. 3, 1925; s. Neville Lamont and Selma Brough (Woodson) A.; student U. Va., 1943-44; B.S. in Mech. Engring., Cornell U., 1946, M. Aero. Engring., 1949, Ph.D., 1953; m. Jane Krist, Feb. 27, 1946; children—Kimberly Sue, Christopher Carter, Kyle Elizabeth. Engr., Ingersoll Rand Co., 1946, NACA, 1946-47, 49-51; design specialist Douglas Airplane Co., 1953-55; dep. dir. Avco-Everett Research Lab., 1955-60; v.p., tech. dir. research and devel. div. Avco, 1960-65; asso. adminstr. Office Advanced Research and Tech., NASA, 1965-68; v.p., dep. group exec. Avco Govt. Products Group, 1968—; mem. NASA spl. adv. com. missile and spacecraft aerodynamics, 1959-62, chmn. spl. adv. com. missile and space vehicle aerodynamics, 1962-65, mem. Mass. Inst. Tech. mech. engring. vis. com., 1967—. Served with USNR, 1943-46. Recipient NASA exceptional Service medal, 1968. Fellow Am. Inst. Aero and Astronautics (chmn. com. vehicle reentry 1963-64, bd. dirs. 1965-68, 70-73); mem. Sigma Xi, Tau Beta Pi. Home: 4 Myopia Hill RD Winchester MA 01890 Office: 201 Lowell St Wilmington MA 01887

ADAMS, MARK, artist; b. Ft. Plain, N.Y., Oct. 27, 1925; s. Earl D. and Edith (Wohlgemuth) A.; student Syracuse U., 1943-46, Hans Hofmann Sch. Fine Arts, 1946, 48; m. Beth Van Hoesen, Sept. 12, 1953. One-man shows include Gump's Gallery, 1953, Stanford, 1957, San Diego State Coll., 1958, deYoung Mus., 1959. San Jose State Coll., 1959, Portland (Ore.) Mus., 1961, Cal. Palace of Legion of Honor, 1961, San Francisco Mus. Art, 1962, French & Co., N.Y.C., 1964, Hansen Galleries, San Francisco, 1966; one-man retrospective Cal. Palace Legion of Honor, 1970; exhibited in numerous group shows, including Mus. Contemporary Crafts, N.Y.C., 1957, 58, 62, 65, Dallas Mus., 1958, San Francisco Art Inst., 1953, 58, 59, 61, 62, 65, San Francisco Mus. Art, 1961, Stanford, 1961, Pasadena Mus., 1962, 66, St. Louis Art Mus., 1964, Norfolk Mus., 1966; rep. permanent collections San Francisco Mus. Art, Dallas Mus. Fine Arts, Chase Manhattan Bank, N.Y.C., San Francisco Pub. Library, also pvt. collections; archtl. commissions in tapestry, stained glass, mural. Instr. San Francisco Art Inst., 1961; painter in residence Am. Acad. in Rome, 1963. Mem. San Francisco Art Inst. (artist com.). Address: 3816 22d St San Francisco CA 94114

ADAMS, MARK HANNA, lawyer; b. Girard, Kan., Sept. 22, 1907; s. Cecil C. and Lucinda Belle (Fowler) A.; LL.B., Kan. U., 1920; m. Helen B. Miller, Dec.. 26, 1924 (dec.); children—Mark Hannah II, Wells Miller; m. 2d, Jeanette C. Cullison, Nov. 6, 1948. Admitted to Okla., bar , 1920; co. atty. Texas Co., Okla., 1921-22; atty. Fed. Land Bank, Wichita, Kan., 1923-24; spl. atty. Office Gen. Counsel of Internal Revenue, Dept. Justice, Washington, 1925-26; gen. practice law, Wichita, 1926—; sr. mem. Adams, Jonce, Robinson & Monka; pres. KAKE TV & Broadcasting Inc.; chmn. bd. Underground Vaults & Storage Co.; mng. partner Stevens Co. Oil & Gas Co. dir. Ortmeyer Lumber Co. Mem. Kan. C. of C. (past dir.), Ind. Natural Gas Assn. (past dir.), Nat. Inst. Logopedics (dir.), Am., Wichita (past pres.), Kan. bar assns., Delta Upsilon (past pres.). Methodist. Mason (Shriner). Clubs: Wichita, Wichita Country, Abraham Lincoln, Farm and Ranch, Petroleum. Home: 345 N Belmont ST Wichita KS 67208. Office: Am Sava Bldg P O Box 1034 Wichita KS 67202

ADAMS, MILFORD MANCHESTER, railroad ofcl.; b. Perry, O., Sept. 1, 1908; s. Quincy and Eva May (Manchester) A.; B.B.A. magna cum laude, Western Res. U., 1958. With Erie Lackawanna Ry. Co., Cleve., 1932—, sec.-treas., 1968—. Served to capt. AUS, 1943-46, 50-52. Mem. Beta Alpha Psi, Beta Gamma Sigma. Unitarian. Home: 11800 Edgewater Dr Lakewood OH 44107 Office: Midland Bldg Cleveland OH 44115

ADAMS, MILTON BERNARD, air force officer; b. Eagle Pass, Tex., May 12, 1917; s. Lewis M. and Marion (Jones) A.; B.S., U.S. Mil. Acad., 1939; grad. Air War Coll., 1950, Nat. War Coll., 1955; m. Jean S. Besson, June 14, 1943; children—Mary S., Milton B., John L., Jean C., Frank L. Commd. 2d lt. USAAF, 1939, advanced through grades to maj. gen. USAF, 1964; fighter pilot and unit comdr., 1940-46, 55-59; dir. mil. schs., 1950-54; adviser to Iranian Air Force, 1947-49; engaged in weapon system devel. and procurement mgmt. Hdqrs. USAF, 1959-62; mil. planner S. Vietnam, 1962- 63; tech. reconnaissance comdr. Shaw AFB, S.C., 1965-66; def. communications planner Def. Communications Agy., 1966-67; with USAF Hdqrs. Command, 1967-68; chief of staff Pacific Air Forces, 1968-70; dep. chief of staff for plans and operations, 1970—. Decorated Legion of Merit, D.F.C., Air medal. Mem. Order Deadalians, K.C., Rotarian. Address: Box 32 Staff CINPAC FPO San Francisco CA 96610

ADAMS, NORMAN ILSLEY, Jr., physicist; b. Winthrop, Mass., Sept. 20, 1895; s. Norman Ilsley and Mabel Estelle (George) A.; B.A., Yale, 1917, Ph.D., 1923; m. Genevieve A. Sloan, July 28, 1926; children—Norman Ilsley III, Harry Bell. Engr. Am. Tel. & Tel. Co., dept. devel. and research, N.Y.C., 1923-24; mem. faculty Yale U., New Haven, 1925—, prof. physics, 1944-64, prof. emeritus, 1964—; vis. prof. U. Ida., 1964, U. Delaware, 1965, Central Wash. State Coll., 1967; cons. engr. in radio broadcasting, 1927. Served as 2d lt., 301st Heavy Tank Bn., A.E.F., France, 1918; dir. Eatontown Signal Lab., Fort Monmouth, N.J., 1941-43; disch. rank of lt. col. Registered profl. engr. (communications), Conn. Awarded Legion of Merit, World War II. Fellow Am. Phys. Soc.; mem. Res. Officers Assn., Ret. Officers Assn., Mil. Order World Wars, Order Lafayette, Gamma Alpha, Phi Beta Kappa, Sigma Xi. Republican. Episcopalian. Clubs: Appalachian Mountain, Yale (N.Y.C.). Author: Principles of Electricity (with L. Page), 1931; Electrodynamics (with L. Page), 1940. Address: 6812 SW 35th Way Gainesville FL 32601

ADAMS, PARK PEPPER, III, musician; b. Highland Park, Mich., Oct. 8, 1930; s. Park II and Cleo (Coyle) A.; student Wayne State U., 1948-50. Profl. baritone saxophonist/clarinetist, 1944—; appearance with Stan Kenton, Theolonious Monk, Benny Goodman, Dizzy Gillespie, others; coleader Quintet with Donald Byrd, 1958-62; recording artist for Blue Note, Solid State records. Served with AUS, 1951-53; Korea. Recipient New Star award Down Beat mag., 1957, Talent Deserving of Wider Recognition, 1967. Author seventeen recorded compositions. Office: care Radio Registry 850 7th Av New York City NY 10019

ADAMS, PAUL DEWITT, retired army officer; b. Heflin, Alabama, Oct. 6, 1906; s. Lovic E. and Ruth (Jacksosn) A.; B.S., U.S. Mil. Acad., 1928; student Inf. Sch., 1930-31, Nat. War Coll., 1946-47; m. Mabel Gertrude Decker, Aug. 5, 1929; children—Robert Thomas, Marjorie Ruth. Commd. 2d lt. inf., U.S. Army, 1928, advanced through grades to general, 1961; served in Panama, 1931-34, Presidio San Francisco, 1934- 38, P.I., 1938-40, Ft. Jackson, S.C., 1940-41, T.H., 1941-42; assigned 1st Spl. Service Force (U.S. Canadian commando-type unit), 1942-43; with 36th U.S. Div., 1944, 45th Div., 1945; faculty Command and Gen. Staff Sch., Ft. Leavenworth, Kan., 1947-50, Army War Coll., 1950-51; asst. div. comdr. 24th Inf. Div., Korea, 1951-52, Japan, 1952; chief staff 10th U.S. Corps, Korea, 1952; comdr. 25th Div., 1952; chief staff 8th Army, Korea, 1952-53; comdg. gen. 101st Airborne Tng. Div., Camp Breckinridge, 1953; dep. asst., asst. chief staff G-3 Dept. Army, 1953-55; comdg. gen. XVIII Airborne Corps, Ft. Bragg, N.C. 1955-57, No. Area Command, Germany, 1957-58, Am. Land Forces, Middle East, Lebanon, 1959; dep. comdg. gen. 7th U.S. Army, Ger., 1958-59, V Corps, Germany, 1959-60, 3d U.S. Army, Fort McPherson, Ga., 1960; comdr.-in-chief U.S. Strike Command, MacDill AFB, Fla., 1961-66; ret., 1966; mgmt. cons. 1966-70; pres. Paul O. Adams & Assos., Inc., mgmt. cons., 1968-70; First Fed. dir. Savs. & Loan Assn. of Tampa (Fla.). Mem. Fla. Judicial Qualifications Commn., 1968-71. Decorated D.S.M. with 2 oak leaf clusters (Army). D.S.M. (USAF), Silver Star, Legion of Merit with 3 oak leaf clusters, Bronze Star with V device and 3 oak leaf clusters, Commendation Ribbon; Order de Bayaca (Columbia); Order of Menelich (Ethiopia); Croix de Guerre with Bronze Star (France). Mem. C. of C. Clubs: Army-Navy (Wash.); Army-Navy Country (Arlington, Va.); Palma Clea Golf (Tampa, Fla.). Home: 5014 San Miguel St Tampa FL 33609

ADAMS, PAUL WINFREY, lawyer, business exec.; b. Ozark, Ark., July 10, 1913; s. Robert Montague and Myrtle (Johnson) A.; B.S., Trinity Coll., Hartford, Conn., 1935; LL.B., Yale, 1938; m. Louise Forbes Barnes, Mar. 21, 1942; childrenSally B. (Mrs. T. V. O'Connor), Thomas Fuller, Edward Montague. Admitted to Conn. bar, 1938, to N.Y. bar, 1964; practiced in Hartford, 1938-42, 45-50; counsel Mfrs. Assn. Conn., 1939-42; pres. The Norden Labs. Corp., 1949-55; chmn. bd. Norden-Ketay Corp., N.Y.C., 1956-58; chmn. Mut. Assurance Co., Hartford, Trans-Mountain Corp.; dir. Abbott Ball Co.; asst. dean Yale Law Sch., 1956-58; sr. partner firm Adams & Eyster, N.Y.C., 1958-66; partner Seward & Kissel, N.Y.C., 1966—. Trustee Trinity Coll., Hartford, Conn., 1958-64. Served as lt. USNR, 1942-45. Mem. Am. Bar Assn. Republican. Clubs: Round Hill (Greenwich); Dauntless (Essex, Conn.); Hartford; N.Y. Yacht, Union League, India House (N.Y.C.); Cruising of America; Royal Swedish Yacht; Royal Bermuda; Indian Harbour. Home: Greenwich CT 06830 Office: 63 Wall St New York City NY 10005

ADAMS, PHELPS HAVILAND, ret. pub. relations exec.; b. Boston, Dec. 14, 1902; s. Henry Ethelbert and Mary Aurora (Haviland) A.; student U. Colo., 1919-22; B.Litt., Columbia, 1924; Pulitzer traveling scholarship, 1924; student London Sch. of Econs., 1924, The Sorbonne, Paris, France, 1925; m. Ruth E. Hollinger, June 18, 1928. Columbia corr. N.Y. Herald, 1923; joined staff of N.Y. Sun as reporter, 1926, Washington corr., 1929-50, sent to Palestine, Trans-Jordan, Syria and Lebanon to do spl. series entitled The Truth About Palestine, Oct.-Dec. 1937, war corr. aboard U.S.S. Enterprise, off Japan, April 1945; spl. asst. to asst. to chmn. U.S. Steel Corp., 1950-55, exec. dir. pub. relations and asst. to chmn., 1955-57, v.p. pub. relations, 1957-63, adminstrv. v.p. pub. relations, 1964-67. Pres. Litchfield Park (Ariz.) Library Assn., 1970-71. Recipient Freedoms Found. Honor award, 1950; Gold Plate award Am. Acad. Achievement, 1967. Mem. Pub. Relations Soc. Am., Pub. Relations Seminar (chmn. 1959-60), Sigma Delta Chi. Clubs: Alfalfa, Gridiron (pres. 1948), Nat. Press (Washington); Wigwam Golf and Country (Litchfield Park, Ariz.). Address: PO Box 881 Litchfield Park, AZ 85340.

ADAMS, PHILIP RHYS, dir. art museum; b. Fargo, N.D., Nov. 19, 1908; s. Charles Ryan and Myra (Oldfather) A.; Wabash Coll., 1925-26; B.A., Ohio State Univ., 1929; M.A., New York Univ., 1930; student Princeton, 1930- 31; Litt.D., Miami U., 1949; Litt.D., Coll.-Conservatory Music, Cin., 1958; D.F.A., Wittenberg U., 1956; L.H.D., U. Cin., 1964, Hebrew Union Coll., 1966; m. Marie Constance LeMercier-duQuesnay. Oct. 4, 1932 (dec.); children—Jeremy deQuesnay, Yvonne Valeric (dec.), Philip Le Mercier; m. 2d, Rosan Krippendorf Clark, Sept., 1947. Instr. in art, Newcomb Coll., Tulane Univ., 1931-34; asst. dir. Columbus (Ohio) Gallery of Fine Arts, 1934-36, dir., 1936-45; dir. Cincinnati Art Museum, 1945—, lectr. with Bur. of Univ. Travel. Mexico and Great Britain, summers of 1935, 36, 37, 38; lectr. Salzburg Seminar in Am. Studies, 1960. Exec. sec. art com., Office of Coordinator of Inter-Am. Affairs, 1941; trustee Am. Fedn. of Arts. Recipient Centennial Achievement award Ohio State U., 1970. Mem. Assn. of Art Museum Dirs., Am. Inst. Decorators (hon.), Omicron Delta Kappa (honorary mem.), Phi Gamma Delta. Contbr. profl. publis.; lectr. Home: 3003 Observatory Av Cincinnati OH 45208

ADAMS, PHOEBE-LOU, journalist; b. Hartford, Conn., Dec. 18, 1918; d. Harold Irving and Alice (Burlingame) Adams; A.B. cum laude, Radcliffe Coll., 1939. Reporter, Hartford Courant, 1942-45; mem. editorial staff Atlantic Monthly, Boston, 1945—. Author: A Rough Map of Greece, 1965. Office: 8 Arlington St Boston MA 02116

ADAMS, RALPH EDWIN, physician; b. Caldwell, Ida., May 30, 1930; s. Edwin E. and Ruth (Shawver) A.; B.Th., N.W. Christian Coll., 1952; B.S., U. Ore., 1954; M.D., 1956; M.B.A., U. Chgo., 1961; m. Patricia Anne Wessels, Sept. 27, 1958; children—Julie, Erik, Laurie. Intern Gorgas Hosp., Ancon, C.Z., 1956-57; resident surgery Mayo Found., 1957-59; asst. sec. Council Med. Edn. and Hosps., A.M.A., Chgo., 1960-62; med. dir. St. Joseph's Hosp., Victoria, B.C., 1962-66; exec. v.p. adminstrn. Presbyn.-St. Luke's Hosp., Chgo., 1966-68; exec. dir. So. Nev. Meml. Hosp., Las Vegas, 1968-69; resident radiology U. Okla. Med. Center, 1969—; cons. Health, Edn. and Welfare, Health Services and Mental Health Adminstrn. Mem. Nev. Comprehensive Health Planning Council, 1968-69. Mem. Am. Hosp. Assn., Am. Protestant Hosp. Assn. (trustee, chmn. Council on Assn. Devel.), Am. Coll. Hosp. Adminstrs. Home: 1515 NW 35th St Oklahoma City OK 73118

ADAMS, RALPH NORMAN, educator; b. Atlantic City, N.J., Aug. 26, 1924; B.S., Rutgers U., 1950; Ph.D. in Analytical Chemistry, Princeton, 1953; married; 1 child. Instr. analytical chemistry Princeton, 1953-55; asst. prof. chemistry U. Kan., 1955-58, asso. prof., 1958-63, prof., 1963—. Served with USAAF, 1943-46. Mem. Am. Chem. Soc. Office: Dept Chemistry Grad Sch U Kan Lawrence KS 66044*

ADAMS, RALPH WYATT, Sr., univ. pres., lawyer; b. Samson, Ala., June 4, 1915; s. Alfred E. and Eunice M. (Clements) A.; A.B., Birmingham-So. Coll., 1937; LL.B., University of Alabama, 1940, LL.D., 1965, J.D., 1969; grad. study University of Colo., 1958, George Washington U., 1960; m. Dorothy Kelly, Sept. 5, 1942; children—Ralph Wyatt, Kelly Clements, Samuel. Admitted to Ala. bar, 1940, also U.S. Supreme Ct. bar; atty., dep. supt. Ala. Dept. Ins., 1945-46; judge, Tuscaloosa, Ala., 1946-47; founder Acad. Life Ins. Co., Denver, 1957; lectr. life ins. U. Colo. Dep. dean, acting dean Air Force Law Sch., Air U., pres. Troy State Univ. 1964—. Dir. Bankers Credit Life Ins. Co., Am. Educators Life Ins. Co. Mem. State Personnel Bd. Ala., State Ins. Bd. Ala. Vice Pres. Ala.-Fla. council Boy Scouts Am., trustee of Lyman Ward Military Academy, Camp Hill, Ala. Served to capt. USAAF, 1941-45; brig. gen. Ala. Ari Nat. (Guard. Mem. Am. Legion, Phi Alpha Delta, Kappa Delta Pi, Pi Delta Phi, Kappa Phi Kappa, Lambda Chi Alpha. Methodist. Mason, Rotarian. Clubs: Alexandria Civitan (past pres.), Army-Navy Country (Alexandria, Va.); Montgomery (Ala.) Country; Trey Country. Home: President's Mansion Troy State U Troy AL 36081

ADAMS, RAYMOND DEL, physician; b. Portland, Ore., Feb. 13, 1911; s. William H. and Eva (Morriss) A.; A.B., U. Ore., 1932, A.M., 1933; M.D., Duke, 1936; M.A., Harvard, 1954; D.Sc. honoris causa, U. Ghent; m. Margaret Elinor Clark, May 19, 1933; children—Mary Elinor, John William, Carol Ann, Sarah Ellen. Intern, asst. resident medicine Duke Hosp., 1936- 38; Rockefeller Found. fellow neurology, 1938-41; now Bullard prof. neuropathology Harvard, also chief neurology service Mass. Gen. Hosp. Fellow French Acad. Neurology, Am. Acad. Arts and Scis. Mem. Am. Neurol. Assn., Am. Assn. Neuropathologists, Am. Soc. Clin. Investigation, Lebanese Neurol. Soc. (hon.), Brit. Assn. Neurologists (hon.), Assn. Research Nervous and Mental Diseases; hon. mem. French, Swiss socs. neurologists, Internat. Brain Research Orgn., German Soc. Neuropathologists. Author textbook on neuropathology, monographs on neurosyphill's, pathology of muscle diseases; numerous articles on neurology and neuropathology; co-author Harrisons's Textbook of Medicine. Home: 320 Adams St Milton MA 02186 Office: Mass Gen Hosp Fruit St Boston MA 02114

ADAMS, RAYMOND F., banker; b. West Haven, Vt., 1907; Sec., v.p. Chem. Bank N.Y. Trust Co., N.Y. C. Home: 465 Doremus Av Glen Rock NJ 07452 Office: 20 Pine St New York City NY 10015

ADAMS, RAY ROOSEVELT, cement co. exec.; b. Slippery Rock, Pa., Feb. 17, 1907; s. Ralph Pearson and Effie Miria (Dible) A.; student Slippery Rock State Tchrs. Coll., 1925-27, U. Buffalo, nights 1933-43; m. Eugenia Grace Goette, May 25, 1932; 1 son, James Dooley. From chemist to supt. rockwool div. Fed. Portland Cement Co., Buffalo, 1928-45; plant mgr. Peerless Cement Co., Pt. Huron, Mich., 1945-58; project mgr. for design, constrn. cement mill Am. Cement Corp., Clarkdale, Ariz., 1958-59, v.p. corp., 1959-71; pres. div. Phoenix Cement Co., 1959-71; pres. Hawaiian Cement Corp., Honolulu. Bd. dirs., pres. Boys Clubs Phoenix. Mem. N.A.M., Ariz. Acad. Elk. Clubs: Cloud (sec.); Executives, Phoenix Country, Arizona (Phoenlx); Outrigger Canoe, Oahu Country (Honolulu). Office: care Hawaiian Cement Corp 1660 Kapiolani Blvd Honolulu HI 96814

ADAMS, RICHARD DONALD, ret. naval res. officer, export exec.; b. Ambridge, Pa., June 14, 1909; s. Arthur David and Mary May (Patterson) A.; B.S. in Mech. and Elec. Engring., U.S. Naval Acad., 1932; m. Lorene M. Hoffer, Nov. 19, 1950; children—David Byron, April Annette. Commd. ensign U.S. Navy, 1932; active duty, 1932-37, 41-46; mem. Res., 1937-41, 46-69; advanced through grades to rear adm., 1963; rep. of comdt. 12th Naval Dist., 1964-66; dep. comander Wester Sea Frontier, 1966-69, ret. With Superior Diesel Engine Co., 1937-41; owner, mgr. Overseas Indsl. Services, exporters machinery and indsl. supplies, San Francisco, 1952—, R.D. Adams Co., mfrs. agts., San Francisco, 1946—. Decorated Arym Distinguished Unit citation, Navy Res. medal with bronze star, other campaign and area ribbons. Registered profl. engr., Cal. Mem. Am. Soc. M.E., Navy League U.S. (national dir.), Naval Reserve Assn. (nat. adv. com.). U.S. Naval Acad. Found., Res. Officers Assn. U.S., U.S. Naval Inst., U.S. Naval Acad. Alumni Assn. Mason (32). Home: 495 Redwood Av San Bruno CA 94066 Office: 681 Market St San Francisco CA 94105

ADAMS, RICHARD LEON, banker; b. Scottsbluff, Neb., July 19, 1921; s. Clyde Charles and Elizabeth (Sullvain) A.; student Okla. A. and M. Coll., 1940; diploma Grad. Sch. Banking of South, La. State U., 1963; m. Mildred Catherine Moody, Oct. 29, 1945; children—Janine Elaine, Richard Leon, Nancy Sue, Charles Clyde III, Donna Jo. Clk., Scottsbluff Nat. Bank, 1937-41; with First Nat. Bank Palm Beach (Fla.), 1947—, sr. v.p., 1965-68, exec. v.p., 1968—; vice chmn. bd. Palm Beach Mall Bank, W. Palm Beach, Fla., 1970—. Treas. Palm Beach County Council P.T.A., 1965-66. Bd. dirs. Fla. Bankers Assn. Ednl. Found., chmn., 1971-72; bd. dirs. Palm Beach County Heart Assn., v.p., 1971-72, treas., 1970-71; bd. dirs. Palm Beach County Comprehensive Community Mental Health Center; adv. bd. Palm Beach County Salvation Army. Served to maj. USAAF, 1941-46, USAF, 1951-53; ETO, Korea. Decorated D.F.C., Air medal with oak leaf cluster. Mem. Am., Fla. (chmn. mortgage div. 1968-69, mem. comml. credit com. 1969—) bankers assns., Homebuilders Soc. Real Estate Appraisers, Air Force Assn., Navy League, Assn. Gen. Contractors. Methodist (mem. ch. bd., trustee 1960—). Clubs: Sailfish (bd. govs. 1970—), Flying Alligators, Quiet Birdmen, Islanders (Palm Beach). Home: 4401 N Terrace West Palm Beach FL 33407 Office: First National Bank 255 S County Rd Palm Beach FL 33480

ADAMS, RICHARD MILLER, airlines exec.; b. Orange, N.J., Apr. 15, 1919; s. Ray Russell and Zoa (Miller) A.; B.S. in Aero. Engring., U. Mich., 1940; m. Annabel VanWinkle, June 20, 1942; children—Annabel, Elisabeth, Christopher. With Pan Am. World Airways, 1940-62, mgr. maintenance, overseas div., 1957- 62; with Continental Air Lines, Inc., 1962—, sr. v.p. operating and tech. services, Los Angeles, 1965—, mem. bd. dirs., 1967-69. Mem. Soc. Automotive Engrs., Tau Beta Pi, Delta Upsilon. Clubs: Lakeside Golf (Hollywood, Cal.). Home: 15960 Valley Wood Rd Sherman Oaks CA 91403 Office: Continental Airlines Inc Los Angeles Internat Airport Los Angeles CA 90009

ADAMS, RICHARD NEWBOLD, anthropologist; b. Ann Arbor, Mich, Aug 4, 1924; s. Randolph Greenfield and Helen Constance (Spiller) A.; A.B., U. Mich., 1947; M.A., Yale, 1949, Ph.D. 1951; m. Betty Virginia Hannstein, Nov 4, 1951; children—Walter Randolph, Tani Marilena, Gina Constance. Ethologist, Inst Social Anthropology Smithsonian Instn, Guatemala City, 1950-51; specialist grantee State Dept. 1951-52; scientist WHO, Guatemala City, 1953-56; prof. sociology and anthropology Mich. State U., 1956-62; vis. prof. anthropology U. Cal. at Berkeley, 1960-61; prof. Anthropology, 1962—, asst. dir. Inst. Latin Am. Studies, Univ. of Texas, Austin, 1962-67, chmn. dept. anthropology, 1964-67; program cons. Latin Am. div. Ford Found., 1967-71. Served to lt. (j.g.), USNR, 1943-46. Fellow Am. Anthrop. Soc. (exec. bd.), A.A.A.S. (v.p., sect. chmn.); mem. Latin Am. Studies Assn. (pres. 1967-68), Soc. Applied Anthropology (pres. 1962-63), Am. Sociol. Assn., Am. Ethnol. Soc., Sigma Xi. Author: Home Made Poems, 1934, Cultural Surveys of Panama-Nicarague-Guatemala-El Salvador-Honduras, 1957; A Community in the Andes, 1959; Introduccion a la Antropologia aplicada, 1964; Second Sowing; Power and Secondary Development in Latin America, 1967; Crucifixion by Power; Essays in the National Social Structure of Guatemala 1944-66, 1970. Co-author: United States University Cooperation in Latin America, 1960; Responsibilities of the Foreign Scholar to the Local Scholarly Community, 1969. Co-editor: Human Organization Research, 1960; Contemporary Cultures and Societies of Latin America, 1964. Office: Dept Anthropology U Tex Austin TX 78712

ADAMS, RICHARD TOWSLEY, coll. dean; b. Chgo., July 15, 1921; s. Ralph Ephraim and IdaBelle (Towsley) A.; B.S., Purdue U., 1942, Ph.D., 1965; m. Joan Burridge, Nov. 2, 1963; children—James Towsley, Michael Ralph. Disposal officer U.S. Dept. State, Brazil, India, 1943-46; v.p. Indamer Corp., Inc., 1946-69, pres., 1958-69; chmn. Indamer Afghan Industries, Inc., Afghanistan, 1960-69; asst. prof. U. Nev., 1963-65; prof., dir. Bus. Research and Service Inst., dir. State Tech. Services Program, Western Mich. U., Kalamazoo, 1965-69; dean Sch. Bus., Ferris State Coll., Big Rapids, Mich., 1969—; chmn. bd. Devel. Cons., Inc., Cin., 1960-66. Active Jr. Achievement; mem. Tippecanoe County (Ind.) Bd. Aviation Commrs., 1954-59, West Lafayette (Ind.) Bd. Sch. Trustees, 1959-63; v.p., dir. Mich. Found. Ednl.-Indsl. Cooperation, 1968-69. Mem. Am. Finance Assn., Ind. Soc. Chgo., Aircraft Owners and Pilots Assn., Am. Assn. U. Profs., Phi Delta Theta, Alpha Kappa Psi. Methodist. Elk, Rotarian. Home: 839 Osburn Circle Big Rapids MI 49307

ADAMS, ROBERT ALLAN, architect; b. N.Y.C., Mar. 27, 1929; s. George Allan and Carolyn J. (Witte) A.; diploma in Bldg. Constrn., U. State N.Y., Farmingdale, 1949, Asso. in Applied Sci., Constrn. Tech., 1957; B.Arch., Pratt Inst., 1958; m. Emily Ann Delventhal, Aug. 25, 1956; children—Eve Ann, Seth Allan. Designer- draftsman Harrison & Abramovitz, Architects, N.Y.C., 1958-59; job capt. Paul Thiry, Architect, Seattle, 1959-63; prin. Architects Workshop, Seattle, 1963-65; chief architect Frankfurter & Assos., cons. engrs., Seattle, 1965-68; asso. architect Sverdrup & Parcel & Assos., Inc., cons. engrs., Seattle, 1968—. Mem. Hawthorne Adv. Council, 1970—. Served with C.E., U.S. Army, 1951-52. Recipient N.Y. Housing Authority Low Cost Housing Design Competition award, 1957, Seattle chpt. A.I.A. Home of the Month Design award, 1964. Mem. A.I.A., Seattle, Bellevue chambers commerce, U.S. Power Squadron. Presbyn. (elder). Club: Corinthian Yacht (Seattle). Important works include Seattle Center Coliseum Design of Fixed and Mobile Stadium Seating, 1963, Design of The Flexible House, Seattle, 1964. Home: 3827 Cascadia Av S Seattle WA 98118 Office: 505 106th St NE PO Box 369 Bellevue WA 98009

ADAMS, ROBERT E., physician. Exec. dir. Research Hosp. and Med. Center, Kansas City, Mo. Office: Meyer Blvd and Prospect Av Kansas City MO 64132*

ADAMS, ROBERT FRANKLIN, lawyer; b. Jackson, Ala., July 10, 1907; s. David and Lucy (Lee) A.; A.B., U. Ala., 1927, LL.B., 1937; m. Margaret Crossley, June 30, 1939; children—Robert Franklin, Mary Elizabeth, Laura (Mrs. Samuel R. Wooldridge, Jr.). Asst. cashier, dir. Jackson Bank & Trust Co., 1927-34; admitted to Ala. bar, 1937; since practiced in Mobile, mem. firm Johnstone, Adams, May, Howard & Hill and predecessor firms, 1937—, partner, 1942—; lectr. continuing legal edn. U. Ala. Pres. Citro, Inc., Mobile Oil Prodn. Corp.; dir. Title Ins. Co., Lerio Corp., So. Elec. & Pipefitting Corp. Pres. Council of Social Agys.; bd. dirs.- trustee Mobile Opera Guild. Served with AUS, 1944-45; ETO. Recipient Algernon Sidney Sullivan award, 1937. Mem. Am., Ala., Mobile (past pres.) bar assns., Internat. Soc. Barristers, Farrah Order Jurisprudence, Mobile Area C. of C. (past treas., dir.). Omicron Delta Kappa, Sigma Chi. Baptist. Kiwanian. Club: Mobile Country. Home: 253 Island Ct Mobile AL 36606 Office: Mchts Nat Bank Bldg Mobile AL 36602

ADAMS, ROBERT MCCORMICK, anthropologist; b. Chgo., July 23, 1926; s. Robert McCormick and Janet (Lawrence) A; Ph.B., U. Chgo., 1947, M.A., 1952, Ph.D., 1956; m. Ruth Salzman Skinner, July 24, 1953; 1 dau., Megan. Archaeol. field tng. in Jarmo, Iraq, 1950-51, Yucatan, Mexico, 1953; field studies history irrigation and urban settlement, Iraq and Iran, 1956—; reconnaissance and excavation ancient Mayan settlement patterns, Chiapas, Mexico, 1958-61; mem. faculty U. Chgo. and staff Oriental Inst., 1955—, asso prof., 1961-62, prof., 1962—; dir. inst., 1962-68; dean div. social scis., 1970—; resident dir. Baghdad School, American Schools of Oriental Research, 1968-69. Served with USNR, 1944-46. Fellow Am. Acad. Arts Scis., Middle East Studio Assn., A.A.A.S., Am. Anthrop. Assn.; mem. Soc. Am. Archaeology, German Archaeol. Inst., Nat. Acad. Scis., Sigma Xi. Author: Land Behind Baghdad, 1965; The Evolution of Urban Society, 1966; The Uruk Countryside, 1971. Editor: (with C. H. Kreling) City Invincible: A Symposium on Urbanization and Cultural Development in the Ancient Near East, 1960. Home: 5201 S Kimbark Av Chicago IL 60615

ADAMS, ROBERT MORFORD, Jr., lawyer; b. Duluth, Minn., Feb. 13, 1916; s. Robert M. and Cherrill (McNeill) A.; A.B., Stanford, 1937, LL.B., 1940; m. Elizabeth Sweet, Mar. 23, 1940; children—Robert M., Clifford S., Richard M. Admitted to Cal. bar, 1941, also U.S. Supreme Ct.; practice law San Francisco, 1941—; asso. firm McCutchen, Olney, Mannon & Greene, 1941-47, firm Athearn, Chandler & Farmer, Hoffman & Angell, 1947-50; partner firm Angell & Adams, 1950-62, firm Angell, Adams and Holmes, 1962-70, firm Busterud, Draper & Adams, 1970—. Served with intelligence USNR, 1942-45. Mem. Am. Bar Assn., Bar Assn. San Francisco, Am. Judicature Soc., Am. Inst. Mining Engrs. (asso.), Engrs. Club San Francisco, Phi Beta Kappa, Theta Delta Chi, Phi Alpha Delta. Episcopalian. Club: Bohemian (San Francisco). Home: 515 Warren Rd San Mateo CA 94402 Office: Russ Bldg 235 Montgomery St San Francisco CA 94104

ADAMS, ROBERT MORTON, lawyer; b. N.Y.C., Jan. 16, 1900; s. Robert A. and Frances (Bennett) A.; M.E., Stevens Inst. Tech., 1921; LL.B., Fordham U., 1924; m. Mercedes M. Cullinan, June 19, 1937;

children—Robert Morton, Richard Holbrook, Stephen Bennett, Mercedes Molyneux. Admitted to N.Y. bar, 1925; asso. firm Pennie, Edmonds, Morton, Taylor & Adams, and predecessor, 1921-30, partner, 1930—. Trustee Norwalk (Conn.) Hosp., New Canaan (Conn.) Library. Served with USNRF, 1918-22. Mem. Am., N.Y. (bd. govs., officer 1938-41, 43-50, pres. 1946-47) patent law assns., Assn. Bar City N.Y. (exec. com. 1947-51), Pilgrims Soc., Alumni Assn. Stevens Inst. Tech. (pres. 1945-46), Beta Theta Pi, Delta Theta Chi. Roman Catholic. Clubs: University (N.Y.C.); New Canaan Country. Home: Weed St New Canaan CT 06840 Office: 330 Madison Av New York City NY 10017

ADAMS, ROBERT WAUGH, Jr., banker; b. Johnstown, Pa., Oct. 26, 1936; s. Robert Waugh and Mary Louise (Pyle) A.; B.S. in Accounting, Pa. State U., 1958; M.B.A., U. Louisville, 1967; grad. Stonier Sch. Banking, 1967; m. Karen Elizabeth Day, June 13, 1964; children—Robert Waugh, Tara Anne, Teller, Cambria Savs. & Loan Assn., Johnstown, Pa., summers 1955, 56, 57, Johnstown Bank and Trust Co., summer 1958; with Citizens Fidelity Bank and Trust Co., Louisville, 1959—, asst. cashier, from 1961, asst. v.p., 1964. comptroller, 1967-69, v.p., comptroller, 1969—; tchr. Am. Inst. Banking, 1969—. Active local United Fund, Louisville Fund, Parkhill Community Center. Vice chmn. bd. trustees St. Catharine Coll., Springfield, Ky. Served to capt., AUS, 1958-59. Mem. Planning Execs. Inst. (pres. 1969-70), Bus. Adminstrn. Inst. (chpt. treas. 1971—), Am. Inst. Banking, Financial Execs. Inst. (chpt. v.p. 1971—), English-Speaking Union, Theta Chi (treas., v.p. 1956-58), Delta Sigma Rho, Delta Sigma Pi, Scabbard and Blade, Skull and Bones. Catholic. Club: Toastmasters (past club pres., area gov. 1967-68). Home: 1302 Abbeywood Rd Louisville KY 40222 Office: 437 W Jefferson St Louisville KY 40202

ADAMS, ROLLAND LEROY, publisher; b. Huntingdon, Pa., Dec. 27, 1904; s. Lemuel B. and Carrie (Snyder) A.; student Dickinson Coll. and Law Sch., 1922-25; LL.D., Dickinson Coll. 1966; m. Pauline S. Homback, June 26, 1930; childrenNancy A. (Mrs. Donald Taylor), Marcia S. (Mrs. George L. Roehr), Mary H. (Mrs. John F. Sitzer, Jr.). Teller, 1st Nat. Bank, Newport, Pa., 1925; bank examiner, Pa., 1925-29; asst. to pres. E.P. Wilbur Trust Co., Bethlehem, Pa., 1929-30; with Bethlehem Globe Pub. Co., 1930-33, gen. mgr., 1933-52, pub., pres., 1952-67, chmn. bd., 1967—; chmn. bd. City News Co. Bethlehem, Inc.; pres. Times Pub. Co., Quaker State Coca-Cola Bottling Co. (all Bethlehem), A.B.E. Broadcasting Co. Chmn. Bethlehem Community Chest Campaign, 1949, St. Luke's Hosp. (Bethlehem) Expansion Campaign, 1952; organizer, chmn. Northampton County Civil Def. Council, 1941-42; mem. Gov's Hosp. Study Commn., 1958—. Trustee St. Luke's Hosp., Dickinson Coll. Carlisle, Pa. Recipient Alumni award Lehigh U., 1956; named Man of Year, Sertoma Club Bethlehem, 1965. Mem. Am., Pa. (pres. 1956; ex-officio mem. exec. com.) newspaper pubs. assns., Bethlehem C. of C., Sigma Delta Chi (hon. mem), Sigma Alpha Epsilon. Methodist Episcopalian. Clubs: Nat. Press (Washington); Pen and Pencil (Phila.); Saucon Valley Country, Bethlehem (Bethlehem). Founder Billy Ney scholarship for Newport (Pa.) Union High Sch. Home: RD 4 Saucon Valley Rd Bethlehem PA 18018 Office: 210 W 4th St Bethlehem PA 19015

ADAMS, RUSSELL BALRD, airline exec.; b. Wheeling, W.Va., Dec. 28, 1910; s. Russell Updegraff and Daisy Dell (Hilton) A.; student Elliott Bus. Coll., Wheeling, 1926, Bethany Coll., 1926-27, U. Ky. 1927; m. Frances Esther Nordin, Oct. 27, 1935; children—Russell Baird, Richard Alan, Marilyn (Mrs. Joseph H. Felter, Jr.), David Anthony. Office mgr. Bradford Supply Co. and clerk, John J. McKay, Sistersville, W.Va., 1927-30; various positions in office of chief post office insp. Post Office Dept., 1930-36, apptd. post office insp., 1936, trans. to CAA (later CAB), 1939, serving in various capacities in econ. bur., apptd. dir., 1945. mem., 1948. Rep. interdept. adv. com. on surplus aircraft disposal, 1944-46; tech. adviser U.S. delegation Internat. Civil Aviation Conf., Chgo., 1944, 1st Interim Assembly, Provisional Internat. Civil Aviation Orgn., Montreal, Can., 1946; mem. U.S. Sect. Com. of Internat. Tech. Aerial Legal Experts, 1946; chmn. econ. div. Air Coordinating Com., 1946-50, alternate rep. CAB, 1946-50, mem. Internat. Civil Aviation Orgn. Panel, 1947-50; alternate del. U.S. delegation First Assembly Internat. Civil Aviation Orgn., Montreal Can., 1947, del. U.S. delegation commn. on multilateral agreement on comml. air rights in Internat. Air Transport, Geneva, Switzerland, 1947, chmn. U.S. delegation, 2d Assembly Internat. Civil Aviation Orgn., Geneva, Swizerland, 1948, singing on behalf of U.S. in accordance with powers given by the pres., Conv. of Internat. Recognition of Rights in Aircraft, 1948; chmn. U.S. delegation Peruvian negotiations, 1948, Canadian negotiations, 1949, U.S. Philippine negotiations, 1950, U.S.- Netherlands negotiations, 1951, 4th Assembly Internat. Civil Aviation Orgn., 1950, U.S.-French Negotiation, Paris, 1951; special assistant to the Sec. State, 1951; v.p. Pan Am. World Airways 1951-. Chairman Davies Memorial Committee. Mem. Bus. Govt. Relations Council, Federal City Council. Decorated Grand Official Merit Ordem Soberana Vera Cruz (Brazil). Mem. Sigma Nu. Democrat. Unitarian. Clubs: Metropolitan, University, National Aviation (v.p. 1955-65, gov.), Circus Saints & Sinners (bd. govs.), Aero (pres. 1960), National Capital Democratic, Congressional Country, Jefferson Islands (gov.), International (bd. govs.; sec. 1966), 1925 F Street (Washington); Burning Tree. Home: 9120 Harrington Dr Potomac MD 20854 Office: 815 15th St NW Washington DC 20005

ADAMS, RUTH MARIE, coll. pres.; b. N.Y.C., July 10, 1914; d. Thomas H. and Hester R. (Dalton) Adams; B.A., Adelphi Coll., 1935, D.H.L., 1961; M.A., Columbia, 1943; Ph.D., Radcliffe Coll., 1951; D.Litt., Russell Sage Coll., 1961; L.L.D., Rutgers U. 1966, U. Mass., 1970; D.H.L., Bates Coll., 1970; L.H.D., St. Lawrence U., 1971. Tchr. English, Mepham High Sch., Bellmore, N.Y., 1938-43; resident Radcliffe Coll., 1943-45; teaching fellow, tutor Harvard, 1944-46; instr., then asst. prof., asso. prof. English, chmn. honors div. U. Rochester, 1946-60; prof. English, dean Douglass Coll., Rutgers U., 1960-66; prof. English, pres. Wellesley (Mass.) Coll., 1966—. Mem. Modern Lang. Assn., Phi Beta Kappa. Address: Wellesley Coll Wellesley MA 02181

ADAMS, SAM, educator; b. Walthall, Miss., Mar. 14, 1916; s. S. F. and Addie A.; B.S., Delta State Tchrs. Coll., Cleveland, Miss., 1936; M.A., La. State U., 1940, Ph.D., 1951; m. Grace Boudreaux, Oct. 22, 1944; 1 dau., Carolyn. High sch. sci. tchr., Miss. and Ala., 1936-38, 40-42; tchr. USAAF and Maritime Service, 1942-43; physicist Oak Ridge Nat. Lab., 1944, 46-49; asso. prof. physics McNeese State Coll., Lake Charles, La., 1951-54; asso. prof. edn. La. State U., 1954-62, prof. edn., 1962—, asso. dean acad. affairs, 1962-65. Served with AUS, 1944-46. Mem. N.E.A., Nat. Sci. Tchrs. Assn., Nat. Council Tchrs. Math., Am. Ednl. Research Assn. Author: Science in Our Environment, 1957; Science in Our World, 1957; Science in the Universe, 1958; Teaching Arithmetic Concepts and Skills, 1963; Educational Measurement for the Classroom Teacher, 1966; To Be A Teacher, 1969; 2010 Glendale Av Baton Rouge LA 70808

ADAMS, SAMUEL CLIFFORD, Jr., fgn. service officer; b. Waco, Tex., Aug. 15, 1920; s. Samuel Clifford and Sarah Catherine (Roberts) A.; B.A., Fisk U., 1940, M.A. (Social Sci. fellow), 1947; Ph.D. (John Hay Whitney Found. fellow), U. Chgo., 1952; postdoctoral student London Sch. Econs. and Polit. Sci., Sch. Oriental and African Studies, also Maxwell Sch. of Syracuse U., 1957; m. Evelyn Baker Adams. Employed as machinist trainee Norfolk (Va.) Navy Yard, 194244; research and teaching asst. grad. dept. Fisk U., 1946-47; dir. Marion Coop. Center, Am. Missionary Assn., 1947-50; research asst., com. on edn., tng. and research race relations, div. social scis. U. Chgo., 1950 51: mass edn. specialist U.S. Spl. Tech. and Econ. Mission to Asso. States Indo-China, 1952-54; acting chief edn. div. USOM, Saigon, Vietnam, 1954-55; chief edn. and community devel. divs. USOM, Phnom Penh, Cambodia, 1955-57; chief edn. adviser Office ICA Rep., Am. Consulate Gen., Lagos, Nigeria, 1958-61; rep. AID, Republic of Mali, Africa, 1961, dir. mission, 1962-64; mem. senior seminar foreign policy Fgn. Service Inst., Dept. State, Washington, 196468; U.S. ambassador to Niger, 1968-69; asst. adminstr. AID, Bur. for Africa, Dept. State, Washington, 1969—. Served as chaplain's asst. AUS, 1944-46. Nominated William A. Jump Meml. award, 1954; recipient Arthur S. Flemming award, 1957. Asso. fellow Royal Anthrop. Inst.: mem. Am. Sociol. Soc., Alpha Phi Alpha. Author articles on race and cultural relations. Home: 3226 N MacGregor Way Houston TX 77021 Office: Bur for Africa AID Dept State Washington DC 20523

ADAMS, SAMUEL PICKENS, ins. co. exec.; b. Indpls., June 21, 1913; s. Henry C. and Mary (Pickens) A.; A.B., Williams Coll., 1935; m. Kathryn E. Koenig, Aug. 31, 1940; children—Elizabeth, Sarah Ann. With Lincoln Nat. Life Ins. Co., Ft. Wayne, Ind., 1935—, actuary, 1955—,, v.p., 1963—, sec., 1967—. Active local chpt. A.R.C.; mem. econ. edn. adv. bd. Purdue U., 1954—. Fellow Soc. Actuaries; mem. Am. Acad. Actuaries, Am. Soc. Corp. Secs., Phi Beta Kappa, Delta Kappa Epsilon. Home: 2340 Indian Village Blvd Ft Wayne IN 46809 Office: 1301-27 S Harrison St Ft Wayne IN 46801

ADAMS, SCOTT, librarian; b. Agawam, Mass., Nov. 20, 1909; s. Scott and Edith Fisher (Ferre) A.; A.B., Yale, 1930; M.L.S., Columbia, 1940; m. Barbara Winn, June 29, 1935; 1 dau., Susanna. Dept. head Tchrs. Coll. Library, Columbia, 1940-42, Providence Pub. Library, 1943-45; acting librarian Armed Forces Med. Library, 1946-50; librarian U.S. Nat. Insts. Health, Bethesda, Md., 1950-59; program dir., fgn. sci. information Office of Sci. Information Service, Nat. Sci. Found., 1959-60; dep. dir. Nat. Library of Medicine, 1960-69; spl. asst. to the fgn. sec. Nat. Acad. Scis., 1970-71, sec. U.S. Book Exchange, Inc., 1952-53. Mem. internat. adv. com. documentation, libraries and archives to UNESCO, 1967-70. Fellow A.A.A.S. (sec. information and communications sect.); mem. District of Columbia (pres. 1948), Med. (mem. bd. dirs. 1952-55, pres. 1967-68) library assns., Council Nat. Library Assns. (sec. 1954-55), Am. Documentation Inst. (pres. 1954-55), Spl. Libraries Assn. Clubs: Yale, Cosmos (Washington). Editor of O. P. Market, 1943. Home: 10401 Grosvenor Pl Rockville MD 20852

ADAMS, SHERMAN, former gov. N.H.; b. East Dover, Vt., Jan. 8, 1899; s. Clyde H. and Winnie Marion (Sherman) A.; A.B., Dartmouth Coll., 1920, A.M., 1940; LL.D., U. N.H., 1950; D.C. L., New Eng. Coll., 1951; LL.D., Coll., St. Lawrence Univ., 1954, Center Coll., Ky., 1955, University Me., Middlebury Coll., 1957; m. Rachel Leona White, July 28, 1923; children—Marion (Mrs. William Freese), Jean (Mrs. William M. Hallager), Sarah, Samuel. Treas., Black River Lumber Co. Vt. 1921- 22; mgr., timberland and lumber operations, The Parker-Young Co., Lincoln, N.H., 1928-45; former dir. Pemigewasset R.R., Concord; pres. Loon Mountain Recreation Corp., 1966—; mem. N.H. Ho. of Reps., 1941-44, chmn. com. on labor, 1941-42, speaker of house, 1943-44; mem. 79th Congress (1945-47), 2d N.H. Dist.; gov. N.H., 1949-53; asst. to Pres. U.S., 1953-58. Chmn. Conf. N.E. Govs., 1951-52. Served with USMCR, 1918. Dir. (life) Northeastern Lumber Mfrs. Assn. Del. Rep. Nat. Conv., 1944, 52. Mem. (sr.) Soc. Am. Forresters, S.A.R. (N.H. soc.), Sigma Alpha Epsilon. Mason (33). Republican. Author: First Hand Report, 1961; also articles in Life, other mags. Lectr. Address: Pollard Rd Lincoln NH 03251

ADAMS, STANLEY, lyricist; b. N.Y.C., August 14, 1907; s. Henry Charles and Nan (Josephs) A.; LL.B., N.Y. U., 1929; m. Janice Schwarts, Sept. 28, 1940 (div.); 1 dau., Barbara Paula; m. 2d, Bernice Halperin. Author of lyrics for Little Old Lady, My Shawl, What A Diffrence A Day Made, There Are Such Things, many others; contributed songs to The Show Is On. A Lady Says 'Yes' (stage shows), Every Day's A Holiday, Duel in the Sun, Strategic Air Command (motion pictures), others, Adv. bd. Am. Fedn. Musicians, Nat. Cultural Center, Washington, Kennedy Cultural Center. Dir. Braille Inst. Mem. Country Music Assn. (v.p.), Songwriters Protective Assn. (v.p. 1943-44), A.S.C.A.P. (dir. 1944—, pres. 1953—), Nat. Music Council (v.p.), Delta Beta Phi. Club: Friars. Home: 3 Orchard Lane Kings Point NY 11024 Office: 575 Madison Av New York City NY 10022

ADAMS, THEODORE FLOYD, clergyman; b. Palmyra, N.Y., Sept. 26, 1898; s. Floyd Holden and Evelyn (Parkes) A. B.A., Denison U., 1921; B.D., Colgate Rochester Divinity Sch., 1924; D.D. (hon.), U. of Richmond, 1938, William and Mary, 1940, Denison U., 1940, Washington and Lee, Baylor, 1958, Stetson University, 1959, McMaster U., 1962, Wake Forest U., 1968; L.H.D., Hampden-Sydney Coll., 1959; LL.D., Keuka Coll., 1964; m. Esther Josephine Jillson, Feb. 26, 1925; children—Betsy Ann (Mrs. Frank K. Thompson), Theodore F., John Jillson. Ordained to ministry of Baptist Ch., 1924; pastor in Cleveland, O., 1924-27, Toledo, O., 1927-36; pastor First Baptist Ch., Richmond, Va., 1936-68, pastor emeritus, 1968—; visting professor Southeastern Sem., Wake Forest, N.C., 1968—; v.p. Baptist Young Peoples Union of Am. 1925-26; mem. bd. promotion, Ohio Baptist Conv., 1928-35; pres. Ohio Baptist Young Peoples Union, 1925-27. V. pres. Bapt. World Alliance, 1947-50, mem. exec. com., 1934—, pres., 1955-60, mem. administrv. com., 1960—; mem. fgn. mission bd. So. Bapt. Conv., 1940-50, 61-67, mem. joint com. pub. affairs; board dirs. Va. Inst. of Pastoral Care; bd. dirs., v.p. CARE, 1960-70; member board directors Rockefeller Brothers Theological Fellowship Program, 1961-70; trustee Council on Religion and Internat. Affairs, 1951—. Mem. bd. Richmond Memorial Hosp.; mem. bd. trustees So. Bapt. Hosp., 1950-53, U. Richmond; trustee, hon. chmn. bd. Va. Union U.; trustee Va. Baptist Children's Home, 1936-57, pres. bd. trustees, 1936-53. Recipient Upper Room citation for leadership, 1960; Nat. Brotherhood citation Nat. Conf. Christians and Jews, 1964. Mem. Phi Beta Kappa. Beta Theta Pi, Phi Mu Alpha, Omicron Delta Kappa. Clubs: Rotary (Richmond). Author: Making Your Marriage Succeed, 1953; Making the Most of What Life Brings, 1957; Tell Me How, 1964; Baptists Around The World, 1967. Contbr. articles to religious jours. Home: 5100 Monument Av Richmond VA 23230 Office: Southeastern Bapt Sem Wake Forest NC 27587

ADAMS, THEODORE LIONEL, clergyman; b. Bangor, Me., Feb. 23, 1915; s. Raphael and Ida (Tomchin) A.; B.A., Yeshiva U., 1936, M.S., 1960, Ph.D., 1962; Rabbi, Rabbi Isaac Elchanan Theol. Sem., 1937; postgrad. Columbia, 1944-47; m. Bernice Nemetski, Jan. 11, 1938; children—Lawrence Myron, Howard Joseph, Sivia Esther, Myril Ita. Rabbi. Congregation Mt. Sinai, Jersey City, 1938-53, Congregation Ohab Zedek, N.Y.C., 1953—. Pres. Rabbinical Council N.J., 1939-52, now hon. pres.; financial sec. Rabbinical Council of Am., 1948-50, v.p., 1950-52, pres., 1952-54, now hon. pres.; v.p. Synagogue Council of Am., 1955-57, pres., 1957-59, hon. pres., 1959—, mem. exec. bd., 1949—, also chmn. internat. affairs com.; nat. vice chmn. Nat. Council of Hapoel Hamizrachi, 1952—. Mem. OPA, 1941-46; mem. Jersey City Planning Commn., 1946-51, Civil Rights Commn., 1950-53; cons. to Gov. of N.J. on N.J. Youth Conf., 1947-50; del., cons. Mid- Century White House Conf. on Children and Youth, 1950; mem. dirs. Jewish Welfare Bd. and rep. to U.S. Mission to UN; mem. Nat. Community Relations Adv. Com.; mem. Pres.' People to People Com., 1957—, Pres.' Com. for Internat. Econ. Growth, 1958—; del. White House Conf. on Children and Youth, 1960—; mem. Stryker's Bay Community Council, Manhattan. Mem. bd. dirs. Commn. on Conf. on Jewish Material Claims Against Germany; chmn. Nat. Exploratory Com. on Jewish Unity. Recipient Mordecai Ben David award Yeshiva U., 1950. Del. World Zionist Congress, Jerusalem, 1956. Mem. Am. Social. Soc., Am. Acad. Polit. and Social Sci. Editor: Sermon Manual of Rabbinical Council of America, 1948. Contbr. Jewish Forum, Jewish Life. Home: 680 West End Av New York City NY 10025 Office: 118-124 W 95th St New York City NY 10025

ADAMS, THOMAS BROOKS, advt. exec.; b. Detroit, Sept. 16, 1919; s. Andrew S. and Louise A. (Brooks) A.; B.A., Wayne State U., 1944; m. Mary E. Bryant, Mar. 22, 1945; children—Janis E., Julie A., Kathleen M. With Campbell-Ewald Co., Detroit, 1945—, chmn. of the bd., 1968—. Vice pres. United Found.; bd. dirs. Wayne State U. Alumni Fund. Served from ensign to lt. comdr., USNR, 1941-45; lt. comdr. Res. Decorated Navy Cross, Distinguished Flying Cross, Air medal Presdl. Unit citation; named Outstanding Young Advt. Man of Year by N.Y. Assn. Advt. Men and Women, 1955. Mem. Wayne State U. Alumni Assn. (v.p., trustee), Advt. Council (dir.), Greater Detroit Bd. Commerce (vice chmn. bd.). Home: 931 W Harsdale Rd Bloomfield Hills MI 48013 Office: Gen Motors Bldg Detroit MI 48202

ADAMS, THOMAS HAMMOND, lawyer; b. Ann Arbor, Mich., Sept. 1, 1901; s. Henry C. and Bertha (Wright) A.; A.B., U. Mich., 1922; LL.B., Harvard, 1925; m. Hortense O. Miller, Sept. 24, 1927; children—Thomas Hammond, Clarlssa Barlow (Mrs. Thomas C. Goad). Reporter, N.Y. Evening Post, 1921-22; admitted to Mich. bar, 1927, since practiced in Detroit; partner in the firm Hill, Lewis, Adams, Goodrich & Tait, 1933-; lectr. Wayne U. Law Sch., 1937-47. Mem. Mich. Bd. Law Examiners, 1948-60; chmn. Nat. Conf. Bar Examiners, 1952- 53. Dir. Michigan Sugar Co. Mem. Am., Mich., Detroit bar assns., Am. Law Inst., Am. Judicature Soc., Alpha Delta Phi, Delta Theta Phi, Sigma Delta Chi. Clubs: Detroit; Orchard Lake Country; Village Players Dirmingham. Home: 746 Puritan Rd Birmingham MI 48009 Office: Penobscot Bldg Detroit 26 MI 48226

ADAMS, THOMAS HINCKLEY, Jr., investment banker; b. Wellesley Hills, Mass., Mar. 6, 1915; s. Thomas Hinckley and Ida (Lincoln) A.; grad. high sch.; m. Margaret Elizabeth Nichols, Jan. 21, 1938; children—Thomas Hinckley III, John Nichols. Clk., N.E. Power Service Corp., 1934-37; stockbroker J.H. Goddard & Co., Inc., Boston, 1937-38; stockbroker Ballou, Adams & Co., Inc., 1938-44; stockbroker Paine, Webber, Jackson & Curtis, Boston, 1944-64, gen. partner, 1965-70, v.p., 1970—. Treas., bd. dirs. Stone Inst., Newton Home for Aged People; treas., trustee Newton Pub. Library. Mem. Investment Bankers Assn. Am. (chmn. New Eng. group), Bond Club Boston. Boston Investment Club, Boston Security Analysts Soc. (past mem. exec. com.), Inst. Chartered Financial Analysts, Longwood Covered Cts. (pres., trustee). Republican. Unitarian. Clubs: Brae Burn Country, Down Town; Rotary (Boston). Home: 133 Dartmouth St West Newton MA 02165 Office: 24 Federal St Boston MA 02110

ADAMS, TOM, sec. state Fla.; b. Jacksonville, Fla., Mar. 11, 1917; s. Thomas Burton and Carolyn (Hamilton) A.; grad. The Hill Sch., Pottstown, Pa., 1936; A.B., U. Mich., 1940; postgrad. U. Fla. Law Sch., 1948; D. Space Edn., Brevard Engring. Coll.; H.H.D., Trinity Coll.; m. Helen Brown, July 30, 1939; children—Carolyn (Mrs. James A. DeHaven, Jr.), Augusta (Mrs. T. Buckingham Bird), Frances. Real estate, property mgmt. H.P. Holmes, Inc., Detroit, 1940-42; plant supt. Foremost Dairies, Jacksonville and Daytona Beach, Fla., 1942-44; owner, operator dairy farm, Orange Park, 1944-48; timber dealer, property mgmt., Orange Park Properties (Fla.), 1948-61; farmer, Fla., 1942-61; mem. Fla. Senate, 29th Dist., 1956-60, chmn. com. reorgn. Fla. Dept. Agr.; sec. state Fla., 1961—. Pres., Leon County United Fund, 1964; state campaign chmn. Fla. Mental Health Assn., 1964. Decorated Order of San Carlos (Colombia); named Most Outstanding Freshman Senator 1957 session, Fla. Legislature, Most Valuable Mem. Legislature 1959 session, Most Effective State Adminstr., 1961, 63, 65; recipient Agrl. award Fla. Legislature, 1957. Mem. U.S. Commn. Southeast River Basins (mem. resources adv. bd.), Nat. Rivers and Harbors Congress (dir.), Nat. Waterways Conf. (chmn. 1964-65, pres. 1965-67), Miss. Valley Assn. (pres. 1968, dir.), Fla.-Colombia Alliance (founder 1963), Fla. State U. Gold Key Soc., Newcomen Soc., U. Fla. Alumni Assn., Blue Key, Phi Delta Theta, Alpa Kappa Psi. Baptist. Moose (state pres. 1966-67), Rotarian. Home: 1702 Golf Terrace Tallahassee FL 32304 Office: State Capitol Tallahassee FL 32304

ADAMS, VIERS WILSON, former univ. dean; b. Braddock, Pa., Jan. 29, 1909; s. Frank T. (Morrow) A.; A.B., U. Pitts., 1930, M.A., 1934; student U. Chgo., U. Fla.; Ed. D. (hon.), Waynesburg Coll., 1961; m. Zella Wallace, July 18, 1932. Student adviser Johnstown Center. U. Pitts., 1930-32, asst. to head, 1932-36, head of center, 1936-45, asst. dir. extension div., 1945- 46, dir. Ellsworth Center, 1947-51, asso. dir. extension div. and summer sessions, also dir. spl. services, 1951-54, dir. extension div. and summer sessions, also dir. spl. services 1951-54, dir. extension div. dir. summer sessions and evening classes, 1958-71, ret., dean emeritus, U.S. Office Edn., 1946-47. Mem. Pa. Dept. Pub. Assistance Bd. for Cambria County, 1941-44, for Allegheny County, 1946-49; mem. Johnstown Municipal Airport Commn., 1942-43. Recipient George Wharton Pepper award U. Pitts., 1930; Distinguished Service award Am. Legion. 1943, Civilian Def. award, 1944. Mem. Assn. U. Evening Colls., Nat. U. Extension Assn., Adult Edn. Assns., Phi Delta Kappa. Omicron Delta Kappa, Theta Chl. Republican. Presbyn. Mason. Home: 1319 NW 28th St Gainesville FL 32601

ADAMS, WALTER HARRIS, coll. dean; b. Springtown, Tex., Nov. 29, 1903; s. Edmund A. and Alice (Moore) A.; A.B., Abilene (Tex.) Christian Coll., 1925; A.M., Stanford, 1927; Ph.D., Columbia, 1932; m. Louise Harsh, Sept. 7, 1927; children—Louise Newby, Nancy, Walter Harris. Instr. math. Abilene Christian Coll., 1925-26, asst. prof. edn., 1927-30, dean of students, 1931-38, coll. Dean prof. secondary edn., 1938-69, acad. v.p., 1969-70, dean emeritus, 1970—. Mem. Texas Bd. Examiners for Tchr. Education, past chmn., mem. adv. com. Tex. Research League. Mem. Assn. Tex. Grad. Schools (past president), Association of Texas Colleges (past pres.), Tex. Conf. on Edn. (past pres.), Phi Delta Kappa. Rotarian (past pres. Abilene). Author: Placement of Students to Teaching Positions, 1932. Home: 650 E N 21st St Abilene TX 79601

ADAMS, WARREN SANFORD 2d, food co. exec., lawyer; b. Cleve., Sept. 4, 1910; s. Otis Howard and Hermine (Weis) A.; A.B., Princeton, 1930; LL.B., Harvard, 1934; J.S.D., N.Y.U., 1941. Admitted to N.Y. bar, 1935; pvt. practice, N.Y.C., 1934- 40; gen. counsel chems. div. WPB, 1941; with Corn Products Co., 1946- -, gen.

counsel, 1960—, v.p., 1962—; pres., dir. 580 Park Av., Inc., N.Y.C., 1957—. Bd. dirs. Washington Sq. Home, N.Y.C.; trustee, gen. counsel Whitehall Found., Inc., N.Y.C. Served to maj. USMCR, 1942-46. Mem. Am., Internat., N.Y. State, Inter Am. bar assns., Bar Assn. City N.Y. Episcopalian. Clubs: University (Washington); Meadow Brook (L.I.); Racquet and Tennis, Church, Metropolitan Opera (N.Y.C.); Nat. Golf Links Am. (Southhampton, L.I.); Royal and Ancient Golf (St. Andrews, Scotland); Royal St. George's Golf (Sandwich, Eng.). Home: 580 Park Av New York City NY 10021 Office: 717 Fifth Av New York City NY 10022

ADAMS, WESTON WOOLLARD, business exec.; b. Springfield, Mass., Aug. 9, 1904; s. Charles Francis and Lillias Mae (Woollard) A.; student Phillips Exeter Acad., 1921-23; B.A., Harvard, 1928; m. Mildred Culver Boyd, Jan. 8, 1933 (div. 1936); children—Abigial Mae (Mrs. Willys K. Silvers), John Weston; m. 2d, Nancy Evelyn Atkins, Sept. 26, 1936; children—Wendy Ann (Mrs. Shelby M. C. Davis), Weston Woollard. Mem. Boston Stock Exchange, 1929-69, bd. govs., 1938-42, 64-69, v.p., 1953-62, pres., 1962-64; mem. N.Y. Stock Exchange, 1946-69; chmn. bd. Adams, Harkness & Hill, Inc., Boston; pres. the Boston Profl. Hockey Assn., Inc., 1936-51, 64-69, chmn. bd., 1958—; chmn. bd. Boston Garden-Arena Corp., 1951—. Mem. bd. govs. Nat. Hockey League. Served from lt. to comdr. USNR, 1942-46. Clubs: The Aleppo Temple, Harvard (Boston); Country (Brookline); Eastern Yacht (Marblehead Neck, Mass.); Caterpillar. Home: 145 Sargent Rd Brookline MA 02146 Office: care Boston Bruins Hockey Club 150 Causeway St Boston MA 02114

ADAMS, WILLIAM ELIAS, surgeon; b. Nichols, Ia., May 1, 1902; s. Frank A. and Alvina W. (Mills) A.; B.S., M.D., U. Ia., 1926; m. Dr. Huberta Livingstone, June 9, 1928; 1 dau., Diana Isabella Livingstone (Mrs. John Morgan, Jr.). Intern surgery U. Ia., 1926-27, instr. anatomy, 1927-28; Douglas Smith research fellow U. Chgo., 1928-29, asst. surgery, 1929-30, asst. resident, 1930-31, instr., resident surgery, 1931- 33, instr., chief resident, 1933-35, asst. prof., 1936-40, asso. prof., 1940-47, prof., 1947-54, Raymond prof., 1954-67, Raymond prof. surgery emeritus, 1967—, chmn. dept. surgery, 1959-65; attending surgeon U. Chgo. Hosps., 1936-67, Billings Hosp., Chgo., 1936-67; asst. dir. A.C.S.; sr. cons. surgeon Municipal Tb Sanitarium, Chgo., Great Lakes Naval Tng. Hosp., instr. surgery Washington U., St. Louis, 1933; guest asst. surgery U. Berlin, 1935-36; hon. prof. surgery U. Guadalajara (Mexico), 1955, U. Madrid (Spain), 1956; Fulbright guest prof. surgery U. Glasgow (Scotland) 1956. Treas. 1st Internat. Congress on Smoking, Health, 1963-66. Recipient Alexander B. Vishnevski medal Inst. Surgery, Moscow, Russia, 1966; certificate merit clin. and research surgery Vishnevski Inst., U. Moscow, 1966. Diplomate Am. Bd. Surgery, Am. Bd. Thoracic Surgery (founding mem., chmn., 1956-57). Fellow A.C.S. (sec. 1959-62), Am. Surg. Assn., Kansas City Acad. Medicine (hon.); hon. mem. Soc. Cancerol Mexico, Sociedad de Cirugia de Guadalajara; mem. Am. Assn. Thoracic Surgery (pres. 1959-60), Central Surg. Society, A.M.A. (chmn. sect. diseases of chest 1965-66), Ill. (chmn. bd. trustees 1964-66, trustee 1958-67), Chgo. (pres. 1970-71) med. socs., Chgo. Surg. Soc. (treas. 1948-52, pres. 1952-53), Chgo. Path. Soc. (pres. 1950), Chgo. Tb Soc. (pres. 1938), Soc. U. Surgeons (founding mem.), Internat. Soc. Surgery, Am. Coll. Chest Physicians (president Ill. chpt. 1960-61, nat. pres. 1967-68), U.S. and Mexico Med. Soc. (hon.), Soc. Clin. Surgery, Pan Am. Med. Assn. (N.Am. v.p. sect. gen. surgery), Am. Thoracic Soc., U. Chgo. Med. Alumni Assn. (pres. 1957-58), Sigma Xi, Alpha Kappa Kappa (grand internat. pres. 1965-71), Alpha Omega Alpha (hon.). Presbyn. Mason. Clubs: Quadrangle, South Shore Country (Chgo.); Chikaming Country (Mich.). Contbr. articles sci. jours., Ency. Brit., also chpts. surg. and physiology textbooks. Asso. editor Diseases of the Chest, 1958—; editorial bd. Jour. Thoracic and Cardiovascular Surgery, 1962—; represented U.S.A. on internat. bd. editors Excerpta Medica, 1960-67. Home: 5805 Dorchester Av Chicago IL Office: 55 E Erie St Chicago IL 60611

ADAMS, WILLIAM F., educator; b. Ozark, Ala., April 2, 1907; s. John Quincy and Vivian Brooking (Brantley) A.; A.B., U. of Ala., 1927, M.A., 1928; m. Martha McCoy Dominick, July 20, 1928; one dau. Ann Brooking (Mrs. William S. Pritchard, Jr.). Instr. math. U. of Ala., 1928-43, asst. and asso. prof. math., 1942-46, asst. to dean, Coll. Arts and Scis., 1943-45, asst. dean, 1945-46, dean of admissions, 1946-60, dean emeritus; regional dir. So. States Am. Coll. Testing Program, Inc., 1960-70, ret. 1970. Recipient Algernon Sydney Sullivan award U. Ala., 1950. Mem. Am. Assn. Collegiate Registrars (pres. 1959-60), Assn. Coll. Admissions Counselors, Am. Assn. U. Profs., Am. Personnel and Guidance Assn., Phi Beta Kappa, Omicron Delta Kappa, Pi Mu Epsilon, Kappa Delta Pi, Kappa Sigma. Club: Country (Tuscaloosa, Ala.). Contbr. profl. jours. Home: 321 Caplewood Terrace Tuscaloosa AL 35401

ADAMS, WILLIAM HENRY, banker; b. N.Y.C., Apr. 18, 1924; s. William G. and Bessie (Shopoff) A.; student N.Y.U.; grad. Exec. Devel. Program, U. Buffalo, also Advanced Mgmt. Program, Harvard, 1963; m. Muriel K. Schmidt, June 3, 1945; 1 son, Douglas W. With Chase Manhattan Bank, N.Y.C., 1941—, v.p., 1959-65, sr. v.p., 1965— Served to capt. USAAF, 1942-45; ETO. Mem. Am. Soc. Corp. Secs., Municipal Finance Officers Assn., Am. Bankers Assn. Home: 6 Adriene Ct Farmingdale NY 11736 Office: 1 Chase Manhattan Plaza New York City NY 10015

ADAMS, WILLIAM HENSLEY, educator; b. Nashville, Aug. 14, 1929; s. William Hensley and Mary Pauline (Vaughn) A.; A.B., U. Tenn., 1951; postgrad. U. Okla., 1951, Tulane U., 1953-54; M.S., La. State U., 1956; Ph.D., Auburn U., 1959; m. Marion Adele Massey, Dec. 27, 1951; children—Deska Lee, Norma Dec, Anita Rice, Patricia Lynn. Grad. research asst. Auburn U., 1956-59; sr. research biologist Tenn. Game and Fish Commn., 1959-60; chmn. dept. biology, prof. biology Tenn. Wesleyan Coll., 1960-64; dean Coll. Arts and Scis., prof. biology Tenn. Technol. U., Cookeville, 1964-66; with div. pre-coll. edn. in sci. NSF, 1966-68, div. undergrad. edn. in sci., 1969—; mem. NSF Research Participation for Coll. Tchrs. Highlands Biol. Sta., 1961, NSF Summer Inst. Radiation Biology Oak Ridge Inst. Nuclear Studies, 1961, NSF Summer Inst. Comparative Anatomy Harvard, 1962, NSF Summer Inst. Marine Biology Duke Marine Lab., 1963, NSF-Tenn. Acad. Sci. Vis. Scientist Program, 1962-66; dir. NSF Coop. Coll.- Sch. Sci. Program, 1963-65; mem. Commn. Undergrad. Edn. in Biol. Scis. Southeastern Regional Conf., 1965, Advanced Placement Reader in Biology, 1965. Oak Ridge Inst. Nuclear Scis. Radiation Biology Conf., 1965. Served to maj., Med. Service Corps, USAF, 1951-53, 68-69. Recipient Sigma Xi-Research Engrng. Soc. Am. grant-in- aid, 1960-61, Tenn. Wesleyan Coll. Faculty award, 1962, Tenn. Technol. U. faculty research grant, 1966. Mem. A.A.A.S., Am. Inst. Biol. Scis., Am. Soc. Mammalogists (honorarium 1959), Am. Ornithologists Union, Cooper, Wilson ornithol. socs., Ecol. Soc. Am., Nat. Assn. Biology Tchrs., Tenn. Acads. Sci., Wildlife Soc. Home: 4004 Moss Dr Annandale VA 22003 Office: NSF Washington DC 20550

ADAMS, WILLIAM HESTER III, lawyer; b. Jacksonville, Fla., May 8, 1926; s. William H. and Florence (Vought) A.; A.B., Duke, 1947, LL.B., 1950; m. Carlie M. Collins, Mar. 30, 1967; 1 son, David Barth; children by previous marriage—William Hester IV, Nancy Lynn; 1 adopted dau., Laura Kurz. Admitted to Fla. bar, 1950, since practiced in Fla.; partner firm Mahoney, Hadlow, Chamber & Adams, 1962—. Sec., dir. Sav-A-Stop, Inc. Fla. Commr. uniform laws, 1967—. Served to lt. USNR, 1944-46, 51-52. Mem. Am., Jacksonville bar assns, Nat. Conf. Commrs. Uniform Laws, Fla. Bar, Order of Coif, Chi Phi. Republican. Universalist. Home: 5843 Point Bayou Jacksonville FL 32211 Office: Barnett Nat Bank Bldg Jacksonville FL 32201

ADAMS, WILLIAM JACKSON, Jr., lawyer; b. Carthage, N.C., Sept. 15, 1908; s. William Jackson and Florence (Wall) A.; student Woodberry Forest Sch., Orange, Va.; A.B., U. N.C., 1930, J.D., 1933; m. Elizabeth Whitehead, May 1, 1937; children—Elizabeth Whitehead (Mrs. R. Edward Morrissett, Jr.), William Jackson III. Admitted to N.C. bar, 1933; practice in Rocky Mount, 1933- 39; chief div. legislative drafting and codification of statutes N.C. Dept. Justice, 1939-41; an asst. atty. gen. N.C., 1941-45; practice in Greensboro, 1945—. Mem. steering com. to establish N.C. Constl. Study Commn., 1968-69. Mem. Am., N.C. (pres. 1968-69), Greensboro (pres. 1957-58) bar assns., Am. Judicature Soc., Nat. Conf. Bar Presidents, Phi Beta Kappa, Order of Coif, Phi Delta Phi. Democrat. Methodist. Clubs: Greensboro Country; Carolina Sailing (charter, 1st commodore; Robinson cup 1959) (Henderson, N.C.); Lake Norman Yacht (charter) (Mooresville, N.C.). Student editor in chief N.C. Law Rev., 1933. Contbr. profl. jours., yachting mags. Home: 615 Woodland Dr Greensboro NC 27408 Office: Jefferson Standard Bldg Greensboro NC 27402

ADAMS, WILLIAM R., paper mfr.; b. Albany, N.Y., Mar. 17, 1907; s. Thomas S. and Elizabeth (Rally) A.; A.B., Union Coll., Schenectady, 1928, LL.D., 1953; m. Florence E. Taggart, July 10, 1937; children—Thomas S., Taggart D., Lucy E. Engine assembler Fulton Iron Works Co., St. Louis, 1928; mgr. diesel engine div. Nat. Supply Co., Springfield, O., 1929-31, sales engr. Superior engine div., 1931-35; v.p. Robert E. Read, Inc., Dexter, N.Y., 1935-37; with St. Regis Paper Co., N.Y.C., 1937—, v.p., 1948-57, pres., 1957-71, chmn. bd., 1971—, dir., 1952—, also chief exec. officer; pres., dir. North Western Pulp & Power, Ltd., St. Regis Paper Co. (Can.), Ltd., Norwood & St. Lawrence R.R. Co.; dir. Greyhound Corp. Bd. dirs. U. Me. Pulp and Paper Found., 1958—; trustee Union Coll., 1954—; trustee, vice chmn. Inst. Paper Chemistry; trustee Am. Forest Inst. Mem. Nat. Indsl. Conf. Bd., Am. Paper Inst. (dir.), N.A.M. (dir.). Clubs: Union League, University, Links, Pinnacle (N.Y.C.); Augusta Nat. Home: Smith Ridge New Canaan CT 06840 Office: 150 E 42d St New York City NY 10017

ADAMS, WILLIAM SPRAGUE, educator; b. Sodus, N.Y., May 28, 1919; s. Ephraim Crawford Brown and Bessie (Granger) A.; student Cornell U., 1936-39; M.D., U. Rochester, 1943; m. Esther Driver Stratton, June 19, 1947; children—Thomas G., Mary B., Nancy Q., Esther S. Intern Medicine Strong Meml. Hosp. Rochester, N.Y. 1943-44, asst. resident, 1944-45; resident Wadsworth Gen. Hosp., VA Center, Los Angeles, 1948-49; instr. medicine U. Rochester Sch. Medicine, 1947-48, research fellow medicine, 1946-47; mem. faculty U. Cal. at Los Angeles Sch. Medicine, 1948—, prof. medicine, 1958—, chief div. metabolism, 1950—; vice chmn. dept. medicine, 1967—; adminstrv. sect. chief. asst. in research VA Hosp., Los Angeles, 1949-50. Mem. adv. com. research pathogenesis cancer Am. Cancer Soc., 1956-60; mem. cancer research tng. com. USPHS, 1960-64. Diplomate Am. Bd. Internal Medicine. Mem. A.M.A. A.C.P., Western Soc. Clin. Research, Western Assn. Physicians, Assn. Am. Physicians. Research purine and pyrimidine biochemistry in man. Home: 206 24th St Santa Monica CA 90402 Office: Dept Medicine U Cal Los Angeles Center Health Sciences Los Angeles CA 90024

ADAMS, WILLIAM WESLEY, petroleum co. exec.; b. Jena, La., July 24, 1908; s. William Wesley and Alice (Davis) A.; student Tyler Comml. Coll., 1926-27; m. Anna Sophie Franks, Sept. 17, 1934; children—William C., Alice Andrine, Carole Ann. With Gulf Oil Corp., 1928—, various accounting jobs Maracaibo, Venezuela, mgr. accounting Mene Grande Oil Co., comptroller, mgr. services, v.p. Mene Grande Oil Co., 1928-59, spl. assignment Gulf Oil Corp., Houston, 1961, sr. v.p., Pitts., 1961—. Mem. bd. Community Chest Allegheny County, Pitts. Hosp. Planning Assn. Mem. Nat. Indsl. Conf. Bd., N.A.M., Internat. C. of C. (trustee U.S. council). Home: 2060 Outlook Dr Pittsburgh PA 15234 Office: Gulf Bldg Pittsburgh PA 15219

ADAMS, WRIGHT ROWE, physician; b. Sheridan, Ill., June 14, 1903; s. Harry H. and Bessie (Law) A.; B.S., U. Ill., 1925, M.D., 1929; m. Ruth Chatfield, Oct. 8, 1927; children—Karen Louise, Judson Chatfield. Intern St. Luke's Hosp., Chgo., 1928-30; vol. in pathology Cook County Hosp., Chgo., 1930; resident Billings Hosp., Chgo., 1930-34; instr. medicine U. Chgo., 1934-37, asst. prof., 1937-43, asso. prof., 1943-49, prof. medicine, 1949-70, prof emeritus, 1970—, asso. dean div. biol. scis., 1947-67, chmn. dept. medicine, 1949-61; chief staff U. Chgo. Hosps. and Clinics, 1961-67; exec. dir. Ill. Regional Med. Program, 1967-70. Mem. Joint Commn. on Accreditation of Hosps., 1968—. Trustee Am. Optical Co. Diplomate Am. Bd. Internal Medicine (chmn. 1961). Fellow A.C.P. (gov. for No. Ill. 1957-66, 1st v.p. 1956-67, regent 1967—); mem. A.M.A. (chmn. sect. internal medicine 1962-63), Am. (bd. dirs. until 1967, exec. com. 1957-59 v.p. 1965-67), Chgo. (pres. 1957-59, chmn. council clin. cardiology) Heart assns., Assn. Profs. Medicine, Am. Soc. Clin. Investigation, Inst. Medicine Chgo. (pres. 1968-70), Ill. (pres. 1968), Chgo. socs. internal medicine, Am. Physiol. Soc., Assn. Am. Physicians, Alpha Omega Alpha, Nu Sigma Nu. Author articles on cardiology, cardiovascular physiology. Editor: Pulmonary Circulation, 1959; editorial bd. Circulation. Home: Box 298 Gulf Shores AL 36542

ADAMSON, HUGH MUNRO, fgn. service officer; b. Akron, O., Aug. 18, 1918; s. James F. and Margaret (Munro) A.; student Akron U., 1941; m. Mary Lea Putnam, June 7, 1947; 1 son, Tod. Engaged in advt., 1937-41, airport personnel and adminstrn. supervision, 1946; orgn. methods examiner VA, 1946-50; orgn. methods examiners State Dept., 1950, adminstrv. officer, 1950-52, adminstrv. mgmt. specialist, 1952-54; assigned embassy, Bonn, Germany, 1954-55; cons. sec. state, 1955; 2d sec., Bonn, 1955-59; dep. exec. dir. U.S. mission to UN, 1959; sec. U.S. delegation 14th session UN Gen. Assembly, 1959-60; dep. exec. dir. Bur. Internat. Orgn. Affairs, State Dept., 1960-62; counselor for adminstrn. embassy, Bangkok, Thailand, 1962-65; consul Am. consulate general, Hong Kong, 1965-69, exec. dir. Bur. Security Consular Affairs, State Dept., Washington, 1969—. Served to capt. AUS, 1941-46, 51-52. Home: Akron OH 44309 Office: Bur Security Consular Affairs Dept State Washington DC

ADAMSON, JOHN FRIECE, automotive co. exec.; b. Chgo., Feb. 16, 1921; s. John Friece and Esther (Sandell) A.; B.S., Purdue U., 1942; m. Joehanna C. Suffrin, Apr. 22, 1944; children—Sandell (Mrs. Denis Clanahan), Kathleen (Mrs. Richard Pierce), Stephanie. Draftsman, Ford Motor Co., 1946; with Nash-Am. Motors Corp., Detroit, 1947—, chief engr., 1959-63, dir. engring., 1963- 67, v.p. engring., 1967—. Served to maj. AUS, 1942-46; ETO. Mem. Soc. Automotive Engrs. Home: 3715 Burning Tree Dr Bloomfield Hills MI 48013 Office: 14250 Plymouth Rd Detroit MI 48232

ADAMSON, JOY, author, painter, illustrator; b. Jan. 20, 1910; d. Victor and Traute Gessner; ed. medicine, Vienna, Austria, 1933-35; m. Victor von Klarwill, 1935; m. 2d, Peter Bally, 1938; m. 3d, George Adamson, 1943. Painter, 1938—; researcher wild animals, 1956—; author, 1958—. Clubs: Nanyuki, Nairobi (Kenya). Author: Born Free: a lioness of two worlds, 1960 (film 1966); Elsa, 1961; Living Free, 1961; Forever Free, 1962; Elsa and her Cubs, 1965; The Story of Elsa, 1966; The Peoples of Kenya, 1967; The Spotted Sphinx, 1969. Illustrator; contbr. articles to mags. Home: Lake Naiyasha PO Naiyasha Kenya•

ADAMSON, OSCAR CHARLES, II, lawyer; b. St. Paul, June 9, 1924; s. Oscar Charles and Dorothy M. (Garlock) A.; B.S.L., U. Minn., 1949, J.D., 1951. Admitted to Minn. bar, 1951, U.S. Supreme Ct., 1960, since practiced in Mpls.; partner firm Meagher, Geer, Markham & Anderson, 1960—; adj. prof. law U. Minn. Law Sch., 1962-63, prof. law, 1963-66. Mem. Minn. Supreme Ct. Adv. Com., 1965—. Served with USAAF, 1942-45. Decorated D.F.C., Purple Heart, Air medal. Mem. Am., Minn., Hennepin County bar assns. Clubs: St. Paul Athletic, Pool and Yacht, North Oaks Golf (all located in St. Paul, Minnesota). Author: (with James L. Hetland, Jr.) Minnesota Practice, Civil Rules Annotated, 1970. Home: 14 Evergreen Rd North Oaks St Paul MN 55110 also Paseo del Conquistador Cuernavaca Morelos Mexico Office: 400 2d Av S Minneapolis MN 55401

ADAMSON, ROBERT EDWARD, Jr., navy officer; b. Chgo., Dec. 28, 1920; s. Robert Edward and Helen Myra (Flinn) A.; student Columbia, 1939-40; B.S., U.S. Naval Acad., 1943; student U.S. Naval Postgrad. Sch., 1947-48; M.S. in Physics, Mass. Inst. Tech., 1948-50; m. Carolyn Nelson Axberg, Aug. 18, 1945; children—Robert Edward III, Gail Agnes, Valerie Helen. Commd. ensign U.S. Navy, 1943, advanced through grades to rear adm., 1968; comdg. officer U.S.S. Naifeh, 1956, U.S.S. Wiltsie, 1961, U.S.S. Mullaney, 1962, U.S.S. Galveston, 1965; comdr. Destroyer Div. 152, 1963, Naval support acitivity, DaNang and Saigon, 1969-70, comdr. So. Atlantic Force, 1970—. Decorated D.S.M., Legion of Merit, Air Force Commendation medal; Korean Order Mil. Merit; Nat. Order Vietnam, Navy Distinguished Service Order (Vietnam). Mem. U.S. Naval Inst., Sigma Xi, Alpha Delta Phi. Clubs: Army-Navy Country (Washington), Collector (N.Y.C.). Home: US Naval Support Activity San Juan PR 09550 Office: So Atlantic Force FPO New York City NY 09501

ADAMY, CLARENCE GORDON, assn. exec.; b. Mineral, Wash., May 18, 1917; s. Judson David and Della (Strange) A.; m. Shirley Allmendinger, Dec. 14, 1946; children—Susan Lyn, Sally Jean, Sherry Ann. Nat. service officer AMVETS, 1947-52; dir. vets. affairs Citizens for Eisenhower, 1952; field dir. Nat. Citizens Ednl. TV, 1953-55; dir. personnel Republican Nat. Com., 1955-59; exec. v.p. Nat. Assn. Food Chains, Washington, 1959-66, pres., 1966—. Mem. Pres.'s Commn. on Vets. Pensions, 1955-56; exec. asst., dir. 1957 Inaugural Com. Served as navigator USAAF, 1942-45. Mem. Am. Soc. Assn. Execs. Home: 3800 Moore Pl Alexandria VA 22305 Office: 1725 Eye St NW Washington DC 20006

ADAWI, IBRAHIM HASAN, educator; b. Palestine, Apr. 18, 1930; s. Hasan and Dabella (Miari) A.; came to U.S., 1951, naturalized, 1961; B.S. in Engring. Physics, Washington U., St. Louis, 1953; Ph.D. in Engring. Physics, Cornell U., 1957; m. Gertrud Obert, Aug. 25, 1956; children—Omar, Nadia, Yasmin, Rhonda. Research physicist RCA Labs., Princeton, N.J., 1956-60; research cons. Battelle Meml. Inst., Columbus, O., 1960-68; adj. prof. elec. engring. Ohio State U., 1965-68; prof. physics U. Mo., Rolla, 1968—. Jr. fellow Cornell U., 1953-54, J. McMullen scholar, 1954-55; Sigma Xi fellow, 1955-56. Mem. Am. Phys. Soc. Home: Route 4 Box 27B Rolla MO 65401

ADDABBO, JOSEPH PATRICK, congressman; b. Queens County, N.Y., Mar. 17, 1925; s. Dominick and Anna (Polizzo) A.; student Coll. City N.Y., 1942-44; LL.B., St. John's Law Sch., 1946; m. Grace Salamone, June 12, 1949; children—Dominic, Dina, Joseph. Admitted to N.Y. bar, 1947; practice law Ozone Park, 1948—; mem. 87th Congress, 5th Dist. N.Y., 88th-91st Congresses, 7th Dist. N.Y. Mem. bldg. com. Ozone Park Jewish Center; regional chmn. Bishop's Diocesan Drive for High Sch. and Old Age Home; past pres. Ferrini Welfare League of Cath. Charities. Mem. Ozone Park Men's Assn. (past pres.), Queen's County Bar Assn. Democrat. Elk, Kiwanian. Home: 132-43 86th St Ozone Park NY 11417 Office: 96-11 101st Av Ozone Park NY 11417 also House Office Washington DC 20515

ADDAMS, CHARLES SAMUEL, cartoonist; b. Westfield N.J., Jan. 7, 1912; s. Charles Huey and Grace M. (Spear) A.;student Colgate U., 1929-30, U. of Pa., 1930-31, Grand Central Sch. of Art, N.Y. City, 1931-32; m. Barbara Day, May 29, 1943 div. Oct. 1951); m. 2d, Barbara Barb, Dec. 1, 1954 (div. 1956). Exhibited in Fogg Art Museum, R.I. Sch. of Design, Mus. of the City of N.Y., 1956, Pa. U. Mus., 1957. Met. Museum of Art (war exhbn., print exhbn.). Cartoons appeared in New Yorker, 1935— (TV show The Addams Family based on original Cartoon Characters). Drawings in biennial New Yorker Album and The New Yorker War Album, 1942, represented in Award, Yale Record, 1954 spl. award Mystery Writers Am., 1961. Served with AUS, 1943-46. Clubs: Coffee House, Vintage Car Club of Am., Armor and Arms. Author: Drawn & Quartered, 1942; Addams and Evil, 1947; Monster Rally, 1950; Home Bodies, 1954; Nightcrawlers, 1957; Dear Dead Days, 1959; Black Maria, 1960; The Groaning Board, 1964; The Charles Addams Mother Goose, 1967, My Crowd, 1970. Contbr. drawings Yorker. Address: 25 W 43d St New York City NY 10036

ADDERLEY, HERB ANTHONY, profl. football player; b. Phila., June 8, 1939; s. Charles and Reva (White) A.; B.S., Mich. State U., 1961; m. Bell Adderley, June 26, 1965; 1 dau., Toni. Mem. Green Bay Pakcers, 1961-69, Dallas Cowboys, 1970—; v.p. Giant Step Record Co., Phila. Served with AUS, 1962-66. Participant Super Bowl, 1967, 68, 71, All-Star Game, 1963, 64, 65, 66, 67; named All-Pro annually 1962-69. Mem. Omega Psi Phi. Home: 5219 Wissahickon Av Philadelphia PA 19144

ADDERLEY, JULIAN EDWIN, (Cannonball), saxophonist; b. Tampa, Fla., Sept. 15, 1928; student U.S. Naval Sch. Music, Washington, 1952, Fla. Agrl. and Mech. Coll.; m. Olga James, June 1962. Dir. band Dillard High Sch., Ft. Lauderdale, Fla., 1948-56; debut Cafe Bohemia, N.Y.C., 1955; with brother, organizer ensemble for tour, 1955, on tour, 1955-57, 59—; joined group Miles Davis, 1957, George Shearing's Band, 1959; rec. artist Em Arcy, 1955, Riverside, 1958-64, Capitol Records, 1964, others; appeared Newport Jazz Festival, Randalls Island, (N.Y.C.) Jazz Festival, Jazz at Philharmonic program, with various tours. Served with AUS, 1950-53; leader 36th Army Dance Band. Recipient citation (with Phil Woods), Ency. Jazz Yearbook, 1956; New Alto Star of Year award Down Beat mag., 1959; named one of Top Artists on Campus poll, 1968; Playboy mag. Poll winnters award (readers) for 1st alto, 1962-71, All Stars award (musicians), 1962-71; Downbeat mag. winner Readers Poll, 1968-70. Home: 112-19 34th Av Corona NY 11368 Office: care John Levy 119 W 57th New York City NY 10019•

ADDERLEY, NATHANIEL, musician, composer; b. Tampa, Fla., Nov 25, 1931; s. Julian and Jessie (Johnson) A.; A.B., B.S., Fla. A. and M. U., 1951; m. Ann James, Apr. 21, 1952; children—Nat, Alison. With bands of Lionel Hampton, Woody Herman and J.J. Johnson, 1954-60; with brother Julian (Cannonball) Adderly, 1960—. Served with AUS, 1951-53. Composer: Work Song, 1961; Jive Samba, 1962; Old Country, 1958; Little Boy with Sad Eyes, 1965; Sermonnette, 1956; others. Home: 50 Beveridge St Teaneck NJ 07666 Office: 119 W 57th St New York City NY 10011

ADDISON, ADELE, soprano; b. N.Y.C., July 24, 1925; d. Julius B. and Janette (Taylor) Addison; B.Mus. (scholar), Westminister Choir Coll., 1946; D.H.V., U. Mass., 1963; m. Norman Berger, June 29, 1958. Recital debut Town Hall, N.Y.C., 1952; ann. recital tours U.S., Can.; tour Soviet Union under cultural exchange program, 1963; appeared with New Eng. City Center, Washington opera cos.; orchestral engagements with symphonies, Boston, Cleve., N.Y. Philharmonic, Nat., Chgo., Pitts., Indpls., Los Angeles, San Francisco; world premiere performances include John La Montaine's Fragments from Song of Songs with New Haven Symphony, 1959, Poulenc's Gloria with Boston Symphony, 1961, Foss' Time Cycle with N.Y. Philharmonic, 1960; faculty artist Aspen Music Festival, 1956; sang role of Bess in Goldwyn's Porgy and Bess, 1958; soloist opening concert Philharmonic Hall of Lincoln Center, 1962. Trustee Westminster Choir Coll., CORE Scholarship, Edn. and Defense Fund.‡

ADDISON, JOHN WEST, Jr., educator, mathematician; b. Washington, Apr. 2, 1930; s. John West and Sue Fisher (Nichols) A.; grad. Phillips Acad., 1947; A.B., Princeton, 1951; M.S., U. Wis., 1953, Ph.D. (Univ. fellow, Knapp resident fellow), 1955; m. Mary Ann Church, Aug. 27, 1955; children—John West III, Thomas Cary, Alonzo Church, Samuel Robbins. Instr. math. U. Mich., Ann Arbor, 1954-56; mem. Inst. Advanced Study, Princeton, and vis. scholar Math. Inst. Polish Acad. Scis., Warsaw, 1956-57; asst. prof. math. U. Mich., 1957-62; vis. lectr. math. U. Cal. at Berkeley, 1959-60, asso. prof., 1962-68, prof., 1968—, chmn. dept., 1968—. NSF postdoctoral fellow, 1956-57. Fellow A.A.A.S.; mem. Assn. Symbolic Logic, Am. Math. Soc., Math. Assn. Am. Episcopalian. Editor (with L. Henkin and Al Tarski) The Theory of Models, 1963 International Symposium at Berkeley, 1965. Pres., chmn. bd. govs. Pacific Jour. Math., 1968—. Home: 7927 Terrace Dr El Cerrito CA 94530 Office: Dept Math U Cal Berkeley CA 94720

ADDLESTONE, NATHAN SIDNEY, metals co. exec.; b. Charleston, S.C., Jan. 16, 1913; s. Abram and Rachel (Lader) A.; grad. pub. high sch.; m. Ruth Axelrod, Dec. 12, 1937; children—Carole Anita, Susan Lader. With Sumter Iron & Metal Co. (S.C.), 1932-45, pres., 1938-45; founding pres. Addlestone & Co., Sumter, 1945—, Addlestone Steel Corp., 1945—; founder, chmn. bd. Steelmet, Inc., Charleston, 1961—; chmn. bd. Steelmet Far East Corp., 1969—, also Metals Processing Co., Providence; dir. L.L. Cohen Co., Inc., Philip L. Buxton, Inc., Tidewater Terminal, Inc., Utility Survey Corp.; pres. Columbia Steel & Metal Co., 1951—, Metro Iron & Metal Corp. (also treas., dir.), 1964—. Mem. fgn. trade com. Inst. Scrap Iron and Steel, 1965—, vice chmn., 1970-71. Bd. dirs. Jewish Community Center Charleston. Mem. C. of C. Sumter (past pres.), Nat. Assn. Secondary Materials (past bd. dirs.), Inst. Scrap Iron and Steel (past bd. dirs.). Jewish religion. Rotarian, Elk, Mason (Shriner). Home: 1455 Burning Tree Rd Charleston SC 29407 Office: 8 Cumberland St Charleston SC 29402

ADDOU, ADBULLAHI AHMED, Somali diplomat; b. Brava, Somalia, May 15, 1933; s. Ahmed and Madina Scek (Ahmed) A.; Biennial Diploma, Mogadiscio U. Inst. Law and Econs., 1957-59; M.A. in Polit. Sci., U. Rome, 1963; postfrad. Econ. Devel. Inst., Washington, 1966-67; m. Asha Mohamud Guled, July 26, 1957; children—Marian, Hodan, Hanad, Habon, Mahad, Mussa. Joined Somali Finance Guards, 1952, advanced through grades to lt. col., 1964; dep. comdr. in chief, 1961; resigned, 1965; dir. gen. Ministry of Finance, 1965-68; gov. Somali Central Bank, 1968-70; pres. Somali Devel. Bank, Mogadiscio, 1970; Somali ambassador to U.S., 1970—. Mem. Soc. for Internat. Devel., Internat. Bankers Assn. Address: 1875 Connecticut Av NW Washington DC 20008

ADDUCI, VINCENT JAMES, assn. exec.; b. Oriolo, Italy, Mar. 1, 1920; s. George and Maria Frances (Panno) A.; student U. Hawaii, 1939-41, Detroit Inst. Tech., 1948-49, Detroit Coll. Law, 1949-50, George Washington U., 1951, U. Mich., 1957; m. Kathleen M. Barron, Nov. 23, 1946; children—Vincent James II, Dawn Maria, Lisa Anne. Enlisted as pvt. USAAF, 1939, advanced through grades to col. USAF, 1954; fighter, bomber pilot; insp. gen.; dep. dir. Office Legislative Liason; ret., 1960; v.p., then sr. v.p. Aerospace Industries Assn., 1960-70; pres. Electronics Industries Assn., Washington, 1970—; pres., chmn. bd. AV-SPA Corp., Washington, 1965-69; v.p. Aero Center, Washington, 1965-67. Decorated Legion of Merit with oak leaf cluster, D.F.C., Air medal, Purple Heart, Bronze Star. Mem. Nat. Quill and Scroll. Clubs: Army and Navy (Washington); Toastmasters (Arlington, Va., pres.). Author: Executive Development, 1950. Home: 6419 Waterway Dr Falls Church VA 22044 Office: 2001 I St NW Washington DC 20036

ADDY, WESLEY, actor; b. Omaha, Aug. 4, 1913; s. John R. and Maren S. Addy; B.A., U. Cal. at Los Angeles, 1934. Theatrical appearances include Panic, 1935; How Beautiful with Shoes, 1935; Hamlet. 1936, 38; King Richard II. 1937; Henry IV, Part 1, 1939, Summer Night. 1939; Romeo and Juliet, 1940; Twelfth Night, 1940; Antigone, 1946; Candida, 1946; Another Part of the forest, 1946; Galileo, 1947; The Leading Lady, 1948; The Traitor, 1949; The Enchanted, 1950; King Lear, 1950; The Strong are Lonely, 1953; The First Gentleman, 1957; A Month in the Country, 1963; With Love and Laughter (tour), 1963: film appearances in The First Legion, 1951; Kiss me Deadly, 1955; The Big Knife, 1955; Timetable, 1956; The Garment Jungle, 1957; Ten Seconds to Hell, 1959; What Ever Happened to Baby Jane, 1962; narrator TV program The Brick and The Rose, 1960. Served to maj. AUS, 1941-45. Mem. Actors Equity Assn., A.F.T.R.A., Screen Actors Guild. Address: care Peter Witt Assos 37 W 57th St New York City NY 10019 *

ADE, ERWIN JEROME, business exec.; b. Norwalk, Conn., Dec. 1, 1908; s. William and Flora (Loweth) A.; B.S., Washington and Lee U., 1932; m. Mary Jane Carroll, Aug. 13, 1949; children—Jerome Carroll, James, John. Mem. firm Tamblyn & Tamblyn, fund raising, N.Y.C. 1936- 38; nat. fund raising dir., commerce and industry div., British Relief Soc., 1939; dir. fund raising, Greater N.Y. Com. Commerce and Industry, Red Cross and United Service Orgns. War Fund Campaigns, 1941-43; asso. dir. John Price Jones Corp., N.Y.C., 1945-47; nat. campaign dir., Planned Parenthood Fedn. Am., 1947-48, Am. Heart Assn., 1948-49; adminstrv. dir. Citizens Com. for the Hoover Report, 1949-52; fund raising dir. Nat. Fund for Med. Edn., 1952-56; pres. Ade & Bliss, Inc., pub. relations counsellors, 1956-57, pres. E. J. Ade & Co., Inc., N.Y.C., 1957-61, 63—; v.p., dir. pub. relations Fuller & Smith & Ross, Inc., N.Y.C., 1961-63; pres. Pointmakers, Inc., Betty Blue Art Centers, Inc.; v.p. Marketing Innovations, Inc., 1970—; chmn. bd. Genie Meals, Inc., 1971—. Bd. dirs. Westchester County Multiple Sclerosis Soc.; fund raising counsellor Nat. Planning Assn.; sec. Com. Am. Industry; chmn. 1960 campaign, trustee Hudson River Speech Center. Served with AUS, 1943-45. Asst. to chmn. Eastern div., Am. Liberty League, 1935; exec. sec. Bronx and Richmond Counties, N.Y.C., 1940; United Rep. Finance Com., 1940. Dir. "Textiles Go to War" celebration, Spartanburg, S.C., 1943; asst. admissions officer, U.N. Conf., San Francisco, 1945. Mem. council on Pub. Relations, Inc (mem. bd. counsellors). Mem. Pub. Relations Soc. Am. Assos. Engr. Corps, Co. K. Vets, 7th Regt., N.Y. Pi Kappa Phi. Republican. Protestant. Clubs: Economics, University, Sleepy Hollow Country (N.Y.C); Explorers. Home: 199 Riverview Av Tappan Landing Tarrytown NY 10591 Office: 551 Fifth Av New York City NY 10017

ADEBO, SIMEON OLAOSEBIKAN, Nigerian diplomat; b. Abeokuta, Nigeria, Oct. 5, 1913; s. Adebo, chief Okanlomo of Itoko, Abeokuta and Fowotade; student King's Coll., Lagos, Nigeria, 1929-32; B.A. in English, London, U., 1939, LL.B., 1946; m. Regina Abimbola Majekodunmi, July 9, 1941; children—Funlayo, Oluwole, Abiodun, Oladipo. Barrister-at-law, 1949; asst. financial sec. Nigeria 1953-55; permanent sec. Ministry Finance, head Civil Service Western Nigeria, 1957-60; chief sec. Govt. Western Nigeria, head Civil Service, 1961-62; ambassador of Nigeria to UN, also commnr.-gen. econ. affairs in U.S., 1962-68; undersecretary general of UN, also executive director United Nations Inst. Tng. and Research, 1968—. Provincial registrar Ch. of Province W. Africa, 1951—. Decorated companion Order St. Michael and St. George. Home: Ademola Rd Ibara Abeokuta Nigeria Office: UN Hdqrs New York City NY 10017

ADEL, ARTHUR, physicist; b. Bklyn., Nov. 22, 1908; s. Morris and Jenny (Schrieber) A.; A.B., U. of Mich., 1931, Ph.D., 1933; m. Catherine Emelia Backus, Sept. 11, 1935. Research asso., Lowell Obs., U. of Mich., 1933-35; astrophysicist, Lowell Obs., Flagstaff, Ariz. 1936-42 asst. prof. of physics, Univ. of Mich., 1942-46, asst. prof. astronomy U. Mich., 1946-48; now prof. physics; also dir. Atmospheric Research Obs., No. Arizona Univ., Flagstaff; research fellow physics and instructory astronomy, Johns Hopkins, 1935-36; leader TWA eclipse expdn., Island of Ceylon, June, 1955. Has specialized in study of planetary atmospheres and infrared spectroscopy of solar system; discovered strong Non-Rayleigh atmospheric infrared scattering, 1949; discovered atmospheric N2O, 1939; also determined temperature and location of the atmospheric nitrous oxide layer, 1949-50 demonstrated relationship of atmospheric nitrous oxide to the Nitrogen Cycle, 1951; origin atmospheric N2O, 1946-51; discovered periodic phenomena in stratosphere, 1956. Fellow Am. Phys. Soc., Am. Astron. Soc., Internat. Astron. Union, Phi Beta Kappa, Sigma Xi. Contbr. to Sci. Jours. on astron. discoveries. Office: No Ariz U Flagstaff AZ 86001

ADELMAN, IRMA GLICMAN (Mrs. Frank L. Adelman), educator; b. Cernowitz, Rumania, Mar. 14, 1930; d. Jacob Max and Raissa (Ettinger) Glicman; came to U.S., 1949, naturalized, 1955; B.S., U. Cal., Berkeley, 1950, M.A., 1951, Ph.D., 1955; m. Frank L. Adelman, Aug. 16, 1950; 1 son, Alexander. Teaching asso. U. Cal., Berkeley, 1955-56, instr., 1956-57, lectr. with rank asst. prof., 1957-58; vis. asst. prof. Mills Coll., 1958-59; acting asst. prof. Stanford, 1959-61, asst. prof., 1961-62; asso. prof. Johns Hopkins, Balt., 1962-65; prof. econs. Northwestern U., Evanston, Ill., 1966—; cons. div. indsl. devel. UN, 1962-63, AID, U.S. Dept. State, Washington, 1963—; Internat. Bank Reconstrn. and Devel., 1968. Fellow Center Advanced Study Behavioral Scis., 1970-71. Mem. Am. Econ. Assn., Econometric Soc., Am. Statis. Assn. Author: Theories of Economic Growth and Development, 1961; (with A. Pepelasis and L. Mears) Economic Development: Analysis and Case Studies, 1961; (with Eric Thornbecke) The Theory and Design of Economic Development, 1966; (with C.T. Morris) Society, Politics and Economic Development—A Quantitative Approach, 1967; Practical Approaches to Development Planning-Korea's Second Five Year Plan, 1969. Home: 805 Central St Evanston IL 60201

ADELMAN, MORRIS ALBERT, economist; b. N.Y.C., May 31, 1917; s. David and Lena (Albert) A.; B.S., Coll. City N.Y., 1938; Ph.D, Harvard, 1948; m. Millicent Linsen, Nov. 23, 1949; children—Lawrence, Barbara. Economist, OPA-WPB, 1941-42, Fed. Res. Bd., 1946; from asst. prof. to prof. econs. Mass. Inst. Tech., Cambridge, 1948—. Served to lt. USNR, 1942-46; PTO. Mem. Am. Acad. Arts and Scis., Am. Econ. Assn., Royal Econ. Soc. Home: 83 Nehojden Rd Waban MA 02168 Office: Mass Inst Tech Cambridge MA 02139

ADELMAN, R.J., real estate exec.; b. Chgo., June 21, 1915; s. Samuel and Rose (Colitz) A.; A.B., U. Mich., 1936; m. Betty Friend, Feb. 4, 1941; children—Jean Ruth, Betty Sue. With Arthur Rubloff & Co., Chgo., 1936—, pres., 1952-70, chmn., chief exec. officer, 1970—; dir. Chgo. Title & Trust Co., Playboy Enterprises, Inc., Great Western United Corp. Trustee Michael Reese Hosp., Chgo. Served as 1st lt. USAAF, World War II. Mem. Am. Soc. Real Estate Counselors, Bldg. Mgrs. Assn. Chgo. (dir.), Soc. Indsl. Realtors. Clubs: Standard (Chgo.); Lake Shore Country. Home: 2255 Egandale Rd Highland Park IL 60035 Office: 69 W Washington St Chicago IL 60602

ADELMANN, FREDERICK JOSEPH, educator; b. Norwood, Mass., Feb. 18, 1915; s. Frederick Michael and Helen Margaret (Casey) A.; A.B., Boston Coll., 1937, M.A., 1942; S.T.L., Weston Coll., 1948; Ph.D., St. Louis U., 1955. Entered Soc. of Jesus; ordained priest R.C. Ch., 1947; instr. math. and physics Army Specialized Tng. Program, Boston Coll., 1942-44, asst. prof. philosophy, 1955-68, asso. prof. philosophy, 1968-70, prof., 1970—, chmn. dept., 1955-65; ascetical theology Exerzitienhaus Rottmannshohe, Germany, 1949-50; teaching fellow philosophy St. Louis U., 1950-54; lectr. philosophy Weston (Mass.) Coll. Mem. Am. Assn. U. Profs., Am. Philos. Assn., Jesuit Philos. Assn., Realist Soc. Author: From Dialogue to Epilogue, 1968. Editor: Demythologizing Marxism, 1969. Editor in chief The Quest for the Absolute, 1966. Address: Boston College Chestnut Hill MA 02167

ADELMANN, HOWARD BERNHARDT, educator; b. Buffalo, May 8, 1898; s. Charles Michael and Louise Henrietta (Kohler) A.; A.B., Cornell U., 1920, A.M., 1922, Ph.D., 1924; student U. Freiburg (Germany), 1927; Sc.D. honoris causa, Ohio State U., 1962. Asst. histology amd embryology Cornell U., 1919-21, instr., 1921- 25, asst. prof., 1925-37, prof., 1937—, chmn. dept. zoology, 1944-59, faculty rep. bd. trustees, 1947-51. NRC fellow biol. sci., 1927-28. Recipient Order Star Italian Solidarity (Italy), 1962. Fellow Internat. d'Embryologie (Amsterdam); mem. Am. Assn. Anatomists, Am. Soc. Zoologists, Hist. Sci. Soc., Am. Assn. History Medicine (William H. Welch medal 1967), Bibliog. Soc. (London), Brit. Soc. for History Sci., Internat. Acad. History Medicine, Phi Beta Kappa, Sigma Xi, Phi Kappa Phi. Republican. Lutheran. Author: The Embryological Treatises of Hieronymus Fabricius (Crofts prize Cornell U. Press); Marcello Malpighi and the Evolution of Embryology, 5 vols., 1966 (Pfizer award History of Science Soc. 1967). Asso. editor: Jour. Morphology, 1948-51. Contbr. sci. papers to profl. jours. Home: 410 Columbia St Ithaca NY 14850

ADELSON, JOSEPH BERNARD, educator, psychologist; b. N.Y.C., July 25, 1925; s. Jack and Clara (Prince) A.; B.S., Coll. City N.Y., 1945; M.A., U. Cal. at Berkeley, 1947, Ph.D., 1950; m. Edna Kamener, Feb. 10, 1946; children—Lawrence, Edward, Paul. Faculty social sci. Bennington Coll., 1951-56; faculty U. Mich., Ann Arbor, 1956—, prof. psychology, 1963—, sr. psychologist Psychol. Clinic, 1956—, co-dir. Psychol. Clinic, 1968—, research asso. Survey Research Center, 1954-60. Cons. psychologist, 1953- -. Bd. dirs. Royce J. Noble Fund. Ford Found. fellow, 1960; grantee Social Sci. Research Council, 1964. Fellow Am. Psychol. Assn., Am. Sociol. Assn. Democrat. Jewish religion. Author: (with Elizabeth Douvan) The Adolescent Experience, 1966; also articles. Cons. editor Jour. Personality and Social Psychology, 1961-67, Merrill-Palmer Quar., 1960—, Contemporary Psychology, 1966-67. asso. editor Jour. Youth and Adolescence, 1971—. Home: 1417 Culver Rd Ann Arbor MI 48103

ADERMAN, RALPH MERL, educator; b. Malinta, O., May 27, 1919; s. Rudolph E. and Stella (Litzenberg) A.; B.Ed., U. Toledo, 1941, M.A., 1945; Ph.D., U. Wis., 1951; m. Alice C. Rath, Nov. 26, 1942; 1 son, Jeffrey. High sch. tchr., Henry County, O., 1941-45; grad. teaching asst. U. Wis., 1945-47; instr. Milw. State Tchrs. Coll., 1947-52, Wis. State Coll., Milw., 1952-56; mem. faculty U. Wis.-Milw., 1956—, prof. English, 1959—, chmn. dept., 1960-62; editor Hist. Messenger publn. Milw. County Hist. Soc., 1956—, trustee, 1952—. Recipient grant in aid Am. Philos. Soc., 1954, 57, 70, Am. Council Learned Socs., 1970; award of merit Milw. County Hist. Soc., 1964. Mem. Modern Lang. Assn., Am. Studies Assn., Nat. Council Tchrs. English, Am. Assn. U. Profs., Coll. English Assn., Midwest Modern Lang. Assn., Wis. Acad. Scis., Arts and Letters, Pi Gamma Mu, Sigma Tau Delta, Phi Kappa Phi. Author: The Letters of James Kirke Paulding, 1962; Aspects of American English, rev. edit., 1971. Home: 2302 E Newberry Blvd Milwaukee WI 53211

ADERS, ROBERT O., food co. exec.; b. Bridgeton, Ind., Apr. 21, 1927; s. Oral M. and Frieda (Howell) A.; B.S., Miami U., 1947; J.D., Ind. U., 1951; m. Marguerite Herschede, July 28, 1951; children—Susan, Linda, Katharine, Robert H., and Jennifer Aders. Began career as a teaching fellow Ind. U., 1951-52; admitted to Ind. bar 1951, Ohio bar, 1958; trial atty. U. S. Dept. Justice, 1954-57; with Kroger Co., 1957—, v.p., gen. counsel, Cin., 1964—, chmn. of bd., 1970—, dir. Ramco Inc. Trustee Cin. Urban League, 1963—, Ohio Wesleyan U., United Appeal Greater Cin.; bd. dirs. Y.M.C.A. of Cin. and Hamilton County; bd. dirs., v.p. Super Market Inst. Served with USNR, 1944-46, 52-54. Mem. Ohio Bar Assn., Delta Tau Delta, Phi Delta Phi. Methodist. Clubs: Queen City; Cincinnati; Hyde Park Golf and Country. Office: 1014 Vine St Cincinnati OH 45201

ADES, HARLOW WHITING, educator, b. Rockford, Ill., Dec. 31, 1911; s. Arthur William and Mary Weston (Thayer) A.; B.S., U. of Ill., 1934, M.S., 1935, Ph.D., 1938; m. Florence Hill Adams, Jan. 4, 1933 (div. May 62); childrenHelen May, Elizabeth Anne, William, Susan; m. 2d, Claire Frenkel McMillan, July 31, 1963. Asst. in physiological optics John Hopkins Sch. of medicine, 1938-39; instr. in anatomy Emory Univ. Sch. of Medicine, 1939-42, asst. prof. anatomy, 1942-47, prof. anatomy and chmn. dept. 1947-54, on leave of absence to serve as first annual research prof. of neurology, Inst. Neurology, Northwestern U. Sch. of Medicine, 1947-48; prof. anatomy U. Tex. Southwestern Med. Sch., 1954-57; chief neurol. scis. div. USN Sch. Aviation Medicine, Pensacola, Fla., 1957-65; prof. elec. engring., prof. physiology and biophysics U. Ill., 1965—, prof. of psychology, 1968—. Mem. Am. Assn. of Anatomists, Am. Physiol. Soc., Am. Neurol. Assn., Sigma Xi. Co-author: Structural Pattern of the Organ of Corti, 1966. Specialist in research in neurophysiology of hearing and vision and motor function, eletroencephalography in relation to aviation physiology and safety, effects of noise on inner ear sensory epithelia. Home: 508 Sunnycrest Ct E Urbana, IL 61801.

ADESKO, THADDEUS VINCENT, judge; b. Chgo., Nov. 5, 1902; s. Walter and Angela (Rylski) A.; student U. Chgo., 1920-23; LL.B., Northwestern U., 1931; m. Clara Rutkowski, June 16, 1928; children—Paul, Alice. Admitted to Ill. bar, 1931, practiced in Chgo. until 1951; asst. judge Cook County Probate Ct., 1938- 46; judge Municipal Ct., Chgo., 1951-53, Superior Ct. Cook County, 1953-60, County Ct., 1960-64; presiding judge County div. Circuit Ct. Cook County, 1964-66; justice Appellate Ct., 1966—. Mem. Pres.'s Com. on Community Relations Service. Mem. Ill. Senate, 1947-51. Bd. dirs. Gen. Woods Boy's Club, Polish Welfare Assn.; trustee Alliance Coll. Mem. Am., Ill., Chgo. bar assns., Am. Judicature Soc., Advs. Soc. (past pres.), Cath. Lawyers Guild (past v.p.), Polish Nat. Alliance, Polish Roman Cath. Guild. Democrat. Moose, K.C., Lion. Clubs: City, Chicago Society, Northwestern University (Chgo.). Home: 818 Na Wa Ta Av Mt Prospect IL 60056 Office: Chgo Civic Center Chicago IL 60602

ADIKES, JOHN, banker; b. Jamaica, N.Y., July 15, 1894; s. Thomas and Catherine (Fitzgibbon) A.; LL.B., N.Y. U., 1915; LL.D. (hon.), St. John's U., 1960; m. Ann Linz, Mar. 17, 1925; children—John (dec.), Avis Ann, Thomas. Mem. firm Street, Hanavan & Adikes, 1923-26; trustee Jamaica Savs. Bank, 1926-44, exec. v.p., 1944-45, pres. 1945-67, chmn. bd. dirs., chief exec. officer, 1967-70; mem. Queens adv. com. Chase Manhattan Bank. Former mem. bd. Higher Edn., N.Y.C. Mem. Queens C. of C. (past pres.), Savs. Bank Assn. State N.Y. (past pres.), Am. Bankers Assn. (past pres. savs. and mortgage div.).

ADINOLFI, ANTHONY GEORGE, state govt. ofcl.; b. New Haven, Nov. 30, 1930; s. Salvatore Anthony and Camille (Barbuto) A.; B.S., So. Conn. Coll., 1952; M.A., Ed.D., Columbia; m. Barbara Scofield Dawes, Nov. 28, 1970; stepchildren—Jefferson Douglas Dawes, Byron Fay Dawes III. Gen. mgr., chief exec. officer State Univ. Constrn. Fund, Albany, N.Y., 1962—. Mem. Boston Mayor's Office and Boston Redevel. Authority, 1964-65; mem. N.Y. State Pure Waters Authority, 1967—, N.Y. State Urban Devel. Corp., 1968—. Trustee State of Conn. State Colls., 1968—, Conn. Commn. Higher Edn., 1968—; mem. Detroit Bd. Edn., 1957-62, White Plains (N.Y.) Bd. Edn., 1956-57. Served with AUS, 1953-55. Recipient So. Conn. coll. award, 1965, spl. client award, N.Y. State Assn. Architecture, 1964, award for excellence in architecture, N.Y. State Council on Arts, 1969, citation, A.I.A., 1969. Mem. Am. Assn. Sch. Adminstrs., Council Ednl. Facility Planners, Assn. Sch. Bus. Ofcls., A.I.A. (hon.), Met. Sch. Facilities Planning Group. Home: 274 E Hackett Blvd Albany NY 12208 Office: 194 Washington Av Albany NY 12210

ADKERSON, JOSEPH CARSON, engr., assn. exec.; b. Lynchburg, Va., Feb. 10, 1892; s. Alonza Thomas and Lizzie Lillian (Carson) A.; student pub. schs. Lynchburg; certificate Indsl. Coll. Armed Forces, 1948, 51; m. Anne Winfield Clower, March 11, 1961. Asst. engr. Piedmont-Manganese Corp., Lynchburg, 1912-13, Oxford Mining & Manganese Corp., Lynchburg, 1913-14; engr., mgr. Powells Fort Manganese Mines, Woodstock, Va., 1915-19; v.p., engr. mgr. Hy-Grade Manganese Co., Woodstock, 1919-36; v.p., engr. Hy-Grade Manganese Prodn. & Sales Corp., Woodstock, 1929-32, Nat. Metals Corp., Damascus, Va., 1940-42; pres. Raw Materials Nat. Council, 1936—; cons. engr. Cuban Am. Manganese Corp., N.Y.C., 1940-45; engaged in investigation and research work, manganese, tungsten, other minerals. Chmn. Joint Conf. of Unfair Russian

Competition, 1930-33. Registered profl. mining engr., Va., D.C. Mem. Am. Inst. Mining and Metall. Engrs., Am. Manganese Producers Assn. (pres. 1927—). Presbyn. Democrat. Mason (Shriner). Home: Woodstock VA 22664

ADKINS, CHARLES EDSON, higher edn. cons.; b. Syracuse, N.Y., Aug. 29, 1909; s. H. Morton and Ida (Hubbard) A.; A.B., Dartmouth, 1932; M.A., Syracuse U., 1940; m. Virginia J. Durning, Sept. 14, 1940; children—Terry D., Jameson H., Leslie M., Allison G. Clk. Syracuse Trust Co., 1929-30; reporter Syracuse Herald, 1933-34; instr. Syracuse U., 1936-40; mem. faculty Millikin U., 1940-45; mem. faculty Colgate U., 1945-54, dir. pub. relations, 1954-57; v.p. Wheaton Coll., 1957-60; pres. Briarcliff Coll., 1960-68, also trustee; dir. studies in higher edn. Inst. for Ednl. Devel., 1968-69; pres. Commn. on Independent Colls. and Universities of Pa., 1969-71; cons., 1971—. Former mem. Gov.'s Adv. Com. on Higher Edn., pres. Coll. Research Center. Trustee Scarborough Sch., Sch. Internat. Tng. Expt. in Internat. Living. Mem. Assn. of Am. Colls., Am. Council Edn., Am. Assn. Univ. Profs., Asso. Coll. and Univs. State N.Y. (exec. com.), Assn. Ind. Colls. and Univs. N.Y. (exec. com.), Newcomen Soc., Chi Phi, Pi Delta Epsilon Republican. Episcopalian. Rotarian. Clubs: Sleepy Hollow Country (Tarrytown); Lake Katonan; University, Dartmouth (N.Y.C.); Adirondack League. Address: RD 3 Katonah NY 10536

ADKINS, DOROTHY C., psychologist; b. Atlanta, O., Apr. 6, 1912; d. George Hoadley and Pearl (James) Adkins; B.S. in Edn., Ohio State U., 1931, Ph.D., 1937. Asst. examiner Univ. Chicago, 1936-38, research asso. psychology, 1938- 40; chief research and test constrn. Social Security Bd., 1940-44; chief social sci. and adminstrv. testing, policy cons., chief test development sect. Civil Service Commn., 1944-48 prof. U. N.C., Chapel Hill, 1948-65, chmn. dept. psychology, 1950-60; prof., research Coll. Edn., U. Hawaii, 1965—. Fellow Am. Psychol. Assn. (rec. sec. 1949-52, mem. policy and planning bd. 1952-55, mem. council reps. 1953-56, bd. dirs. 1955-58, pres. div. evaluation and measurement 1952-53); mem. S.E., N.C. (pres. 1951-52) psychol. assns., N.C. Acad. Sci., Psychometric Soc. (pres. 1949- 50), Elisha Mitchell Sci. Soc., Sigma Xi, Pi Mu Epsilon, Pi Lambda Theta. Author: Construction and Analysis of Achievement Tests, 1947; Factor Analysis of Reasoning Tests, 1952; Test Construction, 1960; Statistics, 1964. Asst. mng. editor Psychometrika, 1937-50, managing editor, 1950-56, council editors, 1956-68; bd. editors, 1956—; mem. board coop. editors Ednl. and Psychol. Measurement, 1940—; editorial cons. Pub. Personnel Review, 1955-58. Home: 921 Kealaolu Av Honolulu HI 96816

ADKINS, HENRY MAURICE, lawyer; b. Lafayette, Tex., Sept. 11, 1900; B.A., State Tchrs. Coll.; LL.B., U. Tex., 1925. Admitted to Tex. bar, 1925; partner firm Gibson, Ochsner, Adkins, Harlan & Hankins, Amarillo, Tex. Mem. Amarillo Bar Assn., State Bar Tex. Office: Fisk Bldg Amarillo TX 79101*

ADKINS, JOHN NATHANIEL, geophysicist; b. Spokane, Wash., July 23, 1911; s. John Dauford and Martha Ellen (Cabbage) A.; student Stanford, 1927-28, Sacramento Jr. Coll., 1930-32; A.B. in Physics, U. Cal., 1936. Ph.D. in Seismology (U. fellow 1936-38), 1939; NRC fellow Mass. Inst. Tech., 1939-41; m. Katherine Owen Jackson, May 18, 1941. Staff div. war research Columbia, 1941-45; supervising engr. antennas Airborne Instruments Lab., Inc., N.Y. C., 1945-46; asst. prof. geophysics Mass. Inst. Tech., 1946-48; head geophysics br. Office Naval Research, 1948-49; dir. earth scis. div. 1949-58, dep. sci. dir., 1954-58, asso. research dir., 1958-59, asst. chief scientist, 1959-. Chmn. div. earth scis. NRC, 1958-60. Trustee Chesapeake Bay Found. Fellow Geol. Soc. Am., A.A A.A.A.S.; mem. Seimol. Soc. Am., Am. Geophys. Union, Phi Beta Kappa, Sigma Xi, Theta Tau. Club: Gibson Island. Home: 2 Olmsted Green Baltimore MD 21210 Office: Office of Naval Research Navy Dept Arlington VA 22217

ADKINS, LISLE WITHNELL, r.r. exec.; b. Oswego, N.Y., Aug. 2, 1908; s. Frederick L. and Ethel (Porter) A.; grad. Powelson Inst. Accountancy, Syracuse, N.Y., 1928; m. Harriett Mullen, Aug. 14, 1929; children—Thomas, Gerald, Carolyn. Various adminstrv. and exec. positions with Reynolds Metals Co. and subsidiaries, 1929-42; controller Crosley Corp., 1942-50; gen. controller Crosley-Bendix divs. Avco Mfg. Corp., 1950-55; comptroller Gen. Dynamics Corp., N.Y.C., 1955-60, v.p. and comptroller, 1960-61; v.p. L. & N. R.R., v.p. accounting and taxation, 1961 Mem. Adv. Council on Federal Reports, 1944-62. C.P.A., N.Y. Mem. Financial Execs. Inst. (nat. dir. 1947-49; adv. council 1949—). Clubs: Pendennis; 6710 Deep Creek Dr Prospect KY 40059 Office: 908 W Broadway Louisville KY 40203

ADKINS, RICHARD EUGENE, cattle breeder, banker, b. Howard, S.D., Oct. 1, 1919; s. John Barney and Margaret Louise (Laurson) A.; student Columbia, 1939; B.A., Grinnell Coll., 1941; postgrad. U. Neb., 1946; m. Mollie Harkness Clasper, May 14, 1942; children—Richard Eugene, Mary Catherine, John Jackson II. Cattle breeder, Osmond, Neb., 1947—; dir. Osmond State Bank, 1947—, pres., 1969—. Bd. regents U. Neb., 1958-70, pres., 1964-70. Served to lt. comdr. USNR, World War II. Mem. Neb. Live Stock Feeders Assn., Neb. Bankers Assn., Neb. Stock Growers, Am. Legion, 40 and 8, Alpha Gamma Rho. Elk. Address: Osmond NB 68765

ADKINSON, BURTON WILBUR, geographer; b. Everson, Wash., Mar. 5, 1909; s. Jason H. and Clara Fannie (Warriner) A.; student Western Wash. Coll. Edn., Bellingham, 1926- 29, summers, 1932, 34; A.B. in Edn., U. Wash., Seattle, 1936, M.A. in Geography, 1939; Ph.D., Clark U., Worcester, Mass., 1942; m. Margaret Louise Klock, Sept. 10, 1942; children—Karen Louise, Margaret Jane. Tchr. pub. schs., Wash., 1929-39; asso. regional asst. Office of Geography, Dept. State 1942-43; asst. dir. U.S. Bd. Geog. Names, 1943-44; asst. chief map intelligence sect., map div. OSS, 1944-45; asst. chief, acting chief map div. Libary of Congress, Washington, 1945-47, chief, 1947-49, dir. reference dept., 1949-57, head sci. Information Service (formerly Office Sci. Information), Nat. Sci. Found., 1957-70; dir. Am. Geog. Soc., N.Y.C., 1970—. Mem. A.A.A.S., Am. Geog. Soc., Am. Documentation Inst. Internat. Fedn. for Documentation (past pres.), A.L.A., Spl. Libraries Assn. (treas. 1954-56, 1st v.p., pres, 1959-60), Assn. (Am. Geographers (sec. 1954-57). Club: Cosmos (Washington). Contbr. profl. jours. Home: Apt 3N Whitehall 3333 Henry Hudson Pkwy Riverdale NY 10463 Office: Broadway at 156th St New York City NY 10032

ADLE, PARVIZ, diplomat of Iran; b. Tehran, Iran, Aug. 13, 1924; s. Fazlollah and Marie Louise (Roze) A.; Ph.D., U. Louvain, Belgium, 1952; m. Homa Ettehadieh, Apr. 28, 1953; children—Dariush, Maria, Azita. Head Iranian Broadcasting and Publ., Tehran, 1954-56; press counselor Iranian Embassy, Cairo, 1956-60, minister counselor, Paris, 1960-65; undersec. Ministry of Information, Tehran, 1955-67; gen. dir. press. and information Ministry of Fgn. Affairs, Tehran, 1967-69; consul gen. of Iran in San Francisco, 1969—. Decorated comdr. Order of Crown (Iran); Order Nationàl de Merite (France); Ordinal Tudor Vladimirescu (Roumania); Benemerentium Praemium (Brazil). Home: 3400 Washington St San Francisco CA 94118 Office: Consulate General of Iran 3400 Washington St San Francisco CA 94118

ADLER, ARTHUR M., Jr., toiletries co. and mfg. exec.; b. Chgo., Jan. 14, 1917; s. Arthur M. and Alma (Radzinski) A.; student Dartmouth, 193538; B.S., Northwestern U., 1939; m. Joan Greenebaum, Aug. 30, 1940; children—Jamie E., Wendy J., Arthur M. III. With Helene Curtis Industries, Inc., Chgo., 1940—, exec. v.p., 1966-67, also dir., pres., 1967—. Mem. budget com. Community Fund, Chgo., 1970—, mem. central rev. com., 1968—. Pres. bd. trustees Highland Park (Ill.) Hosp. Found., 1962-68, life trustee, 1968—. Home: 2385 Egandale Rd Highland Park IL 60035 Office: 4401 W North Av Chicago IL 60639

ADLER, BENJAMIN, cons. engr., b. N.Y.C., Nov. 10, 1903; s. William and Rose A.; E.E., Poly. Inst. Bklyn., 1926, D. Eng. (hon.), 1967; m. Beatrice Ross, June 30, 1938; children—Elizabeth Jan (Mrs. Geoffrey Picket), Susan Lois (Mrs. Victor Bers), Pamela Ann, Jane Winifred. Geophys. research engr. Phillips Petroleum Co., 1926-28; research engr. RCA, 1928-30, comml. engring. mgr., 1931-44; chief facilities engr. ABC, 1944-48, also cons. engr. TV broadcasting and communications; pres., dir. engring. Adler Electronics, Inc., New Rochelle, N.Y., 1948-63; v.p. Litton Industries, 1963-65, pres. Royfax div., Paramus, N.J., 1965-68; self-employed cons. engr., Larchmont, N.Y., 1968—, acting pres. Poly. Inst., Bklyn., 1969-71. Chmn. co. TV 59; chmn. engring. com. Com. All Channel Broadcasting, 1963-64; rep. industry adv. com. FCC, 1961. Trustee, corporation bd. Poly. Inst. Brooklyn. Registered profl. engr., N.Y. Recipient Distinguished Alumnus award Poly. Inst. Bklyn., 1965. Fellow A.A.A.S., I.E.E.E.; mem. Industries Assn. (v.p. 1952-65), Soc. Motion Picture and TV Engrs., Nat. Soc. Profl. Engrs. Home: 15 Monroe Av Larchmont, NY 10538.

ADLER, CHARLES, inventor; b. Balt., June 20, 1899; s. Harry and Carolyn (Frank) A.; student Johns Hopkins, 1917-20; m. Alene Steiger, June 10, 1925; children—Amalie Carol, Harry. Inventor rotating stop-sign, r.r.-highway crossing signal, Adler flasher relay, traffic sound detector, Adler double filament incandescent lamps for r.r. signals, traffic signals and airplane navigation lights, speed control highway signal systems, aircraft double lamp anti-collision light, aircraft flashing position-light system, aircraft studded reflector tall-light, and aircraft reflector lamp, aircraft proximity indicator, traffic-actuated traffic signal, automobile spaceometer, aircraft height light, and others. Bd. dirs. Friendship Internat. Airport Balt. Recipient awards Am. Legion, CAA, USAF, USN, Nat. Aeronautic Assn., Aircraft Owners and pilots Assn. Mem. State Aviation Commn. Md., 1953-59, Md. Traffic Safety Commn. Served with S.A.T.C., 1918. Licensed profl. airplane pilot. Mem. Nat. Aeros. Assn. (life mem., nat. councillor Md.), Inst. Traffic Engrs., Soc. Automotive Engrs., Airways Engring. Soc. Guest appearances on television. Contbr. to nat. mags. Home: Sutton Place Apts 1111 Park Av Baltimore MD 21201 Office: 1506 Sutton Pl Apts Baltimore MD 21201

ADLER, EUGENE MAX, business cons.; b. Elgin, Ill., Mar. 1, 1897; s. Abraham and Helen (Strauss) A.; student U. Ill., 1915-17; m. Eugenie Connolly, Dec. 22, 1933; 1 dau., Constance (Mrs. Fred W. Meyer). Mdsg. exec. Sears, Roebuck & Co., 1920-60; dir. Kellwood Co., Chgo., 1961—, Michaels, Stern & Co., Rochester, N.Y., 1961-70, Standard Shares, Inc. 1963—. Served as ensign U.S. Navy, 1918-19. Clubs: Southern Cross (Little Cayman, B.W.I.); Tavern (Chgo.); Lake Shore Country (Glencoe, Ill.). Home: 1011 Sheridan Rd Glencoe IL 60022 Office: 333 N Michigan Av Chicago IL 60601

ADLER, FRANCIS HEED, medical educator; b. Phila., Feb. 4, 1895; s. Lewis H. and Emma Augusta (Heed) A.; A.B., U. Pa., 1916, M.A., 1918, M.D., 1919; m. Emily Anne MacDonald, July 7, 1970; children by previous marriage—Jeanne Morris (Mrs. William Scott), Lynn. Intern Hosp. U. Pa., 1919-21; mem. faculty U. Pa. Med. Sch., 1921—, prof. ophthalmology, 1937-60, emeritus, 1960—. Served with U.S. Army, World War I. Recipient Luciam Howe medal U. Buffalo, 1960, Proctor medal Assn. Research Ophthalmology, 1967. Diplomate Am. Bd. Ophthalmology (sec.- treas.). Mem. Am. Opthal. Soc. (Howe medal 1951), A.M.A. (medal ophthalmology 1959; editor-in-chief Archives Ophthalmology 1950-60), Am. Acad. Ophthalmology and Otolaryngology. Clubs: Union League, Cricket (pres. 1969) (Phila.). Author: Physiology of the Eye, 1950; Text Book of Ophthalmology, 1941. Cons. editor Jour. Ophthalmology. 1960-65. Home: 8870 Towanda St Philadelphia PA 19118

ADLER, FRANK KURT, architect; b. Frankfurt on Main, Germany, Dec. 21, 1926; s. Wilhelm and Ellie (Frank) A.; came to U.S., 1941, naturalized, 1945; Certificate Architecture, Cooper Union, 1953; m. Lydia Jacobs, Oct. 8, 1951; children—Wendy E., Philip J., Arthur B., Karen L. Progressed from office boy to sr. draftsman archtl. firm E. Schoen & Sons-Schoen & Hennessy, N.Y.C., 1946-55; from project architect to chief architect Engineers Inc., Newark, N.J., 1955-63; propr. Frank Adler, A.I.A., Paramus, N.J., 1963—. Dir. North Jersey Cultural Council, 1970-72, trustee Jewish Community Center of Paramus. Served with AUS, 1945-46. Recipient Architects Vegliante award Architects League N.J., 1967. Mem. A.I.A., N.J. Soc. Architects, Architects League North N.J. (treas.), Paramus C. of C. Kiwanian. Home: E 275 Midland Av Paramus NJ 07652 Office: 54 Rt 17 Paramus NJ 07652

ADLER, FRED PETER, electronics mfg. exec.; b. Vienna, Austria, Mar. 29, 1925; s. Michael and Ellida (Bronner) A.; B.E.E. with honors, U. Cal. at Los Angeles, 1945; M.E.E. (Charles A. Coffin fellow 1947, 48), Cal. Inst. Tech., 1948, Ph.D. magna cum Laude, 1950. Came to U.S., 1942, naturalized, 1947. Elec. engr. Gen. Electric Co. Research and Cons. Labs., 1945-47, project engr. Jet Propulsion Lab., 1950; with Hughes Aircraft Co., 1950-70, sr. staff physicist, dept. mgr., 1954-57, mgr. advanced planning, 1957-59, dir. advanced projects labs., 1959-61, v.p., mgr. space systems div., 1961-66, v.p., asst. group exec., 1966-70; pres. Nadgeco Ltd., 1970—. Fellow Am. Inst. Aeros. and Astronautics; mem. N.Y. Acad. Scis., Sigma Xi, Tau Beta Pi. Co-author: (text) Guided Missile Engineering, 1959; also articles tech. jours. Home: 5 Johnson's Dr Hampton-upon-Thames Middlesex England Office: Nadgeco House The Centre Feltham Middlesex England

ADLER, HERBERT, apparel co. exec.; b. N.Y.C., May 4, 1918; s. Victor M. and Dora (Dumain) A.; B.S., Ohio U., 1939; m. Dorothy Schepps, Oct. 26, 1941; children—Carol (Mrs. Martin Mahler), Michael S., Ellen L. Partner, Clarence, Rainess & Co., C.P.A.'s. 1939-67; pres. Bobbie Brooks, Inc., Cleve., 1967—. Served to capt. AUS, 1942-46. Jewish religion (pres. temple). Club: Beechmont Country. Home: 19425 Van Aken Blvd Shaker Heights OH 44122 Office: 3830 Kelley Av Cleveland OH 44114

ADLER, JACOB HENRY, educator; b. Evansville, Ind., Mar. 26, 1919; s. Hiram J. and Jessica (Oberndorfer) A.; B.A., U. Fla., 1939, M.A., 1947; A.M., Harvard, 1948, Ph.D., 1951; m. Emily Carolyn Rowe, June 1, 1952; children—Jennifer Brooke, James Rowe. Mem. faculty U. Ky., 1949-50, 51-69, prof. English, 1965-69, chmn. dept., 1964-69; prof., head English dept., Purdue U., 1969—; Fulbright lectr. Am. lit. univs. Delhi and Lucknow (India), 1960- 61. Served with AUS, 1942-46; CBI. Decorated Bronze Star medal. Mem. Modern Lang. Assn., Midwest Modern Lang. Assn., Nat. Council Tchrs. English, Am. Assn. U. Profs. Presbyn. Author: The Reach of Art: a Study in the Prosody of Pope, 1964; Lillian Hellman, 1969; also articles, chpts. in books. Home: 1523 Summit Dr West Lafayette IN 47906 Office: Dept English Purdue U Lafayette IN 47907

ADLER, JOHN HANS, economist; b. Tachov, Czechoslovakia, Nov. 16, 1912; s. August and Lilly (Beck) A.; Dr. Jur., German U. (Prague), 1937; M.A., Yale, 1940, Ph.D., 1946; m. Vilma Joan Rabl, Sept. 12th, 1939; children—Catherine M. (now Mrs. Ramsey), Marcia V. Came to U.S., 1938, naturalized, 1945. Instr., Yale, 1941-42, Oberlin Coll., 1942-44; economist Fed. Res. Bd., 1944-45; dep. chief finance div. U.S. element Allied Commn. Austria, 1945-47; economist Fed. Res. Bank, N.Y.C., 1947-50; economist Internat. Bank Reconstrn. and Devel., 1950-57, econ. adviser, 1957-61. Dir. Econ. Devel. Inst., 1962-67, sr. adviser, 1967-68, dir. programming and budgeting dept., 1968—. Clubs: Cosmos (Washington); Edgemoor (Bethesda, Md.); East India and Sports (London). Author: (with H. C. Wallich) Public Finance in a Developing Country, 1951; (with E.R. Schlesinger, E.C. Oslon) Public Finance and Economic Development in Guatemala, 1952; (with E.R. Schlesinger, E. Van Westerborg) The Pattern of U.S. Import Trade 1952; also articles in learned jours. Home: 5620 Western Av Chevy Chase MD 20015 Office: 1818 H St NW Washington DC 20433

ADLER, KURT HERBERT, conductor; b. Vienna, Austria, Apr. 2, 1905; s. Ernst and Ida (Bauer) A.; student Vienna State Acad. Music, 1922-26, U. of Vienna, 1923-27; Doctor of Music (honorary), College of the Pacific, 1956; m. Diantha Warfel, July 7, 1940 (div. Dec. 1963); children—Kristin Diantha, Ronald Huntington; m. 2d, Nancy Miller, Aug. 23, 1965. Came to U.S., 1938, naturalized, 1941. Began as coach, accompanist, chorus dir., instr., conductor Max Reinhardt's theaters, Vienna, 1925-28, various opera houses in Germany and Italy, 1928-34; conductor of the Volksoper, Vienna, 1934-36, Vienna Concert Orchestra, 1934-36; asst. conductor to A. Toscanini at Saizburg Festival, 1936; conductor opera and radio, Czechoslovakia, 1936-38; conductor Chicago Opera Co., 1938-43, Grant Park Concerts, Chicago, 1941, 42; guest conductor Ill. Symphony Orchestra, 1942; engagement with San Francisco Opera Co. since 1943; condr. annual Midsummer Music Festival, San Francisco, opera and symphony, since 1944; with New Opera Co., New York, 1945; lectr., guest condr. symphony orchestra U. Cal. at Berkeley, 1949-50; artistic adviser San Francisco Conservatory Music, 1949-52; condr. youth concerts San Francisco Symphony, 1949-52; guest condr. Standard Hour Symphony broadcasts, NBC; asst. to gen. dir. San Francisco Opera, 1952; guest condr. Pacific Music Camp, 1952—, Hollywood Bowl, 1954-56; artistic dir. San Francisco Opera, 1953-56, gen. dir., 1956—; gen. dir. Western Opera Theater, 1966—, Spring Opera of San Francisco, 1961—, Music Center Opera Assn., Los Angeles, 1969; guest condr. San Carlo Opera, Naples, 1958. Decorated Star of Solidarity (Italy), 1957; Officer's Cross (Germany), 1959; cavaliere Italian Republic, 1965; recipient Great Medal of Honor (Austria), 1961; comdr.'s cross Order Merit (Fed. Republic Germany), 1969. Address: War Memorial Opera House San Francisco CA 94102

ADLER, LARRY, harmonica player; b. Balt., Feb. 10, 1914; s. Louis and Sadie (Hack) A.; student Balt. City Coll., 1925-28; m. Eileen Walser, Apr. 11, 1938; childrenCarole, Peter, Wendy. Harmonica player with Paramount cross country units, 1928, with Gus Edwards Revue, 1929, with Ziegfeld's Smiles, 1930, Max Gordon's Flying Colors, 1932; to England with C. B. Cochran, 1934-39, except for temporary tours in U.S., Africa and Australia, including 1st harmonica performance with symphony in Sydney, Australia, 1939; soloist with various U.S. symphony and philharmonic orchestras, 1939-41; entered concert field with dancer Paul Draper, 1941, then making yearly transcontinental tours; numerous U.S.O. tours to Newfoundland, Africa, Mediterranean countries, Pacific area, Germany, 1942-45. Appeared in motion pictures: Many Happy Returns, 1934, Big Broadcast of 1937, Sidewalks of London, 1938, The Singing Marine, 1937; Music for Millions, 1945; The Birds and the Bees, 1947. Produced own revues, Tune Inn, and In Town Tonight. Made recordings for Columbia and Decca of standard works of various composers. Recipient Outstanding Young Am. award Nat. Jr. C. of C., 1944. Author: How I Play, 1936; Harmonica Favorites, 1944; contbr. articles to Chicago Sun and Collier's mag. on U.S.O. trips.*

ADLER, LUTHER, actor; b. N.Y.C., May 4, 1903; s. Jacob P. and Sarah (Lewis) A.; ed. Lewis Inst., Chgo.; studied for stage with parents; m. Sylvia Sidney (div. 1947); 1 son, Jacob Luther; m. 2d Julie Hadley Roche, Apr. 1959. Stage appearance as child actor, Thalia Theatre, Bowery, N.Y.C., 1908; stage debut Provincetown Theatre, N.Y.C., 1921; appeared in numerous plays, including We Americans, 1927, Success Story, 1933, Awake and Sing, 1935, Paradise Lost, 1936, Golden Boy (N.Y.C. and London), 1938, Rocket to the Moon, 1939, Beggars are Coming to Town, 1945, A Flag in Born, 1946, Tovarich, 1952, A Month in the Country, 1956, A View From the Bridge (toured as Eddie Carbone), 1957-59; Mr. Rochester in Jane Eyre, 1943-44, also The Play's the Thing, N.Y.C., part of Shylock in Merchant of Venice, appearance St. James Theatre, London, part of Chebutykin in the Three Sisters, Lenin in The Passion of Josef D., Tevye in Fiddler on the Roof, 1965—. Home: RD 3 Box 196 Kutztown, PA 19530. Office: care Actors Equity Assn 45 W 47th St New York City NY 10036

ADLER, MICHAEL H.B., fgn. service officer; b. Long Branch, N.J., Aug. 19, 1916; s. Louis and Jenny Adler; student Bklyn. Coll., 1936-38, George Washington U., 1941- 44; M.P.A., Harvard, 1966; m. Ada Stambler, 1962; children—Jane Madeline, Michael Jonathon. With ICC, 1939-43, OPA, 1943-44, UNRRA, 1944-47; staff Am. Mission for Aid to Greece, 1947-48, field adviser, Athens, Greece, 1948-54; spl. rep. Hanoi, Vietnam, 1954-55; chief field service. Saigon, Vietnam, 1955- 56; regional exec. officer Far East region, ICA, Washington, 1956-61; dep. dir. U.S. Operations Misson to Liberia, 1960-63; dep. dir. AID mission to Iran, 1963-65; dir. AID mission to Nigeria, 1966-71; dir. AID Mission to Korea, 1971—. Address: Embassy Seoul Korea

ADLER, MORTIMER JEROME, author; b. N.Y.C., Dec. 28, 1902; s. Ignatz and Clarissa (Manheim) A.; Ph.D., Columbia, 1928; m. 2d, Caroline Sage Pring, 1963. Instr., Columbia, 1923-29; asst. dir. People's Inst., N.Y.C., 1927-29; asso. prof. philosophy law U. Chgo., 1930-42, prof., 1942-52; pres., dir. Inst. for Philos. Research 1952—. Mem. Am. Cath. Philos. Assn., Thomistic Inst. Am. Author: Dialectic, 1927; (with Jerome Michael) Crime Law and Social Science, 1933; (with Maude Phelps Hutchins) Diagrammatics 1935; Art and Prudence, 1937; What Man Has Made of Man, 1938; St. Thomas and the Gentiles, 1938; How to Read a Book, 1940; Problems for Thomists; The Problems of Species, 1940; A Dialectic of Morals, 1941; How to Think About War and Peace, 1944; The Idea of Freedom, 1958; (with Louis Kelso) The Capitalist Manifesto, 1958; (with Milton Mayer) The Revolution in Education, 1958; Conditions of Philosophy, 1965. Asso. editor Great Books of the Western World, 1945—. Editor: The Great Ideas; vol. I, The Idea of Freedom, 1958; Great Ideas from the Great Books, 1961; (with L. Kelso) The Capitalist Manifesto, 1958; The New Capitalists, 1961; (with M.

Mayer) The Revolution in Education, 1958. Contbr. to Thomist, Commonweal, Social Frontier. Home: Heaven Hill Rd Sonoma County CA 95476 Office: 1998 Pacific Av San Francisco CA 94109

ADLER, NORMAN ABNER, lawyer; b. N.Y.C., Oct. 8, 1909; s. Isaac Julius and Anna (Bluestein) A.; B.A., N.Y. U., 1930; LL.B., Yale, 1933; m. Leona Kleban, June 28, 1934; children—John Robert, Louise Rachel. Admitted to N.Y. bar, 1933; asso. mem. firm Rosenberg, Goldmark & Colin, N.Y.C., 1933- 38; spl. asst. to U.S. atty. gen., anti-trust div. Dept. Justice, 1938- 45; asst. gen. atty. RCA, 1945-48; gen. atty. Columbia Records, 1948-55, v.p. charge Columbia Record Club, 1955-60; exec. v.p. Columbia Records (div. CBS), 1960-66; v.p., gen. mgr. CBS Ednl. Services Div., 1966-67; v.p., gen. exec. CBS, 1967-71. Mem. Riverside Pub. Health Com. Recipient Cullen prize for excellence in legal scholarship Yale, 1931. Mem. Am. Civil Liberties Union (acad. freedom com.), Fed. Bar Assn., Assn. Bar City N.Y., Order of Coif, Am. Arbitration Assn. (nat. panel arbitrators), Phi Beta Kappa Assos., Phi Beta Kappa, Tau Kappa Alpha. Clubs: Players, City Athletic (N.Y.C.). Mng. editor Yale Law Jour., 1932-33. Home: 101 Central Park W New York City NY 10023 Office: 51 W 52d New York City NY 10019

ADLER, NORMAN PAUL, food co. exec.; b. San Francisco, May 20, 1929; s. Arnold and Virginia (Decker) A.; B.S., U. San Francisco, 1951, LL.B., 1959; postgrad. Golden Gate Coll. Grad. Sch. Bus., 1951-53; m. Robin Ann Paine, Mar. 5, 1966. Admitted to Cal. bar; various accounting positions, 1951-57; asst. sec. DiGiorgio Corp., San Francisco, 1957-60, sec., gen. counsel, 1960—. Mem. Cal. Bd. Archtl. Examiners. Mem. Am. Soc. Corporate secs., Phi Alpha Delta. Republican. Roman Catholic. Home: 16 Whaleship Plaza San Francisco CA 94111 Office: 1 Maritime Plaza San Francisco CA 94111

ADLER, PETER HERMAN, condr.; b. Jablonee, Czechoslovakia, Dec. 2, 1899; s. Bertold and Rinda (Kopf) A.; student Conservatory Music, Prague, Czechoslovakia; m. Helen George, Sept. 25, 1954. Came to U.S., 1939, naturalized, 1944. Condr., Jablonee, Brono and Tepilce, Czechoslovakia, 1923-26, Bremen and Darmstadt, Germany, 1929-33; guest condr. symphonies, central Europe, Russia, 1933-38; Am. debut N.Y. Philharmonic, 1939; guest condr. symphonies, operas, U.S., 1940-48; music and artisic dir. NBC Opera Co., 1949—; music dir. Balt. Symphony Orch., 1959—; guest condr. European TV operas, 1959—. Home: 123 E 57th St New York City NY 10022 Office: care NBC Rockefeller Plaza New York City NY 10020

ADLER, RENATA, writer; b. Milan, Italy, Oct. 19, 1938; s. Frederick L. and Erna (Strauss) Adler; A.B., Bryn Mawr Coll., 1959; M.A., Harvard, 1960; D.d.E.S., Sorbonne, Paris, 1961. Writer-reporter New Yorker, N.Y.C., 1962—; film critic N.Y. Times, 1968-69. Mem. exec. bd. P.E.N. Club. Author: A Year in The Dark, 1970; Toward A Radical Middle, 1970. Mem. Editorial Bd. Am. Scholar. Address: care The New Yorker 25 W 43d St New York City NY 10036

ADLER, RICHARD, songwriter; b. N.Y.C., Aug. 3, 1921; s. Clarence and Elsa (Richard) A.; A.B., U. N.C., 1943; m. Salley Ann Howes, 1958 (div.); children by previous marriage—Andrew H., Christopher E. Mem. advt. dept. Celanese Corp. Am., 1946-50; collaborator with Jerry Ross on scores for musicals John Murray Anderson's Almanac, 1953, Pajama Game, 1954; composer score musical Damn Yankees, 1955, Kwamina, 1961, TV prodns. Little Woman, 1958, Gift of the Magi, 1958; producer White House Press Corrs. and Photographers show for Pres. Kennedy and Prime Minister MacMillan, 1962, N.Y.'s Birthday Salute for Kennedy, 1962, Inaugural Anniversity Salute to Pres. Kennedy, 1963, Salutes to Pres. Johnson, 1964, Inaugural Gala for Pres. Lyndon Johnson, 1965; White House cons. on the arts, 1965-69; producer, composer, lyricist ABC-TV Stage 67 Musical Olympus 7-0000, fall 1966. Cons. on arts gov. N.C.; adv. bd. Inst. Outdoor Drama, 1968—, N.C. Performing School Arts, 1963—. Trustee John F. Kennedy Center for Performing Arts, 1964—. Served to Lt. (j.g.) USNR, 1943-46. Recipient Antoinette Perry award, Donaldson award, Variety Critics Poll for Pajama Game, 1954, Damn Yankees, 1955; Antoinette Perry nomination Kwamina, 1962. Mem. Dramatists Guild (exec. council 1958-68), Am. Guild Authors and Composers (exec. council 1962), A.S.C.A.P. (dir. chmn. exec. com.), ANTA (bd. dirs., exec. com.). Address: 19 E 72d St New York City NY 10021

ADLER, RICHARD BROOKS, educator, elec. engr.; b. N.Y.C., May 9, 1922; s. Arthur H. and Florence (Brooks) A.; student Harvard, 1939-41; S.B., Mass. Inst. Tech., 1943, Sc.D., 1949; m. Dorothy Gordon, May 31, 1951; children—Gordon, Nicholas, Lucas. Mem. Faculty Mass. Inst. Tech., 1949—, prof. elec. engring., 1959—, chmn. undergrad. admissions and student aid com., 1967-69, research asso. Research Lab. Electronics, 1946-56, group leader solid state and transistor group Lincoln Labs., 1951-53, asso. Center Materials Scis. and Engring., 1963—; cons. in field, 1952—. Served with USNR, 1944-46. Recipient Sloan award Mass. Inst. Tech., 1955, 56; Premium award Royal Aero. Soc., 1955. Fellow Am. Acad. Arts and Scis., I.E.E.E.; mem. Sigma Xi, Eta Kappa Nu, Tau Beta Pi. Author: (with S.J. Fricker) Notes on the Flow Scheduled Air Traffic, 1954; (with H.A. Haus) Limitations on Noise Performance of Linear Amplifiers, 1956; (with H.A. Haus) Circuit Theory of Linear Noisy Networks, 1959; (with others) Electromagnetic Fields, Energy and Forces, 1960; (with others) Electromagnetic Energy Transmission and Radiation, 1960; (with others) Introduction to Semiconductor Physics, 1964; (with others) Multistage Transistor Circuits, 1965; (with others) Electronic Conduction in Solids, 1967; also tech. papers. Office: Elec Engring Dept Mass Inst Tech Cambridge MA 02139

ADLER, RICHARD HENRY, apparel co. exec.; b. Rochester, N.Y., May 24, 1911; s. Milton S. and May (Straussman) A.; student Leland Stanford Jr. U., 1928-30; m. Margaret Freund, Aug. 19, 1935; children—James Richard, Thomas William. Advt. mgr. Braeburn, Inc., Rochester, N.Y., 1930-32; sales mgr. Print House of LeoHart, Rochester, 1932-38; v.p. sales mgr., dir. Michael Stern & Co., Inc., men's clothing mfr., Rochester, 1938-52; exec. v.p., dir. Joseph & Feiss Co., Cleve., 1952-57, pres., dir., 1957-70; chmn. bd., 1970—. Mem. Clothing Mfrs. Assn. Am. (pres. 1969—, dir.) Home: 2560 N Moreland Blvd Shaker Heights OH 44120 Office: 2149 W 53d St Cleveland OH 44102

ADLER, ROBERT, electronics engr.; b. Vienna, Austria, Dec. 4, 1913; s. Max and Jenny (Herzmark) A.; Ph.D. in physics, U. Vienna, 1937; m. Mary F. Buehl, 1946. Came to U.S., 1940, naturalized, 1945. Asst. to patent atty., Vienna, 1937-38; lab. Sci. Acoustics, Ltd., London Eng., 1939-40; lab. Asso. Research, Inc., Chgo., 1940-41; research group Zenith Radio Corp., Chgo., 1941-52, asso. dir. research, 1941-52, research, 1963—; developed various electron beam tubs for frequency modulation transmitters, for TV receivers, electron beam parametric amplifier; pioneer ultrasonic remote control for TV, ultrasonic light deflection for laser projection TV. Fellow Inst. Radio Engr.; mem. Nat. Acad. Engring. Contbr. numerous articles profl. publS. Home: 327 Latrobe Av Northfield IL 60093 Office: Zenith Radio Corp 6001 Dickens Av Chicago IL 60639

ADLER, ROBERT SAMUEL, former mut. fund exec.; b. Chgo., Aug. 21, 1900; s. Max and Sophie (Rosenwald) A.; Ph.B., U. Chgo., 1922; m. Helen Loewenstein, Oct. 9, 1924; children—John Robert, Louise (Mrs. Ralph Eder). Various positions, printing enterprizes, 1922- 25, dept. store, 1925-28; investments counseling, 1928-42; organizer Selected Am. Shares, Inc., mut. investment fund, Chgo., 1933, v.p., treas., 1933-41, pres., 1941-42, dir., 1933-55. Officer, dir. Jewish Community Centers Chgo., 1946-60; bd. govs. Hebrew Union Coll. Jewish Inst. Religion, Cin., 1947—. Trustee Chgo. Planetarium. Served to lt. col. AUS, 1942-45. Jewish religion. Clubs: Standard (Chgo.); Lake Shore Country (Glencoe, Ill.). Home: 1446 Waverly Rd Highland Park IL 60035

ADLER, SAMUEL MARCUS, artist, educator; b. N.Y.C., July 30, 1898; s. Harris Bernard and Rose (Levy) A.; student Nat. Acad. Design; m. Sarah Fox, June 29, 1926. One- man exhbns. include Joseph Luyber Galleries, N.Y.C., 1948, U. Ind., 1950, Louisville Art Center, 1950, Mint Mus., 1951, Grace Borgenicht Gallery, N.Y.C., 1952, 54, Phila. Art Alliance, 1954, U. Ill., 1959, Grand Central Moderns, N.Y.C., 1960, Babcock Gallery (2), 1962; Krannert Art Mus., Urbana, Ill., 1964, Notre Dame U., 1965, Rose Fried Gallery, N.Y.C., 1965, U. Ia., 1966, U. Ga., 1967-68, Rippon Coll., 1969, Frank Rehn Gallery, N.Y.C., 1971, 72; exhibited numerous nat., European shows, including Art Inst. Chgo., U. Ia., Butler Inst. Am. Art, Pa. Acad. Fine Arts, Nat. Acad. Design, Corcoran Inst., Denver Art Mus., U. Ill., Va. Mus. Art, Neb. Art Assn., Met. Mus. Art, Whitney Mus. Am. Art, San Francisco Mus. Art, U. Ia., galleries 18 countries Europe and Orient; rep. permanent collections U. Notre Dame, U. Ill. (Purchase award 1952), Mus. of William Proctor Inst., Clearwater (Fla.) Mus., Whitney Mus. Am. Art (Purchase award 1952), S.I. Inst. Arts and Scis. (Purchase award 1962), N.Y.U., S.C. Johnson Collection, Norfolk Mus., Joseph H. Hirshhorn Collections, Glicenstein Mus., Israel, Bklyn. Mus., Ga. Mus., U. Neb. Mus., Syracuse U. Mus.; Wichita State U., St. Lawrence U., Ill. Wesleyan U.; mem. faculty N.Y.U., 1948—, adj. prof., 1960—; mem. faculty U. Ga., 1967; vis. prof. U. Ill., 1959-60, U. Ga., 1967-68; guest lectr. Nat. Com. Art Edn., U. Mich., 1957, Festival Contemporary Arts, U. Ill., 1953-59, 63, N.Y. State Art Tchrs. Assn., 1958, Museum Modern Art, U. Syracuse, 1961, Washington U., 1963, U. Notre Dame, 1963, Beloit Coll., numerous other schs., museums. Juror, Ford Found., 1963. Recipient J. Henry Schiedt meml. prize Pa. Acad. Fine Arts, 1951; Patron's award Audubon Artists, 1st hon. mention 1956, 57, Medal of Honor 1960; asso. mem. Inst. Advanced Study, U. Ill., Urbana, 1964; Ford Found. grant for Artist in Residence in Mus., U. Notre Dame, 1965. Author articles. Address: 27 E 22d St New York City NY 10010

ADLER, SELIG, educator; b. Balt., Jan, 22, 1909; s. Joseph G. and Della (Rubenstein) A.; B.A., U. Buffalo, 1931; M.A., U. Ill., 1932, Ph.D., 1934; m. Janet M. Sukernek, Aug. 26, 1936; children—Ellen (Mrs. David Krantz), Joseph G. Tchr. High Schs, Buffalo, 1934-47; lectr. history State U. New York at Buffalo (formerly U. Buffalo), 1941—, prof. history, 1952 -, Samuel P. Capen prof. Am. History, 1959—; vis. prof. Cornell U., summer 1951, spring 1959, U. Rochester, 1952-53. Mem. N.Y. State Kosher Law Adv. Bd., 1952—. Mem. Am. Hist. Assn., Orgn. Am. Historians, Am. Jewish Hist. Soc. (exec. council), Phi Beta Kappa. Author: The Isolationist Impulse, 1957; (with T. E. Connolly) From Ararat to Suburbia, 1960; The Uncertain Giant, 1921-1941, 1965; also profl. articles. Contbg. editor: Judaism, 1956. Home: 123 Frontenac Av Buffalo, NY 14216.

ADLERBLUM, NIMA H., author; b. Jerusalem, Palestine, Aug. 4, 1886; d. Hayyim and Eva (Hakohen) Hirschensohn; brought to U.S., 1904; student Barnard Coll., also Paris, France; Ph.D., Columbia, 1926; m. Israel S. Adlerblum, Apr. 9, 1914; 1 dau., Ivria (Mrs. Alexander H. Sackton). Founder, mem. Am. Com. Translation and Dissemination John Dewey's and Am. philosophy in Latin Am.; also translation and dissemination Am. works in philosophy of edn.; founder Hadassah Nat. Cultural work (chmn. nat. com., mem. nat. bd. 1920-33); founder Exchange of Thought Movement, Am. and European scholars, 1920; research work throughout Europe, Near East, for studying problems of minority nationalities, Latin Am. for intercultural relationship and immigration of refugees. Life fellow Internat. Inst. Arts and Letters; mem. Am. Philos. Assn., InterAm. Congress Philosophy (elected editor of contemplated edit. of Contemporary Philos. Tendencies throughout the World), Internat. Congress of Philosophy, League for Indsl. Democracy, Hadassah, many other orgns. Author: A Study of Gersonides in his Proper Perspective, 1926; A Perspective of Jewish Life through its Festivals, 1930 (transcribed into Braille); Memoirs of Childhood in Guardians of Our Heritage (Leo Jung editor), 1958; Sara Bayla and Her Times (Leo Jung editor); chpts. in various publs., articles in philos. jours. Home: 220 Ocean Av Long Branch NJ 07740

ADOLFSON, LORENTZ HENNING, univ. adminstr.; b. Chgo., Oct. 14, 1909; s. August H. and Eva (Bergstrom) A.; student Crane Jr. Coll., Chgo., 1929-30; B.A., Wabash Coll., 1933; Ph.D., U. Wis., 1942; m. Mildred Marie Jensen, Apr. 20, 1940; 1 dau., Carol Ann Rittle. Engaged in ins. bus., Chgo., 1926-29, mfg. and wholesale bus., Chgo., 1933-36; instr. polit. sci. univ. extension div. U. Wis.-Madison, 1938-42, asst. prof., 1942-44, dir., 1944-59, dean, 1959-64, dir. univ. summer sessions, 1954-64, chancellor Univ. center system, 1964—; state- wide lectr. on nat. and internat. affairs, 1938-44; head ICA Ankara (Turkey) project in pub. adminstrn. N.Y.U., 1957-58, head Wis. ednl. survey team, Uganda, also Kenya, 1966. edn. in Armed Forces, Dept. Def., 1961-63. Mem. Joint Interim Legislative Com. to Study County Govt. in Wis., 1945-46; mem. Wis. Radio Council, 1945-65, Youth Service Commn., 1947-49, Gov. Wis. Commn. Human Rights, 1947-57, Gov.'s Com. on UN Day (chmn. 1950-56); chmn. Wis. State Brotherhood, 1960; mem. Wis. Free Library Commn., 1951-57. Mem. Nat. U. Extension Assn. (pres. 1951-52), Assn. State U. and Land Grant Colls., Am. Assn. Jr. Colls. (commn. instrn.), Phi Beta Kappa, Tau Kappa Alpha, Phi Kappa Phi, Kappa Sigma, Blue Key. Club: University (Madison). Home: 5105 Odana Rd Madison WI 53711

ADOMIAN, GEORGE, educator; b. Buffalo, Mar. 21, 1922; s. Haig and Rose (Harutunian) A.; B.S., U. Mich., 1944, M.S., 1948; postgrad. Cal. Inst. Tech., 1948-49; Ph.D., U. Cal. at Los Angeles, 1963; m. Corinne Hodgson, Dec. 23, 1956; children—Haig, Diane, Laura. Sr. scientist Hughes Aircraft Co., 1953-64; prof. engring. research, prof. math. Pa. State U., 1964-66; Distinguished prof., David C. Barrow prof. math. U. Ga., 1966—; cons. applied math., aerospace and def. problems, systems theory. Served as lt. (s.g.) USNR, 1944-46. NASA grantee, 1970, 71. Mem. Am. Math. Soc., Am. Phys. Soc., I.E.E.E., Soc. Insdl. and Applied Math., A.A.A.S., Sigma Xi, Sigma Pi Sigma, Tau Beta Pi, Eta Kappa Nu. Contbr. articles to books and profl. jours. Home: 155 Clyde Rd Athens GA 30601

ADOULA, CYRILLE, ex-prime minister Congo.; b. Leopoldville, Sept. 1921; grad. with distinction St. Joseph Inst., Leopoldville, 1941; m. Julienne Adoula; 5 children. With pvt. firms, Congo, 1941-52; bank clk. Congo Central Bank, 1952-56; sec. Gen. Fedn. Congolese Workers subsidiary Gen. Fedn. Labor, 1956; with Patrice Lumumba and Joseph Ileo, organized Mouvement National Congolais, 1958; active independence meetings, Nigeria, 1958; senator representing Equator Province, Republic of Congo; minister of interior Ileo Cabinet, 1960; mem. Kasavubu delegation Gen. Assembly UN, 1960; premier Republic of Congo, 1961-64; organizer, leader (Rade-Co) Rassemblement des Democrates Congolais; Congolese ambassador to Belgium, Luxembourg, 1966, U.S., 1966-69. Catholic.*

ADREON, HARRY BARNES, Jr., architect; b. Norfolk, Va., July 18, 1929; s. Harry Barnes and Helen Rae (Medairy) A.; B.S., Va. Poly. Inst., 1950, M.S., 1952; m. Beatrice Marie Rice, Dec. 27, 1952. With firm Keyes, Lethbridge & Condon, Washington, 1954-61; partner firm Cross & Adreon, Washington, 1961—. Mem. Washington Episcopal Diocesan Archtl. Commn., 1966—. Served as capt. USMCR, 1952-54. Recipient Design award Nat. Assn. Home Builders, 1965-66; award for architecture Washington Bd. Trade, 1965; Design award Bethesda-Chevy Chase C. of C., 1966, 67; Nat. Honor award Am. Inst. Steel Constrn. Registered architect, Va., Md., D.C. Mem. A.I.A. (House and Home award 1966, 67, Honor award Middle Atlantic region 1967, Nat. Honor award 1968), Washington Bldg.. Congress, Constrn. Specifications Inst. (1st v.p. 1970-72), Tau Sigma Delta. Episcopalian (vestryman 1961-63, 67-69, 71—). Home: 4524 N 19th Rd Arlington VA 22207 Office: 901 27th St NW Washington DC 20037

ADRIAN, BARBARA, artist; b. N.Y.C., July 25, 1931; d. Allen Isaac and Mildred (Brown) Adrian; student Art Students League, 1947-54, Hunter Coll., 1951, Columbia Sch. Gen. Study, 1952-54. Art cons. Doyle-Dane-Bernbach, advt. agy., 1960, A.H. Macy, N.Y.C., 1960-61, Saks Fifth Avenue, 1960, Black, Starr & Gorham, 1960; instr. art workshop, Jamaica, N.Y., 1958-59; pvt. tchr. art, 1960—, instr. Art Students League, N.Y. One man shows G. Gallery, 1957, San Juan, P.R., 1951, Grippi Gallery, N.Y.C., 1963, Banfer Gallery, N.Y.C., 1966; exhibited in group shows G. Gallery, 1955-59, City Center Gallery, N.Y.C., 1954, N.Y.C. Festival, 1957, Portland (Me.) Mus., 1958, Workshop Gallery, N.Y.C., 1959, Grippi Gallery, 1960-63, Lane Gallery, Cal., 1962-63, Mus. Gallery Lubbock, Tex., 1962-63, The Gallery, Norwalk, O., 1962, Gallery 777, Plainview, L.I., N.Y., 1963, N.A.D., 1963, Butler Inst., Youngstown, O., 1963, Gallery Modern Art, N.Y.C., 1969, Child Hassam Fund Purchase Exhbn., N.Y.C., 1968, Orr's Gallery, San Diego, 1968, Capricorn Gallery, Washington, Kenmore Gallery, Phila.; represented in permanent collections Grippi Gallery, Summer Found., Butler Inst., McMay Mus., U. So. Ill., San Antonio, Corcoran Gallery, Washington, also pvt. collections in U.S., P.R., Mex Recipient Benjamin Altman prize, 1968. Mem. artists Equity of N.Y. Address: 304 E 73rd St New York City NY 10021

ADRIAN, CHARLES RAYMOND, educator; b. Portland, Ore., Mar. 12, 1922; s. Harry Raymond and Helen K. (Petersen) A.; B.A., Cornell (Ia.) Coll., 1947; M.A., U. Minn., 1948, Ph.D., 1950; postdoctoral fellow, U. Copenhagen (Denmark), 1954-55; m. Audrey Jean Nelson, Apr. 2, 1946; children—Kristin, Nelson. Instr., then asst. prof. govt. Wayne State U., 1949-55; from asst. prof. to prof. polit. sci. Mich. State U., 1955-66, chmn. dept., 1963-66, dir. Inst. Community Devel., 1958-63; prof. polit. sci. U. Cal. at Riverside, 1966—, chmn. dept., 1966-70; cons. fed., state and local govt.; research cons. Mich. Constl. Conv., 1961-62 Adminstrv. asst. to gov. Mich., 1956-57; mem. Meridian Twp. (Mich.) Planning Commn., 1957-60. Served with USAAF, 1943-46; PTO. Faculty fellow Fund Advancement Edn., 1954-55. Mem. Am. Polit. Sci. Assn., Am. Soc. Pub. Adminstrn., Phi Beta Kappa. Author: (with O. P. Williams) Four Cities: A Comparative Study in Community Politics, 1963; State and Local Governments, 2d edit., 1967, 3d edit, 1971; (with Charles Press) American Political Process, 1965, 2d. edit., 1969, Governing Urban America 3d edit., 1968, also articles. Office: Dept Polit Sci U Cal Riverside CA 92502

ADRIAN, WALTER FREDERICK, paper mfr.; b. Menasha, Wis., Oct. 5, 1906; s. Frank and Augusta (Lux) A.; student Columbia Inst. Commerce, 1925-27, Internat. Accountants Soc., 1928-29; m. Eleanor M. Kessler, Sept. 16, 1932; children—Barton C., Brian W. With Badger Paper Mills, Inc., Peshtigo, Wis., 1928—, successively cost accountant, comptroller, sec.-treas., exec. v.p., 1928- 57, pres., 1957—, chmn. bd., 1959—; v.p. Stephenson Nat. Bank, Marinette, Wis.; chmn. Peshtigo State Bank. Dir., v.p. Trees for Mem. Pulp and Paper Mfg. Assn. (dir.), Nat. Assn. Tax Accountants, Financial Execs. Inst. Lutheran. Home: 201 Emery Av Peshtigo WI 54157

ADRIAN, WILLIAM LAWRENCE, ret. bishop; b. Sigourney, Ia., Apr. 16, 1883; s. Nick and Mary (Paulus) A.; A.B., St. Ambrose Coll., Davenport, Ia., 1906; S.T.L., North Am. Coll., Rome, Italy, 1911; LL.D., St. Ambrose Coll., Davenport, Ia., May 1939; student summer sessions, U. of Ia., 1914, '15. Mem. faculty St. Ambrose Coll., 1911-34, v.p. of coll. and prin. high. sch., 1935; pastor St. Bridget's Parish, Victor, Ia., 1935-36; bishop of Nashville, 1936-69; asst. at Pontifical Throne, 1961. Address: 421 Charlotte Av Nashville TN 37219

ADRIANI, JOHN, physician; b. Bridgeport, Conn., Dec. 2, 1907; s. Nicola and Lucia (Caseria) A.; A.B., Columbia, 1930, M.D., 1934; m. Eleanor Anderson, Dec. 1936 (div. Feb. 1947); 1 son, John Nicholas; m. 2d, Irene Miller, Sept. 7, 1953. Intern surgery French Hosp., N.Y.C., 1934-36; resident anesthesiology Bellevue Hosp., N.Y.C., 1936-37; fellow N.Y.U., 1937-39, instr. anesthesiology dept. surgery, 1939-41; asst., then asso. clin. prof. surgery La. State U. Sch. Medicine, 1941-54, clin. prof. surgery and pharmacology 1954; asst. prof., later asso. prof. anesthesiology Loyola Sch. Dentistry, New Orleans, 1945-56, prof. gen. anesthesiology, 1956—; prof. surgery Tulane U., 1947—, dir. dept. anesthesiology and inhalation therapy, 1941—, dir. blood plasma bank, 1944-70, asst. dir., 1960-64; clin. prof. oral surgery Sch. Dentistry, La. State U., 1971—; asso. dir. Charity Hosp. 1966—, center chmn. regional med. program, 1967-70; cons. anesthesiologist Flint-Goodridge, VA, USPHS, Ochsner Found. hosps., Hotel Dieu, New Orleans; cons. to Touro Infirmary, New Orleans, FDA. Mem. adv. com. div. investigational drugs FDA, 1963-; chmn. adv. com. on anesthetic and respiratory drugs, 1968-70; mem. founders group expansion program Holy Cross Coll., 1963; mem. revision com., chmn. com. on anesthesia, subcom. on scope U.S. Pharmacopoela, 1960-70; mem. Nat. Formulary Admissions Com., 1970—. Bd. dirs. Cancer Soc. New Orleans. Named hon. col. staff Gov. La., 1965; recipient Distinguished Service award Am. Soc. Anesthesiologists, 1949, Internat. Anesthesiology Research Soc., 1957; Guedel medal for anesthesiology 1959; gold medal Assn. Alumni Coll. Physicians and Surgeons, Columbia, 1967; silver medal for achievements in medicine Columbia U. Sch. Medicine; Ralph M. Waters award internat. achievements in anesthesiology, 1968; Knight Comdr. Order of Merit (Italy), 1969; named Nat. Italian Am. of Year, 1969. Diplomate Am. Bd. Anesthesiology, (dir. 1960, chmn. exams. com. 1963-, pres. 1967-68). Fellow Am. Soc. Clin. Pharm. and Chemotherapy, Am. Soc. Clin. Pharm. and Thera., Am. Coll. Anesthesiologists (gov. 1944-50, 56-60); mem. Am. Heart Assn., Assn Colonic Surgeons, A.A.A.S., Soc. Exptl. Biology and Medicine, So. Soc. Clinical Research, Internat. Anesthesia Research Soc., NRC, Columbia U. Alumni Assn., Am. Hosp. Assn., Assn. U. Anesthesiologists (pres. 1955), Assn. Univ. Anesthesiology Departmental Chmn., A.M.A. (chmn. council on drugs, 1968—, vice chmn. 1967, chmn. 1967-71), Internat. Soc. Comprehensive Medicine, Am. La. (pres. 1950), So. (pres. 1952—), Cuban (hon.), Venezuelan (hon.) socs. anesthesiologists, So. Med. Assn.,

Southeastern Surg. Congress, Am. Acad. Anesthesiology, Am. Coll. Angiology, Am. Surg. Assn., Mexican Soc. Anesthesiology (hon. pres. 1954), La. Thoracic Soc., Yucatan Soc. Anesthesiology (hon. pres. 1966), Civil Service League La. (dir.), Assn. Wild-life and Fisheries of La. (asso. mem.). Clubs: Thoracophilis Horse Shoe. Author: Pharmacology of Anesthetic Drugs, rev. edit. 1960; Chemistry of Anesthesia, 1946; Techniques and Procedures of Anesthesia, 3d edit., 1964; Nerve Blocks, 1954; Selection of Anesthesia, 1955; General Anesthesiology For Students and Practitioners of Dentistry, 1958; The Recovery Room, 1958; Chemistry and Physics of Anesthesia, 1961; Appraisal-Current Concepts Anesthesiology (Mosby), Vol. 1, 1961, Vol. 2, 1964, Vol. 3, 1966, Vol. 4, 1969; Revision of Labat's Regional Anesthesia, 1967; also scientific and med. papers. Editor: American Lecture Series in Anesthesiology; cons. editor, Surgery, The Resident G. P. Survey Anesthesiology; editor Anesthesiology, 1964-; cons. editor Excerpta Medica, Audiodigest, Dorland's Illustrated Med. Dictionary, 1969—, Internat. Corr. Soc. Anesthesiology. Home: 67 N Park Pl New Orleans LA 70124 Office: Charity Hospital New Orleans LA 70140 ☆

ADRIAN OF CAMBRIDGE, BARON, (Edgar Douglas Adrian), ednl. administr., univ. chancellor; b. London, Eng., Nov. 30, 1889; s. Alfred Douglas and Flora Lavinia (Barton) A.; ed. Westminster Sch., Trinity Coll.; M.A., M.D., Cambridge; hon. degrees various univs.; m. Hester Agnes Pinsent, June 15, 1923 (dec. 1966); 2 daus., 1 son. Lectr. in physiology, Cambridge U., 1920-29, prof. physiology, 1937-51, master Trinity Coll., 1951-65; chancellor U. Leicester, 1957-70, Cambridge, 1967—; pres. Royal Soc. Medicine, 1960-62; Foulerton research prof. Royal Soc., 1929. Served as capt. Royal Army M.C., 1916-19. Created a Baron, 1956. Recipient Nobel prize for physiology and medicine, 1932. Chevalier Legion of Honour (France); Order of Merit, 1942. Pres. Royal Soc. 1950-55 (fgn. sec. 1946); fellow Academia del Lincei; hon. mem. Am. Physiol. Soc., Nat. Acad. Medicine (Argentina), Acad. Nacional de Medicine (Mexico); fgn. asso. Nat. Acad. Scis. (USA); hon. fgn. mem. Am. Acad. Arts and Scis., Royal Acad. Medicine (Belgium), Royal Acad. Sci (Amsterdam), Royal Flemish Acad. Sci.; corr. mem. Acad. Sci. (Paris); fgn. asso. Acad.' Medicine (Paris), Kungl. Vetenshaps. Soc. (Upsala); mem. Am. Philos Soc. Author: The Basis of Sensation, 1928; The Mechanism of Nervous Action, 1932. Home: Trinity Coll Cambridge England

ADSHEAD, LAWRENCE REGINALD, hosp. exec.; b. Calgary, Alta., Can., Apr. 15, 1911; s. John Robert and Edith (Haymen) A.; student pub. schs.; m. Mary Alexandra Marshall, Aug. 7, 1936; children—John Douglas, Gordon Robert, Lynn Eileen. Accountant, U. Alta. Hosp., Edmonton, 1929-41, bus. adminstr., 1941-52, exec. dir., 1952-61; exec. dir. Foothills Hosp., Calgary, 1961—; dir. Alta. Blue Cross Plan, Canadian Council Hosp. Accreditation. Recipient Queen's Coronation medal, 1953. Mem. Canadian (pres.), Alta. (pres.) hosp. assns., Canadian Assn. Health Care Execs. (v.p.), Am. Coll. Hosp. Adminstrs. Baptist. Rotarian. Home: 1632 Cayuga Dr NW Calgary 42 Alberta Canada Office: Foothills Hospital 29th St and 16th Av NW Calgary Alberta Canada

ADSIT, WILLCOX BROWN, finance co. exec.; b. Balt., May 3, 1909; s. Henry and Peachy Poythress (Brown) A.; B.A., Williams Coll., 1930; m. Harriet J. McNulty, Jan. 28, 1939. With Gen Motors Can., Ltd., Oshawa, Ont., summers 1928-29; with Gen. Motors Acdeptance Corp., N.Y.C., 1930-39, 56—, v.p. charge advt., pub. relations, 1956-60, v.p. charge U.S. borrowings, 1960-63, dir., 1960—, exec. v.p. charge borrowings, overseas operations, pub. relations, 1963—; exec. pub. relations staff, mgr. pub. relations office Gen. Motors Corp., N.Y.C., 1939-56; dir. Motors Ins. Corp. Served to lt. USNR, 1942-45. Mem. Am. Indsl. Bankers Assn. (dir.), Delta Upsilon, Clubs: University, Economic (N.Y.C.); Blind Brook (Portchester, N.Y.); Round Hill (Greenwich). Home: Pecksland Rd Greenwich CT 06830 Office: 767 Fifth Av New York City NY 10022

AECK, RICHARD LEON, architect; b. Council Bluffs, Ia., Feb. 26, 1912; student Morningside Coll., Sioux City, 1929-31; B.Arch., Ga. Sch. Tech., 1936. Chief Designer Ft. Ley & Co., Bogota, Colombia, 1937-38; pvt. practice, Atlanta, 1938-42; chief architect Pan Am. Airways, Brazilian Dist., 1942- 43; organized Aeck Asso., Atlanta, 1944; pres. Aeck Assos., Inc., architects, 1962—; prin. works include H. Grady High Sch. Football Stadium, Atlanta, 1948, Alexander Meml. Basketball Coliseum, Ga. Tech., 1956, Peachtree House Apts., Atlanta, 1958, Holy Family Hosp., Atlanta, 1964, IBM Office Bldg., Tampa, 1965, Research Center, Lockheed Aircraft Co., Marietta, Ga., 1969, Grad. Studies Research Center, U. Ga., 1969, DeSoto-Hilton Hotel, Savannah, Ga., 1969, C & S Nat. Bank and Office Bldg., Atlanta, 1969, Floyd County Jr. Coll., Rome, Ga., 1970. Consultant U.S. Overseas Mission to Cambodia, 1963. Preceptor, Rice Univ. Recipient Modern Hosp. of Month award for Newton County Hospital, Covington, Ga., 1955; Award of Excellence for Howard Callaway Residence, Pine Mountain, Ga., Archtl. Record, 1958. Fellow A.I.A. Home: 2200 W Wesley Rd NW Atlanta GA 30327

AEGERTER, ERNEST, pathologist, educator; b. Randolph, Neb., Jan. 4, 1906; s. Ernest Alfred and Jessie (Dorman) A.; A.B., Yankton Coll., 1928; B.S., U. S.D., 1929; M.D., U. Pa., 1932. Intern United Hosp., Westchester, N.Y., 1932-34; resident pathology Willard Parker Hosp., N.Y.C., 1935; fellow pathology Temple U. Med. Center, 1936, mem. faculty, 1936—. prof. pathology, 1945—, dir. dept., 1945-68, dir. emeritus, 1968—; lectr. orthopedic pathology U. Pa. Sch. Medicine, 1950—; cons. Phila. Gen. Hosp., Frankford Hosp., Phila., VA Hosp., Phila., U.S. Naval Hosp., Phila., Shriners Hosp. Crippled Children, Phila., A. I. dePont Inst., Wilmington, Pa. Hosp. Crippled Children, Elizabethtown. Mem. Am. Acad. Orthopedic Surgery (hon.), Am. Assn. Pathologists and Bacteriologists, Coll. Am. Pathologists. Author: (with John Kirkpatrick) Orthopedic Diseases, 1958-63. Home: RD 1 Chalfont, PA 18914. Office: 3400 N Broad St Philadelphia PA 19140

AERTKER, ROBERT JOSEPH, educator; b. New Orleans, June 22, 1916; s. William Herman and Anna (Garic) A.; B.S., La. State U., 1937, M.A., 1947; m. Caralea Hatchell, Apr. 19, 1941; children—Robert, Michael. Tchr., athletic coach, asst. high sch. prin., high sch. prin., asst. supt., supt. Parish Schs., Baton Rouge, 1937—. Pres., Baker Civic Club, 1948-49; mem. City and Parish Bd. Health, 1948—. Served with AUS, 1941-46. Mem. Nat. Assn. Secondary Prins., N.E.A., La. Tchrs. Assn., So. Assn. Sch. Bus. Ofcls., Baton Rouge C. of C., Am. Legion, Phi Delta Kappa. Presbyn. (elder). Lion. Author: Social and Economic History of Baton Rouge, 1946. Home: 8864 Trinity St Baton Rouge LA 70808 Office: 1050 S Foster Dr Baton Rouge LA 70821

AESCHBACHER, WILLIAM DRIVER, historian; b. Tonganoxie, Kan., Jan. 12, 1919; s. Joseph Edmund and Annie Rose (Driver) A.; B.S., U. Neb., 1940, M.A., 1946, Ph.D., 1948; m. Flavia Ann Tharp, Dec. 20, 1944; children—William Richard, Robert David, Steven Joh. Asso. prof. history Murray (Ky.) State Coll., 1948-56; dir. Neb. Hist. Soc., Lincoln, 1956-63; dir. Eisenhower Library, Abilene, Kan., 1963-66; asso. prof. history U. Utah, 1966-68; head dept. history U. Cin., 1968—. Pres., Council Chs., Lincoln, 1962. Served to 1st lt. AUS, 1942-45. Mem. Am., So. Hist. Assns., Orgn. Am. Historians (sec., treas.), Agrl. History Soc., Am. Assn. State and Local History, Am. Mus. Assn. Presbyn. Editor: Neb. History, 1956-63. Home: 8462 Foxcroft Dr Cincinnati OH 45231

AFFLECK, JAMES GELSTON, lawyer; b. Yonkers, N.Y., Dec. 15, 1892; s. James Gelston and Gertrude Louise (Burns) A.; Ph.B., A.M., Brown U., 1914; LL.B., Columbia, 1919; m. Francelia May Johnson, Sept. 11, 1918; children—James children—James Gelston, May F. Admitted to N.Y. bar, 1919; asso. Masten & Nichols, 1919- 31, Milbank, Tweed, Hope & Webb, 1931-33; became partner Milbank, Tweed, Hope & Hadley, 1934, now Milbank, Tweed, Hadley & McCloy. Dir. Milbank Meml. Fund, 1934-66. Served as 1st lt., inf., U.S. Army, 1917-18. Mem. Assn. Bar City N.Y., Am., N.Y. State bar assns. Home: 320 S Ocean Blvd Delray Beach, FL 33444. Office: 1 Chase Manhattan Plaza New York City NY 10005

AFRO, see Basaldella, Afro.

AFSHAR, AMIR-ASLAN, Iranian diplomat; b. Tehran, Iran, Nov. 21, 1922; s. Amir Massoud and Amir Banou (Aghtaj) A.; student U. Berlin (Germany), U. Greifswald (Germany), U. Geneva (Switzerland); Dr. Polit. Scis., U. Vienna, 1943; m. Camilla Saed, Mar. 1, 1950; children-Fatima, Mohammad. Joined Iranian Ministry Fgn. Affairs, Tehran, 1948; attache Imperial Embassy of Iran, Netherlands, 1950-54; Iranian del. to Asian-African Conf., Bandung, Indonesia, 1955; toured U.S. under Eisenhower Exchange Fellowship Program, 1955-56; dep. 19th session Iranian Nat. Assembly, Majlis, 1956, dep. 20th session, 1960; Iranian del. UN Gen. Assembly, 1957, 58-60; civil adj. to His Imperial Majesty Shahanshah of Iran, 1958; minister E. and P., 1962-67; Iranian ambassador to Austria, 1967-68; Iranian rep. Outer Space Conf., Vienna, 1968; Iranian rep. UNIDO Conf., Vienna, 1968; Iranian rep. Rds. and Traffic Conf., Vienna, 1968; chmn. bd. govs. IAEA, Vienna, 1968-69; ambassador to U.S., Washington, 1969—, also ambassador to Mexico. Decorated Order of Homayoun 2d grade, Order of Taj 3d, 4th, 5th grades, medal of Farhang 2d grade, medal of Pas 1st grade, Commemorative medal for 25 years of reign of His Imperial Majesty Shahanshah of Iran, Coronation medal, also numerous fgn. decorations. Author: Study of the Constitution of the German Third Reich, 1942; Study About the Adminstrative Law of the German Third Reich, 1943; The Possibilities of the Expansion of the Iranian Economy, 1943; The Fall of the Third Reich, 1947; Ways and Means of Iran's Participation in International Organizations, 1949; God Created the World, The Dutch Built Holland, 1954; Report on America, 1956. Home: 3003 Massachusetts Av N W Washington DC 20008 Office: 3005 Massachusetts Av N W Washington DC 20008

AGA KHAN, SHAH KARIM IV, b. Dec. 13, 1936; s. Aly S. and Joan Barbara (Yarde-Buller) Aly Kahn; studied LeRosey, Switzerland, also Harvard; LL.D. (hon.), Peshawar U., Pakistan, 1967; m. Sarah Frances Chrichton-Stuart, 1969. Became Aga Khan, spiritual leader and Imam of Ismalli Mohamedans, on death of grandfather Sir Sultan Mohamed Aga Khan, July 11, 1957. Granted title his highness Queen, 1957; granted title his royal highness, Shah of Persia, 1959; commandeur l'Ordre de Merite Mauritanien, 1960; grand croix de l'Ordre de Croissant Vert des Comores, de l'Ordre Malgache, de l'Ordre Nat. Cote d'Ivoire, de l'Ordre Nat. de la Haute- Vlolta, de l'Ordre du Croissant Vert des Commores; Grand Cordon de l'Order du Tadj de l'Empire d'Iran, 1967. Address: 1 rue des Ursins Paris 4e France

AGAM, YAACOV, artist; b. Rishon Le Zion, Israel, May 11, 1928; s. Yechoshua Gibstein and Yochevet Pombrovsky; student Bezalel Art Sch., Jerusalem, Israel, 1946, Siegfried S. Gideon, Polytechnicum, Zurich, Switzerland, 1951; m. Clila Lusternik, Nov. 29, 1956; children—Ron, Orram. Came to Paris, 1951, first exhibited in one-man show in art history kinetic painting, 1953, since exhibited numerous shows and represented in mnay permanent pub., pvt. collections throughout world; executed ceiling Nat. Conv. Centre, mural for liner S.S. Shalom; participated in exptl. films, 1956-58, including Recherche, Song of the Desert, also expt. photography; pioneer kinetic, optical art movement; creator simultaneous multiscenic theatre; one man show Marlborough-Gerson Gallery, N.Y.C., 1966. Recipient prize for artistic creative research VII Biennale, Sao Paulo, Brazil, 1963. Contbr. to publs.; writer text books on conception kinetic, optical art. Home: 4 rue Charles Divry Paris XIV France Office: 26 rue Boulard Paris XIV France also care Marlborough-Gerson Gallery New York City NY 10017

AGAN, ARTHUR COLUMBUS, Jr., former air force officer; b. San Antonio, Sept. 12, 1915; s. Arthur Colombus and Mattie Belle (Todd) A.; B.S., U. Tex., 1939; grad. Air War Coll., 1953; m. Louise Stovall, Sept. 23, 1939; children—Mary Ethel, Helen Todd, Sarah Louise. Commd. 2d lt. U.S. Army AC, 1937, advanced through grades to lt. gen. USAF, 1955; various squadron duties, 1939- 42; operations and tng. staff officer Hdqrs. 8th Air Force, 1942-44; asst. air chief staff for operations USAAF, MTO, 1944; comdr. 1st Fighter Group, Italy, 1944-45; prisoner of war, 1945; with personnel services div. Hdqrs. USAAF, 1945-46, chief div., 1946; asst. chief staff personnel, later dep. personnel and adminstrn. Hdqrs. Air Def. Command, Mitchel Field, N.Y., 1946-49; comdr. 4th Fighter Wing, Andrews AFB, Washington, 1949, 33d Fighter Wing, Otis AFB, Mass, 1949-51, 32d Air Div. (Def.), Stewart AFB, N.Y., 1951; chief personnel and adminstrn. Air Command and Staff Sch., 1951-52; comdr. 58th Fighter Bomber Wing, Korea, 1953-54; dep. for operations, later chief staff CONAD Forces, Eastern CONAD Region, Stewart AFB, 1954-57; comdr. 26th Air Div. (def.), Roslyn Air Force Sta., N.Y., 1957-58, N.Y. Air Def. Sector, McQuire AFB, 1958- 59; dep. for plans, later dep. chief staff plans Hdqrs. Air Def. Command, Ent AFB, Colo., 1959-63; comdr. 26th NORAD Region, comdr. 26th Air Div., 1963-64 asst. dep. chief of staff plans and operations Hdqrs. USAF, 1964-66; vice comdr. in chief Hdqrs. USAF in Europe, 1966; comdr. Aerospace Def. Command, 1966-70; ret., 1970. Decorated Legion of Merit with 2 oak leaf clusters, D.F.C., Air Medal with 2 oak leaf clusters, Purple Heart, Bronze Star; Croix de Guerre with palm (France and Belgium). Mem. Order Daedalians. Episcopalian. Home: 1408 Santa Fe St Corpus Christi TX 78404 also 762-C Fairview Av Annapolis MD 21403

AGAR, HERBERT SEBASTIAN, author; b. New Rochell, N.Y., Sept. 29, 1897; s. John Giraud and Agnes Louise (Macdonough) A.; A.B., Columbia, 1919; A.M., Princeton, 1920, Ph. D., 1922; Litt.D., Southwestern U., Memphis, 1936; LL.D., Boston U., 1941; m. Adeline Scott, Feb. 6, 1918 (div. 1933); children—William Scott, Agnes; m. 2d, Eleanor Carroll Chilton, Apr. 11, 1933 (div. 1945); m. 3d, Barbara Lutyens Wallace, June, 1945. London corr. Louisville Courier- Jour., Louisville Times, 1929-34; author syndicated daily newspaper column, "Time and Tide" 1935-39; editor Louisville Courier- Jour., 1940- 42; lit. editor English Rev. (London), 1930-34; spl. asst. to Am. ambassador, London; dir. Brit. div. OWI London, 1943-46; dir. Rupert Hart-Davis, Ltd., London, 1951-63. Mem. Phi Beta Kappa. Editor: (with Allen Tate) symposium Who Owns America?, 1936. Served as seaman, later chief q.m. USNR, 1917-18, lt. comdr. 1942. Clubs: National Arts, Century (N.Y.C.); Savile (London). Author: (with Willis Fisher, Eleanor Carroll Chilton) (verse) Fire and Sleet and Candlelight, 1928; Milton and Plato, 1928; (with E.C. Chilton), The Garment of Praise, 1929; Bread and Circuses, 1930; The Defeat of Baudelaire (translation), 1932; The People's Choice, 1933 (Pulitzer prize for Am. History); Land of the Free, 1935; What is America?, 1936; Pursuit of Happiness, 1938; (with Helen Hill) Beyond German Victory, 1940; A Time for Greatness, 1942; The Price of Union, 1950; A Declaration of Faith, 1952; Abraham Lincoln, 1952; The Price of Power, 1957; The Saving Remnant, 1960; The Perils of Democracy 1965. Home: Beechwood Petworth Sussex England

AGAR, JOHN GEORGE, Jr., actor; b. Chgo., Jan. 31, 1921; s. John George and Lillian (Rogers) A., grad. high sch.; m. Loretta Grace Barnett Combs, May 16, 1951; children—Linda Susan, Martin David, John George III. Actor, David O. Selznick, 1946-51, Universal Studio, 1954-56; numerous pictures include Fort Apache, 1947, She Wore A Yellow Ribbon, 1948, Sands of Iwo Jima, 1949, Breakthrough, 1950, Undefeated, 1968, Chisum, 1968, Big Jake, 1970. Speaker, Republican party, 1956-68. Nat. bd. dirs. Vols. Am. Served with USAAF, 1943-46. Mem. Am. Legion. Club: Hollywood (Cal.) Hackers. Home: 4960 Noeline St Encino CA 91316

AGAR, WILLIAM MACDONOUGH, geologist, author: b. N.Y. City, Feb. 14, 1894; s. John Giraud and Agnes Louise (Macdonough) A.; grad. The Newman Sch., Lakewood, N.J., 1912; B.S., Princeton, 1916; A.M., 1920, Ph.D., 1922; D.Sc., L.I. U., 1967; m. Alida Stewart Carter, May 6, 1922; children—Alida Marie, Sylvia Carter, Catherine Macdonough, John Herbert Michael. Geologist, Anaconda Anaconda Copper Co., Butte, Mont., 1922-23; instr. geology Yale, 1923-26, asst. prof., 1926-28; asst. prof. geology Columbia, 1928-35; headmaster, trustee The Newman Sch., Lakewood, N.J., 1935- 40; vis. lectr. geology Columbia U., 1940-41; sr. geol., U.S. Geol. Survey, 1942-45; gen. publicity (writing, radio) with Fight for Freedom House, 1940-41; chmn. bd. Freedom House; with Dept. Pubic Information, UN, 1946-56; chmn. Met. region Am. Assn. for UN, 1956-59, chmn. adv. com. 1959, 60; chmn. Hampton chpt. A.R.C., 1960-63, treas. Southampton dist., 1964—; chmn. exec. council Southampton Coll.; chmn. Coll. Com. Eastern L.I., 1962-63. Author and lectr. Served as sous chef Service Sanitaire (Etats) Unis No. 16 (Am. field Service), 1917; 1st lt. Air Service (pilot), U.S. Army, with A.E.F., 1917-18. Decorated Croix de Guerre (France). Mem. Geol. Soc. Am. Democrat. Roman Catholic. Club: Southampton (N.Y.). Contbr. articles on geology to tech. jours. Formerly mem. editorial advisor bd. and contributor articles and revs. to The Commonwealth. Home: 363 Hill St Southampton NY 11968

AGASSI, JOSEPH, philosopher, educator; b. Jerusalem, Israel, May 5, 1927; s. Samuel M. and Fruma (Reichmann) Birnbaum; M.Sc., Hebrew U., Jerusalem, 1951; Ph.D., U. London, 1956; m. Judith Buber, Aug. 10, 1949; children—Tirzah, Aaron. Came to U.S., 1963. Research asso. Center for Advanced Study in Behavioral Scis., Stanford, Cal., 1956-57; lectr. London Sch. Econs., 1957-60; reader, chmn. philosophy dept. U. Hong Kong, 1960-63; asso. prof. U. Ill., 1963-65; prof. Boston U., 1965—; vis. prof. Tel Aviv, Jerusalem, 1966-67, 70-71. Served with Israeli Def. Army, 1948-49. Mem. A.A.A.S., Am. Philos. Assn., Philosophy of Sci. Assn. Author: Towards an Historiography of Science, 2d edit., 1967; The Continuing Revolution, 1968. Editor: Vol. 1 Philos. Forum New Series, 1968. Contbr. articles profl. jours. Home: 18 Clark Lane Sudbury MA 01776 Office: Boston U Boston MA 02215

AGATE, SANFORD S., corp. exec.; b. 1901; married. With Cohn-Hall-Marx Co., 1918-59; exec. v.p. United Merchants & Mfrs. Inc., also chmn. Cohn-Hall-Marx div., 1959—, also dir. Address: 1185 Park Av New York City NY 10028*

AGEE, DARRELL LEE, food co. exec.; b. Costa Mesa, Cal., June 8, 1930; s. James C. and Ruth (Smith) A.; student Santa Ana Coll., 1948, U. So. Cal., 1950; m. Betty Geladas, May 21, 1950; children—Robert D., David S., Richard R., Debra S. Accountant, Hunt Foods, Inc., Cal., 1951-53; salesman, dist. mgr., regional mgr. Frito-Lay, Inc., Cal., 1954-62, marketing dir., Dallas, 1962-64; asst. to bd. chmn. corporate devel. Pepsi Co., Inc., N.Y.C., 1964-67, v.p. operations, Dallas, 1967-68, sr. v.p., 1968—. Home: 10245 Epping Lane Dallas TX 75229 Office: 400 Frito-Lay Tower Dallas TX 75235

AGEE, SAM WILKERSON, air force officer; b. Silver City, N.M., Sept. 21, 1912; s. Sam Wilkerson and Gertrude (Robertson) A.; B.S., U.S. Mil. Acad., 1937; grad. AC Flying Sch., 1938; children by previous marriage—Robertson, Pamela Landon; m. 2d, Ida Elizabeth Ferguson, Dec. 17, 1958; children—Susan Elizabeth, Amanda Dette. Commd. 2d lt. USAAF, 1937, advanced through grades to maj. gen. USAF, 1958; comdr. 9th Air Div. (Def.), Spokane, 1955-57, 26th Air Div. (SAGE), Syracuse, N.Y., 1958-61; dir. operations, dep. chief staff operations Hdqrs. USAF, 1960- 63, dep. comdr. USAF Communications Service, 1963; now supt. N.M. Mil. Inst. Mem. Army Adv. Panel for ROTC Affairs, 1971. Mem. Assn. Mil. Colls. and Schs. U.S. (pres. 1970). Address: NM Mil Inst Roswell NM 88201

AGEE, TOMMIE, player with N.Y. Mets. Profl. Baseball Team. Address: care William A Shea Stadium Roosevelt Av and 126th St Flushing NY 11368 *

AGEE, WARREN KENDALL, educator; b. Sherman Tex., Oct. 23, 1916; s. Frederic M. and Minnie E. (Logsdon) A.; B.A. cum laude, Tex. Christian U., 1937; M.A., U. Minn, 1949, Ph.D., 1955; m. Edda Robbins, June 1, 1941; children—Kim Kathleen, Robyn Kendall. Mem. editorial staff Ft. Worth Star-Telegram, 1937-48; instr. journalism Tex. Christian U., 1948-50, asst. prof., 1950-55, asso. prof., 1955-57, prof., 1957-58, chmn. dept., 1950-58, faculty adviser student publs., 1949-58; prof. journalism, dean sch. journalism W.Va U., 1958-60; mem. ednl. adv. com. WJPB-TV, Fairmont and Weston, W.Va., 1959-60; nat. exec. officer Sigma Delta Chi, 1960-62; professor journalism, dean Evening Coll., Tex. Christian U., Ft. Worth, 1962-65; prof. journalism, dean William Allen White School of Journalism, U. Kan., Lawrence, 1965-69; dean Henry W. Grady Sch. Journalism, U. Ga., 1969—. Pub. information splst. USCG Res. Hdqrs., 1944-45. Mem. adv. screening com. journalism, com. internat. exchange of persons Conf. Bd. of Asso. Research Councils, Washington, 1958-62; mem. Am. Council on Edn. for Journalism, 1955-60, 65-67, mem. accrediting com., 1969—. Mng. dir. William Allen White Found., 1965-69, trustee, 1970—; mng. dir. George Foster Peabody Radio and TV awards, 1969—. Recipient Journalism award from the Fort Worth (Texas) Press, 1936; outstanding News Writing award Ft. Worth Professional chpt. Sigma Delta Chi, 1946; Carl Towley award, Journalism Edn. Assn., 1969. Mem. Assn. Edn. in Journalism (pres. 1958), Am. Studies Assn., also Sigma Delta Chi (president Fort Worth professional chpt. 1954-55; sec. Texas 1957-58; national v.p. campus chpt. affairs 1966-69), Kappa Tau Alpha, Alpha Chi, Phi Kappa Sigma, Alpha Sigma Lambda. Mem. Christian Church. Rotarian. Clubs: Gridiron (Ft. Worth); University (Athens, Ga.). Author: (with Edwin Emery and Phillip H. Ault) Introduction to Mass Communications, 1960, rev. edit., 1965, 70; also articles. Editor: The Press and the Public Interest, 1968; Mass Media In A Free Society, 1969. Asso. editor, bus. mgr. The Quill, 1960-62; adv. editorial bd. Journalism Quar., 1955-60. Home: 130 Highland Dr Athens GA 30601 Office: Henry W Grady Sch Journalism U Ga Athens GA 30601

AGEE, WILLIAM MCREYNOLDS, corp. exec.; b. Boise, Ida., Jan. 5, 1938; s. Harold J. and Suzanne (McReynolds) A.; B.S. in Bus. with high honors, U. Ida., 1960; M.B.A. with distinction, Harvard, 1963; m. Diane Weaver, Sept. 7, 1957; children—Suzanne E., Kathryn D., Robert W. Controller, Title Ins. Co., Boise, 1960-61; with Boise Cascade Corp., 1963—, treas., 1967-68, v.p., 1968-71, sr. v.p. 1971—; dir. Provident Fed. Savs. & Loan Assn. Trustee Boise Sch. Dist., Reed Coll. C.P.A., Ida. Mem. Am. Inst. C.P.A.'s, Ida. Soc. C.P.A.'s, Financial Execs., Inst., U. Ida. Alumni Assn. (v.p. 1967-68), Young Pres. Orgn. (nat. dir.), Beta Theta Pi. Republican. Presbyn. Home: 4005 Del Monte Dr Boise ID 83704 Office: PO Box 200 Boise ID 83701

AGEMIAN, CHARLES ALEXANDER, banker; b. Aug. 4, 1909; s. Alexander and Mary (Gurgian) A.; grad Grad. Sch. Banking Rutgers U., 1950, D.C.S. (hon.), Pace Coll., m. Mary Plumb, June 13, 1936; children—Sandra (Mrs. Malcolm A. Borg), Mary L. (Mrs. Michael Heath). With Chase Manhattan Bank (merger Bank of Manhattan Co. and Chase Nat. Bank), N.Y.C., 1927-69, v.p., comptroller, 1952-60, comptroller gen., 1959-63, exec. v.p. in charge bank operations, financial, tax depts., 1963-69; chmn. bd., chief exec. officer Garden State Nat. Bank, Hackensack, N.J., 1969—; dir., exec. com. Kinney Services, Inc., N.Y.C. Prof. advanced accounting, trustee Pace Coll., N.Y.C. Mem. Regional Adv. Com. on Banking Policies and Practices. Bd. govs. Hackensack Hosp. Mem. Am. Bankers Assn. (exec. council), Bank Adminstrn. Inst. (pres.), Beta Alpha Psi. Home: 2311 Ocean Av Spring Lake NJ 07762 also 150 Overlook Av Hackensack NJ 07601 Office: 170 Main St Hackensack NJ 07601

AGHA, MEHEMED FEHMY, art cons.; b. Nicolaieff, Russia, Mar. 11, 1896; s. Yossouf and Anna (Khoroz) A.; grad. Emperor Alexander Tech. Sch., Nicolaieff, 1913; grad. in econs., Poly. Inst. Emperor Peter the Great, Petrograd, 1918; grad Ecole Nationale des Langues Orientales Vivantes, Paris, 1923. Came to U.S., 1929, naturalized, 1936. Studio and chief Paris div. Gonde Nast, France, 1924-27, art dir. German edit. Vogue mag., Berlin, 1927-29; art dir., N.Y.C., 1929-42; dir. M. F. Agha studio, N.Y.C., 1943-70. Recipient Am. Inst. Graphic Arts medal, 1957. Hon. mem. Inst. Graphic Arts (pres. 1954-55). Clubs: Dutch Treat, Art Directors (life mem., pres. 1934-35) (N.Y.C.). Author monographs on graphic arts. Home: 140 W 57th St New York City NY 10019 also Hillview RD 2 Malvern PA 19355

AGLE, CHARLES KLEMM, architect, city planner; b. Bloomington, Ill., Oct. 19, 1906; s. Charles F. and Clara (Klemm) A.; Grad. Choate Sch., 1923-25; A.B., Princeton, 1929, M.F.A., 1931; student Am. Sch., Fontainebleau, France, 1931; divorced; children—Charles H., Kenneth C., Alan P.; m. 2d, Jo Ann Sayers, June 22, 1968. Asso., Henry Wright, Sr., city planner, N.Y.C., 1931-34; dir. planning Fed. Pub. Housing Authority, 1934-43; dir. planning Harrison, Ballard & Allen, N.Y.C., 1946-52; propr. own firm in city planning and architecture, Princeton, N.J., 1953—; mem. faculty community planning, U. Pa., 1953-54. Princeton Grad. Sch., 1956-66. Served with USNR, 1943-46. Recipient 1968 Design award U.S. Dept. Housing and Urban Devel. Fellow Am. Inst. Architects; mem. Am. Inst. Planners, Am. Soc. Planning Ofcls., Regional Assn. N.Y., Lambda Alpha. Editor, contbr. Rehousing Urban America, 1934; An Approach to Urban Planning, 1953. Author: Family Sizes and Building Types; Zoning, 1965; Community Appearance, 1969; Planned Residential Neighborhoods, 1970. Home: 247 Elm Rd Princeton NJ 08540 Office: 10 Nassau St Princeton NJ 08540

AGNELLI, GIANNI, mfg. co. exec.; b. Torino, Italy, Mar. 12, 1921; s. Edoardo and Princess Virginia Bourbon (del Monte) A.; Dr. Laws, U. Torino; m. Princess Marella Caracciolo di Castagneto; children—Edoardo, Margaret. Chmn. bd. Fiat Co., 1966—, also RIV-SKF Co., and Istituto Finanziario Industriale. Mayor of Villar Perosa. Decorated Mil. Cross of Valour. Address: 10 Corso Marcoi Torino Italy

AGNEW, ALLEN FRANCIS, geologist; b. Ogden, Ill., Aug. 24, 1918; s. Theodore Lee and Agnes Nona (Faris) A.; A.B. with highest honors, U. Ill., 1940, M.S., 1942; Ph.D., Stanford, 1949; m. Frances Marie Keiffer, Sept. 5, 1946; children—Allen Bruce, Lawrence Paul, Leslie Crae, Heather Lee. Geologist, Ill. Geol. Survey, 1939-42. U.S. Geol. Survey, 1942-55; asst. prof. geology U. Ala., 1948-49; asso. prof. geology U. S.D., 1955-57, prof., 1957-63; dir. S.D. Geol. Survey, 1957-63; prof. geology, dir. Water Resources Research Center, Indiana U., Bloomington, 1963-69; dir. Wash. Water Research Center, also prof. geology Wash. State U., 1969- -. Recipient Robert Peele award Am. Inst. Mining Engrs., 1958. Mem. Am. Inst. Profl. Geologists, Am. Geol. Inst., Nat. Water Well Assn., Nat. Assn.. of Geology Tchrs. Geol. Soc. Am., Soc. Mining Engrs. of Am. Inst. Mining, Metall. and Petroleum Engrs., A.A.A.S., Soc. Econ. Geologists, Am. Geophys. Union, Phi Beta Kappa, Sigma Xi. Home: 1500 Upper Dr Pullman WA 99163

AGNEW, ARNOLD HARVEY, newspaper editor; b. Toronto, Ont., Can., May 22, 1925; s. G. Harvey and Helen (Smith) A.; B.A., U. Toronto, 1948, M.A., 1950; m. Flora Jane Mulligan, Aug. 9, 1952; children—John, Sarah, David, Elizabeth. Reporter, Halifax (N.S., Can.) ChronicleHerald, 1948, The Canadian Press, Halifax, 1949; reporter, editor Western Morning News, Plymouth, Eng., 1950; reporter London (Eng.) Daily Express, 1951, United Press, London, 195153, The Telegram, Toronto, 1953; editorin chief Sherbrooke (Que., Can.) Daily Record, 195760; mng. editor Toronto Telegram, 1960-64, exec. editor, 1964-70, v.p., editor-in-chief, 1970—; dir. Telegram Pub. Co., 1966—. Mem. municipal council Village of Sturgeon Point, Ont., 1968—. Bd. dirs. St. John's Convalescent Hosp. Served with RCAF, 194445. Home: 87 Woodlawn Av W Toronto 190 Ontario Canada Office: 440 Front St W Toronto 135 Ontario Canada

AGNEW, BRUCE ANDRAS, journalist; b. N.Y.C., Nov. 9, 1934; s. Clark Mansfield and Gloria (Bugyi) A.; B.A., Yale, 1957; m. Patricia F. Platt. Apr. 27, 1968; 1 dau., Eleanor Jean. Reporter, Bridgeport (Conn.) Telegram, 1957-58, U.P.I., 1958-64; Washington corr. N.Y. Post, 1964-65; reporter Business Week mag., 1965—, now White House corr. Home: 2013 37th St NW Washington, DC 20007. Office: Nat Press Bldg Washington DC 20004

AGNEW, DONALD CHARLES, former assn. exec.; b. Denver, Feb. 3, 1906; s. Charles Clinton and Ella Josephine (Dunlap) A.; A.B., Park Coll., 1929; M.A., Duke, 1932, Ph.D., 1936; m. Lucile Quillen, Mar. 30, 1934; children—Jocelyn Elizabeth, Edith Lucile. Tchr. English, Joplin (Mo.) Sr. High Sch., 1929-31; faculty edn. Winthrop Coll., Rock Hill, S.C., 1933-34; faculty edn. and psychology, head dept. Lander Coll., Greenwood, S.C., 1936-37; faculty philosophy, psychology, edn. Coker Coll., 1937-38, registrar, 1938-39, acting dean, 1939-40, dean, 1940-44, dir. Summer Sch., 1941, acting pres., 1943-44, pres., 1944- 52; chmn. div. community service Oglethorpe U., Atlanta, 1952, pres. univ., 1957-64; exec. sec. commn. on colls. and univs. So. Assn. Colls. and Secondary Schs., 1955- 57, dir. edn. improvement project, 1964-65, acting dir., 1965-66, dir. edn. improvement project, 1966-68, asso. dir. assn., 1968-71. Mem. UN Assn. (Atlanta pres. 1967-69). Presbyn. Author: The Effect of Varied Amounts of Phonetic Training on Primary Reading (monograph), 1939; Southern Association of Colleges and Schools, Seventy Five Years of Educational Leadership, 1970. Home: 3178 Lanier Dr NE Atlanta GA 30319

AGNEW, DWIGHT LUTHER, univ. dean; b. Grand Junction, Colo., Dec. 28, 1911; s. Charles C. and Ella (Dunlap) A.; A.B., Park Coll., 1935; M.A., State U. Ia., 1938, Ph.D., 1947; m. Elizabeth Godard, Aug. 8, 1938; 1 son, David Bruce. Tchr. Cortez (Colo.) Pub. Schs., 1935-37; mem. faculty Waukon (Ia.) Jr. Coll., 1938-42; mem. faculty Stout State U., Menomonie, Wis., 1947—, chmn. dept. social sci., 1947-65, dean Sch. Liberal Studies, 1965—. Chmn. Menomonie Selective Service Bd., 1964—. Trustee, pres. Mabel Tainter Library, 1970—. Served with AUS, 1942-46. Mem. Assn. Higher Edn., Am. Hist. Assn., Wis. Acad. Scis., Arts and Letters, Menomonie C. of C. (pres. 1969-70). Republican. Conglist. Kiwanian. Author: (with others) History of Wisconsin State Universities, 1968. Contbr. to Ency. Britannica. Home: 907 Oakwood Blvd Menomonie WI 54751

AGNEW, FRANK E., Jr., banker; b. Creston, Ia., Sept. 14, 1903; s. Frank E. and Elizabeth (Larimer) A.; A.B., Knox Coll., 1928, hon. degree, 1967; LL.D., Thiel Coll., 1961; m. Suzanne Kohlstaat, Nov. 29, 1930 (dec. Jan. 1971); children—Frank E. 3d, Gates Kennedy, Hewes DeMuth, Suzanne Kohlsaat II. Bookkeeper, Creston, 1923-27; trainee, traveling rep., credit man Continental Ill. Nat. Bank & Trust Co., Chgo., 1928-32; asst. to pres. Morris Plan Corp. Am., N.Y.C., 1932-33; joined Gen. Am. Life Ins. Co., 1933, asst. treas., 1934, asst. v.p., 1935-40, v.p., 1940-49; dir. Boatmen's Nat. Bank, St. Louis, 1945-53, v.p., 1950-52, exec. v.p., 1952-53; pres., dir. Old Kent Bank, Grand Rapids, Mich., 1953-55; pres., dir. Peoples First Nat. Bank & Trust Co. Pitts., chmn. successor bank Pitts. Nat. Bank, 1963—; Trustee Carnegie Mellon U., Carnegie Inst. Mem. Res. City Bankers Assn., Beta Theta Pi. Republican. Episcopalian. Clubs: Fox Chapel Golf (Pitts.); Duquesne. Home: 105 Royston Rd Fox Chapel Pittsburgh PA 15238 Office: 5th and Wood Sts Pittsburgh PA 15230

AGNEW, FRANKLIN ERNEST, III, mfg. co. exec.; b. St. Louis, Apr. 13, 1934; s. Frank Ernest, Jr. and Susanne (Kohlsaat) A.; A.B. in Econs., Princeton, 1956; M.B.A., Harvard, 1958; C.P.A., 1961; m. Dorothy Powning, Feb. 17, 1962; children—Carolyn W., Timothy S., Jennifer S. With First Nat. Bank Chgo., 1958-62, loan officer, 1960-62; with Rockwell Mfg. Co., 1963—, controller, 1963-66, v.p. mfg. power tool div., 1967-68, v.p. mfg. valve div., 1968- 69, v.p. finance, 1969—. Served with AUS, 1959. Mem. Am. Inst. C.P.A.'s. Financial Execs. Inst., Council Financial Execs., Pitts. C. of C. Clubs: University, Fox Chapel Golf (Pitts.). Home: 170 Forest Dr Pittsburgh PA 15238 Office: 400 N Lexington Av Pittsburgh PA 15208

AGNEW, HAROLD MELVIN, physicist; b. Denver, Mar. 28, 1921; s. Sam. E. and Augusta (Jacobs) A.; A.B., U. Denver, 1942; M.S. U. Chgo., 1948, Ph.D., 1949; m. Beverly Jackson, May 2, 1942; children—Nancy E. (Mrs. Jack B. Owens), John S. With Los Alamos Sci. Lab., 1943-46, alternate div. leader, 1949-61, leader weapons div., 1964-70, dir., 1970—; pres. Blaws Corp., 1967—; sci. adviser Supreme Allied Comdr. in Europe, Paris, France, 1961-64. Chmn., Army Sci. Adv. Panel, 1965—; mem. aircraft panel Pres.'s Sci. Adv. Com., 1965- ; mem. USAF Sci. Adv. Bd., 1957-69, Def. Sch. Bd., 1965—; mem. Gov. N.M. Radiation Adv. Council, 1959-61. Mem. Los Alamos Bd. Ednl. Trustees, 1950-55, pres., 1955. Mem. N.M. Senate, 1955-61; sec. N.M. Legislative Council, 1957-61; chmn. N.M. Senate Corp. Commn., 1957-61. Recipient Ernest Orlando Lawrence award AEC, 1966. Fellow Am. Phys. Soc.; mem. Phi Beta Kappa. Sigma Xi, Omicron Delta Kappa. Home: 1459 46th St Los Alamos NM 87544 Office: PO Box 1663 Los Alamos NM 87544

AGNEW, JAMES BLANCHARD, banker; b. Bklyn., Nov. 4, 1915; s. John Paterson and Roberta (Blanchard) A.; grad. Am. Inst. Banking, 1952, Stonier Grad. Sch. Banking, Rutgers U., 1960; m. Virginia Kerwin, Jan, 28, 1943; children—Nancy (Mrs. Nancy Wimmers), John R. With Chase Nat. Bank, N.Y.C., 1933-37, Mfrs. Trust Co., N.Y.C., 1937-58; with Franklin Nat. Bank, Mineola, N.Y., 1958-68, sr. v.p., 1966-68; sr. v.p. Security Nat. Bank, Huntington, N.Y., 1968—. Mem. Harbour Green Civic Assn., 1960—. Served with USAAF 1941-45. Mem. Robert Morris Assos., N.Y. Credit and Financial Mgmt. Assn., Commerce and Industry Assn. N.Y. (council 1964—). Club: Old Westbury (N.Y.) Golf and Country (bd. govs. 1964—), treas., 1967—). Home: 110 Fairfax Rd Massapequa NY 11758 Office: 280 Park Av New York City NY 10017

AGNEW, JANET MARGARET, ret. librarian; b. St. Paul, Nov. 1, 1903; d. Harry M. and Emmeline Marie (Brigham) A.; A.B., U. Manitoba, 1925, A.M., 1930; B.L.S., McGill U., 1933. Instr. library sch. McGill U., 1933-38; asst. prof. library sch. La. State U., 1939-42; librarian Sweet Briar Coll., 1942-47, Bryn Mawr College, 1947-69, formerly head librarian. Member A.L.A., Am. Assn. U. Profs., Bibliog. Society Am., Am. Assn. U. Women, Phila. Art Alliance. Compiler: Southern Bibliography, 1939-42. Home: 201-1319 Newport Av Victoria British Columbia Canada

AGNEW, MRS. SPIRO THEODORE, b. Balt.; d. W. Lee and Ruth Elinor (Schafer) Judefind; m. Spiro T. Agnew, May 27, 1942; children—Pamela Lee, James Rand, Susan Scott, Elinor Kimberley. Wife of v.p. of U.S. Address: Sheraton Park Hotel Washington DC 20008

AGNEW, SPIRO THEODORE, vice pres. U.S.; b. Balt., Nov. 9, 1918; s. Theodore S. and Margaret (Akers) A.; student Johns Hopkins; LL.B., U. Balt.; m. Elinor Isabel Judefind, May 27, 1942; children—James Rand, Pamela Lee, Susan Scott, Elinor Kimberly. Former claims adjuster Lumbermens Mut. Casualty Co., then personnel mgr. Shreiber Food Stores; admitted to Md. bar; formerly engaged pvt. practice law, Balt. and Baltimore County; then mem. firm Karl F. Steinmann; chmn. Baltimore County Bd. ·Appeals, 1958-61; Baltimore County chief exec., 1962-66; gov. Md., 1967-69; vice pres. U.S., 1969—. Chmn. transp. com. Nat. Assn. Counties, 1963. Served as officer AUS, 1941- 45, 51. Decorated Bronze Star. Mem. Md., Balt. bar assns. Republican. Episcopalian. Kiwanian. Address: 2600 Connecticut Av NW Washington DC 20008

AGNICH, FRED JOSEPH, corp. exec.; b. Eveleth, Minn., July 19, 1913; s. John and Angeline (Jerman) A.; B.A. in Geology, U. Minn., 1938; m. Ruth Harriet Welton, Apr. 19, 1941; children—William F., Richard J., James R. With Geophys. Service, Inc., Dallas, 1937-61, exec. v.p., 1951-56, pres., 1956-59, chmn. bd., 1959-61; v.p., dir. Tex. Instruments, Inc., Dallas, 1959-61; owner, operation Landfall Ranch, Lewisville, Tex., 1958-62, Caddo Creek Ranch, LaRue, Tex., 1961—; chmn. bd. Scama Corp., Dallas; chmn. bd. Western States Gas Producing Co., 1965—, also dir.; dir. Southwest Resources, Inc., Houston. Chmn., Dallas County Republican Party, 1966-69. Mem. U.S. Dept. Interior Nat. Adv. Bd. Sport Fisheries and Wildlife, 1970. Bd. dirs. Dallas Theatre Center, Dallas Pilot Inst. for Deaf; bd. govs. Greehill Sch., Dallas, 1956—, chmn, 1960-64. Mem. Tex. Ho. of Reps., 1970—. Mem. Am. Assn. Petroleum Geologists, Soc. Exploration Geophysicists, Am. Mgmt. Assn., Dallas Council World Affairs (dir. 1959- 60), U. Minn. Alumni Assn. (dir.). Clubs: Dallas Executives (pres. 1960- 61), Petroleum, Country (Dallas). Home: 5206 Kelsey Rd Dallas TX 75229 Office: 1st Nat Bank Bldg Dallas TX 75202

AGOOS, JULIAN ELIHU, leather co. exec.; b. Boston, June 26, 1919; s. Solomon and Florence (Montwid) A.; B.S., Harvard, 1940. With Allied Kid Co., Boston, 1940—. pres., 1964—, also dir. Home: 44 Young Rd Weston, MA 02193. Office: 209 South St Boston MA 02111

AGOR, GEORGE FRANKLYN, banker; b. Mahopac Falls, N.Y., Apr. 2, 1912; s. Alfred D. and Mabel (Morse) A.; grad. Am. Inst. Banking, 1934; m. Dorothy Ives Smith, Aug. 23, 1952. Cashier, Mahopac Nat. Bank, 1934-45; with State Bank Albany (N.Y.), 1945—, trust officer, 1956—, v.p., 1958—. Served with USAAF, 1942-45. Home: 42 Douglas Rd Delmar NY 12054 Office: 69 State St Albany NY 12201

AGOSTA, VITO DANTE, educator; b. N.Y.C., July 26, 1923; s. John and Elizabeth (Alvares) A.; M.S. in Engring., U. Mich., 1949; Ph.D., Columbia, 1959; m. Mary Frago, Aug. 9, 1952; children—John Diana, Charles. Thermodynamicist, DeLaval Steam Turbine Co., 1946-47; mem. faculty Bklyn. Poly. Inst., 1950—, prof. aerospace engring., 1962—; press. populsion Scis., Inc., Huntington, N.Y., 1966—, mem. sci. adv. bd. Camin Labs., N.Y.C. Served with AUS, 1943-45. Mem. Am. Inst. Aero. and Astronautics, Combustion Inst., Am. Assn. U. Profs., Am. Soc. M.E., Sigma Xi. Tau Beta Pi. Research on combustion instability in rocket motors; supersonic combustion of two phase system; air and thermal pollution; air breathing propulsion design; heat transfer analysis. Home: 42 Cherry Lane, Huntington, NY 11743. Office: Route 110 Farmingdale NY 11735

AGOSTINELLI, MARIO, sculptor, painter; b. Arequippa, Peru, Sept. 18, 1923; s. Eugenio Filomena (Fernandez-Davila) A.; student in Argentna, Brazil, France and Italy; m. Lori Nedel, Aug. 15, 1957. Came to U.S., 1953, naturalized, 1962. One- man shows include Berkshire (Mass.) Mus., also numerous shows in Chgo., Detroit, Dallas, Los Angeles, San Francisco, Pitts., Boston, Miami, Fla., N.Y.C., Venice, Italy, Rio de Janeiro, Argentina, China and Spain; nat. exhbns. include Allied Artists, Butler Inst. Am. Art, Conn. Acad., Knickerbocker Artists, Miami Nat. Painting Exhbn., Nat. Acad. Design, Nat. Arts Club, Painters and Sculptors Soc. N.J., State Expn., Norfolk (Va.) Mus., Sarasota Ann. at John and Mabel Ringling Mus., Silvermine Guild ann. Springfield (Mass.) Mus. Eastern State Expn., Berkshire Mus. at Berkshire Art Assn. Ann., Internat. Bienal Sao Paulo, Brazil; rep. permanent collections Acad. de Bellas Artes, Buenos Aires, Mus. Modern Art, Rio de Janneiro. Springfield (Mass.) Mus., also pvt. collections. Recipient prize Allied Artists, Berkshire Mus. (2), Conn. Acad.; 1st prize in oil, hon. mention Nat. Arts Club; Samuel F. Morse medal for oil Nat. Acad. Design; Gold medal for oil, hon, mention Knickerbocker Artists; prize Painters and Sculptors Soc. N.J.; Gold medal Salon of Watercolor, Lima, Peru; Gold medal for oil Salon Nacional Artists and Painters, Rio de Janeiro; Silver medal Societe des Artistes Francaise, Paris; premio acquision Socidad des Artistes Escritores de Buenos Aires; purchase prize Springfield Mus. Home: 420 E 79th SE New York City NY 10021 Office: care Beilin Gallery 655 Madison Av New York City NY 10021

AGOSTINI, PETER, sculptor; b. N.Y.C., Feb. 16, 1913; s. Salvatore and Jeva (Vulicevic) A.; student Leonardo da Vinci Art Sch.; m. Dura Swart, Jan., 1940; m. 2d, Marian Brian, June, 1945 (dec. 1961). Exhibited one man shows including Stephen Radich Gallery, N.Y.C., 1960, Richard Gray Gallery, Chgo.; also numerous group shows; rep. permanent collections U. Tex., U. Cal., U. So. Cal., Internat. Ladies Garment Workers Union, also pvt. collections; lectr. Columbia, 1961. Recipient Longview awards, 1960-62; Brandeis U. award, 1964. Home: 151 Av B New York City NY 10009 Office: 613 E 12th St New York City NY 10009

AGRONSKY, MARTIN ZAMA, radio-TV news analyst; b. Phila. Jan. 12, 1915; s. Isador Nathan and Marcia (Dvorin) A.; B.S., Rutgers U., 1936, M.A. (hon.), 1949; m. Helen Smathers, Sept. 1, 1943; children—Marcia, Jonathan, David, Julie; m. 2d, Sharon Hines, Apr. 22, 1971. Gen. reporter Palestine Post, Jerusalem, 1936-37; free lance contbr. newspapers, mags., 1937-40; NBC corr. Geneva, Belgrade, Sofia, Ankara 1940-43; war corr. Libya, Greece, Singapore, Java, Australia, Pacific, 1940-43; Washington corr. ABC, 1943- 64, former NBC radio and TV corr., Washington corr. Today Show; Washington corr. for CBS, 1964; Paris corr., bur. chief CBS, 1964—. Recipient Peabody award for distinguished reporting, 1952. Heywood Broun award for radio reporting Am. Newspaper Guild, 1948, Alfred Dupont award for distinguished reporting and commentary, TV, 1962, Nat. Headliners award TV reporting, 1962, Venice Film Festival award for documentary Polaris Submarine—Jour. Undersea Voyage, 1963. Mem. Congl. Radio- TV Corr. Assn. (pres. 1953), Omicron Delta Kappa (hon. mem.). Clubs: Federal City, Overseas Writers, Nat. Press (Washington). Home: 2605 Tilden Pl NW Washington DC 20008 Office: CBS Paris Bureau 35 Rue Marfeuf Paris France

AGUS, JACOB BERNARD, clergyman; b. Swislocz, Poland, Nov. 8, 1911; s. Judah Leib and Bela (Bereznitsky) Agushewitz; came to U.S., 1927, naturalized, 1929; A.B., Yeshiva U., 1933; A.M., Harvard, 1938, Ph.D., 1939; m. Miriam Shore, June 16, 1940; children—Zalman, Edna (Mrs. Lawrence Povich), Robert, Deborah. Ordained rabbi, 1935; rabbi Temple Ashkenaz, Cambridge, Mass., 1935-39, Agudas Achim North Shore. Chgo., 1939-41, Beth Abraham, Dayton, O., 1942-50; Beth El Cong., Balt., 1950—; adj. prof. religion, hist. Jewish thought Temple U., 1968-71; prof. Rabbinic Judaism reconstructionist Rabbinical Coll., 1969-71. Mem. bds. Balt. brs. Nat. Conf. Christians and Jews, Am. Jewish Com.; mem. bd. Balt. Asso. Jewish Charities and Welfare Fund. Mem. Rabbiniral Assembly Am., United Synagogues Am. Mem. B'nai B'rith (nat. urban commn.). Author: Modern Philosophies of Judaism, 1940; Guideposts in Modern Judaism, 1954; Banner of Jerusalem, 1946; The Evolution of Jewish Thought, 1959; The Meaning of Jewish History, 2 vols., 1963; The Vision and the Way, 1966; Dialogue and Tradition, 1971. Mem. bd. editors Judaism quarterly, 1950—; cons. editor for Ency. Britannica works on Judaism, Jewish history, 1957-68. Home: 7906 Winterset Av Baltimore MD 21208 Office: 8101 Park Heights Av Baltimore MD 21208

AHEE, JOE, former adj. gen. Ariz.; b. Scranton, Pa., Feb. 2, 1914; s. Solomon and Sarah (Haddad) A.; B.S. in Bus. Adminstrn., U. Ariz., 1938; grad. Command and Gen. Staff Coll., 1944, 51, 58, 59; m. Ann Louise Martin, Dec. 4, 1943; 1 son, Joseph Edward. Joined U.S. Army, 1938, commd. 2d lt., 1939, advanced through grades to col., 1954; asst. mil. attache, Egypt, 1941- 42; tank bn. comdr., Europe, 1943-47; chief tactics dept. Armored Sch., 1948-50; assigned mil. mission to Venezuela, 1952-55; chief tng. div. 5th Army, 1955-57, N.G. Bur., 1960-63; comdr. Ft. Douglas, Utah, 1964-65; ret., 1965; adj. gen. Ariz., 1965-66; now sr. adviser Nat. Tng. Center, Vietnam. Decorated Silver Star, Legion of Merit, Bronze Star with oak leaf cluster, Purple Heart with 2 oak leaf clusters; Croix de Guerre (Luxembourg and Belgium). Mem. N.G. Assn. U.S., N.G. Assn. Ariz., Nat. Rifle Assn., Assn. U.S. Army. Home: 625 N Van Buren Av Tucson AZ 85711

AHERN, JOHN IRENAEUS, Utility exec.; b. Weymouth, Mass., June 28, 1907; s. John W. and Catherine (Leary) A.; B.B.A., Boston U., 1930; m. Marion Whitney Brown, Apr. 22, 1936. Trainee, Weymouth Light & Power Co., 1929-30, sales and advt., 1930-34;

asst. mdse. mgr. New Eng. Power Service & Engring. Corp., 1934-36, editor, 1936-37, publicity dir., 1937-47; asst. v.p., dir. pub. relations New Eng. Electric System, Boston, 1947-50, v.p., 1950- -; pres., dir. Mass. Electric & Gas Assn.; pres. Mass. Electric Co., 1968—; v.p., dir., New Eng. Power Service Co.; mem. investment com. Union Warren Savs. Bank; finance com. dir. Boston Mut. Life Ins. Co.; dir. exec. com. Westville Homes Corp.; trustee exec. com. Amoskeag Co., Union Warren Savs. Bank. Dir., mem. exec. com. Mass. Bus. Devel. Assn., Fed. St. Capital Corp. Mem. exec. com. Mass. Com. Caths., Protestants and Jews; bd. govs. Boston U. Human Relations Center, Mass. Safety Council. Bd. dirs., exec. com. Boston chpt. A.R.C.; bd. dirs. Family Counseling and Guidance Centers, Boston, Eunice K. Shriver Center for Mental Retardation; trustee Regis Coll., Walter E. Fernald State Sch.; bd. advisers Stonehill Coll; mem. pres. council Boston Coll. Served to lt. comdr. USNR, 1942-46. Clubs: Algonquin, Clover (Boston). Home: 32 Hickory Cliff Rd Newton MA 02164 Office: 20 Turnpike Rd Westboro MA 01587

AHERN, JOHN JOSEPH, automotive co. exec.; b. Chgo., Sept. 20, 1913; s. James F. and Loretta (Bradley) A.; B.S., Ill. Inst. Tech., 1935; m. Gladys Curtin, June 24, 1936; children—Owen Curtin, Janet Arlene. Engr. Mich. Inspection Bur., 1935-38; spl. agt. Ins. Co. of N.A., Detroit, 1939-42; chief tng. unit and indsl. safety sect., safety and security div. Office Chief of Ordnance, 1942-45; prof. fire protection and safety engring. Ill. Inst. Technology, 1945-59, dir. dept., 1946-59; dir. security Gen. Motors Corp., Detroit, 1959—; former cons. engr. fires, explosives and tech. safety, fire protection to corps., pvt. and govtl. agencies. Civil service commr., Chgo., 1953-59; fire protection cons. Secretary of Def.; cons. AEC. Vice pres. Greater Chgo. Safety Council, 1950-52, pres. 1952-55; sec. Pres. Conf. Fire Prevention, 1947. Registered profl. engr., Ill. Mem. Nat. Fire Protection Assn. (dir., chmn. electronic computer com. v.p., pres. 1970—), Automobile Mfrs. Assn. (chmn. safety and health com.), Greater Detroit Bd. Commerce (chmn. fire prevention com. 1966-68), Engring. Soc. of Detroit, Internat. Assn. Fire Chiefs, Western Soc. Engrs., Am. Soc. Safety Engrs. (exec. com.), Am. Ordnance Assn., Soc. Fire Protection Engrs. (pres. 1950-53), Am. Assn. U. Tchrs. Ins., Am. Soc. Indsl. Security (past pres., past chmn. bd., past dir.). Contbr. profl. jours. Home: 3485 Bradway Blvd Birmingham MI 48010 Office: Gen Motors Corp Detroit MI 48202

AHERNE, BRIAN, actor; b. Kings Norton, Worcestershire, Eng.; s. William deLacy and Louise (Thomas) A.; student Malvern Coll., U. London (Eng.); m. Eleanor de Liagre. Appeared on English stage, in Brit. films, 1924—; appeared on N.Y. stage in The Barretts of Wimpole Street, Lucrece, Romeo and Juliet, St. Joan, Othello, The French Touch, Escapade, The Constant Wife, Quadrille, My Fair Lady, Dear Liar; starred in motion pictures in What Every Woman Knows, I Live My Life, The Constant Nymph, Beloved Enemy, The Great Garrick, Merrily We Life, Juarez, Captain Furry, My Son, My Son, The Lady in Question, Hired Wife, The Man Who Lost Himself, Skylark, Smilin' Through, My Sister Eileen, A Night to Remember, What A Woman, Smart Woman, The Swan, Titanic, The Best of Everything, Susan Slade. Office: William Morris Agy 151 El Camino Dr Beverly Hills CA 90212

AHERNE, JOHN ROBERT, coll. pres.; b. Phila., July 18, 1912; s. John P. and Anna D. (Bradley) A.; A.B., Villanova U., 1935, Litt.D., 1959; A.M., Cath. U., 1939. Ordained priest Roman Cath. Ch., 1938; tchr. Villanova Sch., Ojai, Cal., 1939-42; vice prin. St. Augustine Sch., San Diego, 1943-53, prin., 1953- 62; v.p., dean Merrimack Coll., North Andover, Mass., 1962-68, pres., 1968- -. Address: Merrimack Coll North Andover, MA 01845

AHIDJO, AHMADOU, pres. Cameroon; b. 1924; ed. Ecole Superieure d'Adminstrn., Yagunde; hon. degrees Univs. Montreal, Duquesne, Pitts., N.Y. Formerly engaged in radio adminstrn.; rep. to Rep. Assembly Cameroon, 1947; formerly sec. Assembly, pres. adminstrv. affairs com. and v.p.; counsellor Assembly of French Union, 1955-58, also former sec.; pres. Territorial Assembly of Cameroon, 1956-57; minister interior, 1957-59; dep. prime minister, 1957-58; prime minister, 1958- 59; prime minister, minister interior Ind. State of Camaroon, 1960; pres. Cameroon, 1960-61, of Fedn. Cameroon, 1961—. Pres., Groupe d'Union Camerounaise. Recipient various fgn. decorations; Titulaire Etoile Noire du Benin. Address: Office of Pres Post Box 1085 Yaoundem Cameroon*

AHL, GEORGE WILLIAM HOWARD, assn. exec.; b. N.Y.C., Feb. 22, 1908; s. C.A. William and Josephine (Johnson) A.; student Pratt Inst. Design, 1926-28, Ecole des Beaux Arts, 1928-29; B.Arch., N.Y.U., 1931; student Columbia; m. Muriel L. Schillinger, Dec. 19, 1936; 1 son, David Howard. Architect, Crow, Lewis & Wick, 1931-33; gen. purchasing agt. Columbia Ribbon & Carbon Mfg. Co., 1933-48; dir. purchases Philip Morris Co., 1948-55; exec. sec.-treas. Nat. Assn. Purchasing Mgmt., 1955-60, exec. v.p., 1960—; lectr. Manhattan Coll., also Columbia Graduate Sch. Bus. Adminstrn. Mem. Nat. Indsl. Conf. Bd.; sec., treas. NAPA Purchasing Ednl. Found., 1968—. Vice pres. bd. edn., Dist. 12, N.Y.C. Decorated knight Royal Rosarians of Rose City, Portland, Ore.; recipient Shipman gold medal, 1965. Mem. Nat. Assn. Purchasing Mgmt. (pres. 1954-55; Harry L. Erlicher award 1962), Purchasing Mgmt. Assn., N.Y. (pres. 1949-50), Am. Soc. Assn. Execs., Am. Ordnance Assn., Am. Mgmt. Assn., Pratt Archtl. Club. Lutheran. Home: 48 Nassau Blvd Malverne NY 11565 Office: 11 Park Pl New York City NY 10007

AHLBERG, CLARK DAVID, univ. pres.; b. Wichita, Kan., May 23, 1918; s. Grant and Sue (McGuire) A.; A.B., U. Wichita, 1939; M.A., Syracuse (N.Y.) U., 1942, Ph.D., 1951, LL.D., 1969; m. Rowena Osborn, Aug. 8, 1941; children—Val Jeanne (Mrs. Marshall A. Blake), Thomas G., John C. Grad. fellow, instr. polit. sci. dept. Syracuse U., 1940-42, research dir., Washington Office, 1948-51, asst. dean Coll. Engring., N.Y., 1951-54, asst. prof., 1951-54, v.p. adminstrn. and research, 1959-68, prof. polit. sci. Maxwell Sch. Citizenship and Pub. Affairs, 1959-68; personnel asst. Panama Canal, 1942-43; staff mem. President's Sci. Research Bd., Washington, 1947; personnel researcher Nat. Bur. Standards, Washington, 1947-48; pres. Syracuse U. Research Corp., 1959-68, Syracuse U. Press, 1959-68; pres. Wichita State U., 1968—. Bd. dirs. Wichita Area Community Action Program, Wichita Com. on Fgn. Relations., Kan. region Nat. Conf. Christians and Jews, NIH. Served with AUS, 1944-46. Mem. Am. Assn. State Colls. and Univs., Am. Council on Edn., Assn. Am. Colls., Assn. Urban Univs., Inst. Internat. Edn., Inst. Logopedics (trustee), Kan. Assn. Colls. and Univs., Nat. Council for Tchr. Accreditation, N. Central Assn. Colls. and Secondary Schs., Wichita State U. Library Assos., Phi Eta Sigma, Phi Kappa Phi. Clubs: University (Wichita), Wichita Books and Authors. Author: (with John C. Honey) Attitudes of Scientists and Engineers About Their Government, 1950. Editor: Agency and Departmental Statements on Research and Development Administration, 1947. Contbr. articles profl. jours. Home: 1820 N Hillside St Wichita KS 67214 Office: 1845 Fairmount St Wichita KS 67208

AHLBERG, JOHN HAROLD, educator, mathematician; b. Middletown, Conn., Dec. 10, 1927; s. John Ludwig and Olga (Anderson) A.; B.A., Yale, 1950, M.A. in mathematics, 1954, Ph.D., 1956; M.A. in physics, Wesleyan U., 1952. Chief math. analysis United Aircraft Research Labs., East Hartford, Conn., 1956-68; prof. applied mathematics Brown U., 1958—; vis. lectr. Soc. Indsl. and Applied Mathematics, 1969-71; grad. lectr. Trinity Coll., 1959-68. Mem. Am. Math. Assn., Am. Math. Soc., Sigma Xi. Author: (with E.N. Nilson and J.L. Walsh) Theory of Splines and Their Application, 1967. Contbr. articles profl. jours. Home: Deepwood Dr Amston CT 06231 Office: Brown Univ Providence RI 02912

AHLBERG, THORSTEN JACOB, pub. co. exec.; b. Des Moines, June 28, 1921; s. Thorsten J. and Mabel (Ruecker) A.; B.S. in Bus. Adminstrn., Northwestern U., 1943; m. Eileen Barrett, Jan. 29, 1945; children—Jan L., Jeanne F., James T. With Row, Peterson & Co., textbook pubs., 1946-62, treas., 1947-62; company merged with Harper & Bros. (1962) to become Harper & Row, treas., 1962-66, sr. financial v.p., 1966-68; bus. mgr., controller Columbia U. Press, N.Y.C., 1968—. Served with USNR, 1943-45. Home: 251 Kensett Rd Manhassett NY 11030 Office: 440 W 110th St New York City NY 10025

AHLBRANDT, ROGER SHERIDAN, steel exec.; b. Middletown, O., Apr. 4, 1912; s. G.F. and Jeannette Helen (Jones) A.; B.S., U.S. Naval Acad., 1934; m. Virginia C. Witherow, Apr. 13, 1940; children—Roger Sheridan, Virginia Crossan. Student observer Ludlum Steel Co., Pitts., 1934, Allegheny Steel Co. merged with Ludlum into Allegheny Ludlum Steel Corp., 1938, dist. mgr., 1939-42, 45- 48, asst. mgr. cutting tools, 1948, mgr. stainless bar sales, 1950, treas. 1951-65, v.p., asst. to pres., 1965-66, exec. v.p., 1966-67, pres., 1967—, chief exec. officer, 1968—, also dir.; dir. Ajax Forging & Casting Co., Titanium Metals Corp. Am., True Temper Corp., Wallingford Steel Co., I.P.M. Corp., Arnold Engring. Co., Carmet Co., Spl. Metals Corp., Mellon Nat. Bank & Trust Co., Regional Indsl. Devel. Corp., Jacobson Mfg. Co. Trustee Shadyside Hosp.; bd. dirs. St. Margaret Meml. Hosp.; bd. dirs., mem. exec. com. Allegheny Conf. on Community Devel. Served from lt. (j.g.) to lt. comdr., USNR, 1942-45. Mem. Am. Iron and Steel Inst. (dir.), Pa. Soc., Newcomen Soc. N.Am. Clubs: Fox Chapel Golf, Duquesne, Rolling Rock (Pitts.); Laurel Valley Golf; Twenty-Nine (N.Y.C.). Home: 9 Edgewood Rd Fox Chapel Pittsburgh PA 15215 Office: Oliver Bldg Pittsburgh PA 15222

AHLEM, LLOYD HAROLD, coll. pres.; b. Moose Lake, Minn., Nov. 7, 1929; s. Harold Edward and Agnes (Carlson) A.; A.A., North Park Coll., 1948; A.B., San Jose State Coll., 1952, M.A., 1955; Ed.D., U. So. Cal., 1962; m. Anne T. Jensen, Dec. 29, 1952; children—Ted, Dan, Mary Jo, Carol, Aileen. Tchr. retarded children Fresno County (Cal.) Pub. Schs., 1953-54; psychologist Baldwin Park (Cal.) Sch. Dist., 1955-62; prof. psychology Stanislaus State Coll., Turlock, Cal., 1962-70; pres. North Park Coll., Chgo., 1970—, dir., 1966-70. Recipient distinguished alumnus award, North Park Coll., 1966. Licensed psychologist, Cal. Mem. Am. Psychol. Assn. Mem. Winnetka (Ill.) Covenant Ch. Home: 2101 Greenwood St Wilmette IL 60091 Office: 5125 N Spaulding St Chicago IL 60625

AHLERS, ELEANOR EMILY, educator; b. Seattle, Washington, May 16, 1911; d. Francis Richard and Elizabeth Frances (Prior) Ahlers; A.B., U. Wash., 1932, M.A., 1957; B.S. in Library Sci., U. Denver, 1942; student U. Cal., summer 1948. Tchr., librarian, South Bend, Wash., 1932-36, Mt. Vernon, 1936-42; high sch. librarian, Everett, Wash., 1942-53, also supr. sch. libraries, 1952-53; asst. prof. library sci., sch. edn. U. Ore., 1953-57; exec. sec. Am. Assn. Sch. Librarians, div. A.L.A., 1957-61; supervisor of library services Washington Dept. of Public Instrn., Olympia, 1961-66; asso. prof. Sch. Librarianship. U. Wash., 1966-70, prof., 1970—; instr. tchr.-librarian courses U. Wyo., summers, 1945, 46, San Jose State Coll., summers 1947, 52; asst. dir. workshop for sch. librarians Central Wash. Coll. Edn., summer 1951; coordinator workshop for sch. librarians U. Ore., summer 1956; dir. sch. librarians workshop Kan. State Tchrs. Coll., summer 1964. Member Am. Assn. Sch. Librarians (president 1965-66), American Library Association, National Edn. Assn., Wash. Sch. Library Assn., Phi Beta Kappa, Pi Lambda Theta, Mortar Board, Kappa Delta. Episcopalian. Contbr. articles library, edn. periodicals; editor bulls. in field. Home: 2360 43rd St E Seattle WA 98102

AHLERT, ROBERT CHRISTIAN, educator; b. N.Y.C., Jan. 22, 1932; s. Christian William and Elma Adelaide (Wessel) A.; B.Chem. Engring., Polytech. Inst. Bklyn. 1952; M.S., U. Cal. at Los Angeles, 1958; Ph.D. (N.Am. Aviation fellow), Lehigh U., 1964; m. Barbara Grace Aldrich, June 5, 1954; children—Christi Ann, William King, Michael David. Jr. engr. chem. constrn. div. Am. Cyanamid Co., Linden, N.J., 1951, jr. chem. engr. Calco div., Bound Brook, N.J., 1952-54; research engr. Rocketdyne div. N.Am. Aviation, Inc., Canoga Park, Cal., 1954-56, sr. research engr., 1956-58, engring. supr., 1958-62, sr. tech. specialist, 1962-64, research group leader, 1964; asso. prof. Rutgers U., 1964-69, prof. chem. and biochem. engring., exec. dir. :Bur. Engring. Research, 1970—. Mem. White Twp. (Warren County) Bd. Edn., 1967—, v.p., 1969, pres., 1970; treas., mem. exec. com. Easton YMCA Aquatic Club, 1969—. Fellow Am. Inst. Chemists; asso. fellow Am. Inst. Aeros. and Astronautics; mem. Am. Inst. Chem. Engrs. (mem. or chmn. various coms.), Am. Soc. Testing and Materials, Am. Soc. Engring. Edn., Sigma Xi, Tau Beta Pi, Phi Lambda Upsilon. Contbr. numerous articles profl. jours. Home: PO Box 27 Buttzville NJ 07829

AHLFORS, LARS VALERIAN, mathematician; b. Helsingfors, Finland, Apr. 18, 1907; s. Karl Axel and Sieva (Helander) A.; Ph.D., U. Helsingfors, 1930; LL.D., Boston Coll., 1951; m. Erna Lehnert, June 22, 1933; children—Cynthia, Vanessa, Caroline. Adj. math. U. Helsingfors, 1932-35, prof., 1938-44, asst. prof. math. Harvard, 1935-38; prof. U. Zurich, 1944-46; asso. prof. Harvard, 1946, prof. math., 1946—, named W.C. Graustein prof., 1964, chmn. math. dept. 1948-50. Recipient Field's medal for math. research Internat. Congress of Mathematicians, Oslo, 1936. Mem. Am. Math. Soc., Am. Math. Assn., Societas Scientiarum Fennica, Academia Scientarum Fennica, Swedish Royal, Nat. acads. sci., Club: Faculty (Harvard). Author: Complex Analysis, 1953. Contbr. papers on conformal mapping, Riemann surfaces, others brs. Theory of Function of a Complex Variable to profl. lit. Home: 236 Beacon St Boston MA 02116 Office: Harvard Cambridge MA 02138

AHLGREN, FRANK RICHARD, editor; b. Superior, Wis., June 25, 1903; s. Oscar John and Beatrice Marie (Gibson-Taylor) A.; student Lane Tech. High Sch., Chgo., 1918- 19, Superior (Wis.) State Tchrs. Coll., 1922-25, Memphis U. Law Sch., 1926-28; Dr. Civil Laws, Southwestern Coll.; m. Elizabeth Alley, Feb. 25, 1932; children—Frank Richard, Gibson-Taylor, Calvin Lane. Reporter, Superior (Wis.) Evening Telegram, 1923-24, Duluth (Minn.) Herald, 1924- 25, Milwaukee (Wis.) Jour. 1925-26, Memphis (Tenn.) Evening Appeal, 1926-33, Tex. Newspaper Publishers Assn., Houston, 1934-36, Cleve. Press, 1936-37; editor Memphis Comml. Appeal, 1937-68. Lectr. journalism Memphis State U. Trustee U. Tenn.; bd. dirs. Methodist Hosp., Memphis Pub. Library; mem. Memphis-Ark. Bridge Commn. Mem. Sigma Delta Chi Kappa Tau Alpha. Episcopalian. Mason. Clubs: Tenn., Rotary, Memphis Country, Hunt and Polo (Memphis); National Press. Pres. Am. Council Edn. for Journalism. Home: 2714 Lombardy Memphis TN 38111

AHLGREN, GILBERT HAROLD, agronomist; b. South St. Paul, Dec. 25, 1913; s. Carl Oscar and Hilda Christina (Peterson) A.; S.B., U. Wis., 1936; S.M., Rutgers U., Ph.D., 1941; m. Mildred Elizabeth Wyers, Sept. 11, 1943; children—Lynn Dianne, Alice, William. Asst. agronomy U. Wis., 1936-37; asst. agronomy Rutgers U., 1937-38, instr. agronomy, 1939-41, asst. agronomist N.J. agrl. expt. sta., 1941-42, asso. agronomist, asso. prof., 1942-43, chmn., farm crops dept. prof., 1943—; agt. U.S. Dept. Agr. 1938-39. Pres., Northeastern Weed Control Conf., 1947, 48; agronomist Internat. Devel. Services, Nigeria, 1957, agrl. edn. adviser, Burma, 1961-62; agronomist U.S. AID, South Vietnam, 1962-66, dep. asst. dir. agr. 1966-67; chief of party IRI Research Inst., Rio di Janeiro, 1967-70; agrl. cons., 1970—. Mem. Am. Soc. Agronomy, Genetics Soc. Am., Sigma Xi (sec. Rutgers chpt. 1945-46), Delta Theta Sigma. Republican. Presbyn. Author: Practical Field Crop Production for the Northeast, 1947, rev. edit. 1952; Forage Crops, 1949, rev. edit. 1956; Principles of Weed Control, 1951; Grassland Farming, 1955. Home: 12 Eggers St East Brunswick NJ 08816

AHLGREN, HENRY L., univ. chancellor, scientist; b. Wyoming, Minn., Oct. 3, 1908; s. Carl Oscar and Hilda Christine (Peterson) A.; B.S., U. Wis., 1931, M.S., 1933, Ph.D., 1935, traveling fellow, Europe, 1936; m. Harriet Gleason, Feb. 1, 1936; children—David Lawrence, Margaret Louise. Mem. faculty U. Wis., 1929—, prof. agronomy 1944—, chmn. dept. agronomy, 1949-52, asso. dir. agrl. extension, 1952—, asst. chancellor univ. extension, 1966-67, vice chancellor univ. extension, 1967-69. chancellor univ. extension, dir. coop. extension service, 1969—; dep undersec. for rural devel. U.S. Dept. Agr., 1970—. Recipient Distinguished Service award Dept. Agr., 1962. Fellow Am. Soc. Agronomy (pres. crops and sci. divs. 1953-54); mem. Royal Swedish Soc. Forestry and Agr., Sigma Xi, Phi Eta Sigma, Alpha Zeta, Phi Kappa Phi, Phi Sigma, Delta Theta Sigma. Author: AgronomyPrinciples and Practices (with R.J. Delorit), 1953. Teaching, research pasture improvement. Home: 24 Park Pl The Highlands Madison WI 53705

AHLSCHWEDE, ARTHUR MARTIN, church ednl. ofcl.; b. Seward, Neb., Dec. 5, 1914; s. Herman F. and Elizabeth (Birky) A.; B.S. in Edn., Concordia Tchrs. Coll., Seward, 1941, Litt.D., 1962; M.A., U. Minn., 1949; m. Marie S. Spomer, Nov. 27, 1942; children—Carol, Kathleen, Nancy. Prin., Luth. elementary schs., Hepler, Kan., 1935-37, Gillett, Ark., 1937-40, Mpls., 1942-49; prin. Concordia High Sch., St. Paul, 1949-53; acad. dean Concordia Coll., St. Paul, 1953-56; asst. exec. sec. bd. higher edn. Luth. Ch.-Mo. Synod, St. Louis, 1956-61, exec. sec., 1961—, chmn. div. higher edn., 1962—; mem. div. edn. Luth. Council U.S., 1966—. Recipient Christus Primus award Concordia Coll., Ann Arbor, Mich. 1965. Mem. Minn. Pvt. Sch. League, Luth. Edn. Assn., Internat. Walther League, Luth. Laymen's League, Gamma Sigma Delta, Phi Delta Kappa. Democrat. Home: 7575 Lindbergh Dr Richmond Heights MO 63117 Office: 210 N Broadway St Louis MO 63102

AHLSTROM, SYDNEY ECKMAN, educator: b. Cokato, Minn., Dec. 16, 1919; s. Joseph T. and Selma (Eckman) A.; B.A. Gustavus Adolphus Coll., 1941; M.A., U. Minn., 1946; Ph.D., Harvard, 1952; m. Nancy Ethel Alexander, Aug. 8, 1953; children—Joseph Alexander, Promise Ann, Constance Burton, Sydney Eckman. Tutor history Harvard, 1948-51, instr., 1952-54; mem. faculty Yale, 1954- -, prof. Am. history and modern ch. history, 1964—; chmn. Am. Studies Program, 1967—; mem. faculty Salzburg Seminar Am. Studies, 1949, 52; vis. prof. Princeton, spring 1962. Trustee Gustavus Adolphus Coll., 1967- -. Served to capt., Transp. Corps, AUS, 1942-46. Mem. Am. Hist. Assn., Am. Soc. Ch. History, Am. Studies Assn. Lutheran. Author: (with G. H. Williams, editor) The Harvard Divinity School, 1954; (with J.W. Smith, editor), The Shaping of American Religion, 1961; The American Protestant Encounter with World Religions, 1962; (with G.L. Hunt, editor) Calvinsim and the Political Order, 1965; A Religious History of the American People; also articles. Author and editor: Theology in America, 1967. Home: 99 Armory St New Haven CT 06511

AHMANN, JOHN STANLEY, educator; b. Struble, Ia., Oct. 17, 1921; s. Henry Frank and Philomena (Wictor) A.; B.A., Trinity Coll., 1943; B.S., Ia. State U., 1947, M.S., 1949, Ph.D., 1951; m. June Vivian Hudek, June 23, 1948; children-Sandi Ann, Sheri Kay, Gregory Steven, Shelly Joan. Instr. profl. studies Ia. State U., 1949-51; asst. prof. div. ednl. psychology and psychol. measurement Cornell U., 1951-54, asso. prof., 1954-58, prof., 1958-60; prof. psychology Colo. State U., 1960—, also asso. dir. Human Factors Research Lab., 1969—, asst. to pres., 1961-64, head dept. psychology, 1962-64, acad. v.p., 1964-69; vis. prof. Colo. State U., 1951, Wash. State U., 1960, Western Wash. State Coll., 1970. Cons. research programs U.S. Office of Edn., Dept. Health, Edn. and Welfare; cons. for evaluation of ednl. programs in Colo., N.Y., La., Hawaii; dir. various fed. and state sponsored research projects. Served with USNR, 1943-46; PTO. Fellow A.A.A.S.; mem. Am. Psychol. Assn., Am. Statis. Assn., Am. Ednl. Research Assn., Nat. Council on Measurement in Edn., Sigma Xi, Phi Kappa Phi, Phi Delta Kappa, Phi Lambda Upsilon, Alpha Chi Sigma, Psi Chi. Author: Statistical Methods in Educational and Psychological Research, 1954; Evaluating Pupil Growth, 4th edit., 1971; Evaluating Elementary School Pupils, 1960; Testing Student Achievements and Aptitudes, 1962; Measuring and Evaluating Educational Achievment 1971. Home: 717 Cherokee Dr Fort Collins CO 80521

AHMANN, MATHEW HALL, social action dir.; b. St. Cloud, Minn., Sept. 10, 1931; s. Norbert T. and Chlotilda (Hall) A.; B.A., St. John's U., 1952; postgrad. student U. Chgo., 1953-54; m. Margaret Cunningham, Sept. 18, 1954; children—Elizabeth Thomas, Teresa, Timothy, Ruth, Katherine. Social worker Chgo. Dept. Welfare, 1954-56; business and circulation mgr. Today mag., 1956-57; field rep. Catholic Interracial Council, Chgo., 1957-59, asst. and acting dir., 1959-60; exec. dir. Nat. Cath. Conf. Interracial Justice, 1959-68; exec. dir. Commn. on Ch. and Society, Archdiocese San Antonio, 1969—, organizer, exec. sec. Nat. Conf. Religion and Race, 1962-63. Pres. Project Equality Tex. Exec. com. Lithurgical Conf., nat. exec. bd. Workers Def. League; bd. govs. Center Research and Edn. in Am. Liberties; adv. bd. Law Students Civil Rights Research Council. Mem. Am. Civil Liberties Union. Editor: The New Negro, 1961; Race: Challenge to Religion, 1963; (with Margaret Roach) The Church and the Urban Racial Crisis; Editorial bd. Integrated Edn. Office: PO Box 13190 San Antonio TX 78213

AHN, KWANG SOO, Korean diplomat; b. Seoul, Korea, Sept. 5, 1925; s. Byong Bum and Ok Shik (Chang) A.; student Japanese Mil. Acad., 1941-45, Am. Lang. Inst., 1946-47, U.S. Inf. Sch., 1954-55, U.S. Command and Gen. Staff Coll., 1958-59; m. Sa Bong Han, Feb. 22, 1949; children—Grace, June, Sukkyu. Commd. 2d lt. Korean Army, 1948, advanced through grades to col., 1955; ret., 1961; joined Korean Fgn. Service, 1961; assigned Fgn. Ministry, Seoul, 1961; consul gen. in Los Angeles, 1961-70. Trustee Korean Community Centre, Los Angeles. Recipient 7 decorations, also 15 awards from Korea. Mem. Los Angeles World Affairs Council, Town Hall Los Angeles, Los Angeles County Mus. Buddhist. Home: 1089 Queen Anne Pl Los Angeles CA 10019

AHOUA, TIMOTHEE N'GUETTA, diplomat of Ivory Coast; b. Aboisso, Ivory Coast, Apr. 25, 1931; s. Moise N'Guetta and Assan (Aka) A.; bachelor degree in Pub. Law and Polit. Sci., U. Paris, 1961; student Nat. Sch. French Magistracy of Paris, 1959-62; diploma Inst. Overseas Higher Studies, U. Paris, 1963, m. Germaine Rochemont; 1 son, Philippe. Tng. in French embassy, Bonn, Germany, Acad. Internat. Law, Hague, Netherlands, WHO, ILO, Geneva, Switzerland, 1962-63; 1st counselor Ivory Coast, Washington, 1964-65; ambassador of Ivory Coast to Morocco, 1965- 66, to U.S., 1966—, to Can., 1967—. Home: 5111 Broad Branch Rd NW Washington DC 20008 Office: 2424 Massachusetts Av NW Washington DC 20008

AHR, GEORGE WILLIAM, bishop; b. Newark, N.Y., June 23, 1904; s. Geoge and Mary (Mueller) A.; A.; student St. Vincent's Coll., 1918-23, Seton Hall Coll., 1923-25, N. American Coll., Rome, 1925-29; A.B., A.M., S.T.D. Ordained priest, Roman Cath. Ch., 1928; asst. St. Mary's Ch., Jersey City, 1929, St. Venantius Venantius Ch., Orange, N.J., 1929-30; faculty mem. Seton Hall Coll., South Orange, N.J., 1930-33, Immaculate Conception Sem., Darlington, N.J., 1933-50; rector, 1948-50; elected bishop Roman Cath. Diocese of Trenton, N.J., Jan. 28, 1950, consecrated, Mar. 20, 1950. Home: 901 W State St Trenton, NJ 08618 Office: 701 Lawrenceville Rd Trenton NJ 08638

AHRENDT, KARL FREDERICK, educator, composer; b. Toledo, Mar. 7, 1904; s. Frederick and Amelia (Manthey) A.; B.Mus., Cin. Conservatory Music, 1936; M.Mus., Eastman Sch. Music, U. Rochester, 1937, Ph.D., 1946; m. Christine Colley, June 10, 1933; 1 dau., Elaine. Music study in Berlin, Germany, 1924-25, Paris, France, 1926-28; violinist, condr. in radio and theatre, 1929-34; asso. prof. violin and theory Fla. State Coll., 1937-44, also dir. Sch. Music, prof. composition and violin; condr. orch. Augustana Coll., Rock Island, Ill., 1946- 50; dir. Sch. Music, Ohio U., Athens, 1950-67, now prof. music. Recipient Eurydice composition prize Arts Alliance Phila., 1946; Mac Dowell colonist, summers 1950, 51, 56, 58, 64-66. Mem. Music Tchrs. Nat. Assn., Am. String Tchrs. Assn., Phi Mu Alpha (Sinfonia). Lutheran. Compositions: Symphonic Prelude for Orchestra, 1937; Suite for String Quartet, 1940; 67th Psalm for women's voices and piano, 1944; Symphony No. 1, 1946; Recitative, Variations and Canzona for String Quartet, 1948; Symphonic Profile, "Johnny Appleseed" for orchestra, 1950; Prelude for Orchestra, Pastorale for Strings, 1958; String Quartet, 1962; 100th Psalm for mixed chorus, 1964; Allelulia for chorus and orch., 1965; Variegations for woodwind quintet, 1967; The Lord Sun cantata for chorus, soloist, narrator and orch., 1968; Textures for String Quartet, 1970. Home: Peach Ridge Rd RD 3 Athens OH 45701

AHRENHOLZ, HERMAN WILLIAM, mining engr., educator; b. N.Y.C., Nov. 1, 1916; s. Herman W. and Louise (Reipschlager) A.; B.A. in Geology, Lehigh U., 1938, B.S. in Mining Engring., 1938, Engr. Mines, 1949; student Colo. Sch. Mines, summer 1937; m. Gladys L. Telleen, Oct. 28, 1939; 1 son, Glenn James. Teaching fellow Mass. Inst. Tech., 1938-39; mining engr. N.J. Zinc Co., 1939-49, mine supt., 1954-57; asst. prof., then asso. prof. mining engring. W.Va., U., 1949-54; prof. mining engring. U. Ala., 1957—, head Sch. Mines, 1961-70, dir. engring. extension, 1970—; mining cons. N.J. Zinc Co., Ga. Marble Co., U.S. Bur. Mines, Ala. Power Co., others, 1957—. Registered profl. engr., W. Va., Ala. Mem. Soc. Mining Engrs., Am. Inst. Mining, Metall. and Petroleum Engrs. (chmn. Rock Mechanics unit 1968—), Sigma Gamma Epsilon. Author articles in field. Home: 281 Woodland Hills Tuscaloosa AL 35401 Office: Box 1466 University AL 35486

AHRENS, EDWARD HAMBLIN, Jr., physician; b. Chgo., May 21, 1915; s. Edward Hamblin and Pauline (Forsyth) A.; grad. Hotchkiss Sch., 1933; B.S. magna cum laude, Harvard, 1937, M.D. cum laude, 1941; m. Gertrude A. Fobes, Sept. 12, 1940; children—Sandra Huntington, Peter Forsyth, Burgess. Intern Babies Hosp. of N.Y., 1942-43, chief resident, 1951-52; research asst. Rockefeller U., 1946-49, asso., 1952-58, asso. prof., 1958-60, prof., 1960—; prof. medicine Cornell U. Med. Coll., 1970—; sci. adv. council Blythedale Children's Hosp., 1965—. Sr. fellow NRC and Nat. Found. Infantile Paralysis, 1949- 52; mem. metabolism study sect. USPHS, 1956-61, chmn., 1959-61; editor Jour. Lipid Research, 1963-69, pres. Lipid Research, Inc., 1963—; mem. bd. sci. counselors National Heart Inst., 1963-67; sci. adv. com. New Eng. Regional Primate Center, 1963-69; tech. adv. com. Inst. Human Nutrition, Columbia, 1966—; mem. Stouffer prize selection com., 1966-69; mem. gen. clin. research centers com. NIH, 1970—; chmn. diet-heart rev. panel NHLI, 1967-68. Diplomate Am. Bd. Pediatrics. Mem. Am. Soc. Biol. Chemists, Assn. Am. Physicians, Am. Soc. Clin. Investigation, Harvey Soc., Soc. Exptl. Biology and Medicine, Phi Beta Kappa. Home: 125 Park Av Bronxville NY 10708 Office: Rockefeller U 66th St and York Av New York City NY 10021

AHRENS, MAURICE RUSSELL, educator; b. O'Fallon, Ill., Nov. 22, 1902; s. Charles Augustus and Victoria (Russell) A.; A.B., Culver Stockton Coll., 1925; M.A., U. Denver, 1938, Ed.D., 1947; student U. Chgo., 1940-41; m. Martha Virginia Carter, Dec. 25, 1924; children—Virginia Anne (wife of Dr. David C. Stone), Mary Jean. Supt. schs., Hunnewell, Mo., 1924-26; tchr. pub. schs., Lamar, Colo., also Denver, 1928-38; supr. pub. schs., Denver, 1938-45, dir. instrn., 1945-49; collaborator Human Devel. Center, U. Chgo., 1940-41; asst. supt. charge instrn. pub. schs., Battle Creek, Mich., 1949-51; dir. curricular services, pub. schs. of Corpus Christi, Tex., 1951-54; prof., head dept. elementary edn. U. Fla. Coll. Edn., 1955-60, prof., asst. dean for curriculum, 1960-66, prof., chmn. dept. curriculum and instrn., 1966-70, prof. edn., 1970—, cons. Childcraft, Field Enterprise, Inc., 1960-63. Mem. N.E.A., Assn. Supervision and Curriculum Devel. (v.p. 1951-52, 53-54, pres. 1952-53), Assn. Childhood Edn. Internat., Am. Assn. U. Profs., Phi Delta Kappa. Author: (with N.F. Bush, R. K. Easley) Laboratory Problems for Living Chemistry, 1959, Living Chemistry, rev. edit., 1961. Editor: The Junior High School Program, 1958, Communications and Learning Skills, 1971. Editorial adv. bd. The Instructor, 1953-67. Contbr. articles ednl. periodicals. Home: 1704 NW 10th Av Gainesville FL 32601

AHRENS, RUDOLF MARTIN, educator; b. St. Louis, Feb. 6, 1928; s. Georg F. and Hildegard (zur Nedden) A.; student Heidelberg U., 1946-47; Ph.D., Washington U., 1952; m. E. Alexandra Bjoenness, May 25, 1953; children—Hanno, Cristofer. Nuclear engr. Convair, Ft. Worth, 1952-54; dept. mgr. nuclear analysis Lockheed Aircraft Corp., Marietta, Ga., 1954-57; faculty Ga. Inst. Tech., Atlanta, 1957—, prof. physics, 1966—; vis. scientist Max Planck, Inst., Munich, 1959-60; vis. prof. U. S.C., Columbia, 1967-68. Vice pres. Advanced Research Corp., 1962-64. Mem. N.Y. Acad. Scis., A.A.A.S., Sigma Xi. Home: 673 Kenilworth Ct Stone Mountain GA 30083 Office: Physics Dept Ga Inst Tech Atlanta GA 30332

AHRENS, WILLIAM HENRY, architect; b. N.Y.C., May 12, 1925; s. John Karl and Sophie (Hashage) A.; A.B. in Architecture, Princeton, 1950, M.F.A., 1953; student R.I. Sch. Design, 1946, Tehran U., 1960; m. Joyce Nolan, Mar. 27, 1951. Chief architect Litchfield, Whiting, Bowne, Iran, 1958-61, Rome, 1961-64; dir. internat. operations Whiting Assos., Rome, 1964-67; prin. partner Ahrens Di Grazia Prizzell, Rome, Italy, 1967—; dir. Internat. Cons. Services, SRL, Rome. Chmn. lay council finance com. Santa Susanna Ch., Rome, 1970—. Served with USAAF, World War II; PTO. Recipient Book award A.I.A., 1953, Pub. Service award Tehran Lions Club, 1961. Mem. A.I.A., N.Y. State Soc. Architects. Clubs: Princeton (N.Y.C.); American (Rome). Prin. archtl. works include ITT Sheraton Hotel, Tunisia, 1971, Kingdom of Saudi Arabia correctional instns., 1970. Home: 6 Via delle Terme Deciane Rome Italy Office: 11 Viale America Rome Italy 00144

AHRENSFELD, THOMAS FREDERICK, lawyer; b. Bklyn., June 30, 1923; s. Frederick Herman and Madeline Florence (Moffett) A.; A.B., Bklyn. Coll., 1948; LL.B., Columbia, 1948; m. Joan Ann McGowan, Mar 17, 1944; 1 son, Thomas Frederick. Admitted to N.Y. bar, 1948; asso., then partner Conboy, Hewitt, O'Brien & Boardman, N.Y.C., 1948-58; sec., asso. gen. consel Philip Morris Inc., N.Y.C., 1959-70, v.p., gen. counsel, 1970—. Served to 1st lt. USAAF, 1942-45. Decorated D.F.C. with clusters, Air medal with clusters. Mem. Assn. Bar City N.Y., Am. Bar Assn. Presbyn. (elder). Club: New York Athletic. Home: 85 Nannahagan Rd Pleasantville NY 10570 Office: 100 Park Av New York City NY 10017

AIBEL, HOWARD JAMES, corp. exec., lawyer; b. N.Y.C., Mar. 24, 1929; s. David and Anne (Fishman) A.; A.B. magna cum laude, Harvard, 1950, LL.B. cum laude, 1951; m. Katherine Walter Webster, June 6, 1952; children—David Webster, Daniel Walter, Jonathan Brown. Admitted to N.Y. bar, 1952; asso. firm White & Case, N.Y.C., 1952-57; with Gen. Electric Co., 1957-64, litigation counsel, 1960-64; with Internat. Tel. & Tel. Corp., 1964—, sr. v.p., gen. counsel; dir. ITT World communications, ITT Continental Baking Co., ITT Canteen Corp., Internat. Standard Electric Co. Home: 21 Berkely Rd Westport CT 06880 Office: 320 Park Av New York City NY 10022

AIKEN, CONRAD POTTER, critic, poet; b. Savannah, Ga., Aug. 5, 1889; s. William Ford and Anna (Potter) A.; A.B., Harvard, 1911; m. Jessie McDonald, Aug. 25, 1912 (div. 1929); children—John Kempton, Jane Kempton, Joan Delano; m. 2d, Clarice Lorenz, 1930 (div. 1937); m. 3d, Mary Augusta Hoover, July 7, 1937. Consultant American letters Library of Congress. Author: (poems) Earth Triumphant and Other Tales, 1914; Turns and Movies, 1916; The Jig of Forslin, 1916; Nocturne of Remembered Spring, 1917; The Charnel Rose, 1918; The House of Dust, 1920; Punch, The Immortal Liar, 1921; Priapus and the Pool, 1922; Pilgrimage of Festus, 1923; Scepticisms—Notes on Contemporary Poetry, 1919; Priapus and the Pool, and Other Poems, 1925; Bring! Bring! and Other Stories, 1925; Blue Voyage (novel), 1927; Costumes by Eros (short stories), 1928; John Deth, and Other Poems, 1930; The Coming Forth by Day of Osiris Jones (poem), 1931; Preludes for Memnon (poems), 1931; Great Circle (novel), 1933; Among the Lost People (short stories), 1934; Landscape West of Eden (poems), 1934; King Coffin (novel), 1935; Time in the Rock (poems), 1936; A Heart for the Gods of Mexico (novel), 1939; The Conversation (novel), 1939; And in the Human Heart (poems), 1940; Brownstone Eclogues (poems), 1942; The Soldier, 1944; The Kid (poem) 1947; The Divine Pilgrim (poem), 1949; Skylight One (poems), 1949; Mr. Arcularis (play, with Diana Hamilton), 1949; The Short Stories of Conrad Aiken, 1950; Ushant: An Essay (an autobiography), 1952; Collected Poems, 1953; A Letter from Li Po (poems) 1956; Mr. Arcularis, 1957; Sheepfold Hill (poems), 1957; A Reviewer's ABC (criticism), 1958 (published as Collected Criticism 1968); The Collected Short Stories of Conrad Aiken, published 1960; Selected Poems, 1961; The Morning Song of Lord Zero (poems), 1963; The Collected Novels of Conrad Aiken, 1964; A Seizure of Limericks (poems), 1964; Cats and Bats and Things with Wings (poems), 1965; Tom, Sue, and the Clock (poem), 1966; Preludes (poems), 1966; Thee (poem), 1968; Collected Poems: 1916-1970, 1970; The Clerk's Journal, An Undergraduate Poem, 1971. Editor: Modern American Poets, 1922; Selected Poems Emily Dickinson, 1924; Am. Poetry (1671-1928), 1929; 2Oth Century American Poetry (anthology), 1963. Contbr. to Poets on Poetry, criticism, 1965. Compiler: Selected Poems, 1929. Contbg. editor, Dial, 1917-19. Awarded Pulitzer prize for best vol. of verse, 1929; Bryher Award, 1952, Nat. Book award for Collected Poems (1954). Apptd. to chair of poetry Library of Congress, 1950-52, fellow in Am. letters, 1947. Awarded Bollingen Prize, 1956; fellowship Am. Acad. Poets, 1957; gold medal for poetry Nat. Inst. Arts and Letters, 1958; Huntington Hartford Found. award in lit., 1961; St. Botolph award, 1964; Brandeis medal for poetry, 1967; National Medal for Lit., 1969. Mem. Am. Acad. Arts and Letters. Home: Brewster MA 02631

AIKEN, GEORGE DAVID, U.S. senator; b. Dummerston, Vt., Aug. 20, 1892; s. Edward W. and Myra A. (Cook) A.; grad. Brattleboro (Vt.) High Sch., 1909; m. Beatrice M. Howard, 1914 (dec.); children—Dorothy Howard (Mrs. Harry Morse), Marjorie Evelyn (Mrs. Harry L. Cleverly), Howard George (dec.), Barbara Marion (Mrs. Malcolm Jones); m. 2d, Lola Pierotti, June 30, 1967. With small fruit farm, 1912; started comml. cultivation of wildflowers, 1926. Sch. dir., Putney, Vt., 1920-37; mem. State Ho. of Reps., 1930-33, speaker 1933-34; lt. gov. Vt., 1935-37, elected Gov., 1937-41; elected to U.S. Senate, 1940, to fill vacancy for term ending Jan. 3, 1945; reelected, 1944—. Mem. Windham Co. Farm Bur., Vt. Hort. Soc. (pres. 1917-18), Putney Grange. Republican. Odd Fellow. Author: Pioneering with Wildflowers, 1933; Pioneering with Fruits and Berries, 1936; Speaking From Vermont, 1938. Home: Putney VT 05346 Address: Senate Office Bldg Washington DC 20510

AIKEN, HENRY DAVID, educator; b. Portland, Ore., July 3, 1912; s. Frank Bethel and Miriam (Boskowitz) A.; A.B., Reed Coll., 1935; M.A., Stanford, 1937; M.A., Ph.D., Harvard; m. Jean Flagler Scott; children—Katharine, Perry; m. 2d, Lillian Woodworth, Feb. 17, 1951; 1 son, David; m. 3d, Helen Rowland Geer, Nov. 17, 1958; children—Paula Hume, Henry David. Asso., Columbia, 1944-45; asst. prof. U. Wash., 1945-46; asso. prof. Harvard, 1946-54, prof. philosophy, 1954-65; prof. philosophy and history of ideas Brandeis U., 1965-67, Charles Goldman prof. philosophy, 1967—. Vis. prof. U. Mich., Ann Arbor, 1953. Guggenheim fellow, 1960- 61; Alfred North Whitehead fellow Harvard, 1968-69. Mem. Am. Soc. Polit. and Legal Philosophy, Am. Philos. Assn., Am. Psychol. Assn., Am. Soc. Aesthetics. Democrat. Author: The Age of Ideology; Value: A Cooperative Inquiry; Reason and Conduct, 1962; The Predicament of the University, 1971. Co- editor: Philosophy in the Twentieth Century, 1962; book editor Jour. Philosopy, 1945-52; cons. editor Philos. Review, 1950-54. Contbr. articles to profl., lit. jours. Home: 110 Deacon Haynes Rd Concord MA 01742 Office: Brandeis U Waltham MA 02151

AIKEN, WILLIAM HAMBLEN, paper co. exec.; b. Salado, Tex., May 24, 1916; s. Carl and Anna (Hamblen) A.; B.S. in Chem. Engring., Tex. A. and M. Coll., 1938; M.S. in Chemistry, Inst. Paper Chemistry, 1940, Ph.D., 1942; m. Rosemary Polk, Aug. 1, 1942; children—Rosemary, William Hamblen. Asst. mgr. chem. div. Goodyear Tire & Rubber Co., 1946-52; tech. dir. Gardner Board & Carton Co., 1952-59; v.p. research and devel. engring., dir. Personal Products Corp., 1959-61; v.p. research and devel. Union Bag-Camp Paper Corp. (now Union Camp Corp.), 1961-70, v.p. tech., 1970—. Served to maj. AUS, 1942-46. Fellow A.A.A.S., T.A.P.P.I. (exec. com. 1961-64, pres. 1967-69, recipient award 1971); mem. Am. Chem. Soc., N.Y. Acad. Sci., Am. Nat. Standards Inst. (dir. 1966-70), Sigma Xi. Home: 87 Brookstone Dr Princeton NJ 08540 Office: Box 412 Princeton NJ 08540

AIKIN, CHARLES, educator; b. Bellefontaine, O., Aug. 27, 1901; s. John Patton and Rebecca Ethel (Gustin) A.; B.A., Muskingum Coll., 1924; LL.B., Ohio State U., 1927; Ph.D. (George Eastman fellow), Brookings Grad. Sch., 1930; m. Audrey Marie Kelly, Sept. 25, 1928. From instr. to asso. prof. polit. sci. U. Cal. at Berkeley, 1928-46, prof. polit. sci., 1946—, chmn. dept. polit. sci. 1956-62, 65-66, asst. dean Coll. Letters and Sci., 1941- 42, 49-55, asso. dean, 1955-56, coordinator U. Cal.-U. Bologna program in pub. administrn., 1958. Editorial cons. Chandler Press, San Francisco, 1962—. Research asst. Cal. Constl. Commn., 1930; dist. price officer OPA, San Francisco, 1942-45; asst. to vice chmn. U.S. Commn. on Orgn. Exec. Br. Govt. (Hoover Commn.), 1948-49; specialist Dept. State for Occupied Germany, summer 1950. Decorated knight Order Merit of Italian Govt. Fed. Rep. Germany grantee for study tour Western Germany, 1954; Rockefeller Found. grantee, 1960. Mem. Internat., Am., Western polit. sci. assns., Am. Econs. Assn., Am. Soc. Pub. Adminstrn., Internat. Inst. Adminstrv. Scis., Royal Inst. Pub. Adminstrn. (London), Ohio Bar Assn., Internat. Law Assn., Soc. for Encouragement Modern Art. Club: Commonwealth (San Francisco); Faculty (Berkeley). Author: National Labor Relations Board Cases, 1939; The Exchange Program for German Leaders, 1953; The Negro Votes, 1962. Contbr. articles, revs. to Am., European polit. sci., legal publs. Home: 2750 Buena Vista Way Berkeley CA 94708

AIKMAN, FRANK, Jr., r.r. ofcl.; b. Bklyn., May 27, 1910; s. Frank and Genevieve (Brown) A.; B.S., Lafayette Coll., 1932; m. Gertrude Daly, July 19, 1936; children—Susan (Mrs. Kenneth Fasick), Gretchen (Mrs. Alan Chapman), Frank III. Engring. apprentice Pa. R.R., 1934-36, asst. supr. track, 1936-39, supr. track, 1939-46; gen. supt., v.p. R.R. Siding Constrn. Co., Pitts., 1946-49; engr. maintenance of way L.I. R.R., Jamaica, N.Y., 1949-55, chief engr., 1955—, v.p., 1962-67, pres., gen. mgr., 1967-69; exec. dir. Ry. Signal and Communications Supplies Assn., N.Y.C., 1970—. Cons. transp., 1970—; adv. bd. chem. Bank N.Y. Mem. Assn. R.R.'s N.Y. State (chmn. engring. com.), Am. Assn. R.R.'s (commn. on grade crossings), Am. Soc. C.E., Am. R.R. Engring. Assn., L.I. Assn. (v.p. exec. com., dir.), Queens (dir.), Bklyn. (dir.) chambers commerce, Tau Beta Pi, Theta Chi. Republican. Methodist. Mason (32, Shriner). Clubs: New York Railroad, Unqua-Corinthian Yacht. (Amityville); Southward Ho Country (Bayshore, N.Y.); Merrywood Country (Smithtown, N.Y.). Home: 29 Braham Av Amityville NY 11701 Office: Suite 62 Statler Hotel New York City NY 10001

AIKMAN, JOHN EDGAR, lawyer; b. Brockway, Pa., Jan. 1, 1919; s. Charles E. and Lena (Smith) A.; B.S., Pa. State U., 1940; J.D., U. Pitts., 1948; m. Barbara C. Curry, Jan. 19, 1951; children—Nancy, Rebecca, John M. Fuel and power engr. U.S. Steel, Pitts., 1940-42; admitted to Pa. bar, 1949; practice in Brookville Pa., 1948-68; gen. counsel, sec. Brockway Glass Co., Inc. (Pa.), 1968—; dir. Brockway Citizens Bank. Republican state committeeman, 1964—. Trustee Clarion (Pa.) State Coll. Served with USAAF, 1942-46. Mem. Pa., Jefferson County bar assns. Home: Northview Dr Brookville PA Office: McCullough Av Brockway PA

AILES, STEPHEN, lawyer; b. Romney, W.Va., Mar. 25, 1912; s. Eugene Elliot and Sallie (Cornwell) A.; grad. Episcopal High Sch., Alexandria, Va., 1929; A.B., Princeton, 1933; LL.B., W.Va. U., 1936; m. Helen Wales, June 24, 1939; children—Hester A. Nettles, Stephen Cornwell, Walter Brady, Richard Arvine. Admitted to W.Va. bar, 1936, D.C. bar, 1946; asst. prof. law W.Va. U., 1937-40; practice in Martinsburg, W.Va., 1936-37, 40-42; mem. legal staff OPA, 1942-46, asst. gen. counsel, 1945-46; counsel U.S. Econ. Mission to Greece, 1947; practice in Washington, 1946-61, 65-70; partner Steptoe & Johnson, 1948-61, 65-70; under sec. Army, 1961-64, sec. Army, 1964-65. Pres. Assn. Am. Railroads, 1971—. Mem. Bar Assn. D.C., Am. Fed. bar assns. Clubs: Chevy Chase (Md.); Burning Tree (Bethesda, Md.); Metropolitan (Washington). Home: 4521 Wetherill Rd Westmoreland Hills Washington, DC 20016

AILEY, ALVIN, dancer; b. Rogers, Tex., Jan. 5, 1931; s. Alvin and Lula E. (Cliff) A.; student U. Cal. at Los Angeles, 1949-50, Los Angeles City Coll., 1950- 51, San Francisco State Coll., 1952-53; Lester Horton Dance Theater, Los Angeles, 1949-51, 53, with Hanya Holm, N.Y.C., 1954- 55, with Martha Graham, 1956, others; acting student with Stella Adler, 1960-62, with Milton Katselas, 1961. Choreographer, Lester Horton Dance Theater, 1953—; formed Alvin Ailey Dance Theater, 1958, performed numerous festivals, 1959—, Australian, S.E. Asian tour, 1962; actor, 1961—; choreographer, dancer TV, 1954—; also motion pictures. Performances include House of Flowers, 1954, Sing, Man, Sing, 1956, Jamaica, 1957, Carmen Jones, 1959, Call Me by My Rightful Name, 1961, My People, 1963. Address: care Dance Theatre Found Inc 229 W 59th St New York City NY 10022

AIMEE, ANOUK, actress; b. Paris, France, Apr. 27, 1932; d. H. Dreyfus and Genevieve Durand; student dance and dramatic arts; m. Nicolas Papatakis, July 21, 1951; 1 dau., Manuela; m. 2d, Pierre Barouh, Apr. 20, 1966. Motion picture appearances include La Maison Sous La Mer, 1947; Les Amants de Verone, 1950; Golden Salamander, 1959; Storm Night, 1950; Le Rideau Cramoisi, 1952; Les Mauvaises Rencontres, 1955; Tous Peuvent Me Tuer, 1957; Pot Bouille, 1957; Montparnasse, 19, 1959; Le Tete Contre Les Murs, 1958; Les Dragueurs, 1959; La Dolce Vita, 1960; Le Farceur, 1950; Lola, 1960; Les Amours de Paris, 1960; L'Imprevu, 1960; Quai Notre Dame, 1960; Le Judgement Dernier, 1961; Sodome et Gomorrhe, 1961; Les Grands Chemins, 1962; Education Sentimentale, 1962; Huit et Demi, 1962; A Man and a Woman, 1966; Un Soir, Un Train, 1967; The Appointment, 1968; The Model Shop, 1968. stage appearance in Sud, 1952. Recipient Brit. Film Acad. award as best fgn. actress, for Un Homme et Une Femme, 1968. Home: 46 Rue de Rennes Paris 6eme France

AIN, GREGORY, educator, architect; b. Pitts., Mar. 28, 1908; s. Baer and Haiah (Weissberg) A.; student physics and math. U. Cal. at Los Angeles, 1924- 26, architecture U. So. Cal., 1928; m. Agnes Budin, June 11, 1929; m. 2d, Ruth March, 1940; children—Emily, Christopher; m. 3d, Florence Page, Jan. 25, 1964. With R.M. Schindler, 1932-33, Richard J. Neutra, 1933- 35; propr. own office, 1935-63; prin. works include garden apts., park housing projects, model houses, prefabrication systems; exhbns. U.S., USSR; vis. critic U. So. Cal; prof. architecture, chmn. dept. Pa. State U., 1963-70. Guggenheim fellow, 1939; recipient prizes housing competitions. Mem. A.I.A., Assn. Collegiate Schs. Architecture. Home: 1771 N Sycamore Av Los Angeles CA 90028

AINBINDER, SEYMOUR, dept. store exec.; b. Bklyn., July 10, 1928; s. Max Z. and Sonia (Alterman) A.; student Upsala Coll., 1955, Rutgers U., 1956; m. Rose B. Cooper, Jan. 14, 1951; children—Michael, Jonathan. Pres. Almart/J.B. Hunter div. Allied Stores Corp., 1962—; v.p. Allied Stores, 1968—. Active Nat. Conf. Christians and Jews, Boy Scouts Am., Friends of Tel Aviv U. Mem. Nat. Retail Mchts. Assn. (bd. dirs.), Young Pres. Orgn. Club:

Shackamaxon Golf and Country (pres.) (Scotch Plains, N.J.). Home: 61 Mohawk Rd Short Hills NJ 07078 Office: 116 W 32d St New York City NY 10001

AINSWORTH, DOROTHY SEARS, educator; b. Moline, Ill., Mar. 8, 1894; d. Harry and Stella (Davidson) Ainsworth; A.B., Smith Coll., 1916, Sc.D. (hon.), 1956; M.A., Columbia, 1923, Ph.D., 1930. Tchr. phys. edn. Moline High Sch., 1916-18; instr. phys. edn. Skidmore Coll., 1925-26; instr. hygiene and phys. edn. Smith Coll., 1921-23, dir., prof. phys. edn., 1926-60, prof. emeritus, 1960—; cons. internat. affairs Am. Assn. Health, Phys. Edn. and Recreation, 1960—. Organizing chmn. 1st Internat. Congress on Phys. Edn. and Sports for Girls and Women, Copenhagen, Denmark, 1949, chmn. continuing com., 1949-53, co- chmn., elected pres., 2d Congress, Paris, France, 1953, pres. London, 1957, pres. Washington, (Pres.), 1961; chmn. U.S. joint council on Internat. Affairs in Health Phys. Edn. and Recreation 1950-57; mem. U.S. Com. Pan Am. Inst. Phys. Edn., 1950-56; organizing chmn. 1st Internat. Congress on Essentials of Phys. Edn. for Youth in the Conn. Valley, 1954; chmn. com. on phys. edn. World Confedn. Orgns. Teaching Profession, 1958; U.S. specialist to South Africa, 1960. Mem. Women's Def. Council, Northampton, Mass., 1942-45; with Smith Coll. Relief Unit, Grecourt, France, 1919-20. Recipient Honor award Am. Assn. Health, Phys. Edn. and Recreation, 1949, Gulick medal, 1960; Ling Gold medal Ling Gymnastic Soc., Sweden, for work in internat. affairs, 1949; Medal of Honor by Minister Edn. French Republic, 1953; Hetherington award, highest award Am. Acad. Phys. Edn., 1962; Cross of Honor from Finnish Govt., 1961; decorated comdr. Order Merite Sportif (France), 1961; recipient Woman Conscience award Nat. Council Women, 1968. Fellow Am. Coll. Sports Medicine, Am. Acad. Phys. Edn.; mem. Am. Assn. Health, Phys. Edn. and Recreation (spl. cons. internat. relations, pres.), internat. Council Health, Phys. Edn. and Recreation (pres. 1959-65, hon. pres. 1965—), Internat. Assn. Phys. Edn. and Sports Women (past pres.), Nat. Assn. Phys. Edn. Coll. Women (pres. 1937-41, hon. life mem. 1963—), New Eng. Assn., Am. Assn. U. Women, Nat. Assn. Health Phys. Edn. and Recreation (pres. 1950), Nat. Council Women U.S.A. (3d v.p. 1958), Phi Beta Kappa. Conglist. Clubs: Smith College, Cosmopolitan, Nat. Womans Republican (N.Y.C.); College (Boston); Sulgrave (Washington). Author: The History of Physical Education in 12 Colleges for Women, 1930. Editor: Individual Sports for Women, 1944, first 4 edits. 1963; (with R. Evans) Basic Rhythms, 1957. Contbr. articles profl. mags. Home: 15 Barrett Pl Northampton MA 01060

AINSWORTH, H. GARDNER, fgn. service officer; b. Charleston, S.C., Mar. 15, 1917; s. Walden Lee and Katharine (Gardner) A.; student St. Paul's Sch., Concord, N.H., 1933-35; A.B., Princeton, 1939; spl. studies Harvard, 1948-49; m. Helen Louise Reed, Aug. 25, 1940; children—Linda Gardner, Lee Thornton (Mrs. Keith C. Johnson). Apptd. fgn. service officer, 1940; service in Winnipeg, 1940, San Salvador, 1941-44, Rome, 1944-48, Washington, 1949- 51; 1st sec., Paris, 1951-54, Helsinki, 1954-57, Washington, 1957-60; Nat. War Coll., 1960; econ. counselor Rome, 1960-63, AID Regional Office Central Am., Guatemala, 1964-65; adviser to asst. sec. commerce for sci. and tech., 1965-66; econ. counselor, AID dir., Mexico City, 1966-69; dir. Office Maritime Affairs Dept. State, Washington, 1969—. Mem. Soc. Cin. Club: Chevy Chase (Md.). Address. 7711 Brookville Rd Chevy Chase MD 20015

AINSWORTH, MARY DINSMORE SALTER, (Mrs. Mary D. Ainsworth), psychologist; b. Glendale, O., Dec. 1, 1913; d. Charles Morgan and Mary (Hoover) Salter; B.A., U. Toronto, 1935, M.A., 1936, Ph.D., 1939; m. Leonard H. Ainsworth, June 10, 1950 (div. Aug. 1960). With U. Toronto, 1935-42; cons. to dir. personnel selection, maj. Canadian Women's Army Corps, 1942-45; supt. Women's rehab. Dept. Vets. Affairs, Can., 1945-46; asst. prof. dept. psychology U. Toronto, 1946-50; sr. research psychologist Tavistock Clinic, London. 1950-54; sr. research fellow E. African Inst. of Social Research, Kampala. Uganda. 1954-55; asso. prof. psychology Johns Hopkins, 1956-63, prof. psychology, 1963—; clin. psychologist Sheppard and Enoch Pratt Hosp., 1956-61. Fellow Center Advanced Study Behavioral Scis., 1967-68. Diplomate Am. Bd. Examiners Profl. Psychology. Fellow Soc. Projective Techniques, Am. Psychol. Assn.; mem. British Psychol. Soc. Author: (with A.W. Ham) Doctor in the Making, 1942; (with B. Klopfer, W. Klopfer, R.R. Holt) Developmein the Rorschach Technique, 1954; (with L.H. Ainsworth) Measuring Security in Personal Adjustment, 1958; Infancy in Uganda, 1967. Home: 7511 Club Rd Ruxton MD 21204

AINSWORTH, OSCAR RICHARD, educator; b. Vicksburg, Miss., July 28, 1922; s. Richard Henry and Harriet (Henley) A.; A.A., Hinds Jr. Coll., 1945; B.A., U. Miss., 1946, M.A., 1946; Ph.D., U. Cal. at Berkeley, 1951; m. Edith Josephine Wetzel, Dec. 20, 1947. Prof. math. U. Ala., 1950—; summer employment Redstone Arsenal, ARGMA, ABMA George C. Marshall Space Flight Center, Huntsville, Ala. 1953-62; research engr. Douglas Aircraft, Long Beach, Cal., summer 1956; applied physicist Boeing Airplane Co., Seattle, summer 1957; cons. G.C. Marshall Space Flight Center, 1962-63, research contract, 1963-64; research contracts NASA, 1965-69. Mem. Am. Math. Soc., Sigma Xi, Pi Mu Epsilon (hon.), Sigma Pi Sigma (hon.), Phi Kappa Psi. Contbr. articles profl. jours. Home: 3102 30th St Northport AL 35476

AINSWORTH, ROBERT ANDREW, Jr., U.S. judge; b. Gulfport, Miss., May 10, 1910; s. Robert Andrew and Catherine (Wursch) A.; LL.B., Loyola U., New Orleans, 1932, LL.D., 1967; LL.D., (hon.), Xavier U., New Orleans, 1953; m. Elizabeth Miern, Oct. 14, 1933; children—Elizabeth (Mrs. Clarence Rareshide), Robert Andrew III, Leslie. Admitted to La. bar, 1932; practice in New Orleans, 1932-61; U.S. judge Eastern Dist. La., 1961-66, U.S. Ct. Appeals, 5th Circuit, New Orleans, 1966—. Chmn. bd. mgrs. Council State Govts., 1955-56; mem. Charter Com. City New Orleans, 1951-52; founder La. Legislative Council, 1952; pres. Nat. Legislative Conf., 1955-56. mem. Presdl. Commn. on Govt. Relations, 1961. Mem. La. Senate from Orleans Parish, 1950-61, pres. pro tem, 1952-56, 60-61. Mem. exec. com., dir. Internat. House, 1951-58; mem. adv. council Loyola U. Law Sch.; adv. bd. Ursuline Acad. Recipient Weiss award Nat. Conf. Christians and Jews; St. Mary's Dominican Coll. medal, 1971. Mem. Jud. Conf. U.S. (chmn. com. on ct. adminstrn. 1969—), Am. Judicature Soc. (dir.), Blue Key. Democrat. Roman Catholic. Author La. Civil Service Act, also Ann. Fiscal Session Law. Adv. editors Tulane Law Rev. Home: 1776 Arabelia St New Orleans LA 70115 Office: 400 Royal St New Orleans LA 70116

AINSWORTH, STANLEY HUMPHREYS, univ. dean; b. Sault Ste. Marie, Mich., Aug. 7, 1913; s. William and Miriam (Humphreys) A.; A.B., Mich. State Normal, 1933; M.A., State U. Ia., 1937; Ph.D., Northwestern U., 1949; m. Helen Margaret Sweet, Apr. 7, 1939; children—Richard Arthur, Susan Lois. Tchr. English, coach Van Buren Consol. Schs., Belleville, Mich., 1934-37; tchr. Redford Union Pub. Schs., 1937-39; supr. speech correction, tchr. psychology and speech Itasca Jr. Coll., Coleraine, Minn., 1939-43; supr. speech correction Ind. State Tchrs. Coll., 1943-45; instr., asst. speech correction Northwestern U., 1945-46; instr. to asst. prof. speech Ohio State U., 1947-49; asso. prof. to prof. speech Fla. State U., 1949-53; prof. speech correction, chmn. program exceptional children, U. Ga., 1953-68, Distinguished prof. speech correction, 1964-68, asso. dean for research and grad. studies, 1968—; dir. research project mental retardation, on grant U.S. Office Edn., 1957-59, cons. dir. tng. Bur. for Edn. Handicapped, 1969—; cons. Nat. Inst. Neurol. Diseases and Blindness, NIH, Washington, 1965-66, Nat. Inst. Child Health and Human Development, 1966—; past mem. neurol. and sensory disease service project rev. panel, div. chronic diseases USPHS. Mem. edn. and tng. bd., sec.-treas., dir. Am. Bds. Examiners in Speech Pathology and Audiology, Bd. dirs. Speech Found. Am. Fellow of the Am. Speech and Hearing Assn. (exec. council 1953-54, exec. v.p. 1954-58, pres. 1960, recipient honors of assn.); member Am. Hearing Soc. (v.p., dir.), Ga. Rehab. Assn. (director, recipient of professional award), Speech Assn. Am., So., Georgia speech associations, American Association University Professors, Ga. Edn. Assn., Nat. Rifle Assn., Council for Exceptional Children (chmn. profl. Standords com. 1969—), Phi Kappa Phi, Pi Kappa Delta. Methodist. Author: Galloping Sounds, 1946; Speech Correction Methods, 1948. Editor: Speech and Hearing Problems in the Secondary School, 1950; asso. editor Jour. Speech and Hearing Disorders, 1949-54. Contbr. articles profl. Jours., chpts. in books. Home: 555 Forest Rd Athens GA 30601

AIRD, JOHN BLACK, lawyer; b. Toronto, Ont., Can., May 5, 1923; s. Hugh Reston and May (Black) A.; B.A., U. Toronto, 1946; LL.B., Osgoode Hall Law Sch.; m. Jane Housser, July 27, 1944; children—Lucille Elizabeth, Jane Victoria, Hugh Housser, Katherine Black. Admitted to Ont. bar, 1949; now partner firm Edison, Aird & Berlis, Toronto; gen. counsel Reed Shaw Osler Ltd.; chmn., dir. Prairie Oil Royalties Co. Ltd.; pres., dir. B.C. Oil Lands Ltd.; v.p., dir. Algoma Central Ry.; dir. Am. Metal Climax Inc., Bank of N.S., Can. Tungsten Mining Corp. Ltd., Maple Leaf Gardens Ltd., Nat. Life Assurance Co. Can., numerous others. Trustee, Hosp. for Sick Children. Served to lt. Royal Canadian Navy, 1942-45. Mem. Canadian Bar Assn., Law Soc. Upper Can., Alpha Delta Phi. Mem. Liberal party. Anglican. Clubs: Toronto, Toronto Golf; Rosedale Golf; Granite. Home: 2 Glenallan Rd Toronto 12 Ontario Canada Office: 111 Richmond St W Toronto 110 Ontario Canada*

AIRD, KENNETH, banker; b. Detroit, June 13, 1925; s. David and Laura (Strang) A.; B.B.A., U. Detroit, 1957; grad. Advanced Mgmt. Program, Harvard, 1965; m. Jean Rodda, May 1, 1948; children—Nancy, David, Brian. With Mfrs. Nat. Bank Detroit, 1942—, exec. v.p., 1970—. Served with AUS, 1943-46. Mem. Financial Execs. Inst., Bank Adminstrn. Inst. Clubs: Harvard Business of Detroit, Detroit Athletic. Home: 16567 Surrey Dr Livonia MI 48154 Office: 151 W Fort St Detroit MI 48226

AIRD, ROBERT BURNS, educator, neurologist; b. Provo, Utah; Nov. 5, 1903; s. Dr. John W. and Emily D. (McAuslan) A.; student Deep Springs (Cal.) Coll., 1921-23; A.B., Cornell U., 1926; M.D., Harvard, 1930; grad. student neurophysiology U. Pa., Mass. Gen. Hosp., Boston City Hosp., Boston Psychopath. Hosp., 1939- 40; m. Ellinor H. Collins, Oct. 4, 1935; children—Katharine, Mary, John, Robert. Intern surgery Strong Meml. Hosp., Rochester, N.Y., 1930-31, asst. resident neurosurgery, 1931-32; asst. resident, research fellow U. Cal. Hosp., San Francisco, 1932-35; instr. U. Cal. Med. Sch., 1935-39, asst. prof., 1939-46, prof., 1949—, chmn. dept. neurology, 1947-66, dir. electroencephalographic lab., 1940—. Fulbright research scholar neurology, France, 1957-58. Trustee Deep Springs Coll. Decorated comdr. Order Hipolito Unanue (Peru); recipient Royer award, 1970, Wm. G. Lennox award, 1970. Diplomate Nat. Bd. Medicine, Am. Bd. Neurology. Mem. A.M.A., Am. Neurol. Assn. (v.p.), Cal. Acad. Medicine, Cal. Acad. Sci., Cal. Med. Assn. (chmn. sect. nervous and mental diseases), San Francisco Neurol. Soc. (pres.), Am. Med. Writers Assn., Am. Acad. Neurology, Am. (pres.), Western (pres.) socs. electroencephalography, San Francisco County Med. Assn. (hon.), Harvey Cushing Soc., Am. Epilepsy Soc. (past pres.), Internat. League Against Epilepsy, Assn. Brit. Neurologists (hon.), Argentine Soc. Neurology, Psychiatry and Neurosurgery (hon.), Argentine Multiple Sclerosis Soc. (hon.); corr. mem. Norwegian Neurol. Assn., Peruvian Soc. Neuro-Psychiatry, German Assn. Neurologists. Cons. Jour. Nervous and Mental Diseases. Contbr. articles med. publns. Home: 80 Summit Av Mill Valley CA 94941 Office: U California Med Center San Francisco CA 94122

AIRHART, JOHN C., former govt. ofcl.; b. Greencastle, Ind., July 4, 1916; s. Jesse Edgar and Bertha (Hovermale) A.; student Central Normal Coll., 1935-39; m. Dorotha A. Ford, Jan. 25, 1940. With Dept. Agr., 1940-42; with RFC, Washington, 1942-53, exec. asst. to gen. counsel, 1950-53; adminstrv. officer criminal div. Dept. Justice, 1953-58; asst. dir. Adminstrv. Office U.S. Cts., 1958-64; dep. asst. sec. def. Dept. Def., Washington, 1964-70; now ret. Home: 3118 Patrick Henry Dr Falls Church VA 22044

AIRIS, THOMAS FERGRIEVE, govt. ofcl.; b. Eau Claire, Wis., May 2, 1906; s. Adam J. and Edna (Thomas) A.; student Carroll Coll., Waukesha, Wis., 1924-25; B.S. in Civil. Engring., U. Wis., 1929, C.E., 1956; m. Marca M. Morse, Oct. 24, 1953; children—Susan, John, Janet. With Corps Engrs., 1929-59, constrn. engr. charge U.S. portion St. Lawrence Seaway, 1954-59; dep. dir. D.C. Dept. Hwys. and Traffic, 1959-63, dir., 1963—. Served to col., C.E., AUS, 1942-47, 50-53. Decorated Army Commendation medal; named one of top ten pub. year men of year, Am. Pub. Works Assn., 1967. Registered profl. engr., Wis. Mem. Soc. Am. Mil. Engrs., Am. Soc. C.E., Am. Assn. State Hwy. Ofcls., Am. Road Builders Assn. (bd. dirs. 1966-68), Assn. Hwy. Ofcls. N. Atlantic States (pres. 1966-67), Sigma Phi Epsilon. Home: 10119 Gary Rd Potomac MD 20854 Office: District Bldg 14th and E Sts Washington DC 20004

AISLEY, HAROLD, fgn. service officer; b. Brockton, Mass., Feb. 22, 1916; s. Julius Aisley; B.A., U. Cal. at Los Angeles, 1939, M.A., 1940, Ph.D., 1949; m. Faye Johnston, Dec. 31, 1943; children—Alice Grace, Merle Rose (Mrs. Michael duMonceau). Teaching fellow U. Cal. at Los Angeles, 1946-49; intelligence specialist State Dept., 1949-54; joined U.S. Fgn. Service, 1954; assigned Oslo, Norway, 1955-59; labor attache Am. embassy, Copenhagen, Denmark, 1960-65; dep. dir. Office Internat. Orgns., U.S. Dept. Labor, 1965-69; regional labor attache Am. embassies, Ankara, Turkey, Tehran, Iran Islambad, Pakistan, 1969—. Served with USAAF, 1941- 1941- 46; CBI, ETO. Mem. Fgn. Service Officers Assn. Address: Am. Embassy Ankara, Turkey

AISSEN, MICHAEL ISRAEL, educator; b. Istanbul, Turkey, Jan. 16, 1921; came to U.S., 1922, naturalized, 1943; s. Oscar Ansil and Judith (Cohen) A.; student Cooper Union Sch. Engring., 1938-41; B.S., Coll. City N.Y., 1947; Ph.D., Stanford, 1951; m. Mildred Davis, Apr. 17, 1944; children—Judith, Louis Claire (Mrs. Dennis Deem). Research scientist radiation lab. Johns Hopkins, 1951-60; asso. prof. Fordham U., N.Y.C., 1961-64, prof. math., 1964-70; prof., chmn. dept. math. Newark Coll. Arts and Scis. Rutgers U., Newark, N.J., 1970—. Cons. aerospace research labs. Air Force Dept., Dayton, O., 1967-68; tchr. AID, Pakistan, 1967, 70; mem. Courant Inst. Math., 1960. Served with AUS, 1943-46. Mem. N.Y. Acad. Scis. (chmn. math. sect. 1970—), Soc. Indsl. and Applied Math. (chmn. Balt. sect. 1957), Am. Math. Soc., Math. Assn. Am. Home: 20 Elm St New Rochelle NY 10805 Office: Math Dept Newark Coll Arts and Scis Rutgers U Newark NJ 07102

AITAY, VICTOR, violinist; b. Budapist, Hungary; s. Sigmund and Irma (Fazekas) A.; pvt. study with father; entered Royal Acad. Music at age 7; studied violin with Imre Waldbauer, theory with Zoltan Kodaly, chamber music with Leo Weiner; artist diploma Franz Liszt Royal Acad. Music, Budapest, 1939; m. Eva Vera Kellner, Nov. 17, 1946; 1 dau., Ava Georgianna. Came to U.S., 1946, naturalized, 1952. Organizer, leader Aitay String Quartet, on tour Europe; recitals, also soloist symphony orchestras, Met. Opera Assn., N.Y.C., 1948-54; assn. concertmaster Chgo. Symphony Orch., 1954-62, associated and co-concertmaster, 1962-; concertmaster Ravinia (Ill.) Music Festival, 1960—; prof. First Internat. String Cong; prof. violin DePaul U., Chgo., 1962—; leader Chgo. Symphony String Quartet; conductor, music dir. Lake Forest (Ill.) Symphony Orch. Numerous performances Casals Festival at invitation of Pablo Casals. Home: 212 Oak Knoll Terrace Highland Park, IL 60035 Office: Chicago Symphony Assn 220 S Michigan Av Chicago, IL 60604

AITKEN, ALEXANDER PHILIP, orthopedic surgeon; b. Barre, Vt., Nov. 26, 1904; s. Alexander and Jane (Philip) A.; M.D., Tufts Med. Sch., 1928; m. Stella Murray, Sept. 6, 1933; children—Alexander R., Patricia J. Clin. prof. orthopedic surgery Tufts U. Med. Sch., 1941-55, prof., 1955—; vis. surgeon Boston City Hosp., 1935-66, acting chief orthopedic service, 1954-55, surgeon in chief, dir. orthopedic service, 1955-66, cons. orthopedic surgery, 1966—; chief orthopedic service Winchester, Chelsea Meml., Brooks hosps.; dir. rehab. New Eng. Rehab. Centre, Woburn, Mass.; cons. orthopedic surgery Brockton (Mass.) Hosp., Bon Secours Hosp., Methuen, Mass., Cable Stickney Meml. Hosp., Ipswich, Mass., Charles Choate Meml. Hosp., Woburn, New Eng. Med. Center, Boston, Boston Dispensary Rehab. Dept.; vis. surgeon Sancta Maria Hosp. Mem. Pres.'s Com. on Nat. Employ the Physically Handicapped. Diplomate Am. Bd. Orthopedic Surgeons. Mem. Mass. Med. Assn., A.M.A., A.C.S. (chmn. subcom. indsl. relations), Am. Assn. Surgery Trauma, Am. Orthopedic Assn., Société Internationale de Chirurgie Orthopedique et de Traumatol Am. Acad. Orthopedic Surgeons, Boston Orthopedic Club, Internat. Soc. Orthopedic Surgery and Traumatology, Middlesex East Med. Soc. (pres. 1959), N.Y. Acad. Scis., Alpha Omega Alpha. Contbr. articles to med. jours. Home: 26 Myopia Rd Winchester MA 01890

AITKEN, GEORGE, ins. co. exec.; b. Winnipeg, Man., Can., Nov. 21, 1906; s. Robert Walker and Margaret (Alexander) A.; grad. parochial schs.; m. Winnifred Kinley, Aug. 15, 1931; children—Diana Mary (Mrs. Cameron L. Eckert), Georgina Gail (Mrs. Robert C. Varah), David Michael. With John Scott & Co., Winnipeg, 1923-29, Price, Waterhouse & Co., Winnipeg, 1929-34; chief accountant Great-West Life Ins. Co., Winnipeg, 1934-43, comptroller, 1943-47, sec., 1947-53, asst. gen. mgr., comptroller, 1953-58, vice-pres., comptroller, 1958-68, v.p. adminstrn., 1968-71; mgmt. cons. Aitken Consulting, 1971—. Pres. Winnipeg Art Gallery, 1966-71; vice-chmn. League of Red Cross Socs. Geneva, 1965—, chmn. permanent bareme commn. 1960—. Trustee Winnipeg Gen. Hosp. Fellow Inst. Chartered Accountants. Clubs: Manitoba, York (Toronto); Winnipeg Squash Racquet. Home: Apt 2703 55 Nassau St Winnipeg Manitoba Canada Office: Box 6000 60 Osborne St N Winnipeg Manitoba Canada

AITKEN, HUGH GEORGE JEFFREY, educator; b. Deal, Eng., Oct. 12, 1922; s. George Jeffrey and Ellen (Hughes) A.; M.A., St. Andrews U., 1947; M.A., U. Toronto, 1948; Ph.D., Harvard, 1951; m. Janice Hunter, July 9, 1955; 1 dau., Ellen Bradshaw. Came to U.S., 1948, naturalized, 1957. Research fellow Harvard, 1951-55; from instr. to prof. econs. U. Cal. at Riverside, 1955-65; prof. econs. Amherst Coll., 1965—. Served with RAF, 1942-46. Mem. Econ. History Assn., Am. Econ. Assn. Author: The Welland Canal Company, 1954; Canadian Economic History, 1956; Taylorism at Watertown Arsenal, 1960; American Capital and Canadian Resources, 1961. Editor: Explorations in Entrepreneurial History, 1948-55; Jour. Econ. History, 1966-69. Home: 85 Dana St Amherst MA 01002

AITKEN, JAMES BERTIN, architect; b. San Francisco, Nov. 26, 1919; s. James Bertin and Margert (Shaine) A.; A.A., Marin Jr. Coll., 1945; A.B., U. Cal. at Berkeley, 1950; m. Janice Elise Erickson, Mar. 30, 1965; children—Eileen, Nancy, Christine. Tchr., Mare Island Navy Yard, 1940-42; archtl. draftsman firm DeLappe & Van Bourc, Berkeley, 1950-54; partner Aitken, Collin & Assos. Architects, Berkeley, 1954—; pres. Instant Structures Inc., Berkeley, 1969—. Tchr., author course essentials of residential design and constrn. U. Cal., Berkeley, 1955-60. Served with USAAF, 1943-45. Ford Found. grantee, 1963. Mem. A.I.A. (chmn. aerospace and undersea archtl. task force), Am. Inst. Aeros. and and Astronautics. Club: Berkeley Yacht. Patentee lunar shelter NASA, S.C.; nation's 1st complete relocatable sch. system; collapsable air born deployable bldgs. capable of self gliding, depolying by remote control; collapsable air cargo containers. Home: 161 Ardmore Rd Kensington CA 94707 Office: 2102 Vine St Berkeley CA 94709

AITKEN, PHILIP MARTIN, lawyer, coal co. exec.; b. Lincoln, Neb., Apr. 1, 1902; s. Martin Inglis and Clara (Carmody) A.; A.B., U. Neb., 1923; LL.B., Harvard, 1926; m. Josephine LaMaster, June 14, 1928; children—Philip M., Jean A. (Mrs. J. Andrew Johnson), James L. Admitted to Neb. bar, 1926; partner Woods, Aitken & Aitken, Lincoln, 1932—; asst. U.S. atty., Dist. Neb., 1927- 29; v.p., dir. Sahara Coal Co.; dir., mem. exec. com. Addressograph- Multigraph Corp.; Cleve.; dir. Lincoln Tel.&Tel. Co., First Nat. Bank & Trust Co. Lincoln. Trustee U. Neb. Found. Mem. Am. Bar Assn., Internat. Assn. Ins. Counsel, Newcomen Soc., N.Am., Phi Kappa Psi. Clubs: Union (Cleve.); Country (Lincoln); Thunder-Bird Country (Palm Springs, Cal.); Chicago. Home: 2733 Sheridan Blvd Lincoln NB 68502 Office: 1241 N St Lincoln NB 68508

AITKEN, WEBSTER, pianist; b. Los Angeles, June 17, 1908; student Emil Sauer and Artur Schnabel. Debut, Vienna, Austria, 1929; recitals in Berlin, Rome, Salzburg, London, and Dumbermline, Scotland; soloist with Vienna Philharmonic Orch., Am. debut Town Hall, N.Y.C., 1935; soloist with orchs. and chamber music ensembles throughout U.S.; performed complete repertory Franz Schubert piano sonatas; pvt. tchr. piano; rec. artist Columbia, Gamut records. Mem. Am. Fedn. Musicians. Home: 128 Christopher New York City NY 10014 also: 330 E 54th St New York City NY 10022

AITKEN, WILLIAM INGLIS, lawyer; b. Lincoln, Neb., Oct. 4, 1896; s. Martin Inglis and Clara Elizabeth (Carmody) A.; A.B., U. Neb., 1918; J.D., Harvard, 1921; m. Helen Mary Cook, Sept. 22, 1923; children—Martha Elizabeth (Mrs. J.T. Greer), Mary (Mrs. R. C. L. Greer, Jr.), Nancy Weir (Mrs. H.L. Senger, Jr.). Admitted to Neb. bar, 1921, since practiced in Lincoln; mem. law firm Woods, Aitken, Smith, Greer, Overeash & Spangler, 1921-; v.p., dir., mem. exec. com. Lincoln Tel. & Tel. Co.; dir., mem. exec. com. Addressograph-Multigraph Corp., Cleve.; Cleve.; dir. Woodmen Accident & Life Co., Sahara Coal Co. (Chgo.). Bd. dirs. State of Neb. Hist. Soc. Found.; v.p., dir. Lincoln Found., Inc. Served as 2d lt., F.A., U.S. Army, 1918- 19; 2d lt. U.S. Army Res., 1919-24. Mem. Greater Lincoln Planning Commn., 1931-35, Lincoln Water Adv. Bd., 1952-53. Bd. trustees U. Neb. Found. Mem. C. of C. (dir. 1949-53), Am., Neb. State, Lincoln bar assns., Ind. Pioneers Telephone Assn., Patriarchs, Newcomen Soc., Phi Gamma Delta, Alpha Kappa Psi. Republican. Conglist. (mem. bd. trustees 1942-45, 47-50, chmn. bd.

trustees ch. trust fund). Clubs: Round Table, Country (dir. 1928-35, treas. 1928-34, pres. 1934-35), University (dir. 1929-35) (Lincoln); Union (Cleve.). Home: 2240 Woodsdale Blvd Lincoln NB 68502 Office: 1241 N St Lincoln NB 68508

AJAMIE, AMIL JOSEPH, lawyer; b. Lockport, Ill., June 30, 1924; s. Tom Nasif and Evelyn (Attalla) A.; student U. Ill., 1942-43, Joliet Jr. Coll., 1946-47; B.S.L., Northwestern U., 1949, J.D., 1951; m. Elizabeth Hart, Sept. 20, 1958; children-Michael J., Simone M., Michelle Y., Paul E., Julie A. Admitted to Ariz. bar, 1951, since practiced in Phoenix. Dir. Ariz. Western Mfg. Corp., Carter Sales, Inc., Central Credit Corp., Farm & Home Food Service, Inc. Bd. dirs. St. Josephs Youth Camp, Ariz. State Council Found. K.C., Padre Kino Found. Served with inf., AUS, 1943-46. Decorated Combat Inf. Badge. Mem. Am., Ariz., Maricopa County bar assns., Delta Theta Phi. K.C., Elk, Moose. Club: Lebanon Syrian American of Arizona (v.p.) (Phoenix). Home: 1234 E Gardenia St Phoenix AR 85020 Office: 3550 N Central Av Phoenix AZ 85012

AJEMIAN, ROBERT MYRON, journalist; b. Boston, July 8, 1925; s. Shahin and Rose (Takvorian) A.; grad. Mt. Hermon Sch., 1943; A.B., Harvard, 1948; m. Ruth MacCrellish, Sept. 6, 1952; children—Robert and Katharine (twins), Peter; m. 2d, Elizabeth Patterson, Nov. 27, 1959; children—David John and Andrew Howell. Sportswriter, Boston Evening Am., 1948-51; reporter Life mag., N.Y.C., 1952-54; corr. Time, Life mags., Denver, 1954-56; asst. nat. affairs editor Life mag., N.Y.C., 1957-59; bur. chief Time- Life, Chgo., 1959-61; chief European bur. Life, Paris, France, 1961- 63, polit. editor, N.Y.C., 1963-67; asst. mng. editor, 1968—. Served to lt. (j.g.) USNR, World War II; PTO. Mem. Sigma Delta Chi. Clubs: Harvard, Lake Shore (Chgo); Millbrook, (N.Y.) Golf and Tennis. Home: 115 Central Park W New York City NY 10023 summer Smithfield Rd Amenia NY 12501 Office: Time-Life Bldg New York City NY 10036

AJL, SAMUEL JACOB, microbiologist, biochemist; b. Poland, Nov. 15, 1923; s. Joseph and Celia (Hertz) A.; came to U.S., 1939, naturalized, 1943; B.A., Bklyn. Coll., 1945; Ph.D., Ia. State Coll., 1949; L.H.D. (hon.), Dropsie U.; m. Adele Davis, Sept. 15, 1946; children—Stephen Ira, Diane Frances, Leslie Judith. Asst. prof. bacteriology Washington U. Sch. Medicine, St. Louis, 1949-52; on leave with Rockefeller U., 1951; chief microbiol. chemistry sect. Walter Reed Army Inst. Research, 1952-56, asst. chief dept. bacteriology, 1956-58; prof., dir. metabolic biology NSF, 1959-60; dir. research Albert Einstein Med. Center, Phila., 1960—; prof. dept. biology Temple U., 1960—, research prof. microbiology Sch. Medicine, 1960—. Mem. metabolic biology panel NSF, 1959—. Chmn. exec. bd., bd. govs. Dropsie U. Hebrew and Cognate Studies, Phila., 1966—, acting pres., 1966-67; bd. dirs. Am. Jewish Com., Nat. Found. Jewish Culture. Recipient commendation for superior service U.S. Army, 1955; NSF sr. postdoctorate fellow, Jerusalem, Israel, Oxford, Eng., 1958; recipient Alumus Honors award for outstanding scientific achievements Bklyn. Coll., 1964. Fellow N.Y. Acad. Sci., Biochem. Soc. (Eng.); mem. Soc. Biol. Chemists Am., Soc. Microbiology, Soc. Exptl. Biology and Medicine, Am. Acad. Microbiology, Jewish Publ. Soc. Am. (v.p. 1969, dir.), Sigma Xi. Contbr. articles profl. jours., papers. Editor: Microbial Toxins, 1970; Archives of Biochemistry and Biophysics, 1969. Home: 2296 Bryn Mawr Av Philadelphia PA 19131 Office: Albert Einstein Med Center York and Tabor Rds Philadelphia PA 19141

AJZENBERG-SELOVE, FAY, educator, physicist; b. Berlin, Germany, Feb. 13, 1926; d. Mojzesz A. and Olga (Naiditch) Ajzenberg; came to U.S., 1940, naturalized, 1946; B.S. in Engring., U. Mich., 1946; M.S., U. Wis., 1949, Ph.D., 1952; m. Walter Selove, Dec. 18, 1955. Research fellow Cal. Inst. Tech., 1952, 54; lectr. Smith Coll., 1952-53; cons., fellow Mass. Inst. Tech., 1952- 53; from asst. prof. to asso. prof. Boston U., 1953-57; mem. faculty Haverford Coll., 1957-70, prof. physics, 1962-70, acting chmn. dept. physics, 1967-69; research prof. U. Pa., 1970—; vis. asst. prof. Columbia, summer 1955, Nat. U. Mexico, summer 1955; lectr. U. Pa., 1957; cons. in field, 1962-63. Exec. sec. com. physics faculties in colls. Am. Inst. Physics, 1962-65, mem. adv. com. manpower, 1963-68, adv. com. vis. scientists program, 1963-67; commr. Commn. on Coll. Physics, 1968—; mem. U.S. delegation low energy nuclear physics to USSR, AEC, 1966. Smith-Mundt fellow, 1955; Guggenheim fellow, 1965-66. Fellow Am. Phys. Soc. (mem. exec. com. div. nuclear physics 1970-72) mem. Am. Assn. U. Profs., Phi Beta Kappa, Sigma Xi. Editor: Nuclear Spectroscopy, vol. A and B, 1960. Home: 118 Cherry Lane Wynnewood, PA 19096 Office: U Pa Philadelphia PA 19104

AKAR, JOHN J diplomat, playwright, broadcaster; b. Rotifunk, Sierra Leone, May 20, 1927; s. Joseph Philip and Tikidankay (Mansaray) A.; student Otterbein Coll., 1946-49; B.A. in Polit. Sci., U. Cal. at Berkeley, 1950; student Lincoln's Inn, London, 1950-53, London Sch. Econs., 1950- 52; Nuffield scholar U. Edinburgh (Scotland); m. Constance Eleanor Wright, Nov. 24, 1956; children-Jacqueline Jasmin, Pamela Juli, Melissa Dankay, Michelle Mayilla, Cynthia Collette, Emily Yama. Freelance broadcaster, 1950-55; with Voice of Am., 1955-56; dir. Sierra Leone Broadcasting System, 1957- 67; sec. Sierra Leone Hotels and Tourist Bd., 1960-67; sec. Commonwealth Broadcasting Secretariat, London, 1967-69; ambassador to U.S. from Sierra Leone, 1969—; high commr. to Can., 1970- -; an actor on stage and films; Danforth vis. lectr. to U.S., 1964-66. Mem. Sierra Leone Mus. Com.; chmn. Sierra Leone Nat. Mus., Monuments, and Relics Commn.; founder Nat. Dance Troupe of Sierra Leone. Chiefdom counsellor Bumpeh Chiefdom, Rotifunk, Sierra Leone. Hon. Trustee Baker U., Baldwin, Kan. Decorated Order Brit. Empire; chevalier Cedars of Lebanon, 1959; recipient Sierra Leone Independence medal, 1961; hon. doctorate Albright Coll., Reading Pa., Otterbein Coll., Westerville, O. Mem. A.F.T.R.A. Rotarian. Author (plays): Valley Without Echo, 1949; Cry Tamba, 1961; The Second Chance, 1954. Composer Sierra Leone nat. anthem. Home: P O Box 3 Rotifunk Sierra Leone West Africa Office: Embassy Sierra Leone, 1701 19th St N W Washington DC 20009

AKE, SIMEON, diplomat of Ivory Coast; b. Jan. 4, 1932; ed. Univs. Dakar and Grenoble. Chief of cabinet to Minister Pub. Service, Ivory Coast, 1959-61; 1st counsellor Ivory Coast Mission to UN, 1961-63; ambassador to U.K., Sweden, Denmark and Norway, 1964-66; permanent rep. of Ivory Coast to UN, 1966—. Decorated officer Nat. Order Republic Ivory Coast. Address: Permanent Mission Ivory Coast to UN 46 E 74th St New York City, NY 10021

AKERMALM, SVEN TURE GUNNAR, Swedish govt. ofcl.; b. Stockholm, Sweden, Feb. 19, 1909; s. Ture and Elin (Peterson) A.; matriculation exam., Stockholm, Sweden, 1929; m. Vera Lindeloef, Sept. 26, 1936; children—Peter, Eva. With Sveriges Riksbank (Central Bank of Sweden), Stockholm, 1929—, gen. mgr., 1952—; with Swedish Fgn. Exchange Office, 1940-41, Swedish Clearing Office, 1942-43, Swedish Trade Commn., 1945-47; alt. mem. mng. bd. European Payments Union; alternate exec. dir. IMF, Washington, 1952-54, exec. dir. for Denmark, Finland, Iceland, Norway, Sweden, 1954-56. Mem. Swedish delegation OEEC. Home: Sollentuna Stockholm Sweden Office: Sveriges Riksbank Stockholm Sweden

AKERS, ANTHONY BOYCE, lawyer; b. nr. Charlotte, Tex., Oct. 19, 1914; s. Ambrose B. and Margaret (Long) A.; B.A., U. Tex., 1936; LL.B., Columbia, 1949; m. Jane Pope, Nov. 28, 1942; children—Andra (Mrs. Ronald Frazier), Ellery Jane. Instr. pub. sch., Tex., 1936-37, Cal., 1938-39; admitted to N.Y. bar, 1950, D.C. bar, 1953; pvt. practice, N.Y.C., 1950—; dep. asst. sec., then dep. under sec. internat. negotiations Office Sec. Air Force, 1951-53; dir. N.Y. State Dept. Commerce for N.Y.C., 1955-58; chmn. N.Y.C. Community Mental Health Bd., 1957-58; U.S. ambassador to New Zealand, 1961-63; of counsel McKenzie, Cabell & Green, 1967—. Latin Am. rep. to Inter-Am. Trade and Cultural Center, 1966. Democratic candidate for Congress, 1954, 56, 58; exec. chmn. N.Y. Citizens for Kennedy-Johnson, 1960. Trustee Freedom House. Served to lt. comdr. USNR, 1940-46; PTO. Decorated Silver Star medal with gold star. Mem. Assn. Bar City N.Y., Fed. Bar Council Bar Assn. D.C., Council Fgn. Relations, Fgn. Policy Assn. (nat. council). Home: 920 Fifth Av New York City, NY 10021 Office: 555 Madison Av New York City NY 10022

AKERS, JOHN, life ins. co. exec.; b. Greenville, Tex., May 27, 1921; s. John W. and Edna (Sandlin) A.; B.B.A., U. Mo., 1949; m. Ann Hale Squires, Oct. 27, 1945; children—John C., Robert D., Jeffrey A. Br. accounting mgr. Gen. Motors Acceptance Corp., Waco, Tex., 1949-50; with Franklin Life Ins. Co., Springfield, Ill., 1951—, treas., 1965—. Served as pilot USAAF, 1942-46. Mem. St. Louis Soc. Financial Analysts. Presbyn. (trustee). Mason. Home: 54 W Hazel Dell Springfield IL 62707 Office: Franklin Life Ins Co Franklin Sq Springfield IL 62701

AKERS, JOHN MCCORKLE, trucking co. exec.; b. Maysville, Ky., Apr. 5, 1907; s. William Wirt and Elizabeth (Scott) A.; A.B. in Econs., Davidson Coll., 1928; M.A. in Econs., U. N.C. at Chapel Hill, 1932; grad. student Duke, 1933, Princeton, 1934; m. Dorothy Amanda Dozier, Feb. 14, 1945; children—Mildred Elizabeth, Dorothy Joanne, Mary Kathleen. Asst. dir. WPA, Washington, 1935-37; v.p., gen. mgr. Akers Motor Lines, Inc., Gastonia, N.C., 1937-55, pres., 1955—; pres. A. & W. Realty Co., Gastonia, 1949—, Akers Realty & Sales Co., Inc., Atlanta, 1950—, Akers Center Hardware & Supply, Inc., Gastonia, 1955—, A.&W Rentals, Inc., Gastonia, 1958-69; partner Akers Sales Co., Gastonia, N.C., 1948—; mem. N.C. advisory bd. Liberty Mut. Ins. Co., Charlotte, 1961—. Mem. N.C. Bd. Conservation and Devel., 1960-68; pres. N.C. Indsl. Devel. Found., 1962, bd. dirs., 1963-65; chmn. Davidson Coll. Alumni Fund, 1955-57. Pres. Akers Found., 1955—; adv. bd. Transp. Center, Northwestern U., 1961-66; bd. visitors Davidson Coll., 1957-64; trus. Queens Coll., Charlotte, 1947—; bd. dirs. N.C. Citizens Assn., 1961—. Mem. Am. Trucking Assn. (bd. govs. regular common carrier conf. 1959—, v.p. N.C. 1945-54, chmn. indsl. relations com. 1962-63, mem. exec. com. 1945—, nat. treas. 1954-62, 1st v.p. 1962-63, pres. 1963-64, chmn. bd. 1964- 65), N.C. Motors Carriers Assn. (bd. mem. 1940—, pres. 1962-63), Transp. Assn. Am. (bd. dirs. 1962—), Carolina Transp. Assn. (pres. 1940-60), Davidson Coll. Alumni Assn. (pres. 1957-58), U.S., Gastonia chambers commerce, Gastonia Traffic and Transp. Club, Phi Beta Kappa, Pi Kappa Alpha, Presbyn. (chmn. deacons 1962, elder 1968—). Eagle, Elk. Clubs: Gaston Country; Ponte Vedra (Fla.). Home: 1102 Belvedere Av Gastonia, NC 28052 Office: PO Box 579 Gastonia NC 28052

AKERS, ROBERT WOOD, former govt. ofcl.; b. Topeka, Oct. 7, 1905; s. Everett B. and Mabel M. (Wood) A.; student Washburn U., 1923-24, U. Chgo., 1924, U. Tex., 1925- 26; m. Edna Margaret Wallace, Jan. 1, 1927 (div.); 1 dau., Margaret Ann; m. 2d, Sibylle de l'Epine, Mar. 9, 1956. Reporter, Topeka State Jour., 1922-23, Chgo. City News Bur., 1924-25, San Antonio Eve. News, 1925; reporter Beaumont (Tex.) Enterprise, 1926, city editor, mng. editor, editor, editor-in-chief, 1953-64; editor-in-chief Beaumont Jour., 1953-64; daily news commentator, radio sta. KRIC, 1939-42, 45; v.p., sec. Enterprise Co., Beaumont, 1956-64; lecture tour, India, Philippines, Japan, Korea, under sponsorship Dept. State, 1953; dep. dir. USIA, 1965-69. Served with inf. AUS, 1942-46. Decorated Purple Heart. Mem. Phi Delta Theta. Roman Catholic. Home: Apartado 264 Ibiza Baleares Spain

AKERS, SUSAN GREY, librarian; b. Richmond, Ky., Apr. 3, 1889; d. James Tazewell and Clara Elizabeth (Harris) Akers; A.B., U. of Ky., 1909; certificate, Library Sch., U. of Wis., 1913; Ph.D., Grad. Library Sch., U. Chgo., 1932. Tchr. grade and high schs., 1909-11; with branch of Pub. Library, Louisville, Ky., 1911-12; librarian, Dept. of Hygiene, Wellesley, 1913- 20; cataloger U. N.D. Library, 1920-22; instr. and asst. prof., Library Sch., U. of Wis., 1922-28, also field visitor Wis. Free Library Commn.; asso. prof. library science, U. N.C., 1931-32, acting dir. and prof., 1932-35, dir., prof., 1935-41, dean and prof. Sch. of L.S., 1942-54, prof. and dean emeritus, 1954—; vis. lectr. library sci. U. of Tehran (Iran), 1954-55; sometime summer instr. several univs.; cons. Civil Information and Edn. Sect. U.S. Army, Tokyo, 1950-51. Recipient of Mann Citation by A.L.A., 1956. Mem. U.S. Dept. of State's Internat. Edn. Exchange Program. Mem. A.L.A., N.C. Library Assn. Republican. Presbyterian. Author: Simple Library Cataloging, 1927, 5th edit. 1969, Spanish transl., 1962. Home: 316 Tenney Circle Chapel Hill NC 27514 ☆

AKERS, WILLIAM WALTER, educator; b. Panola County, Tex., Dec. 31, 1922; s. Oscar Walter and Lela (Malone) A.; B.S., Tex. Tech. Coll., 1943; M.S., U. Tex., 1944; Ph.D., U. Mich., 1951; m. Nancy Tressel, Mar. 1, 1947; childrenSusan Elaine, Carol Lorraine. With Atlantic Refining Co., 1947; mem. faculty Rice U., 1947-, prof. chem. engring., 1956-, chmn. dept., 1955-, dir. Bio-Med. Engring., Lab., 1963-; cons. chem. industries, 1947-. Mem. council Oak Ridge Inst. Nuclear Studies, 1958—, vice chmn., 1962, bd. dirs., 1963—; tech. adviser to Yugoslavia, 1962. Served with C.E. AUS, 1941-43. Mem. Am. Chem. Soc., Am. Inst. Chem. Engrs., Am. Soc. Artificial Organs, Sigma Xi, Tau Beta Pi. Episcopalian. Author papers in field. Home: 5214 Green Tree Rd Houston TX 77027

AKERSON, GEORGE EDWARD, Jr., newspaper publisher; b. Mpls., Apr. 20, 1918; s. George Edward and Harriet (Blake) A.; student Harvard, 1939; m. Anne Abbott, Sept. 5, 1941; children—George Edward III, Stuart A., William N.; m. 2d, Phyllis Chadwick, May 9, 1964. With Boston-Herald-Traveler Corp., 1936—, pres., 1963—, chmn. bd., 1968—; pres. WHDH, Inc., 1963—, chmn. bd., 1968—; chmn. bd. Entron, Inc. Served to lt. col. USAAF, 1940-45. Decorated D.F.C. Clubs: Westport (Mass.) Yacht; Boston Yacht. Home: Far Westport MA 02790 Office: 300 Harrison Av Boston MA 02118

AKHURST, DENYS OSMUND, engring. educator; b. Wakefield, Eng., Mar. 2, 1927; s. Sydney A. and Elizabeth E.E. (Wyatt) A.; B.Sc. with 1st class honours in Elec. Engring., U. Nottingham (Eng.), 1951, Ph.D., 1954; m. Enid Sheila Stokes, Aug. 11, 1951; children—Thomas Henry Wyatt, James Michael Willoughby. Came to U.S., 1955, naturalized, 1963. Ferranti Research scholar Instn. Elec. Engrs., London, Eng., 1951-53; coll. apprentice Metropolitan-Vickers, 1953-55, also part-time lectr. elec. engring. Coll. Tech., U. Manchester (Eng.); pres. Metropolitan-Vickers Apprentice Assn., 1955; lectr., then asst. prof. elec. engring. Mass. Inst. Tech., 1955-59; prof. elec. engring., chmn. dept. U. Miami (Fla.), 1959-61; sr. scientist, semiconductor div. Mpls.-Honeywell, Inc., summer 1960; research engr., research and devel. div. Scott Aviation Corp., summer 1961; prof. elec. engring., head dept. U. Ark., 1961-70; dean Coll. Engring., Fla. Atlantic U., 1970—. Bd. govs. Antaeus Lineal Research Assos., 1969—. Recipient NSF postdoctoral research participation award Radio Sci. Lab., Stanford, summers 1962-63; Fulbright scholar, research and lecturing in U.S., 1955-57. Chartered engr. Council Engring. Instns., London; registered profl. engr., Ark. Fellow Instn. Elec. Engrs.; mem. I.E.E.E. (sr. mem., dir. Ozark sec. 1969-70), Am. Society Engring. Edn., Am. Phys. Soc., N.Y. Acad. Sci., Franklin Soc., Soc. Engring. Sci., I.R.E. (vice chmn. Miami sect. 1961), Am. Assn. U. Profs., Fla. Engring. Soc. (vice chmn. engring. orientation com. 1971—, chpt. rep.), Soc., Fla. Assn. Pub. Jr. Colls., Broward Mfrs. Assn., Met. Opera Guild, Sigma Xi, Tau Beta Pi, Pi Mu Epsilon, Eta Kappa Nu, Theta Tau, Blue Key. Kiwanian. Author papers on plasmas, magnetohydrodynamics, vacuum techniques, solid state, analog computers, electromagnetic field theory. Bd. rev. Genesys, 1971—. Home: 940 Sweetwater Lane Boca Raton FL 33432

AKI, KEIITI, educator, seismologist; b. Tokyo, Japan, Mar. 3, 1930; s. Koichi and Humiko (Kojima) A.; B.S., U. Tokyo, 1952, Ph.D., 1958; m. Haruko Uyeda, Mar. 25, 1956; children—Shota, Zenta. Came to U.S., 1966. Research fellow Cal. Inst. Tech., 1958-60, vis. prof., 1963; instr. Internat. Inst. Seismology and Earthquake Engring., 1961-62; asso. prof. U. Tokyo, 1964-66; prof. geophysics Mass. Inst. Tech., 1966—; vis. prof. U. Chile, 1970; WAE geophysicist U.S. Geol. Survey, 1967—. Fulbright postdoctoral fellow, 1958-60. Mem. Am. Geophys. Union, seismological socs. Am. (dir. 1971—), Japan, Royal Astron. Soc. Author: Stochastic Phenomena in Physics, 1956. Home: 56 Park Lane Newton MA 02159 Office: 77 Massachusetts Av Cambridge MA 02139

AKIHITO, TSUGUNOMIYA, Crown Prince of Japan; b. Dec. 23, 1933; s. Emperor Hirohito and Empress Nagako; student Peers Sch., Gakushuin Jr. High Sch., also pvt. tutors; student Gakushuin U., 1952-56; m. Michiko Shoda, Apr. 10, 1959; 3 children. Rep. Emperor at coronation Queen of Eng.; six month tour of 14 countries, 1953; with Princess visited U.S.A., Iran, Ethiopia, India, Nepal, 1960, Pakistan, Indonesia, P.I., 1962, Mexico, Thailand, 1964, Peru, Argentina, Brazil, 1967, Malaysia, Singapore, 1970. Address: Imperial Palace Tokyo Japan

AKIN, CLARENCE WILLIAM, bag co. exec.; b. Portland, Ore., July 18, 1910; s. James William and Margaret (Martin) A.; B.S., Ore. State Coll., 1931; student Harvard Bus. Sch., 1953; m. Dorothy West Dryer, Sept. 7, 1935; children—Charles R., R., Mary M., Caroline E. Accountant, Jaite Co., St. Helens, Ore., 1932-35, salesman, 1935-39, asst. mgr., 1939-41; salesman Bemis Bros. Bag Co., St. Helens, 1941-54, sales mgr., 1945-48, paper bag product supr., St. Louis, 1948-53, asst. dir. sales, 1953-55, spl. assignment to pres., 1955-56, mgr. Omaha div., 1956-58, dir. allied operations, 1958-59, exec. v.p., Mpls., 1960—, also dir. co., dir. fgn. subsidiaries; dir. Curwood, Inc., New London, Wis. Republican. Episcopalian. Mason, Rotarian. Home: 19 S First St Minneapolis MN 55401 Office: 800 Northstar Center Minneapolis MN 55402

AKIN, EARL, author; b. Cal., 1918; s. Earl and Adeline (Damon) A.; A.B., U. Cal. at Berkeley, 1948, M.A., 1949, B.L.S., 1953; Ph.D., Williams Coll., 1958; LL.B., U. Chgo., 1961; m. Helen Brown, 1940 (div. 1958); 1 dau., Diane; m. 2d, Mary Humphreys, 1970. Free-lance author, 1940—; mem. faculty Notre Dame U.; pres. Tern Pub. Syndicate, Carmel, Cal. Pres. forum World Affairs. Served with USCGR, 1940-45. Recipient Cory award, 1966, Sigma key, 1967. Mem. Authors League, Am. Assn. U. Profs., Internat. Platform Assn., Phi Beta Kappa, Phi Alpha Theta. Clubs: Press, Union League (San Francisco); Overseas Press (N.Y.C.). Author: (column) this an' that, 1960—; (screenplay) The Longest Road, 1959; The Wayfarer, 1965; Sigma, 1966; Don's Story, 1967; Image Maker, 1967; The Open Country, 1967; A Girl Called Susan, 1968; (play) A Man's Beach, 1969; A Time to Gather Stones, 1970; Call Back Yesterday, 1970; Jefferson Thorndyke, 1970. Home: Box 302 Carmel CA 93921 also Kings Castle Incline Village NV 89450

AKIN, JACKSON GROVER, lawyer; b. Lebanon, Ky., Apr. 23, 1919; s. Jackson G. and Nell (Moss) A.; A.B. summa cum laude, Washington and Lee U., 1940; LL.B., Harvard, 1947, J.D., 1969; m. Peggy McCormick; children—Emily Ann, Stephan Jackson, Don Jackson. Admitted to N.M. bar, 1947, since practiced in Albuquerque; asso. Rodey, Dickason, Sloan, Akin & Robb, 1947-51, sr. partner, 1951—; chmn. N.M. State Bar Com. to correlate problems with N.M. Med. Soc. Chmn. legal div. United Fund, 1960. Trustee Albuquerque Boys Acad. Served to lt. comdr. USNR, 1942-46. Recipient certificate of recognition for outstanding service N.M. State Bar, 1963, citation USN for rescue work in Coconut Grove fire, 1942. Mem. Am., Albuquerque bar assns., N.M. State Bar (chmn. medico-dental malpractice panel), Albuquerque Lawyers Club (pres.), Phi Beta Kappa, Delta Tau Delta. Elk. Clubs: Albuquerque Petroleum, Albuquerque Country. Home: 1507 Silver St SW Albuquerque NM 87104 Office: First Nat Bank Bldg W Albuquerque NM 87103

AKIN, PAUL B., steel co. exec.; b. Alton, Ill., Jan. 7, 1921; s. William Markham and Rosalind (Bigelow) A.; grad. Morristown Sch., 1940; student Harvard, 1944; m. Nancy Bigelow, Dec. 9, 1944; children—William Todd, Paul Markham, Samuel Bigelow, Benjamin Perry. With U.S. Steel Corp., 1947-49; with Laclede Steel Co., St. Louis, 1949—, now pres., treas., dir.; dir. 1st Nat. Bank in Alton. Served capt. F.A., AUS, 1943-46; ETO. Mem. Am. Iron and Steel Inst., Am. Inst. Mining and Metall. Engrs., Assn. Iron and Steel Engrs. Home: 305 Conway Hill Rd Creve Coeur MO 63141 Office: Arcade Bldg St Louis MO 63101

AKIN, WALLACE ELMUS, educator, geographer; b. Murphysboro, Ill., May 18, 1923; s. Samuel Elmus and Sarah Elizabeth (Lindsay) A.; B.A., So. Ill. U., 1948; student U. Mich., 1943-44; M.A., Ind. U., 1949; Ph.D., Northwestern U., 1952; m. Peggy Jean Holt, June 11, 1948; children—Dianna Jean, David Wallace. Field investigations in Mexico, 1948; instr. phys. geography Northwestern U., 1950-52; field team chief Rural Land Classification Program for P.R., 1950-51; instr. geography Austin Peay State Coll., summer 1952; instr. U. Ill., Navy Pier Chgo., 1952-53; mem. faculty Drake U., 1953—, prof. geography and geology, 1962—, head dept., 1953- -; cons., geologist Ia. Natural Resources Council, summers 1954-61. Fulbright research scholar Inst. Geography, U. Copenhagen (Denmark), 1961-62. Served to lt. (j.g.) USNR, 1943-46. Mem. Assn. Am. Geographers (chmn. West Lakes div. 1967), Arctic Inst. N.Am., Royal Danish Geog. Soc., Soil Conservation Soc. Am. (chmn. internat. relations com. 1963; ofcl. rep. XIX Internat. Geog. Congress, Stockholm, 1960). Editor, contbr. bulls. Home: 5800 Pleasant Dr Des Moines, IA 50312

AKMAL, KHOSROW, diplomat of Iran; b. Teheran, Iran, Dec. 7, 1934; s. Abdollah and Shamsi (Djalili) A.; B.A., U. Teheran, 1956, Ph.D., 1960; m. Shirine Gharib, Oct. 26, 1965; 1 son, Arya. Attache Embassy of Iran, Berne, 1961-64, 3d sec., 1964-65; pvt. sec. to Vice Minister for Fgn. Affairs, 1965-66; pvt. sec. to Fgn. Minister, 1966-68; 2d sec. embassy of Iran, Washington, 1968-70, 1st sec. charge consular affairs, 1970—. Mem. Iranian UN Delegation to 10th Anniversary of UN Assn., Geneva, 1954. Decorated Order of Homayun 4th Grade, Order of Tady 5th Grade, Medal of Coronation

(Iran); UNESCO fellow, 1954. Author: National Economy and the Iranian Policy (in Persian), 1957. Home: 4201 Cathedral Av NW Washington DC 20016

AKOLT, JOHN PATRICK, lawyer; b. Lena, Ia., Dec. 7, 1891; s. John Conrad and Mary (Reagan) A.; A.B., Regis Coll., 1911, M.A., 1912; LL.B., U. Denver, 1914; m. Alice L. Doyle, June 27, 1917; children—John Patrick, Catherine Anne (Mrs. Dan H. Miller), Mary Jeanne (Mrs. George M. MacCaddon). Admitted to Colo. bar, 1914 and since practiced in Denver, specializing in corp. representation, pub. utility, irrigation, oil and gas; mem. firm Akolt, Shepherd, Dick & Rovira, Denver. Presidential-trustee Rocky Mountain Mineral Law Found. Mem. Am., Colo. State, Denver bar assns., Am. Judicature Soc., Phi Alpha Delta. Roman Catholic. K.C. Clubs: Denver Country, Denver, Petroleum (Denver). Office: Western Federal Savings Bldg Denver CO 80202

AKOLT, JOHN PATRICK, Jr., lawyer; b. Denver, May 16, 1918; s. John P. and Alice (Doyle) A.; student U. Notre Dame, 1936-37, U. Colo., 1937-39; B.S. in Chemistry, U. Denver, 1940, LL.B., 1946; m. Jeanette M. Humphrey, Apr. 28, 1943; children—Janet R., John Patrick, III, Jerri Anne. Admitted to Colo. bar, 1946; with Akolt, Shepherd, Dick & Rovira, Denver, 1946—, partner, 1952—. Vice pres., sec., dir. Marr Co., Denver, 1959—; v.p., dir. Jay G. Brown & Assos., Denver, 1970—. Served with USAAF, 1941-45. Mem. Nat. Assn. Coll. and U. Attys. (exec. bd. 1968-69), Am., Colo., Denver bar assns, Chi Psi, Phi Delta Phi. Clubs: Valley Country, Denver Athletic, Petroleum, Gyro (Denver). Home: 637 Fairfax St Denver CO 80220 Office: Western Federal Bldg Denver CO 80202

AKWEI, RICHARD MAXIMILIAN, Ghana diplomat; b. Accra, Ghana, Nov. 27, 1923; s. Richard M. and Martha (Brunger) A.; student Achimota Coll., Ghana, 1939-45; B.A., Christ Ch., Oxford, 1951; postgrad. London U., 1951-52; m. Josephine Akosua Aphram, May 10, 1956; children—Adjeley Abla, Richard Adote, Adotei. Adminstrv. officer, magistrate in Gold Coast, 1952-56; cadet diplomat U.K. High Commn., Ottawa, 1956-57; first sec. Ghana embassy, Washington, 1957-60; dir. W. and E. European depts. Ministry Fgn. Affairs, Accra, 1960-62, prin. sec. ministry, 1963; Ghana ambassador to Mexico, 1964-65; ambassador, permanent rep. to UN European Office, Geneva, ambassador to Switzerland, rep. to Internat. Atomic Energy Agy., Vienna, 1965-67; ambassador, permanent rep. Ghana to UN, N.Y.C., 1967—, v.p. Gen. Assembly, 1969, chmn. 2d com. Gen. Assembly, 1968. Mem. Ghana delegations Commonwealth Prime Ministers Conf., London, 1960, Goodwill delegation to U.S.S.R., Peoples Republic China, Yugoslavia, Hungary, Poland, Albania, Fed. Republic Germany, 1961, First Conf. Non-Aligned Countries, Belgrade, 1961, Colombo Conf. Sino-India border disputes, 1962, 49th Gen. Conf. ILO, UNCTAD meetings, Geneva, 1965-66, Internat. Sugar Conf., Geneva, 1965; vice-chmn. contracting parties GATT, Geneva, 1966-67; 19th and 22d Sessions UN Gen. Assembly. Home: 111 Overlook Rd New Rochelle NY 10804 Office: Ghana Mission to UN 144 E 44th St New York City NY 10017

ALABART MIRANDA, MANUEL, Spanish diplomat; b. Fraga, Spain, Dec. 6, 1914; s. Manuel Alabart and Carmen Miranda; M.Law, U. Laragoza, 1935; m. Maria Cristina Fernandez- Cavada, Sept. 25, 1946; children—Manuel, Jaimi, Alvaro. Joined Spanish Diplomatic Service, 1943; assigned Berlin, London, Fez, La Habana, Madrid and Paris, 1943-63; ambassador to Panama 1963-64; consul gen. in N.Y.C., 1964-69. Decorated grand cross de Vasco Nunez de Balboa (Panama); grand cross del Merito. Civil (Spain). Home: 1155 Park Av New York City NY 10028

ALACOQUE, SISTER MARGARET, hosp. adminstr. Adminstr., St. Francis Hosp., Trenton, N.J. Office: St Francis Hosp 601 Hamilton Av Trenton NJ 08629*

ALAINI, MOHSIN AHMED, diplomat of Yemen; b. North Yemen, 1932; grad. Faculty of Law, Cairo U., faculte du Droit de la Sorbonne, Paris; m. Aziza Bolohom. July 25, 1962. First fgn. minister Yemen Arab Republic Republic, 1962-63; ambassador to U.S., also permanent rep. to UN, 1963-69; A.E. & P., permanent rep,. to UN, 1969—. Gen. sec. Tchrs. Trade Union Aden; mem. exec. bd. Aden Trade Union Congress; rep. Aden Trade Union Congress in Internat. Confedn. Arab Trade Unions. Cairo. Mem. Free Yemeni Movement. Address: 211 E 43d St New York City NY 10017

ALAJALOV, CONSTANTIN, artist; b. Rostov on the Don, Russia, Nov. 18, 1900; s. Ivan and Izabella (Ivanov) A.; came to U.S., 1923, naturalized, 1928; student Gymnasium, Rostor, 1912-17; U. of Petrograd, 1917; 1st participation in exhibition, 1916; drafted by Soviet Govt. as artist to paint murals, portraits, posters, 1920, sent to Persia, 1921; left Russia for Constantinople, 1921; painted murals in U.S., 1923; with The New Yorker since 1926; also worked on Vanity Fair, Vogue, Town and Country, Fortune, Life and others; covers, Saturday Evening Post, 1945; painted 63; alternate commr. rep. N.J., Delaware River Basin Commn., 1961-70; Archipenko's L' Ecole d'Art, Phoenix Art Inst., etc. One-man shows, Hollywood, 1936, N.Y.C., 1942, Dallas, 1951; paintings in Dallas Art Mus., Bklyn. Mus., Mus. Modern Art, Phila. Mus. of Fine Arts, Mus. of City of N.Y., and others; The Constantin Abajalov Manuscript Collection established at Syracuse U., 1964. Illustrated books: George Gershwin Song Book, 1932; Our Hearts Were Young and Gay, by Cornelia Otis Skinner, 1942; Cinderella, by Alice Duer Miller, 1943; Conversation Pieces; A Collection of Alajalov's Paintings and Drawings, text by Janet Flanner, 1942. Home: Ox Pasture Rd Southampton, NY 11968 Office: 140 W 57th St New York City NY 10019

ALANSON, ANN, (Mrs. Lionel Mason Alanson, Jr.), former mem. Democratic Nat. Com.; b. San Francisco, Sept. 24, 1926; d. David and Eleanor (Patek) Werthelm; student Conn. Coll. for Women, 1944-45; m. Lionel Mason Alanson, Jr., Apr. 27, 1946; 1 dau., Mary. With Books, Inc., San Francisco, 1950-56; book rev. TV weekly show Lets Look at Books, 1951-54; chmn. Cal. Dollars for Democrats, 1957-59; women's chmn. Dem. Central Com. No. Cal., 1962-65; women's chmn. Pres. Johnson campaign No. Cal., 1964; mem. Dem. Nat. com. for Cal., 1965-70. Treas., San Francisco Youth Assn.; mem. auxs. Mt. Zion Hosp., San Francisco Mus. Art, Hebrew Home for Aged. Bd. dirs. Nations, Youth Camp on Fgn. Affairs. Mem. Cal. Hist. Soc. Home: 65 Montclair Terrace San Francisco CA 94109

ALARON DE QUESADA RICARDO, diplomat of Cuba; b. May 21, 1937: ed. U. Havana. Head student sect. Provincial office July 26 Revolutionary Movement, 1957-59; pres. Univ. Students' Fedn., also sec. Union Young Communists; dir. for regional policies (Latin Am.), Ministry Fgn. Affair, 1962-66; mem. gov. council Inst. Internat. Politics, Ministry Fgn. Affairs; now permanent rep. Cuba to UN. Address: 6 E 67th St New York City, NY 10021*

ALASONNE, DONALD ROBINSONmfg. exec.; b. Lima, O., Apr. 1, 1932; B.S., U. San Francisco, 1954; M.S., Stanford University, 1956; m. Rosemarie Lois Brown, May 15, 1955; 1 son, Anthony Robinson. Sales rep. Ames-Brockton Fabricated Products, Akron, O., 1956-58, sales mgr. Coshocton, Ohio, 1959-61, gen. manager plant, 1961-68, v.p. sales, 1968--. Instr. bus. Cosyshocton Jr. College, 1968-69. Secretary Coshocton YMCA, 1960-61; active Boy Scouts of America. Trustee Coshocton Animal Welfare League, Curry Home for the Aged. Named Man of Year, Coshocton Junior Chamber of Commerce, 1968. Mem. Coshocton C. of C. (vice president 1967-68, pres. 1969-70), English Speaking Union, Coshocton Sertoma Club, Nat. Assn. Mfrs., Sales Executives Institute, Phi Beta Kappa, Sigma Chi, Phi Mu. Democrat. Mem. Christian Ch. (lay leader). Mason (32, Shriner). Clubs: Coshocton Country, Coshocton City, Running Deer Country. Home: 2d Av Coshocton OH Office: 3d Av Coshocton OH

ALBA, VICTOR, writer; b. Barcelona, Spain, Jan. 19, 1916; s. Pedro and Elias (Elvira) Pages; ed. in law, U. Barcelona, 1932-36; m. Noemie Boune, Mar. 20, 1947; 1 dau., Christine. Internat. affairs commentator Ultima Hora, daily, Barcelona, 1935-39, La Batalla, daily, Barcelona, 1936-37; Latin Am. corr. Combat, daily, Paris, 1947-50; cultural affairs commentator Excelior, daily, Mexico, 1947-57; dir. Galerias Excessior,Mexico, 1954- 57, Center Social Studies and Documentation, Mexico, 1962-65; prof., lectr. polit. sci. U. Kan., 1965; Am. U., 1966-68, Kent (O.) State U., 1967—. Author: Alliance Without Allies, 1965; The Mexicans, 1967; Nationalists Without Nations, 1968: Politics and the Latin American Labor Movement, 1968; The Latin Americans, 1969. Home: Valencia 184 Barcelona Spain Office: Dept Polit Sci Kent State U Kent OH 44242

ALBAN, OF MARY, BROTHER, educator; b. N.Y.C., Oct. 30, 1902; s. William and Ellen (Nugent) D.; A.B., Manhattan Coll. 1928, A.M., 1930; Ph.D., Fordham U., 1939; A.M. in theology, U. Notre Dame, 1950. Joined order Bros. of Christian Schs., 1916; high sch. tchr., De La Salle, 1927-29, St. Augustine's Bklyn., 1929-32; prof. classics, religion Manhattan Coll., 1932-49, head classics dept., 1947-62, registrar, 1950- 55, dir. grad. studies, 1952-59, acad. v.p., 1962-63, dir. grad. div., 1963-69, trustee, 1955-65. Mem. Cath. Classical Assn. Greater N.Y. (charter mem., past pres.), Cath. Coll. Tchrs. Sacred Doctrine (chmn. N.Y. region 1954-58, nat. pres. 1958-60). Contbr. articles to Classical Weekly, Folia, Lang. Tchrs., La Salle Catechist, Am. Ecclesiastical Rev., Procs. Christian Bros. Edn. Conf., Procs. Soc. Cath. Coll. Tchrs. Sacred Doctrine. Home: Manhattan Coll New York City NY 10471

ALBANESE, LICIA operatic soprano; b. Bari, Italy, July 22, 1913; d. Michele and Maria (Rugusa) Albanese; studied voice under Giuseppina R Baldassare Tedeschi, Milan, Italy, 1932-35; LL.D., Seton Hall U. D.H.L., Manhattan Coll.; D.H.L., Fairfield (Conn.) U.; Mus.D. cum laude, St. Peters U., Jersey City; m. Joseph Gimma, Apr. 7, 1945. Won nat. singing contest, Italy, 1935; made an unexpected debut in role of Madame Butterfly in Milan, Italy, 1934, when the leading soprano became ill; formal debut at Royal Theater, Parma, Italy, in role of Madame Butterfly, Dec. 19, 1935; sang at inauguration of Vatican City radio sta. and was decorated by Pope Pius XI; made records of La Boheme with Beniamino Gigli, 1939; sang at concert in honor of Sir Neville Chamberlin and Lord Halifax, Rome, 1939; sang at Convent Garden for the Festival of King George VI; made debut at Met. Opera House, N.Y.C., in Madame Butterfly and La Traviata, 1940. Adv. council 3d St. Music Sch. Settlement; trustee Bagby Music Lovers Found., N.Y.C. Decorated lady grand cross Order Holy Sepulchre. Home: 800 Park Av New York City NY 10021 Office: 147 W 39th St New York City NY 10018

ALBANESE, NAOMI GERTRUDE, coll. dean; b. Scottdale, Pa., Oct. 17, 1916; d. Gaetano and Emelia (Lubrano) Albanese; B.A., Muskingum Coll., New Concord, O., 1939; M.A., Ohio State U., 1951, Ph.D., 1955. Tchr. home econs., foods and nutrition in schs. in Ohio, Pa., and W. Va., 1939-53; grad. asst., then asst. prof. home econs. edn. Ohio State U., 1953-58; vis. prof. Colo. State U., summer 1957, W.Va. U., summer 1956; prof., dean Sch. Home Econs., U. N.C., Greensboro, 1958—, bd. scientific dirs. Inst. Nutrition; cons. Sch. Home Econs., Wichita U., summer 1960, Sch. Home Econs., W.Va. U., summer, 1962, Urban Inst., Purdue U., summers 1963, 64. Mem. subcom. edn. Gov. N.C. Commn. Status Women, 1963- -. Bd. dirs. Home Econs. Found., Greensboro Cerebral Palsy Sch., U. N.C. at Greensboro. Recipient award of merit Gamma Sigma Delta; Oliver Max Gardner award U. N.C., 1971; Distinguished Service Centennial award Ohio State U. Mem. Nat. Assn. State U. and Land-Grant Colls. (home econs. commn.), Am. (v.p. 1966-69, pres. 1971-72), N.C., Guilford County home econs. assns., Am. Assn. U. Women, N.C. Hist. Soc., Am., N.C. dietetic assns., N.C. Pub. Health Assn., Nat. Council Family Relations, N.C. Council Food and Nutrition (pres. 1960-61), N.C. Future Homemakers Am. (hon.), Omicron Nu, Phi Upsilon Omicron, Phi Delta Gamma, Sigma Kappa Chi, Sigma Kappa Phi, Pi Gamma Mu, Delta Kappa Gamma, Chimes (hon.). Author papers in field. Home: 606 Westover Terrace Greensboro NC 27408 also 308 Mulberry St Scottdale PA 15683

ALBAUGH, FRED WILLIAM, lab. dir.; b. Albia, La., Apr. 17, 1913; s. Loren Eugene and Blanche (Kussart) A.; B.A. in Chemistry, U. Cal. at Los Angeles, 1935; M.S. in Chemistry, U. Mich., 1938, Ph.D. in Phys. Chemistry, 1941; m. Edrey Smith, Nov. 25, 1944; children—Jeffrey S., James F., Jean E. Research chemist Manhattan Project, U. Chgo., 1944-45, Union Oil Co., Wilmington, Cal., 1941-43, 45-47; research mgr. Hanford Plant, Gen. Electric Co., 1947-64; research mgr. Battelle-N.W. Lab., Richland, Wash., 1964-67, dir., 1967-70, corp. dir. environment and energy programs Battelle Meml. Inst., 1970—. Mem. AEC mission to Australia, 1958, to Euratom, 1960, 62; chmn. AEC Internat. Panel Use Plutonium for Power Prodn., 1964; mem. AEC- Gen. Electric Task Force on Hanford Diversification, 1963-64; mem. tech. adv. com. U.S.-Can. Joint Program Heavy Water Reactors, 1961-66. Mem. Wash. Bd. Against Discrimination, 1966-68; mem. exec. bd. Blue Mt. council Boy Scouts Am., 1966-68, mem. nat. adv. com., 1968—. Fellow Am. Nuclear Soc., Am. Inst. Chemists; mem. Am. Chem. Soc., A.A.A.S., Sigma Xi, Phi Lambda Upsilon, Alpha Chi Sigma. Author, patentee in field. Home: 2534 Harris Av Richland WA 99352 Office: PO Box 999 Richland WA 99352

ALBAUM, HARRY G., educator, biologist; b. Odessa, Russia, Feb. 9, 1910; s. Morris and Sonia (Rimberg) A.; came to U.S., 1912, naturalized, 1934; A.B., Bklyn. Coll., 1932; M.Sc., N.Y.U., 1934; Ph.D., Columbia, 1938; m. Frieda Goldberg, Nov. 22, 1936; 1 dau., Judith (Mrs. Robert Gorman). Mem. faculty Bklyn. Coll., 1932—, prof. biology, 1953—, acting chmn. dept., 1961, dean div. grad. studies, 1965-69; asso. dean grad. study City U., 1965-69, biol. cons., 1949—, dean of the faculties, 1969—. Trustee Cold Spring Harbor Lab., 1963-69. Recipient Honors Day award Bklyn. Coll., 1946; fellow NRC, 1941, grantee A.A.A.S., 1947, Am. Philos. Soc., 1947, NIH, 1958-62, Am. Cancer Society, 1948-50, USAF, 1950-55. Fellow Am. Inst. Chemists, N.Y. Acad. Scis.; mem. Am. Soc. Biol. Chemists, Soc. Gen. Physiologists, Soc. Biology and Medicine, Bklyn. Coll. Alumni Assn. (pres. educators affiliate 1967), Phi Beta Kappa, Sigma Xi (past pres. Bklyn. Coll. chpt.). Author articles in field. Home: 108 Seaman Av Rockville Center NY 11570 Office: Brooklyn Coll Bedford Av and Av H Brooklyn NY 11210

AL-BAZZAZ, ABDULRAHMAN, author, lawyer; b. Bagdad, Iraq, Dec. 20, 1913; s. Abdul and Nashmya Latif; grad. Bagdad Law Sch., 1935; LL.B., King's Coll., London (Eng.) U., 1939; m. Wafya Al-Wayid, Apr. 5, 1945; children—Amir, Zahera. Former judge Ct. Correction, Iraq; dir. Inst. High Arab Studies, Cairo, Egypt; Iraq ambassador to Cairo, London; sec.-gen., vice prime minister, minister fgn. affairs, Iraq, then prime minister, minister of interior, until 1966. Mem. Iraqi Bar Assn. Author books on legal topics, Iraqi modern history, politics, including: Arab Nationalism, 1965. Address: 20/11/25 Aramya Bagdad Iraq

ALBEE, ARDEN LEROY, educator, geologist; b. Port Huron, Mich., May 28, 1928; s. Emery A. and Mildred (Tool) A.; B.A., Harvard, 1950, M.A., 1951, Ph.D., 1957; m. Ann M. Hood, July 12, 1953; children—Janet L., Carol A., James H., Mary M. Geologist, U.S. Geol. Survey, 1950-59; prof. geology Cal. Inst. Tech., 1959—. cons. in field, 1950. Mem. Mineral. Soc. Am., Geol. Soc. Am. Home: 1320 Hastings Ranch Dr Pasadena CA 91107

ALBEE, EDWARD FRANKLIN, author; b. Mar. 12, 1928. Plays written include The Zoo Story, 1958, The Death of Bessie Smith, 1959, The Sandbox, 1959, The American Dream, 1960, Who's Afraid of Virginia Woolf?, 1961-62, The Ballad of the Sad Cafe (adaption of Carson McCullers' novella), 1963, Tiny Alice, 1964, Malcolm, 1966, A Delicate Balance, 1966. Mem. Nat. Inst. Arts and Letters ‡

ALBEE, GEORGE WILSON, educator; b. St. Marys, Pa., Dec. 20, 1921; s. George W. and Maude (Allen) A.; A.B., Bethany Coll., 1943; M.S., U. Pitts., 1947, Ph.D., 1949; m. Constance Impallaria, Aug. 6, 1955; children—Alexander, Luke, Maud, Sarah. Research psychologist Western Psychiat. Inst., Pitts., 1949-51; asst. exec. sec. Am. Psychol. Assn., Washington, 1951-53; Fulbright prof. Helsinki (Finland) U., 1953- 54; asso. prof. psychology Western Res. U., 1954-56, prof., 1957-71, chmn. dept. psychology, 1957-60, 63-66, Ladd distinguished prof. psychology, 1959-71; prof. psychology U. Vt., 1971—; cons. psychology VA, Surgeon Gen. Army, State Ohio. Dir. task force on manpower Joint Commn. Mental Illness and Health, Cambridge, Mass. and Cleve., 1957-59; on sabbatical leave in Rome, Italy, 1960-61; cons. on research Peace Corps, 1962-65; profl. adv. com. Cleve. Welfare Fedn., 1963-67; program com. Nat. Assn. for Mental Health, 1968-70. Bd. dirs., exec. com., v.p. Cleve. Mental Health Assn. Served as sgt. USAAF, 1943-46. Fellow Am. Psychol. Assn. (bd. profl. affairs, council reps., bd. dirs. 1965—; pres. div. clin. psychology, nat. pres. 1969-70); mem. Eastern, Midwestern, Ohio (pres. 1963-64), Cleve. psychol. assns., A.A.A.S., Am. Assn. U. Profs., Sigma Xi, Psi Chi. Author: Mental Health Manpower, 1959. Home: 144 Laurel Hill Dr South Burlington VT

ALBEE, GRACE ARNOLD, artist; b. Scituate, R.I., July 28th, 1890; m. Percy F. Albee, May 10, 1913 (dec. 1959); children—Edward F., John F., Nathaniel E., William C., Percy F. Painter and engraver. Represented in Brooklyn Museum by purchase award, 1947; represented in museum of Rhode Island School of Design, Library of Congress; Met. Mus., N.Y. City; Carnegie Inst. Mus., Pittsburgh, Pa.; Okla. A. & M. Coll., Stillwater, Okla.; Nat. Mus. Art, Stockholm, Sweden; Cleveland Mus. Art, Cleveland, O.; Kansas City Mus.; Brooklyn Museum, N.Y.; John Herron Art Mus., N.Y., Boston and Newark pub. libraries, Phila. Museum, Melrose (Mass.) Library, Pa. State Library, Harrisburg; Nat. Gallery Art, Washington, Bethlehem Library, Peacham Library, Peacham, Vt., Lynchburg (Va.) Art Club; collection of King Victor Emmanuel of Italy (1940); Cayuga Mus. Hist. and Art, Auburn, N.Y.; Albany (N.Y.) Print Club, Norton Mus. West Palm Beach, Fla., Portland (Me.) Mus. Art, Nat. Bezalel Museum, Jerusalem Israel, Culver Military Acad., Notre Dame U., Nat. Gallery, various private collections. Nat. Academician, 1946; life fellow Met. Mus. Art, 1962. Recipient 67 awards including Eugenia F. Atwood Purchase prize at Philadelphia Print Club, 1949; print prizes N.A.D., Connecticut Acad., Hunterdon Co. Art Center, 1959; Albany Purchase Prize, 1959, 60; Conn. Acad. Purchase prize, 1961; Trenton Mus. Purchase prize, N.A.D. prize, 1959, 62; gold medal for woodcarving Am. Artists Profl. League, 1961; Oakes-on-the-Hill prize Providence Water Color Club, 1964; Florence Kane prize Providence Art Club, 1964; prize Am. Artists Profl. League, 1965; medal and citation contbn. visual arts, painting and wood engraving, Providence Art Club, 1965, R.I. Sch. Design Alumni Association, 1965; Best of Year award drawing, Non Profl. Inst. Pa., 1965; Bowen Purchase award Albany Print Club, 1967; Helen Gould Kennedy award Academic Artists, 1968; others. Hon. vice chmn. R.I. Sch. Design Alumni Fund, 1960. Mem. Am. Artists Professional League (prize 1961, chmn. jury of Selection and awards 1968), N.A.D. (chmn. graphic art membership com. 1953—), Conn. Acad., Providence Water Color Club, Albany Print Club, Hunterdon County Art Center, Audubon Artists, Providence Art Club, Boston Printmakers, Academic Artists' Assn., Met. Mus. N.Y. (life), Met. Opera Guild. Reproductions in numerous publs. Home and studio: 84-43 123rd St Kew Gardens NY 11415

ALBERDING, CHARLES HOWARD, petroleum, hotel exec.; b. Cleyville, N.Y., Mar. 5, 1901; s. Charles and Doris (Roberts) A.; E.E., Cornell U., 1923; m. Bethine Wolverton, May 2, 1930; children—Beth Ann, Mary Katherine, Melissa Linda, Lab. asst., draftsman, operator Producers & Refiners Corp., Parco, Wyo., 1923-25; engr., cracking plant supt. Imperial Refineries, Ardmore Okla., also Eldorado, Ark., 1925-27; head fgn. operating dept. Universal Oil Products Co., London, Eng., Ploesti, Roumania, Rangoon, Burma, Venice, Italy, 1927-33, head operating, service depts., Chgo. hdqrs., 1933-42; pres., dir. Paradise Inn, Inc., Jokake Inn, Inc., Vinoy Park Hotel Co., Holiday Hotel Corp., Alsonett Hotels, Sabine Irrigation Co., Sabine Canal Co., Tides Hotel Corp., Harmony Oil Corp., London Square Corp., Petroleum Spltys., Lincoln Lodge Corp., Peabody Hotel Corp., Memphis, Hermitage Hotel Co., Nashville, Royal Palms Inn, Inc., Torrey Pines Inn, La Jolla, Cal,, Charleston First Corp. Petroleum cons. WPB, 1942-43; dist. dir. petroleum refining Petroleum Adminstrn. for War, 1943-45. Mem. Scorpion. Republican. Conglist. Clubs: Valley (Phoenix); Kenilworth, Cornell (Chgo.); Sunset Country, Bath (St. Petersburg, Fla.). Home: 99 Tudor Pl Kenilworth IL 60043 Office: 9 E Huron Chicago IL 60611

ALBERGHETTI, ANNA MARIA, singer; b. Pesaro, Italy, May 15, 1936; d. Daniele and Vittoria Alberghetti; studied music with father; m. Claudio Guzman, 1964. Began singing at age of six, appeared concerts various European cities; Am. debut, Carnegie Hall, N.Y.C., 1950; soloist Philharmonic Symphony Orch., 1950; appeared motion picture The Medium Italy, 1951, Here Comes the Groom, Paramount Film Studios, Hollywood, 1951, The Stars are Singing, 1953, 10,000 Bedrooms, 1956, Cinderfella, 1960; concert appearances Red Rocks Theatre, Denver, 1954, Lewisohn Stadium, N.Y.C., 1950, 51, Robin Hool Dell, Phila., 1950-51, Hollywood Bowl, Los Angeles, 1955, Philharmonic Auditorium, The Sahara, Las Vegas, Empire Room, Waldorf Astoria, N.Y.C., Desert Inn, Las Vegas; guest star TV shows including Toast of the Town, 1950, Calvacade of Stars, Arthur Murray Show, Bob Hope, Eddie Fisher, Red Skelton, Dinah Shore, Desilu Playhouse, G.E. Theatre, Du Pont Show, Ed Sullivan, Garry Moore, Perry Como. Andy Williams; star Carnival, Broadway, Chgo, prodns., 1961, 62. Recipient Antoinette Perry award as best actress in musical (Carnival), N.Y.C., 1961. Address: care Wm Morris Agy 153 El Camino Beverly Hills CA 90212

ALBERS, ANNI, artist, textile designer; b. Berlin, Germany, June 12, 1899; d. Siegfried and Toni (Ullstein) Fleischmann (changed name to Farman); student Bauhaus in Weimar, 1922; diploma Bauhaus Dessau, 1930; m. Josef Albers, 1925. Came to U.S., 1933, naturalized,

1937. Free lance work, Dessau and Berlin, 1930-33; asst. prof. art Black Mountain (N.C.) Coll., 1933-49; free lance work, New Haven, 1950-; one-man shows include Mus. Modern Art, 1949, Hartford (Conn.) Atheneum, 1953, Honolulu Acad., 1954, Mass. Inst. Tech., 1959, Carnegie Inst. Tech., 1959, Balt. Mus. Art, 1959. Yale Art Gallery, 1960, Contemporary Arts Mus., Houston, 1960; work in permanent collections Mus. Modern Art, Busch-Reisinger Mus. at Harvard, Balt. Mus. Art, Mus. Cranbrook Acad. Art, Currier Gallery Art, others, also pvt. collections; lectr. Minn. Sch. Art, R.I. Sch. Design, San Francisco Mus. Art, Carnegie Inst. Tech., Phila. Mus. Coll. Art, U. Hawaii, Contemporary Art Mus., Houston, Rice Inst., Yale. Recipient Gold medal in craftsmanship A.I.A., 1961; citation Phila. Mus. Coll. Art, 1962. Author: Anni Albers: on Designing, 2d edit., 1962; also articles‡

ALBERS, CHARLES H., banker; b. Chgo., May 24, 1897 s. William and Sophie (Stueven) A.; student YMCA Coll., 1915-19; LL.D., U. Dubuque, 1951; m. Gladys Moreland, June 16, 1924; children—Hugh, Russell, David. Banker, bank examiner, 1911-42; state bank liquidator, 1932-42; trustee Chgo. Surface Lines, 1942-46; mgr., chief examiner Chgo. Clearing House Assn., 1946—; dir. No. Indiana Pub. Service Co., Hammond, Indiana. Vice moderator of Presbyn. Ch. U.S., 1950-51, moderator Chgo. Presbytery, 1950-51. Trustee U. Dubuque, Presbyn. Home for Aged, Evanston, Ill., United Presbyn. Found., Chgo. Sunday Evening Club. Clubs: Bankers, Union League, Executives, Economic. Home: 407 Trinity Ct Evanston IL 60201 Office: 164 W Jackson Blvd Chicago IL 60604

ALBERS, HENRY, astronomer, educator; b. Andover, Mass., Nov. 17, 1925; s. Henry F. and Edna (Oliver) A.; A.B., Harvard, 1950; M.A., U. Minn., 1952; Ph.D., Case Inst. Tech., 1956; m. Wilma Clarice Smith, Mar. 17, 1950; children—Catherine Helen, Christina Edna, Henry Peter. Instr. astronomy U. Minn., 1953-55; instr. astronomy Case Inst. Tech., 1955-56; asst. prof. astronomy Butler U., 1956-58; asst. prof. astronomy Vassar Coll., Poughkeepsie, N.Y., 1958-61, asso. prof., 1961-68, prof., 1968—. Served with USAAF, 1943-46. NSF Sci. Faculty fellow, 1965. Mem. Am. Astron. Soc., A.A.A.S., Am. Assn. U. Profs., Sigma Xi. Address: Vassar Coll Poughkeepsie NY 12601

ALBERS, JOHN KENNETH, singer, composer; b. Pitman, N.J., Dec. 10, 1924; s. John Frederick and Florence (Cade) A.; grad. Phila. Conservatory Music; m. Alice Ballinger; children—Sandra, Joyce, Kenneth, Kohn, Binnie Jean; m. 2d, Nancy Rzemien; children—Marti Lou, John Joseph. Mem. singing group Four Freshmen, 1956—; partner Viscount Internat. Prodns.; v.p. Rossdon Music Co., Kenbob Music Co. Served with inf. AUS, 1943-45. Mem. A.S.C.A.P., Screen Actors Guild, A.F.T.R.A., Tau Kappa Epsilon (hon.). Rec. artist Capitol Records. Address: care Four Freshmen 6047 Hollywood Blvd Hollywood CA 90028

ALBERS, JOSEF, painter, educator; b. Bottrop, Westphalia, Germany, Mar. 19, 1888; s. Lorenz and Magdalena (Schumacher) A.; student Royal Art Sch., Berlin, 1913-15, Sch. Applied Art, Essen, 1916-19, Art Acad., Munich, 1919-20, Bauhaus, Weimar, 1920-23; A.F.D., U. Hartford, 1957, Yale, 1962, Cal. Coll. Arts and Crafts, 1964, U. N.C., 1967; Dr. phil. h.c., Ruhr. U., Bochum, West Germany, 1967; LL.D., Bridgeport U., 1966; D. Fine Arts, U. Ill., Art Sch. Mpls., Kenyon Coll., 1969; m. Anni Fleischmann, May 25, 1925. Came to U.S., 1933, naturalized, 1939. Prof. art, Bauhaus, Weimar, Dessau and Berlin, Germany, 1923-33, Black Mountain (N.C.) Coll., 1933-49, prof., chmn. art Yale, 1950-58, prof. emeritus, 1958-60, ret. as chmn., 1958, vis. critic in advanced painting, 1958-60. Work exhibited and pub., Germany, Holland, Denmark, Norway, Sweden, Switzerland, Italy, France, Czechoslovakia, Eng., U.S., Cuba, Mexico, Brazil, Chili, Venezuela, Can., Australia and Japan; tchr. lectr. univs. U.S. and fgn. countries, Mus. Modern Art, N.Y.C. Decorated comdr.'s cross Order of Merit (Germany); recipient Ada S. Garret prize Chgo. Art Inst., 1954; 3d prize $1000 exhibit Corcoran Art Gallery, 1957; Konrao von Soest Preis, Westphalia, Germany, 1958; Ford Found. fellow, 1959; Graham Found. fellow, 1962; 1964 medal Am. Inst. Graphic Arts; award for painting Internat. Exhbn., Carnegie Inst., Pitts., 1967; grand prix 3d Arts and Letters Bienal Americana de Grabada, Santiago, Chile, 1968, Grand prix painting Nardrheim-Westfalen, West Germany. Mem. Nat. Inst. Arts and Letters, Am. Abstract Artist. Author: Poems and Drawings, 1958, 61; Interaction of Color, 1963; Search Verses Re-Search, 1969; also articles art edn. to mags., books, U.S., Europe. Home: 508 Birchwood Dr Orange CT 06477

ALBERT, ABRAHAM ADRIAN, educator; b. Chicago, Ill., Nov. 9, 1905; s. Elias Albert and Fannie (Fradkin) A.; B.S., U. of Chicago, 1926, M.S., 1927, Ph.D., 1928; LL.D. (honorary), Notre Dame, 1965; So.D. (honorary), Yeshiva University, 1968; L.H.D., U. Ill. Circle Campus, Chgo., 1971; m. Frieda Davis, December 18, 1927; children—Alan Davis, Roy M. (dec.), Nancy Elizabeth. Fellow Nat. Research Council, Princeton, N.J., and Chicago, 1928-29; instr. in mathematics, Columbia U., 1929-31; asst. prof. mathematics, U. of Chicago, 1931-37; associate professor mathematics, 1937-41, prof. mathematics, 1941—, chmn. dept., 1958-62, dean, division of physical sciences, 1962-71, Eliakim Hastings Moore Distinguished Service Prof., 1960—; asso. dir. applied math. group Northwestern U., 1944-45; with Institute for Advanced Study, Princeton, 1933-34; visiting professor University of Brazil, Rio de Janeiro U. Buenos Aires, 1947, U. So. Cal., 1950; Yale, 1956-57, U. Cal. at Los Angeles, 1958; cons. Nat. Security Agy., Dept. Def., IBM Corp., U.S. Office Edn., 1963-67, Inst. for Defense Analyses. Member of the com. div. math., phys., engring. scis. Nat. Sci. Found., 1952-54; mem. gen. scis. panel Dept. of Def., 1954-61; chmn. div. math. NRC, 1952-55; chairman sect. math. Nat. Acad. Scis., 1958-61; dir. communications research div. Inst. for Defense Analyses, 1961-62, now trustee; trustee Inst. for Advanced Study; v.p. Internat. Math. Union, 1971—. Recipient Cole prize for outstanding research in algebra, 1939. Fellow of American Academy Arts and Scis.; member National Academy Science, Am. Math. Soc. (pres. 1965-66), Math. Assn. Am., Acad. Scis. Buenos Aires, Brazilian Acad. of Sciences (corr. mem.), Phi Beta Kappa, Sigma Xi. Club: Quadrangle (Chicago). Author: Modern Higher Algebra, 1937; Structure of Algebras 1939; Introduction to Algebraic Theories, 1941; College Algebra, 1946; Solid Analytic Geometry, 1949; Fundamental Concepts of Higher Algebra, 1956; (with R. Sandler) An Introduction to Finite Projective Planes, published in 1968. Editor Bull. of Am. Math. Soc., 1939-43, Transactions of Am. Math. Soc., 1943-49, Colloquium Publs., 1951-57. Mathematical Surveys 1941-45. Home: 1359 E Park Pl Chicago IL 60637

ALBERT, CALVIN, sculptor; b. Grand Rapids, Mich., Nov. 19, 1918; s. Philip and Ethel (Schlacht) A.; student Art Inst., Chgo., 1936-37, Inst. Design, Chgo., 1937-39; m. Martha Neff, Dec. 25, 1941. Mem. faculty N.Y.U., 1949-51, Bklyn. Coll., 1948-49, Inst. Design, Chgo., 1942-47; prof. art Pratt Inst., Bklyn., 1950—, head grad. sculpture program, 1960—; exhibited in one man shows at Theobald Gallery, Chgo., 1941, Grand Rapids Art Gallery, 1943, 48, Puma Gallery, N.Y.C., 1944, Art Inst., Chgo., 1945, Palace of Legion of Honor, San Francisco, 1947, Laurel Gallery, N.Y.C., 1950, traveling show Des Moines Art Center, U. Mich., Grand Rapids Art Gallery, Mich. State U., 1957, Grace Borgenicht Gallery, N.Y.C., 1952, 54, 56, 57, Stable Gallery, N.Y.C., 1959, 64, Jewish Mus., N.Y.C., 1960, Galleria George Lester, Rome, Italy, 1962; exhibited in group shows at Houston Mus. Fine Arts, 1958-59, Addison Gallery, 1959, Claude Bernard Gallery, Paris, 1961, Art Inst. Chgo., 1962, Sculpture Biennale, Cararra, Italy, 1962, Pa. Acad., Phila., 1963, FAR Gallery, N.Y.C., 1964, Whitney Mus., 1954-57, 60, 62, 64, U. Ill., 1965; rep. permanent collections Whitney Mus., Bklyn. Mus., Art Inst. Chgo., Detroit Inst. Arts, Met. Mus., Jewish Mus., U. Neb., Chrysler Mus. Art, Wm. Rockhill Nelson Gallery Art. Recipient Haass prize Detroit Inst. Arts, 1944, Forst award for sculpture Audubon Artists Annual, 1954, Anonymous Prize for sculpture Audubon Annual, 1957, Fulbright Advanced Research grant, Italy, 1961-62, Tiffany grant, 1963, 65, Guggenheim fellowship, 1966. Author: (with D.G. Seckler) Figure Drawing Comes to Life, 1957. Home: 222 Willoughby Av Brooklyn NY 11205

ALBERT, CARL, congressman; b. McAlester, Okla., May 10, 1908; s. Ernest Homer and Leona Ann (Scott) A.; A.B., U. Okla., 1931; B.A., Oxford U., Eng. (Rhodes scholar), 1933, B.C.L., 1934; m. Mary Harmon, Aug. 20, 1942; children—Mary, David. Admitted to Okla. bar, 1935; legal clk. FHA, 1934- 37; atty., accountant Sayre Oil Co., Oklahoma City, 1937-38; legal dept. Ohio Oil Co., Marshall, Ill., Findlay, O., 1939-40; gen. practice law, Oklahoma City, 1938, Mattoon, Ill., 1938-39, McAlester, Okla., 1946- 47; mem. 80th to 92d Congresses, 3d Okla. Dist., majority leader, 1962-71, speaker, 1971—. Served with AUS, 1941-46; PTO. Decorated Bronze Star medal. Democrat. Methodist. Home: 827 E Osage McAlester OK 74501 Office: Capitol Bldg Washington DC 20515

ALBERT, EDDIE, (Edward Albert Heimberger), actor; b. Rock Island, Ill., Apr. 22, 1908; s. Frank and Julia (Jones) Heimberger; student U. Minn., 1927-29; m. Maria Margarita Guadelupe Teresa Estella Bolado Castilla y O'Donnell (profl. name Margo); children—Edward, Maria. With singing trio, Mpls., 1930, then St. Louis, Cin., to N.Y.C., 1935, for radio show The Honeymooners; Grace and Eddie; acted in Broadway version Brother Rat, Room Service, Boys from Syracuse, Miss Liberty, Say Darling, Music Man; organized Eddie Albert Prodns. for making ednl. films, 1945, subjects such as sex edn., labor- mgmt. relations; appeared in motion pictures including Brother Rat, Carrie, Roman Holiday (nominated for Acad. award), Oklahoma, Sun Also Rises, Roots of Heaven, Attack, Longest Day, Captain Newman; toured night-club act with wife, 1954; star of television series Green Acres; conducted lecture tour on ecology, 1969-70. Bd. dirs. Film Council Am. Home: 719 Amalfi Dr Pacific Palisades CA 90272

ALBERT, EDWARD JOHN, instrument co. exec.; b. Inghams Mills, N.Y., June 20, 1882; s. Frederick J. and Martina (Pope) A.; student mining U. Toronto, 1915-17; m. Bozen B. Lukes, Apr. 20, 1908; 1 dau., Annette Albert Albeck. Salesman, Ingersoll-Rand Co., 1898-1908; sales, engring., design Canadian Allis Chalmers Co., 1908-18; sec., also gen. mgr. Thwing Instrument Co., Phila., 1918-35; gen. mgr., treas. successor co. Thwing-Albert Instrument Co., 1935-46, pres. 1946-57, chmn. bd., 1957-69. Col., Pa. N.G., ret.; mem. Armory Rd. Fellow A.A.A.S.; mem. Am. Soc. for Testing and Materials (hon. life, dir., award 1961), Sci. Apparatus Makers Assn. (award 1960, pres. 1953-55, dir.), T.A.P.P.I. Instument Soc. Am. (sr.), Am. Inst. Mining Metall. and Petroleum Engrs., Candian Inst. Mining and Metallurgy, Am. Petroleum Inst., Am. Soc. Quality Control, Soc. Exptl. Stress Analysis, Forest Products Research Soc. Clubs: Union League Engineers (Phila.); Cricket (Germantown, Pa.). Home: 1133 Hillcrest Rd Pen Valley Narberth PO PA 19072 Office: 10960 Dutton Rd Philadelphia PA 19154

ALBERT, ETHEL MARY, educator; b. New Britain, Conn., Mar. 28, 1918; d. Zundel and Dorothy (Eisenstadt) Sokolsky; B.A., Bklyn. Coll., 1942; M.A., Columbia, 1947; Ph.D., U. Wis., 1949. Instr. philosophy Bklyn. Coll., 1946-47; instr. philosophy U. Wis., 1947-49; instr. philosophy Syracuse U., 1949-52; prof. speech U. Cal. at Berkeley, 1958-66; prof. anthropology and speech Northwestern U., 1966—. Research asso. Harvard U. Lab. Social Relations, 1953-55; Ford Found. Overseas fellow, Africa, 1955-57; asst. dir. NSF Project on anthropology, 1961; Social Sci. Research Council faculty research fellow, 1962; NSF Sr. postdoctoral fellow, 1965-66. Fellow Am. Anthrop. Assn.; mem. A.A.A.S., Am. Philos. Assn., Philosophy of Sci. Assn., African Studies Assn. Author: (With Peterfreund and Denise) Great Traditions in Ethics, rev. edit., 1969; (with Kluckholm) A Selected Bibliography on Values, Ethics and Esthetics, 1959; (with Mandelbaum and Lasker) Teaching of Anthropology, 1963; (with Vogt) The People of Rimrock, 1966. Contbr. articles profl. jours. Home: 612 Mulford St Evanston IL 60202

ALBERT, JOHN, fgn. service officer; b. Vienna, Austria, Jan. 28, 1912; s. Louis and Mary (Glaser) A.; LL.B., Vienna U., 1936; student Vienna Sch. Journalism; m. Hildegard Janauschek, Oct. 29, 1934; children—Larry J., Carol A. Came to U.S., 1940, naturalized, 1945. Editor, later asst. mng. editor Telegrafen-Compagnie, Vienna, 1932-38; asst. fgn. news editor CBS, 1940-42; propaganda analyst, chief intelligence div. OWI, 1942-45; chief ct. interpreter Internat. Mil. Tribunal, Nuremberg, 1945-46; with USIA, 1947—, chief German service, 1948-53, West Europe br., 1953-57, European div., 1957-58, dir. Munich Program Center, 1958-62, chief central program services div. Voice of Am., Washington, 1962-66, chief news and current affairs, 1966-67, sr. news analyst, 1967—. Recipient Superior Service award USIA, 1955. Home: 709 S Belgrade Rd Silver Spring MD 20902 Office: Voice of Am Washington DC

ALBERT, LEO N., pub. co. exec.; b. St. Agatha, Me., Oct. 9, 1920; s. Felix Nicholas and Azilda (Michaud) A.; student Pace Coll., N.Y. U.; m. Virginia Martha Coffey, June 1, 1946. With Prentice Hall, Inc., 1946—, pres. Prentice Hall Internat., 1962—, also pres., dir. parent co.; chmn. bd. Prentice Hall Japan, Inc., Internat. Book Distbrs., London, Eng.; dir. Prentice Hall India Put. Ltd. Mem. adv. com. on tech. information AEC; chmn. joint internat. trade com., mem. internat. copyright com. Assn. Am. Pubs.; mem. State Dept. adv. panel on copywright. Served with USMCR, 1942-46; PTO. Mem. Am. Inst. Graphic Arts. Home: 511 Grandview Terrace Leonia NJ 07605 Office: Route 9W Englewood Cliffs NJ 07632

ALBERT, ROBERT BERTRAND, chem. co. exec.; b. N.Y.C., June 15, 1932; s. Sylvester and Anna (Kraus) A.; B.B.A., Coll. City N.Y., 1952; LL.B., N.Y.U., 1955; m. Audrey Miller, Feb. 17, 1963; children—Susan Beth, Randi Michelle. Admitted to N.Y. bar, 1955; sr. staff auditor S.D. Leidesdorf & Co., C.P.A.'s, 1956-59; mem. tax staff Eisner & Lubin, C.P.A.'s, 1959-60; tax mgr. Nat. Starch & Chem. Corp., N.Y.C., 1960-62, chief accountant, 1962-64, asst. controller, 1964-66, asst. treas., 1965-70, controller, 1966—, treas., 1970—. Mem. N.Y. Bar Assn., Nat. Assn. Accountants, N.Y. Soc. C.P.A.'s. Home: 1016 The Colony Hartsdale NY 10530 Office: 750 3d Av New York City NY 10017

ALBERTONI, ALBERT EDWARD, labor union ofcl.; b. Sacramento, Oct. 27, 1908; s. Elvezio James and Anne (Coutts) A.; ed. pub. schs.; m. Kathryne Radovan, Mar. 28, 1937. Mem. Oakland (Cal.) Fire Dept., 1939-64; retired as capt., 1964; dir. Civil Service Employees Ins. Co., 1959-65, 1st v.p., 1955-60, sec.-treas., 1960-65; v.p., then pres. leg. rep. Federated Fire Fighters Cal., 1940- 60; v.p. Internat. Assn. Fire Fighters, 1956-60, sec.-treas., 1964—. Mem. speakers panel Nat. Fedn. Poliomyelitis, 1949-57, also Oakland Fire Dept. Served to comdr. USNR, World War II. Decorated Letter of Commendation (4). Mem. Internat. Assn. Fire Chiefs, Cal. Fire Chiefs Assn., V.F.W. Moose, Eagle. Clubs: Touchdown, Capitol (Washington). Author articles. Office: 905 16th St NW Washington DC 20006

ALBERTS, WARREN EBEL, airlines exec.; b. Two Rivers, Wis., Sept. 20, 1916; s. Oscar B. and Hattie (Ebel) A.; B.S. in Mech. Engring., U. Wis., 1938; student Stanford, 1953; m. Betty W. Stephens, Sept. 21, 1941; children—Kristin, Lisa. Chief engr. Midwest Gas Burner Co., Austin, Minn., 1940; with United Air Lines, 1946—, v.p. indsl. engring., v.p., asst. to pres., 1958-60, v.p. mgmt. services and controls, 1961—; cons. sec. of commerce, 1951, Brit. European Airways, 1954. Served to col. USAAF, 1941- 46; col. Res. Decorated Legion of Merit; Order British Empire; Croix de Guerre (France). Fellow Am. Inst. Indsl. Engrs. (chmn. publns. policy bd.); mem. Nat. Indsl. Conf. Bd., Am. Mgmt. Assn., Engrs. Joint Council (v.p., bd. dirs.). Author articles on mgmt., engring. Office: United Air Lines PO Box 66100 Chicago IL 60666

ALBERTSON, FRED WOODWARD, lawyer, radio engr.; b. Fairgrove, Mich., Sept. 29, 1908; s. Charles Elton Eugene and Helen Louise (Woodward) A.; A.B., U. Mich., 1931, LL.B., 1934; m. Catherine Frances Dolan, June 10, 1942; children—Fred Woodward, Helen Dolan. Engineered constrn. and operation several broadcast and radio telegraph stas., 1925-27; radio equipped and handled communications with remote meterol. expdns. and stas., U. Mich., 1927- 34; admitted to Mich. bar, 1934, D.C. bar, 1935; gen. law practice, 1935- -; engaged as radio and communications legal counsel for radio, television, telegraph, telephone and broadcast companies and stas., 1935- -; partner Dow, Lohnes & Albertson, specializing in communications, radio and air law, 1944—; licensed radio operator, 1924-; owner, operator amateur radio sta. W3GZ. Member bd. trustees, dir. Delta Theta Phi Found., 1945-46. Registered profl. elec-communications engr., D.C. Life fellow Am. Bar Found.; mem. I.E.E.E. (sr. mem.; chmn. Washington sect. 1946-47, mem. adminstrv. com. 1943-; bd. editors proc. 1946-54), Broadcast Pioneers, Fed. Communications; (pres. 1953-54), Am. (ho. dels. 1953-54, chmn. standing com. on communications 1957-58), D.C. bar assns., Am. Judicature Soc., Delta Theta Phi. Clubs: Engineers (co- founder, life mem.), Washington Radio (past pres.), Congressional Country, Broadcasters, Capitol Hill, National Lawyers (Washington); University Michigan Radio (co-founder, past pres.) (Ann Arbor, Mich.). Home: 3753 Jenifer St Washington DC 20015 also 240 West Wood Dr Key Biscayne FL 33149 Office: 1225 Connecticut Av Washington DC 20036

ALBERTSON, JACK, actor; b. Malden, Mass.; s. Leo and Flora (Craft) A.; ed. pub. schs.; m. Wallace Thomson, Oct. 31, 1952; 1 dau., Maura Dhu. Engaged in theatrical work, 1930—, including vaudeville, burlesque, radio and theatre, motion pictures, TV. Broadway starring role in The Subject Was Roses, 1965. Recipient Oscar award Acad. Motion Picture Arts and Scis. for best supporting actor, 1968. Mem. Screen Actors Guild, Actors Equity, A.F.T.R.A., Am. Guild Variety Artists. Home: 8948 Rosewood Av Los Angeles CA 90048 Office: care William Morris Agy New York City NY 10020 also Beverly Hills CA 90213

ALBERTY, ROBERT ARNOLD, univ. dean; b. Winfield, Kan., June 21, 1921; s. Luman Harvey and Mattie (Arnold) A.; B.S., U. Neb., 1943, M.S., 1944; Ph.D., U. Wis., 1947; D.Sc., U. Neb., 1967, Lawrence Univ., 1967; m. Lillian Jane Wind, May 22, 1944; children—Nancy Lou, Steven Charles, Catherine Ann. Engaged in research blood plasma fractionation for U.S. Govt., 1944-46; mem. faculty U. Wis., 1947-67, prof. chemistry, 1955-67, asso. dean letters and sci., 1961-63, dean Grad. Sch., 1963-67; dean Sch. Sci., Mass. Inst. Tech., 1967—. Cons. NSF, 1958—, NIH, 1962—. Guggenheim fellow, Cal. Inst. Tech., 1950-51; recipient Eli Lilly award biol. chemistry, 1955. Mem. Am. Chem. Soc., Am. Soc. Biol. Chemists, Nat. Acad. Sci., Am. Acad. of Arts and Scis., Phi Beta Kappa, Sigma Xi. Co-Author: Physical Chemistry, 3d edit., 1966; Experimental Physical Chemistry, 3d edit., 1970. Home: 7 Old Dee Rd Cambridge, MA 02138.

ALBIG, REED HARRISON, banker; b. McKeesport, Pa., Jan. 19, 1906; s. John William and Lenora (Reed) A.; student Gettysburg Coll., 1923; A.B., Amherst Coll., 1926; grad. study Harvard; m. Helen Spaide, May 11, 1940. With McKeesport Nat. Bank, 1924—, v.p., 1929-32, exec. v.p., 1932-37, pres., 1937- -; dir. Spaide Shirt Co., Butler, Pa., 1940-47, v.p., 1941-45, pres., 1945-47; mem. bd. dirs. G. C. Murphy Co. Mem. adv. com. Office Comptroller Currency, 1962. First pres. Mon Yough Conf. on Community Devel. Bd. dirs. McKeesport Community Fund, Passavant Hosp., Pitts. Served with USNR, 1943-45. Mem. Independent Bankers Assn. (pres. 1961-62; chmn. fed. legislative com. 1966-67), McKeesport C. of C. (dir., past pres.). Home: Laurel Lane Allison Park PA 15101 Office: McKeesport Nat Bank McKeesport PA 15132

ALBION, ROBERT GREENHALGH, educator, author; b. Malden, Mass., Aug. 15, 1896; s. James Francis and Alice Marion (Lamb) A.; Schools of Portland, Me., 1904-14; A.B., Bowdoin Coll., 1918, Litt.D., 1948; A.M., Harvard, 1920, Ph.D., 1924; Litt. D., Southampton Coll., 1970; L.H.D., U. Me., 1971; m. Jennie Barnes Pope, Aug. 16, 1923. Teaching fellow, Harvard, 1920-22; with Princeton U., 1922-49, as instr. in history, 1922- 24, asst. prof., 1924-28, asso. prof., 1928-39, prof. of history, 1939- 49, dir. of summer session, 1929-42; asst. dean of the faculty, 1929-43; visiting lecturer in oceanic history and affairs, Harvard, 1948-49. Gardiner prof. oceanic history and affairs, 1949-63, prof. emeritus, 1963—; vis. prof. U. Conn., 1964-65, Emory U., Carleton Coll., 1966, U. Me., 1966—, Bowdoin Coll., 1971—. Cons. U.S. Naval War Coll., 1965, National Research Council, 1968. Pres. American Mil. Inst., 1941-45; trustee Naval Historical Found., 1946-50; consultant Maritime Adminstrn., 1952-53; co-ordinator, Munson Inst. Maritime History, 1955-66, dir. 1966—; with Harvard-Navy Polaris Program, 1964—; lectr. U.S. Mil. Acad., Nat. War Coll., U.S. Naval Acad., U.S. Coast Guard Acad. Served as 2d lt. Inf., 1918. Historian of Naval Administration, asst. dir. naval hist., office sec. of navy, 1943-50; expert consultant, War Dept., 1943; Awarded Presidential Certificate of Merit, 1948. Trustee Penobscot Marine Mus., 1960—; adv. bd. South St. Marine Mus., 1969- -. Mem. Me. Historic Sites Committee, 1960-71; m. Mem. Archives Adv. Bd., 1965—, vice chmn., 1968—. Hon. life mem. Soc., Nautical Research (England), N.J. Historical Soc. Member Maine Historical Society (member exec. com. 1958—, pres. 1963-70), Theta Delta Chi, Phi Beta Kappa. Republican. Clubs: Cumberland (Portland, Maine); Faculty (Cambridge, Massachusetts.) Author: Forests and Sea Power: The Timber Problem of the Royal Navy, 1926; Introduction to Military History, 1929; History of England and the British Empire (with W. P. Hall and J. B. Pope), 1937; Square Riggers on Schedule, 1938; The Rise of New York Port, 1815-60, 1939; Sea Lanes in Wartime (with J. B. Pope), 1942; The Navy at Sea and Ashore (with S.H.P. Read), 1947; Seaports South of Sahara, 1959; Forrestal and the Navy (with R. H. Connery), 1961; New England and the Sea (with W.A. Baker, B.W. Labaree), 1971. Editor: Philip Vickers Fithian; Journ. 1775-1776 (with L. Dodson), 1934; Exploration and Discovery, 1965; American Maritime Reprints, 1970. Editorial bd. Jour. Econ. History Am. Neptune, Essex Inst. Hist. Coll. Publs.,

Business Historical Review; also Maritime and Naval Hist.: an Annotated Bibliography, 1955. Pioneered TV course for acad. credit, Harvard, 1959-60. Home: 15 E Street South Portland ME 04106

ALBJERG, VICTOR L., educator, historian; b. Fergus Falls, Minn., Jan. 24, 1892; s. Niels M. and Karen (Johansen) A.; student Hamline U., 1914-17; A.B., U. Minn., 1918; A.M., U. Wis., 1924. Ph.D., 1926; LL.D. (hon.), St. Norbert Coll., 1967; m. Marguerite Hall, Aug. 13, 1927; 1 dau., Patricia Parks (Mrs. Loren Graham). Supt. city schs., Gary, S.D., 1920-22; asst. prof. Purdue U., 1926-29, asso. prof., 1929-37, prof., 1937-62, now emeritus; vis. prof. George Peabody Tchrs. Coll., summers 1929, 30, 31, St. Norbert Coll., 1963-66. Served with USN, overseas, World War I. Hay-Whitney fellow. Mem. Am., Ind. hist. assns., Phi Beta Kappa, Phi Delta Kappa, Sigma Beta Kappa, Alpha Phi Omega. Clubs: Torch, Parlor, Reamer. Author: Foundations of American Neutrality (with C. R. Fish), 1926; From Sedan to Stresa (with Marguerite Albjerg), 1951; Europe Since 1914, 1951; Richard Owen, 1945; Winston Churchill, Herald of Victory, 1971; also articles profl. jours. Home: 1007 Riverton Dr West LaFayette IN 47906

ALBON, ROSS K., gas co. exec.; b. Holland, O., Jan. 2, 1915; s. Harry and Iva (Box) A.; B.S., Bowling Green U., 1936; m. Mary McAndrews, June 28, 1966; children—John, Robert, Donald, Rosemary Ann, Christine, William. Asst. div. mgr. Phillips Petroleum Co., 1936-52; operations mgr. Protane Corp., 1952-59, then chmn. bd., dir.; v.p. marketing Nat. Propane Corp., 1959-60; pres., dir. No. Propane Gas Co., Omaha, 1960-67, chmn., chief exec. officer, 1967-71; pres., dir. No. Gas Products Co., Hydrocarbon Transp., Inc., No. Helex Co.; exec. v.p., dir. No. Natural Gas Co.; dir. Herman Bros., Inc. Dir. Civilian Def., Springfield Twp., O., 1941-42; mem. Springfield Twp. Sch. Bd., 1941-42. Served with AUS, 1942-46. Mem. Nat. LP-Gas Assn. (pres. 1967-68), Ancient Gassers, Sigma Alpha Epsilon. Home: 10030 Seward St Omaha NB 68114 Office: 2223 Dodge St Omaha NB 68102

ALBRAND, MARTHA, author; b. Rostock, Germany, Sept. 8, 1914; d. Paul Freybe and Paula Freybe Albrand; student U. Zürich; m. Joseph M. Loewengard, 1932; m. 2d, Sydney J. Lamon, Came to U.S., 1937, naturalized, 1947. Recipient Le Grand Prix de Literature Policiere (France), 1950. Author: No Surrender, 1942; Without Orders, 1943; Endure No Longer, 1945; Remembered Anger, 1946; None Shall Know, 1947; Whispering Hill, 1948; After Midnight, 1949; Wait For the Dawn, 1950; Desperate Moment, 1951; Challenge, 1952; The Mask of Alexander, 1955; The Linden Affair, 1956; The Obsession of Emmeth Booth, 1957; A Day in Monte Carlo, 1959; Meet Me Tonight, 1960, A Call from Austria, 1963; A Door Fell Shut, 1966; Rhine Replica, 1969; also short stories in Town & Country, Ladies Home Jour. Office: 953 Fifth Av New York City NY 10021

ALBRECHT, ANDREAS CHRISTOPH, educator, scientist; b. Berkeley, Cal., June 3, 1927; s. Andrew C. and Emma (Dinsmore) A.; B.S., U. Cal. at Berkeley, 1950; Ph.D., U. Wash., 1954; postdoctoral student Mass. Inst. Tech., 1954-56; m. Genia Solomon, Sept. 3, 1951; children—Andreas, Johanna, Maria, Robert. Mem. faculty Cornell U., 1956—. prof. chemistry, 1965—; scientist U.S.-USSR Cultural Exchange Program, 1963-64; vis. prof. chemistry U. Cal. at Santa Cruz, 1971. Served with USNR, 1945-46. NSF sci. faculty fellow, 1970-71. Mem. editorial adv. bd. Spectrochimica Acta, 1964—, Chem. Physics Letters, 1967—, Jour. Chem. Physics, 1970-72. Research in electronic spectroscopy and organic solid state. Home: 119 Clover Lane Ithaca, NY 14850.

ALBRECHT, ERICH AUGUST, educator; b. Magdeburg, Germany, Oct. 13, 1907; s. Karl Alfred and Ida (Dorscht) A.; came to U.S., 1932, naturalized, 1943; student theology, U. Berlin (Germany), 1928-32; A.B., Midland Coll., Fremont, Neb., 1934; B.D., Hamma Div. Sch., 1934; Wittenberg (O.) U., 1935; M.A., U. Neb., 1936; Ph.D., Johns Hopkins, 1941; m. Nancy Noble, June 20, 1945; children—Anthony, Ann, Peter. Asst., Then jr. instr. Johns Hopkins, 1938- 42; asst. prof. U. Man. (Can.), 1945-46; asso. prof. Tulane U., 1946-63, prof. German, 1963-65, chmn. dept., 1957-60, 62-65; prof. German, U. Kan., 1965—, dir. M.A. in Teaching program, 1967—, co-dir. Max Kade German-Am. Document and Research Center, 1968—; vis. prof. Johns Hopkins, 1947, 48, 56, Tex. Tech. U., 1960, Ohio State U., 1962. Chmn. Schiller Bi-Centennial Com., 1959; spl. cons. sec. war 1945. Commnr. elections New Orleans, 1956-65; Dem. precinct capt. 14th ward, New Orleans, 1963-65. Bd. dirs. Family Service Soc. New Orleans, 1960—. Served with AUS, 1942-45. Named hon. col. La., 1958; honor citizen New Orleans, 1965; decorated Order of Merit (Germany), 1960; grantee German Govt., 1957, Am. Council Learned Societies, 1952-53, Am. Philos. Soc., 1961-62, 63-64. Mem. Modern Lang. Assn. (mem. Goethe Bibliography 1949), Nat. Writers Frat., Am. Assn. U. Profs., Kan. Modern Lang. Assn., Am. Assn. U. Profs., Kan. Modern Lang. Assn., Am. Assn. Tchrs. German, Phi Beta Kappa, Sigma Upsilon. Author: Deutschland im Umbruch, 1938; Primitivism and Related Ideas in 18th Century German Literature, 1950. Home: 2524 Harvard Rd Lawrence, KS 66044.

ALBRECHT, GEORGE JACOB, educator, landscape architect; b. Laurel Hill, N.Y., Aug. 8, 1908; s. Jacob and Elizabeth (Glock) A.; B.S., N.Y. State Coll. Forestry, 1931; m. Sarah Virginia Gardner, Aug. 29, 1931; children—Jessie E. (Mrs. Verner W. Clapp, Jr.), Sarah Jane (Mrs. Lawrence B. White). Tchr. tech. drawing N.Y.C. high schs., 1931-33; camp supt. Civilian Conservation Corps, Selkirk Shores State Park, N.Y., 1933-44; Landscape architect Nat. Park Service, 1933-44; prof. landscape architecture, chmn. dept. State U. Sch. Landscape Architecture at Coll. Forestry, Syracuse, N.Y., 1946-68, dir. Sch. Landscape Architecture, 1968-69, emeritus dir. and prof., 1969—; cons. in field, 1950—. Chmn. N.Y. State Bd. Examiners Landscape Architecture, 1961-68; chmn. Onondaga County Natural Resources Council, 1955-59; mem. Onondaga Lake Sci. Council, 1965-68, Served to lt. USNR, 1944-46. Fellow Am. Soc. Landscape Architects (pres. Upstate N.Y. chpt. 1962, nat. trustee 1954-56), Am. Inst. Parks Execs.; mem. Syracuse Soc. Architects (asso.), Nat. Conf. State Parks, Am. Civic and Planning Assn. Home: Henderson NY 13650 also 5885 Crane Rd Melbourne Village FL 32901

ALBRECHT, HERBERT RICHARD, inst. adminstr.; b. Kenosha, Wis., Nov. 14, 1909; s. Herman Walter and Sophie (Schwark) A.; B.S., U. Wis., 1932, M.S., 1933, Ph.D., 1936; D.Agr. (hon.), Purdue U., 1962; m. Helen Virginia Terry, June 27, 1936; children—Terry Lorena (Mrs. Frederick H. Shisler), Helen Virginia (Mrs. John T. Henderson). Began Career as agronomist forage corps breeding Auburn U., 1934-44; asst. agronomist forage crops breeding and genetics Purdue U., 1944-46, asst. chief dept. agronomy, 1946-47; head dept. agronomy Pa. State U., 1947-53, dir. agrl. and home econs. extension service, asso. dean Coll. Agr., 1953-62; pres. N. D. State U., Fargo, 1962-68; dir. Internat. Inst. Tropical Agr., Ibadan, Nigeria, also program adviser Ford Found., 1968- -. Mem. Sigma Xi. Alpha Zeta (scribe 1946-52, chancellor 1952-56), Phi Kappa Phi, Gamma Sigma Delta, Sigma Alpha Epsilon, Phi Sigma, Phi Epsilon Phi, Phi Eta Sigma, Blue Key. Lutheran. Kiwanian, Elk. Home: 2 South Dr Lansdale, PA 19446. Office: 320 E 43d St New York City NY 10017

ALBRECHT, MILTON C., educator; b. Dundee, Ill., Sept. 17, 1904; s. Charles J. and Mary (Wendt) A.; A.B., Antioch Coll., 1929; M.A. in English, U. Cal. at Berkeley, 1931, Ph.D. in English, 1937; m. Evelyn M. Thoman, Jan. 3, 1929. From instr. to asst. prof. English, U. Ida., 1937-46; mem. faculty State U. N.Y. at Buffalo (formerly U. Buffalo), 1946—, prof. sociology, 1955—, dean Coll. Arts and Scis., 1958-65; cons. research Council Community Welfare, Buffalo, 1952-63; contbr. Annual Community Life Conf., 1952-60. Past mem. bd. Buffalo Urban League; bd. dirs. Western N.Y. Nuclear Research Center. Recipient N.Y. State Faculty fellowship, 1966, 68, 71. Fellow Am. Sociol. Assn. (chmn. sect. sociology of lit. 1957, 60); mem. Eastern Sociol. Soc., Nat. Council Family Relations, Nat. Council Study Edn., Middle States Assn. Colls. and Secondary Schs. (evaluating teams 1959-64, 66-67, 68), Am. Assn. U. Profs., Buffalo Chamber Music Soc. (dirs.). Editor: Studies in Sociology, Buffalo Studies series, 1967; co-editor: The Sociology of Art and Literature, 1970. Contbr. articles profl. jours. Home: 16 Lake Ledge Dr Buffalo NY 14221

ALBRECHT, RALPH GERHART, lawyer; b. Jersey City, Aug. 11, 1896; s. J. Robert and Gertrude A. F. (Richter) A.; A.B., U. Pa., 1919; J.D., Harvard, 1923; m. Aillinn Leffingwell; 1 son, Peter Leffingwell. Admitted to N.Y. bar, 1924, also U.S. Supreme Ct.; sr. partner Peaslee, Albrecht & McMahon, 1946-60, of counsel, 1960—; spl. asst. to U.S. atty. gen. and asso. trial counsel to Justice Robert H. Jackson, Nuernberg War Crimes Trial, 1945-46; asst. dir. OSS, 1945; counsel German steel, coal and chem. industries in decartelization proceedings before Allied High Commn., 1950-53. Delegate 1st Internat. Congress Comparative Law, The Hague, 1932. Mem. Harvard Overseers' vis. com. to faculty Germanic langs. and lit., 1949-62. Served as apprentice seaman USNRF, 1918; served with Squadron A, 101st Cav., N.Y. N.G., 1924-30; comdr. USNR, 1941-45. Fellow Am. Geog. Soc.; mem. Assn. Bar City N.Y. (fgn. and internat. law coms.), Municipal Art Soc., Am. (chmn. com. pvt. claims against govts.), Internat. (patron) bar assns., Am. Soc. Internat. Law (chmn. Manley O. Hudson medal com.). Internat. Law Assn. (del. Tokyo conf. 1964), Goethe House, Internat., Nat., N.Y.C. legal aid socs., Nat., Mass. Audubon socs., U.S. Naval Inst., Acad. Polit. Sci. (life), Busch-Reisinger Mus., Ex-mems. Squadron A (gov.), Fellowship U.S.-British Comrades (pres. N.Y. chpt. 1949-50), World Peace Through Law Centre. Republican. Mason. Clubs: University, Harvard, Squadron A, Pilgrims U.S. Co- author: America Next, 1940. Research vocational guidance recent sch., and coll. grads. Home: 520 E 86th St New York City NY 10028 Office: 501 5th Av New York City NY 10017

ALBRECHT, WILLIAM PRICE, univ. dean; b. Wilkinsburg, Pa., June 25, 1907; s. Frederick Carl and Althea Adelaide (Price) A.; B.S., Carnegie Inst. Tech., 1929; M.A., U. Pitts., 1934; Ph.D. (Univ. fellow 1938-39), U. Chgo., 1943; Faculty fellow Fund Advancement Edn., U. Oxford (Eng.), 1952-53; m. Jane Lanier Moses, July 17, 1931; children—William Price, Thomas Frederick, Jane Lanier (Mrs. Jean Louis Alix). Tech. writer, editor Westinghouse Electric Corp., 1929-32, 43; instr. English, then asst. prof. Carnegie Inst. Tech., 1934-37, 46; asst. English, U. Chgo., 1938- 39; instr. U. Pitts., 1939-42; asst. prof. Bucknell U. Jr. Coll., 1942- 43; mem. faculty U. N.M., 1946-57, prof., 1954-57, prof. English, U. Kan., 1957—, chmn. dept., 1957-63, dean Grad. Sch., 1963—. Evaluator cons. N. Central Assn., 1964—; cons. So. Ill. U., 1959, 65, U. Wyo., 1964, U.S. Office Edn., 1962-63, 65-68, Mich. State U., 1968-69. Served to lt. USNR, 1943-46; ret. comdr. Mem. Am. Assn. U. Profs. (pres. N.M. 1955), Modern Humanities Research Assn., Modern Lang. Assn., Midwest Modern Lang. Assn. (pres. 1959-60, exec. com. 1960-63), Internat. Assn. U. Profs. English, Nat. Council Tchrs. English, Phi Kappa Phi, Alpha Tau Omega. Democrat. Presbyn. Club: Lawrence (Kansas) Golf and Country. Author: William Hazlitt and the Malthusian Controversy, 1950; The Loathly Lady in Thomas of Erceldoune, 1954; (with C. V. Wicker) The American Technical Writer, 1960; Hazlitt and the Creative Imagination, 1965. Editor Jour. Proceedings and Addresses of the Assn. of Grad. Schs., 1970—. Contbr. profl. jours. Home: 1633 University Dr Lawrence KS 66044

ALBRECHT-CARRIE, RENE, retired educator; b. Izmir, Turkey, Jan. 20, 1904; s. Ernest and Claire (Carrié) Albrecht-C.; came to U.S., 1920, naturalized, 1923; B.-ès Sc., B.-ès-L., French Lycée, Aixen-Provence, 1920; A.B., Columbia, 1923, M.A., 1923, Ph.D. 1938; m. Eleanor Kingsley, July 23, 1932; children—Claire (Mrs. Michael Tomlinson), Pierre. Instr. math. Coll. City N.Y., also Townsend Harris High Sch., N.Y.C., 1923-42; instr. history Queens Coll., 1942-45; prof. history Barnard Coll., 1945-69; prof. history Sch. Internat. Affairs, Columbia, 1953-69, emeritus, 1969—. Rockefeller grantee, France, 1952-53; Fulbright lectr., Italy, 1960-61; Guggenheim fellow, 1966-67. Mem. Am. Hist. Assn. (George L. Beer prize 1938), Council Fgn. Relations, socs. French, Italian hist. studies, Am.-Italy Soc. Author: Italy at the Paris Peace Conference, 1938; Italy from Napoleon to Mussolini, 1950; Diplomatic History of Europe since the Congress of Vienna, 1958; France, Europe and the Two World Wars, 1960; One Europe, 1965.; The Concert of Europe, 1968, Britain and France: Adaptations to a Changing Context of Power, 1970. Home: 39 Claremont Av New York City NY 10027

ALBRIGHT, ARCHIE EARL, Jr., investment banker; b. Akron, O., Aug. 21, 1920; s. Archie E. and Hazel (Beard) A.; A.B. magna cum laude, Wittenberg Coll., 1942; LL.B., Yale, 1948; children—John, Anne, Catherine. Admitted N.Y. bar, 1948; mem. firm Patterson, Belknap & Webb, 1948-53; asst. to pres. Stauffer Chem. Co., N.Y.C., 1953, v.p., 1958-65, exec. v.p., 1965-68; partner Kuhn Loeb & Co., N.Y.C., 1968-69; pres., chief exec. officer Glore Forgan Staats, Inc., 1969-70, Loeb Rhoades & Co., 1971—; dir. P.R. Mallory & Co., Inc., Mich. Gas. Utilities Co., Bowmar Instruments Co. Trustee Nat. Repertory Theater; mem. adv. council Hampshire Coll., bd. of dirs. Fgn. Policy Assn., Police Athletic League. Mem. Assn. Bar City N.Y. Clubs: Yale, Links, Nat. Golf (N.Y.C.); Bedford (N.Y.) Golf and Tennis. Home: 125 E 63d St New York City NY 10021 Office: 375 Park Av New York City NY 10022

ALBRIGHT, ARNOLD DEWALD, ednl. adminstr.; b. Washington, Mar. 6, 1913; s. Earl J. and Elizabeth (Welch) A.; Rector scholar DePauw U., 1931-32; A.B. (honor scholar 1934- 37), Milligan Coll., 1937; M.S. (grad. fellow 1937-38), U. Tenn., 1938; Ph.D. (Gen. Edn. Bd. fellow 1949-50), N.Y.U., 1950; m. Grace Carroll, June 23, 1939; children—Carl Wesley, Earl Thomas. Field worker U.S. Bur. Plant Industry, 1932-34; supr. Chattanooga pub. schs., 1938-39; supr. Tenn. Dept. Edn., then dir. research, chmn. staff, asst. state commr. edn., 1939-49; prof. edn. George Peabody Coll., 1950- 54; asso. dir. So. States Coop. Program in Ednl. Adminstrn., 1950-54; dir. bur. sch. service, chmn. div. ednl. adminstrn., prof. edn. U. Ky., 1954-57, exec. dean extended programs, 1957-61, provost, 1960-62, exec. v.p., 1962-69, v.p. instnl. planning, 1970—; associate director Asso. Programs in Ednl. Adminstrn., Auburn U., 1954-57; cons. So. Regional Edn. Bd. Atlanta, 1958; cons. local Edn. Commn. Atlanta and Fulton County, 1959; study dir. W.Va. Bd. Edn., 1960. Cons. Tenn. Commn. on Children, 1949. Conn. Gov.'s Fact Finding Commn., 1950, So. Edn. Found., 1954—; cons. Ashmore Study (Fund for Advancement of Edn.), 1952-54; asso. dir. study higher edn. Tenn. Legislative council, 1956-58; Tenn. edn. chmn. A.R.C., 1948. Mem. Nat. Conf. Profs. Ednl. Adminstrn. (chmn. 1957), Nat. Council Chief States Sch. Officers, N.E.A., John Dewey Soc., Am. Assn. Sch. Adminstrs., Assn. Higher Edn., Phi Delta Kappa, Sigma Nu, Omicron Delta Kappa. Methodist. Club: Donelson Civic (pres. 1945-47). Author: (with Truman M. Pierce) A Profession in Transition, 1960. Editor: Administrative Leadership, 1952. Adv. editorial bd. The School Executive, 1957-59. Home: 791 Chinoe Rd Lexington KY 40502

ALBRIGHT, EDWIN CARTER, physician, educator; b. Iowa City, Ia., Oct. 8, 1915; s. George Carter and Anna Smith (Close) A.; B.A., State U. Ia., 1936; M.D., Harvard, 1940; m. Mary Gertrude Braunlich, Oct. 26, 1940; children—John, David, George, William. Intern, Mass. Gen. Hosp., Boston, 1940-42; research fellow, resident U. Wis. Med. Sch., Madison, 1946-48, instr. medicine, 1948-49, asst. prof., 1949-55, asso. prof., 1955-60, prof. medicine, 1960—; chief of staff U. Wis. Hosp., 1965; cons. VA Hosp., Madison, 1951—. Bd. dirs. Family Service Agy. Served with M.C., AUS, 1942-46. Diplomate Am. Bd. Internal Medicine. Mem. A.M.A., Am. Thyroid Assn. (dir. 1962-66), Assn. Am. Physicians, Am. Soc. Clin. Investigation, Central Soc. for Clin. Research, A.C.P., Endocrine Soc., Wis. Med. Soc., Phi Beta Kappa, Sigma Xi. Rotarian. Mem. editorial bd. Jour. Clin. Endocrin and Metabolism, 1963-67. Home: 3901 Euclid Av Madison WI 53711

ALBRIGHT, GEORGE FRANKLIN, former life ins. co. exec.; b. Belmont, N.C., Sept. 13, 1916; s. Claude Lee and Minnie (Tate) A.; grad. Davidson Coll., 1937, Advanced Mgmt. Program Harvard, 1956; m. Dorothy Severs, June 25, 1938; children—Dorothy Jane, Claudia Ann, George Franklin. Agt., Union Central Life Ins. Co., 1938-39; with Life Ins. Co. Va., Richmond, 1939- 71, asst. to pres., 1956-57, v.p. charge agencies, 1957-61, sr. v.p., 1961-71, dir., 1960-71; dir. Harford Mut. Ins. Co., Bank of Va. Served to 1st lt Aus, 1943-46. Presbyn. Rotarian, Mason. Clubs: Commonwealth; Country of Va. Home: Berkshire Rd Richmond VA 23221

ALBRIGHT, HARRY DARKES, educator; b. Lebanon, Pa., July 24, 1907; s. Harry S. and Bertha (Darkes) A.; A.B., Lebanon Valley Coll., 1928; A.M., Cornell U., 1931, Ph.D., 1936; m. Elizabeth O. Nelson, June 24, 1936; children—Judith (Mrs. Patrick Gaetani), Stephen. Instr., Ia. State Tchrs. Coll., 1934- 36; instr. Cornell U., Ithaca, N.Y., 1936-40, asst. prof., 1940-46, asso. prof., 1946-58, prof., 1958—, chmn. theatre arts dept., 1949-57, 65-66. Fellow Am. Ednl. Theatre Assn. (past pres.); mem. Speech Assn. Am., Phi Kappa Phi. Democrat. Presbyn. Author: Working Up A Part, 1947; Principles of Theatre Art, 1955. Gen. editor. Books of the Theatre, 1962- 70. Editor: Ednl. Theatre Jour., 1952-54; The Story of the Meininger, 1963; Memories of the Theatre Libre, 1964; Meyerhold's Theatre of the Grotesque, 1971. Translator: The Work of Living Art, 1960. Home: 129 N Sunset Dr Ithaca NY 14850

ALBRIGHT, HORACE MARDEN, conservationist, corp. cons.; b. Bishop, Calif., Jan. 6, 1890; s. George L. and Mary (Marden) A.; B.L., University of California, 1912; LL.B., Georgetown, 1914; LL.D., U. Montana, 1956, U. California, 1961, U. New Mexico, 1962; m. Grace Marian Noble, December 23, 1915; children—Robert (dec.), Marian (Mrs. Jay B. Ford, Jr.). Asst. econs., U. Cal., 1912-13, mem. staff, sec. interior Franklin K. Lane, 1913-16; admitted to bar, D.C. and Calif., 1914; asst. atty. dept. of interior, assigned to nat. park affairs, 1915-17; asst. dir. Nat. Park Service, Washington, D.C., 1917-19, acting dir., 1917-18; asst. dir. (field) same, and supt. Yellowstone Nat. Park, June 28, 1919-Jan. 12, 1929; temporarily in charge Yosemite Nat. Park, 1927-28; dir. Nat. Park Service, Jan. 12, 1929-Aug. 9, 1933. Mem. Nat. Capital Park and Planning Commn., 1929-33; v.p. and gen. mgr., dir. U.S. Potash Co., 1933-46, president, gen. mgr., dir., 1946-56, retired; member board directors Grand Teton Lodge Company. Member bd. trustees Jackson Hole Preserve, Inc., Mills Coll., 1939-42, 1951-59; mem. Council Save-the-Redwoods League; hon. member American Society Landscape Architects; mem. natural resources com. Hoover Commn. to Organize Exec. Br. of Govt., 1948-49; mem. adv. council Nat. Outdoor Recreation Resources Review Com., 1959-62. Berkeley fellow, 1968. Mem. Nat. Audubon Soc. (Audubon medal 1969), Am. Forestry Assn., Theodore Roosevelt Assn. (trustee, hon. v.p.), Nature Conservancy, Nat. Trust Hist. Preservation, Am. Scenic and Historic Preservation Soc. (hon. pres., trustee), Nat. Parks Assn., Wilderness Soc., Desert Protective Council, Resources for Future (dir., chmn. 1952-61), Am. Plan and Civic Association (president 1936-46), Death Valley 49ers (hon. dir.), Pacific Tropical Bot. Garden (pres. 1964-71, trustee), Am. Pioneer Trails Assn. (v.p.), Phi Delta Phi, Beta Gamma Sigma. Presbyn. Mason. Clubs: Cosmos (Washington); Sierra of San Francisco (hon. life); Boone and Crockett, Explorers, Century, Campfire of America (hon. mem. (N.Y.C.); U.C.L.A. Faculty Center (Los Angeles). Author: (with F. J. Taylor) Oh Ranger (about national parks); also numerous articles on conservation, nat. parks, etc. Awarded Pugsley gold medal, Am. Scenic and Historic Preservation Soc., 1933; Order of the Northern Star (Sweden), 1926; named Alumnus of the Year, U. Cal. Alumni, 1952; Frances K. Hutchinson medal Garden Club Am., 1959; Theodore Roosevelt Distinguished Service medal, 1959; Gold medal Camp Fire Club Am., 1962; Distinguished Service award, Am. Forestry award, 1968.

ALBRIGHT, IVAN, artist; b. Chgo., Feb. 20, 1897; s. Adam Emory and Clara Amelia (Wilson) A.; student Northwestern U., 1915-16, U. Ill., 1916-17; art studies Art Inst. Chgo., 1919-23, Pa. Acad. Fine Arts, Phila., 1923, N.A.D., N.Y.C., 1924; L.H.D., Mundelein Coll., 1969; m. Josephine Medill Patterson; children—Joseph Medill Patterson, Alice Patterson, Adam Medill, Blandina Van Etten. Represented in permanent collections Met. Mus. Art, Mus. Modern Art, N.Y.C., Bklyn. Mus., Guggenheim Mus., N.Y.C., Whitney Mus. Am. Art, N.Y.C., Carnegie Inst., Pitts., Chgo. Art Inst., Phila. Mus. Art., Library of Congress, Washington, Wadsworth Athenaeum, Hartford, Conn., Nat. Mus., Jerusalem, Israel, Detroit Inst. Arts, Phoenix Mus. Art, Finch Gallery Art, N.Y.C., Pushkin Mus., Moscow, Russia, Ark. Arts Center; also in pvt. collections Exhibited group shows Internationals Carnegie Inst., Pitts., Pan-Am. Internat., Balt., Century of Progress, Chgo., Golden Gate Internat., San Francisco, N.Y. World's Fair, Half Century Am. Art, Art Inst. Chgo., Twentieth Century Portraits, Mus. Modern Art, N.Y.C., 50 Prints of the Year, One Hundred Am. Prints, The Artist Looks at People, Chgo. Art Inst., Realists and Magic Realists, Mus. Modern Art, N.Y., Masterpiece of the Month, Chgo. Art Inst.; shown internat. in London, Paris, Stockholm, Oslo, Rome, Venice, Berlin, Dusseldorf, Constantinople, Zurich, Tel Aviv, Arras, Milan, Toronto, Sao Paolo. Recipient John C. Shaffer prize Chgo. Art Inst., 1928, Silver medal, 1930, Brower prize, 1941, Harris bronze medal and award, 1943, print prize, 1945, Watson F. Blair prize, 1949, Cahn prize, 1950; silver medal Chgo. Soc. Artists, 1930, gold medal, 1931; Phila. Water Color Club prize Pa. Acad. Fine Arts, 1940, Temple gold medal, 1942, Fellowship prize, 1942, J. Henry Schiedt Meml. prize, 1956; 1st medal for best painting Met. Mus. Victory for Artists Exhbn., N.Y.C., 1942, Met. Mus. prize, 1952; 1st Altman prize N.A.D., 1944, 61; 1st prize 3d Nat. Print Exhbn., 1946; silver medal and award Corcoran Gallery of Art, Washington, 1955; H.M. 24th Carnegie Internat. Exhbn., Pitts., 1950; Northwestern U. Centennial award Northwestern Ty., 1951; $5000 prize Dunn Internat., Lord Beaverbrook Gallery, Frederickton, N.B., N.S. Tate Gallery, London, Eng., 1962. Academician N.A.D. Mem. Nat. Inst. Arts and Letters, Am. Watercolor Soc., Pa. Acad. Fine Arts Fellowship, Am. Acad. Arts and Letters, Chgo. Soc. Artists (past pres.), Phila. Water Color Club. Clubs: Casino, Saddle and Cycle, Tavern, Arts, Chicago Century (Chgo.); Lotos (N.Y.C.); Wayfarers. Home: 880 Lake Shore Dr Chicago IL 60611

ALBRIGHT, JOSEPH MEDILL PATTERSON, newspaperman; b. New Orleans, Apr. 3, 1937; s. Jay Frederick and Josephine (Patterson) Reeve; adopted by Ivan Albright; B.A., Williams Coll., 1958; m. Madeleine Korbel, June 11, 1959; children—Anne Korbel, Alice Patterson, Katharine Medill. Reporter, Denver Post, summers 1956, 57, Chgo. Sun Times, 1958-61; with Newsday, 1961—, chief Washington bur., 1969—, dir., 1963-71. Pres. Alicia Patterson Fund, Alicia Patterson Fund Fellowship Program. Mem. Phi Beta Kappa, Theta Delta Chi. Club: Nat. Press (Washington). Home: 1318 34th St NW Washington DC 20007 Office: Nat Press Bldg Washington DC 20004

ALBRIGHT, JUSTIN W., lawyer; b. Lisbon, Ia., Oct. 14, 1908; B.S.C., U. Ia., 1931, J.D., 1933. Admitted to Ia. bar, 1933; now mem. firm Simmons, Perrine, Albright & Ellwood, Cedar Rapids. Mem. Am., Ia., Linn County bar assns., Phi Delta Phi. Editor Ia. Law Rev., 1932-33. Office: Mchts Nat Bank Bldg Cedar Rapids IA 52406*

ALBRIGHT, LYLE FREDERICK, educator, chem. engr.; b. Bay City, Mich., May 3, 1921; s. William E. and Isabella (Sidebotham) A.; B.S. in Chem. Engring., U. Mich., 1943, M.S., 1944, Ph.D., 1949; m. Jeannette M. Van Belle, Mar. 4, 1950; children—Christine, Diane. Lab technician Dow Chem. Co., 1939-41; chem. engr. E.I. du Pont De Nemours & Co., Inc., Hanford, Wash., 1944-46; research asso. U. Mich., 1948-49; research chem. engr. Colgate-Palmolive Co., Jersey City, 1950-51; asst. prof., asso. prof. U. Okla., 1951- 55; faculty Purdue U., Lafayette, Ind., 1955—, prof., 1958—. Cons. in industry, 1953—. Mem. Am. Inst. Chem. Engrs., Am. Chem. Soc., Am. Oil Chemists Soc., Am. Soc. Engring. Edn., Am. Gas Assn., Combustion Inst., Internat. Brotherhood Magicians. Presbyn. Contbr. articles to profl. jours. Home: 4773N-250W West Lafayette IN 47906

ALBRIGHT, MALVIN MARR, painter, sculptor (painter, under nom de plume Zsissly); b. Chgo., Feb. 20, 1897; s. Adam Emory and Clara Amelia (Wilson) A.; ed. Art Inst. Chgo., Pa. Acad. Fine Arts; Beaux Arts Inst. Design; m. Cornelia Warren Fairbanks, Dec. 18, 1954. Has exhibited paintings and sculpture, 1927—, at N.A.D., Whitney Mus., Mus. Modern Art (all N.Y.C.), Carnegie Inst. (Pitts.), Pa. Acad. Fine Art, Mus. Art Phila. (both Phila.), Corcoran Gallery Art (Washington), Art Inst. Chgo.; also in many important U.S. cities, Internat. fairs, spl. exhbns.; represented in permanent collections Corcoran Gallery, Pa. Acad. Fine Arts, Toledo (O.) Art Mus., San Diego Art Mus., Butler Art Mus. (Youngstown, O.), Library of Congress, others. Recipient numerous awards and prizes N.A.D., Corcoran Gallery Art, Art Inst. Chgo., Dana Water Color medal Pa. Acad. of Fine Arts, others, 1922—. Fellow Royal Soc. Arts (London), Internat. Inst. of Arts and Letters, Pa. Acad. Fine Arts, Phila. Water Color Club; mem. N.A.D. (academician), Nat. Sculpture Soc. Clubs: Tavern, Art, Saddle and Cycle; Peale (Phila.). Home: 1500 Lake Shore Dr Chicago IL 60610 also Harbor Lights Corea ME 04624 also Villa of the Mango Tree 3500 Vista Park Fort Lauderdale FL 33308 ☆

ALBRIGHT, PENROSE STRONG, educator; b. Winfield, Kan., Dec. 14, 1896; s. P. H. and Emma (Strong) A.; B.S., Rensselaer Polytech. Inst., 1922; M.S., U. of Wis., 1929, Ph.D., 1936; m. Mary Lucas, Apr. 27, 1924; children—Penrose Lucas, James Curtice, John Grover. With Southwestern Coll., Winfield, Kan., 18 yrss.; instr. to prof., chmn. div. natural sci. and coordinator of war training service, faculty rep. armed services; head physics dept. Wichita State Univ., 1943-61, prof. emeritus, 1961—; v.p., dir. Kansas-Oklahoma Oil & Gas Company. Bd. dirs. Congregational Found. theol. studies. Honoree, Penrose Albright chair of physics Southwestern Coll. Mem. Am. Chem. Soc., Am. Phys. Soc., Kan. Acad. Sci. (pres. 1949-50), Am. Inst. Chemists, Am. Assn. Physics Tchrs., Am. Soc. Engring. Edn., Am. Legion. Republican. Clubs: Rotary, Farm and Ranch (pres. 1954) (Wichita). Author sci. articles. Home: 220 N Terrace Dr Wichita, KS 67208.

ALBRIGHT, RAYMOND JACOB, govt. ofcl.; b. Reading, Pa., Apr. 7, 1929; s. Raymond Wolf and Catherine (Sherr) A.; B.A., Yale, 1951; Fulbright scholar U. Vienna (Austria), 1951-52; M.A., Harvard, 1954, Ph.D. in Polit. Sci., 1961; m. Ruthmarie Reich, Sept. 13, 1952; children—Raymond Jacob, David Reich. Fgn. affairs officer (Nat. Security Council) affairs and policy planning Office Asst. Sec. Def. (Internat. Security Affairs), 1954-61; with Office Asst. Sec. State (European affairs), 1961- 62; nat. security affairs adviser Treasury Dept., 1962-67; asst. to sec. treasury (Nat. Security Affairs), Office Sec. Treasury, 1967-69; counselor for econ. affairs Am. embassy, Belgrade, Yugoslavia, 1969—; fgn. service res. officer Dept. State, 1969—. Lectr., Yale, 1959, George Washington U., 1960. Mem. Kensington (Md.) Civic Assn., 1958-60. Bd. dirs. Fgn. Policy Discussion Group, Washington. Club: Yale (bd. dirs., chmn. Yale and govt. com. 1966-69 Washington. Author: (with others) Forging a New Sword, 1958. Home: 3609 Dunlop St Chevy Chase MD 20015 Office: Am embassy Belgrade Dept State Washington DC 20521

ALBRITTAIN, JOHN WARREN, naval med. officer; b. LaPlata, Md., Apr. 30, 1911; s. Warren M. and Alberta M. (Carpenter) A.; B.S., U. Md., 1933, M.D., 1935; m. Lorain Cass. May 30, 1957. Intern Univ. Hosp., Balt., 1935-37, resident obstetrics and gynecology, 1937-39; pvt. practice, Balt., 1939-40; commd. lt. (j.g.), M.C., U.S. Navy, 1940, advanced through grades to rear adm., 1965; assigned U.S. Naval Air Sta., San Juan, P.R., 1941-42, U.S.S. Wyoming, 1945-46; resident dermatology U.S. Naval Hosp., St. Albans, N.Y., 1946-49; assigned U.S.S. Iowa, 1953-54, Naval Hosp., Bethesda, Md., 1954-59; exec. officer U.S. Naval Hosp., Portsmouth, Va., 1962-64; comdg. officer Naval Hosp., St. Albans, 1965-66, Great Lakes (Ill.) Naval Hosp., 1966-69; dep. surgeon gen. Bur. Medicine, Washington, 1969 —; Diplomate Am. Bd. Dermatology. Mem. Am. Acad. Dermatology, Soc. Investigative Dermatology, Soc. Tropical Dermatology, Assn. Mil. Dermatologists, A.M.A. Mailing Address: Office: Bur Medicine and Surgery Dept Navy Washington DC 20390

ALBRITTON, CLAUDE CARROLL, Jr., univ. adminstr.; b. Corsicana, Tex., Apr. 7, 1913; s. Claude C. and Iris (Stapleton-) A.; A.B., B.S., So. Meth. U., 1933; A.M., Harvard, 1934, Ph.D. (J. B. Woodworth fellow 1935-36), 1936; m. Jane Christman, Aug. 5, 1944; children—Jane DeHart, Claude C., Elizabeth Ann. From Instr. to asso. prof. geology Southern Methodist U., 1936-17, prof., 1947—, dean faculty Coll. Arts and Scis., 1952-57, dean Grad. Sch., 1957-71, now W.B. Hamilton prof. geology, chmn. bd. publs., vice provost for library devel., exec. sec., treas. Colophon; dir. Grad. Research Center, Inc., 1961-64; dir. Sci. Information Inst., 1964—; geologist U. S. Geol. Survey, 1942-49. Chmn. scholarship selection com. of the Chance Vought Aircraft Corporation, 1955-63; mem. com. geosci. amd man Internat. Union Geol. Socs., U. Cambridge, Eng., 1971; mem. exec. com. John E. Owens Found. Rosenbach Fellow in bibliography U. Pa., 1969-70. Recipient DeWitt medal, 1933. Mem. Dallas Council World Affairs (past dir.), A.A.A.S. (v.p. 1968, mem. philosophy of sci. and math. edn. 1970), Geol. Soc. Am., (councilor 1957-69, chmn. joint tech. program com. 1973), Paleontol. Soc., Am. Assn. Petroleum Geologists, Am. Geol. Inst. (chmn. Liberal arts panel 1963-66), Soc. Econ. Paleontologists and Mineralogists, Tex. Acad. Sci. Phi Beta Kappa, Sigma Xi. Methodist. Clubs: Critic, Cadence, Cosmos. Co-author: The Midland Discovery, 1955; Guidelines and Standards for the Education of Secondary School Teachers of Science and Mathematics, 1971. Editor and co- author: The Fabric of Geology, 1964, Uniformity and Simplicity, 1965; Filosofia de la Geologia, 1970; Editor Jour. Grad. Research Center. Home: 3436 University Blvd Dallas TX 75205

ALBRITTON, ELMER SANFORD, lawyer; b. Dallas, Apr. 5, 1922; s. Elmer Sanford and Mary (Bierer) A.; B.S. in Chem. Engring., Northwestern U., 1947; postgrad. U. Cal. at Berkeley, 1948-50; LL.B. George Washington U., 1952, J.D., 1969; m. Grace Stribling, Aug. 8, 1948; children—Robert Sanford, John, Paul Bierer, Sue Ann. Admitted to D.C. bar, 1952, Cal. bar, 1953; devel. chemist U.S. Rubber Co., 1947-48; patent examiner U.S. Patent Office, 1950-52; patent atty. A.D. Owen, 1952-54, Miketta & Glenny, Los Angeles, 1954-57; patent atty. Flehr & Swain, San Francisco, 1957-58, partner, 1958-67; partner Flehr. Hohbach, Test, Albritton & Herbert, San Francisco, 1967—. Served to lt. USNR, 1943-46. Mem. Am. Bar Assn., Northwestern U., U. Cal. Law Sch. alumni assns., Phi Delta Phi, Phi Delta Theta. Club: Engineers (San Francisco). Home: 55 Upland Rd Kentfield CA 94904 Office: Hong Kong Bank Bldg 160 Sansome St San Francisco CA 94104

ALBRITTON, ROBERT BYNUM, lawyer; b. Andalusia, Ala., Feb. 1, 1905; s. William Harold and Anne (Mashburn) A.; LL.B., U. Ala., 1930; m. Carrie Veal, Aug. 16, 1928; 1 son, William Harold III. Admitted to Ala. bar, 1930, since practiced in Andalusia; mem. firm Albritton & Rankin, 1930—. Dir., v.p., gen. counsel Ala. Textile Products Corp., Andala Co., Troy Textiles, Inc., Enterprise Mfg. Co., Evergreen Textiles, Inc., Elba Apparels, Inc. Bd. dirs. U. Ala. Law Sch. Found. Mem. Am., Ala. (1st v.p. 1970-71), Covington County (pres.1955) bar assns., Fedn. Ins. Counsel, Kappa Sigma, Phi Delta Phi. Presbyn. (deacon). Rotarian. Club: Andalusia Country. Home: 723 Albritton Rd Andalusia AL 36420 Office: 109 Opp Av Andalusia AL 34620

ALBRITTON, ROBERT SANFORD, life ins. exec.; b. St. Paul, Feb. 19, 1914; s. Elmer Sanford and Mary (Bierer) A.; B.S., Northwestern U., 1935; M.B.A., U. Pa., 1937; C.L.U., 1947; m. Helen Richards, Mar. 14, 1938; children—David Richards, Robert Rapp. Agy. supr. Minn. Mut. Life Ins. Co., Mpls., 1937-40; agt. Provident Mut. Life Ins. Co. Phila., Los Angeles, 1940—; pres. Albritton, Frank & Page, Inc., 1961—; chmn. ins. operations com. Empire Life Ins. Co., 1963—. Pres. Million Dollar Round Table of Nat. Assn. Life Underwriters, 1960, Million Dollar Round Table Found., 1962-64. Mem. Phi Delta Theta. Club: Los Angeles Country. Home: 2012 Mandeville Canyon Rd Los Angeles CA 90049 Office: 11661 San Vicente Blvd Los Angeles CA 90049

ALBRITTON, ROGERS GARLAND, educator; b. Columbus, O., Aug. 15, 1923; s. Errett Cyril and Rietta (Garland) A.; student Swarthmore Coll., 1939-41; A.B., St. John's Coll., Annapolis, 1948; M.A. in Philosophy, Princeton, 1952, Ph.D., 1955. Faculty asso. St. John's Coll., 1948-49; part-time instr. N.J. Coll. Women, 1952-53, also Princeton; instr. Sage Sch. Philosophy, Cornell U., 1953-56; mem. faculty Harvard, 1956—, prof. philosophy, 1962—, chmn. com. higher degrees history and philosophy religion, 1960-62, chmn. dept. philosophy, 1963-70. Served with USAAF, 1943-46. Research fellow Am. Council Learned Socs., 1962-63. Fellow Am. Acad. Arts and Scis.; mem. Am. Philos. Assn. Home: 300 Quincy House Cambridge, MA 02138.

ALBURN, MIRIAM ESTELLE, newspaper writer; b. Bklyn.; d. Wilfred Henry and Miriam (Russell) Alburn; A.B., Vassar Coll. Editorial writer Mpls. Star and Tribune, Mpls. Recipient writing awards Minn. Press Women, Nat. Fedn. Press Women, Newspaper Guild of the Twin Cities. Mem. Minn. Press Women (pres. 1955 -56). Home: 11 Summit Pl Minneapolis MN 55405 Office: Mpls Star and Tribune Co Fifth and Portland Sts Minneapolis MN 55415

ALCALAY, ALBERT S., artist, educator; b. Paris, France, Aug. 11, 1917; s. Samuel and Lepa (Afar) A.; student in Paris and Rome, Italy; m. Vera Eshenazi, Nov. 11, 1950; children—Leor, Ammiel. Came to U.S., 1951, naturalized, 1956. One man show De Cordova Mus., Lincoln, Mass., 1968; exhbns. include Venice (Italy) Biennale, Whitney Mus. Modern Art., Mus. Am. Art, U. Ill. at Urbana; represented Mus. Modern Art, N.Y.C., Boston Mus. Fine Arts, Harvard's Fogg Art Mus., DeCordova Mus., Phillips Acad. Mus. Am. Art, Brandeis U. Rose Art Mus., U. Mass. Mus., Wellesley Coll. Mus., Colby Coll. Mus., Smith Coll., U. Rome. Asst. lectr. design Carpenter Center, Harvard, 1960—. Guggenheim fellow, 1960; recipient prize Boston Arts Festival, 1960—. Home: 66 Powell St Brookline MA 02146 Office: 19 Prescott St Cambridge MA 01238

ALCHIAN, ARMEN ALBERT, educator; b. Fresno, Cal., Apr. 12, 1914; s. Alex H. and Lily (Normart) A.; student Fresno State Coll., 1932-34; A.B., Stanford, 1936, Ph.D. in Econs., 1944; m. Pauline Crouse, Sept. 30, 1939; children—Arline (Mrs. Carlton Hoel), Allen. Asst. prof. U. Ore., 1942; faculty U. Cal., Los Angeles, 1946- -, prof. econs., 1958—. Cons. Rand Corp., 1947-62. Served to capt. USAAF, 1942-46. Mem. Mt. Pelerin Soc. Author: University Economics, 3d edit., 1971; Exchange and Production, 1969. Contbr. articles to profl. jours. Home: 3113 Colby St Los Angeles CA 90066

ALCIATORE, ROY LOUIS, restaurateur; b. New Orleans, Dec. 19, 1902; s. Jules Louis and Marie Althea (Roy) A.; student St. Aloysius Coll., New Orleans, 1913-17, Spring Hill Coll., Mobile, Ala., 1917-18, Chenet Inst., New Orleans, 1918-19, Tulane U., 1919; m. Mary Pearl Duggan, Apr. 9, 1932; 1 dau., Yvonne Elaine; m. 2d, Mrs. Fred N. Blount, Jr. Was an apprentice restaurant worker Pension Alciatore, New Orleans, 1920-23; continued studies in famous restaurants, France, 1923-30; mgr. Antoine's (founded by grandfather in 1840, formerly Pension Alciatore, 1930, proprietor); bd. commrs. New Orleans Pub. Belt R.R. Mem. Mardi Gras carnival orgns., also New Orleans Conv. and Visitors Bur. Bd. curators La. State Mus., 1937-41. Served as warrant machinist USCG. Decorated Grand Officer de la Confrerie du Tastevin (Nuits-Saint-Georges, France). Recipient Chevalier du Merite Touristique, France. Recipient Chevalier Du Merite Commercial, France. Mem. New Orleans Assn. Commerce (mem. council), La. Restaurant Assn. (pres. 1937), Wine and Food Soc. of London, Les Amis D'Escoffier Soc., Gourmet Soc. of N.Y. Clubs: Young Men's Business, Southern Yacht, New Orleans Athletic. Home: 5700 Canal Blvd New Orleans LA 70124 Office: 713 St Louis St New Orleans LA 70124

ALCINDOR, LEW, profl. basketball player; b. N.Y.C., Apr. 16, 1947; s. Ferdinand Lewis and Cora Alcindor; grad. U. Cal., Los Angeles, 1969. Basketball player with Milw. Bucks, 1969—. Address: 700 W Wisconsin St Milwaukee WI 53233*

ALCOCK, BEN, advt. exec.; b. Wooster, O., Dec. 5, 1914; s. Ben and Margaret (Smith) A.; ed. pub. schs., Wooster; m. Mildred de Souza, Feb. 13, 1943; children—Jane Moore, John Worthington. Writer, Sherman K. Ellis & Co., 1934-44; v.p., asso. creative dir. Biow Co., 1944-54; v.p. Cunningham & Walsh, 1954-56; exec. v.p. charge creative services Grey Advt., Inc., N.Y.C., 1957-70. Home: 5253 Sycamore Av Riverdale New York City NY 10471 Office: 777 3d Av New York City NY 10017

ALCOCK, NORMAN ZINKAN, research physicist; b. Edmonton, Alberta, Canada, May 29, 1918; s. Joseph Benjamin and Edith (Zinkan) A.; B.Sc., Queens U., 1940; M.S., Cal. Inst. Tech., 1941; Ph.D., McGill U., 1949; m. Patricia Hunter, June 29, 1948; children—Stephen, Christopher, David, Nancy, Jr. research engr. Nat. Research Council Can., 1941-45; asst. research physicist Atomic Energy Can., Ltd., 1947-50; v.p., dir. Isotope Products, Ltd., 1950-57; gen. mgr. Isotopes Products div. Canadian Curtiss-Wright, Ltd., 1957-58; dir. engring. Canadian Curtiss-Wright, Ltd., 1958-59; cons. engr., 1960; self employed, 1960-61; pres., dir. Canadian Peace Research Inst., 1962—. Served with RCAF; 1941-45. Home: 224 Lakewood Dr Oakville Ontario Canada Office: CPRI 514 Chartwell Rd Oakville Ontario Canada

ALCONCEL, TRINIDAD QUITEVIS, Philippine diplomat; b. Caoayan, Illocos Sur Philippines, Nov. 30, 1915; s. Brigido and Salome (Quitevis) A.; B.S. in Sugar Tech. (Bailon de la Rama scholar), U. Philippines, 1938; LL.B. cum laude, U. Manila 1948; m. Soledad Arre, June 15, 1938; children—Solita (Mrs. Jesus Kangleon), Romeo, Cecilio, Angelina (Mrs. Edward Barrientos), Jenny (Mrs. Paul Quezon), Victoria. Tech. asst. Nat. Devel. Co., 1938; chemist Sugar Rehab. Office, 1941-45; mgr., owner Solita's Store, 1942-46; econ. counselor Dept. Fgn. Affairs, 1947-55 (all Manila); admitted to Philippine bar, 1948; practice in Manila, 1955-58; atty., trade cons., Manila, 1955-58; fgn. trader, Honolulu, 1958-62; mgmt. cons. Manila Mayor's Office, 1962-66; minister, consul gen. Philippine consulate gen., Honolulu, 1966—. Adviser United Filipino Council of Hawaii, 1966—. Mem. Consular Corps Honolulu (dean 1971—), Phi Kappa Phi. Rotarian (hon. Honolulu). Home: 339 Elelupe Rd Honolulu HI 96821 Office: Philippine Consulate Gen 2433 Oali Hwy Honolulu HI 96817

ALCORN, GORDON DEE, educator; b. Olympia, Wash., Apr. 6, 1907; s. John H. and Rachel (Austin) A.; B.S., Coll. of Puget Sound, 1930; M.S., U. Wash., 1933, Ph.D., 1935; m. Rowena Lung, Aug. 8, 1935; 1 dau., Patricia (Mrs. Jack Peterson). Instr. biology Coll. Puget Sound, 1930-35; asst. prof. botany U. Ida., 1935-37; v.p., head biology Grays Harbor Coll., 1937-43, pres., 1945-46; asst. prof. U. Puget Sound, Tacoma, summers 1930-45, asso. prof. biology, 1946, prof., 1947—, chmn. dept. biology, 1951—, dir. grad. studies, 1970—. Regester lectr., 1968; with War Manpower Commn. Div. Edn., 1943-45. Mem. White House Conf. on Natural Beauty, 1965, Gov.'s Task Force on Tacoma Civic Arts. Bd. dirs. Puget Sound Mus. Natural History. Mem. Izaak Walton League Am. (Conservationist of Year, Puget Sound chpt. 1969), Nature Conservancy (gov. 1963-66), Cooper Ornithol. Soc., Am. Ornithol. Union, Pacific N.W. Bird and Mammal Soc. (pres.), Am. Assn. U. Profs., Sigma Xi, Pi Gamma Mu, Phi Sigma. Republican. Baptist. Editor-in-chief Murrelet, 1951—. Contbr. articles to profl. jours. Home: 3806 N 24th St Tacoma WA 98406

ALCORN, HOWARD WELLS, state justice; b. Suffield, Conn., May 14, 1901; s. Hugh M. and Cora Terry (Wells) A.; A.B., Dartmouth, 1923; student Harvard Law Sch., Yale Law Sch.; m. Bertha Eloise Pinney, Oct. 28, 1927; children—Carolyn Hatheway, Elizabeth Wells, Dorcas Terry. Admitted to Conn. bar, 1926; judge Suffield Town Ct., 1929-43; exec. sec. to Gov. Conn., 1943; judge Superior Ct. Conn., 1943-59, chief judge, 1959-61; justice Supreme Ct. Conn., 1961-70, chief justice, 1970—. Dir. First Nat. Bank of Suffield, 1928-51, v.p., 1934-51. Chmn. zoning commn. Suffield, 1928-43. Mem. Conn. Ho. Reps., 1927-29, 31, speaker, 1931, floor leader Conn. Senate, 1933; chmn. Republican Town Com., Suffield, 1928-33; alternate del.-at-large Rep. Nat. Conv., 1932. Mem. Am., Conn., Hartford County (treas. 1934-36) bar assns., S.A.R., Sons Union Vets., Conn. Hist. Soc., Antiquarian and Landmarks Soc. (pres. 1936- 40), Suffield Grange. Mason. Conglist. Club: Hartford. Home: 338 S Main St Suffield CT 06078 Office: State Library and Supreme Court Bldg Hartford CT 06103

ALCORN, HUGH MEADE, Jr., lawyer, former chmn. Republican Nat. Com.; b. Suffield, Conn., Oct. 20, 1907; s. Hugh M. and Cora Terry (Wells) A.; A.B., Dartmouth, 1930; LL.B., Yale, 1933; m. Janet Hoffer, Oct. 21, 1933 (dec.); children—Thomas Glenn (dec.), Janet Eileen; m. 2d, Marcia Powell, Apr. 14, 1955. Admitted to Conn. bar, 1933; partner Alcorn, Bakewell & Smith Hartford, 1933—; asst. state's atty. Hartford County, 1935-42, state's atty., 1942-48; v.p., dir. First Nat. Bank of Suffield; dir. United Bank & Trust Co., Hartford. Mem. Conn. Ho. of Reps., 1937, 39, Rep. floor leader, 1939, speaker, 1941; chmn. Suffield Rep. Town Com., 1938-53, mem. Conn. Rep. State Central Com., 1948-57; del. Rep. Nat. Conv., 1940, 48, 52, 56, 60, alternate, 1964, vice chmn. arrangements com., 1956; mem. Rep. Nat. Com. from Conn., 1953-61, vice chmn., 1956-57, chmn. 1957-59, gen. counsel, 1960-61; Rep. floor leader constl. conv., 1965. Mem. Am. Coll. Trial Lawyers, Am., Conn. (pres. 1950-51), Hartford County bar assns., Sons Union Vets., Inc. Conn. Soc. S.A.R., Suffield Grange, Apollo Lodge, Phi Beta Kappa. Republican. Conglist. Mason. Elk. Clubs: University, Hartford, Rotary (pres. 1949-50) (Hartford). Home: 49 Russell Av Suffield CT 06078 Office: 1 American Row Hartford CT 06103

ALDEN, DOUGLAS WILLIAM, educator; b. Washington, Sept. 11, 1912; s. Alanson G. and Grace Anderson (Hunt) A.; A.B., Dartmouth, 1933; A.M., Brown U., 1934, Ph.D., 1938; student U. Paris (France), 1931-32, 35-36; m. Martha Seaver Bowditch, Sept. 11, 1937; children—Claire Douglas (Mrs. Dennis C. Drehmel), Barbara Bowditch (Mrs. Richard C. Giangiulio). Grad. asst. Brown U., 1936-38; instr. French, Tex. Tech. Coll., 1938-41, asst. prof., 1942; instr. French, Amherst Coll., 1941-42; from instr. to asso. prof. French, Princeton, 1945-61; prof. French, head dept. fgn. langs. U. Md., 1961-64; prof. French, chmn. dept. modern langs. U. Va., 1964-71, prof. French, 1971—, chmn. dept. Romance langs., 1966-71; chmn. adv. council Sweet Briar Jr. Year in France, 1950—. Served to capt. USAAF, 1942-45. Decorated Bronze Star; Croix de Guerre, chevalier de l'Ordre des Palmes Academiques (France). Mem. Modern Lang. Assn., Am. Assn. Tchrs. French (exec. com. 1968-71), S. Central Modern Lang. Assn., Assn. Depts. Fgn. Langs. (pres. 1969-70), Assn. Internat. des Etudes Francaises, Alden Kindred Soc., Alpha Sigma Phi. Clubs: Appalachian Mountain; Keswick of Virginia. Author: Marcel Proust and his French Critics, 1940; Introduction to French Masterpieces, 1948; Cortina's French in 20 Lessons, 1950; Premier Manuel, 1954; Jacques de Lacretelle, an intellectual itinerary, 1958; (with André Maman) Grammaire et Style, 1967. Gen. editor: French XX Bibliography, 1949—; rev. editor French Rev., 1964-71; editor: XX Century Vol., Cubeen Bibliography. Home: 1880 Westview Rd Charlottesville VA 22903

ALDEN, HOWEL HENRY, librarian; b. Topeka, Aug. 12, 1907; s. Thomas Dick and Harriet March (Jones) A.; B.A., Washburn Coll., 1926; M.A., U. Kan., 1928; M.S. in L.S., Columbia, 1950. Fellow in English, U. Kan., 1926-27, instr., 1927, 28; instr. English, Grinnell Coll., 1934-46, asst. prof., 1946-52, librarian, asso. prof. English,

1952—. Served with AUS, 1942-45. Mem. Am. Assn. U. Profs., A.L.A., Modern Lang. Assn., Phi Beta Kappa, Sigma Delta Chi. Home: 833 East St Grinnell IA 50112

ALDEN, JOHN RICHARD, historian; b. Grand Rapids, Mich., Jan. 23, 1908; s. Herman and Ida (Jonkmann) A.; A.B., U. Mich., 1929, A.M., 1930, Ph.D., 1939; m. Pearl B. Wells, Dec. 22, 1934; 1 dau., Anne Maria. Alfred H. Lloyd Meml. Research fellow U. Mich., 1939-40; asst. prof. history Mich. State Normal Coll., 1940-43, Bowling Green (O.) State U., 1943-45; asst. prof. U. Neb. 1945-47, asso. prof. history, 1947-50, prof. history, 1950-55; prof. history Duke, 1955—, James B. Duke prof. history, 1963—. Vis. prof. history U. Chgo., summer 1949, U. Mich., summer 1950; Donald L. Fleming lectr. La. State U., 1960; Commonwealth Fund lectr. Univ. Coll., London, 1961. Guggenheim fellow, 1955-56. Author: John Stuart and the Southern Colonial Frontier, 1944; General Gage in America, 1948; General Charles Lee, 1951; The American Revolution 1763-1789, 1954; The South in the Revolution, 1957; The First South, 1961; The Rise of the American Republic, 1963; other writings. Editor: Christopher Ward, War of the Revolution 1952; (with Alice Maginis) A History of the United States, 1960. Home: 2736 Dogwood Rd Durham NC 27705

ALDEN, LUCAS AVERY, financial cons.; b. Portland, Ore., June 1, 1911; s. Horace Franklin and Mabel Avery (Kells) A.; B.S. cum laude (Blacker scholarship 1928-30, Fgn. Travel Prize fellow 1930), Cal. Inst. Tech., 1931, Ph.D. cum laude, 1935; m. Rita Coté, Mar. 8, 1944 (div. 1961); children—Lynne, Joan, Christopher Kells. Teaching fellow Cal. Inst. Tech., 1931-34; investment counsellor, 1935-37; with actuarial div. Met. Life Ins. Co., 1938-39, with bus. research bur., 1940-41; with WPB, 1941-44, chief transport br., planning div., 1942-44; asso. Nat. Planning Assn., 1942-44; joined W.R. Grace & Co., 1944, editor The Grace Log, 1945-46, asst. treas., 1947-49, asst. v.p., 1949-52, v.p., comptroller, 1952-55, v.p. Latin Am. operations, 1956, policy and planning, 1957-59, Latin Am. finance, 1960-66; v.p. Grace Chem. Co., 1953-55; v.p. Naco Fertilizer Co., 1953-54; pvt. financial cons. 1967—. Bd. dirs. N.Y. Young Republican Club, 1939-41; Willkie campaign mgr., 14th Assembly Dist. N.Y. 1940; mem. N.Y. Rep. County Com., 1939-40; alternate del. N.Y. Jud. Conv., 1939. Mem. Civil Air Patrol, 1941-44. Mem. A.A.A.S., Am. Econ. Assn., Am. Mgmt. Assn. Sigma Xi, Tau Beta Pi. Episcopalian. Clubs: The Creek, India House (N.Y.C.); Villa Country, Los Inkas (Lima, Peru). Author: (booklet) Postwar Merchant Shipping, 1944; also articles bus. publs. Address: PO Box 527 Locust Valley NY 11560

ALDEN, RAYMOND MACDONALD, utility co. exec.; b. Palo Alto, Cal., Nov. 17, 1921; s. Raymond Macdonald and Barbara (Hitt) A.; A.B. in Engring., Stanford, 1944; m. Sara Wills, Aug. 30, 1946; children—David Wills, Merritt Ann, John Lee. Engr., Western Union Telegraph Co., 1946-50; engr. Hawaiian Telephone Co., Honolulu, 1951-62, v.p., 1962-64; exec. v.p. United Utilities, Inc., Kansas City, Mo., 1964—. Served with USNR, 1944-46. Registered profl. engr., Hawaii, Kan. Mem. I.E.E.E., Nat. Soc. Profl. Engrs. Home: 5505 Mission Dr Shawnee Mission KS 66208 Office: P O Box 11315 Kansas City MO 64112

ALDEN, ROLAND HERRICK, univ. dean; b. Champaign, Ill., Feb. 4, 1914; s. Raymond Macdonald and Barbara Genery (Hitt) A.; A.B., Stanford, 1936; Ph.D., Yale, 1941; m. Aimee Neff, Sept. 4, 1937; children—Patricia Ann, Roland Herrick, Peter Macdonald. Rockefeller research asst. Stanford, 1936-37, teaching asst., 1935-36; teaching asst. Yale, 1937-41, Mary Miller fellow, 1940-41, instr. zoology, 1941-42, vis. asst. prof., summer 1946; mem. faculty U. Tenn., 1942—, prof. anatomy, 1949—, chief div. anatomy, 1951-61, asso. dean Grad. Sch., 1960-68, dean Grad. Sch., 1968—, dean Coll. Basic Med. Scis., 1961—, chancellor pro tem med. units, 1970. Cons. USPHS, 1960-64, chmn. anatomical scis. tng. com., 1964-70; sec.-treas. Tenn. Bd. Basic Sci. Examiners, 1963—; mem. anatomy com. Nat. Bd. Med. Examiners, 1959- 62; mem. commn. on grad. edn. Nat. Assn. State Univ. and Land-Grant Colls., 1968—. Bd. dirs. Memphis Soc. Crippled Children, 1950-62, pres., 1960; bd. dirs. Tenn. Crippled Children's Soc., 1949-62, v.p., 1957-59, pres., 1960-62; trustee Memphis Ednl. TV Found.; mem. acad. affairs com. of bd. trustees U. Tenn., 1969—. Fellow A.A.A.S.; mem. Am. Assn. Anatomists (pres. 1969—, mem. exec. com. 1967-71, mem. coms. on publ. and ednl. affairs 1962-68), Am. Physiol. Soc., Soc. Exptl. Biology and Medicine, Am. Soc. Zoologists, Am. Assn. Med. Colls., Memphis Execs. Club, Sigma Xi, Gamma Alpha, Omicron Kappa Upsilon. Rotarian. Author papers anatomy, physiology, endocrinology reprodn. Home: 1466 Harbert Av Memphis TN 38104

ALDEN, VERNON ROGER, financial exec.; b. Chgo., Apr. 7, 1923; s. Arvid W. and Hildur Pauline (Johnson) A.; A.B. magna cum laude, Brown U., 1945, LL.D., 1964; M.B.A., Harvard, 1950; LL.D., Emerson Coll., 1957, Ohio Wesleyan U., 1964, R.I. Coll., 1965, William Jewell Coll., 1965, Loyola U., 1966, Wilberforce U., Ottawa U., 1970; L.H.D., North Park Coll., 1965; Lit.D., Ohio U., 1969; D.P.S., Bowling Green U., 1969; Litt.D., Bethany Coll., 1970; m. Marion Frances Parson, Aug. 18, 1951; children—Robert Parson, Anne Elizabeth, James Malcolm, David Douglas. Admission officer Brown U., 1946-48; asst. dir. admissions Northwestern U., 1950-51; dir. financial aid Harvard Grad Sch. Bus. Adminstrn., asso. dean faculty 1951-61; pres. Ohio U., Athens, 1962-69; chmn. bd., chmn. exec. com. Boston Co. and subsidiary Boston Safe Deposit & Trust Company, 1969—, also dir. Ednl. dir. U. Hawaii Advanced Mgmt. Program, summer 1960, Keio U. Advanced Mgmt. Program, Tokyo, Japan, summers, 1960-61; adv. bd. Loeb awards for distinguished reporting financial and bus. news; mem. exec. com., dir. Mead Corp., Digital Equipment Corp., Kendall Corp., Boston. Nat. adv. bd. Girl Scouts U.S.A.; mem. New Eng. regional exec. com. Boy Scouts Am.; chmn. bd. Inst. Coll. and U. Adminstrn.; chmn. Ohio Council Econ. Edn.; chmn. edn. adv. com. Appalachian Commn.; mem. task force on ednl. disparities Urban Coalition; mem. adv. bd. Nat. Football Hall of Fame Found.; mem. commn. on fed. relations Am. Council on Edn.; chmn. Pres.' Task Force to plan Job Corps program; mem. citizens com. Nat. Library Assn.; mem. fondateur Institut Europea d'Adminstrn. des Affairs, Paris, France; vis. com. Harvard Coll.; com. on resources Harvard Med. Sch.; bd. overseers Boston Symphony Orch.; chmn. pres.' devel. council Wilberforce U., Ohio. Trustee, mem. exec. com. Brown U.; trustee Mus. Sci., Boston; chmn. finance com., trustee French Library, Boston; trustee Beaver Sch., Brookline, Chestnut Hill Sch., Carroll Sch., Bethany Coll., W.Va. Served to lt. USNR, 1943-46. Recipient Gov.'s award State Ohio, 1969; Founder's citation Ohio U., 1969. Mem. Phi Beta Kappa, Phi Kappa Phi, Phi Delta Theta, Beta Gamma Sigma, Omicron Delta Kappa. Presbyn. Clubs: University, Fifth Avenue (N.Y.C.); University (Columbus, O.); Union State, Commercial (Boston); Country (Brookline). Home: 37 Warren St Brookline MA 02146

ALDER, HENRY LUDWIG, educator; b. Duisburg, Germany, Mar. 26, 1922; s. Ludwig and Otti (Gottschalk) A.; came to U.S., 1941, naturalized, 1944; A.B. in Math. and Chemistry, U. Cal. at Berkeley, 1942, Ph. D., in Math., 1947; m. Benne B. Alder, Apr. 8, 1963; 1 son. Instr. math. U. Cal., Berkeley, 1947-48; faculty U. Cal., Davis, 1948—, asso. prof. math., 1955-65, prof., 1965—. Chmn., No. Cal. sect. Math. Assn. Am., 1956-57, nat. sec., 1960—; vice chmn. bd. govs. Pacific Jour. Math., 1957—. Mem. Am. Math. Soc., Inst. Math. Statistics, Sigma Xi, Mu Alpha Theta (nat. pres. 1956-59). Author: (with Edward B. Roessler) Introduction to Probability and Statistics, 1960. Home: 724 Elmwood Dr Davis CA 95616

ALDERFER, HAROLD FREED, educator, pub. adminstr.; b. Souderton, Pa., Feb. 1, 1903; s. Henry A. and Lydia M. (Freed) A.; A.B., Bluffton (O.) Coll., 1922; A.M., Syracuse U., 1926, Ph.D., 1928; m. Ella F. Rohrbach, Sept. 2, 1925; children—Johanna (Mrs. William Harris), Henrietta (Mrs. Alan Helffrich, Jr.), Marianna (Mrs. James E. Wood). Prin. and tchr. Marion (S.D.) High Sch., 1922-23; supt. schs., Marion, 1923-25; asst. dept. polit. sci., Sch. Citizenship and Pub. Affairs, Syracuse U., 1925-28; asst. prof. polit. sci., Pa. State Coll., 1928-31, asso. prof., 1931-35, prof., 1935-60, prof. emeritus, 1960—, head dept. polit. sci., 1953-56, exec. sec. Inst. Local Govt., 1936-56; Lewis M. Stevens prof. pub. affairs Lincoln U., 1964-65, prof. polit. sci., dir. Inst. African Government, 1965; vis. lectr. U. Pa., 1938-39, 43-45, 59-69; Harrisburg Area Community Coll., 1970, Juniata Coll., 1971. Dir. Bur. Municipal Affairs, Dept. Internal Affairs, Commonwealth of Pa., 1944-50; cons. OPA, Washington, 1942; planning cons. Am. Municipal Assn., 1943; local govt. specialist Mut. Security Adminstrn., Athens, Greece, 1950-52; asst. commr. operations Urban Renewal Adminstrn., HHFA, 1956-67; mem. Pub. Service Inst. Bd., Commonwealth Pa., 1937-71, 1st dep. Dept. Pub. Instrn., 1957-62; cons. community devel. ICA, Manila, P.I., 1958. Cons. in local govt. in Near and Middle East, UN, 1962-63; local govt. cons. AID, Brazil, 1967, Panama, 1968; sr. asso. Better Govt. Assos., Inc., 1967—; co-dir. research Pa. Constl. Conv., 1967-68; mem. Gov.'s Com. Revision Pub. Employees Law, 1968. Decorated comdr. Order of Phoenix (Greece). Mem. Am. Soc. Pub. Adminstrn., Am. Municipal Assn. (v.p. 1948). Author: I Like Greece, 1956; American Local Government and Administration, 1956; Local Government in Developing Countries, 1964; Public Administration in New Nations, 1968; Pennsylvania Government for the Seventies, 1971. Home: R D 3 Mechanicsburg PA 17055

ALDERSON, WILLIAM THOMAS, Jr., assn. dir.; b. Schenectady, May 8, 1926; s. William Thomas and Helen Martha (Knowlton) A.; A.B., Colgate U., 1947; student Howard Coll., 1944- 45, Tulane U., 1945-46; M.A., Vanderbilt U., 1949, Ph.D., 1952; m. Sylvia Caldwell Farrell, Sept. 14, 1953; children—William Thomas III, Virginia Ann, Rebecca Louise. Asst. archivist Tenn. State Library and Archives, 1952-57, asst. state librarian and archivist, 1959-61; exec. sec. Tenn. Hist. Commn., 1957-61, state librarian and archivist, chmn. commn., 1961-64; dir. Am. Assn. for State and Local History, editor History News, Nashville, 1964—; asst. editor Tennessee Hist. Quar., 1953, asso. editor, 1954-55, editor, 1956-65. Adv. com. Library of Congress Nat. Union Catalog Manuscript Collections, 1965-70; adv. com. hist. socs. and humanistic museums Nat. Endowment Humanities, 1966—; adv. com. Historic Am. Bldgs. Survey, 1967-71; mem. Nat. Museum Act adv. council Smithsonian Instn., 1971—; instr. extension div. U. Tenn., 1954-61; vis. asst. prof. history Vanderbilt U., 1955-56. Dir. Am. Heritage Pub. Co. Mem. Hist. Commn. Met. Nashville and Davidson County, 1966-70. Served with USNR, 1943-46. Fellow Soc. Am. Achivists (council 1963-67); mem. Am. Assn. State and Local History (council 1959-64), Am. Records Mgmt. Assn. (pres. S.E. chpt. 1963-64), Tenn. Assn. Mus. (pres. 1965-67), Assn. Preservation Tenn. Antiquities (trustee 1964-71), Colgate U. Alumni Assn. (pres. Tenn. chpt. 1962-66), Nashville Rose Soc. (pres. 1963), So., Mississippi Valley hist. assns., Nat. Trust Historic Preservation, Tenn. Hist. Soc. (v.p. 1969-71), Am. Assn. Mus. (chmn. accreditation commn. 1970—). Republican. Methodist. Rotarian. Author: Tennessee Historical Markers 1958; (with R. H. White) A Guide to the Study and Reading of Tennessee History, 1959; (with R. M. McBride) Tennessee Historical Markers, 1962; (with H. G. Thomas) Historic Sites in Tennessee, 1963; Tennessee, A Student's Guide to Localized History, 1966. Co-editor: Landmarks of Tennessee History, 1965. Contbr. encys., profl. jours. Home: 24 Taggart Av Nashville TN 37205 Office: 1315 8th Av S Nashville TN 37203

ALDEWERELD, SIMON, internat. govt. ofcl.; b. Amsterdam, Netherlands, June 23, 1909; s. Gerrit and Marianna (Stodel) A.; DRS of Econs., Amsterdam U., 1930; m. Kitty Madelaine Erwteman, Oct. 12, 1939. With Rotterdam Bank, Amsterdam, 1939-40, Fgn. Exchange Control Curacao, 1940-42; supr. Netherlands E. Indies assets in Western Hemisphere N.Y.C., 1942-44; financial adviser for Netherlands Indies affairs Netherlands embassy, Washington, 1944-46; with Internat. Bank Reconstrn. and Devel., 1946—, dir. dept. tech. operations, 1955-65, v.p., 1965—. Home: 2801 New Mexico Av N W Washington, DC 20007. Office: 1818 H St N W Washington DC 20433

ALDISERT, RUGGERO JOHN, U.S. circuit judge; b. Carnegie, Pa., Nov. 10, 1919; s. John S. and Elizabeth (Magnacca) A.; B.A., U. Pitts., 1941, J.D., 1947; m. Agatha Maria DeLacio, Oct. 4, 1952; children—Lisa Maria, Robert, Gregory. Admitted to Pa. bar, 1947; gen. practice law, Pitts., 1947-61; judge Ct. Common Pleas., Allegheny County, 1961-68; judge 3d U.S. Circuit Ct. Appeals, 1968—; prof. law U. Pitts. Sch. Law, 1964—; faculty Appellate Judges Seminar, N.Y.U., 1971; lectr. internat. seminar legal medicine U. Rome, 1965, Law Soc. London, 1967, Internat. seminar comparative law, Rome, 1971. Mem. Pa. Civil Procedural Rules, Com., 1965—; mem. Jud. Conf. Com. on Adminstrn. Criminal Law, 1971—. Chmn. bd. Grubstake, Inc., 1966-68; Allegheny dist. chmn. Multiple Sclerosis Soc., 1961-68; pres. Italian Sons and Daus. Am. Cultural Heritage Found., 1965-68. Trustee U. Pitts., 1968—; bd. visitors Pitts. Learning Research and Devel. Center, 1968—. Served to maj. USMCR, 1942-46. Recipient Outstanding Merit award Allegheny County Acad. Trial Lawyers, 1964. Fellow Internat. Acad. Law and Sci., Am. Coll. Legal Medicine; mem. Inst. Jud. Adminstrn., Am. Law Inst., Pitts. Legal Med. Inst., Italian Sons and Daus. of Am. (pres. 1954-68), Italian Sons and Daus. Am. Fraternal Assn. (nat. pres. 1960-68), Phi Beta Kappa, Phi Alpha Delta, Omicron Delta Kappa. Democrat. Roman Catholic. Author: Il Ritorno al Paese, 1966-67. Home: 805 Elm Spring Rd Pittsburgh PA 15243 Office: Federal Bldg Liberty Av Pittsburgh PA 15222

ALDRICH, ALEXANDER, coll. pres.; b. N.Y.C., Mar. 14, 1928; s. Winthrop Williams and Harriet (Alexander) A.; A.B., Harvard, 1950, LL.B., 1953; M. Pub. Adminstrn., New York University, 1960; m. Elizabeth Bayard Hollins, Aug. 11, 1951 (div.); children—Elizabeth, Elizabeth Winthrop, Amanda, Alexander. Admitted to N.Y. bar, 1955; practiced, N.Y.C., 1955-56; sec. N.Y.C. Police Dept., 1956-58, dep. commr. charge youth program, 1958-60; dir. N.Y. State Div. Youth Albany, 1960-63; exec. asst. to gov. State of N.Y., Albany, 1963-66; exec. dir. Hudson River Valley Commn., 1966-69; pres. L.I.U., 1969—. Chmn., Taconic State Park Commn. Bd. dirs. Bklyn. Hosp., Bklyn. Inst. Arts and Scis.; governing com. Bklyn. Acad. Music; trustee Tchrs. Coll., Columbia Univ. Mem. Am., N.Y. State bar assns., Bar City N.Y., Soc. Cincinnati, N.Y. Zool. Soc. (trustee). Home: 1 Pierrepont St Brooklyn NY 11201 Office: Long Island U Brooklyn NY 11201

ALDRICH, ANITA, educator; b. Elmo, Mo., Sept. 20, 1914; d. Earl L. and Ethel M. (Bailey) Aldrich; B.S., N.W. Mo. State Coll., Maryville, 1936; M.A., U. Kansas City, 1946; Ed.D., Pa. State U., 1957. Physical edn. instr., King City, Mo., 1937-38, St. Joseph, Mo., 1938-42; elementary instrn. health and phys. edn., pub. schs., also Sacred Heart High Sch. Acad., St. Joseph, Mo., 1940-42; spl. asst. health and phys. edn., 1953-60, dir. elementary phys. edn., secondary girls phys. edn., secondary girls intramurals, 1960-64; prof. and chmn. dept. phys. edn. for women, prof. edn. Ind. U., Bloomington, 1964—; instr. phys. edn., National Coll., Kansas City, Mo., 1956-61, night classes, 1959-60; extension courses Central Mo. State Coll., 1949, 50, 56; vis. prof. Utah State U., 1959, 60, also dir. workshop in phys. edn.; vis. prof. Ind. U., 1961, 62, 63. Bd. dirs. YWCA, 1955-58. Mem. Pres.'s Council on Fitness, 1961-63. Hon. fellow, honor award recipient A.A.H.P.E.R. (pres. 1962-63, chmn. curriculum commn. 1965—); mem. Mo. Assn. Health, Phys. Edn. and Recreation (sec.-treas. 1952-53, pres. 1955- 56), Central Dist. Assn. Health, Phys. Edn. and Recreation (pres. 1959- 60), N.E.A., Mo. Tchrs. Assn., Am. Coll. Sports Medicine, Women's C. of C., Pi Lambda Theta, Delta Kappa Gamma, Alpha Sigma Alpha. Author: (with Dr. Pattric Ruth O'Keefe) Education Through Physical Activities, rev. edit., 1959. Editorial bd. Jour. Health, Phys. Edn. and Recreation, 1958- 60. Contbr. chpt. to Sports Safety. Home: 2301 E 2d St Bloomington IN 47401

ALDRICH, ARTHUR MAGNUS, ednl. pub. co. exec.; b. Northfield, Vt., Oct. 27, 1919; s. Harold R. and Elsie (Biorklund) A.; B.A., Wesleyan U., Middletown, Conn., 1941; M.B.A., Harvard, 1947; m. Elaine MacDonald, Oct. 9, 1948; children—Peter, Steven, Nancy, Barbara. Financial analyst Ford Motor Co., 1947-51; asst. to pres. N.Am. Philips Co., 1952-55; asst. controller Curtiss-Wright Co., 1955-58; asst. controller, gen. auditor Mobil Oil Corp., 1961-66; mgr. financial analysis IBM Corp., Chgo., 1958-61, with subsidiary Sci. Research Assos., Inc., 1966—, treas., controller, 1967- -. Served to capt. USAAF, 1942-46, USAF, 1951-52. Mem. Financial Execs. Inst. Home: 830 Timber Lane Lake Forest IL 60045 Office: 259 E Erie St Chicago IL 60611

ALDRICH, BAILEY, judge; b. Boston, Apr. 23, 1907; s. Talbot and Eleanor (Little) A.; A.B., Harvard, 1928, LL.B., 1932; m. Elizabeth Perkins, Aug. 13, 1932; children—Jonathan, David. Admitted to Mass. bar, 1932; with Choate, Hall Hall & Stewart, Boston, 1932-54; U.S. dist. judge for Mass., 1954-59; judge U.S. Ct. Appeals, 1959-64, chief judge, 1965—. Sec. Univ. Hosp. Sec. Boston U. Med Center. Mem. Am. Law Inst., Am. Acad. Arts and Scis., Soc. of the Cin. Home: 120 Brattle St Cambridge, MA 02138. Office: U S Courthouse Boston MA 02109

ALDRICH, CLARENCE KNIGHT, physician, educator; b. Chgo., Apr. 12, 1914; s. L. Sherman and Bessie A. (Knight) A.; B.A., Wesleyan U., 1935; M.D., Northwestern U., 1940; m. Julie H. Murphy, Feb. 4, 1942; children—Carol K., Michael S., Thomas K., Robert F. Faculty U. Minn. Med. Sch., 1947-55, asst. prof., 1947-52, asso. prof., 1952-55; prof. psychiatry U. Chgo. Sch. Medicine, 1955-70, chmn. dept. psychiatry, 1955-64; vis. prof. psychiatry U. Edinburgh, 1963-64; prof., chmn. dept. Coll. Medicine and Dentistry of N.J., Newark, 1970—. Served from asst. surgeon to surgeon, USPHS, 1940-46. Fellow Am. Orthopsychiat. Assn., Am. Psychiat. Assn.; mem. Group for Advancement Psychiatry. Author: Psychiatry for the Family Physician, 1955; Introduction to Dynamic Psychiatry, 1966; (with C. Nighswonger) A Casebook for Pastoral Counseling, 1968. Home: 39 Alexander Av Upper Montclair NJ 07043

ALDRICH, CLIDE EMREL, educator; b. Corning, Ia., Mar. 5, 1901; s. George and Caroline (Thompson) A.; A.B., U. of Ia., 1922, A.M., 1924, Ph.D., 1941; student McGill U., Montreal, 1926, U. of Grenoble (France), 1928-29; D.H.L., Butler U., 1971; m. Myrtle Hayes, Oct. 3, 1930; children—Alice Anne, Caroline Edith. Instr. Spanish. DePauw U., 1924; prof. Romance langs., Butler U., 1924-71, dir. grad. div., 1947-71, head modern foreign langs. dept., 1951-71, emeritus, 1971—. Mem. Am. Assn. U. Profs., State Teachers of French. Mem. United Ch. of Christ. Club: Alliance Francaise. Home: 842 Cleveland St Oakland CA 94606

ALDRICH, DANIEL GASKILL, Jr., univ. chancellor; b. Northwood, N.H., July 12, 1918; s. Daniel Gaskill and Marian (Farnum) A.; B.S., U.R.I., 1939, D. Sc. (hon.), 1960; M.S., U. Ariz., 1941; Ph.D., U. Wis., 1943; m. Jean Hamilton, Aug. 23, 1941; children—Daniel Gaskill III, Elizabeth, Stuart Hamilton. Research chemist U. Cal. Citrus Expt. Sta., Riverside, 1943-55; chmn. dept. soils and plant nutrition U. Cal., Davis and Berkeley, 1955-59, univ. dean agr., Berkeley, 1959-62, now chancellor U. Cal. at Irvine. Dir. Morlan Pacific Co., Buffum's. Mem. sci. adv. com. Subpanel on Research and Edn., World Food Supply Panel; mem. Carnegie Study on Agrl. Edn. Active Boy and Girl Scouts Am., exec. bd. Orange Empire Boy Scouts; bd. dirs. Big Brothers Orange County, Orange County Philharmonic Soc., Big Bros. Am., Stanford Research Inst., Internat. Vol. Services; mem. agrl. adv. com. W.K. Kellogg Found.; trustee Newport Harbor Found., Pacific Sch. Religion, Fund for Theol. Edn., Pilgrim Place; trustee, pres. Agronomic Scis. Found.; hon. sponsor Orange County Soc. Crippled Children. Served as maj., inf., AUS: lt. col. Res. Mem. A.A.A.S. (past pres. Pacific div.), Western Soc. Soil Sci. (pres.), Am. Soc. Agronomy (dir.), Nat. Acad. Scis. (mem. agrl. edn. policy com., commn. on edn. in agr. and nat. resources), Nat. Assn. State Univs. and Land-Grant Colls. (mem. water resources research com.), Soil Conservation Soc., Soil Sci. Soc. Am., Am. Soc. Hort. Sci. Conglist. Home: 1392 Galaxy Dr Newport Beach CA 92660

ALDRICH, FRANK NATHAN, banker; b. Jackson, Mich., June 8, 1923; s. Frank Nathan and Marion (Butterfield) A.; student U. Md., summer 1943; A.B. in Govt., Dartmouth, 1948; postgrad. Harvard, summer 1948; m. Edna Dora DeJan, Nov. 21, 1956; children—Marion Dolores, Clinton Pershing. Sub-mgr. First Nat. Bank of Boston, Havana, Cuba, 1949-60, Rio de Janeiro, Brazil, 1961-62, sub-mgr., Sao Paulo, Brazil, 1963-64, mgr., 1965, exec. mgr., Rio de Janeiro, 1966, v.p. Brazilian brs., 1966-69, v.p. overseas operations, Boston, 1969-70, v.p. Latin Am.-Asia-Africa-Middle East div., Boston, 1970—; exec. v.p., dir. Boston Overseas Financial Corp., Boston; dir. Corporacion Financiera Boston, Buenos Aires, Argentina, First Leasing Australia Ltd., Melbourne, Bank of Boston Trust Co., (Bahamas) Ltd., Nassau, Corporacion Internacional de Boston S.A., San Jose, Costa Rica, Sociedad Anonima Servicios e Inversiones, Buenos Aires, Randolph-Boston Overseas Holding, Luxembourg, Arrendadora Internacional S.A., Mexico City, Arrendadora Industrial Venezolana C.A., Caracas, Venezuela. Served with USAAF, 1943-46. Decorated Air medal with 4 oak leaf clusters, D.F.C. Mem. Air Force Assn., Res. Officers Assn., Inst. Navigation, Royal Astron. Soc. Canada, Brit. Interplanetary Soc., Md. Hist. Soc., Am. C. of C. Rio de Janeiro, Am. C. of C. Sao Paulo, Sphinx Soc., Beta Theta Pi. Mason (Shriner). Clubs: International (Washington); Dartmouth College (N.Y.C.); American (Miami, Fla.). Home: Indian Spring Rd Dover MA 02030 Office: 100 Federal St Boston MA 02106

ALDRICH, GEORGE DAVENPORT, investment banker; b. Marblehead, Mass., Sept. 12, 1916; s. William T. and Dorothea (Davenport) A.; B.A., Harvard, 1939, LL.B., 1942; m. Alice H. Burrage, July 6, 1940 (div. July 1970); children—Camilla, Alison; m. 2d, Lucy A. Devens, June 1971. Admitted to Mass. bar, 1947; asso. Choate, Hall & Stewart, Boston, 1946-49; asso. Inc. Investors, 1949-64, v.p., 1953-64, treas., vice chmn., dir., 1954-64; treas., dir. Inc. Income Fund, 1954-64; v.p., dir. Winslow, Cohu and Stetson,

Boston, 1964-69; sr. v.p. Weiss Voisin, 1969—; corporator Provident Instn. for Savings, Boston; dir. Pyrotector, J. Ray McDermott & Co., Inc. Bd. overseers Boys' Clubs of Boston. Served as lt. comdr. USNR, World War II. Mem. C. of C. Address: 100 Boylston Boston MA 02116

ALDRICH, HAROLD EUGENE, govt. ofcl.; b. Decatur, Neb., Jan. 17, 1914; s. Carl J. and Mabel (Gannon) A.; B.S. in Civil Engring., U. Neb., 1935; student U. Colo., 1941; m. Mary Frances Kingsley, June 13, 1936; children—Mary Clare (Mrs. Bruce J. Williams), Richard K. With Neb. Dept. Roads and Irrigation, 1935-38, Corps Engrs., Rock Island, Ill., 1938-39; with Bur. Reclamation, 1939—, regional dir., Billings, Mont., 1964—, established bur. office of progress control, new repayment contract concepts sale municipal and indsl. water, mem. Inter-Systems Coordinating Com. Rep. to exec. bd. Nat. Elec. Reliability Council. Registered profl. engr., Mont. Mem. Nat., Mont. socs. profl. engrs., Internat. Com. Large Dams, Internat. Com. Drainage and Irrigation, Am. Soc. Pub. Adminstrn., Sigma Phi Epsilon. Methodist. Elk, Rotarian. Home: 743 Park Lane Billings MT 59102 Office: 326 N 26th St Billings MT 59103

ALDRICH, HULBERT, (Stratton), banker; b. Fall River, Mass., Apr. 3, 1907; s. Stanly Adlen and Jane Stratton (Pratt) A.; grad. Phillips Acad., 1926; Ph.B., Yale, 1930; m. Amy Durfee, Jan. 19, 1934; children—Ann, Jane Stratton. With New York Trust Co., N.Y.C., 1930-59, asst. treas., 1939-43, v.p., 1943-52, pres., dir. 1952-59; vice chmn., dir. Chem. Bank, 1959—; dir. C.T. Wilson Co., Ametek, Inc., Royal-Globe Ins. Cos. (chmn. investment com.), IBM World Trade Corp. (exec. com.), Empire Savs. Bank, N.Y.C., Nat. Distillers & Chem. Corp., Eurofinance, Geo. W. Rogers Constrn. Corp., Adela Investment Co. S.A., Harvey Hubbell, Inc., Peter Paul, Inc., London Multinat. Bank; chmn. bd. Commonwealth Fund. Trustee, Presbyn. Hosp. Clubs: Century, Yale, River, Down Town Assn., Union Links, Links Golf, Sky. Home: 1088 Park Av New York City NY 10028 Office: 20 Pine St New York City NY 10015

ALDRICH, MALCOLM PRATT, found. exec.; b. Fall River, Mass., Oct. 1, 1900; s. Stanley A. and Jane S. (Pratt) A.; B.M.C., Durfee Sch., Fall River, Mass., 1918; A.B., Yale, 1922; m. Ella F. Buffington, June 20, 1925; children—Joan, Shirley, Malcolm. Began in finance and philanthropy with Edward S. Harkness; dir. Equitable Life Assurance Soc., Southern Pacific Co.; hon. chmn. Commonwealth Fund, N.Y.C.; dir. Am. Electric Power Co. Hon. mem. bd. trustees Am. Museum, Met. Museum Art. Served as spl. asst. to asst. sec. of Navy for Air, U.S.N. 1942-45; disch. rank capt. Republican. Clubs: Maidstone (East Hampton, L.I.); Yale, Links, Century Assn. (N.Y.C.). Home: 36 E 72d St New York City NY 10021 Office: 1 E 75th St New York City NY 10021

ALDRICH, NELSON WILMARTH, architect; b. N.Y.C., Apr. 6, 1911; s. William Truman and Dorothea (Davenport) A.; A.B., Harvard, 1934, M.Arch., 1938; L.H.D. (hon.), Tufts U., 1956; LL.D., Emerson Coll., 1962; m. Eleanor Tweed (div.); 1 son Nelson Wilmarth; m. 2d, Frances Turner, Nov. 9, 1940; children—Frances D., Abigail, Rosalie C. Designer, Harrison & Abramovitz, 1939-40; project planner U.S. Housing Authority, 1940-42; now mng. partner Campbell, Aldrich & Nulty, Boston; cons. architect Dartmouth, Bradford Jr. Coll., Phillips Exeter Acad.; asso. architect Boston City Hall. Co-founder, chmn. Boston Arts Festival, 1952-64; dir. Boston Archtl. Center, 1968—; chmn. Bos. Art Commn., 1955—; former mem. planning bd. Town of Marblehead. Pres. Inst. Contemporary Art, 1947-60, trustee, 1960-64; mem. archtl. design adv. com. Boston Redevel. Authority, Boston, 1959—; mem. Mass. Bd. Regional Community Colls., 1961—; trustee Boston Mus. of Fine Arts, 1954—; trustee Radcliffe Coll., 1957—, vice chmn., 1961-66; v.p. Met. Boston Arts Center, 1958-60, pres., 1960-63. Served as lt. comdr. USNR, 1942-46, charge combat aircraft service units Pacific. Fellow A.I.A., Am. Acad. Arts and Scis.; mem. Boston Soc. Architects, Mass. Assn. Architects (dir. 1950-58), Harvard Alumni Assn. (dir. 1962-65). Clubs: Tavern, Somerset, St. Botolph (Boston); Eastern Yacht (Marblehead, Mass.); Century (N.Y.C.). Home: Peach's Point Marblehead MA 01945 Office: 100 Boylston St Boston MA 02116

ALDRICH RICHARD STODDARD, investor, producer; b. Boston, Aug. 17, 1902; s. Edward Irving and Mary Pickering (Joy) A.; student Noble and Greenough Pickering Sch., Boston, 1921; A.B. cum laude, Harvard, 1925; m. Helen Beals, Nov. 5, 1927 (div. 1936); children—Richard Stoddard, David Beals; m. 2d, Gertrude Lawrence, July 4, 1940 (dec. Sept. 1952); m. 3d, Elizabeth Boyd, June 18, 1955; children—Susan Aldrich, Mary Joy, Gen. mgr. Richard Boleslavsky and his Am. Lab. Theatre, 1926; co-presented plays; La Gringa, 1928; Twelfth Night, 1929; Art and Mrs. Bottle; 1930; Lean Harvest, The Lady with a Lamp, 1931; Springtime for Henry, 1932; Three Cornered Moon, 1933; By Your Leave, Pure in Heart, 1934; Petticoat Fever, 1935; Fresh Fields, Aged 26, 1936; Tide Rising, Be So Kindly, 1937; Lorelei, 1938; The Importance of Being Earnest, My Dear Children, Margin for Error, 1939; Cue for Passion, 1940; Plan M, 1942; produced Pygmalion (mng. dir. Theatre Inc.), 1945, Playboy of the Western World, 1946; It Takes Two, 1947; Macbeth, 1948; Goodbye My Fancy, 1948-50; Caesar and Cleopatra, 1949-50; The Devil's Disciple, 1950; The Guardsman, 1950-51; The Moon is Blue, 1951-53; The Love of Four Colonels, 1953; A Girl Can Tell, 1953; Sailor's Delight, 1954-55; presented Tallulah Bankhead in Dear Charles 1954-55; brought Old Vic Theatre from London, 1946, Habimah Players from Tel Aviv, The Dublin Gate Theatre from Ireland, 1948; operator four summer theatres: Cape Playhouse, Dennis, Mass., Falmouth Playhouse, Coonamessett, Mass., Cape Cod Music Circus, Hyannis, Mass., South Shore Music Circus, Cohasset, Mass.; operator Nat. Theatre, Washington, 1952—; dir. A Doll's House, Central City (Colo.) Festivals, 1937, Ruy Blas, 1938; dir. Am. Nat. Theatre and Acad., City Center Music and Drama, Inc. Commd. lt., USNR, 1941, advanced through grades to comdr., 1945; exec. officer U.S.N., Advance Amphibious base, Fowey, Cornwall, Eng., 1943-44; comdg. officer Advance Amphibious Base, Southampton, Eng., staff of comdr. Amphibious Bases, U.K., Plymouth, Eng., 1944-45; attached to staff Adm. H.R. Stark, London, pub. relations officer for all U.S.N.F. in Europe, 1945, disch. 1945.D Dep. dir. U.S. Econ. Mission, Madrid, Spain, 1955- 56, dir. Econ. Mission, 1956-62, minister for econ. affiars Am. embassy, Madrid, Spain, 1957-62; dir. U.S. Agy. Internat. Devel. Morocco, 1962-65. Decorated Grand Cross Isabella the Catholic (Spain), 1962. Mem. Soc. Colonial Wars, Soc. Mayflower Descendants, S.A.R. Clubs: Union, Harvard, Players, Coffee House, Badminton, Dutch Treat (N.Y.C.); Internat. Sportmen's, Buck's (London); Metropolitan, Army and Navy (Washington); The Travellers (Paris); Farmington Country (Charlottesville, Va.). Author: Gertrude Lawrence as Mrs. 'A', 1955 (motion picture entitled Star , 1968). Office: 36 W 44th St New York City NY 10036

ALDRICH, ROBERT, motion picture dir.; b. Cranston, R.I., 1918; ed. U. Va.; m.; children—Mrs. Adell Bravos, William, Mrs. Alida Shaffer, Kelly. TV shows include The Doctor; China Smith; films include Big Leaguer (dir.); World for Ranson (co-producer, dir.); Apache, Vera Cruz; Kiss Me Deadly, Big Knife (producer, dir.); Autumn Leaves (dir.); Attack!, (producer, dir.); Ten Seconds to Hell, Angry Hills, Last Sunset (dir.); What Ever Happened to Baby Jane, 4 For Texas, Hush...Hush Sweet Charlotte, Flight of the Phoenix, Dirty Dozen, The Legend of Lylah Clare (producer, dir.); pres. Assos. & Aldrich Co. Inc., Aldrich Studios; producer, dir. The Killing of Sister George, Too Late The Hero, The Grissom Gang. Home: 901 S Longwood Av Los Angeles CA 90019 Office: Aldrich Studios 201 N Occidental Blvd Los Angeles CA 90026

ALDRICH, ROBERT ANDERSON, physician; b. Evanston, Ill., 1917; M.D., Northwestern U., 1944; m. Marjorie Duttenhofer, 1940, children—Robert Anderson, Stephen M., Frederick G. Intern Evanston (Ill.) Hosp., 1943-44; resident pediatrics U. Minn. Hosps., 1946-48, sr. fellow pediatrics, 1948-49; instr. pediatrics U. Minn. Grad. Sch., 1951; asso. staff Mayo Clinic, Rochester, Minn., 1949-50, cons. pediatrics, 1950—; asst. prof. pediatrics U. Ore. Med. Sch., 1951-53, asso. prof., 1953-56; prof. pediatrics U. Wash., Seattle, 1956-63, 64-70, chmn. dept., 1956-62, head div. human ecology dept. pediatrics, 1967-70, dir. health resources study center, 1966-70; v.p. health affairs U. Colo., Denver, 1970—; dir. Nat. Inst. Child Health and Human Devel., NIH, Bethesda, Md., 1963-64. Mem. Pres.'s Com. on Mental Retardation, 1966—, vice chmn., 1966-71; chmn. Gov.'s Council on Mental Health and Mental Retardation, 1968-70. Served to lt. (s.g.), M.C., USNR, 1944-46. Diplomate Am. Bd. Pediatrics, 1951. Mem. A.M.A., Northwestern Pediatric Soc., Soc. Pediatric Research, Am. Acad. Pediatrics, Am. Pediatrics Soc., Soc. Research in Child Devel. Address: 4200 E 9th Av Denver CO 80202

ALDRICH, VIRGIL CHARLES, educator; b. Narsingpur, India, Sept. 13, 1903 (parents U.S. Citizens); s. Floyd Clemet and Ann (Hanley) A.; B.A., Ohio Wesleyan U., 1925, L.H.D. (hon.), 1963; student Oxford U., 1926-27; Diplome d'Etudes Superieures de Philosophie, La Sorbonne, 1928; Ph.D., U. Cal. at Berkeley, 1931; m. Louise Hafliger, Sept. 3, 1927; 1 son, David Virgil. Instr., asst. prof. Rice Inst., 1931-42; vis. prof. Columbia, 1942-46; prof. philosophy Kenyon Coll., 1946-65; vis. prof. Brown U., 1962-63; prof. U. N.C., 1965—. Dir. Kyoto Am. Studies Inst., Japan. Sterling fellow, Yale, 1931-32. Mem. Am. Philos. Assn. (pres.), Am. Soc. Aesthetics (trustee, pres.), So. Soc. Philosophy and Psychology. Author: Philosophy of Art, 1963. Contbr.: Readings in Philophical Analysis, 1951, Reflections on Art, 1958, Faith and the Philosophers, 1962, Religious EXperience and Truth, 1961. Home: 100 Hoot Owl Lane Chapel Hill NC 27514

ALDRICH, WINTHROP WILLIAMS, former ambassador; b. Providence, Nov. 2, 1885; s. Nelson W. and Abby Pierce Chapman (Greene) A.; A.B., Harvard, 1907, J.D., 1910, LL.D., (hon.), 1953; LL.D., Colgate U., 1937, Northeastern U., 1938, Washington and Jefferson Coll., 1939, Brown U., 1944, Lafayette Coll., 1945, Columbia, 1946, Bryant Coll., 1947, Georgetown U., 1952, Queen's U., Belfast, 1955, U. Liverpool, Eng., 1956; D.Sc., N.Y. U., 1950, Stevens Inst. Tech., 1957, U. R.I., 1965, Tuskegee Inst., 1967; m. Harriet Alexander, Dec. 7, 1916; children—Winthrop Williams (dec.), Mary (Mrs. Robert Homans), Harriet (Mrs. Edgar Bering, Jr.), Lucy (Mrs. Devens), Elizabeth Brewster (Mrs. J. Woodward Redmond), Alexander. Admitted to N.Y. bar, 1912; mem. law firm Byrne, Cutcheon Taylor, 1916-17, Murray, Aldrich & Webb, 1919-29; pres. Equitable Trust Co., 1929; pres. Chase Nat. Bank, 1930-34, chmn. bd. dirs., 1934-53; ambassador to Ct. of St. James's, London, Eng., 1953-57. Mem. adv. com. Columbia Sch. Internat. Affairs. Vis. com. Harvard Center Internat. Affairs. Hon. trustee Presbyn. Hosp., N.Y.C., Riverside Ch., N.Y.C. Served as lt. USNR, 1917-18. Decorated Medal for Merit (U.S.); knight Grand Cross of Order Brit. Empire, asso. knight justice Order of St. John of Jerusalem, King's medal for Service in Cause of Freedom (Gt. Britain); comdr. Legion of Honor (France); comdr. Order of Leopold, grand officer Order of Crown (Belgium); grand officer Orange Nassau (Netherlands); grand officer Oak Crown (Luxembourgh); knight comdr. Order of Plus IX (Vatican). Mem. Pilgrims U.S. (v.p., trustee). Clubs: White's (London); Royal Yacht Squadron (Cowes); Royal and Ancient Golf of St. Andrews (Scotland); Hope (R.I.); Racquet, Harvard, Knickerbocker, Brook, Century, Links, N.Y. Yacht (N.Y.C.). Home: 960 Fifth Av New York City NY 10021 Office: 30 Rockefeller Plaza New York City NY 10020

ALDRIDGE, ALFRED OWEN, educator; b. Buffalo, Dec. 16, 1915; s. Albert and Jane (Ette) A.; B.S. in Edn., Ind. U., 1937; M.A., U. Ga., 1938; Ph.D., Duke, 1942; D.U.P., U. Paris (France), 1955; m. Adriana García Dávila, June 7, 1963; 1 dau., Cecily (Mrs. John Ward). Prof. comparative lit. U. Buffalo, 1942-47, U. Md., 1947-67, U. Ill., 1967—. Fulbright prof., France, 1953; Smith-Mundt prof., Brazil, 1957. Mem. Am. (adv. bd. 1965-71), Internat. (adv. bd. 1970) comparative lit. assns., Am. Soc. 18th Century Studies (adv. bd. 1968). Author: Franklin and His French Contemporaries, 1957; Man of Reason: Life of Thomas Paine, 1959; Jonathan Edwards, 1964; Benjamin Franklin: Philosopher and Man, 1965. Editor: Comparative Lit. Studies, 1963—. Home: 101 E Chalmers St Champaign IL 61820 Office: U Ill Modern Land Bldg Urbana IL 61801

ALDRIDGE, FREDERICK FERDINAND, environmental engr.; b. Skoghole, Finland, Jan. 6, 1912; s. Albert Ferdinand and Selma Lindstedt (Soisalo) A.; came to U.S., 1914, naturalized, 1928; B.S., Mass. Inst. Tech., 1934; M.S., Harvard, 1941; postgrad. U.S. Army Sch. Milt. Govt., U. Va., 1943; m. Jean Cairns Miller, Nov. 3, 1934; children—Karl Ferdinand, Ann Margaret (Mrs. Paul Dahl), John Frederick. Constrn. supr. Cambridge (Mass.) Engring. and Sewer Dept., 1936-39; san. engr. Mass. Dept. Pub. Health, 1939-41; san. engring. officer USPHS, 1941-47, 51-64, regional sanitation dir. UNRRA, Egypt, Palestine and Greece, 1944-45, chief san. engr., 1945-46, regional cons. Nat. Housing Agy., Dallas, 1946-47, chief san. engr. Tech. Cooperation Adminstrn. Mission to Iran, 1951-53, chief program engr., India, 1954-56, asst. regional engr., program dir. USPHS, Dept. Health, Edn. and Welfare, San Francisco, 1956-59, chief san. engring. services div. Internat. Health, Washington, 1959-61, chief pub. health adviser U.S. aid mission to Libya, 1961-64, san. engr., dir. water supply and pollution control program Pacific N.W. region, 1964; dir. sanitation services Seattle- King County Dept. Pub. Health, 1947-51, dir. environmental health, 1965—. Bd. dirs. U. S. Conf. of Environmental Health Adminstrs., 1966—, chmn., 1968; mem. com. on san. engring. NRC, 1946-47; mem. Wash. Environmental Council, Citizens for Clean Air, Seattle Municipal League; mem. Puget Sound Regional Comprehensive Health Planning Bd., chmn. environmental com., 1969-70. Served from 1st lt. to lt. col. USPHS, World War II, Korea. Recipient Commendation medal USPHS, 1964. Diplomate Am. Acad. Environmental Engrs. Fellow Am. Pub. Health Assn.; mem. Am. Pub. Works Assn., Nat. Soc. Profl. Engrs., Am. Water Works Assn., Am. Acad. Pub. Health Adminstrs., Inter-Am. Assn. San. Engring., Nat. Environmental Health Assn., Nat. Air Pollution Control Assn. Home: 2581 N E 107th St Seattle WA 98125

ALDRIDGE, GEORGE MILLARD, ins. co. exec.; b. Ellingwood, Kan., Dec. 24, 1922; s. Claude Newton and Esther (Rader) A.; B.S., Kan. U., 1946, grad. student, 1947; student advanced engring., Tex. A. and M. Coll., 1944; m. Rosemary Ryan, Dec. 28, 1946; children—Millard F., Claude M., Anne L., Kathleen. With Business Men's Assurance Co., 1947—, v.p. adminstrn., 1967—, also dir. Served with AUS. 1943-46. Decorated Purple Heart. Fellow Life Office Mgmt. Assn.; mem. Kansas City (Mo.) C. of C., Alpha Kappa Psi (life). Democratic. Catholic. Clubs: Homestead Country. Home: 4306 Homestead Dr Prairie Village KS 66208 Office: BMA Tower Kansas City MO 64141

ALDRIDGE, GORDON JAMES, educator; b. Toronto, Can., Oct. 19, 1916; s. Eugene Froyard and Alicia (Jourdan) A.; B.A., U. Toronto, 1938, diploma in social work, 1939, M.A., 1948, M. Social Work, 1949; Ph.D., U. Michigan, 1955; diploma in edn. U. London, 1963; m. Gladys Chapman, June 21, 1941; 1 son, Ronald Gordon. Came to U.S., 1950, naturalized, 1956. Caseworker, Family Agy., Toronto, 1939-41, case supr., 1946-50; asst. exec. dir., 1949-50. Lectr. U. Toronto, 1946-50, asso. prof. social work, dir. Human Relations Inst., Fla. State U., 1950-52; asso. prof. social work Mich. State U., 1952-57, prof., 1957—, dir. Sch. Social Work, 1959-66. Active state and nat. health and welfare orgns. Served from 2d lt. to maj., Canadian Army, 1941-46; ETO. Mem. Council on Social Work Edn., Nat. Assn. Social Workers, Gerontological Soc., Internat. Assn. Gerontology, Am. Assn. U. Profs. Author: Social Welfare and the Aged, 1959; Social Issues and Psychiatric Social Work Practice, 1959; (with J. Kaplan) Social Welfare of the Aging, 1962; (with Earl J. McGrath) Liberal Education and Social Work, published in 1965. Contbr. to: Florida State University Studies, 1952; Living in the Later Years, 1952; Education for Later Maturity, 1954; Aging is Everyone's Concern, 1957; also articles profl. jours. Home: 322 Kipling Blvd Lansing MI 48912

ALDRIDGE, JOHN FORNISS, Jr., aircraft mfg. co. exec.; b. Mobile, Oct. 10, 1915; s. John Forniss and Sarah (Van Antwerp) A.; B.S. in Aero. Engring., U. Ala., 1936; M.S. in Aero. Engring., Mass. Inst. Tech., 1939; m. Enid Stevens, Oct. 10, 1941 (dec.); children—John Forniss III, Robert Edward; m. 2d, JoAnn Lock, Dec. 5, 1970; Asst. dir. research United Aircraft Corp., 1939-41; with McDonnell Aircraft Corp., St. Louis, 1946- , v.p., 1952-. Cons. aero and space vehicles panel USAF Sci. Bd., 1959- 63. Served to lt. col. USAAF, 1941-46. Mem. Am. Inst. Aero. and Astronautics, Air Force Assn., Am. Ordnance Assn., Navy League U.S. Democrat. Episcopalian. Club: Old Warson Country (St. Louis). Home: 6 Sherwyn Lane Creve Coeur, MO 63141, Office: P O Box 516 St. Louis, MO 63166.

ALDRIDGE, JOHN WATSON, educator, author; b. Sioux City, Ia., Sept. 26, 1922; s. Walter Copher and Nell (Watson) A.; student U. Chattanooga, 1940-43; fellow Breadloaf Sch. English, summer 1942; B.A., U. Cal. at Berkeley, 1947; m. Leslie Felker, Dec. 10, 1954 (div. June 1968); 1 son, Geoffrey; children by previous marriages—Henry, Stephen, Leslie, Jeremy; m. Alexandra Bertash, July 13, 1968. Lectr. English, U. Vt., 1948-50, asst. prof. 1950-53, 54-55; lectr. Christian Gauss Seminars Criticism, Princeton, 1953-54; mem. lit. faculty Sarah Lawrence Coll., also New Sch. Social Research, 1957; prof. English, Queens Coll., 1957; Berg prof. English, N.Y.U. 1957; Fulbright lectr. U. Munich (Germany), 1958-59; writer-in-residence Hollins Coll., 1960-62; Fulbright lectr. U. Copenhagen (Denmark), 1962-63; prof. English, U. Mich., 1964—; book critic N.Y. Herald Tribune Book Week, 1965-66, Saturday Review, 1970—. Staff, Bread Loaf Writers Conf., 1966-69; chief regional judge Book-of-the Month Writing Fellowship Program, 1966—. Served with AUS, 1943-45; ETO. Decorated Bronze Star medal. Mem. Authors Guild and League of Am., Modern Lang. Assn. Author: After the Lost Generation, 1951; Critiques and Essays on Modern Fiction, 1952; In Search of Heresy, 1956; The Party at Cranton, 1960; Time to Murder and Create, 1966; In the Country of the Young, 1970; also articles. Editor: Selected Stories by P.G. Wodehouse, 1958. Home: 1050 Wall St Ann Arbor MI 48105

ALDRIDGE, MARY HENNEN DELLINGER, educator; b. Brownstown, Ark., Jan. 11, 1919; d. Bonnier and Sadie B. (Reeves) Dellinger; B.S. in Chemistry, U. Ga., 1939; M.A., Duke, 1941; Ph.D. in Biochemistry, Georgetown U., 1954; m. Alfred Owen Aldridge, May 18, 1941 (div. 1956); 1 dau., Cecily Joan (Mrs. John P. Ward, Jr.). Chemist, E.I. duPont de Nemours & Co., 1941-47; asst. prof. U. Md., 1947-55; mem. faculty Am. U., 1955—, prof. chemistry, 1962—; pres. Chemco, Inc., 1962-65, Aldridges & Assos. & Co., Inc., 1965—. Research grantee USPHS, 1967-68, Surgeon Gen.'s Office, U.S. Army, 1961-64, 66-69; Eve. Star faculty research grantee, 1961. Mem. Am. Chem. Soc., Washington Acad. Scis. (chmn. teaching sci. panel for Sci. Achievement awards 1969-70), Chem. Soc. Washington (chmn. nat. com. women's activities 1962, chmn. organic topical group 1962-63, bd. mgrs. 1962-66, sec. 1967-68, councilor 1967-69, pres. 1970), A.A.A.S., Am. Assn. U. Profs., Washington Philos. Soc., Washington Chromatography Discussion Group (bd. govs. 1966-71), Sigma Xi, Sigma Delta Epsilon. Home: 2930 45th St NW Washington DC 20016

ALDRIN, EDWIN EUGENE, Jr., astronaut; b. Glen Ridge, N.J., Jan. 20, 1930; B.S., U.S. Mil. Acad., 1951; Sc.D. in Astronautics, Mass. Inst. Tech., 1963; Sc.D. (hon.), Gustavus Adolphus Coll., 1967, Clark U., 1969, U. Portland, 1970, St. Peter's Coll., 1970; Litt.D., Montclair State Coll., 1969; D.Hum., Seton Hall U., 1970; m. Joan Ann Archer; children—James Michael, Janice Ross, Andrew John. Commd. in USAF, 1951, advanced through grades to col.; served as fighter pilot in Korea; worked with experiments in Gemini-Titan flights at field office Space System Div., Manned Spacecraft Center, Houston, prior to appointment as astronaut; pilot Gemini XII orbital rendezvous space flight, Nov. 11-15, 1966; lunar module pilot on first manned lunar landing Apollo XI; established record over 7 hours and 52 minutes outside spacecraft in extravehicular activity; comdt. Aerospace Research Pilots Sch., Edwards AFB, Cal., 1971—. Dir. Mut. of Omaha Ins. Co. Bd. visitors dept. earth and planetary scis. Mass. Inst. Tech. Decorated D.S.M., D.F.C. with oak leaf cluster, Air Medal with 2 oak leaf clusters; recipient numerous awards including Presdl. Medal of Freedom, 1969. Fellow Am. Inst. Aeros. and Astronautics; mem. Soc. Exptl. Test Pilots, Royal Aero. Soc. (hon.), Sea Space Symposium (charter), Internat. Acad. Astronautics (corr.), Sigma Xi, Sigma Gamma Tau, Tau Beta Pi. Mason (33). Address: Aerospace Research Pilots School Edwards AFB CA 93523

ALECK, ADOLPH WILLIAM, educator; b. Elberfeld, Ind., Aug. 13, 1899; s. Eugene J. and Frederika (Becher) A.; B.A., Oglethorpe U., 1923; B.D., Atlanta Theol. Sem., 1923; M.A., Clark U., 1926; Ph.D., N.Y. U., 1931; m. Leola M. Miner, June 9, 1940. Instr., Oglethorpe U., 1922-23, Clark U., 1925-26; spl. lectr. N.Y. U. Sch. Edn., 1928-40; head dept. edn. and psychology Huntingdon Coll., 1945-47; head dept. gen. edn. Miss. State U., 1947- -, prof., head dept. psychology. Vis. prof. psychology State U. Coll., Fredonia, N.Y. Mem. Am., Miss. psychol. assns., Am. Assn. Mental Deficiency, Nat., Miss. Edn. assns., Phi Kappa Pi, Pi Gamma Mu, Kappa Delta Pi. Mem. Evang. and Ref. Ch. Co-author: Outline of Educational Psychology, 1934; Readings in General Psychology 1935; Educational Psychology, 4th edit., 1959. Home: 705 Sassafras Dr Starkville MS 39759

ALEGI, PETER CLAUDE, lawyer; b. New Haven, July 26, 1935; s. Claude and Margaret (Lettieri) A.; B.A. cum laude, Yale, 1956, LL.B., 1959; m. Nicoletta Barbarito, Dec. 16, 1961; children—Gregory, Daniel, Peter. Admitted to Conn. bar, 1959, R.I. bar, 1962, Ill. bar, 1965, also U.S. Supreme Ct.; practice in Providence, 1961-64; with firm Baker & McKenzie, Chgo., 1964-65, Milan and Rome, Italy, 1965—. Dir. Arbos SpA, Breda Standard SpA, Maynard & Co. SpA,

Purina Italia SpA, Sardanavi SpA, Shulton Italianaa SpA. Bd. dirs. R.I. chpt. Am. Civil Liberties Union, 1963-64; mem. Yale Alumni Bd., 1970—. Served with AUS, 1960-61. Fulbright scholar U. Rome, 1959-60. Mem. Am. Bar Assn. Roman Catholic. Home: Via Salaria 330/B Rome Italy Office: Via Venti Settembre 1 00187 Rome Italy

ALEGRIA, FERNANDO, author, educator; b. Santiago, Chile, Sept. 26, 1918; s. Santiago Alegria Toro and Julia (Alfaro) A.; Profl. E., U. Chile, 1938; M.A., Bowling Green State U., 1941; Ph.D., U. Cal., 1947; m. Carmen Letona Melendez, Jan. 29, 1943; children—Carmen, Daniel, Andrew, Isabel. Editor Pan Am. Union, Washington, 1945; prof. Spanish, U. Cal., 1947-67, Stanford, 1967—; dir. writers workshop U. Concepcion, Chile, 1960-63; prof. Latin Am. and Chilean Literatures U. Chile, 1966. Hon. consul of Chile, Berkeley, 1965. Mem. Am. Assn. Tchrs. Spanish, Am. Assn. U. Profs., Instituto International de Lit. Iberoamericana, Sociedad de Escritores de Chile. Author: Lautaro, 1943; Camaleon, 1950; Caballo de copas, 1957; Manana los Guerreros, 1965; Las noches del cazador; Cataclismo, 1960; El poeta que se volvio gusano, 1956; Viva Chile, 1966; La poesia chilena, 1954; Walt Whitman en Hispanoamerica, 1954; Historia de la novela hispanoamericana, 1966; Las fronteras del realismo, 1964; Ten Pastoral Psalms, 1967; Los dias contados, 1968; Amerika, 1970. Home: 55 Arlmonte Dr Berkeley CA 94707

ALEMAN, ROBERTO RAMON, diplomate of Panama; b. Panama, Republic of Panama, Oct. 2, 1921; s. Julio and Emelia (Zubieta) A.; B.A., La. State U., 1942, J.D., 1943; m. Maria Teresa Healy, July 14, 1951; children—Roberto Ramon, Jaime Eduardo, Carmen, Jose Miguel, Alvaro Antonio, Juan Francisco, Lucas Raul. First sec. embassy, Argentina, 1945-47; partner firm Icaza, Gondalez. Ruiz & Aleman, Panams, 1947—; spl. ambassador for Panama Canal Treaty Negotiations, 1965-68; ambassador of Panama to U.S., 1968—. Pres. Cerveceria Nacional, Bank of Commerce and Finance Inc.; dir. Compania Inversionista Panamena S.A.; alternate dir. Cemento Panama, S.A. Clubs: Union, Panama Golf, Panama Yacht and Fishing (Panama); Chevy Chase (Md.); Internat. (Washington). Home: 2601 29th St Washington DC 20008 Office: 2144 Wyoming Av Washington DC 20000

ALEO, JOSEPH JOHN, scientist, educator; b. Wilkes-Barre, Pa., Oct. 8, 1925; s. Vincent and Martha (Lupino) A.; B.S., Bucknell U., 1948; D.D.S., Temple U., 1953; Ph.D., U. Rochester, 1965; m. Fannie Ocuto, Aug. 28, 1949; children—Joseph John, James Robert. Dental surgeon USPHS, 1953-54; pvt. practice dentistry, Meshoppen, Pa., 1954-60; research fellow U. Rochester, 1960-65; asso. prof., chmn. dept. pathology Temple U., 1965-67, prof., chmn. dept., 1967-70, dir. advanced edn. and research, 1970—; cons. NIH. Served with AUS, 1943-46. Mem. Am. Soc. Exptl. Pathology, Internat. Assn. Dental Research, Pathology Soc. Phila., Omicron Kappa Upsilon. Contbr. articles sci. jours. Office: 3223 N Broad St Philadelphia PA 19140

ALESSANDRO, VICTOR NICHOLAS, symphony condr.; b. Waco, Tex., Nov. 27, 1915; s. Victor and Josephine (Kemendo) A.; Mus.B., U. Rochester, 1937, Mus.D. (hon.), 1948; L.H.D., So. Meth. U., 1956; student Mozarteum Acad., Salzburg, Austria, 1937, Santa Cecilia Acad., Rome, Italy, 1938; m. Ruth Drisko, May 1, 1955; children—Victor Tabbut, Ruth Ann. Mus. dir. Oklahoma City Symphony, 1938-51, San Antonio Symphony Orch. and San Antonio Grand Opera Festival, 1951—, Recipient Alice M. Ditson award Columbia, 1956, Nat. Music Council award, 1964. Mem. Internat. Alliance Theatrical and Stage Employees (hon.), Am. Fedn. Musicals (hon.), Bruckner Soc. Am. (hon.), Phi Mu Alpha (hon.). Club: Torch (San Antonio). Home: 711 Garraty Rd San Antonio TX 78209 Office: San Antonio Symmphony Orchestra 600 Hemisfair Plaza Way San Antonio TX 78205

ALESSANDRONI, VEHAN JOSEPH, lawyer; b. N.Y.C., Mar. 1, 1915; s. Anthony P. and Andromeda (Rossini) A.; A.B., Columbia U., 1937, J.D., 1939; m. Alice Shaughnessy, Feb. 2, 1949. Admitted to N.Y. bar, 1941, also Supreme Ct. of Korea, 1946; announcer, CBS Artists Service, Inc., 1940; U.S. atty. Bd. Econ. Warfare, 1942; mem. U.S. Fgn. Econ. Adminstrn. Mission, Belgian Congo, 1943; with Wormser, Koch, Kiely & Alessandroni, N.Y.C., 1946—, sr. partner, 1959—. Dir. Am. Lurgi Corp. Legal officer Mil. Govt. Korea, 1945-46; legal adviser to provincial gov. Kyunggi-Do, Korea, 1946; chief provost judge City of Seoul, 1946; lectr. various tax insts., univs., profl. assns. Recipient U.S. Army Commendation award, 1946; regional award N.Y. Times, 1932; Curtis medal Columbia, 1936. Mem. Assn. Bar City N.Y. Author: The Executor, 1963; Applied Estate Planning, 1963; also articles. Departmental editor Jour. Taxation, 1955-56. Home: Eggleston Lane Old Greenwich CT 06870 Office: 100 Park Av New York NY 10017

ALETTER, FRANK GEORGE, actor; b. College Point, N.Y., Jan. 14, 1926; s. Henry George and Katherine (Marquardt) A.; grad. Flushing (N.Y.) High Sch., 1940-42; m. Lee Meriwether, Apr. 20, 1958; children—Kyle Kathleen, Lesley Anne. With Dramatic Workshop New Sch. Social Research, 1948-50; appearances on Broadway include Mr. Roberts, 1950, Wish You Were Here, 1952-54, Time Limit, 1955, Bells Are Ringing, 1956-59; star TV series Bringing Up Buddy, 1960, Cara Willaims Show, 1962, It's About Time, 1965. Served with AUS, 1944-48.‡

ALEXANDER, ARCHIBALD FERGUSON, educator; b. Mpls., Oct. 13, 1928; s. Archibald Ferguson and Jean (Smith) A.; B.S., U. Minn., 1951, D.V.M., 1951; M.S., Colo. State U., 1958, Ph.D., 1962; m. Susan MacDonald Hart, Sept. 5, 1953; children—Ian Ferguson, Bruce Hart, Jean MacDonald, Ruth Ellen. Mem. faculty Colo. State U., 1956—, prof. pathology, 1966—, head dept., 1966—; research fellow U. Glasgow (Scotland), 1963-64. Served with Vet. Corps, AUS, 1952- 54. Diplomate Am. Coll. Vet. Pathology; mem. Internat. Acad. Pathology, Am. Vet. Med. Assn., A.A.A.S., Minn., Colo. vet. med. assns., Sigma Xi, Phi Zeta, Gamma Sigma Delta. Contbr. articles in field. Home: 992 Summit View Dr Fort Collins CO 80521

ALEXANDER, ARVIN J., lawyer; b. Lethbridge, Alta., Can., May 10, 1909; s. John M. and Lona (Ledford) A.; J.D., Ohio State U., 1936; m. Anne Lawrie Valentine, Aug. 4, 1934; 1 son, Donald V. Admitted to Ohio bar, 1936; partner firm Alexander, Ebinger, Holschuh, Fisher & McAlister, Columbus, Ohio, 1946—. Mem. exec. bd. Greater Columbus Development Commn.; mem. Columbus City Council, 1939-43; mem. Met. Airport Com., 1956-63; chmn. trustees Columbus Better Bus. Bur. Central Ohio, 1958-61; pres. Citizens Research, Inc. 1962-64, chmn. bd., 1964-66; mem. Downtown Area Commn. Bd., 1965—; trustee Mutual Investing Found., Columbus; trustee Columbus Sinking Fund, 1953-54, pres., 1957-58; Hon. trustee Franklin Forum. Mem. Am., Ohio State, Columbus bar assns., Navy League (judge advocate 1963). Home: 3725 Olentangy Blvd Columbus OH 43214 Office: 17 S High St Columbus OH 43215

ALEXANDER, BENJAMIN, physician, educator; b. Boston, Mar. 20, 1909; s. Harry and Ida (Shumann) A.; A.B., Harvard, 1930, M.D., 1934; m. Marie Martha Mayer, June 25, 1937; children—Millard Henry, Judith Lee, Robert Eugene. Intern, Beth Israel Hosp., 1935, staff physician, 1953-66; teaching, traveling fellow Harvard, 1936-38, asso. prof. medicine, 1953-66; practice medicine specializing in hematology, Boston, 1939-66, N.Y.C., 1966—; sr. investigator N.Y. Blood Center, 1966—; clin. prof. medicine Cornell U., 1966—; asso. attending physician Meml. Hosp., 1966—; attending physician N.Y. Hosp., 1967—; cons. Childrens Hosp. (Boston) Mem. Am. Soc. Clin. Investigation, Am. Chem. Soc., Am. Soc. Biol. Chemists, Assn. Am. Physicians, Interurban Clin. Club, Am. Acad. Arts and Scis. Contbr. articles to profl jours. Home: 185 E 85th St New York City NY 10028 Office: N Y Blood Center 310 E 67th St New York City NY 10021

ALEXANDER, BROOKE, former publisher; b. N.Y.C., May 22, 1912; s. Ludwell Brooke and Mary Breckinridge (Maltby) A.; grad. Kent (Conn.) Sch., 1931; B.A., Princeton, 1935; m. Elizabeth Wise Burnett, Jan. 20, 1940; children—Brooke (Mrs. Bruce E. Leddy), Breck. With W. & J. Sloane, N.Y.C., 1935-36, Batten, Barton, Durstine & Osborn, 1936-39, Paris & Peart, 1939-42; With Time, Inc., 1942-70; now ret., former asst. pub. Fortune mag. Past Citizens Housing and Planning Council, N.Y.C. Trustee Mt. Holyoke Coll.; past dir. Am. Inst. Graphic Arts, Grand Jury Assn. N.Y. County; bd. dirs. Trail Blazer Camps, Frontier Nursing Service, Trustees for Conservation. Mem. N.Y.N.G., 1936-39, N.Y. State Guard, 1940-43. Mem. Soc. Cincinnati. Episcopalian (former). Clubs: Union (N.Y.C.); Nassau (Princeton, N.J.). Home: 65 E 96th St New York City NY 10028

ALEXANDER, CECIL ABRAHAM, architect; b. Atlanta, Mar. 14, 1918; s. Cecil Abraham and Jula (Moses) A.; student Ga. Inst. Tech., 1936; A.B., Yale, 1940; student Mass. Inst. Tech., 1941; M. Arch., Harvard, 1947; m. Hermione Weil, Jan. 20, 1943; children—Therese, Judith, Douglas. Partner Alexander & Rothschild, architects, Atlanta, 1949-58; chmn. bd. Finch, Alexander, Barnes, Rothschild & Paschal, Architects and Engrs., Inc., Atlanta, 1958—; pres. A.S.D. Inc., interior design service; dir. Peoples-American Bank; designing architect Ga. Power Bldg., 1st Nat. Bank (both Atlanta). Chmn. Atlanta Citizens Adv. Com. Urban Renewal, 1958-60; mem. Mayor Atlanta Substitute Met. Planning Commn., 1962—, now vice chmn; past vice chmn. Community Council, Atlanta, Ga. Mem. Mayor's Adv. Com. Race Relations, Nat. Citizens Com. Community Relations; chmn. Atlanta chpt. Am. Jewish Com., 1963; chmn. housing resources com. City of Atlanta; S.E. area chmn. adv. council Urban Am.; pres. Resurgens Atlanta. Bd. dirs. Atlanta Symphony Orch. Member of Yale Nat. Alumni Bd., 1963. Served to lt. col. USMCR, World War II. Decorated Air medal, D.F.C. Recipient Brotherhood award Nat. Conf. Christians and Jews, 1964. Fellow A.I.A. (pres. Ga. 1957); mem. Atlanta C. of C. (past dir.). Jewish religion (2d v.p. temple). Home: 2322 Mt Paran Rd Atlanta GA 30327 Office: 44 Broad St N W Atlanta GA 30303

ALEXANDER, CHALMERS WHITFIELD, banker; b. Jackson, Miss., Sept. 29, 1908; s. H. Chalmers and Marina (Whitfield) A.; A.B., Princeton, 1932; LL.B., Jackson Sch. Law, 1938. Admitted to Miss. bar, 1938; with Internal Revenue Service, Jackson, 1938-42 46-48; practice in Jackson, 1948-52; commr. City of Jackson, 1952-57; v.p., sr. trust officer. First Nat. Bank Jackson, 1957—. Past pres. Miss. Estate Planning Council. Served to capt. USAAF, World War II; CBI. Mem. Am., Miss. bar assns., Am. Newcomen Soc., Jackson C. of C., Kappa Sigma. Democrat. Methodist. Rotarian. Contbr. articles to law publs. Home: 927 Poplar Blvd Jackson MS 39202 Office: Box 291 Jackson MS 39205

ALEXANDER, CHARLES HAYNES, govt. ofcl.; b. Mineral Wells, Tex., Aug. 31, 1916; s. Robert Caesar and Belle (Haynes) A.; student George Washington U., 1935-36; LL.B., Southeastern U., 1939, B.C.S., 1948; m. M. Virginia Creel, Nov. 6, 1942; 1 son, Charles Haynes Alexander. With Fed. Emergency Relief Adminstrn., Works Progress Adminstrn., 1935-40, Navy Dept. 1941, WPB, 1942-46; with Dept. Commerce, 1946—, budget officer, 1966—. Chmn. Interdeptl. Budget Officers Conf., 1969-70. Active local PTA. Mem. town council, Cheverly, Md., 1965-68. Served with USCGR, 1944-45. Mem. Am. Soc. Pub. Adminstrn. Club: Prince Georges Country. Home: 5612 Greenleaf Rd Cheverly MD 20785 Office: Main Commerce Bldg Washington DC 20230

ALEXANDER, CHARLES THOMAS, newspaper exec.; b. Mpls., Sept. 21, 1928; s. Charles Thomas and Mary (Stinson) A.; A.B., Duke U., 1950; student Boston U. Sch. Theology, 1953- 55; M.S. in Journalism, Columbia, 1956; m. Elizabeth Jean Brown, Dec. 29, 1951; children—Elizabeth Stinson, Lucy Bruce. With Stinson Bros. Dry Goods Co., Mt. Vernon, Ind., 1950-51, Washington Star, 1956-61; mng. editor Wilmington (Del.) Morning News, 1961-63, Wilmington Morning News and Eve. Jour., 1963-66; mng. editor Dayton (O.) Jour. Herald, 1966-68, editor, 1968-71, editor and pub., 1971—. Served with AUS, 1951-53. Mem. Am. Soc. Newspaper Editors, Sigma Delta Chi, Phi Kappa Psi. Republican. Presbyn. Clubs: Nat. Press (Washington); Moraine Country, Dayton Racquet. Home: 4761 Mad River Rd Kettering OH 45429 Office: 37 S Ludlow St Dayton OH 45401

ALEXANDER, CLAUDE GORDON, educator; b. San Diego, Sept. 15, 19-4; B.S., Ore. State Coll., 1948, M.S., 1950; Ph.D., U. Cal. at Los Angeles, 1955; married, 1954; two children. Asst. prof. biology San Francisco State Coll, 1955-64, asso. prof., then prof., chmn. dept. physiology and behavioral biology, 1964—. Served with AUS, 1944-46. Mem. Soc. Parasitology. Home: 132 Northam Av San Carlos CA Office: San Francisco State Coll San Francisco CA*

ALEXANDER, CLAUDE LIVINGSTONE, Jr., container mfg. exec.; b. Queens, N.Y., Aug. 27, 1927; s. Claude L. and Dorothy (Kluski) A.; B.A., Colgate U., 1948; m. Bernice M. Lowe, Oct. 27, 1944; children—Leslie, Craig, Kim. Asst. to pres. Sun Tube Corp., 1953-54, gen. sales mgr., 1954-58, v.p. sales, 1958; v.p. sales Bradley-Sun div. Am. Can Co., 1958, v.p. Am. Can Co., gen. mgr. Bradley Sun Div.; now pres. Owens Yacht div. Brunswick Corp.; dir. Sun Tube Can., Ltd.; pres. Plastic Bottle and Tube Inst. Dir. Hillside Indsl. Assn. Mem. N.Y. Bd. Trade. Mem. Toilet Goods Assn., Proprietary Assn., Soc. Plastics Industry, Washington (N.J.) C. of C. (past pres.), N.J. Sales Exec. Club. Office: 181 Long Av Hillside NJ 07205

ALEXANDER, CLIFFORD L., Jr., lawyer; b. N.Y.C., Sept. 21, 1933; s. Clifford L. and Edith (McAllister) A.; A.B. cum laude, Harvard, 1955; LL.B., Yale, 1958; m. Adele Logan, July 11, 1959; children—Elizabeth, Mark Clifford. Admitted to N.Y. bar, 1960, also U.S. Supreme Ct., D.C. bar; asst. to dist. atty. N.Y. County, 1959-61; exec. dir. Manhattanville Hamilton Grange, neighborhood conservation project, 1961-62; exec. and program dir. HARYOU, Inc., also pvt. practice law, N.Y.C., 1962-63; mem. staff Nat. Security Council, 1963- 64; dep. spl. asst. to President Johnson, 1964-65, asso. spl. counsel 1965-66, dep. spl. counsel, 1966-67, chmn. Equal Opportunity Commn., 1967-69; partner firm Arnold & Porter, 1969—. Mem. Pres.'s Commn. on Income Maintenance Programs, 1967—; Pres.'s spl. ambassador to the Independence of Swaziland, 1968. Mem. bd. of dirs. Children's Village, Dobbs Ferry, N.Y., 1963-69, NAACP Legal Def. and Ednl. Fund; trustee Radcliffe Coll., Atlanta U.; bd. overseers Harvard; mem. bd. Alumni Assn. Ethical/Fieldston Schs., 1962-63. Served with AUS, 1958-59. Named hon. citizen Kansas City, Mo., 1965; recipient Ames award Harvard, 1955; Frederick Douglass award, 1970. Mem. Am., N.Y. State bar assns. Club: Reveille (Annual Outstanding Achievement award 1966) (N.Y.C.). Home: 819 C St S E Washington DC 20003 Office: 1229 19th St NW Washington DC 20036

ALEXANDER, EDWARD LAWSON, educator, dean; b. Lewiston, Me., Oct. 22, 1925; s. Irving Edward and Sarah (Drew) A.; B.S., U. Me., 1950, M.S., 1951; Ph.D. in Phys. Chemistry, Vanderbilt U., 1955; m. Phyllis Mary Maxwell, Aug. 20, 1949; children—Bruce E., Steven M., Jeffrey D., Beth L. Research asso. nuclear and radiation chemistry Knolls Atomic Power Lab., Gen. Electric Co., 1955-57; asso. prof., asst. dir. reactor project, radiation safety officer Ga. Inst. Tech., 1957-58; mgr.. radiol. scis., indsl. reactor labs. Columbia, 1958-62; prof., dir. radiation sci. center Rutgers U., 1962-67; prof. radiol. scis., dean Grad. Sch., Lowell Tech. Inst., 1967- -. Chmn. Conf. Radiol. Health, 1964-65. Mem. Health Physics Soc. (pres. Greater N.Y. chpt. 1962), Am. Chem. Soc., Am. Nuclear Soc., Am. Assn. U. Profs. Home: 80 Chestnut St Andover MA 01810 Office: Graduate Sch Lowell Tech Inst Lowell MA 01854

ALEXANDER, EDWARD PORTER, hist. orgn. exec.; b. Keokuk, Ia., Jan. 11, 1907; s. Walter Sheron and Anna Moody (Carter) A.; A.B., Drake U., 1928; A.M., State U. Ia., 1931; Ph.D., Columbia, 1938; m. Alice Wagner Bolton, Nov. 27, 1929; children—Anne (Mrs. John Davidson), John, Mary. Tchr., Am. History secondary schs. Ia. and Minn., 1929-32; exec. dir. N.Y. State Hist. Assn., 1934-41; state supr. Hist. Records Survey of N.Y., 1936-38; dir. Hist. Soc. of Wis., 1941-46; dir. interpretation then v.p. Colonial Williamsburg Found., 1946—. Chmn. Va. Hist. Landmarks Commn., 1966—; chmn. U.S. com. Internat. Council Monuments and Sites, 1966-69. Fellow Rochester Mus. Arts and Scis.; mem. Am. Hist. Assn., Am. Assn. of Museums (pres. 1957-60), Am. Assn. for State and Local History, Phi Beta Kappa. Presbyn. Author: A Revolutionary Conservative: James Duane of New York, 1938; articles on history museums and hist. preservation. Editor: New York History, 1939-41; Wisconsin Magazine of History, 1941-46; The Journal of John Fontaine, 1710-1719, 1971. Address: Colonial Williamsburg Found Williamsburg VA 23185

ALEXANDER, GEORGE JONATHON, univ. dean; b. Berlin, Germany, Mar. 8, 1931; (parents U.S. citizens); s. Walter and Sylvia (Grill) A.; A.B. with maj. honors, U. Pa., 1953, J.D. cum laude, 1969; LL.M., Yale, 1965, J.S.D., 1969; m. Katherine Violet Sziklai, Sept. 6, 1958; children—Susan Katina, George Jonathan II. Admitted to Ill. bar, 1960, N.Y. bar, 1961; instr. law, Bigelow fellow U. Chgo., 1959-60; instr. internat. relations Naval Res. Officers Sch., Forrest Park, Ill., 1959-60; prof. law Syracuse U. Coll. Law, 1960-70, asso. dean, 1968-69; vis. prof. law U. So. Cal., 1963; prof. law, dean U. Santa Clara (Cal.) Law Sch., 1970—; cons. in field. Dir. Domestic and Internat. Bus. Problems Honors Clinic, Syracuse U., 1966-69, Regulations in Space Project, 1968-70; dir., mem. exec. com. U.S. assn. Internat. Inst. Space Laws, 1968—; co-founder, 1970, since dir. Am. Assn. Abolition Involuntary Mental Hospitalization. Served with USN, 1953-56. U.S. Navy scholar U. Pa., 1949-52, Law Boards scholar, 1956-59; Sterling fellow Yale, 1964-65; recipient Ralph E. Kharas Civil Liberties award, 1970. Mem. Am., N.Y. State, Cal. bar assns., Assn. Am. Law Schs., Am. Assn. U. Profs. (chpt. pres. 1962), Am. Civil Liberties Union (chpt. pres. 1965), Order of Coif, Justinian Honor Soc., Phi Alpha Delta (chpt. faculty adviser 1967-70). Author: Civil Rights, U.S.A., Public Schools, 1963; Honesty and Competition, 1967; Jury Instructing on Medical Issues, 1966; Cases and Materials on Space Law, 1971; also articles, chpts. in books, one film. Home: 11600 Summit Wood Rd Los Altos Hills CA 94022 Office: Univ Santa Clara Santa Clara CA 95053

ALEXANDER, GEORGE MOYER, clergyman, univ. dean; b. Jacksonville, Fla., May 15, 1914; s. George and Monimia (Starratt) A.; student U. Fla., 1935; B.A., U. of South, 1938, B.D., 1939, S.T.M., Grad. Sch. Theology, 1957; D.D., Va. Theol. Sem, 1957; S.T.D., Seabury-Western Theol. Sem., 1957, m. Mary Danto Bedell, May 25, 1935; children—Stephen Gray, John Rowell. Priest-in- charge St. Mary's, Green Cove Springs, Fla., 1939-42; rector St. Mark's Palatka, Fla., 1942-44, Holy Trinity Ch., Gainesville, Fla., 1945-48, Trinity Ch., Columbia, S.C., 1949-55; fellow Gen. Theol. Sem., 1955-56; dean Sch. Theology, U. of South, 1956—; lectr. St. Augustine's Coll., Canterbury, 1960. Chmn. County Welfare Bd., Alachua County, Fla. Bd. dirs. Community Chest, United Fund; bd. regents U. of South. Mem. Diocese of Fla. (sec. 1941-48), Diocese of Upper S.C. (sec. 1953-54), Nat. Council Episcopal Ch.; dep. to Gen. Conv. P.E. Ch. Author: The Handbook of Biblical Personalities, 1962; Henry Disbrow Phillips, 1968. Contbr. articles church publs. Office: St Luke's University of the South Sewanee TN 37375

ALEXANDER, HAROLD BELL, govt. ofcl.; b. Mineral Wells, Tex., Oct. 2, 1919; s. Robert Caesar and Belle (Haynes) A.; A.B. in Econs., George Washington U., 1953; student U. Tex., 1936-38; m. Janice Fairfield Saunders, Nov. 26, 1941; children—Peter Baldwin, Kathryn Wynne, Daniel Saunders. Budget analyst Dept. Agr., 1938-42, War Assets Adminstrn., 1946-47, CAA, 1947-54; chief budget div. Dept. Commerce, 1954-59; dir. budget FAA, 1963-67, dep. asso. adminstr., 1967—. Served with USAAF, 1942-45. Episcopalian. Home: 2309 Eccleston St Silver Spring MD 20902 Office: 800 Independence Av Washington DC 20003

ALEXANDER, HARRY WALTER, indsl. engr.; b. Los Angeles; s. Charles and Minnie B. (Dillingham) A.; student N.Y. U.; m. Joey Stock. Reporter, feature and financial writer Chgo. Inter-Ocean, 1911-12; sales mgr. Federal Light and Traction Co., N.Y., 1913-15; mgr. promotion Soc. for Elec. Devel., 1916-17; v.p. Am. Writing Paper Co., Holyoke, Mass., 1917- 20; exec. Goldwyn Pictures Corp., 1920-23, chmn. finance com. Goldwyn chain of theatres, 1923-25; est. bus. counsel service in indsl. engring., marketing, negotiations, 1925—. Vice Pres. Am. Type Founders, Elizabeth N.J., 1933-37; pres. Nat. Paper & Type Co. (S.A.), Havana, Cuba. Mem. Am. Arbitration Assn., Sales Mgrs. Assn. of England (London), Native Sons of the Golden West (Los Angeles), Motion Picture Pioneers, Inc., Chicago Press Vets. Assn., Newcomen Soc., (Am. br.). Creator flood lighting of Statue of Liberty. Address: 101 California Av Santa Monica CA 90403

ALEXANDER, HERBERT M., publisher; b. N.Y.C., Sept. 1, 1910: s. Max and Therese (Rothschild) A.; B.A., N.Y. U., 1931; m. Greta Maren Hinterauer, May 8, 1942; 1 son, Thomas P. Publishers' traveler, 1932-34; social worker City of N.Y., 1935-36; editor N.Y. Graphic Soc., 1936-39; copy chief Norman Warren & Co., 1939-42; asso. editor Pocket Books, Inc., 1947, editor-in-chief, 1948—, v.p., 1953—, dir., 1959—, now pub.; exec. v.p. Washington Sq. Press, 1959—; pres. Trident Press, 1963—; dir., v.p. simon & Schuster, 1966—. Served to 2d lt. USAAF, 1942-46. Mem. Phi Beta Kappa, Pi Lambda Phi, Player's. Author translations, articles and short stories. Home: 280 Riverside Dr New York City NY 10025 Office: 630 Fifth Av New York City NY 10020

ALEXANDER, HOLMES, journalist; b. Parkersburg, W.Va., Jan. 29, 1906; s. Charles Butler and Margaret (Moss) A.; B.A., Princeton, 1928; postgrad Trinity Coll., Cambridge, Eng., 1928-29; Litt.D., Salem (W.Va.) Coll., 1971; m. Mary Barksdale, June 24, 1933; children—Hunter Holmes, Peter Barksdale, Mary Madge (Mrs. Rene

R. Dufour). Mem. Md. Gen. Assembly, 1931-35; writer syndicated column McNaught Syndicate, N.Y.C., 1947—. Served with Md. N.G., 1941-42; maj. USAAF, 1942-45. Mem. Soc. Lees Va., Soc. Cin., Overseas Writers Assn., Sigma Delta Chi. Episcopalian. Clubs: 1925 F Street, Federal City, National Press, Metropolitan (Washington). Author: American Talleyrand: Life of Martin Van Buren, 1935; The Proud Pretender: Life of Aaron Burr, 1937; American Nabob, 1939; Dust in the Afternoon, 1940; Selina, 1942; Tomorrow's Air Age, 1953; The Famous Five, 1958; Shall Do No Murder, 1959; West of Washington, 1962; The Equivocal Men, 1964; The Spirit of '76, 1966; Between the Stirrup and the Ground, 1967; Pen and Politics, 1970; With Friends Possess'd, 1970. Home: 922 25th St NW Washington DC 20037 Office: Nat Press Bldg Washington DC 20004

ALEXANDER, HUBERT GRIGGS, educator; b. Lincoln, Neb., Dec. 8, 1909; s. Hartley Burr and Nelly (Griggs) A.; student U. Neb., 1926-27; B.A. magna cum laude, Pomona Coll., 1930; postgrad. U. Paris, France, 1930-31; Ph.D., Yale, 1934; m. Catharine Mildred Botts, Dec. 21, 1936; children—Robert Kirk, Hartley William, Thomas Milton. Archeologist under grant Fed. Emergency Relief Adminstrn. in excavation nr. Jemez, Springs, N.M., 1934-35; from instr. to prof. dept. philosophy U. N.M., Albuquerque, 1935—, chmn. dept. philosophy, 1948-65; vis. prof. Carnegie internship grant Yale, 1954-55. Chmn. UNESCO Citizens Consultation Program, sponsored by U. N.M., 1955- 56; program chmn. Inter-Am. Congress Philososophy, Washington, 1957. Mem. Am. Philos. Assn., Southwestern Philos. Soc. (past pres.), Mountain- Plains Philos. Conf. (past chmn.), Phi Beta Kappa, Phi Sigma Tau (pres. 1966-68, exec. council 1964—). Author: Time as Dimension and History, 1945; Language and Thinking, 1967; Meaning in Language, 1969. Home: 603 Girard Blvd NE Albuquerque NM 87106

ALEXANDER, IRVING EMANUEL, educator, psychologist; b. N.Y.C., May 16, 1922; s. Alex and May (Nisenson) A.; B.A., U. Ala., 1946, M.A., 1947; A.M., Princeton, 1948, Ph.D., 1949; m. Mirian Pearl Fisher, May 2, 1944; children—Stephen F., David J., Kay Robin. Instr., U. Ala., 1946-47; asst. prof. Princeton, 1949-58; psychologist, chief psychology sect., tng. br. Nat. Inst. Mental Health, 1958-63; prof., dir. clin. tng., chmn. dept. psychology Duke, 1963-70; vis. prof. Harvard, 1966-67; Hebrew U., Jerusaleum, 1971; cons. in field, 1952—. Chmn. United Jewish Appeal Drive, Princeton, 1953-54, Durham, 1968-70. Served to 1st lt. USAAF, 1943-45. Decorated Air medal with 5 oak leaf clusters; recipient Grover Cleveland Hall award U. Ala., 1943; Gordon McDonald fellow Princeton, 1947-48, James Theodore Walker fellow, 1948-49; Bollingen fellow Jung Inst., Zurich, Switzerland, 1954-55. Fellow Am. Psychol. Assn.; mem. N.C., Southeastern psychol. assns. A.A.A.S., Am. Assn. U. Profs., Sigma Xi. Jewish religion (bd. dirs. synagogue 1967-68). Author chpts. in books. Editor: (with C. F. Reed and S. S. Tomkins) Psychopathology: A Source Book, 1958. Home: 1111 Watts St Durham NC 27701

ALEXANDER, JAMES ECKERT, editor; b. Zanesville, O., Sept. 4, 1913; s. James Rufus and Nellie (Hunter) A.; A.B., Washington and Jefferson Coll., 1935; m. Jean Kathryn Crew, July 1, 1940; children—James C., Jean (Mrs. Joseph D. Small III), John R. Reporter, Akron (O.) Beacon Jour, 1937, 47-48, Pitts. Press, 1937-38; editor Zanesville News, 1939-42; Sunday editor Mpls. Star-Jour. and Tribune, 1942-45; pub. relations exec. Minn. and Ont. Paper Co., Mpls., 1946; writer, editor Pitts. Post-Gazette, 1949-65, city editor 1965—; prof. U. Pitts., 1963-65; book critic KDKA-TV, Pitts., 1965-67. Mem. Beta Theta Pi (dist. chief 1942-46). Democrat. Presbyn. Clubs: Press, Montour Heights Country (Pitts.). Home: 633 Rock Springs Rd Pittsburgh PA 15228 Office: 50 Blvd of Allies Pittsburgh PA 15222

ALEXANDER, JAMES HENRY, ins. broker, state ofcl.; b. McKenzie, Tenn., Jan. 2, 1922; s. E. Marvin and Lillis (McElroy) A.; student Bethel Coll., 1939-41; B.S. in Bus. Adminstrn., U. Tenn., 1943; m. Lola Diuguid Chestnut, Dec. 21, 1945; children—Anne Elizabeth, James Henry, Jean. Engaged in gen. ins. bus., McKenzie, 1946—; treas. State of Tenn., Nashville, 1963-67; gov.'s staff dir. for indsl. devel., 1967—. Pres. Tenn. Sch. Bd. Assn., 1961; chmn. Tenn. Heart Fund, 1963-64. Sec., Tenn. Bd. Elections, 1953; campaign mgr. Gov. Frank Clement for gov., 1962, for U.S. Senate, 1964; alternate del. Dem. Nat. Conv., 1956. Trustee Lambuth Coll., Jackson, Tenn. Served to lt. (j.g.) USNR, 1943-46. Mem. Insurors of Tenn. (v.p.), Am. Legion (dist. comdr. 1950), V.F.W. Elk, Rotarian. Home: 714 Stonewall St McKenzie TN 38201 Office: Broadway St McKenzie TN 38201 also Jackson State Office Bldg Nashville TN 37219

ALEXANDER, JAMES RADCLIFFE, zinc co. exec.; b. Cleve., Sept. 9, 1913; s. James Frederick and Iva (Radcliffe) A.; B.A., Kenyon Coll., 1935; m. Kathryn Prenter, Jan. 20, 1940; children—James Prenter, Ann Marie. Sales rep. Glidden Co., Cleve., 1937-44, Quaker Rubber Corp., Phila., 1944-50; with Quaker Rubber div. H. K. Porter Co., 1950-58, gen. sales mgr., 1952-58, v.p. sales Thermoid div., 1958-60; v.p. sales N.J. Zinc Co., N.Y.C., 1960—. Mem. N.J. Rubbers Mfrs. Assn. (pres. 1959-60), Am. Zinc Inst. (pres. 1967—), Internat. Lead Zinc Orgn. (dir.), Nat. Paint Varnish Lacquer Assn. (dir. 1967—), Beta Theta Pi. Presbyn. Mason (Shriner). Club: Union League (N.Y.C.); Saucon Valley Country (Bethlehem, Pa.); Whispering Pines Country (Southern Pines, N.C.). Home: 145 E Market St Bethlehem PA 18018 Office: 2045 City Line Rd Bethlehem PA 18018

ALEXANDER, JAMES WAGNER, educator; b. Jefferson, Ga., May 4, 1914; s. James Curtis and Zula (Waggoner) A.; A.B., U. Ga., 1934, M.A., 1935; postgrad. U. Perugia, summer 1936, U. Padua, 1936-37, U. Grenoble, summer 1937; Ph.D., U. Va., 1940; m. Corinne Walker Ball, Sept. 26, 1944; children-James Wagner, Peter Field, Corinne Ball, Kirk Walker. Instr., Bethany Coll., W.Va., 1940-41; faculty U. Ga., Athens, 1946—, now prof., head classics dept. Served to capt. AUS, 1941-46. Mem. Am. Philol. Assn., Archeol. Inst. Am., Classical Assn. Middle West and South (past pres. So. sect.), Vergilian Soc., Classical and Modern Fgn. Lang. Assn. Ga. (past pres.), Phi Beta Kappa, Phi Kappa Phi. Home: 997 Milledge Av Athens GA 30601

ALEXANDER, JANE, actress; b. Boston, Oct. 28, 1939; d. Thomas Bartlett and Ruth (Pearson) Quigley; student Sarah Lawrence Coll., 1957-59, U. Edinburgh, 1959-60; m. Robert Alexander, July 23, 1962; 1 son, Jason. Appeared prodns. Charles Playhouse Boston, 1964-65; Arena Stage, Washington, 1965-68; Broadway prodn. Great White Hope, 1968-69. Recipient Antoinette Perry award, 1969; Theatre World award; Drama Desk award. Address: CMA 600 Madison Av New York City NY 10022

ALEXANDER, JIMMY EUEL, lawyer; b. Bear Creek, Ala., Aug. 8, 1939; s. Alvin E. and Rosa (Arnold) A.; B.S., U. Ala., 1961, J.D., 1963; m. Rosemary Scheuing, Mar. 26, 1966; 1 son, Jason Eric. Admitted to Ala. bar, 1963, since practiced in Athens; mem. firm Malone, Steele & Alexander, 1963—. Mem. Democratic Exec. Com. of Ala., 1966—. Past pres. Athens Inter Club Council; bd. dirs. Tri-County Appalachian Regional Health Commn. Mem. Am., Ala. Limestone County (past pres.) bar assns., U. Ala. Law Sch. Found., Farrah Law Soc., Beta Gamma Sigma, Phi Eta Sigma, Phi Alpha Delta, Delta Sigma Pi. Methodist. Club: Athens Civitan (past pres.). Home: Vestavia Estates Athens AL 35611 Office: 213 S Jefferson St Athens AL 35611

ALEXANDER, JOHN BRUCE, dean, clergyman; b. North Haven, Me., Sept. 23, 1898; s. George and Sadie Helen (Judkins) A.; A.B. summa cum laude, Bates Coll., 1928; B.D. magna cum laude, Yale Divinity Sch., 1932; Ph.D., Yale, 1935; m. Mildred F. Mitchell, July 24, 1930; children—Ruth Ann, Mary Margaret. Rural mail carrier, North Haven, Me., 1918-22; minister, Litchfield (Me.) Federated Churches, prin., Litchfield Acad., 1928-29; ordained minister, Baptist Ch., North Haven, Me., 1929; minister, Conglist. Ch., Lyme, Conn., 1930- 33; on faculty, Dept. of Christian Leadership, Keuka Coll., also minister, Keuka Park Baptist Ch., N.Y. state, 1937-44; head, Dept. of Religion and Philosophy, Culver-Stockton Coll., Canton, Mo., 1944-69, dean faculty, 1947-56, dean of coll., 1956-58, dean of chapel, 1958-69, chmn. div. humanities, 1961-69, prof. emeritus, 1969—. Mem. Am. Assn. U. Profs., Phi Beta Kappa, Tau Kappa Alpha, Pi Gamma Mu. Club: Kiwanis. Author: Turning on Lights, 1940; Early Babylonian Letters and Economic Texts, 1943. Home: 705 Grant St Canton MO 63435

ALEXANDER, JOHN DAVID, Jr., coll. pres.; b. Springfield, Tenn., Oct. 18, 1932; s. John David and Mary Agnes (McKinnon) A.; B.A., Southwestern at Memphis, 1953; student Louisville Presbyn. Theol. Sem., 1953-54; D.Phil. (Rhodes Scholar 1954), Oxford (Eng.) U., 1957; LL.D., U. So. Cal., Occidental Coll., 1970, Centre Coll. of Ky., 1971; m. Catharine Coleman, Aug. 26, 1956; children—Catherine McKinnon, John David III, Julia Mary. Asso. prof. San Francisco Theol. Sem., 1957- 65; pres. Southwestern at Memphis, 1965-69, Pomona Coll., Claremont, Cal., 1969— Council Edn. Pub. Responsibility, 1966—; mem. commn. liberal learning Assn. Am. Colls., 1966-69; mem. commn. colls. So. Assn. Colls. and Schs., 1966-69. Mem. bd. dirs. Louisville Presbyn. Theol. Sem., 1966-69; trustee Webb Sch., Claremont, Cal., 1970—, Tchrs. Ins. and Annuity Assn., 1970—. Mem. Am. Oriental Soc., Soc. Bib. Lit., Soc. Religion in Higher Edn., Phi Beta Kappa, Omicron Delta Kappa, Sigma Nu. Home: 345 N College Av Claremont CA 91711

ALEXANDER, JOHN FRANK, tenor; b. Meridian, Miss.; s. Charles Curtis and Eva (Ogburn) A.; student Duke, 1941-43; B.Mus., Cin. Conservatory Music, 1949; D. Performing Arts, U. Cin., 1968; m. Sue Travis, Aug. 10, 1952; 1 dau., Cindy Sue. Tenor with NBC TV Opera, 1956- 59, N.Y.C. Opera, 1957-61, Met. Opera Co., 1961—; leading tenor with Phila. Lyric Opera, Pitts. Opera, Ft. Worth Opera, New Orleans Opera, Vancouver (B.C., Can.) Opera, Vienna Staats Opera, Covent Garden, London, Vienna (Austria) Volksoper, San Francisco Opera, others; recording artist for RCA Victor, Columbia, London records. records. Served with USAAF, 1944-46. Mem. Am. Guild Musical Artists (bd. govs.). Conglist. Clubs: Dutch Treat, Bohemians (N.Y.C.). Home: 46 Pickwick Rd Manhasset, NY 11030. Office: Metropolitan Opera Co Lincoln Center New York City NY 10018

ALEXANDER, JOHN GORDON, lawyer; b. Buffalo, Aug. 5, 1904; s. William Gordon and Margaret (Crotty) A.; A.B., Princeton, 1926; LL.B., Harvard, 1933; m. Rachel Sheldon, Nov. 25th, 1964; children—John Gordon, Cecily. Admitted to N.Y. bar, 1933, D.C. bar, 1947; practiced in Buffalo, 1933-41, Washington, 1947-50; counsel Navy Dept., 1941-44, War Assets Adminstrn., 1944-46, gen. counsel, 1946-47; gen. counsel Nat. Prodn. Authority, Washington, 1951; asso. counsel Olin Mathieson Chem. Corp., 1953-56, asst. gen. counsel, 1956-60, sec., 1960-69. Home: Steamboat Rd Irvington VA 22480

ALEXANDER, JOHN H., lawyer; b. Denver, Nov. 15, 1904; A.B., Yale, 1926, LL.B., 1928. Admitted to N.Y. bar, 1929, N.J. bar, 1943, D.C. bar, 1966. Now sr. partner firm Mudge, Rose, Guthrie & Alexander, N.Y.C. Mem. Am., N.Y. State bar assns., Assn. Bar City N.Y. Address: 20 Broad St New York City NY 10005

ALEXANDER, JOHN HARVEY, clergyman, ch. assn. exec.; b. Boston, Oct. 19, 1919; s. John and Elizabeth (Coffin) A.; A.B., Bowdoin Coll., 1948; B.D., Bangor Theol. Sem., 1951; D.D., Piedmont Coll., 1970; m. Donna Eloise Estabrooke, June 27, 1943; children-John Kenneth, Karen Jean (Mrs. Thomas F. Hoffman), Margaret Jane, Elizabeth Ann. Ordained to ministry Congl. Ch., 1948; minister Congl. Ch., Winthrop, Me., 1943-49, Galewood Community Ch., Chgo., 1949-56; asso. minister 1st Congl. Ch., Wauwatosa, Wis., 1956-62; minister 1st Congl. Ch., Marshalltown, Ia., 1962-67; moderator organizational meeting Nat. Assn. Congl. Christian Chs., Detroit, 1955, chmn. exec. com., 1960-61, asso. exec. sec., 1967-69, exec. sec., 1969- -. Del. Internat. Congl. Council, Rotterdam, Holland, 1962; supr. Nat. Pilgrim Fellowship Youth Work-camp to Greece, 1964; pres. Marshall County (Ia.) Council Chs., 1965-66; sec.-treas., bd. dirs. Com. for Continuation of Congl. Christian Chs., 1962—; adminstrv. visitor to World-Wide overseas missions, 1969. Chmn. 36th ward Citizens' Adv. Council, Chgo., 1954-56. Republican. Rotarian (bd. dirs. 1964-67), Mason (32). Active nat., internat. efforts to preserve free chs. as expressed in policy, practices of Cong. Chrisitan Chs. Home: 9993 W North Av Wauwatosa WI 53226 Office: 176 W Wis Av Milwaukee WI 53203

ALEXANDER, JOHN WESLEY, educator; b. Greenville, Ill., Apr. 7, 1918; s. John and Ethel (Cummings) A.; B.A., U. Ill., 1940, M.A., 1941; Ph.D., U. Wis., 1949; m. Elizabeth Worth Vinson, Sept. 5, 1946; children—John Vinson, Elizabeth Lynne, Mary Elizabeth, Douglas Webb. Mem. faculty U. Wis., 1947-65, prof. geography, 1963-65, chmn. dept., 1963-65; pres. Inter-Varsity Christian Fellowship, 1965—; vis. prof. Harvard, summer 1955, U. Cal. at Los Angeles, 1958. Served to lt. USNR, 1942-46. Mem. Am. Assn. U. Profs., Assn. Am. Geographers, Phi Beta Kappa, Phi Kappa Phi. Author: Flight Quarters, 1956; Thoughts From the Sea, 1947; Economic Geography 1963; also articles. Home: 146 N Prospect Av Madison WI 53705 Office: 233 Langdon Madison WI 53703

ALEXANDER, JOHN WINTON, educator; b. Atlanta, Oct. 6, 1917; s. Will Winton and Mabelle A. (Kinkead) A.; grad. George Sch. (Pa.); A.B., Columbia, 1939; postgrad. U. N.C., 1939-41, Columbia, 1946-48; m. Miriam R. Heald, May 11, 1965; children by first marriage—Diane (Mrs. N.H. Vincent), Linda, Carol. With U.S. Dept. Agr., 1941-42; instr. sociology Columbia, 1946-54, asst. dean coll., 1957-59, asso. dean, 1959-67, acting dean, 1962-63; engaged in pvt. business, St. Thomas, V.I., 1954-56; dir. N.C. sch. desegregation program Am. Friends Service Com., High Point, N.C., 1956-57; headmaster Westover Sch., Middlebury, Conn., 1967—. Cons. So. Regional Council sch. desegregation problems, 1958-59; cons. to chancellor U. P.R. univ. adminstrn., 1959, 62; chmn. Columbia U. seminar higher edn., 1963-67. Trustee Spelman Coll., 1961-64, Hewlett Sch., East Islip, N.Y. Served to lt. USNR, 1942-45; ETO. Mem. Phi Beta Kappa (hon.). Democrat. Address: Westover School Middlebury CT 06762

ALEXANDER, KENNETH LEWIS, editorial cartoonist; b. Gridley, Cal., June 16, 1924; s. Zareh and Rose (Affolter) A.; student U. Cal. at Berkeley, 1942-43, Rutgers U., 1943- 44, Cal. Coll. Arts and Crafts, 1946-47; m. Dariel A. Hereford, July 15, 1949; children—Mark Kenneth, Stephen Scott, Peter Neil. Free-lance comml. artist, 1947-58; editor Pictorial Living mag., San Francisco Examiner, 1958-63, Sunday art dir., 1963-66, editorial cartoonist, 1966—; TV editorial cartoonist sta. KGO-TV, 1968-69. Served with AUS, 1943-46. Mem. Soc. Am. Editorial Cartoonists, Am. Newspaper Guild, A.F.T.R.A., Kappa Alpha. Author: (with Andrew Curtin) A Gallery of Great Americans. Home: 1182 Glen Rd Lafayette CA 94549 Office: 110 5th St San Francisco CA 94103

ALEXANDER, LEE, mayor; b. 1927; A.B., LL.B., Syracuse U. Admitted to N.Y. bar, 1955. Now mayor of Syracuse. Mem. Am. Bar Assn. Address: City Hall Syracuse NY *

ALEXANDER, LEONARD CLAYTON, univ. dean; b. Glidden, Wis., Nov. 20, 1916; s. Peter Timothy and Teresa (Lucas) A.; student St. Lawrence Coll., 1930-32, Pio Nono Coll., Milw., 1932-34; D.D.S., Marquette U., 1939; student U. Minn., 1947, U. Pa., 1951, m. Helen Ellis, Aug. 19, 1939; children—Joan, Thomas, James, Peter. Mem. faculty Marquette U., 1948—, prof. medicine Sch. Dentistry, 1959—, dean Sch. Dentistry, 1960—; spl. research dental caries control, tic douleureux. Mem. Community Welfare Council Milw.; mem. adv. com. Wis. Bd. Health. Pres. particular council Washington County chpt. St. Vincent de Paul Soc., 1956-60. Served with AUS, 1942-45. Diplomate Am. Bd. Endodontics. Fellow Am. Coll. Dentists (sec. 1953-60); mem. Am. Dental Assn., Am. Assn. Emdodontists. Am. Acad. Periodontology, A.A.A.S., Fedn. Dentaire Internat., Delta Sigma Delta, Omicron Kappa Upsilon, Alpha Sigma Nu. Contbr. articles profl. jours. Home: Route 1 Box 192A Colgate WI 53017 Office: 604 N 16th St Milwaukee WI 53233

ALEXANDER, LEROY ELBERT, educator; b. West Bend, Wis., Nov. 7, 1910; s. Charles Richard and Lillian May (Bailey) A.; B.E., Wis. State U., 1937; M.S., U. Minn., 1940, Ph.D. (Shelvin fellow), 1943; m. Eleanor Minnie Mestelle, Aug. 24, 1940; children—Kathryn (Mrs. Kenneth Morrison Back), Karen. Research chemist Gen. Electric Co., Pittsfield, Mass., 1943-46; fellow Mellon Inst., 1946-48, sr. fellow, 1948—; prof. chemistry Carnegie-Mellon U., Pitts., 1967—. NSF sr. postdoctoral research fellow, 1962-63. Mem. Am. Crystallographic Assn. (sec. 1958-60), Am. Chem. Soc., A.A.A.S., Sigma Xi, Phi Lambda Upsilon. Republican. Lutheran. Club: Pittsburgh Chemists. Author: (with Harold P. Klug) X-Ray Diffraction Procedures, 1954; X-Ray Diffraction Methods in Polymer Science, 1969. Home: 263 Franklin Dr Pittsburgh PA 15241

ALEXANDER, LEROY MONTGOMERY, steel co. exec.; b. Slater, Mo., Nov. 17, 1906; s. Roy Ancell and May L. (Montgomery) A.; extension student U. Kan., also U. Mo. at Kansas City; m. Arlene Bertino, Jan. 1, 1941; children—Judith Lee (Mrs. Bruce J. Freshwater), Susan Lynne (Mrs. Dennis M. McAllister), Cynthia Jane. Mgr. sales Boltand Nut div. Sheffield Steel Corp., 1925-60; mgr. bolt and forged products Armco Steel Corp., 1960-67, dir. sales Western Mill Products div., 1967—. Bd. dirs. Kansas City (Mo.) chpt. Am. Cancer Soc. Mem. Indsl. Fasterners Inst. (exec. com. 1957-64, v.p. 1965, chmn. bd. govs. 1966—), Am. Ordnance Assn. (dir. Midwest post). Presbyn. (ruling elder). Clubs: Kansas City, Blue Hills Country (Kansas City, Mo.). Home: 7817 Gregory Blvd Kansas City MO 64133 Office: 7000 Roberts St Kansas City MO 64125

ALEXANDER, LEWIS MCELWAIN, geographer, educator; b. Summit, N.J., June 15; 1921; s. Harry Louis and Laura (Stryker) A.; A.B., Middlebury (Vt.) Coll., 1942; M.A., Clark U., 1948, Ph.D., 1949; m. Jacqueline Peterson, Dec. 30, 1950; children—Louise Anne, Lance Stryker. Instr. geography Hunter Coll., 1949- 50; asst. prof. geography Harpur Coll., State U. N.Y., 1950-57, asso. prof., 1957-60; prof. geography, chmn. dept. U. R.I., Kingston, 1960—, dir. M. Marine Affairs program, 1968—. Cons. State Dept., 1963—, exec. dir. Law of Sea Inst., 1965—; dep. dir. Pres.'s Commn. on Marine Sci., Engring. and Resources, 1967-68; cons. Nat. Council for Marine Resources and Engring. Devel., 1968—. Served with the USAAF, 1942-46. Office Naval Research grantee, 1958, 62, 66. Mem. Assn. Am. Geographers, Am. Geog. Soc., Am. Soc. Internat. Law, Marine Tech. Soc. Author: World Political Patterns, 2d edit., 1963; Offshore Geography of Northwestern Europe, 2d edit., 1966; The Northeastern United States, 1966. Home: 28 Beech Hill Rd Peace Dale RI 02879 Office: Washburn Hall U RI Kingston RI 02881

ALEXANDER, LLOYD CHUDLEY, author; b. Phila., Jan. 30, 1924; s. Alan Audley and Edna (Chudley) A.; student W. Chester (Pa.) State Coll., 1942, Lafayette Coll., 1943, U. Paris, 1946; m. Janine Denni, Jan. 8, 1946; 1 dau., Madeleine (Mrs. Zohair Khalil). Free-lance writer and translator, 1946—, cartoonist, pianist, advt. writer, mag. editor, 1948—; author-in-residence Temple U., 1970. Served with AUS, World War II. Mem. Authors League Am. Author: And Let The Credit Go, 1955; My Five Tigers, 1956; Janine is French, 1958; August Bondi (Isaac Siegel Meml. award 1959), 1958; My Love Affair with Music, 1960; Aaron Lopez, 1960; Time Cat, 1963; Fifty Years in the Doghouse, 1964; (with Dr. Louis J. Camuti) Park Avenue Vet, 1962; The Book of Three (A.L.A. notable book 1964), 1964; The Black Cauldron (A.L.A. notable book 1965), 1965; Coll and His White Pig, 1965; The Castle of Llyr (A.L.A. notable book 1966), 1966; Taran Wanderer, 1967; The Truthful Harp, 1967; The High King (Newbery medal 1969), 1968; The Marvelous Misadventures of Sebastian, 1970 (Nat. Book award 1971); The King's Fountain, 1971. Translator from French: (Paul Eluard) Selected Writings, 1950; (Jean-Paul Sartre) The Wall, 1951, Nausea, 1953; (Paul Vialar) The Sea Rose, 1951. Address: 1005 Drexel Av Drexel Hill PA 19026

ALEXANDER, MALCOLM MOSS, Jr., cement co. exec.; b. Oklahoma City, Mar. 5, 1925; s. Malcolm Moss and Patty (Saffell) A.; student Westminster Coll., 1946-50; m. Mary Stella Moss, Sept. 26, 1953; children—Malcolm Moss III, Richard Ryan, Thomas Theodore, Charles Clardy, David Dodson. With Mo. Portland Cement Co., St. Louis, 1950—; v.p., gen. mgr., 1958-59, pres., 1959—, chmn. bd., 1965—; dir. First Nat. Bank St. Louis, American Investment Co. Clubs: Old Warson Country, St. Louis (St. Louis); Media; Memphis Country. Home: 16 Greebriar St Ladue MO 63124 Office: 7751 Carondelet Av St Louis MO 63105

ALEXANDER, MAURICE MYRON, educator: b. S. Onondaga, N.Y., Dec. 18, 1917; s. Myron Lucius and Etta May (Fenner) A.; B.S., N.Y. State Coll. Forestry, 1940; M.S., U. Conn., 1942; Ph.D., State U. Coll. Forestry, Syracuse, N.Y., 1950; m. Annette Reina Blain, Aug. 2, 1943; children—Ralph John, Richard Maurice, Robert Alan. Fish and wildlife biologist Conn. Bd. Fish and Game, summers 1941, 42, 45-46; instr. forestry and wildlife mgmt. U. Conn., 1946-47; mem. faculty State U. Coll. Forestry, Syracuse, 1949—, prof. forest zoology, chmn. dept., 1965—. Adviser N.Y. State Fish and Wildlife Mgmt. Bd., 1964—. Active local Boy Scouts Am. Served to capt. AUS, 1942-46; ETO. Decorated Bronze Star. Fellow A.A.A.S.; mem. Am. Soc. Mammologists (life), Wildlife Soc., Ecol. Soc. Am., Am. Inst. Biol. Scis., Sigma Xi. Home: 4039 Tanner Rd RD 2 Syracuse, NY 13215.

ALEXANDER, MYRL EARLY, educator; b. Dayton, O., Aug. 23, 1909; s. John Lester and Florence (Early) A.; A.B., Manchester Coll., 1930, LL.D., 1956; LL.D., Pacific Luth. U., 1966; m. Lorene Shoemaker, January 18, 1934; children—Nancy (Mrs. Robert B. Hibbs), John Alexander. Warden's asst. U.S. Penitentiary, Atlanta, 1931; parole exec. U.S. Bd. Parole, Washington, 1937-40; asso.

warden U.S. Penitentiary, Lewisburg, Pa., 1940-43; warden Fed. Correctional Instn., Danbury, Conn., 1943-45; chief prisons Mil. Govt. for Germany, 1945-46; asst. dir. Bur. Prisons, Washington, 1947-61; prof. correctional adminstrn., dir. Center for Study Crime, Delinquency and Corrections, So. Ill. U., Carbondale, 1961-64, 70—; dir. Bur. Prisons, Dept. Justice, Washington, 1964-70. U.S. rep., vice chmn. delegation UN Congress on Prevention Crime and Treatment of Offenders, Stockholm, 1965; U.S. corr. sect. on social def. UN; spl. cons. various state correctional systems. Mem. exec. bd. Ill. Synod, Luth. Ch. in Am., 1961-64, mem. bd. social ministry. Recipient Pres.'s award for distinguished fed. service, 1967. Mem. Correctional Adminstrs. Assn., Nat. Council on Crime and Delinquency (dir., profl. adv. council), Am. Correctional Assn. (pres. 1956), Am. Soc. Pub. Adminstrn., Am. Acad. Polit. and Social Sci., Nat. Jail Assn., Osborne Assn. (dir.), Correctional Service Fedn. (dir.) Democrat. Author: Jail Administration, 1957. Home: 604 W Oak St Carbondale IL 62901

ALEXANDER, NORMAN E., chem. corp. exec.; b. N.Y.C., 1914; A.B., Columbia, 1934, LL.B., 1936; m. Marjorie Wulf; four children. Pres. Sun Chem. Corp., N.Y.C., 1957—, also dir. Address: 750 3d Av New York City NY 10017

ALEXANDER, NORMAN JAMES, investment co. exec.; b. Regina, Sask., Can., Feb. 9, 1909; s. Robert Merrilees and Catherine (Clarke) A.; m. Juanita Yvonne Denny, Apr. 25, 1944. With James Richardson & Sons, Ltd., Winnipeg, Man., Can., 1927—, v.p., 1968—; mng. partner Richardson Securities of Can., 1960—; v.p. Richardson Securities, Inc., N.Y.C. and Chgo., 1957—; dir. The Investors Group, Westeel-Roscoe Ltd., Great Plains Devel. Co. Can., Dome Petroleums Ltd.; pres., dir. Armstrong & Taylor Ltd., 1969—; pres. Western Canadian Resources Fund Ltd., 1968—. Mem. Toronto Stock Exchange, Chgo. Bd. Trade; past pres. Vancouver Stock Exchange. Served to lt. comdr. Canadian Navy, 1940-45. Mem. Investment Dealers' Assn. Can. (past pres.). Clubs: Vancouver, Capilano Golf and Country (Vancouver); St. Charles Golf and Country (Winnipeg), Winter, Squash Racquet (Winnipeg). Home: 85 Yale St Winnipeg 9 Manitoba Canada Office: Richardson Bldg 1 Lombard Pl Winnipeg 2 Manitoba Canada

ALEXANDER, ORVILLE, educator; b. Vienna, Ill., Aug. 3, 1909; s. Dolpha and Ethel (Burris) A.; B.Ed., So. Ill. U., 1931; M.A., State U. Ia., 1934, Ph.D., 1936; m. Ola Anderson, Sept. 11, 1936; children—Dee, Jon. Instr. polit. sci. N. Central Coll., 1936-38; faculty So. Ill U., Carbondale, 1938—, prof. govt., 1946—, chmn. dept., 1950-69. Vis. prof. U. Miami (Fla.), 1946, Winston-Salem State Coll., 1965. Dir. research Ill. Legislative Council, 1944-46, Ohio Sch. Survey Com., 1954, Ill. Sch. Problems Com., 1951-63. Mem. Am. Polit. Sci. Assn., Am. Soc. Pub. Adminstrn. Lion (internat. counselor). Author: What Faces Ohio Schools, 1955; Illinois School Problems, 6 vols., 1953, 55, 57, 59, 61, 63. Home: 610 W Main St Carbondale IL 62901

ALEXANDER, PAUL, univ. dean; b. Greensburg, Ind., Nov. 6, 1904; s. Frank Samuel and Mary Elizabeth (Pumphrey) A.; A.B. (Rector scholar 1921-25), DePauw U., 1925; M.S. in Edn., Ind. U., 1934, Ed.D., 1951; summer student Harvard, 1949; m. Vera Bickel, Aug. 24, 1926; children—Ava Jean (Mrs. William B. Chew), Paula Rae (Mrs. Ronald E. Woods). Tchr., Clay Township schs., Decatur County, Ind., 1923-27, prin. high sch., 1927-29; supt. schs., Decatur County, 1929-37; high sch. prin. Greensburg pub. schs., 1937-44; mem. faculty Purdue U., 1944—, prof. edn., 1953-70, head dept., 1960-62, dean edn., 1962-70, also chmn. tchr. edn. council, mem. exec. council, prof. edn. and dean emeritus, 1970—. Mem.Ind. Tchrs. Assn., N.E.A., Ind. Schoolmen's Club, Kappa Delta Pi, Phi Delta Kappa, Delta Chi. Home: 1101 Sunset Ct West Lafayette, IN 47906. Office: Graduate House Purdue U Lafayette IN 47907

ALEXANDER, PAUL JULIUS, educator; historian; b. Berlin, Germany, May 12, 1910; s. Carl and Anna (Mauthner) A.; Dr. iur., U. Hamburg (Germany), 1932; licence en droit, U. Paris (France), 1934; Ph.D. in History, Harvard, 1940; m. Eleanor Eyck, June 21, 1938; children—Ann Margaret, Lawrence Ernest, Michael Charles. Came to U.S., 1935, naturalized, 1943. Prof. history Hobart Coll., 1945-54; prof. history, chmn. dept. Brandeis U., 1954-58; prof. history U. Mich., 1958-68; prof. history and comparative lit. U. Cal., Berkeley, 1968—, Research analyst OSS, 1943-45. Fulbright-Hayes research fellow, Italy, 1965-66; Guggenheim fellow, 1951-52, 65-66. Author: The Patriarch Nicephorus of Constantinople, 1958; Gregorii Nysseni Opera Omnia, VO. V, 1962; The Oracle of Baalbek, 1967. Home: 1521 La Loma Berkeley CA 94708

ALEXANDER, RAYMOND PACE, judge; b. Phila., Oct. 13, 1898; s. Hilliard Boone and Virginia Margaret (Pace) A.; B.S. in Econs. magna cum laude, U. Pa., 1920; postgrad. Columbia, summer 1921-22; LL.B., Harvard, 1923; LL.D., Shaw U., Va. State Coll., 1940; Litt.D., Western U., 1947, Campbell Coll., 1948; m. Sadie Tanner Mossell, Nov. 26, 1923; children—Mary Elizabeth (Mrs. Melvin Frank Brown), Rae Pace (Mrs. Thomas K. Minter). Admitted Pa. bar, 1923; mem. firm Raymond Pace Alexander, Phila., 1923-58; former gen. counsel Nat. Med. Assn., Nat. Bapt. Conv., Gen. Conf. A.M.E. Ch.; counsel Pa. Bapt. Conv., bd. bishops A.M.E. Ch.; counsel Pa., Phila. chpts. NAACP; counsellor Haitian embassy, Washington, 1946-49, hon. Haitian consul, Phila., 1948-56; specialist civil and criminal trial practice, state and fed. cts.; judge Common Pleas Ct. Phila., 1959—, sr. judge, 1970—. Mem. Phila. City Council, 1952-58, chmn. com. pub. property and pub. works. Vice chmn. Phila. County div. United Fund; past nat. dir. March of Dimes; nat. dir. Free Europe Com.; speaker Radio Free Europe to Iron Curtain Countries, 1954, 58; pres. Salute to our Responsible Youth, 1970—. Mem. bd., past chmn. bd. mgrs. S.W. br. YMCA, Phila., 1948-58; vice chmn. capital fund dr. YMCA-YWCA Greater Phila.; founder, chmn. bd. trustees Dr. Virginia M. Alexander Scholarship Found.; bd. dirs. Phila. Grand Opera Company; trustee Phila. Council Chs., Berean Coll., Phila.; nat. bd. dirs. Assn. Study Negro Life and History. Honored for outstanding achievement civil liberties Am. Jewish Congress, 1950; outstanding service to citizens of Phila., Barristers Club, 1951; other awards YMCA Phila., Phila. Assn. Pub. Sch. Tchrs.; C. Francis Stradford award Nat. Bar Assn., 1967; Carter G. Woodson award Assn. Study Negro Life and History, 1968; chancellor of Philadelphia Cotillion Soc., 1958—. Mem. Phila. Council Chs. (past dir.), Nat. (pres. 1929-30), Am., Pa., Phila. bar assns., Brandeis Law Soc., Phila. Crime Prevention Assn. (pres. 1967, dir. 1960—, chmn. exec. com. 1970—), Turkish-Am. Law Assn. (hon.), Am. Judicature Soc.; hon. mem. Bar Republic Haiti, Barrister's Library High Ct. India, Phi Beta Kappa, Beta Gamma Sigma. Baptist (past chmn. trustees). Co-founder, editor Nat. Bar Jour., 1940. Home: 700 Westview St Mt Airy PA 19119 Office: 1004 One East Penn Square Philadelphia PA 19107

ALEXANDER, RICHARD ELMONT, lawyer; b. Yellow Springs, O., Dec. 14, 1924; s. Joseph Arthur and Charlotte (Gunckel) A.; student U. Dayton, 1942-43, Carnegie Inst. Tech., 1943-44, 46-47; J.D., U. Chgo., 1950; m. Mary Waring, Aug. 17, 1950; children-Susan, Amy, Jane. Admitted to Ohio bar, 1951, Ill. bar, 1956; patent atty. Gen. Motors Corp., 1953-55, Wilkinson, Huxley, Byron & Hume, Chgo., 1955-58; patent atty., partner Alexander & Slater, 1958- 59, Dawson, Tilton, Fallon, Lungmus & Alexander, 1959-67, Alexander & Speckman, 1967—, Dir. Stevens Candy Kitchens, Inc., Martha Washington Candy Kitchens, Inc. Pres. Community Edn. Com., Evanston, Ill. Trustee St Leonard's House, Chgo.; bd. dirs., exec-com. Great Books Found., Chgo. Served with AUS, 1944-45. Decorated Purple Heart. Mem. Am., Chgo. bar assns., U.S. Trademark Assn. (editorial bd.), Chgo. Patent Law Assn. (past chmn. trademark com.), Sigma Alpha Epsilon. Episcopalian. Editor: Meditations of Andrew Morehouse, 1952. Home: 1130 Lake Shore Dr Evanston IL 60202 Office: 33 N Dearborn St Chicago IL 60602

ALEXANDER, ROBERT EVANS, architect; b. Bayonne, N.J., Nov. 23, 1907; s. Edwin H. and Clara (Evans) A.; B.Arch., Cornell U., 1930; m. Eugenie Vigneron, June 13, 1931 (dec. 1952); children—Lynne Marie, Timothy Milne; m. 2d, Mary Starbuck, Aug. 29, 1953; 1 son, Robert Evans II. Architect W. Wilson, Merrill & Alexander, 1935-41; architect R. E. Alexander, 1946- 49; partner Richard J. Neutra & Robert E. Alexander, Los Angeles, 1949- 58, Robert E. Alexander, F.A.I.A. & Assos., 1959—; projects include Bunker Hill Towers, Caltech Ct. of Man, Orange Coast Coll., U. Cal. Elementary Demonstration Sch., Los Angeles, Baldwin Hills Village, U. Nev. Library, city plans for El Paso, San Fernando, Norwalk, Vista, Escondido, also dormitories, gen. services bldg., School of Medicine, long-range devel. plans U. Cal. at San Diego, grad. student apartments U. So. Cal., Internat. Student Center, numerous others; architect (with Neutra), Am. Embassy, Karachi, Pakistan, also Gettysburg Lincoln Meml. and Painted Desert Community for Nat. Park Service, art centers for U. Nev. and San Fernando State Coll., Francis Scott Key Meml. and Mellon Sci. labs. St John's Coll., Annapolis, Md., Center of Communicating and Performing Arts for Adelphi Coll., library and residence halls Simpson Coll., redevel. of central bus. dist. Tulsa; (with others) County of Los Angeles Hall of Records; cons. architect Cal. Inst. Tech., Claremont Colls.; faculty Coll. Architecture U. So. Cal., 1952- 61. Mem. UN Mission to India, 1951; cons. Pub. Housing Adminstrn., 1950, Govt. of Guam, 1951-52, Fed. Housing Adminstrn., 1958-59. Mem. Planning Commn. of City Los Angeles, 1945-51, pres., 1948-50. Mem. bd. govs. Town Hall. Recipient distinguished honor award So. Cal. chpt. A.I.A., 1946, 51; honor award A.I.A., 1954, others. Fellow A.I.A. (pres. So. Cal. chpt. 1970); mem. Philippine League Architecture, Internat. Centre Regional Planning and Development, Nat. Assn. Housing and Redevelopment Ofcls., Nat. Arbitration Assn., Tau Beta Pi. Contbr. profl. publs. Home: 750 Moon Av Los Angeles CA 90065 Office: 304 S Broadway Los Angeles CA 90013

ALEXANDER, ROBERT SCOTT, business exec.; b. Chgo., May 13, 1908; s. Warner Franklin and Ida Mae (Scott) A.; student YMCA Central Coll., Chgo.; m. Adelaide E. M. Carlson, June 22, 1929; children—Barbara (Mrs. Keller), Karen Ann (Mrs. Bedeau). Engring. dept. Grigsby Gronow Co., until 1929; with Wells Gardner & Co., 1929-62. engr., chief insp., factory supt., gen. mgr., pres., chmn. bd., now dir.; v.p. U.S. instrumentation and equipments group, v.p. Internat. Tel.&Tel., Chgo., 1962-63; v. p. Zenith Radio Corp., 1963—. Mayor, Village of Deerfield, Ill., 1945- 59. Mem. Am. Ordnance Assn., Electronic Industry Assn. (dir.), C. of C. Mason (Shriner). Home: 2400 Windsor Mall Park Ridge IL 60068

ALEXANDER, RUTH WILBUR, journalist; b. Chgo.; d. Prof. Gross and Arabel (Wilbur) Alexander; Mus. B., Kidd Key Conservatory, Sherman, Tex.; A.B. summa cum laude, Northwestern U., 1920, M.A., 1921, Ph.D., 1932; LL.D., Temple U., 1953; m. Howard Van Sinderern Tracy; 1 dau., Anne (Mrs. H. Austin Lederer); m. 2d, Raymond Lindley Redheffer; 1 son, Joseph. Concert pianist, 1929-30; mem. faculty Freedom Sch., 1959-62; asso. editor Finance, 1942-44; editorial columnist N.Y. Mirror, 1944-63, Hearst Headline Service, 1964—, New Orleans Times Picayune, 1957-59, N.Y. Daily News, 1963-65; research cons. Am. Econ. Found., 1961—; editorial cons. Reader's Digest, 1964—; lectr. U. Wis. Extension Dept., Johnson Found.; vis. lecturer at Temple U.; radio and TV debates, Town Meeting, Meet the Press, Keep Posted, Answers for Americans, others. Mem. bd. Young Americans for Freedom; mem. adv. bd. Am. Security Council. Decorated Order of Lafayette; recipient of the award of merit for outstanding achievement Northwestern U., Evanston, Ill., 1945; Freedoms Found. award (editorials), 1949, (pub. addresses), 1951, 53; hon. brig. gen. and a.d.c. to gov. La., 1957; hon. citizen New Orleans, recipient citations from govs. of Ark., Ala., Miss.; named to Exec. and Profl. Hall of Fame. Mem. Nat. Council on Crime and Delinquency, N.Y. Acad. Scis., Acad. Polit. Sci., Am. Judicature Soc., Authors Guild, Writers Guild West, Order George Washington, Nat. Geog. Soc., Nat. Sheriff's Assn. (hon. life), Internat. Platform Assn., Phi Beta Kappa, Gamma Phi Beta. Clubs: Washington Press, Half-Centruy. Home: 11 E 86th St New York City NY 10028

ALEXANDER, SHANA, editor; b. N.Y.C., Oct. 6, 1925; d. Milton and Cecilia (Rubenstein) Ager; student Vassar Coll., 1942-45; m. Stephen Alexander, 1951 (div.); 1 dau., Katherine. With Harper's Bazaar, 1946-47; with Flair, 1950; reporter Life mag., 1951-54, mem. West Coast staff, 1954-61, staff writer, 1961-64, writer twice monthly column The Feminine Eye, 1964-69; editor-in-chief McCall's mag., N.Y.C., 1969—. Recipient Sigma Delta Chi and U. So. Cal. Nat. Journalism award, 1965, Los Angeles Times Woman of Year award, 1967, Golden Pen award Am. Newspaper Womens Club, 1969. Author: The Feminine Eye, 1970. Office: 230 Park Av New York NY 10017

ALEXANDER, THEODORE MARTIN, ins. and real estate cons.; b. Montgomery, Ala., Mar. 7, 1909; s. James H. and Hattie (Hamilton) A.; B.A. in Bus. Adminstrn. with honors, Morehouse Col., 1931, LL.D. (hon.), 1970; m. Dorothy Hudson, Aug. 31, 1931; children—Theodore Martin, Alvia Elizabeth, Dorothy Gwendolyn. Founder, 1931, since pres. Alexander & Co., gen. ins. agy., Atlanta; chmn. bd. Alexander and Assos., Inc.; founder, 1949, former exec. v.p. Southeastern Fidelity Fire Ins. Co., Atlanta; pres., treas. University Plaza Apts., Inc.; sec., dir., exec. com. Mut. Fed. Savs. & Loan Assn., Atlanta, 1963-68; pres. Univ. Towers, Inc.; vice chmn. Atlanta Univ. Center Corp. Fed. jury commr. No. Dist. Ga. Trustee Atlanta Community Chest; sec. bd. trustees Morehouse Coll.; bd. dirs. Butler St. YMCA, Atlanta, 1958—, mem. race relations com., internat. com., del. world council 1961, mem. nat. bd. Mem. citizens adv. com., chmn. relocation com. Atlanta Urban Renewal; mem. better housing commn., mem. housing appeal bd., vice chmn. ethics bd. City Atlanta; mem. nat. citizens' com. for community relations Dept. Commerce, 1964; mem. adv. com. Met. Planning Commn. Atlanta; asst. treas. Atlanta Community Chest; mem. Atlanta Community relations; pres. Sr. Citizens Met. Atlanta, 1968-69. Candidate Atlanta City Council, 1957; candidate for Senate, State of Ga., 1962. Mem. N.A.A.C.P., Urban League, Alpha Phi Alpha, Delta Sigma Rho. Republican. Baptist. Mason (Shriner). Home: 1345 Hunter Rd NW Atlanta GA 30314 Office: 208 Auburn Av NE Atlanta GA 30303

ALEXANDER, WALTER BOYD, coll. ofcl.; b. Philadelphia, Pa., June 28, 1898; s. George Black and Isabelle Herron (Ferson) A.; student Williamson Free Sch. of Mech. Trades, 1915-18, Drexel Inst., 1918; B.S. in Edn., Univ. of Pa., 1925, M.A., 1927; Litt.D., Antioch Coll., 1963; m. Ellen Priscilla Dunn, August 3, 1918 (dec. Apr. 1964); children—Joanne (Mrs. James L. Stern), Rodney Boyd; m. 2d, Dorothy Hall Smith, May 27, 1965. Journeyman carpenter, 1918-19; building contractor, 1919-20; instructor in mathematics Veteran's Bureau Dept., Temple Univ., 1920-24; instr. indsl. arts high sch., Collingswood, N.J., 1924-25; dir. vocational edn., Norristown, Pa., 1925-26; dir. of edn., Phila. Y.M.C.A., 1926-29; asso. personnel dir., Antioch Coll., 1929-32, vocational counselor and instr. mathematics, 1932-34, assistant professor of education, 1935-36; associate professor, 1936-41, prof., 1941, asst. to the pres., 1936- 38, dean of adminstrn. 1938-55, dean of faculty, 1956-63, acting pres., 1939-40, 1947-48, v.p., 1941-63, v.p., dean faculty emeritus, cons., 1963—, bd. editors Antioch Rev., 1941-54, also staff mem. Carnegie study Future of Liberal Arts Coll.; cons., dean Am. Coll. in Paris (France), 1964-66, mem. Am. exec. com., 1965-69. Cons., So. Colo. State Coll. Trustee, Wilberforce University, 1961-67, cons., 1970—. Cons. N.Y. Govs. Commn. Higher Edn., 1960. Fellow Am. Geog. Soc.; mem. N. Central Assn. Schs. and Colls. (coll. examiner, cons. 1954—, exec. bd. commn. on colls. and univs. 1960-64, dir. 1963-67; hon.), Ohio Coll. Assn. (com. on memberships and inspection 1942-64), Am. Humanist Association (treas. and dir. 1960-61). Unitarian. Lectr., coll. cons. Home: Hayfield Hill Clifton Rd Yellow Springs OH 45387 Office: Antioch College Yellow Springs OH 45387

ALEXANDER, WILLIAM ACEL, transp. exec.; s. Willaim G. and Mary (Peters) A.; LL.B., U. Colo., 1923; m. Flora Margaret Forsythe, Jan. 9, 1922; children—Ann (Mrs. Frank Gardiner), Sydney (Mrs. J. Robert Burns), Joan (Mrs. Thomas Hollenbeck), William Robert, Edward J. Admitted to Colo. bar; with Denver Tramway Corp., 1923—, gen. atty., v.p., 1942-49, pres., 1949-68, now chmn. bd., chief exec. officer; dir. Denver U.S. Nat. Bank, Gt. Western Sugar Co. Bd. dirs. St. Luke's Hosp., Denver. Mem. Sigma Phi Epsilon. Mason. Clubs: Denver Country, Denver, Denver Athletic. Home: 2909 E 7th Av Denver CO 80206 Office: 350 E Santa Fe Dr Denver CO 80223

ALEXANDER, WILLIAM DAVIDSON, III, civil engr.; b. Charlotte, N.C., June 20, 1911; s. William Davidson, Jr. and Elizabeth (Galt) A.; B.S., Va. Mil. Inst., 1934; C.E., N.C. State U., 1953; m. Louise York, Nov. 14, 1936; 1 son, William Davidson IV. Engr., William F. Freeman, cons. engr., High Point, N.C., 1934-40; partner Engring. Services, Boise, Ida., 1945-46; project mgr. Urbahn-Roberts-Seeyle-Moran, N.Y.C., 1962-63; partner, v.p., dir. Seelye Stevenson Value & Knecht, N.Y.C., 1963—. Chmn. Engring. Found., N.Y.C., 1966—. Served to lt. col., C.E., AUS, 1940-45, 46-50; to col. USAF, 1950-62; Decorated Legion of Merit, Air Force Commendation medal; recipient citation Engring. News Record, 1966. Fellow Am. Soc. C.E. (Civil Engr. of Year award met. sect. 1966); mem. Am. Inst. Cons. Engrs., Soc. Am. Mil. Engrs., The Moles, Phi Kappa Phi. Episcopalian. Home: 15 Birch Way Tarrytown NY 10591 Office: 99 Park Av New York City NY 10016

ALEXANDER, WILLIAM HENRY, lawyer; b. Thomson, Ill., Nov. 16, 1902; s. Cyrus Hall and Mary Letitia (Livingston) A.; B.S., Knox Coll., 1926; postgrad. U. Chgo. Law Sch., 1926- 29; m. Jane Ashcraft, Dec. 22, 1934; children—Willa Jane, William Raymond, David Risdon, Sarah Susan and Peter Llewellyn (twins), Edwin Michael, James Livingston. Admitted to Ill. bar, 1930; law clk. to sr. judge U.S. Circuit Ct. Appeals, 1930-35; with firm Ashcraft & Ashcraft, Chgo., 1935—, mem. 1936—. Dir. Sargent-Welch Sci. Co., Law Bull. Pub. Co. Trustee Village of Wilmette, Ill., 1941-45, pres., 1945- 53; hon. mem. Wilmette Hist. Commn. Bd. dirs., pres. Eleanor Assn.; trustee, pres. Chgo. Wesley Meml. Hosp.; trustee Northwestern U. Citizen fellow Inst. Medicine Chgo.; mem. Am., Ill., Chgo. (pres. 1960-61) bar assns., Chgo. Hist. Soc. (life), Chgo. Natural History Mus. (life), Scabbard and Blade, Phi Alpha Delta, Lambda Chi Alpha. Republican. Methodist (trustee). Rotarian. Clubs: Indian Hill (Winnetka); Law (Chgo.). Home: 1025 Mohawk Rd Wilmette IL 60091 Office: 1st Nat Plaza Chicago IL 60670

ALEXANDER, WILLIAM MARVIN, educator; b. McKenzie, Tenn., Feb. 19, 1912; s. E. Marvin and Lillis (McElroy) A.; student U. Tenn., 1930-32; B.A., Bethel Coll., 1934; M.A., Peabody Coll., 1936; Ph.D. (Gen. Edn. Bd. fellow), Columbia Tchrs. Coll., 1940; m. Nell McLeod, June 6, 1935; children—William Marvin, Philip M. Tchr., McKenzie (Tenn.) Schs., 1934- 36; research asst. Peabody Coll., 1936-37, Columbia Tchrs. Coll., 1937- 38; asst. dir. curriculum Cin. Pub. Schs., 1939-41; asso. prof. edn. U. Tenn., 1941-43; asst. supt. schs., Battle Creek, Mich., 1946-49; supt. schs., Winnetka, Ill., 1949-50; prof. edn., coordinator in-service edn. U. Miami, 1950-58; prof. edn. George Peabody Coll. Tchrs., 1958-63, chmn. dept., 1959-63; prof. edn. U. Fla., Gainesville, 1963—, chmn. div. curriculum and instrn., 1963-66, dir. Inst. for Curriculum Improvement, 1966-69. Cons. various pub. schs. systems. Trustee Peabody Coll. Served to lt. USNR, 1943-46. Mem. N.E.A. (nat. com. instrn. 1960-64), Alumni Assn. Peabody Coll. (pres. 1969-71), Assn. Supervision and Curriculum Devel. (pres. 1959-60, mem. commn. current curriculm devel. 1964-67, bd. publs. dept. elementary sch. prins. 1964-67, review council 1970—), Nat. Assn. Secondary Sch. Prins., Am. Ednl. Research Assn., So. Assn. Colls. and Secondary Schs. (past chmn. com. accreditation studies), Fla. Assn. Supervision and Curriculum Devel. (past pres.), Sigma Nu, Phi Eta Sigma, Phi Delta Kappa, Kappa Delta Pi. Presbyn. Author: State Leadership in Improving Instruction, 1940; Are You a Good Teacher?, 1959; Changing Curriculum Content, 1963; Changing Secondary School Curriculum; Readings, 1967. Co- author: Secondary Education, 1950; Curriculum Planning, 1954; Effective Teaching, 1956; Modern Secondary Education, 1959; Curriculum Planning for Modern Schools, 1966; Independent Study in Secondary Schools, 1967; The Emergent Middle School, 1968, rev. 1969; Innovations in Secondary Education, 1970; The High School Today and Tomorrow, 1971. Editor: The High School of the Future, 1969; cons. editor Rinehart Edn. Pamphlets, 1957-62; editorial adv. bd. Am. Ency., 1965—. Contbr. articles to profl. publs. Home: 610 NW 89th St Gainesville FL 32601

ALEXANDER, WILLIAM VOLLIE, Jr., congressman; b. Memphis, Jan. 16, 1934; B.A. in Polit. Sci., Southwwestern at Memphis, 1957; LL.B., Vanderbilt U., 1960; m. Gwendolyn Haven, Feb. 6, 1957; 1 dau., Alyse Haven. Admitted to Tenn. and Ark. bars, 1960; legal research asst. to Fed. Judge Marion Boyd. Memphis, 1960-61; asso. firm Montedonico, Boone. Gilliland, Heiskell & Loch, 1961 -63; partner firm Swift & Alexander, Osceola, Ark., 1963-68; mem. 91st and 92d, Congresses 1st Dist. Ark. Commr. Ark. Waterways Commn.; sec. Osceola Port Authority; mem. Osceola Civic Center Commn.; dir. N.E. Ark. Econ. Devel. Dist.; dir. Miss. County Office Econ. Opportunity; atty. Miss. County Urban Renewal Agy.; mem. Miss. County Quorum Ct. and Budget Commn. Bd. dirs. E. Ark. Area council Boy Scouts Am., Miss. County YMCA. Served with AUS, 1951-53. Mem. Am. Acad. Polit. and Social Sci., Am., N. Ark., Tenn., Ark., Osceola bar assn., Am. Legion, Kappa Sigma. Democrat. Episcopalian. Mason, Rotarian. Address: House Office Bldg Washington DC 20515

ALEXANDRE, D.L., corp. exec.; b. N.Y.C., 1917. Vice pres. Engelhard Minerals & Chem. Corp. Home: Far Hills NJ 07931 Office: 430 Mountain Av Murray Hill NJ 07974

ALEXOPOULOS, CONSTANTINE JOHN, mycologist; b. Chgo., Mar. 17, 1907; s. John Constantine and Chrysoula (Panagopoulou) A.; B.S. with honors U. Ill., 1927, M.S., 1928, Ph.D., 1932; m. Juliet

Catherine Dowdy, Aug. 26, 1939. Instr. botany U. Ill., 1934-35; instr. Kent State U., 1935-36, asst. prof., 1936-40, asso. prof., 1940-43; plant pathologist Institut N. Canellopoulos, Piraeus, Greece, 1938-39; staff RFC Rubber Development Program, Amazon Valley, Brazil, 1943-44; officer agrl. rehabilitation, dep. dir. div. agr. and fisheries UNRRA Mission to Greece, 1944-47; asso. prof. botany Mich. State U., 1947-52, prof., 1952-56; Fulbright research scholar U. Athens, Greece, 1954-55; prof., head dept. botany U. Ia., 1956-62; prof. botany U. Tex., Austin, 1962—, acting chmn. dept. botany, 1965. Mem. NSF Systematic Biology Panel, 1962-65. Trustee American Type Culture Collection, 1965-71. Member Bot. Soc. Am. (pres. 1963), Iowa Acad. Sci. (chmn. botany 1960), Internat. Mycol. Assn. (pres. 1971—), Mycol. Soc Am. (pres. 1959), Brit. Mycol. Soc., Ohio Acad. Sci. (v.p. 1943), Mich. Acad. Sci. Arts and Letters (chmn. botany 1954), Torrey Bot. Club, Sigma Xi. Mem. Greek Orthodox Ch. Author: Introductory Mycology, 1952, 62; (with H. C. Bold) Algae and Fungi, 1967; (with W. D. Gray) The Biology of the Myxomycetes, 1968.; (with G.W. Martin) The Myxomycetes, 1969. Editorial bd. Brittonia, 1963-66, Lloydia, 1963-71. Contbr. McGraw Hill Ency. Sci. and Tech., Ency. Biol. Scis., Ency. Biochemistry, Ency. Brit. Home: 917 Calithea Rd Austin TX 78746 Office: Dept Botany U Texas Austin TX 78712

ALFANGE, DEAN, lawyer; b. Constantinople, Dec. 2, 1900; came to U.S., 1901; A.B., Hamilton Coll., 1922; LL.B., Columbia, 1925; m. Thalia Perry, Aug. 11, 1929; children—Whitman, Dean. Admitted to N.Y., U.S. Supreme Ct. bars, 1925; since practiced in N.Y.C.; gen. counsel Ave. B & East Broadway Transit Co., Inc., Sound Dollar Co., BBC Industries, Inc.; counsel Nat. Assn. Tobacco Distbrs. Chmn., N.Y.C. Appeals Bd. 6, Enemy Allen Hearing Bd. So. Dist. N.Y.; mem. adv. com. N.Y. State Def. Council, N.Y. State Salvage Council; mem. N.Y. State Bd. Inquiry in Longshore Industry; founder Legion for Am. Unity, 1940; mem. exec. com. Citizens for Victory; dir. Better Understanding Found. for Religious and Racial Tolerance, Greek War Relief Assn.; nat. chmn. Emergency Com. to Save Jewish People of Europe; chmn. Am. Christian Palestine Com. of Greater N.Y. Chmn., Fgn. Lang. Speakers Bur. Dem. Presdl. Campaign Com., 1940; Dem. candidate for Congress, 17th N.Y. Dist., 1941; nominated for gov. N.Y., Am. Labor Party, 1942; chmn. Liberal and Labor Com. which founded Liberal party State of N.Y., 1944; chmn. Israel Anniversary Celebration Com., 1949. Trustee Fashion Inst. Tech. (N.Y.), United Greek Orthodox Charities, Archdiocesan Greek Cathedral of Holy Trinity, N.Y. Recipient Freedom Found. Award, 1960; Theodore Roosevelt Meml. award for non-fiction book "The Supreme Court and the National Will," 1937; Donor scholarship endowments Hamilton Coll. to promote democratic govt. and religious understanding. Mem. Nat. Inst. Social Scis., Am. Acad. Polit. and Social Sci., UN Assn. (dir.), N.A.A.C.P., Am., N.Y. bar assns., Am. Legion, Nat. Inst. Social Scis., Am. Hellenic Congress (nat. chmn.), Order of Ahepa (past nat. pres.), Grand St. Boys Assn., United Hunts Assn., Phi Beta Kappa, Pi Delta Epsilon, Delta Sigma Rho. Mason. Elk. Clubs: Turf and Field; Economic of N.Y., Circus Saints and Sinners; Governor's (exec. com. N.Y.). Author: My Creed (This Week mag. and Reader's Digest); What America Means. Home: 65 Central Park W New York City NY 10023 Office: 9 E 40th St New York City NY 10016

ALFARO, VICTOR RICARDO, physician; b. Panama, Republic of Panama, Mar. 14, 1907; s. Ricardo Joaquin and Amelia (Lyons) A.; came to U.S., 1922, naturalized, 1942; B.S. in Medicine, Georgetown U., 1927, M.D., 1929; postgrad. otolaryngology U. Pa., 1930-31, audiology and endaural surgery Northwestern U., 1951, laryngoscopy, laryngeal, surgery and bronchoesophagology Jackson Clinic, Temple U., 1943; m. Nancy Hamilton, June 24, 1929; children—Ricardo Joaquin II, Nancy Hamilton. Pvt. practice otolaryngology, Washington, 1932—; sr. attending otolaryngology Episcopal Eye, Ear and Throat Hosp., 1942-58; sr. attending otolaryngology Washington Hosp. Center, 1958-62; cons. otolaryngology Mt. Alto VA Hosp., 1949-55; cons. NIH, 1948-60, Washington Hosp. Center, 1962—; mem. faculty Sch. Medicine, Georgetown U., 1932- 61, prof., head div. otolaryngology, 1949-61, prof. emeritus, 1961—. Bd. dirs. Deafness Research Found. Served to lt. col. M.C., AUS, 1942-46; ETO. Mem. Am. Soc. Otolaryngol. and Opthalmologic Allergy (past mem. council), A.M.A. (past chmn. sect. laryngol. otol. and rhinol.; past del. ho. dels.), Am. Laryngol., Rhinol. and Otol. Soc. (council, past sec., pres. 1971—), Med. Soc. D.C. (past pres.), Am. Acad. Ophthal. and Otolaryngol., Am. Laryngol. Assn., Am. Otol. Soc., Pan-Am. Soc. Otol., Laryngol. and Rhinol., Internat. Congress Otol. (chmn. com. local arrangements Washington 1957 del. for U.S. in Paris 1961, Tokyo 1965), Washington Hearing Soc. (past mem. bd.). Home: 4210 42d St NW Washington DC 20018 Office: 916 19th St NW Washington DC 20006

ALFERS, GERALD JUNIOR, banker; b. Axtell, Kan., Dec. 12, 1931; s. Joseph and Gerald and Olive (Gates) A.; grad. certificate Am. Inst. Banking, 1964; grad. Pacific Coast Banking Sch., 1967; m. Barbara Ruth Small, Aug. 20, 1955; children—Jerilyn, Joseph, Jean, John, James, Jennifer, Jeffrey. Vice pres., cashier Pacific Nat. Bank, Seattle, 1949—. Mem. Wash. Bankers Assn. (chmn. bank operations com. 1967-69). Adminstrv. Mgmt. Soc., Am. Inst. Banking, Seattle C. of C. Roman Cath. Club: Bayview Golf (Seattle). Home: 9358 California Av SW Seattle WA 98116 Office: 900 2d Av Seattle WA 98111

ALFIERI, JOHN JOSEPH, educator; b. Central Nyack, N.Y., Jan. 25, 1917; s. Giovanni N. and Assunta (Padrone) A.; B.A., U. Southwestern La., 1950; M.A., U. Ia., 1952; Ph.D., 1957; student U. Madrid, 1963-64; m. Graciela Andrade, Aug. 20, 1960. Mem. faculty Lawrence U., Appleton. Wis., 1954—. prof. Spanish, chmn. dept., 1965—. Marie Wollpert prof. Spanish, 1965—. Mem. Modern Lang. Assn., Am. Assn. Tchrs. Spanish and Portuguese. Author articles on Pérez Galdós. Home: 803 E Alton St Appleton WI 54911

ALFIN-SLATER, ROSLYN BERNIECE, biochemist, educator; b. Bklyn., July 28, 1916; d. Sam and Lillian (Rubinsky) Alfin; B.A., Bklyn. Coll., 1936; A.M., Columbia, 1942, Ph.D., 1946; m. Grant G. Slater, July 30, 1948. Asst. in charge lecture div., chemistry dept. Bklyn. Coll., 1938-43, tutor gen. inorganic chemistry, 1943, instr. inorganic chemistry, qualitative analysis, evenings 1946- 48; asst. instr. inorganic chemistry, exptl. phys. chemistry, food analysis Columbia, 1943-45, research fellow Corn Industries Research Found., 1945-46; instr. biochemistry N.Y. U. Coll. Dentistry 1945-46; research chemist indsl. enzymes Takamine Labs., Clifton, N.J., 1946-47; research fellow Sloan Kettering Inst. Cancer Research, 1947-48; research asso. dept. biochemistry and nutrition U. So. Cal. Sch. Medicine, 1948- 42, vis. asst. prof., 1952-56, vis. asso. prof., 1956-59; asso. prof. nutrition U. Cal., Los Angeles, 1959-65, prof., 1965—. Mem. nutrition study sect. NIH, 1968-72. Fellow A.A.A.S., Am. Heart Assn. (council on arteriosclerosis), Am. Pub. Health Assn.; mem. N.Y. Acad. Scis., Am. Soc. Biol. Chemists, Am. Inst. Nutrition (Osborne and Mendel award 1970), Soc. Exptl. Biology and Medicine, Am. Oil Chemists Soc., Internat. Soc. Cardiology, Sigma Xi, Phi Sigma, Iota Sigma Pi. Contbr. to sci. books, jours. Editorial bd. jour. Nutrition, 1966-70, Advances in Lipid Research, 1970—. Home: 986 Somera Rd Los Angeles CA 90024

ALFOLDI, ANDREW, educator; b. Pomáz, Hungary, Aug. 27, 1895; s. Antal and Charlotte (Klein) A.; D.Phil., U. Budapest, 1919; D.Phil. (hon.), U. Utrecht, 1936, U. Ghent, 1949, U. Bonn, 1967, U. Paris, 1967; m. Emma Seidl, Aug. 28, 1917; children—Emma, Andrew; m. 2d, Elisabeth Rosenbaum, Mar. 17, 1967. Came to U.S., 1955, naturalized, 1963. Mem. staff Hungarian Nat. Museum, 1919-23; prof. U. Debreczen, Hungary, 1923-30, Budapest, 1930-47, U. Berne, Switzerland, 1948-52, Basle, 1952-56, Inst. for Advanced Study, Princeton, N.J., 1955—. Recipient Gold Medal of the City of Rome, 1960. Mem. Inst. of France, Royal Swedish Acad., Acad. Lincei Rome, Hungarian Acad.; corr. mem. British, Danish, Bavarian, Austrian, Bulgarian acads. social sci., Acad. Göttingen, Mainz, Lund; hon. mem. Pontificia Accdiarch Rome, Archaeol. Inst. Am., Soc. Antiquaries (London), Soc. for Promotion Roman Studies (London), Soc. Antiquaries of Scotland, Finnish, Spanish archaeol. socs., Royal Numis. Soc. (London), Turkish Hist. Soc., others. Author: Early Rome and the Latins, 1965, numerous others. Home: 272 Mercer St Princeton NJ 08540

ALFORD, A.L., Jr., newspaper publisher. Editor, pub. Lewiston (Ida.) Tribune. Office: Tribune Pub Co 505 C St Lewiston ID 83501*

ALFORD, BOBBY RAY, physician, educator; b. Dallas, May 30, 1932; s. Bryant J. and Edith M. (Garrett) A.; A.S., Tyler Jr. Coll., 1951; postgrad. U. Tex., 1951-52; M.D., Baylor U., 1956; m. Othelia Jerry Dorn, Aug. 23, 1953; children-Bradley Keith, Raye Lynn, Alan Scott. Intern Jefferson Davis Hosp., Houston, 1956-57; resident Baylor Coll., U. Medicine Affiliated Hosps. Program, 1957-60; mem. faculty Baylor U. Coll. Medicine, 1960—, prof. otolaryngology, chmn. dept., 1967—. Mem. rev. panel surgeon gen. on neurol. and sensory disease USPHS, 1965-68; cons. Nat. Inst. Neurol. Disease and Stroke, 1970. Recipient Herman Johnson award Baylor U/Coll. Medicine, 1967; spl. NIH fellow Johns Hopkins Hosp., 1961-62. Diplomate Am. Bd. Otolaryngology. Fellow A.C.S.; mem. Soc. Univ. Otolaryngologists (sec. 1965-69), Am. Otol. Soc., Am. Laryngol., Rhinol. and Otol. Soc., Am. Soc. Head and Neck Surgery, Am. Acad. Ophthalmology and Otolaryngology, Am. Bronchoesophagological Assn., Acoustical Soc. Am., Alpha Omega Alpha. Clubs: Houston Yacht, Doctor's (bd. govs. 1967-70) (Houston). Author: Neurological Aspects of Auditory and Vestibular Disorders, 1964, Chief editor A.M.A. Archives of Otolaryngology, 1970—. Home: 114 Warrenton St Houston TX 77024

ALFORD, FREDERICK FERGUS, Jr., warehouseman; b. Dallas, Mar. 17, 1931; s. Frederick Fergus and Olita (McCoy) A.; B.B.A., So. Methodist U., 1952; m. Bertha Olmsted Worthington, Dec. 18, 1954; children—Frederick Fergus III, Bertha Worthington, Harriet Olita. Asst. to pres. Alford Refrigerated Warehouses, Inc., Dallas, 1953-58, v.p., 1956-58, pres. Gulf Coast div., 1958-64, corp. pres., 1964—, also dir. Sec., dir. Am. Council to Improve Our Neighborhoods, 1959-65; chmn. Citizens Alert, 1961-64. Bd. dirs. Boys City, Inc., 1959-65. Served to 2d lt. USAF, 1952-53. Mem. Quartermaster Assn., Am. Warehousemans Assn., Nat. Assn. Refrigerated Warehouses (past chmn. S.W. chpt.), Nat. Assn. Practical Refrigerating Engrs., A.I.M., So. Inst. Mgmt., Soc. Advancement Mgmt., Nat. Rifle Assn., Navy League U.S., Nat. Frozen Food Distbrs. Assn., Tex. Sprimp Assn., Sheriffs Assn. Tex., Sigma Iota Epsilon, Kappa Sigma. Presbyn. Clubs: Propeller of United States, Kiwanis, Press, Country, Town (Corpus Christi, Tex.); Dallas Country, Dervish, Gun, Brook Hollow Golf, Imperial (Dallas). Home: 3819 McFarlin St Dallas TX 75205 Office: 318 Caldiz St Dallas TX 75222

ALFORD, JACK LELAND, mech. engr., educator; b. Long Beach, Cal., Nov. 19, 1920; s. Leon Otto and Ethelind (Humphrey) A.; student U.S. Naval Acad., 1937-39; B.S., Cal. Inst. Tech., 1942, M.S., 1946, Ph.D., 1950; m. Edith Elizabeth Humann, Mar. 8, 1944; children—Christopher John, Margaret Ann. With Turbodyne Corp., Hawthorne, Cal., 1948-50; postdoctoral fellow Cal. Inst. Tech., 1950-52; research engr. Jet Propulsion Lab., 1957-59; head engring. div. U.S. Naval Ordnance Test Sta., 1952-55; asst. to tech. dir. Technicolor Corp., 1955-57; prof. Harvey Mudd Coll., Claremont, Cal., 1959-65, James Howard Kindelberger Prof. engring., 1965—, chmn. dept. engring., 1967—; cons. Aerojet Gen. Corp., 1959-69. Served to lt. USNR, 1942-46. Registered profl. engr., Cal. Mem. Am. Soc. Mech. Engrs., Earthquake Engring. Research Inst., Am. Soc. Engring. Edn., Am. Assn. U. Profs., Sigma Xi, Tau Beta Pi. Office: Harvey Mudd Coll Claremont CA 91711

ALFORD, JOHN MORRIS, former naval officer; b. Galva, Ill., Apr. 13, 1915; s. John Merlin and Shirley (Foote) A.; grad. Marion (Ala.) Inst., 1932; B.S., U.S. Naval Acad., 1936 ; grad. Armed Forces Staff Coll., 1952, Nat. War Coll., 1960; m. Mary Anne Carlsen, Aug. 30, 1948; children—Douglas Blakeshaw, John Morris III, Stephanie, Glenna Maria. Commd. ensign USN, 1936, advanced through grades to rear adm., 1962; sea duty in combat ships Pacific Ocean area, 1936-46, Atlantic and Mediterranean, 1949-51, 54-57, 66-67, Pacific and Far East, 1948-49, 60-64; staff duty, Washington, 1946-48, 52-54, 57-60, 64-66, 66, 67-69; adminstrv. dir. Navy Marine Coast Guard Residence Found., Inc., U.S. Naval Obs., Washington, 1971—. Decorated Legion of Merit, Bronze Star. Mem. U.S. Naval Inst. Home: 3525 Trinity Dr Alexandria VA 22304 Office: US Naval Obs Washington DC 20390

ALFORD, NEILL HERBERT, Jr., legal educator; b. Greenville, S.C., July 13, 1919; s. Neill Herbert and Elizabeth (Robertson) A.; B.A., The Citadel, 1940; LL.B., U. Va., 1947; J.S.D., Yale, 1966; m. Elizabeth Talbot Smith, June 26, 1943; children—Neill Herbert III, Margaret Dudley, Eli Thomas Stackhouse. Admitted to Va. bar, 1954; faculty law U. Va. Law Sch., Charlottesville, 1947-61, 62—, Doherty Found. prof., 1966—; prof. chair internat. law Naval War Coll., 1961-62, cons., 1962—. Spl. counsel Va. Code Commn., 1954—; dir. Va. Bankers Assn. Trust Sch., 1958-61; summer tchr. George Washington U., U. N.C.; Sterling fellow Yale, 1950-51; Ford fellow U. Wis., 1958; dir. U. Va. Press. Comdr. civil affairs group U.S. Army Res., 1947-66. Served to lt. col. AUS, 1941-46; ETO. Decorated Bronze Star, Combat Inf. badge. Mem. Selden Soc., Am. Soc. Legal History, Am. Judicature Soc., Am. Soc. Internat. Law, Va. State Bar, Va., Am. bar assns., Order of Coif, Phi Alpha Delta, Omicron Delta Kappa. Club: Colonnade (Charlottesville). Author: Cases and Materials on Decedents Estates and Trusts, 4th edit., 1971; Modern Economic Warfare: Law and the Naval Participant, 1967. Contbr. articles to profl. jours. Home: 1868 Field Rd Charlottesville VA 22903

ALFORD, ROBERT ROSS, educator; b. Stockton, Cal., Apr. 18, 1928; s. Ellsworth and Grace (Ross) A.; A.B., U. Cal. at Berkeley, 1950, M.A., 1952, Ph.D., 1961; m. Gloria Kramer, June 18, 1949; children—Heidi, Jonathan, Elissa. Lectr. sociology U. Cal. at Berkeley, 1959-61; mem. faculty U. Wis., 1961—, prof. sociology, 1966—, asso. dir. Survey Research Lab., 1961-63; vis. prof. govt. U. Essex (Eng.), 1966-67; vis. prof. sociology Columbia, 1970-71. Mem. Am. Sociol. Assn., Am. Polit. Sci. Assn., Am. Hist. Assn. Author: Party and Society, 1963; Bureaucracy and Participation: Political Cultures in Four Wisconsin Cities, 1969. Home: 560 Riverside Dr New York City NY 10027

ALFRED, WILLIAM, educator; b. N.Y.C., Aug. 16, 1922; s. Thomas Allfrey and Mary (Bunyan) A.; B.A., Bklyn. Coll., 1948; M.A., Harvard, 1949, Ph.D., 1954. Mem. faculty Harvard, 1954—, prof. English, 1963—. Recipient Lit. Assos. award Bklyn. Coll., 1953; Creative Arts Theatre grantee Brandeis U., 1960; Amy Lowell Travelling Poetry scholar, 1956. Served with AUS, 1943- 46. Awarded grant Nat. Inst. Arts and Letters. Mem. Mediaeval Acad. Am., Modern Lang. Assn., Dramatists Guild. Author: The Annunciation Rosary, 1948; (verse plays) Agamemnon, 1954, Hogan's Goat, 1956. Contbr. poems, articles numerous profl. jours. Co-editor: Of Reformation, The Prose Works of John Milton, 1954; asso. editor American Poet, 1942-44. Home: 31 Athens St Cambridge, MA 02138.

ALFVEN, HANNES OLOF GOSTA, educator, physicist; b. Norrkoping, Sweden, May 30, 1908; s. Johannes and Anna-Clara (Romanus) A.; Ph.D., U. Uppsala, 1934; m. Kerstin Maria Erikson, 1935; children—Cecilia Inger, Gösta Reidun, Berenike. Research physicist Nobel Inst. Physics, Stockholm, Sweden, 1937-40; prof. theory electricity Royal Inst. Tech., Stockholm, 1940-45, prof. electronics,, 1945-63, prof. plasma physics, 1963—; prof. U. Cal. at San Diego, 1967—. Pres. Pugwash Conf., 1970. Recipient Gold medal Royal Astron. Soc., 1967, Nobel prize physics, 1970. Author: Cosmical Electrodynamics, 1948; Origin of Solar System, 1956; (with C.G. Falthammar) Cosmical Electrodynamics, Fundamental Principles, 1963. Home: Emblavägen 29 S-182 63 Djursholm Sweden Office: Royal Inst Tech Dept Plasma Physics Stockholm 70 Sweden also Dept Applied Physics and Information Science Univ San Diego CA 92037

ALGASE, BENJAMIN, lawyer; b. Dubuque, Ia., May 31, 1901; s. Solomon and Clara (Abrahams) A.; B.S.S., Coll. City N.Y., 1922; LL.B., Columbia, 1924; m. Julia Cohn, Sept. 18, 1924; children—Roger Carl, Benji Julie. Admitted to N.Y. bar, 1925, since practiced in N.Y.C.; mem. Hays, Algase, Feuer, Porter & Spanier, until 1968; counsel Hays, Feuer, Porter & Spanier, 1968—. Chmn., N.Y. chpt. Am. Friends of Hebrew U., 1952-54, dir., 1952—. Mem. N.Y. County Lawyers Assn., Nat. Lawyers Guild. Home: 151 Central Park W New York City NY 10023 Office: 445 Park Av New York City NY 10022

ALGE, J.A., business exec. Pres., Fla. Retail Owned Grocers, Inc., Tampa. Office: 1102 N 28th St Tampa FL 33605*

ALGER, CHADWICK FAIRFAX, educator, polit. scientist; b. Chambersburg, Pa., Oct. 9, 1924; s. Herbert and Thelma (Drawbaugh) A.; B.A., Ursinus Coll., 1949; M.A., Johns Hopkins, 1950; Ph.D., Princeton, 1958; m. Elinor Reynolds, Aug. 28, 1948; children—Mark, Scott, Laura, Craig. Internat. relations specialist Dept. Navy, 1950-54; instr. Swarthmore Coll., 1957; faculty Northwestern U., Evanston, Ill., 1958-71, prof. polit. sci., 1966-71, dir. internat. relations program, 1967-71; Mershon prof. polit. sci. and pub. policy Ohio State U., 1971—; vis. prof. UN affairs N.Y.U., 1962-63. Served with USNR, 1943-46. Mem. Am. (council), Internat. polit. sci. assns., A.A.A.S., Internat. Studies Assn., Internat. Peace Research Assn. (council), Midwest Conf. Polit. Scis. (recipient prize 1966), Union Internat. Assns. Author: (with others) Simulation in International Relations, 1963. Contbr. articles profl. jours. Home: 2674 Westmont Blvd Columbus OH

ALGER, JAMES DYCE, army officer; b. Brockton, Mass., Mar. 25, 1912; s. James Henry and Constance (Dyce) A.; B.A., U.S. Mil. Acad., 1935; m. Consuelo Zobel de Ayala, July 20, 1940. Commd. 2d lt., cav. U.S. Army, 1935, advanced through grades to maj. gen., 1956; with 1st Armored Div., World War II; assigned Office Joint Chiefs Staff, 1949-50, Office Sec. Def., 1951-52; chief staff 45th Inf. Div., Korea, mem. Korean Mil. Adv. Group, 1953-54; chief staff 4th Armored Div., 1954-55; mem. Dept. Army Staff, 1956-57; asst. div. comdr. 3d Armored Div., 1957-59; asst. chief staff plans-operations Allied Land Forces, Central Europe, 1959-61; comdg. gen. II U.S. Army Corps, 1961-63; asst. dep. chief staff mil. operations Dept. Army, 1963; spl. asst. to chief staff U.S. Army for Spl. Warfare Activities, 1963; U.S. Army mem. U.S. delegation Joint Bd. Def., Can.- U.S., 1963; chmn. U.S. delegation Inter-Am. Def. Bd., U.S. delegation Brazil-U.S. Def. Com.; chmn. U.S. delegation Mexico-U.S. Def. Com., 1963—. Mem. Bethel (Me.) Area Devel. Corp., Sunday River Skiway Corp. Trustee Gould Acad., Bethel. Decorated Legion of Merit with oak leaf cluster, Bronze Star, Purple Heart, D.S.M. with silver star and oak leaf cluster (U.S.); Legion of Honor (Philippines). Mem. U.S. Armor Assn. (exec. council), Assn. U.S. Army, Res. Officers Assn. Home: Quarters 42 Fort Amador CZ Office: Comdr US Army Forces So Command Fort Amador CZ

ALGER, PHILIP LANGDON, elec. engr., educator; b. Washington, Jan. 27, 1894; s. Philip Rounseville and Louisa (Taylor) A.; B.S., St. John's Coll., Md., 1912, A.M., 1916; B.S., Mass Inst. Tech., 1915; M.S., Union College, Schenectady, 1920; D.Engring., U. Colo., 1968; m. Catharine E. Jackson, June 30, 1918 (dec. Sept. 1945); children—Augusta Jordan (Mrs. David C. Prince, Jr.), John Rodgers Meigs, Andrew Dugald Langdon, Ann Vogdes (Mrs. Gert Ehrlich); m. 2d, Helen Jackson Hubbell. Asst. instr., research asst. Mass. Inst. Tech., 1916-17; induction motor engring. dept., alternating current engring. dept., staff asst. to mgr. engring. apparatus dept. Gen. Electric Co., 1919-51, cons. engr. motor dept., 1951-58; adj. prof. elec. engring. Rensselaer Poly. Inst., 1958-70. U.S. del. plenary meeting Internat. Electrotech. Commn., Torquay, Eng., 1938. Chmn., Schenectady Charter League which sponsored adoption city mgr. govt., 1934; dir. Mohawk Devel. Service, Schenectady Bur. Municipal Research. Served as lt., ordnance dept. U.S. Army, 1917-19. Fellow I.E.E.E. (Lamme medal 1958), Instn. Electrical Engrs., Am. Soc. Quality Control, Am. Soc. M.E., A.A.A.S.; mem. Am. Ordnance Assn., Am. Soc. Engring. Edn., Nat. Municipal League, Am. Math. Soc., Newcomen Soc., N.Y. State Soc. Profl. Engrs., Am. Philatelic Soc., Société Français des Electriciens, Am. Legion, United World Federalists, Va. Soc. Cin., Sigma Xi, Eta Kappa Nu (eminent mem.). Author: The Nature of Polyphase Induction Machines, 1951; Mathematics for Science and Engineering, 1957; The Nature of Induction Machines, 1965; also tech. articles sci. mags. Co-author: Ethical Problems in Engineering, 1965. Co-compiler: Steinmetz-The Philosopher, 1965. Editor: The Life and Times of Gabriel Kron, 1969. Home: 1758 Wendell Av Schenectady NY 12308

AL-GHOUSSEIN, TALAT, diplomat of Kuwait; b. Palestine, May 16, 1924; s. Yacoub and Soriya (Nussibeh) Al-G.; B.A. in Journalism, Am. U. Cairo (Egypt), 1944; m. Bassima Al-Ghoussein, Jan. 4, 1953; children—Yacoub Osama, Tarek. Editor fgn. news As-Shaab Daily Newspaper, Jaffa, Palestine, 1946-47; controller Arab. Nat. Bank Ltd., Jaffa, 1947-48; editor fgn. news. dir. English sect. Ofcl. Broadcasting Sta. Jordan, 1948-49; dir. press and pub. information Ministry Fgn. Affairs, Yemen, 1949-53; sec. gen. Devel. Bd. Kuwait, 1953-60; dep. pvt. sec. to Emir of Kuwait, 1960-61; minister counsel embassy of Kuwait, Washington, 1962-63, A.E. and P., 1963-67; A.E. and P., Morocco, Rabat, 1970—. Clubs: International, Metropolitan (Washington). Address: Pastor St N 48 Al-Laymoun Quarter Rabat Morocco

ALGREN, NELSON, author; b. Detroit, Mar. 28, 1909; grad. U. Ill. Author: Somebody in Boots, 1935; Never Come Morning, 1942; The Neon Wilderness, 1947; The Man with the Golden Arm, 1949; ChicagoCity on the Make, 1951; A Walk on the Wild Side, Never Come Morning, 1958; Neon Wilderness, 1960; Notes from a Sea Diary, 1965; Short Stories in O. Henry Meml. Editor: Lonesome Monsters, 1963. Served with AUS, 1942-45. Awards Vols., 1935, 41, Best Am. Short Stories (Foley), 1942-45, Story Anthology, 1933-34. Contbr. short fiction, popular mags. Home: 1958 W Evergreen Chicago IL 60622

ALHADEFF, DAVID ALBERT, educator; b. Seattle, Mar. 22, 1923; s. Albert David and Pearl (Taranto) A.; B.A., U. Wash., 1944; M.A., Harvard, 1948, Ph.D., 1950; m. Charlotte Pechman, Aug. 1, 1948. Faculty, U. Cal. at Berkeley, 1949—, prof. bus. adminstrn., 1959—. Served with AUS, 1943-46. Mem. Am., Western econ. assns., Am. Finance Assn. Author: Monopoly and Competition in Banking, 1954; Competition and Controls in Banking, 1968. Contbr. articles to profl. jours., chpts. to books. Home: 822 Craft Av El Cerrito CA 94530 Office: U Cal Barrows Hall Berkeley CA 94720

ALI, ANWAR, govt. ofcl., economist; b. Gujranwala, West Pakistan, Feb. 16, 1913; s. Dost Mohamed and Raj Begum; B.A. with honors, Islamia Coll., Lahore, 1932, M.A. in Econs., 1934; m. Saeeda Kausar, Sept. 10, 1939; children—Saeed, Aisha. Asst. financial adviser to under-sec. Ministry Finance, Govt. India, 1943-47; dep. sec. Ministry Finance, Govt. Pakistan, 1947-52, joint sec., 1952-54; dir. Middle Eastern dept. IMF, Washington, 1954—; gov. Saudi Arabian Monetary Agy, Jedda, 1958—; dir. (rep. Govt. Pakistan) State Bank of Pakistan, 1952-54, Nat. Bank of Pakistan, 1949-53; rep. Pakistan various internat. meetings. Treas., Anglo Arabic Coll., New Delhi, 1945-47, Islamia, Coll., Karachi, 1950-51. Decorated Sitara-e-Quaid-Azam, 1961, Sitara-e-Pakistan, 1967. Fellow Internat. Banker Assn. Home: 39 Sharia All Ibn-e-Abi Talih Sharafia Jeddah Saudi Arabia Office: Saudi Arabian Monetary Agy Jedda Saudi Arabia

ALI, RASHIED, drummer, percusianist; b. Phila., July 1, 1933; ed. Granoff Sch., pvt. edn. Played drums with Len Bailey, various local groups, rock and roll combos; also worked with Bill Dixon, Paul Bley, Sonny Rollins, Archie Shepp, Marion Brown, Sun Ra, N.Y.C., 1963—; joined John Coltrane combo, 1965; spl. concert performances; recorded with A. Shepp, John Coltrane, Jackie McLean, Alice Coltrane.‡

ALIBRANDI, JOSEPH FRANCIS, electronics co. exec.; b. Boston, Nov. 9, 1928; s. Paul and Anna (Amendolia) A.; B.S. in Mech. Engring., Mass. Inst. Tech., 1952; m. Lambertha A. Araskiewicz, May 12, 1957; children—Paul, Ann-Marie, Carolyn. Engr., Fairchild Engring. & Aircraft Co., 1951; with Raytheon Co., 1952-70, operation mgr., Bedford, Mass., 1962-64, v.p., div. gen. mgr. 1965-68, sr. v.p., 1968-70; exec. v.p. Whittaker Corp., Los Angeles, 1970-71, pres., 1971—; dir. Riker-Maxson. Chmn., Mass. State Coll. Bldg. Authority; campaign chmn. Lowell (Mass.) United Fund, 1963, bd. dirs., 1962—. Served with AUS, 1946-48. Mem. Am. Soc. Naval Engrs., Am. Ordnance Assn. Def. Supply Assn., Navy League U.S., Air Force Assn., Am. Inst. Aeros. and Astronautics, Assn. U.S. Army (life), Nat. Security Indsl. Assn. Home: 16560 Park Lane Circle Los Angeles CA 90049 Office: 10880 Wilshire Blvd Los Angeles CA 90024

ALIG, CORNELIUS O., Jr., banker; b. Indpls., May 24, 1921; s. Cornelius O. and Cecilia (Wulsin) A.; A.B., Princeton, 1943; m. Emily Norris, July 22, 1954; children—Cornelius, Marion, Frances, Alfred. With Indiana Nat. Bank., Indpls., 1946—, exec. v.p., 1968—; also dir.; v.p. Ind. Nat. Corp., 1971—; chmn. bd. First Nat. Bank & Trust Co., Plainfield, Ind., 1965—; dir. Jenn Air Co., Guarantee Auto Stores, Inc. Treas. Bd. for Fundamental Edn., 1967—, Flanner House, 1964—; v.p. Greater Indpls. Progress Com., 1966; mem. Met. Plan Commn. Marion County, 1966, Ind. Motor Vehicle Inspection Bd., 1967. Clk.-treas. Town of Crows Nest. Trustee Methodist Hosp., Indpls; bd. dirs. Ind. Heart Assn., Indpls Zool. Soc.; adv. bd. Ind. State Sch. for Deaf, 1968—. Served with AUS, World War II. Decorated Bronze Star. Episcopalian (vestry). Clubs: Columbia (bd. dirs.). U.S. Auto (treas.)(Indpls.). Home: 700 W 56th St Indianapolis IN 46208 Office: 1 Indiana Sq Indianapolis IN 46204

ALIMANESTIANU, CALIN, hotel exec.; b. Bucharest, Roumania, Dec. 29, 1925; s. Virgil and Nineta (Leon) A.; ed. in Bucharest, Zurich, Switzerland and Rome; m. Betty Lou Nicholas, Aug. 1, 1959; 1 dau. Simone. Came to U.S., 1953, naturalized, 1961. Mgmt. trainee Woodner Hotel, Washington, 1955, Bismarck Hotel, Chgo., 1957; asst. to gen. mgr. Oxford House, Chgo., 1958-60; gen. mgr. Holiday Inn, Newburgh, N.Y., Plainview, L.I., N.Y., 1960-67; v.p. operation, gen. mgr. Holiday Inn, N.Y.C., 1967—. Vice chmn. Roumanian- Am. Club for Nixon as Pres., 1968; mem. GOP Heritage Groups (nationalties div.). Mem. Julio Maniu Am. Roumanian Relief Found. Mem. Royal Automobile Club Roumania. Mem. Eastern Orthodox Ch. Home: Holiday Inn 440 W 57th St New York City NY 10019

ALINSKY, SAUL DAVID, sociologist; b. Chgo., Jan. 30, 1909; s. Benjamin and Sarah (Tannenbaum) A.; Ph.B., U. Chgo., 1930, postgrad. Grad. Sch., 1930-32; LL.D., Saint Procopius Coll., 1958; m. Helene Simon, June 9, 1932 (dec.); children—Kathryn, David; m. 2d, Jean Graham, May 15, 1952 (div. 1969). Sociologist, Inst. for Juvenile Research, Chgo., 1931-36, 36-39; mem. state prison classification bd., div. criminology Ill. State Penitentiary System, Joliet, 1933-36; co-founder Back of Yards Neighborhood Council, Chgo.; exec. dir. Indsl. Areas Found. and Tng. Inst., 1969—. Vis. prof. Vassar Coll., 1969, Antioch Coll., 1970. Will D. Wood fellow Amherst Coll., 1969. Recipient award for social justice Cath. Youth Orgn. Am., 1950. Mem. Authors League Am. Author: Reveille for Radicals, 1946, 70; John L. Lewis, a Biography, 1949, 70; (with Marion K. Sanders) The Professional Radical, 1970; Rules for Radicals, 1971. Contbr. numerous articles to sociol., psychol., ednl. publs. Office: 8 S Michigan Av Chicago IL 60603 also 528 N Michigan Av Chicago IL 60611

ALIOTO, JOSEPH LAWRENCE, mayor; b. San Francisco, Feb. 12, 1916; s. Giuseppe and Domenica (Lazio) A.; A.B., St. Marys Coll., 1937, LL.D. (hon.), 1965; J.D., Cath. U. Am., 1940; m. Angelina Genaro, June 22, 1941; children—Lawrence E., Joseph M., John I., Thomas R., Angela M., Michael J. Admitted to Cal. bar, 1940; spl. asst. to atty. gen., Bd. Econ. Welfare, San Francisco, 1940-45; practiced in San Francisco, 1945—,; mayor San Francisco, 1967—. Pres. Rice Growers Assn. Cal., 1959—, Alioto Enterprises, 1959—; chmn. bd. 1st San Francisco Bank. 1964—; chmn. Cal. Rice Export Assn., 1959—. Pres. San Francisco Bd. Edn., 1948-54, San Francisco Redevel. Agy., 1955-59. Fellow Am. Coll. Trial Lawyers; mem. Am. Bar Assn. Home: 34 Presidio Terrace San Francisco CA 94118 Office: City Hall San Francisco CA 94102

ALIVISATOS, SPYRIDON GERASIMOS ANASTASIOS, biochemist; b. Cephallonia, Greece, Oct. 18, 1920; s. A. Paul and Maria (Kassapoglou) A.; M.D., U. Athens (Greece) Med. Sch., 1946; M.S. in Biochemistry, McGill U., Montreal, Que., Can., 1949, Ph.D. in Biochemistry, 1951; m. Athanasia Malavazos, Nov. 14, 1953; children—Maria Regina, Armaud Paul. Came to U.S., 1952, naturalized, 1959. Merck postdoctoral fellow N.Y. U., N.Y.C., 1952-53; Damon Runyon Meml. fellow Rockefeller Inst. for Med. Research, N.Y.C., 1953-55; chief dept. biochem. research Mt. Sinai Med. Research Found. and Hosp., Chgo., 1955-62; prof., dir. enzymology div. Chgo. Med. Sch., 1962-68, chmn. dept. biochemistry, 1968—; prof., chmn. dept. biochemistry U. Athens, 1966-67. Served with Greek Royal Army, World War II. Recipient award Greek Acad. Scis., 1946, award Chgo. Med. Sch. Bd. Trustees, 1959. Mem. Am., Canadian biochem. socs., Biochem. Soc. London (Eng.), Am. Chem. Soc., Canadian Soc. Microbiologists, Canadian Physiol. Soc., Soc. Exptl. Biology and Medicine, N.Y. Acad Sci., Sigma Xi. Research in biochemistry biogenic amines. Home: 400 Main St Evanston IL 60202

ALKER, HAYWARD ROSE, Jr., educator, polit. scientist; b. N.Y.C., Oct. 3, 1937; s. Hayward Rose and Dorothy (Fitzsimmons) A.; B.S., Mass. Inst. Tech., 1959; M.S., Yale, 1960, Ph.D., 1963; m. Judith Ann Tickner, June 3, 1961; children—Joan Christina, Heather Jane, Gwendolyn Ann. Instr. to asso. prof. polit. sci. Yale, 1963-68; vis. prof. U. Mich., 1968; prof. polit. sci. Mass. Inst. Tech., 1968—. Chmn. Math. Social Scis. Bd., 1970-71. Congl. intern Office of Chester Bowles, 1960. Fellow Center for Advanced Studies in Behavioral Scis., Stanford, Cal., 1967-68. Mem. Am. Polit. Sci. Assn., Internat. Studies Assn., Peace Research Soc. Democrat. Author: Mathematics and Politics, 1965; World Handbook of Political and Social Indicators, 1966; (with others) World Politics in the General Assembly, 1966. Bd. editors of Jour. Interdisciplinary History, 1969-71, Internat. Orgn., 1970—. Home: 288 Mill St Newtonville MA 02160 Office: Mass Inst Tech Cambridge MA 02139

ALL, HAROLD RICHARD, former govt. ofcl.; b. Terre Haute, Ind., Sept. 22, 1916; s. Virgil Samuel and Alma (Newby) A.; student Franklin U., 1938; m. Atha Watson Phillips, Feb. 17, 1942; children—Harold Richard, Carol Ann. With Internal Revenue Service, 1945-71, dist. dir., Chgo., 1959-62, regional commr., North Atlantic, 1965-71, ret., 1971. Chmn., Boston Fed. Exec. Bd. 1964-65, also mem. policy com.; mblzn. coordinator region I, Treasury Dept. Served with USAAF, 1939-45. Recipient Outstanding Performance award Internal Revenue Service, 1954. Mason. Home: 1111 Bogey Lane Long Boat Key Sarasota FL 33577

ALLABEN, FRED ROLAND, lawyer; b. Rockford, Ill., Sept. 19, 1901; s. John Elmer and Harriet (Strickland) A.; A.B., U. Mich., 1923, J.D., 1925; m. Apr. 17, 1925 (div.); children—Robert, Dorothy (Mrs. Dale L. Talbert), Lawrence; m. 2d, Leona M. Heise, Oct. 15, 1954; 1 son, John Randolph. Admitted to Mich. bar 1925, U.S. Supreme Ct. bar, 1945, other fed. cts.; of counsel firm Allaben, Massie, Vander Weyden & Timmer, Grand Rapids, Mich.; city atty., Grand Rapids, 1946-48. Chmn. Kent County A.R.C., 1946-47, now hon. life mem. bd. dir. Recipient Distinguished Alumni Service award U. Mich. Alumni Assn., 1953, U. Mich. Alumni accolade, 1954. Fellow Am. Coll. Probate Counsel (past mem. bd regents, treas. 1965-66), Am. Bar Found. (life), Am. Coll. Trial Lawyers; mem. Grand Rapids (pres. 1952-53), Mich. (commr. 1947-50), Am. (ho. of dels. 1950-58; Mich. chmn. Am. Bar Center Project, 1953-54; ins. sect. council, 1949-54) bar assns., Internat. Assn. Ins. Counsel, Assn. Ins. Attys. (gov. 1950-58), Fedn. Ins. Counsel, Judicial Conf. Mich. (dir. 1955-68), Mich. Bar Found. (pres. 1954-68, life mem.), C. of C. (past chmn. better bus. bur. and state affairs com.), U. Mich Alumni Assn. (mem. exec. com., nat. dir. 1940-43), Phi Alpha Delta. Republican. Unitarian. Mason (32, Shriner). Clubs: Barristers, Lawyers (U. Mich.); Michigan Union (life; U. Mich.). Author articles in legal and med. jours. Lectr. law insts. Home: 1662 Wealthy St SE Grand Rapids MI 49506 also 719 Waddell St Key West FL 33040 Office: Federal Square Bldg Grand Rapids MI 49502

ALLABY, STANLEY REYNOLDS, clergyman; b. Providence, Dec. 28, 1931; s. Edwin T. and Hope (Swift) A.; A.B., Gordon Coll., 1953, B.D., 1956; m. Marion Arlene Johnson, Dec. 18, 1954; children—Norman R., Darlene R., Kimberly A., Stephen R. Ordained to ministry, 1956; pastor Black Rock Conglist. Ch., Fairfield, Conn., 1956—. Dir. Sudan Interior Mission, N.Y.C., 1970—. Bd. dirs. United Neighbors for Self Devel., Bridgeport, Conn., 1963-64, Christian Freedom Found., 1960-70; trustee Gordon Coll. and Gordon Divinity Sch., Wenham, Mass., 1965-69. Recipient George Washington honor medal Freedoms Found., 1968, 69. Mem. Gordon Coll. Alumni Assn. (past pres.), Bridgeport Pastors Assn. (past pres.), Greater Bridgeport Fellowship Evangelicals (past pres.). Home: 1371 Bronson Rd Fairfield CT 06430 Office: 3685 Black Rock Turnpike Fairfield CT 06430

ALLAIN, EMERY EDGAR, paper co. exec.; b. Northbridge, Mass., Oct. 22, 1922; s. Emery and Florida (Pelletier) A.; student Bentley Coll., 1939-41, Northeastern U., 1941-43; m. Florance Chabot, Feb. 10, 1945; children—Amy Louise Devlin, John Emery. With Arthur Andersen & Co., C.P.A.'s, Boston and N.Y.C., 1944-49; controller Royal Lace Paper Works, 1949-51, treas., 1951-54; with Great No. Paper Co., 1954—, controller, 1962-68, v.p. finance, 1968—; v.p. finance, treas. Gt. No. Nekoosa Corp., 1970—. C.P.A., Mass., Me. Mem. Am. Inst. C.P.A.'s, Financial Execs. Inst., Am. Accounting Assn., Nat. Assn. Accountants. Club: Cloud Home: 27 Frontier Rd Cos Cob CT 06807 Office: 75 Prospect St Stamford CT 06902

ALLAM, MARK WHITTIER, veterinarian, univ. dean; b. Fernwood, Pa., Aug. 17, 1908; s. Clyde Macfarland and Helen (Hubbard) A.; V.M.D., U. Pa., 1932; m. Lila Josephine Griswold, Apr. 15, 1933; children—Shelley Lee, Maryjane Whittier. Gen. practice vet. medicine, 1932-45; instr. vet. surgery Sch. Vet. Medicine, U. Pa., 1943-45, asst. prof., 1945-48, asso. prof., 1948-51, prof., 1951—, chmn. dept. surgery, 1951-55, research Harrison Dept. Surg. Research, Sch. Medicine, 1947-51, dean of faculty, 1952—; cons. Pan Am. San. Bur., WHO; member medical advisory bd. FDA, 1965-69, mem. vet. med. adv. bd., 1967—; president Pa. Health Council, 1969—; member expert panel on veterinary education FAD-WHO, 1966—. Pres. board of edn. Media Borough Sch. Dist., 1941-60; president Medic Civic Forum, 1964-67. Member Veterinary Medicine Alumni Assn., (pres. 1943), Am. (v.p. 1956), American (member exec. bd. 1958-63), Pa. Keystone veterinary med. assns., N.Y. Acad. Scis., Sigma Xi, Phi Zeta (nat. pres. 1948). Republican Presbyn. Contbr. General Surgery (edited by Hoskins and Lacroix), revised edit., 1953. Author articles in field. Home: 211 E 5th St Media PA 19063 Office: 3800 Spruce St Philadelphia PA 19104

ALLAN, DENISON MAURICE, educator; b. Hull, Eng., Sept. 15, 1897; s. Andrew and Mary Townsend (Mowbray) A.; student Brantford (Can.) Collegiate Inst.; A.B., A.M., Hampden-Sydney (Va.) Coll., 1916; postgrad. Columbia, 5 summers; A.M., Harvard, 1922, Ph.D., 1926; m. Sarah Evelyn Smith, Aug. 10, 1932; children—Denison Mowbray, David Blair. Came to U.S., 1910, naturalized, 1918. Prof. modern langs. Hampden-Sydney Coll., 1920-21, prof. philosophy and psychology, 1923-69, coach debating, 1923-35, dir. Presbyn. Guidance Center, 1970—. Sprunt lectr. Union Theol. Sem., Richmond, 1944. Trustee Union Theol. Sem. in Va., Presbyn. Home, Lynchburg. Mem. adv. council on higher edn. Presbyn. Ch. U.S., mem. gen assembly's com. on homes and orphanages; rep. Va. synod on State Council Chs. Served in C.W.S., U.S. Army, 1918. Mem. A.A.A.S., So. Soc. Philosophy Religion (pres. 1966-67), Am. Philos. Assn., So. Soc. Philosophy and Psychology, Va. Acad. Sci. (pres. 1938), Am. Psychol. Assn., Am. Personnel and Guidance Assn., Phi Beta Kappa, Sigma Upsilon, Tau Kappa Alpha, Chi Beta Pi, Sigma Chi, Omicron Delta Kappa. Democrat. Presbyn. Author: The Realm of Personality; co-author: Church and Campus. Contbr. to psychol., philos. jours. Asso. editor Presbyn. Outlook. Home: Hampden-Sydney VA 23943

ALLAN, DONALD ASPINWALL, journalist; b. Washington, Dec. 6, 1922; s. Carlisle Visscher and Margaret Scovill (Aspinwall) A.; B.A., Stanford, 1946; m. Margary Emlay, Aug. 21, 1943 (div. 1956); children—Eve, Cathenne MacGregor, Scovill Viescher Aspinwall; m. 2d, Wanda Malinowska, Apr. 24, 1956 (div. 1963); 1 son, David Masson; m. 3d, Alexandra Temple Emmet, Feb. 19, 1963; 1 son, Peter Cushing. Reporter, Redwood City (Cal.) Tribune, 1946- 47, San Francisco News, 1947-48; U.P. corr., Madrid, Paris, then bur. chief, Brussels, 1948-51; reporter N.Y. Times, 1951-52; Rome corr. Newsweek mag., 1953-55; mng. editor N.Am. Newspaper Alliance, 1956-58, editor, 1958-59; sr. editor Coronet mag., 1959-61; mem. staff Reporter, 1961-68, mng. editor, 1964-68; fgn. editor Sat. Eve. Post, N.Y.C., 1968-69. Served to 1st lt., bombardier USAAF, 1942-43. Decorated D.F.C., Air medal with 3 oak leaf clusters, Purple Heart with oak leaf cluster. Mem. S.A.R., Sigma Delta Chi, Alpha Delta Phi. Democrat. Episcopalian. Club: Overseas Press (N.Y.C.). Contbr. articles nat. magazines. Home: 186 E 75th St New York City NY 10021

ALLAN, FRANK NATHANIEL, physician; b. Proton, Ont., Can., Dec. 26, 1899; s. George and Margaret Jane (Ewing) A.; M.B., U. Toronto, 1922, B. Sc. in Medicine, 1924, M.D. cum laude with award of Starr Silver Medal, 1928; m. Lillian Hunter Christie, September 22, 1934; one daughter, Margaret Christie (Mrs. W. Stephen Piper). Junior member of staff, dept. physiology, U. Toronto, 1922-25; intern Toronto Gen. Hosp., 1924-25; fellow medicine Mayo Clinic, Rochester, Minn., 1925-26, staff, 1927-32; instr. medicine Mayo Found., U. Minn., 1928-32; hon. physician N.E. Bapt. Hosp., Boston City Hosp., New England Deaconess Hosp., Boston; co-dir. med. dept. Lahey Clinic, Boston, 1932-47, exec. dir., chmn., 1948-65; asso. clin. prof. med. Boston U., 1961—; clin, prof. of medicine Georgetown U., 1966—; sr. cons. U.S. FDA, 1965—. Awarded Banting medal Am. Diabetes Assn., 1953. Diplomate Am. Bd. Internal Medicine. Fellow A.C.P., A.A.A.S.; mem. A.M.A., Greater Boston Diabetes Soc. (chmn. exec. com. 1961-63), Am. (pres. 1952-53), New England (president 1951-52, honorary president 1968- -, Joslin medal 1969) diabetes associations, Acad. of Medicine Washington, American Society Clin. Investigation, Am. Soc. Exptl. Pathology, Endocrine Soc., Internat., Am., Mass. socs. internal medicine, Canadian Diabetic Assn. (hon.), Central Soc., Clin. Research, Academia Nacional de Medicina Buenos Aires (hon.), Sigma Xi, Alpha Omega Alpha. Conglist. (moderator). Clubs: Brae Burn Country, Skating of Boston (gov. 1965-68). Editor: Diabetes jour., 1951-55, now adv. editor; editorial bd. New Eng. Jour. Medicine, 1952-68, dep. editor, 1965-66. Author med., sci. articles. Mem. exec. com. Internat. Congress Internal Medicine 1958. Home: 44 Barnstable Rd West Newton Boston MA 02165 Office: FDA Washington DC 20204

ALLAN, HARRY THAIN, univ. dean; b. Saugus, Mass., Aug. 12, 1928; s. William Thain and Florence Louise (Horswell) A.; B.A., Washington and Jefferson Coll., 1953, Mass. Inst. Tech., 1953; J.D., U. Chgo., 1956; postgrad. Carnegie Inst. Tech., 1962-63; m. T. Jane Haught, July 4, 1952; children—Linda J., William H. Well logging engr. Hycalog Co., Sheveport, La., 1952-53; indsl. engr. R.R. Donnelley & Sons Co., Chgo, 1953-55; instr. Ill. Inst. Tech., 1955-56; instr. to asso. prof. Ore. State U., 1956-65; from asso. prof. to prof. U. Mass., 1965-70; dean Sch. Mgmt., Syracuse U., 1970—. Alt. county chmn. Benton County (Ore.) Dem. Central Com., 1964-65; town moderator, Amherst, Mass., 1969-70. Served with AUS, 1946-47. Mem. Am., Ore. bar assns., Am. Bus. Law Assn., Law and Society Assn., Inst. Mgmt. Scis., World Peace Through Law Center, Unitarian-Universalist Assn. Author: (with H. Richard Hartzler) An Introduction to Law: a Functional Approach, 1969. Managerial law editor Am. Bus. Law Jour., 1965-70. Contbr. articles profl. jours. Home: 847 Oakwood St Fayetteville NY 13066 Office: Syracuse Univ Syracuse NY 13210

ALLAN, JOHN HAMILTON, physician; b. Stamford, Conn., Oct. 4, 1907; s. Charles Hamilton and Ann (Patterson) A.; A.B., Johns Hopkins, 1929; M.D., 1933; m. Dorothy Allen Boyd, Jan. 24, 1942; children—David Laird, Susan Blair. Intern, Union Meml. Hosp., Balt., 1934-36; resident physician Princeton, 1936-37; resident orthopaedic surgeon N.Y. Orthopaedic Hosp., 1937-39; orthopaedic surgeon, Phila, 1940-43, 46-50; prof. orthopaedic surgery U. Va. Sch. Orthopaedics, Charlottesville, 1950—, chmn. dept., 1950-67. Served with M.C., USNR, 1942-46; PTO; capt. Res. Fellow A.C.S.; mem. Am. Acad. Orthopaedic Surgeons, Am. Orthopedic Assn., So. Surg. Assn., Delta Upsilon. Home: Ednam Forest Charlottesville VA 22901

ALLAN, ROBERT MOFFAT, Jr., bus. educator, investor; b. Detroit, Dec. 8, 1920; s. Robert M. and Jane (Christman) A.; A.B., Stanford, 1941, postgrad. Bus. Sch., 1941; postgrad. U. Cal., 1942-43, Loyola U., Sch. Law, Los Angeles, 1947-51; m. Harriet Spirer, Nov. 28, 1942; children—Robert Moffatt III, Scott, David, Marilee. Marine sec. Founders Ins. Co., 1947-50; v.p. Zinsco Elec. Products Co., 1950-59; v.p. Times Mirror Co., Los Angeles, 1959-64; pres., dir. Cyprus Mines Corp., Los Angeles, 1965-67; pres. Litton Internat. Devel. Corp.; corporate v.p. Litton Industries; mng. dir. Litton Benelux, Belgium, 1967-71; dir. now prof. mgmt. U.S. Naval Postgrad. Sch., Monterey, Cal.; Internat. Rectifier, Regional head Intercollegiate Yachting Assn., 1940-71, Olympic Games Yachting Com., 1959-60. Trustee Anatolia Coll., Greece, Boys Republic. Served from pvt. to maj. USAAF, 1941-45. Recipient award for service to yachting, service to jrs. Helms Athletic Found., 1947-49. Outstanding So. Cal. Businessman, 1966; Man of Year award Greek Am. Soc., 1968. Mem. Inst. Mgmt. Scis., Newcomen Soc., Phi Gamma Delta, Phi Delta Phi. Episcopalian. Mason. Clubs: Newport Harbor Yacht (comdr. 1960-61) (Newport Beach, Cal.); El Dorado Country; Trans Pacific Yacht; N.Y. Yacht (N.Y.C.). Home: 977 Ocean Rd Pebble Beach CA 93953 Office: 1 Management Systems Center Naval Postgrad School Monterey CA 93940

ALLAN, WALTER SCOTT, insurance co. exec.; b. Saugus, Mass., May 30, 1913; s. Walter S. and Lena (Boynton) A.; B.A., Clark U., 1935; m. Leah Clapp, Aug. 21, 1937; children—Donald, Walter S. With claims dept., later med. and rehab. services div. Liberty Mut. Ins. Co., 1935-59, asst. v.p., mgr. med. services, 1959-64, asst. v.p. pub. relations, 1964—. Pres. Am. Hearing Soc., 1963; bd. dirs., exec. com., chmn. rehab. policy com. Nat. Rehab. Assn., pres., 1966; bd. dirs., exec. com. Nat. Health Council; nat. adv. council Nat. Soc. Crippled Children and Adults; trustee, 1st v.p. Easter Seal Soc. Mass.; mem. Nat. Citizens Adv. Com. on Vocational Rehab.; chmn. Vocational Rehab. Planning Commn.; mem. Adv. Com. on Health Protection and Disease Protection to Sec. Dept. Health, Edn. and Welfare, Presdl. Task Force on Problems Physically Handicapped. Served to lt. (s.g.) USNR, 1943-46. Recipient President's award Nat. Rehab. Assn., 1960, Goodwill award Goodwill Industries Am., 1961. Mem. Pub. Relations Soc. Am., U.S. C. of C. (ins. com.), Phi Beta Kappa. Author:

Rehabilitation-A Community Challenge, 1958. Home: Box 59 Canterbury NH 03224 also 55 Clark Rd Brookline MA 02146 Office: 175 Berkeley St Boston MA 02117

ALLAN, WILLIAM, ins. co. exec.; b. Holyoke, Mass., Nov. 26, 1911; s. Joseph K. and Sophie (Donaldson) A.; B.A., Amherst Coll., 1933; m. Christine K. Cameron, July 17, 1937; 1 dau., Judith C. With Home Life Ins. Co., N.Y.C., 1933—, v.p., actuary 1967-69, sr. v.p., 1969—; v.p. HLI Corp.; dir. Home Life Ins. Co., Home Life Equity Fund, Inc., Home Life Equity Sales Corp., DECO Corp. Fellow Soc. Actuaries, Am. Acad. Actuaries; mem. Math. Assn. Am., mem. N.Y. C. of C., Newcomen Soc. N.Am., Phi Beta Kappa, Phi Kappa Psi. Presbyn. (elder, trustee). Clubs: Amherst (N.Y.C.); Coveleigh (Rye). Home: 532 Harrison Av Harrison NY 10528 Office: 258 Broadway New York City NY 10007

ALLAN, WILLIAM, educator; C.E., Poly. Inst. Bklyn., 1924, M.C.E., 1932. Prof. emeritus civil engring., dean emeritus Sch. Engring., City U. N.Y. Registered profl. engr., N.Y. Address: City Univ NY Convent Av at 138th St New York City, NY 10031.*

ALLAN, WILLIAM ALEXANDER, features editor; b. Turtle Creek, Pa., May 4, 1924; s. Alexander Malcolm and Isabel (Young) A.; student U. Va., 1943; B.S. in Physics and Journalism, U. Pitts., 1949; m. Rita McEvoy, Mar. 17, 1951; children—William Alexander, Jeffrey, Marianne. With McKeesport (Pa.) Daily News, 1947-51; with Pitts. Press, 1951—, bus. and financial editor, 1963-70, features editor, 1970—. Served with USAAF, 1943-45; ETO Decorated Air medal; Croix de Guerre (France); recipient Golden Quill award bus. writing Pitts. chpt. Sigma Delta Chi and Pitts. Press Club, 1966. Home: 26 McKelvey Av Pittsburgh, PA 15218. Office: Pittsburgh Press Pittsburgh PA 15230

ALLARD, CLAUDE HENRY, rubber co. exec.; b. Lowell, Mass., Jan. 5, 1921; s. Joseph J. and Cora (Pratt) A.; B.S. in Chemistry, Lowell Tech. Inst., 1947; m. Eleanor Martin, Apr. 19, 1944; children—Charles D., Joseph, James, Philip, Julia, Edward. With U.S. Rubber Co., 1947—, asst. gen. mgr. textile div., 1963-64, v.p., gen. mgr. 1964-66, v.p. Uniroyal Inc., 1967—, pres. Uniroyal Internal. div., 1967-70, pres. Uniroyal Tire div., 1970—. Mem. Mat. Fgn. Trade Council (dir.), Rubber Export Assn. (dir.), Internat. Road Fedn. (dir.). Served with AUS, 1942-46. Home: 130 Mill Rd Stamford, CT 06903. Office: 1230 Av Americas New York City NY 10020

ALLARD, JEAN MCGUIRE (Mrs. Robert Allard), lawyer; b. Trenton, Mo., Dec. 16, 1924; d. Ben J. and Marion (Watson) McGuire; A.B., Culver-Stockton Coll., 1945; A.M., Washington U., St. Louis, 1947; J.D., U. Chgo., 1953; m. Robert Allard, Sept. 9, 1945; 1 son, John Preston. Dept. counselor, psychology dept. U. Chgo., 1948-51, research asso. Law Sch., 1953-58, asst. dean, 1956-58; admitted to Ill. bar, 1953, Ohio bar, 1959; asso. firm Fuller, Harrington, Seney & Henry, Toledo, 1958-59, Lord, Bissell & Brook, Chgo., 1959-62; sec., gen. counsel Maremont Corp., Chgo., 1962—. Mem. Am., Ill., Chgo. bar assns., Am. Soc. Corporate Secs. Home: 2231 E 67th St Chicago IL 60649 Office: 168 N Michigan Av Chicago IL 60601

ALLARD, JEAN VICTOR, ret. Canadian army officer; b. Nicolet, Que., Can., June 12, 1913; s. Ernest and Victorine (Trudel) A.; student St. Laurent Coll., Montreal, Can., St. Jerome Coll., Kitchener, Ont.; D.Sc., Laval U., 1938; LL.D., U. Ottawa, St. Mary's U., Halifax, N.S., 1969; D. Mil. Service (hon.), Royal Mil. Coll., Kingston, Ont., 1970; m. Simone Piche, 1939; children—Michele (Mrs. J. Lajeunesse), Andree. Commd. in Canadian Army, 1939, advanced through grades to gen., 1966; assigned Mediterranean Theater, also N.W. Europe, 1939- 45; Canadian mil. attaché, Moscow, 1945-47; vice Q.M.G., Army Hdqrs., Ottawa, 1951-53; comdr. 25th Canadian Inf. Brigade Group, Korea, 1953, 3d Canadian Inf. Brigade, 1954-56; comdr. Eastern Que. area, Quebec City, 1948-50, 56-58; vice chief Gen. Staff, Canadian Army Hdqrs., Ottawa, 1958-61; comdr. 4th (Brit.) div., Herford, Germany, 1961-63; maj.-gen. Survival Army Hdqrs., Ottawa 1963-64, chief operational readiness, 1964-65; comdr. Canadian Mobile Command, chief Def. Staff, 1966-69; ret., 1969; P.Q. rep. in N.Y., 1969-70; pvt. bus., Montreal, 1970—. Mem., former chmn. bd. govs. U. Ottawa. Decorated Distinguished Service Order, 1943, 1st bar, 1944, 2d bar, 1945; comdr. Order Brit. Empire, 1946; Legion of Merit (U.S.), 1954; Legion of Honor, Croix de Guerre (France); Bronze Lion (Holland). Fellow Royal Soc. Arts. Clubs: Le Cercle Universitaire (Ottawa); Garrison, Winter (Quebec); Mount Royal, Canadian (Montreal); Laval-sur-le-Lac Golf. Home: Casa Belvedere 251 Chemin du Sommet Bleu Ste Adele Quebec Canada Office: 1015 Beaver Hall Hill Montreal 128 Quebec Canada

ALLARD, JOSEPH, musical educator; b. Lowell, Mass., Dec. 31, 1910; s. Joseph J. and Cora G. (Pratt) A.: student New Eng. Conservatory, 1928; m. Marian Maynard, Oct. 12, 1934. Played saxaphone and clarinet with Red Nichols, 1936; appeared on radio shows Bell Telephone Hour, Andre Kostelanetz, DuPont Cavalcade of Am., several others; saxophone soloist with N.Y. Philharmonic Orch.; prin. clarinetist Bell Telephone TV Show; bass clarinet with NBC Symphony under Toscanini; mem. saxaphone and clarinet faculty Juilliard Sch. Music, 1956—, N.Y.U., 1960—, Columbia Tchrs. Coll., 1956—. Author: Three Octave Scales and Chords, 1947; (transcription) 60 Divertimenti Exercises by Gallucci, 1960. Home: 134 Downey Dr Tenafly NJ 07670 Office: Carnegie Hall 154 W 57th St New York City NY 10019

ALLARD, ROMEO PAUL, educator; b. Franklin, N.H., Nov. 13, 1906; s. Joseph and Marie Louise (LeBlanc) A.; B.S., U. Notre Dame, 1931, M.S., 1932, Ph. D., 1934; m. Anne Marie Dahlem, Dec. 27, 1933; children—William Joseph, Bernard Paul, Mary Ann. Instr. in chemistry, Loyola U. of Los Angeles, asst. prof., prof., chmn. dept. chemistry, 1937—, former dean Coll. Sci. Mem. Am. Chem. Soc., Am. Inst. Chemists. Elk. Home: 4131 Madison Av Culver City CA 90230 Office: Loyola U Los Angeles CA 90045

ALLARD, WILLIAM ALBERT, photographer, writer; b. Mpls., Sept. 30, 1937; s. George Axel and Wilhelmina (Dunbar) A.; student Mpls. Sch. Fine Arts, 1959-60; B.S. in Journalism and Art, U. Minn., 1964; m. Mary Kay Burns, Oct. 5, 1957; children—Scott William, Christine Kay, Theresa Ann, David Douglas. Photographer Nat. Geog. mag. 1964-67; now free-lance photographer; exhbns. include Met. Mus. Art, George Eastman House, Rochester, N.Y. Runnerup Mag. photographer of Year, 1965, 67; Grand award White House News Photographers Assn., 1969. Home and office: Barboursville VA

ALLARI, EVERETT CONWAY, constrn. co. exec.; b. San Francisco, Jan. 4, 1912; s. Herman and Clarice May (Smith) A.; grad. bus. adminstrn., U. Cal. at Berkeley, 1932; m. Neil Marie Goforth, July 30, 1933; children—Robert, Ronald. Dept. mgr. Crocker First Nat. Bank, San Francisco, 1932-37; field auditor Alaska Juneau Gold Mining Co., San Francisco, 1937-41; sec.-treas. Barker Corp., Stockton, Cal., 1941-56; asst. v.p., treas. Williams & Burrows Inc., Belmont, Cal., 1956—; asst. sec., treas. G.W. Williams Co., Belmont, 1956—; controller Am. Homes Devel. Co., Belmont, 1956—; asst. sec., treas. Am. Home Co., Belmont, 1956—, El Camino Apt. Co., 1956—. Bd. dirs. Vis. Nurses Assn., Redwood City, Cal., Sequoia Union High Sch. Dist. Edn., Redwood City, G.W. Williams Found.; trustee Lincoln Sch. Dist., Stockton, 1949-56. Mem. Financial Execs. Inst., Nat. Assn. Accountants. Republican. Presbyn. (elder). Mason (Shriner), Elk, Rotarian. Home: 1504 Edgewood Rd Redwood City CA 94062 Office: 500 Harbour Blvd Belmont CA 94002

ALLAWAY, HOWARD, editor; b. Homer, Neb., Jan. 3, 1912; s. James and Mary (Adams) A.; A.B., U. Neb., 1933; M.Sc., Columbia, 1935; m. Jean Dix, Aug. 13, 1938; children—Betsy, James, Thomas. With Asso. Press, N.Y.C., 1936-40; picture editor, city editor, news editor PM, N.Y.C., 1940-48; asso. editor Popular Sci. Monthly, 1948-50, mng. editor, 1951-57, editor, 1957- 62; mng. editor Consumer Reports mag., Mount Vernon, N.Y., 1962-63; asst. to Sunday editor N.Y. Times, 1950-51; dep. dir., tech. publs. div. NASA, 1963-64, dep. Dir. sci. and tech. information div., 1965-66, pub. affairs officer, 1966—. President board education, Stamford, Conn., 1957-58; mem. bd. finance, Stamford, 1960-63. Served as lt. (s.g.) USNR, 1943-45. Mem. Council Advancement Science Writing, Phi Beta Kappa, Sigma Delta Chi. Home: 612 G St SW Washington DC 20024 Office: Office Pub Affairs NASA Washington DC 20546

ALLAWAY, WILLIAM HUBERT, educator, soil scientist; b. Homer, Neb., Apr. 12, 1916; s. James and Mary Ellen (Adams) A.; B.S., U. Neb., 1938, D.Sc., 1971; M.S., Ia. State U., 1939, Ph.D., 1945; m. Mildred Eloise Holland, Nov. 12, 1939; children—Susan Mary, William Hubert, Nancy Jane. Asst. prof. agronomy U. Neb., 1943-45; prof. soils Ia. State U., 1945-50; soil sci., agrl. adminstr. Dept. Agr., Beltsville, Md., 1950-60; soil sci., dir. U.S. Plant, Soil and Nutrition Lab., prof. soils agronomy dept. Cornell U., Ithaca, N.Y., 1960—. Mem. Sci. Exchange delegation to USSR, 1958. Fellow Am. Soc. Agronomy (Soil Sci. Achievement award 1971), A.A.A.S. (council 1960—); mem. Am. Chem. Soc., Soil Sci. Soc. Am., Animal Sci. Soc. Am. Home: Route 2 Ithaca NY 14850

ALLBECK, WILLARD DOW, educator; b. Millville, Pa., Oct. 5, 1898; s. Montraville McHenry and Lida Belle (Schwartz) A.; A.B., Susquehanna U., 1919, D.D., 1941; B.D., Hamma Divinity Sch., Springfield, O., 1925, S.T.M., 1932; A.M., U. Pittsburgh, 1928, Ph.D., 1936; m. Marie L. Neve, June 6, 1923. Ordained to ministry Evangelical Lutheran Ch., 1922; pastor, St. John's Luth. Ch., Highland Parish, Pitts., 1922-37; prof. historical theology Hamma Div. Sch., 1937-67, prof. emeritus, 1967—. Trustee Thiel Coll., 1935-37. Mem. Am. Soc. Church History. Mem. Lutheran Church in America (member commn. on church papers; archivist, Synod of Ohio, 1949- 62). Author: History of the Lutheran Church in America (with J. L. Neve), 1934; Theology at Wittenberg, 1945; Studies in the Lutheran Confessions, 1952, 2d edit., 1968; A Century of Lutherans in Ohio, 1966. Contbr. numerous articles in religious and theol. jours. Home: 1341 N Plum St Springfield OH 45504

ALLBRITTEN, FRANK F., Jr., physician, surgeon, educator; b. Cunningham, Kan., Dec. 1, 1914; s. Frank F. and Frances E. (Grier) A.; A.B., U. Kan., 1935; M.D., U. Pa., 1938; m. Marjorie Clarkson Batley, May 24, 1940; children—Nancy Grier, Cynthia Clarkson, Marjorie Annette, Frank F., III, Martha Louise. Intern, U. Pa. Hosp., 1938-40; surg. resident Pa. Hosp., 1940-43, adj., 1950-54; asso. prof. surgery Jefferson Med. Coll., 1952-54; asst. surgeon Jefferson Med. Coll. Hosp., 1947-52, surg. dir. Barton Meml. div., 1947-54; prof. surgery, chmn. dept. U Kan. Med. Center, Kansas City, 1954-70, prof. surgery, 1970—; cons. thoracic surgery Valley Forge Army Hosp., 1947-54, cardiovascular surgery Phila. Naval Hosp., 1951-54, thoracic surgery Phila. VA Hosp., 1953-54, VA Hosps., Kansas City, Mo., 1954—, Wichita, Kan., 1955-65; cons. U.S. Army Hosp., Leavenworth, Kan., 1958-68. Served from lt. maj. M.C., AUS, 1943-46. Diplomate Am. Bd. Surgery, Am. Bd. Thoracic Surgery. Fellow A.C.S.; mem. A.M.A., Soc. Clin. Surgery, Soc. U. Surgeons, Am. Assn. Thoracic Surgery, A.A.A.S., Am., Western, Central surg. assns., Am. Assn. Surg. Trauma, Sigma Xi, Alpha Omega Alpha. Home: 9321 Catalina Shawnee Mission KS 66207 Office: U Kan Med Center Kansas City KS 66103

ALLBRITTEN, HERBERT GRAVES, educator; b. Murray, Ky., Apr. 26, 1911; s. Bluford Seymour and Nancy Ann (Winchester) A.; B.S., Murray State U., 1931; M.S., U. Ky., 1941; Ph.D., Pa. State U., 1951; m. Martha B. Harris, Dec. 26, 1939; 1 son, James Franklin. High sch. sci. tchr., 1932-36; soil surveyor U.S. Dept. Agr., S.W., 1941-42; ordnance tng. Picatinny Arsenal, 1942; asst. chief insp. ordnance, 1942-43, civilian instr. ordnance, Ft. Knox, 1944-46; research and extension agronomist R.I. Agrl. Expt. Sta., 1947-50; research agronomist, soil chemist S.C. Agrl. Expt. Sta., 1951-59; prof. soils and crops Murray State U., 1959-63, asso. prof., 1963-68; prof. soil chemistry Memphis State U., 1968—; research soil chemistry and tech., plant nutrition, pesticides related to chlorinated hydrocarbons. Fellow Am. Inst. Chemists; mem. Am. Chem. Soc., Soil Sci. Soc. Am., Am. Inst. Chemists, A.A.A.S., Tenn. Acad. Sci., Sigma Xi, Gamma Sigma Delta, Alpha Zeta, Chi Beta Phi. Democrat. Contbr. articles profl. jours. Home: 4217 Paula Dr Memphis TN 38116

ALLBRITTEN, LEO TAYLOR, coll. dean; b. San Antonio, Nov. 20, 1909; s. James William and Mary Elizabeth (Taylor) A.; A.B., Southwestern U., 1930; M.A., U. Tex., 1936; Ed. D., Colo. State Coll., 1946; vis. scholar, Columbia Tchrs. Coll., summer, 1958; m. Blanche Louise Burbank Aug. 22, 1937; 1 son, William Lee. Prin. Deweyville (Tex.) High Sch., 1930-36; head dept. edn. Brownsville (Tex.) Jr. Coll., 1936-42; supr. secondary social studies Colo. State Coll., 1942-43; asst. prof. psychology, dir. vets. affairs, 1945-46; mem. faculty Northwestern State Coll. La., 1946—, dean Grad. Sch., 1954—, dean instrn., 1959-67. Chmn. So. dist. Norwela area council Boy Scouts of America, 1958-62, vice president Norwela council, 1963-64. Served with AUS, 1943-45. Mem. So. Assn. Colls. and Schs. (commn. secondary schs. 1953-59), Phi Kappa Phi, Pi Kappa Delta, Phi Delta Kappa, Kappa Delta Pi. Kiwanian (pres. Natchitoches 1948). Home: 315 S Court Dr Natchitoches LA 71457

ALLBRITTON, JOE LEWIS, lawyer, ins. co. exec.; b. D'Lo, Miss., Dec. 29, 1924; s. Lewis A. and Ada (Carpenter) A.; LL.B., Baylor U., 1949, LL.D. (hon.), 1964, J.D., 1969; m. Barbara Jean Balfanz, Feb. 23, 1967; 1 son, Robert Lewis. Admitted to Tex. bar, 1949, since practice in Houston, 1949—; mem. firm Clawson, Allbritton & Clawson, 1950-53, Allbritton, McGee & Hand, 1961-64; chmn. bd., chief exec. officer Pierce Nat. Life Ins. Co., 1958—; chmn. bd. Pierce Bros., 1958-66, dir., 1958—, Perpetual Corp., 1958—(all Los Angeles); chmn. bd. Mineral Oil Refining Co., Dickinson, Tex., 1963-68; pres., dir. San Jacinto Savs. Assn., 1956-68, dir. Bank of Southwest Nat. Assn., 1964-69, exec. com., 1965-69, chmn. exec. com., dir. Houston Bank & Trust Co., 1969-70; pres., chief exec. officer, dir. Houston Citizens Bank & Trust Co., 1970—; dir. Citizens State Bank, 1961-63; dir. Southwestern Pub. Service Co., Dallas, 1965—. Mem. Hosp. Adv. Council, Tex. Dept. Health, 1965-66, Fgn. Mission Bd., So. Bapt. Conv., Richmond, Va., 1966—. Trustee Baylor U., 1959-68, mem. exec. com., 1960-68, vice chmn. bd., 1965-68; trustee Baylor U. Coll. Medicine, Houston, 1959-68, chmn., 1965-68. Served with USNR, 1943-46. Recipient Distinguished Alumni award Pi Kappa Delta, 1963. Mem. Am., Houston bar assns., State Bar Tex., Am. Judicature Soc., Pi Kappa Delta. Baptist (chmn. trustees 1953—). Home: Warwick Hotel Houston TX 77001 Office: Houston Citizens Bank Bldg Houston TX 77002

ALLDAY, MARTIN LEWIS, Jr., lawyer; b. El Dorado, Ark., May 30, 1926; s. Martin Lewis and Bess (Kavanaugh) A.; LL.B., U. Tex., 1951; m. Patricia Pryor, May 1, 1954; children—Katherine Anne, Elizabeth Graham, Martin Lewis III. Admitted to Tex. bar, 1951; legal examiner oil and gas div. R.R. Commn. of Tex., Austin, 1951-53; atty. legal dept. Superior Oil Co., Midland, Tex., 1953-57, Houston, 1957-59; partner firm Lynch, Chappell, Allday & Culp, Midland, 1959—.Vice pres. United Fund Midland County, 1967; dir. adv. bd. Salvation Army, 1967. State campaign chmn. for George Bush Republican senatorial campaign, 1964. Served with AUS, 1944-46. Decorated Purple Heart medal. Mem. Am., Tex., Midland, Midland County (past v.p., dir.) bar assns., Midland Jr. (past pres.), Midland (past pres., dir.) chambers commerce. Episcopalian (sr. warden, lay reader). Club: Midland Country (past pres.). Home: 2409 Humble St Midland TX 79701 Office: 201 Wall Towers E Midland TX 79701

ALLDREDGE, LEROY ROMNEY, geophysicist; b. Mesa, Ariz., Feb. 6, 1917; s. Leo and Ida (Romney) A.; B.S., U. Ariz., 1939, M.S., 1940; M.Sc. in Engring., Harvard; 1953; Ph.D., U. Md., 1955; m. Larita Williams, Dec. 27, 1940; children—Carol, David Leroy, Joseph Leo, Gary Dean, Mark Evans, Janice, Luann. Instr. physics U. Ariz., 1940-41; fed. radio insp. FCC, Los Angeles, also Washington, 1941-44; radio engr. dept. terrestrial magnetism Carnegie Inst. of Washington, 1944-45; chief electricity and magnetism div. Naval Ordnance Lab., White Oak, Md., 1945-55; analyst operations research office Johns Hopkins, 1955-59; research geophysicist Coast and Geodetic Survey, Dept. Commerce, Washington, 1959-66, acting dir. Inst. Earth Scis., Environmental Sci. Services Adminstrn., Boulder, Colo., 1966, dir. Earth Sciences Labs., 1967—; gen. sec., dir. central bur. Internat. Assn. Geomagnetism and Aeronomy, 1964—. Mem. Am. Geophys. Union (sect. on geomagnetism and seronomy 1950-56, v.p. sect. 1956-59, pres. sect. 1959-61, chmn. Eastern meeting com. 1962-66), Sigma Xi, Phi Kappa Phi. Mem. Ch. of Jesus Christ of Latter-day Saints. Asso. editor Jour. Geophys. Research, 1966-69. Home: 4475 Chippewa Dr Boulder CO 80303 Office: NOAA Environmental Research Labs Earth Scis Labs Boulder CO 80302

ALLDREDGE, MELVIN WILSON, ret. food chain store exec.; b. Mt. Vernon, Ind., Sept. 30, 1911; s. Elijah E. and Hannah (Webb) A.; student U. Evansville, 1930-31, U. Louisville, 1938-39, Butler U., 1954-55; LL.D., U. Evansville, Bethany Coll.; m. Mary Elizabeth Roeder, May 20, 1931; children—Beverly, Shirley Mae (Mrs. Joseph Gerdenich), Melvin C., Stephen C. With Great Atlantic & Pacific Tea Co. Inc., 1931—, pres. central div., Pitts., 1960-62, pres. company, 1963-64, vice chmn. bd., 1964-66, chairman of the board, 1966- -, chief executive officer, 1968—. Mem. bd. trustees John A. Hartford Found., Com. Econ. Devel. Mem. Nat. Assn. Food Chains (dir.). Clubs: Sky, Siwanoy, Economic of New York. Home: Naples FL Office: 420 Lexington Av New York City 10017

ALLEBAUGH, CARL FRANKLIN, lawyer; b. nr. Findlay, O., Dec. 9, 1896; s. Edwin Mc. and Mary C. (Welty) A.; student Ohio U., 1916-18; LL.B., Ohio State U., 1922; m. Helen H. Hutterly, June 20, 1928; 1 dau., Mary Carol (Mrs. Theodore Barna). Admitted to Ohio bar, 1922; practice in Steubenville, 1924—; mem. bd. commrs. on grievances and discipline Supreme Ct. Ohio 1960-65. Chmn. Steubenville Community Chest, 1940-41; chmn. Jefferson County chpt. A.R.C., World War II. Pres. YMCA, Steubenville Automobile Club. Served with USAAF, World War I. Named Boss of Year, Steubenville chpt. Nat. Secs. Assn., 1967. Fellow Ohio Bar Assn.; mem. Am. Bar Assn., Nat. Assn. R.R. Trial Counsel, Internat. Assn. Ins. Counsel, Steubenville C. of C. (past pres.); Delta Tau Delta. Mason, Rotarian, Elk. Home: 305 South Bend Blvd Steubenville OH 43952 Office: Sinclair Bldg Stuebenville OH 43952

ALLEE, JOHN PERCY, lawyer; b. Greencastle, Ind., Nov. 9, 1899; s. Albert W. and Bertha (Rector) A.; student DePauw U., 1918-19, U.S. Naval Acad., 1919-21; LL.B., Columbia, 1924; m. Dorothy Cooper, June 23, 1941; children—John S., Charles P., Dennis H. Admitted to N.Y. bar, 1926, since practiced in N.Y.C.; partner Carter, Ledyard & Milburn, 1939—, sr. partner, 1950—. Mem. Assn. Bar N.Y.C., Phi Kappa Psi. Clubs: University, Metropolitan, Downtown Association (N.Y.C.) Home: Redding Ridge CT 06876 Office: 2 Wall St New York City NY 10005

ALLEGRO, JOHN MARCO, author, scholar; b. London, Eng., Feb. 17, 1923; s. John Marco and Mabel (Perry) A.; B.A. with honors, Manchester U., 1951, M.A., 1952; postgrad. Magdalen Coll. of Oxford U., 1952-53; m. Joan Ruby Lawrence, June 17, 1948; children—Judith Anne, John Mark. Brit. rep. on internat. editing team for Dead Sea Scrolls, Jerusalem, 1953—; adviser to Jordanian Govt. on Dead Sea Scrolls, 1961—; lectr. comparative Semitic philology, Hebrew, and O.T. studies, 1954-70; leader archaeol. expdns. to Jordan; lectr., broadcaster. Trustee, sec. Dead Sea Scrolls Fund, 1962-70. Served with Royal Navy, 1941-46. Recipient Bles Hebrew prize, 1950, Scarborough sr. studentship, 1951-54, Leverhulme research award, 1958. Mem. Soc. O.T. Study, Glasgow U. Oriental Soc., Soc. Authors. Author: The Dead Sea Scrolls, rev. edit., 1964; The People of the Dead Sea Scrolls, 1958; The Treasure of the Copper Scroll, rev. ed., 1964), Search in the Desert, 1964; The Shapira Affair, 1964; Discoveries in the Judean Desert, Vol. V, 1968; The Sacred Mushroom and the Cross, 1970; The End of a Road, 1970; The Chosen People, 1971. Home: The Old Parsonage St Mark's Isle of Man British Isles

ALLEMANG, PAUL VERNON, paper products mfr.; b. South Bend, Ind., Aug. 1, 1914; s. George William and Effie May (Fishburn) A.; student U. Notre Dame, 1936-37; B.S. in Mech. Engring., Purdue U., 1939; m. Dorothy Conway, May 11, 1940; children—Michael C., Paula A., Sue H., Melissa M., Timothy J. With Internat. Harvester Co., 1939-41; partner Stevenson, Jordan & Harrison, Inc., 1941-57; exec. v.p., dir. Westab, Inc., 1957-61, pres., dir., 1961- 68; exec. v.p. Mead Corp., 1968—, also dir. Mem. Phi Delta Theta. Home: 1115 Oakwood Av Dayton OH 45419 also 4769 Northwood Rd Glen Arbor MI Office: PO Box 768 Dayton OH 45402

ALLEMANO, PETER HENRY, govt. ofcl.; b. Fayette City, Pa., Feb. 4, 1913; s. Ralph and Emily (Girardi) A.; B.S., Carnegie Inst. Tech., 1935; M.A., George Washington U., 1961; m. Irene Prentice, May 2, 1943; children—Eric, Ralph, Peter Henry. Indsl. specialist WPB, Washington, 1942-45; instr. Carnegie Inst. Tech., 1935-41; edn. officer Latin Am. div. Dept. State, 1946—; mem. Latin Am. area study program Georgetown U. Grad. Sch., Washington, 1960. Address: Am Embassy Buenos Aires Argentina

ALLEN, ANITA FORD, govt. ofcl.; b. Washington, Feb. 13, 1925; d. Leonard G. and Jerlean (Reynolds) Ford; A.B. summa cum laude, Howard U., 1945; M.A. with honors, U. Chgo., 1946; postgrad. pub. adminstrn. Am. U., 1955-56; m. Willie B. Allen, Dec. 28, 1959; children—George Ferguson, Stephen Ferguson, Willie Allen, Vincent Allen. Instr., Howard U., 1946-48; preliminary cataloger Library of Congress, 1953-56; mgmt. analyst Dept. Army, 1956-63; instr. GSA Inst., Gen. Services Adminstrn., 1963-65; edn. program officer U.S. Office Edn., 1965—. Mem. D.C. Bd. Edn., 1967—, v.p., 1967-70, pres., 1970—. Recipient Outstanding Performance award Gen. Services Adminstrn., 1964. Mem. Council Adminstrv. Women in

Edn. (v.p. 1969-70), Am. Inst. Parliamentarians, Bapt. Com. Wider Coop., Bapt. Ministers Wives Assn., Delta Sigma Theta. Home: 301 Oneida St NE Washington DC 20011 Office: US Office Edn 7th and D Sts SW Washington DC 20202

ALLEN, ANNA FOSTER, librarian; b. W. Pittston, Pa., Feb. 20, 1901; d. Henry J.. and Mary H. (Ainey) Foster; Ph.B., Mohlenberg Coll., 1927; B.L.S., Drexel Inst. Tech., 1931; m. C. Spencer Allen, Sept. 1, 1927. Asst. reference librarian Bryn Mawr Coll., 1931-36; circulation librarian Temple U., 1936-66; librarian Lehigh County Hist. Soc., Allentown, Pa., 1967—, sec., 1968-71. Pres. Muhlenberg Coll. Aux.; mem. coordinating council Allentown Girls Club and Vol. of Am. Day Care Center. Presbyn. Clubs: Woman's, Athenaeum (Allentown). Home: 1553 Turner St Allentown PA 18102 Office: 414 Walnut St Allentown PA 18102

ALLEN, ARCHIBALD WILLIAM, educator; b. Millbrook, Ont., Can., Dec. 9, 1908; (parents Am. citizens); s. Alexander and Anna (Wood) A.; B.A., Stanford, 1930, Ph.D., 1940; M.A., U. Cal. at Berkeley, 1931; m. Shirley May Seifried, June 1, 1942 (div. 1970); children—Anne, John A., Elizabeth L. Instr. classics Carleton Coll., 1940-42; lectr. English, U. Mich., 1946-47; instr., then asst. prof. Yale, 1947-56; prof. classics Colby Coll., 1956-62, Wesleyan U., Middletown, Conn., 1963—. Lectr. classics Harvard, 1952; asst. prof. Stanford, summer 1954. Served with AUS, 1942-46. Decorated Bronze Star. Mem. Am. Philol. Assn., Classical Assn. New Eng., Am. Assn. U. Profs. Contbr. articles to profl. jours. Address: Dept Classics Wesleyan U Middletown CT 06457

ALLEN, ARTHUR BEVERLY, fgn. service officer; b. Grantsville, W. Va., Nov. 11, 1920; s. Arthur Hamilton and Sarah Eugenia (Whiting) A.; B.S.; Harvard, 1941; postgrad. U. Md., 1945-47, Johns Hopkins, 1951-52; m. Rose Mary Foster, Nov. 23, 1943; children—Arthur William, Robert Boyd, Sherilyn Dee, Kent Whiting. With U.S. Naval Ordnance Lab. Washington, 1941-44, 45-47; 3d sec., Beirut, Lebanon, 1947-49; vice consul, Algiers, Algeria, 1949-51; Arabic lang. tng. Dept. State, 1951-52; 2d sec., Baghdad, Iraq, 1952-54, Benghazi, Libya, 1954, Tripoli, Libya, 1954-57; Tunisian desk officer Dept. State, 1957-59, officer charge N.E. African affairs, 1959-61; consul gen., Aleppo, Syrian Arab Republic, 1961-63, Dhahran, Saudi Arabia, 1964-68; diplomat in residence So. Methodist U., 1968-69; dir. Near Eastern and S. Asian programs Bur. Ednl. and Cultural Affairs, State Dept., 1969—; student Indsl. Coll. Armed Forces, 1963-64. Served to ensign USNR, 1944-45. Recipient Meritorious Civilian Service award Navy, 1945. Home: 3622 Patterson St N W Washington DC 20015 Office: Dept State Washington DC 20520

ALLEN, ARTHUR WRIGHT, Jr., govt. ofcl.; b. Washington, Ind., Nov. 2, 1915; s. Arthur Wright and Willoughby (Stamper) A.; student Ind. U., 1933-35; B.S., U.S. Mil. Acad., 1939; grad. Command and Gen. Staff Coll., 1944; m. Mary Virginia Welsh, Mar. 14, 1940. Commd. 2d. lt. U.S. Army, 1939, advanced through grades to col., 1954; troop offecer, also regimental staff officer U.S. Cav., 1939-42; gen. staff officer 102d Inf. div., Europe, 1942-45; exec. asst. to under sec. war, also mil. aide to sec. war, 1945-48; armored staff officer, then battalion comdr. 14th Armored Cav., Germany, 1948- 51; assigned Armed Forces Staff Coll., also Army War Coll., then gen. staff officer Dept. Army, 1951-56; hospitalized, 1957-60; mil. asst., also spl. asst. to sec. army, 1960-63; ret., 1963; dep. under sec. army, 1963-68; dep. asst. sec. army (manpower and res. affairs), 1968-. Dir. Home Bldg. Savs. & Loan Assn., Wsah., Ind. Decorated D.S.M., Legion of Merit, Bronze Star with oak leaf cluster; Order Orange-Nassau (Netherlands); named Sagamore of the Wabash by Indiana. Mem. Ind. Soc. Washington, Ind. U. Alumni Assn., Assn. U.S. Army, Assn. Grads. U.S. Mil. Acad., Army Athletic Assn., (hon. v.p.), U.S. Armour Assn., 102d Inf. Div. Assn., Phi Gamma Delta, Kappa Kappa Psi. Clubs: Army Navy, Army Navy ;Country (Washington); Indiana University (Bloomington). Home: 510 N St S W Washington, DC 20024 Office: Office Asst Sec Army (Manpower and Res Affairs) The Pentagon Washington, DC 20310.

ALLEN, ASHAEL LESTER, coll. dean; b. Los Angeles, Sept. 24, 1923; s. Charles Ashael and Ida (Lillywhite) A.; A.B., U. Cal. at Los Angeles, 1946, Ph.D., 1951; m. Marilyn Murphy, Dec. 29, 1943; children—Katherine (Mrs. Gordon M. Jennings), Christine, Charles L., Ben M., Jane, Andrew S., Nancy, Barbara, Richard F., Bonnie, Mark D. Instr. life scis. Orange Coast Coll., Costa Mesa, Cal., 1951-54; mem. faculty Brigham Young U., 1954—, prof. zoology, 1965-68, dean Coll. Biol. and Agrl. Scis., 1968—. Served to 1st lt. USAAF, 1943-46. Mem. Ch. of Jesus Christ of Latter Day Saints (bishop 1951-54, 56-60, 63- 66). Home: 570 E 400 N Orem UT 84057 Office: Widtsoe Bldg Brigham Young Univ Provo UT 84601

ALLEN, BOBBIE RAY, govt. ofcl.; b. Winnsboro, Tex., July 26, 1922; s. Bura N. and E. Lorena (Brown) A.; student Kilgore (Tex.) Jr. Coll., 1942, St. Mary's (Cal.) Coll., 1943, U. Akron, 1946, Aviation Safety Sch., U. So. Cal., 1957; m. Arlene Evelyn Allen, Nov. 18, 1944; children—Sandra L. (Mrs. Michael D. Walker), Johm M., William D., Robert P., Patricia L. With Goodyear Tire & Rubber Co., 1946; mem. Wichita (Kan.) Fire Dept., 1947-49; owner, operator retail bus., Berea, O., 1949-52; air safety insp. CAB, 1959-61, supervisory air safety insp., 1962-63, dep. dir. bur. safety, 1963-64, dir. bur., 1964-67; dir. bur. aviation Safety Nat. Transp. Safety Bd., 1967-68, spl. asst. to dir. bur., 1968—. Participant 15th ann. Global Strategy Discussions, 1963; chmn. bd. Nat. Aircraft Accident Investigation Sch., 1963-64; mem. tech. com. Guggenheim Found., head U.S. delegation 3d session accident investigation div. Internat. Civil Aviation Orgn., Montreal, Can., 1965; mem. inter-govt. agy. task force for orgn. and staff Dept. Transp., 1966. Served from aviation cadet to comdr. USNR, 1942-46, 52-59, 61-62. Decorated Air medal. Mason, Kiwanian. Home: 2216 Huntington Lane Fort Worth TX 76110 Office: 819 Taylor St Fort Worth TX 76102

ALLEN, BROOKE EMPLE, association executive, retired air force officer; b. Columbus County, North Carolina, September 1, 1910; s. William Robeson and Mary (Jowers) A.; A.B., Davidson Coll., 1933; m. Helen Smith Frank, Jan. 20, 1937; children—Toni, Nikki. Commd. U.S. Army, 1933, promoted through grades to maj. gen., 1956; flying cadet, 1933-34; served with 9th Bomb Group, Mitchel Field, N.Y., 1934-39, 5th Bomb Group, Hickam Field, Hawaii, 1939- 40, comdr. 42d Bomb Squadron, 11th Bomb Group, 1940-42, flew one of the 2 B-17 bombers that were able to take off from Hickam during Pearl Harbor attack, Dec. 7, 1941; comdr. 5th Bomb Group, Guadalcanal, South Pacific, 1942-43; dep. operations 2d Air Force, Colorado Springs, Colo., 1944-45; comdr. 20th Bomb Wing, 1945; dep. comdr. North Atlantic Wing, Air Transport Command, Westover Field, Mass., 1946; chief staff, Air Force rep. U.N. Mil. Staff Com., 1946-48; chief air targets div., directorate Intelligence Hdqrs. U.S. Air Force, 1948-51; comdg. gen. Air Photog. and Charting Service, 1952; chief of staff Mil. Air Transport Service, Washington, 1952-54, director of Information Services, Hdqrs., USAF, 1954-55; comdr. Continental Div. MATS, 1955-57; comdr. Sixth Tactical Air Force, NATO, 1957-59, Hdqrs. Command USAF, Bolling AFB, Washington, 1959-65, ret., 1965; exec. dir. Nat. Aero. Assn., 1966—. Decorated with the Distinguished Service Cross, Legion of Merit oak leaf cluster, Silver Star, Distinguished Flying Cross, Air Medal, Commendation Ribbon with 3 oak leaf clusters, Purple Heart; Presdl. Citation (Navy); Cloud Banner (China); Order of Daedalians. Mem. Phi Gamma Delta, Omicron Delta Kappa. Presbyn. Clubs: Athletic (N.Y.C.); Racquet (Phila.); National Aviation (Washington). Home: 10829 Stanmore Dr Potomac Falls, MD 20854, Office: Shoreham Bldg 806 15th St N W Washington DC 20005

ALLEN, BYRON PAUL, composer; b. Omaha, Dec. 9, 1939; s. Malcolm Graham and Margaret (Bray) A.; ed. pub. schs.; m. Gloria Ann Borovoy, July 7, 1964; 1 dau., Andreya. Alto saxophone player, 1948—; concert Town Hall, N.Y.C., 1965; recorded album (also composed) The Bryon Allen Trio Performing Serious Improvisational Music, 1964. Served with USAF, 1956-59. Address: Apt 706 66 Cleary Ct San Francisco CA 94109

ALLEN, CARL E., corp. dir.; b. Carbondale, Ill. Mar. 13, 1905; s. Carlos Eben and Maude Vrooman (Willsey) A.; grad. Phillips Andover Acad., 1922; A.B., Dartmouth, 1926; m. Katharine Avery, May 21, 1932; children—Nancy (Mrs. Myron Dunn), Avery, Mary, Katharine (Mrs. Steven H. Kelley), With Nat. City Bank of N.Y., 1926- 50, asst. cashier, 1931-35, asst. v.p., 1935-40, v.p., 1940-50; pres. Campbell, Wyant & Cannon Foundry Co., 1950-56; pres. Fed. Res. Bank of Chgo., 1956-61; v.p. Gen. Motors Corp., 1962-70; dir. Marlennan Corp., Miles Labs., Inc. Chmn. citizens bd. U. Chgo., 1959-61; trustee Com. Econ. Devel.; trustee, chmn. investment com. Alfred P. Sloan Foundation. Clubs: Commercial, Chicago; Muskegon (Mich.) Country; Links (N.Y.C.). Home: 1411 Ruddiman Av North Muskegon MI 49445

ALLEN, CATHERINE LOUISE, educator; b. Columbus, Ga.; d. Aubrey Davidson and Louise (Jessop) Allen; B.S., Ga. State Coll. Women, 1936; M.A., Columbia U. Tchrs. Coll., 1941; Ed.D., N.Y. U., 1955. Faculty phys. edn. and recreation U. Tenn., 1941-55; dir. Tenn. Recreation Tng. Program, 1947-55; chmn. women's phys. edn. N.Y. U., 1955-57; prof. edn., coordinator spl. activities U. Pitts., 1957-60; coordinator spl. activities Tufts U., 1960-63; prof. phys. edn. and recreation, co- ordinator field and community services, Boston-Bouve Coll. Northeastern U., 1960-64, chmn. recreation dept., prof. dept. phys. edn. and recreations, 1965-67, dean coll., 1967—. Vis. scholar Piedmont U. Center N.C., 1966. Dir. spl. activities A.R.C., Pacific Ocean areas, 1944-46; guest speaker World Seminar on Health, Phys. Edn. and Recreation, Finland, 1952; social recreation guest speaker and demonstrator Internat. Recreation Congress, 1956; devel. recreation and leadership workshop on nat. basis; del. Internat. Council on Health, Phys. Edn. and Recreation, 1965, World Confedn. Orgns. Teaching Profession, Ethiopia, Africa, 1965; A.A.H.P.E.R. rep. Congress Internat. Assn. Phys. Ed. and Sports for Girls and Women, Cologne, Germany, 1965, U.S.A. rep., 1966-69, head delegation to Japan, 1969; adviser ednl. policies com. N.E.A., 1966-69. Bd. dirs. Nat. Found. Health, Phys. Edn. and Recreation; bd. council Greater Boston Campfire Girls. Pan-Am. scholar for travel and study in Mexico, 1950. Recipient Woman of Year award, Knoxville, Tenn., 1950; Luther Halsey Gulick medal, 1970; citation United Community Services Met. Boston, 1970. Fellow Am. Acad. Phys. Edn. (Creative award 1949); mem. A.A.H.P.E.R. (nat. honor award 1957, pres. So. dist. 1956, chmn. nat. vocational guidance com. 1956-57, v.p. recreation Eastern dist. 1961-63, nat. v.p. 1962-63, chmn. nat. recreation div. 1962-63, nat. pres. 1964- 65, exec. com. internat. relations council), Internat. Platform Assn., Eastern (pres. 1967- 69), Nat. (v.p. So. dist. 1956, mem.- at-large Eastern dist. 1956-58, pres. Eastern dist. 1968, nat. pres. 1969) assns. phys. edn. coll. women, Am. Coll. Sports Medicine, Internat. Assn. Phys. Edn. and Sports for Girls and Women (exec. bd. 1969—), Future Homemakers Am., Mortar Bd., Chi Omega, Delta Kappa Gamma (Doctoral award 1953), Kappa Delta Pi, Pi Lambda Theta, Beta Sigma Phi (internat. hon. mem.), Alpha Lambda Delta. Author: Fun for Parties and Programs, 1956; (with others) Program in Physical Education for Elementary Schools in Tennesse, 1942, Goals for American Recreation, 1964. Contbr. articles to profl. jours. Home: 1600 Beacon St Brookline MA 02146 Office: Boston-Bouvé Coll Northeastern U Boston MA 02115

ALLEN, CHARLES, Jr., investment banker; b. New York City. Founder, sr. partner, Allen & Co., investment bankers, 1922—; dir. C F & I Steel Corp.; chmn. bd. Allen Rances Inc.; pres. Bayou Interests, Inc.; dir., mem. exec. com AMBAC Industries; dir., mem. exec. com., finance com. PepsiCo Inc.; dir. Real Property Owners, Inc., Evergreen Park Shopping Plaza, N. Kansas City Devel. Co.; dir., mem. exec. com. Ogden Corp. Office: 30 Broad St New York City NY 10004

ALLEN, CHARLES CLAFLIN, lawyer; b. St. Louis, Oct. 5, 1893; s. Charles Claflin and Carrie Louise (Richards) A.; A.B., Princeton, 1915; student Washington U. Law Sch., 1915-16, LL.B., St. Louis U. Law Sch., 1919-20; m. Mary Jane Thomson, Dec. 15, 1917; children—Mary Jane (Mrs. Erich G. Weissenberger), Charles Claflin. Admitted to Mo. bar, 1917; counsel Kauffman Smith & Co., St. Louis, 1920-29; counsel Boatmen's Nat. Bank, St. Louis, 1929-32, v.p., gen. counsel, 1933-35; gen. practice of law, St. Louis, 1934-43; partner Lehmann & Allen, St. Louis, 1943-55, Allen & Allen, 1955-60, Lewis, Rice, Tucker, Allen & Chubb, 1960—. Chmn. St. Louis chpt. A.R.C., 1941-42, established St. Louis Blood Bank; mem. speaker's bur. United Fund of St. Louis. Mem. exec. com. Rehab. Center Greater St. Louis, 1931-43; mem. bd. Episcopal Home for Children, 1945-49; trustee St. Luke's Hosp., St. Louis, 1944-56, Community Music Sch. of St. Louis. Served to capt. U.S. Army, 1917-18. Mem. Bar of St. Louis, Am., Mo., St. Louis bar assns., Am. Law Inst., Round Table, Phi Beta Kappa. Republican. Episcopalian (vestryman). Clubs: Princeton (pres. 1948-49), Noonday, St. Louis Country (St. Louis). Home: 710 S Hanley Rd St. Louis MO 63105 Office: 611 Olive St St Louis MO 63101

ALLEN, CHARLES JOSEPH II, advt. exec.; b. Providence, June 8, 1917; s. John Alfred and Emily (Smith) A.; A.B. with honors, U. Pitts., 1939; m. Fay Eleanore Manne, Nov. 19, 1941; children—Linda Fay (Mrs. Marc D. Constant), June Lee (Mrs. Michael L. Traviolia). Corporate sales service mgr. Kroger Co., Cin., 1945-52; v.p. Gardner Advt., Inc., St. Louis, 1952-56, McCann-Erickson, Inc., Chgo., 1956-58; chmn. bd., chief exec. officer Allen, Anderson, Niefeld & Paley, Inc., Chgo., 1958-69; pres. Charles J. Allen & Assos., Elmhurst, Ill., 1970—; v.p., dir. Grabin-Shaw Advt., Milw., 1960—, Gaffin Market Research, Elmhurst, 1970—; pres., dir. A A Gift Shopper Plan, Elmhurst, 1970—; dir. A/C/T Enterprises, Chgo., Press Syndicate Service, Pitts., Grabin-Shaw Press Bur., Milw.; cons. in field, 1960—. Bd. dirs. Oak Knoll Manor Home Owners Assn., 1959—. Named Outstanding Pa. Pres., Pa. Jr. C. of C., 1948. Mem. Assn. Food Execs. (pres. 1967—), Chgo. Assn. Commerce and Industry, Elmhurst C. of C., U. Pitts. Alumni Assn., Am. Marketing Assn. (past dir.), Indsl. Advt. Club. Clubs: Chicago Press; Executives; Itasca (Ill.) Country. Contbr. articles to profl. jours., speaker in field. Home: 750 E Sherwood Dr Addison IL 60101 Office: 381 N York St Elmhurst IL 60126

ALLEN, CHARLES LAUREL, educator, journalist; b. Berwick, N.D., July 5, 1902; s. Charles and Sarah Ellen (Lowry) A.; A.B., U. N.D., 1924; A.M., U. Ill., 1927; Ph.D., Northwestern U, 1948; m. Lida Mae Grace, June 16, 1926; children—Charles Richard, Patricia. Printers' apprentice, advancing to editor-mgr. Towner (N.D.) News Trib., 1913-20; make-up and asst. city editor Jamestown (N.D.) Daily Alert, 1919-20; printer, later make-up editor Grand Forks (N.D.) Daily Herald, tchr. journalism U. N.D. and U. High Sch., 1922-24; prin. high sch., Norwich, N.D., asst. editor Granville (N.D.) Herald, 1920-22; tchr. printing, English, boys band Jefferson Jr. High Sch., Mpls., 1924-25; asst. to prof. journalism U. Ill., 1925-37; owner, pub. 5 rural Ill. newspapers, 1925-37; dir. dept. journalism Rutgers U., 1937-40; asst. dean, dir. research Medill Sch. Journalism, Northwestern U., 1940-59; dir. Okla. State U. Sch. Journalism, 1960-67; dir. grad. studies Tex. Technol. Coll., Lubbock, 1967-69. Chief rural press sect., news bur. OWI, Washington, 1942, chief news bur. 1943; pres. Dyna Scope Human Dynamics Research Co. Exec. sec. N.J. Press Assn., 1937-40; sec. Ill. Weekly Newspaper Assn., 1934-37, dir. Ill. High Sch. Press Assn., 1928- 37; past pres. Am. Assn. Tchrs. Journalism, Am. Soc. Journalism Sch. Adminstrs.; dir. accounting and cost finding Nat. Editorial Assn., recipient Amos prize, 1941; research cons. Am. Press Inst., Columbia U., Anderson (S. C.) Ind., WAIM-TV, Hong Kong Standard, Chgo. Defender, Wis. Hometown Newspapers, Appleton (Wis.) Post Crescent, Chgo. Sun-Times, Green Bay Press-Gazette, Kansas City Star, Tulsa Tribune, Lee Newspaper Group. Mem Phi Beta Kappa, Sigma Delta Chi, Pi Alpha Mu, Delta Sigma Rho, Alpha Delta Sigma, Kappa Tau Alpha. Mason. Republican. Presbyn. Author: Country Journalism (Nelson), 1927; Journalists' Manual of Printing (Nelson), 1929; Publication Laws of New Jersey, 1939; Free Circulation Newspapers, 1940. Editor: Chicago Daily News Almanac, National Almanac, Denver Post Almanac, Rocky Mountain Empire Year Book, Television Bibliography, 1954; Postal Laws and Regulations; 1964; contbr. numerous articles to Journalism revs. Address: Tex Technol Coll Lubbock TX 79409

ALLEN, CHARLES LIVINGSTONE, clergyman; b. Newborn, Ga., June 24, 1913; s. John Robert and Lula (Franklin) A.; A.B., Wofford Coll., 1933; B.D., Emory U., 1937, D.D., 1960; D.D., Piedmont Coll., 1946; LL.D., John Brown U., 1964; m. Leila Haynes, June 19, 1934; children—Charles Livingstone, John Franklin, Mary Jane (Mrs. Charles W. Miller). Ordained to ministry Methodist Ch., 1933; pastor in Ga., 1934-60, Atlanta, 1948-60, First Meth. Ch., Houston, 1960—; frequent guest speaker. Mem. bd. Meth. Hosp., Houston, Meth. Home, Waco, Tex., Moody House, Galveston, Tex. Mem. Phi Beta Kappa. Kiwanian. Author: The Sermon on the Mount, 1966; God's Psychiatry, 1953; When the Heart is Hungry, 1955; The Touch of the Master's Hand, 1956; In Quest of God's Power, 1952; Roads to Radiant Living, 1951; All Things Are Possible Through Prayer, 1958; When you Lose a Loved One, 1959; Healing Words, 1961; Twelve Ways to Solve Your Problems, 1954; The Twenty- Third Psalm, 1961; The Life of Christ, 1962; The Lord's Prayer, 1963; Prayer Changes Things, 1964; The Ten Commandments, 1965; The Beatitudes, 1967; also newspaper columnist. Home: 3469 Piping Rock Lane Houston TX 77027 Office: 901 Clay St Houston TX 77002

ALLEN, CHARLES RICHARD, financial exec.; b. Cleve., Mar. 10, 1926; s. Charles Ross and Jennie (Harmon) A.; student Occidental Coll., 1942-43; B.S., U. Cal. at Los Angeles, 1945; m. Marion Elizabeth Taylor, Aug. 17, 1946; children—Kathleen, Jeanne, Kenneth. Acounting supr. N. Am. Aviation, Inc., Los Angeles, 1946-55; div. controller TRW, Inc., Los Angeles, 1955- 61, dir. finance, 1961-64, asso. controller, Cleve., 1964-66, controller, 1966-67, v.p., chief financial officer, 1967—. dir. New Court Pvt. Equity Fund, Inc., N.Y.C. Served with USNR, 1943-46. Mem. Financial Execs. Inst., Am. Finance Assn., Am. Mgmt. Assn., Finance Planning Council, Greater Cleve. Growth Assn. Clubs: Clevelander, Shaker Heights Country, Union , Pepper Pike (Cleve.); Wall Street (N.Y.C.). Home: 17503 Shelburne Rd Cleveland Heights OH 44118 Office: 23555 Euclid Av Cleveland OH 44117

ALLEN, CHARLES ROBERT, physician, educator; b. Bowling Green, Ky., June 26, 1911; s. Samuel H. and Eva (Lawrence) A.; B.S., Western Ky. State Tchrs. Coll., 1932, M.A., 1933; Ph.D., U. Wis., 1941, M.D., 1946; m. Lucille Fitzhugh, June 27, 1934; children—Charles Robert, Richard F., Elizabeth (Mrs. John McEldowney). Lab. instr. Western Ky. State Tchrs. Coll., 1933-34; grad. asst. Ohio State U., 1934; sci. tchr. Bowling Green Pub. Schs., 1934-35; sci. tchr. Louisville Pub. Schs., 1935-38; research asst. U. Wis., 1938-40, instr. physiology, 1940-42; asst. prof. anesthesiology U. Tex. Med. Br., Galveston, 1942-46, asso. prof., 1946-53, prof., chmn. dept. anesthesiology, 1953—; intern U. Tex. Med. Br., Galveston, 1946-47; practice medicine, specializing in anesthesiology, Galveston, 1946—; med. cons. U.S. Army, Brooke Army Med. Center, Ft. Sam Houston, Tex., 1945—, Oak Ridge Inst. Nuclear Studies, 1949-54, Wilford Hall USAF Hosp., Lackland AFB, Tex., 1953-67, USPHS Hosp., Galveston, 1953—: chief of staff U. Tex. Med. Br. Hosps., 1966-67; mem. respiratory and anesthetic drugs adv. com. FDA, Washington, 1966-70. Mem. adv. bd. Galveston Citizens Comprehensive Planning, 1964-66. Bd. dirs. William Temple Found. Diplomate Am. Bd. Anesthesiology. Fellow Am. Coll. Anesthesiologists (past bd. govs., chmn. oral exams.); mem. Am. (past com. chmn.), Tex. (past pres.), So. (past pres.) socs. anesthesiologists, A.M.A., Tex., So. med. assns., Galveston County Med. Soc. (mem. exec. com., past chmn. bd. censors), Am. Physiol. Soc., Acad. Anesthesiology, Tex. Gulf Coast Anesthesia Soc., Internat. Anesthesia Research Soc., Soc. Acad. Anesthesia (chmn.), Assn. U. Anesthetists (past mem. adminstrv. council), Am. Assn. U. Profs., Sigma Xi. Contbr. articles profl. jours. Home: 20 Cedar Lawn S Galveston TX 77550 Office: 800 Mechanic St Galveston TX 77550

ALLEN, CHARLES WILLIAM, lawyer; b. Portland, Me., Nov. 14, 1912; s. Neal W. and Margaret (Stevens) A.; A.B., Bowdoin Coll., 1934; J.D., U. Mich., 1937; m. Genevieve Lahee, Sept. 5, 1936; children—Thomas H., Ruth W., William N. Admitted to N.Y. bar, 1938, Me. bar, 1946; practiced in N.Y.C., 1937-41, Portland, 1946—; asso. firm Sullivan & Cromwell, 1937-41; partner Pierce, Atwood, Scribner, Allen & McKusick, 1946—. Trustee Portland Savs. Bank, 1959—. Mem. Portland City Council, 1964-70, Chairman 1966. Treas., trustee Bowdoin Coll., 1959-67, bd. overseers, 1967—; treas. Hebron Acad., 1954-59, trustee, 1953-65; trustee Colby, Bates, Bowdoin Ednl. Telecasting Corp., 1961—; mem. com. visitors U. Mich. Law Sch., 1967-68. Served to lt. comdr. USNR, 1942-46. Mem. Am., Me., Cumberland County bar assns., Order of Coif. Home: 41 Rackleff St Portland ME 04103 Office: 1 Monument Sq Portland ME 04111

ALLEN, CLARENCE MILTON, gas transmission co. exec.; b. Salina, Kan., July 3, 1918; s. Claude M. and Stella A. (Wakefield) A.; B.S. in Bus., U. Kan., 1941; m. Geraldine Crago, Jan. 15, 1946; 1 son, David Milton. Supr., Peat, Marwick, Mitchell & Co., C.P.A.'s, Kansas City, Mo., 1946-52; asst. to controller, asst. sec. Panhandle Eastern Pipe Line Co., Kansas City, Mo., 1952-53, v.p., treas., 1966—; controller, asst. sec. Trunkline Gas Co., Houston, 1953-66; v.p., treas. Nat. Helium Corp., Kansas City, Mo., 1966-67; dir. Kan. Devel. Credit Corp. Served to lt. USNR, 1942-46. C.P.A., Mo., Tex. Mem. Financial Execs. Inst. (pres. Houston 1960, member national board of directors 1963-66, area vice pres. 1966-67, nat. pres. 1970-71, So. Gas Assn. (chmn. accounting com. 1960). Home: 2500 W 65th St Shawnee Mission, KS 66208. Office: PO Box 1348 Kansas City 64141

ALLEN, CLARENCE RODERIC, geologist educator; b. Palo Alto, Cal., Feb. 15, 1925; s. Hollis Partridge and Delight (Wright) A.; B.A., Reed Coll., 1949; M.S., Cal. Inst Tech., 1951, Ph.D., 1954. Asst. prof. geology U. Minn., 1954-55; mem. faculty Cal. Inst. Tech., 1955—, prof. geology and geophysics, 1964—, interim dir. Seismological Lab., 1965-67, acting chmn. division of geological scis., 1967-68. Chmn. cons. bd. earthquake analysis Cal. Dept. Water Resources, 1965—; chmn. geol. hazards adv. com. for program Cal. Resources Agy., 1965-66; mem. earth scis. adv. panel NSF, 1965-68, chmn., 1967-68, mem. adv. com. environmental scis., 1970—; mem. U.S. Geol. Survey adv. panel to Nat. Center Earthquake Research, 1966—; mem. Cal. Mining and Geology Bd., 1969—; mem. task force on earthquake hazard reduction Office Sci. and Tech., 1970—. Served to 1st lt. USAAF, 1943-46. Recipient G.K. Gilbert award seismic geology Carnegie Instn., 1960. Fellow Am. Geophys. Union, Geol. Soc. Am. (counselor 1968—); mem. Am. Association of Petroleum Geologists, Glaciological Soc., Earthquake Engring. Research Inst., Seismological Soc. Am. (dir. 1970—), Assn. Engring. Geologists, Structural Engrs. Assn. So. Cal., Soc. Exploration Geophysicists, Phi Beta Kappa. Home: 1160 Cordova St Pasadena CA 91106

ALLEN, CLAUDE LEROY, Jr., educator; b. Melrose, Mass., Jan. 21, 1906; s. Claude LeRoy and Lovisa A. (Delamater) A.; grad. Phillips Acad., Andover, Mass., 1925; A.B., Harvard, 1929; M.A. (hon.), Colby Coll., 1953, Bowdoin Coll., 1963; m. Eleanor Davy, June 28, 1933; children—Constance, Claude LeRoy III, Jane. Mem. faculty, Deerfield (Mass.) Acad., 1931-45; headmaster Hebron Acad, 1945—. Republican. Baptist. Mason, Kiwanian. Address: Hebron ME 04238

ALLEN, CLAXTON EDMONDS, newspaperman; b. Richmond, Va., Nov. 26, 1910; s. Claxton Edmonds and Lydia Ann (Kimbrough) A.; A.B. cum laude, Washington and Lee U., 1932; m. Helen McCreery, Oct. 4, 1940 (dec. Dec. 1963); children—Alice, Donald, C. Edmonds III, Helen Green. Reporter, Chgo., Tribune, Paris, France, 1933-34, St. Louis Post-Dispatch, 1934-36; reporter, editor, bus. rep., bur. mgr. United Press Internat. Atlanta, Chgo., N.Y.C., 1936-45, dir. spl. services, 1945—, mem. mgmt. com., 1957-63, pub. Ocean Press Newspapers div., 1963—; pres. Folly Beach Ltd. Episcopalian. Club: Players, Dutch Treat (N.Y.C.); Nat. Press (Washington). Home: 405 E 54th St New York City NY 10022 Office: 220 E 42d St New York City NY 10017

ALLEN, CLIFTON JUDSON, clergyman, editor; b. Latta, S.C., Nov. 7, 1901; s. William Benjamin and Theodosia (Cox) A.; B.A., Furman U., 1923, D.D., 1960; Th.M., So. Baptist Theol. Sem., 1928, Ph.D., 1932; m. Hattie Bell McCracken, Aug. 22, 1930; children—Judson Boyce, Rosalind (Mrs. John Barker), Robert Moore. Prin., Minturn (S.C.) High Sch., 1923-25; tutor Greek N.T., So. Bapt. Theol. Sem., 1928-31; ordained to ministry So. Bapt. Ch., 1926; pastor in McHenry, Ky., 1926-29 Utica, Ky., 1929-32, Fairmont, N.C., 1932-36, Statesville, N.C., 1936-37; asso. editorial sec. Sunday sch. bd. So. Bapt. Conv., 1937-44, editorial sec., 1945-68; rec. sec. So. Bapt. Conv., 1966—. Mem. commn. Christian teaching and tng. Bapt. World Alliance, 1965-70; mem. exec. com. Bapt. Conv. N.C., 1935-37; mem. internat. Sunday sch. lesson com. div. Christian edn. Nat. Council Chs., 1942-68, chmn. 1960-67; mem. div. assembly, div. Christian edn. Nat. internat. Sunday sch. lesson com. div. Christian edn. Nat. Council Chs., 1942-68, chmn., 1960-67; mem. div. assembly, div. Christian edn. Nat. Council Chs., 1957-63; radio broadcaster, 1945—. Recipient E.Y. Mullins denominational service award So. Bapt. Theol. Sem., 1970. Dmocrat. Rotarian, Quarternion. Author: The Gospel According to Paul, 1956; Points for Emphasis (ann.) 1953—; also curricular materials. Chmn. editorial com. Ency. So. Baptists, 1958; gen. editor Broadman Bible Commentary, 1969—. Home: 4215 Harding Rd Nashville TN 37205 Office: 127 9th Av N Nashville TN 37203

ALLEN, CUTHBERT EDWARD, ednl. adminstr., clergyman; b. Manchester, N.H., Apr. 28, 1906; s. Arthur Bernard and Mary Anne (McMahan) A.; A.B., Belmont Abbey Coll., 1929; M.A., Cath. U. Am., 1935; postgrad. U. N.C.; LL.D., St. Vincent's Coll., 1950. Professed as Benedictine monk, 1927, ordained priest R.C. Ch., 1933; instr. history and sociology Belmont Abbey Coll., 1929-36, prof., 1936—, rector, v.p., 1936-42, 45-47, dean, 1947-54, pres., 1956-60, vice chancellor, 1960—; pastor, Gastonia, N.C., 1933-35. Mem. N.C. Com. on Elementary Edn., 1950-55. Mem. nat. commn. Conf. on Christians and Jews, 1948-56; bd. dirs. A.R.C.; chmn. Health Facilities Commn. Belmont. Recipient Silver medallion, mem. Nat. Honor Corps, Nat. Conf. Christians and Jews. Member Belmont C. of C. (dir.), So. Assn. Colls. and Secondary Schs. (mem. commn. colls. and univs. 1948-55), Colls. and Univs. N.C. (pres.), Am., Am. Cath. hist. assns., Am., Am. Cath. sociol. socs., Charlotte Philos. Soc., Delta Epsilon Sigma, Pi Gamma Mu. Clubs: Charlotte City, Gastonia Country. Author: Catholic Newspapers During Civil War, 1860-65, 1936. Address: Belmont Abbey Belmont NC 28012

ALLEN, CYRIL GLEN, educator; b. Edgerton, Alta., Can., Jan. 23, 1919; s. Bertram and Hilda Mary (Erickson). A.; came to U.S., 1920, naturalized, 1928; student Bethel Jr. Coll., 1937-38; B.S., Winona State Coll., 1941; M.A., U. Minn., 1946, Ph.D., 1949; m. Marjorie W. Allen, Nov. 3, 1940; children—Alice (Mrs. Milton Messimer), Sarah Jane (Mrs. Harry Wetzel). Instr., Wabasso High Sch., 1941-43; instr. U. Cin., 1947-49; asst. prof. U. Minn. Extension, 1949-50; successively asst. prof., asso. prof., prof. history Mankato (Minn.) State Coll., 1950—, chmn. dept. history, 1965—. Bd. dirs. Minn. Council Social Studies. Served with USNR, 1943-45. Fund for Advancement Edn. (Ford Found.) fellow, 1954-55. Mem. Am., Canadian hist. assns., Conf. on Latin Am. History, Soc. History Discoveries, Latin Am. Studies Assn., Orgn. Am. Historians, Phi Alpha Theta. Author: France in Central America, 1966; also articles. Home: Box 112 Waterville MN 56096 Office: Mankato State Coll Mankato MN 56001

ALLEN, DAVID FRANK, lawyer; b. Richwood, O., June 19, 1937; s. Perry David and Mary (Lehman) A.; B.A., J.D., Ohio State U., 1961; m. Ann E. Evans, June 13, 1959; children-Perry David II, Catherine Ann. With Legislative Reference Bur., Columbus, O., 1960-61; admitted to Ohio bar, 1961; practice in Marysville, 1964—; asst. atty. gen. Ohio, 1961-62. Pres. Union County United Appeal; exec. dir. Community Found., Community Services, Inc. of Marysville; exec. sec. Dana W. Morey Found. Served with U.S. Army, 1962- 64. Mem. Am., Ohio bar assns., Phi Alpha Delta, Tau Kappa Epsilon. Democrat. Methodist (trustee). Mason (Shriner), Elk. Home: 520 W 7th St Marysville OH 43040 Office: 233 W 5th St Marysville OH 43040

ALLEN, DONALD GILSON, lawyer, electric co. exec.; b. Manchester, Mass., Aug. 30 1913; s. Raymond Cleaveland and Carrie Edith (Allen) A.; grad. Phillips Acad., 1930; A.B., Dartmouth, 1934; postgrad. Oxford U., 1935; LL.B., Harvard, 1938; m. Charlotte Jones, June 4, 1946; children—Stephen Church, Thomas Cleaveland. Admitted to Mass. bar, 1938; asso. firm Ropes & Gray, Boston, 1938-50; co. counsel New Eng. Electric System, Boston, 1951—, became gen. counsel, 1964, now v.p.; clk. Yankee Atomic Electric Co., Boston, 1954-67, pres., 1967—. Served to lt. USCGR, 1942-45. Home: 95 Spring Rd Concord MA 01742 Office: 20 Turnpike Rd Westboro MA 01581

ALLEN, DON B., corp. exec.; b. 1928; B.A., Yale, 1950, LL.B., 1953; married. With firm Nixon, Hargrave, Devans & Doyle, 1957-61; with Bausch & Lomb Inc., 1961—; sec., 1967—. Served to 1st lt. AUS, 1953-57. Home: 136 Knickerbocker Rd Pittsford NY 14534 Office: 635 St Paul St Rochester NY 14602

ALLEN, DON CAMERON, author, educator; b. St. Louis, Dec. 5, 1903; s. Alvin James and Anna (Wienmann) A.; A.B., U. Ill., 1926, Ph.D., 1931, D.H.L., 1971; A.M., Washington U., 1927; L.H.D., U. Chgo., 1971; m. Mary Whitney Coble, Feb. 1, 1929; 1 dau., Mary Whitney. Asst. instr. English, U. Ill., 1927-28; instr. Purdue U., 1929-30; prof., head dept. Ill. Wesleyan U., 1931-32; instr. to asst. prof. State Coll. Wash., 1932-38; asst. to asso. prof. Duke, 1938- 42; asso. prof. English, Johns Hopkins, 1942-45, prof., 1945—, Sir William Osier prof., 1950. Vis. summer prof. Ohio U., N.C. Coll., 1939-42, Johns Hopkins, 1941, Northwestern U., 1947, U. Ill., 1949, N.Y. U., 1950; F.I. Carpenter prof. U. Chgo., 1948; Sesquicentennial lectr. U. N.C., 1946, Baskerville Brown U., 1947; Taft lectr. U. Cin., 1950; Scott lectr. Wash. U., 1956; lectr. U. Colo., 1957-61; Johnson prof. U. Wis., 1961-62. Am. Council fellow in Europe, 1935-36; Fulbright Research fellow, Oxford, 1950-51; NEH fellow, 1967-68. Mem. Modern Lang. Assn. (editorial com. 1946-61, v.p. 1966), Am. Acad. Arts and Scis., Renaissance Soc. (council), Internat. Assn. U. Profs. English (exec. com.), Am. Philos. Soc., Am. Acad. Arts and Scis., Phi Beta Kappa, Sigma Delta Chi, Chi Psi. Club: Tudor and Stuart. Author: The Star-Crossed Renaissance, 1942; The Legend of Noah, 1950; Doubt's Boundless Sea, 1964. Editor: Treatise Poetrie (Francis Meres), 1933; Palladis Tamia (Francis Meres), 1939; The Owles Almanacke, 1943; The Essayes of Sir William Cornwallis, 1946 A Strange Metamorphosis, 1950; Recent Literature of the Renaissance, 1939-50; That Soveraine Light (with W. Mueller), 1952; The Harmonious Vision, 1954; Paradoxes, 1956; (with others) A Critical Bibliography of French Literature, 1956; (with others) Masters of British Literature, 2 vols., 1958; Four Poets on Poetry, 1959; Image and Meaning, 1960; Moment of Poetry, 1962; A Celebration of Poets, 1967; The Ph.D. in English and American Literature, 1967; (with H.T. Rowell) The Poetic Tradition, 1968; Mysteriously Meant, 1970. Editor: English Literary History; asso. editor Modern Language Notes, Revista di Litteratuer Moderne, Isis, Studies in English Literature, English Language Notes. Contbr. articles, revs., verse to Am., European philol., lit. jours. Home: 1109 Harriton Rd Baltimore MD 21210 Office: Johns Hopkins Baltimore MD 21205

ALLEN, DURWARD LEON, biologist; b. Uniondale, Ind., Oct. 11, 1910; s. Harley J. and Jennie M. (LaTurner) A.; A.B., U. Mich., 1932; Ph.D., Mich. State Coll., 1937; L.H.D., No. Mich. U., 1971; m. Dorothy Ellen Helling, Sept. 23, 1935; children—Stephen R., Harley W., Susan E. Game research biologist Mich. Dept. Conservation, 1935-46; wildlife research biologist U.S. Fish and Wildlife Service, Laurel, Md., 1946-50, asst. chief br. wildlife research, Washington, 1951-54; prof. wildlife ecology Purdue U., Lafayette, Ind., 1954—. Mem. Adv. Bd. on Nat. Parks, U.S. Dept. Interior, chmn., 1971—. Trustee N. Parks Assn. Recipient medal of honor Anglers' Club of N.Y., 1956. Fellow A.A.A.S.; mem. Wildlife Soc. (life mem., pres. 1956-57, Annual Tech. Publ. award, 1946, Annual Conservation Edn. award, 1955, Leopold Meml. medal 1968), Washington Biologists' Field Club, Am. Soc. Mammalogists, Ecol. Soc. Am., Boone and Crockett Club (life), Outdoors Writers Assn. Am. (Jade of Chiefs award 1968), Seminarium Botanicum, Ind. Acad. Sci., Am. Behavior Soc., Am. Acad. Polit. and Social Sci., Am. Inst. Biol. Scis., Sigma Xi, Phi Sigma, Xi Sigma Pi. Author: Michigan Fox Squirrel Management, 1943; Pheasants Afield, 1953; Our Wildlife Legacy, 1954; The Life of Prairies and Plains, 1967. Editor, Pheasants in North America, 1956. Home: Route 10 Windwood Lane West Lafayette IN 47906

ALLEN, DWIGHT WILLIAM, univ. dean; b. Stockton, Cal., Aug. 1, 1931; s. John William and Valera (Fisher) A.; A.B. with distinction, Stanford, 1953, M.A. in Edn., 1957, Ed.D., 1959; m. Carole Jeanine Swall, Apr. 12, 1953; children—Douglas Bruce, Dwight Dennis, Dana Lee, Carla and Cheryl Elaine (twins). Instr., Athens (Greece) Coll., 1953-54; secondary sch. tchr., 1957-59; faculty Stanford, 1958-67, asso. prof. edn., 1965-67; dean U. Mass. Sch. Edn., Amherst, 1968—. Cons. Cal. Commn. Pub. Edn., 1966-67; pres. Jr. Statesmen Found., 1964-66; chmn. planning coordination com., chief cons. ednl. professions devel. act. U.S. Office Edn., 1967, also dir. ednl. coordinates. Served with AUS, 1954-56. Mem. Assn. Colls. and Schs. Edn. in State Univs. and Land Grant Colls., Am. Edn. Research Assn., Nat. Council, Social Studies, A.A.A.S., N.E.A., Nat. Soc. Coll. Tchrs. Edn., Nat. Soc. Study Edn., Phi Delta Kappa. Mem. Nat. Spiritual Assembly of Baha'is of U.S. Author: (with Robert N. Bush) A New Design for High School Education: Assuming a Flexible Schedule, 1964; (with Don Bushnell) The Computer in American Education, 1967; (with others) Technical Skills of Teaching for Elementary and Secondary Education, 1968. Editor: (with Robert Madgic) Great Issues Series, The Scholastic Press, 1966—. Contbr. numerous articles to profl. jours., chpts. in books. Home: Market Rd Amherst MA 01002

ALLEN, EDWARD LAWRENCE, govt. ofcl., economist; b. Stony Point, N.Y., Feb. 28, 1913; s. Ernest John and Clara Adelaine (Termansen A.; B.S., Columbia, 1935; M.A., Am. U., 1946, Ph.D., 1948; m. Doris Anne Hoffman, March 16, 1963; children—Edward Lawrence, Anne Beatrice. Various statis. and research positions with financial firms, N.Y.C., 1935-41; statis. analyst WPB, 1942-43; dep. for research, target analysis USAF, 1946-51; project leader, weapons systems evaluation group OSD, 1951-53; chief econ. research CIA, 1953—; adj. prof. econs. Am. U., 1949—. Served as officer USNR, 1943-46. Mem. Am. Econ. Assn. Author: Economics of American Manufacturing, 1952; Soviet Progress vs. American Enterprise, 1958; Can the United States Maintain its World Leadership, 1960; also articles. Home: 6028 Woodley Rd McLean, VA 22101. Office: 2430 E St NW Washington DC 20505

ALLEN, EDWARD SEARLE, actuary; b. Westfield, Mass., Jan. 26, 1915; s. Park W. and Dolly (Searle) A.; student Clark U., 1933-35; B.S., Columbia, 1937; m. Mildred J. Carlson, July 7, 1940; children—Park W. II, Robert C., Elizabeth S. With actuarial dept. Nat. Bur. Casualty Underwriters, N.Y.C., 1937-46; casualty rate analyst Conn. Ins. Dept., Hartford, 1946-48; asst. gen. mgr., actuary N.Y. Compensation Ins. Rating Bd., N.Y.C., 1949-59; actuary Phoenix of Hartford Ins. Cos., 1959-69; asso. actuary Travelers Ins. Cos., 1969—. Vice pres. Greenwich YMCA, 1957-59. Fellow Casualty Actuarial Soc.; mem. Am. Acad. Actuaries. Home: 10 Randall Dr Suffield, CT 06078. Office: 1 Tower Sq Hartford CT 06115

ALLEN, EDWARD SWITZER, educator; b. Kansas City, Mo., Dec. 12, 1887; s. Kenneth and Rose (Switzer) A.; A.B., Harvard, 1909, A.M., 1910, Ph.D., 1914; postgrad. U. Rome, 1911-13; m. Minne Elisabeth Müller-Liebenwalde, Aug. 9, 1915; children—Julius W., Rosemarie C. (Mrs. Hans Lechner), Hermann A. Master mathematics and physics Berkshire Sch., 1909-10; instr. mathematics Dartmouth, 1913-14, Brown U., 1914-15, U. Mich., 1915-19; asst. prof. W.Va. U., 1919-21; asso. prof. mathematics Ia. State U., 1921-43, prof., 1943—; vis. prof. Grinnell Coll., 1960-62, Cottey Coll., 1964-65, Wartburg Coll., 1967-69. Charter chmn. Ia. Civil Liberties Union, 1935, dir., 1935—. Recipient annual award, Ia. Civil Liberties Union, 1961. Mem. Am. Assn. Univ. Profs. (chpt. pres.), Am. Math. Soc., Math. Assn. Am., Deutsche Mathematiker-Vereinigung, Circolo Matematico di Palermo, Fellowship of Reconciliation, Phi Beta Kappa, Sigma Xi. Socialist. Mem. Soc. of Friends. Author: Plane Trigonometry, 1936. Editor: McGraw-Hill Six-Place Tables, 6 editions, 1925-47. Translator: (with Mrs. Allen) Atom and Cosmos (Reichenbach), 1932; Lectures on Modern Geometry (Segre), 1961. Home: 427 Hawthorne Av Ames IA 50010

ALLEN, EDWARD WEBER, lawyer; b. Oshkosh, Wis., May 12, 1885; s. Thomas Scott and Natalia (Weber) A.; student Oshkosh State Normal Sch., 1892-1903, U. Chgo., 1903-05; LL.B., U. Wash., 1909; m. Hazel Rebecca Conner, June 1, 1915; children—Natalia (Mrs. George E. McSpadden), Thomas. Admitted to Wash. bar 1909; with Wright & Kelleher, Seattle, 1909-12; dep. pros. atty. Pacific County, mem. Hewen & Allen, 1913-14; asst. atty. gen., Washington, 1914-16; now counsel DeGarmo, Leedy, Oles & Morrison, Seattle. U.S. commr., chmn. or sec. Internat. Fisheries Commn., 1932-55; U.S. commr. Internat. Salmon Fisheries Comm. 1937-51; ex-chmn., adviser U.S. Delegation to UN FAO, Baguio, P.I., 1948, Washington, 1948, 49; mem. Gen. MacArthur Fisheries Mission to Japan, 1949; adviser U.S. delegation to Tokyo to negotiate N. Pacific Fisheries Commn. 1954—, U.S. Delegation to UN Fishery Conv., Rome, 1955, U.S. delegation UN Conf., Law the Sea, Geneva, 1958, U.S. delegation Ottawa Fisheries between U.S., Can., Japan, 1964. Served with OSS, 1942- 45. Awarded Alumnus Summa Laude Dignatus, U. Wash., 1947. Fellow Am. Bar Found.; mem. Am. (ex-chmn. internat. law sect.), Internat., Wash. (pres. 1929-30), Seattle bar assns., Pacific N.W. Trade Assn., Am. Law Inst., Am. Soc. Internat. Law, Inst. World Polity, Seattle C. of C. (chmn. Alaska com. 4 yrs.), Seattle Hist. Soc. (trustee), Bibliog. Soc. Am., Wash. S.A.R. (pres. 1937-38), Mountaineers (sec. or v.p. 16 yrs., exec. com. 1919-29), U. Wash. Law Alumni Assn. (pres. 1920-22), Japan Soc., Order of Coif (hon.), Phi Gamma Delta, Delta Chi. Republican. Episcopalian. Mason (32, Shriner). Clubs: Rainier, Mountaineers, Laurelhurst Community, China, World Trade (pres., 1954-56) (Seattle); Bohemian (San Francisco); Explorers (N.Y.C.); Cosmos (Washington). Author: North Pacific, 1936; Dancing Tails and Other Fishy Jingles, 1951; The Vanishing Frenchman, The Mysterious Disappearance of Laperouse, 1959. Contbr. articles to profl. jours. Home: 3711 48th Av N E Seattle WA 98105 Office: Northern Life Tower Seattle WA 98101

ALLEN, EDWIN BROWN, coll. prof.; b. Westerly, R.I., Nov. 3, 1898; s. John and Mary Frances (West) A.; EE., Rensselaer Poly. Inst., 1920, M.S., 1930, Ph.D., 1934; A.M., Harvard U., 1934; student Columbia U., summer 1933, U. Chicago, summers 1935, 38, 41; m. Helen Cornelia Mackay, Sept. 3, 1927. Instr. mathematics, Rensselaer Poly. Inst., 1920-27, asst. prof. 1927-34, prof. math. and astronomy, 1934-64, head dept. mathematics, 1934-60, dean grad. sch., 1959-64, prof. and dean emeritus, 1964—; dir. Nat. Sci. Found., Summer Inst., 1957-59. Dir. Gen. Electric Mathematics Fellowship Program, summers, 1952-59. Served in United States Army Camp, Plattsburg, New York, July-August 1918, Heavy Arty. O.T.S., Ft. Monroe, Va., Sept.-Nov. 1918. Awarded U.S. Volunteer Life Saving medal and R.I. Boy Scout Life Saving medal. Coordinator Naval Flight Prep. Sch., Rensselaer Polytech Inst., 1942-43, War Research, U.S. Arsenal, Watervliet, N.Y., 1943-45. Cons. various pubs., industries. Mem. coms., N.Y. State Dept. of Education. Mem. Am. Math. Society. Society for Symbolic Logic, Mathematical Assn. America (gov. 1949-52), Am. Oriental Soc., History of Science Soc., Am. Research Center Egypt (trustee 1951-63), Am. Schs. Oriental Research, Sigma Xi, Alpha Tau Omega, Eta Kappa Nu, Tau Beta Pi, Pi Mu Epsilon, Republican. Episcopalian. Mason (honorary 33; past district deputy grand master). Author: Vital Mathematics (with D. Maly and S. H. Starkey), 1944; Papers on Science in Orient; also numerous articles. Home: 6 Fairlawn Lane Troy NY 12180

ALLEN, ELIOT DINSMORE, coll. dean; b. Phila., Nov. 13, 1918; s. Harold Douglass and Mabel (Seeley) A.; grad. William Penn Charter Sch., 1936; B.A., Wesleyan U., Middletown, Conn., 1940; student U. Coll. South West (Eng.), 1938-39; A.M., Harvard, 1941; M.A., Princeton, 1947, Ph.D. in English, 1949; m. Dorothy Lois Douglass, Jan. 25, 1947; children—Lois, Harold, Douglass, Ethan. Instr. English, U. Va., 1947-49; asst. prof., then asso. prof. U. Mass., 1949-60; asso. prof. Stetson U., 1960-62, prof. English, 1962-68, dean humanities, 1968-70; dean humanities N.Y. State U. Coll., Plattsburgh, 1970—. Served with USNR, 1942-46. Mem. Modern Lang. Assn., U.S. Naval Inst., Phi Betta Kappa, Phi Nu Theta, Sigma Phi Epsilon, Co-author; A Short Guide to Writing a Research Paper, MS Form and Documentation, 1963; A Short Guide to Writing a Critical Review, 1964; Effect of Practice and Evaluation on Improvement in Written Composition, 1964; The Student Writer's Guide, 1970. Editor: Challenges of Change to the Christian College, 1966. Home: 71 Beekman St Plattsburgh NY 12901

ALLEN, ELIZABETH, (E Ellen Gillease), actress, singer; b. Jersey City, Jan. 25, 1934; d. Joseph and Viola (Mannion) Gillease: student Traphagen Sch. Design. N.Y.C., 1952-54; m. Carl von Vietinghoff-Scheel, Oct. 23, 1952 (div. 1955). Profl. debut in stock prodn. The Tender Trap, 1955; played Juliet in Romanoff and Juliet, N.Y.C., 1957, Magda in The Gay Life, N.Y.C., 1961; numerous roles in stock prodns. and touring cos. throughout U.S., 1955—; played in Cactus Flower, Chgo., 1967; appeared in motion pictures From the Terrace, 1960, Diamond Head, 1962, Donovan's Reef, 1963; made TV debut on Jackie Gleason Show, 1955-56, later appeared various programs including Jack Paar Show, 1959, Wells Fargo, 1960, The Naked City, 1960, 63, 77 Sunset Strip, 1961, Ed Sullivan Show, 1962, Tonight Show, 1963. Recipient Laurel award as outstanding new female personality, 1963. Mem. Actors Equity Assn., Screen Actors Guild, Am. Guild Variety Artists, A.F.T.R.A. Home: 205 E 78th St New York City NY 10021 Office: care Internat Famous Agy 1301 Av of Americas New York City NY 10019

ALLEN, EMIL WILLIAM, Jr., librarian; b. Raymond, N.H., Mar. 4, 1926; s. Emil William and Thelma Mae (Brown) A.; A.B., Bowdoin Coll., 1950, M.L.S., Pratt Inst., 1952; m. Anna Marilyn Coviello, Feb. 12, 1955; children—Mark Vincent, Megan Elizabeth, Rachel Ann. With sci. div. Bklyn. Pub. Library, 1952-53, stack curator, 1953-54; chief bus. and industry div. Ferguson Library, Stamford, Conn., 1955-56; asst. state librarian N.H. Library, Concord, 1956-64, state librarian, 1964—. Sec., N.H. Library Commn., 1964—; exec. sec., dir. Library Found. N.H., 1970—; chmn. New Eng. Interstate Library Compact Bd., 1967—; cons. S.C. State Library, 1970. Dir. Saban Electric Co. Mem. Warner Town budget com., 1962-68, 70—, chmn., 1966-68; mem. Kearsarge Coop. Sch. Dist. planning bd., 1964-66, Kearsarge Regional Sch. Bd., 1966-69; dir. Warner Fall Foliage Festival, Inc., 1970—; mem. Warner Cemetery Commn., 1970—; precinct commnr. Warner Village Fire Dist., 1971—. Trustee Concord Hosp.; bd. dirs. Concord Mental Health Center, 1969-71. Served with AUS, 1944-46, USAF, 1950-51. Mem. Am. Soc. Pub. Adminstrn., Am. (council 1965-69), New Eng. (pres. 1965-66), N.H. library assns.,

Am. Library Trustees Assn. (v.p. 1969-70), N.H. Library Council, Audubon Soc. N.H., Warner Hist. Soc., Soc. Protection N.H. Forests, N.H. Hist. Assn., Am. Civil Liberties Union, N.H. Meml. Soc. (pres. 1967-69), Republican. Unitarian. Kiwanian (pres. Concord 1962). Club: Bowdoin of N.H. Home: Box 204 Warner NH 03278 Office: N H State Library Concord NH 03301

ALLEN, ERNEST MASON, govt. ofcl.; b. Terrell, Tex., Dec. 1, 1904; s. Louis L. and Ada (Turner) A.; Ph.B. magna cum laude, Emory U., 1926, M.A., 1939, D.Sc. (hon.), 1956; LL.D., Clemson U., 1968; m. Virginia Williamson, June 7, 1928; children—Anton M., E. Raworth, James W. Instr. French, Jr. Coll. of Augusta, Ga., 1926-41; sec., treas. Augusta Bus. Coll., 1930-41; project mgr. NYA, Ga., 1941-43; sr. public health representative division veneral diseases USPHS, 1943-45, operations officer, 1945-46, assistant chief division research grants Nat. Insts. Health, 1946-51, chief div. research grants, 1951-60, asso. dir. 1960- 63; grants policy officer USPHS, 1963-68, dir. Office of Extramural Programs, 1968-69; dep. asst. sec. for grant administration policy Department of Health, Education and Welfare, 1969—. Chairman of gov. bd. BioSciences Information Exchange, 1952-55; mem. adv. com. U.S. sci. exhibit Century 21 Expn.; mem. 1963 Nat. Health Forum Com. Cons. Pres.'s Commn. on Health Needs of Nation, mem. com. on academic sci. and engring., 1968-70. Recipient Yorktown medal Gov. of France, 1932. Mem. Phi Beta Kappa, Phi Sigma Iota, Phi Theta Kappa (Distinguished Service award 1971). Home: 8507 Hazelwood Dr Bethesda MD 20014

ALLEN, FRANCIS ALFRED, educator; b. Kansas City, Kan., Oct. 25, 1919; s. Oliver Boyd and Justa Lee (Wingo) A.; A.B., Cornell Coll., 1941, Doctor of Jurisprudence, (honorary), 1958; LL.B. magna cum laude, Northwestern U., 1946; m. June Florence Murphy, Feb. 16, 1947; children—Neil Walsh, Susan Lee. Admitted to Ill. bar, 1950, Mich. bar, 1968; editor-in-chief Ill. Law Rev., 1942-43; legal sec. Chief Justice Fred M. Vinson, 1946-48: asst. prof. law Northwestern U., 1948-50, asso. prof., 1950-53; prof. law Harvard, 1953-56, U. Chgo., 1956-62, U. Mich., 1962-63; Univ. prof. also prof. law U. Chicago, 1963- 66; dean law U. Mich., Ann Arbor, 1966-71, prof., 1966—; faculty Salzburg Seminar in Am. studies, summer 1963. Spl. cons. ESA, 1951. Chairman citizens adv. com. Ill. Sex Offenders Commn., 1952-53; drafting chmn. Ill. Criminal Code, 1961; mem. citizens advisory committee of the Family Court of Cook County, 1962. Served as sgt. USAAF, 1942-45. Recipient Arthur von Briesen medal National Legal Aid and Defender Association, 1963. Guggenheim fellow, 1971-72. Mem. Am. Bar Association, Am. Law Inst. (mem. council 1969—), Ill. Acad. Criminology (pres. 1961-62), Am. Correctional Assn., Phi Beta Kappa, Order of Coif. Methodist. Author: The Borderland of Criminal Justice, 1964. Editor: Standards of American Legislation (Freund), 1965. Contbr. articles on legal subjects to jours. Home: 414 Huntington Pl Ann Arbor MI 48104

ALLEN, FRANCIS F., Jr., pub. service exec.; b. Berkely, Cal., Dec. 29, 1922; s. Francis F. and Ethel (Dooley) A.; A.B. in History and Polit. Sci., U. Cal. at Berkeley, M.B.A. in Marketing, 1948; B.S. in Commerce, 1947, Naval Sci., Notre Dame, 1943; m. Jean McCloud, July 10, 1947; children—Janice Moore, Sally Ann, Nancy Francis, Lucy Elizabeth. Formerly phys. edn. instr. pub. schs., Berkeley, Cal.; asst. instr. retailing U. Cal. at Berkeley, 1948-49; managerial positions Emporium Capwell Corp., Western Dept. Store, San Francisco; advt. and market devel. asst. U.S. Steel Corp.; chmn. Allen & Dorward, San Francisco, Los Angeles, N.Y.C., Pub. Communications Bur., N.Y.C., San Francisco, Telephone Directory Service, San Francisco and Los Angeles; mng. partner PCB Properties Co., San Francisco; pres. Bermuda Research Corp., Oakland. Active Pub. Playground Depts., Oakland, Cal., Berkeley, Piedmont, Cal.; mem. com. devel. Intra-County Swimming Activity, Contra Costa Co. Youth. Active pub. relations Republican party, 1952, 56, 60; adviser Rep. Central Com. Cal. Served to capt. USN, World War II, Korea. Mem. U.S. Navy League, Res. Officer Naval Services, Assn. Indsl. Advertisers (pres. 1959, also dir.), San Francisco, Los Angeles, Portland ad clubs, Advt. Assn. West, Am. Mgmt. Assn., Am. Inst. Mgmt. (mem. presl. council). Am. Marketing Agy. Network (exec. council), San Francisco C. of C., Commonwealth Club, U.S. Forestry Assn., Sierra Club, Issac Walton League, Redwoods Assn., Duck and Trout Unlimited. Home: 125 Meadow View Rd Orinda CA 94563 Office: Allen & Dorward Advt 1660 Bush St San Francisco CA 94109

ALLEN, FRANCIS PITCHER, ret. librarian; b. Rochester, N.Y., Nov. 12, 1902; s. Edwin P. and Edith (Allerton) A.; B.A., Amherst Coll., 1927; B.S., Columbia, 1929; M.A., U. Mich., 1933; m. Janet McMaster, Sept. 12, 1936; 1 dau., Elizabeth MacMaster. Reference librarian Cornell U., 1929-30; librarian univ. museums U. Mich., 1930-36; prof. bibliography U. R.I., 1936-69, librarian, 1936-69, also university archivist, 1959-69, librarian, prof. bibliography emeritus, 1969—; lectr. Library-Audio Visual Dept., U.S. Fla. at Tampa, 1969—. Mem. R.I. Adv. Board Library Commrs. Mem. A.L.A., R.I. Library Assn. (pres. 1943-45) Am. Assn. U. Profs., Soc. Mayflower Descendants, Theta Delta Chi, Phi Kappa Phi (pres. local chpt. 1956—). Presbyterian. Clubs: Grolier (New York City); University (Providence); Rotary (Wakefield, R.I.); Dunes (Narragansett, R.I.); Field (Sarasota, Fla.). Contbr. to Encyclopedia Americana, 1959. Home: 763 John Ringling Blvd Sarasota FL 35577

ALLEN, FRANCIS V., bishop; b. Toronto, Can., June 25, 1909; s. Valentine and Martha (Malcolm) A.; ed. St. Augustine's Sem. Ordained priest Roman Cath. Ch.; asst. St. Dunstan's Parish. Toronto. 1933-34. Blessed Sacrament Parish. Toronto, 1934-35; sec. St. Augustine's Sem., 1935-36; vice chancellor in Temporalibus, 1936-41; v.p. Cath. Ch. Extension Soc., 1941-42; chancellor in Spirtualibus, 1942-48, in Spirtaulibus et Temporalibus, 1948-51; vicar delegate for religious, archidiocesan consulator, 1951-52; pastor Our Lady of Sorrows Parish, Toronto, 1952-54; now bishop.

ALLEN, FRANK CARROLL, banker; b. Hazlehurst, Miss., Nov. 10, 1913; s. Walter Scott and May (Ellis) A.; A.A. with high honors, Copiah-Lincoln Jr. Coll., Wesson, Miss., 1933; student Am. Inst. Banking, 1935, 36, 37, 47, 49; m. Clara Marnee Alford, June 23, 1937; children—Marnee Louise (Mrs. Buel D. Russell), Susan Carroll, Elizabeth Jane. Bookkeeper, teller Georgetown Bank (Miss.), 1933-34, cashier, dir., 1937-41; bookkeeper Deposit Guaranty Bank & Trust Co., Jackson, Miss., 1934-37; bank examiner, Miss., 1942-46; cashier, dir. Brookhaven Bank & Trust Co. (Miss.), 1947-49; pres., dir. Lawrence County Bank, Monticello, Miss., 1949-65; pres. Monticello Bank, 1966—; chmn. adv. bd. Monticello/Newhebron Bank brs., 1966—; adv. bd. Deposit Guaranty Nat. Bank, Jackson, 1966—; chmn. bd., dir. Ins. & Realty Underwriters. Bd. dirs. Miss. Econ. Council, 1950-53; commnr. Monticello Planning Bd., 1964—; bd. dirs. S.W. Miss. Devel. Assn., 1960—. Chmn. scholarship bd. Monticello Mfg. Co., 1960—; trustee Chapman Trust Fund, 1962—. Served to 1st lt. AUS, 1942-46. Mem. Am. (chmn. Miss. dist. 7 on U.S. Savs. Bonds 1952), Miss. (chmn. bank mgmt. com. 1948-49, group v.p. 1948-49) bankers assns., Monticello C. of C. (pres. 1951-53, 60-61, dir. 1951—). Democrat. Baptist (deacon 1953—, Sunday sch. supt. 1958-60). Lion (pres. Monticello 1957-58). Home: PO Box 297 Monticello MS 39654 Office: PO Box 458 Monticello MS 39654

ALLEN, FRED CARY, army officer; b. Vine Grove, Ky., Apr. 29, 1917; s. Fred P. and Alice (Peterson) A.; B.S., Western Ky. U., 1940; m. Eunice Bond, Jan. 25, 1958; children—Joyce Gail (Mrs. David Schimberg), David Frederick. Commd. 2d lt., U.S. Army, 1940, advanced through grades to brig. gen., 1967; inf. and transp. assignments, U.S., Far East, Korea, Alaska, 1940-58; comdg. officer Transp. Bn., 1st Inf. Div., Ft. Riley, Kan., 1958-60; student Indsl. Coll. Armed Forces, Washington, 1960-61; comdg. officer Army Support Command, Alaska, 1962-63; chief of staff U.S. Army, Alaska, 1964-65; dir. army transp. Dept. of Army, Pentagon, 1966-67; dir. logistics (J-A) U.S. Strike Command, MacDill AFB, Fla., 1967-69; dir. prodn. ships, weapons and electronics system Office Sec. of Def., 1969—. Decorated Legion of Merit with 3 oak leaf clusters, Bronze Star, Army Commendation medal. Mem. Nat. Def. Transportation Assn. (hon. nat. pres., v.p. for Alaska 1963-69), Assn. U.S. Army. Rotarian. Home: 8410 Porter St Alexandria VA 22308 Office: Office Secretary of Defense The Pentagon Washington DC 20301

ALLEN, FRED HAROLD, Jr., physician; b. Holyoke, Mass., Feb. 23, 1912; s. Fred Harold and Harriet (Ives) A.; A.B., Amherst Coll., 1934; M.D., Harvard, 1938; m. Frances Williams Brown, July 16, 1938; children—Philip Brown, Mark Harold, Barbara (Mrs. Donald R. Brewster), Dwight Bickford. Intern Children's Hosp., Boston, 1938-42; practice pediatrics, Holyoke, Mass., 1946-47; asso. dir. Blood Grouping Lab., Boston, 1947-63; sr. investigator N.Y. Blood Center of Community Blood Council Greater N.Y., 1963—; clin. asso. prof. pediatrics Cornell U. Med. Coll., 1963—. Served to maj., M.C., AUS, 1942-46. Recipient Karl Landsteiner Meml. award Am. Assn. Blood Banks, 1963; Joseph P. Kennedy Internat. award research mental retardation, 1966. Bd. dirs., vice pres. Dessoff Choirs, N.Y.C. Author: (with L. K. Diamond) Erythroblastosis Fetalis, 1958; also articles. Chief editor for N. and S. Am., Vox Sanguinis, 1963—. Asso. editor Transfusion. Discovered cause and prevention of brain damage in erythroblastosis fetalis, 1950. Home: 3 Merestone Terrace Bronxville NY 10708 Office: 310 E 67th St New York City NY 10021

ALLEN, FRED TIRRELL, business equipment mfg. co. exec.; b. Providence, Sept 20, 1916: s. Lewis Leprelate and Fannie (Pike) A.; B.S., Brown U., 1938; m. Charlotte Ann MacIntyre, June 21, 1940; children—Fred Tirrell, William C., Richard M., Kathleen. With Pitney-Bowes, Inc., Stamford, Conn., 1938—, prodn. control mgr., 1948-55, v.p. mfg., 1955-63, exec. v.p. products, 1963-69, pres., chief operating officer, 1969—; chmn. bd., pres., dir Collateurs Automatiques, S.A.; dir. Thomas Collators, C.P. Bourg, S.A., Monarch Marking Systems Co., Malco Plastics, Inc., Pitney-Bowes of Can., Ltd., Stamford Fidelity Bank & Trust Co. Campaign chmn. United Fund, 1962, 1st v.p., 1963; chmn. Stamford Citizens Action Council, 1964-65; pres. Mgmt. Council Southwestern Conn., 1959-61, 64-66. Home: 338 Stanwich Rd Greenwich CT 06832 Office: 69 Walnut and Pacific Sts Stamford CT 06904

ALLEN, GAY WILSON, univ. prof.; b. Lake Junaluska, N.C., Aug. 23, 1903; s. Robert Henry and Ethel (Garren) A.; A.B., Duke U., 1926, M.A., 1928; Ph.D., U. of Wis., 1934; m. Evie Allison, July 15, 1929. Instr. in English, Lake Erie Coll., Painesville, O., 1929-31, Shurtleff Coll., Alton, Ill., 1934-35, State Univ., Bowling Green, O., 1935-46; prof. English, N.Y.U., 1946—; tchr. summer schs. Harvard, Duke, U. Tex., U. Hawaii. Fellow Rockefeller Found., 1944-45, Guggenheim fellow, 1952-53, 59-60. Mem. International Assn. U. Profs. English, Am. Studies Assn., Modern Language Assn. Am., Phi Beta Kappa. Club: P.E.N. Author: American Prosody, 1935; Literary Criticism: Pope to Croce (with H. H. Clark), 1941; Walt Whitman Handbook, 1946; Masters of American Literature (with H. A. Pochmann), 1949; The Solitary Singer. A Critical Biography of Walt Whitman, 1955; Walt Whitman Abroad, 1955; Walt Whitman's Poems (with C.T. Davis), 1955; Walt Whitman: Evergreen Profile Book, 1959; Walt Whitman as Man, Poet and Legend, 1961; American Poetry (with Walter Rideout and James K. Robinson), 1965; William James. A Biography, 1967. General editor (with Sculley Bradley) Collected Writings of Walt Whitman, 1961—. Contbr. articles and reviews to nat., internat. jours. Home: 454 Grove St Oradell NJ 07649

ALLEN, GEORGE, football coach; b. Detroit, Apr. 29, 1922; s. Earl R. and Loretta (Hannigan) A.; B.A., M.A., U. Mich.; postgrad. U. So. Cal.; m. Etty L. Lumbroso, May 26, 1951; children—George, Gregory, Gerald, Jennifer. Formerly football coach Morningside Coll., Sioux City, Ia., Whittier (Cal.) Coll.; head coach, gen. mgr. Washington Redskins, Nat. Football Conf. Address: 2924 Via Pacheco Palos Verdes CA

ALLEN, GEORGE EDMUND, Jr., lawyer, corp. exec.; b. Kent, O., 1922; B.A., Yale, 1943, LL.B., 1944; m. Mae Reed, May 2, 1949; 1 son. Admitted to Massachusetts bar, 1944; practiced in Boston, 1947--; gen. counsel Acme Mfg. Co., Boston, 1966--; dir. 1st Nat. Bank. Home: 23 Beacon St Boston MA 02107

ALLEN, GEORGE EDWARD, lawyer; b. Booneville, Miss., Feb. 29, 1896; s. Sam. P. and Mollie (Plaxico) A.; LL.B., Cumberland Univ., 1917, LL.D., 1938; Dr. Humane Letters (hon.) Temple Univ., Phila., 1949; m. Mary Keane, Sept. 10, 1930. Admitted to Miss. bar, 1917; in practice at Okolona, 1917-19; in hotel business, 1919-33; commr. of D.C., 1933-39; vice pres. Home Insurance Co. of N.Y., 1938-45; counsel Alvord & Alvord; p. chmn. bd. Duke Internat. Corp., N.Y., Victor Elec. Co., Cin.; mem. exec. com. and dir., AVCO Mfg. Corp., N.Y.; dir. Occidental Life Insurance Co.; trustee Penn. Mutual Life Insurance member board directors Air fleets, Inc., Borne Scrymser Co., City Products Co. Chgo., Duquesne Light Co., Pittsburgh, Pa., W. L. Maxon Corp., N.Y., Washington Mut. Investors Fund, Inc., District of Columbia, Republic Steel Corporation, Washington Properties, Inc., Central States Edison, Phila. Co., Standard Gas & Elec. Co., Steep Rock Iron Mines, Ltd., also S. Klein Department Stores, Sheraton-Astor and the Sheraton Closed-Circuit Television, Inc. Dir. R.F.C.; pres. R.F.C. Mortgage Co. Fed. Nat. Mortgage Assn., War Damage Corp.; treas. Dem. Nat. Congressional Com. since 1940; sec. Dem. Nat. Com., 1943. Trustee Ga. Warm Springs Foundn. Mem. Am. Red Cross (nat. adv. com.; pres. war. com., 1934-44), Boy Scouts of Am. (nat. exec. com.; awarded Silver Buffalo); mem. Nat. Foundation for Infantile Paralysis (v.p. and dir.), Kappa Sigma. Democrat. Methodist. Clubs: Metropolitan, Recess, Wings; Deepdale, Cloud (N.Y.); Burning Tree, Metropolitan (Washington). Author: Presidents Who Have Known Me, 1950. Home: Wardman Park Hotel Washington DC 20008

ALLEN, GEORGE HOWARD, publishing exec.; b. Boston, June 1, 1914; s. Albert Hacker and Myrtie A. (Lawton) A.; B.S., U. Mass., 1936, LL.D., 1967; M.B.A., Harvard, 1938; m. Virginia Russell, Sept. 7, 1940; 1 son, Russell Lawton. Asst. to pres. Nat. Theatre Supply Co., N.Y.C., 1938-40; research mgr. radio sta. WOR, 1941, asst. dir. promotion and research, 1942-43; radio cons. U.S. Treasury Dept., 1943-45; gen. mgr., sec. bd. Coop. Analysis of Broadcasting, N.Y.C., 1944-46; N.E. sales mgr. N.Y. Herald Tribune, 1946, promotion mgr., 1947- 50; chmn. 20th Nat. Bus. Conf., Harvard, 1950; dir. sales promotion McCall's mag., 1950-57, asst. pub., gen. mgr., 1957-60; pub. Better Living mag., 1956; v.p. Mass Markets Publs., Inc., 1953-54, pres., 1954- 55, dir., 1953-55; spl. asst. to pres. Meredith Pub. Co., N.Y.C., 1960- 61, v.p., 1961-66, dir., 1965-66, gen. mgr. mag. pub. div., Des Moines, 1962-66, pub. Better Homes and Gardens, Successful Farming mags., 1964-66; chmn. bd. Nat. Plan Service, Chgo., 1965-66; pub., v.p. Fawcett Publs., Inc., N.Y.C., 1966—. Bd. dirs. Internat. Exchange Program, Ann Arbor. Recipient leadership award Am. Legion, 1932; Young Advt. Man of Year, 1956; Achievement Award, Wash. Ad Club, 1956; Silver Anvil award, Am. Pub. Relations Assn., 1957; Bell Ringer award, Salt Lake City Ad Club, 1957; Pub. Relations News award, 1957; Mgmt. Man of Year. Mem. Am. Marketing Assn. (pres. N.Y. 1946), N.A.M. (dir.), Mag. Pubs. Assn. (dir.), Advt. Fedn. Am. (dir.), U.S. C. of C. (edn. com. 1964-66), Advt. Research Found. (dir. 1965, sec.-treas. 1971), Am. States. Assn., U. Mass. Alumni (v.p.), Harvard Bus. Sch. Assn. (chmn. publs. com. 1967), Harvard Alumni Assn. (dir. 1958- 59), Sales Promotion Execs. Assn. (mem. nat. bd. 1958), Pub. Relations Soc. Am., Newcomen Soc., Lambda Chi Alpha, Adelphis. Conglist. Clubs: Harvard, Canadian, Economic, Pinnacle (N.Y.C.); International (Chgo.); Contbr. articles profl. mags. Home: 112 Pear Tree Point Rd Darien CT 06820 Office: Fawcett Publs Inc 1 Astor Plaza New York City NY 10036

ALLEN, GEORGE WHITAKER, educator, physician; b. Milledgeville, Ga., Feb. 8, 1928; s. Henry Dawson and Caroline (Reynolds) A.; A.B., Harvard, 1948; M.D., Columbia, 1952; m. Lis Margaret Jensen, Oct. 6, 1951; 1 son, John Whitaker. Intern Presbyn. Hosp., N.Y.C., 1952-53; resident U. Chgo. Clinics, 1955-58; pvt. practice, specializing in otolaryngology, Chgo., 1960—; head otolaryngology dept. Chgo. Wesley Meml. Hosp., 1964-67; mem. staff Cook County Hosp.; dir. teaching, research Dept. Otolaryngology, Northwestern U., Chgo., 1959-63. Mem. adv. group Communicative Scis. Study Sect., USPHS, Bethesda, Md., 1962-65. Served with M.C., AUS, 1953-55 Fellow A.C.S.; mem. A.A.A.S., A.M.A., Acoustical Soc. Republican. Methodist. Club: Lake Shore (Chgo.). Research in auditory physiology. Home: 321 Warwick Rd Kenilworth, IL 60043, Office: Chgo Wesley Meml Hosp 250 E Superior St Chicago IL 60611

ALLEN, GINA, author; b. Trenton, Neb.; d. R.V. and Osa (Hanel) Hunkins; B.A. Northwestern U., 1940; m. T.W. Allen; 1 dau. Ginita Allen Wall. Exec. sec. Youth Commn., 3d Jud. Dist. N.M., 1955-60; mem. bd. San Francisco chpt. Henry George Sch. Social Sci., 1969—, San Francisco chpt. Nat. Orgn. for Women, 1970—, Humanist Assn. of San Francisco, 1970—. Chmn. N.M. Democratic Central Com., 1956-59. Unitarian. Author: Prairie Children, 1941; On the Oregon Trail, 1942; Rustics for Keeps, 1948; (with R. V. Hunkins) Tepee Days, 1941, Trapper Days, 1942; Sod-House Days, 1945; The Forbidden Man, 1961 (Anlsfield-Wolf award 1962), Gold!, 1964; Gold Is, 1969; (with Clement G. Martin) Intimacy, 1971; also short stories, articles in popular mags. Mailing Address Only:

ALLEN, GLEN OLAF, educator; b. Canadaigua, N.Y., Jan. 12, 1920; s. Arthur Augustus and Elsa (Guerdrum) A.; A.B., Cornell U., 1941, A.M., 1946, Ph.D., 1951; m. Jean Nancie Frank, July 6, 1946; children—Glen Frank, Arthur Gregory, Gary Guerdrum. Instr. English and philosophy Wells Coll., Aurora, N.Y., 1951-54; mem. faculty Ida. State U., 1954—, prof. English and philosophy, 1961—, chmn. dept. philosophy, 1955-67. Served with F.A., AUS, 1941-46; PTO. Mem. Modern Lang. Assn., Am. Soc. Aesthetics, Am. Philos. Assn., Mind Assn., Phi Delta Theta. Contbr. profl. jours. Home: Box 364 Johnny Creek Rd Pocatello, ID 83201.

ALLEN, GORDON FORREST, coll. ofcl.; b. Freedom, N.Y., Dec. 23, 1908; s. Earl and Louise (Owens) A.; A.B., Houghton Coll., 1930; M.S. in Edn., Cornell U., 1937; Ed.D., U. Buffalo, 1955; m. Faith Ellinwood, April 11, 1936 (dec. Aug. 1967); children—Christopher G., Douglas F.; m. 2d, Elsa V. Benham, Oct. 9, 1968; stepchildren—Elsa Jane, Jeanne. Tchr. sci. and social studies, coach Groveland (N.Y.) High Sch., 1930-31; prin. Cuylerville (N.Y.) pub. schs., 1931-34; tchr. math., social studies Brighton High Sch., Rochester, N.Y., 1934-39, prin., 1939- 47; prof. edn. State U. Coll. Edn., Brockport, N.Y., 1947-55, chmn. dept. edn., 1955-56, dean coll., 1956-64; acting pres. State U. N.Y. at Brockport, 1964-66, vice president for academic affairs, 1966-70, prof. emeritus, 1970—. Member N.E.A., N.Y. State Tchrs. Assn., Rochester Mus., Rochester Art Gallery, Phi Delta Kappa. Presbyn. Clubs: Torch, Rochester. Home: 74 Lynnwood Dr Brockport NY 14420

ALLEN, HARLAND HILL, economist; b. Loyalton, S.D., Dec. 9, 1888; s. Albert Barnes and Harriet Mabel (Hill) A.; student Dakota Wesleyan U., LL.D. (hon.), 1958; A.B., Colo. Tchrs. Coll., 1916, A.M., 1917; postgrad. U. Chgo., 1920-21, Columbia, 1924, Paris, London, Berlin, Leipzig, summers 1926, 29; m. Florence Brooks, May 28, 1927 (dec. Dec. 1964); children—Franklin (dec.), Rolaine Kay (Mrs. James Groves); m. 2d, Alma Louise Petersen, Aug. 8, 1965. Editor, pub. Roscoe (S.D.) Reveille, 1911-12; supt. pub. schs., Kersey, Colo., 1915-16; prof. econs. N. Tex. State Tchrs. Coll., Denton, 1917-19; fellow, teaching asst. U. Chgo., 1919-21; instr. econs. U. Ill., 1921-22; prof. econs., dean Sch. Commerce, Okla. Agrl. and Mech Coll., 1923-24; economist Halsey, Stuart & Co., Chgo., 1927-29, Foreman State Nat. Bank, 1929-31; pres. Growth Research, Inc., successors to Harland Allen Assos., investment mgrs., 1931-61, chmn. bd., 1961-68; founder, chief exec. Growth Industry Shares, Inc., 1946-64; dean Roosevelt Coll. Sch. Commerce, Chgo., 1947-49, xec. com., chmn. bd., 1959-63; charter mem. bd. La Salle Fund, Chgo. Bd. dirs. Dakota Wesleyan U., Mitchell, S.D., Edward A. Filene Good Will Fund. Chmn., Chgo. chpt. Com. to Defend Am., 1941. Recipient Man of Year citation Dakota Weslyan U., 1961. Mem. Am. Econs. Assn., Am. Statis. Assn. (past pres. Chgo.). Unitarian. Clubs: City (dir.), Mid-America, Investment Analysts (pres. 1932-33). Lectr., writer. Author: Whither Interest Rates, 1939; The Businessman's Stake in American-Soviet Friendship, 1943; Investing for Growth-Why and How, 1957; How the Science Revolution is Changing the Social Order, 1964; series World Economic Perspectives for the 1970's, 1970-71; syndicated newspaper column Your Money Problems, 1924-29, Harland Allen Economic Letter, 1932-44. Contbr. articles to Forbes, Barron's, Bankers Monthly, House and Garden, Rotarian, Am. Bankers Assn. Jour., others. Home: 431 S Alvernon Way Tucson AZ 85711

ALLEN, HAROLD BYRON, educator; b. Grand Rapids, Mich., Oct. 6, 1902; s. Arthur Kingsbury and Edith (Welch) A.; B.A., Kalamazoo Coll., 1924; M.A., U. Mich., 1928, Ph.D., 1941; m. Elizabeth Mitchell, June 19, 1934; children—Marjorie Lyle (Mrs. Alexander G. Russell), Susan Kingsbury. From asst. prof. to prof. rhetoric, also asst. to pres. Shurtleff Coll., Alton, Ill., 1925- 34; asst. editor Early Modern English Dictionary, 1934-39, Middle English Dictionary, 1939-40; asst. prof. English San Diego State Coll., 1940-43; mem. faculty U. Minn., 1944—, prof. English, 1958-68, prof. English and linguistics, 1968-71, prof. emeritus, 1971; vis. summer prof. Mills Coll., 1943, U. So. Cal., 1961; Fulbright lectr. U. Cairo (Egypt), 1954-55; Smith-Mundt vis. prof. linguistics UAR Ministry of Education, Cairo, 1958-59; dir., editor Linguistic Atlas of Upper Midwest, 1947—; linguistic consultant The Economy Co., 1967—; English lang. cons. U. Tehran (Iran), 1971. Chmn. lang. arts adv. com. Minn. Bd. Edn., 1962-67. Am. Council Learned Soc. fellow, summers, 1938-40; fellow Fund Advancement Edn., 1951-52. Mem. Am. Friends of Middle East (exec. bd. Minn. 1957—), Am. Civil Liberties Union, Am. Assn. U. Profs., Nat. Council Tchrs. English (pres. 1961; dir. commn. English lang. 1964-67, chmn. Conf. Coll. Composition and

Communication 1952), Tchrs. English to Speakers of Other Langs. (pres. 1966-67), Linguistic Soc. Am., Am. Dialect Soc. (mem. exec. council 1963-68, v.p. 1968-71, pres. 1971—), Am. Name Soc. (bd. mgrs. 1961-63), Canadian Linguistic Assn., Internat. Assn. U. Profs. English, Speech Communication Assn., Minn. Group Linguistics (chmn. 1948- 64-67), Internat. Linguistic Assn., Phi Delta Kappa, Phi Kappa Phi, Pi Kappa Delta, Sigma Tau Delta, Theta Alpha Phi. Author: An Introduction to English Sound Structure, 1960; (with others) New Dimensions in English, 1966; TENES-A Survey of the Teaching of English to Non-English Speakers in the U.S., 1966, also articles. Editor, compiler in field. Home: 200 Cecil St SE Minneapolis MN 55414

ALLEN, HAROLD C., chmn. bd. Allen Industries, Inc. Home: 16500 N Park Dr Southfield MI 48075 Office: Honeywell Bldg 17515 W 9 Mile Rd Southfield MI 48075

ALLEN, HAROLD G., life ins. co. exec.; b. Mecosta County, Mich., Oct. 9, 1911; s. William and Verna R. (Phelps) A.; B.A., U. Mich., 1933, M.A., 1934; m. Jean D. Crawford, Aug. 1, 1937; children—Margaret D., Nancy R. With Bankers Life Co., Des Moines, 1934—, actuary, 1956-63, 2d v.p., 1956-59, v.p., 1959- 66, sr. v.p., 1966-68, pres., 1968—, dir., 1967—. Served to 1st lt. USMCR, 1943-46. Fellow Soc. Actuaries; mem. Des Moines C. of C. (dir.). Home: 4333 Greenwood Dr Des Moines IA 50312

ALLEN, HARRY CLAY, Jr., chemist, educator; b. Saugus, Mass., Nov. 26, 1920; s. Harry Clay and Sarah Elizabeth (Thorburn) A.; B.S., Northeastern U., 1948; Sc.M., Brown U., 1949; Ph.D., U. Wash., 1951; m. Carolyn A. Bliss, Feb. 2, 1948; children—Carol B., Paul T. Research fellow Harvard, 1951-53; asst. prof. Mich. State U., 1953-54; chemist Nat. Bur. Standards, 1954-61, chief analytical and inorganic chemistry div., 1961-63, chief inorganic materials div., 1963-65, dep. dir. Inst. for Materials Research, 1965-66; asst. dir. minerals research Bur. Mines, 1966- 68; prof. chemistry, chmn. dept. Clark U., 1969—. Research asso. U. Cambridge (Eng.), 1959-60; vis. research prof. U. Wash., 1958. Postdoctoral fellow AEC, 1951-53. Served with AUS, 1942-46. Recipient Samuel Wesley Stratton award Nat. Bur. Standards, 1965. Fellow Am. Phys. Soc. Washington Acad. Scis.; mem. Am. Chem. Soc., Sigma Xi, Phi Lambda Upsilon. Club: Cosmos (Washington). Author: (with P. C. Cross) Molecular Vib-rotors, 1963. Home: 21 Rittenhouse Rd Worchester, MA 01602.

ALLEN, HARRY LEE, steel co. exec.; b. Cleve., July 16, 1908; s. Harry Lee and Nelle Virginia (Hayes) A.; student Case Inst. Tech., U. Ala.; m. Henrietta Pearce, Aug. 17, 1935; children—Patricia (Mrs. John G. Murchie), Nancy (Mrs. Robert F. Ducatte), Harry Lee, Mary (Mrs. Kenneth Graziani), Martha. With Corrigan-McKinney Steel Co., 1933-35; co. merged with Rep. Steel Corp., 1935, asst. v.p. steel operations, 1954-60, v.p. operations, 1960-62, v.p. operating staff services and customer relations, 1962-66, v.p., gen. mgr. operations, dir., 1966—. Trustee St. Luke's Hospital. Mem. Am. Iron and Steel Inst., Inst. Mining, and Metall. Engrs., Phi Kappa Psi. Home: 6121 Shore Dr North Madison OH 44057

ALLEN, HENRY ELLSHA, retired educator; b. Orange, N.J., June 13, 1902; s. E. Hubert and Jane Elizabeth (Durand) A.; A.B., Yale, 1924; A.M., Ph.D., U. Chgo., 1930; m. Helen Elizabeth Davis, June 18, 1927; children—Lenore Elizabeth (Mrs. Richard A. Robertson), Carrolyn Ruth (Mrs. Craig M. Wiester). Tchr., Hill Sch., Pottstown, Pa., 1924-26; mem. faculty dept. religion, dir. Christian assn. Lafayette Coll., Easton, Pa., 1930-41; exchange prof. Occidental Coll., Los Angeles, 1939-40; pres. Keuka Coll., Keuka Park, N.Y., 1941-46; asso. dir. program Planned Parenthood Fedn. Am., 1946-47; coordinator students' religious activities U. Minn., 1947-70, prof., 1951-70; lectr. Haskell Inst., U. Chgo., 1933. Fellow Soc. Religion in Higher Edn., Harris Inst. Round Table, summer 1942; mem. Assn. for Coordination Univ. Religious Affairs, 1960—, v.p., 1960-61, pres. 1962. Chmn. intergroup relations com. Greater Mpls. Council of Chs., 1951-53; mem. Gov. Adv. Council on Children and Youth (chmn. com. on religious values 1953-61), Mpls. Round Table Nat. Conf. Christians and Jews (dir. 1948—); mem. Gov. Minn. Human Rights Com., 1950-67, vice chmn., 1956-61; chmn. com. religious observance Minn. Statehood Centennial Commn., 1958; del. White House Conf. Children and Youth, 1960; mem. Mpls. Mayor's Commn. on Human Relations, 1960-64; mem. nat. adv. com. Indian affairs Am. Civil Liberties Union, 1959-62; chmn. internat. affairs com. Minn. Council Chs., 1971—. Bd. dirs. Minn. Fgn. Policy Assn., 1959-68, Internat. Center Students and Visitors, 1962-65, 70—, Civic Orchestra of Mpls., 1959-62, Community Services for Internat. Visitors, 1971—, Minn. br. Am. Civil Liberties Union, 1952-54, Greater Mpls. Council of Chs., 1948-53. Recipient Order North Star, 1958; WTCN citation for Outstanding Community Service, 1962. Mem. Minn. Soc. Mayflower Descendants (jr. dep. gov. 1960-61), Psi Upsilon. Conglist. Clubs: Skull and Bones, Professional Men's, Elizabethan (Yale); Campus (U. Minn.). Editor: Religion in the State University, 1950; Minnesota's Indian Citizens, 1965. Author: The Turkish Transformation, 1935. Home: 1917 James Av S Minneapolis MN 55403

ALLEN, HENRY FREEMAN, ophthalmologist; b. Boston, Nov. 23, 1916; s. Freeman and Ethel (Gibson) A.; A.B. magna cum laude, Harvard, 1939, M.D., 1943; m. Emily L. Tuckerman, June 7, 1941; children—Emily T., Rosamond W., Freeman. Intern Mass. Gen. Hosp., Boston, 1944; resident Mass. Eye and Ear Infirmary, Boston, 1947-49; practice ophthalmology Boston, 1949-68; chief ophthalmology Mass. Eye & Ear Infirmary, 1968—; chief cons. ophthalmology Mass. Gen. Hosp., 1968—; cons. Children's Hosp. Med. Center, Binder-Schweitzer Amazonian Hosp.; clin. prof., head dept. Harvard Med. Sch., 1968—, Henry Willard Williams clin. prof., 1970—. Pres. Channing Home, Boston, 1951-57. Trustee Episcopal Theol. Sch., Cambridge, Perkins Sch. for Blind, Watertown. Served to capt., M.C., AUS, 1944-45; ETO. Mem. Am. Ophthal. Soc., Am. Assn. Ophthalmology (pres. 1970), Am. Acad. Ophthalmology, A.M.A. (chief editor archives ophthalmology, 1966—, Lucien Howe medal 1967), New Eng. Ophthal. Soc., Phi Beta Kappa. Episcopalian. Office: 243 Charles St Boston MA 02114

ALLEN, HERBERT, steel co. exec.; b. Ratcliff, Tex., May 2, 1907; s. Jasper and Leona (Matthews) A.; B.S. in Mech. Engring., Rice U., 1929; m. Helen Daniels, Aug. 28, 1937; children—David Daniels, Anne (Mrs. Jonathan Taft Symonds), Michael Herbert. Engaged in research, 1929-31; with Cameron Iron Works, Inc., and predecessor, Houston, 1931—, v.p. engring. and mfg., 1942-50, v.p., gen. mgr., 1950-66, pres., 1966—, also dir.; dir. Tenneco, Inc., Tex. Commerce Bank. Trustee Rice U., Houston, Texas; St. Stephen's Episcopal Sch., Southwestern Research Inst.; bd. dirs. Tex. Tech. U.; Registered profl. engr., Tex. Fellow Am. Soc. M.E.; mem. Am. Inst. Mining, Metall. and Petroleum Engrs., Am. Petroleum Inst., Tex. Soc. Profl. Engrs. (Engr. of Year award San Jacinto chpt. 1961), Houston C. of C. (bd. dirs. 1952-54, v.p. 1954-55, dir.-at-large 1962), Philos. Soc. Tex., Houston Philos. Soc., Houston Engring. and Sci. Soc. Newcomen Soc. N. Am., Tau Beta Pi. Episcopalian. Clubs: River Oaks Country, Petroleum, Ramada, Houston; Bayou. Patentee in field. Home: 3262 Huntingdon Pl Houston TX 77019 Office: PO Box 1212 Houston TX 77001

ALLEN, HERBERT, investment banker; b. N.Y.C., 1908; children—Herbert A., Susan Kathleen (Mrs. Floyd Hayes), Partner Allen & Co., N.Y.C. Trustee, v.p. Hackley Sch. Clubs: Ardsley Country, Indian Creek Country, Lucayan Country, Shannon Country, Deepdale Golf, Saratoga Golf, Turf and Field, Water Mill Beach. Home: Roland Rd Ardsley Park Irvington NY 10533 Office: 30 Broad St New York City NY 10004

ALLEN, HORACE EUGENE, lawyer; b. Swanton, Vt., July 19, 1890; s. Clarence Eugene and Minerva Saxe (Drury) A.; A.B., Dartmouth, 1912; LL.B., Harvard, 1915; m. Mary Frances Ballantine, July 13, 1918 (dec. Aug. 1961); children—Hortense Ballantine (Mrs. Warren F. Walker, Jr.), Richard Ballantine, Nancy Ballantine (Mrs. Paul D. Hubbe). Admitted to Mass. bar, 1915 and since practiced in Springfield; mem. Allen, Yerrall, Appleton & Thompson, 1923—. Mem. Mass. Bd. Bar Examiners, 1947-63. Pres., trustee Horace Smith Fund. Served as 1st lt. Army Service Corps, 1918. Mem. Civilian Contracts Review Board Springfield Ordnance Dist., 1951. Chmn. Longmeadow Future Planning Com., 1959-63. Mem. Am. (ho. dels. 1946-50), Mass. (treas., 1931-47), Boston bar assns., Nat. Conf. Bar Examiners (council 1947-48). Republican. Conglist. Clubs: Kiwanis (pres. 1953), Appalachian Mountain, Colony. Home: 28 Brittany Rd Longmeadow MA 01106 Office: Third National Bank Bldg Springfield MA 01103

ALLEN, HOWARD PFEIFFER, electric utility exec.; b. Upland, Cal., Oct. 7, 1925; s. Howard Clinton and Emma Maud (Pfeiffer) A.; B.A. cum laude, Pomona Coll., 1948; LL.B., Stanford, 1951; m. Dixie Mae Illa, May 14, 1948; 1 dau., Alisa Cary. Admitted to Cal. bar, 1952; asst. dean, asst. prof. law Stanford Law Sch., 1951-54; with So. Cal. Edison Co., 1954—, v.p., 1962—, dir. Cal. Fed. Savs. & Loan Assn. Mem. financial investment adv. panel Nat. R.R. Passenger Corp., U.S. Dept. Transp. Mem. Los Angeles County Election Commn. Bd. dirs. Los Angeles County Fair Assn.; trustee Pomona Coll. Mem. Los Angeles C. of C. (dir.), Am., Los Angeles County bar assns., State Bar Cal., Bar Assn. San Francisco., Phi Beta Kappa, Phi Delta Phi. Mason (Shriner). Clubs: Jonathan, California. Home: 2541 Mountain Av Claremont CA 91711 Office: 2244 Walnut Grove Av Rosemead CA 91770

ALLEN, IRWIN, motion picture writer, producer, dir.; b. N.Y.C., June 12, 1916; s. Joseph and Eva (Davis) A.; student Coll. City N.Y., 1935, Columbia 1936. Radio news commentator KLAC, Hollywood, Cal., 1939-50; syndicated newspaper columnist, motion picture editor Atlas Features Syndicate, Hollywood, 1940-52; lit. agt. motion picture sales, works of Rex Beach, Fanny Hurst, P.G. Wodehouse, Louis Joseph Vance, Sigrid Undset, Edwin Corie, also pubs. Duell, Sloan & Pearce, Inc., G.P. Putnam's Sons, Harcourt, Brace & Co., 1943-49; television producer, commentator KLAC-TV, Hollywood, 1948-50; founder, pres. Westwood Prodns., Inc., 1949; asso. producer Where Danger Lives, RKO Radio Pictures, Inc., 1950; co- producer A Girl in Every Port, 1951; producer, screenplay writer The Sea Around Us, 1952; producer Dangerous Mission, RKO Radio Pictures, Inc., 1954; writer, producer, director of the Animal World, Warner Brothers, Inc., 1935, producer, dir., co-writer screenplay, The Story of Mankind, 1956; producer, co-writer The Big Circus, 1960; producer, dir., co-writer The Lost World, 1960, Voyage to the Bottom of the Sea, 1961, Five Weeks in a Baloon, 1962, City Beneath the Sea, 1970. creator, producer TV series Voyage to the Bottom of the Sea, 1964, Lost in Space, 1965, The Time Tunnel, 1966, Land of The Giants, 1968. Recipient Academy Award for The Sea Around US, 1952, Internat. Laurel award Motion Picture Exhibitors, 1953; Blue Ribbon award for excellence motion picture prodn. Box Office mag. (twice); Merit award So. Cal. Fedn. Womans Clubs (3 times). Club: Tamarisk Country (Palm Springs, Cal.). Home: 1050 Stradella Rd Los Angeles CA 90024 Office: 20th Century Fox Studio Los Angeles CA 90028

ALLEN, IVAN, Jr., merchant; b. Atlanta, Mar. 15, 1911; s. Ivan and Irene (Beaumont) A.; grad. Georgia Inst. Tech., 1933; m. Louise Richardson, Jan. 1, 1936; children—Ivan III, Inman, Beaumont. With Ivan Allen Co., Atlanta, 1933—, pres., 1946-57, vice chmn. bd., 1957, chmn. bd., 1969—; dir. National Blank Book Co., Holyoke, Mass., Rich's Inc., Southern Airways, Atlanta, Mead Corp., Equitable Life Assurance Soc., So. Bell Telephone, Rich's, Cox Broadcasting Corp. Scout, scoutmaster, area pres., regional committeeman, mem. nat. exec. bd. Boy Scouts Am., awarded Silver Beaver, Silver Antelope, Silver Buffalo; chmn. Greater Atlanta Community Chest, 1949. Lt. col. Gov.'s Staff, 1936; treas. Ga. State Hosp. Authority, 1936; sec. exec. dept. State Georgia, 1945-46; chmn. Police Found.; mayor of Atlanta, 1961-69. Trustee Ga. Tech. Found., Agnes Scott Coll. Served as maj. inf. AUS, World War II, Recipient Armin Maier award Atlanta Rotary Club, 1952. Mem. Ga. Tech. Alumni Assn. (pres. 1953-54), Atlanta C. of C. (pres. 1961, dir.), Nat. Stationery and Office Equipment Assn. (dist. gov. 1938-40, pres. 1955-56), Sigma Alpha Epsilon. Rotarian. Home: 3700 Northside Dr Atlanta GA 30305 Office: 221 Ivy St Atlanta GA 30303

ALLEN, JACK, educator; b. Prestonsburg, Ky., June 18, 1914; s. Edward L. and Anna (Mayo) A.; A.B., Eastern Ky. State Coll., 1935; M.A., George Peabody Coll. Tchrs., 1938, Ph.D., 1941; m. Cherry Falls, Aug. 16, 1941; children—David E., Robert L., Edward L. High sch. tchrs., Ky., 1935-37; asst. prof. history Eastern Ky. State Coll., 1940-42; asso. prof. history George Peabody Coll., 1946-52, prof., 1952—, head dept., 1954- -, chmn. div. social sci., 1963—; instr. Peabody-in-Athens (Greece), 1968. Asso. dir. for academic programs Nashville U. Center Council, 1969-70. Cons. Nova Sch., Ft. Lauderdale, Fla., 1963-67, Oak Ridge Schs., 1969-70. Cons. Nova Sch., Ft. Lauderdale, Fla., 1963-67, Oak Ridge Schs., 1964-66; social studies cons. Republic of Korea, 1961, 69; cons. Tri-Univ. project U. Wash., 1967-69, Bel air Sch., Mandeville, Jamaica, 1970. Adv. council council Edn. Policies Commn.; adv. bd. Am. Viewpoint, Inc.; adv. bd. Am. Edn. Publs., 1970—; Coordinating Council Tchr. Edn. Alliance for Met., Nashville, 1969—. Board directors Presbyterian Student Center. Served with USNR, 1942-45. Alumnus of Yr., Eastern Ky. State Coll., 1960. Mem. Am. Studies Assn., Nat. Council Social Studies (pres. 1958, chmn. publs. com. 1967), Am. Hist. Assn., Miss. Valley Hist. Assn., Phi Delta Kappa, Kappa Delta Pi, Pi Gamma Mu, Pi Omega Pi. Author high sch. textbooks, workbooks; author; (with Hershel Gower) Pen and Sword, 1960 (received Merit award Soc. State and Local History); A Charter for Social Studies in Korea, 1961; (with Adelene E. Howland) The United States of America, 1964, The Americas, 1964, The Earth and Our States, 1966, Nations Around the Globe, 1966, Nations of Other Lands, 1966; Documents U.S.A., 1967; (with others) The Problems and Promise of American Democracy, 1964, (with John L. Betts) History; USA, 1967, 71; (with others) Contemporary Issues in American Democracy, 1969; (with Russell Farnen) Teachers Manual for Contemporary Issues in American Democracy, 1969; (with Jack W. Miller) Parkway School District; The Social Studies, 1969; American Public School, 1969; (with John L. Betts) USA; History and Documents, 1971. Contbr. articles profl. jours., yearbooks. Home: 3705 Hilldale Dr Nashville TN 37215.

ALLEN, JAMES, defense co. executive; b. N.Y. City, May 17, 1906; s. Isaac and Amy (Wechsler) Moskowitz; A.B., Coll. City N.Y., 1927; M.B.A., Harvard, 1930; m. Sylvia Edlavitch, Oct. 19, 1939; 1 dau., Judith Marian. Newspaper corr., Washington, 1932-34; dir. information Securities and Exchange Commn., 1934-40; dir. pub. relations Dept. Justice, 1940-41; exec. sec. Soc. Ind. Motion Picture Producers, Inc., Los Angeles, 1941- 42; asst. dir. domestic br., O.W.I., 1942-44; asst. to v.p. Warner Bros. Pictures, Inc., Burbank, Cal., 1944-48; management, pub. relations counsel, Los Angeles, 1948-52 spl. asst. to Stuart Symington, adminstr. R.F.C., 1951; cons. The Rand Corp., Santa Monica, Call., 1949-60; vice pres. Atlas Corp., N.Y.C., 1952-59; dir., mem. executive com. Northrop Corp., 1951—, v.p., 1959—. Clubs: National Press (Washington); Town Hall (Los Angeles). Editor: Democracy and Finance, speeches of William O. Douglas, 1940. Home: 9508 Tullis Dr Beverly Hills CA 90210 Office: 1800 Century Park E Century City Los Angeles CA 90067

ALLEN, JAMES BROWNING, U.S. senator; b. Gadsden, Ala., Dec. 28, 1912; s. George C. and Mary Ethel (Browning) A.; student U. Ala., 1928-31, U. Ala. Law Sch.,1932-33; m. Marjorie Jo Stephens, Mar. 16, 1940 (dec. Jan. 1956); children—James Browning, Mary Rebecca, Debbie Allen; m. 2d, Maryon Pittman Mullins, Aug. 7, 1964; stepchildren—J. Sanford III, John Pittman, Maryon Foster. Admitted to Ala. bar, 1935; practice in Gadsden, 1935—; mem. Ala. Legislature from Etowah County, 1939-43, mem. Senate from Etowah, and St. Clair County, 1947-51; lt. gov. State of Ala., 1951-55, 63-66; U.S. senator from Ala., 1969—. Del Democratic Nat. Conv., 1952. Served to lt (j.g.) USNR, 1943-46. Home: 7405 Hallcrest Dr McLean VA 22101 also 1321 Bellevue Dr Gadsden AL 35901 Office: New Senate Office Bldg Washington DC 20510

ALLEN, JAMES CALDWELL, assn. exec.; b. Beaver Falls, Pa., June 23, 1907; s. Albert E. and Mallie (Caldwell) A.; student Davidson Coll., 1926-27, U. Ill., 1927-28; B.A. in Econs., George Washington U., 1931; m. Sally Kriegstedt, June 23, 1934, With Bur. Pub. Roads, Washington 1944-64, successively chief accountant, budget officer, asst. dep. commr., dep. commr., 1944-56, asst. commnr. office adminstrn., 1957-62, dir. adminstrn., 1962-64; asst. dir. adminstrn. Hwy. Research Bd., Nat. Acad. Scis., 1964—. Home: 7400 Leesburg Pike Falls Church, VA 22043. Office: 2101 Constitution Av NW Washington DC 20037

ALLEN, JAMES EDWARD, Jr., educator; b. Elkins, W.Va., Apr. 25, 1911; s. James E. and Susan (Garrott) A.; B.A., Davis and Elkins Coll., 1932, LL.D., 1956; postgrad. econs., pub. finance Princeton, 1939; M.Ed., Harvard, 1942, Ed.D., 1945, LL.D., 1960; D.Ped., Niagara U., 1956; LL.D., Syracuse U., 1955, Union U., William Smith Coll., Alfred U., 1956; Litt.D., Hofstra Coll., 1957; Yeshiva U., 1957; Marshall Coll., 1958; LL.D., Fordham U., 1960, N.Y. U., Yale, 1966, Manhattan Coll., 1968, Hamilton Coll., 1968; D.H.L., Columbia, 1964, Pace Coll., 1966; D.Hum., W.Va. U., 1966, Notre Dame, 1970; others; m. Florence Pell Miller, April 23, 1938; children—James Edward III, Judith Pell (Mrs. John Dolven). Mem. staff W.Va. Edn. Dept., 1933-39; chief div. state aid and statistics W.Va., 1939; research asso. Princeton Surveys, 1939-41; research Center for Research in Ednl. Adminstrn., Harvard, 1941-43, sec. faculty, dir. placement Grad. Sch. Edn., 1943-44; operations analyst USAAF, 1944-45; asst. prof. edn., dir. Bur. Sch. Services, Syracuse U., 1945-47; exec. asst. to N.Y. Commr. Edn., 1947-50; dep. commr. edn. N.Y., 1950-55, commr., pres. State U. N.Y., 1955-69; fed. edn. commr., asst. sec. for edn. U.S. Dept. Health, Edn. and Welfare, Washington, 1969-70; lectr. edn., pub. affairs Princeton, 1970—. Trustee City & County Savs. Bank of Albany. Cons. Pres.'s Commn. on Higher Edn., 1946-47; mem. edn. com. States Ednl. Devel. Center. Mem. council Harvard Found. Advanced Study and Research, 1950-54; nat. adv. com. Nat. Ednl. TV and Radio Center; vis com. Harvard Grad. Sch. Edn.; adv. com. Harvard Program on Sci. and Tech. Trustee Danforth Found., Syracuse U., Cornell U. Recipient Charles Evans Hughes award Am. Soc. Pub. Administrn., 1954. Mem. Am. Assn. Sch. Adminstrs., Am. Council Edn., Phi Delta Kappa. Presbyn. (elder). Rotarian. Clubs: Century; Cosmos. Author: State School Fiscal Policy for New Jersey, 1944. Contbr. articles to ednl. mags. Home: RD 3 Lawrenceville Rd Princeton NJ 08540 Office: Woodrow Wilson Sch Princeton U Princeton NJ 08540

ALLEN, JAMES ELBERT, wholesale druggist, assn. exec.; b. Largo, Fla., Sept. 15, 1915; s. Horace Jackson and Miriam Estelle (Collins) A.; student spl. courses Southeastern U., 1936-37; m. Virginia Joynes McComas, Oct. 5, 1940; children—James Elbert, Richard Austin. Sales rep. Muth Bros. & Co., Balt., 1936-40; salesman Henry B. Gilpin Co., 1940-45, mgr. Washington div., 1947-52, exec. v.p., 1952-57, pres., 1957—, chmn. bd. dirs., 1968—, also dir.; pres. Distbn. Services, Inc.; dir. Alliance Labs., Inc., Druggists Supply Corp.; adv. bd. Am. Security and Trust Co. Chief of med. supply sect. Civil Defense, Washington, 1953-55. Chmn. Distbn. Adv. Council, U.S. Bur. Budget. Mem. Resources Mgmt. Planning Task Group for Health Resources. Mem. Nat. Conf. of Christians and Jews. Served with USNR, 1946-47. Mem. Nat. Wholesale Druggists Assn. (past pres.), Nat. Assn. Wholesalers (past pres.), Nat. Drug Trade Conf. (past pres.), Am., Md., D.C., Del., Va. pharm. assns., Nat. Assn. Retail Druggists, Newcomen Soc. N. Am. Kiwanian (past pres.). Home: 3229 Livingston St NW Washington DC 20015 Office: 901 Southern Av Washington DC 20032

ALLEN, JAMES HAMILTON, food co. exec.; b. San Francisco, Apr. 13, 1907; B.A., Stanford, 1928. With Cal. Packing Corp., 1928—, v.p., 1964—. Home: 43 Amador Av Atherton, CA 94025 Office: 215 Fremont St San Francisco CA 94119

ALLEN, JAMES HARRILL, physician, educator; b. Chattanooga, Jan. 31, 1906; s. George Henry and Mary (Harrill) A.; A.B., U. Tenn., 1926; M.D., U. Mich., 1930; M.S., U. Ia., 1938; m. Ruth Sanford, Aug. 17, 1934; children—Mary Helen, George Sanford, John Robert. Intern, resident Univ. Hosps., 1930-34; fellow ophthalmology U. Ia., 1934-36, research asst., 1936-37, instr. ophthalmology, 1937-38, asst. prof., 1938-45, asso. prof., 1945-46, prof., 1946-50; prof. ophthalmology Tulane U., 1950—, chmn. dept., 1953- 67, asso. dean med. dir., Tulane Clinics, 1967—; cons. Nat. Soc. Prevention Blindness, Nat. Council to Combat Blindness, Eye Bank for Sight Restoration (N.Y.), USPHS Hosp., Carville, La., New Orleans VA Hosp.; cons. ophthalmology to air surgeon, 1952-58. Dir. So. Eye Bank, Gulf States Eye Surgery Found, 1950-60; bd. dirs. Information Council Americas, New Orleans Lighthouse for the Blind. Served from capt. to lt. col., USAAF, 1942-46. Recipient Beverly Meyers Nelson achievement award for meritorious contributions in field of vision, 1958; Legion of Honor, Order of DeMolay, 1962. Diplomate Am. Bd. Ophthalmology. Mem. N.Y. Acad. Scis., Pan Am. Assn. Ophthalmology (asst. sec. 1953—), Aerospace Medical Association, American Society for Microbiology, Assn. Mil. Surgeons, Soc. Am. Bacteriologists, A.A.A.S., A.M.A., Assn. Research Ophthalmology (sec.-treas. 1947-54, trustee 1955-60, chmn. 1960), Association of American Physicians and Surgeons, Am. Acad. Ophthalmology and Otolaryngology, La., Orleans Parish med. socs., So. Ophthalmic Pathology Club, Sigma Xi, Theta Kappa Psi; hon. mem. Minn. Acad. Ophthalmology and Otolaryngology, Ft. Worth Eye, Ear, Nose and Throat Soc., Central Ill., Kansas City socs. ophthalmology and otolaryngology, Ark.-La.-Tex. Otolaryng. and Ophthalmological Soc., Dallas So. Clin. Soc., Chilean Ophthalmology Soc. Mason (Shriner), Elk, Rotarian. Editor: Strabismus, A Symposium, 1950, Strabismus Symposium II, 1958; Proc. Assn. Research in Opthalmology, 1948-54; survey of Opthalmology, 1962- 68, cons. editor 1968; editor Mays Diseases of the Eye, 23d edit, 1963, 24th edit., 1968;

collaborating editor Opthalmologico Ibero Americano, 1958—; associate Archieves of Ophthalmology, 1950-53; editorial bd. Investigative Opthalmology, 1961-68; editorial bd. Annals of Ophthalmology, 1968—; cons. editor Audio Digest, 1963—. Contbr. articles to med. jours. Home: 9104 Quince St New Orleans LA 70118

ALLEN, JAMES LANE, mgmt. cons.; b. Somerset, Ky., Nov. 21, 1904; s. Albert Edward and Lelia (Vanhook) A.; B.S., Northwestern U., 1929; m. Gertrude Blankmeyer, Jan. 11, 1930; children—Ruth Elizabeth (Mrs. George M. Hopfenbeck, Jr.), Martha (Mrs. Dale Park, Jr.), Mary (Mrs. Richard E. Carson). Edwin G. Booz Surveys, 1929-34; sec., treas. Ditto Inc., Chgo., 1934-36; partner Booz, Fry, Allen & Hamilton, 1936-42; v.p., dir. Hall Brothers, Inc., Kansas City, Mo., 1942- 43; partner Booz, Allen & Hamilton, mgmt. cons., 1943-62; chmn. Booz, Allen and Hamilton, Inc., 1962-70, hon. chmn., 1970—; dir. Abbott Labs., Jewel Cos., Inc., S. C. Johnson and Son, Inc. Mem. Chgo. regional panel for selection White House Fellows, 1964-70, chmn., 1970. Hon. dir. Evanston Hosp. Assn.; trustee Northwestern U., chmn. adv. council Grad. Sch. Mgmt.; hon. trustee Com. for Econ. Devel.; trustee The Johnson Found. Nat. honoree Beta Gamma Sigma, 1970. Mem. Sigma Nu. Episcopalian. Clubs: Old Elm (Ft. Sheridan, Illinois); Commercial, Chicago, Attic, Economic (Chgo.); Indian Hill (Winnetka, Ill.); University (N.Y.); Gulf Stream Golf, Delray Beach Yacht (Fla.); Gulf Stream Bath and Tennis. Home: 540 Palm Way Gulf Stream Delray Beach FL 33444 also 1630 Sheridan Rd Wilmette IL 60091 Office: 135 S LaSalle St Chicago IL 60603

ALLEN, JAMES PATRICK Jr., lawyer; b. Bklyn., Mar. 20, 1907; s. James Patrick and Eleonore (Brunner) A.; Ll.B., St. Johns U., 1929; m. Evelyn M. Ulmschneider, June 6, 1931; children—James Patrick III, Roger V., Peter Joseph. Admitted to N.Y. bar, 1929, Mass. bar, 1939; practiced in N.Y.C., 1929-32; mem. legal staff Liberty Mut. Ins. Co., N.Y.C., 1932-39, home office legal staff, asst. gen. counsel, counsel, gen. atty., Boston, 1939-68, v.p., gen. counsel, 1968—. Mem. Am. (co-chmn. Conf. Lawyers and Liability Ins. Cos.), N.Y. State. Mass., Boston bar assns., Internat. Assn. Ins. Counsel (past v.p.). Home: 42 Thackeray Rd Wellesley Hills MA 02181 Office: 175 Berkeley St Boston MA 02117

ALLEN, JAMES SIRCOM, physicist, b. Halifax, N.S., Can., Aug. 11, 1911; s. Samuel James M. and Eva (Sircom) A.; came to U.S., 1911, naturalized, 1965; B.A., U. Cin., 1933; Ph.D., U. Chgo., 1937; m. Mary E. Griswold, Nov. 28, 1936; 1 son, Richard C. Asso. prof. Kan. State U., 1937-42; physicist Radiation Lab., Mass. Inst. Tech., 1942-43; physicist Los Alamos Sci. Lab., 1943-46, cons., 1948-68; asst. prof. U. Chgo., 1946-48; prof. U. Ill., Urbanan, 1948—. Fellow Am. Phys. Soc. Episcopalian. Rotarian. Author: The Neutrino, 1958.‡

ALLEN, JAMES STEWART, educator; b. Henrietta, Tex., Jan. 26, 1921; s. Stayton Powell and Corrie (Walker) A.; B.A., U. Tex., 1942, M.A., 1946; Ph.D., Vanderbilt U., 1954; m. Norma McKinney, Dec. 28, 1946; children—Corrie Elizabeth, Caroline Marie. Prof. English, Arlington (Tex.) State Coll., 1947-56, Sam Houston State Tchrs. Coll., 1956-61; Carnegie fellow U. Mich., 1961- 62; dean Grad. Sch., Sam Houston State Tchrs. Coll., 1962-63; asst. dir. for program Tex. Commn. Higher Edn., 1963-65; v.p. acad. affairs Marshall U., Huntington, W.Va., 1965-67; exec. dir. Assn. Tex. Colls. and Univs., 1967-71, pres., 1971—. Mem. Assn. Higher Edn., Tex. Tchrs. Assn., Phi Kappa Sigma. Presbyn. Rotarian. Author: Legal Education in Texas, 1965; Pluralism and Partnership: A Case for the Dual System of Higher Education, 1969. Home: 2504 Spring Lane Austin TX 78703 Office: Commodore Perry Bldg Austin TX 78701

ALLEN, JOHN BOYLE, constrn. co. exec.; b. South Pasadena, Cal., Sept. 22, 1909; s. Harrison Jessup and Mary Anthony (Boyle) A.; ed. pub. schs., also pvt. engring. instrn.; m. Catherine Ruel Pembroke, Aug. 17, 1935 (dec.); children—Gary P., Margaret Susanne; m. second, Betty Jo Greer, 1968. Engaged as stock and bond broker, 1927-31; engineer with Edison Company, 1931-35; pvt. business as contractor and builder, 1935-40; participating mgr. James I. Barnes Constrn. Co., 1940-58; pres. J. B. Allen & Co., Cal. and Nev., 1959—; pres. A & F Assos., land developers and mobile home park operators, 1958—, A & A Mobile Home Park, Inc., 1952—, Vernon Bros., leasing agts., 1952—, Allen Devel. Co. Cal., investments; chmn. bd. Allen Contracting Co., Inc., Orlando, Fla.; dir. El Dorado Ins. Co.; prime contractor Disneyland, Anaheim, Cal., flying saucers, others, also Walt Disney World, Orlando, Fla.; contractor exhibit, ride at Worlds Fair. Clubs: Press and Union League (San Francisco); Tennis Rance (Carmel, Cal.); Santa Barbara (Cal.); Outrigger Canoe (Honolulu). Home: 2525 Ocean Blvd Newport Beach CA 92661 also Castle Surf Apts Honolulu HI 96815 also 401 El Cielito Santa Barbara CA 93105 Office: 36 E Mason St PO Box 899 Santa Barbara CA 93101 also 808 W Vermont Anaheim CA 92805

ALLEN, JOHN FRANKLIN, paper co. exec.; b. St. Paul, Sept 27, 1911; s. Charles Whitney and Beatrice (Kintner) A.; B.A. in Econs., Carleton Coll., Northfield, Minn., 1934; m. Jane Rankin Fite, May 25, 1941; children—Margaret Bothwell. Jane Kimberly. With Nat. Lead Co., Chgo., 1934-37, Waldorf Paper Products Co., Chgo., 1938-58; v.p. Waldorf Paper Products Co., St. Paul, 1958-66; sr. v.p. Hoerner Waldorf Corp., St. Paul. 1966—, also dir. Served to lt. comdr. USNR, 1942-46. Mem Paperboard Packaging Council (past bd. dirs.). Am. Mgmt. Assn., St. Paul Area C. of C. Club: Mideay Civic (St. Paul). Home: 4208 Sunnyside Rd Minneapolis MN 55424 Office: 2250 Wabash Av St Paul MN 55114

ALLEN, JOHN HORTON, coll. pres.; b. Homer, La., Nov. 9, 1923; s. Robert Baker and Ola Lee (Horton) A.; student Northwestern State U. La., 1940-42; B.A., Southeastern La. U., 1949; M.A., La. State U., 1951; Ph.D., Pa. State U., 1955; m. Sidney Mitchell Gremillion, July 14, 1943; children—John Horton, Lisa Jane. Instructor in sociology Pennsylvania State University, 1952-53; asst. prof. sociology, U. So. Miss., 1953- 54, asso. prof., 1955-56; prof. sociology Southeastern La. U., 1956- 57; prof. sociology U. So. Miss., 1957-69, dean Sch. Arts and Scis., 1957-61, dean of university, 1961-69; pres. Centenary Coll. of La., Shreveport, 1969—. Mem. personnel com. Am. Heart Assn., 1969—. Served to 1st lt., pilot, USAAF, 1942-47. Decorated Distinguished Flying Cross, Air medal with 7 oak leaf Clusters, Distinguished Unit citation, ETO ribbon with 4 battle stars. Mem. Am. Studies Assn. (past pres. lower Miss.), Am., So. sociol. assns., Phi Kappa Phi, Omicron Delta Kappa, Phi Mu Alpha, Sinfonia. Methodist (ofcl. bd.). Mason, Rotarian. Home: 254 Rutherford St Shreveport LA 71104

ALLEN, JOHN MILTON, editor; b. Waukesha, Wis., Oct. 30, 1926; S. John Milton and Margaret (Belknap) A.; grad. Hotchkiss Sch., 1945; B.A., Yale, 1950; m. Marcia Burr; children—John Milton III, Cynthia, Jennifer; m. 2d, Elizabeth Ruth Peale, Oct. 16, 1965; children—Rebecca Belknap, Katheryn Ruth. Corr., Time mag., Chgo., Denver and Los Angeles, 1950-54; tchr. Taft Sch., Watertown, Conn., 1954- 56; asso. editor Reader's Digest, 1956-66, sr. editor, 1966-70, sr. staff editor, 1970—. Co-chmn. Craftsbury Common (Vt.) Village Improvement Soc., 1957—. Trustee Sterling Sch., Craftsbury Common, 1966—; bd. govs. Am. Found. Religion and Psychiatry, 1967—. Served with USMCR, 1944-46. Mem. Phelps Soc. Clubs: Yale (N.Y.C.); Quaker Hill Country (Pawling). Home: Sugar Tree Farm Quaker Hill Pawling NY 12564 Office: Reader's Digest Pleasantville NY 10570

ALLEN, JOHN R., advt. agy. exec. Sr. v.p. McCann-Erickson, Inc., N.Y.C. Office: 485 Lexington Av New York City NY 10017*

ALLEN, JOHN STUART, ednl. adminstr.; b. Pendleton, Ind., May 13, 1907; s. Elwood D. and Stella (Anderson) A.; student George Sch., Newtown, Pa., 1921-24; A.B., Earlham Coll., 1928, LL.D. (hon.), Earlham Coll., 1958; M.A., U. Minn., 1929; student Columbia, summer 1931; Ph.D., N.Y. U., 1936; Sc.D. (hon.), U. Tampa, 1958; L.H.D., U. South Fla., 1970; m. Grace H. Carlton, Aug. 23, 1933. Asst. in astronomy U. Minn., 1928-29; instr. Colgate U., 1930-36, asst. prof. astronomy, 1936-42, chmn. comprehensive phys. sci. course, 1931-42, dean of freshman, 1942; dir. div. higher edn. N.Y. State Edn. Dept., 1942-48; v.p. U. Fla., 1948- 53, acting pres., 1953-55, exec. v.p., 1955-57; pres. U. South Fla., Tampa, 1957-70, pres. emeritus, 1970—; spl. adviser to U. North Fla., 1970—; cons curricular, adminstrv. reorgn. U. Costa Rica, 1955. Dir. Univ. State Bank, Tampa. Bd. dirs. Univ. Community Hosp., Tampa; exec. com. So. Regional Edn. Bd., 1960-64; bd. dirs. Princeton Ednl. Testing Service, 1961-65; mem. Nat. Commn. on Coop. Edn., 1968-71; exec. com. Nat. Commn. on Accreditation, 1968; mem. edn. com. on new instns. Am. Council Edn., 1968. Mem. Franklin Inst. Solar Eclipse Expdn., 1932; guest lectr. Hayden Planetarium, 1935; sci. cons., faculty workshop Assn. of Colls. and Univs. of N.Y. State, June 1941; trustee Dudley Obs., 1944-48; chmn. Com. on Approved Schs. for Vets. for N.Y. State, 1945-48; mem. N.Y. State Com. on Tech. Inst. Curriculums; state coordinator Vets. Edn. Council of N.E.A., 1947-1948; chmn. Fla. Certification Com. for Regional Edn. 1949-57; chmn. Fla. State Fulbright Com. 1950-57; mem. gov. adv. Council on Aging, 1960; mem. White House Conf. Aging, 1971; mem. Fla. council 100; mem. several other profl., ednl., community commns. Recipient Distinguished Alumnus citation U. Minn., 1962; Distinguished Alumni citation N.Y. U., 1971. Fellow A.A.A.S.; mem. Fla. Assn. Colls. and Univs. (pres. 1949-50, Distinguished Service citation 1971), Am. Astron. Soc., Royal Astron Soc. of Can., Astron. Soc. of France, Fla. Acad. Scis., Newcomen Soc. of Eng., Nat. Collegiate Players, N.E.A., Albany Adult Edn. Council (pres. 1944-45), Fgn. Policy Assn., Greater Tampa C. of C. (gov.), Sigma Pi Sigma, Lambda Chi Alpha, Phi Delta Kappa, Sigma Xi, Omicron Delta Kappa, Alpha Kappa Psi, Pi Epsilon Delta, Pi Sigma Epsilon, Sinfonia. Mem. Soc. of Friends. Kiwanian (past pres.). Author or co-author several books, bulls. and articles. Home: 3655 Leewood Lane Jacksonville FL 32217

ALLEN, JOSEPH GARROTT, surgeon, educator; b. Elkins, W.Va., June 5, 1912; s. James Edward and Susan H. (Garrott) A.; student Davis and Elkins Coll., 1930-32; A.B., Washington U., St. Louis, 1934; M.D., Harvard, 1938; m. Dorothy O. Travis, July 15, 1940 (div. 1968); children—Barry Worth, Edward Henry, Nannette Susan, Lester Travis, Joseph Garrott; m. 2d, Kathryn L. Shipley, Dec. 27, 1968. Intern Billings Hosp., U. Chgo., 1939, asst. resident surgery U. Chgo., 1940-44, instr. surgery, 1943-47, asst. prof., 1947-48, asso. prof., 1948-51, prof., 1951-59; research asso. metall. labs. Manhattan Project, 1944-46, group leader Argonne Nat. Lab., 1946-59; prof. Stanford, 1959—, exec. dept. surgery, 1959-61. Mem. surgery study sect. USPHS, 1955-59. Trustee Am. Youth Found., 1954-67. Recipient John J. Abel prize for research irradiation injury Am. Assn. Pharmacology and Exptl. Therapeutics, 1948; Ednl. award Am. Assn. Blood Banks, 1954; Gold medal for original research Ill. Med. Soc., 1948, 52; Samuel D. Gross award Pa. Acad. Surgery, 1955; First John Elliott award Am. Assn. Blood Banks, 1956. Mem. NRC, 1950-54. Mem. standards com. Am. Assn. Blood Banks, 1958. Diplomate Am. Bd. Surgery (mem. bd. 1958-64). Mem. Soc. Exptl. Biology and Medicine, Am. Physiol. Soc., A.C.S. (chmn. com. blood and allied problems), Internat. Surg. Group (founder), A.M.A. (Gold medal for original research 1948), Am. Surg. Assn., Soc. Clin. Surgery (sec. 1958-60), S.F. Surg. Soc., Soc. U. Surgeons, Am. Cancer Soc. (chmn. com. cancer therapy), Western, Pacific Coast surg. assns. Author: (with others) Surgery-Principles and Practice, 1957, 4th edit., 1970; Shock and Transfusion, Therapy, 1959; Surgery, Principles and Practices, 1965; also sci. papers. Editor: Peptic Ulcer, 1959; co-editor: Family Health Ency., 1970; chief editor Archives of Surgery. Home: 583 Salvatierra Stanford CA 94305 Office: Stanford U School Medicine Stanford CA 94305

ALLEN, JOSEPH HENRY, publisher; b. Evanston, Ill., Nov. 9, 1916; s. Joseph Henry and Ann Eugenia (Jansen) A.; B.A., Kenyon Coll., 1938; m. Eleanor Clark, June 14, 1941; children—David, Elisabeth, Melinda. With McGraw-Hill Pub. Co., 1938-66, sucessively salesman, regional editor and advt. space salesman, 1938-48, established S.W. office for advt. sales, 1948, div. mgr., Los Angeles, 1951-55, v.p., dir. advt. sales, N.Y.C., 1955-63, v.p. operations, 1963-66; pres. McGraw-Hill Publs. Co., 1966-70; group v.p. McGraw-Hill, Inc., 1970-71, pres. publs. and bus. services group, 1971—. Served as lt. USNR, 1942-45. Mem. Advt. Council (dir.), Am. Advt. Fedn. (dir.), Common Cause (mem. exec. com.). Clubs: University (N.Y.C.); Wee Burn Country (Darien, Conn.). Home: Salem Straits Darien CT 06820 Office: 330 W 42d St New York City NY 10036

ALLEN, JOSEPH PERCIVAL, astronaut; b. Crawfordsville, Ind., June 27, 1937; s. Joseph P. and Harriet (Taylor) A.; B.A., DePauw U., 1959; student Christian Albrechts U., Kiel, Germany, 1959-60; M.S., Yale, 1961, Ph.D., 1965; m. Bonnie Jo Darling, July 9, 1961. Guest research asso. Brookhaven Nat. Lab., 1962- 65; staff physicist Nuclear Structure Lab., Yale, 1965; research asso. U. Wash., 1966; scientist-astronaut NASA-Manned Spacecraft Center, Houston, 1967—. Rector scholar, 1955-59; Fulbright scholar, 1959-60. Mem. Am. Phys. Soc., Am. Astronautical Soc., N.Y. Acad. Scis., Am. Astron. Soc., A.A.A.S., Phi Beta Kappa, Sigma Xi, Beta Theta Pi, Phi Eta Sigma. Author articles in field. Home: 1410 Antiqua Lane Nassau Bay TX 77058 Office: NASA Manned Spacecraft Center CB Houston TX 77058

ALLEN, JUNIUS FERRALL, corp. ofcl.; b. Coraopolis, Pa., Feb. 28, 1910; s. Harvey S. and Ida (Ferrall) A.; B.A., Ohio Wesleyan U., 1931; m. Zella Irwin, Feb. 14, 1936; 1 son, James M. With H. J. Heinz Co., 1934—, beginning as accounting clk., v.p., dir., 1953, exec. v.p. 1959, sr. v.p. Europe, 1969—; dir. H.J. Heinz N.V.-Holland, Societa del Plasmon S.P.A., Italy, Industrias de Alimentacao Idal LDA, Portugal, H. J. Heinz Co. Ltd. (Eng.), Societadel Plasmon S.A.. Bd. dirs. Sarah Heinz House Assn. Clubs: University, Duquesne (Pitts.). Home: 2120 Greentree Rd Pittsburgh PA 15220 Office: 1062 Progress St Pittsburgh PA 15212

ALLEN, KENNETH LELAND, Jr., concert mgr.; b. Cleve., July 29, 1918; s. Kenneth L. and Gertrude Joyce (Cottingham) A.; student U. Chgo., 1938, Cleve. Inst. Music, 1939-40; 1 son, Kenneth L. III; m. Mrs. Mary Marshall (Scott) Damon, July 5, 1958. Campaign dir. Community Concert Service, 1947-48; exec. asst. Austin Wilder Artist Mgmt., 1948-49; v.p., dir. James A. Davidson Mgmt., Inc., 1949-53; pres., dir. Kenneth Allen Assos., 1953-56, merged with Concert Assos., Inc., N.Y.C., v.p., pres., dir., 1956-60; pres., dir. Kenaller Enterprises Inc., 1960—. Grand jury assn. N.Y. County Fund Corp., 1969- 70. Served from pvt. to capt. AUS, 1941-46. Decorated Bronze Star medal. Home: 125 E 63d St New York City NY 10021 also (summer) 24 Viola Rd Suffern NY 10901 also (winter) 708 SE 2d St Delray Beach FL 33444 Office: 111 W 57th St New York City NY 10019

ALLEN, KENNETH WILLIAM, educator, zoologist; b. St. Stephen, N.B., Can., June 20, 1930; s. Thomas Harold and Marion (Moses) A.; came to U.S., 1930, naturalized, 1959; B.S., Wheaton Coll., 1952; M.S., U. Me., 1956; Ph.D., Rice U., 1959; m. Gloria Helen Schoehherr, June 17, 1952; children—Kimberly Allen, Thomas Donald. Postdoctoral fellow Rice U., 1959-60; asst. prof. zoology U. Cal. at Los Angeles, 1960-63; prof. zoology, chmn. dept. U. Me., 1963—. Served with AUS, 1952-54. Mem. Am. Soc. Parasitology, Am. Soc. Zoology, Sigma Xi, Phi Kappa Phi. Home: 13-A Massachusetts St Orono ME 04473

ALLEN, L. SCOTT, bishop, pres. commn. edn. and cultivation United Methodist Ch. Address: 502 S Gay St S W Knoxville TN 37902*

ALLEN, LAFE FRANKLIN, government ofcl.; b. Fayetteville, Ark., Nov. 29, 1914; s. Lafe and Rosa C. (Niles) A.; B.Journalism, U. Mo., 1934, B.A., M.A., 1947; grad. student U. Chgo., 1947-48; m. Mary R. Duffy, Feb. 13, 1936; 1 dau., Mary Josephine. Reporter, Detroit Times, 1935-38, reporter, rewriteman, editorial writer, 1940-42; sec. to mayor Detroit, 1938-40; corr. Washington bur. United Press, 1948-52; chief policy br. Internat. Press Service, Dept. State, 1952-53; information officer U.S. Information Agy., 1953-57, chief news br. Voice of Am., 1957-58; press attache Am. embassy, Rio de Janeiro, Brazil, 1958-60; chief press service Latin Am. br. USIA, 1961—. Served with AUS, 1942-46; lt. col. Res. Recipient Meritorious Service medal U.S. Information Agy. Member Episcopal Church. Clubs: International, National Press, Washington Athletic (Washington); Overseas Press (N.Y.C.); Ft. Myer (Va.) Officers. Contbr. articles mags., revs. Home: 1702 N Nelson St Arlington VA 22207 Office: 1776 Pennsylvania Av N W Washington DC 20547

ALLEN, LAURENCE EDMUND LARRY, war corr.; b. Mt. Savage, Md., Oct. 19, 1908; s. Laurence Bernard and Mary Caroline (Crowe) A.; student schs. several states, grad. high sch.; m. Helen Fazakerley Quisenberry. Began business career Baltimore News, 1926; later on Washington Herald and Huntington (W.Va.) Evening Herald; reporter and telegraph editor Charleston (W.Va.) Daily Mail, 1927-33; with Associated Press, 1933-60, as reporter and state editor Charleston bureau, 1933-35, reporter Washington bureau, 1935-37, fgn. cables desk, N.Y.C., 1937-38, European war corr., 1938-44, corr. Poland, 1945, 47, 49, chief of bur., in Moscow, 1949, in Tel Aviv, 1950, war corr., S.E. Asia, Singapore, 1951, French Union and Vietminh Indochina, 1951-55, Malaya, Thailand, Burma, 1956, Caribbean area, 1957-61; organized Am. Press Service specializing Latin Am., 1960—. Recipient Bronze Star for defending freedom press as prisoner of war, 1945; Croix de Guerre Fr. High Command, Indo China, frontline reporting, Nov. 1952, Received first award Nat. Headliners Club, 1941, for best news-reporting in covering Brit. Fleet operations; awarded Pulitzer prize for reporting on internat. affairs, May 5, 1942; Order of British Empire by King George VI, 1947. Republican. Contbr. many short stories to various publs., 1925-33. Address: Rio Amazonas 78 Mexico City 5 DF Mexico

ALLEN, LEE NORCROSS, univ. dean; b. Shawmut, Ala., Apr. 16, 1926; s. Leland Norcross and Dorothy (Whitaker) A.; B.S., Auburn U., 1948, M.S., 1949; Ph.D., U. Pa., 1955; m. Catherine Ann Bryant, Aug. 24, 1963; children—Leland Norcross, Leslie Catherine. From instr. to prof. history Eastern Baptist Coll., St. Davids, Pa., 1952-61; prof. history Samford U., Birmingham, Ala., 1961—, grad. dean, 1965—. Served with AUS, 1944-46. Research fellow Auburn U., 1948-49; Harrison fellow U. Pa., 1949-52. Mem. Am., So., Ala. hist. assns., Omicron Delta Kappa, Phi Alpha Theta, Kappa Phi Kappa, Pi Gamma Mu. Southern Bapt. Rotarian (pres. Shades Valley club 1969-70). Author: (with Mrs. E.S. Bee) History of Ruhama, 1969; also articles. Home: 24 Pine Crest Rd Birmingham AL 35223

ALLEN, LELAND CULLEN, educator, scientist; b. Cin., Dec. 3, 1926; s. Chester H. and Helen (Cullen) A.; B.S., U. Cin., 1949, E.E., 1950, Ph.D. in theoretical physics, Mass. Inst. Tech., 1957; m. Carol A. Kiger, July 2, 1960; children—Abigail, Ethan, Emily. Nat. Sci. Found. postdoctoral fellow U. Cal., 1958-59; Nat. Sci. Found. sr. postdoctoral fellow, U. Paris, 1967; Guggenheim fellow, Oxford U., 1967; asst. prof. chemistry Princeton, 1960-63, asso. prof., 1963-65, prof., 1965—. Served with USNR, 1945-46. NIH Spl. fellow, 1971-72. Fellow Am. Phys. Soc.; mem. Am. Chem. Soc., Sigma Xi. Research on electronic structure of molecules and solids. Home: 108 Maclean Circle Princeton NJ 08540

ALLEN, LLOYD M., mayor; b. Bloomfield, Ind., July 26, 1919; s. John Frank and Bessie (Denny) A.; LL.B., Ind. U., 1948; m. Doris Elaine Hall, Nov. 12, 1943; childrenRonald Malcolm, Stephen Preston, Richard Denny. Admitted to Ind. bar; city judge, South Bend, Ind., 1959-63; mayor of South Bend, 1964-. Served to lt. comdr., pilot, USNR, 1941-46. Decorated D.F.C., Air medal with 2 gold stars. Mem. Am., Ind. bar assns., Isaak Walton League, S. Bend C. of C., Hearing and Speech Soc., Mental Health Assn. Republican. Presbyn. Elk, Lion. Home: 2106 E Jefferson Blvd South Bend IN 46601 Office: City Hall South Bend, IN 46601.*

ALLEN, LOUIS G., banker; b. 1929; B.B.A., U. Mich., 1951, M.B.A., 1956; married. Financial analyst Ford Motor Co., 1954-58; with Mfrs. Nat. Bank Detroit, 1958—, v.p. mortgage dept., 1965-66, v.p. adminstrn. mortgage dept., 1966-68, sr. v.p. adminstrn. mortgage dept., 1968—. Served with AUS, 1951-53. Office: 151 W Fort St PO Box 659 Detroit MI 48231*

ALLEN, LOWELL ARCHIBALD, utility exec., lawyer; b. Summerside, P.E.I., Can., Apr. 8, 1926; s. William Arthur and Louise (MacKinnon) A.; B.A., Acadia U., 1948; LL.B., Dalhousie U., 1952; m. Anne MacRae, Jan. 6, 1951; children—Susan, David. Called to bar Ont., 1954; Exec. asst. to minister fisheries Fed. Govt., Ottawa, 1953-59; with law dept. C.P. Ry., Montreal, Que., 1959-64; sec. Brascan Ltd., Toronto, 1964—; dir. Am.-Brazilian Suppliers, Inc., Canadian Brazilian Services, Ltd., Mikas Oil Co., Ltd. Served with Canadian Army, 1943-45. Mem. Law Soc. Upper Can., Canadian Bar Assn. Home: 140 Chatsworth Dr Toronto 12 Ontario Canada Office: 25 King St W Toronto 1 Ontario Canada

ALLEN, LUCILE, ednl. cons.; b. Paris, Tex., Jan. 27, 1906; d. Charles Newton and Enola (Hendrick) Allen; A.B., Trinity U., 1927; A.M., So. Meth. U., 1931; Ed.D., Tchrs. Coll., Columbia, 1945; LL.D., Chatham Coll., 1959; D.Litt., Austin Coll., 1965. Tchr., English and sr. counselor Highland Park High Sch., Dallas, 1930-43; Gen. Edn. Bd. fellow in human devel. U. Chgo., 1943; Grace Dodge fellow Tchrs. Coll., Columbia U., 1943-44; exec. sec. Womans Found., 1944-45; prof. edn. Cornell U., 1945-52, counselor of students, 1945- 48, dean of women, 1948-52; dean, prof. Chatham Coll., Pitts., 1952-59; ednl. cons., spl. asst. to pres. Austin Coll., Sherman, Tex., 1959-61; dean women, asso. prof. edn. Stanford, 1961-65; asst. to pres. Fresno State Coll., 1967-70; tchr. English, East Texas State Coll., summer 1936, N.

Texas State Tchrs. Coll., summers 1937-38; lectr. Trinity U., summer 1940; asso. U. Tex. Grad. Curriculum Workshop, summer 1941; lectr. The Hogg Found. for Mental Hygiene and Higher Edn., 1940-43; chmn., Eastern Hazen Conf., 1948. Trustee Woman's Found., Inc.; bd. dirs. Citizens Council, State of N.Y.; mem. Nat. Commn. Edn. for Am. Council of Edn., 1953-60; mem. Nat. Adv. Bd. Civil Def., 1953-56. Recipient Distinguished Alumnus award So. Meth. U., 1955. Mem. N.Y. Assn. Deans and Guidance Counselors (pres. 1952), Am. Assn. U. Women, Nat. Assn. Deans of Women (sec. 1950; pres. 1953-54), N.E.A., Mortar Board, Alpha Chi, Kappa Delta Pi, Pi Lambda Theta. Presbyn. Author profl. articles and brochures. Home: 1676 Sunset Ridge Dr Laguna Beach CA 92651

ALLEN, M. ROBERT, univ. dean, govt. ofcl.; b. N.Y.C., Dec. 8, 1917; s. B.F. and Lillian (Miller) A.; M.A., Columbia, 1941; Ph.D., U. Va., 1946; m. Mary Jane Ham, Sept. 11, 1943; children—Michael Robert, John Timothy. Asst. prof. prof. U. Va., 1946-49; vis. prof. U. Houston and U. Va., 1950-58; ednl. dir., cons. to Dept. Army, Ft. Lee, Va., 1948-59; exec. dir. Nat. Home Study Council, Washington, 1959-61; v.p. Famous Schs., Westport, Conn., 1961- 64; prof. edn., dean div. continuing edn., dir. summer sessions U. Miami (Fla.), 1964—; ednl. cons. to govt. and industry, 1964—. Chmn. accrediting commn. Nat. Home Study Council, 1963-64; vice chmn. accrediting commn. Nat. Assn. Trade and Tech. Schs. Bd. dirs. Va. Ednl. Corp., Mental Health Assn. Served with USNR, 1941-45; capt. Res. Sr. DuPont research fellow U. Va.; recipient award for exceptional service Dept. Army, 1955; sec. army research and study fellow in edn. and TV, U.S. and Europe, 1957-58. Mem. Adult Edn. Assn., Internat. Conf. on Corr. Edn., Nat. Univ. Extension Assn., Def. Supply Assn. Res. Officers Assn., Am. Univ. Evening Colls. Assn., Richmond Psychol. Assn., Internat. Council Edn., Phi Delta Kappa, Phi Alpha Theta, Omicron Delta Kappa, Sigma Delta Chi. Author: Television, Education and Armed Forces, 1958; founding editor Home Study Rev.

ALLEN, MARYON PITTMAN, (Mrs. James Browning Allen), columnist; b. Meridian, Miss., Nov. 30, 1925; d. John D. and Tellie (Chism) Pittman; student U. Ala., 1944-47; m. Joshua Sanford Mullins, Jr., Oct. 17, 1946 (div. Jan. 1959); children—Joshua Sanford III, John Pittman, Maryon Foster; m. 2d, James Browning Allen, Aug. 7, 1964; 1 stepson, James Browning Allen. Office mgr. Dr. Alston Callahan, Birmingham, Ala., 1959-60; bus. mgr. psychiat. clinic U. Ala. Med. Center, Birmingham, 1960-61; agt. Protective Life Ins. Co., Birmingham, 1961-62; women's editor Sun Newspapers, Birmingham, 1962-64; staff writer, columnist The Birmingham News, 1964—; v.p. Emerald Valley Corp., partner J.D. Pittman Partnership Co., Birmingham. Mem. State at large Ala. Hist. Commn. Democratic presdl. elector Dem. primary, 1968. Bd. dirs. Children's Fresh Air Farm, Birmingham, Mamie Fogarty com. Birmingham Festival of Arts. Recipient 1st place award Ala. Press Assn., 1962, 63, also various awards in typography, fashion writing, food pages. Mem. Birmingham Com. 100 for Woman, Ala. Writers Conclave, Antiquarian Soc. Assn., Relay House. Methodist. Clubs: Gadsden Music; Mountain Laurel Garden. Home: 1321 Bellevue Dr Gadsden AL 35901 also 7405 Hallcrest Dr McLean VA 22101

ALLEN, MAURICE BARTELLE, Jr., architect; b. Lansing, Mich., Mar. 20, 1926; s. Maurice Bartelle and Marguerite Rey (Stahl) A.; student Western Mich. U., 1944, Notre Dame U., 1944-46; B.Arch., U. Mich., 1950; m. Nancy Elizabeth Huff, June 29, 1951; children—Robert (dec.), Katherine, David. Draftsman, designer Smith, Hinchman & Grylls, architects, Detroit, 1950-51; designer, asso. Eero Saarinen & Assos., Bloomfield Hills, Mich., 1951-61; v.p. design and planning Tarapata- MacMahon-Paulsen Corp., architects, engrs. and planners, Bloomfield Hills, 1961—; design critic Coll. Architecture and Design, U. Mich., 1958—. Active Detroit Area council Boy Scouts Am., 1969—; mem. environmental arts com. Mich. Council for Arts, 1970—. Served with USNR, 1944-47. Recipient Honor award Detroit chpt. A.I.A., 1970; Honor awards Mich. Soc. Architects, 1970, 71; citation for design high rise structures Am. Iron and Steel Inst., 1971. Registered profl. architect, Mich., Ohio. Mem. Nat. Council Archtl. Registration Bds., A.I.A., Mich. Soc. Architects, Alpha Tau Omega. Republican. Episcopalian. Mason. Club: Detroit Economic. Prin. archtl. works include Gen. Motors Inst. campus devel. and bldgs., Flint, Mich., Mackinac and Manitou halls, Grand Valley State Coll., Mich. Home: 4325 Derry Rd Bloomfield Hills MI 48013 Office: 1191 W Square Lake Rd Bloomfield Hills MI 48013

ALLEN, MEL, sports broadcaster; b. Birmingham, Ala., Feb. 14, 1913; s. Julius and Anna (Leib) Israel; A.B., U. Ala., 1932, LL.B., 1936. Instr. speech, also debating coach, U. Ala., 1932-37; sports announcer, 1935—, broadcasts over radio and TV in various field of sports, including baseball, football, boxing, tennis, etc.; became staff announcer CBS, 1937; broadcaster Yankee and Giant home baseball games, 1939-42, all Yankee baseball games, 1946—, 24 All Star baseball games, 1939—, 19 World Series, 1938-58; football broadcaster, 1935—, including Nat. Collegiate Athletic Assn. games (radio-TV coast-to-coast NBC), 1951-64; also numerous games in Rose Bowl, Orange Bowl, Sugar Bowl, Blue and Gray Game, East-West Game; commentator Fox Movietone Newsreel, 1946-64, NBC radio sports daily, Sports Report (over ABC), 1956. Recipient many awards, medals, honors for work on radio and TV, 1946—. Chmn. sports div. Boy Scouts Am., 1949-50, Cerebral Palsy Fund, 1951, Greater N.Y. Fund, 1950-54; nat. sports chmn. Fight for Sight campaign, 1952—; chmn. children's summer camp campaign United Jewish Appeal, 1956; mem. President's Citizens Adv. Com. Fitness of Am. Youth, 1959-64; chmn. sports com. Salvation Army, 1963—. Served with inf. AUS, 1943-46, with Armed Forces Radio Service, 1945-46; disch. rank staff sgt. Pres. Sports Broadcasters Assn., 1950-51. Mem. Am. Legion, Jewish War Vets. U.S.A. Clubs: Lambs, Friars. Author: It Takes Heart, 1959; You Can't Beat the Hours, 1964. Address: NBC 30 Rockefeller Plaza New York City NY 10020

ALLEN, MELBA TILL, (Mrs. Marvin E. Allen), state ofcl.; b. Butler County, Ala., Mar. 3, 1933; d. Samuel Ben and Gertrude (Johnson) Till; grad. high sch.; m. Marvin E. Allen, Dec. 24, 1950; children—Judy Kathryn, Randy Earl. With Hass-Davis Packing Co., Mobile, Ala., 1951-52, W.T. Smith Lumber Co., Chapman, Ala., 1953-54, Cooper Stevedoring Co., Mobile, 1956-63, Algernon Blair Inc., Montgomery, Ala., 1963-66; now auditor State of Ala., Montgomery. Mem. Bus. Women's Assn. Democrat. Baptist. Mem. Order Eastern Star. Home: Box 3 Route 1 Grady AL 36036 Office: State Capitol Bldg Montgomery AL 36104

ALLEN, MERLE MAESER Jr., lawyer; b. Prescott, Ariz., June 6, 1932; s. Merle Maeser and Centenna (Haymore) A.; B.A., Brigham Young U., 1954; J.D., U. Ariz., 1960; m. Carol Beckstrand, Aug. 16, 1954; children—Leslie Ann, Shauna, Denise, Colette, Mark M., Brian T. Asst. mgr. Thriftee Wholesale, Prescott, 1954; admitted to Ariz. bar, 1960, since practiced in Phoenix; asso. Moe, Romley, Kaplan, Robbins & Green, 1960-66, partner, 1966—. Dir. Pioneer Bank Life Ins. Co., 1968-69. Supt. Scottsdale Stake Young Men's Mut. Improvement Assn., 1962-63; active membership drive Downtown Phoenix YMCA, 1963-66; instl. rep. Theodore Roosevelt council Boy Scouts Am., 1963-65. Served with USAF, 1954-57. Recipient award for interest in and services to youth of community Boy Scouts Am., 1968. Mem. Am., Ariz., Maricopa County bar assns. Mem. Ch. of Jesus Christ of Latter-day Saints (bishop). Author: Advertising Protection Through Copyright, 1960. Home: 8240 E Sheridan St Scottsdale AZ 85257 Office: Arizona Title Bldg Phoenix AZ 85003

ALLEN, MILLER VAN, truck rental co. exec.; b. Atlanta, Feb. 19, 1930; s. Miller Van and Virginia (McGehee) A.; B.Indsl. Engring., U. Fla., 1951; m. Jean Carol Hattaway, Feb. 26, 1949; children—Van III, Paul, Sandi, Teri. Various mgmt. positions So. Bell Telephone Co., 1950-60; with Ryder System, Inc., Miami, Fla., 1960—, pres., 1971—, also dir.; pres. Ryder Truck Rental, Inc., Miami, 1968—. Bd. dirs. Fla. Kidney Found. Mem. Young Pres.'s Orgn., Phi Delta Theta. Clubs: Coral Reef Yacht (dir.), University, Palm Bay (Miami); Ocean Reef (Key Largo, Fla.). Home: 695 Solano Prado Coral Gables FL 33143 Office: care Ryder System Inc 2701 S Bayshore Dr Miami FL 33133

ALLEN, MORRIS, fgn. service officer; b. Providence, June 4, 1917; s. Abraham and Bessie (Yellin) A.; M.B.A., U. Chgo., 1942; m. Ruth Becker, Mar. 8, 1941; children—Jane Lee (Mrs. Onofre Torres), Leslie Beth. Personnel officer Dept. War and Air Force, Washington, 1942-49; Fed. Inservice intern, 1944-45; budget and mgmt. officer Dept. State, 1949-54, personnel mgmt., 1954-55; financial analyst Commerce Dept., Fgn. Service Insp., 1956-57; U.S. Rep. Emoluments Commn. NATO, OECD, Council Europe, Western European Union, spl. asst. to asst. sec. adminstrn., 1958-61; comml. attache Am. embassy, Chile, 1961-65; mem. Sr. Seminar Fgn. Policy, 1965-66, comml. counselor Am. embassy, Brazil, 1966-71; dir. Am. Republics div. Dept. Commerce, 1971—. Mem. Am. C. of C. in Brazil (dir. 1966—). Home: 3324 Grass Hill Terrace Falls Church VA 22043 Office: Dept Commerce Washington DC 20230

ALLEN, NATHANIEL VINCENT, chemist, educator; b. Chicago, 1928; B.S. in Physics, Yale, 1950; Ph.D. in Chemistry, Harvard, 1956; m. Sally Ann Jones, July 5, 1957; children--Kenneth J., Nancy A. Chemist, Acme Chem. Co., Blue Island, Ill., 1950-51; director of Research Lab., Indsl. Chemicals Corp., Cambridge, Mass., 1956-60; project coordinator environmental sect. Steinmetz Assos., Chgo., 1960-61; v.p. for research Bauer Bros. Chem. Co., Inc., Memphis, 1961-64; asst. prof. chemistry Washington U., St. Louis, 1964-66, asso. prof., 1966-70, prof., 1970--, head of chemistry dept., 1970-71. Vis. prof. So. Ill. U., summer 1967, U. of Ore., 1969. Scoutmaster, Boy Scouts America, University City, Mo., 1968-70. Bd. dirs. Rest Haven Home for Elderly, 1960-61; trustee of the Lutheran Hosp., 1965-71. Served from lt. to capt., AUS, 1951-53. Mem. Am. Chem. Soc., Sci. Research Soc. Am. (chpt. treas. 1967), Am. Assn. Chemistry Tchrs., Am. Assn. U. Profs., Wildlife Soc., American Institute Chemists, Ecological Soc. Am. (chpt. sec.), Sigma Xi. Author: (with others) Basic Inorganic Chemistry, 1971. Contbr. articles to profl. jours., encys., also chpts. to books. Home: Fairfax Apts 7291 Windermere Dr University City MO 63105 Office: Dept Chemistry Washington University St Louis MO 63130

ALLEN, NEAL WOODSIDE, Jr., educator; b. Portland, Me., Dec. 10, 1917; s. Neal Woodside and Margaret Louise (Stevens) A.; A.B., Bowdoin Coll., 1940; M.A., Harvard, 1943, Ph.D. (Danforth fellow 1955-56), 1956; m. Alice Lydia Gamage, Dec. 21, 1940; children—Richard G., Marian L. (Mrs. Charles Fenimore, Jr.), Neal Woodside III, Edward S. Tchr., Mount Hermon (Mass.) Sch., 1941-43, Girard Coll., Phila., 1946-48; instr. history U. Me., 1948-50; faculty Union Coll., Schenectady, 1951, prof. history, 1961—, John Bigelow prof. history, 1968—, chmn. dept., 1961-66, chmn. div. social studies, 1961-66, dean humanities and social scis., 1965-66; fellow in law and history Harvard Law Sch., 1966-67; vis. lectr. Kings Coll., Aberdeen (Scotland) U., 1960-61; lectr. Albany Law Sch., 1968—. Bd. dirs. Schenectady Freedom Forum. Served to 1st lt. AUS, 1943-46. Mem. Am. Hist. Assn., Me. Hist. Soc. (hon.), Am. Assn. U. Profs., Selden Soc., Phi Beta Kappa, Alpha Delta Phi. Editor: Maine Province and Court Records, Vol. IV, 1958, Vol. V, 1964, Vol. VI, 1971. Home: 1125 Oxford Pl Schenectady NY 12308

ALLEN, NED BLISS, educator; b. Carbondale, Ill., Dec. 30, 1899; s. Carlos Eben and Maude Vrooman (Willsey) A.; student Andover Acad., 1917-18; A.B., Dartmouth Coll., 1922; B.A., Oxford Univ. (Rhodes scholarship, N.D., 1923-26); Ph.D., U. of Mich., 1931; m. Alice K. Hall, June 25, 1930 (divorced Aug. 1943); 1 dau., Emily Willsey; m. 2d, Margaret Prosser Allison, Feb. 22, 1947. Instr. of English, U. of Southern Calif., 1927-28; asso. prof. of English, U. of Del., 1931-47, prof. of English 1947-65, emeritus, 1965- -, chmn. English dept., 1946-58; vis. professor Wittenberg U., Springfield. O., 1966, Clarion (Pa.) State Coll., 1966-69. Received Robert Stevenson prize Andover, 1918. Fulbright lecturer, Agra, India, 1959-60. Member Am. Assn. Univ. Profs., Modern Lang. Assn., Shakespeare Assn., Phi Beta Kappa, Phi Kappa Phi. Author: Sources of Dryden's Comedies, 1935. Asso. editor Shakespeare Newsletter. Contbr. profl. publs. Newspaper columnist under pseudonym Alan Edwards, 1956-62. Home: 3617 73d Av S E Mercer Island, WA 98040.

ALLEN, NEWTON PERKINS, lawyer; b. Memphis, Jan. 3, 1922; s. James Seddon and Sarah (Perkins) A.; A.B., Princeton, 1943; LL.B., U. Va., 1948; m. Malinda Lobdell Nobles, Oct. 4, 1948; children—John Lobdell, Malinda Nobles, Newton Perkins, Cannon Fairfax. Admitted to Tenn. bar, 1947; asso. Armstrong, Allen, Braden, Goodman, McBride & Prewitt and predecessor firm, Memphis, 1947—, partner, 1950—. Mem. Chickasaw council Boy Scouts Am., 1958-60, exec. bd. mem., 1961—. Bd. trustees LeBonheur Children's Hosp., Memphis, 1964—, vice chmn. bd., 1965; mem. alumni council Princeton, 1954-64. Mem. Am. Coll. Probate Lawyers, American Bar Assn., Tenn., Memphis, Shelby County bar assns. Republican. Episcopalian (mem. vestry). Club: Memphis Lions (pres. 1956). Home: 950 Audubon Dr Memphis TN 38117 Office: Commerce Title Bldg Memphis TN 38103

ALLEN, NICHOLAS EUGENE, lawyer; b. Atlanta, July 24, 1907; s. Columbus Eugene and Maude Anne (Allen) A.; B.S., Princeton, 1929; LL.B., Harvard, 1932; m. Adelaide Whitford, June 11, 1938; children—Sandra, Susanne. Admitted to bar N.J., 1933, D.C., 1940, Md., 1956; pvt. practice, N.J., 1933-35, D.C., 1953—, Md., 1957—; atty. Solicitor's Office, U.S. Dept. Labor, 1936-42, 1947; asst. gen. counsel Dept. of Air Force, 1948, asso. gen. counsel, 1949-51; steel industry div. adviser Office Gen. Counsel, NPA, 1951-52; spl. asst. to Sec. Commerce, dep. acting asst. sec. of commerce for internat. affairs, 1952-53; now member Armour, Herrick, Kneipple & Allen; lectr. Am. U. and George Washington University law schools, 1954-60. Served in Judge Advocate General's Department, United States Army, 1942-46; parachutist and staff judge advocate of 82d Airborne Division in Ardennes, Rhineland and Central European campaigns; staff judge adv. U.S. Hdqurs., Berlin Dist.; exec. officer ETO Judge Adv. Div., brig. gen. USAF Res. ret.; deputy commander 1st (formerly 2d) Air Force Reserve Region, 1960-67. Decorated Legion of Merit, Bronze Star Medal, commendation award (U.S.); Belgian and Dutch fourrageres. Mem. Am., Fed., Md., D.C. bar assns., 82d Airborne Div. Assn., Judge Advocates Assn. (nat. pres. 1956-57), Phi Beta Kappa. Conglist. Club: Army-Navy Country (Arlington, Va.). Home: 5313 Blackistone Rd Westmoreland Hills (Md) Washington DC 20016 Office: Shoreham Bldg Washington DC 20005 also Barlow Bldg Chevy Chase MD 20015

ALLEN, OSCAR NELSON, educator, bacteriologist; b. Corsicana, Tex., May 15, 1905; s. Oscar Andrew and Lillie Mae (Dugan) A.; B.A., M.A., U. Tex., 1927; Ph.D., U. Wis., 1930; postgrad. Rothamsted Exptl. Sta., Harpenden, Eng., London (Eng.) Sch. Tropical Hygiene, Brown Inst., London; m. Ethel Delia Kullmann, July 11, 1930. Research asst. agrl. bacteriology U. Wis., Madison, 1927-28, instr., 1929-30, prof. bacteriology, 1946—; asst. prof. bacteriology and plant pathology U. Hawaii, Honolulu, 1930-35, bacteriologist Grad. Sch. Tropical Agr., 1931-45, cooperating soil bacteriologist Pineapple Research Inst., 1931-41, collaborator bacteriology and platn pathology Hawaii Agrl. Expt. Sta., 1932-41, asso. prof., 1935-40, bacteriologist Queens Hosp. Nursing Sch., 1935-41, acting chmn. dept. botany, 1934-36, 39-40, prof. bacteriology, 1940-45, chmn. dept. botany, 1940-42, vice chmn. dept. biol. scis., 1942, chmn. dept. bacteriology, 1943-45; chmn., prof. dept. bacteriology U. Md., 1945-46. Vis. prof. bacteriology U. Tex., summers 1937-39; del., mem. various congresses, confs. George Ives Haight Travelling awardee U. Wis., Far East, South Pacific, 1962. Fellow Am. Soc. Agronomy; mem. Am. Soc. for Microbiology (ad hoc com. taxonomy com. 1963—), Soil Sci. Soc. Am. (sect. vice chmn. 1947, chmn. 1948), Stain Tech., Am. Assn. U. Profs., Bot. Soc. Am., Am. Phytopath. Soc., Canadian Soc. Microbiology, Internat. Soc. Soil Sci., Soc. for Gen. Microbiology, Sigma Xi, Phi Sigma, Gamma Alpha, Phi Kappa Phi, Alpha Gamma Rho. Author: Experiments in Soil Bacteriology, 3d rev. edit. 1957; also numerous articles. Asso. editor: Bergey's Manual of Determinative Bacteriology (D.H. Bergey), 1948; cons. soils editor Agronomy Jour., 1948-54; co-editor Microbiology and Soil Fertility, 1965. Home: 4142 Hiawatha Dr Madison WI 53711

ALLEN, PAUL JAMES, educator; b. Stockbridge, Mass., Sept. 28, 1914; s. Edward Bernard and Alice (Ormes) A.; A.B., Harvard, 1936; M.S., U. Rochester, 1938; Ph.D., U. Cal. at Berkeley, 1941; m. Mary Remsen North, Apr. 3, 1943; children—David O., Thomas D., Kathryn H. Instr., U. Pa., Phila., 1941- 43; microbiologist U.S. Dept. Agr., Phila., also Salinas, Cal., 1943-46; asst. prof. botany U. Wis. at Madison, 1946-52, asso. prof., 1952-59, prof. 1959—, prof. plant pathology, 1964—, chmn. dept. botany, 1965-70; vis. prof. botany U. Cal. at Berkeley , 1960-61. Merck post-doctoral fellow, Sheffield, Eng., 1953-54. Mem. Bot. Soc. Am., Am. Phytopathol. Soc., Am. Soc. Plant Physiologists, Am. Inst. Biol. Scis., Sierra Club, Nature Conservancy, Sigma Xi. Contbr. articles, particularly on parasitic fungi, physiology of plant disease, spore germination and devel. in fungi, to profl. jours. Home: Route 2 Verona WI 53593 Office: Dept Botany U of Wis Madison WI 53706

ALLEN, PAUL WHEELER, mining co. exec.; b. Chambersburg, Pa., Feb. 12, 1915; s. Paul P. and Gertrude (Wheeler) A.; grad. William Penn Charter Sch., 1933; B.S.,Mass. Inst. Tech., 1937; m. Marjorie Hanson, Sept. 14, 1940; children—Laurence Michael, Clifton. With Cyprus Mines Corp., 1955-, v.p., 1956-70, sr. v.p., 1970—, pres. affiliate Prima Mining Co., exec. v.p., affiliate Anvil Mining Co.; dir. Goldsworthy Mining Ltd., Perth, W. Australia. Mem. Am. Inst. Mining, Metall. and Petroleum Engrs., Mining and Metall. Soc. Am. Home: 1175 Glen Oaks Blvd Pasadena CA 91105 Office: 523 5th St Los Angeles CA 90014

ALLEN, PETER CHRISTOPHER, chem. co. exec.; b. Ashtead, Surrey, Eng., Sept. 8, 1905; s. Ernest King and Florence Mary (Gellatly) A.; ed. Harrow Sch., also Trinity Coll. U. Oxford (Eng.); m. Violet Sylvester Wingate-Saul (dec. 1951); 2 daus.; m. 2d, Consuelo Mario Linaries Rivas, 1952. Joined Brunner, Mond & Co. Ltd. (predecessor to Imperial Chem. Industries Ltd., Eng.), 1928; chmn. plastics div. ICI Ltd., 1948-51; dir. Brit. Nylon Spinners Ltd., 1954-58; pres., chmn. ICI of Can. Ltd., 1961-68; pres. Canadian Industries, Ltd., 1959-62, chmn., 1962-68; pres. Inst. Sci. and Tech., U. Manchester (Eng.), 1968—; v.p. BACIE, 1969—; v.p. Inst. Manpower Studies, 1968—; dir. Bank of Montreal, 1968—. Bd. govs. Nat. Coll. Rubber Tech., 1964-68; mem. Export Council Europe, 1962-65, Overseas Devel. Inst. Council, 1963-64, Iron and Steel Holding and Realisation Agy., 1963-67, Commonwealth Export Council, 1964-67; chmn. com. for exports B.N.E.C., 1964-67. Created knight, 1967. Fellow Brit. Inst. Mgmt.; mem. Ct. of Brit. Shippers Council, Société de Chimie Industrielle (bd. dirs., vice-chmn.), Instn. Chem. Engrs., Canadian Chem. Producers Assn.; hon. mem. Chem. Industries Assn. (pres. 1965-67, council 1967-68); mem. Mfg. Chemists Assn. U.S. (v.p. 1961-62, bd. dirs. 1959-62), Assn. Brit. Chem. Mfrs. (vice-chmn. council 1963-65), Plastics Inst. (pres. 1950-52), Brit. Plastics Fedn. (pres. 1963-65), Canadian C. of C. in Gt. Britain (council 1964-68). Clubs: Junior Carlton; Mt. Royal (Montreal); Royal and Ancient; Royal Cinque Ports; Rye; Royal St. George's; Oxford and Cambridge Golfing; Augusta (Ga.) Nat. Golf; Pine Valley (N.J.). Author: The Railways of the Isle of Wight, 1928; Locomotives of Many Lands, 1954; On the Old Lines, 1957; (with P.B. Whitehouse) Narrow Gauge Railways of Europe, 1959; Round the World on the Narrow Gauge, 1966; (with R.A. Wheeler) Steam on the Sierra, 1960; (with Consuelo Allen) The Curve of Earth's Shoulder, 1966; (with A.B. MacLeod) Rails in the Isle of Wight, 1967; Famous Fairways, 1868. Address: U Manchester Manchester England

ALLEN, PHILIP DRAKE, pub. exec.; b. Mpls., May 23, 1910; s. Arthur Harrison and Sarah (Gary) A.; student Phillips Andover Acad., 1926; B.A., Ohio Wesleyan U., 1933; m. Elizabeth Forgan, June 26, 1936; children—Philip Drake, Berwick Forgan; m. 2d, Frances Crosby Douglas, June 11, 1960; step- children—Richard, Cynthia, Jane Douglas. Sales engr. Walworth Mfg. Co., 1933-38; Western mgr. Business Week mag., McGraw-Hill Pub. Co., 1938-46, dist. mgr. Western dist., 1946-48; partner Allen & Rutherford, 1950-53; v.p. Maclean-Hunter Pub. Corp., Chgo., 1953-56, pres., 1956-64; sr. v.p. sales and marketing Kingsport Press, Inc. (Tenn.), 1964-66, also dir.; v.p. Ware Bros. Co., Phila., in charge N.Y., office, supr. new devels., 1966-67; v.p., pub. Miller Freeman Publications, 1967—; chairman board and chief executive officer H.A.B. Corp. Served from lt. (j.g.) to lt. comdr., USNR, 1942-45. Mem. Asso. Nat. Advertisers (chmn. business paper sect.), Asso. Bus. Publs. (dir., past chmn), Chgo. Bus. Publishers Assn. (past pres.), Assn. Indsl. Advertisers, Delta Tau Delta. Conglist. Clubs: Singing Hill Game (Volo, Ill.) (pres.); University (New York City); University (Chicago); Nutmeg Curling (Darien, Connecticut); Silver Springs Country (Ridgefield, Connecticut). Home: 105 Signal Hill Rd Wilton CT 06897 Office: 370 Lexington Av New York City NY 10017 also 123A Chaussée de Charleroi Brussels 6 Belgium

ALLEN, PHILLIP ELWOOD, lawyer; b. Joplin, Mo., Jan. 18, 1931; s, Elwood A. and Opal (Calhoun) A.; B.S.U. Ark. 1959, LL.B., 1962; m. Lorraine V. Miller, July 12, 1952; children-Linda Denise, Karen Diane, Bradley Phillip. Admitted to Ark. bar, 1962, since practiced in Little Rock; partner firm Allen & Young, 1968—. Officer, dir. Beaver Creek Industries, Inc. Served with AUS, 1949-52, 52-57. Mem. Am., Ark. bar assns., Tau Kappa Alpha, Beta Gamma Sigma, Omicron Delta Kappa, Phi Eta Sigma, Delta Theta Phi. Home: 48 Coachlight Dr Little Rock AR 72207 Office: 501 Woodlane St Little Rock AR 72201

ALLEN, RAYMOND BERNARD, educator, former govt. ofcl.; b. Cathay, N.D., Aug. 7, 1902; s. Anthony J. and Ellen (Faulkner) A.; B.S., U. Minn., 1924, M.A., 1925, M.B., M.D., 1928, Ph.D., 1934; LL.D., Tulane U., 1946, U. Ill., 1946, Lake Forest Coll., 1946, U.

Hawaii, 1948, Boston U., 1948, Gonzaga U., 1949, U. So. Cal., 1951; D.Sc., Whitman Coll., 1947; m. Dorothy Sheard, Aug. 29, 1931 (div. Dec. 1963); children—Charles Anthony, Raymond Bernard, Willard Sheard (dec.), Blanche E. (dec.), Dorothy, Barbara Jean; m. 2d, Emmy Portman Stone, Aug. 13, 1968. Fellow Mayo Found., 1930- 33; gen. med. practice, Minot, N.D., 1928-30; asso. dean in charge grad. studies Coll. Physicians and Surgeons, Columbia, 1934-36; asso. dir., New York Post-Grad. Med. Sch. and Hosp., Columbia, 1933-36; dean Wayne U. Coll. Medicine, 1936-39; exec. dean Chgo. Colls. of U. of Ill. (medicine, dentistry and pharmacy), 1939-46, dean Coll. of Medicine, 1943-46; pres. U. Wash., Seattle, 1946-52; dir. Psychol. Strategy Bd., 1952; chancellor U. Cal. at Los Angeles, 1952-59; dir. U.S. Operations Mission to Indonesia, 1959-61; chief Office Research Coordination, Pan Am. Health Orgn., Washington, 1962-66, chief office of health and population dynamics, 1966-67; cons. health, edn., population dynamics, 1967—; clin. prof. community medicine and internat. health Georgetown U. Coll. Medicine, 1967-70, lectr., 1970—; cons. health, edn., population dynamics AID, State Dept., 1969—. Dir. med. services Office Sec. of Defense, 1949 (on leave from U. of Wash.), dir. Salary Stblzn. Bd., 1951; nat. cons. U.S. Air Force, Air U.; bd. dirs. Transp. Assn. Am., dir. Los Angeles World Affairs Council; pres. 2d World Conf. Med. Edn., 1959; dir. Freedoms Found.; chmn. bd. trustees Ednl. Testing Service, 1951; trustee Carnegie Found. for Advancement Teaching, 1948-59, Am. Com. on United Europe; mem. Com. (Eberstadt) on Nat. Security Orgn. (Hoover Commn. 1948-49); cons. emeritus Nat. War Coll. Fellow A.C.P.; mem. Sigma Xi, Alpha Omega Alpha, Phi Delta Kappa, Phi Beta Kappa (hon.). Republican. Clubs: Cosmos (Washington). Address: Flint Hill VA 22627

ALLEN, REGINALD, ednl. exec.; b. Phila., Mar. 22, 1905; s. Alfred Reginald and Helen Johnson (Warren) A.; grad. cum laude Phillips Exeter Acad., 1922; B.A., Harvard, 1926; m. Helen Howe, May 31, 1946. With advt. dept. Victor Talking Machine Co., 1926-30; copywriter N.W. Ayer, 1930-32, J. M. Mathes, 1932-35; bd. dirs. Phila. Orch. Assn., 1933-35, mgr., 1935-39; head story dept. Universal Pictures, 1939-42; Pacific Coast rep. J. Arthur Rank Orgn., Universal City, Cal., 1946-49; asst. mgr., bus. adminstr., sec. to bd. dirs. Met. Opera Co., N.Y.C., 1949-57, asst. to pres., gen. mgr., 1962-69; exec. dir. operations Lincoln Center Performing Arts, 1957-62; exec. v.p. Am. Acad. Rome, 1969—, acting dir., 1969-70. Mem. DeSchauensee S. African Expdn. to Kalahari Desert, 1930. Mem. Pres.' Adv. com. Nat. Cultural Center, 1958-63; mem. N.Y. State Council Arts, 1961-65; mem. Pres.' Exec. Com. for Shakespeare Anniversary, 1964. Trustee D'Oyly Carte Opera Trust. Served to lt. comdr. USNR, 1942-45. Life fellow Pierpont Morgan Library. Mem. Phila. Acad. Natural Scis., Century Assn. Club: Grolier. Author: The First Night Gilbert & Sullivan, 1958; W. S. Gilbert, An Anniversary Survey and Exhibition Checklist, 1963. Home: 1158 Fifth Av New York City NY 10029 Office: Am Acad in Rome 101 Park Av New York City NY 10017

ALLEN, REX WHITAKER, architect; b. San Francisco, Dec. 21, 1914; s. Lewis Whitaker and Maude Rex. (Allen) A.; A.B., Harvard, 1936, B.Arch., 1939; student Columbia Arch. Sch., 1936-37; m. Elizabeth Johnson, Oct. 11, 1941 (div. 1949); children—Alexandra A. (Mrs. Daniel D. Fleckles), Frances Lambert; m. 2d, Ruth Batchelor, Apr. 1, 1949 (div. 1971); children—Mark Batchelor, Susan Moore. With Research and Planning Assos., N.Y.C., 1939-42, Camloe Fastener Corp., N.Y.C., 1942-45, Isadore Rosenfield, architect, N.Y.C., 1945-48, Blanchard and Maher, architects, San Francisco, 1949-52; established pvt. practice, San Francisco, 1953; pres. Rex Whitaker Allen & Assos., San Francisco, 1961—; prin. works include French Hosp., San Francisco, 1963, Mercy Hosp., Sacramento, 1963, Roseville (Cal.) Dist. Hosp., 1962, Highland Hosp., Oakland, St. Francis Hosp., San Francisco, Dominican Hosp., Santa Cruz, Alta Bates Hosp., Berkeley, Cal., Boston City Hosp., Stanislaus Meml. Hosp., Modesto, Cal., Madera (Cal.) Community Hosp., Sacred Heart Hosp., Eugene, Ore., St. Joseph Hosp., Mt. Clemons, Mich. Chmn., Mill Valley Avd. Edn. Council, 1956. Mem. A.I.A. (v.p. No. Cal. chpt. 1964, bd. dirs. Cal. council 1955-56, 1962-64, national president 1969-70), Constrn. Specification Inst. (pres. San Francisco 1961), Assn. Western Hosps. (chmn. arch. sect. 1957-58), Cal. Hosp. Assn., Am. Hosp. Assn., Internat. Hosp. Fedn., Am. Assn. Hosp. Planning (pres. 1971-72), Union Internat. des Architectes, San Francisco C. of C., San Francisco Planning and Urban Renewal Assn., San Francisco Museum Art, San Francisco Symphony Found., N.Y. Mus. Modern Art. Clubs: Harvard (N.Y.C. and San Francisco); Sierra (San Francisco). Contbr. profl. jours. Home: 4718 17th St San Francisco CA 94117 Office: 259 Geary St San Francisco CA 94102

ALLEN, RICHARD BLOSE, lawyer, editor; b. Aledo, Ill., May 10, 1919; s. James Albert and Claire (Smith) A.; B.S., U. Ill., 1941, J.D., 1947; m. Marion Treloar, Aug. 27, 1949; children—Penelope, Jennifer, Leslie Jean. Admitted to Ill. bar, 1947; staff editor Am. Bar Assn. Jour., 1947-48, 63-66, exec. editor, 1966-70, editor, 1970—; pvt. practice law, Aledo, 1949-57; gen. counsel Ill. Bar Assn., 1957-63. Served from pvt. to maj., Q.M.C., AUS, 1941-46. Mem. Am., Ill., Chgo. bar assns., Sigma Delta Chi, Kappa Tau Alpha, Phi Delta Phi, Alpha Tau Omega. Club: Michigan Shores (Wilmette). Home: 702 Illinois Rd Wilmette IL 60091 Office: 1155 E 60th St Chicago IL 60637

ALLEN, RICHARD NORMAN, food co. exec.; b. Ossian, Ia., Apr. 15, 1911; s. Ward Malcolm and Fanny (Cornell) A.; B.S.C., State U. Ia., 1932; m. Genevieve H. Sobolik, Aug. 31, 1936 (deceased); children—Kenneth R., Judith A., Robert S., Donald W., Ruthann; m. 2d, Agnes Rothenbuhler, Aug. 17, 1968. Accountant, Arthur Anderson & Co., Chgo., 1933-34, Lybrand, Ross Bros. & Montgomery, Chgo., 1934, Material Service Corp., Chgo., 1935-40; with Central Soya Co., Inc., Ft. Wayne, Ind., 1940—, asst. sec., controller, 1944- 64, sec., 1962—, v.p. planning, 1966—; sec., dir. Ft. Wayne Pub. Transp. Corp. Bd. dirs. Ft. Wayne Ednl. Found., Parkview Meml. Hosp.; trustee Central Soya Found. C.P.A., Ind., Ill., Ia. Mem. Am. Inst. C.P.A.'s, Ind. Soc. C.P.A.'s, Financial Execs. Inst., Delta Upsilon. Methodist (finance com.). Club: Orchard Ridge Country. Home: 4924 S Wayne Av Fort Wayne IN 46806 Office: Fort Wayne Bank Bldg Fort Wayne IN 46802

ALLEN, RICHARD SWEETNAM, univ. prof.; b. Pekin, Ill., Nov. 9, 1896; s. William Henry and Margaret Anne (Olt) A.I., student U. Chgo., 1917-18, 1926-27, 36-37, B.S., U. Rochester, 1922, M.S., 1925; m. Leone M.S. McLoughlin, Aug. 23, 1924; 1 son, William Henry II. Research Asso. U. Rochester, 1922-23, asst., 1923-25; instr. Coll. Medicine, U. Tenn., 1925-26; asst. prof. U. Ky., 1927-29, asso. prof. physiology and anatomy, 1929-36, prof. anatomy and physiology, 1936-67, head dept., 1931-67, prof. physiology Med. Center, 1960-67, prof. emeritus, 1967—, faculty asst. to dean Coll. Arts and Scis., 1966-67; physiol. chemist Wilson Research Lab., Chgo., 1923; phys. chemist Western Electric Co., 1921. Served with Heavy Field Arty., U.S. Army, 1918-19. Mem. Am. Legion (past chmn. jr. athletic com. local state orgns.), Assn. Am. Med. Colls., A.A.A.S., Am. Genetic Assn., Nat. Geog. Soc., 40 and 8, Sigma Xi, Alpha Epsilon Delta. Democrat. Baptist. Past sec. Research Club, U. Ky. Contbr. articles profl. jours. Home: 1836 McDonald Rd Lexington, KY 40503.

ALLEN, ROBERT CLYDE, distbn. and marketing cons.; b. Watertown, Tenn., Feb. 7, 1898; s. Moses Frank and Ellen E. (Hudson) A.; student Trinity U., Waxahachie, Tex., 1915-17; m. Willow Sharp, 1967; children by previous marriage—Robert Clyde, Hal K. Sec. Civil Service Commn., 11th Dist., Ft. Worth, 1919-21; asst. operating supt. Montgomery-Ward Co., Ft. Worth br., 1921-22; head accounting Butler Bros., Dallas, 1922-23; created market research operations for Tex. Farm and Range Pub. Co., Dallas, 1923-29; marketing research and promotional activities Butterick Pub. Co., N.Y.C., 1929-34; pres. Maculette, Inc., N.Y.C., 1935-37; gen. sales mgr. Revlon Products, N.Y.C., 1937-39; gen. sales mgr. Schnefel Brothers, Newark, 1939-41; distbn. cons., marketing analyst Stewart, Dougall & Associates, N.Y.C., 1942-53, exec. v.p., dir., 1953-58; dir. Bulova Watch Co. Recipient citations for service, World War I, U.S. Liberty Loan Com., Am. Nat. Red Cross Soc. Clubs: Economic, Sales Executive, Rockefeller Center Luncheon (N.Y.C.); Exchange (New Canaan, Conn.). Home: Butternut Lane Norwalk CT 06851 Office: 630 Fifth Ave New York City NY 10020

ALLEN, ROBERT DAY, educator, biologist; b. Providence, Aug. 28, 1927; s. Richard Day and Mary (Cottrell) A.; A.B., Brown U., 1949; Ph.D., U. Pa., 1953; m. Margaret Dampman, Dec. 23, 1950 (div. 1970); children—Elizabeth, Wayne; m. 2d, Nina Strömgren, Sept. 12, 1971. Asst. instr. zoology U. Pa., 1950-51; instr. zoology U. Mich., 1954-56; asst. prof., then asso. prof. biology Princeton, 1956-66; prof. biology, chmn. dept. State U. N.Y. at Albany, 1966—; cons. to industry, 1963—. Trustee Marine Biol. Lab., Woods Hole, Mass., 1966—. Guggenheim fellow, 1961, 66; recipient Golden Eagle award for non-theatre motion picture Mitosis, Council Internat. Non Theatrical Events, 1955; USPHS predoctoral fellow U. Pa., 1951-53; USPHS postdoctoral fellow Sweden and Italy, 1953-54. Fellow A.A.A.S., Royal Microscopical Soc. Contbr. profl. jours. Editor: Primitive Motile Systems in Cell Biology, 1964. Home: 60 Thorndale Rd Slingerlands NY 12159 Office: Dept Biol Scis State Univ NY Albany NY 12203

ALLEN, ROBERT EUGENE, advt. exec.; b. Allentown, Pa., May 14, 1913; s. Eugene and Mayme (Sourewine) A.; B.C.S., Temple U., 1935; grad. student Columbia, 1938; m. Dorothy Nelson, July 11, 1936; 1 dau., Patricia Ann. Sales promotion Pennzoil Co., 1935-37; account exec. on Westinghouse Electric Co., Fuller & Smith & Ross, Inc., 1937-42, v.p. in charge Westinghouse Electric Co. account, 1942-50, v.p., mgr., dir., 1950-54, pres., 1954- 66, chmn. bd., chief exec. officer, 1967—; dir. Nat. Outdoor Advt. Bur., Reeves Industries, Inc. Bd. dirs. New Rochelle (New York) Hospital; bd. of dirs. Freedoms Found. at Valley Forge. Recipient Ben Franklin medal Alpha Delta Sigma; Order St. John, Queen of Eng., 1969. Mem. Newcomen Soc. N.Am. Pa. Soc., Am. Assn. Advt. Agys. (dir.), Advertising Council Washington (mem. bd. dirs.). Presbyterian. Clubs: Canadian, Advertising (N.Y.C.); Seaview Country (Absecon, N.J.); Larchmont (N.Y.) Yacht; Advertising, Union (Cleve.); Winged Foot Country (N.Y.); Duquesne (Pitts.); Mid-America (Chgo.); Pa. Soc., Rolling Rock (Ligonier, Pa.). Home: 200 Barnard Rd New Rochelle NY 10801 Office: 666 Fifth Av New York City NY 10019

ALLEN, ROBERT HUTTON, telephone co. exec.; b. Douglaston, N.Y., Nov. 16, 1921; s. Archibald John and Grace Browne (MCGuire) A.; B.A., Williams Coll., 1946; m. Elise Eaton, Oct. 16, 1954; children—Warren Eaton, Janet, Martha, Grace. With Cin. Bell Inc., 1946—, gen. comml. mgr., 1963-65, asst. to pres., 1965-67, pub. relations dir., 1967-68, dir. adminstrn. and planning, 1968-70, v.p., sec., treas., 1970—. Trustee Coll. Prep. Sch., Playhouse in the Park, Cin. Served with USAAF, 1942-46. Republican. Clubs: University, Cincinnati Country; Williams (N.Y.C.). Home: 2285 Grandin Rd Cincinnati OH 45208 Office: 225 E 4th St Cincinnati OH 45202

ALLEN, ROBERT JOSEPH, educator; b. Indpls. Mar. 9, 1902; s. Fiske and Olive (Moore) A.; A.B., U. Ill., 1923; M.A., Harvard, 1928, Ph.D., 1929; m. Helen Mohr Hays, June 18, 1931; 1 dau., Deborah Hays. High sch. tchr., 1923-26; faculty, dept. English, U. Kan., 1929-30, Harvard, 1930-37; faculty Williams Coll. since 1937, prof. English, 1949—, Morris prof. rhetoric, 1950-59, John Hawley Roberts prof. English, 1959-71, head English dept., 1949-63, 65-67. Travelling fellow, Eng., 1929, 31, 37. Mem. Modern Lang. Assn. Am. Author: The Clubs of Augustan London, 1933; Life in Eighteenth Century England, 1941. Editor: Addison and Steele; Selections from the Tatler and Spectator, 1957. Contbr. learned publs. Home: Cluett Dr Williamstown MA 01267

ALLEN, ROBERT SCOTT, educator, biochemist; b. Tabiona, Utah, Nov. 13, 1917; s. Robert Ernest and Genevieve (Michie) A.; B.S., Brigham Young U., 1939, M.S., 1940; Ph.D., Ia. State Coll., 1949; m. Louise Pierce, Sept. 4, 1940; children—Don Robert, Gary Wayne, Ross Michael. Research asso. Ia. State U., Ames, 1947-49, faculty, 1949-67, prof., 1957-67, chmn. dept. biochemistry and biophysics, 1960-63; prof., head dept. biochemistry La. State U., Baton Rouge, 1967—. Recipient Am. Feed Mfrs. award in dairy cattle nutrition, 1955.; named Distinguished Prof. Agr., Ia. State U., 1965. Mem. Am. Chem. Soc. (past chmn. Ames sect.), Am. Dairy Sci. Assn., Am. Inst. Nutrition, Sigma Xi, Phi Kappa Phi, Phi Lambda Upsilon, Gamma Sigma Delta. Editor: (with others) Physiology of Digestion in the Ruminant, 1965. Research, numerous publs. on biochemistry of vitamin A and carotene metabolism, lipid absorption and metabolism, forage preservation and utilization, etiology of bloat in ruminants. Home: 256 Court St Baton Rouge LA 70810

ALLEN, ROBERT SHARON, writer; b. Latonia, Ky.; ed. U. Wis., 1923, U. Munich (Germany), George Washington U., U.S. Cavalry Sch., Ft. Riley, Kan., Command and Gen. Staff Coll.; m. Ruth Finney, Mar. 30, 1929. Reporter, Capital Times, Madison, Wis., 1919; successively reporter Wis. State Jour., Milw. Jour., United Press Assn., Christian Science Monitor, Internat. News Service; Washington corr. Phila. Record; Joined U.S. Cav. 1916, promoted to 2d lt., 1918; also capt. Wis. N.G., 1921-27; recalled to active duty U.S. Army, July 1942, with rank of Major, Cav.; promoted to lt. col., May 1943, col., Mar. 1945; operations exec. G-2 Sect. Hdqrs. 3d Army, throughout its combat operations European Theater Operations. Decorated Silver Star, Legion of Merit, Bronze Star, Purple Heart, Commendation Ribbon with cluster, French Legion of Honor, Croix de Guerre with palm and gold star. Mem. Sigma Delta Chi. Clubs: National Press, National Communications, George Washington University. Author: Washington Merry-Go-Round, 1931; Why Hoover Faces Defeat, 1932; More Washington Merry-Go-Round, 1932; Nine Old Men, 1936; Nine Old Men at the Crossroads, 1937; Our Fair City, 1946; Our Sovereign State, 1949; The Truman Merry-Go-Round, 1950; Lucky Forward; Co-author daily syndicated column Washington Merry-Go-Round, 1932-42; daily syndicated column Inside Washington. Contbr. to mags. Home: 1525 28th St N W Washington DC 20007 Office: National Press Bldg Washington DC 20004

ALLEN, ROGER, architect; b. Grand Rapids, Mich., June 23, 1892; s. Frank Payne and Mary Francis (O'Connor) A.; student Grand Rapids pub. schs.; LL.D., Central Mich. Coll., 1956; D. Sc. (hon.), Ferris Institute, 1957; m. Margaret Katherine Sullivan, Nov. 24, 1923; children—Mary Margaret (Mrs. Robert Peckham), Bridget Irene (Mrs. Irving G. Hunsberger). Pvt. archtl. practice, Grand Rapids, 1921—; works include Central Mich. Coll., Ferris Inst. (Big Rapids, Mich.), Mulick Park Elementary Sch., Hall Elementary Sch., Grand Rapids Pub. Mus., St. Thomas the Apostle Cath. Ch., Grace Episcopal Ch. (Holland, Mich.), Mt. Pleasant (Mich.) State Home and Tng. Sch.; columnist Fired at Random for Grand Rapids Press, 1940—. Served as lt. USN, 1918-21. Recipient gold medal Mich. Soc. Architects, 1954. Fellow A.I.A.; mem. Mich. Soc. Architects (pres. 1948-49), Mich. Engring. Soc., Archtl. League N.Y. Episcopalian. Clubs: Torch, Peninsular (Grand Rapids). Contbr. profl. jours. Home: 2461 Westboro Dr N E Grand Rapids MI 49506 Office: McKay Tower Grand Rapids MI 49506

ALLEN, RONALD WAYNE, airline exec.; b. Atlanta, Nov. 20, 1941; s. Marion E. and Ruth (Bradford) A.; B.S. in Indsl. Engring., Ga. Inst. Tech., 1964; m. Margaret E. Slieper, Apr. 18, 1964; children—Mark Jeffrey, Christine Elizabeth. Methods analyst Delta Air Lines, Inc., Atlanta, 1964, adminstrv. asst. personnel, 1964-66, dir. methods, tng., 1966-67, asst. v.p. adminstrn., 1967-69, v.p. adminstrn., 1969-70, sr. v.p. personnel, 1970—. Active Leadership Atlanta Program, 1969-70. Mem. Christian Ch. (deacon). Home: 2486 Clifton Springs Manor Decatur GA 30034 Office: Delta Air Lines Inc Atlanta Airport Atlanta GA 30321

ALLEN, ROSS LORRAINE, coll. dean; b. Newark, Feb. 28, 1905; s. James and Dora (Pollock) A.; B.S. in Edn., U. Mich., 1927, M.S. in Pub. Health, 1934, D.P.H., 1936; m. Madeline Lucia Hitchcock, July 29, 1927; children—Ross Lorraine, Carolyn Virginia (Mrs. Fred J. Cooney). Engaged in sch. health study Am. Child Health Assn., N.Y.C., 1927-28; health edn. tchr. Washington Jr. High Sch., Rochester, N.Y., 1928-35; asst. editor Jour. Health and Phys. Edn., 1935-36; asst. exec. dir., then exec. dir. Am. Camping Assn., 1936- 41; asst. supr. phys. edn. and athletics U. Mich., 1941-45; prof. health edn., chmn. dept. S.U.N.Y. at Cortland, 1945-54, dir. div. health, phys. edn. and recreation, 1954-65, dean grad. studies and research, 1965—. Recipient Outstanding Adminstrv. award N.Y. State Council Health, Phys. Edn. and Recreation. Mem. Am., N.Y. (State Service award 1962) assns. health, phys. edn. and recreation, Am. Sch. Health Assn., Nat. Soc. Study Edn., N.E.A., Am. Ednl. Research Assn., Am. Nat. Com. Health Edn. of Pub., Am. Assn. Colls. Tchr. Edn. Author: (elementary health textbooks) Health for Better Living, 1954-63; School Health, 1961. Home: 1222 Bell Dr Cortland NY 13045

ALLEN, ROY O., Jr., architect; b. Sayre, Pa., Mar. 14, 1921; s. Roy O. and Lyndall (Harding) A.; B.S. in Arch., Pa. State U., 1943; m. Marion Marshall Taylor, Dec. 12, 1964; children by previous marriage—Jeffrey, Gary, Leslie. Procedures engr. Curtis-Wright Corp., 1942-45; with Skidmore, Owings & Merrill, N.Y.C., 1946—, now gen. partner; prin. works include Lever House, Chase Manhattan Bank, Union Carbide bldg. (all N.Y.C.). Mem. A.I.A., Mus. Modern Art. Clubs: Sleepy Hollow Country (Scarborough, N.Y.); Nat. Golf Links (S. Hampton, L.I.); University; Metropolitan. Home: 7 W 81st St New York City NY 10024 Office: 400 Park Av New York City NY 10022

ALLEN, SANFORD, concert violinist. Address: Care NY Philharmonic Orch Broadway at 65th St New York City NY 10023*

ALLEN, SID, business and financial editor San Francisco Chronicle. Address: 901 Mission St San Francisco CA 94119 *

ALLEN, STEPHEN VALENTINE PATRICK WILLIAM, television humorist, song writer; b. N.Y.C., Dec. 26, 1921; s. Carroll and Isabelle (Donohue) A.; student sch. journalism Drake U., 1941, State Tchrs. Coll., Ariz., 1942; m. Dorothy Goodman, Aug. 23, 1943; children—Stephen, Brian, David; m. 2d, Jayne Meadows, July 31, 1954; 1 s. William Christopher. Radio announcer, sta. KOY, Phoenix, 1942, stas. KFAC and KMTR, Los Angeles, 1944; comedian MBS, 1945; disc jockey CBS, 1948; wrote narration and appeared in movie Down Memory Lane, also appeared in I'll Get By, The Benny Goodman Story, Warning Shot; own TV show, 1950—; appeared in Broadway play The Pink Elephant, 1953; host TV show I've Got A Secret, 1964-66. Recipient Grammy award for Gravy Waltz, 1964. Writer of approximately 3000 songs, including, South Rampart Street Parade, This Could be the Start of Something, Picnic, Impossible, Houseboat. Author: Fourteen for Tonight, 1955; The Funnymen, 1956; Wry on the Rocks, 1956; Mark It and Strike It (autobiography); Not All Your Laughter, Not All Your Tears, 1962; Letter to a Conservative, 1965; The Ground is our Table 1966; Bigger Than A Breadbox, 1967; A Flash of Swallows, 1969. Address: 15201 Burbank Blvd Van Nuys CA 91401

ALLEN, TURNER WHARTON, coll. dean; b. Greensboro, Ala., Oct. 4, 1918; s. Charles Ethelbert and Jessie (Wharton) A.; A.B., Centre Coll., Danville, Ky., 1940; M.A., Ind. U., 1941; Ph.D., U. Ky., 1952; m. Elizabeth Palmer Brewer, June 4, 1941; children—Elizabeth Wharton, Anne Taliagerro. Sales rep. U.S. Tobacco Co., 1941-42, 46-47; grad. instr. history U. Ky., 1948-49; from instr. to prof. history, also chmn. dept. Lincoln Meml. U., 1949-54; prof. history Florence (Ala.) State Coll., 1954-56, dean coll., 1956—. Mem. Ala. Tchr. Edn. Profl. Standards Commn., 1959—. Fulbright fellow, Paris, France, 1950-51. Mem. So. Hist. Assn., So. Assn. Councils Tchr. Edn., Ala. Council Deans, Beta Theta Pi, Omicron Delta Kappa. Episcopalian (vestryman, sr. warden). Rotarian (pres., dir. Florence 1960-62). Home: 223 Circular Dr Florence AL 35630

ALLEN, VICTOR HARVEY, editor; b. Brownville, N.Y., June 28, 1910; s. Harvey H. and Ethel Maude (Dietrich) A.; student Antioch Coll., 1935-38; m. Jennie E. Hoeber, Jan. 20, 1939; children—Peter Paul, Andrew Roger. Laborer, merchant seaman, 1928-35; editor Jour. Am. Water Works Assn., 1938-42; prodn. mgr. Interscience Publs., Inc., 1946-48; book designer, 1949; editor Jour. Soc. Motion Picture and TV Engrs., N.Y.C., 1950—. Mil. Service, 1943-45. Mem. Am. Inst. Graphic Arts. Home: 451 Old Sleepy Hollow Rd Pleasantville NY 10570 Office: 9 E 41st St New York City NY 10017

ALLEN, WARD P., fgn. service officer; b. Battle Creek, Mich., Jan. 18, 1915; s. Ward W. and Alberta J. (Mason) A.; student Battle Creek Coll., 1932-34; A.B. cum laude, U. Mich., 1936, J.D., 1939; m. A. Mildred Small, July 23, 1939; children—Judith A., W. Christopher, Jeanette E., Deborah M. Admitted to D.C. bar; atty. Dept. of Justice, 1939-42; adviser to U.S. mem. Inter-Am. Polit. Def. Commn., 1942-45; with Dept. of State, 1945—; mem. U.S. delegations to Inter-Am. Conf. Maintenance of Peace, 1947, IX Internat. Conf. Am. States, 1948, UN gen. assemblies, 1946, 49, 50, 51, 52, 53, UN Commn. for India and Pakistan, 1950; 1st sec. head polit. sect. Am. embassy, Copenhagen, Denmark, 1955-59, consul general, Guayaquil, Ecuador, 1960-62; dep. U.S. rep. to Council of Orgn. of Am. States, dir. Office Inter-Am. Regional Polit. Affairs, Dept. State, Washington, 1962-67, dep. asst. sec. state for internat. orgn. affairs, 1967-71; dep. chief mission Am. embassy, Bogota, Colombia, 1971—. Home: 1220 Shenandoah Rd Alexandria VA 22308 Office: Dept of State Mail Room Dept of State Washington DC 20521

ALLEN, WILBUR JAMES, former corp. exec.; b. Paterson, N.J., June 5, 1906; s. George W. and Lottie Lozier (Van Buskirk) A.; student Columbia, 1927-31; m. Anna Sabaday, Nov. 20, 1934; children—Barry J., James E. With Necarsulmer & Lehlbach, architects, 1928-31; with Best & Co., Inc., N.Y.C., 1931—, successively draftsman, asst. supt., v.p., supt., 1931-55, 1st vice president, director, 1955-63, president, chief executive officer, 1963-. Former planning bd. Upper Saddle River, N.J., former councilman, police commnr. Mem. Newcomen Society in N. Am. Reformed Ch. (elder). Club: Pennington (Passaic, N.J.). Home: 593 B Lake Point Dr Lakewood NJ 08701

ALLEN, WILBURN RAY, railroad ofcl.; b. Peggs, Okla., Feb. 5, 1917; s. Elmer Hill and Mattie Eythel (Tosh) A.; student Southwest Mo. State Coll., Springfield, 1936; grad. Advanced Mgmt. Program, Harvard, 1960; Command Gen. Staff Coll., 1964; divorced; children—Janice Wileen, Charles Robert. With St.L.-S.F. Ry., 1936-66; asst. to pres. C.B. & Q. R.R., 1966-70; v.p. Burlington Northern Inc. Mpls.; 1970—; chmn. bd. Burlington Truck Lines, Inc.; pres. No. Pacific Transport Co. Kansas City-St. Louis Land Co. Served to capt. AUS, 1942-46; brig. gen. Res. Mem. Ill. C. of C.; Chgo. Assn. Commerce and Industry, Am. Legion, 40 and 8, Nat. Def. Trans. Assn. (life), Assn. U.S. Army, Res. Officers Assn. Mason (32, Shriner). Clubs: Lake Shore (Chgo.); Minnesota (St. Paul). Home: 400 Groveland Av Minneapolis MN 55403 Office: 176 E 5th St St Paul MN 55101

ALLEN, WILLARD MYRON, obstetrics and gynecology; b. Macedon, N.Y., Nov. 5, 1904; s. Lewis F. and Marion E. (Hoag) A.; B.S., Hobart Coll., 1926, Sc.D., 1940; M.S., U. of Rochester, 1929, M.D., 1932; Sc.D. (honorary), U. Rochester, 1957; married Julia Belle Gardner, Sept. 6, 1927 (died Feb. 1, 1941); 1 daughter, Lucille Marion: m. 2d, Dorothy Dunn Esley, April 18, 1946. Research fellow, Dept. of Anatomy, U. of Rochester, 1927-29; fellow, Nat. Research Council and asst. in pathology, 1932-33; fellow of Gen. Edn. Bd. and asst. in obstetrics and gynecology, 1934-36, instr., 1936- 38, and asst. prof. of obstetrics and gynecology, 1938-39, U. of Rochester, Sch. of Medicine; interne, asst. resident and resident in obstetrics and gynecology, Strong Memorial Hosp., 1933-37; obstetrician and gynecologist in chief to St. Louis Maternity Hospital, Barnes Hospital; professor of obstetrics and gynecology Washington University School of Medicine, 1940-71; prof. obstetrics and gynecology U. Md., 1971—. Received Eli Lilly award in biochemistry, 1935; citation U. Rochester, 1950. Diplomate Am. Bd. Obstetrics and Gynecology. Mem. Am. Radium Soc., Am. Association Anatomists, Am. Physiol. Soc., A.A.A.S., A.M.A., Soc. Exptl. Biology and Medicine, Am. Assn. for Study Internal Secretions, Am. Assn. Obstetricians and Gynecologists, Am. Coll. Obstetrica and Gynecology, Am. Gynecol. Soc. Société Francais de Gynecologie (hon.), Sigma Xi, Phi Beta Kappa, Alpha Omega Alpha. Mem. Soc. of Friends. Author articles on physiology and biochemistry of sex hormones in med. jours. Home: 14180 Burntwoods Rd Glenwood MD 21738 Office: Barnes Hosp Plaza St Louis MO 63110

ALLEN, WILLIAM, banker. Vice pres., cashier First Nat. Bank Louisville. Office: PO Box 1019 Louisville KY 40201*

ALLEN, WILLIAM HENRY, dentist, educator; b. New Orleans, Jan. 27, 1917; s. William Henry and Victoria (Battiste) A.; A.B., Tougaloo Coll., 1938; D.D.S., Meharry Med. Coll., 1943; postgrad. study U. Mich., 1944; m. Martha Mae Mosley, Feb. 24, 1945. Instr. prosthetics Meharry Med. Coll., Nashville, 1943-44, asst. prof. prosthetics and clin. dentistry, 1945-47, asst. prof. dental materials, 1945-47, acting dean, 1946-47, dir. div. dental tech., prof. prosthetics since 1947, dean, dir. dental edn., 1949-50, dean Sch. Dentistry, 1950-71. Mem. council Nat. Bd. Dental Examiners; mem. Negro Scholarship program adv. com. Am. Fund for Dental Edn. ; mem. dental tng. com. Nat. Inst. Dental Research, 1971—, also mem. regional med. adv. com. Fellow A.A.A.S.; mem. Capitol City Dental Soc. (pres. 1958-59), Pan-Tenn., Am., Tenn. Nat. dental assns., Ala. State Dental Soc. (hon.), Am. Assn. Cleft Palate Rehab., Am. Assn. Endodontists, Internat. Assn. Dental Research (asso. mem. dental materials group), Am. Assn. Dental Schools (mem. com. projects and studies 1957-60), Nashville Dental Soc., Chi Boule Frat., Kappa Sigma Pi, Omicron Kappa Upsilon, Kappa Alpha Psi. Author articles profl. jours. Home: 4213 Hydes Ferry Pike Nashville TN 37218

ALLEN, WILLIAM M., airplane mfg., co. exec.; b. Lo Lo, Mont., Sept. 1, 1900; s. Charles and Gertrude Maud (Hughes) A.; A.B., Montana State U., 1922, LL.D., 1954; LL.B., Harvard, 1925; LL.D., Seattle U., 1957; m. Dorothy Dixon, Apr. 15, 1927 (dec. Nov. 1943); children—Nancy Dudley, Dorothy Dixon; m. 2d, Mary Ellen Agen, Dec. 28, 1948. Began as lawyer with Donworth, Todd & Higgins, Seattle, Wash., 1925; mem. law firm Holman, Sprague & Allen until 1945; chmn. and dir. Boeing Co., Seattle; dir. Standard Oil Co. of Cal., Pacific Nat. Bank of Wash., Western Bancorp. Mem. Seattle, Wash. State, Am. bar assns., Sigma Chi. Clubs: Seattle Golf, Rainier, University (Seattle); Pacific- Union (San Francisco). Home: The Highlands WA 98177 Office: PO Box 3707 Seattle WA 98124

ALLEN, WILLIAM RICHARD, educator; b. Eldorado, Ill., Apr. 3, 1924; s. Oliver Boyd and Justa Lee (Wingo) A.; A.B., Cornell Coll., 1948; Ph.D., Duke, 1953; m. Frances Lorraine Swoboda, Aug. 15, 1948; 2 daus., Janet, Sandra. Instr. Washington U., 1951-52; lectr. econs. U. Cal. at Los Angeles, 1952-53, asst. prof., 1953-58, asso. prof. 1958-63, prof., 1963—; vis. prof. Northwestern U., U. Wis., U. Mich., So. Ill. U.; economist U.S. Dept. Commerce, summer 1962. Served with USAAF, 1943-45. Recipient research grant Social Sci. Research Council, 1950, 62, Ford Found., 1958, NSF, 1965. Mem. Am., Western (pres. 1970-71), So. econ. assns., Western Finance Assn., Phi Beta Kappa. Author: (with A.A. Alchian) University Economics, 3d edit., 1971. Editor: (with C.L.Allen) Foreign Trade and Finance, 1959; (with J.J. Spengler) Essays in Economic Thought, 1960; International Trade Theory, 1965 (with A.A. Alchian) Exchange and Production, 1969. Contbr. articles profl. jours. Home: 11809 Allaseba Dr Los Angeles CA 90066

ALLEN, WILLIAM STEPHEN, architect; b. Neptune Twp., N.J., July 15, 1912; s. William Stephen and Margaret (Pape) A.; B.Arch., U. Pa., 1935, M.Arch., 1936; m. Jane Eileen Eikelman, Feb. 12, 1952. Traveling fellow U. Pa., 1936-37; archtl. designer Masten & Hurd, San Francisco, 1937-41; partner Anshen & Allen, architects, San Francisco, 1946—; prin. works include Chapel of Holy Cross, Sedona, Ariz., 1956, visitor's center Dinosaur Nat. Monument, Utah, 1957, Internat. Bldg., San Francisco, 1961, Coll. of Chem., U. Cal. at Berkeley, 1962, Good Samaritan Gen. Hosp., San Jose, 1965, Bank of Cal. office bldg., San Francisco, 1968, Portland, Ore., 1970, Lawrence Hall of Sci., U. Cal. at Bekeley, 1969, Nat. Sci. Center, Singapore, 1971. Mem. San Francisco Art Commn., 1952-56; mem. pub. adv. panel on archtl. services Gen. Services Adminstrn., 1967-69. Served to lt. comdr. USNR, 1942-46. Fellow A.I.A. (pres. No. Cal. chpt. 1956-57, pres. Cal. council 1962, mem. jury of fellows 1967-69). Home: 168 Harrison Av Sausalito CA 94965 Office: 461 Bush St San Francisco CA 94108

ALLEN, WOODY, movie, TV satirist; b. N.Y.C., Dec. 1, 1935; s. Martin and Nettie (Cherry) A.; student N.Y.U., 1953, Coll. City N.Y., 1953. Writer TV comedy for Sid Ceasar, 1957, Art Carney, 1958-59, Herb Shriner, 1953; appeared in numerous nightclubs, TV shows, 1961—; author, also appeared in motion pictures What's New Pussycat, 1964-65, Take The Money and Run, Bananas; author film What's Up Tiger Lily?, 1966. Recipient Sylvania award, 1957; nominated for Emmy award as television writer, 1957. Democrat. Contbr. numerous pieces to Playboy and New Yorker mags.

ALLENDESALAZAR, JOSE MANUEL, Spanish diplomat; b. Madrid, Spain, Mar. 3, 1935; s. Andres and Carmen (Valdes-Arguelles) A.; LL.B., U. Madrid, 1957; student Diplomatic Sch. Madrid, 1963-65, Acad. Internat. Law, The Hague, 1961; m. Ursula Bertele von Grenadenberg, Dec. 11, 1965. Second sec., Presidencia del Gobierno, Spain, 1959-62, Ministry Fgn. Affairs, Madrid, 1965-66, Lima, Peru, 1966-69; 1st sec., Washington, 1969—. Decorated knight Maestranza de Caballeria de Granada, knight Civil Merit Order; ofcl. Orden del Sol (Peru). Club: Real Automovil de Espana (Madrid). Home: 4628 Reservoir Rd NW Washington DC 20007 Office: 2700 15th St NW Washington DC 20009

ALLENDOERFER, CARL BARNETT, mathematician; b. Kansas City, Apr. 4, 1911; s. Carl William and Winifred (Barnett) A.; B.A. (Rhodes scholar), Oxford U., 1934; Ph.D., Princeton, 1937; mem. Inst. Advanced Study, 1948-49; m. Dorothy Holbrook, June 26, 1937; children—Robert Duff, James Holbrook, William Barnett. Prof. Math. U. Wash., Seattle, 1951—, exec. officer, 1951-62: Fulbright lectr. Cambridge (Eng.) U., 1957-58, Australia, 1963; mem. div. math. NRC, 1956-58, 62-65, commn. on math. Coll. Entrance Exam. Bd., 1955-59. Operations analyst U.S. Govt., World War II. Fellow A.A.A.S.; mem. Am. Math. Soc., Math. Assn. Am. (pres. 1959-60, chmn. com. on ednl. media 1963-66), Inst. Math. Statistics, Soc. for Indsl. and Applied Math., Nat. Council Tchrs. Math., Beta Kappa, Sigma Xi. Club: Monday (Seattle). Author: Principles of Mathematics, 1955; Fundamentals of Freshman Mathematics, 1959; Mathematics for Parents, 1963; Fundamentals of College Algebra, 1967; Principles of Arithmetic and Geometry, 1971. Editor Am. Math. Monthly, 1952-56. Cons. editor in math. Macmillan Co., 1958—. Contbr. articles profl. jours. Home: 4300 53d Av NE Seattle WA 98105

ALLER, LAWRENCE HUGH, astronomer; b. Tacoma, Sept. 24, 1913; s. Leslie E. and Lenabelle (Davis) A.; A.B., U. Cal., 1936; M.A., Harvard, 1938, Ph.D., 1942; m. Rosalind Duncan Hall, Apr. 24, 1941; children—Hugh Duncan, Raymond Donald, Gwendolyn Jean. Jr. fellow Soc. Fellows, Harvard, 1939-42, instr. physics, 1942-43; research physicist U. Cal. at Berkeley, 1943-45; asst. prof. astronomy Ind. U., 1945-48; asso. prof. U. Mich., 1948-54, prof. astronomy, 1954-62; vis. prof. Australian Nat. U., Canberra, 1960- 61, U. Toronto, 1961-62; prof. astronomy U. Cal. at Los Angeles, 1962—. Guest investigator Dominion Astrophys. Obs., 1951, Mt. Wilson Obs.; vis. prof. U. Sydney, U. Tasmania, 1968-69; guest investigator C.S.I.R.O. Australia. Mem. Internat. Astron. Union, Royal Astron. Soc., Am. Acad. Arts and Scis., Nat. Acad. Scis. Author: (with Leo Goldberg) Atoms, Stars and Nebulae, 1943, rev. edit., 1971; Astrophysics, 1954; Gaseous Nebulae, 1956; Abundances of the Elements, 1961; Atmospheres of the Sun and Stars, 1963. Home: 18118 W Kingsport Dr Malibu CA 90265

ALLERS, FRANZ orchestra condr.; b. Czechoslovakia, Aug. 6, 1905; s. Carl and Paula (Kellner) A.; student Praha Conservatory, Prague, 1920; Berlin Hochschule für Musik, Berlin, 1923-26; m. Carolyn Shaffer, 1941 (div. 1961); 1 dau., Carol Frances; m. 2d, Janne Furch, 1963. Came to U.S., 1938, naturalized citizen. First violinist, Berlin Philharmonic Orchestra, 1924-25; condr. Muncpl. Theatre, Carlsbad, 1926; asst. to gen. dir. of music, Wupperthal, Barmen-Elberfeld, 1926-27; 1st condr. United Municipal Theatres, Wupperthal, 1927-33; asst. at Bayreuth Festival by invitation of Siegfried Wagner, summer, 1927; asst. Wagner Festival, Paris, 1929; chief of opera and condr. Philharmonic concerts, Municipal Theatre, Aussig-on-Elbe, 1933-38, also organized youth concerts, in connection with the theatre; condr. Ballet Russe and Ballet Russe de Monte Carlo, London, 1938; toured U.S., South America and Can. as condr. Ballet Russe de Monte Carlo, 1939-44, musical dir., 1942-44; condr. Met. Opera House, N.Y.C., since 1963—, N.Y. Philharmonic, 1965, Chgo. Symphony, 1966, 67, Nuremberg Philharmonic, 1967, Radio-TV Hilversum-Holland, 1968—; guest condr. Opera Munich and Cologne; musical dir. of the Music Theatre Lincoln Center, N.Y.C., 1964-66. Has conducted radio broadcast concerts of Czech Philharmonic and the Radio Corp. of Prague orchestras; has appeared as guest condr. of opera and concerts, Czechoslovakia; Canada, and U.S. Condr. Day Before Spring, 1945-46; Brigadoon, 1947-49; South Pacific, 1950-51, Paint Your Wagon, 1951-52; moving picture of Humperdinck, Haensel and Gretel, 1953; Plain and Fancy, 1954-55; musical director State Fair Musicals, Dallas, Texas, 1953-56; musical director My Fair Lady, 1956-60 (Antoinette Perry award 1959, tour to Russia 1960, Berlin 1961, Munich 1962, Vienna 1963), Hallmark TV program, 1955-63, also Omnibus, Susskind, Firestone programs, Camelot, 1960-63 (Antoinette Perry award 1961). Has conducted most maj. symphony orchs. of U.S.; also Berlin Philharmonic Orch., 1957, 59, 67, Hamburg Radio Orch., 1958, 59, 62, 64, 65, 66, Munich Radio Orch., 1962-65, Bavaria TV Munich 1962-69, Radio Oslo, 1962, Cologne Radio Orch., 1965, Oslo Philharmonic Orch., 1965, Vienna Tonkuenstler Orch., 1965—, Vienna Symphony Orch., 1967, Opera Geneve, 1968—. Rec. artist Columbia RCA Victor, Vanguard, Phillips, Electrola. Eurodisk. Home: 139 W 94th St New York City NY 10025 Office: Columbia Artists Mgmt 165 W 57th St New York City NY 10019

ALLERUP, PAUL RICHARD, editor; b. N.Y.C., June 11, 1912; s. Peter and Helga (Holm) A.; student Eastman Sch., N.Y.C., N.Y.U.; m. Ellen M. Hostrup, Apr. 8, 1938. With Internat. News Service, 1935-58, successively cub reporter, reporter bur. mgr. Cin., asst. bur. mgr. Columbus, O., asst. Pa. state mgr., asst. night editor Chgo., night editor, Chgo., N.Y.C., gen. news editor, asso. mng. editor, mng. editor, 1955-58; dir. spl. news projects and features editor U.P.I., N.Y.C., 1958-59, London news mgr., 1959-62, European gen. news mgr., U.P.I., 1962-66, editor Newsfeatures, 1966—. Served with AUS, 1944-46; ETO. Mem. Assn. Am. Corrs. (London). Club: Wig and Pen, Curzon (London). Address: 220 E 42d St New York City NY 10017

ALLES, GEORGE JEROME, former mfg. co. exec.; b. Elizabeth, N.J., May 29, 1904; s. George and Anna Maria (Lott) A.; Grad. Rutgers U. Sch. Banking: m. Alice French, Jan. 20, 1934; childrenJane Pierson, George VanWyck. Sec.-treas., dir. Linden Trust Co. (N.J.), 1926-38; treas., dir. Sylvania Indsl. Corp.; plant mgr., Fredericksburg, Va., 1938-46; chmn. bd. Farmers and Merchants State Bank, Fredericksburg, 1942-48; dir. purchases Am. Viscose Corp., Phila., 1948-71, v.p., gen. mgr. film div., 1960-71; pres. Sylvan Plastics, Inc., 1960-71; formerly exec. v.p. FMC Corp.; dir. S.E. Nat. Bank of Pa. Presbyn. (elder). Club: Chemists (N.Y.C.). Home: 723 Great Springs Rd Bryn Mawr PA 19010 Office: 1017 John F Kennedy Blvd Philadelphia PA 19103

ALLEY, CALVIN LANE, cartoonist; b. Memphis, Oct. 10, 1915; s. James Pinckney and Nona (Lane) A.; student Memphis State U., 1933-34, Am. Acad. Arts, 1934-35, Chgo. Acad. Arts, 1935-36; m. Geraldine Jehl, Nov. 28, 1939; children—Jerrianne (Mrs. Harry W. Petrie), Carol Lee (Mrs. Harmon C. Williams), Calvin Lane, Irene Jehl (Mrs. Joseph M. Palvado), Richard Wesley. Cartoonist, Kansas City Jour., 1937-39, Nashville Banner, 1939-45, Memphis Comml. Appeal, 1945—; creator The Ryatts daily comic strip Post-Hall Syndicate, 1954; Sigma Delta Chi distinguished service cartoon Over My Dead Body, Library of Congress Exhibit, 1955. Cons. Memphis Acad. Arts. Recipient Freedom Found. medals, 1960-61, 63-64, 66, 66, 69, Freedom Found. certificate, 1968, Cancer Soc. certificates, 1963-65, 68-69, Memphis and Shelby County Safety Council award, certificate of merit Am. Heart Assn., 1968, Mem. Assn. Am. Editorial Cartoonists (charter), Sigma Delta Chi. Methodist. Kiwanian (award Korean War Meml. services E. Memphis club 1953). Club: Colonial (Memphis). Home: 3943 Poplar Av Memphis TN 38111 Office: 495 Union St Memphis TN 38101

ALLEY, JAMES BURKE, lawyer; b. Bedford County, Tenn., Sept. 13, 1894; s. Albert Rayford and Maud (Wardlaw) A.; prep. edn. Webb Sch., Bell Buckle, Tenn.; student Washington and Lee U., 1909-10; Okla. U., 1910-11; A.B., Columbia, 1914; Harvard Law School, 1925; m. Esther Hall Lowe; children—Jane (Mrs. Anthony Jackson), James, Harrison, Cynthia (Mrs. Woodbury H. Andrews). With 1st Nat. Bank, Muskogee, Okla. 1914-16, J.P. Morgan & Co., N.Y. 1916-17; enlisted in U.S. Naval Res. Force, 1917, resigned 1919 at lt.; asst. sec. to v.p. and gen. counsel Indsl. Finance Corp., 1919-22; mem. Council Fgn. Policy Assn., Boston, 1923-25; practiced law in N.Y.C., 1925-32; partner, Glenn, Alley, Geer & Roberts, 1929-32; counsel Reconstruction Finance Corp., in charge of bank reorgn. and recapitalization work, 1932- 35; gen. counsel Reconstruction Finance Corp., March 1935-June 1937; dir. Commodity Credit Corp., Washington and First and Second Export- Import Banks of Washington, 1935-37; mem. law firm Auchincloss, Alley & Ducan since 1937, firm name changed to Hooker, Alley & Duncan, May, 1944. Rep. banking group in Havana and Washington, defaulted Cuban public works obligations, 1937; dir. Manhattan Life Ins. Co., Barcelona Traction, Light and Power Co., Ltd., Panhandle Eastern Pipe Line Company, Missouri-Kansas Pipe Line Co., Compania Hispano-Americana de Electridad, (Chade) S.A., African Metals Corp., Universitas, Ltd. Specializes in adminstrv. and anti-trust law and in law relating to orgn. and reorganization of banking, business and railroad corporations; writer and speaker on subjects in field. Pres. bd. trustees and trustee Green Vale School, Glenhead, L.I. 1951-54; pres. Bd. Edn., Jericho, N.Y., 1945-46. Mem. Am. Bar Assn., Assn. Bar City N.Y., Am. Judicature Soc., Council on Foreign Relations, Beta Theta Pi. Democrat. Presbyterian. Clubs: University, Pilgrims (N.Y.C.).; Metropolitan, 1925 F Street (Washington); Ausable (St. Huberts, N.Y.); Millbrook Golf and Tennis, Millbrook Hunt (Millbrook, N.Y.). Home: 200 E 66th St New York City NY 10021 Office: 51 W 51st St New York City NY 10019

ALLEY, STEPHEN LEWIS, coll. dean; b. Bancroft, Ida., Sept. 25, 1915; s. George and Henrietta (Johnson) A.; student Ida. State U., 1933-36; B.S., U. Utah, 1947, M.S., 1951; Ed.D., Harvard, 1958; m. Maurine Christensen, Aug. 16, 1939; children—Kathryn (Mrs. Michael Smith), Stephen W., Carol, Lynn D. Chemist, Kalumite Corp., 1942-46; tchr. pub. schs., Maled, Ida., 1946- 47, Downey, Ida., 1947-51, Bountiful, Utah, 1951-54; instr. Brigham Young U., Provo, Utah, 1956-57, asst. prof., 1957-59, asso. prof., 1959- 62, prof., dean Coll. Edn., 1969—; vis. prof. U. Utah, 1962-63; chief of party U.S. AID Mission , Haile Selassie U., Ethiopia, 1962-63. Fellow Nat. Philosophy of Edn. Soc., Found. of Edn. Soc.; mem. N.E.A., Utah Edn. Assn., Far Western Philosophy of Edn. Soc., Phi Delta Kappa. Mem. Ch. of Jesus Christ of Latter-day Saints. Home: 600 E Sumac St Provo UT 84601

ALLEY, WILLIAM EDWARD, economist, educator; b. Geneva, Ind., Mar. 27, 1903; s. Robert L. and Lota Ethel (Brooks) Shrewsbury; A.B., DePauw U., 1926; A.M., U. of Ill., 1932, Ph.D., 1941; m. Helen G. Logan, Nov. 27, 1930; 1 dau., Ethel. High sch. tchr., McLeansboro, Ill., 1926-28, Burney, Ind., 1928-29, Urbana, Ill., 1931-36; prin., Burney Consol. Schs., 1929-31; instr. and asst. prof. econs. Grove City (Pa.) Coll., 1936-40, 1940-42; asst. prof., coll. liberal arts, Drake U., 1942-45, asso. prof., 1945-47, prof. economics since 1947, acting head, dept. economics, 1942-45, dept. head since 1945; acting dean, coll. commerce and finance, 1944-45. Mem. Am. Assn. Univ. Profs. (mem. nat. council, 1950-52, state sec., Ia. Conf., 1943-46), Am. and Midwest economic assns., Am. Finance Assn. Mem. Christian Ch. Home: 2612 Kingman Blvd Des Moines IA 50311 Office: Faculty Liberal Arts Drake University Des Moines IA 50311

ALLFREY, VINCENT GEORGE, educator, biochemist; b. N.Y.C., June 28, 1921; s. Thomas Richard and Margaret Theresa (Ryan) A.; B.A., B.S., Coll. N.Y., 1943; M.S., Columbia, 1948, Ph.D., 1949; m. Joan Lenore Brice, July 9, 1943; children—Barbara Claire, Kevin Mark. Mem. faculty Rockefeller Univ., 1949—, prof. gen. physiology, 1963—; spl. research chemistry cell nucleus, role nucleic acids in protein synthesis, role genetic material in RNA synthesis, nuclear energy metabolism, regulation chromosomal activity. Mem. research adv. com. Am. Cancer Soc. Mem. Am. Soc. Biol. Chemists, Am. Soc. Cell Biology, Phi Beta Kappa, Sigma Xi. Editor Jour. Gen. Physiology, 1958—, Exptl. Zoology, 1964—, Archives Biochemistry and Biophysics, 1970—. Home: 24 Winthrop Ct Tenafly NJ 07670 Office: Rockefeller Univ York Av at 67th St New York City NY 10021

ALLGOOD, CLARENCE WILLIAM, U.S. judge; b. Birmingham, Ala., Sept. 12, 1902; s. Robert Veneable and Patricia (Robinson) A.; student Howard Coll., 1921-23; B.S., Ala. Poly. Inst., 1926; LL.B., Brimingham Sch. Law, 1941; m. Marie Maxwell, June 27, 1927; 1 son, Clarence William. Referee in bankruptcy U.S. Dist. Ct. No. Ala., 1937-61; admitted to Ala. bar, 1941; U.S. dist. judge No. Dist. Ala., 1961—. Dir. Fidelity Mortgage Co. ALA., Fidelity Fed. Savs. and Loan Assn. Mem. counsel profl. relations Am. Hosp. Assn., 1950-52; chmn. Ala. Hosp. Trustee Assn., 1951. Chmn. trustees S. Highland Infirmary, Brimingham, 1945-55; trustee Crippled Childrens Hosp. and Clinic, 1941—, pres., 1958; trustee Ala. Soc. Crippled Children and Adults, 1946-48. Mem. Am., Ala., Brimingham bar assns., Pi Kappa Alpha, Sigma Delta Kappa, Blue Key. Mason (Shriner), Elk. Club: Civitan (Birmingham). Author articles, contbr. textbooks. Home: 3524 Brookwood Rd Birmingham AL 35223 Office: P O Box 155 Birmingham AL 35202

ALLILUYEVA, SVETLANA, (Mrs. William Wesley Peters), author; b. U.S.S.R., 1926; d. Joseph Stalin and Nadezhda Alliluyeva; children (previous marriages)—Katherine, Joseph; m. 3d, William Wesley Peters. Author: Twenty Letters to a Friend; Over One Year. Address: care of Taliesin Architects Asso Taliesin West Scottsdale AZ 85252

ALLIN, J. MAURY, coadjutor bishop Protestant Episcopal Diocese Miss. Address: PO Box 953 Jackson MS 39205

ALLIN, WILLIAM MILLAR, former container mfg. exec.; b. Erie, Pa., Feb. 15, 1910; s. John Bradford and Ida May (Millar) A.; student U. Cin., 1928-31; m. Lucille Leona Menville, Jan. 30, 1937; children—Elizabeth-Kay (Mrs. Lecler), William Bradford. Began as salesman, became partner J.B. Allin & Son, sales agts., 1931-39; sales rep. So. Advance Bag & Paper Co., Inc., 1939-45, gen. sales mgr., Boston, 1945-49, v.p. charge sales, 1949- 55, gen. sales mgr. So. Advance Bag & Paper div. Robert Gair Co., Boston, 1955-57; v.p. Continental Can Co., Inc., N.Y.C., 1957-70, ret., 1970. Mem. Delta Tau Delta, Alpha Kappa Psi. Home: 405 Iona St Metairie LA 70005

ALLING, CHARLES CALVIN, III, dentist, educator; b. Guthrie, Okla., Dec. 27, 1923; s. Charles Calvin, Jr., and Bessie Palmer (Keller) A.; A.B., Ind. U., 1943, D.D.S., 1946; M.S., U. Mich., 1954; m. Laura Esther Freeland, May 10, 1947; children—Elaine Sue (Mrs. Andrew W. Lilliston), Rocklin David, Robert Freeland. Prof., chmn. dept. oral surgery U. Ala. in Birmingham, 1969—; cons. Am. Dental Assn., U.S. Army Med. Research and Devel. Command, Surgeon Gen., VA; vis. prof. and lectr. Howard U., Georgetown U., Seoul U. Dir. Kwang Myung Orphanage and Sch. for Blind. Served with AUS, 1946-69. Decorated Legion of Merit. Fellow Am. Coll. Dentists; mem. Am. Soc. Oral Surgeons (dir.), Am. Dental Assn., Am., Southeastern, Ala., Internat. assns. oral surgeons, Chalmer Lyons Acad. Oral Surgery, 38th Parallel Dental Soc. (charter pres.), Internat. Assn. Dental Research, Phi Kappa Phi. Mason (Shriner). Editor: Facial Pain, 1968. Contbr. articles profl. jours., chpts. in books. Research on repair of maxillofacial osseous tissues. Home: 1509 Panorama Dr Birmingham AL 35216

ALLINSMITH, WESLEY, educator, psychologist; b. London, Eng., May 21, 1923 (parents Am. citizens); s. Harry Bryan and Corinne Elizabeth (Allin) A.; A.B., Princeton, 1947; M.A., U. Mich., 1949, Ph.D. in Psychology, 1954; m. Beverly Balch, June 30, 1947; children—Bryan Balch, Wendy, Craig Lewis. Research asso. Office Pub. Opinion Research, Princeton, N.J., 1947; teaching fellow psychology U. Mich., 1948-49, intern clin. and counseling psychology, 1949-52, staff psychologist counseling service, 1952-53, instr., research asso. psychology, 1953-55; asst. prof., research asso. lab. human devel. Grad. Sch. Edn., Harvard, 1955-56, asst. prof., asst. dir. lab., 1956-57, lectr., asso. dir. lab., 1957-60; project dir. Joint Commn. Mental Illness and Health, 1956-59; asst. prof. psychology dept. psychiatry, coordinator research Center Studies Human Devel., Harvard Med. Sch.-Mass. Gen. Hosp., 1960-61; prof. psychology U. Cin., 1961—, head dept. psychology, 1961-68, prof. psychology psychiatry dept., 1962—. Served with USAAF, 1943-46. Recipient Howard C. Warren sr. prize psychology Princeton, 1947. Fellow Am. Psychol. Assn., Am. Sociol. Assn., A.A.A.S.; mem. Soc. Research Child Devel., Am. Assn. U. Profs., Sigma Xi. Author: (with G.W. Goethals) The Role of Schools in Mental Health, 1962. Editor: (with Judy F. Rosenblith) The Causes of Behavior, 1962; 2d edit., 1966. Home: 3850 Clifton Av Cincinnati OH 45220

ALLINSON, THOMAS, mfg. co. exec.; b. Chgo., July 22, 1921; s. Thomas LeRoy and Katherine (Munster) A.; student Northwestern U., 1939-42; grad. Advanced Mgmt. Program, Harvard, 1960; m. Lucretia Hamm, Dec. 31, 1943; children—Katherine Marie, Thomasina Luise. Prodn. mgr. Marchant Calculating Machine Co., 1947-52; prof. bus. adminstrn., extension night courses U. Cal. at Berkeley, 1949-53; gen. mgr., marketing dir. Beckman Instruments, Inc., 1952-57; pres. indsl. products group Daystrom, Inc., also Weston Elec. Instrument Corp., 1957-62; v.p., exec. asst. to pres. and chmn. Curtiss-Wright Corp., 1962-66, chmn. bd. subsidiaries Abrams Instrument Corp., Electronic Fittings Corp., Target Rock Corp.; exec. v.p., dir. Alco Controls Corp., St. Louis, 1966-67; pres., dir. Astrodata, Inc., 1967-68; v.p. Diebold Group, N.Y.C., 1968- 69, pres., dir. Wall St. Information Services, Inc. 1969—; dir. Berry, Cullen, Cohen, Inc., Four-Seasons Villages, Inc., Chas St. Thomas Group, S. Africa, Lincoln Terrace Corp. Hagan Pub. Corp., Marlette Lake Corp., Datum, Inc., RAM Group. Condr. mgmt. and marketing seminars Nat. Devel. Mgmt. Found. of South Africa, 1963-65; chmn. finance vis. com. Clarkson Coll. Tech. Business Sch.; dir. Bur. Municipal Research, Newark. Served as aviator USNR, 1942-47. Mem. Am. Rocket Soc., Instrument Soc. Am., Air Force Assn., Nat. Indsl. Conf. Bd., Am. Ordnance Assn., Assn. U.S. Army, Newcomen Soc. Clubs: Harvard, Union League, Harbarview (N.Y.C.); Balboa Bay (Newport Beach, Cal.); Essex (Newark); Skytop. Home: 307 E 44th St New York City NY 10017 Office: 100 Wall St New York City NY 10005

ALLIS, WILLIAM PHELPS, educator; b. Menton, France, Nov. 15, 1901 (parents Am. Citizens); s. Edward Phelps Jr. and Amedine (Syrena) A.; B.S., Mass. Inst. Tech., 1923, M.S., 1924; Sc.D., Université de Nancy (France), 1925; student Princeton, 1929-30, U. Munich (Germany), 1930-31; m. Nancy Olive Morison, June 11, 1935; children—Amedine, Edward Morison, John Cotton. Mem. faculty Mass. Inst. Tech., 1925—, prof. physics, 1950-67, emeritus prof., sr. lectr., 1967—. Mem. staff Radiation Lab., OSRD, 1940-42; cons. Los Alamos Sci. Lab., 1952—; asst. sec. gen. for sci. affairs NATO, 1962-64; vis. fellow St. Catherine's Oxford (Eng.), 1968; exchange prof. Faculte des Sciences d'Orsay, 1969; vis. prof. Middle East Tech. U., Ankara, Turkey, 1970, U. South Fla., 1971. chmn., Gaseous Electronics Conf., 1949-62, hon. chmn., 1966—. Served from maj. to lt. col. AUS, 1942-45. Decorated Legion of d'Honneur (France), 1969. Fellow A.A.A.S., Am. Phys. Soc., Phys. Soc. London, Am. Acad. Arts and Scis.; mem. Sigma Xi, Sigma Pi Sigma. Author: Thermodynamics and Statistical Mechanics, 1952; Nuclear Fusion, 1960; Waves in Anisotropic Plasmas, 1963; Electrons, Ions, and Waves, 1967. Contbr. Handbuch der Physik, 1956. Research in elec. discharges in gases. Home: 33 Reservoir St Cambridge MA 02138

ALLISON, DWIGHT LEONARD, Jr., finance co. exec.; b. Boston, Oct. 27, 1929; s. Dwight Leonard and Stella (DeGrasse) A.; A.B., Dartmouth, 1956; M.B.A., Amos Tuck Sch. Bus. Adminstrn., 1952; LL.B., Harvard, 1956; m. Lyona G. Strohacker, June 19, 1954; children—Dwight Leonard III, Barbara Lynn, Laurie. Admitted to Mass. bar, 1956; practiced in Boston, 1956-66; asso. Goodwin, Procter & Hoar, 1956-64, partner, 1965-66; v.p., dir. Gardner Assos., Inc., Boston, 1966-68; chmn. finance com. C.H. Sprague & Son Co., 1968-69; chmn. bd. Sprague Assos., Inc., Boston, 1969—; dir. Westmoreland Coal Co., Sprague Med. Systems Corp., Imperial Smokeless Coal Co., Winding Gulf Coals, Inc., Atlantic World Port, Inc.; trustee Newton Savs. Bank. Bd. overseers Boys Club Boston. Served to 1st lt. USAF, 1952-53. Mem. Am., Mass., Boston bar assns. Home: 76 Royalston Rd Wellesley MA 02181 Office: 100 Charles River Plaza Boston MA 02114

ALLISON, FRAN, radio-TV actress; b. LaPorte City, Ia.; student Coe Coll., Cedar Rapids Ia.; m. Archie Levington. Tchr. pub. schs., Ia.; began entertainment career as radio singer, Ia., 1934, Chicago, 1937; prin. radio role Aunt Fanny on Breakfast Club: TV role Kukla, Fran, and Ollie, 1947-57; Fran Allison show, WGN-TV, 1958-60. Office: care Archie Levington 245 E 30th St New York City NY 10019

ALLISON, GEORGE BOGGS, architect; b. Naini Tal, India (parents Am. citizens); s. Alexander B. and Amy J. (Boggs) A.; B.Arch., U. Pa., 1925, M.Arch., 1926; m. Ada A. Sandin, Sept. 6, 1936; 1 son, George Richard. Woodman fellow for European travel and study, 1928-29; with office of John Russell Pope, N.Y.C., 1929-30; mem. and gen. partner Allison, Rible, Robinson & Ziegler, Architects, and predecessor firms, 1930—, gen. partner, 1944—; officer A-R-R-Z, asso. group Leo A. Daly Co., 1969—. Mem. Los Angeles County Capital Projects Appeal Bd., 1969—. Bd. dirs. So. Cal. chpt. Nat. Assn. Prevention Blindness, 1971—. Fellow A.I.A. (pres. So. Cal. 1948, nat. honor award jury 1956, jury of fellows 1959—, chmn. 1963, past mem., past chmn. ins. trustees Cal. council); mem. Am. Arbitration Assn. (nat. panel 1953), Los Angeles C. of C., Beta Theta Pi. Methodist. Rotarian. Club: Wilshire Town (pres. 1967) (Los Angeles). Home: 2227 Guthrie Dr Los Angeles CA 90034 Office: 500 S Virgil Av Los Angeles CA 90020

ALLISON, GERALD LOU, architect; b. Seattle, Oct. 27, 1932; s. Cecil Jay and Ruth (Basilidas) A.; B.Arch., U. Wash., 1955; m. Charlotte Ann Nelson, July 30, 1955; children—Ruth Anne, Lynn Charlotte. Designer, Decker & Christensen, Seattle, 1955-57; architect Wimberly & Cook, Honolulu, 1957-60, asso., 1960-62; v.p. Wimberly, Whisenand, Allison, Tong & Goo Architects, Ltd., Honolulu, 1962—. Design critic U. Hawaii dept. architecture, 1970-71, guest lectr., East-West Center, 1970-71. Pres., Interprofl. Com. on Environmental Design, 1970; mem. Gov.'s Task Force on Natural Environment, 1970, Mayor's Com. to Preserve Natural Beauty, 1971; mem. steering com. Hawaii Community Design Center, 1970-71; co-founder Constrn. Industry Pub. Arts Program, 1970; mem. Hawaii Nani Loa State Fedn. to Preserve Natural Beauty, 1971. Registered architect, Hawaii. Mahalo award for pub. service Hawaii Wood Products Assn., 1970; named Business of Year, Hawaii Bus. and Indsl. mag., 1967. Fellow A.I.A. (Design awards 1960, 62, 64, 68, treas. 1968, v.p. 1969, pres. 1970, jury mem. Honor awards 1971); mem. Outdoor Circle, Life of Land, Alpha Delta Phi. Methodist. Kiwanian. Club: Outrigger Canoe (Honolulu). Weekly newspaper columnist, 1970, 71—. Home: 1607 Ruth Pl Honolulu HI 96816 Office: 2222 Kalakaua Av Penthouse Honolulu HI 96815

ALLISON, IRL, pianist, music educator; b. Warren, Tex., Apr. 8, 1896; s. John Van and Mary Cleona (Richardson) A.; A.B., Baylor Y., A.M., 1922; Dr. Music, Southwestern Conservatory, Dallas, Doctor of Laws, Hardin-Simmons University, 1954; attended Chicago Mus. Coll., summer 1919, Columbia U., 1920-21, summers , U. Tex., 1943; Doctor of Music (hon.), Houston Conservatory, 1954; piano study Ezra RAchlin, Rudolph Hoffman, Josef Evans, Percy Grainger, Ernest Hutcheson, Harold von Mickwitz, Walter Gilewicz; m. Jessie Johnson, July 3, 1918; childrenMary J. (dec.), John (dec.), Irl, Lucille (Mrs. Therl Ockey). Ockey). Dean of Music, Rusk Coll., 1918-19; instr. piano, Baylor Coll. for Women, 1921-23; dean of fine arts, Montezuma Coll., 1923-27; dean Nat. music Hardin-Simmons U., 1927-34; founder, pres. Nat. Guild Piano Teachers, American Coll. Musicians, 1934-; founder Golden Rule Peace Movement and orignator World Peace Programs (radio), 1948; mamager National Piano-Playing Auditions (founder) since 1929; editor, the Guild Yearbook, 1936-45, Nat. Directory of Piano Teachers, 1936-45, Was the founder, now the editor of Piano Guild Notes, 1951-. Member Outstanding Alumnus, Baylor U., 1970. Mem. Music Tchrs. Nat. Assn., Music Educators Nat. Council, Nat. Music Council. Sinfonia. Through the Years; Our George. Contbr. to newspapers, Miniatures of the Mighty to newspapers, music publs. Editor. Compiler; Irl Allison Piano Library, 33 vols. Co- founder, donor Internat. Piano Competition. Home: 1500 Murray Lane Austin, TX 78703

ALLISON, IRL LESLIE, Jr., educator; b. Las Vegas, N.M., Nov. 18, 1924; s. Irl Leslie and Jessie (Johnson) A.; B.S., U. Tex., 1950; m. Patsy Ruth McClelland, Sept. 12, 1943; children—Margaret (Mrs. L. Randell Burch), Richard Austin. Mgr. Am. Coll. Musicians, Austin, Tex., 1950-60, pres., 1961—. Served with AUS, 1943-45. Mem. Nat. Guild of Piano Tchrs. (pres. 1960—), Nat. Fraternity of Student Musicians (pres. 1960—), Delta Chi. Methodist. Club: Optimist. Home: 6602 Shoal Creek Blvd Austin TX 78757

ALLISON, JAMES RALPH, lawyer; b. Salineville, O., Feb. 14, 1930; s. Samuel O. and Lois M. (Willis) A.; B.A., Maryville (Tenn.) Coll., 1952; J.D., U. Chgo., 1955; m. Eleanor Kathryn Nealis, May 2, 1959; children—James Bradley, Matthew Samuel, Jonathan Alexander, Admitted to Ohio bar, 1955; practiced in East Palestine, 1957—; mem. firm Cohen & Allison, 1957—. Dir. Union Comml. & Savs. Bank, East Palestine. Pres. East Palestine Sch. Dist. Bd. Edn., 1965—. Bd. dirs. Columbiana County Mental Health Assn; mem. alumni bd. Maryville Coll., 1967—. Served with CIC, U.S. Army, 1955-57. Mem. Am., Ohio, Columbiana County (sec.-treas.) bar assns. Presbyn. (deacon, elder). Rotarian (dist. gov. 1967-70). Home: 569 Sugar Camp Dr East Palestine OH 44413 Office: 25 E Rebecca St East Palestine OH 44413

ALLISON, JOHN A., life ins. co. exec.; b. 1914; student Occidental Coll.; married. With Occidental Life Ins. Co. Cal., 1954—. exec. v.p. 1967—. Address: Occidental Center Hill and Oliver at 12th St Los Angeles CA 90054*

ALLISON, JOHN MCLEAN, banking exec., lawyer; b. Greenville, Ky., Oct. 8, 1901; s. John and Minnie (Eaves) A.; LL.B., U. Fla., 1927; m. Virginia Taylor, Apr. 22, 1930; children—John McLean, Nancy Elizabeth (Mrs. John C. Arant). Admitted to Fla. bar, 1927; served as county atty. Hillsboro County, 1943-49; v.p., dir., gen. counsel Peninsula State Bank, Tampa, Fla.; gen. counsel Fla. Assn. Ins. Agts.; dir. Tampa Abstract & Title Ins. Co., Morrison, Inc. Mem. state bd. law examiners Fla., 1941-49. Fellow Am. Bar Found. (life mem.); mem. Am. (chmn. sect. legal edn. and admissions to bar 1953-54, mem. ho. dels. 1948-49, 55- 66), Tampa bar assns., Fla. Bar (pres. 1951-52), Am. Law Inst., S.A.R., Order of Coif, Phi Delta Phi, Phi Kappa Phi, Alpha Tau Omega. Episcopalian. Mason (Jester, Shriner, past potentate). Clubs: University, Tampa Yacht and Country, Gasparilla Krewe. Address: P O Box 1531 3110 Dunwoodie St Tampa FL 33601

ALLISON, JOHN R., financial exec.; b. Peterborough, Ont., Can., May 27, 1913; s. Philip L. and Florence A. (Armstrong) A.; ed. Northwestern U., Am. Inst. Banking, Sophia U., Tokyo, Japan; m. Marion Stuart Sellers, Sept. 12, 1942; children—Jacqueline, James, Elizabeth, William, John. Auditor, State Bank & Trust Co., Evanston, Ill., 1931-36; accountant R.R. Donnelly & Sons Co., Chgo., 1936-43; dir. finance, econ. and sci. sect. SCAP, Tokyo, 1945-51; asst. to treas. Norton Co., Worcester, Mass., 1951-54; treas. Norton Behr-Manning Overseas, Inc., 1954-59; v.p., controller- internat. Richardson Merrell, Inc., N.Y.C., 1959-63; treas. Pepsi-Cola Co., N.Y.C., 1963-65; v.p., controller PepsiCo Inc., N.Y.C., 1965-67, v.p., 1967-70, pres., chief exec. officer PepsiCo Services Industries, 1967-70; former pres. subsidiary Lease Plan Internat. Corp., Great Neck, N.Y.; former chmn. bd. N.Am. Van Lines; sr. v.p., treas. Raytheon Co., Lexington, Mass., 1970—. Former mem. Gov.'s Bus. Adv. Com. on Mgmt. Improvement; mem. exec. com. Pacific Basin Econ. Council. Served from pvt. to 1st lt. AUS, 1943-46. Mem. Financial Execs. Inst. Home: 1 Green Lane Weston MA 02193 Office: 141 Spring St Lexington MA 02173

ALLISON, JUNIUS LANDRUM, lawyer, educator; b. Asheville, N.C., Sept. 2, 1909; s. Floss and Geneva (Hunnicutt) A.; A.B., Maryville (Tenn.) Coll., 1932; postgrad. U. N.C., 1938-39, U. Chgo., summer 1940, U. Ill., 1945; LL.B., Asheville U. 1936; J.D., John Marshall Law Sch., Chgo., 1946; m. Hester Keaton, July 4, 1932; children—Judith, Nancy, Sally. Admitted to N.C. bar, 1936, Ill. bar, 1945, Fed. Cts., 1948; practice law in Asheville, N.C., 1936-43; trial atty., dir. Chgo. Legal Aid Bur., also adminstr. legal clinic, Northwestern U. Law Sch., 1945-56, 67-68; field dir. standing com. legal aid work Am. Bar Assn., 1954-63; asso. dir. Nat. Legal Aid and Defender Assn., Chgo., 1954-61, sec., exec. dir., 1961-71; prof. law, dir. clin. legal edn. Sch. Law, Vanderbilt U., 1971—. Prof. govt. Asheville- Biltmore Coll., 1943-45; part-time instr. U. Chgo., 1947, 48; instr. YMCA Adult Edn. Sch., Chgo., 1948; lectr. Fed. Probation Tng. Center, Chgo., 1963-64, Inst. Def. Attys. N.W. Law Sch., 1955-56, 68—; mem. com. corrections Welfare Council Met. Chgo., 1964-68; mem. nat. adv. bd. for legal research and services for elderly Nat. Council Sr. Citizens; mem. Ill. Gov.'s Adv. Council, 1969—; mem. Pres.'s adv. council Minority Bus. Enterprise, 1970—. Bd. dirs. State Reformatory for Women, Nat. Community Council, 1970—; trustee Nat. Found. for Consumer Credit. Recipient Honor award N.C. Classroom Tchrs. Assn., 1962; Reginald Heber Smith award, 1963. Mem. Am., Ill. Chgo. bar assns., Scribes. Author: Office Management for Legal Aid Societies, 1953; also numerous articles, papers in field. Editor proc. Nat. Legal Aid and Defender Assn., 1957-59, also field service letter, 1953-57, 59, 60; Legal Aid Briefcase, 1956-63. Home: 2310 Hemingway Dr Nashville TN 37215 Office: Vanderbilt U School of Law Nashville TN 37215

ALLISON, MARVIN LAWRENCE, journalist; b. Phoenix, Aug. 8, 1934; s. George Lewis and Dorothy (Kinsella) A.; student Long Beach State Coll., 1953-54, Sorbonne, Paris, France, 1952-53; Nieman fellow, Harvard, 1968-69; m. Patricia Ann Kiley, Apr. 2, 1954; 1 son, Marvin Lawrence. Reporter, Downey (Cal.) Live Wire, 1955-57; copy editor Long Beach (Cal.) Ind., also Press-Telegram, 1957- 62, reporter, 1963-66; copy editor Stars & Stripes newspaper, Darmstadt, Germany, 1962; city editor Ind. Press-Telegram, Long Beach, 1966-68, mng. editor, 1969—. Mem. A.P. Mng. Editors Assn. (bd. dirs.), Sigma Delta Chi. Club: Harvard (Los Angeles). Office: 604 Pine Av Long Beach CA 90801

ALLISON, MARY LUCILLE, editor; b. Maryville, Mo., June 15, 1925; d. Samuel Parker and Lucille (Work) Allison; B.A., Mt. Holyoke Coll., 1947. Evaluation editor Ednl. Film Library Assn., 1950-57; free lance writer, editor, 1950-56; editor, publs. officer Spl. Libraries Assn., 1955-60, publs. and pub. relations dir., 1960-66; editor Citation Press, Scholastic Magazines, Inc., N.Y.C., 1966—. Democrat. Author: (with Estelle Latta) The Mark Hopkins Controversy, 1952; The EFLA Redbook of Audio-Visual Equipment, 1953, Supplement, 1955; (with Emily S. Jones, Edward T. Schofield) A Manual for Evaluators of Films and Filmstrips, 1956; New Educational Materials, 1967. Home: Blinn Rd Croton-on-Hudson NY 10520 Office: 50 W 44th St New York City NY 10019

ALLISON, MOSE JOHN, JR., pianist, composer; b. Tippo, Miss., Nov. 11, 1927; s. Mose John and Maxine (Collins) A.; student U. Miss., 1947-49; B.A. in English Lit., La. State U., 1951; m. Audre Mae Schwartz, Jan. 2, 1951; children—Alissa, Amy, John and Janine (Twins). Performances in night clubs throughout Southeast, 1952-56, N.Y.C. and U.S., 1956-, Europe, 1959—,also coll. concerts, TV appearances; recordings include Back Country Suite, 1957, Local Color, 1958, Transfiguration of Hiram Brown, 1960, Word From Mose, 1963, Mose Alive, 1965, I've Been Doin' Some Thinkin', 1968; Hello There, Universe, 1970. Served with AUS, 1946-47. Address: 34 Dogwood Dr Smithtown, NY 11787.

ALLISON, NOAH DWIGHT, former editor; b. Spencer, Ind., Feb. 9, 1899; s. Clayton Benbridge and Pearl (Coble) A.; A.B., DePauw U., 1921; grad. Command and Gen. Staff Sch., Brit. Sr. Staff Coll.; m. Tomi Charpentier, July 3, 1923 (dec.). Reporter, 1921; news editor Post-Enquirer, Oakland, Cal., 1922-24; Sunday editor The Record, Fort Worth, 1925; mng. editor The Light, San Antonio, 1928-67; Lozano prof. journalism Trinity U., 1967-68. Served as 2d lt. RAF, Gt. Britain, World War I; lt. col. Mil. Intelligence Res., AUS, World War II; 36th Div. V Corps, Hdqrs. ETO, 12th Army Group; chief liaison officer, 12th to 21st Army Group (Brit.) in continental operations; campaigns: Normandy, No. France, Ardennes, Rhineland, Central Europe, brig. gen. AUS (ret.). Decorated Bronze Star, Bronze Service Arrowhead, Order of British Empire. Mem. Tex. Cavaliers, Sigma Delta Chi, Beta Theta Pi. Democrat. Mason. Club: Argyle. Home: 102 Allson Dr San Antonio TX 78212

ALLISON, PRESTON BYRAM, educator; b. Ida, La., Mar. 1, 1914; s. John Richard Preston and Ora (Byram) A.; B.A., Centenary Coll., 1934; M.Ed., La. State U., 1947, Ph.D., 1954; m. Melba March Bernard, Aug. 17, 1946; children—Melanie Kay, Kevin Richard. Tchr., Vivian, La., 1934-41, 46-47; prin., Hosston, La., 1947-52; mem. faculty Southeastern La. U., 1954—, prof. edn., 1960—, head dept., 1961-66, dean Sch. Edn., 1963-70. Mem. adv. com. S.W. Ednl. Devel. Lab., 1965-69; mem. state accreditation com. elementary schs. So. Assn. Colls. and Schs. Bd. dirs. Hammond (La.) United Givers, 1967-69. Served with AUS, 1941-46. Mem. N.E.A., Nat. Soc. Study Edn., Assn. Student Teaching, Am. Assn. Higher Edn., La. Tchrs. Assn., Phi Kappa Phi, Phi Delta Kappa, Kappa Delta Pi. Baptist (deacon). Mason, Rotarian (pres. Hammond 1959-60). Home: 1125 N Gen Pershing St Hammond LA 70401

ALLISON, REX, dept. store exec.; b. Birmingham, Ky., July 30, 1910; s. Edgar Seldon and Josephine (Higgins) A.; B.S., U. Ky., 1931; m. Alice Bruner, May 7, 1932 (div. 1949); children—Ann, Rex, Kenneth; m. 2d, Genevieve Couch; Mar. 23, 1951; children—Gen, Geri. With Gen. Electric Co., Schenectady, 1931, Allied Stores Corp. subsidiary cos., 1931—, v.p., 1950-63, sr. v.p., 1963—; pres. The Bon Marche, Seattle, 1946-57, chmn. bd., 1957—; pres. C. C. Anderson Stores Co., Boise, Ida., The Merk, Inc., Longview, Wash., 1950; exec. v.p. The Northgate Co., Seattle, 1948-58, chmn. bd., 1958-71. Served as lt. USNR, 1944-45. Recipient Sullivan medallion U. Ky., 1931. Mem. Sigma Alpha Epsilon. Home: 4718 Indian Bend Rd Paradise Valley AZ 85251 Office: 251 Western Park Dr Scottsdale IL 85251

ALLISON, RICHARD CLARK, lawyer; b. N.Y.C., July 10, 1924; s. Albert Fay and Anice (Clark) A.; B.A., U. Va., 1944, LL.B., 1948; m. Anne Elizabeth Johnston, Oct. 28, 1950; children—Anne Sidney, William Scott, Richard Clark. Admitted to N.Y. bar, 1948; practiced in N.Y.C., 1948-52, 54-55, 55—; partner firm Reid & Priest, 1961—; with U.S. Govt., 1952-54. Trustee Buckley Country Day Sch. Served to ensign USNR, 1942-46. Mem. Am. (chmn. com. Latin Am. law 1964—), Inter-Am. bar assn., Am. Fgn. Law Assn., N.Y. C. of C., Pan Am. Soc., Assn. of Bar City N.Y., S.A.R., Phi Beta Kappa, Omicron Delta Kappa, Pi Kappa Alpha, Phi Delta Phi. Conglist. Club: Union League. Home: 224 Circle Dr Plandome Manor, NY 11030. Office: 40 Wall St New York City NY 10005

ALLISON, ROYAL BERTRAM, air force officer; b. Harlan, Ore., Apr. 22, 1919; s. Smith William and Bessie (Grant) A.; student Ore. State Coll., 1938-41; grad. Air Corps Flying Sch., 1942, Command and Gen. Staff Sch., 1945; m. Liliane Doulcaris, Jan. 28, 1945; 1 son, Michael William. Commd. 2d lt. USAAF, 1942, advanced through grades to lt. gen. USAF, 1969; various assignments, U.S. and Combat duty ETO, 1942-45; comdr. Squadron K, 426th SSFBU, March AFB, Cal., 1945-46; dep. asst. chief staff A-3 and A-5, Hdqrs. 12th Air Force, March AFB, 1947-48; comdr. 11th Reconnaissance Squadron, March AFB, 1948; staff planning officer, dep. chief staff operations Hdqrs. USAF, 1948-50; chief policy div., dir. plans USAF Europe, Germany, 1950-52; chief policy br. J-3, U.S. European Command, Germany, and France, 1952-54; asst. dep. chief staff personnel Air Tng. Command, Scott AFB, Ill., 1954-56; comdr. 3615 Flying Tng. Group, Craig AFB, Ala., 1957-58; asst. for Nat. Security Council affairs, dep. chief staff policy and planning Hdqrs. USAF, 1958-59, exec. to chief staff USAF, 1959-61; dir. plans Hdqrs. USAF, Germany, 1961-63, asst. dep. chief staff operations, 1963-64; dep. chmn. joint chiefs staff spl. studies group, Washington, 1964-67; dep. chief staff plans and operations CINCPAC, 1967-68; asst. to chmn. joint chiefs staff for strategic arms negotiations, 1968—. Decorated D.S.M., Silver Star, D.F.C., Soldiers medal, Air medal with 13 oak leaf clusters, Legion of Merit, Air Force Commendation medal with oak leaf cluster. Croix de Guerre with palm (France). Mem. Scabbard and Blade, Delta Upsilon. Address: 3153 S 14th Arlington VA 22204

ALLISON, STANLEY FREDERICK, paperboard co. exec.; b. Mpls., Apr. 5, 1917; s. Carl J. and Amelia (Marohn) A.; B.B.A., U. Minn., 1939; m. Elizabeth H. Spielman, May 15, 1942; children—Richard B., David K. With Ohio Boxboard Co., 1945-58, v.p., 1953-58; v.p. Pakcaging Corp. Am., Evanston, Ill., 1958-63, sr. v.p., 1963-66, dir., 1965—, pres., chief exec. officer, 1966—; sr. v.p. Tenneco, Inc., 1966—; dir. Tenn. River Pulp & Paper Co., 1969—, chmn. bd., 1970—. Trustee, Paperboard Packaging Council, 1969. Served with USNR, 1942-45. Mem. Fibre Box Assn. (dir. 1958, pres. 1966), Am. Paper Inst. (dir.), Fourdrinier Kraft Bd. Inst. (dir.). Home: 365 E Foster Pl Lake Forest IL 60045 Office: 1603 Orrington Av Evanston IL 60201

ALLNER, WALTER HEINZ, designer, painter, art dir.; b. Dessau, Germany, Jan. 2, 1909; student Bauhaus-Dessau, 1927-30; m. Colette Vasselon, Mar. 8, 1938 (div. June 1951); 1 son, Michel; m. 2d, Jane Booth Pope, Apr. 4, 1954; 1 son, Peter. Came to U.S., 1949, naturalized 1957. Designer Gesellschafts-und Wirtschafts-Museum Vienna, Austria, 1930; asst. to typographer Piet Zwart, Wassenaar, Holland, 1931; editorial, painting and advt. design, Paris, France, 1933-49; art dir. Omnium Graphique, Paris, 1933-36, Omnium Formes, Editions d'Art Graphique et Photographique, Paris, 1933-36; Paris editor Swiss art mag., Graphis, 1945-48; founder, editor Internat. Poster Ann., 1948-52; co-dir. Editions Paralleles, Paris, 1948-51; mem. staff Fortune mag., N.Y.C., 1951—, art dir., 1962—; free-lance designer, design cons. companies; designer poster for traffic safety campaign Outdoor Advt. Assn. Am., 1959-60; exhbt. Salon des Surindependants, Paris, Salon des Réalités Nouvelles, Paris, numerous others, Germany, Austria, U.S. Recipient awards Chgo. Art Dirs. Club, 1952, 60, Art Dirs. Club N.Y.C., 1956, 58, 60. Compiler, editor: A.M. Cassandre, Peintre d'Affiches, 1948. Editor: Posters, 1952. Author numerous articles on poster art. Home: 110 Riverside Dr New York City NY 10024 summer Castle Rd Truro MA 02666 Office: Time and Life Bldg New York City NY 10020

ALLOTT, GORDON LLEWELLYN, senator; b. Pueblo, Colo., Jan. 2, 1907; s. Leonard John and Bertha Louise (Reese) A.; B.A., U. Colo., 1927, LL.B., 1929; LL.D., Colo. Coll., 1963, Colo. State Univ., 1968; Dr.Eng. (hon.), Colorado School of Mines, 1967; m. Welda O. Hall, May 15, 1934; children—Roger Hall, Gordon Llewellyn. Admitted to Colo. bar, 1929, since practiced in Lamar; co. atty., Lamar, 1934, 41-46, city atty., 1937-41; dist. atty., 1946-49; atty., dir. First Fed. Savs. and Loan Assn. of Lamar since 1934; local counsel Amity Mut. Irrigation Co., Brown Lumber Co., Kan.-Colo. Utilities, Inc., C.H. Habern, Inc., State Bank of Wiley (Colo.), Town of Wiley and various ins. cos.; prim. practice irrigation, trial and probate law; lt. gov. of Colo. 1950-54; U.S. senator from Colo., 1955—. Am. delegate to Inter-Parliamentary Union, vice chairman Am. delegation; U.S. rep. 17th Assembly UN; Am. del. Institut D'Etudes Politiques, Vaduz, Lichtenstein; member of National Monuments Commn. Mem. Colo. Bd. Bar Examiners, 1948-50. Nat. chmn. Young Republican Nat. Fedn., 1941-46. Served as maj., U.S.A.F., South Pacific, World War II. Mem. Southeastern Colo. Bar Assn. (pres., 1940-42), Am., Colo. bar assns., Am. Legion, Vets. Fgn. Wars, Airplane Owners and Pilots Assn., Phi Gamma Delta, Delta Sigma Pi. Episcopalian. Mason. Rotarian. Home: Lamar CO 81052 Office: Senate Office Bldg Washington DC 20510

ALLOWAY, LAWRENCE, writer, educator; b. Wimbledon, London, Eng., Sept. 17, 1926; s. Francis Lawrence and Nora (Hatton) A.; m. Sylvia Sleigh, June 28, 1954. Came to U.S., 1961. Asst. lectr. Nat. Gallery, London, 1948-54; lectr. Tate Gallery, London, 1952-55; British corr. Art News mag., N.Y.C., 1954-57; contbg. editor Art Internat. mag., Zurich, Switzerland, 1957-65; dep. dir. Inst. Contemporary Arts, London, 1957-60; instr. art history Bennington (Vt.) Coll., 1961-62; curator Guggenheim Mus., N.Y.C., 1962-66; writer, mem. artist-in-residence program So. Ill. U., Carbondale, 1966-67; chmn. div. of fine arts Sch. Visual Arts, N.Y.C., 1967-68; prof. State U. at Stony Brook (N.Y.), 1968—. Mem. com. London County Council Open Air Exhbn., 1960; juror Carnegie Inst. Internat., 1961; Fgn. leader grantee State Dept., 1958; recipient 2d Fgn. Critics prize 30th Venice Biennale, 1961. Mem. Assn. Internat. Art hon. joint-sec. British sect. 1957-60). Author: Nine Abstract Artists, 1954; Ettore Colla, 1960; The Metalization of a Dream, 1963; The Venice Biennale: 1895-1968, 1969; Violent America: The Movies, 1946-64, 1970. Home: 330 W 20th St New York City NY 10019

ALLPORTER, JOHN WILLIAMS, mfg. exec.; b. Lima, O., Apr. 1, 1932; B.S., U. San Francisco, 1954; M.S., Stanford University, 1956; m. Rosemarie Lois Brown, May 15, 1955; 1 son, Anthony Robinson. Sales rep. Ames-Brockton Fabricated Products, Akron, O., 1956-58, sales mgr. Coshocton, Ohio, 1959-61, gen. manager plant, 1961-68, v.p. sales, 1968--. Instr. bus. Coshocton Jr. College, 1968-69. Mem. Coshocton C. of C. (vice president 1967-68, pres. 1969-70), English Speaking Union, Coshocton Sertoma Club, Nat. Assn. Mfrs., Sales Executives Institute, Phi Beta Kappa, Sigma Chi, Phi Mu. Democrat. Mem. Christian Ch. (lay reader). Mason (32, Shriner). Clubs: Coshocton Country, Coshocton City, Running Deer Country. Home: 2d Av Coshocton OH Office: 3d Av Coshocton OH

ALLPRESS, HENRY A., fgn. service officer; b. Neb., Oct. 18, 1931; LL.B., U. Neb., 1939, M.A., 1949. Mrg., operator feeds processing firm 1931-34; dispatcher-foreman aircraft corp., 1940-45; mgr. feed millfood locker, 1945-46; asst. agrl. economist U. Neb., 1946-50; agrl. economist Bur. Reclamation, 1950-51, Point 5 program, Asunción, 1951-53, FOA, 1953-54; internat. relations officer State Dept., 1954-55; agrl. economist. Bogota, Colombia 1955; with ICA, 1955-61; with AID, 1961—, dir., Equador, 1969—. Address: American Embassy AID Quito Ecuador*

ALLRED, ALBERT LOUIS, educator; b. Mount Airy, N.C., Sept. 19, 1931; s. Caleb Haynes and Bessie (Brown) A.; B.S. in Chemistry, U. N.C., 1953; A.M., Harvard, 1955, Ph.D., 1956; m. Nancy Jean Willis, Aug. 30, 1958; children—Kevin Scott, Gregg Warren, Sarah Elaine. Chemist, E.I. du Pont de Nemours Co., Wilmington, Del., 1952, 55, Mallinckrodt Chem. Works, St. Louis, 1954, Argonne Nat. Lab., 1958; mem. faculty Northwestern U., 1956—, prof., 1969—, asso. dean Coll. Arts, Scis., 1970—. Alfred P. Sloan fellow, 1963-65, postdoctoral fellow U. Rome (Italy), 1967; hon. research asso. Univ. Coll., London (Eng.), 1965. Mem. Am. Chem. Soc., Chem. Soc. (London), Am. Assn. U. Profs. (pres. Northwestern U. 1968-69), Phi Beta Kappa, Phi Lambda Upsilon, Sigma Xi, Alpha Chi Sigma. Home: 820 Milburn St Evanston IL 60201

ALLRED, EVAN LEIGH, educator; b. Deseret, Utah, May 22, 1929; s. Leigh Richmond and Louise (Cowley) A.; B.S., Brigham Young U., 1951, M.S., 1956; Ph.D., U. Cal., 1959; m. Barbara Klea Hawkins, Apr. 21, 1955; children—Kevin Michael, Richard Paul, Steven Leigh and Craig Lynn (twins). Research chemist Phillips Petroleum Co., Bartlesville, Okla., 1951-54; instr. chemistry U. Wash., 1960-61; sr. research chemist Rohm & Haas Co., Phila., 1961-63; asst. prof. chemistry U. Utah, 1963-67, asso. prof., 1967-70, prof., 1970—. NSF fellow, 1959-60. Mem. Am. Chem. Soc., Sigma Xi, Phi Kappa Phi. Research physical and organic chemistry; organic reaction mechanisms; synthesis of molecules of theoretical interest. Home: 3255 Margie Av Salt Lake City UT 84109

ALLRED, GEORGE EDWARD, assn. exec., coll. dean; b. St. Charles, Mo., Mar. 8, 1922; s. George W. and Adele A. (Beck) A.; B.A., Rutgers U., 1951; B.S., Washington U., 1957; M.A., Nat. Christian U., 1968, Lit.D., 1969; m. Lydia V. Esposito, June 30, 1947. Exec. trainee William Ryle Import-Export Co., Inc., 1947-48; instr. English, history and social studies St. Louis and St. Charles counties, 1951-62; dir. edn. Lakeside Center Boys of St. Louis County, 1962-64; pres. Pens for Hire, 1964-65; exec. dir. Asso. Cooperage Industries of Am., Inc., 1965-68; exec. adminstr. Nat. Assn. Execs. and Adminstrs., St. Louis, 1968—; dean of students St. Mary's Coll. of O'Fallon. Served with AUS, 1943-46; CBI. Mem. Am. Soc. Assn. Execs., St. Louis Assn. Execs., Assn. Jr. Coll. Adminstrs., Fund Raising Mgmt. Assn. Club: Washington University (St. Louis). Home: Rt 4 Box 180 O'Fallon MO 63366 Office: 1000 Washington St St Louis MO 63101

ALLRED, JOHN CALDWELL, univ. dean, physicist; b. Breckenridge, Tex., Apr. 24, 1926; s. Oran Henderson and Katherine (Miller) A.; B.A., Tex. Christian U., 1944; M.A., U. Tex., 1948, Ph.D., 1950; m. Mary Elizabeth Bode, June 4, 1950; children—Susan Elizabeth, Katherine Anne, John Renne. Staff mem. Los Alamos Sci. Lab., 1948-55; research scientist Convair Co., 1955-56; mem. faculty U. Houston, 1956—, prof. physics, 1961—, v.p., dean faculties, 1962-68. Mem. Am. Phys. Soc., Am. Nuclear Soc. (charter), Acoustical Soc. Am., Sigma Xi, Alpha Chi, Sigma Pi Sigma. Home: 1300 Antigua Lane Houston TX 77058

ALLSOPP, THOMAS, ins. exec.; b. Newark, May 17, 1918; s. Thomas and Amy A. (Hart) A.; A.B., Princeton, 1939; m. Margaret Jean Johnson, Sept. 28, 1940; children—Carol, Barbara, Susan. With Prudential Ins. Co. Am., 1939—, successively sr. methods analyst, asst. personnel dir., gen. mgr. home office, dir. adminstrn. Canadian head office, exec. gen. mgr. South- Central home office, 1939-55, 2d v.p., 1955-62, sr. v.p. Northeastern home office, Boston, 1962—. Trustee Boston U. Mem. Am. Coll. Life Underwriters. Author: (with Harry J. Volk) Life Insurance Company Organization, 1955. Home: 790 Boylston St Boston MA 02199 Office: Prudential Ins Co Am Boston MA 02199

ALLTOP, JAMES HOWARD, ins. co. exec.; b. Glenville, W.Va., Nov. 28, 1905; s. Evan and Ida (Miller) A.; A.B., Ind. U., 1929; m. Lillian O'Bannon, June 11, 1930; children—James H., William O'Bannon. With Eli Lilly Co., 1929-31, Am. United Life Ins. Co., Indpls., 1931—, personnel dir., 1932-52, sec., 1952-61, sr. v.p., dir., 1961—; lectr. Butler U., 1936-52. Gen. chmn. Community Chest, Indpls., 1953-54. Mem. Ind. U. Alumni Assn. (past pres.), Beta Theta Pi. Home: 1720 E 80th St Indianapolis IN 46240 Office: Am United Life Ins Co Box 368 Indianapolis IN 46204

ALLWORK, RONALD, architect, designer, writer; b. Bklyn., Jan. 23, 1905; s. Roland and Winifred Mary (Breslin) A.; A.B., Columbia, 1928, B.Arch., 1934; m. Eleanor Wallace Bloom, Oct. 17, 1941; 1 dau., Winifred. Exec. engr. Am. Radiator Co., N.Y.C., 1934-38, Red. Hook Housing Project, N.Y.C., 1939; writer, cons. tech. pubs., 1939-42; dep. dir., acting dir. plumbing and heating div. WPB, 1942-43; exec. officer conservation com. Combined Prodn. and Resources Bd.; sec. Anglo-Am. Screw Thread Standardization, 1943-45; archtl. practice N.Y.C., 1946—; sec. Sponsor's Council for Anglo-Am. Screw Thread Unification; furniture designer; adviser and author Am. Inst. Decorator's Manual of Profl. Practice for Decorators, 1950—. Fellow Pierpont Morgan Library. Chmn. N.Y. State Bd. Examiners Architects, 1968-70. Fellow A.I.A. (treas. N.Y. chpt. 1953-56, nat. jud. bd. 1970-75); mem. Alumni Fedn. Columbia U. (v.p. 1953-54), New York Soc. Architects, Nat Council Archtl. Registration Bds. (2d v.p. 1971-72), Am. Soc. Mech. Engrs., Archtl. League N.Y. (pres. 1964-66), Century Assn. N.Y.C., Alpha Delta Phi. Republican. Clubs: Grolier, University (N.Y.C.); Lake Placid (N.Y.); Chevy Chase (Washington); Country of Florida. Author of booklets for Good Housekeeping Mag. Contbr. to Pencil Points, Architectural Record, House Beautiful. Received Columbia Alumni medal, 1952. Home: 25 Sutton Pl South New York City NY 10022 Office: 1 E 57th St New York City NY 10022

ALLY, CARL JOSEPH, advt. exec.; b. Detroit, Mar. 31, 1924; s. Carl and Mary (Miglio) A.; A.B., U. MIch., 1949, student Grad. Sch., 1953; certificate Georgetown U. Sch. Fgn. Service, 1952; m. Patricia M. Nusco, Jan. 15, 1952; children Christopher Jonathan, Patricia Ann, Matthew Carl. Advt. exec. Gen. Electric Co., Schenectady, 1948-51; mgr. N.Y.C. office Campbell- Ewald co., 1955-60; v.p. Papert, Koening, Lois, Inc., N.Y.C., 1960-62; founder, 1962, since chmn. bd., chief exec. officer Carl Ally Inc., N.Y.C.; lectr. New Sch. Social Research, 1964-; cons. marketing, 1959- . Mem. N.Y. Bus. Council Clean Air, 1966-. Hon. trustee Citizens for Clean Air, 1966-; bd. dirs. Fair Campaign Practices Com., 1962-. Served to capt. USAAF and USAF, 1942-45, 50-52. Decorated D.F.C., Air medal with 3 oak leaf clusters. Mem. Sigma Nu. Clubs: Wings (N.Y.C.), Pequod Yacht. Home: 290 Long Meadow Rd Fairfield, CT 06431. Office: 437 Madison Av New York City NY 10022

ALLYN, ARTHUR CECIL, epidopterist, museum dir.; Chgo., Dec. 24, 1913; s. Arthur Cecil and Nelle (Musick) A.; student Dartmouth, 1931-35, Beloit Coll., 1935; m. Dorothy DeWitt, Mar. 21, 1938; children—Dorothy Ann (Mrs. Christopher J. Lavick, Jr.), David D., William N. (adopted). Chmn. bd. A.C. Allyn & Co., Chgo., 1969—; dir. Hart-Carter Corp., Eastman Oil Well Survey Corp., Eastman Internat. GMBH., Allyn Precision Tools (PTY) LTD, Mono Container (PTY) Ltd.; pres., dir. Chgo. White Sox, 1961-70; now mng. dir. Mus. Entomology. Trustee Nat. Coll. Edn. Fellow Royal Entomol. Soc.; mem. Lepidopterists Soc., Sigma Chi. Presbyn. Clubs: Field, University (Sarasota). 201 Seagull Lane Sarasota FL 33580

ALLYN, HENRY GREGORY Jr., r.r. exec.; b. Phila., Dec. 4, 1920; s. Henry Gregory and Frances H. (Steen) A.; grad. Lawrenceville Sch., 1939; B.A., Princeton, 1943; m. Elizabeth Kendrick Burrows, Sept. 20, 1947; children—Henry Gregory III, Florence Elizabeth, John Steen. With Pa. R.R., 194768; asst. v.p. freight sales Penn Central Co., N.Y.C., 1968-69; pres., dir. P. & L.E. R.R., Pitts., 1969-70, chmn., chief exec. officer, pres., dir., 1970—; pres., dir. Lake Erie & Eastern R.R. Co., Pitts., Chartiers & Youghiogheny R.R. Co., Mahoning State Line R.R. Co., Youngstown & So. R.R. Co., Monongahela Ry. Co.; v.p., dir. Montour Land Co., Montour R.R. Co., Dir. Boys Clubs Western Pa. Served with Hosp. Corps, USNR, 1943-46. PTO. Mem. Nat. Def. Transp. Assn., Nat. Freight Traffic Assn., Traffic Club N.Y., Traffic Club Pitts., Ry. Club Pitts. Republican. Clubs: Duquesne, Harvard-Yale-Princeton (Pitts.); Allegheny Country, Edgeworth (Sewickley); Princeton (N.Y.C.); Capitol Hill (Washington). Home: Country Club Rd RD 1 Sewickley PA 15143 Office: P & LE Terminal Bldg Pittsburgh PA 15219

ALLYN, JOHN W., formerly mng. partner A.C. Allyn & Co.; owner Chgo. White Sox; gen. partner Francis I. du Pont & Co.; v.p., dir. Artnell Co.; dir. Eastman Oil Well Survey Co., Trans- Continental Bus Sustem Inc., J. & R Motor Supply Corp., Hitchcock Pub. Co., Aetna State Bank, Pepsi Cola Bottling Co. of Washington. Address: 120 S La Salle Chicago IL 60603*

ALLYN, STANLEY CHARLES, corp. official; b. Madison, Wis., July 20, 1891; s. Charles Herbert and Anna Louise (Cook) A.; A.B., U. Wis., 1913, LL.D., 1946; LL.D., Miami U., Oxford, Ohio, 1952; L.H.D., U. Dayton, 1954, U. Cin., 1956; D.B.A. (hon.) Otterbein Coll., 1966; m. Helen Probasco Compton, Sept. 29, 1917 (dec. 1967); children—Charles Stanley, Mary Louise Compton; m. 2d, Patricia von Krell Turnbull, 1968. Accountant, asst. comptroller, comptroller, treas., exec. v.p., gen. mgr., Nat. Cash Register Co., Dayton, O., 1913-40, dir., 1918-61, pres., 1950-57, chmn. bd., chief exec. officer, 1957-61, chmn. exec. com., 1962-64, dir. emeritus, 1964-70; dir. Dayco Corp., Mead Corp. (Dayton), Western Allegheny R.R. Co., Master Consolidated, Inc., Dayton, Ohio; trustee Northwestern Mutual Life Ins. Co. (Milw.). Bd. dirs. Nat. Conf. Christians and Jews; trustee Dayton Air Force Mus., Logistics Mgmt. Inst., Washington; vice pres. Grand Central Art Galleries; bd. trustees Com. for Econ. Development, N.Y., Thomas Alva Edison Found., N.Y.; mem. bus. adv. council Dept. of Commerce; trustee U.S. Council of Internat. C. of C., Nat. Aviation Hall Fame, Cox Coronary Heart Inst.; industries adv. com. The Adv. Council; pres., Community Chests and Councils of America, 1950-51; vice chmn. 1960, United Community Campaigns; dir. U. Wis. Found.; hon. trustee Inst. Internat. Edn., N.Y.C.; trustee Asia Foundation, San Francisco; hon. mem. nat. council Boy Scouts Am. Head U.S. delegation Econ. Commn. Europe, 1956, 57, 9th gen. session Gen. Conf., UNESCO, 1956, chmn. com. on 6th nat. conf. of U.S. Nat. Commn. for UNESCO, 1957; mem. adv. council U.S. Com. for UN. Decorated Officer French Legion of Honor; recipient Presdl. Certificate of Merit; USN award Distinguished Pub. Service; named Industrialist of Year by Soc. Indsl. Realtors, 1961; recipient Good Citizenship medal S.A.R., 1962; named honorary citizen Athens, Greece. Mem. Psi Upsilon. Clubs: Blind Brook (Port Chester, New York), Lyford Cay, East Hill (Nassau, Bahamas); Buz Fuz, Moraine Country (Dayton); Everglades (Palm Beach, Fla.). Home: 2021 Ridgeway Rd Dayton OH 45419 Died Oct 31 1970

ALLYSON, JUNE, (born Jan Allyson), actress; b. Lucerne, N.Y.; d. Arthur and Clare Allyson; student pub. schs., N.Y.C.; m. Dick Powell, Aug. 19, 1945 (dec.); children—Pamela (adopted), Richard Keith; m. 2d, Glenn Maxwell, 1963. Actress, stage appearances include: Sing Out the News; Very Warm for May; Higher and Higher; Panama Hattie; Best Foot Forward; motion pictures include: Girl Crazy, 1943; Best Foot Forward, 1943; Thousands Cheer, 1943; Meet the People, 1943; Two Girls and a Sailor, 1944; Music for Millions, 1944; Her Highness and the Bellboy, 1945; The Sailor Takes a Wife, 1945; Two Sisters From Boston, 1945; Till the Clouds Roll By, 1946; The Secret Heart, 1946; High Barbaree, 1947; Good News, 1947; The Bride Goes Wild, 1947; Words and Music, 1948; The Three Musketeers, 1948; Little Women, 1948; The Stratton Story, 1948; The Reformer and the Redhead, 1949; Right Cross, 1950; Too Young to Kiss, 1951; The Girl in White, 1951; The Glenn Miller Story, 1954; Remains to be Seen, 1953; Executive Suite, 1954; Strategic Air Command, 1955; You Can't Run Away From It, The Opposite Sex, 1956; Interlude, 1957; My Man Godfrey, 1957; Stranger in My Arms, 1958; star June Allyson Show, 1960-61.

ALMAND, BOND judge; b. Lithonia, Ga., Jan. 13, 1894; s. Alexander James and Clara Emily (Bond) A.; Ph.B., Emory U., 1913, LL.B., Columbia, 1916, A.M., 1916; m. Helen Whitefoot Barnett, June 18, 1932; children—Helen (Mrs. Roy F. Morgan Jr.), Bond. Admitted to Ca. bar 1916; practiced in Atlanta, 1916-42; asst. city atty., 1939-42, judge Fulton Superior Ct., 1942-43, 1945-49, asso. justice Supreme Ct. Ga., 1949-67, presiding justice, 1967-69, chief justice, 1969—. Solicitor Criminal to Fulton County, 1939-42; lectr. Emory U. Sch. Law 1951—. Rep. Ga. Gen. Assembly, 1935-38. Served as 1st lt., Inf., U.S. Army, with 82d and 9th divs., A.E.F., World War I. Mem. Am. Bar Assn. Inst. Jud. Adminstrn., Phi Beta Kappa, Sigma Nu, Phi Alpha Delta, Omcron Delta Kappa, Episcopalian. Home: 3291 Rilman Rd NW Atlanta GA 30327 Office: Judicial Bldg Atlanta GA 30303

ALMEIDA, LAURINDO, guitarist, composer; b. Brazil, Sept. 2, 1917; s. Benjamin and Placedina (Araujo) A.; student Escola Nacional de Muscica do Rio de Janeiro; m. Maria M. Ferreira May 20, 1944 (dec. Aug. 1970). Came to U.S., 1947, naturalized, 1961. Featured soloist Stan Kenton Orch., 1947-50; guitarist motion picture prodns., 1949—; composer musical scores for TV, also motion pictures Maracaibo, 1956, Goodbye My Lady, 1957; recording artist for Capitol, World Pacific and Decca records; owner, operator Brazilliance Music Pub. Co., 1952—. Mem. A.S.C.A.P., Am. Songwriters Assn., Composers Guild Am., Nat. Acad. Recordings Arts and Scis. (bd. govs. classical music). Home: 4104 Witzel Dr Sherman Oaks CA 91403 Office: PO Box 5265 Sherman Oaks CA 91403

ALMEN, GEORGE DANIEL, Jr., oil co. exec., lawyer; b. Bartlesville, Okla., Aug. 9, 1918; s. George Daniel and Opal Jeanne (Harned) A.; A.B., U. Okla., 1940, LL.B., 1942; grad. Advanced Mgmt. Program, Harvard, 1958; m. Dorothy Jeanne Lambert, Sept 1, 1942. Admitted to Okla. bar, 1942; atty. legal dept. Sinclair Oil & Gas Co., 1946-53, asst. to pres., 1953-56, v.p., 1956-64, also div. mgr. New Orleans, Houston, Midland, Tex., dir., 1959-64, v.p. Sinclair Oil Corp., N.Y.C., 1959-64; former pres. chief exec. officer Sinclair Pipe Line Co.; pres., dir. Sinclair Oil & Gas Co., 1965—, Sinclair Can-Oil Co.; dir., exec. v.p. Nat. Bank of Tulsa. Trustee Hillcrest Med. Center, Tulsa U. Served 2d lt. to capt., AUS, 1942-46. Mem. Okla. Bar Assn., Tulsa C. of C. (dir.), Am. Mgmt. Assn., Rocky Mountain Oil and Gas Assn., Am. Petroleum Inst., Mid-Continent Oil and Gas Assn., Newcomen Soc., Phi Gamma Delta, Phi Delta Phi. Clubs: Southern Hills Country (Tulsa), The Tejas (Houston); Independence Country; Tulsa. Home: 2117 E 60th Pl Tulsa OK 74105 Office: Sinclair Oil Bldg Tulsa OK 74103

ALMGREN, HERBERT PHILIP, banker; b. Fairfield, Ala., Oct. 22, 1916; s. O. Philip and Lillie (Becker) A.; B.S. magna cum laude, Springfield Coll., 1938; grad. student Clark U.; m. Jean C. Cleveland, June 10, 1939; children—Caroline (Mrs. Douglas N. Ellis Jr.), Nancy B. (Mrs. Robert A. Killman). Tchr. Rectory Sch., Pomfret, Conn., 1938-40; with Monarch Life Ins. Co., and predecessor, 1940-63, v.p., 1958-63; with First Bank & Trust Co. Hampden County, 1963—, sr. v.p., 1964-65, pres., 1965—, also dir.; pres. Springfield Area Devel. Corp. Treas. Springfield Armory Mus.; trustee Springfield Hosp.; corporator Springfield Boys Club, Wesson Meml. Hosp.; bd. dirs. Springfield Jr. Achievement. Served to lt. (j.g.) USNR, 1943-46. Mem. Mass. Bankers Assn., Greater Springfield C. of C. (v.p.)

Rotarian. Clubs: Colony (Springfield); Longmeadow Country. Home: 42 Dartmouth Rd Longmeadow MA 01106 Office: 127 State St Springfield MA 01103

ALMIRALL, LLOYD VINCENT, lawyer; b. Bklyn., Nov. 9, 1907; s. Juan A. and Emma (Kuntz) A.; A.B., Hamilton Coll., Clinton, N.Y., 1929; LL.B., Harvard, 1932; m. Catherine Lewerth, Sept. 17, 1937; children—Danne, Jan (Mrs. Anthony Olmer), Paul L., Irene. Admitted to N.Y. bar, 1932, since practiced in N.Y.C.; partner firm Breed, Abbott & Morgan, 1946—. Trustee Lenox Sch., N.Y.C., 1946-59, pres., 1951-56; trustee Harvey Sch., Katonah; N.Y., 1948—, Hamilton Coll., 1958-64. Mem. Mr. Haight Jr.'s Litchfield County Hounds (M.F.H.), Chi Psi. Clubs: Players, Downtown Assn., Harvard (N.Y.C.). Home: Bouton Rd South Salem NY 10590 Office: 1 Chase Manhattan Plaza New York City NY 10005

ALMON, CLOPPER, lawyer; b. Tuscumbia, Ala., July 31, 1895; s. Edward Berton and Lucy Jane (Clopper) A.; A.B., Vanderbilt U., 1919; LL.B., Georgetown U., 1921; m. Louise Howell, Aug. 19, 1935 (dec.); 1 son, Clopper; m. 2d, Martha Nathan, Sept., 1953 (dec.); m. 3d, Katharine Graham, Nov. 1961. Admitted Ala. bar, 1920, since practiced in Sheffield as partner firm Almon & McAlister. Mem. Ala. Bd. Bar Commrs. Past pres. Sheffield Bd. Edn. Served to 1st lt. U.S. Army, 1917-18. Mem. Am., Ala. (past pres.), Colbert County (past pres.) bar assns., Vanderbilt Alumni Assn. (past bd. dirs.). Home: 820 River Bluff Dr Sheffield AL 35660 Office: 322 Montgomery Av Sheffield AL 35660

ALMOND, GABRIEL ABRAHAM, educator; b. Rock Island, Ill., Jan. 12, 1911; s. David Moses and Lisa (Elson) A.; Ph.B., U. Chgo., 1932, Ph.D., 1938; m. Maria Dorothea Kaufmann, Apr. 29, 1937; children—Richard J., Peter O., Susan J. Fellow Social Sci. Research Council, 1935-36, 46; instr. polit. sci. Bklyn. Coll., 1939-42; with OWI, Washington, 1942-44, War Dept., ETO, 1945; research asso. Yale U. Inst. Internat. Studies, 1947-49, asso. prof. polit. sci., 1949-51, prof. polit. sci., 1959-63; asso. prof. internat. affairs Princeton, 1951-54, prof., 1954-57, prof. politics, 1957-59; prof. polit. sci. Stanford (Cal.) U., 1963—, exec. head dept. polit. sci., 1964-68. Cons. Air U., 1948, Dept. State, 1950, Office Naval Research, 1951, Rand Corp., 1954-55, Sci. Adv. Bd. USAF, 1960-61; vis. prof. U. Tokyo (Japan), 1962. Recipient Travel and Study award Ford Found., 1962-63; fellow Center for Advanced Study in the Behavioral Scis., 1956-57. Fellow Am. Acad. Arts and Scis.; mem. Am. Philos. Soc., Social Sci. Research Council (bd. dirs., chmn. com. comparative politics), Am. Polit. Sci. Assn. (pres. 1965-66), Am. Assn. Public Opinion Research, Acad. Polit. Sci. Author: The American People and Foreign Policy, 1950; The Appeals of Communism, 1954. Editor, author: The Struggle for Democracy in Germany (with others), 1949; (with others) The Politics of the Developing Areas, 1960; (with Sidney Verba) The Civic Culture, 1963; (with R. Bingham Powell) Comparative Politics: A Developmental Approach, 1966; Political Development, 1970. Home: 4135 Old Trace Rd Palo Alto CA 94305 Office: Stanford Univ Stanford CA 94306

ALMOND, JAMES LINDSAY, Jr., judge; b. Charlottesville, Va., June 15, 1898; s. James Lindsay and Eddie Nicholas (Burgess) A.; LL.B., U. Va., 1923; LL.D., Coll. William and Mary, 1959; m. Josephine Katherine Minter, Aug. 15, 1925. Admitted to Va. bar, 1921; practiced in Roanoke, 1923-32; prin. Zoar High Sch., 1921-22; asst. pros. atty., Roanoke, 1930-33; Judge Hustings Ct., Roanoke, 1933-45; mem. 79th Congress, 2d session (fill vacancy), elected 80th Congress, mem. post office and civil service com.; atty. gen. Va., 1948-57; gov. State of Va., 1958-62; apptd. interim judge U.S. Ct. Customs and Patent Appeals, Washington, 1962-63, asso. judge, 1963—. Served with U.S. Army, World War I. Mem. Am. Va., Roanoke bar assns., faculty, 1970—. Served to Unived Comml. Travelers, Delta Theta Phi. Democrat. Lutheran tchr. men's bible class. Mason (Shriner). Home: 208 Wexleigh Dr Richmond VA 23229 Office: US Court of Customs and Patent Appeals Washington DC 20439

ALMQUIST, ELMER HUGO, Jr., army officer; b. Louisville, May 17, 1919; s. Elmer Hugo and Victoria (Williams) A.; student Johns Hopkins, 1936-37, Auburn U., 1937-40; grad. Advanced Mgmt. Program, Harvard, 1963; m. Dorothy Jeanne Knight, July 27, 1946; children-Deborah Knight, Dorothy Victoria. Commd. 2d lt., U.S. Army, 1940, advanced through grades to maj. gen., 1967; assigned U.S. and Pacific, 1940-45, U.S., 1945-49; student Command and Gen. Staff Coll., 1949-50; assigned U.S., 1950-51, Far East Command, 1951-53; student Armed Forces Staff Coll., 1954; assigned Dept. of Army, 1954-57; student Army War Coll., 1957-58; assigned U.S. Army, Europe, 1958-62, Dept. of Army and Joint Chiefs of Staff, 1962-64, 7th Inf. Div., Korea, 1964-65, Dept. of Army, 1965-67; comdg. gen. So. European Task Force, 1967-68; assigned Hdqrs. U.S. Army, Europe, 1968-69; comdg. gen. 8th Inf. Div., Germany, 1969-70; chief staff U.S. Army Europe 1970—. Decorated D.S.M., Legion of Merit, Joint Services Commendation medal, Bronze Star. Mem. Assn. U.S. Army, Alpha Tau Omega, Tau Beta Pi. Episcopalian. Home: 55 S Buell Av Aurora IL 60506 Office: Hdqrs USAREUR APO New York NY 09403

AL-MUDHAF, MUHALHEL MOHAMMAD, diplomat of Kuwait; b. Kuwait, Sept. 19, 1927; s. Mohamad and Dalal Al- Mudhaf; ed. in Kuwait, UAR and Eng.; spl. course internat. affairs Oxford (Eng.) U., 1961-62. With Kuwait Ministry Edn., 1953-61; charge d'affaires, Lebanon, 1962-65, Syrian Arab Republic, 1964-65; ambassador of Kuwait to Pakistan, 1965-67; ambassador, permanent rep. Kuwait to UN, N.Y.C., 1967-. Office: Kuwait Mission 235 E 42d St New York City, NY 10017

ALMY, GERALD MARKS, educator, physicist; b. Ewing, Neb., Apr. 24, 1904; s. Billings Grinnell and Ada (Marks) A.; B.S., U. Neb., 1924, M.S., 1926; Ph.D., Harvard, 1930; m. Ruth Virtue, July 21, 1930; children—Cynthia (Mrs. T.K. Landauer), Catherine (Mrs. P.N. Hineline).. Mem. faculty U. Ill., Urbana, 1930—, prof. physics, 1943-70, head dept., 1964-70, prof. emeritus, 1970—. Fellow Am. Phys. Soc.; mem. Am. Inst. Physics, A.A.A.S., Am. Assn. U. Profs., Phi Beta Kappa, Sigma Xi. Author articles molecular spectroscopy and fluorescence, betatron devel., photonuclear processes. Home: 509 S Ridgeway Champaign IL 61820 Office: Physics Dept U Ill Urbana IL 61801

ALMY, THOMAS PATTISON, educator, physician; b. N.Y.C., Jan. 10, 1915; s. Don Robinson and Marie (Pattison) A.; A.B., Cornell U., 1935. M.D., 1939; m. Katharine Whitin Swift, Nov. 12, 1943; children—Susan, Anne, Christine. Intern N.Y. Hosp., 1939-40; resident medicine, 1940-43; from asst. prof. to prof. medicine Cornell U. Med. Coll., 1946-68; Nathan Smith prof. medicine, chmn. dept. Dartmouth Med. Sch., 1968—; cons VA Hosps., NIH, NRC, Am. Cancer Soc. Bd. dirs. Digestive Disease Found. Recipient awd. of distinction Cornell U. Med. Coll. Alumni Assn., 1967. Fellow A.C. P. (bd. regents 1968—); mem. Assn. Am. Physicians, Am. Soc. Clin. Investigation, Am. Gastroenterol. Assn. (pres. 1964). Author articles in clin. physiology gastrointestinal disease. Home: Stevens Rd Etna NH 03750 Office: Dartmouth Med Sch Hanover NH 03755

ALNES, ELLIS STEPHEN, journalist; b. Thief River Falls, Minn., Dec. 1, 1926; s. Lloyd T. and Shirley (Anderson) A.; B.A., U. Minn., 1949; m. Margaret Elizabeth Grinols, Dec. 17, 1948; children—Susan, Karen, Judith, Lee. U.P.I. reporter, Bismarck, N.D., 1949-54; reporter, bus. editor, Sunday editor Pioneer Press & Dispatch, St. Paul, 1954-67; editorial writer Mpls. Star, 1967—. Served with USNR, 1944-46. Home: 908 Park Av Mahtomedi MN 55115 Office: 425 Portland Av Minneapolis MN 55415

ALONSO, ALICIA, ballerina; b. Havana, Cuba; d. Dr. Antonio and Ernestina (Hoyo) Martinez; student Sociedad Pro-Arte Musical Havana; studies with Alexandra Fedorova, Anatole Vilzak, Leon Fokine, Vera Volkova, London; student Sch. Am. Ballet, N.Y.C.; m. Fernando Alonso, 1937; 1 dau., Laura. Profl. debut, mus. Great Lady, 1938; appeared in Stars In Your Eyes, 1938, soloist with Ballet Caravan, 1939-40, Ballet Theater, 1940; guest ballerina with Sociedad Pro-Arte Musical, Havana, 1940-48, dancing Giselle, General's Daughter, Concerto, others; with Ballet Alicia Alonso, Ballet de Cuba, 1948-56, appeared for several seasons with Am. Ballet Theater from 1945; guest prima ballerina Ballet Russe, 1955-57; starred in spl. Coppelia, Giselle, Greek Theatre, Los Angeles, 1957-58; with partner Igor Youskevitch tour N. and S. Am., 1957-58; guest ballerina Riga, Leningrad, Kiev, Moscow, USSR, partnered with Leonid Zdanov, V. Simeonov, 1958; with Igor Youskevitch toured S.Am. with Ballet Nacional de Cuba, 1959; an organizer, danced title roles ballets Internat. Festival of Ballet, Havana, 1960; guest star 20th ann. celebration Am. Ballet Theatre at Met. Opera, N.Y.C., 1960; toured Europe, Asia, Mexico, Can. with Ballet Nacional de Cuba, 1961; partner Rodolfo Rodriguez at Pablo Picasso's 80th birthday, France, 1961; chosen spl. del. by Cuban Govt. to participate in celebrations Rabindranath Tagore's Centennial, India, 1961; participant with husband in creation state sponsored Nat. Sch. of Ballet, Cuba, 1962-63; guest artist Les Grande Ballets Canadiens, Montreal, 1967, Royal Danish Ballet, Copenhagen, 1969; now prima ballerina, artistic adviser Ballet Nacional de Cuba, Ballerina, Giselle, Swan Lake, Princess Aurora, Romeo and Juliet, Pas de Quatre, Les Sylphides, Apollo, Jardin aux Lilas, Gala Performance, Peter and the Wolf, On Stage, Theme and Variations, Billy the Kid, Fall River Legend, Undertow, Bluebeard, Coppelia, La Fille MalGardee, Three Cornered Hat, Carmen, Nos Veremos Ayer Noche, Margarita, others; choreographes Ensayo Sinfonica y Lydia, El Pillete, El Circo, others with Ballet Alicia Alonso; partners include premier danseurs, Anton Dolin, Andre Eglevsky, Igor Youskevitch. Named one of ten outstanding women Mademoiselle Mag., 1946; Dance Mag. award as one of 15 outstanding women in world, 1958; granted Medal of Carlos Manuel de Cespedes by Cuban govt. Home: Calzada 510 Havana Cuba Office: care Betty A Ferrell 525 S Gramercy Pl Los Angeles CA 90005

ALOU, MATTY, center fielder for Pitts. Pirates Profl. Baseball Team. Address: care Forbes Field Bouquet St S Pittsburgh PA 15213*

ALPENFELS, ETHEL J., educator, anthropologist; b. Denver, Aug. 21, 1907; d. Julius Henry William and Jennie Annette (Johnson) Alpenfels; student U. Wash.; field work among Am. Indians, fellow Ency. Britannica U. Chgo.; Ph.D., Colo. State Coll. Tchr. anthropology pub. high schs., Chgo.; mem. faculty Beloit Coll., U. Wis. in Milw.; tchr., dir. research on racial origins of Europeans, U. Innsbruck (Austria), summer 1955, now prof. ednl. anthropology, N.Y. U., also dir. grad. workshops in anthropology; distinguished prof. Danfort Found., summmer 1968; Jennings scholar, spring 1968; chmn. faculty and student affairs, trustee Cazenovia Coll. Rockefeller grantee. Named Woman of the Year, also Tchr. of Year, Am. Women's Assn., 1956, Women of the Year, Nat. Assn. Negro Women, 1955; recipient medal of eminence for teaching, Nat. Pan-Hellenic Soc., 1958, Mankind award Alpha Kappa Delta, 1964; Apfenfels award established by Montclair (N.J.) State Coll., 1964; recipient Judy award 1959, Dorothy Hutchinson award Child Welfare League Am., 1964, Colo. Silver Dollar award Albert Einstein Med. Center, Phila., 1965, Distinguished Service to Humanity award Hebrew Home and Hosp. for Chronic Sick, 1965. Author: Sense and Nonsense about Race, 1965; also numerous articles. Home: Pine Cobble Roxbury CT 06783 Office: 239 Greene St New York City NY 10003

ALPENFELTS, HERSCHELL, Jr., chemist, educator; b. Chicago, 1928; B.S. in Physics, Yale, 1950; Ph.D. in Chemistry, Harvard, 1956; m. Sally Ann Jones, July 5, 1957; children--Kenneth J., Nancy A. Chemist, Acme Chem. Co., Blue Island, Ill., 1950-51; director of Research Lab., Indsl. Chemicals Corp., Cambridge, Mass., 1956-60; project coordinator environmental sect. Steinmetz Assos., Chgo., 1960-61; v.p. for research Bauer Bros. Chem. Co., Inc., Memphis, 1961-64; asst. prof. chemistry Washington U., St. Louis, 1964-66, asso. prof., 1966-70, prof., 1970--, head of chemistry dept., 1970-71. Vis. prof. So. Ill. U., summer 1967, U. of Ore., 1969. Scoutmaster, Boy Scouts America, University City, Mo., 1968-70. Bd. dirs. Rest Haven Home for Elderly, 1960-61; trustee of the Lutheran Hosp., 1965-71. Served from lt. to capt., AUS, 1951-53. Mem. Am. Chem. Soc., Sci. Research Soc. Am. (chpt. treas. 1967), Am. Assn. Chemistry Tchrs., Am. Assn. U. Profs., Wildlife Soc., American Institute Chemists, Ecological Soc. Am. (chpt. sec.), Sigma Xi. Author: (with others) Basic Inorganic Chemistry, 1971. Contbr. articles to profl. jours., encys., also chpts. to books. Home: Fairfax Apts 7291 Windermere Dr University City MO 63105 Office: Dept Chemistry Washington University St Louis MO 63130

ALPENMEIR, GEORGE KEITH mfg. exec.; b. Lima, O., Apr. 1, 1932; B.S., U. San Francisco, 1954; M.S., Stanford University, 1956; m. Rosemarie Lois Brown, May 15, 1955; 1 son, Anthony Robinson. Sales rep. Ames-Brockton Fabricated Products, Akron, O., 1956-58, sales mgr. Coshocton, Ohio, 1959-61, gen. manager plant, 1961-68, v.p. sales, 1968--. Instr. bus. Coshocton Jr. College, 1968-69. Mem. Coshocton C. of C. (vice president 1967-68, pres. 1969-70), English Speaking Union, Coshocton Sertoma Club, Nat. Assn. Mfrs., Sales Executives Institute, Phi Beta Kappa, Sigma Chi, Phi Mu. Democrat. Mem. Christian Ch. (lay reader). Mason (32, Shriner). Clubs: Coshocton Country, Coshocton City, Running Deer Country. Home: 2d Av Coshocton OH Office: 3d Av Coshocton OH

ALPERN, MATHEW, educator; b. Akron, O., Sept. 22, 1920; s. Aaron Harry and Goldie (Ray) A.; student U. Akron, 1937-38, 42, No. Ill. Coll. Optometry, 1938-41; B.M.E., U. Fla., 1946; Ph.D., Ohio State U., 1950; m. Rebecca Ann Elsner, Aug. 17, 1951; children—Bowen Lewis, Goldie Ann, Barbara Rachel, Aaron Harry. Asst. prof. optometry Pacific U., 1951-55; instr. ophthalmology U. Mich., 1955-56, asst. prof. physiol. optics Med. Sch., also asst. prof. psychology Coll. Lit., Scis. and Arts, 1956-58, asso. prof. physiol. optics, also asso. prof. psychology, 1958-63, prof. physiol. optics dept. ophthalmology and physiology, also prof. psychology, 1963—. NIH spl. fellow, physiol. lab. U. Cambridge (Eng.), 1961-62; vis. prof. psychobiology Fla. State U., 1968-69; vis. scientist study sect. NIH dir. research grants, Bethesda, Md., 1970—; mem. Am. Com. on Optics and Visual Physiology, 1969—. Fellow Optical Soc. Am.; mem. Am. Physiol. Soc., Am. Psychol. Assn., Assn. Research Opthalmology, Biophys. Soc. Jewish religion. Author: (with others) Sensory Processes, 1966. Contbr. profl. jours. Home: 3545 Woodland Rd Ann Arbor MI 48104

ALPEROVITZ, GAR, author; b. Racine, Wis., May 5, 1936; s. Julius and Emily (Bensman) A.; B.S. in History, U. Wis., 1958; M.A. in Econs., U. Cal. at Berkeley, 1960; Ph.D. in Polit. Economy, U. Cambridge (Eng.), 1964; m. Guillemette Caron, Nov. 6, 1966; children—Kari Fai, David Joseph. Congl. asst., 1961-62; mem. U.S. Senate staff, 1964-65; spl. asst. State Dept., 1965- 66; fellow King's Coll., Cambridge (Eng.) U., 1964-68, Inst. Politics Harvard, 1965-68, Inst. Policy Studies, 1968—; co-dir. Cambridge (Mass.) Inst., 1968—. Author: Atomic Diplomacy: Hiroshima and Potsdam, 1965; Cold War Essays, 1970; also articles. Home: 17 Hubbard Av Cambridge MA 02140

ALPERT, DANIEL, univ. dean, physicist; b. Hartford, Conn., Apr. 10, 1917; s. Elias and Dora (Prechepa) A.; B.S. Trinity Coll., Hartford, 1937, D.Sc. (hon.), 1957; Ph.D. Stanford, 1942; m. Natalie L. Boyle, Jan. 12, 1942; children—Amy Vincell, Laura Jane. Teaching, research asst. Stanford, 1939-41; research physicist Westinghouse Research Lab., Pitts., 1942-50, mgr. physics dept., 1950-55, asso. dir., 1955-57; prof. physics U. Ill. at Urbana, 1957—, dir. Coordinated Sci. Lab., 1959-65, dean Grad. Coll., 1965—. Mem. Ill. Sci. Adv. Council. Mem. Wilkins Twp. Sch. Bd., 1946-56, Allegheny County Sch. Bd., 1956-57, Def. Sci. Bd., 1963—. Trustee Trinity Coll., Inst. Def. Analyses, Argonne Univs. Assn. Recipient Newcomb Cleveland award A.A.A.S., 1954. Mem. Am. Phys. Soc., A.A.A.S., Phi Beta Kappa, Sigma Xi. Author articles ultrahigh vacuum tech., surface physics, computer based edn. Home: 402 W Pennsylvania Av Urbana IL 61801

ALPERT, HARRY, sociologist, univ. dean; b. N.Y.C., Oct. 12, 1912; s. Morris and Mary (Levine) A.; A.B., Coll. City N.Y., 1932; Certificat de Sociologie U. Bordeaux (France), 1933; M.A., Columbia, 1935, Ph.D., 1938; student U. Paris, 1932, U. Chgo., 1940-41; m. Anitra Fink, June 15, 1936; children—Spencer Ward, Geoffrey Philip. Instr., asst. prof. sociology Coll. City N.Y., 1933-47; research cons. bur. applied social research Columbia, 1946-48; professorial lectr., adj. prof. sociology Am. U., 1947, 1950-58; prof. sociology Yale, 1947, U. Washington, 1955; asso. prof. sociology, chmn. dept. anthropology and sociology Queens Coll., 1948-50; research scientist social psychiatry Cornell U. Med. Coll., 1951-56; dean Grad. Sch., prof. sociology U. Ore., 1958-64, dean of faculties, prof. sociology, 1964—; dir. dept. social scis. UNESCO, 1967-70. Public opinion analyst O.W.I., 1943-44; pub. opinion, rationing statistics analyst OPA, 1944-45; analytical statistician Bur. Budget, 1945-48, 50-53; cons. USAF, research and devel. bd. Dept. Def., 1948-50, program dir. social sci. research NSF 1953-58; fellow Center for Advanced Study in Behavioral Scis., 1963-64. Fellow A.A.A.S., Am. Statis. Assn., Am. Sociol. Assn. (v.p. 1958); mem. Pacific Sociol. Assn. (pres. 1962-63), Am. Assn. Pub. Opinion Research (pres. 1955-56), Am. Anthrop. Assn., Population Assn. Am., Sociol. Research Assn. (pres. 1961), World Assn. Pub. Opinion Research, Washington Statis. Soc. (pres. 1954-55), Soc. Psychol. Study Social Issues. Author: Emile Durkheim and His Sociology, 1939 (Spanish edit. 1945). Editor Am. Sociol. Rev., 1960-62. Home: 1766 Alder St Eugene OR 97401

ALPERT, HERB, record co. exec., musician; b. Los Angeles, Mar. 31, 1935; s. Louis and Tillie (Goldberg) A.; student U. So. Cal.; m. Sharon Mae Lubin, Aug. 5, 1956 (div.); children— Dore, Eden. Leader, trumpeter, arranger mus. group Tijuana Brass, 1962—; co-owner A & M Record Co., 1962—. Served with AUS, 1955-57. Named one of Top Artists on Campus (album sales), 1968. Home: Malibu CA 90265

ALPERT, HOLLIS, writer; b. Herkimer, N.Y., Sept. 24, 1916; s. Abram and Myra (Carroll) A.; student New Sch. Social Research, 1946-47, Book reviewer Sat. Review, N.Y. Times, others, 1947-59; film critic Sat. Review, 1950—, Woman's Day, 1953-60; asso. fiction editor New Yorker, 1950-56; contbg. editor Woman's Day, 1956-69, Sat. Rev., 1959—. Past dir. Edward MacDowell Assn. Served to 1st lt. AUS, 1942-46. Recipient Critic's award Screen Director's Guild Am., 1957. Author: The Summer Lovers, 1958; Some Other Time, 1960; The Dreams and the Dreamers, 1962; For Immediate Release, 1963; The Barrymores, published in 1964; The Claimant, 1968; The People Eaters, 1971; also numerous short stories in New Yorker, Harper's Town and Country, Cosmopolitan, Harper's Bazaar. Address: 166 E 61st St New York City NY 10021

ALPERT, NORMAN ROLAND, educator; b. Stamford, Conn., July 28, 1922; A.B., Wesleyan U., 1943; Ph.D. in Physiology, Columbia, 1951; married. Asst. in physiology Columbia, 1948-51, instr., 1951-53; asst. prof. Coll. Medicine, U. Ill., 1953-58, asso. prof., 1958-68; prof., chmn. dept. physiology and biophysics U. Vt., Burlington, 1968—. Served to 1st. lt. AUS, 1944-46. Mem. Am. Soc. Exptl. Biology, N.Y. Acad. Sci., Am. Physiol. Soc., Am. Biophys. Soc., Harvey Soc., Am. Soc. Gen. Physiology. Office: Coll Medicine U Vt Burlington VT 05401*

ALPERT, WARREN, corp. exec.; b. Boston, Dec. 2, 1920; s. Goodman and Tena (Horowitz) A.; B.S., Boston U., 1942; M.B.A., Harvard, 1947. Mgmt. trainee Standard Oil Co. of Cal., 1947-48; financial specialist The Cal. Oil Co., 1948-52; pres. Warren Petroleum Co., 1952-54; pres., chmn. bd. Warren Equities, Inc., 1954—; pres., chmn. Ritz Tower Hotel, Warren Petroleum Corp., Warren Terminals Corp., Alwar Equities, Inc., Potter Fuel Co., Kenyon Oil Co., Inc., The Grove Corp. Petroleum Marketers, Inc., Cazeault Oil Corp., Puritan Oil Co., Inc., Burns Realty Co., Barron Corp., Drake Petroleum Co., Inc., Drake Fuel Corp.; chmn. Nat. Propane Corp., Garden City, N.Y., 1968; trustee Alcott Mgmt. Co. Asst. sec. of state U.S. AID, 1968. Mem. of U.S. Com. for UN, 1958; exec. com. Small Bus. Adminstrn., 1958; mem. Nat. Bd. Field Advisers, 1957. Trustee Boston U. Served with Signal Intelligence, AUS, 1943-45. Mem. Young Presidents Orgn. Clubs: Harvard Business School (exec. com., dir., bd. govs., pres. 1960-61), Friars (N.Y.C.); Metacomet Country (Providence). Home: 465 Park Av New York City NY 10022 Office: Warren Equities Inc 375 Park Av New York City NY 10022

ALSAKER, ELWOOD CECIL, meat packer; b. Rosholt, S.D., Oct. 31, 1924; s. Conrad Peter and Edla Victoria (Wass) A.; B.B.A., U. Minn., 1948; m. Virginia Cumming, Sept. 8, 1947 (dec.). With George a Hormel & Co., Austin, Minn., 1948—, asst. treas., 1962-69, treas., 1969—, dir., 1969—; dir. 1st Nat. bank of Austin. Dir. Austin YMCA; sec.-treas. Hormel Found., 1970—, dir., 1970—. Served with AUS, 1944-46. Mem. Austin C. of C. (dir.). Elk. Club: Austin Country (dir.). Patentee various games. Home: 800 1st Dr NW Austin MN 55912 Office: 501 NE 16th Av Austin MN 55912

ALSCHULER, JACOB EDWARD, lawyer; b. Aurora, Ill., July 9, 1902; s. Benjamin Philip and Lillian (Reinheimer) A.; A.B., U. Wis., 1923; J.D., U. Chgo., 1926; m. Carolyn Strauss, Jan. 11, 1927; children—Rosalie A. (Mrs. Bernard Goldstein), Benjamin Philip, George Arthur. Admitted to Ill. bar, 1926, since practiced in Aurora; partner Alschuler, Putnam, McWethy, Weiss & Weiler and predecessor firms, 1926—. Mem. Ill. Tchrs. Coll. Bd., 1935-43. Chmn. Kane County Democratic Central Com., 1932-42. Mem. Am., Ill., Kane County (past pres.) bar assns., Am. Judicature Soc., Artus, Zeta Beta Tau (past nat. v.p.). Jewish religion. Mason; mem. B'nai B'rith,

Elk, Moose. Clubs: Aurora Country, Union League (Aurora). Home: 143 LeGrande Blvd Aurora IL 60506 Office: 32 Water St Aurora IL 60507

ALSCHULER, SAM, lawyer; b. Aurora, Ill., June 16, 1913; s. Benjamin P. and Lillian (Reinheimer) A.; A.B., U. Wis., 1933; J.D., U. Chgo., 1935; m. Winifred King, Feb. 8, 1939; children-Albert W., Therese A. (Mrs. Richard N. Hale). Admitted to Ill. bar, 1935, since practiced in Aurora; partner Alschuler, Putnam, McWethy, Weiss & Weiler, 1935—. Dir. Aurora Bleachery, Inc. Mem. Aurora Planning Commn., 1954—; chmn. United Fund, 1966; vice chmn., dir. Kane County Council for Econ. Opportunity, 1966- 69. Corp. counsel City of Aurora, 1961-65. Pres., trustee Aurora chpt., pres., bd. dirs. Ill. Assn. Crippled, 1948-63; v.p., bd. dirs. United Community Services Aurora, 1959-68; governing mem., bd. dirs. Aurora Hosp. Assn., 1940—. Served with AUS, 1944-45. Mem. Am., Ill., Kane County bar assns., Am. Judicature Soc., Greater Aurora C. of C. (past pres., dir.), Sigma Delta Chi, Zeta Beta Tau. Democrat. Elk, Moose, Rotarian. Club: Union League. Home: 119 S Buell Av Aurora IL 60506 Office: 32 Water St Aurora IL 60504

ALSDORF, JAMES REED, machinery mfr.; b. Mt. Vernon, O., July 8, 1909; s. Saurin W. and Helen S. (Patterson) A.; B.A., Wesleyan U., 1931; LL.B., Bklyn. Law Sch., 1938; m. Norma L. Lockwood, June 26, 1943; children—Susan Reed, Stephen Brooks. Tax advisor Central Hanover Bank, N.Y.C., 1931-39; admitted to N.Y. bar, 1939; staff atty. Graflex, Inc., Rochester, N.Y., 1939-40; staff atty. Garlock, Inc., Rochester, 1940-60, sec., counsel, 1960-69, v.p., sec., gen. counsel, 1969—; dir. Ortman Miller Machine Co., Inc., Stemco Mfg. Co., Inc., Fluid Power, Ltd., Garlock de Mexico, S.A. Trustee Eisenhower Coll. Served as 1st lt. AUS, 1942-45. Decorated Bronze Star. Mem. N.Y., Fed. bar assns., Am. Soc. Corporate Secs., Am. Judicature Soc., Alpha Delta Phi, Phi Delta Phi. Presbyn. (moderator Geneva Presbytery). Club: University (Rochester). Home: 125 Jackson St Palmyra NY 14522 Office: Midtown Tower Rochester NY 14604

ALSDORF, JAMES WILLIAM, mfg. exec.; b. Chicago, Aug. 16, 1913; s. Anthony James and Camilie (Lederer) A.; student Wharton Sch. Finance and Commerce, U. Pa., 1932- 34; m. Barbara Brach, Aug. 17, 1935 (div. Jan 2, 1950); children—Gregg, Lynne, Jeffery, James; m. 2d, Marilynn Markham, 1952. Pres, and dir. A.J. Alsdorf Corp., Chgo., exporters and internat. mchts., Condor Motors, Inc.; pres., treas., dir. Cory Corp., mfrs., Chgo., also officer and dir. subsidiary cos. and divs.; pres., dir. Mitchell Mfg. Co., & subsidiaries, Chgo., Ill.; treas., dir. of Cory Sales Corp., Chgo., Cory Coffee Service Plan, Inc.; chmn. bd. Flavor- Seal Corp., Chgo.; pres., dir. Cory AG, Zurich, Switzerland; treas., dir. Cory Corp. (Can.) Ltd., Toronto, Ont.; dir. Unarco Industries, Incorporated, L.A. Darling Co., NK Cory AB, Stockholm, Sweden. Mem. nat. com. U. Art Mus., U. Cal. at Berkeley; adv. council U.Art Gallery, U. Notre Dame; mem. of Gov. Ill.'s Com. Trade Expansion. Pres., dir. Alsdorf Found., Chgo.; bd. dirs. World Wildlife Fund, Washington; bd. govs. Menninger Found. of Topeka, Kan.; mem. Brand Wames Found., v.p., trustee, life gov., exec. com., Art Inst. Chgo. Dir., v.p., Sarah Siddons Soc., Chgo.: Juvenile Protective Assn. of Chgo. Benefactor, John Herron Art Inst. Art Assn., Indpls., Ravinia Festival Assn. Mem. art adv. com. McCormick Pl. Art Gallery, Chgo., subscribing mem. Am. Craftsmen's Council, N.Y.C.; vis. com. div. humanities U. Chgo. Mem. Chgo. Hort. Soc., Oriental Ceremics Soc., Am. Assn. Mus.'s Archaeol Inst. Am., Nat. Geog. Soc., Newcomen Soc. N.Am., Nat. Housewares Mfrs. Assn. Chgo. (pres. 1949-51; dir., mem. exec. com.), Gen. Alumni Bd. U. Pa. Northwestern U. Assos., Ordre des Compagnons du Beaujolais, Chgo. Pres.'s Orgn., Newberry Library Association, Chgo. Hist. Soc. (life, gov.), Chinese Art Soc. Am. Inc., Sigma Chi. Episcopalian. Clubs: Execs., The Arts, University of Pa. (past dir.), Internat. Trade (Chgo.); Sunset Ridge Country (Northbrook, Ill.); Post and Paddock (dir., exec. com.) (Arlington Heights, Ill.); Tavern, Key, Internat. (Chgo.). Home: 301 Woodley Rd Winnetka IL 60093 Office: 3200 W Peterson Av Chicago IL 60645

ALSEVER, JOHN B., physician; born in Syracuse, N.Y., Nov. 24, 1908; s. William Dewey and Clara (Bellows) A.; A.B., Syracuse U., 1930; M.D., Harvard, 1934; m. Janet N. Gilbert, Aug. 27, 1938; children—John Dewey, Robert Nichols, Margery Bradner. Intern and asst. resident, Peter Bent Brigham Hosp., 1935-37; practice internal med., Syracuse, N.Y., 1937-42; instr. coll. med., Syracuse U., 1937-42; dir. transfusion service, Syracuse U. Med. Center Hosps, 1940-42; tech. dir. blood plasma sect., med. div., O.C.D., 1942-44, development and control civilian blood plasma reserves, U.S., establishing blood banks in 180 hosps.; dir. Civilian Blood Donor Serv., Am. Nat. Red Cross, 1944-46, development state and local blood and blood derivatives programs, distbn. surplus Army-Navy blood plasma. Served Med. O.R.C., U.S. Army, 1935-42; served as surgeon, U.S. Pub. Health Service, 1942-44, sr. surg., 1946-49, med. dir. since 1949, dir. training and profl. standards, hosp. div., 1946-49, asst. chief, 1949-51; dir. blood program Health and Spl. Weapons Defense Div., Fed. Civil Defense Adminstrn., 1951-53, deputy director, 1953-54, chief hygiene of the aging, Chronic Disease program USPHS, 1954-55, med. dir., 1949-55; med. dir. Blood Services, Scottsdale, Ariz., 1955-68, v.p. med. affairs, 1968—; med. dir. Plasma Services, 1968—, BSP Ins. Co., Scottsdale, 1962—. Diplomate Am. Bd. Internal Med. Fellow A.C.P.; mem. American, Cal., South Central assns. blood banks, Am. Soc. Clin. Pathologists, Ariz., Phoenix pathology socs., Delta Kappa Epsilon, Nu Sigma Nu, Sigma Xi. Republican. Episcopalian. Co-author: Blood Transfusion (textbook), 1948; author sci. articles profl. jours. Home: 3518 N 25th Pl Phoenix AZ 85016 Office: 6401 E Thomas Rd PO Box 1030 Scottsdale AZ 85252 ☆

ALSOP, JOSEPH WRIGHT, newspaperman, author; b. Avon, Conn., Oct. 11, 1910; Wright and Corinne Douglas (Robinson) A.; grad. Groton Sch., 1928; A.B., Harvard, 1932; m. Mrs. Susan Mary Jay Patten, February 16, 1961. Mem. N.Y. Herald Tribune staff, N.Y.C., 1932-35, Washington, 1936-37; with Robert E. Kintner, author of syndicated column on politics, "The Capital Parade", for North Am. Newspaper Alliance, 1937-40; commd. lt., U.S. Navy, 1940; sent to India from Navy, joined Am. Volunteer Air Force as aide to Gen. Chennault; captured by Japanese at Hong Kong and held prisoner until June 1942, when was exchanged and returned to U.S.; became chief of Lend Lease Mission to China at Chunking, Dec. 1942; capt. 14th Air Force and mem. staff of Gen. Chennault, 1943-45. Decorated Legion of Merit, Chinese Cloud Banner. Clubs: Links (N.Y.C.); Turf (London); Travellers' (Paris, France); Metropolitan (Washington). Author: The 168 Days (with Turner Catledge), 1938; Men Around the President (with Robert E. Kintner), 1938; American White Paper (with Robert E. Kintner), 1940; (with Steward Alsop) We Accuse, 1955; The Reporter's Trade, 1958; From the Silent Earth, 1964. Author (with brother, Stewart J. O. Alsop) column Matter of Fact, syndicated through N.Y. Herald Tribune Syndicate, 1945-58, sole author, through Los Angeles Times Syndicate, 1964—. Contbr. Sat. Eve. Post, Life, Atlantic Monthly, New Yorker. Address: 2720 Dumbarton Av Washington DC 20007

ALSOP, STEWART JOHONNOT OLIVER, mag. columnist; b. Avon, Conn., May 7, 1914; s. Joseph Wright and Corrine Douglas (Robinson) A.; grad. Groton Sch., 1932; A.B., Yale, 1936; m. Patrica Hankey, Oct. 1944; children—Joseph Wright, Ian Alexander Douglas, Elizabeth Winthrop, Stewart Johonnot Oliver, Richard Nicholas, Andrew Christian. Began as editor Doubleday Doran, N.Y.C.; after World War II, partner with brother, Joseph, to write column, Matter of Fact, for N.Y. Herald Tribune Syndicate, 1945-58; nat. affairs contbg. editor Sat. Eve. Post, 1958-62, Washington editor, 1962-68; columnist Newsweek mag. 1968—. Enlisted in Kings Royal Rifle Corps, British Army, 1942; inf. platoon comdr. Italy, 1943; transferred to Am. Army as parachutist OSS, 1944; parachuted into France to join Maquis shortly after D-Day; resigned commn., 1945. Decorated Croix de Guerre with palm (France); mentioned in dispatches. Clubs: River (N.Y.C.); Metropolitan (Washington). Contbr. articles to Sat. Eve. Post, Life, Atlantic Monthly mags. Author: (with Thomas Braden) Sub Rosa, 1945; (with Joseph Alsop) We Accuse, 1955; (with Joseph Alsop) The Reporter's Trade; Nixon and Rockefeller, 1960; The Center, 1968. Home: 3520 Springland Lane Washington DC 20008 Office: 1750 Pennsylvania Av Washington DC 20006

AL-SOWAYEL, IBRAHIM, diplomat of Saudi Arabia; b. Unayzah, Najd, Saudi Arabia, Aug. 31, 1916; s. Abdallah and Hessah Al-S.; grad. Saudi Inst., Mecca. 1936; Cairo (Egypt) U., 1940; m. Ebitissam Lutfiyah, May 11, 1944; three sons and three daughters. Engaged as teacher of Arabic lit. Sch. Prep. Student Mission Abroad, Mecca, 1942; 1st sec. Saudi Arabian legation, Cairo, 1943-52; charge d'affaires, Beirut, Lebanon, 1952; counselor Ministry Fgn. Affairs, 1954- 56, acting dep. fgn. minister, 1956-57; 1st Saudi Arabian ambassador to Iraq, 1957-60; fgn. minister Saudi Arabia, 1960-62; mem. legal com. Council Ministers, 1962; minister agr., 1962-64; ambassador to U.S., 1964—. Del. 11th session Arab League, Cairo, 1949; rep. Saudi Arabia Fgn. Ministers Conf., Baghdad, Iraq, 1961; head Saudi Arabia delegation Conf. Non- Aligned Countries, Belgrade, Yugoslavia, 1961; head polit. br. Royal Diwan, 1962; spl. adviser to king, 1962. Decorated Order Independence (Libya); Order Star (Nat. China); Order Nile (Egypt); Order Republic (UAR); Order Crown (Iraq); Order Lebanon. Home: 2800 Woodland Dr NW Washington DC 20008 Office: 1520 18th St NW Washington DC 20036

ALSPACH, PHILIP HALLIDAY, mfg. co. exec.; b. Buffalo, Apr. 19, 1923; s. Walter L. and Jean E. (Halliday) A.; B.Engring. in Mech. Engring., Tulane U., 1944; m. Jean Edwards, Dec. 20, 1947; children—Philip Clough, Bruce Edwards, David Christopher. With Gen. Electric Co., 1945-64, mgr. indsl. electronics div. planning, 1961-64; v.p., gen. mgr. constrn. machinery div. Allis Chalmers Mfg. Co., Milw., 1964-68; exec. v.p., dir., mem. exec. com. Jeffrey Galion, Inc., 1968-69; sr. v.p. I.T.E. Imperial Corp., Phila., 1969—; dir. Winnebago Industries, Inc. Registered profl. engr. Mass., Wis., La. Mem. Soc. Automotive Engrs. (sr.), I.E.E.E., Soc. Mfg. Engrs., Am. Mgmt. Assn. Clubs: Canadian (N.Y.C.); Mohawk (Schenectady, N.Y.). Author papers in field. Home: 825 Andorra Rd Lafayette Hill PA 19444 Office: 1900 Hamilton St Philadelphia PA 19130

ALSPACH, RUSSELL KING, former army officer, educator; b. Phila., Feb. 22, 1901; s. Charles Bennett and Elizabeth (Varwig) A.; B.A., U. Pa., 1924, M.A., 1931, Ph.D., 1932; m. Sara Catharine Campion, May 10, 1924; children—Ann Jane (Mrs. James Fitzcharles), Sally Campion (Mrs. Philip Anderson). Appraisal engr., 1918-20; mem. English dept. U. Pa., 1924-42, 45-47; commd. lt. col. U.S. Army, 1947, advanced to brig. gen.; ret. 1965; prof. English, U.S. Mil. Acad., 1947-65, head dept., 1961-65; lectr. English, U. Mass., 1965-66, prof. English, 1966—, head dept. English, 1967-69. Vis. prof. Grad. Sch. U. Pa., 1962-63. Served to lt. comdr. USNR, 1942-45. Mem. Modern Lang. Assn., Am. Folklore Soc. (council), Nat. Council Tchrs. English, English Inst., Coll. Conf. Communication. Club: The Army-Navy Country (Washington). Author: Poetry of the Celtic Renaissance, 1932; Irish Poetry from the English Invasion to 1798, rev. edit., 1959. Co- editor: The Variorum Edition of the Poetry of W. B. Yeats, 1957; editor: The Variorum Edition of the Plays of W.B. Yeats, 1965; Wade's Bibliography of Yeats, rev. edit., 1968; asst. editor Winston Dictionary, 1926-28, 37-39. Contbr. articles profl. jours. Address: Dept English U Mass Amherst MA 01002

ALSPAUGH, JOHN FRANK, state indsl. devel. exec.; b. Winston-Salem, N.C., Feb. 23, 1921; s. William T. and Elizabeth (Hester) A.; B.S., U. N.C., 1947; m. Frances Rousseau, Mar. 1, 1952; childrenJohn F., Nancy R., David A. With indsl. relations dept. Western Electric Co., Winston-Salem, 1947-48; 48; accounting machine sales rep. Nat. Cash Register Co., Winston-Salem, 1948-54; mgr. indsl. dept. Winston-Salem C. of C., 1954-60; exec. dir. Va. Peninsula Indsl. Com. and Peninsula Ports Authority of Va., Newport News, 1960-67; dir. gov.'s Div. Indsl. Devel., Commonwealth Va., Richmond, 1967—. Served to capt. USMCR, 1943-46. Mem. Am. (bd. dirs. 1969—), So. (bd. dirs. 1961, 63) indsl. devel. councils, Nat., So. assns. state devel. agys. Democrat. Methodist. Clubs: Golden Horseshoe (Williamsburg, Va.), Downtown (Richmond, Va.). Home: 208 Santa Clara Dr Richmond, VA 23229. Office: State Office Bldg Richmond, VA 23219

ALSTADT, WILLIAM ROBERT, dentist; b. Thebes, Ill., Oct. 7, 1916; s. Henry Lee and Gradie (Cole) A.; student Ark. State Coll., 1933-34; D.D.S., Washington U., 1938, Carnegie postgrad. fellow orthodontics, 1938-39; M.S.D. and D.D.S. (hon.), Nihon U. Sch. Dentistry, Tokyo, Japan; D.M.D. (hon.), Nippon Dental College, Tokyo; D.Sc. (hon.), Kansas City U.; m. Harriet Marie Smith, September 3, 1938 (dec. Feb. 1962); children—Richard Lee, Mary Lynn, Thomas Henry, m. 2d, Laura May Goodness, Aug. 31, 1962. Practice of orthodontia, Little Rock, 1939—; vis. lectr. U. Tenn. Sch. Dentistry; vis. prof. Osaka Dental Coll., Tokyo Dental College; cons. Army and Navy Hosp., Hot Springs, 1947-55; mem. Denver Orthodontic Seminar, 1946-53; cons. Ark., Welfare Dept., Ark. Ednl. TV Commn. Mem. Ark. bd. dental examiners, 1946-50, pres. 1949-50. Mem Little Rock Civil Service Commn., 1949—, chmn., 1955-57, 65-67; ex-chmn. Safety Council; mem. Ark. Civil Def. Bd., 1950-54, Ark. Bd. Health, 1958-62, pres., 1959- 60, Jr. Dep. Sheriffs. Hon. lectr. Tokyo Dental Coll.; hon. prof. Nihon U. Sch. Dentistry. Served to lt. col., AUS, World War II. Recipient Alumni citation Washington University St. Louis; 1st diploma award Buenos Aires U. Dental Sch., 1968. Named hon. col., Miss., Kentucky, Tennessee, hon. adm., Neb., commodore, Okla., hon. traveller by Gov. Ark. Diplomate Am. Bd. Orthodontics. Fellow International (president of the U.S.A. section 1968-69), American colleges of dentists; mem. American Dental Association (pres. 1957-58, trustee), Arkansas Dental Association (past chairman legislative council), Pierre Fauchard Acad., Fedn. Dentaire Internationale, United Comml. Travelers, Little Rock, North Little Rock chambers commerce, A.A.A.S., Am. Soc. Dentistry for Children, Acad. Internat. Dentistry, Community Concert Assn. (v.p.), Little Rock Civic Music Assn. (past exec. v.p.), Fifty for Future, Inc., Little Rock C. of C. (dir.); honorary mem. Japan, Philippine, Australian, Mexican dental assns., Soc. Francaise D'Orthopedic Dento-Faciale, Pan Am Med. Association (honorary chairman dental section 1967—), Thailand Dental Assn. (hon.), Circulo Argentino de Odontologia (hon.), Omicron Kappa Upsilon. Methodist. Mason (32, Shriner). Clubs: Civitan (past pres.), Hi-12 (past pres.), Little Rock Country, (Little Rock), Top of the Rock, North Hills Country. Asso. editor Orthodontic Directory of World. Adviser to Funk & Wagnall's Ency., 1958—. Contbr. articles to profl. jours. Home: 11 Edgehill St Little Rock AR 72207 Office: 121 E 4th at Scott Little Rock AR 72201

ALSTON, ANGUS SORENSEN, telephone co. exec.; b. Salt Lake City, Dec. 22, 1914; s. Clinton A. and Martha Helen (Sorensen) A.; student Colo. Coll., 1933-36; LL.D., So. Colo. State Coll., 1968; m. Fanny Christian, July 1, 1938 (dec. Sept. 1968); children—Clinton Angus, Joan Elizabeth; m. 2d, Darlene Norder, Sept. 27, 1969; step-children—Bonnie Sue Norder, Donna Lee Norder (Mrs. Korchun). With Mountain Tel. & Tel. Co., 1936-61, v.p., Colo., 1954-58, v.p. co. personnel, 1958-61; v.p., gen. mgr. Bell Telephone Co. Pa., Pitts., 1962-64; exec. v.p. Am. Tel. & Tel. Co., 1967-70; pres. Southwestern Bell Telephone Co., 1970—; dir. Pepsico., Inc., Gen. Steel Industries, Inc., Gen. Am. Life Ins. Co., Civic Center Redevel. Corp., First Nat. Bank, St. Louis, St. Louis Union Trust Co. Bd. dirs. Nat. Safety Council, St. Louis and St. Louis County YMCA, St. Louis Area council Boy Scouts Am., Civic Progress, Mo. Pub. Expenditure Survey, United Fund, Arts and Edn. Council, Nat. Indsl. Pollution Council; charter trustee Colo. Coll.; trustee Washington U.; adv. trustee St. Louis Ednl. TV Commn. Mem. U.S., St. Louis chambers commerce, Phi Gamma Delta. Clubs: Baltusrol Golf (Springfield, N.J.); Old Warson Country; St. Louis; Bogey; Racquet, Noonday. Home: 28 Williamsburg Rd Creve Coeur MO 63141 Office: 1010 Pine St St Louis MO 63101

ALSTON, ANNIE MAY, Joint Com. on Def. Prodn., Washington, 1969—. Chmn. com. librarian; b. Henning, Tenn., Nov. 26, 1917; d. Willis and Eddie May (Roy) Alston; student David Lipscomb Coll., Nashville, 1935-37; B.A., Harding Coll., Searcy, Ark., 1939; M.A., U. Chgo., 1952; B.S. in Library Sci., George Peabody Coll., 1943; M.A., Harding Grad. Sch. Religion, President's, 1967. Tchr., Gibson, Tenn., 1939-41; tchr.-librarian West Memphis High Sch., 1941-44; asst. prof. English, Harding Coll., Memphis 1944-47, librarian, 1947-62, librarian Sch. Bible and Religion, Harding Coll., 1962—. Exec. dir. Nat. Library Week for Ark., 1959. Mem..Am., Ark. (chmn. coll. library sect. 1957, pres. 1958), Southeastern, Am. Theol., Tenn. (chmn. coll. and univ. sect. 1966-67, sec. 1969-) library assns. Home: 1000 Cherry Rd MeOhis TN 38117

ALSTON, CHARLES HENRY, painter, sculptor, educator; b. Charlotte, N.C., Nov. 28, 1907; s. Primus Priss and Anna (Miller) A.; B.A., Columbia, 1929, M.A., 1931; m. Myra Adele Logan, Apr. 8, 1944. One man show include Oppenheimer Gallery, Chgo., 1950, John Heller Gallery, N.Y.C., 1953-57, Feingarten Gallery, N.Y.C., 1958, Dunbarton Gallery, Boston, 1960, Gallery Modern Art, N.Y.C., 1969; group exhbns. include Met. Mus. Art, Whitney Mus. Am. Art, Mus. Modern Art, Pa. Acad. Fine Arts, Corcoran Gallery, Washington, Balt. Mus. Art, High Mus., Atlanta; rep. permanent collects Met. Mus., Whitney Mus., Detroit Mus., U. Neb., Atlanta U., Howard U., Art Students League, N.Y.C., IBM Corp.; executed murals Golden State Mut. Life Ins. Co., Los Angeles, 1948, Harlem Hosp., N.Y.C., 1969, Mus. Natural History, N.Y.C., 1960, Coll. City N.Y., 1960, Abraham Lincoln High Sch., N.Y.C., 1961, Harriet Tubman Jr. High Sch., N.Y.C., 1962; illustrator Fortune mag., 1943—, New Yorker mag., 1937—, Red Book, 1936—, Colliers, 1935—, Madamoiselle, 1940—, others; artist-critic Mus. Modern Art, 1956-57, New Sch. Social Research, 1961-62; artist OWI, 1940-41; instr. Arts Students League, 1950—; asso. prof. Coll. City N.Y., 1970—. Mem. adv. bd. Nat. Council Arts, 1968-69; artist mem. N.Y.C. Art Commn., 1970—; mem. screening com. painting Inst.. Internat. Edn., 1968; co-dir. State Dept. and Mus. Modern Art art program Brussels World Fair, 1958. Bd. dirs. Nat. Soc. Mural Painters. Served with AUS, 1943-44. Grantee Inst. Arts and Letters, 1958; recipient Lowe award painting Joe and Emily Lowe Found., 1960; DeWitt Clinton Alumni award DeWitt Clinton Alumni Assn., 1961; Thomas B. Clakre award Nat. Acad. Design, 1971; Arthur Wesley Dow fellow Columbia, 1930; Rosenwald fellow, 1938-40; bronze heads of Dr. Martin Luther King commd. by Community Ch., N.Y.C., 1971. Address: 1270 Fifth Av New York City NY 10029

ALSTON, JAMES O., corp. exec.; b. 1922; married. With Dixie Bldg. Supply Inc., Tampa Fla., 1947-53; partner Walter Constrn. Co., 1953-55; pres., dir. Jim Walter Corp., 1955-70, vice chmn. bd., 1970—; pres. Jim Walter Homes, Inc., 1970—; dir. Celotex Corp., Marine Bank & Trust Co., First Fla. Bancorp. Address: 1500 N Dale Mabry Hwy Tampa, FL 33607

ALSTON, PHILIP HENRY, Jr., lawyer; b. Atlanta, Apr. 19, 1911; s. Philip Henry and May (Lewis) A.; A.B., U. Ga., 1932; LL.B., Emory U., 1934; student Harvard Law Sch., 1935; m. Elkin Goddard, June 27, 1939; children—Elkin Goddard (Mrs. James E. Cushman), John Goddard. Admitted to Ga. bar, 1934, since practiced in Atlanta; with firm Alston, Miller & Gaines, 1940—, now partner. Mem. Atlanta adv. bd. Citizens and So. Nat. Bank; dir. Printpack, Inc., Inc., So. Iron & Equipment Co., Nat. Data Corp. Trustee Fulton-DeKalb Hosp. Authority; sec. U. Ga. Found., Charles Loridans Found.; treas. Vasser Woolley Found. Served to lt. USNR, World War II. Fellow Am. Bar Found.; mem. Am. Law Inst., U. Ga. Alumni Soc. (pres. 1963-64), Atlanta C. of C. (bd. dirs.), Sigma Alpha Epsilon. Episcopalian (past sr. warden). Home: Office: Citizens & So Nat Bank Bldg Atlanta GA 30303

ALSTON, ROBERT A., banker; b. Thomasville, Ga., 1909; student U. Ga.; LL.B., Atlanta Law Sch., 1931; grad. Rutgers U. Grad. Sch. Banking, 1951; m. Caroline Hardin; children—Lansing, Victoria Elizabeth, Former sr. v.p. trust officer, dir. Hamilton Nat. Bank, Chatanooga, now cons.; pres., dir. Highland Co., Russ Realty Co.; dir. King Enterprises, Inc., Porter Warrer Industries, Inc., Atlas Paper Box Co., sec., trustee Caldsted Found., Inc.; asso. Fletcher Bright Co., real estate, Chattanooga. Mem. Bar Assn. Tenn., Ga., Chattanooga bar assns. Kiwanian. Home: Wood Nymph Trail Lookout Mountain TN 37350 Office: 1701 Market St Chattanooga TN 37401

ALSTON, WALLACE MCPHERSON, educator, clergyman; b. Decatur, Ga., July 16, 1906; s. Robert Augustus and Mary (McPherson) A.; A.B., Emory U., 1927, A.M., 1929; B.D., Columbia Theol. Sem., 1931; Th.M., Union Theol. Sem., 1937, Th.D., 1943; grad. work U. of Chicago, 1929, Coll. of the Bible, Lexington, Ky., 1933-35, Columbia, 1930 and 1947; D.D., hon., Hampden-Sydney Coll., 1939; LL.D., Davis and Elkins Colls., 1942, Emory U., 1954; m. Madelaine McNall Dunseith, May 27, 1931; children—Wallace McPherson & Mary McNall (Mrs. John L. Parish, Jr.). Ordained to the ministry of the Presbyterian Ch., 1931; prin. Avondale Estates (Ga.) High Sch., 1925-26, 1928-29: instr. New Testament Greek, Columbia Theol. Sem., 1929-31; pastor Rock Spring Ch., Atlanta, 1931-33, Maxwell St. Ch., Lexington, Ky., 1933-35; dir. young people's work, Presbyn. Ch. U.S., hdqrs. Richmond, Va., 1935-38; pastor 1st Ch., Charleston, W.Va., 1938-44, Druid Hills Ch., Atlanta, 1944-48; vice pres. and prof. philosophy, Agnes Scott Coll., Decatur, Ga. 1948, now pres., trustee. Moderator Presbyn. Church in United States, 1961-62. Member of the Nat. Commn. Accrediting; mem. commn. on religion in higher edn. Assn. Am. Colls.; mem. Dekalb County Merit System Council. Bd. sponsors Atlanta Sch. Art; bd. trustees Westiminister Sch., Atlanta, Protestant Radio and TV Center, Inc., Columbia Theol. Sem., Decatur. Mem. Southern U. Conf. (exec. com.), Alpha Tau Omega, Omicron Delta Kappa, Phi Beta Kappa (dir.

Georgia assn.), Tau Kappa Alpha, Pi Delta Epsilon, Democrat. Clubs: Piedmont Driving, The Ten, Rotary, Atlanta Athletic. Author: The Throne Among the Shadows, 1945; Break Up The Night, 1947; Mirrors of the Soul, 1953. Home: 213 S Candler St Decatur GA 30030

ALSTON, WALTER EMMONS, major league baseball mgr.; b. Butler County, O., Dec. 1, 1911; s. William Emmons and Lenora (Neanover) A.; B.S. in Phys. Edn., Miami U., Oxford, O., 1935; m. Lela Vaughn Alexander, May 10, 1930; 1 dau., Doria La Verne (Mrs. Harry Ogle). Mgr. Los Angeles Dodgers, and predecessor Bklyn. Dodgers, 1954—, Nat. League championship team 1955, 56, 59, 63, comml. announcer, Chgo., 1945, sports World's Championship team 1955, 59, 63. Named Major League Mgr. of Year, Sporting News, 1955, 59, 63. Author: Alston and the Dodgers, 1966. Home: Route 2 Oxford OH 45056 Office: Dodger Stadium 1000 Elysian Park Av Los Angeles CA 90012

ALSTON, WILLIAM PAYNE, educator; b. Shreveport, La., Nov. 29, 1921; s. William Payne and Eunice (Schoolfield) A.; B.M., Centenary Coll., 1942; Ph.D., U.Chgo., 1951; m. Mary Frances Collins, Aug. 15, 1943 (div.); 1 dau., Frances Ellen; m. 2d, Valerie Tibbetts Barnes, July 3, 1963. Instr philosophy U. Mich., 1949- 52, asst. prof., then asso. prof., 1952-61, prof., 1961-71, acting chmn. dept., 1961-64; prof. philosophy Rutgers U., 1971—; vis. asst. prof. U. Cal. at Los Angeles, 1952-53; vis. lectr. Harvard, 1955-56. Served with AUS, 1942-46. Rackham Summer Research fellow 1955-56). Mem. Mich. Acad. Sci., Arts and Letters (chmn. philosophy sect. 1958). Author: Religious Belief and Philosophical Thought, 1963; (with G. Nakhnikian), Readings in twentieth Century Philosophy, 1963; Philosophy of Language, 1964; (with R.B. Brandt) The Problems of Philosophy; Introductory Readings, 1967, numerous articles in field, chpts. in books. Home: 1332 Prospect Av Plainfield NJ 07060

ALSTRIN, W.L., drug stores exec. Comptroller Walgreen Co., Chgo. Office: 4300 Peterson Av Chicago IL 60646*

ALT, HOWARD LANG, physician; b. Chgo., July 28, 1900; s. Frank Henry and Clara (Lang) A.; M.D., Northwestern U., 1924, Ph.D., 1934; m. Patricia Drew, June 19, 1935; children—Leslie (Mrs. John G. Mott), Abby Lynn (Mrs. L. Russell Cartwright), Robin Julie (Mrs. Crocker Snow, Jr.), Howard Lang, Winston Drew, Patricia Brooke (Mrs. Peter Kountz). House officer Wesley Meml. Hosp., Chgo., 1923-25; asst. resident and resident physician Peter Bent Brigham Hosp., Boston, 1925-29; teaching fellow in medicine Harvard Med. Sch., 1927-29; asst. to Prof. O. Warburg, Kaiser Wilhelm Inst. fur Biologie, Berlin-Dahlen, Germany, 1929-30; asst. Medizinische Klinik, Wuerzburg, Germany, 1930; asso. in medicine Northwestern Med. Sch., 1930-36; dir. hematology clinic, 1931-58, dir. labs. and in charge clin. pathology, 1935-39, instr. chemistry 1931-50, asst. prof..medicine, 1936-46, asso. prof., 1946-56, prof., 1956-68, prof. emeritus, 1968—; mem. staff Passavant Hosp., Chicago, chief of medicine, 1958-63; cons. hematologist Children's Meml. Hosp., 1940—, VA Research Hosp., 1954—. Dir., Hosp. Service Corp. Served as expert cons. in internal medicine, U.S. Army, 1946-47. Diplomate Am. Bd. Internal Medicine. Mem. A.C.P., Internat., Am. socs. hematology, Assn..Am..Physicians, Central Soc. for Clin, Research, Inst..Medicine Chgo., Chgo. Soc. Internal Medicine, Sigma Xi, Delta Upsilon, Alpha Kappa Kappa. Contbr. to profl. jours. on hematology; made discoveries relating to pathologic physiology of anemia. Home: 1144 N Michigan Av Evanston IL 60202 Office: 707 Fairbanks Ct Chicago IL 60611

ALTAZAN, JOHN EDWARD, coll. dean; b. Port Allen, La., Sept. 17, 1926; s. Edward E. and Daisy (Thibodeaux) A.; B.S., La. State U., 1950, M.B.A., 1951; Ph.D., U. Ill., 1954; m. Marie Anne Hayes, June 1, 1957; children—Alison Marie, Kerrin Anne. Asst. prof. econs. Loyola U., New Orleans, 1954-58; dir. div. bus. adminstrn., asso. prof. econs. La. State U., New Orleans, 1958-63, dean Coll. Bus. Adminstrn., prof. econs., 1963—. La. corr. So. Econ. Jour., 1956-70. Pres. bd. dirs. Friends of New Orleans Pub. Library, 1965-66. Served with USNR, 1944-46. U. Ill. fellow, 1951-54; Ford Found. Faculty research seminar, 1958. Mem. Am., So. econ. assns., Southwestern Social Sci. Assn., So. Bus. Adminstrn. Assn. (pres. 1969-70), Southwestern Assn. Bus. Sch. Deans (pres. 1967-68), Omicron Delta Kappa, Phi Kappa Phi, Beta Gamma Sigma, Phi Eta Sigma, Delta Sigma Pi, Beta Alpha Psi, Tau Kappa Epsilon. Rotarian. Author: Interstate Commerce Commission Concerning Consolidations and Acquisitions of Control in the Motor Carrier Industry, 1956. Contbr. articles to profl. jours. Home: 1443 Pressburg St New Orleans LA 70122

ALTEMEIER, WILLIAM ARTHUR, surgeon; b. Cin., July 6, 1910; s. William A. and Carrie (Moore) A.; B.S., U. Cin., 1930, M.D., 1933; M.S. in Surgery, U. Mich., 1938; m. Edna Wyss, June 16, 1934; children—William Arthur, Ann, George. Intern, Cin. Gen. Hosp., 1933-34; surg. resident Henry Ford Hosp., 1934-39, asst. resident, 1937-38, resident surgeon, 1938-39, asso. surgeon, 1939- 40; instr. surgery U. Cin., 1940-43, asst. prof., 1943-52, Christian R. Holmes prof., chmn. dept., 1952—, dir. research surg. bacteriology lab., 1940—; dir. surg. services Cin. Gen. Hosp., 1952—, clinician out-patient dept., 1943—; surgeon-in-chief Holmes and Children's Hospitals, 1952—; consulting surgeon Dunham, Drake Meml., Cin. VA hosps.; limited pvt. practice, Cin., 1940—. Responsible investigator contract subcoms. Surgeon Gen.'s Office, U.S. Army, numerous phys. conditions related to armed services, 1942—; mem. div. med. scis. Nat. Research Council, 1950- 53, mem. subcom., burns, 1948-53, shock, 1950-53, trauma, 1953-59; surg. cons. Surgeon Gen. of U.S. Army, Japan and Korea, 1953. Recipient Theodore Andrews McGraw award Queen City Optimist Club. Diplomate of the American Bd. Surgery (bd. 1953-59, v. chmn. 1958-59). Fellow A.C.S.; mem. Central Surg. Assn. (treas. 1953-56, president-elect 1957, president 1958), Society Clinical Surgery (pres. 1962-64), Soc. University Surgeons, Southern Surg. Soc., Am. Surg. Assn. (pres. 1969- -), Am. Protologic Soc., Queen City Optimists (pres. 1960—), Roy D. McClure Surg. Soc. (pres. 1966—), A.A.A.S., American Assn. Surgery of Trauma, Am. Cancer Soc., A.M.A., Am. Soc. Clin. Investigation, Assn. Am. Med. Colls., Cin. Acad. Medicine, Cin. Surg. Soc. (pres. 1956-57), Henry Ford Hosp. Med. Assn. (v.p. 1952-54, pres. 1954-56), Halsted Soc., Hist. and Philos. Soc., Internat. Soc. Surgery, Mont Reid Surg. Soc., (president elect), Society of Surgical Chairmen, New York Acad. Sci., Ohio State Med. Assn., Ohio State Surg. Assn., Okla. Clin. Soc., Omaha Mid-West Clin. Soc., Western Surg. Assn. (council 1954-55. 1st v.p. 1957), Pan Pacific Surg. Assn., Surg. Biology Club, Soc. for Surgery Alimentary Tract, Alpha Omega Alpha. Clubs: Commonwealth, Rotary, Cincinnati, Queen City, Western Hills Country, Optimist. Author articles in field. Contbr.: Christipher's Textbook of Surgery, 1947, 56-68; Nelson's Looseleaf of Surgery, 1948; Advances in Military Medicine, 1948; Surgery of Trauma, 1953; The Thyroid Gland, 1956; Surgery: Principles and Practice, 1957, 61, 66; Textbook of General Surgery, 1958; Complications in Surgery and Their Management, 1960; Cole and Elman's Textbook of Surgery, 1959, 1964, The Thyroid Gland, 1964; Surgical Bleeding, 1966. Mem. editorial boards of American Surgeon, 1953- -; Annals of Surgery, 1955—; Surgery, 1952; Current Therapy, 1958; Jour. Surg. Research, 1961—. Home: 1368 Neeb Rd Cincinnati OH 45238 Office: Cin Gen Hosp Cincinnati OH 45229

ALTENBERND, AUGUST LYNN, educator; b. Cleve., Feb. 3, 1918; s. Adolf Carl and Lucy M. (Cheyney) A.; B.S. in Edn., Ohio State U., 1939, M.A., 1949, Ph.D. in English, 1954; m. Mary Blazekovich, Apr. 19, 1941; children—Toni (Mrs. Andrew J. Gold), Mark, Nicholas. Relief visitor, Cleve., 1939-42; tchr. English, John Bryan High Sch., Yellow Springs, O., 1942-44; supply clk. Wright- Patterson AFB, 1944, asst. buyer spl. aircraft Procurement div., 1946- 48; instr. Ohio State U., 1949-54; mem. faculty U. Ill. at Urbana, 1954—, prof. English, 1965—, head dept., 1966—; cons. English, Macmillan Co., 1962—. Served to 2d lt. AUS, 1944-46. Mem. Modern Lang. Assn., Nat. Council Tchrs. English. Editor: (with Leslie L. Lewis) Introduction to Literature: Stories, Poems, Plays, 3 vols., 2d edit., 1969; (with Leslie L. Lewis) Handbooks for the Study of Fiction, Poetry, Drama, 3 vols., 1966; Exploring Literature: Fiction, Poetry, Drama and Criticism, 1970. Home: 710 W Washington St Urbana IL 61801

ALTER, CHESTER M., U. chancellor; b. Rush Co., Ind., Mar. 21, 1906; s. David O. and Maggie (Brookbank) A.; B.S., Ball State Teachers Coll., Muncie, Ind., 1927; A.M., Indiana U., 1928; student U. of Pittsburgh, 1928-29; Ph.D., Harvard, 1936; LL.D., Ball State Teachers College, 1954, Colorado College, 1955, Northeastern U., 1956, Boston U., 1959, U. Colo., 1963. U. Denver, 1967; D.P.S., Ohio Wesleyan U., 1961; L.H.D., Okla. city U., 1965; D.Sc. (hon.), Colorado State U., 1967; m. Arvilla Norrison, July 1, 1933; children—Katherine Jane (dec.), Richard David. Tchr. pub. schs., Ind., 1923-25; Austin teaching fellow, Harvard, 1929-30, univ. scholar, 1930-32, research asso., 1932-33; instr. chemistry Boston U., 1934-37, asst. prof., 1937-40, prof., 1940-53, acting dean grad. school, 1944-45, dean, 1945-53, chancellor U. Denver, 1953-67; chancellor emeritus, since 1967—; tech. cons., 1938-53. Research adv. com. Nat. Planning Assn., 1946-48; cons. research and development bd. Dept. of Def., 1949. Pres. Newton Community Chest, 1947- 49, N.E. Conf. Grad. edn., 1948-49. Mem. gen. bd. edn. Meth. Ch., also del. Gen. Conf., 1956, 1960, 1964, 1968. Mem. adv. com. Inst. Internat. Edn.; mem. Colo. Com. on Fulbright Scholarships, Colo. Instl. Devel. Council. Bd. dirs. Nat. Conf. Christians and Jews for Colo.; Central City Opera House Assn.; trustee Alaska Methodist U., Ill. Sch. Theology, Loretto Heights Coll.; chmn. bd. visitors USAF Air U. Recipient Alumni Distinguished Service award Ball State Tchrs. Coll., 1961, Evans award U. Denver, 1964. Fellow Am. Acad. Arts and Scis.; mem. Am. Chem. Soc. (sec. div. analysis and micro-chem., 1944-46; dir. N.E. sect., chmn. 1947-48), Ind. Acad. Sci., N.E. Conf. Grad. Edn. (sec. treas.), Assn Urban Univs. (pres. 1958-59), Assn. Am. Colls., Am. Council on Edn., Am. Assn. U. Profs., Phi Beta Kappa, Phi Delta Kappa, Omicron Delta Kappa, Alpha Chi Sigma, A.A.A.S., Sigma Xi, Phi Lambda Upsilon, Beta Gamma Sigma. Clubs: Rotary (dir., pres. 1958-59), Denver Country. Contbr. tech. papers sci. publs. Home: 3131 E Alameda Av Denver CO 80209

ALTER, DAVID, lawyer; b. Izka, Czechoslovakia, Oct. 31, 1923 (derivative citizen); s. Morris and Bertha (Davidovic) A.; B.S., Coll. City N.Y., 1947; LL.B., Harvard, 1950; m. Deborah B. King, Dec. 25, 1955; children—Lisa, Amy. Admitted to N.Y. bar, 1950; practice in N.Y.C., 1951—; asso. Simons, Schur & Strauss, 1951-54; partner Squadron & Alter, 1954-60; partner Squadron, Alter & Weinrib, 1960-66; partner Pross, Halpern, Lefevre, Raphael & Alter and predecessor firm, 1966—; N.Y. counsel Screen Actors Guild; counsel Motion Picture Players Welfare Fund. Trustee Screen Actors Guild, Producers Pension and Welfare Plans. Served with USAAF, 1943-46. Mem. Assn. Bar City N.Y., Am., N.Y. State bar assns. Home: 51 Fifth Av New York City NY 10003 Office: 530 Fifth Av New York City NY 10036

ALTER, DAVID EMMET, Jr., govt. ofcl.; b. Mussoorie, U.P., India, July 14, 1921; s. David Emmet and Mary Martha (Payne) A. (parents U.S. citizens); B.A., Coll. Wooster, 1943; M.A., Mills Coll., 1950; m. Edith Marie Coapman, Dec. 8, 1943; children—Dismore J., David Emmet III. Fgn. service officer AID, 1954—, program adviser U.S. Mission to OAS, 1967—; author, artist, pub. The Wanderers Almanac, 1969—. Served with AUS, 1943-46, 50-54. Recipient meritorious honor award AID, 1959. Home: PO Box 1101 Silver Spring MD 20910 Office: AID Department State Washington DC 20523

ALTER, GERALD MILTON, internat. agy. ofcl., economist; b. Mason City, Ia., Dec. 15, 1919; s. William and Rebecca (Levinson) A.; S.B., Harvard, 1941, M. Pub. Adminstrn., 1948, M.A., 1949, Ph.D. in Econs., 1954; m. Charlotte Mae Kivo, Dec. 17, 1943; children—Gregory, Michael, Linda. Fiscal analyst Bur. Budget, 1942-45; economist bd. govs. Fed. Res. System, 1945-46, 48-51, Dept. Commerce, 1946-47; with Internat. Bank Reconstrn. and Devel., 1951—, econ. adviser Western hemisphere dept., 1958-64, dir. dept., 1964-69, dir. S. Am. dept., 1970—. Mem. Am. Econ. Assn., Phi Beta Kappa. Home: 5124 Linnean Terrace NW Washington DC 20008 Office: 1818 H St NW Washington DC 20433

ALTER, JEAN VICTOR, educator; b. Warsaw, Poland, Oct. 7, 1925; s. Victor and Melanie (Lorein) A.; M.A., U. Brussels (Belgium), 1948; doctorate, U. Paris, 1951; Ph.D., U. Chgo., 1956; m. Maria Pospischil, Sept. 16, 1956; 1 dau., Nora. Came to U.S., 1951. Instr., then asst. prof. Howard U., 1952- 58; asst. then asso. prof. U. Md. 1958-67; prof., chmn. dept. Romance langs. Case Western Res. U., 1967- 69; prof. French, U. Pa., 1970—; lectr., writer in field. Recipient Fulbright award, 1951; Smith-Mundt grantee, 1951. Mem. Modern Lang. Assn., Am. Assn. Tchrs. French, Am. Assn. U. Profs., Aesthetic Soc., Soc. des Prof. Francais en Am., Author: Les origines de la satire antibourgeoise en France, 1966; La vision du monde d'Alain Robbe-Grillet, 1966; L'Esprit antibourgeois sous l'ancien regime, 1970. Home: 56 Waterloo Rd Devon PA 19333 Office: Dept Romance Languages Univ Pa Philadelphia PA 19104

ALTER, KARL JOSEPH, archbishop; b. Toledo, Aug. 18, 1885; s. John and Elizabeth (Kuttner) A.; M.A., St. John's U., Toledo, 1902, Ph.D., 1929; student St. Mary's Sem., Cleve., 1904-10; LL.D., Notre Dame U., 1937. Ordained priest Roman Catholic Ch., 1910; pastor St. Mary's Parish, Leipsic, O., 1910-12; asst. pastor St. John's Parish, Lima, O., 1912-14, dir. Diocesan charities, 1914-29, also prof. sociology all colls. St. John's U.; dir. Nat. Sch. Social Service, Washington, 1929-31; apptd. bishop of Toledo (O.), 1931, consecrated, 1931; archbishop Cin., 1950-69; titular archbishop of Minora, 1969—; named asst. to the Papal Throne, 1950. Asst. bishop, social action dept. Nat. Cath. Welfare Conf., 1935-42, mem. adminstrv. bd., chmn. social action dept., 1942-50, treas., vice chmn. adminstrv. bd., 1950-52, chmn. adminstrv. bd., 1952-55, 58-62, sec. adminstrv. bd., 1962-66, vice chmn. adminstrv. bd., Chmn. Dept. Lay Orgns., 1956-58; mem. central prep. commn. II Vatican Council, 1959-62; mem. Commn. for Bishops and Govt. of Dioceses, 1962-65. Home: 5870 Belmont Av Cincinnati OH 45224

ALTER, ROBERT B., educator, critic; b. N.Y.C., Apr. 2, 1935, s. Harry and Tillie (Zimmmerman) A.; B.A., Columbia, 1957; M.A., Harvard, 1958, Ph.D., 1962; m. Judith Berkenbilt, June 4, 1961; children—Miriam, Dan. Instr., then asst. prof. English, Columbia, 1962-66; mem. faculty U. Cal. at Berkeley, 1967—, prof. Hebrew and comparative lit., 1969—, chmn. dept. comparative lit., 1970-72; columnist Commentary mag., 1965—. Guggenheim fellow, 1966-67; Nat. Endowment for the Humanities sr. fellow, 1972-73. recipient English Inst. Essay prize, 1965. Mem. Am. Comparative Lit. Assn. Jewish religion. Author: Rogues Progress: Studies in the Picaresque Novel, 1964; Fielding and the Nature of the Novel, 1968; After the Tradition, 1969. Home: 1735 Highland Pl Berkeley CA 94709

ALTERMAN, DAVID F., food co. exec.; b. 1917; married. With Alterman Foods Inc., Atlanta, 1946—, now sr. v.p. sales, dir.; sec., treas. Atlantic Preserving Co. Inc. Office: 933 Lee St SW Atlanta GA 30310*

ALTERMAN, MAX C., food co. exec.; b. 1919; married. With Alterman Foods Inc., Atlanta, 1946—, now sr. v.p. warehousing, dir. Office: 933 Lee St SW Atlanta GA 30310*

ALTHANS, WILLIAM RIECK, railroad exec., lawyer; b. St. Louis, June 27, 1908; s. Emile H. and Della (Althans) A.; A.B. with high distinction, U. Mich., 1930, J.D. with distinction, 1932; m. Margaret Elder, Feb. 21, 1942. Admitted to Mich. bar, 1932, Ohio bar, 1957; asso. with Goodenough, Voorhies, Long & Ryan, Detroit, 1932-34; pvt. practice, 1934-38; atty. P.M. R.R., 1938-43, asst. gen. atty., 1943-45, gen. atty., 1945-47; with C. & O. Ry., 1947—, successively gen. atty., asst. gen. counsel, gen. solicitor, Detroit, 1947-56, gen. solicitor, Cleve., 1956-58, gen. counsel, 1958-66; gen. counsel C. & O., B. & O. Ry.,1966—. Regional v.p. Nat. Assn. R.R. Trial Counsel, 1957. Mem. Am., Mich., Ohio, Detroit, Cleve. bar assns., Mich., Detroit hist. socs., Detroit Mus. Art Founders Soc., C. & O. Recreation Assn., P.M. Athletic Assn. (pres. 1944-45), Newcomen Soc., Order of Coif, Phi Beta Kappa, Phi Kappa Phi, Phi Eta Sigma. Republican. Presbyn. Mason. Clubs: Detroit Yacht; Shaker Heights Country; Rowfant; Nat. Lawyers (Washington). Home: 2680 West Park Blvd Shaker Heights OH 44120 Office: Terminal Tower Cleveland OH 44113

ALTHEIMER, ALAN J., lawyer; b. St. Louis, Sept. 2, 1903; A.B., Columbia, 1923, J.D., 1925. Admitted to Ill. bar, 1926, since practiced in Chgo.; mem. firm Altheimer, Gray, Naiburg & Strasburger. Dir. Conveyor Systems, Inc., Edward Gray Corp., Max Stern's Sons Co., Franklin Picture Frame Co., Pick Hotels Corp., Park Forest Savs. & Loan Assn. Bd. dirs. Nat Jewish Welfare Bd., Union Am. Hebrew Congregations. Recipient 1st Professional Merit award Columbia U. Law Sch. Alumni Assn.; Frank L. Weil award Nat. Jewish Welfare Bd. Mem. Am., Ill., Chgo. bar assns., Zeta Beta Tau. Clubs: Standard, Harmonie, Northmoor. Office: 1 N LaSalle St Chicago IL 60602

ALTHOLZ, JOSEF LEWIS, educator; b. N.Y.C., Aug. 14, 1933; s. Carl Hyman and Rae (Huberfeld) A.; B.A., Cornell U., 1954; M.A., Columbia, 1955, Ph.D., 1960. Instr. U. Minn., 1959-61, asst. prof. history, 1961-64, asso. prof., 1964-67, prof., 1967—; vis. prof. U. Wis., 1970-71. Precinct and ward chmn. Democratic Party, 1964-68. Served with AUS, 1955-57. Guggenheim fellow, 1964-65. Mem. Am. Hist. Assn,., Conf. Brit. Studies, Am. Cath. Hist. Assn., Upper Midwest History Conf. (sec. 1968-70), Am. Assn. U. Profs., Am. Civil Liberties Union, Phi Beta Kappa. Jewish religion. Author: Liberal Catholic Movement in England, 1962; Chruches in the Nineteenth Century, 1967; Victorian England, 1970. Co-editor Correspondence of Lord Acton and Richard Simpson, Vol. 1, 1971; adv. editor Cath. Hist. Rev., 1966-69. Home: 2 River Terrace Ct Minneapolis MN 55414

ALTHOUSE, ERNEST E., utility co. exec.; b. Strausstown, Pa., Sept. 24, 1904; s. Adam Joseph and Minnie (Burkey) A.; E.E., Lehigh U., 1926; m. Elizabeth Righter Plank, May 29, 1935. With Central Hudson Gas & Electric Corp., Poughkeepsie, N.Y., 1928—, pres., 1968—, alsodir.; dir. Utilities Mut. Ins. Co. Bd. dirs. Mid-Hudson Pattern for Progress, Inc. Registered profl. engr., N.Y., Pa. Mem. I.E.E.E., Soc. Gas Lighting. Mason. Home: 1 Alden Rd Poughkeepsie, NY 12603. Office: 284 South Av Poughkeepsie, NY 12602.

ALTHOUSE, H.J., chain drug co. exec.; b. Glen Rock, Pa., Nov. 16, 1909; s. John J. and Emma (Smith) A.; student accounting, Thompsons Sch. Bus., 1927-29; m. Lillian A. Winter, May 20, 1936; children—Alice Ann (Mrs. Francis L. Dugan), Harold J., William F. With Peoples Drug Stores Inc., Washington, 1928—, comptroller, 1949-51, treas., 1951—, also dir. Mem. Washington Bd. Trade. Mem. Financial Inst. Am., D.C. Pharm. Soc. Kiwanian. Home: 5532 Charles St Bethesda MD 20014 Office: 60 Florida Av NE Washington DC 20002

ALTHOUSE, PAUL MARCKS, educator; b. Reading, Pa., Oct. 9, 1916; s. Solomon A. and Katie (Marcks) A.; B.S., Pa. State Coll., 1938, M.S., 1940, Ph.D., 1943; m. Virginia F. Feick, Aug. 16, 1941; childrenPaul Richard, Nancy Jean. Mem. faculty Pa. State U., 1942-, prof. agrl. and biol. chemistry, 1951- -, dir. gen. edn., 1962-65, asst. v.p. resident instrn., 1965-67, v.p. resident instrn., 1967-70; v.p. for academic affairs, 1970—. Mem. A.A.A.S., Am. Chem. Soc., Am. Oil Chemists Soc., N.E.A., Assn. Gen. and Liberal Studies. Home: 1001 Saxton Dr State College PA 16801 Office: 203-C Old Main University Park PA 16802

ALTIZER, THOMAS JONATHAN JACKSON, educator, theologian; b. Cambridge, Mass., Sept. 28, 1927; s. Jackson Duncan and Frances (Greetham) A.; student St. John's Colls., 1944-45; A.B., U. Chgo., 1948, A.M., 1951, Ph.D., 1955; m. Alma Rose Barker, Aug. 26, 1967; children—John Jackson, Katherine Blake. Asst. prof. religion Wabash Coll., 1954- 56; asst. prof., then asso. prof. religion Emory U., 195668; prof. English State U. N.Y. at Stony Brook, 1968—. Served with AUS, 1945-46. Author: Oriental Mysticism and Biblical Eschatology, 1961; Mircea Eliade and the Dialectic of the Sacred, 1963; The Gospel of Christian Atheism, 1966; The New Apocalypse, 1967; Descent into Hell, 1970. Home: 210 Chestnut St Port Jefferson NY 11777 Office: Religious Studies State U NY Stony Brook NY 11790

ALTMAN, HAROLD, artist, educator; b. N.Y.C., Apr. 20, 1924; s. Morris and Anna (Sperling) A.; student Florence Cane Sch. Art, N.Y.C., 1936-41, Art Students League, 1941-42; B.F.A., Cooper Union Art Sch., 1947; student New Sch. Social Research, 1947-48, L'Academie de la Grande Chaumiere, Paris, 1949-52; m. Anita Maria Schulz, on July 15, 1948 (div.); children—Evan, Toby, and Ann; m. 2d, to Linda Plotkin, 1962. Asst. prof. N.Y. State Coll. Ceramics, Alfred U., 1952-54; asst. prof. Woman's Coll. U. N.C., 1954-56; asst. prof. Ind. U., summer 1956. U. Wis., Milw., 1956-62; asso. prof. Pa. State U., 1962- 67, prof., 1967—; Fulbright research scholar for France, 1964-65; rep. permanent collections Mus. Modern Art, Art Inst. Chgo., Cleve. Mus Art, Nat. Gallery Art, Whitney Mus. Art, Detroit Inst. Fine Arts, Pa. Acad. Fine Arts, Boston Mus. Art, Walker Art Center, Met. Mus. Art, N.Y.C., Library Congress, also Mus. Modern Art, Haifa, Israel, Royal Mus. Fine Arts, Copenhagen, Denmark, Mexico City, Bonn, Germany, Smithsonian Instn., Los Angeles County Art Mus.; one man shows Gallerie 8, Paris, 1951, Martha Jackson Gallery, N.Y.C., 1958, Peter Deitsch Gallery, 1958, 60, Contemporaries Gallery, 1959, 63, Art. Inst. Chgo., 1960, San Francisco Mus. Art, 1961, Santa Barbara Mus. Art, 1961, Escuela Nacional Artes Plasticas, Mexico, 1961, numerous others; exhibited group shows including First Bienniale de Paris, 1959, 2d Biennial Interamericanna, Mexico City, 1960, 3d Internat. Print Biennial, Tokyo, Japan, 1962, others. Served with C.E., AUS, 1943-46.

Recipient Wards Boston Printmaker exhbn., 1960, 61, Am. Graphic Artists Ann., 1961, 62, Audubon Artists Am., 1961, 62, Nat. Acad. Design Am., 1962, numerous other awards; Guggenheim fellow, 1960, 61, Tamarind Lithography Workshop fellow, 1961; Fulbright fellow to France, 1964-65. Home: Lemont PA 16851

ALTMAN, IRWIN, educator; b. N.Y.C., July 16, 1930; s. Louis L. and Ethel (Schonberg) A.; B.A., N.Y.U., 1951; M.A., U. Md., 1954, Ph.D., 1957; m. Gloria Seckler, Jan. 2, 1953; children—David Gary, William Michael. Asst. prof. Am. U., Washington, 1957-58, sr. research scientist, asso. prof., 1960- 62, adj. prof., 1962-69; research scientist human scis. research, Arlington, Va., 1958-60; research psychologist Naval Med. Research Inst., Bethesda, Md., 1962-69; adj. prof. U. Md., 1968-69; prof., chmn. psychology dept. U. Utah, Salt Lake City, 1969—; cons. VA, USPHS, Batelle Meml. Inst. Served to 1st lt. Adj. Gen. Corps., U.S. Army, 1954- 56. Mem. Am., Eastern, D.C., Utah psychol. assns., A.A.A.S., Soc. Exptl. Social Psychology, Soc. Psychol. Study Social Issues, Assn. for Study Man Environment Relations (dir.). Author: (with J.E. McGrath) Small Groups, 1966. Mem. editorial bd. Comparative Group Studies, 1970—, Man-Environment Systems, 1969—. Contbr. articles profl. jours. Home: 2827 Commonwealth Av Salt Lake City UT 84109

ALTMANN, ALEXANDER, educator; b. Kassa, Hungary, Apr. 16, 1906; s. Adolf and Malvine (Weisz) A.; Dr.phil., Berlin (Germany) U., 1931; rabbi, Rabbinical Sem., Berlin, 1931; M.A. (hon.), Manchester (Eng.) U., 1943; D.H.L., Hebrew Union Coll.-Jewish Inst. Religion, 1967; m. Judith Frank, Dec. 20, 1932; children—Fay Aviva (Mrs. Raphael A. Lunzer), Michael, Eve (Mrs. Yigal Yardeni). British subject, 1946. Rabbi, Berlin Jewish Community, 1931-38; prof. Jewish philosophy Rabbinical Sem., Berlin, 1932-38; communal rabbi, Manchester, 1938-59; dir. Inst. Jewish Studies, Manchester, 1953- 58; Philip W. Lown prof. Brandeis U., 1959—. Hon. pres. Inst. Jewish Studies, Univ. Coll., London, Eng., 1959—. Fellow Am. Acad. Arts and Scis., Am. Acad. Jewish Research. Author books and articles in German, English, Hebrew on medieval philosophy and mysticism, 18th Century philosophy, modern Jewish thought. Editor: Jour. Jewish Studies, 1954-59; Scripta Judaica, 1957—; Brandeis Studies and Texts, 1963-67. Home: 126 Glen Av Newton Center, MA 02159. Office: Brandeis Univ Waltham, MA 02159.

ALTMANN, ANDREW TAYLOR, lawyer; b. Balt., May 9, 1918; s. Andrew J. and Sara (McCauley) A.; B.S., U. Md., 1941; J.D., George Washington U., 1948; m. Marjorie W. Kerbey, Dec. 9, 1944; children-Kerbey Taylor., Andrew Taylor, Elizabeth Anne, Penny. Admitted to D.C. bar; practiced in Washington, 1949—; gen. counsel McLachlen Nat. Bank, Equitable Life Ins. Co., Wilkins-Rogers, Inc. Served to capt. AUS, 1941-46. Mem. Sigma Nu, Phi Delta Phi. Clubs: Columbia Country (Chevy Chase); University (Washington). Home: 32 W Kirke St Chevy Chase MD 20015 Office: Washington DC 20001

ALTON, RALPH TAYLOR, bishop; b. Deerfield, O., Aug. 10, 1908; s. John Taylor and Roberta Hazel (Schwartz) A.; A.B., Ohio Wesleyan U., 1928, D.D. (hon.), 1951; S.T.B., Boston U., 1932; m. Marian Bannon Black, July 23, 1931; children—Phyllis Ann (Mrs. Harold Thor Hansen), Bruce Taylor. Ordained to ministry Meth. Ch., 1932; pastor in Mass., Ohio and Wis., 1932- 60; elected bishop, 1960; assigned Wis. area, 1960—. Mem. Gen. Conf. Meth. Ch., 1956, 60; res. mem. Meth. Jud. Council, 1956-70. Trustee Lawrence Coll.; bd. dirs. Bellin Hosp., Green Bay, Wis., Meth. Hosp., Madison, Wis., Meth. Manor, W. Allis, Wis.; exec. bd., chmn. Meth. Com. Overseas Relief; vice chmn. Meth. Bd. Homes and Hosps.; trustee N. Central Coll., Evangelical Theol. Sem.; pres. Wis. Council Chs., 1966-67. Home: 702 Morning Star Lane Madison WI 53711 Office: 325 Emerald Terrace Sun Prairie WI 53590

ALTSCHUL, ALFRED SAMUEL, transp. co. exec.; b. Chgo., Oct. 16, 1939; s. Herman and Lillian (Ginsburg) A.; B.S., U. Wis., 1961; M.B.A., U. Chgo., 1963; m. Lynn Silverman, Sept. 8, 1968; 1 son, Howard. With Gen. Am. Transportation Corp., Chgo., 1964—, asst. treas., 1967-70, treas., 1970—; lectr. financial mgmt. Active Talent Assistance Program; dir. young people's div. Jewish Fedn. Chgo. Served with AUS, 1963-69. Mem. Financial Mgrs. Assn. (pres.), Alpha Epsilon Pi. Jewish religion. Clubs: Fullerton Tennis, Covenent (Chgo.). Home: 2626 N Lake View Chicago IL 60614 Office: 120 S Riverside Plaza Chicago IL 60680

ALTSCHUL, ARTHUR GOODHART, investment banker; b. N.Y.C., Apr. 6, 1920; s. Frank and Helen (Goodhart) A.; grad. Deerfield Acad., 1939; A.B., Yale, 1943; m. Stephanie Wagner, Apr. 29, 1956 (dec. July 1961); children—Stephen Frank, Charles; m. 2d, Siri Sylvia Patricia von Reis, June 11, 1963; children—Arthur Goodhart, Emily Helen, Serena von Reis. Partner Goldman, Sachs & Co., N.Y.C., 1959—; chmn. bd. Gen. Am. Investors Co., Inc.; dir. Data-Control Systems, Inc., Asso. Dry Goods Corp., Cleary Petroleum Corp.; mem. adv. bd. Lord & Taylor. Pres. bd. trustees St. Bernard's Sch., N.Y.C.; mem. council Yale; trustee Whitney Mus. Am. Art, Am. Assembly, Assos. in Fine Arts of Yale U. Art Gallery. Served to 1st lt. USMCR, 1943-45. Asso. fellow Pierson Coll., Yale. Mem. Council Fgn. Relations, Am. Fedn. Arts (trustee). Clubs: Century Assn., Recess, Yale (N.Y.C.); Stanwich; Century Country; Madison Square Garden; Turf and Field; Vineyard Haven Yacht; Bond. Home: 993 Fifth Av New York City NY 10028 Office: 55 Broad St New York City NY 10004

ALTSCHUL, FRANK, ret. exec.; b. San Francisco, Apr. 21, 1887; s. Charles and Camilla (Mandlebaum) A.; B.A., Yale, 1908, LL.D., 1967; LL.D., Bates Coll., 1952; m. Helen Lehman Goodhart, 1913; children—Charles II (dec.), Margaret (Mrs. Daniel Lang), Edith (Mrs. Robert C. Graham), Aruthur Goodhart. Bd. dirs. Gen. Am. Investors Co., Inc. Asso. fellow Pierson Coll., Yale, New Haven, honorary fellow University Coll., Oxford. Vice pres., sec. Council on Fgn. Relations, Inc., N.Y.C.; vice chmn. Nat. Planning Assn. and chmn. internat. com. Served to apt. U.S. Army, 1917-19; A.E.F.; maj. O.R.C., 1924. Decorated officer Legion of Honor (French). Mem. Union Interalliee, Le Compagnie Typographique (Paris). Clubs: Pilgrims U.S., Century Assn., Grolier, Lotos, Nat. Arts, Yale, Fifth Ave., Recess (N.Y.C.); Odd Volumes (Boston); Elizabethan (New Haven); Rowfant (Cleveland); Cosmos, Army and Navy, Metropolitan, 1925 F Street (Washington). Author: Let No Wave Engulf Us, 1941. Home: Overbrook Farm 356 Riverbank Rd Stamford CT 06903 Office: 730 Fifth Av New York City NY 10019

ALTSCHUL, HELEN G., (MRS. FRANK ALTSCHUL), civic worker; b. N.Y.C., May 9, 1887; d. Philip J. and Hattie (Lehman) Goodhart; A.B., Barnard Coll., 1907; m. Frank Altschul, Jan. 9, 1913; children—Charles, II (dec.), Margaret A. Lang, Edith A. Graham, Arthur Goodhart. Mem. bd. N.Y. Infirmary, 1935-; hon. v.p. Girls' and Boys' Service League N.Y.; trustee Barnard Coll. Mem. Am. Assn. U. Women. Clubs: Women's University (pres. 1947-49), Barnard College (pres. 1932-35), Cosmopolitan, Women's City. Address: 356 Riverbank Rd Stamford, CT 06903 also 781 Fifth Av New York City NY 10022

ALTSCHUL, ROLF, educator, chemist; b. Duesseldorf, Germany, Jan. 24, 1918; naturalized U.S. citizen; A.M., Harvard, 1939, Ph.D. in Chemistry, 1941; m.; 2 children. Fellow, Harvard, 1941; Pitts. Plate Glass Co. fellow, 1941-44; lectr. Bryn Mawr Coll., 1944-45; prof. chemistry Sarah Lawrence Coll., 1945—; research asso. Brandeis U., 1954—; spl. research kinetics and mechanisms liquid phase reactions. Mem. Am. Chem. Soc. Address: care Dept Chemistry Sarah Lawrence Coll Bronxville NY 10708*

ALTSCHULE, MARK DAVID, physician; b. N.Y.C., July 16, 1906; s. Benedict and Clara (Feldman) A.; B.S., Coll. City N.Y., 1927; M.D., Harvard, 1933; m. Julia Diamant, July 6, 1934. House officer pathology Peter Bent Brigham Hosp., Boston, 1932; house officer medicine Beth Israel Hosp., Boston, 1932-34, resident med. research, 1934-35, vis. physician, 1946—; dir. internal medicine and research clin. physiology McLean Hosp., Belmont, Mass., 1947-68, cons., clin. physiologist, 1968—; asso. Thorndike Lab., Boston City Hosp., 1955—; attending physician Boston VA Hosp., 1953—; staff cons. Boston City Hosp., North Adams (Mass.) Hosp., Haverford (Pa.) State Hosp., Lab. Clin. Psychophamacology Nat. Inst. Mental Health, 1964-67, Chelsea Naval Hosp., 1968—, Yale-Haven Hosp., 1969—, Children's Hosp. Med. Center, Boston, 1964-67; lectr. medicine Yale Sch. Medicine, 1966; asst. clin. prof. medicine Harvard Med. Sch., 1952-70, asso. clin. prof. medicine, 1970—; editor-in-chief Lippincott's Med. Sci., 1959-68, Med. Counterpoint, 1969—. Diplomate Am. Bd. Internal Med. Hon. curator prints, photographs Francis A. Countway Library of Medicine, Harvard, 1969—. Mem. Assn. Am. Physicians, Soc. Exptl. Biology and Medicine, N.Y. Acad. Scis., Am., New Eng. heart assns., Am. Coll. Clin. Pharmacology and chemotherapy, Am. Soc. Clin. Investigation, Internat. Cardiology Found., History Sci. Soc., Medieval Acad. Am. Mass. Med. Soc., Alpha Omega Alpha. Author: Physiology in Diseases of the Heart and Lungs, rev. edit., 1954, Japanese edit., 1956; Bodily Physiology and Mental and Emotional Disorders, 1953; Acute Pulmonary Edema, 1954; The Pineal Gland: A Review of the Physiologic Literature, 1954; Essays in the History of Psychiatry, 1957; Roots of Modern Psychiatry, 2d edit., 1965; (with A. Osol and R. Pratt) The United States Dispensatory Physicians' Pharmacology, 1967. Home: 74 The Fenway Boston MA 02115 Office: 115 Mill St Belmont MA 02178

ALTSHUL, HAROLD MILTON, drug co. exec.; b. N.Y.C., June 19, 1909; s. Victor I. and Fannie (Kosven) A.; student Cornell U., 1928-29; m. Anne Majette Grant, Feb. 13, 1959; children—Victor Anthony, Lindsey Grant. With Ketchum & Co., Inc., N.Y.C., 1930—, sales mgr., 1933, operations mgr., 1934, pres., 1935—, dir., 1935—; chmn. bd. dirs. Success Chem. Co., Bklyn., 1965—. Fellow Aspen Inst. for Humanistic Studies; mem. Nat. Wholesale Druggists Assn. (v.p. 1938, mem. bd. control 1957-59), Am. Arbitration Assn. (mem. nat. panel 1946-59), Drug, Chem. and Allied Trades Assn. (exec. com. 1942-50, chmn., 1946, adv. council 1947-50) N.Y. Bd. Trade (dir. 1943-51, v.p. 1948-50), Young Presidents Orgn. (dir. 1951-55, chmn. exec. com. 1951-52, v .p. 1952-53), Chief Execs. Forum (dir. 1958—, pres. 1962). Clubs: North Shore Country (Glen Head, N.Y.); City Athletic (N.Y.C.); East Hampton (N.Y.) Yacht (gov. 1965—, commodore 1967-68). Home: 1020 Park Av New York City NY 10028 Office: 16 E 40th St New York City NY 10016

ALTSHULER, NATHAN, educator, anthropologist; b. Detroit, Oct. 31, 1925; s. Aaron and Sylvia (Spitzer) A.; B.A., U. Mich., 1951; postgrad. U. Ariz., 1951-52; Ph.D., Harvard, 1956; m. Meredith Treene, Apr. 14, 1959; children—Anthea, Linnea, Alyssa. Research asst. Am. Mus. Natural History, 1947-49; research asst., teaching fellow Harvard, 1952-56; instr. Boston U., 1956-57; research asso. Joint Com. Mental Illness and Health, 1958-59; postdoctoral Nat. Inst. Mental Health fellow Harvard, 1959-60; asst. prof. to prof., chmn. dept. anthropology Coll. William and Mary, 1960—. Served wih inf., AUS, 1944-46. Recipient alumni research award, Coll. William and Mary, 1963, faculty award, Phi Beta Kappa, 1963, faculty award, Student Assn., 1967. Fellow Am. Anthropol. Assn.; mem. Phi Beta Kappa. Research on Cree and Eskimo at Hudson Bay, health programs various African nations and Guyana. Home: 202 Tyler Brooks Dr Williamsburg VA 23185

ALTUS, WILLIAM DAVID, psychologist, educator; b. Burlington, Kan., May 28, 1908; s. Samuel Abraham and Cora Jane (Burch) A.; A.B., B.S., Kan. State Tchrs. Coll., 1930, M.S., 1932; Ph.D., N.Y.U., 1941; m. Mary Agnes Atkinson, Dec. 14, 1929; m. 2d, Grace Merriman Thompson, Dec. 24, 1951; children—Martha, Elizabeth, Deborah. Instr., Santa Barbara Coll., 1941-44, asst. prof., 1944-47, asso. prof., 1947-54, prof., 1954—, chmn. dept. psychology, 1950-55; faculty research lectr. U. Cal. at Santa Barbara, 1961—. Served from 2d lt. to capt. AUS, 1942-46. Fellow Am. Psychol. Assn., A.A.A.S.; mem. Am. Assn. U. Profs. Club: Sierra. Contbr. articles jours. Home: 767 Las Palmas Dr Santa Barbara CA 93105

ALTWEGG, AL, journalist. Business and financial editor Dallas News. Office: A H Belo Corp Communications Center Dallas TX 75222*

ALVARES, ALBERT HAMILTON, chemist, educator; b. Chicago, 1928; B.S. in Physics, Yale, 1950; Ph.D. in Chemistry, Harvard, 1956; m. Sally Ann Jones, July 5, 1957; children--Kenneth J., Nancy A. Chemist, Acme Chem. Co., Blue Island, Ill., 1950-51; director of Research Lab., Indsl. Chemicals Corp., Cambrige, Mass., 1956-60; project coordinator environmental sect. Steinmetz Assos., Chgo., 1960-61; v.p. for research Bauer Bros. Chem. Co., Inc., Memphis, 1961-64; asst. prof. chemistry Washington U., St. Louis, 1964-66, asso. prof., 1966-70, prof., 1970--, head of chemistry dept., 1970-71. Vis. prof. So. Ill. U., summer 1967, U. of Ore., 1969. Bd. dirs. Rest Haven Home for Elderly, 1960-61; trustee of the Lutheran Hosp., 1965-71. Served from lt. to capt., AUS, 1951-53. Mem. Am. Chem. Soc., Sci. Research Soc. Am. (chpt. treas. 1967), Sigma Xi. Author: (with others) Basic Inorganic Chemistry, 1971. Home: Fairfax Apts 7291 Windermere Dr University City MO 63105 Office: Dept Chemistry Washington University St Louis MO 63130

ALVARES, ALFRED VICTOR JORGE, architect; b. Macau, Sept. 14, 1910; s. Luis Maria and Emklia (Jorge) A.; ed. Philippine schs., Internat. Corr. Schs.; m. May Bulldeath, Aug. 1, 1945; children—Andrea (Mrs. Edward Sinclair), Alfred, Brenda (Mrs. Daryll Patton). Pvt. archtl. practice, 1937—; prin. A.V. Alvares & Assos., 1946—, specializing hosp. design. Hon. fellow A.I.A., mem. Hongkong Soc. Architects (past pres.). Home: 20 Repulse Bay Rd Hongkong Office: 16 Ice House St Hongkong

ALVAREZ, LUIS W., physicist; b. San Francisco, June 13, 1911; s. Walter C. and Harriet S. (Smyth) A.; B.S., U. Chgo., 1932, M.S., 1934, Ph.D., 1936, Sc.D. 1967; Sc.D., Carnegie-Mellon U., 1968, Kenyon Coll., 1969; m. Geraldine Smithwick, 1936; children—Walter, Jean; m. 2d, Janet L. Landis, 1958; children—Donald and Helen. Research asso., instr., asst. prof., asso. prof. U. Cal., 1936-45, prof. physics, 1945—, asso. dir. Lawrence Radiation Lab., 1954-59; radar research and devel. Mass. Inst. Tech., 1940-43, Los Alamos, 1944-45. Recipient Collier Trophy, 1946; Medal for Merit, 1948; John Scott medal, 1953; Einstein medal, 1961; Nat. Medal of Sci., 1964; Michelson award, 1965; Nobel prize in physics, 1968; named Cal. Scientist of Year, 1960. Fellow Am. Phys. Soc. (pres. 1969); mem. Nat. Acad. Scis., Nat. Acad. Eng., Am. Philos. Soc., Am. Acad. Arts and Scis., Phi Beta Kappa, Sigma Xi. Home: 131 Southhampton Av Berkeley CA 94707

ALVAREZ, WALTER CLEMENT physician; b. San Francisco, Calif., July 22, 1884; s. Luis Fernandez and Clementina (Schuetze) A.; M.D., Cooper Med. Coll. (Stanford), 1905; post-grad. student Harvard Med. Sch., 1913; m. Harriet Skidmore Smyth, Feb. 22, 1907; children—Gladys (Mrs. Raymond Archibald), Luis Walter, Robert Smyth, Bernice (Mrs. Bradley Brownson). Asst. in clinic pathology, Cooper Med. Coll., Stanford U., 1906-07; physician Cananea, Mexico, 1907-09; internist San Francisco, 1910-25; asst. in medicine, Stanford, 1911-12; asst. in research medicine, U. Cal., 1915-16, instr., 1916-20, asst. prof., 1920-24, asso. prof., 1924-26; successively asso., head of sect. and sr. consultant, Div. Medicine, Mayo Clinic, Rochester, Minn., since 1926, emeritus since 1950; asso. prof. medicine, Mayo Found., U. of Minn., 1926-34, prof., 1934-51, emeritus; professorial lectr. medicine U. Ill. Med. Sch., 1951- 52, emeritus. Diplomate Am. Bd. Internal Medicine, Am. Bd. Gastroenterology. Trustee Josiah Macy, Jr., Foundn., 1930-32. First Caldwell Lecturer, Am. Roentgen Ray Society. Fellow Am. Coll. Physicinas; mem. Assn. Am. Physicians, Am. Physiol. Soc., Am. Soc. for Clin. Investigation, Soc. Expt. Biology and Medicine, Am. Gastroenterol. Assn. (pres. 1928; Friedenwald medallist 1951), Am. Soc. Pharmacology Exptl. Therapeutics, A.M.A., Am. Anthropol. Assn., Am. Assn. Phys. Anthropologists, A.A.A.S., Alpha Kappa Kappa, Sigma Xi, Alpha Omega Alpha. Republican. Club: University (Chgo.). Author: The Neuroses, 1951; Danger Signals, 1953; Nervousness, Indigestion and Pain, 1954, An Introduction to Gastroenterology, 1948; Danger Signals, 1957; Live at Peace with Your Nerves, 1958; Practical Leads to Puzzling Diagnosis, 1958; Minds that Came Back, 1961; Incurable Physician, An Autobiography, 1963; Little Strokes, 1966. Emeritus editor-in-chief Modern Medicine, also Geriatrics. Syndicate med. columnist, 1951—. Office: 700 N Michigan Av Chicago IL 60611 ☆

ALVAREZ-TOSTADO, CLAUDIO, educator; b. Durango, Mexico, June 4, 1912; B.S., U. Ariz., 1934, M.S., 1935; Ph.D. in Chemistry, Stanford, 1939; m. 1943. Jr. research asso. chemistry and medicine Stanford, 1939-40; asst. prof. chemistry Santa Clara, 1941-44; lectr. Stanford, 1943-44, acting asst. prof., 1944-46, asst. prof. phys. sci., 1946-49, asso. prof., 1949-58, prof. phys. sci. and chemistry, 1958—. Vis. prof. chemistry U. Mayor de San Andres, Bolivia, 1956. Research in reaction kinetics, ultracentrifugation, inorganic chemistry of silicon. Address: 761 Stanford Av Palo Alto CA 94305 *

ALVARY, LORENZO, bass singer; b. Hungary, Feb. 20, 1909; s. William and Elizabeth (Kras) A.; B.L., U. Geneva (Switzerland), 1930; LL.M., U. Budapest (Hungary), 1932; m. Hallie Carr Fox, 1959. Came to U.S., 1938, naturalized, 1944. Made debut Royal Opera House, Budapest, Hungary, 1934; toured in concerts and operas throughout world, 1934—; with Vienna State Opera under Bruno Walter, 1937; Met. Opera Co., N.Y.C., 1942—; soloist N.Y. Philharmonic Symphony under Bruno Walter and Arturo Toscanini, Leonard Bernstein, others, 1942—; has appeared in Rio de Janiero, Sao Paula, Brazil, Mexico City, Montivideo, Uruguay, Teatro Colon, Buenos Aires, 1956, Opera Paris, 1957, San Francisco Opera, 1940-71, Stuttgart, Berlin, Naples, Venice, Genoa, 1956—; producer Scarlatti Spectacle, Venice, Brussels, Paris, 1961, 62; host weekly program Opera Topics, Sta. WNYC, 1964—. Judge internat. vocal contests Met. Opera Auditions, Busseto, Enna, Vercelli (all Italy). Calvinist. Home: 205 W 57th St New York City NY 10019 Office: Metropolitan Opera Co New York City NY 10023

ALVEN, WESLEY OGDEN, educator, psychologist; b. Chgo., May 28, 1915; s. Wesley Ruben and Mary (Odgen) A.; Th.B., No. Bapt. Theol. Sem., Chgo., 1939; Ph.B., Loyola U., Chgo., 1940; M.A., U. Akron, 1944; Ph.D., Western Res. U., 1950; m. Katherine Norton, Dec. 26, 1953. Ordained to ministry Evang. Congl. Ch., 1938; minister Evang. Congl. Ch., Akron, O., 1938-46; instr. Western Res. U., 1946-47; asst., then asso. prof. U. Akron, 1947-58, dir. univ. measurement service, 1951-54; me. faculty Fairleigh Dickinson U., Rutherford, N.J., 1958—, prof. psychology, 1962—, chmn. dept., 1958-63. Mem. Am., N.J. psychol. assns., Psi Chi, Delta Epsilon Sigma, Kappa Delta Pi, Omicron Delta Kappa. Home: 11 Cooper Pl Rutherford NJ 07070

ALVEY, EDWARD, Jr., educator; b. Richmond, Va., June 13, 1902; s. Edward and Ida Floyd (Huffman) A.; B.A., U. Va., 1923, M.A., 1928, Ph.D., 1931; m. Frances Ellen McClintic, June 16, 1927; 1 dau., Frances Ellen (Mrs. Joseph J. Montllor). High sch. prin., Hot Springs, Va., 1924-28; supr. student teaching, instr. secondary edn. U. Va., 1928-34, dean Mary Washington Coll. U. Va., 1934-67, prof. edn., 1967—. Pres. Historic Fredericksburg, 1971. Mem. Assn. Va. Colls. (pres. 1953-54), Va. Acad. Sci. (past pres. edn. sect.), Va. Edn. Assn. (past pres. tchr. edn. dept.), Jamestown Soc., Am. Assn. Academic Deans, Raven Soc., Conf. Academic Deans So. States (chmn. 1966), Phi Beta Kappa, Phi Delta Kappa, Alpha Phi Sigma, Alpha Psi Omega. Presbyn. (elder). Kiwanian (past pres. Fredericksburg). Contbr. Ann. Rev. Edn., Americana Corp., Americana Ency., Reader's Digest Yearbook. Home: 1104 College Av Fredericksburg VA 22401

ALWAY, ROBERT HAMILTON, pediatrician, educator; b. University Place, Neb., Dec. 10, 1912; s. Frederick J. and Eva M. K. (Cook) A.; B.S., U. Minn., 1937, M.D., 1940; m. Sophia Chamberlin, May 21, 1942; children—Anne, Mary K., Frederick R., Joan, Theodore. Instr., asso. prof. U. Utah, 1942-49; asso. prof. pediatrics Stanford, 1949-52; prof. pediatrics U. Colo., 1953-55; prof. pediatrics Stanford, 1955—, acting dean med. sch., 1957, dean, 1958-64; med. dir. Stanford Convalescent Home, 1956-60; Commonwealth Fund fellow Guy's Hosp., London, Eng., 1964-65. Nat. adv. council Nat. Inst. Child Health and Human Devel., 1963-67. Mem. Am. Acad. Pediatrics, Am. Pediatric Soc., Cal. Acad. Medicine. Chi Psi, Nu Sigma Nu, Alpha Omega Alpha. Home: 10 Mapache Ct Portola Valley CA 94025 Office: Stanford Med Center Stanford CA 94305

ALWORTH, E. PAUL, educator; b. Cleveland, Okla., Dec. 17, 1917; s. Paul and Clara (Dickson) A.; A.B., U. Mo., 1939, M.A., 1940, Ph.D., 1958; grad. student U. Grenoble (France), 1946; m. Virginia Swain, June 28, 1947; 1 son, Kelly James. Instr. English, Okla. Mil. Acad., 1940-41; mem. faculty U. Tulsa, 1948-, prof. English, chmn. dept., 1959-; cons. bus. communications, 1958-. Served with AUS, 1942-46, Mem. Am. Assn. U. Profs., Nat. Council Tchrs. English, S. Central Modern Lang. Assn., Internat. Soc. Gen. Semantics, Sigma Chi. Author: (with D. E. Hayden) A Semantics Workbook, 1956, Classics in Semantics, 1964; Will rogers, 1965; (with Hayden and Tate) Classics in Linguistics, 1967. Home: 5924 E 49th St Tulsa, OK 74135.

ALWYNE, HORACE, educator; b. Lancashire, Eng., Oct. 13, 1891; s. Thalberg and Mary M. (Whittaker) A.; student Manchester (Eng.) Grammar Sch. and Royal Coll. of Music; m. Mildred Sewall Avery, Dec. 15, 1938. Came to U.S., 1913. Concert pianist since 1906; condr. orchestra and chorus, Manchester Grammar Sch., 1910-12; concert pianist and student, Berlin, Germany, 1912-13; head of piano dept., Skidmore Sch. of Arts (now Skidmore Coll.), Saratoga Springs, N.Y., 1914-21; asso. prof. music, Bryn Mawr Coll., 1921-27, Alice Carter

Dickerman prof. music and dir. dept. of music 1927-57; John Hay Whitney Found. vis. prof. Grinnell Coll., 1957-58; prof. emeritus music Bryn Mawr Coll., 1957—, vis. prof., 1958-65; head piano dept. Bryn Mawr Conservatory of Music, 1962- -; dir. music, Shipley Sch., Bryn Mawr, Pa., 1933-40; mem. faculty Surette Summer Sch. Music, Concord, Mass., 1922-26; lecturer in music, Curtis Inst. of Music, Philadelphia, Pa., 1926-28; Swarthmore Coll., summer 1943; concert pianist has appeared in recitals in England, Germany, Austria, Sicily and U.S.; soloist with Phila. Orchestra, New York Philharmonic, Detroit Symphony, Russian Symphony, Philadelphia String Sinfonietta (several times with each orgn.), in England with British Broadcasting Corp. Orchestra, Hallé orchestra and Bournemouth Symphony, also with well known quartets and chamber orgns. in U.S. Mem. bd. dirs. Settlement Music Sch. of Phila., Phila. Chamber String Sinfonietta, 1931-34. Hon. fellow Royal Coll. of Music (Manchester), 1924, gold medallist, 1912. Sir Charles Hallé Memorial Scholar, 1909-12; recipient Christian R. and Mary F. Lindback award for distinguished teaching ($1,000 grant), 1962. Pres. Soc. Contemporary Music, Phila., 1928-29; hon. dir. Tri-County Jr. Concerts Assn., Wayne, Pa. Home: 1512 Montgomery Av Rosemont PA 19010 Office: Bryn Mawr College Bryn Mawr PA 19010

ALY, BOWER, educator; b. Crystal City, Mo., Feb. 20, 1903; s. Otto and Alice (Bowers) A.; B.S., Southeast Mo. State Coll., 1925; A.M., U. Mo., 1926; student U. Cal., 1929; Ph.D., Columbia, 1941; m. Addie Johnson, Aug. 9, 1926 (dec. 1936); children—Joanna, Barbara, Bower Johnson, Martha Alice and Charles Ernest; m. 2d, Lucile Folse, Feb. 7, 1943; 1 son, Stewart F. Tchr. English, S.E. Mo. State Coll., 1926-30; instr. English, U. Mo., 1930-35, asst. prof. English, 1935-40, asso. prof. speech, 1940-44, prof. speech 1944-57; prof. speech U. Ore., 1957—; vis. prof. speech, Columbia, summers 1938, 41, U. of Wis., summer, 1939, Coll. City of N.Y., 1940; prof. English, U. Hawaii, 1946-47, 55, 65, La. State U., 1950, Cornell U., 1964, Cal. State Coll., Los Angeles, 1968. Recipient of the Julius M. Nolte award, 1965. Mem. Speech Assn. Am. (mem. exec. council; 1st v.p., 1943, pres. 1944), Am. Assn. U. Profs., Western Speech Assn.; hon. mem. Delta Sigma Rho, Tau Kappa Alpha. Democrat. Author: (with Gilman and Reid) A Course Book in Public Speaking, revised 1939; The Rhetoric of Alexander Hamilton, 1941; (with Gilman and White) Fundamentals of Speaking, 1963 (with L.F. Aly) Speeches in English, 1968, American Short Speeches, 1968. Editor: The Discussion and Debate Manual, 1934-64, Quarterly Journal of Speech, 1950-53; Alexander Hamilton; Selections Representing His Life, His Thought, and His Style, 1957. Home: 1138 E 22d Av Eugene OR 97403

AL YASIRI, KAHTAN ABBASS, coll. dean; b. Hindia, Iraq, Jan. 20, 1939; s. Abbass and Fakria Al Y.; came to U.S., 1958; B.Sc., U. Neb., 1962; M.S., 1963; Ph.D., Ia. State U., 1965; m. Ann M. Johnson, June 8, 1961; children—Jeanan, Shawn. Research asst. U. Neb., Lincoln, 1961-63; inst. Ames (Ia.) pub. schs., 1963-65; instr. Ia. State U., Ames, 1964-65; asso. prof., head dept. bus. and econs. Wis. State U. at Platteville, 1965-66, prof. econs. dean Coll. Bus. and Econs., 1966—. Mem. Am., Midwest, Western econ. assns., Agr. Econ. Assn., Omicron Delta Epsilon. Author: Economic Work and Program Study, 1966; Growth and Progress in Business, 1966. Home: 1555 N Elm St Platteville WI 53818

ALYEA, EDWIN PASCAL, surgeon; b. Clifton, N.J., Feb. 4, 1898; s. Joseph P.S. and Sarah Mae (Dinsmore) A.; B.S., Princeton, 1919; M.D., Johns Hopkins, 1923, postgrad., 1923-29; m. Nancy B. Anderson, June 9, 1926; children—Edwin Pascal, Nancy. Resident in medicine and instr. in surgery Johns Hopkins U. Sch. Medicine, 1923-26; resident, instr. in urology Brady Urol. Inst., Johns Hopkins Hosp., 1926-29; successively instr., asst. prof., asso. prof. surgery in charge urologic div. Duke U. Med. Sch., 1942, prof. urology, 1947-65, prof. emeritus, 1965—; past chief urology Duke U. Med. Center, Durham, N.C.; cons. Watts, Lincoln, VA hosps., Durham, 1953. Mem. venereal disease com. NRC, Washington, 1940-42; mem. Nat. Med. Com. on Birth Control, 1933. Served with A.R.C., 1917; with heavy arty., O.T.C., U.S. Army, 1918. Diplomate Nat. Bd. Med. Examiners, Am. Bd. Urology. Fellow A.C.S. (gov. 1954); mem. Clin. Soc. Genito-Urinary Surgeons, Am. Assn. Genito-Urinary Surgeons, Am. Urol. Assn., Urosurg. Soc., Johns Hopkins Surg. Soc., Am. Neisserian Med. Soc., Am., N.C. med. socs., So. Med. Assn., Southeastern (hon.), N.C., Fla. urol. socs., Phi Beta Kappa, Alpha Omega Alpha. Contbr. numerous articles to profl. jours. Address: Duke Hospital Durham NC 27706

ALYEA, ETHAN DAVIDSON, lawyer; b. Clifton, N.J., Feb. 2, 1896; s. Joseph Pascal Strong and Sarah May (Dinsmore) A.; A.B., Princeton, 1916, M.A., 1917; LL.B., Harvard, 1922; m. Dorothy Collins, Aug. 2, 1924; children—Jane D., Ethan Davidson. Admitted to N.Y. bar, 1923, since practiced in N.Y.C.; mem. firm Dewey, Ballantine, Bushby, Palmer & Wood. Dir. Royal Bank Can. Trust Co., Fairbanks Co. Pres. Montclair (N.J.) Council Social Agys., 1948-50. Bd. dirs. Grand Central Art Galleries, Inc., 1961-69; pres., dir. Cintas Found.; trustee Montclair Community Chest, 1954-57; pres. Montclair Adult Sch., 1946-48, trustee, 1946—; trustee Montclair Library, 1947-57; v.p., trustee Montclair Art Mus., 1953-67. Served as sgt. U.S. Army, 1918-19. Mem. Am., Inter-Am., Internat., N.Y. bar assns., Assn. Bar City N.Y., N.Y. County Lawyers Assn., Phi Beta Kappa. Clubs: University, Downtown Assn. (N.Y.C.). Home: 77 Highland Av Montclair NJ 07042 Office: 140 Broadway New York City NY 10005

AMACK WILLIAM SHELDON, diversified mfg. co. exec.; b. Cin., May 21, 1910; grad. Phillips Acad., Andover, Mass., 1927; B.S., Princeton, 1931; postgrad. Mass. Inst. Tech., 1931-33; m. Jean R. Holland, June 16, 1935; children--Lois A., Andrew M., James. Salesman, Brown Mfg. Co., Boston, 1932-33; jr. engr. Ball Metals Co., Carson City, Nev., 1933-36, engr., 1936-37, sr. engr., 1937-40; project engr. Kingston Engring. Co., Los Angeles, 1940-43; with dept. engring. City of Denver, 1946-50, dep. head, 1950-52; 2d v.p. Johnson Mfg. Co., Kansas City, Kansas, 1952-54, v.p. for engring., 1954-57; v.p. research Consol. Industries, Inc., South Bend, Ind., 1957-60, exec. v.p., 1960-65, pres., 1965-70, chmn. bd., chief exec. officer, 1970–, also dir.; dir. ABC Chem. Co., 2d Nat. Bank, Country Food Storage Co., Providence Indsl. Corp. (Ind.), Wilson Investment Co., Inc., Hammond Life Ins. Co., Inc. (Ind.), Prudential Ins. Co., Haverford Mfg. Co., Leader Pub. Co. Pres., Dewey High Sch., Kansas City, Mo., 1953-54; fund chmn. local div. Salvation Army, 1959-60. Mem. South Bend Republican Com., 1964-68. Bd. dirs. Ind. council Boy Scouts Hosp., 1965-71. Served from lt. to capt., AUS, 1951-53. Mem. Am. Chem. Soc., Sci. Research Soc. Am. (chpt. treas. 1967), Am. Assn. Chemistry Tchrs., Am. Assn. U. Profs., Wildlife Soc., American Institute Chemists, Ecological Soc. Am. (chpt. sec.), Sigma Xi. Author: (with others) Basic Inorganic Chemistry, 1971. Contbr. articles to profl. jours., encys., also chpts. to books. Home: Fairfax Apts 7291 Windermere Dr University City MO 63105 Office: Dept Chemistry Washington University St Louis MO 63130

AMADEUS, SISTER M., educator; b. Detroit; b.A., Marygrove Coll., 1931; M.A., Notre Dame U., 1941; Ph.D., Cath. U. of Am., 1947. Tchr., Saint Mary Acad., Monroe, Mich., 1927-38; supr. schs. Archdiocese of Detroit, 1938-44; dean Marygrove Coll., 1947-69; dean of studies IHM Community, Monroe, 1969—. Mem. Am. Psychol. Assn., Am. Assn. U. Profs., Adult Edn. Assn. U.S.A Address: 610 W Elm Monroe, MI 48161.

AMADO, JORGE, author; b. Bahia, Brazil, Oct. 8, 1912; s. Joad Amado Frank and Eulalia Leal; lawyer, U. de Brazil, 1935; m. Zelia Cattai, July 14, 1945; children—Joad Jorge, Paloma. Deputado nacional, 1946-48. Author: Pais do Carnaval, 1931; Cacou, 1933; Suor, 1934; Julialia, 1935; Mar Morto, 1936; Capitues da Areia, 1937; ABE de Castro Alues, 1941; Tenos do Sem Fin, 1943; Sao Jorge dos Illreus, 1944; Bahia de Tados es Lantos, 1945; O Amor do Soldado, 1947; Seara Vermellai, 1946; Os Subterraneas da Leilerdade, 1954; Gabriela cravo e canela, 1958; Os Velhos Marinheiros, 1961; Os Pastores de Noite, 1964; Dana Flor e Seus dais Maridos, 1966. Address: 33 Rua Alagoinhas Salvador Bahai Brazil

AMADO, RALPH DAVID, educator; b. Los Angeles, Nov. 23, 1932; s. Richard Joseph and Suzanne (Nahoum) A.; B.A., Stanford, 1954; Ph.D. (Rhodes scholar), Oxford U., 1957; m. Carol Stein, May 28, 1961; children—Richard Lewis, David Phillip. Research asso. U. Pa., 1957-59, asst. prof., 1959-62, asso. prof., 1962-65, prof. physics, 1965—. Cons., Arms Control and Disarmament Agy., 1962-65, Los Alamos Sci. Lab., 1965—. Fellow Am. Phys. Soc.; mem. A.A.A.S. Home: 509 Latmer Rd Merion PA 19066

AMADON, DEAN, ornithologist; b. Milw., June 6, 1912; s. Arthur and Mary (Evenson) A.; B.S., Hobart Coll., 1934, Sc.D. (hon.), 1960; Ph.D., Cornell U., 1947; m. Octavia Gardella, 1940; children—Susan, Emily. With Conn. Bd. Fisheries and Game, 1936-37; mem. staff Am. Museum Natural History, N.Y.C., 1937—, now chmn. staff, also Lamont curator birds. Served with AUS, 1943-46. Fellow Am. Assn. for Advancement Science; mem. Am. Ornithologists Soc. (pres.), Linnaean Soc. N.Y. (pres.), Author: (with R. C. Murphy) Land Birds of America; Birds Around the World. Home: 25 Kenwood Rd Tenafly NJ 07670 Office: American Museum Natural History Central Park West at 79th St New York City NY 10024*

AMALDI, EDOARDO, physicist; b. Carpaneto, Piacenza, Italy, Sept. 5, 1908; s. Ugo and Luisa (Basini) A.; Dr. Physics, U. Rome, 1929; m. Ginestra Giovene, Oct. 19, 1933; children—Ugo, Franceso, Daniela. Became prof. physics U. Rome, 1937; sec.-gen. European Orgn. for Nuclear Research, 1952-54; pres. Internat. Union Pure and Applied Physics, 1957-60. Fellow Lincei Nat. Acad.; mem. Royal Soc. for Scis. Uppsala, Acad. Scis. USSR, Royal Inst. Gt. Britain, Am. Philos. Soc., Am. Acad. Arts and Scis., Nat. Acad. Scis. U.S.A., Royal Acad. Netherlands, Acad. Leopoldina, Royal Swedish Acad. Scis., Royal Soc. London. Research and publs. on atomic, molecular and nuclear physics. Home: Viale Parioli 50 Rome Italy

AMANDES, RICHARD BRUCE, univ. dean; b. Berkeley, Cal., Mar. 29, 1927; s. F. Frederic and Nellie (McHoul) A.; A.B., U. Cal. at Berkeley, 1950; J.D., Hastings Coll. Law, 1953; LL.M., N.Y. U., 1956; m. Joanne Vivien Beran, June 9, 1950; children—Christopher Bruce, Robin Michelle. Admitted to Cal. bar, 1954; pvt. practice law, San Francisco, 1954; instr. U. Wash. Sch. Law, 1954-55, vis. asst. prof., 1956-57, asst. prof., asst. dean, 1958-60, asso. prof., asst. dean, 1960-64; asst. prof. U. Wyo. Sch. Law, 1957-58; asso. dean, Robert W. Harrison prof. law Hastings Coll. of Law, U. Cal., 1964-66; dean, prof. law Tex. Tech U., Lubbock, 1966—. Vis. asst. prof. So. Meth. U. Sch. Law, summer 1957; adminstr. Continuing Legal Edn., State of Wash., 1959-64; participant Summer Workshop for Internat. Legal Studies, U. Cal., Berkeley, 1958. Chmn., Conf. Western Law Schs., Seattle, 1959, Lubbock, 1971; mem. exec. com. Law Sch. Admission Test Council, 1962-64; chmn. Bar Exam. Revision Com. Tex., 1969—; sec.-treas.. Tex. Tech. Law Sch. Found. Served with AUS, 1945-47. Teaching fellow N.Y. U. Sch. Law, 1955-56. Mem. Am. (chmn. com. on significant real property decisions 1965-66), Wash. bar assns., State Bar Cal., State Bar Tex., Assn. Am. Law Schs. (council on new and expanding law schs.), Edward S. Thurston Honor Soc., Order of Coif, Phi Alpha Delta, Lambda Alpha Epsilon, Phi Kappa Phi. Contbr. articles to profl. publs. Home: 3306 39th St Lubbock TX 79413

AMAR, HENRI, educator, physicist; b. Casablanca, July 14, 1920; s. Jacob and Zora (Elbaz) A.; B.A., B.S., Acad. Paris, 1940; M.A., U. Algiers, 1942; M.A., Ohio State U., 1948,, Ph.D., 1952; m. Mary Helene Genissieux, Dec. 23, 1952; children—Jacques G., Francois C., Yvette Anne. Asst. prof. physics Lafayette Coll., 1952-56; sr. research physicist Franklin Inst., 1956-60; asso. prof. physics Temple U., 1960-66, prof., 1966—, co-dir. AEC research contract, 1964—. Recipient award for excellence in teaching and research, Lindback Found., 1966. Fellow Am. Phys. Soc.; mem. Am. Assn. Physics Tchrs., Am. Assn. Univ. Profs., Franklin Inst. Research and publs. on theoretical physics, magnetism and metallic alloys. Home: 330 Euclid Av Ambler PA 19002 Office: Barton Hall Temple Univ Philadelphia PA 19122

AMARACK, BENJAMIN JOSEPH mfg. exec.; b. Lima, O., Apr. 1, 1932; B.S., U. San Francisco, 1954; M.S., Stanford University, 1956; m. Rosemarie Lois Brown, May 15, 1955; 1 son, Anthony Robinson. Sales rep. Ames-Brockton Fabricated Products, Akron, O., 1956-58, sales mgr. Coshocton, Ohio, 1959-61, gen. manager plant, 1961-68, v.p. sales, 1968--. Instr. bus. Coshocton Jr. College, 1968-69. Named Man of Year, Coshocton Junior Chamber of Commerce, 1968. Mem. Coshocton C. of C. (vice president 1967-68, pres. 1969-70), English Speaking Union, Coshocton Sertoma Club, Nat. Assn. Mfrs., Sales Executives Institute, Phi Beta Kappa, Sigma Chi, Phi Mu. Democrat. Mem. Christian Ch. (lay leader). Mason (32, Shriner). Clubs: Coshocton Country, Coshocton City, Running Deer Country. Home: 2d Av Coshocton OH Office: 3d Av Coshocton OH

AMAREL, SAUL, educator, computer scientist; b. Thessaloniki, Greece, Feb. 16, 1928; s. Albert and Sol (Pelossof) Amario; B.Sc., Israel Inst. Tech., Haifa, 1948, Ingenieur EE, 1949; M.S., Columbia, 1953, D.Eng. Sci., 1955; m. Marianne Kroh, Dec. 20, 1953; children—Dan, David. Came to U.S., 1957, naturalized, 1962. Sci. dep. Israel Ministry Def., Israel, 1948-52, project leader control and computer systems, 1955-57; research engr. Electronic Research Lab., Columbia, 1953-55; head computer theory research RCA Labs., Princeton, N.J., 1957-69; prof., chmn. computer sci. dept. Rutgers U., New Brunswick, N.J., 1969—. Vis. prof. computer sci. Carnegie Mellon U., 1966; cons. RCA Labs., Princeton, 1969—. Mem. chem./biol. information handling rev. com. NIH, 1971—; Columbia Seminar asso. on relations between research, edn. and computers, 1965—. Trustee Ramapo Coll. N.J. Mem. I.E.E.E. (sr.), Soc. Indsl. and Applied Math., Assn. Computing Machinery, A.A.A.S., Sigma Xi. Mem. editorial bd. Artificial Intelligence, Internat. Jour., 1969—. Contbr. articles to sci. jours. Home: 25 White Pine Lane Princeton NJ 08540 Office: Rutgers U New Brunswick NJ 08903

AMATEIS, EDMOND ROMULUS, sculptor; b. of Am. parents, Rome, Italy, Feb. 7, 1897; s. Prof. Louis and Dora (Ballin) A.; art edn., Beaux Arts Inst. Design, N.Y. City, 1916- 17, 1920-21, Academie Julian, Paris, 1919, Am. Acad. in Rome, 1921-24; m. Mildred Denison, Aug. 10, 1942 (dec. 1966). Prin. works include busts, garden figures, folklore groups; Kansas City Liberty Meml., Baltimore War Memorial, U.S. Govt. Memorial, Draguignan, France; also reliefs and portrait studies, Polio Wall of Fame, Georgia. Warm Springs Found. Asso. in sculpture, Columbia. Served in F.A., U.S. Army, Apr. 1917-Aug. 1919, participating in battles of Chateau-Thierry, St. Mihiel, Meuse Argonne. Asso. of Nat. Acad., 1936, Nat. Academician, 1943; mem. Nat. Sculpture Soc. (pres. 1942-44), Alumni Assn. Am. Acad. in Rome, Nat. Inst. Arts and Letters. Fellowship Am. Acad. in Rome, 1921-24; Henry O. Avery prize, Archtl. League of N.Y., 1929; James E. McClese prize, Pa. Acad. Fine Arts, 1933, Lindsey Sterling Morris Medal, Nat. Sculptor Soc. Designer of medal of Society of Medalists, 1940; U.S. Govt. medals for Typhus Commn. and Pacific Theatre of Operations, Liberty Hyde Bailey medal, 1958. Club: University (Winter Park, Fla.). ☆

AMATO, VINCENT VITO, financial exec.; b. Bklyn., Oct. 14, 1929; s. Anthony and Josephine (Maniscalco) A.; B.B.A., Coll. City N.Y., 1951, M.B.A., 1958; m. Marie Dioguardi, Apr. 24, 1955; children—Stephanie, Janine, Anthony, Christopher. Liaison to div. controller Allied Chem. Corp., N.Y.C., 1951- 59; accounting systems rep. Olivetti-Underwood, N.Y.C., 1959-61; v.p. planning, controller, acquisitions exec. SuCrest Corp., N.Y.C., 1961—; adj. asst. prof. N.Y.U., also Am. Mgmt. Assn. seminars. Pres. Lakeridges Civic Assn. Mem. Financial Execs. Inst., Assn. for Corporate Growth, Am. Mgmt. Assn. (tech. adviser). Home: 7 Alder Ct Matawan NJ 07747 Office: 120 Wall St New York City NY 10005

AMAYA, RENE D., librarian; A.A., B.A., A.M. in L.S. With Detroit Pub. Library, 1957-61; asst. librarian Detroit Inst. Tech., 1961-65, head librarian, 1965-67; asst. prof., librarian Orchard Ridge campus Oakland Community Coll., Farmington, Mich., 1967—. Mem. A.L.A., Mich. Library Assn., Mich. Community and Jr. Coll. Assn. Home: 1465 Chicago Blvd Detroit MI 48206 Office: Orchard Ridge Campus Oakland Community Coll Farmington MI 48024

AMAZEEN, EDWARD SUTHERLAND, investment co. exec.; b. Melrose Mass., Dec. 23, 1909; s. Edward Clifton and Evelyn Maria (Sutherland) A.; A.B. cum laude, Harvard, 1931; M.B.A., 1935; m. Elizabeth Childs Taylor, Apr. 14, 1934; children—Elizabeth Anne (Mrs. Edward R. Hammond, Jr.), Edward Sutherland, Nancy Jane. Grad. sec. Phillips Brooks House Assn., Harvard, 1931-36; mgr. billing dept. Carter's Ink Co., Cambridge, Mass., 1935; with Coffin & Burr, Inc., investment bankers, Boston, 1935-41, 47-58, v.p., mgr. investment trust dept., 1947-58; co-founder Importsales, Inc., also Loire Imports, Inc., N.Y.C., 1947; with One William St. Fund, Inc., N.Y.C. 1959-65. v.p. 1962-65; dir. sales One William dept. Lehman Bros., 1960-65; v.p. dir. William St. Sales Inc. 1959-64; pres. dir. Willimington Capitol Services Corp 1965—; v.p. Blue Ridge Mut. Fund, 1965—; dir. Loire Imports Inc.; trustee S. Scituate Savs. Bank, Norwell, Mass. Pres., trustee Woodlawn Cemetery, Everett, Mass., 1949—. Chmn. Republican Town Com., Hanover, Mass., 1940-58; chmn. planning bd., Hanover, 1948-60; mem. Mass. Rep. Exec. Com., 1954-59. Served to comdr. USNR, 194147; ETO. Mem. Nat. Assn. Securities Dealers (past chmn. New Eng. dist.), Investment Bankers Assn. Am. (past vice chmn. New Eng. group, past chmn. investment companies com.), Investment Co. Inst. Clubs: Bond (past bd. govs.), Down Town (Boston); Harvard (N.Y.C.); Old Colony Harvard (Brockton, Mass.). Home: Main and Cedar Sts Hanover MA 02113 Office: 111 Broadway New York City NY 10006

AMBLER, ERIC, author; b. London, Eng., June 28, 1909; s. Alfred Percy and Amy Madeline A.; student Colfe's Grammar Sch.; student (engring. scholarship), London U., 1925; m. Louise Crombie, Oct. 5, 1939 (div. May 1958); m. 2d, Joan Harrison, Oct. 11, 1958. Apprentice in engring. firm, London, 1928; advt. copy writer, 1933-37; dir. advt. agy., 1937-38; full time writer, 1938—. Served as Air Raid Precautions stretcher bearer during defense of London, Aug.-Oct. 1940; joined Brit. Army (arty.), Nov. 1940; served in N. Africa, Italy, later as lt. col. on Brit. Army staff, charge prodn. army morale, ednl., tng. films. Decorated Bronze Star (U.S.). Author: The Dark Frontier, 1936; Background to Danger, 1937; Cause for Alarm, 1939; A Coffin for Dimitrios, 1939; Journey into Fear, 1940; Intrigue, 1943; Judgment on Deltchev, 1951; Epitaph for a Spy, 1952; The Schirmer Inheritance, 1953; State of Siege, 1956; Passage of Arms, 1960; The Light of Day, 1962; The Ability to Kill, 1963; A Kind of Anger, 1964; Dirty Story, 1967; The Intercom Conspiracy, 1969; Love Hate Love, 1970; movies: The Way Ahead, 1945; United States (Army documentary), 1945; The October Man, 1947; One Woman's Story, 1948; Highly Dangerous, 1950; The Magic Box, 1951; Encore, 1952; The Promoter, 1952; Roughshoot, 1953; The Cruel Sea, 1953; Lease of Life, 1954; The Purple Plain, 1955; Yangtse Incident, 1957; A Night to Remember, 1958; The Wreck of the Mary Deare, 1959; Topkapi, 1964. Home: Chem Ile de Salagnon 1 1815 Clarens Switzerland

AMBRECHT, WILLIAM H., banker. Chmn. bd. First Nat. Bank of Mobile. Office: 31 Royal St PO Drawer 1467 Mobile AL 36601*

AMBRIDGE, D.W., former paper mfr.; b. Mexico City, Mexico, Jan. 5, 1898; s. Charles Theodore and Frances (White) A.; B.Sc. in Chem. Engring., McGill U., Montreal, Can., 1923; LL.D., Waterloo Luth. U., 1962; m. Jessie Louise Barlow, June 10, 1924; children—Cicely Barlow (Mrs. N. B. Bell), Janet White (Mrs. J.M.G. Scott), Shirley Sinclair, Charlotte. Control engr. Abitibi Power & Paper Co., Ltd., Iroquois Falls, Ont., Can., 1923-27; gen. supt. Anglo-Canadian Pulp and Paper Mills, Ltd.; asst. gen. mgr. Anglo-Newfoundland Devel. Co., 1927-36; asst. to pres. Ontario Paper Co., Thorold, Ont., 1936; asst. gen. mgr., v.p., 1943-46; dir. Polymer Corp., Ltd., 1942-50, pres., 1945; pres., also gen. mgr. Abitibi Paper Co., Ltd., 1946-59, pres., 1959-63, chmn. bd., 1963-68, hon. chmn., 1968—, also hon. dir.; dir. Canadian Gas & Energy Fund Ltd., Can. Malting Co., Ltd., Canadian Security Growth Fund Ltd. Served with C.F.A., 2d Division C.E.F., World War I; dir. gen. shipbldg. br. Dept. Munitions and Supply, Ottawa, Ont., World War II. Decorated comdr. Order Brit. Empire. Councillor Nat. Indsl. Conf. Bd. Mem. Phi Delta Theta. Club: York (Toronto). Home: 19 Wychwood Park Toronto Ontario Canada

AMBROSE, MYLES JOSEPH, lawyer; b. N.Y.C., July 21, 1926; s. Arthur P. nd Anna (Campbell) A.; student New Hampton Sch., N.H., 1944; B.B.A., Manhattan Coll., 1948; J.D., N.Y. Law Sch., 1952; m. Elaine Miller, June 26, 1948; children—Myles Joseph, Kathleen Anne, Kevin Arthur, Elise Mary, Nora Jeanne, Christopher Miller. Personnel mgr. Devenco, Inc., 1948-49, 51-54; admitted to N.Y. bar, 1952, U.S. Supreme Ct. bar, 1959, U.S. Ct. Customs and Patent Appeals, 1970; adminstrv. asst. U.S. atty. So. dist. N.Y., 1954-57; instr. econs. of labor Manhattan Coll., 1955-57; asst. to sec. U.S. Treasury, 1957-60; exec. dir. Waterfront Commn. of N.Y. Harbor, 1960-63; chief counsel N.Y. State Joint Legislative Com. for Study Alcoholic Beverage Control Law, 1963-65; dir. Am. Materials & Mfg. Corp.; asst. to commr. U.S. Bur. Customs, Washington; 1969—. U.S. observer 13th session UN, Geneva, Switzerland, 1958, chmn. U.S. delegation, 27th Gen. Assembly, Internat. Criminal Police Orgn., London, 1958, 28th Extraordinary Gen. Assembly, Paris, 1959, U.S. observer 29th Gen. Assembly, Washington, 1960; chmn. U.S.-Mexico Conf. on Narcotics, Washington, 1960; cons. U.S.-Mexico Conf. on Narcotics, Mexico, 1969; Interpol Conf. del Mexico City, 1969; U.S. del. Customs Coop. Council, Brussels, 1970, Interpol Conf., Brussels, 1970. Bd. dirs. Manhattan Coll. Alumni Adv. Council; trustee New Hampton Sch. Recipient Presdl. Mgmt. Improvement certificate Pres. Nixon, 1970, Sec. Treasury Spl. award. Mem. N.Y.C., N.Y. State bar assns., N.Y. State Dist. Atty. Assn., Guild Cath. Lawyers N.Y., Internat. Assn. Chiefs Police, Alpha Sigma Beta, Phi Alpha Delta (hon.). Club: Knollwood Country. Home: 5506 Uppingham St Chevy Chase MD 20015 Office: U S Bureau Customs 2100 K St NW Washington DC 20226

AMBRUS, JULIAN L., medical educator; b. Budapest, Hungary, Nov. 29, 1924; s. Alexander and Elizabeth A.; student U. Budapest, 1942-47; M.D., U. Zurich, 1949; postgrad. Sorbonne, 1949-50; Ph.D. in Med. Sci., Jefferson Med. Coll., 1954; m. Clara M. Bayer, Feb. 18, 1945; children—Madeline, Peter, Julian, Linda, Steven, Katherine, Charles. Came to U.S., 1949, naturalized, 1955. Research asst., instr. histology U. Budapest, 1943-45, demonstrator pharmacology, 1946-47; asst. pharmacology U. Zurich, 1947-49; asst. dept. therapeutic chemistry, virology Inst. Pasteur, Paris, 1949; asst. prof., asso. prof., Phila. Coll. Pharmacology and Sci., 1950-55; prin. cancer research scientist Roswell Park Meml. Inst. and Hosp., 1955—, asst. to the dir., 1961-65, dir. Springville Labs., 1965—; asst. prof. pharmacology U. Buffalo Med. Sch., 1955-61, asso. prof. pharmacology, 1961-65, prof., 1965—, chmn. Roswell Park div. exec. com. Grad. Sch., 1955-65; prof. biochem. pharmacology State U. N.Y. at Buffalo, 1964—, asso. in internal medicine, 1961—, asst. prof. internal medicine, 1964-66, asso. prof. internal medicine, 1966-71, prof., 1971—; dir. Instnl. Cancer Tng. Program USPHS, 1956-65. Mem. USPHS, NIH; mem. com. Thrombalytic agts., 1960-66; cons. A.M.A. Council Drugs, Adv. Com. on Blood Coagulation Components Protein Found., Cambridge, Mass., Bur. Drugs, Food and Drug Adminstrn. Commnr. Lake Erie chpt. U.S. Pony Clubs. Trustee Calasanctius Prep. Sch. for Acad. Gifted, Buffalo Chamber Music Soc., Internat. Inst. Buffalo; bd. regents Am. Coll. Law and Sci. Recipient first prize med. student paper Hungarian Med. Sch., 1947, 1st prize surgery U. Budapest, 1947. Diplomate in clin. chemistry Am. Bd. Clin. Chemistry. Fellow Am. Coll. Angiology, Royal Soc. Medicine, Am. Coll. Pharmacology and Chemotherapy, Council on Clin. Cardiology, Am. Heart Assn., Internat. Coll. Angiology, Am. Geriatrics Soc., N.Y. Acad. Sci., A.A.A.S., Internat. Soc. Hematology; mem. Am. Soc. Hematology, Am. Soc. Nuclear Medicine, Am. Soc. Pharmacology and Exptl. Therapeutics, Am. Soc. Physiology, Am. Assn. Cancer Research, Am. Soc. Clin. Uncalogy, Fedn. Clin. Research, Soc. Exptl. Biology and Medicine, Assn. Am. Med. Colls., Cath. Physicians Guild, Sigma Xi, Rho Chi, Physiol. Soc. Phila., Radiation Research Soc., Buffalo Zool. Soc. (chmn. Sci. Council 1965-66), Buffalo Acad. Medicine. Contbr. articles profl. jours. Editor-in- chief Jour. Medicine, Hematology Revs.; editorial bd. Folia Hematologica, Rev. Communications in Clin. Pathology and Pharmacology. Home: 143 Windsor Av Buffalo NY 14209 also West Hill Farm Emmerling Rd Boston NY 14025 Office: 666 Elm St Buffalo NY 14203 also 571 E Main St Springville NY 14141

AMEEL, DONALD JULES, retired zoologist; b. Detroit, Apr. 24, 1907; s. Jules T. and Selma Ida (Beer) A.; A.B., Wayne U., 1928; A.M., U. Mich., 1930, Ph.D., 1933; m. Henrietta Ruth Zezula, Aug. 3, 1937; children—John Jules, Donna Ruth, George Robert. Asst. in zoology U. Mich., 1928-32, fellow, 1932-33, temporary instr., 1935-36; asso. prof. biology Augustana Coll., 1933-35; instr. zoology Kan. State U., 1937-42, asst. prof., 1942-45, prof., head dept., 1945-67; ret. Former zoologist Kan. Bd. Agr. Fellow A.A.A.S.; mem. Am. Soc. Parasitologists, Am. Microscopical Soc., Kan. Acad. Sci. (pres. 1956), Sigma Xi, Phi Sigma, Phi Kappa Phi, Gamma Sigma Delta. Conglist. Home: 411 Edgerton Av Manhattan KS 66502

AMELL, ALEXANDER RENTON, educator, chemist; b. Clarksburg, Mass., Mar. 3, 1923; s. Louis and Agnes (Renton) A.; B.S., U. Mass., 1947; Ph.D., U. Wis., 1950; m. Allison Hamlin Moore, Sept. 5, 1945; children—A. Renton, Nancy Allison, Jane Anderson, Rebecca Susan. Instr. chemistry Hunter Coll., N.Y.C., 1950-52; asst. prof. Lebanon Valley Coll., 1952-55; research asso. Brookhaven Nat. Lab., 1955; mem. faculty U. N.H., Durham, 1955—, prof. chemistry, 1962-, chmn. dept., 1961-. Active Durham Youth Assn. Served to 1st lt. AUS, 1942-45. Decorated D.F.C., Air medal with 4 oak leaf clusters. Home: 4 Chesley Dr Durham, NH 03824.

AMEN, IRVING, artist; b. N.Y.C., June 25, 1918; s. Benjamin and Bessie (Glusack) A.; student Pratt Inst., N.Y.C., 1933-35, Art Students League, N.Y.C., 1946- 48, Academie de la Grande Chaumiere, Paris, France, 1949-50; m. Dora Beck, May 21, 1941. Tchr., Pratt Inst., 1957, 58, U. Notre Dame, 1962; one man shows N.Y.C., sann Francisco, Denver, Washington, Louisville, Detroit, Albuquerque, Cleve., Phila., Memphis, Salt Lake City, numerous other cities in U.S., also in Jerusalem, Israel; rep. permanent collections Met. Mus. Art, Mus. Modern Art, Library of Congress, Smithsonian Instn., Bibliotheque Nationale (Paris), Bibliotheque Royale (Brussels, Belgium), Bezalel Nat. Mus. (Jerusalem), Victoria and Albert Mus. (London, Eng.), Stadtische Mus. (Wilberfeld, Germany), N.Y. Pu. Library, Phila. Mus. Art, Boston Mus. Fine Art, Balt. Mus. Art, Cambridge (Mass.) Pu. Library, Cin. Mus. Art, de Cordova and Dana Mus. (Lincoln, Mass.), numerous others. Served with USAAF, 1942-45. Mem. Artists Equity (dir.), Soc. Am. Graphic Artists (dir.), Internat. Inst. Arts and Letters, Internat. Soc. Wood Engravers, Am. Color Print Soc., Audubon Artists, Boston Printmakers, L'Accademia Fiorentia delle arti del disegno Florence (Hon.). Home: 120 E 90th St new York City, NY 10029. Studio: 153 Waverly Pl New York City NY 10014

AMEN, PAUL JOHN, banker; b. Lincoln, Neb., July 6, 1916; s. Henry J. and Barbara (Wacker) A.; B.A., U. Neb., 1938, M.A., 1941; m. Florence Moll, June 12, 1943; children—Karen Sue, Mary Kathryne, Barbara Alice, Paul John. Instr., English dept. U.S. Mil. Acad., 1943-46, head baseball coach, 1943-52, asst. football coach, 1943-55; head football coach Wake Forest Coll., Winston-Salem, N.C., 1956-59; v.p. Wachovia Bank & Trust Co., Charlotte, N.C., 1960-67; pres., dir. Nat. Bank Commerce Trust & Savs. Assn., Lincoln, 1967-; dir. Lincoln Bank South, Kearney First Nat. Bank, Fremont First Nat. Bank, Fremont First State Bank. Dir., treas. Salt Valley Watershed Dist.; mem. Lincoln Water adv. bd. Chmn. Mecklenburg County chpt. A.R.C., 1965; chmn. United Arts Fund, Charlotte, 1966. Bd. dirs. Tax Research Council; trustee U. Neb. Found.; trustee, pres. Assos. Doane Coll. Served with AUS, 1942-46. Named Coach of Year, 1956, 59. Mem. Neb. Assn. Commerce and Industry (dir.), Neb. Bankers Assn. (mem. exec. council), Lincoln C. of C., Delta Tau Delta. Conglist. Elk, Rotarian. Clubs: Country, University (Lincoln). Home: 2770 Woodscrest St Lincoln, NB 68502. Office: 13th and O Sts Lincoln, NB 68501.

AMENT, ARTHUR ROBERT GEORGE, utility exec.; b. Seaforth, Ont., Can., Feb. 17, 1907; s. William and Janet Elizabeth (Winter) A.; B.Commerce, U. Toronto, 1928; m. Margaret McKay, Sept. 11, 1935; children—Janet Anne, Catherine Elizabeth. With Clarkson, Gordon, Gilforth, Guilfoyle & Nash, chartered accountants, Toronto, 1928-35; office mgr. Robson Leather Co., Ltd., Oshawa, Ont., 1935-40; chief accountant Research Enterprises, Ltd., Leaside, Ont., 1940-42, asst. comptroller, 1942-44, treas., 1944-46; treas. Turbo Research, Ltd., Leaside, 1944-46; asst. to comptroller British Am. Oil Co., Ltd., Toronto, 1946-48; with Brascan Ltd. (formerly Brazilian Light & Power Co., Ltd.), Toronto, 1948, asst. treas. controls, budget comptroller, dir. adminstrn., 1948-55, comptroller, 1955-61, treas., 1961; dir. Brazilian Light Ltd., Canadian Brazilian Services Ltd., Am. Brazilian Suppliers Inc., Brascan Internat. Finance Co. Ltd. Decorated Order British Empire. Chartered accountant, Ont. Mem. Inst. Chartered Accountants Ont. Presbyn. Clubs: Toronto Hunt, The Arts and Letters (Toronto); Albanyo Home: 25 Dunbar Rd Toronto 5 Ontario Canada Office: 25 King St W Toronto 1 Ontario Canada

AMERASINGHE, HAMILTON SHIRLEY, Ceylon diplomat; b. Colombo, Ceylon, Mar. 18, 1913; student Royal Coll., Colombo, 1921-30, Univ. Coll., Ceylon, 1930-34; B.A. with honours, London U., 1934. Entered Ceylon Civil Service, 1937; resident mgr. Gal Oya Devel. Bd., 1950-52; counseller Ceylon embassy, Washington, 1953-55; Ceylon del. 5th Com. UN Gen. Assembly 12th Session, 1957; permanent sec. Ministry Nationalized Services and Rd. Transp., chmn. Port Corp., 1958; additional permanent sec. Ministry External Affairs, 1960; sec. to Treasury, permanent sec. Ministry Finance, mem. monetary bd. Central Bank Ceylon, alternate gov. for Ceylon in Internat. Bank for Reconstrn. and Devel., 1961-63; high commr. for Ceylon in India, Ceylon ambassador to Nepal and Afghanistan, 1963; mem. Ceylon delegation to prep. meeting 2d Conf. Non Aligned Nations, Colombo, 1964; leader Ceylon delegation to Prep. Meeting Fgn. Ministers, 2d Afro. Asian Conf., Jakarta, 1964; leader Ceylon delegation, vice chmn. Ann. Session ECAFE, New Delhi, 1966; permanent rep. to UN, N.Y.C., 1967, chmn. Ceylon delegation to 22d to 25th sessions of Gen. Assembly, 1967-70, chmn. Com. Peaceful Uses of Sea-Bed and Ocean Floor beyond Limits Nat. Jurisdiction, 1966-71. Home: 1000 Park Av New York City NY 10028 Office: 630 3d Av New York City NY 10017

AMERELLER, HORST GEORG, lawyer; b. Munich, Germany, Oct. 15, 1934; s. Otto and Therese (Simmet)) A.; LL.B., U. Munich, 1957; diploma European Research Inst., Saarbrücken, 1958; LL.M., Harvard, 1960; S.J.D., U. Saarbrücken, 1963; m. Almut Peters, Sept. 19, 1964; children—Florian, Stefanie. Law clk., atty., Munich, 1960-63; practice in Frankfurt, Germany, 1963—; partner firm Baker & McKenzie, Chgo., 1966—. Officer Christian-Democrat Students Assn., U. Munich, 1954-56. Mem. Frankfurt Bar Assn., Harvard Law Sch. Assn. Europe. Home: 3 A Burgerstrasse Kronberg Germany 6242 Office: 42 44 Niddastrasse Frankfurt Germany 6000

AMERINE, MAYNARD ANDREW, educator, enologist; b. San Jose, Cal., Oct. 30, 1911; s. Roy Reagan and Tennie (Davis) A.; B.S., U. Cal. at Berkeley, 1932, Ph.D. in Plant Physiology, 1936. Mem. faculty U. Cal. at Davis, 1935—, prof. enology, enologist Exptl. Sta., 1952—, chmn. dept. viticulture and enology, 1957-62. Served to maj. AUS, 1942-46. Decorated chevalier de Merite Agricole (France), 1947; recipient diplome d'honneur l'Office Internat. du Vin, 1952, 65; 2d prize Oberly award A.L.A., 1953; Guggenheim fellow, 1954-55; Merit award Am. Soc. Enologists, 1967. Mem. Am. Soc. Enologists (pres. 1958-59), A.A.A.S., Am. Soc. Hort. Sci., Am. Chem. Soc., Inst. Food Technologists. Republican. Baptist. Clubs: Sutter (Sacramento); Bohemian (San Francisco). Author: (with M. A. Joslyn) Table Wines; The Technology of their Production in California, 1951; (with Louise Wheeler) A Check-List of Books and Pamphlets on Grapes and Wines and Related Subjects, 1951; A Short Check-List of Books and Phamphlets in English on Grapes, Wine and Related Subjects, 1949-1959, 1959; (with others) The Technology of Wine Making, 2d edit., 1967; (with G. L. Marsh) Wine Making at Home, 1962; (with M.A. Joslyn) Desert. Appetizer and Related Favored Wines: The Technology of Their Production, 1964; (with V.L. Singleton) Wine: An Introduction for Americans, 1965; (with Rose M. Pangborn and E. B. Roessler) Principles of Sensory Evaluation of Food, 1965; A Check List on Grapes and Wines, 1960-68, with supplement for 1949-59, 1969; (with M.A. Joslyn) Table Wines: the Technology of Their Production, 1970. Home: 2840 Spring Mountain Rd St Helena CA 94574

AMES, ALFRED CAMPBELL, journalist; b. Spokane, Wash., July 21, 1916; s. William Porter and Anna (Campbell) A.; A.B., U. Kan., 1936; A.M., U. Ill., 1937, Ph.D., 1943; m. Elanor Alice Holliday, Feb. 4, 1951. Asst. English, U. Ill., 1937-43, instr., 1943-44; instr. English, Ill. Inst. Tech., 1944-46, asst. prof., 1946-51; asso. editor book sect. Chgo. Tribune, 1951-56, editorial writer, 1956—; lectr. bus. English, Northwestern U., 1945-64, lectr. journalism, 1964—. Mem. Modern Lang. Assn., Phi Beta Kappa. Mem. Soc. of Friends. Home: 734 Noyes St Evanston IL 60201 Office: 435 N Michigan Av Chicago IL 60611

AMES, AMYAS, investment banker; b. Sharon, Mass., June 15, 1906; s. Oakes and Blanche (Ames) A.; student Country Day Sch., Newton, Mass.; A.B., Harvard, 1928, M.B.A., 1930; D.H.L., Pace Coll., 1970; m. Evelyn I. Perkins, June 14, 1930; children—Oakes, Edward Amyas, Olivia, Joan Evelyn. Analyst, Stone, Webster, Inc., 1930-32; security analyst Kidder, Peabody & Co., Inc., 1932-34, sales mgr., syndicate mgr., 1934-41, partner, 1941, now vice chmn. exec. com. Adminstrv. officer War Shipping Adminstrn., Washington, 1941-44. Gov. N.Y. Stock Exchange, 1949-55. Trustee, Carnegie Corp. N.Y. Bd. dirs. Rockefeller Center, Inc. chmn. Concerned Citizens for the Arts, N.Y.C.; chmn. bd. Lincoln Center for Performing Arts. Chmn. Joint Com. Edn. 1951-69. Chmn., Philharmonic Symphony Soc. N.Y. Mem. Investment Bankers Assn. Am. (pres. 1963, chmn. exec. com. 1964), Beta Gamma Sigma (hon.). Clubs: Somerset (Boston); Century, Recess (N.Y.C.). Home: Moore's Hill Rd Cold Spring Harbor Long Island NY 11724 also 535 Park Ave New York City NY 10021 Office: 20 Exchange Pl New York City NY 10005

AMES, MRS. BOBBIE HACKNEY, mem. Republican Nat. Com.; b. Washington, N.C., July 23, 1930; d. James Acra and Mae (Ayers) Hackney; student Greensboro (N.C.) Coll., 1948-49, E. Carolina Coll., Greenville, N.C., 1949-50; m. John Brewer Ames, Dec. 30, 1950; children—Elizabeth, John Brewer II, Laurie and David (twins), James Hackney. Pres. Ala. Fedn. Rep. Women, 1965-67; mem. Rep. Nat. Com. for Ala., 1968- -. Prin. Perry Christian Sch., Marion, Ala., 1965-66, 69. Dir. Ames Bag & Packaging Corp., Marion. Pres. Dallas County Fedn. Ch. Women, 1952. Bd. dirs. Occupational Rehab. for Central Ala., 1970—, Ala. Assn. Pvt. Schs., 1971—. Recipient Woman of Year award Rep. Women, Ala., 1967. Woman of Achievement award Bus. and Profl. Women's Club, 1969. Mem. Ala. Hist. Soc. Mem. Westminster Community Ch. Club: Selma (Ala.) Garden (past pres.) Home: Amesmont Marion AL 36756 Office: Box 670 Marion AL 36756

AMES, BRUCE NATHAN, biochemist, geneticist; b. N.Y.C., Dec. 16, 1928; s. Maurice U. and Dorothy (Andres) A.; B.A., Cornell U., 1950; Ph.D., Cal. Inst. Tech., 1953; m. Giovanna Ferro-Luzzi, Aug. 27, 1960; children—Sofia, Matteo. Chief sect. microbial genetics NIH, Bethesda, Md., 1953-68; prof. biochemistry U. Cal. at Berkeley, 1968—. Recipient Eli Lilly award Am. Chem. Soc., 1964; Washington Acad. Sci. award, 1965; Flemming award, 1966. Mem. Am. Soc. Biol. Chemists, Am. Soc. Microbiology, Am. Acad. Arts and Scis., Genetics Soc., Am. Soc. Microbiologists, Am. Acad. Arts and Scis. Research, publs. on histidine biosynthesis and its control; operon regulation; mutagenisis. Home: 1324 Spruce St Berkeley CA 94709

AMES, CHARLES OAKES, investment banker; b. N.Y.C., Oct. 28, 1926; s. Charles Edgar and Eleanor (King) A.; A.B., Harvard, 1948; m. Shirley Avril Foerderer, May 19, 1951; children—Charles Foerderer, Shelley Foerderer, Percival Foerderer. Salesman, Glidden Co., 1949-53; registered rep. Merrill Lynch, Pierce, Fenner & Smith, 1953-56; with Paine, Webber, Jackson & Curtis, Inc., N.Y.C., 1956—, gen. partner, 1961-70, v.p., 1970—. Trustee E. Woods Sch., Oyster Bay, 1962-68, Percival E. and Ethel Brown Foerderer Found., 1969—, Milton (Mass.) Acad., 1969—; mem. adv. com. Soc. for Relief of Women and Children, 1966—; dir. Eagle Dock Found., Cold Spring Harbor, N.Y., 1965-69. Served with USNR, 1944-46. Republican. Episcopalian. Clubs: Downtown Assn., Winter, Harvard of N.Y.C., Cold Spring Harbor Beach (bd. mgrs. 1962-64, 69—). Home: 8 Wawapek Rd Cold Spring Harbor NY 11724 Office: 140 Broadway New York City NY 10005

AMES, ELIZABETH, former art dir.; b. Montevideo, Minn.; d. Theodore F. and Sarah (Macfarlane) Knappen; B.A., U. Minn.; D.Arts, Skidmore Coll., 1947; m. John Carroll Ames, June 19, 1918. Organized plan for hospitality to composers, writers, other artists, for purpose of working in arts, at estate of Yaddo; exec. dir. Corp. of Yaddo, Saratoga Springs, N.Y., 1924-70, exec. dir. emeritus, 1970—, also mem. corp. Recipient Distinguished Service award Nat. Inst. Arts and Letters, 1959. Mem. Am. Assn. U. Women. Mem. Soc. Friends. Home: Yaddo Saratoga Springs NY 12866

AMES, FISHER, lawyer; b. Oklahoma City, July 6, 1905; s. Charles Bismark and Elizabeth P. (Allen) A.; A.B., Harvard Coll., 1926; LL.B., U. Okla., 1930; m. Jewell Turner, Nov. 5, 1934; children—Judith (Mrs. James P. Rhoads), Sarah (Mrs. Bruce B. Lenz). Admitted to Okla. bar, 1930, since practiced in Oklahoma City; sr. partner firm Ames, Daugherty, Bynum, Black, Ashabranner & Rogers, 1950—. Served to comdr. USNR, 1941-45. Home: 821 NW 38th St Oklahoma City OK 73118 Office: 219 Couch Dr Oklahoma City OK 73102

AMES, HAROLD TAYLOR, indsl. engr.; b. Antioch, Ill., Feb. 16, 1894; s. Chester C. and Mary Josephine (Taylor) A.; ed. pub. schs.; m. Katharine Fetrow, Mar. 21, 1925; children—Harold Fetrow, Janet Virginia. Identified with mfg. of automobiles, 1926-37; at various times pres. Duesenberg, Inc. of Ind., exec. v.p. Auburn Automobile Co. (Ind.), v.p. Cord Corp.; dir. King-Seeley Thermos Co.; pres., dir. The La Porte Corp., 1940—, Chgo. Electric Mfg. Co., 1945—, Nat. Stamping & Electric Works, 1948—. Served as 1st lt. U.S. Air Service, 1917-19. Republican. Mason. Clubs: Chicago Athletic, Bob O'Link Golf; Thunderbird Country. Home: 1630 Sheridan Rd Wilmette IL 60091 Office: Prudential Plaza Chicago IL 60601

AMES, JOHN DAWES, banker; b. May 7, 1904; s. K.L. and S.S. Ames; grad. Princeton, 1928; m. Charlotte Schoonmaker, Nov. 9, 1928; children—John D., William S., Knowlton; m. 2d, Constance Hasler, Oct. 1, 1949. Pres. Chgo. Jour. Commerce, 1929-50; exec. dir. midwest div. Dow Jones & Co., Inc., Pubs. Wall St. Jour., 1951-53; partner Bacon, Whipple & Co., 1953—; dir. Home Owners Ins. Co., Pyle-Nat. Co., Clark Equipment Co. Served as lt. col. U.S. Army. Presbyn. Home: 600 N Washington Rd Lake Forest IL 60045 Office: 135 So LaSalle St Chicago IL 60603

AMES, JOHN LELAND, educator; b. Freedom, Wyo., July 14, 1907; s. John C. and Emma (Wolfley) A.; B.A., U. Wyo., 1946, M.A., 1948; Ed.D., U. Utah, 1952; m. Ann Golden, Oct. 5, 1935; children—James Golden, John David. Tchr., prin. elementary sch., Star Valley, Wyo., 1927-35; tchr. elementary sch., Lyman, Wyo., 1935-41, Cheyenne, 1941-43; field exec. Pikes Peak council Boy Scouts Am., 1943-44; prin. elementary sch., supr., Cheyenne, 1945-47; asst. prin. elementary sch., Rochester, Minn., 1947-48; asst. prof. U. Utah, 1948-53; prin. elementary sch., La Mesa, Cal., 1953-54, asst.. supt. Spring Valley Sch. Dist., La Mesa, 1954-55; prof. edn. Queen's Coll., N.Y.C., 1955-57, dir. tchr. edn. 1957-66, dir. grad. program preparation sch. adminstr., prof. sch. adminstrn., program coordnator. Mem. N.Y. State Adv. Com. Proficiency Exams., 1962-64; Mid Atlantic regional evaluator NDEA Reading Inst.; cons. Title I Reading Survey, 1966-67. Served with USNR, 1944-45. Mem. N.E.A., Am. Assn. U. Profs., Am. Assn. Colls. Tchr. Edn., Am. Assn. Sch. Adminstrs., Nat. Council Tchrs. English, Phi Delta Kappa, Phi Kappa Phi, Kappa Delta Pi. Contbr. articles profl. mags. Home: 7 Laura Lane East Setauket NY 11733 Office: Queens College Flushing NY 11367

AMES, JOHN LEWIS, lawyer, advt. exec.; b. Norfolk, Va., July 15, 1912; s. Harry Lee and Catherine I. (Betty) A.; A.B., Randolph-Macon Coll., 1933; LL.B., U. Richmond (Va.) 1937; postgrad. N.Y. U. Law Sch., 1939-40; m. Margaret Kilbon, Apr. 8, 1939; children—Margaret Lee, John Lewis. Admitted to Va. bar, 1936, N.Y. bar, 1940; mem. tax div. Home Life Ins. Co., N.Y.C., 1937-38; trial atty. Tanner, Sillocks & Friend, N.Y.C., 1938-41; house counsel Ruthrauff & Ryan, Inc., N.Y.C., 1941-42, house counsel and asst. to pres., 1945-48, sec., counsel, 1948-50, v.p., sec., 1950-55, v.p., sec., treas., 1955-57, also dir.; v.p., sec. Erwin, Wassey, Ruthrauff & Ryan, Inc., 1957-59; asst. dir. bus. affairs CBS TV Network, Inc., N.Y.C., 1959-62; v.p., sec., treas. Kudner Agy., Inc., 1962-65, also dir.; sr. v.p. adminstrn. and finance West, Weir & Bartel, Inc., N.Y.C., 1966, exec. v.p., dir., until 1968; v.p., sec. Lennen & Newell, Inc., 1968-; dir. Carroll Products, Inc.; spl. agt. FBI, Washington and N.Y.C., 1942-45. Spl. dep. atty. gen. N.Y. State, 1946- 48. Life trustee Randolph-Macon Coll. Mem., now pres. Massapequa Bd. Edn.; past pres. Nassau-Suffolk Sch. Bds. Assn. Past chmn. trustees Am. Assn. Advt. Agencies Group Ins. Mem. N.Y. County Lawyers Assn., Eastern Inter-Coll. Basketball Ofcls. Assn., Am. Arbitration Assn. (mem. nat. panel), Soc. Former Spl. Agts. F.B.I., Alumni Soc. Randolph-Macon Coll. (pres.), Phi Kappa Sigma, Omicron Delta Kappa, Tau Kappa Alpha. Methodist. Clubs: Southward Ho Country (Bay Shore, L.I.); Murray Hill (N.Y.C.). Home: 129 Rumson Rd Harbour Green Massapequa NY 11758 Office: 380 Madison Av New York City, NY 10017.

AMES, JOSEPH LYNN, labor union ofcl.; b. DeSoto, Mo., July 24, 1925; s. Walker and Edith (Farley) A.; B.A., Washington U., St. Louis, 1951; m. Billie Gene Coil, Jan. 11, 1944; children-Gregory A., Theresa J.; m. 2d, Lillian Recant, Oct. 29, 1955; 1 dau., Victoria E. Organizer, Internat. Ladies Garment Workers Union, 1948-49; staff rep. Local 688, Teamsters, 1951-53; organizer Am. Fedn. State, County and Municipal Employees, 1953-54, sec.- treas. Local 410, St. Louis, 1955-66, pres. Mo. Council 72, 1965-66, internat. v.p., 1965-66, asst. to internat. pres., 1966, internat. sec.- treas., 1966—. Mem. Mo. Ho. of Reps., 1960-62. Served with AUS, 1943- 46; ETO. Decorated Bronze Star medal, Purple Heart, Combat Inf. Badge. Home: 3801 Gramercy St N W Washington DC 20016 Office: 1155 15th St N W Washington DC 20005

AMES, LOUISE BATES, child psychologist; b. Portland, Me., Oct. 29, 1908; d. Samuel Lewis and Annie Earle (Leach) Bates; A.B., U. Me., 1930, M.A., 1933, Sc.D., 1957; Ph.D., Yale, 1936; D.Sc., Wheaton, 1967; m. Smith Ames, May 22, 1930 (div. (div. 1937); 1 dau., Joan Ames (Mrs. Robert Clifford Chase). Research sec., personal asst. to Dr. Gesell, Yale Clinci Child Devel. Yale Med. Sch., 1933-36, instr., 1940-44, asst. prof., 1944-50; curator Yale Films of Child Devel. 1944-50; co-founder Gesell Inst. Child Devel., dir. research. sec.- treas., 1950—, asso. dir., chief psychologist, 1968; collaborator (with Dr. Frances L. Ilg) daily syndicated newspaper column Child Behavior; weekly TV broadcast on child behavior WBZ, Boston, 1952-55. Certified psychologist, Conn. Mem. Conn. Psychol.

Soc., Am. Psychol. Assn., Soc. Research Child Devel., Internat. Council Women Psychologists (bd. dirs. 1945-47), Soc. Projective Techniques (pres. 1970) Sigma Xi. Author: (with Arnold Gesell and others) First Five Years of Life, Infant and Child, Child from Five-to-Ten, Years Ten to Sixteen, Child Behavior, Child Rorschach Responses, Rorschach Responses in Old Age, Adolscent Rorschach Responses, Mosaic Patterns of American Children, Parents Ask, Guidance Nursery School, School Readiness, Is our Child in the Wrong Grade?, Child Care and Development. Editorial bd. Jour. Genetic Psychology, Jour. Learning Disabilities, Edn. Digest. Home: 283 Edwards St New Haven CT 06051 Office: 310 Prospect St New Haven CT 06051

AMES, MILTON BENJAMIN, Jr., aerospace researcher; b. Norfolk, Va., Sept. 21, 1913; s. Milton B. and Mabel (Roberts) A.; student William and Mary Coll., Va. Poly. Inst., 1931-32, Ga. Inst. Tech., 1933-34; B.S. in Aero. Engring., Guggenheim Sch. Aeros., Ga. Inst. Tech., 1936; m. Martha Nuland, Jan. 22, 1944; children—Carol Diane, Linda Anne, Milton Stephen. Aero. research engr. Langley Meml. Aero. Lab., Langley Field, Va., 1936- 41; instr. aeros. Norfolk div. Va. Poly. Inst., 1940-41; engring. asst. to G. W. Lewis, dir. NACA, Washington, 1941-43, engring. asst. to chief mil. research NACA hdqrs., 1943-46, chief aerodynamics div. NACA hdqrs., 1946-58; asst. dir. aero. and space research NASA, 1959-60, dep. dir. advanced research, 1960-61, dir. space vehicles Office Advanced Research and Tech., 1961-70, sr. engr. research mgmt. council, 1970—, dir. NASA hdqrs. projects Fire, Pegasus and Lifting Body flight research program; partner Ames Bros., Norfolk. Mem. fluid dynamics panel, adv. group aero. research and devel. NATO. Recipient NASA award for projects Fire and Pegasus, 1966; named Distinguished Alumnus Old Dominion U., 1966. Fellow Inst. Aeros. and Astronautics (chmn. Washington sect. 1948-49); mem. A.A.A.S., Nat. Aeros. Assn. (policy com. of contest and record bd.), Theta Chi. Clubs: University (Washington); Belle Haven Country (Alexandria, Va.). Author research publs., tech. summaries. Home: 1605 River Farm Dr River Bend Estates Alexandria VA 22308 Office: NASA Washington DC 20546

AMES, VAN METER, educator; b. De Soto, Ia., July 9, 1898; s. Edward Scribner and Mabel (Van Meter) A.; Ph.B., U. Chgo., 1919, Ph.D., 1924; m. Betty Breneman, June 12, 1930; children—Sanford Scribner, Christine (Mrs. Judson E. Cornish), Damaris. Faculty U. Cin., 1925, head dept. philosophy, 1959- -, Obed J. Wilson prof. ethics, 1960-66, Obed J. Wilson prof. ethics emeritus, 1966—, fellow Grad. Sch., 1957—. Vis. prof. Cornell U., summer 1931, U. Tex., 1934-35, U. Hawaii, 1947-48. Faculté des Lettres, U. Aix-Marseille (France), spring 1949, Columbia, summer 1957. Mem. 3d East-West Philosophers Conf., U. Hawaii, summer 1959. Rockefeller grantee, France, 1948; Fulbright research prof. philosophy Komazawa U., Tokyo, Japan, 1958-59. Mem. Am. Philos. Assn. (pres. Western div. 1959- 60), Am. Soc. Aesthetics (pres. 1961-62), Am. Humanist Assn. Author: Aesthetics of the Novel, 1928; Introduction to Beauty, 1931; (poetry) Out of Iowa, 1936; Proust and Santayana, 1937; Andre Gide, 1947; (with Betty B. Ames) Japan and Zen, 1961; Zen and American Thought, 1962. Editor: Beyond Theology: The Autobiography of Edward Scribner Ames, 1959. Home: 448 Warren Av Cincinnati OH 45220

AMES, WALTER IRVING, lawyer; b. Perry County, Ill., Dec. 4, 1892; s. George M. and Emma (Johnston) A.; A.B., Stanford, 1919, J.D., 1921; m. Marguerite Roberts, Apr. 22, 1922; children—Nancy (Mrs. Petersen), Forbes R. Admitted to Cal. bar, 1921; mem. firm Gray, Cary, Ames & Frye, and predecessor, San Diego, 1926—. Pres. bd. Putnam Found., Fleet Found. Mem. Am., San Diego (pres. 1932) bar assns., State Bar Cal. Republican. Club: Cuyamaca. Home: 7740 Hillside Dr La Jolla CA 92037 Office: Union Bank Bldg San Diego CA 92101

AMEY, RONALD LEROY, fashion designer; b. Globe, Ariz., May 18, 1932; s. Ronald L. and Martha (Siofeld) Amey; student Chouinard Art Inst., 1951-52; student Parson's Sch. Design, 1957-67. Asst. designer Jane Derby, 1958-59. Arnold Scaasi, 1959; designer, partner, v.p. Burke-Amey, N.Y.C., 1959-69; pres. Ronald Amey, Inc., N.Y.C., 1970—; lectr., fashion cons. Mt. Mary Coll., Milw., F.I.T., Tobe-Coburn, Pa. State U., Bennington Coll., Cazenovia Coll. pioneer pattern exploitation, combining geometrics and florals and discordant colors. Mem. com. fund raising for charity Leukemia Found. Served with USAF, 1952-56. Recipient 1st Golden Needle award Mt. Mary Coll.; Gold Coast fashion award, Chgo., 1970. Home: 419 E 57 St New York City NY 10022 Office: 16 W 57th St New York City NY 10019

AMIDON, ELLSWORTH LYMAN, physician, educator; b. West Barnet, Vt., Apr. 3, 1906; s. Freeman Ellsworth and Mary Ann Ward (Walker) A.; student Goddard Sem., 1922-23; B.S., Tufts Coll., 1927; M.D., U. Vt., 1932; M.S., U. Pa. Grad. Sch., 1936; m. Mae Agnes Elizibeth Liddle, June 29, 1932; childrenRoger Lyman, Cynthia Jean. Intern Mary Fletcher Hosp., Burlington, Vt., 1932- 33, med. dir., 1934; instr. pathology U. Vt. Med. Coll., 1933-35, instr. pathology and internal medicine, 1936-37, asst. prof. internal medicine, 1937-40, asso. prof., 1940-45, chmn. dept., 1945-64, prof., 1945-. Med. chmn. fund-raising Chittenden unit Vt. Heart Assn. Surgeon USPHS Res. Recipient Distinguished Service award Vt. Med. Soc., 1965. Diplomate Am. Bd. Internal Medicine. Master A.C.P. (regent 1957—, 1st v.p. 1963); mem. Am. (dir. 1958-63), Vt. (liaison to Am. Heart Assn.; pres. 1956-57) heart assns., Am. Diabetic Assn., Am. Fedn. Clin. Research, Vt., Montreal med. socs. Mem. editorial bd. Book of Health, 1953. Contbr. articles profl. jours. Home: 144 Deforest Rd Burlington VT 05401 Office: Mary Fletcher Hosp Burlington VT 05401

AMIDON, GEORGE BRIGGS, paper co. exec.; b. Houston, Minn., Nov. 30, 1910; s. Edmound Perry and Julia M. (Briggs) A.; B.S. in Forestry, U. Minn., 1936; m. J. Erma Teters, Feb. 26, 1932 (dec. Feb. 1971); children—G. Keith, Judith (Mrs. Richard Dougherty), James S. With Minn. Forestry Dept., also U.S. Forest Service, 1935-44; with Minn. and Ont. Paper Co., 1944—, dir. woodlands, 1956-63, v.p. woodlands, 1963—. Mem. adv. com. Inst. Agr., U. Minn.; chmn. Minn. Forest Industries Information Com. Mem. Soc. Am. Foresters (sec., chmn. upper Miss. Valley sect.), Am. Pulpwood Assn. (pres., dir.). Conglist. (trustee, bd. deacons, chmn. bldg. com.). Rotarian. Home: 118 Riverview Blvd International Falls MN 56649 Office: Boise-Cascade Corp International Falls MN 56649

AMINI, JOHARI M., (Jewel C. Latimore), poet; b. Phila., Feb. 13, 1935; d. Vol William and Alma (Bazel) McLawler; A.A., Chgo. City Coll., 1968; student U. Chgo., 1968-69; B.A., Chgo. State Coll., 1970. Treas. Orgn. Black Am. Culture, 1969. Author: Images in Black, 1967; Black Essence, 1968; A Folk Fabel, 1969; Let's Go Some Where, 1970. Address: 8229 Emerald Av Chicago, IL 60620.

AMINO, LEO, sculptor, designer; b. Japan, June 26, 1911; s. Ichiju and Yufu A.; came to U.S., 1929; student N.Y.U., Am. Artists Sch.; m. Julie Blumberger, 1947; 1 dau., Erilo. One man shows include Montross Gallery, 1940, Artists' Gallery, 1940-43; Clay Club Gallery, 1941-49, Bonestell Gallery, 1945, Sculptors Gallery, 1947-49, Sculpture Center, 1951, 52, 54, 57, 71, Art Alliance, Phila., 1951, East Hampton Gallery, 1969, 70; represented in Mus. of Modern Art, Massillon Mus., Addison Gallery Am. Art, U. Neb., Grand Rapids Mus., Olsen Found., New Haven, Tex. State Coll. Women, Des Moines Art Center, Whitney Mus. Am. Art, pub. and pvt. collections; tchr. sculpture Block Mountain (N.C.) Coll., 1946, 50; now tchr. sculpture Cooper Union, N.Y.C. Studio: 58 Watts St New York City NY 10013

AMIRIKIAN, ARSHAM, engring. co. exec.; b. Armenia, May 17, 1899; s. Paravon and Pearl (Delbarian) A.; came to U.S., 1919, naturalized, 1927; B.S., Ecole Superiore des Ponts de Chaussees, Constantinople, 1919; C.E., Cornell U., 1923; D.Tech.Sc., Technische Hochschule, Vienna, 1960; m. Philomena Elizabeth Boardman, Aug. 8, 1925; children—Richard Armen, Joyce Eleanor (Mrs. Robert A. Harrison). Steel fabricator draftsman and designer, 1923-28; various engring. positions to chief engring. cons. Naval Facilities Engring. Command, U.S. Navy Dept., Washington, 1928-71; pres. Amirikian Engring. Co., Arlington, Va., 1971—; cons. engr. shore and floating structures, harbor and docking facilities; adjunct prof. engring. George Washington U., 1965-66. Recipient Fuertes Grad. gold medal Cornell U., 1943, Lincoln gold medal Am. Welding Soc., 1949, A.E. Lindau award Am. Concrete Inst., 1958, Distinguished Service award Dept. of Navy, 1966, Distinguished Service award Def. Dept., 1969, Goethals medal Soc. Am. Mil. Engrs., 1971. Mem. Am. Soc. C.E. (hon.), Am. Welding Soc. (hon.), Am. Concrete Inst., Soc. Naval Architects and Marine Engrs., Internat. Inst. Welding, Sigma Xi. Author: Analysis of Rigid Frames, 1942. Contbr. articles tech. periodicals. Inventor of Ammi lift dock and transfer system, biserrated rib framing, split-beam prestressing, thin-shell hollow-rib and cellular precast concrete framing systems. Home: 6526 Western Av Chevy Chase MD 20015 Office: 1401 Wilson Blvd Arlington VA 22209

AMIS, EDWARD STEPHEN, educator, chemist; b. Himyar, Ky., Nov. 9, 1905; s. Jack and Artie (Southard) A.; B.S., U. Ky., 1930, M.S., 1933; Ph.D., Columbia, 1939; m. Annie Velma Birdwhistle, Sept. 2, 1934; children—Edward Stephen, Velma Dianne. Mem. faculty La. State U., 1939-45, asso. prof., 1943-45; staff Carbide & Carbon Chems. Corp., Oak Ridge, 1945-47; prof. chemistry U. Ark., Fayetteville, 1947—. Recipient Distinguished Research award U. Ark., 1967. Fellow N.Y. Acad. Scis.; mem. Am. Chem. Soc. (So. Chemist award 1959, S.W. award 1960), Chem. Soc., Ark. Acad. Scis., Sigma Xi, Alpha Chi Sigma, Pi Mu Epsilon, Phi Lambda Upsilon, Sigma Pi Sigma. Author: Kinetics of Chemical Change in Solution, 1949; A Book of Verse and Prose, 1965; Solvent Effects on Reaction Rates and Mechanisms, 1966, Russian edit., 1968; (with James F. Hinton) NMR Studies of Ions in Solution, 1972; Saga of Racehorse and Other Items, 1969; A Novice in Europe and Other Writings, 1971; also numerous articles. Research on electromotive chemistry, conductance and transference of electrolytes in solution, kinetics and mechanism of chem. reactions in pure and mixed solvents, solvation of ions in pure and mixed solvents using conductance, transference and nuclear magnetic resonance procedures, theories of ion-diplolar molecule reactions, temperature coefficients of reaction rates, electron exchange reactions. Home: 1655 Woolsey St Fayetteville AR 72701

AMIS, KINGSLEY, English novelist; b. Apr. 16, 1922; s. William Robert and Rosa Amis; ed. City of London Sch., also St. John's, Oxford; m. Hilary Ann Bardwell (div. 1965); 3 children; m. 2d, Elizabeth Jane Howard, 1965. Lectr. English, U. Coll. Swansea, 1949-61; vis. fellow creative writing Princeton, 1958-59; fellow in English, Peterhouse, Cambridge U., Eng., 1961-63. Served with Army, 1942-45. Author: (verse) A Frame of Mind, 1953; Lucky Jim, 1954 (filmed 1957); That Uncertain Feeling, 1955 (filmed as Only Two Can Play, 1961); (verse) A Case of Samples, 1956; I Like it Here, 1958; Take a Girl Like You, 1960; New Maps of Hell, 1960; My Enemy's Enemy, 1962; One Fat Englishman, 1963; The James Bond Dossier, 1965; (with Robert Conquest) The Egyptologists, 1965; The Anti-Death League, 1966; A Look Round the Estate (verse), 1967; I Want It Now, 1968; The Green Man, 1969; What Became of Jane Austen, 1970. Contbr. to publs. Home: Lemmons Hadley Common Barnet Hertfordshire Office: care A D Peters 10 Buckingham St London WC2 England

AMISANO, JOSEPH, architect; b. N.Y.C., Jan. 10, 1917; B. Arch., Pratt Inst., 1940, M. Arch., 1941. Draftsman, Sanders & Breck. N.Y.C., 1940-41; Harrison, Abramovitz & Fouilhoux, N.Y., 1941-42; draftsman, structual designer Pan Am. Airways, Brazil, 1942-44; gen. designer Ketchum, Gina & Sharp, N.Y.C., 194450; with Toombs & Co., 1950-52; partner firm Toombs, Amisano & Wells, Atlanta, 1953—; prin. Works include Cyrus W. Strickler Doctors bldg., Atlanta, childrens ward Ga. Warm Springs Found., Charles Heyman residence, Rome, Ga.; design critic Pratt Inst., 1952. Recipient Prix de Rome, 1950-52; certificate Progressive Architecture, 1954. Home: 1028 Nawench Dr NW Atlanta GA 30327* Office: 148 Cain St N E Atlanta GA 30303

AMLING, FREDERICK, educator; b. Cleve., Dec. 23, 1926; s. Gustav and Elsie (Fisher) A.; B.A., Baldwin Wallace Coll., 1948; M.B.A., Miami U., Oxford U., 1949; Ph.D., U. Pa., 1957; m. Gwendolyn Stewart, Feb. 17, 1951; children—Jeffrey, Scott, Terrence. Instr. U. Me., 1948-50, U. Pa., 1950- 52, U. Conn., 1952-55; prof. finance and investment chmn. dept. Miami U., Oxford, 1955-66; prof. finance U. R.I., Kingston, 1966—, dean Coll. Bus. Adminstrn., 1966-69; now prof. bus. finance George Washington U.; cons. finance and investment, 1959—. Dir. Apollo Fund, Keystone-Custodian, Boston. Chmn. local Cancer Crusade 1964. Served with USNR, World War II. Mem. Washington Soc. Financial Analysts, Financial Mgmt. Assn., Investment Club Miami U (pres. 1962), Am. Finance Assn., Beta Gamma Sigma, Delta Sigma Pi, Lambda Chi Alph. Presbyn. (elder 1962- 66). Clubs: University (pres. 1964) (Miami U., Oxford); Turks Head (Providence). Author: Investments: An Introduction to Analysis and Management, rev. edit. 1970. Contbr. articles in field finance to profl. jours., newspapers. Home: 7312 Masters Dr Potomac MD 20854 also 17 New Salt Rd Ocean Park ME 04063 Office: Hall of Govt and Business 21st St and G St Washington DC 20006

AMMARELL, JOHN SAMUEL, Jr., security services exec.; b. nr. Reading, Pa., Mar. 21, 1920; s. John Samuel and Marie (Rothermel) A.; A.B., Muhlenberg Coll., 1941; postgrad. George Washington U., 1942-43; m. Florence Rebecca Althouse, June 27, 1942; children—John, David, Robert Lynn. Spl. agt., asst. chief liaison FBI, Washington, 1942-54; asso. Gt. Am. Tchrs. Agy., Allentown, Pa., 1955-56; mgr. personnel, dir. security Air Products & Chems., Inc., Trexlertown, Pa., 1956-58; exec. v.p. Wackenhut Corp., Coral Gables, Fla., 1958—, also dir.; exec. v.p. Wackenhut Services, Inc., 1960—; pres., dir. Wackenhut Electronics, 1966-67; dir. Gor-Bac Security Systems, Inc., Wackenhut Protective Systems, Inc. Bd. dirs. Asso. Industries Fla., 1966-68, sec., 1968-69 treas., 1969-70, v.p., 1970-71. Trustee Newberry Coll., 1970—. Recipient Alumni Achievement award Muhlenberg Coll., 1971; named Community Leader Am., 1970-71. Mem. Soc. Former Spl. Agts. FBI (pres. Pan Am. chpt. 1967-68), Lambda Chi Alpha, Omicron Delta Kappa, Phi Alpha Theta. Lutheran. Elk. Club: Country of Coral Gables. Home: 13001 SW 71st Av Miami FL 33156 Office: 3280 Ponce de Leon Blvd Coral Gables FL 33134

AMMARELL, RAYMOND ROBERT, JR., publisher; b. Paterson, N.J., Sept. 30, 1917; s. Raymond Robert and Effie (Hahn) A.; A.B., Dartmouth, 1938, M.C.S., Amos Tuck Sch., 1939; m. Barbara Ramsey, Mar. 6, 1942; children—Robert, Natalie, Raymond Robert III. Accountant, Patterson & Ridgeway, N.Y.C., 1939-41; with Time, Inc., 1941-63, gen. mgr. Sports Illus. mag., 1961-63; gen. exec. Doubleday & Co., Inc., 1964-65, v.p., 1965-67, sr. v.p., 1967-. Served to capt. USAAF, 1942-45. Office: 277 Park Av New York City, NY 10017.

AMMERMAN, ALBERT MERLIN, coll. pres.; b. Coldwater, Mich., Sept. 21, 1914; s. Jay B. and Vera (Crandall) A.; A.B., U. Mich., 1937, M.A., 1940; Ed.D., Wayne State U., 1960; m. Ruth Irene Lennox, Aug. 17, 1940; children—Albert Jay, Kathleen Ruth (Mrs. Roger Wall), John Edgar, David William. Tchr., Fordson High Sch., Dearborn, Mich., 1937-44; dean instrn. Henry Ford Community Coll., Dearborn, 1946-61; pres. Suffolk County Community Coll., Selden, N.Y., 1961—. Dir. Tinker Nat. Bank, Setauket, N.Y. Mem. Nat. League for Nursing-Am. Assn. Jr. Colls. Commn. on Nursing Edn., 1966, Brookhaven Indsl. Commn., 1963—. Bd. dirs. Suffolk County council Boy Scouts Am. Served as officer USNR, World War II; PTO. Recipient Distinguished Edn. Service award Suffolk Community Coll., 1966. Mem. N.E.A., Nat. Assn. Collegiate Registrars and Admissions Officers, Adult Edn. Assn., Am. Assn. Jr. Colls. (cons.), Phi Delta Kappa. Presbyn. Rotarian. Club: St. George's Golf and Country (bd. dirs.) (Stony Brook, N.Y.). Author: Sociological Survey of Dearborn, Michigan, 1942. Home: 545 College Rd Selden NY 11784

AMMIDON, HOYT, banker; b. Balt., June 30, 1909; s. Daniel Clark and Estelle H. (Hoyt) A.; student Loomis Sch., Windsor, Conn., 1923-25, 1926-28, Le Rosey Sch., Rolle, Switzerland, 1925-26; B.A., Yale, 1932; LL.D., Hofstra U., 1968; m. Elizabeth MacI. K. Callaway, May 19, 1933; children—Hoyt, Lee Thorne. With Central Hanover Bank (now Mfrs. Hanover Trust Co.), 1932—, asst. sec., 1937-43, v.p., 1950-52, trustee, 1957; presently dir. Howard Johnson Co.; chmn. U.S. Trust Co., N.Y.C., 1958—; chmn. bd. U.S. Trust Investment Fund, U.S. Internat. Adv. Co.; dir., mem. exec. com. Nypen Co., Inc.; dir., exec. com., chmn. audit com. Perkin- Elmer Corp.; dir., mem. finance com., credit com. Am. Express Co., Am. Express Banking Corp.; dir. Gt. No. Paper Co., Gen. Am. Transp. Co., trustee, securities com. Greenwich Savs. Bank. Mem. devel. bd. Yale U., mem. com. N.Y. Clearing House Assn., citizen's adv. co. of N.Y.C. Pub. Library; bd. dirs. Music Theater Lincoln Center, Inc., Lincoln Center Performing Arts, chmn. Lincoln Center Fund; bd. dirs. Fed. Hall Meml. Assos., N.Y.C., N.Y.C. Nat. Shrines Assos.; bd. govs. Hundred Year Assn. of N.Y.; trustee, pres. emeritus bd. Loomis Sch.; trustee Cooper Union Advancement Sci. and Art; fellow Pierpont Morgan Library; bd. dirs. adv. council Am. Ditchely Found.; council Friends Music Theatre of Lincoln Center; adv. com. Marine Hist. Assn. Served as lt. USCGR, 1942-45. Decorated grand ofcl. Order Crown of Italy; Fundacion Internacional Eloy Alfaro (Panama). Mem. Soc. Colonial Wars, Soc. Mayflower Descs., Am. Inst. Banking (adv. council N.Y. chpt.), Assn. Res. City Bankers, Council Fgn. Relations, English-Speaking Union U.S. (dir.), Down Town Assn., Grad. Club Assn. New Haven, Assn. Internat. Anciens Roseens, Pilgrims, U.S. Srs. Golf Assn., Chi Psi. Clubs: Racquet and Tennis, Bond, Economic (N.Y.C.); Cold Spring Harbor Beach, Cove Neck Tennis Courts, Cruising of America; Elihu (Yale) (grad. pres. 1958-60); River, Links, Piping Rock, St. Nicholas Hockey, Mory's Assn., Nat. Golf Links of America; Wyanranch Sportsmans; Royal and Ancient Golf of St. Andrews (Scotland); Augusta Nat. Golf. Home: Juniper Hill 74 Goose Hill Rd Cold Spring Harbor Long Island NY 11724 Office: 45 Wall St New York City NY 10005

AMMON, JAMES BROWN, drug co. exec.; b. Reading, Pa., June 26, 1922; s. Adam C. and Emily (Brown) A.; A.B., Amherst Coll., 1944; M.B.A. with distinction, Harvard, 1951; m. Martha M. Sutton, May 21, 1955; children—Cynthia H., Sarah C., David S. With Gulf Oil Corp., 1951-53, Westinghouse Air Brake Co., 1953- 55, Chrysler Corp., 1955-58; with Baxter Labs., Inc., Morton Grove, Ill., 1958—, v.p., treas., 1967-70, v.p. corp. devel., 1970—. Mem. Chgo. Crime Commn., 1965—. Served with AUS, 1943-46. Mem. Am. Mgmt. Assn., Chi Phi. Republican. Mem. Glenview Community Ch. Home: 645 Woodmere Lane Glenview IL 60025 Office: 6301 Lincoln Av Morton Grove IL 60053

AMMONS, ARCHIE RANDOLPH, poet, educator; b. Whiteville, N.C., Feb. 18, 1926; s. Willie M. and Lucy Della (McKee) A.; B.S., Wake Forest Coll., 1949; student U. Cal. at Berkeley, 1951-52; m. Phyllis Plumbo, Nov. 26, 1949; 1 son, John Randolph. Prin., Hatteras (N.C.) Elementary Sch., 1949-50; exec. v.p. Freidrich & Dimmock, Inc., biol. glassware mfr., Millville, N.J., 1952- 61; asst. prof. English, Cornell U., 1964-68, asso. prof., 1968—. Served with USNR, 1944-46. Guggenheim fellow 1966; traveling fellow Am. Acad. Arts and Letters, 1967; recipient Levinson prize Poetry mag., 1970. Author: Ommateum, 1955; Expressions of Sea Level, 1964; Corsons Inlet, 1965; Tape for the Turn of the Year, 1965; Northfield Poems, 1966; Selected Poems, 1968; Uplands, 1970; Briefings, 1971.

AMMONS, EUGENE, (Gene), tenor saxophonist; b. Chgo., Apr. 14, 1925; s. Albert Ammons. Played with Billy Exkstine and Woody Herman bands during 1940's; mem. twotenor combo with Sonny Stitt, later on own during 1950s; night club performances around Chgo., 1960-61; recording artist for Prestige, Argo, Verve records. Address: 5517 S Justine St Chicago IL*

AMON, JOHN WILLIAM, advt. exec.; b. Grand Rapids, Mich., May 11, 1919; s. Willis R. nd Martha B. (Williams) A.; B.F.A., Am. Acad. Art, 1940; student Art Inst. Chgo., 1936-40, Harrison Sch. Art, Chgo., 1937, Northwestern U., evenings 1938-39; m. Hilma A. Wheling, Sept. 22, 1942; children—Janice, Susan, Peggy. Art dir. Henri, Hurst & McDonald advt., Chgo., 1946; art dir. Grant Advt., Chgo., 1947; exec. art dir. Needham, Harper & Steers, Chgo., 1948-68; exec. creative dir. Campbell-Mithun, Inc., Chgo., 1968—; instr., Northwestern U., 1962-64; lectr. instr. painting colls. and profl. schs., 1960—; exhibited in Door County (Wis.) permanent Gallery, Sister Bay, Artist Guild Chgo., Mt. Prospect (Ill.) Bank, Art Fair, Oak Park, Ill., Art Fair, Mt. Prospect, Arts Club Membership Show, Chgo. Served with AUS, 1940-45. Decorated Bronze Star with oak leaf cluster. Mem. Art Dirs. Club Chgo. (pres.), Nat. Soc. Art Dirs. (v.p.), Arts Club Chgo. (membership chmn.), Artists Guild, Chgo. Communicative Arts. Club: Tavern (Chgo.). Home: 707 Glendale Mount Prospect IL 60056 Office: 111 E Wacker Dr Chicago IL 60601

AMORY, CLEVELAND, writer; b. Nahant, Mass., Sept. 2, 1917; s. Robert and Leonore (Cobb) A.; ed. Milton Acad., 1935; A.B., Harvard, 1939; L.H.D., New Eng. Coll.; m. Cora Fields Craddock, 1941 (div. 1947); m. 2d, Martha Hodge, 1953; 1 dau., Gaea McCormick. Newspaper reporter Nashua (N.H.) Telegraph, Ariz. Daily Star, Tucson, then mng. editor Prescott (Ariz.) Evening Courier; asso. editor Sat. Eve. Post, 1939-41, 43; free lance writer, 1943—. Pres. The Fund for Animals. Clubs: Harvard, Dutch Treat (N.Y.C.). Author: The Proper Bostonians, 1947; Home Town, 1950; The Last Resorts, 1952; Who Killed Society?, 1960; Vanity Fair (anthology), 1960. Editor-in-chief Celebrity Register, 1963.

Columnist for Saturday Rev., TV Guide; lectr.; radio and TV commentator. Home: 150 E 72d St New York City NY 10021 Office: 140 W 57th St New York City NY 10019

AMORY, HAROLD IRVIN, physician; b. Battery Park, Va., Dec. 3, 1905; s. Alfonso Franklin and Anne (Bishop) A.; student Randolph-Macon Coll., 1927; M.D., Med. Coll. Va., 1931; m. Nellie Thompson, July 16, 1932; childrenShirley Mae (Mrs. George Herbert Chappelear, Jr.), George Franklin, Intern St. Vincent DePaul Hosp., Norfolk, Va., 1931-32: commd. 1st lt. M.C., U.S. Army, 1932, advanced through grades to col., 1943; radiol. resident Letterman Gen. Hosp., San Francisco, 1939-41, chief radiol. service, 1941-42; comdg. officer 78th Gen. Hosp., 348th Sta. Hosp., World War II; chief radiol. service Walter Reed Army Hosp., Washington, 1946-53; chief radiol. consultants div. Office Surgeon Gen., 1950-53; ret., 1954; dir. radiol. service Beckley Meml. Hosp., 1955-60; prof., chmn. dept. radiology W.Va. U. Sch. Medicine, 1960-70; staff Kettering (O.) Meml. Hosp., 1970—. Decorated Bronze Star medal; recipient Silver medal Am. Roentgen Ray Soc. Diplomate Am. Board Radiology. Fellow Am. College Radiology; mem. A.M.A., Radiol. Soc. N.Am. (2d v.p. 1953), Assn. U. Radiologists, W.Va. Radiol. Soc. (pres. 1964), Phi Beta Pi, Sigma Phi Epsilon, Alpha Omega Alpha. Home: 200 Jamestown Circle Centerville OH 45459 Office: Kettering Meml Hosp Kettering OH 45429

AMORY, ROBERT, Jr., lawyer; b. Boston, Mar. 2, 1915; s. Robert and Leanore (Cobb) A.; A.B., Harvard, 1936, LL.B., 1938; m. Mary Armstrong, June 17, 1938. Admitted to N.Y. bar, 1939, N.H. and Mass. bars, 1946, D.C. bar, 1965; practiced in N.Y.C., 1938-40; prof. law and accounting Harvard Law Sch., 1946-52; dep. dir. CIA, 1952-62; chief internat. div. Bur. Budget, 1962-65; mem. NSC Planning Bd., 1953-61; now mem. Corcoran, Roley, Youngman & Rowe, Washington. U.S. del. Bermuda Conf., 1953, Bangkok, 1955. Trustee, Arena Stage; bd. overseers Harvard U.; mem. adv. council Sch. Advanced Internat. Studies, Johns Hopkins U.; mem. Cambridge Sch. Com., 1949-51; treas. Washington Cathedral Found. Entered Army as pvt., 1941; commanded amphibian engr. battalion and regiment, New Guinea and Philippine campaigns; discharged as col., 1946; lt. col. Armor, Mass. N.G., 1946-51; active service 1951. Mem. Am. Law Inst., Council on Fgn. Relations, Harvard Alumni Assn. (pres. 1961-62, dir. 1959-63). Clubs: Century (N.Y.C.); Cosmos (Washington), Chevy Chase; Cruising of America. Author: Surf and Sand, 1947; Materials on Accounting, 1949. Home: 4833 Dexter Terrace Washington DC 20020 Office: 1511 K St NW Washington DC 20005

AMOS, FRANKLYN BOOTHROYD, physician; b. Chittenango, N.Y., July 16, 1906; s. Henry Edward and Jennie Leuella (Cramer) A.; M.D., Syracuse U., 1931; M.P.H., Johns Hopkins, 1937; m. Gladys Boardman, June 26, 1930; children—Susanne (Mrs. John Williamson), Franklyn Boothroyd, Sarah (Mrs. Darryl Bradt), Penelope (Mrs. Gary Baitsholts). Intern Syracuse Meml. Hosp., 1931-32; gen. practice medicine, Central Sq., N.Y., 1932-35; asst. dist. health officer N.Y. State Dept. Health, Batavia, 1936-38, dist. health officer, 1938-40, asst. dir. local health services, 1940-47, dir. profl. tng., 1948-67, asst. commr., 1967-71; instr. Harvard Sch. Pub. Health, 1946-62; asso. prof. community health Albany Med. Coll., 1950-69; lectr. Columbia Sch. Pub. Health, 1956—; adj. prof. environmental engring. Rensselaer Poly. Inst., 1961-70. Mem. nat. adv. com. on pub. health traineeships, 1956-61; spl. cons. ICA Mission to Colombia, 1956. Diplomate Am. Bd. Preventive Medicine (trustee 1968, vice chmn. pub. health 1969—). Fellow A.M.A., Am. Coll. Preventive Medicine (vice chmn. pub. health 1969-70), Am. Pub. Health Assn. (chmn. com. profl. tng. health officers sect. 1963-68); mem. Med. Soc. State of N.Y. (chmn. com. on continuing edn. 1961-66, chmn. com. on health manpower 1966-69), Assn. Am. Med. Colls., Albany County Med. Soc., Sigma Alpha Epsilon, Alpha Kappa Kappa. Club: University (Albany). Contbr. articles profl. jours. Address: 38 E Bayberry Rd Glenmont NY 12077

AMOS, JOHN ELLIS, lawyer; b. Charleston, W.Va., July 16, 1905; s. John Ellison and Louise Hampton (Delaney) A.; student Augusta Mil. Acad.; LL.B., W.Va. U., 1929; m. Edith Johnston, Oct. 5, 1935; children—John Delaney, Mary Amos Kolstad. Admitted to W.Va. bar, 1929, since practiced in Charleston; mem. firm Amos & Brotherton. Dir. Vulcan Materials Co. (Birmingham, Ala.), Consolidation Coal Co., Am. Electric Power Co. Mem. W.Va. Ho. Dels. from Kanawha County, 1935-47, speaker, 1943-45, 47; mem. W.Va., Senate, 1947-56. Mem. Dem. Nat. Com. from W.Va., 1959-68. Pres. W.Va. Bd. Regents, 1969, sec., 1970. Mem. Am. Trucking Assn. (pres. 1965, chmn. bd. 1966, v.p. at large). Home: 1 Morris St Charleston WV 25301 Office: Kanawha Valley Bldg Charleston WV 25301

AMOSOFF, NIKOLAI MIKHAYLOVICH, surgeon; b. Olchovo, Russia, Dec. 1913; s. Mikhail Ivanovich and Elyzaveta (Nikanorova) A.; grad. Archangelsky Med. Inst., 1939, (by corr.), Moscow Politech. Inst., 1940; m. Lidia Vasliievna Denisenko, Apr. 15, 1944; 1 dau., Ekaterina Nikolaevna Amosova. Technician, Archangelsk Power-Sta., 1932-35; postgrad. student Archangelsk 1935-41; chief surgeon Bryansk region, 1946-52; chief dept. thoracic surgery Kiev Inst. TB and Thoracic Surgery, 1952—; chief thoracic surgery Inst. Advanced Tng., 1955—; chief dept. biol. cybernetics Inst. Cybernetics, Acad. Scis. USSR, 1957—. Dept. Supreme Soviet of USSR, 1962—. Served as mil. surgeon, 1941-45, Decorated Order Lenin, 1961; recipient Lenin prize, 1961; named Merited Scientist of Ukranian Republic, 1959. Corr. mem. Acad. Med. Scis. USSR; fellow All Union Soc., Ukranina Soc. Surgeons and Cardiologists, European Soc. Cardiac Surgeons, Internat. Soc. Surgeons; mem. Acad. Scis. Ukranian Republic. Author: Thoracic Surgery, 1958; Cardiac Operations with Artificial Circulation, 1962; Control of Vital Functions and Cybernetics, 1964; Modeling of Thinking and Mind, Am. edit., 1967; The Open Heart, 1964; Papers from Future (pub. in 21 countries), 1966; Notes from the Future, 1970; also articles. Home: 42 Lenina Kiev 30 Russia Office: 7 Stepan Rasin spusk Kiev Russia

AMPARAN, BELEN, opera singer; b. El Paso, Tex., Sept. 11, 1931; s. Rafael Arriola and Aurora Amparan Iturbide; student Franco-Ingels Sch., Mexic City, 1939- 44; faculty music Conservatory Music and Dramatic Arts Sch., Bellas Artes, Mexico City, 1944-50; m. Bruno Berte, Sept. 18, 1954. Profl. debut, Milan, Italy, 1952; appeared with Opera of Bellas Artes of Mexico, 1953; concerts with conductor Celibidache, 1954; Italian tour, Carmen, Norma, Orfeo, Trovatore, also several modern operas, 1955; debut Royal Theatre Rome, 1955; concert tour, France, 1955; TV premiere of Carmen, Italy, 1955; tour as Carmen in Spain, 1955; debut Met. Opera, 1956, mem. company, 1957-; other appearances include theatres in Washington, San Francisco, Phila., Chgo., Balt., Cin., Boston, also Canada; concert for UN clebration, 1957; debut 10 Thousand People Theatre in Caracalla, also in Rome with Aida, at Arena Flegrea, Naples with Gioconda, 1959. Recipient award Bach contest Conservatory of Mexico, 1948, scholarship for Italy, 1950. Home: Torre Velasca 5 Milan, Italy. Office: Metropolitan Opera House 147 W 39th St New York City NY 10018

AMPER, ALAN, metals co. exec.; b. Brownsville, Pa., Sept. 20, 1923; s. Robert and Lillian (Ehrenpreis) A.; student U. Va., 1941-43; m. Shirley Moskowitz, Oct. 20, 1946; children-Neil, Martha, Leslie. With Southwest Steel Corp., Pitts., 1946-61, v.p., 1948-61; founder, 1961, since pres., chief exec. officer Steelmet, Inc., Pitts. Bd. dirs. Montifiore Hosp., United Jewish Fedn. Served with AUS, 1943-46. Mem. Inst. Scrap Iron and Steel, Nat. Assn. Secondary Material Industries, Pi Lambda Phi. Clubs: Westmoreland Country (Export, Pa.); Concordia (Pitts). Home: 1046 Lyndhurst Dr Pittsburgh PA 15206 Office: Grant Bldg Pittsburgh PA 15219

AMRAM, DAVID WERNER III, composer, conductor, musician; b. Phila., Nov. 17, 1930; s. Philip and Emilie (Weyl) A.; student Oberlin Conservatory Music, 1948-49, Manhattan Sch. Music, 1955-56; B.A. in European History, George Washington U., 1952; student composition with Vitorio Giannini, horn with Gunther Schuller, N.Y.C. Composer incidental music prodns. N.Y. Shakespeare Festival, 1956-67, Broadway plays, 1958—, films, 1957—, also TV; first composer-in-residence N.Y. Philharmonic Orch., 1966-67. Served with AUS, 1952-54. Recipient Obie award for compositions for Phoenix Theater and N.Y. Shakespeare Festival, 1959. Compositions for orch. include The American Bell, Autobiography for Strings, Shakespearean Concerto, Horn Concerto, King Lear Variations, Third Concerto, numerous others; operas include Twelfth Night, The Final Ingredient. Recording artist for RCA-Red Seal. Home: 461 6th Av New York City NY 10011 Office: Care Barna Ostertag 501 Fifth Av New York City NY 10017

AMRAM, PHILIP WERNER, lawyer; b. Phila., Mar. 14, 1900; s. David Werner and Beulah (Brylawski) A.; A.B., U. Pa., 1920; B.S.A., Pa. State Coll., 1922; LL.B. cum laude, U. Pa., 1927; m. Emilie S. Weyl, Dec. 18, 1924; children—Mariana B., David Werner, III. Admitted to Pa. bar, 1927, practiced as mem. law firm of Wolf, Block, Schorr & Solis-Cohen, Phila., 1927-42; admitted to D.C. bar, 1945; now mem. Amram, Hahn, Sundlun & Sandground, Washington; tchr. Pa. practice and practice ct. U. Pa. Law Sch., 1929-42; in charge aviation activities, as chief internat. air transport div. Bd. Econ. Warfare, Washington, 1942; chief rep. S. Pacific area, 1943; spl. asst. to Atty. Gen. U.S. in charge litigation against Standard Oil Co. (N.J.), 1943- 45, also spl. adviser to Alien Property Custodian. Mem. civil procedural rules com. Supreme Ct. Pa. 1938—, chmn., 1958—; chmn. adv. com. to U.S. Commn. on Internat. Rules of Jud. Procedure, 1959-66; mem. adv. rules com. U.S. Dist. Court, Eastern Dist. Pa., Circuit Ct. of Appeals, 1939-42. Ofcl. U.S. observer Hague Conf. Internat. Pvt. Law, 1956, 60, mem. ofcl. delegation, 1964, 68. Asso. trustee law sch. U. Pa. Served as 2d lt. inf. U.S. Army, World War I. Pres., United Community Services of Washington, 1956-68, La Fondation de l'Ecole Française Internationale de Washington. Decorated chevalier French Legion of Honor. Mem. Am. Law Inst., Mil. Order Fgn. Wars, Am., Fed., Internat., state and local bar assns., Order of Coif, Phi Kappa Phi. Club: Cosmos. Author: Amram's Pennsylvania Common Pleas Practice, 7th edit. 1970; New Federal Rules in Pennsylvania, 1938; Goodrich-Amram Pennsylvania Procedural Rules Service, 1940—. Editor-in-chief, U. Pa. Law Rev., 1926-27. Lectr.; contbr. law revs. Home: 2601-31st St Washington DC 20008 also Loveladies NJ 08008 Office: Colorado Bldg Washington DC 20005

AMREIN, YOST URSUS LUCIUS, zoologist, educator; b. Arosa, Switzerland, Jan. 3, 1918; s. Otto Friederich and Anna Elisabeth (Beerli) A.; came to U.S., 1938, naturalized, 1942; B.A., U. Cal. at Los Angeles, 1947, M.A., 1948; Ph.D., 1951; m. Margaret Cuthbertson Brown, Dec. 28, 1948; 1 son, Lucius George. Asst. ranch supr. Teesdale Ranch, nr. Ndola, No. Rhodesia, 1937-38; from instr. to asso. prof. zoology Pomona (Cal.) Coll., 1951-59, prof. zoology, chmn. dept., 1959-68, Willard G. Halstead prof., 1961—. Research fellow Swiss Tropical Inst., Basel, 1964-65. Served with AUS, 1942-45; CBI. Decorated Bronze Star with one cluster. Pub. Health fellow Nat. Inst. Med. Research, London, Eng., 1957-58, research grantee, 1959—; recipient Outstanding Grad. Achievement award Phi Sigma, U. Cal. at Los Angeles, 1951. Fellow Royal Soc. Tropical Medicine and Hygiene, A.A.A.S.; mem. Western Soc. Naturalists (pres. 1969), Ecol. Soc. Am., Am., So. Cal. socs. parasitologists, Soc. Protozoologists, Am. Soc. Zoologists, Sigma Xi, Phi Sigma. Contbr. articles profl. jours. Home: 456 Harrison Av Claremont CA 91711

AMRINE, HAROLD THOMAS, educator; b. Moline, Ill., June 9, 1916; s. Earl T. and Ada (Klein) A.; B.S. in Mech. Engring., State U. Ia., 1938, M.S. in Mech. Engring., 1939; m. Jean Alice Marvin, May 27, 1942; 1 dau., Joan Elizabeth (Mrs. John B. Russell). Indsl. engr. Swift & Co., Sioux City, Ia., 1939-40; planning engr. W. A. Sheaffer Pen Co., Ft. Madison, Ia., 1940; instr. engring. drawing dept. Ohio State U., 1940-41, 45-46; asst prof., asso. prof., prof. Purdue Univ., 1946—, head Sch. Indsl. Engring., 1955-69, asso. dir. div. sponsored programs Purdue Research Found., 1970—, interim head Sch. Elec. Engring., 1962. Chmn. Nat. Council Indsl. Engring. Acad. Dept. Heads, 1965-66; Fulbright lectr. U. Melbourne (Australia), 1959; vis. prof. Ariz. State U., 1969-70. Served from 1st lt. to lt. col. Ordnance Corps, AUS, 1942-45. Fellow Am. Inst. Indsl. Engrs. (past v.p., dir., v.p. edn. and student affairs 1969-71); mem. Am. Soc. M.E., Am. Soc. Engring. Edn. (chmn. indsl. engring. div. 1960-61), Sigma Xi, Tau Beta Pi, Alpha Pi Mu. Methodist. Elk, Rotarian. Co-author: Manufacturing Organization and Management, 2d edit., 1966. 107 Sunset Lane West Lafayette IN 47906 Office: Sch Engring Purdue U Lafayette IN 47907

AMSTER, HARVEY JEROME, educator, physicist; b. Cleve., Sept. 30, 1928; s. Sidney Nelson and Hilda (Klein) A.; B.S. in Physics, Cal. Inst. Tech., 1950; Ph.D., Mass. Inst. Tech., 1954. Sr. scientist Bettis Atomic Power Lab., Westinghouse Electric Corp., 1954-57, fellow scientist, 1957-60, adv. scientist, 1960-61; mem. faculty U. Cal. at Berkeley, 1961—, prof. nuclear engring., 1965—; physicist Lawrence Radiation Lab., Livermore, Cal., 1961; sr. physicist Northrop Space Labs., Hawthorne, Cal., 1963; vis. prof. U. Wis., 1963, Western Res. U., 1965; staff Inst. Def. Analyses, Arlington, Va., 1969; cons. to industry, 1962—. Mem. Am. Phys. Soc., Am. Nuclear Soc. (exec. com. reactor physics and Benchmark com. math. and computation div.), A.A.A.S. Author articles models of atomic nucleus, neutron cross sections, thermal neutron spectra, spatial distbns. and environmental consequences of nuclear tech. Home: 1338 Shattuck Av Berkeley CA 94709

AMSTERDAM, ANTHONY GUY, legal educator; b. Phila., Sept. 12, 1935; s. Gustave G. and Valla (Abel) A.; A.B., Haverford Coll., 1957; LL.B., U. Pa., 1960; m. Lois P. Sheinfeld, Aug. 29, 1968. Law clk. to U.S. Supreme Ct. Justice Felix Frankfurter, 1960-61; admitted to D.C. bar, 1960; asst. U.S. atty., 1961-62; prof. law U. Pa. Law Sch., 1962-69, Stanford Law Sch., 1969—; cons. litigating atty. numerous civil rights groups; cons. govt. commns. Mem. Commn. to Study Disturbances at Columbia, 1968. Trustee Center Law and Social Policy, Calif. Indian Legal Services, Am. Civil Liberties Union No. Cal., Lawyers Constl. Defense Com., James Madison Constl. Law Inst. Named Outstanding Young Man of Year, Phila. and Pa. Jaycees, 1967; recipient First Distinguished Service award U. Pa. Law Sch., 1968, Haverford award, Haverford Coll., 1970. Author: The Defensive Transfer of Civil Rights Litigation From State to Federal Courts, 1964; (with B. Segal and M. Miller) Trial Manual for the Defense of Criminal Cases, 1967; also numerous articles. Editor-in-chief U. Pa. Law Rev., 1959-60. Home: 1104 Laureles Dr Los Altos CA 94022 Office: Stanford Univ Law Sch Stanford CA 94305

AMSTERDAM, GUSTAVE GERALD, lawyer; b. Phila., Aug. 25, 1908; s. Benjmain and Anna (Feld) A.; student Inst. for Auslander, U. Berlin, Germany, 1929-30; A.B., U. Pa., 1930, LL.B., 1933; m. Valla Abel, July 3, 1933; 1 son, Anthony G. Admitted to Pa. bar, 1933; pvt. practice law, 1934-35; chief counsel 3d Res. Dist., RFC, Phila., 1935-38; with firm Sundheim, Folz & Sundheim, Phila., 1933-42. Vice pres. Albert M. Greenfield & Co., 1938- 56; v.p. Bankers Securities Corp., 1946-51, exec. v.p., 1951-55, pres., 1955-70, chmn., 1959—; chmn. City Stores Co., N.Y.C.; chmn. Albert M. Greenfield & Co., Inc., 1968—; pres., dir. Benjamin Franklin Hotel Corp., Phila., Land Title Bldg. Corp., Phila.; pres., trustee Albert M. Greenfield Found., Phila.; v.p., dir. Bankers Realty Corps., Phila., City Stores Found., Inc., Phila.; dir. Yellow Cab Cos. of Phila. and Camden; chmn., mem. exec. com. B. Lowenstein & Bros., Inc., Memphis; dir. Bonwit Teller & Co., Atlantic Theatres, Inc., Gold Trading Stamp Co., Phila., Kaufman-Straus Co., Louisville, Phila. Electric Co.; chmn., dir. Bankers Bond & Mortgage Guaranty Co. of Am., W. & J Sloane Co.; dir. Loft Candy Corp., Sloane-Mayer Co., 1st Pa. Bank & Trust Co., 1st Pa. Corp., Horn & Hardart Baking Co., Western Savs. Fund Soc. Vice pres., mem. exec. bd. Phila. council Boy Scouts Am.; v.p., mem. exec. com. Old Phila. Devel. Corp. Dir. Bur. Municipal Research, Pa. Economy League, Fedn. Jewish Agencies Phila., United Fund of Phila., Albert Einstein Med. Center; trustee Jefferson Med. Coll. and Hosp.; bd. dirs. Phila. Orch. Assn., Greater Phila. Movement, Phila. Port Corp., U. City Sci. Center; trustee U. Pa., U. Mus.; mem. bd. Franklin Inst. Research for Better Schs., Inc. Served from 2d lt. to maj. USAAF, 1942-46. Mem. Am., Pa., Phila., Fed. bar assn., Am. Law Inst. Democrat. Home: 5209 Woodbine Av Philadelphia PA 19131 Office: 1315 Walnut St Philadelphia PA 19107

AMSTERDAM, MOREY, actor, writer, producer; b. Chgo., Dec. 14, 1914; s. Max and Jenny (Finder) A.; student U. Cal. at Berkeley; m. Catherine Amayia Patrick, Dec. 17, 1941; children—Geoffrey, Cathy. Boy soprano radio sta. KPO, San Francisco; cellist with theatre orchs. and concert ensembles; vaudeville appearances; gag and song writer for comedians. Author: Keep Laughing; Betty Crocker's Crock Book. Address: 1012 N Hillcrest Rd Beverly Hills CA 90210

AMSTUTZ, EDWARD DELBERT, educator; b. New Athens, O., May 1, 1909; s. Platte T. and Louise (Allison) A.; B.S., Coll. of Wooster (O.), 1930, Sc.D (hon.), 1969; M.S., Inst. Paper Chemistry, 1931; Ph.D., Cornell U., 1936; m. Frances Van Schaack; Aug. 30, 1935; children—Edward Allison, Jean Louise, William Platte. Research scholar Inst. Paper Chemistry, Appleton, Wis., 1930-32; teaching asst. Cornell U., Ithaca, N.Y., 1933-36; instr. chemistry Union Coll., 1936-38; instr. chemistry Lehigh U., Bethlehem, Pa., 1938-41, asst. prof., 1941- 43, asso. prof., 1943-47, prof. organic chemistry, 1947-70, Howard S. Bunn Distinguished prof. chemistry, 1970—, head dept. chemistry, 1960-68. Fulbright lectr., Spain, 1963. Mem. Am. Chem. Soc., A.A.A.S., Sigma Xi. Republican. Presbyn Home: 3465 Altonah Rd Bethlehem PA 18017

AMUNDSEN, LAWRENCE HARDIN, educator; b. Pine River, Wis., Sept. 23, 1909; s. Albert and Cora Elizabeth (Hardin) A.; B.S., Coll. of Ozarks, 1931; Ph.D., U. Fla., 1935; m. Helen Francis Langslow, Dec. 16, 1934; children—Albert Lawrence, Ralph Francis, Franklin Hardin, Bruce Langslow. Instr., Adelphi Coll., Garden City, N.Y., 1935-36; instr. U. Conn., Storrs, 1936-38, asst. prof., 1938-41, asso. prof., 1941-46, prof., 1946—. Research fellow Purdue U., 1942; chemist USPHS, S.I., N.Y., 1943-44; vis. prof. Fla. Atlantic U., Boca Raton, 1968. Mem. Bd. Edn., Scotland, Conn., 1948-61. Fellow A.A.A.S.; mem. Am. Chem. Soc., New Eng. Assn. Chemistry Tchrs., Conn. Acad. Arts and Scis., Sigma Xi, Phi Lambda Upsilon. Republican. Conglist. Club: Chemists (N.Y.C.). Author textbook and articles in chemistry field. Home: RFD 1 Storrs CT 06268

AMUNDSON, NEAL RUSSELL, chem. engr.; b. St. Paul, Jan. 10, 1916; s. Oscar and Hazel (Cottrell) A.; B.Chem. Engring., U. Minn., 1937, M.S., 1941, Ph.D. in Math., 1945; m. Shirley Dimond, Sept. 25, 1941; children—Gregg Russell, Beth Eva, Erik Neal. Postdoctoral fellow applied math. Brown U., 1944-45; asst. prof. math. U. Minn., 1945-47, asso. prof. chem. engring., 1947-51, prof., head dept., 1951—, Regents' prof. chem. engring., 1967—. Fulbright scholar, Guggenheim fellow, Cambridge (Eng.) U.; 1954-55. Mem. Am. Chem. Soc. (recipient indsl. and engring. chemistry award 1960), Am. Inst. Chem. Engring. (William H. Walker award 1962, Warren K. Lewis award 1971), Nat. Acad. Engring., Am. Soc. Engring. Edn. (Vincent Beudix award 1970), Sigma Xi, Tau Beta Pi, Phi Lambda Upsilon, Alpha Chi Sigma. Editor Internat. Series on Phys. and Chem. Engring. Sci. Contbr. Research papers profl. jours. Home: Lily Pond Lane North Oaks Farm St Paul MN 55110

AMUSSEN, ROBERT MARTIN, editor; b. Washington, Feb. 18, 1924; s. Theodore Smith and Lorna (Russell) A.; B.A., Swarthmore Coll., 1949; m. Diane Duke, Dec. 9, 1949 (div.); children—Gretchen Duke, Susan Dwyer, John Russell. Asso. editor G. P. Putnam's Sons 1950-54, editor McGraw Hill Book Co., Inc., 1954-57; sr. editor E. P. Dutton & Co., N.Y.C., 1958-62; J.B. Lippincott Co., 1963-65; dir., editor-in-chief Bobbs-Merrill Co., Inc., 1966—. Office: 3 W 57th St New York City NY 10019

AMUSSEN, THEODORE SMITH, publisher; b. Salt Lake City, Aug. 15, 1915; s. Theodore S. and Lorna Addison (Russell) A.; student Brooks Sch., North Andover, Mass., 1930-35, Sorbonne, Paris, 1935-36, Harvard, 1936-37; m. Anne Nelson Cutler, Oct. 14 1939 (dec. Nov. 1958); children—Deborah, Daniel, David, Timothy Dwyer. Asst. editor Rinehart & Co., Inc. (formerly Farrar & Rinehart Inc.) N.Y.C., 1938-45, asso. editor, 1945-47, v.p., gen. mgr. trade dept., editor-in-chief gen. book dept., 1953-60; exec. editor Reynal, Hitchcock & Co., Inc., 1947; editor Harcourt, Brace & Co., Inc., also Reynal & Hitchcock when merged, 1948; editor-in-chief Henry Holt & Co., Inc., 1950-53; v.p. Peters Co., Inc., 1961-65; editor spl. publs. div. Nat. Geog. Soc., 1966-68; chief div. books Nat. Park Service, 1968-70; editor-in-chief Nat. Gallery of Art, 1970—; dir. Rinehart & Co., Inc., Fred Feldkamp Prodns., Inc. Served as pub. relations specialist USNR, 1945-46. Mem. P.E.N. Clubs: Harvard (N.Y.C.); Overseas Press; Publishers Lunch; Coffee House. Home: 3133 University Blvd W Kensington MD 20795 Office: Nat Gallery of Art Washington DC 20565

AMUZEGAR, JAHANGIR, diplomat of Iran; b. Tehran, Iran, Jan. 13, 1920; s. Habibollah and Turan (Azemudeh) A.; B.A., U. Tehran, 1941; M.A., U. Washington, 1948; Ph.D., U. Cal. at Los Angeles, 1955; m. Eleanor R. Horn, Sept. 27, 1958. Econ. adviser, plan orgn. Govt. Iran, 1956-57; minister commerce, 1961-62; minister finance, 1962; ambassador-at-large, chief Iranian econ. mission Washington, 1962—; asst. prof. econs. Mich. State U., 1957-58; asso. prof. Occidental Coll., Los Angeles, 1958-60, U. Cal. at Los Angeles, 1960; research prof. Brookings Instn., Washington, 1960-61. Mem. Pi Gamma Mu. Author: Technical Assistance in Theory and Practice,

1966; Iran: Economic Development under Dualistic Conditions, 1971. Contbr. profl. jours. Home: 6713 Tulip Hill Terrace Washington DC 20016 Office: 5530 Wisconsin Av NW Washington DC 20015

AMY, ERNEST VALENTINE, cons. engr.; b. N.Y.C., Feb. 11, 1892; s. Ernest H. J. and Isabelle (O'Donohue) A.; E.E., Columbia, 1917; m. Jessie Marie Mercier, May 15, 1943. Engr. test dept., New York Edison Co., 1919-20; engr. research dept. Marconi Wireless Telegraph Co., 1920-21; with RCA, 1922-28, in engring. dept. design div. 1921-22, in charge first installation 2-way radio telephone (on S.S. America), 1922-23; engr. in charge Radio Relay Station, Belfast, Me., 1923-25, engr. design sect., in charge constrn. antennae, Rocky Point, L.I., 1926-27, and Bolinas, Cal., 1928; cons. engr., 1928—; dir. Mercier Realty & Investment Co. Dir. Armstrong Meml. Research Found., Inc., 1955—. Served as 1st lt. 302d Engrs., 77th Div., U.S. Army, 1917-18. Recipient Armstrong medal Radio Club of Am., Inc., 1965. Registered profl. engr., N.Y. Mem. Am. Numis. Soc., Am. Inst. Elec. Engrs., I.R.E., Soc. Am. Mil. Engrs., Radio Club Am., Theta Delta Chi. Democrat. Roman Catholic. Clubs: Columbia U. (N.Y.); Atlantic Beach (L.I.). Inventor, co- inventor of sound absorber blocks and many basic radio devices for noise reduction and radio aerial systems. Address: 1890 Bay Blvd Atlantic NY 11509

AMYX, DARRELL ARLYNN, educator; b. Exeter, Cal., Apr. 2, 1911; s. Buford Elmore and Maude (Kirkman) A.; A.B. in Classics, Stanford, 1930; M.A. in Latin, U. Cal. at Berkeley, 1932, Ph.D. in Latin and Classical Archaeology, 1937; m. Eleanor Wilkinson, July 6, 1936; 1 dau., Ellen Anne. Instr. Latin, U. Chgo., 1937-39; successively asst., research asso., instr. classics, U. Cal. at Berkeley, 1939-42; with U.S. Office Censorship, San Francisco, 1942-45; mem. faculty U. Cal. at Berkeley, 1946—, prof. art, 1958—, chmn. dept., 1966-71, asst. dean Coll. Letters and Scis., 1964-65, curator classical art univ. art museum, 1965-71, curator ancient Mediterranean art R.H. Lowie Mus. Anthropology, 1958—, humanities research prof., 1969. Fellow, Am. Sch. Classical Studies, Athens, Greece, 1935-36; Guggenheim fellow, 1957-59; Fulbright sr. research grantee to Greece, 1957-58; grantee Am. Council Learned Socs., 1941, 62, fellow, 1965-66. Mem. Archaeol. Inst. Am.,.Am. Philol. Assn., Coll. Art Assn., Phi Beta Kappa. Asso. editor Cal. Studies in Classical Antiquity, vol. 1, 1968—. Author: An Amphora with a Price Inscription, 1941; Corinthian Vases at San Simeon, 1943; (with W.K. Pritchett), The Attic Stelai (with W.K. Pritchett), 1958; also articles. Home: 671 Oberlin Av Kensington, CA 94708. Office: Dept of Art Univ California Berkeley CA 94720

ANAGNOST, CATHERINE COOK, lawyer; b. Tegea, Greece,.Feb. 10, 1919; d. Peter and Athena (Reppas) Cook; diploma Northwestern U., 1942; m. Themis Anagnost, Aug. 15, 1942; children—Maria, Alexander, James. Certified pub. accountant, 1943; admitted to Ill. bar, 1948, since practiced in Chgo.; mem. Anagnost & Anagnost, 1948—. Mem. Nat. Panel of Arbitrators. Alternate del. Republican Nat. Conv., 1964; Rep. candidate for judge Circuit Ct. Cook County, 1964. Mem. bd. women's adv. council N.Y. World's Fair for 1964-65; v.p., dir. Beverly Farm Found.; past dir. Chgo. chpt. Girl Scouts Am. Chmn. 1966 Founders Day Program Northwestern U. Recipient Merit award Northwestern U., 1964. Mem. Northwestern U. Alumni Assn., Am. (del. ho. of dels. 1965-67), Ill., Chgo., West Suburban (past pres., chmn. bd.), Hellenic (past pres. Ill.) bar assns., Women's Bar Assn. Ill. (past dir.), Hellenic Profl. Soc. Ill. (past v.p.), Internat. House Assn. (past treas. Chgo.), Nat. Assn. Women Lawyers (pres. 1963- 64), Internat. Fedn. Women Lawyers, Am. Trial Lawyers Assn. (past asso. editor jour.), Nat. Platform Assn., Nat. Fedn. Bus. and Profl. Women's Clubs, Nat., Internat. councils women, Assn. Plaintiff's Lawyers Ill., Greek Women's U. Club. Mem. Order Eastern Star, White Shrine Jerusalem. Home: 2345 N Oak Park Av Chicago IL 60635 Office: 11 S LaSalle St Chicago IL 60603

ANASTASI, ANNE, (Mrs. John Porter Foley, Jr.), educator; b. N.Y.C., Dec. 19, 1908; d. Anthony and Theresa (Gaudiosi) Anastasi; A.B., Barnard Coll., 1928; Ph.D., Columbia, 1930; Litt.D. (hon.), U. Windsor (Can.), 1967; Sc.D., Cedar Crest Coll., 1971; Ph.D., Villanova U., 1971; m. John Porter Foley, Jr., July 26, 1933. Instr. psychology Barnard Coll., N.Y.C., 1930-39; asst. prof. Queens Coll., N.Y.C., 1939-46; asso. prof. Fordham U., N.Y.C., 1947-51, prof., 1951—, chmn. dept. psychology, 1968—. Intermittently dir. research projects USAF; mem. NRC, 1952-55. Pres., Am. Psycholo. Found., 1965-67. Mem. Am. (rec. sec. 1952-55, pres. div. gen. psychology 1956-57, bd. dirs. 1956-59, 68-70, pres. div. evaluation and measurement 1965-66, pres. 1971—), Eastern (pres. 1946-47, dir. 1948-50), psychol. assns., Psychonomic Soc., Psychometric Soc., Phi Beta Kappa, Sigma Xi. Author: Differential Psychology, 1937, rev. edit., 1949, 58; Psychological Testing, 1954, rev. edit. 1961, 68; (with J.P. Foley, Jr.) Human Relations and the Foreman, 1951; Fields of Applied Psychology, 1964; also articles in field. Editor: Individual Differences, 1965; Testing Problems in Perspective, 1966. Home: 121 E 38 St New York City NY 10016

ANASTOS, GEORGE, educator, zoologist; b. Akron, O., Jan. 9, 1920; s. Peter and Kaliroy (Kakarakis) A.; B.S. with distinction, Akron U., 1942; M.A., Harvard, 1947, Ph.D., 1949; m. Angelica Pappas, Sept. 8, 1946; children—Phyllis Catherine, Barbara Ann. Teaching fellow biology Harvard, 1947-49; asst. prof. zoology Miami U., Oxford, O., 1949-51; mem. faculty U. Md., 1951—, prof. zoology, 1958—, head dept., 1961-68, exec. sec. Inst. Acarology, 1953-58, asst. dir., 1958-61; lectr. Inst. Acarology, Ohio State U., 1962-68. Spl. cons. USPHS, 1954; cons. Dept. Def., 1955-65, NSF, 1961-68; prin. investigator grants and contracts NIH and Dept. Army, 1953; sci. adviser WHO, Geneva, Switzerland, 1968—, dir. WHO Regional Reference Center, 1970—. Served to lt. USNR, 1942-46. Guggenheim fellow, 1958. Mem. Washington Acad. Sci., Am. Soc. Parasitologists, Helminthological Soc. Washington, Soc. Systematic Zoology, Entomol. Soc. Am., Sigma Xi (pres. Md. chpt. 1962), Phi Sigma Kappa, Alpha Sigma Omicron (pres. Akron U. 1941-42). Author: The Scutate Ticks of Indonesia, 1950; The Ticks of the USSR, 1957; Index Catalogue to Russian, Central and Eastern European and Chinese Literature in Medical Entomology, vols. 1-12, 1963-67; Ixodid Ticks of Central Africa, vols. 1-4, 1966-67. Editor: Jour. Econ. Entomology, 1970—. Home: 3021 Crest Av Cheverly MD 20785

ANASTOS, MILTON VASIL, educator; b. N.Y.C., July 10, 1909; s. Vlassios and Stella Hope (Spartali) A.; A.B. (First Boylston prize 1929), Harvard, 1930, (Latin oration 1931), S.T.B., 1935, Ph.D., 1940, student Law Sch., 1932-33; m. Sept. 7, 1935; div. 1938; 1 son, Milton Vasil; m. 2d, Rosemary Park, July 31, 1965. Asst. history Harvard, 1935-37, 40-41, asst. English, 1939-41, Jr. fellow Dumbarton Oaks Research Library and Collection, 1941-43, fellow, 1944-46, asst. prof. Byzantine theology, 1946-51, asso. prof., 1951-59, prof., 1959-64, librarian Div. Sch., 1936-39, vis. asso. prof. church history, 1956-59, vis. prof., 1959-64, sec. Harvard Theol. Rev., 1937-39; prof. Byzantine Greek, U. Cal. at Los Angeles, 1964-67, prof. Byzantine Greek and history, 1967—; instr. bibl. history Wellesley Coll., 1937; lectr. U. Munich, U. Thessalonika, Conn. Coll. Women, U. Wash., univs. Cal. at Berkeley and Los Angeles, Manhattanville Coll. Vice chmn. Harvard Found. Advanced Study and Research, Washington, 1951-52; mem. U.S. Commn. Preservation Monuments; 1942-43; research analyst. OSS, 1943-45. Mem. bd. scholars Harvard U. Dumbarton Oaks Research Library and Collection, 1952—. Grantee Am. Council Learned Soc., 1948; Fulbright sr. research fellow, 1954-55; Guggenheim fellow, 1954-55, 66-67. Fellow Mediaeval Acad. Am., Am. Numis. Soc.; mem. Soc. Macedonian Studies (corr. mem.), Am. Hist. Assn., Internat. Com. Für den Nachdruck griechischer Handschriftenkataloge, Am. Philos. Soc., Phi Beta Kappa (pres. U. Cal. at Los Angeles 1967-68). Democrat. Mem. Greek Orthodox Ch. Author: Pletho's Calendar and Liturgy, Dumbarton Oaks Papers, 1948; Byzantine Influence on the Latin Culture of the Twelfth Century, 1961; Nestorius Was Orthodox, 1963. Co-editor: Vigiliae Christianae, 1966—, Viator, 1969—. Home: 969 Hilgard Av Los Angeles CA 90024

ANCERL, KAREL, conductor; b. Tucapy, Czechoslovakia, Apr. 11, 1908; s. Leopold and Ida (Pseiz) A.; student master class composition and conducting, Conservatoire Music, Prague; m. Hana Glücklich, Oct. 5, 1946; children—George, Ivan. Condr., Liberated Theatre, Prague, 1930-33, Czechslovakia Radio Orch., 1933-39, Opera of 5th May, Prague, 1946-49; head conductor Czech Philharmonic Orch., 1950-68, Toronto Symphony Orch., 1969-70; prof. conducting class Acad. Music, Prague, 1948-52; guest condr., Europe, U.S., Asia, Australia. Recipient Laureate of State prize Czechoslovakia, 1958; Klement Gottwald State prize, 1958; Charles Cross Acad. prize, 1960, 64; Artist of Merit, 1965; Nat. Artist, 1967. Hon. member Royal Academy Of Music (London). Home: Narodmi 25 Prague 1 Czechoslovakia Office: Czech Philharmonic Orchestra Prague Czechoslovakia

ANCKER, CLINTON JAMES, Jr., educator; b. Cedar Falls, Ia., June 21, 1919; s. Clinton James and Fern (Lalan) A.; B.S. in Mech. Engring., Purdue U., 1940; M.S., U. Cal. at Berkeley, 1949, Mech. Engr., 1950; Ph.D., Stanford, 1955; m. Margaret Wright Rees, Apr. 11, 1947; children—Clinton James III, Evan Randolph, Megan Lalan, Scott Rees. Jr. engr. Detroit Edison Co., 1941, 46; instr. Purdue U., 1946-47; asst. prof. U. Cal. at Berkeley, 1947-55; operations analyst Operations Research Office, Chevy Chase, Md., 1955-56; sr. engr. Booz-Allen Applied Research, Inc., Chgo., 1956-58; mgr. Analco Services Co., Chgo., 1958-59; head math. and operations research program System Devel. Corp., Santa Monica, Cal., 1959-67; dir. Nat. Hwy. Safety Inst., Dept. Transp., 1967-68; prof., chmn. dept. indsl. and systems engring. U. So. Cal., 1968—. Served to capt. AUS, 1941-46. Mem. Am. Soc. M.E., Operations Research Soc. Am. (nat. council 1970-73), Soc. Indsl. and Applied Mathematics, Am. Inst. Indsl. Engrs., Mil. Operations Research Soc. (exec. com. 1964-65), Sigma Xi, Tau Beta Pi, Pi Tau Sigma. Author papers in field. Home: 23908 Malibu Knolls Rd Malibu CA 90265 Office: Dept Indsl and Systems Engring Univ So Cal Los Angeles CA 90007

ANDA, GEZA, pianist; b. Budapest, Hungary, Nov. 19, 1921; s. Géza and Mathilde (von Tomosvary) A.; ed. Budapest Acad. Music; m. Hortense Buhrle, Dec. 17, 1964. Became Swiss citizen, 1955. Debut with Mengelberg, 1939; appearances with Berlin, Vienna, N.Y. philharmonic orchs., Amsterdam Concertgebouw, Philharmonia London, Paris Conservatoire, Santa Cecillia Rome, Phila., Chgo., San Francisco symphony orchs., also Edinburgh, Vienna, Montreux, Besancon festivals; pianist Salzburg and Lucerne festivals 12 consecutive seasons; ann. appearances Festival Hall London; frequent U.S., Canadian tours. Decorated chevalier ~~de l'Ordre~~ des Arts et des Lettres (France); recipient Grand Prix des Disques, 1961, 62, 63, 66; Franz Liszt prize, 1940; Grand Prix des Discophiles Paris, 1966; Prix of German critic, Berlin, 1966; Schallplattenpreis Wiener Flotenuhr, 1969, 70. Hon. mem. Royal Acad. Music (London). Address: Zollikerstr 178 Zurich Switzerland

ANDEEN, GUSTAV KENNETH, univ. pres.; b. Mt. Vernon, Wash., June 23, 1918; s. Gustav Knut and Esther (Miller) A.; B.A., Upsala Coll., 1939; student Brown U., 1939-40, U. Minn., 1940-41; B.D., Lutheran Sch. Theology, 1945; M.A., Columbia, 1947, Ph.D., 1952; m. Constance Yvonne Carlson, June 22, 1945; children—Gerhardt Kenneth, Timothy Robert, Kathryn Joy. Ordained to ministry Luth. Ch., 1945; minister in Bergenfield, N.J., 1945-47, Barstow, Ill., 1947-58; prof. Augustana Coll., Rock Island, Ill., 1947- 65; pres. Bethany Coll., Lindsborg, Kan., 1965-67; acad. dean William Rainey Harper Coll., Palatine, Ill., 1967-69; pres. Wittenberg U., Springfield, O., 1969-; vis. prof. Luth. Sch. Theology, 1962-64. Chmn. Luth. Commn. Ch. Vocations, 1960-65, Central States Exam. Com., 1965-67; vice chmn. bd. parish edn. Luth. Ch., 1954-58. Mem. Am. Assn. U. Profs. (pres. Augustana chpt. 1962-63), Am. Scandinavian Found. (pres. Augustana Coll. chpt. 1960-61), Am. Acad. Religion, Religious Edn. Assn., Am. Assn. Higher Edn. Author: Education in the Augustana Lutheran Church, 1952; Genesis, Book of Beginning, 1965. Home: 644 N Wittenberg Av Sprigfield OH 45504

ANDELMAN, SAMUEL LOUIS, city health commr.; b. Chgo., Mar. 7, 1916; s. Isaac and Ida (Shapiro) A.; B.S., Northwestern U., 1938; M.D., M.S., U. Ill., 1942; M.P.H., U. Mich., 1954; m. Joan K. Hunt, Feb. 19, 1944; children—Margaret Joan, Barbara Joyce, Janet Marie, Nancy Jean. Intern U.S. Marine Hosp., Chgo., 1942-43; sr. asst. surgeon USPHS, 1943-46; gen. practice medicine, Harlan County, Ky., 1946-52, county health officer, 1945-52; regional health officer So. Ill. Dept. Health, Carbondale, 1952-56; asst. commr. health Chgo. Bd. Health, 1956-60, commr. health, 1960—; prof. pub. health St. Xavier Coll. Sch. Nursing, Chgo., 1958—; dir. health Skokie, Ill., 1968—. Mem. regional conf. com. Cook County (Ill.) Com. White House Conf. Aging, 1960-; appeal bd. Air Pollution Control Com., Chgo., 1960—; mem. Pres.'s Commn. on Health and Health Facilities; mem. adv. com. Medic Alert Found. Internat. Bd. dirs. Lawson YMCA, Chgo.; active local Girl Scouts Am., Am. Legion, P.T.A. Mem. Ill. N.G., 1933-39, Ky. N.G., 1946-56, U.S. Army Res., 1958-69; now col. ret. Mem. Am., Ill. med. assns., Chgo. Med. Soc., Am. Coll. Preventive Medicine, Nat. Bd. Med. Examiners, Am., Ill. pub. health assns., Am. Soc. Pub. Adminstrn., Am., Chgo. heart assns., Ill. Assn. Med. Health Officers (past pres.), Chgo. Assn. Commerce and Industry, Am. Legion (citation local post 1960). Home: 7842 N Kedvale Av Skokie IL 60076 Office: 54 W Hubbard St Chicago IL 60610

ANDERBERG, EDWARD CLARENCE, banker; b. N.Y.C., Nov. 28, 1918; s. Eberhard I. and Selma (Bogren) A.; B.S., N.Y.U., 1951, M.B.A., 1966; m. Carol Kirkwood, Oct. 12, 1951; children—Thomas, Robert, Karen, Stephen. With The Green Point Savs. Bank, Bklyn., 1935—, asst. sec., 1954-60, asst. v.p., 1960-66, v.p., 1966-67, exec. v.p., 1967—. Bd. mgrs. Greenpoint br. YMCA, 1970—, chmn. world service com., 1967—. Served with AUS, 1942-46. Home: 571 Stanton Av Baldwin NY 11510 Office: 807 Manhattan Av Brooklyn NY 11222

ANDEREGG, DOYLE EDWARD, educator; b. Uhrichsville, O., Jan. 19, 1930; s. Edward Hiram and Alice (Sproul) A.; B.Sc., Ohio State U., 1952, M.Sc., 1957, Ph.D., 1959; m. Jeanne Carolyn Walker, Feb. 9, 1957; children—Alice Elizabeth, Carolyn Myra. Mem. faculty U. Okla., 1959-67, asso. prof., 1965-67, chmn. dept. botany and microbiology, 1963-67; prof., head dept. biol. scis. U. Ida., 1967—, asst. grad. dean, 1969-70. Served with AUS, 1953-55. Fellow A.A.A.S.; mem. Am. Inst. Biol. Scis., Am. Phytopathol. Soc., Bot. Soc. Am., Am. Bryological and Lichenological Soc., Mycol. Soc. Home: 825 West C St Moscow ID 83843

ANDERER, JOSEPH HENRY, textile co. exec.; b. Phila., Oct. 12, 1924; s. Joseph L. and Catherine (Fleck) A.; B.M.E., Ga. Inst. Tech., 1947, B.I.E., 1948; m. E. T'Lene Brinson, Apr. 4, 1948; children—Joseph D., Mark H., Nancy T. Chem. engr. Atlantic Richfield Corp., 1947-55; fiber research mgr., textile devel. lab. mgr. Am. Viscose Corp., 1955-62; with Celanese Corp., 1962-69, exec. v.p. textile mktg., 1967-69; pres., dir. cosmetic and fragrance div. Revlon, N.Y.C., 1969-71; pres. M. Lowenstein, 1972—; dir. ALRAC Corp. Served to lt. USMCR, 1943-45. Mem. Tau Beta Pi, Pi Tau Sigma. Methodist. Clubs: N.Y. Athletic; Tamarack Country. Patentee fiber technology. Home: 41 Lake Wind Rd New Canaan CT 06840 Office: 1430 Broadway New York City NY

ANDERHALTER, OLIVER FRANK, educator; b. Trenton, Ill., Feb. 14, 1922; s. Oliver Valentine and Catherine (Vollet) A.; B.Ed., Eastern Ill. State Tchrs. Coll., 1 1943, Ped.D. (hon.), 1956; A.M., St. Louis U., 1947, Ph.D., 1949; m. Elizabeth Fritz, Apr. 30, 1945; childrenSharon, Stephen, Dennis. Mem. faculty St. Louis U., 1947—, prof. edn., 1957—, dir. Bur. Instl. Research, 1949-65, 1949-65, Univ. Computer Center, 1961-69, chmn. research methodology dept., 1968—; v.p. Scholastic Testing Service, Chgo., 1951-. Chmn. finance com. Greater St. Louis Campfire Girls Orgn., 1958- 59. Served as pilot USNR, 1943-46. Mem. Am. Ednl. Research Assn., Nat. Council Measurement, Am. Statis. Assn., N.E.A. Author, editor standardized standardized tests. Home: 2305 Shirley St Jennings, MO 63136. Office: 3690 W Pine St St Louis MO 63108

ANDERS, CURTIS LANGFORD, financial exec., author; b. Commerce, Tex., Sept. 22, 1927; s. Curtis Langford and Viola (Bell) A.; B.S., U.S. Mil. Acad., 1949; M.A., Columbia, 1955; m. Martha Louise Buie, June 8, 1949. Commd. 2d lt. U.S. Army, 1949, advanced through grades to capt., 1951; served with 7th Div., Korea, 1950-51; instr. English, U.S. Mil. Acad., 1953-56; ret., 1956; asst. mgr. Brown Bros. Harriman & Co., pvt. bankers, N.Y.C., 1958-66; v.p., mgr. investor relations Carl Byoir & Assos., Inc., N.Y.C., 1966—. Decorated Bronze Star with combat V, Purple Heart with oak leaf cluster. Episcopalian. Author: The Price of Courage, 1957; Fighting Generals, 1965; Fighting Airmen, 1966; Warrior: The Story of George S. Pattoh, 1967; Fighting Confederates, 1968; (with Charles Boswell) Now I See, 1969. Office: 800 2d Av New York City NY 10017

ANDERS, EDWARD, educator, chemist; b. Libau, Latvia, June 21, 1926; s. Adolph and Erica (Leventals) Alperovitch; student U. Munich (Germany), 1949; A.M., Columbia, 1951, Ph.D., 1954; m. Joan Elizabeth Fleming, Nov. 12, 1955; children—George Charles, Nancy Elizabeth. Came to U.S., 1949, naturalized, 1955. Instr. U. Ill., 154-55; mem. faculty U. Chgo., 1955- -, prof. chemistry, 1962—; vis. prof. Cal. Inst. Tech., 1960, U. Berne (Switzerland), 1963-64, 70; resident research asso. NASA, 1961, cons., 1961- 69, mem. lunar sample analysis planning team, 1967-69; research asso. Field Mus. Natural History, Chgo., 1968—; spl. research origin and age meteorites, composition lunar rocks, origin moon and planets. Recipient Univ. medal for excellence Columbia, 1966; J. Lawrence Smith medal Nat. Acad. Scis., 1971. Fellow A.A.A.S. (Newcomb Cleveland prize 1959), Meteoritical Soc. (v.p. 1970—), Am. Geophys. Union; mem. Am. Astron. Soc. (chmn. div. planetary scis. 1971—), Internat. Union Geodesy and Geophysics, Internat. Astron. Union, Am. Chem. Soc., Geochem. Soc., Sigma Xi. Asso. editor Geochimica et Cosmochimica Acta, 1966—, Icarus, 1970—. Contbr. profl. jours. Home: 5415 S Hyde Park Blvd Chicago IL 60615 Office: Enrico Fermi Inst 5630 S Ellis Av Chicago IL 60637

ANDERS, WILLIAM A., astronaut; b. Hong Kong, Oct. 17, 1933 (parents Am. citizens); s. Arthur F. Anders; B.S., U.S. Naval Acad., 1955; M.S., Air Force Inst. Tech.; m. Valerie Elizabeth Hoard; children—Alan Frank, Glen Thomas, Gayle Alison, Gregory Michael. Commd. 2d lt. USAF, 1955, advanced through grades to maj.; nuclear engr., instr. polit. Air Force Weapons Lab., Kirtland AFB, N.M.; astronaut with Manned Spacecraft Center NASA; back up pilot Gemini II mission; lunar module pilot Apollo 8 mission, 1968; back-up crew Apollo 11; exec. sec. Nat. Aeros. and Space Council, 1969—. Recipient Collier trophy Nat. Geog. Soc. Samuel Hubbard medal, Gen. Thomas D. White USAF Space trophy and Harmon trophy; NASA Distinguished Service award, Air Force Distinguished medal. Mem. Soc. Exptl. Test Pilots, Am. Nuclear Soc., Tau Beta Pi. Office: Nat Aeros and Space Council Houston TX 77058

ANDERSEN, ANDREAS STORRS, educator, artist; b. Chgo., Oct. 6, 1908; s. Arthur Olaf and Mary (Storrs) A.; student Carnegie Inst. Tech., 1928-30, Acad. di Belli Arti, Rome, Italy, 1930-31. Art Inst. Chgo., 1931-34; diploma British Acad. Fine Arts, Rome, 1931; m. Louise Susan Spaulding, Oct. 6, 1934; children—Frances Stinson, Mary Ader. Mem. faculty U. Ariz., 1935-61. prof. art, head dept., 1940-61, dir. univ. art gallery, 1949- 56; dir. Otis Art Inst. of Los Angeles County, 1961—, pres., 1968—; co-dir. Southwestern Indian Art Project, 1960-61; paintings exhibited Met. Mus. Art, Whitney Mus. Art, Cocoran Gallery Art, M.H. De Young Meml. Mus.; represented in permanent collections IBM Corp., U. Ariz., pvt. collections. Pres. emeritus Tucson Art Center. Mem. Nat. Assn. Schs. Art (dir. 1967—), Am. Assn. U. Profs., Coll. Art Assn., N.E.A., Nat. Art Edn. Assn., Beta Theta Pi. Episcopalian. Art editor: Signs and Symbols in Christian Art, 1954. Home: 6661 Maryland Dr Los Angeles CA 90048 Office: 2401 Wilshire Blvd Los Angeles CA 90057

ANDERSEN, ARTHUR JAMES, lawyer; b. N.Y.C., July 4, 1929; s. Arthur J. and Isabelle C. (Beggs) A.; A.B., St. John's U., 1950, LL.B., 1952; LL.M., N.Y. U., 1957; grad. advanced mgmt. program Harvard; m. Deborah Ann White, Nov. 29, 1958; childrenArthur James III, David Beggs, Matthew White, Timothy Chappel. Admitted to N.Y. bar, 1952; law asst. to N.Y. County Surrogates, 1956-57; asso. firm Debevoise, Plimpton & McLean, 1958-61; v.p., sec., counsel James Talcutt Inc., finance co., 1961-66; gen. counsel, sec. Wallace-Murray Corp., mfg. gen. indsl. products, N.Y.C., 1966—. Served with USCGR, 1952-54. Mem. Am., N.Y. State bar assns., Assn. Bar City N.Y., Am. Soc. Corporate Secs., Nat. Rev. (bd. dirs.). Clubs: University (N.Y.C.). Home: 19 Hawthorne Rd Bronxville, NY 10708. Office: 299 Park Av New York City NY 10017

ANDERSEN, ELMER L., mfg. exec., former gov. Minn.; b. Chgo., June 17, 1909; s. Arne and Jennie (Johnson) A.; B.B.A., U. Minn., 1931; LL.D. (hon.), Macalester College, St. Paul, 1965; m. Eleanor Johnson, 1932; children—Anthony L., Julian L., Emily E. With H. B. Fuller Co., mfrs. indsl. adhesives, 1934—, sales mgr., 1937- 41, pres., 1941-61, 63-71, chmn., 1961-63, 71—, chief exec. officer, 1971—; mem. Minn. Senate, 1949-58; gov. of Minn., 1961-63. Campaign chmn. St. Paul Community Chest, 1959—; exec. com. Boy Scouts Am.; mem. Nat. Parks Centennial Commn., 1971. Bd. dirs., pres. Child Welfare League of America; pres. St. Paul Gallery and Sch. of Art; trustee Augsburg Coll., Mpls.; regent U. Minn., chmn. bd., 1971. Recipient Outstanding Achievement award U. Minn., 1959. Mem. Adhesive Mfrs. Assn. Am. (past pres.), Minn. Hist. Soc. (exec. council, pres.). Republican. Lutheran. Rotarian (past pres. St. Paul, past dist. Home: 2230 W Hoyt Av St Paul MN 55111 Office: 2400 Kasota Av St Paul MN 55108

ANDERSEN, ERIC, composer, singer; b. Pitts., Feb. 14, 1943; s. Harold Andrew and Janis (Gallatin) A.; student Hobart Coll., 1961-63. Folk singer, composer, guitarist, pianist; rec. artist for Vanguard Records, 1964; composer folk songs recorded by Judy Collins, Pete Seeger, Johnny Cash, Peter, Paul and Mary, Joan Baez, others; composer theme for movie version of Blues for Mr. Charlie; actor Andy Warhol's exptl. films, 1965. Mem. A.S.C.A.P. Composer: Come to My Bedside, My Darlin', 1965; Violets of Dawn, 1965; Thirsty Boots, 1965; The Hustler, 1965; My Land is a Good Land, 1964; The Looking Glass, 1964; 'Bout Changes and Things, 1966; Take 2, 1967; Avalanche, 1968. Office: care Arthur Gorson 850 7th Av New York City NY 10019

ANDERSEN, FRED C., window mfg. co. exec.; b. Spring Valley, Minn., Sept. 1, 1886; s. Hans J. and Mary (Cummings) A.; grad. high sch.; m. Isabel Holmes Barnhart, Nov. 28, 1919 (dec. 1937); foster children—Mrs. A.D. Hulings, Hugh J. Andersen; m. 2d, Katherine Dyer Blount, June 24, 1941. With Andersen Corp., window mfr., Bayport, Minn., 1903—, v.p., 1907-14, pres., 1915-60, chmn. bd., 1960—; chmn. bd. dir. First State Bank of Bayport; dir. First Nat. Bank, Stillwater. Pres. Andersen Found., past pres. Indianhead council Boy Scouts Am.; dir. Tozer Found., Stillwater, Minn. Recipient Silver Beaver award Boy Scouts Am. Mem. Minn. Employers Assn. (past pres.), Am. Legion. Republican. Conglist. Clubs: Rotary (past pres.); Minnesota; Minneapolis, Home: Bayport MN 55003 Office: Andersen Corp Bayport MN 55003

ANDERSEN, FREDERICK PETER, ins. co. exec.; b. Jersey City, Nov. 2, 1910; s. Marinou and Meta (Rover) A.; m. Frances Isabelle Newbury, May 12, 1939; childrenF. Peter, Stephanie G., Karen S. With Equitable Life Assurance Soc. U.S., N.Y.C., 1927—, asso. controller, 1961, 2d v.p., 1962-65, v.p., auditor, 1965-. Pres. Bd. Health, Cranford, N.J., 1952-56; chmn. Inter-Municipal Water Commn., 1953-56. Mayor, Cranford, 1952-56; freeholder Union County, N.J., 1955-56. Mem. Harvard Advanced Mgmt. Assn. (dir., past pres. N.Y.), Hist. Soc., Chartered Life Underwriters Assn. Republican. Club: Swim (Cranford). Home: 9 Dartmouth Rd Cranford, NJ 07016. Office: 1285 Av of Americas New York City NY 10019

ANDERSEN, HAROLD WAYNE, publishing co. exec.; b. Omaha, July 30, 1923; s. Andrew B. and Grace (Russell) A.; B.S. in Edn., U. Neb., 1945; m. Marian L. Battey, Apr. 19, 1952; children—David, Nancy. Reporter, Lincoln (Neb.) Star, 1945-46; with Omaha World-Herald, 1946—, pres., 1966—; dir. Peter Kiewit Sons, Inc. Pres., Downtown Omaha, Inc. Bd. dirs. U. Neb. Found., United Community Services, Jr. Achievement Omaha (pres. 1964-65). Mem. Am. Newspaper Pubs. Assn. (bd. dirs.; v.p. found.), Omaha C. of C. (v.p. 1964-65, bd. dirs. 1970—), Phi Beta Kappa, Phi Gamma Delta. Republican. Presbyn. Home: 6545 Prairie Av Omaha NB 68132 Office: Omaha World-Herald World-Herald Sq Omaha NB 68102

ANDERSEN, KENNETH BENJAMLN, assn. exec.; b. Jamestown, N.Y., Apr. 6, 1905; s. Benjamin Gaylord and Esther Lydia (Nelson) A.; B.S., Dartmouth, 1927; grad. student N.Y.U., 1930-31; m. Mildred Mary Cederquist, June 1, 1935; children—Richard Tyler, Mary Gaylord, Kendal Elizabeth. Budget supr., mgr. sales estimating dept. Dahlstrom Metallic Door Co., Jamestown, N.Y., 1927-30, 33-34; sec. Am. Management Assn., N.Y.C., 1930-33, asst. to pres., 1939- 41; asst. sec. Rubber Mfrs. Assn., 1934; adminstrv. asst. Office of Sec. Dept. Commerce, Washington, 1935-39; adminstrv. sec. Nat. Elec. Mfrs. Assn., N.Y.C., 1941-46; asst. to pres. Sci. Apparatus Makers Assn., 1947-48, exec. v.p., 1948-67; pres. Assn. Mem. Services, Inc., Chgo., 1967—. Mem. Winnetka Planning Commn., 1966-71; chmn. of Winnetka Caucus Com. 1964-65, chmn., 1970—. Pres. bd. mgrs. Nat. Inst., Mich. State U., 1956-57; regent Inst. Orgn. Mgmt. Mem. Trade Assn. Execs. Forum Chgo. (pres. 1954-55), Am. Soc. Assn. Execs. (pres. 1958), Nat. Indsl. Council (chmn. 1950), Phi Beta Kappa, Zeta Psi. Episcopalian (vestryman). Club: The Tower (Chgo.). Asso. editor: Handbook of Business Administration, 1931; contbg. author Association Management, 1958. Home: 607 Oak St Winnetka IL 60093 Office: 435 N Michigan Av Chicago IL 60611

ANDERSEN, KENNETH KAAE, educator; b. Perth Amboy, N.J., May 13, 1934; s. Anton Carl and Kristine (Kaae) A.; B.S., Rutgers U., 1955; Ph.D., U. Minn., 1959; student Pa. State U., 1959-60; m. Barbara Estelle Fowler, July 20, 1957; children—David Kaae, Peter Carl, Joyce Karen. Prof. chemistry U. N.H., 1960—; vis. prof. Tech. U. Denmark, Lyngby, Denmark, 1971; vis. prof. U. East Anglia, Norwich, Eng., 1966-67. NSF fellow, 1966-67; Fulbright lectr. 1971. Mem. Am. Chem. Soc. Research organic sulfur chemistry. Home: 16 Garden Lane Durham NH 03824

ANDERSEN, LAIRD BRYCE, coll. dean; b. Madison, S.D., Sept. 16, 1928; s. Andrew Christopher and Alyce (Farrington) A.; B.S., U. Minn., 1950 M.S., 1951, M.A., 1961; Ph.D., U. Ill., 1954; m. Joan Roberta Westwood, Nov. 23, 1961; 1 son, Christopher Frederick. Asst. prof. Lehigh U., 1954-59; asso. prof. Rice U., 1959-60, U. Neb., 1961-63; prof., asso. dean engring. Newark Coll. Engring., 1963-66, prof., dean engring., 1966—. Registered profl. engr., engr., N.J. Mem. Am. Soc. Engring. Edn. (chmn. chem. engring. div. 1967), Am. Inst. Chem. Engrs., Sigma Xi, Phi Lambda Upsilon, Tau Beta Pi, Alpha Chi Sigma, Triangle. Co-author: Principles of Unit Operations, 1960; Introduction to Chemical Engineering, 1960. Home: 280 Hillside Av Chatham, NJ 07928. Office: 323 High St Newark NJ 07102

ANDERSEN, WAYNE V., art historian; b. Hinton, Ia., July 7, 1928; s. Henry Vesti and Anna (Marie) (Steinhagen) A.; student Los Angeles City Coll., 1949-50; B.A., U. Cal. at Berkeley, 1959; M.A., Columbia U., 1961, Ph.D., 1966; m. Ebba Stoll-Andersen, Apr. 9, 1951; children—Maja, Mark; m. 2d, Phyllis Sutton, July 17, 1968. Archtl. designer and builder, also art tchr. and critic, Berkeley, Cal., 1953- 59; instr. art history Columbia, 1960-61; sr. curator Walker Art Center, Mpls., 1961-62; asso. prof. history of art Mass. Inst. Tech., 1964-68, prof. history art, 1968—; vis. lectr. art history U. Minn., 1961-62; William Bayard Cutting travelling fellow Columbia, 1962-63; Beigian-Am. CRB fellow, summer 1963; Ford Found. fellow in humanities, 1963-64; vis. prof. Yale, 1969. Arts cons. Urban Redevel. Authority, City of Boston, 1968-. Mem. Coll. Art Assn. Am., Am. Soc. Aesthetics. Author: The Sculpture of Herbert Ferber, 1962; Cezanne's Portrait Drawings, A Study in the Evolution of His Graphic Style, 1968; Takis-Evidence of the Unseen, 1968; Gauguin's Paradise Lost, Lost, 1970; also articles and revs. in art publs. Office: Dept Architecture Mass Inst Tech Cambridge MA 02139

ANDERSON, ADOLPH GUSTOF, coll. pres.; b. Salem, S.D., Sept. 7, 1913; s. Carl Adolph and Sigrid (Traneus) A.; B.S., U. Pitts., 1934, Ph.D. in Phys. Chemistry, 1940; student Juilliard Grad. Sch. Music, 1942-44; m. Margaret Elizabeth Laird, Nov. 25, 1937; childrenChristopher Laird, Peter Tranus. Tchr. chemistry Geneva Coll., Beaver Falls, Pa., 1936-40, U. Pitts., 1940-42, City Coll. N.Y., 1942-44, 46-60; with div. war research Columbia, 1944- 46; mem. faculty Hofstra U., 1960-69, prof. chemistry, 1963-69, dean New Coll., 1962-69, dir., trustee Scandinavian Seminar, 1962-; pres. Hartwick Coll., Oneonta, N.Y., 1969—. Trustee Scandinavian Seminar Coll., Coll., Denmark. Mem. Am. Chem. Soc., A.A.A.S., N.Y. Acad. Scis. Home: Thornwood Draper St Oneonta NY 13820

ANDERSON, ALAN ROSS, educator; b. Portland, Ore., Apr. 11, 1925; s. Ross E. and Selma (Wetteland) A.; B.A., Yale, 1950, Ph.D., 1955; M.Litt., Cambridge U., Eng., 1952; m. Carolyn Reed Willson, June 11, 1949; children-Nicholas George, Jeffrey Joseph, Elizabeth Grace, Timothy John. Faculty, Dartmouth Coll., 1954-55; faculty Yale, 1955-64, prof., 1962-64; Fulbright Lectr. U. Manchester, 1964-65; faculty U. Pitts., 1965—, chmn. philosophy dept., 1967—, prof., 1965—. Dir. Basic Edn., Inc., 1958-64. Mem. selection com. Woodrow Wilson Fellowship Found., 1961-64, Am. Council Learned Socs., 1970—. Served with Signal Corps, AUS, 1943- 46. Mem. Kingsley Trust Assn., Am. Philos. Assn. (bd. officers 1970—), Symbolic Logic, Mind Assn., Phi Beta Kappa, Chi Delta Theta. Contbr. articles profl. jours. Home: 4215 Bigelow Blvd Pittsburgh PA 15213

ANDERSON, ALBERT ESTEN, publisher; b. Mpls., Aug. 29, 1921; s. Albert and Viola (Gullickson) A.; B.A., St. Olaf Coll., 1944; postgrad. Luther Theol. Sem., 1945, U. Minn., 1946; m. Delores Wennblom, July 17, 1954; children—Barbara, David. Sales mgr. Augsburg Pub. House, Mpls., 1947-68, asst. gen. mgr., 1963-70, gen. mgr., 1970—; dir. Fourth Northwestern Nat. Bank, Mpls., 1967—. Bd. dirs. Lutheran Student Found. Minn., 1960-68; regent Augsburg Coll., 1964-70. Served with USMCR, 1943, USNAC, 1944. Recipient Distinguished Alumnus award St. Olaf Coll., 1970. Mem. Protestant Ch.-Owned Pubs.'s Assn. (dir. 1963—). Republican. Lutheran. Home: 4809 Hibiscus Av Minneapolis MN 55435 Office: 426 S 5th St Minneapolis MN 55415

ANDERSON, ALLAN CROSBY, hosp. exec.; b. Jamestown, N.Y., Sept. 18, 1932; s. Emmons E. and Gertrude (Sweet) A.; B.S., Syracuse U., 1954; M.H.A., U. Minn., 1956; m. Pauline Culver, June 24, 1956; children—Todd Culver, Emily Ann. Asst. adminstr. Highland Hosp., Rochester, N.Y., 1959-62, adminstr., 1965-68; asst. dir. Presbyn. Hosp., Phila., 1962-65; exec. dir. Strong Meml. Hosp., U. Rochester, 1968—; asst. prof. health services U. Rochester Sch. Medicine and Dentistry. Mem. exec. com. Sub-Regional Adminstrs. Group, Adminstrs. Conf., Sub-Regional Exec. Conf., bd. dirs. Rochester Regional Hosp. Council; mem. manpower com. and hosp. planning com., bd. dirs. Genesee Region Health Planning Council; mem. med. policy adv. com. Monroe County Dept. Health and Social Services; chmn. pub. relations com., bd. dirs. Rochester Hosp. Service Corp. Bd. dirs. Rochester Presbyn. Home, 1967-70, Home Care Assn. Rochester and Monroe County, Health Council Monroe County. Served to 1st lt., Med. Service Corps, USAF, 1957-59. Mem. Am. Coll. Hosp. Adminstrs., Hosp. Assn. N.Y. State (dir.). Presbyn. (ruling elder). Home: 301 Landing Rd S Rochester NY 14610 Office: 260 Crittenden Blvd Rochester NY 14620

ANDERSON, ALLAN W., educator; B.A., Wash. Missionary Coll.; M.A., Trinity Coll.; Ph.D., Columbia. Prof. philosophy San Diego State U. Office: Dept Philosophy San Diego State U San Diego CA 92115*

ANDERSON, ALVIN GEORGE, educator; b. Duluth, Minn., Apr. 21, 1911; s. August and Sigrid (Fogelberg) A.; B.C.E. with distinction, U. Minn., 1933, M.S., 1935, Ph.D., 1950; m. Dorothy Erickson, July 9, 1938 (dec. 1955); childrenShirley D. (Mrs. Donald H. Mills), Judith K. (Mrs. Ronald H. Spielbauer), Gail D.; m. 2d, Geneva Nygren, Aug. 2, 1958. Asso. hydraulic engr. Dept. Agr., 1938-43; tech. aid OSRD, 1943-45; mem. faculty U. Minn., 1945—, prof. civil engring., 1959—; cons. in field, 1952-. Fellow Am. Soc. C.E. (Norman medal 1961, Stevens award 1965); mem. Internat. Assn. Hydraulic Research, Am. Geophys. Union, Am. Soc. Engring. Edn., Sigma Zi, Tau Beta Pi. Lutheran. Author research papers on air entrainment, sediment transp., hydraulic structures. Home: 3625 22d Av S Minneapolis, MN 55407.

ANDERSON, ARNOLD HERBERT, life ins. co. exec.; b. Chgo., Oct. 3, 1915; s. Hilding A. and Alma (Johnson) A.; A.B., Western Mich. U., 1937; M.A., U. Mich., 1941; m. Christine Mitchell, Jan. 11, 1947; children—Robert N. Power (step-son), Betsy E. Instr. math., Dundee, Mich., 1938-40; with Life & Casualty Ins. Co., Nashville, 1946—, chief actuary, 1955-66, exec. v.p. adminstrn., 1966—, also mem. exec. com., dir.; chmn. World-Wide Assurance Co. Ltd., Eng., 1969—. Served to lt. (s.g.) USNR, 1941-46. Mem. Southeastern Actuaries Club, Nashville Actuarial Club (pres. 1966-67), Am. Mgmt. Assn., Am. Acad. Actuaries, Life Office Mgmt. Assn. (dir.), Am. Legion (post comdr. 1948-49). Home: Route 2 Ramsgate Ct Brentwood TN 37027 Office: Life and Casualty Tower Nashville TN 37219

ANDERSON, ARTHUR L., banker. Exec. v.p., sec. San Diego Trust & Savs. Bank. Office: 540 Broadway San Diego CA 92112*

ANDERSON, ARTHUR N., utility co. exec.; b. N.Y.C., Jan. 18, 1912; s. Nels and Mathilda (Sandlund) A.; B.S. in Mech. Engring., N.Y.U., 1933; m. Marion A. Olson, Aug. 8, 1937; childrenMarian Elaine, Nils A. With Consol. Edison Co. of N.Y., Inc., 1933-50, 54-, various engring. and supervisory positions, gas and electric prodn. depts., engring. and constrn. depts., v.p. construction, 1961-; power engr. indsl. devel. atomic energy AEC, 1950- 52; with Atomic Power Devel. Assos., Detroit, 1952-54. Mem. Am. Soc. M.E., Soc. Gas Operators N.Y.C., Engrs. Club N.Y., Queens C. of C. (dir.). Club: Manhattan. Home: 7 Elm Sea Lane Plandome Manor Long Island, NY 11030. Office: 4 Irving Pl New York City, NY 10003.

ANDERSON, AXEL GORDON, educator; b. Chgo., Dec. 24, 1904; s. Axel Walter and Wilma Adolphina (Oberg) A.; D.D.S., Loyola U., Chgo., 1927; m. Edith Catherine Hein, Nov. 28, 1928 (dec. 1959); childrenCharles Peter, David John; m. 2d, Gladys A. Turley, Oct. 27, 1962; stepchildrenRonald L. Turley, Thomas A. Turley, Jean C. Turley. Pvt. practice dentistry, Hinsdale, Ill., 1927- 42; oral surgeon VA Hosp., Hines, Ill., 1946-57; lectr. clinician to med. and dental socs., 1946-57; prof. oral and maxillofacial surgery, head dept. U. Ill. Coll. Dentistry, 1957-, clin. prof. surgery Coll. Medicine, 1957-, dir. Hosp. Oral Surgery, 1957-; cons. Hinsdale Hosp., West Side VA Hosp., Chgo., 1967—. Served to lt. comdr. Dental Corps, USNR, World War II. Diplomate Am. Bd. Oral Surgery. Fellow Am. Coll. Dentists; mem. Am., Ill. dental assns., Chgo. Dental Soc., Chgo. Soc. Oral Surgeons, Omicron Kappa Upsilon, Delta Sigma Delta. Home: 6 W Ayres St Hindsdale IL 60521 Office: 808 S Wood St Chicago IL 60612

ANDERSON, BERNHARD WORD, educator, clergyman; b. Dover, Mo., Sept. 25, 1916; s. Arthur Lincoln and Grace (Word) A.; B.A., Coll. of Pacific, 1936; B.D., Pacific Sch. Religion, Berkeley, California, 1939, M.A., 1938, Dr. Divinity, 1960; Ph.D., Yale, 1945; S.T.D., U. Pacific, 1961; D.D., Colgate U., 1965; m. Joyce Griswold, Sept. 22, 1936; children—Carol Joyce, Sylvia Joan, Ronald Bernhard, Ruth Anne. Ordained to ministry of United Methodist Ch., 1939; pastor Meth. chs. of Cal. at Pittsburg, 1936-37, Sunnyvale, 1937-41, Millbrae, 1944-46, of Wauregan and Central Village Congl. Ch., Conn., 1942-44, Community Ch., Columbus, N.Y., 1946-48; instr. dept. philosophy and religion Colgate U., 1946-48; James A. Gray asso. prof. Bibl. lit. U. N.C., 1948-50; Joseph B. Hoyt prof. O.T. interpretation Colgate Rochester Div. Sch., 1950-54; dean Theol. Sch., Drew U., 1954-63, Henry Anson Buttz prof. Bibl. theology, 1954- 68; prof. O. T. theology Princeton Theol. Sem., 1968—; ann. prof. Am. Sch. of Oriental Research, Jerusalem, Jordan, 1963-64; Burns lectr. Knox Coll., Dunedin, N.Z., 1969; Haskell lectr. Oberlin U., 1970. Chmn. study dept. United Student Christian Council, 1951-54; leader youth movements YMCA, YWCA, Student Christian Movement; speaker Religious Emphasis Week various colls. Fellow Society for Religion in Higher Education; mem. Soc. Bibl. Lit., Am. Acad. Religion, Biblical Colloquium, Biblical Theologians, Am. Theol. Soc., Pi Gamma Mu. Author: Rediscovering the Bible, 1951; The Unfolding Drama of the Bible, 1953, 71; Understanding the Old Testament, 1957-66; Creation Versus Chaos, 1967; Out of the Depths—Studies of the Psalms, 1970. Editor, translator: A History of Pentateuchal Traditions (M. Noth), 1971. Chmn. editorial bd. Christian Scholar, 1956-58; mem. editorial bd. Theology Today, 1969—. Contbr. Interpreter's Bible. Author articles. Adminstrv. dir. Drew-McCormick Archaeol. Expdn., Bibl. City Shechem. Co-editor Israel's Prophetic Heritage, 1962. Editor: The Old Testament and Christian Faith, 1963. Home: 89 Mercer St Princeton NJ 08540

ANDERSON, BERTIL GOTTFRID, ret. educator; b. Escanaba, Mich., Jan. 5, 1904; s. August Bernhard and Bernhard Anna Matilda (Johnson) A.; A.B., Augustana Coll., 1926; M.S., State U. Ia., 1929, Ph.D., 1930; m. Lorraine Dorothy Ossian, June 9, 1931; childrenLouise E., John D., James B. Instr. high sch., Andover, Ill., 1926-27; instr. biology Western Res. U., 1930-38, asst. prof., 1938-41; research asso. Franz Theodore Stone Labs., Ohio State U., 1941-42, summer staff, 1938-50; faculty zoology W.Va. U., 1942-53, prof., 1949- 53; prof. zoology Pa. State U., 1953-69, prof. emeritus zoology, 1969—, head dept. zoology and entomology, 1953-63, head dept. zoology, 1963-67; vis. prof. Transylvania U., summers 1933-34. Mem. aquatic life adv. com. Ohio River Water Sanitation Commn., 1952-; research Fedn. Sewage and Indsl. Wastes Assns., 1949-; mem. nat. tech. adv. com. on water quality criteria to sec. of interior, 1967-68. Recipient Outstanding Achievement award Augustana Coll. Alumni Assn., 1970. Fellow A.A.A.S.; mem. Am. Inst. Biol. Scis., W. Va. (pres. 1952-53), Ohio, Pa. acads. sci., Am. Soc. Zoologists, Am. Soc. Naturalists, Am. Soc. Limnology and Oceanography, Am. Fisheries Soc. (asso. editor trans. 1949-53), Nat. Assn. Biology Tchrs., Entomol. Soc. Am., Sigma Xi, Gamma Sigma Delta, Phi Sigma, Gamma Alpha. Lutheran. Author articles in field. Home: 315 Hillcrest Av State College PA 16801 Office: Life Sciences Bldg Pa State U University Park PA 16802

ANDERSON, BRADLEY JAY, cartoonist; b. Jamestown. N.Y., May 14, 1924; s. Perle J. and Jennie (Solomonson) A.; B.F.A., Syracuse U., 1951; m. Barbara Marie Jones, Sept. 8, 1945; children—Christine Dorothy (Mrs. Ruben Castandeda, Jr.), Craig Bradley, Paul Richard, Mark Stephen. Art dir. audio visual dept. Syracuse U., 1950-51; free-lance mag. cartoonist, 1950—; art dir. Ball & Grier, pub. relations, Utica, N.Y., 1952-53; syndicated cartoonist Marmaduke, 1954—, Grandpa's Boy, 1954—; exhbns. include San Deigo Fair Fine Arts and Cartoons, 1966, Punch mag. exhbn., 1954, Selected Cartoons of 14 Sat. Eve. Post Cartoonists, 1958, Americana Overseas exhbn., 1957; rep. permanent collections Albert T. Reid Coll., William Allen White Found., Syracuse U. Manuscripts Library. Served with USNR. 1943-46. Mem. Mag. Cartoonists Guild, Newspaper Comics Council, Nat. Cartoonists Soc., Am. Legion. Mason. Author: Marmaduke, 1955; More Marmaduke, 1958; Marmaduke, 1966; Marmaduke Rides Again, 1968. Home: 1316 York Dr Vista, CA 92083.

ANDERSON, BRUCE MURRAY, educator; b. Detroit, July 14, 1929; s. Harold Bruce and Elizabeth (Miller) A.; B.S., Ursinus Coll., 1953; M.S., Purdue U., 1954; Ph.D., Johns Hopkins, 1958; m. Constance Burchard Derr, June 29, 1950; children—David Bruce, Marcia Anne, Nancy Louise. Postdoctoral fellow Brandeis U., 1958-60; asst. prof. biochemistry U. Louisville, 1960-63; asso. prof. biochemistry U. Tenn., 1963-67, prof., 1967-70; prof., head dept. biochemistry and nutrition Va. Poly. Inst. State U., 1970—. Served with USAAF, 1946-49. Mem. Am. Chem. Soc., Am. Soc. Biol. Chemists, Sigma Xi, Phi Lambda Upsilon. Research and publs. on enzymology and pyridine nucleotide chemistry. Home: 1013 Highland Circle SE Blacksburg VA 24060

ANDERSON, BUIST MURFEE, lawyer; b. Marion, Ala., Nov. 17, 1904; s. Edward Buist and Mary Agnes (Murfee) A.; student Marion (Ala.) Inst.; B.S., U. Va., 1924; LL.B., Yale, 1929; m. Dorothy Mary Craford, February 27, 1932; children—Mary Jeanne (Mrs. Richard F. Jones III), David Craford, Dudley Buist. Began as statistician U.S. Department Agr., 1924-27; admitted to Ala. bar, 1928, Conn. bar, 1930, U.S. Supreme Ct., 1937; atty. with Conn. Gen. Life Ins. Co., 1929-39, counsel 1939-69, v.p., 1949-69; with firm Murtha, Cullins, Richter & Pinney, Hartford, 1969—; dir. Am. Leasing Corp., Am. Republic Life Ins. Co. N.Y.; mem. adv. com. Bloomfield br. Conn. Bank and Trust Co. Chmn. bd. finance Met. Dist. Commn. Mem. Am. Arbitration Assn. (dir.), Am. Bar Assn., Assn. Life Ins. Counsel (pres. 1959-60), Am. Life Convention (chmn. legal sect. 1948). Baptist. Editor: Vance on Insurance, 3rd edit. 1951. Editor of Legal Notes, Transactions (Soc. Actuaries), 1941-64. Home: Gale Rd Bloomfield CT 06002 Office: 101 Pearl St Hartford CT 06103

ANDERSON, BURNETT, fgn. service officer; b. Grantsburg, Wis., July 13, 1919; s. Hjalmar Andrew and Emma (Johnson) A.; A.B., U. Rochester, 1940; m. Maria (Pia) Troell, Aug. 3, 1954; children—Mark Bo, Lee Troell. Salesman, Vick Chem. Chem. Co., 1940-41; clk. N.Y. Herald Tribune, 1941; press sec. to govs. H.E. Stassen, Edward J. Thye, Minn., 1941-44; staff writer Mpls. Daily Times, 1944-47, fgn. corr., Scandinavia, 1947-52; press officer Mut. Security Agy., Germany, 1953; dep. dir. pub. relations USIA, 1954, dep. chief Press and Publs. Service, 1955-57; counselor for pub. affairs Am. embassy, Tehran, Iran, 1957-60, asst. dep. dir., 1961-64; asso. dir. policy and plans, 1964, dep. dir., 1965-66; counselor for public affairs Am. embassy, Madrid, Spain, 1967-69, Paris, France, 1969—; with Nat. War Coll., 1960-61. Recipient Arthur S. Fleming award for outstanding fed. service, 1955. Mem. Theta Delta Chi. Club: Fort McNair Officers. Author: Stockholm, Capital and Crossroads, 1953. Author, translator vols. on Scandinavia. Home: 97 Blackburn Rd Summit NJ 07901

ANDERSON, C. E., pulp and paper co. exec.; b. Coos Bay, Ore., Feb. 7, 1929; s. Eldin H. and Marian Rae (Anderson) A.; A.B., Whitman Coll., 1950; spl. certificate Yale, 1952; M.B.A., Harvard, 1956; m. Margery Irene Botts, Dec. 22, 1950; children—Thomas, Joanne, Patricia. With Rayonier, Inc., N.Y.C., 1956-70, gen. mgr. indsl. relations, N.Y.C., 1963-67, v.p. adminstrn., 1967-68, sr. v.p., 1968-70; pres. ITT Rayonier, Inc., 1970—. Served with USAF, 1950-54. Home: 102 Glen Hill Rd Wilton CT 06897 Office: 161 E 42d St New York City NY 10017

ANDERSON, C. J., savs. and loan assn. exec. Pres., First Fed. Savs. and Loan Assn. New Haven. Office: 80 Elm St New Haven CT 06503*

ANDERSON, CARL DAVID, scientist; b. New York, N.Y., Sept. 3, 1905; s. Carl David and Emma Adolfina (Ajaxson) A.; B.S., Calif. Inst. of Tech., 1927, Ph.D., magna cum laude, 1930; hon. Sc.D., Colgate U., 1937, Gustavus Adolphus Coll., 1963; LL.D. (hon.), Temple University, 1948; m. Lorraine Elvira Bergman; children—Marshall

David, David Andrew. Coffin research fellow Calif. Inst. Tech., 1927-28, teaching fellow in physics, 1928-30, research fellow in physica, 1930-33, asst. prof. physics, 1933-37, asso. prof., 1937-39, prof., 1939—; chmn. div. physics, math. and astronomy, 1962—. Research on X-Ray photoelectrons, 1927-30; research on gamma rays and cosmic-rays since 1930; discoverer of positron, 1932. Awarded gold medal Am. Inst. of City of N.Y., 1935; Nobel prize in physics, 1936; Elliott Cresson medal of the Franklin Inst., 1937; John Ericsson medal Am. Soc. Swedish Engrs., 1960. Mem. Am. Phys. Soc., Am. Philos. Soc., Nat. Acad. Scis., Tau Beta Pi, Sigma Xi. Address: California Institute of Technology Pasadena CA 91109

ANDERSON, CARL E., business exec.; b. Pitts., Dec. 10, 1912; s. Carl A. and Esther J. (McCarrell) A.; student State Tchrs. Coll., Indiana. Pa.; m. Dolores Leadbeater; children—Carl E., Nancy Lee (Mrs. Judge), David W. With Bethlehem Steel Corp., then Westinghouse Electric Corp., 1937-43, Warren City Mfg. Co. (O.), 1943-46; v.p. operations C.R. Squibb & Sons, 1946-56, Revlon, Inc., 1956-57; gen. mgr. Cornish Wire Co., Williamstown, Mass., 1957-58; dir. mgmt. consultation Ebasco Service, Inc., 1939-61; pres., chief exec. officer, dir., mem. exec. com. E. W. Bliss Co., Canton, O., 1961-65, chmn., pres., chief exec. officer, 1963—; dir. Heppenstall Co., Pitts., Harter Bank & Trust Co., Canton, Gulf & Western Industries, Inc., E W Bliss Co. Bd. advisers Walsh Coll. Recipient Horatio Alger award, 1967. Mem. Am. Iron and Steel Inst., Greater Canton C. of C. (pres.), Am.-Israel C. of C. Home: 3025 Woodcliffe Dr NW Canton OH 44718 Office: 229 Wells Av NW Canton OH 44703

ANDERSON , CARL MAGNUS, lawyer; b. Gary, S.D., Jan. 10, 1905; s. H.A. and Emma (Johnson) A.; A.B. cum laude, U. Minn., 1927; J.D., 1930; LL.D., Wagner Coll., 1966, Upsala Coll., 1970; m. Ida Johnson, Aug. 16, 1930; children—Eric Hall, John Anders, Mary Lisa. Bookkeeper, First Nat. Bank, Grantsburg, Wis., 1922 - 24; admitted to Minn. bar, 1930, N.Y. bar, 1932, U.S. Supreme Ct. bar, 1938; asso. Root, Clark, Buckner & Ballantine, N.Y.C., 1930-34; head legal dept. Merck & Co., Inc., Rahway, N.J., 1934-48, asst. sec., 1937-48, asst. to pres., 1942- 50, dir. fgn. activities, 1950-52, sec., 1956-70, dir., 1969-70; v.p. Merck (N.A.), Inc., 1952-54, Merck-Sharp & Dohme Internat. Div., 1954-56. Pres., Merck Co. Found., 1964-70. Bd. dirs. United Negro Coll. Fund, nat. campaign chmn., 1964, 65; trustee Clara Maass Meml. Hosp.; bd. fellows Union Coll., chmn. bd. trustees Upsala Coll. Treas. Lutheran Ch. in Am., dir. Common Investing Fund. Recipient Outstanding Achievement award U. Minn., 1968. Mem. Assn. Bar City N.Y., Am. Bar. Assn., Am. Soc. Corporate Secs. (past v.p., dir.), Phi Beta Kappa Assos., Iron Wedge, Phi Beta Kappa, Theta Delta Chi, Phi Delta Phi, Phi Sigma Phi. Republican. Lutheran. Clubs: University (N.Y.C.); Beacon Hill (Summit, N.J.). Home: 97 Blackburn Rd Summit NJ 07901

ANDERSON, CARL WILSON, social worker; b. Glenside, Pa., Dec. 19, 1912; s. William E. and Isoline (Pessenger) A.; A.B., Pa. State Coll., 1934; M.S.W., U. Pa., 1936, D. Social Work, 1953; J.D., William Mitchell Coll. Law, 1957; m. Katherine Jane Lee, Feb. 14, 1934; children—Carl Wilson, Susan Jane (Mrs. G. Thomas Page), Katherine Lee. Caseworker, Pa. Prison Soc., Phila., 1936-38; with Cambridge-Somerville (Mass.) Youth Study, 1938-41; dir. Home Service Boston Met. chpt. A.R.C., 1941-47; dir. Family Ct. for New Castle County, Wilmington, Del., 1947-53; exec. dir. Family and Children's Service, Mpls., 1953-59; commr. Office for Children and Youth Pa. Dept. Pub. Welfare, Harrisburg, 1959-66; dean, prof. Sch. Social Work U. N.C., Chapel Hill, 1966-71; exec. dir. Center for Human Services, Cleve., 1971—; cons. Childrens Bur., Dept. Health, Edn. and Welfare, council Nat. Council on Crime and Deliquency, 1964-67. Recipient citation Nat. Probation and Parole Assn., 1959, Career Service award Pa. League for Civil Service, 1965. Mem. Am. Bar Assn., Nat. Assn. Social Workers, Acad. Certified Social Workers. Author: (with Arthur E. Fink and Merrill B. Conover) The Field of Social Work, 5th edit., 1968. Home: 3167 Linden Rd Rocky River OH 44116

ANDERSON, CARLYLE ELMER, finance co. exec.; b. Erhard, Minn., Dec. 21, 1909; s. Christian M. and Emma (Paulson) A.; B.B.A., U. Minn., 1932; m. Elizabeth Hervey Wyckoff, Oct. 16, 1936; children—William Christian (dec.), Elizabeth Leslie, Meredith (dec.), Judith Wyckoff, Robert David (dec.). Sales promotion dept. Marshall Field & Co., Chgo., 1933-35; creative editor Hart Publs., Inc., Chgo., 1936-38, v.p. charge creative and sales dept., 1938-42; pres., dir. Wyckoff-Anderson, Inc., Merdith, Inc.; chmn. Monogram Glass Co. of Can., Ltd.; dir. First Nat. Bank & Trust Co. of Evanston, several corps. Life trustee Community Hosp. of Evanston, Evanston Hosp. Assn.; asso. Northwestern U.; trustee, chmn. U. Minn. Found. Recipient outstanding achievement award U. Minn., 1959. Mem. Kappa Sigma. Alpha Delta Sigma. Methodist. Clubs: Merchants and Manufacturers, Economic (Chgo.); University, Kiwanis (Evanston); Glen View (Golf, Ill.). Home: 2425 Lincoln St Evanston IL 60201 Office: 1st Nat Bank Bldg Evanston IL 60201

ANDERSON, CARROLL SUMMER, banker; b. Mercer, Pa., Nov. 18, 1915; s. William V. and Elma (Carroll) A.; B.B.A., Westminster Coll., 1937; m. Jean C. Smith, Aug. 1, 1942; children—Stephen, William, Christine, Thomas, Amy; m. 2d, Shirley H. Houser, Oct. 28, 1968. Investment analyst Cleve. Trust Co., 1943-51; asst. v.p. Pitts. Nat. Bank, 1952-54; asst. v.p. Toledo Trust Co., 1954- 56; with Mfrs. Nat. Bank, Detroit, 1956—, now exec. v.p., chmn. trust com.; dir. Crowley Milner & Co. Mem. Detroit Financial Analysts Soc., Mich. C. of C. (member bd.), Sigma Phi Epsilon. Clubs: Detroit; Dearborn (Mich.) Country. Home: 1 Crescent Ct Dearborn MI 48124 Office: Mfrs Nat Bank Detroit MI 48226

ANDERSON, CHARLES ARNER, physician; b. in Cortland, Ohio, June 13, 1907; s. James Cossatt and Halle Lenore (Clark) A.; student Miami U., 1927, Cleve. Coll., 1928, Ohio Wesleyan U., 1929-31; M.B., Ch.B., U. Edinburgh, 1937, L.R.C.P., 1938, D.N.B., 1939; m. Mary Pond Hughes, July 9, 1949; children—Charles Arner, David James, Grayson Carroll, Warren Rice. Postgrad. tng. urology Genesee Hosp., U. Rochester, St. Francis Hosp., Peoria, Ill., Watts Hosp., U. N.C., 1937-42; asso. urology St. Louis U., 1946-47; pvt. practice urology, Warren, O., 1947—; chief urol. service St. Joseph Riverside Hosp., Warren, 1948-62, asso. staff, 1962—; asso. staff Trumbull Meml. Hosp., Warren, 1962-64, staff urologist, 1964—. Pres., treas. Warndeer Land Co., Inc., 1962—; president, treasurer Denusurg Corp., 1967—. President Patriotic Edn., Inc., 1968-69, chmn., 1970—. Mem. Ohio Republican Cent. Com. Served as capt., M.C., AUS, 1942-46; chief urol. and surg. service 29th Evacuation Hosp. Recipient Minute Man award Nat. Soc. S.A.R.; named Ky. col., Miss. col. Mem. Am. Urol. Assn., Trumbull County Hist. Soc. (v.p. 1964-68, pres. 1969—) A.M.A., Ohio, Trumbull County med. socs., Am. Soc. Clin. Hypnosis, S.A.R. (nat. pres. 1962-63), Order Ky. Cols., Order Miss. Cols., Symposiarchs (nat. pres. 1968-69), Kappa Sigma (dist. grand master 1964- 67, nat. alumni commr. 1967-70). Mason (Shriner, Jester). Clubs: Buckeye, Trumbull Country. Home: 125 Golf Dr N E Warren OH 44483 Office: 546 Washington N E Warren OH 44483

ANDERSON, CHARLES ARNOLD, educator; b. Platte, S.D., Jan. 13, 1907; s. Edward Thomas and Edith (Orvis) A.; B.A., U. Minn., 1927, M.A., 1928, Ph.D., 1932; m. Mary Jean Bowman, July 18, 1942; 1 son, Lloyd Barr. Faculty U. Minn., 1929, Harvard, 1930-35, 43, Ia. State U., 1936-43, U. Ky., 1945-58; various U.S. Govt. assignments, 1944-45; faculty U. Cal. at Berkeley, 1948-49; vis. prof. U. Lund (Sweden), 1954-55; Fulbright scholar Uppsala (Sweden) U., 1955-56; prof. U. Chgo., 1958—, also dir. Comparative Edn. Center; cons. UNESCO, Ford Found., DEDC. Mem. Comparative Edn. Soc. (pres.), Phi Beta Kappa, Sigma Xi. Editor: Am. Jour. Sociology, 1967—. Joint editor Edn., Economy and Soc., 1961; Edn. and Econ. Growth, 1965. Contbr. articles profl. jours. Home: 5650 Dorchester St Chicago IL 60637

ANDERSON, CHARLES BURROUGHS, bookseller; b. Washington, Ia., Mar. 4, 1905; s. Marion T. and Lucy (Burroughs) A.; Ph.B., U. Chgo., 1926; M.A., Columbia, 1929; student U. Paris, 1931; diplomiert U. Berlin, 1932; m. Herta Lindke, Sept. 16, 1938 (div.); m. 2d, Frances L. Wallace, May 28, 1946. Faculty, Edgewood Sch., 1926-28; instr. English, Columbia, 1929-31, faculty Horace Mann Sch., 1934-45; supr. Coll. Entrance Exam. Bd., 1933-39; pres. Anderson's Book Shop, Inc., Larchmont, N.Y., 1946-; lectr. Grad. Inst. Book Publishing, N.Y.U., 1959-62. Bd. dirs. Am. Booksellers Assn., 1954-62, 64-, pres., 1958-60, chmn. bd. dirs., 1960-62, bd. judges Carey-Thomas Book award, 1958; bd. dirs. Library Club Am., 1959; steering com. Nat. Library Week, Dohme Internat. Div., 1954-56. Pres., Merck Co. Foound., 1964-70; bd. , Nat. Com. for Florence Agreement, 1960-68; Am. del. Internat. Community Booksellers, Wiesbaden, Germany, 1962; rep. R.R. Bowker Co. to Internat. Book Fair, Frankfurt, 1965—. Mem. Alpha Delta Phi, English Grad. Union (Columbia). Clubs: Lions (pres. 1951); Columbia University. Author: Common Errors in English Corrected; Rapid Vocabulary Builder; Guide to Good Pronunciation. Co-translator: World History of Dance (Sachs), 1938. Editor: Manual on Bookselling. Contbr. articles to profl. publs. Home: 554 Riverside Dr Ormond Beach FL 32074 Office: 96 Chatsworth Av Larchmont NY 10538

ANDERSON, CHARLES ROBERTS, educator; b. Macon, Ga., Oct. 17, 1902; s. Robert Lanier and Gertrude (Roberts) A.; A.B., U. Ga., 1924, A.M., 1928; Ph.D., Columbia, 1939; m. Eugenia Blount, June 1, 1935; m. Mary Pringle, May 3, 1963. Instr. English, U.Ga., 1927-30; instr. English, Duke U., 1930-35, asst. prof., 1935-39, asso. prof., 1939-41; asso. prof. Am. lit. Johns Hopkins, 1941-45, prof., 1946—, chmn. dept., 1950-56, Caroline Donovan prof. Am. lit., 1957-69, prof. emeritus, 1969—; Lamar Found. lectr., Wesleyan Coll., 1957; vis. prof., summers, George Washington U., 1938, Johns Hopkins, 1940, U.Cal., 1946, Columbia, 1947-48, U. So. Cal., 1950, U. Hawaii, 1956; guest prof., U. Heidelberg, Germany, 1949; vis. lectr. Nagano Seminar, Japan, summer, 1954, auspices U.S. Dept. State, Am. specialist lectr., Singapore, Manila, Taiwan and Japan, 1965-66; mng. editor Am. Lit., 1932-33; Rosenwald fellow, 1938-39; asso. editor Modern Lang. Notes, 1942—; fellow Huntington Library, summer 1952; Fulbright fellow U. Rome, 1952-53, U. Torino, Italy, 1959- 60, Kyoto U., also Doshisha U., 1969; Guggenheim fellow, 1965-66. Fellow Soc. Am. Studies; mem. Modern Lang. Assn. (chmn. Am. lit. group 1957), Am. Assn. U. Profs., Soc. of Am. Historians, Melville Soc. Am. (pres. 1946), Phi Beta Kappa, Phi Delta Theta, Sigma Upsilon. Author: Melville in the South Seas, 1939; Emily Dickinson's Poetry; Stairway of Surprise (Christian Gauss award Phi Beta Kappa), 1960; The Magic Circle of Walden, 1968. Editor: Journal of a Cruise in the Frigate United States with notes on Melville, 1937; Sidney Lanier: Poems and Letters, 1970; Thoreau's World: Miniatures from his Journal, 1971; Melville's Typee, Greylock Edition, 1971. Gen. editor: Centennial Edition of Sidney Lanier (10 vols.), 1945; American Literary Masters, 2 vols., 1965. Contbr. profl. jours. Adv. bd. Jour. Am. Lit., 1955-58, editorial bd., 1959-62. Home: 7523 Club Rd Ruxton MD 21204 Address: Johns Hopkins U Baltimore MD 21218

ANDERSON, CLIFTON A., educator; b. nr. Vermillion, S.D., July 2, 1911; s. John A. and Selma (Hoyer) A.; B.S., U. S.D., 1932, A.B., 1933; M.S., Pa. State U., 1946; Ph.D., Ohio State U., 1952; m. Lillian Kennedy, Aug. 17, 1938; children—Robert Bruce, John Kennedy. Engring. trainee, time study engr. Westinghouse Elec. Corp., Pitts., 1933-38; instr. to prof. indsl. engring. Pa. State U., 1938-57; prof., head dept. indsl. engring. N.C. State U., 1957—; prof. Inst. Advanced Study in Bus. Orgn., Torino, Italy, 1953; cons. indsl. firms. Mem. vol. arbitration panel N.C. Dept. Labor, 1961—. Served to capt. AUS, 1942-45. Fellow Am. Inst. Indsl. Engrs. (regional v.p. 1967-69); mem. Operations Research Soc. Am., Am. Soc. Engring. Edn., Phi Beta Kappa, Sigma Xi, Tau Beta Pi, Alpha Pi Mu (nat. pres. 1956-58). Contbr. Indsl. Engring. Handbook, 1971. Home: 320 Yadkin St Raleigh NC 27609

ANDERSON, CLINTON PRESBA, senator; b. Centerville, S.D., Oct. 23, 1895; s. Andrew Jay and Hattie Belle (Presba) A.; student Dakota Wesleyan U., 1913-15, U. Mich., 1915-16; L.H.D. (hon.), Dakota Weslyan U., 1933; D.Agr., N.M. Coll. Agr. and Mechanic Arts, 1946; LL.D., U. Mich., St. Lawrence U., 1946, Mo. Valley Coll., 1949, U. Alaska, 1965; m. Henrietta McCartney, June 22, 1921; children—Sherburne Presba, Nancy (Mrs. Ben L. Roberts). Reporter, editor, Albuquerque, 1918-22; mgr. ins. dept. Loan & Mortgage Co., 1922-24; owner ins. agy., Albuquerque, 1925-63. Treas., State of N.M., 1933-34; mem. 77th to 79th U.S. congresses from N.M. at large; sec. U.S. Dept. Agr., 1945-48; U.S. senator from N.M., 1949—. Mem. Sears-Roebuck Found. Mem. Delta Theta Phi. Democrat. Presbyn. Mason, Elk, Rotarian (pres. Rotary Internat. 1932-33). Home: 3621 Camino Alameda S W Albuquerque NM 87105 also 6 Wesley Circle N W Washington DC 20016 Office: 215 5th S W Albuquerque NM 87101 also Senate Office Bldg Washington DC 20510

ANDERSON, CORLISS DORAN, educator, financial cons.; b. New Windsor, Ill., July 24, 1904; s. Martin Charles and Mamie (Rumbeck) A.; B.S., U. Ill., 1926, M.S., 1927, Ph.D., 1929; m. Catherine Maude Dunlop, Aug. 18, 1928; children—Corliss Dunlop, Brierly Wadsworth, Judith Louise (Mrs. Charles M. Stuart). Investment analyst Bonbright & Co., Chgo., 1929-31; investment research U. Chgo. Endowment Fund, 1931-45; co-founder, mng. partner Duff, Anderson & Clark, indsl. investment and financial analysts, Chgo., 1945-56; prof. finance Northwestern U., 1956- 66, chmn. dept. finance Sch. Bus., 1959-64. Member of the board of dirs. Hammond Corp., Halsey, Stuart & Co., Signode Corp., Chgo. Title & Trust Co., Littelfuse, Inc. Pres. high sch. bd. edn., Barrington, Ill., 1946-50; mem. gen. bd. pensions Methodist Ch. Trustee Garrett Theol. Sem., U. Ill. YMCA, Chgo. Wesley Meml. Hosp. C.F.A. Mem. Investment Analysts Soc. Chgo (pres. 1937-38), American Econ. Assn., Phi Gamma Delta, Tau Beta Pi, Beta Gamma Sigma, Phi Eta Sigma (charter member). Republican. Club: University (Chgo.). Author: Corporate Reporting for the Professional Investor, 1962; co-author Managerial Problems in Finance, 1964. Home: 217 Linden Rd Barrington IL 60010

ANDERSON, CURTISS MARTIN, editor, writer; b. Mpls., July 16, 1928; s. Otto and Hilda Marie (Holman) A.; B.A., U. Minn., 1951; m. Anne Sonopol, December 12, 1953. With Meredith Pub. Co., Des Moines, 1951-60, editor Vacation Ideas book, also Home Building Ideas book for Better Homes & Gardens mag. 1951-52, asso. editor, sr. writer mag., 1956-57, spl. features editor mag., 1957-60; asso. editor, staff writer Ladies Home Jour., Phila., 1960, mng. editor, 1961-62, editor-in-chief, 1962- 63; contract writer McCall's mag., 1963; editor Venture-The Traveler's World, N.Y.C., 1963-71, v.p., 1967-71; editor Hallmark Cards, Inc., Kansas City, Mo., 1971—. Served with USN, 1946-48. Recipient award for best article on architecture in non-profl. mag. A.I.A., 1955; named one of ten outstanding young men of year U.S. Jr. C. of C., 1963. Mem. Am. Soc. Mag. Editors, Sigma Delta Chi. Home: 5205 W 96th St Shawnee Mission KS 66207 Office: Hallmark Cards Inc Kansas City KS 64141

ANDERSON, DALE KENNETH, lawyer; b. Toledo, O., May 30, 1922; s. Ture B.G. and Astrid (Pearson) A.; student Miami U., Oxford, O., 1940-41, 45; J.D., U. Toledo, 1950; m. Barbara Phillips, Apr. 1, 1950; children—Sherri (Mrs. Richard Sleight), Hollis Ruth. Admitted to Ohio bar, 1950, since practiced in Toledo; sr. partner firm Anderson, Holder, Herschel & Barkenquast; liaison officer coordinator USAF Acad., 1965—. Dir. Service Products, Inc., Toledo. Served with USAAF, 1941-45, now col. Res. Recipient USAF Acad. citation, 1966, Hon. Doctorate, U. Toledo, 1968. Mem. Toledo, Lucas County bar assns., Am. Arbitration Assn., Phi Kappa Tau, Delta Theta Phi. Republican. Lutheran. Clubs: Inverness (Toledo); Hull-Prairie (Perrysburg, O.); Springbrook Riding (trustee, past pres.) (Lambertville, Mich.). Home: 4725 Penridge Rd Toledo OH 43615 Office: Spitzer Bldg Toledo OH 43604

ANDERSON, DANIEL VIRDEN, ret. govt. ofcl.; b. Dover, Del., Dec. 31, 1908; s. James Hall and Blanche Virden (Brown) A.; A.B., U. Va., 1930; student Nat. War Coll., 1950; m. Joy Virginia Grubbs, Nov. 21, 1942; children—Scott Virden, Joy Greer (Mrs. Robert V. Weston). Fgn. service officer Dept. of State from 1931, vice consul, Rome. 1931-32, Lisbon, 1933-36, Bombay, 1936-40; vice consul, 2d sec. of embassy Bogotá, 1941-43; consul Barranquilla, Colombia, 1943-44, Valencia, Spain, 1944-47; 2d sec., consul, Habana, 1947-48, 1st sec., 1948-49; 1st sec., Lisbon, 1950-51, Madrid, 1951-52; dir. politico-mil. affairs Hdqrs. Supreme Allied Comdr. Atlantic, Norfolk, Va., 1952-55; dep. chief of mission and counselor of embassy, Saigon, Vietnam, 1955-57; evaluation officer ICA, Washington, 1957-59; dir. Office S.E. Asian Affairs, Dept. State, 1959-62; Am. consul gen., Marseilles, France, 1962-68, dean Consular Corps., 1965-68. Mem. Phi Beta Kappa, Pi Kappa Alpha, Raven Soc. Home: 1609 Forest Lane McLean VA 22101

ANDERSON, DAVID F., lawyer; b. Wilmington, Del., Aug. 12, 1908; s. David A. and Elizabeth L. (Houghton) A.; B.A., U. Del.; LL.B., U. Pa.; m. Anne Barlow, Oct. 19, 1940; children—David A., Anne C. Admitted to Del. bar, 1933, since practiced in Wilmington; partner firm Potter, Anderson, & Caroon; city solicitor, Wilmington, 1945-49. Gen. counsel, dir. Delaware Trust Co. Served to capt. AUS, 1943-45. Mem. Am., Del. bar assns. Club: Wilmington. Editor: Delaware Corporation Law, Annotated. Home: 517 W 18th St Wilmington DE 19802 Office: Delaware Trust Bldg Wilmington DE 19801

ANDERSON, DAVID REY, financial exec.; b. Ft. Wadsworth, S.I., N.Y., Sept. 12, 1898; s. John Scott and Carlotta (Bloss) A.; B.A., U. Pa., 1917; m. Shirley Bennett Locke, Nov. 4, 1934; 1 dau., Ronalda. Office mgr. George J. Kelly Co., 1917-18; staff mem. Lybrand, Ross Bros. & Montgomery, C.P.A.'s, 1918-27; sec., treas. Wilbur-Suchard Chocolate Co., 1927-29; asst. treas., controller Kendall Co., Boston, 1929-48; treas. W.B. Saunders Co., Phila., 1948-52; controller Niles-Bement-pond Co., West Hartford, Conn., 1952-55; controller Pratt & Whitney, Inc., West Hartford, 1955-56, v.p., controller, 1956; controller Stanley Works, New Britain, Conn., 1956-66, dir. financial planning, 1966-69; v.p. finance Gearhart- Owen Industries, Inc., Ft. Worth, 1970—. C.P.A., Pa. Mem. Financial Execs. Inst., Am. Inst. C.P.A.'s, Nat. Assn. Accountants, Am. Accounting Assn., Phi Beta Kappa. Unitarian. Author: Practical Controlership, 1947, co-author 2d edit., 1961. Home: 3208 W Biddison St Fort Worth TX 76109 Office: PO Box 1936 Fort Worth TX 76101

ANDERSON, DEWEY, economist, cattle rancher; b. Grand Forks, N.D., Jan. 14, 1897; s. Hans D. and Amalia B. (Peterson) A.; A.B., Stanford U., 1927, M.A., 1928, Ph.D., 1932; m. Erma Sams, June 30, 1920; children—Harry, June; m. 2d, Shirley Nichols, Nov. 14, 1969; step-children—Isabel Swisher, Alan Nichols. Exec., Prisoner of War Work and Relief, Poland and Baltic States, 1921-24; exec. Am. sect. European Student Relief, Russia, 1924-27; mem. faculty Stanford U. and dir. Stanford-Alaska Ednl. Study, 1930-34; mem. Calif. legislature, 1935-37; dir. research econ. problems John Randolph and Dora Haynes Foundation, Los Angeles, 1936-38; co-dir. (with Prof. Percy E. Davidson) Inst. Occupational Research, Stanford University; budgeteer, by appointment Gov.-Elect, Calif., 1938-39; adminstr. State Relief Adminstrn., Calif., 1939; econ. counsel, exec. sec. Temporary Nat. Econ. Com., 1939-41; chief Am. hemisphere div. Board of Economic Warfare, Washington, D.C., 1942; chief supply and transport div., Office of Fgn. Relief and Rehabilitation Operations, Dept. of State, 1943; mem. food adv. com. War Food Adminstrn., 1943; founding mem., chief of field operations, U.N.R.R.A., 1944; exec. sec. Small Bus. com., U.S. Senate, 1945; exec. dir., Public Affairs Institute, Washington; mem. bd., treas. Citizens Com. on Natural Resources, Washington. Sr. phys. dir. Coast Defenses Puget Sound, Washington 1917-18. Granted commission as lt. colonel, U.S. Army, Jan. 1943; Commn. deferred for other govt. wartime assignment. Chmn. unemployment com., legislation interim com. on real property taxation, v. chmn. legislative com. on study of health insurance (Calif.), 1935- 38; pres. Calif. Conf. on Social Work, 1938-39. Mem. Am. Economics Assn., Am. Political Science Assn., Phi Delta Kappa (pres. nat. council del.), Phi Beta Kappa. Democrat. Methodist. Club: National Press (Washington). Author or co-author of numerous books, among the later titles being: Ballots and the Democratic Class Struggle (with Percy E. Davidson), 1943; Recent Trends in Am. Labor, 1945; principal author: Future of Independent Business, Govt. Printing Office, 1947; A Policy and Program for Success, 1950; Aluminum for Defense and Prosperity, 1952; To Make a Free World, 1955; Health Service is a Basic Right of All the People, 1956; Meeting California Water Needs, 1958; Natural Resources-Their Protection and Development, 1959; Always To Start Anew; The Making of a Public Activist, 1969. Home: 206 Del Mesa Carmel CA 93921 ☆

ANDERSON, DILLON, lawyer; b. McKinney, Texas, July 14, 1906; s. Joseph and Elizabeth (Dillon) A.; B.S., U. Okla., 1928; LL.B., Yale, 1929; LL.D., Tex. Christian U., 1954, Allegheny Coll., 1956; m. Lena Carter Carroll, May 30, 1931; children—Susan (Mrs. Charles A. Whiteford, Jr.), Lena (Mrs. Jerry Van Kyle), and Elizabeth (Mrs. Ronald E. Martin). Admitted to Tex. bar, 1929; with firm Baker and Botts, (formerly Baker, Botts, Parker & Garwood), Houston, 1929-, partner 1940-; spl. asst. to Pres. U.S. for nat. security affairs, 1955-56; dir. Westinghouse Electric Corp., U.S. Plywood-Champion Papers, Inc., also Fed. Dept. Stores, Inc., Monsanto Co.; cons. Nat. Security council, 1953-60. Trustee Schlumberger Found., Foley Found., Carnegie Endowment Internat. Peace, The Brookings Instn. Mem. U.S. delegation to Summit Conf. at Geneva, 1955. Served as col. U.S. Army, 1942-45. Decorated Legion of Merit, Army Commendation Ribbon. Fellow Am. Acad. Arts and Scis.; mem. Council Fgn. Relations, Inc., Fgn. Policy Assn. (dir.), World Affairs Council Houston (adv. bd.), Houston Com. Fgn. Relations (pres. 1950-51),

Am. Bar Assn., Am. Law Inst. (council), Tex. Inst. Letters. Clubs: Houston Country (pres., dir. 1948-49), Eagle Lake Rod and Gun (Houston); Bayou, Texas, Metropolitan (Washington); Chevy Chase (Bethesda, Md.); The Brook (N.Y.C.). Author: I and Claudie, 1951; Claudie's Kinfolks, 1954; The Billingsley Papers, 1961. Home: 3414 Del Monte St Houston TX 77019 Office: One Shell Plaza Bldg Houston TX 77002

ANDERSON, DONALD BERNARD, oil co. exec.; b. Chgo., Apr. 6, 1919; s. Hugo August and Hilda (Nelson) A.; B.S. in Mech. Engring., Purdue U., 1942; m. Patricia Gaylord, 1945. Vice pres. Hondo Oil & Gas Co. (formerly Malco Refineries, Inc.), Roswell, N.M., and subsidiary corps., 1946-63; pres. Anderson Oil Co., Roswell, 1963—; pres. Cotter Corp., 1966-70, chmn. bd., 1966—. Curator fine arts, mem. acquisitions com. Roswell Mus. and Art Center, 1949-56, trustee, 1956—, pres. bd., 1957- -; bd. dirs. Sch. Am. Research, Santa Fe; regent Eastern N.M. U. Served to lt. USNR, 1942-46. Home: Route 1 Box 214-A Roswell NM 88201 Office: Box 1000 Roswell NM 88201

ANDERSON, DONALD EDWARD, research and devel. exec.; b. Delsvan, Minn. Sept. 16, 1931; s. Levi Edward and Sarah (Hillman) A.; B.S., U. Minn., 1952, M.S., 1954, Ph.D. in Elec. Engring., 1958; m. Cynthia Jane Luedtke, June 16, 1954; children—Scott Mark, Gwen Marie, Bruce Alan, Gail Diane. Ressearch asst. U. Minn., 195254, research fellow, 195458, mem. faculty, 1958-68, prof. elec. engring., 1967-68; with G.T. Schjeldahl Co., Northfield, Minn., 1967—; v.p., dir. corp. research and devel., 1968—; cons. in field, 1958—. Mem. I.E.E.E., Am. Phys. Soc., Sigma Xi. Tau Beta Pi., Eta Kappa Nu, Kappa Eta Kappa. Research elctron emission, superconductivity, phys. electronics; patentee electronmagnetic energy storage, direct energy conversion, teaching elec. circuit theory field theory. electronics. Home: Route 2 Northfield MN 55057 Office: GT Schjeldahl Co Northfield MN 55057

ANDERSON, DONALD GEORGE, educator; b. Burlington, Ia., Oct. 11, 1930; s. George H. and Esther (McCaleb) A.; A.A., Burlington Jr. Coll., 1950; B.S., U. Ia., 1956, M.A., 1957, Ph.D., 1962; m. Beulah Esther Fargo, June 6, 1959; children—David A., Susan R. Instr. U.S.D., 1957-59; instr. mktg. U. Ia., 1959-61; asst. prof. mktg. U. N.D., 1961-62; asst. prof. marketing U. South Fla., 1962-63; prof., chmn. marketing U. N.D., 1963—. Chmn. New Indsl. Devel. Subcom. N.D. Economic Devel. Commn., 1967. Served with USN, 1951-54. Mem. Am., So. mktg. assns., So., Midwest econ. assns., V.F.W., Beta Gamma Sigma, Order Artus, Delta Sigma Pi. Mason. Elk. Home: 2910 Clover Dr Grand Forks ND 58201

ANDERSON, DONALD GRIGG, physician, educator; b. N.Y.C., Aug. 2, 1913; s. James Hewston and Myra Esther (Grigg) A.; grad. Phillips Exeter Acad., 1930; A.B., Harvard, 1935; M.D., Columbia, 1939; m. Erna Louise Goettsch, June 25, 1938; children—Patricia Gail, Roberta Vail, James Henry. Intern. Boston City Hosp., 1939-41; resident St. Luke's Hosp., N.Y.C., 1941; asst. resident in medicine Presbyn. Hosp., N.Y.C., 1941-42; resident in medicine Evans Meml., Mass. Meml. hosps., Boston, 1942-43, research fellow, 1943-45; vis. physician Mass. Meml. Hosps., 1945-47, also asst. mem. Evans Meml.; dean Boston U. Sch. Medicine, 1945-47; sec. Council on Med. Edn. and Hosps., A.M.A. Chgo., 1947-53; dean sch. medicine and dentistry U. Rochester, 1953-66, prof. medicine, 1953-; vis. prof. medicine U. Va., 1965, Columbia U., 1966. Pres., Nat. Fund for Med. Edn., 1966-69; sec. Com. Survey Med. Edn., 1948-53; mem. Pres. Sci. Adv. Com. on Bioastronautics, 1961- 64; sec. Joint Com. on Med. Edn. in Time of Nat. Emergency, 1947-53; mem. mem. healing arts ednl. adv. com. to dir. Selective Service System, 1947-63; mem. Citizens Fed. Com. on Edn., U.S. Office Edn., 1947-52; bd. dirs. Am. Med. Edn. Found., 1950-60, Rochester Regional Hosp. Council, 1954-66. Cons. edn., tng. div., Office Surgeon Gen. Army, 1950-56. Diplomate Am. Bd. Internal Medicine. Mem. A.M. A., Am. Fedn. for Clin. Research, N.Y. Med. Soc., Assn. Am. Med. Colls. (pres 1961-62), Mountain View C. of C., Alpha Omega Alpha (pres. 1966-68), Nu Sigma Nu, Sigmet Omega. Clubs: Pundit (Rochester). Home: 151 Panorama Trail Rochester, NY 14625. Office: 260 Crittenden Blvd Rochester NY 14620

ANDERSON, DONALD NICHOLAS, adj. gen. Ore.; b. Portland, Ore., Sept. 6, 1915; s. Andrew Nicholas and Helen Lucille (Churchley) A.; B.S., U. Ore., 1939; m. Margaret Kathryn Byrne, Nov. 15, 1944; 1 son, Donald Nicholas. Apptd. 2d lt., inf., AUS, 1939; called to active duty, 1941; served in PTO, 1942-45; released from active duty as maj., 1946; joined Ore. N.G. as maj., 1947, advanced through grades to maj. gen., 1964; asst. adj. gen. Ore., 1962-63, adj. gen., 1963-. Decorated Silver Star, Bronze Star with oak leaf cluster, Air medal, Combat Inf. badge. Mem. Adj. Gen. Assn., N.G. Assn. U.S., N.G. Assn. Ore., Mil. Order World Wars, Association of the United States Army, Vets. of Foreign Wars, Am. Legion, Alpha Tau Omega. Home: 1845 Brookside Av N W Salem, OR 97304. Office: care Mil Dept Salem, OR 97310.

ANDERSON, DONALD RENE, ins. co. exec.; b. Hoquiam, Wash., Oct. 23, 1928; s. Earl R. and Clara (Cooper) A.; B.B.A., U. Wash., 1953; m. Iris A. Gilbreath, July 15, 1951; children—Karen, Susan, Gayle, Brian. Staff accountant Price Waterhouse & Co., Seattle, 1953-56; resident auditor Allstate Ins. Co., 1956-57; sr. accountant Safeco Life Ins. Co., 1957-58; chief accountant Balfour, Guthrie & Co., 1958-62; sr. accountant Peat Marwick Mitchell & Co., Seattle, 1962-64; treas., controller Farmers New World Life Ins. Co., Mercer Island, Wash., 1964—. Financial adviser to King County Jr. Achievement Clubs. Served with AUS, 1946-48. C.P.A., Wash. Fellow Life Office Mgmt. Inst.; mem. Am. Inst. C.P.A.'s, Wash. Soc. C.P.A.'s, Financial Execs. Inst., Tax Execs. Inst. (sec. 1971-72), Beta Alpha Psi, Sigma Phi Epsilon. Home: 4419 138th St SE Bellevue WA 98006 Office: 9611 Sunset Hwy SE Mercer Island WA 98040

ANDERSON, DON LYNN, educator, geophysicist; b. Frederick, Md., Mar. 5, 1933; s. Richard Andrew and Minola (Phares) A.; B.S., Rensselaer Poly. Inst., 1955; M.S., Cal. Inst. Tech., 1959, Ph.D., 1962; m. Nancy Lois Ruth, Sept. 15, 1956; children—Lynn Ellen, Lee Weston. With Chevron Oil Co., Mont., Wyo., Cal., 1955-56; with Air Force Cambridge Research Center, Boston, 1956-58; with Arctic Inst. N.Am., Boston, 1958; mem. faculty Cal. Inst. Tech., Pasadena, 1962—, asso. prof. geophysics, 1964-68, prof., 1968—, dir. seismol. lab., 1967—. Sloan Found. fellow, 1965-67. Mem. Am. Geophys. Union (James B. Macelwane award 1966), A.A.A.S., Soc. Exploration Geophysics, Seismol. Soc. Am., Sigma Xi. Asso. editor Jour. Geophys. Research, 1965-67. Home: 669 E Alameda St Altadena CA 91001 Office: 1201 E California Blvd Pasadena CA 91109

ANDERSON, E. B., drug co. exec.; b. Michigan City, Ind., Aug. 30, 1926; s. A.B. and Esther (Nicholson) A.; A.B. cum laude Ind. U., 1949, J.D., 1952; grad. Advanced Mgmt. Program, Harvard, 1970; m. Adrienne Scotchbrook, Aug. 6, 1955; children—Rebecca J., Katherine V. Admitted to Ind. bar, 1952; partner firm Butt, Bowers & Anderson, Evansville, Ind., 1952-60; head gen. law dept. Baxter Labs. Inc., Morton Grove, Ill., 1961-65; v.p., sec., gen. counsel, dir., mem. exec. com. Hoffmann-La Roche Inc., Nutley, N.J., 1965—. Corp. counsel City of Evansville, Ind., 1956-58. Served with AUS, World War II. Mem. Phi Beta Kappa. Home: 201 Fells Rd Essex Falls NJ 07021 Office: 340 Kingsland St Nutley NJ 07110

ANDERSON, EARL JENNINGS, plant pathologist; b. Roy, Wash., June 8, 1908; s. Albert and Henrikka (Jensen) A.; B.S., Wash. State Coll., 1932, M.S., 1934; Ph.D., U. Md., 1937; m. Marion Louise Preston, Aug. 18, 1934; 1 son, David Preston. Instr. botany N.D. Agr. Coll., 1938; asso. plant pathologist Pineapple Research Inst. Hawaii, Honolulu, 1939-43; prof., head dept. plant pathology Wash. State Coll., and head div. plant pathology Wash. Expt. Sta., 1943-45; pathologist Pineapple Research Inst., U. Hawaii, Honolulu, 1945-50, head pathology dept., 1950-61, head pest control sect., 1961-66, head plant pathology dept., 1964-66, affiliate staff Grad. Sch., 1960-66; research Dole Philippines, Inc. 1966—. Mem. Emergency Prodn. Comm., Honolulu, 1941-43, mem. exec. com. Wash. State Postwar Planning Co., 1943. Recipient Fulbright Research Award, Australia, 1957; NRC fellow, 1937. Mem. A.A.A.S., Am. Phytopath. Soc., Am. Inst. Biol. Scis., Hawaiian Bot. Soc., Alpha Zeta, Phi Kappa Phi, Sigma Xi. Office: Dole Philippines Inc PO Box 362 Commercial Center PO Makati Rizal Philippines

ANDERSON, EDDIE (Rochester), actor; b. Oakland Cal., Sept. 18, 1905; s. Ed and Ella Anderson. Vaudeville and night club apperances; featured on Jack Benny radio and TV programs; films include Transient Lady, Three Men on a Horse, Jezebele, You Can't Take it With You, Thanks for the Memory. Gone With The Wind, Tales of Manhattan, Cabin in the Sky, Broadway Rhythm, I Love a Band Leader, The ShowOff. Address: care Screen Actors Guild, 7750 Sunset Blvd Los Angeles CA.*

ANDERSON, EDWARD CLIFFORD, investment banker; b. Richmond, Va., Nov. 26, 1893; s. George Wayne and Estelle Marguerite (Burthe) A.; student U. Va., 1914-16, Mass. Inst. Tech., 1916-17; m. Isabel Walker Scott, Jan. 12, 1922; childrenGeorge Wayne, Elisabeth Strother (Mrs. Jonathan Bryan III), Isabel Scott (Mrs. Harvie W. Fitzgerald). Began with Imperial Tobacco Co., Great Britain and Ireland, 1919; with Scott & Stringfellow, investment bankers, Richmond, 1919-47, mem. firm, 1927-47; organizer, 1948, since sr. partner Anderson & Strudwick, investment bankers, Richmond; mem. N.Y. Stock Exchange, 1956-70; dir. So. Dept. Stores. Exec. mgr. Victory Fund Com. 5th Fed. Res. Dist., also 5th Fed. Res. Dist. War Finance Com., World War II; civilian aide to sec. of army, 1952-57; hon. chmn. Va. Army Adv. Com., 1952-57. Bd. visitors U. Va., 1942-52. Served to 1st lt. F.A., U.S. Army, 1917-19; AEF in France; capt. Va. N.G., 1921-24. Decorated Croix de Guerre with silver star, Fourragere (France). Mem. Investment Bankers Assn. Am. (vice chmn. S.E. Group 1941-42, nat. bd. govs. 1941-42), U. Va. Alumni Assn. (past pres. Richmond, past nat. bd. mgrs.), Assn. U.S. Army, Assn. Descs. Signers Declaration of Independence, Monticello Assn., Assn. Officers First Div. U.S. Army, Arundel Assn., Delta Phi. Democrat. Episcopalian (vestry). Clubs: Cape Arundel Golf (dir., Kennebunkport, Me.); Country of Va. (past dir.), Commonwealth (past dir.), Fishing Bay Yacht, Soldiers Lodge (pres.), Richmond. Home: 1234 Rothesay Rd Richmond, VA 23221. Office: 913 E Main St Richmond VA 23212

ANDERSON, EDWARD PARK, business exec.; b. Pitts., Dec. 12, 1908; s. Cocus and Ids (Mackey) A; A. B. Harvard, 1930; m. Elizabeth Edwards, Apr. 29 1933; children—Hope (Mrs. K. J. Dalgleish), Elizabeth (Mrs. E. P. Sheridan), Jane. Sr. v.p., dir. Richardson-Meerrell, Inc. (formerly Vick Chem. Co.), N.Y.C. Mem. Phi Beta Kappa. Home: Old Farm Rd Darien CT 06820 Office: 122 E 42d St New York City NY 10017*

ANDERSON, EDWIN JOHN, brewing co. exec.; b. Rockford, Ill., Aug. 3, 1902; s. John A. and Emma (Wallin) A.; A.B., Beloit (Wis.) Coll., 1927; m. Isabelle B. Bort, Mar. 31, 1928; children—Suzanne Jane (Mrs. Harold J. Stenglein, Jr.) (dec.), Marynell (Mrs. Richard G. Williams). Advt. mgr. ABC Washing Machine Co., Peoria, Ill., 1927; with Goebel Brewing Co., Detroit, 1938—, pres., 1941-58; pres. Goebel Brewing Co. of Cal., Oakland; dir., mem. adv. bd. Lumberman's Mut. Casualty Ins. Co.; pres., gen. mgr. dir. Detroit Lions Football Co., 1949-62, exec. v.p., 1962—. Former mem. bd. dirs. Detroit Community Fund, United Found., Detroit Bd. Commerce, Met. Bldg. Com. of Detroit; past pres. Children's Hosp. of Mich. Episcopalian. Clubs: Detroit Athletic, Bloomfield Hills Country, Detroit (Detroit). Home: 235 Harlan Dr Bloomfield Hills MI 48013 Office: Detroit Lions Inc Detroit MI 48226

ANDERSON, ELMER EBERT, educator; b. Ottawa, Ill., June 28, 1922; s. Oscar Elmer and Ruth (Ebert) A.; A.B., Occidental Coll., 1950; M.S., U. Ill., 1956; Ph.D., U. Md., 1964; m. Amelia Gabriel, Oct. 30, 1943; children—Kenneth, Mark, Scott, Ruth, Carl. Instr. Deep Springs Coll., 1952-53, dean, 1953-55; teaching asst. U. Ill., 1955-57; research physicist Electromagnetics div. U.S. Naval Ordnance Lab., White Oak, Md., 1957-62, chief, 1962-65; asso. prof. physics Clarkson Coll. Tech., 1965-68, prof., 1968—, chmn. dept., 1966—. Served with USN, 1940-46, 1950-52. Mem. Am. Phys. Soc., Am. Assn. Physics Tchrs. Author: Modern Physics and Quantum Mechanics, 1971. Home: 18 Broad St Potsdam NY 13676

ANDERSON, ERICA, documentary film maker; b. Vienna, Austria, Aug. 8, 1914; d. Edvard and Ilona Kellner; student photo school in Vienna, Austria; L.H.D. (hon.); m. Larry Collier Anderson, June 20, 1940. Came to U.S., 1940, naturalized, 1945. Documentary films on persons such as Henry Moore, Grandma Moses, Albert Schweitzer, Carl Jung, Thomas Dooley, and others in Poland, Peru, Laos, Indochina, Haiti, Belgium. Established Albert Schweitzer Friendship House and library, Great Barrington, Mass., pres. Author: World of Albert Schweitzer, 1955; The Schweitzer Album; Albert Schweitzer's Gift of Friendship. Address: Hurlburt Rd Great Barrington MA 01230

ANDERSON, ERIC ALBERT, educator; b. S. St. Paul, Minn., Dec. 9, 1907; s. Andrew and Hannah (Nelson) A.; B.S. in Forestry, U. Wash., 1932; Ph.D., N.Y. State Coll. Forestry, 1949; m. Edna Vivian Barrie, Dec. 25, 1934; childrenBarrie, Eric Anthony, Jan Elizabeth. With Nat. Paper Products Co., also Dept. Agr., 1929-34; jr. forester U.S. Forest Service, 1935-39; grad. teaching asst. N.Y. State Coll. Forestry, 1939-42; forest products technologist U.S. Forest Service, 1942-50; prof. State U. Coll. Forestry, Syracuse U., 1950-, chmn. dept. wood tech., 1951-59, dept. wood products engring., 1959-. Mem. U.S. delegation 5th FAO Conf. Wood Tech., 1963; mem. evaluation team Forestry Sch., Pa. State U., 1961; vis. scientist Soc. Wood Sci. and Tech., 1961-62, 62-63, mem. edn. study com., 1961-64; mem. evaluation wood tech. program needs of Chilean univs. Nat. Acad. Sci., 1961; mem. FAO Forest industries mission to Bosnia-Herzegovina and Montenegro, 1966. Mem. Soc. Wood Sci. and Tech., Soc. Am. Foresters, Internat. Assn. Wood Anatomists, N.Y. Acad. Sci., Forest Products Research Soc. (pres. 1968-69), Sigma Xi. Contbr. profl. jours. Home: 561 Cumberland Ave Syracuse, NY 13210.

ANDERSON, ERNEST CARL, chemist; b. Rock Island, Ill., Aug. 23, 1920; s. Ernest Axel and Mary (McGaughey) A.; A.B., Augustana Coll., 1942; Ph.D., U. Chgo., 1949; m. Catherine D. Payne, June 21, 1942; childrenChristopher F., Nicholas J., Catherine J. Analytical chemist Metall. Lab., U. Chgo., 1942-44; analytical chemist Los Alamos Sci. Lab., U. Cal., 1944-46, staff mem. biophysics, 1949-. Rask-Orsted fellow U. Copenhagen, 1951-52; cons. Metrix, Inc., 1961—. Recipient E.O. Lawrence award AEC, 1966. Fellow A.A.A.S.; mem. Biophys. Soc. Research on natural radiocarbon and radiocarbon dating, human body composition, cellular biochemistry. Home: 1610 S Sage St Los Alamos NM 85744 Office: Los Alamos Sci Lab Box 1663 Los Alamos NM 87544

ANDERSON, ERNEST W., aero. engr., educator; b. Fargo, N.D., Aug. 23, 1905; s. George Ernest and Isabelle (Lawrence) A.; B.S., N.D. Agrl. Coll., 1926; M.S., Ia. State Coll., 1928, Ph.D., 1933; postgrad. Cal. Inst. Tech., 1934; m. Florence Evelyn McCarthy, June 12, 1928; children—James Robert, John Ernest, Mary Ellen Jill. Mem. teaching and research staff Ia. State U., Ames, 1926—, prof. math., 1947—, prof. aero. engring., 1951-71, head dept., 1955—, Anston Marston distinguished prof. engring. 1959—; asso. Ames Lab. of AEC; owner, operator Certification Hybrid Seed Co., 1935-47. Operations analyst USAF, 1951—. Mem. Central Ia. Airport Authority Bd; mem. exec. com., vice chmn. bd. Ia. State U. Meml. Union. Recipient Faculty citation Ia. State U., 1964. Mem. Inst. Aeros. and Astronautics, Am. Math. Assn., Am. Soc. Engring. Edn., Soc. Indsl. and Applied Math., Ia. Engring. Soc., Aerospace Edn. Council Ia., Osborn Research Club , Sigma Xi, Phi Kappa Phi, Pi Mu Epsilon, Tau Beta Pi. Rotarian. Home: 2318 Donald St Ames IA 50010

ANDERSON, EUGENE I., auto parts co. exec.; b. Crothersville, Ind., Oct. 5, 1917; s. Irving and Grace (Rawlings) A.; B.S. in Indsl. Engring., Purdue U., 1939; m. Rosemary Tulley, Oct. 9, 1941; childrenDavid E., John F., Carol, Judy J. Indsl. engr. Goodyear Tire & Rubber Co., Akron, O., 1939-43, P.R. Mallory Co., Indpls., 1946-47; indsl. engr., plant mgr., works mgr., gen. gen. mgr., exec. v.p., now pres., dir. Arvin Industries; dir. Irwin Union Bank & Trust Co., Columbus. Served with USNR, 1943-46. Home: 214 19th St Columbus IN 47201 Office: 1531 E 13th St Columbus IN 47201

ANDERSON, EUGENE NEWTON, educator; b. Tehuacana, Tex., July 24, 1900; s. Jesse and Luda Lee (Newton) A.; A.B., U. Colo., 1921; Ph.D., U. Chgo., 1928; student Trinity U. (Tex.), 1918-19, U. Berlin, 1924-25; m. Pauline Relyea, June 25, 1932; 1 son, Eugene Newton. Instr., U. Chgo., 1925- 32, asst. prof. European history, 1932-36; prof. European History, Am. U., Washington, 1936-41; coordinator information, 1941-42; Office Strategic Services, 1942-45; asst. chief division cultural cooperation State Dept., Washington, 1945, asso. chief German-Austrian activities div. occupied areas, 1946-47; expert on humanities in German and Austrian univs. for War Dept. and Am. Council Learned Socs., summer 1949; prof. European history U. Neb. 1947-55; prof. European history U. Cal. at Los Angeles, 1955-68, emeritus prof. European history, 1968—; vis. prof. U. Cal. at Santa Barbara, 1968-70; faculty Peshawar U., West Pakistan, summer 1961; vis. prof. U. Cal. Santa Barbara, 1968-70. Fellow Soc. Sci. Research Council, studying in Germany, 1930-31, and summer 1937. Served with U.S. Army, 1918. Mem. Am. Assn. U. Profs., Am. Hist. Assn. (chmn. program com. 1939), Phi Beta Kappa, Phi Delta Theta. Presbyn. Author: The First Moroccan Crisis, 1904-06 (1930); Nationalism and the Cultural Crisis in Prussia, 1806-15 (1939); The Humanities in the German and Austrian Universities, 1950; Process versus Power, 1952; The Prussian Elections of 1862 and 1863, 1954; The Social and Political Conflict in Prussia, 1858-64, 1954; Modern Europe in World Perspective, 1958; European Issues in the 20th Century, 1958; co-author; Political Institutions and Social Change in Continental Europe in the 19th Century, 1968. Co-editor: Medieval and Historiographical Essays in Honor of J. W. Thompson, 1940; Europe in the 19th Century; A Documentary Analysis, 2 vols., 1961. Bd. editors Jour. Modern History, 1952-55. Home: 552 Pintura Dr Santa Barbara CA 93105

ANDERSON, EUGENIE MOORE, former govt. ofcl.; b. Adair, Ia., May 26, 1909; d. Ezekiel Arrowsmith and Flora Belle (McMillen) Moore; student Stephens Coll., 1926-27, Simpson Coll., 1927-28, Carleton Coll., 1929-30, Julliard Inst. Musical Art, 1930-32; m. John P. Anderson, Sept. 9, 1930; children—Elizabeth Johanna (Mrs. Ghei), Hans Pierce. Am. ambassador to Denmark, 1949-53, Am. minister to Bulgaria, 1962-65; U.S. rep. on UN Trusteeship Council 1965-68; alternate U.S. del. to 20th and 21st sessions UN Gen. Assembly, 1965-68; spl. asst. to sec. of state, Washington, 1968—. U.S. rep. to Third session UN ad hoc commn. on prisoners of war, 1952; mem. Zellerbach Commn., toured Iron Curtain country refugee camps in Western Europe, 1957; mem. Am. delegation Atlantic Congress, London, 1959; mem. bd. U.S. Com. for Refugees, 1959-60; mem. ednl. policy com. Inst. Internat. Edn., 1959-62; lectr. in India, auspices Asia Found. and Indian Council World Affairs, 1961; vice chmn. Citizens Com. for Internat. Devel., 1961-62. Chmn. Democratic Farm Labor party, Goodhue County, 1944-48; mem. Dem. Nat. Com. for Minn., 1948-49; del.-at-large for Minn., Dem. Nat. Conv., 1948, 60, 68; chmn. Minn. Commn. Fair Employment Practices, 1955-60; mem. Dem. Nat. Adv. Com. on Fgn. Policy, 1957-61. Trustee Am. Freedom from Hunger Found.; bd. dirs. Minn. World Affairs Center. Mem. Am. Assn. UN (bd. dirs.), League Women Voters, Am. Assn. U. Women, Pi Beta Phi. Methodist. Home: Tower View Red Wing MN 55066

ANDERSON, FELIX SYLVESTER, bishop; b. Wilmington, N.C., Oct. 3, 1893; s. Charles and Betty (Foye) A.; A.B., Livingstone Coll., 1920; student Hood Theol. Sem., 1920-21, Western Theol. Sem., 1922-24; m. Bessie Bezzell, Apr. 28, 1920; children—Felix Sylvester, Herman Leroy, Mrs. Wright P. Robinson, Joseph D., Theodore M., Mrs. Alfred Haney. Ordained to ministry A.M.E. Zion Ch.; pastor in N.C., Ala. and Ky., 1916-60; bishop of Louisville, 1960—; tchr. P.W. Moore High Sch., Elizabeth City, N.C., 1929-31. Pres. Mobile Civic Orgn., 1942-48, chmn. Louisville Civic Orgn., 1950-54. Mem. Ky. Ho. of Reps., 1954-60. Recipient plaque for service Ky. Gen. Assn. A.M.E. Zion Ministerial Alliance, 1954-58. Mem. N.A.A.C.P. (life), Ky. Tchrs. Assn., Ky. Fraternal Police Officers. Democrat. Home: 741 S 44th St Louisville KY 20520

ANDERSON, FLORENCE, found. exec.; b. Bklyn., Oct. 29, 1910; d. Charles Albert and Florence (Gould) Anderson; A.B., Mt. Holyoke Coll., 1931; spl. student N.Y. U., New Sch. Social Research; LL.D. (hon.), Western Coll. for Women, 1967. With Carnegie Corp., N.Y.C., 1934—, administrv. asst., 1939-47, asst. sec., 1947-51, asso. sec., 1951-54, sec., 1954—. Sec. Carnegie Found. for Advancement Teaching, 1955—. Served from 2d lt. to capt. USMCR, 1943-45, asst. adj. Marine Corps Schs., dir. Nat. Info. Bur. Mem. Adult Edn. Assn. U.S., Marine Corps. Res. Officers Assn., Phi Beta Kappa. Clubs: Cosmopolitan, Mount Holyoke (N.Y.C.); Washington (Conn.). Home: 235 E 50th St New York City NY 10022 Office: 437 Madison Av New York City NY 10022

ANDERSON, FLOYD EDWARD, author, newspaperman; b. Superior, Wis., July 15, 1906; s. John Elmer and Paula (Hagen) A.; m. Joy Eder, Oct. 29, 1932; children—Joan (Mrs. J. Anderson Doviak), Peter, Thomas, Martin, Joseph, Mary Teresa, Stephen. Editorial asst. Am. mag., N.Y.C., 1932-36; engaged in pvt. bus., 1936-45; sales mgr. Am. Press, N.Y.C., 1945-48; mng. editor Catholic Light, Scranton,

Pa., 1948-51, Advocate, Newark, 1951-61, Register system of papers, Denver, 1961-62, Central Cal. Register, Fresno, 1962- 63; dir. NC News Service (U.S. Catholic Conf.), Washington, 1963-68; v.p. Internat. Fedn. Cath. Press Agys., 1968-69; editor The New World, Chgo., 1969—. Recipient award Cath. War Vets N.J., 1956; decorated knight of St. Gregory, 1959. Mem. Cath. Press Assn. (bd. dirs. 1954-63, sec. 1954-59, v.p. 1959-61, pres. 1961-63; St. Francis de Sales award 1963), Internat. Fedn. Dirs. Cath. Publs. (v.p. 1967-69), Internat. Cath. Fedn. Newspapers and Pubs. (v.p. 1971). Clubs: Chicago Press, Headline (Chgo.). Author: The Bishop's Boy, 1957; Father of the American Navy, 1959; Father Baker, 1960; Gold Rush Bishop, 1962; The Birth Control Encyclical, 1969. Editor: Council Daybook, Vatican II, sessions 1 and 2, 1965, session 3, 1965, session 4, 1966. Home: 508 W Hintz Rd Arlington Heights IL 60002 Office: 109 N Dearborn St Chicago IL 60602

ANDERSON, FORREST HOWARD, gov. of Mont.; b. Helena, Jan. 30, 1913; s. Oscar A. and Nora (O'Keefe) A.; student U. Mont.; LL.B., Columbia, 1938; m. Margaret Evelyn Samson, Jan. 24, 1941; children—Margaret Louise, Arlee Joan, Newell Burke. Admitted to Mont. bar, 1938; practice of law, Helena, 1938-52; co. atty., Lewis and Clark Co., 1945-47; spl. counsel indsl. accident fund State of Mont., 1947-49; asso. justice Supreme Ct. Mont. 1953-57, atty. gen., Mont., 1957-69; gov. of Mont., 1969—. Mem. Mont. State Legislature, 1943-45. Mem. Phi Delta Theta. Methodist. Mason (32, Shriner), Elk, Eagle, Moose. Home: 2 Carson Helena MT 59601 Office: State Capitol Helena MT 59601

ANDERSON, FRANK ABEL, educator; b. Bridgeport, Conn., June 22, 1914; s. Frank Fabian Andre and Anna Elizabeth (Olson) A.; B.S., U. So. Cal., 1936; M.S., U. Me., 1940; Ph.D., La. State U., 1947; m. Mary Alla Courtney, June 11, 1942; children—Frank, Phyllis. Technologist, Shell Oil Co., Dominguez, Cal., 1936-38; asst. prof. chemistry U. Miss., 1940-45; prof., acting chmn. dept. chemistry and chem. engring. U. Miss., 1947-48, prof., chmn. dept. 1948-55, prof., chmn. dept. chem. engring., 1955- 65, prof. chem. engring., asso. dean. engring., 1965—. Gaylord fellow La. State U., 1945-47. Mem. Am. Inst. Chem. Engrs., Am. Chem. Soc., Am. Soc. Engring. Edn., Miss. Acad. Scis., Phi Kappa Phi, Phi Eta Sigma, Phi Lambda Upsilon, Alpha Chi Sigma, Phi Theta Kappa. Methodist. Rotarian. Author: Fundamentals of Chemistry (with Glenn H. Brown), 1944. Compiler: Chemical Engineering Problems-1946 (with H.J. Garber), 1946. Home: 410 S 11th St Oxford MS 38655 Office: University of Mississippi MS

ANDERSON, FRANK WHITTEN, banker; b. Jersey City, June 6, 1902; s. Frank Cobb and Elizabeth (Whitten) A.; m. Helen-Mary Hockman, Apr. 30, 1927; 1 son, Frank Whitten. With Trust Co. of N.J., Jersey City, 1929-39, asst. v.p., 1936- 39; asst. v.p. First Nat. Bank, Wilkes-Barre, 1939-45; v.p. Miners Nat. Bank of Wilkes-Barre, 1945-50, former president, dir. Past pres., dir. Wyoming Valley Community Chest; dir. Greater Wilkes-Barre Indsl. Devel. Fund. Trustee YWCA; bd. dirs. Wilkes-Barre Gen. Hosp. Mem. Greater Wilkes-Barre C. of C. (dir.), Miss. Acad. Scis. (pres. 1962- 63). Presbyn. Clubs: Westmoreland (Wilkes-Barre). Home: 539 Ford Av Kingston PA 18704 Office: 8-18 W Market St Wilkes-Barre PA 18701*

ANDERSON, FREDERIC DUCEY, lawyer; b. Gloucester City, N.J., June 19, 1914; s. Howard Clifford and Bertha (Ducey) A.; A.B. magna cum laude, Princeton, 1935; J.D., Harvard, 1938; m. Barbara Fowler, Oct. 16, 1940; children—Mary Howard, Frederic Fowler. Admitted to Ind. bar, 1938, also U.S. Supreme Ct.; practice in Indpls., 1938—; partner firm Barnes, Hickam, Pantzer & Boyd, and predecessor, 1942—. Dir. Mchts. Nat. Bank and Trust Co. Indpls., Hillenbrand Industries, Inc. Bd. dirs. Ind. State Symphony Soc., Children's Mus. Served to lt. (j.g.) USNR, 1943-46. Mem. Am. (council sect. labor relations law 1962—, chmn. 1971-72), 7th Circuit, Ind., Fed., Indpls. bar assns., Phi Beta Kappa, Phi Beta Kappa Assos. Republican. Presbyn. Clubs: University, Woodstock, Players, Contemporary, Lawyers, Columbia, Harvard, Princeton (past pres.) (Indpls.); Princeton (N.Y.C.); Nat. Lawyers (Washington). Contbr. legal jours. Home: 3543 Delaware Common Indianapolis IN 46220 Office: Merchants Bank Bldg Indianapolis IN 46204

ANDERSON, FRED WOODROW WILSON, educator; b. Lisco, Neb., June 14, 1918; s. George Washington and Etta (Smith) A.; B.S., Neb. State Coll., Chadron, 1940; M.A., U. Neb., 1949, Ed.D., 1959; m. Mary Louella Lindsay, Aug. 29, 1942; childrenBarbara Elaine, Lorraine Sue. Tchr., coach Cairo (Neb.) pub. schs., 1940-41; prin., tchr. Alma (Neb.) pub. schs., 1941, Walton (Neb.) consol. schs., 1946; supt. schs., Cairo, 1946-51, Cambridge, Neb., 1951-60; dean, prin. Jefferson County (Colo.) schs., 1960-62; prof. edn. So. State Coll., Springfield, S.D., 1962-64, dir. student personnel, 1963-64; vis. instr. Black Hills State Coll., Spearfish, S.D., summers 1959-62, prof. edn. chmn. div. edn. and psychology, 1964—. Mem. S.D. Commn. Tchr. Edn. and Profl. Standards, 1964-67, S.D. Com. Evaluation Tchr. Edn. Programs, 1966-67. Served with USMCR, 1942-46. Mem. Nat., Neb. (treas. Dist. V, 1958), Furnas County (sec. 1953, pres. 1959) edn. assns., Am. Legion (past post comdr.), Black Hills State Coll. Edn. Assn. (pres. 1967-68). Methodist (chmn. ofcl. bd. 1967-68). Rotarian (pres. Cambridge 1953), Mason (Shriner). Home: 1311 W Jackson St Spearfish SD 57783

ANDERSON, GAYLORD WEST, public health educator; b. Mpls., Dec. 31, 1901; s. Frank Maloy and Mary Gertrude (Steele) A.; A.B., Dartmouth, 1922; student Sorbonne, Paris, 1922-23, U. Zurich, 1923; M.D., Harvard, 1928, Dr. Pub. Health, 1942; m. Viola Dennis, Oct. 26, 1929; one dau., Gail Elizabeth (Mrs. Harvey Safeer). Teaching asst. chemistry Harvard, 1923-24; interne Albany (N.Y.) Hosp., 1928-29, epidemiologist, div. of communicable diseases, Mass. Dept. of Health, 1929-30, asst. dir., 1930- 31, dir. and dep. commr. of public health, 1931-37; asst. in public health adminstrn., Harvard Sch. Pub. Health, 1931-37; exec. sec. Mass. Legislative Commn. to Investigate Pub. Health Laws and Policies, 1935-37; prof., head dept. of preventive medicine and pub. health U. of Minn., 1937-44, dir. Sch. Public Health, 1944-46, Mayo prof. and dir. 1946-69, dean, 1969-70, dean emeritus, 1970—; cons. govtl. orgns. and depts.; spl. cons. to Dept. of State in missions to Brazil, Argentina, Chile and Peru, 1948, Colombia and Ecuador, 1949, Chile, 1950, Korea, 1954, for WHO to Egypt, 1953, India, Iran and Egypt, 1958. Served from major to col., M.C., U.S. Army, 1942- 45. Decorated Legion of Merit; comdr. Order of Hipolito Unanue (Peru); recipient Harrington award Mpls. Jr. C. of C., 1959; Sedgwick Meml. award Am. Pub. Health Assn., 1963. Diplomate Am. Bd. Preventive Medicine. Hon. fellow Royal Soc. Health (Eng.); mem. Am. Coll. Preventive Medicine, Am. Epidemiol. Soc. (pres. 1951), American College Preventive Medicine, Am. Pub. Health Assn. (pres. 1952), Canadian (hon.) pub. health assns., Mass. Med. Soc., Phi Beta Kappa, Alpha Omega Alpha, Sigma Xi, Delta Omega, Alpha Chi Sigma. Conglist. Clubs: Campus; University (St. Paul). Author: Communicable Disease Control (with M.G. Arnstein), 1941; chapter on "Regulation in Public Health" in Regulatory Administration (by Graham & Reining), 1943; Global Epidemiology (with J. S. Simmons, T.F. Whayne and H.H. Horack), 1944, Vol. II, 1951, Vol. III, 1954; chpt. on Principles of Epidemiology in Bacterial and Mycotic Infections of Man (by Dubos and Hirsch), 1965. Contbr. articles med. jours. Home: 2261 Folwell St St Paul MN 55108 Office: Sch Pub Health U Minn Minneapolis MN 55455

ANDERSON, GEORGE EDWARD, ret. physician; b. Bklyn., Aug. 29, 1897; s. Frederick William and Julia (Von Greiff) A.; A.B. magna cum laude, N.Y. U., 1919, M.D., 1922; m. Katherine Clifford Doherty, Sept. 27, 1924. Attending physician Bklyn. Hosp., 1933, dir. medicine, 1955-64, chief metabolic clinic, also acting dir. medicine Bklyn. Hosp.-Cumberland Hosp. Center; cons. physician Bethany Deaconess Hosp., 1950-65; dir. out-patient services Bklyn. Cumberland Med. Center, 1964-68; cons. Lutheran and Methodist hosps.; clin. prof. emeritus medicine State U., N.Y. Coll. Medicine; curator and asso. directing librarian Library of Kings County Med. Soc. Fellow N.Y. Acad. Medicine, A.C.P.; mem. Am. Rheumatism Assn., Am. Diabetes Assn. (mem. council, sec. 1942-48), N.Y. Heart Assn., Endocrine Soc., N.Y. Diabetes Assn. (dir.; pres. 1944-45), Bklyn. Soc. Internal Medicine (pres. 1941-46), Phi Beta Kappa, Alpha Omega Alpha. Conglist. Home: 590 Flatbush Av Brooklyn NY 11225

ANDERSON, GEORGE HARDING, broadcasting co. exec.; b. Buffalo, Mar. 6, 1931; s. Gordon and Addine (Harding) A.; B.A., Harvard, 1954; m. Sandra Bradley, Aug. 24, 1957; 1 son, Geoffrey Bradley. With First Nat. Bank Boston, 1955-58, Randolph Assos., Wellesley, Mass., 1959-61; pres. Precision Products Co. Inc., Waltham, Mass., 1961-64; sales mgr. WBI-TV, Boston, 1964-66; office mgr. Blair Radio, Boston, 1966-67; sales mgr. WHDH-TV, Boston, 1967-68; exec. v.p. Guy Gannett Broadcasting Services, WGAN-AM-FM-TV, Portland, Me., WHYN-AM-FM-TV, Springfield, Mass., 1968—; dir. Me. Nat. Bank; incorporator Portland Savs. Bank. Pres. Me. Audubon Soc., 1971—, Portland Soc. Natural History, 1971—; maj. Portland United Fund Drive, 1971. Trustee Osteopath. Hosp. Me.; incorporator Me. Med. Center; bd. dirs. Me. Cancer Soc. Served with USAF, 1951-53. Mem. New Eng. Broadcasters (dir.). Clubs: Portland Country; Harvard (Boston); Harvard Varsity, Owl (Cambridge, Mass.). Home: 11 Lantern Lane Cumberland Foreside ME 04110 Office: 390 Congress St Portland ME 04111

ANDERSON, GEORGE K., educator; b. Springfield, Ill., Oct. 20, 1901; s. George Everett and Mary Aletta (Kumler) A.; student Tome Sch., 1912-14, Phillips Exeter Acad., 1914-16; A.B., Harvard, 1920, A.M., 1921, Ph.D., 1925; A.M. (hon.), Brown U., 1947; Litt.D., Middlebury Coll., 1966; m. Ethel Mary Humphrey, Oct. 30, 1933; children—Margaret, John. Instr. English, George Washington U., 1924-27; mem. faculty Brown U., 1927—, prof. English, 1947—, chmn. dept. English, 1950-60; vis. prof. English, Breed Loaf Sch. English, Middlebury Coll., 1931-33, 36-37, 40-42, 44, 47-55, 57-58, 60-61, 63-70, N.Y. State Tchrs. Colls., 1938-39. Guggenheim fellow, 1945. Mem. Medieval Acad. Am., Renaissance Soc. Am., New Eng. Coll. English Assn. (pres. 1968), Modern Lang. Assn. Am., R.I., Vt. hist. socs. Author: The Literature of England, 1936; This Generation, 1939; The Literature of the Anglo-Saxons, 1949; The World in Literature, 1950-51; English Literature from the Beginnings to 1485, 1962; The Legend of the Wandering Jew, 1965; The First Fifty Years, 1969. Contbr. chpts. to books, articles to profl. publs. Home: 169 Power St Providence RI 02906

ANDERSON, GEORGE LAVERNE, educator; b. Blue Rapids, Kan., Feb. 27, 1905; s. Anders and Mary (Pitman) A.; A.B., U. Kan., 1926, A.M., 1931; Ph.D., U. Ill., 1933; m. Caroline Miek, June 8, 1928; childrenMarianne, James LaVerne. Tchr., adminstr. Kan. Pub. Schs., 1926-30; mem. faculty Colo. Coll., 1934-45, No. Mont. Coll., summer 1934, N.M. Highlands U., summers 1939, 40, 42; asso. prof. history U. Kan., 1945-49, prof. history, 1949-70. Mem. Am., So., Western hist. assns., Orgn. Am. Historians, Agrl. Hist. Soc., Phi Beta Kappa. Lutheran. Author: General William J. Palmer-A Decade of Colorado Railroad Building, 1870-1880, 1936; Kansas West, 1963; The Widening Stream: The History of the Exchange National Bank of Atchison; Variations on a Theme: History as Knowledge of the Past. Editor: Issues and Conflicts: Studies in Twentieth Century American Diplomacy, 1959. Contbr. articles to profl. jours. Home: 1702 University Dr Lawrence KS 66044

ANDERSON, GEORGE LESTER, educator; b. Chadron, Neb., Feb. 4, 1911; s. Emil M. and Beulah (Wilson) A.; A.B., Neb. State Tchrs. Coll., 1932; M.A., Colo. State Coll. Edn., 1937; Ph.D., U. Minn., 1941; D.H.L., Bradley U., 1962; Dr. honoris causa, Nat. U. Asuncion (Paraguay), 1965; m. Margaret Wefso, May 24, 1934; children—Judith Clark, Gerald Wesley. High sch. prin., Haigler, Neb., 1932-35, Gordon, Neb., 1935-37; supt. schs., Hay Springs, Neb., 1937-38; research asst. and instr. Coll. Edn., U. Minn., 1938-41, asst. prof. edn., dir. Univ. High Sch. and student teaching, 1941-45, asso. prof., 1945-46, asso. prof. edn., 1946-48, prof. edn., 1948-49; dean tchr. edn., prof. edn. N.Y. City Colls., 1949-51; dean adminstrn., prof. edn. U. Buffalo, 1951-55; vice chancellor ednl. affairs, U. Buffalo (now State U. N.Y. at Buffalo), 1955-62, v.p. ednl. affairs, 1962-65, prof. higher edn., 1965-66, distinguished service prof. higher edn., 1966-69; prof., dir. Center for Study Higher Edn., Pa. State U., 1969—; lectr. U. Mich., 1945, Harvard, 1946, U. Colo., 1951, U. Cal. Berkeley, 1957, 60, 67. Cons. tchr. edn. U.S. Office Mil. Govt. for Germany, 1947. Del. White House Conf. Edn., 1955, exec., N.Y. State com. Recipient Outstanding Achievement award U. Minn., 1956. Mem. Am. Assn. U. Profs., N.E.A., Am. Ednl. Research Assn., Am. Psychol. Assn., Nat. Soc. Study Edn., Nat. Council Social Work Edn. (dir. 1958-64), Am. Assn. Higher Edn. (dir. 1966-69), Phi Beta Kappa. Editor reports, yearbooks. Contbr. to ednl. jours. Home: 111 Grandview Rd State College PA 16801 Office: Willard Bldg Pa State U University Park PA 16801

ANDERSON, GEORGE W., Jr., govt. ofcl.; b. Bklyn., Dec. 15, 1906; s. George W. and Clara (Green) A.; B.S., U.S. Naval Acad., 1927; student Nat. War Coll., 1949- 50; m. Muriel Buttling, Oct. 3, 1933 (dec. 1947); children—George W. III, Mary A. Coughlin, Thomas P.; m. 2d, Mary Lee Lamar Sample, May 15, 1948; 1 dau., Carolyn Sample Abshire. Commd. ensign USN, 1927, advanced through grades to adm., 1961; ships officer U.S.S. Cincinnati; naval aviator and ships officer Fleet, U.S.S. Lexington, U.S.S. Yorktown; comdg. officer U.S.S. Mindoro, U.S.S. Franklin D. Roosevelt; assigned Bur. Aero.; successively assigned staffs Comdr. Air Force Pacific, comdr.-in-chief Pacific, comdr.-in-chief U.S. Fleet, comdr. 6th Fleet, Supreme Allied Comdr. Europe; chmn. Office U.S. Joint Chiefs of Staff; comdr. Taiwan Patrol Force, chief staff to Comdr. in Chief, Pacific; then comdr. U.S. 6th Fleet Com. Car Div. Six, and then chief of naval operations, 1961-63; U.S. A.E. and P. to Portugal, 1963-66; now chmn. Pres.'s Intelligence Adv. Bd.; dir. Crown Cork & Seal, Value Line Funds, Nat. Airlines, other corps. Decorated D.S.M. with gold star, Legion of Merit, Bronze Star, (U.S.); Order of Precious Tripod (China); Order of Prince Henry the Navigator, Maltese Cross, grand cross of Mil. Merit (Portugal); Order Brit. Empire; cross knight comdrs. Royal Order King George I, grand cross Royal Order of Phoenix (Greece); Great Star of Mil. Merit (Chile); grand ofcl. Order of Naval Merit (Brazil); comdr. Legion of Honor (France); recipient Laetare medal U. Notre Dame, 1963; Sovereign Order Malta. Mem. Naval Acad. Alumni Assn. (pres.), Council Fgn. Relations. K.C. Clubs: The Brook (N.Y.C.); Chevy Chase; N.Y. Yacht; Alfalfa, Metropolitan (Washington). Home: 5907 Frazier Lane McLean VA 22101

ANDERSON, GLENN ELWOOD, investment banker; b. Asheville, N.C., July 24, 1914; s. James Garrett and Lottie Lee (Alexander) A.; A.B., Duke, 1934; m. Grace Elizabeth Curtis, Oct. 10, 1936; children—Glenn Elwood, Charlotte Alexander. With Kirchofer & Arnold, Inc., and successor firm Carolina Securities Corp., Raleigh, N.C., 1934—, beginning as sec., successively v.p., dir., asst. to pres. and dir., exec. v.p. and dir., 1934-55, pres., dir., 1955—; dir. Hydra Computer Corp., Raleigh, Carolina Wholesale Florists, Inc., Sanford, N.C. Natural Gas Co. Fayetteville, N.C., Securities Investor Protection Corp., Washington, Food Town Stores, Inc., Salisbury, N.C. Mem. N.C. Securities Adv. Com. Past v.p. United Fund of Raleigh and Wake County. Mem. Nat. Assn. Securities Dealers (bd. govs. 1958-60, chmn. bus. conduct com. 1959, chmn. bd. 1960), Investment Bankers Assn. Am. (chmn. southeastern group 1962, bd. govs. 1967- 69), Securities Dealers Carolinas (organizer, 1st pres.), Sigma Phi Epsilon. Methodist (trustee). Clubs: Raleigh-Durham Bond (past pres.); Raleigh City, Sphinx (pres. 1965), Carolina Country (Raleigh). Home: 121 Pasquotank Dr Raleigh NC 27609 Office: Carolina Securities Corp P O Box 1071 Raleigh NC 27602

ANDERSON, GODFREY TRYGGVE, educator; b. Chgo., Sept. 4, 1909; s. Andrew and Lottie Bornes A.; Ph.D., Chicago U., 1944; m. Idalene Skillern, 1930; childrenDennis, Marilyn, Constance, Donald. Dean of men, Kingsway Coll., 1937-39; prof. history Atlantic Union Coll., 1939-46; acad. dean, 1944-46; pres. La Sierra Coll., 1946-54; pres. Loma Linda U. (formerly Coll. Med. Evangelists), 1954-67, prof. history, 1967—. Mem. Am. Hist. Assn., Orgn. Am. Historians, World Affairs Council Inland So. Cal. (past pres.). Mem. Seventh-day Adventists. Home: 24783 Lawton Loma Linda CA 92354 Office: Loma Linda CA 92354

ANDERSON, GRANT THRALLS, lawyer; b. Portland, Ore., Apr. 5, 1910; s. James Clifford and Nettie Avis (Thralls) A.; B.A., U. Ore., 1933, J.D., 1936; m. Mildred Lucille Shields, June 19, 1937 (dec. July 1961); children—Sharon Shields (Mrs. John R. Greiner), Franklin Vance (killed in action); m. 2d, Maryesther Agnew, July 1, 1967. Adm. to Ore. bar, 1936, since practiced in Portland; asso. firm Miller, Anderson, Nash, Yerke & Wiener, and predecessors, 1936—, partner, 1948—; instr. Northwestern Coll. Law, 1944-48; atty. Portland pub. schs., Beaverton pub. schs., Multnomah County Intermediate Edn. Dist.; atty., trustee of Pacific U. Mem. Am., Multnomah County bar assns., Am. Judicature Soc., Ore. State Bar, Nat. Pilots Assn., Northwest Aviation Council, Phi Delta Phi. Republican. Mason (32). Clubs: Waverly Country, Multnomah Athletic (Portland); Rotary. Home: 6326 S E Reed College Pl Portland OR 97202 Office: Georgia Pacific Bldg Portland OR 97204

ANDERSON, GUSTAVE THEODORE, physician; b. Gothenburg, Neb., Nov. 5, 1917; s. Joel and Brita (Larson) A.; A.B., U. Neb., 1939, M.D., 1942; postgrad U. Pa. Grad. Sch. Medicine, 1952-53; m. Thelma Ruth Olson, Feb. 12, 1942; children—Douglas Theodore, Joel Edward. Intern St. Luke's Hosp., Denver, 1942-43; commd. lt. (j.g.), M.C., U.S. Navy, 1943, advanced through grades to capt., 1956; jr. med. officer U.S.S. Macdonough, 1943, U.S.S. Gen. John Pope, 1944-45; preceptorship internal medicine with Dr. O.V. Calhoun, Lincoln, Neb., 1946-47; gen. practice medicine, North Platte, Neb., 1947-48; resident dermatology U.S. Naval Hosp., San Diego, 1949-50; comdr. collecting and clearing company, also regtl. surgeon 1st Marines, and exec. officer med. batallion 1st Marine Div., Korea, 1950- 51; resident dermatology U.S. Naval Hosp., Phila., 1951-52; asst. chief dermatology U.S. Naval Hosp., Portsmouth, Va., 1953-58; chief dermatology, port surgeon U.S. Naval Hosp., Yokosuka, Japan, 1958-61; chief dermatology U.S. Naval Hosp., Bethesda, Md., 1961-66; research asst. for advanced med. programs Bur. Medicine, U.S. Navy, 1966-67; ret., 1967; practice medicine specializing in dermatology, Annapolis, Md., 1967—; clin. asst. prof. dermatology Georgetown U. Med. Sch., 1966—. Decorated Legion of Merit, Bronze Star with combat device, Navy Commendation medal with combat device; recipient James Clarke White award Assn. Mil. Surgeons U.S. Diplomate Am. Bd. Dermatology. Mem. A.M.A., Am. Acad. Dermatology, Soc. Investigative Dermatology, Internat. Soc. Tropical Dermatology, Assn. Mil. Dermatologists, Washington, Md. dermatology socs. Home: The Tecumseh Annapolis MD 21403 Office: 16 Murray Av Annapolis MD 21401

ANDERSON, GWEN ODEGAARD, (Mrs. Harlan J. Anderson), mem. Republican Nat. Com.; b. Legnite, N.D., June 3, 1930; d. Adolph and Beatrice (Shannon) Odegaard; student U.S.D., 1948-51; m. Harlan J. Anderson, June 4, 1951; children—Mark Harlan, Barbara Shannon. Precinct committeewoman Benton County Rep. Central Com., Hart, Wash., 1958-60, dist. chmn., Kennewick, Wash., 1959-60, Benton County vice chmn., 1960- 62, state committeewoman, 1962-65; treas. 4th Congl. Dist. Rep. Club, 1963-65; vice chmn. exec. bd., state vice chmn. Wash. Rep. Central Com., Olympia, 1965-68, dir. state precinct tng. program, 1966—; Wash. chmn. Women for Nixon, 1968; mem. Rep. Nat. Com. from Wash., 1968—; del. Wash. Rep. Convs., 1960, 62, 64; adviser to exec. bd. Wash. Fedn. Rep. Women, 1965—. Edn. dir. Ben-Franklin Heart Assn. Bd., 1957-59, dir. compliation Heart Referral Booklet, 1959; mem. Benton Franklin Mental Health and Mental Retardation Com., 1966; publicity chmn. Kennewick Gen. Hosp. Aux. Bd., 1960; patrol leader Columbia Basin council Girl Scouts U.S.A., 1965-67. Mem. Am. Assn. U. Women (past ways and means chmn., sec. Richland br.), Alpha Phi. Lutheran. Clubs: Tri City Country (Kennewick), Tri Cities Alpha Phi Alumnae (past pres.). Editor: (with L. Kramer) A Guide For Good Political Manners, 1965. Editorial bd. Republican Report, 1965-68. Home: 819 W 23d Pl Kennewick WA 99336 Office: Republican State Central Com 497 Tyee Dr Olympia WA 98501

ANDERSON, HARALD, chem. co. exec.; b. Riga, Latvia, May 3, 1926; s. Harry Siegfried and Anna Amalia (Grundins) A.; B.S., Goethe U., Frankfurt/Main, Germany, 1948; m. Aelita Arija Geske, Sept. 22, 1953; children—Ilse, Harald, David, Christine. Came to U.S., 1955, naturalized, 1966. Controller, Cancit, Caracas, Venezuela, 1949-55; pres. Inversiones El Corozo, Caracas, 1956-61, Bridgewater Realty Corp., 1968—; adminstrv. dir. Hoechst Remedia, Caracas, 1962-64; v.p., treas. Am. Hoechst Corp., Bridgewater, N.J., 1964—, dir., 1965—; dir. chmn. bd. Behring Diagnostics, Inc., Woodbury, N.Y.; dir. Azoplate Corp., Murray Hill, N.J., Tri-Point Industries, Inc., Commack, L.I., N.Y., Hystron Fibers, Inc. Lutheran. Address: PO Box 2500 Somerville NJ 08876

ANDERSON, HAROLD ALBERT, engring. and bldg. exec.; b. Beverly, Mass., Jan. 19, 1908; s. John Albert and Ann (Westerberg) A.; C.E., Tufts Coll., 1928; m. Grace Whittaker, Apr. 24, 1936; children—Harold Albert, Richard A., Robert W. With Austin Co., Cleve., 1928—, exec. v.p., gen. mgr., 1958—, pres., 1963—, also chief exec. officer, 1969—. Registered profl. engr. 47 states, P.R., Nfld., N.S., N.B. Mem. Euclid Gen. Hosp. Assn. Am. Soc. C.E., Nat. Soc. Profl. Engrs. Clubs: Union, Hermit Mayfield Country (Cleveland); Bay Head (N.J.) Yacht. Home: 2731 Chesterton Rd Shaker Heights OH 44122 Office: 3650 Mayfield Rd Cleveland OH 44121

ANDERSON, HAROLD E., business exec.; b. Jamestown, N.Y., 1916; grad. Benjamin Franklin U., 1937; married. With Eagle-Picher Industries, Inc., Cin., 1946—, comptroller, chief accounting officer, 1960—. Office: 800 Am Bldg Cincinnati OH 45202*

ANDERSON, HAROLD H., publisher; b. Princeton, Ill., June 27, 1901, s. A. Clarence and Hilda (Linder) A.; B.S., Northwestern, 1924; m. Virginia Copeland, Feb. 20, 1926; 1 dau., Carolyn. Sales mgr. Asso. Editors, Inc., Chgo., 1924-25; partner Publishers Syndicate, Chicago, 1925-62; pres., exec. editor Publishers Newspaper Syndicate, 1963-67; chmn. Publishers-Hall Syndicate, 1967-68; co-founder Am. Inst. Pub. Opinion, 1935; dir. Am. Hosp. Supply Corp. Trustee Northwestern U., Wesley Hosp. Mem. Phi Gamma Delta. Methodist. Clubs: University, Chicago (Chicago); Glen View (Golf, Ill.); Indian Hill (Winnetka, Ill); Ocean-Country of Fla. (Delray). Home: 1420 Sheridan Rd Willmette IL 60091 Office: 111 W Monroe St Chicago IL 60603

ANDERSON, HAROLD HOMER, psychologist; b. Dakota City, Neb., Oct. 23, 1897; s. Samuel Lilley and Mary (Inglis) A.; S.B., Harvard, 1922; Diplome, Rousseau Inst., Geneva, Switzerland, 1928; Certificat de Pédagogie, U. of Geneva, 1928, Ph.D., 1929; m. Gladys Marie Lowe, June 30, 1927 (dec. June 17, 1965); children—Janet Lowe (Mrs. John W. Twente, Jr.), Theodore Inglis Anderson, m. 2d, Thelma Chapman Jean, Apr. 28, 1969. Research assistant prof. psychology Ia. Child Welfare Research Sta., State U. Ia., 1929-36; specialist in emergency nursery schs., U.S. Office Edn. and Fed. Emergency Relief Adminstrn., Washington, 1934; asst. prof. psychology U. Ill., 1936-41, asso. prof., 1941- 46; prof. psychology, head dept. Mich. State U., 1946-55, research prof., 1955-66, research professor emeritus, 1966—; summer sch. faculty Okla. A. and M. Coll., 1937, State U. Ia., 1937, U. Cal., 1942; guest dir. Summer Mental Hygiene Workshop, U. Omaha, 1951-53; sabbatical leave from U. Ill. at U. Cal., 1942-43; specialist U.S. Dept. State, Frankfurt-Main, Germany, Workshop Modern Psychologies and Edn., 1952; research, Karlsruhe, Germany, project dir. U.S. HICOG and Hochschule for International Padagogische Forschung, Sept. 1952: sabbatical from Mich. State U. for research in Mexico, 1953, 63; Fulbright research prof. psychology U. Frankfurt Main, Germany, 1953-54; internat. research lectr. in psychology U. Stockholm, Oslo and Helsinki, 1954; prin. investigator Research in Creativity, 1956—; cons. White House Conf. Children and Youth, 1960, Centro de Investigaciones Sociales, Monterrey, Mexico, 1960-63. Bd. dirs. Ingham County (Mich.) Rehab. Center, 1953-61, chmn., 1959- 61. Served with S.A.T.C., Harvard, 1918. Diplomate in clin. psychology Am. Bd. Examiners in Profl. Psychology, 1948. Fellow Am. Psych. Assn., Am. Orthopsychiat. Assn. (dir. 1948-50, v.p. 1952-53), A.A.A.S., Am. Edn. Research Assn.; mem. Midwestern, Mich. (pres. 1950-51) psychol. assns., Soc. for Research in Child Devel., Soc. for Psychol. Study Social Issues, Nat. Com. for Mental Hygiene, Mich. Acad. Sci., Inter-Am. Soc. Psychology (treas. 1957-61, pres. elect 1961-63, pres. 1963-64), Sociedad Argentina Piscologia (hon. mem.), World Fedn. for Mental Health, Nat. Gerontological Assn., Sigman Xi. Unitarian. Editor: (with Gladys L. Anderson) Introduction to Projective Techniques, 1951. Creativity and its Cultivation, 1959; Creativity in Childhood and Adolescence, 1965. Contbr. tech., profl. publs. Home: 282 Maplewood Dr East Lansing MI 48823

ANDERSON, HAROLD O'NEILL, banker; b. Paducah, Ky., May 22, 1909; s. Isaac O'Neill and Rose (Smith) A.; student business coll., also banking courses; m. Victoria E. LaBat, Aug. 20, 1933; childrenHarold Thomas, Donna Jean (Mrs. Anthony A. Post), Carol Lee, Vicky Lynn. With Bank of Am., 1927-29; with First Nat. Bank Denver, 1929-, auditor, 1950-; tchr. in field, 1958-. Chartered bank auditor. Mem. Bank Adminstrn. Inst. (past chmn. various coms.). Methodist. Author articles. Home: 32 Morningside Dr Denver, CO 80215. Office: First Nat Bank Denver Denver CO 80217

ANDERSON, HARRY FREDERICK, Jr., architect; b. Chgo., Feb. 4, 1927; s. Harry Frederick and Sarah Matilda (Anderson) A.; B.Arch., Ill. Inst. Tech., 1953; m. Frances Annette Zeilstra, Jan. 27, 1951; children—Scott H., Mark S., Robert R., Grant Alan. Chief draftsman Stade & Cooley, Chgo., 1953-55; partner firm Stade, Dolan & Anderson, Chgo., 1955-65; project architect Perkins & Will Partnership, Chgo., 1965-67, partner, v.p., 1967—; prin. works include Rockford Coll. (Ill.) Library, 1967, Sci. Bldg., 1968, Arts Complex, 1970, Women's Dormitory, 1969; Silver Cross Hosp., Joliet, Ill., 1971; Westlake Hosp., Melrose Park, Ill., 1970; Am. Soc. Clin. Pathologists bldg., Chgo., 1971. Chmn. adv. council Booth Meml. Hosp., Chgo., 1969—; adv. bd. Chgo. Salvation Army, 1969—. Served with USNR, 1944-47. Mem. A.I.A., Internat. Hosp. Fedn., Am. Pub. Health Assn., Am. Hosp. Assn., A.L.A., Am. Assn. Jr. Colls., Ill. Assn. Profls., Guild Religious Architecture, Ill. Pub. Health Assn., Am. Arbitration Assn. Lutheran (dir. Mo. Synod). Club: University (Chgo.). Home: 1001 Hastings St Park Ridge IL 60068 Office: 309 W Jackson Blvd Chicago IL 60606

ANDERSON, HARRY LOY, banker, lawyer; b. Palmetto, Fla., Oct. 15, 1907; s. Harry Sigler and Margaret (Loy) A.; LL.B., Stetson U., 1928; m. Therese Vivienne Areeneaux, Oct. 17, 1935; children—Andrea, Therese, Harry Loy, Denise. Admitted to Fla. bar, 1928, D.C. bar, 1938, U.S. Supreme Ct., 1934; practiced in Ocala, Fla., 1928-34, Washington, 1942-56; pros. atty. Marion County, Fla., 1930-32; partner firm Duckett, Gill & Anderson, Washington, 1953-56, Bowie & Anderson Co., Washington, 1953-56; pres., dir. First Fed. Savs. & Loan Assn., West Palm Beach, Fla., 1958—; dir. Riggs Bank, Washington, Fairfax County Nat. Bank (Va.), Atlantic Nat. Bank, West Palm Beach, Walker & Dunlop Co., Washington, Washington Mut. Ins. Co., Washington Life Ins. Devel. Corp., Anderson & Co., Inc., Washington, Szemco, Inc., Molecular Research, Inc. (both West Palm Beach), Fed. Home Loan Bank Greensboro, Nat. Life Ins. Co. Fla., Financial Fire & Casualty Co., Key Biscayne Bank (Fla.), Blvd. Nat. Bank, Miami, Fla. Bd. dirs. Fla. Indsl. Devel. Corp.; mem. S. Fla. Regional Export Expansion council U.S. dept. Commerce; mem. Small Bus. Adminstrn., Small Bus. Adv. Council for Fla.; mem. Fla. World's Fair Authority; adv. council naval affairs Sixth Naval Dist. State dir. Orange Bowl Com., Miami. Pres. elect Heart Assn. of Palm Beach, Martin counties; chmn. bd. Heart Assn. West Palm Beach. Mem. Fla. Council of 100. Treas. Fla. Kennedy-Johnson Campaign, 1960. Bd. dirs. Boys Club Am., Met. Police Boys Club, Father-Son Boys Clubs; tustee St. Mary's Hosp., Palm Beach County Trust Fund; mem. exec. adv. com. Fla. Atlantic U. Recipient Pop Warner award. Mem. Fla., D.C. bar assns., Home Builders Assn. Am., Nat. Assn. Real Estate Bds., Mortgage Bankers Assn. Am., Nat. Assn. Ins. Agys., Fla. C. of C. (dir.), U.S., (legislative com.), Fla. (legislative com.), Nat. savs. and loan leagues, S.A.R., Sigma Nu. Democrat. Methodist. Mason (Shriner). Clubs: Rotary (West Palm Beach); Burning Tree, Congressional (pres. 1952-56) (Washington); Seminole, Bath and Tennis, Everglades, Beach, Coral Beach (Palm Beach); Country of Fla.; Metropolitan (N.Y.C.). Home: 196 Banyan Rd Palm Beach FL 33480 Office: 215 S Olive Av West Palm Beach FL 33480

ANDERSON, HARRY ROBERT, govt. ofcl., rancher; b. Hilmar, Cal., May 21, 1910; s. Emil and Emma (Franson) A.; B.S. in Bus. Adminstrn., U. Cal. at Berkeley, 1934; m. Merle Kueny, Aug. 12, 1941; 1 dau., Bettina (Mrs. Stephen F. Sims). With Cal. Dept. Finance, 1935-52, budget analyst, adminstrv. officer, 1952-61; dep. dir. Cal., Dept. Fish and Game, 1961-65; asst. sec. Dept. Interior for pub. land mgmt., 1965-69; adminstrv. asst. to Congressman Glen Anderson, 17th dist. Cal., 1969—. Served to capt. USAAF, 1942-46. Democrat. Lutheran. Mason (Shriner). Clubs: Valley Hi Country (Sacramento); Army-Navy Country (Arlington, Va.). Home: 729 S Pitt St Alexandria VA 22314 Office: House Office Bldg Washington DC 20240

ANDERSON, HENRY BRACKENRIDGE, lawyer; b. Wilkinsburg, Pa., May 30, 1918; s. Henry B. and I. Adella (Stewart) A.; B.A., Wesleyan U., Middletown, Conn., 1940, M.A., 1948; LL.B, cum laude, U. Conn., 1948; m. Audrey E. Matthews, June 25, 1952; children- William H. Buker III (stepson), David Lowell, Brooke Stewart (Mrs. Pacifico S. Uminga), Bettina Stewart. Asst. to dean freshman Wesleyan U., 1940-41; admitted to Conn. bar, 1948; trial justice Town of Sherman, 1948-50; partner Cramer & Anderson and predecessor firms, New Milford, 1951—; town counsel, Sherman, 1948—; judge Probate Dist. Sherman, 1951-58. Bd. dirs. deSherbinin Products, Inc., Hawleyville; corporator New Milford Savs. Bank; regional dir. Union Trust Co. of New Haven, Danbury, Conn. Mem. exec.com. Conn. Probate Assembly. Chmn. Bd. Edn., Sherman, 1967—. Bd. dirs. Conn. Attys. Title Guaranty Fund, Hartford; trustee New Milford Hosp. Served to lt. comdr. USNR, 1941-46; PTO. Decorated Silver Star medal, Bronze Star medal. Mem. Am., Conn. (mem. exec. com. real properties sect.), Litchfield County (past pres.) bar assns., Alpha Chi Rho. Republican. Conglist. Home: Route 55 Sherman CT 06784 Office: 21 Main St New Milford CT 06776

ANDERSON, HERBERT ADOLPH, univ. dean; b. Jeffries, Wis., May 15, 1918; s. Andrew and Anna (Carlson) A.; B.S., Stout State U., 1944; M.A., U. Minn., 1947; Ed.D., U. Mo., 1953; m. Merle Irene Hansen, Feb. 21, 1943; children—Nancy Jane (Mrs. Douglas Milner), Deanna Mae, Gary Lee. Tchr. heat treating USAAF, Chanute Field, Ill., 1942-43; tchr. Central High Sch., Red Wing, Minn., 1944-47, Stanford U. contract, Philippines, 1957-60; with Stout State U., 1948-57, 60—, dean Sch. Applied Sci. and Tech., 1966—. Dir. Stout State U. Found., 1967-70. Eichelberger scholar, 1940-41. Mem. Wis. Indsl. Edn. Assn. (pres.), N.E.A., Am. Vocational Assn., Am. Indsl. Arts Assn., Nat. Assn. Indsl. Tchr. Educators. Editorial bd. School Shop, 1969—. Home: 1001 N Shore Dr Menomonie WI 54751

ANDERSON, HERBERT E., clergyman; b. Madrid, Ia., Mar. 1, 1916: s. Oscar Albim and Ellen (Peterson) A.; B.A., Wheaton (Ill.) Coll., 1941; B.D., Princeton Theol. Sem., 1947; D.D. (hon.), Western Baptist Theol. Sem., Portland, Ore., 1962; m. Alice Elizabeth Johnson, Sept. 28, 1943; children—Mark, Karen, Stephen, Timothy, James, Peter. Ordained to ministry Bapt. Ch., 1948: dir. Salem (Ore.) Youth Center, 1947-48; pastor in Gladstone, Ore., 1948- 52, The Dalles, Ore., 1952-58, Lebanon, Ore., 1958-62; gen. dir. Conservative Bapt. Fgn. Mission Soc., Wheaton, Ill., 1967-71; pastor Hinson Meml. Bapt. Ch., Portland, Ore., 1971—. Mem. bd. Conservative Bapt. Assn. Am. 1958-63, pres., 1963-67; moderator Conservatie Bapt. Assn. Ore., 1961-62. Bd. dirs. Western Bapt. Theol. Sem., Judson Bapt. Coll., Portland. Home: 1137 S E 20th St Portland OR 97214 Office: 1137 SE 20th St Portland OR 97214

ANDERSON, HERBERT HENRY, naval officer; b. Campbell, N.Y., Nov. 21, 1918; s. Walter and Grace M. (Axtell) A.; student Bucknell U., 1936-37; B.S., U.S. Naval Acad., 1941; M.B.A., Harvard, 1953; grad. Nat. War Coll., 1959; m. Marguerite Cornell, Dec. 18, 1949. Commd. ensign U.S. Navy, 1941, advanced through grades to rear adm., 1967; comdg. officer U.S.S. George, 1946-47, U.S.S. Zellars, 1953-55; dir. Navy Mgmt. Sch., Monterey, Cal., 1959-62; comdg. ofcr. U.S.S. Halsey, 1963-64; comdr. Destroyer Squadron 17, 1964-65; dir. program change div. Navy Dept., 1965-67; asst. chief naval personnel for edn. and tng., Navy Dept., 1967-69; comdr. Cruiser-Destroyer Flotilla 11, U.S. Pacific Fleet, 1969-70; comdr. U.S. South Atlantic Force, 1970-71; dir. Policy Plans and NSC Affairs Office of Sec. Def., Washington, 1971—. Decorated Navy Commendation medal with gold star, Legion of Merit with gold star. Mem. Nat. Acad. Mgmt., Sigma Chi. Methodist Episcopalian. Home: 1151 W Water St Elmira NY 14905 Office: Dir Policy Plans NSC Affairs OASD (ISA) Pentagon Washington DC 20350

ANDERSON, HERBERT LAWRENCE, physicist; b. N.Y.C., May 24, 1914; s. Joseph and Sima (Goldberg) A.; A.B., Columbia, 1935, B.S., 1936, Ph.D., 1941; m. Jean Betty Clough, Jan. 11, 1947; childrenFaith Alexandra, Clifton Leon, Kelley Pierce, Dana Zachary. Research asst. Columbia, 1940-42; physicist, metall. lab. U. Chgo., 1942-45, asst. prof., 1946, asso. prof., 1947-50, dir. constrn. 170 inch synchrocyclotron, 1947-51, prof., 1950—; sr. physicist physicist Los Alamos Lab., U. Cal., 1945-46; chmn. subcom. neutron standards NRC, 1947-49; cons. U.S. Naval Ordnance Test Sta., Inyokern, 1953; prof. physics, dir. Enrico Fermi Inst. Nuclear Studies, U. Chgo., 1958-63. Guggenheim fellow, 1956; Fulbright lectr., Italy, 1957. Fellow Am. Phys. Soc.; mem. Nat. Acad. Scis. Home: 4923 Kimbark Av Chicago, IL 60615.

ANDERSON, HERBERT R., ret. bus. exec.; b. Elizabeth, N.J., Aug. 20, 1903; s. August and Charlotte (Berglund) A.; student pub. schs.; m. Laurette Elsesser, Feb. 16, 1929; two children. With Group Securities, Inc., Jersey City, 1934—, dir., 1939—, pres., 1950-64, chmn., 1964-71; cons., former vice chmn. Distbrs. Group, Inc.; former sr. v.p., dir. US Life Corp. Pres. Investment Co. Inst., 1958-60. Mem. Investment Bankers Assn. Am. (chmn. investment cos. com 1961-63, gov. 1966-69), Nat. Assn. Securities Dealers. Home: 503 Colonial Av Westfield NJ 07090 also 12169 Turtle Beach Rd North Palm Beach FL 33408

ANDERSON, HOWARD CLEVENGER, utility exec., lawyer; b. Gloucester, N.J., Dec. 3, 1910; s. Howard C. and Bertha M. (Ducey) A.; A.B., Princeton, 1931; LL.B., Harvard, 1934. Admitted to N.Y. bar, 1934, D.C. bar, 1958; asso. firm Root, Clark, Buckner & Ballantine, N.Y.C., 1934-46; atty. Western Electric Co., Inc., N.Y.C., 1946-56, gen. solicitor, 1956-58; v.p., gen. counsel Chesapeake & Potomac telephone cos. of Washington, Va., Md. and W.Va., 1958—. Mem. Am. Bar Assn., Bar Assn. of D.C., Bar Assn. City N.Y., Phi Beta Kappa. Clubs: Metropolitan, Columbia (Washington); Princeton (N.Y.C.). Home: 5302 Elliott Rd Washington 16 DC Office: 1710 H St NW Washington DC 20006

ANDERSON, HOWARD RICHMOND, educator, cons. editor; b. N.Y.C., Oct. 1, 1898; s. Lars Gustav and Charlotte (Johnson) A.; A.B., Augustana Coll., 1922; A.M., U. Chgo., 1928; Ph.D., U. Ia., 1930; m. Greta Karling. June 27, 1923 (div. 1951); children—William Howard, Douglas Gustav; m. 2d, Monica Luffman, Dec. 2, 1951; children—Monica Jane, James Stewart. Head social studies Theodore Roosevelt High Sch., Wyandette, Mich., 1922-28; head social studies Univ. High Sch., also asst. prof. history U. Ia., 1930-37; dir. social studies Ithaca pub. schs. and prof edn. Cornell U., 1937-44; dir. Sch. Edn., also dir. summer sessions Cornell, 1944-46; specialist for social scis. U.S. Office Edn., Washington, 1946-48, chief instrnl. problems, 1948-51, chief for social scis., 1951-54; dean Univ. Sch., dir. summer session U. Rochester, 1954-60, provost, 1960-61 sr. cons. editor, secondary school dept. Houghton Mifflin-Co., Boston, 1961—. Served as 1st sgt. inf. U.S. Army, 1917-19, AEF one yr. Decorated Croce dir Guerra (Italy). Mem. com. edn. for dem. citizenship Nat. Assn. Secondary Sch. Principals and Nat. Council for Social Studies, 1941-45; mem. U.S. delegation to UNESCO seminar on improvement of textbooks, Belgium, 1950. Member of staff, UNESCO seminar on teaching of history, France, 1951. Member Nat. Council for Social Studies (pres. 1940), N.E.A., Am. Ednl. Research Assn., Nat. Soc. for Study Edn., Am. Hist. Assn., Phi Delta Kappa. Democrat. Lutheran. Co-author serveral books, 1931-; The History of Our World, 1959. Editor 13th and 25th yearbooks Nat. Council Social Studies. Home: 40 Arrowhead Rd Weston, MA 02193. Office: 110 Tremont St Boston MA 02107

ANDERSON, HOWARD STONE, clergyman; b. Durand, Wis., July 2, 1905; s. Frank Howard and Ada (Stone) A.; A.B., U. Omaha, 1925; B.D., Chgo. Theol. Sem., 1928; D.D., Doane Coll., 1942; m. Marlowe Addy, Mar. 23, 1927; children—Polly Jo (Mrs. Roger K. Graham), Marlowe Mercedes (Mrs. Alan R. Kidston), Chloe Sylvia (Mrs. Paul D. Nassau). Ordained to ministry Congl. Ch., 1927; student pastor Peoria Heights Congl. Ch., Peoria, Ill., 1927-28; pastor First Congl. Ch., Williston, N.D., 1928-32, Warren Av. Congl. Ch., Chgo., 1932-36, First Congl. Ch., Washington, 1936-47, United Ch., Bridgeport, Conn., 1947-51 Searsdale (N.Y.) Congl. Ch., 1951-62; minister and supt. So. Cal. and Southwest Conf. United Ch. of Christ, 1962-65; sr. minister Old First Ch., Springfield, Mass., 1965-68; minister First Congregational United Church of Christ, Washington, 1968-70, emeritus, 1970—; minister parish life Second Congl. Ch., Greenwich, Conn., 1970—; lecturer at annual ministers conferences Hampton Institute, 1942, 1944, School of Methods, Morgan Coll., 1943, 44, 45, Sch. Religion, Howard U., 1944; coll. preacher George Washington U., Md. U., Hampton Inst., Howard U., Am. U., Talladega, West Point Mil. Acad., Middlebury Coll., Conn. Coll. Dir. Middle Atlantic Conf. Congl. Christian Chs., 1937-43, exec. com., pres. bd. dirs., 1938-43; dir. bd. home missions congl. Christian Chs., 1946- 54, exec. com., 1946-54, pres. bd., 1952-54; dir. Am. Missionary Assn.; exec. com. Internat. Council Congl. Christian Chs.; mem. gen. commn. on Army and Navy chaplains, 1937-47, exec. com., 1939-41; mem. commn. on evangelism and devotional life Congl. denomination, 1938-44, com. on religious life in nation's capital, 1936-47; del. gen. council Congl. Christian Chs., 1938, 40, 46, 48, 50; exchange preacher to Holland and British Isles, auspices Nat. Council Chs. in U.S. and Brit. Council Chs., 1958. Trustee Howard U., also vice chmn., chmn. exec. com. Mem. Washington Ministerial Union (pres. 1941-42), Theta Phi Delta. Rotarian. Home: 2 Putnam Hill Greenwich CT 06830 Office: 139 E Putnam Av Greenwich CT 06830

ANDERSON, HOWELL WHITEHEAD, banker; b. Wilson, N.C., Aug. 19, 1906; s. Wilson Puryear and Lucy (Whitehead) A.; student U.N.C., 1927; m. Mary Frances Herring, Jan. 23, 1935; children—Howell Whitehead, Frances Lynwood. Pres. Watson Warehouse, Inc., Wilson, 1938-52, chmn. bd., 1952-67, dir., 1935-67; pres., dir. Wilson Radio Co., 1948-67, Greenville Radio Co. (N.C.), 1954-67, Anderson Creech Oil Co., Greensboro, N.C., 1948-67, Anderson Creech Transp. Co., Greensboro, 1956-67; v.p. Brunswick Navigation Co., Southport, N.C., 1936-52, pres., dir., 1952-67; v.p. N.C. TV Co., 1954-55; pres. Coastal Gas Corp., Goldsboro, 1955-56; partner Kenwood & Co., real estate, Wilson, 1953-67; chmn. exec. com. First Union Nat. Bank, Charlotte, N.C., 1967—; chmn. exec. com., vice chmn. bd. First Union Nat. Bancorp., Charlotte, 1968—; dir. Nat. Bank Wilson. Dir. Wilson Civil Def., 1953-67; mem. Eastern Carolina Airport Authority, 1954, Wilson Airport Authority, 1957-67. Served to capt. USAAF, 1942-45. Mem. Wilson C. of C. (pres. 1950), Zeta Psi. Methodist. Clubs: Charlotte City; Gulf Stream Golf, Gulf Stream Bath and Tennis (pres.) (Delray Beach). Home: 1117 Beach Dr Delray Beach FL 33444 Office: 301 S Tryon St Charlotte NC 28201

ANDERSON, HUGH HANSON, hotel cons.; b. Dallas, Oct. 4, 1914; s. Robert C. and Ellen (Wilkins) A.; student U. Houston, 1946-47; m. Dorothy L. Knudsen, Aug. 4, 1949; childrenAnn L., David A. With Adolphus Hotel, Dallas, 1934-39; asst. mgr. Biltmore Hotel, Oklahoma City, 1939-41; resident mgr. White Plaza Hotel, Dallas, 1946-50; mgr. Hotel Texas, Ft. Worth, 1950-57; mng. dir. Adolphus Hotel, 1956-66; gen. mgr. Roosevelt Hotel, New Orleans, 1966-69; 1966-69; hotel-motel cons., developer, 1969—; dir. Dallas Hotel Co. Served with USAAF, 1941-46. Mem. Tex. Hotel Assn. (dir.), New Orleans Hotel-Motel Assn. Clubs: Lakewood Country, City, Lions (Dallas), New Orleans Athletic. Address: Willow Lakes Farm Lewisville TX 75067

ANDERSON, HURST ROBINS, univ. pres.; b. Cleveland, Sept. 1904; s. Foster C. and Ora Estelle (Robins) A.; A.B., Ohio Wesleyan Univ., 1926; student Mich. Law Sch., 1927-28; M.S., Northwestern U., 1934; LL.D., Ohio Wesleyan U., 1949; Litt.D., Simpson Coll., 1958; Ed.D., U. Chattanooga, 1960; L.H.D., DePauw U., 1963, Neb. Wesleyan U., 1966; LL.D., Albright Coll., 1965; D.P.S., Ohio No., 1966; workshop in higher edn. Chgo., summer 1939, Gen. Edn. Bd. Rockefeller Found. fellows in Higher Edn., 1941; m. Marian Charlene Powell, Aug. 24, 1932; children—Sarah Jane, Powell Robins, Kathleen Ruth. Asst. alumni sec., Ohio Wesleyan, 1926-27; instr. English lang. and debate Allegheny Coll., 1928-31, asst. prof., 1931-32, asst. prof. speech, 1932-39, asso. prof., 1931-40, prof., 43, registrar, 1940; pres. Centenary Jr. Coll., 1943-48: pres. Hamline U., St. Paul, 1948-52; pres. Am. U., Washington, 1952—, hon. chancellor, 1968—; v.p. U. Senate Meth. Ch.; exec. dir. Methodist Corp., 1969—. Pres., Jr. coll. council Middle Atlantic States Assn., 1947-48, N.J. Assn. Colls. and Univs., 1946-48; pres. Nat. Assn. Schs. and Colls. Meth. Ch., 1964-65; exec. bd. World Meth. Council; past pres. Assn. Am. Colls.; bd. dirs. D.C. League for Nursing. Dir. United Tanker Corp., 1st Nat. Bank Washington. Mem. Fed. City Council, Washington. Trustee Washington Center Met. Studies, Wesley Jr. Coll., Dover, Del., Internat. Found.; mem. bd. govs. Wesley Theol. Sem., Washington; bd. regents Am. Found. for Greece; hon. chmn. Sino-Am. Cultural Com.; past chmn. com. Inter Am. Schs. Service: vice chmn. 1960 White House Conf. on Children and Youth; vice chmn. Bd. Fgn. Scholarships; exec. com. Am. Friends Middle East; v.p. Nat. Council of Churches, U.S.A., 1966-69; bd. dirs. Council Protestant Colls. and Univs. Named Ky. col. Member N.A.T.S., Kappa Phi Kappa, Delta Sigma Rho, Omicron Delta Kappa, Sigma Alpha Epsilon, Pi Sigma Alpha, Alpha Phi Omega, Phi Kappa Phi. Republican. Methodist. Clubs: Cosmos, University (hon.) (Washington). Author: Practical Speaking; many articles in ednl. publs. Home: 4100 Cathedral Av NW Washington DC also 1317 Harsh Rd Lakeside OH 43440

ANDERSON, IAIN MAIR, automobile mfg. co. exec.; b. Calcutta, India, May 11, 1931; s. Ian Hoyle and Elizabeth (Wilson) A.; chartered accountant, Glasgow (Scotland) U., 1953; m. Joan Gordon Sutherland, Oct. 30, 1954; childrenIan Gordon, Kenneth Sutherland, Joan Elizabeth. Came to U.S., 1963. Chartered accountant, 1948-53; asst. treas. Boynton Acceptance Co., Toronto, Can., 1954-55; financial, mfg. and purchasing positions with Ford Motor Co. Cn., 1955-63; with Am. Motors Co., 1963—, operations control dir., 1965-66, controller, 1966—, v.p., 1967—; dir. Holmes Foundry, Sarnia, Ont., Can. Home: 1295 Chesterfield St Birmingham MI 48009 Office: 14250 Plymouth Rd Detroit MI 48232

ANDERSON, IRA DENNIS, educator; b. Mentone, Ind., Sept. 8, 1907; s. Emra D. and Lenna (Coplen) A.; B.S., Ind. U., 1929; M.B.A., Northwestern U., 1930, Ph.D., 1944; m. Virginia McCarty, Aug. 22, 1931; children—Dennis M., Michael C. Acting asst. prof. merchandising U. N.D., 1931-32, instr. accounting, 1932; instr. marketing and merchandising Ind. U., summer 1932, acting asst. prof., 1933; asst. prof. bus. adminstrn. Ohio Wesleyan U., 1933-35; asst. chief retail trade U.S. Bur. of Census, 1935-37; asst. prof. marketing Northwestern U., 1937-44, asso. prof. marketing, 1944-49, prof. marketing, 1949-, chmn. marketing dept., 1950-53, asso. dean, dir. undergrad div., 1953-63; vis. asso. prof. marketing U. Cal. at Los Angeles, summer 1949. Am. cons. to Spl. Com on Commerce Edn., India, summer 1959. Mem. Am. Marketing Assn. (pres. 1955), American Association University Professors, Alpha Kappa Psi, Beta Gamma Sigma frats., also Acacia. Clubs: Northwestern University Faculty; University (Evanston). Author: Principles of Retailing (with C. W. Barker), 1935, rev., 1941 (with C. W. Barker, J. D. Butterworth) rev. 1956. Home: 1930 Orrington Av Evanston IL 60201

ANDERSON, IRVING CHARLES, oil co. exec.; b. Morton, N.Y., Aug. 25, 1916; s. Charles and Bessie (Altpeter) A.; B.S. in Chem. Engring., Syracuse U., 1937; grad. Northwestern U. Inst. Mgmt., 1956; m. Lucille Stothard, Aug. 21, 1941; children—Stephen Stothard, Debra Lee. Refinery engr. affiliate of Standard Oil Co. (N.J.), Aruba, Netherlands Antilles, head control group, 1937-42; with Esso Research & Engring. Co., 1942-47, with Creole Petroleum Corp., 1947-61, mgr. export sales, 1958-60, v.p., 1960-61; v.p. cargo sales dept. Esso Internat., Inc., 1961-66, v.p. dir., 1966-69, sr. v.p., dir., mem. exec. com., 1969-70; fuel oil coordinator Standard Oil Co. (N.J.), 1970—. Active Cub Scouts Am., Little League Baseball. Mem. Am. Petroleum Inst., Pi Kappa Alpha, Alpha Chi Sigma. Conglist. (trustee). Clubs: Echo Lake Country (Westfield, N.J.); Touchdown, N.Y. Athletic, Hemisphere (N.Y.C.). Home: 50 Birch Lane Short Hills NJ 07078 Office: 15 W 51st St New York City NY 10020

ANDERSON, J. BLAINE, lawyer; b. Trenton, Utah, Jan. 19, 1922; s. Leslie Howard and Theo Ellen (Stocking) A.; student U. Ida., 1940-41, U. Wash., 1945-46; LL.B., U. Ida., 1949; m. Grace Little, Nov. 14, 1944; children—J. Eric, J. Blaine, Leslie Ann, Dirk Brian. Admitted to Ida. bar, 1949, since practiced in Blackfoot; partner firm Furchner and Anderson, and predecessor law firms, 1955—. Chmn. Ida. Air Pollution Commn., 1959-60. Fellow Am. Coll. Trial Lawyers; mem. Am. Bar Assn. (mem. ho. of dels. 1959-60, 64—, gov. 1971—, mem. council gen. practice sect. 1962-66, 70—, mem. adv. bd. editors Jour. 1969—), Am. Coll. Trial Lawyers, Ida. State Bar (bd. commrs. 1958-61, pres. 1960-61, chmn. unauthorized practice of law com. 1955-58), S.E. Ida. Dist. Bar (pres. 1957-58), Am. Judicature Soc. (dir. 1961-66), Am. Coll. Probate Counsel. Mason, Elk. Home: 658 Airport Rd Blackfoot ID 83221 Office: 178 W Judicial St Blackfoot ID

ANDERSON, J. D., ins. co. exec.; b. Hobart, Okla., Sept. 2, 1913; s. William D. and Grace (Underwood) A.; student Okla. U., 1931-32; B.A., Central State Coll., Edmond, Okla., 1936; LL.D. (hon.), Neb. Wesleyan U., 1966; m. Kathleen Joy Jones, July 25, 1940; children—Ann (Mrs. Don Cavaleri), Kay (Mrs. Jerry Rekers), Mary, James D. Prin., coach Ryan (Okla.) High Sch., 1936-39; dist. rep. Mid-Continent Life Co., Chickasha, Okla., 1939-45, agy. dir., Oklahoma City, 1946-49, agy. v.p. and dir., 1950-54; agy. v.p., dir. Guarantee Mut. Life Co., Omaha, Neb., 1954-59, exec. v.p., 1959-61, pres., 1961—; dir. Pullman Co., Chgo., U.S. Nat. Bank. Bd. dirs. Mid-Am. council Boy Scouts Am., Met. YMCA, Jr. Achievement, Omaha Symphony Assn., Girls Town, Nat. Conf. Christians and Jews, Neb. Meth. Hosp.; gen. chmn. United Appeal, 1968; trustee Omaha Indsl. Found.; pres. trustees Neb. Wesleyan U. Served to lt. comdr. UNSR, 1942-45; ETO, PTO. Mem. Omaha Met. Assn. Churches (pres.), Omaha C. of C. (pres. 1969, dir.), Am. Life Conv. (dir.), Life Office Mgmt. Assn. (dir.), Omaha Sales and Marketing Execs. (pres. 1957), Navy League, Ad-Sell, Air Force Assn. Methodist. Clubs: Downtown Rotary (pres.), Oak Hills Country (dir.), Happy Hollow, Plaza, Omaha (Omaha). Home: 9511 Westchester Lane Omaha NB 68114 Office: 8721 Indian Hills Dr Omaha NB 68114

ANDERSON, JACK NORTHMAN, newspaper columnist; b. Long Beach, Cal., Oct. 19, 1922; s. Orlando N. and Agnes (Mortensen) A.; student U. Utah, 1940-41, Georgetown U., 1947- 48, George Washington U., 1948; m. Olivia Farley, Aug. 10, 1949; children—Cheri, Lance F., Laurie, Tina, Kevin N., Randy, Tanya, Rodney, Bryan. Reporter, Salt Lake Tribune, 1939-41; war corr. Deseret News, 1945; reporter Washington Merry-go-Round, 1947—, partner, 1965—; Washington editor Parade mag., 1954-68, bur. chief, 1968—. Missionary in Southern states for Church Jesus Christ of Latter Day Saints, 1941- 44; sec., trustee Chinese Refugee Relief, 1962—. Served with U.S. Mcht. Marine, 1944-45; with AUS, 1946-47. Mem. White House Corr. Assn. Club: National Press (Washington). Author: (with Ronald May) McCarthy the Man, the Senator, The Ism, 1952; (with Fred Blumenthal) The Kefauver Story, 1956; (with Drew Pearson) U.S.A.Second Class Power?, 1958; Washington Expose, 1966; Case Against Congress (with Drew Pearson), 1968. Home: 7300 Burdette Ct Bethesda MD 20034 Office: 1612 K St NW Washington DC 20006

ANDERSON, JACK ROY, health care mgmt. co. exec.; b. Mansfield, O., Feb. 14, 1925; s. Roy L. and Katherine (Munson) A.; B.S., Miami U., 1947; M.S., Columbia, 1949; m. Rose-Marie J. Garcia, June 24, 1950; childrenGail Ellen, Neil Robert, Barbara Ann. Accounting mgr. Time, Inc., N.Y.C., 1950-59; asst. to controller W.R. Grace & Co., N.Y.C., 1959-62; v.p., treas. Hartford Publs., Inc., N.Y.C., 1962-65; controller McCall Corp., N.Y.C., 1965-68; v.p., controller Leasco Data Processing Equipment Corp., N.Y.C., 1968-70; pres., dir. Hosp. Affiliates, Inc., Nashville, 1970—. Vice pres. Greenwich (Conn.) Council Parent-Tchr. Assn., 1961-62. Served as lt. (j.g.) USNR, 1943-46. Mem. Columbia Bus. Assos., Financial Execs. Inst., Sigma Chi, Beta Alpha Psi. Clubs: Board Room (N.Y.C.); Richland (Nashville); Stamwich (Greenwich, Conn.), Towers (Oxford, O.). Home: 110 Lynwood Terrace Nashville TN 37205 Office: Parkway Towers Nashville TN 37205

ANDERSON, JAMES DONALD, oil co. exec.; b. Cheyenne, Wyo., Nov. 22, 1909; s. Paul L. and Maude (McIver) A.: C.E., U. Wyo., 1933; m. Rhea Wadsworth, July 27, 1935; children—Barbara Kay, Michele Jean. With Marathon Oil Co., 1936—, dir. v.p. prodn. subsidiary Marathon Internat. Oil Co., 1962—, sr. v.p. parent co., 1969—, also dir. Bd. mgrs. Rose-Hulman Inst., 1964—. Mem. Am. Petroleum Inst., Am. Inst. M.E. Republican. Presbyn. Mason (Shriner). Home: 120 Beechmont Dr Findlay OH 45840 Office: 539 S Main St Findlay OH 45840

ANDERSON, JAMES G., educator; b. Portland, Ore., Oct. 22, 1914; s. James G. and Julia E. E. (White) A.; A.B., U. Notre Dame, 1937, Ph.D., 1946; student Catholic U., 1937- 41, Holy Cross Coll., 1937-41. Ordained priest Roman Cath. Ch., 1941; instr. chemistry U. Notre Dame, 1946; instr. U. Portland, 1946-48, asso. prof., head dept., 1948-52, v.p. 1952-55, dean Coll. Sci.; 1956-68, prof. chemistry, 1959-68, 70—, dean Coll. Arts and Sci., 1968-70. Mem. Am. Chem. Soc. Address: U Portland Portland OR 97203

ANDERSON, JAMES HENRY, univ. dean; B.S., U. Ga., 1949; M.A., N.C. State Coll., 1955; Ph.D., Ia. State U., 1957. Prof. agr. and biol. engring. Miss. State U., State College, also dean Coll. Agr. Office: Coll Agr Miss State State College MS 39762

ANDERSON, JAMES RICHARD, educator; b. Whitaker, Ind., Nov. 20, 1919; s. Pearl and Sarah Ethel (Potter) A.; B.S. with high distinction, Ind. U., 1941, A.B. with honors, 1947; M.A., 1947; student McGill U., 1947; Ph.D., U. Md., 1950; m. Joy Elaine Worstall, Feb. 14, 1945; children—James Richard, Judyth Sue, Janine Joy, John Worstall. Asst. prof. geography U. Md., 1950-52; geographer Agrl. Research Service, Dept. Agr., 1952-60; head prof. dept. geography U. Fla., Gainesville, 1960-69, Mem. Assn. Am. Geographers (pres. Southeastern division) 1965-67, chmn. commn. geog. applications of remote sensing 1967- 69, councilor 1969—), Florida Society of Geographers, Agrl. History Soc., National Council Geog. Edn., Am. Geog. Soc., Phi Beta Kappa, Sigma Xi, Phi Delta Kappa. Baptist. Author: A Geography of Agriculture, 1970. Mem. internat. com. for preparing World Atlas of Agr. Home: 3211 N W 21st Av Gainesville FL 32601

ANDERSON, JAMES SENCABAUGH, business cons.; b. Dayton, O., Apr. 6, 1910; s. Harold N. and Dorcas (Sencabaugh) A.; B.S. in Mech. Engring., Case Inst. Tech., 1932; m. D. Margaret McBride, 1955; children—David T., Jane, Elizabeth, James M. Mem. sales staff Republic Steel Corp., 1932-41; with Babcock & Wilcox Co., 1941-66, successively sales staff tubular products div., asst. gen. sales mgr., gen. sales mgr., v.p. sales, 1941-59, v.p., gen. mgr. tubular products div., 1959-63, vice pres., gen. mgr., 1963-65, pres., 1965-66, dir. cons., 1966—; pres. Allied control Co., Inc., 1966-69; mgmt. cons., 1969—; chmn. bd. Skodco Inc., Greenwich, Conn., 1970—; dir. Emerson Electric Co., St. Louis; mem. adv. com. Bankers Trust Co., N.Y.C. Mem. Am. Iron aand Steel Inst., Am. Soc. for Metals, Am. Ordnance Assn. Clubs: University (N.Y.C.); Greenwich Country. Home: 1 Putnam Hill Greenwich CT 06830

ANDERSON, JAMES TREAT, univ. ofcl.; b. Washington, June 18, 1921: s. Richard James and Dorothy (Pettit) A.; B.S., Mich. State U., 1943, M.S., 1948; Ph.D., U. London (Eng.), 1952; postgrad. Imperial Coll., London, 1952; m. Margaret Elizabeth Dick, Feb. 25, 1945; children—James Maynard, Janice Elizabeth, Robert Stephen, Nicholas William. From instr. to asso. prof. mech. engring. Mich. State U., 1946-59, prof., 1959-60; vis. prof. Tulane, 1960; chmn. dept. mech. engring. W.Va. U., 1960-63; dean engring. U. Nev., Reno, 1963—, v.p. acad. affairs, 1970—. Cons. jet engine dept., aircraft nuclear propulsion dept. Gen. Electric Co., Cin., 1957-61, Alleghany Ballistic Missile Lab., 1961-63. Served to 1st lt. Signal Corps, OSS, 1943-46. Registered profl. engr., Mich., Nev. Mem. Am. Soc. M.E., Am. Soc. Engring. Edn., Sigma Xi, Pi Tau Sigma, Tau Beta Pi, Phi Kappa Phi, Sigma Tau. Home: 2170 Royal Dr Reno NV 89503

ANDERSON, JEREMY R., artist; b. Palo Alto, Cal., Oct. 28, 1921; student San Francisco Art Inst., 1946-50; m. Frances W. Whitney, 1947; children—Timothy and Bruce (twins), Jennifer. Tchr., San Francisco Art Inst.; one-man exhbns. at Metart Gallery, San Francisco, 1949, Allan Frumkin Gallery, Chgo., 1954, Stable Gallery, 1954, Dilexi Gallery, San Francisco, 1960, 61, 62, 64, Dilexi Gallery, Los Angeles, 1962, Quay Gallery, San Francisco, 1970; one-man retrospective show San Francisco Mus. Art, 1966, annuals, 1948, 49, 51, 52, 53, 58, 59, 63, Whitney Mus. Am. Art Ann., 1956, 64, also 50 Cal. Artists exhbn., 1962-63, U. Ill., 1955, 57, Stanford U., 1962, Kaiser Center, Oakland, Cal., 1963, 2ieme Salon Internat de Galerias Pilotes, Lausanne, Switzerland, 1966, Portland Mus., 1968, Funk Show, U. Cal. at Berkeley, 1967, Los Angeles Mus., 1967, Expo '70, Osaka, Japan, 1970, others; represented in perm. coll. Pasadena Art Mus. San Francisco Mus. Art, U. Cal. at Berkeley, Mus. Modern Art, N.Y.C. Served with USNR, 1941-45. Recipient I.N. Walter Sculpture prize San Francisco Mus. Art, 1948; Abraham Rosenberg Found. Traveling Fellowship, 1950, Sculpture prize San Francisco Art Assn., 1959. Address: 534 Northern Av Mill Valley CA 94941

ANDERSON, JERRY MAYNARD, educator; b. Deronda, Wis., Sept. 16, 1933; s. Jens B. and Mamie P. (Hanson) A.; B.S., Wis. State U. at River Falls, 1958; M.S., No. Ill. U., 1959; Ph.D., Mich. State U., 1964; m. Betty Lou Schultz, Feb. 7, 1959; 1 son, Gregory Jens. Instr. speech U. Me., 1959-61; asst. prof. speech, dir. forensics Mich. State U., 1961-68; prof., chmn. dept. speech and dramatic arts Central Mich. U., Mt. Pleasant, 1968—. Mem. State adminstrv. bd. Democratic Party of Wis., 1959; chmn. 6th Congl. Dist. Mich. Dem. Orgn., 1966-67. Served with USNR, 1952-54. Recipient Sr. Distinguished Professionalism award Central Mich. U., 1971. Research fellow Harry S. Truman Found., 1965; fellow Am. Council on Edn. Acad. Adminstrn. Internship Program, 1971—. Mem. Central States (v.p. 1971; Outstanding Young Tchr. award 1966), Mich. (pres. 1967-68) speech assns., Am. (chmn. finance com. 1968-70), Midwest (pres. 1969—) forensic assns., Speech Communication Assn. (mem. Legislative Assembly 1969-70), Rotarian. Author: (with Paul J. Doure) Readings in Argumentation, 1968; also articles. Home: 1022 Glenwood Pl Mount Pleasant MI 48858

ANDERSON, JOHN, Jr., ex-gov. of Kansas; b. Olathe, Kan., May 8, 1917; s. John and Ora May (Bookout) A.; A.B. in Econs., Kansas U., 1943, LL.B., 1944; m. Arlene Auchard, May 22, 1943; childrenJohn III, King David and Kerry Diann (twins). Admitted to Kan. bar, 1944; practiced law, 1946-56, mem. firm Hodges, Hambleton and Anderson, Olathe, Kan., 1953-55; county attorney, Johnson County, Kan., 1947-53; atty. gen., Kan., 1956-61; gov. State of Kansas, 1961-64; mem. firm Hackler, Anderson, Chipman, Speer & Vader. Mem. Kan. Senate, 1953-56. Mem. Am., Kan. bar assns. Home: Route 1 DeSoto KS 66018 Office: Park-Cherry Bldg Olathe, KS 66061.

ANDERSON, JOHN ADOLPH, prof. pediatrics; b. Sioux Falls, S.D., Oct. 28, 1908; s. Lars and Minnie (Olson) A.; student U. of S.D., 1926-28; B.S., U. of Minn., 1933, M.D., 1933, Ph.D., 1940; student graduate school University of Colorado, 1935-37; m. Albertine Agatha Arth, September 8, 1934; children—Judith Kay, Robert John. Intern, pediatrics, University of Minnesota, 1933-34, research assistant, 1934-35; fellow, Child Research Council, Denver, Colo., 1935-37; instr. in pediatrics, U. of Minn., 1937-40, asst. prof., 1940-43; prof. and head of dept. pediatrics and communicable diseases, U. Utah Med. Sch., 1943; prof., exec. head dept. pediatrics Stanford, 1949-54; prof., head dept. pediatrics U. Minn., 1954—. Diplomate Am. Bd. Pediatrics (pres.). Fellow Am. Pub. Health Soc. A.A.A.S., Soc. Pediatric Research. Assn. Study Internal Secretions, Am. Fedn. for Clin. Research, A.M.A., Minn., Hennepin County med. socs., Northwestern Pediatric Soc., Nat. Physicians Council (v.p.), Western Clin. Research Soc., Western Soc. for Pediatric Research, Am. Pediatric Soc., Sigma Xi, Delta Chi, Phi Chi, Phi Kappa Phi. Contbr. to Nelson Textbook of Pediatrics, Brennemans Practice of Pediatrics, Holt and McIntosh Textbook Pediatrics. Mem. editorial bd. Pediatrics; asso. editor Advances Pediatrics. Home: 2298 Folwell St St Paul MN 55108 Office: U Minn Minneapolis MN 55455

ANDERSON, JOHN BAYARD, congressman; b. Rockford, Ill., Feb. 15, 1922; s. E. Albin and Mabel Edna (Ring) A.; A.B., U. Ill., 1942, J.D., 1946; LL.M., Harvard, 1949; hon. doctorates, U. Ill., Wheaton Coll., Shimer Coll., Biola Coll., Geneva Coll.; m. Keke Machakos, Jan. 4, 1953; children—Eleanora, John Bayard, Diane, Karen. Admitted Ill. bar, 1946; practice in Rockford, 1946-52; with U.S. Fgn. Service, 1952-55; assigned West Berlin, Germany, 1952-55; mem. 87th -92d Congresses, 16 Dist. Ill., mem. joint com. atomic energy, rules com.; chmn. Ho. Republican Conf., 1969—. Past mem. bd. edn. Trinity Coll., Chgo. Past mem. bd. dirs. Vols. Am., Board of Rockford. Served with F.A., AUS, World War II. Mem. Phi Beta Kappa. Republican. Mem. Evangel. Free Ch. (past trustee). Author: Between Two Worlds: A Congressman's Choice, 1970. Editor: Congress and Conscience, 1970. Home: 115 James Av Rockford IL 61107 also 5616 Ogden Rd Washington DC 20016 Office: Longworth Bldg Washington DC 20515

ANDERSON, JOHN BOWLING, tobacco co. exec.; b. Dundas, Va., Sept. 30, 1913; s. John H. and Margaret (Bowling) A.; student Croft's Accounting Sch., Durham, N.C.; m. Fay Thompson, July 12, 1936; 1 son, John Craig. With Liggett & Myers Tobacco Co., Durham, N.C., 1934-47, N.Y.C., 1947-50, St. Louis, 1950-51, Richmond, Va., 1951-53, asst. treas., N.Y.C., 1954-58, treas., dir., 1958-61, now exec. v.p. Served with USAAF, 1942-45. Mem. Am. Legion, N.J. C. of C., N.Y. So. Soc. Methodist (mem. ofcl. bd.). Clubs: Pelham (N.Y.) Country, Pelham Men's; Rockefeller Center Luncheon (N.Y.C.). Home: 101 Iden Av Pelham Manor NY 10803 Office: 630 Fifth Av New York City NY 10020*

ANDERSON, JOHN DENTON, educator; b. Didsbury, Alta., Can., July 15, 1912; s. William Ray and Nina (Denton) A.; brought to U.S., 1913; B.A., U. Colol., 1938, M.A., 1940; postgrad. U. Okla., 1940-41; Ph.D. in Biology, Stanford, 1949; m. Jane Graybill Collier, Apr. 12, 1943; children—Sibyl A. (Mrs. William Les Pellum), Richard Rox, George Collier, Donald Denton. Instr. physiology U. Ill., 1949-53, asst. prof., 1953-57, asso. prof., 1957-65, prof., 1965—, asst. dir. med. program, 1969-71, asso. dean Sch. Basic Med. Scis., Urbana, 1971—. Served to 1st lt. M.C., AUS, 1942-46. Home: 1305 W Clark St Champaign IL 61820 Office: 533 Burrill Hall U Ill Urbana IL 61801

ANDERSON, JOHN EDWARD, lawyer; b. Mpls., Sept. 12, 1917; s. William Charles and Myrtle (Grosvenor) A.; B.S. cum laude, U. Cal. at Los Angeles, 1940; M.B.A. with distinction (Baker scholar), Harvard, 1942; J.D. cum laude, Loyola U., 1950; m. Margaret Stewart, Sept. 14, 1942 (dec.); children—Margaret Susan, Judith Grosvenor, John Edward, Deborah Lee (dec.), William Stewart; m. 2d, Marion Redding, Mar. 3, 1967. Accountant, Arthur Andersen & Co., C.P.A.'s, Los Angeles, 1945-48; admitted to Cal. bar, 1950, since practiced in Los Angeles and Santa Ana; partner firm Kindel & Anderson, 1953—; dir. Cam-Stat Inc., Gates, Kingsley & Gates, Inc., Canoga Industries, Nat. Accomodation, Inc., Pinehurst Corp., Applied Magnetics Corp., Sloan Tech. Corp., Founders Life Ins. Co., Shapell Industries, Inc., Nat. First Corp., Indsl. Tools, Inc., Bourns, Inc. Trustee Claremont Mens Coll., Eternal Valley Meml. Park. Served to lt. USNR, 1942-45. C.P.A., Cal. Mem. Am. Bar Assn., State Bar Cal., Am. Inst. Accountants, Cal. Soc. C.P.A.'s, Phi Delta Phi, Beta Gamma Sigma, Beta Theta Pi. Presbyn. (elder). Clubs: Los Angeles Country, California, Stock Exchange of Los Angeles (Los Angeles); Eldorado Country (Palm Desert, Cal.); The Beach (Santa Monica, Cal.). Home: 340 N June St Los Angeles CA 90004 Office: 510 S Spring St Los Angeles CA 90013 also 1016 N Broadway Santa Ana CA 92701

ANDERSON, JOHN F., clergyman; b. Dallas, May 27, 1920; s. John Franklin and Jewel (Thomason) A.; B.A., Austin Coll., Sherman, Tex., 1941; B.D., Union Presbyn. Theol. Sem., Richland, Va., 1944; Th.M., Austin Presbyn. Theol. Sem., 1953; m. Nancy Lee Love, Aug. 31, 1943; children—William Earl, Paul Burris, Rebecca Sue. Ordained to ministry Presbyn. Ch.; pastor in Tyler, Tex., 1946-51, Dallas, 1951-52, 52-58, Orlando, Fla., 1958-65; exec. sec. bd. nat. ministries Presbyn. Ch. U.S.A., 1965—. Served as chaplain USNR, 1944-46; PTO. Recipient Distinguished Service award Dallas Jr. C. of C., 1955. Kiwanian (pres. Tyler 1951), Rotarian (pres. Downtown Dallas 1958). Author weekly column Dallas Morning News, 1953-58, Orlando Sentinental, 1958-65. Home: 958 Castle Falls Dr NE Atlanta GA 30329 Office: 341 Ponce de Leon Av NE Atlanta GA 30308

ANDERSON, JOHN FIRTH, librarian; b. Saginaw, Mich., Oct. 5, 1928; s. Harlan Firth and Irene Martha (Bowser) A.; B.A., Mich. State U., 1949; M.S. in L.S., U. Ill., 1950; m. Patricia Ann Goble, June 18, 1950; children—Douglas Firth, Elizabeth Ann. Young people's librarian Enoch Pratt Free Library, Balt., 1950-52; with Balt. County Pub. Library, 1952-58, supr. adult work, 1955- 56, asst. county librarian, 1956-58; dir. Knoxville (Tenn.) Pub. Library System, 1958-62, Tucson Pub. Library, 1962-68; city librarian San Francisco Pub. library, 1968—. Charter mem. Freedom to Read Found.; mem. San Francisco Symphony Found. Mem. Am. (mem. at large council 1961-65, 66-70, bd. dirs. pub. library assn. 1961-65, bd. dirs. library adminstrn. div. 1964-65, chmn. library orgn. and mgmt. sect. 1964-65, pres. library adminstrn. div. 1968-69), Cal. (mem. council 1970-71), Tenn., Southwestern, Ariz. (pres. pub. libraries div. 1964-65, pres. 1967-68, Librarian of Year 1968) library assns., San Francisco Opera Guild, Beta Phi Mu. Presbyn. (elder). Clubs: Kiwanis (pres. Tucson 1968); Torch (v.p. Knoxville 1962); Commonwealth of Cal. Contbr. profl. publs. Home: 280 San Benito Way San Francisco CA 94127 Office: Civic Center San Francisco CA 94102

ANDERSON, JOHN H., Jr., lawyer; b. Fayetteville, N.C., Dec. 28, 1907; B.A., LL.B. with honors, U. N.C. Admitted to N.C. bar, 1929, since practiced in Raleigh; mem. firm Smith, Anderson, Dorsett, Blount & Ragsdell. Fellow Am. Coll. Trial Lawyers; mem. Am., N.C. (mem. exec. com. 1941), 7th Jud. Dist. (pres. 1947-48), Wake County bar assns., Internat. Assn. Ins. Counsel (exec. com. 1953- 59), Am. Counsel Assn., Order of Coif, Phi Delta Phi. Office: Wachovia Bank Bldg Raleigh NC 27602

ANDERSON, JOHN MUELLER, educator; b. Cedar Rapids, Ia., July 29, 1914; s. Arthur G. and Lois A. (Mueller) A.; B.A., U. Ill., 1935, M.A., 1936; Ph.D., U. Cal. at Berkeley, 1939; m. Mary A. Gale, June 11, 1936. Credit mgr. retail store Sears, Roebuck & Co., New Albany, Ind., 1939-41; research engr. Elgin Nat. Watch Co. (Ill.), 1941-42; chief spl. project Mpls.-Honeywell Co., 1942-43, asst. to chief engr., 1943-45; lectr. math. U. Minn., 1945-46; mem. faculty Pa. State U., 1946-, prof. philosophy, 1951-68, Evan Pugh Research prof. philosophy, 1968-; head dept., 1948-49, 52-55, 58-67, acting asst. dean for research, 1964, summer 1965, dir. Inst. Arts and Humanistic Studies, 1966-68, liberal arts editor Pa. State Studies; vis. lectr. U. Ill., summer 1965; guest prof. U. Otago (New Zealand), 1955, Free U. Berlin (Germany), 1961-62, cons. operations research, computer design. Mem. Am., Western Pa. philos. assns., Am. Assn. U. Profs., Assn. Am. Studies, Assn. Symbolic Logic, Soc. Phenomenology and Existential Philosophy (exec. com. 1965-68), Am. Soc. for Aesthetics, Am. Math. Soc., Phi Beta Kappa, Sigma Xi, Pi Gamma Mu, Alpha Tau Omega. Author: (with Anderson and Maudeville) Industrial Management, 1942; CalhounBasic Documents, 1952; The Individual and the New World, 1955; (with H.W. Johnstone, Jr.) Natural

Deduction, 1962; The Realm of Art; also articles. Editor, Man and World. Patentee computers. Home: 269 S Osmond St State College, PA 16801. Office: Sparks Bldg University Park PA 16802

ANDERSON, JOHN WEIR, editor; b. Phila., Sept. 29, 1928; s. Henry Ince and Marian (Carter) A.; A.B., Williams Coll., 1950; m. Madelyn Anne Streeter, Apr. 28, 1956; children—Hilary Elissa, Adam Weir. Reporter, York (Pa.) Dispatch, 1953- 55, Reading (Pa.) Times, 1955-56; reporter Washington Post, 1957-61, editorial writer, 1961-67, city editor, 1968-69, fgn. editor, 1970—. Served with AUS, 1946-48. Author: Eisenhower, Brownell and the Congress, 1964. Home: 514 Prince St Alexandria VA 22314 Office: 1515 L St NW Washington DC 20005

ANDERSON, JOSEPH NORMAN, mdsg. co. exec.; b. Mpls., May 12, 1926; s. Joseph E. and Helen (Larson) A.; B.B.A. with distinction, U. Minn., 1947; m. Ruth E. Anderson, Sept. 6, 1952; children—Peter, Timothy, Paul, Matthew, Robin, Kathryn. With Sears, Roebuck & Co., 1947-49, Gamble-Skogmo, Inc., 1950-64; v.p. finance, dir. Nat. Bellas Hess, Inc., 1964-67, pres., chief exec. officer, dir., 1967-69, now chairman of board, pres., chief executive officer. Pres. Merchants Research Council, 1961-62. Served with AUS, 1953-55. Mem. Phi Beta Kappa, Beta Gamma Sigma. Republican. Presbyn. Home: 11335 Jarboe St Kansas City MO 64114 Office: 715 Armour Rd North Kansas City MO 64116

ANDERSON, JOSEPH TOMLINSON, educator, biochemist; b. Hilton, N.Y., Dec. 10, 1909; s. Arthur R. and Grace (Tomlinson) A.; B.S., U. Rochester, 1930, M.S., 1932, Ph.D., 1947; m. Gwendolyn R. Peck, Nov. 27, 1935; children—Owen L., Jan Ellen. Instr., Med. Sch., U. Rochester, 1947-50; from asst. prof. to prof. Lab. Physiol. Hygiene, U. Minn., Mpls., 1950—, prof. biochemistry, 1959—. Mem. Am. Chem. Soc., Am. Inst. Nutrition, Am. Oil Chemists Soc., Fellowship of Reconciliation, Phi Beta Kappa, Sigma Xi. Research, publs. on relationships between diet and type and amount of lipids in blood serum and their correlation to coronary heart disease. Home: 1965 Autumn St St Paul MN 55113 Office: Lab Physiol Hygiene U Minn Stadium Gate 27 Minneapolis MN 55455

ANDERSON, JUDITH, actress; b. Adelaide, Australia; d. James Anderson- Anderson and Jessie Margaret (Saltmarsh) Anderson; student Rose Park, South Australia, 1908-12, Norwood, South Australia, 1913-16; D.F.A. (hon.), Northwestern U., L.H.D., Fairfield U., 1964; m. Benjamin H. Lehman, 1937 (div. 1939); m. 2d, Luther Greene, July 11, 1946 (div. 1950). Played in The Royal Divorce, Sign of the Cross, Monsieur Beaucaire, Under Fire, The Three Musketeers, Turn to the Right, The Dove, 1925, Behold the Bridegroom 1927, Strange Interlude, 1930, Mourning Becomes Electra, 1931, Firebird, Divided by Three, 1932, Conquest, 1933, Mask and the Face, Come of Age, 1934, The Old Maid, 1935, Hamlet, 1936, Macbeth (London), 1937, Family Portrait, 1939, Tower Beyond (tragedy by Robinson Jeffers), 1941, Macbeth, 1941, Three Sisters, 1942, Medea, 1947-49; toured with stage show John Brown's Body, 1951-52, in pictures: Rebecca, 1939, Kings Row, 1942, Edge of Darkness, 1943, Cinderfella, 1960, And Then There Were None, Strange Love of Martha Ivers, Specter of Roses, Diary of Chambermaid, Tycoon, Red House; appeared on TV in Macbeth, 1955, 60 (recipient Emmy Award, 1961). Decorated dame comdr. Order Brit. Empire. Rancho Verde Carpenteria CA 93013

ANDERSON, KARL WALTER, physician; b. Mpls., Nov. 5, 1900; s. Andrew and Wilhelmina (Peterson) A.; B.S., U. Minn., 1922, B.M., 1923, M.D., 1924; fellowship in internal medicine under Dr. Hilding Berglund, 1925, 26, 27; m. Crystal Justus, Sept. 23, 1925; children—Alice Crystal (Mrs. R.N. Berry), Karen Justus (Mrs. E. K. Boberg). Began practice medicine Mpls., 1924; mem. faculty U. Minn., 1928—, asso. clin. prof., 1942—, asst. med. dir. Northwestern Nat. Life Ins. Co. 1931-41, chief med. officer, 1941-46, med. dir., 1946—, 2d v.p., 1952-57, v.p., 1957-64, sr. v.p. 1964-66; chief med. cons. Minn. Div. Ednl. Rehab., 1967—. Past chmn. finance com. WHO-U.S.A.; treas. Mpls. meeting Pan Am. Health Orgn., 1962; chmn. health and med. care div. Community Chest and Council Hennipen County; mem. commn. to study problems on aging in State of Minn. Bd. dirs. Goodwill Industries, Met. Med. Center. Recipient Harold S. Diehl gold medal award U. Minn. Med. Sch., 1966, Minn. Med. Assn. gold medal. Diplomate Am. Bd. Internal Medicine. Mem. Am. Life Conv. (bd. mgrs. med. sect., 1951), Am. Diabetes Assn., Assn. Life Ins. Med. Dirs. Assn., Minn. Med. Found. (v.p.), A.R.C. (local dir.), Minn. Med. Assn. (treas.), Life Ins. Medicine (mem. bd.), A.A.A.S., A.M.A., Am. Public Health Assn., Central Soc. Clin. Research, Minn. Soc. Internal Medicine, Minn. Path. Soc., Mpls. Acad. Medicine (pres. 1946). Minn. Heart Assn. (pres. 1959). Clubs: Rotary; Mpls. Lafayette; Illinois Athletic. Contbr. articles mags. Mem. Olympic team to Paris, France, 1924 (nat. champion of 120 hurdles, 1923-24, indoor high hurdles, 1923, 24). Baptist. Home: Linwood Rd Excelsior MN 55331

ANDERSON, KENNETH ELLSWORTH, univ. dean; b. Ithaca, N.Y., Dec. 21, 1914; s. Grover M. and Bessie (Hunt) A.; B.S., Cornell U., 1937, Ph.D., 1943; M.S., U. N.H., 1940; m. Agnes E. Schickel, Feb. 7, 1942; children-Kenneth, Vincent, Joan, Mary, Paul, Kathleen, Agnes, Patricia, William, John, Theresa. Chemist, bacteriologist N.Y. Water Service Corp., N.Y.C., 1937-38; bacteriologist Genesse Brewing Co., Rochester, NY., 1946; mem. faculty St. Bonaventure (N.Y.) U., 1946—, prof., chmn. dept. biology, 1949-68, mem. bd. instrn., 1952—, dean Sch. Arts and Scis., 1966-69, dean Sch. Grad. Studies, 1969—. Cons. microbiology problems relating to oil prodn. Mem. A.A.A.S., Soc. Am. Microbiologists, U.S. Pub. Health Assn., N.Y. Acad. Scis. Editor Sci. Studies, 1947-69. Research bactericides and oil floods, physiology of Desulfovibrio desulfuricans. Home: 96 Rock City Rd Olean NY 14760 Office: Dept Biology St Bonaventure Univ St Bonaventure NY 14778

ANDERSON, KENNETH EUGENE, educator; b. Mpls., Mar. 2, 1910; s. Peter Wilhelm and Alma Annette (Ekstrum) A.; B.S., U. Minn., 1932, M.A., 1934, Ph.D., 1949; m. Dorothy Woodruff Smith, Aug. 1, 1934; children—Peter Alden, Philip Norman. Tchr., adminstr. pub. schs., Minn., 1934-44; instr. U. Minn. High Sch., 1944-46, dir., 1946-47; prin. Campus High Sch., Ia. State Tchrs. Coll., 1947-48; asst. prof. edn. U. Kan., 1948-50, asso. prof. edn., dir. bur. edn. research service, 1950-52, prof. edn., 1952—, dean sch. edn., 1952-69; exec. dir. Kan. Master Planning Commn. on Post High Sch. Edn., 1970—. Recipient Outstanding Achievement award U. Minn., 1965; Master Tchr. award Kan. State Tchrs. Coll., Emporia, 1971. Fellow A.A.A.S. (v.p. Sect. Q 1961-62); mem. N.Y. Acad. Scis., Nat. Assn. Research Sci. Teaching (pres. 1954-55), North Central Assn. Colls. and Secondary Schs. (dir., exec. com. 1961-65), N.E.A., Am. Psychol. Assn., Nat. Soc. Study Edn., Am. Statis. Assn., Am. Ednl. Research Assn. (pres. 1959). Author: Anderson-Fisk Chemistry Test, 1966; (with Collister, Ladd) The Educational Achievement of Indian Children, 1953; (with others) The Indian Child Goes to School, 1957; (with H.A. Smith) Topics In Statistics for Students in Education, 1959. Exec. editor Bull. Edn. and Kan. Studies in Education, 1953-68. Contbr. profl. publs. Home: 2014 Clifton Ct Lawrence KS 66044

ANDERSON, KENNETH NORMAN, assn. exec.; b. Omaha, July 10, 1921; s. Duncan McDonald and Latitia Jane (Steed) A.; student U. Omaha, 1939-41, Ore. State Coll., 1943-44, Stanford, 1944-45, Northwestern U. coll. Medicine, 1945-46, U. Chgo., 1958-60; m. Lois Elaine Harmon, Jan. 12, 1945; children—Eric Stephen, Randi Laine, Jani Jill, Douglas Duncan. With U.S. Army Finance Office, Neb. and Mont., 1941-42; engring. aid U.S. Army Engrs., Omaha, 1946; radio news editor sta. KOIL, Omaha, 1946-47; bur. mgr. Internat. News Service, Omaha and Kansas City, Mo., 1947-56; spl. features editor Better Homes and Gardens mag., 1956-57; asso. editor Popular Mechanics mag., 1957-59; editor Today's Health mag., pub. by A.M.A., Chgo., 1959- 65; editor Holt, Rinehart & Winston, 1965-70; exec. dir. Coffee Information Inst., 1970—; lectr. mag. writing New Sch. Social Research, 1959. N.Y.U., 1960, Omaha U., 1961, Rennselaer Poly. Inst., 1964. Sec. Douglas County (Neb.) Dist. Bd. Edn., 1954-56. Served with AUS, 1942-46. Recipient citation Nat. Poetry Assn., 1946. Mem. Nat. Assn. Sci. Writers, A.A.A.S., Am., N.Y. pub. health assns., N.Y. Acad. Scis., Soc. Illustrators, Am. Inst. Biol. Scis., Outdoor Writers Assn. Am., Sigma Delta Chi. Methodist. Clubs: Omaha Press (co-founder); Overseas Press, Deadline (N.Y.C.). Co-author: Lawyers' Medical Cyclopedia, 1962; The Family Physician, 1963; Today's Health Guide, 1965; Pictorial Medical Guide, 1967. Adv. editor Nutrition Today, 1965—. Contbr. med. and nature articles to Funk & Wagnall Ency. Home: 23 McQueen St Katonah NY 10536 Office: 18 E 48th St New York City NY 10017

ANDERSON, KENNETH THEODORE, mem. Dem. Nat. Com; b. Burdick, Kan., June 22, 1909; s. Emil Theodore and Cora Florentine (Bjorkback) A.; student Wichita U.; B.S., U. South, 1931; m. Norma Jean Denny, February 6, 1958; children—Lisa Nell, Mary Michelle, Eric Theodore. Manager of a hotel, 1931-33; prodn. dept. Skelly Oil Co., 1933-35, sales depts., Chgo., 1935-38; organizer, operator Universal Butane Corp., Centralia, Ill., 1938-40; in cattle bus. since 1940, v.p. Anderson Cattle Co., Inc., Emporia, Kansas; chairman Kansas Soya Products. Mem. Federal Farm Credit Board, 1963—. Elected mem. Kan. State Ho. of Reps., 1948; Dem. candidate for gov. Kan., 1950; mem. Dem. Nat. Com. from Kan., 1952—. Chmn. bd. govs. Agrl. Hall of Fame and Nat. Center. Served as lt., gunnery officer (s.g.), USNR, 1944-46. Mem. Am. Legion, Vets. Fgn. Wars, Amvets (charter mem.), Phi Gamma Delta. Lutheran. Rotarian. Home: 6111 Expressway NW San Antonio TX 78227 Office: Box 399 Emporia KS 66801

ANDERSON, KINSEY A., physicist; b. Preston, Minn., Sept. 18, 1926; s. Melvin R. and Allene (Michener) A.; B.A., Carleton Coll., 1949; Ph.D., U. Minn., 1955; m. Lilica Athena Vassiliades, May 29, 1954; children—Danae, Sindri. Guggenheim fellow Royal Inst. Tech., Stockholm, Sweden, 1959-60; faculty U. Cal. at Berkeley, 1960—, prof. physics, 1966—. dir. Space Sci. Lab., 1970—. Cons., NSF, NASA. Mem. Am. Geophys. Union, Am. Phys. Soc., Am. Astron. Soc., Internat. Astron. Union, Phi Beta Kappa, Sigma Xi. Contbr. numerous articles to profl. jours. Research in direct measurement of low energy solar cosmic rays, auroral zone particles with balloons and rockets, satellite measurements of radiation zones and solar particles in interplanetary space. Home: 8321 Buckingham Dr El Cerrito CA 94530 Office: Space Sci Lab U Cal Berkeley CA 94720

ANDERSON, LAURENS, educator; b. Belle Fourche, S.D., May 19, 1920; s. Adolph and Mary Elizabeth (Slaughter) A.; B.S. in Chemistry, U. Wyo., 1942, M.S. in Biochemistry, 1947, Ph.D. in Biochemistry, 1950; m. Doris Elaine Young, Sept. 15, 1945; children—Eric Edward, Karl Arnold, Kristin Elaine. Faculty biochemistry U. Wis., Madison, 1951—, prof., 1961—. Served with USAAF, 1942-45. Merck fellow natural scis. Eidgenössiche Tech. Hochscule, Zurich, Switzerland, 1950-51; NIH sr. postdoctoral fellow Ind. U., 1971. Mem. Am. Chem. Soc., Am. Soc. Biol. Chemists, Sigma Xi. Mem. United Ch. of Christ (mem. council higher edn.). Contbr. articles to profl. jours. Home: 5639 Lake Mendota Dr Madison WI 53705

ANDERSON, LAWRENCE BERNHART, architect, educator; b. Geneva, Minn., May 7, 1906; s. Andrew S. and and Lena (Christianson) A.; B.S., U. Min., 1926, B.S. in Architecture, 1927; M.Arch., Mass. Inst. Tech., 1930; student Ecole des Beaux-Arts, Paris, 1930-32; m. Rosina DuPont, July 30, 1936; childrenJudith, Karen, Lawrence. Practice architecture, 1936—; partner H.L. Beckwith, Cambridge, 1938-54, Anderson, Beckwith and Haible, 1954—; mem. faculty Mass. Inst. Tech., 1933-, prof., 1945-, charge dept. architecture, 1946-67, dean Sch. Architecture and Planning, 1965—. Asso. N.A.D. Fellow Am. Acad. Arts and Sci., Royal Acad. Fine Arts, Copenhagen, A.I.A.; mem. Assn. Collegiate Schs. Architecture (pres. 1953-55). Address: Mass Inst Tech Cahbridge MA 02139

ANDERSON, LAWREN food co. exec.; b. Mataredonda, Vera., Mexico, Apr. 5, 1930 (parents Am. citizens); s. Lawrence Leslie and Barbara Graham (Ryan) A.; grad. Kent Sch., 1948; A.B., Princeton, 1952; M.A., Columbia, 1956; M.A., Yale, 1957; M.B.A., N.Y. U., 1966; m. Stella Lee Edwards, Aug. 26, 1958; children—Lawrence L. III, John Edwards, Elizabeth Hope, Stella Lee Graham. Salesman, Procter & Gamble, 1954-55; account rep. J. Walter Thompson, N.Y., Colombia, 1957-61; asst. product mgr., then product devel. mgr. Gen. Foods, White Plains, N.Y., 1961-63; product mgr. Corn Products, N.Y.C., 1963-67; asso. Innotron Imperial Tobacco, Montreal, Que., Can., 1968-69; pres. Growers Wine Co., Victoria, B.C., Can., 1969-70; pres. S & W Fine Foods, Inc., San Francisco, 1970—. Served with USMCR, 1952-54. Mem. Young Pres's. Orgn. Lion. Clubs: Commonwealth of California (San Francisco); University Cottage (Princeton, N.J.). Home: 200 Menlo Oaks Dr Menlo Park CA 94025 Office: 333 Schwerin St San Francisco CA 94134

ANDERSON, LEE, author; b. Saxton, Pa., July 19, 1896; s. Samuel Andrew and Myra Agnes (Brode) A.; m. Helen Anderson White, Dec. 27, 1941; 1 dau., by previous marriage, Mary Jane. Self-employed as publisher, farmer, lectr. contemporary poetry, also reader of own poems on coll. campuses; research asso. Yale, 1959—; vis. lectr. U. Cal. at Berkeley, 1963-65; recordings of 155 Am. and Brit. poets reading own works, 1948—; coordinated Yale Series of Recorded Poets, 1959-61; distinguished vis. lectr. Frostburg (Md.) State Coll., 1966-67; poet in residence U. Wis., Eau Claire, 1967. Served with USNRF, World War I. Scholar, U. Pitts., 1916. Author: Prevailing Winds, 1944; The Floating World, 1953; The Floating World and Other Poems, 1956; Nags Head and Other Poems, 1960; Nags Head (recording), 1960; Eye Versus Ear, 1961; Bearstone Tetralogy, 1969. Address: RD Glen Rock PA 17327

ANDERSON, LEE STRATTON, newspaper editor; b. Trenton, Ky., Dec. 15, 1925; s. Herbert Love and Corinne (Kirkpatrick) A.; A.B., U. Chattanooga, 1948; m. Elizabeth McDonald, June 10, 1950; children—Corinne Elizabeth, Mary Stewart. Reporter Chattanooga News-Free Press, 1942-48, asso. editor, 1948-58, editor, 1958—; pres. Anderson-Meyers Enterprises, Inc., operator Confederama; pres. Trail of Tears, Inc., Gatlinburg, Tenn. Pres., Chattanooga Conv. and Visitor's Bur., 1958; chmn. Chattanooga chpt. A.R.C., 1968-70. Served with USAAF, World War II; maj. Army Res. Recipient Freedoms Found. awards for editorial writing, 1959, 60, 63-69; Freedoms Found. award speech 1962. Mem. Sigma Chi. Presbyn. (elder). Rotarian (pres. Chattanooga 1964-65). Author: Valley of The Shadow; Battles of Chickamauga and Chattanooga 1863. Home: 220 N Crest Rd Chattanooga TN 37404 Office: 400 11th St Chattanooga TN 37401

ANDERSON, LEE WILLIAM, educator; b. West Palm Beach, Fla., Nov. 15, 1926; s. Hjalmer Lawerance and Lillian (Betzinger) A.; B.A., Reed Coll., 1952; M.S., Tulane U., 1955, Ph.D., 1956; m. Jacqueline Downing, Apr. 6, 1951; children—Kimberly, Alan, Lars. Asst. prof. U. Ore., 1956-60; asso.prof. U. Ga., 1960-62; asso. prof. Pa. State U., 1962-64, prof. math., 1964—; math. cons. Naval Ordnance Testing Sta., China Lake, Cal., 1959. Served with USNR, 1944-46. Republican. Episcopalian. Elk. Contbr. sects. to text books, articles to math. jours. Home: 246 E Hamilton Av State College PA 16801

ANDERSON, LEIGH CHARLES, ret. educator; b. Muskegon, Mich., Mar. 28, 1899; s. Rudolph Pere and Josephine (Torgeson) A.; B.S., U. Mich., 1921, M.S., 1922, Ph.D., 1924; m. Alloa Caviness, Feb. 2, 1925; children—Leighton Charles, Peter Caviness, Robert Keith. Mem. faculty U. Mich., 1924-69, prof. chemistry 1944-69, chmn. dept., 1948-66. Served pvt. U.S. Army, 1918. Fellow A.A.A.S.; mem. Am. Chem. Soc., Sigma Xi, Phi Lambda Upsilon, Alpha Chi Sigma, Gamma Alpha. Mason. Author: A Manual for the Organic Chemistry Laboratory (with W.E. Bachman), 1953, rev. edit. (with Robert C. Elderfield, P.A.S. Smith, W.E. Bachmann), 1960. Contbr. to sci. jours. Home: 1120 Lincoln Av Ann Arbor, MI 48104.

ANDERSON, LELAND DALE, ret. educator, dentist; b. Watertown, Wis., Dec. 6, 1899; s. Wilbur Leland and Emma Adelaide (Handy) A.; D.D.S., State U. Ia., 1924; m. Margaret Ruth McAllister, Nov. 20, 1922; 1 dau., Margery Jean (Mrs. Leonard B. Vranicar). Gen. practice dentistry, Monroe, Ia., 1924-40; faculty Coll. Dentistry, State U. Ia., from 1940, prof., head dept. dental tech., from 1955. Mem. city council, sch. bd., also city clk., Monroe, Ia. Served with U.S. Army, 1918-19. Mem. Am. Coll. Dentists, Am. Dental Assn., Johnson County, Dist., Ia. dental socs., Am. Legion (past adj., comdr.), Omicron Kappa Upsilon (sec.-treas. supreme chpt. 1955-60, pres. 1962-63), Sigma Phi Alpha (hon.). Mason (Shriner), Elk; mem. Order Eastern Star. Home: 211 Highland Dr Iowa City IA 52240

ANDERSON, LEMOYNE W., librarian; b. Wheaton, Minn., Aug. 16, 1923; s. Walter E. and Ruth (Lundquist) A.; student Gustavus Adolphus Coll., 1942, 46; A.B., U. Minn., 1948, B.S. in L.S., 1948; M.S., U. Ill., 1951, Ph.D., 1970; m. Hollis Annetta Pearson, June 2, 1950; children—Kristine Marie, Victoria Annetta. Serials librarian Ia. State U., 1948-50; counselor librarian U. Ill., Chgo., 1951-55, reference librarian, asst. prof. library sci., 1955-57; dir. libraries, prof. library sci. Colo. State U., 1957—. Served to sgt. AUS, 1942-45. Decorated Bronze Star medal, Purple Heart. Mem. Am., Mountain-Plains, Colo. (pres. 1971—) library assns., Assn. Coll. and Research Libraries, Am. Assn. U. Profs., Am-Scandinavian Found., Alpha Tau Omega. Lutheran. Club: Lions. Home: 2000 Orchard Pl Fort Collins CO 80521

ANDERSON, LEO E., lawyer; b. Gettysburg, S.D., Feb. 20, 1902; s. Laurits Martin and Leonora (Ellis) A.; student U. Redlands, 1921-22; B.S., B.A., U. So. Cal., 1924, LL.B., 1927; m. Hollis Norris, Nov. 1, 1931 (dec. 1959); childrenDenise, David H.; m. 2d, Pauline Murray, Feb. 12, 1961. Admitted to Cal. bar; with firm Meserve, Mumper & Hughes, Los Angeles, 1927-, partner, 1938-Vice pres., dir. Lennox Industries; pres., dir. Slobe Avenue Corp., Saybrook Corp.; treas., dir. Prairie Oil Co., Ill. Crude Oil Co. Chmn. Los Angeles County Republican Central Com., 1936- 40, Cal. Rep. Central Com., 1946-48. Trustee U. Redlands (Cal.). Mason (grandmaster Cal. 1958). Home: 1215 S Orange Grove Blvd Pasadena CA 91105 Office: 612 S Flower St Los Angeles CA 90017

ANDERSON, LEONARD GUSTAVE, railroad ofcl.; b. Danville, Ill., Jan. 16, 1919; s. Andrew John and Hedvig (Engstrom) A.; B.S., U. So. Miss., 1947; LL.B., Emory U., 1949; m. Perrin Louise Johnston, Aug. 25, 1946. Admitted to Ga. bar, 1949; lawyer Atlantic Coast Line R.R. Co., 1950-67; lawyer Seaboard Coast Line R.R. Co., 1967-68, treas., 1968—; dir. Seacoast Transp. Co., Tampa and Gulf R.R., Trailer Train Co. mem. finance com. Fruit Growers Express Co., Norfolk & Portsmouth Belt Line R.R. Co. Served to capt. AUS, 1942-46; maj. Res. Mem. Am. Bar Assn., State Bar Ga., Phi Delta Phi. Democrat. Methodist. Club: Ponte Vedra (Ponte Vedra Beach, Fla.). Home: 300 W Franklin St Richmond VA 23220 Office 3600 W Broad St Richmond VA 23213

ANDERSON, LEROY, composer, conductor; b. Cambridge, Mass., June 29, 1908; s. Brewer A. and Anna M. (Johnson) A.; A.B., Harvard, 1929, M.A., 1930, postgrad., 1930-34; m. Eleanor Jane Firke, Oct. 31, 1942; children—Jane M., Eric R., Rolf F., Kurt A. Tutor div. music Radcliffe Coll., 1930-32; music dir. Harvard Band, 1932-35; organist, choirmaster East Congl. Ch., Milton, Mass., 1929-35; guest condr. own rec. orch., 1950-; guest condr. many symphony orchs. Served as capt. M.I., AUS, 1942-46, 51-52. Mem. A.S.C.A.P., Dramatists Guild, Am.-Scandinavian Found., Assn. Ex-Mems. Squadron A, Am. Guild Authors and Composers, Phi Beta Kappa. Club: Harvard (Boston). Composer: Jazz Pizzicato, Jazz Legato, The Syncopated Clock, Fiddle-Faddle, Irish Suite, Sleigh Ride, Serenata, A Trumpeter's Lullaby, The Waltzing Cat, A Christmas Festival, Belle of the Ball, Blue Tango, The Typewriter, Bugler's Holiday, Forgotten Dreams, Clarinet Candy, Home Stretch, Arietta, Balladette, The Golden Years, The Captains and the Kings, and others. Office: care ASCAP 575 Madison Av New York City NY 10022

ANDERSON, LESLIE PAUL, educator; b. Shorewood, Wis., Sept. 21, 1926; s. Alonzo Herman and Martha (Peterson) A.; B.S., U. Wis., 1951, M.S., 1954, Ph.D., 1960; m. Joanne Inglefield, Dec. 4, 1954; children—Clinton Mark, Kurt David, Jean Nicole. Credit analyst U.S. Steel Co., 1954-55; staff asst. to pres. Evert Container Corp., Milw., 1955-57; instr. U. Wis.- Madison, 1958-60; asst. prof. U. Ariz., 1960-62; economist, cons. SEC, 1962-64; asso. prof. finance U. Ore., 1964-69; vis. asso. prof. Harvard, 1967-69; prof. finance, chmn. dept. finance and real estate Colo. State U., Fort Collins, 1969—. Chmn. Colo. Recreation Corp.; pres. Leslie P. Anderson & Assos.; cons. Mountain States Telephone Co., J.I. Wells & Co. Inc., Soft-Pac, Inc. Tchr. creative photography to disadvantaged children, 1967—. Served with USNR, 1944-46, to 1st lt. USAF, 1951-53. Earhart Found. fellow, 1957-58, Ford pre-doctoral fellow, 1958-59, Ford doctoral dissertation fellow, 1959-60. Mem. Am., Western (dir. 1970-71) finance assns., Financial Mgmt. Assn. (v.p. 1970-71), Am. Econ. Assn. Author: Financial Analysis, 1970; The Finance Function, 1971; Capital Structure Analysis, 1971. Contbr. articles profl. jours. Home: 21 Forest Hills Lane Fort Collins CO 80521

ANDERSON, LUTHER CARLETON, business exec.; b. Scandinavia, Wis., Aug. 3, 1898; s. Peter B. and Carrie A. (Thompson) A.; A.B., U. Wis., 1922; m. Meryl A. Halsted, Aug. 4, 1923; children—Edith L. (Mrs. Beatty H. Ramsay), Janet C. (Mrs. Thomas A. Butler). Tchr., Washburn, Wis., 1917, Weyauwega, Wis., 1918-20; investment banker Spencer-Trask Co., 1922-29; investment counsel H.S. and S.G. Mudd Co., 1936-68; pres. Bowie Pie Co., 1943-65, Sutter Basin Corp. Ltd., 1946—; pres., chief exec. officer

Arden-Mayfair Inc., 1967-70, also dir.; dir. Cyprus Mines Corp. Commr. Los Angeles City Employees Retirement System, 1938-53; dir. Los Angeles Met. Water Dist., 1953—. Trustee Seeley W. Mudd Found. Served with U.S. Army, World War I. Club: Los Angeles Country, California, Bel-Air Bay (Los Angeles); La Quinta (Palm Desert, Cal.); DeAnza Desert Country (Borrego Springs, Cal.). Home: 12837 Highwood St Los Angeles CA 90049 Office: 523 W 6th St Los Angeles CA 90014

ANDERSON, MARIAN, contralto; b. Phila., Feb. 17, 1902; ed. Phila. pub. schs.; mus edn. pvt. study in Phila., N.Y. and abroad; hon. degreees 23 Am. ednl. instns., 1 Korean; m. Orpheus H. Fisher, July 24, 1943. As child sang in Union Bapt. Ch. choir, Phila.; a fund raised through a church concert enabled her to take singing lessons under an Italian instr.; won 1st prize in competition with 300 others at N.Y. Lewisohn Stadium, 1925; began singing career, 1924; debut in Un Ballo in Maschera, Met. Opera, 1955; has made many concert tours of the U.S. and Europe; one of the leading contraltos in world; appearances in all famous concert halls, stadia; U.S. del. to UN, 1955. Recipient Bok Award, 1940; awarded Finnish decoration "probenignitate humana," 1940; decorations from Sweden, Philippines, Haiti, Liberia, France, numerous states and cities in U.S.; Yokus Lo medal (Japan). U.S. del. 13th Gen. Assembly, UN. Mem. Alpha Kappa Alpha. Home: Danbury CT 06810

ANDERSON, MARQUARD JOHN, mfg. exec.; b. Clairton, Pa., Apr. 15, 1920; s. Carl J. and Anna C. (Carlson) A.; B.S., U. Pitts., 1942; m. Catherine Markey, June 2, 1945; childrenCarl, John, Ruth C. With Aro Corporation, Bryan, O., 1945-. successively asst. sales mgr., asst. to v.p., v.p., 1945-56, pres., 1956—, also dir.; dir. Reliance Electric Co., Cleve., Citizens Nat. Bank, Bryan, Union Pump Co., Battle Creek, Mich. Served as capt. USAAF, 1942-45. Mason (Shriner). Home: Center Ridge Rd Bryan OH 43506 Office: Aro Corp 1Aro Center Bryan OH 43506

ANDERSON, MARTIN, educator, govt. ofcl.; b. Lowell, Mass., Aug. 5, 1936; s. Ralph and Evelyn (Anderson) A.; A.B. summa cum laude, Dartmouth, 1957; M.S. in Engring. and Bus. Adminstrn., Thayer Sch. Engring. and Amos Tuck Sch. Bus. Adminstrn., 1958; Ph.D. in Indsl. Mgmt., Mass. Inst. Tech., 1962; m. Annelise Graebner, Sept. 9, 1965. Asst. to dean, instr. engring. Thayer Sch. Engring., 1959; research fellow Joint Center Urban Studies, Mass. Inst. Tech. and Harvard, 1961-62; asst. prof. finance Grad. Sch. Bus., Columbia, 1962-65, asso. prof. bus., 1965-68; spl. asst. to Pres. of U.S., 1969-70, spl. cons. to Pres. U.S. for systems analysis, 1970—. Dir. research Nixon presdl. campaign, 1968. Served as 2d lt. AUS, 1958. Mem. Am. Econ. Assn., Am. Finance Assn., Phi Beta Kappa. Author: The Federal Bulldozer: A Critical Analysis of Urban Renewal, 1949-62, 1964. Home: Watergate Washington DC 20009 Office: White House Washington DC 20500

ANDERSON, MILTON HENRY, psychiatrist, hosp. adminstr.; b. Omaha, July 31, 1919; s. Milton Henry and Emma Fay (Anderson) A.; student Northwestern U., 1937-38; A.B., Omaha U., 1941; M.D., U. Neb., 1943; m. M. Margaret Cushing, July 24, 1943 (dec. 1960); children—Gregory Cushing, Milton Henry III, Herbert Clark, Eric Austin; m. J. Sue Roberts, September 12, 1966. Intern Long Island Coll. Medicine, 1943-44; resident Lenox Hill Hosp., N.Y.C., 1944-45; clin. dir. Hastings (Neb.) State Hosp., 1948-51; med. supt. Osawatomie (Kan.) State Hosp., 1951-53, Evansville State Hosp., 1953-69; dir. psychiatry Welborn Meml. Hosp., 1969—. Cons. Deaconess, St. Mary's hosps., regional VA hosps., states Ill. and Ind.; bd. dirs. Evansville Child Guidance Clinic, 1953-62, Vanderburgh County Mental Health Clinic, 1964; active local health fund drives, YMCA. Served to capt., M.C., AUS, 1945-47. Bishop Clarkson resident physician, 1947-48; fellow Bennett Found., 1947-48. Diplomate Am. Bd. Psychiatry and Neurology. Fellow Am. Psychiatric Assn., Am. Orthopsychiat. Assn., A.A.A.S., Am. Geiratric Soc.; mem. Central Neurophyschiat. Assn., Western Electroencephalographic Soc., Am. Epilepsy Soc., Am. Group Psychotherapy Assn., Assn. Research Nervous and Mental Diseases, Sigma Chi, Phi Rho Sigma. Mason (Shriner). Clubs: Indpls. Athletic; Evansville Country; Rotary (pres. 1968-69). Address: 3700 Bellemeade St Evansville IN 47715

ANDERSON, NILS, Jr., mcht., exec.; b. Plainfield, N.J., Jan. 28, 1914; s. Nils and Marguerite (Stephens) A.; ed. Lawrenceville, Loomis schs.; B.A., Williams Coll., 1937; student Colo. Sch. Mines, George Washington U. Law Sch.; m. Jean Derby Ferris, July 30, 1938; children—Nils III, Derby Ferris, Stephens Massie, Ward Reynolds. With Koppers Co., summers 1933-37, Bakelite Corp., 1937-41; dir. Deveboise-Anderson Co., Inc., 1937—, pres., 1950-58, chmn. bd., 1965—; pres., dir. Debanders, Inc., 1950—; v.p. Casein Co. Am. (subsequently chem. div. Borden Co.), 1945-50 (also dir. Am., S.Am. cos. during this period); pres., dir. Fairfield Sales Corp., 1953—; pres. Port Ore Processing Co. With WPB, 1941-45, chief adhesives unit, 1942, chief plastics br., 1944-45, also govt. presiding officer adhesives, plastics industry adv. coms., chem. div. adviser to Dept. Agr.; combined Raw Materials Bd., Stock Pile and Shipping Br. during World War II; mem. U.S. Trade Mission to Rumania and Poland, 1965. Mem. Am. Soc. M.E., Am.. Inst. Mining, Metall. and Petroleum Engrs., Am. Coke and Coal Chems. Inst., Am. Iron and Steel Inst., Newcomen Soc. N. Am., Pa. Soc., Soc. Colonial Wars, Soc. War 1812, Pilgrims Soc., Alpha Delta Phi. Clubs: Links, University, Pinnacle (N.Y.C.); Country (Fairfield); Duquesne (Pitts.); Travellers (Paris); Rolling Rock (Pa.); Pequot Yacht. Author tech. articles on adhesives and plastics. Home: 1100 Pequot Rd Southport CT 06490 Office: 60 E 42d St New York City NY 10017

ANDERSON, NORMAN J., marine corps officer; b. Manitowoc, Wis., Feb. 7, 1913; s. Anton O. Anderson; A.B., U. Cal. at Los Angeles, 1934; postgrad. student Stanford; m. Irene Fernandez, June 12, 1954; children—Norman, Kirk. Flight tng., 1936; commd. 2d lt. USMCR, 1937, advanced through grades to maj. gen. USMC, 1965; aide to comdg. gen. 1st Marine Aircraft Wing; combat missions in Solomons World War II; comdr. VMB-423, Bismarck and Philippines areas, World War II; comdr. aircraft engring. squadion, El Toro, Cal.; head air sect. Amphibious Warfare Sch.; dep. comdr. MAG-33, Korea; assigned Pacific Fleet Evaluation Group; grad. Nat. War Coll., 1953; head air sect., tactics and techniques bd. Devel. Center, Quantico, Va., 1953-56, Policy Analysis Div., Hdqrs. USMC, 1956-59; comdg. officer MAG-11, Japan; assigned Nat. War Coll., also mem. bd. to examine orgn. Hdqrs. USMC, 1961; asst. wing comdr. 2d Marine Aircraft Wing, 1963-64; comdg. gen. Marine Corps Air Bases Eastern Area, also Marine Corps Air Sta., Cherry Point, N.C. 1964-66. 2d Marine Aircraft Wing, 1966-67, 1st Marine Wing, Vietnam, 1967-68; dep. comdr. Fleet Marine Force, Atlantic 1968-69; dep. chief staff Atlantic Command, 1969—. Decorated D.S.M., Silver Star; recipient Profl. Achievement award U. Cal. at Los Angeles. 1967. Mem. Theta Xi. Home: Arlington VA Office: Hdqrs USMC Washington DC 20380

ANDERSON, NORMAN RICHARDS, advt. agy. exec.; b. New Rochelle, N.Y., Mar. 17, 1914; s. F. Richard and Gertrude (Saye) A.; grad. Worcester (Mass.) Acad., 1934; m. Irene Smith, Nov. 21, 1962; 1 dau., Judith Lovejoy. Sales mgr. Internat. Silver Co., N.Y.C., 1935-41; asst. plant mgr. Douglas Aircraft Co., Long Beach, Cal., 1942-45; buyer R.H. Macy & Co., N.Y.C., 1945-47; sales, advt. mgr. Gen. Foods Corp., N.Y.C., 1947-51; pres. Allen, Anderson, Niefeld & Paley, Inc., Chgo., 1952-; dir. Grabin-Shaw Advt., Milw. Bd. govs. Met. Housing and Planning Council. Club: Lake Shore (Chgo.). Home: 850 Dewitt Pl Chicago IL 60611 Office: 351 E Ohio St Chicago, IL 60611.

ANDERSON, O. KELLEY, ins. exec.; b. Lamoni, Ia., May 11, 1907; s. Oscar and Ella Belle (Kelley) A.; B.A., U. Ia.; M.B.A., Harvard; m. Alma Weichel, Jan. 21, 1933; 1 son, O. Kelley, Jr. With Stone & Webster, Inc., 1929-31; v.p., clk. Kidder Peabody Acceptance Corp., 1931-33; v.p., sec. Consol. Investment Trust, Boston, 1933-35, pres., trustee, 1935-50; pres. New Eng. Mut. Life Ins. Co., 1951-66, chmn., 1966—, dir., 1947—; pres., dir., founder Boston Fund, Inc., 1939-50, now dir.; dir. Daniel Green Co., Boston Edison Co., Gillette Co.; dir. Capital Exchange Fund, Inc., Depositors Fund Boston, Inc., Fiduciary Exchange Fund, Inc., Leverage Fund Boston, Inc., Second Fiduciary Exchange Fund, Inc., Ritz-Carlton Hotel Co., Exchange Fund Boston, Inc., Diversification Fund, Inc., Boston Common Stock Fund, Inc.; trustee Real Estate Investment Trust Am., Century Shares Trust, Provident Instn. for Savs., Consol. Investment Trust. Trustee Com. for Econ. Devel. Fellow Am. Acad. Arts and Scis.; mem. Nat. Indsl. Conf. Bd. Home: 15 Chestnut St Boston MA 02108 Office: 501 Boylston St Boston MA 02117

ANDERSON, ODIN WALDEMAR, sociologist, educator; b. Mpls., July 5, 1914; s. Edwin and Anna (Ormbreck) A.; B.A., U. Wis., 1937, M.A., 1938; B.A. in L.S., U. Mich., 1940, Ph.D., 1948; m. Helen Hay, June 24, 1939; children—Kristin Alice, Thor Edwin. Instr., U. Mich. Sch. Pub. Health, 1944-49; asso. prof. dept. clin. preventive medicine, med. faculty U. Western Ont., London, 1949-52; research dir. Health Information Found., N.Y.C., 1952-62; research dir. Health Information Found., U. Chgo., 1962-64, research dir. Center Health Adminstrn. Studies, 1964-66, asso. dir., 1966—, asso. prof. sociology, dept. sociology and Grad. Sch. Bus., 1962-64, prof., 1964—. Mem. research com. Nat. Tb Assn., 1959- 64; mem. U.S. Nat. Com. Vital and Health Statistics, 1959-63; mem. research com. Am. Hosp. Assn., 1959—. Fellow Am. Sociol. Assn. (past chmn. sect. med. sociology), Am. Pub. Health Assn., Am. Coll. Hosp. Adminstrs. (hon.). Author: (with Jacob J. Feldman) Family Medical Care and Voluntary Health Insurance, 1956; (with others) Family Medical Care and Health Insurance, 1963; (with Ronald Andersen) A Decade of Health Services: Social Survey Trends in Use and Expenditures, 1968; The Uneasy Equilibrium: Private and Public Financing of Health Services in the U.S., 1875-1965, 1968. Home: 1325 E 55th St Chicago IL 60615

ANDERSON, ORSON LAMAR, educator, physicist; b. Price, Utah, Dec. 3, 1924; s. Orson B. and Elda (Edwards) A.; B.S., U. Utah, 1948, Ph.D., 1951; m. Dorothy C. Gage, July 3, 1946; children—Bonnie, Sherri, Chester. Physicist mechanics research Bell Telephone Labs., Murray Hill, N.J., 1951-60; mgr. materials research Am.-Standard Research Labs., New Brunswick, N.J., 1960-63; sr. research asso. Lamont Geol. Obs., Columbia, 1963—, adj. prof., 1963-66, prof. geology, 1966—. Served with USAAF, 1942-45. Fellow Am. Phys. Soc., Am. Ceramic Soc. Editor-in-chief Jour. Geophys. Research, 1966—. Contbr. articles profl. jours. Home: Route 9 W Box 178 Palisades NY 10964 Office: Geology Dept Columbia New York City NY 10027

ANDERSON, OSCAR ALFRED, coll. pres.; b. Mpls., Apr. 19, 1916; s. Alfred B. and Pearl (Gulack) A.; student Augsburg Coll., Mpls., 1934-36; B.A., St. Olaf Coll., Northfield, Minn., 1936-38; Th.B., Luther Theol. Sem., St. Paul, 1942; student Lutheran Bible Inst., Mpls., 1933-34, Union Theol. Sem., N.Y.C., 1962; LL.D., Concordia Coll., Moorhead, Minn., 1963; m. Leola Stime, Aug. 14, 1943; children—Donna Margaret, Randall, Sheldon, Gracia. Ordained to ministry Luth. Ch., 1942; pastor Lake Harriet Luth. Ch., Mpls., 1942-48; exec. dir. Internat. Young People's Luther League, 1948- 54; pastor Trinity Luth. Ch., Moorhead, 1954-63; pres. Augsburg Coll., 1963—. Dir. Fourth Northwestern Nat. Bank, Mpls. Mem. Mpls. Indsl. Devel. Commn., 1966-70. Mem., dir. Minn. Council on Econ. Edn., 1967—; bd. dirs. Mpls. Urban Coalition, 1968—; bd. regents Luther Theol. Sem., 1960—, chmn., 1960-64; bd. dirs. Univ. Community Devel. Corp., 1966—; pres. Minn. Pvt. Coll. Council, 1967-69; bd. dirs. Breck Sch., Mpls. Urban Coalition, 1968—, Twin City Inst. Talented Youth, 1966—; bd. govs. Met. YMCA, Mpls., 1967—; exec. com. Norwegian-Am. Hist. Assn., 1969—; adv. council UN Assn. of Minn., 1971—. Rotarian. Club: Minneapolis. Author: With Him All the Way, 1948; Baptism and its Relations to Lutheran Evangelism, 1955. Address: Augsburg Coll Minneapolis MN 55404

ANDERSON, OSCAR V., clergyman; b. N.Y.C., Feb. 24, 1903; s. August and Augusta (Gustafson) A.; A.B., Upsala Coll., East Orange, N.J., 1929; B.D., Augustana Theol. Sem., 1932, Th.M., 1933, D.D., 1953; postgrad. Union Theol. Sem., Columbia U., U. Chgo.; m. Lilly V. Flodden, June 20, 1933; childrenSandra Ruth (Mrs. Robert C. Sanderson), Bruce Timothy. Prof. Christianity, Augustana Coll., 1932-35; pastor Calvary Luth. Ch., Chgo., 1935-39, Grace Luth. Ch., LaGrange, Ill., 1939- 1939- 54, Bay Shore Luth. Ch., Milw., 1963-; pres. Central Conf. Augustana Luth. Ch., 1954-63. Mem. and officer numerous bds. and commns. Augustana Luth. Ch., Nat. Luth. Council, Luth. Council U.S. Am., Nat. Council Chs. of Christ U.S.A., study com. World Council of Chs.; bd. dirs. Luth. Sch. Theology, Chgo.; exec. council Luth. Ch. in Am. Mem. Am. Soc. Church History, Augustana Hist. Soc. Author pamphlets and articles in church history and related fields. Home: 5303 N Santa Monica Blvd Milwaukee WI 53217 Office: 1200 E Hampton Rd Milwaukee WI 53217

ANDERSON, PAUL EDWARD, cement co. exec.; b. Pottsville, Pa., Aug. 19, 1921; s. Thomas and Virginia (Nolan) A.; grad. Peirce Sch. Bus. Adminstrn., Phila., 1948; m. Florence Joan White, Oct. 16, 1948; childrenPaul Edward, Barbara Jane. With Lehigh Portland Cement Co., Allentown, Pa., 1948-, credit mgr., 1957-64, treas., 1958-67, v.p. corporate devel., 1967-70, mgr. real estate 1970—. 1970. Bd. dirs. Pa. Economy League. Roman Catholic. Home: 3756 Turner St Allentown PA 118104 Office: 718 Hamilton St Allentown PA 18101

ANDERSON, PAUL F., bishop; b. Boston, Apr. 20, 1917; s. Philip Leo and Mary Elizabeth (Doyle) A.; B.A., St. John's Sem., Brighton, Mass., 1943. Ordained priest Roman Cath. Ch., 1943; pastor Sioux Falls (S.D.) Cath. Diocese, 1946-68; coadjutor bishop of Duluth, 1968-69, bishop, 1969—. Home: 2215 E 2d St Duluth MN 55812 Office: 215 W 4th St Duluth MN 55806

ANDERSON, PAUL HERMAN, metallurgist, educator; b. Rapid City, S.D., Dec. 14, 1920; s. Albert and Hannah (Johnson) A.; B.S., Sch. Mines, 1943; M.S., U. Minn., 1949, Ph.D., 1954; m. Genevieve Carol Carson, June 18, 1943; children—Paul Carroll (dec.), Lois Ellen, Ruth Elaine, Daniel Howard. Supt. heat treatment dept. Am. Hammered Piston Ring div. Koppers Co., Balt., 1943- 46; teaching asst., research fellow U. Minn., Mpls., 1946-51; instr. Colo. Sch. Mines, Golden, 1951-54; prof. metallurgy S.D. Sch. Mines and Tech., 1954—, head dept. metallurgy, 1954-70; prof. metallurgy Istanbul Tech. U., Turkey, 1964-66; guest metallurgist Brookhaven Nat. Lab., summers 1956- 57; staff mem. Los Alamos Sci. Lab., summers 1958-63. Pres. Meadowbrook P.T.A., Rapid City, 1961-62, USAF Dependents' Sch. P.T.A., Istanbul, 1965-66. Mem. bd. edn. Rapid City Ind. Sch. Dist., 1969—; v.p., 1970-71, pres., 1971—. Registered profl. engr., Cal. Mem. Am. Inst. Mining, Metall. and Petroleum Engrs. (chmn. Black Hills sect. 1963, com. mem. at large council edn. 1964-66), Am. Soc. Metals (sec. edn. com. 1960-63, adv. com. jour. 1967-70), Am. Soc. Engring. Edn. (materials sci. com. 1962- 63), Inst. Metals (Brit.), A.A.A.S., Am. Assn. U. Profs., S.D. Acad. Sci., Sigma Xi, Sigma Tau, Gamma Alpha, Gamma Delta. Republican. Lutheran. Home: 2020 Stirling St Rapid City SD 57701

ANDERSON, PAUL O., newspaper editor; b. Tacoma, Jan. 9, 1916; s. Oscar and Edith (Johnson) A.; student U. Puget Sound, 1935-39, St. Martins Coll., 1938; m. Kathleen Murphy, Sept. 18, 1943; children—Sandra (Mrs. Joseph G. Gordon), Virginia Lee. With Tacoma Daily Ledger, 1935; with Tacoma News Tribune, 1935—, mng. editor, 1964-69, editor, 1969—. Served with USNR, 1940-45, 51-53. Mem. Naval Res. Officers Assn., Sigma Delta Chi. Lutheran. Mason. Home: 617 N Stadium Way Tacoma WA 98403 Office: 713 St Helens Av Tacoma WA 98401

ANDERSON, PAUL RUSSELL, univ. pres.; b. Akron, O., Sept. 27, 1907; s. Foster Cookman and Ora Estelle (Robins) A.; B.A. cum laude, Ohio Wesleyan U., 1928; Ph.D., Columbia U., 1933; student Union Theol. Sem., N.Y., 1930-31, New Sch. for Social Research, N.Y., 1932-33; LL.D., Ohio Wesleyan U., 1949, U. Pitts., 1950, Allegheny Coll., 1957, Lake Erie Coll., 1960. Phila. Coll. Osteopathy, 1967, Villanova U., 1968, Dropsie Coll., 1969; D.Sc., Wilkes Coll., 1968; L.H.D., Elmira Coll., 1958; D.Litt., Chatham Coll., 1960; m. Betty Ann Brown, July 26, 1934; 1 son, Bayard Dick. Instr., Am. U. of Beirut, Syria, 1928-30; asso. prof. MacMurray Coll., Jacksonville, Ill., 1933-34; prof., Lake Erie Coll., Painesville, O., 1934-40; on leave at Oberlin Coll., 1938-30; asso. prof. philosophy Lawrence Coll., 1940-41, dean of coll., prof. philosophy, 1941-45, on leave as cons. Am. Council on Edn., 1944-45; pres. Chatham Coll., Pitts., 1945-60; v.p. univ., prof. philosophy Temple U., Phila., 1960-67, pres., 1967—. Hon. mem. Ninth Internat. Congress Philosophy, Paris, 1937, Internat. Seminar, India, 1950; lectr. Dept. of State, India, 1953; mem. com. on measurement and evaluation Am. Council on Edn. (chmn. 1953-60); bd. dirs. Pitts. Symphony Orch., 1950-60; mem. Civic Bd. of Pitts. Playhouse, 1945-60, Pa. State Council Edn., 1952-62; chmn. Com. Pub. Health, 1948-58. Trustee Beaver Coll.; pres. Pa. Found. Independent Colls., 1959-60. Mem. Pa. Assn. Colls. and Univs. (pres. 1948-49), Am. Philos. Assn., A.A.A.S., Am. Assn. U. Profs., Sigma Alpha Epsilon, Omicron Delta Kappa, Phi Beta Kappa, Delta Sigma Rho, Pi Delta Epsilon. Republican. Episcopalian. Clubs: Racquet, Union League (Phila); Century (N.Y.C.). Author: Science in Defense of Liberal Religion: A Study of Henry More's Attempt to Link Seventeenth Century Religion with Science, 1933; Platonism in the Midwest, 1963. Co-author: Philosophy in America from the Puritans to James, 1939. Edtor: Universal Military Training and National Security, 1945. Home: 250 S 18th St Philadelphia, PA 19103.

ANDERSON, PEYTON TOOKE, Jr., former newspaper pub.; b. Macon, Ga., Apr. 9, 1907; s. Peyton Tooke and Nell Brown (Griswold) A.; grad. Riverside Mil. Acad., Gainesville, Ga., 1924; student, Columbian Prep. Sch. Washington, 1924-25, U.S. Naval Acad., 1925-27; m. Katherine McClure, June 10, 1930; children—Katherine (Mrs. Katherine A. Bleibtreu), Deyerel (Mrs. Deyerle A. Hanson). With Macon Telegraph and News, 1916-69; dir. Southern Co., Ga. So. and Fla. R.R., Knight Newspapers, Inc. Served with USN, 1941- 45. Decorated Bronze Star. Episcopalian.

ANDERSON, PHILIP SIDNEY, lawyer; b. Little Rock, May 9, 1935; s. Philip Sidney and Frances (Walt) A.; B.A., U. Ark., 1959, LL.B., 1959; m. Rosemary Gill Wright, Sept. 26, 1959; children—Sidney Walt, Philip Wright, Catherine Gill. Admitted to Ark. bar, 1960, since practiced in Little Rock; partner Wright, Lindsey & Jennings; lectr. Ark. Law Sch., 1963-65; mem. Ark. Supreme Ct. Com. on Jury Instrns., 1962—. Past pres., now mem. bd. dirs. Friends of Little Rock Pub. Library; bd. dirs. Little Rock Unlimited Progress, Inc., Ark. region Nat. Conf. Christians and Jews, Pulaski County chpt. Nat. Found.; sponsor Little Rock Chamber Music Soc. Served to 2d lt. U.S. Army, 1959-60. Recipient Spl. award Ark. Bar Assn., 1966. Mem. Am. Judicature Soc., Am., Ark., Pulaski County bar assns., Ark. Bar Found. (dir.), Blue Key, Kappa Sigma. Co-author: Arkansas Model Jury Instructions, 1965. Home: 4716 Crestwood St Little Rock AR 72207 Office: 2200 Worthen Bank Bldg Little Rock AR 72201

ANDERSON, QUENTIN, educator, critic; b. Minnewaukan, N.D., July 21, 1912; s. Maxwell and Margaret E. (Haskett) A.; student Dartmouth, 1931-32; A.B., Columbia, 1937, Ph.D., 1953; M.A., Harvard, 1945; m. Margaret Pickett, May 27, 1933 (div. Aug. 1946); 1 dau., Martha Haskett; m. 2d, Thelma Ehrlich, Dec. 13, 1947; children—Abraham Bruce, Maxwell Lincoln. Mem. faculty Columbia, 1939—, prof. English, 1961—; vis. prof. U. Sussex (Eng.), 1966-67. Fulbright grantee, France, 1962-63. Mem. Modern Lang. Assn., Author's League. Editor: Henry James, Selected Short Stories, 1950; The American Henry James, 1957; (Hawthorne) Twice Told Tales, 1960; (with Joseph A. Mazzeo) The Proper Study, 1962; The Imperial Self, 1971. Home: 29 Claremont Av New York City NY 10027

ANDERSON, RALPH ALEXANDER, Jr., architect; b. Houston, Jan. 1, 1923; s. Ralph Alexander and Ruby (Ellison) A.; B.A. in Arch., Rice Inst., 1943, B.S., 1947. With firm Wilson, Morris & Crain, Houston, 1947-52, partner, 1952-62; partner firm Wilson, Morris, Crain & Anderson, Houston, 1962—; prin. works include World Trade Center, Houston, 1962, Kelsey-Seybold Clinic, Houston, 1963, WISH-TV, Indpls., 1966, Western Nat. Bank, Houston, 1967, Houston Post Bldg., 1969. Pres. Contemporary Art Mus. Houston, 1957, Houston Bot. Soc., 1967-68; chmn. Billboards, Ltd., action group, 1967-71. Served with inf. AUS, 1943-45; ETO. Fellow A.I.A. (pres. Houston 1966); mem. Phi Beta Kappa. Home: 1638 Banks St Houston TX 77006 Office: 3456 W Alabama St Houston TX 77027

ANDERSON, RAYMOND HAROLD, journalist; b. Barnum, Wis., June 11, 1926; s. James C. and Gusta (Krugrud) A.; B.A., U. Wis., 1951, M.A., 1952; student (Fulbright scholar), Slavic Inst., U. Aarhus (Denmark), 1952-53; m. Alevtina Ledovskikh, Apr. 29, 1963; 1 son, Alexander Harold. With Staunton (Va.) News Leader, 1955-56, Richmond (Va.) Times-Dispatch, 1956-60; mem. staff N.Y. Times, 1960—, fgn. corr., 1966—; instr. Russian and German langs. U. Richmond, 1959-60. Served with USNR, 1943-46. Home: Sadovo-Samotechnaya 1224 Moscow

ANDERSON, RAYMOND QUINTUS, mfg. co. exec.; b. Jamestown, N.Y., Nov. 27, 1930; s. Paul N. and Cecille (Ogren) A.; grad. Phillip Acad., Andover, Mass., 1949; B.S. in Engring., Princeton, 1953; postgrad. Grad. Sch. Indsl. Mgmt., Mass. Inst. Tech.; m. Sondra Rumsey, June 5, 1954; children—Heidi, Kristin, Gerrit, Mitchell, Tracy, Brooks. With Dahlstrom Mfg. Corp., Jamestown, 1957—, exec. v.p., 1965, pres., 1968—; dir. Jamestown Mut. Ins. Co., Bank of Jamestown, Jamestown Furniture Mart, Inc. Jamestown Industries, Inc. Chmn. Jamestown United Fund drive, 1964. Trustee Jamestown Community Coll. Served with USNR, 1954-57. Mem.

Mfrs. Assn. Jamestown Area (pres. 1967—). Republican. Episcopalian. Clubs: Moon Brook Country (Jamestown); Sportsmen's (Chautaguo, N.Y.). Patentee in field. Home: 121 Arlington Av Jamestown NY 14701 Office: Dahlstrom Mfg Corp Jamestown NY 14701

ANDERSON, REX HERBERT, ins. co. exec.; b. Rockford, Ill., Jan. 18, 1920; s. Herbert E. and Ethel V. (Helin) A.; A.B., Beloit Coll., 1941; m. Martha Jean Baker, Sept. 11, 1943; 1 son, Rex Herbert. Group field rep. Wash. Nat. Ins. Co., 1951-52, advt. and sales promotion, 1946-50; supr. Great West Life Assurance Co., 1950-52, br. office supr., St. Louis, 1952-53; dir. accident and sickness sales N.Y. Life Ins. Co., 1953-55, dir. sales promotion, 1955-56, asst. v.p. charge sales devel., 1956-57; v.p. marketing Life Ins. Co. N. Am., Phila., 1957-62, charge Individual sales and agy. operations, 1962-64, exec. officer charge individual life and health lines, life reins. dept., 1964—, sr. v.p., 1970—; dir. INA Security Corp., INA-Life of N.Y., INA Life Ins. Co. (Cal.). Trustee Phila. Coll. Art, 1966—. Served with USAAF, 1942-46. Mem. Life Ins. Agy. Mgmt. Assn., Health Ins. Assn. Am., Tau Kappa Epsilon, Delta Sigma Rho. Republican. Presbyn. Home: 1210 Pine Wood Rd Villanova PA 19085 Office: 1600 Arch St Philadelphia PA 19101

ANDERSON, RICHARD AUGUST, trade assn. exec.; b. Oberon, N.D., May 31, 1915; s. Carl and Gerda (Werssell) A.; B.A., Gustavus Adolphus Coll., 1938; student Mich. State U., 1958, Syracuse U., 1963; m. Virginia Trepanier, July 24, 1943; childrenDavid, Marcia, Robert, Thomas. Div. mgr. U.S. C. of C., Chgo., 1957-61; exec. dir. Alumninum Extruders Council, LaGrange, Ill., 1961-, Open Die Forging Inst., 1965-; pres. Anderson Mgmt., 1965-, Virdic Distbrs., LaGrange, 1965-. Sec., dir. Am. Soc. Assn. Execs. Found. Served with USAAF, 1942-46. Mem. Am. Soc. Assn. Execs. (dir., pres. 1967-68), Assn. Execs. Forum Chgo. (pres. 1965-66), Inst. for Orgn. Mgmt. (bd. regents, 1965-). Home: 116 Stirrup Pl Burr Ridge Hinsdale, IL 60521. Office: 440 Sherwood Rd La Grange Park IL 60525

ANDERSON, RICHARD DAVIS, mathematician; b. Hamden, Conn., Feb. 17, 1922; s. John Edward and Dorothea (Lynde) A.; B.A., U. Minn., 1941; Ph.D., U. Tex., 1948; m. Jeanette Olliver, Apr. 12, 1943; children—Susan Courtney, Virginia Dale, Richard Davis, Charlotte Marie, David Montgomery. Instr., U. Tex., 1941-42, 45-48; from instr. to asso. prof. U. Pa., 1948-56; prof. La. State U., 1956-59, Boyd prof. Math., 1959—, acting dean Grad. Sch., 1968-69; mem. Inst. Advanced Study, Princeton, 1951-52, 55-56; colleague Mathematisch Centrum, Amsterdam, 1962-63. Vis. lectr. Math. Assn. Am., 1959, 60; vis. prof. U. Amsterdam, 1970-71; Alfred P. Sloan research fellow, 1960-63; panel mem., writer Sch. Math. Study Group; chmn. Com. on Undergrad. Program in Math., 1965-67. Served to lt. USNR, 1942-45. Mem. Am. Math. Soc. (council 1967-69), Math. Assn. Am. (bd. govs. 1963-65), A.A.A.S. (council 1965-67). Home: 2954 Fritchie Dr Baton Rouge LA 70809

ANDERSON, RICHARD WILLIAM, educator, psychiatrist; b. Brainerd, Minn., Sept. 11, 1919; s. John Peter and Christine (Erichsen) A.; student Carleton Coll., 1936-38; B.S., U. Minn., 1941, M.B., M.D., 1943; m. Bette Ann Simonson, July 31, 1943; children—Peter, John, Erik. Intern, U.S. Marine Hosp., Seattle, 1943; grad. tng. Mass. Mental Health Center, 1946-47, part-time 1949-50; resident psychiatrist Baldpate, Inc., Georgetown, Mass., 1947-50; dep. commr. mental health Minn., 1950-51; pvt. practice, St. Paul, 1951-53; mem. faculty U. Minn. Med. Sch., 1953—, prof. psychiatry, 1961—; chief psychiatry service Mpls. Gen. Hosp., 1953-57, dir. adult psychiatry clinic, 1958-70, chief clin. services, dept. psychiatry, 1970—. Served with AUS, 1943-46. Commonwealth Fund fellow, Ipswich, Eng., 1963-64. Diplomate Am. Bd. Psychiatry and Neurology. Fellow Am. Psychiat. Assn.; mem. Minn. Med. Assn., Hennepin County Med. Soc., Minn. Psychiat. Soc. Contbr. profl. jours. Home: 1318 W 47th St Minneapolis MN 55409

ANDERSON, ROBBIN COLYER, coll. dean; b. DeRidder, La., June 8, 1914; s. Ward and Elizabeth (Richardson) A.; B.S. in Chem. Engring., La. State U., 1934, M.S. in Chemistry, 1936; Ph.D. in Phys. Chemistry, U. Wis., 1939; m. Margaret Foster Ball, July 20, 1946; children—Charles Ward, Robbin Bruce, Richard Ball. Mem. faculty U. Tex., 1939-67, asso. dean Grad. Sch., 1966-67; head insts. sect. div. sci. personnel and edn. NSF, 1960-61; dean Coll. Arts and Sci., prof. chemistry U. Ark., 1967—; cons. in field, 1942—. Mem. Am. Chem. Soc., Tex. Acad. Sci. (pres. 1966-67), Faraday Soc., A.A.A.S., Fayetteville C. of C., Ark. Acad. Sci., Sigma Xi, Phi Kappa Phi, Omicron Delta Kappa, Lambda Chi Alpha. Rotarian. Author articles. Home: 1599 Halsell Rd Fayetteville AR 72701

ANDERSON, ROBERT, mfg. co. exec.; b. Columbus, Neb., Nov. 2, 1920; s. Robert and Lillian (Devlin) A.; B.S. in Mech. Engring., Colo. A. and M. Coll., 1943; M. Automotive Engring., Chrysler Inst., 1948; m. Constance Dahlun Severy, Oct. 2, 1942; children-Robert, Kathleen D. With Chrysler Corp., 1965-67, v.p., gen. mgr. Chrysler-Plymouth div., 1965-67, v.p. corp., 1967-68; with N. Am. Rockwell Corp., 1968—, pres. comml. products group, v.p. corp., 1968-69, exec. v.p. corp., 1969-70, pres., chief operating officer, 1970—, also dir.; adv. dir. Security Pacific Nat. Bank, Los Angeles, 1970—. Served to capt., F.A., AUS, 1943-46. Mem. Soc. Automotive Engrs., Newcomen Soc. N. Am., Phi Kappa Psi, Sigma Tau, Tau Beta Pi, Sigma Nu. Clubs: Detroit Athletic; Bloomfield Hills (Mich.) Country; Duquesne (Pitts.); Rolling Rock, Laurel Valley Golf (Ligonier, Pa.); Los Angeles Country; Eldorado Country (Palm Desert, Cal.). Home: R D 4 Ligonier PA 15658 Office: N Am Rockwell Bldg Pittsburgh PA 15222

ANDERSON ROBERT, sports editor N.Y. Daily News. Address: 220 E 42nd St New York City NY 10017*

ANDERSON, ROBERT ALBERT, mfg. exec.; b. Lima, O., Apr. 1, 1932; B.S., U. San Francisco, 1954; M.S., Stanford University, 1956; m. Rosemarie Lois Brown, May 15, 1955; 1 son, Anthony Robinson. Sales rep. Ames-Brockton Fabricated Products, Akron, O., 1956-58, sales mgr. Coshocton, Ohio, 1959-61, gen. manager plant, 1961-68, v.p. sales, 1968—. Instr. bus. Cosyhocton Jr. College, 1968-69. Secretary Coshocton YMCA, 1960-61; active Boy Scouts of America. Trustee Coshocton Animal Welfare League, Curry Home for the Aged. Named Man of Year, Coshocton Junior Chamber of Commerce, 1968. Mem. Coshocton C. of C. (vice president 1967-68, pres. 1969-70), English Speaking Union, Coshocton Sertoma Club, Nat. Assn. Mfrs., Sales Executives Institute, Phi Beta Kappa, Sigma Chi, Phi Mu. Democrat. Mem. Christian Ch. (lay leader). Mason (32, Shriner). Clubs: Coshocton Country, Coshocton City, Running Deer Country. Home: 2d Av Coshocton OH Office: 3d Av Coshocton OH

ANDERSON, ROBERT ALEXANDER, ret. corp. exec.; b. Honolulu, June 6, 1894; s. Robert Willis and Susan Alice (Young) A.; M.E., Cornell U., 1916; m. Margaret Leith Center, Nov. 14, 1919; children—Robert Alexander, David Leith, Allen Willis, Pamela Susan. Apprentice, Westinghouse Electric & Mfg. Co., East Pittsburgh, Pa., 1916-17; research dept. Isko Co., Chgo., 1919-21; chief engr. McClellan Refrigerating Co., Chgo., 1921-23; successively sales engr., dept. mgr., treas., v.p., pres., chmn. bd. The Hawaii Corp. (formerly Von Hamm-Young Co., Inc.), Honolulu, 1923-68, chmn. emeritus, 1968-70, now dir.; pres. Alex Anderson Music, Inc.; dir. Bishop Investment Corp. Chmn. Hawaii Aeros. Commn., 1929-32, Hawaii Visitors Bur., 1945. Bd. dirs., past pres. Honolulu Symphony; bd. dirs. Oahu Devel. Conf.; pres. Leahi Found. Served to 1st lt. USAAF, 1917-19. Decorated Purple Heart; named Hawaii Citizen of Year, 1969. Mem. Am. Soc. Refrigeration Engrs., A.S.C.A.P., Downtown Improvement Assn. (past pres.), Am. Guild Authors and Composers, Hawaiian Sugar Planters Assn., Order Daedalians (founder mem.), Quiet Birdmen, Pi Kappa Alpha, Eta Kappa Nu. Mason. (33, Jester, Shriner). Clubs: Savage of Ithaca, Bohemian, Rotary (past pres., dist. gov. 1956-57), Pacific, Oahu Country, Waialae Country, Mid-Pacific Country, Kani Ka Pila, Outrigger Canoe. Composer 100 songs, including Lovely Hula Hands. Home: 2954 Makalei Pl Honolulu HI 96815 Office: Alexander Young Bldg Honolulu HI 96813

ANDERSON, ROBERT BERNARD, ex-sec. treasury; b. Burleson, Texas, June 4, 1910; s. Robert Lee and Elizabeth (Haskew) A.; grad. Weatherford (Tex.) Coll., 1927; LL.B., U. of Tex., 1932; LL.D., McMurry Coll. (Tex.), Tex. Christian U.; Litt.D., Mid-Western U. (Tex.); m. Ollie Mae Adnerson, Apr. 10, 1935; children—James Richard, Gerald Lee. Admitted to Texas bar, 1932, and began practice of law Fort Worth, Texas, 1932; elected to Texas Legislature, 1932; became assistant atty. gen. of Tex., 1932; prof. of law, U. of Tex., 1933; state tax commr., Tex., 1934; racing commr., Tex., 1934; mem. state tax bd., 1934; chmn. and exec. dir. Tex Unemployment Commn., 1936; Sec. of Navy, 1953-54; deputy secretary defense, 1954-55; pres. Ventures, Ltd., and dir. various affiliated and other cos., 1955-57; sec. of treasury, 1957-61; ltd. partner Carl M. Loeb, Rhoades & Co., 1961—; partner Robert B. Anderson & Co.; chmn. Robert B. Anderson & Co., Ltd.; co-chmn. Yugoslav Am. Corp., Romanda Devel. Co., Ltd.; dir. C.I.T. Financial Corp., Planning Research Corp., State Nat. Bank of Conn., Clinton Internat. Corp., Lease-A-Car, Inc., IMODCO, Inc., Pan Am. Airways, Goodyear Tire & Rubber Co. Trustee Eisenhower Exchange Fellowships. Mem. nat. exec. bd. Boy Scouts Am., Am. Council on NATO, Bus. Adv. Council Dept. Commerce. Recipient Texas Award, 1954; Cross of the Order of Boyaca, Columbia, 1954; Most Exalted Order of the White Elephant, Thailand, 1954; Texan of the Year, 1955; Medal of Freedom, 1955; Navy Distinguished Pub. Service Award, 1955; Army Exceptional Service Award, 1955; Air Force Civilian Service Award, 1955; Grand Cross Ct. of Honour, 1959. Mem. Nat. Geog. Soc. (life), Washington Nat. Cathedral, Navy League Am., Am. Bar Assn., Bar State N.Y., Assn. Bar City N.Y., The Chancellors, Phi Delta Phi. Mason (33), Supreme Council Order DeMolay. Clubs: Dallas Athletic; Links, Metropolitan, University (N.Y.C.); Greenwich Country, The Field, Round Hill (Greenwich, Conn.); Metropolitan (Washington); Toronto (Toronto, Can.). Home: 2 E 67th St New York City NY 10021 Office: One Rockefeller Plaza New York City NY 10020

ANDERSON, ROBERT CLETUS, educator; b. Birmingham, Ala., July 18, 1921; s. Allie Cletus and Dana (Hilliard) A.; B.S., Auburn U., 1942; M.A., U. N.C., 1947; Ph.D., N.Y.U., 1950; m. Margaret Campbell Spidle, June 2, 1942; children—Margaret Campbell, William Robert. Research asst. Inst. for Research in Social Sci., U. N.C., 1946-47; asst. to dean Sch. of Edn., N.Y.U., 1948-50; dir. Grad. Sch., Memphis State U., 1950-53; exec. asso. So. Regional Edn. Bd., 1953-55, asso. dir., 1955-57, dir., 1957-61; exec. v.p. Auburn U., 1961-65; v.p. research U. Ga., Athens, 1965—, prof. sociology, 1965—. Dir. So. Regional Project on Ednl. TV, So. Regional Edn. Bd., 1952, So. Regional Conf. on Edn. Beyond the High Sch., 1957; mem. nat. council Nat. Planning Assn., 1958-68; mem. Surgeon Gen.'s cons. group on Med. Edn., 1958-59; mem. W.K. Kellogg Found. Ednl. Adv. Com., 1960-64, Joint Council on Ednl. Telecommunications, 1961-70, v.p., 1965-67; chmn. council for research policy and adminstrn. Nat. Assn. State Univs. and Land-Grant Colls., 1965-67. Chmn. exec. com. Skidaway Inst., Oceanograph, 1968-69. Served from 2d lt. to capt., AUS, 1942-46; ETO. Decorated Purple Heart. Mem. Am. Council on Edn. (mem. council on fed. relations 1963-67), Am. Assn. for Higher Edn., Nat. Council Univ. Adminstrs., Phi Kappa Phi, Alpha Tau Omega, Alpha Kappa Delta, Kappa Delta Pi, Omicron Delta Kappa, Phi Delta Kappa, Phi Eta Sigma, Pi Gamma Mu. Democrat. Presbyn. Home: 640 Glenwood Dr Athens GA 30601

ANDERSON, ROBERT EARLE, Jr., elec. appliance co. exec.; b. New Haven, Sept. 12, 1916; s. Robert Earle and Emily Hays (Farr) A.; grad. Phillips Exeter Acad., 1934; A.B., Princeton, 1948; LL.B., Yale, 1941; m. Barbara Louise Porter, Jan. 5, 1944; children—Peter B., Michael P., Susan (Mrs. Robert E. Murphy), Timothy F. Admitted to N.Y. bar, 1945, Mass. bar, 1956; asso. Simpson, Thacher & Bartlett, N.Y.C., 1941, 45-51; with Sylvania Elec. Products, Inc., N.Y.C., 1951—, v.p., gen. counsel, sec., 1969—; dir. various corps. Served with USNR, 1942-45. Mem. Am., Mass., Boston bar assns., Order of Coif. Home: 72 Brook Run Lane Stamford CT 06905 Office: 730 3d Av New York City NY 10017

ANDERSON, ROBERT FERDINAND, mining co. exec.; b. Hibbing, Minn., Apr. 26, 1921; s. A.G. and Anna (Tanquist) A.; B. Engring., Mich. Tech. U., 1944; m. Marjorie Mahon, Mar. 9, 1944; children—Judith A., Christopher R., Mark M. With Hanna Mining Co., 1947—, exec. v.p., 1969—, also dir.; v.p., dir. Ida Mining Co., 1967—, Morton Ore Co., 1962—, S. Agnew Mining Co., 1962—, Nat. Steel Corp. Can. Ltd., 1962—. Bd. dirs. Am. Lutheran Ch. Served with USAAF, 1943-46. Mem. Am. Inst. Mining, Metall. and Petroleum Engrs., Am. Iron and Steel Inst., Am. Iron Ore Assn. Lutheran (trustee). Clubs: Cleve. Athletic, Union (Cleve.); Duquesne (Pitts.). Home: 3585 Eldorado Dr Rocky River OH 44116 Office: 100 Erieview Plaza Cleveland OH 44114

ANDERSON, ROBERT GREGG, diversified industry exec.; b. St. Joseph, Mo., Oct. 3, 1928; s. Clarence William and Marie Louise (Newman) A.; student U. Okla., 1948-49, U. Tulsa, 1950. Pres. Gregg Anderson Realty, San Diego, 1959-63; v.p. Trousdale Constrn. Co., Los Angeles, 1963-67, cons., 1967—; pres. Amfac Properties div., v.p. Amfac, Inc., Honolulu, 1967-69, sr. v.p., 1969—; pres., chmn. bd. Accent Enterprises, Inc., Amfac Silverado Corp., Neilson Way Corp., 745 Fort St. Corp.; dir. Central Oahu Land Corp.; v.p. Silverado Country Club & Resort, Inc.; dir. Kekaha Sugar Co., Lihue Plantation Co., Ltd., Oahu Sugar Co., Ltd., Pioneer Mill Co., Ltd., Puna Sugar Co., Ltd., Waiahole Water Co., Waiahole Irrigation Co., Ltd. Served with USNR, 1950-54. Mem. Hawaii Sugar Planters Assn. Clubs: Waialae Country, Pacific, Outriggers Canoe (Honolulu). Office: PO Box 3230 Honolulu HI 96801

ANDERSON, ROBERT HENRY, educator; b. Milw., July 28, 1918; s. Robert Dean and Eleanor (Weil) A.; B.A., U. Wis., 1939, M.A., 1942; Ph.D., U. Chgo., 1949; A.M. (hon.), Harvard, 1959; m. Mary Jane Hopkins, July 19, 1941; children—Dean Robert, Lynn Mary, Scott William, Carol Jane. Tchr., Oconomowoc, Wis., 1940-43; research asst. ednl. field service U. Chgo., 1946-47; prin. Roosevelt Sch., River Forest, Ill., 1947-49; supt. schs. dist. 163, Park Forest, Ill., 1949-54; mem. faculty Grad. Sch. Edn., Harvard, 1954-, prof. edn., 1962-; vis. summer prof. U. Ia., 1953, U. Wis., 1960, U. Hawaii, 1962, U.S. Dependents' Schools, Heidelberg, 1966; lectr., cons. sch. orgn., adminstrn., architecture. Served USNR, 1943-46. Mem. Nat. Soc. Study Edn., Am. Assn. Sch. Adminstrs., N.E.A., Am. Ednl. Research Assn., Assn. Supervision and Curriculum Devel., Phi Delta Kappa. Episcopalian. Author: Teaching in a World of Change, pub. 1966. Co-author: The Nongraded Elementary School, rev. edit., 1963. Co-editor: As the Twig is Bent, 1971. Contbr. chpts. books. Home: 8 Winslow Rd Winchester, MA 01890. Office: Longfellow Hall Harvard U Cambridge MA 02138

ANDERSON, ROBERT J., ins. co. exec.; b. St. Stephen, N.B., Can., Oct. 24, 1914; s. Frank R. and Gladys (MacDermott) A.; student Northeastern U.; m. Carol Roth, June 28, 1941; childrenDavid Stewart, Joan Stewart. Naturalized U.S. citizen, 1943. With Household Fuel Corp., Worcester, Mass., 1938-39; with Nat. Fire Ins. Co., Hartford, Conn., 1940-, sec., 1955-57, v.p., 1957-60, exec. v.p., 1960-66, sr. v.p., 1966-68; v.p. Continental Casualty Co., 1965-68; exec. v.p. Ter Bush & Powell, Inc., Schenectady, 1968—. Mem. Newcomen Soc. N. Am. Mason. Clubs: Fort Orange (Albany, N.Y.) N.Y.) ; Mohawk Golf (Schenectady); Hartford; Wampanoag Country (West Hartford); Wall Street (N.Y.C.). Home: 2163 Orchard Park Dr Schenectady, NY 12309. Office: 148 Clinton St Schenectady NY 12305

ANDERSON, ROBERT JEWELL, former govt. ofcl.; b. Marshall, Tex., Oct. 16, 1910; s. Robert Jewell and Maude (Hill) A.; D.V.M., Tex. A. and M. Coll., 1935; m. Verlyn Benskin, Apr. 22, 1932; children—Jann Patricia Hall, Robert Jewell III. Tech.-co-dir. Mexico-U.S. Commn. Eradication Foot and Mouth Disease, 1947-52; asst. chief Bur. Animal Industry, Dept. Agr., 1953-54, dir. animal disease eradication div. Agrl. Research Service, 1954-61, asst. adminstr., 1961-63, dep. adminstr., 1963-66, asso. adminstr., 1966-70. Mem. U.S.-Mexico Foot and Mouth Disease Commn. Trustee S.W. Animal Research Found. Member American Vet. Medicine Assn. (mem. council biologics and therapeutics 1960, mem. sci. program com. 1970—), U.S. Livestock San. Assn. Home: Route 2 Box 70 Marshall TX 75670

ANDERSON, ROBERT JOHN, physician; b. Winona, Minn., Sept. 12, 1913; s. Adolph Ingvald and Julia Marie (Blekre) A.; A.B., Carleton Coll., 1935; M.B. and M.D., U. Minn., 1939; M.S. in Pub. Health, Columbia, 1943; m. Ruth Eleanor Kittleson, June 26, 1940; children—Robert J., Julia Ann. Health officer, Texas County, Mo., 1941, Newton County, Mo., 1942; Tb control officer San Antonio (Tex.) City Health Dept., 1944-45; chief bur. Tb, Cal. Dept. Pub. Health, 1946; asst. chief div. Tb, USPHS, 1947-48, chief, 1948-51, chief chronic disease and Tb, 1951-54, asst. chief spl. health services, Washington, 1954-56, chief Communicable Disease Center, Atlanta, 1956-60, dep. chief Bur. State Services, 1960- 62, chief, 1962-66; commd. officer regular Corps USPHS, promoted asst. surgeon gen., 1957-66, ret., 1966; med. dir. Am. Thoracic Soc., 1966-70; mng. dir. Nat. Tb and Respiratory Disease Assn., 1970—. Diplomate Am. Bd. Preventive Medicine and Pub. Health. Mem. Am. Coll. Chest Physicians, A.M.A., Am. Pub. Health Assn., Am. Thoracic Soc., Assn. Mil. Surgeons, Am. Coll. Preventive Medicine, Phi Beta Kappa, Phi Rho Sigma. Home: 3624 N 36th Rd Arlington VA 22207 Office: Nat Tb and Respiratory Disease Assn 1740 Broadway New York City NY 10019

ANDERSON, ROBERT NELSON, lawyer; b. Roanoke, Va., May 6, 1899; s. Thomas Gerald and Lena Stuart (Nelson) A.; A.B. cum laude, George Washington U., 1921, LL.B., 1923; m. Mary Rogers, Mar. 24, 1926; children—Mary Elizabeth, Robert Nelson, William Gerald. Admitted to Va. bar, 1922, D.C. bar, 1923; spl. atty. Office Solicitor of Internal Revenue, Washington, 1922-25; asso. law firm Humphreys & Day, Washington, also N.Y.C., 1925-32; sr. mem. firm Anderson, Lawrence & Anderson, 1932-34; spl. asst. to U.S. Atty. Gen., 1934-57, reviewing officer, legal coordinating counsel, 1957-69; mem. firm Delany, Robertson & Anderson, Washington, 1969—. Specialist in tax litigation for U.S. govt.; tried test cases involving constitutionality of Agrl. Adjustment Act, Civilian Conservation Corps Acts, Kerr-Smith Tobacco Act, Bankhead Cotton Control Act. Mem. Ho. Deps. representing Am. Bar Assn., 2d Internat. Conf. Legal Profession, The Hague, 1948, 3d Conf., London, 1950, 4th conf., Madrid, 1952, 5th conf., Monte Carlo, 1954; rep. Fed. Bar Assn., 7th Conf., Cologne, 1958, 8th conf., Salzburg, Austria, 1960, 9th Conf., Edinburgh, Scotland, 1962, 10th Conf., Mexico City, 1964, 11th Conf., Lausanne, Switzerland, 1966, 12th Conf., Dublin, 1968, 13th Conf., Tokyo, Japan, 1970; mem. plan com. 4th Nat. Conf. Citizenship, N.Y.C., 1949, 5th, 6th, 7th, 8th, 9th confs., Washington, 1950-54; mem. atty. gen.'s Adv. Com. Citizenship, 1949-54; incorporator, dir., gen. counsel Nat. Conf. on Citizenship, 1953—; sec. Friends of Law Library of Congress, 1953-66, pres., 1966—; an incorporator Found. of Fed. Bar Assn., 1954. Chmn. bd. govs. Lyon Village Community House, 1961-65. Mem. Fed. (nat. pres. 1942-43; nat. council 1949—), Am. (ho. dels., rep. Fed. Bar Assn. 1944-45; chmn. com. that organized Internat. Bar Assn. 1944-47), Internat. (council 1947-52, 58—, chmn. mem. com. 1952-58, 67—), D.C., Va., Inter-Am. (del. 1st Conv. Havana, 1941), bar assns., Ilustre y Nacional Colegio de Abagados Mexico (hon.), Legal Aid Bur. D.C., Arlington Hist. Soc. (editor mag. 1956-58, pres. 1958-59), Delta Tau Delta, Phi Alpha Delta. Democrat. Methodist. Clubs: Nat. Lawyers (founder mem. 1962) (Washington); Washington Golf and Country (Arlington County, Va.). Home: 2732 N 18th St Arlington VA 22201; also Penrith Orlean VA 22128 Office: 815 15th St NW Washington DC 20005 also 2060 N 14th St Arlington VA 22201

ANDERSON, ROBERT ORVILLE, industrialist; b. Chgo., Apr. 13, 1917; s. Hugo A. and Hilda (Nelson) A.; B.A., U. Chgo., 1939; m. Barbara Phelps, Aug. 25, 1939; children—Katherine, Julia, Maria, Robert Bruce, Barbara Burton, William Phelps, Beverly. With Am. Mineral Spirits Co., Chgo., 1939-41; asso. Malco Refineries, Inc., now Hondo Oil and Gas Co., Roswell, N.M., 1941- 63, former pres.; chmn. bd. Atlantic Richfield Co., N.Y.; owner, pres. Lincoln County Livestock Co., Roswell; dir. Chase Manhattan Bank, Chase Manhattan Corp., Pan Am. World Airways, Columbia Broadcasting System, Inc. Mem. Com. Econ. Devel., Nat. Petroleum Council, Washington. Chmn., Aspen Inst. for Humanistic Studies; adv. bd. Inst. Internat. Edn., Denver; vice chmn. bd. John F. Kennedy Center for Performing Arts, Washington, chmn. Lovelace Found.; chmn. bd. Eisenhower Fellowships, Resources for Future; trustee Anderson Found. N.M., Cal. Inst. Tech., U. Chgo. Mem. Am. Petroleum Inst. (dir.). Clubs: Century (N.Y.C.); California (Los Angeles); Philadelphia. Home: 612 N Kentucky Av Roswell NM 88201 Office: 717 Fifth Av New York City NY 10022

ANDERSON, ROBERT PALMER, judge; b. Noank, Conn., Mar. 27, 1906; s. Arthur Pickett and Jessie Palmer (Ashby) A.; grad. Phillips (Andover) Acad., 1923; A.B., Yale, 1927, LL.B., 1929; m. Elizabeth Paffard, Jan 5, 1935; children—Robert Palmer, Frederic P. Admitted to Conn. bar, 1929; pub. defender New London Co., Conn., 1936-47, states atty., 1947-53; judge Superior Ct., State Conn., 1953-54; judge U.S. Dist. Ct., Conn., 1954-60, chief judge, 1960-64; judge U.S. Ct. Appeals, 2d circuit, N.Y.C., 1964-71, sr. judge, 1971—. Mem. State Bar Examining Com., 1936-54; mem. Conn. Senate, 1947-48. Served as comdr. USCG Res., 1942-45, capt. Res., 1955—. Decorated Bronze Star medal; Order Brit. Empire. Fellow Jonathan Edwards Coll., Yale U. Mem. Marine Hist. Assn. (trustee). Home: Brook St Noank CT 06340 Office: US Ct House Foley Sq New York City NY 10007

ANDERSON, ROBERT WOODRUFF, playwright; b. N.Y.C., Apr. 28, 1917; s. James Hewston and Myra Esther (Grigg) A.; grad. Phillips Exeter Acad., 1935; A.B. magna cum laude, Harvard, 1939, M.A., 1940; m. Phyllis Stohl, June 24, 1940 (died 1956); m. 2d, Teresa Wright, Dec. 11, 1959. Tchr. playwriting Am. Theatre Wing, 1946-50; playwright Love Revisited, produced Westport Country Playhouse, 1951, All Summer Long, Arena Stage, Washington, 1953, N.Y.C., 1954, Tea and Sympathy, N.Y.C., 1953; mem. Playwrights Co., 1953-60; faculty Salzburg Seminar in Am. Studies, 1968; writer in residence U. N.C., 1969. Bd. govs. Am. Playwrights Theatre. Served as lt. USNR, 1942-46. Recipient 1st prize for Come Marching Home, Army-Navy Playwriting Contest for servicemen overseas, 1945. Mem. Dramatists Guild (pres.), New Dramatists Com. (past pres.). Clubs: Coffee House, Century Assn., Harvard (N.Y.C.). Author: (screenplays) Tea and Sympathy, 1956, Until They Sail, 1957, The Nun's Story, 1959. The Sand Pebbles, 1965; (plays) Silent Night, Lonely Night, 1959, The Days Between, 1965, You Know I Can't Hear You When the Water's Running, 1967; I Never Sang for My Father (play) 1968, (screenplay), 1970; Solitaire/Double Solitaire (play), 1971. Home: Bridgewater CT 06752

ANDERSON, ROGER E., banker; b. 1921; B.S., Northewstern U., 1942; married. With Continental Ill. Nat. Bank and Trust Co., Chgo., 1946—, exec. v.p., 1968—, also dir.; dir. Continental Bank Internat., Continental Internat. Finance Corp., Internat., Continental Internat. Finance Corp., Banco Atlantico, Barcelona, Spain, Banque Americano-Franco-Suisse Pour le Marco, Casablanca, Morocco, E.D. Sassoon Banking Co. Ltd., London, Eng. Served with USNR. 194246. Address: 231 S LaSalle St Chicago IL 60690*

ANDERSON, ROLAND BENNETT, army officer; b. Duncan, Okla., Oct. 23, 1913; s. Charles Mansfield and Prebble (Griffith) A.; student petroleum engring. U. Okla., 1930-34; B.S., U.S. Mil. Acad., 1934-38; postgrad. Mass. Inst. Tech., 1940-41, Army War Coll., 1953-54; m. Gene Cox, Oct. 6, 1945; children—Bruce, Gene. Commd. 2d lt. U.S. Army, 1938, advanced through grades to maj. gen., 1965; comdr. Boston Ordnance Dist., 1954-57; dep. chief indsl. div., chief ordnance, 1957-60; asst. chief staff G-4 Communications Zone, U.S. Army in Europe, Orleans, France, 1960-62; comdg. gen. U.S. Army Weapons Command, Rock Island Arsenal, Ill., 1962-66; dir. material acquistion Office Sec. Army, 1966-70; dir. Def. Supply Agy., 1970-71; ret. 1971. Decorated Legion of Merit, Purple Heart, Order Brit. Empire, D.S.M. Mem. Am. Ordnance Assn., Assn. Grads. U.S. Mil. Acad. Address: 450 16th Av South Naples FL 33940

ANDERSON, ROSE GUSTAVA, cons. psychologist; b. Gothenberg, Neb.; d. Mathew and Emily (Axling) Anderson; A.B., U. Neb., 1917, M.A., 1918; Ph.D., Columbia, 1925; studied in Vienna, 1929-30. Asst. psychology U. Neb., 1917-18; asst. psychologist Psychol. Clinic, Cleve. Bd. Edn., 1918-19; research asst., mental examiner Minn. State Bd. Control, also State Dept. Edn., 1919-23; psychologist Mpls. Child Guidance Clinic, 1925-30, psychol. lab. Boston Psychopathic Hosp., summer 1930; psychol. dir. Ednl. Adjustment Bur., Westchester County Children's Assn., 1930-32; instr. Inst. Edn. N.Y.U., 1931-32; dir. child adjustment and sch. service div., cons. to women Psychol. Service Center, N.Y.C., 1932—, dir. Psychol. Service Center, 1942-58; edn. dir. Camp Wah-Na-Gi, Lake George, N.Y., summer 1934; instr. Tchrs. Coll. Columbia, summer, 1936-37, instr. extension div., 1940-42; instr. U. Cal. at Berkeley, summers 1940-42; v.p. Psychol. Corp., 1943-56; independent research, 1958—. Diplomate Am. Bd. Examiners. Fellow Am. Psychol. Assn. (division pres.), Am. Orthopsychiat. Assn.; mem. N.Y. State Assn. Applied Psycholoy, Phi Beta Kappa. Clubs: Green Mountain; Appalachian Mountain. Co-author: Kuhlman-Anderson Intelligence Tests; Kuhlmann-Anderson Measure of Academic Potential. Author articles on test scoring methods, clin. and counseling psychology. Home: Meadow Lakes Village Hightstown NJ 08520

ANDERSON, ROSS E., bakery co. exec.; b. 1898. With Campbell Taggart Assos. Bakeries Inc., 1938—, now chmn. exec. com., dir.; chmn. bd. Colonial Baking Co., Little Rock. Address: 6211 Lemmon Av Dallas TX 75201*

ANDERSON, ROY ARNOLD, aerospace co. exec.; b. Ripon, Cal., Dec. 15, 1920; s. Carl Gustav and Esther (Johnson) A.; A.B., Stanford, 1947, M.B.A., 1949; m. Betty Leona Boehme, June 10, 1948; children—Ross David, Karyn Dale, Debra Elayne, James Patrick. With Westinghouse Electric Corp., 1952-56; mgr. accounting and finance, then dir. mgmt. controls Lockheed Missiles & Space Co., 1956-65; dir. finance Lockheed-Ga. Co., 1965-68; asst. treas. Lockheed Aircraft Corp., 1968-69, v.p., controller, 1969-71, sr. v.p. finance, 1971—; dir. Avantek, Santa Clara, Cal., Granite Rock Co., Watsonville, Cal. Served with USNR, 1942-46, 50-52, C.P.A., Cal. Mem. Financial Execs. Inst., Nat. Assn. Accountants, Phi Beta Kappa. Home: 4367 Shepherds Lane La Canada CA 91011 Office: 2655 N Hollywood Way Burbank CA 91502

ANDERSON, ROY GENE, naval officer; b. Neosho, Mo., Dec. 24, 1915; s. Roy Godfred and Ilagene (Bowers) A.; B.S. in Elec. Engring., U.S. Naval Acad., 1940; student U.S. Naval Postgrad. Sch., 1945-46; engring. degree in aero. engring., Cal. Inst. Tech., 1947; grad. Indsl. Coll. Armed Forces, 1963; m. Olivia Langston Ratlif, Dec. 26, 1942; children—Jean (Mrs. David E. Radford), Philip Ratlif. Commd. ensign U.S. Navy, 1940, advanced through grades to rear adm., 1965; assigned U.S.S. Minneapolis, 1940-42, Submarine Sch., New London, Conn., 1942-43, U.S.S. Flying Fish, 1943-44, U.S.S. Kingfish, 1944-45, Bur. Ordnance, Washington, 1947-48; exec. officer guided missile submarine Cusk, 1948-49; comdg. officer guided missile submarine U.S.S. Carbonero, 1949-51; assigned Office Chief Naval Operations, 1951-53; mem. staff of comdr. Submarine Squadron 5, 1953-55; comdr. Submarine Div. 51, 1955; plans officer Polaris submarine program Navy Dept., 1955-58; chief staff to comdr. Polaris Submarine Squadron 14, 1958-60; Polaris officer on joint staff comdr. in chief Atlantic, 1960-64; comdr. U.S.S. Taconic, 1964-65, Amphibious Group 4, 1965-67; sr. navy mem., weapons systems evaluation group Office Dir. Def. Research and Engring., Office Sec. Def., 1967-71; dir. systems analysis div. Chief Naval Operations, 1971; comdr. service force Atlantic Fleet, 1971—. Sec. U.S. Naval Acad. Class 1940, 1967-71. Decorated Legion of Merit with 3 gold stars, Bronze Star with gold star and combat V, Commendation ribbon with bronze star and combat V, numerous area and unit ribbons. Mem. Am. Ordnance Assn., U.S. Naval Acad. Alumni Assn. Club: Army-Navy Country (Arlington, Va.).

ANDERSON, ROY MARTIN, food co. exec.; b. Bklyn., June 22, 1921; s. John and Mary E. (Martinsen) A.; A.B., Duke, 1944; LL.B., Columbia, 1946; m. Mary Sievers Woody, May 28, 1944; children—Roy Martin, Susan Jane, Thomas Woody. Admitted to N.Y. bar, 1948, practiced in Hempstead until 1951; with Continental Baking Co. (name changed to ITT Continental Baking Co.), Rye, N.Y., 1951—, v.p., 1961—, gen. counsel, 1962-69, dir., 1964—; pres., gen. mgr. ITT Food Products Europe, 1969—; dir. Hong Kong Food Products Mfg. Co., Ltd. Served with USAAF, 1942-44. Mem. Am., Internat. bar assns., Am. Judicature Soc., Sigma Alpha Epsilon, Phi Delta Phi. Home: 22 Wesskum Wood Rd Riverside CT 06878 Office: ITT Food Products Europe 11 Blvd de L'Empereur Brussels 1 Belgium

ANDERSON, ROY STUART, univ. dean, physicist; b. Springfield, Mass., Oct. 16, 1921; s. O. William and Gladys (Merry) A.; B.A., Clark U., 1943; A.M., Dartmouth, 1948; Ph.D., Duke, 1951; m. Barbara Anne Norris, June 11, 1944; childrenKaren Jana, Loring Dodd, Scott William. Research engr. Stanford Research Inst., 1951-52; asst. prof. physics, then asso. prof. U. Md., 1952-60; prof. physics, chmn. dept. Clark U., 1960-70, dean Grad. Sch., 1970—; research asso. Duke, 1951, 53, 54, U. Cal. at Berkeley, 1958-59, Woods Hole Oceanographic Instn., 1961; cons., lectr. in field; spl. research radio spectroscopy of atoms and molecules. Served to lt. USNR, 1943-46. Fellow Am. Phys. Soc.; Mem. Am. Assn. Physics Tchrs., Am. Assn. U. Profs., Philos. Soc. Washington, Sigma Xi, Sigma Pi Sigma. Conglist. Clubs: Bohemians (Worcester); U.S. Power Squadron (Worcester County); Five Islands (Me.) Yacht. Author articles in field. Home: 13 Algonquin Rd Worcester, MA 01609.

ANDERSON, RUDOLPH EMIL, lawyer; b. Porter Mills, Wis., Nov. 18, 1896; s. Carl R. and Thea M. (Andersen) A.; J.D., U. Wis., 1924; m. Dorothy C. McKay, Jan. 4, 1933; m. 2d, Nellie B. Russell, Dec. 26, 1959. Admitted to Minn. bar, 1925; practice in Duluth, 1925; admitted to Wis. bar, 1924; practice of law, Superior, 1925-; mem. firm Hughes, Anderson & Davis, 1950—. Past pres. Superior-Douglas County Community Fund, Gitche Gumee Area council Boy Scouts Am. Bd. dirs. Wis. Bar Found., Superior State U. Found.; mem. World Peace Through Law Center. Fellow Am. Bar Found., Am. Coll. Trial Lawyers; mem. Am. (ho. of dels. 1960-), 7th Fed. Circuit, Wis. (ho. govs. 1955-57, dir. ins. sect. 1953-57, pres. 1957-58), Douglas County (pres. 1940) bar assns., Internat. Assn. Ins. Counsel, Am. Arbitration Assn. (nat. panel arbitrators), U. Wis. Law Alumni Assn. (mem. Benchers Soc.), Am. Legion. Mason (Shriner, Jester). Clubs: Madison (Wis.); Gitche Gumee, Northland Country (Duluth). Home: 1719 Hammond Av. Superior WI 54880 Office: Telegram Bldg Superior WI 54880

ANDERSON, RUTH LEILA (Mrs. D.C. Maxwell), ret. educator; b. nr. Albia, Ia., Oct. 7, 1897; d. Amandus and Susan Christene (Johnson) Anderson; A.B., U. Ia., 1918, A.M., 1923, Ph.D., 1927; m. David Crawford Maxwell, Oct. 7th, 1943 (dec.). High sch. tchr. in Iowa, 1918-22; grad. asst. in English, U. Ia., 1924-26, instr., 1926-29; prof., head dept. English, William Penn Coll., 1929-30; prof. English, dean women Central Coll., Fayette, Mo., 1930-43; instr. English, U. Wis., 1944-45; asso. prof. English, dean women Millikin U., Decatur, Ill., 1945-48, prof. English, chmn. humanities div., also chmn. English dept., 1948-64, prof. emeritus, 1964—; prof. English, former chmn. dept. Carthage Coll., Kenosha, Wis., 1964-70; vis. asso. prof. Northwestern U., summer 1947. Mem. Modern Lang. Assn., English, Shakespeare Assn. Am., Phi Beta Kappa. Methodist. Author: Elizabethan Psychology and Shakespeare's Plays, Humanistic Studies, Vol. III, 1927, rev. edit., 1966; also articles. Home: 310 N Clinton St Iowa City IA 52240

ANDERSON, SIGURD, judge; b. Arendal, Norway, Jan. 22, 1904; s. Karl and Bertha (Broten) A.; brought to U.S., 1906, became citizen upon father's naturalization, 1915; B.A., U. S.D., 1931, LL.B., 1937; LL.D., Yankton Coll., 1953, Gettysburg Coll., 1958; m. Vivian Walz, Apr. 3, 1937; 1 dau., Kristin Karen. States atty. Day Co., S.D., 1939-41; asst. atty. gen. S.D., 1941-43; atty. gen., 1947-51; gov. S.D., 1951-55; mem. FTC, 1955-64; pvt. practice law, Webster, S.D., 1964-67; judge 5th Jud. Circuit S.D., 1967—. Chmn., Mo. River States Com., 1953-55. Bd. dirs. Am. Norwegian Mus. Served as officer USNR, World War II. Recipient D.A.R. Americanism medal for contbns. to state and nation by fgn.-born citizen, 1958; Freedoms Found. award, 1963. Mem. adv. council Civil War Centennial Commn. Mem. Am. Judicature Soc., Fed., Am., S.D. bar assns., V.F.W., Am. Legion, Phi Beta Kappa, Delta Theta Phi, Pi Kappa Delta, Lambda Chi Alpha (hon.). Republican. Lutheran. Mason (33, Shriner). Home: Webster SD 57274

ANDERSON, STANLEY CLIFFORD, health products co. exec.; b. Greeley, Colo., Dec. 22, 1918; s. Eric E. and Selma (Carlson) A.; B.B.A. summa cum laude, Pace Coll., 1948; m. Virginia C. Heeb, Nov. 24, 1945; children-Susan A. (Mrs. Theodore Johnson), Wayne C. Sr. auditor Peat, Marwick, Mitchell & Co., N.Y.C., 1948-51; asst. controller, gen. auditor, gen. controller, asst. treas., treas., dir., mem. exec. com. Johnson & Johnson, New Brunswick, N.J., 1952—. Treas., trustee Middlesex Gen. Hosp., Francie E. Parker Meml. Home. Served with USNR, 1941-45. C.P.A., N.J. Mem. Financial Exeos. Inst., Am. Inst. C.P.A.'s. Presbyn. (trustee). Home: 225 Golf Edge Westfield NJ 07090 Office: 501 George St New Brunswick NJ 08903

ANDERSON, STANLEY ROBERT, univ. dean; b. Rudyard Mich., Mar. 11, 1920; s. John Leslie and Henrietta (Farrish) A.; B.S., Mich. State U., 1946, M.S., 1949; Ph.D., Ia. State U., 1954; m. Dorothy Anne Austin, Aug. 27, 1946; children—Anne (Mrs. Donald A. Leake), William, Carol. Field rep. Mich. Crop Improvement Assn., 1946-49; instr. Charlevoix (Mich.) pub. schs., 1949- 50; instr. agronomy Ia. State U., 1950-54; mem. faculty Ohio State U., 1954-67, prof. agronomy, 1963-67; dean, prof. agr. Tex. A. and I. U., Kingsville, 1967—. Pres. Make and Keep Kingsville Beautiful, Inc., 1968; active local Boy Scouts Am. Served to 1st lt. USAAF, 1943-45. Decorated D.F.C., Air medal with 3 clusters; Named Prof. of Year, Ohio State U., 1958—, Distinguished Adviser, 1967; recipient Merit Tchr. award Ohio State U., 1967; named State Farmer Ohio, 1958. Fellow Am. Soc. Agronomy (bd. dirs. 1956-58, chmn. seed prodn. and tech. div. 1955-56, chmn. resident teaching div. 1957-58, chmn. physiology and metabolism div. 1965-66); mem. Crop Sci. Soc. (bd. dirs. 1955-57-67, tech. editor jour. 1966-69), Gamma Sigma Delta, Alpha Zeta, Phi Delta Kappa, Farmhouse Frat. Methodist. Kiwanian. Clubs: Kingsville Country. Contbr. profl. jours. Home: 1115 Elizabeth Av Kingsville, TX 78363.

ANDERSON, STEFAN STOLEN, banker; b. Madison, Wis., Apr. 1934; s. Theodore M. and Siri (Stolen) A.; A.B. magna cum laude, Harvard, 1956; M.B.A., U. Chgo., 1960; m. Joan Timmermann, Sept. 19, 1959; children—Sharon Jill, Theodore Peter. With Am. Nat. Bank & Trust Co. of Chgo., 1960—, v.p., 1966-68, group v.p., 1968, exec. v.p., 1969—; v.p. Am. Nat. Corp.; dir. Am. Nat. Overseas Corp. Vice pres. Nat. Youth Adv. Council for White House Conf. on Children and Youth, 1950. Pres., bd. dirs. U. Chgo. Grad. Bus. Assn.; v.p., bd. dirs. Lyric Opera Guild; bd. dirs. Talent Assistance Program, Nat. Conf. Christians and Jews, Mental Health Assn. of Chgo., Met. Crusade Mercy, Chgo. council Boy Scouts Am. Served with USNR, 1956-58. Mem. Cosmopolitan C. of C., Robert Morris Assos., Am. Inst. Banking, Phi Beta Kappa, Beta Gamma Sigma. Clubs: Economic, University, Harvard (dir.) (Chgo.); Sunset Ridge Country. Home: 712 Glenayre Dr Glenview IL 60025 Office: 33 N LaSalle St Chicago IL 60625

ANDERSON, STUART LEROY, clergyman, coll. chancellor; b. Elmore, O., Jan. 24, 1912; s. George Alfred and Grace Pearl (Longfellow) A.; A.B., Albion Coll., 1933, D.D. honoris causa, 1945; B.D., Chicago Theol. Sem., 1936; M.A., U. Chgo., 1936; Litt.D., Pacific U., 1960; m. Raezella Tom Klepper, Sept. 25, 1935; children—Philip, Catherine. Ordained to ministry Congl. Ch., 1936; minister First Ch., Argo, Ill., 1935-36, Glendale, Cal., 1938- 43, Long Beach, 1943-50; minister youth First Ch., Los Angeles, 1936-37; pres., prof. homiletics Pacific Sch. Religion, Berkeley, Cal., 1950-71, chancellor, 1971—. Moderator Los Angeles Assn. Congl.-Christian Chs., 1943-44, Congl. Conf. So. Cal. and S.W., 1949-50, Northern Cal. Congl. Conf., 1952-53; mem. Congl. Commn. on Theol. Edn., 1956—; mem. nat. com. war victims and reconstrn. Congl. Christian Chs.; mem. Prudential com. Am. Bd. Commrs. for Fgn. Missions, 1943-46, v.p., 1946-53; mem. U.S. conf. for World Council Chs., 1961—; asst. moderator for Gen. Synod United Ch. Christ, 1961-63; protestant observer Second Vatican Council, 1965; mem. theol. commn. United Ch. of Christ, 1971—. Bd. dirs. Rockefeller Bros. Theol. Fellowship Program, 1958-64. Mem. Tau Kappa Epsilon, Alpha Phi Gamma, Delta Sigma Rho. Clubs: Rotary, U. Cal. Faculty (Berkeley); Commonwealth (San Francisco). Author: A Faith to Live By, 1959. Home: 344 Quincy Av Long Beach CA 90814

ANDERSON, THEODORE ROBERT, educator; b. Mpls., Nov. 3, 1927; s. John Edward and Dorothea (Lynde) A.; B.S., U. Minn., 1948; M.S., U. Wis., 1951, Ph.D., 1953; m. Beverly Ann Simpson, Aug. 30, 1952; children—O. Craig, Theodore L., Lincoln E. Instr. dept. sociology U. Wis., 1951-53; asst. prof. dept. sociology Yale, 1953-59; asso. prof., acting chmn. dept. sociology U. Ia., 1960-66; prof. U. Ore., 1966-69; prof. sociology U. Minn., Mpls., 1969—. Mem. rev. panelist NSF, 1966-68. Served with USNR, 1944-46. Recipient NSF research grant, 1965-69. Mem. Am. Sociol. Assn., Am. Statis. Assn., Population Assn. Am. Author: (with J.H. Parker) The Participation of Teachers in School and Professional Affairs, 1964; (with M. Zelditch) A Basic Course in Statistics: With Sociological Applications, 1968. Home: 4816 Aldrich Av S Minneapolis MN 55409

ANDERSON, THEODORE WILBUR, Jr., math. statistician; b. Mpls., June 5, 1918; s. Theodore Wilbur and Evelynn (Johnson) A.; B.S. with highest distinction, Northwestern U., 1939; M.A., Princeton, 1942, Ph.D., 1945; m. Dorothy Fisher, July 8, 1950; children—Robert Lewis, Janet Lynn, Jeanne Elizabeth. Asst., dept. math. Northwestern U., 1939-40; instr. Princeton, 1941-43, research asso. 1943-45; research asso. Cowles Commn., U. Chgo., 1945-46; staff Columbia, 1946-67, successively instr. math. statistics, asst. prof., asso. prof., 1946-56, prof., 1956-67, chmn. math. statistics dept., 1956-60, 64-65, acting chmn., 1950-51, 63; prof. statistics and econs. Stanford, 1967—. Vis. prof. math. Imperial Coll. Sci. and Tech., London, U. Moscow, also vis. prof. statistics U. Paris 1967-68. Dir. project Office Naval Research, Columbia; cons. Rand Corp.; mem. com. on basic research adv. to Office Ordnance Research, Nat. Acad. Scis.-NRC, 1955-58, mem. panel on applied math. adv. to Nat. Bur. Standards, 1964-65; chmn. com. on statistics NRC, 1961-63; mem. com. on support research in math. scis. Nat Acad. Scis., 1965-68; mem. com. Presidents Statis. Socs., 1962-64. Guggenheim fellow, 1947-48; fellow Center for Advanced Study in Behavioral Scis., 1957-58. Fellow Am. Statis. Assn. (v.p. 1971—), Econometric Soc., Royal. Statis. Soc., A.A.A.S., Inst. Math. Statistics (pres. 1963); mem. Am. Math. Soc., Biometric Soc., Indian, Internat. statis. insts., Conf. Bd. Math. Scis. (exec. com.), Am. Assn. U. Profs., Psychometric Soc., Sigma Xi. Editor, Annals of Math. Statistics, 1950-52; editorial bd. Psychometika. Home: 746 Santa Ynez St Stanford CA 94305

ANDERSON, THOMAS ALBERT, oil co. exec.; b. Bradford, Pa., Oct. 16, 1910; s. Anton Michael and Edna (Thomas) A.; B.S. in Petroleum Engring., Pa. State U., 1932; m. Mildred Aldine Northrop, Dec. 28, 1935; children—Sara Louise, Micaela Aldine. With Quaker State Oil Refining Co., Oil City, Pa., 1932—, pres., 1970—, also dir.; dir. Gen. Electric & Telephone Pa. Bd. dirs. Venango Devel. Corp., 1965—. Recipient High Achievement award Ohio River Valley Water Sanitation Commn., 1958. Mem. Ohio Oil and Gas Assn. (trustee 1954—), Pa. Grade Crude Oil (bd. dirs. 1961—), Am. Petroleum Inst. Home: 8 Crestview Dr Oil City PA 16301 Office: Quaker State Oil Refining Co Center St Oil City PA 16302

ANDERSON, THOMAS DUNAWAY, lawyer; b. Oklahoma City, Mar. 9, 1912; s. Frank Ervin and Burdine (Clayton) A.; LL.B., Washington and Lee U., 1934; student Rice Inst., 1930-31; m. Helen Sharp, Feb. 21, 1938; children—Helen Sharp, Lucille Clayton, John Sharp. Admitted to Tex. bar, 1934; asso. Andrews, Kurth, Campbell & Bradley, attys., 1934-41, 46-47; v.p., trust officer Tex. Nat. Bank, 1947-56; pres., dir. Tex. Fund Mgmt. Co., 1956-60; sr. v.p., trust officer Texas Commerce Bank, 1960-65; partner Anderson, Brown, Orn, Pressler & Jones, attys., 1965—; pres., dir. Boston Co. of Tex., 1966—; dir. Columbia Sci. Industries Corp. Trustee Kelsey & Leary Found., Foley Bros. Store Found., U. (Tex.) Cancer Found., Arts and Scis. Found., Episcopal Ch. Found., Lambuth Coll.; mem. bd., past chmn. Houston Grand Opera Assn.; trustee, past pres. Mus. Fine Arts of Houston. Mem. Am., Houston bar assns., State Bar Tex. Episcopalian. Clubs: Coronado, Eagle Lake Rod and Gun, Bayou, Houston Country, Texas. Co-author: How to Live and Die with Texas Probate, 1968. Home: 3925 Del Monte Houston TX 77019 Office: Southwest Tower Houston TX 77002

ANDERSON, THOMAS FOXEN, educator, scientist; b. Manitowoc, Wis., Feb. 7, 1911; s. Anton Oliver and Mabel (Foxen) A.; B.S., Cal. Inst. Tech., 1932, Ph.D., 1936; student U. Munich (Germany), 1932-33; m. Wilma Fay Ecton, Dec. 28, 1937; children—Thomas Foxen, Jessie Dale. Instr. chemistry U. Chgo., 1936-37; investigator botany U. Wis., 1937-39, instr. phys. chemistry, 1939-40; RCA fellow of NRC, 1940-42; asso. Johnson Found., U. Pa., 1942-46; mem. faculty U. Pa., 1946—, prof. biophysics, 1958—; sr. mem. Inst. Cancer Research, 1958—, chmn. dept. molecular biology, 1963—; spl. research raman spectra, molecular structure, surface chemistry, biol. applications electron microscopy, genetics and structure viruses and bacteria. Fulbright and Guggenheim fellow Inst. Pasteur, Paris, France, 1955-57, recipient Silver medal, 1957. Mem. Nat. Acad. Sicis. (chmn. U.S. nat. com. pure and applied biophysics), Electron Microscope Soc. Am. (pres. 1955), Internat. Fedn. Electron Misroscope Socs. (pres. 1960-64), Biophys. Soc. (pres. 1965), Am. Soc. Naturalists, A.A.A.S., Soc. Gen. Physiologists, Deutsche Gesellschaft für Elektronenmikroskopie, Soc. Francaise de Microscopie Electronique (hon. mem.), Am. soc. for Microbiology, Sigma Xi. Home: 326 Zane Av Philadelphia PA 19111

ANDERSON, THOMAS LEIGHTON, advt. exec.; b. Lindsay, Ont., Can., Dec. 19, 1895; s. Thomas and Margaret A. (Stuart) A.; m. Gladys A. Blake, Sept. 20, 1918; children—Joan P., Richard J. Jeweller, P.W. Ellis & Co., Toronto, 1912-15; Jeweller, optician Vandusen & Anderson, Toronto, 1915-20, copywriter, account exec. Advt. Service Co., Toronto, 1920-28; v.p., mgr. Cockfield, Brown & Co., Ltd., Toronto, 1928-42, v.p., mng. dir., 1942-56, pres., 1956-58, chmn. bd., 1958—; pres. Gaylord Lithographing Ltd., Toronto. Served with RAF, 1918. Club: Granite (Toronto). Home: 7 Thornwood Rd Toronto 289 Ontario Canada Office: Gaylord Lithographing Co Ltd 11 Southport St Toronto 3 Ontario Canada

ANDERSON, THOMAS PATRICK, engring. educator; b. Chgo., Oct. 22, 1934; s. Clarence Kenneth and Anne (Moran) A.; B.S. in Mech. Engring., Northwestern U., 1956, M.S., 1958, Ph.D., 1961; m. Elizabeth Ann Toof, July 9, 1960; children—Patricia, James. Engr., Askania Regulator Co., Chgo., 1953-55; research engr. Cook Research Labs., Skokie, Ill., summer, 1956, ARO Inc., Tullahoma, Tenn., summers 1958, 59; asst. prof., then asso. prof. Northwestern U., 1960- 66; prof. mech. engring. U. Ia., 1966—; chmn. dept., 1966-70; cons., asso. dep. dir. interdeptl. energy study Office Sci. and

Tech., 1963-65. Named One of Ten Outstanding Young Men, Chgo. Jr. Assn. Commerce and Industry, 1964. Registered profl. engr., Ill., Ia. Fellow Ia. Acad. Sci.; mem. A.A.A.S., Am. Assn. U. Profs., Am. Geophys. Union, Am. Inst. Aero. and Astronautics, Am. Phys. Soc., Am. Soc. Engring. Edn., Am. Soc. M.E., N.Y. Acad. Scis., Soc. Automotive Engrs., Sigma Xi. Author numerous articles in field. Home: 1013 Tower Ct Iowa City IA 52240

ANDERSON, TOTTON JAMES, educator; b. Beirut, Lebanon, May 26, 1909; s. Samuel M. and Agatha (Totton) A.; A.B., U. Cal. at Berkeley, 1930, M.A., 1931; Ph.D., U. So. Cal., 1946; m. Frances Elizabeth Moore, Aug. 17, 1934. Registrar, dean Ventura (Cal.) Coll., 1935-42, 46-47; mem. faculty U. So. Cal., 1947—, prof. polit. sci., 1958—, asso. dean div. social scis. Coll. Letters, Arts and Scis., 1966-69; vis. prof. U. Hawaii, summer 1958; polit. cons., 1960—. Exec. com. Cal. Constl. Revision Commn., 1964—; chmn. exec. com. Cal. Legislative Intern Program, 1957—; mem. Mayor Los Angeles Community Redevel. Adv. Com., 1966-68; asso. dir. Nat. Center Edn. in Politics, 1954-55; regional dir. Citizenship Clearing House, 1959-63. Trustee Coro Found., 1959—. Served to lt. col. USAAF, 1943-45; col. Res. Decorated Bronze Star. Mem. Am., Western (pres. 1952-53) polit. sci. assns., Am. Acad. Polit. and Social Scis., Phi Beta Kappa, (pres. Alpha Alumni Assn. in So. Cal. 1964-66). Co-author: Introduction to Political Science, 2d edit., 1967; Western Politics, 1958; Bibilography on Western Politics, 1958; Politics in the American West, 1969; Political Dynamiting, 1970; contbg. author: Cooperation and Conflict: Readings in American Federalism, 1969. Contbr. profl. jours. Home: 5523 S Verdun Av Los Angeles, CA 90043.

ANDERSON, TRUMAN EDGAR, oil and gas company exec.; b. Almena, Wis., Apr. 15, 1920; s. Peter C. and Hazel Ann (Cristman) A.; B.A., U. Wis., 1942; m. Marjorie Ann Hempy, Dec. 24, 1942 (div. 1966); children—Truman Edgar, Sue Ann, Stephen Wiles, and Sarah Lou; m. 2d, Doris A. Carlson, 1967. Life Ins. agent, Mpls., 1946-52; partner Anderson-Plank-Arnao, specialized investments, Mpls., 1952-55; exec. v.p. Apache Corp., Mpls., 1955-59, chmn. bd., 1959-64; cons. to oil and gas industry, 1964-67; with Petro Search Oil and Gas Fund, 1967—; became pres. Devcoa Internat., Inc., 1964. Mem. bd. dirs. Hennepin County Cancer Crusade; trustee Fairview Hosp., Mpls., Direction, Inc., Mpls.; bd. regents, mem. exec. com. St. Olaf Coll., Northfield, Minn.; bd. trustees bd. pensions Lutheran Ch. Am. Served to capt., pilot, USAAF, 1942-46; mem. Air N.G., 1947-51. Mem. Am. Mgmt. Assn., Presidents Profl. Assn. Club: Minneapolis. Home: 2723 Benedict Canyon Dr Beverly Hills CA 90210 Office: Wall St at Herschel Box 1814 LaJolla CA 90237

ANDERSON, VERNON ELLSWORTH, educator; b. Atwater, Minn., June 15, 1908; s. Frank E. and Johanna (Pearson) A.; B.S. with distinction, U. Minn., 1930, M.A., 1936; Ph.D., U. Colo., 1942; m. Alice Parker, Sept. 1, 1931; 1 dau., Mary M. (Mrs. L.F. Bayhi). Prin., tchr. English and social studies Askov (Minn.) High Sch., 1930-34; prin. Elk River (Minn.) High Sch., 1934-37; dean Worthington (Minn.) Jr. Coll., 1937-40; adminstrv. asst. to dean U. Colo., 1940-42, instr., summer 1941; state curriculum dir. Dept. Pub. Instrn., Olympia, Wash., 1942-44; dir. curriculum Portland (Ore.) pub. schs., 1944-46; dir. curriculum center, asso. prof. to prof. edn. U. Conn., 1946-55; prof. edn. U. Md., 1955—, dean Coll. Edn., 1955-70; tchr. U. Wash., summer 1943, U. Minn., summers 1945, 49, U. Colo., summer 1952, U. Cal. at Berkeley, summer 1959, U. So. Cal., summer 1961, U. P.R., summer 1967; cons. curriculum work schs.; conf. speaker workshop leader. Mem. Minn. Ednl. Policies Com., 1939-40; chmn. jr. coll. com. State of Wash., 1943-44; mem. Com. Action Research Com., 1954-55; co-chmn. Conn. Regional Conf. Edn., 1954-55; mem. Md. Com. for Fulbright Hayes Grad. Fellowships, 1967—; mem. Gov.'s Job Corps Task Force, 1969—; mem. Tchr. Edn. Adv. Council Md., 1968-71, chmn., 1970-71; mem. commn. on edn. for teaching profession Nat. Assn. State Univs. and Land Grant Colls., 1968—. Mem. Assn. for Supervision and Curriculum Devel. (dir. 1945-56, 59-63, 65-68, mem. exec. com. 1953- 55, 65-68, 2d v.p. 1954-55, chmn. com. exhibits and instructional materials 1960 conf., chmn. conf. com. 1962-63), N.W. (exec. sec. 1943-56), New Eng. (exec. sec. 1949-52), Md. (program chmn. 1957-59) assns. for supervision and curriculum devel., Nat. Assn. Secondary School Prins. (chmn. prin.'s self-survey com. Minn. 1937-38), Minn. Secondary Sch. Prins. Assn. (exec. bd. 1939-40), Minn. Jr. Coll. Dean's Assn. (sec. 1938-40), Eastern Conn. Schoolmen's Assn. (president 1953-54), Am. Ednl. Research Assn., John Dewey Soc., Nat. Soc. Study Edn., Md. Tchrs. Assn. N.E.A., Am. Assn. Higher Edn., Am. Assn. U. Profs., Am. Assn. Sch. Adminstrs., Fed. Schoolmen's Club, Kappa Delta Pi, Phi Kappa Phi, Phi Delta Kappa. Lutheran (exec. bd. Lutheran Student Found. for Md., D.C. 1957-60, bd. parish edn. Luth. Ch. in Am., since 1963—. Author: Principles and Procedures of Curriculum Improvement, 1956, rev. 1965; Before You Teach Children, also Teachers Guide; Before You Teach Children, 1962. Co-author: Principles and Practices of Secondary Education, 1951, revised edition, 1962; Instructor's Manual: Principles and Practices of Secondary Education, 1951; Curriculum Guidelines in an Era of Change, 1969. Author numerous articles, monographs, reviews, chapters in books. Editor: School and University, 1940-42; Washington State Curriculum Journal, 1942-44; School Bulletin Portland, Oregon, 1944-46; assoc. editor Jour. Ednl. Research, 1945-65. Home: 7006 Wells Parkway West Hyattsville MD 20782 Office: Coll Edn U Md College Park MD 20742

ANDERSON, VICTOR ELVING, educator, geneticist; b. Stromsburg, Neb., Sept. 9, 1921; s. Edwin L. and Olga (Elving) A.; A.A., Bethel Jr. Coll., 1941; student Bethel Theol. Sem., 1941-43; B.A., U. Minn., 1945, M.S., 1949, Ph.D., 1953; m. Carol Esther Rexion, Aug. 31, 1946; children—Catherine, Carl, Christine, Martha. Faculty dept. biology Bethel Coll., 1946-60; asst. dir. Dight Inst. for Human Genetics, U. Minn., 1954—, asso. prof. zoology and genetics, 1961-66, prof. genetics and cell biology, 1966—. Cons. Nat. Inst. Neurol. Disease and Blindness, 1961-68. Bd. regents Bethel Coll. and Sem. Named Alumnus of Year, Bethel Coll. and Sem., 1965. Mem. A.A.A.S. (pres. Acad. Conf. 1967), Am. Soc. Human Genetics (dir. 1967-70), Minn. Acad. Sci. (pres. 1964-65), Am. Sci. Affiliation (pres. 1963-65), Phi Beta Kappa, Sigma Xi. Author: (with H.O. Goodman and S.C. Reed) Variables Related to Human Breat Cancer, 1958; also articles. Research on gentics in human behavior and mental retardation. Home: 1775 N Fairview Av St Paul MN 55113 Office: Dight Inst Human Genetics U Minn Minneapolis MN 55455

ANDERSON, VIRGIL LEE, statistician, educator; b. North Liberty, Ind., May 2, 1922; s. George W. and Mabel (Schrader) A.; B.S., Ia. State U., 1947, Ph.D., 1953; m. Avis E. Harbaugh, Dec. 4, 1943; children—Cheryl E. (Mrs. Robert D. Shadley), Michael, Denise J. Asst. prof. statistics Purdue U., 1951-56, asso. prof., 1956-60, prof., 1960—; cons. U.S. Naval Ammunition Depot, Crane, Ind., 1959—; univ. asso. Bayer & McElrath, Inc., mgmt. cons., Detroit, 1965—. mem. adv. com. Nat. Coop. Hwy. Research Program, Washington, 1963—. Served with AUS, 1943-46. Fellow Am. Statis. Assn.; mem. Inst. Math. Statistics, Am. Inst. Biol. Scis., Sigma Xi. Home: 337 Leslie Av West Lafayette IN 47906 Office: Math Scis Bldg Purdue U Lafayette IN 47907

ANDERSON, WALLACE ERVIN, physicist, educator; b. Scranton, S.C., Oct. 28, 1913; s. Miles Hannibal and Laura (Wallace) A.; B.S., The Citadel, 1934; M.S., U. Ky., 1936; Ph.D. (Rackham fellow 1947), U. Mich., 1949; m. Rheta M. Frierson, Sept. 12, 1939; children—Sarah Graham, Mary Wallace. Mem. faculty The Citadel, 1936-42, 46—, prof. physics, head dept., 1953—, acad. dean, 1966—, v.p. for acad. affairs, 1970—; spl. tutor Med: Coll. S.C. Teaching Hosp., Charleston, 1959-67; research asso., Duke, 1949, 50. Served to lt. col. AUS, 1942-46; col. Res. Decorated Legion of Merit. Mem. Am. Phys. Soc., Am. Assn. Physics Tchrs., Am. Soc. Engring. Edn., S.C. Acad. Sci., Mil. Order World Wars, Sigma Xi, Sigma Pi Sigma. Episcopalian. Rotarian. Home: Quarters 2B The Citadel Charleston SC 29409

ANDERSON, WALLACE LUDWIG, educator; b. Hartford, Conn., Sept. 9, 1917; s. Emanuel and Greta (Askerbloom) A.; B.A., Trinity Coll., Conn., 1939, M.A., 1945; Ph.D., U. Chgo., 1948; m. Mary Elizabeth Belden, Mar. 10, 1943; children—Hale, Whit. Tchr. pub. schs. Conn., 1939-42; asst. prof. English, U. No. Ia., Cedar Falls, 1948-54, asso. prof., 1954-58, prof., 1958—, asst. dean instr., 1959-63, asso. dean instrn., 1963-65, dean undergraduate studies, 1965—. Mem. intercultural edn. com. Edn. and World Affairs, Served with USAAF, 1942-45. Recipient Fulbright award The Netherlands, 1957-58. Guggenheim fellow, 1967-68. Mem. Am. Assn. U. Profs., Assn. Higher Edn., Modern Lang. Assn., Nat. Council Tchrs. English. Author: (with N.C. Stageberg) Poetry as Experience, 1952, Introductory Readings on Language, 1962; Edwin Arlington Robinson: A Critical Introduction, 1967. Contbr. articles profl. jours. Home: 1034 W 15th St Cedar Falls IA 50613

ANDERSON, WALTER STRATTON, Jr., business exec.; b. N.Y.C., Apr. 21, 1912; s. Walter Stratton and Virginia Miller (Ewing) A.; student Loomis Sch., Windsor, Conn., 1927- 29; B.S., Harvard, 1933; postgrad. U. Chgo., 1949-50; m. Mary McIntire Betts, Sept. 30, 1944; children—Virginia Randolph, Thomas Stratton. Vice consul, Le Havre, France, 1937-38; with Fgn. Service Officers' Tng. Sch., Dept. State, 1939; vice consul, Johannesburg, South Africa, 1939-41, Lagos, Nigeria, 1941-42, Accra, Gold Coast, 1942; with Dept. State, 1942-43; 3d and 2d sec., vice consul, Lima, Peru, 1943-46; 2d sec., consul, London, 1946-49; with Dept. State, 1949-52; first sec., Rangoon, Burma, 1953-54, Oslo, Norway, 1954-58; asst. dir. for program operations Internat. Ednl. Exchange Service, Dept. State, 1958-60, dep. dir. Office of Ednl. Exchange, 1960-61, dep. examiner Bd. Examiners for Fgn. Service, State Dept., 1961-62, ret.; sec. Center for Internat. Affairs, Harvard, 1962-63; v.p. GTE Internat., Inc. subsidiary Gen. Telephone & Electronics Corp., Washington, 1963—; dir. Gen. Telephone Co. Alaska. Adviser, U.S. delegation to fifth meeting Consultative Com. on Econ. Devel. in South and S.E. Asia, New Delhi, 1953; mem. Bus.-Industry Polit. Action Com. Mem. Am. Fgn. Service Assn., Armed Forces Communications and Electronics Assn. Roman Catholic. Club: International (Washington). Home: 5310 Albemarle St Washington DC 20016 Office: 1120 Connecticut Av NW Washington DC 20036

ANDERSON, WARREN DEWITT, educator; b. Bklyn., Mar. 19, 1920; s. Cyril DeWitt and Susan (Olsen) A.; B.A., Haverford Coll., 1942; M.A., Harvard U., 1947; B.A., Oxford (Eng.) U., 1949; Ph.D., Harvard, 1954; m. Anne Bacon Worden, June 14, 1947; children—Claudia, Eric Worden, Peter DeWitt. Classics master Loomis Sch., Windsor, Conn., 1947; instr. Greek and Latin, Coll. of Wooster, 1950-54, asst. prof., 1954-55, asso. prof., 1955-60, prof., chmn., 1960-67; prof. English and comparative lit. U. Ia., 1967-70, chmn. program comparative lit., 1968-70; prof. comparative lit. U. Mass. at Amherst, 1969—, chmn. program in comparative lit., 1970—. Served with AUS, 1942-46. Mem. Am. Assn. Rhodes Scholars, Modern Language Assn., Am. Comparative Lit. Assn., Phi Beta Kappa. Democrat. Episcopalian. Author: Matthew Arnold and the Classical Tradition, 1965; Ethos and Education in Greek Music, 1966; co-editor, contbr. Victorian Essays, 1967; translator: Theophrastus: The Character Sketches, 1970. Home: 27 High Point Dr Amherst MA 01002

ANDERSON, WARREN ROLAND, hotel exec.; b. Kalispell, Mont., Nov. 2, 1929; s. Adolphe E. and Marion (Freer) A.; B.A., Wash. State U., 1951; m. Susan L. Merrow, Feb. 2, 1952; children—John Frederick, Jaynee Sue. Asst. mgr. Davenport Hotel, Spokane, Wash., 1953-56, gen. mgr., 1964-68, asst. mgr. Finlen Hotel, Butte, Mont., 1956-57; exec. asst. mgr. Benjamin Franklin Hotel, Seattle, 1957-59; resident mgr. Multnomah Hotel, Portland, Ore., 1959; mgr. Rainbow Hotel, Great Falls, Mont., 1960; gen. mgr. Northern Hotel, Billings, Mont., 1961-64; gen. mgr. Hotel Dusit Thani, Bangkok, 1968—; v.p. Anderson's, Inc., Kalispell, Mont.; pres. Downtown Parking Garage, Inc.; now gen. mgr. Hotel Bonaventure, Montreal, Que. Dir. Gt. Falls Trade Promotion Assn., Great Falls Community Chest, Billings United Fund, Flying Cloud Guest Ranch, Spokane U.S.O., United Neighbors. Served to capt. inf. AUS, 1951-53. Decorated Bronze Star medal. Mem. Mont. Taxpayers Assn. (dir.), Mont. (v.p.), Wash. (v.p.), Am. (dir.) hotel and motel assns., Billings C. of C. (dir.), Montreal Bd. Trade, Montreal C. of C. Mason (Shriner), Elk, Rotarian. Clubs: petroleum (dir.) (Billings); Optimist (Seattle). Home: 40 Soi 11 Sukhumuit Bangkok Thailand Office: Hotel Dusit Thani Rama IV Rd Bangkok Thailand

ANDERSON, WAYNE JEREMY, educator; b. Salt Lake City, Aug. 30, 1908; s. Parley Pratt and Sarah Ettie (Jeremy) A.; B.A., U. Utah, 1934, M.A., 1937, Ph.D. in Ednl. Psychology and Family Life, 1954; postgrad. U. Minn., 1954; m. Ruth Elise Mace, June 14, 1938; children—Annette (Mrs. William A. Rifley), Cherie (Mrs. Robert L. Muirbrook), James, Julie (Mrs. David Curle), Jill. Tchr. schs., Salt Lake City, 1934-41; div. head expediting dept. Salt Lake Dist. U.S. Engrs., War Dept., 1941-45; exec. sec. Utah Social Hygiene Assn., 1945-49; prof. family living U. Minn., 1949—. Cons. Minn. Gov.'s Adv. Com. on Children and Youth, 1957-67. Pres., Minn. Council Family Life, 1962-64; mem. Internat. Adv. Com. Parents Without Partners, 1966-70. Mem. Nat. Council Family Relations, Am. Psychol. Assn., Am. Assn. Marriage and Family Counselors, Am. Assn. U. Profs. Mem. Ch. of Jesus Christ of Latter-day Saints (bishop, mem. high council dist. presidency). Author: Meeting the Needs of Today's Family, 1962; Design for Family Living, 1964; How to Understand Sex, 1966; How to Discuss Sex with Teen-Agers, 1969; Living, Loving and Marrying, 1969; How to Explain Sex to Children, 1971; Harmon Killebrew, Baseball's Superstar, 1971. Home: 4715 Girard Av S Minneapolis MN 55409 Office: 30B Nicholson Hall U Minn Minneapolis MN 55455

ANDERSON, WENDELL RICHARD, gov. of Minn.; b. St. Paul, Feb. 1, 1933; s. Theodore M. and Gladys (Nord) A.; B.A., U. Minn., 1954, LL.B., 1960; m. Mary Christine McKee, Aug. 11, 1963; children—Amy, Elizabeth, Brett. Admitted to Minn. bar, 1960; mem. Minn. Ho. of Reps., 1959-63, Minn. State Senate, 1963-71; gov. State of Minn., 1971—. Mem. U.S. Olympic Hockey Team, 1956, U.S. Nat. Hockey Team, 1955, 57. Dir. St. Paul Sister City Corp. Chmn. Minn. Humphrey for Pres. campaign, 1968. Served as 1st lt. inf., AUS, 1955-56. Named one of two outstanding legislators from Minn., Eagleton Inst. Politics of Rutgers U., 1967. Mem. Minn., Ramsey County bar assns., U.S. Olympians, Minn. Alumni Club. Mem. Minn. Dem. Farm Labor Party. Office of the Governor State Capitol St Paul MN

ANDERSON, WILBUR CHARLES, railroad equipment mfg. co. exec.; b. Bklyn., Jan. 11, 1919; s. Charles and Augusta M. (Johnson) A.; B.S., N.Y. U.; m. Shirley Edith Hale, Dec. 22, 1945; children—David Alan, Barbara Carol. With ACF Industries, Inc., 1938—, treas., 1963—, sec., from 1965. Served to capt. AUS, 1941-46. Home: 222 Valley Ct Haworth NJ 07641 Office: 750 3d Av New York City NY 10017

ANDERSON, WILLIAM, ret. educator; b. Mpls., Oct. 25, 1888; s. Edward and Maren (Olausen) A.; A.B., U. Minn., 1913; A.M., Harvard, 1914, Ph.D., 1917; m. Morgia DeLaittre Mansur, Dec. 28, 1915; children—Morgia Jeanette (Mrs. Howard Penniman), Marian Ruth (Mrs. Robt. L. Olson). Instr. govt., Harvard University, 1915-16; successively instr. polit. sci., asst. prof., asso. prof. and prof. U. Minn., 1916-57, chmn. dept. polit. sci., 1927-32, 35-47, dir. Bur. for Research in Govt., 1919-28. Mem. Social Science Research Council, 1932- 36; mem. Council's Com. on Pub. Adminstrn., 1933-45, chmn. 1939-45; chmn. Council's Com. on Gov., 1941-45. Mem. Mpls. Charter Commn., 1926-36, 45-48, Minn. State Planning Bd., 1935-38, Minn. Resources Commn., 1939-43; mem. com. on fed.-state relations Commn. on Orgn. Exec. Br. Govt., 1947-48. Commn. on Intergovtl. Relations, 1953—. Pres., Mpls. Research Bur. 1941-47. Fellow A.A.A.S.; mem. Am. Polit. Sci. Assn. (1st v.p. 1929, pres. 1942). Am. Soc. Pub. Adminstrn., Am. Assn. U. Profs., Phi Beta Kappa. Author: A History of the Constitution of Minnesota, 1921; City Charter Making in Minnesota, 1922; American City Government, 1925; The Units of Government in the United States, 1934, rev. edit., 1943; Local Government and Finance in Minnesota, 1935; American Government, 1938, rev. edit., 1946; Fundamentalss of American Government, 1940; The National Government of the United States, 1946; Federalism and Intergovernmental Relations, 1946; The Nation and the States, Rivals or Partners?, 1955; Intergovernmental Fiscal Relations, 1956; Man's Quest for Political Knowledge: The Study and Teaching of Politics in Ancient Times, 1964. Editor: Local Government in Europe, 1939; Intergovernmental Relations Series, 1950-60. Contbr. to Minn. Law Rev., National Municipal Rev., Am. Polit. Science Rev., others. Home: 111 Belbourne Av SE Minneapolis MN 55414

ANDERSON, WILLIAM, lawyer; b. Sharpsburg, Pa., Oct. 8, 1905; s. William and Mildred B. (Moore) A.; A.B., Cornell U., 1926; LL.B., Harvard, 1929; m. Mary E. Powell, Dec. 29, 1934; children—Carolyn (Mrs. Walter P. Orbin), Jane P. (Mrs. Roger S. Blair). Admitted to Pa. bar, 1930; asso., jr. partner Dickie, McCamey & Chilcote, Pitts., 1930-37; counsel Pitts. Rys. Co., 1937-52; sec., gen. counsel, dir. Pitts. Group Cos. of Columbia Gas System, Inc., 1952-70; of counsel Thorp, Reid & Armstrong, Pitts., 1970—. Mem. Am., Pa., Allegheny County, Fed. Power bar assns., Am. Judicature Soc., Pitts. C. of C., Pa. Gas Assn., Am. Soc. Corporate Secs. Home: 749 Gypsy Lane Pittsburgh PA 15228 Office: Grant Bldg Pittsburgh PA 15219

ANDERSON, WILLIAM ARNOLD DOUGLAS, physician; b. Ontario, Can., Aug. 27, 1910; s. Thomas H.P. and Lottie H. (Cook) A.; A.B., Victoria Coll., U. Toronto, 1931; M.D., U. Toronto, 1934, M.A., 1936; m. Harriott I. Gates, Sept. 1934; children—Douglas Richard, Mary Carolyn, Joan, Judith. Came to U.S., 1936, naturalized, 1941. Intern St. Michael's Hosp., Toronto, 1934-35, fellow pathology Banting Inst., 1935-36; asst. pathology Duke U., 1936-37; instr. pathology U. Tenn., 1937-40; asst. prof. pathology St. Louis U., 1940- 44, asso. prof., 1944-45; prof. pathology, dir. dept. pathology, sch. medicine, Marquette U., 1945-53; prof. pathology, U. Miami Sch. Med., also director department pathology, 1953—; director laboratories St. Joseph's Hospital, Milwaukee, 1945-53; dir. labs. Jackson Meml. Hosp., Miami, 1953—; vis. prof. pathology U. Capetown (S. Africa), 1961; consultant Armed Forces Institute Pathology. Director-at-large American Cancer Society, 1966—. Recipient Sci. Products Found. award, 1959; Ward Burdick award Am. Soc. Clin. Pathologists, 1965; Distinguished Service award Coll. Am. Pathologists and Am. Soc. Clin. Pathologists, 1969. Fellow A.C.P., Coll. Am. Pathol. (president 1956-57), Am. Soc. Clin. Pathologists, American Medical Writers Assn. (pres. 1966-67), Internat. Acad. Cytology; mem. Path. Soc. Gt. Britain and Ireland, Am. Assn. Pathologists and Bacteriologists, Am. Soc. Exptl. Pathol., A.M.A., Wis. Soc. Pathologists (pres. 1949-51), American Cancer Society (dir.-at-large 1966-71). Methodist. Author: Synopsis of Pathology, 1942, 7th edit., 1968; Pathology, 1948, 6th edit., 1971; Pathology Seminars, 1955, Asso. editor Am. Jour. Clin. Pathology, 1951-55, Lab. Medicine, 1969-71; mem. editorial bd. Excerpta Medica, sect. V (Pathology), 1949—, Cancer, 1964—. Home: 2701 Columbus Blvd Coral Gables FL 33134 Office: Jackson Meml Hosp Miami FL 33136

ANDERSON, WILLIAM BANKS, ophthalmologist; b. Haw River, N.C., Dec. 18, 1897; s. William Holt and Mary (Banks) A.; A.B., U. N.C., 1920; M.D., Johns Hopkins, 1924; m. Mildred Everett, Oct. 18, 1927; children—William Banks, Edward Everett, Charles Alexander. Intern Union Meml. Hosp., Balt., 1924-25; resident Mass. Eye and Ear Infirmary, Boston, 1925-27; practice medicine, specializing in ophthalmology, Durham, N.C., 1927—; asso. McPherson Hosp., 1927-45; asso. prof. surgery charge ophthalmology Duke Med. Center, 1930-49, prof., chief div. ophthalmology, 1949-65, prof. ophthalomolgy emeritus, chief div., 1965—; cons. VA Hosp., Durham, 1950- -. Mem. neurol. and sensory disease service adv. com. Neurol. and Sensory Disease Service Project Rev. Panel, Dept. Health, Edn. and Welfare, 1963-64, cons. Div. Hosp. and Med. Facilities, 1968. Examining physician SSS, 1941-47. Served as 2d lt., inf. U.S. Army, 1917; with USPHS, 1943. Diplomate Am. Bd. Ophthalmology (chmn. 1965-66). Fellow A.C.S. (past chmn. adv. council for ophthalmology); mem. A.M.A. (past chmn. sci. sect. ophthalmology), So. Med. Assn. (chmn. sect. ophthalmology), N.C., Durham-Orange County med. socs., Am. Ophthal. Soc., Am. Acad. Ophthalmology and Otolaryngology (v.p.), Assn. for Research in Ophthalmology, N.C. Soc. For Research in Ophthalmology, N.C. Soc. For Prevention Blindness (chmn. med. adv. com.), N.C. Eye, Ear, Nose and Throat Soc. (past chmn.). Home: 502 E Forest Hills Blvd Durham, NC 27707. Office: PO Box 8707 Durham NC 27707

ANDERSON, WILLIAM ERNEST, lawyer; b. Chgo., July 31, 1895; s. Andrew and Mary (Lofqvist) A.; LL.B., Webster Coll., 1920; LL.M., Loyola U., Chgo., 1926; m. Marjorie Allen, June 18, 1927; children—Laurel Joyce, Lois Winifred; m. 2d, Beatriz Hernandez del Valle. Admitted to Ill. bar, 1920, since practiced in Chgo., specializing in patents, unfair competition, trade- marks and copyrights; counsel to firm Fitch, Even, Tabin, and Luedka, and predecessor firm, Chgo., 1931—. U.S. claims commr. for Morocco, Algeria, Tunisia, 1943-45. Served to lt. col. AUS, 1942-46. Mem. Soc. Internat. Law, Inter-Am., Internat., Am., Ill., Fed., Chgo. bar assns., Am. Fgn. Law Assn., Am., Chgo. patent law assns., Copyright Soc. Clubs: Union League (Chicago); University (Evanston). Author: Spanish Adjectives and Adverbs, 1941. Home: 7212 Oak Av River Forest IL 60305 Office: 135 S LaSalle St Chicago IL 60603

ANDERSON, WILLIAM F., newspaper editor; b. Greeneville, Tenn., Feb. 16, 1927; s. Nicholas and Fuschia (Stine) A.; ed. Ia. State Coll., U. Tenn. Reporter, Knoxville (Tenn.) Jour., 1949, Nashville Banner, 1950; aviation writer Dayton (O.) Jour. Herald; bur. chief Pacific Stars and Stripes, 1955; city editor Chgo. Tribune, 1968-70; nat. news corr. 1970—. Served with USNR, World War II. Recipient Navy Civilian Merit award. Club: Nat. Press (Washington). Office: 1750 Pennsylvania Av NW Washington DC 20006

ANDERSON, WILLIAM GAIN, accountant; b. East St. Louis, Ill., July 15, 1932; s. William G. and Marie (Gain) A.; B.S. magna cum laude, St. Louis U., 1954; student U. Wichita, 1962-63; m. Kathryn Sue Hammitt, June 18, 1955; children—Mark William (dec.), Laura Ashton, Kristin Claire. With Ernst & Ernst, C.P.A.'s, 1956—, resident mgr., Wichita, Kan., 1961-67, partner, St. Louis, Mo., 1967—. Treas. Jr. Achievement Wichita, 1961-67. Served with AUS, 1954-56. C.P.A., Mo., Kan., La., N.C. Mem. Nat. Assn. Accountants (bd. dirs. Wichita 1964-66, treas. 1965-66, v.p. 1967), Am. Inst. C.P.A.'s, Kan. Soc. C.P.A.'s (dir. 1965-67). Republican. K.C. Home: 362 Gascony Way St Louis MO 63122 Office: 10 Broadway St Louis MO 63102

ANDERSON, WILLIAM HARRY, economist, educator; b. Marinette, Wis., June 9, 1905; s. John and Anna (Olsen) A.; B.A., U. Wis., 1928, LL.B., 1938, Ph.D., 1945; m. Ione E. Swanson, Sept. 2, 1936; 1 son, Harland. Security analyst Halsey Stuart, Chgo., 1928-29; chmn. social sci. dept. W. Chgo. Community High Sch., 1929-36; admitted to Wis. bar, 1938; practice in Madison, 1938-46; atty. Woodward & May, 1938-45; asst. prof. econs. U. Wis., 1945-46; asso. prof. econs. U. So. Cal., 1946-52, prof., 1952-66, chmn. dept. econs., 1957-61; John C. Lincoln prof. pub. finance Claremont (Cal.) Men's Coll. and Grad. Sch., 1966—, chmn. dept. econs., 1968-71; finance cons. Inst. Adminstrv. Affairs, Tehran, Iran, 1956-57; dir. Lincoln Sch. Pub. Finance, 1968—. Mem. Am., Western econ. assns., Nat. Tax Assn., Western Finance Assn., Wis., Cal. bar assns., Artus. Author: Taxation and the American Economy, 1951. Home: 539 Wesley Way Claremont CA 91711

ANDERSON, WILLIAM HENRY SCHOEN, banker; b. Renovo, Pa., Feb. 27, 1911; s. Arthur C. and Lenore (Gist) A.; B.S., Temple U., 1935, M.B.A., 1948; m. Elizabeth Laverty, June 4, 1938 (dec. 1951); 1 son, William Henry; m. 2d, Catherine Erskine, June 28, 1958; 1 dau., Patricia Anne. With State Bank Renovo, 1928-29; with First Pa. Banking & Trust Co., Phila., 1929—, asst. comptroller, 1949- 61, auditor, 1961-63, gen. auditor, 1963—; instr. finance Temple U. Evening Sch., 1948-49. Scoutmaster, mem. troop com. Barren Hill (Pa.) council Boy Scouts Am., 1951-56. Mem. Bank Adminstrn. Inst. (gov., past pres. Phila. chpt., nat. chmn. accounting commn.), Inst. Internat. Auditors, Co. Mil. Historians, Brigade Am. Revolution, Delta Sigma Pi. Contbr. profl. jours. Home: 4029 MacNiff Dr Lafayette Hill PA 19444 Office: SE Corner 15th and Chestnut Sts Philadelphia PA 19101

ANDERSON, WILLIAM J., lawyer; b. Oakville, Man., Can., Apr. 20, 1918; B.A., U. Man., 1942; J.D., Osgoode Hall. Admitted to Ont. bar, 1948; partner firm Gardiner, Roberts, Anderson, Conlin, Fitzpatrick, O'Donohue & White, Toronto, Ont., Can. Mem. County York Law Assn., Canadian Bar Assn., Advocates Soc. (dir. 1969—), Lawyers Club Toronto. Office: Canadian Imperial Bank Commerce Bldg Toronto 1 Ontario Canada*

ANDERSON, WILLIAM PINCKNEY III clergyman; b. Clinton, S.C., Dec. 9, 1918; s. William Pinckney Jr. and Clayte (Bailey) A.; B.A., Furman U., 1939; B.D., Union Theol. Sem. Va., 1942; spl. student Columbia, 1956; m. Betty Kline, Apr. 18, 1942; children—John Stuart, Nancy. Ordained to ministry Presbyn. Ch. U.S., 1942; pastor, Williamsburg, Va., 1945-49; asso. pastor Westminster Ch., Miami, Fla., 1949-50; dir. young adult work Presbyn. Ch. U.S., 1950- 52, dir. adult and family edn., 1952-56, sec. Christian teaching, 1957-60; pastor Forest Hills Presbyn. Ch., Tampa, Fla., 1960- 64; exec. sec., stated clerk, treas. Presbytery of Winchester (Va.), 1964-67; pastor St. Andrews Presbyn. Ch., Dunedin, Fla., 1967—; moderator Norfolk Presbytery, 1948. Leader planning staff Covenant Life Curriculum for Christian Edn., Presbyn. Ch. U.S. Served as lt. comdr. Chaplains Corps USNR, 1942-45. Recipient distinguished citizenship award Williamsburg Jr. C. of C., 1947. Home: 2373 Harrison Dr Dunedin FL 33528 Office: 705 Michigan Blvd Dunedin FL 33528

ANDERSON, WILLIAM ROBERT, congressman; b. Bakerville, Tenn., June 17, 1921; s. David Hensely and Mary (McKelvey) A.; grad. Columbia Mil. Acad., 1939; B.S. in Elec. Engring., U.S. Naval Acad., 1942; D.Sc., Defiance Coll., 1958; m. Yvonne Etzel, June 10, 1943; children—Michael David, William Robert. Commd. ensign U.S. Navy, 1942, advanced through grades to capt., 1960; assigned submarines Tarpon, Narwhal, Trutta, Pacific combat patrols, World War II, postwar service submarines Sarda, Trutta, Tang; comdr. attack submarine U.S.S. Wahoo, Pearl Harbor, 1953-55; head tactical dept. Submarine Sch., 1955-56; staff naval reactors br. AEC, Washington, 1956-57; comdr. U.S.S. Nautilus, 1957-59; ret. 1962; cons. to Pres. J.F. Kennedy, until 1963; mem. 89th-92d Congresses, 6th Tenn. Dist. Decorated Bronze Star, Legion of Merit; recipient Stephen Decatur prize Navy League U.S., Distinguished Service award N.Y.C., Christopher Columbus medal Genoa, Italy; Elisha Kent Kane medalist Geog. Soc. Phila., 1959; Patron's medal Royal Geog. Soc., 1959; Leadership award Freedoms Found., 1960. Mem. Am. Legion, Amvets. Club: Explorers (N.Y.C.). Author: Nautilus 90 North, 1959; First Under the North Pole, 1959; The Useful Atom, 1966. Contbr. articles nat. mags., profl. publs. Home: Waverly TN Office: House Office Bldg Washington DC 20515

ANDERSON, WILLIAM SCOVIL, educator; b. Brookline, Mass., Sept. 16, 1927; s. Edgar Weston and Katrina (Brewster) A.; B.A., Yale, 1950, Ph.D., 1954; A.B., Cambridge (Eng.) U., 1952, M.A., 1955; m. Lorna Candee Bassette, June 12, 1954; children—Judith, Blythe, Heather, Meredith, Keith. Prix de Rome fellow Am. Acad. in Rome, 1954-55; instr. classics Yale, 1955-59; resident in Rome, Morse fellow, 1959-60; mem. faculty U. Cal. at Berkeley, 1960—, prof. Latin and comparative lit., 1966—; prof. charge Intercollegiate Center Classical Studies, 1967-68, chmn. classics, 1970—. Served with AUS, 1946-48; Korea. Mem. Am. Philol. Assn., Danforth Assos., Soc. Religion. Mem. P.E. Ch. Contbr. profl. jours. Mem. editorial bd. Classical Jour., Vergilius, Satire Newsletter. Home: 1424 Lincoln St Berkeley, CA 94702.

ANDERSON, WILLIAM STATON, pediatrician; b. Wilson, N.C., 1906; M.D., Johns Hopkins, 1931. Intern, Johns Hopkins Hosp., 1931-32; asst. resident, then resident pediatrics N.Y. Hosp., 1932-35; instr. pediatrics Cornell U. Med. Coll., 1933-35; mem. sr. attending pediatric staff Children's Hosp., Washington, Washington Hosp. Center; civilian cons. U.S. Navy Hosp., Bethesda, Md., NIH; clin. prof. pediatrics George Washington U. Sch. Medicine. Diplomate Am. Bd. Pediatrics. Mem. A.M.A., Am. Pediatric Soc., Am. Acad. Pediatrics (former pres.). Address: 5300 Westbard Av Washington DC 20016

ANDERSON , WILTON THOMAS, educator; b. Richland, Tex., Nov. 29, 1916; s. William Nix and Ruth (Skipper) A.; B.S., Northwestern State Coll., Alva, Okla., 1938; M.C.E., U. Okla., 1941; Ed.D., U. Colo., 1953; m. Gwendolyn Hollis, Dec. 10, 1938; children—Kaye Lynn, Wilton Thomas. Bus. tchr. Cyril (Okla.) High Sch., 1938-40; asso. prof., head dept. bus. No. Okla. Jr. Coll., 1940-46; prof., head dept. bus. adminstrn. Bowling Green Coll. Commerce, 1946- 47; asso. prof. accounting U. Colo., 1947-57; dir. edn. Am. Inst. C.P.A.'s, N.Y.C., 1957-60; prof., head dept. accounting Okla. State U., 1960—. Named Outstanding Bus. Adminstrn. Tchr., Okla. State U., 1963, 64, 70, Outstanding U. Tchr., 1970. C.P.A., Okla., Colo. Mem. Am. Inst. C.P.A.'s, Okla. Soc. C.P.A.'s, Am. Accounting Assn. (v.p. 1964-65), Beta Gamma Sigma, Beta Alpha Psi (nat. council 1964-68, nat. pres. 1966-67), Delta Sigma Pi. Author: (with C.A. Moyer and A.R. Wyatt) Accounting: Basic Financial, Cost and Control Concepts. Contbr. articles profl. publs. Home: 60 Yellowbrick Rd Stillwater OK 74074

ANDERSON, WOODROW S., corp. exec.; b. Chgo., May 27, 1913; s. Swan and Louise V. (Peterson) A.; student U. Cal. at Los Angeles. 1933-34 m. Grace Jacobson, Oct. 23, 1939; children—Mrs. Karen Schwarz, Richard L., Kathe; m. 2d, Marian Lincoln, Mar. 18, 1967. Dist sales rep. Am. Safety Razor Co., Bklyn., 1939; salesman Nat. Cash Register Co., Chgo., 1939-45; with Addressograph Multigraph Corp., Chgo., 1945-49, Cleve., 1949—, asst. mgr. methods and sales tng., 1951-53, asst. nat. sales mgr. multigraph div., 1953-57, nat. sales mgr., 1957-65, v.p. marketing, 1965-67, adminstrv. v.p. corp., 1967-70, v.p. corporate sales and marketing, 1970—. Home: 1040 Canyon View Rd Northfield OH 44067 Office: 20600 Chagrin Blvd Shaker Heights OH 44122

ANDERSON-IMBERT, ENRIQUE, educator, author; b. Cordoba, Argentina, Feb. 12, 1910; s. Jose Enrique and Honorina (Imbert) Anderson; M.A., Universidad Nacional de Buenos Aires, 1940, Ph.D., 1946; m. Margarita Di Clerico, Mar. 30, 1935; children—Carlos Eduardo, Anabel. Came to U.S., 1947, naturalized, 1953. Prof. lit. Universidad Nacional de Cuyo (Argentina), 1940, Universidad Nacional de Tucuman (Argentina), 1941-46; lectr. Spanish lit. Smith Coll., Northampton, Mass., 1944; prof. Spanish lit. Mich. U., 1947-65; Victor S. Thomas prof. hispanic lit. Harvard, 1965—. Mem. Am. Acad. Arts and Scis. Author: La Flecha en el Aire, 1937; Tres novelas de Payro con picaros en tres miras, 1942; Ensayos, 1946; Ibsen y su tiempo, 1946; El arte de la prosa en Juan Montalvo, 1948; Estudios sobre escritores de America, 1954; Historia de la literatura hispanoamericana, 1954; Los grandes libros de Occidente y otros ensayos, 1957; Que es la prosa, 1958; El cuento espanol, 1959; Critica interna, 1961; El grimorio, 1961; Vigilia Fuga, 1963; Los domingos del profesor, 1965; El gato de Cheshire, 1965; Genio y figura de Sarmiento, 1967; La originalidad de Rubén Dario, 1968; Análisis del Tabaré, 1968; Analisis del Fausto, 1968; La Sandia y otros cuentos, 1969; Una aventura de Sarmiento en Chicago, 1969; Metodos de critica literaria, 1969; La locura juega al ajedrez, 1971. Home: 20 Elizabeth Rd Belmont MA 02178 Office: Boylston Hall Harvard Cambridge MA 02138

ANDERSSEN, HAROLD ARTHUR, diversified mfg. co. exec.; b. Cin., May 21, 1910; grad. Phillips Acad., Andover, Mass., 1927; B.S., Princeton, 1931; postgrad. Mass. Inst. Tech., 1931-33; m. Jean R. Holland, June 16, 1935; children--Lois A., Andrew M., James. Salesman, Brown Mfg. Co., Boston, 1932-33; jr. engr. Ball Metals Co., Carson City, Nev., 1933-36, engr., 1936-37, sr. engr., 1937-40; project engr. Kingston Engring. Co., Los Angeles, 1940-43; with dept. engring. City of Denver, 1946-50, dep. head, 1950-52; 2d v.p. Johnson Mfg. Co., Kansas City, Kansas, 1952-54, v.p. for engring., 1954-57; v.p. research Consol. Industries, Inc., South Bend, Ind., 1957-60, exec. v.p., 1960-65, pres. 1965-70, chmn. bd., chief exec. officer, 1970--, also dir.; dir. ABC Chem. Co., 2d Nat. Bank, Country Food Storage Co., Providence Indsl. Corp. (Ind.), Wilson Investment Co., Inc., Hammond Life Ins. Co., Inc. Pres., Dewey High Sch., Kansas City, Mo., 1953-54; fund chmn. local div. Salvation Army, 1959-60. Mem. South Bend Republican Com., 1964-68. Bd. dirs. Ind. council Boy Scouts Am., 1969-71; trustee Lovell Found. Served to lt., Corps Engrs., AUS, 1943-45. Decorated Bronze Star medal. Member N.A.M., South Bend C. of C. (v.p. 1963-65, dir. 1965-70), Am. Mgmt. Assn., Ind. Engrs. Soc. (program com. 1961-62), Princeton Alumni Assn. Episcopalian. Rotarian, Optimist. Clubs: South Bend Golf; Links (N.Y.C.). Home: 6823 Broad Terrace Av South Bend IL 46505 Office: PO Box 1019 South Bend IN 46501

ANDERSSON, THEODORE, educator; b. New Haven, Feb. 18, 1903; s. Seth Samuel and Anna Erika (Johnson) Levine; B.A., Yale, 1925, M.A., 1926, Ph.D., 1931; m. Harriet Josephine Murdock, Apr. 8, 1930; children—Theodore Murdock and Margit, (Mrs. Timothy R. Clifford) (twins). Instr. French, Yale, 1927-37; prof. Romance langs., chmn. dept. Am. U., 1937-41; asso. prof. Romance langs. Wells Coll. Aurora, N.Y., 1941-43, prof., chmn. dept., 1943-45; head Western European sect., div. cultural coop., State Dept., 1945-46, edn1. adviser Office Internat. Ednl. Exchange, 1946; asso. prof. French, dir. undergrad. instrn. French, Yale, 1946-51, dir. master in arts teaching program, 1951-54, asso. dir. program, 1954-55; asso. sec., asso. dir. fgn. lang. program Modern Lang. Assn. Am., 1955-56, dir. fgn. lang. program, 1956-57; prof. Romance langs. U. Tex., 1957-65, chmn. dept., 1959-68, prof. Romance languages and edn., 1965—; summer tchr. U. State N.Y. College Tchrs., Albany, 1937, Harvard, 1948, Middlebury Coll., 1954, U. Wis., 1954, 55, Stanford, 1955, U. Wash., 1958. Ednl. adviser Mut. Security Agy., 1952; dir. UNESCO seminar, Nuwara Eliya, Ceylon, 1953; U.S. del. UNESCO Inst. for Edn., Hamburg, Germany, 1959, 62; dir. research study conf. on leadership role of state; supr. modern fgn. langs., George Washington U., 1960; Ford Foundation program specialist for modern languages, Santiago, Chile, 1964-65; dir. bilingual design project S.W. Ednl. Devel. Lab., U.S. Office Edn., Austin, Texas, 1968- 69, director of bilingual section, 1969-70, resource specialist, 1970-71. Decorated chevalier Legion of Honor (France). Member of the Am. Council on Teaching of Foreign Languages, Modern Lang. Assn. Am., Am. Assn. Tchrs. French, Am. Assn. Tchrs. Spanish and Portuguese, N.E.A., International Institute Ibero-American Literature (pres. 1961-63). Author: Carlos María Ocantos, Argentine Novelist, 1934, translation, 1935; The Teaching of Foreign Languages in the Elementary School, 1953; (with F.H. Walter) The Teaching of Modern Languages, 1955; (with others) The Education of the Secondary School Teacher, 1962; Foreign Languages in the Elementary School: A Struggle Against Mediocrity, 1969; (with Mildred Boyer) Bilingual Schooling in the United States, 1970. Editor: (with T.G. Bergin) French Plays, 1941; Tex. Fgn. Langs. Assn. bull., 1958-63. Home: 1006 Lund Austin TX 78704

ANDERTON, FARRIS NORMAN, bldg. materials and chem. co. exec.; b. Town Creek, Ala., Apr. 22, 1917; s. Julius Floyd and Myrtle (Bowling) A.; B.S., U. Ala., 1939; m. Mary Margaret Mims, Aug. 3, 1946; children—Norma Gayle, Mary Ann, Keith Mims. Mgmt. accounting trainee U.S. Steel Corp., Birmingham, Ala., 1939-46; various positions, 1946-52; controller Hohenberg Bros. Co., Memphis, 1952-55; sec., treas., dir. Birmingham Paper Co., 1955-60; treas. Vulcan Materials Co., Birmingham, 1960-70, controller, 1970—. Speaker to profl. groups, colls., 1956—. Served to capt. AUS, 1941-45. Mem. Financial Execs. Inst. (past pres., nat. dir.), Nat. Assn. Accountants (past treas., dir.), Beta Alpha Psi. Baptist (chmn. bd. deacons). Clubs: Lions (past treas., dir.), Vestavia Country, The Club. Home: 3356 Faring Rd Birmingham AL 35223 Office: 1 Office Park Circle Birmingham AL 35223

ANDES, JOHN WILBUR, Jr., assn. exec.; b. Knoxville, Tenn., July 18, 1928; s. John Wilbur and Irene (Garrett) A.; A.B., Princeton, 1948; m. Patricia Jane Guy, Nov. 20, 1954; children—Alan Patrick, Jane Alison. With Blue-Cross-Blue Shield of Fla., 1948-50, 52-57, profl. relations mgr., 1955-57; asst. exec. sec. Am. Soc. Anesthesiologists, Park Ridge, Ill., 1957-58, exec. sec., 1958—. Served with USNR, 1950-52. Mem. Am. Assn. Med. Soc. Execs., Med. Soc. Execs. Conf. Greater Chgo., Park Ridge C. of C., Am. Soc. Assn. Execs. Clubs: Princeton (Chgo.); Court (Princeton). Home: 1810 Walnut St Park Ridge IL 60068 Office: 515 Busse Hwy Park Ridge IL 60068

ANDES, KEITH, actor, singer; b. Ocean City, N.J., July 12, 1920; s. William G. and Elsie (Metzger) A.; student St. Edwards Sch., Oxford, Eng., 1938; B.S. in Edn., Temple U., 1943; studied voice with Clyde Dengler, Luigi Cuiffrida, Rosalie Snyder, J. Mebane Beasley; m.; 2 sons. Debut in Winged Victory, N.Y.C., 1943; appeared in Chocolate Soldier, 1947, Kiss Me, Kate, 1948-50, Maggie, 1953, Wildcat, 1960, 63, Don Quixote in Man of La Mancha, 1967; motion pictures include Winged Victory, 1944, The Farmer's Daughter, 1947, Project X, 1949, Clash by Night, 1952, Blackbeard the Pirate, 1952, Split-Second, 1953, Key Man, 1954, The Second Greatest Sex, 1955, Away All Boats, 1956, Pillars of the Sky, 1956, Interlude, 1957, Damn Citizen, 1958, Surrender, 1959, Hells Bloody Devils; frequent TV guest appearances, 1955—; appeared on TV in This Man Dawson, Glynis. Served with USAAF, World War II. Mem. Screen Acotrs Guild, A.F.T.R.A., Actors Equity Assn. Address: 10836 Kingsland St Los Angeles CA 90052*

ANDLAUER, EDGAR LOUIS, restaurant chain exec.; b. Newark, Mar. 10, 1923; s. Frederick Charles, Sr., and Anna Maria (Lowenberg) A.; B.S., Rutgers U., 1948, M.B.A., 1954; m. A. Virginia Brown, Nov. 3, 1956; children—Phillip, Lynn, Eric. Accountant, mgr. mgmt. adv. services Price-Waterhouse & Co., N.Y.C., 1948-65; v.p., treas. Howard Johnson Co., Boston, 1965—. Served with AUS, 1943-46; ETO. C.P.A., N.J., Ohio, N.Y. Mem. Financial Execs. Inst., Am. Inst. C.P.A.'s, Ohio Soc. C.P.A.'s. Home: 234 Bristol Rd Wellesley MA 02181 Office: 250 Granite St Braintree MA 02184

ANDOLSEK, CHARLES FRANCIS, ins. co. exec.; b. N.Y.C., Jan. 17, 1910; s. Louis and Julia (Glotts) A.; m. Muriel Winifred Merrick, June 16, 1934; children—Sheila Armstrong, Charles Merrick. With Equitable Life Assurance Soc. U.S., N.Y.C., 1929—, beginning as clk., successively supr., office mgr., mgr. claims, 2d v.p., 1929-59, v.p., 1959—. Served from lt. (j.g.) to lt. comdr., USNR, 1943-45. Home: East Saddle River Rd Hohokus NJ 07423 Office: 1285 Av of Americas New York City NY 10019 wME

ANDOLSEK, LUDWIG JOHN, govt. ofcl.; b. Denver, Nov. 6, 1910; s. Ludvig and Frances (Gouze) A.; B.Ed., St. Cloud (Minn.) State Tchrs. Coll., 1935; m. Regina A. Burnett, Nov. 25, 1945; 1 dau., Kathryn M. With Nat. Youth Adminstrn., 1936-42, area dir., No. Minn., 1940-42; asst. to personel officer charge personal relations and grievance procedures VA Hosp., St. Cloud, 1947- 50; civilian personnel officer Ellsworth AFB, Weaver, S.D., 1950-51; adminstrv. asst. to Congressman J.A. Blatnik, 1951-62; chief clk. com. pub. works Ho. of Reps., 1963; commr. U.S. Civil Service, 1963—, vice chmn. commn., 1963-69. Served to capt. AUS, 1942-46. Recipient Silver Helmet, Civil Servant of Year, Amvets, 1966. Mem. Am. Legion, Amvets (life). Eagle (dist. dir. central Minn. 1948-50). Home: 9609 Bulls Run Pkwy Bethesda, MD 20034. Office: 1900 E St NW Washington DC 20415

ANDONYADIS, AVYERIS CHRISTOS, architect; b. Istanbul, Turkey, Jan. 29, 1928; s. Christos and Evdoksiya (Ksidis) A.; student Lyceum of Zografyon, Istanbul, 1942-48; M.Sc. Engring. and Architecture, Tech. U. Istanbul, 1953; M.Arch., U. Mich., 1964; m. Elly Zauraki, July 22, 1956; children—Nephelie, Christos. Came to U.S., 1960, naturalized, 1970. Partner, H. Vapurciyan, A. Andonyadis, E. Kortan & N. Yaubyan, Istanbul, 1953-58; with Doxiadis Assos., internat. cons. on devel. and ekistics, Athens, Greece, 1958-60; with Doxiadis Assos., Inc., Phila. and Washington, 1960—, now asst. v.p. Served to res. lt., C.E., Turkish Army, 1954. Recipient Daverman Merit award in architecture, 1963. Teaching fellow U. Mich., 1963-64. Mem. Turkish Inst. Architects, A.I.A., Am. Inst. Planners (asso.), U. Mich. Alumni Assn. Clubs: American Hellenic League. Important works include Govt. Hall Adapazari, Turkey, 1963, Govt. halls of Urfa, Gaziantep, Gumushane, Coll. and State Hosp. of Samsun, Turkey, Hdqrs. Hwy. Dept. Turkey, Kocatepe Mosque, Turkish Pavillion Internat. Expn. 58, Brussels, Belgium, Court House, Thesaloniki, Greece, housing projects in Pakistan, Iraq, Phila., Cin., Hampton, Va., 1960-71; riverfront redevel. in Louisville, Georgetown, D.C., 1965-71; environmental studies for power plants, Mich., 1969-71. Home: 1602 44th St NW Washington DC 20007 Office: 1058 Thomas Jefferson St NW Washington DC 20007

ANDRAS, ROBERT KNIGHT, Canadian cabinet minister; b. Lachine, Que., Can., Feb. 20, 1921; s. John Donald and Angela Eva (Knight) A.; grad. Wesley Coll., Winnipeg, 1938; D. Pub. Service, Northland Coll., Ashland, Wis., 1970; m. Frances Hunt, Oct. 20, 1945; children—Robert Hunt, Angela Knight. Exec. Ford Motor Co., 1946-58; elected Liberal mem. Fed. Parliament, 1965, re-elected, 1968; apptd. mem. Queen's Privy Council for Can., cabinet minister without portfolio with responsibility for Indian policy, 1968, minister responsible for housing, 1969, minister of state for urban affairs, 1971—. Served to maj. Canadian Army, 1942-46. Decorated Voluntary Medal, France and Germany Medal, Def. Medal, War Medal 39-45, Centennial Medal. Mem. Thunder Bay C. of C. (charter pres.), Inter-Parliamentary Union, NATO, Commonwealth parliamentary assns., Alta, Indian Assn. (hon. pres. 1969). Club: Gyro (Thunder Bay). Home: 318-33 Court St Thunder Bay Ontario Canada Office: House of Commons Ottawa Ontario Canada

ANDRE, CARL, artworker; b. Quincy, Mass., Sept. 16, 1935; s. George Hans and Margaret (Johnson). One man shows include Tibor de Nagy Gallery, N.Y.C., 1965, 66, Dwan Gallery, Los Angeles, 1967, Dwan Gallery, N.Y.C., 1967, bei Konrad Fischer, Dusseldorf, Germany, 1967, Mönchengladback, Germany, 1968, The Hague, Primary Structure, N.Y.C., 1966, Sculpture of the Sixties, Los Angeles, 1967. Address: Box 540 Cooper Sta New York City NY 10003.

ANDRE, FLOYD, coll. dean; b. New Sharon, Ia., Sept. 13, 1909; s. Graham and Alice (Fox) A.; B.S. in Agronomy, Ia. State Coll., 1931; M.S. in Entomology, 1933, Ph.D., 1936; m. Hazel May Beck, June 22, 1935 (dec. Apr. 1956); childrenJacqueline, Alice, Richard Graham. Asst., Ia. State Coll., 1932-34, instr. entomology and zoology, 1936-38, asst. entomologist, expt. sta., 1934-38, asso. entomologist Bur. Entomology and Plant Quarantine, U.S. Dept. Agr., 1938-40, entomologist and expt. sta. adminstr. Office Expt. Stations, 1940-43, sr. entomologist and expt. sta. adminstr., 1943-46; prof. econ. entomology U. Wis., also asst. dir. state agr. expt. sta., 1946-48, asst.

dean Coll. of Agr., asst. dir. state agr. expt. sta. and agr. extension service, 1948-49; dean of agr. Ia. State Coll. and dir. state agr. expt. sta. and agr. extension service, 1949—. Dir. Union Story Trust & Savs. Bank. Adviser on agrl. edn. to Argentina, 1960, 61 Paraguay, 1964, Brazil, 1964, 65, 67. Mem. Entomol. Soc. Am., Assn. Econ. Entomologists, Biol. Soc. Washington, Phi Kappa Phi, Alpha Zeta, Sigma Xi, Gamma Delta. Presbyn. Author of articles and bulls. on agrl. and entomol. subjects. Home: 2109 Ashmore Circle Ames IA 50010

ANDRE, OSCAR JULES, lawyer; b. Charleroi, Belgium, May 15, 1900; s. Oscar Jean and Aline (Bastin) A.; came to U.S., 1908, naturalized, 1914; A.B. magna cum laude, Salem Coll., 1925; LL.B., U. Va., 1929; m. Ruby E. Cox, June 14, 1932; children—Nancy A. (Mrs. Oakah L. Jones, Jr.), Marcia E., David J. Admitted to W.Va. bar, 1929; mem. firm Steptoe & Johnson, Clarksburg, 1929—, partner, 1934—, sr. partner, 1950—. Vice pres., dir. Clarksburg Theatre Co.; dir. First Nat. Bank, Salem, W. Va. Pres. Clarksburg Community Concert Assn.; past pres., bd. dirs. W.Va., Harrison County Tb and health assns.; bd. dirs. Salem Coll., 1930-51, Union Protestant Hosp., United Hosp. Center, Clarksburg; adv. bd. Clarksburg YWCA. Fellow Am. Coll. Trial Lawyers; mem. W. Va. State Bar (bd. govs. 1957-60, v.p. 1960-62, pres. 1962-63), Am., W.Va., Harrison County (past pres.) bar assns., Fed. Jud. Conf., Am. Judicature Soc., Phi Beta Kappa, Order Coif. Republican. Methodist (chmn. ofcl. bd.). Kiwanian (past pres.). Home: 424 Holden Av Clarksburg WV 26301 Office: Union Bank Bldg Clarksburg WV 26301

ANDRE, PETER J., banker. Sr. v.p. Bowery Savs. Bank, N.Y.C. Office: 110 E 42d St New York City NY 10017*

ANDREAE, ROBERT EDWARD, textile co. exec.; b. Yale, Mich., Apr. 29, 1911; s. Edward and Marcia (Beecher) A.; grad. Mercersburg Acad., 1929; B.A., U. Mich., 1933, M.B.A., 1934; m. Betty Van Slambroock (dec. July 1962); children—Melanie, Elizabeth, Robert Edward, Laura; m. 2d, Laura Weston Cansfield, Nov. 29, 1968. Sec.-treas., dir. Yale Woolen Mills (Mich.); dir. Ex-Cello-O-Corp., Mich. Nat. Bank. Bd. dirs. Henry MacMorran Found. Home: 4426 Gratiot Av Port Huron MI 48060 Office: 3 First St Yale MI 48097

ANDREANO, RALPH LOUIS, educator, economist; b. Waterbury, Conn., Apr. 11, 1929; s. John and Loretta (Creasia) A.; A.B., Drury Coll., 1952; M.A., Washington U., St. Louis, 1955; Fulbright scholar U. Oslo (Norway), 1952-53; Ph.D., Northwestern U., 1960; m. Carol Jean Wessbecher, Sept. 5, 1955; children—Maria Carol, Nicholas George. Instr. econs. Northwestern U., 1959-60; asst. prof. econs. Earlham Coll., 1961, asso. prof., chmn. dept., 1962-65; asst. prof. bus. adminstrn. Harvard Bus. Sch., 1961-62; Brookings Nat. Research prof., 1964-65; asso. prof. econs., dir. undergrad. program econs. U. Wis., 1965-67, prof., 1967—, dir. Health Econs. Research Center, 1969—. Ofcl. del. Am. Econ. Assn. to Am. Council Learned Socs., 1964-70. Ford Faculty Research fellow, 1968- 69. Mem. Am., Midwest econ. assns., Am. Assn. U. Profs., Econ. History Assn. Author: (with H.F. Williamson and others) A History of American Petroleum Industry, 2 vols., 1959, 63; No Joy in Mudville: The Dilemma of Major League Baseball, 1965; Student Economists Handbook, 1967. Editor, author: New Views on American Economic Development, 1965. Editor: Economic Impact of the Civil War, 1963, rev. 1967; The New Economic History: Papers on Methodology, 1971. Editor, founder: Explorations in Entrepreneurial History, 2d series, 1963-71. Contbr. profl. jours. Home: 1815 Vilas Av Madison WI 53711

ANDREAS, DWAYNE ORVILLE, agrl. products processing and milling co. exec.; b. Worthington, Minn., Mar. 4, 1918; s. Reuben P. and Lydia (Stoltz) A.; student Wheaton (Ill.) Coll., 1935-36; m. Dorothy Inez Snyder, Dec. 21, 1947; children—Sandra Ann, Terry Lynn, Michael D. Vice pres.. dir. Honeymead Products Co., Cedar Rapids, Ia., 1936-46; chmn. bd. First Interoceanic Corp., Mpls.; dir., chmn. exec. com. Nat. City Bank Mpls.; v.p. Cargill, Inc., Mpls., 1946-52; dir., chmn. exec. com., chief executive officer Archer Daniels Midland Co., Mpls.; dir. ADM Milling Co., Kansas City, Gooch Feed Mills, Lincoln, Neb., Sterling Precision Co., N.Y.C., Fleischman Malting Co., Mpls., Northwestern Nat. Life Ins. Co., Mpls. Mem. Pres.'s Gen. Adv. Commn. on Fgn. Assistance Programs, chmn. food and population subcom.; mem. Pres.'s Adv. Council on Mgmt. Improvement. Mem. exec. com. Washington, Radio Free Europe, N. Star Research and Devel. Inst., Mpls.; trustee Mpls. Art Inst.; trustee U.S. Naval Acad. Found., Freedom from Hunger Found.; pres., Andreas Found. Mem. Chemurgic Council (past pres.), Chgo. Bd. Trade. Clubs: Union League (Chgo.); Indian Creek Country (Miami Beach, Fla.); Minneapolis, Minikahda (Mpls.); Blind Brook Country (Purchase, N.Y.). Home: Shore Hills Excelsior MN 55331 also Sea View Hotel Miami Beach FL 33154 also Waldorf Towers 50th and Park Av New York City NY 10022 Office: Archer Daniels Midland Co Exec Office Minneapolis MN 55440

ANDREAS, JOHN LOUIS, Jr., agrl. processing co. exec.; b. nr. Pierceton, Ind., Nov. 23, 1910; s. John Louis and Ida Ann (Brower) A.; student Purdue U., 1928-29, Ind. U. extension, 1933-36, 39; C.P.A., 1942; m. Ann Bratt, Sept. 1, 1933; 1 dau., Mary Ann. Farm and service sta. worker, 1930-33; bakery worker Kroger & Co., 1933-35; bookkeeper Schiefer Auto Co., 1935-36; accountant Pease & Sanford, Ft. Wayne, Ind., 1936-42, W.C. Pease, C.P.A., Ft. Wayne, 1942-50, J.L. Andreas, C.P.A., Ft. Wayne, 1950-52, J.L. Andreas, C.P.A., Ft. Wayne, 1950-52; with Central Soya Co., Inc., Ft. Wayne, 1952—, asst. sec., asst. treas., 1952-62, treas., 1962-70, v.p., 1966-70, v.p. finance, 1970—, also dir.; treas., dir. F.P. C. Realty Corp., 1959—; sec., treas., dir. Growth Industries, Inc., 1961-68. Bd. dirs., past pres. Vis. Nurse Service, Ft. Wayne; sec., dir. Wildcat Recreation Assn., Ft. Wayne. Mem. Chgo. Bd. Trade. Mem. Am. Inst. C.P.A.'s, Ind. Soc. C.P.A.'s. Presbyn. (elder, trustee, treas.). Mason (32, Shriner). Home: 2601 Westbrook Dr Fort Wayne IN 46805 Office: Fort Wayne Nat Bank Bldg Fort Wayne IN 46802

ANDREAS, LOWELL WILLARD, mfg. co. exec.; b. Lisbon, Ia., Feb. 24, 1922; s. Reuben P. and Lydia (Stoltz) A.; student Wheaton (Ill.) Coll., 1939-41, U. Ia., 1941-42; m. Nadine B. Hamilton, May 30, 1943; children—Pamela Jane (Mrs. Richard Lee), David Lowell. With Honeymead Products Co., Mankato, Minn., 1947- 67, pres., 1952-67; treas., dir., mem. exec. com. First Interoceanic Corp., Mpls., 1960—; exec. v.p. Archer Daniels Midland Co., Mpls., 1967-68, pres., Decatur, Ill., 1968—, also dir., mem. exec. com.; chmn. bd. Kayot, Inc.; dir., mem. exec. com. Nat. City Bank Mpls.; dir. Interoceanic Commodities Corp., Mankato Citizens Telephone Co. Mem. Chgo. Bd. Trade, Mpls. Grain Exchange. Bd. dirs., exec. v.p. Andreas Found. Served with AUS, 1942-46. Mem. Phi Delta Theta. Presbyn. Clubs: Union League (Chgo.); Minneapolis. Home: 83 N Country Club Rd Decatur IL 62526 Office: 4666 Faries Pkwy Decatur IL 62526

ANDREAS, PERRY W., business exec.; b. DeKalb, Ill., Nov. 8, 1924; s. Albert M. and Dorothy (Achenbach) A.; student State U. Ia.; m. Grace Hurd, May 24, 1925; children—Cynthia, Beth, Albert Mark. With N.Am. Cement Corp., N.Y.C., 1949-63, pres., 1957-63; pres., dir. Nat. Portland Cement Corp., 1963-68; chmn. bd. Tech. Accessories Co., Princeton, N.J., 1968—. Mem. Young Pres., Orgn. (chmn. N.Y. chpt.), Phi Delta Theta. Club: Westchester Country. Home: Round Hill Rd Greenwich CT 06830

ANDREE, RICHARD VERNON, educator, mathematician; b. Mpls., Dec. 16, 1919; s. Richard A. and Marguerite (Eigner) A.; B.S., U. Chgo., 1942; Ph.M., U. Wis., 1945, Ph.D., 1949; m. Josephine Peet, Dec. 15, 1944; children—David, Peter, Suzanne, Jeanne. Grad. asst. U. Wis.-Madison, 1942-47, acting instr., 1947-49; asst. prof. math. U. Okla., 1949-55, asso. prof., 1955-57, prof., 1957—, prof. information and computing scis., 1970—, research asso. computer sci., 1960—, acting dir. Computer Lab., 1960, chmn. dept. math., 1961-69. Prin. lectr. Inst. for Coll. Tchrs. Math., AID, India, 1965; vis. mathematician Math. Assn. Am., 1962—; lectr. various workshops, insts., 1957—. Dir. Computer Systems, Inc., Math. Computer Consultants, 1961—. Bd. govs. Center Research Coll. Instrn. in Sci. and Math. Fellow Okla. U. Research Inst. Recipient C.C. MacDuffee Distinguished Service award Pi Mu Epsilon, 1966; Nat. fellow numerical analysis Nat. Bur. Standards. Fellow A.A.A.S.; mem. Am. Math. Soc., Math. Assn. Am., Assn. Symbolic Logic, Assn. Computing Machinery, Am. Soc. Engring. Edn. (chmn. math div.), Data Processing Mgmt. Assn., Soc. Indsl. and Applied Math., Nat. Council Tchrs. Math., Okla. Council Tchrs. Math., Assn. Ednl. Data Systems, Sigma Xi, Pi Mu Epsilon (nat. sec., treas. 1957—), Mu Alpha Theta (founder). Author: (with John C. Brixey) Fundamentals of College Mathematics, rev. edit., 1961; Modern Trigonometry, 1957; Selections from Modern Abstract Algebra, 2d rev. edit., 1971; Programming the IBM 650 Computer, 1958; Tables of Indices and Power Residues, 1962; Introduction to Calculus with Analytic Geometry, 1963; Computer Programming and Related Mathematics, 1966; Programming the 1130 computer with Related Mathematics, 1969; Computer Programming—Techniques, Analysis and Mathematics, 1972. Contbr. numerous articles profl. jours. Home: 627 E Boyd St Norman OK 73069

ANDREN, JOHN H., banker; b. May 30, 1908; s. John M. and Augusta (Anderson) A.; student Grad. Sch. Banking. Rutgers U.; m. Lillian Rehberg, Oct. 11, 1934; children—Dorothy J., John H. Asst. mgr. fgn. dept. Hanover Bank, 1946-51, asst. v.p., 1951-56, v.p. 1956-61; v.p. Mfrs. Hanover Trust, 1961-63, became sr. v.p., 1963, now exec. v.p. dir. Mfrs. Hanover Internat. Banking Corp., Mfrs. Hanover Internat. Finance Corp. C. of C. Mfrs. Hanover Ltd. Bd. dirs. Nat. Fgn. Trade Council. Inc; vice chmn. fgn. exchange com. N.Y. Money Market. Mem. Norwegian Am. C. of C. (dir.). Home: 179 Brookville Rd Brookville NY 11545. Office: 350 Park Av New York City NY 10022

ANDRES, FREDERICK WILLIAM, lawyer; b. Alexandria, Egypt, Sept. 21, 1906 (parents U.S. citizens); s. Frederick Henry Augustus and Laura Edith (Beazell) A.; grad. Phillips Exeter Acad., 1925; A.B., Dartmouth, 1929, A.M. (hon.), 1963; LL.B., Harvard, 1932; m. Katherine Pratt Weeks, Sept. 9, 1931; children—Katherine Weeks (Mrs. Jonathan Moore), Anita (Mrs. David S. Rogerson), William McKenzie. Admitted to Mass. bar, 1932, since practiced in Boston; mem. firm Sherburne, Powers & Needham, 1940—. Sec. Concert Network, Inc.; clk., dir. George B.H. Macomber Co., H.A. Johnson Co., London Harness Co., Granet Corp., Hamilton Constrn. Corp.; dir. Investors Bank & Trust Co. Regional chmn. Dartmouth Capital Fund campaign, 1958-61; sec.-chmn. Dartmouth class 1929, 1929-63; trustee Dartmouth, 1963—; pres. Dartmouth Alumni Assn. Boston, 1950; chmn. Dartmouth Athletic Council, 1956-61. Regional chmn. United Negro Coll. Fund, 1960. Mem. Brookline (Mass.) Town Meeting, 1947-53, Brookline Personnel Bd., 1957-66. Bd. dirs. Brookline Citizens Com., 1948-57; trustee Phillips Exeter Acad., 1962—, pres. bd., 1965—; trustee Champlain Coll., 1966-70, Bennington Coll., 1956-63; trustee Beaver Country Day Sch., Chestnut Hill, Mass., 1947-64, pres., 1949-64; trustee Elizabeth Carleton House, Boston, 1954—, pres., 1957- 66; mem. corporation New Eng. Deaconess Hosp., 1963—. Recipient Alumni award Dartmouth, 1963. Mem. Am., Boston bar assns., Dartmouth Alumni Assn. Boston (pres. 1950), Phi Gamma Delta, Casque and Gauntlet Sr. Soc., Gen. Alumni Assn. Phillips Exeter Acad. (pres. 1962-63), Nisi Pruis Club. Republican. Episcopalian (vestry 1957-60). Clubs: The Country (Brookline); Harvard, Union (Boston): Dartmouth (N.Y.C.); Beverly Yacht (Marion, Mass.). Author: (with others) The College on the Hill-A Dartmouth Chronicle, 1964. Home: 106 Laurel Rd Chestnut Hill Brookline MA 02167 Office: 225 Franklin St Boston MA 02110

ANDRESEN, HELMUT, banker; b. Flensburg, Germany, Jan. 14, 1909; s. August W. and Ingeborg A. (Holm) A.; B.S., Columbia, 1939; LL.B. cum laude St. John's U., 1935, LL.M, 1936; m. Florence B. Webersinn, June 22, 1935; children—Florence, Frances. With U.S. Trust Co. N.Y., 1929-51, asst. v.p., 1948-51, v.p. Bank Manhattan Co., 1951-55, Chase Manhattan Bank, 1955-61; exec. v.p. U.S. Trust Co. N.Y., 1961—. Admitted to N.Y. bar, 1938. Mem. Am., N.Y. State bar assns., Assn. Bar City N.Y., Corp. Fiduciaries Assn., N.Y. State Bankers Assn., Alumni Assn. Sch. Gen. Studies Columbia. Club: Nassau Country (Glen Cove, N.Y.). Author: Estate Taxes and Tax-Exempt Residues, 1962. Home: Mill Neck NY 11765 Office: 45 Wall St New York City NY 10005

ANDRESON, EVERETT HARLAN, food marketing cons.; b. Abilene, Kan., Jan. 23, 1907; s. Henry A. and Ada A. (Goodnow) A.; student Kan. State U., 1923-25, U. Cal. at Los Angeles, 1927, U. Wash., 1927; A.B, Stanford, 1929; grad. Harvard Advanced Mgmt. Course, 1958; m. Jeanette Rickey, July 30, 1932; children—Francis E., Clara (Mrs. Donald G. Kurgan), Arlene (Mrs. R. J. Des Jardins, Jr.). With Gen. Mills, Inc., Mpls., 1929-69, beginning as auditor, successively sales supr., dist. sales mgr., hdqrs. adminstrv. exec., sales mgr. new products, merchandising mgr., 1929-53, dir. sales, 1953-57, v.p., 1955-69, dir. marketing, 1957-60, dir. trade and customer relations, 1960-69; now food marketing cons. Cons., U.S. Dept. Agr., 1965-68. Active local chpts. A.R.C.; mem. adv. council Harvard Bus. Sch. Fund. Trustee, Food Industry Ednl. Council; bd. dirs. Shamrock Found. Mem. Mpls. Inst. Fine Arts (patron), Minn. Orchestral Assn., Friends of Symphony, Kappa Sigma, Kappa Kappa Psi. Republican. Episcopalian. Clubs: Minneapolis Athletic, Meadowlark Country. Home: Stoney Beach Ranch Grey Eagle MN 56336 Office: Grey Eagle MN 56336

ANDRESON, WILBUR REEVES, moving and storage co. exec.; b. Lincoln, Neb., June 21, 1915; s. Robert D. and Bessie (Reeves) A.; B.S., U. Cal., Los Angeles, 1937; m. Georgia Jane Price, Aug. 12, 1938; 1 dau., Sally (Mrs. George O. Bergstrom). With L.H. Penney & Co., C.P.A.'s, Los Angeles, 1938-41; with Ford Motor Co., Dearborn, Mich., 1946; pres., dir. Bekins Moving & Storage Co., Los Angeles, 1946—. Served with USAAF, 1941-46. Decorated Bronze Star medal. Mem. Moving and Storage Nat. Tech. Assn. (chmn., dir.), Financial Execs. Inst. (past pres. Los Angeles). Home: 12636 Homewood St Los Angeles CA 90049 Office: 1335 S Figueroa St Los Angeles CA 90015

ANDRESS, SAMUEL COE, lawyer; b. Hayesville, O., June 27, 1906; s. Upton Samuel and Millicent Alma (Coe) A.; A.B., Wittenberg U., 1925; LL.B., U. Cin., 1928. Admitted to Ohio bar, 1928, since practiced in Akron; sr. partner firm Wise, Roetze, Maxon, Kelly & Andress. Dir. Akron Controller & Motor, Inc., Mac Allied Tools Corp., Wright Tool & Forge Co., R.H. Downing, Inc., Jay Em Corp., R.J. Music, Inc., Hardware & Supply A.C. Williams Co., Yoder Bros., Inc. Trustee Akron Beacon Jour. Charity Fund. Served to lt. USNR, 1942-45. Mem. Am., Ohio, Akron bar assns., Akron C. of C. (past pres.), Order of Coif, Lambda Chi Alpha, Delta Sigma Rho, Phi Alpha Delta. Episcopalian. Clubs: Rotary, City, University, Sharon, Portage Country (Akron). Home: 161 E Fairlawn Blvd Akron OH 44313 Office: 1 Cascade Plaza Akron OH 44308

ANDREW, DEAN CAROL, educator; b. Trenton, Utah, June 23, 1922; s. Alexander Leroy and Lydia May (Lott) A.; B.S., Utah State U., 1946, M.S., 1947, Ph.D., 1951; m. Ann Damstedt, Dec. 22, 1943; children—Judy Ann, Larry Dean. Counselor- tchr. Ida. State Coll., 1947-49; mem. faculty So. State Coll., 1952- 68, acad. dean, 1957-68; dir. ednl. planning Magnolia (Ark.) Pub. Schs., 1968—. Tchr. summers Williamette U., U. Utah, No. State Tchrs. Coll., U. Ark., N.M. State U., N.C. State U.; vocational cons. govt. agys. Vice pres. S.W. Econ Devel. Dist. Ark. Bd. dirs. Magnolia Boys Club. Served with USMCR, 1942-45. Mem. Am., Ark. psychol. assns., Nat. Vocational Guidance Assn., Am., Ark. personnel and guidance assns., Am., So. coll. personnel assns., Nat., Ark. edn. assns. Mem. Ch. of Jesus Christ of Latter-day Saints (pres. Ark). Rotarian. Author: (with R.D. Willey) Modern Methods and Techniques of Guidance, 1955; (with Lester N. Downing) Selected Readings in Guidance, 1955; (with R.D. Willey) Administration and Organization of a Guidance Program, 1958; (with Francis Stroup) Barriers to College Attendance, a Study of Factors Involved in the Educational Discontinuance of High School Graduates, 1959; also articles. Home: 814 Smith St Magnolia AR 71753

ANDREW, THOMAS, choreographer, ballet dir.; b. Mt. Carmel, Pa., Mar. 11, 1932; s. Theophil and Mary (Wasilewski) Andrulewiez. Solo dancer Met. Opera Assn., 1956- 63, also choreographer operas Martha, 1961, Un Ballo in Maschera, 1962; dir., choreographer Santa Fe Opera Ballet, 1960-62, N.Y.C. Opera Ballet, 1963-71, Phila. Lyric Opera Ballet, also Balt. Civic Opera Ballet, 1964- 67, My Fair Lady in Warsaw, Poland, 1964, San Francisco Opera Ballet, 1967; choreographer Radio City Music Hall, 1967; dir. ballet Newport Music Festival, Newport, R.I., 1970; founder, dir., chief choreographer Ballet Brio with tours in U.S. and V.I.; staged opera ballets Filene Center, Washington, 1971, Traviata ballet for accoustical testing Kennedy Center, Washington, 1971.

ANDREW, WARREN, educator; b. Portland, Ore., July 19, 1910; s. John and Alice (Lucke) A.; B.A. summa cum laude, Carleton Coll., 1932; fellow Brown U., 1932- 33, M.S., 1933; Ph.D., Yale, 1936, U. Ill., 1936; M.D., Baylor Med. Coll., 1943; m. Nancy Valerie Miellmier, Aug. 18, 1936; 1 dau., Linda Nancy. Asst. instr. zoology Yale, 1933-34, U. Ill., 1934-36; teaching fellow U. Ga., 1936-37, instr., fellow anatomy, 1937-39; instr. anatomy, sch. medicine Baylor U., 1939-41, asst. prof. anatomy, 1941-43; asso. prof. histology Southwestern Med. Coll., Dallas, 1943-45, prof., 1946- 47; vis. prof. U. Montevideo, Uruguay, 1945-46; prof. anatomy, chmn. dept. sch. medicine George Washington U., 1947-48, 49-52, cons. anatomy George Washington U. Hosp., 1947-52; vis. prof. Washington U., St. Louis, 1948-49; cons. cytology VA Hosp., Martinsburg, W.Va., 1950-52; Am. Mus. Natural History vis. investigator, Lerner Marine Biol. Lab., Bimini, Bahamas, B.W.I., 1951; vis. scientist Barro Colorado Island, C.Z., 1952; advisor anatomy, mem. exhibits com. Second Internat. Geronotological Congress, 1951; prof. anatomy dir. dept. Bowman Gray Sch. Medicine, 1952-57; prof., chmn. dept. anatomy sch. medicine Ind. U., Indpls., 1957—; lectr. Tokyo and Kyoto med. schs. Japan, summer 1960, Karachi, Pakistan, also Bombay and Jamnagar, India, summer 1962; vis. scientist U. Coll. Hosp. Med. Sch., London, 1970, U. Capetown, 1970, Bernice P. Bishop Mus., Honolulu, 1971. Ofcl. del. Pan-Am. Congress Gerontology, editorial, bd. Gerontologia, Basel, 1957—; rep. biology Internat. Research Com. for Gerontology; participant IX Internat. Congress Cell Biology; IV Internat. Congress Gerontology, 1957; conf. aging of nervous system Nat. Neurol. Diseases and Bindness, 1957; conf. Aging Process, 1957; mem. Ind. Commn. on Aging, 1958—; Ind. del. White House Conf. on Aging, 1961. Research Bermuda Biol. Sta., 1959; mem. corp. Reicipient Distinguished Service Award, U.S. Jr. C. of C., 1946; research award Gerontological Found., 1959. Mem. Gerontological Soc. (mem. council and corp., 1950-53, 57—), Internat. Assn. Gerontology (vice chmn. for biology, research com.), Am. Assn. Anatomists, Am. Society Zoologists, A.A.A.S., Soc. Exptl. Biol. and Medicine, Philos. Soc. Washington, Tex. Med. Assn., Tissue Culture Assn., Washington Soc. Pathologists, Washington Acad. Medicine, N.Y. Acad. Sci., Internat. Com. for Standardization in Hematology, Biol. Soc. Montevideo, Amigos de la Naturaleza de Montevideo, Am. Soc. Electron Microscopists, Internat. Soc. Cell Biology, Am. Med. Soc. Vienna (life), Sigma Xi, Phi Beta Kappa, Phi Chi. Club: Cosmos. Author: Comparative Histology, 1959; Comparative Hematology, 1965; Microfabric of Man; One World of Science, 1966; The Anatomy of Aging in Animals and Man, 1971; Contbg. author, Ency. Britannica. Mem. editorial bd. Gerontological Newsletter, 1959—, Quar. Bull. Ind. U. Med. Center, 1959. Columnist, Poets' Corner of Indpls. Contbr. sci. articles, profl. publs. Home: 5275 N Capitol Av Indianapolis IN 46208

ANDREWES, CHRISTOPHER HOWARD, pathologist; b. London, Eng., June 7, 1896; s. Frederick William and Phyllis Mary (Hamer) A.; M.B., B.S., U. London, 1921, M.D., 1923; LL.D., Aberdeen U., 1963; m. Kathleen Helen Lamb, Mar. 26, 1927; children—John Frederick, Michael Robert, David Anthony. House physician, clin. asst. St. Bartholomews Hosp., London, 1921-23, 25-26; asst. resident physician Rockefeller Hosp., N.Y.C., 1923-25; mem. sci. staff Nat. Inst. for Med. Research, London, 1927-61, dep. dir., 1952-61. Served with Royal Naval Vol. Res., 1918-19. Created knight bachelor, 1961; recipient Bisset-Hawkins medal Royal Coll. Physicians; Steward prize Brit. Med. Assn., 1952; William Julius Mickle fellow U. London, 1931. Fellow Royal Soc., Royal Entomol. Soc.; mem. Nat. Acad. Sci. (fgn. asso.), Am. Philos. Soc. (fgn.), Soc. for Gen. Microbiology (hon., U. K.), Soc. Pathology. Author: Viruses of Vertebrates, 1964; The Common Cold, 1965; also over 200 articles on influenza and common cold viruses. Address: Overchalke Coomba Bissett Salisbury England

ANDREWS, ALBERT H., Jr., physician; b. Chgo., June 20, 1907; s. Albert H. and Hattie (Frazey) A.; B.S., Northwestern U., 1929, M.S. in Physiology, 1932, M.D., 1933; m. Jane Olson, June 25, 1938. Intern St. Luke's Hosp., Chgo., 1932-33; practice medicine, specializing in bronchoesophagology and laryngeal surgery; mem. staff Presbyn.- St. Luke's Hosp., Children's Meml. Hosp., VA West Side Hosp., Skokie Valley Community Hosp.; cons. Edgewater Hosp., Englewood Hosp., St. Francis Hosp., DuPage County Tb Case and Treatment Bd., Municipal Tb Sanitarium, all Chgo. area; clin. asst. Northwestern U., Chgo., 1933-38, research asst., 1933-40; mem. faculty Coll. Medicine, U. Ill., Chgo., 1939—, clin. asso. prof. bronchoesophagology, 1955-63, clin. prof., 1963-65, prof., 1965—, head dept. otolaryngology, 1967—. Served to lt. comdr., M.C., USNR, 1942-45; ETO. Diplomate Am. Bd. Otolaryngology. Fellow A.M.A., Am. Coll. Chest Physicians (treas., past pres. Ill.), Inst. of Medicine of Chgo.; mem. Chgo., Ill. med. socs., Am. Acad. Ophthalmology and Otolaryngology, Am.

Laryngological, Rhinological and Otological Soc., Am. Broncho-esophagological Assn., Am. Laryngological Assn., Am. Council Otolarynology, Indsl. Med. Assn., Am. Assn. Ry. Surgeons, Internat. Bronch-esophagological Soc., Internat. Corr. Soc. Ophthalmalogists and Otolaryngologists, Pan-Am. Assn. Oto-Rhino-Laryngology and Bronchoesophagology, Chgo. Laryngological and Otological Soc. (pres. 1962-63), A.A.A.S., Am. Registry Inhalation Therapists, Inc (pres. bd. trustees), Am. Assn. for Inhalation Therapy (mem. bd. med. advisers 1954-66), Kansas City Soc. Ophthalmology and Otolaryngology (hon.), Am. Med. Writers Assn. Club: Union League (Chgo.). Home: 1131 W Monroe Av Chicago IL 60626 Office: 122 S Michigan Av Chicago IL 60603

ANDREWS, ALBERT O'BEIRNE, found. exec.; b. N.Y.C., Feb. 17, 1912; s. Champe and Henriette (Korber) A.; grad. Choate Sch., Wallingford, Conn., 1930; B.S., Yale, 1934; LL.B., Harvard, 1937; m. Frances Jennings Hall, Apr. 2, 1938; children—Albert O'Beirne, Sarah Hall. Admitted to N.Y. bar, 1937; asso. firm Sullivan & Cromwell, N.Y.C., 1937-50; with Am. Radiator & Standard San. Corp., N.Y.C., 1950-67, dir. pub. affairs, 1964-67, pres. indsl. div., 1960-64, asst. to pres., 1965-67; v.p., sec. Andrew W. Mellon Found., N.Y.C., 1967—. Served with USCGR, 1942-45. Mem. Assn. Bar City N.Y., Newcomen Soc. N.Am. Clubs: Knickerbocker, Yale (N.Y.C.); Silver Spring Country (Ridgefield, Conn.). Home: Box 201 Wilton CT 06897 Office: Andrew W Mellon Found 140 E 62d St New York City NY 10021

ANDREWS, ARCHIE MOULTON, govt. ofcl.; b. Greenwich, Conn., July 29, 1919; s. Archie M. and Eleanor (Underwood) A.; grad. Phillips Acad., 1937, Rugby (Eng.) Sch., 1938; A.B., Princeton, 1941; m. Margaret Jane Jones, Mar. 3, 1944; childrenArchie Moulton III, Peter Underwood, Duncan Trumbull. Exec. trainee W.R. Grace & Co., 1941-42; econ. analyst State Dept., 1942-43; U.S. rep. blacklist com. Ministry Econ. Warfare, Am. embassy, London, Eng., 1943-45; with Dictograph Products, Inc., Danbury, Conn., 1946-63, pres., 1962-63, also dir.; pres. Acousticon-Dictograph Co. Ltd., Can., 1963, dir., 1958-63; dir. Gen. Acoustics Ltd., Eng., 1950-63; dep. dir. Bur. Internat. Commerce, Dept. Commerce, 1964-69; comml. counsellor Am. to North Africa, 1966. Club: Princeton (Washington). Home: 55 Great Cumberland Pl London W1 England Office: U S Embassy London England

ANDREWS, ARTHUR J.F., constrn. machinery co. exec.; b. Swansea, Gt. Britain, May 15, 1906; s. Arthur and Gertrude (Francis) A.; ed. Malvern, Eng., also Ecole Piqier Paris, France; m. Elsy Maud Johns, Aug. 5, 1936; 1 dau., Jane Frances (Mrs. Job Hünerwadel). Devel. engr. A.C. Cars, Ltd., Thames Ditton, Eng.; with Gardner Diesel Engines, Manchester, Eng., All Wheel Drive, Ltd., Camberley, Eng.; dir. Clark Equipment, Ltd., England; vice chmn. Clark Equipment Co. A.C., Zurich, Switzerland; chmn. Cheshire Utilities Ltd., Camberly, Eng. Served with Royal Navy. Clubs: Royal Yachting Assn., Royal Berkshire Golf, Royal Thames Yacht. Home: Pembroke House Valley End Chobham Surrey England Office: 2 place Champs de Mars Brussels Belgium

ANDREWS, BENNY, artist; b. Madison, Ga., Nov. 13, 1930; s. George Cleveland and Viola (Perryman) A.; student Ft. Valley State Coll., 1948-50, U. Chgo., 1956-58; B.F.A., Chgo. Art Inst., 1958; m. Mary Ellen Jones Smith, Apr. 3, 1957; children—Christopher, Thomas Michael, Julia Rachael. Instr. art New Sch. for Social Research, N.Y.C., 1967-70, Queens Coll., N.Y.C., 1968—; vis. artist Cal. State Coll. at Hayward, 1969; one man shows Kessler Gallery, Provincetown, Mass. 1960-70, Forum Gallery, N.Y.C. 1962-64-66, Henri Gallery, Alexandria, Va. 1963-64, Studio Museum, N.Y.C. 1970; exhibited in group shows at Detroit Inst., 1959, Phia. Acad. of Art, 1960, Brooklyn Museum, 1963, Butler Inst. Am. Art, 1967, Museum of Modern Art, N.Y.C. 1968-71, High Museum, Atlanta 1971; represented in permanent collections Mus. Modern Art, N.Y.C., High Mus., Atlanta, African Mus., Washington, Norfolk Mus., (Va.), Butler Inst. Am. Art, Youngstown, O., Chrysler Mus., Provincetown, Mass., Lajolla Mus. (Cal.). Served with USAAF, 1950-54. Co-chmn. Black Emergency Cultural Coalition, 1969—. Served with USAAF, 1950-54. John Hay Whitney fellow, 1965-67; Dorne Professionship, U. Bridgeport (Conn.), 1970; N.Y. Council Arts grantee, 1971. Contbr. articles on black art, culture to profl. jours. Home: 463 West St New York City NY 10014 Office: 31 Beekman St New York City NY 10038

ANDREWS, BURTON HOWELL, naval officer; b. Los Angeles, July 14, 1916; s. Herbert Burton and Margaret Hill (Howell) A.; B.S., U.S. Naval Acad., 1941; M.S., U.S. Naval Postgrad. Sch., 1948; m. Eurith Linthicum Maynard, Aug. 6, 1942; children—Eurith Lynne, Virginia Howell, Scott Foster. Commd. ensign USN, 1941, advanced through grades to read adm., 1969; dep. dir. tactical electromagnetic programs OPNAU, 1971—. Decorated Bronze Star medal with combat V (2). Mem. I.E.E.E. (sr. mem.), Am. Soc. Naval Engrs., U.S. Naval Inst., Soc. of Cin. Mason. Club: Harvard Business School (Washington). Home: 11713 Milbern Dr Potomac MD 20854 Office: Op-093B Chief of Naval Operations The Pentagon Washington DC 20350

ANDREWS, CARL WILLIS, Jr., headmaster; b. New Bethlehem, Pa., Mar. 5, 1921; s. Carl Willis and Helen L. (Smith) A.; grad. Haverford (Pa.) Sch., 1939; B.A., Amherst Coll., 1943, L.H.D.; student U. Rochester, 1950; M.A., Bucknell U., 1952; 1952; m. Margaret C. Stewart, Dec. 7, 1946; childrenStewart Scott, Margaret Lathrop, Mary Bunker. With Graybar Electric Co., 1947-49; head history dept. Allendale Sch., 1949-50; dir. admissions Friends Central Sch., Phila., 1950-58; headmaster Collegiate Sch.., N.Y.C., 1959-. Bd. dirs. Center Programmed Instrn., Independent Schs. Fund N. Y. Guild Ind. Schs. N.Y.; trustee Nightingale Bamford Sch.; pres. Guild of Ind. Schs. Served to 1st lt., Signal Corps, AUS, 1943-46. Ford Found. travel-study grant, 1969. Mem. Country Day Headmasters Assn., N.Y. State Assn. Pvt. Schs. (trustee), Headmasters Assn., Cum Laude Soc. (regent dist. 3). Club: University. Home: 315 E 72d St New York City NY 10021. Office: 241 W 77th St New York City NY 10024

ANDREWS, CARVER DANA, actor; b. Collins, Miss., Jan. 1, 1909; s. Rev. Charles Forrest and Annis (Speed) A.; student Sam Houston State Tchrs. Coll., 1926-29; m. Janet Murray (dec.); one son, David (dec.); m. 2d, Mary Todd, 1939; children—Katharine, Stephen, Susan. Actor in motion pictures since 1939; including roles in Berlin Correspondent, 1942, Ox Bow Incident, 1942, Crash Dive, 1942, The Purple Heart, 1943, Wing and a Prayer, 1944, Laura, 1944, Walk in the Sun, 1944, State Fair, 1945, Fallen Angel, 1945, Canyon Passage, 1945, Best Years of Our Lives, 1946. Boomerang, 1946, Night Song, 1947, Daisy Kenyon. 1947, Deep Waters, 1947, The Iron Curtain, 1948, No Minor Vices, 1948, Forbidden Street, 1948, Sword in the Desert, 1949, My Foolish Heart, 1949; Edge of Doom, 1950; Sealed Cargo, 1950; Where the Sidewalk Ends, 1950, The Frogmen, 1951, I Want You, 1951, Assignment Paris, 1952, Elephant Walk, 1953, Duel in the Jungle, 1953, Three Hours to Kill, 1954, Smoke Signal, 1954, Strange Lady in Town, 1954, While the City Sleeps, 1955; Comanche, 1955, Beyond a Reasonable Doubt, 1956, Spring Reunion, 1956, Night of the Demon, 1956, Zero Hour, 1957, Enchanted Island, 1957, The Fearmakers, 1958, The Crowded Sky, 1959, Madison Avenue, 1960, The Satan Bug, The Crack in the World, Harm's Way, The Loved Ones, 1964; (TV) The Right Hand Man, 1958, Alas Babylon, 1960, The Play-off, 1960, Alcoa Premiere, Checkmate, Twilight Zone, Dick Powell Show, 1962, Bob Hope Show, Twilight Zone, Bing Crosby Prodns., 1963; (Broadway) Two for the Seesaw, 1959, The Captains and the Kings, 1962; Pres. Malabar Properties, Inc.; dir. Apt. Assos. Los Angeles County. Mem. Screen Actors Guild (pres. 1963-65). Home: Box B Palos Verdes Peninsula CA 90274 Office: 2018 N Vine St Hollywood CA 90028

ANDREWS, CHARLES LUTHER, educator, physicist; b. Berkshire, N.Y., May 6, 1908; s. George Luther and Edna (Bush) A.; A.B., Cornell U., 1930, Ph.D., 1938; m. Kathlyn Clara Merrill, June 17, 1934; children—Merrill Leroy, Louise Catherine. Instr., N.Y. State Coll. Tchrs., Albany, 1931-44; mem. faculty State U. N.Y. at Albany, 1944—, prof. physics, 1944—, chmn. dept., 1944-69. Cons. Gen. Electric Research and Devel. Center, Schenectady, 1943-. Recipient Distinguished citation Am. Assn. Physics Tchrs., 1963. Mem. Am. Phys. Soc., Optical Soc. Am. (pres. Hudson-Mohawk sect. 1970-71), Albany Inst. History and Art, Sigma Xi, Sigma Pi Sigma. Club: University (Albany). Author: Optics of Electromagnetic Spectrum, 1960. Research, patentee microwave optics, electronic devices. Home: 556 Washington Av Albany NY 12203

ANDREWS, CLIFFORD MARTIN, ceramic products and chem. mfg. co. exec.; b. Butte, Mont, Dec. 31, 1912; s. Joseph Martin and Bessie (Veale) A.; B.S. in Ceramic Engring., U. Ill., 1934; m. Mary Savilla George, May 23, 1936; children—Robert Lee, Joseph Edwin. Ceramic engr. Altorfer Bros., Peoria, Ill., 1934-36; enameling plant supt. Ingersoll Steel & Disc div. Borg Warner Co., Chgo., 1936-38; enameling plant supt. McCray Refrigerator Co., Kendallville, Ind., 1938-42; asso. research prof. ceramic engring. U. Ill., 1942-45; tech. mgr. Internat. div. Ferro Corp., Cleve., 1945-51, mng. dir. Ferro-Brazil, Sao Paulo, 1951-56, v.p. internat. operations, Cleve., 1956-65, exec. v.p., dir., 1965—; dir. Ferro-Australia, Ferro- Can., Ferro- France, Ferro-Holland, Ferro Far East Ltd. Hong Kong, Ferro-India, Ferro Far East, Inc. Japan, Ferro-Mexico, Eriez Mfg. Co., Erie, Pa., Harris Calorific Co., Cleve. Mem. Greater Cleve. Growth Assn., Cleve. Council World Affairs, Nat. Fgn. Trade Council, Am. Ceramic Soc., Keramos, Sigma Xi. Mem. Christian Ch. Clubs: Union, Chagrin Valley Country. Home: 25495 Bryden Rd Beachwood Cleveland OH 44122 Office: 1 Erieview Plaza Cleveland OH 44114

ANDREWS, DALE WALKER, ednl. adminstr.; b. San Bernardino, Cal., Dec. 22, 1919; s. Charles Walker and Bessie Edrena (Wallen) A.; B.S., U. Cal. at Davis, 1941; M.A., Cal. State Polytech. Coll., 1952; Ph.D., U. Minn., 1957; m. Mary Louise Terhaar, July 16, 1943; children—John Thomas, Mary Clare, David Charles, Fred Nicholas. Dir. agr., supervising tchr. Merced (Cal.) Union High Sch., 1946-49, Arroyo Grande Union High Sch., 1949-50; agrl. tchr. trainer, instrl. materials. coordinator, spl. ednl. services coordinator Cal. State Polytech. Coll., 1950-61, dean Coll. San Luis Obispo, 1961- 66, v.p., chief adminstrv. officer, 1966-67, acad. v.p., 1967—. Pres., chmn. bd. Bd. Education, Monterey Diocese, 1969—; bd. dirs., v.p. Cal. Polytech. Found. Served to maj. USMCR, World War II. Mem. Cal. Agr. Tchrs. Assn. (pres. region-at-large 1953-54), Cal. Polytech. Staff Assn. (bd. dirs.), Phi Delta Kappa (v.p. Beta Gamma chpt. 1960- 61), Gamma Sigma Delta, Alpha Zeta. Danforth tchr. grantee, 1955- 56; Danforth asso., 1956-60, sr. Danforth asso., 1960-; Hon. State Farmer, 1952; K.C. lectr., San Luis Obispo, 1953. Co-author: Selected Lessons in Agricultural Science, 1961. Co-author, editor, prodn. mgr. color filmstrips, other instrl. materials. Home: 324 Highland Dr San Luis Obispo CA 94301

ANDREWS, DAVID KNEELAND, coll. pres.; b. Wauwatosa, Wis., July 28, 1914; s. George A. and Frances (Kneeland) A.; grad. Upper Sch., The Principia, St. Louis, 1932, B.A., Principia Coll., Elsah, Ill., 1936; M.A., Columbia, 1944, Ed.D., 1961; m. Helen D. Hance, Dec. 28, 1940. Tchr. math and French, Principia Upper Sch., 1937-45, prin. Principia Lower Sch., 1945-53, headmaster Lower and Upper Schs., 1953-58, supr. St. Louis campuses, 1958, asst. to pres., 1956-59, v.p., 1959-61; pres. The Principia, 1961—. Mem. Assn. Childhood Edn., Phi Delta Kappa, Kappa Delta Pi. Christian Scientist. Address: Principia College Elsah IL 62028

ANDREWS, DAVID TALLMADGE, banker; b. Yonkers, N.Y., Aug. 13, 1920; s. Charles Sperry and Alice (Peterson) A.; grad. Kent Sch., 1939; A.B., Williams Coll., 1943; M.A., Harvard, 1949; m. Kathryn M. Shaffer, Oct. 14, 1956; children-Alice P., Melville D., David Tallmadge. With 1st Westchester Nat. Bank, New Rochelle, N.Y., 1949-63; with Nat. Comml. Bank & Trust Co., Albany, N.Y., 1963-67; v.p., sr. trust officer Nat. Bank of Westchester, White Plains, N.Y., 1967—; dir. Davis & Lawrence Co.; trustee, dir. Riverside Cemetery Assn., Norwalk, Conn.; instr. Am. Inst. Banking. Served to maj., inf., AUS, 1942-46; PTO. Decorated Bronze Star medal. Mem. Phi Beta Kappa, Psi Upsilon. Home: Garlen Rd Katonah NY 10536 Office: 31 Mamaroneck Av White Plains NY 10601

ANDREWS, DONALD HATCH, chemist; b. Southington, Conn., June 11, 1898; s. Russell Gad and Mary Boies (Hatch) A.; grad. Phillips Acad., Andover, Mass., 1916; B.A., Yale, 1920, Ph.D., 1923; m. Josephine Adair Veeder, June 20, 1939 (div. 1950); m. 2d Elizabeth Howland, Sept. 23, 1950; 1 son, Donald Hatch. Research asst. in chemistry, Yale, 1923; nat. research fellow, U. Cal. at Berkeley, 1924-25; internat. research fellow U. Leiden, 1925-26; research fellow Bartol Research Found., 1926-27; with Johns Hopkins U., Balt., 1927—, prof. chemistry, 1930—, chmn. dept., dir. chem. laboratory, 1936-44, dir. Cryogeny Lab., 1943-48. B. N. Baker prof. chemistry, 1957-63, prof. emeritus, 1963—; prof. chemistry Fla. Atlantic U., Boca Raton, 1963-64, distinguished prof. chemistry, 1964-67, distinguished prof. emeritus 1967—. Mem. div. chemistry NRC, 1933; chmn. Calorimetry Conf., 1957-58. Mem. 1st sci. commn. L'Inst. Internationale de Froid. Fellow Royal Chem. Soc. (Eng.), N.Y. Acad. Scis., A.A.A.S., Am. Philos. Soc., mem. Am. Chem. Soc. (sec. div. phys. and inorganic chemistry, 1932, vice chmn., 1933, chmn. 1934), Am. Math. Soc., Am. Math. Assn., Am. Phys. Soc., Philosophy of Sci. Assn., Brit. Assn. Philosophy of Sci., Phi Beta Kappa, Sigma Xi. Republican. Episcopalian. Club: Appalachian Mountain. Author: Fundamental Chemistry, 1962; Quimica Fundamental, 1964; Symphony of Life, 1967; Quimica Geral., 1968; Notions Fondamentales de Chimie 1968; Introductory Physical Chemistry, 1970. Home: 750 NE 33d St Boca Raton FL 33432

ANDREWS, EARLE TOPLEY, civil and cons. engr., corp. exec.; b. Fowlerville, N.Y., Jan. 9, 1902; s. Fred Earle and Florence Virginia (Topley) A.; ed. U.S. Naval Acad., Washington and Lee U.; m. Rosalie Esther Exline, Oct. 2, 1925; children—Hale Earle, Fred Hayes, Patricia Rosalie (Mrs. Charles E. Middlekauff). With Pa. Glass Sand Corp. (ITT) and subsidiaries, Berkeley Springs, W.Va., 1925—, sr. exec. v.p., 1962-63, pres., chief exec. officer, 1963-68, chmn. bd. dirs., 1968—; civil and cons. engr. Mem. Susquehanna Valley Flood Control Commn., 1939-45; chmn. Warm Springs Pub. Service Commn.; mem. Citizens Adv. Commn. Legislation W.Va. Pres. W.Va. Bd. Regents; trustee Indsl. Health Found.; vis. com. Coll. Engring. of W.Va. U., 1963-65, Appalachian Center of W.Va. U., 1964-68; mem. adv. bd. Morgan County War Meml. Hosp. Col. Civil Air Patrol, 1950-56. Named centennial engr. W.Va. Soc. Profl. Engrs., 1963; elected Robert E. Lee asso. Washington and Lee U., 1968; recipient Profl. Achievement award W.Va. Soc. Profl. Engrs., 1970. Fellow Am. Soc. C.E. (pres. 1966-67); mem. Engrs. Joint Council (dir. 1967-70), Nat., W.Va. (past pres.) socs. profl. engrs., Am. Inst. Mining and Metall. Engrs., Internat. Assn. Hydraulic Research, Am. Soc. Testing and Materials, A.A.A.S., Am. Concrete Inst., Md. Assn. Engrs., Nat. Indsl. Sand Assn. (past pres.), W.Va. Mfrs. Assn. (dir.), Def. Orientation Conf. Assn., Pa. Soc., Engrs. Club Phila., Chi Epsilon. Republican. Presbyn. Mason. Clubs: Palmetto (Charleston, S.C.); Fifth Avenue (N.Y.C.); Fountain Head Country (Hagerstown, Md.). Home: PO Box 245 Berkeley Springs WV 25411 Office: Pa Glass Sand Corp Berkeley Springs WV 25411

ANDREWS, EDWARD CLINTON, Jr., univ. pres.; b. Rockland, Me., Jan. 9, 1925; s. Edward C. and Ruth (Grafton) A.; A.B., Middlebury Coll., 1946; M.D., Johns Hopkins, 1951; m. Jean Lyndes, Nov. 8, 1947; children—Leslie Jan (Mrs. James Freeman), Dawn Kristy, Dale Allison, Edward Clinton III, Scott Stanley. Intern Johns Hopkins Sch. Medicine and Johns Hopkins Hosp., Balt.; asso. prof. pathology U. Vt. Coll. Medicine, Burlington, 1958-67, prof. pathology, 1967—, asso. dean, 1964-66, dean, 1966-67, dean div. health scis., 1967-70, pres. univ., 1970—. Cons. specialist pathology Med. Center Hosp. Vt, Mem. A.M.A., Vt., Chittenden County med. socs., N.Y. Acad. Scis. Home: 112 S Williams St Burlington VT 05401 Office: U Vt Burlington VT 05401

ANDREWS, ELLIOTT ELLSWORTH, librarian; b. Springfield, Mass., Nov. 28, 1921; s. Arthur A. and Rachel (Thompson) A.; A.B., Brown U., 1947, A.M., 1949; M.L.S., U. R.I., 1966; m. Constance Karen Hurley, June 21, 1949; childrenGuy Benjamin, Charlotte. Charge social studies Brown U., 1949- 51; librarian Providence Jour. Library, 1951-62, R.I. State Library, 1962-; state librarian, state record commr. Served with AUS, 1942-45, 51-52. Mem. Am., R.I. (dir. 1955-57) library assns., Spl. Libraries Assn. (chmn. newspaper div. 1958-59), Am. Assn. State Libraries, Am. Assn. Law Libraries, Soc. Am. Archivists, R.I. Hist. Soc. Club: Brown of R.I. Home: 272 Morris Av Providence RI 02906 Office: Rhode Island State Library Providence RI 02903

ANDREWS, ELMORE LYNNWOOD, lawyer; b. Mpls., Nov. 19, 1892; s. Frederick Grove and Jennie (Kelly) A.; student U. Mich., 1912-13; LL.B., U. Va., 1916; m. Florence C. Stafford, Sept. 14, 1920 (dec. 1942); children—Stafford E., David L.; m. 2d Ruth S. Moak, Apr. 23, 1945. Admitted to Va. bar, 1916, Ohio bar, 1916; practice in Cleve., 1916-; mem. firm Thompson, Hine & Flory, 1916- , partner, 1926-, sr. partner, 1960-. Dir. Medusa Portland Cement Co., Osborn Mfg. Co., Land Title Guarantee & Trust Co., Curtis Noll Corp., Motch & Merryweather Machinery Co., Am. Vitrified Products Co., Cleve. Punch & Shear Works Co., Clauss Cutlery Co., Parsons & Co., Inc. Past pres., trustee Citizens League Cleve.; mem. vis. com. Western Res. U. Law Sch. Served with U.S. Army, 1917-19. Mem. Am., Ohio, Cleve. bar assns., Raven Soc., Order of Coif, Nisi Prius. Clubs: Union, Nisi Prius (Cleve.), Country (Pepper Pike, O.); Hunting Valley Gun (Solon, O.). Home: 2995 Courtland Blvd Shaker Heights, OH 44122. Office: Nat City Bank Bldg Cleveland OH 44114

ANDREWS, ELWOOD F., steel co. exec.; b. Indpls., Nov. 1, 1921; s. D. Lee and Fern (Gooch) A.; B.S., Butler U., 1942; student Exec. Program, Carnegie Inst. Tech.; m. Elvira Marie Hiland, Sept. 6, 1940; children—Nancy Lee, Dennis Dee (dec.), Betsy B. Instr. purchasing Butler University, 1949-58; dir. purchase Pitman, Moore Co. div. Allied Lab., Indpls., 1946-58; v.p. purchases Allegheny Ludlum Industries, Inc., Pitts., 1961—. Served to lt. USNR, World War II. Decorated Silver Star, Bronze Star. Mem. Nat. Assn. Purchasing Agts. (pres. 1953-54, chmn. bus. survey com.). Mem. Christian Ch. Clubs: Duquesne, Highland Country (Pitts.). Office: Oliver Bldg Pittsburgh PA 15222 ‡

ANDREWS, FLETCHER REED, ret. ednl. adminstr.; b. N.Y.C., Jan. 22, 1894; s. Addison Fletcher and Ella (Reed) A.; A.B., Dartmouth, 1916; LL.B., Western Res. U., 1925; J.S.D. (Sterling fellow), Yale, 1941; m. Marguerite Jeavons, Aug. 8, 1917; children—Jeanne (Mrs. Jacob B. Perkins), Fletcher Reed. With advt. dept. Crowell Pub. Co., 1916-17; asst. to gen. mgr. J.H.R. Products Co., Willoughby, O., 1919-22; admitted to Ohio bar, 1925 and practiced law with Copeland and Quintrel, Cleve., 1925-27; prof. law Western Res. U. Sch. Law, 1927-64, dean, 1948-58; impartial chmn. Thompson Products, Inc., Pension Bd., 1952-58; referee Probate Ct., 1961—. Trustee, v.p. Cleve. Bar Found., Cleve. Community Fund, Council World Affairs. Adviser spl. com. bar exam. Supreme Ct. Ohio.; Ohio annotator Restatement of Conflict of Laws. Pres. League of Ohio Law Schs., 1949; gen. chmn. Cleve. Community Fund, 1941-42; mem. exec. com. Legal Aid Soc. of Cleve., 1935-40, treas., 1963-65; fiscal trustee Dorcas Soc., 1955—; mem. Dartmouth Coll. Alumni Council, 1935- 41; formerly trustee Univ. Sch., Cleve., Bennett Jr. Coll., Millbrook, N.Y. Served U.S. Army, 1917-19, with A.E.F.; commd. maj., promoted lt. col. Judge Adv. Gen.'s Dept., 1942-45. Decorated Medal of Honor (France), Legion of Merit (U.S.), Distinguished Service award Cleve. Community Fund, 1943, Alumni award Dartmouth Coll., 1957. Mem. Am., Cleve. (pres. 1960-61, chmn. uniform comml. code com.), Ohio (com. on banking and comml. law), Cuyahoga County bar assns., Am. Arbitration Assn. (arbitration law com. 1955-58), Am. Law Inst. (council 1947-52), Order of Coif, Alpha Delta Phi, Phi Delta Phi. Republican. Unitarian. Clubs: Union, University, Country (Cleve.); Army-Navy (Washington). Asso. editor Throckmorton's Ohio General Code, 1929; editor Baldwins Ohio Law Review, 1931; also several chpts. in Ohio Annotations to the Restatement of Conflict of Laws, 1935-38. Contbr. to law jours. Home: 2542 Stratford Rd Cleveland Heights OH 44118 Office: 2145 Adelbert Rd Cleveland OH 44106

ANDREWS, FRANK ARLAND, educator; b. Newport, R.I., June 30, 1921; s. Frank and Helen (Fallon) A.; B.S., U.S. Naval Acad., 1941; M.A., Ph.D., Yale, 1950; m. M. Maxine Andrews, June 14, 1958; children—Patrick, Jeffrey, Philip, Jean, James, Mary, Thomas, Frank, Theresa, Daniel, Timothy, Susan. Commd. ensign USN, 1941; assigned destroyers, 1942-43, submarines, 1943-64; chmn. sci. dept. U.S. Naval Acad., 1959- 62; retired; asso. prof. Cath. U. Am., 1964—, prof. mech. and ocean engring., 1967—. Dir. Chesapeake Instrument Corp., Gen. Physics Corp. Decorated Silver Star, Marine Corps medal, Bronze Star, Letter of Commendation. Mem. Acoustical Soc. Am., U.S. Naval Inst., Am. Soc. M.E. Author articles in field. Home: Homewood Rd Ferry Farms Annapolis MD 21402 Office: Cath U Am Michigan Av Washington DC 21117

ANDREWS, FRANK EMERSON, author, found. cons.; b. Lancaster, Pa., Jan. 26, 1902; s. Harry and Ellen (Wiggins) A.; A.B., Franklin and Marshall Coll., 1923, L.H.D., 1952; m. Edith Lillian Severance, July 5, 1932; children—Frank M., Peter Bruce, Bryant. Free-lance writer of articles in magazines and books, 1918—; mgr. advt. printing The Macmillan Co., pubs., 1923-26, dir. mail service dept., 1926-28; dir. publs. Russell Sage Found., 1928-56; pres. Found. Library Center, N.Y.C., 1956-67, cons., 1967-; cons. publs. Twentieth Century Fund, 1941-56; cons. NSF, 1958-68. Mem. Tenafly Planning Bd., 1936-62. Trustee Franklin and Marshall Coll., Tenafly Library Bd. Mem. Duodecimal Soc. Am. (pres. 1944-50, chmn. bd. 1950-63),

Authors League Am., Phi Beta Kappa, Lambda Chi Alpha. Mem. Riverside Church, N.Y.C. Author numerous books including: New Numbers, 1935; Philanthropic Giving, 1950; Corporation Giving, 1952; Grugan's God, 1955; Philanthropic Foundations, 1956; Upside-Down Town, 1958; Legal Instruments of Foundations, 1958; Numbers Please, 1961; (with John M. Glenn and Lilian Brandt) Russell Sage Foundation 1907-46, 1947; Knights and Daze, 1966; Patman and Foundations, 1968; the Tenafly Public Library, A History, 1970. Home: 34 Oak St Tenafly, NJ 07670.

ANDREWS, FRED CHARLES, educator; b. Aylesbury, Sask., Can., July 13, 1924; s. Henry Marmaduke and Margaret (Van de Bogart) A.; B.S. in Math., U. Wash., 1946, M.S. in Math. Statistics, 1948; Ph.D., U. Cal., Berkeley, 1953; m. Joyce Davenny, Apr. 5, 1944; children—Linda (Mrs. Pierre Dunn), David W., Gail E. Research asso. Applied Math. and Statistics Lab., Stanford, 1952-54; asst. prof. math., asso. statistician U. Neb., 1954-57; asso. prof. math. U. Ore., 1957-66, dir. Statistics Lab. and Computing Center, 1960-69, prof. math., 1966—. Pres., Met.-Civic Club Eugene-Springfield, 1967-68. Trustee, Ore. Grad. Center. Served to lt. (j.g.) USNR, 1943-46. Sr. Fulbright-Hays lectr. U. Tampere (Finland), 1969-70. Mem. Inst. Math. Statistics, Am. Statis. Assn., Biometric Soc., A.A.A.S., Am. Assn. U. Profs., Sigma Xi. Contbr. articles profl. jours. Home: 2705 Emerald St Eugene OR 97403

ANDREWS, FREDERICK NEWCOMB, univ. dean; b. Boston, Feb. 5, 1914; s. Frederick Huntoon and Gertrude (Macomber) A.; B.S., U. Mass., 1935, M.S., 1936, D.Sc., 1962; Ph.D., U. Mo., 1939; m. Gertrude Evelyn Martin, Sept. 3, 1938; childrenFrederick Martin, Donna Elaine. Instr. animal husbandry U. Mass., 1936; coop. agt. U. Mo.-U.S. Dept. Agr., 1936-40; asst. prof. animal sci. Purdue U., 1940-45, asso. prof., 1945-49, prof., 1949-, asst. to dean Grad. Sch., 1949-54, dir. Herrick Lab. Environmental Studies, 1960-, head dept. animal scis., 1962, dean Grad Sch., v.p. research, 1963—; v.p. Purdue Research Found., 1964—. Spl. cons. Latin Am. programs in agrl. sci. Rockefeller Found., 1956, 61, bd. cons. agrl. programs, 1962-; mem. Ford Found. ednl. mission to Mexico, 1962; mem. Fulbright award com.; research grant reviewer NSF-NIH; mem. numerous coms. nutrition and animal physiology Nat. Acad. Scis.; mem. Internat. Conf. on Use Isotopes in Animal Biology and Med. Scis., Mexico City, 1961. Recipient research award Sigma Xi, 1949, Morrison research award Am. Soc. Animal Sci., 1961. Fellow A.A.A.S.; mem. Am. Soc. Zoologists, Am. Soc. Animal Sci., N.Y. Acad. Scis., Am. Dairy Sci. Assn., Poultry Sci. Assn., Ind. Vet. Med. Assn. (hon.), Am. Assn. Anatomists, Sigma Xi, Phi Kappa Phi, Gamma Sigma Delta. Author: Breeding Better Liverstock, 1953; Breeding and Improving of Farm Animals, rev. edit., 1967; Swine Production, rev. edit., 1962. Editorial bd. Jour. Animal Sci. Home: 691 Sugar Hill Dr West Lafayette IN 47906 Office: Grad House Purdue U Lafayette IN 49707

ANDREWS, GEORGE WILLIAM, congressman, b. Clayton, Ala., Dec. 12, 1906; s. George William, Sr., and Addie Bell (King) A.; LL.B., U. Ala., 1928; m. Elizabeth Bullock, Nov. 25, 1936; children—Jane M. (Mrs. Thomas M. Hinds), George William III. Practiced in Union Springs, Ala., 1928- 43; circuit solicitor 3d Jud. Circuit State of Ala. (Bullock, Barbour, Dale and Russell counties), 1931-43. Mem. 78th Congress (elected 1944 to fill vacancy), member 79th-87th, 89-92d congresses, 3d Ala. Dist., mem. 88th Congress Ala. at-large. Served as lt. (j.g.), USNR World War II; released from active duty following election as mem. Congress. Mem. Third Jud. Circuit, Ala. bar assns., Sigma Nu. Phi Delta Phi, Omicron Delta Kappa. Democrat. Baptist. Home: Union Springs AL 36089 Office: House Office Bldg Washington DC 20525

ANDREWS, GLENN, former congressman; b. Anniston, Ala., Jan. 15, 1909; s. Roger Lee and Beryl Elizabeth (Jones) A.; student Mercersburg Acad., 1926-27; A.B., Princeton, 1931; m. Ethel Standish Jackson, Jan. 1937; children—Ethel Houston (Mrs. George Kilby), Arthur Glenn, Frank Scott. With IBM, Nat. City Bank, N.Y.C., 1931-37; salesman, dist. mgr. subsidiary Eastman Kodak Co., New Orleans, 1937-47; advt. exec., pres. Andrews Advt., Inc., Anniston, 1947—; mem. 89th Congress 4th Dist. Ala.; farmer Anniston, Ala., 1960—. Mem. James Madison Commn., 1964—. Chmn., Republican Party, Calhoun County, 1952—; candidate sec. state, 1956; candidate Ala. Ho. of Reps., 1958; regional coordinator Rep. Party, 1960-64, dist. chmn., del. state conv. 1962, del. nat. conv., 1964; Rep. chmn. 4th Congrl. Ala. Dist. Mem. com. sponsors MacArthur Meml. Com. Episcopalian. Rotarian, Mason (32, K.T.). Clubs: Anniston Country; The Club (Birmingham, Ala.); Nassau (Princeton, N.J.). Home: 1205 Champaign St Anniston AL 36201 Office: Andrews Advt Inc PO Box 1589 Anniston AL 36201

ANDREWS, HELEN RILLING, ret. librarian; b. Erie, Pa., Mar. 4, 1909; d. Emil Louis and (Cameron) Rilling; B.A., Lake Erie Coll., 1931; B.S., Columbia, 1932; m. C.B. Andrews, Sept. 27, 1963. With Erie Pub. Library, 1937-70, 1949-70. Bd. dirs. Erie Guidance Center, 1959-65, Erie County Hist. 1960-62, 64-66, 69—; bd. dirs. Erie Art Center, 1960-62, mem. adv. assns., Am. Assn. U. Women (bd. dirs. Erie chpt. 1949-59, 1st v.p. 1950- 51), Mental Health Assn. Erie County, Internat. Inst. Erie, Booker T. Washington Center, Pa. Hist. Assn., Jr. League Erie. Republican. Home: 630 W 9th St Erie PA 16502.

ANDREWS, HENRY NATHANIEL, Jr., scientist; b. Melrose, Mass., June 15, 1910; s. Henry Nathaniel Florence Clara (Hollings) A.; B.S., Mass. Inst. Tech., 1934; M.S., Washington U., St. Louis, 1937, Ph. D., 1939; student Cambridge (Eng.) U., 1937-38; m. Elisabeth Claude Ham, Jan. 12, 1939; childrenHollings T., Henry III, Nancy R. Mem. staff Washington U., 1939-64, Prof. Bot. Garden, St. Louis, 1941-64, asst. to dir., 1944-47; part time employee U.S. Geol. Survey; chmn. botany Dept. U. Conn., Storrs, 1965- 67, head systematic and environmental biol. sect., 1967-70. NSF post doctoral fellow Swedish Mus. Natural History, Stockholm, 1964-65; Fulbright teaching fellow Poona Univ., India, 1960-61. Mem. Bot. Soc. Am., Paleontol. Soc., Torrey Bot. Club, Phi Beta Kappa, Sigma Xi. Research work deals primarily with fossil plants of central coal fields, Devonian age Fossils, Arctic paleobotany. Home: 33 Lynwood Rd Storrs, CT 06268.

ANDREWS, J. FLOYD, airline exec.; b. 1919; student Wichita U., also Friends U.; married. With Pacific Southwest Airlines, 1949—, pres., chief exec. officer, 1962—, also dir.; dir. San Diego Gas and Electric Co., Bank of La Jolla, So. Cal. First Nat. Bank. Served with USAAF, 1944-48. Address: 3225 N Harbor Dr San Diego CA 92101*

ANDREWS, JAMES, Jr., assn. exec., lawyer; b. Phila., Oct. 21, 1911; s. James and Edith (Kenderdine) A.; B.S., Haverford Coll., 1933; LL.B., U. Pa., 1936; m. Elisabett Bardsley, Aug. 31, 1940. Admitted to Pa. bar, 1937; atty. Penn Mut. Life Ins. Co., 1937-38; asso. counsel Strawbridge & Clothier, Phila., 1938-43; exec. asst. Am. Friends Service Com., 1943-47; sec. Gen. Milk Co., 1947-48; dir. health ins. Life Ins. Assn. Am., 1948-56, asst. gen. counsel, 1957-62, sec., 1962-68, v.p. adminstrn., 1969—. Vice chmn. Health Ins. Council, 1949-56. Recipient medal for humanitarian work in Finnish Lapland, 1946. Mem. Phila. Bar Assn., Triangle Soc. Mem. Soc. of Friends (trustee Scarsdale Mountain (Boston); Sharswood Law (U. Pa. Law Sch.). Home: 15 Manor Dr Yonkers NY 10710 Office: 277 Park Av New York City NY 10017

ANDREWS, JAMES ALVAN, investment banker; b. Laurel, Miss., Dec. 26, 1904; s. Adolphus G. and Grace (Montgomery) A.; student Harvard, 1926; m. Barbara Tompkins, Oct. 30, 1928; children—Patricia (Mrs. John L. Ashby, Jr.), James M. With State Dept., 1927-29, various N.Y. investment security dealers, 1930-49; pres. Andrews & Wells, Inc., N.Y.C., 1949-59, James A. Andrews & Co., Inc., 1960—. Mem. Municipal Bond Club N.Y.C., Bond Club N.J., Municipal Forum, Bankers Club Am. Republican. Presbyn. Home: 301 Orange Av Cranford NJ 07016 Office: 70 Pine St New York City NY 10005

ANDREWS, JAMES NEWTON, paperboard co. exec.; b. Cleve., Feb. 13, 1914; s. Lloyd E. and Martha Jane (Hunt) A.; A.B., Wittenberg U., 1936; m. Janet Zieger, May 20, 1939; 1 son, James Douglas. With Ohio Boxboard Co., 1936-59; company merged with Central Fibre Products Co. and Am. Box Board Co. to form Packaging Corp. Am., 1959; exec. v.p. Packaging Corp. Am., 1959-63, pres., 1963-65, chmn. bd., 1966-70; pres. Fibre Box Assn., Chgo., 1970—; dir. State Nat. Bank, Evanston, Ill. Bd. dirs. Wittenberg U., Springfield, O. Mem. Beta Theta Pi. Home: 207 Woodstock Av Kenilworth IL 60043 Office: 224 S Michigan Av Chicago IL 60604

ANDREWS, JAMES WILLIAM, food co. exec.; b. Chgo., Mar. 15, 1918; s. James Roy and Evalyn Marie (Funkey) A.; A.B., DePauw U., 1940; M.B.A., Harvard, 1942; m. Joan Lawson, Sept. 4, 1943; children—Faith, Ellen, Elisabeth. With Gen. Foods Co., 1953—, marketing mgr. Jell-O div., 1962-64, marketing mgr. Post div., 1964, pres., gen. mgr. Canadian subsidiary Gen. Foods, Ltd., 1964- 68, v.p. parent co., White Plains, N.Y., 1965—, v.p., gen. mgr. Jell-O div., 1968, pres. Maxwell House div., 1969—, group v.p., 1971—; dir. Kimberly-Clark Co. Served as lt. USNR, World War II. Home: Lone Tree Farm Rd New Canaan CT 06840 Office: 250 North St White Plains NY 10605

ANDREWS, JAY D., marine ecologist, educator; b. Bloom, Kan., Sept. 9, 1916; s. Jay S. and Eva (Dilley) A.; B.S. in Agr., Kan. State Coll., 1938; M.S. in Zoology, U. Wis., 1940, Ph.D., 1947; m. Mary Stuart Hornsby, Mar. 1948; children—Donna Gay, Jay Stuart. With Va. Inst. Marine Sci., Gloucester Point, 1946—, now sr. marine scientist; asso. prof. U. Va.; now prof. marine sci. Coll. William and Mary. Served with inf. AUS, 1941-45. Mem. Nat. Shellfisheries Assn. (past pres.), Ecol. Soc. N. Am., Am. Soc. Limnology and Oceanography, Atlantic Estuarine Research Soc., Am. Inst. Fisheries Research Biologists, Sigma Xi, Phi Kappa Phi, Alpha Zeta. Research on epizootiology of oyster diseases. Home: 11 Cornwallis Rd Yorktown VA 23490 Office: Va Inst Marine Sci Gloucester Point VA 23062

ANDREWS, JOHN CHARLES, lawyer; b. Duncan, Okla., Oct. 24, 1926; s. John Charles and Eva L. (Loos) A.; student Okla. City U., 1944; LL. B., Okla. U., 1949; m. Patricia Ellen Coffey, Nov. 22, 1952; children—John Charles III, Patricia Kathleen, Michael Joseph, Margaret Ann, Daniel Coffey, Timothy Jerome. Admitted to Okla. bar, 1949; asst. ins. commnr. Okla., 1949-50; sr. partner Andrews, Mosburg, Davis, Elam, Legg & Kornfeld, and predecessors, Okla. City, 1967—. Dir. United Founders Life Ins. Co., Founders Bank & Trust Co., Carey Lumber Co., Balliet's Inc., N.M. Transp. Co.; trustee Central Cemetary Co. of Ill. Served with AUS, 1944-46. Mem. Am., Okla. bar assns., Phi Delta Phi. Democrat. Roman Catholic. Clubs: Oklahoma City Golf and Country, Serra (pres. 1963) (Oklahoma City); Beacon; Tower. Home: 1709 Wilshire Blvd Oklahoma City OK 73116 Office: United Founders Tower Oklahoma City OK 73112

ANDREWS, JOHN FONTAINE, lawyer; b. Montgomery, Ala., Jan. 6, 1938; s. James Warren and Mary (McCormick) A.; B.S., Auburn (Ala.) U., 1959; LL.B., Tulane U., 1962. Admitted to Ala. bar, 1962; practiced in Montgomery, 1963—; mem. firm Capell, Howard, Knabe & Cobbs, 1963—, partner, 1967—; prof. Jones Law Sch., 1964—. Served with Ala. N.G., 1962-64; to capt. U.S. Army, 1964- 68. Mem. Am., Ala., Montgomery County bar assns., Montgomery Jr. C. of C., Order of Coif, Phi Delta Theta, Phi Alpha Delta. Mem. bd. editors: Tulane Law Review, 1960-62. Home: 2036 Ellen St Montgomery AL 36106 Office: 57 Adams Av Montgomery AL 36103

ANDREWS, JOHN HAMILTON, architect; b. Sydney, Australia, Oct. 29, 1933; B.Arch., Sydney U., 1956; M.Arch., Harvard, 1958; m. Rosemary Andrews; 4 sons. Chief designer John B. Parkin Assos., Toronto, Ont., Can., 1958-61; pvt. practice, Toronto, Can., 1962—; mem. staff U. Toronto Sch. Architecture, 1962-69, prof., chmn. archtl. devel., 1967-69. Recipient Centennial medal (Can.), 1967, Massey medal for architecture (Can.), 1967, Arnold Brunner prize for architecture Nat. Inst. Arts and Letters and Am. Acad. Arts and Letters, 1971. Fellow Royal Archtl. Inst. Can., Royal Australian Inst. Architects; mem. Royal Inst. Brit. Architects (asso.). Prin. works include: Scarborough Coll., U. Toronto, African Place, Expo 1967, Montreal, Que., Can., Weldon Library, U. Western Ont., Harvard Grad. Sch. Design, Smith Coll. Art Center, Belconnen Govt. Offices, Canberra, Australia, Dade County Port Devel., Miami, Fla., numerous others. Home: 32 Florida Rd Palm Beach New South Wales 2108 Australia Office: 47 Colborne Toronto 1 Ontario Canada

ANDREWS, JOHN JACOBS, mathematician, educator; b. Ann Arbor, Mich., Jan. 10, 1906; s. Frank Eugene and Ada May (Benedict) A.; A.B., Westminster Coll., 1929; M.A., St. Louis U., 1940, Ph.D., 1950; m. Anna Kubasta, June 4, 1929. Actuarial student Gen. Am. Life Ins. Co., St. Louis, 1930-34; spl. instr. St. Louis Bd. Edn., 1935-39, tchr. high sch., 1940-43; faculty St. Louis U., 1946—, prof. math., 1963—; dir. NSF SSTP, 1960-67, NSF In-Service Insts., 1961—. Served with USNR, 1943-46. Mem. Math. Assn. Am. (gov. Mo. sect. 1964-67), Am. Math. Soc., Sigma Xi, Pi Mu Epsilon. Home: Elmcrest Farm Route 2 Hillsboro MO 63050 Office: 221 N Grand St Louis MO 63103

ANDREWS, JOHN ROBERT, physician; b. Kent, O., June 10, 1906; s. William Baird and Anna (Doyle) A.; Ph.B., Brown U., 1928; M.D., Western Res. U., 1932; D.Sc. in Medicine, U. Pa., 1948; m. Anne Cosgrove, June 15, 1935; children—Catherine Firth (Mrs. Albert Kapikian), William Baird, John Robert; m. 2d. Jeannette Welsh, Mar. 7, 1951; m. 3d, Nicole Croizier, Dec. 31, 1962. Intern Cleve. City Hosp., 1932-33; resident U. Pa. Hosp., 1933-35, Meml. Hosp., N.Y.C., 1937; prof., dir. radiology Bowman Gray Sch. Medicine, 1950-55; with Nat. Cancer Inst., NIH, 1955-64, chief radiation br., 1955-64; clin. prof. oncology Georgetown U. Sch. Medicine, 1958-64, prof. radiology, 1964—; dir. radiotherapy Georgetown U. Hosp., 1964—; cons. Sibley Meml., Providence hosps., Washington, Clin. Center of NIH, Gordon Friesen Assos.; chief radiotherapy service Washington VA Hosp. Mem. A.M.A., Am. Roentgen Ray Soc., Radiol. Soc. N.A., Am. Radium Soc., Am. Coll. Radiology, D.C. Med. Soc., Radiation Research Soc., Am. Assn. Cancer Research, Am. Assn. for Cancer Edn. Author: The Radiobiology of Human Cancer Radiotherapy, 1968. Contbr. articles to profl. jours. Home: 4428 Volta Pl NW Washington DC 20007 Office: 3800 Reservoir Rd NW Washington DC 20007

ANDREWS, JOHN STEWART, retail co. exec.; b. Salem, O., Oct. 28, 1919; s. William W. and Lora (Ressler) A.; student U. Dayton, 1939-40, U. Queensland (Australia), 1945-46; grad. Harvard Grad. Sch. Bus. Advanced Mgmt. Program, 1965; m. Marie Louise Adams, Mar. 22, 1944; children—William Douglas, Jeffrey Lynn, Kathleen Margaret, Richard Dale, John Michael (dec.). Exec. vice-pres. Rike-Kumler Co., Dayton, O., 1965-69; exec. vice-pres. Shillitos, Cin., 1969, pres., 1970—; dir. Asso. Mdsg. Corp. Mem. exec. com. Social Planning Council Cin.; v.p. Family Service Assn. Trustee Community Chest and Council of Cin. Area. Served to lt. USAAF, 1940-45. Presbyn. (elder 1961—). Clubs: Bankers, Cincinnati Athletic, Harvard Business School (Cin.). Home: 8625 Hopewell Rd Cincinnati OH 45242 Office: Shillito's 7th and Race St Cincinnati OH 45202

ANDREWS, JOHN W., chem. co. exec.; b. 1936; grad. Stanford; B.A., U. Cal. at Los Angeles. With Purex Corp. Ltd., Lakewood, Cal., 1967—, controller, 1968—, v.p., 1970—. Office: 5101 Clark Av Lakewood CA 90712*

ANDREWS, JOHN WILLIAMS, writer, lawyer; b. Bryn Mawr, Pa., Nov. 10, 1898; s. Charles McLean and Evangeline (Walker) A.; ed. Taft Sch., Watertown, Conn.; A.B., Yale, 1920, LL.B., 1926; m. Elizabeth Robert, July 14, 1934 (div. 1953); 1 son, John Douglas Walker; m. 2d, Miriam Benton Wise, Oct. 30, 1953. Mgr. Chung Mei News Agency, Internat. News corr., Peking, China, 1921-22; legislative corr. New Haven (Conn.) Journal Courier, 1922-23; admitted to N.Y. State bar, 1927, practiced with firm Root, Clark, Buckner & Ballantine, N. Y. City, 1926-32; free-lance writer since 1932; asso. with history dept. Yale, 1938-40, special instr. honor students in thesis writing; asst. to adminstr. Conn. State Defense Council, 1940-42; chief Fed. State Relations Sect., U.S. Dept. Justice, Washington, 1942-48; adminstrv. vice chmn. Nat. Conf. on Prevention and Control of Juvenile Delinquency, 1947-48; trial atty., Anti-Trust Division Dept. Justice, Washington, 1948-50; cons. N.P.A. 1952; with Hill & Knowlton, Inc., pub. relations council, 1952-53; pres. Andrews Assos., Inc., 1954-62; pres. Lit. publs. Found., Boston. Dir. Cooper Hill Writers' Conference, East Dover, Vermont. Served as 2d lt. Army Air Service, World War I. Co-recipient Robert Frost Narration Poetry award, 1963. Fellow Timothy Dwight Coll. (Yale U.), 1938-40. Vice chmn. and mem. bd. trustees Lingnan U., Canton, China. Vice pres. and mem. bd. dirs. Washington Housing Assn., 1947-52, pres., 1952; dir. Washington Inst. Mental Hygiene, 1951-52. Member Poetry Soc. Am., Catholic Poetry Soc. of Am., Alpha Delta Phi, Wolf's Head. Clubs: Aviation Country of Long Island; Elizabethan (Yale U.); Cosmos (Washington); Rowfant (Cleve.); Yale (N.Y.C.). Author: History of the Founding of Wolf's Head, 1934; Prelude to "Icaros." 1936; Georgia Transport (verse play for radio), 1938; A Ballad of Channel Crossings, 1940; First Flight, the Story of the Wright Brothers at Kitty Hawk, N.C.; Hill Country North, a Vermont Cycle, 1965; A.D. Twenty-One Hundred, A Narrative of Space, Legends of Flight, Triptych for the Atomic Age. Editor-in-chief Poet Lore. Editor St. Lawrence Sea Way Fact Sheet, 1958-61. Contbr. articles and poems to various publs. Address: 52 Cranbury Rd Westport CT 06830

ANDREWS, JULIE, actress, singer; b. Walton-on-Thames, Eng., Oct. 1, 1935; d. Edward C. and Barbara Wells; m. Tony Walton May 10, 1959; 1 dau. Emma; m. 2d, Blake Edwards; studied with pvt. tutors; studied voice with Mme. Stiles-Allen. Debut as singer Hippodrome, London, 1947; appeared in pantomime Cinderella, London, 1953; appeared Broadway prodn. The Boy Friend, New York City, 1954, My Fair Lady, 1956-60, Camelot, 1960-62; films include Mary Poppins (academy award for best actress, 1964), 1964, The Americanization of Emily, 1964, Torn Curtain, 1966, The Sound of Music, 1966, Hawaii, 1966, Thoroughly Modern Millie, Star!, Darling Lili. Made TV debut in High Tor, 1956. Recipient N.Y. Drama Critics award My Fair Lady, 1955-56; Golden Globe award Hollywood Fgn. Press Assn., 1964, 65; named World Film Favorite (female) 1967. Home: The Old Meuse Walton-on-Thames Surrey England Office: Chasin-Park-Citron Agy 10889 Wilshire Blvd Los Angeles CA 90024

ANDREWS, JULIO ANTONE, govt. ofcl.; b. New Bedford, Mass., Oct. 15, 1934; s. Antone and Antonia (Travis) A.; A.B. in Edn., San Jose State Coll., 1957; M.A. in Adminstrn., San Francisco State Coll., 1964; m. Eve Marie Cunha, Aug. 24, 1957; children—Lisa Marie, David Alan. Tchr., Palo Alto (Cal.) Unified Sch. Dist., 1957-63, intern coordinator, 1963-64, prin., 1964-65; contractor's overseas rep. San Francisco State Coll., Liberia, 1965-67; country dir. U.S. Peace Corps, Ethiopia, 1967-70, Thailand, 1970—. Bd. govs. Am. Community Sch., Monrovia, Liberia, 1965-67, Addis Ababa, Ethiopia, 1968-70. Home: 525 Hilbar Lane Palo Alto CA 94303 Office: 42 Soi Somprasong II Petchburi Rd Bangkok Thailand

ANDREWS, KENNETH RICHMOND, educator; b. New London, Conn., May 24, 1916; s. William John and Myrtle (Richmond) A.; A.B., Wesleyan U., 1936, M.A., 1937; Ph.D., U. Ill., 1948; M.A. (hon.), Harvard, 1957; m. Edith May Platt, Apr. 29, 1945 (div. 1969); children—Kenneth Richmond, Carolyn; m. 2d, Carolyn Erskine Hall Feb. 14, 1970. Tchr. English, U. Ill., 1937-41; instr. bus. adminstrn. Harvard Grad. Sch. Bus. Adminstrn., 1946-47, asst. prof., 1947-52, asso. prof., 1952-57, prof., 1957-65, Donald K. David Prof. bus. adminstrn., 1965—, faculty chmn. Advanced Mgmt. Program, 1967-70, Master Leverett House, 1971—; vis. prof. Univ. Lausanne (Switzerland), 1958-59; cons. on mgmt. devel. and policy problems. Dir. John Wiley & Sons, Inc., Reed & Barton, Harbridge House. Trustee Wesleyan U. Served from pvt. F.A. to maj. USAAF, 1941-46. Mem. Phi Beta Kappa. Author: Nook Farm, 1950; (with others) Problems of General Management, 1962; (with others) Business Policy Text and Cases, 1965; The Effectiveness of University Executive Development Programs, 1966; The Concept of Corporate Strategy, 1971. Editor: The Case Method of Teaching Human Relations and Administration, 1953. Home: 23 DeWolfe St Cambridge MA 02138 Office: Soldiers Field Boston MA 02163

ANDREWS, LAVONE D., architect; b. Beaumont, Tex., Sept. 18, 1912; d. Charles and Lavone (Lowman) Dickensheets; student Miss Hamlin's Sch., San Francisco, Marlborough Sch., Los Angeles; A.B., Rice Inst., 1933, B.S. in architecture, 1934; m. Mark Edwin Andrews, July 23, 1948; 1 son, Mark Edwin, III. Asso. with outstanding architects in Southwest, 1934-37; opened own office, Houston, 1937-41; architect firm Anderson, Clayton & Co., cotton firm, 1941-51, also pvt. work, museum in Washington, Naval Hist. Found. & Health Center, schs. for City of Houston. Selected as 3d of the 10 outstanding women architects in Am., Archtl. Record, 1947. Licensed architect, Tex. and D.C. Trustee Museum of Fine Arts in Houston. Mem. A.I.A., Royal Inst. Architects Ireland, Pallas Athene Literary Soc. of Rice Inst. Episcopalian. Clubs: River, Colony (N.Y.C.); Houston, Houston Country. Home: 8 Shadder Way Houston TX 77019 also Knappague Castle County Clare Ireland also (summer) Sea Wynde Fisher's Island NY 06390 Office: Bank of Southwest Bldg Houston TX 77002

ANDREWS, LAWRENCE JAMES, educator; b. San Diego, Sept. 27, 1920; s. Elmer James and Florence (Brown) A.; B.S., U. Cal. at Berkeley, 1940; M.A., U. Cal. at Los Angeles, 1941, Ph.D., 1943; m. Elizabeth Merriam Heggelund, Apr. 24, 1944; children—Robin

Elizabeth, Carol Jeanne. Lectr. chemistry U. Cal. at Los Angeles, 1943-44; chemist Clinton Engr. Works, Tenn. Eastman Corp., Oak Ridge, 1944-45; from instr. to asso. prof. chemistry U. Cal. at Davis, 1945-57, prof., 1957—, chmn. dept. chemistry, 1959-62, acting dean Coll. Letters and Sci., 1962-63, dean, 1964—. Cons., Kasetsart U., Bangkok, Thailand, 1966-68. Faculty fellow Fund Advancement Edn. (Ford Found.), Harvard, also Mass. Inst. Tech., 1953- 54; Fulbright research scholar U. Hull (Eng.), 1967-68. Mem. Nat. Assn. State Univs. and Land-Grant Colls. (commn. on arts and scis. 1968—), Am. Chem. Soc. (chmn. Sacramento sect. 1958-59), Sigma Xi, Pi Mu Epsilon, Phi Lambda Upsilon, Alpha Chi Sigma, Phi Kappa Phi. Author (with R. M. Keefer) Molecular Complexes in Organic Chemistry, 1964. Contbr. articles to sci. publs. Home: 350 W 8th St Davis CA 95616

ANDREWS, MARGARET SUSANNA, lawyer, librarian; b. Pine Island, Minn., Apr. 28, 1901; d. Jacob A. and Mary Alice (Finn) Bringgold; LL.B., U. Minn., 1926; m. Raymond C. Andrews, June 30, 1927; childrenMary Ellen (Mrs. Robert Anderson), Susan Margaret (Mrs. Robert Wilson), Charles Bringgold. Admitted to Minn. bar, 1926; asst. Clk. jud. com. Minn. Hos. of Reps., 1927; office mgr. Chicago County Coop. Assn., Lindstrom, Minn., 1938-52; gov.'s legislative clk., 1953; law librarian Minn., 1953—. State sec. Republican Party, 1946-53, dir. speaker's bur. state and nat. campaigns, 1952. Mem. St. Paul Bus. and Profl. Women's Club, Minn. Congress Parents and Tchrs., Inc. (state parliamentarian 8 yrs., chmn. state office procedure 3 yrs., sec. 3 yrs.), Archdiocesan Council Catholic Women (parliamentarian 4 yrs.), Am. Legion Aux. (state conv. parliamentrian 5 yrs.). Home: Lindstrom MN 55045 Office: State Capitol St Paul MN 55103

ANDREWS, MARIE SCHERER, nursing educator; b. Boston, Sept. 12, 1914; d. William Francis and Elizabeth Theresa (Fitzgerald) Scherer; R.N., Mass Gen. Hosp., 1936; student Simmons Coll., Boston, 1937-39; B.S. in Edn., Boston U., 1941, M.S., 1949, fellow Sch. Nursing, 1947-49; m. Joseph William Andrews, Feb. 20, 1943; 1 son, William Richard. Mem. staff Mass. Gen. Hosp. and Mass. Eye and Ear Infirmary, 1936-41, supr., instr. nursing and nursing edn., 1937-41; pvt. duty nurse, 1941-42; pub. health nurse, summer 1941; parttime instr. nursing Bouve Sch. Phys. Therapy, Tufts U., 1941-44; instr. nursing, supr. field practice and teaching Boston U. Sch. Nursing, 1943-48; mem. faculty Boston Coll. Sch. Nursing, 1948—, prof. nursing edn., 1960—, chmn. dept. nursing Grad. Sch., 1958—. Mem. Watertown (Mass.) Bd. Health, 1956—, sec., 1956-58, chmn., 1958-62; chmn. nursing edn. com. Nat. Found. Infantile Paralysis, 1956; civilian cons. to surgeon gen. U.S. Navy, 1962—; tech. cons. Bay State Rehabn. Clinic, 1956—; lectr. Walter Reed Army Hosp., 1962-64; civilian cons. Murphy Army Hosp., 1944; clin. cons. VA Hosps., 1962—; cons. to trustees Boston City Hosp., 1962-70; tech. cons. Mass. State Hosp. Sch., Canton, 1952—, chmn. adv. council, 1969—; cons. Nat. Soc. For Prevention Blindness, 1968—; cons. schs. nursing Peter Bent Brigham, Worcester City, Cambridge-Mt. Auburn hosps.; mem. Mass. Bd. Registration in Nursing, 1969—. Recipient citation Nat. Found. Infantile Paralysis, 1950, 59; named Nurse of Year, Archdiocesan Council Catholic Nurses, Boston, 1960; recipient 150th Anniversary medal and citation Mass. Gen. Hosp., 1961. Mem. Am., Mass. (pres. 1958-62, bd. dirs. 1962—) nurses assns., Nat. League Nursing, A.R.C. Nurses Assn., Northeastern Assn. Bds. Health, Nat. Found. Grad. Nurse Edn., Boston U., Mass. Gen. Hosp. (bd. dirs.) alumni assns., Nat. Council Cath. Nurses, Mass. Cath. Womens Guild, League Cath. Women, Sienna Soc. (hon.), Am. (chmn. edn. com. 1970—), Mass. (chmn. nursing edn. com. 1966-67) heart assns., Sigma Theta Tau. Contbr. articles profl. jours. Co- editor: Current Concept in Cardiac Nursing, 1963—. Home: 48 Green St Watertown MA 02172 Office: Cushing Hall Boston Coll Chestnut Hill MA 02167

ANDREWS, MARK, farmer, congressman; b. Fargo, N.D., May 19, 1926; s. Mark and Lillian (Hoyler) A.; student U.S. Mil. Acad., 1944-46; B.S., N.D. State Coll., 1949; m. Mary Willming, June 28, 1949; children-Mark III. Sarah Jane, Karen Louise. Farmer, Mapleton, N.D., 1949-; exec. com. Garrison Diversion Conservancy Dist., adminstrn. irrigation from Garrison Dam, 1955—; mem. 88th-92d congresses 1st Dist. N.D. Mem. Rep. Nat. Com. for N.D.; Rep. nominee for gov. N.D., 1962. Dir. Cass County chpt. A.R.C. Mem. Rep. Nat. Farm Council, Young Rep. Nat. Fedn. (past vice chmn.), N.D. Young Republicans (past chmn.), Nat. Reclamation Assn. (chmn. land limitations com.), Farm Bur., Am. Legion, N.D. Stockmen's Assn., N.D. Crop Improvement Assn. (pres.), Greater N.D. Assn., Northwest Farm Mgrs., N.D. Water Users Assn., Sigma Chi. Episcopalian. Home: Mapleton ND 58059

ANDREWS, MARK EDWIN, lawyer and industrialist; b. Houston, Oct. 17, 1903; s. Jesse and Celeste (Bujac) A.; grad., Lawrenceville Prep. Sch., 1923; A.B., Princeton, 1927; LL.B., So. Tex. Coll. of Law, 1934; post grad., U. of Colo., 1931-34; m. Marguerite McLellan (dec., 1946); m. 2d, Lavone Dickensheets, July 23, 1948; children—Marguerite McLellan, Mark Edwin III. Pres. Andrews, Loop & Co., 1928-34, Ryan & Andrews, 1936-42, Westmoreland Mfg. Co., 1936-42, M.E. Andrews, Ltd., since 1951, Ancon Oil & Gas, Inc., 1951—. Dixel Manufacturing Co.; faculty So. Texas Coll. of Law, 1943-42. Served U.S.N.R., 1942-46, advancing lt. to capt., serving in Office of Procurement and Material, Exec. Office of the Sec., Navy Dept.; chief of procurement, U.S.N., 1945-46; Asst. Sec. of Navy, 1947-49. Decorated, Legion of Merit, U.S.N., 1946. Mem. Houston Com. on Fgn. Relations (Carnegie Found.). Republican. Episcopalian. Clubs: Houston Country, Bayou. Allegro, Houston (Houston); Links, Recess; River (N.Y.C.); Tiger Inn, Right Wing (Princeton, N.J.); Fishers Island Country, Hay Harbor Country (Fishers Island, N.Y.); Lahinch (Ireland); Kildare St. (Dublin, Ireland). Author: Law vs. Equity in The Merchant of Venice, 1936; Buying a Navy (pub. by USN), 1946; Wildcatters Handbook, 1952. Contbr. articles to law publs. Home: 8 Shadder Way Houston TX 77019 also Sea Wynde Fishers Island NY Knappogue Castle County Clare Ireland Office: Bank of Southwest Bldg Houston TX 77002

ANDREWS, MICHAEL FRANK, educator; b. Cairnbrook, Pa., Mar. 4, 1916; s. Frank and Libra (Testa) A.; student Juniata Coll., Huntingdon, Pa., 1935-37; B.F.A., U. Kan., 1940, M.S., 1948; postgrad. Ia. State U., 1946; Ph.D., Ohio State U., 1952; postgrad. Syracuse U., 1964; m. Helen W. Baker, Dec. 30, 1940; children—Judith Lynn, Connee Jean, Michael Curtis. Tchr. pub. sch., Lawrence and Hays, Kan., 1940-42, U. Kan., 1946-48, Ohio State U., 1948-50. U. So. Cal., 1950-52, U. Wis., 1952-55; Dual prof. art and edn., head synaesthetic edn., Syracuse (N.Y.) U., 1955—. Vis. prof. U. Hawaii, summer 1967. Pres. Kan. Art Tchrs. Assn., 1947-49; v.p. Cal. Art Tchrs. Assn., 1951-52. Served to 1st lt. USAAF, 1942-46. Recipient Profl. Div. for Sculpture award, Columbus. O., 1949: Nat. Decorative Arts and Sci. award Syracuse, 1949; Sculpture award Columbus Art League, 1950; Wis. Salon of Art award Madison, 1954. Mem. N.E.A., Nat. Art Educators Assn. (pres. Eastern region 1966-68), Internat. Soc. Edn. through Art. Author: Creative Printmaking, 1964; Creative Education: The Liberation of Man, 1965; Sculpture and Ideas, 1966. Editor: Creativity and Psychological Health, 1961. Home: 6657 Woodchuck Hill Rd Jamesville NY 13078 Office: Skytop Syracuse U Syracuse NY 13210

ANDREWS, MILDRED MORFORD, educator; b. Hominy, Okla., Sept. 25, 1915; d. George Frederick and Clara (Parks) Andrews: student Bethany Coll., Lindsborg, Kan., 1933-34; B.F.A., U. Okla., 1937; M.Mus., U. Mich., 1940. Mem. faculty Sch. Music, U. Okla., Norman, 1938—, prof. music, 1953—, David Ross Boyd distinguished prof., 1964—. Vis. prof. organ Union Theol. Sem., N.Y.C., summers 1963, 66, Episcopal music confs., Evergreen Colo., 1940-64. Eugene, Ore., 1965, Sewannee, Tenn., 1960, 62, 65; organ concerts throughout U.S., 1939—; organist-choirmaster St. John's Episcopal Ch., Norman, 1936-64; cons. music and fine arts. Bur. Higher Edn., Wash. Chmn. Episcopal Diocese Okla. Music Com., 1945-63. Named Outstanding Faculty Woman, U. Okla., 1948, One of 10 Outstanding Faculty Mems., 1953; recipient Career Achievement award Profl. Panhellenic Assn.; Distinguished Service citation U. Okla.; named to Okla. Hall of Fame, 1971. Mem. Am. Guild Organists (chmn. Okla. 1962-64, nat. dir. student guild groups 1966—, nat. council 1966-69), Music Tchrs. Nat. Assn. (nat. chmn. organ and ch. music com. 1956-64), Nat. Fedn. Music Clubs (nat. organ chmn. 1956-60), Mortar Bd., Phi Beta Kappa, Mu Phi Epsilon (dist. dir. 1966-68, nat. v.p. 1966—), Pi Kappa Lambda, Alpha Lambda Delta, Delta Kappa Gamma. Home: 712 Mockingbird Lane Norman OK 73069

ANDREWS, OLIVER, Jr., educator; b. Montclair, N.J., May 26, 1917; s. Oliver and Rosamund (Capen) A.; B.S. cum laude, Harvard, 1939; diplome, Institut de Phonetique, Paris, 1948; M.A., Middlebury Coll., 1947; Ph.D., McGill U., 1956; m. Ann Roberta Wright, Sept. 4, 1953; children—Oliver III, Elizabeth W., Rosamund C., Michael C., Anthony W. Tchr., Gov. Dummer Acad., Byfield, Mass., 1939-43; asst. prof. Bates Coll., 1948-52; asst. prof. Purdue U., 1956-58, asso. prof., 1958-60; prof., head dept. modern langs. St. Lawrence U., 1960-66, founder, dir. jr. year in France, 1964; prof., head dept. Romance and classical langs. U. Conn., Storrs, 1966—, founder, dir. jr. year in France, 1967. Exec. dir. Charles I. Travelli Fund, Boston, 1960—; cons. Dept. Health, Edn. and Welfare, 1962-67. Bd. dirs. Council on Internat. Ednl. Exchange. Served with AUS, 1943-45. Decorated Bronze Star medal with oak leaf cluster (U.S.); Chevalier Ordre des Palmes Academiques, Commandeur Societe Vinicole de Medoc. Mem. Am. Assn. U. Profs., Modern Lang. Assn. Am. (cons. 1964-68, chmn. com. N.E. Conf. 1968, dir. Conf. 1969—), Am. Assn. Tchrs. French. Club: Harvard (N.Y.C.). Contbr. articles lang. jours. Home: Dog Lane Storrs CT 06268

ANDREWS, PAUL BENJAMIN, metal marketing cons.; b. Decatur, Ill., July 17, 1901; s. Forrest William and Ida L. (Morgan) A.; student U. Ill.; m. Lucille Georgeanne Chaille, June 9, 1928. Asst. sales mgr. Mueller Co., Decatur, Ill., 1924- 30; asst. sales mgr. Revere Copper & Brass, Inc., Rome, N.Y., 1930-40, asst. gen. sales mgr., N.Y.C., 1940-42, mgr. mdse. sales, 1946-50, 52- 65, v.p., 1965-66; pres. Ando Pub. Co., Cold Spring, N.Y., 1966—; metal marketing cons. Dir. copper div. NPA, Dept. Commerce, Wash., 1950-52; Pres. Highland Public Soc., Garrison Station Plaza, Inc. Served to comdr. USNR, 1942-46; chief copper sect. Exec. Office Navy Dept. Decorated Legion of Merit. Clubs: Copper (founder, past pres.); Highlands Country (dir.), Garrison (N.Y.) Yacht. Contbr. articles profl. publs. Pioneered use of copper tubing for piping. Home: Rocklawn Upper Station Rd Garrison-on-Hudson NY 10524 Office: 80 Main St Cold Spring NY 10516

ANDREWS, PAUL REVERE, publisher; b. Toronto, Ont., Can., Aug. 6, 1906 (parents U.S. citizens); s. Carroll Benjamin and Grace (Dolan) A.; B.A. cum laude, Norwich U., 1930, D.Litt., 1966; m. Virginia Prentice Ettinger, Jan. 20, 1940; children—Gail (Mrs. John Whelan), Carole Prentice, Joan Prentice, Jane Prentice (Mrs. Mark Talon), Paul Richard Prentice. Engaged in ins. bus., 1930-35; with Prentice-Hall, Inc., 1935—, pres. co., 1965-71, chmn. bd., 1971—, also dir.; founder, now chmn. bd. Prentice-Hall Can., Ltd.; chmn. bd. P-H of Australia, Ltd.; dir. Winthrop Pubs., Inc., Prentice Hall India, Prentice-Hall Internat., Warren Schloat Prodns., Inc., Sylvan Properties, Inc., Prentice Hall Corp. Systems, Inc., Living Color Financial Displays, Inc., Prentice-Hall Japan, Inc., N.Y. Inst. Finance Corp. Chmn. coll. sect. Am. Textbook Pubs. Inst., 1956, bd. dirs., 1960-63, mem. sect. chmn.'s council, 1961-62, treas., 1962-63; trustee Nat. Assn. Coll. Stores, 1960. Alumni rep. to bd. trustees Norwich U., 1958, trustee, 1965, Mem. Theta Chi. Club: Stanwich (Conn.). Home: 13 Aiken Rd Greenwich CT 06830 Office: Prentice-Hall Inc Route 9-W Englewood Cliffs NJ 07632

ANDREWS, PETER FERGUSON, author; b. N.Y.C., May 23, 1931; s. Bert and Nadine (Wright) A.; grad. Deerfield Acad., 1950; student Hamilton Coll., 1950-51; m. Marjorie Key, Jan. 12, 1960; 1 dau., Regan. Nat. corr. Hearst Publns., Washington, 1959-62; asso. editor Playboy mag., 1963-66; sr. editor Reader's Digest, 1967-70; free-lance writer, 1962—; contbg. editor Gallatin Report, 1962- -. Mem. Author's Guild, Soc. Mag. Writers. Clubs: Nat. Press, Metropolitan (Washington): Overseas Press (N.Y.C.); Waccabuc Country Author: A Tragedy of History, 1963; In Honored Glory, 1966; The Reluctant Hero, 1970. Address: Lime St Old Lyme CT 06371

ANDREWS, PRESCOTT RICHARDSON, lawyer; b. N.Y.C., Jan. 16, 1901; s. Walter Edson and Henrietta (Richardson) A.; A.B., Amherst Coll., 1922, LL.B., Harvard, 1925; m. Virginia Hawkins, June 4, 1931; children—Tabitha (Mrs. Pehr C. Buber), Prescott Richardson. Admitted to N.Y. bar, 1926; law asst. Humes, Buck & Smith 1925-31; mem. firm., Humes, Buck, Smith & Stowell and successor firm Humes, Andrews, Botzow & Wagner, N.Y.C., 1931—; dir. sec., treas. Moose Mtn. Ltd. Mem. Am. Bar Assn., Assn. Bar City N.Y. Presbyn. Clubs: Down Town Assn., University; Seabright Lawn Tennis and Cricket (gov.), Seabright Beach. Home: 1192 Park Av New York City NY 10028 also Black Point Rd Rumson NJ 07760 Office: 50 Broadway New York City NY 10004

ANDREWS, RALPH MORELAND, lawyer; b. Oil City, Pa., July 28, 1903; s. Hugh B. and Elizabeth (Moreland) A.; A.B. cum laude, Oberlin Coll., 1925; LL.B., Harvard, 1928; m. Katheryn Rickenbrode, Aug. 27, 1935. Admitted to N.Y. and Pa. bars, 1929; since practiced in Buffalo; mem. firm of Hodgson, Russ, Andrews, Woods & Goodyear 1946-71. Trustee Oberlin Coll., 1949-55. Fellow Am. Bar Found.; mem. Am. Judicature Soc., Am. (tax sect.), N.Y. (exec. com.; v.p. 1953-55, chmn. sect. on taxation 1954-56), Erie Co. (chmn. taxation com. 1950-55) bar assns., Asso. Industries N.Y. State Inc. (chmn. tax com. 1955-62), Nat. Alumni Assn. Oberlin (pres. 1936-39), Oberlin Alumni Assn. Western N.Y. (pres. 1931-32); U.S. (chmn. taxation com. 1939-40) and Buffalo (pres. 1935-36, chmn. bd. dirs. 1936- 37, mem. exec. com., 1936-37, chmn. taxation com., 1934-35, chmn. civic affairs com., 1934-35), Jr. C. of C., Buffalo C. of C. (pres. 1947-48, exec. v.p., 1943-45, v.p. 1942-43, mem. bd. dirs. 1940-43, 1946-48, chmn. taxation com. 1938-43; mem. municipal affairs adv. com., mem. taxation com), Y.M.C.A. (dir.). United Presbyn. Clubs: Buffalo (dir. 1960-63), Wanakah Country (dir. 1961-63). Home: 1217 Delaware Av Buffalo NY 14209 Office: 1 M&T Plaza Buffalo NY 14203

ANDREWS, RICHARD HALE, found. exec.; b. White Plains, N.Y., June 23, 1917; s. Robert Horrace and Katherine Isabel (Burt) A.; student Phillips Exeter Acad., 1936-37; A.B., Harvard, 1941; m.. Philadelphia Masters Carpenter, Nov. 17, 1945; children—Richard Hale, David Gage, Philadelphia Masters; m. 2d, Mary Ellen Reynolds, July 14, 1970. Reporter Boston Record, 1940-41; asst. counselor vets. Harvard, 1946-48; spl. fgn. corr. Mpls. Star and Tribune, 1948; sec. Am.-Scandinavian Found., 1948-53; exec. dir. Corning Glass Works Found. (N.Y.), 1953—, v.p., 1959—, mgr. spl. projects pub. relations dept., 1969—; mgr. nat. pub. relations Corning Glass Works, 1959-65, mgr. econ. research, 1965-69. Adviser, Sanctuary, Inc. Founding trustee Jamestown Glasshouse Found., Inc. Mem. research adv. council Found. for Research on Human Behavior. Served as capt. AUS, World War II. Mem. Nat. Indsl. Conf. Bd. (chmn. council exec. on co. contbns. 1958), Better Bus Bur. (nat. adv. com. on solicitations). Presbyn. Home: Black Oak Farm RFD 2 Watkins Glen NY 14891 Office: Corning Glass Works Houghton Park Corning NY 14830

ANDREWS, ROBERT VINCENT, univ. dean; b. Portland, Ore., July 4, 1916; s. Merrill Grover and Mildred Gertrude (Snelling) A.; B.S. in Chem. Engring., Ore. State Coll., 1938; M.S., Tex. A. and M. Coll., 1940, Ph.D., 1952; postgrad. Harvard, Mass. Inst. Tech., 1942; m. Marjorie Louise Kibbe, July 11, 1942. Chem. engr. Tidewater Asso. Oil Co., 1938-40; from instr. to prof. chem. engring. Tex. A. and M. Coll., 1938-55, research, design Monsanto Chem. Co., 1948-49; design, constrn. Hanford Works, Gen. Electric Co., also prof. co. sch. nuclear engring., 1951-52; research Tex. Engring. Expt. Sta., also Tex. A. and M. Research Found., 1953-55; vis. lectr. Dow Chem. Co., 1954; dean engring., dir. Lamar Research Center, Lamar State Coll. Tech., Beaumont, Tex., 1955-61; dean engring. Trinity U., San Antonio, 1961—. Mem. research adv. com. to coordinating bd. Tex. Coll. and U. System. Trustee, S.W. Research Inst., Tex. Mil. Inst., San Antonio. Served to capt. USAAF, 1942-46. Registered profl. engr., Tex., Ohio. Mem. Am. Inst. Chem. Engrs. (past chmn. Sabine Area sect.), Am. Chem. Soc. (past chmn. Tex. A. and M. sect.), Am. Soc. Engring. Edn., Tex. Soc. Profl. Engrs. (pres. Bexar chpt. 1967—, engr. of year award 1967), Sigma Xi, Tau Beta Pi, Sigma Tau, Alpha Tau Omega. Episcopalian. Author articles in field. Home: 146 Oakmont St San Antonio TX 78212

ANDREWS, SCHOFIELD, lawyer; b. N.Y.C., Aug. 7, 1889; s. Avery De Lano and Mary Campbell (Schofield) A.; grad. St. Paul's Sch., Concord, N.H., 1906; A.B., Harvard, 1910; LL.B., U. Pa., 1913; m. Lillian Forsyth Brown, Apr. 21, 1921 (died May 1927); children—Schofield, Stuart Brown, Stockton Avery; m. 2d, Marie D. Grant, May 9, 1929. Admitted to Pa. bar, 1913, since practiced in Phila., mem. firm Ballard, Spahr. Andrews and Ingersoll, Phila., 1919—. Served with U.S. Army, 1917-19; lt. col., asst. chief of staff, 90th Div., with A.E.F. Decorated D.S.M. Republican. Episcopalian. Club: Philadelphia. Home: Chestnut Hill Philadelphia PA 19118 Office: Land Title Bldg Philadelphia PA 19110

ANDREWS, SEWALL DUBOIS, Jr., corp. exec.; b. Mpls., Aug. 18, 1908; s. Sewall D. and Lilla student Hill Sch., Pottstown, Pa.; student Amherst Coll., 1928-29, U. Minn., 1931, advanced mgmt. program, Harvard Bus. Sch., 1951; m. Katherine Dodge, Oct. 1, 1931; children—Katherine M. (Mrs. C.A. Nalen), Laura H. (Mrs. John Crosby), Lilla Finch (Mrs. John F. Patterson). Dir. purchases Gen. Mills, Inc., Mpls., 1937-43, gen. mgr. chem. div., 1947- 55, gen. mgr. soybean div., 1955-60, v.p., 1955-, gen. mgr. splty. Products div., 1960-66, adminstr. internat. activities, 1966—; dir. Northwest Internat. Bank, Mpls., Gt. No. Ins. Co., Mpls., Twin City Co., Nat. Connector Co., Mpls. Bd. dirs. Episcopal Ch. Found., Mpls. Symphony Orchestral Assn.; pres. bd. trustees Northrop Collegiate Sch., Mpls. Served as lt. col. AUS, 1943-45. Decorated Bronze Star, Legion of Merit. Mem. Nat. Fatty Acid Assn. (chmn. steering com. 1954), Nat. Soybean Processors Assn. (exec. com., dir. 1954-), Nat. Squash Racquets Assn. (exec. com.), Am. Legion, Psi Upsilon. Episcopalian. Clubs: Minneapolis; Woodhill Country (Wayzata, Minn.); Yacht (Commodore 1956-57) (Minnetonka, Minn.). Home: Wayzata MN 55391 Office: General Mills Inc Minneapolis MN 55426

ANDREWS, T. COLEMAN, accountant; b. Richmond, Va., Feb. 19, 1899; s. Cheatham William and Dora Lee (Pittman) A.; ed. pub. schs., schs., Richmond; D.C.S., Pace Coll., 1954; LL.D., U. Mich., 1955, Grove City Coll., 1963; Sc.D., U. Richmond, 1955; m. Rae Wilson Reams, Oct. 18, 1919; children—Thomas Coleman, Wilson Pittman. Entered pub. accounting profession, 1918; founder T. Coleman Andrews & Co., C.P.A.'s Richmond, 1922; co-founder Bowles, Andrews & Towne, actuaries, Richmond, 1948; chmn. bd., pres., Am. Fidelity & Casualty Co., Inc., 1955-63; chmn. bd., pres. Fidelity Bankers Life Ins. Co., 1955-63, chmn. bd., 1963-65; chmn. bd. Nat Liberty Life Ins. Co., Valley Forge, Pa., 1965- 67; chmn. Service Enterprises, Inc., Richmond, 1967—; dir. Hardi-Gardens, Inc. auditor pub. accounts Commonwealth of Va., 1931- 33; comptroller, dir. finance, dir. utilities bus. office, exec. sec. sinking fund commn., City of Richmond, 1938-40; mem. staff dir. fiscal div. War Dept., 1941, contract renegotiation office Dept. Navy, 1942; officer USMC, 1943-45, on loan to Dept. State as chief accountant, dir. transp. North African Econ. Bd., Algiers, 1943; mem. (G-2) Gen. Staff, 4th Marine Aircraft Wing, Central Pacific, 1944-45; organizer, dir., corp. audits div. U.S. Gen. Accounting Office, 1945-47; commr. Internal Revenue Service, Dept. Treasury, 1953-55. Chmn. accounting and auditing study group 1st Hoover Commn., 1948. Decorated Bronze Star Medal; recipient Alexander Hamilton award Dept. Treasury, 1955, 1st award Tax Execs. Inst., 1955, award for pub. service Virginians of Md. C.P.A., Va. Mem. Richmond C. of C. (pres. 1958), Am. Inst. C.P.A.'s (award for outstanding service 1947; pres. 1950-51), Va. Soc. C.P.A.'s, Am. Accounting Assn., Fed. Govt. Accountants Assn. Ind. Democrat (independent candidate for president 1956). Episcopalian. Mason. Clubs: Commonwealth (Richmond); Bohemian (San Francisco); Country of Va. Home: 6 Iris Lane Richmond VA 23226 Office: 1508 Willow Lawn Dr Richmond VA 23230

ANDREWS, THELMA, ret. librarian; b. Lampass, Tex., Mar. 10, 1904; d. Athelston and Emily (Adams) Andrews; B.A., Hardin-Simmons U., 1925; M.A., State U. Ia., 1928, U. Chgo., 1945. Librarian Hardin-Simmons U., 1926-56; dir. Abilene Pub. Library, 1956-71; vis. lectr. Grad. Sch. Library Sci., U. Tex., summers 1964-67. Mem. Tex. Library Assn. (past pres.), A.L.A. Home: 1841 Grape St Abilene TX 79601

ANDREWS, THEODORE HENDERSON, army officer; b. Caldwell, Tex., Aug. 22, 1916; s. Theodore Edward and Eva Elizabeth (White) A.; B.S., Tex. A. and M. Coll., 1938; postgrad. Queens Coll., 1948, Command and Gen. Staff Coll., 1945, Armed Forces Staff Coll., 1955, U.S. Army War Coll., 1958; m. Mildred Gardenia Mills, Apr. 3, 1942. Commd. 2d lt. U.S. Army, 1938, advanced through grades to brig. gen., 1964; asst. dir. dept. mil. psychology and leadership, 1951-52; group comdr. 1st Battle Group, 18th Inf., Ft. Riley, Kan., 1958-59; comdg. officer 7th Army Support Command, Europe, 1960-61; asst. div. comdr. Combat Operations 7th Inf. Div. USARPAC- Korea, 1964-65; dep. dir. operations NMCC J-3 Joint Staff, Office Joint Chief of Staff, Washington, 1965-66; chief Far East Div., plans and policy dir. J-5, Joint Chief of Staff, 1966-68; asst. dep. chief of staff for individual tng. Hdqrs. CONARC, Ft. Monroe, Va., 1968—. Decorated Silver Star medal with oak leaf cluster, Bronze Star medal with 2 oak leaf clusters, Legion of Merit with oak leaf cluster; French Croix de Guerre; Iranian medal for service. Mem. Assn. U.S.

Army, Am. Mgmt. Assn. Methodist. Home: 804 W Alligator St Caldwell TX 77836 Office: Hdqrs Continental Army Command Fort Monroe VA 23351

ANDREWS, W. EDWARD, lawyer; b. Toccoa, Ga., Sept. 9, 1923; A.B., U. Ga., 1949, LL.B., 1949. Admitted to Ga. bar, 1949; now mem. firm Candler, Cox & Andrews, Atlanta. Served to lt. (j.g.) USNR, 1943-46. Mem. Am., Atlanta (sec. 1969-70) bar assns., State Bar Ga., Lawyers Club of Atlanta, Phi Delta Phi. Office: Atlanta Gas Light Tower Atlanta GA*

ANDREWS, WAYNE, author; b. Kenilworth, Ill., Sept. 5, 1913; s. Emory Cobb and Helen (Armstrong) A.; grad. Lawrenceville Sch., 1932; A.B., Harvard, 1936; Ph.D., Columbia, 1956; m. Elizabeth A. Hodges, June 12, 1948; 1 dau., Elizabeth Waties. Curator manuscripts N.Y. Hist. Soc., 1948-56; editor Charles Scribner's Sons, 1956-63; Archives of Am. Art prof. Wayne State U., 1964—. Mem. Société Chateaubriand (Paris), Victorian Soc. in Am. (v.p.). Author: The Vanderbilt Legend, 1941; Battle for Chicago, 1946; Architecture, Ambition and Americans, 1955; Architecture in America, 1960; Germaine: A Portrait of Madame de Staël, 1963; Architecture in Michigan, 1967; Architecture in Chicago and Mid-America, 1968; Architecture in New York, 1969; (pseudonym Montagu O'Reilly) Who Has Been Tampering With These Pianos, 1948. Editor: Concise Dictionary of American History, 1962; Best Short Stories of Edith Wharton, 1957. Home: 521 Neff Rd Grosse Pointe MI 48230 Office: 5200 Woodward Av Detroit MI 48202

ANDREWS, WILLIAM DOREY, educator; b. N.Y.C., Feb. 25, 1931; s. Sidney Warren and Margaret (Dorey) A.; A.B., Amherst Coll., 1952; LL.B., Harvard, 1955; m. Shirley May Herrman, Dec. 26, 1953; childrenHelen Estelle, Roy Herrman, John Frederick, Margaret Dorey, Susan Louise, Carol Mary. Admitted to Mass. bar, 1959; practice in Boston, 1959-63; asso. Ropes & Gray, 1959-63; lectr. Harvard Law Sch., Cambridge, Mass., 1961-63, asso. prof., 1963- 65, prof., 1965-; asso. reporter for accessions tax proposals Am. Law Inst. Fed. Estate and Gift Tax Project; cons. U.S. Treasury Dept. Mem. Zoning Bd. Appeals, Concord, 1966—. Served to lt. USNR, 1955-58. Mem. Am. Bar Assn., Am. Assn. U. Profs. Home: 26 Elm St Concord MA 01742 Office: Harvard Law Sch Cambridge MA 02138

ANDREWS, WILLIAM GEORGE, educator; b. Windsor, Colo., Aug. 5, 1930; s. Nathan Edwin and Ellen (Samson) A.; B.A., Colo. State U., 1952; C.E.P., U. Bordeaux (France), 1955; Ph.D., Cornell U., 1959; div.; children—Donna Ellen, William George, Jennifer Louise, Edwin Bartilon; m. 2d, Monika Wickert; 1 son, Christopher Scott. Teaching asst. Cornell U., 1955-58; instr., asst. prof. Dartmouth, 1958-61; asst. prof., asso. prof. govt. Tufts U., 1961-67; research asso. Inst. Polit. Studies, U. Paris (France), also prof. Am. Coll. in Paris and Inst. Am. Studies, Paris, 1962-63; prof. polit. sci. State U. N.Y. at Brockport, chmn. dept., 1967-71, dean social scis., 1970—. Served to 1st lt. USAF, 1952-54. Mem. Am., N.Y. (exec. com. 1968-69) polit. sci. assns., Rochester Com. Fgn. Relations. Republican. Lutheran. Author or editor: American National Political Institutions, 1962; French Politics and Algeria, 1962; European Political Institutions, 2d edit., 1966; Soviet Institutions and Policies, 1966; European Politics I, 1966; Poliitcs and Civil Liberties in Europe, 1967; Constitutions and Constitutionalism, 3d edit., 1968; European Politics II, 1969; Politics of International Crises, 1969; Coordinate Magistrates, 1969; The Politics of Coups d'etat, 1969; also numerous articles. Gen. editor: (series) New Perspectives in Political Science, 1960—. Home: 46 College St Brockport NY 14420

ANDREWS, WILLIAM HENRY, Jr., ins. cons.; b. Tarboro, N.C., July 18, 1899; s. William Hyman and Dollie (Savage) A.; A.B., U. N.C., 1920; C.L.U., Am. Coll. Life Underwriters, 1937; m. Pearle Balsley Humphrey, Oct. 23, 1923; 1 son, William Humphrey. Treas. Univ. Agy., Jefferson Standard Life Ins. Co., Chapel Hill, N.C., 1920-22, life underwriter, Greensboro (N.C.) br., 1922-28, mgr., Greensboro, 1928-64; now engaged in sales and consultation; dir. Gate City Savs. and Loan Asso. former dir. Eastern Music Festival. Vis. com. Guilford Coll; former mem. nat. exec. com., former state chmn. Savs. Bond div. Treasury Dept.; former mem. Greensboro Study Commn., Greensboro Safety Council; former chmn. budget and finance com., campaign com. United Fund. Former chmn. bd. overseers C.L.U. Devel. Fund Commn. Recipient John Newton Russell Meml. award, 1962. Mem. Am. Coll. Life Underwriters (trustee), Am. Soc. C.L.U.'s (past pres.), Nat. Assn. Life Underwriters (past pres., vice chmn. nat. industry relations com.), Def. Orientation Conf. Assn. U.S. Army, Delta Tau Delta (past 2d v.p. distinguished service chpt., past nat. sec.). Presbyn. (elder). Mason (Shriner). Clubs: Civitan (past president), Greensboro Country (past pres.), Merchants and Manufacturers (Greensboro). Cons. editor Life and Health Ins. Handbook. Home: 618 Woodland Dr Greensboro NC 27408 Office: O Henry Sq Greensboro NC 27405

ANDREWS, WILLIAM STUART, lawyer; b. Phoenix, Aug. 20, 1927; s. Lloyd J. and Francie (Webb) A.; student Phoenix Coll., 1945-48; LL.B., J.D., U. Ariz., 1952; m. Marilys Ann Benigni, Oct. 14, 1961; children-Lloyd James III, William Stuart, Chester D., Teresa Lee, Julie Ann, Elizabeth Francie. Admitted to Ariz. bar, 1952; since practiced in Phoenix, mem. firm Andrews, Marenda & Moseley and predecessor firms, 1958—; dep. Maricopa County atty., 1952- 57; asst. atty. gen. Ariz., 1959. Chmn. Maricopa County Bd. Suprs., 1966. Served with USNR, 1946-48. Mem. Am., Ariz. (past bd. govs.), Maricopa County (past dir.) bar assns., Sigma Alpha Epsilon, Phi Delta Phi. Democrat. Roman Catholic. Home: 902 W El Camino Dr Phoenix AZ 85021 Office: Luhrs Tower 45 W Jefferson St Phoenix AZ 85003

ANDREYCHUK, THEODORE, educator, psychologist; b. Detroit, Dec. 1, 1916; s. Fred and Martha (Naluskovich) A.; B.M., Mich. State Coll., 1943; M.A., U. Redlands, 1951; Ph.D., U. Tex., 1954; m. Virginia A. Morse, Nov. 13, 1943. Band instr., Mason, Mich., 1946-47; counseling intern U., Tex., 1952-53; postdoctoral intern, counseling psychologist VA, 1953-57; mgmt. psychologist firm Rohrer, Hibler & Replogle, 1957-62; prof. psychology, chmn. dept. Tex. Tech U., 1962—. Served with USAAF, 1943-46. Mem. Am., Southwestern, Tex. psychol. assns. Home: 3815 53d St Lubbock, TX 79413.

ANDRIC, IVO, novelist; b. 1892; ed. univs. Zagreb, Vienna, Cracow; Doctorate in Philosophy, Graz U. Former mem. Young Bosnia, Yugoslav revolutionary nat. movement; mem. Diplomatic Service, World War I to World War II, ambassador to Berlin at outbreak World War II; writer numerous books on history and conditions of Bosnia and the struggle of the Serbian people against Turkish occupation. Recipient the Nobel prize for literature in 1961. Mem. Serbian Acad. Belgrade, Yugoslav Acad. Zageeb, Slovenian Acad. Ljubljana. Author: The Spinster (English transl. The Woman from Sarajevo 1965; Bosnian Story, English transl. 1959, Bridge on the Drina, English transl. 1959, Devil's Yard English transl. 1962, The Vizier's Elephant, English transl. 1962, The Pasha's Concubine and Other Tales, English transl., 1968, others. Address: Ulica Proleterskin brigada 2-a Belgrade Yugoslavia

ANDRIE, GEORGE JOSEPH, profl. football player; b. Grand Rapids, Mich., Apr. 20, 1940; s. Stanley E. and Clara Rita Andrie (Dzierwa) A.; A.B., Marquette U., 1962; m. Mary Lou Lorscheider, Dec. 29, 1962; children—George, Michael, Margaret, Deborah. With Dallas Cowboys football team, 1962—; real estate asso. Phil Ross Realty, Dallas, 1965—. Named Nat. Football League All-Star player, 1966-70. K.C. Office: 6116 N Central Expressway Dallas TX 75206

ANDRINGA, CALVIN BRUCE, hotel exec.; b. Omro, Wis., Mar. 2, 1941; s. Cornelius and Bessie Irene (McKenzie) A.; B.B.A., U. Wis., 1963, J.D., 1966; m. Patricia Ann Perkins, July 7, 1968; 1 dau., Deborah Rene. Tax accountant Arthur Andersen & Co., Milw., summer 1966; treas. Wausau Paper Mills Co. (Wis.), 1968-70; v.p., treas. Marriott Corp., Washington, 1970—. Bd. dirs. Durango Orthopedic Assn. Served to capt. U.S. Army, 1966-68. Decorated Army Commendation medal. Mem. Am., Wis. bar assns., Am. Soc. Mil. Comptrollers (nat. sec. 1968). Home: 6205 Plainview Rd Bethesda MD 20034 Office: 5161 River Rd Washington DC 20016

ANDROS, DEE GUS, univ. football coach; b. Oklahoma City, Oct. 17, 1924; s. Gus D. and Harriett (Roberts) A.; B.S. in Edn., Okla. U., 1950, M.A. in Edn., 1952; m. Luella Thomas, Jan. 24, 1949; 1 dau., Jeanne. Coach, Okla., 1954-55; Kan. U., 1953, Tex. Tech. Coll., 1954-55, U. Neb., 1956, U. Cal., 1957-59, U. Ill., 1960-61, U. Ida., 1962-64; prof. edn., head football coach Ore. State U., 1965—. Served with USMCR, 1943-46, PTO. Decorated Bronze Star. Mem. Acacia. Methodist. Mason. Home: 715 Elizabeth Way Corvallis OR 97330

ANDRUS, CECIL D., gov. of Ida.; b. Hood River, Ore., Aug. 25, 1931; s. Hal Stephen and Dorothy (Johnson) A.; student Ore. State U., 1948-49; m. Carol Mae May, Aug. 27, 1949; children—Tana Lee, Tracy Sue, Kelly Kay. State gen. mgr. Paul Revere Life Ins. Co., 1969-70; gov. State of Ida., 1971—. Mem. Ida. Senate, 1961-66, 69-70. Served with USNR, 1951-55. Mem. Am. Legion, V.F.W., Ida. Taxpayers Assn. (dir. 1964-66). Democrat. Elk. Home: 1805 N 21st St Boise ID 83702 Office: Office of Governor Boise ID 83707

ANDRUS, EDWIN COWLES, physician; b. Kaatsban, N.Y., Feb. 28, 1896; s. Jonathan Cowles and Margaret (De Witt) A.; A.B., Oberlin Coll., 1916, A.M., 1917, hon. Sc.D., 1941; M.D., Johns Hopkins, 1921; m. Miriam Jay Wurts, June 10, 1933. House officer Johns Hopkins Hosp., 1921-23; fellow in medicine Nat. Research Council, London and Vienna, 1923-25; resident physician Johns Hopkins Hosp., 1925-27; asso. in medicine Johns Hopkins Med. Sch., 1926- 31, asso. prof., 1931-61, prof. emeritus, 1961—, asst. dean med. faculty, 1929-34; physician Johns Hopkins Hosp.; cons. cardiology Walter Reed Army Hosp., 1954-62. Asst. to chmn. com. med. research OSRD, 1942-44, chief div. medicine 1944-46; chmn. com. med. problems in civil aviation NRC, 1944-46, mem. com. aviation medicine, 1945-46, subcom. cardiovascular diseases, 1946-51; spl. cons. to surgeon gen. USPHS, 1946-51; chmn. cardiovascular study sect. Nat. Adv. Heart Council, 1946-51, mem. council, 1953-62; sr. spl. cons. Nat. Heart Inst., 1957-62; mem. med. exchange mission to Russia, 1961; dir. 2d Nat. Conf. Cardiovascular Disease, 1963. Bd. dirs. Passano Found., 1955—. Master A.C.P.; mem. Inter-Am. (council 1954-68, v.p. 1960-68), Internat. (council 1958-66) cardiological socs., Sociedad Peruana de Cardiologia (hon.), A.M.A., Am. Physiol. Soc., Am. Soc. Study Arteriosclerosis, Am. Heart Assn. (pres. 1954-55), Am. Soc. Clin. Investigation, Am. Clin. and Climatol. Assn., Assn. Am. Physicians, Med. and Chirurgical Faculty Md., A.A.A.S., Phi Beta Kappa, Sigma Xi, Alpha Omega Alpha. Republican. Clubs: Elkridge, Fourteen West Hamilton Street (Balt.). Home: 209 E Highfield Rd Baltimore MD 21218 Office: 550 N Broadway Baltimore MD 21205

ANDRUS, ELWIN A., lawyer; b. Troy Center, Wis., Mar. 28, 1904; s. Francis Leroy and Mary V. (Watrous) A.; LL.B., U. Wis., 1927; m. Florence R. Stetson, June 15, 1925 (dec.); 1 son, Frank Stetson; m. 2d, Marion R. Olson, Aug. 9, 1952. Admitted to Wis. bar, 1927, also U.S. Patent Office and U.S. Supreme Ct.; practice with Edwin B.H. Tower, Jr., Milw., 1927-28; with patent dept. A.O. Smith Corp., 1928-29, charge patent dept., 1929-39; pvt. practice patent, trade-mark and copyright law, 1939—; asso. Andrus, Sceales, Starke, Sawall, Milw.; lectr. U. Wis. Law Sch., 1947-49. Fellow Am. Coll. Trial Lawyers; mem. Inter- Am., Am. (chmn. sect. patent, trademark and copyright law 1958-59), Milw. County, 7th Fed. Circuit (pres. 1961-62) bar assns., Wis. State Bar (chmn. sect. patent trademark, copyright law 1960- 62), Am. Patent Law Assn., Chgo., Milw. (pres. 1938-39) patent law assns., Internat. Patent and Trade Mark Assn. (exec. bd. 1955-57), Canadian Patent Inst., Milw. Engrs. Soc., Am. Judicature Soc. Christian Scientist (ch. pres. 1960-63, 70—). Mason (32, Shriner). Clubs: University, Athletic. Home: 1610 N Prospect Av Milwaukee WI 53202 Office: 735 N Water St Milwaukee WI 53202

ANDRUS, GERALD LOUIS, utilities holding co. exec.; b. Crowley, La., Nov. 15, 1904; s. Charles D. and Rosa C. (Ramoin) A.; B.B.A., Tulane U., 1928; m. Lucile G. Isacks, Apr. 22, 1930; 1 dau., Marion L. (Mrs. Andrew McCollam, Jr.). With New Orleans Pub. Service, Inc., 1928-62, comptroller, 1947-52, v.p., 1952-59, pres., 1959-62, dir., 1959—; pres. Middle South Utilities, Inc., N.Y.C., 1962- 70, chmn. bd., chief exec. officer, 1970—; dir., 1960—; pres., dir. Middle South Services, Inc., New Orleans, 1963-70, chmn. bd., chief exec. officer, 1970—; dir. La. Power & Light Co., Miss. Power & Light Co., Ark. Power & Light Co.; dir. New Orleans br. Fed. Res. Bank of Atlanta, 1959-61, chmn., 1960. Mem. Bd. City Trusts, 1954-62. Chmn. finance United Fund Drive, 1954. Bd. adminstrs. Tulane U. Clubs: New Orleans Country (pres. 1959-60), Boston (pres. 1967-68), Stratford, Pickwick (New Orleans); Blind Brook, Racquet and Tennis, Links, Recess (N.Y.C.). King of New Orleans Mardi Gras, 1960. Home: 1309 Nashville Av New Orleans LA 70115 Office: 225 Baronne St New Orleans LA 70161 also 280 Park Av New York City NY 10017

ANDRUS, JAMES ROMAN, art educator; b. St. George, Utah, July 11, 1907; s. Alex B. and Rozilla (Brooks) A.; student Dixie Jr. Coll., 1925-26, Otis Art Inst., Los Angeles, 1934-39; B.S., Brigham Young U., 1942, M.S., 1943; art student Colorado Springs Fine Arts Center, Columbia, also Art Students League; Ed.D., U. Colo., 1958; m. Irva Rose Pratt, July 3, 1933; children—Roman Raphael, James Gregory, Aniene, Aniece, Alee Veigh. Prof. art and edn. Brigham Young U., 1959—, former chmn. dept.; exhibited group shows Boston Mus. Drawing Ann., Wichita Print Ann., Asso. Am. Artist Galleries, Forum Gallery, Los Angeles Mus., Cal. State Fair, So. Cal. Festival of Allied Arts, Dixie Coll. Fine Arts Festival, Municipal Art Gallery, Jackson, Miss., others. Mem. Utah State Fine Arts Com. Recipient purchase prize Utah Inst. Fine Arts, 1945, 50, 54. Mem. Nat., Western art edn. assns., Art Students League N.Y., Utah Acad. Sci. Arts and Letters (Distinguished Service award 1968), Central Utah Art Counsel (mem. bd.). Mem. Ch. Jesus Christ of Latter Day Saints. Home: 1765 N 651 E Provo UT 84601

ANDRUSHKIW, JOSEPH WASYL, educator, mathematician; b. Horodok, Ukraine, Mar. 21, 1906; s. Wasyl and Apollonia (Jachowski) A.; Maturity Diploma with excellence, State Gymnasium, 1924; M.S., State U. Lviw, 1930, M.Ed., 1932; Ph.D. in Math.. Ukranian Free U., Munich, Germany, 1946, Dr. Habilitatus, 1947, Dr. Philosophiae (hon.), 1962; m. Sophie Kovalchuk, July 16, 1932; children—Bohdan, Roman. Came to U.S., 1949, naturalized, 1955. Prof. State Tchrs. Coll. State Gymnasium and Lyceum, Kenty, Poland, 1930-39; instr. math. U. Lviw. 1939-40; instr. math. Tchrs. Coll., Jaworiw, Ukraine, 1942-44; dir. Tchrs. Coll., Mittenwald, Germany, 1945-48; asst. prof. Ukrainian Free U., Munich, 1947-49; mem. faculty Seton Hall U., S. Orange, N.J., 1949—, prof. math., 1955—, chmn. dept., 1962—. Dir. sect. math. and physics Shevchenko Sci. Soc., N.Y.C., 1969—. Fellow N.Y. Acad. Scis.; mem. Am. Math. Soc., Math. Assn. Am., Soc. Mathematique de France, Indian Math. Soc., A.A.A.S., Edinburgh, Glasgow, London math. socs., Deutsche Mathematiker Vereinigung, Schweizerische, Osterreichische math. gesellschafts, Polskie Towarzystwo Matematyczne, Unione Mateenmatica Italiana, Australian Mathematic Soc. Author numerous articles, editor proc. profl. socs. Home: 149 Milton Pl South Orange, NJ 07079.

ANDRUSS, HARVEY ADOLPHUS, ret. coll. pres., author; b. Ft. Worth, Feb. 19, 1902; s. Edward Hamilton and Myrtle (McDaniel) A.; A.B., U. Okla., 1924; M.B.A., Northwestern U., 1926, postgrad., 1928; Ed.D., Pa. State Coll. (now Pa. State U.), 1949; m. Elizabeth Archibald, June 12, 1929; 1 son, Harvey Adolphus. Prin. high schs, Okla., 1921-24; head commerce dept. Ponca City (Okla) High Sch., 1924-25; lectr. Northwestern U. Sch. Commerce, 1925-27; prof. dept. commerce Indiana (Pa.) U., 1927-30; organizer and dir. dept. bus. edn. State Tchrs. Coll., Bloomsburg, Pa., 1930-37, dean instrn., 1937-39, pres., 1939-69; pres. Bloomsburg State Coll., 1960-69, pres. emeritus, 1969—. Spl. lectr. N.Y.U., 1937, U. Okla., 1939, Okla. A. & M. Coll., 1942, 43, 49; ednl. cons. and head dept. accounting Army U., Shrivenham, Eng., 1945-46; cons. higher edn. Pa. State Coll., 1948; cons. citzenship edn. Tchrs. Coll., Columbia, 1950; vis. prof. Pa. State U., summer 1957. Dir. Bloomsburg Bank & Columbia Trust Co. Represented Am. Assn. Tchrs. Colls. in hearings before both House and Senate (78th Congress) on legislation to extend Civil Pilot Tng. Act of 1939. Editorial cons. Southwestern Pub. Co., Gregg Pub. Co., Macmillan Co., Lyons & Carnahan. Mem. Victory Fund Com., 3d Fed. Res. Dist., Phila; cons. bus. problems com. Investment Bankers Assn. Am., Chgo.; adviser on civil service exam. Unemployment Compensation Bd. Rev., Dept. Labor and Industry, Harrisburg; sec. Coop. Commn. on Tchr. Edn. in Pa.; chmn. budget and fees com. bd. Presidents Pa. State Colls.; cons. ednl. policies com. N.E.A., Washington; pres. Alpha Alumni Asso. of Phi Beta Kappa in Pa.; dir. Bloomsburg Hosp.; mem. exec. com. Bloomsburg chpt. A.R.C., chmn., 1933-35; mem. exec. com. Consumer Edn. Round Table; Pa. State Edn. Assn. (v.p. coll. and univ. sect.); mem. exec. com. Salvation Army (Bloomsburg); past pres. and v.p. comml. sect. Pa. Edn. Assn.; v.p. Coll. Insts. Round Table Nat. Comml. Tchrs. Fedn.; mem. N.E.A., Pa. Edn. Assn., Eastern Comml. Tchrs. Assn., Nat. Bus. Tchrs. Fedn., So. Bus. Edn. Assn. Presbyn. Mason (33). Kiwanian. Author books including: Burgess Business Law, 1952. Home: Country Club Dr Bloomsburg PA 17815

ANDRY, E. ROBERT, educator; b. nr. Huntingburg, Ind., Sept. 24, 1907; s. George and (Mason) A.; A.B., Butler U., 1930, A.M., 1934, B.D., 1934; Ph.D., Southern Baptist Theol. Sem., 1942; m. Oma Belle Alvey, Aug. 30, 1931; childrenRobert Bruce, Oma Kathryn. Ordained to ministry of the Christian Ch., 1934, and served rural chs. in Ind., 1930-34; minister Madison, Ind., 1934-38, Downey Av. Ch. Indpls., 1938- 44; head dept. religion Coll. Liberal Arts and Scis., Butler U., also prof. Bibl. history and lit., 1944—; youth leader and counselor. Ford Found. fellow, Jerusalem, 1952-53. Mem. Soc. Bibl. Lit. and Exegesis, Am. Acad. Religion, Am. Schs. Oriental Research, Kappa Delta Rho, Tau Kappa Alpha, Phi Kappa Phi, Theta Phi. Club: Lions (Westfield). Home: Westfield IN 46074 Office: Butler University Indianapolis IN 46208

ANDRZEJEWSKI, JERZY, author, screenplay writer; b. Warsaw, Poland, Aug. 19, 1909; s. Jan and Eugenia (Glinojecka) A.; grad. Warsaw U., 1931; m. Maria Abgarowicz, Jan. 31, 1946; children—Martin, Agnes. Recipient Cross of Work Banner 1st class, 1949. Author: (novels) Harmony of the Heart (award Youngs of Polish Acad. Lit. 1939), 1938; Ashes and Diamonds (Odrodzenie award 1948. Red Rose award 1964. Golden Ear award 1965, both for best book written in Poland postwar period), 1947; The Inquisitors, 1957; The Gates of Paradise, 1961; A Sitter for a Satyr, 1963; The Appeal, 1968; (stories) The Inevitable Ways, 1937; Night, 1945; The Golden Fox, 1955; As if the Grove, 1961; The Mash, 1970; Prowetheus, 1971; others. Address: 53/4 Swierczewskiego Warsaw Poland

ANDY, ORLANDO JOSEPH, educator, surgeon; b. New Britain, Conn., Jan. 21, 1920; s. Jack and Josephine (Berloni) A.; B.S., Ohio U., 1942; M.D., U. Rochester, 1945; m. Louise C. Murphy, June 11, 1960; childrenMaria, Orlando Joseph, Patrick Murphy, John Christopher, Paul Marlin. Intern St. Francis Hosp., intern Baptist Meml. Hosp.. Memphis, 1948-49; fellow neuropathology U. Ill. Neuropsychiat. Inst., Chgo., 1949-50; neurosurg. resident Bapt. Meml. Hosp. and John Gaston Hosp., Memphis, 1950-52; fellow, resident neurol. surgery John Hopkins, 1952-53, intstr. neurol. surgery, also USPHS fellow div. neurol. surgery, 1953-55; prof., head div. neurosurgery U. Miss. Med. Center, Jackson, 1955-60, prof., head dept. neurosurgery, 1960-. Served with AUS, 1946-48. Diplomate Am. Bd. Neurol. Surgery. Mem. Am. Acad. Cerebral Palsy, Am. Acad. Neurology, A.C.S., Am. Epilepsy Soc., Am. Fedn. Clin. Research, Am. Heart Assn., Am., So. med. assns., Assn. Research Nervous and Mental Diseases, Carribean, So. neurol. socs., Congress Neurol. Surgeons, Am., Eastern, So. electroencephalagraphic assns., Cushing Soc., Law-Sci. Acad., Midwestern Psychol. Assn., Neurol. Soc. Am., N.Y. Acad. Scis., Pavlovian Soc., Sigma Xi, Alpha Omega Alpha. Home: Route 1 Box 131 Madison MS 39110

ANET, FRANK ADRIEN LOUIS, educator; b. Doulcon, France, Oct. 24, 1926; s. Adrien Louis and Anna (Giorcelli) A.; B.Sc. (hon.), U. Sydney, 1949, M.Sc., 1950; D.Phil., U. Oxford, 1952; m. Reginni Phadke, May 29, 1955. Postdoctoral fellow Nat. Research Council of Can., 1953-54; asst. prof. U. Ottawa, 1954-55, asso. prof., 1955-62, prof., 1962-64; vis. prof. U. Cal. at Los Angeles, 1963, prof. chemistry, 1964—. Fellow Chem. Soc. London; mem. Am. Chem. Soc., Sigma Xi. Editorial bd. of Jour. Magnetic Resonance. Contbr. articles sci. jours. Home: 10501 Wilshire Blvd Los Angeles CA 90024

ANFINSEN, CHRISTIAN BOEHMER, biochemist; b. Monessen, Pa., Mar. 26, 1916; s. Christian Boehmer and Sophie (Rasmussen) A.; B.A., Swarthmore Coll., 1937, D.Sc., 1965; M.S., U. Pa., 1939; Ph.D., Harvard, 1943; D.Sc., Georgetown U., 1967; m. Florence Bernice Kenenger, Nov. 29, 1941; children—Carol Bernice, Margot Sophie, Christian Boehmer. Am.- Scandinavian Found. fellow Carlsberg Lab., Copenhagen, 1939. Rockefeller fellow, 1954-55; sr. cancer research fellow Med. Nobel Inst., Stockholm. Sweden. 1947; asst. prof. biol. chemistry, Markle scholar Harvard Med. Sch., 1948-50, prof. biochemistry, 1962-63; Guggenheim fellow Weizmann Inst., Rehovot, Israel. 1958; chief lab. cellular physiology and metabolism Nat. Heart Inst., Bethesda, Md., 1950-62; chief lab. chem. biology Nat. Inst. Arthritis and Metabolic Diseases. Bethesda, 1963—. Bd. govs. Weizmann Inst. Sci., Rehosot, Israel. Mem. Am. Soc. Biol. Chemists (pres. 1971-72), Am. Acad. Arts and Scis., Nat. Acad. Scis., Washington Acad. Scis., Fedn. Am. Scientists (treas. 1958-59, vice chmn. 1959-60). Author: The Molecular Basis of Evolution, 1959. Contbr. to sci. publs. Home: 8 West Dr Bethesda MD 20014 Office: National Inst Arthritis and Metabolic Diseases Bethesda MD 20014

ANG, ALFREDO HUA-SING, engring educator; b. Philippines, July 4, 1930; s. Tiong and Khio (Lim) A.; came to U.S., 1955, naturalized, 1968; B.S. in Civil Engring., Mapua Inst. Tech., Manila, Philippines, 1954; M.S., U. Ill., 1957, Ph.D., 1959; m. Myrtle Be Lim, Dec. 23, 1954; children—Evelyn Lim, Irene Beatrice, James Alfred. Structural designer Mulvaney-McMillan Co., Manila, 1954- 55; research asst., then research asso. U. Ill. at Urbana, 1955-59, mem. faculty, 1959—, prof. civil engring., 1965—, asso. mem. Center Advanced Study, 1964-65; cons. in field, 1960. Recipient Walter L. Huber civil engring. research prize Am. Soc. C.E., 1968. Asso. fellow Am. Inst. Aeros. and Astronautics; mem. Internat. Assn. for Bridge and Structural Engring. (mem. safety commn. European concrete com.), Am. Soc. M.E., Am. Soc. C.E. (chmn. task com. structural safety, probabilistic methods in engring; chmn. com. plasticity, math. methods), Am. Soc. Engring. Edn., Sigma Xi (treas. U. Ill. 1966-68), Phi Kappa Phi. Author papers in field. Mem. editorial bd. Jour. Structural Mechanics. Home: 2204 Combes St Urbana IL 61801

ANGEL, GROVER LAMARR, educator; b. Mars Hill, N.C., July 2, 1909; s. Samuel W. and Sue (Gardner) A.; A.B., High Point Coll., 1929; M.A., George Washington U., 1946, Ed. D., 1952; spl. student U. N.C., summer 1930, Northwestern U., 1950; m. Mary Nell English, Dec. 27, 1937; 1 dau., Carolyn Sue. Tchr. English, sci. Denton (N.C.) High Sch., 1929-31; tchr. English. Spring Creek (N.C.) High Sch., 1931-35; tchr. sci. Beech Glen (N.C.) High Sch., 1935-37; head English dept. Marshall (N.C.) High Sch., 1937-39; prin. Hot Springs (N.C.) High Sch., 1939-42; corr. Asheville (N.C.) Citizen-Times, 1931-42; spl. investigator Dun & Bradstreet, Inc., Washington, 1942-44, mgr., 1944-46; cons. Office of Naval Research, Navy Dept., 1946; employment adviser sci. personnel div. Navy Dept. and Naval Research Lab., 1946-47; research asso. Am. Council on Edn., 1947-50; asst. to dean Coll. Gen. Studies, George Washington U., 1950-51, asst. dir. off-campus div., 1951-53, dir., 1954-56, asst. dean, 1956-57, dean, 1957-66, lectr. edn. Sch. Edn., 1950-55, professorial lectr. edn. 1955-57, asso. prof. edn., 1957-59, prof., 1959—. Lectr. Edn. Am. Council Edn., Internat. House, 1954-55. Mem. Naval Labs. Adv. Com. on Sci. Personnel, 1946-50; pres. Washington chpt. Nat. Cystic Fibrosis Research Found., 1959-61, 65-67, pres. region IV, 1960-62, nat. trustee, 1962—; mem. steering com. Tng. Officers Conf., 1960-62; U.S. del. World Congress U. Adult Edn., Denmark, 1965. Recipient High Point Coll. alumnus of year award, 1957. Mem. A.A.A.S., Am. Edn. Research Assn., Nat. Vocational Guidance Assn., Am. Assn. Higher Edn., Assn. U. Evening Colls. (pres. region 5, 1963), Nat. U. Extension Assn., Adult Edn. Assn. U.S.A., Soc. Advancement Mgmt., Soc. Personnel Adminstrn., N.E.A., N.C. Edn. Assn., Am. Assn. U. Profs., Fed. Schoolmen's Club, Jr. Order of United Am. Mechanics, Phi Delta Kappa (chpt. pres. 1953-54, area coordinator dist. VI 1955-58, faculty sponsor 1955—), Alpha Sigma Lambda (faculty sponsor 1965), Epsilon Eta Phi. Democrat. Methodist. Mason (Shriner). Author: Poetry in Contemporary American Poets, 1937-38; Teacher Application Forms, 1946; The Management of Internal School Finance, 1952. Home: 10108 Green Forest Dr Hillandale Forest Silver Spring MD 20903 Office: George Washington U Washington DC 20006

ANGEL, HERBERT EDMUND, govt. ofcl.; b. Roanoke, Va., Apr. 12, 1907; s. Lewis Cabell and Mary (Pearce) A.; A.B., George Washington U., 1930, M.A., 1932; postgrad. Johns Hopkins U., 1932-33, Am. U., 1938-43; m. Virginia Katherine Burbank, Apr. 18, 1936; 1 dau., Dorothy Pearce. Staff State Dept., 1932- 36; asst. to dir. publs., later asst. to archivist U.S., Nat. Archives, 1936-43; dir. records mgmt. div. Nat. Archives and Records Service, Gen. Services Adminstrn., 1950-56, asst. archivist of U.S. in charge of Office Records Mgmt., 1956-59, 62-64, asst. archivist Office Fed. Records Centers, 1964-68; dep. archivist of U.S., 1968—; dir. of adminstrn. Gen. Services Adminstrn. 1959-62; dir. office methods div. Adminstrv. Office, Navy Dept., 1946-50; lectr. Am. U., 1938-42, 52, 60- 61, adj. prof., 1961-68; dir. Inst. on Records Mgmt., 1956-59, 64. Mem. task force on records mgmt., paperwork mgmt. Hoover Commns., 1948-54. Served from lt. to comdr. USNR, 1943-46; asst. dir., then dir. records adminstrn. Recipient Career Service award Nat. Civil Service League, 1955. Mem. Soc. Am. Archivist. (pres. 1966-67), Sigma Alpha Epsilon. Mason. Home: 8919 Brickyard Rd Potomac MD 20854 Office: Nat Archives and Records Service Gen Services Adminstrn Washington DC 20408

ANGEL, JOHN LAWRENCE, anthropologist; b. London, Eng., Mar. 21, 1915; s. John and Elizabeth Day (Seymour) A.; came to U.S., 1928, naturalized, 1937; grad. Choate Sch., 1932; A.B. magna cum laude, Harvard, 1936, Ph.D., 1942; m. Margaret Seymour Richardson, July 1, 1937; children—Elizabeth Richardson (Mrs. Joel H. Feigon), Stephen Bearne, Jonathan Seymour. Asst. anthropology Harvard, 1939-41; instr. anthropology U. Cal. at Berkeley, 1941-42, U. Minn., 1942-43; mem. faculty Jefferson Med. Coll., Phila., 1943-62, prof. anatomy, phys. anthropology, 1962, vis. prof., 1962-71; curator phys. anthropology Smithsonian Instn., 1962—; field work Greece, Turkey, Cyprus, 1937-39, 49, 54, 57, 65, 67, 69; professorial lectr. George Washington U., 1962—; vis. prof. Howard U. Sch. Medicine, 1965-70; Johns Hopkins Sch. Pub. Health, 1965—. Cons. surg. anatomy U.S. Naval Hosp., Phila., 1957-62; mem. adv. panel anthropology NSF, 1960-62. Guggenheim fellow, 1949. Mem. Am. Assn. Phys. Anthropologists (sec.- treas. 1952-56), Am. Anthropol. Assn., Am. Soc. Human Genetics, Am. Assn. Anatomists, Archaeol. Inst. Am., Council Old World Archaeology (trustee), A.A.A.S., N.Y. Acad. Sci., Greek Anthrop. Soc. (corr.). Author: Troy, The Human Remains, 1951; Lerna, the People, 1971; also articles. Home: 5311 Wriley Rd Washington DC 20016 Office: Div Physical Anthropology Smithsonian Instn Washington DC 20560

ANGELAKOS, DIOGENES JAMES, educator; b. Chgo., July 3, 1919; s. James and Georgia B.S., U. Notre Dame. 1942; M.S., Harvard, 1946, Ph.D., 1950; m. Helen Hatzilambrou, Dec. 29, 1946; childrenErica, Demetri. Engr., Westinghouse Electric Co., 1942-43; instr. U. Notre Dame, 1943-46; teaching fellow Cruft Labs., Harvard, 1947-49, research asst. at univ., 1949-50; asst. prof. U. Notre Dame, 1950-51; mem. elec. engring and computer scis. dept. U. Cal. at Berkeley, 1951-, prof., 1960-, dir. Electronics Research Lab., 1964-, vice chmn. dept., 1964-; liaison scientist Office Naval Research, Am. embassy, London, 1961-62. fellow, 1957-58. Fellow I.E.E.E.; mem. Sigma Xi, Eta Kappa Nu, Tau Beta Pi, Author: (with T.E. Everhart) Microwave Communications, 1968: also numerous articles. Home: 978 Euclid Av Berkeley, CA 94708.

ANGELL, DONALD KINNEY, found. exec.; b. Cortland, N.Y., Nov. 14, 1906; s. Walter Halbert and Harriet (Kinney) A.; B.S. in econs., U. Pa., 1930; children—Donald, Margaret, Stephen; m. Madelon Cunningham, 1955; stepchildren—Mary Cunningham, Frank Cunningham, Victoria C. Baldwin. Editor field service State Mut. Life Ins. Co., 1930-33, asst. gen. agt., N.Y.C., 1933-37; exec. sec. U. Pa., 1937-38, asst. to dir. Bicentennial Celebration, 1939- 40, asst. mgr. U. Council on Devel., 1941, dir. Houston Hall, 1941-45, gen. mgr. Council on Devel., 1945-46, sec. corp., 1946- 51, v.p. charge univ. fund, sec. corp., 1951-55, v.p., asst. to pres., 1956-70; sr. v.p. U. Pa. Found., 1970—. Dir. Bellevue-Stratford Co., West Phila. Corp. Bd. dirs. Phila. Civic Center, Conv. and Visitors Bur., Pathway Sch. Mem. Ams. Competitive Enterprise System (dir.), Kappa Alpha (trustee). Republican. Episcopalian. Clubs: Bachelors Barge: Philadelphia Country, Rittenhouse. Home: 1930 Rittenhouse Sq Philadelphia PA 19103 Office: Franklin Bldg U Pa Philadelphia PA 19104

ANGELL, ERNEST lawyer; b. Cleve., June 1, 1889; s. Elgin Adelbert and Lily (Curtis) A.; A.B., Harvard, 1911, LL.B., 1913; LL.D., Bard Coll., 1954; m. 1915 (div. 1929); children—Nancy (Mrs. Stableford), Roger, Christopher C., Abigail B.; m. 2d, Elizabeth B. Chapin, 1939. Admitted to Ohio bar, 1914, N.Y. bar, 1920; practiced in Cleve., 1913-17, in N.Y.C., 1920—; mem. firm Hardin, Hess & Eder, 1922-36; regional adminstr. for N.Y., SEC, 1936-38; mem. firm Spence, Hotchkiss, Parker & Duryee, 1938-54. Served to capt., inf. U.S. Army, 1917-19; A.E.F. Trustee Briarcliff Coll. Chmn. N. Y. area Loyalty Rev. Bd., 1948-50. Mem. Am., N.Y. State bar assns., N.Y. County Lawyers Assn., Assn. Bar City N.Y., Am. Civil Liberties Union (past chmn.), Am. Assn. for Free Jurists (chmn. bd.), Phi Beta Kappa. Clubs: Century Assn., Harvard, River (N.Y.C.). Author: Supreme Court Primer, 1937; Les Aspects Constitutionnels des Libertés Publiques aux Etats-Unis, 1964. Editor: The Rule of Law in the United States, 1958, 62. Contbr. articles to lit. jours. and law revs. Home: 156 E 66th St New York City NY 10021

ANGELL, GEORGE WARD, univ. pres., educator; b. Ilion, N.Y., June 19, 1912; s. Earl Warren and Lily (Ward) A.; B.S., Ohio State U., 1934, M.A., 1939; Ph.D., Syracuse U., 1947, LL.D., 1956; m. Ruth Theodora Humphrey, June 29, 1939; children—Susan, Eric, Carol. High sch. math. tchr., Chillicothe, O., 1934-37; high sch. math. and phys. edn. tchr., Earlville, N.Y., 1937-42; supervising prin. Central Sch., Earlville, 1942-45; asst. dir. Evaluation Service Center, Syracuse U., 1945-47; chmn. dept. higher edn. Mich. State Coll., 1947-49; dean State U. Coll., New Paltz, N.Y., 1949-53; pres. State U. N.Y. Coll. at Plattsburgh, 1954—. Mem. Am. Psychol. Assn., Am. Ednl. Research Assn., Nat. Soc. for Advancement of Teaching, N.E.A., Nat. Soc. Study Edn., A.A.A.S., Am. Assn. Sch. Adminstrs. Contbr. articles to ednl. jours. Home: 133 Court St Plattsburgh NY 12901

ANGELL, JAMES BROWNE, engring. educator; b. Staten Island, N.Y., Dec. 25, 1924; s. and Jessie (Browne) A.; S.B., S.M., Mass. Inst. Tech., 1946, Sc.D. in Elec. Engring., 1952; m. Elizabeth Isabelle Rice, July 22, 1950; childrenCharles Lawrence, Carolyn Corson. Research asst. Mass. Inst. Tech., 1946-51; mgr. solid-state circuit research, research div. Philco Corp., Phila., 1951-60; mem. faculty Stanford, 1960-, prof. elec. engring., 1962—, dir. Solid-State Electronics Lab., 1964-71, asso. industry and govt., 1960-. Mem. electronics adv. group for comdg. gen. U.S. Army Electronics Command, 1964—; mem. U.S. Army Sci. Adv. Panel, 1968-. Carillonneur, Stanford, 1960-; area chmn. town incorporation com. Portola Valley, Cal., 1963-64. Bd. dirs. Portola Valley Assn., 1964-67. Fellow I.E.E.E. (chmn. internat solid state circuits conf. 1964); mem. Am. Guild Organists, Guild Carillonneurs in N. Am. (dir. 1969—, rec. sec. 1970—), Am. Assn. U. Prof., A.A.A.S. Author sect. book. Home: 30 Shoshone Pl Portola Valley, CA 94025. Office: Stanford Electronics Lab Stanford CA 94305

ANGELL, JAMES WATERHOUSE, economist; b. Chgo., May 20, 1898; s. James Rowland and Marion Isabel (Watrous) A.; A.B., Harvard, 1918, A.M., 1921, Ph.D., 1924; student U. Chgo., 1919-20; m. Jane Norton Grew, Oct. 19, 1923; children—James Grew, Edward Dexter (dec.). Asst. in econs. U. Chgo., 1919-20; instr. in econs. Harvard, 1921-22, 23-24; lectr. in econs. Columbia, 1924-26, asso. prof., 1926-31, prof., 1931-66, prof. emeritus, 1966—; vis. prof. New Sch. Social Research, 1966-67; Office Civilian Requirements, WPB and predecessor units, 1941-43; with Fgn. Econ. Adminstrn., 1943-45, asst. adminstr., 1945; U.S. rep. with rank of minister Allied Commn. on Reparations, Germany, 1945-46; dir. United Funds-Can. Internat., 1961-70. Vice chmn. Anthracite Coal Industry Commn., Pa., 1937-38. Tech. adviser U.S. delegation to UN Monetary-Financial Conf., 1944; U.S. del. to Paris Conf. on Reparations, 1945; cons. Nat. Security Resources Bd., 1948-50, UN, 1951. Fellow Am. Acad. Arts and Scis.; mem. Am. Econ. Assn. (v.p. 1940), Royal Econ. Soc. (Eng), Acad. Polit. Sci., Council on Fgn. Relations, Phi Beta Kappa. Episcopalian. Club: Century Assn. (N.Y.C.). Author: The Theory of International Prices, 1926; The Recovery of Germany, 1929, 32; Der Wiederaufbau Deutschlands, 1930; Financial Foreign Policy of the U.S., 1933; The Behavior of Money, 1936; Investment and Business Cycles, 1941; co-author, Measures for International Economic Stability, 1951. Contbr. articles to profl. jours. Home: West Chop MA 02573

ANGELL, PHILIP HAROLD lawyer; b. Newark Valley, N.Y., Mar. 21, 1896; s. Charles Everett Adelaide C. (Turner) A.; B.A., U. Cal., 1919; LL.B., Harvard, 1921; m. Ethel F. Chappelka, Sept. 14, 1921; childrenDorothy F., Philip Harold. Admitted to Cal. bar, 1921, since practiced in San Francisco; partner Athearn, Chandler, Hoffman & Angell, 1922-50; sr. partner firm Angell, Adams & Holmes. Pres., sec., dir. S.D.E. Corp.; dir. Fidelity Savs. & Loan Assn., Tracy Drilling Corp. Mem. Cal. Bd. Bar Examiners, 1942-45, chmn. bd., 1944-45. Mem. bd. edn., Berkeley, 1935; chmn. adv. panel Cal. Youth Correction Authority, 1941-42; mem. Personnel Bd., Berkeley, 1937-59, chmn., 1937-58: former vice chmn. Nat. Loyalty Bd., 12th Regional Office, Civil Service Commn. Mem. State Bar Cal. (gov. 1939-42, pres. 1941-42), Am., Fed., San Francisco bar assns., Am. Judicature Soc., Nat. Legal Aid Assn., Am. Soc. Internat. Law, Cal. Alumni Assn., Harvard Law School Assn., Lambda Chi. Clubs: Harvard, Olympic (San Francisco), Lawyers; Los Angeles Athletic. Home: 50 Florida Av Berkeley CA 94707 Office: 200 Bush St San Francisco CA 94104

ANGELL, RICHARD BRADSHAW, educator; b. Scarsdale, N.Y., Oct. 14, 1918; s. Stephen LeRoy and Alice (Angel) A.; B.A., Swarthmore Coll., 1940; M. Govt. Adminstrn., U. Pa., 1948; M.A. in Philosophy, Harvard, 1948, Ph.D. in Philosophy, 1954; m. Imogene Lucille Baker, June 4, 1949; children—John Baker, Paul McLean, James Bigelow, David Bradshaw, Kathryn Elizabeth. Acting asst. prof. Fla. State U., 1949-51; asst. prof. Ohio Wesleyan U., 1954-58, asso. prof., 1958-63, prof., 1963-68; prof., chmn. philosophy dept. Wayne State U., 1968—. Served to capt., Med. Adminstrv. Corps, AUS, 1942-45. Mem. Am. Assn. U. Profs., Am. Philos. Assn., Am. Civil Liberties Union. Mem. Soc. of Friends. Home: 1297 E Maple Rd Birmingham MI 48008 Office: 691 Merrick Detroit MI 48202

ANGELL, ROBERT COOLEY, sociologist, educator; b. Detroit, Apr. 29, 1899; s. Alexis Caswell and Fanny Carey (Cooley) A.; A.B., U. Mich., 1921, A.M., 1922, Ph.D., 1924; Hum.D., Western Mich. U., 1967; m. Esther Robbins Kennedy, Dec. 23, 1922; children—James Kennedy, Sarah Caswell. Instr. sociology U. Mich., Ann Arbor, 1922-26, asst. prof., 1926-30, asst. prof., 1930-35, prof., 1935-69, prof. emeritus, 1969—, chmn. dept. sociology, 1940-52, dir. Coll. Honors Program, 1957-61; co-dir. Center for Research on Conflict Resolution, 1961-65; exec. dir. Sociol. Resources for Secondary Schs., 1966-71. Dir. Tensions Project, UNESCO, Paris, 1949-50; mem. U.S. Nat. Commn. for UNESCO, 1950-56, vice chmn. commn., 1953; Deiches lectr. Johns Hopkins, 1957. Mem. Charter Study Commn., Ann Arbor, 1953-55. Aviation cadet, 1918-19; capt., lt. col. A.C., 1942-45, Decorated Bronze Star. Mem. Internat. (pres. 1953-56), Am. (pres. 1951) sociol assns., Mich. Sociol. Soc., Am. Civil Liberties Union, Am. Assn. U. Profs., Sociol. Research Assn., Mich. Acad. Scis., Arts and Letters, Internat. Studies Assn., Research Club (U. Mich.), Phi Beta Kappa, Delta Kappa Epsilon. Democrat. Club: Ann Arbor Golf and Outing. Author: The Campus, 1928; A Study in Undergraduate Adjustment, 1930; The Family Encounters the Depression, 1936; The Integration of American Society, 1941; The Moral Integration of American Cities. 1951; Free Society and Moral Crisis, 1958; Peace on the March, 1969; also articles in sociol. jours. Editor Am. Sociol. Rev., 1946-48. Home: 1007 Berkshire Rd Ann Arbor MI 48104 ☆

ANGELL, WARREN MATHEWSON, music educator; b. Bklyn., May 13, 1907; s. Earl Warren and Lily (Ward) A.; B.Mus., Syracuse U., 1929, M.Mus., 1933; Ed.D., Columbia, 1944; summer study Eastman Sch. Music, 1937, with Eisenberger, Vienna, 1931; m. Evalyn Juliette Wells, Sept. 6, 1934; children—Richard Franz, Sally, Juliette. Head piano dept. Murray (Ky.) Tchrs. Coll., 1935-36; dean coll. fine arts Okla. Bapt. U., also dir. Bison Glee Club, 1936—; mem., condr., arranger and soloist Fred Waring's Pennsylvanians, also mem. and soloist Robert Shaw's Collegiate Chorale, 1942-44. Mem. bd. So. Baptist Theol. Sem. Honored by resolution of Okla. Senate, 1971. Fellow Am. Inst. Vocal Pedagogy, Internat. Inst. Arts and Letters, Nat. Assn. Tchrs. Singing; mem. A.S.C.A.P. (award 1970-71), Am. Choral Dirs. Assn. (founder mem.), So. Bapt. Ch. Music Conf. (hon. life), Nat. Assn. Schs. Music, Sigma Phi Epsilon, Phi Mu Alpha, Kappa Delta Pi, Phi Delta Kappa. Elk, Lion (coach Shawnee Quartet). Author: Vocal Approach, 1950; Choir Clinic Manual, 1952; The Beginning Vocalist, 1956; The Progressing Vocalist, 1957; The Advanced Vocalist, 1958. Composer many choral works. Contbr. music jours. Dir. clinics, festivals Midwest, South, S.W. U.S. Dir. Tuneclippers, U.S.O. coll. touring group, Far East, 1963, Europe, 1965. Home: 1920 N Bell St Shawnee OK 74801

ANGELO, BONNIE (Mrs. Harold R. Levy), newspaper corr.; b. Winston-Salem, N.C.; d. Ernest J. and Ethel (Hudgins) Angelo; B.A., U. N.C.; m. Harold R. Levy, Aug. 19, 1950; 1 son, Charles Christopher. Reporter, women's editor Winston-Salem Jour. & Sentinel, 1944-50; women's editor Richmond Times-Dispatch, 1950; feature writer Newsday, 1953-55, Washington corr., 1955-63; syndicated columnist Newhouse Nat. News Service, 1963-66; Washington corr. Time mag., 1966—, weekly feature WTTG-TV, 1967—. Pres. Women's Nat. Pres. distinguished reporting in civil rights Paul Tobenkin Meml. Found., 1961. Mem. White House Corrs. Assn. Home: 5401 Edgemoor Lane Bethesda MD 20014 Office: 888 16th St NW Washington DC 20006

ANGELO, FRANK, newspaperman; b. Detroit, Sept. 6, 1914; s. Nicolo and Ida (Carini) A.; B.A., Wayne State U., 1934; m. Elizabeth Paton Stoll, Feb. 25, 1950; children—Frank, Andrew. From copy boy to copy reader sports dept. Detroit News, 1934-41; sports writer, copy reader, feature editor Detroit Free Press, 1941-52, asst. to exec. editor, 1952-55, mng. editor, 1955-71, asso. exec. editor, 1971—. Mem. A.P. Mng. Editors (past nat. exec. bd.). Mich. A.P. Assn. (pres. 1967), Mich. Press Assn. (pres. 1969), Mackenzie Honor Soc., Sigma Delta Chi (pres. Detroit, 1956-57, nat. pres. 1969-70). Home: 14424 Rutland St Detroit MI 48227 Office: Detroit Free Press 321 W Lafayette Av Detroit MI 48226

ANGELO, HAROLD EDWARD, banker; b. Edwards, Miss., Aug. 30, 1924; s. Victor Joseph and Mary (McPhearson) A.; B.S., Miss. State U., 1947; LL.B., U. Mich., 1951, M.B.A., 1954; m. Margaret Alice Hodges, Jan. 31, 1953; children—Elizabeth Margaret, Mary, Paul, Jane. Asso. prof. bus. adminstrn., asst. dean Amos Tuck Sch., Dartmouth 1955-59; dean men U. Colo., 1959-63; sr. v.p., trust officer Colo. Nat. Bank, Denver, 1963-71. Served to capt. USMCR, 1943-46, 51-52. Mem. Gov.'s Econ. Research Com. Mem. Blue Key, Beta Gamma Sigma, Omicron Delta Kappa, Phi Delta Phi, Phi Kappa Tau (nat. pres. 1959-62). Clubs: Serra, University. Home: 3400 E 7th Av Pkwy Denver CO 80206 Office: Colorado Nat Bank PO Box 5168 TA Denver CO 80202

ANGER, FRANK GEORGE, banker; b. Muskegon, Mich., Aug. 2, 1906; s. Frank H. and Lillian (Stroemer) A.; student Northwestern U., 1925-28; LL.B., Chgo. Kent Coll. Law, 1936; m. Julia Vrooman, Sept. 7, 1934; children—Arthur, Frank D. With Indsl. Nat. Bank of Chgo., 1926, asst. sec., 1937, v.p., 1942, pres., dir., 1946; admitted to Ill. bar, 1936; v.p. Chgo. Nat. Bank, 1948-54, dir., 1953-61, pres., 1955-61; sr. v.p. Harris Trust & Savings Bank, 1961; with Winters Nat. Bank, Dayton, O., 1961—, now chmn. bd. Commr., Glen Ellyn Park Dist., 1949-54, pres., 1954-; bd. mgrs. Chgo. YMCA, treas. 1957; chmn. Chgo. council Boy Scouts Am., received Silver Beaver award, 1955; pres. Air Force Mus. Found. Mem. Ill. Bankers Assn. (v.p. 1958—). Clubs: Executive, Economic, Attic, Commonwealth (Chgo.). Home: 351 Fawnwood Rd Dayton OH 45429 Office: 40 N Main St Dayton OH 45402

ANGEVINE, DANIEL MURRAY, physician; b. Saint John, N.B., Can., Oct. 8, 1903; s. James Edwin and Mary Edna (Irvine) A.; B.A., Mt. Allison U., 1924; M.D., C.M., McGill U., 1929; m. Dorothy Edna Shepherd, July 8, 1933; children—James Murray, Charles Douglas, Judith Melanie. Came to U.S., 1932, naturalized, 1942. Resident pathologist Montreal Gen. Hosp., 1929-30; intern U. Pa. Hosp., 1930-32; asst. pathologist N.Y. Hosp., also instr. and asst. prof. pathology, med. coll. Cornell U., 1932-40; pathologist A.I. duPont Inst., Wilmington, Del., 1940-45; vis. asst. prof. path. U. Pa., 1940-45; prof. pathology, dept. chmn. med. sch. U. Wis., 1945-68; pathologist U. Hosps., 1945-68; asso. dir. research Armed Forces Inst. Pathology, 1968—; area cons. pathology VA, 1946-68; cons. pathologist Surgeon Gen. U.S. Army, 1948-68, NRC, 1949-52, USPHS, 1947-52; mem. com. on skeletal system NRS, 1959-66; mem. study group in host factors in lung cancer Am. Cancer Soc., 1959; chief research pathologist Atomic Bomb Casualty Commn., Hiroshima, Japan, 1962-63. Served from maj. to col. AUS, 1942-45; ETO. Mem. Am. Assn. Path. and Bact. (pres. 1961-62), Soc. Med. Consultants to Armed Forces, Am. Soc. Exptl. Path. (council, pres. 1953), Soc. Exptl. Biol. and Medicine (council 1950-52), Am. Soc. Clin. Investigation, Harvey Soc., A.M.A., Am. Rheumatism Assn. (exec. council), Am. Socs. for Exptl. Biology (chmn. fed. bd. 1954), Assn. Mil. Surgeons, Washington Acad. Medicine. Author: Atlas of Orthopedic Pathology, 1943. Contbr. to Confs. on Connective Tissue Macy Found., 1950-54; Mechanism of Inflammation (Jasm and Robert), 1954; Diseases of Connective Tissue (Asboe-Hansen), 1954; Recent Trends in Pathology (Collins), 1959. Chief editor Archives of Pathology. Home: 1220 East West Hwy Silver Spring MD 20910 Office: Armed Forces Inst Pathology Washington DC 20305

ANGEVINE, ERNEST GROESBECK, lawyer; b. Highland, N.Y., June 15, 1901; s. Jay Ferris and Sarah (Bernard) A.; B.A., Williams Coll., 1923; LL.B., Harvard, 1927; m. Helen Crosby, Oct. 6, 1928; children—William, Faith (Mrs. Jan D. Curran), Helen (Mrs. Howard E. Smith, Jr.), Richard. Admitted to Mass. bar, 1927, since practiced in Boston; partner firm Hutchins & Wheeler, 1936—. Trustee W. Newton Savs. Bank (Mass.), 1940—, v.p., 1966—; treas., dir.

Acme-Walnut, Inc. Chmn., Newton (Mass.) Retirement System, 1954—; mem. Newton Licensing Bd., 1969—. Alderman, City of Newton, 1946-54; v.p. bd., 1948-54; mem. Republican ward and city com., also city finance com. Trustee Children's Mus., Boston, 1934—, pres., 1964-66; trustee Newton YMCA, Newton-Wellesley Hosp.; trustee, v.p. Newton Cemetery. 1970—. Mem. Am., Boston bar assns., Phi Gamma Delta. Mem. United Ch. Christ (deacon 1956-62). Mason. Club: Brae Burn Country (bd. dirs. 1966-70) (West Newton). Home: 95 Prince St West Newton MA 02165 Office: 1 Boston Pl Boston MA 02108

ANGLE, JOHN ELMER, steel exec.; b. Mansfield, O., Oct. 3, 1909; s. John Elmer and Nellie Laverne (McClelland) A.; B.S., Lehigh U., 1932; m. Gertrude Fletcher, Mar. 29, 1935; childrenPeter Fletcher, Anthony John, Jeffrey David, Burleigh Paul. Metallurgist, Gary Sheet Mill, Am. Sheet & Tin Plate Co., 1932-36; div. supt. Gary Sheet & Tin Mill, U.S. Steel Corp., 1936-44, asst. gen. supt., 1944-52, gen. supt., 1952-55, v.p. indsl. engring. U.S. Steel Corp., Pitts., 1955-60, adminstrv. v.p.- prodn., steel producing divs., 1960-64, adminstrn. v.p. prodn. services, 1964-67, adminstrv. v.p. steel operations, 1967-69, exec. v.p. prodn., 1969—. Past pres. Gary Pub. Library Bd.; pres. Pitts. Symphony Soc. Mem. Am. Mgmt. Assn., Am. Iron and Steel Inst., Phi Gamma Delta, Tau Beta Pi. Republican. Presbyn. Home: Persimmon Rd RD 3 Sewickley PA 15143 Office: 525 William Penn Pl Pittsburgh PA 15230

ANGLE, PAUL MCCLELLAND, historian, writer; b. Mansfield, O., Dec. 25, 1900; s. John Elmer and Nellie Laverne (McClelland) A.; student Oberlin Coll., 1918-19; A.B., Miami U., Oxford, O., 1922, Litt.D., 1966; A.M., U. Ill., 1924; Litt.D., Augustana Coll., 1941 LL.D., Knox Coll., 1944; L.H.D., Ill. Coll., 1947; LL.D., Lake Forest, 1965; m. Vesta Verne Magee, June 17, 1926; children—Paula, John Edwin. Rep., Am. Book Co., 1924-25; exec. sec. Abraham Lincoln Assn. (formerly Lincoln Centennial Assn.), 1925-32; historian Ill. State Hist. Library and sec. Ill. State Hist. Soc. 1932-45; dir. Chgo. Hist. Soc., 1945-65, sec., 1965-70. Mem. Am., Mississippi Valley hist. assns., Phi Beta Kappa, Sigma Chi. Clubs: Tavern (Chicago), Author: (with Carl Sandburg) Mary Lincoln, Wife and Widow, 1932; Lincoln—1854 to 1861, 1933; Here I Have Lived—A History of Lincoln's Springfield, 1935; (with Richard L. Beyer), Handbook of Illinois History, 1943; A Shelf of Lincoln Books, 1946; The Lincoln Reader, 1947; Bloody Williamson, 1952; By These Words, 1954; (with Earl S. Miers) The Living Lincoln, 1955; The Chicago Historical Society, 1856-1956, 1956 Created Equal? The Complete Lincoln-Douglas Debates, 1958: The American Reader, 1958; (with Earl Schneck Miers) Tragic Years 1860-1865, 1960; Crossroads; 1913, 1963; The Civil War Years in Pictures, 1967; A Portrait of Abraham Lincoln in Letters by his Oldest Son, 1968; Prarie state, 1968. Home: 1802 Lincoln Park W Chicago IL 60614

ANGLE, STACY L., mfg. exec.; b. Berlin, Wis., Jan. 30, 1900; s. Stacy and Emma A.; student high sch. and normal sch.; supplementary courses Mpls. Y.M.C.A. schs., 1921-25; m. Helen Ford, June 25, 1927; childrenMargaret Helen, Stacy Latham. Successively accountant, auditor, controller Minneapolis-Moline Co., 1920-43, treas., 1939-59, 63-, v.p., 1952-60, sr. v.p., 1960-; sr. v.p., treas. Motec, Inc., 1962-; dir. First Nat. Bank, Hopkins, Minn. Mem. Controllers Inst. Am., Nat. Assn. Cost Accountants. Republican. Lutheran. Club: Minikahda (Mpls.). Office: Minneapolis-Moline Co Hopkins MN 55343

ANGLEMIRE, KENNETH NORTON, ret. publishing co. exec., writer, conservationist; b. Chgo.; s. Fred Rutherford and Isabel (Alguire) A.; B.S., U. Ill.; J.D., Chgo.-Kent Coll. Law; m. Anne Hayes. Admitted to Ill. bar; pvt. practice of law to 1936; atty. Chgo. Title and Trust Co., 1936-42; chief accountant, office mgr. Graphic Arts Displays, Inc., Chgo., 1942-50; comptroller Marshall Industries, Chgo., 1950-53; comptroller Marquis-Who's Who, Inc., Chgo., 1953-58, v.p., comptroller, 1958-59, exec. v.p. charge operations, dir., 1959-69, chmn. bd., pub., 1969-70; pres., dir. A.N. Marquis Co., Inc., Chgo., 1964-69. Mem. Ill. State Scholarship Commn., 1966-69; charter mem. bus. adv. council Chgo. Urban League, until 1970. Hon. mem. Staff of N.M. Atty. Gen. Mem. Adult Edn. Council Greater Chgo. (dir. 1968-70), Ill. Audubon Soc. (v.p. finance, dir. 1961-65), Friends of Earth, A.I.M. (fellow pres.'s council), Greater North Michigan Av. Assn. (dir. 1966-70), Dickens Fellowship, N.M. Opera Guild, Old Santa Fe Assn., N.M. Ornithol. Soc., Pi Kappa Alpha, Delta Theta Phi. Mason. Club: Sierra (founder and chmn. Great Lakes chpt. 1959-61, 64-66, mem. exec. com. 1959-69); N.M. Mountain. Writer articles on music, natural history, mountain adventure. Home: 221 Spruce St Santa Fe NM 87501

ANGLIN, JAMES P., lawyer; b. Westmount, Que., Can., Jan. 28, 1912; s. James Penrose and Florence E. (Christy) A.; B.A., McGill U., 1933, B.C.L., 1936; postgrad. U. Paris (France); m. Julia Elizabeth Moore, Sept. 14, 1938; children—Susan Elizabeth (Mrs. Eric W. Winn), Julia Christine, James Penrose. Admitted to Que. bar, 1936; now partner firm Smith, Davis, Anglin, Laing, Weldon & Courtois, Montreal. Chmn. Canadian Schenley Distilleries Ltd.; dir. Fabco Mfg. Ltd., Crown Trust Co. Mem. exec. com. Bishop's U. Mem. Canadian Bar Assn. (v.p. Que. 1967, exec. com. 1968-69), Psi Upsilon. Clubs: University; St. James's Royal Montreal Golf; Royal and Ancient Golf (St. Andrew's, Scotland). Home: 1115 Sherbrooke St W Montreal Quebec Canada Office: 630 Dorchester Blvd W Montreal 101 Quebec Canada*

ANGLUND, JOAN WALSH, author, illustrator; b. Hinsdale, Ill., Jan. 3, 1926; d. Thomas F. and Mildren(Pfiefer) Walsh; student Art. Inst. Chgo., 1944, Am. Acad. Art, 1945; m. Robert Lee Anglund, Nov. 9, 1947; childrenJoy Ann, Todd Emerson. Author, illustrator: A Friend is Someone Who Likes You(N.Y. Times selection as 1 of 10 best illus. books 1958), 1958; The Brave Cowboy, 1959; Look Out the Window, 1959; Love is a Special Way of Feeling, 1960; In a Pumpkin Shell, 1960; The Cowboy and His Friend, 1961; Christmas is a Time of Giving, 1961; Nibble Nibble Mousekin, 1962; Spring is a New Beginning, 1963; Cowboy's Secret Life, 1963; A Pocketful of Proverbs, 1964; Childhood is a Time of Innocence, 1964; A Book of Good Tidings, 1965; What Color is Love, 1966; A Year is Round, 1966; A Cup of Sun, 1967; Amor Est Semsus Quidam Peculiaris, 1968; Hacourt Brace & Jovanovich 757 3d Av New York City NY 10017.

ANGNEY, DAVID HARRY, banker; b. Elk River, Ida., Feb. 23, 1912; s. Haughey H. and Mary E. (Berry) A.; B.A., U. Ida., 1932; M.A., Brown U., 1934, doctoral study, 1934-39; student Brookings Instn., 1934-35; m. Edna M. Rydberg, June 17, 1939; children—David H., Mark N., Brett R. Instr., Brown U., 1939-41, 47-48; research economist R.I. Textile Assn., 1941-46; asst. mgr. Coventry Co. (R.I.), 1946-47; with Fed. Res. Bank Boston, 1948—, sr. v.p., 1970- -; mem. adminstrv. com. Greater Boston Exec. Program, Mass. Inst. Tech.; edn. com. Boston chot. Am. Inst. Banking. Mem. personnel com. Greater Boston YMCA. Mem. personnel bd., Wellesley, Mass., 1960-68. Mem. corp. Perkins Sch. for Blind; bd. govs. Huntington Av. br. YMCA. Mem. Phi Beta Kappa, Delta Sigma Rho, Lambda Chi Alpha. Mem. United Ch. Christ. Home: 8 Riverdale Rd Wellesley Hills MA 02181 Office: 30 Pearl St Boston MA 02106

ANGOFF, CHARLES, educator, author; b. Minsk, Russia, Apr. 22, 1902; s. Jacob Joseph and Anna (Pollack) A.; brought to U.S. 1908, naturalized, 1923; A.B., Harvard; Litt.D., Fairleigh Dickinson U., 1966; m. Sara F. Freedman, June 13, 1943; 1 dau., Nancy Carol (Mrs. Richard G. Gallin). Newspaperman on Boston papers, 1923; mem. editorial staff American Mercury, 1925-31, editor, 1931-34, mng. editor 1934-35; mem. editorial bd. Nation, 1935-36; editor Am. Spectator, 1936; contbg. editor North Am. Rev., 1938-40; Am. commentator The Living Age, 1938-40; mng. editor Am. Mercury 1943-50; exec. editor Mercury Publs. 1950-51; adv. editor True Crime Detective, 1950-51; mng. editor Book of Wit and Humor, 1950-51; lectr. English, U. Kansas City, 1949, 50; lectr. U. N.H., 1951-61; adj. prof. English, Wagner Coll., 1956; prof. English, Fairleigh Dickinson U., 1957—; chief editor Fairleigh Dickinson U. Press, 1967—; adj. prof. lit. N.Y.U., 1958-66. Advisor Jewish Book Guild, 1949—. Fellow Boston U. Libraries, 1964—. Fellow Jewish Acad. Arts and Scis.; mem. Poetry Soc. Am. (pres. 1969—). Author: A Literary History of the American People, vols. I and II, 1931; Palestrina, Savior of Church Music, 1944; (play) Something to Sing About (produced Pasadena Playhouse), 1940; (play) Moment Musical (produced N.Y.C.), 1943; Adventures in Heaven (short stories), 1945; The Book of Libel, 1946; When I Was a Boy in Boston (short stories), 1947; The Fathers of Classical Music, 1947; Journey to the Dawn, 1951; In the Morning Light, 1953 (Daroff Fiction award 1954); The Sun at Noon, 1955; Something About my Father and Other People, 1956; H.L. Mencken, A Portrait from Memory, 1956; Between Day and Dark, 1959; The Bitter Spring, 1961; Summer Storm, 1963; Memory of Autumn (Davoff Fiction award 1969), 1968; Winter Twilight (novel) (Author award N.J. Assn. Tchrs. English 1970), 1970; Season of Mists (novel), 1971; Prayers at Midnight (poems), 1971. Editor: Arsenal for Skeptics (pen name Richard W. Hinton), 1934; Stradivari, The Violin Maker (by Helen Tinyanova), 1938; (with Joseph Hilton Smyth) The World Over, 2d edit., 1939; (with Leon Bryce Bloch) The World Over, 2d edit., 1940; (with Lawrence E. Spivak) The American Mercury Reader, 1944; The World of George Jean Nathan, 1952; (with Clarence R. Decker) Modern Stories from Many Lands, 1963; The Tone of the Twenties, 1966; The Bell of Time, 1966; The Humanities in the Age of Science, 1968; Memory of Autumn (Daroff Fiction award 1969), 1968; George Sterling: A Centenary Memoir, 1969. Editor The Lit. Review, 1957—. Home: 140 W 86th St New York City NY 10024

ANGRIST, ALFRED ALVIN, pathologist; b. Bklyn., Mar. 25, 1902; s. Isaac and Fannie (Levine) A.; B.S., Coll. City N.Y., 1922, also postgrad.; M.D., L.I. Coll. Medicine 1926; postgrad. Columbia, Rutgers U., N.Y. Eye and Ear Infirmary, McGill U., Poly. Inst., Oak Ridge Inst. Nuclear Studies, Cornell U.; m. Sylvia Maude Kasden, June 9, 1932; 1 son, Burton M. Intern, resident, Bronx, City, Met. hosps.; instr., asst. prof. pathology N.Y. Med. Coll., 1929- 34, asso. prof. pathology, 1934-54; prof., chmn. emeritus dept. pathology Albert Einstein Coll. Medicine, 1954-69; dir. lab. services Bronx Municipal Hosp. Center, 1954-69; cons. Dist. Atty. of Queens County; cons. pathologist Queens Hosp. Center, other hosps. Bd. dirs. Health Ins. Plan Greater N.Y.; bd. govs. Isaac Alpert Research Inst. Fellow Coll. Am. Pathologists (founder); mem. Am. Assn. Pathology and Bacteriology, Am. Soc. Exptl. Pathology, Am. Soc. Clin. Pathology, N.Y. Acad. Medicine, N.Y. Pathol. Soc. (past pres.), Queens County Med. Soc. (past pres.), Queensboro Council Social Welfare (past pres.), Queensboro Tb and Health Assn. (dir.), Internat. Acad. Pathology, N.Y. State Med. Soc., N.J. Soc. Pathology, A.A.A.S., Am. Acad. Forensic Sci., Harvey Soc., Am. Fedn. Clin. Research, N.Y. Acad. Scis., N.Y. State Assn. Approved Pub. Health Labs., A.M.A. Home: 162-01 Powells Cove Blvd Whitestone NY 11357 Office: Albert Einstein College of Medicine Eastchester Rd and Morris Park Av Bronx NY 10461

ANGST, JOHN EDWARD, transp. co. exec.; b. Buhl, Minn., Feb. 21, 1919; s. Robert A. and Virginia (de Haas) A.; A.B., Princeton, 1940; grad. Advanced Mgmt. Program, Harvard, 1956; m. Louise Woodruff, Aug. 14, 1945; children—Robert Woodruff, Carlton Clough, Louise. With Oglebay, Norton & Co., Cleve., 1940-41; v.p. Am. Car & Foundry div. ACF Industries, Inc., 1945-61; gen. mgr. Freight Car div. Gen. Am. Transp. Corp., Chgo., 1961-63, v.p., 1963-64, group v.p., 1964-68; v.p. M.P.R.R., T. & P. Ry., St. Louis, 1968—; chmn. bd. Am. Refrigerator Transit Co., Mo. Improvement Co.; pres., dir. Sebastian County Coal & Mining Co. Trustee Lake Forest Acad., 1953. Served as maj. F.A., AUS, 1941-45. Mem. Newcomen Soc., Am. Soc. M.E. Clubs: Glen View Golf, Chicago, Union League (Chgo.); Cloud (N.Y.C.); Bohemlan (San Francisco); Wings of St. Albans, Old Warson Country, Noonday, St. Louis (St. Louis). Home: 1 Bridle Creek Rd St Louis MO 63124 Office: 210 N 13th St St Louis MO 63103

ANGSTADT, EARLE KERN, Jr., business exec.; b. Reading, Pa., Feb. 16, 1926; s. Earle Kern and Katharine (Auman) A.; A.B., Dartmouth, 1946; m. Suzanne Ferris, Jan. 27, 1951; children—Katharine, Elizabeth. With R.H. Macy & Co., N.Y.C., 1946-51; buyer,dept. mgr., 1948-51; with Young & Rubicam, N.Y.C., 1951-64, v.p., stockholder, 1958-61, sr. v.p., div. mgr., 1961-64; pres., chief exec. officer Abercrombie & Fitch Co., N.Y.C., 1964-70, also chmn. bd., dir; pres. McCall Pattern Co., N.Y.C. 1970—; dir. Theo. C. Auman, Inc.; trustee Manhattan Savs. Bank. Trustee Madison Sq. Boys Club. Clubs: Camp Fire of Am.; Union League, Woodway Gun, N.Y. Yacht (N.Y.C.); Wee Burn Country (Darien, Conn.). Mason (Shriner). Home: Contentment Island Rd Darien CT 06820 Office: 230 Park Av New York City NY 10017

ANGULO, ALBERT WILLIAM, holding co. exec.; b. Madrid, Spain, Aug. 5, 1936; s. Guillermo and Maria Luisa (Urgoiti) A.; came to U.S., 1945, naturalized, 1951; B.S., Lehigh U., 1959; M.B.A., Temple U., 1968; m. Elizabeth Timmins, Mar. 23, 1964; children—Geoffret, Marisa. Trainee to rep. S.A., Girard Trust Bank, Phila., 1959-66; asst. treas., officer charge Latin Am. div. Fidelity Bank, Phila., 1966-70; treas. Internat. Systems & Controls Corp., Houston, 1970—; v.p. Applied Tech. Co., AmVen Corp.; v.p., treas. ISC World Trade Corp., ISC Devel. Corp.; sec., treas. Internat. Rice Marketing Assos.; treas. Rhodes Tech. Corp., Lang Engring. Inc.; dir. Almancenadora Araure (Venezuela). Mem. Internat. Trade Devel. Assn. Bucks County (pres. 1969-70). Home: 12118 Mossycup St Houston TX 77024 Office: 2727 Allen Pky Houston TX 77001

ANGULO, MANUEL RAFAEL, lawyer; b. N.Y.C., Sept. 5, 1917; s. Charles and Ysabel (Piedra) A.; B.A., Yale, 1939; LL.B., Harvard, 1942; postgrad. Columbia, 1952; m. Carolyn Louise Bonin, Nov. 6, 1937; children—Charles B., M. Ralph; m. 2d, Diana Hutchins Rockwell, June 12, 1970. Admitted to N.Y. bar, 1947; practice in N.Y.C., 1942-48, 61—; asso. Davis, Polk, Wardwell, Sunderland & Kiendl, 1942-48; attaché, econ. analyst Am. embassy, Santo Domingo, 1943-44; attaché embassy, Lisbon, Portugal, 1944-46; with OSS, London, 1944; gen. solicitor Creole Petroleum Corp., Caracas, Venezuela, 1948-54; partner Escritorio J.M. Travieso Paul, Caracas, 1954-61; partner Curtis, Mallet-Prevost, Colt & Mosle, N.Y.C., 1961—; lectr. Law Sch. U. Va., 1963—. Mem. council Boy Scouts Am., Venezuela, 1955-59; pres. N. Am. Assn. Venezuela, 1957-59. Mem. Am., Internat., Inter Am., N.Y. State, N.Y.C. bar assns., N.Y. County Lawyers Assn., Am. Fgn. Law Assn., Societe de Legislation Comparee, Pan Am. Soc. U.S., Sigma Xi. Clubs: Yale, Union League, Broad Street, Metropolitan Opera (N.Y.C.); Metropolitan (Washington); Farmington Country, Redlands (Charlottesville, Va.). Contbr. profl. jours. Home: One Gracie Sq New York City NY 10028 Office: 100 Wall St New York City NY 10005

ANIEVAS, AGUSTIN, musician; b. N.Y.C., Nov. 6, 1934; s. Agustin and Ofelia (Arias) A.; B.S., Juilliard Sch. Music, 1958, M.S., 1959; m. Carol Kreisberg, Apr. 13, 1957; children—David, Marc. Concerts include world-wide recital and orchestral concerts, readings, radio and TV appearances. Served with AUS, 1959. Recipient Michael award, Chgo., 1958, Concert Artists Guild, N.Y.C., 1959, Reine Elizabeth Concors, 1960, Dimintri Mitropoules Internat. award, N.Y.C., 1961. Home: 207 Chaussee de Malines Wezembeck ophem Belgium Office: care Angel Records 1290 Av of the Americas New York City NY 10019

ANIGSTEIN, LUDWIK, educator, lab. dir.; b. Warsaw, Poland, Feb. 2, 1891; s. Isidore and Helen (Steinkalk) A.; Ph.D. magna cum laude, U. Heidelberg, 1913; med. diploma U. Dorpat, 1915; M.D., U. Poznan, 1923; certificate London Sch. Tropical Medicine, 1923; m. Luba Heller, Apr. 16, 1916; children—Alice Helen (Mrs. Bruce Grynbaum), Robert; m. 2d, Dorothy M. Whitney, May 2, 1958. Came to U.S. at Invitation of NRC, 1939, naturalized, 1945. Head parasitology State Inst. Hygiene, Warsaw, 1919-30; lectr. pub. health State Sch. Hygiene, Warsaw, 1926-39; lectr. parasitology U. Warsaw, 1929-39; research asso. U. Calif., 1940; asso. in preventive medicine U. Tex., Galveston, 1940-42, asst. prof., 1942, asso. prof. tropical medicine, 1943, prof. preventive medicine and pub. health, 1946-70, emeritus prof. preventive medicine and community health, 1970—; dir. Rickettsial Research Lab.; cons. geog. medicine Med. Br. Hosps.; cons. med. div. Oak Ridge Inst. Nuclear Studies. Research student in tropical medicine, Britain Colonial Service, Malay States, 1929-31; malaria expert Siamese Govt., 1931; health expert Govt. of Liberia, 1935-36. Served as med. officer, Russian Red Cross, 1915-18. Mem. malaria commn. League of Nations, 1924- 39, typhus experts commn., 1937; chmn. sec. tropical pathology Internat. Congress Tropical Medicine, Amsterdam, Netherlands, 1938. Mem. UNRRA med. mission to Poland, 1946. Fellow Royal Soc. Tropical Med. and Hygiene (London), Am. Pub. Health Assn., A.A.A.S., Tex., N.Y. acads. scis., Am. Acad. Microbiology; mem. Royal Soc. Health (London), Am. Soc. Exptl. Pathology, Am. Assn. Cancer Research, Am. Soc. Tropical Medicine and Hygiene, Tex. Pub. Health Assn., Soc. Am. Bacteriologists (also Tex. br.), Soc. Exptl. Biology and Medicine, Sci. Research Soc. Am., Sigma Xi, Phi Delta Epsilon, Mu Delta. Contbr. many articles on protozoology, bacteriology, epidemiology, immunology, tropical disease to sci. jours. Specialist in research in rickettsial diseases. Home: 28 Manor Way Galveston TX 77550

ANIN, T.E., banker. Dep. mng. dir. Ghana Comml. Bank, Accra. Office: Cor High St and Thorpe Rd Accra Ghana*

ANIXTER, ALAN B., elec. machinery co. exec.; b. Chgo., July 25, 1920; s. Julius B. and Zelda (Rogoff) A.; B.S. in Econs., U. Pa., 1941, M.B.A., 1943; m. Gail Annenberg, Nov. 6, 1943; children—James, Scott. With Webster-Chgo. Corp., 1941-43; partner Telmor Engring. Co., Chgo., 1943-46; v.p. sales R.I. Insulated Wire Co., Cranston, R.I., 1946-52; partner Mfrs. Agy., Chgo., 1953-57; pres. Anixter Bros., Inc., Skokie, Ill., 1957—; dir. Cregier Elec. Mfg. Co., Mark Products, Royal Elec. Co., Patterson Steel Co., Turmac, Ltd., Telewire, Inc. Clubs: Standard (Chgo.); Briarwood Country (Deerfield, Ill.). Home: 1323 Holly Winnetka IL 60093 Office: 8707 Skokie Blvd Skokie IL 60076

ANKA, PAUL, singer, composer; b. Ottawa, Can., July 30, 1941; s. Andrew and Camilia (Tannis) A.; ed. pub. schs., Ottawa; m. Anne de Zogheb, Feb. 16, 1963; 1 dau., Alexandra. Came to U.S., 1959. Appeared maj. cities S.Am., Caribbean, Europe, U.S., 1956—; motion pictures include the Longest Day (author title song), 1961; TV appearances include Ed Sullivan, Danny Thomas, Perry Como, Johnny Carson, Dean Martin TV Shows, Hollywood Palace, Open Mind; replacement in Broadway musical What Makes Sammy Run?, 1954; appeared at Copacabana, N.Y.C., Sands Hotel, Las Vegas, Caribe Hilton Hotel, San Juan, P.R., Waldorf Astoria, N.Y.C.; participated San Remo Music Festival, 1964; recording RCA Victor Records; propr. Spanks Music Corp., 1958—, Flanka Music Corp., 1958—, Camy Prodns., Inc., 1961-66. Holder 15 gold records for million dollar world-wide sellers. Club: Friars (N.Y.C.). Composer: Diana, 1957; Crazy Love; Lonely Boy, 1959; Put Your Head on My Shoulder, 1959; Time to Cry, 1959; The Longest Day, 1962; Tonight Show theme music, others, also compositions for other artists. Office: 200 W 57th St New York City NY 10019

ANKER, HERBERT S., educator, biochemist; b. Danzig, Sept. 16, 1912; s. Arthur and Helene (Raczinski) A.; student U. Freiburg (Germany), 1932-36, U. Vienna (Austria), 1936-38; M.D., U. Basel (Switzerland), 1939; Ph.D., Columbia, 1943; m. Dorothy Goldberg, Apr. 25, 1960; 1 son, Anthony; children by previous marriage—Martin R., Wendy. Came to U.S., 1941, naturalized, 1945. Postdoctoral fellow Columbia, 1943-45; mem. faculty U. Chgo., 1945—, prof. biochemistry, 1958—. Fellow Columbia, 1942-43. Mem. Am. Chem. Soc., Am. Soc. Biol. Chemists, Sigma Xi. Home: 5509 S Kenwood Av Chicago IL 60637

ANKRUM, LEONARD DOYLE, trading co. exec.; b. Fort Dodge, Ia., Nov. 28, 1928; s. William and Velma Elsie (Seamonds) A.; B.S.C., U. Ia., 1951; m. Marion Jean Davis, June 23, 1951; children—James D., Carol D. Head accounts payable dept., Montgomery Ward, Oakland, Cal., 1953-55; comptroller, Overseas Nat. Airways, Washington, 1955-61; treas., P.A. & S. Small Co., York, Pa., 1961-71, exec. v.p., 1964-71, pres., chief operating officer, 1971—, also dir.; dir. Super Thrift Markets, Inc., York, D.F. Stauffer Biscuit Co., Inc., York. Bd. dirs. York County Easter Seal Soc. Served to lt. USAF, 1951-53. Mem. Nat. Assn. Accountants, (past bd. dirs.), Phi Kappa Sigma. Presbyn. Clubs: York Country, Lafayette, University (York). Home: 2060 N Brook Circle York PA 17403 Office: Box 589 York PA 17405

ANLIKER, MAX, educator; b. Zurich, Switzerland, Dec. 25, 1927; M.S. in Physics, Swiss Fed. Inst. Tech., 1952, Ph.D. in Natural Scis., 1955; m. Gertrud M. Schibli, Apr. 2, 1953; children—Verena G., Susan B., Mark D. Came to U.S., 1955, naturalized, 1963. Teaching asst. mechanics Swiss Fed. Inst. Tech., 1951-55; research asso., instr. Bklyn. Poly. Inst., 1955-56; sr. research engr. Convair, San Diego, 1956-58; mem. faculty Stanford, 1958- -, now prof. biomechanics. Fellow Nat. Acad. Scis., 1965- 67. Mem. Am. Soc. Engring. Edn. (chmn. space engring. com. 1966-68), Am. Heart Assn. (exec. com. basic sci. council 1966-68), Am. Math. Soc., Am. Physiol. Soc., Sigma Xi. Spl. research vibration, surface tension phenomena and biomechanics. Office: Dept Aeros and Astronautics Stanford Univ Stanford CA 94305

ANLYAN, WILLIAM GEORGE, surgeon, univ. ofcl.; b. Alexandria, Egypt, Oct. 14, 1925; s. Armand and Emmeraude (Nazar) A.; B.S. magna cum laude, Yale, 1945, M.D., 1949; m. Constance Louise Lucier, June 19, 1948; children—William George, John Peter, Louise. Intern, resident, instr., asso. in surgery Duke Hosp., Durham, N.C., 1949-53, asst. prof. surgery, 1958-61, prof. surgery, 1961—; asso. dean

Sch. Medicine Duke, 1963, dean, 1964-69, v.p. health affairs, 1969—. Chmn. Durham VA V.P.'s Com.; surg. cons. Durham VA Hosp. Markle scholar med. sci., 1953-58. Chmn. regents Nat. Library Medicine, 1971-72. Diplomate Am. Bd. Surgery, Am. Bd. Thoracic Surgery. Fellow A.C.S.; mem. Soc. U. Surgeons, Soc. Vascular Surgery, Internat. Cardiovascular Soc., Soc. Clin. Surgery, Am. Heart Assn., So. Med. Assn., Surg. Biology Club II, Am., So. surg. assns., Halsted Soc., Allen O. Whipple Surg. Soc., Assn. Am. Med. Colls. (chmn. 1970-71), Sigma Xi, Alpha Omega Alpha. Rotarian. Home: 1516 Pinecrest Rd Durham NC 27705

ANNABLE, WELDON GRANT, devel. co. exec.; b. Evanston, Ill., Jan. 28, 1937; s. Weldon Grant and Julia (Howell) A.; B.S., Purdue U., 1959; M.B.A., Harvard, 1965; m. Eleanor Jane Scott, June 26, 1960; children—David Ross, Susan Elizabeth. Marketing cons. Booz, Allen & Hamilton, Inc., N.Y.C., 1964; mgr. spl. financial projects, controller Columbus (Ind.) operations, dir. product financial analysis Cummins Engine Co., Inc., 1965-68; div. controller Irwin Mgmt. Co., Columbis, 1968-69; v.p., controller Gen. Signal Corp., N.Y.C., 1969-71; sr. v.p. Whittaker Devel. Corp., 1971—; pres. Bldg. Products Corp., Knoxville, Tenn., 1971—. Served to lt., C.E.C., USNR, 1959-63. Named Outstanding Young Am., 1970. Mem. Machinery and Allied Products Inst., Financial Execs. Inst. Home: 10109 Tan Rara Dr Concord TN 37720 Office: 1111 North Shore Dr Knoxville TN 37919

ANNAKIN, KEN, film dir., writer; b. Beverly, Eng., Aug. 10, 1914. Former journalist, actor, stage producer; made 1st feature film, Holiday Camp, 1946; recent films include: Across the Bridge, Swiss Family Robinson, The Longest Day, Those Magnificent Men in Their Flying Machines, The Battle of the Bulge, Monte Carlo or Bust. Prod., dir., co-author: Those Darling Young Men in Their Jaunty Jalopies. Address: care Warner Bros Pictures Inc 666 Fifth Av New York City NY 10019*

ANNAN, LORD (Noel Gilroy), coll. provost; b. London, Eng., Dec. 25, 1916; s. James and Fannie student Stowe Sch., Buckingham, 1930-35; B.A., King's Coll. Cambridge U., 1938, M.A., 1943; m. Gabriele Ullstein, June 30, 1950; children—Amanda Lucy, Juliet Louise. With Brit. Army, 1939-46, ended mil. career as lt. col. polit. div. Control Commn. Germany, 1946; fellow Kings Coll., Cambridge, 1946, asst. tutor, 1947, provost, 1956-66; provost Univ. Coll., London, 1966-; univ. lectr. politics Cambridge, U., 1948-66; mem. Pub. Schs. Commn. Trustee Churchill Coll., Cambridge Brit. Mus.; chmn. acad. planning bd. U. Essex; mem. acad. planning bd. U. East Anglia, Brunel U. Decorated Order Brit. Empire. Author: Leslie Stephen, 1951; The Intellectual Aristocracy, 1955; Roxburgh of Stowe, 1965. Address: University Coll Gower St London WCIE 6 BT England

ANNEAR, PAUL RICHARD, educator; b. Cedar Rapids, Ia., Jan. 19, 1915; s. Richard Floyd and Hortense Beatrice (Camp) A.; B.A. in Astronomy, Drake U., 1936; M.S., Case Inst. Tech., 1938; Ph.D., U. Mich., 1949; m. Elizabeth Jane Barkley, Sept. 2, 1939; children—Sandra Sue (Mrs. Robert McMillan Thompson), Marcia Louise (Mrs. Kenneth Eugene Beery), Craig Barkley. Instr. physics, astronomy Hunter Coll., 1940-41; prof. dept. math. and astronomy Baldwin-Wallace Coll., Berea, O. 1941—, head dept., 1942-71. Data reduction analyst RCA Missile Test Project, Patrick AFB, Fla., summers 1957, 58, NASA Lewis Research Center, Cleve., 1959, Goodyear Aerospace Corp., Akron, O., 1966. Councilman, Berea, 1956-60. Mem. Am., Cleve. astron. Socs., Math. Assn. Am., Am. Assn. U. Profs., Am. Contract Bridge League, Phi Beta Kappa, Kappa Mu Epsilon. Club: Oakwood Tennis (Strongsville, O.). Home: 66 Barberry Dr Berea OH 44017

ANNENBERG, WALTER H., U.S. ambassador; b. Milw., 1908; ed. The Peddie Sch., Wharton Sch., U. Pa.; D. Journalism (hon.), Temple U.; L.H.D., Pa. Mil. Coll.; LL.D., La Salle Coll., U. Pa., Dropsie Coll.; L.H.D., Albert Einstein Coll. Medicine; m. Veronica Dunkelman (div.); 1 dau., Wallis; m. 2d, Leonore Cohn. Pres. Triangle Publs., Inc., Phila., Seventeen Mag., TV Guide, Morning Telegraph, Daily Racing Form. United States ambassador to Great Britain. Pres. M.L. Annenberg Found., Annenberg Fund; founder, pres. Annenberg Sch. Communications, Grad. Sch. U. Pa. operates stas. WNBF-TV and radio (Binghamton, N.Y.), WFBG-TV and radio (Altoona-Johnstown, Pa.), WLYH-TV (Lebanon). Trustee Dermatology Foundation, Philadelphia Mus. Art, United Fund Phila. area; trustee-at- large Found. for Ind. Colls., Inc.; founder, mem. bd. overseers Albert Einstein Coll. Medicine; dir., trustee Eisenhower Med. Center, Palm Desert, Cal.; bd. govs. Academy Food Marketing of St. Joseph's College; bd. corporators The Peddie Sch.; adv. bd. lay trustees Villanova Univ.; mem. Nat. Neiman Fund Committee; member Navy national committee Army- Navy Mus.; trustee, co-chmn. devel. adv. com. U. Pa.; a founder, trustee Eisenhower Exchange Fellowships. Former comdr. USNR. Decorated Officer French Legion of Honor; commander of Order of the Lion (Finland); commander of Order of Crown of Italy, comdr. of the Order of Merit (Italy); recipient of the Russell H. Conwell award Temple University; Gold medal award Freedoms Found., Pa. Meritorious Service medal; Man of Year award Del. Valley Coun., 1964; gold medal award Phila. Club of Printing House Craftsmen; Samuel S.Fels medal award, 1968. Fellow Pa. Academy Fine Arts; mem. Navy League, Newcomen Soc., Alliance Francaise de Phila., Confrerie des Chevalier du Tastevin, Am. Soc. Newspaper Editors, Internat. Press Inst., Inter Am. Press Assn., Frairs Sr. Soc., Cum Laude Soc., English-Speaking Union, Am. Swedish Hist. Found., Am. Newspaper Pub. Assn., Phi Sigma Delta, Sigma Delta Chi. Clubs: Green Valley Country (Lafayette Hill); Poor Richard, Midday, Faculty U. Pa. (Phila.); Hillcrest County (Beverly Hills); Tamarisk Country (Palm Springs); Lynford Cay (Nassau, Bahamas); Overseas Press (N.Y.C.); Nat. Press (Washington); Century Country (White Plains, N.Y.). Donor Walter H. Annenberg Library and The Masters' House to the Peddie Sch., Hightstown, N.J. Home: Llanfair Rd Wynnewood PA 19096 Office: 4000 N Broad St Philadelphia PA 19101

ANNIS, EDWARD ROLAND, physician; b. Detroit, Mar. 27, 1913; s. Edward Roland and Ethel Mary (Graham) A.; B.S., U. Detroit, 1933, D.Sc., 1963; M.D., Marquette U., 1938; postgrad. Cook County Grad. Sch., Chgo.; D.Sc., U. San Diego, Hahnemann Med. Coll.; LL.D., U. Scranton; Litt.D., Barry Coll. of Miami, 1966; m. Betty McCue Starck, June 16, 1941; children—Joseph Payne, Brian Roland, Paul Starck, Barbara Mary, Marjorie Joan, Kathleen Deborah, Timothy John, Roberta Marie. Intern, Milwaukee County Hosp., 1937-38; practice medicine specializing in surgery, Tallahassee, 1938-46, Miami, Fla., 1946—; chief dept. gen. surgery Mercy Hosp., 1953- 64; med. cons. Home Life Ins. Co. N.Y.; attending surgeon North Shore Hosp.; vis. surgeon Jackson Meml. Hosp., Variety Children's Hosp., Christian Hosp. (all Miami), St. Francis Hosp., Miami Beach, Fla.; med. cons. Houston Oilers, 1970—. Dir., Boulevard Nat. Bank; Royal Resources Exploration, Inc., Regency Income Corp., Inc. (Denver), Medequlp Corp., Chgo., pres. Denver Corp., 1969-71; exec. v.p. Physicians Planning Service Corp., N.Y.C., 1971—. Chmn. Fla. Gov.'s Citizens Med. Com. on Health, 1959. Trustee Nat. Assn. Interns and Residents; bd. dirs. Imperial-Am. Resources Fund Inc. Recipient Distinguished Service award Creighton U., 1963, Outstanding Alumnus of Year award Marquette U., 1964. Fellow Internat. Coll. Surgeons (pres. U.S. sect. 1964-65), Am. Acad. Gen. Practice (hon. life), Air Force Soc. Clin. Surgeons (hon.), Flying Physicians Assn. (hon.), Am. Profl. Practice Assn. (chmn.), Southeastern Surg. Soc.; mem. A.M.A. (pres. 1963-64, trustee 1967- 69), World (pres. 1963-64, council emissary 1964-66), Fla. (chmn. legislative com. 1960-65), Dade County med. assns., Miami, U.S. (dir.) chambers commerce, Nat. Assn. Professions (dir.). Roman Catholic. K.C. Clubs: Bath (Miami Beach); Palm Bay, Jockey (Miami). Home: 4425 Banyan Lane Bay Point Miami FL 33137 Office: 2121 Biscayne Blvd Miami FL also Physicians Planning Service Corp 292 Madison Av New York City NY 10017

ANNIS, MORTON LAWRENCE, cigar co. exec.; b. N.Y.C., Mar. 24, 1917; s. Julius Benjamin and Minnie (Brosow) A.; B.S. in Econs., Wharton Sch. of U. Pa., 1938; m. Marion Roberts, Aug. 14, 1941; children—Morton Lawrence, Susan Barbara. Exec. v.p. Gradiaz, Annis & Co., Inc., Tampa, Fla., 1946-58, pres., 1959-62; sr. v.p., dir. Gen. Cigar Co., Inc., N.Y.C., 1963—; dir., exec. com. Founders Life Assurance Co. Fla., 1963—; dir. Capitol National Bank, Tampa, Florida, 1963—, vice chmn. bd., 1964—. Vice pres., chmn. exec. Fla. Downs & Turf Club, Oldsmar. Mem. Tampa Com. 100, 1963—; mem. Anti-Defamation League of B'nai B'rith, 1959—, nat. cabinet mem. appeal, 1963. Bd. dirs. Tampa United Fund, 1963; trustee U. Tampa, Berkeley Prep. Sch., Tampa Art Inst. Served to maj., ordnance dept., AUS, 1941-45. Decorated Army Commendation medal. Mem. Cigar Mfrs. Assn. Tampa (dir. 1963), Cigar Inst. Am. (dir. 1960), Cigar Mfrs. Assn. Am. (bd. govs. 1963), Greater Tampa C. of C. Home: 108 Martinique St Tampa FL 33606 Office: PO Box 1 Tampa FL 33605

ANNUNZIO, FRANK, congressman; b. Chgo., Jan. 12, 1915; s. Ralph and Rose (Malizzio) A.; B.S., M.Ed., DePaul U.; m. Angeline Alesia, Dec. 28, 1935; children—Jacqueline (Mrs. Frank Lato), Linda (Mrs. William O'Donnell), Susan (Mrs. Kevin Tynan). Asst. supr. Nat. Defense Training Program Austin Evening Sch., Chgo.; lesiglative, ednl. dir. United Steelworkers of Am., Chgo.; mem. 89th to 92d Congresses, Ill. 7th Dist. Dir. Ill. Dept. Labor; chmn. War Ration Bd. 40-20; mem. adv. com. on Unemployment Compensation; mem. adv. com. to Ill. Indsl. Commn. on Health and Safety; mem. adv. bd. Cook County (Ill.) Health and Survey; chmn. Community Services Com.; mem. Chgo. Commn. on Human Relations; regional dir. All Am. Council. chmn. Italian Am. Democratic Com. Cook County. Gen. chmn. Villa Scalabrini Devel. Fund; v.p., lay adv. bd. Villa Scalabrini Italian Old People's Home; mem. sponsors' com. Glenmary Home Missions. Mem. Little Flower Soc., Am. Com. Italian Migration (dir.), Catholic Youth Orgn. K.C. (4). Club: City (Chgo.). Office: Longworth Bldg Washington DC 20515

ANOPOL, GEORGE, orthopedic surgeon; b. Stretynsk, Siberia, Mar. 24, 1893; s. Walter and Gitel (Gershenovich) A.; came to U.S., 1900, naturalized, 1907; ed. Coll. City N.Y.; M.D., U. of Bellevue Hosp. Med. Coll., N.Y., 1920; m. 1946. Intern N.Y. Post Grad. Hosp., 1920-22; gen. practice, N.Y.C., 1922-25; instr. gen. surgery, N.Y. Post Grad. Med. Sch. and Hosp., 1922-25; asso. in orthopedic surgery Columbia U., 1925-30, asst. prof., 1930-36, asso. clin. prof. orthopedic surgery, 1938-39, clin. prof., 1939, prof. clin. orthopedic surgery, 1940-41; dir. orthopedic surgery N.Y. Post Grad. Hosp., now prof. clin. orthopedic surgery and chief orthopedic med. service Univ. Hosp.; cons. orthopedics, Yonkers Profl. Hosp.; cons. orthopedic surgery Norwalk (Conn.) Gen. Hosp.; cons. orthopedic surgery, chief leg lengthening clinic Yonkers Gen. Hosp.; orthopedic cons., attending, VA Hosp., Bklyn. Bd. dirs. Am. Rehab. Com. Lt. comdr., orthopedic surgery USNR, 1934—, on active duty as comdr. with Naval Base Hosp. No. 4; capt. M.C., USN Hosp., Bklyn., 1943-45; disch. 1945., capt. USNR, ret. Diplomate orthopedic surgery Internat. Coll. Surgeons. Fellow A.C.S., Am. Acad. Orthopedic Surgeons, N.Y. Acad. Medicine, A.M.A., Am. Acad. Compensation Medicine; mem. N.Y. State, N.Y. County med. socs., N.Y. Post Grad. Alumni Assn., N.Y. Post Grad. Conf., Interurban Orthopedic Club, Yonkers Acad. Medicine. Contbr. numerous articles on orthopedic surgery to jours. Office: 237 Valentine Lane Yonkers NY 10705

ANOUILH, JEAN, playwright; b. Bordeaux, France, June 23, 1910; m. Monelle Valentin; 1 dau.; m. Nicole Lancon, 1953; 2 daus., 1 son. Plays include, Mandarine, 1932, Le Voyageur sans bagages, 1937, Wild Girl, 1938, Euridice, 1942, Antigone, 1944, Oreste, 1945, Ring Around the Moon, 1948, Rehearsal, 1950, The Waltz of the Toreadors, 1951, The Lark, Medea, 1953, Poor Bitos, 1956, Becket, 1959, La Grotte, 1961, L'Orchestre and La Foire D'Empoigne, 1962; Writer ballets for Les Bailets de Paris; films include Deux Sous les Violettes, Monsieur Vincent (awarded Grand Prix du Cinema Francais), Madame de, La Morte de Belle, Richard III, Pattis Blances, Caprice de Caroline, Becket; TV plays include: Monsieur Barnett. Recipient Prix Dominique de la mise en scéne, 1959. Address: care Les Editions de la Table Ronde 40 rue du Bac Paris VII France*

ANSARY, HUSHANG, ambassador of Iran to U.S.; b. 1928; ed. schs. in Eng., Japan and U.S.A. Spl. reporter Internat. News Service and Internat. News Photos; press attaché Publ. and Propaganda Dept. Japan; comml. attaché Japan; econ. attaché Tokyo; chief supervisory Com. Pub. Supplies, mem. High Council Iranian Aviation; tech. under-sec. Ministry Commerce; spl. ambassador in African countries; ambassador to Pakistan and Ceylon, 1965-66; minister information, 1966-67; ambassador to U.S.A., 1967-69; minister economy, Teheran, Iran, 1969—. Address: Ministry Economy Maidan Arg Teheran Iran

ANSBRO, JOHN J., clergyman. Roman catholic vicar gen., Archdiocese of Newark. Address: 113 Elmwood Av East Orange NJ 07018*

ANSCHUETZ, NORBERT LEE, banker; b. Leavenworth, Kan., May 16, 1915; s. Otto William and Irma (Hilpert) A.; A.B., U. Kan., 1936; LL.B., Harvard, 1939; grad. Nat. War Coll., 1957, State Dept. Sr. Seminar, 1967; m. Roberta Cook, Mar. 13, 1943; children—Carol, Ellen (Mrs. W.W. Lewis III), Susan, Nancy. Admitted to Mo. bar, 1939; practice in Kansas City, Mo., 1939-41; with Dept. State, 1946-68, fgn. service officer, 1951-68; assigned successively, Washington, Athens, counselor Bangkok, 1954-56; minister-counselor Cairo, 1958-62, Paris, 1962-64, Athens, Greece, 1964-67; rep. for Middle East and Africa, First Nat. City Bank N.Y., Beirut, 1968-70, fgn. affairs rep., internat. banking group N.Y.C., 1971—. Served to lt. col. AUS, 1941-46. Hon. citizen Athens, 1967. Mem. Council Fgn. Relations. Address: First Nat City Bank 399 Park Av New York City NY 10022

ANSCOMBE, FRANCIS JOHN, statistician; b. Elstree, Hertfordshire, Eng., May 13, 1918; s. Francis Champion and Honoria Constance (Fallowfield) A.; student Brighton Coll., 1931-36; B.A., U. Cambridge, 1939, M.A., 1943; m. Phyllis Elaine Rapp, June 16, 1954; children—Francis Rossiter, Anthony John, Frederick, Elizabeth. Came to U.S., 1956. With the British Ministry of Supply, 1940-45; staff Rothamsted Exptl. Sta., Harpenden, Hertfordshire, Eng., 1945-47; lectr. math. Cambridge U., 1948-56; research asso. Princeton, 1953-54, asso. prof. math., 1956-60, prof., 1960-63; prof. statistics, Yale, New Haven, 1963—; vis. asso. prof. U. Chgo., 1959-60. Chmn. Nat. Acad. Scis-NRC adv. panel applied math. div. Nat. Bur. Standards, 1966-67. Fellow A.A.A.S., Am. Statis. Assn., Inst. Math. Statistics, Royal Statis. Soc.; mem. Internat. Statis. Inst. Author: Curso de Aplicaciones Industriales de la Estadistica, 1957. Contbr. articles to sci. jours. Office: Dept Statistics Box 2179 Yale Sta New Haven CT 06520

ANSELL, GEORGE STEPHEN, metallurgist, educator; b. Akron, O., Apr. 1, 1934; s. Frederick Jesse and Fanny (Soletsky) A.; B.Met.E.,Rensselaer Poly. Inst., 1954; M.Met.E., 1955, Ph.D., 1960; m. Marjorie Boris, Dec. 18, 1960; children—Frederick Stuart, Laura Ruth, Benjamin Jesse. Phys. metallurgist U.S. Naval Research Lab., Washington, 1957-58; faculty Rensselaer Poly. Inst., Troy, N.Y., 1960—, Robert W. Hunt prof. metall. engring., 1965—, chmn. materials div., 1969—. Dir. Ilikon Corp., Natick, Mass.; cons. to pvt. cos. Recipient Curtis W. McGraw award Am. Soc. for Engring. Edn., 1971. Mem. Am. Inst. Mining, Metall. and Petroleum Engrs. (Hardy Gold medal 1961), Am. Soc. for Metals (Alfred H. Geisler award Eastern N.Y. chpt. 1964, Bradley Stoughton award 1968), Electron Microscope Soc. Am., N.Y. Acad. Scis., Internat. Assn. for Dental Research, Sci. Research Soc. Am., Sigma Xi, Tau Beta Pi, Phi Lambda Upsilon. Research, publs. on theoretical and exptl. analysis of relationships between defect structure and properties of crystaline solids. Home: 6 Colonial Green Loudonville NY 12211 Office: Dept Materials Engring Rensselaer Poly Inst Troy NY 12181

ANSELL, JULIAN SAMUEL, physician; b. Portland, Me., June 30, 1922; s. Jacob M. and Anna (Fieldman) A.; B.A., Bowdoin Coll., 1947; M.D., Tufts U., 1951; Ph.D., U. Minn., 1959; m. Eva R. Ballin, June 17, 1951; children—Steven, Jody, Carol, Ellen, Peter. Intern U. Minn. Hosp., 1951-52, resident urology, 1952-53, sr. resident, 1955-56; instr. urol. surgery U. Minn. Med. Sch., 1956-59; mem. faculty and staff U. Wash. Sch. Medicine and affiliated hosp., 1959—, prof. urology, chmn. dept., 1965—; chief urol. div. VA Hosp., Mpls., 1956-59; mem. staff urol. div. U. Minn. Hosp., 1956-59; chief urology Univ. Hosp., Seattle, 1959—, USPHS Hosp., Seattle, 1966—, King Country Hosp., Seattle, 1959—. Served with USAAF, 1943-46. Fellow USPHS, 1955-56. Diplomate Am. Bd. Urology. Fellow A.C.S.; mem. Am., Western, N.Western urol. socs., Am., Wash. med. assns., King County Med. Soc., Seattle Acad. Surgery, Am. Assn. U. Profs., A.A.A.S., Soc. Univ. Urologists. Club: Am. Alpine. Home: 3831 49th Av NE Seattle WA 98105

ANSELME, JEAN-PIERRE LOUIS MARIE, educator, chemist; b. Port-au-Prince, Haiti, Sept. 22, 1936; s. Pierre F. and Jeanne (Kieffer) A.; came to U.S., 1955, naturalized, 1960; B.A., St. Martial Coll., Haiti, 1955; B.S., Fordham U., 1959; Ph.D., Poly. Inst. Bklyn., 1963; m. Marie-Celine Carrie, Dec. 31, 1960; children—Fabiene, Veronika, Vanessa. Research asso. Poly. Inst. Bklyn., 1963, 65, sr. instr., 1965; Nat. Sci. Found. fellow Institut fur Organische Chemie, Munich, 1964; asst. prof. chemistry U. Mass. at Boston, 1965-68, asso. prof., 1968-70, prof., 1970—; pres. Organic Preparations and Procedures, Inc. (Newton, Mass.). Recipient Seymour Shapiro award as outstanding grad. student organic chemistry Poly. Inst. Bklyn., 1963; Sloan fellow, 1969-71. Mem. Am. Chem. Soc., Chem. Soc. London, Chem. Soc. Japan, Gesellschaft Deutscher Chemiker, Sigma Xi, Phi Lambda Upsilon. Author: (with others) Organic Compounds with Nitrogen-Nitrogen Bonds, 1966. Founder, editor of Organic Preparations and Procedures, 1969-70, Organic Preparations and Procedures Internat., 1971—. Contbr. articles profl. jours. Office: 100 Arlington St Boston MA 02116

ANSFIELD, FRED JOSEPH, educator; b. Milw., Aug. 30, 1910; s. Joseph and Toby (Hoffman) A.; B.S., U. Wis., 1931, M.D., 1933; m. Ruth L. Beaser, Feb. 22, 1940; children—Valentine J., Toby A. Intern Milw. County Hosp., 1933-34, resident, 1934-35, mem. faculty cancer research div. U. Wis. Med. Sch., 1957—, prof. surgery, 1964—; cons. cancer chemotherapy VA Hosp., Madison. Pres. Glidden Sch. Bd., 1953-55. Served with M.C., AUS, 1944-46; ETO. Decorated Bronze Star, Silver Star, Purple Heart. Mem. Am. Assn. Cancer Research, N.Y. Acad. Scis., A.A.A.S., James Ewing Soc., Am. Soc. Clin. Oncology (past pres.), Sigma Xi, Alpha Omega Alpha. Author: Chemotherapy of Disseminated Solid Tumors. Home: 5118 Juneau Rd Madison WI 53705

ANSHEN, MELVIN, educator; b. Boston, July 2, 1912; s. Zalkend and Fanny (Kogan) A.; A.B., Harvard, 1933, M.B.A., 1935, D.C.S., 1940; m. Gertrude Lakson, Sept. 14, 1936. Prof. Ind. U., 1937-51, grad. sch. indsl. adminstrn. Carnegie Inst. Tech., Pitts., 1951-62; prof. bus. Grad. Sch. Bus., Columbia, 1962—; dir. research coordination staff WPB, 1942-46; acting dep. adminstr. program and requirements Defense Prodn. Adminstr., 1951; vis. lectr. bus. sch. Harvard, 1947; vis. prof. Stanford, 1950. Mem. Am. Econ. Assn. Author: Wartime Production Controls, 1949; Modern Marketing, 1939; An Introduction to Business, 1942; Private Enterprise and Public Policy, 1953. Home: 205 West End Av New York City NY 10023

ANSLEY, William Bonneau, lawyer; b. Charleston, S.C., Apr. 30, 1908; s. Francis Wilcox and Ellen Whitredge (Bennett) A.; LL.B., U. Ga., 1930; m. Florence Jackson Bryan, Oct. 2, 1934; children—Ellen Bennett (Mrs. Edward Hooper Hardison), Shepard Bryan, William Bonneau. Admitted to Ga. bar, 1930; city atty., Decatur, Ga., 1934; mem. Bryan, Carter, Ansley & Smith, Atlanta, 1941-; pres., chmn. bd. DeKalb County Fed. Savs. & Loan Assn. Mem. Ga. Savs. and Loan League (treas. 1951-53), Ga., Atlanta bar assns., Chi Phi, Phi Delta Phi, Episcopalian. Clubs: Lawyers, Piedmont Driving, Nine O'clocks, Peachtree Golf (Atlanta). Home: 3590 Paces Valley Rd NW Atlanta GA 30327 Office: First Nat Bank Bldg Atlanta GA 30303

ANSLINGER , HARRY JACOB U.S. commr. of narcotics; b. Altoona, Pa., May 20, 1892; s. Robert J. and Christina (Fladtt) A.; student Pa. State Coll., 1913-15; LL.B., Washington Coll. Law, 1930; LL.D., U. Md.; m. Martha Denniston; 1 son, Joseph. Attached to Am. Legation, The Hague, 1918-21; vice-consul, Hamburg, Germany, 1921-23; consul, La Guaira, Venezuela, 1923-25, Nassau, Bahamas, 1926; chief div. of foreign control, Treasury Dept., 1926-29; asst. commr. of prohibition, 1929-30; U.S. commr. of narcotics, 1930-62. Mem. efficiency bd., Ordnance Div., War Dept., 1917-18. Del. of U.S. to Conf. on Suppression of Smuggling, London, 1926, Paris, 1927, to Internat. Congress against Alcoholism, Antwerp, 1928, Conf. to Revise Treaty with U.S., Ottawa, Can., 1928, Conf. of Limitation of Mfr. of Narcotic Drugs, Geneva, 1931; co-observer of U.S. at League of Nations Opium Adv. Com., 1932, 33, 34, 36, 37, 38, 39; U.S. del. Internat. Conf. for Suppression Illicit Traffic in Narcotic Drugs, League of Nations, Geneva, 1936; U.S. rep. commn. on Narcotic Drugs of U.N. Recipient Pa. Ambassador, Proctor Gold Medal Awards, 1952; One of ten outstanding career men, Federal Govt., Nat. Civil Service League, 1958; Alumni Recognition award Am. U., 1959; Distinguished Alumnus award Pa. State U., 1959; Alexander Hamilton medal, Remington medal, Presdl. Citation. Mem. Com. drug addiction NRC. Hon. mem. Terre Haute Acad. Medicine; asso. mem. Internat. Police Chief Assn.; mem. adv. com. Internat. Cooperation Criminal Law, Am. Bar Assn.; life mem. Pa. and Blair County Pharm. Assn.; adv. bd. Mil. Police Assn. Mem. Am. Fgn. Service Assn., Diplomatic and Consular Officers Ret. (bd. govs.), Sigma Nu Phi. Co- author: The Traffic in Narcotics, The Murderers, The Protectors. Address: 612 Pine St Holidaysburg PA 16648

ANSOFF, HARRY IGOR, univ. dean; b. Vladivostok, Russia, Dec. 12, 1918; s. Samuel Ernest and Eva (Vagin) A.; M.E., Stevens Inst. Tech., 1941, M.S., 1943; Ph.D., Brown U., 1948; m. Dorothy Webster, Oct. 1, 1948; children—Peter, Eve, Ricky, Christopher. Mem. faculty Stevens Inst. Tech., 1941-43, U.S. Naval Acad., 1946-48; project officer Rand Corp., 1948-56; devel. planning specialist Lockheed Aircraft Corp., 1956-57; dir. Divers Task Force, 1957-61; v.p., gen. mgr. Lockeed Electronics Co., 1961-63; prof. indsl. adminstrn. Carnegie Mellon U., 1963-68; dean Grad. Sch. Mgmt., Vanderbilt U., 1968—; cons. in field. Dir. New Mgmt. Center, Inc., 1968—. Fellow A.A.A.S., Am. Acad. Mgmt.; mem. Am. Math. Soc., Operations Research Soc. Am., Inst. Mgmt. Scis., N.Y. Acad. Scis., Sigma Xi, Tau Beta Pi. Author: Corporate Planning, 1965; Business Strategy, 1969. Home: 1824 Laurel Ridge Nashville TN 15215

ANSON, ABRAHAM, govt. ofcl.; b. N.Y.C., Jan. 21, 1912; s. Emil and Ida (Glazer) A.; student Coll. City N.Y., 1928-33, N.Y.U., 1940, Manhattan Coll., 1942-43, George Washington U., 1957-58, 61-62; m. Stella Anna Greenstein, Oct. 22, 1938; children—Myra Leah. Salesman Hagelstein Bros., N.Y.C., 1932-42; jr. engring. aide U.S. Coast and Geodetic Survey, 1942-43; topographical engr. U.S. Geol. Survey, 1946-57; gen. engr. photogrammetry U.S. Army Engrs., 1957-64; gen. engr. geog. scis. U.S. Army Engrs. Topographic Lab., Ft. Belvoir, Va., 1964—; guest lectr. U. Ill., 1969, Okla. State U., 1971, Nat. Research Council, 1971; mem. photog. team NASA, 1964-65. Served with AUS, 1943-46. Recipient hon. mention Talbert Abrams award, 1971; named Engr. of Distinction, Engring. Joint Council, 1970. Mem. Am. Soc. Photogrammetry (dir., exec. com. 1966-69, 69-72), Intersoc. Color Council, Optical Soc. Am., A.A.A.S. Asso. editor: Manual of Color Aerial Photography, 1968. Contbr. articles tech. jours. Home: 6066 Munson Hill Rd Falls Church VA 22044 Office: Geol Scis Div US Army Ft Belvoir VA 22060

ANSON, CHARLES PHILLIPS, economist, educator; b. Chgo., July 1, 1902; s. Clinton Ellsworth and Icy Dora (Phillips) A.; student Hiram Coll., 1920-22; A.B., U. Wis., 1924; A.M., Ohio State U., 1930; Ph.D., U. N.C., 1940; m. Floris Carmene Roush, May 20, 1929 (dec. Jan. 1950); 1 dau., June Esther; m. 2d, Mary Hellen Dodson, Dec. 20, 1951. Asst. prof. econs. Potomac State Sch., Keyser, W.Va., 1930-35; lectr. Western Md. Coll., summers 1932-35; teaching fellow U. N.C., 1936-38; prof., head dept. econs. Roanoke (Va.) Coll., 1938-42; lectr. econs. U. N.C., 1946; head dept. econs., bus. adminstrn. and sociology Auburn (Ala.) U., 1946-67, prof. econs., 1967—. Labor arbitrator Am. Arbitration Assn., U.S. Mediation and Conciliation Service, 1955—; dist. price exec. OPA, Roanoke, 1942-45. Mem. Am., So. econ. assns., Indsl. Relations Research Assn., Delta Sigma Pi, Omicron Delta Kappa, Phi Kappa Phi. Home: 354 Chewacla Dr Auburn AL 36830

ANSTREICHER, KURT, physician; b. Oderberg, Austria, 1911; M.D., U. Vienna (Austria), 1936. Intern, U. Vienna Med. Sch. Inst. Internal Medicine, 1936-38; resident Provincial Hosp. for Mental Disease, Brandon, Man., Can., 1945-52, dir. Mental Hygiene Clinic of Western Man.; resident U. Pa. Grad Sch., 1952-53, Pa. Inst., Phila., 1953-54; acting supt. Del. State Hosp., New Castle, 1964-65, asst. supt., 1965—. Instr. U. Pa., 1952—. Diplomate in psychiatry Am. Bd. Psychiatry and Neurology. Fellow Am. Psychiat. Assn., A.A.A.S.; mem. A.M.A. Office: Del State Hosp Dupont Hwy New Castle DE 19720*

ANTELL, BERTEL WALDEMAR, mgmt. cons.; b. Bklyn., Oct. 20, 1907; s. Edward John and Anna Iliamna (Hornborg) A.; A.B., Cornell U., 1928. With Comml. dept. N.J. Bell Telephone Co., 1929-33; personnel dept. R.H. Macy & Co., 1933-37; with Equitable Life Assurance Soc., 1937-41, Am. Cyanamid Co., 1941-42, Gulf Oil Corp., 1946-48; with Rogers, Slade & Hill, mgmt. cons., 1948-50; partner Sorzano, Antell & Wright, 1950-55, Antell, Wright & Assos., 1955-60, Antell, Wright & Nagel, N.Y.C., 1960—; dir. Gourdine Systems, Inc. Spl. personnel cons. ECA, 1948. Mem. Cornell U. Council. Served with USNR, 1942-46; chief personnel procurement OSS, 1944-45. Mem. Delta Upsilon. Rep. Lutheran. Clubs: Racquet and Tennis, Twenty-Nine, Cornell, Players, Union League (N.Y.C.); Bohemian (San Francisco). Home: 1 Pierrepont St Brooklyn, NY 11201. Office: 230 Park Av New York City NY 10017

ANTHIS, FAY WRIGHT, (Mrs. Austin F. Anthis), educator; b. Belton, Tex., Nov. 16, 1896; d. Franklin Alexander and Nancy Adeline (Atkins) Wright; B.S., Kan. State Coll., 1917; M.S., U. Tex., 1939; postgrad. Cornell U., 1945, Columbia, 1947; Dr. Nutrition, Tex. Woman's U., 1955; m. Austin Forrest Anthis, Aug. 11, 1917 (dec. 1930); children—Fay Evelyn (Mrs. Dean Couch), Barbara Jane (Mrs. James H. Wagner), Austin Forrest. Tchr. home econs. Okla. high schs., 1937-40; adminstrv. intern dietetics U. Tex., 1940; dietitian U. Houston, 1942, instr., 1942, prof., adminstr., chmn. home econs., 1944—. Nutritional adviser to Civil Def. rep., 1st Internat. Dietetic Congress, Amsterdam, 1952; lecture tour, Brazil, 1953; rep. 9th Internat. Home Econs. Congress, Washington, 1958. Recipient Matrix award for outstanding contribution to education, Theta Sigma Phi, 1969. Mem. Am. Assn. U. Profs., Inst. Food Technologists, Am. Dietetic Assn., Am. Home Econs. Assn., Acad. Sci., Am. Assn. U. Women, D.A.R., U.D.C., P.E.O., Alpha Chi Omega, Alpha Delta Kappa, Alpha Lambda Delta, Phi Upsilon Omicron, Kappa Delta Pi. Baptist. Author articles profl. jours. Home: 3711 San Felipe Rd Houston TX 77027

ANTHIS, ROLLEN HENRY, air force officer; b. Navina, Okla., Dec. 4, 1915; s. Leo L. and Pearl Emily (Stapleton) A.; student Okla. U., 1933-37; grad. primary, basic and advanced pilot tng., Randolph and Kelly Fields, Tex., 1939, Air War Coll., 1949, Nat. War Coll., 1959; m. Evelyn Barnhart, May 26, 1939; children—Penelope, Jane, Deborah, Sally. Commd. 2d lt. USAAF, 1939, advanced through grades to maj. gen., 1963; various assignments, U.S., 1939-44; comdr. 1257th Air Base Unit, Air Tactical Corps, Marrakech, Morocco, 1944-45, 1252d Air Base Unit, Casablanca, Morocco, 1945-46; exec. officer to dep. chief staff A-1, Air Tactical Corps, 501st AFB Unit, Washington, 1946-47; asst. chief staff A-1, Hdqrs. Air Tactical Corps, 1947-48, Hdqrs. Mil. Air Transp. Service, 1948-49; mem. faculty Air War Coll., 1949-52; comdr. 1603d Air Transp. Wing USAFE, 1952-55; dep. chief, operations control div. Dep. Chief Staff Operations, Hdqrs. USAF, 1955-56, chief manpower div., 1956-58; vice comdr. 13th Air Force, Clark Air Base, Philippines, 1959-61; comdr. 2d ADVON, also chief air force sect. MAAG, Saigon, Vietnam, 1961-62; comdr. 2d Air Div., Tan Son Nhut Air Base, Saigon, Vietnam, 1962-64; spl. asst. for counterinsurgency and spl. activities Office Joint Chiefs Staff, 1964-66; comdr. Hdqrs. Command, USAF, 1966- 67, 17th Air Force, Ramstein, Germany, 1967-69; chief of staff, combined mil. planning staff, CENTO, 1969—. Decorated D.S.M., Legion of Merit with three oak leaf clusters, Air medal, Army Commendation medal with 2 oak leaf clusters, also numerous area and service ribbons; Alawite medal of 3d order with bronze loop (France); medal of independence (Libya); Nat. Order Vietnam medal; recipient French, Vietnamese and Royal Thai air force wings; citation of honor award Air Force Assn.; Legion of Honor, Internat. Supreme Council, Order DeMolay. Home: 320 S Barker St El Reno OK 73036 Office: Hdqrs USAF Washington DC 20332

ANTHONY, CHARLES, (Charles Anthony Caruso), singer; b. New Orleans, July 15, 1929; s. Anthony and Anna (Caruso) Caruso; student Tulane U., 1946; Mus.B., Loyola U. of South, New Orleans, 1951; m. Eleanor Trentacosta, July 17, 1949; children—Anna Elizabeth, Barbara Marie. Singer leading tenor roles New Orleans Opera Assn., New Orleans Recreation Dept. Scorsone Ensemble, Theater of Music in New Orleans, Teatro Comunale, Florence, Italy, 1952, Rome and Milano Radio Italiano, 1953, Am. Chamber Opera, N.Y.C., Opera Cameos, N.Y.C.; winner auditions Met. Opera Co., 1952, mem. company 1953—.

ANTHONY, CHARLES R., merchant; b. nr. Trenton, Tenn., Aug. 10, 1885; s. Zachary Cicero and Elvira Ann (Pennington) A.; student Indianola Bus. Coll., Holdenville; Dr. Laws (hon.), Oklahoma City U.; Dr. Humanities (hon.), Beth Nazarene Coll., m. Lutie L. Mauldin, July 10, 1910; children—Helen (Mrs. Galloway), Ray T., Guy M., Betty (Mrs. Zahn), Dana (Mrs. Clasby). Organized C.R. Anthony Co., Oklahoma City, Okla., 1922, pres. and chmn. bd.; co. now operating 309 stores in 21 states; chmn. bd. Citizens Nat. Bank, Oklahoma City; dir. Southwestern Bell Telephone Co. Pres. United Fund, 1952; mem. Okla. State Fair Bd. Bd. dirs. Frontiers of Sci. Found. Okla.; bd. dirs., treas. YMCA; trustee Nat. Cowboy Hall of Fame and Western Heritage. Recipient Horatio Alger award, 1963; named to Okla. Hall Fame; citation Nat. Conf. Christians and Jews, 1965. Hon. mem. Telephone Pioneers Am. Club: Rotary (hon. mem.). Home: Skirvin Tower Hotel Oklahoma City OK 73102 Office: 701 N Broadway Oklahoma City OK 73102

ANTHONY, CLOYD, ret. educator; b. Nashville, Ind., Sept. 11, 1901; s. George W. and Cora (Freese) A.; A.B., Ind. State U., 1925; M.A., Ind. U., 1929, Ph.D., 1935; m. Hazel Dillman, Dec. 27, 1926; children—Mark, John, Mary (Mrs. Donald G. Gardner). Tchr., adminstr. rural and urban schs., Ind., 1920-36; asso. prof. social scis. Central Mo. State Coll., Warrensburg, 1936- 44; asst. prof. Mich. State U., 1944-45; prof. sociology Ind. State U., 1945-68, prof. emeritus, 1968—, chmn. div., 1955-67. Mem. Am. Sociol. Assn., Am. Acad. Polit. and Social Sci., Ind. Acad. Social Sci., Ind. Council Social Studies, Alpha Kappa Delta, Phi Delta Kappa. Home: 2701 Wallace Av Terre Haute IN 47802

ANTHONY, DONALD ELLIOT, ret. educator; b. Oakland, Cal., Nov. 30, 1899; s. Arthur Kellog and Minnie (Buckelew) A.; B.A., Leland Stanford U., 1922, Ph.D., 1928; M.A., Cornell, 1923; student U. Cal., 1923-25; m. Arvella M. Coffin, June 24, 1929; 1 son, Donald Bruce. Instr. econs., bus., sociology U. Nev., 1926- 28; asst. prof. econs. Lehigh U., 1928-29; asst. prof. dept. econs. U. Akron, 1929-34, asso. prof., 1934-35, prof., head dept., 1935-36; prof., head dept. bus. adminstr. Kent State U., 1936-65, asst. dean Coll. Bus. Adminstrn., 1965-70, prof. mgmt. emeritus, 1970—. Chmn. Portage County chpt. A.R.C., 1951. Mem. Am. Econ. Assn., Indsl. Relations Research Assn., Am. Arbitration Assn., Soc. Advancement Mgmt., Omicron Delta Gamma, Beta Gamma Sigma, Delta Sigma Pi. Episcopalian (lay reader). Kiwanian (hon.). Club: Torch (Akron). Contbr. articles profl. publs. Home: 118 Wilson Av Kent OH 44240

ANTHONY, E. JAMES, educator; B.S., U. London, 1938, M.B., B.S., 1942, D.P.M., 1947, M.D., 1949. Now Blanche Ittleson prof. child psychiatry Washington U. Med. Sch., St. Louis; lectr. U. Chgo. Mem. Royal Coll. Surgeons, Internat. Assn. Child Psychiatry (pres.); licentiate Royal Coll. Physicians. Address: Sch Medicine Washington U St. Louis, MO 63130.

ANTHONY, EDWARD, writer; b. N.Y.C., Aug. 4, 1895; s. Robert and Rose (Friedman) A.; ed. pub. schs.; m. Esther H. Howard, Dec. 17, 1928; 1 son, Richard W. Started newspaper work on Bridgeport (Conn.) Herald, 1917; stationed at Camp Merritt, 1918-19, World War; with N.Y. Herald, 1920-23; asso. editor Farm and Fireside, 1923-28; asso. editor of "Judge," 1923; staff American Magazine, 1929; press service dir. Crowell Group (American Magazine, Collier's, Woman's Home Companion), 1930-42; publisher Woman's Home Companion, 1942-52, Collier's mag., 1949-54; cons. to Am. Girl mag. 25 yrs.; now writer; editorial cons. Book div. Reader's Digest, 1968—. Publicity dir. Hoover presdl. campaign, 1928. Served as dir. pub. relations War advt. Council, World War II. Trustee Herbert Hoover Birthplace Found. Clubs: Dutch Treat, Nat. Press, P.E.N., Players. Author: Merry-Go- Roundelays, 1921; The Pussycat Princess, 1922; The Fairies Up-to-Date, 1923; Razzberry, 1924; How to Get Rid of a Woman, 1928; Bring 'Em Back Alive (with Frank Buck), 1930; Wild Cargo (with Frank Buck), 1932; The Big Cage (with Clyde Beatty), also screen version of same, 1933; Nowhere Else in the World (with Gordon Enders), 1935; I Live on Air (with A.A. Schechter), 1941; The Sex Refresher, 1943; Every Dog Has His Say, 1947; Oddity Land, 1957; This Is Where I Came In, 1960; O Rare Don Marquis, 1962; (with Clyde Beatty) Facing the Big Cats, 1965; (with Henry Trefflich) Jungle for Sale, 1967; (with Eric Sloane) Mr. Daniels and the Grange, 1968. Author book and lyrics of mus. comedy Good Luck Sam; also numerous mag. articles. Home: Aspetuck Ridge Rd CT 06776

ANTHONY EDWARD MASON, educator; b. Cleve., Sept. 1, 1922; s. Edward Mason and Elsie (Haas) A.; A.B., U. Mich., 1944, M.A., 1946, Ph.D., 1954; m. Ann Louise Terbrueggen, Sept. 18, 1946; children—Lynn Diane (Mrs. Roland Higgins), Janice Louise, Edward Mason IV. From instr. English to prof. linguistics U. Mich., 1945-64; prof., chmn. dept. gen. linguistics U. Pitts., 1964- -, acting dir. Lang. Acquisition Inst., 1970—; vis. lectr., Afghanistan, 1951, Thailand, 1955-57, Mexico, 1964-65; dir. S.E. Asian English Project, Thailand, Laos, Vietnam, 1958-61, Rockefeller Found. Thai Project, 1968—; cons. in field. Mem. Nat. Adv. Council Teaching English as a Fgn. Lang. Resource person Detroit Bd. Edn., 1964, Pitts. Bd. Edn., 1965. Smith- Mundt grantee, 1951; recipient Fulbright award, 1955-57; Nat. Def. Edn. Act Lang. Research grantee, 1965-67; State Dept. grantee, 1964, 65. Mem. Linguistic Soc., Assn. Asian Studies, Siam Soc. (life), Assn. Tchrs. English to Speakers of Other Langs. (pres. 1967), Nat. Council Tchrs. English. Democrat. Presbyn. Author: Reading Thai Syllables, 1962; (with others) Foundations of Thai, 2 vols., 1968. Book rev. editor Lan. Learning, 1948, editor, 1949. Home: 4118 Northampton Dr Allison Park PA 15101 Office: Dept Gen Linguistics Univ Pittsburgh Pittsburgh PA 15213

ANTHONY, HARRY ANTONIADES, city planner, educator; b. Skyros, Greece, July 28, 1922; s. Anthony G. and Maria G. (Ftoulis) Antoniades; B.Arch., Nat. Tech. U., Athens, Greece, 1945; student Ecole Nat. Supérieure des Beaux Arts, Paris, France, 1945-46; M.City Planning U. Paris, 1947; Docteur d'Universite, Sorbonne, Paris, 1949; Ph.D. in Arch. and Urban Planning, Columbia, 1955; m. Anne C. Skoufis, Sept. 23, 1950; children—Mary Anne, Kathryn Harriet. Came to U.S., 1951, naturalized, 1954. Architect-planner with Constantinos A.Doxiadis, Athens, 1943-45, LeCorbusier, Paris, 1946-47, ECA, Paris, 1949-51; city planner with Maurice E.H. Rotival, N.Y.C., 1951-52; chief planner Brown & Blauvelt, N.Y.C., 1952-54; city planner Skidmore, Owings & Merrill, N.Y.C., 1954-56; prin. planning cons. Brown Engrs. Internat., N.Y.C., 1956-60; prin. Brown & Anthony City Planners, Inc., N.Y.C., 1960-69; mem. faculty Columbia, 1953—, prof. urban planning, 1963—, dir. grad. planning program Sch. Architecture, 1962-65; vis. prof. urban design Tulane U., 1967-68; vis. speaker Dartmouth, Tulane U., U. City N.Y., U. Okla., Ohio U., Auburn U., Cal. State Polytech. Coll., 1960—; vis. lectr. U. Cal., also San Diego State Coll., 1969-70; planning, zoning, urban renewal and urban design cons. to several cities, U.S. and abroad, 1956—, also cons. to UN, to govt. and univs.; planning commr., Leonia, N.J., 1958-64. Recipient Premier Grand Prix Internat. Exhbn. Housing and City Planning, Paris, 1947; William Kinne Fellows travelling fellow in planning N.Am., 1956; Urban Center of Columbia U. research award, 1969. Mem. A.I.A. (Arnold W. Brunner scholar 1958), Am. Inst. Planners, Am. Soc. Planning Ofcls., Regional Plan Assn., Nat. Assn. Housing and Redevel. Ofcls., Am. Assn. U. Profs. Author: Lectures on Planning Urban America, 1962. Contbr. master plans, reports, zoning ordinances, articles to various publs. Home: 475 Grand View Terrace Leonia NJ 07605 also 766665 Caminito Avola LaJolla CA 92037 Office: Sch Architecture Columbia Univ New York City NY 10017

ANTHONY, JOSEPH, theatrical dir.; b. Milw., May 24, 1912; s. Leonard Deuster and Sophie (Herts) A.; student U. Wis., 1929-31, Pasadena (Cal.) Playhouse, 1931-35, Daykarhanova Sch. Stage, N.Y.C., 1935-37; m. Perry Wilson, Aug. 3, 1942; children—Peter Dean, Ellen Roe. Appeared in amateur theatres, Milw., 1930, Pasadena Playhouse, 1931-35; 1st profl. appearance with Helen Gahaganin in Mary Queen of Scots, Los Angeles; Lady in the Dark, 1939, other appearances include Professor Mamlock, 1936, Truckline Cafe, 1946, Peer Gynt, 1947, Skipper Next to God, 1948, Anastasia, 1954-55, Country Girl, 1951, Camino Real, 1953, Flight into Egypt, 1952; motion picture appearances include Shadow of a Thin Man, Joe Smith, American, also TV dramatic prodns.; dancing partner to Agnes de Mille, 1940-41; dir. theatrical prodns. Bullfight, 1954, The Lark, 1955, The Rainmaker, 1954, Clearing the Woods, 1957, Marriage-go-Round, 1958, Winesburg, Ohio, 1959, The Best Man, 1960, The Most Happy Fella, 1956, Mary, Mary, 1961, Under the Yum-Yum Tree, 1960, Romulus, 1962, 110 in the Shade, 1963, The Last Analysis, 1964, Slow Dance on the Killing Ground, 1964, Rhinoceros, 1961; Mrs. Dally, 1965; The Playroom, 1965; Weekend, 1967; Jimmy, 1969; dir. motion pictures The Rainmaker, 1956, The Matchmaker, 1959, Career, 1959, All in a Night's Work, 1961, The Captive City, 1962, Tomorrow, 1971, also TV prodns.; dir. Am. Shakespeare Festival, 1965, 66, Guthrie Theatre, 1969, Ahmondson Theatre, Los Angeles, 1968; lectr. Am. Theatre Wing, Daykarhanova Sch. Stage; tchr. Vassar Coll., 1966, N.Y. U., 1968-69, Hunter Coll., 1967-70. Served with AUS, 1942-46. Mem. A.F.T.R.A. (bd. 1950), Actor's Equity (council 1951-56), Screen Dirs. Guild (bd. 1961), Soc. Stage Dirs. and Choreographers (pres. 1963-65), Am. Actors Co. (founding mem.), Actor's Studio. Address: Winding Road Farm Ardsley NY 10502

ANTHONY, JOSEPH GARNER, lawyer; b. Phila., Dec. 19, 1899; s. Charles Howard and Rachel Edith (Humphreys) A.; A.B., Swarthmore Coll., 1923; LL.B., Harvard, 1926; m. Dorothy McClaren, June 29, 1926; children—Patricia A., Garner A. Admitted to Hawaii bar, 1926, Supreme Ct. of U.S., 1936; atty. gen. of Hawaii, 1942-43; in pvt. practice, Honolulu, 1943-. Vice pres. Queen's Hosp., Honolulu. Served with F.A., U.S. Army, World War I. Fellow Am. Bar Found.; mem. Am. Coll. Trial Lawyers, Am. Bar Assn. (state del. 1944- 47, 53-62, bd. govs. 1961-64). Episcopalian. Clubs: Pacific, Oahu Country. Author: Hawaii Under Army Rule. Contbr. articles to legal jours. Home: 3251 Pacific Heights Rd PO Box 3199 Honolulu, HI 96801. Office: 333 Queen St Honolulu HI 96813

ANTHONY, ROBERT L., educator; b. Ft. Recovery, O., May 6, 1912; s. William H. and Frances (Phillips) A.; A.B., Miami U., Oxford, O., 1933; Ph.D. in Physics, Yale, 1936; m. Marcella Huerkamp, Aug. 20, 1938; children—Mary J., James R., Elizabeth A., Catherine M., Paul L., Barbara J. Research asso. physics Yale, 1936-37; mem. faculty physics U. Notre Dame, 1937-, prof., 1953—; on leave as mem. tech. staff-physics Ground Systems Group, Hughes Aircraft Co., Fullerton, Cal., 1962-63; with applied research sect. Martin Co.-Titan missile program, summer 1959; research high-polymer physics, ultrasonic attenuation in liquids, gen. solid state physics. Fellow Am. Phys. Soc.; mem. Am. Assn. Physics Tchrs., Phi Beta Kappa, Sigma Xi. Roman Catholic. Contbr. articles profl. jours., chpts. books. Home: 17382 Cleveland Rd South Bend, IN 46635. Office: Dept Physics Notre Dame IN 46556

ANTHONY, ROBERT NEWTON, educator; b. Orange, Mass., Sept. 6, 1916; s. Charles H. and Grace (Newton) A.; A.B., Colby Coll., 1938, M.A. (hon.), 1959, L.H.D., 1963; M.B.A., Harvard, 1940, D.C.S., 1952; m. Gretchen Lynch, Aug. 28, 1943; children—Robert N., Victoria Stewart. Faculty Bus. Sch., Harvard, 1940-42, 46—, now Ross Graham Walker prof. mgmt. control, Leatherbee lectr. 1967; pres. Mgmt. Analysis Center, Inc., 1955-63; asst. sec., controller Def. Dept., 1965-68; prof. Mgmt. Devel. Inst., Switzerland, 1957-58; mem. Stanford Exec. Devel. Program, 1962; mem. adv. bd. IMEDE, Switzerland, 1961-65, 68—; spl. asst. to sec. of Air Force. Trustee Lexington Savs. Bank; dir. Systems Audit Corp. Bd. nominations Ohio State U. Accounting Hall of Fame, 1959-65; mem. bd Mgmt. Internat., 1961-65; trustee Colby Coll., 1959—. Served from ensign to lt. comdr. USNR, 1941-46. Recipient Distinguished Leadership award Fed. Govt. Accountants Assn., Distinguished Pub. Service medal Dept. Def. Fellow Acad. Mgmt., mem. Internat. Univ. Contact, IMEDE Alumni Assn., Am. Accounting Assn. (v.p. 1959), Accounting Principles Round Table (moderator 1963), Financial Execs. Inst., Nat. Assn. Accountants (chmn. cost concepts subcom.), Fed. Govt. Accountants Assn.; Am. Soc. Mil. Comptrollers, Phi Beta Kappa, Pi Gamma Mu. Club: Harvard Business School (dir. 1966—). Author: Cases, Problems and Questions in Practical Controllership, 1949; Management Controls in Industrial Research Organization, 1952; (with Dearborn and Kneznek) Spending for Industrial Research, 1951-52; Shoe Machinery: Buy or Lease?, 1955; Management Accounting, Text and Cases, 1956, 4th edit., 1970; Office Equipment, Buy or Rent?, 1957; (with Dearden) Supplementary Cases and Problems in Management Accounting, 1960, 3d edit. as Accounting Problems and Cases, 1970; (with Mason and Hunt) Cases in Financial Management, 1960; Essentials of Accounting, 1964; Management Accounting Principles, 1965, rev. edit., 1970; Planning and Control Systems: A Framework for Analysis, 1965; (with Dearden and Vancil) Management Control Systems, 1966; (with Hekimian) Operations Cost Control, 1967; Plaid in Management Accounting, 1970. Editor: Automatic Data Processing 1956; cons. editor Richard D. Irwin, Inc. Mem. bd. Harvard Bus. Rev., 1947-59. Home: 39 Meriam St Lexington MA 02173

ANTOINE, MARCEL, diplomat, Haitian lawyer; b. Port-au-Prince, Feb. 8, 1900. Lawyer, Haiti, 1929—; former govt. commr. Civil Ct. Petit Goave, Haiti; consul-gen., Santiago, Cuba, 1947-57; chargé d'affaires, Santiago, Chile, 1957-59; ambassador to Panama, 1959-62, to Venezuela, 1962-64, to Argentina, 1964-67; permanent rep. to UN, 1967—. Address: 801 2d Av New York City NY 10017*

ANTON, DAVID MICHAEL, hosp. dir.; b. Bklyn., Jan. 27, 1911; s. Sol and Grace Anton; m. Audrey Keller, Oct. 16, 1941. Chief hosp. operations VA br. office, Columbus, O., 1946-47; asst. dir. VA Hosp., Dearborn, Mich., 1947-53, VA Hosp., Bklyn., 1953-54, VA Hosp., N.Y.C., 1954-57; hosp. dir. VA Hosp., Castle Point, N.Y., 1957-58; area dir. adminstrv. services VA Area Med. Office, Boston, 1958-63;

dir. bldg. mgmt. service VA Central Office, Washington, 1963-66; hosp. dir. VA Hosp., West Haven, Conn., 1966-70, VA Hosps., St. Louis, 1970—. Mem. policy com. Fed. Exec. Bd.; mem. Gov.'s Adv. Council on Comprehensive Health Planning; mem. regional adv. com. Bi-State Regional Med. Program. Served to maj. Med. Service Corps, AUS, USAAF, 1942-46; ETO. Recipient citations Am. Legion, U.S. Customs Port N.Y., 1957, Am. Legion dept. N.Y., 1957, dept. Conn., 1970, AMVETS Spl. Meritorious Commendation Nat., 1967, United Spanish War Vets dept. Conn., 1968, Vets. World War I dept. Conn., 1968, 70, D.A.V. dept. Conn., 1970, others; Adminstrs. Outstanding award and Chief Med. Dirs. Spl. Achievement award VA, 1970. Fellow Royal Soc. Health Eng.; mem. Am. Coll. Hosp. Adminstrs., Am. Pub. Health Assn., Assn. Mil. Surgeons U.S., Fed. Hosp. Inst. Alumni Assn. Am. Med. Colls., Am. Hosp. Assn., Am. Legion, Ret. Officers Assn., Fed. Bus. Assn. Rotarian, Mason. Address: VA Hosp St Louis MO 63125

ANTON, HECTOR ROQUE, educator; b. El Paso, Tex., Mar. 14, 1919; s. Roque and Luisa (Guerra) A.; student Los Angeles City Coll., 1938-39; B.S., U. Cal. at Los Angeles, 1942, M.S., 1947; Ph.D., U. Minn., 1953; m. Lois Miriam Triggs, 1949; children—John R., David L., Mary F., Susan C. Jr. accountant Ivar Pally, C.P.A., Beverly Hills, Cal., 1946; instr. U. Minn., 1947-50, vis. prof. Sch. Bus. Adminstrn., 1958-59; asst. prof. U. Wash., 1950-54; mem. faculty U. Cal. at Berkeley, 1954—, prof. accounting, chmn. dept., 1964- 68, asso. dean Grad. Sch. Bus., 1969—, mem. faculty council Center for Research, 1957—; Fulbright prof. Svenska Handelshogskolan, Helsingfors, also Kauppakorkeakoulu, Helsinki, Findland, 1961-62; vis. prof. Turun-Kauppakorkeakoulu, Finland, spring 1962, Victoria (New Zealand) U., 1966; Ford Found. distinguished vis. prof. U. Chgo., 1968-69; cons. to govt. and industry. Grantee Ford Found., 1957, 59, 64; fellow Wallenberg Found., Stockholm, Sweden, 1965; NSF grantee, 1968-69. Mem. Am. Accounting Assn. (exec. com. 1969, dir. research 1969—), Am. Econ. Assn., A.A.A.S., Nat. Assn. Accountants, Inst. Mgmt. Scis., Alpha Kappa Psi, Beta Alpha Psi, Beta Gamma Sigma. Author: (With others) Accounting Teachers, 1953; Accounting for the Flow of Funds, 1962; (with W.S. Boutell) Fortran and Business Data Processing, 1964; (with P.A. Firmin) Contemporary Issues in Cost Accounting, 1966; Fortran and Business Data Processing, 1968 (Japanese edit. 1971); (with R.K. Jaedicke) Fund and Cash Flows, 1970; also numerous articles, monographs, chpts. in books. Contbr. to Handbook of Modern Accounting, 1970. Home: 1062 Mariposa Av Berkeley CA 94707

ANTON, JOHN PETER, educator; b. Canton, O., Nov. 2, 1920; s. Peter C. and Christine (Giannopoulos) A.; B.S., Columbia, 1949, M.A., 1950, Ph.D., 1954; m. Helen Vezos, Nov. 26, 1955; children—James, Christopher, Peter. Instr., Pace Coll., 1953-54; vis. lectr. U. N.M., 1954-55; asst. prof. U. Neb., 1955-58; asso. prof. Ohio Wesleyan U., 1958-62; prof. State U. N.Y., Buffalo, 1962-67, asso. dean Grad. Sch., prof., 1967-69; Fuller E. Callaway prof., chmn. dept. philosophy Emory U., 1969—. Served with AUS, 1946-47. Mem. Modern Greek Studies Assn. (v.p. 1969—), Soc. Macedonian Studies (hon.), Am. Philos. Assn., Soc. Ancient Greek Philosophy, Am. Soc. Aesthetics, Medieval Acad. Am., Phi Beta Kappa (hon.), Eta Sigma Phi (hon.), Phi Sigma Tau (hon.). Author: Aristotle's Theory of Contrariety, 1957; Science, Philosophy and Educational Tasks, 1966; Naturalism and Historical Understanding, 1967; Philosophical Essays, 1969; Essays in Ancient Greek Philosophy, 1971. Editorial cons. Jour. History of Philosophy, 1968—, The Humanist, 1967—; editorial bd. Arethusa: Jour. Classical Studies, 1967—, Neo-Hellenica, 1970—. Home: 2582 Sugarplum Ct NE Atlanta GA 30345

ANTON, MARK, corp. exec.; b. Chgo., Dec. 3, 1892; s. Bryon and Jane (Olwell) A.; ed. pub. schs., Newark, N.J.; m. Adele Buecke, Sept. 19, 1923 (dec. Feb. 6, 1961); children—Mark John, Jane. Asst. to works mgr. Hyatt Roller Bearings, 1916-20; formed Circle Stamping & Mfg. Co., later called Mark Anton Mfg. Co., 1920; established Suburban Gas Co., 1928, Inc., 1929; established Warren County Gas Co., 1931; organized Nat. Bottled Gas Assn. (now Liquefied Petroleum Gas Assn.), 1931, pres., 1931-34; bought Eastern Seaboard retail properties from Phillips Petroleum Co. and formed Suburban Propane Gas Corp., 1945, pres. and dir., 1945, now chmn. bd.; treas. and dir. Warren County Gas Co.; dir. Federal Trust Co., SBN Gas Co., Gas- Oil Exploration Co., The Lionel Corp., Found. Life Ins. Co. Am., and Liquigas (Milan, Italy). Essex County freeholder, 1950-52; served as state senator from Essex County, 1953; mem. N.J. State Planning and Devel. Council, 1957; chmn. N.J. Navigation Com.; trustee Seton Hall U., N.J. Citizens Hwy. Com., N.J. Safety Council, Orange Meml. Hosp., Westminster Choir Coll.; vice pres., bd. trustees Kessler Inst. Rehab.; nat. trustee, exec. chmn. N.J. region Nat. Conf. Christians and Jews; bd. dirs. N.J. chpt. Arthritis and Rheumatism Found., Am. French Found., Essex County Service Chronically Ill.; county crusdae chmn. Am. Cancer Soc., 1965; drive chmn. United Cerebral Palsy of North Jersey, 1966, 1967. Served as lt. U.S. Army, World War I; nat. chmn. N.R.A. Code Authority for Liquefied Petroleum br. industry, 1933; chief fuel oil for Atlantic Coast, Petroleum Adminstrn. for War, 1942; N.J. mgr. Smaller War Plants Corp., 1943-44. Mem. Marymount Coll. Fathers' Council, N.J. C. of C. (dir.), Liquefied Petroleum Gas Assn. (dir.), Am. Legion, Clubs: Bankers, N.Y. Athletic, Circus Saints and Sinners (treas.), Economic (N.Y.C.) Lucullus Circle, Bayhead Yacht, Downtown, Rock Spring Country (N.J.); Capitol Hill; Manhasset Bay Yacht.; Great Oaks Yacht; Circumnavigators; Marco Polo; 744 Broad St. Home: Claridge House Verona NJ 07044 Office: Suburban Propane Gas Corp Mt Pleasant Av Whippany NJ 07981 also 20 Exchange Pl New York City NY 10005

ANTON, MARK JOHN, gas co. exec.; b. Newark, Feb. 12, 1926; s. Mark and Adele (Beucke) A.; B.A., Bowdoin Coll., 1951; m. Elizabeth Flower, Oct. 31, 1953. With Suburban Propane Gas Co., Whippany, N.J., 1949—, v.p. charge sales, asst. sec., 1958-61, exec. v.p., 1961-63, pres., 1963—, also dir.; dir. Am. Nat. Bank & Trust, Morristown, N.J. Trustee, Hosp. Center Orange (N.J.), Kent Place Sch., Summit, N.J. Served with USNR, 1944-46. Mem. Nat. LP-Gas Assn., Assn. Young Gassers (pres. 1961-62). Clubs: Baltusrol Golf (Springfield, N.J.); Beacon Hill (Summit). Home: 31 Washington Av Short Hills NJ 07078 Office: Suburban Propane Gas Corp Whippany NJ 07981

ANTONAKOS, STEPHEN, sculptor; b. So, Greece, Nov. 1, 1926; came to U.S., 1930; ed. Bklyn. Community Coll., Bklyn. Mus. Art Sch. Sculptor, working primarily in neon; one-man show U. Me., 1958, Avant-Garde Gallery, N.Y., 1958, Miami Mus. Modern Art, 1964, Schramm Gallery, Ft. Lauderdale, 1964, Byron Gallery, N.Y.C., 1964, Fischbach Gallery, N.Y.C., 1967-69; exhibited Miami Mus. Modern Art, 1958, Martha Jackson Gallery, N.Y., 1960, Allan Stone Gallery, 1961, 62, 64, Byron Gallery, 1963, 64, PVI Gallery, N.Y., 1964, 65, WMAA, 1966 (2), 68, 69, Newark Coll. Engring., 1968, U. N.C., 1968, R.I. Sch. Design, 1969, U. Cal. at Los Angeles Art Gallery, 1969, numerous others; represented in permanent collections Whitney Mus. Am. Art, N.Y.C., Larry Aldrich Mus., Ridgefield, Conn., Finch Coll. Mus., N.Y., Miami Mus. Modern Art. Instr. painting and sculpture U. N.C. at Greensboro.*

ANTONELLI, THEODORE, army officer; b. New Haven, Jan. 6, 1920; s. Michael and Gilda (Iezzi) A.; A.B., U. Conn., 1941; M.A., George Washington U., 1965; grad. Command and Gen. Staff Coll., 1955, Army War Coll., 1959, Indsl. Coll. Armed Forces, 1963; m. Margaret Genevieve Smith, July 7, 1945; 1 son, William Michael. Commd. 2d lt., inf., U.S. Army, 1941, advanced through grades to maj. gen., 1970; served 1st Inf. Div. and Hdqrs. 6th Corps, Europe and N. Africa, World War II; liaison officer to West German R.R., 1948-51; chief research Trans Arctic Group, Ft. Eustis, Va., and Greenland Ice Cap, 1953-54; mem. staff Office Dep. Chief Staff Logistics, 1955-58; with 1st Cav. Div., Korea, 1959-60; chief staff transp. Office Army Missile Command, 1960-62; with Office Joint Chiefs Staff, Mil. Assistance Affairs Africa region, 1963-66; vice dir. Def. Communications Planning Group, Washington, 1968-69; dir. distbn. and transp. U.S. Army Materiel Command, Washington, 1969— Decorated Silver Star with oak leaf cluster, Legion of Merit, Army Commendation medal with 2 oak leaf clusters, Joint Service Commendation medal, B.S.M., Purple Heart, Combat Inf. badge. Mem. Nat. Def. Transp. Assn., Am. Ordnance Assn., Assn. U.S. Army. Home: 822 Empress Ct Alexandria VA 22308 Office: US Army Materiel Command Washington DC 20315

ANTONINI, LUIGI, first v. p. Internat. Ladies' Garment Workers Address: 3 William St Newark NJ 07102*

ANTONIO, ADOLPH LOUIS, aerospace co. exec.; b. Beckley, W.Va., Aug. 19, 1913; s. John Paul and Florence (Alois) A.; B.S., Pa. State U., 1935; M.S., Mass. Inst. Tech., 1937, Ph.D., 1939; m. Marie Elizabeth Light, Aug. 22, 1957; children—David Hugh, Frederick Bryant, Christopher John, Dean Francis. Devel. engr. Standard Oil Devel. Co., 1939-43; with Aerojet-Gen. Corp., 1944—, v.p. chems., 1958-64, group v.p. research and tech., 1964—. Recipient Hickman award Am. Rocket Soc., 1952. Mem. Am. Mgmt. Assn., Am. Chem. Soc., Am. Inst. Chem. Engrs., Am. Inst. Aeros. and Astronautics. Home: 1019 W Foothill Blvd Arcadia CA 91006 Office: 9100 E Flair Dr El Monte CA 91731

ANTONIONI, MICHELANGELO, motion picture dir.; b. Ferrara, Italy, Sept. 29, 1912; s. Ismaele and Elisabetta Roncagli; degree in Econs. and Commerce, U. Bologna (Italy). Formerly asst. dir., also film critic for newspapers; films dir. include 8 documentaries, 1945-50; Cronaca di un Amore, 1950; I Vinti, 1952; La Signora Senza Camelie, 1953; Le Amiche, 1955; Il Grido, 1957; L'Avventura, 1960; La Notte, 1961; L'Eclisse, 1962; Il Deserto Rosso, 1964; Blow Up (Golden Palm Cannes Film Festival 1967), 1967; Zabriskie Point, 1970. Address: Via Vincenzo Tiberio 18 Rome Italy

ANTRIM, MALCOLM BURROWS, steel co. exec.; b. W. Pittston, Pa., June 29, 1916: s. Hiram H. and Mabel (Burrows) A.; B.E.E., Rensselaer Poly. Inst., 1938; student U. Pa., 1952-53; m. Ruth Alice Shultz, Aug. 30, 1941; children—Richard Douglas, Barbara Ellyn, Janice Ruth. With Repp & Menzies, engrs., Scranton, Pa., 1938-39, Westinghouse Electric Co., 1939-41; with Lukens Steel Co., Coatesville, Pa., 1941—, mgr. engring. and construction, 1959-66, mgr. engring. services, 1966-67, director engineering and planning, 1967—. Vice pres. Coatesville Area Sch., 1964—; treas. E. Fallowfield Sch. Bd., 1954-59, pres., 1960-64; sec. operating adv. com. Central Chester County Vocational Tech. Sch., 1965-70; mem. Pa. Adv. Council for Vocational Edn., 1969-70. Bd. mgrs. Coatesville Hosp., 1954-60; life mem. W. End Fire Company, Coatesville. Registered profl. engr., Pa. Mem. Assn. Iron and Steel Engrs. (chmn. Phila. 1958; nat. chmn. research com. 1961-64, nat. pres. 1965), Am. Inst. Elec. and Electronic Engrs., Am., British iron and steel insts., Verein Deutscher Eisenhuttenleute, Am. Ordnance Assn., Franklin Inst., Coatesville C. of C., Nat., Pa. socs. profl. engrs., N.A.M. (ednl. com., telecommunications com.), Coatesville C. of C., Air Pollution Control Assn., Theta Chi. Republican. Presbyn. Clubs: Coatesville Country; Wellwood Yacht (Charlestown, Md.). Home: RD 3 Box 68 Coatesville PA 19320 Office: Lukens Steel Co Coatesville PA 19320

ANTUPIT, SAMUEL NATHANIEL, art dir.; b. West Hartford, Conn., Feb. 14, 1932; s. Louis and Sylvia (Feinberg) A.; grad. Loomis Sch., 1950; B.A. in English, Yale, 1954, B.F.A. in Graphic Design, 1956; m. Rosalie Jane Littman, Dec. 30, 1956; children—Lisa Ruth, Jennifer Carol, Stephen Michael, Peter Louis. Asst. art dir. Harper's Bazaar mag., 1958-61, Show mag., 1961-63; asst. corp. art dir. Conde Nast Publs., 1963, Pushpin Studios, 1963-64; art. dir. Art in Am., 1963-64, N.Y. Rev. Books, 1963—, Esquire mag., 1964-68; pres. Hess and/or Antupit, designer, publs., and cons., 1968-70; lectr. pub. procedures course Harvard-Radcliffe Coll., 1965—; propr. Cycling Frog Press, Pound Ridge, N.Y., 1961—, Antupit & Others Inc., 1971—, Subsistence Press, 1971—. Trustee Hiram Halle Meml. Library. Served with AUS, 1956-58. Recipient Design awards Art Dirs. Club, N.Y.C., 1960—, Type Dirs. Club, N.Y.C., 1961—, Soc. Illustrators, 1961—, Art Dirs. Club, Boston. Mem. Nat. Acad. Rec. Arts and Scis., Am. Inst. Graphic Arts (bd. dirs. 1968—. v.p. 1970-71; Design awards 1965—) . Home: East Woods Rd Pound Ridge NY 10576 Office: 27 E 62d St New York City NY 10021

ANTWI, LAWFORD ODAI, diplomat of Ghana; b. Accra, Ghana, Aug. 13, 1932; s. Obo and Mary (Quaye) A.; student St. Augustine's Coll., 1951-52; B.A., U. Coll. of Gold Coast, 1958; m. Comfort Mavis Tackie, Feb. 7, 1959; children—Captain, Moira, Patricia, Mavis, Theodore, Charity. 1st sec., acting resident minister to Guidea, 1959-61; adminstrv. officer Ministry of Def., 1962-63; counsellor/charge d'affaires, Tokyo, 1964-67; dir. Africa div. Fgn. Ministry, 1967-69; counsul gen.; N.Y.C., 1969-70; minister to Bonn, 1970—. Del. to China and Korea, 1963, Presdl. entourage, Upper Volta and Niger, 1968, West African Econ. Community, Monrovia, 1968, OAU summits, Algiers, 1968, Addis Ababa, 1969; rep. 5th com. UN Gen. Assembly, 1969; chmn. spl. com. for evacuation and rehab. of Ghanian fishermen expelled from Sierra Leone, 1968-69; spl. Ghana rep. Bur. Placement and Edn. of Refugees of Orgn. African Unity, 1969. Home: 14 Arndtstrasse 532 Bad Godesberg West Germany Office: Embassy of Ghana 73 Adenauerallee 53 Bonn West Germany

ANUSZKIEWICA, RICHARD JOSEPH, artist; b. Erie, Pa., May 23, 1930; s. Adam Jacob and Victoria (Jankowski) A.; B.F.A., Cleve. Inst. Art, 1953; M.F.A., Yale, 1955; B.S. in Edn., Kent State U., 1956; m. Sarah Feeney, Nov. 26, 1960; children—Adam John, Stephanie. Exhibited one man shows at Butler Art Inst., Youngstown, O., 1955, The Contempories, N.Y.C., 1960, 61, 63, Sidney Janis Gallery, New York City, 1965-67, Dartmouth College, 1967, Cleveland Museum of Art, 1967, Kent State University, 1968; exhbt. in group shows at Museum Modern Art, 1960-61, 63, 65, U. Ill., 1961, N.Y. U., 1961, Pa. Acad. Design, 1962, Whitney Mus. Am. Art, 1962, 63-64, 70, 71, Inst. Contemporary Arts, Boston, 1962, Columbus (O.) Gallery Fine Arts, 1962, City Art Mus., St. Louis, 1962, Munson-Williams-Proctor Inst., Utica, N.Y., 1962, Tweed Gallery U. Minn., 1962, Silvermine (Conn.) Guild Artists, 1962, 63, Atheneum Sch., Helsinki, Finland, 1962, Mus. Modern Art, Sarasota, Fla., 1962, J.B. Speed Art Mus., Louisville, 1962, Meml. Art Gallery, Rochester, N.Y., 1962, Allentown (Pa.) Art Mus., 1963, Krannert (Ill.) Art Mus., 1963, De Cordova Mus., Lincoln, Mass., 1963, Washington Gallery Modern Art, 1963, U. Mich. Mus. Art, 1964, Sidney Janis Gallery, N.Y.C., 1964, 65, Art Inst., Chgo., 1964, 71, Tate Gallery, London, 1964, Far Gallery, 1964, Carnegie Inst., Pitts., 1964, Carnegie Inst., Pitts., 1964, Corcoran Gallery Art, Washington, 1965, Art Fair Cologne (Germany), 1967, Larry Aldrich Mus., Ridgefield, Conn., 1968, 71, Hopkins Center Art Galleries Dartmouth Coll., Hanover, N.H., 1969, Denver Art Mus., 1969, Va. Mus. Fine Arts, Richmond, 1970, Ind. State U., Terre Haute, 1970, Masur Modern Art, Monroe, La., 1970, Birmingham (Ala.) Mus., 1971, others; rep. permanent collections at Mus. Modern Art, Whitney Mus. Am. Art, Cleve. Mus. Art, Corcoran Gallery Art, Allentown Art Mus., Albright-Knox Art Gallery, Butler Art Inst., Akron (O.) Art Inst., Yale Art Gallery, Chgo. Art Inst., Larry Aldrich Mus., Ridgefield, Conn. Contbr. articles profl. jours. Home: 76 Chestnut St Englewood NJ 07631 Office: Sidney Janis Gallery New York City NY 10017

APARICIO, LUIS, shortstop for Boston Red Sox Profl. Baseball Team.*

APEL, HAROLD WILLIAM, librarian; b. Portsmouth, O., June 19, 1921; s. John and Ida (Stock) A.; A.B., Miami U., Oxford, O., 1950; student U. Chgo., 1952; M.S. in L.S., Western Res. U., 1954; m. Catherine Marie DeLay June 20, 1954; 1 son, John Frank. Radio announcer-operator sta. WPAY, Portsmouth, 1939-42, program dir., 1945-46; staff positions Miami U. Library, Oxford, O., 1948-55; librarian Marshall U. Library, Huntington, W.Va., 1955-. Exec. dir. W.Va. Com. for Nat. Library Week, 1958-60. Civilian insp. Signal Corps Material, 1942-45. Served with AUS, 1946-47. Mem. W.Va. (pres. 1957-59), Am. (councilor 1959-63) library assns., Phi Beta Kappa. Rotarian. Home: 249 Forest Rd Huntington, WV 25705.

APEL, WILLI, musicologist; b. Konitz, Germany, Oct. 10, 1893; s. Max and Ida (Schoenlank) student U. Bonn, 1912-13, U. Munich, 1913-14; Ph.D., U. Berlin, 1936; m. Ursula Siemering, Sept. 22, 1928. Came to U.S., 1936, naturalized, 1944. Prof., Freie Schulgemeinde, Wickersdorf, 1922-28, Luisenstädtisches Gymnasium, Berlin, Germany, 1928-36, Longy Sch. Music, Cambridge, Mass., 1936-43; lectr. music Harvard, also Radcliffe Coll., 1938-42; lectr. Boston Center for Adult Edn., 1938-50; prof. music Ind. U., Bloomington, 1950-64, prof. emeritus, 1964—. Fellow Mediaeval Acad. Am.; mem. Am. Musicol. Soc., Internat. Gesellschaft für Musikwissenschaft. Author: The Notation of Polyphonic Music, 800-1600, 1942; Harvard Dictionary of Music, 1944. 2d edit., 1969 (with A.T. Davison) Historical Anthology of Music (2 vols.), 1946, 50; Masters of the Keyboard, 1947; French Secular Music of the Late 14th Century, 1950; Gregorian Chant, 1958; Geschichte der Orgel-und Klavier-musik bis 1700, 1967; French Secular Compositions of the 14th Century, Vol. I, 1970, Vol. II, 1971. Contbr. articles Am., fgn. periodicals. Home: 1018 E 2d St Bloomington IN 47401

APGAR, VIRGINIA, physician; b. Westfield, N.J., June 7, 1909; d. Charles Emory and Helen (Clarke) Apgar; A.B., Mt. Holyoke Coll., 1929; M.D., Columbia, 1933; M.P.H., Johns Hopkins, 1959; Med.Sc.D., Womans's Med. Coll., 1964, N.J. Coll. Medicine and Dentistry, 1967; Sc.D., Mt Holyoke Coll., 1965, Boston U., 1969. Intern in surgery Presbyn. Hosp., N.Y.C., 1933-35; resident anesthesiology U. Wis. and Bellevue Hosp., N.Y.C., 1937; clin. dir. dept. anesthesiology Columbia-Presbyn. Med. Center, 1938-59; prof. anesthesiology Columbia, 1949-59; med. staff Nat. Found., March Dimes, 1959—, chief div. congenital malformations, 1959-68, v.p. for med. affairs, 1968—; lectr. pediatrics (teratology) Cornell Med. Sch., 1965-71, adj. prof. pediatrics, 1971—. Mem.-at-large Methodist Bd. Hosps. and Homes, 1965—; alumnae trustee Mt. Holyoke Coll., 1965—. Recipient Alumnae award Mt. Holyoke Coll., 1954, Elizabeth Blackwell award, 1960. Diplomate Am. Bd. Anesthesiology, 1939. Fellow Am. Coll. Anesthesiology (chmn. bd. govs. 1950-52), N.Y. Acad. Medicine, Am. Acad. Pediatrics (hon. asso.), Am. Coll. Obstetrics and Gynecology (asso.), N.Y. Acad. Scis.; mem. Am. Pediatric Soc., A.A.A.S., Am. Eugenics Soc., Cong. Anomalies Research Assn. Japan, Catgut Acoustical Soc. (v.p.), Am. Soc. Human Genetics, Teratology Soc., Am. Pub. Health Assn., Pan-Am. Soc. Anesthesiology (hon.), Am. Soc. Anesthesiology (treas. 1939-45, distinguished service award 1961, hon. mem.), Harvey Soc., A.O. Whipple Surg. Soc., 25 Year Club Presbyn. Hosp., Amateur Chamber Music Players, Am. Philatelic Soc., Ubiquiteers (treas. 1959), Alpha Omega Alpha; hon. mem. N.Y. State Soc. Anesthesiology, Wash. State Obstet. Soc., Alaska Med. Soc., Irish-Am. Pediatric Soc., Alumni Soc. Sloane Hosp., Pediatric Soc. Dominican Republic. Home: 30 Engle St Tenafly NJ 07670 Office: PO Box 2000 White Plains NY 10605

APLAN, FRANK FULTON, educator; b. Boulder, Colo., Aug. 11, 1923; s. Frank Fulton and Helen Elizabeth (Fischer) A.; B.S., S.D. Sch. Mines and Tech., 1948; M.S., Mont. Coll. Mineral Sci. and Tech., 1950, Mining Engr. (hon.), 1968; Sc.D., Mass. Inst. Tech., 1957; m. Clare Marie Donaghue, June 30, 1955; children—Susan M., Peter D., Lucy A. Engr., Climax Molbydenum Co., 1950-51; asst. prof. U. Wash., 1951-53; sr. scientist Kennecott Copper Corp., 1957; group mgr. mineral engring., mining and metals div. Union Carbide Corp., 1957-67; prof., head dept. mineral preparation Pa. State U., 1968—; v.p., dir. Fischer Bros., Ft. Pierre, S.D., 1968-71. Served with AUS, 1942-46. Mem. Am. Inst. Mining. Metall. and Petroleum Engrs. (asso. chmn. minerals beneficiation div. 1971-72), Am. Chem. Soc., Am. Inst. Chem. Engrs., Sigma Xi. Contbr. profl. jours. Home: 432 W Fairmount Av State College PA 16801 Office: Mineral Sci Bldg Pa State Univ University Park PA 16802

APOLINAR, DANNY, writer, composer; b. Bklyn., Mar. 15, 1934; s. Archie and Dorothy (Beckhardt) A.; student Pratt Inst., 1954. Comml. artist-designer, 1952; pianist, vocalist, dancer, 1959—; recording artist for Atlantic, RCA records; composer, author, lyricist Your Own Thing, 1968. Served with AUS, 1957-59. Recipient Drama Critics Circle award, Outer Circle award, A.S.C.A.P. Pacesetter award, all for Your Own Thing, 1968. Mem. Am. Fedn. Musicians, A.F.T.R.A., Actors Equity, A.S.C.A.P. Home: 888 8th Av New York City NY 10023 Office: care Louis P Randell 1501 Broadway New York City NY 10026

APOLLONIO, UMBRO, art critic; b. Trieste, Apr. 20, 1911; s. Virgilio and Angela (Pensalfine) A.; Bachelor's degree; m. Fabiola Zanini; children—Marina, Gabriella. Prof. history contemporary art U. Padua; dir. rev. La Biennale de Venezia; editor Art Internat. of Lugano; writer in internat. cultural revs., mem. art juries, organizer exhbns. and meetings on modern art; curator Archivio Storico d'Arte Contemporanea, Venice; pub. Seurat, Venice, 1947, Chagall, Venice, 1949, Pittura Italiana Moderna, 1950, Marini, Milan, 1953, la Cultura Dell' Espressionismo, 1952, Picasso, Novare, 1954, Consagra, Rome, 1956, Delacroix, 1956, Sant' Elia, 1958, Mondrian, 1965, Braque, 1966, Hartung, 1967, Fauves E Cubisti, 1959, Miró, Florence, 1969, Mondrian e L'Astrattismo, Milan, 1970, Futurismo, Milan, 1970; pub. unprinted Works of Italo Svevo. Decorated Order of Merit of Italian Republic, Order Cross of South (Brazil); recipient laureate prize Le stanze del Libro, Rome, 1935, prize Ministry Pub. Instrn. for art criticism, 1946, 58, prize 24th Venice Biennial, 1948, prize Cortina Ulisse for art criticism, 1951, Gold medal for culture and art, 1962. Mem. Acad. Raffaello Urbino, Conseil Intern. Cinema et Télévision, Centro Intern. Ricerche Strutture Amrientali, Verucchio, Centre

Intern. Tapisserie, Lau Sonne, Intern. Center Communication and Sci. Home: via Candia 19 Venice Italy Office: Cà Giustinian-San Marco Venice Italy

APONE, CARL ANTHONY, journalist; b. Brownsville, Pa., July 9, 1923; s. Peter P. and Carmelia (Puglia) A.; B.A. cum laude, U. Notre Dame, 1949; M.A., Boston U., 1950; m. Kathleen King, Jan. 23, 1965; 1 dau., Elizabeth. Asst. prof. Journalism and Am. lit. St. Mary's Coll. for Women, Notre Dame, Ind., 1950-53; staff writer, U.P. Detroit, 1953; city editor Brownsville Telegraph, 1953-57; staff writer Pitts. Sun- Telegraph, 1958-60; music editor Pitts. Press, 1960—; mem. faculty journalism Duquesne U., 1967—; free-lance writer, 1950—. Mem. panel com. St. Vincent DePaul Soc., 1963—. Served with inf., AUS, 1943-46. Recipient Golden Quill Journalism awards; Pa. Newspaper Pubs. Assn. awards. Mem. Third Order St. Francis. Home: 2016 Worcester Dr Pittsburgh PA 15243 Office: Pitts Press Blvd of Allies Pittsburgh PA 15230

APONTE, GONZALO ENRIQUE, physician, educator; b. P.R., July 15, 1929; s. Gonzalo and Lalita (Socorro) A.; came to U.S., 1945; B.S., Georgetown U., 1948; M.D., Jefferson Med. Coll., 1952; m. Barbara Ann Bockus, June 15, 1963. Intern Jefferson Med. Coll. Hosp., 1952-53, resident pathology, 1953-57; fellow Nat. Cancer Inst., Jefferson Med. Coll., 1955-57, mem. faculty, 1959—, coordinator cancer teaching, 1960-68, asst. dir. cancer tng. program, 1968—, prof. pathology, head dept., also dir. clin. labs., 1967-; research collaborator Brookhaven Nat. Lab., 1960-67. Mem. exam. com. Edn. Council Fgn. Med. Students, Nat. Bd. Med. Examiners. Served to lt. comdr. M.C., 1957-59. Markle scholar med. sci., 1960-65; recipient Lindback award Distinguished Teaching, Christian R. and Mary F. Lindback Trust, 1961; named Clin. Sceintist of Year, Assn. Clin. Scientists, 1967. Mem. Coll. Am. Pathologists, Am. Soc. Clin. Pathologists, Internat. Acad. Pathology, Am. Assn. Blood Banks, Assn. Clin. Scientists, Am. Soc. Cytology, Phila. County Med. Soc., Sigma Xi, Alpha Omega Alpha. Home: 506 Pine St Philadelphia, PA 19106.

APONTE, JOSE C., atty. gen. P.R.; b. Guayama, P.R., Oct. 18, 1909; s. Jose J. and Candelaria (Garcia) A.; B.A., LL.B. magna cum laude, U. P.R; m. Divina Lebro, July 5, 1936; children—Jose C., Ubaldo, Nahir (Mrs. de Casanova), Nayra (Mrs. de Zerr), Ina R., Aviles. Admitted to P.R. bar; pvt. practice, 1933-41; asst. dist. atty., 1941-43; dist. atty., Caguas, 1943- 45, San Juan, 1945-47; spl. prosecutor and criminal div. Dept. Justice San Juan, 1946-67; atty. gen. P.R., 1967—. Recipient Manuel A. Perez award, 1967. Mem. P.R., Internat., Inter-Am. bar assns. Author articles on drug addiction. Home: 863 Las Marias Av Hide Park Pio Piedras, PR. Office: 150 Fortaleza St San Juan PR 00902

APONTE MARTINEZ, LUIS, archbishop; b. Lajas, P.R., Aug. 4, 1922; s. Santiago E. Aponte and Rosa Martinez; student San Ildefonso Sem., San Juan, P.R., 1944, St. John's Sem., Boston, 1950; LL.D. (hon.), Fordham U., 1965. Ordained priest Roman Cath. Ch., 1950; asst. in Patillas, P.R.; pastor in Maricao, P.R., Sta. Isabel, P.R., 1953-55; sec. to bishop of Ponce, P.R., 1955-57; pastor in Aibonito, P.R., 1957-60; aux. bishop of Ponce, 1960-63, bishop, 1963-64; archbishop of San Juan, 1964—. Chancellor Cath. U. P.R., Ponce, 1963—. Served as chaplain P.R. N.G., 1957-60. Lion. Address: Box 1967 San Juan PR 00901

APOSHIAN, HURAIR VASKEN, educator; b. Providence, Jan. 28, 1926; s. Leo and Manishag (Aghajanian) A.; B.S., Brown U., 1948; M.S., U. Rochester, 1950, Ph.D., 1953; m. Mary Mobareket Zaidan, Apr. 7, 1948; children—Christine Manishag, David Leo, Mary Ann. Mem. faculty Vanderbilt U. Sch. Medicine, 1954-59, asst. prof., 1956-59; USPHS research fellow Stanford Sch. medicine, 1959-62; asso. prof. microbiology Tufts U. Sch. Medicine, 1962-67; prof., chmn. cell biology and pharmacology U. Md. Sch. Medicine, 1967—. Mem. Am. Soc. Biol. Chemists, Am. Soc. Pharmacology and Exptl. Therapeutics, Am. Assn. Cancer Research, Am. Chem. Soc., N.Y. Acad. Scis., A.A.A.S. Research enzymology virus infections, oral agts for heavy metal poisoning, gene therapy. Office: 660 Redwood St Baltimore MD 21201

APOSTLE, HIPPOCRATES GEORGE, educator; b. Tyrnavos, Greece, Jan. 1, 1910; s. George C. and Aspasia (Tzartzanos) A.; came to U.S., naturalized, 1922; B.A., Columbia, 1933, M.A., 1935; postgrad. U. Chgo., 1935-39; Licence en Philosophie, Laval U. (Can.), 1941; Ph.D. in Philosophy, Harvard, 1943; m. Margaret Wylie, 1968. Asst. prof. math. and physics W. Va. Wesleyan U., 1942-43; asst. prof. math. U. Rochester, 1943-45; asst. prof. math. and philosophy Amherst Coll., 1945-47; asst. prof. philosophy U. Chgo., 1947- 48; prof. math. Grinnell Coll., 1948—, Steele prof., 1961—. Author: Aristotle's Philosophy of Mathematics, 1952; College Algebra, 1954; A Survey of Basic Mathematics, 1960; Aristotle's Metaphysics, 1967; Aristotle's Physics, 1969. Home: 817 East St Grinnell IA 50112

APOSTOL, TOM MIKE, educator, mathematician; b. Helper, Utah, Aug. 20, 1923; s. Mike A. and Florence (Papathanasopoulos) A.; B.S., U. Wash., 1944, M.S., 1946; Ph.D., U. Cal. at Berkeley, 1948; m. Jane Clark Thornton, Sept. 16, 1959. Lectr., U. Cal. at Berkeley, 1948-49; C.L.E. Moore instr. Mass. Inst. Tech., 1949-50; mem. faculty Cal. Inst. Tech., 1950—, prof. math., 1962—; vis. lectr. Math. Assn. Am., 1958-60. Mem. Am. Math. Soc., Math. Assn. Am. (bd. govs. 1962-65, chmn. So. Cal. sect. 1965-66), A.A.A.S. Author: Mathematical Analysis, 1957; Calculus, vol. I, 1961, vol. II, 1962; Calculus with Linear Algebra, Vol. I, 1967, Vol. II 1969; also articles. Editor: Selected Papers on Calculus, 1969. Office: Cal Inst Tech Pasadena CA 91109

APOSTOLAKOS, PETER CONSTANTINE, educator; b. Mpls., Mar. 14, 1915; s. Gust and Theodora (Zotalis) A.; B.B.A., U. Minn., 1940, B.S., 1947, M.A., 1949, Ph.D., 1957; m. Ruth Ziegler, Sept. 13, 1947; children—Diane, Constance, Margo. Lectr., asso. prof. and head dept. psychology U. Minn., Duluth, 1950-59; dir. tng., cons. Duluth, Missabe & Iron Range Ry., 1957-62; asso. prof. psychology Tex. Womans U., Denton, 1962-63; prof. head dept. psychology Chico (Cal.) State Coll., 1963-67, dean Sch. Behavioral and Social Scis., prof. psychology, 1967—. Pres. Butte County Coordinating Council for Mentally Retarded, 1969-70. Served with USAAF, 1942-46. Mem. Am. Psychol. Assn., Am. Statis. Assn., Assn. for Tng. and Devel., Am. Personnel and Guidance Assn., Phi Delta Kappa, Kappa Delta Pi, Psi Chi. Home: 1572 Filbert Av Chico CA 95926

APPEL, ALFRED, lawyer; b. N.Y.C., May 8, 1906; s. Samuel and Sadie (Niedermann) A.; A.B., Cornell U., 1926, J.D., 1928; m. Beatrice C. Hoffman, Sept. 3, 1931; children-Alfred, Elizabeth (Mrs. Paul Schaffer), John S. Admitted to N.Y. bar, 1928, since practiced in N.Y.C.; asso. Proskauer, Rose, Goetz & Mendelsohn and predecessor firms, 1928-40, partner, 1940—, now sr. partner. Dir. McGregor Doniger, Inc., 1954-70. Mem. Bd. Edn. Union Free Sch. Dist. 7, Great Neck, N.Y., 1954-60; mem. Cornell Law Sch. Adv. Council, 1967—. Bd. dirs. S.L. Hoffman Found., Inc.; trustee Soc. of Hillside Hosp.; mem. Charles H. Oestreich Found. Mem. Assn. Bar City N.Y., N.Y. County Lawyers Assn., Am., N.Y. State bar assns., Order of Coif, Sigma Alpha Mu, Phi Kappa Phi. Jewish religion. Club: Cornell (N.Y.C.). Editor, bus. mgr. Cornell Law, 1927-28. Home: 200 E 57th St New York NY 10022 Office: 300 Park Av New York NY 10022

APPEL, BENJAMIN writer; b. N.Y.C., Sept. 13, 1907; s. Louis and Bessie (Mikofsky) A.; student U. Pa., 1925-26, N.Y. U., 1926-27; B.S., Lafayette Coll., 1929; m. Sophie Marshak, Oct. 31, 1936; children—Carla, Willa Suzie, Marianna Consideration. Writer, 1929—; mechanic Republic Aviation Corp., Farmingdale, N.Y., 1943; with Office Civilian Def., Washington, 1943-44; spl. writer to Paul V. McNutt, chmn. War Manpower Commn., Washington, 1944-45; spl. asst. to U.S. High Commr. McNutt, Manila, P.I., 1945-46; spl. cons. to Sec. of Interior Julius A. Krug, 1946; asso. with John Steelman, dir. Office War Mblzn. and Reconversion, 1946-47. Author numerous books, 1934—; latest being: Fortress in the Rice, 1951; Hell's Kitchen (short stories), 1952; Plunder, 1952, Dock Walloper (short stories), 1953; Sweet Money Girl, 1954; Life and Death of a Tough Guy, 1955; In the Klondike Gold Rush (juvenile), 1956; At The Battle for Bataan (juvenile), 1957; The Raw Edge, 1958; The Funhouse, 1959; With Cortes and Montezuma (juvenile), 1959; A Big Man, A Fast Man, 1961; A Time of Fortune, 1963; With Many Voices: Europe Talks About America, 1963: Man and Magic, 1966; Why the Russians Are the Way They Are, 1966; Why the Chinese Are the Way They Are, 1968; Age of Dictators, 1968; The Fantastic Mirror, 1969. Stories have appeared in O. Henry and O'Brien anthologies. Home: Roosevelt NJ ☆

APPEL, GERSION, educator, clergyman; b. Budapest, Hungary, Jan. 13, 1916; s. Juda and Celia (Perl) A.; came to U.S. 1924, naturalized, 1930; B.A., Yeshiva Coll., 1938, D.H.L., 1945; Rabbi, Isaac Eichanon Theol. Sem., 1941; Ph.D., Harvard, 1962; m. Miriam Cohen, May 4, 1942; children—Dvora (Mrs. Michael Nussbaum), Shlomo, Ziporah (Mrs. Zev Wilon), Yakov, Rebecca, Esther. Rabbi, Worcester, Mass., 1941-46, N.Y.C., 1946-48, Seattle, 1948-58, Kew Gardens, N.Y., 1958-68; prof. Jewish philosophy Stern Coll., Yeshiva U., N.Y.C., 1961—, chmn. dept. philosophy, 1970—; adj. prof. Hebrew studies N.Y. U. Grad. Sch. Arts and Scis., 1968—. Chaplain, VA Hosp., Rutland, Mass., 1942-46, Young Israel Inst. for Jewish Studies, N.Y.C., 1946-48. Recipient Bernard Revel Meml. award religious edn., 1959; Honor award United Jewish Appeal, 1957, Am. Jewish Tercentenary, 1955, Yeshiva U., 1962. Mem. Rabbinical Council Am. (v.p. 1952), Mediaeval Acad. Am., Yeshiva U. Alumni Assn. Author: Sefer Ha-Neyar: A Thirteenth Century Code of Jewish Law, 1960. Editor: Studies in Jewish Law, Philosophy and Literature, 1970.

APPEL, JAMES ZIEGLER, physician; b. Lancaster, Pa., May 15, 1907; s. Theodore Burton and Mary Hurford (Calder) A.; B.S., Franklin and Marshall Coll., 1928, Sc.D., 1952; M.D., U. Pa., 1932; m. Florence Burch, Aug. 4, 1933; children—Florence (Mrs. Joseph A. Pontius), Mary (Mrs. Crosby Smith), Nancy (Mrs. William Hess), Charlotte (Mrs. E. Hollihan), James. Intern, Robert Packer Hosp., Sayre, Pa., 1932-33; gen. practice medicine, Lancaster, 1933-35, surgery, 1935—; tng. surgery Lancaster Gen. Hosp., 1935-42; organizer, dir. health dept. Franklin and Marshall Coll., 1943—. Adv. bd. Sears-Roebuck Found., 1955-61; sec. Am. Med. Research Found. of A.M.A., 1961-67, pres., 1964-66; trustee Sci. and Ednl. Trust, Med. Soc. Pa., pres., 1960—. Served as lt. col. Pa. N.G., 1946. Fellow A.C.S.; mem Med. Soc. Pa. (trustee 1948-58), Med. Service Assn. Pa. (dir. 1945-57), A.M.A. (trustee 1957-67, mem. commn. hosp. accreditation; pres. 1965-66), Lancaster City and County Med. Soc., Phi Beta Kappa, Chi Phi, Phi Alpha Sigma. Mem. United Church of Christ. Home: 1939 Pine Dr Lancaster PA 17601 Office: 305 N Duke St Lancaster Pa 17602

APPEL, JOHN GLENN, army officer; b. Terre Haute, Ind., June 4, 1918; s. Randolph B. and Kathryn (Glenn) A.; B.S., Rose Poly. Inst., 1941; grad. Army Command and Gen. Staff Coll., 1946, Air Command and Staff Coll., 1948, Armed Forces Staff Coll., 1958, Army War Coll., 1962; postgrad. U. Pitts., 1963; m. Mary Jane Delgar, May 16, 1942; children—Kathryn Anne (Mrs. Jack F. Lane, Jr.), John Glenn, Robert D. Commd. 2d lt. U.S. Army, 1941, advanced through grades to maj. gen., 1970; comdg. gen. Deseret Test Center, Ft. Douglas, Utah, 1966-69; dir. plans Office Dept. Chief of Staff for Logistics, Dept. of Army, Washington, 1969-70; dir. chem. and nuclear operations Office Asst. Chief of Staff for Force Devel., Dept. of Army, Washington, 1970—; instr. Armed Forces Staff Coll. Active A.R.C., Boy Scouts Am. Decorated Legion of Merit with oak leaf cluster, Army Commendation medal. Mason (Shriner). Home: 1608 Oakcrest Dr Alexandria VA 22302 Office: Asst Chief Staff Force Development Dept Army Washington DC 20310

APPEL, KAREL, artist; b. Amsterdam, Netherlands, Apr. 25, 1921; s. Jan and Johana (Chevallier) A.; student Nat. Acad. Fine Arts, Amsterdam, 1940-43. Painter, 1936—, in Paris, 1950—; one-man shows Municipal Mus., Amsterdam, Museum Schiedam, Holland, Kunst Halle, Bern, Switzerland, also Martha Jackson Gallery, N.Y.C., Gallery Stadler, Paris, others; works included various group exhbns., 1946—. Recipient UNESCO prize Venice Biennale, 1953; Lissone prize, Italy, 1958; Acquisition prize Sao Paulo Biennale, Brazil, 1959; Graphique Internat. prize Ljubjiana, Jugoslavia, 1959; Guggenheim Nat. prize Holland, 1961; Guggenheim Internat. prize, 1961. Illustrator: De Blijde en Onvoorziene Week (Hugo Claus), 1950; Atonaal (Simon Vinkenoog), 1951; De Ronde Kant van de Aarde (Hans Andreus), 1952; Het Bloed Stroomt Door (Bert Schierbeek), 1954; Unteilbare Teil (Andre Frenaud), 1960; Een Dier Heeft een Mens Getekend (B. Schierbeek), 1961; others. Home: 7 rue Brezin Paris 14e France Office: care Galerie Stadler Tableaux 51 rue de Seine Paris France

APPEL, KENNETH ELLMAKER, psychiatrist; b. Lancaster, Pa., May 15, 1896; s. John Wilberforce and Ella Julia (Roberts) A.; A.B., Franklin and Marshall Coll., 1915, D.Sc. (hon.), 1935; A.M., Harvard, 1916, Ph.D., 1918, M.D., 1924; m. Madeleine Hunt, Sept. 2, 1921; children—Joan, Katharine. Resident physician U. Pa. Hosp., Phila., 1924-26; asst. physician dept. nervous and mental diseases Pa. Hosp., 1926-29, cons. dept. mental and nervous diseases, chief neuro-psychiat. clinic Out-Patient Dept., 1930; psychiatrist Inst. of Pa. Hosp., 1930; asst. prof. psychiatry Med. Sch., U. Pa., 1931-45, prof. clin. psychiatry, 1941-64, prof. emeritus Dept. Psychiatry, 1964—; cons. psychiatrist to ednl. instns. Diplomate Am. Bd. Psychiatry and Neurology (pres. 1954). Fellow A.C.P.; mem. A.M.A., Am. Psychiat. Assn. (pres. 1953-54), Coll. Physicians Phila., Am. Neurol. Soc., Am. Psychoanalytical Soc., Phi Beta Kappa, Phi Kappa Psi, Alpha Omega Alpha. Mem. Reformed Ch. Am. Author books in field, latest being Psychiatry in Modern Warfare (with Dr. E. A. Strecker), 1946; Living Wisely and Well, 1949. Editorial bd., contbr. Am. Handbook of Psychiatry, 1959. Contbr. med. jours., chpts. books. Home: 206 Glenn Rd Ardmore PA 19003

APPL, FREDRIC CARL, educator; b. Mt. Hope, Kan., Nov. 17, 1932; s. Frederick Carl and Vida Jane (Gates) A.; B.S. in Mech. Engring., Carnegie Mellon U., 1954, M.S. in Mech. Engring., 1956, Ph.D. in Mech. Engring., 1958; m. Esther Natalie Simpson, June 13, 1954; children—Sandra Lee, Charlotte Joann, Cynthia Lucille. Research asst. Carnegie Inst. Tech., 1954-57, instr.-asst. prof., 1957-58; cons. Mine Safety Appliances Co., Pitts., 1957-58; research engr. Jersey Prodn. Research Co., Tulsa, 1958-60; asso. prof. engring. Kan. State U., 1960-64, prof., 1964-65, Jennings prof., 1967—; cons. Christensen Diamond Products Co., Salt Lake City, 1965-67. NSF grantee, 1961-63, 63-65. Mem. Am. Soc. M.E., Soc. Petroleum Engrs., Sigma Xi, Tau Beta Pi, Pi Tau Sigma, Phi Kappa Phi, Pi Mu Epsilon. Reviewer Applied Mechanics Revs., 1968—. Contbr. articles profl. jours. Patentee in field. Home: 1916 Indiana Lane Manhattan KS 66502

APPLBAUM, KARL, rabbi, lawyer; b. Hungary, Feb. 10, 1910; s. Rabbi Emanuel and Goldie (Eckstein) A.; B.S., State Tchrs. Coll., California, Pa., 1932; M.S., Coll. City N.Y., 1935; LL.B., St. Lawrence U., 1937, J.D., 1939; M.A., N.Y. U., 1952; D.H.L., Yeshivah U., N.Y.C., 1957; Ph.D., St. Andrews' Ecumenical U. Coll., London, Eng., 1956, D.D. with honors, 1956; LL.D. Honoris Causa, Phoenix Acad., Bari, Italy, 1957; J.D., Bklyn. Law Sch., 1967; m. Heleh Siegel, June 9, 1934; children—Elaine Claire (Mrs. I. David Feldman), Florence Rene (Mrs. Ephraim Laifer), Joseph Stewart. Came to U.S., 1922, naturalized, 1922. Ordained rabbi, 1936; rabbi Avenue M Jewish Center, Brooklyn, 1938-50, 57—, Jewish Community, Bayside, L.I., 1950-53; prof. practical rabbinics, history various theol. sems., 1950-56; chaplain 307th Gen. Hosp., Jamaica, L.I.; spiritual advisor Assn. Jewish Employees N.Y.C. Dept. Social Services. Admitted to N.Y. bar, 1939, Fed. Dist. Cts. So. and Eastern dists., 1955, U.S. Supreme Ct., 1956, Ct. Mil. Appeals, 1956; practice of law, 1938—; spl. dep. attorney general State of N.Y., 1958—. Active United Jewish Appeal, Fedn. Jewish Philanthropies, Young Israel of Kew Gardens Hills; chaplain, trustee Ind. Buakrester Sick Aid Assn.; trustee Sherishower Benevolent Assn. Chmn., The Queens Civic Improvement Council; treas. N.Y. Community Local Sch. Bd. Served as 1st lt., Chaplains Corps., AUS, 1945; col. Res., ret. Mem. Hapoel Hemizrachi Am., Am. Legion, Acad. Scis., Zionist Orgn. Am., Royal Arcanum, Am. Pub. Welfare Assn., N.Y. State Welfare Conf., Queens County Bar Assn., Rabbinical Alliance Am., Jewish War Vets (state chaplain), Affiliated Young Democrats, Mil. Chaplains Assn. U.S., Res. Officers Association (state chaplain, vice president, national chaplain 1965-66, 70-71, exec. v.p. Queens chpt. 1970—), Navy League U.S., Mil. Order World Wars, Association of U.S. Army (president Long Island chpt., chaplain 1st region), Hon. Order of Ky. Cols., Internat. Platform Assn., N.Y. State Bar Assn., Am. Acad. Polit. and Social Sci., Amvets, N.A.A.C.P., Assn. Jewish Chaplains Armed Forces, Am. Judicature Soc., Assn. Orthodox Jewish Scientists. Odd Fellow, K.P. (past chancellor); member B'nai B'rith, Sinai Fraternal Order. Clubs: Democratic; American Israeli; Roslyn Country Forest Hills County. Home: 13680 71st Rd Flushing NY 11367 Office: 1898 Bay Av Brooklyn NY 11230

APPLE, B. NIXON, lawyer; b. Toronto, Ont., Can., 1924; ed. U. Toronto, Osgoode Hall Law Sch. Partner firm Salter, Reilly, Jamieson & Apple, Toronto. Dir., Midrim Mining Co., Ltd., Multi-Minerals, Ltd., Texmont Mines, Ltd., Tallsman Mines, Ltd. Home: 171 St Leonards Av Toronto Ontario Canada Office: 302 Bay St Toronto Ontario Canada

APPLE, RAYMOND WALTER, Jr., journalist; b. Akron, O., Nov. 20, 1934; s. Raymond Walter and Julia (Albrecht) A.; student Princeton, 1952-56; A.B., Columbia, 1961; m. Edith Smith, Oct. 1, 1966. Reporter, Wall St. Jour., 1956-57, 59-61; writer, corr. NBC News, 1961-63; mem. staff N.Y. Times, 1963—, Albany bur. chief, 1964-65, Vietnam corr., 1965-66, Vietnam bur. chief, 1966-68, Africa bur. chief, 1969, nat. polit. corr., 1970—. Served with AUS, 1957-59. Recipient Krout prize history Columbia, 1961; award Acad. TV Arts and Scis., 1963; George Polk Meml. award, 1967; Overseas Press Club award, 1967. Mem. Am. Newspaper Guild. Club: Federal City (Washington). Contbr. nat. mags., books. Home: 413 N St NW Washington DC 20024 Office: 1920 L St NW Washington DC 20036

APPLE, SPENCER BUTLER, Jr., educator; b. Kansas City, Mo., June 11, 1912; s. Spencer Butler and Edith Elizabeth (Kurtz) A.; B.S. in Agr., Tex. A. and M. U., 1933, M.S. in Horticulture, 1936; Ph.D. in Horticulture, Wash. State U., 1953; m. Mary Anne Holland, Sept. 1, 1940; children—Judy, Susan, Steven. Instr. horticulture Tex. A. and M. U., 1935-42; research and extension horticulturist Mich. State U., 1942-43, 46; asso. horticulturist Ore. State U., 1950-55, prof. horticulture, head dept., 1955—. Served to lt. (s.g.) USNR, 1943-46. Fellow A.A.A.S.; mem. Am. Soc. Hort. Sci., Sigma Xi. Home: 1460 NW 12th St Corvallis OR 97330

APPLE, WALTER EUGENE, lawyer; b. Cin., Mar. 8, 1931; s. Otis R. and Zora (Bertram) A.; B.S., Ohio State U., 1954, J.D. summa cum laude, 1956; m. Dorothy A. McGuffey, May 26, 1951; children—Mark, Dianne Michael. Admitted to Ohio bar, 1957, since practiced in Toledo; partner Fuller, Seney, Henry & Hodge, 1964—. Served with USMC 1951-53. mem. Am., Ohio, Toledo bar assns., Order of Coif, Phi Delta Phi. Home: 2549 Underhill Rd Ottawa Hills Toledo OH 43615 Office: 405 Madison Av Toledo OH 43604

APPLE, WILLIAM SHOULDEN, assn. exec. b. Spokane, Wash., July 28, 1918; s. Harry and Ann (Chon) A.; student Wayne State U., 1945-46; B.S. in Pharmacy, U. Wis., 1949, M.B.A., 1951, Ph.D., 1954; D.Sc. (hon.), U.L.I., 1966, Union U., 1969; m. Lucille Harriet Josephs, May 3, 1942; children—Chandra Eden, Hugh Charles Instr. pharmacy U. Wis., 1951-53, asst. prof., 1953-56, asso. prof., chmn. dept. pharmacy adminstrn., 1956-58; asst. sec. Am. Pharm. Assn., Washington, 1958-59, sec., gen. mgr., 1959, exec. dir., 1959—. Del. U.S. Pharmacopeial Conv., Washington, 1960; mem. Com. 100 for Nat. Health Ins. Charter bd. dirs. Community Health Inc.; bd. dirs. Am. Assn. World Health Inc., U.S. com. for WHO. Served to maj. AUS, 1941-46; lt. col. Res. Named Am. Druggist of Yr., 1961, 67, Rho Pi Phi Man of Yr., 1961; recipient J. Leon Lascoff Meml. award, 1961, Wayne State U. Distinguished Service award, 1962, Hugo H. Schaefer medal, 1966, Remington Honor medal, 1967; Colegio de Quimico Farmaceuticos de Chili, 1961; U. Wis. citation, 1965. Fellow A.A.A.S., Am. Soc. Hosp. Pharmacists; mem. National Drug Trade Conference (secretary- treas., pres. 1970), Am., Wis. (pres. 1956-57, chmn. bd. 1957-58) pharm. assns., Am. Council Pharm. Edn. (past pres.), Internat. Pharm. Fedn. (U.S. rep.), N.Y. Acad. Scis., Japan Pharm. Assn. (hon.), Rho Chi, Phi Lambda Upsilon, Phi Kappa Phi. Home: 6423 Crosswoods Dr Falls Church VA 22044 Office: 2215 Constitution Av NW Washington DC 20037

APPLEBAUM, MEYER, food stores exec. Vice chmn. Applebaum's Food Markets, Inc., St. Paul. Office: 860 Vandalia St Paul MN 55114*

APPLEBAUM, SIDNEY, food stores exec. Exec. v.p., sec. Applebaum's Food Markets, Inc, St. Paul. Office: 860 Vandalia St Paul MN 55114*

APPLEBEE, FRANK WOODBURY, ret. art educator; b. Boston, June 2, 1902; s. Albert and Hattie (Hart) A.; diploma Mass. Coll. Art, 1925; B.S., Auburn U., 1931, M.A., 1937; m. Alice Macy, June 2, 1928; 1 dau., Phyllis Macy; m. 2d, Martha Stubblefield, June 3, 1951; adopted children—Donald Robert, Gloria Anne. Mem. faculty Auburn (Ala.) U., 1926—, prof. art, 1932-69, acting dean Sch. Architecture, Fine Arts, 1961-62, head art dept., 1932-69, prof. art emeritus, 1970—. Paintings represented in permanent collections Auburn U., U. Montevallo, Montgomery Mus. Art. Mem. Ala. Art Commn., 1961-63. Mem. Water Color Soc. Ala., Ala. Art League, Phi Kappa Phi, Kappa Delta Pi. Home: 316 Chewacla Dr Auburn AL 36830

APPLEBY, JACK JESTINY, retired naval officer; b. Ozark, Mo., Aug. 22, 1915; s. Felix J. and Francis (List) A.; B.S., U. Cal. at Berkeley, 1938; grad. Naval War Coll., 1956; grad. Advanced Mgmt. Program, Harvard, 1963; m. Amy Hart Butler, Sept. 14, 1940; 1 dau., Linda (Mrs. Phillip Stubblefield). Commd. ensign USN, 1938, advanced through grades to rear adm., 1964; various assignments as supply officer, ships and stas., until 1945; supply officer U.S.S. Tarawa, 1945-46; dir. personnel div., bur. supplies and accounts Navy Dept., Washington, 1946-50; supply and fiscal officer Naval Air Sta., Alameda, Cal., 1950-54; supply officer, comptroller, staff Comdr. Naval Air Force, Pacific Fleet, 1956-58; exec. officer Aviation Supply Office, Phila., 1958-60; comdr. Navy Ship's Store Office, Bklyn., 1960-65; dep. chief Naval Material, Washington, 1965-66; dep. comdt. Indsl. Coll. Armed Forces, 1966-69; comdg. officer Naval Supply Corps, Oakland, Cal., 1969—. Home: 687 Christine Dr Danville CA 94526

APPLEGARTH, MARGARET TYSON, author and lecturer; b. New Brunswick, N.J., July 8, 1886; d. Henry C. and Mary (Tyson) Applegarth; A.B., U. Rochester, 1908; L.H.D. , Denison U., 1942. Mem. Phi Beta Kappa. Presbyn. Author: Joy To The World, 1945; Right Here, Right Now, 1950; Men as Trees Walking, 1952; Moment By Moment, 1955; Twelve Baskets Full, 1957; Heirlooms, 1966; also articles in mags. Home: 20 E 76th St New York City NY 10021 ☆

APPLEGATE, ARTHUR LOWRIE, investment banker; b. Sewickley, Pa., 1914; ed. Princeton, 1937. Pres., dir. Hulme, Applegate & Humphrey, Inc., Pitts.; dir. Allegheny Plastics Co., Polavision Co. Am. Mem. Investment Bankers Assn. Am. (bd. govs.). Club: Iron City Fishing (dir.). Home: RD 1 Scaife Rd Sewickley PA 15143 Office: Union Trust Bldg Pittsburgh PA 15219

APPLEGATE, IRVAMAE VINCENT, coll. dean; b. Beulah, N.D., Sept. 18, 1920; d. Irving Joseph and Helen (Engberg) Vincent; B.S., N.D. State U., 1941, D.Sc. (hon.), 1963; M.A., U. Minn., 1951, Ph.D., 1957; m. Dwain William Applegate, Apr. 13, 1944. Tchr. pub. schs., Cass Lake, Minn., 1941-43; tchr., high sch. prin. pub. schs., Hazen, N.D., 1943-46; reporter-writer Independent Age, Aitkin, Minn., 1946-47; tchr., then high sch. prin. pub. schs., Princeton, Minn., 1947-56; mem. faculty St. Cloud (Minn.) State Coll., 1956—, asso. dean tchr. edn., 1961-62, dean Sch. Edn., 1962—. Mem. Minn. Adv. Com. Tchr. Edn., 1961-66, Minn. Mental Health Planning Council, 1963-65; mem. edn. com. Gov. Minn. Adv. Council Children and Youth, 1964; subcom. non- med. resources Minn. Mental Health Planning Council, 1964-65; employment com. Gov. Minn. Commn. Status Women, 1964-65; del. World Confedn. Orgns. Teaching Profession, 1967—, exec., 1969—; cons. U.S. Office Edn., 1969—. Recipient Presdl. citation Audio-Visual Coordinators Assn. Minn., 1963; Hon. Awards certificate Minn. Elementary Prins. Assn., 1964; Outstanding Achievement award U. Minn., 1965. Mem. Minn. Assn. Supervision and Curriculum Devel. (bd. dirs., editor 1959-62), Zonta, Am. Assn. U. Women, Minn. (pres. 1963-65), Nat. (life mem., pres. 1966-67, chmn. compliance com. 1966-69, chmn. urban task force 1966-69) edn. assns., Minn. Press Woman, Nat. Council State Assn. Presidents (exec. com., 1963-64), Am. Legion Aux., St. Cloud C. of C., Kappa Delta, Pi Lambda Theta, Delta Kappa Gamma (pres. Eta chpt. 1960-62), Delta Psi Kappa. Author monthly column Assignment Education, 1963-66. Home: Route 2 Sauk Rapids MN 56379 Office: St Cloud State Coll St Cloud MN 56301

APPLEGATE, ORAL LESTER, mfg. exec.; b. Maysville, Ky., Jan. 4, 1914; s. Earl and Marguerite (Macy) A.; m. Ruth D. Hensgen, Sept. 14, 1935; childrenRuth Ann, Oral L. Mem. bd. edn., City of Cin., 1938-42; chief plant engr. Standard Brands, 1942-45, staff engr., 1945-49, plant mgr., 1949-55, v.p. engring., 1955-58, v.p. mfg., 1958-67, sr. v.p., 1967—, also dir. Mason (Shriner). Home: 28 Doris Dr Scarsdale NY 10583

APPLEMAN, JOHN ALAN, lawyer; b. Webster Groves, Mo., May 14, 1912; s. Milo Donaldson and Emma Catherine (Faust) A.; A.B., U. Ill., 1932, LL.D., 1935, M.A. 1950; m. Jean Gerber, Jan. 9, 1935; 1 dau., Jean, 1 son (dec.). Admitted to Ill., Ky., Mass., D.C., U.S. Supreme Ct., other bars. Speaker, lectr. at univs., bar convs.; legal adv. bd. Traumatic Medicine and Surgery for Atty. Condr. Profl. Trial Lawyers Seminar, 1963—. Fellow Internat. Acad. Trial Lawyers (gov. 1958-64, dean 1959-60), Internat. Soc. Barristers; mem. Am. (life), Ill. (life), Ky., Champaign County (gov. 1958-61, pres. 1959-60), Chgo. bar assns., Fedn. Ins. Counsel (pres. 1950-52, chmn. bd. govs. 1952-53), Phi Beta Kappa, Phi Eta Sigma. Republican. Presbyn. Author: Automobile Liability Insurance, 1938; Insurance Law and Practice, 25 vols., 1940-46, Vols. 1-6, 7, 8, 16, 20, 21, rev. 1961-71; Preparing and Trying Cases in Illinois (2 vols.), 1950; Illinois Dramshop Briefs, 1951, 60; Successful Jury Trials, 1952; Successful Appellate Techniques, 1953; Military Tribunals and International Crimes, 1954, 71; How To Use Life Insurance in Estate Analysis, 1954; Basic Estate Planning, 2 vols. 1957; Approved Appellate Briefs, 1958; How To Increase Your Money Making Power, 1959, rev. edit. 1964. Long playing records and tapes entitled: Examples of Cross Examination, 1960, 69, Cross-Examination, 1963; Preparation and Trial, 1967; Your Psychic Powers and Immortality, 1968; The Elusive Song, 1969. Contbr. to numerous law jours. and revs., Ency. Brit., World Book Ency. Address: The Maples Urbana IL 61801

APPLEMAN, MILO DON, bacteriologist, educator; b. Wellston, Mo., Dec. 3, 1909; s. Milo Donaldson and Emma Catherine (Faust) A.; A.B., U. Ill., 1931, M.S., 1935, Ph.D., 1940; m. Lucille Elizabeth Mieher, July 28, 1936; 1 son, Milo Don. Research, teaching asst. soil bacteriology dept. agronomy U. Ill., 1936-40, asso. soil bacteriology, studying quick-freezing and vacuum-drying of bacteria, 1940-43, asst. prof., 1943-47; asso. prof. dept. bacteriology U. So. Cal., Los Angeles, 1947-50, chmn. dept. bacteriology, 1950-63, prof. bacteriology, dept. biol. scis., 1963—. Cons., v.p. Daylin Labs., Inc., Los Angeles; cons. in food bacteriology. Fellow, Fund for Advancement Edn. 1954-55; hon. research fellow U. Aberdeen, Scotland, 1954-55; spl. fellow NIH, 1962-63; adv. com. Cal. Dept. Health, 1952-58. Diplomate Am. Bd. Med. Microbiology, Am. Intersoc. Acad. Fellow Royal Soc. of Medicine, Am. Acad. Microbiology (charter); mem. Med. Research Assn. (dir.), Inst. Food Technologists, Am. Soc. Microbiology (pres. So. Cal. 1957, councilor 1958-60), Am. Assn. U. Profs., Societe de Diplomes of U. Nantes (France) (hon.), Sigma Xi, Alpha Sigma Lambda, Phi Sigma, Gamma Sigma Delta. Author numerous publs. on bacterial physiology, food and dental bacteriology to univ. sta. publs., manuals, sci. publs., Ency. Brit. Home: 4315 San Rafael Av Los Angeles CA 90042 Office: Daylin Labs Inc Los Angeles CA 90042

APPLEQUIST, DOUGLAS EINAR, educator, chemist; b. Salt Lake City, Oct. 29, 1930; s. Einar I. and Margaret (Musser) A.; B.S., U. Cal. at Berkeley, 1952; student Mass. Inst. Tech., 1952-53; Ph.D., Cal. Inst. Tech., 1955; m. Linda Joanne Donlon, Feb. 5, 1966; 1 dau., Wendy Linn. Mem. faculty U. Ill., Urbana, 1955—, prof. organic chemistry, 1964—. Arthur and Ruth Sloan vis. prof. chemistry Harvard, spring 1964; cons. to industry, 1956—. Mem. Am. Chem. Soc., Chem. Soc. (London, Eng.), Am. Civil Liberties Union, Am. Assn. U. Profs., Phi Beta Kappa, Sigma Xi. Spl. research on mechanisms of organic reactions, small-ring compounds, bridgehead displacements, organic photochemistry. Home: 204 Pell Circle Urbana IL 61801

APPLEQUIST, HARRY C., lawyer; b. Mpls., Jan. 1, 1904; LL.B., U. Minn., 1927. Admitted to Minn. bar, 1927; practice in Duluth; mem. firm Applequist, Lyons, Nolan, Donovan, Larson & Barnes. Mem. Am., Minn., 11th Jud. Dist. bar assns., Duluth C. of C. (pres. 1949-50). Office: 1000 Alworth Bldg Duluth MN 55802*

APPLETON, ARTHUR IVAR, mfr. electric products; b. Chgo., Oct. 14, 1915; s. Albert Ivar and Lillian (Wihk) A.; B.A., Dartmouth, 1936; m. Martha O'Driscoll, July 20, 1947; children—Thomas Albert, Arthur Ivar (by previous marriage), James Kenneth, John Stephen, Linda Charlotte, William Paul. With Appleton Electric Co., 1936—, pres., chmn. bd., 1947—; dir. Zenith United Corp., Gulfstream Park Racing Assn.; propr. Appleton Oil Co. Served with USNR, 1943-45. Decorated Letter of Commendation. Mem. Phi Delta Theta. Presbyn. (trustee 1958-59). Clubs: Chgo. Athletic Assn., Mid-Am. (Chgo.); Bob O'Link Golf; Exmoor Country (Highland Park, Ill.); Surf (Surfside, Fla.); Indian Creek (Miami Beach, Fla.). Home: 1 Bridlewood Rd Northbrook IL 60062 Office: 1701 W Wellington Av Chicago IL 60657

APPLETON, FRANCIS RANDALL, Jr., lawyer; b. Lenox, Mass., July 9, 1885; s. Francis Randall and Fanny (Lanier) A.; A.B. cum laude, Harvard, 1907, LL.B. cum laude, 1910; m. Joan Mary Egleston, May 29, 1935. Admitted to N.Y. bar, 1911; asso. firm Winthrop & Stimson, 1910-16; mem. firm Appleton, Rice & Perrin, 1916— (both N.Y.C.). Hon. life pres. Ipswich (Mass.) Hist. Soc., 1943—; pres. N.Y. Farmers, Inc., 1940-47; bd. mgrs. Am. Soc. Prevention Cruelty to Animals, N.Y.C., 1922-43. Commd. capt., inf. O.R.C., 1916; active duty U.S. Army, 1917-19, A.E.F., 1918-19; advanced from capt. to lt. col., inf.; lt. col. inf. Res., 1919-46; Officers' Hon. Ret. List, 1946, ret., 1952. Mem. Assn. Bar City N.Y., N.Y. State Bar Assn., N.Y. Soc. Colonial Wars, S.R., Am. Legion (founder mem.). Mem. Ascension Meml. Ch. (Vestryman 1929-70, churchwarden 1942-71). Clubs: Meadow Brook (past v.p., treas., sec.) (Westbury, L.I.); Racquet and Tennis, Westminster Kennel, Harvard (N.Y.C.); Somerset, Myopia (Boston); Porcellian (Harvard); Army and Navy (Washington); White's (London, Eng.). Breeder registered Guernsey and Polled Hereford cattle and Shropshire sheep at Appleton Farms, Ipswich, Essex County, Mass., a 1000 acre farm granted to ancestor Samuel Appleton, 1638; owner Barberry Kennels (registered Am. Kennel Club, 1899), breeders of Smooth Fox Terriers; horse trainer, fox hunter. Home: 700 Park Av New York City NY 10021 also Appleton Farms Ipswich MA Office: 63 Wall St New York City NY 10005

APPLETON, JOSEPH HAYNE, educator; b. Collinsville, Ala., Aug. 5, 1927; s. Shelton and Helen (Gower) A.; B.C.E., Auburn U., 1947; M.S., U. Ill., 1949, Ph.D., 1959; m. Patricia Ann Zimmerman, May 8, 1954; children—Joseph F., Sandra K., Jeffrey T., Tricia A., Kevin L., Kathryn L. Research asst. U. Ill., Urbana, 1947-49, research asso., 1951-54; structural engr. U.S. Bur. Pub. Rds., Washington, 1949-50; instr. N.C. State Coll., 1950-51; structural engr. Ala. Cement Tile Co., Birmingham, 1954-59; prof. engring. U. Ala., Birmingham, 1959—, asso. prof. dentistry, 1960—, asso. prof. physiology and biphysics, 1966—, chmn. div. engrin Cons. structural analysis and design, 1959—. Mem. Am. Soc. C.E., Am. Soc. Engring. Edn., Am. Concrete Inst., Nat. Soc. Profl. Engrs., Am. Assn. U. Profs., Sigma Xi, Tau Beta Pi, Phi Kappa Phi, Chi Epsilon. Methodist. Author numerous articles in field. Home: 4237 Antietam Dr Birmingham, AL 35213

APPLETON, JULIUS HENRY, lawyer; b. Springfield, Mass., Feb. 8, 1907; s. Allen Lansing and Lydia Dexter (Owen) A.; student Middlesex Sch., Concord, Mass.; A.B., Harvard, 1929; J.D., Boston U., 1933; LL.D., Springfield Coll., 1966; m. Louise Elizabeth Briggs, June 25, 1949; children—Allen Edmund, Stephen Briggs. Admitted to Mass. bar, 1933; with firm Allen, Yerrall, Appleton & Thompson, Springfield, 1951—. Vice pres., dir. Holyoke Water Power Co., 1955-68; dir. Third Nat. Bank Hampden County, Monarch Capital Corp.; clk., trustee Springfield Instn. Savs. Pres. Springfield Boys' Club, 1941-43; pres. corp. Springfield Coll., 1941-55, now trustee; past trustee Springfield Library and Museums Assn.; trustee Springfield Hosp. Mem. Am. (Mass. del. ho. of dels. 1939, 40), Mass., Hampden County bar assns. Republican. Conglist. Clubs: Harvard, Longmeadow Country, Colony, Appalachian Mountain, Gladden, The Club. Home: 77 E Greenwich Rd Longmeadow MA 01106 Office: 1387 Main St Springfield MA 01103

APPLETON, OLIVER DAYTON, broker; b. N.Y.C., Jan. 10, 1905; s. Charles W. and Harriet (Ferry) A.; grad. Kent Sch., 1923; B.S., St. Lawrence U., 1927; m. Elsa Gunnison, Dec. 3, 1927; children—Joan (Mrs. Charles B. Stone, Jr.), Frederic G., Charles W. II. With Electric Bond & Share Co., 1927-31; with Cyrus J. Lawrence & Sons, N.Y.C., 1931-69, partner, 1950-69; pvt. practice, 1969—. Mem. N.Y. Stock Exchange, 1954- 62. Trustee St. Lawrence University. Served as captain 4th Infantry Division, AUS, World War II. Decorated Bronze Medal with cluster. Mem. Alpha Tau Omega. Episcopalian. Clubs: Bedford Golf and Tennis (Bedford Villege, N.Y.); University (N.Y.C.). Home: McLain St Mt Kisco NY 10549 Office: 115 Broadway New York City NY 10006

APPLETON, WILLIAM WORTHEN, educator; b. N.Y.C., Dec. 31, 1915; s. William Henry and Noel (Johnston) A.; B.A., Harvard, 1938; Ph.D., Columbia, 1949. Mem. faculty Columbia, 1945—, prof. English, 1960—. Served with AUS, 1942-45. Author: A Cycle of Cathay, 1951; Beaumont and Fletcher, 1956; Charles Macklin, 1960. Home: 39 E 79th St New York City, NY 10021 Office: Lewisohn Hall Columbia Univ New York City NY 10021

APPLEWHITE, ROBERT METZLER, orgn. exec.; b. Newport News, Va., June 21, 1921; s. Edgar Jarrat and Mabel Agnes (Metzler) A.; student Coll. William and Mary, 1940-42. Internat. scholarship Am. Field Service, 1946-49, 57—; sec. Am. Field Service, Inc., 1962—; with B.H. Lawson Assos., fund raising counsel, Rockville Centre, N.Y., 1949-56. Volunteer ambulance driver Am. Field Services, 1942-45. Decorated Bronze Cross of Merit with swords (Poland), 1944. Home: 34 Gramercy Park New York City NY 10003 Office: 313 E 43d St New York City NY 10017

APPLEY, LAWRENCE A., assn. exec.; b. Nyack, N.Y., Apr. 22, 1904; s. Rev. Joseph Earl and Jessie (Moore) A.; A.B., Ohio Wesleyan U., 1927, LL.D., 1946; LL.D., Bethany Coll., 1951, St. Lawrence U., 1951, Colgate U., 1955; Litt.D., Bryant Coll., 1970; m. Ruth G. Wilson, Sept. 1, 1927; children—Ruth Ann (Mrs. Albert Gleaves Cohen), Judith (Mrs. Karl Otto Grutter). Served as instr. Colgate U., 1927-30; personnel mgr. Buffalo div. Socony Mobil Oil Co., Inc., 1930-34, ednl. dir., N.Y.C., 1934-41; v.p. Vick Chem. Co., N.Y.C., 1941-46, dir., 1945-47; v.p., dir. Montgomery Ward & Co., Chgo., 1946- 48; pres. Am. Mgmt. Assn., 1948-68, chmn, 1968—; dir. Brunswick Corp., Nat. Can Corp., Nat. Biscuit Co., Standard Oil Co. Ohio, Harris-Intertype Corp., Oneida, Ltd., Howard Swink Advertising, D.W. Phillips Internat., Am. Precision Industries, Barber-Colman Co. Adviser, U.S. Civil Service Commn. on adminstrv. orgn., 1938-41; expert cons. to Sec. of War on civilian personnel, 1941- 42; exec. dir., later dep. chmn. War Manpower Commn., Washington, 1943- 44; mem. personnel policy com. Hoover Commn. 1948, personnel adv. com. AEC. 1948-52. Pres. Truman's Adv. Com. on Mgmt. 1949-52, U.S. Commn. on Intergovtl. Relations, 1953-54; mem. U.S. Bus. Ethics Adv. Council, 1961- 63. Pres. Glen Ridge (N.J.) Bn. Forum, 1945-46. Bd. of Edn., 1940-46. Trustee Thunderbird Grad. Sch. Internat. Mgmt., Colgate U., The Northfield Schs. Recipient War Dept. citation for meritorious civilian service, 1944; Presdl. citation Medal for Merit, 1946; Skipper Allen award Nat. Assn. Train Directors, 1958; Human Relations award, 1952, Taylor Key Soc. Advancement Mgmt., 1961; Henry Laurence Gantt medal, 1963. Fellow Internat. Acad. Mgmt. Mem. Am. Mgmt. Assn. (v.p. charge personnel div. 1942-44, dir., mem. exec. com. 1944-47), Am. Soc. M.E. (chmn. exec. com. mgmt. 1945), Soc. Advancement Mgmt., Nat. Morgan Horse Club (pres., dir.), Phi Beta Kappa Assos., Phi Beta Kappa, Omicron Delta Kappa, Chi Phi, Delta Sigma Rho, Sigma Iota Epsilon. Baptist. Clubs: Marco Polo (N.Y.C.); Deerfield Beach Golf and Country. Author: Management in Action; Management Evolution; Values in Management; A Managers Heritage. Home: West Lake Moraine Rd Hamilton NY 13346 also 1541 SE 9th St Deerfield Beach FL 33441 Office: Box 88 Hamilton NY 13346

APPLEY, MORTIMER HERBERT, psychologist, educator; b. N.Y.C., Nov. 21, 1921; s. Benjamin and Minnie (Alber), Applezweig; B.S., Coll. City N.Y., 1942; M.A., U. Denver, 1946; Ph.D., U. Mich., 1950; m. Dee Gordon, June 5, 1942 (div. Oct. 1969); children—Richard Gordon, John Benton; m. 2d, Mariann B. Hundahl, Jan. 10, 1970; stepchildren—Scott, Eric, Heidi. Instr., U. Denver, 1945-47; instr. U. Mich., 1947-49; asst. prof. Wesleyan U., Middletown, Conn., 1949-52; prof., chmn. psychology Conn. Coll., New London, 1952-60; prof., chmn. psychology So. Ill. U., Carbondale, 1960-62; prof., chmn. psychology York U., Toronto, Ont., Can., 1962-67, dean faculty grad. studies, 1965-68; prof., chmn. psychology U. Mass., Amherst, 1967-69, dean Grad. Sch., 1969—; cons. NSF, Nat. Insts. Mental Health, NRC of Can., Can. Council, VA. Served with USAAF, 1942-45. Fellow Am. Psychol. Assn. (past chmn. edn. and tng. bd.); mem. Canadian, Conn. (past pres.) psychol. assns., Internat. Council Psychologists, A.A.A.S., Sigma Xi, Psi Chi, Phi Sigma. Democrat. Unitarian (chmn. bd. mgrs. congregation). Author: (with C.N. Cofer) Motivation: Theory and Research, 1964; (with R. Trumbull) Psychological Stress, 1967; (with J. Rickwood) Psychology in Canada, 1967. Editor: Adaption Level Theory: A Symposium, 1971; asso. editor: Psychol. Abstracts, 1961-62. Editorial cons. Psychol. Rev., Physiology and Behavior, Canadian Jour. of Psychology, Jour. of Personality and Social Psychology. Contbr. articles profl. jours. Home: 315 Lincoln Av Amherst MA 01002

APPLEYARD, MILTON HERBERT, hosp. exec.; b. Johnstown, Pa., Apr. 30, 1929; s. Milton A. and Leona (Cook) A.; B.S., U. Pa., 1956, postgrad., 1959-60; M.S., Columbia, 1964; m. Anne Sandberg, Aug. 19, 1950; children—Lorraine Marie, Karl Wallace, Milton John. Asst. dir. Presbyn.-U. Pa. Med. Center, Phila., 1957-66; exec. dir. United Hosp., Inc., Beaver Falls, Pa., 1966-70, Harrisburg (Pa.) Hosp., 1970—. Dir. Dauphin County Mental Health/Mental Retardation Program, 1970—; mem. Commonwealth of Pa. Comprehensive Health Planning Adv. Council, 1970—. Served with USMCR, 1948-52. Fellow Am. Coll. Hosp. Adminstrs.; mem. Am. Hosp. Assn., Hosp. Assn. Pa. (dir. 1969-72). Rotarian. Home: 322 Laurel Dr Laurel Woods RD 1 Hershey PA 17033 Office: Harrisburg Hospital S Front St Harrisburg PA 17101

APPLEYARD, ROBERT BRACEWELL, bishop; b. Jamestown, N.Y. Nov. 17, 1917; s. Albet Edward and Elizabeth (Sharp) A.; A.B., Allegheny Coll., Meadville, Pa., 1940, D.D., 1955; B.D., Union Theol. Sem., 1943; D.D., Trinity Coll., Hartford, Conn., 1962; m. Katharine Louise Gelbach, Sept. 12, 1942; children—Robert Bracewell, Jonathan Briggs, Jane Sharp, Daniel Scott. Ordained priest Episcopal Ch., 1947; asst. dean, dir. program returning service men Union Theol. Sem., 1945-48; asst. minister in N.Y.C. 1945-48; rector Christ Ch., also chaplin Taft Sch., Watertown, Conn., 1948-52; rector Christ Ch., also chaplain Rosemary Hall Sch., Greenwich, Conn., 1952-65; rector in Palm Beach, Fla., 1965- 68; bishop Eiscopal Diocese Pitts., 1968—; hon. canon Christ Ch. Cathedral, Hartford, St. Luke's Cathedral. Orlando, Fla. Bd. dirs. Action Housing, Hosp. Planning, St. Margaret's Meml. Hosp., Episcopal Ch. Home, A.R.C., YMCA, Planned Parenthood, Religious Leaders, Nat. Safety Council; trustee Book Common Prayer and Hymnal Soc., Am. Ch. Bldg. Fund, Seabury House, Rosemary Hall Sch., Pomfret Sch.,' St. Andrews Sch., Sanford Coll.; mem. men's com. Japan Internat. Christian U. Served as chaplain USNR, 1943-46. Mem. Am. Guild Organists, Acad. Religion and Mental Health, Gen. Conv. Episcopal Ch., Nat. Council Chs. Phi Beta Kappa, Phi Delta Theta, Clubs: Fox Chapel Golf, Longue Vue, Duquesne (Pitts.). Home: 715 Amberson Av Pittsburgh PA 15232 Office: 325 Oliver Av Pittsburgh PA 15222

APPLING, HUGH GUERNSEY, fgn. service officer; b. Oakdale, Cal., Apr. 12, 1921; s. Hugh L. and Mary E. (Guernsey) A.; A.B., U. Cal. at Berkeley, 1941; M.A., Stanford, 1947; m. Mary L. Bess, Mar. 23, 1947; children—Gregory B., Mary B., Hugh B., Jane B. Bank clk., 1941-42; vice consul, sec. Am. embassy, Vienna, Austria, 1947-50; staff U.S. rep. to N. Atlantic Council, London, 1951, Paris, 1952; assigned to Dept. State, 1953-56; sec. of embassy consul, Bonn, Germany, 1956-60; spl. asst. to under sec. for polit. affairs Dept. State, Washington, 1960-61, spl. asst. to dep. undersec. of state for adminstrn., 1961-63, dep. dir. Office West European Affairs, 1964-65; dep. chief mission Am. embassy, Damascus, Syria, 1965-66; sec. of Am. embassy, Manila Philippines, 1967- 68; province sr. adviser, Viet Nam, 1968-70; dep. chief mission Am. embassy, Canberra, Australia, 1970—. Served with AUS, 1942-45. Mem. Am. Fgn. Service Assn., Lambda Chi Alpha. Mem. United Ch. Christ. Home: 625 Pine Av Oakdale CA 95361 Office: care Dept State Washington DC 20525

APRISON, MORRIS HERMAN, educator, biochemist; b. Milw., Oct. 6, 1923; s. Henry and Ethel (Mollin) A.; B.S. in Chemistry, U. Wis., 1945, tchrs. certificate, 1947, M.S. in Physics, 1949, Ph.D. in Biochemistry, 1952; m. Shirley Reder, Aug. 21, 1949; children—Barry, Robert. Grad. teaching asst. in physics U. Wis., Madison, 1947-49, grad. research asst. in pathology Sch. Medicine, 1950-51, grad. research asst. in biochemistry, 1951-52; tech. asst. in physics Inst. Paper Chemistry, Appleton, Wis., 1949-50; biochemist, prin. investigator, head biophysics sect. Galesburg (Ill.) State Research Hosp., 1952-56; prin. research investigator in biochemistry, asst. prof. depts. biochemistry and psychiatry and Inst. Psychiat. Research, Ind. U. Med. Sch., Indpls., 1956-60, asso. prof., 1960-64, prof. biochemistry, 1964—, chief neurobiology sect., 1969—. Co-chmn. session on neurotransmitters 23d Internat. Physiol. Congress, 1966, chmn. session neurochemistry and neuropharmacology 25th Congress, 1971; ad hoc mem. study sect. psychopharmacology Nat. Inst. Mental Health, 1967-71, mem. neuropsychology study sect., 1970—. Served with USNR, 1944-46. Mem. Am. Chem. Soc. (chmn. biann. symposium Ind. sect. 1962), Am. Physiol. Soc., Biophys. Soc., Soc. Biol. Psychiatry, Soc. Exptl. Biology and Medicine, Internat. Brain Research Orgn., Internat.

(co-chmn. 1st internat. meeting Strasbourg, France 1967), Am. (council 1971—), socs. neurochemistry, Sigma Xi. Contbr. articles profl. jours. Adv. editorial bd. Neurosci. Research, 1968—, Biol. Psychiatry, 1969—, Neuropharmacology, 1969—; regional editor Life Scis. Home: 5810 N Dearborn St Indianapolis IN 46220

APT, CHARLES, artist; b. N.Y.C., Dec. 10, 1933; s. Gustav Lee and Tami Vera (Salzman) A.; B.F.A., Pratt Inst., 1956; m. Ursula Edith Betz, July 24, 1959; children—Gregory, Sam. Exhibited in group shows at Mus. Fine Art, Springfield, Mass., 1966, Expn. Intercontinentale, Monaco, France, 1966, 68, N.A.D., 1965, 68, Am. Watercolor Soc., 1965, 66, 68, 69, Allied Artists Am., 1964, 65, 67, 69, 70, Nat. Mus. Racing, Saratoga, N.Y., 1967, Atlantic City Race Track, 1967, Nat. Arts Club, 1967; one-man show Ground Floor Art Gallery, N.Y.C., 1967, 68, 69, Aquedect Race Track Art Gallery, N.Y.C., 1967, Grand Central Art Galleries, 1969. Served with AUS 1956-58. Recipient Gold medal Am. Vets. Soc. Artists, 1965, Best in Show award Saratoga Mus. Racing Ann., 1967, 2d Benjamin Altman award for figure painting N.A.D. 1968, Le Prix Prince Souverain, Monaco, 1968, hon. mention Allied Artists Am., 1970. Mem. Artists Fellowship (trustee), Grand Central Art Galleries. Clubs: Salmagundi, Nat. Arts (N.Y.C.). Home: 280 9th Av New York City NY 10001 Studio: 400 W 23d St New York City NY 10011

APTER, DAVID ERNEST, educator, author; b. N.Y.C., Dec. 18, 1924; s. Herman and Bella (Steinberg) A.; B.A., Antioch Coll., 1950; M.A., Princeton, 1952, Ph.D., 1954; m. Eleanor Selwyn, Dec. 28, 1947; children—Emily, Andrew. Asst. prof. polit. sci. Northwestern U., 1954-57; asso. prof. U. Chgo., 1957- 61, exec. sec. Com. ofr Comparative Study of New Nations, 1959-61; prof. U. Cal. at Berkeley, 1962-69; prof. polit. sci. and sociology Yale, 1969—; cons. in field, 1954—. Asso. dir. Inst. Internat. Studies, U. Cal. at Berkeley, 1961-66, dir., 1966-69; dir. Peace Corps tng. program for Ghana, 1962, 63; adv. com. African affairs State Dept., 1962-69; mem. Pres. Kennedy's Task Force on Africa, 1960; mem. com. comparative sociol. research Social Sci. Research Council, 1968. Served with AUS, 194346. Fellow Center Advanced Studies Behavioral Scis., 1958-59; Social Sci. Research Council area tng. fellow for research in Ghana, 1952-53; Guggenheim fellow, 1967-68; aux. research tng. fellow Social Sci. Research Council, 1959; Ford fellow for research in Uganda, 1955-56; Rockefeller grantee, 1968; vis. fellow All Soul's Coll., Oxford (Eng.) U., 1967-68 asso. fellow St. Anthony's Coll., 1968—. Fellow Am. Acad. Arts and Scis., Am. Sociol. Assn., Am. Soc. Philol. and Legal Philosophy; mem. N.Y. Acad. Sci., Am. Polit. Sci. Assn., A.A.A.S., African Studies Assn. (bd. dirs. 1963-66). Author: The Gold Coast in Transition, 1955; The Political Kingdom in Uganda: A Study in Bureaucratic Nationalism. 1961; (with Harry Eckstein) Comparative Politics: A Reader, 1963: The Policies of Modernization, 1965; Some Comceptual Approaches to the Study of Modernization, 1968; A Structural Theory of Politics, 1971; (with Charles Andrain) Contemporary Analytical Theory, 1971; also articles. Editor: Ideology and Discontent, 1964; (with James Joy) Contemporary Anarchism, 1971. Home: 2800 Ridge Rd North Haven, CT 06473.

APTHEKER, HERBERT, historian; b. Bklyn., July 31, 1915; s. Benjamin and Rebecca (Komar) A.; B.S., Columbia, 1936, A.M., 1937, Ph.D., 1943; Ph.D. (hon.), Martin Luther U., Halle, Germany, 1966; m. Fay Aptheker, Sept. 4, 1942; 1 dau., Bettina. Editor, Masses and Mainstream, 1948-52, Polit. Affairs, 1952-63; dir. Am. Inst. Marxist Studies, N.Y.C., 1964—; lectr. throughout U.S. and Europe, 1946—; vis. lectr. dept. history Bryn Mawr Coll., 1969—; vis. lectr. U. Mass., 1971-72. Ind. Peace candidate for U.S. Congress, 1966. Served to maj., F.A., AUS, 1942-46; ETO. Guggenheim fellow, 1946-47; grantee Social Sci. Research Council, 1961, Rabinowitz Found., 1965. Mem. Am. Hist. Assn., Assn. Study Negro Life (History award 1939, 69). Author: To Be Free: Studies in American Negro History, 1948; World of C. Wright Mills, 1960; Soul of the Republic, 1964; Negro Slave Revolts in the United States, 1939; Negro in the Civil War, 1938; Nat Turner's Slave Rebellion, 1966; Mission to Hanoi, 1966; Labor Movement in the South During Slavery, 1954; The Truth about Hungary, 1957; The Nature of Democracy, Freedom and Revolution, 1967; History of the American People, 2 vols., 1959, 60; Essays in the History of the American Negro, rev. edit., 1964; Era of McCarthyism, 1955; Dare We Be Free?, 1960; American Foreign Policy and the Cold War, 1962; American Negro Slave Revolts, 1943; rev. edit., 1963; American Civil War, 1961; Urgency of Marxist- Christian Dialogue, 1970; Afro-American History: the Modern Era, 1971. Editor: Disarmament and American Economy, 1960; One Continual Cry, 1965; Marxism and Democracy, 1964; And Why Not Every Man?, 1961; Marxism and Alienation, 1965; Documentary History of the Negro People in the United States, 2 vols., 1951; Marxism and Christianity, 1967; Autobiography of W.E.B. DuBois, 1968. Home: 32 Ludlam Pl Brooklyn NY 11225 Office: 20 E 30th St New York City NY 10016

AQUADRO, CHARLES D., union ofcl. Pres., United Slate, Tile and Composition Roofers, Damp and Waterproof Workers Assn., AFL-CIO. Office: 1125 17th St NW Washington DC 20036*

AQUILINO, DANIEL, banker; b. Needham, Mass., Feb. 4, 1924; s. Michael Aquilino and Anna (Bruno) A.; B.S. magna cum laude, Northeastern U., 1949; grad. Stonier Grad. Sch. Banking, Rutgers U., 1962; m. Theresa H. Barberio, Nov. 9, 1946; children—Donna Lee (Mrs. Herbert F. Fraser), Daniel C., Michael D. With Fed. Res. Bank Boston, 1949—, sr. v.p., 1970—. Served with AUS, 1943-45. Home: 3 Bakers Hill Rd Weston MA 02193 Office: 30 Pearl St Boston MA 02106

ARAFEH, MEHADIN KAMEL, hosp. supt., physician; b. Damascus, Syria, Aug. 22, 1931; s. Kamel Bakri and Suad Khalil (Beiruty) A.; P.C.B., U. Damascus, 1949, M.D., 1955; postgrad. U. Pa., 1957, Yale, 1959-60; m. Barbara Mary Waterman, July 9, 1960; children—Susan, Adnan, Joyce. Came to U.S., 1955, naturalized, 1965. Intern Emory U. Hosp., 1955-56; resident Mercy Hosp., Phila., 1956-57, N.Y.U. Bellevue Med. Center, 1957-59; sr. psychiatrist Conn. Valley Hosp., Middletown, 1959-63, clin. dir., 1963-64, dir. psychiat. tng., 1964-65, asst. supt., 1965- 67, supt., 1967—; asst. clin. prof. psychiatry Yale Sch. Medicine, 1965-68, lectr. in psychiatry, 1968—; cons. Middlesex Meml. Hosp. Corporator Middletown Savs. Bank. Chmn. Conn. Postgrad. Seminar Corp. in Neurology and Psychiatry, 1970—. Bd. dirs. Middlesex United Fund, Gilead House, Elmcrest Manor; corporator Middlesex Meml. Hosp. Fellow Am. Psychiat. Assn.; mem. Conn. Psychiat. Soc. (past counsellor), A.M.A., World Med. Assn., World Psychiat. Assn., A.A.A.S. Rotarian. Home: Harvey Dr Middletown CT 06457 Office: Conn Valley Hosp PO Box 351 Middletown CT 06457

ARAGON, LOUIS, author; b. Paris, France, Oct. 3, 1897; ed. faculty medicine, U. Paris; m. Elsa Kagan Troilet, Feb. 1928, 39. A founder of Surrealism; joined Communist Party, becoming leading exponent of Socialist Realism; formerly sec. Internat. Assn. Writers of Def. of Culture; formerly mem. editorial staff L'Humanite newspaper; mng. editor eve. paper Ce Soir before and after World War II; editor Community Weekly Les Lettres Francaises. Mem. central com. French Communist Party; v.p. Assn. des Ecrivains combattants, 1945-60; mem. Lenin Peace Prize Com. Served in French Army, 1919; served in tank troop French Army, 1939-40; taken prisoner, but escaped and went underground; worked in Resistance and edited clandestine paper Les Etoiles. Decorated Croix de Guerre (2), Medaille Militaire; recipient Prix Renaudot, 1936. Author: Anicet, 1920; Le Mouvement Perpetuel, 1925; The Bells of Basel, 1933; Residential Quarter, 1936; Passengers of Destiny, 1942; Aurelian, 1945; Les Communistes, 1949-50; Literature Sovietique, 1955; History of the USSR, 1962; also popular war poems. Translator: (Lewis Carroll) The Hunting of the Snark, 1928; Five Sonnets of Petrarch, 1947. Address: 21 rue de Richelieu Paris 1e France

ARAKAWA, SHUSAKU, painter; b. Nagoya City, Japan, 1936; studied medicine. Came to U.S., 1961. Became asso. with Yomiuri independents and Neo-Dada Organizers, Tokyo, 1959; participated Tokyo Arts Festival, 1960; one man shows Muramatsu Gallery, Tokyo, 1959, Mudo Gallery, Tokyo, 1961, Galerie Schmela, Düsseldorf, Germany, 1963, 65, 66, Dwan Gallery, Los Angeles, 1964, 66, Palais des Beaux-Arts, Brussels, Belgium, 1964, Minami Gallery, Tokyo, 1965, Galleria dell'Ariete, Milan, Italy, 1965, Württembergischer Kunstverein, Stuttgart, Germany, 1965, Dwan Gallery, N.Y.C., 1966, Wide White Space Gallery, Antwerp, Belgium, 1966, Stedelijik van Abbemuseum, Eindhoven, 1966-67, Von der Heydt Mus., Wuppertal, 1967; also exhibited numerous group shows, Los Angeles, N.Y.C., Ill., Japan, Europe. Address: care of Dwan Gallery 29 W 57th St New York City NY*

ARAM, ABBAS, diplomat of Iran; b. Yazd, Iran; s. Ali Reza and Monavvar (Bibi) A.; B.A., U. Calcutta. Joined Fgn. Service Iran, 1935; sec. consulate gen., New Delhi, India, 1935-38; 3d sec., embassy, London, Eng., 1938-43; asst. chief 3d polit. dept. Ministry Fgn. Affairs, Teheran, 1943-45; 1st sec. embassy, Berne, Switzerland, 1945-46; 1st sec., counsellor, charge d'affairs embassy, Washington, 1946, 49, 50; chief 4th polit. dept. Ministry Fgn. Affairs, 1951-53; counsellor, counsul, gen., Baghdad, Iraq, 1953; minister embassy, Washington, 1953-57; dir. gen. polit. affairs Ministry Fgn. Affairs, 1957-58; ambassador to Tokyo, also rep. to China, 1958-59; minister fgn. affairs, 1959-60; ambassador to Iraq, 1960-62; minister fgn. affairs, 1962-67; leader Iranian delegation gen. assemblies UN, 1959, 60, 63, 64, 66; ambassador to Court of St. James, 1967-69; Ministry Fgn. Affairs, Teheran, Iran, 1969—. Address: Ministry of Foreign Affairs Teheran Iran

ARAM, JOHN LORENZO, lumber co. exec.; b. Joseph, Ida., Sept. 19, 1912; s. James Henry and Phebe (Smith) A.; B.S., U. Ia., 1936; m. Mary Jane Pace, June 14, 1936; children—Frances Jane, John David, James Pace. Trainee, employment mgr., asst. shipping supt., shipping supt. Potlatch Forests, Inc., Lewiston, Ida., 1936-49; mgr. mfg. Boise Payette Lumber Co., Boise, Ida., 1949-50. v.p. mfg., 1950-53, exec. v.p., 1953-55, pres., 1955-56, also dir., pres., dir. Morrison-Merrill & Co., Salt Lake City, Constrn. Finance Co., Boise; v.p. Weyerhaeuser Timber Co., Tacoma, 1957-64, v.p. operations, 1964, spl. studies, 1965-67, v.p. transp. and materiel; pres., chmn. bd. Willapa Cedar Products Co., Weyerhaeuser, N.M.: dir. Hauserman Inc., Weyerhaeuser Can., Ltd., Weyerhaeuser, Que., Ltd., Heath Tecna Corp., Educators Mfg. Co., Nat Bank Wash.; mem. exec. com. Lakewood, Unlimited, Tacoma. Vice chairman Western Wood Products Study Com.; mem. Ida. Bd. Forestry, 1949-55. Former dir. St. Luke's Hosp., Children's Home Finding and Aid Soc., Boise; past trustee Tacoma YMCA; trustee Mills Coll., Ft. Steilacoom Community Coll.; marketing adv. council U. Ore., mem. industry adv. com. Nat. Housing Center; bd. regents nat. tng labs. Gonzala U. Past dir., Western Pine Assn., So. Ida. Forestry Assn., N.A.M., West Coast Lumbermen's Assn., Western Forestry and Conservation Assn. (pres. 1955), Western Wood Products Assn. (dir. 1964—), Nat. Assn. Purchasing Agts. Republican. Episcopalian. Elk. Clubs: Wash. Athletic; Tacoma, Tacoma Country and Golf. Home: 11315 Butte Terrace SW Tacoma WA 98498 Office: Tacoma Blvd Tacoma WA 98401

ARAM, NATHAN WALTER, electronics co. exec.; b. Moline, Ill., Oct. 5, 1916; s. Walter and Elizabeth (Rumsey) A.; student Augustana Coll., 1935-37; B.S. in Elec. Engring., Purdue U., 1939; evening student Northwestern U., 1940-42; m. Shirley Dellinger, Apr. 29, 1944; children—Robert L., Stephen P., Alan W., Richard B. With Zenith Radio Corp., 1939—, chief engr., v.p., 1961—. Recipient Distinguished Alumnus citation Purdue U., 1964. Registered profl. engr., Ill. Fellow I.E.E.E.; mem. Chgo. Radio Engrs. Club, Sigma Xi (asso.), Eta Kappa Nu. Methodist. Home: 221 Oak St Tower Lakes Barrington, IL 60010 Office: 6101 W Dickens Av Chicago IL 60639

ARAND, LOUIS A., educator; b. Pitts., Nov. 3, 1892; s. Jacob J. and Josephine M. (Arand) A.; A.B., A.M., S.T.B., St. Mary's Sem. and U. Balt., 1912-17; S.T.L., Catholic U. Am., Washington, 1919; S.T.D., Angelico U., Rome, Italy, 1921; student in Paris, France, 1919-20. Prof. philosophy St. Mary's U., 1921-24, dogmatic theology Sulpician Sem., Washington, 1924-39, sacramental theology, 1926-39, dogmatic theology Cath. U., 1936—; pres. Div. Coll., Cath. U., 1932—, also trustee. Republican. Author: (with Fr. Tanguerov) Doctrine and Devotion, 1933. Editor, The Spiritual Life, 1932; St. Augustine: Faith, Hope and Charity, 1947.

ARANGO, JORGE SANIN, architect; b. Bogota, Colombia, Nov. 29, 1916; s. Fernando Isaza and Maria Jaramillo (Sanin) A.; student Universidad Catolica de Chile Sch. Architecture, 1935-42, Harvard Grad. Sch. Design, 1942-43; m. Elizabeth Leighton, 1944; 1 son, Peter Arango-Wolff; m. 2d, Judith Brooks Wolpert, Dec. 14, 1951; children—Richard, Virginia. Head archtl. firm Arango & Murtra, Bogota, 1946-59; prof. architecture and urban design Nat. U., Bogota, 1945-47; vis. lectr. Sch. Architecture, U. Cal., Berkeley, 1956, 58. Pub. bldgs. dir. Colombia, 1948-49; co-author basic plan for devel. Bogota, 1948; pres. Colombian Soc. Architects, 1946-51, Colegium for Engrs. and Architects of Colombia, 1955. Recipient Excellence in Design awards Miami and Fla. chpts. A.I.A., 1967; selected by Archtl. Record for one of best designed residences in U.S.A., 1970. Mem. A.I.A. Author: (with C. Martinez) Architecture in Colombia, 1951; The Urbanization of the Earth, 1970. Home: 3920 Wood Av Miami FL 33133 Office: 3141 Commodore Plaza Miami FL 33133

ARANOW, EDWARD ROSS, lawyer; b. N.Y.C., Apr. 30, 1909; s. Harry and Sarah (Rosenfield) A.; A.B., Columbia, 1929, J.D., 1932; m. Rita Abrons, July 11, 1941; children—Vicki (Mrs. Donald Klein), Judith, Robert L. Admitted to N.Y. bar, 1933; asso. firm Colby, Brown & Pollack, N.Y.C., 1932-34, Szold & Brandwen, N.Y.C., 1934-39; practiced in N.Y.C., 1939-42; sr. partner Aranow, Brodsky, Bohlinger, Benetar, Einhorn & Dann, N.Y.C., 1946—, dir. Barbizon Plaza Hotel, Inc., Union Terminal Cold Storage Co., Inc. Lectr. Practicing Law Inst., N.Y.C. Bd. dirs., sec. Cejwin Camps, Inc., 1946—; bd. visitors Columbia Law Sch., 1957—; trustee Scarsdale (N.Y.) Adult Sch., 1967—. Served to maj. AUS, 1942-46. Decorated Royal Order of Vasa (Sweden), 1967; recipient medal for conspicuous alumni service Columbia U. 1962. Mem. Am., Internat., N.Y., New York County, Judge Adv. General's bar assns., Columbia Law Sch. Alumni Assn. (pres. 1965-67), Bar Assn. City N.Y., Phi Beta Kappa, Zeta Beta Tau. Co-author: Proxy Contests for Corporate Control, rev. edit., 1968. Contbr. articles profl. jours. Home: 47 Colby Lane Scarsdale NY 10583 Office: 469 Fifth Av New York City NY 10017

ARANT, WILLIAM DOUGLAS, lawyer; b. Waverly, Ala., May 19, 1897; s. William Jackson and Emma (Baker) A.; B.S. and M.S., Univ. of Va., 1920; LL.B., Yale, 1923; m. Letitia Tyler McNeel, Dec. 31, 1929; children—Adele (Mrs. Richard J. Stockham, Jr.), Letitia Christian, Frances Fairlie. Instr. polit. sci., U. Va., summers 1920-22; admitted to Alabama bar, 1923; with Tillman, Bradley & Baldwin, Birmingham, Ala.; mem. successor firms 1927—, now Bradley, Arant, Rose & White; spl. asst. to atty. gen. of U.S. and chief counsel for Petroleum Administrative Bd. (N.R.A.), Washington, D.C., 1933-34; chmn. Regional Labor Bd., 6th Dist., N.R.A., 1934-35; public mem. 4th Regional Labor Board, Atlanta, 1942-44; mem. nat. com. study Anti-Trust Laws, 1953-54. Enlisted as pvt. U.S. Army, June 1918; later assigned Field Arty., C.O.T.S., Camp Taylor, Ky., 2d lt., 1919. Mem. Bd. Appeal, Dist. 2, Ala. Selective Service system, 1940-45. Pres. Birmingham Civic Symphony Assn., 1936-38; pres. Birmingham Civic Opera Assn., 1957-60. Trustee Brooke Hill Sch., Eye Found., Inc. Mem. Am. Bar Assn. (com. on bill of rights 1938-45, chmn. 1941-43), Ala. State Bar Assn. (pres. 1936-37; mem. bd. commrs. 1931-40), Birmingham Bar Assn., Am. Law Inst., Assn. Bar City of N.Y., Beta Theta Pi, Phi Delta Phi, Phi Beta Kappa, Order of Coif. Democrat. Episcopalian. Clubs: Redstone, Mountain Brook Country; Yale (N.Y. City). Editor in chief, Yale Law Jour., 1922-23. Home: 2815 Argyle Rd Birmingham AL 35213 Office: Brown-Marx Bldg Birmingham AL 35203

ARANYOS, ALEXANDER SANDOR, international operations exec.; b. Zillina, Czechoslovakia; s. Ludwig and Ethel (Wilhelm) A.; Degree Comml. Engring. cum laude, Grad. Sch. Commerce U. Prague, 1931; m. Gertrude Reisman, Aug. 22, 1937; children—Alexander Paul, Vivian Jane. With Mine & Foundry Co. (formerly Coburg, Ltd.), Bratislava, Czechoslovakia, 1933-40; adminstrv. asst. to pres. and export mgr. Gen. Motors Distbrs., Republic of Panama, 1940-41; mgr. Latin Am. div. Van Raalte Co., N.Y.C., 1941-53; with Fruehauf Corp., Detroit, 1953-, v.p. internat. operations, 1956-; pres., dir. Fruehauf Internat. Ltd., 1957—; mem. consultative council Fruehauf do Brasil, S.A. (Sao Paulo); dir. Deutsche Fruehauf GMBH & Co. Kg., Gravenbruch, Germany, Trailers South Africa Ltd., Johannesburg, Fruehauf Trailers (Australasia Pty. Ltd., Melbourne, Crane Fruehauf Trailers Ltd., Dereham, Norfolk, Eng., Fruehauf France, S.A., Ris-Orangis, France, Fruehauf de Mexico, S.A., Coacaleo, Nippon Fruehauf Co., Ltd., Tokyo, NETAM, N.V. Nederlandsche tank Apparaten-en Machinefabriek, Kotterdam; asso. dir. Clyde Industries Ltd., Sydney. Mem. regional export expansion council U.S. Dept. Commerce, 1970-71. Mem. Research Inst. Am., A.I.M., Detroit Bd. Commerce, Am. Australasian Assn. N.Y., Internat. Execs. Assn. N.Y., U.S. C. of C. (mem. internat. com.) Clubs: Rotary, Rockefeller Center Luncheon (N.Y.C.); World Trade (Detroit). Home: 2 Bridle Lane Sands Point NY 11050 Office: 10900 Harper Av Detroit MI 48232 also 30 Rockefeller Plaza New York City NY 10020

ARATA, BLAKE GEORGE, lawyer; b. New Orleans, Aug. 15, 1931; s. George Galway and Marion (Giraud) A.; B.B.A., Loyola U., New Orleans, 1952, J.D., 1953; m. Jo-Ann P. Graffagnino, July 3, 1954; children—Cynthia, Blake George, Elizabeth, Patrick, Michael, Jo-Ann. Admitted to La. bar, 1953, since practiced in New Orleans; partner firm Gordon, Arata & McCollam, 1970—; city atty., New Orleans, 1970—. Campaign mgr. for New Orleans Mayor Moon Landrieu, 1969. Served to lt. comdr. USNR, 1953-57. Mem. Am., La. (chmn. mineral law sect. 1968), New Orleans bar assns. Catholic. Clubs: Southern Yacht, Loyola L (pres. 1960) (New Orleans). Home: 548 Emerald St New Orleans LA 70124 Office: Bank of New Orleans Bldg New Orleans LA 70112

ARATENBURG, JOHN EUGENE, mfg. exec.; b. Lima, O., Apr. 1, 1932; B.S., U. San Francisco, 1954; M.S., Stanford University, 1956; m. Rosemarie Lois Brown, May 15, 1955; 1 son, Anthony Robinson. Sales rep. Ames-Brockton Fabricated Products, Akron, O., 1956-58, sales mgr. Coshocton, Ohio, 1959-61, gen. manager plant, 1961-68, v.p. sales, 1968--. Instr. bus. Coshocton Jr. College, 1968-69. Mem. Coshocton C. of C. (vice president 1967-68, pres. 1969-70), Sales Executives Institute, Phi Beta Kappa, Sigma Chi, Phi Mu. Democrat. Mem. Christian Ch. (lay leader). Mason (32, Shriner). Clubs: Coshocton Country, Coshocton City, Running Deer Country. Home: 2d Av Coshocton OH Office: 3d Av Coshocton OH

ARBANAS, FREDERICK VINCENT, profl. football player; b. Detroit, Jan. 14, 1939; s. Francis Vincent and Lucille Cathrine (Stromback) A.; student Mich. State U., 1961; m. Sharon Ann Duff, Aug. 20, 1960; children—Michael, Lisa, JoBeth. Tight end Kansas City (Mo.) Chiefs, 1961—; pres. Fred Arbanas & Co.-Nat. Yellow Page Advt. Agy. Mem. Jackson County (Mo.) Sheriff Dept., 1970. Bd. dirs. Big Brothers, Kansas City, Mo., 1969—. Home: 11700 E 139th St Kansas City MO 64149 Office: 3130 Broadway Kansas City MO 64111

ARBAUGH, GEORGE BARTHOLOMEW, educator, clergyman; b. Frankfort, Ind., Dec. 28, 1905; s. Alonzo Harvey and Nora Leone (Bartholomew) A.; A.B., Carthage Coll., 1926; A.M., State U. Ia., 1927, Ph.D., 1931; B.D., Hamma Div. Sch., Wittenberg Coll., 1930; student Leipzig U., Germany, 1928-29; m. Catherine R. Evans, July 31, 1927; 1 son, George Evans. Ordained to ministry United Lutheran Ch. in Am., 1931; pastor Redeemer Luth. Ch., Hartford, Wis., 1931-34, St. Mark's Luth. Ch., Dubuque, Ia., 1934-36; prof. philosophy, psychology Carthage Coll., 1936-43; pastor 1st Luth. Ch., West Allis, Wis., 1943-45; prof. philosophy, psychology Augustana Coll., Rock Island, Ill., 1945—, dean, 1947-67, also v.p. coll., 1961-67. Mem. Am. Philos. Assn., Am. Soc. Ch. History, Phi Beta Kappa. Author: Revelation in Mormonism, 1932; Growth of a Christian, 1959; Gods, Sex and Saints, 1957; co-author; Oriental Philosophy, 1949; Kierkegaard's Authorship, 1967; contbr. to jours. Home: 3426 7th Av Rock Island IL 61201

ARBEGAST, NEIL RICHARD, physician, educator; b. Lancaster, Pa., Mar. 27, 1934; s. Clyde Emerson and Helen (Meyer) A.; student U. Md., 1955-57, M.D., 1961; postgrad. Baylor U. Coll. Medicine, 1962-67; m. Marilyn D. Madigan, May 27, 1955; children—Fred Richard, Duane Emerson, Michele Ann, Ann Elizabeth, Melissa Lynn. Intern, Univ. Hosp., Balt., 1961-62; resident Baylor U. Coll. Medicine, 1962-66, instr. surgery, 1966-67, asst. prof. surgery, 1967-69; asst. dep. chief surgery Ben Taub Gen. Hosp., Houston, 1966-67; dir. dept. surgery Kern County Gen. Hosp., Bakersfield, Cal., 1970—; asst. clin prof. dept. surgery U. Cal. at Los Angeles, 1971—. Participated in first successful heart transplant by Tex. Heart Inst. Cardiovascular Team, 1968. Served with AUS, 1953-55. Fellow A.C.S., Am. Coll. Chest Physicians, Am. Coll. Cardiology; mem. Am. (Billing Gold medal 1967), Cal., So. med. assns., Kern County Med. Soc., Contbr. articles to profl. jours. Home: 708 Elsey St Bakersfield CA 93309

ARBEIT, ARNOLD ARVIN, cons. architect, artist; b. N.Y.C., Oct. 1, 1916; s. Carl and Caroline (Puretz) A.; grad. Beaux Arts Inst. Design, 1936; B.Arch., N.Y.U., 1938, M.Arch., 1940; M.A. in Edn., N.Y.U., 1955; diploma Mass. Inst. Tech., 1945; Ph.D., Burton Coll., 1965; Ed.D., Brantridge, Sussex, 1966; Sc.D., Johnson C. Smith U., 1969; m. Amelia U. Feibush, Sept. 18, 1938; 1 son, Stuart Carl David. Architect, N.Y. Navy Yard, Bur. Naval Architecture, 1935-38, Bur.

Constrn., Bd. Edn., N.Y.C., 1938-43; pvt. practice, 1950—; mem. faculty Cooper Union, 1947-65, N.Y.U., 1952-53; now prof., dir. dept. coll. planning programming services, campus planning and devel. City U. N.Y., also univ. architect; cons., regional dir. Univ. facilities, Westchester; instr., lectr. Exhibits, Laurel Gallery, Bklyn. Mus., 8th St. Gallery, Delgado Art Mus.; one man art shows New York every year. Mem. Mayor's Panel Architects, 1952—; supr. Civil Def. Manhattan 2d Dist. Registered profl. architect, N.Y., N.J., Conn., R.I., Pa., Mass., Md., N.C.A.R.B. Served with Transp. Corps, AUS, 1942-46; col. U.S. Army Res.; chief Monument, Fine Arts and Archives Civil Affairs. Recipient Morse medal design N.Y.U., also Armstrong medal watercolor. Mem. A.I.A. (chmn. hdqrs. com.), N.Y. Soc. Architects (chmn. arts and architecture com.), N.Y. State Assn. Architects, Nat. Inst. Archtl. Edn. (chmn., trustee), Soc. Coll. and Univ. Planning, N.Y.U. Archtl. Alumni Assn. (pres.). Contbr. articles profl. publs. Address: 116 Fox Meadow Rd Scarsdale NY 10538

ARBIB, MICHAEL ANTHONY, educator, cybernetician; b. Eastbourne, U.K., May 28, 1940; s. John R. and Helen (Arbib) A.; B.Sc., U. Sydney, 1960; Ph.D. in Math., Mass. Inst. Tech., 1963; m. Prue Hassell, Dec. 29, 1965; children—Phillipa Jane, Benjamin Giles. Came to U.S., 1966. Vis. lectr. U. New South Wales, 1962, 65, 68, Mont. State U., summers 1963, 65, Imperial Coll. London, 1968; lectr. tours U.S., Europe, USSR, 1963-64; mem. faculty Stanford, 1965-70, asso. prof. elec. engring., 1969-70; prof. psychology and computer sci., chmn. computer sci. U. Mass., 1970—; editorial bd. Internat. Jour. Man-Machine Studies, Jour. Cybernetics. Mem. Am. Math. Soc., Assn. Computing Machinery, I.E.E.E., A.A.A.S. Author: Brains, Machines and Mathematics, 1964; Theories of Abstract Automation, 1969; The Metaphorical Brain, 1971; author (with others) Topics in Mathematical System Theory, 1969. Editor Algebraic Theory of Machines, Languages and Semigroups, 1968. Home: 164 Aubinwood Rd Amherst MA 01002

ARBOGAST, WILLIAM FREDERICK, educator; b. Pueblo, Colo., Aug. 6, 1906; s. William Theodore and Lottie Drusilla (Larson) A.; student Westminster Coll., Salt Lake City, 1924-26; B.S., U. Utah, 1928, Ed.D., 1952; M.A., U. Denver, 1938; m. Edna Domgaard, Nov. 26, 1930; childrenEdna Mae (Mrs. Ronald F. Delparte), Frederick Theodore, Anne Louise. Sr. high sch. tchr. Sevier Dist., Utah, 1928-31; jr. high and elementary sch. tchr., Salt Lake City, 1931-42; prin. Jefferson Elementary Sch., 1942-45, Irving Jr. High Sch., 1945-52, East High Sch., 1952-56, Highland High Sch., 1956-63 (all Salt Lake City); pres. Westminster Coll., 1963-68, trustee, 1963-68, coordinator fed. govt. programs, 1968—; occasional tchr. edn. adminstrn., summers and extension classes U. Utah, Westminster Coll. Bd. dirs. Salt Lake City YMCA, Pro-Utah, Inc. Mem. Nat., Utah edn. assns., Nat. Assn. Secondary Sch. Prins., Salt Lake City C. of C., Phi Delta Kappa. Methodist. Clubs: Kiwanis, University (Salt Lake City); Rotary (Sugarhouse, Utah). Home: 990 Fairclough Dr Salt Lake City UT 84106

ARBOGAST, ZOLLIE O., Jr., lawyer; b. Kansas, Ill., June 6, 1929; s. Zollie O. and Helen (Ryan) A.; student Eastern Ill. State U., 1947-49; LL.B., Chgo.-Kent Coll. Law, 1952, J.D., 1969; m. Mary Anita Stewart, June 2, 1951; children-Daniel Steven, Alane Annette. Admitted to Ill. bar, 1952; practiced in Marshall, 1952-63, Casey, 1967—; county judge Clark County, Ill., 1958- 64; asso. judge 5th Judicial Circuit Ill., 1964-67; partner Partlow & Arbogast, 1967—. Mem. Ill., Clark County bar assns., Phi Alpha Delta. Republican. Mem. Christian Ch. Mason. Home: 801 E Alabama St Casey IL 62420 Office: 110 E Main St Casey IL 62420

ARBUCKLE, DUGALD SINCLAIR, educator; b. Estevan, Sask., Can., June 28, 1912; s. John Finley and Margaret (Sinclair) A.; B.S., U. Alta., 1940, B.Ed., 1942; Ph.D., U. Chgo., 1947; m. Margaret May Redmond, Oct. 10, 1942; children—Donald Redmond, Margaret Ann, Mary Elizabeth, Jane Katherine, Judith Ellen. Naturalized, 1952. Tchr., personnel worker Alta. schs., 1931-41; lab. instr. U. Alta., 1941-43; ednl. officer RCAF, 1943-45; ednl. cons. Internat. Harvester co., 1946-37; prof. edn., chmn. counselor edn. Boston U., 1947—. Cons. numerous univs., 1951—; vis. prof. Wash. State Coll., Central Coll. Wash., Brigham Young U., N.Y.U., U. Hawaii, U. Tex., 1951-59, Ore. State U., Ariz. State U., U. So. Cal.; cons. psychology Harvard, 1959-60; cons. U.S. Dept. of Def., U.S. Office Edn., U.S. Dept. Vets. Affairs. Fellow Am. Psychol. Assn.; mem. Am. Personnel and Guidance Assn. (past pres.), Student Personnel Assn. Tchr. Edn. (past pres.), Mass. Council Tchrs. Edn. (past pres.), Mass. Soc. Social Hygiene (past pres.). Am. Social Hygiene Soc. (past dir.), Am. Acad. Psychotherapists, Am. Coll. Personnel Assn., Nat. Vocational Guidance Assn., N.E., Mass. psych. assns., Am. Edn. Research Assn., Am. Assn. U. Profs., Alumni Assns. U. Alta., U. Chgo. Club: Alpine, Author: Industrial Counseling, 1949; Teacher Counseling, 1950; Student Personnel Services in Higher Education, 1951; Guidance and Counseling the Classroom, 1954; Counseling: An Introduction, 1961; Personnel Services in American Schools, 1962; Counseling: Philosophy, Theory Practice, 1965; Personnel Services in the Modern School, 1966; Counseling and Psychotherapy: An Overview, 1967, Counseling: Philosophy and Theory, 1970. Contbr. articles to profl. publs. Home: 101 Billings St Sharon MA 02067 Office: Boston U Boston MA 02215

ARBUCKLE, ERNEST COMINGS, banker; b. Lee, N.H., Sept. 5, 1912; s. Frank Albert and Ernestine C. (Weeden) A.; A.B., Stanford, 1933, M.B.A., 1936; m. Katherine Norris Hall, Dec. 10, 1942; children—Ernest C., Joan, Katherine, Susan. Personnel specialist Standard Oil of Cal., 1937-41, orgn. analyst, 1945- 46; dir. procurement, asst. to pres. Golden State Co., Ltd., 1946-50; asst. v.p. W.R. Grace & Co., N.Y.; exec. v.p. Grace & Co. (Pacific Coast); v.p. Grace & Co. C.Am., 1950-58; dean Grad. Sch. Bus., Stanford, 1958-68; chmn. bd. Stanford Research Inst., 1966-70, now bd. dirs.; chmn. Wells Fargo Bank, San Francisco, 1968—; dir. Owens-Ill., Inc., Safeway Stores, Inc., Castle & Cooke, Inc. Hewlett Packard Co., Utah Constn. & Mining Co. Mem. Commn. on White House Fellows, 1964-68; mem. Adv. Com. on Pvt. Enterprise in Fgn. Aid, 1964-65; mem. Pres.'s Commn. on Internat. Trade and Investment Policy; mem. industry adv. council Dept. Def. Bd. dirs. Nat. Center for Vol. Action, San Francisco Opera Assn.; trustee Com. for Econ. Devel., San Francisco Bay Area Council, Stanford; incorporator Nat. Corp. for Housing Partnerships. Served as lt. comdr. USNR, 1941-45. Decorated Silver Star; recipient Freedoms Found. award, 1950; Adminstrv. Excellence award Stanford Bus. Sch. Assn., 1968; Bus. Leadership award U. Mich. Grad. Sch. Bus. Adminstrn. Mem. San Francisco C. of C. (dir.). Republican. Clubs: Pacific Union, Bohemian. Home: 12 Arastradero Rd Menlo Park CA 94025 Office: 464 California St San Francisco CA 94120

ARBUCKLE, JOHN WILLIAM, communications co. exec.; b. Indpls., Apr. 29, 1925; s. William S. and Inez (Smith) A.; B.A. in Bus. Adminstrn., Butler U., 1948; m. Maxine Demlow, Aug. 18, 1946; children—Nancy Lynn, John Richard. With Ind. Bell Telephone Co., 1949—, v.p., sec., treas., 1968-71, v.p. operations, dir., mem. exec. com., 1971—. Dir., 2d v.p. Better Bus. Bur. Indpls. Mem. President's Club, Butler U. Served with AUS, 1943-46, 50-52. Mem. Indpls. C. of C., Newcomen Soc. N. Am., Ind. C. of C. Clubs: Indpls. Athletic; Woodland Country (dir., treas.). Home: 6440 Knyghton Rd Indianapolis IN 46220 Office: 240 N Meridian St Indianapolis IN 46204

ARBUS, DIANE, photographer; b. N.Y.C., Mar. 14, 1923; d. David Irwin and Gertrude (Russek) Nemerov; grad. high sch.; m. Allan Arbus, Apr. 10, 1941; children—Doon, Amy. Exhibited in group shows at Mus. Modern Art, 1965, Guggenheim Group Show Phila. Coll. Art, 1966, Mus. Modern Art New Documents, 1967, Fogg Mus., 1967; represented in permanent collections Mus. Modern Art, George Eastman House, Rochester, N.Y.; tchr. Parsons Sch. Design, 1965-66, Cooper Union 1968-69. Guggenheim fellow, 1963, 66. Contbr. articles mags., newspapers. Home: 463 West St New York City NY 10014

ARCENEAUX, THOMAS JOSEPH, univ. dean; b. Lafayette, La., June 13, 1908; s. Emilien and Aline (Martin) A.; B.S., Southwestern La. Inst., 1929; M.S., Tex. A. & M. Coll., 1931; Ph.D., Ia. State Coll., 1934; Dr.Sci.Agr., Laval U., Que., 1955; m. Carita Melchior, Aug. 27, 1936. Tchr. Sci., Crowley (La.) High Sch., 1929-32; research fellow Ia. State Coll., 1932-34; mem. faculty Southwestern La. Inst., 1934-35, La. State U., 1935-41; dean Coll. Agr., prof. agronomy U. Southwestern La., Lafayette, 1941—. Agrl. cons. ECA Mission to France, charge agrl. survey of Madagascar, summer 1950, France; also survey of French West Africa, summer 1951. Decorated knight Saint Gregory The Great, 1949; officier d'Academie Republic of France, 1955. Mem. Am. Soc. Agronomy, Am. Genetic Assn., La. Acad. Scis., La. Teachers Assn., S.A.R., Phi Kappa Phi, Phi Kappa Theta, Phi Delta Phi. Democrat. Roman Catholic. K.C. (4). Rotarian. Home: 217 St Joseph St Lafayette LA 70501

ARCHAMBAULT, BENNETT, corp. exec.; b. Oakland, Cal.; s. Albert Joseph and May (Smales) A.; student Ga. Inst. Tech.; S.B., Mass. Inst. Tech.; m. Margaret Henrietta Morgan, Feb. 19, 1948; children—Suzanne Morgan, Michele Lorraine, Steven Bennett. Vice pres., gen. mgr. M. W.Kellogg Co., N.Y.C., 1946-54; pres. Stewart-Warner Corp., Chgo., 1954—, chmn. bd., 1959—; dir., chmn. exec. com. Thor Power Tool Co.; dir. Kemperco, Inc., Lumbermens Mut. Casualty Co., Am. Motorists Ins. Co., Union Tank Car Co., Trans Union Corp., Harris Trust & Savs. Bank. Head, London Mission for OSRD, 1942-45. Mem. Mayor's Com. Econ. And Cultural Devel. Chgo. Mem. gov.'s com. United Republican Fund Ill.; chmn. for Ill., Rep. Nat. Finance Com. Trustee Ill. Inst. Tech., also mem. exec. com. Research Inst.; trustee, mem. exec. com., nominating com. Mus. Sci. and Industry; past mem. corp. and com. on devel. Mass. Inst. Tech., 1960-65, mem. standing com. on devel. sr. adv. bd. Am. Security Council; bd. dirs. Greater Chgo. Safety Council; trustee Better Govt. Assn.; bd. dirs. Chgo. council Invest-in-Am., Chgo. Central Area Com., Protestant Found. Greater Chgo. Decorated Medal Merit (U.S.); His Majesty's Medal for Service in Cause of Freedom (Brit.). Mem. Employers Assn. Greater Chgo. (dir.), Newcomen Soc. N.Am., Research Soc. Am., C. of C. U.S. (policy com.), Ill. Mfrs. Assn. (dir., exec. com.), N.A.M. (exec. com., dir., nominating com.), Am. Ordnance Assn. (dir. Chgo. post). Republican. Clubs: Broad Street (N.Y.C.); Racquet, Saddle and Cycle, Commercial, Westmoreland, Executives, Chicago (Chgo.). Home: 3240 Lake Shore Dr Chicago IL 60657 Office: 1826 Diversey Pkwy Chicago IL 60614

ARCHAMBAULT, GEORGE FRANCIS, editor; b. Springfield, Mass., Apr. 29, 1909; s. George Charles and Catherine V. (Mayette) A.; Ph.G., Mass. Coll. Pharmacy, 1931, Ph.C., 1933, Pharm.D., 1960; LL.B., Northeastern U., 1941; D.Sc., Phila. Coll. Pharmacy, 1951; LL.D., Temple U., 1961; m. Lillian Herbert, Sept. 3, 1934; children—Joan Anne (Mrs. Joseph Rubis), Lillian Kathleen (Mrs. Anthony Matan), Patricia Gay (Mrs. Andrew Kachik), Frances Helen (Mrs. Robert Parks), George Francis, William Herbert. Registered pharmacist in Mass., 1932—; mem. faculty Mass. Coll. Pharmacy, 1933-45, lectr. pharmacy and bus. adminstrn., 1945-47; admitted to Mass. bar, 1942; pvt. practice, Belmont, Mass., 1945-47; dir. profl. relations in New Eng. states Liggett Drug Co., 1945-47; commd. pharmacist USPHS, 1947-67, pharmacist dir., 1952; chief pharmacy br., div. hosps. Bur. Med. Services, also pharmacy liasion officer Office Surgeon Gen., USPHS, 1960-67, medicare pharmacy planning cons. div. med. care adminstrn., 1965-67; dean, prof. pharmacy adminstrn. Coll. Pharmacy, U. Fla., Gainesville, 1967; cons. on pharmacy and instnl. drug distbn. system. Mem. revision com. U.S. Pharmacopeia, 1950-60, trustee, 1960-70; mem. faculty Inst. Hosp. Law of Am. Hosp. Assn., 1954-69; chmn. joint com. Am. Soc. Hosp. Pharmacists and Am. Hosp. Assn., 1955-68; pharm. cons. Catholic Hosp. Assn., 1950—; pharmacy cons. profl. exam. service Am. Pub. Health Assn., 1949-59; adv. pub. health service pharmacy and prescription trend, div. prices and cost of living Bur. Labor Statistics, 1955-67; mem. nat. adv. com. Law-Medicine Research Inst., Boston U., 1960-65; lectr. law hosp. pharmacy and use investigative drugs. Life mem. Am. Pharm. Assn. (chmn. council 1959-60, com. publs. 1958-59, pres. Washington 1950, nat. pres. 1962-63); mem. Am. Soc. Hosp. Pharmacists (charter, past pres.), A.A.A.S. (v.p. 1958, mem. council 1959-68), Commd. Officers Assn. USPHS, Mass. Soc. Hosp. Pharmacists (founder, hon.), La. Soc. Hosp. Pharmacists (hon.), Kappa Psi, Rho Chi. Author numerous articles, chpts. in books. Editor: Hosp. Formulary Mgmt. Jour. Home: 5916 Melvern Dr Bethseda MD 20034

ARCHAMBAULT, LOUIS, sculptor; b. Montreal, Que., Can., Apr. 4, 1915; s. Anthime Sergius and Annie (Michaud) A.; student Coll. Jean-de-Brebeuf, Montreal; B.A., U. Montreal, 1936; m. Mariette Provost, June 7, 1941; children—Aubert, Eloi, Patrice. Works exhibited Internat. Sculpture Exhbn., Festivals of Gt. Britain, London, Eng., 1951, 10th Triennale, Milan, Italy, 1954, 18th Biennial, Venice, 1956, 11th Triennale, Milan, 1957, Brussels Universal and Internat. Exhbn., 1958, Pitts. Internat., 1958, Internat. Exhbn. Contemporary Sculpture, Expo '67, Montreal; represented in permanent collections Nat. Gallery, Ottawa, Museo Internatzionale Dalla Ceramica, Faenza, Italy, Art Gallery Ont., Sun Life Bldg. Toronto, Uplands Air Terminal, Ottawa, Place des Arts, Montreal, Malton Airport, Toronto, Scarborough Coll., Toronto, others; executed free-standing sculptured and mural wall Canadian Pavillion, Brussels Exhbn., 1958, sculptures for Canadian Pavillion and Arts Gallery Plaza, Expo '67. Resident artist U. Que., Montreal. Canadian Govt. fellow for travel in France, 1953-54, Can. Council grantee, 1959, 62, 69; recipient Arts medal Royal Archtl. Inst. of Can., 1958; Service medal Order Can., 1968. Academician Royal Canadian Acad. Arts. Address: 278 Sanford Av St Lambert, Quebec Canada.

ARCHBOLD, RICHARD, mammalogist, explorer; b. N.Y.C., Apr. 9, 1907; s. John F. and May (Barron) A.; ed. pvt. schs and spl. studies at Columbia; unmarried. Mammalogist, Mission Zoologique Franco-Anglo-Americaineà Madagascar, 1929-31; leader and sponsor New Guinea Expdn., 1933-34, 1936- 37; leader Indisch-Amerikaansche Expeditie (in cooperation with Netherlands Indies Govt.), 1938; expdn. to Ariz., 1940; pres. Archbold Expdns., 1935—; resident dir. Archbold Biol. Sta., 1941—. Trustee John D. Archbold Meml. Hosp., Thomasville, Ga. Decorated officer Order Orange Nassau, 1940. Mem. Inst. Aeros. and Astronautics, Soc. Naturalists, Ecol. Soc., German Soc. Mammalogists, Am. Mammalogists Soc., Am. Ornithologists Union. Clubs: Explorers, Am. Alpine (N.Y.). Contbr. to sci. jours. Home: Route 2 Box 380 Lake Placid FL 33852

ARCHER, E. JAMES, educator; b. Chgo., Oct. 2, 1925; B.S., Northwestern U., 1949, M.S., 1950, Ph.D., 1952; m. Marian Ann Cisar, June 18, 1949 (dec. Jan. 1969); m. 2d, Barbara Staner Uehling, May 2, 1969 (div. July, 1971). Mem. faculty U. Wis., 1952-65, prof. psychology, 1961-65, chmn. dept., 1962-65; prof. psychology, dean Grad. Sch., U. Colo., 1965-69; v.p. acad. affairs U. R.I., 1969-71, prof. psychology, 1971—. Mem. psychobiology panel NSF, 1963-66; chmn. region X selection com. Woodrow Wilson Fellowship Found., 1960-65; mem.-at-large exec. com. Midwest Conf. Grad. Study and Research, 1967-68; mem. personality and cognition research rev. com. Nat. Inst. Mental Health, 1968-72. Served with USNR, 1943-46. Fellow A.A.A.S., Am. Psychol. Assn.; mem. Midwest Psychol. Assn. (council 1962- 65, sec.-treas. 1968-70), Nat. Assn. State Univs. and Land Grant Colls. (exec. com., council acad. affairs). Cons. editor Jour. Exptl. Psychology, 1957-62. Author articles. Home: 54 Dockray Rd Wakefield RI 02879

ARCHER, EDMUND MINOR, artist; b. Richmond, Va., Sept. 28, 1904; s. William Wharton and Rosalie (Pleasants) A.; student Nora Houston and Adele Clark Studio, Richmond, 1911-18; grad. St. Christopher's Sch., Richmond, 1921; student U. Va., 1921-22, Art Students League N.Y., 1923-25; ind. study in Europe, including Academie Colarossi, Paris, 1925-26. Asso. curator Whitney Mus. Am. Art, N.Y.C., 1930-40; instr. drawing, painting composition Corcoran Sch. Art, also faculty George Washington U., 1944-68 emeritus, 1968—. Mem. bd. control Art Students League N.Y., 1924-25. One-man shows various U.S. cities; works exhibited prin. museums and nat. exhbns., N.Y. and Chgo. world fairs, 1930—, N.A.D., 1956, Corcoran Gallery of Art, Washington, 1959; paintings in collections Boston Museum Fine Arts, Corcoran Gallery Art, Fisk U., Naval Acad. Mus., Va. Mus. Fine Arts, Whitney Mus. Am. Art, Valentine Mus., Va. Commonwealth U., U. Va.; portraits represented in collections of univs. Va., Princeton, Richmond, Mich., Va. State Capitol, Med. Coll. Va.; portraits include Charles C. Abbott, Herbert C. Moseley, J. Phillips Coleman, Fred M. Carroll, Justice Thomas C. Gordon; executed mural Hopewell (Va.) Post Office. Served with 603d Engrs., AUS, World War II. Recipient Corcoran bronze medal, 3d William A. Clark prize Corcoran Gallery Art, 1930, Purchase award Va. Mus. Fine Arts, 1941; painting prize, also popular prize Norfolk Mus. Arts and Scis., 1950. Fellow Internat. Inst. Arts and Letters, Switzerland, 1961. Address: : 13 S Foushee St Richmond, VA 23220

ARCHER, EVAN CHANDLEE, banker; b. Haddonfield, N.J., Nov. 15, 1913; s. F. Morse and Bessie (Chandlee) A.; B.A., Princeton, 1934; m. Helen Frances Allen, Feb. 22, 1935; children—Evan Chandlee, Helen R. (Mrs. G. Michael Crawford), Katherine H. (Mrs. James M. Smith). With Phila. Nat. Bank. 1934—, sr. v.p., 1964—, exec. v.p., 1970—. Treas., dir. Delaware Valley Council, 1956. Served to lt. (j.g.) USNR, 1944-45. Mem. Robert Morris Assos., Assn. Res. City Bankers. Clubs: Pine Valley Golf (Clementon, N.J.); Seaview Country (Absecon, N.J.). Home: Munn Lane Cherry Hill, NJ 08034. Office: Phila Nat Bank Broad and Chestnut Sts Philadellphia PA 19101

ARCHER, FRANKLIN MORSE, Jr., lawyer; b. Camden, N.J., Sept. 17, 1902; s. Franklin Morse and Bessie (Chandlee) A.; grad. Phillips Exeter Acad., 1919; A.B., Princeton, 1923; LL.B., Harvard, 1926; m. Mary Joy G. Reeve, Sept. 22, 1928; children—Franklin Morse III, Mary Joy, Elizabeth A. (Mrs. Dow Drukker), William Reeve. Admitted to N.J. bar, 1928, since practiced in Camden; partner firm Archer, Greiner, Hunter & Read, 1928—; asso. prof. U. Pa. Law Sch., 1933-49. Dir. Provident Mut. Life Ins. Co., Phila., Twitchco Inc., Blatt Investment Co.; dir., chmn. exec. com. South Jersey Nat. Bank. Pres. N.J. Bd. Child Welfare, 1957-63; mem. regional adv. com. NLRB, 1960-61. Mem. N.J. Supreme Ct. Com. on Appellate and Civil Rules. Pres. Phila. Skating Club, Humane Soc., Ardmore, Pa., 1951-53; pres. bd. mgrs. Cooper Hosp., Camden, 1958-66, chmn. bd. mgrs., 1966—; former trustee United Fund Camden County, Moorestown (N.J.) Community House; bd. dirs. World Wildlife Fund, Inc. Fellow Am. Coll. Probate Counsel; mem. Am. (comml. arbitration com; membership com. sect. real property, probate - trust law), N.J. (com. removal judges), Camden County bar assns., World Affairs Council Phila. (past dir.), Phi Beta Kappa. Clubs: Princeton, Philadelphia, Sunday Breakfast (Phila.); Moorestown Field; Camden Rotary (past pres.); Barnegat Light Yacht; Nassau (Princeton, N.J.). Home: 515 Chester Av Moorestown NJ 08057 Office: 518 Market St Camden NJ 08101

ARCHER, GLENN LEROY, lawyer, educator, business exec.; b. Densmore, Kan., Mar. 29, 1906; s. Garfield Joseph and Adah Maude (Burnap) A.; diplomas, Central Acad. and Coll., McPherson, Kan., 1923 and 1925; B.S., Greenville (Ill.) Coll., 1927, LL.D., 1966; M.S., U. Colo., 1938; LL.B. magna cum laude, Washburn U., 1946; postgrad. Northwestern U., 1947; m. Ruth Agnes Ford, June 16, 1928; children—Glenn LeRoy, Marilyn Jean. Supt. schs., Densmore, Kan., 1927-34, Almena, 1934-39; county supt. schs. Norton County, hdqrs. Norton, 1939; adminstrv. asst. to gov. of Kan., 1939-42; dir. profl. relations Kan. State Tchrs. Assn., 1942-43; asso. dir. legislative and fed. relations div. N.E.A., Washington, 1943-44, special counsel, 1946; admitted to Kan. bar, 1946; dean and prof. of law Washburn Law Sch., 1947-48; exec. dir. Nat. Commn. on Church and State, Washington, 1948—; pres. Home Lumber Coal and Grain Co., Densmore, 1940-47; partner law firm Allen, Ascough and Archer, Topeka, 1946; operator ranch near Densmore, 1928—. Mem. Kan. State Bd. Edn., 1942, White House Conf. on Rural Edn., 1944; mem. Nat. War Labor Bd. (regional), 1942. Holder life teaching certificate, Kan. Mem. Internat. Law Soc., Nat. and Kan. edn. assns., Am., Kan. State and Shawnee County bar assns., Kappa Delta Pi, Pi Alpha Delta. Republican (mem. state and nat. speakers bur. 1932-44; county chmn. Norton County 1934). Methodist (holder local preachers license). Clubs: Lions (sec. 1928; dir. 1942), Kansas Schoolmasters. Asso. editor Kansas Teacher, 1941-42; asst. editor Legislative News Flash, 1943; editor Church and State Review, 1948-64, pub., 1964-. On world tour, 1961. Home: 9507 Monroe St Silver Spring MD 20910 Office: 8120 Fenton St Silver Spring MD 20910

ARCHER, JAMES ELSON, educator; b. Hedley, Tex., Dec. 1, 1922; s. James M. and Mary Minerva (Bolles) A.; B.S., Tex. Tech. U., 1947; Ph.D., Mass. Inst. Tech., 1950; m. Reta Faye Turner, Nov. 8, 1942; 1 son, James Elson. Instr., Mass. Inst. Tech., 1950-52, Sloan fellow in indsl. mgmt., 1963-64; researcher Pitts. Plate Glass Co., Pitts., 1952-53, asst. dir., 1953-54, asso. dir., 1954-56, dir. research, 1956-62; mng. partner Archer Assos., Dallas, 1963-64; corporate dir. mgmt. systems Tex. Instruments, Dallas, 1964-68; prof. Tex. Tech. U., Lubbock, 1968—. Served with USAAF, 1943-46. Home: 6208 Lynnhaven St Lubbock TX 79413 Office: P O Box 4200 Lubbock TX 79409

ARCHER, JEROME WALTER, educator; b. Milw., May 23, 1907; s. James A. and Anne (Herkens) A.; A.B. cum laude, Marquette U., 1930, M.A., 1932; postgrad. U. Chgo., 1936; Ph.D. (Univ. fellow 1939-40), Northwestern U., 1942; m. Anne Stanish, Aug. 19, 1933; 1 son, Robert Hugh. Chmn. dept. English, West Milwaukee High Sch.,

1930-36; mem. faculty Marquette U., 1936-63, prof. English, 1952-63, chmn. dept., 1948-63; chmn. dept. English, Ariz. State U., Tempe, 1963-71, prof., 1963—. Cons., U.S. Office of Education, 1966-71. Mem. Nat. Council Tchrs. English (2d v.p., program chmn. 1956, dir. 1953-62, 69-72, dir. European study tour 1960, adv. bd. Coll. English 1963-65. Modern Lang. Assn., Conf. Coll. Composition and Communication (chief exec. officer 1955), Medieval Acad. Am., Am. Dialect Soc., Am. Assn. U. Profs., English Club Greater Milw. (pres. 1949-51), Ariz. English Tchrs. Assn., English-Speaking Union (pres. Phoenix 1966-69, dir. 1969—), Assn. Depts. of English, Phi Kappa Phi. Roman Catholic. Clubs: Phoenix press, University, Camelback Tennis and Swim. Co-author: A Reader for Writers, 3d edit., 1971; Exposition, 2d edit., 1971. Editor: Research and Development of English Programs in the Junior College, 1965. Author articles, contbr. profl. jours. Home: 5146 N 68th Pl Scottsdale AZ 85253 Office: Ariz State U Tempe AZ 85281

ARCHEY, HARRY LEE, Jr., ret. ins. co. exec.; b. Cin., Apr. 12, 1908; s. Harry Lee and Elsa (Roll) A.; B.S., Wharton Sch., 1928; m. Charlotte Hicks, Oct. 1, 1932. With Fidelity Mut. Life Ins. Co., Phila., 1928—, supr. policy holders service div., 1932-43, statistician, 1943-47, asst. sec., 1947-48, sec., 1948-61, v.p. adminstrn., 1961-67, v.p., 1967-71. Active in United Fund Phila., United Cerebral Palsy Assn. Served with USAAF, 1943. Mem. Life Office Mgmt. Assn. (past pres., past dir.), Geog. Soc. Phila. (past pres., past dir.). Presbyn. (elder). Rotarian. Home: 819 Glendalough Rd Philadelphia PA 19118

ARCHIBALD, A. EDWARD, cons. actuary; b. Seaforth, Ont., Can., Nov. 1, 1902; s. Andrew and Margaret (Wallace) A.; B.A., U. Toronto, 1926; m. Dorothy E. Burns, Aug. 31, 1935; 1 dau., Ellen Radcliffe. With State Mut. Life Assurance Co., Worcester, Mass., 1926-28, Woodward, Fondiller & Ryan, cons. actuaries, N.Y.C., 1928-33; actuary Vol. State Life Ins. Co., Chattanooga, 1933-43, v.p. and actuary, 1943-55; dir. mgmt. controls Investors Diversified Services, Inc., Mpls., 1955-58, v.p., 1958-67; v.p., actuary Investors Syndicate Life Ins. & Annuity Co., Mpls., 1957-59, dir., 1957—, exec. v.p., 1959-66, pres., 1966-67; cons. actuary, 1968-70. Fellow Soc. Actuaries; mem. Casualty Actuarial Soc. Home: 200 Richardson St Lookout Mountain TN 37350

ARCHIBALD, ADAMS GORDON, utility exec.; b. Truro, N.S., Can., Jan. 7, 1911; s. Harry Adams and Willana A.; B.Comm., Dalhousie U (Can.); m. Marion D. Muggah, Sept. 14, 1938; 3 sons, 1 dau. Salesman, Maritime Telegraph & Telephone Co., Ltd., Halifax, N.S., 1934-35, chief clk., Sydney, N.S., 1935-39, local mgr., Amherst, N.S., 1939-40, gen. comml. supr., Halifax, 1940-43, gen. comml. mgr., 1943-56, gen. plant mgr., 1956-58, gen. mgr., 1958-59, v.p., gen. mgr., 1959-63, pres., 1963-70, chmn., pres., chief exec. officer, 1970—; dir. Eastern Can. Savs. & Loan Co., Eastern Tel. and Tel. Co., N.S. Trust Co. Past pres., mem. council Halifax Bd. Trade; vice chmn. bd. govs. Dalhousie U. Bd. dirs. N.S. Hwy. Safety Council. Mem. Canadian C. of C. (v.p. for N.S.). Clubs: Saraguay; Halifax. Home: 6083 Belmont Rd Halifax Nova Scotia Canada Office: 88 Hollis St Halifax Nova Scotia Canada*

ARCHIBALD, ARNOLD ADAMS, ret. steel co. exec.; b. Truro, N.S., Can., Sept. 16, 1905; s. Lewis Edgar and Elizabeth May (McCallum) A.; student Chauncy Hall Sch., Boston, 1923-24; B.S., Mass. Inst. Tech., 1930; m. Clara West Butler, Dec. 24, 1937; children—Lewis Edgar II, Roger Williams, John Baird. Came to U.S., 1923, naturalized, 1942. With Jones and Laughlin Steel Corp., Pitts., 1935—, beginning as metall. asst., successively asst. works metallurgist, metall. engr., salesman, asst. to v.p., v.p., 1954-65, adminstrv. v.p., 1965-70, now ret. Served as dollar-a-year man on WPB, 1942-44, 45, Civilian Prodn. Adminstrn., 1946-47. Mem. Am. Iron and Steel Inst., Am. Iron and Steel Engrs., Am. Soc. for Metals. Clubs: Pittsburgh Athletic Assn., Duquesne (Pitts.); Union (Cleve.). Home: 1327 Coraopolis Heights Rd Coraopolis PA 15108 Office: Union Trust Bldg Pittsburgh PA 15222

ARCHIBALD, BRYAN FREDERICK, sem. pres.; b. Brockton, Mass., May 8, 1912; s. Arthur C. and Nelly B. (Purdy) A.; B.Sc., Acadia U., 1934; B.D., Colgate-Rochester Div. Sch., 1933; postgrad. Boston U., 1944-52; D.D., Keuka Coll., 1950; m. Jane Louise Walter, Dec. 27, 1937; children—Sara Jane (Mrs. Douglas L. Hawthorne), Mary Nell (Mrs. Daniel D. Ebaugh), Nancy Louise, Arthur Frederick. Ordained to ministry Baptist Ch., 1938; pastor in Brockton, 1938-45, Springfield, Mass., 1945-56, Washington, 1956-63, Haddonfield, N.J., 1963-65; pres. No. Bapt. Theol. Sem., 1965—. Bd. dirs. Chgo. Bapt. Assn.; mem. council theol. edn. Am. Bapt. Conv.; mem. com. on Christian higher edn. Ill. Bapt. Conv. Address: 100 W Butterfield Rd Oak Brook IL 60521

ARCHIBALD, CARL BRICE, petroleum co. exec.; b. Hiteman, Ia., Feb. 3, 1915; s. Russell B. and Minnie (Johnson) A.; student Augustana Coll., 1933-35; B.S., U. Ill., 1937; div.; 1 son, Carl Brice. Accounting mgr., various positions controllers office Pure Oil Co., Chgo., 1937-66; controller Clark Oil & Refining Corp., Milw., 1966—. Served with USAAF, World War II. Mem. Am. Petroleum Inst., Financial Execs. Inst., Systems and Procedures Assn. Am., Am. Legion. Baptist. Home: 6741 W Keefe Av Pkwy Milwaukee WI 53216 Office: 8530 W National Av Milwaukee WI 53227

ARCHIBALD, FRED IRWIN, publisher; b. McCook, Neb.; s. William Wallace and May (Irwin) A.; student U. Neb. Coll. Engring., 1911-13; LL.D. (honorary), Morgan State Coll., Balt., 1967; m. Edna Esther Olson, Aug. 11, 1921; 1 son, Fred John. Began career as advt. salesman, 1913; advt. mgr. Lincoln (Neb.) Star, 1913-17, bus. and advt. mgr., sec. and treas., 1919-27; advt. dir. Omaha (Neb.) World Herald, 1927-31; gen. mgr. Omaha Bee-News, 1931-33; advt. dir. and asst. pub. New York American, 1934-35; pub. Omaha Bee-News, 1936-37; pres. and pub. Albany (N.Y.) Times Union, 1938- 53; pub. and editorial supr. Balt. News-Post and Am., 1953-64; dir. Hearst Corp.; former v.p., dir., mem. radio and TV, finance coms. Hearst Publishing Co., Inc., Hearst Consol. Publs., Inc.; sec. Armadale Farms, Inc.; partner Archibald-Armadale Assos., New Market, Md. Adv. bd. Nat. Conf. Christians and Jews; mem. adv. com. Ch. Home and Hosp., Balt. Chmn. Balt. Civic Center Commn., Md. Pub. Broadcasting Corp.; mem. adv. com. Seton Inst.; pres. Balt. Civic Opera Co.; chmn. Md. Higher Edn. Loan Corp.; mem. Md. Cruises Commn. Trustee Balt. Mus. of Arts, United Student Aid Fund, Inc., N.Y.C.; bd. dirs. Com. for Downtown, Balt. Served as lt. 346th F.A., 91st Div., 1917-18; maj. Mil. Govt. Div., U.S. Army, 1943; col. N.Y. N.G. Res. ret. Mem. N.Y. Pubs. Assn. (past Pres., hon. life mem.), Chesapeake Assn. A.P. (past pres.), Am. Legion (life), Sigma Alpha Epsilon, Sigma Delta Chi (past state chmn.). Episcopalian. Mason (32). Clubs: Omaha Athletic; National Press (Washington); Advertising, Maryland, Merchants (Balt.); Gulf and Bay (Sarasota, Fla.). Home and office: 830 W University Pkwy Baltimore MD 21210

ARCHIBALD, JOHN CRAIG, ret. ins. exec.; b. Seaforth, Ont., Can., Aug. 30, 1905; s. William R. and Jessie (Craig) A.; A.B., U. Toronto, 1928; m. Helen Clement, Aug. 16, 1933; children—Jean Bruce. Came to U.S., 1929, naturalized, 1936. Mem. acturial dept. North Am. Life Ins. Co., Toronto, 1928-29, Equitable Life Assurance Soc. U.S., N.Y.C., 1929-34; asso. with Bankers Life Co., Des Moines, 1934-70, asst. acturary, 1936-43, underwriting sec., 1943-46, underwriting v.p., 1946-56, v.p., 1956-61, sr. v.p., 1961- 70, dir., 1960-71. Fellow Soc. Actuaries (gov.); mem. Home Office Life Underwriters (pres. 1953-54). Club: Actuaries (Des Moines). Home: 1704 Luin Lane Des Moines IA 50322

ARCHIBALD, KALMAN DALE, biologist, educator; b. Brockton, Mass., Jan. 19, 1910; s. Arthur Crawley and Nellie Beth (Purdy) A.; B.A., Denison U., 1933; M.A., Ohio State U., 1934, Ph.D., 1954; B.D., Colgate-Rochester Div. Sch., 1946; m. Marjorie Frances Davis, Feb. 21, 1935; children—Kay Dale (Mrs. Donald A. McDaniel), Carol Diane (Mrs. Gunars K. Neiders), Marjorie Lois (Mrs. M. Lois Sauma). Scholar, Frans Theodore Stone lab. Ohio State U., 1935, asst. zoology, then instr. Ohio State U., 1935- 36, 40-41; asso. prof. biology, head dept. Ouachita Coll., Arkadelphia, Ark., 1936-43, instr. physics, 1942-43; instr. zoology Keuka Coll., Keuka Park, N.Y., 1946-47; asso. prof. biology Acadia U., Wolfville, N.S., Can., 1947-48; faculty Denison U., 1948—, prof. biol. scis., 1959—, chmn. dept. biology, 1960-63, dir. gen. edn. course life sci., 1949-60, 64-66; dir. forest insect research Nova Scotia Research Found., 59; spl. research age determination ictalurus punctatus and noturus flavus, histogenesis blood cells fresh-water fishes, forest aphidae of N.S., embryology Japanese Medaka fish, Oxyzias latipes, embryology Congo Cichlid fish, Cichlosoma nigrofasciatum; research behavioral genetics Ohio State U., 1967-68; Research Corp. grant, 1968—. Ordained to ministry Baptist Ch., 1943; pastor N.Y. State, 1943-47, interim supply pastor, 1948—. Fellow Ohio Acad. Sci.; mem. A.A.A.S., Am. Genetic Soc., Entomol. Soc. Am., Am. Inst. Biol. Scis., N.E.A. N.S. Inst. Scis., Assn. Midwest Biology Tchrs., Ohio Conf. Biology Tchrs., Ohio Edn. Assn., Denison Sci. Soc., Am. Assn. U. Profs., Sigma Xi, Alpha Epsilon Delta, Kappa Sigma. Mason, Lion. Author monographs, articles. Home: RD 2 Granville OH 43023

ARCHIBALD, RALPH GEORGE, educator; b. Sackville, N.B., Can., May 23, 1901; s. Herbert Dixon and Amelia Milligan (George) A.; B.A., U. Man., 1922; M.A., U. Toronto, 1924; Ph.D., U. Chgo., 1927; postdoctoral, U. Göttingen, 1930-31; m. Norma Gwendolyn Jones, July 8, 1941; 1 son, John Duncan. Came to U.S., 1925, naturalized, 1949. Demonstrator in physics U Man., 1921-22; lectr. math. Wesley Coll., Winnipeg, Man., 1922-23; asso. Columbia, 1927-28, asst. prof., 1928-38; asst. prof. Queens Coll., City U. N.Y., Flushing, 1938-43, asso. prof., 1943-48, prof., 1948-71, emeritus, 1971—. Mem. Am. Math. Soc., Math. Assn. Am., Am. Sci. Affiliation, Sigma Xi. Presbyn. (elder 1970—). Author: An Introduction to the Theory of Numbers, 1970; also articles. Home: 43-19 192d St Flushing NY 11358

ARCHIBALD, REGINALD MAC GREGOR, physician, chemist; b. Syracuse, N.Y., Mar. 2, 1910; s. Eben Henry and Minnie (Archibald) A.; B.A., U. B.C., 1930, M.A., 1932; Ph.D., U. Toronto, 1934, M.D., 1939; m. Evelyn Stroh, June 12, 1948; children—Ruth, Lawrence. Tchr., research asst. U. B.C., 1930-32; teaching and research asst. U. Toronto, 1932-33, fellow pathol. chemistry, 1933-35; intern Hosp. for Sick Children, Toronto, 1937, surgery, 1938, medicine, 1939; intern Toronto Gen. Hosp., 1939-40; fellow div. med. scis. Nat. Research Council, 1940-42; asst. resident physician Rockefeller Hosp., 1941-46; asso. Rockefeller U., 1946, mem., 1948—, prof., 1955—, sr. physician Rockefeller Hosp., 1955—; prof. biochemistry, sch. hygiene and pub. health Johns Hopkins, 1946-48; med. research in pediatric endocrinology and biochemistry, devel. clin. lab. methods, study of influence of hormones on enzymes. Fellow A.A.A.S.; mem. Am. Chem. Soc., Am. Soc. Biol. Chemists, Harvey Soc., Am. Fedn. Clin. Research, Coll. Phys. and Surg. Ont., Med. and Chirurg. Faculty Md., Endocrine Soc., Soc. Exptl. Biology and Medicine, Soc. Research in Child Devel., Brit. Biochem. Soc., Sigma Xi. Mem. editorial bd. Jour. Biol. Chemistry, 1948-58, Jour. Clin. Endocrinology & Metabolism, 1952-60, Child Development, 1954-56; adv. bd. Analytical Chemistry, 1957-60. Home: 266 Ancon Av Pelham NY 10803 Office: Hospital of Rockefeller U 66th St and York Av New York NY 10021

ARCHIE, JAMES LEE, artist; b. Orlander, N.C., June 14, 1924; s. Eddie and Elizabeth (Mitchell) A.; ed. Cath. schs.; m. Marjorie Ann Booth, June 7, 1959; children—Victoria Esther, Olivia Rebecca, Daniel James, Enoch Lee. Exhbtd. group shows Africa l'Leto Galleries, N.Y.C., 1970, Youth Devel. Agy. Exhbt., 1970, Countee Cullen Library, N.Y.C., 1970, Studio Museum, N.Y.C., 1969, Mary Rogers Coll., 1969, Afro-American Art Festival, 1969, Tucker Galleries, N.Y.C., Freedom Bank, N.Y.C., 1969, Harlem Hosp., 1968; dir. Creative Community Workshop, N.Y.C.; decorator Broadway Producer David Merrick also Actress Leslie Uggams; designer Apollo Theater, Harlem, N.Y., dressing rooms; dir. Tucker Galleries, N.Y.C.; Vol. art therapist for adults in disadvantaged areas; art instr. elem. schs.; vol. cons. to tchrs. to improve their understanding of problems facing slum-bred youngsters; vol. community cons. Museum Arts Projects in slum areas. Mem. Museum Art N.Y.C., Federated Cultural Commn. Mem. Seventh-day Adventist Ch. Author: Destitute Meets Tranquility, 1969, Cry of Hunger at Midnight; Strength of Black Beauty, 1969. Address: 138 Edgecombe Av New York City NY 10030

ARCHIE, WILLIAM COUNCILL, found. exec.; b. Salisbury, N.C., June 23, 1908; s. George W. and Sarah (Beard) A.; B.A., Davidson Coll., 1929; M.A., Wake Forest Coll., 1935; M.A. (Bergen fellow), Princeton, 1940, Ph.D., 1949; m. Ruth Toms Newby, Sept. 1, 1934; children—Suzanne (dec.), William Councill. Tchr. Gulf Coast Mil. Acad., Gulfport, Miss., 1929-31; tchr. Oak Ridge (N.C.) Mil. Inst., 1931-33; instr. Wake Forest Coll., 1935-38, asst. prof. romance langs., 1940-42, asso. dean, 1956-57, dean, 1957-58; asso. prof. romance langs. Duke, 1946-56, dean freshmen, 1949-51, acting dean instrn., 1951- 52, asst. dean Trinity Coll., Duke, 1952-56; dean Coll. Arts and Scis., Emory U., 1958-61; dir. higher edn. State of N.C., Raleigh, 1961-65; dean Coll. Arts and Science, U. Delaware, 1965-66; exec. dir. Mary Reynolds Babcock Found., Winston-Salem, N.C., 1966—. Bd. dirs. Boys Club, Winston-Salem, 1956, Learning Inst. N. C. Bd. visitors Davidson Coll.; former trustee Warren Wilson Coll. The College Found.; chmn. bd. trustees Southeastern Council Founds., 1970—. Served from first lieutenant to major Intelligence Corps, AUS 1942-46. Decorated Merito Militar (Mexico). Mem. Am. Assn. U. Profs., Modern Lang. Assn. Am., Am. Assn. Tchrs. French, Pi Kappa Phi, Omicron Delta Kappa. Democrat. Presbyn. Clubs: Forsyth Country, Rotary (Winston-Salem, N.C.); Cosmos; Torch. Home: 511 Roslyn Rd Winston-Salem NC 27110 Office: 102 Reynolds Village Winston-Salem NC 27106

ARCINIEGAS, GERMAN, editor, author; b. Bogota, Colombia, Dec. 6, 1900; s. Rafael and Aurora (Angueyra) A.; LL.D., Universidad Nacional Bogotá, 1925; Dr. Honoris Causa, Mills Coll., 1944; m. Gabriela Vieira, Nov. 19, 1926; children—Aurora, Gabriela. Editor, El Tiempo, Bogotá, 1928; vice consul, London, 1930; prof. Universidad Nacional Bogotá, 1931-38, charge d'affaires, Buenos Aires, 1939-41; minister of edn. of Colombia, 1941- 46, vis. prof. Columbia, 1943, 47-54, U. Chgo., 1944, Mills Coll., 1945, U. Cal. at Berkeley 1945, prof. Columbia, 1954; served as ambassador of Colombia at Rome, Italy; former editor Cuadernos, Paris, France; now ambassador of Colombia to Venezuela. Past v.p. Am. Com. Cultural Freedom. Mem. Academia Colombiana, Academia Colombiana de Historia; corr. mem. acads. of Madrid, Mexico, Venezuela, Cuba; hon. asso. Nat. Inst. Arts and Letters. Author: El Estudiante de la Mesa Redonda, 1932; The Knight of El Dorado, 1942; Germans in the Conquest of America, 1943; The Green Continent, 1944; Este Pueblo de America, 1945; Caribbean, Sea of the New World, 1946; The State of Latin Aemrica, 1952; Amerigo and the New World, 1955; Italia, Guia para Vagabundos, 1959; America Magica, 1959; America Magica II, 1961; Cosas Del Pueblo, 1962; El Mundo de la Bella Simoneta, 1962; Entre el Mar Rojo y el Mar Muerto, 1964. Home: Embassy of Colombia Urbanización Campo Alegre Avenida El Parque 18 Caracas Venezuela

ARDEN, DEAN NORMAN, educator; b. Mpls., Oct. 3, 1925; s. Wesley and Clare (Newton) A.; B.S. in Elec. Engring., U. Mich., 1946, B.S. in Engring. Math., 1946; Ph.D. in Math., Purdue U., 1957; m. Marguerite Mackey, Sept. 12, 1954; children—Karen, Lynn, Eric, Amy. Asst. prof. Mass. Inst. Tech., 1955-60, asso prof., 1960-64; prof. Rensselaer Poly. Inst., Troy, N.Y., 1964—, chmn. elec. engring. curriculum, 1967-; tech. expert for UN, Taiwan, China, 1962- 63; cons. Raytheon Co., Bedford, Mass. Pres. Schenendehowa Central Sch. Bd., 1967, 1968; pres. Saratoga County Shch. Bds. Assn., 1968-70. Served with USMCR, 1943-46. Mem. I.E.E.E., Am. Math. Soc., Soc. for Indsl. and Applied Math. Home: 20 Locust Lane Elnora, NY 12065 Office: Rensselaer Poly Inst Troy NY 12181

ARDEN, EUGENE, univ. dean; b. N.Y.C., June 25, 1923; s. Harry and Gussie (Shevach) A.; B.A., N.Y.U., 1943; M.A., Columbia, 1947; Ph.D., Ohio State U., 1953; m. Sandra E. Rose, July 11, 1948; children—Stacey, Jonathan. Mem. faculties Ohio State U., Queen's Coll., also Hofstra U., 1947-56; from asst. prof. to prof., chmn. dept. English and humanities div. C.W. Post Coll., Greenvale, N.Y., 1956-62, dean, 1962-64; dean grad. faculties L.I. U., 1964-70, dean Conolly Coll., 1970-71, exec. dean Bklyn, Center, 1971—. Bd. dirs. Mid-Island YM and YWHA, 1962-64. Served with AUS, 1943- 46; ETO. Mem. Modern Lang. Assn., Eastern Deans Assn., Conf. Acad. Deans. Mem. B'nai B'rith (pres. Central Nassau lodge 1966-68). Contbr. articles to profl. jours., mags. Home: 92 Lancia Dr East Norwich NY 11732 Office: Long Island U Brooklyn NY 11201

ARDEN, EVE, actress; b. Mill Valley, Cal., Apr. 30, 1912; d. Charles Peter and Lucille (Frank) Quedens; student pub. schs.; m. Edward G. Bergen (div. 1948); children (adopted)—Liza, Constance; m. 2d, Brooks West, Aug. 24, 1951; 1 son, Douglas Brooks; 1 adopted son, Duncan Paris. Actress N.Y. shows, Shubert Ziegfield Follies, 1933, Very Warm for May, Two for the Show, Let's Face It, 1941; motion pictures include Stage Door, 1938, Cover Girl, The Doughgirls, Mildred Pierce, Goodbye My Fancy, We're Not Married, Anatomy of a Murder, Dark at the Top of the Stairs; began in radio series Our Miss Brooks 1948, TV series, 1952; television series The Eve Arden Show, 1957-58, Mothers-in-Law, 1967—; star nat. company Butterflies Are Free, Chgo. and Los Angeles, 1970. Recipient Emmy (Acad. TV Arts and Sci.) award, 1953; Sarah Siddens award for Actress of Year in Hello Dolly, Chgo., 1967-68. Home: Westhaven Ranch Hidden Valley Ventura County CA 91360 Office: P O Box 1065 Studio City CA 90164

ARDEN, JOHN, playwright; b. Barnsley, Eng., Oct. 26, 1930; s. Charles Alwyn and Annie (Layland) A.; B.A., King's Coll., Cambridge (Eng.) U., 1953; diploma architecture Edinburgh (Scotland) Coll. Art, 1955; m. Margaretta Ruth D'Arcy, May 1, 1957; children—Gwalchmei (dec.), Finn, Adam, Jacob, Neuss. Author (plays): Live Like Pigs, 1958; Sergeant Musgrave's Dance, 1959; The Happy Haven, 1960; The Workhouse Donkey, 1963; Armstrong's Last Good Night, 1964; Left Handed Liberty, 1965; (with wife) The Business of Good Government, 1960; Ars Longa Vita Brevis, 1964; The Royal Pardon, 1966; The Hero Rises Up, 1968. Annual fellow playwriting Bristol (Eng.) U., 1959; lectr. drama and politics N.Y.U., 1967. Address: Ramsay Ltd 14A Goodwin's Ct London WC2 England

ARDEN, THOMAS T., mfg. exec.; b. Chgo., Nov. 9, 1905; s. James J. and Jeannette (Brown) A.; student U. Ill., 1923-25, Carnegie Inst. Tech., 1926-27; m. Ruth M. Clovis, Sept. 26, 1927; 1 dau., Marilyn R. (Mrs. A. C. Geldner). Br. mgr. Ruud Mfg. Co., Indpls., Milw., 1926-31; gen. sales mgr. Milw. Gas Splty. Co., 1931-36; sales mgr. Robertshaw-Fulton Controls Co., Greensburg, Pa., 1936-41, pres. Grayson Controls div., Long Beach, Cal., 1941-43, exec. v.p. Western operations, 1943-57, pres., dir., 1957—; dir. Central Nat. Bank, Reynolds Metals Co. (both Richmond, Va.). Office: 1701 Byrd Av Richmond VA 23226

ARDERY, JULIA HOGE SPENCER, civic worker, ex-Dem. nat. committeewoman; b. Richmond, Va., Sept. 16, 1889; d. Issac J. and Sally L. (Pendleton) Spencer; grad. Hamilton Coll., 1908; student Transylvania Coll., 1908-09; m. William B. Ardery, Apr. 14, 1910; children—William B., Winston B., Philip p. Vice chmn. Paris (Ky.) Sesquicentennial, 1939, Sesquicentennial Commn., Commonwealth of Ky., 1940-42; curator, chmn. restoration Duncan Tavern Historic Center, D.A.R., 1940—; mem. Ky. Historic Markers Com., 1949-64; mem. Ky Commn. Preservation Historic and Archtl. Assets, 1951—; mem. exec. com. Ky. Civil War Centennial Com., 1958-65; Gov's Adv. Com. Ky. Hwys. Program, 1957-60. County chmn. fund drives A.R.C., World War II. Nat. elector sec. Electoral Coll., 1944—; del. Dem. Nat. Conv., mem. platform and resolutions com., 1956; Dem. nat. committeewoman for Ky., 1956-60. Trustee Kate McClintock Home for Aged Women, 1930-47. Mem. Bourban County (Ky.) Health and Welfare League (past pres.), Ky. Hist. Soc. (hon. v.p., mem. exec. com. 1932-61; distinguished service award Ky. 1968), Nat. Soc. Daus. of Founders and Patriots of Am., Order First Families Va. (burgess Ky. 1935-71), Soc. Descs. King William I the Conqueror (life founder), Brit.-Am. Soc. (life), Nat. Soc. Colonial Dames Am. in Commonwealth Ky., Internat. Soc. Daughters Barons Runnemede, D.A.R., Delta Delta Delta (outstanding alumnae award Ky. 1957). Mem. Disciples of Christ Ch. Club: Filson (Louisville). Author hist., general books, records. Address: Bourbon Heights Lexington Rd Paris, KY 40361.

ARDERY, PHILIP PENDLETON, lawyer; b. Lexington, Ky., Mar. 6, 1914; s. William Breckenridge and Julia (Spencer) A.; A.B., U. Ky., 1935; LL.B., Harvard, 1938; M.B.A., U. Louisville, 1957; m. Agnes Stuyvesant Tweedy, Dec. 6, 1941; children—Peter Brooks, Philip Pendleton, Joseph Lord Tweedy, Julia Spencer. Admitted to Ky. bar, 1938; practice in Frankfort, 1938-40, 45- Louisville, 1952—; partner firm Brown, Ardery, Todd and Dudley, 1959—. -. Sec. Ky. Aero. Commn., 1946; commr. Jefferson County, 1958-61. Pres. Ky. Heart Assn., 1955, chmn. bd., 1956; chmn. bd. Am. Heart Assn., 1966- Served to col. USAAF, 1941-45, USAF, 1950-52; now maj. gen. USAF-Res. Res. ret. Decorated Silver Star, D.F.C. (2), Air medal (4); Croix de Guerre with palm (France). Mem. Am., Ky., Louisville bar assns., Phi Beta Kappa. Democrat. Episcopalian. Club: Pendennis (Louisville). Home: 424 Pennington Lane Louisville, KY 40207 Office: Ky Home Life Bldg Louisville KY 40202

ARDIS, MARK BURKETT, psychiatrist; b. Ann Arbor, Mich., June 15, 1929; s. Emberson Robert and Ethel (Layer) A.; B.S., U. Mich., 1951, M.D., 1955; m. Jacquelyn J. Rau, June 21, 1952; children—Jan E., Robert J., Ann L., David M. Intern St. Luke's Hosp., Cleve., 1955-56; resident in psychiatry VA Hosp., Topeka, 1958-61; psychiatrist VA Hosp., St. Cloud, Minn., 1961-62; asst. chief of staff

VA Hosp., Downey, Ill., 1962-63; chief of staff VA Hosp., Danville, Ill., 1963-67; asst. prof. psychology U. Ill., 1963-67; asst. chief psychiatry VA Central Office, Washington, 1967-69; asst. clin. prof. psychiatry Georgetown U., 1967-69; dir. VA Hosp., Topeka, 1969—. Mem. Kan. Gov.'s Adv. Commn. on Instl. Mgmt. and Community Mental Health, 1969—. Bd. dirs. Shawnee Community Mental Health Corp. Served to capt. USAF, 1956-58. Recipient VA Chief Med. Dir.'s Commendation award, 1967. Mem. A.M.A., Am. Psychiat. Assn., Phi Lambda Upsilon, Alpha Omega Alpha. Home: 1940 Pembroke Lane Topeka KS 66604 Office: VA Hosp Topeka KS 66622

ARDLEIGH, JOSEPH D., research inst. exec.; b. Scranton, Pa., May 24, 1914; s. Hugh Granville and Pauline (Danvers) A.; ed. N.Y.U.; m. Susan Bell; children—Paul, Carl, Hugh, Teri. With Milbank, Tweed, Hope & Webb, New York City, 1923- 33; successively devel. mgr., operating mgr. and personnel mgr., Hoover Co., North Canton, O., 1933-37; sec.-treas., Sales Methods, Inc. (business established by himself), N.Y. C., 1937-39; membership dir. Research Inst. of Am., 1939—, v.p., 1944-53, exec. v.p., 1953-67, pres., 1967-68, pres., chief exec. offier, 1968—; pres. Nat. Law Press; dir. Emery Air Freight Corp. Mem. Nat. Soc. Sales Tng. Execs., Nat. Sales Execs., C. of C., Sales Execs. Club of New York (pres.). Clubs: Greenwich Country; Union League (gov.) (N.Y.C.). Author books and articles on marketing and human relations. Home: Greenwich CT 06830 Office: Research Inst Bldg 589 Fifth Av New York City NY 10017

ARDOIN, JOHN LOUIS, newspaperman; b. Alexandria, La., Jan. 8, 1935; s. Louis and Ruth (Herren) A.; Mus.B., U. Tex., 1955; Mus.M., U. Okla., 1956; postgrad. Mich. State U., 1958-59. Asst. editor Mus. Am. mag., 1959-63, asso. editor, 1963-64, editor, 1964; mng. editor Philharmonic Hall program, mem. music staff Sat. Rev., 1965-66; music editor, amusements critic Dallas Morning News, 1966—; N.Y. music critic London Times, 1964-66, Opera mag., 1965-66. Mem. N.Y. Music Critics Circle; 1960-64. Author articles. Home: 4318 Abbott Av Dallas TX 75205 Office: Communications Center Dallas TX 75222

ARDREY, ROBERT, author; b. Chgo., Oct. 16, 1908; s. Robert Leslie and Marie (Haswell) A.; Ph.B., U. Chgo., 1930; m. Berdine Grunewald, Aug. 11, 1960; children—Ross, Daniel. Lectr., cons. evolution human behavior, 1963—. Guggenheim fellow, 1937-38; recipient Sidney Howard Meml. award, 1940; Theresa Helburn Meml. award, 1961. Mem. Phi Beta Kappa. Author: (plays) Star-Spangled, 1936, Casey Jones, 1938, How to Get Tough about It., 1938, Thunder Rock, 1939. Jeb, 1946, Sing Me No Lullaby, 1954, Shadow of Heroes, 1958, Plays of Three Decades, 1968; (screenplays) They Knew What The Wanted, 1940, Lady Takes a Chance, 1943, The Green Years, 1945, The Three Musketeers, 1947, Madame Bovary, 1948, Khartoum, 1966; (novels) Worlds Beginning, 1944, The Brotherhood of Fear, 1952; (evolutionary behavior) African Genesis, 1961, The Territorial Imperative, 1966, The Social Contract, 1970. Address: Via Garibaldi 88 Trastevere Rome Italy

ARDREY, WILLIAM BOYLE, educator; b. Denver, Feb. 2, 1912; s. William George and Hessie (Boyle) A.; B.S., Monmouth Coll., 1934; M.S., Mich. State Coll., 1936, Ph.D., 1939; m. Catherine Michael, Aug. 16, 1940; children—William Boyd, Kathleen Ann. Fellow and asst. Mich. State Coll., 1934-39; instr. U. of Ida., 1939-40; asst. prof. and asst. bacteriologist Expt. Sta., U. of Ida., 1940-44, asso. prof. and asso. bacteriologist, 1944-45; prof. bacteriology and asso. bacteriologist, 1945-49, prof., pathologist, 1949-68, prof., vet. microbiologist, 1968—. Mem. Poultry Sci. Assn., A.A.A.S., Am. Soc. Microbiology, Am. Pub. Health Assn., Sigma Xi, Alpha Epsilon Delta. Methodist. Home: 308 S Hayes St Moscow ID 83843

ARDUSER, RAYMOND A., mfr. wood products; b. Dubuque, Ia., July 19, 1902; s. Paul and Margaret (Wally) A.; M.E., Ia. State U., 1926; m. Marjorie Leinard, Sept. 25, 1928; 1 son, John Alan. With Farley & Loetscher Mfg. Co., Dubuque and Springfield, Ore., 1926-62, v.p., 1960-62; exec. v.p., dir. E.L. Bruce Co., Inc., Memphis, 1963; chmn. bd. Royal Oak Charcoal Co., Memphis; exec. v.p., dir. Cook Industries, Inc. (merger E.L. Bruce Co., Inc. and Cook & Co.), 1969—; pres., dir. Miss. & Skuna Valley R.R. Co., Memphis, Robbins Flooring Co., Memphis; dir. Riverside Industries, Marks, Miss. Bd. dirs. Shelby United Neighbors, Memphis. Vice pres., dir. Dubuque C. of C., 1953-56; active indsl. div. Dubuque Community Chest, 1935-55; cons. Dubuque Boys Club, 1950-55. Mem. Nat. Mgmt. Assn. (pres. 1950-52). Kiwanian (pres. Dubuque 1949), Elk. Home: 5468 Collingwood Cove Memphis TN 38101 Office: 2185 Democrat Rd Memphis TN 38116

AREEDA, PHILLIP, educator, lawyer; b. Detroit, Jan. 28, 1930; s. Elias Herbert and Selma (Cope) A.; A.B., Harvard, 1951, LL.B., 1954; Harvard travelling fellow, 1954-55. Admitted to Mich. bar, 1954; mem. White House staff, asst. spl. counsel to Pres. U.S., 1956-61; mem. faculty Harvard Law Sch., 1961, prof. law, 1963—. Exec. dir. U.S. Cabinet Task Force on Oil Import Control, 1969. Served to 1st lt. USAF, 1955-57. Mem. Am. Law Inst. Author: Antitrust Analysis, 1967. Office: Langdell Hall Cambridge MA 02138

AREF, ABDUL RAHMAN MOHAMMED, Iraqi army officer, politician; b. 1916; ed. Baghdad Mil. Acad. Head of armoured corps, until 1962; comdr. 5th Div., 1963; mem. Regency Council, 1965; asst. chief of staff Iraqi Armed Forces, 1963-64, acting chief of staff, 1964, chief of staff, 1964-68, rank of maj.-gen.; pres. of Iraq, 1966-68, prime minister, 1967. Address: care of Embassy of Iraq 22 Queen's Gate London SW7 England

AREL, BULENT, composer. Has engaged in teaching, compositon symphonies, ballets, chamber and theatre music, electronic music; formerly research asst. (Rockefeller Found. grantee) Columbia-Princeton Electronic Music Center. Composer: Music No. 1, 1960; Music for a Sacred Service, also Prelude and Postlude, 1961; Stereo Electronic Music No. 1, 1964. Home: 310 W 97th St New York City NY*

ARELLANO, OTILIO AUSBERTO, architect; b. Manila, P.I., Feb. 8, 1916; s. Arcadio and Amalia (Ocampo) A.; B.S., Mapua Inst. Tech., 1940; m. Liwayway Almario, Jan. 6, 1940; children—Carlos Jose, Maria Lourdes (wife of Dr. Brigido Carandang), Maria Felicitas, Maria Agnes, Deogracias Andres. Pvt. archtl. practice, Manila Philippines, 1940—; chief architect for 1st Philippine Internat. Fair, 1952; architect Internat. Inst. Rural Reconstrn., 1958, Nat. Bur. Investigation, 1963; nat. architect Philippine Pavilion, N.Y. World's Fair, 1964-65; architect, v.p. operations Philippine Monorail Transit System, 1968-71; dir. Project Technologists, Inc. Mem. Bd. Examiners for Architects, 1949-52. Pres. Philippine Youth Welfare Coordinating Council, 1955-71, Philippine Mental Health Assn., 1958-60; chmn. Manila 4th Centennial Commn., 1969-72. Vice chmn. Rizal Youth Devel. Found. Recipient Manila Kalinangan award for architecture, 1970, Cavaliere award Rep. of Italy, 1954. Fellow A.I.A. (hon.) Philippine Inst. Architects (pres. 1959-60); mem. Philippine Architects and Engrs., United Tech. Orgns of Philippines (pres. 1958-59), Confedn. Sci. and Tech. Orgns. of Philippines (pres. 1960-63), Archtl. Centre Club, Inc. (pres. 1971-72). Club: Manila Lions, (pres. 1955-56, dep. gov. internat.). Address: 154 J Arellano San Juan Rizal D-724 Republic Philippines

ARENA, JAY M., pediatrician; b. Clarksburg, W.Va., Mar. 3, 1909; s. Anthony M. and Rose (Sandy) A.; B.A., W.Va. U., 1930; M.D., Duke U., 1932; m. Pauline Elizabeth Monteith, July 10, 1931; children—Rosanne (Mrs. Oscar Green), Jay Morris Jr., Carolyn Jean, Mary Margaret (Mrs. Harry Anderson), Katherine (Mrs. Arthur Prosser), Pauline (Mrs. William Myers), Regina. Intern Strong Meml. Hosp., Rochester, N.Y. 1932, Johns Hopkins Hosp., 1932-33; asst. resident Duke Hosp., 1933-34, resident, 1934-35; instr. pediatrics Vanderbilt U., 1936; asst. prof. pediatrics Duke Hosp., 1936-50, asso. prof., 1951-56, prof., 1956—, prof. community health scis., 1970—, dir. Poison Control Center, 1953—; editorial bds. Council Family Health, Clin. Pediatrics, Nutrition Today, Pediatric News, Highlights, Reportes Medicos. Chmn. Z 66 standards com. Nat. Standards Inst., 1969—; pres. Am. Assn. Poison Controls Centers, 1968-70. Mem. Am. Acad. Pediatrics (exec. bd. 1965-71, pres.-elect 1970-72), Am. Pediatric Soc., Phi Beta Kappa, Sigma Xi, Alpha Omega Alpha. Author (with James W. Hardin) Human Poisoning from Native and Cultivated Plants, 1969; Poisoning: Toxicology-Symptoms-Treatments, 2d edn., 1970; Dangers to Children and Youth, 1971. Home: 1403 Woodburn Rd Durham NC 27705

ARENDALL, CHARLES BAKER, Jr., lawyer; b. Portsmouth, Va., Feb. 13, 1915; s. Charles B. and Kate (Peacock) A.; A.B., U. Richmond, 1935; LL.B. cum laude, Harvard, 1938; m. Nan Eager Boone, Oct. 26, 1944; children—Nan Boone, Lawrence Barclay, Kathryn, Elizabeth. Asso. Root, Clark, Buckner & Ballentine, N.Y.C., 1937; admitted to Ala. bar, 1938; asso. Smith & Johnston, Mobile, 1938- 41; mem. firm Hand, Arendall, Bedsole, Greaves & Johnston and predecessor, Mobile, 1941—. Adv. bd. Cumberland Law Sch. Howard Coll.; trustee Mobile Coll. Fellow Am. Coll. Trial Lawyers; mem. Am., Ala., Inter-Am., Mobile bar assns., Internat. Assn. Ins. Counsel, Am. Law Inst., Assn. Railroad Trial Counsel, Omicron Delta Kappa, Pi Delta Epsilon, Alpha Psi Omega, Kappa Sigma. Baptist. Clubs: Athelstan, Lakewood Country. Home: Kingsway Springhill Mobile AL 36608 Office: First Nat Bank Bldg Mobile AL 36601

ARENDS, LESLIE CORNELIUS, congressman; b. Melvin, Ill., Sept. 27, 1895; s. George Teis and Talea (Weiss) A.; student Oberlin Coll., 1912- 13; LL.D., Ill. Wesleyan U.; m. Betty Tychon; 1 dau., Leslie. Formerly pres. Comml. State Bank, Melvin; mem. 74th to 92d Congresses 17th Ill. Dist., Rep. whip, ranking minority mem. Armed Services Com. U.S. del. N. Atlantic Assembly, 1961-70. Served with USN, 1918-19. Trustee emeritus Ill. Wesleyan U., Mem. Am. Legion, Republican. Methodist. Mason (33). Home: Melvin IL 60952 Office: Rayburn Office Bldg Washington DC 20515

ARENDT, HANNAH, author, polit. scientist; b. Hannover, Germany, Oct. 14, 1906; d. Paul and Martha (Cohn) Arendt; B.A., Königsberg Pr., 1924; student univs. Marburg, Freiburg; Ph.D., Heidelberg U. (Germany), 1928; H.L.D., Bard Coll., 1959, Goucher Coll., 1960; hon. degree Smith Coll., 1966, York U., Toronto, 1968, Loyola U., Chgo., 1970, Yale, 1971; m. Heinrich Bluecher, 1940 (dec.). Came to U.S., 1941, naturalized, 1951. Social worker, Paris, France, 1934-40; research dir. Conf. on Jewish Relations, 1944-46; chief editor Schocken Books, Inc., 1946-48; exec. dir. Jewish Cultural Reconstrn., N.Y.C., 1949-52; vis. prof. U. Cal. at Berkeley, 1955, Princeton, 1959, Columbia, 1960, others; prof. U. Chgo., 1963-67; univ. prof. New Sch. for Social Research, N.Y.C., 1967—; lectr. Recipient award Nat. Inst. Arts and Letters, 1954; Lessing Preis, Hamburg, 1959; Freud preis Deutsche Akademie für Sprache und Dichtung, 1967. Guggenheim fellow, 1952-53. Rockefeller fellow, 1959-60, 69-70. Fellow Am. Acad. Arts and Scis. (Emerson-Thoreau medal 1969); mem. Am. Acad. Polit. Sci., Am. Soc. Polit. and Legal Philosophy, Nat. Inst. Arts and Letters, mem. Deutsche Akademie für Sprache und Dichtung (corr. mem.). Author: The Origins of Totalitarianism, 1968; Rahel Vornhagen, 1957; The Human Condition, 1958; Between Past and Future, 1968; On Revolution, 1963; Eichmann In Jerusalem, 1964; Men In Dark Times, 1968; On Violence, 1970; others. Home: 370 Riverside Dr New York City NY 10025

ARENS, RICHARD FRIEDERICH, educator; b. Iserlohn, Germany, Apr. 24, 1919; s. Louis H. and Hedwig (Aldag) A.; came to U.S., 1925, naturalized, 1934; B.A., U. Cal. at Los Angeles, 1941; M.A., Harvard, 1942, Ph.D., 1945; m. Helen Cornfeld, Oct. 28, 1943; 1 son, Philip. Mem. Inst. for Advanced Study, Princeton, N.J., 1945-47; prof. math. U. Cal. at Los Angeles, 1947—. Mem. Am. Math. Soc., A.A.A.S., Am. Assn. U. Profs., Phi Beta Kappa, Sigma Xi. Mng. editor: Pacific Jour. Math., 1965—. Home: 12436 Deerbrook Lane Los Angeles CA 90049

ARENSBERG, CHARLES F. C., lawyer; LL.B., Harvard. Admitted to Pa. bar, 1905; former mem. firm Patterson, Crawford, Arensberg & Dunn, Pitts.; now counsel Tucker, Burke, Campbell & Arensberg, Pitts. Dir. Pitts. Nat. Bank. Pres. Pa. Bar Assn., 1950-51. Address: 600 One Oliver Plaza Pittsburgh PA 15222 also 1100 Peoples Bank Bldg Pittsburgh PA 15222*

ARENSBERG, CONRAD MAYNADIER, anthropologist, sociologist, educator; b. Pitts., Sept. 12, 1910; s. Charles F. C. and Emily Wright (Maynadier) A.; A.B., Harvard, 1931, Ph.D., 1934; m. Margaret Jacklin Walsh, June 13, 1935; children—Emily Maynadier, Margaret Farrell, Cornelius Wright. Jr. Fellow Harvard, 1934- 37; with indsl. relations sect. Mass. Inst. Tech., 1937-40; chmn., organizer dept. sociology and anthropology Bklyn. Coll., 1940-42; chmn. sociology Barnard Coll., 1946-50; cons. research in Ruhr, Socialforschungstelle, Dortmund, Germany, 1950-51; research dir. UNESCO Inst. for Social Scis., Cologne, 1952; prof. anthropology Columbia, 1953- -. Served from capt. to maj. AUS, 1943-45. Mem. Soc. Applied Anthropology (founder). Episcopalian. Clubs: Harvard (N.Y.C.); St. Botolph (Boston). Author: Irish Countryman, 1936; Family and Community in Ireland, 1940; Measuring Human Relations (with Eliot D. Chapple), 1942. Editor of Human Organization, 1946-52, Am. Anthropol. Assn. Manual for Point 4 Workers, 1953. Indsl. Relations Research Assn. Summary Human Relations Research, 1955; (with Karl Polanyi) Trade and Markets in the Early Empires, 1957; (with Solon T. Kimball) Culture and Community, 1965; (with Arthur Niehoff) Introducing Social Change, 1964. Home: 445 Riverside Dr New York City NY 10027 Office: Schermerhorn Hall Columbia U New York City NY 10027

ARENSBERG, GEORGE HOWARD, Jr., banker; b. Pitts., Mar. 22, 1930; s. George Howard and Thelma (Ciegler) A.; student Robert Morris Jr. Coll., 1948-52, U. Pitts., 1954-60; grad. Stonier Grad. Sch. Banking, Rutgers U., 1961-63. Bookkeeper, F.J. Kress Box Co., 1948-50; asst. comptroller Mellon Nat. Bank & Trust Co., 1950- 63; v.p., comptroller Western Pa. Nat. Bank, 1963-71; exec. v.p. First Nat. Bank, Albuquerque, 1971—. Served with AUS, 1952-54. Mem. Am. Mgmt. Assn., Bankers Adminstrv. Inst., Planning Execs. Inst. Home: 2212 Lester Dr NE Albuquerque NM 87112 Office: 223 Central Av NW Albuquerque NM 87101

ARENSMEYER, ROBERT MARK, chain drugstore co. exec.; b. St. Louis, Sept. 1, 1921; s. Arthur W. and Florence (Burgee) A.; B.S.C., St. Louis U., 1943; M.B.A., Washington U., 1958; m. Regina Mack, Feb. 7, 1948; children—Mark Arthur, Margaret Mary, John Robert, Ellen Anne, Robert Mark. Accountant, Price Waterhouse & Co., St. Louis 1946-50; asst. to sec.treas. Granite City Steel Co., 1950-58; controller Town & Country Shops, Inc., Sedalia, Mo., 1958-63; treas. controller Katz Drug Co., 1963-67; v.p.; controller Lansburgh's Dept. Stores, 1967-68; comptroller Peoples Drug Stores, Inc., Washington, 1968—. Served with AUS, 1943-46. C.P.A., Mo. Mem. Am. Inst. C.P.A.'s. C.D. Soc. C.P.A.'s, Financial Execs. Inst. Home: 8300 Raymond Lane Potomac, MD 20854 Office: 60 Florida Av NE Washington DC 20002

ARENT, ALBERT EZRA, lawyer; b. Rochester, N.Y., Aug. 25, 1911; s. Hyman J. and Sarah (Weller) A.; A.B., Cornell, 1932, LL.B., 1935; m. Frances Feldman, Nov. 23, 1939; children—Stephen Weller, Margery Jane (Mrs. Peter Oliver Safir). Admitted to N.Y. bar, 1935, D.C. bar, 1945; research asst. N.Y. State Law Revision Commn., 1934; atty. U.S. Bur. Internal Revenue, 1935-39; spl. asst. to Atty. Gen. U.S., 1939-44; chief trial atty. Alien Property Unit, U.S. Dept. Justice, 1942-44; pvt. law practice specializing in taxation; partner firm Arent, Fox, Kintner, Plotkin and Kahn and predecessor firms, Washington, 1944—; lectr. taxation Am. U., 1948-52; prof. taxation Georgetown Law Sch., 1951—; also lectr. tax subjects before Practicing Law Inst., N.Y.U., U. Chgo. tax insts., Am., Fed., various local and state bar assns. Dir. Macke Co., Madison Nat. Bank, Kent Washington, Inc. Prosecuted leading fgn. agt. registration act cases, World War II. Vice pres. Jewish Community Council of Greater Washington, 1953-57, pres., 1957-61; mem. adv. council Cornell Law Sch.; mem. exec. com., steering com. Nat. Urban Coalition, 1970—; mem. policy council and exec. com. Common Cause, 1970—. Bd. dirs. Overseas Edn. Fund of League Women Voters, 1961—; vice chmn. Nat Jewish Community Relations Adv. Council, 1967-70, pres., 1970—; vice chmn. Conf. Pres.' Major Jewish Orgns., 1970—. Mem. Am. Law Inst., Am. Judicature Soc., Am., Fed., D.C. bar assns., Telluride Assn., Phi Beta Kappa, Phi Kappa Phi. Contbr. articles to legal publs. Home: 3108 Rolling Rd Chevy Chase MD 20015 Office: Federal Bar Bldg Washington DC 20006

ARENTS, CHESTER ABBO, engr., educator; b. Leonardville, Kan., Apr. 19, 1910; s. Abbo Edward and Hazel Amanda (Johnson) A.; B.S., Ore. State Coll., 1932, M.S., 1946; M.E., Ore. State U., 1953; D.Sc., Marshall U., 1968; m. Edna Louisa Van Vleet, Feb. 18, 1935. Test engr. (automotive), City of Portland, Ore., 1936-41; asso. elec. engr. Bonneville Power Adm., 1941-43; asst. prof. mech. engring. Ore. State Coll., 1943-46; asso. prof. mech. engring. in charge machine design and heat power engring. Mont. State Coll., 1946- 47; asso. prof. mech. engring. and asst. dept. dir. Ill. Inst. Tech., Chgo., 1947-49, asst. dean engring., 1949-51, coordinator research and prof. mech. engring. in charge sponsored research program, 1951-55; dean Coll. Engring., W.Va. University, 1955—, also dir. of engring. Expt. Sta. Cons. Nat. Insts. Health Div. of Air Pollution. Past sec. Nat. Conf. Indsl. Hydraulics; member Bldg. Research Adv. Bd.; mem. bd. rev. Marine Engring. Lab., U.S. Navy; mem. State Planning Com. Mem. Pub. Land Corp. W.Va. Pres. W.Va. Registration Bd. Profl. Engrs. Past dir. N.E. zone Nat. Council State Board of Engineering Examiners. Registered profl. engr., Ore., Ill., W.Va. Mem. Am. Assn. of Land Grant Colleges and Universities, Am. Soc. Testing Materials, W.Va. Soc. Profl. Engrs., Am. Soc. M.E., Am. Soc. Engring. Edn., Am. Inst. E.E., Am. Assn. U. Profs., Nat. (dir.), W.Va. socs. profl. engrs., Morgantown C. of C. (pres. 1962), Morgantown Community Assn. (trustee), Am. Standards Assn., Sigma Xi, Pi Tau Sigma, Tau Beta Pi, Eta Kappa Nu, Alpha Pi Mu. Methodist. Author manuals on insulation. Past editor Industrial Bull. Home: 1244 Oxford Pl Morgantown WV 26505 Office: West Virginia U Morgantown WV 26505

ARENTZEN, EDWARD SENTMAN, ret. educator and naval officer; b. Stratford, N.J., Jan. 7, 1916; s. Edward and Mamie (Vogel) A.; B.S., US Naval Acad., 1937; S.M. in Naval Architecture and Marine Engring., Mass. Inst. Tech., 1943; m. Marcia Brooks Eddy, Mar. 29, 1941; children—Marcia J. (Mrs. Stephen Root), Karen C. Commd. ensign USN, 1937, advanced through grades to capt., 1956, now capt. USN (ret.); with preliminary design br., initiating all new submarine designs Bur. Ships, Navy Dept., 1953-58; developed basic features for Skate, Triton, Skipjack, Polaris; prof. naval constrn. Mass. Inst. Tech., 1958-62, adminstrv. officer physics dept., 1962-67; project leader advance engring. Quincy division of General Dynamics Corp., 1967-69. Recipient commendation medal Sec. Navy, 1962. Mem. Soc. Naval Architects and Marine Engrs. (Capt. J.H. Linnard prize 1961), Am. Soc. Naval Engrs., Sigma Xi, Tau Beta Pi. Episcopalian. Mason. Home: 75 Thornberry Rd Winchester MA 01890

AREY, LESLIE BRAINERD, anatomist; b. Camden, Me., Feb. 15, 1891; s. Arthur Brainerd and Mary Josephine (Page) A.; A.B., Colby Coll., Waterville, Me., 1912, D.Sc., 1937; Ph.D., Harvard Univ., 1915; LL.D., Chgo. Med. Sch., 1934; m. Edith Holt, 1926. Asst. in zoölogy, 1912-13, teaching fellow, 1913- Harvard; asst. in zoölogy Radcliffe, 1913-14; instr. anatomy, 1915- 17, asso. prof., 1917-19, prof. microscopic anatomy, 1919-24, Robert L. Rea prof. anatomy, and chmn. dept. anatomy, 1924-56, Northwestern U. Med. Sch., emeritus prof. anatomy, 1956—; mem. staff Wesley Meml. Hosp., Passavant Hosp., Children's Meml. Hosp; spl. cons. NIH. Sometime investigator U.S. Bureau Fisheries; sometime chmn. Com. Basic Scis., White House Conf. on Child Health and Protection; sometime guest lectr. Chgo. Jr. Colls; vis. prof. U. P.R., 1963, 64. Subchmn. Internat. Anatomical Nomenclature Co., 1962-. Chmn., Internat. Com. on Embryological Terminology, 1963. Recipient Alumni medal Northwestern Univ., 1959; named to City of Chicago Hall of Fame, 1967. Fellow Chgo. Acad. Sci. (pres., 1956—); mem. Am. Soc. Zoologists (sec. 1928, treas. 1925-30), Am. Assn. Anatomists (exec. com. 1930-34, v.p. 1942-46, pres., 1952-54), Phi Beta Kappa, Sigma Xi, Delta Upsilon, Phi Beta Pi (praetor 1932-34 and 1940-47; supreme archon, 1934-41; trustee and supreme councillor, 1934-; supreme editor, 1942, moderator 1951—), Alpha Omega Alpha (hon.), Pi Kappa Epsilon, Pi Delta. Sec.-treas. Interfraternity Confs., 1938-42, pres. 1944-47; mem. exec. com. Profl. Interfraternity Conference, 1942-44. Republican. Mason (K.T., 32, Shriner). Clubs: University, Chaos. Author: Tratado de Endocrinologia Clinica, 1951; Word Book Encyclopedia, 1949; Morris Human Anatomy, 1966; Developmental Anatomy, 1965; Human Histology, 1968; Medical Dictionary, 1957; Anatomy Desarrollo, 1958; Histologia Humana, 1958; Centennial History of Northwestern University, Medical School, 1959. Asso. editor: Jour. Morphology, Excerpta Medica; editor: Northwestern U. Med. Sch. Mag., 1963—. Writer papers and monographs on anatomy and physiology. Address: 3440 Lake Shore Dr Chicago IL 60657 ☆

AREY, MARY EDITH, former orgn. exec.; b. Cin., Oct. 25, 1902; d. William Day and Lillian (Bezell) Holt; Ph.B., U. Chgo., 1923; m. Leslie Brainerd Arey, July 1, 1926. Mem. bd. mgrs. Woman's Am. Bapt. Fgn. Mission Soc., 1937-54, v.p., 1942-44, pres., 1944-46, v.p., 1946-50, pres., 1950-54; mem. Council on Missionary Cooperation, 1950-54; mem. council finance and promotion No. Baptist Conv., 1942-48, vice chmn., 1946-47, program com., 1946-47; chmn. Nat. Com. on Woman's Work, 1947-49, member Commn. on Rev., 1947-50, mem. gen. council Am. Baptist Conv., 1954-60, exec. com.,

1956-60, mem. finance com., 1960-69; pres. Women's Bapt. Mission Union Chgo., 1941-43; bd. mgrs. United Council Ch. Women, 1944-46; mem. Chgo. Girl Scout Council, 1932-38; bd. dirs. Bapt. Missionary Tng. Sch., 1941- 50; mem. gen. bd. Nat. Council Chs. of Christ U.S.A., 1952-54. Republican. Club: Cordon (1933-45). Contbr. articles Bapt. pubs. Home: 3440 Lake Shore Dr Chicago IL 60657

ARFKEN, GEORGE BROWN, Jr., physicist, educator; b. Jersey City, Nov. 20, 1922; s. George B. and Ann Barbour (Hill) A.; B.E. in Chem. Engring., Yale, 1943, M.S., 1948, Ph.D. in Physics, 1950; m. Carolyn Irene Dines, June 18, 1949; children—Bruce, Peter, Cynthia. Faculty Miami U., Oxford, O., 1952—, prof., chmn. dept. physics, 1956—. Cons., Los Alamos Scientific Lab., 1962-66. Served as lt. (j.g.) USNR, 1943-46. Mem. Am. Inst. Physics, Am. Assn. Physics Tchrs., Sigma Xi. Author math. physics text, also articles profl. jours. Home: 5301 Coulter Lane Oxford OH 45056

ARGERSINGER, WILLIAM JOHN, Jr., educator; b. Chittenango, N.Y., Apr. 14, 1918; s. William John and Elsie M. (Hosley) A.; A.B., Cornell U., 1938, Ph.D., 1942; m. Marjorie R. Hayes, Sept. 12, 1942; children—William John III, Peter Hayes, Ann Elizabeth II. Instr. chemistry Cornell U., 1942-44; chemist, research chemist, group leader Monsanto Chem. Co., 1944-46; with U. Kan., 1946— , from asst. to asso. prof. chemistry, 1946-56, prof., 1956—, asso. dean Grad. Sch., 1956-63, asso. dean Faculties, 1963-70, dean research adminstrn., 1970—. Fellow A.A.A.S., Am. Inst. Chemists; mem. Soc. Engring. Sci., Am. Chem. Soc., Am. Assn. U. Profs., Kan., N.Y. acads. sci., Phi Beta Kappa, Sigma Xi, Phi Pappa Phi, Phi Lambda Upsilon, Alpha Chi Sigma. Author textbook in advanced inorganic chemistry; articles on thermodynamics of electrolytes, physical chemistry. Home: 325 Park Hill Terrace Lawrence, KS 66044

ARGUELLES, JAIME, Spanish diplomat; b. Madrid, Spain, Apr. 22, 1910; s. Manuel and Maria Josefa (Armada) A.; student Faculty Law, Diplomatic Sch., 1931-32; m. Margarita Salaverria, Jan. 16, 1937; children—Jacobo, Isabel (Mrs. Alonso Alvarez de Toledo), Margarita (Mrs. Juan Carvajal), Pedro, Ines, Jose Patricio, 3d sec. in Ministry, 1933-36; 3d sec. Consulate Gen., Buenos Aires, Argentina, 1936-38; vice-consul Consulate Gen., Vienna, Austria, 1938; comml. attache Ministry Industry and Commerce, 1939, 2d sec., 1939; comml. attache in Lisbon, Portugal, 1940-43; comml. attache for Nr. East in commn. at Comml. Office, London, 1943-45; comml. attache Embassy, London, 1945-47; comml. attache Ministry Industry and Commerce, 1947; sec. of embassy 1st class, Ministry Fgn. Affairs, 1948-52; under- sec. Fgn. Economy, 1952-55; minister plenipotentiary, 1955; pres. Spanish delegation OEEC, 1955-58; minister plenipotentiary in ministry, 1958-61; cons. mem. Superior Council, Ministry Fgn. Affairs, Washington, 1961—. Chmn. bd. La Union y el Fenix Espanol; dir. Banco Espanol de Credito. Decorated Red Cross of Mil Merit, Civil War medal, grand cross comdr. Order Civil Merit, Comdr. Isabel la Catolica; comdr. Polar Star of Sweden; officer Order of Christ, officer Order of Benemerance (Portugal); officer Order of Crown (Italy). Address: 2801 16th St N W Washington DC 20009

ARGYRES, PETROS NICHOLAOS, educator; b. Lefkas, Greece, Mar. 9, 1927; s. Nicholaos Constantinos and Georgia (Aretha) A.; came to U.S., 1947, naturalized, 1956; A.B. with highest honors, U. Cal., Berkeley, 1950, M.A., 1952, Ph.D., 1954; m. Nita M. Dressler, Aug. 2, 1958; children—Peter N., Philip C., Anneta Z. Research physicist Westinghouse Research Lab., Pitts., 1954-58; with Lincoln Lab., Mass. Inst. Tech., 1958-66; mem. faculty Mass. Inst. Tech., 1966-67; mem. faculty Northeastern U., Boston, 1967—, prof. physics, 1967—. IBM fellow 1952-53; U. Cal. fellow, 1953-54. Fellow Am. Phys. Soc.; mem. A.A.A.S., Sigma Xi, Phi Beta Kappa. Contbr. articles profl. jours. Home: 39 Meriam St Lexington MA 02173

ARIAS, DAME MARGOT FONTEYN DE, (Margot Fonteyn), ballerina; b. Reigate, Eng., May 18, 1919; Litt.D. honoris causa, Leeds U.; Mus. D. honoris causa, U. London; Mus. D., Oxford, 1959, U. of Manchester, 1966; LL.D. Cambridge, 1962; m. Roberto E. Arias, 1955. Joined Sadler's Wells Ballet, 1934, now guest artist Royal Ballet and other Cos. Decorated Comdr. Order of Brit. Empire, 1951, Dame Comdr. Order Brit. Empire, 1956; Order Finnish Lion, 1960. Pres. Royal Acad. Dancing, 1954—. Address: Royal Opera House Convent Garden London WC2 England

ARIAS, SALVO ROBERT, ret. stock broker; b. Smyrna, Turkey, July 4, 1900; s. Rabeno and Sultana (Cohen) A.; student Alliance Sch., Smyrna, Lycee de St. Joseph, Smyrna; m. Hilda Bennett, Aug. 1, 1929; 1 son, Robert R. Office boy Meridional Trading Corp., 1920-21; freight solicitor N. Am. Forwarding Corp., 1921-24, freight broker, 1924-26; customers man for Newman Brothers and Worms, 1926-47; mem. N.Y. Stock Exchange, 1947-61; pres., dir. S.R. Arias, Inc., 1961-66 (merged with A.G. Becker & Co., Inc.), sr. v.p., 1966-70; now cons.; dir. C., R.I. & P. Ry., Norris Food Corp., Chgo. Clubs: Scarsdale Town; Bankers (N.Y.C.). Home: 13 Brookby Rd Scarsdale NY 10583

ARIE, RAFFAELE, bass singer; b. Sofia, Bulgaria, 1922; ed. Sofia Conservatory. Formerly with N.Y. City Opera; appeared as Simon Boccanegra, Chgo. Lyric Opera, 1965; other roles include Don Giovanni, Mephistopheles. Address: Largo O Murani No 2 Milan Italy*

ARIES, LEON JUDAH, surgeon; b. Chgo., Feb. 25, 1909; s. Frank and Lizzie (Narensky) A.; B.S., U. Ill., 1927, M.D., 1931, M.S., 1931; Ph.D., Northwestern U., 1940; m. Marie Dorothy Levine, Sept. 26, 1945; children—Jane (Mrs. Richard Levin), Elizabeth, Nancy. Intern, Cook County Hosp., Chgo., 1931-33, resident, 1933-35; practice medicine, specializing in surgery, Chgo., 1935—; asst. prof. surgery Northwestern U. Med. Sch., 1940-55; prof. surgery Chgo. Med. Sch., Cook County Grad. Sch., 1940-65, Chgo. Med. Sch., 1957-71; attending surgeon Cook County Hosp., St. Joseph Hosp., Edgewater Hosp., Mt. Sinai Hosp. Sec. br. Jewish Childrens Bur.; trustee Francis Parker Sch. Served to maj. AUS, 1943-45. Recipient Chgo. Surg. Soc. award, 1940. Mem. A.C.S., Internat. Coll. Surgeons, Sigma Xi, Alpha Omega Alpha. Contbr. articles profl. jours. Home: 3920 Lake Shore Dr Chicago IL 60613 Office: 30 N Michigan Av Chicago IL 60602

ARING, CHARLES DAIR, physician; b. Dent, O., June 21, 1904; s. Fred and Alice (Dair) A.; B.S., U. of Cin., 1929, M.D., 1929; m. Mary Shroder, October 16, 1931; children—Dair (Mrs. David Rausch), Charles S. Rotating intern Cin. Gen. Hosp., 1929-30; resident in psychiatry and receiving physician, 1930-31, Longview State Hospital, 1931; was house officer in neurology, Boston City Hosp., 1932; voluntary asst., Children's Hosp., Boston, 1933; resident, Boston City Hospital, 1933-34; fellow in neurophysiology dept. physiology, Yale, 1934-35; Rockefeller fellow in neurology Nat. Hosp., London, Univ. of Madrid, Breslau U., 1935-36; instr. in neurology, U. Cin. Coll. of Medicine, 1935-38, asst. prof., 1938-41, asso. prof., 1941-46, prof., 1947—; prof. of neurology, U. Calif. Med. School, 1946-47; asst. attending neurologist Cin. Gen. Hosp., 1935-38, attending neurologist, 1938-46, dir. neurol. clinic, 1941-46; dir. neurol. div. Univ. Hosp., San Francisco, 1946-47; dir. neurol. service Cin. Gen. Hosp., 1947—. Mem. commission on neurotropic virus disease of Bd. for Investigation and Control of influenza and other epidemic diseases in the army, 1941-46; com. on neurology NRC, 1947—; med. adv. bd. Nat. Multiple Sclerosis Soc., 1950-56; bd. dirs. Founds. Fund for Research in Psychiatry, 1953-55; mental health study sec. USPHS, 1953-57; primate research study sect., 1961-64. Mem. Am. Epilepsy Soc. (v.p. 1942-43, pres. 1944-46), A.M.A., Am. Neurol. Assn. (pres. 1962-63, mem. council 1951-53, 61-68), Am. Psychiat. Assn., Am. Psychosomatic Soc. (council 1947), Assn. for Research in Nervous and Mental Disease (v.p. 1947, 52), Soc. for Exptl. Biology and Medicine, Sigma Xi, Alpha Omega Alpha. Club: Literary. Editorial bd. Archives of Neurology and Psychiatry, 1943-62, 64—, Psychosomatic Medicine, 1961—, Jour. Nervous and Mental Diseases, 1962-69; editor Am. lectures in neurology, 1946—. Home: 2401 Ingleside Av Cincinnati OH 45206 Office: Cin Gen Hosp Cincinnati OH

ARIS, EARL MAYNARD, educator; b. Pontiac, Mich., Sept. 12, 1914; s. Leslie and Rachel (Kennedy) A.; A.B., Albion Coll., 1937; M.B.A., U. Mich., 1939, Earhart fellow, 1962, Ph.D., 1966; m. Marjorie Bunney, Aug. 28, 1937; 1 son, David Earl. Lectr. accounting Ohio Wesleyan U., 1939-40; research accountant Mich. Consol. Gas Co., 1940-42; plant comptroller liquid-cooled engine div. Aviation Corp., 1942-43; 43; mem. financial staff Fruehauf Trailer Co., 1943-45; faculty Albion Coll., 1945—, chmn. dept. econs. and bus. adminstrn., 1953—, prof. econs., bus. adminstrn., 1955—, chmn. social sci. div., 1958—, dir. overseas summer program, 1961. Pub. utility rate adviser Albion City Council, 1951-70; sec. Mich. Colls. Study Abroad, 1961; mem. scholarship com. Inst. European Studies, 1960—. Bd. dirs. Alliance Assos. Mem. Albion and Marshall Accountants Assn. (chmn. 1950), Mich. Coll. Tchrs. Accounting (chmn. 1959), Am. Accounting Assn., Am. Assn. U. Profs., Phi Gamma, Delta Sigma Rho, Omicron Delta Kappa. Methodist (bd. missions). Author: Outlines to Essentials of Accounting, 1957. Home: 504 Linden Av Albion MI 49224

ARIS, RUTHERFORD, applied mathematician; b. Bournemouth, Eng., Sept. 15, 1929; s. Algernon Pollock and Janet (Elford) A.; B.Sc. (spl.) with 1st class honours in Math., London (Eng.) U., 1948, Ph.D., 1960, D.Sc., 1964; student Edinburgh (Scotland) U., 1948-50; m. Claire Mercedes Holman, Jan. 1, 1958. Came to U.S., 1955, naturalized, 1962. Tech. officer Billingham div. I.C.I. Ltd., 1950-55; research fellow U. Minn., 1955-56; lectr. tech. math. Edinburgh U., 1956-58; mem. faculty U. Minn., 1958—, prof. chem. engring., 1963—; cons. to industry, lectr., 1961—. Sr. research fellow NSF, 1964-65; recipient E. Harris Harbison award for distinguished teaching, 1969. Fellow Inst. Math. and Its Applications; mem. Soc. Nat. Philosophy, Soc. Indsl. and Applied Math., Am. Chem. Soc., Mediaeval Acad. Am. Lutheran. Author: Optimal Design of Chemical Reactors, 1961; Vectors, Tensors and the Basic Equations of Fluid Mechanics, 1962; Discrete Dynamics of Chemical Reactors, 1965; Elementary Chemical Reactor Analysis, 1969.

ARIYOSHI, GEORGE RYOICHI, lt. gov. Hawaii; b. Honolulu, Mar. 12, 1926; s. Ryozo and Mitsue (Yoshikawa) A.; student U. Hawaii, 1944-45; A.B., Mich. State U., 1949; LL.B., U. Mich., 1952; m. Jean Miya Hayashi, Feb. 5, 1955; children—Lynn Miye, Todd Ryozo, Donn Ryoji. Admitted to Hawaii bar, 1952, since practiced in Honolulu. Mem. T.H. Ho. of Reps., 1954-58, T.H. Senate, 1958, Hawaii State Senate, 1959-70; chmn. Senate Ways and Means Com., 1963-64, Senate majority leader, 1965-66, majority floor leader of State Senate, 1969-70; lt. gov. Hawaii, 1970—. Dir. Hawaiian Ins. & Guaranty, Ltd., 1966-70, First Hawaiian Bank, 1962-70, Honolulu Gas Co., Ltd., 1964-70. Chmn. Small Bus. div. Community Chest, 1963; fund raiser pub. employees div. Aloha United Fund; exec. bd. Aloha council Boy Scouts Am., 1970-71; chmn. Citizenship Day Com., 1971. Mem. bd. mgrs. YMCA, 1955-57. Served with M.I. Service, AUS, 1945-46. Mem. Am. (ho. dels. 1969—), Hawaii (pres. 1969) bar assns., Hawaii Bar Found. (charter mem., pres. 1969—). Democrat. Club: Military Intelligence Service Vets (pres. 1968-69). Home: 29 Kawananakoa Pl Honolulu HI 96813 Office: State Capitol Honolulu HI 96813

ARKFELD, LEO, bishop; b. Butte, Neb., Feb. 4, 1912; s. George and Theresa (Siemer) A.; ed. Divine Word Sem., Techny, Ill. Ordained priest Roman Catholic Ch., 1943; missionary to New Guinea, 1945; bishop of Wewak, New Guinea, 1945—. Address: Wewak New Guinea

ARKHURST, FREDERICK SIEGFRIED, Ghanaian diplomat; b. Sekondi, Ghana, Oct. 13, 1920; s. Frederick and Hagar (Crankson) A.; M.A., Aberdeen (Scotland) U., 1952; m. Joyce Eileen Cooper, Oct. 3, 1959; children—Reginald, Cecile Nanaba. Regional information officer Ghana Govt., 1953-54; attaché Brit. embassy, Rome, 1955-56; counsellor Ghanian Mission to UN, 1957-60; economist Econ. Commn. for Africa, 1960-62; prin. sec., head Ghana Fgn. Ser., Accra, 1963-65; ambassador, permanent rep. UN, N.Y.C., 1963-67; dir. African programs Adlai Stevenson Inst. Chgo., 1967-68, Phelps-Stokes Fund N.Y., 1970—; adviser UN Conf. on Human Environment, 1971—. Dir. tng. courses in diplomacy UN Inst. for Tng. and Research, 1969, 71. Served with 82d W. African Div., 1940-45; CBI. Decorated British Empire medal. Faculty fellow Center for Internat. Affairs Harvard, 1962-63. Asso. mem. Royal Inst. Internat. Affairs, London. Author: Africa in the Seventies and Eighties. Editor: Issues in Development, 1970. Home: 2500 Johnson Av Riverdale NY 10463 Office: Phelps-Stokes Fund 22 E 54th St New York City NY 10022

ARKIN, ALAN WOLF, actor; b. N.Y.C., Mar. 26, 1934; s. David I. and Beatrice (Wortis) A.; student Los Angeles City Coll., 1951-53, Bennington Coll., 1954-55; m. Barbara Dana, June 16, 1964; 1 son, Anthony; children by previous marriage—Adam, Matthew. Broadway appearances include From The Second City, 1961, Enter Laughing, 1963, LUV, 1964; motion picture appearances include The Russians are Coming, The Russians Are Coming (Golden Globe award as best actor in musical or comedy 1967), 1966, Woman Times Seven, 1967; Wait Until Dark, 1967, Inspector Clouseau, 1968, The Heart is a Lonely Hunter, 1968, Popi, 1969, Catch-22, 1970; mem. theatre group Second City Chicago and Off-Broadway, 1961; recording of childrens music, The Babysitters, 1958, Songs and Fun with The Babysitters, 1960, The Family Album, 1965, The Babysitters Menagerie, 1968; short motion pictures include That's Me, 1963, The Last Mohican, 1965; dir. movie shorts Thank God It's Friday, People Soup; dir. motion picture Little Murders, 1971. Address: 200 W 57th St New York City NY 10019

BEGIFORE, LAWRENCE STONER, mfg. exec.; b. Lima, O., Apr. 1, 1932; B.S., U. San Francisco, 1954; M.S., Stanford University, 1956; m. Rosemarie Lois Brown, May 15, 1955; 1 son, Anthony Robinson. Sales rep. Ames-Brockton Fabricated Products, Akron, O., 1956-58, sales mgr. Coshocton, Ohio, 1959-61, gen. manager plant, 1961-68, v.p. sales, 1968--. Instr. bus. Cosyhocton Jr. College, 1968-69. Secretary Coshocton YMCA, 1960-61; active Boy Scouts of America. Trustee Coshocton Animal Welfare League, Curry Home for the Aged. Named Man of Year, Coshocton Junior Chamber of Commerce, 1968. Mem. Coshocton C. of C. (vice president 1967-68, pres. 1969-70), English Speaking Union, Coshocton Sertoma Club, Nat. Assn. Mfrs., Sales Executives Institute, Phi Beta Kappa, Sigma Chi, Phi Mu. Democrat. Mem. Christian Ch. (lay leader). Mason (32, Shriner). Clubs: Coshocton Country, Coshocton City, Running Deer Country. Home: 2d Av Coshocton OH Office: 3d Av Coshocton OH

ARKUS, LEON ANTHONY, museum dir.; b. Passaic, N.J., May 6, 1915; s. Mayer and Elizabeth (Hoffman) A.; Townsend Harris Prep., Coll. City N.Y. Asst. to dir. Masterpieces of Art Exhbn., N.Y. World's Fair, 1939-40; cons. fgn. relief orgns. Art Aid Corp., N.Y.C., 1941; personnel mgr. Foley Bros., Inc., also Spencer, White & Prentice, Inc., Ahwaz, Iran, 1942-43; mgr. Douglas Curry Assos., Inc., N.Y.C., 1946-47; spl. asst. to pres. Am. Fedn. Arts, 1948; v.p., dir. Raymond & Raymond, Inc., N.Y.C., 1949-54; asst. dir. Mus. Art, Carnegie Inst., 1954-62, asso. dir., 1962-68, dir., 1968—. Mem. contemporary arts adv. com. Northwood Inst. Bd. govs. Pitts. Plan for Art, 1958—. Served to capt. AUS, 1943-45. Decorated Bronze Star. Hon. mem. Am. Inst. Interior Designers, Asso. Artists Pitts.; mem. Am. Assn. Museums, Assn. Art Mus. Dirs. Author: Three Self-Taught Pennsylvania Artists: Edward Hicks, John Kane, Horace Pippin, 1966; Carl-Henning Pedersen, 1968; Art of Black America, 1969; Pittsburgh International Exhibition of Contemporary Art, 1970; John Kane Painter, A Catalogue Raisonne, 1971. Home: 420 Coventry Rd Pittsburgh PA 15213 Office: 4400 Forbes Av Pittsburgh PA 15213

ARKUSH, ARTHUR SPENCER, editor, publisher; b. Chgo., June 22, 1925; s. Herbert Edgar and Rose (Hirsch) A.; student U. Ill., 1942-43; B.A., DePaul U., 1949; m. Betty Waldman, Mar. 20, 1948; children—Daniel Robert, Herbert Barry, Richard Mitchell. Reporter, Chgo. Sun-Times, 1948-49, asst. picture editor, 1949- 53; founder, dir. Lamb Publs., pubs. TV Tab mag., 1953-56; editorial dir. Publishers Devel. Corp., pubs. Guns mag., Shooting Industry mag., Boats and Motors mag., Arts and Activities, Modern Man mag., Players Showcase mag., Skokie, Ill., 1957-58, asst. to pub., gen. mgr., 1958-62, v.p., 1962-68; v.p. Transamerican & Export News Co., 1962-68; founder, pub. Pro Football Weekly, 1968—; pres. Pro Football Weekly, Inc., 1968—, Pro Sports Weekly, Inc., 1969—. Served with USAAF, 1943-46. Home: 698 Ridge Rd Highland Park IL 60035 Office: 5608 N Western Av Chicago IL 60645

ARKWRIGHT, GEORGE ALFRED, ret. jurist; b. Bklyn., Sept., 1888; s. George A. and Mary Augusta (McKeever) A.; A.B., Pa. U., 1911; LL.B., Fordham U., 1917; LL.D., St. John's U., 1951; m. Loretta Marie Cleary, Aug. 20, 1924; children—George Alfred, Harold Joseph, Evelyn A. Benson, Marjorie Marie, Richard Thomas. Taught pub. schs. N.Y. City, 1912-17; admitted to bar, 1917, clerked with Grout & Grout and Lewis & Kelsey; began gen. practice in Brooklyn, 1919; admitted to courts of N.Y. State, U.S. Dist., Circuit, and Supreme courts; mem. N.Y. Public Service Commn., 1943-50; justice Supreme Court of N.Y. State, 1950-58, 61-64, ofcl. referee, 1959-60; mem. Appellate Term, Supreme Ct., 2d Dept. N.Y., 1954-56; presiding judge Kings County Spl. Inquiry, 1956-58; trustee Kings Hwy. Savs. Bank (Bklyn.). Nat. council, exec. com. region 2, hon. mem. Greater N.Y. councils, mem. and past pres. Brooklyn council Boy Scouts of America. Am. Chmn., Law Library Bklyn.; former chmn. Del. Water Project Commn.; Prize Commr. for duration of war (apptd. by U.S. judges); former head Rep. Speaker's Bur. in city, state, nat. campaigns. Served With A.E.F. at Toule, St. Mihiel, Argonne. Recipient Silver Beaver and Antelope awards Boy Scouts Am. Mem. Am., Fed., N.Y. State, Bklyn. (3 times pres.; life trustee) bar assns., Bklyn-Manhattan Trial Lawyers' Assn., Catholic Lawyers Guild, A.A.A.S., Am. Legion, Travelers Aid Soc. (bd. dirs.), St. Patrick's Soc., St. Edmund's Holy Name Soc., Emerald Soc., Supreme Ct. Judges Assn., Am. Ordnance Assn., Pa. Alumni Assn., National Geographic Society, Fordham Alumni Assn. Roman Catholic. K.C., Rotarian. Clubs: Automobile of New York, Lawyers of Bklyn., Cathedral, Breezy Point Surf, The Brooklyn. Home: 1868 E 24th St Brooklyn NY 11229

ARLEDGE, ROONE PINCKNEY, TV exec.; b. Forest Hills, N.Y., July 8, 1931; s. Roone and Gertrude (Stritmater) A.; B.B.A., Columbia Coll., 1952; m. Joan Heise, Dec. 27, 1953 (div. 1971); children—Elizabeth Ann, Susan Lee, Patricia Lu, Roone Pinckney. With Dumont TV, 1952-53; producer-dir. children's and pub. affairs programming NBC, 1955-60; producer network sports ABC-TV, 1960-61, vice pres. charge sports, 1963-68; president ABC Sports, Inc., 1968—, executive producer 1964, 1968, 1972 Olympic games; initiated the Wide World of Sports program, 1961. Served with AUS, 1953-54. Recipient Emmy award, 1966, 67, 68, 69, 70, TV Guide award, 1964, Cannes Film Festival award, 1965, 66, George Foster Peabody awards internat. understanding (2); Certificate of Merit Outdoor Writers Assn. Am., Nat. Headlines spl. citation, 1968; Saturday Rev. award; Distinguished Service award N.Y. chpt. Broadcast Pioneers, 1968; named Man of Yr., Nat. Assn. TV Program Execs., Phila. Advt. and Sales Club, Football News, Gallagher Report. Home: 240 Central Park S New York City NY Office: 1330 Av Americas New York City NY 10019

ARLEN, HAROLD, composer; b. Buffalo, Feb. 15, 1905; s. Samuel and Celia (Orlin) Arluck; ed. Hutchinson High Sch., Buffalo; m. Anya Taranda. Began as boy singer in choir conducted by his father, a cantor; profl. pianist at age 15; organized orchs. and played in clubs and lake steamers, Buffalo; went to N.Y.C., 1927, and became arranger, pianist and singer for Arnold Johnson, band leader, first composition, Get Happy, sung in the 9:15 Revue, 1928; asso. with Ted Koehler, 1930, and since wrote songs for Cotton Club revues, etc. Received Acad. award for Over the Rainbow, 1939. Composer: Hitting the Bottle, One Love, You Said It, I Gotta Right to Sing the Blues, Satan's Little Lamb, It's Only a Paper Moon, Let's Fall in Love (complete score for motion picture), I Love a Parade, Kickin' the Gong Around, Minnie Moocher's Wedding Day, I've Got the World on a String, Stormy Weather (sung by Ethel Waters), Happy As the Day is Long, Life Begins at 8:40 (complete score), Strike Me Pink, Last Night When We Were Young (written for Lawrence Tibbett), Sing My Heart (for Irene Dunne), Wizard of Oz complete score for motion picture), A Day at the Circus (motion picture), American Minuet, Americanegro St Suite (4 spirituals), 1941; The Sky's the Limit (Fred Astaire); Up in Arms (Danny Kaye); That Old Black Magic, Blues in the Night, Accentuate the Positive, Let's Take the Long Way Home (for Bing Crosby), My Shining Hour (for Fred Astaire and Joan Leslie), Hit the Road to Dreamland, Happiness is Just a Thing Called Joe (for Ethel Waters), Calabash Pipe (for Eddie Cantor), The Eagle and Me, Evalina, I've Got a Song (all for Bloomer Girl), Come Rain, Come Shine, L'il Augie is a Natchal Man (St. Louis Woman), Lydia, Sweet and Hot, Devil and Deep Blue Sea, The Man That Got Away, I Could Go on Singing (for Judy Garland), The Morning After (for Eileen Farrell), So Long, Big Time (for Tony Bennett), The Silent Spring (for Lena Horne), Fine Kind of Freedom (for Barbara Streisand). Broadway shows include: Americana, Hooray for What, Bloomer Girl, St. Louis Woman, House of Flowers, Jamaica, Saratoga, Free and Easy (a blue opera), also several editions Earl Carroll's Vanities: motion picture scores include: Star Spangled Rhythm, Love Affair, The Sky's the Limit, Here Come the Waves, Cabin the the Sky, Out of this World, A Star is Born, The Country Girl, Gay Purr-ee. Contbr. of an article to book on George Gershwin. Address: care Al Berman 551 Fifth Av New York City NY 10017

ARLEN, MICHAEL J., writer; b. London Eng., Dec. 9. 1930; s. Michael and Atlanta (Mercati) A.; student St. Paul's Sch., Concord, N.H. 1944-48, Harvard 1948-52; m. Ann Warner, Mar. 11, 1957 (div. Apr. 1971); children—Jennifer, Caroline, Elizabeth, Sally. Came to U.S., 1940. Reporter, Life mag., 1952-56. Juror, Alfred DuPont-Columbia Survey Broadcast Journalism, 1968-70; staff writer The New Yorker mag. Author: Living-Room War, 1969; Exiles, 1970. Home: 168 E 68th St New York City NY 10021 Office: care The New Yorker 25 W 43d St New York City NY 10036

ARLING, EMANIE NAHM, writer, artist; b. Bowling Green, Ky.; d. Max B. and Sunshine (Friedman) Nahm; ed. Potter Coll. (Bowling Green), Belmont Coll. (Nashville, Tenn.), Western Ky. State Normal Sch. (Bowling Green), Bowling Green Business U., and spl. courses at Columbia; m. Walter E. Sachs, July 10, 1917 (div. 1939); 1 dau., Jane (Mrs. Hodes); m. 2d, August Philips, April 4, 1963. One man show of paintings The Iolas Gallery, 1957, 58, 59, Bodley Gallery (N. Y. C.), Portal Gallery (London, Eng.), Ror Volmar (Paris, France), Galerie Forum, (Madrid, Spain), 1963; also exhibited Sagittarius and Collectors' galleries. Mem. Authors' League Am., P.E.N., York Club, Sigma Iota Chi. Author: Talk, 1924; Red Damask, 1926; The Terrible Siren-Victoria Woodhull (1838-1927), 1929; The Octangle, 1930; A Pot With Feeling, 1960. Contbr. short stories and book revs. to mags. Address: 175 S Bald Hill Rd New Canaan CT 06840

ARLING, LEONARD SWENSON, indsl. physician and surgeon; b. Chicago City, Minn., Nov. 25, 1910; s. Charles Emil Swenson and Emily Charlotte (Carlson) A.; B.S., U. of Minn., 1933, M.B., 1934, M.D., 1936; m. Marion Arline Schroeder, June 24, 1938; children—Heather Marion (Mrs. Frank Louis Greenagel), Pamela Jill (Mrs. Walter A. Simmons), Bryan Jeremy. Served as intern, Receiving Hosp., Detroit, 1935-36; gen. practice medicine, Mpls., 1936-44, practice limited to indsl. medicine and surgery 1944—; physician Twin Cities assembly plant, Ford Motor Co. 1936—; founder, co-owner and pres. N.W. Indsl. Clinic P.A., 1944—; mem. staff, chief of staff Met. Med. Center, Mpls., 1954. Mem. Govs. Adv. Com. on Employment of Physically Handicapped in Minn., 1948-55; mem. bd. United Hosp. Fund of Mpls. and Hennepin County. Regional cons. R.R. Retirement Bd. for Minn., N.D., S.D., Mont., Wis. Bd. dirs. Jr. Achievement Mpls. and Hennepin County. Pillsbury fellow U. Minn. Found., E.T. Bell Assos., U. Minn. Diplomate Am. Bd. Preventive Medicine in occupational medicine. Fellow Indsl. Med. Assn. (chmn. small plants services com., sec. 1957-60); mem. A.M.A. (chmn. joint conf. council indsl. health, chmn. state com. 1954, 55), Central States Soc. Indsl. Medicine and Surgery (gov., pres. 1956- 57), Minn. Med. Assn. (chmn. com. indsl. health 1948-55), Minn. Acad. Occupational Medicine and Surgery (pres. 1964), Medical Alumni Assn. of U. Minn. (pres. 1969), Am. Cancer Soc. (unit dir.; pres. Hennepin County unit 1964-65), C. of C. (chmn. health sect., indsl. com.), A.A.A.S., Citizens League Greater Mpls., Isaac Walton League, Swedish-Am. Inst. Mpls., Photog. Soc. Am. Phi Rho Sigma. Lutheran. Mason (32, K.T. Shriner). Clubs: Minneapolis, Probus (past pres.) (Mpls.); Midway (St. Paul). Home: 2310 E 43d St Minneapolis MN 55406 Office: 3033 University Av SE Minneapolis MN 55414

ARLINGHAUS, FRANCIS ANTHONY, educator; b. Cin., June 13, 1905; s. Francis Joseph and Anna Mary (Rosswinkel) A.; A.B., Xavier U., Cin., 1926; A.M. (Taft fellow), U. Cin., 1929; A.M. (Edward Austin, Thayer fellows), Harvard, 1931, Ph.D., 1933; L.H.D., Detroit U., 1971; m. Blanche Terese Stolinski, Jan. 25, 1940; children—Francis Joseph, William Charles. Tchr. history St. Xavier High Sch., Cin., 1926-29; instr. history U. Detroit, 1933-34, asst. prof., 1934-40, asso. prof., 1940-46, prof., 1946-68, Distinguished Univ. prof., 1968—; dir McNichols Evening and Summer Sessions, 1950-64, asso. dean Coll. Arts, 1960-64, v.p. for student affairs, 1964-68. Vis. prof. Xavier U., summers 1931-35; mem. civilian faculty Nat. War Coll., Washington, 1953. Mem. Am. Hist. Assn., Am. Catholic Hist. Assn. (pres. 1948), Alpha Sigma Nu, Phi Alpha Theta. Roman Catholic. Home: 1122 Hillside Dr Birmingham MI 48009

ARLOW, JACOB A., psychiatrist; b. N.Y.C., Sept. 3, 1912; s. Adolph A. and Ida (Feldman) A.: B.S., N.Y. U., 1932, M.D., 1936; m. Alice Diamond, Oct. 31, 1936; children—Michael Saul, Allan Joseph, Seth Martin, Jonathan Bruce. Rotating intern Harlem Hosp., N.Y.C., 1936-38; resident neuropsychiatrist USPHS Hosp., Ellis Island, N.Y., 1938-39; resident psychiatrist Kings County Hosp., Bklyn., 1939, asst. psychiatrist mental hygiene clinic, 1941; asst. resident neurologist Montefiore Hosp., Bronx, N.Y., 1940, asst. neurologist, 1942-45; resident psychiatrist N.Y. State Psychiatric Inst. and Hosp., N.Y.C., 1940-41; cons. psychiatrist Pride of Judea Children's Home, Bklyn., 1940-45; pvt. practice parttime, N.Y.C., 1941, full time, 1942; student psychiatrist Profl. Sch., N.Y. Psychoanalytic Inst., N.Y.C., 1941-47, lectr. psychomatic medicine, 1948-50, instr. psychoanalysis and religion Sch. Applied Pschoanalysis of inst., 1951-52; instr. neurology Columbia Coll. Phys. and Surg., 1942-44, instr. psychiatry psychomatic service of psychoanalytic clinic for tng. and research, 1947-51, Turner visiting prof. psychiatry, 1967-68; research asso, instr. psychiatry Presbyn. Hosp.-Columbia Med. Center, 1944-51; clin. asst. prof. psychiatry State U. N.Y. Coll. Medicine at N.Y.C., 1952-55, clin. asso. prof., 1955-62, clin. prof., 1962—; faculty N.Y. Psychoanalytic Inst., 1956—; John B. Turner vis. professor psychiatry College Physicians and Surgeons, Columbia; vis. prof. psychiatry La. State U. Sch. Medicine, 1969-70, Yeshiva U.-Albert Einstein Coll. Medicine, 1971-72. Vice pres. Great Neck (L.I.) Coop. Sch.; trustee, sec. N.Y. Psychoanalytic Inst., 1956-59. Diplomate Am. Bd. Neurology and Psychiatry. Mem. A.M.A., Am. Psychoanalytic Assn. (pres. 1960-61, chmn. COPE 1962-66, bd. editors jour.; chmn.- elect bd. profl. standards 1967- -), Am. Psychiat. Assn., Psychosomatic Soc., N.Y. Psychoanalytic Inst. (pres. 1966-68), Internat. Psycho-Analytic Assn. (treas.; vice pres.). Author: Legacy of Sigmund Freud, 1956; (with Charles Brenner) Psychoanalytic Concepts and the Structural Theory, 1964. Editorial bd. Psychoanalytic Quar., Annual Survey Psychoanalysis, Psyche. Home: 94 Wildwood Rd Great Neck NY 11024 Office: 120 W 58th St New York City NY 10019

ARLT, GUSTAVE OTTO, ednl. exec.; b. Lock Haven, Pa. May 17, 1895; s. Hans and Helene Bertha (Hoffman) A.; student Elmhurst Coll., 1910-11, LL.D.; A.B., U. Chgo., 1915, A.M., 1929, Ph.D., 1931; LL.D., U. Cal.; Litt.D., Brown U.; L.H.D., Claremont U.; m. Gusti Herrman, June 25, 1920; 1 dau., Marlene. Instr. German, Ind. U.; 1923-24; asst. prof. of German, De Pauw U., 1924-29; asso. prof., Ind. U. 1931-35; prof. German, U. Cal. at Los Angeles, 1935-61, asso. dean grad. div., 1950-57, dean, 1958-61, dean emeritus, 1962, chmn. dept. Germanic langs., 1935-44, chmn. fgn. lang. group, 1940-44; pres. Council Grad. Schs. in U.S., Washington, 1961-70, pres. emeritus, 1970—. Dir. Cal. Lit. Centennial, 1950. Served with 302d Bn., Tank Corps, U.S. Army, with A.E.F. and as civilian employee, Provost Marshal Gen.'s Dept., Am. Forces in Germany, 1917-23. Decorated officers cross Order of Merit (Fed. German Republic). Mem. Hist. Soc. So. Cal. (pres. 1956-62), Los Angeles Chamber Symphony Soc. (pres. 1956-57), Modern Lang. Assn. Am., Nat. Humanities Council, Soc. Advancement Scandinavian Study, Am. Musicol. Soc., Calif. Folklore Soc., (pres. 1952-54), Am. Assn. Tchrs. German (v.p. 1943-44), Delta Phi Alpha, Pi Delta Phi, Phi Mu Alpha. Clubs: Rotary, Faculty, Cosmos. Auhor: Trutznachlgall, 1936. Editor: Das Schiff des Heils, 1933; Jabcobowsky und der Oberst, 1945; Der Abituriententag. 1948. Editor: Modern Lang. Forum, 1937-42; asso. editor, Cal. Folklore, 1942—; compiler and editor Kleiner Liederfreund, 1938. Translator: Jacobowsky and the Colonel (Franz Werfel), 1944; Star of the Unborn (Franz Werfel), 1946; Mirrorman (Franz Werfel), 1949. Editor: Hist. Soc. So. Cal. 1953-62. Contbr. articles to profl. jours. Address: 3900 Watson Pl N W Washington DC 20016

ARMACOST, GEORGE HENRY, ret. univ. pres.; b. Upperco, Md., May 6, 1905; s. Joshua Franklin and Matilda Frances (Nolte) A.; A.B., Dickinson Coll, 1926, LL.D., 1947; postgrad. Johns Hopkins, summers 1926, 1927, 1930; A.M., Columbia, 1930, Ph.D., 1940; L.H.D., Coll. Osteo. Phys. and Surgeons, Los Angeles, Denison U., 1957, U. Redlands, 1970; m. Verda Gay Hayden, June 14, 1933; children—Peter Hayden, Michael Hayden, Samuel Henry, Mary Cole (Mrs. Jack Hulst). Tchr. sci. Kane (Pa.) High Sch., 1926-29, prin., 1932-36; asso. in secondary edn., Tchrs. Coll., Columbia, 1930-32, mem. staff summer sessions, 1931- 36; prin. Shore Sch., Euclid, O., 1936- 37; asso. prof. edn. Coll. William and Mary, 1937-42, prof., 1942-45, acting dean of men, 1943-45, dir. summer sch. and chmn. dept. edn., 1944-45; pres. U. Redlands (Cal.), 1945-70, pres. emeritus, 1970—; prof. edn., chmn. profl. div. Alderson-Broaddus Coll., 1971—. Mem. accreditation com. Cal. Bd. Edn. Mem. adv. bd. Redlands br. Bank of Am., 1968—. Mem. bd. So. Cal. Baptist Conv., pres., 1960-61; trustee Berkeley Baptist Div. Sch.; bd. A.K. Smiley Pub. Library; council of regents Forest Lawn, Glendale, Cal. Mem. Lincoln Shrine Assn. (pres.), Ind. Colls. So. Cal. Inc. (pres.), Western Colls. Assn. (pres.), Council Protestant Colls. and Univs. (pres. 1963), Assn. Ind. Cal. Colls. and Univs. (pres. 1966-68), N.E.A., Nat. Assn. Deans and Advisors of Men, Nat. Council for Social Studies, Kappa Delta Pi, Phi Delta Kappa, Phi Beta Kappa (pres. So. Cal. alumni 1960-62), Omicron Delta Kappa. Rotarian. Club: Redlands Country. Author High School Reports, 1940. Home: Greystone Alderson-Broaddus Coll Philippi WV 26416

ARMANNI, ARMANDO, hotel exec.; b. Rome, Italy, Dec. 2, 1902; s. Romolo and Emilia (Danesi) A.; student U. Rome; m. Gabrielle Monnet, Feb. 22, 1945. With Hotel Savoy, London, Eng., 1920, then Hotel Meurice, Paris, France, Hotel Badrutt Palace, St. Moritz; with Italian Gradn Hotels Co., 1924—, gen. mgr. Hotel Excelsior, Rome, Italy, 1948—. Decorated commendatore Italian Republic. Home: 32 Via Valdagno Rome Italy 00191. Office: Hotel Excelsior Rome Italy 00100

ARMBRECHT, FRANK MAURICE, controller; b. Richmond, Va., Nov. 13, 1912; s. John H. and Ada (Shell) A.; m. Jean Frances O'Leary, Oct. 21, 1939; children—Frank Maurice, David Lee. With So. States Coop., Inc. Richmond, 1930—, now controller; dir. Coop. Mills, Inc., Cin. Mem. Nat. Assn. Accountants (past chpt. pres.), Financial Execs. Inst. (past chpt. pres), Nat. Soc. Accountants for Coops (past pres.), Nat. Council Farmer Coops., Am. Inst. C.P.A.'s. Home: 7666 Yarmouth Drive Richmond VA 23225 Office: So States Coop Inc 7th and Main St Richmond VA 23213

ARMBRECHT, WILLIAM H., lawyer, business exec.; b. Mobile, Ala., Nov. 1, 1908; s. William H. and Anna Bell (Paterson) A.; LL.B., U. Ala., 1932; m. Katherine Little, Oct. 8, 1927; children—William H. III, Katherine, Anna Bell, Conrad Paterson, Clara. Admitted to Ala. bar, 1932, since practiced in Mobile; partner Armbrecht, Jackson & DeMouy; pres., gen. counsel, dir. Ala., Tenn. 138 No. R. R., 1950—; gen. counsel McLean Industries; gen. counsel, dir. Taca Airways; dir. title Ins. Co. Mobile, Grand Hotel Co., Mobile Towing Co., So. Industries Corp.; chmn., dir. 1st Nat. Bank of Mobile. Mem. Mobile Indsl. Devel. Bd.; dir. Found. for Pub. Higher Edn. Mem. Am., Ala., Mobile (pres. 1954) bar assns., C. of C. (dir.), Ala. C. of C. (dir.), Dauphin Island Property Owner's Assn. (dir.), Phi Delta Phi, Alpha Tau Omega. Episcopalian (trustees board). Clubs: Lakewood Country (Point Clear, Ala.); Country, Athelstan, Propeller, Kiwanis (Mobile); Lunch (N.Y.C.). Home: 112 Pinebrook W Spring Hill AL 36608 Office: Mchts Bank Bldg Mobile AL 36602

ARMBRUSTER, JOHN HENRY, corp. exec.; b. St. Louis, Sept., 10, 1895; s. Frank and Mary (Osher) A.; student Tulane U., U. Denver; m. Eleanor L. Doepke, Apr. 3, 1919; children—Priscilla (Mrs. John A. Hoel), Elizabeth (Mrs. Q. Williams Johns, Jr.), Alice (Mrs. Stanley Hafer), Joan (Mrs. Kenneth Fiala). Organizer, pres. Community Fed. Savs. & Loan Assn., St. Louis, 1932—; chmn. bd. John H. Armbruster & Co., realtors, St. Louis, 1940—; pres. Armbruster Ins. Agy., St. Louis, 1945—; v.p. Holmes Realty & Investment Co, St. Louis, 1965—; dir. St. John's Community Bank, St. Louis County, Nat. Home Life Assurance Co., St. Louis, St. Paul Title Ins. Co., Bank Bldg. & Equipment Co., St. Louis. Pres. St. Louis Jr. C. of C., 1929, Police and Firemen's Fund St. Louis, 1962; sec. St. Louis YMCA, 1958—, memb. internat. com, 1960—; mem. exec. com. St. Louis council Boy Scouts Am., 1957—. Trustee Williams Woods Coll., 1958—, St. Louis U.S.O., 1965—, bd. dirs. Central Inst. for Deaf. Served with U.S. Navy, World War I. Recipient Silver Beaver award Boy Scouts Am., 1958, Service to Youth award YMCA, 1960. Mem. C. of C. Met. St. Louis (dir.), Nat. League Insured Savs. Firms (dir.), Am. Inst. Appraisers (past pres. St. Louis), Real Estate Bd. St. Louis County (past pres.). Rotarian (past pres. Clayton, Mo.). Home: 13 High Acres Dr St Louis MO 63132 Office: 8944 St Charles Rd St Louis MO 63114

ARMENTI, CARMEN JOHN, former mayor; b. Trenton, N.J., Apr. 11, 1929; s. Carmine and Ermelinda (Cenamo) A.; student Pennington (N.J.) Prep. Sch., 1948; m. Hope Vulgaris, Oct. 1, 1966; 1 dau., Melinda. Recreation supr., Trenton, 1955-62; spl. asst. to N.J. commr. labor and industry, 1962-66; mayor of Trenton, 1966-71. Served with AUS, 1951-53. Democrat. Home: 944 Edgewood St Trenton NJ 08608

ARMERDING, HUDSON TAYLOR, coll. pres.; b. Albuquerque, June 21, 1918; s. Carl and Eva May (Taylor) A.; A.B., Wheaton (Ill.) coll., 1941; A.M., Clark U., 1942; Ph.D., U. Chgo., 1948; postgrad. Harvard, 1949-50; m. Miriam Lucille Bailey, Dec. 26, 1944; children—Carreen, Taylor, Paul, Miriam, Jonathan, Instr. social sci. Wheaton Coll, 1946-48; successively prof. history, dean, also acting pres. Gordon (Mass.) Coll. 1948-49, 50-61; ordained to ministry Baptist Ch., 1951; minister in Manchester, N.H., 1949-50, Brockton, Mass., 1951-54; prof. history Wheaton Coll., 1961—, provost, 1963-65, pres. 1965—. Dir. North Conway (N.H.) Inst., 1959-67. Mem. home council Overseas Mission Fellowship, also China Inland Mission, Phila. Served with USNR, 1942-46; comdr. Res. Mem. Nat. Assn. Evangelicals (pres.), Assn. Asian Studies, Officers Christian Union, U.S. Naval Inst., Pi Gamma Mu, Pi Kappa Delta. Author: Christianity and the World of Thought, 1968. Address: 326 N Washington St Wheaton IL 60187

ARMFIELD, CLAUDE CLARK, Jr., banker; b. Winston-Salem, N.C., Nov. 3, 1918; s. Claude Clark and Mozelle (Phillips) A.; B.S., U. N.C., 1939; grad. Stonier Sch. Banking, Rutgers U., 1960; m. Mary Sue Wall, July 27, 1941; children—Janice (Mrs. John M.M. Gregory, III), Claude Clark III, Phillip Wall. With Charlotte br. Fed. Res. Bank Richmond, 1939-48, examiner, 1946-48; successively v.p., exec. v.p., pres. Bank of Lenoir (N.C.), 1951-58; exec. v.p., dir. First Union Nat. Bank, Lenoir, 1958-69, Western region First Union Nat. Bank N.C., Asheville, 1969—. Mem. Morehead Scholarship Com., 1957—; chmn. Caldwell dist. Boy Scouts Am., 1961-62; pres. Lenior C. of C., 1961-62. Chmn. trustees Blowing Rock Hosp.; trustee Patterson Sch. Boyd, Broyhill Edn. Fund; bd. visitors Appalachian State U. Served to maj. USMCR, 1940-45. Named Caldwell County Man of Year, 1966. Mem. N.C. Bankers Assn. (pres. 1971), V.F.W., Am. Legion. Methodist (steward). Mason. Clubs: Blowing Rock Country (pres. 1970); Asheville Country, Biltmore Forest Country (Asheville). Home: 3 Sunset Summit Asheville NC 28804 Office: PO Box 2450 Asheville NC 28802

ARMINGTON, RALPH ELMER, educator; B.S., Tufts U.; M.S., N.Y.U.; Ph.D., U. Pitts. Prof. elec. engring. Ill. Inst. Tech., Chgo. Office: Dept Elec Engring 3300 Federal St Chicago IL 60616

ARMINGTON, RAYMOND Q., road machinery mfg. exec.; b. Wickliffe, O., Jan. 12, 1907; s. George A. and Clara O. (Pritchard) A.; B.Indsl.Engring., Ohio State U., 1928; m. Elizabeth Cole Rieley, Sept. 22, 1932; children—Charles R. (dec.), George A., Steven E., Linda E. Engr. time study dept. B. F. Goodrich Co., Akron, O., 1928, Miller Rubber Co, Akron, 1929-30; engr. Armington, Engring. Co. (later absorbed by Euclid Road Machinery Co.), Euclid, O., 1931; v.p. gen. mgr. Euclid Road Machinery Co., 1937-51, pres., 1951-53 (Euclid Road Machinery Co. acquired by Gen. Motors 1953), gen. mgr. Euclid div. Gen. Motors Corp., 1953-60; chmn. Triax Co., 1960—, Euclid (Great Britain) Ltd., Glasgow, Scotland, 1950-60; dir. White Motor Corp., Addressograph-Multigraph Co., Lubrizol Corp. Harris Calorific Co., ARDAC Corp. Trustee, Bluecoats, Inc., Case-Western Res. U., Holden Arboretum, U. Circle Devel. Found., Ednl. Research Council Greater Cleve. Mem. Soc. Automotive Engrs. Presbyn. Clubs: Union (Cleve.); Kirtland. Home: RD 3 7921 Eagle Rd Willoughby OH 44094 Office: 1361 Chardon Rd Cleveland OH 44117

ARMISTEAD, MOSS WILLIAM, III, newspaper exec.; b. Suffolk, Va., Sept. 7, 1915; s. Moss William, Jr., and Mary Judith (Smith) A.; student Randolph-Macon Coll., 1933-36; LL.D., Washington and Lee Univ., 1967; m. Mary Ragan Bridges, Dec. 30, 1939; 1 dau., Elfeda Bridges (Mrs. Peter Huff Ring). Served as a reporter for the Covington Virginian, 1936; reporter, state editor utility editor, legislative corr. Roanoke Times, 1936-42; exec. sec. to Gov. of Va. and Sec. of Commonwealth, 1946-47; asst. to pub. Times & World-News, Roanoke, Va., 1947-51, asso. pub., 1951, v.p., pub., 1954; pres., dir. Times-World Corp., also pub. Roanoke Times and World-News, 1954—, chmn. bd., 1955-69; pres. Roanoke Valley Devel. Corp., 1957-59; dir. Landmark Communications, Inc., Nelson-Roanoke Corp., First National Exchange Bank, Chesapeake & Potomac Telephone Co. Va., Dominion Bankshares Corp., Roanoke, Va. Mem. State Bd. Welfare and Instns., 1947-51. Pres. Roanoke Community Fund. 1952, Central YMCA, 1957-58; pres. Community Hospital Roanoke Valley. Mem. Va. Port Authority, Norfolk. Served from pvt. to 1st Lt. Inf., AUS, 1942-46; capt. Va. N.G., 1947-50. Decorated Purple Heart. Mem. U.S., Va. (v.p.), Roanoke (pres.1953) C.'s of C., Va. Press Assn., Am. Newspaper Pub. Assn. (dir., sec.), So. Newspaper Pubs. Assn., Phi Kappa Sigma, Sigma Delta Chi, Alpha Kappa Psi. Club: Shenandoah (Roanoke). Office: 201 Campbell Av Roanoke VA 24011

ARMISTEAD, PARKES, banker; b. Franklin, Tenn., July 21, 1893; s. George Harrison and Jessie (Parkes) A.; student Vanderbilt U.; m. Katherine Moore, Apr. 12, 1917. Asst. cashier Broadway Nat. Bank, 1918-23, asst. cashier First Am. Nat. Bank, Nashville, 1923-27, asst. v.p., 1927-29, v.p., 1929-35. exec. v.p., 1935-48, pres., 1948-57, chmn. bd., 1957-69, hon. chmn., 1969—, also dir.; dir. United Cities Gas Co., Nashville Indsl. Corp., Dyersburg Cotton Prod. Corp., Keith, Simmons 138 Co., Gen. Box Co., Rockford Textile Mills, Inc., McMinnville, Tenn. Trustee Vanderbilt U. Rotarian. Clubs: Bellemeade Country, Cumberland. Home: Abbot Martin Rd Nashville TN 37215 Office: 4th Av and Union Sts Nashville TN 37201

ARMISTEAD, THEUS NICHOLSON, hosp. supt.; b. Shreveport, La., Aug. 5, 1916; s. William Wilchia and Lillian (Willis) A.; student Acad. Sch., Centenary Coll., Shreveport, 1934-37; M.D., La. State U., 1946; M.P.H., Tulane U., 1960; m. Lola Pearl Horton, Nov. 26, 1947; children—William Clinton, Susan Garland, John Nicholson. Intern Tri-State Hosp., Shreveport, 1946-47; gen. practice State Line Clinic, Waskom, Tex., 1947-48; dir. Webster Parish Health Unit, Minden, La., 1950-51; gen. practice Plain Dealing, La., 1951-56; dir. Red River, DeSoto and Claiborne Parish Health Units, 1955- 60; area med. cons. parishes N.W. La., 1960-64; La. health officer, pres. La. Bd. Health, 1964-66; supt. E. La. State Hosp., Jackson, 1966- Surgeon, USPHS, 1962, sr. surgeon, 1964. Served to capt. AUS, 50. Episcopalian. Address: East Louisiana State Hosp Jackson, LA 70748.

ARMISTEAD, WILLIAM HOUSTON, research adminstr.; b. Nashville, July 28, 1916; s. William Houston and Gayle (Tigert) A.; B.E., Vanderbilt U., 1937, M.S., 1938, Ph.D., 1941; m. Mary Elizabeth Gratzer, Aug. 30, 1936; children—Gayle Kimbrell (Mrs. Harold Byerly, Jr.), Katherine Elise (Mrs. Gus Hancock), John Elbert, Thomas H., William G., Thaniel E. With Corning Glass Works, 1941—, successively research chemist, sr. research asso. in chemistry, mgr. melting dept., dir. research and devel., 1941-56, v.p., dir. research and devel., 1956-61, v.p., 1961-71 dir. tech. staffs, 1961—, vice chmn. bd., 1971— also dir.; dir. Corhart Refractories Co., Signetics Corp., Dow-Corning Corp. Trustee Corning Mus. Glass; mem. vis. com. Materials Sci. Center, Cornell U.; mem. com. visitors Engring. Sch., Vanderbilt U. Fellow Am. Ceramic Soc.; mem. Indsl. Research Inst., Dirs. Indsl. Research, Am. Chem. Soc., C. of C., Sigma Xi, Tau Beta Pi. Clubs: University (N.Y.C.). Home: 240 Delevan Av Corning NY 14830 Office: Corning Glass Works Corning NY 14830

ARMISTEAD, WILLIS WILLIAM, coll. dean; b. Detroit, Oct. 28, 1916; s. Eber Merrill and Josephine Brunell (Kindred) A.; D.V.M., Tex. A. and M. Coll, 1938; M.Sc., Ohio State U., 1950; Ph.D., U. Minn., 1955; m. Martha Sidney Clark, Sept. 17, 1938 (dec. 1964); children—Willis William, Jack Murray, Sidney Merrill; m. 2d, Mary Wallace Nelson, 1967. pvt. practice vet. medicine, 1938-40; instr. Sch. Vet. Medicine, Tex. A. and M. Coll, 1940-42, asst. prof. to prof., 1946-53; dean Sch. Vet. Medicine, 1953-57; dean Coll. Vet. Medicine, Mich. State U., East Lansing, 1957—. Collaborator animal diseases and parasite research div. Dept. Agr., 1954-65; cons., adviser commn. vet. edn. of South, So. Regional Edn. Bd., 1953-56; mem. gov.'s sci. adv. bd., 1958-60; nat. cons. to Air Force Surgeon Gen., 1960-62; mem. adv. council Inst. Lab. Animal Resources, NRC, 1962-66; pres. Assn. Am. Vet. Med. Colls., 1964- 65; vet. med. resident investigators selection com. U.S. VA, 1967-70; vet. medicine rev. com. Bur. Health Professions Edn. and Manpower Ting., U.S. Dept., Health, Edn. and Welfare, 1967-71; mem. Nat. Bd. Vet. Med. Examiners, 1970—. Served from 1st lt. to maj. Vet. Corps, AUS, 1942-64. Mem. A.A.A.S., U.S. Livestock San. Assn., Am. (pres. 1957-58), Tex. (pres. 1947-48), Mich. (trustee Edn. and Sci. Trust 1970—), vet. med. assns., N.Y. Acad. Scis., Sigma Xi, Phi Kappa Phi, Phi Zeta, Omega Tau Sigma (nat. Gamma Award Ohio State U. 1962). Contbg. author; Canine Surgery, rev. edit. 1957; Canine Medicine, rev. edit., 1959. Editor:

The North Am. Veterinarian, 1950-56; asso. editor Jour. Am. Animal Hosp. Assn., 1964-70. Contbr. tech. articles to profl. jours. Home: 1840 Northgate Dr East Lansing MI 48823

ARMITAGE, ARTHUR LLEWELLYN, univ. ofcl.; b. Marsden, Eng., Aug. 1, 1916; s. Kenyon and Lucy Amelia (Beaumont) A.; B.A. (Found. Bachelor scholar), Queens' Coll., Cambridge U., 1937; Commonwealth Fund fellow, Yale, 1937-39, LL.B., 1937, M.A., 1940, LL.D., 1970; m. Joan Kenyon Marcroft, Aug. 20, 1940; children—Ann Kenyon, Katherine Mary. Called to bar Inner Temple, 1940; fellow Queens' Coll., 1945-58, from asst. tutor to sr. tutor, 1945-58, pres., 1958-70, vice chancellor univ., 1965-67, univ. lectr. law, 1947-70, hon. fellow, 1970—; vice chancellor Manchester U., 1970—; dep. chmn. quarter sessions County Huntingdon and Peterborough, 1965—; justice of peace, Cambridge, 1950-70. Chmn. Wages Council, 1955-70; mem. chmn.'s papel Indsl. Ct., 1962—; Chmn. trustees Sav. Bank Arbitration Tribunal, 1964- -; chmn. Com. Pay Postmen, 1964; chmn. Agrl. Wages Bd., 1968—. Served to maj. Kings Royal Rifle Corps and 2d Army, 1940-45. Decorated Order of Andrès Bello (Venezuela); hon. bencher Middle Temple, 1968. Mem. Soc. Pub. Tchrs. Law (pres. 1967-68). Author: (with J.W.C. Turner) Case Book on Criminal Law, 3d. edit., 1964. Co-editor: Clerk and Lindsell on Torts, 2d edit., 1961. Address: Vice-Chancellor's Office The University Manchester M13 9PL England

ARMITAGE, JOHN AUSTIN, fgn. service officer; b. Greenville, Tenn., Aug. 4, 1919; s. Leighton and Madeline Elizabeth (Noell) A.; B.S., U. Tenn., 1940; M.B.A. with distinction, Northwestern U., 1942; student Russian Inst., Columbia, 1946-47; m. Patricia Sue Weiss, Jan. 7, 1950; children—Lewis Leighton, John Marshall. Joined U.S. Fgn. Service, 1947; 3d sec. embassy, Prague, Czechoslovakia, 1947-50; 2d sec. legation, Bern, Switzerland, 1950; chief Eastern European br. Voice of Am., USIA, 1951-54; 2d sec. embassy, Moscow, USSR, 1955-57; officer charge multilateral polit. relations, Office Soviet Union Affairs, Dept. State, 1957-61; assigned Nat. War Coll., 1961-62, 1st sec. Am. Embassy, Teheran, Iran, 1962-65; counsellor, Am. embassy, Moscow, USSR, 1966-67; polit. conselor Am. embassy, Teheran, Iran, 1967-69; dir. Office UN Polit. Affairs Dept. State, 1970—. Mem. Vice Presdl. Party vis. USSR, 1959; mem. U.S. group accompanying Khrushchev on U.S. tour, 1960. President's ofcl. party for conf. with Khrushchev, Vienna, 1961. Served to lt. (s.g.) USNR, 1942-46. Mem. Phi Kappa Phi, Beta Gamma Sigma, Phi Gamma Delta. Address: 5016 Hawthorne Pl NW Washington DC 20016

ARMITAGE, MERLE, writer; b. Mason City, Ia., Feb. 12, 1893; s. Elmer E. and Lula May A.; ed. pub. schs.; m. 2d, Elsa Stuart, 1943; 1 dau., Chama Armitage; m. 3d, Isabelle Heymann, 1953; stepchildren—Agnes, Marc. Engaged civil engring., then designer of modern stage decorations until 1911; impresario, asso. with Charles L. Wagner, 1911-15; publicity dir. Diaghilev Ballet, 1915; asst. to pres. Nat. Soc. for Broader Edn., 1916-17; managed tours of Scotti Grand Opera Co., Russian Grand Opera Co., The Beggars Opera, concert courses of leading artists, 1919-21; mgr. Fitzgerald Concert Direction, Los Angeles, 1921; a founder, Los Angeles Grand Opera Assn., 1924, Gen. mgr., 1924-30; mgr. Philharmonic Auditorium, 1933—; editorial and art dir. Look mag. Commd. lt. col. AAF, World War I. Decorated Legion of Merit; recipient Cordon Bleu from Wine and Food Soc. Regional chmn. PWA Project. Author-designer many items, 1929—; works produced since 1945, include among others: Burro Alley (Corle), Saints and Saint Makers (Boyd), First Penthouse Dwellers of America (Underhill), 1946; Merle Armitage Dance Memoranda, Paintings of Russell Cowles, 1947; Smile at the Foot of the Ladder (Miller), 1948; Operations Santa Fe, 1948; Murder and Mystery in N.M., 1948; Paul Klee, 1950; Claude Debussy, 1950; Gershwin, man and legend, 1958; Fit for a Queen; Stella Dysart of Ambrosia Lake; Railroads of America, Dynamic Dissonance (Danz), Operatic Masterpieces (Downs), 1952; Neighborhood Frontiers, 1954; Photographs of Brett Weston, 1956; Two books on Igor Stravinsky, 1956. Address: Box 519 Santa Fe NM

ARMITAGE, RICHARD, univ. ofcl.; b. Ravenna, O., Apr. 15, 1918; s. Harry and Inez (Hughes) A.; A.B., Oberlin Coll., 1939; M.A., Ohio State U., 1940, Ph.D. (Univ. scholar 1940-41), 1945; postdoctoral student U. Tex., 1951-52; m. Janet Plummer, May. 28, 1942; children—Bruce, Suzanne, Barry, Daniel, Douglas, John. Faculty Ohio State U., Columbus, 1941-70, 71—, prof. Romance langs., 1966-70, 71—, asst. dean Coll. Arts and Scis., 1954-55, asst. dean Grad. Sch., 1956-60, asso. dean, 1960-63, dean, 1963-70, univ. ombudsman, 1971—; provost, dean faculties U. Mo., Kansas City, 1970-71. Vis. prof. Kenyon Coll., fall 1947. Cons. Minn. State Coll. Bd., 1968, Inst. Internat. Ed. 1967—. Chmn. region VIII, Woodrow Wilson Fellowship Found., 1961-65; bd. dirs. Ohio State U. Research Found.; chmn. editorial bd. Ohio State U. Press; trustee Children's Hosp., 1967-70; mem. adv. com. on grad. programs Ohio bd. Regents, 1965-70. Ford Fellow, 1951-52, Mem. Modern Lang. Assn. (planning and adv. com. coll. lang. manual project 1958-60, commn. on trends in edn. 1968-71), Am. Assn. Tchrs. Spanish and Portuguese. Club: Torch. Author: (with W. Meiden) Beginning Spanish; also articles, reviews. Office: 340 Ohio Union Ohio State Univ Columbus OH 43210

ARMITAGE, ROBERT E., electronic component mfg. co. exec.; b. 1926; grad. Bentley Coll. Accounting and Finance, 1946; married. Sr. auditor Patterson, Teele & Dennis, 1946-53; with Sprague Eleectric Co., 1953—, treas., sr. financial officer, 1968— ; dir., 1969— Address: 87 Marshall St North Adams, MA 02147

ARMITAGE, ROBERT EMERY, architect; b. Portland, Me., Sept. 2, 1932; s. William O. and Edna (Emery) A.; student Boston U., 1950-51; student Syracuse U., 1951-53, 55-58; m. Nancy Ann Schwarz, Oct. 18, 1958; children—Alan S., Neil E., William O. II. Archtl. draftsman William O. Armitage, Portland, Me., 1958-64; architect, partner William O. & Robert E. Armitage, Portland, 1964—. Mem. Citizens Urban Renewal Effort, 1963-64; bd. dirs. N.E. Hearing & Speech Center, Portland's Childrens Theatre. Served with U.S. Army, 1953-55. Recipient 1st place award New Eng. sect. applied lighting contest Illuminating Engring. Soc., 1967. Mem. A.I.A. (corp. mem. Me. chpt.), Constrn. Specification Inst. (pres. Portland chpt., region I awards corr.), Illuminating Engring. Soc. Episcopalian (sr. warden). Club: Young Republican (Portland). Archtl. work includes State Me. Pavilion Expo 67, Montreal, Can. Home: Reef Rd Cape Elizabeth ME 04107 Office: 666 A Congress St Portland ME 04101

ARMKNECHT, RICHARD FREDERICK, Jr., apparel co. exec.; b. Troy, N.Y., Dec. 2, 1928; s. Richard Frederick and Rebecca (Graham) A.; B.A., Colby Coll., 1950; M.B.A., Harvard, 1954; m. Ruth Berglund, Sept. 3, 1955; children—Beth, Richard Frederick III, Carl, John. Research asso. Harvard Bus. Sch. 1954-57; cons. Arthur D. Little Inc., 1957-59; project leader Harbridge House Inc., Boston, 1959- 61; treas. William Carter Co., 1961—, also dir. Served to lt. (j.g.) USNR, 1951-53. Mem. Financial Execs. Inst. Club: Treasurers (Boston). Home: 51 Plainfield Rd Concord MA 01742 Office: 962 Highland Av Needham MA 02194

ARMOR, RAYMOND HUGHES, chem. co. exec.; b. Pitts., Jan. 24, 1920; s. Raymond and Nell (Hughes) A.; B.S., Bucknell U., 1941; student Robert Morris Sch. Bus., Pitts., 1946-48; M.B.A., Western Res. U., 1954; m. Dorothy McKinley, Jan. 14, 1944; children—Paul R., Gail A., Joyce, Nancy K. With Diamond Shamrock Corp. (merger Diamond Alkali Co. and Shamrock Oil & Gas 1967), 1941-70, asst. treas., Cleve., 1953-57, treas., 1957-60, controller, 196O-69, asst. to financial v.p., 1969-70; v.p. finance Terra Chems. Internat., Inc., Sioux City, Ia., 1970—. Served as 1st lt. USAAF, 1942-45. Decorated Air medal with three oak leaf clusters. Mem. Phi Beta Kappa, Kappa Sigma. Club: Sioux City Country. Home: 4860 Skyline Dr Sioux City IA 51104 Office: 507 6th St Sioux City IA 51101

ARMOUR, ANDREW WATSON, III, mfg. exec.; b. Chgo., Oct. 22, 1908; s. A Watson and Elsa (Parker) A.; student Northwestern U., 1928, Princeton, 1929-31; m. Jean Shedd Schweppe, Feb. 22, 1936 (dec. Jan. 1963); children—Laura (Mrs. G. B. Cook), Andrew Watson IV; m. 2d, Sarah Wood Addington, Apr. 6, 1966. Sales exec. Armour & Co., Chgo., 1936-46; exec. v.p. Huck Mfg. Co., Chgo., 1946-52, pres., 1952—. Mem. Chgo. adv. bd. Salvation Army; trustee Shedd Aquarium, Presbyn.-St. Luke's Hosp. Republican. Episcopalian. Clubs: Ivy (Princeton); The Chicago, Racquet (Chgo.); Onwentsea Country (Lake Forest, Ill.); River (N.Y.C.). Home: 850 E Deerpath Rd Lake Forest IL 60045 Office: 141 W Jackson Blvd Chicago IL 60604

ARMOUR, LAURANCE HEARNE, Jr., banker; b. Chgo., May 20, 1923; s. Laurance Hearne and Frances Lacy (Withers) A.;grad. Hotchkiss Sch., 1941; A.A., Princeton, 1945; student Northwestern U., 1947-48; m. Margot Caroline Boyd, Apr. 7, 1954; childrenLaurance Hearne, Steven Shelby, Margot Brooks, With LaSalle Nat. Bank, Chgo., 1948-, dir., 1951-, vice chairman, 1953-, chairman exec. com., 1964-, Dir. Espiscopal Charities Chgo., Passavant Meml. Hosp.; mem. corp. Seabury-Western Theological Sem. Served from pvt. to 1st lt., AUS, 1943-46. Home: 930 Rosemary Rd Lake Forest IL 60045 Office: 135 S LaSalle St Chicago IL 60603

ARMOUR, LLOYD ROWLAND, newspaper editor; b. Greene County, Ark., May 17, 1922; s. William Velt and Oma (Rowland) A.; A.B., Lambuth Coll., Jackson, Tenn., 1948; grad. student, Vanderbilt U., 1949-50; m. Barbara Joan Link, Oct. 9, 1954; children—Christopher, Mark Richard. Bur. chief Memphis Comml. Appeal, 1947-48; v.p., asso. editor Nashville Tennessean, 1948—. Bd. dirs. Day Care Center for Retarded Children. Served with USMCR, 1941-45. Mem. Nat. Conf. Editorial Writers (treas.), Sigma Delta Chi. Democrat. Presbyn. Club: City (Nashville). Contbr. nat. magazines. Home: 1105 Stonewall Dr Nashville TN 37220 Office: 1100 Broadway Nashville TN 37201

ARMOUR, NORBERT FRED, dept. store exec.; b. Spencer, S.D., Nov. 23, 1914; s. Fred and Marie C. (Muller) A.; grad. Advanced Mgmt. Program, Harvard, 1958; m. Cecelia M. Skripek, Sept. 11, 1937; children—Kenneth Allan, Barbara Sue. With Carson Pirie Scott Co., Chgo., 1934—, store mgr., 1952-58, gen. mdse. mgr., sr. v.p., 1958-64, exec. v.p., 1964-69, pres., 1969—, also dir.; dir. Evergreen Plaza Bank, Roxbury Carpet Co., Concord Ins. Co. Bd. dirs. State Street Council. Served with AUS, 1943-45, Mem. Chgo. Federated Advt. Club. Clubs: Chicago Athletic Assn., Economic, Executives, Midlothian Country, Chicago, Commercial (Chgo.). Home: 12504 Navajo Dr Palos Heights, IL 60463. Office: 1 S State St Chicago IL 60603

ARMOUR, RICHARD Willard, prof., author; b. San Pedro. Calif., July 15, 1906; s. Harry Willard and Sue (Wheelock) A.; A.B., Pomona Coll., Claremont, Calif., 1927; A.M., Harvard, 1928, Ph.D., 1933; Litt.D., Coll. of Ozarks, 1944; L.H.D., Whittier College, 1968; LL.D., Coll. Ida., 1969; m. Kathleen Fauntleroy Stevens, Dec. 25, 1932; children—Geoffrey Stevens, Karin Elizabeth. Instr. in English, U. of Texas, 1928-29, Northwestern University, 1930-31; Dexter Scholar (research fellow) from Harvard, at John Forster Library, Victoria and Albert Museum, London, 1931; professor of English and head div. of modern langs., Coll. of the Ozarks, 1932-33; Am. lecturer, U. of Freiburg, Germany, 1933-34; asst. prof. asso. prof. and prof. English, Wells Coll., 1934-45; prof. English, Scripps Coll. and Claremont Grad. Sch., 1945-63; dean of faculty Scripps Coll., 1961-63, Balch lectr. in English lit., 1963-66, prof. emeritus, 1966—; served as Am. specialist abroad for U.S. State Dept., 1964, 66, 67, 68, 70; Fund Advancement Edn. faculty fellow, 1953-54; Carnegie visiting prof. English, U. Hawaii, 1957; leader of European tours, summers, 1926-31. Trustee Claremont Men's College. Served as 2d lt., inf., Res. Corps, U.S. Army, 1927-37; active duty in Antiaircraft Arty., 1942-46; lt. col., detailed to War Dept. Gen. Staff (mem. 1944-46); col. U.S. Army Res. Decorated Legion of Merit with Oak Leaf Cluster. Mem. Modern Lang. Assn. Am., Am. Assn. Univ. Profs., California Writers Guild, P.E.N., Phi Beta Kappa. Conglist. Author of numerous books, including Coleridge the Talker, 1940; Yours for the Asking, 1942; Golf Bawls, 1946; Writing Light Verse, 1947; For Partly Proud Parents, 1950; It All Started with Columbus, 1953; Light Armour, 1954; It All Started With Europa, 1955; It All Started With Eve, 1956; Twisted Tales From Shakespeare, 1957; Nights with Armour, 1958; It All Started With Marx, 1958; Drug Store Days, 1959; The Classics Reclassified, 1960; Golf Is A Four-Letter Word, 1962; Armour's Almanac, 1962; The Medical Muse, or What to Do Until the Patient Comes, 1963, Through Darkest Adolescence, 1963; Our Presidents, 1964; The Year Santa Went Modern, 1964; American Lit Relit, 1964; An Armoury of Light Verse, 1964; The Adventures of Egbert the Easter Egg, 1965; Going Around in Academic Circles, 1965; Animals on the Ceiling, 1966; Punctured Poems, 1966; It All Started with Hippocrates, 1966; It All Started with Stones and Clubs, 1967; A Dozen Dinosaurs, 1967; Odd Old Mammals, 1968; My Life With Women, 1968; English Lit. Relit, 1969; On Your Marks: A Package of Punctuation, 1969; A Diabolical Dictionary of Education, 1969; All Sizes and Shapes of Monkeys and Apes, 1970; A Short History of Sex, 1970; Who's in Holes? 1971; Out of My Mind, 1971. Member editorial bd. The Writer; dept. ed. Quote: The Weekly Digest. Contbr. articles and poems to nat. mags. Home: 460 Blaisdell Dr Claremont CA 91711

ARMS, BREWSTER LEE, bus. exec.; b. Pasadena, Cal., Dec. 18, 1925; s. Louis Lee and Mae Warne (Marsh) A.; B.A., Stanford, 1948, LL.B., 1951; m. Shirley Smallwood, Mar. 17, 1962; children—Emily Diane, Stephen, Andrew. Admitted to Cal. bar, 1952; with Bankline Oil Co., 1952-59, atty., corp. sec., 1955-59; atty. The Signal Companies, Inc. (formerly Signal Oil and Gas Co.), Los Angeles, 1959-63, atty., corp. sect. 1963-70, v.p., gen. counsel, 1970—. Served with inf. AUS, 1944-45. Mem. Am., Cal., Los Angeles bar assns., Am. Soc. Corp. Secretaries. Home: 2104 Via Fernandez Palos Verdes Estates CA 90274 Office: 1010 Wilshire Blvd Los Angeles CA 90017

ARMS, GEORGE WARREN, educator; b. La Grande, Ore., Feb. 1, 1912; s. George Wells and Marguerite (Shattuck) A.; A.B., Princeton, 1933; student univs. Zurich and Munich; Ph.D., N.Y. U., 1939; m. Elizabeth Tanner, June 27, 1936. Tchr. prep. schs., 1933-34, 1935-38, Bennett Jr. Coll., 1939; asst. prof. English, Mary Washington Coll., U. Va., 1939-44; prof. English, U. N.M., Albuquerque, 1945—, chmn. dept., 1951-56; vis. prof. English, N.Y.U., summer 1949. Bd. dirs. Explicator Lit. Found., 1969—, pres., 1969-70. Fellow Ford Found., 1954-55; recipient grant-in-aid Am. Council Learned Socs., 1964; Am. Philos. Soc. grantee, 1968. Mem. Modern Lang. Assn., Coll. English Assn., Nat. Council Tchrs. English, Am. Assn. U. Profs., Phi Beta Kappa, Phi Kappa Phi. Democrat. Presbyn. Author: A Bibliography of William Dean Howells, 1948; Readings for Liberal Education, 1948; Poetry Explication, a Checklist, 1950; The Fields Were Green, 1953; Symposium, 1954. Editor The Explicator, 1942- -; The Hazard of New Fortunes, 1952; The Rise of Silas Lapham, 1940; Howells' Prefaces to Contemporaries, 1957; Twelve American Writers, 1962. Mem. bd. editors Am. Lit., 1960-69; exec. com. Howells Edit. Editorial Bd.; bd. consultants Am. Lit. Realism, 1967—. Home: 607 Vassar Dr N E Albuquerque NM 87106

ARMSTRONG, A. JAMES, bishop United Methodist Ch. Address: Capitol Bldg., Aberdeen, SC 57401.*

ARMSTRONG, ALFRED RINGGOLD, educator; b. Washington, July 6, 1911; s. Frank Miller and Lulu (Reichert) A.; B.S., Coll. William and Mary, 1932; postgrad. U. Mich., 1935-36; Ph.D. (Gen. Edn. Bd. fellow), U. Va., 1944; m. Martha Wallace Barber, Oct. 6, 1934; children—Robert Miller, Alfred Barber. Instr., Coll. William and Mary, 1933-36, asst. prof., 1936-45, asso. prof., 1945- 61, prof., 1961—. Mem. Am. Chem. Soc., Phi Beta Kappa, Sigma Xi. Author: (with Hogness and Johnson) Qualitative Analysis and Chemical Equilibrium, 1966. Home: 512 Newport Av Williamsburg VA 23185

ARMSTRONG, ALLAN LEROY, physician; b. Miami, Fla., Nov. 19, 1923; s. Roy Armstrong and Clara Lillian (Harvey) A.; student Western Md. Coll., 1943-44, U. Md., 1944- 45; M.D., U. Va., 1949; m. Sylvia Jane Jander, Sept. 10, 1949; children—Marcia Jane, Janet Anne, Helen Hughes, Michael Allan. Intern U. Va. Hosp., 1949-50; jr. physician Blue Ridge Sanatorium, Charlottesville, Va., 1950-53, sr. physician, 1954-58; course pulmonary function Boston City Hosp., 1956, 61; mem. staff S.W. Fla. Tb Hosp., Tampa, 1959-66, instr. Tb and chest diseases, 1958-66, med. dir., 1960-66; asso. staff Tampa Gen. Hosp., 1964-65, active staff, 1966—, chmn. infections com., 1966—, attending physician Chest Clinic, 1969—; mem. staff Univ. Community Hosp., 1968—, chmn. med. records com., 1968—, dir. medicine, 1970—, exec. com., 1970—; mem. staff St. Joseph's Hosp., Tampa, 1966—; spl. cons. Tb, USPHS, 1960—; clin. asso. prof. Coll. Medicine, U. Fla., Gainesville, 1967—; instr. chemistry Blue Ridge Sanatorium Sch. Nursing, 1950-58, instr. microbiology, 1950-58; postgrad. lectr. Tb, U. Va. Sch. Nursing, 1954-58, instr. Tb, Sch. Medicine, 1950-58, lectr. health studies Coll. Arts and Scis., 1957. Served with AUS, 1943-46, USAF, 1953-54. Grantee NIH, 1965-68. Mem. Am., So., Fla. med. assns., Hillsborough County Med. Soc., Am., Fla. (pres. 1963-64) thoracic socs., Nat. Tb Assn., Hillsborough County Tb and Health Assn. (dir. 1960-63), Gulf Coast Tb and Respiratory Disease Assn. (dir. 1963-71, exec. com. 1966-70, adv. com. 1963—), Fla. Tb and Respiratory Disease Assn. (adv. dir. 1964-66, dir. 1964-70). Author numerous articles in field. Home: 10222 Valle Dr Tampa FL 33612 Office: 3000 Medical Park Dr Tampa FL 33612

ARMSTRONG, ANNE LEGENDRE (Mrs. Tobin Armstrong,) mem. Republican Nat. Com.; b. New Orleans, Dec. 27, 1927; d. Armant and Olive (Martindale) Legendre; grad. Vassar Coll., 1949; m. Tobin Armstrong, Apr. 12, 1950; children—John Barclay, Katharine A., Sarita S., Tobin and James L. (twins). Pres. Drink-O-Mat Corp., Ft. Jackson, S.C., 1964—. Trustee Kenedy County (Tex.) Sch. Bd., 1968—. Chmn. Kenedy County Republican Party, 1958-61; mem. Tex. Rep. Exec. Com. from 20th dist., 1961-66; Republican dep. vice chmn., 1965-66; Rep. state vice chmn., 1966-68; mem. Rep. Nat. Com. from Tex., 1968—; mem. exec. com. Rep. Nat. Com., 1971—; del. Rep. Nat. Conv., 1964, 68, mem. platform com., 1964, 68. Mem. Phi Beta Kappa. Home: Armstrong Ranch Armstrong TX 78338

ARMSTRONG, ARTHUR FRANCIS, paper co. exec.; b. Windsor, N.S., Apr. 2, 1913; s. Arthur Francis and Ethel Eugene (Shand) A.; student Kings Coll. Sch., Windsor; B.A., U. Toronto, 1936; m. Meredith Stampfer Armstrong, Oct. 17, 1959; children—Thomas, John, Ceclia. Salesman with Scott Paper Co., Chester, Pa., 1936-42, dir. indsl. relations, 1957-58; personnel mgr. Falls Paper & Power Co., Oconto Falls, Wis., 1946-51, asst. to plant mgr., 1951; vice president Westminster Paper Co. (now named Scott Paper Limited), New Westminster, B.C., Canada, 1956-58, president, 1958—, also mng. dir.; dir. B.C. Forest Products, Ltd. Bd. trustees Camp Tecumseh, boys camp; bd. govs. Crofton House Sch., Trinity Coll. Sch., Port Hope, Ont., Can. Served to lt. Royal Canadian Navy, 1942-45. Mem. Phi Kappa Pi. Clubs: Rittenhouse (Phila.); Philadelphia Skating (Ardmore); Shaughnessy Golf and Country, Vancouver (Vancouver); Capilano Golf and Country (West Vancouver). Home: 630 Southborough Dr West Vancouver British Columbia Canada Office: Scott Paper Ltd PO Box 760 New Westminster British Columbia Canada

ARMSTRONG, ARTHUR JAMES, clergyman; b. Marion, Ind., Sept. 17, 1924; s. Arthur J. and Frances (Green) A.; A.B., Fla. So. Coll., 1948; B.D., Candler Sch. Theology, 1952; D.D., Fla. So. U., 1960, DePauw U., 1965; L.H.D., Ill. Wesleyan U., 1970, Dakota Wesleyan U., 1970; m. Phyllis Jeanne Shaeffer, Feb. 26, 1942; children—James, Teresa (Mrs. John Etchison), John, Rebecca (Mrs. Doug LeMaster), Leslye. Ordained to ministry Meth. Ch., 1947; minister in Fla., 1945-58; sr. minister Broadway Meth. Ch., Indpls., 1958-68; bishop United Meth. Ch., Dakotas area, 1968—; instr. Christian Theol. Sem., Indpls., 1961-68; del. 4th Gen. Assembly World Council Chs., 1968; del. Nat. Council Chs., 1970, mem. dept. internat. affairs, 1970—; mem. bd. Christian social concerns United Meth. Ch., 1968—. Vice- chmn. Hoosiers for Peace, 1968; mem. Ind. State Platform Com. Democratic Party, 1968; mem. Nat. Coalition for a Responsible Congress, 1970. Trustee Dakota Wesleyan U., Meth. Hosp., Mitchell, S.D. Served with USNR, 1942. Recipient distinguished service award Indsl. Jr. C. of C., 1959. Author: The Journey That Men Make, 1969; The Urgent Now, 1970; Mission: Middle America, 1971. Contbg. author The Pulpit Speaks on Race, 1966; War Crimes and the American Conscience, 1970. Home: 1419 N Main St Aberdeen SD 57401 Office: Capitol Bldg Aberdeen SD 57401

ARMSTRONG, ARTHUR SOPER, mfr.; b. N.Y.C., Feb. 2, 1911; s. Arthur Soper and Mabel (Rinker) A.; A.B., Harvard, 1932; m. Janet Morrill, Apr. 5, 1932; children—Joan, Virginia; m. 2d, Jean Harvey, Aug. 17, 1940; children—Jennifer, Arthur; m. 3d, Ann Hale Dickinson, Nov. 17, 1951; children—Elizabeth, Peter; m. 4th, Halina Kogutowska, Aug. 8, 1970. With Cleve. Twist Drill Co. since 1932, dir. since 1947, gen. mgr. since 1951, pres., now chmn. bd. dirs.; chmn. bd., pres. Acme-Cleve. Corp., 1968—; chmn. bd. dirs. Cleve. Twist Drill (G.B.) Ltd., Cleve. Twist Drill (Can.); dir. Cleve. Trust Co., Wean United Inc., Reliance Electric Co. Pres. Acme-Cleve. Found.; trustee St. Luke's Hosp.; overseer Case Western Res. U. Presbyn. (pres. trustees). Home: 2914 W Park Blvd Shaker Heights OH 44120 Office: 1242 E 49th St Cleveland OH 44114

ARMSTRONG, CHARLES JOHNSTONE, univ. pres.; b. Victoria, B.C., June 11, 1911; s. Charles Leland and Jessie Agnes (McKilligan) A.; grad. Victoria (B.C.) Coll., 1930; A.B., U. B.C., 1932, LL.D., 1961; Ph.D. (William Watson Goodwin fellow), Harvard, 1936; LL.D., Coll.

Ida., 1960, McGeorge Coll. Law (Cal.), 1966; Litt.D., Pacific U., 1963; m. June Eulalie Herren, Aug. 31, 1937 (dec. Nov. 1969); children—Judith E., Christopher A., Charles Stuart, Michael John Alston. U. S. citizen since 1925. Instr. in classics Rollins Coll, Winter Park, Fla., 1936-38, asst. prof., 1938-39; instr. in classics Dartmouth, 1939-41; instr. classics Brown U., 1941-43, asst. to dean coll., 1942-43; asst. prof. classics Whitman Coll., Walla Walla, Wash., 1943-45, dir. Navy V 12 Coll. Tng. Program, 1943-45, vets. counselor 1944-53, asso. prof. classics, 1945-47, dean adminstrn., chmn. bd. counselors, 1945-51, chmn. div. letters and arts, 1947-48, Clement Biddle Penrose prof. Latin, 1947-53, v.p., dean faculty, 1951-53; pres. Pacific U., forest Grove, Ore., 1953-58, U. Nev., Reno, 1958-67, Dayton-Miami Valley Consortium, 1967—. Exec. commr. for State of Nev., Western Interstate Comm. on Higher Edn., 1959-67, vice chmn., 1961-62, chmn., 1962-63; chmn. bd. Asso. Rocky Mountain Univs., 1962-63; mem. exec. com. Nat. Assn. State Univs., 1961-64. Air raid warden Providence Civilian Def., 1942-43. Mem. Walla Walla Council U.S.O., 1944-45; vice chmn. Vets. Service Council 1944-48; steering com. N.W. Conf. Higher Edn., 1949-52, conf. chmn. 1951-52. A founder, chmn. exec. bd. and actor in numerous plays, Little Theatre of Walla Walla, 1944-48; mem. exec. com. Pacific N.W. Conf. on Arts and Scis. 1947-50; chmn. Ore. Colls. Found., 1956-57; vice chmn. Gov.'s Com. on Higher Edn. for Ore., 1956-58; mem. nat. adv. council Religion in Edn. Found., 1956-60; mem. Gov. Nev. Adv. Com. on Indian Affairs, 1961-64; Nev. vice-chmn. Nat. Conf. Christians and Jews, 1962-64; mem. Pacific Coast com. Am. Council on Edn. Recipient Outstanding Civilian Service medal Dept. Army, 1965. Mem. Internat. Assn. U. Pres., Assn. Ind. Colls. Ore. (chmn. 1956-57), Assn. Am. Colls. (commn. pub. relations 1956-58), N.W. Assn. Secondary and Higher Schs. (exec. com. 1955-67, chmn. com. on coop. research 1956-60), Pacific North West Intercollegiate Athletic Assn. (chmn. presidents council 1956-57), Am. Philol. Assn., Newcomen Soc. Eng., Psi Upsilon. Republican. Episcopalian. Editor, contbr. publs. in field. Home: 4975 Woodman Park Dr Dayton OH 45432

ARMSTRONG, CLYDE ALLMAN, lawyer; b. New Kensington, Pa., June 14, 1898; s. Ulysses S. and Anna M. (Allman) A.; A.B., Westminster Coll., 1919; LL.B., U. Pitts., 1922; m. Ethlyn W. Logan, Dec. 27, 1923; children—Dale L., Clyde W., Carolyn Lee. Admitted to Pa. bar, 1922, since practiced in Pitts., mem. firm Thorp, Reed & Armstrong; prof. comml. law Carnegie Inst. Tech., 1923-30. Dir. Nat. Storage Co. Past pres. Columbia Hosp.; past dir. Hosp. Service Assn. Pitts. (Blue Cross); v.p., past pres. bd. trustees Westminster Coll.; pres. United Presbyn. Bds. Served as 2d lt., F.A., U.S. Army, 1918. Mem. Am., Pa., Allegheny County bar assns., Am. Judicature Soc., Am. Coll. Trial Lawyers, Acad. Trial Lawyers Allegheny County, Delta Theta Phi. Republican. Mason. Clubs: Duquesne, Fox Chapel Golf, Williams Country (Pitts.). Home: 405 Buckingham Rd Pittsburgh PA 15215 Office: Thorp Reed & Armstrong Grant Bldg Pittsburgh PA 15219

ARMSTRONG, DEWITT CLINTON, III, army officer; b. Ancon, Canal Zone, June 13, 1921; s. Brig. Gen. Clare Hibbs and Mary (Coombs) A.; B.S., U.S. Mil. Acad., 1943; grad. Command and Gen. Staff Coll., 1956, Nat. War Coll., 1965; M.A., M.P.A., Princeton, 1958, Ph.D., 1960; m. Kate Peters Johnson, May 17, 1948; children—DeWitt Clinton IV, Kate Ellen. Commd. 2d lt. U.S. Army, 1943, advanced through grades to brig. gen., 1968; combat with 14th Armored Div., World War II; strategic planner Depts. of Army, Def. and State, 1959-64, Vietnam, 1965-66; command duties 2d Armored Div., 1967-69; dep. chief Army intelligence, 1969-70; advisor to Vietnamese III Corps comdr., 1970-71; comdg. gen. U.S. Army Forces, Mil. Region 2, Vietnam, 1971—. Mem. U.S. delegation Fgn. Ministers Conf., Paris, 1961; mem. Berlin Task Force, 1961-63; mem. Policy Planning Council of U.S. Dept. of State, 1963-64. Decorated Legion of Merit with oak leaf cluster. Mem. Council Fgn. Relations. Episcopalian. Club: Army-Navy (Washington). Contbr. articles profl. jours. Home: 1109 N Howard St Alexandria VA 22304 Office: APO San Francisco CA 96350

ARMSTRONG, DONALD BUDD, Jr., advt. exec.; b. N.Y.C., June 23, 1915; s. Donald Budd and Eunice (Burton) A.; B.A., Harvard, 1937; m. Marion Lee Rising, Aug. 9, 1940 (div. Jan. 1955); children—Judith Lee (Mrs. Duncan Keir Alexander), Donald Budd III; m. 2d, Eleanor Dippel Sinclair, Jan. 1955. Jr. exec. trainee Lehn & Fink, Inc., N.Y.C., 1937-39; advt. research Young & Rubicam, Inc., 1939-45; asso. dir. research McCann- Erickson, Inc., N.Y.C., 1946-48, dir. research, 1949-51, v.p. charge research, mem. adv. com. advt. plans, 1951-55, chmn. creative plans bd., 1956, v.p. for marketing services, chmn. marketing plans bd., 1957, asst. to the pres. and coordinator of profl. services, 1958, v.p. in charge account planning and marketing services, 1959-63; chmn. bd. McCann-Erickson (Can.) Ltd., 1959-63, Communications Affiliates, Inc., N.Y.C., 1960-61; member of the corporate staff, sr. v.p., asso. dir. J. Walter Thompson Co., N.Y.C., 1963—. Member Am. Marketing Association (vice pres. 1952), Copy Research Council, Advt. Research Found., Am. Assn. Advt. Agencies (standing com. on research), Am. Assn. Pub. Opinion Research. Clubs: Hasty Pudding of 1776, D. U., Lampoon, Harvard (N.Y.C.); Sleepy Hollow Country. Author: Dynamics of Mass Media. Home: 450 E 63d St New York City NY 10021 Office: 420 Lexington Av New York City NY 10017

ARMSTRONG, EDWARD GABRIEL, banker; b. Enfield, Conn., Sept. 16, 1897; s. G. Allingham and Harriet (Hurlburt) A.; B.S., Trinity Coll., 1921; m. Barbara Morrison Eaton, July 24, 1922; children—Edward A., Lucia (Mrs. Donald R. Williams, Jr.). With Lomas & Nettleton Co., New Haven, 1921-25; with Union & New Haven Trust Co., 1925-69, head trust dept., 1945-65, dir., 1947-69, sr. v.p., 1959-63, vice chmn. bd., chmn. trust com., 1963-69; chmn. trust bd. Union Trust Co., 1970—. Charter mem. New Haven Preservation Trust, also mem. com. standards; dir. Conn. League Hist. Socs, 1965-67. Mem. Conn. Bankers Assn. (v.p., exec. com., chmn. trust com. 1951-52), Soc. Colonial Wars Conn. (gov. 1968-70, dep. gov. gen. 1970—), New Haven Colony Hist. Soc., Antiquarian and Landmarks Soc., Psi Upsilon. Epicopalian (vestryman, past chmn. finance com.). Clubs: Lawn (pres. 1940-43), Graduate (New Haven). Home: 3 Briar Lane Hamden CT 06511 Office: 205 Church St New Haven CT 06502

ARMSTRONG, ELLIS LEROY, engr., govt. ofcl.; b. Cedar City, Utah, May 30, 1914; s. Leroy Smith and Mary Ada (Wood) A.; B.S. in Civil Engring., Utah State U., 1936, postgrad. Colo. State U.; Eng. D., Newark Coll. Engring., 1966; Sc.D. (hon.), So. Utah State U., 1971; m. Florine Clark, June 8, 1937; children—Ellis Bruce, Dale Clark, Larry Leroy, Elaine, Diane Kay, David Kent. Design, constrn. projects Western states U.S. Bur. Reclamation, 1936-45, charge design sect. on dam and hwy. work Engring. Center, Denver, 1945-47; charge of Trenton Dam Project, Neb., 1948-53; engr. mem. Egyptian-Am. Rural Improvement Commn., Cairo, also spl. cons. Egyptian Govt. on High Aswan Dam Project, 1953; project engr., dep. project mgr. St. Lawrence Power and Seaway Project, Power Authority State of N.Y., 1954-57; dir. hwys. State of Utah, 1957-58; U.S. commr. pub. roads Dept. Commerce, Washington, 1958-61; pres. Better Highways Information Found., 1961-62; sr. partner Porter, O'Brien & Armstrong, cons. engrs., 1962-65; pres. Porter, Armstrong, Ripa & Assos., 1965-68, Armstrong Assos., engrs. and cons., Salt Lake City, 1968—. Asst. regional dir. U.S. Bur. Reclamation, 1969-70; U.S. commr. reclamation Dept. Interior, Washington 1970—. Mem. of U.S. com. large dams World Power Conf. Adv. bd. Newark Coll. Engring. Recipient Distinguished Service award Utah State U., 1959, Royce J. Tipton award Am. Soc. C.E., 1970; named Profl. Engr. of Year, State of Utah, 1969, pub. works mem. of year, 1971. Registered profl. engr., Utah, N.Y., D.C., N.J., Me., Ariz., Vt., Nev., Cal. Fellow Am. Soc. C.E.; mem. of Nat. Soc. Profl. Engrs., Newark C. of C. (past dir.), Am. Concrete Inst., Am. Road Builders Assn. (life), Phi Kappa Phi, Chi Epsilon (nat. hon. mem.). Mem. Ch. of Jesus Christ of Latterday Saints. Rotarian. Author numerous articles on design and constrn., mgmt. earth dams, water resources and hwys. Home: 12821 Huntsman Way Potomac MD 20854 Office: Interior Bldg Bur Reclamation Washington DC 20240

ARMSTRONG, FRANK A., mgmt. exec.; b. Hillsdale, N.J., Dec. 19, 1921; s. Joseph M. and Mae (Parker) A.; B.S., Rutgers U.; postgrad. Princeton, N.Y.U.; m. Dorothy Armstrong, July 5, 1947; children—Mark, Christine, Michael. Mng. dir. Amos Parrish Co., N.Y.C., 1953-56; pres. Sales Communication, Inc., N.Y.C., 1956-60, Communications Affiliates, Inc., N.Y.C., 1960-62; exec. v.p., mgr. N.Y. office, chmn. exec. com. McCann-Erickson, Inc., 1962-68; pres. Moxie-Monarch-Nu Grape Co., 1968—. Lectr. marketing N.Y.U. Mem. Sales Promotion Execs. Assn., Direct Mail Advt. Assn., Internat. Advertisers Assn., Sales Execs. Club N.Y. (Speakers award). Author: Idea Tracking, 1960; The Modern Sales Manager's Secret Weapon, 1966. Home: 2950 Rivermead Dr NW Atlanta GA 30327 Office: 3742 Northeast Expressway Doraville GA 30340

ARMSTRONG, FRANK GOODELL, automobile co. exec.; b. Waukesha, Wis., Sept. 19, 1913; s. Howard G. and Frances (Seely) A.; student U. Wis., 1931-33; A.B., U. Mich., 1935; J.D., Detroit Coll. Law, 1946; m. Betty Van Dyne, June 27, 1936; children—David, Kirk, Judith. With Detroit Edison Co., 1935-41; dir. research Employers' Assn. Detroit, 1941-46; with Burroughs Corp., 1946- 63, v.p., 1959-63; v.p. Crown Zellerbach Corp., 1963-65; v.p. Indsl. Relations Counselors, Inc., 1965-66; v.p. Am. Motors Corp., Detroit, 1966—. Home: 629 Overbrook Rd Bloomfield Hills MI 48013 Office: 14250 Plymouth Rd Detroit MI 48232

ARMSTRONG, FREDERICK STEWART, Jr., corp. exec; b. Cleve., Sept. 22, 1908; s. Frederick Stewart and Adelaide Margaret (Koster) A.; diploma in commerce, Northwestern U., 1939; m. Mary Ann Kennedy, June 5, 1937; children—Julia Adelaide (Mrs. David J. Long), Jane Ann (Mrs. Philip L. Renowden), Patricia Kay (Mrs. Mark A. Davis), Catherine Marie. With Pullman Inc., Chgo., 1952-71, comptroller, 1959-71. C.P.A., Ill. Mem. Am. Inst. C.P.A.'s, Financial Execs. Inst.

ARMSTRONG, GEORGE ELLIS, univ. adminstr., surgeon; b. Lawrence Co., Ind., Aug. 4, 1900; s. Frank T. and Jennie G. (Norvell) A.; A.B., U. of Ind., 1922, M. D., 1925, LL.D., 1952; grad. Army Med. Sch., Med. Field Service Sch., 1927, Advanced Course, 1940; Command and Gen. Staff Sch., Ft. Leavenworth, Kan., 1941; m. Lillian T. Ott, Mar. 20, 1937; 1 son, George B. Intern, Letterman Gen. Hosp., San Francisco, 1925; med. officer, U.S. Army, 1926- 55; asst. chief, surg., Walter Reed Hosp., 1931-35; asst. chief Surg. Service, Fort Benning, Ga., 1935-37; asst. surgeon and chief, Surg. Service, Tienstsin, China, 1937-38; chief, Surg. Service, chief, venereal disease ward, Fort Stotsenburg, P.I., 1938-39; asst. theater surgeon, CBI, Jan.-June, 1944; theater surgeon, CBI, later surgeon China Theater, 1944-46; dep. surgeon gen. with rank of brig. gen. 1947, maj. gen., 1948, surgeon gen. army 1951-55; v.p. for med. affairs N.Y.U., 1955-69, also dir. of N.Y.U. Med. Center, Mem. Pres.' Health Resources Adv. Com.; med. adv. com. MEDICO: pres. Am. Bur. for Med. Aid to China; active Am. Emergency Com. for Tibetan Refugees; bd. dirs. Am.-Philippine Sci. Found. Decorated Legion of Merit, Am. Def. Service medal, Asiatic Pacific Campaign medal with three bronze stars, World War I and II victory medals, Army Commendation medal (U.S.); Cloud Banner, Hon. Nobility medal, Legion of Honor (China); Order of the Crown of Italy, Order of St. Maurice and St. Lazarus, Korean Order of Mil. Merit TAEGUK, French Medaille d'Honneur du Service de Sante Militarie d'Or. Fellow A.C.S., A.C.P.; mem. A.M. A., Am. Hosp. Assn., Am. Vet. Med. Assn. (hon), Am. Pharm. Assn. (hon.), Am. Assn. Surgery Trauma (hon.). Am. Found. Trop. Medicine (hon.), Internat. Coll. Surgeons (hon.), Am. Coll. Chest Physicians (hon.), Am. Coll. Hosp. Adminstrs. (hon.), Assn. Mil. Surgeons, Council Pan-Pacific Surg. Assn., Ind. Pub. Health Assn. (hon.), Brazilian Acad. Mil. Medicine (hon.), Nat. Resuscitation Soc. (pres.), N.Y. Medico-Surg. Soc., Nat. Health Council (dir., v.p.), N.Y.C. Hosp. Soc., Soc. Med. Cons. to Armed Forces, Nat. Bd. Med. Examiners, Phi Kappa Psi (exec. com. N.Y.U. alumni chpt.), Phi Rho Sigma, Alpha Omega Alpha, Scabbard and Blade, Mason (33 Shriner), Sojourner. Clubs: N.Y. University; Lotos. Home: Dane-Allen Beach Santa Rosa Beach, FL 32459.

ARMSTRONG, GEORGE LOWTHER, ins. co. exec.; b. Newcastle-on-Tyne, Eng., Mar. 21, 1910; s. John George and Else (Pedersen) A.; student Rutherford Coll., Newcastle, 1921-26; m. Gertrude Alice Smith, Aug. 19, 1950. Came to U.S., 1945. With Caldonian Ins. Co., Newcastle, Worcester, 1926-34, chief clk., 1934-39, asst. mgr., Calcutta, India, 1939-42, Eng. brs., 1946-47; pres. Caledonian Am. Ins. Co., Hartford, Conn., and chmn. U.S. bd. Caledonian Ins. Co., 1946-57; v.p. Peerless Ins. Co., 1957-58; v.p. and mgr. for Can., Continental Ins. Co., Fidelity Casualty Co., Niagara Ins. Co., 1958—, Dominion Ins. Corp., Royal Gen. Ins. Co. Can., 1966—. Served as lt. Royal Navy, 1942-45. Clubs: Royal Montreal Golf; St. George's Golf and Country. Home: 1 Darling Brook Crescent Islington Ontario Canada Office: 18 King St E Toronto Ontario Canada

ARMSTRONG, GEORGE ROBERT, utility exec.; b. Terre Haute, Ind., Oct. 6, 1898; s. Fred and Cornelia (Woolsey) A.; B.S., Rose Poly. Inst., 1921, D.Eng., 1969; m. Emma Thorne, May 20, 1930. Engr. constrn. Louisville Gas & Electric Co., 1922-29, gen. supt. constrn., 1929-39, gen. supt., 1939-48, exec. v.p., 1948-57, president, 1957-63, chmn. bd., 1963—; chmn. bd. Ohio Valley Transmission Corp.; v.p. Ind.-Ky. Electric Corp.; dir. East Central Nuclear Group, Ohio Valley Electric Corp., Cherokee Equity Corp.; dir. emeritus First Nat. Bank of Louisville, Ky. Trust Co., 1st Ky. Co. Mem. Louisville Zoo Commn., Louisville and Jefferson County Air Bd. Bd. dirs. Cumberland Coll., Leabon, Tenn., Louisville Indsl. Found. Served with U.S. Army, World War I. Mem. Am. Inst. E.E., Engrs. and Architects Club. Home: 1412 Willow Av Louisville KY 40204 Office: 311 W Chestnut St Louisville KY 40202

ARMSTRONG, GRANT, lawyer; b. Raymond, Wash., Sept. 30, 1907; s. Oren G. and Clara (Knutson) A.; LL.B., U. Wash., 1929; m. Elbertine Adams, Jan. 25, 1933. Admitted to Wash. bar, 1930; practice in Chehalis, 1930—; mem. firm Murray, Armstrong and Vander Stoep. 1946—. Dir. Pacific Nat. Bank Wash., Seattle . Bd. regents U. Wash., 1950-57. Served to lt. comdr. USNR, 1943-46. Fellow Am. Coll. Trial Lawyers, Am. Bar Found; mem. Am. (state del. 1965—), Wash. (bd. govs. 1958-61, pres. 1964-65) bar assns., Sigma Nu, Phi Delta Phi, Order of the Coif (honorary). Republican. Episcopalian. Rotarian. Clubs: Seattle Golf; Tacoma. Home: 1080 Glen Rd Chehalis WA 98532 Office: 969 Pacific Av Chehalis WA 98532

ARMSTRONG, HAMILTON FISH, editor, author; b. N.Y.C., Apr. 7, 1893; s. D. Maitland (artist; consul gen. to Italy) and Helen (Neilson) A.; A.B., Princeton, 1916, Litt.D., 1961; LL.D., Brown U., 1942, Columbia, 1963; Litt.D., Yale, 1957, Harvard, 1963; Dr. Hon. Causa, U. Basel, 1960; m. Helen Mac G. Byrne, Dec. 31, 1918; 1 dau., Gregor; m. 2d, Carman Barnes, Dec. 27, 1945; m. 3rd, Christa Von Tippelskirch, July 11, 1951. Commd. 2d lt. U.S. Army, Oct. 26, 1917, and assigned 22nd Inf.; 1st lt., 17, 1917; apptd. mil. attaché to Serbian War Mission in U.S., 1917; apptd. acting mil. attaché, Am. legation, Belgrad, Serbia, Dec. 1918; mem. editorial staff N.Y. Evening Post, 1919-21; spl. corr. in Eastern, Europe, 1921-22; mng. editor Fgn. Affairs (quar. rev.) 1922-28, editor 1928—; mem. adv. com. on Post-War Fgn. Problems, State Dept., 1942-44; spl. asst. to U.S. ambassador in London, with personal rank of minister, 1944; spl. adviser to sec. of state, 1945; adviser U.S. delegation, San Francisco Conf., 1945; dir. Council Fgn. Relations, Inc. Trustee N.Y. Soc. Library (pres. 1944-58), Woodrow Wilson Found. (v.p. 1928-30; pres. 1935-37); mem. President's Adv. Com. on Polit. Refugees. Decorated Order of St. Sava, 1918, Order of White Eagle (with swords), 1919, (both Serbian); Order of Crown (Rumania), 1924; Comdr. Legion of Honor (France), 1947; Order of White Lion (Czechoslovakia), 1947. Mem. Am. Philos. Soc. Club: Century. Editor: Book of New York Verse, 1918; (with W.L. Langer) Foreign Affairs Bibliography, 1933; The Foreign Policy of the Powers, 1935; The Foreign Affairs Reader, 1947. Author: New Balkans, 1926; Where the East Begins, 1929; Hitler's Reich-the First Phase, 1933; Europe Between Wars? 1934; (with A.W. Dulles) Can We Be Neutral? 1936, Can America Stay Neutral? 1939; We or They, 1937; When There Is No Peace, 1939; Chronology of Failure, 1940; The Calculated Risk, 1947; Tito and Goliath, 1951; Those Days 1963; Peace and Counterpeace: From Wilson to Hitler, 1971. Contbr. to mags. Home: 58 W 10th St New York City NY 10011 Office: 58 E 68th St New York City NY 10021

ARMSTRONG, HARRIS, ret. architect; b. Edwardsville, Ill., Apr. 6, 1899; s. Henry Clair and Leone (Weir) A.; spl. student Ohio State U., 1924-25; m. Louise McClelland, Jan. 1, 1926; children—Joan, Jeffrey, John Harris. Pvt. practice architecture, Kirkwood, Mo., 1931-69; executed Shanley Bldg., 1934, Grant Med. Clinic, 1938, Am. Stove Co. Adminstrn. Bldg., 1948, Cancer Research Labs., Clayton br. dept. store, adminstrv. group for McDonnell Aircraft Corp., St. Louis Airport, U.S. Consulate at Basra, Iraq. Design cons. G.S.A. Bldg., Kansas City, Mo. Chmn. St. Louis County Bldg.Com. Recipient silver medal Paris Expn., 1936, award of merit Epiphany Ch., Kirkwood, Mo., 1961. Fellow A.I.A. Home: 200 Sappington Rd St Louis MO 63122 Office: 180 S Sappington Rd St Louis MO 63122

ARMSTRONG, HENRY BOLDEN, III, ins. co. exec.; b. New Haven, Dec. 12, 1919; s. Henry Bolden and Mabel I. (Finley) A.; grad. Roxbury Sch., 1937; B.A., with honors, Yale, 1941, LL.B., 1943; m. Frances Porter Farsworth, May 11, 1968; children by previous marriage—Christopher Story, Mary Cameron. Admitted to N.Y. bar, 1946, Conn. bar, 1947; with Sullivan & Cromwell, N.Y.C., 1946-47; with Travelers Ins. Cos., Hartford, Conn., 1947—, counsel, 1963-66, asso. gen. counsel, 1966-69, gen. counsel, 1969—; dir. J. Wadson Beach, Inc., Caribbean Atlantic Life Ins. Co. Chmn. Farmington (Conn.) Republican Town Com., 1966-67. Served to 1st lt. AUS, 1944-46. Mem. Conn., Hartford bar assns. Republican. Conglist. Home: 290 Mountain Spring Rd Farmington CT 06032 Office: 1 Tower Sq Hartford CT 06115

ARMSTRONG, HENRY CONNER, Canadian diplomat; b. Winnipeg, Man., Can., June 16, 1925; s. William Arthur Laird and Archena May (Conner) A.; B.Sc. in Metall. Engring., Queen's U., Kingston, Ont., 1949; M.B.A. (Kresge fellow), U. Toronto, 1954; diploma in Indsl. Adminstrn., Centre D'Etudes Industrielles, Geneva, Switzerland, 1958; m. Barbara Fay Jackson, May 20, 1950; children—Barbara E., Nancy M., Scott J. Various sales and marketing positions Aluminum Co. of Can., Ltd., 1954-64; commodity officer Dept. Trade and Commerce, Ottawa, Ont., 1964-66; comml. counsellor Canadian Embassy, Washington, 1966—. Tchr. course in prodn. mgmt. Carleton U., Ottawa, 1966. Served with RCAF and Royal Navy, 1944-45. Mem. Assn. Profl. Engrs. Ont., Canadian Inst. Mining and Metallurgy, Am. Soc. Metals. Methodist. Club: University (Washington). Home: 9710 Carriage Rd Kensington MD 20795 Office: Canadian Embassy 1746 Massachusetts Av NW Washington DC 20036

ARMSTRONG, HENRY IRWIN, Jr., lawyer; b. Detroit, July 19, 1887; s. Henry Irwin and Sarah (Aikman) A.; A.B., U. Mich., 1909; LL.B., Havard, 1912. Admitted to Mich. bar, 1912, since practiced in Detroit; mem. firm Bodman, Longley, Bogle, Armstrong & Dahling. Served to capt., inf. U.S. Army, 1917-18. Mem. Am., Mich., Detroit bar assns., Phi Beta Kappa, Psi Upsilon. Clubs.: Detroit, Detroit Athletic, Detroit Boat, University (Detroit). Home: 415 Burns Dr Detroit MI 48214 Office: Buhl Bldg Detroit MI 48226

ARMSTRONG, HERBERT DEUEL, oil co. exec.; b. San Rafael, Cal., Sept. 20, 1907; s. Thomas S. and Nancy E. (Deuel) A.; J.D., U. Cal., 1933; m. Muriel H. Cunningham, June 27, 1931; 1 dau., Alice Lynn. Admitted to Cal. Bar, 1933; asso. Agnew & Boekel, San Francisco, 1934-39; mgr. credit dept., asst. cashier Fed. Res. Bank, San Francisco, 1939-43, dir., 1966—; asst. treas. Standard Oil Co. of Cal., 1943-47, asst. to chmn. bd., 1947, now treas.; treas. Chevron Oil Co. Home: 125 Lakeview Dr Woodside CA 94062 Office: 225 Bush St San Francisco CA 94104

ARMSTRONG, HERBERT STOKER, univ. dean; b. Toronto, Ont., Can., Nov. 23, 1915; s. George Readie and Ethel (Stoker) A.; B.A., U. Toronto, 1938, M.A., 1939; Ph.D., U. Chgo., 1941; D.Sc., McMaster U., 1967; m. Kathleen Halbert, Sept. 6, 1941; children—Catherine, Margaret. Mem. faculty McMaster U., 1941-62, prof. geology, 1948-62, dean arts and scis., 1960- 62; dean sci. U. Alta., 1962-63, v.p. acad., 1963-64; pres. U. Alta. at Calgary, 1964-66; pres., vice chancellor U. Calgary, 1966-68; dean grad. studies and research U. Guelph (Ont.), 1968—; from asst. to field geologist Ont. Dept. Mines, summers 1937-46, 55, 56. Mem. bd. mgmt. Art Gallery Hamilton, 1949-62, pres., 1957-59; mem. council Hamilton Assn., 1946-53, pres., 1951-52; chmn. camp com. Hamilton YMCA, 1958-61, bd. dirs., 1961-62; bd. dirs. Hamilton Philharmonic Orch., 1959- 62, Edmonton Symphony Soc., 1963-64, Calgary Philharmonic, Fellow Royal Soc. Can., Royal Canadian Geog. Soc., Geol. Assn. Can. (charter); mem. Canadian Geol. Fedn., Canadian Inst. Mining and Metallurgy, Alta. Soc. Petroleum Geologists, Geol. Soc. Finland, Geochem. Soc. Mem. United Ch. Can. Mason. Contbr. articles to profl. jours, Home: 2 Ardmay Crescent Guelph Ontario Canada

ARMSTRONG, JAMES CLIFFORD, advt. exec.; b. Jackson, Tenn., Feb. 15, 1918; s. James Clifford and Alice Rebecca (Diffee) A.; student U. Tenn., 1936-41; m. Phyllis Frankland, Dec. 29, 1953; children—Leonard, Todd, Alice, Cliff. With Gross Advt., Chgo., 1945-46; with Armour & Co., Chgo., 1946-50, advt. and sales promotion mgr. canned foods div., 1948-50; successively marketing plans writer, account service, account mgmt. N.W. Ayer & Son,

1950-58; with Young & Rubicam, Los Angeles, 1958-70, v.p., 1960-64, gen. mgr., Los Angeles, 1962-68, sr. v.p. in charge West Coast, 1968-70; owner Armstrong & Co., San Marino, Cal., 1970—. Mem. Am. Assn. Advt. Agys. (past gov. So. Cal. council), Los Angeles C. of C., Advt. Club Los Angeles. Episcopalian. Club: Jonathan (Los Angeles). Home: 1375 Pasqualito Dr San Marino CA 91108 Office: 475 Huntington Dr San Marino CA 91108

ARMSTRONG, JAMES ISBELL, coll. pres.; b. Princeton, N.J., Apr. 20, 1919; s. William Park and Rebekah Sellars (Purves) A.; grad. Taft Sch., Watertown, Conn., 1937; A.B., Princeton, 1941, Ph.D., 1949, LL.D., 1967; L.H.D. (hon.), Bates Coll., 1967; Litt.D. (hon.), Grinnell College; m. Carol Penrhyn Aymar, Nov. 1, 1942; children—Carol Park, James Isbell, Elizabeth Logan. Instr. classics Ind. U., 1949-50; mem. faculty Princeton, 1947-48, 50-63, asso. prof. classics, 1960-63, asst. and asso. dean Grad. Sch., 1958-62; pres. Middlebury Coll., 1963—. Pres. New Eng. Colls. Fund, 1966-68. Trustee Princeton Theological Seminary, 1964-70, Miss Fine's Sch., Princeton, N.J., 1956-63, Westminster Found., 1953-63, Hazen Found., 1967—; alumni trustee Princeton U. Served to captain AUS, 1941-46, 51-52. Decorated Bronze Star; Woodrow Wilson Nat. fellow, 1946-47; sr. fellow Am. Acad. in Rome, 1955-56. Mem. Am. Philol. Assn., Vt. High Edn. Council, New Eng. Assn. Colls. and Secondary Schs., Inc. (commn. on institutions on higher edn.), Phi Beta Kappa. Presbyn. (elder). Clubs: Princeton, University (N.Y.C.). Home: 3 South St Middlebury VT 05753

ARMSTRONG, JAMES SINCLAIR, banker, Lawyer; b; N.Y.C., Oct. 15, 1915; s. Sinclair Howard and Katharine Martin (LeBoutillier) A.; grad. Milton (Mass.) Acad., 1934; A.B. cum laude Harvard, 1938, LL.B., 1941; postgrad. Northwestern Univ., 1942-44, 46-48; married Joan Shepard Miller, 1960; 5 children by previous marriage. Admitted to Ill. bar, 1941, N.Y. bar 1959; asso. firm Isham, Lincoln & Beale, Chgo., 1941-45, 46-49, mem., 1950-53; mem. SEC. Washington, 1953-57, chmn. commn., 1955-57; asst. sec. navy for financial mgmt., also comptroller Dept. Navy, Washington, 1957-59; exec. v.p. U.S. Trust Co. of N.Y., 1959—; dir. Gen. Adjustment Bur., Inc., Broadway Savs. Bank, Riegel Paper Corp., N.Y.C., Berger Brunswrg Corp., Los Angeles, Trustee, treas. N.Y.U. Medical Center; trustee Samuel Rubin Found., N.Y.C, Ch. Pension Fund, N.Y.C., The Gunnery Sch., Washington, Conn. Fellow Pierpont Morgan Library. Served as lt. (j.g.) USNR, 1945-46. Mem. Am. Bar Assn., Am. Law Inst., Am. Bankers Assn., Am. Soc. Corporate Secs., Assn. Am. Railroads, Assn. Bar City of N.Y., Fgn. Policy Assn. (asso.), Nat. Trust for Scotland (Edinburgh), New Eng. Soc., Navy League U.S. (life), N.Y. C. of C., N.Y. Hist. Soc. (life), Pilgrims U.S., St. Andews Soc. State N.Y. (life, standing com.), Huguenot Soc. Am., St. Nicholas Soc. City N.Y., Soc. Colonial Wars of N.Y. Clubs: Church, Century, Down Town, Bond, Harvard, (N.Y.C.); Chevy Chase (Md.); Legal, Saddle and Cycle (Chgo.); Capitol Hill, Metropolitan (Washington). Home: 211 E 18th St New York City NY 10003 Office: 45 Wall St New York City NY 10005

ARMSTRONG, JOHN ALEXANDER, educator, polit. scientist; b. St. Augustine, Fla., May 4, 1922; s. John Alexander and Maria (Hernandez) A.; Ph.B., U. Chgo., 1948, M.A., 1949; student U. Frankfurt (Germany), 1949-50; Ph.D., Columbia, 1953; m. Annette Taylor, June 14, 1952; children—Janet Ann, Carol Louise, Kathryn Marie. Research analyst War Documentation Project, Alexandria, Va., 1951, 53-54; asst. prof. internat. relations U. Denver, 1952; vis. asst. prof. internat. relations Columbia, 1957; mem. faculty U. Wis., Madison, 1954—, prof. polit. sci., 1960—, exec. sec. Russian area studies program, 1959- 63, 64-65, acting dir. Western European area studies program, 1966-67. Mem. adv. panel European affairs State Dept., 1966-69. Served with AUS, 1942-46; ETO. Guggenheim fellow, 1967-68. Mem. Am. Assn. Advancement Slavic Studies (pres. 1965-67), Council Fgn. Relations, Am., Midwest polit. sci. assns., Phi Beta Kappa. Author: Ukrainian Nationalism, 2d edit., 1963; The Soviet Bureaucratic Elite, 2d edit., 1966; The Politics of Totalitarianism, 1961; Ideology, Politics and Government in the Soviet Union, 2d edit., 1967. Editor: Soviet Partisans in World War II, 1964. Home: 2118 Chamberlain St Madison WI 53705

ARMSTRONG, JOHN ARCHIBALD, oil co. exec.; b. Dauphin, Man., Can., Mar. 24, 1917; s. Herbert H. and Louisa I. (McDonald) A.; B.Sc. in Geology, U. Man., 1937; B.Sc. in Chem. Engring., Queen's U., 1942; m. June Keith, Oct. 7, 1943; children—David Duncan, Douglas Keith, Willard Drew, With Imperial Oil Ltd., 1940—, gen. mgr. producing dept. now exec. v.p., dir.: asst. coordinator producing coordination dept. Standard Oil Co. (N.J.), 1959; dir. Alta. Gas Trunk Line Co. Ltd., 1958-59, Home: 14 Sandfield Rd Willowdale, Canada. Office: 111 St Clair Av W Toronto 7 Ontario Canada

ARMSTRONG, JOHN CHACE, indsl. engr.; b. Rochester, N.Y., Nov. 25, 1918; s. George Simpson and Dorothy (Miller) A.; B.A., Williams Coll, 1940; B.S. in Chem. Engring., N.Y.U., 1942; m. Helga Evensen, Dec. 28, 1950; children—Karin C., Christine F., Elizabeth Anne. Research chemist, indsl. engr. E.I. duPont de Nemours & Co., Niagara Falls, N.Y., 1942-46; cons. indsl. engr. Geo. S. Armstrong & Co., Inc., N.Y.C., 1946—, pres., 1961—, also dir. Pres. alumni assn. Coll. Arts and Scis., N.Y.U., 1969. Trustee, treas. Stoneleigh-Burnham Sch., Greenfield, Mass.; bd. dirs. Greenwich Community Chest. Mem. Am. Chem. Soc., Am. Inst. Cons. Engrs., Am. Inst. Chem. Engrs., N.Y. Soc. Security Analysts, Zeta Psi, Conglist. Clubs: Williams (N.Y.C.); Riverside Yacht; Chemical. Home: 35 Lockwood Av Old Greenwich CT 06870 Office: 2 Park Av New York City NY 10016

ARMSTRONG, JOHN HENRY, mgmt. cons.; b. Kewanee, Ill., Sept. 15, 1908; s. Robert and Mary Esther (Johnston) A.; B.S., U. Ill., 1931, M.S., 1932; m. Charlotte Theodora Baer, June 10, 1935; children—John Henry, Robert Elliot, Beverly Joyce. With A.T. Kearney & Co. (now A. T. Kearney & Co., Inc.), Chgo., 1935—, became partner, 1949, now v.p., dir.; partner A.T. Kearney Personnel Services; v.p., dir. A.T. Kearney Internat., Inc., A.T. Kearney, G.m.b.H.; dir. A.T. Kearney, S.p.A., A.T. Kearney, Ltd., Norcross & Partners, Ltd. Mem. Ill. C. of C., Am. Mgmt. Assn., Am. Marketing Assn., Tau Beta Pi, Kappa Delta Rho. Republican. Presbyn. Clubs: Union League, Executive (Chgo.). Home: 288 Vine Av Highland Park IL 60035 Office: 100 S Wacker Dr Chicago IL 60606

ARMSTRONG, JOHN KENASTON, mfr.; b. Springfield, Mass., Sept. 2, 1929; s. Ralph A. and Avice E. (Bliss) A.; B.A. (Olin scholar), Wesleyan U., Middletown, Conn., 1950; M.B.A. (Baker scholar), Harvard, 1956; m. Katharine Kipp, Dec. 17, 1955; children—Leigh, Kipp. Asst. controller Ford div. Ford Motor Co., Dearborn, Mich., 1958-64, dir. market representation, 1964-68; financial and group v.p. Keene Corp., N.Y.C., 1968—; chmn. bd. Fed. Home Loan Bank N.Y., United Chem. Corp. Served with Signal Corps, AUS, 1950-53. Mem. Harvard Bus. Sch. Consulting Vols., Phi Beta Kappa. Home: 56 Winfield Lane New Canaan CT 06840 Office: 345 Park Av New York City NY 10022

ARMSTRONG, JOHN WALLACE, contractor; b. Grand Rapids, Mich., June 16, 1905; s. Wallace A. and Grace H. (Laubach) A.; B.S., U. Mich., 1926; m. Virginia C. Holler, Aug. 26, 1931; children—Margaret Ann, Gail Elizabeth. Constrn. engr. J.A. Utley Co., gen. contractors, Detroit, 1926-36; v.p. Darin & Armstrong, Inc., gen. contractor, Detroit, 1936-53, pres., 1954—; dir. Mich. Mut. Liability Ins. Co., 1953—. Bd. dirs. Detroit YMCA, United Found., Detroit. Mem. Asso. Gen. Contractors Am. (pres. Detroit 1955- 56). Club: Detroit Golf. Home: 18 Oakland Park Pleasant Ridge MI 48069 Office: 2041 Fenkell St Detroit MI 48238

ARMSTRONG, JON STEPHEN, banker; b. Elkhart, Ind., Jan. 23, 1938; s. Lewis S. and Marcella (Kern) A.; B.S. in Bus., Ind. U., 1960; m. Mary E. Conrad, June 13, 1959; children—Elizabeth Ann, Wendy Suzanne. Sr. credit analyst Nat. Bank Detroit, 1960-63; with St. Joseph Bank & Trust Co., S. Bend, Ind., 1963- 68; sr. v.p.; 1966-68; pres., dir. St. Joseph Valley Bank, Elkhart, 1968- -, SJV Corp., Elkhart, 1968—. Trustee Elkhart Community Schs., 1969, v.p., 1970. Adv. bd. Goshen (Ind.) Coll., 1969—. Recipient Distinguished Service award S. Bend Jaycees, 1967. Distinguished Service award Elkhart Jaycees, 1970. Mem. Greater Elkhart C. of C. (pres., dir. 1971). Home: 3 Kim Ct Elkhart IN 46514 Office: 431 S Main St Elkhart IN 46514

ARMSTRONG, MARSHALL SMITH, accountant, assn. exec.; b. Indpls., June 13, 1914; s. William A. and L. Fern (Smith) A.; ed. Ind. U., Butler U.; m. Marjorie L. Thompson, Sept. 24, 1939; children—David F., Julie Beth (Mrs. Philip Alexander), Kristi Lee. Mng. partner Geo. S. Olive & Co., Indpls., 1942—; lectr. Ind. U., also Am. Inst. Banking, 1948-55. Pres. Am. Inst. C.P.A.'s, 1970-71. Mem. adv. bd. St. Francis Hosp., Indpls., 1969-72; pres. exec. devel. program Ind. U., 1954-55; adv. com. Ind. Mgmt. Inst., 1956-57. Mem. Am. Group of C.P.A. Firms (charter chmn. bd. govs.), Ind. Assn. C.P.A.'s (pres. 1961-62). Mem. Christian Ch. Contbr. articles profl. jours. Home: 5381 Shorewood Dr Indianapolis IN 46220 Office: 320 N Meridian St Indianapolis IN 46204

ARMSTRONG, MARVIN DOUGLAS, biochemist; b. Wilmington, N.C., Apr. 15, 1918; s. Marvin Dolphus and Marie (Curry) A.; B.S., U. S.C., 1938; M.S., U. Ill., 1939, Ph.D., 1941; m. M. Josephine Stahl, Feb. 28, 1946; children—Penelope, Joel, Peter, Douglas, Alan. Research asst. dept. biochemistry Cornell U. Med. Coll., 1941-42, 46; asst. research prof. biochemistry U. Utah, 1946-51, asso. research prof., 1951-57; chmn. biochemistry dept. Fels Research Inst., Yellow Springs, O., 1957—. Cons. metabolism and nutrition, metabolism study sects. NIH, USPHS, 1957-60. Served to lt. USNR, 1942-46. Decorated Air medal (Navy), D.F.C. Mem. A.A.A.S., Am. Chem. Soc., Am. Soc. Biol. Chemists, Biochem. Soc., Soc. Exptl. Biology and Medicine, Phi Beta Kappa, Sigma Xi, Phi Kappa Phi, Alpha Chi Sigma. Home: 139 E Limestone St Yellow Springs OH 45387 Office: Fels Research Inst Yellow Springs OH 45387

ARMSTRONG, NEIL A., astronaut, educator; b. Wapakoneta, O., Aug. 5, 1930; s. Stephen Armstrong; B.S. in Aero. Engring., Purdue U., 1955; M.S.A.E., U. So. Cal.; m. Janet Shearon; children—Eric, Mark. With Lewis Flight Propulsion Lab., NACA, 1955; then aero. research pilot for NACA, later NASA, High Speed Flight Sta., Edwards, Cal.; astronaut Manned Spacecraft Center, NASA, Houston, 1962-70; command pilot Gemini 8, March 1966; comdr. Apollo II, 1st man to walk on moon, 1969; dep. asso. adminstr. (aeros.) office Advanced Research and Tech., Hdqrs. NASA, Washington, 1970-71; prof. aerospace engring. U. Cin., 1971—. Served as aviator with USN, 1949-52; Korea. Recipient Octave Chanute award Inst. Aero. Scis., 1962, Presdl. medal for freedom, 1969, Exceptional Service medal NASA, Hubbard Gold medal Nat. Geographic Soc., 1970, Kitty Hawk Meml. award, 1969, Pere Marquette medal, 1969, Arthur S. Fleming award, 1970, numerous others. Fellow Am. Inst. Aeros. and Astronautics (Astronautics award 1966), Am. Astronaut. Soc., Soc. Exptl. Test Pilots; mem. Soaring Soc. Am. Office: Coll Engring U Cin Cincinnati OH 45221

ARMSTRONG, OLIVER WENDELL, oil co. exec.; b. Mound Valley, Kan., July 13, 1919; s. Charles Eugene and Elva (Williams) A.; student Kan. State U., 1937-40; B.S., Kan. State Coll., Pittsburg, 1941; m. Betty Jane Nichols, June 24, 1945; 1 dau., Julia Anne. With Phillips Petrolium Co., 1944—, div. credit mgr., Chgo., 1951-55, regional credit mgr., Bartlesville, Okla., 1955-59, adminstrv. asst., 1959-60, asst. treas., 1960-65, sec., treas., 1965—. Mem. Am. Petroleum Inst., Financial Execs. Inst. Republican. Presbyn. Elk, Mason (Shriner, Jester), Rotarian. Home: 2000 Skyline Dr Bartlesville OK 74003 Office: Phillips Bldg Bartlesville OK 74003

ARMSTRONG, OSCAR VANCE, fgn. service officer; b. Hsuchowfu, China, Apr. 19, 1918 (parents Am. citizens); s. Oscar V. and Lena (Stutzman) A.; B.S., Davidson Coll., 1939; m. Camilla Sorley, June 15, 1945; children—Stephen V., Brian C. Engaged in ins. bus., 1939-41; joined U.S. Fgn. Service, 1946; vice consul, Canton, 1946-47, Peiping, 1947-49, Saigon, 1950, Singapore, 1950- 52; consul, Kuala Lumpur, Malaya, 1953-55, Hong Kong, 1955-57; div. chief State Dept., Washington, 1957-61; assigned Nat. War Coll., 1961-62; 1st sec. Am. embassy, London, Eng., 1962-64; Am. consulate gen., Hong Kong, 1964-66; assigned State Dept., 1966-68; dep. chief mission, Taipei, 1968-71; polit. adviser Comdr.-in-chief Pacific, 1971—. Served to 1st lt. pilot, USAAF, 1941-45; prisoner of war, Germany, 1943-45. Mem. Phi Beta Kappa. Office: Polit Adviser Comdr in Chief Pacific Honolulu HI

ARMSTRONG, PHILIP BROWNELL, med. educator; b. Rutherford, N.J., Mar. 26, 1898; s. Samuel Eugene and Isabella Augusta (Gott) A.; B.S., Mass. State Coll., 1921; M.D., Cornell U., 1926; m. Marion Louise Schmuck, Sept. 7, 1932; children—Peter Brownell, Samuel Currie. Instr. Cornell U., 1926-28, asst. prof., 1928-37; Rockefeller fellow Cambridge U., Sir William Dunn Inst. Bichem., 1934-35; prof. anatomy U. Ala. Sch. Med., 1937-38; prof. anatomy State U. N.Y., Syracuse, 1938-69, prof. emeritus, 1969—. Anatomist, Nat. Bd. Med. Examiners, 1939-55; clk. Corp. Marine Biol. Lab., 1940-42, trustee, 1946—, dir., 1950- 66, pres. corp., 1966-67; dir. Gen. Biol. Supply House: mem. corp. Woods Hole Oceanographic Instn., 1950—. Mem. Fulbright Fellowship com. NRC, 1960. Mem. Am. Zool. Soc., Am. Anat. Assn., Am. Physiol. Soc., Harvey Soc., Sigma Xi, Phi Sigma Kappa, Nu Sigma Nu, Alpha Omega Alpha. Contbr. articles on exptl. embryology and physiology on original research in 45 publs. Home: 1338 Westmoreland Av Syracuse NY 13210

ARMSTRONG, ROBERT BAKER, textile co. exec.; b. Montgomery, Pa., July 5, 1914; s. Robert Griffey and Savilla (Baker) A.; B.S. in Econs., U.Pa., 1936; M.A., 1939; m. Elizabeth Brownell Nicely, June 8, 1940; children—Robert Nicely, Richard Brownell, Bruce Griffey. Research asst. indsl. research dept. U. Pa., 1936-39; instr. econs. Gettysburg Coll., 1939-41; economist OPA, 1942- 43, prize exec. textile br., 1946-47; mgr. bus. analysis dept. N. Am. Rayon Corp., also Am. Bemberg Corp., 1947-49; with Am. Enka Corp. (N.C.), 1949—, asst. v.p. mfg., 1957-60, treas. 1960—, v.p., 1969—, also dir. Cons. OPS, 1950-51. Mem. bd. Montreat Anderson Coll., Montreat, N.C., Highland Hosp., Asheville, N.C. Served to lt. (s.g.) USNR, 1943- 46. Mem. Soc. Advancement Mgmt., Nat. Assn. Bus. Economists. Presbyn. Mason, Rotarian (bd. dirs. Asheville). Clubs: University (N.Y.C.); Biltmore Forest Country and Mountain City (Asheville). Home: 23 Amherst Rd Asheville NC 28803 Office: Am Enka Corp Enka NC 28728

ARMSTRONG, ROBERT DOUGLAS, mining co. exec.; b. Ottawa, Ont., Apr. 25, 1916; s. William Allan and Jennie (Berry) A.; B. Commerce, Queen's U., 1937; chartered accountant, 1941; m. Dorothea Christine Fairleigh, Dec. 29, 1943; children—Robert Michael, Reginald Brock, Barbara Elizabeth, Robert Douglas II. With Price Waterhouse & Co., C.P.A.'s, Toronto, 1937-41, Imperial Oil Ltd., Toronto, 1941-50, A. V. Roe Can., 1951-53; comptroller Canadian Nat. Rys., Montreal, 1953-56, v.p., 1956-59; with Chrysler Corp., 1959-62; pres. Chrysler Leasing Corp., 1962-64; pres. Canadian Found. Co., Ltd. Toronto, 1964-66; pres., chief exec. officer Rio Algom Mines Ltd., Toronto, 1966—. Served with Canadian Army, World War II. Home: 30 Glenorchy Rd Don Mills Ontario Canada Office: 120 Adelaide St W Toronto 1 Ontario Canada

ARMSTRONG, ROBERT MARKLE, sugar refinery exec.; b. Oklahoma City, Apr. 28, 1908; s. Oscar Raymond and Cora (Markle) A.; B.S., Tex. A. and M. Coll., 1930; m. Louise Z. Armstrong, May 2, 1936; children—Robert David, Marguerite Jean, John Markle. With Westinghouse Electric & Mfg. Co., Pitts., Phila., also Mansfield, O., 1930-37; sales rep. W. W. Overton & Co., sugar brokers, Dallas, 1937-42; with Imperial Sugar Co., Sugar Land, Tex., 1946—, now president, director; v.p. Ft. Bend Utilities Co., Sugar Land, 1953- -. Served as capt. Signal Corps, AUS, 1942-46. Mem. Tex. Mfrs. Assn. (v.p., director). Presbyterian (elder). Lion. Clubs: Riverbend Country (Sugar Land); Fort Bend Country; Petroleum, Fork (Houston). Home: 1 Cleveland Dr Sugar Land TX 77478 Office: Imperial Sugar Co Sugar Land TX 77478

ARMSTRONG, ROBERT PLANT, editor; b. Wheeling, W.Va., May 19, 1919; s. Clarence Warren and Dorothy Johanna (Green) A.; B.A., U. Ariz., 1944; M.A., U. Ia., 1946; Ph.D., Northwestern U., 1957. Traveler, Houghton Mifflin & Co., 1945-46; field editor Harper and Bros., 1956-58; editor Alfred A Knopf, N.Y.C., 1958-59; dir. U. Ariz. Press, 1959-60; dir. Northwestern U. Press, 1960—, prof. Coll. Arts and Scis., 1967—; vis. prof. art history State U. N.Y., Buffalo, summer 1970; vis. curator African art Buffalo Mus. Sci., summer 1970. Served with USNR, 1940-43. Fellow African Studies Assn., Am. Anthrop. Assn.; mem. Assn. Am. Univ. Presses, Modern Lang. Assn., Assn. Am. U. Profs. Author: The Affecting Presence: An Essay in Humanistic Anthropology, 1971, Forms and Processes in Africa, 1970. Home: 1625 Ridge Av Evanston IL 60201 Office: 1735 Benson Evanston IL 60201

ARMSTRONG, ROBERT THEXTON, chemist, chem. co. exec.; b. Chadron, Neb., Dec. 27, 1909; s. William D. and Alice (Cole) A.; B.S., Mass. Inst. Tech., 1931, Ph.D., 1935; m. Jane Botsford, July 3, 1960; 1 son, Robert Thexton. Teaching asst. chemistry Mass. Inst. Tech., 1928-35, instr., 1935-37; research on synthetic rubber, polymers, rubber chems. U.S. Rubber Co., 1937-44; research on tire cord N.Am. Rayon Corp., 1944-46; fiber devel., prodn. control Celanese Corp. Am., N.Y.C., 1946-51, asso. dir. research, 1952- 53, tech. dir. textile div., 1953-56, v.p., tech. dir., 1956—, sr. v.p. research, 1967—; dir. de Vegh Mut. Fund, Inc. Trustee, So. Vt. Art Center; bd. govs. N.C. Research Triangle Inst., 1955—. Mem. Am. Chem. Soc., Soc. Chem. Industry, Sigma Xi. Contbr. sci. papers to profl. publs. Patentee synthetic polymers and rubber chems. Home: High Meadows Manchester Center VT 05255 Office: 522 Fifth Av New York City NY 10036

ARMSTRONG, THOMAS GEORGE, advt. agy. exec.; b. Boston, June 28, 1931; s. Thomas George and Harriet (Hastings) A.; B.A., Colgate U., 1952; m. Martha Allen, Mar. 24, 1956; 1 dau., Melissa Woods. Trainee, Richardson-Merrill, 1952-56; exec. v.p. internat. operations, dir. Grey Advt., Inc., N.Y.C., 1956-71; sr. v.p. J. Walter Thompson Co., 1971—; chmn. Grey & Internat. Partners. Sec., Colgate U. Alumni Class, 1952-67. Served to 1st lt., arty. AUS, 1953-56. Mem. Internat. Advt. Assn. (dir. at large). Episcopalian. Clubs: Westchester Country (Rye, N.Y.); Wentworth (Eng.). Home: 22 Althea Lane Larchmont NY 10538 Office: 875 N Michigan Av Chicago IL 60611

ARMSTRONG, VICTOR, broadcasting exec.; b. Pauls Valley, Okla., June 24, 1921; s. Henry Harrison and Rea (Baker) A.; 1 dau., Valorie Field. Advt. mgr. of Consol. Vultee Aircraft Corp., 1946-48; account exec. J. Walter Thompson Co., N.Y.C., San Francisco, Detroit, 1949-53; v.p. Kenyon & Eckhardt, Inc., Detroit, also N.Y.C., 1954-58, sr. v.p., 1959, also dir.; sr. v.p. Ted Bates & Co., Inc., N.Y.C.; pres. Valjon, Inc., Mpls., 1968—. Served to capt. USAAF, 1942-45. Decorated D.F.C. with clusters, Air medal with clusters, Purple Heart. Clubs: Minneapolis, Hazletine Nat. Golf; Sleepy Hollow Country (Scarborough, N.Y.). Author: The Long Green. Home: 19 S 1st St Minneapolis MN 55401 Office: 63 S 1st St Minneapolis MN 55401

ARMSTRONG, WALTER PRESTON, Jr., lawyer; b. Memphis, Oct. 4, 1916; s. Walter Preston and Irma Lewis (Waddell) A.; grad. Choate Sch., Wallingford, Conn., 1934; A.B., Harvard, 1938, LL.B., 1941; D.C.L., Southwestern at Memphis, 1961; m. Alice Kavanaugh McKee, Nov. 3, 1949; children—Alice Kavanaugh, Walter Preston III. Admitted to Tenn. bar, 1940, practiced in Memphis, 1941—; asso. firm Armstrong, Allen, Braden, Goodman, McBride & Prewitt and predecessor firms, 1941—, partner, 1948—. Commr. for Promotion of Uniformity of Legislation in U.S. for Tenn., 1947-67. Pres. bd. edn. Memphis City Schs., 1956-61; mem. Tenn. Higher Edn. Commn. , 1967—, Tenn. Hist. Commn., 1969—. Served from pvt. to maj. AUS, 1941-46. Fellow Am. Bar Found. (sec. 1960-62), Am. Coll. Trial Lawyers; mem. Am. (ho. of dels. 1952—), Tenn. (bd. govs. 1967—), Memphis & Shelby County, Inter-Am., Internat. bar assns., Assn. Bar City N.Y., Am. Law Inst., Am. Judicature Soc., Nat. Conf. Commns. on Uniform State Laws (pres. 1961-63), Harvard Law School Assn. (sec. 1957-58), Order of Coif, Scribes (pres. 1960-61), Omicron Delta Kappa. Author law rev. articles. Home: 1530 Carr Av Memphis TN 38104 Office: Commerce Title Bldg Memphis TN 38103

ARMSTRONG, WARREN BRUCE, coll. dean; b. Tidioute, Pa., Oct. 16, 1933; s. Mead C. and Mary (Griffin) A.; Th.B., Bapt. Sem., Johnson City, N.Y., 1956; A.M., U. Mich., 1958, Ph.D., 1964; m. Elizabeth Ann Fowler, Aug. 7, 1954; children—Linda Susan, Heidi Jo. Instr. history Olivet Coll., 1961-63, asst. prof., 1963-65, chmn. dept., 1964-65; asst. prof. Wis. State U., Whitewater, 1965-66, asso. prof., 1966-69, prof., 1969-70, asst. dean Coll. Arts and Scis., 1966-69, asso. dean, 1969-70; dean St. Cloud (Minn.) State Coll., 1970- -, prof. history, 1970—. Councilman, Whitewater, 1968-70. Mem. Am. Assn. U. Profs., Orgn. Am. Historians, Am. Conf. Acad. Deans., Am. Assn. Higher Edn., Phi Kappa Phi. Democrat. Contbr. articles profl. jours. Home: 1755 Cherry Lane St Cloud MN 56301

ARMSTRONG, WILLIAM H., lawyer; b. Neosho, Mo., Oct. 3, 1902; s. Willard P. and Zoe (Hatler) A.; A.B., U. Mo., 1924; LL.B., Harvard, 1927; m. Ellen Atwood, Oct. 31, 1929; children—William H., Ellen, A. Wallace. Admitted to Mo. bar, 1927, since practiced in St. Louis; partner firm Armstrong, Teasdale, Kramer & Vaughan. Dir. A.B. Chance Co., Centralia, Mo.; dir., mem. exec. com. Standard Brands, Inc., N.Y.C.; dir. Mississippi Valley Structural Steel Co., Cupples Co., mfrs., Hubbell Metals, Inc., 800 North 12th Inc. (all St. Louis). Bd. dirs., past chmn. St. Louis Bi-State chpt. A.R.C.; bd. dirs. Lindenwood Coll., sec., treas. bd. 1944—; bd. dirs. emeritus, past sec.

Episcopal-Presbyn. Found. for Aging. Mem. Am., Mo., St. Louis bar assns., Am. Judicature Soc., Am. Law Inst. Clubs: Racquet, Noonday, Log Cabin, St. Louis Country. Home: 625 Skinker Blvd St Louis MO 63105 Office: 611 Olive St St Louis MO 63101

ARMSTRONG, WILLIAM HOWARD, educator, author; b. Lexington, Va., Sept. 14, 1914; s. Howard G. and Ida (Morris) A.; A.B., Hampden-Sydney Coll., 1936; postgrad. U. Va., 1937-38; m. Martha Stonestreet Williams, Aug. 24, 1942; children—Christopher, David, Mary. Tchr. history Kent (Conn.) Sch., 1945- -. Recipient Nat. Sch. Bell award for distinguished service in interpretation of edn., 1963. Author: Through Troubled Waters, 1956; Study is Hard Work, 1957; Peoples of the Ancient World, 1959; 87 Ways to Help Your Child in School, 1961; Sounder (Newbery award), 1969; Barefoot in the Grass (Life of Grandma Moses), 1970; Sour Land, 1971. Home: Kimadee Hill Kent CT 06757

ARMSTRONG, WILLIS COBURN, assn. exec., educator; b. Bklyn., Apr. 2, 1912; s. James Claude and Hattie Amelia (Fairchild) A.; grad. Phillips Acad., Andover, Mass., 1929; A.B., Swarthmore Coll., 1933; A.M., Columbia, 1934, postgrad., 1934-39: postgrad. U. Cal. at Berkeley, summers 1936, 37; m. Louise Schaffner, May 2, 1959; 1 son, Ian. Tchr. social sci. Horace Mann Sch., Columbia, 1934-39; staff Am. embassy, Moscow, 1939-41; ofcl. Lend-Lease Adminstrn. and Fgn. Econ. Adminstrn., Washington, 1941-45, War Shipping Adminstrn., 1945-46; adviser on state trading U.S. Dept. State, 1946-48, asst. chief div. comml. policy, 1948-49, asso. chief econ. resources staff, 1949-51, spl. asst. office internat. materials policy, 1951- 52, dep. dir., 1952-54, acting dir., 1954-55, dept. dir. Office of Internat. Trade and Resources, 1955-57, dir. Office Internat. Resources, 1957-58; econ. counselor Am. embassy, Ottawa, Ont., Can., 1958-60, dep. chief of mission, minister, 1960-62; dir. Office Brit. Commonwealth and No. European Affairs, Washington 1962-64; minister for econ. affairs Am. embassy, London, Eng., 1964-67; asso. dean Sch. Internat Affairs, Columbia U., 1967-69, sr. lectr. in diplomacy, 1969—; pres. U.S. Council, Internat. C. of C., N.Y.C., 1969—. Lectr. Am. U., 1945-46; lectr. Soviet affairs Sch. Advanced Internat. Studies, Washington, 1946-58; U.S. del. to internat. rubber meetings, 1950-58, other internat. meetings on trade, wool, inter- Am. affairs. Recipient Rockefeller Pub. Service award, 1956. Mem. Council Fgn. Relations, Delta Upsilon. Presbyn. Clubs: Reform (London); Columbia University (N.Y.C.); DACOR (Washington). Author articles in field. Home: 163 Brookstone Dr Princeton NJ 08540 Office: 1212 Av of Americas New York City NY 10036

ARNABOLDI, LEO PETER, Jr., lawyer; b. Paterson, N.J., Dec. 28, 1924; s. Leo Peter and Stella (Sandes) A.; A.B. summa cum laude in Econs., Amherst Coll., 1947; J.D., Yale, 1950; m. Sheila Gallagher, Dec. 27, 1958; children—Lee, Clinton, Lilla. Admitted to N.Y. bar, 1951; asso. firm Willkie Farr & Gallagher, N.Y.C., 1950-52; asso. firm Olwine, Connelly, Chase, O'Donnell & Weyher, N.Y.C., 1952-59, partner, 1960—; sr. partner, 1969—. Chmn. exec. com. Lionel Corp., N.Y.C., 1958—; dir., mem. exec. com. Seabrook Foods, Inc., Alpex Computer Corp. Served to lt. USAAF, 1944-46. Mem. Phi Beta Kappa, Beta Theta Pi. Clubs: Greenwich Country, Stanwich (Greenwich). Editor Yale Law Jour., 1949-50. Home: 26 Cedarwood Dr Greenwich CT 06832 Office: 299 Park Av New York City NY 10017

ARNALL, ELLIS GIBBS, lawyer, former gov. Ga.; b. Newnan, Ga., Mar. 20, 1907; s. Joe Gibbs and Bessie Lena (Ellis) A.; student Mercer U., 1924; A.B., U. of South, 1928, D.C.L., 1947; LL.B., U. Ga., 1931; LL.D., Atlanta Law Sch., 1942, Piedmont Coll., 1943, Bryant Coll., 1948; m. Mildred DeLaney Slemons, Apr. 6, 1935; children—Alvan Slemons, Alice Slemons. Admitted to Ga. bar, 1931; mem. Ho. of Reps., Coweta County, Ga., and speaker pro tem, 1933-37; atty. gen. Ga., 1939-43; gov. Ga., 1943-47; pres. Columbus Nat. Life Ins. Co. (formerly Dixie Life Ins. Co.), Newnan, 1946-60, Soc. Ind. Motion Picture Producers, Beverly Hills, 1948-60, Ind. Film Producers Export Corp., Beverly Hills, 1953-60; sr. partner law firm Arnall, Golden & Gregory, Atlanta; chmn. bd. Coastal States Life Ins. Co., Atlanta, 1956—, Atlanta Americana Motor Hotel Corp. Dir. OPS, Feb.-Sept. 1952. Mem. Nat. Commn. for UNESCO, 1947-51, 63—; mem. U.S. delegation Fifth Conf. UNESCO, Paris, France, 1949; mem. U.S. delegation Anglo- Am. Film Conf., London, Eng., 1950, 53-56. Mem. Franklin D. Roosevelt Warm Springs Meml. Commn., 1970—. Trustee U. South, 1946-50, Mercer U., 1960-70. Fellow Internat. Inst. Arts and Scis.; mem. Am. Judicature Soc., Nat. Assn. Life Ins. Co., Inc. (chmn. bd. 1955—), Am., Fed., Ga. Bar assns., Soc. Motion Picture Arts and Scis., Phi Beta Kappa, Phi Delta Phi, Kappa Alpha. Democrat. Club: Atlanta Lawyers. Author: The Shore Dimly Seen, 1946, What the People Want, 1947. Home: 213 Jackson St Newnan GA 30263 Office: Fulton Federal Bldg Atlanta GA 30303

ARNALL, PAUL MCGREW, ret. assn. exec.; b. Elk Falls, Kan., Aug. 4, 1895; s. Millard F. and Mary (Dinkle) F.; student Kan. U., 1919-20, Kan. State Tchrs. Coll., 1916-17; m. Edna Chain, Oct. 14, 1922; 1 dau., Patricia Ann (Mrs. J. David Lynch, Jr.). From salesman to gen. sales mgr. Graton & Knight Co., Worcester, Mass., 1920-33, Chgo. mgr., N.Y. mgr. F.A. Whitney Co., Leominster, 1933-38; gen. sales mgr., v.p. charge sales, then exec. v.p., dir. Ohio Injector Co., Wadsworth, O., 1938-49; v.p., general mgr. The Lunkenheimer Co., Cin., 1950-51, dir., 1950—, pres., gen. mgr., 1951-68; exec. vice pres., chief exec. officer Elizabeth Gamble Deaconess Home Assn., Cin., 1968-69; trustee emeritus Central Trust Co. Mem. adv. bd. Gen. Protestant Orphan Home; mem. lay adv. bd. Good Samaritan Hosp., 1969—. Trustee, past pres. Greater Cin. Hosp. Council; trustee Meml. Homes Found. Served with USMC, World War 1. Mem. Sigma Alpha Epsilon. Episcopalian. Mason (Shriner). Clubs: Queen City, Camargo, Cincinnati Country (Cin.); Commercial. Home: Kugler Mill Rd Indian Hill Cincinnati OH 45243

ARNASON, ALBERT FREEMAN, university dean; b. Hensel, N.D., Mar. 12, 1908; s. Arni and Gudrun (Baldwin) A.; B.S., U. N.D., 1929, M.A., 1935; LL.D., Jamestown Coll., 1948; m. Maude Thorsgard, Aug. 10, 1933; 1 dau., Ruth Mary. High sch. instr., Bottineau, N.D., 1929-30; head social scis. dept. N.D. Sch. Forestry, 1930-38, pres. sch., 1938-43; state commr. higher edn., 1943- 58, state dir. vocational edn., 1954-58; asst. dean school medicine Univ. N.D., 1958—; educational consultant in Germany, Department of State, 1950. Mem. Pres.' Com. on Edn. Beyond the High School. Past pres. Bottineau Community Service Club, N.D. Intercollegiate Athletic Assn., Bottineau U. of N.D. Alumni Assn. Mem. Nat. Edn. Assn., N.D. Acad. Sci., Am. Assn. Sch. Adminstn., N.D. Edn. Assn., Phi Delta Kappa. Lutheran. Mason, Rotarian. Club: Executives. Home: 410 18th Av S Grand Forks ND 58201

ARNASON, HJORVARDUR HARVARD, art historian; Winnipeg, Man., Can., Apr. 24, 1909; s. Sveinbjorn and Maria (Bjarnadottir) A.; student U. Man., 1925-27; B.S., Northwestern U., 1930, A.M., 1937; M.F.A., Princeton, 1939; m. Elizabeth Hickox Yard, July 25, 1936; children—Eleanor Atwood, Jon Yard; m. 2d, Elinor Lane Franklin, June 9, 1966. Came to U.S., 1927, naturalized, 1940. Instr., Northwestern U., 1936-38; research asst. and lectr. Frick Collection, N.Y.C. 1938-42; lectr. Hunter Coll, 1939-42; field rep., OWI, Iceland, 1942-44, asst. dep. dir. for Europe, hdqrs. Washington, 1944-45; chief, program planning and evaluation unit Office of Internat. Information and Cultural Affairs, Dept. State, Washington, 1945-46; vis. asso. prof. art U. Chgo., 1947; prof., chmn. dept. art U. Minn., 1947-61; dir. Walker Art Center, Mpls., 1951-61; v.p. for art adminstrn. Solomon R. Guggenheim Found., N.Y.C., 1961-69. Fulbright fellow, France, 1955-56; Carnegie vis. prof. U. Hawaii, 1959; sr. research fellow Nat. Endowment for Humanities, 1971-72. U.S. rep. Prep. Commn. on UNESCO, London and Paris, 1946. Trustee Am. Fedn. Arts, Solomon R. Guggenheim Found., T.B. Walker Found., Inc., Joseph H. Hirshhorn Mus., Washington, Jacques Lipchitz Found. Decorated chevalier de l'Ordre des Arts et des lettres (France); knight Order St. Olav (Norway). Mem. Coll. Art Assn., Am. Assn. Mus., Internat. Council Museums, U.S. Nat. Com. for History of Art, Am. Assn. U. Profs., Am. Soc. for 18th Century Studies, Societ é Francaise d'Etude du 18 eEe Siècle. Clubs: Century, Princeton (N.Y.C.). Author: Modern Sculpture, 1962; Conrad MarcaRelli, 1962; Sculpture by Houdon, 1964; Alexander Calder, 1966; History of Modern Art, 1968; Jacques Lipchitz: Fifty Years of Sketches in Bronze, 1969; (with Ugo Mulas) Alexander Calder, 1969; also monographs, catalogues, articles on medieval, 18th Century and modern art. Home: 1075 Park Av New York City NY 10028

ARNAUD, LEOPOLD, architect, educator; b. N.Y.C., March 2, 1895; s. Leopold and Fortunëe (Zarcharie) A.; grad. Lyceé Janson de Sailly (U. Paris), 1914; B.Arch., Columbia, 1918, M.S. in architecture, 1933; student École des Beaux Arts, Paris, 1919-24 (Architecte Diplomé par le Governement Francais); m. Blanchette Stearns, Nov. 5, 1927; children—Blanche Fortunée, Anthony Leopold. Archtl. designer Warren & Wetmore, architects, N.Y., 1924-29; designer Voorhees, Gmelin & Walker, N.Y., 1929-32; lectr. history of architecture Columbia, 1929-32, instr. in architecture, 1933-35, asst. prof. and acting dean, sch. of architecture, 1935-37, prof. history of architecture, 1937-42, Ware prof. architecture, 1942, dean architecture, 1937-60; dean emeritus and Ware prof. emeritus, 1960, dir. Sch. Painting and Sculpture, 1948-56, Sch. Dramatic Arts, 1948-53; dir. Casa Italiana, Columbia, 1950-55; vis. Carnegie prof. to S.A., 1943; Dept. State lectr. S.A., 1954; with USIA, 1959-64; cultural attache Am. embassy, Brazil, 1960-62, Am. embassy, Spain, 1962-64. Served with F.A., U.S. Army U.S. Army, 1917-19, A.E.F., 13 months; wounded at Pexonne, 1918. Decorated Silver Star citation; recipient Silver medal Soc. des Architectes Diplómés par le Govt. Francais; Medaille du Proféssurat, Soc. des Architectes Provinciaux, France; chevalier Legion of Honor (France), 1949; cav. officer Merito della Repubblica (Italy), 1955; knight Order Corpus Christi, Toledo (Spain), 1966. Fellow A.I.A.; mem. Assn. Collegiate Schs. Architecture (pres. 1940-42), Sch. Art League of N.Y. (pres. 1941-45), Theta Delta Chi; hon. mem. Instituto de Cultura Hisánica, Madrid, socs. architects of Peru, Mexico, Buenos Aires, Ecuador and Colombia; corr. mem. Nat. Acad. Fine Arts, Argentina, Academie d'Archtecture de Paris. Clubs: Century, Columbia U., Ex-mems. of Squadron A. Contbr. to archtl. jours. Address: Calle Pedro de Valdivia 6 Madrid 6 Spain

ARNAZ, DESI, actor, producer; b. Santiago, Cuba, Mar. 2, 1917; s. Desiderio Alberto Arnaz y de Acha and Dolores A.; student pub. schs. Miami, Fla.; m. Lucille Ball, Nov. 30, 1940 (div. May 1960); m. 2d, Edith Mack Hirsch. Appeared Roney Plaza Hotel, Miami, 1936; introduced La Conga dance to US, Miami, 1938; starred La Conga Club, N.Y.C., 1938; with R.K.O., Hollywood, Cal, 1940, M.G.M. studios, 1942; mus. dir. Bob Hope radio show, 1946; under contract to Columbia Records, 1953; star (with Lucille Ball) TV show I Love Lucy, C.B.S.-TV, 1950-57; star (with Lucille Ball) Long, Long, Trailer, 1953, Forever Darling, 1955; former co-star Lucille Ball-Desi Arnaz Show (for Westinghouse); host Westinghouse Desilu Playhouse; pres. Desilu Productions Inc. until 1962; now independent producer; pres. Desi Arnaz Prodns., Inc. Served AUS, 1944-46. Address: Desi Arnaz Prodns 9336 Washington Blvd Culver City CA 90230

ARNDT, JOHN FALKNER, ret. advt. exec.; b. Phila., Dec. 6, 1898; s. Charles Henry and Helen Moore (Falkner) A.; A.B., Kenyon Coll, 1921; m. Helen Chapman; children—John Falkner, Willis Chapman, Helen Collings, Charles Henry, II. Salesman, Hagan Corp., Pitts., 1921-22; asst. sales mgr. Franklin Sugar Refining Co., Phila., 1922-23; prodn. dept. F. Wallace Armstrong Advt. Agy., 1923-24; pres. John Falkner Arndt & Co., advt. agy., 1924-54; pres., treas. Arndt, Preston, Chapin, Lamb & Keen, Inc., 1954-59, chmn. bd., 1959-70; founder Continental Advt. Agy. Network, pres., 1933-55, chmn., 1955-57. Trustee, Episcopal Acad., 1948-66; bd. dirs. Valley Forge Hist. Soc.; past dir. United Fund, Crime Prevention Assn.; mem. exec. com., v.p. Ind. Schs. Fund, 1955-66. Served with U.S. Army, 1918. Mem. S.R., Psi Upsilon. Republican. Home: 527 St Davids Av St Davids PA 19087

ARNDT, KARL, physician; b. Denver, Dec. 9, 1908; s. Rudolph William and Elizabeth (Waugh) A.; A.B., Williams Coll., 1929; M.D., U. Colo., 1933; m. Helen Millett, Dec. 30, 1933; children—Nicholas A., Sarah M., Karl D., Burnham W. Instr. pathology Columbia Coll. Phys. and Surg., 1933-34; intern in medicine Presbyn. Hosp., N.Y.C., 1934-36; pvt. practice of medicine, 1936—; asso. clin. prof. medicine U. Colo. Sch. Medicine, 1944—. Chmn. bd. censors Denver Med. Soc.; mem. Denver Art Commn.; pres. bd. trustees Denver Art Mus.; trustee Music Assos. of Aspen, Seabury-Western Theol. Sem., Evanston, Ill. Served to maj., M.C., AUS, 1942-45. Diplomate Am. Bd. Internal Medicine. Fellow A.C.P.; mem. Denver Clin. and Pathol. Soc. A.M.A., Colo., Denver med. socs., Alpha Omega Alpha, Delta Upsilon. Republican. Episcopalian (standing com. Diocese of Colo.; dep. to gen. conv. Episcopal Ch., 1955, 58, 61, 64, 67, 69, 70; vestryman, sr. warden). Clubs: Denver Country, Mile High (Denver). Home: 860 Vine St Denver CO 80206 Office: 3705 E Colfax Av Denver CO 80206

ARNDT, RAYMOND HENRY, utilities co. exec.; b. Rock Island, Ill., Dec. 3, 1898; s. Henry C. and Elizabeth (Jensen) A.; B.S. in M.E., U. Ill., 1923; student gas engring., Columbia, 1928; student indsl. mgmt., Johns Hopkins, 1943; m. Madge Shephard, June 20, 1925. Engr. Am. gas Co., Rockford, Ill., 1923- 27; plant supt. United Gas Improvement Co., Rockford, 1927-31; with Balt. Gas & Electic Co., 1931—, beginning as asst. supt., successively supt., asst. gen. supt. gas. gen. supt., 1931-57, vice president in charge of the Gas division, 1957—. Served with U.S. Navy, World War I. Mem. Am. Gas Assn., Soc. Gas Lighting, Am. Soc. M.E., Nat. Soc. Profl. Engrs., Balt. Assn. Commerce. Presbyn. Mason (Shriner). Clubs: Engineers, Baltimore Country, Baldric (Balt.). Home: 4302 N Charles St Baltimore MD 21218 Office: Balt Gas & Electric Co Lexington and Liberty Sts Baltimore MD 21203

ARNDT, ROBERT NORTON DOWNS, ret. advt. exec.; b. Phila., Sept. 11, 1904; s. Charles H and Helen (Falkner) A.; grad. Germantown Friends Sch.; A.B., Kenyon Coll., 1927; m. Alice Sumner, June 7, 1929; children—Robert Ewins Sumner, Thomas Moore, Judith Channing (Mrs. Theodore S. Ingalls). Partner, account exec. Arndt, Preston, Chapin, Lamb & Keen, Inc., advt., Phila., 1928-65, exec. v.p., 1929-65. Trade adviser to govt. and people Poland in collaboration with U.S. Dept. State, auspices Dept. Commerce, 1959. Former publicity chmn., regional chmn. Phila. United Fund; mem. Nat. Council Protestant Episcopal Ch. Am.; chmn. gen. div. 3d province, Episcopal Laymen's Work; chmn. dept. communications Episcopal Diocese Pa.; vestryman St. Stephen's Episcopal Ch., Cohasset, Mass.; dir. parish relations, asst. promotion dir. Episcopalian Mag. Chmn., Republican Town Finance Com. Bd. dirs. Neighborhood League, Wayne, St. Davids, Ithan Civic Assn.; mem. exec. council Brotherhood St. Andrews. Recipient certificate of service U.S. Dept. Commerce. Mem. Nat., Eastern (past. dir.) indsl. advertisers assns., Phila. Jr. C. of C. (past pres.), Nat. Sales Execs. Assn., Newcomen Soc., Cohasset Hist. Soc. (dir.), Psi Upsilon. Club: Church (Phila.). Editor: The Citizen, Hanover, Mass. Contbr. articles to trade jours. Home: 391 S Main St Cohasset MA 02025

ARNDT, WALTER WERNER, educator; b. Constantinople, Turkey, May 4, 1916; s. Fritz Georg and Julia (Heimann) A.; Dipl.Econ.Pol.Sc., Oriel Coll., Oxford (Eng.) U., 1936; cand. mag., Sch. Bus. Adminstrn., Warsaw (Poland) U., 1939; B.S. summa cum laude, Robert Coll., Istanbul, Turkey, 1943; Ph.D., U. N.C., 1956; m. Sophie Miriam Bach, Jan. 6, 1945; children—Robert Michael, Joachim David, Prudence Joy, Corinne Constance. Came to U.S., 1949, naturalized, 1955. Asst. dir. Turkey office Internat. Rescue and Relief Com., 1942-49, Intergovtl. Com. Refugees, 1945-47, UN Internat. Refugee Orgn., 1947-49; instr. Robert Coll., Istanbul, 1945-48; corr. The Economist, 1946-48; instr., then asst. prof. classical and modern langs. Guilford Coll., 1950-56, asst. prof., then asso. prof. Slavic and linguistics U. N.C., 1957-66, chmn. dept. linguistics, Slavic and Oriental langs., 1965-66; prof. Russian, Dartmouth, 1966—, chmn. dept. Russian lang. and lit., 1967-70; Fulbright prof. U. Münster (Germany), 1961- 62; guest prof. Polish, U. Colo., summer 1965. Served with OSS, 1943-45. OWI, 1945. Ford fellow U. Mich., 1952, Harvard, 1956-57; research grantee Am. Philos. Soc., 1967; co-recipient Bollingen prize for translation poetry, 1963. Mem. Linguistic Soc. Am., Am. Assn. Advancement Slavic Studies, S. Atlantic Modern Lang. Assn. (chmn. Slavic sect. 1959- 60, sec. 1962-63, chmn. 1963-64), Am. Assn. Tchrs. Slavic and E. European Langs. (v.p. 1964—), Nat. Slavic Honor Soc. (v.p. 1964-65), S. Conf. Slavic Studies (v.p. 1964-65, pres. 1965-66). Author: Alexander Pushkin: Eugene Onegin, 1963; Wilhelm Busch, Clement Dove, The Thwarted Poet, 1967; (with L. Levine) Grundzüge moderner Sprachbeschreibung, 1969; Pushkin Threefold, 1971. Home: 38 Maple St Hanover NH 03755

ARNER, CHARLES EDWARD, banker; b. St. Paul, June 16, 1922; s. George Henry and Alice (Schroeder) A.; student U. Minn., 1946-48; m. Barbara Estelle Mannheimer, Jan. 22, 1948; children—Stephanie (Mrs. Michael F. Thompson), Cort William. Vice pres. 1st Nat. Bank of St. Paul, 1952-66, sr. v.p., 1968—; pres. 1st Computer Corp., 1966-68. Served with USNR, 1942-46, 50-52. Mem. Bank Adminstrn. Inst. (1st v.p.). Episcopalian. Home: 5 W Shore Rd St Paul MN 55110 Office: 332 Minnesota St St Paul MN 55101

ARNER, DOUGLAS GENE, educator; b. McCook, Neb., Dec. 16, 1926; s. John Erwin and Marie Alice (Trivelpiece) A.; B.S., Creighton U., 1948; M.A., U. Mich., 1952, Ph.D., 1955; m. Blanche Virgina DeJong, Apr. 23, 1949; 1 son, John DeJong. Teaching fellow U. Mich., 1950-51; instr., then asst. prof. Princeton, 1952-59; mem. faculty Ariz. State U., 1959—, prof. philosophy, 1963—; lectr. Ariz. Inst., 1965—. Served with AUS, 1944-46. Recipient Alumni Distinguished Teaching award Ariz. State U., 1965. Mem. Ariz. Acad., Phi Kappa Phi. Club: University (Phoenix). Home: 8045 E Windsor Av Scottsdale AZ 85257 Office: Dept Philosophy Ariz State Univ Tempe AZ 85281

ARNER, SAMUEL DEWALT, archaeologist; b. Vandergrift, Pa., June 17, 1900; s. George William and Elizabeth (deWalt) A.; diploma in law LaSalle Extension U.; student Bellvue Coll., Westminister, Colo.; diploma Zarephath Bible Inst. N.J.; studied poetry U. Cal. Extension; m. Violet Stewart, Apr. 2, 1935 (div. Oct. 1953); children—Paul C., David D., Jon Peter; m. 2d, Irene C. de Lopez de Santa Anna, May 31, 1957. Writer many poems pub. in various periodicals, including The Woodland Ghost, and Oteen, 1917-27; theol. articles to ch. mags., 1923-27; theol. lectr., 1926-31; Western landscape artist engaged in many expdns. to various parts of Western Am., Mexico, C.Am., S.Am. in interest of archaeol. research, 1931—; archaeol. research in Egypt, Lebanon, Israel, Turkey, Greece, 1969; founder, curator Mus. of Antiquities and Art, Cathedral City, Cal., now painting series oil portraits of famous Old West characters for mus.; owner Desert Realty Co. Pres. Taxpayers and Civic Improvement Assn. Dir. Palm Springs Republican Assembly, 1959; candidate for Congress, 1942. Trustee Desert Estate Co. Recipient award Merit for archaeol. research; diploma for distinguished achievement. Mem. Internat. Platform Assn., C. of C., Smithsonian Instn. (nat. mem.), Nat. Hist. Soc. (founding), Am. Acad. Polit. and Social Sci. (founding) Internat. Oceanographic Found., Am. Assn. Museums, D.A.V. (past chpt. comdr.), Am. Inst. Fine Arts, Presbyn. Home: P O Box 687 Cathedral City CA 92234 Office: 68-615 Broadway Cathedral City CA 92234

ARNESON, AXEL NORMAN, physician; b. Ft. Worth, July 5, 1905; s. Axel and Leonora (Keeble) A.; B.S., Tex. Christian U., 1924; M.D., Washington U., St. Louis, 1928; m. Ruth Leach, Dec. 12, 1931; 1 son, Normon Arne. Fellow, Meml. Hosp., N.Y.C., 3 yrs.; now prof. clin. obstetrics and gynecology, also asso. prof. clin. radiology Washington U. Sch. Medicine; asso. attending gynecologist Barnes & St. Louis Maternity Hosp., St. Louis. Served as lt. col. M.C., AUS, 1942-45. Fellow Am. Assn. Obstetricians and Gynecologists, Am. Coll. Obstetricians and Gynecologists (treas. 1958-64, pres. 1965), Am. Gynecol. Soc.; mem. St. Louis Med. Soc. (pres. 1953), Washington U. Alumni Assn. (pres. 1951-52, med. alumni rep. to univ. bd. dirs. 1952-55), Am. Radium Soc. (pres. 1947-48, Janeway lectr. 1963), Central Assn. Obstetricians and Gynecologists (pres. 1958-59), Radiol. Soc. N. Am. (Carman lectr. 1955), St. Louis Gynecol. Soc. (pres. 1948-49), St. Louis Surg. Soc. (pres. 1951-52), Am. Coll. Radiology (chancellor 1953- 56). Home: 6314 Waterman Av St Louis MO 63130 Office: 4511 Forest Park Blvd St Louis MO 63108

ARNESON, GEORGE STEPHEN, corp. exec.; b. St. Paul, Apr. 3, 1925; s. Oscar and Louvia Irene (Clare) A.; B. Elec. Engring., U. Minn., 1949; B.S. in Marine Transp., U.S. Mcht. Marine Acad., 1945; m. Maria Fernanda Suarez; children—George Stephen Fernando, Deborah Clare Fernanda, Diane Elizabeth Fernanda, Frederick Oscar Fernando. Sales engr. Hubbard & Co., Chgo., 1949-54; cons. Booz, Allen & Hamilton, Chgo., 1954-57; mgr. marketing cons. services, dir. marketing, plant mgr. Borg-Warner Corp., 1957-60; asst. gen. mgr., then v.p., gen. mgr. Delta-Star Electric div. H.K. Porter Co., Inc., Pitts., 1960-63, v.p., gen. mgr. elec. div., 1963-65; v.p. marketing Wheeling Steel Corp., 1965-66; pres. Vendo Co., Kansas City, Mo., 1966—, chief exec. officer, 1967—, also dir., chmn. exec. com. Bd. dirs. Civic Council Greater Kansas City, Heart of Am. United Fund. Served with USNR, 1943-46. Mem. U. Minn. Alumni Assn. (dir.), Phi Gamma Delta (life), Alpha Phi Omega (life). Republican. Presbyn. Mason (K.T., Shriner). Club: Kansas City. Home: 801 W 65th St Kansas City MO 64113 Office: 7400 1 12th St Kansas City MO 64126

ARNESON, HOWARD FREDERIC lawyer, corp. exec.; b. Kent, O., 1922. Home: 23 Beacon St Boston MA 02107

ARNESS, JAMES, TV actor; b. Mpls., May 26, 1923; s. Rolf C. and Ruth (Duesler) Arness; student Beloit Coll., 1942; m. Virginia Chapman, Feb. 12, 1948; children—Craig, Jenny Lee, Rolf. Motion pictures include: The Farmer's Daughter, People Against O'Hara, Hellgate, Battleground, Hondo, Island in the Sky, Big Jim McLaine, Many Rivers to Cross, A Foreign Affair, Sea Chase, Wagon Master, Her Twelve Men, The First Traveling Saleslady, Flame of the Islands, Gun the Man Down; actor live and filmed TV shows, 1954—; star Gunsmoke series CBS-TV, 1955—. Served as pvt. AUS, World War II. Mem. Beta Theta Pi. Home: Pacific Palisades 90272 Office: 1456 N Bronson Hollywood 28, CA

ARNEST, BERNARD, artist; b. Denver, Feb. 19, 1917; s. Bernard Patrick and Marie (Kaelin) A.; student Colorado Springs Fine Arts Center; m. Barbara Maurin, June 5, 1948; children—Paul, Lisa, Mark. Instr., Mpls. Sch. Art, 1947-49; asst. prof., then asso. prof. dept. art U. Minn., 1949-57; prof., head dept. art Colo. Coll. and Sch. Art, Colorado Springs Fine Arts Center, 1957-71; U.S. Dept. State grantee to Afghanistan, 1960; exhibited Whitney Ann., Pitts. Internat., Corcoran Biennial; commd. for murals New Vets. Bldg., St Paul State Capitol, First Nat. Bank Southdale, Mpls.; one-man exhbns. San Francisco Mus., 1940, Mpls. Art Inst., 1948, Walker Art Center, 1954, Kraushaar Galleries, N.Y.C., 1948, 52, 59, 62; represented in various pvt., nat. art collections. Co-chmn. advanced placement in art examining com. Coll. Entrance Exam. Bd., 1970. Chief war artist hdqrs. U.S. Army, ETO, 1943-45. Guggenheim fellow for creative work in painting, 1940. Mem. Am. Assn. U. Profs., Coll. Art Assn. Am. Home: 1502 Wood Av Colorado Springs CO 80907 Office: Art Dept Colo College Colorado Springs CO 80903

ARNEST, HENRY CLAY, food co. exec.; b. Seattle, July 5, 1911; s. Leslie B. and Julia C. (Prentice) A.; grad. Advanced Mgmt. Program, Harvard, 1935; m. Pauline L. Philbrick, Oct. 19, 1911; children—Henry Clay, Katie Ellen (Mrs. Robert W. Blew). Sr. v.p. Carnation Co., Los Angeles, 1967—. Home: 818 N Doheny Dr Los Angeles CA 90069 Office: 5045 Wilshire Blvd Los Angeles CA 90036

ARNETT, DENVER FLOYD, retired educator; b. Cairo, W.Va., Jan. 19, 1905; s. Alva Dora and Nancy Jane (Scott) A.; A.B. in Secondary Edn., Marshall Coll., 1930; A.M., U. W. Va., 1937; postgrad. U. Pitts., 1939—; m. Gertrude Ann Butler, July 28, 1932; 1 dau., Nancy Carol. Elementary sch. tchr., 1923-24, prin., 1924-29; prin. Greenbrier High Sch., Ronceverte, W. Va., 1930-36, Sistersville (W.Va.) High Sch., 1936-52; registrar, dir. admissions Glenville (W.Va.) State Coll., 1952-55; dean West Liberty (W.Va) State Coll., 1955-70, prof. edn., 1970-71; instr. W.Va. U. grad. extension courses, 1963—; tchr. history Greenbrier Coll., Lewisburg, W.Va., summers 1935-37. Mem. Nat. Council Tchr. Edn. and Profl. Standards, 1955-70, W.Va. Council Aging, 1960—. Mem. N.E.A., W.Va. Assn. Acad. Deans (pres. 1965-66), Kappa Delta Pi. Republican. Presbyn. Elk (past exalted ruler), Lion (past pres.). Office: West Liberty State Coll West Liberty WV 26074

ARNETT, FOSTER DEAVER, lawyer; b. Knoxville, Tenn., Nov. 28, 1920; s. Foster Greenwood and Edna (Deaver) A.; B.A., U. Tenn., 1946; LL.B., U. Va., 1948; m. Jean Medlin, Mar. 3, 1951; children—Melissa Lee, Foster Deaver. Admitted to Va. and Tenn. bars, 1948; with firm Cates, Fowler, Long & Fowler, Knoxville, 1948-55; partner firm Arnett, Draper & Hagood, and predecessors, Knoxville, 1955—. Pres. Knox Children's Found., 1959-61, U. Tenn. Hearing and Speech Center, 1963-65; chmn. nat. alumni annual giving program U. Tenn., 1962-63. Bd. dirs. Knoxville chpt. A.R.C., E. Tenn. Children's Rehab. Center, Knoxville chpt. Am. Cancer Soc. Del. Republican Nat. Conv., 1964. Served to 1st lt. AUS, 1942-46; PTO; Lt. col. USAR ret. Decorated Silver Star, Purple Heart. Fellow Am. Coll. Trial Lawyers, Internat. Soc. Barristers, Scribes; mem. Tenn. (pres. 1968-69), Knoxville (pres. 1959-60) Am. bar assns., Internat. Assn. Inc. Counsel, Fedn. Ins. Counsel, S.E. Def. Counsel Assn. (v.p. 1966), Am. Trial Lawyers Assn., Soc. Hosp. Attys. (charter), Am. Hosp. Assn. (charter), U. Tenn. Gen. Alumni Assn. (pres. 1961-62). Phi Gamma Delta, Phi Delta Phi, Scarabbean Secret Soc., Omicron Delta Kappa, Scabbard and Blade. Clubs: Civitan, Cherokee County, Racquet, City, U. Tenn. Faculty, Men's Cotillion, Appalachian, Elks (Knoxville). Home: 4636 Alta Vista Way S W Knoxville, TN 37919. Office: Hamilton Bank Bldg Knoxville TN 37902

ARNETT, JUDD, journalist; b. Russell, Ky., Nov. 11, 1911; s. Thomas Frank and Claudia (Dillon) A,; student U. Toledo; m. Fern Haver, Dec. 22, 1934. Owner, Tuscola (Ill.) Rev.; bur. chief St. Petersburg (Fla.) Times; editor Savannah (Ga.) Morning News; now columnist, mem. editorial bd. Detroit Free Press. Served with USNR, World War II. Mem. Sigma Delta Chi. Clubs: Lakelands Golf and Country. Home: 14456 Grandmont St Detroit, MI 48227. Office: 321 W Lafayette St Detroit MI 31

ARNETT, PETER GREGG, newspaper corr.; b. Riverton, New Zealand, Nov. 13, 1934; s. Eric Lionel and Jane (Gregg) A.; ed. pub. schs., New Zealand; m. Nina Nguyen Thu-Nga, September 17, 1964; children—Andrew Kim, Elsa Christina. Reporter Southland Times, Invercargill, New Zealand, 1951-54. The Standard Wellington, New Zealand, 1955-56, The Sun, Sydney, Australia, 1957; asso. editor Bangkok (Thailand) World, 1958-60; editor Vientiane World, Vientian, Laos, 1960; corr. A.P., Jakarta, Indonesia, 1961-62, Vietnam, 1962-70, N.Y., 1970—. Served with New Zealand Army, 1952-54. Recipient Pulitzer prize for internat. reporting, 1966; Sigma Delta Chi award for fgn. correspondence, 1967; Overseas Press Club citation, fgn. reporting, 1968, 70; George Polk Meml. award Overseas Press Club, 1970. Address: care AP 50 Rockefeller Plaza New York City NY 10020

ARNETT, ROSS HAROLD, Jr., entomologist; b. Medina, N.Y., Apr. 13, 1919; s. Ross Harold and Hazel Dell (Oderkirk) A.; B.S., Cornell U., 1942, M.S., 1946, Ph.D., 1948; m. Mary Catherine Ennis, Feb. 16, 1942; children—Ross Harold III, Michael J., Mary Anne, Barbara E., Frances X. C., Joseph A., Bernadette T., Matthew C. Instr., Cornell U., 1945-48; entomologist U.S. Nat. Mus., Washington, 1948-54; asso. prof. St. John Fisher Coll., Rochester, N.Y., 1954-58; prof. biology Cath. U. Am., Washington, 1958-66, head dept. biology, 1962-66, dir. Inst. Study Natural Species, 1961-66; prof. entomology Purdue U., Lafayette, Ind., 1966-70; Henry L. Beadel fellow Tall Timbers Research Sta., Tallahassee, Fla., 1970—. Vice pres. Am. Entomol. Inst., Ann Arbor, Mich.; v.p. Bio-Rand Found., Inc., Balt. Mem. Entomol. Soc. Am., Entomol. Soc. Am., Am. Soc. plant Taxonomists, Am. Ornithol. Soc., Am. Entomol. Soc., A.A.A.S., Am. Inst. Biol. Sci., Soc. Systematic Zool., Sigma Xi, Phi Kappa Phi. Author: Beetles of the United States, 1962; (with D.C. Braungart) Introduction to Plant Science, 1962, 2d edit., 1965, 3d edit., 1970; also numerous articles. Standardized classification beetles U.S. and families beetles world; research on study speciation as it affects evolutionary process. Home: Route 1 Box 161 Tallahassee FL 32303

ARNETT, RUSSELL EUGENE, lawyer; b. Oak Park, Ill., July 28, 1927; s. Roy E. and Evelyn (Hall) A.; student Central Coll., 1946-48; LL.B., Northwestern U., 1951; m. Betty J. Epps, Aug. 7, 1954; children—April, Heather, Hans. Admitted to Alaska bar, 1955, since practicd in Anchorage; U.S. commr., Nome, Alaska, 1952. Pres. Anchorage Republican Club, 1957. Served with USNR, 1945-46. Mem. Alaska (bd. govs.). Anchorage (past pres.) bar assns. Home: Star Route A Box 43 Anchorage AK 99502 Office: 1016 W 6th Av Anchorage AK 99501

ARNETT, WILLIAM TOBIAS, architect, educator; b. Pontiac, Ill., Sept. 24, 1905; s. William Ross and Carrie Belle (Tobias) A.; B.S. in Architecture, U. Fla., 1929, M.A. in Arch., 1932; postgrad. Columbia, summer 1929; m. Anna Margurite Baker, June 3, 1929; children—Sarah Belle, William Dale. Asso. Rudolph Weaver, architect, 1925-39; instr. architecture, U. Fla., 1932-36, asst. prof., 1936-41, prof. architecture, 1945—, dean Coll. Architecture and Fine Arts, 1946-56, dean emeritus, 1956—, mem. council Inst. Gerontology, 1951-57, dir. bur. Archtl. and Community Research, 1949-56, chmn. grad. faculty in community planning, 1953-60. Mem. Plan Bd., Gainesville 1948-60, chmn., 1957-60; dir. Fla. Planning and Zoning Assn., 1953, 55, 62, pres., 1959; mem. Fla. Bd. Architecture, 1946-49, pres., 1948; mem. com. on archtl. edn. So. Regional Edn. Bd., 1953-55. Served from capt. to lt. col., inf. AUS, 1941-46. Decorated Legion of Merit. Registered architect, Fla. Mem. A.I.A. (pres. Fla. N. chpt. 1947-48, exec. bd. S. Atlantic regional council 1954-55), Fla. Assn. Architects (dir. 1938, 53, chmn. com. redistricting 1953-55, chmn. com. planning and zoning 1956-57, chmn. com. community devel. 1958-61, v.p. 1962-64, pres. 1965), Am. Inst. Interior Designers (hon.), Beta Theta Pi, Phi Kappa Phi, Sigma Tau, Scabbard and Blade. Democrat. Methodist. Mason, Kiwanian. Research in coll. campus planning; developed Fla. Project Method in architectural edn. (with Rudolph Weaver). Home: 2105 NW 3d Pl Gainesville FL 32601

ARNEY, RICHARD DALE, meat packing co. exec.; b. Marshalltown, Ia., Feb. 6, 1911; s. W.M. and Ruth (Binford) A.; B.A., Carleton Coll., 1935; m. Muriel MacKay, Mar. 25, 1934; children—Richard M., Natalie (Mrs. Earl Williams), Jan (Mrs. Michael Kresky). Tchr., coach Austin (Minn.) High Sch., 1933-36; with George A. Hormel & Co., Austin, 1936-69, v.p., 1956-57, v.p. grocery products div., 1957-62, v.p. marketing, 1962-66, exec. v.p., 1966-69, also dir.; exec. v.p. food products group Swift & Co., 1969—. Mem. Grocery Mfrs. Am. (dir.), Gelatin Mfrs. Inst. (dir.), Nat. Meat Canners Assn. (v.p.), Am. Meat Inst. Republican. Conglist. (trustee). Home: 1000 Lake Shore Plaza Chicago IL 60611 Office: 115 W Jackson Blvd Chicago IL

ARNHART, JAMES RHYNE, hosp. adminstr.; b. Asheville, N.C., Jan. 26, 1924; s. James W. and Eula (Rhyne) A.; B.S., Maryville (Tenn.) Coll., 1951; M.H.A., Washington U., St. Louis, 1953; J.D., YMCA Law Sch.; m. Bobbye Lynn Brooks, Nov. 18, 1952. Adminstr. Rutherford Hosp., Murfreesboro, Tenn., 1954—. Mem. adv. council Tenn. Licensed Practical Nurses Assn., 1962—; mem. Tenn. Hosp. Licensing Bd., 1963—; mem. citizens adv. com. Dept. Pub. Welfare Tenn., Murfreesboro, 1964. Bd. dirs. Tenn. Cancer Soc., 1960, Blue Cross-Blue Shield Tenn., 1963—. Fellow Am. Coll. Hosp. Assn. (chmn. council 1960-61, dir. 1966, chmn. legislative com. 1966). Methodist (ofcl. bd.). Rotarian. Home: 1710 Riverview Dr Murfreesboro TN 37131 Office: Rutherford Hosp Murfreesboro TN 37131

ARNHEIM, RUDOLF, educator, psychologist; b. Berlin, Germany, July 15, 1904; s. Georg and Betty (Gutherz) A.; Ph.D., U. Berlin, 1928; m. Mary Elizabeth Frame, Apr. 11, 1953, 1 dau., Margaret. Came to U.S., 1940, naturalized, 1946. Asso. editor publs. Internat. Inst. Ednl. Films, Rome, Italy, 1933-38; lectr., vis. prof. Grad. Faculty, New Sch. Social Research, 1943-68; mem. Faculty Sarah Lawrence Coll., 1943-68; prof. psychology of art Carpenter Center for the Visual Arts, Harvard U., Cambridge, Mass., 1968- -; Guggenheim fellow, 1941-42; Fulbright lectr. Ochanomizu U., Tokyo, Japan, 1959-60. Mem. Am. Psychol. Assn. (pres. div. psychology and arts 1957-58, 65-66, 70-71), Am. Soc. Aesthetics (pres. 1959-60), Coll. Art Assn. Author: Art and Visual Perception, 1954; Film as Art, 1957; Picasso's Guernica, 1962; Toward A Psychology of Art, 1966: Visual Thinking, 1969; Entropy and Art, 1971; Radio, 1971. Home: 19 Garden St Cambridge, MA 02138.

ARNIM, SUMTER SMITH, educator; b. Hallettsville, Tex., Oct. 9, 1904; s. Charles William and Lydia Katherine (Smith) A.; B.A., Rice Inst., 1926; D.D.S. (Montgomery Ward fellow), Northwestern U., 1930; Ph.D. (Rockefeller fellow), Yale, 1935; m. Dorothy Mildred Brownlee, Sept. 8, 1945; children—Susan Smith (Mrs. Leonard Campbell Smyth II), Leslie Anne (Mrs. Leslie Arnim Gibson). Instr., Yale Sch. Medicine, 1934-35; asst. prof. operative dentistry U. Ill., 1937-39; prof. Med. Coll. Va. Sch. Dentistry, 1939-45; prof. Ohio State U. Sch. Dentistry, 1945-47; prof. pathology, dir. Postgrad. Sch. Dentistry, U. Tex. Dental br., Houston, 1947-66, asso. dean grad. studies, 1964-66, dean Grad. Sch. Biomedical Scis., 1966-70, dean emeritus, prof. pathology, 1970—; gen. practice dentistry, New Haven, 1935-37, Houston, 1953-56; cons. Proctor & Gamble, VA, Surgeon Gen. USAF. Recipient certificates of appreciation USAF, 1966, 68, U. Tex. System, 1970, Gold medal award Am. Soc. Periodontists, 1967. Fellow Acad. Sci.; mem. Am. Dental Assn., Internat. Assn. for Dental Research, Am. Assn. U. Profs., A.A.A.S., Am. Acad. Oral Pathology. Contbr. articles profl. jours. Home: 6407 Ella Lee Lane Houston TX 77027 Office: PO Box 20367 Houston TX 77025

ARNOLD, ALLEN MYRON, railroad exec.; b. Telford, Pa., July 28, 1912; s. Frank and Marie (Bergey) A.; student Taylor Bus. Sch., also Wharton Sch., U. Pa.; m. Olga Vivian Reed, Sept. 20, 1939; children—David Myron, Jean Elizabeth. Asst. to sec and treas. Reading Co., Phila., 1955-59, asst. sec., 1959- 62, asst. sec., asst. treas., 1962-66, sec.-treas., 1966—, also sec.- treas. subsidiary cos. Mem. Assn. Am. Railroads, Am. Soc. Corporate Secs. Mason. Home: 588 Hillside Dr Lansdale, PA 19446. Office: Reading Terminal 12th and Market Sts Philadelphia PA 19107

ARNOLD, ARTHUR OLOF, clergyman, educator, sem. ofcl.; b. San Francisco, Oct. 7, 1912; s. John August and Emily Louise (Peterson) Anderson; A.B., Gustavus Adolphus Coll., 1935; B.D., Augustana Theol. Sem., 1939; postgrad. U. Chgo., 1949-50; D.D.; Pacific Lutheran U., 1957; M.A., Northwestern U., 1960; m. Eleanor Olson, June 21, 1939; children—Cheryl Corinne, Kent Arthur, Jacqueline Miriam. Ordained to ministry Lutheran Ch., 1939; pastor Grace Luth. Ch., Davenport, Ia., 1939-44, Gloria Dei Luth. Ch., Duluth, Minn., 1944-46; asst. prof. Gustavus Adolphus Coll., 1946-49; prof. Luth. Sch. Theology at Chgo., 1949—, adminstrv. v.p., 1965-67, dean of students, 1967—. Member executive bd. Ill. Conf., Augustana Luth. Ch., 1943-44, mem. bd. parish edn., 1945-51; weekly columnist Luth. Companion, 1961-62; mem. bd. publs. Luth. Ch. in Am., 1964—. Bd. dirs. Augustana Book Concern, 1958-62; trustee Gustavus Adolphus Coll., 1945-46. Author: You and Yours. Home: 5401 Hyde Park Blvd Chicago IL 60615 Office: 1100 E 55th St Chicago IL 60615

ARNOLD, CARROLL CLYDE, educator; b. Lake Park, Ia., Apr. 29, 1912; s. Clyde Byron and Juliette (Hornbeck) A.; B.A., Sioux Falls (S.D.) Coll., 1933; M.A., State U. Ia., 1940, Ph.D., 1942; m. Ruby Swenson, Aug. 27, 1936. Tchr. English and history Sioux Falls High Sch., 1935-39; asst. State U. Ia., 1939-41; instr. speech U. Akron, 1941-42, Chatham Coll., 1942-43; instr. speech Cornell U., 1946, asst. prof., 1946-52, asso. prof., 1952-60, prof., 1960-63, chmn. dept. speech and drama, 1957-63; prof. speech Pa. State U., 1963—; vis. lectr. State U. Ia., 1946, U. Wis., 1955, U. So. Cal., 1959. Recipient J.A. Winans award for distinguished scholarship in rhetoric, 1969. Mem. Speech Assn. Am., Speech Assn. Eastern States (pres. 1963-64), Pa. Speech Assn., Am. Assn. U. Profs., Phi Kappa Phi, Pi Kappa Delta. Author: (with R.H. Wagner) Handbook of Group Discussion, 1950, rev. edit., 1964; (with J.F. Wilson) Public Speaking as a Liberal Art, 1964, rev. edit., 1968. Editor: (with D. Ehninger, J.C. Gerber) The Speaker's Resource Book, 1960, rev. edit., 1966; Speech Monographs, 1966-68; asso. editor Quar. Jour. Speech, 1952-62, Philosophy and Rhetoric, 1968—. Home: 492 Sierra Lane Park Forest Village State College PA 16801

ARNOLD, CHARLES WOOD, life ins. co. exec.; b. Kansas City, Mo., Nov. 20, 1907; s. Wood and Daisy (Dunskin) A.; student Mo. U., 1929. With Kansas City Life ins. Co. (Mo.), 1921-, sec., 1964-, also dir. Pres. Kansas City Civic Ballet Assn. Mem. Life Ins. Agy. Mgmt. Assn. (bd. dirs.). Clubs: Mission Hills (Kan.) Country; Native Sons, Mercury (Kansas City, Mo.). Home: 611 W 49th St Kansas City, MO 64113. Office: 3520 Broadway Kansas City, MO 64141.

ARNOLD, CHESTER A., paleobotanist; b. Leeton, Mo., June 25, 1901; s. Elmer and Edith (Funderburg) A.; B.S., Cornell U., 1924, Ph.D. 1929; m. Jean Davidson, Aug., 1933; children—David Graeme, Eric Bruce, Patricia Ann. Instr. botany U. Mich., 1928-35, asst. prof., 1935-41, asso. prof., 1941-47, prof. 1947-71, emeritus, 1971—, curator fossil plants, 1929-71, emeritus, 1971—. Author: Introduction to Paleobotany, 1947. Home: 1911 Mershon Dr Ann Arbour MI 48103

ARNOLD, CHESTER LEE, chemist; b. Sacramento, Sept. 10, 1904; s. Emery Claude and Jennie (Hunter) A.; B.S., U. Cal., 1929; Ph.D., U. Pitts., 1932; m. Florence B. Pos, June 3, 1950; children—Elizabeth Sue, Chester Lee. Chief glass tech. Phoenix Glass Co., 1935-43; dir. research western div. Stauffer Chem. Co., San Francisco, 1943-49, dir. research, 1947—, v.p., 1956-64, v.p. technical, 1964-65, v.p., gen. mgr. plastics div., 1965-69, dir., 1968—, cons., 1969—. Mem. Soc. Plastics Industry, Am. Chem. Soc. Home: Scout Trail Darien CT 06820 Office: 299 Park Av New York City NY 10017

ARNOLD, DAVID B., with Gray & Rogers, Inc., 1946-, partner, 1956-, v.p., mem. exec. com., 1963-65, exec. v.p., 1965-67, pres., 1967-. Address: Gray & Rogers Inc 12 S 12th St Philadelphia, PA 19107.

ARNOLD, DAVID CLEMENT, electronics co. exec.; b. Farson, Ia., Sept. 28, 1919; s. David Edwin and Hazel (Brown) A.; B.S. in Elec. Engring., Ia. State U., 1942; m. Ann Robel, Mar. 20, 1941; children—Nancy, Susan, John David, Robert Edwin. Engr., Gen. Electric Co., 1942-45, Gilfillan Bros., Los Angeles, 1945- 48; chief engr., then dir. research and devel. Collins Radio Co., 1948- 59; v.p. Alpha Radio, Richardson, Tex., 1959-61; operations mgr. RCA, Burlington, Mass., 1961-65; v.p., gen. mgr. Hoffman Electronics Corp., El Monte, Cal., 1965, exec. v.p., dir., 1965-66, pres., 1966-70; pres. Conductron Corp., 1970-71; corporate v.p. McDonnell Douglas Corp., 1971—; pres. McDonnell Douglas Electronics Co., 1971—. Mem. I.E.E.E., Am. Astronautical Soc., Am. Ordnance Assn., Electric Industries Assn. Home: RFD 1 Box 72 Portage Des Sioux MO 63373 Office: 2300 N 3d St St Charles MO 63301

ARNOLD, DAVID RUDD, business exec.; b. Galesburg, Ill., June 26, 1916; s. Ray Mortimer and Helen Massey (Rudd) A.; A.B. cum Laude, Knox Coll., 1937; M.B.A., Harvard, 1939; m. Jean Gebhart, Apr. 4, 1942; children—Steven Ferris, Nancy Babbitt, Judith Massey, Scott Gebhart; m. 2d, Joan Miller, Aug. 2, 1969. Pub. accountant Price Waterhouse & Co., C.P.A.'s, N.Y.C., 1939-44; mgmt. cons. A.T. Kearney & Co., Chgo., 1945-49; dir. mgmt. planning Gardner Board & Carton Co., Middletown, O., 1950-54, controller, 1954-58; gen. auditor C., R.I. & P. Ry., 1959-60, v.p., 1961-62; comptroller Continental Can Co., N.Y.C., 1962-64, v.p., 1964—. Bd. dirs. Chgo. City Soc. Congl. Ch., 1959-61, Chgo. Goodwill Indsutries, 1960-61; nat. bd. dirs. Jr. Achievement, 1954- 58; bd. dirs. N.Y.C. Mission Soc.; trustee Knox Coll. C.P.A., N.Y., Ill. Mem. Financial Execs. Inst., Nat. Assn. Accountants, Phi Beta Kappa, Beta Theta Pi. Clubs: Union League; Wee Burn Country (Darien, Conn.). Home: 63 Dorchester Rd Darien CT 06830 Office: 63 3d Av New York City NY 10017

ARNOLD, DUANE, utility exec.; b. Sanborn, Ia., Nov. 12, 1917; s. Grant D. and Beatrice (Short) A.; B.A., Grinnell Coll., 1942; m. Henrietta Dows, Apr. 27, 1946; children—Margaret Helen, Duane, Elizabeth, Mary. Dist. mgr. Ia. Electric Light & Power Co., Cedar Rapids, 1948-49, operations supt., 1949-50, v.p. operations, 1950-54, v.p., gen. mgr., 1954-61, pres., 1961- 69, chmn., pres., 1969—; chmn., dir. Perpetual Savs. & Loan Assn.; dir. Merchants Nat. Bank, Cedar Rapids, Banks of Ia.; pres., dir. Cedar Rapids & Ia. City R.R. Chmn. Community Chest, 1953. Dir. Cedar Rapids YMCA, pres., 1959- 60; dir. Pub. Welfare Bur.; trustee Midwest Research Inst., Mercy Hosp., Cedar Rapids; pres. Hall Radiation Center; trustee, treas. Herbert Hoover Birthplace Found. Served with USMCR, 1942- 45; lt. col. Res. Decorated Purple Heart, Bronze Star. Mem. Mo. Valley Elec. Assn. (pres. 1958), C. of C. (pres.). Presbyn. (trustee, deacon. elder). Mason (Shriner). Club: Cedar Rapids Country. Home: 321 Crescent SE Cedar Rapids IA 52403 Office: PO Box 351 Cedar Rapids IA 52406

ARNOLD, EDDY, singer; b. Henderson, Tenn., May 15, 1918; m. Sally, Nov. 28, 1941; children—Dick, Jo Ann (Mrs. Pollard). Appeared on WSM Radio, Nashville with Pee Wee King's western band Golden West Cowboys, 1940-43; co-host Grand Ole Opry radio program, 1943-48; guest appearances on numerous radio shows, including RCA Victor Show, We The People, Spike Jones Show, Luncheon at Sardi's, Paul Whiteman Show, Breakfast Club, Western Theatre; own radio show Checkerboard Square, 1947-55; made first television appearnce on Milton Berle Show, 1949; appeared in motion pictures Feudin Rhythm, 1949, Hoedown, 1950; N.Y.C. debut at Carnegie Hall, 1966; debut at Coconut Grove nightclub, Los Angeles, 1967; television appearances include shows hosted by Ed Sullivan, Perry Como, Danny Kaye, Dinah Shore, Danny Thomas, Mike Douglas, Jackie Gleason, Johnny Carson, Les Crane, Dean Martin and Red Skelton; featured on TV spls. Am. Music, Profile from the Land, 1968, Kraft Music Hall Spls., 1968, 69, 70; appeared with symphony orchs. of Hartford, Memphis, Nashville, 1967-68; recordings include Mommy, Please Stay Home With Me, 1944, That's How Much I Love You, Bouquet of Roses, Anytime, I'll Hold You In May Heart, Don't Rob Another Man's Castle, What's He Doing in My World?, Make the World Go Away, The Last Word in Lonesome is Me, Misty Blue, Turn the World Around, Here Comes Heaven. Owner, Eddy Arnold's Tenn. Fried Chicken, Inc., 1968—. Hon. chmn. Tenn. Young Democrats. Named to Country Music Hall of Fame, 1966, Entertainer of Year, 1967. Author: It's a Long Way from Chester County, 1969. Address: c/o Gerard W Purcell Assos 150 E 52d St New York City NY 10022*

ARNOLD, EDMUND CLARENCE, educator, writer; b. Bay City, Mich., June 25, 1913; s. Ferdinand M. and Ann J. (Begick) A.; A.A., Bay City Jr. Coll., 1934; A.B., Mich. State U., 1954; student Cite Universitie, Paris, France, 1945; m. Viola I. Burtzloff, Apr. 19, 1940; children—Kathleen Anne, Bethany, Bruce. Co- publisher

Frankenmuth (Mich.) News, 1945-67; picture editor Saginaw (Mich.) News, 1946-52; dir. trade relations Mergenthaler Linotype Co., Bklyn., 1958-60; night editor State Jour., Lansing, Mich., 1953-54; editor Linotype News Bklyn., 1954-67; contbg. editor Editor and Publisher, 1964—, The Publisher's Auxiliary, 1952-65, Canadian Printer and Pub.; editor and pub. Editorial Bd. Indsl. Arts Methods; staff lectr. Am. Press Inst.; asst. editor Quill mag., 1958- -; dir. Am. Metal Market, 1958-68; prof. journalism, chmn. graphic arts and publ. depts. Syracuse U., 1960—; mem. bd. cons. Communications Inst., Acad. Ednl. Devel. cons. publs. newspaper design. Mem. commn. on church papers Lutheran Ch. Am. Served as sgt. AUS, 1943-45; stafff Stars and Stripes, 1944-45. Recipient George A. Polk Meml. award, 1957; Voight Meml. award, 1964; Towley Meml. award, 1968; Journalism Pioneers medal, 1970; George Washington medal, 1970; Friars award St. Bovaventure U., 1971. Mem. Nat. Editorial Assn. (spl. award of merit 1958), Inter-Am. Press Assn., Am. Inst. Graphic Arts, Am. Acad. Advt. (regional dean 1965-70), Sigma Delta Chi, Alpha Delta Sigma, Phi Theta Kappa, Phi Kappa Phi. Author: Functional Newspaper Design, 1956; Profitable Newspaper Advertising, 1960; Feature Photos That Sell, 1960; Ink on Paper; A Handbook of the Graphic Arts, 1963; (with Hillier Krieghbaum) The Student Journalist; Typografia por Periodicas Latinoamericanos, 1964; Type and Typography, 1964; Processes of Printing and Engraving, 1964; The Yearbook, 1966; Modern Newspaper Design, 1969; Ink on Paper 2, 1971. Contbg. editor Random House Dictionary English Language, Ency. Americana, 1969—. Home: 312 Wedgewood Terrace DeWitt NY 13214 Office: Newhouse Communications Center Syracuse NY 13210

ARNOLD, ELLIOTT, author; b. N.Y.C., Sept. 13, 1912; s. Jack and Gertrude (Frank) A.; m. Helen Emmons (div., 1957); children—Thomas Guy, Mary Jean; m. 2d, Julie Kennedy, Sept. 1958 (div. Jan. 1961); m. 3d, Jacqueline Harris Stephens, Feb. 1961 (div. 1963); m. fourth, Glynis Johns, October 1964. Newspaperman on New York World-Telegram, 1934-42; mem. editorial staff The American Indian, 1948—. Served as capt. AUS, 1942-45. Decorated Bronze Star medal. Clubs: Players, Lotos, Wings: American (London, Eng.). Author: Two Loves, 1934; Personal Combat, 1936; Only the Young, 1939; Nose for News, 1941; Finlandia, The Story of Sibelius, 1941; The Commandos, 1942; Mediterranean Sweep (with Richard Threulsen), 1944; Big Distance (with Donald Hough), 1945; Tomorrow Will Sing, 1945; Blood Brother, 1947; Everybody Slept Here, 1948; Deep in My Heart, 1949; Walk with the Devil, 1950; Time of the Gringo, 1953; Broken Arrow, 1954; White Falcon, 1955 (William Allen White award 1958); Flight from Ashiya (Commonwealth Club of Cal. fiction award for 1960), 1959; A Night of Watching (Commonwealth Club of Cal. fiction award 1967), 1967; A Kind of Secret Weapon, 1969; Code of Conduct, 1970; also short stories, articles for mags. Office: care Robert H Ginter Co 120 El Camino Dr Beverly Hills CA 90212

ARNOLD, ELTING, lawyer; b. Staatsburg, N. Y., Aug. 1, 1912; s. Harry and Adelaide (Elting) A.; A.B., Williams Coll., 1934; LL.B., Columbia, 1937; m. Hannah Burr Polk, Aug. 24, 1936; children—Sarah Burr, Patricia. Editor, Columbia Law Rev., 1935-37; admitted to N.Y. bar, 1938, D.C. bar, 1949; asso. firm Root, Clark, Buckner and Ballantine, New York, 1937-39; atty. U.S. Treasury Dept., 1939-47, chief counsel Fgn. Funds Control, 1947, asst. to asst. gen. counsel, 1947-48, asst. gen. counsel in charge of internat. finance and monetary matters 1948-60; acting dir. Foreign Assets Control, 1950-60; gen. counsel Inter-Am. Development Bank, 1960—. Mem. Am. Soc. Internat. Law, N.Y., D.C. bar assns., Am. Ornithologists Union, Phi Beta Kappa. Home: 4914 Dorset Av Chevy Chase MD 20015 Office: Inter-Am Development Bank Washington DC 20577

ARNOLD, ERNEST, lawyer; b. Upland, Neb., Jan. 13, 1913; s. Ernest and Bess (Barber) A.; A.B., U. Neb., 1935, LL.B., 1937. Admitted to Neb. and Cal. bars, examiner Neb. Ry. Commn., 1937-40; claims atty. Gen. Ins. Co. Am., 1940- 42; partner firm Keith, Creed & Sedwick, San Francisco, 1946-58, Sedgwick, Deteret, Moran & Arnold, San Francisco, 1958—. Served to lt. USNR, 1942-46. Mem. Am. Bar Assn., State Bar Cal., Bar Assn. San Francisco, Internat. Assn. Ins. Counsel, Assn. Def. Counsel (bd. dirs. 1965-66), Am. Bd. Trial Advocates, Phi Alpha Delta. Club: Olympic. Home: 1890 Broadway San Francisco, CA 94109. Office: 111 Pine St San Francisco CA 94111

ARNOLD, FREDERIC EBERHARD, Jr., architect; b. Salt Lake City, July 3, 1920; s. Frederic Eberhard and Ethyl Belle (Martin) A.; student U. Utah, 1937-38; B.S. in Architecture, U. Mich., 1942; M.Arch., Washington U., St. Louis, 1947; m. Mary Ellen Dieter, June 8, 1946; children—Mary Katherine (Mrs. Dominique de Moncuit), William Frederic, Michael John, David Robert, Paul Raymund, Joseph Lee. Design architect Wittenberg, Delony & Davidson, Little Rock, 1947-52, asso., 1952-58, partner, 1958—, sec., dir. corp., 1964—. Patron, mem. Ark. Arts Center, 1965—; mem. Pulaski County Mental Health Assn., 1962—; mem. Greater Little Rock Cath. Interracial Council, 1965—, pres., 1968-69, 69-70; mem. Ark. Council on Human Relations, 1966—; mem. adv. council Econ. Opportunity Agy. Pulaski County, 1969-71; rep. Ark. Prison Ministry, 1970-71. Bd. dirs. Cath. High Sch. for Boys, Little Rock. Served with M.C. AUS, 1942-46. Registered profl. architect, Ark. Mem. A.I.A. (design group for Little Rock 1970, 1961), C. of C., Tau Sigma Delta. Roman Catholic. Project architect Riceland Foods, Stuttgart, Ark., Ark. State Hosp., Ark. Power & Light Co., Ark. Blue Cross- Blue Shield. Home: 10115 Rodney Parham Rd Little Rock AR 72207 Office: 510 Center St Little Rock AR 72201

ARNOLD, G. DEWEY, Jr., accountant; b. Montgomery, Ala., Jan. 30, 1925; s. G. Dewey and Janie Esther (Terry) A.; B.A. in Econs., U. of South, 1949; grad. student accounting, U. Tenn.; m. Dorothy Louise Wenger, Dec. 4, 1954; children—Susan O., G. Dewey III. With Aladdin Industries, Inc., Nashville, 1949-50; with Price Waterhouse & Co., C.P.A.'s, 1950-, partner, 1961-, partner charge Washington office, 1965-; instr. accounting Robert Morris Sch. Accounting, 1952-53; lectr., course dir. mgmt. accounting Inst. Mexicano de Administracion de Negocias, A.C. 1958- 64. Bd. dirs. Jr. C. of C., 1954-55; exec. com. Fed. City Council, 1966- -; bd. dirs. Greater Washington Ednl. TV Assn., Inc.; mem. Washington Bd. Trade. Served with USNR, 1943-45. C.P.A., Pa., D.C., Md. Mem. Am., D.C., Md. insts. C.P.A.'s Nat. Assn. Accountants, Am. Arbitration Assn. Episcopalian. Clubs: Rotary; Congressional Country, Burning Tree, Nat. Press, University (Washington). Home: 7107 Helmsdale Rd Bethesda, MD 20034. Office: 1707 L St N W Washington DC 20036

ARNOLD, GARY HOWARD, film critic; b. Princeton, Ind., Aug. 22, 1942; s. Charles Howard and Ferris (Smith) A.; student N.Y.U., 1959-60, U. Cal. at Berkeley, 1960-63; m. Sue Datz, Dec. 29, 1967; 1 dau., Pauline. Film critic Diplomat mag., 1966; film critic, reporter Ind. Film Jour., 1968-69; film critic Washington Post, 1969—. Home: 1230 13th St NW Washington DC 20005 Office: 1515 L St NW Washington DC 20005

ARNOLD, HARRY BARTLEY, lawyer; b. Columbus, O., Aug. 27, 1912; s. Harry Bartley and Grace (Russell) A.; A.B. summa cum laude, Princeton 1933; LL.B., Yale, 1936; m. Mary Jane Hubbard, July 8, 1936; children—Thomas Bartley, Susan Hubbard (Mrs. Richard B. Baumgartner), Nancianne (Mrs. R. Barclay Below), Katherine. Admitted to Ohio bar, 1936, since practiced in Columbus; partner firm Wright, Harlor, Dir. Midland Mut. Life Ins. Co., Columbus, 1951-, asst. counsel, 1956-62, asso. counsel, 1962-69, now gen. counsel. Chmn. screening com. Columbus United Appeal, 1965; chmn. budget and admissions com. United Community Council Columbus, 1958-59, trustee, 1958-65, pres., 1961-63; mem. Nat. Budget and Consultation Com. Nat. Health and Welfare Agencies, 1958-61. Trustee, v.p. Childrens Hosp., Columbus; trustee Columbus Acad., 1938-62, pres., 1948-55; trustee Columbus Symphony Orch., 1964- 67; mem. grad. bd. Yale Law Sch., 1957-59; trustee Columbus YMCA, 1937- 63, exec. com., 1948-56, 1st v.p., 1956. Served to lt. USNR, 1942-46; PTO Recipient George Meany Community Service award Franklin County (O.) AFL-CIO, 1962. Fellow Am. Coll. Trial Lawyers; mem. Am., Ohio, Columbus bar assns., Assn. Life Ins. Counsel, Internat. Assn. Ins. Counsel, Am. Judicature Soc. Republican. Clubs: Columbus Country, University (Columbus); Castalia (O.) Trout; Princeton of Central Ohio (pres. 1959- 62). Home: 9351 Harlem Rd Westerville, OH . 43081. Office: Huntington Trust Bldg Columbus OH 43215

ARNOLD, HARRY LOREN, Jr., dermatologist; b. Owosso, Mich., Aug. 7, 1912; s. Harry L. and Meda (Sheldon) A.; A.B. cum laude, U. Mich., 1932, M.D. cum laude, 1935; M.S., 1939; m. Jeanne M. Prevost, July 11, 1942; children—Sara Joan, Charles R., Harry Loren III, John P., Susan M. Intern, U. Mich. Hosp., 1935-36, resident, 1936-37, instr. dermatology, 1937-39; chief dermatology Straub Clinic, Honolulu, 1939-69; clin. prof. dermatology U. Hawaii. Pres. Straub Med. Research Inst., 1961-63. Diplomate Am. Bd. Dermatology (mem. bd.). Fellow A.C.P., A.A.A.S.; mem. Hawaii (past pres.), Honolulu County (past pres.) med. assns., Hawaiian Acad. Sci. (past pres.), Am. Acad. Dermatology (past v.p.), Internat. Soc. Tropical Dermatology (past v.p.), Internat. Leprosy Assn., Hawaii, Pacific (pres. 1968) dermatol. socs., A.M.A. (past del., sec., chmn., alternate del. sect. dermatology), Am. Dermatol. Assn. (bd. dirs. 1969-70, pres. 1971), Sociedad Argentina de Leprologia, Sociedad Cubana de Dermatologia y Sifilografia, Asociacion Argentina de Dermatologia, Sociedad Venezolana de Dermatologia, Venereologia y Leprologia, Honolulu Wine and Food Society, Social Sci. Assn. Honolulu, Sigma Xi, Kappa Beta Phi, Alpha Omega Alpha, Nu Sigma Nu, Phi Kappa Psi, Zeta Psi. Author: Modern Concepts of Leprosy, 1953; Raibyo Gentaiteki Gainen, 1956. Editor: Hawaii Med. Jour., 1941—, Straub Clinic Proc., 1941-; corr. editor; Internat. Jour. of Leprosy, 1950-; editorial bd. Cutis, 1965-, Group Practice, 1966-. Home: 4340 Pahoa Av Honolulu HI 98616 Office: 888 S King St Honolulu HI 96813

ARNOLD, HENRY FREDERICK, ret. fgn. service officer; b. Newark, Nov. 13, 1908; s. Henry Cyrus and Ernestine Caroline (Kiefer) A.; Litt. B., Rutgers U., 1929; M.A., Columbia, 1932; Ph.D., N.Y.U., 1942; grad. Nat. War Coll., 1956; m. Dorothy Moore, Oct. 7, 1953 (dec. Dec. 1970); one son, David Henry. Instr., Bordentown (N.J.) Mil. Inst., 1929-30; asso. prof., pub. relations officer Upsala Coll., East Orange, N.J., 1930-43; instr. several adult edn. schs., 1933-40; with O.W.I., N.Y.C., 1943-45; U.S. pub. affairs officer, Helsinki, Finland, also 2d sec., 1945-50; dep. pub. affairs adviser Bur. European Affairs, Dept. State, Washington, 1951-52, dir. Office European Programs, 1952-53; country pub. affairs officer and attache USIA, Vienna, Austria, 1953-55, asst. dep. dir. for plans, Washington, 1956-67, country pub. affairs officer, Seoul, Korea, 1957-60, fgn. service insp., 1960-62, insp. gen., 1962; counselor of embassy for pub. affairs, Teheran, Iran, 1962-66, Belgrade, Yugoslavia, 1966-70; ret., 1970. Home: 10273 Jerabach Dr San Diego CA 92131

ARNOLD, JACKSON DOMINICK, adm. U.S. Navy. Address: Chief of Naval Material Dept Navy Washington DC 20360*

ARNOLD, JAMES ELISHA, univ. dean; b. Sneedville, Tenn., Mar. 18, 1906; s. William and Dicy (Purkey) A.; B.A., Carson-Newman Coll., 1928; M.A., U. Tenn., 1932, Ed.D., 1955; m. Grace Harrison, Sept. 27, 1930; children—Edwin Harrison, Judith Grace. Tchr. English and Latin, Hancock County (Tenn.) High Sch., 1928-34; prin. Horace Maynard High Sch., Maynardville, Tenn., 1934-40, Claiborne County (Tenn.) High Sch., 1940-43; specialist sch. and community service extension div. U. Tenn., 1943-49, coordinator services, 1949-55, dean. univ. extension, 1955-70, dean continuing edn. Statewide System, 1970—. Past pres. E. Tenn. Community Improvement Program; chmn. Tenn. Ednl. TV Commn., 1954. Senator Tenn. Legislature, 1943-47. Bd. dirs. Adult Edn. Action Council, 1970. Mem. Internat. Platform Assn., Southeastern Adult Edn. Assn. (pres. 1952-53), N.E.A., Tenn. Edn. Assn., Nat. U. Extension Assn. (chmn. govtl. relations com. 1969), Am. Assn. State Univs. and Land-Grant Colls. (chmn. council gen. extension 1960), Adult Edn. Assn. U.S.A. (exec. com. 1957-59), Newcomen Soc., Acacia (alumni pres.), Phi Delta Kappa. Republican. Baptist. Kiwanian. Author: A Study of Adult Education through University Extension with Special Reference to the University of Tennessee, 1955. Home: 4701 Holston Hills Rd Knoxville, TN 37916.

ARNOLD, JAMES RICHARD, educator, chemist; b. New Brunswick, N.J., May 5, 1923; s. Abraham Samuel and Julia (Jacobs) A.; A.B., Princeton, 1943, M.A., 1945, Ph.D., 1946; m. Louise Clark, Oct. 11, 1952; children—Robert C., Theodore J., Kenneth C. Postdoctorate fellow Inst. Nuclear Studies, U. Chgo., 1946- 47, mem. faculty, 1948-55; NRC fellow Harvard, 1947-48; mem. faculty chemistry Princeton, 1955-58; asso. prof. chemistry U. Cal. at San Diego, 1958-60, prof., 1960—, chmn. dept. chemistry, 1960-63; asso. on Manhattan Project, 1943-46. Mem. lunar and planetary missions bd. of NASA; mem. space sci. bd. Nat. Acad. Sci.; chmn. sub-com. radio-chemistry NRC. Pres. Torrey Pines Elementary Sch. P.T.A., 1964-65. Pres. La Jolla Democratic Club, 1965-66. Mem. Nat. council World Federalists-U.S.A., 1970—. Remsen Meml. lectr. Am. Chem. Soc., 1965; recipient E.O. Lawrence medal AEC, 1968. Mem. Nat. Acad. Sci., Am. Acad. Arts and Scis., Am. Chem. Soc., A.A.A.S., Nat. Council Fedn. Am. Scientist. Asso. editor Jour. Chem. Physics, 1953-56. Contbr. articles profl. jours. Home: 9505 Poole St La Jolla CA 92038

ARNOLD, JOHN A., ins. exec.; b. Lake Geneva, Wis., Oct. 2, 1890; s. Clifton S. and Anna E. (Alfred) A.; student Middlebury Coll., 1913, M.A., 1954; m. Lucy M. Kelley, Dec. 22, 1917; 1 son, John A. Spl. agt. Fitchburg Mut. Fire Ins. Co. (Mass.), 1915-17; sec. Mut. Ins. Agy., Inc., Fitchburg, 1917-23, Merrimack Mut. Ins. Co., Andover, Mass., 1923-32; sec. Fed. Mut. Fire Ins. Co., Boston, 1932-37, v.p., dir., 1937—, gen. mgr., 1952-56, sr. v.p., 1956-70; v.p. Am. Mfrs. Mut. Ins. Co., N.Y.C., 1941-70, exec. v.p., 1953-56, sr. v.p., 1956- 70; treas., dir. Am. Mut. Reins. Co., Chgo., 1941-65; pres., dir. Mut. Loss Research Bur., 1946-60; v.p. Lumbermens Mut. Casualty Co., 1948-58, sr. v.p., 1963-70; v.p. Am. Motorists Ins. Co., 1949-65, sr. v.p., 1963-70; exec. asst. to chmn. bd. Kemper Ins. Group; dir. Asso. Mutuals, Inc. Mem. exec. com. Transp. Ins. Rating Bur., 1946-66. Past trustee Middlebury Coll. Mem. Mut. Ins. Inst. (pres., dir. 1962-70) Mut. Ins. Adv. Assn. (dir.), Associated Alumni Middlebury Coll. (past pres.), Delta Kappa Epsilon. Republican. Conglist. Mason (32, K.T., Shriner). Clubs: Tower (Chicago); University (Evanston). Contbr. profl. jours. Home: 1704 Hinman Av Evanston IL 60201

ARNOLD, JOHN HENRY, chem. co. exec.; b. Hyde Park, Mass., Sept. 11, 1909; s. Henry Freeman and Agnes (Bigelow) A.; B.S., Mass. Inst. Tech., 1931, M.S., 1932; m. Urania Marie Bernadas, Jan. 12, 1946; children—John Henry, Kathryn (Mrs. Alan Sheppard), Susan, Mary. Dir. research and devel. Kellex Corp., N.Y.C., 1943-45; v.p., dir. Hydrocarbon Research, Inc., N.Y.C., 1945-54; cons. engr., N.Y.C., 1959-61; v.p. No. Chem. Co., Balt., 1957-59; cons. engr., Searsport, Me., 1959-61; v.p. Air Products & Chems., Inc., Allentown, Pa., 1961—; dir. Tektran; mem. vis. com. chem. engring. dept. Lehigh U. Financial v.p. Lehigh Valley Assn. for Retarded Children, 1965—; mem. planning com. Allentown Community Coll., 1966; mem. coll. coordinating council Fairleigh Dickinson U.; mem. men's maintenance com. Allentown Symphony Orch., 1969-70. Mem. Am. Chem. Soc., Am. Soc. Mech. Engrs., A.A.A.S., N.Y. Acad. Sci. Roman Catholic. Home: 69 Lehigh Pkwy N Allentown PA 18103 Office: Air Products & Chems Inc Allentown PA 18101

ARNOLD, JOHN PHILLIP, educator; b. Elmore, Minn., Feb. 5, 1911; s. Archie Vernon and Eva Mattie (Kircher) A.; student Alexandria Jr. Coll., 1934-35; D.V.M., Ia. State U., 1941, M.S., 1948; Ph.D., U. Minn., 1956; m. Margaret Hazel Crom, June 6, 1944; children—Phillip Marshall, Mary Margaret. Pvt. practice vet. medicine, Blooming Prairie, Minn., 1941-46, Mora, Minn., 1948-50; mem. staff Ia. State U., 1947-48; instr. U. Minn., St. Paul, 1950-56, asso. prof., head vet. surgery and radiology, 1956-57, prof., head vet. surgery and radiology, 1967-71, prof., acting head vet. hosps., 1971—. C.I.A. adviser vet. medicine Seoul Nat. U., 1960-61; cons. A.I.D., Colombia, 1963. Mem. Am., Minn. (pres. 1970) So. Minn., Twin City vet. med. assns., Am. Assn. Equine Practitioners, Minn. Acad. Equine Practitioners, Conf. Research Workers Animal Disease., Minn. Territorial Pioneers (dir.). Methodist. Mason. Contbr. articles to profl. jours., chpt. to book. Research on surgery bovine mammary gland, innveration of abdominal wall of cattle. Home: 5406 E Bald Eagle Blvd White Bear Lake MN 55110 Office: Vet Hosps U Minn St Paul MN 55101

ARNOLD, JULEAN, ret. govt. ofcl.; b. Hankow, China, Oct. 8, 1914 (parents U.S. citizens); s. Julean and Gertrude (Davis) A.; B.A., Pomona Coll., 1936; A.M. Fletcher Sch. Law and Diplomacy, 1938; student Sch. Advanced Internat. Studies, Johns Hopkins, 1959; m. June Carl, Dec. 2, 1944; children—Judith T., Christine W., Richard B. Comml. agt. Dept. of Commerce, 1939-41; internat. trade economist Dept. of State, Washington, 1946-52; with U.S. Tech Coop. mission to Brazil, 1952-57, ICA-AID, Washington, 1958-61, 65-67; mem. Internat. Secretariat, Orgn. for Econ. Cooperation and Devel., Paris, France, 1962-65; assigned AID Mission to Vietnam, 1967-69. Mem. U.S. delegations Internat. Tariff Confs. conducted under Gen. Agreement on Tariffs and Trade, Geneva, Switzerland, 1947, Annecy, France, 1949; mem. U.S. delegation 32d Session UN Econ. and Social Council, Geneva, 1961. Served to lt. col., AUS, 1941-46. Home: 6631 Park Ridge Blvd San Diego CA 92120

ARNOLD, LEE, engr., educator; b. Chgo., Dec. 26, 1912; s. George Edward and Sarah (Elbaum) A.; B.S. with honors, Duke, 1937; M.S. (fellow), Cal. Inst. Tech., 1938; Ph.D., Columbia, 1947; m. Muriel Streich, July 6, 1941 (dec. Oct. 2, 1962); children—Joan Holly, Jane Susan. Research engr. Glenn L. Martin Co., 1938-40; chief vibrations group Republic Aviation Co., 1940-41; cons. United Aircraft Co., 1941- 42; head structural dynamics and development Bur. Aeros., USN, 1942-45; partner Biot & Arnold, cons. applied mathematics and physics, 1945-50; pres. Lee Arnold Assos., Inc., N.Y.C., 1950—; prof. Inst. Flight Structures, Columbia, 1953-58; prof. aero. and astronautical engring., dir. Guggenheim sch. aeros. N.Y. U., 1958—; president Kahf Company, Inc., engring. sci. and research development, N.Y.C., 1955; v.p. Gen. Applied Sci. Labs.; pres. Pan Tech. Cons., Inc., 1969—. Mem. nat. adv. com. aeros.; member seminar group for aero. research and development NATO, 1954; cons. NASA, 1966-69, to Sec. Dept. Transp., 1966—. Asso. fellow Inst. Aero. Scis.; mem. Am. Inst. Aeros. and Astronautics, Acoustical Soc. Am., Phi Beta Kappa. Mem. editorial staff Jour. Aero. Scis. Address: 177 E 77th St New York City NY 10021

ARNOLD, LIONEL KENNETH, educator; b. Bristow, Ia., Dec. 30, 1895; s. Arthur Albert and Caroline (Jakeway) A.; A.B., Ellsworth Coll., 1920; B.S., Ia. State U., 1921, M.S., 1926, Ph.D., 1930; m. Lora Annette Killius, May 14, 1923; children—Charlotte (Mrs. Steven J. Honet), Lionel Charles. Emeritus prof. chem. engring. dept. Ia. State U.; cons., expert witness on agrl. by-product utilization and fires, explosions (gas). Served with AUS, World War I. Mem. Am. Inst. Chem. Engrs., Ia. Acad. Sci., Sigma Xi, Phi Kappa Phi, Phi Lambda Upsilon. Author: Introduction to Plastics, 1968. Home: 635 Agg Av Ames IA 50010

ARNOLD, MALCOLM, musician; b. Northampton, Eng., Oct. 21, 1921; s. William and Anne (Hawes) A.; student Royal Coll. Music, London; study (Mendelsohn scholar) Italy, 1948; D. Mus. (hon.), Exeter Coll., 1970. Prin. trumpet London Philharmonic Orchestra, 1941- 43, 1945-48; composer coronation ballet Homage to the Queen, 1953; composer 6 symphonies. Recipient Academy Motion Picture Arts and Scis. award for music Bridge on the River Kwai, 1958. Decorated comdr. Order Brit. Empire, 1970. Home: Primrose Cottage St Merryn Padstow Cornwall England

ARNOLD, MARGARET LONG, (Mrs. Dexter Otis Arnold), club woman; b. Lusk, Wyo., Aug. 15, 1914; d. S. Burman and Margaret M (Hock) Long; A.B., Syracuse U., 1934; H.H.D., New Eng. Coll., 1951; m. Dexter Otis Arnold, June 27, 1939. Dir. of speech and dramatics Syracuse schs., 1935-39; pres. N.H. Fedn. Women's Clubs, 1950-52; chmn. UN specialized agys. Gen. Fedn. Women's Clubs, 1952-54, communications dept., 1954-56, recording sec., 1956—, 1st v.p., 1960, pres., 1962-64, hon. pres., 1964—; also daily radio commentator. Chmn. N.H. Council Problems of Aging; mem. nat. adv. com. White House Conf. on Aging; vice chmn. Nat. Conf. on Citizenship; chmn. Def. Adv. Com. on Women in the Services; N.Y. State chmn. Continuing Edn. Council; mem. N.Y. Council Women, N.Y. Council on Aging, U.S. Interdepartmental Adv. Council on Status of Women, Citizens Council Status of Women, N.Y. State Council Continuing Edn.; dir. Council World Affairs; dir., v.p. CARE, N.H. Social Welfare Council, Old Ft. No. 4, N.Y. World's Fair; bd. govs. Arthritis and Rheumatism Found.; bd. visitors Am. Freedom Center, Freedoms Found. at Valley Forge; trustee Am. Freedom from Hunger Found., Inc.; chmn. bd. Outstanding Young Women in Am.; bd. dirs. Girls Clubs Am., USO, Mid Hudson Patterns for Progress; alumni council rep. Syracuse Univ. Named N.H. Dist. Citizen; recipient Pettee medal U. N.H.; Arents medal U. Syracuse; Nat. Recognition award Freedoms Found.; Alumni award 4-H, 1966. Mem. Ch. Women's Assn., Concord Hosp. Assn. (v.p. 1952-53), League Women Voters, Am. Assn. U. Women, Nat. Laymens League (dir.), Delta Gamma (past nat. officer). Conglist. Home: 15 Dewitt Dr Saugerties NY 12477

ARNOLD, MARTIN, journalist; b. N.Y.C., May 14, 1929; s. A.M. and Evelyn (Goodman) A.; B.A., Adelphi Coll., 1951; m. Irmgard Alexy, May 25, 1952; children—Mark William, Christopher Curt. With Newsday, 1952-54, N.Y. Herald Tribune, 1954-59; reporter N.Y. Times, 1959—. Fellow Robert F. Kennedy Meml. Found. Served with AUS, 1946-48. Recipient George Polk award for polit.

reporting, 1968; Page One award for feature writing N.Y. Newspaper Guild, 1970. Home: 2710 S St Marks Av Bellmore NY 11710 Office: 229 W 43d St New York City NY 10036

ARNOLD, MELVIN CHESTER, mfg. co. exec.; b. Toledo, Mar. 8, 1923; s. Chester E. and Esther (Lauffer) A.; B.S., Ohio State U., 1944; LL.B., U. Toledo, 1948; m. Julia McDonald, Sept. 27, 1947; children—Douglas McDonald, David Lauffer, Barbara Jean, Melvin Chester, Mark Emerick, Wendy Lauretta, Francis John, Julie Ann. Admitted to Ohio bar, 1949, Neb. bar, 1953; legal counsel Toledo Scale Corp., 1946-52; sec., dir. Omaha Retinning Corp., 1955-59; sec., treas., dir. Omaha Foods Inc., 1957-59; legal consel Omar, Inc., Omaha, 1953-59; sec., asso. counsel Eaton Corp., Clev., 1959-67, v.p., gen. counsel, 1967—. Bd. dirs. Welfare Fedn.; trustee of Hill House, Cleve.; bd. trustees Family Service Assn. Mem. Am., Ohio, Cleve. (chmn. corp. law dept. com.) bar assns., Am. Soc. Corp. Secs., Cleve. C. of C., Alpha Tau Omega. Rotarian. Clubs: Mayfield Country, Union, Cleveland Playhouse, Clevelander, Mid-Day (Cleve.); Wequetonsing Golf (Harbor Springs, Mich.). Home: 22500 Shelburne Rd Shaker Heights OH 44122 Office: 100 Erieview Plaza Cleveland OH 44114

ARNOLD, MELVIN LUXTON, editor; b. Portland, Ore., Aug. 23, 1913; s. Daniel and Letitia (Luxton) A.; student pub. schs. of Portland; m. Valerie Hendricksen, May 13, 1933; 1 dau., Alexandra. Reporter News-Telegram, Portland, 1930-35; advt. and pub. relations work, 1935-43; on leave to exec. office Pres. of U.S., U.S. Treasury campaign, 1943-44; head publs. group, pub. relations dept. Standard Oil Co. (N.J.), 1944-45; dir., editor-in-chief Beacon Press, Boston, 1947-56; asso. dir. Harper & Row, 1956—, editor, 1956-65, sr. v.p., dir., 1966-67, pres., 1967-70, sr. editor, 1970—; editor Harper Torchbooks, 1956-65. Unitarian. Club: Century Assn. (N.Y.C.). Author (with C.R. Joy), Africa of Albert Schweitzer, 1948, rev. edit., 1959. Office: 28 Tavistock St London WC2E 7PN England

ARNOLD, MILTON WYLIE, air transportation; b. Troup County, Ga., May 23, 1907; s. Abner Reeves and Anita (Hightower) A.; student A. Inst. Tech., 1924-27; B.S., U.S. Mil. Acad., 1931; grad. Advanced Flying Sch., Kelly Field, Tex., 1932; M.S., Calif. Inst. Tech., 1937, spl. research, 1941; m. Sallie Elliott Jesse, December 12, 1932; m. 2d, Dorothy De Golyer, May 15, 1954 (dec. 1969); children—Felicia De Golyer and Douglas de Golyer Arnold. Commd. 2d lt., U.S.A.A.F., 1931, advanced through grades to brig. gen., 1945; assigned directorate of weather, Office Chief of Air Force, Washington, D.C., 1941; assigned Operations, Air Transport Command, 1942, in charge development of No. Atlantic ferry route, 1942, in charge planning and operations of presidential air transp., Casablanca Conf., and later round the world flights, 1943; with 8th Air Force, Eng., 1943-45, wing comdr. 2d Combat Bomb Wing, 1944-45; chief of staff Air Transport Command, Washington, D.C., 1945; voluntarily retired, 1946; v.p. in charge operations and engring. Air Transport Assn. Am., 1946-58; pres. Gen. Aircraft and Leasing div. Gen. Dynamics Corp., 1958-62; dir. Middleburg Nat. Bank, Air Express Internat. Trustee and founder Anglo-Am. Meml. Library, Norwich, Eng. Mem. President's Spl. Bd. of Inquiry on Air Safety, 1947. Decorated Silver Star, Legion of Merit, Distinguished Flying Cross with 3 oak leaf clusters. Bronze Star Medal, Air Medal with 4 oak leaf clusters (U.S.), Croix de Guerre with palm (France and Belgium), Distinguished Flying Cross (Gt. Britain). Asso. fellow Inst. Aeronaut. Scis.; Sigma Xi, Chi Phi. Episcopalian. Author, lectr. in field. Clubs: Army-Navy Country, Army and Navy, Metropolitan (Washington); Eastward Ho Country; Chathan Beach and Tennis; Stage Harbor Yacht. Home: Middleburg VA 22117

ARNOLD, PHILIP MILLS, oil co. exec.; b. Springfield, Mo., Feb. 9, 1911; s. Anthony L. and Mary Genevieve (Hodnett) A.; B.S., Washington U., 1932, Chem. E., 1941. Chem. engr. research div. Philips Petroleum Co., 1937-45, asst. mgr. chem. engring. div., 1946-48, asst. mgr. chem. dept., 1948-50, mgr. research and devel. dept., 1950-64, v.p. research and devel., 1964—. Exec. com. div. chemistry and chem. tech. NRC, 1961-65; mem. U.S. Nat. Com., Internat. Union Pure and Applied Chemistry, 1961-, chmn., 1964-68; mem. bur. Internat. Union Pure and Applied Chemistry, 1969—; dir. Coordinating Research Council, 1964, pres., 1969-71; pres. Indsl. Research Inst., 1964-65. Fellow Am. Inst. Chemists, Am. Inst. of Chem. Engrs; mem. Nat. Acad. Engring., Soc. Chem. Industry, World Petroleum Congresses (perm. council), Am. Chem. Soc., A.A.A.S., Dirs. Indsl. Research, Am. Petroleum Inst., Am. Soc. Testing Materials, Atomic Industrial Forum (dir. 1966-69), Ind. Natural Gas Assn., Ind. Petroleum Assn., Sigma Chi, Tau Beta Pi, Alpha Chi Sigma. Republican. Home: Box 1457 Bartlesville OK 74003 Office: Phillips Petroleum Co Bartlesville OK 74004

ARNOLD, REMMIE LEROY, mfr., Masonic Lodge ofcl.; b. Petersburg, Va., Jan. 25, 1894; s. Andrew Alexander and Mary Virginia (Longworth) A.; student pub. schs.; m. Charlia Sears, Apr. 27, 1918; children—Remmie Le-Roy, Dorothy Lawrence (Mrs. Robert J. Waite). Founder Edison Pen Co., pres., 1915-35; founder, owner, R. L. Arnold Pen Co., Inc., Petersburg, Va., 1935—, pres. Remmie Arnold Pen Co., Inc., 1955—; exec. dir. So. States Indsl. Council, 1941-44, pres., 1946-48; mem. industry com. Dept. Labor, 1941. Active all phases of Masonry, 33, Shriner; leader Shrine hosp. work; trustee Crippled Children Hosp. Bd. of the Shriners Hosp. of N. Am., since 1965; past imperial potentate, N.Y.C. Mem. Nat. Register Prominent Ams., Va. Agrl. Extension Service, Wisdom Hall of Fame. Mem. Am. War Dads (nat. pres. 1943-44), Va., Petersburg (dir.) chambers commerce, Va. Mfrs. Assn. (dir. 1938-39), Va. Aviation Flying Corps, U.S.N. League, League Va. Municipalities, Newcomen Soc. Eng., Square and Compass, Sigma Alpha Chi, and others. Democrat. Baptist. Elk (exalted ruler, 1939-41, dist. dep. Grand exalted ruler, 1944), Eagle, Red Man, Kiwanian. Clubs: Circus Sinners and Saints (organizer, 1st pres. Will Rogers Tent, 1937, nat. pres. 1938- 39, trustee), Ruritan (Prince George), Commonwealth (Richmond, Va.); Country, Indian Swamp Fishing (Petersburg) and others. Home: 12 Saddleback Lane Petersburg VA 23803 Office: 15 N Union St Petersburg VA 23803 ☆

ARNOLD, RICHARD KEITH, research adminstr.; b. Long Beach, Cal., Nov. 17, 1913; s. H. Park and Mayme (Swan) A.; A.A., Glendale Jr. Coll., 1935; B.S., U. Cal. at Berkeley, 1937; M.F., Yale, 1938; Ph.D., U. Mich., 1950; m. Helen Louise DuBose, Feb. 7, 1942; children—Bruce Gaillard, Richard Park, Jay Ross; m. 2d, Lillian C. DeAngelis, Oct. 24, 1970. Asso. in forestry U. Cal., Berkeley, 1939-42, asst. prof., 1946-51, 53-55; forester, fire research Forest Service, Dept. Agr., Berkeley, 1951-53. chief of fire research, 1955-57, dir. Pacific S.W. Forest Expt. Sta., 1957-63. dir. div. forest protection research Forest Service, Washington, 1963-66, dep. chief of research, Washington, 1969—; dean Sch. Natural Resources, U. Mich., 1966-69; cons. civil def. and fire research State of Cal.; cons. Fed. civil Def., Pacific Sci. Assn.; U.S. rep. Forestry, 1957-62; U.S. mem. FAO Com. on Forestry Edn., 1968-69; mem. adv. com. Yale U. Sch. Forestry; mem. fire research com. Nat. Acad. Sci., 1968—. Chmn. fire working group N.Am. Forestry Commn., 1965-66, chmn. com. of alternates, 1970—. Mem. Mich. Gov.'s Commn. on Urban Affairs, 1968. Served to lt. USNR, 1942-46. Fellow Soc. Am. Foresters (past mem. governing council); mem. Internat. Union Forestry Research Orgns. (sect. chmn.), Internat. Union Socs. of Foresters (exec.dir.), A.A.A.S., Am. Forestry Assn., Phi Beta Kappa, Sigma Xi. Kiwanian. Club: Cosmos (Washington). Home: 6303 Cedell Ct Camp Springs MD 20031 Office: Forest Service US Dept Agr Washington DC 20250

ARNOLD, RICHARD SHEPPARD, lawyer; b. Texarkana, Tex., Mar. 26, 1936; s. Richard Lewis and Janet (Sheppard) A.; grad. Phillips Exeter Acad., 1953; B.A. summa cum laude, Yale, 1957; J.D. magna cum laude, Harvard, 1960; m. Gale Ann Palmer Hussman, June 14, 1958; children—Janet Sheppard, Lydia Palmer. Admitted to D.C. bar, 1961, Ark. bar, 1960; practiced in Washington, 1961-64, Texarkana, 1964—; law clk. to Justice Brennan, Supreme Ct. of U.S., 1960-61; asso. Covington & Burling, 1961-64; partner Arnold & Arnold, 1964—; part-time instr. U. Va. Law Sch., 1962-64. Mem. Ark. Constl. Revision Study Commn., 1967-68; gen. chmn. Texarkana United Way Crusade, 1969-70; pres. Texarkana Community Chest, 1970-71. Candidate for Congress, 4th Dist. Ark., 1966; del. Democratic Nat. Conv., 1968; del. Ark. Constl. Conv., 1969-70; chmn. Ark. Dem. Party Com. on Presidential Primaries, 1968 Bd. Dirs. Lake Texarkana Water Supply Corp Mem. Cum Laude Soc., Phi Beta Kappa. Episcopalian. Case editor: Harvard Law Review, 1959-60. Contbr. articles profl. jours. Home: 305 E 20th Texarkana AR 75501 Office: 507 Hickory St Texarkana AR 75501

ARNOLD, RICHARD THOMAS, educator; b. Indpls., June 18, 1913; s. Robert Henry and Sarah Anne (Jones) A.; B.E., So. Ill. State Tchrs. Coll., 1934; M.S., U. Ill., 1935, Ph.D., 1937; m. Doris Marie Madsen, Sept. 1, 1939; children—Mary Lyn, Robert Henry. Research fellow U. Ill., 1936-37; became mem. faculty U. of Minn., 1937, prof. chemistry, 1946, head dept. of chemistry, 1953-55; program adminstr., basic research in phys. sci. Alfred P. Sloan Found., N.Y.C., 1955-60; dir. research Mead Johnson & Co., 1960, v.p. in charge research, 1961-62, v.p., chmn. sci. adv. bd., 1968—; pres. Mead Johnson Research Center, 1962—; prof., chmn. dept. chemistry So. Ill. U., 1969—. Recipient award in pure chem. Am. Chem. Soc., 1949. Guggenheim fellow, 1948; sci. adviser to U.S. High Commr., Germany, 1952-53. Mem. Am. Chem. Soc., A.A.A.S., Phi Beta Kappa, Sigma Xi, Alpha Chi Sigma. Editor: Organic Syntheses, 1952. Home: 5 Heritage Rd Carbondale IL 62901

ARNOLD, ROBERT OLIVER, textile mfr.; b. Hampton, Ga., Oct. 24, 1888; s. Robert Johnson and Nellie (Curry) A.; B.S., U. Ga., 1908; LL.D., Mercer U., 1961; m. Florence Turner, Mar. 20, 1930. With Arnold Grocery Co., Athens, Ga., 1908-14, Athens Mattress & Spring Bed Co., 1908-17; sec. Hampton (Ga.) Cotton Mills, 1919, pres., 1920-24; v.p., gen. mgr. Mallison Braided Cord Co., Athens, 1924-32; treas., gen. mgr. Covington (Ga.) Mills, 1932-45, pres. 1945—, dir.; mem. bd. dirs. Ga. Railroad & Banking Co. since 1935, Cotton-Textile Inst., N.Y.C., 1944-47; dir. Mobile (Ala.) Gas Service Corp. 1945—, chmn. bd., 1970—; dir. Atlanta Gas-Light Co., 1948—, Henry Grady Hotel Corp., Phoenix Ins. Corp., Phoenix Investment Co., Atlanta; trustee First Atlantic Realty Fund. Mayor, Athens, 1916-17. Trustee Ga. Baptist Children's Home; chmn. bd. regents U. Ga., 1949-63. Served as capt. U.S. Army, 1917-19. Mem. Cotton Mfrs. Assn. Ga. (pres. 1939-40). Am. Legion (past comdr.), Newcomen Soc. Eng. Baptist. Home: Covington GA 30209 Office: P O Box 191 Covington GA 30209

ARNOLD, RUCKER DEAN, telephone co. exec.; b. Granite City, Ill., Apr. 29, 1933; s. Glen Andrew and Malinda (Squires) A.; B.S., Washington U., 1957; M.B.A., Ohio State U., 1960; m. LuWayne Judith Eskelin, Apr. 8, 1961; children—Tamara Judith, Andrea LuWayne, Dean Michael. Mem. sr. staff Arthur Andersen & Co., St. Louis, 1957-62; controller Continental Telephone Corp., St. Louis, 1962-71, v.p., controller, 1971—. Served with AUS, 1953-55. Mem. Am. Inst. C.P.A.'s, U.S. Ind. Telephone Assn. (accounting com.), Am. Accounting Assn., Mo. Soc. C.P.A.'s. Office: 222 S Central St St Louis MO 63105

ARNOLD, STANLEIGH, Sunday editor Chronicle Features. Address: 555 Sutter St San Francisco CA 94102*

ARNOLD, STANLEY NORMAN, business cons.; b. Cleve., May 26, 1915; s. Morris L. and Mildrd (Stearn) A.; B.S. in Econs., Wharton Sch. U. Pa., 1937; m. Barbara Anne Laing, Aug. 31, 1946; 1 dau., Jennifer Laing. Co-founder, exec. v.p. Pick-N-Pay Super Markets, Inc., Cleve., 1937-51; v.p., dir. Cottage Creamery, Co., Cleve., 1937-51; dir. sales promotion div. Young & Rubicam, Inc., N.Y.C., 1952-58; founder, pres. Stanley Arnold & Asso., Inc., N.Y.C., 1958—; cons. Ford Motor Co., United Air Lines, General Electric, Nat. Cash Register, Phillip Morris, Continental Can Co., Am. Express, Hunt Foods, Quaker Oats, Goodyear, Republic Steel, numerous others. Founding mem. Nat. Businessmen for Humphrey, 1968, Nat. Citizens for Humphrey, 1968; chmn. White House Library Fund Raising Com., 1961-63. Bd. govs. Nat. Arthritis Found.; pres. Ind. Sch. Fund N.Y.C. Clubs: Lotos, Dutch Treat, Les Amis D'Escoffier, Fifth Avenue (N.Y.C.); Racquet, Tennis, Seven Lakes Country, Tamarisk Country (Palm Springs). Author: Tale of the Blue Horse, 1968; also contbr. periodicals. Home: 1020 Park Av New York City NY 10028 Office: 375 Park Av New York City NY 10021

ARNOLD, TERRELL E. S., fgn. service officer; b. Bluefield, W.Va., Dec. 14, 1925; s. Carl Eugene and Mary Elizabeth (Craven) A.; A.B., Stanford, 1953; M.A., San Jose (Cal.) State Coll., 1957; m. Yvonne Iris Wright, Nov. 25, 1951. Tchr. English and pub. speaking Fremont High Sch., Oakland, Cal., 1954-56; joined U.S. Fgn. Service, 1957; analyst Bur. Intelligence and Research, State Dept., 1958- 59; econ. officer embassy, Cairo, 1960-61, consulate gen., Calcutta, 1962-64; economist Bur. Econ. Affairs, State Dept., 1965-67, chief food for freedom div., 1967-69; dep. chief mission embassy, Colombo, Ceylon, 1969-70; assigned Nat. War Coll., 1970-1. Served with USNR, 1943-46, 51- 52. Recipient Meritorious Service award State Dept., 1966. Mem. Am. Fgn. Service Assn. Episcopalian. Home: 1425 4th St SW Washington DC 20024 Office: Dept State Washington DC 20520

ARNOLD, TOM, lawyer; b. Houston, Nov. 20, 1923; s. Thomas Jewel and Georgia (Buck) A.; B.S. in Elec. Engring., U. Tex., 1943, LL.B., 1949; m. Grace Gordon, Dec. 8, 1956; children—Vivian Gordon Thomas. Admitted to Tex., D.C. bars, 1949; practice in Houston, 1951—; lawyer patent sect. U.S. Dept. Justice, 1949-51; asso., partner Hutcheson, Taliaferro & Hutcheson, 1951-56; partner Arnold & Roylance, 1957-66, Arnold, Roylance, Kruger & Durkee, 1966-69, Arnold, White & Durkee, 1969—; sometime lectr. patent, trade mark and copyright law U. Tex., U. Houston, S. Tex. Coll. Law. Dir. South Tex. Law Jour., Inc., 1960—, pres., 1966. Chmn. Nat. Council Patent Law Assns., 1969-70; mem. adv. com. Crews Lecture Series 1965—, Patent, Trademark and Copyright Research Inst., George Washington U., 1966—, Tex. Legislative Council, 1966-67; mem. patent adv. com. U.S. Dept. Commerce, 1968-71. Bd. dirs. Houston Tennis Patrons, 1965—. Served to lt. (j.g.) USNR, 1943-46. Fellow Tex. Legal Found.; mem. Am. (past chmn. patent, trademark, copyright sect.), Tex. (past sec. and chmn. patent, trademark, copyright sect.) Houston bar assns., Am. (bd. mgrs.), Houston patent law assns., Houston C. of C., U. Tex. Ex-student's Assn. (exec. council, 1970—), Tex. Execs. of Houston (pres. 1969-70), Practising Law Inst. (adv. council 1968—), Order of Coif, Phi Gamma Delta, Phi Eta Sigma. Republican. Methodist. Kiwanian. Asst. editor: Tex. Law Rev., 1948-49. Contbr. articles profl. jours. Home: 6014 Deerwood St Houston TX 77027 Office: Post Oak Tower Houston TX 77027

ARNOLD, VICTOR CLAYOUS, coll. dean; b. Kalamazoo, Mich., Sept. 29, 1925; s. George P. and Clara (Crowe) A.; B.A., Western Mich. U., 1949; M.A., U. Wis., 1950, Ph.D., 1958; m. Margie Lee Hartleroad, Oct. 23, 1944; children—Victoria Lee (Mrs. Wayne Williams), Sandra M. (Mrs. Thomas F. Johnson), Brandley C., Elizabeth Anne. Asst. dean letters and sci. U. Wis., 1952-60, 1962-63; dean liberal arts U. Dubuque, 1960-62; dean coll. North Central Coll., 1963-71; dean coll. St. Andrews Presbyn. Coll., 1971—, prof. European history, 1971—. Served with AUS, 1943-47. Mem. Am. Hist. Assn., Am. Conf. Academic Deans, Phi Alpha Theta. Presbyn. (elder 1956-68). Home: Route 1 Lakewood Hills Laurinburg NC 28352

ARNOLD, WALTER MARTIN, educator, govt. ofcl.; b. Steelton, Pa., June 14, 1906; s. Philip and Ella (Sullenberger) A.; B.S., Pa. State U., 1929, M.Ed., 1935; Ed.D., Okla. State U., 1957; m. Evelyn Reeser, June 5, 1931; children—Jean Elizabeth (Mrs. Francis A. Rudolph, Jr.), Philip Elbert, Marilyn Ethel (Mrs. James A. Miller). Instr., Lancaster (Pa.) Boys High Sch., 1929-37; supt. Stevens Trade Sch., Lancaster, 1937-41; spl. rep. trade and indsl. edn. U.S. Office Edn., 1941-43; dir. vocational edn. Allentown (Pa.) city schs., 1943-45; personnel mgr. Mack Mfg. Corp., 1945-49; asso. H. W. Beyer Assos., pension cons., Allentown, 1949-50; supr. trade and indsl. edn., Okla., 1950-54; dir., exec. officer vocational edn., Kan., 1954-59; dir. area vocational edn. br., div. vocational and tech. edn., U.S. Office Edn., 1959-61, asst. commnr. vocational and tech. edn., 1961- 67; cons. vocational and tech edn., also dir. of Pa. Study of Vocational Edn., 1967-69; Pres. Am. Vocational Research Corp., 1969—. Pres. Kan. Adult Edn. Assn., 1958-59; mem. Gov. Kan. Com. Mental Retardation, 1958, Gov. Kan. Inter-Deptl. Com. Aging, 1956-59, Kan. Adv. Council Edn., 1954-59; chmn. planning com. Four State Conf., 1957; tng. dir. Kan. Survival Plan Project, 1956-59. Mem. Am. Soc. Engring. Edn., Am. Tech. Edn. Assn., Council Local Admistrs. Vocational Edn. and Practical Arts, Am. Vocational Assn., N.E.A., Pa. State U. Alumni Assn., Okla. State U. Alumni Assn., Nat. Assn. State Directors Vocational Edn., A.A.A.S., Am. Soc. for Tng. and Devel., Alpha Chi Rho, Kappa Phi Kappa, Kappa Delta Pi, Phi Delta Kappa, Iota Lambda Sigma. Home: 1301 S Scott St Arlington VA 22204 Office: 1510 H St NW Washington DC 20005

ARNOLD, WALTER HAROLD, lawyer; b. Woodruff, S.C., May 1, 1907; s. Walter Hardin and Carrie (Anderson) A.; LL.B. cum laude, Furman U., Greenville, S.C., 1931; m. Lucy Hoyt Furman, Mar. 2, 1935; children—Caroline (Mrs. Carlisle Ragland Davis Jr.), Walter Harold. Admitted to S.C. bar, 1930; since practiced in Greenville; city atty., Greenville, 1951—; spl. S.C. state circuit judge Anderson County, 1955, Richland County, 1961. Mem. S.C. Bd. Commrs. on Grievances and Discipline, 1968—. Recipient Distinguished Pub. Service award Nat. Inst. Municipal Law Officers, 1960. Mem. Am., S.C. (past mem. exec. com.), Greenville County (past pres.) bar assns., Internat. Assn. Ins. Counsel, Pi Kappa Phi, Tau Kappa Alpha. Mason, Lion. Home: 1732 N Main St Greenville SC 29609 Office: Lawyers Bldg Greenville SC 29603

ARNOLD, WILLIAM ARCHIBALD, biologist; b. Douglas, Wyo., Dec. 6, 1904; s. William Archibald and Nellie Agnes (O'Brien) A.; B.S., Cal. Inst. Tech., 1931; Ph.D., Harvard, 1935; m. Jean Irving Tompkins, Sept. 11, 1929; children—Elizabeth Irving (Mrs. G. Lew Choules) and Helen Holbrook (Mrs. David Kent Herron). Served as a research asst., also asst. prof. Stanford, 1937-42; physicist Eastman Kodak Co., Rochester, N.Y., 1942-44, Oak Ridge, 1944- 46; with Oak Ridge Nat. Lab., 1946—, prin. biologist, 1946-69, cons. biology div., 1970—. Sheldon fellow, 1935-36; Gen. Edn. Bd. fellow, 1936-37; Rockefeller fellow, Copenhagen, Denmark, 1938-39; recipient Charles F. Kettering research award Kettering Found., 1963. Mem. Nat. Acad. Scis. Home: 115 Tabor Rd Oak Ridge TN 37830 Office: Biology Div Oak Ridge Nat Lab Oak Ridge TN 37830

ARNOLD, WILLIAM EDWIN, educator; b. Louisville, Mar. 30, 1899; s. William E. and Elizabeth (Strother) A.; A.B., Ky. Wesleyan Coll., 1921; M.A., Columbia, 1928; Ph.D., Ohio State U., 1932; L.H.D., Ky. Wesleyan U., 1959; m. Ruth Hisle, Aug. 16, 1922; 1 son, William Edwin. High Sch. tchr., Buffalo, Wyo., 1921-22; prin., Hinton, W.Va., 1922-24; prof. Ky. Wesleyan Coll., 1924-30; research asst. Ohio State U., 1931-35, vis. prof., summer 1935; asst. prof. U. Pa., 1935-40, asso. prof., 1940-43, prof. edn., 1943-69, emeritus prof. edn., 1969—, dean Graduate Sch. Edn., 1956-63; vis. prof. summers U. Wis., 1948, U. Tex., 49, U. Cal., 50, 64, 66, Tchrs. Coll. Columbia, 1952-53. Ednl. specialist, , West Germany, 1953; cons. Office Edn., Dept. Edn., Pa., Del., Md.; adv. com. U.S. Civil Service Commn. for Dept. Health, Edn., Welfare; gov.'s adv. council Pa. Dept. Pub. Instruction. Mem. of Phi Delta Kappa. Author articles profl. publs. Home: 110 Madison Rd Lansdowne PA 19050 Office: 3700 Walnut St Philadelphia PA 19104

ARNOLD, WILLIAM H., broker; b. Dyersburg, Tenn., Jan. 18, 1901; s. Luther Coleman and Lockie (Dufford) A.; student Castle Heights Mil. Acad., Lebanon, Tenn., 1917- 19; B.S., Mil. Acad., 1924; grad. Inf. School, Ft. Benning, Ga., 1928, Command and General Staff Sch., Ft. Leavenworth, Kan., 1938; m. Elizabeth Welsh Mullen, Feb. 17, 1926; children—Elizabeth, Emily (dec.), William H., Joseph C. Served in Hawaii, 1928-30; in Tiensin, China, 1934-36; detailed to Gen. Staff Corps, Sept. 1941, G-1 of IV Corps until Mar. 1942, G-3 of IV Corps until Apr. 1943; then chief of staff of XIV Corps, overseas; comdr. Americal Div., Bougainville, 1944, later Cebu, Negros, Philippines; dep. dir., Plans and Operations War Dept. Gen. Staff, 1946; chief budget dir., Dept. of Army, 1948; chief Joint Mil. Mission for Aid to Turkey, 1950-53; comdg. gen. U.S. Forces, Austria, 1953-55; comdg. gen. 5th U.S. Army, 1955-61; partner Betts Borland & Co., Chgo., brokers, 1961—. Mem. Ill. State Police Merit Bd., 1961-64. Decorated D.S.M. with oak leaf cluster, Silver Star, Legion of Merit with oak leaf cluster, Bronze Star with oak leaf cluster, Air Medal (U.S.) officer Legion of Honor (France), chief comdr. Legion of Honor (P.I.); Grand Gold Badge of Honor (Austria). Home: 261 S Bluffs Edge Dr Lake Forest IL 60045 Office: 111 S LaSalle Chicago IL 60603

ARNOLD, WILLIAM STRANG, lawyer; b. Yonkers, N.Y., Feb. 5, 1921; s. L. J. and Hazel (Strang) A.; A.B., U. Ark., 1942, J.D., 1947; LL.M., Columbia, 1948; m. Mary Ellen Gittinger, Sept. 17, 1943; children—Patricia (Mrs. Neil S. West), Richard L. Admitted to Ark, bar, 1947; practice in Crossett and Hamburg, 1948—; sr. partner Arnold, Hamilton & Streetman. Dir. Ashley Life Ins. Co., MonArk Boat Co., First Nat. Bank of Crossett, Ashley County Abstract Co. Mem. adv. bd. DeSota Area council Boy Scouts Am., 1970, Mem. Crossett Health Found. Served with USAAF, 1942-45. Mem. Am., Ark. (past pres.) bar assns., Am. Coll. Probate Counsel, Am. Judicature Soc. Address: PO Drawer A Crossett AR 71635

ARNOLD, WINTON CUMBERLAND, lawyer; b. Walla Walla, Wash., Apr. 11, 1903; s. John Schuyler and Minnie (Blackard) A.; student U. Ida., 1920-24; m. Minnie Wiley, Nov. 4, 1927 (dec.); children—Winton Cumberland, Alice Anne (Mrs. John S. Calvert);

m. 2d Vivien Click, Oct. 19, 1961. Admitted to Ida. bar, 1924, Alaska bar, 1927, Wash. bar, 1945; practice in Grangeville, Ida., 1925- 27, Hyder and Ketchikan, Alaska, 1929-45, Seattle, 1945-60, Anchorage, 1960—; U.S. commr., Hyder and Ketchikan, 1927-33. Mem. Alaska Planning Council, 1935-39; chmn. Salmon cons. com. to Sec. Interior, 1943-44; dir. Alaska Salmon Industry, 1945-60, chmn. coordinating com., 1949-60; mem. adv. com. on fisheries Dept. State, 1954-63; mem. adv. com. on fisheries and conservation Dept. Interior, 1939-41, 55-60; mem. adv. com. Am. sect. Internat. North Pacific Commn., 1953-62; mem. Dept. State exchange group to visit Siberian Fisheries, 1959; mem. Alaska Temp. Claims Commn., 1964. mem. Alaska (past dir.), Anchorage (past dir.) chambers commerce, Pioneers of Alaska, Pioneers of Wash., Nat. Lawyers Club, Kappa Sigma, Phi Alpha Delta. Republican. Episcopalian. Mason, Elk, Rotarian. Clubs: Petroleum (Anchorage), Washington Athletic, Artic (Seattle). Home: Turnagain Arms Anchorage AK 99501 Office: Lathrop Bldg Anchorage AK 99501

ARNON, DANIEL ISRAEL, biochemist; b. Poland, Nov. 14, 1910; s. Leon and Rachel (Chodes) A.; naturalized Am. citizen; B.S., U. Cal., 1932, Ph.D., 1936; m. Lucile Jane Soule, Feb. 24, 1940; children—Anne (Mrs. Jonathan Hodge), Ruth, Stephen, Nancy, Dennis. Instr., U. Cal. at Berkeley, 1936-41, asst. prof., asso. prof., 1941-50, prof. plant physiology, 1950- 60, prof. cell physiology, 1960—, chmn. dept. cell physiology, 1961—; biochemist, Cal. Agrl. Expt. Sta., 1958—. Guggenheim fellow U. Cambridge (Eng.), 1947-48; lectr. Belgian Am. Found., U. Liège, Belgium, 1948; Fulbright research scholar Max-Planck Inst., Berlin- Dahlem, Germany, 1955-56. Served from lt. to maj., AUS, 1943-46. Recipient Gold medal Univ. Pisa, 1958; Charles F. Kettering award photosynthesis research; Stephen Hales prize award Am. Soc. Plant Physiologists; Guggenheim fellow, 1962-63. Fellow Am. Acad. Arts and Sciences, A.A.A.S. (co-recipient Newcomb Cleveland prize 1940), Am. Inst. Chemists; mem. Nat. Acad. Scis., Royal Swedish Acad. Scis., Acad. d'Agriculture de France, Am. Chem. Soc., Am. Soc. Biol. Chemists, Biochem. Soc. (London), Am. Soc. Plant Physiologists (pres. 1952-53), Scandianavian Soc. Plant Physiologists, Sigma Xi. Clubs: Sierra (San Francisco); Faculty (Berkeley). Author articles tech. jours.* Editor: Annual Review of Plant Physiology, 1948-55. Home: 28 Norwood Av Berkeley CA 94707

ARNON, MICHAEL, Israeli govt. ofcl.; b. Vienna, Austria, Apr. 10, 1925; s. Israel and Mela (Luft) Garfunkel; Diploma Internat. Affairs, London U.; m. Hadara Strod, Feb. 24, 1948; children—Ehud, Dorit. Mem. editorial staff Palestine Post, 1945-48; with Govt. of Israel, 1949—; ambassador to Ghana, 1962-65; consul gen. Israeli Consulate Gen., N.Y.C., 1965-68; sec. to Govt. of Israel, 1968—. Served with Israel Def. Army, 1948-49. Home: 2 Haportzim St Jerusalem Israel Office: HaKirya Jerusalem Israel

ARNOTT, HERMON JOHN, savs. banker; b. Mpls., Mar. 3, 1904; s. Hermon J. and Laura (McIntosh) A.; B.A., U. Minn., 1924; M.B.A., Harvard, 1926; m. Helen V. Kanne, Feb. 22, 1949. With Farmers and Mechanics Savs. Bank, Mpls., 1933—, pres., chmn. bd. Trustee Mpls. United Hosp. Fund; pres. Mpls. Family and Childrens Service, Minn. chpt. Nat. Hemophilia Found.; mem. adv. com. Minn. Trust and Retirement Funds, Mpls. Tchrs. Retirement Fund. Mem. Nat. Assn. Mut. Savs. Banks (mem. bd.), Financial Analysts Fedn., Phi Beta Kappa. Mem. Universalist Ch. Clubs: Minneapolis, Six O'Clock, Evergreen, Apollo (Mpls.); Le Seuer (Minn.) Country; St. Paul Athletic. Home: 3846 Zenith Av S Minneapolis MN 55410 Office: 90 S 6th St Minneapolis MN 55402

ARNOW, LESLIE EARLE, research cons.; b. Micanopy, Fla., June 22, 1909; s. Joseph Leslie and Mable Annie (Thrasher) A.; Ph.G. and B.S., U. Fla., 1930; Ph.D., U. Minn., 1934, M.B. and M.D., 1940; m. Jennie Martin, July 17, 1933, 1 son, Peter Leslie. Grad. asst. in physiol. chemistry and biophysics U. Minn., 1931-34, instr. physiol. chemistry, 1934-40, asst. prof., 1940- 42; dir. biochem. research, med.-research div. Sharp and Dohme, Div. Merck & Co., Inc., 1942-44, dir. research 1944-53, v.p., dir. research 1953-56; v.p. Merck Sharp & Dohme Research Labs. div. Merck & Co., Inc.; exec. dir. Merck Inst. for Therapeutic Research, 1956-58; pres. Warner-Lambert Research Inst., 1958-65, senior scientific cons., 1965—; v.p. Warner-Lambert Pharm. Co., 1958-65. Past pres. bd. trustees Morris County Easter Seal Soc. Recipient Centennial award U. Fla., 1953, Outstanding Achievement award U. Minn., 1955. Fellow A.A.A.S., N.Y. Acad. Sci.; A.M.A., Morris County Med. Soc., Research Dirs. Assn., Am. Chem. Soc., Am. Soc. Biol. Chemists, Am. Therapeutic Soc., Soc. Experimental Biology and Medicine, Phi Beta Kappa, Sigma Xi, Alpha Omega Alpha, Phi Beta Pi, Gamma Sigma Epsilon, Rho Chi, Phi Sigma, Alpha Epsilon Delta, Gamma Alpha, Sigma Chi. Clubs: Morris County Golf; Phila Art Alliance. Author: Introduction to Physiological and Pathological Chemistry, 1966; Introduction to Laboratory Chemistry, 1966; Introduction to Organic and Biological Chemistry (with H.C. Reitz), 1949; Health In A Bottle, 1970; also articles in tech. pub. Home: 14 Fairfield Dr Convent Station NJ 07961 Office: Morris Plains NJ 07950

ARNOW, WINSTON EUGENE, U.S. judge; b. Micanopy, Fla., Mar. 13, 1911; s. Joseph Leslie and Mabel (Thrasher) A.; B.S. in Bus. Adminstrn., U. Fla., 1932, J.D., 1933; m. Frances Day Cease, Jan. 11, 1941; 1 dau., Ann. Research clk. Supreme Ct. of Fla., 1932; admitted to Fla. bar, 1933; gen. practice Gainsville, Fla., 1935-42; mem. firm Clayton, Arnow, Duncan, Johnston, Clayton & Quincey, Gainesville, 1946-67; judge U.S. Dist. Ct., No. Dist. Fla., Pensacola, 1968—. Chmn. steering com. Fla. Civil Practice before trial. Served to maj. AUS, 1942-46. Fellow Am. Coll. Probate Counsel; mem. Am. Bar Assn., Fla. Bar; Am. Law Inst., Soc. Bar 1st Jud. Circuit, Order of Coif (hon.), Scabbard and Blade, Florida Blue Key, Sigma Phi Epsilon, Phi Delta Phi, Tau Kappa Alpha, Phi Delta Epsilon. Clubs: Pensacola Country, Pensacola Rotary. Contbr. articles profl. jours. Home: San Carlos Hotel Pensacola FL 32502 Office: US Dist Ct Pensacola FL 32502

ARNOWITT, RICHARD LEWIS, educator, physicist; b. N.Y.C., May 3, 1928; s. Leon and Belle (Feinberg) A.; B.S., Rensselaer Poly. Inst., 1948, M.S., 1948; Ph.D., Harvard, 1953; m. Young In Rhee, Apr. 21, 1961; children—Michael, Myron. Research asso. U. Cal. Radiation Lab., Berkeley, 1952-54; mem. Inst. for Advanced Study, Princeton, N.J., 1954-56; asst. prof. Syracuse U., 1956-59, asso. prof., 1959-62; prof. physics Northeastern U., 1962—. Mem. Am. Phys. Soc. Studies and numerous publs. on high energy physics in the theories used to understand interactions between particles and resonances that arise in high energy scattering; relativity, on structure of Einstein's gravitational theory concerning the quantization of the theory and the nature of gravitational radiation. Home: 7 Wheeler Rd Lexington MA 02173 Office: Dept Physics Northeastern U Boston MA 02115

ARNSTEIN, JOSEPH M., publisher; b. Chgo., Jan. 4, 1913; s. Julius and Sophie (Neuman) A.; Ph.B., U. Chgo., 1933; m. Helen Gallagher, Jan. 4, 1941; children—Joseph M., Hugh J., Mary, Judee. Statistician Walgreen Drug Co., 1934; statistician Esquire, Inc., N.Y.C., 1935-51, circulation dir., 1951-55, v.p. circulation, 1955-60, sr. v.p., 1960—; dir. Hudgeons, EZ Products Inc., Cleve., Esquire, Inc., N.Y.C., Precise Imports Corp., Suffern, N.Y. Mem. U. Chgo. Alumni Assn. Home: 37 Ridge St Crestwood Tuckahoe NY 10707 Office: 488 Madison Av New York City NY 10022

ARNSTEIN, KARL, design and constrn. of airships; b. Prague, Bohemia (now Czechoslovakia), Mar. 24, 1887 s. Wilhelm and Ida (Feigl) A.; Dr. Tech. Sciences, U. of Prague, 1912; hon. Dr. Engring., U. of Aix-La-Chapelle, 1927; D.Sc. (hon.), U. of Akron, 1967; m. Bertl Maria Jehle, Sept. 18, 1919; children—Marian Renee, Ruth Suzanna, Karl Frank, William Gerald. Came to U.S., 1924, naturalized 1930. Asst. prof. bridge design, U. of Prague, 1912; designed reconstruction of found. of Cathedral of Strassburg; with engring. staff of Zeppelin Co., builders of aircraft, Friedrichshafen, Germany, 1914-24; designed about 70 mil. and comml. airships, including the American ship, Los Angeles, supervising constrn. and participating in major trial flights of most of the ships; tech. dir. aircraft constrn., Goodyear Tire & Rubber Co., Akron, O., 1924; v.p. and chief engr. Goodyear-Zeppelin Corp., 1925-39; v.p. and chief engr., Goodyear Aircraft Corp., 1940-57, cons., 1957-59; engaged in practice as independent cons., 1959—. Developed designs for two mil. rigid airships of 6,500,000 cubic feet capacity for U.S. Navy, directed design and construction of U.S.S. Akron and U.S.S. Macon, Large airship dock near Goodyear factories, pressure type airships, stratosphere balloons, lightweight streamline train and heavier-than-air craft. Recipient Distinguished Pub. Service award USN, 1957, Naturalized Am. award Akron Bar Assn., 1959. Registered profl. engr., State of Ohio. Fellow Am. Soc. Mech. Engrs., Am. Inst. Aeros. and Astronautics; mem. Soc. Automotive Engrs., Soc. Exptl. Stress Analysis, Sigma Tau. Club: Exchange. Author: Einflusslinien, 1912. Co-Author: Joseph Melan. 1923; Aerodynamic Theory, Vol. 6. Contbr. to Th. von Karman Applied Mechanics Anniversary Volume, 1941; also numerous articles to Am. and European tech. mags. on theory of structures and gen. engring. subjects, particularly on airships. Home: 817 Delaware Av Akron, OH 44303.

ARNSTEIN, LEO H., lawyer; b. Chgo., Aug. 2, 1906; s. Julius and Sophie (Neumann) A.; Ph.B., U. Chgo., 1926, J.D., 1928; m. Citron, Apr. 27, 1934; children—Julie, Marcia, Nicki. Admitted to Ill. bar, 1928; practice of law, Chgo., 1928—, mem. firm Lederer, Livingston, Kahn & Adsit, 1941- 63, Kahn, Adsit & Armstein, 1963, now Arnstein, Gluck, Weitzenfeld & Minow; dir. Koehler Mfg. Co. Trustee Village Glencoe, Ill. Mem. Am., Ill., Chgo. bar assns. Home: 880 Forest Way Glencoe IL 60022 Office: 120 LaSalle St Chicago IL 60603

ARNSTEIN, MARGARET G., nurse, coll. dean; b. N.Y.C., Oct. 27, 1904; d. Leo and Elsie (Nathan) Arnstein; A.B., Smith Coll., 1925, D.Sc. (hon.), 1950; R.N., Presbyn. Hosp. Sch. Nursing, N.Y.C., 1927; A.M., Columbia, 1929; M.P.H., Johns Hopkins, 1934; D.Sc., Wayne State University, 1962. Staff nurse No. Westchester (N.Y.) Dist. Nursing Assn., 1929-20; county staff nurse and supr. Westchester County Dept. Health, 1930-33; cons. nurse, Communicable Disease Div., N.Y. State Dept. Health, 1934-37; asso. prof. and dir. course in pub. health nursing U. Minn., 1937-40; cons. nurse (dist. supervision), N.Y. State Dept. Health, 1940-46; chief nurse Balkan Mission in UNRRA, 1943-45; apptd. sr. nurse officer in USPHS, 1946, chief Div. Nursing Resources, 1949-57, chief div. pub. health nursing, 1958-60, chief div. nursing, 1960-64, assigned health manpower study conducted by Rockefeller Found. with AID, 1965, sr. nursing adviser internat. health Office Surgeon Gen., 1965; prof. pub. health nursing U. Mich., 1965-67; dean Sch. Nursing, Yale U., 1967—. Recipient Rockefeller Pub. Service award, 1965. Mem. Nat. League Nursing, Am. Nurses Assn., Am. Pub. Health Service, Fgn. Policy Assn., Phi Beta Kappa. Club: Cosmopolitan (N.Y.C.). Author: (with Gaylord Anderson and Mary Lester) Communicable Disease Control, 1962. Contbr. numerous articles in profl. jours. Home: 435 Whitney Av New Haven CT 06511 Office: 333 Cedar St New Haven CT 06510

ARNSTEIN, WALTER LEONARD, educator; b. Stuttgart, Germany, May 14, 1930; s. Richard and Charlotte (Heymann) A.; came to U.S., 1939, naturalized, 1944; B.S.S., Coll. City N.Y., 1951; M.A., Columbia, 1954; Ph.D., Northwestern U., 1961; postgrad. U. London (Eng.), 1956-57; m. Charlotte Culver Sutphen, June 8, 1952; children—Sylvia, Peter. Asst. prof. history Roosevelt U., Chgo., 1957-62, asso. prof., 1962-66, prof., acting dean grad. div., 1966-67; prof. history U. Ill., 1968—; vis. asso. prof. history Northwestern U., 1963-64, spring 1966. Served with AUS, 1951-53; Korea. Fulbright scholar, 1956-57; fellow Am. Council Learned Socs., 1967-68. Mem. Am. Hist. Assn., Brit. Hist. Assn, Conf. Brit. Studies, Am. Assn. U. Profs., Phi Beta Kappa, Phi Alpha Theta. Author: The Bradlaugh Case: A Study in Late Victorian Opinion and Politics, 1965; Britain Yesterday and Today, 1966, 71. Mem. bd. advisers Victorian Studies, 1966—. Contbr. articles profl. jours. Home: 1506 Maplecrest Dr Champaign IL 61820 Office: Dept History 309 Gregory Hall U Ill Urbana IL 61801

ARON, RAYMOND CLAUDE FERDINAND, educator, author; b. Paris, France, Mar. 14, 1905; s. Gustave and Suzanne (Levy) A.; Agregation de Philosophie, Ecole Normale Superieure and Faculty of Letters, Paris U., 1928, Doctorat es Lettres, 1938; LL.D., Harvard, 1958, U. Bale, 1960, U. Bruxelles, 1963, Columbia U., 1966, Southampton, 1968; m. Suzanne Grouchon, Sept. 5, 1933; children—Dominique (Mrs. Antoine Schnapper), Laurence. Sec., Center Social Studies, Ecole Normale Superieure, 1934-39; lectr. faculty letters U. Toulouse (France), 1939; editor Le France Libre, London, Eng., 1940-44; columnist Figaro, 1947—; prof. faculty letters Paris U., 1955-68; Andrew D. White prof.-at-large Cornell U., 1965; prof. Collège de France, 1970. Author: Introduction to the Philosophy of History, 1938; Century of Total War, 1951; Opium of the Intellectuals, 1955; Peace and War Among Nations, 1962. Home: 87 Blvd Saint-Michel Paris 5e France Office: 6 rue de Tournon Paris France

ARONOFF, BILLIE LOUIS, surgeon; b. Dallas, May 28, 1914; s. Joseph and Julia (Rubenstein) A.; student U. Chgo., 1931-33, So. Methodist U., 1933-34; M.D., Baylor U., 1938; m. Valerie Kirk Rosenthal, Feb. 7, 1942; children—Gail Jon (Mrs. Harold Granek), Stephen Louis, Nancy Frances, Ronald Joseph. Intern, then resident surgery Parkland Meml. Hosp., Dallas, 1939-41; fellow surgery Lahey Clinic, Boston, 1943-44; fellow surgery Oschner Clinic, New Orleans, 1944; resident surgery Meml. Hosp. for Cancer, N.Y.C., 1944- 45; practice surgery, Dallas, 1945—; pres. staff Gaston Hosp. Pres. Dallas County unit and Tex. div. Am. Cancer Soc., also nat. bd. dirs., mem. sci. exec. com.; chmn. cancer com. Tex. Med. Assn. and Baylor U. Med. Center; adv. com. Tex., exec. com., chmn. task force cancer Regional Med. Program. Recipient Unit and Divisional award Am. Cancer Soc. Fellow A.C.S. (Tex. chmn. liaison fellows for cancer). Club: Columbian (bd. dirs.) (Dallas). Home: 5551 Drane Dr Dallas TX 75209 Office: 712 N Washington St Dallas TX 75246

ARONOFF, MAX, music sch. exec.; b. N.Y.C., Dec. 25, 1907; s. Abraham and Rose (Zunikoff) A., student Curtis Inst., 1924-34; hon. degree, Combs Coll. Music, 1963; m. Reba Hoffstein, May 24, 1931; children—Mrs. William Katzenstein, Mrs. Milton Katz. Instr. viola Curtis Inst. Music, Phila., 1929-42, 55—; founder, dir. New Sch. Music, Inc., Phila., 1943-; concert artist in U.S., 1944-45. Can., 1927—; Ambler Festival, Temple U., 1970-71; mem. Phila Orch., 1944- Mem. adv. bd. Berkshire Festival; lectr. numerous convs. and workshops for string tchrs. assns.; summer instr. in residence Inter-Am. U., P.R. Mem. Phila. Art Alliance (music com., Achievement medal). Home: 1019 Keystone Av Upper Darby PA 19082 Office: 301 S 21st St Philadelphia PA 19103

ARONOWITZ, SAMUEL ETTELSON, lawyer; b. Albany, N.Y., 1890; s. Max and Dora (Ettelson) A.; A.B., Dartmouth, 1911; LL.B., Albany Law Sch., 1914, St. Rose Coll., 1971. Admitted to N.Y. bar, 1914; partner O'Connell & Aronowitz, Albany, 1924—; counsel, hon. dir. Nat. Comml. Bank & Trust Co. of Albany, 1939—; gen. counsel, trustee City & County Savs. Bank, 1924—; pres. Better Albany Living, Inc., 1966—. Mem. bd. fellows Brandeis U., 1952—; bd. Albany Med. Center Hosp., nat. exec. com. Am. Jewish Com., Jewish Welfare Bd., Joint Distbn. Com. Served as sgt. 309th Mach. Gun bn. 78th Div., World War I; col. judge adv. N.Y. Guard, 1940-48. Mem. Am., N.Y. State, Albany County bar assns., Federated Bar Assns. 3d Jud. Dist. (past pres.), Am. Legion (past comdr. dept. N.Y.). Republican. Jewish religion. Mason (Shriner). Clubs: Albany, Coloine Country (Albany); Dartmouth (N.Y.C.). Home: DeWitt Clinton Hotel Albany NY 12207 Office: 100 State St Albany NY 12207

ARONS, ARNOLD BORIS, physicist; b. Lincoln, Neb., Nov. 23, 1916; s. Solomon and Esther (Rosen) A.; M.E., Stevens Inst. Tech., 1937, M.S., 1940; Ph.D., Harvard, 1943; A.M. (hon.), Amherst Coll., 1953; m. Jean Rendall, Aug. 17, 1942; children—Marion, Janet, Kenneth, Paul. Asst., later asso. prof. physics Stevens Inst. Tech., 1946-52; research asso. phys. oceanography Woods Hole Oceanographic Inst., 1948—; prof. physics Amherst Coll., 1952-68; prof. physics U. Wash., 1968—; charge underwater blast measurments Operation Crossroads; cons. Naval Ordnance Lab., Waterways Expt. Sta. Research explosion phenomena, phys. oceanography Woods Hole Oceanographic Instn., World War II, trustee, 1964—. Mem. Commn. on Coll. Physics, 1962-68. Guggenheim fellow, 1957-58; NSF sci. faculty fellow, 1962-63. Fellow A.A.A.S.; mem. Am. Phys. Soc., Am. Meteorol. Soc., Am. Assn. Physics Tchrs. (pres. 1967), Am. Geophys. Union, Am. Geochem. Soc. Author: Development of Concepts of Physics, 1965; also sci. articles. Home: 10313 Lakeshore Blvd N E Seattle, WA 98125.

ARONSOHN, ALAN JAY BABIN, lawyer; b. Williamsport, Pa., Nov. 8, 1924; s. Cornelius K. and Micky (Babin) A.; B.A., Alfred U., 1947; LL.B., Columbia, 1949; m. Ellen Levy, May 30, 1948; children—Lee, Judith, Abby. Admitted to N.Y. bar, 1950, since practiced in N.Y.C.; research asst. Am. Law Inst. Income Tax Revision Project, 1949-50; asso. Rabkin & Johnson, 1951-52; partner Robinson, Silverman, Pearce, Aronsohn & Sand, 1952—; lectr. Practicing Law Inst.; mem. adv. com. N.Y.U. Ann. Inst. on Fed. Taxation. Dir. Nyhaco Credit Corp., Ltd., Union Fed. Savs. & Loan Assn. Served with USNR, 1943-46. Mem. Am. Bar Assn. (spl. adviser real property tax problems com.). Author: Partnership and Income Taxes, 1970. Contbr. articles profl. jours. Mailing Address: Office: 230 Park Av New York City NY 10017

ARONSON, BORIS, artist, stage designer; b. Kiev, Russia, Oct. 15, 1900; s. Solomon and Deborah (Turfsky) A.; ed. State Art Sch., Kiev, also pvt. schs., Moscow and Kiev; student art, Moscow, Kiev, Paris; m. Lisa Jalowetz, June 5, 1945; 1 son, Marc. Came to U.S., 1923. A founder Mus. Modern Art, Kiev; in U.S. worked with Unser Theatre and Yiddish Art Theatre; designer for stage and ballet, including sets for N.Y.C. prodns.: Cabin in the Sky; Sadie Thompson; The Country Girl, 1951; I've Got Sixpence, 1952; The Crucible, 1953; My Three Angels, 1953; The Rose Tattoo, 1955; A View from the Bridge, 1955; The Diary of Anne Frank, 1955; Bus Stop, 1955; Hole in the Head, 1956; Orpheus Descending, 1956; Small War on Murray, Hill, 1956; The Firstborn, 1958; J.B., 1958; The Cold Wind and The Warm, 1958; Do Re Mi, 1960; A Gift of Time, 1962; (for Stratford, Eng.) Coriolanus, 1959; (London, Eng.) Judith, 1962; Incident of Vichy, 1964; Fiddler on the Roof, 1964; Cabaret, 1966; Mourning Becomes Electra, 1967; The Price, 1968; Zorba, 1968; Company, 1970; (Met. Opera House) Fidecio, 1970; Follies, 1971; commnd. to do art work for interior of Temple Sinai, Washington, 1961, also Community Center Synogogue, Sands Point, N.Y.; numerous exhbns. of paintings; represented in pvt. colls., also exhibited stage designs, and model with projected slides, called Painting with Light. Recipient Guggenheim fellowship, 1950, Am. Theatre Wing award for stage designs, 1950-51; Tony award, 1955, 66, 67, 68, 69, 70, Joseph Maharam award 4 times; Brandeis U. Creative Arts award commn., 1969; New Eng. Theatre Conf. Spl. award, 1970. Mem. United Scenic Artists Union. Author: Marc Chagall, 1923; Modern Graphic Art, 1923. Home: 1 W 89th St New York City NY 10024

ARONSON, DAVID, artist; b. Shilova, Lithuania, Oct. 28, 1923; s. Peisach Leib and Gertrude (Shapiro) A.; came to U.S., 1929, naturalized, 1931; certificate Boston Mus. Sch., 1946; m. Georgianna B. Nyman, June 10, 1956; children—Judith, Benjamin, Abigail. Instr. painting Boston Mus. Sch., 1943-54; prof. art Boston U., 1962—, chmn. div., 1954-62; one man shows include Niveau Gallery, N.Y.C., 1945, 56, Mus. Modern Art, 1946, Boris Mirski Gallery, Boston, 1951, 59, 64, 69, Downtown Gallery, N.Y.C., 1953, Nordness Gallery, N.Y.C., 1960, 63, 69, Rex Evans Gallery, Los Angeles, 1961, Long Beach (Cal.) Mus., 1961, Westhampton (N.Y.) Gallery, 1961, J. Thomas Gallery, Provincetown, Mass., 1964, Zora Gallery, Los Angeles, 1965, Hunter Gallery, Chattanooga, 1965, Kovler Gallery, Chgo., 1966, Bernard Danenberg Galleries, N.Y.C., 1969; represented in perm. colls. Art Inst. Chgo., Va. Mus. Fine Arts, Richmond, Bryn. Mawr. Coll., Brandeis U., Tupperware Mus., Orlando, Fla., Decordova Mus., Lincoln, Mass., Mus. Modern Art, Atlanta U., Atlanta Art Assn., U. Neb., Krannert Art Mus. of U. Ill., Whitney Mus. Am. Art, Colby Coll., U. N.H., Portland Mus. Art, Corcoran Gallery Art, Washington, Munson Williams Proctor Art Inst., Ithaca, N.Y., Boston Mus. Fine Arts, Smithsonian Instn., Washington, Milw. Art Inst., Pa. Acad. Fine Arts, Johnson Found., Racine, Wis., Worcester (Mass.) Art Mus., Brockton (Mass.) Mus. Art, Longy Sch. Music, Cambridge, Mass., Boston U., Joseph Hirschhorn Collection, Hebrew Tchrs. Coll., Brookline, Mass.; sculpture commns. Container Corp. Am., 1963, 65. Academician elect Nat. Acad. Design, 1970. Recipient 1st Judges prize Inst. Modern Art, Boston, 1944, 1st Popular prize, 1944; Choice Friends of Art, Art Inst. Chgo., 1946, Purchase prize Va. Mus. Fine Arts, 1946, Travelling fellow Boston Mus. Sch., 1946; Grand prize Boston Arts Festival, 1952, 54, 2d prize, 1953; 1st prize Tupperware Art Fund, 1954; grantee in art Nat. Inst. Arts and Letters, 1958, Purchase prize, 1961, 62, 63; Guggenheim fellow, 1960; Adolph and Clara Obrig prize for painting N.A.D., 1968; purchase prize Pa. Acad. Fine Arts, Asso. mem. N.A.D. Home: Brimstone Lane Sudbury MA 01776 also Fairview Prince Edward Island Canada Office: 855 Commonwealth Av Boston MA 00215

ARONSON, DAVID, rabbi; b. Vitebsk, Russia, Aug. 1, 1894; s. Jekuthiel Zalman and Yetta (Kudritzin) A.; brought to U.S., 1906, naturalized, 1918; A.B., N.Y. U., 1916; A.M., Columbia, 1917; Rabbi, Jewish Theol. Sem. of Am., 1919, D.H.L. (honoris causa), 1946; D.D., U. Judaism, 1969; m. Bertha Friedman, May 1, 1927; children—Raphael, Hillel. Served with the Jewish Welfare Bd., camp rabbi, Camp Upton, L.I., 1917-19; rabbi, Salt Lake City, 1920-22, Duluth, Minn., 1922-24, Beth El Synagogue, Mpls., 1924-59, since emeritus; prof. rabbinics grad. sch. U. Judaism, Los Angeles, 1959—; vis. lectr. Jewish Theol. Sem. Asso. editor of the Am. Jewish World, 1930-59. Mem. Gov.'s Human Relations Commn., 1943-59, Mayor's Council on Human Relations, Citizen's Charter Commn.; rep. Am. Jewish Conf., 1943; pres. Rabbinical Assembly of Am., 1948-50; bd. dirs., bd. overseers Jewish Theol. Sem. and others. Contbr. articles relating to Jewish affairs to profl. jours. Author: The Jewish Way of Life. Home: 8555 Saturn St Los Angeles CA 90035 Office: 6525 Sunset Blvd Los Angeles CA 90028

ARONSON, HARRY BERNARD, watch mfg. co. exec.; b. Bklyn., May 29, 1901; s. Bernard and Mary (Palakoff) A.; ed. pub. schs., Chgo.; m. Alice Levin; 1 dau., Faith Audry (Mrs. Donald Pollack). With A. Hirsch & Co., Chgo., 1919-24; successively clk., salesman, sec. Manheimer Watch Co., Chgo., 1924-39; founder, partner Hampden Watch Co., Chgo., 1939-49; former founder, pres. Hallmark, Inc., Chgo.; pres., dir. Waltham Watch Co., Chgo. Active in Community Fund, A.R.C., United Jewish Appeal. Rotarian; mem. B'nai B'rith. Home: 1550 Lake Shore Dr Chicago IL 60610 Office: 231 S Jefferson St Chicago IL 60606

ARONSON, LESTER RALPH, biologist; b. Bklyn., Apr. 9, 1911; s. Samuel and Hannah (Besthoff) A.; B.A., Cornell (N.Y. State Tuition Scholarship), 1932, M.A., 1933; postgrad. Columbia, 1938-40; Ph.D., N.Y. U., 1945; m. Evelyn Rappaport, Sept. 26, 1936; children—Carl Henry, Frederick Richard. Mem. faculty sch. gen. studies Hunter Coll., 1946-53; asst. dept. animal behavior Am. Mus. Natural History, N.Y.C., 1938-42, staff asst., 1942-43, asst. curator, 1943-46, acting chmn., asso. curator, 1946-49, chairman, associate curator, 1949-56, chairman and curator, 1956—, dean council of scientific staff, 1958-60, 69; adjunct asso. prof. biology, N.Y. U., 1951-58; adj. prof., 1958—. U.S. Fulbright Research scholar, 1953. Fellow N.Y. Acad. of Sciences, N.Y. Zoological Soc., A.A.A.S., Animal Behavior Soc.; mem. Am. Soc. Anatomists, Ecol. Soc. Am., Am. Soc. Zoologists, Am. Soc. Naturalists, Am. Soc. Ichthyologists and Herpetologists. Author articles sci. publs. Mem. editorial bd. Animal Behaviour, 1958-62, asso. editor, 1962-66, editor, 1965-68. Editorial bd. Curator, 1958—, Copcia, 1960-62. Home: 47 Cedar St Hillsdale NJ 07642 Office: 79th St at Central Park W New York City NY 10024

ARONSON, LOUIS VINCENT, II, mfg. exec.; b. Newark, Jan. 18, 1923; s. Alexander H. and Leona L. (Lazarus) A.; B.S., U.S. Naval Acad., 1945; m. Joan Barbara Fisch, Nov. 2, 1945; children—James Richard, Robert A., Kathryn Ann, Diane. Methods engineer Ronson Corporation, 1947-48, supervisor prodn. control, 1948- 50, v.p. charge material procurement, 1950-52, v.p. charge operations, 1952, dir. 1952—, president 1953—. Bd. dirs. Nat. Conf. Christians and Jews. Served as ensign USN 1945-47. Mem. Am. Naval Acad. Athletic Assn., Am. Ordnance Assn. Club: 24 Karat. Home: PO Box 548 Far Hills NJ 07931 Office: 1 Ronson Rd Woodbridge NJ 07095

ARONSON, STANLEY MAYNARD, educator, physician; b. N.Y.C., May 28, 1922; s. Eliuh and Lena (Hassner) A.; B.S., Coll. City N.Y., 1943; M.D., N.Y.U., 1947; m. Betty Ellis, June 3, 1947; children—Susan, Lisa, Sarah. Faculty, Columbia Coll. Phys. and Surg., 1951-54, Yale Sch. Medicine, 1964-65; prof. pathology, asst. dean State U. N.Y., Bklyn., 1960-70; dir. labs. Kings County Hosp. Center, Bklyn., 1965-70; prof. med. sci. Brown U., 1970—. Cons. physician neuropathology Jewish Chronic Disease Hosp., Bklyn., 1951, NIH, 1962—, N.Y. regional office VA, 1965-70. Mem. A.M.A., Am. Neurol. Assn., Am. Assn. Neuropathology, N.Y. Acad. Medicine, Am. Acad. Neurology, Am. Assn. Pathologists and Bacteriologists, N.Y. Neurol. Soc. Author: (with B.W. Volk) Cerebral Sphingolipidoses, 1962; Inborn Disorders of Sphingolipid Metabolism, 1966; also numerous articles. Research on genetics pathology and diagnostic features of infantile cerebral degenerative diseases, population dynamics, pathology and epidemiology of cerebral vascular disease and stroke. Home: Elm St Rehoboth MA 02769 Office: Dept Med Sci Brown U Providence RI 02912

ARONSZAJN, NACHMAN, educator; b. Warsaw, Poland, July 26, 1907; s. Judel and Anna (Wernikowska) A.; Ph.D., U. Warsaw, 1930; D.Sc., U. Paris, 1935; m. Sylvia Lee, Jan. 25, 1951; 1 son, Mark. Came to U.S., 1949, naturalized, 1954. Chargé de reserches Centre Nat. de la Recherche Scientifique, Paris, 1936-45, Maitre de recherches, 1945-49; research prof. math. Okla. State U., 1949-51; prof. math. U. Kan., Lawrence, 1951-63, Solon E. Summerfield distinguished prof., 1963—. Mem.-at-large NRC, 1960-63. Served with Polish Army, 1939-45. Mem. Am. Math. Soc., Am. Math. Assn., Sigma Xi. Home: 1015 Tennessee St Lawrence, KS . 66044.

AROVA, SONIA, ballerina; b. Sofia, Bulgaria, June 20, 1928; d. Albert and Rene (Melamedov) A.; certificate d'etude with honors, Ballet World Championship of Ballet, Paris, France; tchr. diploma with honors, Paris Conservatoire Music and Dance; m. Thor Sutowski; 1 child, Ariane. Mem. first company Internat. Ballet of Eng.; first Le Lac des Cygnes with Rambert Company, London; guest with original Ballet Russe; performed in Japan; guest Royal Ballet Company; mem. Nat. Ballet Company, Washington; singer Opera Comique, Paris; appeared in 3 films on ballet; dir. ballet Norwegen Opera, 1966-70, State Opera, Hamburg, Germany, 1971—. Home: 16 Rue Le Cluse Paris 17eme France Office: 1060 E Main St El Cajon CA 92021

ARPE, JOHN EDWIN, metal products co. exec.; b. Milw., June 10, 1916; s. Walter C. and Amanda (Bruck) A.; student U. Wis., 1938-42, Marquette U., 1943-46; Advanced Mgmt. Program, Harvard, 1966; m. Germaine M. Brewer, Aug. 10, 1940; children—James F., John E., Christine Mary, Janet Emily. Various depts. including gen. accounting, govt. accounting, contract adminstrn., mfg. Heil Co., Milw., 1934-61, v.p. in charge mfg., 1961, v.p. adminstrn. and finance, 1962-68, dir., 1964—, treas., v.p., 1968, exec. v.p., treas., 1968—. Bd. dirs. Luth. Hosp. Milw. Mem. Financial Execs. Inst. Home: 12520 Stephen Pl Elm Grove WI 53122 Office: 3000 W Montana St Milwaukee WI 53201

ARPS, LESLIE HANSEN, lawyer; b. Leipzig, Germany, July 14, 1907; parents Am. citizens; s. George F. and Alice (Black) A; A.B., Stanford, 1928; LL.B., Harvard, 1931; m. Ruth Collicott, Oct. 26, 1959. Admitted to N.Y. bar, 1932; asso. Root, Clark, Buckner & Ballantine, N.Y.C., 1931-42, 46-48; mem. firm Skadden, Arps, Slate, Meagher & Flom, N.Y.C., 1948—; spl. asst. atty. gen. State of N.Y.; asst. chief counsel N.Y. State Crime Commn., 1951-52; asst. gen. counsel to N.Y. State Moreland Commn. to Investigate State Agys. in relation to Pari-Mutuel Harness Racing, 1953-54; cons. N.Y. State Moreland Commn. on Alcoholic Beverage Control law, 1963-64. Chmn. bd. trustees Gateway Sch. N.Y., 1965-67. Served to lt. col. USAAF, 1942-45. Mem. Am., N.Y. State, N.Y.C. bar assns., N.Y. County Lawyers Assn., Phi Beta Kappa. Clubs: Union League, Harvard (N.Y.C.). Home: 530 Park Av New York NY 10021 Office: 551 Fifth Av New York NY 10017

ARRABAL, FERNANDO, author, playwright; founder artistic movement El Panico. Author: Baal Babylon, 1961; La Pierre de la Folie; L'Enterrement de la Sardine; Fêtes ed Rites de la Confusion; Fando and Lis; L'Architecte et L'Empereur D'Assyrie; Exiled from Spain by Franco govt. Address: care Grove Press Inc 53 E 11th St New York City NY 10003

ARRAJ, ALFRED ALBERT, dist. judge; b. Kansas City, Mo., Sept. 1, 1906; s. Elias and Mary (Dervis) A.; LL.B., U. Colo., 1928; m. Madge L. Connors, Nov. 12, 1929; 1 dau., Sally Marie. Admitted to Colo. bar, 1928; gen. practice law, Denver. Springfield, Colo., 1928-36; county atty., Beca County, Colo., 1936-42, 46-48, dep. dist. atty., 1946-48; dist. judge 15th Jud. Dist. Colo., 1949-57; U.S. judge Dist. of Colo., 1957-59, chief judge, 1959—. Served from 1st lt. to maj. USAAF, 1942-46; CBI. Recipient Norlin Recognition award for distinguished achievement U. Colo., 1968, William Lee Knous award U. Colo. Sch. Law, 1970. Mem. Am. Judicature Soc., Am. Colo., S.E. Colo. (pres. 1940). Fed., Denver bar assns., Am. Legion, Order of Coif, Judicial Conf. U.S., Phi Delta Phi. Episcopalian. Club: University. Home: 200 Ivy Street Denver, CO 80220. Office: U S Courthouse Denver CO 80202

ARRAU, CLAUDIO concert pianist; b. Chillan, Chile, Feb. 6, 1903; began piano study in Chile, endowed as child prodigy by Chilean govt. to study at Stern Conservatory, Berlin, with Martin Krause; m.; children—Carmen, Mario, Christopher. Made successful debut, Berlin, 1915, toured Germany extensively; returned to Chile; achieved great reputation in Europe, South America, concertized annually U.S. since 1941; 1st tour of Australia, 1947; South Africa, 1949, 53, 56, also India, Ceylon, Singapore; toured Germany, 1954; toured Israel, 1951, 53, 57; presented 32 Beethoven Piano Sonatas in N.Y., 1953. Awarded Ibach prize for piano playing, 1917; 1st pl. Internat. Congress Pianists, Switzerland, 1925; also Liszt prize twice, and the Schulhoff prize. Recorded major piano works of Beethoven, Bach, Mozart, Weber and pieces of Liszt, Chopin, Busoni and Stravinsky many collectors' items.

ARRICK, LAWRENCE, producer-director; b. N.Y.C., Sept. 12, 1928; s. Harold and Alyce (Glinsky) A.; m. Rose Arrick, Nov. 2, 1952. Asso. producer Pyramid Film Prodns., N.Y.C., 1959; story editor Screen Gems, Inc., 1959; producer East Size/West Side TV series, 1963-64, Mr. Broadway TV series, 1964-65; theatricals directed include The Death of Bessie Smith, Ivanoff, The Maids, The Bald Soprano, The Chairs, The Sandbox, Two Executioners, The Chip, The Zoo Story, 1962, Second City Revue, 1962-63, Looking for Action (London, Eng.), 1963, The Heroine, 1963, numerous others; mem. director's unit Actor's Studio; tchr. Bennington Coll., 1953-54, Herbert Berghof Sch., N.Y.C., 1954-55, Bard Coll., 1954-55, Dramatic Workshop, N.Y.C., 1957-58, Stella Adler Sch., N.Y.C., 1959. Address: 1200 Fifth Av New York City NY 10029

ARRIES, LESLIE GOODWIN, Jr., broadcasting exec.; b. Evanston, Ill., Dec. 22, 1924; s. Leslie Goodwin and Dorothy (Carney) A.; B.S., Northwestern U., 1945; m. Elizabeth B. Logan, Sept. 17, 1949; children—Leslie Goodwin III, Linda, Lauren, Lisabeth. Broadcast engr. WTTG, Washington, 1946-47, dir. remote programs and spl. events, 1947-48; program operations mgr. WDTV, Pitts., 1948-50; asst. dir. programming and prodn. Dumont Television Network, WABD-TV, N.Y.C., 1950-53; gen. mgr. WTTG, 1953-56; account exec. CBS Television Spot Sales, Chgo., 1956-57; dir. television WHDH-TV, Boston, 1957-64; gen. mgr. KYW-TV, Cleve., 1964-65; pres. WBC Prodns., N.Y.C., 1965-67; v.p., gen. mgr. WBEN, Inc., Buffalo, 1967—. Chmn., All Industry Television Sta. Music Licensing Com.; dir. Assn. Broadcast Engring. Standards, Inc.; mem. television information council Television Information Office; television bd. dirs. Nat. Assn. Broadcasters. Bd. dirs. Nat. Conf. Christians and Jews, Jr. Achievement of Niagara Frontier. Mem. civic adv. com. State U. N.Y. at Buffalo, State U. Coll. at Buffalo; mem. men's adv. com. Children's Hosp., Studio Arena Theatre. Served with USNR, 1943-46. Mem. Internat. Radio and Television Soc., Nat. Acad. Television Arts and Scis., Broadcast Pioneers, Navy League U.S., Buffalo Area C. of C. (dir., exec. com.), Sigma Delta Chi, Delta Tau Delta. Clubs: Buffalo, Country of Buffalo, Northwestern University Alumni (Buffalo); Orchard Park (N.Y.) Country. Home: 1 Smokes Creek Rd Orchard Park NY 14127 Office: 2077 Elmwood Av Buffalo NY 14207

ARRIGONI, LOUIS, coop. food distbr.; b. S. Cle Elum, Wash., Aug. 4, 1916; s. Joseph and Esther (Paganelli) A.; B.S., U. Wash., 1938, M.S., 1940, Ph.D., 1945; m. Evelyn L. Pierson, Apr. 26, 1944; children—Nancy, Evelyn, James. Asst. prof. chemistry U. Wash., 1943-49; with Consol. Dairy Products Co., 1949-67, 71—, v.p., 1962-67, dir., 1964—, pres., 1971—; pres. Asso. Grocers Inc., Seattle, 1967-71, also dir., chmn. exec. com.; dir. Internat. Bank Commerce, Western Family Foods, Tips Ins. Inc., Dairy Export Co. Inc. Mem. Am. Pharm. Assn., Sigma Xi. Elk. Clubs: Wash. Athletic, Rainier (Seattle). Home: 3623 NE 115th St Seattle WA 98125 Office: 635 Elliott Av Seattle WA 98119

ARRINGTON, JAMES HUGH, oil producer; b. Jethro, Arkansas, May 23, 1904; s. William H. and Laura T. (Fulks) A.; L.I., Ark. Tech. Jr. Coll., 1927; B.S., Okla. A. and M. Coll., 1930; m. Veneta C. Berry, July 5, 1930; children—Harriet V. (Mrs. Jack Griffith), Aneta, Laura B. (Mrs. Luke Leon Nigliazzo, Jr.). Superintendent, Alix public schools, 1927-29; athletic coach, teacher Ripley (Ark.) High Sch., 1931-33, also partner newspaper Ripley Rev. and mgr. 2000 acre ranch; buyer Lake Carl Blackwell project, 1933-35; pres. The Marco Corp., The Amco Corp., The Jim Arrington Corp.; dir. Okla. Fracturing Service, Thomas N. Berry & Co. Mem. Oklahoma Ho. of Reps. from Payne County, 1942-60; chmn. Okla. Dem. Party, 1940-46; Dem. nat. committeeman for Okla., 1956-63. Pres. Nat. Happy Groundhog Day Assn.; mem. local council Boy Scouts Am.; hon. mem. Okla. Semi-Centennial Commn., 1956-57. Hon. col. various Okla. govs.; named to Okla. State U. Alumni Hall of Fame Ark. Tech. Alumni Hall of Distinction. Mem. Mid-Continent Oil and Gas Assn., Am. Petroleum Inst., Isaac Walton League, Stillwater, Oklahoma City chambers commerce, Oklahoma City Press Assn., Okla. Jack and Jennet Assn., Red Red Rose, Sigma Nu. Presbyn. Clubs: Oklahoma, Tower, Oklahoma City Golf and Country (Oklahoma City); Fifty, Lions (Stillwater). Home: 1724 Kingsbury Lane Oklahoma City OK 73116 Office: Cravens Bldg Oklahoma City OK 73102

ARRINGTON, WILLIAM RUSSELL, lawyer, corp. exec.; b. Gillespie, Ill., July 4, 1906; s. William Parnell and Ethel Louise (Fanning) A.; A.B., U. Ill., 1928, J.D., 1930; m. Ruth Browne, Oct. 8, 1932; children—Patricia Lee, Michael Browne. Admitted to Ill. bar, 1930, sr. mem. Arrington, Healy & Wilson, Chgo., 1944—; v.p., dir., gen. counsel Combined Ins. Co. of Am. and related cos. 1939—, sec., 1962—; acting pres. and dir. Soy Bean Products Co., 1942-45; vice pres., dir. Alberto-Culver Company, 1964—; dir. Bank of Chgo., 1954—. Gen. atty. Ridgeville Park Dist., 1941-57; mem. Nat. Legislative Conf. Intergovernmental Relations Com., 1965—; mem. Gov.'s Ill. Revenue Study Commn., 1968-69; mem. U.S. Adv. Commn. on Intergovernmental Relations, 1969—. Mem. Ill. Ho. of Reps., 4th Senatorial Dist., 1944-54, Ill. Senate, 1954—; chmn. Ho. judiciary com., 1951-53, mem. Ill. Legislative Commn. to revise Ill. Constitution Revenue Article, 1951, mem. joint legislative commission to revise Ill. Constitution Jud. Article, 1951-53; mem. Ill. Legislative Council, 1955—; chmn. Ill. Legislative Audit Commn., 1957—; mem. Ill. Revenue Laws Study Commn., 1961-63. pres. protem, majority leader Ill. Senate, 1964—. Adv. com. Ill. Masonic Hosp., 1964—; chmn., bd. mgrs. Robert R. McCormick Boys Club, 1960—. Bd. dirs. Am. Found. Religion and Psychiatry, 1962—, Found. Study of Cycles, 1962—, Found. Research on Nature of Man, 1964—, Chgo. Boys' Clubs. 1962—, Mental Health Assn. Greater Chgo., 1964—, Stone-Brandel Center, 1966—, W. Clement and Jessie V. Stone Found., 1958—, Evanston Hosp., 1968—. Mem. U.S. C. of C. (com. 1959—), Internat. Assn. Ins. Counsel, Am., Ill., Chgo. (bd. mgrs. 1952-54) bar assns., Ins. Fedn. Ill., Nat. Conf. State Legislative Leaders (mem. exec. com. 1965—), Nat. Soc. State Legislators (bd. govs. 1966—), Phi Beta Kappa, Phi Eta Sigma, Gamma Eta Gamma. Clubs: Law (life), Union League, Economic, Chicago Press, Sangamo. Home: 929 Edgemere Ct Evanston IL 60202 Office: 135 LaSalle St Chicago IL 60603

ARROL, JOHN, corp. exec.; b. Scotland, Aug. 6, 1923; s. William and Isabella (Gordon) A.; brought to U.S., 1924, naturalized, 1934; B.S. in Bus. Adminstrn., Xavier U., 1953; M.A., Vanderbilt U., 1964; m. Jane Trice, June 18, 1949; children—Robert, Nancy, David, William. Cost supr. Ford Motor Co., 1950-57; planning supr. Curtiss Wright Corp., 1957-58; with Avco Corp., 1958-64, asst. controller, 1962-64; corporate controller Globe-Union, Inc., Milw., 1964-70, v.p., controller, 1970—; pres. Data Automation Services; instr. cost accounting U. Tenn., 1960-62, bus. adminstrn. Ind. U., 1964. Bd. dirs. Milw. capt. A.R.C. Mem. Nat. Assn. Accountants, Financial Execs. Inst. Rotarian. Home: 12530 N Jacqueline Ct Mequon WI 53092 Office: 5757 N Green Bay Av Milwaukee WI 53201

ARROM, JOSE JUAN, educator, author; b. Holguin, Cuba, Feb. 28, 1910; s. Jose Arrom March and Marina Gonzalez Solis; came to U.S., 1932, naturalized, 1942; B.A., Yale, 1937, M.A., 1940, Ph.D., 1941; m. Silvia Ravelo, Apr. 19, 1946; children—Jose Orlando, Silvia Marina. Mem. faculty Yale, 1937—, prof. Spanish, 1954—, curator Latin Am. collection, 1942-62, adviser, 1962—, dir. grad. studies Spanish, 1952-68; lectr. OAS in Colombia, summer 1960; vis. prof. Hispanic Am. lit. Havana U., summer 1946, U. Ariz., fall 1961, Rice U., summer 1964. Mem. nat. screening com. Fulbright-Hays Awards, 1962-63. Sterling fellow Yale, 1944-45; Guggenheim fellow, 1947-48, 64-65; Fulbright Research fellow, Spain, 1968. Fellow Conn. Acad. Arts and Scis., Ateneo Americano, Inst. de Historia del Teatro Americano; corr. fellow Real Academia de Cordoba, Academia Cubana de la Lengua, also Academia de Artes y Letras de Cuba; mem. Modern Lang. Assn. Am., Am. Assn. Tchrs. Spanish and Portuguese, Inst. Internat. de Lit. Hispanoamericana, Assn. Internat. de Hispanistas, Phi Beta Kappa. Author: Historia de la literatura dramatica cubana, 1944; Estudios de literatura hispanoamericana, 1950; El Principe jardinero y fingido Cloridano, 1951; El teatro de Hispanomerica en la epoca colonial, 1956; Certidumbre de America, 1959; Esquema generacional de las letras hispanoamericanas, 1963; Historia de la invencion de las Yndias, 1965; Hispanoamerica; Panorama Contemporaneo de su Cultura, 1969. Contbg. editor: Handbook of Latin American Studies, 1945-52. Home: 70 High Lane Hamden CT 06517 Office: Yale Univ New Haven CT 06520

ARROW, KENNETH JOSEPH, economist; b. N.Y.C., Aug. 23, 1921; s. Harry I. and Lillian (Greenberg) A.; B.S. in Social Sci., City Coll. N.Y., 1940; M.A., Columbia, 1941, Ph.D., 1951; LL.D., U. Chgo., 1967; m. Selma Schweitzer, Aug. 31, 1947; children—David Michael, Andrew. Research asso. Cowles Commn. for Research in Econs., 1947-49; asst. prof. econs. U. Chgo., 1948-49; acting asst. prof. econs. and statistics Stanford, 1949-50, asso prof., 1950-53, prof. econs. and statistics, 1953-68; prof. of econs. Harvard, 1968—, exec. head dept. econs., 1954-56, acting exec. head dept., 1962-63; economist Council Econ. Advisers, U.S. Govt., 1962; cons The RAND Corp. Served as capt. AUS., 1942-46. Social Sci. Research fellow, 1952; fellow Center for Advanced Study in the Behavioral Scis., 1956-57; fellow Churchill Coll., Cambridge, Eng., 1963-64. Recipient John Bates Clark medal American Economic Assn., 1957. Fellow Am. Acad. Arts and Scis., Econometric Soc. (v.p. 1955, pres, 1956), Am. Statis. Assn., Inst. Math. Statistics; mem. Am. Econ. Assn. (mem. exec. com. 1967-69), Nat. Acad. Sciences, Am. Philos. Soc., Inst. Mgmt. Scis. (pres. 1963, chmn. council 1964). Author: Social Choice and Individual Values, 1951; Essays in the Theory of Risk Bearing, 1970. Co-author: Mathematical Studies in Inventory and Production, 1958; Studies in Linear and Nonlinear Programming, 1958; Time Series Analysis of Inter-industry Demands, 1959; Public Investment, The Rate of Return and Optimal Fiscal Policy, 1970. Office: 1737 Cambridge St Harvard U Cambridge MA 02138

ARROWSMITH, MARVIN, newspaper corr.; b. Detroit, Aug. 8, 1913; grad. U. Detroit, 1935; m. Mary Frances Haule, 1938; 6 sons, 1 dau. Editor high sch., coll. papers; reporter, composing room staff Detroit newspapers; with A.P., 1942—, successively mem. staff Detroit bur., Grand Rapids bur., Washington bur., Senate staff, then White House corr. assigned nat. and polit. convs. and presdl. campaign coverage, 1948, 52, 56, 60, news editor Washington bur. A.P., 1961-65, asst. chief of bur., 1965-69, chief of bur., 1969—. Home: 1501 Trombone Ct Vienna VA 22180 Office: Asso Press Washington DC

ARROWSMITH, WILLIAM AYRES, educator, writer; b. Orange, N.J., Apr. 13, 1924; s. Walter Weed and Dorothy (Ayres) A.; grad. Hill Sch., 1941; B.A., Princeton, 1947, Ph.D., 1954; B.A. (Rhodes scholar 1948-51), Oxford (Eng.) U., 1951, M.A., 1958; LL.D., Loyola U., 1968, Dickinson Coll., 1971; L.H.D., St. Michael's Coll. Burlington, Vt., 1968; D.Litt., Westminster Coll., Fulton, Mo., 1969; D.Litt., Dartmouth, 1970; m. Jean Reiser, Jan. 10, 1945; children—Nancy, Beth. Instr. classics Princeton, 1951-53; instr. classics and humanities Wesleyan U., Middletown, Conn., 1953-54; asst. prof. classics and humanities U. Cal. at Riverside, 1954-56; mem. faculty U. Tex., 1958-70, prof. classics, 1959-70, chmn. dept., 1964-66, Univ. prof. arts and letters, 1965-70; ednl. cons. Ford Found., 1970-71; cons. Leadership Tng. Inst., Office of Edn., 1970-71; vis. prof. Mass. Inst. Tech., spring 1971; fellow Center Advanced Studies, Wesleyan Univ., 1967, Battelle Meml. Inst., Seattle, 1968; founding editor Chimera, 1942-44, Hudson Rev., 1948-60. Arion, Jour. Classical Culture, 1962—; adv. editor Tulane Drama Rev., 1960-67; adv. bd. Mosaic, 1967—; mem. exec. com. Nat. Translation Center, 1965—. Served with AUS, 1943-46. Woodrow Wilson fellow, 1947-48; Guggenheim fellow, 1957-58; Prix de Rome sr. research fellow Am. Acad. Rome, 1956-57; Phi Beta Kappa vis. scholar, 1964-65; recipient Longview award criticism, 1960; Bromberg award excellence teaching U. Tex., 1959, Morris L. Ernst award excellence teaching, 1962, Piper prof. for distinguished teaching, 1966, Harbison award distinguished teaching, 1971. Mem. P.E.N., Assn. Am. Rhodes Scholars, Phi Beta Kappa. Democrat. Translator: (Petronius) The Satyricon, 1959; (Euripides) Bacchae, Cyclops, Heracles, Orestes and Hecuba, 1960; (Aristophanes) Birds. 1961; Clouds, 1962; (with R. Shattuck) The Craft of Context of Translation, 1962; (with D. S. Carne-Ross) (Cesare Pavese) Dialogues with Leucó, 1965. Editor: Image of Italy, 1961; Five Modern Italian Novels, 1964; also author numerous articles profl. jours. Home: RD 1 Bristol VT 05443

ARROYO, MARTINA, soprano; m. Emilio Poggioni. Leading soprano Met. Opera, N.Y.C., in roles including Il Trovatore, Aida, Madama Butterfly, Un Ballo in Maschera, Cavalleria Rusticana, La

Forza del Destino, Don Giovanni; performed opening night Met. season, 1970-71; performed at Vienna State Opera, Convent Garden, Teatro Colon, Buenos Aires, San Francisco and all maj. opera houses; Soloist N.Y., Vienna, Berlin, Royal (London) philharmonics, San Francisco, Pitts. symphonies, Concertgebouw, other maj. orchs.; frequent performer Saratoga, Ravinia, Tanglewood festivals and festivals Vienna, Berlin, Helsinki; oratios include Verdi and Dvorak Reguiems, Beethoven Missa Solemnis and Choral Fantasy, Judas Maccabaeus, others. Recs. for Columbia, London, Angel, DGG records. Named Outstanding Alumna Hunter Coll., N.Y.C. Address: care Maurice Feldman 745 Fifth Av New York City NY 10022

ARRUPE, PEDRO, clergyman; b. Bilbao, Spain, Nov. 14, 1907; s. Marcelino and Dolores (Gondra) A.; student State U. Madrid, 1922-27, Jesuit Seminaries at Oña Spain, 1931-32, Marneffe, Belgium 1932-33, Valkenburg, Holland, 1933-36, also St. Louis U., St. Mary's Coll., Kan., 1936-37, St. Stanislaus Tertianship, Cleve., 1937-38. Entered Soc. of Jesus at Loyola, Spain, 1927; ordained priest Roman Catholic Ch., 1936; rector, master of novices, Jesuit Novitiate, Hiroshima, Japan, 1942-54; provincial superior, Japan, 1954-65; vice chancellor Sophia U., Tokyo, 1956-64, prof., 1956-64; gen. Soc. of Jesus, Rome, Italy, 1965-; pres. Union Superiors Gen., 1967—. Decorated Comendador de Isabel la Católica. Author: Yo Vivi La Bomba Atómica, 1952; Este Japón increible, 1954; Christo no Michi; Kyosan-Shugi; Miyo Sono Hito Wo; Xaverio No Shingen; Xaverio No Sugata; Wakaki Seidai No Atau. Home: Borgo S Spirito 5 00193 Rome Italy

ARSEM, ALVAN DONALD, equipment mfg. co. exec.; b. Schenectady, July 3, 1923; s. William Collins and Helen Theresa (Moran) A.; B.S. in Elec. Engring., Mass. Inst. Tech., 1945; postgrad. Syracuse U., 1950-52, U. Buffalo, 1963-65; m. Katharine L. Brooks, June 30, 1945; children—Nancy (Mrs. R. Ray Osborn), Marilyn, Harold, Beverly. Devel. engr. RCA, Camden, N.J., 1945-48; mgr. advanced product devel. Gen. Electric Electronics Lab., Syracuse, N.Y., 1948-55; mgr. engring. Stewart-Warner Electronics, Chgo., 1955-58; mgr. engring. and research Wurlitzer Co., North Tonawanda, N.Y., 1958-60, v.p. engring. and research, 1960-68, exec. v.p., 1968—. Served with AUS, 1942-43. Mem. I.E.E.E. (sr.), N.Y. Acad. Sci., U.S. Naval Inst., Am. Inst. Aeros. and Astronautics, Acoustical Soc. Am., Sci. Research Soc. Am. Clubs; Chicago Yacht; Town (Tonawandas); Olcott (N.Y.) Yacht. Home: 5119 Shimerville Rd Clarence NY 14031 Office: Wurlitzer Co North Tonawanda NY 14120

ARSHT, S. SAMUEL, lawyer; b. Wilmington, Del., July 4, 1910; s. Morris and Elizabeth (Handler) A.; B.S. in Econs., U. Pa., 1931, LL.B., 1934; m. Roxana Cannon, May 9, 1940; children—Adrienne, Alison. Admitted to Del. bar, 1934, since practiced in Wilmington; partner firm Morris Nichols, Arsht & Tunnell. 1942—. Gen. counsel Del. Hwy. Dept., 1955-69; dir., sec. Brandywine Raceway Assn. (Del.). Mem. adv. com. New Castle (Del.) County, 1956-60; mem. Gov. Del. Tax Adv. Comm., 1953; chmn. Del. Revised Code Commn., 1949-65. Pres. Wilmington Child Guidance Center, 1957-58. Bds. dirs. Oakebourne Hosp., W. Chester, Pa., 1959-66. Kutz Home, Wilmington, Del., 1960—. Mem. Am. Law Inst., Am. Judicature Soc., Nat. Council Jud. Confs., Am., Del. (v.p. 1963-65) bar assns. Democrat. Clubs: Greeneville Country, Brandywine Country (Wilmington, Del.). Editorinchief Del. Code Annotated, 1953, biennial supplements to 1965; chmn. drafting of Del. corp. law, 1967, also revs. Del. decedents estate law. Contbr. articles on corp. law. Home: 415 Old Kennett Rd Wilmington, DE 19807. Office: Du Pont Bldg Wilmington DE 19899

ARTERBURN, NORMAN FRANK, judge; b. Bicknell, Ind., May 31, 1902; s. Clay H. and Anna (Hoover) A.; A.B. cum laude, Ind. U., 1923; J.D., U. Chgo., 1926; LL.D., Vincennes U., 1971; m. Lois E. Richards, 1926 (dec.); children—Joan, Linda, Faith. Admitted to Ind. bar, 1923, practiced in Vincennes, 1927-55, mem. Arterburn & Hart, 1946- 55; pros. atty. 12th Jud. Dist. Ind., 1928-30; justice Supreme Ct. of Ind., 1955-71, chief justice, 1971—; vis. prof. law Ind. U., 1949, 53-54. Mem. Ind. Bd. Law Examiners, 1938-44, pres., 1944. Bd. govs. Good Samaritan Hosp. Mem. Am., Ind., Vincennes bar assns. Methodist. Mason (32). Home: 1529 Old Orchard Rd Vincennes IN 47591 Office: Supreme Court State House Indianapolis IN 46204

ARTHOS, JOHN, educator; b. Wilmington, Del., July 18, 1908; s. James and Norma (Bennett) A.; A.B., Dartmouth, 1930; A.M., Harvard, 1933, Ph. D., 1937; m. Martha Rose Ennen, May 10, 1952; children—Lydie, John, James, Maria, Martha. Mem. faculty English dept. U. Mich., Ann Arbor, 1938- 42, 45—, asso. prof., 1949-54, prof., 1954—; faculty U. Wash., Seattle, 1963; research prof. U. Florence, 1949-50, U. Rome, 1970-71. Served with AUS, 1942-45. Decorated 1942-45. Decorated Bronze Star. Guggenheim fellow, 1956-57; Am. Council Learned Socs. fellow, 1963-64; Henry Russell lectr. U. Mich., 1970. Mem. Modern Lang. Assn. Am., Milton Soc., Dante Soc., Assn. Am., Milton Soc., Dante Soc., Renaissance Soc. Author: Minturno to The Apennines, 1946; Language of Natural Description in Eighteenth Century Poetry, 1949; On a Mask Presented at Ludlow-Castle, 1954; On the Poetry of Spenser and the Form of Romances, 1956; Dante, Michelangelo and Milton, 1963; The Art of Shakespeare, 1964; Milton and the Italian Cities, 1968. Editor: Love's Labor's Lost, 1965; Life of Adam (G. B. Lordane), 1968; Selected Poetry of John Dryden, 1970. Home: of John Dryden, 1970. Home: 2026 Hill St Ann Arbor MI 48104

ARTHUR, BEATRICE, actress; b. N.Y.C.; d. Philip and Rebecca Frankel; student Blackstone Coll., also Franklin Inst. Sci. and Arts; student acting with Erwin Piscator, Dramatic Workshop, New Sch. Social Research; m. Gene Saks, May 28, 1950; 2 sons. Theatrical appearances include Lysistrata, 1947, Dog Beneath the Skin, 1947, Gas, 1947, Yerma, 1947, No Exit, 1948, The Taming of the Shrew, 1948, Six Characters in Search of An Author, 1948, The Owl and the Pussycat, 1948, Le Boungeois Gentil Homme, 1949, Yes is For a Very Young Man, 1949, Creditors, 1949, Heartbreak House, 1949, Three Penny Opera, 1954, 55, Shoestring Revue, 1955, Seventh Heaven, 1955, The Ziegfeld Folliers, 1956, What's The Rush?, summer 1956, Mistress of the Inn, 1957, Nature's Way, 1957, Ulysses in Nightown, 1958, Chic, 1959, Gay Divorcee, 1960, A Matter of Position, 1962, Mame (Tony award best supporting mus. actress), 1966, Fiddler on the Roof, 1964; stock appearances with Circle Theatre, Atlantic City, summer 1951, State Fair Music Hall, Dallas, 1953, Music Circus, Lambertville, N.J., 1953; resident commedienne Tamiment (Pa.) Theatre, 1953; numerous TV and nightclub appearances, 1948—; motion picture appearances in That Kind of Woman, 1959, Lovers and Other Strangers, 1970. Mem. Artists Equity Assn., Screen Actors Guild, A.F.T.R.A. Address: 271 Central Park W New York City NY 10024

ARTHUR, FRANKLIN KILNORE, Jr., newspaperman; b. Redlands, Cal., June 27, 1910; s. Franklin K. and Helen (Williams) A.; A.B., U. Redlands, 1931; m. Mardelle Ann Simpson, Apr. 12, 1946; children—Rita, Franklin Kilnore II. Successively sports writer, reporter, polit. reporter, night city editor San Bernardino (Cal.) Sun, 1931-38; reporter, city editor A.P., Los Angeles, 1938-53, news editor Newsfeatures, N.Y.C., 1953-58, adminstrv. asst. to gen. mgr. A.P., 1958, chief bur., N.Y.C., 1958-63; editor, pub. Monterey (Cal.) Peninsula Herald, 1963—. Mem. Pulitzer Prize bd., 1964-66. Served to lt. comdr. USNR, 1942-45. Mem. Cal.-Nev. A.P. Assn. (pres. 1968-69), Cal. Newspaper Pubs. Assn. (chmn. Central Coast Counties unit 1968-69), Sigma Delta Chi (pres. No. Cal. profl. chpt. 1969-70). Baptist. Rotarian. Clubs: Los Angeles Press (dir., treas. 1951-53); Deadline (treas. 1959-60), Dutch Treat (N.Y.C.); Old Capitol (Monterey); Beach (Pebble Beach). Office: Toledo Times 541 Superior St Toledo OH 43604

ARTHUR, GEORGE ROLAND, electronics engr., assn. ofcl.; b. Phila., Feb. 22, 1925; s. George Gardner and Laura (Mager) A.; student Webb Inst., 1944-45; B.Eng., Yale, 1948, M.Eng., 1949, Ph.D., 1952; m. Madeline Wilma Alby, Feb. 23, 1946; children—George Roland, Stephen, Lesley, Randy, Gail. Instr. elec. engring. Yale, 1949-52; sect. head missile guidance Sperry Gyroscope, 1952-56; mgr. airborne missile electronics RCA, Camden, N.J., 1956-59; mgr. adv. manned systems engring. Gen. Electric Co., Phila., 1959-63; dep. dir. aerospace ITT Labs., Nutley, N.J., 1963-66, tech. dir. ITT U.S. Def. Group, 1966-67; v.p. ITT-Europe, 1967—. Served with USNR, 1943-46. Fellow Brit. Interplanetary Soc., A.A.A.S., Am. Astron. Soc. (pres. 1959, 60); sr. mem. I.E.E.E., Am. Inst. Aeros. and Astronautics; mem. Sigma Xi, Tau Beta Pi. Home: 69 Av de l'Armee Brussels Belgium Office: 11 Blvd de L'Empereur Brussesl Belgium

ARTHUR, HAROLD RICHARD, banker; b. St. Louis, Sept. 17, 1920; s. Corrie Lenox and Martha (Bradford) A.; student San Mateo (Cal.) Jr. Coll., 1938-39; m. Rosemarie Hamlin, Feb. 8, 1947; children—Diane, Janet, Linda. With Am. Trust Co., San Francisco, 1939-51; with Brenton Companies. also asst. cashier Brenton State Bank and State Bank Des Moines, 1951-53; with Am. Trust Co. (name changed to Wells Fargo Bank, N.A., 1960), San Francisco, 1954—, v.p., cashier, 1968—. Served with USNR, 1942-45. Mem. Cal. Bankers Assn., Bank Administrn. Inst., Am. Inst. Banking (instr., past pres. Stanislaus County chpt.). Club: San Francisco Commercial. Office: 464 California St San Francisco CA 94120

ARTHUR, HENRY BRADFORD, economist; b. Gloversville, N.Y., Apr. 24, 1904; s. Bradford Harlan and Minnie E. (Simmons) A.; A.B., Union Coll., 1926, LL.D., 1952; M.A., Harvard, 1931, Ph.D., 1935; m. Charlotte Beals, June 21, 1931; children—H. Bradford, Janice S. (Mrs. Bowen H. McCoy). In statis. and econ. research for Harvard Econ. Soc. 1928-32; instr. econs. Harvard, 1930-32; research in Div. of Research and Planning, N.R.A., Washington, D.C., 1933, Com. on Govt. Statistics and Information Services, 1933-34, Consumers Div., Nat. Emergency Council, 1934-35; asst. dir. Div. of Research, W.P.A., 1935-36; lectr. Am. U., 1935-36; in comml. research dept. Swift & Co., 1936-39, economist, 1939-60; Moffett prof. agr. and bus. Harvard Grad. Sch. Bus. Adminstrn., 1960-70, prof. emeritus, 1970—; vis. prof. Salzburg Seminar in Am. Studies, 1966. Cons. Ho. of Reps. com. on postwar econ. policy, 1944-46; cons. on rationing O.P.A., 1942-43; chief Program Review Div., European Office E.C.A., Paris, 1948-49; industry mem. WSB, 1950-51; mem. E.C.A. evaluation mission to Denmark, 1953. Mem. Hinsdale (Ill.) Bd. of Edn., 1945-53; mem. Hinsdale Plan Commn., 1959-60; trustee Union Coll., 1953-61; mem. council Harvard Found. Adv. Studies and Research, 1958-61. Fellow Am. Statis. Assn. (v.p. 1942, dir. 1943-45)); mem. Conf. Bus. Economists (chmn. 1958-60), Am. Econ. Assn., Phi Beta Kappa, Sigma Xi, Theta Delta Chi. Club: Cosmos (Washington). Co-author: Futures Trading Seminar, vol. II, vol. III; Dynamics of Adjustment in the Broiler Industry; Theory in Marketing; Tropical Agribusiness Structures and Adjustments—Bananas; Commodity Futures as a Business Management Tool. Contributor of articles to Am. Econ. Rev., Jour. Am. Statis. Assn., Harvard Bus. Rev. Home: 28 Tyler Rd Belmont MA 02178 Office: Harvard Grad Sch Bus Adminstrn Boston MA 02163

ARTHUR, HOWARD L., Jr., banker. Sr. auditor First Union Nat. Bank N.C., Charlotte. Office: Box 10498 301 S Tryon St Charlotte NC 28201*

ARTHUR, JOHN BURWELL, refractories co. exec.; b. Poplar Bluff, Mo., Jan. 29, 1889; s. Hiram David and Sophronia Carruthers (Jackson) A.; student pub. schs., Poplar Bluff, Mo., also Birmingham, Ala.; D.Engring., honoris causa, U. Mo. Sch. Mines and Metallurgy, 1958; m. Greeta B. Lawson, May 10, 1913; children—Dorothy E. (Mrs. Carl Bachmann), Betty Jane (Mrs. Robert G. Hook, Jr.). Office mgr. Sandoval Zinc Co., East St. Louis, Ill., 1910- 11; office mgr. Cypress Lumber Co., Apalachicola, Fla., 1911-13; office mgr. Leach Lumber Co., Poplar Bluff, Mo., 1913-14; v.p., gen. mgr. A.P. Green Fire Brick Co. Mexico, Mo., 1914-29; pres., chmn. Mexico Refractories Co. (Mo.), 1929—; chmn. Nat. Refractories Co., Phila., 1935—; pres. Big Savage Refractories Co., Frostburg, Md., 1938—, Fire Brick Engrs., Inc. Cleve., 1936—, Niles Fire Brick Co. (Ohio), 1954—, Mexico Refractories Co. of Cuba, Havana, 1955—; dir. Refractories Engring. & Supplies, Ltd., Hamilton, Ont., Can., First Nat. Bank, Mexico, Mo., New Orleans Ct. Northern Ry. Co., St. Louis. Pres. KXEO Radio Sta., Mexico, Mo., 1959. Dir. Refractories Institute, Pitts., pres., 1959. Mem. Christian Ch. Clubs: Duquesene (Pitts.); Mexico City Country; Jefferson City Country; Merion Golf (Ardmore, Pa.). Home: 718 E Monroe St Mexico MO 65265 Office: Mexico Refractories Co Mexico MO 65265

ARTHUR, JOHN KENNETH STUART, accountant; b. London, Eng., Nov. 18, 1918; s. John F. Stuart and Ethelwyn (Hurst) A.; brought to U.S., 1919, naturalized, 1942; B.A., Rice U., 1941; M.B.A., Harvard, 1947; m. Marian Smedes, Jan. 16, 1943; children—John Kenneth Stuart II, David Stuart, Bruce Smedes. With Lybrand, Ross Bros. & Montgomery, C.P.A.'s, 1947—, partner-in-charge, Dallas, 1958—. Vice chmn. Dallas County crusade Am. Cancer Soc., 1966, bd. dirs., 1966-67, chmn., 1967; bd. dirs. Dallas Symphony Orch., 1966. Served to capt. AUS, 1942-46; ETO, PTO. C.P.A., Tex. Mem. Am. Inst. C.P.A.'s (council 1966-67), Tex. Soc. C.P.A.'s (pres. 1966-67), Nat. Assn. Accountants. Kiwanian. Clubs: Preston Trail Golf (treas.), Brook Hollow Golf (bd. govs. 1966-67). Home: 5806 Glen Falls Lane Dallas TX 75209 Office: First Nat Bank Bldg Dallas TX 75202

ARTHUR, JOHN MORRISON, utility exec.; b. Pitts., Aug. 17, 1922; s. Hugh Morrison and Ann Matilda (Crowe) A.; B.S. in Elec. Engring., U. Pitts., 1944, M.S. in Elec. Engring., 1947; m. Sylvia Ann Martin, June 19, 1948; children—William Robert, John Martin, Advrew Scott. With Duquesne Light Co. Pitts., 1945-, v.p., asst. to chmn. bd. and pres., 1966-67, pres., 1967-68, chmn. bd., 1968—, also dir.; dir. Mellon Nat. Bank & Trust Co., Allegheny County Steam Heating Co., Cheswick and Harmar R.R. Served with AUS, 1942-43. Recipient Outstanding Alumni award U. Pitts., 1968. Mem. I.E.E.E., Edison Electric Inst., Assn. Edison Illuminating Cos., Pa. Electric Assn., Engrs. Soc. Western Pa. Clubs: Duquesne (Pitts); Montour Heights Country (Coraopolis). Home: 1401 Coraopolis Heights Rd Coraopolis PA 15108 Office: 435 6th Av Pittsburgh PA 15219

ARTHUR, MAX, hosp. adminstr.; b. Maynard, Ia., Dec. 25, 1921; s. William Leonard and Marie (Meyer) A.; student Upper Ia. Coll., 1940-42, Albright Coll., 1943-44; m. Anita Delores Blake, Nov. 4, 1944; children—Bradley Kent, Gregory Len, David Alan. Sales rep. Ohio Equipment Co., Madison, Wis., 1951-57; adminstr. Grundy County Hosp., Grundy Center, Ia., 1957-60, Summit Hosp., Oconomowoc, Wis., 1960-62; hosp. and phys. relations Asso. Hosp. Services, Milw., 1963-65; adminstr. Waukesha (Wis.) County Instns., 1965—; mem. adv. com. Wis. Dept. Health and Social Services. Served with USAAF, 1942-44. Licensed nursing home adminstr., Wis. Lutheran. Mason. Address: 25042 W Northview Rd Waukesha WI 53186

ARTHUR, ROBERT ALAN, author; b. N.Y.C., June 10, 1922; s. William and Margaret (Brock) A.; B.A. in Journalism with highest honors, U. Pa., 1946; m. Jane Wetherell, May 27, 1966; 1 dau., Kate; children by prev. marriage—Jonathan, Gretchen, Timothy. Contbr. short stories to magazines, 1948-52; free-lance TV writer, 1952-56; asso. producer Philco TV Playhouse, 1955, producer, 1956; film writer, 1957-59; producer NBC Sunday Showcase, 1959-60; v.p. Talent Assos. Ltd., 1961-62; charge prodn. United Artists TV, 1963-64; film writer, 1965-66; author Broadway prodns. A Very Special Baby, 1956, Kwamina, 1961, Carry Me Back to Morningside Heights, 1968; author screen plays Grand Prix, 1967, For Love of Ivy, 1968, Trespass, 1971; writer-dir.. The Lost Man, 1968-69. Served to 1st lt. USMCR, 1942-46. Recipient Sylvania award for best original TV play, 1954, 55; Emmy award, 1955. Mem. Am. Civil Liberties Union, N.A.A.C.P., TV Acad. Arts and Scis. (bd. govs. 1958-59), Actor's Studio, Writers Guild of America-West, Acad. Motion Picture Arts and Scis., Sigma Nu. Author: The History of the Third Marine Division, 1947; (novel) The Glorification of Al Toolum, 1952. Home: 968 Fireplace Rd East Hampton NY 11937

ARTHUR, ROBERT JAMES, editor; b. Scranton, Pa., Aug. 18, 1904; s. James C. and Anna (Mannix) A.; LL.B., Columbia (extension), 1921; m. Dorothy M. Edmunds, July 28, 1941; 1 son, Robert James. Reporter, Scranton Tribune and Scrantonian, 1921-40, columnist, 1926-48, editor, 1946—. Chmn., Scranton Redevelopment Authority. Mem. Am. Soc. Newspaper Editors, Am., Pa. newspapers pubs. assns., Scranton C. of C. (dir.); hon. mem. Am. Newspaper Guild, Internat. Typog. Union. Republican. Roman Catholic. Contbr. to mags. Home: 1819 Monsey Av Scranton PA Office: 332-38 N Washington Av Scranton PA

ARTHUR, ROBERT MILTON, educator, biol. engr.; b. Fond du lac, Wis., Mar. 21, 1924; s. Simon Albert and Irma Minnie (Spielberg) A.; B.A., Ripon Coll., 1949; B.S., Northeastern U., 1953; M.S., Harvard, 1956; Ph.D., State U. Ia., 1963; m. Sally K. McMillan, Mar. 13, 1965; 1 son, Robert McMillan. Asst. engr. City of Fond du Lac, 1949-52; asst. engr. Chgo. Pump Co., Chgo., 1953-56; prof., chmn. dept. biol. engring. Rose-Hulman Inst. Tech., Terre Haute, Ind., 1956—. Pres., Arthur & Assos., Cons. Engrs., Fond du Lac, 1957—, Arthur Bros. Co., instrument mfrs., Fond du Lac, 1965—, Biotech. Research Center, Fond du Lac, 1971—. Served with AUS, 1943-46; ETO. Mem. Water Pollution Control Fedn. (chmn. instrumentation com. 1970—), Am. Soc. Engring. Edn. (biomed. com. 1964-66, 71—), Tau Beta Pi. Editor 3d, 4th, 5th Bioengring. Symposia Rose- Hulman Inst. Tech. Patentee in field; developer biol. engring. dept. Rose- Hulman Inst. Tech., 1967. Home: 344 Potomac Av Terre Haute IN 47803

ARTHUR, WALLACE, physicist, educator; b. N.Y.C., Nov. 22, 1932; s. Adolph Heimlich and Helen (Beckerman) A.; B.E.E., N.Y.U., 1957, B.E.S., 1957, Ph.D., 1962; m. Lois Shiller, Jan. 17, 1960; children—David A., Edward S., Stephen D. Research asst. N.Y.U., 1957-61; lectr. Rutgers U., 1961-62; prof. physics Fairleigh Dickinson U., Teaneck, N.J., 1962—; cons. Canrad Precision Industries, Nuclear Research Assos. Served with Signal Corps, U.S. Army, 1952-54. Mem. A.A.A.S., Am. Phys. Soc., Am. Assn. Physics Tchrs., Am. Assn. U. Profs. (past chpt. chmn.), Sigma Xi. (chpt. chmn.). Author: (with S.K. Fenster) Mechanics, 1969. Home: 22 Raymond St Harrington Park NJ 07640 Office: 1000 River Rd Teaneck NJ 07666

ARTHUR, WILLIAM BOLLING, mag. editor; b. Louisville, Sept. 6, 1914; s. Stanley H. and Margaret (Carter) A.; A.B., U. Ky., 1937, LL.D., 1967; m. Frances Lee Young, Aug. 19, 1939; children—William Bolling, Richard Houghton. Asst. state editor Louisville Courier-Jour., 1939-41; asst. mng. editor Look mag., 1949-54, mng. editor, 1954-66, editor, 1966- -; v.p. Cowles Magazine & Broadcasting Inc., 1962-70; v.p., dir. Cowles Communications, Inc., 1970—. Chief press br. Bureau Public Relations, War Dept., 1944-46. Nat. council Boy Scouts Am. Trustee, Berea Coll. (Ky.). Decorated Legion Merit. Recipient Freedom's Found. award, 1948. Mem. Am. Soc. Mag. Editors (chmn.), English-Speaking Union, Nat. Council Chs. (v.p. at large), Sigma Delta Chi (nat. pres. 1968-69). Presbyn. (bd. nat. missions). Home: 715 Bleeker Av Mamaroneck NY 10543 Office: 488 Madison Av New York City NY 10017

ARTINIAN, ARTINE, scholar French lit.; b. Pazardjick, Bulgaria, Dec. 8, 1907; s. Peter and Akaby (Berberian) A.; brought to U.S., 1920, naturalized, 1930; A.B., Bowdoin Coll., 1931; diploma U. Paris (France), 1932; A.M., Harvard, 1933; Ph.D., Columbia, 1941; Litt.D., Bowdoin Coll., 1966; grad. work U. Grenoble (France), 1931, U. Poitiers (France), 1932; m. Margaret Willard Woodbridge, June 27, 1936; children—Margaret (Mrs. Otto Laske), Robert W., Ellen (Mrs. David Strickland). Asst. French, Bowdoin Coll., 1930-31; ednl. worker dept. correction organizing inmate sch. Welfare Island Penitentiary, N.Y.C., 1934-35; prof. French, John Marshall Coll. Law, N.J., 1935-36; chmn. French dept. Bard Coll., Annandale, N.Y., 1935-64, chmn. div. langs., lits., 1939-40, 44-45, 56-57, 58-59, 60-64, prof. emeritus French, 1964—, head instr. French, A.S.T.P. unit, 1943-44; prof.-in-charge Sweet Briar (Va.) Jr. Year in France, 1953-55; acting dir. U.S. house Citè Universitaire, Paris, summers, 1955, 56, 58. Mem. Com. Examiners (French sect.) Coll. Entrance Exam. Bd., 1962-64. Trustee Am. Students Center, Paris. Compiler of an extensive Guy de Maupassant collection permanently on exhibit U. Tex.; exhibited collection drawings and paintings of French writers U.S. tour sponsored by French govt., 1968-70; exhibited Century and a Half of French Illustrators, Cornell U., Brandeis U., Harvard, 1968; The French Visage, A Century and a Half of French Portraits, Bowdoin Coll. Mus. Art, Hopkins Art Center, Dartmouth Coll., others, 1969; exhibited Music in Art at Henry Morrison Flagler Mus., Palm Beach, Fla., Brandeis U., Wellesley Coll., 1971; also exhibited other collections numerous other univs. U.S. including Columbia, Harvard French Inst. N.Y.C. Guest of French govt., summer 1946. Decorated officer d'Academie (France), 1948; fellow Am. Council Learned Socs., 1943-44; Fulbright research scholar, France, 1949-50; grantee research Am. Philos. Soc., Paris, 1960. Mem. Société des Amis de Guy de Maupassant (v.p. 1950—), Modern Lang. Assn. Am. (sec. 19th Century French sect. 1947, chmn. 1948), Am. Assn. Tchrs. French, Nat. Fedn. Modern Lang. Tchrs., Am. Assn. U. Profs. (pres. Bard Coll. chpt. 1951-52), Sociètè Litteraire des Amis d'Emile Zola (U.S. rep. bd. dirs. 1954—), Theta Delta Chi, Pi Delta Epsilon. Author: Maupassant Criticism in France, 1880-1940; With an Inquiry into His Present Fame and a Bibliography, 1941, 69. Editor: La Correspondance inèdite de Guy de Maupassant, 1951; Pour et Contre Maupassant, 1955; Complete Short Stories of Guy de Maupassant, 1955; La Queue de la Poire de la Boule de Monsigneur (Flaubert), 1958; La-Haut (Hysmans), 1963; From Victor Hugo to Jean Cocteau, 1965. Contbr. profl. jours., books. Office: Bard Coll Annandale-on-Hudson NY

ARTSCHWAGER, RICHARD, artist; b. Washington, Dec. 26, 1924; s. Ernst and Eugenia (Brodsky) A.; A.B., Cornell U., 1948; pupil of Amedee Ozenfant, N.Y.C., 1949-50; m. Elfriede Wejmelka, Feb. 6, 1948; 1 dau., Eva. One-man shows include Leo Castelli Gallery, N.Y.C. 1965, 67, Konrad Fischer, Dusseldorf, Germany, 1968; numerous gallery and museum group shows, 1963—; works represent permanent collections Milw. Art Center, also Mus. Modern Art, Whitney Mus., The Rockhill-Nelson Mus., Kansas City, Mo., Detroit Art Center, Stroer Mus., Darmstadt, Germany, Aachen (Germany) Mus., also pvt. collections; originated abstract illusion in sculpture and reliefs. Address: 20 E Broadway New York City NY 10004

ARTZ, FREDERICK BINKERD, historian; b. Dayton, O., Oct. 19, 1894; s. J. Elam and May (Binkerd) A.; A.B., Oberlin Coll., 1916, D.Litt., 1966; student U. Toulouse, 1919, U. of Paris, 1922-23; Ph.D., Harvard, 1924; D.Litt., Carthage Coll., 1970. Instr. history, Antioch Coll., 1916-17, Harvard, 1923-24; asst. prof. history, Oberlin 1934—; vis. prof. Harvard, 1930-31; lectr. Harvard Summer Sch., 1931 and 34. Served with A.E.F., France, 1917-19. Fellow Social Sci. Research Council, 1928- 29. Mem. Am. Hist. Assn., Am. Assn. Univ. Profs., Royal Hist. Soc., Société d'Histore Moderne, Phi Beta Kappa. Author: France Under the Bourbon Restoration, 1931; Reaction and Revolution, 1814-32 (W.L. Langer series of " Rise of Modern Europe"), 1934; The Intellectual History of Europe from St. Augustine to Marx-a Guide, 1941; The Mind of the Middle Ages, 200-1500 A.D., an Historical Survey, 1954; From the Renaissance to Romanticism A.D. 1300-1830, 1962; Renaissance Humanism, 1300-1550; Development of French Technical Education, 1500-1850; The Enlightenment in France, published 1968. Contbr. Am. History Rev., Saturday Rev. Lit., Jour. of Modern History, Revue d'Histore Moderne, Ency. of Soc. Sciences. Mem. bd. editors Jour. of Modern History, 1932-35; Jour. of Central European Affairs since 1940. Home: Oberlin OH 44074

ARTZ, KENNETH BUCKLEY, publishing co. exec.; b. Reading, Pa., July 14, 1928; s. Clarence Bright and Naomi (Floyd) A.; B.S. in Econs., Albright Coll., Reading, 1957; m. Ann Louise Wildermuth, June 2, 1956. Sr. accountant Price Waterhouse & Co., Phila., 1957-63; asst. to controller Curtis Pub. Co., Phila., 1963- 66, treas., 1966-69, v.p., treas., 1969-71; v.p. finance and adminstrn. Ballantine Books, Inc. subsidiary Internat. Textbook Corp., N.Y.C., 1971—. Served with AUS, 1951-53, C.P.A., Pa., D.C. Mem. Am. Inst. C.P.A.'s. Home: Hopkinson House Philadelphia PA 19106 Office: Ballantine Books 101 Fifth Av New York City NY 10003

ARTZY, RAFAEL, educator, mathematician; b. Konigsberg, Germany, July 23, 1912; s. Eduard I. and Ida (Freudenheim) Deutschlander; student Konigsberg U., 1930-33; M.A., Hebrew U., 1934, Ph.D., 1945; m. Elly Iwiansky, Oct. 12, 1934; children—Ehud, Michal, Barak. Came to U.S., 1960, naturalized, 1967. Tchr., prin. Israel High Schs., 1934-51; instr., asso. prof. Israel Inst. Tech., 1951-60; research asso., lectr. U. Wis., Madison, 1956-58; asso. prof. U. N.C., Chapel Hill, 1960-61; prof. Rutgers U., 1961-65, State U. N.Y., Buffalo, 1965-67; prof. math. Temple U., Phila., 1967—; with Inst. for Advanced Study, 1964. Mem. Am. Math. Soc., Math. Assn. Am., Israel Math. Union, Am. Assn. U. Profs. Author: Linear Geometry, 1965. Contbr. research papers to Am., Israeli, German, Swiss jours. Hebrew Ency. Home: 415 Wischman Av Oreland PA 19075 Office: Dept Math Temple U Philadelphia PA 19122

ARUNDELL, FRANK VICTOR, Jr., advt. exec.; b. N.Y.C., Feb. 25, 1930; s. Frank Victor and Anne (Hughes) A.; m. Doris T. Smith, Sept. 26, 1954; children—Frank Victor III, Denise, Andrea Ellen. Artdir. Cecil Presbrey; art dir., producer Dancer Pitzgerald-Sample, 1955—, v.p., 1968—. Served with AUS, 1951-53. Mem. Broadcaster Advertisers Producers Soc. (bd. dirs. 196869). Home: 500 8th Av New Hyde Park, NY 11040. Office: 347 Madison Av New York City NY 10017

ARUTUNOFF, ARMAIS SERGEEVICH, pump mfg. co. exec.; b. Tiflis, Caucasus, Russia, June 21, 1893; s. Sergei Lasarevich and Varvara (Esaibekova) A.; B.S., Poly. Inst., Petrograd, Russia, 1917; m. Claudia G., Apr. 12, 1917; children—Sergei, Anait, Anatoly. Came to U.S., 1923, naturalized, 1932. Designer elec. equipment for oil wells, 1914—; v.p., mgr. Electrobur, Baku, Russia, 1914-17; v.p. Russki Electro-Dvigatel Arutunova, Ekaterinslov, Russia, 1917-21, Reda Motoren Verwertung G.M.B.-H., Berlin, Germany, 1921-23; chief engr., v.p. Bart Mfg. Co., Bartlesbille, Okla. 1927-30; pres. Reda Pump Co., Bartlesville, 1938—, chmn., 1930—, Mem. A.A.A.S., Am. Inst. E.E., Am. Petroleum Inst., Mid-Continent Oil and Gas Assn., U.S. C. of C. Episcopalian. Clubs: Tulsa; Hillcrest Country (Bartlesville); Marco Polo (N.Y.C.); California (Los Angeles). Home: 1200 Cherokee St Bartlesville OK 74003 Office: 509 W 1st St Bartlesville OK 74003

ARVEY, JACOB M., lawyer; b. Chgo., Nov. 3, 1895; s. Israel and Bertha Arvey; ed. Crane High Sch., John Marshall Law Sch.; m. Edith Freeman, June 11, 1915; children—Erwin, Howard, Helen Sue. Began practice, Chgo., 1916; asst. state's atty. Cook County, 1918-20; mem. law firm Raber, Kostner, Herr & Arvey, 1920-25; now mem. firm Arvey, Hodes & Mantynland; master in Chancery Circuit Court of Cook County, 1930-34. Chmn. bd. Marina City Bank Chgo.; dir. Republic Nat. Bank, Miami, Fla. Alderman 24th Ward, Chgo., 1923-41; chmn. Cook County Central Com. of Democratic Party; elected Ill. Democratic Nat. Committeeman, 1950. Bd. dirs. Am. Israel Pub. Affairs Com., Am. Friends Tel Aviv U., Am. Com. Weizmann Inst. Sci., Eleanor Roosevelt Cancer Found., Am. ORT Fedn., Asso. Talmud Torahs Chgo. (hon.), Jewish Burial Soc. Chgo., Louis Weiss Meml. Hosp., Home for the Aged, Miami, Home for the Aged, Chgo., Mt. Sinai Hosp., Miami Beach, Fla.; bd. dirs., adv. bd. Am. Friends of Hebrew U.; adv. council Brandeis U., World Jewish Congress, Synagogue Council America, Emotionally Disturbed Children; mem. Cath. Interracial Council Citizens Bd., Chgo.; adv. bd. Israeli Pub. Inst.; internat. hon. bd. Ency. Judaica Press, Inc. Hon. chmn. Israel Bonds. Served with AUS, World War II. Mem. Am., Fed., Ill., Chgo. bar assns., Am. Legion (vice chmn. distinguished guests com.). Mason, Elk, Odd Fellow, K.P.; mem. B'nai B'rith. Clubs: Bryn Mawr Country, Covenant (Chgo.); Westview Country (Miami); Nat. Capitol Democratic (Washington); Nat. Democratic (N.Y.C.). Home: 2300 Lincoln Park W Chicago IL 60614 Office: 1 N LaSalle St Chicago IL 60602

ARVEY, MARTIN DALE, educator; b. Los Angeles, Dec. 6, 1915; s. David and Bessie (Tarkovsky) A.; student U. Cal., Los Angeles, 1933-35, B.A., Berkeley, 1937; M.S., U. Ida., 1939; Ph.D., U. Kan., 1949; div.; children—William D., Richard D., Michael T. Mem. faculty U. Okla., 1949-50, Long Beach State Coll., 1953-62; spl. asst. NSF, 1962-67; prof. U. of Pacific, Stockton, Cal., 1967—. Served to lt. USNR, 1944-46, 50-53. Recipient Rockefeller grant, 1962, NSF Inst. grants, 1961, 68, 70, 71. Mem. A.A.A.S., Am. Inst. Biol. Scis., Am. Ornithologists Union, Cooper Ornithol. Soc., Sigma Xi, Phi Sigma. Home: 1350 Buckingham Way Stockton CA 95207

ARVIN, MARTIN JOSEPH, educator, physicist; b. Montgomery, Ind., Apr. 9, 1902; s. Robert Francis and Margaret (McDonald) A.; A.B., Ind. State U., 1926; M.S., U. Ill., 1930, Ph.D., 1934; m. Margaret Elizabeth Rowland, Aug. 17, 1936; children—William Francis, Ann Margaret, Jane Rowland. Tchr., Morgan Park Jr. Coll., Chgo., 1935-36, Chgo. high schs., 1936-43; instr. U. Ill., 1943-45; cons. Milw. Gas Specialty Co., 1943-45, research physicist, 1945-49; prof. physics So. Ill. U., Carbondale, 1949—, acting chmn., 1964-66. Mem. Am. Assn. U. Profs., Am. Inst. Physics, Am. Assn. Physics Tchrs., Sigma Xi. Patentee thermoelectric generator. Home: RR 3 Carbondale IL 62901

ARZT, MAX, rabbi, educator; b. Poland, Mar. 20, 1897; s. Hyman and Anna (Grossbach) A.; B.S., Coll. City. N.Y., 1918; M.A., Columbia, 1921; M.H.L., Jewish Theol. Sem. Am., 1921, D.H.L., 1934, D.D., 1950; m. Esther Podolsky, Mar. 7, 1922; childrenMiriam (wife Dr. Saul Teplitz), David, Raphael. Came to U.S., 1902, naturalized, 1915. Rabbi, Temple Beth El, Stamford, Conn., 1921-24, Temple Israel, Scranton, Pa., 1924-39; dir. field activities, asso. prof. practical theology Jewish Theol. Sem., 1939-51, vice chancellor, 1951-, Israel Goldstein prof. practical theology, 1962- . Pres. Rabbinical Assembly Am., 1939, exec. com. United Synagogue Am.; mem. editorial com. Jewish Publ. Soc., mem. com. translators of Hebrew scriptures into English for Jewish Publ. Soc. Am.; mem. Pa. Gov.'s Commn. on Pub. Assistance and Relief, 1934; charter mem. Adv. Council Internat. Movement for Atlantic Union, Inc.; U.S. del. to NATO Congress, London, summer 1959. Mem. exec. com. N.Y. Bd. Rabbis. Author: Justice and Mercy, 1963. Contbg. editor Judaism, quar. Home: 280 Riverside Dr New York City, NY 10025. Office: 3080 Broadway, New York City, NY 10027.

ARZT, SHOLOM, educator, mathematician; b. N.Y.C., May 3, 1929; s. Morris and Dorothy (Schwartz) A.; A.B., N.Y.U., 1946, M.S., 1948, Ph.D., 1951; m. Esther Lerman, Sept. 1, 1960; 1 son, Jonathan. Sr. mathematician Applied Physics Lab., Johns Hopkins, 1951-54; project engr. Specialty Electronics Corp., 1954-58; asst. prof. mathematics Cooper Union, 1958-63, asso. prof., head dept., 1963-69, prof., 1969—. Mem. Am. Math. Soc., Math. Assn. Am., Soc. Indsl. and Applied Mathematics, Am. Assn. Univ. Profs., Am. Civil Liberties Union. Home: 340 W 28th St New York City NY 10001

ASAO, SHINICHIRO, diplomat of Japan; b. Tokyo, Japan, Jan. 1, 1928; s. Shinsuke and Hiroe (Higuchi) A.; B.A., Faculty Law U. Tokyo, 1951; m. Michiko Mitani, Nov. 17, 1956; children—Kiyoko, Keiichiro. With Fgn. Service Japan, 1951—; dir. security div. Ministry Fgn. Affairs, 1965-67; 1st sec. Japanese embassy, Washington, 1968—, counselor, 1971—. Fellow Center Internat. Affairs, Harvard, 1967-68. Clubs: Internat., Nat. Press (Washington). Home: 5312 Westpath Way Washington DC 20016 Office: 2520 Massachusetts Av NW Washington DC 20008

ASBELL, BERNARD, author: b. Bklyn., May 8, 1923; s. Samuel and Minnie (Zevin) A.; student U. Conn., 1943-44; m. Mildred Sacarny, Jan. 2, 1944; children—Paul, Lawrence, Jonathan, Jody; m. 2d, Marjorie Baldwin Farrell, June 11, 1971. Reporter, Richmond (Va.) Times-Dispatch, 1945- 47; engaged in pub. relations, Chgo., 1947-55; mng. editor Chgo. mag., 1955-56; free lance author, 1956—; tchr. non-fiction writing U. Chgo., 1956-60, Bread Loaf Writers Conf., Middlebury (Vt.) Coll., 1960, 61, U. Bridgeport, 1961-63; cons. Ednl. Facilities Labs., 1963, U. Ill., 1964, Ford Found., 1965, 1968-69; cons. to sec. of health, edn. and welfare, 1965-68, Sci. Research Assos. div. IBM, Carnegie Corp. N.Y. Justice of peace, Wilton, Conn., 1966-67. Chmn. Wilton Democratic Party, 1964-66. Served with AUS, 1943-45. Recipient Sch. Bell award N.E.A., 1965; Edn. Writers Assn. 1st prize mag. coverage, 1965, spl. citation, 1966. Mem. Soc. Mag. Writers (pres. 1963, exec. council 1964-66), Edn. Writers Assn. Author: When F.D.R. Died, 1961; The New Improved American, 1965; What Lawyers Really Do, 1970; Careers in Urban Affairs, 1970. Contbr. nat. magazines. Address: 116 Harbor Pkwy Clinton CT 06413

ASBILL, MAC, lawyer; b. Ridge Spring, S.C., Nov. 19, 1893; s. Burdette McKendrie and Emma (Nicholson) A.; A.B., Wofford Coll., 1913; LL.B., Harvard, 1917; m. Jennie Sutherland, June 1, 1921; 1 son, Mac. Admitted to D.C. bar, 1919, Ga. bar, 1920, U.S. Supreme Ct., 1923; partner firm Watkins, Russell & Asbill, Watkins & Asbill and Watkins, Asbill & Watkins, Atlanta, 1920- 34; partner firm Cummings & Stanley, and successor firm Cummings, Stanley, Truitt & Cross, Washington, 1945-49, Sutherland, Tuttle & Brennan, Atlanta and Washington, 1949-53, mem. successor firm Sutherland, Asbill & Brennan, 1953-70, counsel, 1970—; spl. asst. to atty. gen. U.S., 1934-41, chief, trial sect. anti-trust div., 1936-37, 1st asst. lands div., 1937-39, tax div., 1939, anti-trust div. in charge oil litigation, 1939-41. Served as lt., U.S. Army, 1917-18. Mem. Am., D.C., Ga., bar assns. Club: Columbia Country (Washington). Home: 2101 Connecticut Av Washington DC 20008 Office: Farragut Bldg Washington DC 20006

ASBURY, R.L., utility co. exec. Controller, Duke Power Co., Charlotte, N.C. Office: 422 S Church St Charlotte NC 28202*

ASBURY, WILBUR FRANCIS, diversified industry exec.; b. Winslow, Ariz., Nov. 13, 1911; s. Harry Wilber and Fannie May (Klooz) A.; B.S., U. Ariz., 1933; m. Angela Lane, July 5, 1949; children—Harry W., Frank B., Craig T., Wilbur Francis, Donald James; Richard L. Beck, Robert Beck (foster sons). With City Products Corp., Phoenix, 1933—, mgr. Western div., 1941—, v.p., 1957—; dir. Valley Nat. BAnk, Phoenix. Chmn. Maricopa County Better Govt. Assn., 1956; co-dir. civil def., Maricopa County-City Phoneix, 1950-60; mem. Ariz. Hwy. Commn., 1959-64. Mem. Aircraft Owners and Pilots Assn., Phoenix C. of C. (past pres.), Thunderbirds, Sigma Chi. Episcopalian. Maon (Shriner) Clubs: Phoenix Country, Kiva (Phoenix). Home: 3209 W Manor Dr Phoenix, AZ 85014. Office: PO Box 4366 Phoenix AZ 85030

ASCANI, FRED JOHN, air force officer; b. Beloit, Wis., May 29, 1917; s. Gino and Maria (Franciñi) A.; student Beloit Coll., 1935-37; B.S., U.S. Mil. Acad., 1941; grad. Air War Coll., 1954; m. Catherine Marie Hanretta, Jan. 9, 1942; children—John F., William G., Carole Jo, Susan C., Stephen, Clare, Mary Elizabeth, David. Commd. 2d lt. U.S. Army, 1941, advanced through grades to maj. gen. USAF, 1962; rated pilot, 1942; squadron comdr. 483d Comb Group, 1944-45; comdr. 816th Squadron, 1944-45; chief bomber test, Wright-Patterson AFB, O., also dep. chief flight test div., 1945-50; dir. flight test and engring. Edwards AFB, Cal., 1950-51; vice comdr. Air Force Flight Test Center, 1951-53; group comdr. 86th Fighter Interceptor Wing, 1954-55; wing comdr. 50th Fighter Bomber Wing, 1955- 57; dep. chief staff plans and operations Wright Air Devel. Center, 1957- 59, dir. labs., 1959, dir. systems engring. Wright air devel. div., 1959- 61; systems program dir. B-70, 1961-64; comdr. systems engring. group, dep. comdr. research and tech. div. Wright-Patterson AFB, 1964-66; vice comdr. 5th Air Force (PACAF), 1966-68; dep. chief staff-operations Air Force Logistics Command, Wright-Patterson AFB, Ohio, 1968—. Systems engring. chmn. Dayton (O.) Muscular Dystrophy campaign, 1964-65. Decorated D.F.C. with 7 oak leaf clusters, Air medal with 4 oak leaf clusters, Legion of Merit (U.S.); Croix de Guerre (France); recipient McKay trophy USAF, 1952; Benemerenti medal Pope Paul VI, 1965. Mem. Greater Dayton Area, Rockford chambers commerce, Order Daedalians, V.F.W., Air Force Assn. Home: 2525 Cero Vista Dr Rockford IL 61107 Office: Hdqrs Air Force Logistics Command Box 196 Wright-Patterson AFB OH 45433

ASCH, JULES THEODORE, credit card co. exec.; b. N.Y.C., Jan. 19, 1912; s. Jacob and Augusta (Salinger) A.; B.S. in Econs., Wharton Sch. of U. Pa., 1932; children by previous marriage—Peter, Geraldine; m. 2d, Isabelle Marcus, Sept. 9, 1955; 1 dau., Barbara. With Diners' Club, Inc., N.Y.C., 1954—, exec. v.p. finance, 1965-71, v.p. planning, 1971—, also dir. Home: 215 E 68th St New York City NY 10021 Office: 10 Columbus Circle New York City NY 10019

ASCH, STAN, (Stanley William Aschemeier), cartoonist; b. St. Paul, Aug. 31, 1911; s. Luther Wesley and Amy Katherine (Koempel) A.; grad. Cathedral Sch., St. Paul, 1927; studied commercial art Mills Acad., St. Paul, also privately; unmarried. Began as cartoonist, 1926; created cartoons for The Farmer, Farm, Stock and Home and The Farmer's Wife, St. Paul (latter with circulation above one million); drew daily comic feature for St. Paul Daily News, 1931-32; contbr. to Popular Magazines, Inc., New Yorker and other mags., 1933-60; formerly asso. with McClure Newspaper Syndicate. Made exhibit and handled exhibits of other Am. cartoonists, St. Paul Pub. Library, 1932 and 1934; instr. cartooning U. of Minn., 1934, 35, 36 and 37; lectured on cartooning, Columbia U., 1941; Art Student's League, N.Y., 1943; lectr. various New York art schools, 1949; asso. with newspaper syndicate field. Hon. mem. Eugene Field Soc. Roman Catholic. Clubs: Nat. Press (Washington); Benson Players (N.Y.). Address: 362 Riverside Dr New York City NY 10025

ASCHAFFENBURG, E. LYSLE, hotel exec.; b. St. Louis, Jan. 9, 1892; s. Albert and Elvine (Schaefer) A.; M.E., Cornell, 1913; m. Helene Bloom, Jan. 21, 1918; children—Albert Lyle, Jean; m. 2d, Josye K. Wagner, Oct. 16, 1953. President, manager Lafayette Hotel, New Orleans, 1919-27; v.p. Standard Bond & Mortgage Co., 1925-30; pres. Pontchartrain Hotel, New Orleans, since 1927, mng. dir. since 1936, chmn. bd., 1968—; editorial adv. staff Hotel Management since 1940; pres. New Orleans Little Theatre Prodns., Inc., 1946-61; chmn. bd. Le Petit Theatre du Vieux Carre, 1957—, Pontchartrain Hotel, New Orleans, 1968—; bd. dirs. Fair Grounds Corp., New Orleans, 1948; bd. of dirs., founder member Internat. House, New Orleans, 1949; bd. dirs. New Orleans Crime Commn., New Orleans Safety Council; v. chmn. Mayor's Com. on Juvenile Delinquency; pres. Metropolitan New Orleans Safety Council, 1958. 1st lt. Ordnance Corps, U.S. Army, 1917, with 82d div., France, 1918-19. Recipient Gold Plate award Internat. Food service Mfrs. Assn., 1969. Mem. Inter-Am. (sec. since 1949), Am. (bd. govs. 1949, chmn. residential hotels com. 1948), La. (pres. 1944), New Orleans (pres. 1948) hotel assns., C. of C. New Orleans Area (dir.), Cornell Soc. Hotelmen, Confrerie des Chevaliers du Tastevin (grand ofcr.). Hotel Sales Mgmt. Assn. (chmn. so. dist. 1951), New Orleans Opera Assn. (bd. dirs. 1944-51), Am. (mem. bd. 1966), Greater New Orleans (pres. 1966) hotel and motel assns., Shakespeare Soc. New Orleans, Confrerie de la Chaine des Rotisseurs (grand council); maitre New Orleans. Office: Pontchartrain Hotel New Orleans LA 70140

ASCHAFFENBURG, WALTER EUGENE, composer; b. Essen, Germany, May 20, 1927; s. William Arthur and Margarete (Herz) A.; came to U.S. 1938, naturalized, 1944; diploma, Hartford Sch. Music, 1945; B.A., Oberlin Coll., 1951; M.A., Eastman Sch. Music, 1952; m. Nancy Dandridge Cooper, Aug. 14, 1951; children—Ruth Margareta, Katherine Elizabeth. Prof. music theory and composition Oberlin (O.) Coll. Conservatory Music, 1952—, also chmn. dept. music theory. Served with the AUS, 1945-47. Recipient award Fromm Music Found., 1953, Nat. Inst. Arts and Letters, 1966. Guggenheim fellow, 1955-56, Mem. Am. Civil Liberties Union, Am. Assn. U. Profs. (past chpt. pres.), Am. Soc. U. Composers, Am. Music Center, Nat. Opera Assn. Composer: Ozymandias-Symphonic Reflections for Orch., 1952; Cello Sonata, 1953; Sonata for Solo Violin, 1954; Piano Sonatina, 1954; String Quartet, op. 9, 1955; Bartleby-opera, op. 10, 1962; Elegy for Strings, op. 12, 1961; Three Dances for Orch., op. 15, 1966; Three Shakespeare Sonnets, op. 14, 1967; Quintet for Winds, op. 16, 1967; Proem for Brass and Percussion, op. 17, 1969; Duo for Violin and Cello, op. 18, 1971. Home: 49 Shipherd Circle Oberlin OH 44074

ASCHENBENNER, ALBERT JOSEPH, coll. dean; b. Idaho Falls, Ida., Nov. 28, 1913; s. Joseph A. and Mary E. (Wenzel) A.; A.B., Whitman Coll., 1940; M.S., U. So. Cal., 1947, Ed.D., 1961; m. Ruth G. Freeman, June 5, 1943; children—Joyce Carol, Michael J., Dorothy Ann. Tchr., coach Custer County High Sch., Miles City, Mont., 1940-41; instr. English and history Cal. State Poly. Coll., 1947-52, registrar, admissions officer, 1952-56, asso. dean students, counselling, 1956-64, dean sch. arts and scis., 1964—. Served with AUS, 1941-46; ETO. Home: 1678 N 2d Av Upland CA 91786 Office: Cal State Poly Coll Pomona CA 91166

ASCHENBRENNER, KARL, educator, philosopher; b. Bison, Kan., Nov. 20, 1911; s. John and Elisabeth Nathalia (Schnell) A.; A.B., Reed Coll., 1934; M.A., U. Cal. at Berkeley, 1938, Ph.D., 1940; m. Margaret Marie Kerr, Jan. 19, 1937; children—Lisbeth, Peter, John. Instr. philosophy Reed Coll., 1940-42; mem. faculty U. Cal. at Berkeley, 1946—, prof. philosophy, 1959—, chmn. philosophy, 1960-63, chmn. dept. design, 1964-65; vis. lectr. Amerika Inst., U. Munich, 1950. Del. Internat. Congresses Aesthetics, 1956, 60, 64. Served to lt. USNR, 1943-46. Guggenheim fellow, Vienna and London, 1956-57; Fulbright research fellow U. Munich, 1963-64. Mem. Am. Soc. Aesthetics, Brit. Soc. Aesthetics, Phi Beta Kappa. Club: University Faculty (Berkeley). Co-editor, translator: (Baumgarten) Reflections on Poetry 1954; Aesthetic Theories, 1965. Author: The Concepts of Value, 1971; also articles, reviews in field. Home: 1616 La Vereda Rd Berkeley CA 94709

ASCHER, CHARLES STERN, pub. adminstr.; b. N.Y. City, Apr. 20, 1899; s. Ernst and Josephine (Stern) A.; student Ethical Culture Sch., New York, 1904-14; A.B., Columbia, 1920, LL.B., 1921; m. Helen Shire, May 25, 1921 (dec. March 1960); children—Joan, Robert. Admitted to New York State bar, 1921, Illinois State bar, 1933; practiced in New York, 1921-25; asst. counsel War Finance Corp., Washington, D.C., 1922; sec. and gen. counsel City Housing Corp., New York, 1926-31, mem. bd. dirs. 1940-47; sec. Pub. Adminstrn. Clearing House, Chgo., 1932-36, asso. dir., N.Y.C. office, 1952-55; sec., dir. publs. Pub. Adminstrn. Service, 1933-35; exec. dir. Nat. Assn. Housing Ofcls., 1934; sec. com. pub. adminstrn. Social Sci. Research Council, 1935-42, com. housing research, 1949-51; regional rep. of adminstr. expediter region 2 Nat. Housing Agy., 1942-47, dir. urban devel. for entire agency, 1945-46; exec. officer for program Office Dir. Gen. UNESCO, Paris, 1947-48; prof. polit. sci. Bklyn. Coll. of City U. N.Y., 1948-69, prof. emeritus, 1969—; chmn. of dept. of polit. sci., 1949-66; internat. rep. Inst. Pub. Adminstrn., 1956—; lectr. polit. sci. U. Chgo., Columbia, Syracuse U.; rep. at UN of Internat. Inst. Adminstrv. Sci., Internat. Union Local Authorities, Internat. Fedn. Housing and Planning, 1949—, Inter Am. Planning Soc., 1959—, Internat. Information Centre Local Credit, 1965—, Eastnern Regional Orgn. Pub. Adminstrn., 1965—, Internat. Assn. Supreme Audit Instns., 1970—; cons. N.Y. N.Y. State Dept. Health, WHO, Nat. Resources Planning Bd.; dir. Citizens Housing and Planning Council, N.Y. City, 1941—, pres., 1963-64; pres. Conf. Non-governmental Orgns. in Consultative Status with the UN, 1961-63. Mem. Am. Soc. Pub. Adminstrn. (past pres.), Am. Soc. Planning Ofcls. (past treas.), Soc. Internat. Development, Am. Inst. Planners, Lambda Alpha, Phi Beta Kappa, Union of Internat. Assns.,

Nat. Assn. Housing and Redevel. Ofcls. (sec. internat. com. 1955—), Inter. Am. Planning Soc. (adv. council), Radburn Assn. (trustee 1929-32, hon. trustee 1967—). Club: Adirondack Mountain. Author: Program Making in UNESCO; The Private Covenant in Urban Development. Contbr. Periodicals. Home: 75 Central Park W New York City NY 10023 Office: 55 W 44th St New York City NY 10036 ☆

ASCHER, HANS ALBERT, investment banker; b. Springfield, Mass., Nov. 14, 1895; s. Moritz and Amalie (Boedlander) A.; B.A., Yale, 1916; m. Germaine Samuel, Aug. 23, 1945; 1 son, John Albert. With Hallgarten & Co., 1916-22; gen. partner R.W. Pressprich & Co., 1922-40; cofounder William E. Pollock Co., Inc., 1940, chmn. bd., 1965-70, now cons. Home: 415 E 52d St New York City NY Office: 160 Water St New York City NY 10005

ASCHER, MARY (Goldman), artist, author; b. Leeds, Eng., Dec. 24, 1900; d. Jacob and Naomi (Goldsand) Goldman; B.B.A., Coll. City N.Y., 1923; M.A., N.Y. U., 1934; postgrad. Columbia U. Tchrs. Coll.; art studies pvt. instr., also Grand Central Sch. Art, Art Students League, Famous Artists Sch., N.Y. Sch. Applied Design for Women; m. David Ascher, Dec. 24, 1926. Tchr. high schs., N.Y.C., 1925-39, chmn. dept., 1939-46; dean, guidance dir., adminstrv. asst. William Howard Taft High Sch., 1946-53; lectures and limited folio edits. of lithographs on Women of Old Testament and Apocrypha; designed and executed stained glass window of Lot's wife. Paintings exhibited N.Y. galleries, Argentina, Japan, Can., Mexico, Eng., Scotland, France, also Provincetown, 1958, Art USA 58, Coliseum-Art USA 59; one man shows Charels Barzansky Galleries, N.Y.C., 1959, Advt. Club N.Y., 1968, Fordham U., Bronx, 1968, B'nai B'rith Mus., Washington, 1970; one man traveling show, lithographs in U.S.A., 1965-70; traveling group show, 1963-65; paintings represented in permanent collections Alfred Khouri Meml. collection, Norfolk (Va.) Mus., Israel, U.S. Nat. Mus. Sports, N.Y.C., Fordham U., N.Y.C., B'nai B'rith Mus., others, also pvt. collections. Recipient gold medal of honor Painters and Sculptors Soc. N.J. Nat. Ann., 1958; winner group show Prix de Paris, 1959; Marcia Brady Tucker award Nat. Assn. Women Artists, 1960; Huntington Hartford Found. fellow, 1961; 1st prize modern watercolor N.Y. State Biennial, Nat. Biennial, Nat. League Am. Pen Women, Washington, 1962; McBurndy Corp. award 18th New Eng. Ann., 1967; 1st prize for poetry N.Y.C. br. Nat. League Am. Pen Women, 1968, 70; invited to submit all realia to Archives Am. Art, Smithsonian Inst. Fellow Royal Soc. Arts London; mem. Internat. Platform Assn., Nat. League American Pen Women, Nat. Assn. Women Artists (Seligson Meml. award 1968), Artist Equity Assn., Am. Soc. Contemporary Artists, N.Y. Soc. Women Painters, Nat. Soc. Arts and Letters, Am. Fedn. Artists, Met. Mus. Art, Mus. Modern Art, Art Students League (life), Am. Assn. U. Women. Author: Poetry-Painting, 1958. Home: 336 Central Park W New York City NY 10025

ASCHER, ROBERT, archeologist, educator; b. N.Y.C., Apr. 28, 1931; s. Alfred and Claire (Euscue) A.; Ph.D., U. Cal., 1960; m. Marcia Alper, Mar. 28 Prof. archaeology Cornell U., 1960—; excavations in U.S., Mexico, Turkey. Author: Origins of Man. Home: 524 Highland Rd Ithaca NY 14850

ASCHMANN, HAROLD HOMER, educator, geographer; b. San Francisco, May 5, 1920; s. George Henry and Julia (Keay) A.; A.B. U. Cal. at Los Angeles, 1940, M.A., 1942; Ph.D., U. Cal., 1954; m. Katharine Louise Goodale, Sept. 1, 1943: children—Stefanie Gail, Erika Louise, Jean Elise, Sara Margaret, Harold Konrad, Carl Edward. Asst. prof. geography San Diego State Coll., 1946- 48; instr. geography U. Neb., 1950-51; asst. prof. geography Los Angeles State Coll., 1951-54; asst. prof. geography U. Cal. at Riverside 1954- 58, asso. prof., 1958-64, prof., 1964— with USAAF, 1942-46. Mem. Assn. Am. Geographers, Southwestern Anthrop. Assn. (pres. 1954-55), Assn. Pacific Coast Geographers (pres. 1965-66). Author: The Central Desert of Baja California: Demography and Ecology, 1959: The Natural and Human History of Baja California, 1966. Home: 4757 Kansas Av Riverside CA 92507

ASCOLI, MAX, writer; b. Ferrara, Italy, June 25, 1898; s. Enrico and Adriana (Finzi) A.; LL.D., U. Ferrara (Italy), 1920; Ph.D., U. Rome, 1928; m. Marion Rosenwald, Oct. 5, 1940; 1 son, Peter. Came to U.S., 1931, naturalized, 1939. Prof. jurisprudence Italian univs., 1926-31; mem. grad. faculty New Sch. for Social Research, N.Y.C., 1933-50, dean. grad. faculty, 1940-41, asst. dir. cultural relations, coordinator inter- Am. affairs, 1940-42; pres. Handicraft Devel. Inc., 1944-54; editor, pub. The Reporter, 1949-68. Mem. Council on Fgn. Relations. Author: Intelligence in Politics, 1936; (with Arthur Feiler) Fascism for Whom, 1938; The Power of Freedom, 1948. Editor: (with Fritz Lehmann) Political and Economic Democracy, 1938; The Fall of Mussolini, 1948; Our Times, The Best From the Reporter, 1960. Home: 23 Gramercy Park S New York City NY 10003 Office: 660 Madison Av New York City NY 10021

ASELTINE, WALTER MORLEY, canadian senator; b. Nappanee, Ont., Canada, Sept. 3, 1886; s. George S. and Harriet T. (Goldsmith) A.; B.A. Manitoba U., 1909; m. France A. Derby, July 20, 1911; 1 son, John M.; m. 2nd, Laura I. King, Aug. 8, 1923; children—Morley G., Elaine (Mrs. Mervyn Johnson), Kenneth, Adele (Mrs. Fred Herbert). Called to Sask. bar, 1913: made King's Counsel, 1930; practice law, Rosetown, Sask., 1913—; mem. firm Aseltine and Aseltine. Mayor of Rosetown, 1930-34; mem. Canadian Senate, 1933—, leader govt. in Senate, 1958-62; mem. Privy Council, 1961—. Sec. Rosetown Board Trade, 1920-34. Mem. Can., Sask. (sr. life mem.) bar assns. Mem. United Ch. of Can. Mason. Home: Rosetown Saskatchewan Canada

ASGEIRSSON, ASGEIR, former Pres. Iceland; b. Koranes, Iceland, May 13, 1894; s. Asgeir Eythorsson and Jensina Bjorg (Mattiasdottir) A.; grad. Reykjavik High Sch., 1912; grad. theology U. Iceland, 1915; m. Dora Thorhalls-dottir. Mem. of Althing (Icelandic Parliament), 1923-52, mem. fgn. relations com., 1928-31, 38-52: rep. Iceland on bd. dirs. Internat. Monetary Fund, 1947-52; mem. Icelandic del. to Un Assembly. Paris, 1948; Minister of Finance, 1931-34, Prime Minister, 1932-34; President Republic of Iceland, 1952-68. Grand Master Order of Icelandic Falcon. Decorated Grand Crosses Order of Vasa (Sweden), White Rose (Finland), Orange Nassau Order (Netherlands); Order of Merit of German Fed. Republic: Knight of Royal Danish Elephant Order; Royal Swedish Serafimer Order. Home: Aragata 14 Reykjavik Iceland

ASH, FRED CALBERT, lawyer, corp. exec.; b. Clinton, Ia., Mar. 2, 1916; s. John Thomas and Inger (Davidsen) A.; A.B., U. Chgo., 1938, J.D., 1940; m. Winifred L. Lee, Oct. 26, 1946; children—Frederick Lee, John, Stephen. Admitted to Ill. bar, 1940; asst. to dean law sch. U. Chgo., 1946-47; with firm Kirkland, Fleming, Green, Martin & Ellis, Chgo., 1947-57; sec., treas., gen. counsel Reuben H. Donnelley Corp., 1957-62; v.p. Dun and Bradstreet, Inc., 1961-62; gen. counsel Wilson Co., Inc.; now sec. Ling-Temco-Vought, Inc., Dallas. Served to maj., inf., AUS, 1941- 46. Mem. Am., Chgo. bar assns. Conglist. Clubs: University, Law (Chgo.); Indian Hill (Winnetka). Home: 10111 Waller Dallas TX Office: Ling-Temco-Vought Inc PO Box 5003 Dallas TX 75222

ASH, PHILIP, educator, psychologist; b. N.Y.C., Feb. 2, 1917; s. Samuel Kieval and Estella (Feldstein) A.; B.S. in Psychology, U. City N.Y., 1938; M.A. in Personnel Adminstrn., Am. U., 1949; Ph.D. in Psychology, Pa. State U., 1949; m. Ruth Clude, Sept. 16, 1945; children—Peter, Sharon. Analyst to unit chief occupational research Labor Dept., 1940-47; research fellow Pa. State U., 1947-49, asso. prof., 1949-52; asst. to v.p. indsl. relatons Inland Steel, 1952-68; prof. psychology U. Ill. at Chgo. Circle, 1968—; cons. Manplan Cons., Chgo., 1968—, John E. Reid Assos., Chgo., 1969—; dir. Vernon Psychol. Labs. Mem. pub. adv. com. Chgo. Commn. Human Relations, 1957—, retirement com. Chgo. Commn. Sr. Citizens, 1960—; chmn. Ill. Psychologist Examining Com., 1963—. Diplomate Indsl. Psychlogy Am. Bd. Profl. Psychology. Fellow Am. Psychol. Assn. (pres. div. indsl. psychology 1968-69), A.A.A.S., Internat. Acad. Forensic Psychology; mem. Ill. (pres. 1963-64), Chgo., Midwest psychol. assns., Am. Personnel and Guidance Assn., Am. Psychology-Law Soc., Indsl. Relations Research Assn., Internat. Assn. Applied Psychology, Internat. Gerontol. Assn., Phi Beta Kappa, Sigma Xi, Psi Chi. Author: Guide for Selection and Placement of Employees, 1971; also articles. Home: 645 S Bruner St Hinsdale IL 60521 Office: U Ill Box 4348 Chicago IL 60680

ASH, ROBERT, lawyer; b. Buffalo, Oct. 1, 1894; s. John Robert and Lucretia Elizabeth (Kingston) A.; LL.B., George Washington U., 1918; m. Frances Halliburton Luna, Oct. 5, 1926; 1 dau., Fanchon. Admitted to D.C. bar, 1918, since practiced in Washington; sr. partner Ash, Bauersfeld, Burton & Mooers, and predecessor firms, 1956—, specializing taxation; Washington counsel Prentice-Hall, Inc. Mem. adv. com. on appellate rules Com. on Rules of Practice and Procedure, Jud. Conf. U.S., 1960-68. Dir. Potomac Nat. Bank (Md.). Fellow Am. Bar Found; mem. Am. (tax counsel 1969-70, standing com. on fed. judiciary 1962-68), Dist. of Columbia bar assns., Am. Law Inst. Mem. Episcopal Church. Clubs: Metropolitan (Washington); Chevy Chase (Md.); Burning Tree (Bethesda). Author: How to Write a Tax Brief, 21st edit., 1971; Preparation and Trial of Tax Cases, 1955; Tax Problems Encountered in the General Practice of Law, 1960. Home: 6817 Bradley Blvd Bethesda MD 20034 Office: 39 Wisconsin Av NW Washington DC 20016

ASH, ROY LAWRENCE, busines exec.; b. Los Angeles, Oct. 20, 1918; s. Charles K. and Fay E. (Dickinson) A.; M.B.A. Harvard, 1947; m. Lila M. Hornbek. Nov. 13, 1943; children—Loretta (Mrs. Truman T. Ackerson), James, Marilyn (Mrs. R. Stanley Hodge), Robert, Charles. With Bank of Am., 1936-42. 47-49; chief financial officer, Hughes Aircraft Co., 1949-53; co-founder Litton Industries, Inc., Beverly Hills, Cal., 1953-, dir., 1953—, pres., 1961—; dir. various Litton subsidiaries; bd. dirs. Bank Am. Corp.; bd. dirs., mem. exec. and trust coms. Bank of Am., Global Marine, Inc., Pacific Mut. Life Ins. Co. Chmn. President's Adv. Council on Exec. Orgn., 1969-71; co-chmn. Japan-Cal. Assn. Trustee Cal. Inst. Tech., Com. for Econ. Devel., Urban Inst.; pres., bd. dirs. Los Angeles World Affairs Council. Mem. Am. Mgmt. Assn., Financial Execs. Inst., The Conf. Bd. Clubs: Bel Air Country, Harvard (Los Angeles). Home: 655 Funchal Rd Los Angeles CA 90024 Office: 360 N Crescent Dr Beverly Hills CA 90213

ASHABRANNER, BRENT KENNETH, ednl. fund exec.; b. Shawnee, Okla., Nov. 3, 1921; s. Dudley and Rose Thelma (Cotton) A.; B.S. in Edn., Okla. State U., 1948, M.A. in English, 1951; m. Martha White, Aug. 9, 1941; children—Melissa Lynn, Jennifer Ann. Free lance writer, 1947-52; instr. English Okla. State U., 1952-55; ednl. materials devel. adviser ICA, Addis Ababa, Ethiopia, 1955-57; chief ednl. material devel. program ICA, Tripoli, Libya, 1957-59; edn. program officer AID, Lagos, Nigeria, 1960-61; dep. dir. Peace Corps, Nigeria 1961-62, India, 1962-64, dir., 1965-66, dir. univ. relations and tng., Washington, 1966-67, dep. dir. Peace Corps, Washington, 1967-69; research asso. Center for Studies in Edn. and Devel., Harvard, 1969-70; dir. Near East-South Asia program Pathfinder Fund, Boston, 1970—. Served with USNR, 1942-45. Recipient Career Service award Nat. Civil Service League, 1968. Author: (with Russell Davis) Point Four Assignments, 1959; Ten Thousand Desert Swords, 1960; The Choctaw Code, 1961, Chief Joseph, 1962; Land in the Sun: the Story of West Africa, 1963; Strangers in Africa, 1963; A Moment in History: the First Ten Years of the Peace Corps, 1971; (with Milburn and Williams) A First Course in College English, 1961. Home: 9508 Byeforde Rd Kensington MD 20795 Office: 850 Boylston St Boston MA 02167

ASHBERY, JOHN LAWRENCE, author; b. Rochester, N.Y., July 28, 1927; s. Chester Frederick and Helen (Lawrence) A.; grad. Deerfield Acad., 1945; B.A. Harvard, 1949; M.A. Columbia, 1951. Art critic European edit. N.Y. Herald Tribune, 1960- 1960-65; exec. editor Art News, 1965—; editor quar. rev. Art and Lit., 1963—; spl. research life and work Raymond Roussel. Author: (poems) Some Trees, 1956, 70, The Tennis Court Oath, 1962, Rivers and Mountains, 1966, The Double Dream of Spring, 1970; (one act play) The Heroes, 1952; (three act play) The Compromise, 1956; Selected poems, 1967; (novel with James Schuyler) A Nest of Ninnies, 1969; also numerous articles art criticism. Home: care Art News 444 Madison Av New York City NY 10022

ASHBROOK, CHARLES GARNER, ins. exec.; b. Granville, O., Nov. 22, 1899; s. Milan Pratt and Lucy (Shepardson) A.; grad. Doane Acad., Granville, O., 1917; A.B., Denison U., Granville, 1921; m. Lois Teeter, June 8, 1923; children—Lois Anne (Mrs. Walter Lorimer), Charles Garner. With North Am. Life Ins. Co. of Chgo., 1921—, successively med. clk., mgr. renewals, asst. supt. agencies, supt. agencies, dir., 1938-70, v.p., 1944-51, dir. agencies, 1947-51, exec. v.p. 1951, pres. 1955-61, chmn. bd., 1961-68, hon. chmn., 1968—. Trustee Ohio Bapt. Conv., Denison U., Granville, O. Served with S.A.T.C., World War I. Recipient Distinguished Alumni citation, Denison U., 1956. Mem. Am. Legion, Beta Theta Pi, Republican. Baptist. Mason (Shriner, K.T.), Elk Clubs: University (Chgo.). Rotarian. Home: PO Box 358 129 S Mulberry St Granville OH 43023 Office: 35 E Wacker Dr Chicago IL 60601

ASHBROOK, JOHN MILAN, congressman; b. Johnstown, O., Sept. 21, 1928; A.B. with honors, Harvard U. 1952; J.D., Ohio State U. 1955; LL.D., Ashland Coll., 1963; children—Barbara, Laura, Madeline. Admitted to Ohio bar, 1955, since practiced in Johnstown; pub. Johnstown Ind. weekly, 1953—; mem. 87th- 92d congresses 17th Dist. Ohio; mem. 101st, 102d Ohio Gen. Assemblies. Past chmn. Young Republican Nat. Fedn. Served with USN. Home: 8513 Hempstead Av Bethesda MD 20034 Office: House Office Bldg Washington DC 20515

ASHBURY, HOWARD HICKS, hosp. supt., physician; b. Balt., Dec. 1, 1904; s. Howard Elmer and Ellen Lizette (Hicks) A.; B.S. U.Va., 1930, M.D., 1931; m. Emily Caroline Strohman, Dec. 20, 1929; children—Mary Lee, Allan Banister; m. 2d, Helen Powell Martin, May 1, 1952. Tng. in radiology Church Home Hosp., Balt., also Meml. Hosp., New York City, 1931-34; practice radiology and oncology, Balt., 1935-52; tng. in psychiatry U. Va., 1953- 56, instr., then asst. prof. psychiatry, 1956-58; clin. dir. Western State Hosp., Staunton, Va., 1958-60; supt. Eastern State Hosp., Williamsburg, Va., 1960—. Diplomate Am. Bd. Radiology, Am. Bd. Psychiatry and Neurology. Fellow Am. Psychiat. Assn.; mem. Am. Radium Soc., Neuropsychiat. Soc. of Va. (pres. 1962- 63), Williamsburg C. of C. (bd. dirs.), Phi Kappa Psi, Phi Chi. Episcopalian. Home: Drawer A Williamsburg VA 23185

ASHBY, CLARENCE GARNETT, lawyer; b. Newport News, Va., Apr. 24, 1900; s. Charles Avlett and Evelyn Willis (Garnett) A.; A.B., U.N.C., 1922. LL.B., 1922; m. Eloise Roberts, Dec. 30, 1925. Admitted to Fla. bar, 1922, since practiced in Jacksonville; mem. firm Ulmer, Murchison, Kent, Ashby and Ball, 1955-. Home: 1836 Montgomery Pl Office: Florida Nat. Bank Bldg Jacksonville, FL

ASHBY, DONALD WAYNE, Jr., accountant; b. Camden, N.J., Feb. 17, 1926; s. Donald Wayne and Dorothy (Childers) A.; B.S., Ohio State U., 1949; m. Anne Chester, Dec. 2, 1950; children—Pamela Anne and Donald Wayne III. Parnter, Haskins & Sells, Certified Pub. Accountants. 1961M, partner charge Columbus (O.) office, 1963—. Served with USNR, 1944-46; with USAF 1950-51. C.P.A., N.Y., Ohio, Mem. Am. Inst. C.P.A.'s, Ohio Soc., C.P.A.'s Phi Gamma Delta. Episcopalian. Clubs: Scioto Country, Columbus Athletic (pres. 1968), Columbus, The Golf (Columbus). Home: 4906 Riverside Dr Columbus OH 43221. Office: 250 E Broad St Columbus OH 43215

ASHBY, EUGENE CHRISTOPHER, educator; b. New Orleans, Oct. 25, 1930; s. Anthony and Ida (Bruno) A.; B.S., Loyola U. of South, 1951; M.S., Auburn U., 1953; Ph.D., U. Notre Dame, 1956; m. Carolyn Bruce Turner, Sept. 13, 1952; children—Chris, Stephen, Terry, Marie, Julie, Angela, Rachel. Research asso. Ethyl Corp., Baton Rouge, 1956-63; asst. prof. Sch. Chemistry, Ga. Inst. Tech., Atlanta, 1963-65, asso. prof., 1965-68, prof., 1968—. Cons. Continental Oil Co., E.I. DuPont Corp. Recipient Sigma Xi Research award, 1968, Lavoisier medal French Chem. Soc., 1971. Sloan fellow, 1964-66. Mem. Am. Chem. Soc., Sigma Xi. Roman Catholic. Contbr. articles profl. jours. Home: 2516 Flair Knoll Dr Atlanta GA 30329

ASHBY, JACK LANE, steel exec.; b. Berkeley, Calif., Apr. 3, 1911; s. Dr. Shirley Joshua and Lola (McKellips) A.; A.B., Stanford, 1933; m. Patricia Robbins, June 17, 1936; children—Peter Robbins, Robert Lane, Richard William, Charlotte Ashby, Sarah Robbins. Investment banker with E.F. Hutton & Co., San Francisco, 1933-35, Eastland & Co., 1935-39, Irving Lundborg & Co., 1939-40; indsl. financing with comml. Investment Trust Co., 1940- 41; with Kaiser Steel Corp., Oakland, 1941—, v.p. gen. mgr., 1948-59, pres., 1959, now vice chairman, dir.; chmn. Kaiser Resources Ltd., dir. Kaiser Industries Corporation, United International Shipping Corporation, Hamersley Iron Pty. Limited (Australia). Dir. Nat. Indsl. Conf. Bd. Member Los Angeles, San Francisco and Oakland C's of C., Cal. State Chamber Commerce (dir.), Am. Iron and Steele Institute (director). Delta Kappa Epsilon. Episcopalian. Clubs: California, (Los Angeles); Claremont Country (Oakland); The Family, Pacific-Union, Commonwealth (San Francisco); Laurel Valley Golf (Ligonier, Pa.); Silverado Country (Napa, Cal.) Home: 2210 Soda Canyon Rd Napa CA 94558 Office: Kaiser Center 300 Lakeside Dr Oakland CA 94612

ASHBY, LYLE WALTER, ednl. cons.; b. Guide Rock, Neb., May 16, 1905; s. Ernest W. and Virginia (Walsh) A.; B.A., Hastings Coll., 1927, LL.D., 1949; M.A. Am. U., 1931; Ph.D., Columbia, 1936; m. Annetta Anderson, July 20, 1928; children—Harold, Lyle Walter, Coralyn Virginia. Field man Hastings Coll., 1927; tchr. Kearney Sr. High Sch., 1927-28; asst. dir. div. publs. N.E.A., 1928, asst. editor jour., 1942-48, asst. sec. profl. relations, 1948-55, asst. exec. sec. ednl. services, 1955-58, dep. exec. sec., 1959-70; pvt. cons., 1970—; vis. instr. Wash. State Coll., 1937. Chmn. Conf. Nat. Orgns., White House Conf. Edn., 1960-62; chmn. Nat. Com. Children and Youth, 1967-69; mem. exec. com. Joint Council Ednl. TV, 1957-61; cons. to profl., ednl. orgns. in India on short term Fulbright Scholarship, 1961-62. Mem. Nat. Commn. on TV, Radio and Films, Meth. Ch., 1960-64, Commn. on Higher Edn., Balt. Conf., 1963—. Trustee Am. U., 1944—. Mem. N.E.A., Nat. Conf. Social Work (dir. 1955- 58), Ednl. Press Assn. Am. (sec. treas. 1935-45, v.p. 1947-48), Fed. Schoolmen's Club (pres. 1971-72), World Confederation Orgn. of Teaching Profession Australia and New Zealand (del. 1970). Methodist. Author: THe Efforts of the States to Support Education, 1936; also articles various mags. Editor: The Public and Education, 1945-48. Observer Bikini atomic bomb tests, 1946. Home: 540 N St SW Washington DC 20024

ASHBY, MABEL KATHLEEN, writer; b. Tysoe, Warwickshire, Eng., May 16, 1892; d. Joseph and Hannah (Ashby) Ashby; B.A., U. Birmingham, 1914; M.Ed., U. Manchester, 1930. Engaged in rural edn., Eng., 1915-19; tchr. tng. colls. Eng., 1925- 28; prin. Hillcroft Coll., Surbiton, Eng., 1933-46. Pres. Womens Inst., Bledington, Oxford, 1960—. Chmn. council Bledington Parish, 1958-61. Author: The Country School, 1929; Joseph Ashby of Tysoe (James Tait Black prize for biography 1962, Leverhulme research award 1962), 1961. Home: Peglers Barn Bledington Oxford England Office: care Cambridge Univ Press 32 E 57th St New York City NY 10022

ASHBY, NEAL TURNER, writer; b. Des Moines, Ia., Oct. 28, 1924; s. Ted R. and Eva (Meyer) A.; student State U. Ia., Drake U.; m. Joan Millhaem, June 7, 1945 (dec. 1969); children—Laurel Louise, Lucianne Lee, Lawrence T. Staff, Des Moines Register, 1940-43, feature writer 1944-45; reporter Kansas City Star, 1943-44; staff N.Y. Mirror, 1945-63, Sunday editor, 1957-63, columnist, 1952-63; asso. editor Parade Mag., 1963-69; mng. editor Family Week Mag., 1970; free lance writer, 1971—; contbr. to nat. mags. Pres. Williston Park (N.Y.) Library Bd., 1962-67. Episcopalian. Address: 119 Cornwell Av Williston Park NY 11596

ASHBY, PHILIP HARRISON, educator; b. Lynden, Wash., Sept. 28, 1916; s. Paul Hardin and Tressie (Flesher) A.; student Whitman Coll., 1934-36, U. Wash., 1936-37; B.A., U. Puget Sound, 1938; B.D., Pacific Sch. Religion, 1943; Ph.D., U. Chgo., 1950; m. Mabel Clare Kelley, Aug. 30, 1936; children—Joan C. (Mrs. Llewelyn G. Pritchard), Philip K. Ordained to ministry Methodist Ch., 1940; minister in Wash. and Cal., 1936-44; mem. faculty Princeton, 1950—, prof. religion, 1965—, chmn. dept., 1968—; vis. prof. Perkins Sch. Theology, 1952, Drew Theol. Sch., 1955, Pacific Sch. Religion, 1964, U. Cal. at Santa Barbara, 1968. Served as chaplain USNR, 1944-46. Jonathan Edwards bicentennial preceptor Princeton, 1953-56, McCosh faculty fellow, for study in India, 1967-68. Fellow Soc. Religion in Higher Edn.; mem. Am. Acad. Religion, Am. Soc. Study Religion. Home: 478 Lake Dr Princeton NJ 08540 Office: 1879 Hall Princeton NJ 08540

ASHBY, ROBERT SAMUEL, lawyer; b. Crawfordsville, Ind., July 9, 1916; s. William Wallace and Nellie (Graybill) A.; A.B. with highest honors, Ind. U., 1938; LL.B. magna cum laude (editor law rev.) Harvard, 1941; m. Susan Gatch, June 4, 1949; children—Jean G., Willis G. Admitted to Ind. bar, 1941, N.Y. bar, 1942; with firm Carter, Ledyard & Milburn, N.Y.C., 1941-42; partner firm Barnes, Hickam, Pantzer & Boyd, Indpls., 1946—; gen. counsel Peoples Home Life Ins. Co. Ind. Dir. Ind. Nat. Bank, Inland Container Corp., Altamil Corp. Trustee Indpls. Mus. Art, 1960—. Served to lt. comdr. USNR, 1942-46. Mem. Am., Ind., Indpls. bar assns., Assn. Bar City New York, Bar Assn. Seventh Fed. Circuit, Indpls. Lit. Soc. Phi Beta Kappa, Sigma Nu. Clubs: The Indianapolis Dramatic, Contemporary,

University. Contbr. articles tax, legal jours. Home: 7248 Pennsylvania St Indianapolis IN 46240 Office: Merchants Bank Bldg Indianapolis IN 46204

ASHCRAFT EDWIN MAURICE III ret. govt. ofcl.; b. Chgo., Sept. 20, 1905; s. Edwin Maurice, Jr. and Anna Louise (Strawbridge) A.; grad. Phillips Exeter Acad., 1925; student Princeton, 1925-28; B.S.L., Northwestern U., 1931; m. Jane McNeely Cochran, Sept. 6, 1928 (dec. Sept. 1961); 1 dau., Avis Ann (Mrs. John V. Mungesser); m. 2d, Mildred Virginia Winslow, June 19, 1962. Admitted to Ill. bar, 1931; partner firm Ashcraft & Ashcraft, Chgo. 1931-48; dir. Street & Smith Publs. Inc., 1937-48, Am. Coating Mills, 1936-47, Weco Products Co., 1935-45; with contact div. Officer Operations, CIA, 1948-65, dir. Domestic Contact Service, 1965-66. Mem. Chgo. Bar Assn., Phi Delta Phi. Clubs: Legal, Univerity, Racquet (Chgo); Nat. Lawyers, University (Washington); Princeton (N.Y.C.) Home: 3900 Watson Pl NW Washington, DC 20016.

ASHCRAFT, GEORGE GRADY, corp. exec.; b. Eamar County, Ala., 1899; m. Alice Faye Ashcraft; 1 dau., Bettye Faye (Mrs. Willian J. Senter). Exec. v.p., dir. Ala. Dry Dock & Shipbldg. Co. Mem. C. of C. (dir.). Mason. Clubs: Seamens (dir.), Country, Lakewood. Home: 1742 Hunter Av Mobile AL 36604 Office: PO Box 1507 Mobile AL 36601

ASHE, ARTHUR, tennis player; b. Richmond Va., 1944; grad. U. Cal. at Los Angeles, 1966. Winner two U.S. Inter-collegiate championships during coll.; winner U.S. Men's Hard Court Championship, 1963, U.S. Amateur title, 1968, U.S. Open championship, 1968; now mem. U.S. Davis Cup Team; Australian open winner U.S. Men's Clay Ct., 1967; pres. Players Enterprises, Inc., Washington. Served with AUS. Address: 888 17th St N W Washington DC 20006

ASHE, DAVID IRVING, labor lawyer; b. Brooklyn, Nov. 13, 1910; s. Morris and Bessie (Newman) A.; B.S.S. magna cum laude, Coll. City of N.Y., 1929; J.D., Columbia U., 1932; m. 1934 (div. 1959); children—Judith (Mrs. Walter J. Handelman), Deborah Lucy (Mrs. Steven B. Warheit); m. 2nd., Amelia H. Wexler, Dec. 26, 1962; stepchildren—Richard, Susan (Mrs. Stuart Lahn). Admitted to the N.Y. state bar in 1933, since practiced in N.Y.C. specializing in law of labor relations and representing internat. and local labor unions; mem. firm Ashe & Rifkin since 1940; instr. labor law and labor problems Trade Union Inst. of Rand Sch. of Social Sci., 1936-45, dir., 1940-44; mem. bd. dirs. New Leader (pub.), 1944-50. Labor law cons. Am. Civil Liberties Union. Mem. state adv. com. for study of vocational edn. in N.Y. City schs. 1949-52; mem. com. (N.Y. City bd. edn.) to study impact of increased birth rate on N.Y. City schs. 1948-49. Dir. Civic Legislative League of N.Y., 1948-52. Mem. adminstrv., nat. exec. coms. Jewish Labor Com. 1965—, chmn. N.Y. Div., 1966—; mem. Nat. Jewish Com. Relations Adv. Council, 1965—; mem. edn. com. United Negro Coll. Fund, 1960-62; mem. Nat. Conf. Christians and Jews; mem. com. on legislation Citizens Union, N.Y.C., 1960-64. Mem. Bd. Higher Edn., N.Y.C., 1966—. Bd. dirs. Research Found. City Coll. City U. N.Y.; bd. dirs. New York Adult Edn. Council, Inc. Pres. of Musicians Service Corp. Mem. Nat. Panel Arbitrators, Am. Arbitration Assn., Workers Def. League (nat. com. 1956-58), Nat. Planning Assn. (nat. council), Workmen's Circle, (gen. counsel), The Alumni Assn. of the Columbia School of Law, Bar Assn. N.Y.C. (mem. labor and social security legislation com., 1951-54, 67—), Alumni Assn. of City Coll., United Parents Assns. of N.Y.C. (counsel, past pres., chmn. exec. council and legislative com. and v.p.), Pub. Edn. Assn. (mem. legislation and sch. administration com. 1950-62), N.Y. County Lawyers Assn., Phi Beta Kappa. Author: Yellow Dog Contracts, Legal and Social Aspects, 1931: The Taft-Hartley Law: How It Affects Unions and Workers, 1947; The Labor-Management Reporting and Disclosure Act of 1959; An Analysis, 1959. Adv. editor, Parents mag. 1948-50. Contbr. to labor ednl. publs. Home: 201 E 79th St New York City NY 10021 Office: 253 Broadway New York City NY 10007

ASHE, WILLIAM J., exec. v.p. Witco Chem. Co. Home: 277 Park Av New York City NY 10017*

ASHEIM, LESTER EUGENE, librarian, educator; b. Spokane, Jan. 22, 1914; s. Sol and Bertha (Bergman) A.: A.B., U. Wash., 1936, B.A. in Librarianship, 1937, M.A., 1941; Ph.D., U. Chgo. (Grad. Library Sch. fellow), 1949. Jr. reference asst. Library U. Wash., 1937-41; librarian U.S. Fed. Penitentiary, McNeill Island, Wash., 1941-42; regional librarian Fed. Pub. Housing Authority, 1946; vis. lectr., library sch. U. Ill., summer 1949; asst. prof., grad. library sch. U. Chgo., 1948-52, dean students, 1951-52, dean, asso. prof. 1952-62; dir. Internat. Relations Office, A.L.A., 1962-66, dir. office for library edn., 1966-71; prof. Grad. Library Sch., U. Chgo., 1971—. Served with Signal Intelligence, A.U.S., 1942-45. Recipient Distinguished Alumnus award U. Wash. Sch. of Librarianship, 1966; Intellectual Freedom award Ill. Library Assn., 1966; Scarecrow Press award for library lit., 1968. Mem. Am. Library Assn., Am. Assn. U. Profs., Phi Beta Kappa, Zeta Beta Tau. Author: The Library's Public (with Bernard Barelson), 1949; Librarianship in the Developing Countries, 1966. Editor: A Forum on the Public Library Inquiry, 1950; The Core of Education for Librarianship, 1954, The Future of the Book, 1955; Humanities and the Library, 1957; New Directions in Public Library Development. 1957; Persistent Issues in American Librarianship, 1961. Home: 253 E Delaware Chicago IL 60611 Office: 1100 E 57th St Chicago IL 60637

ASHEN, ROBERT MORTON, mfr.; b. Chgo., Mar. 14, 1934; s. Benjamin and Dorothy (Gurevitz) A.; B.S., Purdue U., 1956; J.D., Harvard, 1958; m. Rita Joan Saunders, June 11, 1961; children—Jon Benjamin, Ceth Augusta. Admitted to Cal. bar, 1962; atty. Anderson, Luedeka, Fitch, Even & Tabin, Chgo., 1958-61, 63-65, Herzig & Walsh, Los Angeles, 1961-63, 65-66, Miketta, Glenny, Poms & Smith, Los Angeles, 1966-67; sec., gen. counsel VSI Corp., Pasadena, Cal., 1967—; dir. Growth Tech. Corp. (Los Angeles). Mem. Am. Civil Liberties Union. Served with USAF, 1959. Mem. Am., Los Angeles County, Beverly Hills bar assns., Harvard Law Sch. Assn., Patent Law Assn. Los Angeles, Pi Tau Sigma, Tau Beta Pi, Sigma Alpha Mu. Mason. Home: 348 N Highland Av Los Angeles CA 90036 Office: 600 N Rosemead Blvd Pasadena CA 91107

ASHENHURST, ROBERT LOVETT, educator; b. Paris, France, Aug. 9, 1929 (parents Am. citizens); A.B., Harvard, 1950, S.M., 1954, Ph.D., 1956; m. Julia Brewster Brown, June 18, 1949; (div. Feb. 1964); children—Julia Brewster, John Cobden, David Russell, Martha Lovett. Research asso. Harvard, 1950-56, instr., 1956- 57; asst. prof. U. Chgo., 1957-60, asso. prof., 1960-65, prof., 1965—, marshal of univ., 1968—, dir. Inst. for Computer Research, chmn. com. on information scis., 1969—, asso. dir. Computation Center, 1965-69. Mem. Woodlawn Hosp. Corp., Chgo., 1965—; treas. Hyde Park-Kenwood Community Conf., 1969—. Mem. Assn. for Computing Machinery (editor monograph series 1964—), Soc. Indsl. and Applied Math., I.E.E.E., Inst. Mgmt. Scis., A.A.A.S., N.Y. Acad. Sci., Phi Beta Kappa, Sigma Xi. Clubs: Tavern, Quadrangle (Chgo.). Home: 5539 S Woodlawn Av Chicago IL 60637 Office: 5640 S Ellis Av Chicago IL 60637

ASHER, ESTON JACKSON, psychologist, educator; b. London, Ky., June 25, 1901; s. Silas Wootson and Margaret (Tuttle) A.; A.B., U. Ky., 1923, M.A., 1924; grad. study U. Tex., 1927-28, Ohio State U., 1935-36; m. Bertha Smith, Dec. 30, 1922; children—Eston Jackson, Frank Woodson, Emma Jean (Mrs. Ralph Meckling), Margaret Rae (Mrs. Donald Lyon). Instr. U. Tex., 1924-28; instr. U. Ky., 1928-29, asst. prof., 1929-37, asso. prof. psychology, 1937-45; asso. prof. Purdue U., 1945-48, prof. psychology, 1948-69, prof. emeritus, 1969, head dept., 1954-64; vis. lectr. psychology High Point (N.C.) Coll., 1969—. Dir. Ky. Coop. Testing Service, 1932-45. Fellow Am. Psychol. Assn.; mem. Midwestern Psychol. Assn., Ind. Acad. Sci., Phi Beta Kappa, Sigma Xi. Author: (with J. Tiffin, F.B. Knight) The Psychology of Normal People, rev. edit., 1946: Introduction to General Psychology, 1953. Home: 1513 McGuinn Dr High Point NC 27262

ASHER, FREDERICK, mail order co. exec; b. Chgo., Mar. 6, 1915; s. Louis Eller and Alice (Wormser) A.; B.A. cum laude, Dartmouth, 1937; student U. Wis., 1938; m. Frances Reitler, June 30, 1938; children—Frederick Matheson, Alice (Mrs. Taylor G. White), Deborah Helene. Gen. mgr. Louis G. Cowan, Chgo., 1939- 41; advt. mgr. Consol. Book Publ. Co., Chgo., 1945-50; pres. Frederick Asher, Inc., advt., Chgo., 1950-55; pres. John Plain & Company, mail order, Chgo., 1955-66, pres., chief exec. officer, 1966—; dir. Glencoe Nat. Bank, Zenith Life Ins. Co., Chgo. Bd. dirs. Travelers Aid Soc., John Plain Found., HIghland Park Hosp.; trustee Lake Forest (Ill.) Acad. Served AUS, 1944-45. mem. Mail Order Assn. Am. (dir.). Clubs: Mid-America (Chgo.); Ojai (Cal.) Valley Country; Northmoor Country (Highland Park, Ill.). Home: 405 Moraine Rd Highland Park IL 60035 Office: 444 W Washington St Chicago IL 60606

ASHER, ROBERT ELLER, internat. relations specialist; b. Chgo., Oct. 18, 1910; s. Louis Eller and Alice (Wormser) A.; student Dartmouth, 1927-30, U. Berlin (Germany), 1930-31; Ph.B., U. Chgo., 1932, M.A., 1934; m. Ethel Stuart Watson, Feb. 2, 1935; children—Robert L., Vicki A. (Mrs. J.D. Lambert). Researcher, Am. Pub. Welfare Assn., Chgo., Fed. Emergency Relief Administrn., Washington, 1934-35; research WPA, Washington, 1935-37, chief of procedures and statistics sect., div. profl. and service projects, 1937-39; asst. to dep. adminstr. Nat. Youth Adminstrn., 1939- 42; chief clearance sect. office civilian supply WPB, 1942-43; exec. asst. chief of import div. N. African Econ. Bd., Lend-Lease Adminstrn., 1943; dep. chief planning and control staff liberated areas br. Fgn. Econ. Adminstrn., 1944; civilian staff mil. displaced persons br. SHAEF, spl. asst. to chief liaison officer UNRRA, 1944-45, dir. div. procedural co-ordination, 1945-46; joined Dept. of State, 1946; served as spl. asst. to chief Mission Econ. Affairs, London, Eng., 1946-47, to asst. sec. state for econ. affairs, 1951-54, as dep. chief U.S. Resident Delegation, Econ. Commn. for Europe, Geneva, Switzerland, 1947-49, as chief, 1949-50, as adviser to dir. European Regional Affairs, 1950-51; sr. fellow fgn. policy studies staff Brookings Instn., Washington, 1954—. Vice pres. Internat. affairs Americans Democratic Action, 1956-58; v.p. Center Internat. Econ. Growth, 1961-63; cons. various internat. agys. Mem. Am. Econ. Assn., Soc. Internat. Devel. (editorial bd. rev. 1958-65, mem. council 1962-65, v.p. 1966-68), Am. Soc. Internat. Law (rev. and devel. bd. 1965-68), Phi Beta Kappa. Author: Grants, Loans and Local Currencies: Their Role in Foreign Aid, 1961; Development of the Emerging Countries: An Agenda for Research, 1962; Development Assistance in the Seventies: Alternatives for the United States, 1970; The UN and Promotion of the General Welfare, 1957: The UN and Economic and Social Cooperation, 1957; also spl. reports for UN, FAO, other agys. Contbr. articles profl. jours. Home: 3838 Cathedral Av NW Washington DC 20016 Office: 1775 Massachusetts Av NW Washington DC 20036

ASHFORD, HOWARD JOHN, Jr., fgn. service officer; b. Lockport, N.Y., Apr. 8, 1923; s. Howard John and Doris (Saunders) A.; A.B., Washington and Jefferson Coll., 1946; postgrad. U. Minn., 1946-47, Princeton, 1950-51; Distinguished grad. U.S. Air War Coll., 1965; m. Virginia Allen, July 15, 1950. Asst. office mgr. Gen. Mills, Inc., Buffalo, 1947-48; entered U.S. Fgn. Service, 1948; assigned Am. Consulate Gen., Dhahran, Saudi Arabia, 1948, vice consul, 1948-49; vice consul Am. Consulate, Berlin, Germany, 1949-50; Turkish area and lang. tng. Dept. State and Princeton U., 1951-52; 2d sec. Am. Embassy, Ankara, 1952-56; consul Am. Consulate, Adana, Turkey, 1961-63; polit. counselor Am. Embassy, Kabul, 1963-65; with Office Sec. Def., 1966-68; counselor Am. Embassy, Ankara, 1968—. Served with AUS, 1943-45; ETO. Decorated Bronze Star medal, Purple Heart; recipient U.S. Dept. State Superior Honor award, 1969. Mem. Am. Fgn. Service Assn., Middle East Inst., Phi Kappa Psi. Presbyn. Address: Am Embassy APO New York City NY 09254

ASHFORD, LAPLOIS, social worker; b. McCool, Miss., July 18, 1934; s. Hazel and Amie Ashford; B.A. (Ralph Bunche scholar), U. Rochester, 1957; postgrad. U. Alaska, 1959; M.A., State U. N.Y. at Albany, 1960. Tchr. children with learning problems, Rochester, N.Y., 1960-62; group worker, asst. dir. day camp Montgomery Neighborhood Center, Rochester, 1960-62; nat. dir. Youth and Coll. div. N.A.A.C.P. 1962-65; dep. commr. pub. safety, Rochester, 1965-67; exec. dir. Urban League Rochester, 1967-70; Chgo. Urban League, 1970—. Treas., Deluxer Devel., Inc. Pres. Bd. Edn., City Sch. Dist. Rochester, 1968; chmn. Action for Survival, Chgo., 1970. Bd. dirs. Rochester Gen. Hosp., Planned Parenthood, Met. Housing Com., Boy Scouts Am., Opera Theatre, Blue Cross and Blue Shield, Adv. Panel to Com. Inner City Health Services, Adv. Com. to Youth Home of Rochester, 1968; mem. exec. bd. N.A.A.C.P. Served with U.S. Army, 1957-59. Recipient Omega Psi Phi award for outstanding community service, 1961, Rochester N.A.A.C.P. citation for outstanding service to orgn., 1961, LeRoy E. Snyder award for outstanding community contbns. and involvement, 1967; named Outstanding Man of Year, N.Y. State Jr. C. of C., 1965. Mem. N.E.A., N.Y. State, Rochester tchrs. assns., Rochester C. of C., Beta Delta Gamma. Democrat. Rotarian. Home: 1023 E Hyde Park Blvd Chicago IL 60615 Office: 4500 S Michigan Av Chicago IL 60653

ASHFORTH, ALDEN BANNING, composer, educator; b. N.Y.C., May 13, 1933; s. Henry Adams and Mariana (Richardson) A.; grad. St. Paul's Sch., 1950; student Harvard, 1950-52; A.B., Oberlin Coll., 1958, Mus.B., 1958; M.F.A., Princeton, 1960; m. Nancy Regnier, June 12, 1956; children—Robyn Richardson, Melissa Adams, Lauren Elizabeth. Instr. music Princeton, 1961; instr. music theory Oberlin (O.) Coll. Conservatory Music, 1961-64; instr. music Washington Square Coll., N.Y. U., 1965-66; lectr. music City Coll. of N.Y., 1966-67; asst. prof. music U. Cal. at Los Angeles, 1967—. Composer of: Variations for Orchestra, 1958: Fantasy-Variations, 1959; Tanka Songs, 1959; Episodes, 1963; (electronic compositions) Carousel, All the Lovers, Vocalise, Cycles, 1965. Home: 8336 Wonderland Av Los Angeles CA 90046 Office: 405 Hilgard Av Los Angeles CA 90024

ASHIDA, JAMES HARUSO, fgn. service officer; b. Kent, Wash., Feb. 4, 1920; s. Rinzo and Mineyo (Kurisu) A.; B.A., U. Wash., 1946; M.A., U. Pa., 1947, U. Chgo., 1948; student Johns Hopkins, 1958-59; m. Sachiko Kashiwagi, Sept. 1, 1951; children—Ellyn R., Mark C. Joined U.S. Fgn. Service, 1955; assigned polit. consular officer, Athens, 1955-56; econ. officer, Tehran, Iran, 1956-58; Arab lang. area trainee, Beirut, Lebanon, 1959-60, econ. officer, 1960-63; chief econ. sect., Khartoum, Sudan, 1964-67; assigned Dept. Commerce, 1967-69; consul Fukvaka, Japan, 1970. Served with AUS 1942-46. Mem. Am. Fgn. Service Assn. Presbyn. Home: AM Consulate 5 26 Ohori 2 Chome Fukuoka Japan 810 Office: AM Consulate APO San Francisco CA 96502

ASHIN, MARK, educator; b. N.Y.C., Mar. 1, 1917; s. Max and Zina (Rudin) A.; B.A., U. Chgo., 1937, M.A., 1938, Ph.D., 1950; m. Alice Elaine Froyd, Jan. 9, 1949; 1 son, Paul. Instr., Mich. State Coll., East Lansing, 1938-41; instr. U. Chgo., 1947-51, asst. prof., 1951-57, asso. prof., 1957-67, prof. English, 1967—; vis. prof. Rochester U., 1961, N.Y. U., 1964. Dir. Nat. Defense Edn. Act Special Inst. for Advanced Study in English, 1968; dir. Special Summer Session Disadvantaged Students, U-Chgo., 1970. Served to 2d lt. OSS, AUS, 1943-46. Recipient Quantrell Distinguished Teaching award U. Chgo., 1954. Mem. Modern Lang. Assn., Nat. Council Teachers English, Shakespeare Assn., Renaissance Soc. Am. Home: 5541 Dorchester Av Chicago IL 60637

ASHKENAZI, ELY EZRA, electronics co. exec.; b. Mexico City, Mexico, Sept. 13, 1922; s. Ezra E. and Sefia (Hakim) A.; accounting degree Am. Acad. Accounting, 1941; m. Grace France, June 18, 1950; children—Ezra, Issac, Ronald, Shefie, David, Allegra. Came to U.S., 1936, naturalized, 1944. Partner E.S. & E. Ashkenazi, Charlotte, N.C., 1939-56; partner Nanasi Co., West New York, N.J., 1953-68; pres. Realtone Electronics, N.Y.C., 1960-68, Soundesign Corp., Jersey City, 1968—. Trustee Hillel Sch., Wanamassa, N.J.; bd. govs. Monmouth YM-YWHA, Ocean Twp., N.J. Served with USAAF, 1943-45. Home: 77 Monomouth Dr Deal NJ 07723 Office: 34 Exchange Pl Jersey City NJ 07302

ASHKENAZY, VLADIMIR, concert pianist; b. Gorky, Russia, July 6, 1937; ed. Central Music Sch., Moscow, also Moscow Conservatory; studies with Sumbatyan, Lev Oborin; m. Thorunn Johannsdoffir, Feb. 25, 1961; children—Vladimir, Nadya, Dimitri. London debut London Symphony Orch. under George Hurst, later solo recital Festival Hall, 1963; performed concets all over world; recordings. Winner 2d place Internat. Chopin Competition, Warsaw, 1955, 1st place Queen Elizabeth Internat. Piano Competition, Brussels, 1956; with John Ogdon, winner Tchaikovsky Piano Competition, Moscow, 1962. Home: Brekkugerdi 22 Reykjavik Iceland Office: care of Hurok Concerts Inc 1370 Av of Americas New York City NY 10019

ASHKIN, JULIUS, educator, physicist; b. Bklyn., Aug. 23, 1920; s. Isadore and Anna (Fishman) A.; A.B., Columbia, 1940, A.M., 1941, Ph.D. in Physics, 1943; m. Claire Ruderman, Sept. 1, 1946; children—Beth, Laura. Mem. staff Los Alamos Sci. Lab., 1943-46; asst. prof. U. Rochester, 1946-50; faculty Carnegie-Mellon Univs., 1950—, prof. physics, 1958—, chmn. dept., 1961—. Fellow Am. Phys. Soc.; mem. Am. Assn. Physics Tchrs., A.A.A.S. Home: 5136 Beeler St Pittsburgh PA 15217

ASHLER, PHILIP FREDERIC, ednl. adminstr.; b. N.Y.C., Oct. 15, 1914; s. Philip and Charlotte (Barth) A.; B.B.A. cum laude, St. Johns Coll., 1935; M.B.A., Harvard, 1937; grad. Indsl. Coll. Armed Forces, 1956; Sc.D., Fla. Inst. Tech., 1969; LL.D., U. W. Fla., 1969; m. Jane Porter, Mar. 4, 1942 (dec. 1968); children— Philip Frederic, Robert Porter, Richard Harrison; m. 2d, Elise Barrett Duvall, June 21, 1969; stepchildren—Richard Edward, Jeffries Harding. Enlisted USMCR, 1932; commd. ensign USN, 1938, advanced through grades to rear adm., 1959; served in Normandy, So. France, Iwo Jima; dir. Office Small Bus. Dept. Def., Washington, 1948-51; mem. joint staff Joint Chiefs Staff, 1957-59; ret., 1959; dir. devel. Pensacola Jr. Coll., 1960-68; vice chancellor adminstrn. State U. System Fla., 1968-70, exec. vice chancellor, 1970—. Mem. Fla. Edn. Council, 1967-68; commr. from Fla., Edn. Commn. States, 1967-68; legislative adv. council So. Regional Edn. Bd., 1966-68; chmn. Fla. Bd. Ind. Colls. and Univs., 1971—; chmn. Fla. Civil Def. Adv. Council, 1966-69; mem. Select Council on Post-High Sch. Edn., 1967-68. Mem. Fla. Ho. Reps., 1963-68. Chmn. bd. dirs. Fla. Heart Assn., 1969-71; bd. dirs. Easter Seal Soc., 1963-68, Am. Heart Assn., 1971—, LeMoyne Art Found., Tallahassee, Fla. Decorated Bronze Star with Combat V; recipient Internat. Distinguished Service award Kiwanis Internat., 1965; Distinguished Service award Am. Heart Assn., 1965, 71; Legislative award St. Petersburg Times, 1967. Mem. Kappa Delta Pi. Episcopalian (licensed lay reader). Democrat. Mason (32, Shriner), Elk, Nat. Sojourne Rotarian. Clubs: Capital City Country, Capital City Tiger Bay (v.p.) (Tallahassee). Home: 1506 Argonne Rd Tallahassee FL 32303 Office: 107 W Gaines St Tallahassee FL 32304

ASHLEY, BENEDICT, educator, clergyman; b. Neodesha, Kan., May 3, 1915; s. Arthur Burton and Bertha (Moore) A.; M.A., U. Chgo., 1938; Ph.D., U. Notre Dame, 1941; S.T.L., Aquinas Inst., 1949, Ph.D., 1950. Joined Dominican Order, 1941, ordained priest Roman Catholic Ch., 1948; prof. philosophy Aquinas Inst., 1952—, pres. Aquinas Inst. Philosophy and Theology, 1962- -; chmn. div. theology and philosophy St. Xavier Coll. 1960-61, prof. Theology Inst. Religion and Human Devel., Tex. Med. Center, Houston, 1970—. Cons. Center Liberal Studies in Edn., St. Xavier Coll., Danforth Found. Bishops Com. on Priestly Formation; dir. Albertus Magnus Lyceum. Mem. Am. Cath. Philos. Assn., Nat. Cath. Ednl. Assn., Midwest Assn. Theol. Schs. (pres.), Am. Philos. Assn. Author: (with Kane and Corcoran) Science in Synthesis, 1952; The Arts of Learning and Communication, 1957; Aristotle's Sluggish Earth, 1959. Home: 1702 Bolsover St Houston TX 77005

ASHLEY, FLETCHER, architect; b. Orange, N.J., May 28, 1926; s. Raymond Eliot and Hilda Fletcher (Brazer) A.; grad. Phillips Acad., Exeter, Mass., 1944; A.B cum laude in Archtl. Sci., Harvard, 1950, M. Arch., 1953; m. Joan Shepard, June 10, 1948; children—Hilda B. (Mrs. Stanley L. Rideout), Karen S., Gail H., Alison F. Asso. Hugh Stubbins, architect, Cambridge, Mass., 1954-59; self- employed architect, Lexington, Mass., 1954-64; partner firm Ashley & Myer, Cambridge, 1961-64; prin. dir., treas. Ashley, Myer & Assos., Inc., Cambridge, 1964-69; prin., dir., treas. Ashley/Myer/Smith Inc., Cambridge, 1969—. Trustee, corporator Cambridge Savs. Bank, 1969—, Corporator Barn Gallery, Ogunquit, Me.; treas. Orchard Tennis Cts., Lexington. Served with USNR, 1944-45. Recipient Progressive Architecture design award, 1958; A.I.A. Homes for Better Living award, 1962, Nat. award merit, 1970; 1st prize Internat. Archtl. Design competition New Boston Archtl. Center, 1964; Dept. Housing Urban Devel. nat. award, 1970, Archtl. Record award excellence for low income housing project, Boston, 1971. Mem. A.I.A., Mass. Assn. Architects, Boston Soc. Architects, Boston Archtl. Center. Clubs: Harvard (Boston); Belmont Hill (Mass.); Cliff Country (Ogunquit). Archtl. commns. for Harvard, Babson Coll., Hampshire Coll., Marlboro Coll., Boston Redevel. Authority, Mass. Bay Transit Authority, Lowell State Coll., Worcester State Coll. Home: 6 Moon Hill Rd Lexington MA 02173 Office: 14 Arrow St Cambridge MA 02138

ASHLEY, FLOYD C., corp. exec.; b. Jackson, Minn., 1909. Treas., dir. Nash-Finch Co., Merchants Finance Co., Walt & Eddies, Inc., Williams- Unimart, Inc. Home: 15720 Highway 7 Minnetonka MN 55343 Office: 3381 Gorham Av Minneapolis MN 55426

ASHLEY, HOLT, educator; b. San Francisco, Jan. 10, 1923; s. Harold Harrison and Anne (Oates) A.; student Cal. Inst. Tech., 1940-43; B.S., U. Chgo., 1944; S.M., Mass. Inst. Tech., 1948, Sc.D., 1951; m. Frances M. Day, Feb. 1, 1947. Faculty, Mass. Inst. Tech., 1946-67, prof. aero., 1960-67; 67; prof. aeros. and astronautics Stanford U., 1967-; spl. research aeroelasticity, aerodynamics; cons. govt. agencies, research orgns., indsl. corps. Mem. sci. adv. bd. USAF, 1958-; research adv. com. structural dynamics NASA, 1952-60; research adv. com. on aircraft structures, 1962—; mem. Kanpur Indo-American program, Indian Inst. Tech., 1964-65. Mem. Greater Boston coordinating council Boy Scouts Am., also mem.-at-large, and adviser air explorer squadron. Recipient Goodwin medal Mass. Inst. Tech., 1952; named one of 10 outstanding young men of year Boston Jr. C. of C., 1956. Fellow Am. Acad. Arts and Scis., Am. Inst. Aeronautics and Astronautics (asso. editor jour., v.p. tech. 1971); mem. Am. Meterol. Soc. (profl., recipient 50th Anniversary medal, 1971), A.A.A.S., Nat. Acad. Engring., Phi Beta Kappa, Sigma Xi, Tau Beta Pi. Co-author: Aeroelasticity, 1955; Principles of Aeroelasticity, 1961; Aerodynamics of Wings and Bodies, 1965. Home: 475 Woodside Dr Woodside CA 94062

ASHLEY, JAMES MANSFIELD, glass co. exec.; b. Toledo, Oct. 15, 1908; s. Charles Sumner and Emily Lindsay (Bellman) A.; grad. Ashville (N.C.) Boys Sch., 1926; student Williams Coll. 1926-29; m. Ruth Stewart Sloan, May 29, 1933; children—Clark C. Sarah L. (Mrs. David Dolgenos). James Mansfield IV, Susan E. Clk., Office Pub. Defender, Cook County, Ill., 1930-33; with Libbey Owens Ford Glass Co., Toledo, 1934—, dir. pub. relations, 1946- 59, v.p., 1959—. Pres., dir., mem. exec. com. Producers Council U.S., 1947-59; dir. Bldg. Research Inst. of Nat. Acad. Sci., 1952-55; v.p. Trades Relations Council U.S., 1957-60, dir., 1954—, chmn. bd., 1960—; dir. Downtown Toledo Assos., 1957—. Mem. Toledo Chamber of Commerce (vice pres., dir.), Delta Upsilon. Conglist. Clubs: Toledo, Toledo Country, Contbr. encys. Home: 3327 Pelham Rd Toledo OH 43606 Office: Libbey Owens Ford Glass Co 811 Madison Av Toledo OH 43624

ASHLEY, LEE CHRISMAN, banker; b. Denver, Nov., 25, 1908; s. Frank R. and Carolyn (Roberts) A.; m. Elizabeth Bratton, Oct. 20, 1937; 1 dau., Jean D. (Mrs. Thomas M. Francis). With First Nat. Bank Denver, 1930—, sr. v.p., cashier, 1948—; dir. First Nat. Bank Southglenn, Colo., First Nat. Bank Bear Valley, Colo.; dir., treas. First Nat. Bank Bancorp. Inc., 1968—. Bd. dirs. Downtown Denver Improvement Assn., 1964—; bd. dirs., v.p. Boys Clubs Denver, 1962—; bd. mgrs., treas. St. Luke's Hosp., Denver, 1960—. Served to maj. USAAF, 1942-46. Decorated Bronze Star. Home: 983 S Adams Way Denver CO 80209 Office: First Nat Bank Denver CO 80217

ASHLEY, PAUL PRITCHARD, lawyer; b. Fostoria, O., July 2, 1896; s. Dr. John P. and Della (Gust) A.; student U. Cal., 1919; LL.B., U. Wash., 1925; m. Katherine Macrae Smith, Aug. 20, 1932; children—Mary Macrae, Katherine Cooper, Admitted to Wash. bar, 1926, since practiced in Seattle; now mem. Ashley, Foster, Pepper & Riviera. Asso. prof. bus. adminstrn. U. Wash., 1928-30; lectr. Pacific Coast Banking Sch., 1939-66. Active civic activities; co-chmn. Wash. chpt. Nat. Conf. Christians and Jews; pres. Seattle Symphony Orch., 1963-66. War and Community Chest, 1944, Municipal League Seattle and King County, Wash., 1958-60. Estate Planning Council, 1960. Trustee World Affairs Council, Seattle Opera Assn., China Club; pres. Seattle Found., 1952-54, 56. Fellow Am. Bar Found.; mem. Am. Judicature Soc., Wash. Bar Assn. (bd. govs. 1949-52, pres. 1961), Wash. Civil Def. Council, Am. Law Inst., Am., Seattle (pres. 1941) bar assns., English Speaking Union (pres. 1942- 43), Nat. Conf. Bar Presidents (exec. com. 1962-, chmn. 1967-68), Order Coif, Acacia, Phi Beta Kappa, Phi Delta Phi. Clubs: Lawyers (N.Y.C.): Rainier. College (pres. 1938), Harbor (Seattle). Author: Cases on Business Law, 1935; Essential of Libel, 1948; Say it Safely, 1956, rev. 3d edit., 1966, 4th edit., 1969. 1st editor Wash. Law Rev. Contbr. articles legal publs. Home: 2009 Broadmoor Dr Seattle WA 98102 Office: Exchange Bldg Seattle WA 98104

ASHLEY, ROBERT PAUL, Jr., coll. dean; b. Balt., Apr. 15, 1915; s. Robert Paul and Ethel (Rice) A.; A.B., Bowdoin Coll., 1936; M.A., Harvard, 1937, Ph.D., 1949; m. Virginia Woods, June 24, 1939; children—Virginia (Mrs. Michael Hager), Dianne (Mrs. C.W. Per-Lee, Jr.), Cynthia, Robert Paul III, Jacquelyn. Tennis coach and instr. English, Portland (Me.) Jr. Coll., 1938-39; instr. English, Colby Jr. Coll., 1939- 43; tng. instr. Boston Q.M. Depot, 1944; teaching fellow English, Harvard, 1946-48, coach tennis, 1946; asst. prof. English, asst. dean, coach tennis Washington and Jefferson Coll., 1948-51; asst. prof. English U.S. Mil. Acad., 1951-55; dean of coll., prof. English, Ripon Coll., 1955—, tennis coach, 1955-64, acting pres., 1966, v.p., 1968—; vis. prof. U.S. Naval Acad. 2d Sem., 1968-69. Dir. news and records Midwest Athletic Conf., 1956-61, v.p. 1957-58, pres. 1958-59, commr., 1960-66; examiner, cons. North Central Assn., 1963—; mem. Commn. on Colls. and Univs., 1968—. mem. Wis. Commn. Higher Ednl. Aids, 1964-67, chmn., 1965-66. Served as lt. (j.g.) USNR, 1944-46; maj. U.S. Army Res., 1951-55, now col. Mem. Am. Assn. U. Profs., Modern Lang. Assn. Am., Wis. Tennis Assn., Phi Beta Kappa, Zeta Psi. Author: Wilkie Collins, (juveniles) The Stolen Train, Rebel Raiders. Editor: (anthologies) Elizabethan Fiction, Tales of Suspense; Faulkner at West Point, Civil War Poetry. Contbr. articles profl. jours. Home: 510 Lincoln St Ripon WI 54971

ASHLEY, THOMAS WILLIAM LUDLOW, congressman; b. Toledo, Jan. 11, 1923; s. William Meredith and Mary Alida (Ludlow) A.; student Kent (Conn.) Sch., 1939-42; A.B., Yale, 1948; LL.B., Ohio State U., 1951. Admitted to Ohio bar, 1951, practiced in Whitehouse. 1951-52; gen. counsel Formed Steel Products, 1951-52; co- dir, pres sect., asst. dir. spl. projects Radio Free Europe Com., 1952- 54; mem. 84th to 92d Congresses, 9th Ohio Dist. Del. Ohio State Democratic Conv., 1954. Trustee Boys Club of Toledo. Served with AUS, 1942-46. Home: Waterville OH 43566 Office: 2427 Rayburn Bldg Washington DC 20515

ASHLEY, WARREN HENRY, architect; b. East Longmeadow, Mass., Oct. 8, 1909; s. Henry Simeon and Jennie (Coomes) A.; B.Arch., Syracuse U., 1931; m. Barbara Ann Ashley. Owner-architect firm Warren H. Ashley, West Hartford, Conn., 1951—. Recipient Top Honor awards Wilbert Snow Elementary Sch., Middletown, Conn., Sch. Exec. Competition for Better Sch. Design, 1955, Boston Arts Festival, 1956; Top Honor award Edgemont Jr.-Sr. High Sch., Greenburgh, N.Y., A.I.A., 1957, Spl. citation Sch. Exec. Competition for Better Sch. Design, 1957, hon. mention, 1958; Interior award Instns. Mag., 1959; citation Herricks High Sch. Library, New Hyde Park, L.I., N.Y., N.Y. Library Assn., 1964; award of excellence Am. Inst. Steel Constrn., 1961; citation Am. Assn. Sch. Adminstrs., 1967; also other archtl. awards. Latest prin. works include: elementary schs. in Granby, Mass., 1964, Armonk, N.Y., 1962, Rochester, N.H., 1967, Sydney, N.Y., 1968; middle schs. Ossining, N.Y., 1965, Ticonderoga, N.Y., 1967, Longmeadow, 1967, Somerset, Mass., 1966; high schs. in Buzzards Bay, Mass., 1965, Nanuet, N.Y., 1962, Cresskill, N.J., 1960, Oneonta, N.Y., 1965, Plattsburgh, N.Y., 1965, Cooperstown, N.Y., 1967, Little Falls, N.Y., 1967, New Ipswich, N.H., 1967. Mem. Nat. Pilots Assn., Aircraft Owners and Pilots Assn. Home: 361 Mountain Rd West Hartford CT 06117 Office: 740 N Main St West Hartford CT 06117

ASHMAN, JAMES ERNEST, corp. ofcl.; b. East Palestine, O., July 19, 1902; s. Jacob and Camella (Atchison) A.; student Geneva Coll., Beaver Falls, Pa., 1920-21, U. N.C., 1922-23; m. Lena Frances Core, Dec. 5, 1925. Salesman, Ashman Coal Co. East Palestine, 1924-29; salesman, sales promotion mgr. Burroughs Adding Machine Co., Detroit, 1929-40; procedures dir. U.S. Steel & Carnegie Ill. Steel Corp., Pitts., 1940-46; controller, Rockwell Mfg. Co., 1948-51, v.p., 1951, exec. v.p., 1952; pres., dir. Air Assos., Inc., Teterboro, N.J., 1953-56, Ultrasonic Corp. (now Advance-Wilson Industries, Inc.), Cambridge, Mass., 1956-62; chmn. bd., pres., chief exec. officer Gray Mfg. Co., N.Y.C., 1962—. Mem. A.I.M. (pres. council). Clubs: Wings, Farmington County (Charlottesville, Va.). Home: Shadwell VA Office: 641 Lexington Av New York City NY 10022

ASHMEAD, JOHN, Jr., educator, author; b. N.Y.C., Aug. 22, 1917, s. John and Mildred (Hinkel) A.; B.A. magna cum laude, Harvard, 1938, M.A., 1941, Ph.D., '1950; m. Ann Wheeler Harnwell, Oct. 15, 1949; children—John III, Graham Gaylord, Gaylord Harnwell, Louisa Harral, Theodora Wheeler. Mem. faculty Haverford Coll., 1947—, prof. English, 1961—; lectr. English Bryn Mawr Coll., 1949; lectr. English and history Athens (Greece) Coll., 1956- 57; Fulbright lectr. Am. studies Osaka (Japan) U. Fgn. Studies, 1955-56, Nat. Chengchi U. and Taiwan Normal U., Taipei, 1960-61, Banaras (India) Hindu U., 1964-65. Mem. Nat. Adv. Council Teaching English as a Fgn. Lang., 1962-67; pres. Fellows of Am. Studies Phila., 1968-69; chmn. Sch. and Coll. Conf. English, N.Y.C., 1966-68; U.S. del. British Council Cof. Teaching English Lit. Overseas, Cambridge, Eng., 1962; chief regional judge for Pa. and N.Y., Book of Month Club Writing Fellowship contest, 1966. Served to lt. USNR, 1942-46; PTO. Decorated Commendation medal; grantee Am. Council Learned Societies, 1960, Am. Inst. Indian Studies, 1964-65, Asia Soc., 1964-65, Ford Found., 1964. Mem. Modern Lang. Assn. (chmn. Oriental-Western lit. relations conf. group 1966), Am. Studies Assn., Assn. Asian Studies, Machine Transp. Soc., Soc. Archtl. Historians, Nat. Council Tchrs. English, Phi Beta Kappa. Author: (novel) The Mountain and the Feather, 1961; (textbook) English 12, 1967. Editor short stories, articles, revs. Home: 9 College Lane Haverford PA 19041

ASHMORE, CLINTON N., U.S. atty.; b. Wakulla County, Fla., 1913; B.A., U. Fla.; LL.B., Cumberland Sch. Law of Howard Coll.; m. Katherine Ashmore; 1 son, Chap. Admitted to Fla. bar, 1934; pros. atty., Leon County, 1950-60; now U.S. atty. No. Dist. Fla. Recipient Good Govt. award C. of C. Home: 1005 E 7th Av Tallahassee FL 32303 Office: Fed Bldg 429 E 6th Av Tallahassee FL 32303

ASHMORE, FRANK LEON, univ. ofcl.; b. Greenville, S.C., Dec. 12, 1925; s. Frank Little and Lemma Leone (Burdette) A.; student Duke, 1943-44; A.B., Furman U., 1947; student Candler Sch. Theology, Emory U., 1950-53; m. Nancy Price Hall, Sept. 4, 1948; children—Elaine Anne, Hall Burdette, Louise Leona. Asst. news editor Greenville News, 1947-49; life ins. salesman, 1949-50; theol. student assigned also to churches in S.C. Ann. Conf., 1951-53; copy editor Atlanta Jour., 1953; staff pub. relations and devel. Emory U., 1953-57, asst. dir. devel. and pub. relations, 1956-57; dir. devel. and pub. relations Randolph-Macon Woman's Coll., 1957- 59; exec. dir. Am. Coll. Pub. Relations Assn., Washington, 1959-61; asst. v.p. for devel. Duke, Durham, N.C., 1961-63, v.p. for instl. advancement, 1963—. Mem. Nat. adv. com. Council Advancement Small Colls., 1959-61; pub. relations adv. com So. Regional Edn. Bd., 1959-62, chmn., 1961-62. Mem. devel. adv. com. Nat. Urban Coalition. Trustee Bennett Coll., Paine Coll., N.C. Symphony. Served to ensign USNR, 1943-45. Mem. Am. Coll. Pub. Relations Assn., Am. Alumni Council, Delta Tau Delta. Democrat. Methodist. Kiwanian. Contbr. articles to profl. publs. Home: 2637 McDowell St Durham NC 27705

ASHMORE, HARRY SCOTT, editor, found exec.; b. Greenville, S.C., July 27, 1916; s. William Green and Nancy Elizabeth (Scott) A.; B.S., Clemson Coll., 1937; Nieman fellow journalism, Harvard, 1941-42; LL.D., Oberlin Coll., 1958, Grinnell Coll., 1963; m. Barbara Edith Laier, June 2, 1940; 1 dau., Anne Rogers. Reporter-columnist Greenville (S.C.) Piedmont, 1937-39; polit. writer Greenville News and Charlotte (N.C.) News, 1939-41; asso. editor Charlotte News, 1945-47, editor, 1947; editor editorial page Ark. Gazette, Little Rock, 1947, exec. editor, 1948-59, on leave to serve as asst. Stevenson for presdl. campaign, 1955-56; cons. Center for Study of Democratic Instns., Fund for Republic, 1959-60; editor in chief Ency. Brit., 1960-63, editor Britannica Perspectives, 1964-68; exec. v.p. Center for Study Democratic Instns., 1967-69, pres., 1969—. Mem. bd. Nat. Com. for an Effective Congress, 1966—; vice chmn. adv. council Am. Civil Liberties Union, 1970—. Bd. dirs. Fund for Republic. Served from 2d lt. to lt. col. inf. AUS, 1942-45; mem. War Dept. Gen. Staff, 1945. Decorated citation for spl. duty as chief staff Task Force Faith, Ruhr Pocket, 1945; Bronze Star with two oak leaf clusters; recipient Sidney Hillman award, 1957; Pulitzer Prize, editorial writing, 1958; Freedom House award, 1958. Author: The Negro and the Schools, 1954; An Epitaph for Dixie, 1957; The Other Side of Jordan, 1960; The Man in the Middle, 1966; (with William C. Baggs) Mission to Hanoi, 1968. Home: PO Box 4068 Santa Barbara CA 93103

ASHMORE, HENRY LUDLOW, coll. pres.; b. Tallahassee, July 4, 1920, s. John Henry and Nursie (Whaley) A.; B.A. with honors, U. Fla., 1942, Ed.M., 1948, Ed.D. (grad. fellow 1947-50), 1950; m. Clarice Langston, Aug. 16, 1946; children—Randan Ludlow, Jerri. Prin., St. Marks (Fla.) Sch., 1946-47; dir. student teaching Ga. Tchrs. Coll., 1950-53; pres. Pensacola Jr. Coll., 1954-64; pres. Armstrong State Coll., Savannah, Ga., 1964-. Dir. Candler Hosp., Savannah. Served to 1st lt., AUS 1942-46. Mem. Kappa Delta Pi, Phi Delta Kappa, Phi Kappa Phi. Democrat. Baptist (chmn. bd. deacons). Rotarian. Home: 1416 N Camden Circle Savannah GA 31406

ASHMORE, JACK PEARCE, Jr., lawyer, real estate developer; b. Graceville, Fla., June 9, 1930; s. Jack Pearce and Gracie (Flournoy) A.; A.B., Emory U., 1952, LL.B., 1958; m. Margaret Blythe Posey, Nov. 1, 1957; children—Blythe Gentry, Margaret Blain. Admitted to Ga. bar, 1957; mem. firm Alston, Sibley, Miller, Spann & Shackelford, Atlanta, 1957-63; partner successor firm Alston, Miller & Gaines, 1963-65; founder, partner firm Ashmore & Boozer, Atlanta, 1965-68; founder, partner firm Sanders, Hester, Holley, Ashmore & Boozer, Atlanta, 1968—; mng. partner Investment Properties, Ltd., Atlanta and Athens, Ga., 1965—, Ashmore Bros. Properties, Atlanta, 1968- -; pres. Candler Bldg. Inc., Atlanta, 1970—; dir. Ashmore Realty Co., Atlanta Hawks Basketball, Inc., Profl. Athletes Land Fund, Inc., Peoples Am. Bank Atlanta; trustee Cousins Mortgage and Equity Investments; lectr. Emory U. Sch. Law, 1959-65. Bd. visitors Emory U., 1970—. Served with AUS, 1952-55. Mem. Am., Ga., Atlanta bar assns., Mortgage Bankers Assn., Phi Delta Phi, Phi Delta Theta. Democrat. Episcopalian. Clubs: Lawyers, Commerce, Piedmont Driving (Atlanta). Home: 200 Blackland Rd N W Atlanta GA 30342 Office: The Candler Bldg Atlanta GA 30303

ASHMORE, JAMES, educator; b. Russellville, Ark., June 6, 1926; s. Ira Ashmore; B.S., N. Tex. State Coll., Denton, 1947, M.S. in Chemistry, 1948; Ph.D. in Biochemistry, St. Louis U., 1953; m. Lottie Holt, Jan. 27, 1948; children—David, Robert Jane, Edward. Shering fellow Endocrine Soc., 1953- 54; tutor biochem. scis. Harvard, then asst. prof. biochemistry Med. Sch., 1957-58; asso. prof. biochemistry Ind. U. Med. Sch., 1958-60, prof., chmn. dept. pharmacology, 1961-68, 69—; prof. chmn. dept. biochemistry U. Mass. Med. Sch., 1968-69; spl. research endocrine regulation metabolism, use isotopes in biology and medicine, metabolism of neoplastic tissues. Mem. A.A.A.S., Endocrine Soc., Am. Soc. Biochemistry, Am. Soc. Pharamcology and Exptl. Therapeutics, Biochem. Soc. (London), Soc. Exptl. Biology and Medicine, Central Soc. Clin. Research, Am. Diabetes Assn., Sigma Xi. Contbr. articles profl. jours. Office: 1100 W Michigan St Indianapolis IN 46202

ASHMORE, ROBERT THOMAS, lawyer; b. on farm, Greenville County, S.C., Feb. 22, 1904; s. John Thomas and Lena (Smith) A.; grad. Furman U., 1927; m. Willie Vance Linthicum; 1 dau., Nancy Vance. Practiced law, Greenville, since 1928; elected pros. atty. Greenville County Ct., 1930, 13th Jud. Circuit of S.C. (Greenville and Pickens counties), 1936, 40, 44, 48, 52; elected mem. 83d Congress, 4th S.C. Dist., June 1953, to fill vacancy; mem. 84th to 90th Congresses, 4th S.C. Dist.; pvt. practice law, 1968—. Chmn. S.C. Appalachian Regional Planning and Devel. Commn. Served with U.S. Army, 1942-46; now col. U.S. Army Res. Mem. S.C. Jr. C. of C. (organizer, past pres.), Greenville Jr. C. of C. (past dir., v.p., pres.), U.S. Jr. C. of C. (v.p.), Jr. Order United Am. Mechanics, Res. Officers Assn., Am. Legion (vice comdr. Greenville). Democrat. Baptist. Odd Fellow, Woodman of World. Clubs: Greenville Exchange (pres.), Men's Garden. Home: Manly Dr R9 Greenville SC 29609

ASHTON, DORE, educator, author: b. Newark, May 21, 1928; s. Ralph N. and Sylvia (Ashton) Shapiro; B.A., U. Wis., 1949; M.A., Harvard, 1950; m. Adja Yunkers, July 8, 1952; children—Alexandra Louise, Marina Svietlana. Asso. editor Art Digest, 1951-54; asso. critic N.Y. Times, 1955-60; lectr. Pratt Inst., 1962-63; head humanities dept. Sch. Visual Arts, 1965-68; head dept. art history Cooper Union, 1968—; art critic, lectr., dir. exhbns. Recipient Mather award for art criticism Coll. Art Assn. 1963; Guggenheim fellow, 1964; Graham fellow, 1963; Ford Found. fellow, 1960. Mem. Internat. Assn. Art Critics (governing bd.), Phi Beta Kappa. Author: Abstract Art Before Columbus, 1957; Poets and the Past, 1959; Philip Guston, 1960; The Unknown Shore, 1962; Rauschenberg's Dante, 1964; Modern American Sculpture, 1968; A Reading of Modern Art, 1970; Richard Lindner, a full-length study, 1969; Pol. Bury, 1971. Co-editor: Redon, Moreau, Bresdin, 1961. N.Y. contbg. editor Studio Internat., 1941—, Opus Internat., 1968—, XXième Siecle, 1955—. Contbr. Vision and Value series (Gyorgy Kepe), 1966, The New Art anthology (Gregory Battcock), 1966. Home: 217 E 11th St New York City NY 10003

ASHTON, EUGENE SAMUEL, educator, clergyman; b. Lewiston, Me., June 5, 1913; s. Albert William and Hattie (Flower) A.; student U. Ia., 1930-31; B.S., Bates Coll., 1934; B.D., Union Theol. Sem., N.Y.C., 1937, S.T.M., 1938, Th.D., 1939; m. Hildred Millet Peck, Sept. 11, 1934: children—Stephanie, Peter. Ordained to ministry of Congl. Ch., 1939; instr. dept. religion Goucher Coll., 1939-47; minister of worship Mount Vernon Pl. Meth. Ch., Balt., 1942-47; Lee S. McCollester prof. Bibl. lit. Tufts Coll. Sch. Religion, 1947—, acting dean, 1953-54, chaplain Tufts College, 1954—, chairman department religion, 1955—; vis. lectr. Pacific School Religion, summer 1945, Westminster (Md.) Theol. Sem., 1946-47; chaplain Vets. Assn. Lawrence Light Guard Medford. Bd. dirs. Gen. Theol. Library, Boston, 1954—. Mem. Soc. Sci. Study Religion, Assn. Asian Studies, Nat. Assn. Bibl. Instrs. (mem. council 1949-52, placement sec. 1944-46), Soc. Bibl. Lit. and Exegesis (pres. N.E. sect. 1953-54), N.E. Alumni Union Theol. Sem. (pres. 1951), Phi Beta Kappa. Rotarian. Home: 55 Talbot Av Somerville MA 02144 Office: Tufts College Medford MA 02155

ASHTON, FREDERICK, choreographer; b. Guayaquil, Ecuador, Sept. 17, 1906 (parents British citizens); s. George and Georgina (Fulcher) A.; ed. Dover (England) College: Litt.D. (honorary), Durham College; D.Litt. (honorary), East Anglia, 1967; D.Mus. (hon.), U. London, 1970. Director of the opera 4 Saints in 3 Acts, N.Y.C., 1934; prin. choreographer and director Royal Ballet Co., London, England; creator ballets for Royal Ballet: Ondine, Cinderella, Sylvia, Fille and Gardee, Les Patineurs, Symphonic Variations, Scenes de Ballet, Facade, Wedding Banquet, Enigma Variations; for N.Y. City Ballet: Illuminations, Picnic in Tintagel; (film) Tales of Beatrix Potter, 1970. Served to flight lt. RAF, World War II. Decorated Legion Honour; comdr. Order Brit. Empire: comdr. Order of the Dannebrog; knighted 1962; Companion Honour, 1970. Home: 8 Marlborough St Chelsea London SW3 England

ASHTON, GEOFFREY CYRIL, educator, geneticist; b. Croydon, Eng., July 5, 1925; s. Cyril Hanniss and Ethel (Pate) A.; B.Sc., Liverpool U., 1943, Ph.D., 1958, D.Sc, 1967; m. Kathleen J. Stanley, Feb. 25, 1951; children—Carolyn Joy. Kathryn Alison, Melinda Jane, Jonathan Geoffrey. Research asst. U. Toronto, Ont., Can., 1948-50; sect. leader Glaxo Labs., Eng., 1951-56; sr. sci. officer Farm Livestock Research Centre, Eng., 1956-58; prin. research officer Commonwealth Sci. and Indsl. Research Orgn., Australia, 1958-64; prof. genetics U. Hawaii, 1964—, chmn. dept., 1965—. Mem. blood group scientists panel FAO, 1963—, chmn. subcom. on protein polymorphism nomenclature, 1963—. Mem. Genetics Soc. Am., Am. Soc. for Human Genetics, Am. Soc. Naturalists. Home: 5414 Kirkwood Pl Honolulu HI 96821

ASHTON, HARRIS JOHN, corp. exec.; b. Elizabeth, N.J., June 21, 1932; s. Earle S. and Dorothy (Black) A.; B.A., Yale, 1954; LL.B., Columbia, 1959; m. Angela Murphy, Oct. 20, 1962; children—Kelly Elizabeth, Victoria Catherine. Admitted to N.Y. bar, 1960, asso. atty. Breed, Abbott & Morgan, 1959-62, Lovejoy, Wasson, Lundgren & Huppich, 1962-64; partner Lovejoy, Wasson, Lundgren & Ashton, 1964—; pres., chief exec. officer Gen. Host Corp., 1967-70, chmn., chief exec. officer, 1970—; sec., dir. Franklin Custodian Funds, Inc., Express Funds, Inc., Am. Internat. Service Corp. Served to lt. AUS, 1955-57. Mem. Am. Bar Assn., Bar Assn. CIty N.Y., Delta Kappa Epsilon. Clubs: Yale (N.Y.C.): Sleepy Hollow Country. Home: Clapboard Ridge Rd Greenwich CT 06830 Office: 245 Park Av New York City NY 10017

ASHTON, JOHN WILLIAM, educator; b. Lewiston, Me., July 11, 1900; s. Albert William and Hattie Manetta (Flower) A.; A.B., Bates Coll., 1922, LL.D., 1952; Ph.D., U. Chicago, 1928; m. Florence Elizabeth Huber, Nov. 1, 1925; 1 dau., Elizabeth Mary Breatrice. Instr. English and speech Yankton (S.D.) Coll., 1922-23; instr. English State U. Ia., 1923-26,, asst. and asso. prof. English, 1927-40; Internat. Research fellow Huntington Library, 1932-33; prof. English and chmn. dept. U. Kan., 1940-45; br. head English Shrivenham American U., County Berkshire, Eng., 1945; prof. English, dean Coll. Arts and Scis. Ind. U., 1946-52, v.p., 1952-58, v.p., dean grad. sch., 1958-65, prof. English and folklore, 1966-70, prof. emeritus, 1970—. Mem. adv. com. on Nat. Def. Edn. Act fellowships under Office of Edn., 1962-66, dir. div. grad. programs, 1965-66, cons., 1966—; mem.

tng. grants com. Nat. Inst. Dental Research. Served C.O.T.S., Camp Lee, Va., 1918. Mem. Am. Folklore Soc., Modern Lang. Assn., Nat. Council Tchrs. of English, Religious Edn. Assn. (dir.), Council Grad. Schs. U.S. (chmn. 1964), Ch. Hist. Soc., N.E., Hoosier, Cal. folklore socs., Renaissance Soc. Am., N. Central Assn. Colls. and Secondary Schs., Phi Beta Kappa, Delta Sigma Rho. Episcopalian (mem. standing liturgical commn.). Editor: Trends in Graduate Work, 1931; Types of English Drama, 1940. Home: 1115 Brooks Dr Bloomington IN 47401

ASHTON, SISTER MARY MADONNA, hosp. adminstr.; b. St. Paul; d. Avon B. and Ruth (Fehring) Ashton; B.A., St. Catherine's Coll., St. Paul, 1944; M.S., St. Louis U., 1946; M.H.A., U. Minn., 1958. DIr. med. social service dept. St. Joseph's Hosp., St. Paul, 1949-56; dir. out-patient dept. St. Mary's Hosp., Mpls., 1958-59, asst. adminstr., 1959-62, adminstr., 1962-68, exec. v.p., 1968—; preceptor, mem. faculty U. Minn. Program in Hosp. Adminstrn. Trustee Minn. Blue Cross Assn. Recipient Sabra Hamilton award Program in Hosp. Adminstrn., U. Minn., 1958. Fellow Am. Coll. Hosp. Adminstrs.; mem. Nat. Catholic Hosp. Assn., Congregation of Sisters St. Joseph of Carondelet. Home: 2414 S 7th St Minneapolis MN 55406

ASHTON, RAYMOND J., ret. architect; b. Salt Lake City; s. Edward T. and Effie (Morris) A.; student sch. engring. U. Utah, Ecole des Beaux Arts Sch. Archtl. Design; m. Winnie Richards. June 18, 1913; children—Yvonne R. (Mrs. Richard Willey), Joy R., Leila R. (Mrs. J.P. Collier), Janet R. (Mrs. Wesley J. Gransden). Traveled in Europe, 1909-12; archtl. draftsman, 1913-16; architect Rutherford & Ashton, 1918; formed partnership with Raymond L. Evans, 1922. Pres. bd. Utah Symphony; mem. bd. Utah Art Inst. Fellow A.I.A. (past pres.; past pres. jury of fellows); mem. Am. Archtl. Found. (pres.), Utah Bldg. and Constrn. Congress (pres. 1933-54). Mem. Church of Jesus Christ of Latter-Day Saints. Clubs: University, Alta (Salt Lake City). Home: 1145 Copper Basin Rd Prescott AZ 86301

ASHWORTH, JOHN LAWRENCE, lawyer; b. Hunington, W.Va., Apr. 15, 1934; s. W.L.J. and Johnnie (Summers) A.; B.A., Ohio Wesleyan U., 1956; J.D., U. Mich., 1959; m. Rosemary L. Baxter, Aug. 10, 1957; children-Julie, Amy, Molly. Admitted to Ky. bar 1962, Ohio bar, 1960; practice in Ashland, 1960-64, Marion, 1964—; staff atty. Ashland Oil & Refining Co., 1960-64. Chmn. Nat. Found. March of Dimes, 1970; chmn. profl. div. Marion County United Appeal, 1970. Bd. dirs. Marion County United Community Services. Recipient award of merit Ohio Legal Center Inst., 1964. Mem. Am., Ohio (past com. chmn.), Ky. bar assns. Baptist. Rotarian. Home: 725 King Av Marion OH 43302 Office: 148 W Center St Marion OH 43302

ASHWORTH, MAYNARD RICHARD, newspaper pub.; b. Holden, Mo., July 21, 1894; s. Henry Brinkley and Eunice Mary (West) A.; ed. State Tchrs. Coll., Warrensburg, Mo., 1912- 15, U. Chgo., summer 1916, U. Minn., summer 1917; m. Annie Laurie Page, Jan. 26, 1926; children—Maynard Richard, Peggy. Tchr., Guthrie, Okla., 1915-16, Mpls., 1917; dept. store work, Pitts., 1919-24; real estate, Pitts., Los Angeles, Miami, 1924-26; in newspaper work 1927—; with Ledger-Enquirer, Columbus, Ga., 1927-28, Durham (N.C.) Sun. 1929; gen. mgr. Wilmington (N.C.). Star- News, 1929-30, Long Beach (Cal.) Sun, 1930-31; newspaper broker, Los Angeles, 1932; with San Pedro News Pilot, 1932-34; gen. mgr. Ledger- Enquirer, Columbus, 1934-36; pub. Columbus Ledger and Columbus Enquirer, 1936—; pres. R.W. Page Corp., 1961; dir. Columbus Bank & Trust Co. Inc.; sec.-treas. Columbus Broadcasting Inc. Served to 2d lt. U.S. Army, 1917-19; commd. 1st lt. inf., Res. Corps, 1919, capt., 1924; served in World War II, Aug. 1941-Oct. 1944; capt. to lt. col. inf.; 17 months Africa and Italy. Democrat. Methodist. Mason (32, Shriner). Clubs: Rotary (dist. gov., 165th dist., 1939-40), Country, Big Eddy (Columbus); Officers' (Fort Benning, Ga.). Home: 821 Peachtree Dr Columbus GA 31906 Office: Ledger-Enquirer Columbus GA 31901

ASIMOV, ISAAC, author, educator; b. Petrovichi, Russia, Jan. 2, 1920; s. Judah and Anna Rachel (Berman) A.; brought to U.S., 1923, naturalized 1928; B.S., Columbia, 1939, M.A., 1941, Ph.D., 1948; m. Gertrude Blugerman, 1942; children—David, Robyn Joan. With Boston U. Sch. Medicine, 1949—, asso. prof. biochemistry, 1955—. Recipient James T. Grady award Am. Chem. Soc. 1965, A.A.A.S.-Westinghouse sci. writing award, 1967. Author: Pebble in the Sky, 1950; I, Robot, 1950; The Stars, Like the Dust, 1951; Foundation, 1951; Foundation and Empire, 1952; Currents of Space, 1952; Second Foundation, 1953; Caves of Steel, 1954; End of Eternity, 1955; Races and People, 1955; The Naked Sun, 1957; (textbook) Biochemistry and Human Metabolism, rev. edit., 1957; World of Carbon, 1958; World of Nitrogen, 1958; Nine Tomorrows, 1959; The Words of Science, 1959; Realm of Numbers, 1959; The Living River, 1960; Kingdom of the Sun, 1960; Realm of Measure, 1960; Wellsprings of Life, 1960; Words from Myths, 1961; Realm of Algebra, 1961; Life and Energy, 1962; Words in Genesis, 1962; Fact and Fancy, 1962; Words on the Map, 1962; Search for the Elements, 1962; Words from the Exodus, 1963; The Human Body, 1963; The Genetic Code, 1963; Intelligent Man's Guide to Science, 1960; View from a Height, 1963; Kite that Won the Revolution, 1963; Human Brain, 1964; A Short History of Biology, 1964; Quick and Easy Math, 1964; Adding a Dimension, 1964; A Short History of Chemistry, 1965; The Greeks, 1965; Of Time and Space and Other Things, 1965; The New Intelligent Man's Guide to Science, 1965; An Easy Introduction to the Slide Rule, 1965; Fantastic Voyage, 1966; The Noble Gases, 1966; The Neutrino, 1966; The Roman Republic, 1967; Understanding Psyics, 1966; Is Anyone There?, 1967; To the Ends of the Universe, 1967; Mars, 1967; Egyptians, 1967; Asimov's Mysteries, 1968; Science, Numbers and I, 1968; Stars, 1968; Galaxies, 1968; A Whiff of Death, 1968; Near East, 1968; Asimov's Guide to the Bible, vol. 1, 1968; The Dark Ages, 1968; Words from History, 1968; Photosynthesis, 1969; The Shaping of England, 1969; Twentieth Century Discovery, 1969; Nightfall and Other Stories, 1969; Asimov's Guide to the Bible, vol. 2, 1969; Opus 100, 1969; ABC's of Space, 1969; Great Ideas of Science, 1969; Solar System and Back, 1970; Asimov's Guide to Shakespeare (2 vol.), 1970; Constantinople, 1970; ABC's of the Ocean, 1970; Light, 1970. Address: Oliver Cromwell Hotel 3-K 12 W 72d St New York City NY 10023

ASKEW, HAROLD COCHRAN, educator; b. Hattiesburg, Miss., Dec. 10, 1923; s. John Wells and Carrie Elizabeth (Cochran) A.; B.S., U. Chgo., 1947; D.D.S., Washington U., 1951; M.S., U. Ala., 1958; m. Billy Jacquelin Childers, Feb. 2, 1952; 1 dau., Lenora Jean. Pvt. practice dentistry, Hattiesburg, 1954-55; prof. dentistry U. Ala. at Birmingham Sch. Dentistry, also chmn. dept. odontology, 1958—. Served with AAC, 1943-46, with Dental Corps. USAF, 1951-54. Mem. Am. Dental Assn., Internat. Assn. Dental Research, Am. Prosthodontics Soc. Home: 2200 Garland Dr Birmingham AL 35216

ASKEW RALPH KIRK, Jr., art dealer; b. Kansas City, Mo., Nov. 19, 1903; s. R. Kirk and Marion (Ess) A.; grad. Phillips (Andover) Acad., 1921; student architecture Mass. Inst. Tech., 1921-23; B.S., Harvard, 1925, postgrad. history of art, 1926-27; m. Constance Atwood, May 18, 1929; children—Pamela, Phoebe (Mrs. Des Marals), Atwood (Mrs. Charles Allaire). Agt., Durlacher Bros., art dealers, London and N.Y.C., 1927-37, owner, 1937-; specializes in old and modern paintings and drawings. Publisher: Oedipus by Meyer Schapiro with original etchings by Kurt Seligmann, 1944; also definitive catalogues on loan exhbns. of Tintoretto, Poussin, Claude, Magnasco, Caravaggio and the Caravaggisti, Domenico Fetti, others. Home: RD 1 East Greenville PA 18041 Office: 110 E 57th St New York City NY 10022

ASKEW, REUBIN O'DONOVAN, gov. of Fla.; b. Muskogee, Okla., Sept. 11, 1928; s. Leo Goldberg and Alberta (O'Donovan) A.; B.S., Fla. State U., 1951; LL.B., U. Fla., 1956; m. Donna Lou Harper, Aug. 11, 1956; children—Angela Adair, Kevin O'Donovan. Admitted to Fla. bar, 1956; pvt. practice law, Pensacola, Fla., 1956-70; gov. Fla., 1970—. Asst. solicitor Escambia County, 1956-58; mem. Fla. Ho. Reps., 1958-62, Fla. Senate, 1962-70. Mem. Fla. Exec. Com. Tb and Health Assn., 1960-65, Children's Home Soc., 1965-70. Served with AUS, 1946-47, to capt. USAF, 1946-53. Mem. Fla., Am. bar assns., Am. Legion. Democrat. Presbyn. (elder 1960—). Mason, Rotarian. Home: Governor's Mansion Tallahassee FL 32303 Office: The Capitol Tallahassee FL 32304

ASKEW, WILLIAM CLARENCE, historian, educator; b. Hamilton, Ga., Nov. 23, 1910; s. John David and Sallie (Dean) A.; A.B., Mercer U., 1931; M.A., Duke, 1934, Ph.D., 1936; m. Alice Washburn, Dec. 30, 1936; 1 dau., Elizabeth Anne. Prin., Cataula (Ga.) Sch., 1931-33; instr. U. Ark., 1936-39, asst. prof., 1939-43; asst. prof. Colgate U., Hamilton, N.Y., 1946-49, asso. prof., 1949-55, prof. history, 1955—, chmn. dept., 1967-69; vis. lectr. history U. Tex., summer 1949; vis. prof. history Duke, summer 1962, U. Ky., summer 1965; asso. Columbia Seminar on Modern Italy, 1966—. Served to lt. comdr. USNR, 1943-46. John Simon Guggenheim Meml. fellow, 1952, Fulbright grant for Italy, 1952-54. Mem. Am. Assn. U. Profs., Am. Hist. Assn., Soc. for Italian Hist. Studies, N.Y. State Assn. European Historians (pres. 1970-71), Phi Beta Kappa, Pi Kappa Phi, Phi Alpha Theta. Democrat. Baptist. Author: Europe and Italy's Acquisition of Libya, 1911-1912, 1942. Co-editor, contbr. Power, Public Opinion and Diplomacy, 1959. Contbr. articles profl. jours. Home: 9 E Kendrick Av Hamilton NY 13346

ASKEY, EDWIN VINCENT, surgeon; b. Sligo, Pa., Aug. 15, 1895; s. Edwin Nelson and Pauline (Williams) A.; B.S., Allegheny Coll., 1917, D.Sc., 1958; M.D., U. Pa., 1921; L.H.D., Cal. Coll. Medicine, 1963; m. Martha Kirk Nebinger, July 10, 1923; children—Jane Elizabeth (Mrs. Walter Edwin Moore, Jr.), Edwin Vincent, David Harrison. Surgeon, Los Angeles, 1924—. Mem. bd. edn., Los Angeles, 1937-43, pres., 1941. Diplomate Am. Bd. Surgery. Fellow A.C.S.; mem. A.M.A. (speaker ho. of dels. 1955—, nat. pres. 1960-61), Cal. (past pres.), Los Angeles County (past pres.) med. assns., Los Angeles Surg. Soc., Alpha Omega Alpha, Delta Tau Delta, Alpha Chi Sigma, Nu Sigma Nu. Methodist. Address: 757 Malcolm Av Los Angeles CA 90024

ASKIN, SIMON, corp. exec.; b. Charlotte, N.C., Mar. 18, 1910; s. Charles and Goldie (Nairin) A.; B.S. Lehigh U., 1932; m. Lucille Bunin, Dec. 24, 1939; children—Neil Zachary, Glenn Nairn. Vice pres., dir. Heyden Chem. Corp., 1948-52, pres. 1952-57; pres., chief exec. officer Heyden Newport Chem. Corp. (merger of Heyden Chem. Co. and Newport Industries, Inc.; name changed to Tenneco Chems., Inc. 1965), 1957-65, pres., dir., 1965-66; vice chmn. bd. Tenneco, Inc., 1966-70, exec. v.p., 1970—; chmn. bd., pres. Tenneco Properties, Inc.; chmn. bd. Tenneco Realty, Inc., Tenneco West, Inc., Heggblade-Marguleas-Tenneco, Cal. Almonds, Inc., Cal. Date Co., Wheeler Ridge Farming Co., Stockdale Devel. Corp., Pine Mountain Club; dir. Tenn. Gas Transmission Co., Tenneco Oil, Tenneco Chems., Inc., Petro-Tex Chem. Corp., Packaging Corp. Am., Palmetto Corp., J. I. Case Co., Newport News Shipbldg. & Dry Dock Co., Walker Mfg., Deepsea Ventures, Inc.; adv. bd. Chase Manhattan Bank. Fellow Inst. Dirs. (Eng.); mem. Fgn. Policy Assn., Nat. Indsl. Conf. Bd., Synthetic Organic Chem. Mfrs. Assn., Soc. Chem. Industry, Am. Ordnance Assn. (mem.-at-large council), Newcomen Soc. N.Am., Pi Lambda Phi. Clubs: Chemists', Ramada (Houston); Pinnacle, Sales Executives of N.Y.; Board Room, Raffles, Economic (N.Y.). Home: 2016 Main St Houston TX 77002 Office: 1010 Milam St Houston TX 77002

ASKWITH, HERBERT, editor, pub. relations counselor; b. Boston, May 6, 1889; s. Barry and Gertrude (Aron) A.; A.B. magna cum laude, Harvard, 1907; m. Margaret A. Long, June 30, 1910; children—Bertram, Edna Abbey, Jean, Marjorie Louise. Asst. English, comparative lit. Harvard, 1907; mem. editorial staff Good Health Pub. Co., Battle Creek, Mich., 1908-12; publ. mgr. The Independent, N.Y.C., 1916-21; editor, pub. World Rev., 1922-26; v.p. Horace Liveright, Inc., book publishers, 1927-29; pub. relations counselor, N.Y.C., 1935—; cons. to pres. New Haven R.R., 1954-56. Mem. N.Y. Gov.'s Panel Commuting Problems, 1959; initiator plan r.r. terminal and shopping center New Rochelle, N.Y.; chmn. Westchester Commuters Group; mem. Larchmont Park Commn.; promotion Garden of a Million Tulips, N.Y. World's Fair, 1939. Twice recipient Bowdoin Lit. prize Harvard. Mem. Phi Beta Kappa. Clubs: Harvard (Westchester); Publicity (v.p.) (N.Y.C.). Author: Encyclopedic Guide to Garden Flowers and Garden Planning; Seven Keys To A Happy Retirement; A Common-Sense Guide to Children's Reading. Editor: Macaulay's Life of Johnson: Boswell's Johnson (Modern Library Giants): Keeping Mentally Fit (Jastrow); (with Arnold Herrick) This Way to Unity. Author mag., newspaper articles. Lectr.; frequent radio-TV guest speaker. Home: 57 N Chatsworth Av Larchmont NY 10538 Office: 545 Fifth Av New York City NY 10016

ASLESON, JOHAN ARNOLD, educator; b. Stoughton, Wis., Sept. 13, 1918; s. Jacob A. and Clara (Gunderson) A.; B.S., U. Wis., 1942, M.S., 1947, Ph.D., 1957; m. Barbara Amble, Oct. 12, 1943; children—Stephen Johan, JoAnn, Carol Jane. Mem. faculty, research in soils Mont. State U., 1947-54, asst. to dir. Agrl. Expt. Sta., 1954-56, asst. dir. sta., 1956-58, asso. dir., 1958-62, dir. sta., 1962-65, dean agr., dir. Agrl. Expt. Sta., 1965—. Dir. Gallatin Nat. Life Ins. Co., Bozeman. Served with AUS, 1942, USNR, 1943-45. Mem. A.A.A.S., Soil Sci. Soc. Am., Am. Soc. Agronomy, Sigma Xi, Alpha Zeta, Phi Kappa Phi. Rotarian. Home: 2419 Spring Creek Dr Bozeman MT 59715

ASLESON, ROBERT FREEMAN, pub. co. exec.; b. New Ulm, Minn., Oct. 11, 1935; s. Raymond and Florence Elvina (Anderson) A.; B.S., B.B.A., U. Minn., 1958, M.S. in Indsl. Engring., 1958; LL.B., George Washington U., 1961; m. Patricia Gail Starnes, Sept. 10, 1960; children—Robyn, Kristin, Gail. Asst. to pres. Xerox Corp., Rochester, N.Y., 1961-62, sales rep., N.Y.C., 1963-64; marketing mgr. Univ. Microfilms, a Xerox subsidiary, Ann Arbor, Mich., 1964-65, v.p. operations, 1966-67, gen. mgr., 1967-68, pres., 1969—; v.p. Xerox Edn. Group, 1971. Mem. citizens' adv. bd. St. Joseph's Hosp., 1970—. Campaign chmn. Ann Arbor United Fund, 1969, bd. dirs., 1969-70. Served with USNR, 1958-61. Recipient Distinguished Service award Ann Arbor Jr. C. of C., 1967. Mem. Tau Beta Pi, Pi Tau Sigma, Beta Gamma Sigma. Rotarian. Home: 2630 Englave Dr Ann Arbor MI 48103 Office: 300 N Zeeb Rd Ann Arbor MI 48106

ASMAN, ROBERT JOSEPH, mfg. co. exec.; b. St. Louis, Feb. 7, 1924; s. Robert J. and Anna M. (Spaeth) A.; student Holy Cross Coll., 1941-43; A.B., Cath. U. Am., 1948; LL.B., Georgetown U., 1951; m. Mary Elizabeth Kane, Sept. 8, 1948; children—Kathryn Anne, Robert Joseph III, Peter Kane, Teresa Elizabeth, Susan Marie, Elizabeth Jane. Admitted to D.C. bar, 1952, Ohio bar, 1961; asso. firm Cummings, Truitt & Reeves, Washington, 1956; trial atty. anti-trust div . Dept. Justice, 1952-53; asst. U.S. atty. D.C., 1953-60; counsel flight propulsion lab. dept. Gen. Electric Co., 1960-63; v.p., sec., gen. counsel Pneumo Dynamics Corp., Cleve., 1963-70; pres., chief exec. officer, exec. dir., Ohio State Bar Assn. Automated Research, Cleve. Mem. mental health planning com. Cleve. Welfare Fedn., 1966. Trustee Hill House, Cleve., 1964—, Cleve. Mental Health Assn., 1966-68, St. John's Coll. Served with AUS, 1943-45; ETO. Decorated Bronze Star. Mem. Am. Soc. Corp. Secretaries, Am., Fed., D.C., Ohio bar assns., Greater Cleve. Growth Assn., Phi Delta Phi. Clubs: Clevelander, Skating (Cleve.). Home: 2676 Berkshire Rd Cleveland Heights OH 44106 Office: Hanna Bldg Cleveland OH 44115

ASMUSSEN, SVEND, violinist; b. Copenhagen, Feb. 28, 1916. Profl. musician, 1933—; appeared in act known as Three Danes, 1960s; recording artist for Atlantic, Warner Bros. records. Address: care Warner Bros. Records, 4000 Warner Blvd Burbank, CA 91503.*

ASNER, EDWARD, actor; b. Kansas City, Mo., Nov. 15, 1929; s. Morris David and Lizzie (Seliger) A.; grad. high sch.; student U. Chgo., 1947-49; m. Nancy Lou Sykes, Mar. 23, 1959; children—Matthew and Liza (twins), Kathryn. Debut at Playwrights Theatre, Chgo., 1953; appeared on television, in Off-Broadway and Broadway shows, N.Y.C., 1955-61; appeared in numerous motion pictures and television shows, Los Angeles, 1961—; now appearing on Mary Tyler Moore Show, CBS-TV. Served with Signal Corps, U.S. Army, 1951-53. Office: care Jack Fields & Assos 9255 Sunset Blvd Los Angeles CA 90069

ASPER, SAMUEL PHILLIPS, physician, educator; b. Oak Park, Ill., July 14, 1916; s. Samuel Phillips and Amanda (Groth) A.; A.B., Baylor U., 1936; M.D., Johns Hopkins, 1940; fellow in medicine Harvard, 1941-42, 46-48; m. Ann Carver, Mar. 13, 1942; children—Ann Carver, Lucy Lawrence (Mrs. J.S. Wurts). Resident physician Johns Hopkins Hosp., 1948-49, physician, 1949—, v.p. for med. affairs, 1970—; prof. medicine Johns Hopkins U., 1960—, asso. dean Sch. Medicine, 1957-68. Trustee Baptist Home Md. Served to capt. M.C., AUS, 1942-45; ETO. Diplomate Am. Bd. Internal Medicine. Fellow A.C.P. (pres. 1969-70); mem. Am. Diabetes Assn., Endocrine Soc., Am. Soc. Clin. Investigation, Assn. Am. Physicians, Am. Clin. and Climatol. Assn., Interurban Med. Club, Peripatetic Club, Alpha Epsilon Delta, Alpha Omega Alpha. Baptist (trustee). Home: 213 Kemble Rd Baltimore MD 21218

ASPERGER, PAUL, lawyer; b. Tucson, Apr. 26, 1928; s. Otto and Dorothy (Heckman) A.; B.A., U. Cal. at Berkeley, 1949, J.D., 1952; m. Esther Weakley, July 23, 1950; children—James, Donald, Robert, Anne. Admitted to Cal. bar, 1953, since practiced in Fresno; partner firm Thomas, Snell, Jamison, Russell, Williamson & Asperger, Fresno, 1956—. Served with AUS, 1945. Mem. Am., Fresno, Kern County bar assns., State Bar of Cal., Am. Judicature Soc. Home: 5655 N Thorne St Fresno CA 93705 Office: Del Webb Bldg Fresno CA 93705

ASPIN, LES, congressman; b. Milw., July 21, 1938; s. Leslie and Marie (Orth) A.; B.A. summa cum laude, Yale, 1960; M.A., Oxford (Eng.) U., 1962; Ph.D., Mass. Inst. Tech., 1965; m. Maureen Shea, Jan. 11, 1969. Mem. staff Sen. William Proxmire, 1960, campaign dir., 1964; staff asst. to Walter Heller chmn. Pres. Kennedy's Council Econ. Advisers, 1963; mem. 92d Congress 1st Wis. Dist. Served to capt. AUS, 1966-68. Mem. Jr. C. of C., Am. Legion, Phi Beta Kappa. Episcopalian. Home: 206 15th St #11 Racine WI 53403 Office: Cannon Office Bldg Washington DC 20515

ASPINALL, CARL EDWARD, food co. exec.; b. Lima, O., Sept. 7, 1934; s. Derward Ernst and Genevieve Beatrice (Arnold) A.; B.S. in Bus. Adminstrn., Miami U., Oxford, O., 1956; m. Mary Lou Allshouse, June 16, 1956; children—Scott Edward, Mark Steven, Todd Carlton. Staff accountant Arthur Andersen & Co., C.P.A.'s, Chgo., 1958-62; accounting mgr. Curtiss Candy Co., Chgo., 1962-66; mgmt. finance Booz, Allen & Hamilton, Inc., mgmt. cons., Chgo., 1966-68; v.p. Hollywood Brands div. Consol. Foods Corp., Centralia, Ill., 1968-70; corporate controller Am. Bakeries Co., Chgo., 1970—. Served to 1st lt. USMCR, 1956-58. Mem. Financial Execs. Inst., Delta Tau Delta. Elk. Club: Torguatus Gun (Chgo.). Home: 2400 Greenwood Av Wilmette IL 60091 Office: 10 S Riverside Plaza Chicago IL 60606

ASPINALL, OWEN STEWART, gov. Am. Samoa; b. Grand Junction, Colo., Sept. 21, 1927; s. Wayne N. and Julia (Kuns) A.; B.A., U. Denver, 1949; LL.B., American U., 1955; m. Taotafa Lutu, Dec. 24, 1966; 1 son, Robert Stewart. Admitted to D.C. bar, 1955, Colo. bar, 1956, Am. Samoa bar, 1962; dep. dist. atty Mesa County, Colo., 1957-61; atty. gen. Am. Samoa, 1961-62, territorial sec., 1962-67, gov., 1967—. Chmn. Mesa County chpt. A.R.C., 1959-61. Served with AUS, World War II. Mem. Am., Colo., Am. Samoa bar assns., Am. Legion, Beta Theta Pi, Delta Theta Phi. Lion (dist. gov. 1961). Home: Govt House Pago Pago American Samoa

ASPINALL, WAYNE NORVIEL, congressman; b. Middleburg, O., Apr. 3, 1896; s. Mack and Jessie Edna (Norviel) A.; A.B., U. of Denver, 1919; LL.B., Denver Law Sch., 1925; LL.D., U. Alaska, U. Denver, Colo. State U., also Colo. Sch. Mines; m. Julia E.Kuns, (dec. July 1969); children—Wayne Norviel, Owen Stewart, Richard Daniel, Ruth JoAnne (Mrs. Essie Jeffers Best). Admitted to Colo. bar, 1925; practiced law, also engaged in peach orchard industry; mem. Colo. Ho. of Reps., 1931-38, speaker, 1937, 38; state senator, 1939-48; mem. 81st to 92d congresses, 4th Colo. Dist.; chmn. Interior and Insular Affairs Com., Pub. Land Law Rev. Commn.; mem. Joint Com. Atomic Energy. Apptd. mem. Mo. Basin Survey Commn. by Pres. Truman. Served with Signal Corps, AUS, World War I; capt., assigned to mil. govt. service, World War II; legal expert with U.S. and English forces; participated in Normandy drive as Am. officer with Brit. 2d Army. Mem. Am., Colo., Mesa County bar assns., Am. Legion, 40 and 8. Democrat. Meth. Mason (33, K.T., Shriner), Odd Fellow, Elk, Lion. Home: Palisade CO Office: Rayburn House Office Bldg Washington DC 20515

ASPINWALL, ROBERT ASHTON, aviation co. exec.; b. Bklyn., Apr. 13, 1915; s. John Ashton and Susan (Boggs) A.; student Pace Coll., 1932-36; C.P.A., N.Y., 1939; m. Marguerite DuBois Abrew, Oct. 7, 1939; children—Carol (Mrs. Martin C. Miller), John Forest, Susan Edith. Pub. accountant Hurdman & Cranstoun, N.Y.C., 1935-43; asst. gen. mgr. Sikorsky Aircraft Co., 1943-58; gen. mgr. Norden div. United Aircraft Corp., 1958-62, asst. treas. United Aircraft Corp., 1962-65, treas., 1965—; dir. United Aircraft Internat. Inc.; adv. bd. Hartford Nat. Bank and Trust; incorporator Farmington Savs. Bank. Bd. dirs. Farmington Found.; incorporator Hartford Hosp. Mem. Financial Exec. Inst., Am. Soc. C.P.A.'s. Home: 16 Main St Farmington, CT 06032. Office: United Aircraft Corp Hartford CT 06108

ASPIS, SAMUEL LOUIS, physician, hosp. adminstr.; b. N.Y.C., June 1, 1916; s. Morris Benjamin and Emma (Liverant) A.; B.S., Coll. City N.Y., 1937; M.D., Middlesex U., Waltham, Mass., 1941; m. Laura Elizabeth King, June 3, 1943. Intern, then resident Beth David Hosp., N.Y.C.; with VA, 1946—, chief staff, VA Hosp., Birmingham,

Ala., 1955-57, VA Hosp., Poplar Bluff, Mo., 1957-59, dir. VA Hosp., Kansas City, Mo., 1959-67, VA Hosp., Cleve., 1967—. Chmn. Fed. Exec. Bd., 1966; mem. exec. com. A.R.C., Cleve. Trustee U. Circle, Cleve. Served with M.C., AUS, 1942-46. Decorated Bronze Star. Fellow Am. Coll. Hosp. Adminstrs.; mem. A.M.A., Jackson County Med. Soc., Am. Hosp. Assn., Mo. Pub. Health Assn., Mil. Order World Wars. Address: 10701 East Blvd Cleveland OH 44106

ASPLIN, EDWARD WILLIAM, packaging co. exec.; b. Mpls., June 25, 1922; s. John E. and Alma (Carlbom) A.; B.B.A., U. Minn., 1943; postgrad, U. Mich., 1947-48, Wayne State, 1949-50, Rutgers U. Sch. Banking, 1957-59; m. Eleanor Young Rodgers, Oct. 20, 1951; children—Sarah E., William R., Lynn E. Cost accountant Nat. Bank Detroit, 1947-50; asst. v.p. adminstrn. Northwest Bancorp., Mpls., 1950-59; v.p. marketing Northwestern Nat. Bank, Mpls., 1959-67; v.p. organizational planning Bemis Co., Inc., Mpls., 1967—, also dir. Active Mpls. Assn. for Mentally Retarded Children, Urban Coalition. Bd. dirs. Eitel Hosp. Served with USNR, 1943-46. Clubs: Hazeltine Golf (dir.) (Chaska, Minn.); Minneapolis. Home: 17524 Hampton Ct Minnetonka MN 55343 Office: 800 Northstar Center Minneapolis MN 55402

ASPLUND, HANS, architect; b. Stockholm, Sweden, Aug. 16, 1921; s. Gunnar and Gerda (Sellman) A.; m. Dagny Bjorner, 1946. With UN archtl. officer, N.Y.C., 1947-48; pvt. archtl. practice, 1950—; chmn. Swedish Archtl. Soc., 1959-62; architect for ofcl. projects bldgs. in Peru, Sudan, Kuwait, also civic hall, Eslöv, 1957, department store, Stockholm, 1962, parking garage, Stockholm, 1964. Prof. Faculty Architecture U. Lund (Sweden). Mem. Bldg. Soc. So. Sweden (pres.), Royal Acad. Art, Stockholm. Address: Borgeby Slott 23050 Bjerred Sweden

ASPLUND, TORE, artist; b. Stockholm, Sweden, July 16, 1903; s. Arvid and Dagmar (Moltrecht) A.; brought to U.S., 1904, naturalized, 1930; student Art Students League, Nat. Acad., Grand Central Art Sch.; unmarried. Mem. faculty Nat. Acad. Design Sch. Fine Arts. Water color mural, also teakwood mural Bank of N.Y.; executed mural for N.Y. Telephone Co., 1969. Served as combat artist, U.S. Coast Guard, rating, chief boatswain's mate. Recipient Zabriskie purchase prize, Am. Water Color Soc.; Audubon purchase prize, Audubon artist Busch prize, Allied Artists; Sonn, Shaw and Ididor prizes, Salmagundi Club; Adolph & Clara Obrig award, Nat. Acad., 1956; Lena Newcastle Meml. award, 1956, Herb Olsen award, American Watercolor Society, 1957; Gold Medal Honor, National Arts Club, 1969. N.A. Mem. Am. Water Color Soc., Audubon Artists, Allied Artists. Clubs: Philadelphia Water Color, Salamagundi. Home: 10 E 16th St New York City NY 10003 Studio 853 Broadway New York City NY 10003

ASPREY, WINIFRED ALICE, educator; b. Sioux City, Ia., Apr. 8, 1917; d. Peter and Gladys (Brown) Asprey; A.B., Vassar Coll., 1938; M.S., State U. Ia., 1943, Ph.D., 1945. Student tchr. Brearley Sch., N.Y.C., 1938-40; tchr. Girls Latin Sch., Chgo., 1940-42; asst. instr. math. State U. Ia., 1942-45; faculty math. Vassar Coll., Poughkeepsie, N.Y., 1945—, prof., chmn. dept., 1958-62; now Elizabeth Stillamn Williams prof. math., dir. Computer Center; vis. asso. math. Ednl. Testing Service, summer 1959; dir. an acad. year inst. in math. under N.Y. State Edn. Dept., 1962-63, computer inst. high sch. tchrs., 1964, 66, 67; vis. prof. on exchange program IBM, Poughkeepsie, 1969-70. Bassar Coll. fellow, 1950-51; NSF grantee summer inst., Eugene, Ore., 1954, U. Cal. at Los Angeles, 1962; IBM post-doctoral indsl. research fellow, 1957-58; NSF faculty fellow, 1964-65. Fellow A.A.A.S., Ia. Acad. Sci.; mem. American Math. Soc., Math. Assn. Am., Soc. Indsl. and Applied Math., Am. Assn. U. Profs., Ia. Acad. Scis., Am. Statis. Assn., Assn. Computing Machinery (nat. lectr. 1970-71), Nat. Council Tchrs. Math., Phi Beta Kappa, Sigma Xi. Address: Computer Center Vassar Coll Poughkeepsie NY 12601

ASSARO, DOMINICK, mayor; b. Utica, N.Y., Apr. 8, 1926; s. Nicholas and Josephine (Sciortino) A.; grad. high sch. Mayor, Utica, 1968—. Mem. devel. com. Nat. League Cities-Conf. Mayors. K.C., Lion. Home: 629 Pleasant St Utica NY 13501 Office: City Hall Utica NY 13502

ASSELIN, PIERRE, Canadian govt. ofcl.; b. Montreal, Can., Jan. 14, 1910; s. Oliver and Alice (LeBoutillier) A.; B.A., U. Montreal, 1931, M.Commerce, 1934; m. Marcelle Lacroix, Dec. 12, 1936; children—Huguette (Mrs. J.B. Smith), Michelle (Mrs. J.E. Hyndman), Andre, Marie (Mrs. Jean Maury), Pierre. Engaged in newspaper mgmt., 1934-36; sec. Que. Dept. Lands and Forests, 1936-48; pvt. sec. to prime minister Can., 1949-58; with Dept. External Affairs, Ottawa, 1958-65; consul gen. in San Francisco; now consul gen. in New Orleans. Office: Canadian Consulate 2 Canal St New Orleans LA 70130

ASSELL, LEO NICHOLAS, railroad ofcl.; b. Aurora, Ill., Dec. 22, 1916; s. Frank Albert and Elizabeth (Reuland) A.; student Met. Bus. Coll., Aurora, 1936; m. Viola Marie Wallers, June 14, 1941; children—Diane (Mrs. Robert H. Tuma), Kenneth, Robert Michael. With C., B. & O. R.R., 1936—, asst. sec., asst. treas., 1962-64, sec.-treas., 1964—; treas. Burlington No. Inc., 1970—; treas., asst. sec., dir. St. Louis and Kansas City Land Co., 1964—; treas. Burlington Truck Lines, Inc., Glacier Park Co., Keokuk Union Depot Co., Ore., Cal. & Eastern Ry. Co., Ore. Electric Ry. Co., Ore. Trunk Ry., Paducah & Ill. R.R. Co., Ruth Realty Co., Spokane, Portland & Seattle Ry. Co., Walla Walla Valley Ry. Co.; asst. sec., treas. Winona Bridge Ry. Co., 1964—; asst. treas. Burlington Equipment Co., 1964—. Treas. Burlington No. Found. Mem. Ill. C. of C., Chgo. Assn. Commerce and Industry. Home: 527 Aberdeen Dr St Paul MN Office: 176 E 5th St St Paul MN

AST, RAYMOND JOHN, Jr., educator; b. Buffalo, N.Y., Sept. 4, 1918; s. Raymond John and Meroita (Andrle) A.; B.Ed., State U. Coll. N.Y., 1939, M.Ed., 1940; student Columbia U. Tchrs. Coll., 1946-51; m. Doris A. Paynter, Oct. 11, 1943; 1 son, Richard J. Tchr. secondary sch. history Morristown (N.Y.) High Sch., 1940-42; tchr. secondary sch. history Amherst Central High Sch., Snyder, N.Y., 1942-43; tchr. social studies Maplewood Jr. High Sch., Maplewood, N.J., 1946-65; adminstr. So. Orange Maplewood (N.J.) Adult Sch., 1947-66; field dir. N.J. Council on Economic Edn. Montclair State Coll., 1965-66, adminstr. adult continuing edn. center, 1966—; project dir. Spl. Demonstration Adult Basic Edn. Learning Center Project Office of Adult Edn. N.J. Dept. Edn., Upper Montclair, N.J., 1968-70; project dir. Nat. Multimedia Center for Adult Basic Edn., Washington, 1970—. Mem. Nat. adv. com. Project Step-up, San Diego Community Colls., 1970-71. Bd. dirs. Inst. for Lifetime Learning, Long Beach, Cal.; bd. dirs. Adult Edn. Action Council. Served with AUS, 1943-46. Mem. adult edn. assns. N.J., U.S., Assn. Adult Edn., Nat. Assn. Pub. Continuing Adult Edn., N.J. Edn. Assn., N.J. State Coll. Faculty Assn., Am. Assn. U. Profs., Essex County Edn. Assn., Phi Delta Kappa, Delta Kappa. Home: 74 Woodland Av Verona NJ 07044 Office: Adult Continuing Edn Center Montclair State Coll Upper Montclair NJ 07043

ASTAIRE, FRED, actor and dancer; b. Omaha, Neb., May 10, 1899; s. Frederic and Ann (Gelius) A.; ed. pub. schs.; m. Phyllis Baker, July 12, 1933 (died 1954); children—Fred, Ava, Peter Potter (step-son). Co-starred with sister as team of Fred and Adele (Mrs. Kingman Douglas) Astaire, 1916-32; appeared in Over the Top, Passing Show of 1918, Apple Blossoms, Lady Be Good, The Bandwagon, Funny Face, following sister's marriage to Lord Charles Cavendish, starred alone in musical comedies later motion pictures, including Gay Divorcee, Roberta, Follow the Fleet, Swingtime, Top Hat, Shall We Dance?, Damsel in Distress, Carefree, The Story of Vernon and Irene Castle, Broadway Melody of 1940, Second Chorus, You'll Never Get Rich, Holiday Inn, You Were Never Lovelier, The Sky's the Limit, The Ziegfeld Follies', Yolanda and the Thief, Blue Skies, Easter Parade, Barkleys of Broadway, Three Little Words, Let's Dance, Royal Wedding, The Belle of New York, The Bandwagon, Daddy Long Legs, Silk Stockings, Funny Face, On the Beach, The Pleasure of His Company, Notorious Landlady, Finian's Rainbow, 1967 Midas Run, 1968; star Fred Astaire Show, 1968; appeared on TV in It Takes A Thief; starred in TV specials; host, occasional star Alcoa Premier. Recipient 9 Emmy awards; Acad. award for raising standards all musicals, 1949. Episcopalian. Clubs: Racquet and Tennis, Lambs, The Brook (N.Y.C.). Author: Steps In Time, 1950.‡

ASTIN, ALLEN VARLEY, physicist; b. Salt Lake City, June 12, 1904; s. John Andrew and Catherine (Varlye) A.; A.B., U. Utah, 1925; M.S., N.Y.U., 1926, Ph.D., 1928; D.Sc., Lehigh U., 1953, Geo. Washington U., 1958, N.Y.U., 1960; m. Margaret L. Mackenzie, Aug. 31, 1927; children—John Allen, Alexander William. Nat. Research Council fellow Johns Hopkins, 1928-30; research asso. utilities research com. Nat. Bur. Standards, 1930-32, physicist, 1932-69, asst. chief ordnance devel. div., 1944-48, chief electronics and ordnance div., 1948-50, asso. dir., 1951-52, dir., 1952-69, dir. emeritus, 1969—, cons., chmn. inter-departmental com. scientific research and devel., 1954-55. Mem. NACA, 1952-58. Mem. Internat. Com. Weights and Measures, 1954-69, Naval Research Adv. Com., 1953-59, Def. Sci. Board, 1956-69; chmn. com. on fed. labs. Fed. Council Sci. and Tech., 1962-69; mem. Nat. Motor Vehicle Safety Adv. Council; U.S. coordinator U.S.-France Sci. Cooperation Program, 1969. Decorated President Certificate of Merit (U.S.); King's Medal (United Kingdom); recipient Rockefeller Pub. Service award; Distinguished Alumni award U. Utah, 1968; Standards medal Am. Nat. Standard Inst., 1969; Harry Diamond award I.E.E.E., 1970. Fellow Am. Phys. Soc., A.A.A.S., Inst. of Radio Engrs.; mem. Am. Soc. Testing Materials, Am. Acad. Arts Scis., Instrument Soc. Am., Nat. Acad. Scis. (home sec. 1971), Am. Philos. Soc., Washington Philos. Soc., Washington Acad. Scis., Am. Ordnance Assn., Inst. of Aeronautical Scis., Armed Forces Electronics and Communications Assn., Standards Engr. Soc. (hon.), Am. Dental Assn. (hon.), Am. Soc. Heating, Ventilating and Air Conditioning Engrs., Sigma Xi, Phi Kappa Phi. Club: Cosmos. Home: 5008 Battery Lane Bethesda MD 20014

ASTMAN, JOSEPH GUSTAV, educator; b. Willimantic, Conn., Nov. 8, 1916; s. Joseph and Helen (Mueller) A.; B.A., Trinity Coll., Hartford, Conn., 1938; M.A., Yale, 1942, Ph.D., 1948; grantee Am. Council Learned Socs., U. Mich., summer 1956; m. Dorothy Rennie, Dec. 31, 1941; children—Joseph Gustav 3d, William Rennie, Dorthe Rennie. Tchr. German Trinity Coll., 1941-42, 46-48; tchr. English and German Avon (Conn.) Old Farms Sch., 1942-43; tchr. German St. Joseph Coll., West Hartford, Conn., 1947-48; mem. faculty Hofstra U., Hempstead, N.Y., 1948—, prof. German, chmn. dept. fgn. langs. and lit., 1954-66, dean Coll. Liberal Arts and Scis., 1966—, dir. Nat. Def. Edn. Act Summer Lang. Inst., 1960-63. Asso. Yale Library, 1955—; dir. testing Modern Lang. Assn., N.Y.C., 1964-65; mem. Woodrow Wilson fellowship selcetion com., 1966-70; mem. Middle-States Evaluation Teams. Active local Boy Scouts Am., Little League, P.T.A. Mem. bd. Friends Nassau County Hist. Mus. Bd. fellows Trinity Coll., Hartford. Served with AUS, 1944-46; ETO. Mem. Am. Assn. U. Profs. (pres. Hofstra chpt. 1951-52), Modern Lang. Assn. Am., Assn. Tchrs. Slavic E. European Langs. (v.p. N.Y. State 1951-55), Nat. Assn. Standard Med. Vocabulary, Am. Legion (past post vice comdr.), Early Trades and Crafts Soc., Maynard Hill Hist. Soc. (charter), Sigma Kappa Alpha, Sigma Delta Pi. Contbr. articles in field. Home: 2 Border Lane Levittown NY 11756 Office: Hofstra U Hempstead Turnpike Hempstead NY 11550

ASTON, A.D., Sr., savs. and loan assn. exec. Pres., San Fernando Valley Fed. Savs. and Loan Assn. Office: 6842 Van Nuys Blvd Van Nuys CA 91405*

ASTON, JAMES WILLIAM, banker; b. Farmersville, Tex., Oct. 6, 1911; s. Joe A. and Jimmie Gertrude (Jackson) A.; B.S. in C. E., A.&M. U. Tex., 1933; m. Sarah Camilla Orth, June 29, 1935; 1 son, James William. Asst. city mgr., Dallas, 1935-39, city mgr., 1939-41; city mgr., Bryan, Tex., 1939; v.p. Republic Nat. Bank of Dallas 1945-55, exec. v.p., 1955-57, dir., pres., 1957-65, chmn., chief exec. officer, dir., 1965—; dir. Am. Airlines, Inc., Lone Star Steel Co., Gen Portland Cement Co., Times Mirror Co., Zale Corp., Group Hosp. Service, Inc., Group Med., Surg. Service Neuhoff Brothers Packers, Gibraltar Life Ins. Co. of Am., Dallas Times Herald. Mem. Greater Dallas Planning Council; treas. City of Dallas. Trustee, treas., Tex. Research Found.; trustee Wadley Insts. Molecular Medicine, S.W. Legal Found., Hoblitzelle Found.; dir., treas. State Fair Texas; bd. govs. So. Meth. U., United Way of Am. Served from lt. to col. USAAF, 1941-45; air. orgn. planning, hdqrs. A.A.F., asst. chief, later chief staff Air Transport Command. Awarded D.S.M., Legion of Merit. Registered profl. engr. Mem. Nat. Indsl. Conf. Bd., Assn. Res. City Bankers, Trinity Improvement Assn. (v.p.), Newcomen Soc. N. Am., Am. Bankers Assn. (exec. council 1965-68), Tex. Bankers Assn. (past pres.), Internat. C. of C. (trustee U.S. council), Tau Beta Phi. Mem. Christian Ch. Clubs: City, Dallas, Northwood Country, Athletic, Petroleum Country, Dallas Country (Dallas); Army-Navy Country (Washington); Brook, Marco Polo (N.Y.C.); Preston Trail Golf; Lancers; Las Colinas Country; Chaparral, Southwest; Cherokee (Longview, Tex.). Home: 5000 Royal Lane Dallas TX 75229 Office: PO Box 5961 Dallas TX 75222

ASTON, R.G., advt. agy. exec. Sr. v.p., sec., treas. McCann Erickson Advt. of Can. Ltd. Office: Britannica House 151 Bloor W Toronto 5 Ontario Canada*

ASTON, RICHARD DOUGLAS, savs. and loan exec.; b. Bakersfield, Cal., July 8, 1901; s. Frank C. and Grace (Rigby) A.; student Cal. State Poly., 1920-21, U. Cal. at Berkeley, 1921-24; m. Ruth Elizabeth Hoffman, Jan. 1, 1924; 1 son, Robert D. Asst. mgr. Oak Knoll br. Security First Nat. Bank, Pasadena, Cal., 1924-28; sec.-treas. West Coast Bond & Mortgage Co., Pasadena, 1928-41, exec. v.p., 1945-49, pres., 1949—; sec.-treas. Mut. Savs. & Loan Assn., Pasadena, 1930-41, cons., 1941-45, exec. v.p., 1945-49, pres., 1949-59, chmn. bd., pres., 1959-61, chmn. bd., 1961—; pres. Wesco Financial Corp., 1959-61, chmn. bd., 1961—. Served to maj. AUS, 1941-45. Clubs: Rotary, University, Annandale Golf (Pasadena). Home: 1015 Fallen Leaf Rd Arcadia, CA 91006. Office: 315 E Colorado Blvd Pasadena CA 91109

ASTOR, GERALD MORTON, journalist; b. New Haven, Aug. 3, 1926; s. Louis and Leah (Cohen) A.; A.B., Princeton, 1949; grad. student Columbia, 1949-51; m. Sonia Judith Sacoder, Nov. 23, 1949; children—Theodore Alan, Laurence Philip, Andrew Michael. Researcher, writer Look mag., 1951-54; writer, picture editor Sports Illustrated, 1954-62; editor Sat. Eve. Post, 1962-63; sr. editor Look mag., 1963—. Chmn. Scarsdale Fair Housing Group, 1962-63; cons. Nat. Adv. Commn. Civil Disorder, 1967. Served with AUS, 1944-46. Recipient Albert Lasker Med. Journalism award, 1966, Best Mag. Sports Story award, 1966. Mem. N.Y. Newspaper Guild (chmn. Look unit 1966—), Phi Beta Kappa. Author: The New York Cops, 1971. Home: 50 Sprain Valley Rd Scarsdale, NY 10583. Office: 488 Madison Av New York City NY 10022

ASTOR, MARY LUCILE LANGHANKE, actress; b. Quincy, Ill., May 3, 1906; d. Otto and Helen (Vasconcellos) Langhanke; ed. pub. schs. and pvt. tutors; m. Kenneth Hawks, Feb. 28, 1928 (dec. 1930); m. 2d, Dr. Franklyn Thrope, June 29, 1931 (div. 1935); 1 dau., Marylyn Hauoli; m. 3d, Manuel del Campo, Feb. 18, 1937 (div. 1942); 1 son, Anthony Paul; m. 4th Thomas G. Wheelock, Dec. 24, 1945. Appeared in numerous motion pictures, 1920—, including Beau Brummel, Ladies Love Brutes, Lost Squadron, Red Dust, World Changes, Page Miss Glory, Dodsworth, The Prisoner of Zenda, The Hurricane, 1937, Listen Darling, Midnight, 1938, Brigham YoungFrontiersman, 1940, The Great Lie, 1941, Maltese Falcon, Across the Pacific, 1942, Fiesta, Claudia and David, Meet Me in St. Louis, Desert Fury, The Rich Full Life, Act of Violence, Little Women, Return to Peyton Place, Hush, Hush Sweet Charlotte; actress appearing various roles in stage plays; Among the Married, Tonight at Eight Thirty, The Male Animal, Time of the Cuckoo, Don Juan in Hell (on the road), Starcross Story (on Broadway); dramatic roles TV shows, 1953—. Recipient Oscar for best supporting role in The Great Lie, 1941. Author: Mary Astor, My Story; The Incredible Charlie Carewe, The Image of Kate; The O'Conners; Goodbye Darling-Be Happy!; Place Called Saturday, 1968. Home: Malibu CA 90265

ASTOR, MRS. VINCENT, trustee Metropolitan Mus. Art. Former feature editor House and Garden. Vice chmn. State Park Commn. N.Y.; mem. Art Commn. City N.Y. Pres. Vincent Astor Found.; trustee N.Y. Pub. Library, N.Y. U., Pacific Bot. Tropical Garden. Recipient plaque achievement for contbg. to enhancement N.Y., Women's Aux. A.I.A., 1968. Author: Patchwork Child; The Bluebird Is At Home. Office: Met Mus Art Fifth Av at 82d St New York City NY 10028

ASTROLOGES, FRANK A., pres. Oak Electro/Neties Corp., 1968—. Address: Oak Electro/Neties Corp Chrystal Lake, IL 60014.*

ASTROM, C. SVERKER, Swedish diplomat; b. Uppsala, Sweden, Dec. 30, 1915; s. John and Brita (Kugelberg) A.; B.A., U. Uppsala, 1935, LL.B., 1939. Joined Swedish Fgn. Service, 1939; assigned Moscow, USSR, 1940-43, Fgn. Ministry, 1943-46, Washington, 1946-48, Stockholm, 1948-53, London, Eng., 1953-56; head polit. dept. Ministry Fgn. Affairs, 1956-64; permanent rep. Sweden to UN, 1964-70; chief Swedish negotiator for entry into Common Market, Stockholm, 1970—. Office: care Swedish Foreign Service Stockholm Sweden

ASTURIAS, MIGUEL ANGEL, author; b. Oct. 19, 1899; ed. Inst. Nacional de Guatemala, U. de Guatemala, also U. de Paris a la Sorbonne. Founder Gen. Students Assn. Guatemala, also U. Popular de Guatemala; founder periodical El Diario del Aire; cultural attache Guatemalan embassy, Mexico, 1946-47; minister-counsellor counsellor embassy, Buenos Aires, 1947-52; minister, Paris, 1952-53; ambassador to El Salvador, 1953, to France, 1966—; lectr. on lit., S. Am. and Europe. Recipient Prix Sylla Mnosegur, Paris, 1931; Pris du Meilleur Roman Etranger, Paris, 1952; Lenin Peace prize, 1966; Nobel prize in lit., 1967. Author: El Problema Social del Indio, 1923 (lectures) Argultecture de la Vida Nueva, 1928; Leyendas de Guatemala, 1930; El Senor Presidente, 1946; (poetry) Sien de Alondra, 1948; Hombres de Maiz, 1949; Viento Fuerete, 1950; El Papa Verde, 1953; Week-End en Guatemala, 1955; Los Ojos de los Enterrados, 1960; El Alha Jadito, 1961; Mulata de Tal, 1963; Antologia Teatral, 1964; (poem) Clarivigilia Primaveral, 1965; Le Miroir de Lida Sal, 1967; Mulata, 1967; Strong Wind, 1969; Talking Machine, 1970; (essay) Latinoamerica y otros. ensayos, 1968. Address: rue de Courcelles 73 Paris 8e France*

ASTUTO, PHILIP LOUIS, educator; b. N.Y.C., Jan. 5, 1923; s. Salvatore and Anna (Insalaco) A.; B.A., St. John's U., 1943; M.A., Columbia, 1947, Ph.D., 1956; m. Natella M. Digia, July 4, 1953; children—Philip, Anne Marie. Mem. faculty St. John's U., 1947—, prof. Spanish, 1958—, dir. Latin Am. studies, 1957-60, chmn. dept. modern fgn. langs., 1961-65. Participant Prof.-Student Summer Seminar, sponsored State Dept., 1950. Served to 1st. lt., inf., AUS, 1943-46; ETO. Mem. Am. Assn. Tchrs. Spanish and Portuguese, Am. Hist. Assn., Assn. Latin Am. Studies Modern Lang. Assn. Contbr. articles profl. jours. Home: 11 Steuben Dr Jericho NY 11753 Office: St John's U Jamaica NY 11432

ASTWOOD, EDWIN BENNETT, physician; b. Bermuda, Dec. 29, 1909; s. Ernest Millard and Imogene C. (Doe) A.; B.S., Columbia Union Coll., 1929; student Loma Linda U., 1929-31; M.D. and C.M., McGill U. Med. Sch., 1934; fellow surgical path. lab., Johns Hopkins Hosp., 1935-37; Rockefeller Found. fellow, 1937-39; research fellow in biology Harvard, 1938-39, Ph.D., Harvard, 1939; Sc.D. (hon.), U. Chgo., 1967; m. Sara Merritt, June 3, 1937; children—Philip Merritt, Nancy Bennett (Mrs. Robert F. Lindsey). Med. house officer Royal Victoria Hosp., Montreal, 1934-35; asso. in obstetrics Johns Hopkins U., and asst. obstetrician Johns Hopkins Hosp., 1939-40; asst. prof. pharmacotherapy Harvard Med. Sch., 1940-45, vis. prof. biol. chemistry, 1958; asso. in medicine Peter Bent Brigham Hosp., 1940-45; research prof. medicine Tufts U. Sch. Medicine, 1945-52, prof. medicine 1952—; endocrinologist J.H. Pratt Diagnostic Hosp., 1945-48; sr. physician New Eng. Med. Center Hosps.; physician Boston Dispensary, 1945—; lectr. Australian Postgrad. Fedn. Medicine, 1954. Adv. council Nat. Insts. Arthritis and Metabolic Diseases, 1965-69; chmn. Laurention Hormone Conf., 1968—. Recipient Ciba award Assn. Study Internal Secretions, 1944; Cameron prize U. Edinburgh, 1948; John Phillips Meml. award A.C.P., 1949; Borden award Assn. Am. Med. Colls., 1951; Claude Bernard medla U. Montreal, 1953; Lasker award Am. Pub. Health Assn., 1954; Nat. Inst. Arthritis and Metabolic Disease research career award, 1962—; Gordon Wilson medal Am. Clin. and Climatological Assn., 1966. Mem. Am. Physiol. Soc., A.A.A.S., Am. Chem. Soc., Endocrine Soc. (pres. 1961-62; Koch award 1967), Assn. Am. Physicians, Am. Soc. Clin. Investigation, A.C.P., Am. Acad. Arts and Scis., Nat. Acad. Scis.. Am. Coll. Clin. Pharmacology and Chemotherapy (regent 1964-67), Brit. Soc. Endocrinology, Harvey Soc. (lectr. 1945), Mass. Med. Soc., Alpha Omega Alpha. Research, publis. on mammary gland devel., sex hormones, corpus luteum function, radioactive iodine, pituitary hormones, metabolism of fat; introduced use of antithyroid in treatment hyperthyroidism, 1943. Home: 30 Irving St Brookline MA 02111 Office: 171 Harrison Av Boston MA 02111

ATCHESON, JAMES EDWARD, architect; b. Terrell, Tex., Jan 26, 1906; s. Frank and Bessie (Barton) A.; B. Arch., Tex. Tech. Coll., 1936; m. Armista Lucille Heggen, June 20, 1936; children—Michael Edward, Daniel Benn, Timothy Jon, Anne Louise. Draftsman, Eickenroht & Cocke, architects, San Antonio, also part-time instr.

Tex. Tech. Coll., 1928-34; designer O.R. Walker, architect, Lubbock, Tex., 1935-40; asso. archt. engr., C.E., U.S. Army, Albuquerque and Pyote, Tex., 1942-44; partner Walker & Atcheson, architects, Lubbock, 1941-46; prin. James Atcheson, architects, Lubbock, 1947-48; partner Atcheson & Atkinson architects, Lubbock, 1949-55, Atcheson, Atkinson & Cartwright, architects and engrs., Lubbock, 1956—; prin. works include Lubbock Country Club, 1960, Citizens Nat. Bank, Lubbock, 1963, First Christian Ch., Lubbock, 1964, Bell System Telephone Bldg., Lubbock, Tex. (merit award for architectural excellence), 1967, Am. State Bank, Lubbock, 1969, Courthouse and Fed. office bldg., Lubbock, 1971. Mem. A.I.A. (pres. Panhandle chpt. 1945, Lubbock chpt. 1963), Tex. Soc. Architects (v.p. 1960); Constn. Specifications Inst. (pres. Lubbock chpt. 1966), Phi Delta Theta. Lutheran (pres. 1966-67). Kiwanian. Club: Lubbock Country. Home: 3203 26th St Lubbock, TX 79410. Office: 1214 14th St Lubbock TX 79401

ATCHISON, WILLIAM FRANKLIN, educator; b. Smithfield, Ky., Apr. 7, 1918; s. William Duncan and Mary Lou (Beatty) A.; A.B., Georgetown Coll., 1938; M.A., U. Ky., 1940; Ph.D., U. Ill., 1943; postgrad. Harvard, 1950-51; m. Lois Ethel Bruinkool, June 7, 1947; children—Allen Franklin, Glen Ray, Mary Beth, David Duncan. Physics lab. asst. Georgetown Coll., 1936-38; teaching asst. math. U. Ky., 1939-40; teaching asst., instr. math. U. Ill., 1940-44, instr., asst. prof. math., 1946-55; research asso. prof. math. Ga. Inst. Tech., 1955-63, research prof. math., 1963-66, head programming and coding group Rich Electronic Computer Center, 1956-57, chief Rich Electronic Computer Center, 1957-66, acting dir. Sch. Information Sci., 1963-64; dir. Computer Sci. Center, U. Md., 1966—, also prof. computer sci. U. Md. Mem. curriculum com. on computer sci., chmn. adv. panel computer sci., chmn. council on computer centers and computer sci. edn. and research So. Regional Edn. Bd.; chmn. edn. com. Assn. Computing Machinery; chmn. working group on computer sci. edn. at secondary sch. level Internat. Fedn. Information Processing, also mem. edn. com. Contbr. articles profl. jours. Home: 10711 Gatewood Av Silver Spring MD 20903 Office: Computer Sci Center U Md College Park MD 20742

ATCHLEY, DANA WINSLOW, Jr., electronics mfg. co. exec.; b. N.Y.C., Oct. 27, 1917; s. Dana Winslow and Mary Cornelia (Phister) A.; grad. Loomis Sch., 1935; B.S., Harvard, 1940; m. Barbara Welch, Aug. 26, 1939 (div. 1953); children—Dana Winslow III, Mary Babcock, Elizabeth Ross, Sarah Ross; m. 2d, Barbara Standish Payne, May 1, 1954; children—Marion Woodward, Abigail Adams, Cornelia Phister, Katherine Saltonstall. Engr., Hygrade-Sylvania, Inc., 1940-41; govt. sales mgr. electronics div. Sylvania Electric Products, 1945-47; sales mgr. Tracerlab, Inc., 1947-50, dir. engring., 1950-51; tech. coordinator United Paramount Theatres, Inc., 1951-52; pres., dir. Microwave Assos., Inc., Burlington, Mass., 1952-69, chmn., chief exec. officer, dir., 1969—; dir. Spectra Metrics, Inc. Mem. exec. com. Yacht Racing Union of Mass. Bay. Served to lt. comdr. USNR, 1941-45. Mem. I.E.E.E., Am. Radio Relay League, Radio Club of Am. Clubs: St. Botolph (Boston); New York Yacht; Marblehead Frostbite Sailing (sec.); Appalachian Mountain (Boston) . Home: Concord Rd Lincoln MA 01773 Office: Microwave Assos Inc Burlington MA 01803

ATEPOR, BONIFACE KWAME, diplomat; b. Sovie, Dzigbe, Ghana, May 14, 1934; s. William K. and Paula (Yawa Zaku) A.; student U. Bordeaux (France), 1956-58; B.A., Ghana U., 1960; Carnegie fellow in diplomacy Columbia, 1966-67; m. Isabelle Kwame, July 14, 1960; children—Christine, Margaret, Regina, Alice. Assistant Secretary Ghana Congo Co-ordinating Office, Leopoldville, Congo, 1960; asst. sec. Afrian affairs secretariat Pres.'s Office, Accra, 1961-62; 1st sec. Ghana embassy, Senegal, 1962-63; Algeria, 1963, Tunisia, 1963-65; counselor Ghana embassy, Washington, since 1968—. Leader Ghana delegation to Washington Diplomatic Conf. on Patent Cooperation, Treaty, 1970, to Intelsat Conf. Washington, 1969-70. Roman Catholic. Home: 2254 Sudbury Rd NW Washington DC 20012 Office: 2460 16th St NW Washington DC 20009

ATHA, STUART KIMBALL, Jr., banker; b. Newark, May 28, 1925; s. Stuart Kimball and Katharine Grosvenor (Dixon) A.; B.A., Princeton, 1950; m. Eleanor Hendry, July 6, 1946; children—Stuart Kimball III, Susan Hendry, Peter William. With Hanover Bank, N.Y.C., 1950-62, asst. sec., 1955-56, asst. treas., 1956-62; asst. sec. Chem. Bank N.Y. Trust Co., N.Y.C., 1962, asst. v.p., 1962-65, v.p., 1965—. Served to 1st lt. USAAF, 1943-46. Clubs: Canadian of New York, Princeton of New York, Cannon (Princeton). Home: Russet Rd Valley Cottage NY 10989 Office: 277 Park Av New York City NY 10017

ATHAY, RUSSELL GRANT, educator, astrophysicist; b. Smithfield, Utah, Dec. 5, 1923; s. Henry Elzo and Mabel (Jacques) A.; student U. Wash., also U. Cal. at Los Angeles, 1943-44; B.S. in Radio Enging. and Physics, Utah State U., 1947; Ph.D. in Astrophysics, U. Utah, 1953; m. Twila Jensen, Apr. 20, 1945; children—Russell Jay, Carol Jane, Luann, Darrell, Renee. Chief observer High Altitude Obs., Climax, Colo., 1950-52; sr. research staff High Altitude Obs., Boulder, Colo., 1952-63; research asso. Harvard Coll. Obs., 1955-58; guest lectr. Cal. Inst. Tech., 1958; adj. prof. U. Colo., 1961-63, chmn. dept. astrophysics and atmospheric physics U. Colo., 1962-63; prof., head dept. physics U. Utah, 1963-64; sr. research staff high altitude obs. Nat. Center for Atmospheric Research, Boulder, 1964—, also prof. adjoint U. Colo., Boulder, 1964—; vis. prof. Coll. de France, summer 1965. Solar reporter U.S. nat. com. Internat. Year of Quiet Sun, also mem. astronomy and Internat. Year of Quiet Sun panels, NSF, 1962-65; mem. solar physics com. NASA, 1962-64; sci. adviser astronauts projects Gemini and Apollo, 1963-64; mem. vis. com. div. 95 and 13, Nat. Bur. Standards, 1963-66; mem. Geophysics Research Bd., 1970—. Served to 1st lt. USAAF, 1943-46. Mem. Internat. Astron. Union (U.S. nat. com. 1970—, pres. Commn. 12 1970—), Am. Astron. Soc., Am. Geophys. Union. Mem. Ch. of Jesus Christ of Latter Day Saints (bishop). Co-author: Physics of the Solar Chromosphere, 1961. Home: 1029 Paragon Dr Boulder CO 80303 Office: High Altitude Observatory Boulder CO 80302

ATHENAGORAS, HIS ALL HOLINESS, Archbishop of Constantinople, New Rome and Ecumenical Patriarch; b. 1886; grad. Orthodox Theol. Sem., Halki, Istanbul, 1910. Ordained deacon, 1910, later served as gen. sec. Athens Archdiocese; elected by Holy Synod as Metropolitan of Corfu and Paxos; apptd. archbishop of Greek Orthodox Ch. of N. and S. Am. with offices in N.Y.C., 1931; elected Patriarch of Constantinople by Holy Synod, 1948. Address: Greek Orthodox Patriarchate Fener Istanbul Turkey

ATHENAGORAS, THEODORITOS, (born Theodoros G. Kokkinakis), bishop; b. Patmos, Dodecanese Islands, 1912; student schs. Patmos, Revelation Sch., Cyprus, Gen. Theol. Sem., N.Y.C., 1936; grad. Patriarchal Theol. Sem., 1934; M.S.T., Master Philosophy, Northwestern U., Chgo. Came to U.S., 1936. Ordained priest, Greek Orthodox Ch., 1940; served Patriarchal Ch. of St. Sava, Alexandria, St. Andrew's Ch., Chgo., St. Demetrios Ch., Astoria, Li., N.Y.; tchr. Theol. Acad. of Pomfret (Conn.), Acad. of St. Basil; consecrated bishop Western State Diocese, 1950; was pres. Holy Cross Theol. Sch., Brookline, Mass.; bishop Met. Can. St. George Ch., 1960-63; met. archbishop Thyateria and Gt. Britain and primate of Scandinavia, 1963; rep. to World Chs. Confs., Amsterdam, Evanston, New Delhi, Uppsala; pres. 4th Panorthodox Conf., Belgrade, 1967; vice pres. Nat. Council Chs. Christ in U.S. Author: Theological Research on Christian Unity. Former editor Orthodox Observer. First Orthodox prelate sent to Vatican after 9 centuries of silence between Roman Cath. and Orthodox chs. to arrange meeting of Pope Paul VI and Patriarch Athenagoras in Jerusalem, 1964. Address: 5 Craven Hill London W2 England

ATHERTON, ALEXANDER SIMPSON, newspaper exec.; b. Honolulu, Mar. 29, 1913; s. Frank Cooke and Eleanore Alice (Simpson) A.; grad. Tabor Acad., Marion, Mass., 1931; B.A., Dartmouth, 1936; m. LeBurta Marie Gates, Oct. 8, 1941; children—Burta Lee, Frank Cooke II, Marjory Gates. With Hawaiian Trust Co., Honolulu, 1954-66, asst. v.p., 1958-66; pres. Honolulu Star-Bull., 1963—; pres. Guam Publs.; dir. Hawaiian Trust Co., Castle & Cooke, Inc. Pres. Mid-Pacific Inst., 1955—; past campaign chmn. Honolulu Community Chest. Trustee Hawaii Loa Coll., F.C. Atherton Trust, Juliette M. Atherton Trust; bd. dirs. Hawaii div. Am. Cancer Soc., Honolulu Council Social Agencies, Africare, Inc. Jr. Achievement Hawaii. Mem. Navy League U.S., Theta Delta Chi. Republican. Mem. United Ch. Christ. Clubs: Kaanapali Golf; Pacific, Adventurers, Waialae Country, Oahu Country (Honolulu); Collectors (N.Y.C.). Home: 2150 Puualii Pl Honolulu, HI 96822.

ATHERTON, ALFRED LEROY, Jr., fgn. service officer; b. Pitts., Nov. 22, 1921; s. Alfred Leroy and Joan (Reed) A.; grad. Phillips Exeter Acad., 1940; B.S., Harvard, 1944, M.A., 1947; spl. student economics U. Cal. at Berkeley, 1961-62; m. Betty Wylie Kittredge, May 16, 1946; children—Lynne Kittredge, Michael Anton, Reed Wylie. Joined U.S. Fgn. Service, 1947; vice consul, Stuttgart, Germany, 1947-50, Bonn, Germany, 1950-52; 2d sec., Damascus, Syria, 1953-56; consul, Aleppo, Syria, 1957-58; internat. relations officer Bur. Near Eastern and S. Asian Affairs, State Dept., 1959-61; consul, Calcutta, India, 1962-65; dep. dir. Office Near Eastern Affairs, State Dept., 1965-66, country dir. Arab States North, 1966-67, country dir. Israel and Arab Israel Affairs, 1967-69; dep. asst. sec. Bur. Near Eastern and S. Asian Affairs, 1970—. Served to 1st lt., F.A., AUS, 1943-45; ETO. Decorated Air medal, Silver Star. Mem. Fgn. Service Assn. Unitarian. Home: 3400 Ordway St N W Washington DC 20016 Office: Dept of State Washington DC 20037

ATHERTON, FLORA CAMERON, polit. worker, found. exec.; b. Waco, Tex.; d. William Waldo and Helen Emelyn (Miller) Cameron; A.B., Sweet Briar Coll., 1946; children—Ike Simpson III, Megan Cameron. Dir. Certain-Teed Products Corp. Mem. exec. com. San Antonio World's Fair, 1968; mem. Pres.'s Mission to Latin Am. headed by Gov. Rockefeller; U.S. del. Inter-Am. Commn. Women, 1969—; mem. citizens stamp adv. com. U.S. Postal Service. Active Rep. Party of Tex., 1952—, mem. hdqrs. com., 1957-58, vice chmn. state exec. com., 1958-60; mem. Rep. Nat. Com. for Program and Progress, 1959; mem. Rep. Nat. Com. for Tex., 1960-65; asst. to exec. dir. platform com., del. Rep. Nat. Conv., 1960, del., 1960, 64, alternate del., 1968; mem. Rep. Nat. Finance Com., 1965—. Pres. Kamko Found.; adv. trustee Southwest Found. Research and Edn.; trustee Trinity U., San Antonio, Sweet Briar Coll., Witle Mus., San Antonio; mem. nat. council Met. Opera. Mem. Jr. League San Antonio, Colonial Dames Am. Home: 315 Westover Rd San Antonio TX 78209 Office: 4600 Broadway San Antonio TX 78209

ATHERTON, JAMES KENNETH WARD, photographer; b. Washington, Dec. 16, 1927; s. Fairfax Malcolm, Sr., and Mildred (Herrcher) A.; ed. pub. schs., Nat. Sch. Photography; m. Patricia Ann Hall, Oct. 18, 1949; children—Michael, Robin, Jamie, Steven. Telephoto operator Acme Newspictures, 1949-50; photographer U.P.I., Washington, 1950-70; picture editor Washington Post, 1970—. Served with U.S. Navy, 1946-47. Recipient 2d prize feature class, World Photo Exhbn., Hague, Netherlands, 1966, Bill Pryor Meml. award, Washington-Balt. Newspaper Guild, 1962, 63, 64, 66, 69; award for newsfeature picture Nat. Headlines Club, 1969; 1st prize gen. news category, Pictures of Year competition, Nat. Press Photographers Assn., 1964, 1st prize annual photo contest, White House Press Photographers Assn., 1952, 57, 61, 62, 63, 64, 1st prize presdl. class, 1970, grand award, White House contest, 1961, Ernest E. Grass Meml. award Kent State U., 1957. Mem. Nat. Press Photographers Assn., White House News Photographers Assn. Home: 2913 Stanton Av Silver Spring MD 20910 Office: 1515 L St N W Washington DC 20005

ATHERTON, LEWIS E., univ. prof.; b. Bosworth, Mo., Mar. 1, 1905; s. Caleb Franklin and Ethel (France) A.; student U. of Okla., 1923-25; A.B., U. of Mo., 1927, A.M., 1930, Ph.D., 1937, Guggenheim fellow, 1940; m. Mary Louise Webb, June 5, 1929; children—Barbara Lee, Mary Ann. Instr. in history N.M. Mil. Inst., 1928-29. St. Joseph Jr. Coll., 1930-31, Wentworth Mil. Acad., Lexington, Mo., 1931-36; instr. U. of Mo., 1936-39, asst. prof., 1939-42, asso. prof., 1942-46, prof. since 1946, chmn. dept. history, 1944-50. Newberry Library fellow, 1950-51. Mem. Agrl. History Soc. (pres. 1952), Phi Beta Kappa, Delta Sigma Rho. Presbyn. Author: The Pioneer Merchant in Mid-America, 1939; The Southern Country Store, 1949; Main Street on The Middle Border, 1954; The Cattle Kings, 1962. Home: 600 Crestland Rd Columbia MO 65201

ATHERTON, WARREN HENDRY, lawyer; b. San Francisco, Dec. 28, 1891; s. Dwight C. and Elizabeth (Hendry) A.; m. Anne Holt, July 7, 1917 (dec.); children—Holt, Warren, Dwight Copeland, Nancy Anne; m. 2d, Marietta Monachino Cochran, Aug. 17, 1952. Admitted to Cal. bar, 1914, since practiced in Stockton; gen. counsel, dept. vets. affairs State Cal.; mem. law firm Atherton & Dozier; legislative counsel Port of Stockton. Pres. Westwarehouses, Inc., Inland Harbor Storage Co., Madera Factors; vice chmn., dir. San Joaquin First Fed. Savs. & Loan Assn.; dir. Lilval, Inc., Sims Grupe Mgmt. Co., Inc., Lincoln Properties, Inc., B.F.B., Inc.; owner, operator Delta Farm. Pres. Stockton Community Chest, 1938; mem. San Francisco Bay Ports Commn., 1952-57; pres., founder Stockton (Cal.) Opera Assn.; mem. Nat. Security Tng. Commn., 1953-59; chmn. Stockton chpt. A.R.C., 1949-50, No. Cal. chmn. Vets for Eisenhower, 1952, 56; pres. Nat. Rep. Vets. League; past chmn. Rep. Central Com. San Joaquin County. Cons. to sec. of War, World War II. Served as pvt., Co. D., 363d Infantry, 91st Div.; with A.E.F., Apr. 1918-Aug. 1919; capt., Ordnance, Feb.-Sept. 1919. Mem. State Bd. Paroles of Calif., 1933-35. Trustee Counsel for Inter-Am. Affairs, 1945-47. Pres. San Joaquin County Bar Assn., 1921; pres. Stockton C. of C., 1933-35. Mem. Am. Legion (past nat. comdr., mem. exec. com. 1937-38, 1944-70, chmn. Inter-Am. affairs com. 1944-57), Am. Bar Assn., State Bar of Cal., Cal. C. of C., Disabled Am. Vets. Presbyn. Clubs: Rotary (hon.), Kiwanis (pres. 1924), Commonwealth, Army and Navy; Monterey Peninsula Golf and Country. Stockton Golf and Country, St Francis Yacht. Home: 12 Atherton Island Stockton CA 95204 Office: Wells Fargo Bank Bldg Stockton CA 95202

ATHOS, ANTHONY GEORGE, educator; b. Detroit, Jan. 29, 1934; s. George Anthony and Emma (McSween) A.; grad. Gen. Motors Inst., 1956; M.B.A., Harvard, 1958, D.B.A., 1964. Asst. prof., then asso. prof. U. So. Cal., 1962-66; asst. dean Harvard Grad. Sch. Bus. Adminstrn., 1966-68, lectr. organizational behavior, 1968-70, asso. prof., 1970-71, prof. organizational behavior, 1971—. Recipient Distinguished Tchr. award U. So. Cal., 1964; named Great Tchr. by Time mag., 1966. Co-author: Behavior in OrganizationsA Multidensional View, 1968. Home: 81 Raymond St Cambridge MA 01773 Office: Humphrey House Harvard Grad Sch Bus Adminstrn Boston MA 02163

ATIYA, AZIZ SURYAL, educator, historian; b. Egypt, July 7, 1898; M.A., U. Liverpool (Eng.), 1933, D. Litt., 1938; Ph.D., U. London, 1933; D.H.L., Baldwin Wallace Coll., 1962; L.H.D., U. Utah, 1968; LL.D., Brigham Young, m. Lola H. Messiha, July 31, 1941; children—Nayra, Ramez. Came to U.S., 1955. Tutor, U. London, 1932-33, Bonn prof. history, 1935-38, Cairo and Alexandria prof. history, also vice dean and chmn. dept., 1939-52; prof. history U. Zurich (Switzerland), 1951-54, U. Beirut (Lebanon), 1954-55, U. Mich., 1955-56, Columbia, 1956-57, Ind. U., 1957, Princeton, 1957-59; prof. history U. Utah, 1959-, distinguished prof. history, 1968-. First hist. insp., Cairo, 1938-39; cons. Library of Congress, 1950-51; pres. Inst. Coptic Studies, Cairo, 1952-54; dir. Middle East Center, U. Utah, 1961-67; corr. mem. UNESCO, 1953-; mem. Orthodox Coptic Community Council, Cairo, 1953-54. Charles Beard and Univ. fellow U. Liverpool, 1931-33; first Fulbright exchange scholar from Egypt, 1950-51; Patten lectr. Ind. U., 1957; decorated knight order St. Catherine Mt. Sinai, 1953. Mem. Am. Assn. Middle East Studies (trustee), Acad. Mediteranean Studies (corr.). Coptic Christian. Author Crusade of Nicopolis, 1934; Crusade in the Later Middle Ages, 1938; Egypt and Aragon, 1938; Qawanin al-Dawawin, 1943; Arabic MSS of Mt. Sinai, 1950; History of Patriarchs, 2 vols. 1948-59; Crusade Commerce and Culture, 1962; Crusade Historiography, 1962; History of Eastern Christianity, 1968; also numerous articles, monographs. Home: 1335 Perry Av Salt Lake City UT 84103

ATKESON, THOMAS CONNER, educator; born Columbia, Ala., Nov. 21, 1897; s. Clarence Lee Crawford and Annie May (Conner) A.; student, Southern U., 1916-17, U. of Ala., 1917-18; B.S., Georgetown U., 1927, M.S. cum laude, 1928, Ph.D., 1931; m. Helen Douglas Whiting, July 20, 1920; 1 dau., Helen Douglas (Mrs. Wm. F. Phillips). Asso. prof. accounting and bus. administrn. Georgetown U. 1931-32; sr. econ. analyst, Bur. Internal Revenue, 1935; mem. exec. com. conf. of income and wealth, Nat. Bur. of Econ. Research, 1941-42, asst. to commr. of internal revenue in charge of research and statistics, 1945, asst. to commr. of internal revenue and dir. mgmt. staff, 1948-52; asst. commr. internal revenue, 1952-54; apptd. to chair of taxation, Marshall Wythe Sch. of Law, William and Mary Coll., 1954-68, Chancellor prof. taxation emeritus, cons. Law Sch.'s tax program, 1968—, head div. social scis., 1959-62. Mem. State Revenue Resources and Econ. Study Commn., 1968-70, commn. cons., 1970—; pres. Williamsburg Citizens Assn. Mem: financial advisory commn. City of Williamsburg, Va., 1958—. Dir. of Ann, William and Mary Tax Conference, Coll. William and Mary. Recipient Gold Medal award Sec. of the Treasury, 1954. Fellow Am. Statis. Assn.; hon. mem. Tax Execs. Inst., Inc.; mem. Pi Kappa Alpha. Episcopalian. Mason. Clubs: Rotary, Cosmos (Washington); Middle Plantation. Contbr. treatises on taxation to profl. jours; also active participant in programs nat. tax orgns. Home: 703 Goodwin St Williamsburg VA 23185

ATKIN, J. MYRON, coll. dean; b. Bklyn., Apr. 6, 1927; s. Charles Z. and Esther (Jaffe) A.; B.S., City Coll. N.Y., 1947; M.A., N.Y. U., 1948, Ph.D., 1956; m. Ann Spiegel, Dec. 25, 1947; children—David, Ruth, Jonathan. High Sch. sci. tchr., N.Y.C., 1948-50; elementary sch. sci. cons. Great Neck (N.Y.) pub. schs., 1950-55; prof. sci. edn. Coll. Edn., U. Ill. at Urbana, 1955—, asso. dean, 1966-70, dean, 1970—. Served with USNR, 1945-46. Fellow A.A.A.S. (sec. sect. Q 1968-70); mem. Council Elementary Sci. Internat. (pres. 1969-70). Author children's sci. textbooks. Home: 1109 S Westlawn St Champaign IL 61820 Office: Coll Edn Univ Ill Urbana IL 61801

ATKIN, KENWARD LOUIS, educator; b. Houghton, Mich., Mar. 12, 1919; s. Charles W. and Ella W. (Young) A.; A.B., U. Mich., 1942, M.B.A., 1952; Ph.D., Mich. State U., 1961; m. Jane Follis, Dec. 16, 1945; children—Charles, Thomas, Penelope, David. Partner, mgr. C.W. Atkin & Son, Soo, Mich., 1946-51; marketing specialist Ford Motor Co., Detroit, 1952; merchandising mgr. Ex-Cell-O Corp., Detroit, 1953-56; instr. to prof., chmn. dept. advt. Mich. State U., East Lansing, 1956—; cons. State of Mich., Gen. Motors Co., Foote, Cone & Belding Advt. Agy. Served to maj. AUS, 1942-46; with Mich. N.G., 1946-50. Fellow Am. Assn. Advt. Agys. (educator coordinator), Econ. Found.; mem. Am. Marketing Assn., Assn. for Edn. in Journalism (chmn. advt. div.), Am. Acad. Advt. (dean), Kappa Tau Alpha. Author: Communications and Consumer Behavior, 1961. Contbr. articles profl. jours. Home: 313 Droste Circle East Lansing MI 48823

ATKINS, CARL CLYDE, judge; b. Washington, Nov. 23, 1914; s. C. C. and Marguerite (Criste) A.; student U. Miami (Fla.), 1931-32; LL.B., U. Fla., 1936, J.D., 1967; LL.D., Barry Coll., Miami Shores, 1966; LL.D., Biscayne Coll., Miami, 1970; m. Esther Castillo, Jan 18, 1937; children—Sister Julie Atkins, Carla Schulte, Carl Clyde. Admitted to Fla. bar, 1936; practice in Stuart, 1936-41, Miami, 1941-66; partner firm Walton, Lantaff, Schroeder, Atkins, Carson & Wahl, and predecessors, 1941-66; U.S. dist. judge So. dist. Fla., 1966—. Founder-trustee Lawyers Title Guaranty Fund, 1948—, treas., 1963-66. Pres. St. Augustine Diocesan Union Holy Name Societies, 1950-51, Miami Archdiocesan Council Cath. Men, 1959-70. Recipient Outstanding Cath. award Nat. Conf. Christians and Jews, 1959. Fellow Am. Coll. Trial Lawyers; mem. Fedn. Ins. Counsel, Am. (ho. of dels. 1960-66), Dade County (pres. 1953-54) bar assns., Fla. Bar (bd. govs. 1954-59, pres. 1960-61), Internat. Assn. Ins. Counsel, Tau Kappa Alpha, Phi Kappa Tau, Phi Alpha Delta. Kiwanian (past dir. Miami). Clubs: Miami; Coral Gables Country. Author articles profl. jours. Home: 2040 Country Club Prado Coral Gables FL 33167 Office: U S Ct House Miami FL 33132

ATKINS, CHET, named best instrumentalist of year. 1967. Address: care ARCO Enterprises 806 17th Av S Nashville, TN.*

ATKINS, CRAIG STARBUCK, judge, lawyer; b. Greensboro, N.C., Aug. 17, 1903; s. Benjamin F. and Neva O. (Starbuck) A.; student U. N.C., 1920-21; A.B., George Washington U., 1923, LL.B., 1925; m. Margaret Elinor Denty, June 30, 1926; children—Craig Starbuck, Constance (Mrs. John E. McShulskis). Admitted to D.C. bar, 1925; atty. U.S. Bd. Tax Appeals, 1927-37; atty. Office of Chief Counsel Internal Revenue Service, 1937-49, asst. chief counsel, 1954-55; tax adviser to Greek Govt. and ECA Mission to Greece, 1949-51; judge Tax Ct. of U.S., 1955—. Mem. Am. Bar Assn., Sigma Phi Epsilon. Mason. Home: 7004 Florida St Chevy Chase MD 20015 Office: U S Tax Ct Washington DC 20044

ATKINS, DALE MORRELL, physician; b. Somerset, Colo., Jan. 20, 1922; s. James Perry and Lura May (Morrell) A.; B.A., U. Colo., 1943, M.D., 1945, M.S., 1953; m. Loretta Ilene Davidson, June 20, 1943; children—Loretta, Linda, Peter, John. Intern Mass. Meml. Hosp., 1945-46; resident medicine Colo. U. Sch. Medicine, 1948-50, resident urology, 1950-53; pvt. practice genitourinary surgery, Denver, 1953—; clin. asst. prof. surgery U. Colo. Sch. Medicine, 1955—. Mem. bd. regents U. Colo. Served to capt., M.C., AUS, 1946-48.

Mem. Phi Beta Kappa. Republican. Methodist. Rotarian. Home: 3982 S Chase Way Denver CO 80235 Office: 1855 Gaylord St Denver CO 80206

ATKINS, EDWARD J., lawyer; b. Miami, Fla., July 16, 1926; s. Carl Clyde and Marguerite (Criste) A.; student U.S. Mcht. Marine Acad., 1944-46; B.A., U. Fla., 1949; LL.B., U. Miami, 1951; m. Helen Marie Graymas, Jan. 5, 1957; children—Edward J., Marguerite Ann, Amy Marie, Carol Patricia, Michael John. Admitted to Fla. bar; asso. firm Walton, Lantaff, Schroeder, Carson & Wahl, and predecessors, Miami, 1954-59, partner firm, 1959—. Served with AUS, 1951-54. Recipient Distinguished Service award Armed Forces League. Mem. Am., Fed., Dade County (pres. jr. bar 1961-62, pres., 1965-66) bar assns., Fla. Bar (gov.), Internat. Assn. Ins. Counsel, Judge Advs. Assn., Holy Name Soc. (diocesan union pres. 1959- 61), Sierra Club, Phi Alpha Delta, Sigma Tau Delta, Tau Kappa Alpha, Kappa Alpha. Kiwanian, K.C. (dist. dep. 1962-64, Fla. adv. 1964-67). Home: 5755 S W 111th Terrace Miami FL 33156 Office: Du Pont Bldg Miami FL 33131

ATKINS, ELISHA, educator, physician; b. Belmont, Mass., Nov. 16, 1920; s. Robert Wrisley and Ruth (Hornblower) A.; A.B. magna cum laude, Harvard, 1942; M.D., U. Rochester, 1950; m. Elizabeth Potter, Nov. 17, 1944; children—Ruth G., Elisha H., Warwick P., Natasha, David. Intern, asst. resident Barnes Hosp., St. Louis, 1950-52; research fellow, then instr. medicine Washington U. Sch. Medicine, St. Louis, 1952-55; mem. facutly Yale Med. Sch., 1955—, prof. medicine, 1967—; sabbatical leave Radcliffe Inf., Oxford, Eng., 1962-63; attending physician Yale-New Haven Hosp.; cons. W. Haven (Conn.) VA Hosp. Served to 1st lt. USMCR, 1942-45. Research grantee USPHS. Mem. Am. Soc. Clin. Investigation, Assn. Am. Physicians, Interurban Clin. Club. Author articles on pathogenesis of fever with spl. emphasis on exptl. fevers induced by microbial agts. and antigens in specifically sensitized animals. Home: 33 Westward Rd Woodbridge CT 06525 Office: 333 Cedar St New Haven CT 06510

ATKINS, IRVIN MILBURN, educator, agronomist; b. Corning, Kan., July 24, 1904; s. Irvin Daniel and Dora Mae (Hollowell) A.; B.S., Kan. State U., 1928, M.S., 1936; Ph.D., U. Minn., 1945; m. Mary Ruth Loveless, Aug. 28, 1932; children—Mary Virginia (Mrs. William E. Lyles), Irvin Milburn. With Dept. Agr., 1928-54, plant breeder small grains, Denton, Tex., 1930-54; small grain sect. leader Tex. A. and M. U. in coop. with Dept. Agr., 1954—; prof. agronomy Tex. A. and M. U., 1954-69, prof. emeritus, 1969—. Fellow Am. Soc. Agronomy; mem. Sigma Xi, Alpha Zeta, Phi Kappa Phi, Gamma Sigma Delta. Methodist. Kiwanian (pres. Denton 1948; chmn. agrl. com. Tex.-Okla. 1950). Author numerous articles, research bulls. Home: 1215 Marsteller St College Station TX 77840

ATKINS, OLIVER OLLIE F., photographer; b. Hyde Park, Mass., Feb. 18, 1916; s. Oliver Fraser and Annie Sally (McLeod) A.; grad. Huntington Sch. for Boys, Boston; A.B., U. of Ala., 1938; m. Marjorie Neola Deakin, Aug. 10, 1940; children—Randie Claire (Mrs. Shumate), Dale Ann (Mrs. Wheeler). Served as staff and chief photographer for the Birmingham (Ala.) Post, 1939-40; staff photographer, Washington Daily News, 1940-42; fgn. correspondent photographer, 1942-45; Washington photographer, Sat. Eve. Post, Washington office, 1945-69, fgn. correspondent, photographer, Japan and Korea, 1951; photography columnist, Washington Post, 1947-50; personal photographer to Pres. of U.S., chief White House photographer, 1969—; photography 2 photo books, Washington Portrait and Potomac Portrait. Recipient Grand award, White House News Photographers' Assn., 1943; portrait award Graflex All-American Photo Contest, 1946; received citation from A.R.C. for overseas service. Mem. White House News Photographers Assn. (pres. 1964, exec. com.); U.S. Senate Photographers Gallery, (chmn. inaugural com.), Nat. Press Photographers' Assn. (personalities award, 1952; fellowship award, chmn. freedom of information com.), Am. Overseas Assn. (pres.). Author: Camera on Assignment. Home: 1364 MacBeth St McLean VA 22101 Office: The White House Washington DC 20500

ATKINS, ORIN ELLSWORTH, oil co. exec.; b. Pitts., June 6, 1924; s. Orin E. and Dorothy (Whittaker) A.; student Marshall Coll., Huntington, W. Va., 1942-43, 46- 47, LL.D., 1970; student U. Pa., 1943-44; LL.B., U. Va., 1950; m. Kathryn Agee, Nov. 25, 1950; children—Randall, Charles. Admitted to W. Va. bar, 1950, Ky. bar, 1952; with Ashland Oil Inc. (Ky.), 1950—, exec. asst., 1956- 59, adminstrv. v.p., 1959-65, pres., 1965-69, pres., chief exec. officer, 1969—, also dir.; dir. Cin. br. Fed. Res. Bank Cleve., 1968-71. Mem. Nat. Pub. Adv. Com. on Regional Econ. Devel., Ky. Council Econ. Advisers. Pres. adv. bd. Marshall U. Served with AUS, 1942-46. Mem. Am., W. Va., Ky. bar assns., Am. Petroleum Inst. (dir.), Nat. Planning Assn. (nat. council), Nat. Petroleum Refiners Assn., Nat. Petroleum Council. Presbyn. Home: 602 Amanda Dr Bellefonte Ashland KY 41101 Office: 1409 Winchester Av Ashland KY 41101

ATKINS, PAUL MOODY, financial and mgmt. cons.; b. Boston, Apr. 3, 1892; s. Edward and Martha Moody (Williams) A.; A.B., Yale, 1914; A.M., 1915; postgrad. Armour Inst., Chgo., U. Chgo., N.Y. U.; Docteur de l'Universite de Paris, 1925; m. Genevieve Bergier, June 15, 1920; children—David Pierre, Henri Bergier, Edward Moody. Cost accountant Acme Wire Co., 1914-15, Gray & Davis, Inc., 1915; prodn. engr. Square D Co., 1916; mgmt. engr. Acme Wire Co., 1916-17; cons. engr. L.V. Estes, Inc., indsl. engrs., 1919-20; instr. mfg. U. Chgo., 1920-26; engr.-economist Ames, Emerich & Co., 1926-31; spl. liquidator securities U.S. Comptroller of Currency, 1932-37; treas. Alfred P. Sloan Found., 1937-38; v.p., dir. Grant & Atkins, Inc., 1939-40; financial and mgmt. cons., 1938—; lectr., radio commentator on internat. affairs, 1960—; adj. prof. bus. adminstrn. Rutgers U., 1956-62. Specialist, Am. Com. to Negotiate Peace, Paris, 1919; Am. sec. sub-com. on Czechoslovakian Affairs, Peace Conf. pub. credit com. Kemmerer Financial Mission to Peru, 1931; chief Argentina-Paraguay unit Am. Hemisphere div. Bd. Econ. Warfare, 1942; econ. adviser Ministry of Finance, Imperial Govt. of Iran, 1943; specialist banking and fgn. exchange Am. Mission for Aid to Greece, 1947-48; temp. banking adviser for Japan to sec. army, 1948. Trustee Internat. Coll., Beirut, 1937-42; bd. dirs. Seamen's House YMCA, N.Y.C., 1939-42. Served with U.S. Army, 1917-19; instr. U.S. Army Arty. Sch., Clermont-Ferrand, France, 1918; maj. to lt. col. M.I. Res., 1924-35. Mem. Am. Econ. Assn., Intercultural Assn., Phi Beta Kappa, Beta Theta Pi, Pi Gamma Mu. Conglist. Author books in field; latest being Bank Bond Investment and Secondary Reserve Management, 1940. Contbr. articles gen., financial and indsl. jours. Address: 199 Inwood Av Upper Montclair NJ 07043 ☆

ATKINS, SAMUEL DECOSTER, educator; b. Madison, N.J., Oct. 25, 1910; s. Oscar and Elizabeth (DeCoster) A.; A.B., Princeton, 1931, A.M., 1932, Ph.D., 1935; m. Jeannette Guerin, Aug. 31, 1935; children—Samuel DeCoster, Pamela G., Bowman K. Asst. prof. Latin, Baylor U., 1935-37; instr. classics and Sanskrit, Princeton, 1937-41, asst. prof., 1941-48, asso. prof., 1948-58, prof., 1958—, chmn. dept. classics, 1961—; Fulbright research scholar in linguistics, Thailand, 1959-60. Served from lt. (j.g.) to lt. comdr., USNR, World War II; as comdr., 1950-52. Mem. Am. Philol. Assn., Am. Oriental Soc., Linguistic Soc. Am., Linguistic Soc. India, Phi Beta Kappa. Author: Pushan in the Rigveda, 1941. Contbr. articles learned jours. Home: 78 Alexander St Princeton NJ 08540

ATKINS, STANLEY HAMILTON, bishop; b. Newcastle, Eng., Mar. 8, 1912; s. George Thomas and Ethel (Williams) A.; AKCL, King's Coll., London, 1938; D.D., Nashotah House, Wis., 1969; m. Mildred Maureen March, May 5, 1942; children—Frances Mary (Mrs. Del J. Johnson), Paul, Elizabeth. Ordained to ministry Episcopal Ch., 1938; served Diocese of Durham, Eng., 1938-49, Rupert's Land, Can., 1949-55, St. Paul's, Hudson, Wis., also St. Thomas Ch., New Richmond, Wis., 1955-62; archdeacon of Milw., 1962-69; coadjutor bishop of Eau Claire, Wis., 1969-70, bishop, 1970—. Chaplain Western Province of the Community of St. Mary (Kenosha, Wis.). Trustee Nashotah House Sem., 1969—. Served as chaplain, lt. col., Brit. Army, 1941-46. Club: Rotary (Eau Claire). Home: 145 Marshton Av Eau Claire WI 54701 Office: 510 S Farwell St Eau Claire WI 54701

ATKINS, STUART PRATT, educator; b. Balt., Mar. 8, 1914; s. (George) Robert and Huldah M. (Pratt) A.; A.B., Yale, 1935, Ph.D., 1938; A.M. (hon.), Harvard, 1948; m. Lillian E. Reed, June 7, 1946; 1 son, Stuart Reed. Instr. Dartmouth, 1938-41, Harvard, 1941-43, Princeton, 1946; asst. prof. German, Harvard, 1946-48, asso. prof., 1948-56, prof. 1956-65, chmn. dept. Germanic langs. and lits., 1952-57, 60-65; prof. German, U. Cal., 1965—; -; Guggenheim fellow, 1955, 68; vis. prof. U. Goettingen (Germany), 1962; guest prof. Ripon Coll., 1964. Served USAAF, 1943-46. Decorated Bronze Star, Croix de Guerre; recipient gold medal Goethe Institut, 1968. Mem. Am. Council on German Studies, Inc. (chmn. bd. dirs. 1968-70), Faust-Gesellschaft, Internationale Vereinigung füer Germanische Sprach und Literaturissenschaft, Am., Internat. comparative lit. assns., Modern Lang Assn. Am. (1st v.p. 1971), Modern Humanities Research Assn., Am. Assn. Tchrs. German (exec. council, 1966-68), Philol. Assn. Pacific Coast, Harvard Mus. Assn. Dante Soc. Am., Nat. Carl Sohurz Assn., Phi Beta Kappa. Club: Faculty (U. Cal. Santa Barbara). Author: The Testament of Werther, 1949; Goethe's Faust: A Literary Analysis, 1958; The Age of Goethe, 1969; editor, author revision Bayard Taylor's Faust, trans., 1962, and Goethe's Faust, Part I, bilingual edit., 1963, also articles. Editor: German Quar., 1952-57. Home: 752 Woodland Dr Santa Barbara CA 93108

ATKINSON, ANDY RAYMOND, ret. electronics co. exec.; b. Upland, Ind., May 20, 1907; s. Oscar E. and Lizzie (Ferguson) A.; B.S., Ind. U., 1933; m. Madeline F. Nelson, Dec. 24, 1936; children—Stanley and Stephen (twins), Ronald. Cost Accountant Marion Machine & Foundry Co. (Ind.), 1926-29; accountant Chevrolet div. Gen. Motors Corp., 1933-38; asst. treas. Talon, Inc., Meadville, Pa., 1938-43; chief accountant Am. Steet & Wire Co., Cleve., 1943-49; div. controller Ford Motor Co., 1949-55; controller-treas. Kwikset Locks Co., Anaheim, Cal., 1955-57; dir. finance Cannon Electric Co., Los Angeles, 1957-61; controller Varian Assos., Palo Alto, Cal., 1961-71. Mem. Nat. Assn. Accountants, Financial Execs. Inst. Home: 980 Palo Alto Av Palo Alto CA 94501

ATKINSON, ARTHUR JOHN, physician; b. Chgo., Dec. 4, 1900; s. William James and Bertha (Behn) A.; B.S. and M.S., U. Chgo., 1921; M.D., Rush Med. Coll., 1924; m. Inez Hill, Apr. 27, 1929; children—Inez, Arthur John. Asso. in pharmacology and physiology U. Chgo., 1920-24; intern Presbyn. Hosp., 1924-25; med. residency, Cook County, 1926-27; asso. in medicine Rush Med. Coll., 1925-31; asst. physician Presbyn. Hosp., 1926-30; asst. prof. medicine Northwestern U. since 1931; attending physician Passavant Memorial Hosp. since 1931; specializing in internal medicine since 1926. Mem. Am. Gastroenterol. Assn., A.M.A., Central Soc. for Clin. Research, Inst. of Medicine of Chgo., Chgo. Soc. Internal Medicine, Am. Coll. Gastroenterology, Chgo. Med. Soc. Clubs: Mid-America Chiselers, Chicago Yacht (Chgo.). Home: 54 E Division St Chicago IL 60610 Office: Prudential Bldg Prudential Plaza Chicago IL 60601

ATKINSON, BYRON HARRY, univ. adminstr.; b. Montreal, Ont., Can., Apr. 16, 1917; s. Harry Byron and Isabel (Thomson) A.; B.A., U. Cal. at Los Angeles, 1940, M.A., 1949, Ed.D., 1958; m. Dorothy Rae Fuge, Jan. 3, 1940; children—Byron Scott, Barry Clarke, Shelley, and Craig Jay. Mem. faculty U. Cal. at Los Angeles, 1943—, prof. edn., 1950—, dean students, 1960—. Mem. Cal. Bd. Edn., 1946-64, Cal. State Coll. Bd. Trustees, 1961-64, Gov. Cal. Rehab. Commn., 1945-48. Served to 1st lt., inf., AUS, 1940-43. Mem. Phi Eta Sigma, Sigma Nu, Phi Delta Kappa. Democrat. Conglist. Author articles, monographs. Home: 1621 Idlewood Rd Glendale, CA 91202. Office: 405 Hilgard Av Los Angeles CA 90024

ATKINSON, CARROLL HOLLOWAY, educator; born Fairbury, Nebraska, October 24, 1896; s. Charles Raymond and Florence (Bennie) Atkinson; A.B., Lawrence Coll., 1920; student U. of Grenoble (France), 1919, Pacific U., 1922, U. of Ore., 1922, U. of Washington, 1923, U. of Calif. at Los Angeles, 1926, U. of Southern Calif. (M.A.), 1926-30, U. of Tex., 1937, George Peabody Coll. for Teachers (Ph.D.), 1937-38; m. Ruby Baker, Aug. 23, 1921 (died 1925); children—Yvonne Dorothy, Carroll Holloway; m. 2d, Mary Hanse, 1926 (died 1941); m. 3d, Carol Mary Gonzales, 1959; children—Ardith Anne, Alicia Arthurita, Arthur Amigo. Jr. clerk Metropolitan Life Ins. Co., 1915-16; steno. Sheridan (Wyo.) Iron Works, 1917-18; statistician Kimberly-Clark Paper Co., Wis., 1920-21; athletic coach Lawrence Coll., 1915-17 and 1919-21; prof. and athletic coach, Coll. of Ida., 1921-22; prin. and coach, Forest Grove, Ore., 1922-23, Thorp, Wash., 1923-24, North Bend, Ore., 1924-25; salesman Acme Fast Freight Service, 1925-26; teacher Pasadena Pub. Schs., 1926-30; prin. and coach San Luis Obispo, Calif., 1930-35; ednl. advisor Civilian Conservation Corps, 1935-36; asso. prof. North Texas State Teachers Coll., 1936-37, Edinboro (Pa.) State Teachers Coll., 1938-39; asso. prof. and dir. radio Jersey City and Newark (N.J.) State Teachers colls., 1939-41; dir. Nelson and McLucas Memorial Libraries, Detroit, 1941-45; pub. relations dept., Key System., Oakland, Calif., 1945-46; columnist Honolulu star-Bulletin and radio producer, 1946-47; columnist Santa Fe New Mexican, 1951-52; dean of men, Southwestern U., 1947-49; dir. tchr. tng. Dakota Wesleyan U., 1949-51; lectr. St. Michaels College, Santa Fe, 1951-54, also summer; supervising prin. public schools, Projoaque, New Mexico, 1951-54 teacher (summers) U. of Wash., 1940, U. of Wyo., Northern Mont. Coll. and Eastern Mont. State Normal Sch., 1941, U. of Utah, 1943, N.M. Highlands University, 1949, supervising prin. Belen (N.M.) pub. schs., 1954-57; tchr. pub. schs., Grants, New Mexico, 1957-60; prof. edn., psychology, Tex. Luth. Coll., Sequin, Tex., 1960-61; chmn. psychology dept. Pacific U., 1961-64; vis. prof. history Fla. Meml. Coll., 1964-66; asso. prof. edn. Bethune-Cookman Coll., 1966—. Extension staff faculty, N.M. Western Coll., 1954-57; radio producer, 1931—; with Wally Gluck Enterprises. Mem. exec. com. Boy Scouts Am. Served with A.E.F., World War I. Life mem. N.E.A.; mem. A.A.A.S., Tex. Acad. Sci., Texas Psychol. Assn., Am. Assn. Sch. Adminstrs., Soc. Advancement Learning, Am. Legion, Acad. Polit. Sci., United Comml. Travelers, Portland Psychol. Assn., Am. Assn. of Croix de Guerre, Vets. Fgn. Wars, Am. Assn. U. Profs., Daytona Beach Psychol. Association, International Platform Association. Methodist. Author 19 books, 1938—, including; Intellectual Tramp, 1955; Story of Education, 1962, 65. Address: 3021 N Oleader Av Daytona Beach, FL 32018.

ATKINSON, DANIEL EDWARD, educator, biochemist; b. Pawnee City, Neb., Apr. 8, 1921; s. Max and Amy (Neiswanger) A.; B.Sc., U. Neb., 1942; Ph.D., Ia. State U., 1949; children—Kristine Ruth, Owen Rolf, Joyce Elaine, Ellen Lee, David Eric. Research fellow Cal. Inst. Tech., 1949-50; asso. scientist Argonne Nat. Lab., 1950-52; mem. faculty U. Cal. at Los Angeles, 1952—, prof. chemistry, 1962—. Served with USNR, 1943-46. Guggenheim fellow, 1966-67. Mem. Am. Soc. Biol. Chemists, Am. Chem. Soc., Am. Soc. Microbiology, Am. Soc. Plant Physiologists. Home: 3123 Malcolm Av Los Angeles CA 90034

ATKINSON, FREDERICK GRISWOLD, former dept. store exec.; b. Aspinwall, Pa., Dec. 5, 1904; s. John Frederick and Dee (Griswold) A.; student Columbia Coll., 1922-26; m. Joyce Mallory Hill, May 25, 1934; 1 son, Frederick (dec.). With Cities Service Co. N.Y., 1926-34; with Procter & Gamble Co. of Cin., 1935-40; with R. H. Macy & Co., Inc., N.Y. City, 1940-70, v.p. for personnel administrn., 1948-67, sr. v.p., 1967-70, cons., 1970—; dir., cons. THinc. Career Planning Corp., N.Y.C.; dir. Garden State Plaza Corp.; trustee Seamen's Bank for Savings (N.Y.C.); cons. Econ. Devel. Council N.Y.C. Trustee Roosevelt Hospital, N.Y.C. Chmn. Am. Retail Fedn. Employee Relations Com., 1951-55, chmn. personnel adv. council Nat. Indsl. Conf. Bd., 1952-53. Treas. U.S. Com. UNICEF; mem. labor-mgmt. Manpower Policy Com., ODM; mem. Sec. Labor Adv. Com. Wage Stabilization. Pres. bd. trustees St. Paul's Am. Ch., Rome, Italy, St. James Am. Ch., Florence, Italy; pres. bd. of fgn. parishes P.E. Ch. of U.S. Served as col. USAF, 1942-45; brig. Gen. USAF Res., 1954—; spl. cons. to Sec. of Air Force, 1950-51. Awarded Distinguished Service medal for military service in Air Force personnel adminstrn., World War II. Mem. Am. Mgmt. Assn. (dir., v.p. personnel div. 1954-56, hon. life mem.), Delta Upsilon. Clubs: Union, Wings (N.Y.C.); Army and Navy (Washington). Home: 530 E 72d St New York City, NY 10021. Office: 151 W 34th St New York City NY 10001

ATKINSON, GEORGE HERRING, contractor; b. Colorado Springs, Colo., Apr. 10, 1905; s. Guy F. and Myrtle L. (Herring) A.; A.B. cum laude in Econs., Stanford, 1926; D.Bus. Adminstrn. (hon.), U. Pacific, 1959; m. Mildred McKillican, July 28, 1926 (dec. 1967); children—Duane E., Ray N., Earl H., Lois M.; m. 2d, Lavina Parsons, Apr. 1968. With Guy F. Atkinson Co., contractors and engrs., S. San Francisco, Cal., 1926—, v.p., 1934-43, gen. mgr., 1938-64, pres., 1943-70, chmn., 1970—; mng. dir. Mangla Dam Contractors, bldrs. hydroelectric and irrigation project in W. Pakistan, 1961-68; dir. Hyster Co., 1954—; gen. mgr. Grand Coulee Dam constrn., 1936-38. Pres. San Mateo County Community Chest, 1949-50, The Beavers, Los Angeles, 1958; mem. Gen. Conf. Methodist Ch., 1948, 52, 56, 60, 64, 66, 68, 70; vice chmn. Commn. Interjurisdictional Relations Meth. Ch., 1964-68. Pres. bd. trustees Willamette U., 1964—; trustee Pacific Sch. Religion, Berkeley, Cal., 1944—, San Francisco YMCA, 1945-55. Recipient Golden Beaver award The Beavers, 1965; Moles award The Moles, N.Y.C., 1966. Mem. Asso. Gen. Contractors Am. (gov. bd. 1949-67), Phi Beta Kappa. Republican. Clubs: Arlington (Portland, Ore.); Bankers, Stock Exchange (San Francisco). Author articles in field. Home: 1655 Floribunda Av Hillsborough, CA 94010. Office: 10 W Orange Av South San Francisco CA 94080

ATKINSON, JOHN WILLIAM, educator, psychologist; b. Jersey City, Dec. 31, 1923; s. Frank Gray and Wilhelmina (Meyer) A.; B.A., Wesleyan U., Middletown, Conn., 1947; M.A., U. Mich., 1948, Ph.D., 1950; m. Mary Jane Wanta, Apr. 15, 1944; children—Ann Mina, David John, William Frank. Asst. prof. Wesleyan U., 1949-50; successively asst. prof., prof. psychology, research asso. Survey Research Center U. Mich., Ann Arbor, 1950—. Served to 2d lt. USAAF, 1943-45. Social Sci. Research Council fellow, 1952-55, Center for Advanced Study in Behavioral Scis. fellow, 1955-56, Guggenheim fellow, 1960-61, USPHS spl. research fellow, 1969-70. Fellow Am. Psychol. Assn.; mem. A.A.A.S., Am. Assn. U. Profs. Author: (with others) The Achievement Motive, 1953; An Introduction to Motivation, 1964; (with David Birch) The Dynamics of Action, 1970. Editor: Motives in Fantasy, Action and Society, 1958; (with N. T. Feather) A Theory of Achievement Motivation, 1966.

ATKINSON, JUSTIN BROOKS, journalist; b. Melrose, Mass., Nov. 28, 1894; s. Jonathan H. and Garafelia (Taylor) A.: A.B., Harvard, 1917; L.H.D., Williams Coll., 1941; D.H.L., Adelphi Coll., 1960; LL.D., Pace Coll., Franklin and Marshall Coll., Brandeis Univ., 1965, Clark Univ., 1965, Washington Coll., 1966, Long Island Univ., 1967; m. Oriana MacIlveen, Aug. 18, 1926; 1 step-son-Bruce T. MacIlveen. Began as reporter on Springfield Daily News, 1917; instr. in English, Dartmouth Coll., 1917-18; reporter and asst. to drama critic Boston Evening Transcript, 1919-22; asso. editor Harvard Alumni Bull., 1920-22; editor Book Review, N.Y. Times, 1922-25, drama critic, 1925-42, 46-60; war corr., Chungking, China, 1942-44; news corr. Moscow, 1945-46, critic at large, 1960-65. Cpl., Devel. Batt., Co. Y, Camp Upton, 1918. Awarded Pulitzer prize for journalism, May 1947. Fellow Am. Acad. Arts and Scis. Democrat. Club: The Players (New York City, N.Y.). Author: Skyline Promenades, 1925; Henry Thoreau, Cosmic Yankee, 1927; East of the Hudson, 1931; The Cingalese Prince, 1934; Broadway Scrapbook, 1947; Once Around the Sun, 1951; Tuesdays and Fridays, 1963; Brief Chronicles, 1966; Broadway, 1970. Editor: Walden and other writings of Henry David Thoreau, 1937; Complete Essays and other writings of Ralph Waldo Emerson, 1940; College in a Yard, 1957; The Pace Report, 1966; Sean O'Casey Reader, 1968. Home: Durham NY 12422

ATKINSON, MILTON ANSON, Jr., orgn. exec.; b. nr. Gatesville, Tex., Oct. 27, 1917; s. Milton Anson and Georgia (Wilson) A.; student N.Tex. Agrl. Coll., 1935-37; B.A., Tex. Christian U., 1940; m. Helen Gwendolyn Brower, July 30, 1940; children—Anson Kelley, David Kevin, Dana Christopher. Reservations agt. Am. Airlines, Inc., Dallas, 1941-44, sales rep., Dallas, Memphis, Tulsa, 1946-48, dist. sales mgr., Ft. Worth, Phoenix, 1948-60, city mgr., Phoenix, 1960-63; exec. v.p. Ft. Worth C. of C., 1963-67, C. of C. of Met. St. Louis, 1967—; exec. v.p. St. Louis Regional Commerce and Growth Assn., 1971—. Served to ensign USNR, 1944-46; PTO. Mem. Am. C. of C. Execs. Methodist. Home: 14040 Calcutta Dr Chesterfield MO 63017 Office: 10 Broadway St Louis MO 63102

ATKINSON, PAUL E., shipbuilding co. exec.; b. Mineola, N.Y., 1921; ed. Webb Inst. Naval Architecture, 1942. Pres., dir. Sun Shipbldg. & Dry Dock Co. Home: Route 202 and Warren St Malvern PA 19355 Office: Sun Shipbldg & Dry Dock Co Chester PA 19013*

ATKINSON, RICHARD C., educator; b. Oak Park, Ill., Mar. 19, 1929; s. Herbert and Margaret (Feuerbach) A.; Ph.B., U. Chgo., 1948; Ph.D., Ind. U., 1955; m. Rita Loyd, Aug. 20, 1952; 1 dau., Lynn Loyd. Lectr. applied math. and stats. labs. Stanford (Cal.) U., 1956-57; asst. prof. psychology U. Cal. at Los Angeles, 1957-61; prof., chmn. dept. psychology Stanford, 1961—. Served with AUS, 1954-56. Guggenheim fellow, 1967; fellow Center for Advanced Study in Behavioral Scis., 1963; recipient Distinguished Research award Social Sci. Research Council, 1962. Mem. Soc. Exptl. Psychologists. Author: Introduction to Psychology, 1971; Computer Assisted Instruction, 1969; An Introduction to Mathematical Learning Theory, 1965. Home: 724 Santa Ynez Stanford CA 94305

ATKINSON, STERLING KRICK, retired univ. adminstr.; b. Bellaire, O., Feb. 11, 1904; s. Frank Gillespie and Amelia Caroline (Krick) A.; student Juniata Coll., Huntingdon, Pa., 1921-23; B.S.C., Temple U., 1926; M.A., U. Pa., 1929; Ph.D., Columbia, 1934; m. Mildred Catharine Miller, Dec. 28, 1927; 1 son, Sterling Krick. Mem. faculty and staff Temple U., 1926-69, prof. accounting, 1934-56, v.p., treas., 1956-69; dir. edn. Crown Can Co., 1940-43; research staff Nat. Assn. Accountants, 1943-46; partner Hart, Fry, Atkinson and Rule, C.P.A.'s, Phila., 1947-50; mgmt. specialist Lybrand Ross Bros. & Montgomery, C.P.A.'s, Phila., 1953-56. Mem. Gov. Pa. Adv. Council Statistics, 1955-59, Citizens Budget Com. Phila., 1955-70, C.P.A., Pa. Mem. Am., Pa. insts. C.P.A.'s, Nat. Assn. Accountants (v.p. 1955-56, chmn. research com. 1957-59, chmn. ad hoc com. recognition ednl. attainment 1970-71), Am. Econ. Assn., Am. Accounting Assn., Controllers Inst. Am., Beta Gamma Sigma, Beta Alpha Psi. Contbg. author: Industrial Accountant's Handbook, 1954; The Cost Accountants' Handbook, 1944. Contbr. articles profl. jours. Home: 13402 N 107th Dr Sun City AZ 85351

ATLAS, DAVID, educator; b. Bklyn., May 25, 1924; s. Isadore and Rose (Jaffee) A.; B.Sc., N.Y.U., 1946; M.Sc., Mass. Inst. Tech., 1951, D.Sc. in Meteorology, 1955; m. Lucille Rosen, Sept. 26, 1948; children—Joan Linda, Robert Fred. Chief weather radar br. Air Force Cambridge Research Labs., Bedford, Mass., 1948-66; prof. meterology U. Chgo., 1966—. Chmn. Nat. Acad. Scis. Panel Remote Atmospheric Probing. Served as 1st lt. USAAF, 1943-46. Recipient Loeser award Air Force Cambridge Research Labs., 1957, O'Day award, 1964; Robert M. Losey award Am. Inst. Aero. and Astronautics, 1966. NSF sr. postdoctoral fellow Imperial Coll., London, Eng., 1959-60. Fellow Am. Meteorol. Soc. (councilor 1961-64; Meisinger award 1957; asso. editor publs. 1957—); mem. Am. Geophys. Union, Royal Meteorol. Soc., Internat. Radio Sci. Union (pres. inter- union commn. on radio meteorology 1969—). Inventor weather radar devices. Home: 5131 S Cornell Av Chicago IL 60615

ATOMAN, DANIEL, hosp. adminstr.; b. Lynn, Mass., Mar. 1, 1915; s. Wolff and Rose (Kushner) A.; M.D., Middlesex U., Waltham, Mass., 1939; m. Juanita Katherine McPhate, Nov. 22, 1939; children—Judith (Mrs. Darl Schoonover), Jean (Mrs. Robert Feldman). Intern, Natchez (Miss.) Charity Hosp., 1939-40; resident So. Miss. Charity Hosp., Laurel, 1940-41, King Meml. Hosp., Selma, Ala., 1941-42; mem. staff VA Hosp., Chillicothe, O., 1946-63, chief staff, 1960-63; dir. VA Hosp., Ft. Lyon, Colo., 1963-68, VA Hosp., Pitts., 1968—. Served with M.C., AUS, 1942-46. Mem. A.M.A., Am. Psychiat. Assn., A.A.A.S., Fed. Hosp. Inst., Am. Coll. Hosp. Adminstrs., Assn. Mil. Surgeons U.S. Address: VA Hosp Leech Farm Rd Pittsburgh PA 15206

ATTAWAY, DOUGLAS F., newspaper pub. co. exec.; b. Shreveport, La., 1910. Pres., dir. Journal Pub. Co., Shreveport, pub. Shreveport Journal. Home: 957 Sheridan St Shreveport LA 71104 Office: 222 Lake St Shreveport LA 71102*

ATTEBERRY, MAXINE, univ. dean; b. Du Quoin, Ill., July 15, 1905; d. Albert S. and Lela (Eaton) Atteberry; grad. White Meml. Sch. Nursing, 1933; B.S., Pacific Union Coll., Angwin, Cal., 1939; M.S., U. So. Cal., 1950. Supr. phys. therapy Kern Gen. Hosp., Bakersfield, Cal., 1934-36; instr. pre-nursing La Sierra Coll., Arlington, Cal., 1938-46; dir. bursing Service White Meml. Hosp., 1946-56, dir. Sch. Nursing, 1946-49; asst. dir. Loma Linda U. Sch. Nursing, 1949-54, dean Sch. Nursing, 1954—. Mem. Cal. Bd. Nursing Edn. and Nurse Registration, 1952-60, then pres.; mem. Western Council Higher Edn., 1958—, then pres. Mem. Nat. League Nursing, Am. Nurse Assn. Mem. Seventh Day Adventist Ch. Home: 25795 Lomas Verdes St Redlands CA 92373 Office: Sch of Nursing Anderson St Loma Linda CA 92354

ATTEBERRY, ROY LEIGHTON, army officer; b. Dallas, Mar. 30, 1917; s. Roy Leighton and Maggie (Redman) A.; B.S., U.S. Mil. Acad., 1941; postgrad. Columbia, 1946, Georgetown U., 1956; grad. Brit. Imperial Def. Coll., 1961; m. Priscilla Ropes, Dec. 25, 1941; children—Leighton Chapman, Miriam Gail (Mrs. Robert Fusco), Priscilla Trois, Carol Redman. Commd. 2d lt. U.S. Army, 1941, advanced through grades to brig. gen., 1967; command and staff Pacific and European theaters, World War II, Korea, Vietnam; mem. gen. staff Dept. of Army, SHAPE, 1961-64; chief of staff Theater Army Support Command, Europe, 1968-70; now assigned U.S. Army Tng. Command. Decorated Silver Star with oak leaf cluster, Legion of Merit with 2 oak leaf clusters, Bronze Star with 2 oak leaf clusters (U.S.); Croix de Guerre (France and Belgium). Mem. West Point Alumni Assn., Assn. U.S. Army. Club: University (N.Y.C.). Home: Meredith Neck Rd Meredith NH 03253 Office: Hdqrs US Army Tng Command Fort Dix NJ 08640

ATTEBERRY, WILLIAM DUANE, diversified mfg. co. exec.; b. Decatur, Ill., Mar. 24, 1920; s. William Herman and Lucile (Hunter) A.; B.E., U. So. Cal., 1943; m. Doris Jean Walker, Dec. 19, 1946; children—William Thomas, James Norman, Thomas Hunter. Engr., P.R. Mallory & Co., Indpls., 1946; v.p. Western Lead Products Co., Los Angeles, 1946-51; pres. chems. and metals div. Eagle-Picher Co., Cin., 1951, 60-65; exec. v.p. Eagle-Picher Co., 1965-67, also dir.; pres. Eagle-Picher Industries, Inc., 1967—; dir. Fifth-Third Union Trust Co., Cin., 1st Nat. Bank Joplin, Mo., Empire Dist. Electric Co. Bd. dirs. Joplin YMCA; trustee Boys Club Cin. Served to capt. USMCR, 1943-46; PTO. Mem. Am. Inst. Mining, Metall. and Petroleum Engrs., Am. Zinc Inst. (dir., v.p.), Sigma Chi. Republican. Presbyn (trustee). Clubs: Queen City, Cincinnati Country, Tippecanoe Lake (Ind.) Country. Home: 7956 Indian Hill Rd Cincinnati OH 45203

ATTENBOROUGH, RICHARD SAMUEL, actor; b. Aug. 29, 1923; s. Frederick L. Attenborough; ed. (Leverhulme scholar; Bancroft medal) Royal Acad. Dramatic Art; m. Sheila Beryl Grant Sim. Theatrical appearances include Ah Wilderness, 1941, Awake and Sing, 1942, The Little Foxes, 1942, Brighton Rock, 1943, Journey Together, 1945, The Way Back (Home of the Brave), 1949, To Dorothy, a son, 1950, Sweet Madness, 1952, The MouseTrap, 1952-54, Double Image, 1956-57, The Rape of the Belt, 1957-58; motion pictures include In Which We Serve, School for Secrets, The Man Within, Dancing with Crime, Brighton Rock, London Belongs to Me, The Guinea Pig, The Lost People, Boys in Brown, Morning Departure, Hell's Sold Out, The Magic Box, Gift Horse, Father's Doing Fine, The Eight O'Clock Walk, The Ship That Died of Shame, Private's Progress, The Baby and the Battleship, Brothers in Law, the Scamp, Dunkirk, The Man Upstairs, Sea of Sand, Danger Within, I'm All Right Jack, Jet Storm, S.O.S. Pacific, Only Two Can Play, All Night Long, Trial and Error, The Great Escape, The Third Secret, The Guns of Batasi, The Flight of the Phoenix, The Sand Pebbles; Doctor Dolittle, The Bliss of Mrs. Blossom, Only When I Larf, The Last Grenade, A Severed Head, David Copperfield; co- founder, co-producer Beaver films and appeared in their The Angry Silence, 1959; formed Allied Makers and appeared in first production The League of Gentlemen; producer Whistle Down The Wind, 1961, The L-Shaped Room, 1962; dir. Oh! What a Lovely War, 1968; Young Winston, 1971. Recipient Best Actor award Brit. Film Academy, 1964. Clubs: Garrick; Beefsteak; Green Room. Address: Old Friars Richmond Green Surry England

ATTERBERG, KURT MAGNUS, Swedish composer, condr., critic, violoncellist; b. Göteborg, Sweden, Dec. 12, 1887; s. Anders Johan and Elvira (Uddman) A.; Diploma in Elec. Engring., Royal Tech. High Sch., Stockholm, 1911; student composition with Anders Hallén, 1910-11; m. Margareta Dalsjö, 1925. Condr. Dramatic Theatre, Stockholm, 1915-21; music critic Stockholm-Tidningen, 1919-57; sec. Royal Swedish Acad. Music, 1940-53; condr. orchs. in Sweden, Berlin, Hamburg, Heidelberg, Helsingfors, Vienna, Wiesbaden, Paris, Warsaw, Bremen, Braunschweig, Dresden, Oslo, Bergen, Brussels, Ostende, Vicy. Composer 9 symphonies (Symphony No. 6 recieved Schubert Centenary Meml. Contest award); (operas) Herwarth the Harper, 1919, Bäckahästen, 1925, Fanal, 1934, Aladdin, 1941, The Tempest, 1948; (pantomime ballets) Peter the Swineherd, 1921, The Wise and the Foolish Virgins, 1920; incidental music to Shakespeare's Tempest; three cantatas: Requiem, Jarnbaraland and Songen; 8 suites for orch.; five concertos for solo instruments with orch.; various chamber music and chorus works. Recipient decorations from Sweden, Denmark, Finland, Austria, France, Germany, Norway. Mem. Soc. Swedish Composers (a founder, hon. pres. 1947), Fedn. Conféderation Internationale des Sociétés d'Auteurs et Compositeurs (hon. pres.). Address: Ridogatan 25 11536 Stockholm Sweden

ATTERHOLT, FRANK MARION, cons.; b. Denver, Jan. 24, 1907; s. Frank Marion and Florence (Post) A.; student Phillips Acad., Andover, Mass., 1923-34; B.A., Yale, 1928; m. Emma Link Findlay, Nov. 9, 1929. With Irving Trust Co., N.Y. City, in various capacities, 1928-55, asst. sec. 1939, asst. v.p., 1946, v.p. in charge Rockefeller center office, 1948-55; ind. financial cons., 1955—. Served as capt. CAC, U.S. Army, 1942-45. Mem. Phi Beta Kappa. Republican. Episcopalian. Clubs: Clarksburg (W. Va.) Country; University (N.Y.C.); Tucson Country. Author several short stories. Home: 115 S 5th St Clarksburg WV 26301 Office: 115 S 5th St Clarksburg WV 26301

ATTHAKOR, BUNCHANA, Thailand govt. ofcl.; b. Mahasarakam, Thailand, July 15, 1910; s. Tongdee and Kaew (Namanasarakam) A.; LL.B., Chulalongkorn U., Thailand, 1933, Ph.D., 1966; M.A. in Govt. and Pub. Finance, Ind. U., 1955, LL.D., 1966; m. Sae Sirishinha, July 20, 1936; children—Mrs. Taksina Savanavanda, Mrs. Uttara Rasmussen, Mrs. Burapa Atthakor. Prof. Thammasat U., Thailand, 1956-67; rector Nat. Inst. Devel. Adminstrn., Thailand, 1966-67; dir.-gen. Dept. Tech. and Econ. Coop., Thailand, 1963- 67; former ambassador of Thailand to U.S.; minister econ. affairs. Bd. Govs. Found. Poor Students Thailand. Decorated knight grand cordon Most Exalted Order White Elephant (Thailand); Order Grand Cross (Fed. Republic Germany). Author: Public Finance Administration of Thailand, 1962. Home: 55 S01 65 Sukumvit Rd Bangkok Thailand Office: 2300 Kalcrama Rd NW Washington DC 20008

ATTINELLO, JOHN SALVATORE, aero. engr.; b. Phillipsburg, N.J., Aug. 2, 1920; B.M.E. cum laude, Lafayette Coll., Easton, Pa., 1943; student Cal. Inst. Tech.; M.S. in Aero. Engring., Cath. U. Am., 1950; grad. student U. Md., 1950-55; married, four children. Engring. officer overhaul and repair div. Naval Air Sta., Kodiak and Attu, Alaska, 1943-45; spl. project officer service test dept. Naval Air Sta., Patuxent River, Md., 1945-46; aircraft design, research div. Bur. Aeros., Navy Dept., Washington, 1946-48, asst. head supersonic aerodynamics, 1949-52, head supersonic aerodynamics, 1952-56; asst. chief research Fairchild Aircraft div., Hagerstown, Md., 1955-57, asst. to chief engr. tech. Fairchild Aircraft and Missiles div. Fairchild Engine & Airplane Corp., 1957-59, corp. sci. adv. bd., 1958- 60, asst. to dir engring., 1959-60; chief Scout Class vehicles NASA, 1961, chief exptl. devel., 1961-62; sr. tech. staff Inst. Def. Analyses, research and engring. support div., 1962—, cons. weapons systems evaluations div., 1962—, projects mgr. sr. tech. staff systems evaluation div., 1966-71; numerous sci. lectures. Cons. Brit. Ministry Supply and Royal Navy, 1952-53; cons. U. Mich., 1958, AEC, 1962—. Active Boy Scouts Am.; sec. Franklin County Authority, Greencastle, Pa., 1957-60; v.p. Pinecrest Citizens Assn., 1962-63; bd. dirs. Pincrest Community Center, Inc., 1963, pres., 1964. Recipient Meritorious Civilian Service award devel. highlift BLC system jet aircraft, U.S. Navy, 1953, citation and award for co-invention recording gun camera for use in Korea, 1954. Asso. fellow Inst. Aerospace Scis. (council 1958- 60, 60-62), Royal Aero. Soc.; mem. Nat. Security Industries Assn., Inst. Aero. Scis. (chmn. Hagerstown sect. 1958-59), Tau Beta Pi. Presbyn. (ruling elder). Club: Toastmasters Internat. Contbr. articles tech. publs. Patents in field. Home: 6474 Woodridge Rd Alexandria VA 22312

ATTINGER, ERNST OTTO, educator; b. Zurich, Switzerland, Dec. 27, 1922; s. Ernst and Martha (Padrutt) A.; M.D., U. Zurich, 1949; M.S., Drexel U., 1961; Ph.D., U. Pa., 1965; m. Francoise M.L. Daubige, Feb. 4, 1947; children—Christophe M. E., Nathalene C.M., Joelle M.E. Came to U.S., 1952, naturalized, 1966; Intern and resident San. Du Midi Davos, 1949-52, Lincoln Hosp., N.Y.C., 1952-53, Nat. Jewish Hosp., 1953-54, Boston City Hosp., 1954-56; asst. prof. medicine Tufts U. Sch. Medicine 1956-59; asst. prof., then asso. prof. physiology U. Pa. Vet. Med. Sch., 1961-67; research dir. Presbyn.- U. Pa. Med. Center, 1963-67; prof. biomed. engring., chmn. dept. U. Va. schs. med., engring. and applied Sci., 1967—, prof. physiology, 1967—; cons. in field. Mem. Am. Physiology Soc., Biophys. Soc., I.E.E.E., Biomed. Engring. Soc., Sigma Xi. Editor: Pulsatile Blood Flow, 1964; Global Systems Dynamics, 1970. Home: Blair Park Route 1 Box 277 Crozet VA 22932 Office: Box 224 Medical Center Charlottesville VA 22901

ATTWOOD, WILLIAM, publisher; b. Paris, France, July 14, 1919; s. Frederic and Gladys (Hollingsworth) A.; grad. Choate Sch., 1937; A.B., Princeton, 1941; m. Simone Cadgene, June 22, 1950; children—Peter, Janet, Susan Attwood. Corr., New York Herald Tribune in Paris and with UN bur., 1946-49; European corr. Colliers mag., 1949-51: European editor Look mag., 1951-54, nat. editor, 1955-57, fgn. editor, 1957-61; U.S. ambassador to Guinea, 1961-63; spl. adviser U.S. delegation to UN, 1963-64; U.S. ambassador to Kenya, 1964-66; editor-in-chief, v.p. Cowles Communications, Inc., N.Y.C., 1966-70; pres., pub. Newsday, Inc., Ganden City, N.Y., 1970—. Mem. John F. Kennedy presdl. campaign staff, 1960. Regional alumni trustee Princeton, 1967-71. Served to capt. AUS, 1941-45. Recipient Nat. Headliners award, 1955, 57, George Polk Meml. award, 1956, N.Y. Newspaper Guild Page One award, 1960. Mem. Council Fgn. Relations. Am. Fgn. Service Assn., Nat. Acad. Social Sci. Democrat. Club: Century. Author: The Man Who Could Grow Hair, 1949; Still the Most Exciting Country, 1955; (with George B. Leonard, Jr. and J. Robert Moskin) The Decline of the American Male, 1958; The Reds and the Blacks, 1967; The Fairly Scary Adventure Book, 1969. Home: 423 Carter St New Canaan CT 06840 Office: 550 Stewart Av Garden City NY 11530

ATTWOOD, WILLIAM ELIJAH, Jr., banker; b. New Britan, Conn., Feb. 9, 1913; s. William Elijah and Fannie (Wetmore) A.; A.B., Princeton, 1936; m. Elsa Morgan Frisbie, Sept. 9, 1939; children—William Elijah III, Suzanne M., Polly F. Clk. Goldman, Sachs & Co., N.Y.C., 1936-38; asst. sec. Burritt Mut. Savs. Bank. New Britain, 1938-40, sec., 1940-42, sec.-treas., 1942-49, pres., 1949-54; exec. v.p. New Britain Bank & Trust Co., 1954-58, pres., 1958—; dir. Stanley Works, Allied Thermal Corp. Republican. Episcopalian. Home: 37 Windsor Rd New Britain CT 06052 Office: 235 Main St New Britain CT 06051

ATWATER, A. G. COX, business exec.; B.S.E., Wharton Sch. Commerce, U. Pa., 1931. With Wm. Wrigley Jr. Co., Chgo., since 1933, became sales mgr., 1946, v.p., 1952- 65, hon. sr. v.p., dir.; dir. Uarco Industries, Inc., Wm. Wrigley Jr. Co. Ltd. (Can.). Served with USNR, 1942-46, overseas assignment with O.S.S., 1943-45, now capt. Res. Clubs: Arlington Park Jockey (dir., pres.), Post and Paddock; Chicago Athletic; Tavern (pres.); Lake Geneva (Wis.) Country; Balboa Bay (Newport Beach, Cal.); Lyford Cay (Nassau). Office: 410 N Michigan Av Chicago IL 60611

ATWATER, ELTON, educator; b. Rochester, N.Y., Dec. 22, 1912; s. Lucius C. and Florence (Andrews) A.; A.B., U. Rochester, 1934; M.A., Am. U., 1936, Ph.D., 1939; diploma, Grad. Inst. Internat. Studies, Switzerland, 1938; m. Alice Elizabeth Weitz, Sept. 14, 1945; children—David, Andrew Charles, Ellen Marie, Kevin Robert. Asst. prof. polit. sci. Elmira Coll., 1939-43; asso. prof. internat. affairs Am. U., 1947-50; asso. prof. polit. sci. Pa. State U., 1950-57, prof., 1957—, head dept., 1956-57, 60-63. Asso. dir. Quaker Program at UN, 1957-59, cons., 1971—. Mem. Am. Polit. Sci. Assn., Am. Soc. Internat. Law. Mem. Soc. of Friends. Author: American Regulation of Arms Exports, 1941; (with others) World Affairs, Problems and Prospects, 1958; World Tensions; Conflict and Accomodation, rev. edit., 1972. Contbr. World Book Ency. Home: 450 E Irvin Av State College PA 16801 Office: Dept Polit Sci Pa State U University Park PA 16802

ATWATER, FRANKLIN SIMPSON, ball bearing co. exec.; b. New Britain, Conn., Aug. 24, 1916; s. George Franklin and Ida (Simpson) A.; B.S., Mass. Inst. Tech., 1938; m. Marion Jane Brian, May 9, 1947; children—Mary-Jane, Brian, Sally. Mem. staff Mass. Inst. Tech., 1938-39; with Fafnir Bearing Co. div. Textron, Inc., New Britain, 1939—. prodn. engr., indsl. engring. mgr., asst. gen. works mgr., gen. works mgr., 1939-59, v.p. mfg., 1959-63, v.p. operations, 1963-67, exec. v.p., 1967-69, pres., 1969—; dir. New Britain Nat. Bank, Goss & DeLeeuw Machine Co., Conn. Natural Gas Co. Conglist. Club: Shuttle Meadow Country New Britain). Author: (with L.L. Bethel and others) Industrial Organization and Management, 1945; Essentials of Industrial Management, 1954; Production Control, 1942. Home: 116 Hickory Hill Rd New Britain CT 06052 Office: Fafnir Bearing Co Booth St New Britain CT 06050

ATWATER, GORDON INGHAM, geologist; b. Milw., June 17, 1907; B.A. in Econs., U. Ia., 1929, M.S. in Geology, 1930; Ph.D., U. Wis., 1936; m. Emogene Chapman, June 25, 1934. Instr., U. Ia., 1930; geologist U.S. Geol. Survey, summers 1931- 32; asst, geology Columbia, 1931-32; Emmons econ. fellow Harvard, Yale and Columbia, 1932-33; mem. Ia. Geol. Survey, 1932-34; instr. geology U. Buffalo, summers 1934, 35; geologist N.Y. Geol. Survey, summers 1934, 35, Amerada Petroleum Corp., 1936-37, Skelly Oil Co., 1937-38; chief geologist, head land dept. William Helis Oil Co., 1938-46; cons. geologist, sr. mem. Atwater, Cowan, Carter, Miller & Heffner, New Orleans; pres. Royalties Assos., New Orleans, 1948-63; dir. Plaquemines Oil & Devel. Co. Cons. Ala. Dept. Conservation, 1951-56; spl. cons. La. Mineral Bd., 1957-62; cons. prof. geology La. State Univ., 1965—. Fellow Geol. Soc. Am.; mem. Am. Geol. Inst. (pres. 1961-62), Am. Assn. Petroleum Geologists (v.p. 1958; distinguished lectr. 1957, 65; hon.), New Orleans Geol. Soc. (hon. life), Am. Arbitration Assn. (nat. panel arbitrators), Am. Inst. Mining and Metall. Engrs., Soc. Exploration Geophysicists, A.A.A.S., Am. Geophys. Union, Seismological Soc. Am., Sigma Xi. Home: Osceda Point Lynn Haven FL Office: Whitney Bldg New Orleans LA 70130

ATWATER, HORACE BREWSTER, Jr., food co. exec.; b. Mpls., Apr. 19, 1931; s. Horace Brewster and Eleanor (Cook) A.; A.B., Princeton, 1952; M.B.A., Stanford, 1954; m. Martha Joan Clark, May 8, 1955; children—Elizabeth C., Mary M., John C., Joan P. Divisional v.p., dir. marketing Gen. Mills, Inc., 1958-65, marketing v.p., 1965-70, exec. v.p., 1970—; dir. S & A Co., Foley Mfg. Co. Bd. dirs. Mpls. Soc. Blind, Mpls. Urban League, Hennepin County A.R.C. Served to lt. (j.g.) USNR, 1955-58. Club: Woodhill Country (Wayzata, Minn.). Home: 234 Edgewood St Wayzata MN 55391 Office: 9200 Wayzata Blvd Minneapolis MN 55426

ATWATER, JAMES DAVID, journalist b. Westfield, Mass., Oct. 25, 1928; s. William Henry and Vesta Buffum (Gannett) A.; B.A., Yale, 1950; m. Patricia Anne Levington, Jan. 15, 1955; children—Mary Elizabeth, Stephen Gannett, Christopher Perry, Andrea, Katharine, Jennifer. Corr., writer Time mag., 1953-62; contbg. editor Sat. Eve. Post, 1963-66, sr. editor, 1966-69; mag. writer, 1971—. Spl. asst. to Pres. U.S., 1969-70. Mem. sch. bd. Union Free Sch. Dist. 2, Town Greenburgh, N.Y., 1965-69, pres., 1968. Served to 1st lt. USAF, 1950-53. Address: 81 Abingdon Villas London W8 England

ATWATER, VERNE STAFFORD, banker; b. Pitts., Aug. 22, 1920; s. Verne L. and Priscilla (Brodeur) A.; B.A. Heidelberg Coll., 1942; M.B.A. Harvard, 1943; Ph.D. in Econs., N.Y.U., 1961; m. Evelyn Lowe, May 29, 1943; children—Lynda, Louise. Dir. placement, asst. prof. bus. adminstrn. Syracuse U., 1946-50; asst. to chmn. bd. N.J. Bank, Paterson, 1950-56; dir. adminstrn. Ford Found., 1956-61, rep., Argentina/Chile, 1961-63, dir. Latin Am. and Caribbean Program, 1963-65, v.p., 1964-68; pres. Westinghouse Learning Corp., N.Y.C., 1968-71; pres., chief exec. officer, trustee Central Savs. Bank, N.Y. Mem. Pres.'s Task Force Career Devel., 1967-68, N.Y. State Bus. Adv. Council, N.J. Housing Finance Agy., 1966-70. Trustee Heidelberg Coll., Paterson State Coll. Served to lt. USNR, 1943-46. Clubs: Arcola County (Paramus, N.J.): University (N.Y.C.); Harvard Business School of N.Y. (dir.). Home: 6 Maynard Ct Ridgewood NJ 07450 Office: 2100 Broadway New York City NY 10023

ATWELL, ROBERT JAMES, medical educator; b. Gary, Ind., Sept. 1, 1919; s. Oswald B. and Helen N. (Neuding) A.; A.B., Duke, 1941; M.D., 1944; m. Paula Mozelle Mitchell, Apr. 28, 1945; children—Robert, David M., Paul N. Intern Duke Hosp., 1944-45; resident Duke Hosp., 1945-47, Bellevue Hosp., N.Y.C., 1947-48; chief med. service Ohio Tb Hosp., Columbus, 1950-66; mem. faculty Coll. Medicine, Ohio State U., 1951—, prof., 1966—; mem. attending staff U. Hosp., Columbua, 1952—, dir., prof. Sch. Allied Med. Professions, 1966—. Cons. asst. sec. health affairs Dept. Health, Edn. and Welfare, 1971—, Nat. Library Medicine, 1970—, A.M.A., 1969—, Regional Med. Programs, Dept. Health, Edn. and Welfare, 1969—, Bur. Health Manpower Edn., NIH, 1968-70, Nat. Inst. Arthritis and Metabolic Diseases, 1962, VA, 1954—. Chmn. med. adv. coms. State Tchrs. Retirement System, State of Ohio, 1966—. Fellow A.C.P.; mem. Assn. Schs. Allied Health Professions (sec.-treas. 1969, pres. 1971), A.M.A., Am. Thoracic Soc., Central Soc. Clin. Research, Am. Fedn. Clin. Research. Contbr. articles profl. jours. Home: 1964 Collingswood Rd Columbus OH 43221

ATWELL, WEBSTER, lawyer; b. Dallas, July 8, 1900; s. William Hawley and Susan (Snyder) A.; B.A., Williams Coll., 1921; LL.B., Harvard, 1924; m. Laura Burgher, Apr. 27, 1928; children—William Webster, Anthony. Admitted to Tex. bar, 1924; asst. U.S. Atty., No. Dist. Tex., 1924-25; pvt. practice gen. civil law, Dallas, 1925—; sr.

partner firm Atwell, Grayson & Atwell, 1961-69; of counsel Atwell, Malouf, Mussel-White & Bynum, Dallas, 1969—. Dir. Southland Corp., Great Nat. Life Ins. Co. Exec. com. Soc. Alumni Williams Coll., chmn. Alumni Fund, 1953-54, also mem. development com. bd. trustees. Active World Peace Through Law Center. Bd. visitors So. Meth. U. Served with R.O.T.C., World War I. Mem. Dallas C. of C., Assn. Life Ins. Counsel (pres. 1958-59), Internat., Am. (ho. dels. 1964-65), Tex., Dallas bar assns., Am. Judicature Soc., Am. Life Conv., Nat. Legal Aid and Defenders Assn., Tex. Bar Found., Phi Delta Theta, Delta Sigma Rho. Methodist (mem. ofcl. bd., trustee). Clubs: Lawyers, Williams (N.Y.C.); Petroleum, Brook Hollow Country (Dallas). Author: The Case for Oil and Gas Loans, 1942; The Life Insurance Law of Texas, 1948. Home: 3630 Overbrook Dr Dallas TX 75205 Office: Republic Nat Bank Tower Dallas TX 75101

ATWOOD, ANN MARGARET, author; b. Heber, Cal., Feb. 12, 1913; d. Howard C. and Marie (Jones) Atwood; B.A., U. Redlands, 1934; student Art Center Sch., Los Angeles, summer 1935. Owner, mgr. Ann Atwood Studio Children's Portraiture, Riverside, Cal., 1937-40, San Marino, Cal., 1940-60, S. Laguna, Cal., 1960-67; founder, dir. adult edn. class in poetry writing, Riverside, 1938-40; tchr. poetry Hollywood (Cal.) High Sch., 1943-44. Mem. Sierra Club, Wilderness Soc. Republican. Author, illustrator (or author-photographer) (poetry) Being Made of Earth, 1940; The Little Circle, 1967; author, illustrator: New Moon Cove (awards 1969, 70), 1969; The Wild Young Desert, 1970; Haiku: The Mood of Earth, 1971; author-photographer: (filmstrips) Sea, Sand and Shore, 1969; The Art of the Sea, 1969; Signatures in the Sand, 1969; The Making of a Desert, 1970; Life Conquers the Desert, 1970; The Little Circle (Silver medal Internat. Film and TV Festival 1970), 1970; The Heart of Haiku, 1971; Haiku: A Photographic Interpretation, 1971; (filmstrips with Elizabeth B. Hazelton) Sammy, the Crow, 1970; Tahiti is my Island, 1969; Teeka, the otter, 1971; photographer: Sammy, The Crow Who Remembered, 1969. Address: 32013 Point Pl South Laguna CA 92677

ATWOOD, EDWARD CHARLES, JR., univ. dean; b. N.Y.C., Dec. 2, 1922; s. Edward Charles and Bertha Margaret (Moloney) A.; A.B., Princeton, 1946, M.A., 1950, Ph.D. in Econs., 1959; m. June Matilda Ruschmeyer, Mar. 30, 1946; children—Edward Charles III, Jeffrey Terrell. Teaching fellow U. Buffalo, 1946-47; part-time instr. Princeton, 1948-50; instr. Denison U., 1950-52; from asst. to asso. prof. Washington and Lee U., 1952-60, dean students, 1961-69, dean Sch. Commerce, 1969-, also prof. econs.; econ. cons. Bankers Trust Co., N.Y.C., 1956; economist Gen. Electric Co., 1960-61; tchr. courses Am. Inst. Banking, Va., Sch. Banking, 1957-59. Dir. Rockbridge Nat. Bank, Lexington, Va. Served with USNR, 1942-46. Mem. Am., So. econ. assns., Beta Gamma Sigma, Omicron Delta Kappa, Omicron Delta Epsilon. Presbyn. Home: 203 W Preston St Lexington VA 24450

ATWOOD, EDWARD WILSON, lawyer; b. Portland, Me., June 27, 1897; s. Thomas W. W. and Grace E. (Tobie) A.; student Bowdoin Coll., 1916-17; LL.B., Boston U., 1922; m. Luena Hutchinson, Sept. 1, 1927; children—Thomas W. W. (U.S. Army), Luena A. (Mrs. Howard W. Whitaker). Admitted to Me. bar, 1922, since practiced in Portland; now mem. firm Pierce, Atwood, Scribner, Allen & McKusick. Mem. Maine Bd. Bar Examiners, 1935-51. Dir. Keyes Fibre Co., Waterville, Me. Mem. Me. Ho. of Reps. from Portland Dist., 1923-25. Corporator Me. Med. Center, Portland. Served to 2d lt. U.S. Army, 1917- 19; AEF in France. Mem. Am., Me. (pres. 1951-52) bar assns., Psi Upsilon, Woolsack Soc. Republican. Clubs: Portland Country, Cumberland (Portland). Home: 223 Western Promenade Portland ME 04102 Office: One Monument Square Portland ME 04111

ATWOOD, FELIX, lawyer; b. Ennis, Tex., Mar. 4, 1908; s. Harry and Bessie (Craig) A.; A.B., Tex. Christian U., 1931; LL.B., Tex. U., 1931; m. Martha Ellen Templeton, Aug. 4, 1934; 1 son, Felix Michael. Admitted to Tex. bar, 1931, practiced in Ennis, 1931-39, city atty., 1936-39; spl. atty. Bur. Internal Revenue, Washington, 1939-42, counsel charge tech. staff, St. Louis office, 1946; pvt. practice specializing in fed. income taxation, Dallas, 1946—; sec., dir. Ennis Business Forms, Inc.; lectr. tax matters Southwestern Legal Inst., former chmn. 4th ann. inst. U. Tex. Law Sch. Served as lt. col. Judge Adv. Gen's. Dept., AUS, 1942-45. Mem. Am. (tax sect.), Fed., Tex., Dallas bar assns., Sigma Alpha Epsilon. Presbyterian. Woodman of the World, Mason. Clubs: Engineers, Lancers (Dallas). Lectr. before various bar, accountants assns. Home: 307 N Sherman St Ennis TX 75119 Office: Republic Nat Bank Bldg Dallas TX 75201

ATWOOD, GEORGE ELLIOT, mining co. exec.; b. Savannah, Ga., July 21, 1918; s. Jules Epping and Mary Jane (McIntosh) A.; B.S., N.M. Inst. Mining and Tech. 1939, Met. Engr., 1945, Eng. D., 1968; m. Mildred Kayser, Mar. 1, 1954; children—Mary Elizabeth, Mary Ellen, George Elliot, Barbara Ann, Thomas Jules. Metall. supt. Potash div. Internat. Minerals & Chem. Corp., Carlsbad, N.M., 1940-50; asst. resident mgr. Potash div. Duval Corp., Carlsbad,N.M., 1950-54, resident mgr., 1954-57, resident mgr. Copper div., Tucson, Ariz., 1957-58, v.p., dir., 1958-64; exec. v.p., dir. Duval Corp., Tucson, Ariz., 1964—, also Duval Sierrita Corp., Duval Sales Corp. Mem. Am. Inst. Metall. Engrs., Mining and Metall. Soc. Am. Clubs: Tucson Country Club, Tucson Nat. Golf Club, Presidents Club U. Ariz. Patentee mineral dressing and solubility chemistry. Home: 4101 E Poe St Tucson AZ 85711 Office: 4715 E Fort Lowell Rd Tucson AZ 85712

ATWOOD, HARRY ERWIN, life ins. exec.; b. Park Rapids, Minn., Aug. 29, 1910; s. Erwin W. and Louise (Berg) A.; A.B. cum laude, U. Minn., 1931; m. Margaret A. White, Nov. 19, 1932; children—Roger, Nancy. With Northwestern Nat. Life Ins. Co., Mpls., 1931—, beginning as staff publicity advt., successively agy. sec., 2d v.p., 1931-56, exec. v.p., dir., 1956-69, now pres., dir.; pres., dir. N. Atlantic Life Ins. Co., Jericho, N.Y.; dir. 1st Hennepin state Bank, Mpls. Mem. pub. relations council Inst. Life Ins. Pres., trustee Bapt. Hosp. Fund, St. Paul; trustee United Hosp. Fund.; bd. dirs. Mpls. area chpt. A.R.C.; bd. pres.' assos. Bethel Coll., St. Paul. Recipient Francis E. Harrington award for outstanding service in field pub. health in Minn., 1967. Mem. Health Ins. Assn. Am. (dir.), Beta Theta Pi, Sigma Delta Chi. Republican. Baptist. Rotarian. Clubs: Wayzata (Minn.) Country: Minneapolis, Skylight (Mpls.). Home: 4465 Ellerdale Rd Hopkins MN 55343 Office: 20 Washington Av S Minneapolis MN 55440

ATWOOD, JOHN LELAND, corp. exec.; b. Walton, Ky., Oct. 26, 1904; s. Elmer Bugg and Mabel (Bagby) A.; A.B., Hardin Simmons Coll., 1926; B.S., U. of Tex., 1928; D.Eng., Stevens Inst. Tech., 1955, Carnegie-Mellon U., 1965; m. M. Saxon Songer, Oct. 26, 1968 (dec.); 1 dau. by prev. marriage, Marian. Jr. aeroplane engr. with Army Air Corps, Wright Field, Dayton, O., 1928-29; design engr. Douglas Aircraft Co., Santa Monica, Cal., 1930-34; v.p. and chief engr. North Am. Aviation, Inc., 1934-38, v.p. and asst. gen. mgr., 1938-41, 1st v.p. 1941, pres., 1948-67, chief exec. officer, 1960-67, chmn. bd., 1962-67; pres., chief exec. officer N. Am. Rockwell Corp., 1967-70, sr. cons., dir., 1970—; dir. Times Mirror Co., Pacific Indemnity Co. Chmn. industry adv. com. NACA, 1958. Recipient Presidential Certificate Merit, 1948, Pub. Service award NASA, 1969, Distinguished Engring. Grad. award Coll. Engring., U. Tex., 1960; named comdr. of merit, Italy, 1955. Hon. fellow Am. Inst. Aero. and Astronautics; mem. Soc. Automotive Engrs., Aerospace Industries Assn. (hon. adv. com.), Tau Beta Pi. Baptist. Office: 1700 E Imperial Hwy El Segundo CA 90245

ATWOOD, KIMBALL CHASE III, geneticist; b. N.Y.C., May 15, 1921; s. Kimball Chase, Jr. and Mary Evelyn (Girdner) A.; A.B., Columbia, 1942; M.D., N. Y. U., 1946; m. Barbara F. Drew, Mar. 31, 1945; children—Barbara J., Jane E., Kimball C., Nathaniel B. Asst. zoology Columbia, 1942, vis. asst. prof., 1950- 51; intern Bellevue Hosp., N.Y.C., 1946-47; sr. biologist Oak Ridge Nat. Lab., 1951-58; asso. prof. med. genetics U. Chgo., 1958-60; prof. microbiology, 1960-69, head dept. U. Ill., 1960-63; prof. genetics Columbia, 1969—. Corporate mem. Marine Biol. Lab., Woods Hole, Mass. Diplomate Nat. Bd. Med. Examiners. Fellow A.A.A.S., N.Y. Acad. Scis.; mem. Genetics Soc. Am., Soc. Am. Naturalists, Radiation Research Soc., Sigma Xi, Phi Kappa Phi, Alpha Omega Alpha. Club: Woods Hole (Mass.) Yacht. Home: 560 Riverside Dr New York City NY

ATWOOD, PAUL WILLIAMS, Investment co. exec.; b. Winona, Ida., Jan. 4, 1903; s. Thomas Melvin and Della Dain (O'Neal) A.; B.S. in Bus. Adminstrn., U. Idaho, 1927; m. Ethel Bache, Dec. 24, 1932; 1 dau., Eloise Jean (Mrs. Richard W. Barlow). Engaged in advt. and mdsg. Call-Bulletin, San Francisco, 1927-29; dir. research Assn. Nat. Advertisers, N.Y.C., 1929- 34; dir. marketing E. T. Howard Co., N.Y.C., 1934-37; mgmt. cons., 1937- 41; partner Stewart, Dougall & Assos., mgmt. cons., N.Y.C., 1941-52; pres. U B S Chem. Co., Cambridge, Mass., 1953-62; pres. Fed. St. Capital Corp., Boston, 1964-68, now dir.; dir. Design Pak, Inc., Marlboro, Mass., Trans-Sonics, Inc., Burlington, Mass., Atkins and Merrill, Inc., Maynard, Mass., Transworld Adhesives & Chems., Rockland, Mass.; trustee The Home Savings Bank of Boston. Mem. Newcomen Soc., S.A.R., Kappa Sigma, Alpha Kappa Psi. Conglist. Clubs: Algonquin, Down Town (Boston); Winchester Country. Author articles on mgmt. and marketing. Home: 21 Pilgrim Dr Winchester MA 01890 Office: 75 Federal St Boston MA 02110

ATWOOD, ROBERT BRUCE, editor and publisher; b. Chicago, Ill., Mar. 31, 1907; s. Burton H. and Mary Beach (Stevenson) A.; A.B., Clark U., 1929; Doctor of Letters, Alaska Meth. Univ., 1967; m. Evangeline Rasmuson, Apr. 2, 1932; children—Marilyn A. Odom, Sara Elaine. Reporter Worcester (Mass.) Telegram, 1926-29 and 1934-35, Ill. state Journal, Springfield, 1929-34; editor and pub. Anchorage (Alaska) Daily Times; pres. The Anchorage- Westward Hotel Company; director of Alaska Airlines. Chairman of the Alaska Statehood committee, 1949-59. Norwegian vice consul at Anchorage, Alaska. Mem. Asso. Press, American Newspaper Pubs. Assn., Internat. Press Inst., Am. Polar Soc. (gov.), Am. Soc. Newspaper Editors, C. of C. (pres. 1944, 48), Inter-Am. Press Assn., Sigma Delta Chi. Republican. Presbyterian. Rotarian. Club: National Press. Author pamphlets, articles, editorials published in various jours. Office: 820 Fourth Av Anchorage AK 99501

ATWOOD, ROLLIN SALISBURY, ret. educator; b. Chgo., June 19, 1903; s. Wallace Walter and Harriet Towle (Bradley) A.; B.S., U. Chgo., 1924; M.S., Clark U., 1925, Ph.D., 1928; postgrad. U. Manchester, 1926-27; m. Ruth Letitia Cox, May 24, 1930; children—Frances Patricia, Ruth Letitia. Tchr. geogrpahy high schs., Trenton, N.J., 1925-26; prof. geography Bucknell U., summer 1926, 29; asst. prof. geography U. Fla., 1928-29, asso. prof., 1929-35, asst. dean coll. bus. adminstrn., 1930-31, dir. Inst. Inter-Am. Affairs, 1930-42, prof. geography, 1935-42, chmn. social sci. courses gen. coll., 1935-40, chmn. div. geography and geology, 1940-42; prof. geography Clark U., summer 1928, U. Ia., summer 1940; research asso. Carnegie Instn. of Washington, 1932-34; sr. econ. analyst, asst. comml. attache U.S. Fgn. Service, Am. embassy, Quito, Ecuador, 1942-44; econ. policy officer div. North and West Coast Affairs, Office Am. Republic Affairs, State Dept., Chief research br. div. Geography and Cartography, 1945-46, asst. chief div. River Plate Affairs, 1947, acting dir. Office North and West Coast Affairs, 1950, dep. dir. Office S. Am. Affairs, 1950, dir., 1951-55; dir. Office Latin Am. Operations, 1955-61, dir. office spl. operations Inter-Am. Devel. Bank, Washington, 1961-62; prof. geography Am. U. Sch. Internat. Service, Washington, 1962-68, prof. emeritus, 1968—; spl. lectr. geog. factors in world economy Fgn. Service Ednl. Found., Washington, spring semesters, 1945, 46, Am. U., 1945. Mem. Dept. of State Adv. Com. Adjustment Fgn. Students in U.S., 1940-42; U. Fla. del. to Pan Am. Reciprocal Trade Conf., Sacramento, Fla., 1930, 4th Pan Am. Comml. Conf., Washington, 1931, 2d Annual Conf. Pan Am. Inst. Geography and History, Washington, 1935; U.S. del. 5th Pan Am. Inst. Geography and History, Santiago, Chile, 1950; del. Inter-Am. Econ. and Social Council, Brazil, 1954, Internat. Geog. Congress, Brazil, 1956. Mem. bd. Instituto de las Espanas, 1938-42; trustee Bradley Elementary Sch. (Bethesda, Md.). Recipient Cervantes medal Instituto de las Espanas, 1942. Fellow Swedish Anthropology and Geography Soc. (hon.); mem. Assn. Clark Geographers, Am. Geog. Soc., Pan Am. Soc., Geography Soc. Eng., Assn. Am. Geographers, Fla. Assn. Colls. and Univs. (council mem. 1936-42), Fla. Acad. Scis. (chmn. social sci. div. 1936-38, v.p. 1936-37), Fla. State C. of C. (chmn. Pan Am. com., 1938-42), Delta Kappa Epsilon. Author: The Localization of the Cotton Industry in Lancashire, England, 1930; Workbook in Geography, 1935; numerous articles profl. jours. Home: 19107 Roman Way Gaithersburg MD 20760

ATWOOD, SANFORD SOVERHILL, univ. pres.; b. Janesville, Wis., Dec. 3, 1912; s. C. Starr and Cora (Soverhill) A.; B.A., U. Wis., 1934, M.A., 1934, Ph.D., 1937; L.H.D. (hon.), Gettysburg Coll., 1966; m. Nora Elizabeth Long, Aug. 15, 1936; children—Charles Starr, Elizabeth Ann, Phoebe Ellen, Richard Jay. Teaching fellow, asst. U. Wis., 1934-37; asst., asso. agronomist U.S. Regional Pasture Research Lab., State Coll., Pa., 1937-44; asst. prof., asso. prof. plant breeding Cornell, 1944-48, prof., 1948-63, head dept. plant breeding, 1949-53, dean grad. sch., 1953-55, provost, 1955-63; pres. Emory U., Atlanta, 1963—. Chmn. So. dist. com. selection Rhodes scholarships, 1967, 68, 69; mem. adv. council Marshall Scholarships, 1966—; mem. adv. panel for sea grant instnl. support Nat. Oceanic and Atmospheric Adminstrn., 1966—; chmn. com. agrl. land use and wildlife resources NRC-Nat. Acad. Scis., 1965-70; mem. Council So. Univs., 1964—, pres., 1967-68. Bd. dirs. Oak Ridge Asso. Univs, 1965—, Council for Financial Aid to Edn., 1969—, Nat. Med. Fellowships, 1968—, Met. Atlanta Rapid Transit, 1965—; bd. vis. Air U., 1969-71, chmn., 1970-71; mem. So. regional adv. com. Inst. Internat. Edn., 1966—; trustee Com. for Econ. Devel., 1965—, mem. research and policy com., 1971—; trustee Alpha Chi Rho Ednl. Found., 1962—. Fellow Am. Soc. Agronomy, N.Y. Acad. Sci.) A.A.A.S.; mem. Am. Soc. Naturalists, Atlanta C. of C. (dir. 1963-67), Am. Genetic Assn., Am. Assn. U. Profs., Genetics Soc. Am., Bot. Soc. Am., Biometrics Soc., Atlantic Council of U. S., Phi Beta Kappa, Sigma Xi, Phi Kappa Phi, Omicron Delta Kappa, Phi Sigma, Gamma Alpha, Phi Eta Sigma, Alpha Chi Rho. Rotarian. Clubs: Atlanta Athletic, Piedmont Driving, Capital City, Druid Hills Golf; University (N.Y.C.); Cosmos (Washington). Contbr. articles sci. jours., books. Home: 1463 Clifton Rd NE Atlanta GA 30329

ATYEO, HENRY CLAY, educator; b. Belleville, Mich., May 5, 1905; s. Oliver C. and Emily (Newberry) A.; B.S., Wayne U., 1926; diploma Am. Acad. Classical Studies, Rome, Italy, 1929; M.A., U. Mich., 1931; Ph.D., Columbia, 1939; m. Violet M. Rodriguez, Dec. 20, 1940 (dec.); 1 son, James Henry Atyeo. Tchr. of social studies Southwestern High School, Detroit, 1926-34; tchr. history White Plains (N.Y.) High Sch., 1934-47, chmn. dept., 1941-47; inst. history Hampton Inst., summers, 1944-45; part-time instr. Sch. Commerce, N.Y.U., 1945-46, asst. prof., 1947-52, asso. prof., 1952-58, prof., 1958-64, vice chmn. gen. course group, 1952-59, chmn. 1959-64, mem. commn. coordinated liberal studies, 1963—; prof. history Washington Square Coll. N.Y.U., 1964—. Guest appearances, radio program Headlines in Perspective, NBC, 1954-55; dir., instr. hist. closed-circuit TV expt., 1957. Chmn. N.Y.U. Interfaith Council, 1957, 59; mem. White Plains Civil Def. Council, 1942-45, Bd. mgrs., mem. exec. com., br. YMCA, 1955-65; rep. (Methodist) U. Christian Found. of N.Y.U. Fellow, Hebrew U., Jerusalem, Israel, 1967, Confs. in E. Africa countries: Kenya, Uganda, Tanzania, 1970. Mem. Am. Assn. U. Profs. Am. Hist. Assn., Phi Delta Kappa, Kappa Delta Pi, Sigma Eta Phi, Alpha Phi Sigma. Methodist (lay preacher 1940-69). Clubs: Arch and Square, New York U. Faculty. Author: The Excursion as a Teaching Technique, 1939. Author articles on Middle East, 1950—. Home: 90 Bryant Av White Plains, NY 10605. Office: New York U Washington Sq New York City NY 10003

ATZMON, ISRAELI MOSHE, condr.; b. Budapest, Hungary, July 30, 1931; ed. Tel-Aviv Acad. Music, Guildhall Sch. Music, London; m. Niza Atzmon; 2 daus. Played horn for various orchs.; Chief condr. Sydney (Australia) Symphony Orch., 1969—; condr. in Israel, Eng., Australia, Germany, Sweden, Norway, Switzerland, Spain, Finland, Italy, Austria, Turkey and U.S.A.; guest condr. Ravinia Festival, Chgo., 1968. Recipient Leonard Berstein prize, 1963; 1st prize Internat. Condrs. Competition, Liverpool, Eng., 1964. Address: 16 Canfield Gardens London NW 6 England*

AU, TUNG, educator; b. Hong Kong, Sept. 8, 1923; s. Tung C. and Fuk K. (Leung) A.; came to U.S., 1947, naturalized, 1963; B.S., St. John's U., 1943; M.S., U. Ill., 1948, Ph.D., 1951; M. Sci. Engring., U. Mich., 1954; m. Isabel Szeto, June 18, 1955; children—Thomas, Yolande. Structural engr., 1951-55; asst. prof. U. Detroit, 1955-57; asso. prof. Carnegie-Mellon U., 1957-64, prof., 1964—, acting head civil engring. dept., 1971; engring. cons. Registered profl. engr., Pa., Ill. Mem. Am. Soc. C.E., Nat. Soc. Profl. Engrs., Am. Soc. Engring. Edn., Am. Concrete Inst., Operations Research Soc. Am., Sigma Xi, Phi Kappa Phi, Tau Beta Pi. Author: Elementary Structural Mechanics, 1963; Introduction to Systems Engineering-Deterministic Models, 1969. Contbr. reports: Keystone Corridor Transportation Study, 1965; Testing and Evaluation of Transit Expressway, 1966. Home: 625 Driftwood Dr Pittsburgh PA 15238

AUBARET, PIERRE-HENRI, diplomat of Switzerland; b. Geneva, Jan. 9, 1913; s. Charles and Jane (Chevallier) A.; Licencie en droit, U. Geneva, 1935; lawyer's diploma, U. Berne (Switzerland), 1937; m. Madeleine Barbier-Revaclier, Jan. 25, 1941; children—Francois, Olivier. With bank in Berlin, 1937-38, solicitor in London, 1938-39; attache legation Fed. Polit. Dept., Berne, 1940-44; dep. comml. attache legation, London, 1944-45, 2d sec., 1945-47, 1st sec. polit. sect., 1947-48; 1st sec. acting counsellor legation, New Delhi, India, 1948-51; with div. commerce, Berne, 1951-52, counsellor legation, head sect. Latin Am. div. commerce, 1952-55; consul gen., Wellington, New Zealand, 1955-59; Swiss mem. Neutral Nat. Supervisory Commn., Korea, 1957; ambassador to Indonesia, 1959-63, to Fedn. Malaya, 1961-62, to Norway and Iceland, 1963-69; consul gen., N.Y.C., 1969—. Served as capt., F.A., Swiss Army. Home: 640 Park Av New York City NY 10021 Office: 444 Madison Av New York City NY 10022

AUBERGER, KENNETH JAMES, govt. ofcl.; b. Rochester, N.Y., Sept. 23, 1926; s. Joseph and Evelyn (McGinness) A.; B.B.A., St. Bernadine-Siena Coll., 1950; J.D., Am. U., 1959, M.B.A., 1961; m. Patricia Frances Sacco, Apr. 14, 1951. Accountant-auditor Carl Thomy & Co., Rochester, 1950-51, U.S. Gen. Accounting Office, 1952-64; chief examiner Farm Credit Adminstrn., 1965—; admitted to D.C. bar, 1960. Served with USNR, 1945-46, 51-52. C.P.A., Md. Mem. Am., D.C. bar assns., Am. Inst. C.P.A.'s, Md. Soc. C.P.A.'s. Home: 10410 Gary Rd Potomac MD 20854 Office: Farm Credit Adminstrn Washington DC 20578

AUBREY, JAMES THOMAS, Jr., radio and TV exec.; b. LaSalle, Ill., Dec. 14, 1918; s. James Thomas and Mildred (Stever) A.; grad. Phillips Exeter Acad., 1937; A.B. cum laude, Princeton, 1941; m. Phyllis St. Felix Thaxter, Nov. 16, 1944 (div.); children—Susan Schuyler, James Watson. Account exec. Street & Smith Publs. and Conde Nast, 1946-48; account exec. CBS Radio Sta. KNX, 1948- 50, account exec., gen. sales mgr., gen. mgr. TV sta, KNXT, 1951-55; program mgr. CBS TV Network, Hollywood, 1955-56, v.p. in charge creative services CBS, Inc., 1958-59, executive vice president CBS Television Network, 1959, president, 1959-65; vice president in charge of programs, talent ABC TV Network, 1956-58; pres. MGM, 1969—. Co-chmn. Heart Com. of Broadcasting Industry. Adv. bd. Mus. Theater Acad.; bd. dirs. Brand Names Found., American Shakespeare Festival Theatre and Acad. Served as maj. USAAF, 1941-45. Mem. Newcomen Soc. N. Am. Episcopalian. Clubs: Brook (N.Y.C.); Sleepy Hollow Country (Pleasantville, N.Y.); Nat. Golf Links of Am.; Bel-Air Country (Los Angeles); LaQuinta (Cal.) Country. Home: 116 Central Park S New York City NY 10019

AUBREY, STEVER, advt. exec.; b. LaSalle, Ill., Aug. 31, 1920; s. James Thomas and Mildred (Stever) A.; grad. Phillips Exeter Acad., 1939; B.A., Princeton, 1943; m. Sally Hixon, May 23, 1947; children—Lynne, Jennifer, Catherine, Stever H., Michael R. With Anderson, Davis & Platte, N.Y.C., 1946-50, J. Walter Thompson Co., 1950-58, McCann Erickson, 1958-59, Doherty, Clifford Steers & Shenfield, Inc., 1959-61; exec. v.p., dir. exec. com. J. Walter Thompson Co., 1961—. Trustee St. Vincent's Hosp. Clubs: Racquet and Tennis (N.Y.C.); Country (New Canaan, Conn.). Home: 545 West Rd New Canaan CT 06840 Office: 420 Lexington Av New York City NY 10017

AUBRY, EUGENE EDWARDS, architect; b. Galveston, Tex., Nov. 15, 1935; s. Frank J. and Christine C. (Anderson) A.; B.S., U. Houston, also B.Arch.; m. Elizabeth Hunter, July 12, 1958; children—Camilla Elizabeth, Christine Eugenia. Partner firm Barnstone and Aubry, 1966-70, Wilson, Morris, Crain & Anderson, Houston, 1970—; prin. works include Harris County Center for Retarded, 1967, John F. Mather residence, 1967, offices of Schlumberger Ltd., N.Y.C., 1967, offices of Paul, Weiss, Goldberg, Rifkind, Wharton and Garrison, N.Y.C., 1968, Inst. for Arts and Media Center, Rice U., Houston. Mem. Contemporary Art Assn., Mus. Fine Arts Houston, Mus. Fine Arts N.Y.C., A.I.A., Tex. Soc. Architects. Home: 2219 Dickey Pl Houston TX 77019 Office: 3465 W Alabama Houston TX 77027

AUBURN, NORMAN PAUL, university pres.; b. Cincinnati, O., May 22, 1905; s. Joseph and Huldah Auburn; A.B., U. Cin., 1927, student Law Sch., 1927-28, Grad. Sch., 1934-35; LL.D., 1952; LL.D., Parsons Coll., 1945, U. Liberia, 1959; D.Sc., U. Tulsa, 1957; Litt.D., Washburn U., 1961; L.H.D., Coll. of Wooster, 1963; m. Kathleen Montgomery, June 28, 1930; children—Ames (Mrs. M. L. Latta, Jr.), Richard, Mark, David Bruce. Editor Cincinnati Constructor, 1928-33;

asst. mgr. Asso. Gen. Contractors of Am., 1928-33; publicity mgr. Allied Construction Industries, 1930-33; exec. sec. U. of Cincinnati Alumni Assn., 1933-36; editor Cincinnati Alumnus, 1929-36; asst. dir. and asst. prof. U. of Cin., Evening Coll., 1936-38; asso. prof. U. of Cin., 1938-40, acting dean, 1940-41, dean and prof., 1941-43, dean of univ. adminstrn., clk. bd. dir. 1943-51, v.p. 1943-51, acting pres. 1949; exec. U. Cin. Research Found., 1943-51; mem. Ohio Higher Edn. Assistance Com., 1963-65; pres. U. Akron, 1951—; acting pres. Council Financial Aid to Edn., N.Y.C., 1957-58, bd. dirs., 1957-71; spl. asst. univ. relations A.I.D., U.S. State Dept., 1965-66, cons., 1966—; cons. Academy Ednl. Development, Inc., N.Y.C., 1965-70, v.p., dir. studies for urban affairs, 1971—; chmn. Univ. Council on edn. for Pub. Responsibility, 1965-66; dir. Great Lakes Megalopolis Research Project, 1968—; vice chmn. Am. Council Edn., 1963-64, dir., 1969-72. Dir. First Fed. Savs. and Loan Assn., Akron, 1st Nat. Bank Akron. Exec. com. Akron Area Progress Bd.; dir. Akron Gen. Hosp.; trustee of Greater Akron Musical Assn., 1967—. Trustee Lane Theological Seminary McCormick Theol. Sem., Akron Art Inst., Ohio Coll. Assn. (pres. 1960-61); mem. Air Force ROTC Adv. Panel to Dept. of USAF, 1960-64; mem. exec. com. Ohio Research and Devel. Bd., 1962-65; pres. Herman Muehlstein Found., 1965—. Fellow A.A.A.S.; mem. Assn. Am. Colls. (vice chmn. commn. coll. adminstrn. 1965-68), Am. Soc. Engring. Edn., Am. Assn. State Colls. and Univs. (chmn. com. on internat. programs 1970-71), Assn. of Univ. Evening Colls. (pres. 1944), Assn. Urban Univs. (pres. 1955-56, sec.-treas. 1956-65), Newcomen Society Eng., Cincinnatus Soc., Queen City Assn., Alpha Kappa Psi, Phi Alpha Delta, Lambda Chi Alpha, Omicron Delta Kappa, Scabbard and Blade. Presbyn. Clubs: Rotary (pres. Akron, 1958-59), Commonwealth (Cin.); University (Akron and Columbus, O.), Torch; City (Akron). Contbr. ednl. jours. Home: 856 Mayfair Rd Akron OH 44303

AUCHINCLOSS, HUGH D, business exec.; b. Newport R.I., 1897; ed. Yale. Partner, Auchincloss, Parker & Redpath, Washington; now v.p. Thompson; McKinnon & Auchincloss, Inc. Bd. dirs. Boys Clubs Am. Mason. Home: 3044 O St N W Washington DC 20007 Office: 1705 H St N W Washington DC 20006

AUCHINCLOSS, LOUIS STANTON, author; b. Lawrence, N.Y., Sept. 27, 1917; s. Joseph Howland and Priscilla (Stanton) A.; grad. Groton Sch., 1935; postgrad. Yale, 1939; LL.B., U. Va., 1941; m. Adele Lawrence, Sept. 1957; children—John, Blake, Andrew. Admitted to N.Y. bar, 1941; asso. firm Sullivan & Cromwell, 1941-51; asso. Hawkins, Delafield & Wood, N.Y.C., 1954-58, partner, 1958—. Trustee St. Bernard's Sch., Josiah Macy, Jr. Found.; mem. adminstrv. com. Dumbarton Oaks Research Library and Collection; pres. Mus. City of N.Y. Served as lt. USNR, 1941-45. Mem. Am. Coll. Probate Counsel, Nat. Inst. Arts and Letters. Episcopalian. Club: Century Assn. Author: The Indifferent Children, 1947; The Injustice Collectors, 1950; Sybil, 1952; A Law for the Lion, 1953; The Romantic Egoists, 1954; The Great World and Timothy Colt, 1956; Venus in Sparta, 1958; Pursuit of the Prodigal, 1959; The House of Five Talents, 1960; Reflections of a Jacobite, 1961; Portrait in Brownstone, 1962; Powers of Attorney, 1963; The Rector of Justin, 1964; Pioneers and Caretakers, 1965; The Embezzler, 1966; Tales of Manhattan, 1967; A World of Profit, 1968; Motiveless Malignity, 1969; Second Chance, 1970; Elizabeth Wharton, 1971. Home: 1111 Park Av New York City NY 10028 Office: 67 Wall St New York City NY 10005

AUCHINCLOSS, SAMUEL SLOAN, mfg. exec.; b. N.Y.C., Oct. 12, 1903; s. Samuel Sloan and Anne S. (Agnew) A.; student Mass. Inst. Tech., 1927; m. Lydia K. Garrison, Feb. 18, 1939; children—Robert G., Philip S., Samuel Sloan. Vice pres. N.Y. Quotation Co., 1938-40; v.p. operations, pinspotters div. Am. Machine & Foundry Co., 1946-52; pres. DeWalt, Inc., 1952-55, Cleve. Welding Co., 1954-57, AMF Cycle Co., 1955-57; pres., chmn. bd., dir. Tracerlab, Inc., Boston, 1957-; pres., dir. Keleket X-Ray Corp., 1957-; dir. AMP Inc. and subsidiaries, 1962—, pres., 1965—. Served from lt. col. to col. Signal Corps, AUS, World War II. Decorated D.S.M., Legion of Merit, Silver Star, Bronze Star. Home: RD 3 Mechanicsburg PA 17055 Office: P O Box 3608 Harrisburg PA 17105

AUCOIN, CLAYTON VERL, coll. dean; b. Lincoln, Neb., Oct. 26, 1930; s. Marcel Joseph and Lillie (Fettin) A.; B.S., La. Coll., 1951; M.S., Auburn U., 1953, Ph.D., 1956; postgrad. Stanford, 1960-61; m. Claire Russell, Sept. 6, 1952; children—Leslie Rae, Marcia Jean, Ralph Clayton. Asst. prof. math. Auburn U., 1955-57; sr. engr. Martin Co., Orlando, Fla., 1957-58; from asst. prof. to asso. prof. U. Southwestern La., 1958-63; mem. faculty Clemson U., 1963—, prof., head dept. math., 1964-69, dean Coll. Phys. and Math. Scis., 1969—. Served with USMC, 1948. Mem. Am. Math. Soc., Math. Assn. Am., Soc. Indsl. and Applied Math., Sigma Xi, Phi Kappa Phi. Co-author: Elementary Contemporary Mathematics, 1964; Elementary Contemporary Algebra, 1965; College Algebra, 1966; Modern Mathematics for Elementary School Teachers, 1966. Home: 333 Woodland Way Clemson SC 29631

AUDE, THEODOR RENDTORFF, pipeline exec.; b. Middletown, N.Y., June 18, 1909; s. Herman T. R. and Alice (Hopkins) A.; A.B., Colgate U., 1930; student advanced mgmt. program Harvard, 1950; m. Katherine Stradling, Dec. 27, 1932; children—Thomas C., John R. With Service Pipe Line Co., Tulsa, 1930-71, successively laborer, timekeeper, engr., asst. chief engr., chief engr., asst. gen. mgr. engring. and constrn., mgr. planning and econs., 1930- 49, v.p. traffic, v.p. operations, 1930-68, pres., 1968-69, dir., 1949-71, ret., 1971; pres. Amoco Pipeline Co., Chgo., 1970-71; gen. mgr. transp. Am. Oil Co., 1969-71. Mem. Am. Soc. Corrosion Engrs., Nat. Soc. Profl. Engrs., Am. Petroleum Inst., Phi Beta Kappa, Delta Upsilon. Home: 3233 E 57th St Tulsa OK 74105

AUDEN, WYSTAN HUGH, poet; b. Feb. 21, 1907; s. George Augustus A.; ed. Gresham's Sch., Holt, and Christ Ch., Oxford; Litt.D. (hon.), Swarthmore Coll. Author: Poems, 1930; Orators, 1932; Dance of Death (play), 1933; (with Christopher Isherwood) Dog Beneath the Skin, 1935; (with Christopher Isherwood) Ascent of F. 6, 1936; (with Louis MacNeice) Letters from Iceland, 1937; Spain, 1937; On This Island, 1937; Selected Poems, 1938; (with Christopher Isherwood) Journey to a War, 1939; (with Christopher Isherwood) On the Frontier, 1939; (with T. Worsley) Education, Today-and Tomorrow, 1939; Some Poems, 1940; Another Time, 1940; Double Man, 1941; For the Time Being, 1944; Collected Shorter Poems, 1930-44, 1950; Enchafèd Flood, 1950; R. Hoggart (An Introduction Essay), 1951; Nones, 1952; The Dyer's Hand and Other Essays, 1962; About the House, 1966. Editor: (with John Garrett) Poets Tongue, 1935; Oxford Book of Light Verse, 1938; Selections from Tennyson, 1944; Nineteenth Century Minor Poets, 1967; Secondary Worlds, 1968; City Without Walls (poems), 1969. Recipient Rollingen prize for poetry, 1953; National Book award for vol. poetry The Shield of Achilles, 1956; Times Three, 1960; Alexander Droutsky Meml. award, 1959; Guinness poetry award, 1959; Nat. Medal for Lit., 1967.‡

AUDET, LIONEL, clergyman; b. Ste.-Marie de Beauce, Que., Can., May 22, 1908; s. Louis and Eugenie (Turcotte) A.; Ph.L., Grand Seminaire de Que., 1931; D.Th., Angelicum, Rome, 1936. Ordained priest Roman Catholic Ch., 1934; prof. theology Grand Seminaire de Que., 1936-52, dir. spiritual, 1945-47, superieur, 1950-52; aux. bishop Que., 1952—. Author: Notre Participation au Sacerdoce du Christ, 1945. Address: Archbishop's House CP 459 Quebec 4 Canada

AUDETTE, LOUIS DE LA CHESNAYE, govt. ofcl.; b. Ottawa, Ont., Can., Apr. 7, 1907; s. Justice Louis Arthur and Mary Grace (Stuart) A.; B.A., Ottawa U., 1927, Licentiate in Philosophy, 1927; LL.B., U. Montreal, 1931. Called to bar P.Q., 1931, created Queen's Counsel, 1953; practiced as Audette & O'Brien, later Audette & McEntyre, Montreal, 1931-39; 1st sec. Dept. External Affairs, Can., 1945-47; commr. Canadian Maritime Commn., 1947-54, chmn., 1954-59; chmn. Tariff Bd. Can., 1959—. Dir. Park S.S. Co., Ltd., 1948-54, pres., 1954-59; dir. Export Devel. Corp., 1947-71. Mem. Court Martial Appeal Bd., 1951-59, N.W. Tys. Council, 1947-59. Served with Royal Canadian Navy; comdr. various ships North atlantic, Mediterranean; ret. lt. comdr., 1945. Mentioned in dispatches. Mem. Que. Bar Assn. Roman Catholic. Clubs: Rideau, Cercle Universitaire; Canadian (pres. 1953-54) (Ottawa). Home: 451 Besserer St Ottawa KIN 6C2 Ontario Canada Office: 219 Argyle Av Ottawa KIA 0G7 Ontario Canada

AUDY, JACK RALPH, educator, med. ecologist; b. Eng., Dec. 24, 1914; s. Alphonse William and Hannah (Whitemore) A.; L.M.S.S.A., Guy's Hosp. Med. Sch., U. London, 1937, M.B., B.S., 1939, Ph.D., 1952; M.D., 1971; m. Catherine Florence Murray, Mar. 24, 1947; 1 dau., Helen M. Intern Hull (Eng.) Royal Infirmary, 1937-39, E. African Med. Service, Brit. Somaliland, 1940; head div. virus research and med. zoology Inst. Med. Research, Kuala Lumpur, Malaysia, 1947-59; dir. George Williams Hooper Found. Med. Research, U. Cal. at San Francisco, 1959—, prof. internat. health and human ecology, chmn. dept. internat. health, 1967—; program dir. U. Cal. Internat. Center Med. Research and Tng., 1960—; Health Clark lectr. U. London. Served to lt. col., M.C., Brit. Army, 1940-47. Fellow Am. Pub. Health Assn., Cal. Acad. Sci., Royal Entomol. Soc., Royal Soc. Tropical Medicine and Hygiene (Chamler's Meml. award 1959); mem. A.A.A.S., Am. Soc. Parasitologists, Am. Soc. Tropical Medicine and Hygiene, Brit. Ecol. Soc., N.Y. Acad. Sci., Royal Soc. Medicine, Sigma Xi. Author: Red Mites and Typhus, 1968. Editor: Malaysian Parasites I-XV, 1953, XVI-XXXIV, 1957; Public Health and Medical Sciences in the Pacific, 1964. Home: 355 Pacheco St San Francisco CA 94116

AUER, BERNHARD MACHOLD, publishing co. exec.; b. Mt. Vernon, N.Y., Aug. 3, 1915; s. George J. and Lily (Machold) A.; grad. Taft Sch., 1935; A.B., Williams Coll., 1939; m. Carol McCoy, May 26, 1941; childrenSusan, Sally, William B. With Time, Inc., 1939—, circulation dir. Time mag., 1951-60, circulation and promotion dir., 1960, pub., 1960-66, v.p., 1962-66, sr. v.p., 1966-69; exec. v.p. for mag. pub., 1970—; chmn. bd. Select Mags., Inc., 1959-60, Pres. Bronxville Community Fund, 1956; mem. Marshall Scholarship Selection Com. Trustee Com. for Econ. Devel.; bd. dirs. Advt. Council; trustee Taft Sch., 1953-57, 63-67, Williams Coll., 1962-67, Sarah Lawrence Coll., 1965-69; chmn. bd. trustees Fleming Coll. & Inst. European Affairs, 1969-70. Mem. Nat. Inst. Social Scis. (v.p.), Mag. Pubs. Assn. Clubs: Williams, Hemisphere, N.Y. Yacht (N.Y.C.); Belle Haven, Round Hill (Greenwich, Conn.). Home: Meadow Wood Dr Greenwich CT 06830 Office: Time Inc Time & Life Bldg Rockefeller Center New York City NY 10020

AUER, EDWARD DANIEL, ins. exec.; b. Ft. Wayne, Ind., Feb. 8, 1903; s. Daniel and Matilda S. (Peters) A.; student Heidelberg Coll., 1922, Ind. U., 1923; m. Ione Breeden, Sept. 8, 1923; children—Daniel (dec.), Edward David. Real estate bus., Ft. Wayne, Ind., 1923-39; asst. mgr. mortgage loan dept. Lincoln Nat. Life Ins. Co., 1939-43, 2d v.p. mgr. mortgage loan dept., 1943-45, v.p., mgr. mortgage loan dept., 1945-54, v.p., 1954-58, sr. v.p., 1958-68, dir., 1947-68, chmn. investment com., 1956-68; chmn. bd. Dominion Life Assurance Co., Waterloo, Ont., Can., 1957-63, Am. States Ins. Co., Am. States Life Ins. Co., Am. Economy Ins. Co. (all Indpls.), 1963-68, Am. Union Ins. Co. N.Y., 1964-68, Superior Ins. Co., Dallas, 1965-68, Sentinel Indemnity Co., Dallas, 1965-68, Utilities Ins. Co., St. Louis, 1967-68, Preferred Fire Ins. Co., 1967-68, Western Pacific Ins. Co., Western Pacific Life Ins. Co., Seattle, 1967-68; pres. Auer Investment Co., Inc., Ft. Wayne, Sharberg Realty Corp., Ft. Wayne; v.p., dir. Auer Mortgage Co., Detroit; dir. Old Ft. Industries, Inc., Transcontinenal Motor Inns, Inc., Theo. H. Davies & Co., Ltd., Peter Eckrich & Sons, Inc., Ill. Brick Co., Chgo., Pioneer Western Corp., Clearwater, Fla., Gen. Telephone Co. Ind., Inc., Ft. Wayne Nat. Bank. Mem. investment com. Aid Assn. for Lutherans, Appleton, Wis., 1968—; mem. State Ind. Policy Commn. Post High Sch. Edn.; pres. bd. dirs. Parkview Meml. Hosp., Ft. Wayne, 1966-69. Trustee DePauw U., 1965—, chmn. investment and real estate com., 1966—, Trustee, Malpas Scholarship Trust, DePauw U. Mem. Mortgage Bankers Assn., Ft. Wayne Med. Soc. Ednl. Found., Inc., Hosp. Planning Council Ft. Wayne, Ind. Soc. Chgo., Am. Inst. Real Estate Appraisers, Nat., Ind. and Ft. Wayne real estate bds., C. of C., Beta Gamma Sigma. Methodist. Mason (Shriner, Jester). Clubs: Country, Quest, Junto (Ft. Wayne). Home: 1624 Wood Moor Dr Fort Wayne, IN 46804. Office: 2304 Ft Wayne Nat Bank Fort Wayne IN 46802

AUER, EDWARD THOMAS, psychiatrist; b. Phila., Jan. 18, 1919; s. William Harper and Anna (Maguire) A.; B.A., U. Rochester, 1940; M.D., Temple U., 1943; m. Mary Hedesh, Sept. 23, 1944; children—Robert, Thomas, Kenneth, Mary Ann, Edward. Intern, Abington (Pa.) Meml. Hosp., 1943-44, chief resident, 1947-48; fellow psychiatry U. Pa. Med. Sch., 1948-50, mem. faculty, 1950-62, asso. prof. psychiatry, 1956-62, asst. instr. medicine, 1950-53; pvt. practice with Dr. Kenneth Appel & Assos., Phila., 1950-56, with Drs. Edward T. Auer, William T. Donner & Assos., Pa., 1956-62; cons. psychiatry Coatesville VA Hosp., Phila., 1954-56; prof. psychiatry, chmn. dept. neurology and psychiatry St. Louis U. Sch. Medicine, 1962—, Samuel W. Fordyce prof. psychiatry, 1967—; cons. John Cochran VA Hosp., St. John's Mercy Hosp., St. Louis. Mem. Nat. Task Force Human Sexuality, 1967-70; vice chmn. Mental Health Planning Com., St. Louis, 1966-69. Served to capt. M.C., AUS, 1944-47. Fellow Am. Psychiat. Assn.; mem. A.M.A., Mo., St. Louis med. socs., Group Advancement Psychiatry (dir. 1966-68), Eastern Mo. Psychiat. Soc. (pres. 1967-68), So. Psychiat. Assn., A.A.A.S., Central Neuropsyhciat. Assn., Sigma Xi, Alpha Omega Alpha. Cons. editor Jour. Human Sexuality. Contbr. med. jours. Home: 9 Clayton Terrace St Louis MO 63131 Office: David P Wohl Meml Mental Health Institute 1221 S Grand Blvd St Louis MO 63104

AUER, PETER LOUIS, plasma physicist, educator; b. Budapest, Hungary, Jan. 12, 1928; s. Laszlo and Irma (Morgenstern) A.; came to U.S., 1937, naturalized, 1942; A.B., Cornell U., 1947; Ph.D., Cal. Inst. Tech., 1951; m. Rheta E. Siegel, Aug. 27, 1952; children—Deborah, Douglas, Andrea, Matthew. Physicist, Gen. Electric Research Lab., Schenectady, 1954-61; head plasma physics Sperry Rand Research Center, Sudbury, Mass., 1961-64; dep. dir. Ballistic Missile Def., Office Sec. Def., Washington, 1964-66; prof. aerospace engring. Cornell U., Ithaca, N.Y., 1966—, dir. lab. plasma studies, 1967—; cons. Office Sec. Def., Inst. for Def. Analyses, Gen. Electric Co., Riverside Research Inst., AEC, NRC, Nat. Acad. Scis. Guggenheim fellow, 1960-61. Fellow Am. Phys. Soc. Editor: Plasma Physics, 1970. Contbr. articles profl. jours. Pantentee in field. Home: 220 Devon Rd Ithaca NY 14850

AUERBACH, ARNOLD, ("Red"), profl. basketball exec.; b. N.Y.C., Sept. 20, 1917; s. Hyman and Marie (Thompson) A.; B.S. in Phys. Edn., George Washington U., 1940, M.A. in Edn., 1941; m. Dorothy Lewis, June 6, 1941; children—Nancy, Randy. Pres., gen. mgr., v.p., Boston Celtics Basketball Team; coach 9 Consecutive all star games; winner 9 Eastern div. titles, 7 world titles; rep. State Dept. for clinics, demonstrations, exhbns.; dir. basketball sch., Camp Milbrooms, Marshafield, Mass.; dir. activities Rutgers Country Club; sports commentator, lectr. New Eng. rep. Cello- Craft Products, Inc.; dir. Seacrest Hotel, N. Falmouth, Mass. Chmn. in Mass. for Easter seals. Recipient Boston's Medal Distinguished Achievement; Sports Achievement award B'nai B'rith. Mem. Nat. Coaches Assn., Omicron Delta Kappa, Colonials (George Washington U.). Club: Touchdown (award) (Washington). Author: Basketball for the Player, Fan and Coach. Home: 3101 Legation St NW Washington DC 20015 Office: 150 Causeway St Boston MA 02114

AUERBACH, CARL ABRAHAM, educator; b. N.Y.C., Oct. 2, 1915; s. Moritz and Rose (Auerbach) A.; A.B., L.I. U., 1935; LL.B., Harvard, 1938; m. Laura Kron, Sept. 12, 1940; children—Linda Eugenie, Eric Hart. Admitted to N.Y. bar, 1938, also U.S. Supreme Ct.; with firm Ansell, Ansell & Marshall, Washington, 1938; atty. Dept. Labor, 1938-40; asst. gen. counsel OPA, 1940-43, gen. counsel, 1946-47; asso. gen. counsel Office Econ. Stblzn., 1946; prof. law U. Wis. Law Sch., 1947-61, U. Minn. Law Sch., 1961—. Staff dir. com. internal orgn. and procedure Adminstrv. Conf. U.S., 1961-62; cons. AID, 1963, 66; mem. Commn. Marine Sci., Engring. and Resources, 1966-69; mem. Div. Behavioral Scis., NRC (exec. com.); mem. Nat. Hwy. Safety Adv. Com., 1968-71; mem. Citizens League Mpls.; mem. Adminstrv. Conf. U.S., 1970—. Served with AUS, 1943-46; ETO. Fulbright fellow, 1953-54; fellow Center Advanced Study Behavioral Scis., 1958-59. Mem. Am. Law Inst., Law and Soc. Assn. (trustee), Am. Bar Assn., Am. Soc. Internat. Law. Author: (with others) The Legal Process, 1961; (with Nathanson) The Federal Regulation of Transportation, 1953; also articles. Home: 3230 Kyle Av N Minneapolis MN 55422

AUERBACH, EUGENE K., business exec.; b. 1905; B.A., U. N.H., 1928; M.B.A., Harvard, 1930; married. Warehouse supt. Great Atlantic & Pacific Tea Co., 1930-36; placement dir. U. N.H., 1936-42; commd. ensign USN, 1942, advanced through ranks to capt., ret., 1969; treas. Wackenhut Corp., Coral Gables, Fla., 1969—; treas. Wackenhut Services, Inc., Wackenhut Protective Systems Inc. Office: 3280 Ponce de Leon Blvd Coral Gables FL 33134*

AUERBACH, ISAAC LEVIN, computer scientist; b. Phila., Oct. 9, 1921; s. Philip and Rose (Levin) A.; B.S. in Elec. Engring., Drexel U., 1943; M.S. in Applied Physics, Harvard, 1947; 1 son, Philip B.; m. 2d, Nina K. Auerbach. Research engineer with computer div. Remington-Rand Univac, 1947-48; dir. spl. products div. Burroughs Corp., 1949-57; pres. Auerbach Corp. for Sci. and Tech., Phila., 1957—; chmn. bd. Comp Data Services Corp., 1969; pres. Auerback Pubs, Inc., 1969; pioneered devel. and use magnetic cores in digital communications; computer memory systems; dir. devel. Atlas ICMB guidance computer, SAGE radar target detection equipment, real time information processing, numerical control systems data systems in BMEWS bus. information systems. U.S. cons. on information processing and automation UNESCO, 1957-60, chmn. U.S. com. 1st Internat. Conf. Information Processing, 1959; founder, 1st pres. Internat. Fedn. for Information Processing, 1960-65, hon. life mem., 1969. Tech. adviser Internat. Computation Centre, Rome, Italy; bd. tech. advisers Center Strategic Studies, Georgetown U., Washington; mem. nat. council Nat. Planning Assn.; member Phila. Bd. Edn. Citizen's Policy Adv. Com. Trustee Fedn. Jewish Agencies, Jewish Publ. Soc. Served as lt. (j.g.), USNR, 1943-46; radar and communications officer Destroyer Escort Div., Atlantic Fleet; radio and radar engr. Naval Research Lab., Washington. Recipient Grand medal City of Paris, 1959, alumni citation Drexel U., 1961, Tower of David award State of Israel, 1969. Fellow I.E.E.E. (award Phila. sect. 1961), A.A.A.S., Brit. Computer Soc.; mem. Instrument Soc. Am., Am. Soc. for Cybernetics, Assn. for Computing Machinery, Research Soc. Am., Franklin Inst., Am. Technion Soc., Nat. Acad. Sci. (com. sci. and tech. communication), Eta Kappa Nu. Mem. B'nai B'rith. Asso. editor: Handbook on Automation Computation and Control, 1959, Computer Handbook, 1961. Holder patents on computer systems, magnetic memory, magnetic circuitry, electronic circuitry, electronic packaging techniques, elec. connectors. Home: 480 N Latches Lane Merion PA 19066 Office: 121 N Broad St Philadelphia PA 19107

AUERBACH, ROBERT, educator; zoologist; b. Berlin, Germany, Apr. 12, 1929; s. Richard J. and Ella (Levi) A.; A.B., Berea (Ky.) Coll., 1949; A.M., Columbia, 1950, Ph.D., 1954; m. Wanda Virginia Irwin, June 18, 1950; children—Richard J., Emily K. Research asso. Oak Ridge Nat. Lab., 1954-55; postdoctoral fellow Nat. Cancer Inst., 1955-57; mem. faculty U. Wis., 1957-, prof. zoology, 1964—. Guggenheim fellow, 1967-68. Mem. Soc. Develtl. Biology, Am. Soc. Zoologists, Am. Assn. Immunologists, Transplantation Soc. Home: 4334 Upland Dr Madison, WI 53705.

AUERBACH, STANLEY IRVING, ecologist; b. Chgo., May 1921; s. Abraham and Carrie (Friedman) A; B.S., U. Ill., 1946, M.S., 1947; Ph.D., Northwestern U., 1949; m. Dawn Patricia Davey, June 12, 1954; children—Andrew J., Anne E., Jonathan B., Alison M. Instr., then asst. prof. Roosevelt U., Chgo., 1950-54, asso. scientist, then scientist, health physics div. Oak Ridge Nat. Lab., 1954-59, sr. scientist, sect. leader, 1959-70, dir. ecol. sci. div., 1970—; lectr. radio-ecology U. Tenn., 1958—; adj. research prof. radiation ecology U. Ga., 1963—. Mem. U.S. exec. com. Internat. Biol. Program, co-chmn. program coordinating com., dir. decid. forest biome project, 1969—; mem. Nat. Acad. Sci. Adv. Commn. on Research to sec. agr., 1969—; mem. NAE Power Plant Siting Program Commn., 1970—; mem. aquatic biology com. ORSANCO; mem. ecol. adv. bd. Bur. Reclamation. Mem. Tenn. Citizens Wilderness Planning (dir. 1968), Planned Parenthood Assn. Dir., treas. Oak Ridge Nursery Sch.; bd. dirs. Oak Ridge Civic Music Assn., 1963-66; trustee Inter-Am. Inst. Ecology. Served to 2d lt. AUS, 1942-44. Fellow A.A.A.S.; mem. Am. Inst. Biol. Scis. (bd. govs.), Soc. Zoology (chmn. ecology div.), Am. Soc. Agronomy, Brit. Ecol. Soc., Health Physics Soc., Entomol. Soc. Am., Research Soc. Am., Soc. Systematic Biology, Ecol. Soc. Am. (chmn. com. radioecology 1963-65, sec. 1964-69, chmn. finance com. 1969—, pres. elect 1970-71), Sigma Xi, Alpha Epsilon Pi. Spl. research ecology centipedes, radioecology and radioactive waste disposal, environmental behavior of radionuclides. Home: 24 Wildwood Dr Oak Ridge TN 37830 Office: P O Box X Oak Ridge TN 37830

AUGELLI, ANTHONY THOMAS, U.S. judge; b. Italy, Mar. 27, 1902; s. Lorenzo and Lucia (Aquilino) A.; brought to U.S., 1904, naturalized, 1910; LL.B., N.J. Law School, 1929; LL.M., Mercer Beasley Sch. Law, Newark, 1934; m: Mary Carroll, Oct. 28, 1936; children—Kathleen, Robert, Marie, Patricia. Admitted to N.J. bar, 1930, U.S. Supreme Ct., 1939, other fed. and state cts.; with firm

Milton, Augelli & Keane, and predecessors, Jersey City, 1930-61, partner, 1935-61; U.S. dist. judge for N.J., 1961-68, chief judge, 1968—. Dir. Hudson County Nat. Bank, Jersey City, 1943-61. Park commnr., Hudson County, 1955-61. Mem. Am., N.J., Hudson County, N.Y., N.J. and Conn. Fed. bar assns., N.Y. County Lawyers Assn., Dante Alighieri Soc. Elk. Office: U S Court House Federal Sq Newark NJ 07101

AUGENSTEIN, BRUNO W., research exec.; b. Germany, Mar. 16, 1923; s. Wilhelm C. and Emma (Nina) A.; brought to U.S., 1927, naturalized, 1935; Sc.B. in Physics and Math., Brown U., 1943; M.S. in Aero., Cal. Inst. Tech., 1945; m. Kathleen Greenlaw, May 30, 1950; children—Karen, Eric, Christopher, Supr., North Am. Aviation Co., 1946-48; asst. prof. Purdue U., 1948-49; sr. sci. Rand Corp., 1949-58; dir. planning Lockheed Missiles & Space Co., 1958-61; spl. asst. Office Sec. Def., 1961-65, now cons.; research adviser Inst. Def. Analyses, 1965-68; v.p. research Rand Corp., Santa Monica, Cal., 1968-71, chief scientist, 1971—; cons. Nat. Acad. Sci., Bur. Budget, 1965—, Nat. Bur. Standards, 1971—. Bd. regents Nat. Library of Medicine, Dept. Health, Edn. and Welfare. Recipient Distinguished Pub. Service award Dept. Def. Mem. Am. Inst. Physics, Am. Geophys. Union, Am. Inst. Aeros. and Astronautics, N.Y. Acad. Scis., A.A.A.S., Am. Nuclear Soc., Pattern Recognition Soc., Philosophy of Sci. Assn., Symbolic Logic Assn. Club: Cosmos (Washington). Home: 1144 Tellem Dr Pacific Palisades CA 90272 Office: 1700 Main St Santa Monica CA 90406

AUGENSTEIN, PAUL M., mfg. co. exec.; b. Warren, O., Mar. 30, 1913; s. Church Brenard and Nancy (Shrimplin) A.; A.B., Hiram (O.) Coll., 1935; m. Jean Thompson McKibbin, Aug. 13, 1937; children—Don C., Janice K., Nancy L. With Gen. Electric Co., 1935-58; pres. Airtemp div. Chrysler Corp., 1958-61; former exec. v.p. charge U.S. operating Divs. Am. Radiator & Standard San. Corp.; chairman board Gulfstan Corp., Miami, Fla.; dir. Am.-Standard Products (Can.) Ltd., Toronto, Ontario, Canada; member Grand Central adv. bd. Chem. Bank N.Y. Trust Co. Mem. spl. gifts com. N.Y. chpt. Am. Cancer Soc. Bd. dirs., vice pres. Air Conditioning and Refrigeration Inst. Mem. Exec. Golf Assn. Internat. (a sponsor), Newcomen Soc. N.Am. Clubs: Engineers, Union League (N.Y.C.); Fairmount Country (Chatham). Home: 171 Main St Madison NJ 07940 Office: 40 W 40th St New York City NY 10018

AUGER, FRED SAUNDER, newspaper pub.; b. Alberta, Can., June 7, 1907; s. Albert R. and Mabel (Saunders) A.; B.S. in Bus., U. Ida.; m. Dorothy K. Hill, June 18, 1934; children—Barry, Timothy. Formerly advt. mgr. Procter & Gamble Co., Ltd., mgr. Vancouver br. McKim Advt. Agy., v.p., pub., Winnipeg Tribune; pub. Vancouver Province, 1958—. Mem. Canadian Daily Newspaper Pubs. Assn., Phi Gamma Delta. Address: Vancouver Daily Provincel Vancouver British Columbia Canada

AUGER, PIERRE V., physicist; b. Paris, France, May 14, 1899; s. Victor E. and Eugenie (Blanchet) A.; student Ecole Normale Superieure, Paris, 1919-22; Docteur es Sciences, U. Paris, 1926; m. Suzanne Motteau, July 7, 1921. Asst. U. Paris, 1922-32, prof., 1932-41; research asso. U. Chgo., 1941-44, mem. Anglo-Canadian team atomic energy research; dir. higher edn., Paris, 1945-48; dir. nat. sci. dept. UNESCO, 1948-59; chmn. French Com. for Space Research, 1959-61; exec. sec. European Commn. for Space Research, 1961-64; dir. gen. European Space Research Orgn., 1964-68; dir. Laboratoire de Physique Cosmique, 1968—. Decorated great officer Legion of Honor, 1962; recipient Antonio Feltrinelli international prize for science, 1961. Fellow American Physical Society; member Society Francaise de Physique. Author: What Are Cosmic Rays, 1943; L'Homme Microscopique, 1952; Current Trends in Scientific Research, 1961. Discoverer Auger-effect, 1926; Auger-Showers, 1938. Address: 12 Rue Emile Faguet Paris 14 France

AUGHINBAUGH, HENRY E., Jr., banker; b. Harrisburg, Pa., Sept. 19, 1908; s. Henry E. and Edythe (Seiders) A.; grad. Nat. Assn. Bank Auditors and Controllers Sch., 1931; m. Ethel R. Myers, Aug. 19, 1929; children—Harry Elwood, Donna Lee. With East End Trust Co., 1927-31; with Allison-East End Trust Co., 1931-57, asst. sec., asst. treas., 1948-52, sec., treas., 1952-57; asst. v.p., comptroller Central Trust Co., 1957-58; comptroller Central Trust-Capital Bank, 1958-61; auditor Nat. Bank & Trust Co. of Central Pa., Harrisburg, 1961-70; regional auditor Nat. Central Bank, Lancaster, Pa., 1970—, Dir. bd. pensions Central Pa. Conf. United Meth. Ch., 1966—. Mem. Am. Legion, V.F.W. Methodist (adminstrv. bd.). Served with F.A., AUS, 1945-46; ETO. Home: 405 Alden St Harrisburg PA 17109 Office: 222 Market St Harrisburg PA 17108

AUGUST, ROBERT OLIN, journalist; b. Ashtabula, O., Oct. 6, 1921; s. Frank and Lillian (Olin) A.; B.A., Coll. of Wooster, 1943; m. Marilynn Eccles, Sept. 23, 1943; 1 dau., Allson. With Cleve. Press, 1946—, staff sports dept., 1950—, covered profl. football, 1953-58, exec. sports editor, 1957-58, sports editor, 1958-64, sports columnist, 1964-67, sports columnist, sports editor, 1967—. Served from ensign to lt. (j.g.), USNR, 1943-46. Recipient Cleveland Newspaper Guild awards, 1958, 61. Mem. Sigma Delta Chi. Home: 5608 Chelmsford Dr Lyndhurst OH 44124 Office: Cleveland Press Plaza Cleveland OH 44113

AUGUSTINCIC, ANTUN, sculptor; b. Klanjec, Yugoslavia, May 4, 1900; s. Adam and Katarina (Kralj) A.; grad. Acad. of Arts, Zagreb, Yugoslavia, 1924; French Govt. scholar, Ecole des arts decoratifs and Acad. des beaux arts, Paris, 1924- 26; m. Nada Mickacic, Sept. 17, 1924; 1 dau., Rosa. Exhibited Salon des Independants, Paris, 1925, Salon des artistes francais (2d prize internat. competition London 1925), Paris. 1925; sculptor meml. to Sumadija fighters killed in World War I, Kragujevac, Yugoslavia, 1928, Peter Kocic meml., Banja Luka, Yugoslavia, 1929. equestrian statues at Tsar Dusan bridge, Skoplje, Yugoslavia, 1938, figure of miner Internat. Bur. Labor bldgs., Geneva, Switzerland, 1936, meml. to radicals shot at Zajecar, Yugoslavia, 1937, group, carrying away a wounded partisan, Beograd, 1944, monumental meml. to Red Army at Batina Skela, Danube River, 1947, statue of Marshall Tito, Kumrovec, Yugoslavia, 1946, monumental meml. The Bordermen, Banja Luka, 1955-61, meml. to victims of fascism, Addis Ababa, Ethiopia, 1955, meml. to Ras Makonem, Harrar, Ethiopia, 1959, meml. to partisan fighters, Moleta, Ethiopia, 1958, numerous others; created equestrian statue Yugoslavia presented in UN, 1954; recipient first prize competition for meml. fighters of Nice killed in World War I, 1930, first prize competition monument at Split, 1936, first prize meml. Silesian uprising, Katowice,, Poland, 1937, 4th prize internat. competition meml. Justo Jose Urquiza, 1937, first prize internat. competition meml. Albanian war hero Scanderberg, 1937; prof. Acad. Fine Arts, Zagreb, 1945—. Active People's Liberation Movement, 1941-; vice chmn. Anti-Fascist Council of Nat, Liberation, Yugoslavia, 1943; mem. Yugoslav mil. mission to Moscow, 1944-45. Mem. Yugoslavian Acad. Sci. and Arts. Home: Bulatova 14 Zagreb, Yugoslavia Office: Jabukovac 6 Zagreb, Yugoslavia

AUJALEU, EUGENE, physician; b. Negrepelisse, France, Oct. 29, 1903; s. Eugene Henri and Claire (Pailler) A.; grad. Faculty Medicine U. Toulouse (France), 1927; m. Nadine Dumas, Nov. 8, 1937; children—Claire, Suzanne. Prof. Val de Grace (Army Health Service), 193639; physician in mil. hosps., 193639; insp. gen. pub. health, 1941-42; dir. health service French Com. Algerian Nat. Liberation, 1943-44; dir. social health French Health Dept., 1945-56; dir. gen. French Pub. Health, 1956-64; dir. gen. Nat. Health Inst. and Med. Research, Paris 1964-69, hon. dir. gen., 1969—. Pres. exec. council WHO, 1959; pres. World Health Assembly, 1968, French state counsellor, 1966. Served with French Army, 1939-45. Decorated grand officer Legion of Honor. Author articles social medicine, physiology, epidemiology, pub. health. Home: 144 Blvd Montparnasse Paris 14, France.

AULD, DAVID VINSON, civil engr.; b. Washington, Dec. 18, 1907; s. Robert Edgar and Elizabeth (Vinson) A.; B.S. in Civil Engring., Princeton, 1929; m. Saranell Wilson, Nov. 21, 1931; 1 son, David. With Govt. D.C., 1929-64, supt., chief engr. water div., 1946-53, dir. dept. san. engring., 1953-64; pvt. practice engring., 1965—. Commr. Interstate Commn. Potomac River Basin, 1953-64, chmn., 1959-61; chmn. Washington Sanitation Conf., 1947-48. Recipient Merit citation for outstanding career pub. service Nat. Civil Service League, 1957, Career Service award, 1962. Registered profl. engr., D.C., Md. Diplomate Am. Acad. Environmental Engrs. Fellow Am. Soc. C.E.; mem. Water Pollution Control Fedn., Am. Water Works Assn. (nat. dir. 1954-57; George Warren Fuller award 1962), Am. Pub. Works Assn. (Pub. Works Man-of-the-Year award 1961), Washington Soc. Engrs. (dir. 1959-60; award 1962) Princeton Engring. Assn. Presbyn. (elder). Clubs: Cosmos (Washington); Chesapeake Bay Yacht. Home: Doncaster Manor Easton MD 21601 Office: Box 698 Route 1 Easton MD 21601

AULT, PHILLIP H., editor; b. Maywood, Ill., Apr. 26, 1914; s. Frank W. and Bernda (Halliday) A.; A.B., DePauw U., 1935; m. Karoline Byberg, June 5, 1943; 1935-37; 1935- corr. editor U.P.I., Chgo., N.Y.C., Iceland, North Africa, London, Eng., 1938-48, bur. chief, London, 1944-45; asst. mng. editor, dir. editorial page Times-Mirror Co., Los Angeles, 1948; editorial page editor Los Angeles Mirror-News, 1948-57; exec. editor Asso. Desert Newspapers, 1958-68; asso. editor South Bend Tribune, 1968—. Mem. asso. faculty Ind. U. Mem. Sigma Nu. Author: This Is The Desert, News Around the Clock; Wonders of the Mosquito World; How to Live in California; Home Book of Western Humor. Co-author: Springboard to Berlin, 1943; Reporting the News; Introduction to Mass Communications. Home: 1615 Riverside Dr South Bend IN 46616 Office: South Bend Tribune South Bend IN 46626

AULT, BROMWELL, chem. corp. exec.; b. Wyoming, O., June 28, 1899; s. George C. and Helene (Bromwell) A.; grad. Phillips Acad., 1918, Yale, 1922; m. Allie Burchenal, Oct. 18, 1923; children—J. Burchenal, Bromwell. Chem. engr. Ault & Wilborg Co., 1922-25 pres., gen. mgr. Ault & Wilborg Varnish Works, Inc., 1925-31 (both Cincinnati); v.p., dir. Internat. Printing Ink Corp., 1931-36, pres., dir., mem. exec. com. 1936-44; v.p., dir., mem. exec. com. Inmont Corp., 1944-64, ret., 1971; cons. chem. engring. and marketing, N.Y.C., 1971—; trustee Bowery Savings Bank; former dir. Procter & Gamble (Cin.). Vice chmn. Episcopal Ch. Found., N.Y.C. Trustee Phillips Andover Acad. Mem. Mfg. Chemists assn., Nat. Indsl. Conf. Bd., Bus. Council Internat. Understanding, Advt. Council Bd. (past dir.). Clubs: Yale, Yacht (N.Y.C.); St. Elmo (New Haven); Piping Rock (Locust Valley, N.Y.); Edgartown (Mass.) Yacht. Home: 980 Fifth Av New York City NY 10021 Office: 1133 Av Americas New York City NY 10036

AULT, JAMES MASE, clergyman, educator; b. Sayre, Pa., Aug. 24, 1918; s. Tracey Everett and Bessie (Mase) A.; A.B. magna cum laude, Colgate U., 1949; B.D. magna cum laude, Union Theol. Sem., N.Y.C., 1952, S.T.M., 1964; postgrad. St. Andrews U., Scotland, 1966; D.D., Am. U., Washington, 1968; m. Dorothy Mae Barnhart, Dec. 22, 1943; children—James Mase, Kathryn Louise, Elizabeth Ann, Christopher John, (dec.) Tool engr. Ingersoll-Rand Co., 1936-42; ordained to ministry Methodist Ch., 1950; pastor Meth. Ch., Preston, N.Y., 1946-49; pastor Carlton Hill Meth. Ch., East Rutherford, N.J., 1951-53; pastor Meth. Ch., Leonia, N.J., 1953-58; pastor First Meth. Ch., Pittsfield, Mass., 1958-61; dean students, asso. prof. practical theology Union Theol. Sem., N.Y.C., 1961-64, prof. practical theology, dir. field edn., 1964-68; dean, prof. pastoral theology Theol. Sch., Drew U., Madison, N.J., 1968—. Served to 1st lt. AUS, 1942-46. Faculty fellow Am. Assn. Theol. Schs., 1965-66. Mem. Am. Assn. U. Profs., Acad. Polit. and Social Sci., Phi Beta Kappa. Author: Responsible Adults for Tomorrow's World, 1962. Home: 8 Campus Dr Madison NJ 07940

AULT, LEE ADDISON, art dealer, publisher b. Cin., Sept. 30, 1915; s. Lee Brownell and Hildegard (von Steinwehr) A.; grad. St. Paul's Sch., 1933; student Princeton, 1933-35; m. Dorothy Perin Smith, Aug. 5, 1935 (div. 1958); childrenLee Addison 3d, Dorothy Perin; m. 2d, Isabel Biddle Henry, Aug. 15, 1958. Pres., Quadrangle Press, Inc., 1946-50; dir., exec. com. Vision, Inc., N.Y.C., publishers Vision (Latin Am. news mag.), 1953-; pres. Art in Am. Co., 1956-69, Lee Ault & Co., art gallery, N.Y.C., 1970—. Trustee Skowhegan Sch. of Painting and Sculpture. Served as vol. Am. Field Service, attached Brit. Eighth Army, 1942-43; as capt. USMCR, air combat intelligence, 1943-45. Mem. Am. Fedn. Arts. Home: 141 E 72d St New York City NY 10021 Office: 25 E 77th St New York City NY 10021

AULT, RICHARD LEROY, govt. ofcl.; b. Wichita, Kan., July 13, 1917; s. Clement Leroy and Una (McClain) A.; student Long Beach (Cal.) Jr. Coll., 1934-35, 37-39; B.S., U. Md., 1952; m. Virginia Ilene Jasper, June 22, 1940; children—Richard Leroy, Ann Elizabeth, James Bryson. Commd. 2d lt. USAAF, 1940, advanced through grades to brig. gen. USAF, 1966; ret., 1970; exec. officer Office of Under Sec., Smithsonian Instn., Washington, 1970—; comml. pilot. Decorated Legion of Merit with 2 oak leaf clusters, Air Force and Army commendation medals (U.S.), Order of Rising Sun (Japan). Mem. Am. Soc. Pub. Adminstrn., Air Force Assn., Daedalian Soc. Methodist. Mason. Club: Quantico Flying. Home: 9115 Volunteer Dr Alexandria VA 22309 Office: Smithsonian Institution Washington DC 20560

AULT, THOMAS JEFFERSON, mfg. exec.; b. Portland, Ind., June 23, 1911; s. Ross Earl and Olga (Sattler) A.; grad. Los Angeles Stock Exchange Inst., 1931, Cumnock Coll., 1932; A.B., U. Cal. at Los Angeles, 1934; m. Mary Carr, June 30, 1938; 1 son, Brian Carr. Trainee Warner Gear div. Borg-Warner Corp., 1935-37, buyer, 1937-41, asst. purchasing agt., 1941-51, purchasing agt., 1951-52, v.p., 1952-53, v.p., asst. gen. mgr. Detroit Gear div., 1953-54, pres., gen. mgr., 1954-56, pres., gen. mgr. Long Mfg. div., 1954-58; pres. Long Mfg. Co., Ltd., 1954-57, pres., gen. mgr., 1957-58; pres., gen. mgr. Cello Products, Ltd. (Can.), 1957-58; pres., dir. Saco-Lowell Shops, 1958-60; pres. automotive division Budd Company, Detroit, 1960-64; v.p. corporate devel., dir. McCord Corp., Detroit, 1965-68; pres., chief exec. officer, mem. bd. Avis Indsl. Corp., Madison Heights, Mich., 1968-69; pres., chief exec. officer, owner Western Flyer Coach, Ltd., Winnipeg, Can., 1970—; pres., chief exec. officer Ault Industries, Inc., Detroit, 1970-71; pres., dir. Bryan Metals, Inc. (O.). Mem. adv. council Jr. Achievement of S.W. Mich. Mem. Soc. Automotive Engrs., U.S. C. of C., Am. Ordnance Assn., Mich. Mfrs. Assn., Canadian Mfrs. Assn., N.A.M., Am. Mgmt. Assn. (mem. planning council), Employers Assn. Detroit (dir., exec. bd.). Detroit C. of C., Mich. Ambassadors, Farm Equipment Inst., Sigma Nu. Mason. Clubs: Detroit Athletic, University, Country of Detroit, Recess, Economic (dir.) (Detroit); Grosse Pointe (Grosse Pointe Farms, Mich.); Boat, Algonquin (Boston); Indiana Society (Chgo.); Winter Harbor Yacht, (N.H.); The Old (Sans Souci, Mich.); University (Toronto). Home: 8200 E Jefferson Detroit MI 48214 Office: Western Flyer Coach Ltd 6 Otter St Winnipeg 19 Manitoba Canada

AULT, WARREN ORTMAN, historian; b. Lenexa, Kan., Jan. 8, 1887; s. Addison and Mary Aleja (McElwain) A.; A.B., Baker U., 1907, LL.D., 1937; Rhode scholar from Kan., Oxford U., 1900-10, B.A., 1910, M.A., 1917; Univ. fellow in history, Yale, 1911-14, Ph.D., 1919; D.Litt., Boston U., 1960; m. Myrtle Lavina Wilcock, June 12, 1931; children—Addison, Mary Myrtle. Instr. history Baker U., 1910-11; instr. history Boston U., 1913-19, asst. prof., 1919-24, Wm. Edwards Huntington prof. history, chmn. dept., 1924-57, emeritus; Bacon lectr., 1933, Univ. lectr., 1951-52; Distinguished scholar-in-residence Baker U., 1968-69; vis. prof. Kansas City regional Council Higher Edn. Served with M.C., U.S. Army, later 2d lt. F.A., 1919. Guggenheim fellow, 1926-27; hon. fellow Jesus Coll., Oxford U., 1971. Fellow Am. Acad. Arts and Scis. Royal Hist. Soc.; mem. Am. Hist. Assn., N.E. History Tchrs. Assn. (pres. 1934-35), Phi Beta Kappa, Zeta Chi. Republican. Methodist. Clubs: University, Appalachian Mountain (Boston). Author: Private Jurisdiction in England, 1923; Court Rolls of the Abbey of Ramsey and the Honor of Clare, 1927; Europe in the Middle Ages, 1932; Europe in Modern Times, 1947; Open Field Husbandry and the Village Community, 1965. Contbr. to hist. publs. Home: 22 Fairlee Rd Waban MA 02168 ☆

AULTMAN, RICHARD EUGENE, editor; b. Moline, Ill., Dec. 21, 1933; s. Chester Clyde and Margaret Augusta (Klouser) A.; B.A. in Journalism, Northwestern U., 1956, M.S., 1957; m. Joyce Engelhard, Sept. 8, 1956; children—Kimberly Ann, Michael Stewart. Sports reporter Decatur (Ill.) Herald-Rev., 1957-59; copy editor Chgo. Sun Times, 1959; asso. editor Golf Digest, Norwalk, Conn., 1959-61, exec. editor, 1961-64, editor, 1964—. Collaborator (with Arnold Palmer) column Golfing with Arnold Palmer, 1964—. Recipient MacGregor-Brunswick Golf Writers' award mag. div., 1967, Nat. Golf Writers' championship, 1963. Mem. Golf Writers Assn. Am., Beta Theta Pi. Conglist. Author: (with Gary Player) Golf Secrets, 1962; (with Bob Toski) Touch System for Better Golf, 1971; Learn to Play Golf, 1966; Square-to-Square Golf Swing: Model Method for the Modern Player, 1970. Home: 6 Highwood Lane Westport CT 06880 Office: 88 Scribner Av Norwalk CT 06856

AUMONT, JEAN-PIERRE, actor, author; b. Paris, France, Jan. 5, 1913; m. Maria Montez, July 13, 1943 (dec. Sept. 1951); 1 dau., Maria-Christina; m. 2d, Marisa Pavan, Mar. 27, 1956; children—Jean-Claude, Patrick. Motion pictures include: Assignment in Brittanny, 1943, The Cross of Lorraine, 1943, Heartbeat, 1945, Sheharazade, 1946, Atlantis, 1947, Lilli, 1952, Charge of Lancers, 1954, Hilda Crane, 1956, The Seventh Sin, 1957, John Paul Jones, 1958, The Enemy General, 1959, The Blonde From Buenos Aires, 1960, The Devil at 4 O'Clock, 1960, The Horse Without A Head, 1962, Incident at Vichy, 1965, Gigi, The Tempest, 1967, Blind Man's Bluff, 1967, Castle Keep, 1968; Theatrical appearances include: My Name is Aquilon, 1949, Heavenly Twins, 1955, Design for Living, 1948, A Second String, 1960, As You Like It, 1953, Julius Caesar, 1956, Tovarich, 1963, Incident at Vichy, 1965, The Tempest, 1967, Blind Man's Bluff, 1967, So. Pacific, 1967, Hostile Witness, 1967, A Girl in My Soup, 1969, Camino Real, 1970; television appearances: Arms and the Man, No Time for Comedy, A Month in the Country, Hold Back the Dawn, The Imposter, Patty Duke Show, The Name of the Game. Served French Army, 1939-45. Decorated Legion of Honour, Croix de Guerre. Address: 15 W 72d New York City NY 10023

AUNE, BRUCE ARTHUR, educator; b. Mpls., Nov. 7, 1933; s. Arthur Berg and Doris (Bowler) A.; B.A., U. Minn., 1955, M.A., 1957, Ph.D., 1960; postgrad U. Cal. at Los Angeles, 1957-58; m. Ilene Mae Carlson, Sept. 20, 1955; children—Alison Judith, Patricia Marion, Kirsten Marie. Research asst. Minn. Center Philosophy Sci., 1960; instr. Oberlin (Ohio) Coll., 1960-62; asst. prof. U. Pitts., 1963-65, asso. prof., 1965-66; prof head dept. philosophy, U. Mass., Amherst, 1966—. Charles E. Merrill fellow, 1963-1964, Guggenheim fellow, 1963-64, Mem. Am. Philos. Assn., Am. Psychol. Assn., Mind Assn., Phi Beta Kappa. Author: (with others) Philosophy in America, 1966; Knowledge, Mind and Nature, 1967; Rationalism, Empiricism and Pragmatism, 1970. Home: 91 Blackberry Lane Amherst MA 01002

AURAND, CALVIN WILLIAM, banker; b. Minneapolis, Apr. 15, 1904; s. William H. and Jane (Kyte) A.; A.B., U. Minn., 1925; m. Eleanor Kingman, Sept. 8, 1928; children— Calvin W., Elizabeth K., Benjamin K. Clerk credit dept. Midland Nat. Bank & Trust Co., Minneapolis, 1925-33, asst. cashier, 1933-38, v.p., 1938-41; v.p., treas., Northwest Bancorporation, 1941-45; v.p., dir. Midland Nat. Bank, 1945-50; past pres. Iowa-Des Moines Nat. Bank, now dir.; dir. Meredith Corp., Northwestern Bell Telephone Co. Trustee Drake U., Des Moines, Ia. Mem. Association of Reserve City Bankers. Home: Rt 3 Des Moines IA 50321 Office: Iowa-Des Moines Nat Bank 6th and Walnut Sts Des Moines IA 50309

AURAND, CHARLES HENRY, Jr., univ. dean; b. Battle Creek, Mich., Sept. 6, 1932; s. Charles Henry and Elisabeth D. (Hoekstra) A.; B. Mus., Mich. State U., 1954, M. Mus., 1958; Ph.D., U. Mich., 1971; m. Donna M. Erb, June 19, 1954; children—Janice, Cheryl, Sandra, Charles, William. Mem. faculty Hiram Coll., 1958-61, acting chmn. dept. music, 1960-61; dean Dana Sch. Music, Youngstown (O.) State U., 1961—. Bd. dirs. Youngstown Philharmonic Soc. Served to 1st lt. USAF, 1954-56, Mem. Music Educators Nat. Assn., Am. Assn. for Higher Edn., Phi Mu Alpha. Home: 578 Green Garden Dr Youngstown OH 44512

AURAND, EVAN PETER, naval officer; b. N.Y.C., June 10, 1917; s. Henry Spiese (U.S. Army) and Margaret (Decker) A.; B.S., U.S. Naval Acad., 1938; student Flight Sch., Pensacola, Fla., 1940; m. Patricia L. Riley, Dec. 27, 1941; 1 dau., Margaret L. Commd. ensign USN, 1938, advanced through grades to vice adm., 1969; various assignments Pacific Fleet, World War II; comdr. Night Fighter Sqdn. 76, 1943, Fighter Sqdn. 1-A, 1947, 48, 51; exec. officer U.S.S. Hancock, 1955; naval aide to Pres. U.S., 1957-61; comdg. officer USS Greenwich Bay, 1961, U.S.S. Independence, 1961-62; comdr. Antisubmarine Warfare Group I, 1965-67; dir. Long Range Objectives Group, Navy Dept., 1967-69; comdr. Antisubmarine Warfare Force, U.S. Pacific Fleet, 1969—. Decorated Navy Cross, Legion of Merit with 2 gold stars, D.F.C. with gold star, Air Medal. Mem. Naval Inst. Office: COMASW FORPAC FPO San Francisco CA 96610

AURBACH, LESTER PHILLIP, publisher; b. Cleve., Dec. 11, 1906; s. Alexander and Della (Zuckerman) A.; A.B., Cornell U., 1928; m. Matjorie Ruth Weil, Sept. 10, 1933; children—Laurence Jay, Leslie Ruth (Mrs. Matthew J. Harris). With advt. dept., refrigeration div. Gen. Electric Co., 1929-33; sales corr. Master Builders Co., Cleve., 1933-34; sales rep. Snap-Out Form Co., Chardon, O., 1934-35; with

Indsl. Pub. Co., Cleve., 1935—, pres., 1960-68, chmn. bd., 1968—; v.p., dir. Pittway Corp., Northbrook, Ill. Mem. Cornell U. Council; chmn. adv. council Bus. Adminstrn. Sch., Cleve. State U. Mem. Cleve. Area Commn. Older Persons. Bd. dirs. Montefiore Home, Cleve. Mem. Ecol. Soc. Am., Nat. Fluid Power Assn., Am. Welding Soc., Phi Epsilon Pi. Home: 2547 Warwick Rd Shaker Heights OH 44120 Office: 614 Superior Av W Cleveland OH 44113

AURELIUS, MARCUS JAMES, steel co. exec.; b. Los Angeles, June 30, 1910; s. Thomas and Emily (Ireland) A.; A.B., U. Denver, 1931, LL.B., 1963; m. Almina Epperson, Aug. 8, 1936. With Colo. Fuel and Iron Co., Denver and Chgo., 1931-37; salesman r.r. materials Carnegie-Ill. Steel Corp., Chgo., 1937-43, sales engr., 1943-44, asst. to mgr. r.r. materials, Pitts., 1944-46; v.p. sales U.S. Steel Supply Div., Chgo., 1946-50, Columbia-Geneva Steel Div., San Francisco, 1950-54; v.p., gen. mgr. sales U.S. Steel Corp., 1955-57, adminstrv. v.p. comml., 1957—. Bd. dirs. of Keep Am. Beautiful; trustee Carnegie Hero Fund Commn., Pitts. Mem. Pa. Soc., Am. Iron and Steel Inst., Western Pa. Engrs. Soc., Kappa Sigma, Alpha Kappa Psi. Presbyn. Clubs: Duquesne (Pitts.); Fox Chapel Golf; Pine Valley Golf (Clementon, N.J.); Cypress Point (Pebble Beach, Cal.). Home: 560 Squaw Run Rd Pittsburgh PA 15238 Office: 600 Grant St Pittsburgh PA 15230

AURELL, RANDOLPH CARL, educator; b. Worcester, Mass., Apr. 4, 1908; s. Carl E. and Anna (Jansson) A.; B.S., N.Y. U., 1933; M.S., U. Pa., 1940; Ph.D., Yale, 1955; m. Abbie R. Usher, Aug. 13, 1938; 1 dau., Abbie A. (Mrs. Garry M. Brown, Jr.). Mem. faculty Conn. State Coll., 1955—, dean arts and scis., 1965-70. Home: 111 Rogers Rd Forestville CT 06010 Office: Central Conn State Coll New Britain CT 06050

AURIOL, JACQUELINE, French pilot; b. Chalans, France, Nov. 5, 1917; m. Paul Auriol; children—Jean-Claude, Jean-Paul. Social emissary French pres. Vincent Auriol; obtained pilot's license, 1948, mil., comml. pilot licenses, 1950, helicopter license, 1950, test pilot license, 1956; holder world speed record for women, 1951, 63, speed record for women in Mirage III, 1962, became second woman to break sound barrier with jet plane, 1955. Recipient Harmon trophy, 1952, 53; Grand Gold medal F.A.I., 1964; decorated officier Legion d'honneur. Address: 2 quai de Gesvres Paris France

AURNER, ROBERT RAY, corp. exec., author; b. Adel, Ia., Aug. 20, 1898; s. Clarence Ray and Nellie (Slayton) A.; B.A. summa cum laude, University of Iowa, 1919, Master of Arts in 1920, Ph.D., 1922; m. Kathryn Dayton, June 16, 1921; 1 son, Robert Ray 11. Dir. customer relations, new business The State Bank, Madison, Wis., 1925-28; research dir., The Walker Co., 1925-30; established Aurner and Associates, cons. mgmt., bus. adminstrn., market distribution and human relations, pres., exec. dir., 1938—; dir. Carmel Savs. & Loan Assn., 1960—, v.p., dir. Pacific Futures, Inc., 1962—; dir., chmn. bus adv. com. VNA Corp., 1959-62. Lectr. NBC Station WTMJ, 1929-30. State commr., Wis. Library Certification Bd., 1931-38; vice- pres. Nat. Assn. of Marketing Teachers, 1931; pres. Am. Bus. Communication Assn., 1939-40. Mem. Faculty, U. of Wis. 1925-48, ranking research prof. of bus. adminstrn., chairman adminstrn. and mgmt. div., 1930-48; prof. bus. mgmt. U. Pitts., 1934, 36, 39; administrative consultant Internat. Cellucotton Products Co., Chgo., 1947-52; consultant, dir. Communications Div., Fox River Paper Corp., Appleton, Wis., 1947-60; v.p., gen. consultant, dir. Scott, Inc., Milw. annd Carmel, 1949—; cons. U.S. Naval Postgrad. Sch., Management School Division, Department of the Navy, Dept. Def., 1957—, Jahn & Ollier Corp., Morris, Schenker, Roth, Inc., First Nat. Bank (Chgo.), Allis- Chalmers Corp., Milw.; ltd. partner Salinas-Peninsula Investment Co., 1963—; cons. Wis. Div. Vital Statistics, 1930-48. Dean, Coll. of Commerce, Biarritz American University, France, U.S. Army Univ. Center No. 2, European Theater, 1945-46; special lecturer, Netherlands School of Economics, Rotterdam, Holland, 1945; U.S. State Dept. rep., Dutch-American Conf., The Hague, Holland, 1945, member national advisory com. Conference of American Small Business Organizations since 1947. Dir. SAE Corp., Evanston, Ill., 1943-53, pres., chmn. bd., 1951-53; mem. nat. adv. counsel Atlantic Union, Inc., 1949—. Trustee Levere Meml. Found., Chgo., 1943-53, pres., chmn. bd., 1951-53; finance exec. Carmel Found. (Cal.), dir., chmn. finance com., mem. internal trusteeship com., exec. com., 1954—; mem. bd. investment mgmt. Hazeltine Fund California, 1963- -; adv. gov., bd. dirs. Monterey Fund Edn.; dir., chmn. com. endowments York Sch., 1966-69. Recipient Distinguished Service award, Sigma Alpha Epsilon, 1967. Fellow of the American Business Communication Association (honorary.); member American Marketing Assn., Wis. Acad. Scis., Arts and Letters, State Historical Society of Iowa, Phi Beta Kappa, Delta Sigma Rho, Alpha Kappa Psi (vice chairman com. profl. programs, exec. group 1955—), Sigma Alpha Epsilon (supreme council, 1943-53, national president 1951-53). Clubs: The Continental (Chicago); The Highlands, Decemvir, Convivium (Monterey Peninsula); The Stateseman's (Los Angeles); The Group (Pebble Beach, Cal.). Author books, publs. relating to field; latest being: Development in Management; Specialized Field Approach, 1963; Language Control for Business, 1965; Success Factors in Executive Development, 1960; Effective English for Business Communication, 6th edit., 1970; Effective Communication in Business with Management Emphasis, 5th edit., 1967. Contbg. editor: Am. Bus. Practice, 4 vols., Am. Ency. Social Scis. Home: San Antonio and Inspiration Avs Carmel Point Carmel-by-the Sea CA 93921 Office: PO Box 3434 Carmel CA 93921

AUSE, MARSHALL GERHARD, assn. exec.; born Fairbault, Minn., July 2, 1919; s. Oscar and Anna (Hope) A.; B.A., St. Olaf Coll., 1941; M.H.A., U. Minn., 1953; m. Ruth Mauldin, Dec. 27, 1951; 1 son, Marshall Craig. Med. adminstrv. officer VA Hosps., Northport, L.I., N.Y., St. Cloud, Minn., N. Little Rock, Ark., 1945-51; adminstrv. resident Mary Hitchcock Hosp. Dartmouth, 1952- 53; asst. dir. St. Lukes Hosps., Milw., 1953-55; adminstr. Lutheran Med. Center, Bklyn., 1955-62, Orange County Med. Center, Orange, Cal., 1962-68, dir. bur. mgmt. services Am. Hosp. Assn., Chgo., Ill., 1968—; lectr. Sch. Pub. Health, U. Cal. at Los Angeles, Cal. Coll. Medicine; vis. lectr. various colls. and univs.; preceptor Center for Continuing Edn. in Health Scis., U. Cal. at Berkeley; vis. lectr. U. Colo.; cons., course hosp. adminstrn. U. of Tehran (Iran). Member Commn. on Hosps. Nat. Luth. Council, 1956-62; mem. state hosp. adv. council Cal. County Suprs. Assn. Pres., dir. Bklyn., L.I., S.I. Hosp. Council; bd. dirs. Childrens Hosp., Orange. Trustee Norwegian Childrens Home. Served to rank of 1st lt. in the Med. Adminstrn. Corps, AUS, 1942-46. Recipient Distinguished Service award Luth. Med. Center, 1961. Mem. Am., Cal., Luth. (past pres., dir.) hosp. assns., Am. Assn. Pub. Health, Am. Coll. Hosp. Adminstrs., Am. Mgmt. Assn., U. Minn. Hosp. Adminstrs. Alumni Assn. (past pres.). Clubs: Desert (Palm Springs); Kiwanis; Lake Shore. Contbr. articles to trade publs. Home: 910 N Lake Shore Dr Chicago IL 60611 Office: 840 N Lake Shore Dr Chicago IL 60611

AUSE, ORVAL HOPE, dairy co. exec.; b. Kenyon, Minn., Aug. 15, 1909; s. Oscar A. and Anna (Hope) A.; student St. Olaf Coll., 1928-29; B.S., Ia. State U., 1932; M.S., U. Minn., 1934; m. Maurine Brogmus, Sept. 17, 1932; children—Orval Craig, Robert G., Marianne (Mrs. Alan Mitchell), Carol Jean. Instr. dairy industry Ia. State U., 1934-35; butter insp. Dept. Agr., 1935; with H.C. Christians Co., Chgo., 1935-70, pres., 1960-70; pres. Gt. Lakes Packing Co., 1970—. Pres. West Suburgan council Boy Scouts Am., 1959-60, mem. exec. com. Region XII; pres. Oak Park (Ill.) Elementary Sch. Bd., 1945-48, Hinsdale (Ill.) Community Chest, 1953-55, Hinsdale Community House, 1955-60; v.p., mem. council Suburban Community Chest; mem. Hinsdale Plan Commn., 1962-64, Hinsdale Zoning Bd. Appeal, 1965-70. Bd. govs. Ia. State U. Found.; trustee Chgo. Met. Crusade of Mercy. Mem. Nat. Dairy Council (dir. 1963-67), Am. Butter Inst. (dir. 1962-68), Chgo. Dairy Tech. Soc. (pres. 1942), Am. Dairy Sci. Assn., Chgo. Assn. Commerce and Industry, Chgo. Mercantile Exchange, Audubon Soc., Wilderness Soc., Sierra Club, Izaak Walton League, Alpha Sigma Phi, Alpha Zeta. Republican. Lutheran. Clubs: Hinsdale Golf; Diarymens Country (Boulder Junction, Wis.). Home: 949 N Madison St Hinsdale IL 60521 Office: 1535 W 43d St Chicago IL 60609

AUSLAND, JOHN CAMPBELL, fgn. service officer; b. La Crosse, Wis., July 14, 1920; s. John Engebo and Margaret (Weir) A.; B.A., Princeton, 1947, student Grad. Sch., 1947- 49; student Laval U., Quebec, Can., 1946; m. Malory Campbell, Aug. 15, 1946; children—Anne, Hayden, Steven. Radio announcer, 1939-42; joined U.S. Fgn. Service, 1949; assigned Germany, 1949-51, State Dept., 1951- 54, 61-69, Belgrade, Yugoslavia, 1954-56, Australia, 1956-61; dep. chief mission, Oslo, Norway, 1969—. Served to capt. AUS, 1942-45. Decorated Bronze Star, Silver Star; recipient Superior Service award State Dept., 1965; Sec. Def. Civilian Meritorious Service award, 1967. Mem. Am. Fgn. Service Assn. Author articles in field. Home: 32 Hoffsjef Lovenskioldsvei Oslo Norway Office: American Embassy Oslo Norway

AUSLANDER, GEORGE, engr., banker; b. N.Y.C., May 15, 1904; s. Alfred and Rougea (Foster) A.; ed. Pratt Inst., 1925; m. Evelyn Foster Steiner, Nov. 29, 1935; children—June Foster, Diane Evelyn. With Pub. Service Heat & Power Co., Inc., Valley Stream, N.Y., 1925—, chmn. bd., 1947—; chmn. bd. Valley Nat. Bank L.I., Valley Stream, 1948—; L.I. chmn. U.S. Treasury Savs. Bond Program; chmn. L.I. chpt. Nat. Conf. Christians and Jews. Mayor, Village of Hewlett Harbor, L.I. Mem. Nassau County Village Ofcls. Assn. (pres. 1965), Nassau Clearing House Assn., Am. Inst. Banking, Am., N.Y. State bankers assns., Ex-Mems. Assn. Squadron A, Order Lafayette. Episcopalian. Mason (32). Clubs: Metropolitan (N.Y.C.); Lawrence Beach (Atlantic Beach, L.I.); Lake Placid (N.Y.); Pratt Architectural (Bklyn.); Rockville Links (Rockville Center, N.Y.); Beach (Palm Beach, Fla.) Home: 1325 Harbor Rd Hewlett Harbor L I NY 11557 Office: 235 Rockaway Av Valley Stream NY 11582

AUSLEY, CHARLES SAXON, lawyer; Tallahassee, Jan. 15, 1907; s. Charles Merit and Elizabeth (Saxon) A.; LL.B., U. Fla., 1930; m. Loranne DuBose, June 28, 1933; children—Anne (Mrs. Ryals Lee), Charles DuBose, Nancy Mitchell (Mrs. Joe Hannon). Admitted to Fla. bar, 1930; since practiced in Tallahassee; sr. mem. firm Ausly, Ausly, McMullen, McGehee & Carothers and predecessors, 1935—. Dir. Capital City 1st Nat. Bank, Capitol City 2d Nat. Bank, Tallahassee. Mayor, Tallahassee, 1937-42. senator, 1943-45. Fellow Am. Bar Found.; mem. Am. Bar Assn., Am. Coll. Trial Lawyers, Internat. Acad. Trial Lawyers. Presbyn. Home 1410 Betton Rd Tallahassee FL 32303 Office: Washington Square Bldg Tallahassee FL 32303

AUSMUS, JAMES TIPTON, lawyer, co. exec.; b. Mexico, Mo., Sept. 10, 1937; s. R. E. and Barbara Miller (Beck) A.; A.B., U. Mo., 1959, LL.B., 1962, J.D., 1962; m. Joan Johnson, Aug. 16, 1959; children—James Tipton II, Jeffrey K., Joseph Andrew. Admitted to Mo. bar, 1962, since practiced in Centralia; with legal dept. A.B. Chance Co., 1962-64, 69—, sec., corporate atty., 1969—; pvt. practice, 1964-69; city atty. Centralia and Sturgeon, Mo., 1964-69. Chmn. Centralia United Fund, 1966-70, local Salvation Army com., 1965—. Mem. bd. aldermen City of Centralia, 1971—. Served to 2d lt. U.S. Army, 1959-61; capt. Res. ret. Mem. Centralia C. of C., Centralia Jr. C. of C., Alpha Tau Omega, Phi Delta Phi. Republican. Methodist. Kiwanian. Home: 1 Leabrook Dr Centralia MO 65240 Office: 210 N Allen St Centralia MO 65240

AUST, JOE BRADLEY, surgeon, educator; b. Buffalo, Sept. 8, 1926; s. Joe Bradley and Edith (Derby) A.; M.D., U. Buffalo, 1949; M.S. in Physiology, U. Minn., 1957, Ph.D. in Surgery, 1958; m. Constance Ann MacMullin, June 18, 1949; children—Jay Bradley, Bonnie Jean, Barbara Ann, Linda Lee, Mary Louise, Tracey Roberta. Intern U. Minn. Hosps., 1949-50, resident, 1950-58; scholar Am. Cancer Soc., U. Minn., 1957-62, mem. faculty, 1957-66, prof. surgery, 1964-66; prof. surgery, chmn. dept. U. Tex. Med. Sch. at San Antonio, 1966—; cons. Minn. State Prison, 1958-62, Anoka State Hosp., 1962-65, Brooke Army Med. Hosp., 1967—, Wilford Hall USAF Hosp., 1967—. Served with M.C., USNR, 1950-52. Diplomate Am. Bd. Surgery, Am. Bd. Thoracic Surgery. Fellow A.C.S.; mem. Am., Western, Central surg. assns., Soc. Univ. Surgeons, Soc. Head and Neck Surgeons, Am. Assn. Cancer Research, Am. Soc. Exptl. Pathologists, San Antonio Surg. Soc., N.Y. Acad. Scis., Halsted Soc., Soc. Clin. Oncology, Transplantation Soc., Soc. Exptl. Biology and Medicine, Sigma Xi, Alpha Omega Alpha, Phi Chi. Spl. research cancer immunity, regional cancer chemotherapy, shock, homotransplantation. Home: 902 Serenade Dr San Antonio TX 78213

AUSTELL, EDWARD CALLAWAY, banker; b. Spartanburg, S.C., Aug. 9, 1937; s. Edward and Frances Roberta (Glenn) A.; A.B., Davidson Coll., 1959; M.B.A., U.N.C., 1960; postgrad. Nat. Trust Sch. Northwestern U., 1968; m. Louise Arnold Zimmerman, May 14, 1966; 1 dau., Frances Barrett. Vice pres. trust dept. First Nat. Bank S.C., 1964-71; v.p. trust dept. Ga. R.R. Bank & Trust Co., Augusta, 1971—. Trustee Augusta Symphony League, Augusta Opera Assn. Served with AUS, 1960-62. Mem. Am. Inst. Banking, Augusta Estate Planning Council, Atlanta Soc. Financial Analysis, Beta Theta Pi. Presbyn. (vice chmn. bd. deacons). Mason. Clubs: Pinnacle, Augusta Country (Augusta); Palmetto, Tarantella (Columbia, S.C.). Home: 2206 Crestwood Dr Augusta GA 30904 Office: PO Box 1211 699 Broad St Augusta GA 30902

AUSTELL, ROBERT RHETT, Jr., pub. co. exec.; b. Middletown, N.Y., May 7, 1925; s. Robert Rhett and Mary Van Etten (Stivers) A.; grad. Hotchkiss Sch., 1943; B.A., Williams Coll., 1948; M.B.A., Harvard, 1950; m. Madeleine Pohlmann, Sept. 27, 1947; children—Elizabeth, Robert Rhett III, Sarah. With Time, Inc., 1950 - -, v.p., 1965-69, exec. v.p., 1969—, gen. mgr. Time Mag., 1960-64, pub. Time-Life Books, 1964-69; dir. Gen. Learning Corp., Sterling/Manhattan, Little, Brown & Co. Trustee Hotchkiss School, 1967—, v.p. bd. trustees, 1970—. Served with inf., AUS, World War 11. Mem. Phi Beta Kappa, Sigma Phi. Clubs: Williams, The Harvard (N.Y.C.); The Sleepy Hollow (Scarborough, N.Y.). Home: 47 Quinn Rd Briarcliff Manor NY 10510 Office: Time and Life Bldg Rockefeller Center New York City NY 10020

AUSTEN, KARL FRANK, physician, educator; b. Akron, O., Mar. 14, 1928; s. Karl and Bertle (Jehle) A.; A.B., Amherst Coll., 1950; M.D., Harvard, 1954; m. Joycelyn Chapman, Apr. 11, 1959; children-Leslie Marie, Karla Ann, Timothy Frank, Jonathan Arthur. Intern in medicine Mass. Gen. Hosp., 1954-55, asst. resident, 1955-56, sr. resident, 1958-59, chief resident, 1961, asst. in medicine, 1962-63, asst. physician, 1963-66, chief pulmonary unit, 1964- 66, also cons. in medicine; practice medicine, specializing in internal medicine, Boston, 1962—; USPHS postdoctoral research fellow Nat. Inst. Med. Research, Mill Hill, London, Eng., 1959-61; asst. in medicine Harvard Med. Sch., 1961; instr., 1961-62, asso. in medicine, 1962-64, asst. prof., 1965-66, asso. prof., 1966-68, prof., 1969—; physician-in- chief Robert B. Brigham Hosp., 1966—; physician Peter Bent Brigham Hosp., 1966—. Mem. fellowship subcom. Arthritis Found., 1968—; mem. council Infectious Disease Soc. Am., 1969—; mem. arthritis tng. grants com. Nat. Inst. Arthritis and Metabolic Diseases, NIH, 1970—. Mem. Masconomet Regional Sch. Com., 1966-69. Served to capt., M.C., U.S. Army, 1956-58. Mem. Am. Soc. Pharm. and Exptl. Therapeutics, Am. Soc. Exptl. Pathology, Am. Assn. Immunologists, Brit. Soc. Immunology, Am. Soc. Clin. Investigation, Assn. Am. Physicians, Am. Acad. Allergy (mem. exec. com.). Contbr. articles profl. jours. Home: 34 Bradford Rd Wellesley Hills MA 02181 Office: Robert B Brigham Hosp 125 Parker Hill Av Boston MA 02120

AUSTEN, WILLIAM GERALD, surgeon, educator; b. Akron, O., Jan. 20, 1930; s. Karl A. and Bertl (Jehle) A.; B.S., Mass. Inst. Tech., 1951; M.D., Harvard, 1955; m. Patricia Ramsdell, Jan. 28, 1961; children—Karl Ramsdell, William Gerald, Christopher Marshall. Intern, then resident surgery Mass. Gen. Hosp., Boston, 1955-60, chief surgery, 1969—; prof. surgery Mass. Gen. Hosp. and Harvard Med. Sch., 1966—. Served as surgeon USPHS, 1960-62. Markle scholar acad. medicine, 1963-68. Mem. Soc. U. Surgeons (sec. 1967-70), Mass. Heart Assn. (pres. elect 1970). Author articles in field. Home: 41 Myopia Rd Winchester MA 01890 Office: Mass Gen Hosp Boston MA 02114

AUSTERLITZ, ROBERT PAUL, educator; b. Bucharest, Rumania, Dec. 13, 1923; s. Otto and Rose (Zellenka) A.; came to U.S., 1938; naturalized, 1946; A.B., New Sch. Social Research, 1950; M.A., Columbia, 1950, Ph.D., 1955; student Finland, 1951-53, Japan, 1953-54, 56-58; m. Sylvi Nevanlinna, Mar. 21, 1953; children—Monica, Paul. Mem. faculty Columbia, 1958—, prof. linguistics and Uralic studies, 1965—, chmn. dept. linguistics, 1965-68; vis. faculty mem. Linguistic Inst., U. Wash., Seattle, summers 1962-63; vis. asso. prof. Yale, 1964-65; vis. prof. U. Cal. at Berkeley, 1969. Cons. map lang. families Eurasia, Smithsonian Instn., 1967. Served with AUS, 1943-45. Decorated knight 1st class Order Lion Finland; sr. fellow Nat. Endowment for Humanities, 1971-72. Mem. Linguistics Soc. Am. (life), Soc. Finno-Dugrienne (corr.), Linguistic Soc. Japan. Author: Ob-Ugric Metrics, 1958. Co-editor: Jour. Word, 1960-65; Readings in Linguisitics II, 1966. Address: Philosophy Hall Columbia Univ New York City NY 10027

AUSTERN, HERMAN THOMAS, lawyer; b. N.Y. City, Sept. 19, 1905; s. Lester and Gertrude (Phillips) A.; B.S., N.Y.U., 1926; LL.B. magna cum laude, Harvard (Langdell fellow), 1929; m. Esther Kramer, Oct. 16th, 1934; children—Helen Theresa (Mrs. Earl Colson), and David Thomas. Admitted to bar, 1931; legal sec. to U.S. Circuit Judge Julian W. Mack, 1929, Justice Louis D. Brandeis. 1930; lectr. bus. law N.Y.U., 1947-48, adj. professor law, 1957—; lecturer at Harvard Law School, 1968; practice law, Washington, 1931—; partner Covington & Burling, 1936—; chief counsel Nat. Canners Assn., 1942—; dir. The Ludlow Corp., Boston. Mem. Patent Adv. Panel AEC, 1949-56; adv. council Food Law Inst., 1949—. Mem. Am. Bar Assn. (council antitrust sect. 1959-62, chmn., 1963-64; chmn. com. food standards, banking, comml. law sect.), N.Y. State Bar Assn. (chmn. Fed. Trade Commn. com., antitrust law sect.), D.C. Bar Assn., A.A.A.S., Alpha Lambda Phi, Delta Kappa Delta, Phi Beta Kappa. Clubs: Metropolitan, Harvard (D.C., N.Y.); Nat. Lawyers. Author articles. Editorial adv. bd. Food Drug Cosmetic Law Jour.; adv. bd. Jour. of Reprints for Antitrust Law and Econs. Home: 3506 Garfield St NW Washington DC 20007 Office: 888 16th St NW Washington DC 20006

AUSTILL, ALLEN, univ. dean; b. Newton, Mass., June 22, 1927; s. William E. and Anna (Pifer) A.; B.A., U. Chgo., 1948, M.A., 1951; m. Joan Mildred Sellery, June 4, 1950; children—Randolph Allen, Christopher Scott, Lara Anne. Research asso. Council State Govts., Chgo., 1951-52; dir. admissions and placement St. Johns Coll., 1953-55; dir. student housing U. Chgo., 1955-57; dean students State U. N.Y. at Stony Brook, 1957-61; cons. Ford Found., Middle East, Amman, Jordan, 1962; asso. dean New Sch. Social Research, 1962-64, dean, 1964—. Cons. title I, Higher Edn. Act, State N.Y. Pres. Friends of Cresskill Library, 1969-71. Served with AUS, 1945-46. Author: (with others) Higher Education in the Forty-Eight States, 1952; Summary of State Legislation and Elections, 1953. Home: 1 Lambs Lane Cresskill NJ 07626 Office: 66 W 12th St New York City NY 10011

AUSTIN, ALLAN STEWART, engr., constrn. exec.; b. Cleve., Apr. 1, 1905; s. Wilbert J. and Ida M. (Stewart) A.; B.S., Yale, 1927; m. Margaret Stroup, July 29, 1929; 1 son, Richard C.; m. 2d, Winifred Nienhouse, Mar. 11, 1947; 1 son, James W. With Austin Co., Cleve., 1928—, successively labor foreman and clk., Los Angeles, field engr., supt. and sales engr., Cleve., dist. mgr., London, Eng., sec., v.p., gen. sales mgr., 1928-58, pres., 1958-63, chmn. bd., 1963—, chief exec. officer, 1963-70; dir. Austin Internat. Corp., Austin Co. Found., Central Nat. Bank, Cleve. Trustee Lake Erie Coll., Cleve. Inst. Music, Hiram (O.) Coll. Served from capt. to maj. AUS, 1943-46, Presbyn. Clubs: Yale (N.Y.C.); Kirtland (O.) Country; Gulfstream (Fla.) Golf; Union (Cleve.); Ocean, Little (Delray Beach, Fla.). Home: 2731 Sherbrooke Rd Shaker Heights OH 44122 Office: 3650 Mayfield Rd Cleveland OH 44121

AUSTIN, ALVIN EDWARD, educator, journalist; b. Grand Forks, N.D.; s. Raymond Easton and Kathryn Veronica (Mayer) A.; A.B., U. of N.D., 1931; grad. Mil. Intelligence Center, Camp Ritchie, Md., 1944; m. Ellen Jane Megivern, June 4, 1946; children—Suellen, Sheila Ann. Night city editor Grand Forks Herald, 1931-33, night editor, 1933-42, condr. column, Looking Around, 1938-57, mem. editorial staff, 1946-57; asst. in journalism U. of N.D., 1940-42, prof. journalism, 1946—, chmn. journalism dept., 1946-69; visiting prof. journalism Univ. of Vt., 1967-68; director Model Cities Project, Fargo, N.D., 1969-70. Mem. bd. control student publs. U. N.D. Alderman Grand Forks, 1962-64; v.p. Grand Forks City Bd. Health, 1962-64; mem. N.D. Vets. Aid Commn., 1965-71, chmn., 1970-71. Pres. Grand Forks City Council, 1962- 64. Served with G-2 Sect., X Corps, U.S. Army, 1942-46, 39 mos.; participated in occupation of Japan, 1945-46; discharged with rank of 1st lt.; member Organized Reserve Corps, 1947-50. Decorated Bronze Star medal; recipient Wells Meml. Key Sigma Delta Chi, 1955. Mem. Am. Assn. Journalism Sch. Adminstrs. (pres. 1953; chmn. summer faculty fellowships com.), Association Education Journalism, V.F.W., Am. Legion, Inland Daily, N.D. press assns., Blue Key, Sigma Delta Chi (nat. v.p. 1952-55; vice chmn. nat. freedom information com. 1959-71; mem. nat. press ethics com. 1947-49), Kappa Sigma. Roman Catholic. Elk, K. of C. Home: 525 25th St Grand Forks ND 58201 Office: Merrifield Hall Univ North Dakota Grand Forks ND 58202

AUSTIN, ATWOOD, corp. exec.; b. Leavenworth, Kan., June 3, 1904; s. Col. William A. and Helen (Atwood) A.; B. Ceramic Engring., Ohio State U., 1925; m. Mary R. McEvoy, May 11, 1940; children—John Atwood, Helen L. McCord, Stephen M., Ann McEvoy. Investment banking with Van Grant & Co., Detroit, 1937-41; treas., dir. Harlan Electric Co., Detroit, 1939-45; asso. Henry J. Kaiser activities 1945—; v.p., treas. Kaiser Steel Corp., Oakland, Cal., 1950-63; v.p. Kaiser Industries, 1963-70; dir. Centerbury Woods. Adviser Chinese Govt. Mission, 1944. Bd. dirs. Episcopal Homes Found., Kula Bot. Garden. Mem. Phi Delta Theta, Keramos. Episcopalian. Clubs: Beach (Pebble Beach); Lahaina (Maui, Hawaii) Yacht. Box 213 Pebble Beach CA 93953

AUSTIN, BERNARD LIGE, naval officer; b. Wagener, S.C., Dec. 15, 1902; s. Elijah Andrew and Loula Ola (Gant) A.; student The Citadel, 1918-20; B.S., U.S. Naval Acad., 1924; student U.S. Nat. War College, 1946-47, Imperial Def. Coll., 1949; LL.D., Long Island U., University Rhode Island; m. Isabella Murray Leith, Apr. 16, 1925; children—Alexandra (Mrs. Nathaniel Willis James, III), Jane Stuart (Mrs. Frank Thomas Watkins, Jr.), Isabella Leith (Mrs. William Walter Warlick, Junior). Commissioned ensign U.S. Navy, 1924, advanced thru grades to vice adm., 1956; jr. officer U.S.S. New York, 1924-26; student torpedo sch., Newport, submarine sch., New London, 1926-27; submarine duty, Pearl Harbor, T.H., 1927-31; instr. physics, chemistry Naval Acad., 1931-34; comdr. submarine U.S.S. R-11, 1934-37; exec. officer presdl. yacht Potomac, 1937; press relations officer Navy Dept., 1937-40; spl. naval observer, London, Eng., 1940-41; comdr. U.S.S. Woolsey, 1942, U.S.S. Foote, Destroyer Div. 46 South Pacific, 1943, Destroyer Squadron 14, Marshall Islands campaign, 1944; operations officer Comdr. Destroyers Pacific, 1944, asst. chief staff for adminstrn. Cincpac, 1944-45; Navy mem. secretariat State, War, Navy Coordinating Com., 1945-46; Navy mem. staff Nat. Security Council, 1947- 48, dep. to Joint Chiefs Staff rep. on sr. staff NSC, 1951; comdr. Service Squadron 1, West Coast, 1950, Service Squadron 3, Western Pacific, 1950-51; dep. and dir. internat. affairs div. Navy Dept., 1951- 54; comdr. Cruiser Div. 2, 1954-55, dir. joint staff Joint Chiefs of Staffs, 1956-58; comdr. 2d Fleet and striking fleet, Atlantic, 1958-59; dep. chief Naval Operations for Plans and Policy, 1959-60; pres. Naval War Coll., 1960-64; chmn. Inter-Am. Def. Bd., 1964-67. Decorated Navy Cross, Gold Star, D.S.M. with gold star, Legion Merit, Bronze Star, Presdl. Unit Citation. Home: Rockville MD 20850

AUSTIN, BILL, formerly asst. coach Los Angeles Rams Profl. Football Team, and head coach Pitts. Steelers Profl. Football Team, now asst. coach Chgo. Bears Football Team. Address: 173 W Madison St Chicago IL*

AUSTIN, BURTON FORSYTHE, physician; b. Geneva, Ala., Jan. 12, 1895; s. James Weldon and Minnie (Keith) A.; M.D., U. Ala., 1917; M.P.H., Harvard, 1933; married Molly Mack, Oct. 9, 1917; m. 2d, Elizabeth P. Sealy, June 17, 1950; m. 3d, Rubby Folsom Ellis, Apr. 4, 1959. Health officer Morgan County, Alabama, 1920-23, Madison County, Ala., 1923-25; asst. to state health officer, Montgomery, Ala., 1925-35; dir. bureau of hygiene and nursing State Health Dept., Montgomery, 1935-41; acting state health officer, Ala., 1941-42, state health officer, 1942-47; adminstr. health services and med. dir. South Eastern Area Am. Red Cross (La., Miss., Tenn., Ala., Fla., Ga., S.C. and N.C.) 1947; dir. Palm Beach County Health Dept., 1948; sr. doctor VA Regional Office, Montgomery, now chief div. pulmonary diseases. Served as 1st lt. med. sect. ORC, 1917-20; lt. col., Med. Corps, State Guard, 1942-46; lt. col., Ala. Nat. Guard, since 1946. Awarded Mil. Cross by U.D.C., 1937; certificate of merit and Selective Service medal by the President, 1946. Diplomate Am. Bd. Preventive Med. Pub. Health. Fellow Med. Assn.; mem. Ala., So. med. assns., Montgomery County Med. Soc., Am., Ala. thoracic socs., Ala. Tb Assn., New Orleans Grad. Med. Assembly (asso.), Am. Legion (past dept. comdr.), 40 and 8, V.F.W., D.A.V., Mil. Order World War, Newcomen Soc. Eng. (N.Am. br.), Theta Kappa Psi, Delta Omicron Alpha. Democrat. Presbyn. (elder). Kiwanian. Clubs: Executives (past pres.), Knife and Fork (Montgomery). Home: 1916 S Hull St Montgomery AL 36104 Office: 474 S Court St Montgomery AL 36104

AUSTIN, DARREL, artist; b. Raymond, Wash., June 25, 1907; s. Albert and Ella (Caruthers) A.; ed. pub. schs.; studied art at Oregon and Notre Dame univs. and with Emile Jacques; m. Margot Helser Feb. 24, 1933; 1 son, Darrel. Began painting, 1925; painted murals for Med. Coll. U. Ore., 1934. Rep. in nat. shows at Whitney Museum (N.Y.C.), Carnegie Inst. (Pitts.), Art. Inst. (Chgo.), Inst. Modern Art (Boston), City Art Mus. (St. Louis), Springfield (Mass.) Mus. of Fine Arts, Soc. of Four Arts (Palm Beach, Fla.); also rep. in spl. exhbn. "Contemporary Painting in the U.S." at Met. Mus., New York, later on tour of Latin Am. countries; also rep. in coll. of Met. Mus of Fine Arts, Boston, Detroit Inst. of Art, Albright Art Gallery, Buffalo, Smith Coll. Mus. of Art, Phillips Meml. Gallery, Washington, D.C., Nelson Gallery of Art, Kansas City, Mo., Rochester Meml. Art Gallery, Clearwater (Fla.) Museum. Address: Rte 3 New Fairfield CT 06430

AUSTIN, EDWIN CHARLES, lawyer; b. Barrington, Ill., Mar. 28, 1892; s. Charles Henry and Luella (Hawley) Austin; B.A., U. of Wis., 1912; LL.B., Northwestern U., 1915, M.A., 1917; m. Marion Roberts, June 9, 1917; children—Barbara (Mrs. Robert L. Foote), Patricia (Mrs. Renslow D. Sherer), Elizabeth (Mrs. David A. Lindsay). Admitted to bar by Ill. Supreme Court, 1915, since practiced law, Chicago; mem. firm Sidley & Austin; counsel Chgo. Community Trust, 1944-64. Dir. Brooks-Scanlon, Inc., The Hoover Co., Leath & Co. Served as lt. U.S. Navy, 1917-19. Mem. New Trier High Sch. Bd., 1919-20; mem. Glencoe School Bd., 1927-31 (pres. 1929-31); mem. Ill. State Bd. of Bar Examiners, 1925-27, Ill. State Bd. of Examiners in Accountancy, 1934- 37. Pres. Roycemore Sch., 1934-40; pres. Cook County Sch. of Nursing, 1943-44; trustee Am. Library Assn., Old Peoples Home, Evanston Hospital; past member bd. trustees Vassar Coll. and Northwestern U.; bd. dirs. Lyric Opera Chgo., governing mem. Chgo. Orchestral Assn. Fellow Am., Chgo. bar founds.; mem. Am., Ill., Chgo. bar assns., Law Club (pres. 1966-67), Legal Club (Pres. 1944- 45), Order of Coif, Delta Sigma Rho, Sigma Phi, Phi Delta Phi. Republican. Congregationalist. Clubs: Chgo., Commercial, Commonwealth, Mid-Day, Old Elm, Union League (pres. 1935), University, Executives (Chgo.); Glen View (Ill.); Indian Hill (Winnetka, Ill.); Wausaukee (Wis.); Army and Navy (Washington). Home: 1171 Whitebridge Hill Rd Winnetka IL 60093 Office: One First National Plaza Chicago IL 60670

AUSTIN, FREDERICK PASQUA, Jr., tool mfg. exec.; b. Leadville, Colo., Aug. 1, 1909; s. Frederick Pasqua and Mary Eliza (Henderson) A.; A.B., Stanford, 1931; m. Elizabeth Merriam, July 11, 1936; children—Judith M. (Mrs. George F. Kilborn), Bethany. Staff accountant Lybrand, Ross Bros. & Montgomery, Los Angeles, 1931-35, Boston, 1935-39; with Brown & Sharpe Mfg. Co., Providence, 1939—, successively comptroller, asst. treas., dir., 1939-47, v.p., treas., 1947-69, v.p. finance, 1969—. Republican. Conglist. Clubs: Hope (Providence); Little Compton Golf (Warrens Point Beach). Home: 5300 Post Rd East Greenwich RI 02818 Office: Precision Park PO Box 456 North Kingstown RI 02853

AUSTIN, GEORGE THOMAS, educator, chem. engr.; b. Salem, Ill., June 6, 1914; s. Charles E. and Eunice (Hord) A.; B.S. in Chem. Engring., U. Ill., 1936; Ph.D., Purdue U., 1943; m. Helen E. Frost, Apr. 23, 1937; children—Mary (Mrs. J. Hautamaki), Thomas, Jane. Jr. engr. Socony-Vacuum Oil Co., 1936- 39; chief chem. engr. Mallinckrodt Chem. Co., 1943-47; vis. prof. Indian Inst. Sci., Bangalore, India, 1954-55; mem. faculty Wash. State U., 1947—, prof. chem. engring., 1950—, chmn. dept., 1950; cons. in field. Registered profl. engr., Wash. Mem. Am. Inst. Chem. Engrs., Am. Chem. Soc., Am. Soc. Engring. Edn., Alpha Chi Rho, Alpha Chi Sigma, Kiwanian (pres. Pullman 1960). Author articles in field. Home: 1600 Landis Pl Pullman WA 99163 Office: Chem Engirng Bldg Wash State Univ Pullman WA 99163

AUSTIN, GORDON HARRISON, assn. ofcl.; b. Davenport, Ia., Sept. 1, 1913; s. Fred T. and Lenore Lenore (Harrison) A.; B.S. in Engring., U.S. Mil. Acad., 1936; grad. USAAF Flying Schs., 1937, Air War Coll., 1948, Nat. War Coll., 1953; m. Joyce Tedman, Dec. 12, 1949; 1 dau. Elizabeth Jean. Commd. 2nd lt. U.S. Army, 1936, advanced through grades to maj. gen. USAF, 1964; various assignments, U.S. and Hawaii, 1936-42; exec. officer Boston Air Def. Wing, 1942; comdr. 325th Fighter Group, MTO, 1942-43, 319th Bombardment Group, MTO, 1943; dep. chief staff operations 42d Bombardment Wing, MTO, 1943-44; chief fighter br., operations and requirements div. Hdqrs. USAAF, 1944-47; dir. operations Hdqrs. First Air Force, Ft. Slocum, N.Y., 1948-49; USAF rep. Western Union Mil. Hdqrs., Fontainebleau, France, 1949-50; USAF mem. So. European-Western Mediterranean Regional Planning Group (NATO), Paris, France, 1950; chief air force sect. Mil. Assistance Adv. Group, France, 1950-52; mem. joint strategic plans group Joint Staff, 1952-55; mem. war plans div. Hdqrs. USAF, 1955; dep. chief staff operations Hdqrs. Central Air Def. Force, 1955- 58; comdr. 20th Air Div., Richards-Gebaur AFB, 1958; comdr. 11th Air Div., Ladd AFB, Alaska, also dep. comdr. Alaskan Air Command, 1958-60; dep. dir. operational requirements Hdqrs. USAF, 1960-62; dep. chief staff operations, also sr. USAF rep. Hdqrs. Allied Air Forces Central Europe (NATO), 1962-65; comdr. Eastern NORAD Region/1st Air Force, Stewart AFB, N.Y., 1965-66; v.p. operations Nat. Security Indsl. Assn. Decorated Silver Star, Legion of merit with oak leaf cluster, D.F.C., Air medal with 13 oak leaf clusters; Legion of Honor, Croix de Guerre (France). Home: 6202 Foxcroft Rd Alexandria VA 22307 Office: 740 15th St N W Washington DC 20005

AUSTIN, GRANVILLE SEWARD, govt. ofcl., author; b. Boston, Apr. 10, 1927; s. Albert Murray and Madeline (Power) A.; B.A., Dartmouth, 1950; D. Phil., Oxford (Eng.) U., 1964; m. Nancy McConnell, Aug. 20, 1954; children—Andrea Kristen, Craig Moffatt, Geoffrey Granville, Hilary Mac. Free-lance reporter/photographer, with Valley News, N.H., 1950-54; provincial pub. affairs officer, press attache, Vietnam and Lebanon, 1954-58; fellow Inst. Current World Affairs, Oxford, England and New Delhi, India, 1960-66, mem. 1968—; dir. Office Research and Analysis for Near East and S. Asia, State Dept., 1966-69; fgn. policy adviser Senator Clifford P. Case, 1970; writer, cons., 1971; spl. asst. internat. affairs to sec. Dept. Heatlh, Edn. and Welfare, 1971—. Served with AUS, 1945-46. Mem. Asian Studies Assn., Middle E. Studies Assn. Author: The Indian Constitution, Cornerstone of a Nation, 1966; also articles. Home: 7413 Rebecca Dr Alexandria VA 22307 Office: Dept Health Edn and Welfare Washington DC

AUSTIN, HARRY GUIDEN, engring. and constrn. co. exec.; b. Belton, Tex., Dec. 10, 1917; s. Harry Guiden and Emma Lena (Brown) A.; B.S. in Elec. Engring., Tex. A. and M. Coll., 1938; M.B.A., Harvard, 1940; m. Elizabeth Ann Heard, Aug. 31, 1940; children—Lucy Ann, Elizabeth Austin Page, Catherine Marshall. With Pan Am. Airways, Miami, Fla., 1940-41; elec. engr. Brown Shipbldg. Co., Houston, 1941-45; with Brown & Root, Inc., Houston, 1945—, v.p., 1960-65, sr. v.p., 1965-68, sr. group v.p., 1968-70, exec. v.p. constrn., 1970—, also dir.; chmn. bd. Bank of Harris County; dir. Atlas Travel, Inc., Highland Ins. Co. (both Houston). Adv. bd. Houston Salvation Army. Registered profl. engr., Tex. Mem. Nat. Soc. Profl. Engrs., I.E.E.E., Houston Engring. and Sci. Soc. (past pres.), Houston Com. Fgn. Relations, Harris County Heritage Soc., Mus. Nat. Sci., Mus. Fine Arts. Methodist. Clubs: Petroleum, Houston Country, Ramada, World Trade (Houston). Home: 267 Pine Hollow Lane Houston TX 77027 Office: PO Box 3 Houston TX 77001

AUSTIN, JAMES ALBERT, lawyer, banker; b. Boston, Apr. 5, 1902; s. Thomas Francis and Mary Ellen (Punch) A.; student Erasmus Hall High Sch., Bklyn., 1914-19; LL.B., Cornell, 1925; m. Virginia Glass, Feb. 17, 1951; children—Ann, Mary Jane (by previous marriage), James Albert, Susan Virginia. Practiced law, New York City, 1925-27, since 1938; gen. counsel Atlantic Pub. Utilities, Inc., Boston, 1928-31; asst. U.S. atty. So. Dist. N.Y., 1932-34; counsel FTC and Securities and Exchange Commn., Washington, 1934-37; v.p. charge corporate trust div. Irving Trust Co., 1949—; director United States Banknote Co. Mem. Pilgrim Soc. Clubs: University, Down Town Association (New York City). Home: 131 Ardsley Rd Scarsdale NY 10583 also the Quarter Deck Paul's Point Martha's Vineyard MA 02169 Office: One Wall St New York City NY 10015

AUSTIN, JAMES WILLIAM, airline ofcl.; b. Fountain Run, Ky., Nov. 5, 1905; s. James William and Leighton (Barr) A.; A.B., Colo. Coll., 1929; LL.D., New Eng. Coll., 1966; m. Esther Amick, Nov. 11, 1934. Investment banker, 1931-41; v.p., dir. Capital Airlines, 1948-58; pres., dir. N.E. Airlines, Inc., 1958- 1958-64, chmn., 1966-68, dir., 1958—. Served as col. USAAF, 1942-46. Mem. Air Transport Assn. Am. (dir.), Beta Theta Pi. Clubs: Nat. Aviation, Metropolitan, Chevy Chase, Aviation, Army and Navy (Washington); Sky (N.Y.C.). Home: 249 E 48th St New York City NY 10017 Office: 250 Park Av New York City NY

AUSTIN, JOHN DAVID, banker; b. Memphis, Jan. 16, 1936; s. Thomas L. and Vela (Davis) A.; B.B.A., Ga. State U., 1961; m. Dorothy Clemans, Dec. 31, 1959; children—Laura Jan, David John. Jr. accountant Windham, Brannon, Simons & Cashion, Atlanta, 1959-61; jr. accountant Price Waterhouse & Co., Atlanta, 1961-64, sr. tax accountant, Miami, Fla., 1964-67; audit mgr. N.C. Nat. Bank, Greensboro, 1968, v.p., gen. auditor, Charlotte, 1969—. Served with U.S. Army, 1957-59. C.P.A., Ga. Mem. Am. Inst. C.P.A.'s, Inst. Internal Auditors. Office: PO Box 120 Charlotte NC 28201

AUSTIN, JOHN F., Jr., corp. exec.; b. Palestine, Tex., 1908; ed. U. Tex., 1930. Pres., dir. T.J. Bettes Co.; chmn. bd. Business Funds, Inc.; dir. First City Nat. Bank, Houston, Harrisburg Nat. Bank, First State Bank, Frankston, Tex., Benjamin Franklin Savs. & Loan Assn. Mason. Home: 11039 Delford Houston TX 77007 Office: 201 Main St Houston TX 77002*

AUSTIN, JOHN HOGG, Jr., utilities exec.; b. Bryn Mawr, Pa., Apr. 16, 1928; s. John Hogg and Helen Elizabeth (Miner) A.; B.S., Yale, 1950; m. Joan Dorothy Bickel, Oct. 14, 1950; children—Nancy, Thomas, Patricia, Katherine. With Phila. Electric Co., 1950—, asst. mgr.-mgr. financial div., 1964-66, comptroller, 1967-71, v.p. finance and accounting, 1971—; dir. Central Penn Nat. Bank. Trustee Southern Home for Children. Mem. I.E.E.E., Edison Electric Inst., Financial Execs. Inst., Am. Gas. Assn., Franklin Inst. Episcopalian. Club: Yale (Phila.). Home: 1435 Potter Lane Wayne PA 19087 Office: 1000 Chestnut St Philadelphia PA 19105

AUSTIN JOHN PAUL beverage co. exec.; b. La Grange, Ga., Feb. 14, 1915; s. Samuel Yates and Maude (Jernigan) A.; A.B., Harvard, 1937. LL.B., 1940; m. Jeane Weed, July 14, 1950; children—John Paul, Samuel Weed. Admitted to N.Y. bar, 1940; practiced in N.Y.C., 1940-41, 45-49; mem. legal dept. Coca-Cola Co., 1949-50, exec. v.p., 1961-62, pres., dir., 1962—, chief exec. officer, 1966—; chmn. bd., 1970—; exec. v.p. Coca-Cola Export Corp., 1958-59, pres., dir., 1959—; dir. Continental Oil Co., Morgan Guaranty Trust Co., N.Y.C., Gen. Electric Co., Trust Co. Ga., Atlanta, Dow Jones & Co., Inc. Served as lt. comdr. USNR, 1942-45. Clubs: Racquet and Tennis, Links (N.Y.C.); Blind Brook Golf (Purchase, N.Y.); Capital City, Peachtree Golf (Atlanta). Office: PO Box 1734 Atlanta GA 30301

AUSTIN, KENNETH RALPH, ins. co. exec.; b. Keosauqua, Ia., Mar. 15, 1920; s. James Clayton and Nancy M. (Landreth) A.; B.C.S., Drake U., 1941; M.S., U. Ia., 1942; m. LaVerne Eleanor Turin, May 9, 1942; children—Marilyn Ruth, Alan Karl. With Equitable Life Ins. Co. Ia., Des Moines, 1947—, asst. sec., 1953-59, supt. policy issue, 1959-60, agy. v.p., 1960-64, v.p., controller, 1964-66, exec. v.p., 1966-69, pres., 1969—, past trustee. Bd. dirs. S. Ia. Methodist Home, Am. Assn. Homes for Aging; trustee Simpson Coll., Indianola, Drake U. Served to comdr. USNR, 1942-45. Fellow Life Office Mgmt. Assn. Inst.; mem. Life Ins. Agy. Mgmt. Assn., Am. Life Conv. (bd. dirs.), Life Ins. Assn. Am. Home: 111 30th St Des Moines IA 50312 Office: PO Box 1635 Des Moines IA 50306

AUSTIN, LAWRENCE WILBUR, bldg. material co. exec.; b. Crystal Lake, Ia., Dec. 11, 1908; s. Andrew and Julia (Johnson) A.; B.S. in Commerce, U. Ia., 1930; m. Mary J. Jamieson, Aug. 27, 1938; children—William Lawrence, John Andrew. In charge accounting Haskins & Sells, Chgo., 1930-39; sec., treas. Western Foundry Co., Chgo., 1939-46; with U.S. Gypsum Co., Chgo., 1946—, sec., 1966—, asst. treas., 1956—. Mem. Am. Soc. Corp. Secretaries, Delta Sigma Pi. Club: Union League (Chgo.). Home: 291 Longacres Lane Palatine IL 60067 Office: 101 S Wacker Dr Chicago IL 60606

AUSTIN, LEROY SYL, coll. dean; b. Oklahoma City, Nov. 13, 1922; s. Roy S. and Nina (Myers) A.; student U. Cal. at Berkeley, 1943-44; B.S., U. Tulsa, 1946; M.B.A., U. Mich., 1947; Ed.D., Columbia Tchrs. Coll., 1960; m. Betty Ruth Smith, Dec. 27, 1948; children—Dana LeRoy, Amy Lena. Indsl. relations research Standard Oil and Gas Co., Tulsa, 1947-50; dir. residence U. Tulsa, 1950- 51; dir. student personnel Quinnipac Coll., Hamden, Conn., 1953-56; dean students Pratt Inst., 1956-59; asso. dean men Pa. State U., 1959-65; v.p. student affairs State U. N.Y., 1965—. Served with AUS, 1943-46. Mem. Am. Coll. Personnel Assn., Am. Personnel and Guidance Assn., Phi Delta Kappa. Unitarian. Home: 27 N Manheim Blvd New Paltz NY 12561

AUSTIN, LOIS MARINTHA, nurse educator; b. Hinsboro, Ill., May 8, 1903; d. Homer Moon and Lenora Anne (Clipson) Austin; student Ia. State Tchrs. Coll., Cedar Falls, 1921-22; B.S. in Liberal Arts and Nursing, State U. Ia., 1931; M.A. in Edn., Ohio State U., 1939; postgrad. Columbia Tchrs. Coll., 1940, Ohio State U., 1949; Ph.D., U. Chgo., 1957. Tchr. elementary schs., Ia. and Ill., 1921-29; prof. grad. programs nursing edn. U. Pitts., 1958—, spl. asst. to the dean Sch. Nursing, 1968-69, acting chmn. dept. nursing edn., 1959-64. Mem. women's adv. com. N.Y. World's Fair, 11963—. Recipient U. Ia. All Alumni Distinguished Service award, 1967; Certificate Merit, Key award Alpha Tau Delta, 1968. Mem. Nat. League Nursing (pres. 1963-67, dir.), U. Pitts. Nursing Alumni Assn. (hon.), Pa. (bd. dirs. ednl. and adminstrs. tchrs. and counselors sect., bd. dirs. area 6, chmn. com. research and studies), Am. nurses assns., Sigma Theta Tau (pres. 1955-58), Pi Lambda Theta, Kappa Delta Pi. Author articles. Home: 400 N Negley Av Pittsburgh PA 15206

AUSTIN, MAURICE, tax lawyer, educator; b. N.Y.C., Nov. 29, 1905; s. Isaac and Sophie (Teitel) A.; B.S., B. Social Sci. cum laude, Coll. City of N.Y., 1925, M.B.A., 1925, B.B.A., 1929; LL.B. magna cum laude, St. Lawrence U., Bklyn. Law Sch., 1937; m. Jennie Ginsburg, June 16, 1929; children—Alice May (Mrs. Alex J. Soled), Irvin Alan. Instructor in accountancy and taxation Coll. City of N.Y. since 1928; mem. Klein, Hinds & Finke, C.P.A.'s, 1929-53; admitted to N.Y. bar, 1937; mem. Klein, Finke & Austin, attys., 1937-53; mem. Austin & Diamond, attys. specializing in taxation, 1955—; prof. law Bklyn. Law Sch., 1942-53; adj. prof. taxation, City Coll. of N.Y., 1954—. Mem. Treasury Dept. Adv. Com. on Income Tax; conducted investigation on behalf Am. bankruptcy trustees of Ivar Kreuger Match "Empire," Europe and U.S. Recipient City College Townsend Harris medal for distinguished post- graduate achievement, 1968, Bernard M. Baruch medal, 1970. Mem. Am., N.Y. State bar assns., N.Y. Co. Lawyers Assn., Am. Law Inst. Am. Inst. Accts. (v.p. 1949-50), N.Y. State Soc. C.P.A.'s (pres. 1951-52), Nat. Tax Assn., Tax Inst., Philonomic Council, Phi Beta Kappa, Alpha Beta Psi, Beta Gamma Sigma. Clubs: City, Assn. Alumni Coll. City N.Y. (N.Y.C.); Accountants. Author: Outline Federal Income and Excess Profits Taxes on Corporations, 1943; also articles profl. jours. Home: 1175 York Av New York City NY 10021 Office: 350 Fifth Av New York City NY 10001

AUSTIN, RICHARD BAKER, III, army officer, physician; b. Knoxo, Miss, Apr. 28, 1915; s. Richard Baker, Jr., and Jessie (Morse) A.; B.S., Miss. State Coll., 1937; M.D., Tulane U., 1941; grad. Command and Gen. Staff Coll., 1957; m. Hazle Keene, Mar. 22, 1942; children—Jean, Richard Baker IV. Commd. 1st lt. U.S. Army, 1943, advanced through grades to col., 1965; intern Bapt. Hosp., Memphis, 1941; resident protestant Hosp., Nashville, 1946-47; resident obstetrics and gynecology St. Thomas Hosp., Nashville, 1947-48, Nashville Gen. Hosp., 1948-50; comdg. officer 30th Med. Group, 1962-64, Lyster Army Hosp., Ft. Rucker, Ala., 1964-68, 68th Med. Group, Vietnam, 1968-69, Womack Army Hosp., Ft. Bragg, N.C., 1969—; dep. comdr. 44th Med. Brigade, Vietnam, 1969. Decorated Legion of Merit with oak leaf cluster, Air medal, Army Commendation medal. Diplomate Am. Bd. Obstetrics and Gynecology. Fellow Am. Coll. Obstetricians and Gynecologists; asso. fellow Aerospace Med. Assn.; mem. Assn. U.S. Army, Am. Coll. Hosp. Adminstrs., A.M.A., Assn. Mil. Surgeons, Beta Beta Beta, Theta Kappa Psi. Home: 5 Dyer St Ft Bragg NC 28307 Office: Hdqrs WAHSTC Ft Bragg NC 28307

AUSTIN, RICHARD BEVAN, U.S. dist. judge; b. Chgo., Jan. 23, 1901; s. Harry Plumer and Alice (Bevan) A.; Ph.B., Denison U., 1923; J.D., U. Chgo., 1926; m. Louise Crew, June 20, 1925; children—Richard William, David Crew, Robert Bevan. Admitted to Ill. bar, 1926, since practiced in Chgo.; with firm Osborne, Kline & McGurren, 1926-32; asso. Dwight H. Green, 1949-52; asst. state's atty., Chgo., 1933-47, 1st asst. state's atty., 1947-48, 52-53; judge Superior Ct. of Cook County, 1953-60; chief justice Criminal Ct. of Cook County, 1954-55, 60-61; U.S. Dist. Ct. judge, Chgo., 1961—. Democratic candidate for gov. Ill., 1956. Mason. Club: Olympia Field Country (pres. 1970-71). Home: 808 Argyle Flossmoor IL 60422 Office: U S District Ct 219 S Dearborn St Chicago IL 60604

AUSTIN, RICHARD ERWIN, elec. mfg. co. exec.; b. Albany, N.Y., Dec. 10, 1914; s. A. Hoyt and Bessie Dean (Erwin) A.; B.A. in Bus. Adminstrn., Duke, 1937; m. Florence M. Rickert, June 25, 1938; 1 dau., Barbara Deane. With Westinghouse Electric Corp., 1937—, group dir. mgmt. services dept., 1958-63, v.p. mgmt. services, 1963-66, v.p., asst. controller, 1966—, dir. bus. devel. programs, 1968—, sr. cons. growth programs, corporate devel., 1970. Mem. pub. recreation com., Lakewood, O., 1940-55, pres., 1952. Mem. McCandless Twp. Republican County Com., 1957—. Mem. Nat. Assn. Accountants (pres. Cleve. 1950-51, nat. bd. dirs. 1958-60, nat. v.p. 1963-64), Budget Execs. Inst. (charter), Stuart Cameron McLeod Soc., Pi Eta Sigma, Alpha Kappa Psi, Delta Tau Delta. Presbyn. (elder). Mason (32, K.T., Shriner). Home: 140 Pine Rd Pittsburgh PA 15237 Office: 3 Gateway Center Pittsburgh PA 15230

AUSTIN, ROBERT WINTHROP, lawyer, educator; b. New York City, January 24, 1908; s. Charles Alan and Edith Jane (Bunten) A.; grad. Horace Mann School for Boys, 1925; A.B., Dartmouth Coll., 1929; LL.B., Harvard 1932; LL.D., Hanover College, 1964; m. Mary L. Carpenter, Aug. 31, 1933; children—Lewis, Linda, Jane, Mary. Admitted to N.Y. State bar, 1935, Mass. bar, 1949; asso. Breed, Abbott, & Morgan, N.Y.C., 1932-44, partner 1944-46; v.p., sec., dir. Penick & Ford, Ltd., Inc., N.Y.C., 1946-51; lectr. Harvard Bus. Sch., 1951-53, prof., 1953-67, Charles Edward Wilson prof. bus. adminstrn., 1967—; dir. of Warren Pumps, Inc., Sperry & Hutchinson Co., McCord Corp. Mem. Am... (past chmn. FTC com. sect. antitrust law), N.Y. (past chmn. food and drug law com.) bar assns., Delta Kappa Epsilon. Clubs: Harvard (N.Y.C.); Country (Brookline, Mass.). Author: (with J. Peter Williamson) Law in Business Administration. Home: 1010 Memorial Dr Cambridge MA 02138 Office: Harvard U Grad Sch Bus Adminstrn Boston MA 02163

AUSTIN, RUBEN VARGAS, educator; b. San Antonio, July 28, 1915; s. Joseph Jonathan and Aurelia (Vargas) A.; B.A., U. Dubuque, 1936; M.A., State U. Ia., 1940, Ph.D., 1958; m. Mabel Rhetta Edwards, May 15, 1938; children—Ann (Mrs. Patrick H. Coffey), Sara Ellen (Mrs. Bryon H. Jefferson), Sharon (Mrs. James L. Reynolds). Instr. secondary schs., Ia., 1936-42; chmn. dept. econs. U. Dubuque, 1946-53; staff econs. dept. State U. Ia., 1953-55; asst. dean Coll. Bus. and Pub. Service, co-ordinator ICA programs in Brazil and Vietnam, 1955-61; chmn. dept. econs. and bus. adminstrn. U. Del., 1961-70, dean Coll. Bus. and Econs., 1963-70, H. Rodney Sharpe prof. econs. and bus. adminstrn., 1962; prof., dean Coll. Bus. and Pub. Service, Governors State U., Park Forest South, Ill., 1970—. Mem. city council, Dubuque, 1950-55, mayor, 1953-54; candidate U.S. Congress, 2d Dist. Ia., 1954. Trustee Brandywine Jr. Coll. Served to lt. comdr. USNR, 1942-46. Mem. Am. Econ. Assn., Am. Mgmt. Assn., Order Artus, Beta Gamma Sigma. Home: 22512 Lakeshore Dr Lakewood Richton Park IL 60417

AUSTIN, SAM M., educator; b. Columbus, Wis., June 6, 1933; s. Alec Wright and Mildred (Reinhard) A.; B.S., U. Wis., 1955, M.S., 1957, Ph.D., 1960; m. Mary Ellen Herb, Aug. 15, 1959; children—Laura Gail, Sara Kay. Research asso. U. Wis., 1960; postdoctoral fellow Oxford (Eng.), U., 1960-61; asst. prof. physics Stanford, 1961-65; asso. prof. physics Mich. State U., 1965-69, prof., 1969—. NSF fellow, 1960-61; Alfred P. Sloan fellow, 1963-66. Mem. Am. Phys. Soc., Am. Assn. Physics Tchrs., Am. Assn. U. Profs. Research in nuclear physics and nuclear astrophysics. Home: 4789 Ardmore St Okemos MI 48864 Office: Cyclotron Lab Mich State U East Lansing MI 48823

AUSTIN, SPENCER PETER, clergyman; b. Lone Wolf, Okla., Dec. 15, 1909; s. Otis Frank and Bertha Ethel (Sinclair) A.; A.B., Phillips U., 1931, M.A., 1932, B.D., 1933, D.D., 1957; student Boston U. Sch. Theology, 1943-45; m. Margaret Ellen Wolfinger, Dec. 15, 1932 (dec. Apr. 1968); children—Roy Frank, Jack Spencer, Margaret Anna; m. 2d, Kathleen B. Bailey, Dec. 30, 1969. Ordained to ministry Christian Ch. (Disciples), 1931; pastor in Cedardale and Tangier, Okla., 1929-33, Sayre, Okla., 1933-36, Mangum, Okla., 1937, Duncan, Okla., 1937-43, Everett, Mass., 1943-45; nat. dir. evangelism United Christian Missionary Soc., 1945-50, exec. resources dept., 1950-56; exec. Unified Promotion Christian Chs., 1957—, chmn. com. relief appeals, 1957—, adminstrv. sec. com. fraternal aid to British chs., 1954; chmn. Week of Compassion com., 1963—. Pres. Christian Ch. Found., 1961-69. Trustee Nat. Christian Missionary Conv., 1957-69; exec. com. Council Christian Unity; mem. grad. sem. council Phillips U., 1962-70; denomination rep. Nat. Council Chs., also mem. exec. com. dept. stewardship and chmn. benevolence promotion com.; mem. exec. com. Ch. World Service, chmn., 1966-70; interim com. Council Agencies Christian Chs., 1952-68. Mem. Disciples of Christ Hist. Soc. (life). Rotarian, Kiwanian (pres. Sayre 1936). Odd Fellow. Author: Evangelism. 1947. Home: 287 S Downey Av Indianapolis IN 46219 Office: 222 S Downey Av Indianapolis IN 46219

AUSTIN, T. L., utility exec.; b. 1919; B.S. in Mining Engring., U. Ala., 1942; married. With Indsl. Generating Co., 1953-59; with Tex. Power & Light Co., 1959—, pres., chief exec. officer, 1967—, also dir. Served with USNR, 1942- 45. Address: Fidelity Union Life Bldg., Dallas, TX 75201.*

AUSTIN, THEODORE ARNOLD, educator; b. Potter Hill, R.I., July 3, 1915; s. Charles W. and Ellen (Thorp) A.; R.N., Hudson River State Hosp. Sch. Nursing, Poughkeepsie, N.Y., 1940; B.S. in Hosp. Adminstrn., Northwestern U., 1947; M.B.A., Northeastern U., 1954; M.P.A., Harvard, 1955; Ed.D., Boston U., 1968; m. Winifred Caire, Aug. 8, 1941; children—Michael Francis, Kathryn Mary, Thomas Andrew, Peter Jerome, Christopher Charles, John Joseph, Ann Bernadette. From adminstrv. asst. to supt. Worcester (Mass.) City Hosp., 1947-63; dir. Cambridge (Mass.) City Hosp., 1963-66; exec. dir. Jersey City Med. Center, 1966-68; asso. dean, prof. hosp. adminstrn. N.J. Coll. Medicine and Dentistry, 1968—. Bd. incorporators Bay State Savs. Bank, Worcester, 1960. Mem. Nat. council Boy Scouts Am., 1964—, pres. Mohegan council, 1960, mem. exec. com. region one, 1964; mem. def. council Civil Def. and Disaster Control, Newark, 1968—; mem. exec. com. Worcester Community Chest, 1950-64; chmn. hosp. div. A.R.C. campaign, Worcester, 1958-60. Served with AUS, World War 11. Fellow Am. Coll. Hosp. Adminstrs.; mem. Am. Hosp. Assn., Am. Pub. Health Assn. Home: 11 Skyline Dr Jersey City NJ 07305 Office: 65 Bergen St Newark NJ 07107

AUSTIN, TOM NOELL, tobacco co. exec.; b. Greeneville, Tenn., May 11, 1916; s. Clyde Bernard and Felice (Noell) A.; student U. Cal. at Los Angeles, 1936; B.A., U. Tenn., 1937; m. Emily Donaldson, Nov. 19, 1938; children—Tom Noell, Merrily (Mrs. Charles L. Teasley, Jr.), Jay Donaldson, Richard Lyon. Shipping clk. Douglas Tobacco Co., 1937; with Austin Co., Greeneville, 1940—, v.p., 1944-48, pres., 1948-70, chmn. bd., 1970—; dir. First Nat. Bank, Greeneville; v.p. Unaka Co., Greeneville, Moss Tobacco Co., Horse Cave, Ky., Austin Carolina Co., Kinston, N.C., Mullins Leaf Tobacco Co. (S.C.), Sanford Tobacco Co. (N.C.). Trustee Tusculum Coll.; mem. devel. council U. Tenn. Mem. Young Pres. Orgn., Chief Execs. Forum, Phi Gamma Delta, Omicron Delta Kappa. Elk. Club: Exchange (Greeneville). Home: R F D 7 Greeneville TN 37743 Office: Austin Co Hall and Willis St Greeneville TN 37743

AUSTIN, WALTER JAMES, educator; b. St. Louis, Feb. 6, 1920; s. Walter James and Florence (Knappmeier) A.; B.S. in C.E., Rice U., 1941; M.S., U. Ill., 1946, Ph.D., 1949; m. Helen Evelyn Green, June 18, 1949; children—James Randall, Elaine Kathryn. Structural designer Chgo. Bridge & Iron Co., 1942-46; mem. faculty U. Ill. at Urbana, 1947-60, asso. prof. civil engring., 1952-60; prof. civil engring. Rice U., 1960—, chmn. dept. of civil engring., 1963-64; cons. structural analysis and design, plates and shells, reinforced concrete. Fellow Am. Soc. C.E. (Moisseiff award 1958); mem. Column Research Council, Am. Soc. Engring. Edn., Internat. Assn. for Shell Structures, Sigma Xi, Tau Beta Pi. Author tech. papers. Home: 5211 Rutherglenn Dr Houston TX 77035

AUSTIN, WHITLEY, newspaper editor; b. Emporia, Kan., Feb. 12, 1910; s. Jason Rugg and Sabra (Whitley) A.; student Kan. State Tchrs. Coll., Emporia, 1927-29; A.B., U. Wis., 1931; m. Mary Danforth, June 2, 1941; children—Danforth W., Catherine S. Reporter, Emporia Gazette, 1931-32; reporter, editor Hutchinson (Kan.) News, 1933-48; editor, pub., pres. Salina (Kan.) Jour., 1949—. Pres. Kan. A.P., 1957-58. Vice pres., dir. Enterprises, Inc., Hutchinson, 1962—; pres. Riverside Investments, Inc., Salina, 1961—. Mem. adv. com. Schilling AFB, Kan., 1951-65; mem. Kan. Govtl. Ethics Com., 1970—. Trustee, exec. com. William Allen White Found., 1950—; bd. regents ednl. instns. Kan., 1958-65, chmn., 1961; trustee Kansas Wesleyan U., 1966—. Served with AUS, 1942-46. Decorated Bronze Star medal. Recipient William Allen White award, 1964. Member Am. Soc. Newspaper Editors, Internat. Press Inst., Am. Legion, Salina C. of C., Phi Delta Theta. Episcopalian. Mason, Rotarian, Elk. Home: 133 Overhill Rd Salina KS 67401 Office: Journal Bldg Salina KS 67401

AUSTIN, WILLIAM MANDEVILLE, educator; b. Phila., Jan. 31, 1914; s. William M. and Marcella (McCreary) A.; A.B., Princeton, 1935, M.A., 1937, Ph.D., 1938; Sterling fellow, Yale, 1940-42. Instr. classics U. Minn., 1938-39; instr. classics N.Y.U., 1946-47; lang. technician OWI, 1942-43; fellow Am. Council Learned Socs., 1947-48; asso. prof. internat. relations Johns Hopkins, 1948-53; asso. prof. linguistics Georgetown U., 1953-61; prof. linguistics Ill. Inst. Tech., Chgo., 1962—. Fellow A.A.A.S.; mem. Linguistic Soc. Am. (mem. exec. com.), Am. Oriental Soc., Phi Beta Kappa. Author: A Basic Course in Rumanian, 1958; Papers in Lingusitics, 1966. Contbr. Ency. Brit. Contbr. articles profl. jours. Home: 330 Diversey Pkwy Chicago IL 60657

AUSTIN, WILLIAM WEAVER, educator; b. Lawton, Okla., Jan. 18, 1920; s. William McKinley and Leone Elizabeth (Weaver) A.; A.B., Harvard, 1939, A.M., 1940, Ph.D., 1951; m. Elizabeth Jane Hallstrom, June 20, 1942; children—Ann Elizabeth, Margery Jane. Asst. prof. music U. Va., 1946-47; with Cornell U., 1947—, chmn. music dept., 1958-63, prof., 1960-69, Goldwin Smith prof. musicology, 1969—; vis. asso. prof. Princeton, 1957-58. Guggenheim fellow, 1961-62. Served from ensign to lt., USNR, 1942-46. Mem. Am. Musicological Soc., Soc. Ethnomusicology, Music Tchrs. Nat. Assn., Music Educators Nat. Conf., Am. Assn. U. Profs., Coll. Music Soc. (pres. 1960-62), Internat. Musicological Soc., Am. Acad. Arts and Scis., Gesellschaft für Musikforschung. Author: Music in the Twentieth Century, 1966. Editor: New Looks at Italian Opera, 1968; Debussy, Prelude à "L'Après-midi d'un faune", 1970. Contbr. articles music publs. Home: 205 White Park Rd Ithaca NY 14850

AUSTIN, WILLIAM WYATT, Jr., educator; b. Vicksburg, Miss., May 29, 1915; s. William Wyatt and Ethel Catherine (Davis) A.; B.S. in Chemistry, Birmingham-So. Coll., 1935; M.S., Vanderbilt U., 1939, Ph.D., 1948; m. Lucia Meade Patton, June 28, 1939; children—William Wyatt III, Lynda Meade (Mrs. James Harold Rouse), Elizabeth, Frank. Teaching fellow Vanderbilt U., 1938-41; supr. materials and process control labs. Convair, Inc., Nashville, 1941-45; sr. research metallurgist So. Research Inst., Birmingham, Ala., 1945-52; asso. prof. N.C. State U., Raleigh, 1952-54, prof. metall. engring., head dept. materials engring., 1954—. Industry cons. metal failure, corrosion, foundry problems; research grantee U.S. Navy Bur. Ships, Texaco, Inc., Gen. Electric Found. Mem. Am. Soc. Metals (nat. trustee, treas. 1967—), Am. Inst. Mining and Metall. Engrs., Sigma Xi, Phi Kappa Phi, Alpha Sigma Mu, Tau Beta Pi. Methodist (v.p. commn. world service and finance N.C. Conf. United Meth. Ch.). Optimist. Contbr. research and sci. publs., tech. reports. Home: 3221 Birnam Wood Rd Raleigh NC 27607

AUSTRIAN, ROBERT, physician; b. Balt., Apr. 12, 1916; s. Charles Robert and Florence (Hochschild) A.; A.B., Johns Hopkins, 1937, M.D., 1941; m. Babette Friedmann, Dec. 29, 1963; stepchildren—Jill Bernstein, Toni Bernstein. House officer Johns Hopkins Hosp., 1941-50, asst. dir. med. out-patient dept., 1951-52; asso. prof. medicine, then prof. medicine State U. N.Y. Coll. Medicine, 1952-62; John Herr Musser prof., chmn. dept. research medicine U. Pa. Sch. Medicine, 1962—; attending physician Hosp. U. Pa.; cons. medicine Phila. Gen. Hosp.; Tyndale vis. lectr. and prof. Coll. Medicine U. Utah, 1964; spl. research infectious diseases, bacterial genetics. Mem. com. meningococcal infections Commn. Acute Respiratory Disease and Commn. Streptoccal and Staphylococcal Diseases, Armed Forces Epidemiological Bd.; cons. surg. gen. U.S. Army Research and Devel. Command, 1966-69; subcom. streptococcus and pneumococcus Internat. Com. Bacteriol. Nomenclature; mem. allergy and immunology study sect. Nat. Inst. Allergy and Infectious Diseases, 1965-69; bd. sci. counselors Nat. Inst. Allergy and Infectious Diseases, 1967-70, chmn., 1969-70. Trustee Johns Hopkins, 1963-69. Served to capt., M.C., AUS, 1943-45. Recipient U.S. Typhus Commn. medal, 1947. Diplomate Am. Bd. Internal Medicine. Fellow A.C.P., N.Y. Acad. Scis., Am. Acad. Microbiology; mem. Assn. Am. Physicians, Am. Soc. Clin. Investigation, Am. Clin. and Climatol. Assn., Am. Soc. Microbiology (v.p. N.Y. br. 1961-62), Soc. Exptl. Biology and Medicine, Harvey Soc., Am. Fedn. Clin. Research, Balt. Med. Soc., Am. Assn. Immunologists, N.Y. Acad. Medicine (sec. sect. microbiology 1961- 62), Phila. County Med. Soc., Coll. Physicians Phila., Interurban Clin. Club (pres. 1970), Infectious Disease Soc. Am. (pres. 1971), Phi Beta Kappa, Sigma Xi, Alpha Omega Alpha, Omicron Delta Kappa. Clubs: 14 W. Hamilton Street, Suburban, Center (Balt.). Mem. editorial bd. Jour. Bacteriology, 1964-69; Am. Rev. Respiratory Diseases, 1963-66, Bacteriol. Rev., 1967—; Jour. Infectious Diseases, 1969—. Address: Dept Research Medicine U Pa Sch Medicine Philadelphia PA 19104

AUTEN, JOHN HAROLD, govt. ofcl.; b. Ames, Ia., June 29, 1922; s. John T. and Dorothy (Davis) A.; B.Sc., Ohio State U., 1947; Ph.D., Mass. Inst. Tech., 1954; m. Ethel Anne Pye, Jan. 20, 1951; children—Susan Irene, John Aaron, Joanne Marie. Instr., Ohio State U., 1952; from instr. to prof. econs., Rice U., 1952- 64; with Office Financial Analysis, Treasury Dept., 1963—, dir., 1966- -. Served with USAAF, 1943-46. Mem. Am. Econs. Assn., Am. Finance Assn. Contbr. profl. jours. Home: 5100 Talbot Pl Alexandria VA 22304 Office: Treasury Dept Washington DC 20220

AUTIAN, JOHN, educator, researcher; b. Phila., Aug. 20, 1924; s. Zaker and Minnie (Castian) A.; B.S., Coll. Pharmacy, Temple U., 1950; M.S., U. Md., 1952, Ph.D., 1954; m. Ginny Darlene Langford, Nov. 19, 1962; 1 son, Zaker John. Asst. prof. Coll. Pharmacy, Temple U., 1954-56, Coll. Pharmacy, U. Md., 1956-57, U. Mich., 1957-60; asso. prof. U. Tex., 1960-65, prof., dir. drug-plastic research and toxicology lab., 1965-67; prof. pharmaceutics, prof. dentistry, also dir. Material Sci. Toxicology Lab., U. Tenn. Med. Center, 1967—; cons. Clin. Center, NIH, 1960—; spl. research plastics for med. and para-med. applications. Served with AUS, 1943-46. Recipient Distinguished Alumni award Temple U., 1964; citation for research U. Md. Sch. Medicine, 1964. Mem. A.A.A.S. (v.p. 1962), Am. Pharm. Assn. Author numerous articles in field. Contbr. textbooks. Home: 3756 Albatross Cove Memphis TN 38128.

AUTORI, FRANCO, orchestra condr.; b. Naples, Italy, Nov. 29, 1903; s. Michelangelo and Marta (Martucci) Autoriello; m. Paola Lawn, 1928 (dec. 1946); m. 2d, Lygia Berezynska, Jan. 27, 1948. Came to U.S., 1928, naturalized, 1936. Orchestra condr. Pa. Grand Opera Co., 1928, Chgo. Civic Opera Co., Ravinia Opera Co., 1928-32; condr. Dallas Symphony, summers 1932-34; condr. Sinfonietta of Dallas, 1932-34; staff conductor The Federal Music Project, N.Y.C., 1934-36; musical director, conductor Philharmonic Orchestra, Buffalo, 1936-45; mus. dir., condr. Chautauqua Symphony Orchestra, summers 1944-52; guest condr. NBC Symphony, 1946, State Radio Symphony Orchestra, Buenos Aires, others; condr. concerts, opera, Poland, 1947-48; asso. condr. N.Y. Philharmonic Symphony Soc., 1949-59; musical dir., condr., Tulsa Philharmonic Soc., 1961-71. Home: 2825 E 48th St Tulsa OK 74105

AUTRY, JAMES ARTHUR, editor; b. Memphis, Mar. 8, 1933; s. Ewart Arthur and Ruth Edna (Eubanks) A.; B.A. in Journalism, U. Miss., 1955; m. Dorothy Gillery Kalins, Feb. 14, 1971; children (by previous marriage)—James A., Richard R. Editor, Courier-Chronicle, Humboldt, Tenn., 1959-60; copy chief Better Homes & Gardens mag., Des Moines, 1960-62, mng. editor, 1962-67, editor, 1970—; editor, pub. New Orleans mag., 1967-68; editorial dir. Meredith Spl. Interest Publs., Des Moines, 1968-70; instr. English, writing, evening classes. Served with USAF, 1955-59. Democrat. Conglist. Home: Rural Route 1 West Des Moines IA 50265 Office: 1716 Locust St Des Moines IA 50303

AUTRY, ORVON GENE, singer, actor, radio entertainer; b. Tioga, Tex., Sept. 29, 1907; s. Delbert and Elnora (Ozment) A.; grad. Tioga (Tex.) High Sch., 1925; m. Ina Mae Spivey, Apr. 1, 1932. Began as railroad telegraph operator, Sapulpa, Okla., 1925; made first phonograph record of cowboy songs, 1929; radio artist Sta. WLS, Chicago, 1930-34; motion picture actor since 1934; first picture "In Old Santa Fe"; has since starred in 82 musical Western feature pictures; just completed 52 half-hour television pictures; pres. Flying A Prodns., Challenge Records, Inc.; owner TV stas. KOOL-TV, Phoenix, KOLD-TV, Tucson, radio stas. KMPC, Hollywood, KSFO, San Francisco, KVI, Seattle, Wash., KEX, Portland, Oregon. Chmn. Los Angeles American League, Los Angeles Angels. Joined U.S. Army Air Force as tech. Sgt., July 26, 1942, commd. as flight officer in Air Transport Command, discharged June 17, 1945. Member International Footprinters. Mason (32, Shriner), Elk. Has written over 250 songs including That Silver-Haired Daddy of Mine, 1931; You're the Only Star in My Blue Heaven, 1938; Dust, 1938; Tears On My Pillow, 1941; Be Honest With Me, 1941; Tweedle O'Twill, 1942; Here Comes Santa Claus, 1948.

AUWERS, STANLEY JOHN, motor carrier exec.; b. Grand Rapids, Mich., Mar. 22, 1923; s. Joseph T. and Cornelia (Moelhoek) A.; student Calvin Coll., 1940-41; B.B.A., U. Mich., 1943; m. Elizabeth Kruis, Apr. 6, 1946; children—Ellen (Mrs. William Northway), Stanley John, Thomas. With Ernst & Ernst, Detroit, 1943-51; controller Interstate Motor Freight System, Grand Rapids, Mich., 1951-61, v.p., controller, 1961-65, v.p. finance, 1965-69, exec. v.p., 1969—, also dir. Chmn. cost com. Mich. Trucking Adv. Bd. to Mich. Pub. Service Comm., 1958-63; mem. citizens com. to study Mich. tax structure advisory Mich. Ho. Reps., 1958. C.P.A., Mich. Mem. Am. (gov. regular common carrier conf.), Mich. (sec., gov.), Motor Carriers Central Freight Assn. (dir.), Tax Execs. Inst., Am. Inst. C.P.A.'s, Trucking Employers. Presbyn. Home: 2712 Darby St SE Grand Rapids MI 49506 Office: 134 Grandville St SW Grand Rapids MI 49502

AUXIER, GEORGE WASHINGTON, educator; b. nr. Paintsville, Johnson County, Ky., Nov. 27, 1905; s. Isaac Lincoln and Jemima Catherine (Wheeler) A.; A.B., Miami U., 1930, M.A., 1934; Ph.D., Ohio State U., 1938; postgrad. Georgetown U. Law Sch., 1941; grad. Nat. War Coll., 1957; m. Fernallen Arnold, Apr. 5, 1942; children—George Calvert, Catherine Fern, John Wheeler. Asst., dept. history, Ohio State U., 1934-36; supt. survey fed. archives, Ohio State, 1936-37; research asst. Library of Congress, 1937-40; asst. editor Territorial Papers of U.S. Dept. State, 1940-1942; liaison officer Office of Censorship, 1942; hist. officer, War Dept. Gen. Staff (G-2), 1942-44, prin. policy analyst Office of Exec. Sec., WPB, 1944-45, chief policy analysis staff. bur. of demobilization, Civilian Prodn. Adminstrn., 1945-46, WPB historian and chief policy analysis and records br., 1946-47, prin. policy analyst, asst. gen. mgr.'s office, U.S. AEC, 1947, dir. gen. research and reports, program officer, and occasionally acting sec. of the Nat. Security Resources Bd., Exec. Office of the Pres., 1947-51; exec. sec. DPA and NPA, 1951-53, Bus. and Def. Service Adminstrn., Dept. Commerce, 1953-56; with Exec. Office of Pres., 1957-68; cons., research contractor, 1968—; lectr. U.S. history and diplomacy Am. U., 1940-41, George Washington U., 1945-46; prof. bus. adminstrn. U. Md., 1970—. Mem. Am. Soc. for Pub. Adminstrn., Am. Polit. Sci. Assn., Am. Econs. Assn., Am., Miss. Valley hist. assns., Am. Acad. Polit. and Social Scis., Soc. Am. Archivists, Phi Alpha Theta, Beta Theta Pi. Mason. Clubs: Cosmos (Washington); Officers (Fort Leslie J. McNair); Argyle Country. Author numerous books, 1934—. Directed preparation several moblzn. studies pub. by U.S. Govt. Home: 12315 Fernmont Lane Silver Spring MD 20902

AUYB, MUHAMMAD, govt. ofcl. Pakistan; b. June 15, 1914; ed. Univ. Coll., London, London Sch. Econs., Gray's Inn. Joined Indian Civil Service, 1936; asst. commr., Punjab, 1936-41; under sec. and dept. sec., dept. supply and commerce, Govt. India, 1942-47; dep. sec. and joint sec. Ministries Commerce, Kashmir Affairs and Finance, Govt. Pakistan, 1947-54; sec., adviser Pakistan Delegation to UN, 1947-52; dir. Pakistan Indsl. Devel. Corp., 1955-60; sec. Ministry Finance, Govt. Pakistan, 1960-61; ambassador to Fed. Germany, 1961-64, to European Econ. Community, 1962- 67, to Belgium and Luxembourg, 1964-67, to European Coal and Steel Community, 1964-67; permanent rep. European Office UN and specialized agencies, Geneva, 1965-67; exec. dir. World Bank, 1967—. Mem. Order Brit. Empire; decorated star Quaid-i-Azam; Eisenhower exchange fellow, 1954-55. Author: United Nations at Work, 1952. Address: 1818 H St N W Washington DC .*

AVAKIAN GEORGE phonograph recording co. exec.; b. Armavir, Russia, Mar. 15, 1919; s. Mesrop and Manoush (Avedisian) A.; came to U.S., 1923, naturalized, 1928; B.A., Yale, 1941; student Harvard, 1943-44; m. Anahid Ajemian, May 22, 1948; children—Maro, Anahid, Gregory. Produced first jazz album, Chicago Jazz, 1939; researcher-producer Columbia Records, 1940-41, prod.-exec., 1946-58, dir. internat. dept., 1948-51, dir. popular album dept., 1951-58; dir. artists and repertoire dept. Warner Bros. Records, 1956-62; mgr. popular record dept. RCA Victor, 1960-62; jazz critic, columnist, 1938-50; dir. Avakian Bros., Inc., Teheran, Brussels,

N.Y.C., 1952-; ind. record producer, 1962-. Trustee Walden Sch. Served with AUS, 1941-46. Mem. Nat. Acad. Recording Arts and Scis. (trustee; pres. N.Y.C. chpt. 1963-64, nat. pres. 1965-66). Editor (with Walter Schaap) Hot Discography, 1948. Home: 285 Central Park W New York City NY 10024 Office: 10 W 33d St New York City NY 10001

AVALLE-ARCE, JUAN BAUTISTA, educator; b. Buenos Aires, Argentina, May 13, 1927; s. Juan B. and Maria (Avalle-A); came to U.S., 1948; A.B., Harvard, 1951, M.A., 1952, Ph.D., 1955; m. Constance Marginot, Aug. 20, 1956 (dec. 1969); children—Juan Bautista III, Maria Martina, Alejandro Alcantara; m. 2d, Diane Janet Pamp, Aug. 30, 1969. Tutor, Harvard, 1953-55; asst. prof., then asso. prof. Spanish, Ohio State U., 1955-62; prof. Spanish, Smith Coll., 1962-66, Sophia Smith prof. Hispanic studies, 1966-69; William Rand Kenan, Jr. prof. Spanish, U. N.C., 1969—; lectr. in field, 1961—. Recipient Bonsoms medal, Spain, 1961, Community Leader Am. award, 1969; Guggenheim Fellow, 1961; grantee Am. Council Learned Socs., 1965, 68, Nat. Endowment Humanities, 1968, Am. Philos. Soc., 1961, 67; recipient Susan Anthony Potter Lit. prize, 1951; Centro Gallego Lit. prize, 1947. Mem. Soc. de Bibliofilos Espanoles, Assn. Internat. de Hispanistas, Modern Lang. Assn., Renaissance Soc., Inst. d'Etudes Medievales, Inst. de Lit. Iberamericana. Clubs: Triangle Hunt (Durham); U. N.C. Pole; Combined Training Events Assn. Author: Conocimiento y vida en Cervantes, 1959; La pastoril espanola, 1959; La Galatea de Cervantes, 2 vols., 1961; Gonzalo Fernandez de Oviedo, 1962; El Inca Garcilaso en sus Comentarios, 1961; Deslindes cervantinos, 1961; Three Exemplary Novels, 1964; Bernal Frances y su Romance, 1966; El Persiles de Cervantes, 1969; Los entremeses de Cervantes, 1969; Don Juan Valera y Morsamor, 1970. Home: Euskaletxea Garrett Rd Durham NC 27707

AVANT, DONALD W., hosp. adminstr. Adminstr., Olive View Med. Center. Office: Olive View Med Center Box 501 Olive View CA 91330*

AVE, PAUL E., electronics co. exec.; b. Clinton, Ind., June 2, 1933; s. Anthony and Louise (Buffo) A.; B.S., Ind. U., 1954, J.D., 1959; m. Betty Jean Richardson, June 7, 1958; children—Karen Louise, James Brett, Gregroy Richardson. Admitted to Tex. bar; practiced in Dallas; asso. atty. Turner, White, Atwood, Meer & Francis, 1959-62; asst. legal counsel aerospace div. Ling-Temco-Vought, Inc., Dallas, 1962-65, asso. gen. counsel, 1965-68; v.p., sec., gen. counsel LTV Ling Alter, Inc., Dallas, 1968—; dir. Tamar Electronics, Inc. Served to 1st lt. USAF, 1954-56. Mem. Am., Tex. bar assns., Am. Corporate Secretaries Soc., Sigma Pi. Home: 10807 Pinocchio St Dallas TX 75229 Office: PO Box 30385 Dallas TX 75230

AVEDISIAN, ARMEN G., constrn. co. exec.; b. Chgo., Oct. 28, 1926; s. Karekin Der and Kardovil (Ignatius) A.; B.S., U. Ill., 1949; m. Dorothy D. Donian, Nov. 22, 1952; children—Guy A., Vann A., Donna A. Civil engr. Standard Paving Co., Chgo., 1949; constrn. supt. Gallagher Asphalt Corp., Thornton, Ill., 1950-55; v.p., dir. Am. Asphalt Paving Co., Chgo., 1956-64; chmn. bd., pres. Lincoln Stone Quarry, Inc., Joliet, Ill., 1964—, Avedisian Industries, Inc., Hillside, Ill., 1964—; chmn. bd. Delta Constrn. Corp., Joliet, 1968—, Swenson, Inc., Joliet, 1970—, Midstate Stone Corp., Gillespie, Ill., 1970—; chmn. bd., chief exec. officer Hillside (Ill.) Stone Corp., 1969—. Mem. pres.'s com., guarantor Lyric Opera, Chgo., 1968—; gov. life mem. Men's Council, Art Inst. Chgo., 1961—. Trustee Avery Coonley Sch. Served with AUS, 1944-45. Mem. Nat. Limestone Inst. (chmn. bd. 1971—), Midwest Crushed Limestone Inst. (pres. 1966-67), Ill. Rd. Builders Assn. (dir., treas. 1963), Am., Western socs. civil engrs., Ill. Assn. Aggregae Producers (dir., pres. 1968), Sigma Nu. Clubs: Chicago Athletic, Chicago Yacht; Butterfield Country (Hinsdale, Ill.); Dunham Woods Riding (Wayne, Ill.); Lake Geneva (Wis.) Country. Home: 701 Taft Rd Hinsdale IL 60521 Office: Eisenhower Expressway and Mannheim Rd PO Box 669 Hillside IL 60162

AVEDISIAN, EDWARD, painter; b. Lowell, Mass., 1936; student Boston Museum Sch. Art. One-man exhbns. include Boyston Print Center Gallery, Cambridge, Mass., 1957, Hansa Gallery, 1958, Tibor de Nagy Gallery, 1959, 60, Robert Elkon Gallery, N.Y.C., 1962, 64-68, Galerie Zigler, Zürich, 1964, Nicholas Wilder Gallery, Los Angeles, 1966, 68, 69, Kasmin Gallery, London, 1966, 67; group exhbns. includes Tibor de Nagy Gallery, Hansa Gallery, Boston Mus. Art, Mus. Modern Art, Washington. Whitney Mus. Art, Dayton (O.) Art Internat., Kasmin Gallery, Mus. Modern Art, N.Y.C., Jewish Mus., N.Y.C., Larry Aldrich Mus., San Francisco Mus. Art, Paintings From Expo '67, Boston Inst. Contemporary Art; rep. permanent collections Guggenheim Mus., Whitney Mus. Art, Mus. Modern Art, Los Angeles Mus. Art. Pasadena (Cal.) Mus. Art, Larry Aldrich Mus., Wadsworth Atheneum. Chrysler Mus. Art; artist-in-residence U. Kan., 1969; instr. Sch. Visual Arts, N.Y.C., 1969-70. Address: care Robert Elkon Gallery 1063 Madison Av New York City NY 10028*

AVEDON, RICHARD, photographer; b. N.Y.C., May 15, 1923; s. Jack and Anne (Polonsky) A.; student Columbia; m. Dorcas Nowell, 1944; m. 2d, Evelyn Franklin, Jan. 29, 1951; 1 son, John. Staff photographer Harper's Bazaar, 1946-65; photographer French fashions, 1947—; staff photographer Vogue mag., 1966—; contbg. photographer Life, Look, Graphis mags., U.S. Camera ann.; work exhibited Mus. Modern Art, Phila. Mus. Modern Art; spl. visual cons. Paramount film Funny Face; TV cons.; advt. photographer; a founder, mem. faculty Famous Photographers Sch. Westport (Conn.); one man show, photographs in perm. coll. Smithsonian Inst.; one man retrospective exhbn. Mpls. Inst. Arts, summer 1970. Recipient highest achievement medal awards Art Directors Show, 1950—; voted one of world's ten greatest photographers Popular Photography, 1958. Mem. Am. Soc. Mag. Photographers. Author: Observations, 1959; Nothing Personal, 1964. Editor: Diary of a Century (photographs by Jacques Henri Lartique), 1970. Address: 407 E 75th St New York City NY 10021

AVERBACH, ALBERT, lawyer, author, lectr.; b. Bender Bessarabia. Feb. 22, 1902; s. Matus and Eva (Kirchen) A.; LL.B., Albany Law Sch., Union U., 1923. Admitted N.Y. bar 1924; mem. firm Freshman & Averbach, Syracuse, 1924-30; Averbach & Goldstein, 1930-32; pvt. practice 1932-41; Averbach & Bonney, Seneca Falls, 1941-55; mem. firm Gair, Finley, Averbach, Mahley & Hoffmann, Syracuse, Seneca Falls, N.Y.C., 1955-62, Gair and Averbach, 1962—; pvt. practice Syracuse, Seneca Falls, N.Y.C., Buffalo, 1955—; v.p., gen. counsel to Rumsey Mfg. Corp., also Rumsey Products, Inc., 1941- 47. Asso. editor personal injury and tort law Nat. Assn. Claimants Compensation Attys. law jour. Mem. adv. bd. editors Oleck's Negligence and Compensation Service. Hon. fellow Am. Coll. of Legal Medicine; fellow of Internat. Acad. Law and Sci.; mem. Am. Trial Lawyers Assn. (past v.p., bd. govs.), Internat. Acad. Trial Lawyers (pres. bd. dirs.), Legislative Com. N.Y. State Assn. Plaintiffs Trial Lawyers, Inc. (bd. dirs.), Federal bar assns. of N.Y., N.J., Conn., Am., Internat., Onondaga County, N.Y. State (trial lawyers sect.) bar assns., Am. Judicature Soc., Justinian Legal Soc., Soc. Med. Jurisprudence Scribes. Author numerous profl. publs., including: Handling Accident Cases, 8 vols.; Handling Automobile Cases, 2 vols., Tort and Medical Yearbook (co-editor with M.M. Belli), 2 vols. Mem. legal adv. bd. Traumatic Medicine and Surgery for the Attorney, 10 vol. ency. Asso. editor Internat. Jour. Law and Sci. Lectr. numerous law instns. Home: R D 6 Auburn NY 13021 Office: 30 State St Seneca Falls NY 13148 also 350 Fifth Av New York City NY 10001 and 333 E Onondaga St Syracuse NY 13202

AVERBACH, BENJAMIN LEWIS, educator; b. Rochester, N.Y., Aug. 12, 1919; s. George and Lillian (Yves) A.; B.S., Rensselaer Poly. Inst., 1940, M.S., 1942; Sc.D., Mass. Inst. Tech., 1947; m. Gertrude Mary McCarthy, Sept. 6, 1947; children—Paul Vincent, Anne Louise, Clare Frances. Chief metallurgist U.S. Radiator Corp., 1942-44; metallurgist Gen. Electric Co., 1944-45; mem. faculty Mass. Inst. Tech., 1947—, prof. metallurgy, 1960—; pres. Alloyed Research Corp., Cambridge, Mass., 1955-63; dir. Beryllium Metals and Chem. Corp., 1960-63; cons. in field, 1947—. Vice pres. Internat. Conf. on Fracture, 1969—. Fellow Am. Soc. Metals (Howe medal 1959); mem. Am. Phys. Soc., Am. Inst. Metall. Engrs., Brit. Inst. Metals, Brit. Iron and Steel Inst. Editor: Fracture, 1959. Contbr. articles profl. jours. Patentee in field. Home: 45 Orchard St Belmont MA 02178 Office: 13-5082 Mass Inst Tech Cambridge MA 02139

AVERETT, ELLIOTT, banker; b. Chatham, N.J., Jan. 6, 1918; grad. Phillips Exeter Acad., 1936, Advanced Mgmt. Program, Harvard, 1958; m. Julia Bancroft Fletcher; children—Elliott 111, Thomas Hamlett, Julia Hall. With Bank of N.Y., 1940—, asst. treas., 1949-52, asst. v.p., 1952-56, v.p., 1956-63, exec. v.p., 1963-66, sr. exec. vice president, 1966-68, chief administrative officer, 1967, pres., 1968—, also dir.; pres., chief exec., dir. Bank of N.Y. International Corporation; dir. Albany Ins. Company; trustee Greenwich Savings Bank. Pres., trustee The Seeing Eye, Inc., Morristown, N.J.; trustee Far Brook Sch., Short Hills, N.J.; mem. bd. mgrs. N.Y. Bot. Garden, N.Y.C. Served to capt. AUS, 1941-46, ETO, Decorated Purple Heart, Silver Star. Clubs: Down Town Assn., Chicago; Amateur Ski, Anglers (N.Y.C.); Somerset Hills Country. Home: Youngs Rd New Vernon PO Basking Ridge NJ 07920 Office: 48 Wall St New York City NY 10015

AVERILL, LLOYD JAMES, Jr., clergyman, educator; b. Warrenville, Ill., Apr. 5, 1923; s. Lloyd James and Dorothy Mae (Rogers) A.; student Central YMCA Coll., Chgo., 1941-42, Beloit Coll., 1942-43; B.A. with honors, U. Wis., 1947; B.D., Colgate Rochester Divinity Sch., 1950, M.Th., 1966; M.A. in Sociology, University Rochester, 1952; grad. student Garrett Bib. Inst., 1953, 56, 57; postgrad. Westminster Coll. Cambridge U., 1965-66; L.H.D., Lewis and Clark Coll., 1962; Doctor of Laws, Carroll Coll., 1967, William Jewell Coll., 1967; Litt.D., Augustana (Ill.) Coll., 1968; D.D., Tusculum Coll., 1968; m. Shirley Mae Karr, Feb. 9, 1944 (div. June 1968); childrenShelley Ann, Leslie Jean, Scott Alan; m. 2d, Carol Anne White, July 13, 1968. Ordained to ministry Baptist Ch., 1949; pastor, Rochester, N.Y., 1947-51; asso. dir. field work, instr. practical theology Colgate Rochester Div. Sch., 1951-54; dean chapel Kalamazoo Coll., 1954-67, asst. prof. religion, then asso. prof., 1954-62, prof., 1962-67, asst. to pres., 1957-63, v.p. coll., 1963-67; pres. Council Protestant Colls. and Univs., 1967-68; vis. distinguished prof. sociology Ottawa U., Baker U., Park Coll., 1968-69; frequent speaker, lectr. Cons. asso. Assn, Am. Colls., 1967-68; cons. commn. on fed. relations Am. Council on Edn., 1967-68; mem. Colloquium on New Directions on Higher Edn.; mem. adv. council on campus ministry programs Danforth Found.; cons. Kansas City Regional Council for Higher Edn., 1968-69. Exec. chmn. Bach Festival Soc. Kalamazoo, 1959-62; v.p. Kalamazoo County Council Chs., 1961-65; exec. com. Community Caucus Kalamazoo, 1961-65. Recipient Campus Ministry grant Danforth Found., 1958-59; grad. fellow Colgate Rochester Div. Sch., 1950. Served with USAAF, 1943-46. Mem. Am. Assn. UN (pres. Kalamazoo 1957-58), Am. Acad. Religion, Am. Soc. Ch. History, Am. Assn. Higher Edn. Democrat. Kiwanian. Club: Torch. Author: A Strategy for the Protestant College, 1966; American Theology and the Liberal Tradition, 1967; Between Faith and Unfaith, 1968. Author articles, book revs.‡

AVERILL, PAUL NEAL, newspaper pub.; b. Cleve., Sept. 30, 1906; s. George W. and Cora Mae (Palmer) A.; student U. Mich., 1925-26; m. Mae Frances Coakley, Apr. 18, 1930; children—Barbara Ann (Mrs. Henry M. Hogan, Jr.), Judith Louise (Mrs. David Otis). Pub. Birmingham (Mich.) Eccentric, 1926—; dir. Synercom Communications, Birmingham-Bloomfield Bank; pres. Suburban Newspapers of Mich., Averill Press; pub. Southfield (Mich.) Eccentric. Bd. dirs. Oakland County Mental Health Services Bd., 1963—, South Oakland United Community Services, Detroit United Found., Family Service Oakland County, Mich. Welfare League; Bloomfield Art Assn., Suburban Press Found., Friends of Modern Art, Friends Adv. Com. of Oakland U.; chmn. Tri County Family Service Agencies; pres. Family Service Assn. Am. Mem. Mich. Assn. Community Mental Health Bds. (dir.), Mich. Soc. Gerontology, Printing Industry Am., Adcraft Club Detroit, Graphic Arts Assn. Mich. Club: Detroit Press. Contbr. articles profl. jours. Home: 1497 Lochridge Rd Bloomfield Hills MI 48013 Office: 1225 Bowers St Birmingham MI 48008

AVERITT, ROBERT TABOR, educator; b. Kaufman, Tex., July 12, 1931; s. James Ted and Tina (Young) A.; B.A., North Tex. State Coll., 1951; M.A., U. Tex., 1957; Ph.D., 1961; m. Brett Thomas, Sept. 16, 1957; children—Mark Harrison, Angela Lee. Tchg. asst. U. Tex., 1956-59; asst. prof. Smith Coll., 1961-66, asso. prof., 1966-69, prof., 1969—. Served with USNR 1953-55.NSF fellow, 1959, 1960; Southern Fellowship fellow, 1960-61; NDEA fellow, 1962. Mem. Am. Econ. Assn., Assn. Evolutionary Economists, Am. Assn. U. Profs. (pres. Smith chpt. 1969—). Author: The Dual Economy, 1968. Home: 85 Washington Av Northampton MA 01060

AVERY, GEORGE SHERMAN, Jr., botanist, adminstr.; b. Benton Harbor, Mich., Aug. 3, 1903; s. George Sherman and Georgia (Pattison) A.; B.S., Tulane U., 1924; M.S., Dartmouth Coll., 1925; Ph.D., U. of Wis. 1927; D.Sc., U. of British Columbia, 1950; D.Litt., Long Island U., 1956; m. Mary Virginia Kellogg, March 4, 1926; children—Mary Virginia (Mrs. L. E. Craig), William Pattison. Instr. botany, Duke U., Durham, N.C., 1927-29, asst. prof., 1929-31, on leave of absence as Nat. Research fellow, Columbia U., 1930-31; prof. of botany, Conn. Coll., New London, and dir. Conn. Arboretum, 1931-44; foreign fellow, Rockefeller Found., 1938; dir. Brooklyn Botanic Garden, 1944-70; adj. prof. biology N.Y. U., 1967—. Mem. Museums Council of N.Y.C. (pres. 1954-55, 67-68), Botanical Soc. of Am. (pres. 1957, treas. 1044-46), Am. Soc. Plant Physiologists, A.A.A.S., Am. Assn. Univ. Profs., Sigma Xi, Kappa Sigma. Co-author: Growth Hormones in Plants, 1936; Hormones and Horticulture, 1947; author or co-author of original researches and other scientific articles. Editor-in-chief Survey Biol. Progress, vols. 1 and 2. Contbr. Ency. Britannica. Home: Quaker Hill CT 06375 Office: 35 Clark St Brooklyn NY 11201

AVERY, HARRY COSTAS, educator; b. Phila., Apr. 9, 1930; s. Costas George and Eugenia (Geraleas) A.; A.B. in Classics, U. Pa., 1953; M.A. in Byzantine History, U. Ill., 1956; Ph.D. in Classics, Princeton, 1959; m. JoAnn McDonald, Aug. 18, 1962; children—Eugenia, Anna, Constantine, William. Instr. Greek, Bryn Mawr Coll., 1959-61; asst. prof. classics, U. Tex., Austin, 1961-66, asso. prof., 1966-67; jr. fellow Center Hellenic Studies, Washington, 1963-64; prof., chmn. dept. classics U. Pitts. 1967—. Vis. prof. Am. Sch. Classical Studies, Athens, Greece, 1971-72, mem. mng. com., 1968—; chmn. adv. council to com. on Classical Sch., Am. Acad. in Rome. Served to sgt. AUS, 1948-49. Recipient Bromberg award for teaching excellence U. Tex., 1966; Fulbright fellow to Greece, 1953-54. Mem. Am. Philol. Assn. (dir. 1970—), Soc. Promotion Hellenic Studies, Assn. Guillaume Bude. Contbr. articles profl. jours. Home: 213 Tennyson Av Pittsburgh PA 15213

AVERY, KENNETH WILLIAM, profl. football player; b. N.Y.C., May 23, 1944; s. Paul Rigby and Diana (Bridge) A.; B.S. in Phys. Edn., U. So. Miss., 1967; student N.Y. Inst. Finance, 1970; m. Margaret Theo Wannamaker, June 1, 1969. Profl. football player; mem. Boston Patriots, 1966, N.Y. Giants, 1967-68, Cin. Bengals, 1969—; pres. All Pro-Mgmt., Inc., Miami, Fla., 1971—; v.p. Corporate Adminstrs., Inc., Miami, 1971—, Tax Shelters Cons. for Pro Athletes, Miami, 1971—; agt. Manhattan Life Ins. Co., 1971—. Recipient 19 coll. scholarship offers; named Most Valuable Player Cleve. versus N.Y., 1967, Phila. versus N.Y. Giants, 1967, Houston versus Cin. Bengals, 1970. Mem. Homestead (Fla.), Homestead Jr. chambers commerce, Booster Club South Dade High Sch., Nat. Football League Players Assn., U. So. Miss. Alumni Assn. Roman Catholic. Home: 6900 N Kendall Dr Miami FL 33156 Office: Riverfront Stadium Cincinnati OH 45202

AVERY, MARY ELLEN, medical educator; b. Camden, N.J., May 6, 1927; d. William Clarence and Mary (Miller) Avery; A.B., Wheaton Coll., Mass., 1948; M.D., Johns Hopkins, 1952. Intern Johns Hopkins Hosp., 1953-54, resident, 1954-57; practice medicine, specializing in pediatrics, Boston, 1957-59, Balt., 1959-69; asso. prof. pediatrics Johns Hopkins, 1964-69; prof., chmn. dept. pediatrics McGill U. Med. Sch., 1969—; physician-in-chief Montreal Children's Hosp., 1969—. Mem. council Med. Research Council Can.; mem. study sect. NIH, 1967—. Trustee Wheaton Coll. Recipient Mead Johnson award in pediatric research, 1968. Markle scholar in med. scis., 1961-66. Fellow Am. Acad. Pediatrics; mem. Am. Pediatric Soc., Am. Physiol. Soc., Soc. Pediatric Research (pres. elect), Phi Beta Kappa. Author: The Lung and Its Disorders in the Newborn Infant, 2d edit., 1968; (with A. Schaffer) Diseases of the Newborn, 1971. Editorial bd. Pediatrics, 1965-71, Am. Rev. Respiratory Diseases, 1969—, Am. Jour. Physiology, 1967—; also articles. Home: 3545 Redpath St Montreal Quebec Canada Office: Montreal Children's Hosp 2300 Tupper St Montreal Quebec Canada

AVERY, NOYES LATHAM, Jr., physician; b. Grand Rapids, Mich., May 31, 1909; s. Noyes Latham and Evelyn (Leonard) A.; A.B., Williams Coll., 1932; M.D., Harvard, 1936; m. Ann Edmunds, Nov. 28, 1942; 1 son, Noyes Latham III. Resident pathology Mallory Inst., Boston City Hosp., 1936-37; intern Univ. Hosp., Ann Arbor, Mich., 1937-38, asst. resident, then resident, 1938-40; instr. U. Mich. Med. Sch., 1940-41; pvt. practice internal medicine and cardiology, Grand Rapids, 1946—; mem. cons. staff Blodgett Meml. Hosp., Grand Rapids, 1948—, chmn. dept. medicine, 1964—; mem. vis. staff St. Marys, Butterworth, Mary Free Bed hosps. Mem. adv. bd. Grand Rapids dist. Mich. Consol. Gas Co., 1949—. Served to lt. col., M.C., AUS, 1941-46. Diplomate Am. Bd. Internal Medicine. Fellow A.C.P. (bd. govs. for Mich, 1959-68); mem. A.M.A., Am. Heart Assn., Mich. (pres. 1957), Am. socs. internal medicine, Mich. (councilor 5th Dist 1970—), Kent County (del. to Mich. soc. 1962-71) med. socs., Alpha Omega Alpha. Republican. Conglist. Rotarian. Clubs: University, Kent Country (Grand Rapids). Home: 2747 Bonnell Dr Grand Rapids MI 49506 Office: 515 Lakeside Dr SE Grand Rapids MI 49506

AVERY, RALPH HILLYER, artist; b. Savannah, Ga., Sept. 3, 1906; s. Van Brunt and Lila Bell (Cherry) A.; grad. Rochester Inst. Tech., 1928; scholarship Louis Comfort Tiffany Found., Oyster Bay, N.Y., summers 1930-31. Represented in Charles and Emma Frye Free Art Mus., Seattle, Meml. Art Gallery, Rochester; one-man exhbns. Smithsonian Instn., Nat. Coll. Fine Arts, Washington, 1944, Telfair Acad. Arts and Scis., Savannah, Ga., 1952, Arnot Art Gallery, Elmira, N.Y., 1953. Served with USNR, 1942-45. Recipient 1st prize First Ann. Picturesque Rochester competition, 1929; bronze medal Buffalo Soc. Artists, 1939, Marian Stratton Gould purchase prize Rochester Finger Lakes exhbns., 1948, Henry Projansky prize for watercolor, 1952, for group of watercolors, 1953, James Hogarth Dennis award, 1954, Charles L. Rumrill popular award, 1954, Suzanne Morgan Macy award, 1955, Barnard, Porter Remington and Fowler Co. award, 1957, Lillian Fairchild award for creative work in art, poetry, lit., U. Rochester, 1954, Herbert L. Pratt purchase prize, Am. Mag. citation 87th ann. exhbn. Am. Watercolor Soc., 1954, M. Grumbacher purchase prize for Spring Night, Rudolf Lesch Fine Arts purchase prize for Umbrella Parade, both 90th ann. exhbn. Am. Watercolor Soc. Fellow Rochester Mus. of Arts and Scis.; mem. Am. Watercolor Soc., Nat. Acad. Design. Club: Rochester Art (past pres.). Contbr. articles profl. publs. Home: 11 Livingston Park Rochester NY 14608 Office: 60 N Fitzhugh St Rochester NY 14614

AVERY, RAY STANTON, self-adhesive mfg. co. exec.; b. Oklahoma City, Jan. 13, 1907; s. Oliver Perry and Emma (Dickinson) A.; A.B., Pomona Coll., 1932; m. Dorothy Durfee, Aug. 7, 1935 (dec. Oct. 1964); children—Judith C., Dennis S., Russell D.; m. 2d, Ernestine Onderdonk, Dec. 26, 1965; children—J. Lawrence and Stephen R. Onderdonk. Founder, Avery Products Corp., San Marino, Cal., 1935, now chmn. bd., chief exec. officer; dir. Bus. Internat. and Ameron, Inc. Chmn. bd. fellows Claremont (Cal.) Grad. Sch. and Univ. Center; trustee Huntington Library, Cal. Tech.; bd. dirs. Friends of Claremont Colls., Los Angeles County Mus.; bd. govs. Performing Arts Council Music Center. Clubs: California (Los Angeles); Newport Harbor Yacht; Valley Hunt; Annandale Golf. Home: 430 Laguna Rd Pasadena CA 91105 Office: 415 Huntington Dr San Marino CA 91108

AVERY, THOMAS EUGENE, educator; b. Thomson, Ga., Nov. 18, 1925; s. Henry Thomas and Gladys (Smith) A.; B.S. in Forestry, U. Ga., 1949; M.F., Duke, 1950; Ph.D. (Peavy-Van Dusen-Harrington scholar 1955-56), U. Minn., 1958; m. Marianna Gay Morre, Nov. 24, 1966. Mgmt. forester Armstrong Cork Co., 1950-51; asst. prof. forestry Ark. A. and M. Coll., 1951-55, Mich. State U., 1960-62; research photogrammetrist U.S. Forest Service, New Orleans, 1956-60; asso. prof. forestry U. Ga., 1962-66; former prof. forestry, head dept. U. Ill.; tech. cons. Abrams Aerial Survey Corp., Lansing, Mich., 1962-66. Served with USNR, 1943-46. Recipient Unit award for superior service Dept. Agr., 1957. Mem. Soc. Am. Foresters (council 1968- 69), Am. Soc. Photogrammetry (chmn. photo interpretation com., 1966-67), Sigma Xi, Phi Kappa Phi, Xi Sigma Pi, Alpha Zeta, Blue Key. Author: Interpretation of Aerial Photographs, 2d edit., 1968; Forest Measurements, 1967; also articles. Home: PO Box 261 Philadelphia IL 61864

AVERY, WALLACE ELROY, oil exec.; b. St. Anthony, Ida., Apr. 30, 1905; s. Frank and Jennie Belle (Buck) A.; student Ida. Tech. Inst., 1923-24; B.S., U. Cal., 1929, LL.B., 1933; m. Viola Rohrs, Dec. 23, 1933; children—Susan Irene, Sara Eleanor (Mrs. JJohn Gregory), John. Admitted to Cal. bar, 1933; oil business, Cal., 1933-42; asst. chief counsel Petroleum Adminstrn. for War, 1942-45; atty., asst. gen. mgr. indsl. and business relations dept., asst. sec., sec. Texaco Inc., N.Y.C., 1945-61, v.p. West Coast, 1961-70; ret., 1970. Clubs:

California (Los Angeles); San Gabriel Country; One Hundred (Los Angeles). Home: 688 Canterbury Rd San Marino CA 91108 Office: 3350 Wilshire Blvd Los Angeles CA 90005

AVERY, WILLIAM HENRY, former gov. Kan., oil co. exec.; b. Wakefield, Kan., Aug. 11, 1911; s. Herman W. and Hattie M. (Coffman) A.; A.B., U. Kan., 1934; m. Hazel Bowles, June 16, 1940; children—Bill, Barbara Ann (Poore), Bradley Eugene, Martha Sue. Farmer, stockman, nr. Wakefield, Kan., 1935-55; mem. 84th to 88th Congresses, 2d Kansas dist., gov. Kan., 1965-67; Garvey Enterprises, 1967-68; asst. to pres. Clinton Oil Co., 1969, exec. v.p. adminstrn., 1971—, also mem. exec. com.; pres. Real Petroleum (merged with Clinton Oil Co. 1971), 1969-71. Mem. Kan. Legislature, 1951-55, Legislative Council Kan., 1953- 55. Dir. bd. edn. Wakefield High Sch. Mem. Kan. Farm Bur., Delta Upsilon. Republican. Methodist. Mason. Club: Lions (Wakefield). Home: 19 Douglas Wichita KS 67207

AVERY, WILLIAM HERBERT, lawyer; b. Jacksonville, Fla., July 16, 1905; s. William Herbert and Annelyle (Graves) A.; B.S. magna cum laude, Princeton, 1927; J.D., Harvard, 1930; m. Eugenie Petrequin, Oct. 6, 1934; children—Nancy (Mrs. H. Paul Pressler), Cameron Scott, Richard Manchester. Admitted to bar, 1930, since practiced in Chicago with Cutting, Moore & Sidley and successor firms, now partner Sidley & Austin, 1944—; lectr. Nat. Trust Sch., 1947-64; dir. Acme Printing Ink Co., Chgo. Title & Trust Co., Carson, Pirie, Scott and Co., Equitable Life Assurance Soc. of U.S. Mem. adv. council Ill. Dept. Public Welfare, 1948-52; pres. Kenilworth Sch. Bd., 1950-53; mem. citizens' bd. U. Chgo., Northwestern U. Assos. Trustee or dir. Civic Fedn. (past v.p.), George Williams Coll., Legal Aid Bur. Chgo. (past chmn.), Nat. Legal Aid and Defender Assn. (past pres.), Sunday Evening Club, United Charities (past pres.), YMCA (pres.), Ravinia Festival Assn. Mem. Am., Ill., Chgo., Internat. bar assns., Am. Acad. Polit. Sci., Am. Judicature Soc., Am. Law Inst., Chgo. Estate Planning Council. Presbyn. (elder). Clubs: Commercial (past pres.), Commonwealth (past pres.), Economic (past pres.), Harvard Law (past pres.), Law, Legal, Princeton (past pres.), Tax (past pres.), Mid-Day, University (Chgo.); Indian Hill (Winnetka, Ill.); Old Elm (Lake Forest, Ill.). Home: 99 Indian Hill Rd Winnetka IL 60093 Office: One First Nat Plaza Chicago IL 60670

AVERY, WILLIAM TURNER, educator; b. East Cleveland, O., Sept. 9, 1912; s. Leland Charles and Lela Grace (Gott) A.; B.A., Western Res. U., 1934, M.A., 1935, Ph.D., 1937; m. Frances Elizabeth Jordan, Mar. 28, 1948; 1 dau., Frances Elizabeth. Instr. classics, Western Res. U., 1939-40; instr. romance langs. and German, Fenn Coll., Cleve., 1940-42; instr. to asso. prof. classics Dickinson Coll., 1946-48; asso. prof. to prof. La. State U., 1948-55; prof., head dept. classical langs. and lits. U. Md., 1955—. Served as sgt. USAAF, 1942-45. Fellow Am. Academy in Rome; mem. Dante Soc. Am., Nat. Assn. on Standard Med. Vocabulary, Classical Assn. of the Atlantic States, Am. Philol. Assn., Sigma Chi, Eta Sigma Phi, Phi Sigma Iota, Phi Eta Sigma. Contbr. to scholarly jours. in U.S., Europe. Home: 4324 Van Buren St University Park Hyattsville MD 20782

AVERY, WILLIS FRANK, lawyer, business exec.; b. Manchester, N.H., Jan. 31, 1881; s. Frank Winfield and Hannah (Quinn) A.; student Brown U., U. Me.; LL.B. Washington Coll. Law, 1920; m. Annice Robinson Hill, Aug. 25, 1904 (died Sept. 11, 1949); children—Mrs. Dorothy A. Campbell, Frank W., Mrs. Edythe A. Warburton, and Mrs. Mary Elizabeth Coates; m. second, Mildred Priscilla Bell on December 30, 1950 (dec. Mar. 26, 1962). Prin. Westmoreland (N.H.) High Sch., 1904-05, Wiscasset (Me.) Acad., 1905-06, Limington (Me.) Acad., 1906-15; asst. examiner U.S. Patent Office, 1915-20; mem. legal staff Westinghouse Electric & Mfg. Co., South Philadelphia, Pa., 1920-24; patent atty. The B. F. Goodrich Co., Akron, O., 1924-36; asst. sec., patent counsel, 1936-44, gen. counsel, 1944-48, sec., 1944-49, retired 1950; entered pvt. practice law, Project Research Service, Rubber Industry Problems, 1950—; v.p., gen. mgr. Industry Inventions Inc. Trustee Sr. Citizens Center of Summit County, Inc. Mem. Am., Ohio, Akron bar assns., Bar Assn. D.C., Cleve. Patent Law Assn., (hon.), Ohio, D.C., U.S. Supreme Ct. bars, S.A.R. Republican. Episcopalian. Mason, Rotarian. Clubs: Akron City, Franklin (Akron). Address: 64 Waldorf Dr Akron OH 44313

AVIDAR, ABRAHAM, diplomat of Israel; b. Poland, Dec. 5, 1918; s. Avigdor and Sara (Prost) A.; student U. London (Eng.), 1944; history and lit. degree, Hebrew U., Jerusalem, 1953; m. Malka Kastner, Mar. 10, 1950; children—Giora, Raanan, Zafrira. Member of Kibbutz, 1947-58; diplomatic mission to Poland and USSR, 1958-61; mem. U.S. div. Ministry Fgn. Affairs, Jerusalem, 1962, dep. spokesman, 1963; sr. consul polit. affairs, N.Y.C., 1965-66; consul gen. of Israel for Midwest, Chgo., 1966-69; now minister information embassy Israel. Office: 1621 22d St NW Washington DC*

AVILA, CHARLES FRANCIS, utility co. exec.; b. Taunton, Mass., Sept. 17, 1906; s. Charles I. and Annie (Vera) A.; B.S. in Elec. Engring. and Bus. Adminstrn., Harvard, 1927; LL.D., U. Mass., 1963; m. Elizabeth A. McLean, Feb. 12, 1934; children—Donald F., Carolyn L. (Mrs. Michael Ferber). With Boston Edison Co., 1929—, asst. to pres., 1954- 56, v.p. engring. and constrn., 1956-57, v.p., asst. gen. mgr., 1957-59, corporate vice president, 1959-60, pres., gen. mgr., 1960-67, chmn. bd., mem. exec. com., 1967—, chief exec. officer, 1960-70; v.p., dir., exec. com. Yankee Atomic Electric Co.; dir., mem. policy, exec., audit coms. Raytheon Co.; dir. John Hancock Mut. Life Ins. Co., Conn. Yankee Atomic Power Co., Nat. Shawmut Bank Boston, Shawmut Assn., Liberty Mut. Fire Ins. Co.; dir., exec. com. Liberty Mut. Ins. Co.; corporator Boston Five Cents Savs. Bank, Milton Savs. Bank; dir. Central Bus. Dist., Pub. Utilities Reports, Inc. Mem. nat. adv. council World Energy Conf.; ofcl. observer 4th UN Internat. Conf. on Peaceful Uses of Atomic Energy. Bd. dirs. Mass. Bay United Fund; trustee, mem. corp., adv. bd., com. devel. Northeastern U. Registered profl. engr., Mass. Fellow I.E.E.E. (Edison medal 1968); mem. Edison Electric Inst. (dir., exec. com., past pres.), Electric Research Council (past chmn.), Soc. Harvard Engrs. and Scientists (exec. com.), Elec. Council New Eng. (dir., exec. com., past pres.), Assn. Edison Illuminating Cos. (exec. com.), Asso. Industries Mass. (dir.), Newcomen Soc., Electric Coordinating Council New Eng. (exec. com.), New Eng. Electric Utilities Presidents' Conf., U.S. Naval Inst., N.E. Power Coordinating Council (exec. com.), Nat. Acad. Engring., Nat. Indsl. Conf. Bd., U.S. Nat. Com. C.I.G.R.E. Clubs: Beacon Soc. (pres. 1966), Commercial, Algonquin, Harvard (Boston). Designer high-altitude mil. cameras. Home: 75 Martin Rd Milton MA 02186 Office: 800 Boylston St Boston MA 02199

AVILA, ROGUE J., ambassador of Paraguay to U.S. Address: 2400 Massachusetts Av NW Washington DC 20008*

AVIRETT, JOHN WILLIAMS, 2d, lawyer; b. Cumberland, Md., May 13, 1902; s. John Williams and Sarah Donnell (Roemer) A.; grad. Episcopal High Sch., Alexandria, Va., 1919; A.B., U. Va., 1923, M.A., 1924; LL.B., Harvard, 1927; m. Barbara Brooke Dennis, July 22, 1947; stepchildren—G.R. Dennis Rawlins, William Murray Rawlins. Admitted to Md. bar, 1927, since practiced in Balt.; partner firm Piper & Marbury, and predecessors, 1933—. Active in passage Md. Fireworks Law, 1941, med. research on stray dogs in Balt. law, 1949. First pres. pub. relations council Community Fund Balt., 1936-37; counsel, dir. Jr. Assn. Commerce Balt., 1936-38. Trustee Balt. Mus. Art (pres. 1962-68), St. James Sch., Hagerstown, Md.; bd. dirs. Md. Soc. Prevention Blindness, 1935—, pres. 1935-41; bd. dirs. Nat. Soc. Prevention Blindness, 1937-68, Balt. Council Social Agencies, 1939-42; an organizer, mem. exec. com. Md. Soc. Med. Research, 1950—; bd. mgrs. Uplands Home Church Women, Balt., 1953-63, v.p., 1957-63. Mem. standing com. Episcopal Diocese Md., 1954-55. Served to capt. USNR, 1943- 46. Decorated Legion of Merit. Fellow Md. Bar Found.; mem. Am., Md., bar assns., Am. Law Inst., Balt. Assn. Commerce (bd. dirs.), Raven Soc., Phi Beta Kappa, Phi Gamma Delta. Clubs: Maryland, Elkridge, 14 West Hamilton Street, Merchants, Center, Bachelors Cotillon (Balt.). Home: 7205 W Bellona Av Baltimore MD 21212 Office: First Nat Bank Bldg Baltimore MD 21202

AVITABILE, GIUSEPPE, Italian diplomat; b. Naples, Italy, Sept. 10, 1920; s. Luigi and Letizia (Muzzioli) A.; D. Modern Letters. U. Rome, 1946, D.Law, 1952; m. Milena Hendrich, Dec. 21, 1949; children—Daniela, Elena. Joined Italian Fgn. Service, 1955; assigned Innsbruck, Austria, 1957-59, Oral, Algeriaa, 1959- 61. Bonn, Germany, 1961-65, Rome, Italy. 1965-68; consul gen. in Chgo., 1968—. Served with Italian Army, World War II. Decorated knight Order Merit Italian Republic; officer's cross Order Merit Fed. Republic Germany. Home: 625 N Lake Shore Dr Chicago IL 60611 Office: 625 N Michigan Av Chicago IL 60611

AVITHAL, THEODOR, conductor; b. Bacau, Roumania, Jan. 13, 1933; s. Meyer and Roza (Culer) Leibovici; Diploma of Merit, Conservatory Music Ciprian Porumbescu, Bucharest, Roumania, 1955; m. Ursula Reyher, May 18, 1963; children—Nicole, Christian. Permanent condr. Filarmonica Moldova, Iasi, Roumania, 1955-59; guest condr. various orchs., Belgium, Holland, Israel, U.S., Switzerland, West Germany; regular condr. St. Louis Philharmonic Soc., 1963-70; resident guest condr., acting music dir. Wichita Symphony Soc., 1970-71; asst. prof. Wichita State U., 1970-71; conductor, music dir. U. Ark.-Fayetteville Symphony Orch., 1971—; vis. asst. prof. music U. Ark., 1971—. Home: 1522 Hotz Dr Fayetteville AR 72701

AVON, EARL OF, (Sir Robert Anthony Eden), former prime minister; b. June 12, 1897; s. Sir William and Sybil Frances (Grey) E.; student Eton; B.A. with 1st class honours, Christ Church Coll., Oxford, 1922; hon. D.C.L., Oxford, 1936, Durham 1937, Cambridge, 1938; LL.D., Cambridge, Birmingham, Leeds, Sheffield, Belfast, Toronto, Cal., McGill, Columbia, Denver, Bristol univs.; m. Beatrice Beckett, Nov. 5, 1923; children—Simon (killed in action in Burma, 1945), Nicholas; m. 2d, Clarissa Spencer Churchill, Aug. 1952. Served as capt. with King's Royal Rifle Corps, as brig. maj., World War I; justice of peace, Durham County, 1923; mem. Brit. Ho. of Commons, 1923-57, leader of House, 1942-45; parliamentary pvt. sec. to the sec. of state for fgn. affairs, 1926-29; parliamentary under-sec. Fgn. Office, 1931-33; privy councillor, 1934; Lord Privy Seal, 1934-35; minister without portfolio League of Nations Affairs, 1935; sec. of state for fgn. affairs, 1935-38, 1940-45, 1951-55, for dominion affairs, 1939-40, for war, 1940; deputy prime minister, 1951- 55. prime minister 1955-57. Rep. Gt. Britain at Am. British-Russian Conf., Moscow, 1943, signer of 4- power declarn. agreed upon at that conf.; chancellor U. Birmingham. Decorated Mil. Cross; created Knight Order of Garter, 1954. Author: Places in the Sun; Foreign Affairs, 1939; Freedom and Order; Days for Decision; Full Circle, 1960; Facing the Dictators, 1962; The Reckoning, 1965; Toward Peace in Indochina, 1966. Address: Manor House Alvediston Salisbury Wiltshire England

AVRAMOVIC, DRAGOSLAV, govt. ofcl., economist; b. Skoplje, Yugoslavia, Oct. 14, 1919; s. Nikola and Jelena (Sahovic) A.; Ph.D., U. Belgrade, 1956; m. Maria Jovanovic, May 23, 1943; children—Zoran, Mila, Dora. Came to U.S., 1953. Sec. Yugoslav Monetary Reform Commn., 1945-46; dep. sec. Yugoslav Nat. Bank, 1946-47; sec. planning and negotiating team Fgn. Financial Resources, 1948-50; lectr. econs. part-time U. Belgrade, 1947-50, full time, 1950- 53; mem. staff Internat. Bank Reconstrn. and Devel., 1953—, asst. dir. econs. dept., 1964-65, dir. spl. econs. studies, office of the pres., 1965-68, dir. commodity stabilization studies, 1968-69, dir. industrialization studies, 1969-70; chief economist S. Am. dept., 1970—; head of the World Bank econ. missions to Philippines, 1961-62, Nigeria, 1965, Algeria, 1966, Brazil, 1967, Iran, 1969, Pakistan, 1969, Colombia, 1970-71. Author: Debt Servicing Capacity and Postwar Growth in International Indebtedness, 1958; Debt Servicing Problems of Low Income Countries, 1960; Economic Growth and External Debt, 1964. Home: 13200 Cleveland Dr Rockville MD 20850 Office: 1818 H St N W Washington DC 20433

AVRUTICK, ABRAHAM NOAH, rabbi; b. Russia, Nov. 19, 1909; s. Fishel and Sosel (Shimshilevitch) AvR.; B.A., Yeshiva Coll., 1934; grad. Rabbi Isaac Elchanan Theol. Sem., Yeshiva U., 1929-36; D. Hebrew Letters, Yeshiva U., 1966; m. Frances Ruth Feldman, Nov. 8, 1938; children—Rena (Mrs. Richard S. Barth), Judith (Mrs. Meyer Berkowitz), Naomi (Mrs. Harold L. Rosenbaum). Came to Can., 1921, naturalized Am. citizen, 1943. Rabbi, 1936; pulpits held, Fitchburg, Mass., 1936-38, Newburgh, N.Y., 1938-46; rabbi Agudas Achim Synagogue, Hartford, Conn., 1946—. Successively sec., treas., v.p. Rabbinical Council Am., pres., 1962-64, hon. pres., 1965; v.p. Yeshiva of Hartford; dir. Union of Orthodox Jewish Congregations Am. Active Community Chest, North End Citizens Com.; mem. Conn. Safety Commn.; mayor's mem. Com. on Hartford. Bd. dirs. Hartford Jewish Fedn., Jewish Centre, Hebrew Home for Aged, Jewish Social Service. Recipient Mr. Success award radio sta. WCCC, Rabbinic Leadership award Union Orthodox Jewish Congregations Am., 1964. Editor: RCA Sermon Manual, 1960. Contbr. articles to religious periodicals. Home: 2 Old Field Rd West Hartford CT 06007

AVSHALOMOV, JACOB, composer, conductor, educator; b. Tsingtao, China, Mar. 28, 1919; s. Aaron and Esther (Magidson) A.; came to U.S., 1937, naturalized, 1944; student Reed Coll., Portland, Ore., 1939-41; Mus. B., Eastman Sch. Music, 1942, M.A., 1943; Hon. degree, U. Portland, 1965; m. Doris Felde, Aug. 31, 1943; children—David, Daniel. Mem. music dept. Columbia, 1947-54, asst. prof., 1954; condr. Portland Jr. Symphony Orchestra, 1954—. Condr. U.S. premier of Michael Tippett's oratorio A Child of Our Time, Columbia U. Chorus and Orchestra, 1952; Sinfonietta premiered by Thos. Scherman at Town Hall, 1949, Taking of T'ung Kuan by Stokowski with Detroit Symphony, 1952, Evocations by Stokowski at Museum of Modern Art, 1953, Tom of Bedlam by Robert Shaw at Carnegie Hall, 1953; The Oregon, Symphony for Ore. Centennial, 1962. Mem. Nat. Council For Humanities, 1968. Served with inf. AUS, 1943-44, ETO. Alice M. Ditson fellow, 1946, Guggenheim fellow, 1951-52; recipient N.Y. Critics Circle award for Tom O' Bedlam, 1953; Naumberg recording award for Sinfonietta, 1956. Mem. League of Composers, Am. Composer Alliance, Internat. Soc. Contemporary Music. Champion, North China fancy diving, 1934-37. Home: 2741 SW Fairview Blvd Portland OR 97201 Office: Portland Jr Symphony Park Bldg Portland OR 97201

AWADALLAB, ABUBAKR, govt. ofcl. Sudan; b. 1915. Formerly chief justice Sudan, now premier and minister fgn. affairs. Address: care House of Constituent Assembly Office of Prime Minister Khartoum, Republic of Sudan.*

AWES, GERALD A., chain store exec.; b. Colorado Springs, Colo., 1914; m.; 3 children. Chmn. exec. com. Lucky Stores, Inc., San Leandro, Cal., also dir. Mem. Nat. Assn. Food Chains (past chmn. bd.). Office: 1630 Newell Av Walnut Creek CA 94596

AXE, LEONARD HENRY, lawyer; b. Council Grove, Kan., Oct. 9, 1900; s. Joseph Henry and Minnie (Burdick) A.; A.B., Baker U., 1923, L.L.D. (hon.), 1953; LL.B., U. Kan., 1929; S.J.D. U. Mich., 1942; m. Hermia Massey, Aug. 19, 1929. Instr. bus. law U. Kan., 1929-31, asst. prof., 1931-36, asso. prof., 1936-40, prof., 1940-57, asst. to the chancellor, 1945-47, acting dean sch. bus., 1947-48, dean, 1948-57; fellow human relations, grad. sch. bus. adminstrn. Harvard, 1948; exec. dir. Dept. Adminstrn., State Kan., 1953-55; pres. Kan. State Coll. of Pittsburg, 1957-65, pres. emeritus, 1965—; dir. revenue State of Kan., 1965-67; dean of coll. Cottey College, Nevada, Mo., 1967-68; atty.-in- residence Schroeder, Heeney, Groff & Spies. Mem. Order of Coif, Omicron Delta Kappa, Kappa Sigma, Phi Delta Phi, Beta Gamma Sigma. Rotarian. Author: Aviation Insurance, 1931. Contbr. law publs. Home: 2136 W 30th St Topeka KS 66611 Office: 704 KPL Tower Topeka KS 66612

AXEL, PETER, physicist; b. Bklyn., May 12, 1923; A.B., Bklyn. Coll., 1943; M.S., U. Ill., 1947, Ph.D. in Physics, 1949; m. Shirley Thomas, 1954; 1 dau., Sarah. Mem. staff elec. devel., radiation lab. Mass. Inst. Tech., 1943- 46; asst. prof. physics U. Ill., 1949-55, asso. prof. physics, 1955-59, prof. physics, 1959-; spl. research nuclear physics, radioactivity, photon induced reactions, electronics, nuclear instrumentation. Mem. Am. Phys. Soc. Bd. dirs. Bull. Atomic Scientists. Home: 1109 S Douglas Urbana IL 61801.

AXELRAD, NORMAN DAVID, restaurant exec.; b. Chgo., Nov. 13, 1929; s. Samuel and Bessie (Young) A.; B.A. in Econs., U. Mich., 1951; J.D., Northwestern U., 1954; m. Sandra Ann Gault, Aug. 26, 1964; 1 son, John E. Admitted to Ill. bar, 1955; mem. firm Chapman, Anixter & Delaney, Chgo., 1955-60; v.p., sec., dir. McDonald's Corp., Oak Brook, Ill., 1960—; lectr. in legal symposiums. Served with U.S. Army, 1954-56. Mem. Am., Ill., Chgo. bar assns. Contbr. articles profl. jours. Office: McDonald's Plaza Oak Brook IL 60521

AXELRAD, SIDNEY, social psychologist; b. N.Y.C., May 25, 1913; s. Harris and Bessie (Ehrenworth) A.; B.S.S., Coll. City N.Y., 1933; M.A., N.Y.U., 1937; D.S.S., New Sch. Social Research, 1943; postgrad, N.Y. Psychoanalytic Inst., 1948-52; m. Sylvia Brody, May 11, 1949. Research asso. N.Y.U., 1933-34, N.Y. State Tng. Sch. Boys, 1934-38; supr. N.Y.C. Bd. Child Welfare, 1938-41; fellow Rockefeller Found., 1941-42; staff Research Project on Totalitarian Communications, 1942-43; from tutor to vis. prof. grad. faculty New Sch. Social Research, 1946-54; from instr. to asso. prof. Queens Coll., 1948-60, prof., 1960, chmn. anthropology-sociology dept., 1950-64, dir. grad. studies, 1962-67, dean of grad. studies, 1967—; asso. dean grad. studies City U. N.Y., 1962—; research cons. Social Work and Mental Health Agys., 1946—; psychol. pediatric psychiatry service Lenox Hill Hosp., 1961-67, co-dir. child devel. research project, 1963—. Served with USAAF, 1943-46. Fellow Am. Social Assn., Royal Soc. Health, A.A.A.S.; mem. Am. Psychol. Assn., Sigma Xi. Author: (with others) German Radio Propaganda, 1944; Occupational Choice, 1950; Anxiety and Ego Formation in Infancy, 1970; also articles in profl. jours. Asso. editor: Psychoanalysis and the Social Sciences, 1954-58; editorial bd. Am. Jour. Orthopsychiatry, 1957-62; co-mng. editor Psychoanalytic Study of Society, 1958-70. Home: 1148 Fifth Av New York City NY 10028 Office: Queens Coll Flushing NY 11367

AXELROD, ABRAHAM E., educator, chemist; b. Cleve., June 10, 1912; s. Max and Rose (Leiken) A.; B.A., Western Res. U., 1933, M.A., 1936; Ph.D.,U. Wis., 1939; m. Velma Hellerstein, Sept. 12, 1939; children—Nancy, Philip. Research chemist Western Pa. Hosp., 1942-50; asso. prof. chemistry U. Pitts., 1945-50; asso. prof. Western Res. U., Cleve., 1950-54; prof. biochemistry Sch. Medicine, U. Pitts., 1954—, asso. dean Sch. Medicine, 1965-70. Mem. Am. Chem. Soc., Am. Inst. Nutrition, Am. Soc. Biol. Chemists, Am. Assn. Immunologists, Biochem. Soc. (London, Eng.). Home: 5821 Walnut St Pittsburgh PA 15232

AXELROD, BERNARD, educator, biochemist; b. N.Y.C., Oct. 16, 1914; s. Alex and Rose Axelrod; B.S., Wayne State U., 1935; M.S., George Washington U., 1939; Ph.D., Georgetown U., 1943; m. Sara Feingersh, 1934; children—Eugene, Judith Ann. Chemist, U.S. Dept. Agr., Washington, 1938-43, Cal., 1943-50, chief enzyme sect. Western regional research lab. Bur. Agr. and Indsl. Chemistry, 1952-54; asso. prof. biochemistry Purdue U., Lafayette, Ind., 1954-58, prof., 1958—, head dept. biochemistry, 1965—. Sr. research fellow Cal. Inst. Tech., 1950-52, NSF sr. research fellow Carlsberg Laboratorium, Copenhagen, 1960, U. Cal. at Santa Cruz, 1970-71. Fellow A.A.A.S.; mem. Am. Soc. Biol. Chemists, Am. Chem. Soc., Am. Inst. Biol. Sci., Am., Japanese socs. plant physiology. Contbr. articles profl. jours. Home: 337 Hollywood Dr West Lafayette IN 47906 Office: Purdue U Sch Agr Lafayette IN 47907

AXELROD, GEORGE, author; b. N.Y.C., June 9, 1922; s. Herman and Beatrice (Carpenter) A.; m. Gloria Washburn, Feb. 28, 1942 (div. June 1954); children—Peter, Steven; m. Joan Stanton, Oct. 1954; 1 dau., Nina. Radio and TV script writer, 1947—, including sketches for comedians, and TV Celebrity Time series, also films. Mem. Authors League Am., Dramatists Guild. Author: Beggar's Choice, 1947; Blackmailer, 1952; Small Wonder (revue with Max Wilk), 1948; (plays) The Seven Year Itch, 1953, Will Success Spoil Rock Hunter, 1955; (films) Phffft, The Seven Year Itch, Bus Stop; producer (with Clinton Wilder) Visit to a Small Planet (play), 1957; Goodbye, Charlie (play) 1959 (also dir.); Breakfast at Tiffany's (film), 1959; author screenplays; The Manchurian Candidate (produced with John Frankenheimer), 1962, and Paris When it Sizzles (produced with Richard Quine), 1963; How To Murder Your Wife, 1965; dir. Once More, With Feeling (play), 1958; producer, dir., co-author screen play Lord Love a Duck; dir. play Star Spangled Girl; writer, producer, dir. The Secret Life of an American Wife. Home: 301 N Carolwood Dr Los Angeles CA 90024

AXELROD, JULIUS, biochemist, pharmacologist; b. N.Y.C., May 30, 1912; s. Isadora and Molly (Leichtling) A.; B.S., Coll. City N.Y., 1933; M.A., N.Y.U., 1941, D.Sc. (hon.), 1971; Ph.D., George Washington U., 1955, LL.D. (hon.), 1971; D.Sc., U. Chgo., 1965; D.Sc. (hon.), Med. Coll. Wis., 1971; m. Sally Taub, Aug. 30, 1938; children—Paul Mark, Alfred Nathan. Chemist, Lab. Indsl. Hygiene, 1935-46; research asso. 3d N.Y.U. research div. Goldwater Meml. Hosp., 1946-49; asso. chemist sect. chem. pharmacology Nat. Heart Inst., NIH, 1949-50, chemist, 1950-53, sr. chemist, 1953-55, acting chief sect. pharmacology Lab. Clin. Sci., Nat. Inst. Mental Health, 1955, chief sect. pharmacology, 1955—; Otto Lowei meml. lectr. N.Y.U., 1963; Karl E. Paschkis meml. lectr. Phila. Endocine Soc., 1966; NIH lectr., 1967; Nathanson meml. lectr. U. So. Cal., 1968; James Parkinson lectr. Columbia, 1971; Wartenberh lectr. Am. Acad. Neurology, 1971; Arnold D. Welch lectr. Yale, 1971; Harold Carpenter Hodge distinguished lectr. toxicology U. Rochester, 1971; Bennett lectr. Am. Neurol. Assn., 1971. Cons. George Washington U., 1959—; panelist U.S. Bd. Civil Service Examiners, 1958—; mem. research adv. com. United Cerebral Palsy Assn., 1966-69; mem.

psychopharmacology study sect. Nat. Inst. Mental Health, 1970—; mem. Population Crisis Com., Internat. Brain Research Orgn. Recipient Meritorious Research award Assn. Research Nervous and Mental Diseases, 1965; Gairdner award distinguished research, 1967; Nobel prize med. physiology, 1970; Alumni Distinguished Achievement award George Washington U., 1968; Superior Service award Dept. Health, Edn. and Welfare, 1968, Distinguished Service award, 1970; Claude Bernard professorship and medal U. Montreal, 1969; Distinguished Service award Modern Medicine mag., 1970; Albert Einstein award Yeshiva U., 1971. Fellow Am. Soc. Neuropsychopharmacology; mem. German Pharmacol. Soc. (corr.), Am. Chem. Soc., Am. Soc. Pharmacology and Exptl. Therapeutics, Am. Soc. Biol. Chemists, A.A.A.S., Sigma Xi, hon. mem. Am. Psychopathol. Assn. Contbr. articles profl. jours. Editorial bd. Jour. Pharmacology and Exptl. Therapeutics, 1956—, Jour. Medicinal Chemistry, 1962—, Circulation Research, 1963—, Currents in Modern Biology, 1966—; editorial adv. bd. Communication in Behavioral Biology, 1967, Jour. Neurobiology, 1968—, Jour. Neurochemistry, 1969, Jour. Neurovisceral Relation, 1969, Rassegna di Neurologia Vegetativa, 1969—, Internat. Jour. Psychobiology, 1970—; hon. cons. editor Life Scis., 1961—. Co-author: The Pineal, 1968. Home: 10401 Grosvenor Rd Rockville MD 20852 Office: NIH Bethesda MD 20014

AXELROD, LEONARD RICHARDSON, biochemist, educator; b. Bklyn., Mar. 31, 1927; s. Philip and Rose (Richardson) A.; B.S., Coll. City N.Y., 1948; Ph.D., U. Rochester (N.Y.), 1951; m. Phyllis Thelma Seiden, Aug. 18, 1951; children—Douglas Wayne, Judith Ellen, Mitchell Brian, Janet Ann. Cons. Atomic Energy Project AEC, Rochester, 1953-55; chmn. dept. biochemistry S W Found. Research and Edn., 1955—, dir. of div. biol. growth and devel., 1965—; research prof. chemistry St. Mary's U., 1961—. Mem. Am. Mus. Natural History, N.Y.C.; mem. nat. adv. bd. Cystic Fibrosis Found. Fellow Am. Inst. Chemists, Chem. Soc. (London); mem. Am. Endocrine Soc., Am. Chem. Soc., N.Y. Acad. Scis., Soc. Nutrition and Endocrine-Mexico, Sigma Xi. Contbr. articles profl. jours. Patentee in field. Home: 122 Rio Bravo St San Antonio TX 78216 Office: 7480 W Commerce St San Antonio TX 78284

AXELROD, PHILIP, fgn. service officer; b. N.Y.C., Aug. 28, 1918; s. Thomas and Miriam (Cummins) A.; B.A., Coll. City N.Y., 1938; M.A., Columbia Teachers Coll., 1939; m. Dorothy Mardar, Nov. 11, 1945; children—Barbara Helen, Nancy Rae, Roy David. Vocational appraiser U. Del., 1946-48; joined U.S. Fgn. Service, 1948; vice consul, Marseille, France, 1948-50; 2d sec. Am. embassy, Athens, Greece, 1951-56; internat. relations officer State Dept., 1957-60; polit. counselor Am. embassy, Bangkok, Thailand, 1961-63; dep. dir. Operations Center, Dept. State, 1963-64; mem. faculty Nat. War Coll., 1965-67; spl. liaison officer NATO so. region comdr., Naples, Italy, 1967-69; polit. counselor Am. embassy, Madrid, Spain, 1969—. Served to capt. AUS, 1941-46. Mem. Am. Fgn. Service Assn., Phi Beta Kappa. Address: care Am Embassy Madrid Spain

AXELROD, SOLOMON JACOB, physician, educator; b. Gloversville, N.Y., Sept. 25, 1912; s. Max and Ray (Semser) A.; A.B. magna cum laude, Dartmouth, 1934; M.D., Jefferson Med. Coll., 1938; M.P.H., U. Mich., 1948; m. Pearl Guttman, June 30, 1935; children—Peter, Joan. Intern Phila. Gen. Hosp., 1938-40; research fellow U. Pa., 1940-41; med. officer Tenn. Dept. Health, 1941-43; med. dir. Mich. Rapid Treatment Center, 1948-49; mem. faculty U. Mich. Sch. Pub. Health, 1949—, resident lectr., 1949-51, asso. prof., 1951-54, prof., 1954—, dir. bur. pub. health econs., 1959-70, chmn. dept. med. care orgn., 1965-70; asso. health and med. care Community Research Assos., 1952-54. Served as sr. surgeon, USPHS (R), 1943-50; chief med. officer migrant labor health program War Food Adminstrn., 1945-47; rural health cons., 1947-48. Diplomate Am. Bd. Preventive Medicine. Fellow Am. Pub. Health Assn.; mem. Phi Beta Kappa, Delta Omega. Author: (with Darsky and Sinai) Comprehensive Medical Services Under Voluntary Health Insurance, 1958. Editorial bd. Public Health Economics, 1951-66, Med. Care Rev., 1966—. Home: 457 Barton North Dr Ann Arbor MI 48105

AXELSON, CHARLES FREDERIC, Jr., food co. exec.; b. Chgo., Apr. 24, 1917; s. Charles Frederic and Katherine (Strong) A.; A.B., M.B.A., U. Chgo., 1937; m. Dorothy L. Jepson, July 23, 1940; children—Linda (Mrs. Michael Hoy), Fred, Lori. Staff accountant Lybrand, Ross Bros. & Montgomery, Chgo., 1938-41; with U.S. Gypsum Co., Chgo., 1941-70, asst. controller, 1946-52, controller, 1952-60, controller, asst. treas., 1960-70; v.p. controller Libby, McNeill & Libby, Chgo., 1970—; lectr. accounting Northwestern U., 1946-53. Chmn. assos., trustee Nat. Coll. Edn. Mem. Am. Inst. C.P.A.'s, Financial Execs. Inst. (past pres. Chgo. chpt., past nat. dir., past v.p. Midwestern area), Phi Delta Theta. Presbyn. Clubs: Executives, Economic, University Tower (Chgo.); Shore (Northbrook, Ill.). Home: 1230 Lee Rd Northbrook IL 60062 Office: 200 S Michigan Av Chicago IL 60604

AXELSON, JOSEPH ALLEN, profl. athletic corp. exec.; b. Peoria, Ill., Dec. 25, 1927; s. Joseph Victor and Florence Ealen (Massey) A.; B.S. in Journalism, Northwestern U., 1949; m. Malcolm Rae Smith, Oct. 7, 1950; children—David Allen, Mark Stephen, Linda Rae. Sports information dir. Georgia So. Coll., 1954-55; sports information dir. Furman U., 1956; public relations dir. Georgia So. Coll., 1957-60, Nat. Assn. Intercollegiate Athletics, Kansas City, Mo., 1961-62, Bowling Proprietor's Assn. Am., Park Ridge, Ill., 1963-64; asst. exec. sec. Nat. Assn. Intercollegiate Athletics, 1965-68; exec. v.p., gen. mgr. Cin. Royals Profl. Basketball Team, 1969—; mgr. Cin. Gardens, 1970—. Served to capt., Signal Corps, AUS, 1952-54. Mem. Phi Kappa Psi. Republican. Presbyn. Home: 5809 Kugler Mill Rd Cincinnati OH 45236 Office: 2250 Seymour Av Cincinnati OH 45212

AXELSON, KENNETH STRONG, corp. exec.; b. Chgo., July 31, 1922; s. Charles F. and Katherine (Strong) A.; A.B. (John Crerar scholar 1939-43), U. Chgo., 1944; postgrad. Va. Poly. Inst., 1943-44; m. Roberta Bearhope, Jan. 23, 1943; children—Kenneth Strong, Jerrold Frederick, Stephen Robert, John Christian. Accountant, Arthur Andersen & Co., C.P.A.'s, Seattle, 1946- 48; controller Columbia Lumber Co. of Alaska, Juneau, 1948-50; mgmt. cons. McKinsey & Co., Chgo., 1950-52; mgr. mgmt. controls dept. Peat, Marwick, Mitchell & Co., C.P.A.'s, N.Y.C., 1952-53, partner, 1953-63; v.p. finance J.C. Penney Co., Inc., N.Y.C., 1963-67, v.p. finance and adminstrn., 1967—, also dir.; chmn. bd. J.C. Penney Financial Corp., 1964—; dir. J.C. Penney Ins. Co., J.C. Penney Life Ins. Co., Sarma, S.A., Brussels, Belgium, Protection Mut. Ins. Co. Served as warrant officer AUS, 1943-46. C.P.A., N.Y., Ill., Wash., Ia., N.M., Va. Mem. Am. Inst. C.P.A.'s (accounting principles bd. 1968-70), Financial Execs. Inst., Nat. Assn. Accountants, N.Y. Soc. C.P.A.'s, U. Chgo. Sch. Bus. Assn. (pres. 1957-58), Phi Delta Theta. Baptist. Club: Alumni Club U. Chgo. (pres. N.Y.C. 1961-62). Author: Responsibility Reporting, 1961. Editor Mgmt. Controls Jour., 1958-63. Contbr. articles on uses of accounting for mgmt. Home: 115 Central Park W New York City NY 10023 Office: 1301 Av of Americas New York City NY 10019

AXEN, RICHARD FREDERICK, educator; b. Berwyn, Ill., Nov. 24, 1920; s. Fred I. and Bertha (Madison) A.; student Morton Jr. Coll., Cicero, Ill., 1939-41, U. Chgo., 1941-42; B.A., Miami U. of Ohio, 1943; Ed.D., U. Cal. at Los Angeles, 1952; m. Doris L. Ingram, Aug. 23, 1950; 1 dau., Laurie. Chemist Universal Oil Products, Riverside, Ill., 1946-48; research asst. to pres. Union Coll., Schenectady, N.Y., 1950-51; dean of students State U. N.Y., Fredonia, 1952-53; dir. admissions, registrar U. Kansas City, 1954-56; asso. dean students and admissions San Francisco State Coll., 1956-68, prof. higher edn., 1958—. Served with USAAF, 1943-46. Mem. Assn. Higher Edn., Am. Civil Liberties Union, Assn. Cal. State Coll. Profs. Democrat. Author: (with Robert Smith and Devere Pentony) By Any Means Necessary, 1970, Unfinished Rebellions, 1971. Contbr. articles profl. jours. Home: 1659 Lexington St San Mateo CA 94402 Office: 1600 Holloway St San Francisco CA 94132

AXENE, DEAN LANE, naval officer; b. Kansas City, Mo., Aug. 1, 1923; s. Oscar Frederick and Marlow (Gross) A.; B.S., U.S. Naval Acad., 1944; B.S. in Elec. Engring., Mass. Inst. Tech., 1948; m. Sally Ann Haas, June 7, 1944; children—Eric Christopher, Kristen (Mrs. Ronald R. Wenning). Commd. ensign USN, 1944, advanced through grades to rear adm., 1969; electronics officer, engring. officer, naviagation officer U.S.S. Tiru, 1948-50; electronics officer of staff Comdr. Submarine Squadron 1, 1950-51; electronics officer of staff Comdr. Submarine Force, U.S. Pacific Fleet, 1951-52; exec. officer U.S.S. Sea Robin, 1952-53; tng. at Westinghouse Bettis Plant, AEC, Pitts., 1953, Naval Reactor Testing Sta., Arco, Ida., 1953; commissioning exec. officer U.S.S. Nautilus, 1954-55; comdr. U.S.S. Croaker, 1955-57; dir. nuclear dept. Submarine Sch., New London, 1957- 59; instrn. at Naval Reactors br. AEC, Washington, 1959-60; prospective comdg. officer U.S.S. Thresher, Portsmouth (N.H.) Naval Shipyard, 1960- 61, comdr., 1961-63; attended Polaris command course Naval Guided Missiles Sch., Dam Neck, Va., 1963; prospective comdg. officer U.S.S. John C. Calhoun, Newport News (Va.) Shipbuilding & Drydock Co., 1963-64, comdr., 1964-66; mem. State Dept. Sr. Seminar in Fgn. Policy, 1966-67; head policy coordination, diplomatic clearance and internat. aviation br., Politico-Mil. Policy div. Office Chief Naval Operations, Navy Dept., Washington, 1967-69, dir. Pan-Am. affairs, Naval Missions and Adv. Group div., 1969-70; dep. chief of staff, asst. chief of staff for plans, policy and operations Staff of NATO's Supreme Allied Comdr. Atlantic, Norfolk, Va., 1970—. Decorated Bronze Star medal with combat V, Legion of Merit, Gt. Star of Mil. Merit (Chile). Mem. U.S. Naval Acad. Found., U.S. Naval Hist. Found., U.S. Naval Inst., Nat. Geog. Soc. Home: 2257 Oxford Rd Columbus OH 43221 Office: Dep Chief of Staff Supreme Allied Comdr Atlantic Norfolk VA 23511

AXFORD, HIRAM WILLIAM, librarian, educator; b. Butte, Mont., Apr. 7, 1925; s. Harold Frederick and Della (Albert) A.; A.B., Reed Coll., 1950; M.A., U. Denver, 1958, Ph.D., 1968; m. Lavonne Brady, Nov. 11, 1956. Head librarian Denver Post, Inc., 1958-60; adj. prof. Grad. Sch. Librarianship, U. Denver, 1959-67, asst. dir. libraries, 1960-65, dir. libraries, 1965-67; dir. libraries, prof. history Fla. Atlantic U., Boca Raton, 1967-70; univ. librarian, prof. library sci. Ariz. State U., 1970—. Mem. Urban U. Library Com., 1966—; project dir. Intermountain Union List of Serials, 1970—. Fulbright lectr. U. Punjab, Lahore, West Pakistan, 1963-64. Served with AUS, 1943-46. Mem. A.L.A. (com. vice chmn. resources and tech. services div.), Ariz. Library Assn., Am. Assn. U. Profs. Library Automation, Research and Cons. Assn. (pres. 1970). Author: Gilpin County Gold, 1971. Home: 13020 N Hayden St Scottsdale AZ 85281

AXFORD, ROY ARTHUR, educator; b. Detroit, Aug. 26, 1928; s. Morgan and Charlotte (Donaldson) A.; B.A., Williams Coll., 1952; B.S., Mass. Inst. Tech., 1952, M.S., 1955, Sc.D., 1958; m. Anne-Sofie Langfeldt Rasmussen, Apr. 1, 1954; children—Roy Arthur, Jr., Elizabeth Carole, Trevor Craig. Supr. theoretical physics group Atomics Internat., Canoga Park, Cal., 1958-60; asso. prof. nuclear engring. Tex. A. & M. U., 1960-62, prof., 1962-63; asso. prof. nuclear engring. Northwestern U., 1963-66; asso. prof. U. Ill. at Urbana, 1966-68, prof., 1968—; cons. Los Alamos Sci. Lab., 1963—. Vice-chmn. Mass. Inst. Tech. Alumni Fund Drive, 1970—. Mem. Am. Nuclear Soc., Am. Soc. M.E., Am. Inst. Aeronautics and Astronautics, Sigma Xi. Home: 2017 S Cottage Grove Urbana IL 61801

AXINN, SIDNEY, educator; b. N.Y.C., Jan. 30, 1923; s. Hyman and Celia (Schneider) A.; student Horace Mann Sch. for Boys, 1936-40; student U. Pa., 1940-42, A.B., 1947, Ph.D., 1955; m. June Morris, June 21, 1947; children—Constance, David. From instr. to prof. philosophy Temple U., Phila., 1948—, lectr. Med. Sch., 1956-66, adj. prof. psychiatry, 1966- -; cons. Dept. Labor. Served with AUS, 1943-46. Mem. Am. Philosophic Assn., Am. Soc. Polit. Legal Philosophy, Assn. for Symbolic Logic, Internat. Soc. for Philosophies of Law (Am. Sec.). Contbr. articles in field to profl. jours. Home: 722 Wyndale Rd Jenkintown PA 19046 Office: Temple U Broad and Montgomery Sts Philadelphia PA 19122

AXLEY, RALPH EMERSON, lawyer; b. Seymour, Wis., Jan. 12, 1902; s. Frederick William and Jennie C. (Gallagher) A.; B.A., U. Wis., 1923, LL.B., 1926; m. Katharine Nella Hartman, Sept. 10, 1928 (dec., Mar. 1967); children—Hartman, Francesca Jane; m. 2d, Elizabeth Kauffman Hahn, Jan. 21, 1968. Admitted to Wis. bar, 1925; with firm Schubring, Ryan, Clarke & Petersen and sucessor firms Madison, 1925—; partner Schubring, Ryan, Petersen & Sutherland, 1940-58; partner Petersen, Sutherland, Axley & Brynelson, 1959-69; partner Petersen, Axley, Brynelson & Herrick, 1969—. Vice pres., dir. W.T. Rogers Co. Mem. Am. (council pub. utilities sect. 1953-57, chmn. standing com. 1952-53), Wis., Dane County bar assns., Am. Judicature Soc., Selden Soc., Delta Sigma Rho, Phi Delta Phi. Republican. Conglist. Mason (Shriner). Clubs: Madison, Maple Bluff Country, Optimist (Madison). Contbr. articles profl. jours. Home: 3515 Sunset Dr Shorewood Hills Madison WI 53705 Office: 122 W Washington Av Madison WI 53703

AXMAN, LAURENCE HENRY, lawyer; b. Kansas City, Mo., July 30, 1890; s. Charles David and Sophia (Cahn) A.; A.B., Columbia, 1911, LL.B., 1913. Admitted to N.Y. bar, 1913, D.C. bar, 1958, U.S. Supreme Ct. bar, 1923; pvt. practice of law, 1913-17, 1942; asst. U.S. atty., So. Dist. of N.Y., 1917-19, spl. asst. to U.S. atty. gen. in charge trial sect., 1948-52; trial atty. civil div., Dept. Justice, Washington, 1952- 61, employment policy officer, 1957-61; practice law, Washington, 1962—. Tech. consultant White House Conf. Children and Youth, 1960; mem. adv. com. hearing examiners Civil Service Commn. Dir. Fed. Bar Assn. Found., 1954-58. Member Federal (pres. 1957-58, mem. nat. council, vice chmn. com. ct. claims, vice chmn. com. juvenile and youth problems, chmn. 50th anniversary commn. 1970, chmn. constn. and bylaws com.; mem. jud., selections, ethics coms.), Internat. (v.p. 1958), D.C. bar assns., Bar Assn. City N.Y., Nat. Lawyers Club. Home: 3636 16th St NW Washington DC 20010

AXTELL, DEAN ROBERT, steel co. exec.; b. Kenosha, Wis., Apr. 11, 1927; s. Albert E. and Martha (Sorenson) A.; student Mich. State U., 1945, Carroll Coll., Waukeshaw, Wis., 1947-48; B.B.A. cum laude, U. Wis., 1950; m. Marion J. Speaker, Dec. 30, 1950; children—Stephen, David, Thomas. Auditor, Ernst & Ernst, C.P.A.'s, Milw., 1951-55; with Inland Steel Products Co., Milw., 1955—, regional sales mgr., 1962-63, treas., 1963-68, v.p. operations, 1968—, also mem. bd. dirs. Served with USAAF, 1945-47, USAF, 1950-51. C.P.A., Wis. Mem. Am. Inst. Accountants, Financial Execs. Inst., Wis. Soc. C.P.A.'s. Home: 617 E Lexington Blvd Whitefish Bay WI 53217 Office: 4101 W Burnham St Milwaukee WI 53201

AXTELL, GEORGE CLIFTON, marine corps officer; b. Ambridge, Pa., Nov. 29, 1920; s. George C. and Cora (Perrine) A.; student U. Ala., 1938-40; student U.S. Navy Post Grad. Sch., 1941-42; LL.B., George Washington U., 1952, M.A., 1954; student Nat. War Coll., 1963-64; m. Phyllis Crafton, Mar. 21, 1942; children—Grey C., Guy C. Commd. 2d lt. USMC, 1940, advanced through grades to maj. gen., 1965; squadron comdr., group tactical officer, Korea, 1952; personnel plans AVN Programs, 1954-59; comdr. fighter group MAG-12, Japan, 1959-60; asst. chief staff G-4, Hdqrs. USMC, 1966-70; comdg. gen. 2d Marine Wing, 1970—. Decorated Air medal with six stars, D.F.C. with gold star, Navy Cross, Legion of Merit with combat V and 2 gold stars. Mem. Am. Bar Assn., Bar Assn. D.C., Nat. Lawyers Club, Nat. Congress Parents and Tchrs., Marine Corps Assn., Toastmasters, Armed Forces Mgmt. Assn., Arlington Symphony Assn., Inst. Aero. Scis., U.S. Naval Inst., Am. Ordnance Assn., Theta Chi, Phi Beta Phi. Club: Aviation Yacht and Country (Chaptico, Md.). Office: Comdg Gen 2d Marine Aircraft Wing FMF MCAS Cherry Point NC 28533

AXTELL, WILLIAM BATES, educator; b. Schenectady, N.Y., Jan. 6, 1908; s. George William and Kathryn (Chadsey) A.; student Purdue U., 1928-30; A.B., Union Coll. (Schenectady), 1934; M.A., Syracuse U., 1939, Ed.D., 1949; m. Ruth Gordon, Aug. 22, 1936; 1 son, John William. Sci. tchr. Central Sch., Sharon Springs, N.Y., 1935-37, pub. schs., Ithaca, N.Y., 1937-42; asst. prof. edn. Union Coll., Schenectady, N.Y., 1946-47; research asst., instr. edn. Syracuse U., 1947-49; asso. prof. edn., chmn. dept. St. Lawrence U., 1949-53, prof. edn., head dept. edn., 1964—, acting dean of coll., 1967; pres. W. Va. Inst. Tech., Montgomery, 1953-61; prof. edn., chmn. dept. edn. Davis and Elkins Coll., Elkins, W.Va., 1961-64. Ednl. adviser Q.M. Sch., U.S. Army, Ft , Lee, Va., 1962. Exec. bd. St. Lawrence council Boy Scouts Am. Bd. dirs. Kanawha Valley Mining Inst., 1954-61. Served with AUS, 1942-46; lt. col. Res. Mem. N.E.A., Phi Delta Kappa, Sigma Alpha Epsilon. Republican. Presbyn. Mason, Rotarian. Author: (with Myles Rodehaver, Richard Gross) The Sociology of the School, 1957. Home: 20 Judson St Canton NY 13617.

AXTMANN, ROBERT CLARK, educator; b. Youngstown, O., Feb. 25, 1925; s. Charles Frank and Marguerite (Conklin) A.; A.B., Oberlin Coll., 1947; Ph.D., Johns Hopkins, 1950; m. Annabell Hoxie, Apr. 9, 1949; children—Connelle Marguerite, Tyrrell Charles, Ellen Virginia. Instr. Johns Hopkins, 1949; physicist Aberdeen Proving Ground, 1950; from scientist to sr. research supr. E.I. duPont de Nemours & Co., 1950-59; mem. faculty Princeton, 1959—, chmn. program nuclear studies in engring., 1960-68, chmn. Council Environmental Studies, 1970—, Mobil prof. chem. engring., 1959—; vis. fellow Israel Atomic Energy Commn., 1964, Comision Nacional de Energia Nuclear, Mexico, 1969. Mem. N.J. Commn. Radiation Protection, 1966-70. Served with USNR, 1944-46. Mem. Am. Phys. Soc., Am. Inst. Chem. Engrs., Am. Chem. Soc., A.A.A.S. Club: Indian John Point (Ont., Can.) Yacht. Contbr. profl. jours. Home: 272 Hartley Av Princeton NJ 08540

AYARS, ALBERT LEE, supt. schs.; b. Kettle Falls, Wash., Sept. 17, 1917; s. Glen Garrison and Ama Belle (Jennings) A.; B.A., Wash. State U., 1939, B.Ed., 1940, M.A., 1942, D.Ed., 1956; m. Frances Louise Schaaf, June 21, 1941; children—Cheron Marie (Mrs. Howard Holman), Judith Louise, Albert Lee, Danielle Jo (Mrs. Richard Alexander), Garrison Hubert, Debora Ann, Theodore Ama, Virginia Darlene. Tchr., Davenport (Wash.) High Sch., 1940-42; prin. Colville (Wash.) High Sch., 1942-45; supt. Omak (Wash.) pub. schs., 1945-49, Sunnyside (Wash.) pub. schs., 1949-52; asso. dir. Joint Council Econ. Edn., N.Y.C., 1952-53; dir. edn. dept. Hill and Knowlton, Inc., also v.p. John W. Hill Found., N.Y.C., 1953-65; supt. schs., Spokane, 1965—; vis. prof., lectr. sch. adminstrn., curriculum and pub. relations Wash. State U., Mich. State U., No. Mich. U., Gonzaga U., U. Del., others; cons. in field, mem. adv. coms., speaker and panelist. Adv. bd. Seven Colls. Vocational Workshops, 1962-65, Robert A. Taft Inst. Govt., 1961- -, W.E. Upjohn Inst. Employment Research, 1963—; pres. council nat. orgn. adult edn. Nat. Assn. Industry-Edn. Coop., 1959, hon. life mem., 1965—; chmn. bd. advisers, pres. Assn. Internat. des Etudiants en Sciences Economiques et Commerciales, 1960. Bd. dirs. Inland Empire council Boy Scouts Am., Inland Empire YMCA, Spokane Lilac Festival Assn., Inland Empire chpt. A.R.C., Spokane County March Dimes, Spokane Council P.T.A., Inland Empire Sci. Fair Assn., Northwest Regional Edn. Lab., United Crusade and Council Spokane County, Joint Council Econ. Edn. Recipient service recognition Council Nat. Orgns. Adult Edn., 1959; first service citation Nat. Workshop Dirs. Conf., 1962; service plaque Whitworth Coll., 1963; Coronat medal St. Edwards U., 1963; first life membership, service plaque Nat. Assn. Industry-Edn. Coop., 1965. Life fellow Internat. Inst. Arts and Letters; fellow A.A.A.S.; mem. N.Y. Acad. Scis., Am. Acad. Polit. and Social Sci., Internat. Platform Assn., Internat. Assn. Parliamentarians (hon.), Inland Empire Edn. Assn. (pres. 1968-69), Wash. State U. Alumni Assn. (pres. N.Y. area 1949-50, 54- 65), Am. Assn. Sch. Adminstrs. (dir., mem. exec. com 1969—), Phi Kappa Phi, Phi Delta Kappa, Kappa Delta Pi. Baptist. Rotarian. Clubs: University, Knife and Fork, Manito Golf and Country (Spokane). Author: Administering the People's Schools, 1957; How to Plan Community Resources Workshops, 1954; The Teenager and Alcohol, 1970; also articles, chpts. in books. Home: 4407 S Madelia Spokane WA 99203 Office: 825 W Trent Av Spokane WA 99201

AYARS, ANN, opera singer. Address: care London Records Inc 521 W 25th St New York City NY 10010.*

AYCOCK, CLARENCE C. TADDY, lt. gov. La.; b. Franklin, La., 1916; LL.B., Loyola U. of South, 1937; m.; 6 children. Mem. La. Ho. of Reps., 1952-60, speaker, 1952-60; lt. gov. State La., 1960—. Dir. Comml. Bank & Trust Co., Franklin, La.; mem. firm Aycock, Horne, Caldwell & Coleman, Franklin. Mem. La. Bar Assn. Democrat. Home: 608 Palfrey St Franklin LA 70538 Office: State Capitol Baton Rouge LA 70804

AYCOCK, WILLIAM BRANTLEY, educator; b. Lucama, N.C., Oct. 26, 1915; s. William P. and Myrtle (Moore) A.; B.S., N.C. State Coll., 1936; M.A., U. N.C., 1937, J.D., 1948; LL.D., Atlantic Christian Coll., 1959, Wake Forest Coll., 1959, Duke, 1963; m. Grace Mewborn, Oct. 25, 1941; children—William Preston 11, Nancy W. Tchr. pub. schs., Greensboro, N.C., 1937-40; adminstr. FSA, 1940-42; prof. law U. N.C., 1948-57, 64- 66, chancellor, 1957-64, Kenan prof. law, 1966—. Served from 1st lt. to lt. col., inf. AUS, 1942-45; col. Judge Adv. Gen.'s Corps, Res., 1956. Decorated Silver Star, Legion of Merit, Bronze Star. Mem. Order of Coif, Omicron Delta Kappa, Phi Kappa Tau. Author: (with Seymour Wurfel) Military Law Under the Uniform Code of Military Justice, 1955. Home: 902 Arrowhead Rd Chapel Hill NC 27514

AYCOCK, WILLIAM FRANK, Jr., newspaper pub. co. exec.; b. Selma, Ala., Jan. 6, 1909; s. William Frank and Mamie (Finlayson) A.; B.S., Samford U., 1930; m. Margaret O'Dell, June 15, 1935; 1 dau., Peggy (Mrs. Malcolm L. Prewitt, Jr.). With Birmingham News Co. (Ala.), 1937-56, v.p., asst. to gen. mgr., 1953- 56; pres., bus. mgr.

Memphis Pub. Co., 1957—. Mem. exec. com. Future Memphis. Bd. dirs. Danny Thomas Memphis Classic Golf Tournament, Memphis Cotton Carnival Assn., Mid- South Fair; adv. com. Baptist Meml. Hosp., Memphis; vice chmn., trustee So. Newspaper Pub. Assn. Found. Served as officer USNR, World War II. Decorated Legion of Merit with V device, Air medal with gold star, Purple Heart. Mem. So. Newspaper Pubs. Assn. (pres.-elect), Pi Kappa Alpha. Baptist. Rotarian. Home: 50 Cherry Rd Memphis TN 38117 Office: 495 Union Av Memphis TN 38101

AYDELOTT, ALFRED LEWIS, architect; b. Brassfield, Ark., May 30, 1912; s. Herbert Raymond and Louise (Vaden) A.; student U. Ill., 1933-36; m. Hope Galloway, May 31, 1952; children—Alfred Lewis III, Martin Vaden. Head A. L. Aydelott & Assos, Memphis, Tenn., 1946—; vis. design critic Yale, 1947, Carnegie Inst. Tech., 1953-54, Mem. Ala. Poly. Inst. adv. bd., 1958-59; mem. U.S. Navy archtl. rev. and adv. panel, 1966-68; mem. Gen. Services Adminstrn. adv. panel, 1968-69; mem. Memphis Bd. Adjustment, 1957-58. Served with USMCR, World War II. Fellow A.I.A. (pres. Memphis 1958), Alpha Tau Omega. Club: University (Memphis). Architect Hospital para Empleades, Lima, Peru, 1951; U.S. Embassy Bldg., Manilla, P.I., 1961; Internat. Hdqrs. Bldg. Pet, Inc., St. Louis, Mo., 1968. Home: 150 Waring Rd Memphis TN 38117 Office: 2080 Peabody Av Memphis TN 38104

AYDELOTT, GALE BENTON, railroad exec.; b. LaGrange, Ill., July 22, 1914; s. James H. and Pearl (Buck) A.; B.S., U. Ill., 1936; student Inst. for Mgmt., Northwestern U., 1953; m. Estella Schooley, Feb. 6, 1938; children—Mary, Stephen, Roger. With D. & R. G.W. R.R. Co., Denver, 1936-, successively welder helper, track insp., engring. asst., roadmaster, trainmaster, div. supt., v.p. and gen. mgr., exec. v.p., 1936-56, pres., dir., 1956-; dir. First Nat. Bank of Denver, Ideal Cement Co., First Security Corp. Salt Lake City, Am. Crystal Sugar Co., Rio Grande Industries. Trustee U. Denver. Mem. Am. Assn. R.R. Supts.,·Nat. Def. Transp. Assn. Clubs: Alta (Salt Lake City); Rotary, Denver (Denver); Union League (Chgo.). Home: 919 Vine St Denver CO 80206 Office: 1531 Stout St Denver CO 80202

AYDELOTTE, JAMES ROBERT, mfg. co. exec.; b. Ft. Scott, Kan., Jan. 10, 1918; s. James B. and Gertrude (Canatsey) A.; B.S. in Bus. with honors, U. Kan., 1939; m. Virginia W. Schryver, Oct. 27, 1940; children—James Edward, Kevin Robert. With Gen. Electric Co., 1939-42, 48-60, mgr. budgets and measurements, 1955-60; controller Spanish subsidairy of Armstrong Cork Co., 1946-48; controller Nat. Standard Co., Niles, Mich., 1960-64; sec., controller Koehring Co., Milw., 1965-68; controller Schwitzer div. Wallace Murray Corp., Indpls., 1968-70; controller Wallace-Murray Corp., N.Y.C., 1970—. Chmn. budget com. Niles Community Fund, 1961-64. Bd. dirs. Jr. Achievement, Niles, 1961-64. Served to capt. AUS, 1942-46. Mem. Financial Execs. Inst., Beta Gamma Sigma. Republican. Conglist. (past deacon, treas., trustee). Home: Morehouse Lane Darien CT 06820 Office: 299 Park Av New York City NY 10017

AYER, ALFRED JULES, educator, philosopher; b. London, Eng., Oct. 29, 1910; s. Jules and Reine (Citroen) A.; M.A., Christ Church, Oxford (Eng.) U., 1936; D.Honoris Causa, U. Brussels (Belgium), 1962; m. Renee Lees, Nov. 25, 1932. children—Julian, Valerie Jane; m. 2d, Alberta Constance Chapman, July 15, 1960; 1 son, Nicholas Hugh. Lectr. philosophy Christ Church, Oxford U., 1933-40, fellow, dean Wadham Coll., 1945-46; Grote prof. philosophy of mind and logic Univ. Coll., U. London, 1946-59; Wykeham prof. logic U. Oxford, 1959, now fellow of New College. Served with British Army, 1940-45. Fellow British Acad.; hon. mem., American Academy of Arts and Sciences. Author: Language, Truth and Logic, 1936; The Foundations of Empirical Knowledge, 1940; Philosophical Essays, 1954; The Problem of Knowledge, 1956; The Concept of Person, 1963; The Origins of Pragmatism, published 1968; Metaphysics and Common Sense, 1969. Home: 10 Regent's Park Terrace London N W 1 England.

AYER, BERNARD FREDERICK, paper mfg. co. exec.; b. Malden, Mass., Jan. 29, 1913; s. George Frederick and Clementine M. (Barchard) A.; B.B.A., Northeastern U., 1940; m. Constance Okell, Oct. 19, 1940; children—Mark F., Bruce M., Gordon C. Asst. treas. Rumford Falls Power Co., also Rumford Light Co. (Me.), 1942-51, treas., 1951-60; treas. Oxford Paper Co., Rumford, 1960—. Chmn. Me. Republican Com., 1958-60; mem. Rep. Nat. Com., 1959-60; del. Rep. Nat. Conv., 1960. Vice chmn. trustees Nat. Commn. Coop. Edn. Mem. Nat. Assn. Accountants, Stuart Cameron McLeod Soc. Mason. Club: Canadian (N.Y.C.). Home: 321 Ocean Dr Kennebunk Port ME 04046 Office: 49 Congress St Rumford ME 04276

AYER, HUGH MASON, educator, historian; b. Livia, Ky., Mar. 8, 1924; s. Henry Cashman and Myrtle (Thomasson) A.; A.B., Western Ky. State Coll., 1948; M.A., Ind. U., 1950, Ph.D., 1957; m. Elizabeth Heisler, Aug. 17, 1946; children—Margaret Mason, David Hugh. Instr. history Culver Mil. Acad., 1952-58; mem. faculty N. Tex. State U., Denton, 1958—, prof. history, 1960—, chmn. div. social sci., 1965-69, asso. dean Coll. Arts and Scis., 1969—. Mem. Denton Planning and Zoning Commn., 1962-66, chmn., 1964-66; mem. Denton City Council, 1969—. Served with USNR, 1943-45; PTO. Mem. Am. Hist. Assn., Orgn. Am. Historians, Am. Assn. U. Profs., So. Hist. Assn., Southwestern Social Sci. Assn., Danforth Assos. Mem. Christian Ch. Home: 425 Mimosa Dr Denton TX 76201

AYER, JOHN, Jr., railroad ofcl.; b. Newton, Mass., Oct. 6, 1912; s. John and Josephine (Stevens) A.; B.S. in Elec. Engring., Mass. Inst. Tech., 1936; m. Rosemary Horstmann, Sept. 14, 1940; children—Susan Emilyn, Mary Josephine, John III With Pa. R.R., 1936-38; with D. & R.G.W. R.R. Co., 1938—, chief engr., 1951-62, v.p. operations, 1962-69, v.p. tech. services, 1969—, pres., dir. Denver Union Terminal Ry. Co., Rio Grande Land Co.; v.p. Salt Lake City Union Depot Co.; dir. Pueblo Union Depot Co. Mem. Am. Ry. Engring. Assn., Colo. Soc. Engrs., Am. Mgmt. Assn., Am. Assn. R.R. Supts., Nat. Rifle Assn., Western Ry. Club, Denver, Salt Lake City, Pueblo chambers commerce, Mass. Inst. Tech. Alumni Assn. (hon. sec.), Pi Tau Pi Sigma. Republican. Conglist. Mason (Shriner). Home: 1263 S Jackson St Denver CO 80210 Office: P O Box 5482 Denver CO 80217

AYERS, ARCHIE RAYMOND, govt. ofcl.; b. Anderson, S.C., Oct. 5, 1910; s. Claude M. and Callie Lola (Moss) A.; B.S., U. of S.C., 1935; A.M., Duke U., 1937; Ph.D., George Peabody Coll. for Tchrs., 1944; m. Valla Evelyn Young, June 27, 1939; children—William Claude, Evelyn Valla. Scholarship asst., U. of S.C., 1933-35; mathematics tchr., football coach, Belton (S.C.) High Sch., 1935-36; scholarship asst., Duke U., 1936-37; adminstrv. asst. and dir. audio-visual edn., New Hanover Schs., Wilmington, N.C., 1937-41; head physics, George Peabody Coll. for Tchrs., 1941-46; asso. prof. edn. and prin. lab. sch., Eastern Ill. State Coll., Charleston, 1946-49; academic dean, Lycoming Coll., Williamsport, Pa., 1949-50; dean of univ., Kan. Wesleyan U., Salina, 1950-51; pres. Detroit Inst. Tech., 1951-56; prof. adminstrn. and ednl. services Mich. State U., 1956-58; specialist for coll. and univ. orgn. U.S. Office of Edn., Washington, 1958-66, chief faculty devel. br., 1966- -. Dir. Evaluative and Planning Survey, Howard Coll., 1960. Mem. N.E.A., Am. Phys. Soc., Am. Assn. Sch. Adminstrs., A.I.M. (life mem. President's Council), A.A.A.S., Assn. Student Tchrs., Blue Key, Kappa Pi Kappa, Pi Mu Epsilon, Sigma Pi Sigma, Kappa Delta Pi. Methodist. Author: (with others) An Evaluation and Planning Survey of Oklahoma Baptist University, 1959, Survey of Higher Education in the Tidewater Area of Virginia, 1959, Survey of Higher Education in South Dakota, 1960, Survey of Higher Education in Hawaii, 1962, Organization and Administration of Institutions of Higher Education, Internal Structure, 1962; co-author: Survey of Higher Education in Connecticut, 1964, Case Studies in Liberal Arts Colleges, Academic Administration, 1964, Student Services Administration in Higher Education, 1966. Contbr. articles to Ency. Modern Edn., 1943. Home: P O Box 229 McLean VA 22101 Office: Office of Edn Dept Health Edn and Welfare Washington DC 20203

AYERS, JAMES R., Jr., lawyer; b. Petersburg, Va., 1907; LL.B., U. Va., 1930; also ad. Hampden Sydney Coll.; m. Barbara Willcox; 1 son, James Riley IV. Gen. counsel, sec. So. States Coop., Inc. Mem. Am., Va., Richmond bar assns. Episcopalian (vestryman, past warden, trustee ch. schs. Va. diocese). Home: Rose Hill Route 2 Montpelier VA 23192 Office: So States Bldg Richmond VA 23219*

AYERS, JOHN CARR, educator, oceanographer; b. Marcellus, Mich., Oct. 4, 1912; s. Harve and Mabel (Finch) A.; A.B., Kalamazoo Coll., 1934; M.S., Kan. State Coll., 1936; Ph.D., Duke, 1939; m. Catherine Elizabeth Goffin, June 20, 1938; children—Jane (Mrs. William J. Walsh), Mary (Mrs. James R. Stockard), Patricia Ann, Helen Elizabeth. Asst. prof. U. S.C., 1939-44; asso. biology Woods Hole (Mass.) Oceanographic Instn., 1944-49; asso. prof. Cornell U., 1949-56; prof. oceanography U. Mich., 1956—. Mem. Am. Soc. Limnology and Oceanography (pres. 1962), Sigma Xi. Author articles in field. Home: 8120 Huron St Dexter MI 48130 Office: North Univ Bldg Univ Mich Ann Arbor MI 48104

AYERS, MAURICE THURBER, educator; b. Irvington, N.J., Nov. 21, 1908; s. Maurice Cecil and Harriett (Thurber) A.; B.S., Mass. Inst. Tech., 1931; M.S., Columbia, 1942; m. Cathryn Marie Allers, May 4, 1956; children—Ralph E. (by prev. marriage), E. Stuart Ling (foster son), Douglas F. Math. tchr. Milburn (N.J.) High Sch., 1933-36; instr. machine design dept. Cooper Union, N.Y.C., 1936-42; prof. Rutgers U., 1942—, prof. gen. engring., chmn. dept. gen. engring., asso. dean coll. engring., 1959-60, asst. to pres. of the univ., 1961—. Served from lt. (j.g.) to lt. comdr., USNR, 1944-46. Mem. Am. Soc. Engring. Edn. (chmn. Middle Atlantic sect. 1948), Am. Soc. C.E., Tau Beta Pi. Rotarian. Home: 241 Fairview Av Long Valley NJ 07853 Office: Rutgers University New Brunswick NJ 08903

AYERS, THOMAS G., utility exec.; b. Detroit, Feb. 16, 1915; s. Jule C. and Camilla (Chalmers) A.; A.B., U. Mich. 1937; LL.D., Elmhusrt Coll., 1966; m. Mary Andrew, Nov. 25, 1938; children—Catherine Mary (Mrs. James W. Allen), Thomas G., William Charles, Richard James, John Stevens. With Pub. Service Co. No. Ill., 1938-52, mgr. indsl. relations, 1948-52; asst. v.p. Commonwealth Edison Co., Chgo., 1952, v.p., 1953-62, exec. v.p., 1962-64, pres. 1964—, also dir.; dir. 1st Nat. Bank Chgo., Zenith Radio Corp., Sears, Roebuck & Co., G.D. Searle & Co. Mem. Electric Research Council, 1970. Chmn. Ill. Com. Selection for Rhodes Scholarships, 1967-70. Met. Crusade of Mercy, 1969, Leadership Council for Met. Open Communities. Bd. dirs. Community Fund Chgo., Central DuPage Hosp.; trustee Presbyn.-St. Luke's Hosp., Northwestern U. Mem. Chgo. Assn. Commerce and Industry (dir., past pres.), Electric Heating Assn. (dir.). Clubs: Chicago, Economic, Mid-Day, Commercial, Commonwealth (Chgo.); Glen Oak Country. Home: 199 Montclair Av Glen Ellyn IL 60137 Office: One 1st Nat Plaza PO Box 767 Chicago IL 60690

AYLER, DON, musician; b. Cleve., Oct. 5, 1942; studied music Miller Acad. Music, Cleve., Cleve. Inst. Music. Trumpet player since age 7; mem. Albert Ayler Quintet, 1964—; performed in Europe, 1963; guest performer of John Coltrane at Philharmonic Hall concert, N.Y.C., 1966. Recording: Spiritual Unity. Address: 2978 Ripley Rd Cleveland OH 44120*

AYLOR, JOHN HAMILTON, lawyer; b. Brightwood, Va., Aug. 30, 1917; s. Roy Cleveland and Nellie Y. (Weaver) A.; LL.B., U. Va., 1940; m. Jean Andrea Miller, Jan. 17, 1948; children—Cheryl Jean, Joan Hamilton, John Roy Brainard. Admitted to Va. bar, 1940; mem. firm Phillips, Kendrick, Gearheart & Aylor, Arlington and Fairfax, Va., 1941—, partner, 1953—. Served with AUS, 1941-46, 50-51. Mem. Am., Fairfax County (pres. 1961-62) bar assns., Va. State Bar, No. Va. Builders Assn. (past dir., sec.), Sigma Nu Phi. Lion (past v.p. Fairfax), Rotarian (bd. dirs. Fairfax 1967—, v.p. 1968, pres. 1969-70). Club: Fairfax Country (bd. dirs. 1968—, sec. 1969, v.p. 1970). Home: 3329 Pensa Dr Falls Church VA 22041 Office: 4017 Chain Bridge Rd Fairfax VA 22030

AYLWARD, RONALD LEE, lawyer; b. St. Louis, Mo., May 30, 1930; s. John Thomas and Edna (Ketcherside) A.; A.B., Wash. U., 1952, J.D., 1954; student U. Va., 1955; m. Margaret Cecilia Hellweg, Aug. 10, 1963; children—Susan Marie, Stephen Ronald, Carolyn Ann. Admitted to Mo. bar, 1954; asso. firm Henghan, Roberts & Cole, St. Louis, 1958-59; asst. counsel Olin Corp., East Alton, Ill., 1960-64; asst. gen. counsel INTERCO, Inc., St. Louis, Mo., 1964-66, asso. gen. counsel, mgr. law dept., 1966-69, asst. sec., 1966—, gen. counsel, 1969—, mem. operating bd., 1970—. Served with AUS, 1955-58. Mem. Am., Mo. bar assns., St. Louis (chmn. bus. law 1970-72, corp. law 1964-67, spl. projects 1964-65, Moot Court Coms. 1966-67) bar assns., Am. Footwear Mfrs. Assn. (nat. affairs vice-chmn. 1970, chmn. 1971), Nat. Assn. Mfrs. (mem. taxation com. 1970—), St. Louis C. of C. (mem. legislation and tax com. 1966—, vice chmn. 1970-71), Am. Soc. Corp. Secs., Delta Theta Phi. Clubs: Elks, Missouri Athletic Club. Home: 5 Williamsburg Rd Creve Coeur MO 63141 Office: 1509 Washington Av St Louis MO 63166

AYMAR, GORDON CHRISTIAN, portrait painter; b. East Orange, N.J., July 24, 1893; s. William Howard and Maud (Christian) A.; A.B., Yale, 1914; postgrad. Sch. Mus. Fine Arts, Boston, 1917; m. Margaretta Kneass White, Jan. 24, 1920 (dec.); children—Carol Penrhyn (Mrs. James Isbell Armstrong), Barbara (Mrs. Harry Woodward Earle, Jr.), Gordon Christian (dec.). Art dir. J. Walter Thompson, N.Y.C., 1920-30; art dir., v.p. Compton Advt. Agy., N.Y.C., 1930-45; cons. designer, portrait work, 1945-59; exhibited Darien Library, Darien Art Festival, Rowayton (Conn.) Art Center, Conn. Classic Arts, Nat. Acad., Christ Ch., Redding, Conn., Bridgeport (Conn.) Mus. Art, Sci. and Industry, Am. Watercolor Soc., Canton (O.) Art Inst., Boise (Ida.) Art Inst., Charles and Emma Frye Mus., Seattle, Abilene (Tex.) Fine Arts Mus., Orlando (Fla.) Art Assn., Columbia (S.C.) Mus. Art, Davenport (Ia.) Municipal Art Gallery, Moore Coll. of Art, Phila., Arnot Art Gallery, Elmira, N.Y., Baldwin-Wallace Coll., Berea, O., Brooks Meml. Art Gallery, Memphis, Tenn., Phoenix Art Mus., Century Assn., Yale Club of N.Y.C., Nat. Arts Club, Dayton Art Inst., Montreal (Can.) Mus. Art, Royal Soc. Painters in Water Colour, London, Eng., Washington (Conn.) Art Assn., Kent (Conn.) Art Assn.; portraits in permanent collections of Am. Cyanamid Co., N.Y., Madison Av. Presbyn. Ch., N.Y., Nat. Council Chs., N.Y. Phillips Acad., Andover, Mass., South Kent (Conn.) Sch., Temple of Justice, Olympia, Wash., Yale U. Art Gallery, New Haven, Neurol. Inst., N.Y.C., Middlebury (Vt.) Coll., photographs in perm. study coll. Mus. of Modern Art N.Y.; art dir. Darien Hist. Soc. Chmn. Park and Recreation Com., rep. town meetings, Darien, Conn., 1952-58. Served as lt. (j.g.) USNR, World War I. Recipient award Nat. Soc. Art Dirs., 1951. Mem. N.Y. Art Dirs. Club (adv. bd., past pres.), Nat. Soc. Art Dirs. (charter pres., bd.), Am. Watercolor Soc. (bd. dirs. 1960-61, 1st v.p. 1961-62). Author: An Introduction to Advertising Illustration, 1930; Bird Flight, 1934; Start 'Em Sailing, 1941; Treasury of Sea Stories, 1944; (with Gordon C. Aymar, Jr.) Second Book on Sailing, 1960; (with Margaretta W. Aymar) Michael Sails the Mud Hen, 1960; Yacht Racing Rules and Tactics, 6th edit., 1970; The Art of Portrait Painting, 1967. Address: R F D 1 Flat Rock Rd South Kent CT 06785

AYME, MARCEL, author; b. Joigny, Burgundy, France, Mar. 29, 1902; s. Joseph and Emma (Monamy) A.; ed. U. Paris; m. Marie-Antoinette Arnaud, Apr. 6, 1932. Author: (novels) Brulebois, 1926, La table aux créves, 1929, La jument verte, 1933 (The Green Mare 1938), The Hollow Field, 1933, Travelingue, 1941, Uranus, 1948, The Transient Hour, 1948, The Barkeep of Blemont, 1950, The Miraculous Barber, 1951, The Second Face, 1953, The Secret Stream, 1954, Le passe-muraille, 1959, Conscience of Love, 1962; (short stories) The Proverb, and other Stories, 1961, Across Paris and Other Stories, 1963; (plays) Vogue la Galerie, 1944, Lucienne et le Bondrer, 1947, Clerambard, 1950 (transl. Count of Clerambard 1955), Tete des Autres, 1952, Les oiseaux de la lune, 1955 (transl. Moonbirds 1959), Louisiaue, 1962, Les Maxitules, 1962, Quatre Verites, 1956, La Mouche bleue, 1957, Patron, 1960, Consommation, 1963, le Ninantore, 1963, la Convention, 1963, Belzevoir, 1966; (films) Les Sorcieres de Salem (adaptation of Arthur Miller's The Crucible), Papa, Mama, the Maid and I, 1956, Love and the Frenchwomen, 1961. Address: 26 rue Novins Paris 18e France*

AYMOND, ALPHONSE HENRY, pub. utilities ofcl., lawyer; b. St. Louis, Sept. 27, 1914; s. Alphonse H. and Anne (Putz) A.; A.B., Northwestern U., 1936; J.D., U. Mich., 1939; LL.D., Olivet Coll., 1970; m. Elizabeth Shierson, Sept. 30, 1939; children—Charles H., Robert D., William G. Admitted to Ill. bar, 1939, Mich. bar, 1947; with firm Miller, Gorham, Wescott & Adams, Chgo., 1939-44; with Commonwealth & So. Corp., N.Y.C., 1946-47; atty. Consumers Power Co., Jackson, Mich., 1947- 51, gen. atty., 1951-55, v.p., gen. counsel, 1955-57, exec. v.p., dir. 1957-60, chmn. bd., chief exec. officer, 1960—; pres., dir. Mich. Gas Storage Co., 1960—; dir. City Bank & Trust Co., Jackson, Nat. Bank Detroit, Am. Seating Co., Kellogg Co.; trustee Northwestern Mut. Life Ins. Co., Northwestern Mut. Life Mortgage & Realty Investors. Former mem. Jackson Planning Commn.; regional exec. com. Boy Scouts Am. Chmn. Mich. Found. for Arts; trustee W.K. Kellogg Found., Citizens Research Council, Mich. Colls. Found., Jackson Found. Served to lt. (j.g.), Supply Corps, USNR, 1944-46. Mem. Am. Bar Assn., Edison Electric Inst. (dir., past pres.), Assn. Edison Illuminating Cos. (exec. com.), Am. Gas Assn. (dir.), Order of Coif. Club: Economic (dir.) (Detroit). Episcopalian (trustee Diocese Mich.). Home: 1912 4th St Jackson MI 49203 Office: 212 W Michigan Av Jackson MI 49201

AYNESWORTH, HORACE DANIEL, air force officer; b. Childress, Tex., Nov. 6, 1915; s. Joseph Hickman and Mary (Timmons) A.; student W. Tex. State Coll., 1933-34, U. Tex., 1934-36, Armed Forces Staff Coll., 1947-48, Air War Coll., also Air U., 1952-53; m. Marian DuLongpre Heckscher, June 22, 1940; children—Daniel Valantine, Peter Timmons. Commd. 2d lt. USAAF, 1937, advanced through grades to grig. gen., 1959; comdr. Travis AFb, 1945-47; Dept. Defense staff, 1948-52; formerly inspector gen. Alaskan Air Command, comdr. Elmendorf AFB, Alaska, then dep. comdr. Field Command Defense Atomic Support Agy., Washington, now dep. dir.; formely comdr. 837th Air div., comdr. Tactical Air Reconnaissance Center, dep. dir. operations Hdqrs. USAF, Washington. Decorated Silver Star, Legion of Merit, D.F.C., Air medal; Croix de Guerre (France). Mem. Phi Kappa Psi. Home: 5721 Robinwood Lane Falls Church VA 22041 Office:Hdqrs USAF Washington DC .

AYOUB, RAYMOND GEORGE DIMITRI, mathematician, educator; b. Sherbrooke, Que., Can., Jan. 2, 1923; s. George F. and Nazeera (Rizk) A.; came to U.S., 1949, naturalized, 1956; B.S., McGill U. (Can.), 1943; M.S., U. Pa., 1946; Ph.D., U. Ill., 1950; m. Christine Sykes Williams, July 1, 1950; children—Cynthia, Daphne. Prof. math. Canadian Meteorol. Service, Goose Bay, Labrador, 1943-45; Benjamin Peirce instr. Harvard, Cambridge, Mass., 1950-52; asst. prof. Pa. State U., University Park, 1952-55, asso. prof., 1955-60, prof., 1955-60, prof. math., 1960—, also chmn. dept., 1968—; vis. research scholar Oxford U. (Eng.), 1962; vis. prof. U. Frankfurt (Germany), 1966- 67. Mem. Am. Math. Soc., Math. Assn. Am., Canadian Math. Congress, Société Mathématique de France, London Math. Soc., Deutsche Mathematik Verein. Author: An Introduction to the Analytic Theory of Numbers, 1964. Research in analytic, algebraic theory of numbers. Home: 120 Ridge Av NE State College PA 16801 Office: McAllister Bldg Pennsylvania State University University Park PA 16802

AYRE, ROBERT STEVENSON, educator; b. Monticello, Ill., Mar. 11, 1912; s. Joseph William and Laura (Stevenson) A.; A.B., Stanford, 1934, C.E., 1936, Ph.D., 1942; m. Barbara W. Vaughan, June 15, 1940; children—Margaret, Mary, Richard. Mech. engr. Naval Ordnance Lab., Washington, 1942-45; research engr. Standard Oil Co. (Ind.), Chgo., 1945-46; asso. prof. mech. engring. Stanford, 1946-52; asso. prof. to prof. civil engring., chmn. dept., Johns Hopkins, 1952-58; prof. civil engring., chmn. dept. Robert Coll. Istanbul, Turkey, 1958- 59, Yale, 1959-65; prof. civil engring., chmn. dept. U. Colo., 1965—. Mem. Am. Soc. C.E., Am. Soc. M.E. Author: (with Jacobsen) Engineering Vibrations, 1958. Research vibrations, structures, exptl. mechanics. Home: 1645 Sunset Blvd Boulder CO 80302.

AYRES, CHARLES BURGESS, headmaster; b. Wallingford, Conn., Feb. 2, 1920; s. Russell Romeyn and Jean (Burgess) A.; grad. cum laude, Choate Sch., 1938; S.B., Harvard, 1942, A.M., 1950; m. Katharine George, Dec. 3, 1942; children—Burgess Nelson, Robert George, Susan and Margo (twins). Instr. history Choate Sch., Wallingford, 1946-56, head Lower Forms, 1956-62, dean, 1962-64; headmaster Shattuck Sch., Faribault, Minn., 1964-69, The Gunnery, Washington, Conn., 1969—. Reader, Am. history Ednl. Testing Service, Princeton, N.J.; developed merit exams. Police Dept., Wallingford; co-leader student groups to USSR, summers 1959, 62, 64. Mem. Ct. of Burgesses, Borough of Wallingford, 1949-53, mem. Town Council, 1962-64. Bd. dirs. YMCA, Wallingford; bd. dirs. St. Andrew's Camp, Wallingford, 1948-55, Conn. Assn. Ind. Schs., 1971—. Served to lt. USNR, 1942-46. Mem. Headmasters Assn. Episcopalian. Clubs: Litchfield County (Conn.) University; Fox, Varsity (Harvard). Home: The Gunnery Washington CT 06793

AYRES, GILBERT HAVEN, educator; b. Upland, Ind., Aug. 29, 1904; s. Burt Wilmot and Mary (Huggins) A.; A.B., Taylor U., 1925; Ph.D., U. Wis., 1930; m. Helen Jane Shoemaker, Aug. 17, 1926 (dec.); children—Margaret Jane (Mrs. Robert G. Petersen), Alice Barbara (Mrs. Donald L. Baeder); m. 2d, Katherine Holly Mills, Dec. 22, 1960. Instr. chemistry Taylor U., 1925-27, U. Wis., 1930-31; asst. prof. to asso. prof. chemistry Smith Coll., 1931-47; from asso. prof. to prof. chemistry U. Tex., Austin, 1947—; cons. analytical chemistry. Served with USNR, 1943-46. Recipient analyst of the year award Dallas Soc.

Analytical Chemists, 1970. Fellow A.A.A.S.; mem. Am. Chem. Soc., Sigma Xi, Alpha Chi Sigma, Phi Lambda Upsilon. Author: Quantitative Chemical Analysis, 2d edit, 1968. Contbr. articles profl. jours. Home: 3307 Perry Lane Austin TX 78731

AYRES, JOHN FEARHAKE, newspaper editor; b. Houston, Tex., Sept. 27, 1900; s. Warren E. and Susan (Fearhake) A.; LL.B., U. of Texas, 1923; m. Nell Reese, May 13, 1945. Teacher of English, Galveston High Sch., 1923-24; editor Cleburne (Tex.) Times, 1924-26; special writer Port Arthur (Tex.) News, 1926-37, became editor, 1937, exec. editor 1967. Admitted to Tex. bar, but has never practiced. Mem. Sigma Nu. Democrat. Mem. Disciples of Christ Ch. Mason. Club: Rotary. Home: 301 Emory Lane Port Arthur TX 77641 Office: Port Arthur News Box 789 Port Arthur TX 77641

AYRES, JOHN SAMUEL, chem. engr.; b. Kansas City, Mo., Oct. 12, 1914; s. William I. and Jessie C. (Heinlein) A.; B.S., U. Mo., 1935; m. Dorothy Rule Fritts, Jan. 19, 1939. With Cook Paint & Varnish Co., 1936—, successively chemist Kansas City, Mo., mgr. research Detroit div., v.p. indsl. sales, Kansas City, 1936-60, pres., 1960—, also dir.; dir. North Kansas City State Bank, Marley Co., Gas Service Co., Asso. Industries Mo. Bd. govs. Am. Royal Assn.; exec. com. Midwest Research Inst.; trustee U. Kansas City, Midwest Research Inst., Rehab. Inst. Recipient engring. honor award U. Mo., 1962, Faculty-Alumni award U. Mo., 1970. Mem. Greater Kansas City C. of C. (past pres.), Nat. Paint Varnish and Lacquer Assn. (treas.), Am. Chem. Soc. (Citizen Chemist award 1968), Detroit Soc. Paint Tech., Engring. Soc. Detroit, Kansas City Paint Varnish and Lacquer Assn. Clubs: Kansas City River, Mission Hills Country; Detroit Athletic, Orchard Lake Country (Detroit). Home: 1238 W 63d Terrace Kansas City MO 64113 Office: P O Box 389 Kansas City MO 64141

AYRES LYMAN S merchant; b. Indpls., July 5, 1908; s. Frederic Murray and Alma (Hoegh) A.; Ph.B., Yale, 1930; LL.D., Franklin (Ind.) Coll., 1962; m. Isabel Ferguson,Sept. 22, 1934; 1 dau., Elise. With L.S. Ayres & Co., Indpls., dept. store, 1930-, mdse. mgr., 1938-42, v.p., 1940-54, pres. 1954-62, chmn. bd., 1962—, alsodir.; dir. Mchts. Nat. Bank Indpls., Indiana Bell Telephone Co., Indpls. Water Co., John Bressmer Co., Springfield, Ill., Ayr-Way Stores, Indpls. Bd. dirs. Ind. Library and Hist. Soc., Indpls. United Fund; trustee Hanover (Ind.) Coll., Crown Hill Cemetery, YMCA, Indpls. Served as lt. USNR, 1942-44. Episcopalian. Home: 5656 Sunset Lane Indianapolis IN 46208 Office: 1 West Washington St Indianapolis IN 46204

AYRES, ROBERT MOSS, Jr., investment banker; b. San Antonio, Sept. 1, 1926; s. Robert Moss and Florence (Collett) A.; student Tex. Mil. Inst., 1944; B.A., U. of South, 1949; postgrad. Oxford U. (Eng.), 1949; M.B.A., U. Pa., 1952; m. Patricia Ann Shield, Sept. 10, 1955; children—Robert Atlee, Vera Patricia. With Kidder, Peabody & Co., Phila., N.Y.C., 1950-52; with Dittmar & Co., San Antonio, 1952-53; pres., dir. Russ & Co., Inc., San Antonio, 1953—; dir. River Properties, Inc., Key Allegro Devel. Co., Howell Corp., Main Savs. Assn., Nat. Edn. Systems Corp., Air S.W. Co. Allied mem. N.Y. Stock Exchange, Am. Stock Exchange. Past pres. Asso. Alumni U. of South; past pres. bd. dirs. Bexar County chpt. A.R.C.; past pres. bd. trustees Tex. Mil. Inst., trustee, chmn. bd. regents U. of South. Served with USNR, 1944-46. Mem. San Antonio Soc. Financial Analysts (past pres.), Order of Alamo, Tex. Cavaliers, Argyle, Bankers Club Am. (N.Y.C.), Investment Bankers Assn. Am. (chmn. Tex. dist.; bd. govs.), Sigma Alpha Epsilon. Episcopalian (mem. exec. bd. diocese W. Tex.; vestryman). Clubs: San Antonio German, San Antonio Country, San Antonio, San Antonio Petroleum. Home: 100 Alameda Circle San Antonio TX 78212 Office: Alamo Nat Bldg San Antonio TX 78205

AYRES, SAMUEL, III, physician; b. Kansas City, Mo., May 1, 1919; s. Samuel and Helen (Lowry) A.; A.B., Stanford, 1940, M.D., 1944; m. Norma Jean Pritchard, Jan. 1957; 1 son by previous marriage, Richard Lowry. Intern Los Angeles Gen. Hosp., 1943; resident dermatology and syphilology Cleve. City Hosp., 1944-45; pvt. practice dermatologic and cosmetic surgery (now limited to hair transplantation and dermobrasion), 1947—; mem. sr. attending staff dermatology U. So. Cal.-Los Angeles County Med. Center, 1947—, chmn., 1962-63, dir. Surg. Skin Planing (dermobrasion) Clinic, 1955—; attending staff Hosp. Good Samaritan, Los Angeles; mem. faculty U. So. Cal. Med. Sch., 1947—, asso. clin. prof. dermatology, 1961—. Served to capt., M.C., AUS, 1945-47. Diplomate Am. Bd. Dermatology. Mem. Am., Cal. (chmn. sect. dermatology 1967-68), Los Angeles County (councillor 1956- 58) med. assns., Pacific Dermatol. Assn., Los Angeles Dermatol. Soc. (pres. 1963-64), Am. Acad. Dermatology (dir. cutaneous surgery course 1961-65), Am. Dermatol. Assn., Soc. Investigative Dermatology, Hollywood Acad. Medicine, Med. Symposium Soc. Los Angeles (pres. 1965), Los Angeles Acad. Medicine, N. Am. Clin. Dermatol. Soc., Noah Worchester Dermatol. Soc., Med. Research Assn. Cal., Beverly Hills Acad. Medicine, Am. Acad. Facial and Plastic and Reconstructive Surgery, Los Angeles Art Assn., Los Angeles County, Los Angeles County Mus. Natural History, Alpha Kappa Kappa. Author numerous articles in field. Home: 2251 Fern Dell Pl Los Angeles CA 90028 Office: 405 N Bedford Dr Beverly Hills CA 90210

AYRES, WILLIAM HANES, former congressman; b. Eagle Rock, Va., Feb. 5, 1916; s. William H. and Loatie Emma (Welch) A.; A.B., Western Reserve U., 1936; m. Mary Helen Coventry, Apr. 1, 1937; children—Virginia, Frank, Judith. Salesman, heating equipment, Akron, 1936-44; pres. William H. Ayres, Inc., Akron, O., 1946—. Mem. 82d to 91st Congresses, 14th Ohio Dist. Served as private U.S. Army, 1945-46. Mem. Am. Legion, Amvets. Republican. Methodist. Eagle, Moose. Home: 5709 Kirkwood Dr Washington DC 20016 Office: 1400 Wilson Blvd Arlington VA

AYRES, WILLIAM LEAKE, educator; b. Gatesville, Tex., June 26, 1905; s. Matthias Leake and Myrtie (Buckley) A.; A.B., Southwestern U., 1923; postgrad. U. Tex., 1923-25, U. Vienna, 1928-29; Ph. D., U. Pa., 1927; m. Juliette Pagenstecher, Sept. 3, 1926; children—Juliette (Mrs. D. G. Spears), Dorothy (Mrs. R. G. Rutishauser), William Leake III. Nat. Research fellow, 1927-29; asst. prof. math. U. Mich., 1929-33, asso. prof., 1933-41; prof. math. Purdue U. 1941-62, head dept. math., 1941-48, asst. dean Grad. Sch. 1943-47, acting dean Sch. Sci., Edn. and Humanities, 1946-47, dean, 1947-62; v.p., provost So. Meth. U., Dallas, 1962-66, prof. math., 1962-70, Findlay prof. math., 1970—. Vis. prof. U. Va., summer 1938, U. Cal. at Los Angeles, summer 1939. Mem. Ind. Commn. on Pub. Employee Retirement, 1953-54. Served as operations analyst USAAF, 1944-45. Recipient Gold Honor medal Am. Rose Soc., 1969. Mem. Am. Rose Soc. (pres. 1950-51), Am. Math. Soc. (asso. sec. 1938-46), Math. Assn. Am. (v.p. 1946-47), Phi Delta Theta. Rotarian. Author: (with C.G. Fry and H. F. S. Jonah) General College Mathematics, 1952, 60, 70. Editor: (with R. L. Wilder) Lectures in Topology, 1941. Home: 5440 Del Roy Dr Dallas TX 75229

AZAR, LARRY, educator; b. Boston, Aug. 18, 1923; s. Samuel and Sadie (Moses) A.; B.Sc., Boston Coll., 1949, M.A., 1950; Ph.D., U. Toronto, 1953; m. Bedea Raffoul, June 22, 1947; children—Elizabeth, Thomas, Janet, George, Robert. Mem. faculty in philosophy Fordham U., 1953-62, chmn.-dept., 1960-62; mem. faculty St. John's U., Jamaica, N.Y., 1962-66; prof. philosophy, chmn. dept. Iona Coll., New Rochelle, N.Y., 1966—. Served with inf., AUS, World War II; ETO. Mem. N.Y. Acad. Scis., A.A.A.S., Am. Metaphys. Soc., Am. Philos. Assn., Am. Cath. Philos. Assn. Author: Introduction to Philosophy Quiz Book, 1965; (with F.F. Centore) Philosophy Today, 1967. Contbr. articles profl. jours. Home: 119-58 27th Av Flushing NY 11354 Office: Iona Coll New Rochelle NY 10806

AZAR, RAYMOND GEORGE, mfr.; b. Cleve., Mar. 29, 1924; s. Sam G. and Lydia (Fetlha) A.; B.S., George Pepperdine Coll., 1949; m. Eleanor Swezea, Oct. 6, 1945; children—Michelle, Sidneye, Robert. Chief cost accountant Garrett Corp., Los Angeles, 1953-56, chief accountant, 1956-59; controller Garrett Corp., 1959-61, adminstrv. asst. to pres., 1961-63, v.p. contracts-pricing, license agreements, 1963-69; chmn., chief exec. officer Dunham-Bush, Inc., West Hartford, Conn., 1969—; dir. Garrett Corp., Garrett Micro-Circuits Corp., Aero Hydrolics, Normalair-Garrett, Ltd. (Eng.); chmn., chief exec. officer Aerial Transit Systems, Inc. Served with USAAF, 1942-45; PTO. Decorated Air Medal. Mem. Am. Mgmt. Assn., Nat. Assn. Accountants. Home: 60 Elizabeth St Hartford CT 06104 Office: 175 South St West Hartford CT 06110

AZAROFF, LEONID VLADIMIROVITCH, educator; b. Moscow, Russia, June 19, 1926; s. Vladimir Ivanovitch and Maria Yulievna (Odlen) A.; came to U.S., 1939, naturalized, 1945; B.S. cum laude, Tufts Coll., 1948; Ph.D., Mass. Inst. Tech., 1954; m. Carmen Wade, Mar. 9, 1946 (div. July 1968). Research physicist Armour Research Found., Chgo., 1953-54, sr. scientist, 1954-57; asso. prof. metall. engring. Ill. Inst. Tech., 1957-61, prof., 1961-62; prof. physics, dir. Inst. Material Sci., U. Conn., 1966—; guest physicist Brookhaven Nat. Lab., 1961,62,64; cons. Owens-Ill., Phillips Electronics, Hilger-Watts, Inc. U.S. del. Internat. Union Crystallographers, teaching commn., 1963-69. Served with AUS, 1944-46. Fellow Am. Phys. Soc. (cons. editor), Mineral. Soc. Am.; mem. A.A.A.S., Am. Crystallographic Assn., Am. Inst. Mining Engrs., Sigma Xi, Phi Kappa Phi, Sigma Pi Sigma. Author 5 books, including Elements of X-Ray Crystallography, 1968; also articles. Home: PO Box 103 Storrs CT 06268

AZIZ, PHILIP JOHN ANDREW FERRIS, artist; b. St. Thomas, Ont., Can., Apr. 15, 1923; s. Charles and Cecelia (Fakhoury) A.; B.F.A., Yale, 1947, M.F.A., 1949; student Harvard, 1949. Lectr. art U. Western Ont., 1950-55; one man exhbns. include Montreal Mus. Fine Arts, 1952, Eatons Fine Art Galleries, Toronto, 1950, 57, U. Waterloo, 1967, Gallery Modern Art, N.Y.C., 1968,69, Meredith Long Houston Gallery, 1970, Internat. Freedoms Festival, Detroit, 1971, Grosse Pointe (Mich.) War Meml. Centre, 1971; numerous group shows, U.S., Can. and Europe; rep. permanent collections Montreal Mus. Fine Arts, Detroit Art Inst., Vatican Mus., Met. Opera, also pvt. collections. Trustee Nat. Pollution Found. Served with RCAF, 1942-45. Hon. adm. Tex. Navy, 1970. Fellow Internat. Inst. Arts and Letters; mem. Yale Alumni Assn. Can., Phi Alpha. Clubs: Yale (N.Y.C.); University (Toronto). Address: 1180 Western Rd London Ontario Canada

AZNAVOUR, CHARLES, (Varenagh Azanavourian) singer, actor; b. Paris, France, May 22, 1924; s. Micha Azanourian; ed. Ecole centrale de T.S.F., Centre de spectacle, Paris, France; m. Micheline Rigal, 1945; 1 dau., Patricia; m. 2d, Evelyne Plessis; 1 son, Patrick; m. 3d, Ulla Thursel, Jan. 11, 1967. Mem. Jean Daste Co., 1941; with Pierre Roche in Les Facheux, also Arlequin, 1944; song recitals in France, Europe, U.S.; motion picture appearances include La Tete Contre Les Murs, 1959; Tirez sur le pianiste, 1960; Un taxi pur Tobrouk, 1964; Le testament d'Orphee, 1964; Le Diable et les Dix Commandements, 1964; Hasute- Fidelite, 1965; La Metamorphose Des Cloportes, 1965; Paris Au Mois D'Aout; Le Facteur S'en Va-T-En Guerre, 1966; Caroline Cherie, 1967; L'Amour; Les Aventuriers, 1968; composer music for motion pictures includes Soupe au lait, l'Ile du bout du monde, Ces Dames preferent le lambo, Le cercle vicieux, De quoi tu te meles Daniela, Douce Violence, Les Parisiennes; author music for operetta Monsieur Carnaval, 1965; also author, composer, interpreter numerous songs. Co-mgr. Editions Musicales, 1965—. Hon. v.p. Maison de Retraite des Vieux Comediens (retirement home for old actors). Address: 124 rue La Boetic Paris 8e France*

AZPEITIA, ALFONSO GIL, educator, mathematician; b. Madrid, Spain, Feb. 22, 1922; s. Alfonso Gil and Nieves Azpeitia; B.S., U. Madrid, 1941, M.S., 1948, Ph.D. 1952. Came to U.S., 1955, naturalized, 1963. Research asso., vis. prof. math. Brown U., 1955-57, 61; prof. math. U. Mass. at Amherst, 1957-65, U. Mass. at Boston, 1965—; mathematician USN Civil Engr. Lab., Port Hueneme, Cal., 1964, 66, 68; Fulbirght lectr. Colombia, 1969, Peru, 1970. Mem. Am. Math. Soc., Math. Assn. Am., Soc. Indsl. and Applied Mathematics, Operations Research Soc. Am., Am. Assn. U. Profs. Contbr. articles profl. jours. Home: 650 Huntington Av Boston MA 02115

AZPEITIA, MARIO, labor ofcl.; b. Key West, Fla., Nov. 22, 1899; s. Armando H. and Andrea (Esquinaldo) A.; student San Carlos Sch., Key West; m. Rosalia C. Azpeitia, Oct. 30, 1967; children—Mario, Jr., Armando, Evelio, Eloy, Mary. Mem. Cigar Makers Internat. Union, A.F. of L., pres. since 1948. Home: 2703 St John St Tampa FL 33607 Office: 815 15th St Washington DC 20005

AZZINI, JUAN EDUARDO, banker. Second v.p. Banco dela Republica Oriental del Uruguay, Montevideo. Office: Calies Cerrito Zabala Solis and Piedros Montevideo Uruguay*

BAAR, EMIL N., lawyer; b. Vienna, Austria, Sept. 9, 1891; s. Jacob and Fannie (Sonnenschein) B.; A.B., Columbia, 1913, J.D., 1915; D.H.L., Hebrew Union Coll.; m. Amelia A. Wasch, June 19, 1919. Admitted to N.Y. State bar, 1915, mem. firm Baar, Bennett & Fullen, N.Y.C., 1926—; justice state Supreme Ct., 1951. Trustee Met. Savs. Bank, Bklyn.; adv. bd. Mfrs. Trust Co. Hon. chmn. bd. Jewish Hosp., Bklyn.; trustee Bklyn. Inst. Arts and Scis. (hon.), United Hosp. Fund, Inc., Jewish Braille Inst. Am. (pres.), Fedn. Jewish Philanthropies; governing com. Bklyn. Mus., hon. pres. Union Temple; gov. Hebrew Union Coll.-Jewish Inst. Religion, World Union for Progressive Judaism, Ltd. (life mem.). Served with 49th Inf., AUS, World War I. Mem. Union Am. Hebrew Congregations (hon. chmn. bd.), Am., N.Y., Bklyn. Bar assns., Assn. Bar City N.Y., Am. Legion (past county comdr.). Mason (32), Elk. Clubs: Sojourners; Unity (Bklyn.); Bankers (N.Y.C.); Fresh Meadow Country (pres. chmn. bd. 1936-46); Columbia University. Home: 225 E 57th St New York City NY 10022 Office: 1 Battery Park Plaza New York City NY 10004

BAAS, CHARLES WILLIAM, religious orgn. exec.; b. Atlantic City, May 28, 1920; s. George J. and Grace (Hart) B.; B.S., Rutgers U., 1950; M.B.A., N.Y. U., 1954; Litt. D., Wagner Coll., 1971; m. Gertrude Rosenast, June 17, 1944; children—Charles W., Bruce Warren. Cost accountant Alco-Gravure div. Publ. Corp., 1938- 42; plant accountant, gen. accountant Koppers Co., Inc., 1942-45; with S.D. Leidesdorf & Co., C.P.A.'s, 1945-46; asst. to treas., then treas. Am. Bible Soc., 1946—; dir., pres. Astor Place Real Estate Co., Inc. Mem. Luth. Laymen's Movement; treas. United Bible Socs., London, 1960; chmn. Conf. on Gift Annuities; mem. Bd. Am. Missions, Luth. Ch. Am. Mem. Nat. Assn. Accountants, Beta Gamma Sigma. Home: 565 Beech St Haworth NJ 07641 Office: 1865 Broadway New York City NY 10023

BABB, ALBERT LESLIE, educator, cons. engr.; b. Vancouver, B.C., Can., Nov. 7, 1925; s. Clarence Stanley and Mildred (Guttridge) B.; came to U.S.; 1948, naturalized, 1954; B.A.Sc., U. B.C., 1948; M.S., U. Ill., 1949, Ph.D., 1951; student Internat. Sch. Nuclear Sci. and Engring., Argonne Nat. Lab., 1956, 57; m. Lois Marguerite Henderson, Dec. 21, 1948; children—Eugene Matthew, Philip Leslie, Christine Louise. Chem. engr. Nat. Research Council Can., 1948; research engr. Rayonier, Inc., 1951- 52; faculty U. Wash., Seattle, 1952—, chmn. nuclear engring. group, 1957-65, prof. chem. engring., 1960—; dir. nuclear reactor labs., 1962—, prof., chmn. dept. nuclear engring., 1965—; cons. in field, 1952—. Dir. Thermodynamics, Inc., Seattle. Active local Services to Children's Orthopedic Hosp., Seattle Artificial Kidney Center. Recipient citation Wash. Joint Legislative Com. Nuclear Energy, 1968; named Engr. of Year, Wash. State Profl. Engrs. Assn., 1969. Mem. Am. Nuclear Soc. (dir.), Am. Chem. Soc., Am. Inst. Chem. Engrs., Am. Soc. Engring. Edn. (chmn. nuclear engring. div. 1965-66), Am. Nephrology Soc., Am. Soc. Artificial Internal Organs, Sigma Xi, Tau Beta Pi, Pi Mu Epsilon, Alpha Chi Sigma. Presbyn. Club: Sand Point Country (Seattle). Contbr. chpts. to books, profl. jours. Co-developer continous central artificial kidney system for low cost treatment in hosps., also devel. automatic artificial kidney system for overnight unattended hemodialysis of patients in homes, and mass screening techniques for early diagnosis of cystic fibrosis in children. Home: 8218 Crest Dr NE Seattle WA 98115

BABB, HAROLD, educator, psychologist; b. Mosheim, Tenn., Sept. 4, 1926; s. Ray Edward and Mary Louise (Brown) B.; B.A., Wayne State U., 1950; M.A., Ohio State U., 1951, Ph.D., 1953; m. Marjorie Craig Leask, Sept. 27, 1947; children—Patricia Craig, Barbara Lou, David Edward. From asst. to asso. prof., chmn. dept. psychology Coe Coll., Cedar Rapids, Ia., 1953-58; prof., chmn. dept. Hobart and William Smith Colls., Geneva, N.Y., 1958- 63; exec. sec., grants specialist NIH, 1963-64; prof. psychology, chmn. dept. U. Mont., Missoula, 1964-71, State U. N.Y. at Binghamton, 1971— Served with USNR, 1944-46. Mem. Am. Assn. U. Profs., Psychonomic Soc., Am., Midwestern, Rocky Mountain, Mont. psychol. assns., Sigma Xi. Contbr. articles to jours. Home: 2309 Hemlock Lane Vestal NY 13850

BABB, HOWARD SELDEN, educator; b. Portland, Me., May 14, 1924; s. Hugh Webster and Persis (Conant) B.; B.A., Kenyon Coll., 1948; M.A., Harvard, 1949, Ph.D., 1955; m. Corinna Meyer, Feb. 14, 1951; 1 son, Stephen D. Instr., Kenyon Coll., 1951-52; asst. instr., asso. prof. Ohio State U., 1952-65; asso. prof. U. Cal. at Irvine, 1965-67, prof., 1967—, chmn. dept. English, 1969—. Served to lt. (j.g.) USNR, 1943-46. Author: Jane Austen's Novels: The Fabric of Dialogue, 1962; The Novels of William Golding, 1970. Home: 2507 Via Marina Newport Beach CA 92660 Office: Dept English U Cal Irvine CA 92664

BABB, JERVIS JEFFERIS, business cons.; b. State College, Pa., Apr. 28, 1902; s. Maurice Jefferis and Blanche Elsiegood (Vincent) B.; A.B., Haverford Coll., 1921; postgrad. U. Pa., 1921-22; M.B.A., Harvard, 1924; m. Ruth Hutchinson, June 5, 1926; 1 dau., Phyllis Elizabeth (Mrs. Donald Sheldon Perkins). Exec. v.p., dir. S.C. Johnson & Son, Inc., Racine, Wis., 1944-50; pres. Lever Bros. Co., N.Y.C., 1950-55, chmn. bd., 1955-58, now dir.; dir. SuCrest Corp., Universal Foods Corp., Gruen Industries, Inc., Guardian Life Ins. Co., Nepture Meter Co., Am. Can Co.; Bank of N.Y., Bank of N.Y. Co., Inc.; trustee Dry Dock Savs. Bank. Trustee Com. Econ. Devel. Clubs: University, Economic (N.Y.C.); Duxbury (Mass.); Yacht: Kittansett. Home: 110 E 57th St New York City NY 10022 also Duxbury MA 02332 Office: 100 Park Av New York City NY 10017

BABB, STANLEY ERNEST, Jr., educator; b. Galveston, Tex., Sept. 22, 1934; s. Stanley Ernest and Alma Emelia (Buchan) B.; B.S., U. Tex., 1954, M.A., 1955, Ph.D., 1957; m. Mary Rheims Dunn, June 8, 1956; children—Stanley, Harold, Andrew, Michael, Matthew. Mem. faculty U. Okla., 1958—, prof. physics, 1968—. Bd. dirs. U. Okla. Research Inst., 1969—. Postdoctoral fellow U. Ill., 1957-58. Mem. Am. Phys. Soc., No. Nut Growers Assn., Sigma Xi, Sigma Pi Sigma. Author articles high pressure techniques and phenomena. Home: 803 S Berry Rd Norman OK 73069

BABBIDGE, HOMER DANIELS, Jr., univ. pres.; b. West Newton, Mass., May 18, 1925; s. Homer Daniels and Allalie Lavinia (Adams) B.; B.A., Yale, 1945, M.A., 1948, Ph.D., 1953, LL.D., 1969; LL.D., Ithaca Coll., 1960, Trinity Coll., 1969, Am. Internat. Coll., 1970; L.H.D., U. Hartford, 1963, Fairfield U., 1968, Rosary Hill Coll., 1969; D.Pub. Adminstrn., Rollins Coll., 1971; m. Marcia Joan Adkisson, Dec. 22, 1956; children—Amy Allison, Sandra Allalee, Alexander Adams. Dir. financial aids, lectr. edn. Yale, mem. bd. admissions, 1954-57, exec. fellow Pierson Coll., 1949-57, head resident counselor of freshmen, 1948-49, co-founder Am. studies at Yale for fgn. students, 1948; spl. asst. U.S. Commr. Edn., 1955-56; asst. to sec. Dept. Health, Edn. and Welfare, 1957-58, dir. program financial assistance to higher edn., 1958-59, asst. commr., dir. div. higher edn., 1959-61, now cons. to sec.; pres. U. Conn., Storrs, 1962—. Trustee, N.E. Utilities; dir. Security Corp., Hartford Nat. Bank. Trustee Hazen Found., Gannett Found.; chmn. U.S. Adv. Commn. on Internat. Ednl. and Cultural Affairs; mem. Conn. Ednl. TV Corp.; mem. faculty-student-adminstrv. affairs com. Assn. State Univs. and Land-Grant Colls.; mem. council advisers Nat. Scholarship Fund for Negro Students; mem. nat. bd. advisers Nat. Assn. for Retarded Children; mem. Edn. Commn. of States. Asso. fellow Pierson Coll. Named One of 10 Outstanding Young Men of Nation, U.S. Jr. C. of C., 1959, recipient Distinguished Service medal Dept. Health, Edn. and Welfare, 1961, Human relations award Nat. Conf. Christians and Jews, 1970. Mem. Am. Hist. Assn., Am. Studies Assn., Aurelian Soc., Conn. Council on Higher Edn., Marine Hist. Assn. (hon. chmn.), Scroll and Key. Clubs: Elizabethan, Fence (Yale); Hartford Twentieth Century, Monday Evening; Century (N.Y.C.). Author: Student Financial Aid: A Manual for Colleges and Universities, 1960; Noah Webster: On Being American, 1967; (with W.R. Rosenzweig) The Federal Interest in Higher Education, 1962. Home: Oak Hill Rd Storrs CT 06268

BABBITT, MILTON BYRON, educator, composer; b. Phila., May 10, 1916; s. Albert E. and Sarah (Potamkin) B.; A.B., N.Y.U., 1935; M.F.A., Princeton, 1942; D.Mus., Middlebury Coll., N.Y. U., Swarthmore Coll.; m. Sylvia Miller, Dec. 27, 1939; 1 dau., Betty Ann. Music faculty Princeton, 1938—, math. faculty, 1943-45, bicentennial preceptor, 1953-56, William Shubael Conant prof. music, 1966—; faculty Salzburg Seminar in Am. Studies, 1952, Princeton Seminar in Advanced Msuical Studies; dir. Columbia-Princeton Electronic Music Center; faculty Internationale Ferienkurse, Darmstadt, 1964. Recipient Joseph A. Bearns Prize, 1942, N.Y. Music Critic's Citation, 1949, 64; Nat. Inst. Arts and Letters award, 1959; Gold medal Brandeis U., 1970. John Simon Guggenheim fellow, 1960-61. Mem. Internat. Soc. Contemporary Music (pres. 1951-52, del., 1952 Festival), League of Composers, Nat. Inst. Arts and Letters, Am. Inst. Physics. Phi Beta Kappa. Author: The Function of Set Structure in the Twelve Tone System, 1946; also articles in mus. jours. Composer: Music for the Mass, 1940; String Trio, 1941; Three Compositions for Piano, 1947; Composition for Four Instruments, 1948; Composition for Twelve Instruments, 1948; Composition for Viola and Piano, 1950;

Woodwind Quartet, 1953; String Quartet No. 2, 1954: Composition for Synthesizer, 1961; Vision and Prayer, 1961; Ensembles, 1964; Philomel, 1964. Home: 76 Western Way Princeton NJ 08540

BABBS, CHARLES FREDERICK, lawyer; b. Brandon, O., July 25, 1903; s. Carl R. and Maude L. (Conaway) B.; Ph.B., Denison U., 1925; J.D., Ohio State U., 1928; m. Mary E. Bitner, Aug. 17, 1935; 1 son, Charles Frederick. Admitted to Ohio bar, 1928; asso. firm Tracy, Chapman & Welles, Toledo, 1928-35, Welles, Kelsey & Coburn, 1935-37; partner firm Welles, Kelsey, Cobourn & Harrington, 1937-45, Welles, Kelsey, Fuller, Cobourn & Harrington, 1945-49, Fuller, Harrington & Seney, 1949-53; asst. gen. counsel Owens-Ill. Glass Co. (name changed to Owens-Ill. Inc. 1965) Toledo, 1953-68, sec. 1958-69, v.p., 1963-69; counsel Fuller, Seney, Henry and Hodge, 1969—. Served from capt. to maj., Judge Adv. Gen.'s Dept., AUS, 1943-45. Mem. Am., N.Y. State, Ohio, Fed., Inter-Am., Toledo bar assns., Am. Judicature Soc., Judge Advs. Assn., Am. Soc. Corporate Secs., Order of Coif, Delta Theta Phi. Unitarian. Clubs: Toledo, Toledo Country. Home: 3853 Sulphur Spring Rd Toledo OH 43606 Office: Edison Plaza 300 Madison Av Toledo OH 43604

BABCOCK, CHARLES LUTHER, educator; b. Whittier, Cal., May 26, 1924; s. Robert Louis and Margarette (Fuller) B.; A.B., U. Cal., Berkeley, 1948, M.A., 1949, Ph.D., 1953; m. Mary Ayer Taylor, Aug. 6, 1955; children—Robert Sherburne, Jennie Rownd, Jonathan Taylor. Instr. classics Cornell U., 1955-57; asst. prof., asso. prof. classical studies U. Pa., 1957-66, asst. dean to vice dean Coll. Arts and Scis., 1960-64, acting dean, 1964; prof. classics Ohio State U., Columbus, 1966—, chmn. dept., 1966- 68, dean Coll. Humanities, 1968-70; Fulbright scholar in classics, fellow Am. Acad. in Rome, 1953-55, prof.-in-charge Summer Sch., 1966. Served to capt., inf., AUS, 1943-47. Decorated Bronze Star medal with V device. Mem. Am. Philol. Assn. (dir.), Vergilian Soc. (v.p.), Classical Assn. Midwest and South (mem. exec. com.), Classical Soc. of Am. Acad. Rome (past pres.), Phi Beta Kappa, Phi Sigma Kappa. Contbr. articles profl. jours. Home: 973 Lynbrook Rd Worthington OH 43085 Office: 154 N Oval Dr Columbus OH 43210

BABCOCK, CONRAD STANTON, ret. army officer, research inst. exec.; b. Leavenworth, Kan., Jan. 12, 1904; s. Conrad Stanton and Marion (Eells) B.; grad. Groton Sch., 1922; B.S., U.S. Mil. Acad., 1925; student Inst. Far Eastern Studies, U. Mich., 1937-38; m. Jadwiga Noskowiak, Nov. 12, 1928; children—Barbara, Conrad Stanton III. Commd. 2d lt. cav., U.S. Army, 1925, advanced through grades to maj. gen., 1956; mem. U.S. Army Olympic Equestrian Team, 1936; asst. mil. attaché to Ambassador Grew, Japan, 1941-42; mem. joint strategic plans com., Joint Chiefs of Staff, 1944; comdg. officer 7th Cav. Regt., 1947-48; dep. chief staff for Gen. MacArthur, 1949-50; mil. adviser to John Foster Dulles on Japanese Peace Treaty, 1950; adviser to Arthur Dean at Panmunjon, Korea, 1953; asst. div. comdr. 7th U.S. Inf. Div., Korea, 1954; counselor of mission U.S. Mission to UN, 1954-55; asst. div. comdr. 2d U.S. Armored Div., 1955-56, comdg. gen., 1956-57; chief Mil. Assistance Adv. Group, France, 1957-59; comdg. gen. 8th U.S. Army Corps, 1959-60; dir. Mut. Weapons Devel. Team, U.S. Mission to NATO, Paris, France, 1960-61; ret., 1961; dir. operational tech. div. Stanford Research Inst., Menlo Park, Cal., 1961-64, spl. asst. to pres. for mil. affairs, 1964-69, asst. to pres., 1969—. Decorated Legion of Merit, Bronze Star with gold device, Purple Heart, Commendation Ribbon with 2 oak leaf clusters. Mem. Inst. Strategic Studies, Council Fgn. Relations. Club: Knickerbocker. Home: 138 Hacienda Carmel CA 93921 Office: Stanford Research Inst Menlo Park CA 94025

BABCOCK, DAVID EDWARD, dept. store exec.; b. Manitowoc, Wis., Nov. 15, 1914; s. David E. and Eleanor (Pelnar) B.; ed. pub. schs., Kan.; m. Dorothy Viner, Nov. 7, 1940; children—David Edward, Michael, Christine. Enlisted in U.S. Army, 1936, commd., 1942, advanced through grades to maj., 1944; resigned, 1945; asst. personnel dir. Remington Rand, Inc., 1945-47; personnel dir. Gladdings Dept. Store, Providence, 1947-49; store supt. Brown-Dunkin Dept. Store, Tulsa, 1949-51; v.p., personnel dir. Dayton Co., Mpls., 1951-67, dir., 1957-67; sr. exec. v.p. May Dept. Stores Co., St. Louis, 1967—, also dir. Mem. Mpls. Fair Employment Practice Commn., 1954-47, Minn. Retail Fedn., 1962-67. Bd. dirs. Minn. Blue Cross, 1965-67, Minn. Employment Assn., 1964-67. Mem. indsl. relations adv. council U. Minn., 1965-67. Decorated Legion of Merit. Mem. Am. Mgmt. Assn., Am. Retail Fedn. (dir., exec. com., employee relations com.). Kiwanian (dir. Mpls. 1965-67). Home: 35 Overhills Dr St Louis MO 63124 Office: 601 Olive St St Louis MO 63101

BABCOCK, FREDERIC, author, editor lectr.; b. Ord, Neb., Oct 31, 1896; s. Henry Ernest and Jennie (Powell) B.; student U. Neb., 1913-17; m. Helen Reber, Oct. 20, 1935; 1 dau., Susan. Reporter, Neb. State Jour., 1913-17; city editor Wyo. State Tribune, 1917-24; drama editor Denver Post, 1924-26; mem. editorial staff Seattle Times, 1926, Mpls. Journal, 1927; travel editor Chgo. Tribune, 1928-42, editor Mag. of Books, 1942-60. Mem. Pulitzer fiction award jury, 1949-51. Served with U.S. Army, World War I. Mem. Authors League Am., Orlando Art Assn., Thoreau Soc., Alpha Sigma Phi, Sigma Delta Chi. Mem. Soc. of Friends. Mason (32, Shriner). Clubs: University (Winter Park, Fla.); Greater Orlando (Fla.) Press. Author: Blood of the Lamb, 1932; Hang Up the Fiddle, 1954. Contbr. to Sat. Rev., The Nation, Christian Century, N.Y. Times Book Rev., other mags., 1928—. Home: 1231 Via Estrella Winter Park FL 32789

BABCOCK, HORACE WELCOME, astronomer; b. Pasadena, Cal., Sept. 13, 1912; s. Harold Delos and Mary Geddie (Henderson) B.; B.S., Cal. Inst. Tech., 1934; Ph.D., U. Cal., 1938; D.Sc., U. Newcastle-upon-Tyne (England), 1965; m. 1940 (div. 1958): children—Anne Lucille, Bruce Harold; m. 2d, Elizabeth Mae Aubrey, 1958; 1 son, Kenneth L. Asst., Lick Obs., Mt. Hamilton, Cal., 1938-39; instr. Yerkes and McDonald Observatories, Williams Bay, Wis., Ft. Davis, Tex., 1939- 41; with Radiation Lab., Mass. Inst. Tech., 1941-42; with Cal. Inst. Tech., 1942-45; staff mem. Mt. Wilson and Palomar Observatories, Carnegie Instn. of Washington, Cal. Inst. Tech., Pasadena, 1946—, asst. dir. Mt. Wilson and Palomar Obs., 1957-63, asso. dir., 1963-64, dir. Hale Observatories (formerly Mt. Wilson and Palomar), 1964—. Recipient Draper medal Nat. Acad. Scis., 1957; Eddington medal Royal Astron. Soc., 1958, Gold medal, 1970; Bruce medal Astron. Soc. Pacific, 1969. Mem. Royal Astron. Soc. (asso., Gold medal 1970), Societé Royale des Sciences de Liege (corr. mem.), Am. Philos. Soc., Am. Acad. Arts and Scis., Nat. Acad. Scis., Am. Astron. Soc. (councilor 1956-58), Astron. Soc. Pacific, Internat. Astron. Union, Sigma Xi, Tau Beta Pi. Author sci. and tech. papers in profl. jours. Home: 2189 N Altadena Dr Altadena CA 91001 Office: Hale Observatories 813 Santa Barbara St Pasadena CA 91101

BABCOCK, HOWARD WILLIAM, judge; b. Austin, Minn., Apr. 7, 1917; s. Clarence S. and Irene Mildred (Orrin) B.; student Luther Coll., Decorah, Ia., 1935-37; B.S.L., LL.B., William Mitchell Coll. Law, St. Paul, 1941; m. Leontyne Najgrodzka , Nov. 12, 1946. Admitted to Minn. bar, 1941, Nev. bar, 1948, U.S. Supreme Ct., 1959; pvt. practice, Reno Nev., 1948- 55, Las Vegas, Nev., 1948-55, 61—; asst. U.S. atty. for Nev., 1955-58, U.S. atty., 1958-61; now state dist. judge Eighth Dist. Active, The City of Hope; mem. Las Vegas council Camp Fire Girls. Served to lt. USNR, 1941-45. Mem. Am., Nev. bar assns., Am. Judicature Soc., Sigma Nu Phi. Clubs: Las Vegas Optimist. Home: 1107 Orange Av Las Vegas NV 89108 Office: 300 Fremont St Las Vegas NV 89101

BABCOCK, JAMES CHESTER, educator; b. Fayetteville, Ark., Feb. 25, 1908; s. George Edward and Hannah (Muncy) B.; A.B., U. Ark., 1929; M.A., State U. Ia., 1930, Ph.D., 1934; M.A. (hon.), Dartmouth, 1951; studied at Centro de Estudios Históricos, Madrid, Spain, 1932, Sorbonne, Paris, 1933; m. Helen Alberta Wood, June 2, 1930 (div. 1961); children—Janet Elizabeth, James Stephen, Arthur E., Helen L.; m. 2d, Sandra Eileen Scharff, Dec. 30, 1961. Instr. Romance langs. U. Chgo., 1936-43, asso. prof., 1943-50; vis. prof. of the humanities Dartmouth, 1949, prof. Romance langs., 1950-57, chmn. dept., 1953-57; professor Romance langs., Ohio State U., Columbus, 1957- -, chmn. dept. of Romance languages, 1957-65. Mem. of Modern Language Assn. Author: (with P.K. Hartstall) Sinous écrivions, 1937: (with S.N. Treviño) Introduction to Spanish, 1944; also contbr. book chpt. Editor: (with M.B. Rodriguez); Amilia, 1949; Contigo pay y cebolla, 1953. Editorial adviser in Spanish for Houghton Mifflin Co., 1945—. Home: 2451 Fishinger Rd Columbus OH 43221 Office: Dept Romance Languages Ohio State U Columbus OH 43210

BABCOCK, RICHARD FELT, lawyer; b. Evanston, Ill., Nov. 3, 1917; s. William Frank and Gertrude (Felt) B.; A.B. magna cum laude, Dartmouth, 1940; J.D. cum laude, U. Chgo., 1946, M.B.A., 1950; m. Elizabeth Vaughn Burlingham, June 12, 1943; children—Rebecca, Richard, Elizabeth, Catherine, David, John. Admitted to Ill. bar; asso. firm Sidley, Austin, Burgess & Harper, Chgo., 1946-48; partner Overton & Babcock, Chgo., 1948-51, Taylor, Miller, Busch & Wagner, Chgo., 1951-56, Ross, Hardies, O'Keefe, Babcock, McDugald & Parsons, Chgo., 1957—. Lectr. bus. law Northwestern U. Sch. Commerce, 1951-58; lectr. U. Chgo. Grad. Sch. Bus., Chgo., 1953-54; cons. on land use law Ford Found., 1960-62. Dir. Met. Housing and Planning Council, Chgo.; commr. Northeastern Ill. Met. Planning Commn. Asso. dir. Nat. Vols. for Stevenson, 1952; chmn. adv. com. Land Use project Am. Law Inst. Served with Am. Field Service, 1941-43, with Brit. 8th Army, Western Desert, 1942-43, then with N.Z. Divisional Cav. Mem. Am. Inst. Planners, Am. Soc. Planning Ofcls. (pres. 1970-71), Order of Coif, Phi Beta Kappa, Lambda Alpha. Democrat. Clubs: Mid-America, University (Chgo.). Author: The Zoning Game, 1966. Contbr. articles to profl. revs. Home: 1314 S Fleming Rd Woodstock IL 60098. Office: 122 S Michigan Av Chicago IL 60603

BABCOCK, RICHARD JOSEPH, publisher; b. Blue Point, L.I., N.Y., Aug. 5, 1911; s. Charles Joseph and Mary Agnes (Wray) B.; student La Salle Acad., 1926-27; m. Genevieve Ackerman, Mar. 26, 1932; 1 dau., Wray Ann. Sales mgr., Northwest Airlines, 1935-36; mem. sales dept. Farmer's Wife mag., 1936-39; with Farm Jour., Inc., Phila., 1939—, pres., dir., 1951—, pub., 1962—; v.p. Family Circle mag., 1941-42, pres. WGYN FM Broadcasting Sta., 1942; pres., dir. Rec-Chek Inc. Vice chmn. bd. dirs. Audit Bur. Circulations; bd. dirs. Found. for Am. Agr.; past chmn. Advt. Research Found. Mem. Mag. Pubs. Assn. (dir. , former chmn.). Home: 2401 Pennsylvania Av Philadelphia PA 19130 Office: 230 Washington Square Philadelphia PA 19105

BABCOCK, ROBERT ANDERSON, banker; b. Saybrook, Conn., Sept. 20, 1907; s. Robert Anderson and Emma (Edwards) B.; student Yale, 1926-27, Rutgers U. Sch. Banking, 1950-51; m. Elsie Theresa Schmitt, Feb. 2, 1935; children—Linda (Mrs. William C. Munson), Robert Anderson IV. With Conn. Savs. Bank, New Haven, 1928—, asst. treas., 1938-46, sec., 1946—. Mem. S.A.R. (historian Gen. David Humphreys br.). Republican. Episcopalian. Mason. Home: 31 Ridgewood Av North Haven CT 06517 Office: 47 Church St New Haven CT 06501

BABCOCK, ROBERT SHILLINGFORD, educator; b. Chgo., July 22, 1915; s. Oliver M. and Martha (Shillingford) B.; A.B., U. Rochester, 1937; B.A., Oxford U., Eng., 1939, M.A., 1943; Ph.D., Northwestern U., 1949; LL.D., Marlboro Coll., 1957, U. Vt., 1969; m. Alice-Anne Hanchett, Aug. 20, 1940; children—Robert Shillingford, Ann, Julie, Peter Trowbridge, Martha Rena, Inst., Black Mountain Coll., N.C., 1940-42; econ. analyst Treasury Dept., Washington, 1942; mem. Bd. Econ. Warfare, 1942-43; asst. prof. polit. sci. U. Vt., 1946-54. asso. prof., 1954-59, prof. polit. sci., 1961- -; provost (pres.) Vermont State Colls., 1965—; mem. Vt. Senate, 1951, 53, 57, pres. pro tem, 1957-59; sec. to gov. Vt., 1955; lt. gov. Vt., 1959-61. Served as lt. (j.g.) USNR, 1943-46. Rhodes scholar, 1937. Mem. Am. Polit. Sci. Assn., Phi Beta Kappa. Author: State and Local Government and Politics, 1957, rev. edit., 1962. Home: RD 1 South Burlington VT 05401 Office: Vermont State Colls 322 S Prospect Burlington VT 05401

BABCOCK, SUMNER HOVEY, lawyer; b. Waterbury, Conn., May 15, 1902; s. William Sumner and Edith Hovey (Carter) B.; B.S. in Mech. Engring., Lafayette Coll., 1924; LL.B., Harvard, 1927; m. Catharine Bushnell Jones, Apr. 13, 1937 (dec. Mar. 1965); children—William S., Barbara; m. 2d, Margaret Bassick Munier, Oct. 15, 1967. Admitted to Mass. bar, 1927, since practiced in Boston; partner firm Bingham, Dana & Gould, 1939—. Past pres. Mass. Correctional Assn. Past chmn. library trustees and various coms. Town of Wellesley, Mass. Trustee Lafayette Coll. Fellow Am. Coll. Trial Lawyers; mem. Am., Mass. (v.p. 1960-62), Boston (pres. 1953-55) bar assns., Tau Beta Pi, Theta Delta Chi. Republican. Conglist. Home: 113 Abbott Rd Wellesley Hills MA 02181 Office: 1 Federal St Boston MA 02110

BABCOCK, WILLIAM DANIEL, Jr., ins. co. exec.; b. Phila., Feb. 14, 1912; s. William Daniel and Elsie (Ritter) B.; B.S., U. Pa., 1933, M.B.A., 1948; m. Selma Virginia Press, Oct. 26, 1935; children—Donna V. (Mrs. Terrance Farley), Janice C. (Mrs. James J. Johnson). Treas., Mfrs. Casualty Ins. Co., Phila., 1934-50; treas. Keystone Ins. Co., Phila., 1950-59; sr. v.p., treas. Gen. Accident Group, Phila., 1959—; instr. accounting Wharton Sch., U. Pa., 1946-48. Mem. Ins. Accounting and Statis. Assn. (past pres.), Soc. Ins. Accountants. Home: 255 E Waverly Rd Wyncote PA 19095 Office: 414 Walnut St Philadelphia PA 19106

BABER, POWHATAN MILLER, govt. ofcl.; b. Clarksburg, W.Va., Feb. 19, 1917; s. Powhatan Miller and Elsie (Christie) B.; student Bethany Coll., 1935, Tex. Christian U., 1936; B.A., W.Va. U., 1939; m. Dorothy Louise Woodson, Apr. 6, 1946; children—Stephen Christie, Susan Wood, Alexander Powhatan. Adminstrv. asst. Am. embassy, Ankara, Turkey, 1942-1944; vice consul Am. consulate gen., Istanbul, Turkey, 1946-48, Madras, India, 1948-49; attache-adminstrv. officer Am. embassy, Lisbon, Portugal, 1950-53, Prague, Czechoslovakia, 1954-55; first sec., adminstrv. officer Am. embassy, Lima, Peru, 1955-59; dep. exec. dir. Latin Am., Dept. of State, 1959-65; counselor adminstrv. affairs Am. embassy, Mexico City, 1965-69, Am. mission, Seoul, Korea, 1969—. Served with AUS, 1945-46. Mem. Fgn. Service assn. Episcopalian. Office: US Mission to Korea APO San Francisco CA 96301

BABIARZ, JOHN EDWARD, orgn. exec.; b. Wilmington, Del., June 6, 1915; s. Stanley and Maryanne (Feret) B.; B.A., U. Del., 1937; m. Adele F. Barczuk, June 4, 1939; children—John Edward, Francis. With Del. Bedding Co., Wilmington, 1939- -, treas., mgr., 1941—; register in chancery, clk. orphans ct., New Castle County, 1948-52; chief clk. Del. Ho. of Reps., 1955-56; pres. Wilmington City Council, 1956-60; mayor of Wilmington, 1960-69; exec. dir. Better Bus. Bur. Del., Inc., 1969—. Chmn., Regional Conf. Elected Ofcls., 1963-65. Del. Democratic Nat. Conv., 1956, 60, 64, 68. Served with AUS, World War II. Mem. V.F.W. (condr. Del 1950- 51), Am. Legion, Holy Name Soc., Polish Falcons, Pulaski Legion. K.C., Eagle, Kiwanian. Club: Businessmens Lucheon (Wilmington). Home: 303 Lea Blvd Wilmington DE 19802 Office: 1609 Delaware Av Wilmington DE 19806

BABICH, LEO B., banker; b. New Zealand, 1911. Vice pres. Bank of Am., N.T. & S.A., Los Angeles. Bd. govs. Am. Stock Exchange, Investment Bankers Assn. Am., mem. N.Y. Stock Exchange. Home: 1032 W Orange Grove Av Arcadia CA 91006 Office: 650 S Spring St Los Angeles CA 90014*

BABIN, CLAUDE HUNTER, univ. chancellor; b. Baton Rouge, Feb. 6, 1924; s. Ventress Victor and Essie (Bond) B.; B.A., La. State U., 1945; M.A., U. Wis., 1946; Ph.D., Tulane U., 1954; LL.D., Hendrix Coll., 1965; m. Barbara Ann Murphy, Dec. 29, 1947; 1 son, Claude Hunter. Instr. history U. Miami (Fla.), 1946-49; grad. fellow Tulane U., 1949-54; asst. prof., asso. prof., then prof. history Ark. A. and M. Coll., College Heights, 1954-60, acad. dean, 1960-62, pres., 1962-71, chancellor U. A. and M., 1971—. Ford fellow, 1951-52. Mem. Coll. Presidents Com. for Study Higher Edn. in Ark.; sec. Drew County Health, Edn. and Cultural Corp. Bd. dirs. U. A. and M. Wesley Found. Mem. Am., So. hist. assns., Am. Assn. U. Profs. (asso.), Ark. Edn. Assn., State Coll. Presidents Orgn., Assn. State Colls. and Univs., Ark. Farm Bur. Fedn., Acad. Polit. Sci., C. of C., Kappa Sigma, Phi Alpha Theta, Pi Sigma Alpha. Democrat. Methodist. Kiwanian. Home: UAM Campus AR 71655

BABIN, DONALD ALFRED, banker; b. White Castle, La., Sept. 4, 1920; s. Cyrille and Etta (LaBiche) B.; student U. Houston, 1954-55; m. Mary Sutherland, Aug. 16, 1946; children—Karen (Mrs. James Michael Mallette), Robert C., William C., Donald Alfred, Michael I. With Bank of Southwest N.A., Houston, 1939- -, auditor, 1957-66, v.p., cashier, 1966—; mem. faculty Am. Inst. Banking, 1961-62. Served with USAAF, World War II. Mem. Bank Adminstrn. Inst. (pres. Gulf Coast chpt. 1967—, state dir. 1968-69, sch. key award 1965), Am. Inst. Banking, Inst. Internal Auditors, Am. Soc. Corporate Secs., St. Vincent de Paul Soc., Spring Br. Sports Assn. Roman Catholic. Clubs: Memorial Valley Civic, Westchester Booster (Houston). Home: 1805 Laurel Oaks Dr Richmond TX 77469 Office: 910 Travis St Houston TX 77001

BABIN, VICTOR, pianist, composer; b. Moscow, Russia, Dec. 13, 1908; s. Heinrich and Rosalie (Wolk) B.; student State Conservatory, Riga, Latvia, 1921-27, Berliner Hochschule fur Musik, Berlin, Germany, 1928-31; A.F.D., U. N.M., 1961; m. Vitya Vronsky, Aug. 31, 1933. Came to U.S., 1937, naturalized, 1944. Appeared on concert stage, Europe, 1928-37; Am. debut as two-piano team with Vitya Vronsky, N.Y.C., 1937; transcontinental concert tour Am., 1937—; soloist symphony orchs., appeared radio and TV; mem. Aspen (Colo.) Festival, 1949—, dir. Aspen Inst. Music, 1952-54; mem. Festival Quartet (with Goldberg, Primrose, Graudan), 1956-62; dir. Cleve. Inst. Music, 1961—; chmn. Tanglewood Inst. Berkshire Music Center, Lenox, Mass., 1965-67. Served with AUS, World War II. Recipient Cleve. Creative Arts award, 1966. Mem. Am. Guild Musical Artists, A.S.C.A.P., Pi Kappa Lambda. Composer: String Quartet, Piano Trio, Song Cycle "Beloved Stranger" to lyrics by Witter Bynner; Sonata for Cello and piano; Konzertstück for violin and orch.; Two Concerti for two pianos and orch.; Six Bach Sonatas and Stravinsky's Petrouchka Suite transcribed for 2 pianos; Three Concertos da Camera. Home: 19101 Van Aken Blvd Shaker Heights Cleveland OH 44120 Office: Cleveland Inst Music Cleveland OH 44106

BABINGTON, SUREN H., surgeon, author; A.B., U. Cal., 1922, M.D., 1925; postgrad. Cook County Grad. Sch. Medicine, Stanford, U. Cal., Harvard Med. Sch.; m. Mary Dieckmann, 1937; children—Suren F., Mary Lee, Nancy, Anne. Chief surgery Mendocino State Hosp., 1926-28; pvt. practice medicine, Berkeley, Cal., 1928—; vis. surgeon Alameda County Instns., 1929-41, Highland Hosp., 1937-41; cons. vascular surgery Fairmont Hosp., 1941-43; staff phys. Rainbow Bridge and Monument Valley Expdns., 1934-36; mem. staff Herrick Meml. Hosp.; former mem. staff Alta Bates hosps., Berkeley, Samuel Merritt, and Childrens hosps., Oakland; chief staff, chief surgery, 1948-56, chmn. acad. council for interns and residents, 1946-56, Herrick Meml. Hosp. Med. examiner SSS, 1940-45. Founder, pres. Berkeley Med. Center; Cal. del. to Assn. Am. Phys. and Surg., 1954-56; chmn. exec. com., pres. bd. trustees Herrick Meml. Hosp. Active Boy Scouts Am. (Silver Beaver Award; mem. nat. council, mem. Region XII com.); pres. Berkeley High School P.T.A., 1966-67; pres. Berkeley YMCA, 1966-70; mem. City of Berkeley Welfare Commn., 1961-62; past v.p. Community Chest; pres. Berkeley Community Concerts Assn., 1960-71. Awarded Congl. Medal Merit, 1944-46; Pres. Cup Am. Physicians Writers Guild; Benjamin Franklin award High Twelve Internat. Community Service award Berkeley C. of C., Cal. Assembly and Senate awards; Internat. Inst. award as an outstanding immigarnt to U.S. Diplomate Intern at Bd. Surgery Am. Bd. Abdominal Surgery. Fellow Internat. Coll. Surgeons (del. Internat. sci. assembly, Lima, Peru, 1946, Madrid, Spain 1952. Sao Paulo, Brazil 1954, Tokyo 1968: vice-regent Cal.; del. 4th Pan Pacific Surg. Assn., Honolulu, 1948), Am. Med. Writers Assn., Am. Med. Authors, Internat. Acad. Proctology, Am. Geriatic Soc. mem. A.M.A., Am. Soc. Abdominal surgeons (program vice chmn. 1960), Alameda County, Pan. Am. (past pres. San Francisco br., regional adminstr.; nat. adv. v.p.), Cal. (ho. of dels., 1944-46) med. assns., Doctors Hist. Soc. (founder and pres.), Am. Physicians Art Assn., Am. Physicians Lit. Guild, Abraham Lincoln Fellowship (life mem.), Oakland Forum and Oakland Symphony (founding mem.), Pan Pacific Surg. Assn.; hon. mem. Peruvian Acad. Surgery and Acad. Medicine, San Paulo, Brazil, Cal. Congress P.T.A. (hon. life). Episcopalian. Mason (32, Shriner). Clubs: City Commons (past pres., life dir.), Lions (past pres. Berkeley; del. Internat. conv. Nice, France, 1962, Alumni Iceland (founder, pres.), High Twelve (past pres., dir. Berkeley, internat. rep.; past pres. Cal. assn.), Cal. Writers (past pres.). Author: Human Sexual Sterilization; Management of Post-operative Pain; Surgery of Diverticulitis: Phenobarbital-Rash and other Toxic Effects; Simple Ulcers of Jejuno-eileum; Surgical Treatment of Varicose Veins and other technical and sci. publs.; Among the Navajo Indians of Arizona; Navajos, Gods and Tom-Toms; Medical Practices Among the Navajos; Juvenile Delinquents-How Come; Herrick Hospital Manual; The Boomerang that Landed a Navajo; The Mysteries of the Boomerang: Why I Could Not Quit. Home: 81 Hillcrest Rd Berkeley CA 94705 Office: 2340 Ward St Berkeley CA 94705

BABLER, BERNARD JOSEPH, chemist, educator; b. Humbird, Wis., Mar. 19, 1914; s. John and Mary (Benish) B.; B.S. in Chemistry, U. Wis., 1935; M.S., 1936; Ph.D., La. State U., 1940; m. Berenice A. Brunk, June 9, 1942; children—Susan M. (Mrs. Robert W. Powers),

James Harold, Maribeth Anne, Pamela Jane. Asst. limnology U. Wis., 1935-36; teaching fellow La. State U., 1936-39; from instr. chemistry to prof., chmn. dept. DePaul U., 1940-47; faculty U. Ill. at Chgo. Circle, 1947—, prof. chemistry, 1957—, acting head div. phys. sci., 1961-62, exec. sec. Chemistry Dept., 1965—; cons. in field, 1941—. Mem. Am. Chem. Soc., Alpha Chi Sigma, Phi Eta Sigma, Phi Lambda Upsilon, Omega Beta Pi. Elk. Home: 1847 W Chase Av Chicago IL 60626.

BABLER, WAYNE ELROY, telephone co. exec.; b. Orangeville, Ill., Dec. 8, 1915; s. Oscar E. and Mary (Bender) B.; B.A., Ind. Central Coll., 1936; J.D., U. Mich., 1938; LL.D., Ind. Central Coll., 1966; m. Mary Blome, Dec. 27, 1940; children—Wayne Elroy, Marilyn Anne, Sally Jane. Admitted to Mich. bar, 1938, N.Y. bar, 1949, Mo. bar, 1955, Wis. bar, 1963, also U.S. Supreme Ct.; with firm Bishop & Bishop, Detroit, 1938-42; chief price atty. OPA, Detroit, 1942-44; contract sec. Fisher Body div. Gen. Motors Corp., 1944- 45; partner firm Bishop & Babler, Detroit, 1945-48; atty. Am. Tel. & Tel Co., 1948-55; gen. solicitor Southwestern Bell Telephone Co., St. Louis, 1955-63, v.p., gen. counsel, 1965—; v.p., gen. counsel Wis. Telephone Co., Milw., 1963-65. Part-time prof. torts and restitution Detroit Coll. Law, 1938-48. Bd. dirs., pres. St. Louis Soc. Crippled Children. Mem. Am., Fed. Communications, Wis., Milw. bar assns., Mo. Bar, Bar Assn. St. Louis. Clubs: Noonday, Bellerive Country. Home: 17 Ridge Creek Creve Coeur MO 63141 Office: 1010 Pine St Saint Louis MO 63101

BABSKIE, ROBERT F., psychiatrist, hosp. supt.; b. Glen Lyon, Pa., Feb. 27, 1922; s. Peter J. and Angeline (Gull) B.; student Bucknell U., 1940-43; M.D., Jefferson Med. Coll., 1947; m. Catherine M. Domanovsky, Jan. 19, 1950; children—Robert, John. Intern Gen. Hosp., Wilkes-Barre, Pa., 1947-48; house physician Nanticoke State Gen. Hosp., Nanticoke, Pa., 1948-49, resident obstetrics and gynecology, 1949-51; pvt. practice medicine, Nanticoke, Pa., 1952-64; resident psychiatry Danville (Pa.) State Hosp., then Eastern Pa. Psychiat. Inst., Phila., 1965-68; acting med. dir., Scranton, Pa., 1971—; supt. Retreat State Hosp., Hunlock Creek, Pa., 1968—; prof. psychology Wilkes Coll., 1968—; cons. psychiatry Nanticoke State Gen. Hosp.; psychiatrist Malabar Youth Drug Center, Wilkes Barre, Pa., St. Stanislaus Orphanage, Sheatown, Pa. Served with AUS, 1943-46, 51-52. Mem. Luzerne County, Pa. med. socs., A.M.A., Am. Psychiat. Assn., Am. Hosp. Assn., Am. Acad. Hosp. Adminstrn., Med. Supts. Assn. Pa. (sec. 1969—). Home: 246 E Washington St Nanticoke PA 18634 Office: Retreat State Hospital Hunlock Creek PA 18621

BABSON, ARTHUR CLIFFORD, economist; b. Portland, Ore., July 19, 1909; s. Sydney Gorham and Grace Bowditch (Campbell) B.; B.S., U. Ore., 1931; m. Margery Tindle Grey, Aug. 3, 1946; children—John Pell, Robert Grey. With Union Terminal Coldstorage Co., Jersey City, 1932-36, asst. supt., 1935-36; with Babson's Reports, Inc., Babson Park, Mass., 1936—, v.p., 1940—; dir., mem. fiduciary com. Cape Ann Nat. Bank & Trust Co. of Gloucester; dir. Sierra Pacific Power Co., City Investing Co., N.Y.C.; dir., mem. exec. com. Home Ins. Co.; v.p. Babson Ranch Co. Chmn. Sherborn (Mass.) Bd. Selectmen. U.S. Naval rep. lt. comdr., Ceylon and Southern India, 1942-45. Mem. Pilgrims of U.S., Chi Psi. Episcopalian. Lectr. on econ. and social trends. Home: Sherborn MA 01770 Office: Babson's Reports Inc Babson Park MA 02157

BABSON, DAVID LEVEAU, investment counsel; b. Gloucester, Mass., Sept. 16 1911; s. Elmer W. and Emma G. (Leveau) B.; B.S., Harvard, 1932; m. Katherine L. Allen, 1934; children—David Leveau, Susan A. (Mrs. Young), Katherine L. Vice pres., dir. Babson's Reports, Inc., 1932-40; pres., dir. David L. Babson & Co., Inc., 1940—; dir. Jones Plans Inc., Sierra Pacific Power Co., David L. Babson Investment Fund, Inc. Mem. Wellesley Bd. Pub. Works, 1964—. Trustee, Commonwealth Housing Found.; trustee, treas. Grimes-King Found. for Elderly, Inc. Mem. Boston Security Analysts Soc., Investment Counsel Assn. Republican. Conglist. Co-author: Investing for a Successful Future, 1959. Home: 27 Clovelly Rd Wellesley Hills MA 02181 Office: 1 Boston Pl Boston MA 02108

BACALL, LAUREN, actress; b. N.Y.C., Sept. 16, 1924; d. Natalie Bacall; student pub. schs., m. Humphrey Bogart, May 21, 1945 (dec. 1957); children—Stephen, Leslie; m. 2d, Jason Robards, July 1961; 1 son, Sam. Actress Broadway plays, Johnny 2x4, Franklin Street, 1942, Goodbye Charlie, 1959; motion picture actress, 1942—, pictures include: To Have and Have Not, The Big Sleep, 1944, Confidential Agent, 1945, Dark Passage, 1947, Key Largo, 1948, Young Man With a Horn, 1949, Bright Leaf, 1950, How To Marry a Millionaire, 1953, Woman's World, 1954. The Cobweb, Blood Alley, 1955; Written on the Wind, Designing Woman, The Gift of Love; Flame Over India, 1959; Sex and the Single Girl, 1965; Harper, 1966; appeared in Broadway play Cactus Flower, 1966-67, Applause, 1969-71; TV spl. The Paris Collections, 1968. Address: care Morgan Marcee Jr Inc 6363 Wilshire Blvd Los Angeles CA 90048

BACCI, ALEXANDER HUGO, architect; b. Chgo., Mar. 17, 1904; s. Joseph A. and Adele (Del Osso) B.; B.S. in Architecture, Armour Inst. Tech., 1926; fellow Chgo. Archtl. Club for postgrad. work, Europe, 1930; m. Felice Frances Tomei, Nov. 16, 1927. Exec. partner Schmidt, Garden & Erikson, architects-engrs., Chgo., 1946—; prin. works include Silvain and Arma Wyler Children's Hosp., U. Chgo. Med. Center, 1967, hdqrs. bldg. Allstate Ins. Co., Skokie, Ill., 1967, Children's Meml. Hosp., Chgo., 1957, Loyola U. Med. Center, Maywood, Ill., 1968, tech. center Procter & Gamble Co., Cin., 1960, tech. and research center Carrier Corp., Syracuse, N.Y., 1956, tech. center Continental Can Co., Chgo., 1956, Hdqrs. Bldg., Allstate Ins. Co., Skokie, Ill., 1967. Mem. Ill. Architect Exam. Com., 1961-65, chmn., 1966-67; mem. vis. com. Nat. Archtl. Accrediting Bd., 1965-67; mem. vis. com. Nat. Council Archtl. Registration Bds., 1966-69. Trustee U. Chgo. Cancer Research Found., 1961-69. Served to lt. col. C.E., AUS, World War II; ETO. Fellow A.I.A.; mem. Ill. Soc. Architects. Clubs: Cliff Dwellers, Arts, Chicago Athletic (Chgo.); Lake Zurich (Ill.) Golf. Home: 250 Old Farm Rd Northbrook IL 60062 Office: 104 S Michigan Av Chicago IL 60603

BACCIGALUPPI, HARRY, wine co. exec.; b. N.Y.C., Aug. 2, 1901; s. John B. and Theresa Baccigaluppi; B.S. in Civil Engring., Cooper Union, 1923; student Columbia, 1923-26; m. Ethel Hutcheon, Nov 25, 1930; children—Roger John, Carol Adele (Mrs. Frank P. Clarke). Pres. Cal. Grape Products Corp., San Francisco, 1946—, Calgrape Wineries, Inc., San Francisco, 1964—. Pres. Wine Inst., 1948-50, sec., 1955—; vice chmn. Wine Conf. Am., 1953-67, Fed. Grape Crush Adv. Bd., 1961-63. Home: 2205 Ray Dr Burlingame, CA 94011. Office: 55 New Montgomery St San Francisco CA 94105.

BACH, GEORGE LELAND, economist; b. Victor, Ia., Apr. 28, 1915; s. James Everett and Ethel (Sies) B.; A.B., Grinnell Coll., 1936, LL.D., 1956; Ph.D., U. Chgo., 1940; LL.D., Carnegie Inst. Tech., 1967; m. Ruth Bartoo, Sept. 7, 1939; children—Christopher Leland, Barbara Kathleen, Susan Louise, Timothy Lee. Instr. Ia. State Coll., 1939-41; spl. asst. and sr. economist Bd. Govs. Fed. Res. System, 1941-44; prin. economist U.S. Dept. Commerce, 1946; prof., head dept. econs. Carnegie Inst. Tech., 1946-62, dean Grad. Sch. Indsl. Adminstrn., 1949-62, Maurice Falk prof. econs., 1962-66; Ford research prof. Stanford U., 1963-64, Frank Buck prof. econs., 1966—; chmn. bd. Pitts. br. Fed. Res. Bank Cleve., 1961-66; cons. Commn. on Orgn. of Exec. Br. Govt., U.S. Treasury and bd. govs. Fed. Res. System. Trustee Joint Council on Edn. Ford Found. Faculty Research Fellow, 1958-59. Served with USNR, 1944-46, Fellow Am. Acad. Arts and Scis.; mem. Am. Finance Assn., Am. Econ. Assn. (exec. com. 1959-62), Nat. Task Force Econ. Edn. (chmn.), Inst. Mgmt. Sci., Phi Beta Kappa, Phi Kappa Phi. Author: Economic Analysis and Public Policy, 1943, 1949; Federal Reserve Policy Making 1950; Economics, 1954, latest edit., 1971; Inflation: A Study in Economics, Ethics, and Politics, 1958; Making Monetary and Fiscal Policy, 1971. Co-author: Management and Corporations, 1960; Economic Analysis and Policy, 1963, 66; Microeconomics, 1966, 70; Macroeconomics, 1966, 70. Contbr. articles various profl. jours. Home: 661 Cabrillo Av Stanford CA 94305

BACH, MARCUS, author, educator; b. Sauk City, Wis., Dec. 15, 1906; s. Louis P. and Albertina (Buerki) B.; student Wis. Sch. Music, Madison, 1920-22, Mission House Coll. and Sem., Plymouth, Wis., 1924-25; A.M., U. Ia., 1937, Ph.D., 1942; m. Lorena Ernest, Aug. 17, 1932. Engaged in research and study, Ky., N.M., Cal., Mexico, 1933-35 (Rockefeller fellowship in research and creative writing, 1934-36); instr. dramatic lit. Carleton Coll., Northfield, Minn., 1937; research among Am. religious and folk groups, 1938-40; asso. dir. and prof. Sch. Religion, U. Ia., 1942—; Found. for Spiritual Understanding. Recipient Charles Sergel Nat. Playwriting award for Happy Merger, 1937, Nicholas Copernicus award, 1943. Mem. Am. Acad. Polit. and Social Sci. Commd. to write dramatic spectacles and dramas for centennial observances, including Light of Ages, City of Chgo., 1937; Timothy Alden, Allegheny Coll., Meadville, Pa., 1940; The Path of Faith, Iowa Methodism, 1944. Author: (religious and folk plays) Flag Stop; While Mortals Sleep, 1935; Within These Walls, 1936; Champion of Democracy, 1940; Who is Mrs. Chimpsie?, 1940: Common Ground, 1943; Sunrise By Request, 1944; (books) They Have Found a Faith, 1946; Report to Protestants, 1948; The Dream Gate, 1949; Faith and My Friends of Faith and Learning, 1951; Strange Altars, 1952; The Will to Believe, 1955; The Circle of Faith, 1956; God and the Soviets, 1958; Major Religions of the World, 1959; Adventures in Faith, 1959; Strange Sects and Curious Cults 1961; Had You Been Born in Another Faith, 1962; The Unity Way of Life, 1963; Let Life Be Like This, 1964; Spiritual Breakthroughs for our Time, 1965; The Power of Perception, 1966; The Wonderful Magic of Living, 1968; The World of Serendipity, 1970; Strangers at the Door, 1971. Contbr. to ency. and nat. mags. Lectr. on interfaith understanding, contemporary religious movements and Am. religious scene with emphasis on America's little- known religions. Home: 100 Via Alameda Palos Verdes Estates CA 90274

BACH, MILTON FRANCIS (Mickey Bach) sports writer, cartoonist; b. Waconia, Minn., Sept. 30, 1909; s. Christ H. and Lucy (Raddee) B.; high school and university edn.; B.S., and M.S., U. of Wis. (1928-31); majored in art and history (including cartooning) Federal Schs., Mpls.; m. Virginia Sherwood Fletcher, March 6, 1944. Advertising artist, Lee Larson Advt., Waukesha, Wis., 1934-35; cartoonist and sports art dir. Mpls. Star Jour., 1935-41, Chgo. Sun, Nov. 1941-Jan. 1942. Served from 2d lt. to capt. AUS, June-Oct. 1941, 1942-45; pub. relations officer Fort Benning, Ga., 1942, later assigned to army newspaper, South Pacific Area. Mem. Nat. Cartoonists Soc. Sigma Chi. Clubs: Masquers; Greater Los Angeles Press. Author: Word-A-Day. Author "Word-a-Day" daily cartoon feature distributed by Pubs.-Hall Syndicate. Home: 2430 OceanView Av Los Angeles CA 90005 Office: Publishers-Hall Syndicate 30 E 42d St New York City NY 10017

BACH, OTTO KARL, mus. dir., lectr.; b. Chgo., May 26, 1909; s. Otto Carl and Louise (Gatter) B.; A.B., Dartmouth, 1931; postgrad. U. Paris, 1937; A.M., U. Chgo., 1941; H.H.D., U. Denver, 1955; m. Cile Miller, June 9, 1937; 1 son, Dirk Palmer. Mus. asst. Dartmouth Coll. Mus., 1930; asst. dir. Milw. Art Inst., 1932-33; dir. Grand Rapids (Mich.) Art Gallery, 1933-44, Denver Art Mus., 1944—; tchr. art history, 1933—; artist. Mem. art adv. com. USAF Acad. Recipient citation for Extraordinary Services by city and county of Denver; Am. Creativity award May Co., 1961; chevalier des Arts et Lettres, 1969. Member Am. Fedn. Art, Am. Assn. Museums, Assn. Art Mus. Dirs. Author: New Way to Paul Klee, 1945; Am. Heritage, 1949; Under Every Roof, 1950; Pre Colombian Gold. 1951. Organized, established Living Arts Center, 1958. Home: 140 Krameria St Denver CO 80220 Office: 100 W 14th Av Pkwy Denver CO 80204

BACH, RALPH EDWARD, publisher; b. Orange, N.J., Jan. 26, 1903; s. Edward John and Minnie (Clarke) B.; B.S., N.Y.U., 1925; m. Henrietta Steenman, July 3, 1926; children—Ralph E., Peter H. Analyst trust dept. Bankers Trust Co., N.Y.C., 1925-28; asst. mgr. trust dept. Bank of Am., 1928-29; financial writer Financial World, pub. by Guenther Pub. Corp., 1929-33, research editor, 1933-40, v.p., 1941-49, exec. v.p., 1949-55, pres., 1955—, also dir. Mem. arbitration panel Am. Stock Exchange. Mem. N.Y. C. of C., Psi Upsilon. Clubs: Maplewood (N.J.) Country; Whitehall (N.Y.C.). Home: 244 Long Hill Dr Short Hills NJ 07078 Office: 17 Battery Place New York City NY 10004

BACHARACH, BERT, columnist Chgo. Today; writer column Now Hear This, King Features Syndicate and Central Press Assn.; author Bert Bacharach's Book for Men, 1953; Right Dress, 1955. Address: 200 E 57th St New York City NY 10022*

BACHARACH, BURT, pianist, composer; b. Kansas City, Mo., May 12, 1929; s. Bert and Irma (Freeman) B.; studied McGill U., Montreal, 3 years, with Darius Milhaud at New Sch. for Social Research, with Henry Cowell at Music Acad. West, Santa Barbara, Cal.; m. Paula Stewart; m. 2d, Angie Dickinson; 1 dau., Lea Nikki. Accompanist Vic Damone, 1952, later Polly Bergen, Georgia Gibbs, Joel Gray, Ames Bros., Marlene Dietrich; now composer songs, film scores, stage musicals; frequent collaborator Hal David. Served with AUS, 1950-52. Composer: Magic Moments, The Story of My Life, 1957, Don't Make Me Over, 1962, Walk on By, Trains and Boats and Planes, Anyone Who Had a Heart, What the World Needs Now, 1965, I'll Never Fall in Love Again, Do You Know the Way to San Jose?, The Look of Love, Raindrops Keep Fallin' on My Head (Acad. award 1970); Composer scores The Man Who Shot Liberty Valence, Wives and Lovers, Send Me No Flowers, A House is Not a Home, What's New Pussycat?, The April Fools. Recs. for A&M Records, Kapp Records. Named (with David) Entertainers of Year Cue mag., 1969. Author: The Bacharach-David Song Book, 1970. Address: 166 E 61st St New York City NY 10021*

BACHAUER, GINA, concert pianist; b. Athens, Greece, May 21, 1913; d. John and Ersilia Bachauer; studied with Woldemar Freeman at Athens Conservatoire, with Alfred Cortot at Ecole Normale, Paris, France, later with Sergei Rachmaninoff; m. John Christodoulo, 1937; m. 2d. Alec Sherman, 1951. Debut in Athens with Nat. Symphony orchestra of Athens, 1935; toured Europe, 1937-39; gave more than 600 concerts for Allied Forces 1940-45; debut in London, Eng., 1947, in N.Y.C., 1950; annual concert tours in U.S., 1951—; tours in Can., S.Am., Australia, New Zealand, Africa, many European countries, Israel, Cuba, P.R., Hong Kong; recipient Gold medal Athens Conservatoire, 1929, Prix d' Honneur, Internat. Music Competition, Vienna, Austria, 1933. Decorated comdr. Order of Golden Phoenix, comdr. Order of Welfare (Greece). Home: 6 Cumberland Terrace Regent's Park London NW 1 England also: care Hurok Concerts Inc 1370 Av of Americas New York City NY 10019

BACHELLER, JOSEPH HENRY, Jr., banker; b. Newark, Feb. 25, 1905; s. Joseph Henry and Edith (Smith) B.; B.S., Princeton, 1926; m. Helen Boott, Nov. 8, 1957; children—Barbara Lamb, Joseph Henry III, Sherman Boott Russ. Cadet engr. Pub. Service Corp. N.J., 1926-30; with Prudential Ins. Co. Am., 1931-41; exec. v.p. Suffolk Franklin Savs. Bank, Boston, 1941-63, pres., 1963-71, chmn., trustee, 1971—; dir., clk. Worcester Bus. Co., Inc. (Mass.). Chmn. Community Fund, Hingham, Mass., 1942-43, sect. chmn., Boston Charitable Trust; corporator New Eng. Deaconess Hosp., Morgan Meml. Mem. Savs. Banks Assn. Mass. (chmn. mortgage com.), Nat. Assn. Mut. Savs. Banks. Unitarian. Clubs: Union (Boston); Hingham Tennis; Golf, Squash and Tennis (bd. dirs.), (Cohasset, Mass.). Home: 179 Main St Hingham MA 02043 Office: 45 Franklin St Boston MA 02110

BACHER, EDWARD LEONARD, ret. polit. party exec.; b. Gilbertville, Mass., Nov. 14, 1889; s. John Michael and Anna Maria (Mueller) B.; A.B., Williams Coll., 1911; m. Corinda LaRocca, May 24, 1920. Fgn. trader, Java, Sumatra and Straits Settlements, Standard Oil Co. of N.Y., 1911-15; editor, sec. fgn. trade course Bus. Tng. Corp., N.Y.C., 1916-17, Pacific Comml. Co., 1917-18, Quaker City Corp., Phila., 1919-20; asst. mgr. fgn. commerce dept., U.S. C. of C., 1920-27, mgr., 1927-45; mgr. war service div., 1941-45; sec. U.S. Sect. Can.-U.S. Com. (U.S. and Canadian chambers commerce), 1933-45; mgr. Am. sect. Internat. C. of C., and U.S. sect. Inter-Am. Council of Commerce and Prodn., 1943-45. Exec. sec. Republican Nat. Finance Com. 1944- 61; exec. dir. Rep. Nat. Com., 1945-49, asst. treas., 1949-61, comptroller, 1952-61; treas. Nat. Recount and Fair Elections Com., 1960-61. Trustee, past treas. Phi Gamma Delta Ednl. Found. Expert Internat. C. of C. del. to League of Nations Conf. on Customs Formalities, Geneva, 1923. Served as lt. F.A., U.S. Army, 1918. Recipient award of merit. Constrn. Bn., U.S. Navy, 1943. Mem. Com. on Internat. Econ. Policy, N.Y.C., 1944-45. Mem. Internat. C. of C. (trade terms com. 1927-39; Am. sect. subcom. to review Europe-U.S. trade 1931), U.S. C. of C. (sec. nat. defense com. 1933-45, com. on edn. 1938-40, cattlemen's com. of Can.- U.S. chambers of commerce 1937, nat. policy council 1940-41, win the war 1933-36, on com. 1941-42, spl. com. on internat. postwar problems, 1941-45), Am. Philatelic Soc., Phi Beta Kappa Assos., Phi Beta Kappa, Phi Gamma Delta (Distinguished Fiji award in 1967), Gargoyle. Conglist. Clubs: University, Congressional Country (Washington); Rehoboth Beach Country; Henlopen Acres Beach Club. Author: Export Technique, 1916; Doing Export Business, 1927; Foreign Trade Promotion, 1930. Editor Fgn. trade course by mail, 1916-18; editor Our World Trade, series of quarterly reviews (U.S. C. of C.), 1927-45. Condr. Nat. Fgn. Trade week throughout U.S., 1935-45. Lectr. N.Y. Bd. Edn., 1918; lect. Fgn. Trade Sch., Georgetown U., 1923-27. Compiler: Republican Fact Book (Rep. Nat. Finance com.). 1947-50. Home: 4523 Hawthorne St NW Washington DC 20016 also 8 Zwaanendael Heniopen Acres Rehoboth Beach DE 19971

BACHER, ROBERT FOX physicist; b. Loudonville, O., Aug. 31, 1905; s. Harry and Byrl (Fox) B.; B.S., U. Mich., 1926; Ph.D., 1930, Sc.D., (hon.), 1948; m. Jean Dow, May 30, 1930; children—Martha, Andrew Dow. Nat. Research fellow Cal. Inst. Tech., 1930-31, Mass. Inst. Tech., 1931-32; Alfred Lloyd fellow U. Mich., 1932-33; instr. physics Columbia, 1934-35; instr. to prof. physics Cornell, 1935-49; radiation lab. Mass. Inst. Tech., 1940-45; head exptl. physics div. Los Alamos Lab. atomic bomb project, 1943-44, bomb physics div., 1944-45; mem. AEC, 1946-49; mem. President's Sci. Adv. Com., 1957-60, Naval Research Adv. Com., 1957-62; prof. physics Cal. Inst. Tech., 1949—, dir. Norman Bridge lab. physics, chmn. div. physics, math., astronomy, 1949-62, provost coll., 1962-70; dir. Detroit Edison Co., Bell & Howell Co., TRW Inc. Pres. Internat. Union Pure and Applied Physics, 1969—. Trustee Univs. Research Assn., chmn., 1970—; trustee Asso. Univs., Inc., Atoms for Peace Awards. Power Reactor Devel Corp., Carnegie Corp. of N.Y., Inst. Def. Analysis, Rand Corp., 1950-60; bd. fellows Claremont U. Center. Recipient Medal for Merit, 1946. Mem. Am. Acad. Arts and Scis., Am. Phys. Soc. (pres. 1964), Nat. Acad. Sci., Am. Assn. U. Profs., Am. Philos. Soc., A.A.A.S., Sigma Xi, Kappa Sigma. Home: 345 S Michigan Av Pasadena CA 91106

BACHERT, RAYMOND PAUL, utility co. exec.; b. Aurora, Ill., Nov. 14, 1924; s. William C. and Mary (Lindenmeyer) B.; B.S., U. Ill., 1950; m. Marjorie Elaine Miller, June 24, 1950; children—Linda, Paula, Nancy. Accountant, Commonwealth Edison Co., Chgo., 1950-55, accounting supr., 1955-65, asst. comptroller, 1965-66, asst. v.p., 1966-71, treas., 1971—. Served with USAAF, 1943-46. C.P.A., Ill. Home: 222 Hartway Ct Montgomery IL 60538 Office: P O Box 767 Chicago IL 60690

BACHKO, NICHOLAS, shipping co. exec.; b. Keystone, Pa., Dec. 7, 1919; s. William and Jilia (Eustachie) B.; B.S., U.S. Merchany Marine Acad., 1942; postgrad. Columbia, 1946-49; m. Helen Mary Jadwin, Apr. 25, 1942; children—Nicholas (dec.), William (dec.), Laura Helen. With United States Lines, Inc., N.Y.C., 1946—, chmn. permanent planning group, 1968-69, sr. v.p. for corporate planning and devel., 1969—. Served to chief engr. USNR, World War II; PTO. Recipient Outstanding Achievement award U.S. Maritime Acad., 1957. Mem. Soc. Nav. Architects and Marine Engrs., Am. Mgmt. Assn., Nat. Def. Transp. Assn. Clubs: Downtown Athletic (N.Y.C.); Port Washington Yacht (N.Y.). Patentee in field. Home: 67 Bogart Av Port Washington NY 11050 Office: 1 Broadway Av New York City NY 10004

BACHMAN, EDWARD K., lawyer; b. Bristol, Tenn., Feb. 2, 1907; s. Edward K. and Mary (Martin) B.; A.B., Princeton, 1928; LL.B., Yale, 1931; m. Elinore Lincoln, Nov. 13, 1943; children—Winifred R., Laura L. Admitted to N.Y. bar, 1932; asso. Kelley Drye Warren Clark Carr & Ellis and predecessor firms, N.Y.C., 1931-48, partner, 1948—. Dir. Nat. Marine Service, Inc., Red Hand Compositions Co. Sec., Coe Found. Trustee Planting Fields Found., Bklyn. Inst. Arts and Scis.; mem. governing com. Bklyn. Botanic Garden. Mem. Am., N.Y. bar assns., Assn. Bar City N.Y. Republican. Episcopalian (vestryman). Mason. Clubs: Brook, Knickerbocker, Racquet and Tennis (N.Y.C.); Rembrandt (Bklyn). Home: 2 Montague Terrace Brooklyn Heights NY 11201 also S Country Rd Remsenburg NY 11960 Office: 350 Park Av New York City NY 10022

BACHMAN, EUGENE, trust co. exec. Auditor, exec. officer of bank Mercnatile Trust Co., St. Louis. Office: 721 Locust St St Louis MO 63166*

BACHMAN, G. BRYANT, educator, chemist; b. Kansas City, Mo., Aug. 18, 1905; s. Gustave William and Madge (Bryant) B.; B.A., U. Colo., 1926; Ph.D., Yale, 1930; m. Nancy Powell, Mar. 12, 1929; children—William P., Madge (Mrs. Edwin H. Harrison, Jr.), John B. Faculty, Ohio State U., 1930-36; chemist Eastman Kodak Co., Rochester, N.Y., 1936-39; faculty Purdue U., Lafayette, Ind., 1939—, prof. chemistry, 1941—, emeritus, 1971—; cons. to chem. industries.

Fellow Ind. Acad. Sci., Am. Inst. Chemists; mem. Am., Ind. chem. socs., A.A.A.S. Author: Organic Chemistry, 1949. Bd. editors Jour. Organic Chemistry, 1936-56. Contbr. articles profl. jours. Research in organic synthesis, drugs, plastics, rubbers, nitro compounds, combustion. Home: 923 N Chauncey Av West Lafayette IN 47906 Office: Dept Chemistry Purdue U Lafayette IN 47907

BACHMAN, HAROLD EARL, Jr. diversified mfg. co. exec.; b. Cin., May 21, 1910; grad. Phillips Acad., Andover, Mass., 1927; B.S., Princeton, 1931; postgrad. Mass. Inst. Tech., 1931-33; m. Jean R. Holland, June 16, 1935; children--Lois A., Andrew M., James. Salesman, Brown Mfg. Co., Boston, 1932-33; jr. engr. Ball Metals Co., Carson City, Nev., 1933-36, engr., 1936-37, sr. engr., 1937-40; project engr. Kingston Engring. Co., Los Angeles, 1940-43; with dept. engring. City of Denver, 1946-50, dep. head, 1950-52; 2d v.p. Johnson Mfg. Co., Kansas City, Kansas, 1952-54, v.p. for engring., 1954-57; v.p. research Consol. Industries, Inc., South Bend, Ind., 1957-60, exec. v.p., 1960-65, pres., 1965-70, chmn. bd., chief exec. officer, 1970--, also dir.; dir. ABC Chem. Co., 2d Nat. Bank, Country Food Storage Co., Providence Indsl. Corp. (Ind.), Wilson Investment Co., Inc., Hammond Life Ins. Co., Inc. (Ind.), Prudential Ins. Co., Haverford Mfg. Co., Leader Pub. Co. Pres., Dewey High Sch., Kansas City, Mo., 1953-54; fund chmn. local div. Salvation Army, 1959-60. Mem. South Bend Republican Com., 1964-68. Bd. dirs. Ind. council Boy Scouts Am., 1969-71; trustee Lovell Found. Served to lt., Corps Engrs., AUS, 1943-45. Decorated Bronze Star medal. Member N.A.M., South Bend project coordinator environmental sect. Steinmetz Assos., Chgo., 1960-61; v.p. for research Bauer Bros. Chem. Co., Inc., Memphis, 1961-64; asst. prof. chemistry Washington U., St. Louis, 1964-66, asso. prof., 1966-70, prof., 1970--, head of chemistry dept., 1970-71. Vis. prof. So. Ill. U., summer 1967, U. of Ore., 1969. Bd. dirs. Rest Haven Home for Elderly, 1960-61; trustee of the Lutheran Hosp., 1965-71. Served from lt. to capt., AUS, 1951-53. Mem. Am. Chem. Soc., Sci. Research Soc. Am. (chpt. treas. 1967), Sigma Xi. Author: (with others) Basic Inorganic Chemistry, 1971. Home: Fairfax Apts 7291 Windermere Dr University City MO 63105 Office: Dept Chemistry Washington University St Louis MO 63130

BACHMAN, KENNETH LEROY, govt. ofcl., economist; b. Eddy, Okla., Nov. 14, 1913; s. Albert Odin and Mary Elizabeth (Trekell) B.; B.S., Okla. State U., 1936; M.S., U. Ill., 1938; M.P.A., Harvard, 1947, Ph.D., 1952; m. Audrey Theresa Torrence, Aug. 16, 1941; 1 son, Kenneth Leroy. With Dept. Agr., 1938-52, 54—, asst. to adminstr. Agrl. Marketing Service, 1960-61, dir. devel. and trade div. Econ. Research Service, 1961-67, dir. econ., analysis div. FAO, Rome, 1967—. Mem. Social Sci. Com. on Agrl. Econs., 1958-63; adv. com. Agrl. Policy Inst., N.C. State U., 1960-62; mem. Agrl. Exchange Delegation to USSR, 1963. Mem. parents adv. com. Ohio U., 1962—. Mem. Am. Agrl. Econs. Assn. (pres. 1965- 66; award for published research 1951), Internat. Conf. Agrl. Econs., Farm House Frat., Phi Kappa Phi. Mem. Ch. fo Christ. Home: Via Girolamo Dandini 8 Rome Italy Office: FAO Rome Italy

BACHMAN, PAUL WILLIAM, ret. chemist; b. Newport News, Va., Aug. 28, 1899; s. Ernest and Hedwig (Schmidt) B.; B.S., Johns Hopkins, 1923, Ph.D., 1926; m. Nancy George Hazell, Oct. 29, 1932; children—Ann, Rebecca Elizabeth. Mgr. tech. devel. Comml. Solvents Corp., Terre Haute, Ind., 1942-49; v.p. Davison Chem. Co., Balt., 1949-55, Koppers Co., Inc., Pitts., 1955-64; sr. partner Siems, Bachman & Assos., Balt., 1964-66: trustee, past vice chmn. Indsl. Hygiene Found,; vis. com. physical scis. Johns Hopkins. Mem. N.A.M. (dir., chmn. research com. 1962-64), Am. Chem. Soc., Am. Inst. Chem. Engrs., Sigma Xi, Omicron Delta Kappa, Gamma Alpha, Phi Gamma Delta. Clubs: Gibson Island (Md.); Chemists (N.Y.C.); Merchants (Balt.). Home: Gibson Island MD 21056

BACHMAN, STANDISH K., state ofcl.; b. Maplewood, N.J., Mar. 16, 1918; s. Stanley M. and Ruth (Kennedy) B.; student Brown U., 1936-38, N.Y.U., 1938-40; m. Meredith E. Tauck, Apr. 9, 1940; children—Standish K., Elaine, Judith, Merleyn. Sales rep. Ladies Home Jour., 1944-49; N.Y. slaes mgr. Look mag., N.Y.C., 1949-61; gen. bus. mgr. Am. Home mag., N.Y.C., 1961-63; commr. Me. Dept. Econ. Devel., Augusta, 1963-69. Dir. N.Y. Worlds Fair Corp.; treas. Me. Indsl. Bldg. Authority. Bd. dirs. New Eng. Council. Served to ensign USNR, 1942-43. Home: River Rd Bowdoinham ME 04008

BACHMANN, ERNEST THEODORE, clergyman; b. Philadelphia, Oct. 13, 1911; s. Ernest Frederick and Lydia (Brezing) B.; student Penn Charter Sch., Phila., 1925-29; B.A., Haverford (Pa.) Coll., 1933; M.A., Harvard, 1934; B.D., Lutheran Theol. Sem., Phila., 1937, S.T.M., 1942; Ph.D., U. of Chicago, 1946; grad. study U. of Tuebingen and Erlangen, Germany, 1937-38; D.D., Thiel Coll., 1963; D.S. Ed., Midland Coll., 1964; m. Mercia J. Brenne, Oct. 5, 1941; children—Frederick Brenne, Mary Lydia. Ordained minister of United Lutheran Ch., 1938; asst. pastor Trinity Lutheran Ch., Pottsville, Pa., 1938-40; pastor St. Stephen's Lutheran Ch., Wilmington, Del., 1940-42; prof. ch. history, Chicago Lutheran Sem., Maywood, Ill., 1942-48; dep. chief Religious Affairs Branch. Office of U.S. High Commr. for Germany, 1948-51; guest prof. church history Luther Theol. Sem., St. Paul. 1951- 52; prof. ch. history and missions, also director of graduate studies Pacific Lutheran Theological Seminary, Berkeley, 1952-61; sec. theol. edn. United Lutheran Ch. Am., 1961-62; exec. sec. bd. coll. edn. Luth. Ch. in Am., 1962-64, exec. secretary board of theol. education, 1964—. Chairman commission on Theological education dept. ministry Nat. Council of Churches, 1965-69. Liaison rep. between World Council of Chs. (Geneva hdqrs.) and chs. in Germany, 1946-47; prisoner of war work under Internat. Y.M.C.A. War Prisoners' Aid Program, 1945-46. Mem. Social Service Commn., Church Fedn. of Greater Chicago, Am. Soc. Ch. History, Am. Hist. Association, Luther Association, American Theological Society, also Phi Beta Kappa. Independent. Author: They Called Him Father—the Life Story of Christian Frederick Heyer, 1942; Epic of Faith, 1952; Word and Sacrament, 1960; Lutherans in Brazil, 1970; contbr. theol. and religious jours. Home: 73 Philip Dr Princeton NJ 08540 Office: 231 Madison Av New York City NY 10016

BACHMANN, INGEBORG, writer; b. Klagenfurt, Austria, June 25, 1926; ed. univs. Graz, Innsbruck and Vienna. Writer for Vienna Broadcasting Co., 1952; vis. prof. poetry U. Frankfurt, 1959-60. Recipient prize Group 47, 1953; prize Fedn. Assn. German Ind., 1954; prize Assn. German Critics, 1960; Radio Play prize, 1959; Büchner prize, 1964. Mem. German PEN-Center, Berlin Acad. Arts. Author: Die gestundete Zeit (poetry), 1953; Das 30 Jahr (short stories), 1960; (radio plays) Die Zikaden, 1954, Der Gute Gott von Manhattan, 1958; Ein Ort für Zufälle, 1965; librettos for ballet Der Idiot, 1952, opera Der Prinz von Homburg, 1960, opera Der Junge Lord, 1964. Address: care R Piper & Co Verlag 8 Munich 13 Georgenstrasse 4 German Fed Republic also Via Bocca di Leone 60 Rome Italy*

BACHMANN, RAPHAEL OTTO, univ. dean; b. Granville, Ia., Jan. 28, 1921; s. Joseph Franz and Eleanor Elizabeth (Bunkers) B.; B.S., Creighton U., 1942; Ph.D. (fellow Am. Found. Pharm. Edn. 1947-49), Purdue U., 1950; m. Mary Eleanor Mather, June 12, 1948; children—Linda Ann, Carolyn Sue, Richard Allen. Grad. asst. Purdue U., 1942-44, asst. prof. pharm. chemistry, 1949-51, asso. prof., 1951-54; prof. pharm. chemistry U. Ark., 1954-61; dean, prof. Sch. Pharmacy, W.Va. U., Morgantown, 1961—. Bd. dirs. Am. Found. for Pharm. Edn. Served to lt. USNR, 1944-46. Recipient Lehn & Fink medal, 1942. Mem. Am. Pharm. Assn., Am. Assn. Colls. Pharmacy (chmn. chem. tchrs. sect. 1955-56, pres. 1969-70), Am. Chem. Soc., Am. Acad. Pharm. Sci., W.Va. Pharm. Assn. (dir.), Am. Inst. History Pharmacy (W.Va. rep.), A.A.A.S., Iowa, Monongalia County, Pulaski County (v.p.) Pharm. assns., Am. Coll. Apothecaries, Am. Soc. Pharmacognosy, U.S. Pharm. Conv., Am. Bd. Diplomates in Pharmacy (charter, regional dir.), Nat. Drug Trade Conf. (del.), Morgantown C. of C., Sigma Xi, Rho Chi, Kappa Psi, Phi Sigma Kappa, Phi Lambda Upsilon, Alpha Chi Sigma, Alpha Sigma Nu. Rotarian. Home: 1281 Dogwood Av Morgantown WV 26505

BACHMEYER, ROBERT WESLEY, assn. exec.; b. Cin., Jan. 11, 1915; s. Arthur C. and Lulu K. (Troeger) B.; A.B., U. Cin., 1939; M.B.A., U. Chgo., 1947; m. Margaret L. Knickerbocker, Jan. 25, 1942; children—Susan Lee, Janet Lynne, Margaret Ann, Asst. dir. Hosp. for Spl. Surgery, N.Y.C., 1941; hosp. specialist USPHS, Washington, 1942; asst. dir. Children's Hosp., Boston, 1946; dir. Aultman Hosp., Canton. O., 1947-54. St. Barnabas Hosp. and St. Andrews Hosp., Mpls., 1954-63; mem. faculty, course hosp. adminstrn. U. Minn., 1955-63; preceptor course hosp. adminstrn. U. Chgo., 1949—; exec. dir. Youngstown Hosp. Assn., 1963-68; prin. Herman Smith Associates, hospital consultants, Hinsdale, Ill., 1968-71; v.p. adminstrn. Am. Coll. Hosp. Adminstrs., Chgo., 1971—. Lectr. hosp. adminstrn. George Washington U., Med. Coll. Va. Secretary- treasurer St. Barnabas Hosp. Research Foundation; assistant treas. board trustees Youngstown Hospital; mem. bd. of trustees Blue Cross, Youngstown, O., 1963-68; bd. trustees Mpls. War Meml. Blood Bank, 1955-63. Served to lt. AUS, 1943- 46. Fellow Am. Coll. Hosp. Adminstrs. (regional regent 1957-62, pres. 1963-64); mem. Am. Protestant Hosp. Assn. (trustee 1954-63), Am. Hosp. Assn. (life), U. Chgo. Program Hosp. Adminstrn. Alumni Assn. (pres. 1964-65), Am. Pub. Health Assn., Royal Soc. Health (Eng.), Hosp. Adminstrs. Study Soc. Home: 314 N Bruner Av Hinsdale IL 60521 Office: 840 N Lake Shore Dr Chicago IL 60611

BACHRACH, ALICE (Mrs. Alfred R. Bachrach), volunteer social welfare; b. N.Y.C.; d. David and Dora (Stern) Rothschild; student N.Y. schs., Parsons Sch. Design; m. Alfred R. Bachrach, Dec. 3, 1924; children—John David and Robert Lee (twins), Ellin (Mrs. Baron J. Gordon). Began volunteer work, 1920; was active in organizing women's div. Nat. Jewish Welfare Bd., chmn. women's div., mem. bd. dirs. and exec. com., 1942-55, hon. chmn., 1955—, v.p. Nat. Jewish Welfare Bd., 1945-64; mem. bd. Nat. U.S.O., 1942—, v.p., 1951-64, exec. com., 1951-64; former mem. Women's Adv. Council, Dept. Def.; former mem. Nat. Civilian Adv. Com., W.A.C.; former sec., mem. bd. A.S.A.F.; former mem. Women's adv. com. information M.S.A.; mem. Conf. on Vol. Services to Psychiat. Patients, 1957-58; gov. Hebrew Union Coll., Jewish Inst. Religion; past sec. Com. Frank L. Weil Inst. Advanced Studies of Religion and Humanities; past mem. VA Voluntary Service Nat. Adv. Com., chmn. study on recruitment and retention of vols.; past v.p. YWHA, N.Y.C.; exec. com. nat. bd. Girl Scouts, 1946, v.p., 1953-57; former chmn. Am. Girl Mag. Girl Scouts; former mem. bd. Fedn. Jewish Philanthropic Orgns. of N.Y.C.; mem. Blood Center Devel. Com. of N.Y., 1962-; dir., mem. exec. com. N.Y. Blood Center, also sec., 1969—; former trustee, mem. exec., devel. coms. Parsons sch. Design. Recipient Frank L. Weil award for contbn. to service for men and women in armed forces, 1952. Club: Women's City (N.Y.C.). Home: 33 E 70th St New York City NY 10021

BACHRACH, BRADFORD K., photographer; b. Worcester, Mass., Nov. 8, 1910; s. Louis Fabian and Dorothy Deland (Keyes) B.; grad. Phillips Exeter Acad., 1929; A.B., Harvard, 1933; m. Rosamond Esselen, Feb. 19, 1939; children—Susan Prentiss, William Bradford, Dorothy Locke, Laura Keyes. With Bachrach, Inc., portrait photographers, Watertown, Mass., 1933—, v.p., dir., 1938—, pres, 1955—. Served to lt. USNR, 1943-45. Mem. Mass. Soc. Mayflower Descs. Unitarian. Clubs: Harvard (N.Y.C.); Wellesley Country. Home: 50 Windsor Rd Wellesley Hills MA 02181 Office: 44 Hunt St Watertown MA 02172

BACHRACH, LOUIS FABIAN, Jr., portrait photographer; b. Newton, Mass., Apr. 9, 1917; s. Louis Fabian and Dorothy Deland (Keyes) B.; grad. Phillips Exeter Acad., 1935; A.B., Harvard, 1939; m. Janice Rose Daugherty, Dec. 27, 1941; children—Pamela Keyes, Gretchen Burdie, Louis Fabian III, Robert Deland. With Bachrach, Inc., Watertown, Mass., 1939—, v.p., 1950—, treas., 1959—; dir. First Fed. Savs. & Loan Assn., Boston. Served to lt. USNR, 1942-45. Unitarian. Home: 215 Highland Av Newtonville MA 02160 Office: 44 Hunt St Watertown MA 02172

BACHRACH, PETER, educator; b. Chgo., June 19, 1918; s. Walter and Alice (Loeb) B.; A.B., Reed Coll., 1942; Ph.D., Harvard, 1952; m. Florence Helena Rice, Mar. 15, 1946; children—Lorein (Mrs. James JeDon), Catherine, Sarah, Ruth, Molly, David. Teaching fellow, tutor dept. govt. Harvard, 1945-46; mem. faculty Bryn Mawr Coll., 1946-67, prof. polit. sci., 1963-68, chmn. dept., 1965-68; prof. polit. sci. Temple U., Phila., 1968—; vis. prof. Swarthmore Coll., 1954, U. P.R., 1957, Haverford Coll., 1962. Mem. selection com. region IV, Woodrow Wilson Fellowship Found., 1967—; cons. to Commn. Population Growth and the American Future, 1970-71. Bd. dirs. Greater Phila. br. Am. Civil Liberties Union. Ford Found. fellow, 1952-53; Rockefeller Found. fellow, 1957-58, 64-65. Mem. Am. Polit. Sci. Assn. (mem. com. on status women in profession 1969—), Am. Soc. Polit. and Legal Philosophy, Am. Assn. U. Profs. Author: Problems in Freedom, 1954; The Theory of Democratic Elitism, 1967; (with M. Baratz) Power and Poverty, 1970. Editor, contbr. Roles of Elites in a Democracy, 1971; adv. editor Politics and Society, 1970—. Contbr. profl. jours., encys. Home: 673 Ardmore Av Ardmore PA 19001 Office: Dept of Political Science Temple Univ 1947 N Broad St Philadelphia PA 19122

BACK, PAUL WILLIAM, art dir., artist; b. Bklyn., Feb. 9, 1929; s. William and Edna (Olmstead) B.; B.F.A., Pratt Inst., 1952; Centre D'Arte scholar Centre D'Arte, Haiti, summer 1951; m. Ursula Susan Weinand, May 9, 1965; children—Stacey Lee, Alicia Ursula. Polit. cartoonist Newsday, 1957-58, art. dir., 1959—; one man shows include Vera Lazuk Gallery, N.Y.C., 1961, 64; rep. permanent collections Frick Family, Scripps Family; archtl. designer 43 bldgs. Dairy Barn Stores, 1960—; advt. cons. Dairy Barn Stores, Inc., 1960—. Named Polit. Cartoonist of Year, Oberlin Coll., 1958; recipient Art. Dir. of Year award L.I. Art Dirs Club, 1963. Mem. L.I. Art Dirs. Club (v.p. 1964). Home: 87 Bayview Av Northport NY 11768 Office: 550 Stewart Av Garden City NY 11530

BACKE, JOHN DAVID, corp. exec.; b. Akron, O., July 5, 1932; s. John A. and Ella A. (Enyedy) B.; B.S. in Bus. Adminstrn., Miami U., 1954; M.B.A., Xavier U., 1961; m. Katherine A. Elliott, Oct. 22, 1955; children—Kim, John. Various managerial positions in engring., financial and marketing functions Gen. Electric Co., 1957-66; v.p., dir. marketing Silver Burdett Co. div. Gen. Learning Corp., 1966-68, pres., 1968-69; exec. v.p. Gen. Learning Corp., Morristown, N.J., 1969, pres., chief exec. officer, 1969—. Chmn. employee and pub. relations Gen. Electric Park Commn., Cin., 1960; mem. Phoenix City Planning Bd., 1963-64. Trustee United Fund Morris County, 1971—. Served to 1st lt. USAF, 1954-57. Home: 43 Penwood Rd Basking Ridge NJ 07920 Office: 250 James St Morristown NJ 07960

BACKER, WILLIAM M., advt. agy. exec. Sr. v.p. McCann-Erickson, Inc., N.Y.C. Office: 485 Lexington Av New York City NY 10017*

BACKLAR, MARSHAL, motion picture producer; b. St. Louis, Aug. 13, 1935; s. Joseph and Rosemary (Shuchart) B.; A.B., Princeton, 1957; postgrad. U. Paris (France), 1957-58. Producer Skaterdater, 1st prize winning motion picture in Cannes (1966) and Moscow (1967) film festivals; pres. Byway Prodns., Inc., 1965—; co-producer TV spl. trilogy: The American Boy, 1966-67 (Silver Dove winner Monte Carlo TV Festival 1968); feature motion picture producer Twentieth Century Fox, 1967-69, Pretty Poison, 1968; co- producer film The River Boy (1st prize Venice and Vancouver film festivals), 1967. Served with AUS, 1959-61. Nominated for Acad. award, 1965. Office: Columbia Pictures 1438 N Gower Av Hollywood CA 90028

BACKLUND, BRANDON HAZE, cons. engr.; b. Amarillo, Tex., June 13, 1918; s. Francis Victor and Nancy (Haze) B.; student Neb. U., 1937-40, Omaha U., 1948: B.S. in Civil Engring., Ia. State Coll., 1941; m. Emily Louise Hess, June 5, 1941; children—Nancy Lee, Mark Haze, Gregory. Structural engr. Ceco Steel Products Corp., Omaha, 1947-49; dist. structural engr. Portland Cement Assn., Omaha, 1949-51; pres. B.H. Backlund & Assos., architects, engrs., Omaha, Grand Island 1951-68, Backlund Caribbean Engring. Corp., St. Croix, V.I. 1961—, World Wide Consultants, Washington 1964-66; v.p., gen. mgr. McGaughy, Marshall, McMillan & Backlund, architects, engrs., Omaha, Grand Island, 1968—. Chmn. adv. council Neb. State Tech. Services, 1966—; pres. Neb Transp. Inst., 1967- 71. Served from 2d lt. to lt. col. C.E., AUS 1941- 47; dep. comdr. Neb. N.G., 1967—. Decorated Bronze Star medal. Registered profl. engr., Neb., Ia., Minn., N.D., S.D., Wyo., Colo., Kan., P.R., Va., Cal. Fellow Am. Soc. C.E.; mem. Omaha Bus. Men's Assn., Soc. Am. Mil. Engrs., Colegio de Ingenieros, Arquitectos y Agramenseres de P.R., Am. Inst. Cons. Engrs., Water Resources Assn., Nat. (v.p. 1959-61, dir. 1953-55, pres. 1964-65), Neb. (pres. 1956-57, dir. 1950-54) socs. profl. engrs., Omaha (chmn. hwy. com. 1956), U.S. chambers commerce, Am. Pub. Works Assn., Omaha Engrs. Club, Profl. Engrs. of Neb., Am Waterworks Assn., Nat. Fedn. Ind. Businessmen. Mason (Shriner), Rotarian, Elk. Home: 13114 Leavenworth Rd Omaha NB 68154 Office: 8610 Cass St Omaha NB 68114

BACKMAN, CARL WARD, educator; b. Canandiagua, N.Y., July 1, 1923; s. Carl Fritios and Edna Lillian (Ward) B.; B.A., Oberlin Coll., 1948; M.A., Ind. U., 1950, Ph.D., 1954; m. Shirley Louise Bennett, June 25, 1947; children—Carl, Lorraine, Elaine, Valerie. Instr., U. Ark., Fayetteville, 1951-55; prof. sociology U. Nev., Reno, 1955-64, 67—; program dir. sociology and social psychology NSF, Washington, 1965-67. Cons. NSF, NIH, Nat. Inst. Mental Health. Served with AUS, 1943-46. Grantee Nat. Inst. Mental Health, 1958-62, U.S. Office Edn., 1963-64. Fellow Am. Sociol. Assn., Am. Psychol. Assn., A.A.A.S.; mem. Pacific Sociol. Assn. (pres. 1969-70), Soc. Exptl. Social Psychology. Author: (with P.F. Secord) Social Psychology, 1964, Problems in Social Psychology, 1966, A Social Psychological View of Education, 1968. Editor: Sociometry, 1969-72. Home: 1225 Hoge Rd Reno NV 89503

BACKMAN, JULES, economist, educator, author; b. N.Y.C., May 3, 1910; s. Nathan and Gertrude (Schall) B., B.C.S., N.Y. U., 1931, A.M., 1932, M. B.A., 1933, D.C.S., 1935; m. Grace Straim, Oct. 18 1935; children—Susan Frank, John Randolph. Statistician Sydeman Bros., stock brokers, 1932-33; v.p. editor Econ. Statistics, Inc., 1933-35; with SEC, 1935; pub. utility research Madden & Dorau, 1936-37; instr. econs. Sch. Commerce, N.Y.U., N.Y.C., 1938-44, asst. prof., 1944-46, asso. prof. 1946-50, prof., 1950-60, research prof., 1960—. Dir. Scarsdale Nat. Bank. Head econ. cons OPA, 1942, Brooking Inst., 1943; econ. advisor Steel Wage Cases, 1944, 49, 52; tech. adv. to industry mems. President's Cost of Living Com., 1944; econ. adv. to r.r. in wage and rate cases 1946-60, N.Y. Joint Legis. Com. on Rents, 1953; mem. N.Y. Milk Shed Price Com., 1947-49; mem. Gov's. Com. on Milk Marketing, 1961-65. Gen. chmn. Reform Jewish Appeal, 1966-69; mem. Nat. Marketing Adv. Com., 1967-69; cons. Gen. Accounting Office, 1971—. Mem. N.Y.U. Senate, 1962-65; vice chmn. bd. govs. Hebrew Union Coll. Recipient N.Y. Univ. Meritorious Service award, 1943, Madden award 1960, Man of Year 1961 award Alumni N.Y.U.; Presidential citation N.Y. U., 1964; Am. Judaism award, 1970. Hon. fellow Am. Statis. Assn.; mem. Am. Econ. Assn., Soc. Bus. Adv. Profs. (pres. 1955), N.Y. U. Alumni Fedn (pres. 1954-56), Beta Gamma Sigma, Phi Lambda Delta, Lambda Gamma Phi, Sigma Eta Phi (hon.) Alpha Phi Sigma (hon.). Clubs: N.Y.U. (chmn. bd. 1961-65), Metropolis Country (dir.). Author: Adventures in Price Fixing, 1936; Government Price Fixing, 1938; Investment Dynamics, 1939; Rationing and Price Control in Great Britain 1943; Price Contorl and Subsidy Program in Canada 1943; Economics of the Potash Industry, 1946; Surety Rate Making, 1949; Bituminous Coal Wages, Profits, and Productivity, 1950; Economics of Armament Inflation, 1951; (ed. and co-author) War and Defense Economics, 1952; Price Practices and Price Policies, 1953; Rate Policies and Rate Practices of the Post Office, 1954; Administered Prices, 1957; Wage Determination, 1959; Pricing: Policies and Practices, 1960; Advertising and Competition, 1967; The Economics of the Machinery Industry, 1962; Economics of the Chemical Industry, 1970; (with M.R. Gainsbrugh) Economics of the Cotton Textile Industry, 1946, Inflation and the Price Indexes, 1966. Econ. editor: Trust & Estates mag., 1938-46; editorial writer N.Y. Times, 1943-48. Home: 59 Crane Rd Scarsdale NY 10583 Office: NYU Sch Commerce Washington Square New York City NY 10003

BACKOFEN, WALTER ALAN, educator: b. Rockville, Conn., Dec. 8, 1925; s. Walter P. and Bertha (Pfau) B.; S.B., Mass. Inst. Tech., 1946, Sc.D., 1950; m. Elizabeth W. Warren, Aug. 6, 1950. Faculty Mass. Inst. Tech., 1950—, prof. metallurgy and materials sci., 1968-. Mem. Am. Soc. Metals (Bradley Stoughton award 1959, Henry Marion Howe medal 1965), Am. Inst. Metall. Engrs., Brit. Inst. Metals. Home: 2 Lee St Marblehead, MA 01945 Office: 77 Massachusetts Av Cambridge MA 02139

BACKRASS, ERWIN, physician; b. Frankfurt/Main, Germany, July 3, 1922; s. Wilhelm C. and Elisabeth (Michels) B.; M.D., Johann W. Goethe U., 1951; postgrad. N.Y. Polyclinic Med. Sch. and Hosp., 1953-54. Came to U.S., 1951, naturalized, 1956. Intern St. John's Riverside Hosp., Yonkers, N.Y., also No. Westchester Hosp., Mt. Kisco, N.Y., 1951-53; psychiat, resident State Hosp., Howard, R.I., also Norwich, (Conn.) State Hosp., 1954-56, 58-59; staff physician State Hosp., Howard, 1956-58, 59-61; clin. dir. R.I. Inst. Mental Health, Howard, 1961-64, supt., 1964-67; div. chief Ft. Logan Mental Health Center, Denver, 1968-. Diplomate Am. Bd. Psychiatry and Neurology. Mem. Am. Psychiat. Assn., New Eng. Soc. Psychiatry. Address: 3520 W Oxford Av Denver CO 80236.

BACKSTROM, FREDERICK THURE, savs. and loan assn. exec.; b. Lidkoping, Sweden, July 18, 1903; s. Carl Victor and Eva Maria (Utberg) B.; came to U.S., 1907, naturalized, 1914; diploma Am. Savs. and Loan Inst., 1931; m. Ethel M. Erickson, June 19, 1927; 1 son, Alan George. Br. mgr. Century Fed. Savs. & Loan, N.Y.C., 1926-40; with First Fed. Savs. & Loan Assn., New Haven, 1940—, pres., 1955-69, chmn. bd., 1969—; dir. FHLB Bank, Boston, 1949- 52; mem. adv. council FHLB, Washington, 1950-52; dir. Tradesmens Nat. Bank, New Haven, Underground Protective Vault, Inc., Stafford Springs, Conn., 1962-68. Pres. New Haven Council Chs., 1955-56. Trustee Arnold Coll., Milford, Conn., 1947-50; sec., trustee Quinnipiac Coll., Hamden, Conn., 1963—; bd. dirs. Quinnipiack council Boy Scouts Am., 1961—; adv. council Sch. Exec. Devel. New Haven Coll., 1963-68. Mem. U.S. (bd. dirs., exec. com. 1948-51), Conn. (pres. 1951) savs. and loan leagues, Fed. Savs. and Loan Council Conn. (pres. 1942-43), Council Mut. Savs. Instns. (chmn. bd. 1965-69), Am. Savs. and Loan Inst. (pres. N.Y.C. chpt. 1930-31), Conn. (bd. dirs. 45-49), New Haven (bd. dirs. 1952-55) chambers commerce. Clubs: Rotary (pres. 1957-58), Quinnipiack (pres. 1963-64) (New Haven). Home: 1040 Ridge Rd Hamden CT 06517 Office: 80 Elm St New Haven CT 06503

BACKUS, DANA CONVERSE, lawyer; b. Bayonne, N.J., Feb. 26, 1907; s. Henry M. and Mary E. (Neilson) B.; A.B., Harvard, 1927, LL.B., 1929; m. Louise B. Laidlaw, Sept. 16, 1933; children—Mary (Mrs. Douglas Rankin), Janet (Mrs. E. Blythe Stason, Jr.), Elizabeth (Mrs. Stephen Stuart Girard Jr.), Harriet Meredith (Mrs. Conrad H. Todd), Anne Converse (dec.). Admitted to N.Y. bar, 1930, since practiced N.Y.C.; partner Kramer, Marx, Greenlee & Backus. Sec., dir. J.R. Wood & Son, Inc., 1958-70; Allied English Potteries, Inc., 1970—. Exec. com. Citizens Union; pres. Citizens Union Research Found Am. del. Assn. UN to World Fedn. UN Assns., 1946-47; mem. secretariat UN Conf., San Francisco, 1945; mem. exec. com. Com. for Def. of Constn. by Preserving Treaty Power, 1952-54. Served from capt. to lt. col. Judge Adv. Gen.'s Dept., AUS, 1943-46. Mem. Assn. Bar City N.Y., Mayflower Soc., Phi Beta Kappa. Clubs: Downtown Assn., Lunch, Harvard (L.I. v.p., N.Y.C., L.I.); Manhasset Bay Yacht, Appalachian Mountain. Contbr. many articles to profl. jours. Home: 1158 Fifth Av New York City NY 10029 also 180 Middle Neck Rd Sands Point Port Washington NY 11050 Office: 29 Broadway New York City NY 10006

BACKUS, JIM, (James Gilmore Backus), actor, writer; b. Cleve., Feb. 25, 1913; s. Russell Gould and Daisy (Gilmore-Taylor) B.; student Ky. Mil. Sch., Louisville, U. Sch., Cleve., Am. Acad. Dramatic Arts, N.Y.C.; m. Henriette Kaye (Henny Backus), Jan. 14, 1943. Broadway, radio, Bel Air CA Office: 8810 Sunset Blvd Los Angeles CA 90069

BACKUS, MYRON PORT, educator, mycologist; b. Madison, Wis., Apr. 14, 1908; s. Edward W. and Elizabeth (Port) B.; A.B., U. Wis., 1928, A.M., 1929, Ph.D., 1931; m. Ingrid Simley, Aug. 17, 1931; 1 son, Bernard M. NRC fellow N.Y. Bot. Garden and Columbia, 1931-33; asso. mycology Boyce Thompson Inst. Plant Research, 1933-34; mem. faculty U. Wis.-Madison, 1934—, prof. botany and plant pathology, 1947—, emeritus, 1971—; collaborator in penicillin project under Office Prodn. Research and Devel., WPB World War II. Mem. 3d Internat. Congress Microbiology, N.Y., 1939. Mem. Mycol. Soc. Am., Brit. Mycol. Soc., Am. Phytopathol. Soc., Wis. Acad. Scis., Arts and Letters. Torrey Bot. Club, Phi Beta Kappa (treas. Alpha chpt. Wis. 1938-50), Sigma Xi, Phi Sigma, Gamma Alpha. Editorial bd. Mycologia, 1949-53; chmn. editorial bd. Mycologia Memoirs, 1953-56; adv. editor in mycology Bot. Rev., 1947-65. Contbr. articles sci. jours. Home: 1811 Regent St Madison WI 53705

BACON, CECIL HENRY, Jr., forest products co. exec.; b. Seattle, May 26, 1909; s. Cecil Henry and Ellen (Cook) B.; B.A., U. Wash., 1930; Velma Payne, June 11, 1945; children—Terry Payne (Mrs. Frank Calver, Jr.), Barbara Ann. Engaged in retail bldg. material business, 1930-41; pres. Henry Bacon, Inc., 1941-45; with Simpson Logging Co., Shelton, Wash., 1945-58, v.p., gen. mgr., 1953-58; with Simpson Timber Co., Seattle, 1958—, pres., 1962-70, vice chmn., 1970—, also dir.; dir. Simpson Lee Paper Co., Simlog Corp., Seattle br. Fed. Res. Bd. San Francisco. Trustee Va. Mason Hosp., Ryther Child Center (both Seattle). Served with USAAF, 1941-45. Mem. N.A.M. (bd. dirs.), Nat. Forest Products Assn. (bd. dirs.), Seattle C. of C. (trustee 1961-64, 65-68, 70-73). Episcopalian. Clubs: Rainier, Seattle Golf, Seattle Yacht, University (Seattle); Tacoma. Home: The Highlands Seattle WA 98177 Office: Washington Bldg Seattle WA 98101

BACON, CHARLES LANGSTON, lawyer; b. Marshall, Mo., Oct. 14, 1909; s. Charles B. and Nettie (Fry) B.; A.B., Missouri Valley Coll., 1930, LL.D., 1962; LL.B., Mo. U., 1934; m. Helen Elizabeth Selvidge, Dec. 28, 1941; children—Sharon Ruth, Charles Langston. Admitted to Mo. bar, 1933, Fed. Ct., 1934, Supreme Ct., 1949; partner Judge Robert D. Johnson, 1934; mem. firm James & Bacon, 1941-52; chief counsel Marketing div. Skelly Oil Co., 1952; now partner firm Shook, Hardy, Ottman, Mitchell & Bacon. Sec. Jackson County Bd. Park Commrs.; mem. Mo. Citizens Commn. for Study Pub. Schs., 1951-53; pres. Greater Kansas City Armed Forces Council, Mo. Boys' State, 1950-51; trustee Missouri Valley Coll., 1938—; pres. Liberty Meml. Assn., 1969—. Served with USNR, 1942-46 Decorated commandeur Croix de Merite Combattant (France), 1962; recipient Legion of Honor, Order de Molay, 1963; Meritorious Pub. Service citation U.S. Navy, 1962. Mem. Mo. Bar (gov.), Mil. Order World Wars, Am. Legion (Mo. comdr. 1950, nat. comdr. 1961-62, Acad. Mo. Squires, Phi Delta Phi, Omicron Delta Kappa, Sigma Nu, Mason. Editorial bd. Mo. Law Rev., 1932-33. Home: 1263 W 67th Terrace Kansas City MO 64113 Office: 915 Grand Av Kansas City MO 64116

BACON, CHARLES SUMNER, educator; b. Chgo., Dec. 13, 1901; s. Charles S. and Maria F. E. (von Rosthorn) B.; B.S., U. Chgo., 1922, M.S., 1923; Ph.D., U. Vienna, 1926; m. Virginia Dare Dillon, July 30, 1963; children—John Arthur, Robert Charles, Mary Frances (Mrs. Gilbert Escandon). Field geologist Huasteca Petroleum Co., 1926; refinery engr. Pure Oil Co., 1927; instr. geology Riverside (Cal.) Coll., 1928-36; instr., asso. prof. geology Tex. A. and M. Coll., 1936-42; geologist U.S. Geol. Survey, Salt Lake City, 1942-45; cons., San Bernardino, Cal., 1945-47; prof., dept. head Case Inst. Tech., 1947-61; prof. geology Case Western Res. U., 1961-68, emeritus, 1968—; Fulbright exchange prof. geology U. Vienna, 1955-56; exchange prof., head mining engring. Bandung (Indonesia) Inst. Tech., 1959-61; vis. prof., chmn. dept. geology Am. U., Beirut, Lebanon, 1968-70. Fellow Ohio Acad. Sci., A.A.A.S.; mem. Am. Assn. Petroleum Geologists, Mineral. Soc. Am., Mineral. Soc. Can., Assn. Geology Tchrs. Author: Lab. Manual College Geology, 2d edit., 1962; Application of the Niggli-Becke Projection for Rock Analyses, 1947; Geology of Confusion Range, Utah, 1948; Comparison of Higher Education in America, Indonesia and Europe, 1960. Home: 6073 Wedgewood Dr Mentor OH 44060

BACON, DAISY SARAH, editor, writer; b. Pennsylvania; d. E. Ellsworth and Jessie M. (Holbrook) Bacon; educated by pvt. tutors. Editor: Love Story mag. since 1928: Ainslee's Mag., 1934-38; Smart Love Stories, 1937-39; Pocket Love mag., 1937; Detective Story and Romantic Range mags. since 1940; special overseas edition Detective Story mag. for armed forces distributed by Special Services Div., A.S.F. U.S. Army, 1942-June 1946; publisher of Gemini Books, 1963—. Spur Awards judge Western Writers Am., 1967-68. Mem. Daus. Am. Revolution. Republican, Episcopalian. Compiler of four prize story anthologies annually: Detective Story Annual, All Fiction Detective Stories, All Fiction Stories, Love Story Annual. Author: Love Story Writer, 1953, 2d edit., 1959; Love Story Editor, 1963; The Fiction Years (to be published). Contributor of articles magazines. Desc. Gov. William Bradford of Plymouth Colony, and Capt. John Holbrook of Weymouth. Home: 7 Hillside Av Port Washington NY 11050 Office: 520 Fifth Av New York City NY 10036

BACON, DONALD WALTER, govt. ofcl.; b. Cin., Aug. 28, 1914; s. Frank B. and Laura (Claassen) B.; A.B., Antioch Coll., 1939; m. Lois Neuhart, June 8, 1946; children—Janet, Anne, David, Susan. With Lybrand, Ross Bros. & Montgomery, C.P.A.'s, Chgo., 1939-40; asst. budget dir. Studebaker Corp., South Bend, Ind., 1940-42; staff Office Comptroller Gen., Washington, 1946-53, Dept. Army, Washington, 1953-54; with Internal Revenue Service, 1954—, regional commr., 1956-62 asst. commr., 1962—. Served as lt. comdr. USNR, 1942-46. Mem. Am. Inst. C.P.A.'s, Mass. Soc. C.P.A.'s, Fed. Govt. Accountants Assn. (nat. pres. 1962-63). Home: 1440 Cola Dr McLean VA 22101 Office: US Internal Revenue Service 12th and Constitution Avs Washington DC 20225

BACON, DOROTHY CAROLIN, economist; b. Beloit, Wis., Feb. 25, 1902; d. George Preston and Hanna (Churchill) Bacon; student Simmons Coll., 1918-19; A.B., Radcliffe Coll., 1922, A.M., 1924, Ph.D., 1928. Statistical asst., div. research and statis. Fed. Res. Bd., 1922-23; asst in econs. Vassar Coll., 1924- 25, instr., 1925-26; with Smith Coll., 1927—, prof., 1938-70, prof. emeritus, 1970—, Robert A. Woods prof. econs., 1956-70; head statis. lab., Bur. Bus. Research, Met. Life Ins. Co., summer 1928; research asso. Nat. Bur. Econ. Research, 1930-31; sr. research asst. Fed Deposit Ins. Corp., 1934; fed. dir. research project on effects of fed. benefits on nat. economy WPA, 1935, 36; head research sect., copper price br., O.P.A., 1941-43; asst. div. economist Food Price Div., 1943- 45, cons., 1945-47; cons., food div. OPS, 1951; cons. internat. study group Brookings Instn., 1952; Fulbright prof. econs. U. Philippines, 1956-57; Ford Found. study grantee, Manila, Philippines, 1971. Mem. Am. Econ. Assn., Assn. Asian Studies, Asia Soc., Phi Beta Kappa Republican. Conglist. Author: Recent Economic History of Five Small Towns, 1937; also articles on econ. and statis. subjects in Rev. Econ. Statistics and Am. Statis. Jour. Home: Norton Hill Rd Ashfield MA 01330 Office: Smith College Northampton MA 01060

BACON, EDMUND NORWOOD, city planner; b. Phila., May 2, 1910; s. Ellis W. and Helen (Comly) B.; B.Arch., Cornell U., 1932; m. Ruth Holmes, Sept. 16, 1938; children—Karin Ellis, Elinor Ruth, Hilda Holmes (Mrs. Frederick W. Badenoch), Michael Comly, Prudence Ann, Kevin Norwood. Archtl. designer, Shanghai, China, 1934; with W. Pope Barney, architect, Phila., 1935; supr. city planning Inst. Research and Planning, Flint, Mich., 1937-39; mng. dir. Phila. Housing Assn., 1940-43; co-designer Better Phila. Exbn., also sr. land planner Phila. City Planning Commn., 1946-49; exec. dir. Phila. City Planning Commn., 1949-70, also devel. coordinator, 1968-70; prof. adviser in Franklin D. Roosevelt Meml. Competition, 1959; vis. lectr. U. Pa., 1950—. Mem. Pres.'s Citizen's Adv. Com. Recreation and Natural Beauty, 1966-69. Trustee Am. Acad. in Rome, 1965—. Recipient Art Alliance Phila. medal achievement, 1961; Man of Year award City Bus. Club Phila., 1962; Brown medal award Franklin Inst., 1962. Ford Found. travel fellow, 1959; Rockefeller fellow, 1963. Fellow A.I.A., Am. Inst. Planners. Author: Design of Cities, 1967. Address: 2117 Locust St Philadelphia PA 19103

BACON, ERNST, musician; b. Chicago, Ill., May 26, 1898; s. Dr. Charles S. and Maria von (Rosthorn) B.; student Northwestern U.; U. of Chicago; M.A., Univ. of California, 1935; studied privately with Alexander Raab, Glenn D. Gunn, Ernest Bloch, Karl Weigl; m. Mary Prentice Lillie, 1927; children—Margaret Frances and Joseph Rosthorn; m. 2d., Analee Camp, 1937; children—Paul Ernest Bacon, Arthur Bacon; m. 3d, Moselle Camp, 1952; 1 dau., Madeline K. Appeared in concerts in U.S. and Europe; served on faculties of Eastman School, Hamilton College and Converse College; founder Bach festival of Carmel, California, 1935; supervisor and conductor, Federal Music Project, San Francisco, 1935-37; dean Sch. of Music, Converse Coll., Spartanburg, S.C., 1938-45; dir. New Spartanburg Festival, 1939-45; dir. Sch. Music, Syracuse U., 1945-47, composer-in-residence, now prof. emeritus Syracuse (N.Y.) Univ. Bispham Award, Ditson and League of Composers Commns. Pulitzer fellowship, 1932, Guggenheim fellowship, 1939, 1942, Campion citation; grant-citation Nat. Inst. of Arts and Letters, American Society Authors, Composers and Publishers. Composer 3 symphonies; 4 orchestral suites; The Ecclesiastes; By Blue Ontario's Shore (choral); Great River (orchestra); 4 series orchestral songs; music to The Tempest, and Yours, A. Lincoln (Paul Horgan); (opera); A Tree on the Plains (Paul Horgan); Take Your Choice (musical comedy in collaboration); Drumlins Garden (opera); Riolama (piano-orchestra); Spirits and Places (organ); also works for piano, 2 pianos, ch. music and songs; Requiem (choral). Author: Words on Music; Notes on the Piano; Fables. Home: 57 Claremont Av Orinda CA 94563

BACON, FRANCIS, artist; b. Dublin, Ireland, 1909. Self-taught painter; one man exbns. include Hanover Gallery, London, Eng., 1949, Durlacher Bros., N.Y.C., 1953; one of three British reps. 27th Venice Biennale, 1954; other exhbns. include Mus. Modern Art, 1955, Paris, Turin, Milan and Rome, 1957-58, Marlborough Fine Art Gallery, London, 1960, Tate Gallery, London, 1962, Solomon R. Guggenheim Mus., 1963, Art Inst. Chgo., 1964, travelling exhbns. Hamburg Kunsthalle, Stockholm Modern Mus., Dublin Mus. Modern Art, 1965, Galerie Maeght, Paris, Marlborough Galleria d'Arte, Rome, Milan, Toninelli, London, 1966-67, Marlborough-Gerson, N.Y.C., 1968; retrospective show Grand Palais, Paris, 1971, Kunsthalle, Düsseldorf, 1972; represented in permanent collections Tate Gallery, Mus. Modern Art, Contemporary Art Soc. London, numerous others. Recipient Rubens prize City of Siegen (Germany), 1967. Address: care Marlborough Fine Art Gallery 39 Old Bond St London W1 England

BACON, HAROLD MAILE, mathematician, educator; b. Los Angeles, Jan. 13, 1907; s. Robert Harold and Lura (Maile) B.; A.B., Stanford, 1928, A.M., 1929, Ph.D., 1933; m. Rosamond Clarke, Feb. 23, 1946; 1 son, Charles Robert. Clk. actuary's dept. Pacific Mut. Life Ins. Co., Los Angeles, 1929-30; asst. in math. Stanford, (Cal.), 1930-31, acting instr., 1931-32, instr., 1932-36, asst. prof., 1936-43, asso. prof., 1943-50, prof. math., 1950—; Instr. math. San Jose (Cal.), State Coll., winter 1934- 35; prof. Math. Inst., U.S.C., summer 1959. Fellow A.A.A.S.; mem. Math. Assn. Am. (gov. 1941-43, 57-60, sec. No. Cal. sect. 1939-45, chmn. 1949-50), Am. Math. Soc., Nat. Council Tchrs. Math. Am. Assn. U. Profs., Cal. Math. Council, Phi Beta Kappa, Sigma Xi, Phi Delta Kappa, Theta Delta Chi. Democrat. Episcopalian. Author: Differential and Integral Calculus, 1942, 2d edit., 1955; (with C. G. Jaeger) Introductory College Mathematics, 1954, 62. Home: PO Box 4144 Stanford CA 94305

BACON, HARRY ELLICOTT, intestinal surgeon; b. Phila.; Aug. 25, 1900; s. H. Augustus and Minnie S. (Thomas) B.; grad. Friends Central Sch., 1918; B.S., Ursinus and Villanova Coll., 1921; M.D., Temple U., 1925; D.So., U. Argentina and Ursinus Coll.; postgrad. St. Marks Hosp. (London), Hosp. St. Antoine (Paris), U. Pa.; hon. degree U. Bologna, Italy; LL.D., U. Montevideo, Uruguay, 1963; m. Althea Perot Patrician, June 21, 1935; children—Andrea Perot, Harry Ellicott. Fellow in proctology U. Pa., 1928-30; clin. asst. anatomy Temple U. Med. Sch., 1930-1931, asso. prof. proctology Grad. Sch. Medicine 1936-1942, prof, head dept. proctology Med. Sch. and Temple U. Hosp., 1942—, pres. Temple U. Med. Staff; asst. chief surgeon radiologic dept. Phila. Gen. Hosp., 1934-38; cons. Mercy, Douglas, Nat. Stomach, Shriners, Rush hosps. (Phila.), St. Christopher's, Kimbal hosps. (Lakewood, N.J.), Frankford, Northeastern hosps. Guest lectr. med. colls., univs. Served as lt. comdr. USNR, 1941. Decorated Commando order la Courrone (Belgium); Cross Alfonso X-the Wise (Spain); Commando Carlos Finlay Cross (Cuba); recipient Gold Key, U. Vienna, Austria; La Societe de Cherurgie de Lyon, France and Soredad Chilena de Proctologia hon. fellow. Diplomate Am. Bd. Surgery, Am. Bd. Colon and Rectal Surgery (pres.). Hon. fellow fgn. med., surg. socs., Japan, Turkey, Brazil, P.I., Mexico, Italy, Chile, Cuba, Gt. Britain, France, Belgium, Germany, Egypt, Greece, also Internat. Coll. Surgeons. Am. Proctologic Soc. (pres. 1948); fellow A.C.S., Am. Gastroent. Research Soc.; mem. Internat. Soc. Surgery A.M.A., Am. Therapeutic Soc., Path. Soc., Nat. Gastroent. Soc., Soc. for Advancement Gastroenterology, Assn. Mil. Surgeons U.S., Franklin Inst., Am. Legion, Alpha Omega Alpha, Phi Chi. Republican. Presbyn. Mason (32). Clubs: Union League (N.Y.C., Phila.); University, Philadelphia Country, Plays and Players, Orpheus, Physicians Motor, Naval Officers, Medical, Aesculapian, Quarterbacks, Penn (Phila.); Racquet, Seaview Country. Author: Anus, Rectum and Sigmoid Colon, 3d edit., 1949; Essentials of Proctology, 1943; Atlas Surgery of Collon, 1955; Proctology, 1956; Surgical Anatomy of Rectum and Colon, 1956; Ulcerative Colitis, 1958; Surgical Anatomy, 1962; Cancer of Rectum and Colon, 1964. Home: 344 Laurel Lane Haverford PA 19041 Office: 255 S 17th St Philadelphia PA 19103

BACON, HELEN HAZARD, educator; b. Berkeley, Cal., Mar. 9, 1919; d. Leonard and Martha (Stringham) Bacon; B.A., Bryn Mawr Coll., 1940, Ph.D. , 1955; postgrad. U. Cal. at Berkeley, 1940-41, Radcliffe Coll., 1941-42, Litt.D., Middlebury Coll., 1970. With communications div. U.S. Navy Dept., 1942; instr. Greek and Freshman English, Bryn Mawr Coll., 1946-49; instr. Latin, N.C. Women's Coll., Greensboro, 1951-52; from instr. to asso. prof. Classics, Smith Coll., 1953-61; faculty Barnard Coll., N.Y.C., 1961—, prof. Greek and Latin, 1965—, chmn. dept., 1962—. Scholar in residence Am. Acad. in Rome, 1968-69. faculty Bread Loaf Sch. English, summers 1966, 68. Served to lt. WAVES, USNR, 1942-46. Fulbright fellow Am. Sch. Classical Studies, Athens, Greece, 1952-53; Founders fellow Am. Assn. U. Women, 1963-64. Mem. Am. Philol. Assn., Archaeol. Inst. Am., Classical assns. Empire State, Atlantic States, N.Y. Classical Club (v.p. 1965-67), Am. Civil Liberties Union (dir. Hampshire-Hamden chpt. 1959-60), Phi Beta Kappa (hon.). Author: Barbarians in Greek Tragedy, 1961; also articles, revs. Home: 464 Riverside Dr New York City NY 10027

BACON, ISAAC, coll. dean; b. Czechoslovakia, Sept. 3, 1914; s. Joshua Heschel and Rebecca (Klappholz) B.; Ph.D., Masaryk U., 1939; postgrad. Johns Hopkins, 1946; m. Esther Liebb, Jan. 4, 1942; childrenStephen J., Joshua H., Ari D. Came to U.S., 1939, naturalized, 1943. Faculty, U. Colo., 1946-60, instr., 1946-50, asst. prof., 1950-56, asso. prof., 1956-60; vis. lectr. Johns Hopkins, summer 1950; acting dean Yeshiva Coll., 1959, dean, 1960-, also prof. linguistics; faculty fellow Fund for Advancement Edn., 1954-55. Served with AUS, 1943-45. Mem. Mediaeval Acad. Am., Modern Lang. Assn., Renaissance Soc. Am. Linguistic Soc. Am., Am. Assn. Tchrs. German, Am. Assn. U. Profs. Office: Yeshiva College Amsterdam Av at 186th St New York City NY 10033

BACON, JAMES EDMUND, brokerage co. exec.; b. Mt. Vernon, N.Y., Feb. 27, 1931; s. John Anderson and Charlotte (Robb) B.; A.B., Harvard, 1952, LL.B., 1958; m. Edith Williamson, Oct. 5, 1963; children—Charlotte, Rachel, Nicholas. Admitted to N.Y. bar, 1966, D.C. N.Y. bar, 1959; with firm Steadman, Collier & Shannon, Washington, 1958-61; atty. spl. study SEC, 1961-63; v.p. surveillance Am. Stock Exchange, 1963-68; with G.H. Walker & Co., N.Y.C., 1968—, gen. partner, 1970—, v.p., sec., 1971—. Served to lt. (j.g.) USNR, 1952-55. Mem. U.S. C. of C., Met. Squash Racquets Assn. (pres.). Republican. Episcopalian. Clubs: Racquet and Tennis (N.Y.C.); University (Washington). Home: 1112 Park Av New York City NY 10028 Office: 45 Wall St New York City NY 10005

BACON, OSCAR GRAY, educator; b. Sanger, Cal., Nov. 8, 1919; s. Oscar F. and Julia (Gray) B.; A.B., Fresno State Coll., 1941; M.S., U. Cal. at Berkeley, 1944, Ph.D., 1948; m. Barbara Conover, June 25, 1970; children by previous marriage—Bonnie (Mrs. Stephen Krisiak), Gayle E. Faculty, U. Cal., Davis, 1948—, asso. prof., 1956-63, prof. econ. entomology, entomologist, 1963—, chmn. dept entomology, 1967—. Mem. Entomol. Soc. Am., Pacific Coast Entomol. Soc., A.A.A.S., Sigma Xi. Home: 615 Cordova Pl Davis CA 95616

BACON, PEGGY, artist, writer; b. Ridgefield, Conn., May 2, 1895; d. Charles Roswell and Elizabeth (Chase) Bacon; diploma Kent Place Sch., Summit, N.J., 1913; student Art Students' League, Sch. Fine and Applied Arts, N.Y.C.; m. Alexander Brook, May 4, 1920 (div.); children—Belinda, Alexander Bacon. Began as artist, 1920; tchr. art Fieldston Sch., N.Y.C., 1933-39; former tchr life drawing, painting and composition Art Students League, tchr. drawing Hunter Coll., Stella Elkins Tyler Coll. Fine Arts, Phila., Corcoran Art Sch., Washington; past tchr. New Sch. Social Research, New Art Center, Kennebunk, Me., summers; tchr. Summer Sch. Music and Art, Stowe, Vt.; work represented in permanent collection Met. and other museums. Guggenheim fellow, 1934; grant Nat. Acad. Arts and Letters, 1942. Mem. Nat. Inst. Arts and Letters. Author and illustrator: Funeralities, 1925; Lion-hearted Kitten, 1927; Mercy and the Mouse, 1928; Ballad of Tangle Street, 1929; The Terrible Nuisance, 1931; Animosities, 1931; Mischief in Mayfield, 1933; Off with Their Heads, 1934; The True Philosopher, 1919; Catcalls, 1935; The Mystery of East Hatchett or Eric the Pink Viking, 1939; Starting from Scratch, 1945, The Good American Witch, 1957. Author: The Inward Eye (novel), 1952; The Oddity, 1962; The Ghost of Opalina, 1967; author, illustrator The Magic Touch, 1968. Illustrator more than 60 books. Contbr. verse, drawings and stories to leading mags. Home: Box 156 Cape Porpoise ME 04014

BACON, PHILLIP, educator, author; b. Cleve., July 10, 1922; s. Hollis Phillip and Emma (Schneider) B.; student The Citadel, 1940-41; A.B., U. Miami, 1946; M.A., George Peabody Coll. for Tchrs., 1951, Ed.D., 1955; m. Dorothy Willey, Aug. 16, 1951; children—Laura Jane (Mrs. Robert C. Fraser), Phillip Everett. Tchr. social studies Castle Heights Mil. Acad., Lebanon, Tenn., 1946-47, Army and Navy Acad., Carlsbad, Cal., 1948-53; grad. asst. geography George Peabody Coll., for Tchrs., 1953-55, dean Grad. Sch., 1963-64; asst. prof. geography U. Pitts., 1955-56; vis. asst. prof. geography Columbia Tchrs. Coll., 1956-57, asso. prof., 1957-60, prof., 1960-63, 64-66; prof. geography U. Wash., Seattle, 1966-71, co-dir. tri-univ.

project in elementary edn., 1967-71; prof. geography U. Houston, 1971—; Mem. editorial adv. bd. World Book Ency., 1965—; bd. cons. World Book Atlas, 1965-70; cons. editor Golden Press, 1958-61; cons. book div. Time, Inc., 1960-69; cons. social sci. project Ednl. Research Council Am., 1962-70; mem. steering com. High Sch. Geography Project, 1965-70; cons. U.S. Office Edn., 1964—; mem. Wash. Social Studies Adv. Commn., 1968-71; curriculum cons. Served with USNR, 1942-45. Fellow Royal Geog. Soc., Am. Geog. Soc. N.Y.; mem. Assn. Am. Geographers, Nat. Council for Geog. Edn. (pres. 1966), Nat., Wash. edn. assns., Am. Assn. Higher Edn., Nat. Council Social Studies, Sigma Alpha Epsilon, Phi Delta Kappa, Kappa Delta Pi, Pi Gamma Mu. Presbyn. Clubs: Men's Faculty of Columbia; Mercer Island Country. Author: Australia, Oceania, and the Polar Lands, 1961; North America, 1961; Children's Picture Atlas of the World, 1966; (with Norman Carls and Frank E. Sorensen) Knowing Our Neighbors in the United States, 1966; Knowing Our Neighbors in the United States and Canada, 1966; Regions Around The World, 1970; (with R.R. Boyce) Towns and Cities, 1970; (with others) The United States and Canada, 1970; (with P.V. Greco) The Story of Latin America, 1970. Editor: Focus on Geography, Key Concepts and Teaching Strategies, 1970; co-editor: Foundations of World Regional Geography Series, 1970—. Cons. editor Life Pictorial Atlas of the World, 1961, Jour. of Geography, 1967-70. Contbr. articles profl. jours. Home: 18601 Point Lookout Dr Nassau Bay Houston TX 77058

BACON, ROBERT M., investment banker; b. Alameda, Cal., June 5, 1913; s. William Robert and Alice (Maurer) B.; A.B., Stanford, 1935; m. Francesca Murrieta, June 12, 1937; children—Robert Lawrence, William Robert II, Peter Van Nuys, Gen. partner Bacon & Co., 1935-50; resident mgr. Francis I. duPont & Co., 1950-52; with E.F. Hutton & Co. Inc., 1952—, now sr. v.p., San Francisco, also mem. exec. com., dir.; dir. Charter Pacific Corp. Bd. govs. Pacific Coast Stock Exchange, 1964-66. Pres., dir. Internat. Inst.; mem. budget com. United Bay Area Crusade. Served to lt. comdr. USNR, 1942-45. Mem. Beta Theta Pi (pres. alumni assn.). Clubs: Pacific-Union, Bond (bd. dirs. 1958-59), Bohemian, Municipal Bond (San Francisco); Cal. Tennis. Home: 3236 Pacific Av San Francisco CA 94118 Office: 160 Montgomery St San Francisco CA 94104

BACON, ROBERT STILLWELL, banker; b. Mobile, Ala., Apr. 8, 1907; s. Robert Stillwell and Venetia (Danner) B.; B.S., Washington & Lee U., 1929; m. Susanne Robinson, June 21, 1957; children—Perrin (Mrs. William E. Drew), Robert Stillwell, Richard Lee. Pres. First Nat. Bank, Mobile, 1967—, also dir.; dir. Lerio Corp., Ala. D.D. & S.B. Co. Bd. dirs., chmn. drive Mobile Community Chest, 1943. Mem. Mobile C. of C. (dir.). Clubs: Mobile Country, Athelstan (Mobile); Lakewood Country (Point Clear, Ala.); Isle Dauphine (Dauphin Island, Ala.). Home: 2157 Venetia Rd Mobile AL 36605 Office: 31 N Royal St Mobile AL 36602

BACON, ROGER VICTOR, lawyer; b. St. Louis, Aug. 26, 1941; s. Victor Edward and Edna (Wisdom) B.; B.S., U. Mo., 1963, J.D., 1966; m. Susan Joan Black, Aug. 25, 1962; children—Dawn Ann, Stacy Marie. Admitted to Ohio bar, 1966, since practiced in Defiance; partner Weaner, Hutchinson & Zimmerman, 1966—; lectr. Peace Officers Tng. Course. City solicitor, Defiance, 1968-71; village solicitor Villages of Hicksville, Ney and Sherwood, O., 1969; asst. county prosecutor Defiance County, 1969—. Chm. County March of Dimes Drive, 1969-70. Bd. dirs. Defiance County Humane Soc. Recipient certificate of appreciation Ohio State Hwy. Patrol, 1969. Mem. Am., Ohio (local gov. law com.), Northwestern, Defiance County (pres.) bar assns., Alpha Kappa Psi, Phi Delta Phi, Lambda Chi Alpha. Republican. Presbyn. (deacon). Rotarian (dir. Defiance). Home: 368 Wilson St Defiance OH 43512 Office: State Bank Bldg Clinton St Defiance OH 43512

BACON, ROY M., educator; B.S. in Bus. Adminstrn., Youngstown U.; M.Ed., Kent State U.; Ed.D., U. Tenn.; postgrad. U. Ky. S.S. Rickly prof. edn. Heidelberg Coll., Tiffin, O. Office: Dept Edn Heidelberg Coll Tiffin OH 44883

BACON, SELDEN D., educator; b. Pleasantville, N.Y., Sept. 10, 1909; s. Selden and Josephine Dodge (Daskam) B.; A.B., Yale, 1931, A.M., 1935, Ph.D., 1939; m. Cornelia Howard, Dec. 20, 1934; 1 dau., Cornelia Anne; m. 2d, Margaret Keller, May 25, 1946; children—Selden Daskam, Michael McAlpine.. With dept. sociology Pa. State Coll., 1937-39; prof. sociology, dir. sect. on alcohol studies, dir. summer sch. alcohol studies, Yale, 1939- 62; prof. sociology, dir. Center Alcohol Studies, Rutgers U. New Brunswick, N.J., 1962—. Dir. dept. behavioral scis. of div. research Lankenau Hosp., Phila., 1959-60. Sec.- treas. Nat. Com. for Edn. Alcoholism, 1945-50; bd. dirs. Council Social Agencies, 1947-51, Conn. Prison Assn., 1944-54: chmn. Conn. Commn. Alcoholism, 1945-60; com. on alcohol and drugs Nat. Safety Council, 1961—; bd. dirs. N.Am. Assn. Alcoholism Programs, 1964-68, v.p., 1967—, Recognition award, 1970; program chmn. 18th Internat. Congress on Alcohol and Alcoholism, Washington, 1968; mem. Nat. Adv. Com. on Alcoholism, 1966- 68; mem. assembly of dirs. Internat. Council Alcohol and Alcoholism; mem. exec. com. Internat. Council on Alcohol and Addictions, 1968—. Mem. Am, Eastern sociol. socs., A.M.A. (mem. sub-com. on alcoholism), Conn. Acad. Arts and Scis. Author: (with R. Straus) Drinking in College, 1953. Editor Quar. Jour. Studies on Alcohol, 1946—. Contbr. 3 chpts. to Alcohol, Science and Society, 1947; also contbr. profl. jours. Office: Center of Alcohol Studies Rutgers University New Brunswick NJ 08903

BACON, WALLACE ALGER, educator, author; b. Bad Axe, Mich., Jan. 27, 1914; s. Russell Alger and Mana (Wallace) B.; A.B., Albion Coll., 1935, Litt. D., 1967; A.M., U. Mich., 1936, Ph.D., 1940. Instr. English, U. Mich., 1941-47; chmn. dept. interpretation Northwestern U., Evanston, Ill., 1947—, asso. prof. English and speech, 1950-55, prof. speech, 1955—; Fulbright lectr., Philippines, 1961-62; Fulbright-Hays lectr., 1964-65. Served with AUS, 1942-46. Decorated Legion of Merit; Alfred Lloyd postdoctoral fellow U. Mich., 1940-41; Rockefeller fellow, 1948-49; Ford Found. fellow, 1954-55; recipient Hopwood Major award writing drama U. MIch., 1936; spl. citation U. Philippines, 1965, 70; spl. commendation Ednl. Found. Philippines, 1965. Mem. Speech Communication Assn. (past pres. com. interpretation; chmn. com. publs. 1966; Golden Anniversary Prize Fund award 1965), Shakespeare Assn. Am., Renaissance Soc. Am., Central States Speech Assn., Malone Soc., Am. Assn. U. Profs. Phi Beta Kappa, Delta Sigma Rho, Theta Alpha Phi. Author: (verse play) Savonarola (Bishop Sheil award 1946), 1950; William Warner's Syrinx, 1950; (with Robert S. Breen) Literature as Experience, 1959, Literature for Interpretation, 1961;(with N. Crame-Rogers and C. V. Fonacier) Spoken English, 1962; The Art of Oral Interpretation, 1965; The Art of Interpretation, 1966, Asso. editor Quar. Jour. Speech, 1957-59, 63-65; Speech Monographs, 1966-71; also articles, poetry, monographs. Home: 315 Linder Av Northfield IL 60093 Office: 1822 Sheridan Rd Evanston IL 60201

BACON, WARREN HOLLIS, steel co. exec., b. Chgo., Jan. 12, 1923; s. Robert P. and Belle B. (Blackshear) B.; A.B., Roosevelt U., 1948; M.B.A., U. Chgo., 1951; m. Mary Lou E. Webb, Sept. 9, 1946; children—Warren Hollis, Roger Hollis, Randall Hollis. With Supreme Life Ins. Co., Chgo., 1946-66, indsl. relations dir., 1956-58, v.p., 1958-66; asst. dir. indsl. relations Inland Steel Co., Chgo., 1966—; dir. Hyde Park Fed. Savs. & Loan. Mem. bd. Welfare Council Met. Chgo. Mem. Chgo. Bd. Edn., 1963—. Trustee Russell Sage Found.; trustee-at-large Univ. Research Assn. Served with AUS, 1943-46. Fellow Life Mgmt. Inst. of Life Office Mgmt. Assn.; mem. Nat. Ins. Assn. (v.p.). Episcopalian (vestry). Home: 316 E 89th Pl Chicago IL 60619 Office: 30 W Monroe St Chicago IL 60603

BACOPULOS, GEORGE JOHN, clergyman; b. Decatur, Ill., Dec. 25, 1921; s. John George and Agnes (Johns) B.; student Tex. Tech. Sch., 1943; diploma theology, Holy Cross Greek Orthodox Theol. Sch., Pomfret, Conn., 1953; m. Evelyn Bardis, June 2, 1946; childrenJohn, Dorothy, Maria, Chris. Ordained priest Greek Orthodox Ch., 1952; asst. dean Boston Cathedral, 1952-57, acting dean, 1955-57; pastor St. Constantine Ch., Detroit, 1957-60; dir. interch. relations Archdiocese N.Y., 1960-62, acting chancellor, 1962-64, chancellor, 1964-. Mem. gen. bd. Nat. Council Chs., 1960-69. dir. chaplains affairs, mem. study and planning commn., also ecumenical commn. conf. Orthodox Bishops Ams., 1961-; commnr. chs. on internat. affairs. World Council Chs., 1961-; del. 3d assembly World Council Chs., New Delhi, India, 1961; mem. com. civil rights Nat. Council Chs., 1963-. Served with AUS, 1943-45; ETO. Decorated Bronze Star with oak leaf cluster, Purple Heart with oak leaf cluster; cross of Holy Sepulchre (Jerusalem). Home: 86 Rockledge Rd Bronxville, NY 10708. Office: 10 E 79th St New York City NY 10021.

BACSIK, JOSEPH GEORGE, mfg. co. exec.; b. Ansonia, Conn., Oct. 20, 1917; s. Michael J. and Catherine (Sebas) B.; student U. Tampa (Fla.), 1940-41, Bridgeport (Conn.) Engring. Inst., 1941-43; m. Helen Ann Halat, Nov. 23, 1945; children—Joseph, Susan Elizabeth, Michael James, James Joseph. With United Aircraft Corp., 1941-53, engring adminstrv. supr. Chance Vought Aircraft div., 1943-53; with Chance Vought Inc., 1953-62, mgr. contract adminstrn. and pricing, 1959-62; with Ling-Temco-Vought, Inc., 1962—, controller, 1965—, v.p., 1967—; dir. LTV Aerospace Corp., LTV Electrosystems, Inc., LTV Ling Altec Inc. Served with USAAF, 1937-41. Mem. Am. Mgmt. Assn., Financial Execs. Inst., Aerospace Industries Assn. (vice chmn. procurement and finance com.). Nat. Security Indsl. Assn., Dallas Council World Affairs, Holy Name Soc. K.C. Club: Oak Cliff Country (Dallas). Home: 1608 Hanging Cliff Dr Dallas TX 75224 Office: PO Box 5003 Dallas TX 75222

BACZEWSKI, EDWARD THOMAS, advt. exec.; b. Great Neck, N.Y., Oct. 12, 1921; s. Klemens Stanislaus and Honorata (Wysocka) B.; B.A., Fordham U., 1943; M.B.A., Harvard, 1947; m. Marie Theresa Moore, May 14, 1949; children—Barbara Ann, Constance Marie (Mrs. Alphonsus Gerard Collins), David Jan, Joanne Theresa, Mark Edward, Jan Paul, Judith Ann, Christopher, Peter Matthew. Research asst. Kenyon Research Corp., N.Y.C., 1946, Newsweek mag., N.Y.C., 1947; media dir. Paris and Peart Advt., N.Y.C., 1947-50; asso. media dir. Cunningham & Walsh Advt., N.Y.C., 1950-62, v.p., 1957, dir., 1968—, sr. v.p., 1969, sec., 1969—. Councilman, Borough Harrington Park, N.J., 1954-59, mayor, 1960-67; mem. Bergen County Housing Authority, 1963-64. Trustee Pascack Valley Hosp., Westwood, N.J., 1969—. Served with AUS, 1943-45. Decorated Purple Heart. Republican. Roman Catholic. Home: 163 Bogert's Mill Rd Harrington Park NJ 07640 Office: 260 Madison Av New York City NY 10016

BADDOUR, RAYMOND FREDERICK, educator; b. Laurinburg, N.C., Jan. 11, 1925; s. Frederick Joseph and Fannie (Rizk) B.; B.S., U. Notre Dame, 1945; M.S., Mass. Inst. Tech., 1949, Sc. D., 1951; m. Anne M. Bridge, Sept. 25, 1954; children—Cynthia Anne, Frederick Raymond, Jean Bridge, Asst. dir. Engring Practice Sch., Oak Ridge, 1948-49; asst. prof. Mass. Inst. Tech., 1951-57, asso. prof., 1957-63, prof. chem. engring, 1963—, head dept., 1969—, dir. Environmental Lab., 1970—. Mem. project separation AEC, 1954; Am. Inst. Chem. Engrs. del. Mendeleev Conf. on pure and applied chemistry Moscow U., 1959; lectr. Max Planck Insts., Germany, 1962; Shell Lectr. Cambridge (Eng.) U., 1962; P.C. Riley lectr. Notre Dame U., 1964; mem. sci. adv. com. Gen. Motors Corp., 1971—. Co-founder, chmn. bd. Abcor, Inc., Cambridge, Mass., 1963—; dir. Raychem Corp., 1971—; cons. Mobil Chem. Co., N.Y.C., 1963—, U.S. Dept. Commerce, 1960-62. Mem. corp. Boston Museum Sci.; trustee Buckingham Sch., Cambridge, mem. sci. and tech. adv. bd. Field Enterprises, Chgo. (World Book Ency.), 1966-68. NSF post-doctoral fellow, 1967-68. United Engrs. and Constructors preceptorship, 1956. Fellow Am. Inst. Chemists; mem. Am. Acad. Arts and Scis., Am. Inst. Chem. Engrs., Am. Chem. Soc., N.Y. Acad. Scis., A.A.A.S., Sigma Xi. Research publs. and patents in field. Home: 96 Fletcher Rd Belmont MA 02178 Office: 77 Massachusetts Av Cambridge MA 02139

BADE, WILLIAM G., educator. Prof. math. U. Cal. at Berkeley. Office: 301 Campbell Hall U Cal Berkeley CA 94720*

BADEAU, JOHN LACY, accountant, cons.; b. Osyka, Miss., Mar. 21, 1904; s. George Thomas and Edith (Locke) B.; ed. high sch., LaSalle Extension U.; m. Ruth Hill Carr, Jan. 26, 1934. Accountant Laurel Wholesale Dry Goods Co. (Miss.), 1922-27; office mgr. George A. Hormel & Co., Birmingham, Ala., 1927-35; with Ernst & Ernst, C.P.A.'s, Birmingham, 1936-68, partner, 1956-68, now cons.; instr. evening classes accounting U. Ala., 1942, also Birmingham chpt. Am. Inst. Banking, 6 years. Chmn. bond study com., Birmingham, 1960. Chmn. bd. trustees Civitan Internat. Found., bd. govs. Ala. Assn. Independent Colls.; bd. dirs. Ala. Soc. C.P.A.'s Ednl. Found.; treas. Birmingham Symphony Assn.; pres. bd. dirs. Carraway Meth. Hosp. C.P.A., Ala. Mem. Am. Inst. C.P.A.'s (council 1950), Nat. Assn. Accountants, Ala. Soc. C.P.A.'s (past pres., sec. Birmingham chpt. 1950), Beta Alpha Psi. Republican. Methodist (vice chmn. ofcl. bd. 1951). Clubs: Civitan (pres.), Vestavia Country (bd. govs. 1960), Relay House, The Club, Downtown (Birmingham). Home: 4549 Dolly Ridge Rd Birmingham AL 35243 Office: First Nat Bldg Birmingham AL 35203

BADEAU, JOHN STOTHOFF, ex-ambassador, educator; b. Pitts., Feb. 24, 1903; s. Charles C. and Mary Lyles (Stothoff) B.; B.S., Union Coll., Schenectady, 1924, D.D., 1942; postgrad. New Brunswick Theol. Sem., 1925-28; B.D., Rutgers U., 1928; S.T.M., Union Theol. Sem., 1936; LL.D., Riker Coll., 1958, Alma Coll. 1966, Dickinson Coll. 1966; m. Margaret Louise Hathaway, Sept. 7, 1924; children—Jeanne Hathaway, Roger Carroll, Peter Weekes. Tchr., Lyndhurst, L.I., N.Y., 1924-25; student pastor Mariners Harbor Reformed Ch. (S.I.), 1926-28; ordained ministry Ref. Ch. in Am. 1928; missionary service under United Mission in Mesopotamia, mosul, Iraw, 1928-30, Baghdad, Iraq, 1930-35; asso. prof. religion, philosophy Am. U., Cairo, 1936-38, dean faculty arts, scis., 1938-44, pres., 1945-53; pres. Near East Found., 1953-61; U.S. ambassador to UAR 1961-64; transferred to ministry of Presbyn. Ch. of U.S.A., 1953; dir. Middle East Inst., Columbia, N.Y.C., 1964-71, also prof. modern Middle East studies, 1966-71, prof. emeritus, 1971—; professorial lectr. Georgetown U., Washington, 1971—; regional chief Middle E., OWI, Washington, 1943-45; lectr. Fgn. Policy Assn. Mem. com. fgn. schs. Egyptian Ministry Edn.; com. religious liberty Fed. Council Chs.; chmn. edn. com. New East Christian Council; mem. Near East com. Nat. Councill Chs.; exec. com. Am. Council Voluntary Agys.; mem. edn. com. Iran Found., mem. internat. com. YMCA. Trustee Union Theol. Sem., Am. U. of Cairo, Near East Found. (chmn.), Middle East Inst., Washington. Mem. Egyptian Assn. Social Studies, Middle East Studies Assn. (pres. 1970), Fellowship of Unity, Cairo, Egypt, Sigma Xi, Tau Kappa Alpha. Club: Cosmos (Washington). Author: East and West of Suez (Fgn. Policy Assn. Headline Book); The Emergence of Modern Egypt, 1953; The Lands Between, 1958; The American Approach to the Arab World, 1968. Home: 220 Garfield St Haworth NJ 07641 Office: Kent Hall Columbia U New York City NY 10027

BADER, ARNO LEHMAN, educator; b. Grand Rapids, Mich., Jan. 13, 1902; s. George Julius and Clara (Lehman) B.; A.B., U. Mich., 1924, A.M., 1925, Ph.D., 1933; m. Marian C. Hernam, Sept. 9, 1927; children—Thomas Hernam, James Daniel, Instr. rhetoric U. Mich., Ann Arbor, 1925-30, instr. English, 1930-38, asst. prof., 1938-45, asso. prof., 1945-51, prof. English, 1951—; exchange prof. Nat. Central U., Nanking, China, 1936-37. Mem. Modern Lang. Assn., Am. Assn. U. Profs., Nat. Council Tchrs. English, Coll. English Assn., Theta Chi. Co-editor: Prose Patterns, 1933; Essays of Three Decades, 1939; Essays for our Time, 1947. Editor: To The Young Writers: Hopwood Lectures Second Series, 1965, Contbr. articles to profl. publs. Home: 285 Orchard Hills Dr Ann Arbor MI 48104

BADER, CHARLES HENRY, ins. co. exec.; b. Nashville, Aug. 23, 1909; s. Harry H. and Mabel (Beall) B.; student Vanderbilt U., 1927-28; B.B.A., U. Wash., 1931; M.S., U. Mich., 1935; m. Margaret L. Hutcheson, Dec. 25, 1936; children—Mary Hutcheson (Mrs. David G. Brooks), Inez Gwin. Actuary, Acme Life Ins. Co., Tulsa, 1936; actuary Interstate Life & Accident Ins. Co., Chattanooga, 1936-49, v.p., 1949-55, adminstrv. v.p., 1955-64, sr. v.p., 1964-68, exec. v.p., 1968—, also dir.; dir. Interstate Corp. Pres. Chattanooga Jr. Achievement, 1967. Served to capt. USAAF, 1942-45; CBI. Mem. Nat. Alliance Businessmen (dir. Chattanooga met. div. 1969-70), Life Office Mgmt. Assn. (pres. 1959-60). Home: 204 Sylvan Dr Lookout Mountain TN 37350 Office: 540 McCallie Av Chattanooga TN 37402

BADER, HENRI, glaciologist; b. Brugg, Switzerland, Jan. 15, 1907; s. Walter and Leonie (Bel) B.; Ph.D. in Minerology, U. Zürich (Switzerland), 1935; m. Adele Christen, Sept. 24, 1938. Came to U.S., 1945, naturalized, 1951. Engaged in avalanche research for Swiss Govt., 1935-38; mineralogist Lab. Quinico Nacional, Bogota, Columbia, 1940-41; quarry supt. Curacao Mining Co., N.W.I., 1941-45; asso. research specialist Bur. Mineral Research, Rutgers U., 1945-49; chief scientist snow, ice and permafrost research establishment U.S. Army, Wilmette, Ill., 1952-60; research prof. Sch. Engring., U. Miami (Fla.), 1960-63; sci. attache Am. embassy, Bonn, Germany, 1963-64, Bern, Switzerland, 1965-66, sr. research scientist, 1967-, spl. research snow and ice, snow mechanics, glaciology, glaciological engring., research and devel. polar regions. Mem. Geol. Soc. Am., Geophys. Union, Glaciological Soc., Sigma Xi. Home: 2451 Brickell Av Miami, FL 33129. Office: U Miami Coral Gables FL 33124

BADER, JACK LANI, coll. dean, lawyer; b. Honolulu, Hawaii, Dec. 11, 1932; s. Oliver Jones and Thelma Loraine (Springer) B.; B.A., U. Hawaii, 1956; J.D., U. Chgo., 1960; m. Arelene Marie Bufka, Mar. 14, 1959; children—Miles Gordon, Laura Elizabeth, Graham. Admitted to N.Y. bar, 1961, Cal. bar, 1962; asso. Sherman & Sterling, N.Y.C., 1960-62, Pillsbury, Madison & Sutro, San Francisco, 1962-64; mem. firm. Rosenak & Bader, San Francisco, 1964-68; prof. law Golden Gate Sch. Law, San Francisco, 1968-69, prof., dean Sch. Law, 1969—. Dir., mem. exec. com. Sentinel Life Ins. Co. Mem. dean's adv. com. to continuing edn. of Bar U. Cal., 1969—. Trustee San Francisco Consortium. Mem. Am., N.Y., Cal., San Francisco bar assns., San Francisco Lawyers Club. Democrat. Contbr. articles profl. jours. Home: 101 Cornilia St Mill Valley CA 94941 Office: 536 Mission St San Francisco CA 94105

BADER, ROBERT SMITH, coll. dean; b. Falls City, Neb., June 18, 1925; s. Ray Jay and Grace (Smith) B.; B.S., Kan. State U., 1949; Ph.D., U. Chgo., 1954; m. Virginia Sue Baertch, Aug. 22, 1948; children—Douglas, Jonathan, Eric, Joel. Instr., then asst. prof. biology U. Fla., 1952-56; from asst. prof. to prof. zoology U. Ill. at Urbana, 1956-68; prof. biology, dean Coll. Arts and Scis., U. Mo.-St. Louis, 1968—. Served with USNR, 1943- 45. Mem. Soc. Study Evolution, Am. Inst. Biol. Scis., Am. Soc. Zoologists, N.Central Assn. Colls. and Univs., Sigma Xi. Research variation in dentition of mammals. Home: 7241 Kingsbury St St Louis MO 63130

BADGER, GEORGE FRANKLIN, educator; b. Everett, Mass., May 14, 1907; s. Benjamin F., Jr., and Elizabeth (Bensen) B.; B.S., Mass. Inst. Tech., 1929; M.P.H., Johns Hopkins, 1932; M.D., U. Mich., 1938; m. F. Loyola Collins, Aug. 30, 1934; children—George F., Robert L., James M. Asst. epidemiologist Detroit Dept. Health, 1929-34; asso. biostatistics Johns Hopkins, 1938- 45, asst. prof., 1945-46; asso. prof. biostatistics Case Western Res. U. Med. Sch., Cleve., 1946-49, prof., 1949—, dir. div. biometry, 1963-67, dir. dept. biometry, 1967-69. Mem. adv. com. on epidemiology and biometry NIH, 1958-62, mem. Mem. study sect. on human ecology, 1963-65. Cons. Sec. War Commn. on Acute Respiratory Diseases, 1942-44; mem. commn. on acute respiratory diseases Armed Forces Epidemiol. Bd., 1944-65; cons. to surgeon gen. U.S. Army, 1954-59; mem. med. adv. com. Nat. Found. 1959-61. Served as maj. AUS, 1944- 46. Mem. Am. Statis. Assn., Am. Epidemiol. Soc. (pres. 1960-61), Am. Pub. Health Assn., Biometric Soc. Mem. editorial bd. Am. Rev. Respiratory Diseases, 1966-70. Home: 750 Spafford Oval Northfield OH 44067 Office: Wearn Research Bldg University Hosps Cleveland OH 44106

BADGER, JAMES GOLVIN, ret. lumber co. exec.; b. La Fontaine, Ind., Feb. 8, 1895; s. Job and Emma (Summers) B.; student Marion (Ind.) Normal, summer 1912, Ind. U., 1913; m. Charlotte Lucille Blodgett, May 29, 1918; children—James Golvin, Frank Kelly. Tchr. pub. schs., 1912-14; instr., mgr. Fitzgerald's Bus. Coll., Schenectady, N.Y., also Noblesville (Ind.) Bus. Coll., 1914-16; accounting clk., 1916-17; with Edward Hines Lumber Co., 1919—, successively bookkeeper, auditor So. operations, gen. auditor, sec.-treas., v.p., 1927-54, executive vice president, 1955-60, mem. board directors 1957- 69; past dir. Ore. & Northwestern R.R. Co.; pres., dir., Southern Mineral Corp. Pres. Wilmette Sch. Bd., 1944-46. Served as 2d lt. 135th F.A., U.S. Army, 1917-19. Mem. Indiana Soc. Chgo. (v.p.), Am. Legion, Son of American Revolution. Mason. Clubs: Union League (pres. 1957-58), Rotary (treas. 1959-60) (Chgo.); Westmoreland Country (Wilmette); Lauderdale Yacht (Ft. Lauderdale, Fla.). Home: 1508 Hinman Av Evanston IL 60201

BADGETT, JAMES L., mfg. co. exec.; b. 1928; B.S., U. Ill., 1953; married. Vice pres. operations Eversharp, Inc., 1965-69; pres. Schick Electric Inc., Lancaster, Pa., 1969—, also dir. Served with USAF. Office: 216 Greenfield Rd Lancaster PA 17604*

BADILLO, HERMAN, congressman; b. Caguas, P.R., Aug. 21, 1929; s. Francisco and Carmen (Rivera) B.; B.B.A. magna cum laude, City Coll. N.Y., 1951; LL.B. cum laude, Bklyn. Law Sch., 1954; C.P.A., 1956; m. Irma Deutsch, May 18, 1961; children—Loren, Mark, David. Admitted to N.Y. bar, 1955; with Ferro, Berdon & Co., C.P.A.'s, N.Y.C., 1951-55; mem. firm Permut & Badillo, N.Y.C., 1955-62; dep. commnr. N.Y.C. Dept. Real Estate, 1962-65; commnr.

N.Y.C. Dept. Relocation, 1962-65; pres. Borough of Bronx, 1966-69; mem. 92d Congress from 21st dist. N.Y. Del. N.Y. State Constl. Conv., 1966; del., mem. credentials com. Nat. Democratic Conv., 1968. Recipient First Scholarship prize Bklyn. Law Sch., 1954, Dean's Evidence prize, 1954; William Payton Richardson Meml. prize, 1953. C.P.A., N.Y. Mem. Beta Gamma Sigma. Alpha Beta Psi, Sigma Alpha. Home: 405 W 259th St Riverdale Bronx NY 10471 Office: 840 Grand Concourse Bronx NY 10451 also Cannon House Office Bldg Washington DC 20515

BADINGS, HENK, composer; b. Bandoeng, Indonesia, Jan. 17, 1907; s. Herman Louis Johan and Marie (Polvliet) B.; Dr.Engr., Tech. U. Delft (Netherlands), 1931; self taught as composer; m. Jeannette M. Tukke, Oct. 1, 1946; 1 dau., Yvonne. Asst., Tech. U. Delft, 1931-34; prof. mus. composition Rotterdam (Netherlands) Conservatory, 1934-35; prof. mus. composition Musiclyceum Amsterdam (Netherlands), 1935-37, co-dir., 1937-41; dir. State Conservatory, The Hague, 1941-45; free-lance composer, 1945-62; guest prof. U. Adelaide (Australia), 1962-63; prof. mus. composition Musikhochschule Stuttgart (Germany), also acoustics and information- theory U. Utrecht (Holland), 1962—; spl. work with octotonality, 31 tone temperament, electronic devices; electronic ballets, performed opera houses Western Europe. Recipient A.O. Prix Italia for opera Orestes, 1954; Paganini prize for violin sonata, 1953; Chigiana prize for quintet, 1952; Radio prize Paris for Choral work, 1951; Salzburg award for electronic opera Salto Mortale, 1959; Premio Marzotto prize for concerto for 2 pianos, 1964. Mem. Royal Flemish Acad. Arts. Rotarian. Compositions include 14 symphonies, 20 concertos, 24 other symphonic works, 6 operas, 10 ballets, 4 oratorios, 7 cantatas, 6 theatre or film works, 60 chamber music works, 24 piano works, 12 organ works, 6 carillons, 24 electronics music works, 90 chorus a cappella, 16 chorus with accompaniment, 75 songs. Home: Einsiedelstr 14 7405 Dettenhausen West Germany Office: Musikhochschule Urbansplatz Stuttgart West Germany

BADOUD, JOHN JAMES, labor union exec.; b. McDonald, Pa., Feb. 11, 1912; s. James J. and Maggie (James) B.; student Kiski Prep. Sch., Saltsburg, Pa., 1932; m. Agnes Marie Rodichok, June 7, 1934; children—Constance Margaret (Mrs. Richard B. Parks), Gary David, John James, Dale Thomas, Karen Louise (Mrs. Terrell B. Bridges), William Alan, Keith Lynn. Truck driver, lab. technician Am. Briquet Co., Lykens, Pa., 1934-42; mem. United Mine Workers America, 1937, president local union 13010, dist. 50, 1940-42, traveling auditor dist. 50, 1942, regional dir. Mich. dist. 1944-54, assistant to pres. dist. 50, Washington, 1954-57, sec.-treas. dist 50, 1957—. Mem. labor panel region II, NWLB, 1944-45. Mem. Mich. Commn. Study Problems of Aging, 1951-52. Home: 3945 Military Rd NW Washington DC 20015 Office: 1435 K St NW Washington DC 20005

BADURA-SKODA, PAUL pianist; b. Vienna, Austria, Oct. 6, 1927; s. Ludwig and Margarete (Winter) Badura; pvt. piano lessons with Viola Thern, also Conservatory of Vienna, 1945-48: summer classes with Edwin Fischer, Lucern, Switzerland, 1948, 1950, 51, 54; m. Eva L. Halfar, Sept. 19, 1951; children—Ludwig, Maria Christina, Elisabeth, Michael. Concert debut, Vienna, 1948; concerts with condrs. Furtwangler and Karajan, 1949; pianist Salzburg Festival, 1950; concert tours Western Europe, 1950-52, Australia, 1952, U.S. and Can., 1952-53, South and Central Am., U.S., Can., 1953, Western Europe, U.S., 1954-55; U.S., Canada, Australia, New Zealand, 1956, Far East, 1960-61, 63, regular concert tours through all European countries, 1956—, S.Am., 1962, 63, N.Y.C., 1964; vis. prof. U. Wis., spring 1964, Stanford, summer 1965; artist in residence U. Wis., 1966—. Recipient 1st award in Austrian competition, Vienna, 1947; 2d award Internat. Bartok Competition, Budapest, 1948. Author: (with Dr. E. Badura) Mozart Interpretation, 1957, Interpreting Mozart on the Keyboard, 1962; cadenzas for several Mozart Concertos, 1962; numerous LP recordings. Completion of Mozart's Larghetto and Allegro for two pianos, 1960, of five unfinished Schubert piano sonatas, 1968. Editor several Urtext edits. (Mozart concerti, Schubert piano compositions. Chopin studies, others), 1964—. Owner collection of historic pianofortes. Home: 5802 Julia St Madison WI 53705

BAECHLE, JAMES JOSEPH, lawyer; b. Lancaster, O., Nov. 25, 1932; s. Robert John and Helen (Kennedy) B.; B.S. in Bus. Adminstrn. cum laude, Ohio State U., 1954; LL.B., Harvard U., 1957. Admitted to N.Y. bar, 1960; practice in N.Y.C., 1960-62, 65—; asso. firm White & Case, N.Y.C., 1959-62, 65-67, Paris, 1962-65; v.p., sec., gen. counsel Brown Co., N.Y.C., 1967—. Mem. pres.' council Center Internat. Studies N.Y. U., 1967—. Served with USAF, 1957-59; capt. Res. Mem. Am., N.Y. State, N.Y.C. bar assns. Clubs: Travellers (Paris), Harvard (N.Y.C.). Home: 190 E 72d St New York City NY 10021 Office: 277 Park Av New York City NY 10017

BAECHTOLD, HARRY WILLIAM, banker; b. Union City, N.J., Oct. 15, 1919; s. Henry and Mildred (Stegelandt) B.; student N.Y. U., 1938-40; m. Mildred L. Notton, July 18, 1942; 1 dau., Barbara Joyce. With Marine Midland Bank, N.Y.C., 1945—, sr. v.p., 1969—. Served to capt. USAAF, 1942-45. Kiwanian (bd. dirs. N.Y.C.). Home: 20 Martha Blvd Parlin NJ 08859 Office: 140 Broadway New York City NY 10015

BAEHR, GEORGE, physician, health officer; b. N.Y.C., Apr. 16, 1887, s. Herman and Sara (Gusky) B.; M.D., Columbia, 1908; student exptl. pathology U. of Freiburg (Germany), 1911-12, exptl. pharmacology U. Vienna, 1912-13; m. Francine Gordon, Oct. 6, 1917; 1 dau. Barbara. Internship and research fellowship Mt. Sinai Hosp., N.Y.C., 1908-11; mem. A.R.C. San. Commn. in Russia and Balkans, 1915-16; lt. col. M.C., U.S. Army, in command U.S. Base Hosp. No. 3, France, 1918; chief, 1st med. service, Mt. Sinai Hosp., 1927-50, dir. clin. research, 1944-50; clin. prof. medicine Columbia, 1929-50; Distinguished Service prof. Mt. Sinai Sch. Medicine, City U. N.Y., 1966—; cons. physician La Guardia Hosp., St. Joseph Hosp. Monmouth Meml. Hosp., Long Branch, N.J.; mem. Pub. Health Council, State of N.Y., 1935—, chmn. 1955-69 Bd. Hosps. N.Y. City, 1944-69; pres. med. dir. Health Ins. Plan Greater N.Y., 1950-57; spl. med. cons., 1957—; adminstrv. cons. Dept. Hosps., N.Y.C., 1933-45; mem. sci. bd., Pub. Health Resrch. Inst.; bd. dirs. mem. tech. bd. Milbank Meml. Fund; med. dir. USPHS and chief med. officer U.S. Office Civilian Defense, 1941-44; del. from U.S. State Dept. to 4th, 5th and 6th Decennial Internat. Confs. to revise internat. list of causes of death, Paris, 1938-48. Trustee, Community Service Soc.; bd. dirs. N.Y. State Communities Aid Assn.; mem. nat. adv. health council NIH, USPHS, 1945-50. Fellow A.C.P.; mem. A.M.A., Assn. Am. Physicians, Am. Heart Assn., (hon.) Am. Hosp. Assn., Am. Pub. Health Assn. (v.p. 1952-53), Soc. for Clin. Investigation, Am. Assn. Pathologists and Bacteriologists. A.A.A.S., N.Y. Acad. Medicine (pres. 1945-48, trustee 1950-60), Sigma Xi; Alpha Omega Alpha. Clubs: Cosmos, Army and Navy (Washington); Players (N.Y.C.). Co-author: Cecil's Textbook of Medicine, 8th edit., 1952. Co-editor; Convalescent Care, 1940; Preventive Medicine, 1942; Medical Uses of Cortisone, 1954; Oxford Loose- Leaf Medicine, vol. IV, 1955; chmn. adv. editorial bd. Standard Nomenclature of Diseases and Operations, 1932-60. Contbr. articles to pub. health and med. jours. Home: 45 Sutton Pl S New York City NY 10022 Office: 110 E 80th St New York City NY 10021

BAEHR, HARRY WILLIAM newspaperman; b. Bklyn., Nov. 9, 1907; s. Harry William and Hilda Ruth (Kornmaier) B.; A.B., Dartmouth, 1929; M.A., Columbia, 1930. Ph.D., 1936; m. Jean Campbell Bogart, June 27, 1934 (dec. 1963); m. 2d, Joann Elizabeth Price, May 8, 1964. Feature writer N.Y. Herald Tribune, 1937-40, editorial writer, 1940-52, asst. chief editorial writer, 1952- 56, chief editorial writer, dir., 1956-58, editorial writer, 1958- 66; editorial writer World Jour. Tribune, N.Y.C., 1966-67, Herald Tribune Internat., 1967—; instr. journalism N.Y. U., 1944-45; asso. in journalism Columbia, 1946-58. Dir., v.p. Bklyn. Eye and Ear Hosp. Decorated officer Order St. John of Jerusalem; recipient Journalism award Finlandia Found., 1958. Mem. Naval Hist. Found., Company Mil. Historians, Phi Beta Kappa. Clubs: Century Assn. (N.Y.C.); Brooklyn. Author: The New York Tribune since the Civil War, 1936. Home: 135 Willow St Brooklyn NY 11201 Office: 229 W 43d St New York City NY 10036

BAENSCH, WILLY E., physician; b. Magdeburg, Germany, 1893; M.D., Halle (Germany) U., 1910. Intern surg., med. and univ. clinics Halle U., 1914-19; clin. tng. Curie Inst., Paris, France, Radiumhemmed, Stockholm, Sweden, 1926, also Central Roentgen Inst., Vienna Austria, 1926; dir. radiology and cancer research, prof. radiology Leipzig U., 1926-45; dir. dept. roentgenology Georgetown U., Washington, also prof., 1947—, now chmn. dept. radiology; sr. cons. VA, Washington. Recipient Gold medal Georgetown U., 1967. Diplomate Am. Bd. Radiology. Hon. mem. German Roentgen Soc. (Rieder medal 1969). Address: 5911 Onondoga Rd Glen Echo Heights MD 20768

BAER, ARTHUR A., banker; b. Chgo., 1896; grad. U. Chgo., 1918. Chmn. bd. Beverly Bank, Chgo.; chmn. Riverdale Bank, Gary-Wheaton Bank, Mt. Greenwood Bank, Alsip Bank. Home: 9001 S Damen Av Chicago IL 60620 Office: 1357 W 103d St Chicago IL 60643*

BAER, BEN KAYSER, cotton merchant; b. Charleston, W.Va., June 26, 1926; s. Frank Adler and Helen (Kayser) B.; grad. Phillips Exeter Acad., 1944; A.B. summa cum laude, Princeton, 1947; LL.B., Yale, 1949; m. Eleanor Hirsch, Nov. 5, 1953; children—Julie Anne, Ben Kayser III, Frank Edward. Admitted to W.Va. bar, 1950; partner firm McClintic, James, Wise & Dadisman, Charleston, W.Va., 1951-56; with Allenberg Cotton Co., Memphis, 1957—, pres., 1965—; pres., dir. 104 S. Front St. Corp., 1965—, Allen Warehouse of Cal., Inc., 1965—; pres., dir. Allenberg Internat. Cotton Co. Treas., dir. Memphis Symphony Orch., 1963-71; bd. dirs. Memphis Arts Council, 1962-70. Served to ensign USNR, 1944-46. Mem. Am. (bd. dirs. 1967), So. (pres. 1969) cotton shippers assns., Phi Beta Kappa. Jewish religion. Clubs: Ridgeway Country (Memphis); Quadrangle (Princeton). Home: 5026 Greenway Rd Memphis TN 38117 Office: 104 S Front St Memphis TN 38103

BAER, DONALD G., ret. naval officer, marketing exec.; b. Uniontown, Pa., July 4, 1915; s. Jacob Ayers and Elizabeth Anne (Fike) B.; B.S., U.S. Naval Acad., 1937; grad. Indsl. Coll. Armed Forces, 1957; m. Phoebe McLeod Nibbs, June 18, 1942; children—Sandra (Mrs. Judley G. Eaton), Geoffrey Clark. Commd. ensign U.S. Navy, 1937, advanced through grades to rear adm., 1965; various assignments in ships and ashore, 1937-70; comdr. U.S.S. Lapon, 1944-45, U.S.S. Remora, 1946, U.S.S. Seacat, 1947; staff engr. Submarine Squadron 2, 1947-48; repair officer submarine base, New London, Conn., 1948-52; exec. officer U.S.S. Orion, 1953; comdr. Submarine Div. 63, 1954; assigned progress analysis div. Office Chief Naval Operations, 1954, polit.-mil. div., 1958; comdg. officer U.S.S. Fulton, 1957-58; spl. asst. to chief naval operations, 1958-59; comdr. Submarine Squadron 1, 1960; spl. asst. to chief Bur. Naval Personnel, 1961-62; chief staff, dep. comdr. Submarine Force, Atlantic Fleet, 1963-64; comdr. Naval Base, Subic Bay, Philippines, 1964-66, Submarine Flotilla 6, 1966-67; dep. chief naval material (program and financial mgmt.), 1967-70, ret. 1970; dir. marketing research and planning Meloy Labs., Inc. Decorated Navy Cross, Legion of Merit (2), Bronze Star with V. Sec. Navy Commendation. Registered profl. engr. Episcopalian (lay reader). Club: Army Navy (Washington). Home: 5944 Oakdale Rd Mclean VA 22101

BAER, ERIC, educator; b. Nieder-Weisel, Germany, July 18, 1932; s. Arthur and Erna (Kraemer) B.; came to U.S., 1947, naturalized, 1952; M.A., Johns Hopkins, 1953, D.Engring., 1957; m. Ana Golender, Aug. 5, 1956; childrenLisa. Michelle. Research engr., polychems. dept. E.I. du Pont de Nemours & Co., Inc., 1957-60; asst. prof. chemistry and chem. engring. U. Ill., 1960-62; asso. prof. engring. Case Inst. Tech., 1962- 66; prof., head dept. polymer sci. Case Western Res. U., 1966-; cons. to industry, 1961-. Mem. Am. Chem. Soc., Am. Phys. Soc., Am. Inst. Chem. Engring., Soc. Plastics Engring., Plastics Inst. Am. (trustee). Author articles in field. Editor: Engineering Design for Plastics, 1963; Polymer Engineering and Science, 1967-. Home: 2 Mornington Lane Cleveland Heights, OH 44106. Office: Case Western Res Univ Cleveland OH 44106

BAER, GEORGE ROBERT, diversified mfg. co. exec.; b. Cin., Jan. 20, 1919; s. George and Margaret (Evans) B.; B.A., U. Cin., 1940; m. Mary Margaret Newkirk, Sept. 25, 1944; children—Barbara Ann, George Robert II. Employment mgr. Wright Aero. Corp., 1940-42; with Perfect Circle Corp. (now Perfect Circle div. of Dana Corp., Hagerstown, Ind., 1942-68, v.p. operations, 1960-63, pres., 1963-68; chmn. bd. Schellens True Corp., Ivoryton, Conn., 1963-68; v.p. Ball Corp., Muncie, Ind., 1969—. Mem. exec. bd. Whitewater Valley council Boy Scouts Am., 1955—, pres. vice chmn. 10th Dist. Republican Finance Com., 1962-66. Served to lt. (j.g.) USNR, 1944-46. Mem. Soc. Automotive Engrs., Ind. C. of C. (v.p., dir.). Sigma Chi, Omicron Delta Kappa. Mem. United Ch. Christ. Home: 605 Tyrone Dr Muncie IN 47304 Office: 509 S Macedonia Av Muncie IN 47302

BAER, HERBERT RALPH, lawyer, educator; b. Paterson, N.J., Apr. 18, 1901; s. H. Walter and Amelia (Schmutz) B.; A.B., Cornell U., 1923; LL.B., Harvard, 1926; m. Elizabeth Severn, June 24, 1924; children—Elizabeth Shirley (Mrs. Daniel Curtis Lewis, Jr.), Bruce Lawrence. Admitted to N.J. bar, 1927, N.Y. State bar, 1940, N.C. bar, 1950; trial counsel firm McCarter & English, Newark, 1927-38; teaching fellow Cornell Univ. Law Sch., 1939-40; prof. law Wake Forest Coll., 1940-45, acting dean for Wake Forest Coll. at combined Duke-Wake Forest Law Sch., 1944-45; prof. law, U. N.C., Chapel Hill, 1945—, Alumni distinguished prof. law, 1961—. Rationing atty. OPA, Washington, 1942, dist. price atty., Raleigh, N.C., 1942-44. Mem. Am., N.C. bar assns. Maritime Law Assn. U.S., Order of Gimghouls, Delta Theta Phi. Presbyn. Club: Harvard. Author: Admiralty Law of the Supreme Court, 1963; also articles in law revs. and jours. Home: 903 Arrowhead Rd Chapel Hill NC 27514

BAER, JOHN WILLARD, air force officer; b. Lewiston, Ida., July 24, 1919; s. John and Lillie (Hollingsworth) B.; student U. Ida., 1937-39; B.S., U.S. Mil. Acad., 1943; M.A., Georgetown U., 1950; m. Jane Elizabeth Sykes, June 18, 1949; children—John Willard, William Dashiell, Robert Sykes. Commd 2d lt., USAAF, 1943, advanced through grades to brig. gen. USAF, 1965; pilot, World War II; mem. U.S. planning team NATO Standing Group, Office Sec. Def., 1952-55; command assignments various fighter units, Far East and Europe, 1955-67; dep. comdr. U.S. Mil. Assistance Command, Thailand, 1969; dir. Near East and S.E. Asia region Office Sec. Def., 1969-70; dep. dir. strike forces Hdqrs. USAF, Washington, 1970—. Decorated Silver Star, Legion of Merit, D.F.C. with 2 oak leaf clusters, Air medal with 19 oak leaf clusters, Commendation medal. Episcopalian. Club: Army Navy City (gov.). (Washington). Home: 4915 Loughboro Rd Washington DC 20016 Office: The Pentagon Washington DC 20330

BAER, JULIUS ARTHUR, II, merchant; b. St. Louis, Apr. 18, 1921; s. Arthur B. and Lucile (Calisch) B.; grad. St. Louis Country Day Sch., 1939; A.B., Duke Univ., Durham, North Carolina, 1943; children—Julius Arthur III, Patricia Anne. Assistant field dir. A.R.C., 1943-46; with Stix, Baer & Fuller Co., dept. store, St. Louis, 1946—, div. mdse. mgr., 1955-57, br. store mgr., 1957-59, v.p. charge total store mdsg. and publicity, 1959-61, exec. v.p., 1961-63, pres., 1963—, also dir.; vice pres., Asso. Dry Goods; dir. Merc. Trust Co. Mem. pres.'s council St. Louis U.; bd. dirs., pres. Downtown St. Louis, Inc.; bd. dirs. St. Louis area council Boy Scouts Am., City Art Mus., KETC-TV ednl. network, Govtl. Research Inst., St. Louis Municipal Opera, St. Louis Jewish Hospital, St. Louis Symphony Society, Herbert Hoover Boys Club of St. Louis, Civic Progress, Inc., United Fund of Greater St. Louis. Recipient Medal of Honor, Centre Nationale du Commerce Exterieur, French Govt., 1960; Ordre de L'economie French Govt., 1965; Al Merito Turistico, Spanish Govt., 1968; Am. Legion citation, 1969. Mem. C. of C. Met. St. Louis (dir.), Nat. Retail Mchts. Assn. (dir.), Omicron Delta Kappa, Theta Alpha Phi, Zeta Beta Tau. Office: Stix Baer and Fuller Co 603 Washington Av St Louis MO 63101

BAER, REXFORD LEVERING, inst. exec.; b. Los Angeles, Nov. 25, 1931; s. Joseph Levering and Eunice Marguerite (Richardson) B.; B.A., Los Angeles State Coll., 1954; M.A. in Internat. Relations (Herman fellow 1957-59), U. So. Cal., 1959; m. Cornelia Van Natta Goodwin, Aug. 21, 1959; children—Marianne Benora, Kathleen Goodwin. Asst. to dir. Sch. Internat. Relations, U. So. Cal., 1957-59; with USIA, 1959-68, dep. policy dir. Latin Am. and Cuban affairs, 1967-68; dir. so. Cal. region Inst. Internat. Relations, 1968- 71, dir. W. coast region 11E, 1971—. Mem. World Affairs Council, Town Hall, Com. Fgn. Relations, Los Angeles County Mus. Art. Served with AUS, 1954-57. Recipient Meritorious Service award USIA, 1961, 66. Mem. Delta Upsilon. Republican. Conglist. Home: 1944 La Fremontia St South Pasadena CA 91030 Office: 1212 Wilshire Blvd Los Angeles CA 90017

BAER, RUDOLF LEWIS, physician, educator; b. Strasbourg, France, July 22, 1910; s. Ludwig and Clara (Mainzer) B.; M.D., U. Basel (Switzerland), 1934; postgrad. dermatology N.Y. Postgrad. Med. Sch., 1937-39; m. Louise Jeanne Grumbach, Nov. 6, 1941; children—John Reckford, Andrew Rudolph. Came to U.S., 1934, naturalized, 1940. Intern Beth Israel Hosp., N.Y.C., 1934- 35; resident dermatology Montefiore Hosp., N.Y.C., 1936-37; faculty Columbia Sch. Medicine, 1939-48; dir. dept. dermatology Univ. Hosp. 1961—; faculty N.Y.U. Sch. Medicine, 1948—, chmn. dept. dermatology, 1961—, George Miller MacKee prof., 1961—; dir. dept. dermatology Bellevue Hosp. Center, 1961—; sr. cons. VA Hosp., N.Y.C.; cons. Goldwater Meml. Hosp., N.Y.C., Monmouth Meml. Hosp., Long Branch, N.J., Elizabeth A. Horton Meml. Hosp., Middletown, N.J., Jewish Home and Hosp. for Aged, N.Y.C., surgeon gen. U.S. Army, FDA; mem. Internat. Com. Dermatology; mem. com. on revision U.S. Pharmacopeia, 1970—; mem. commn. cutaneous diseases Armed Forces Epidemiologic Bd.; Dohi lectr., also recipient Dohi medal Japanese Dermatol. Soc., 1965; Von Zumbusch lectr., Munich, 1967; Hellerstrom lectr., Stockholm, 1970; O'Leary lectr., Rochester, 1971. Diplomate Am. Bd. Dermatology (mem. 1964—, pres. 1967-70). Fellow N.Y. Acad. Medicine (chmn. sect. dermatology 1963-64), Am. Acad. Dermatology, Am. Acad. Allergy, Am. Coll. Allergists; mem. A. M.A. (chmn. section dermatology 1965-66), Am. Dermatol, Assn., Soc. Investigative Dermatology (pres. 1963-64), A.A.A.S., Bronx (pres. 1952), N.Y. dermatol. socs., N.Y. Allergy Soc., N.Y. Acad. Scis., N.Y. County and State Med. Soc.; hon. mem. Austrian, Brit., Brazilian, Danish, Finnish, Iranian, Israeli, Polish, Swedish, Venezuelan dermatol. socs.; corr. mem. Argentinian, Cuban, French, Italian dermatol. socs., French Allergy Soc. Editor: Office Immunology, 1947; Atopic Dermatitis, 1955; Year Book Dermatology, 1955-65; also past mem. numerous editorial bds. Author over 240 articles. Home: 1185 Park Av New York City NY 10028 Office: 566 1st Av New York City NY 10016

BAER, THOMAS J., lawyer; b. N.Y.C., May 11, 1927; s. Edward J. and Catherine (Long) B.; B.S., Columbia, 1955, LL.B., 1957; m. Margaret C. Hill, Aug. 28, 1951; children—Thomas James, Stephen Michael, Margaret Jane, Julie Ellen, Maura Beth. Admitted to N.Y. bar. 1958, since practiced in N.Y.C.; partner firm Hawkins, Delafield & Wood, 1967-. Mem. Am., N.Y. State bar assns., Municipal Forum N.Y., Municipal Finance Officers Assn. (asso.). Roman Cath. Clubs: Bankers, Columbia (N.Y.C.). Home: 523 White Av Northvale NJ 07647 Office: 67 Wall St New York City, NY 10005.

BAERREIS, DAVID ALBERT, educator; b. N.Y.C., Nov. 2, 1916; s. Philip George and Anna M. (Schomaker) B.; B.A., U. Okla., 1941, M.A., 1943; Ph.D., Columbia, 1949; m. Margaret Brandenburg, May 21, 1943. Project supr., then asst. state supr., archeol. projects WPA, Okla., 1947-40, 41-42; faculty U. Wis., Madison, 1947—, prof. anthropology, 1955—, chmn. dept. sociology and anthropology, 1956-58, 59-60. Mem. div. anthropology and psychology NRC, 1958-61. Served with AUS, 1943-46; ETO. Recipient Increase Lapham research medal Wis. Archeol. Soc., 1955, Fellow Am. Anthrop. Assn., Royal Anthrop. Inst., A.A.A.S. (v.p., chmn. sect. H 1963); mem. Central States Anthrop. Soc. (pres. 1956), Soc. Am. Archaeology (sec. 1957-60, pres. 1962-63), Am. Indian Ethnohistoric Conf. (pres. 1957), Am. Folklore Soc. (v.p. 1958, exec. com. 1959-61), Phi Beta Kappa, Sigma Xi (asso.). Author articles, monographs archaeology, ethnohistory, gen. anthropology. Home: 1233 Sweet Briar Rd Madison, WI 53705.

BAERWALD, JOHN EDWARD, educator, traffic engr.; b. Milw., Nov. 2, 1925; s. Albert John and Margaret (Brandt) B.; student Valparaiso U., 1943, 46-48; B.S. in Civil Engring., Purdue U., 1949, M.S., 1949, Ph.D., 1956; m. Elaine Shirley Eichstaedt, Apr. 3, 1948; children—Thomas John, James Kurt, Barbara Lynn. Research asst. Purdue U., 1949-50, research asso., 1950-52, research engr., instr. hwy. engring., 1952-55; asst. prof. U. Ill. at Urbana, 1955-57, prof. transp. and traffic engring., 1960—, dir. Hwy. Traffic Safety Center, 1961—, staff asso. Police Tng. Inst., 1969—; pres. Inst. Traffic Engring., 1970—; cons. traffic engr., 1952—. Chmn. Parking and Traffic Commn., Champaign, Ill., 1960-69; mem. Gov.'s Ofcl. Traffic Safety Coordinating Com., 1962-69. Registered profl. engr., Ill., Ind. Served with AUS, 1943-46. Mem. Inst. Traffic Engrs. (dir. 1964-65, sec.-treas. 1967 tech. v.p. 1968, adminstrv. v.p. 1969), Am. Soc. C.E., Nat. Safety Council, Hwy. Research Bd., Transp. Assn. Am., Sigma Xi, Chi Epsilon. Lutheran. Mason, Lion. Contbr. articles profl. jours. Home: 1421 Mayfair Rd Champaign IL 61820 Office: Engring Hall U Ill Urbana IL 61801

BAERWITZ, HERBERT G., lawyer; b. Bklyn., May 29, 1920; s. Sam and Belle (Schenck) B.; student Brown U., 1936-37; B.A., U. Cal. at Los Angeles, 1940; LL.B., U. So. Cal., 1947; m. Eva Cathey, May 4, 1944; children—Vicki, Stephen. Resident counsel Edward Small Prodns., Inc., 1947-49, also dir.; pvt. practice, 1949-66; mem. firm Baerwitz & Gordon, 1966-70; mem. firm Ball, Hunt, Hart, Brown & Baerwitz, Beverly Hills, Cal., 1970—. Dir. Aubrey Schenck Enterprises, Inc., William Castle Prodns., Inc., Esco Realty Corp. Served to lt. USNR, 1941-45. Mem. Am., Cal., Beverly Hills bar assns., Am. Judicature Soc., Los Angeles Copyright Soc. Home: 17211 Rancho St Encino CA 91316 Office: 450 N Roxbury Dr Beverly Hills CA 90210

BAESEL, STUART OLIVER, architect; b. Charlotte, N.C., Feb. 5, 1925; s. Edward Franklin and Rose (Engel) B.; student U. N.C., 1940-42, Ecole des Beaux Arts (Fountainbleau, France), 1948; B.Arch., N.C. State U., 1950; M.Arch., Cranbrook Acad. Art, 1951; m. Betsey London Cordon, Nov. 23, 1949; children—Stuart Oliver, Betsey London, Cordon Telfair. Architect firm A.G. Odell, Jr. & Asso., Charlotte, N.C., 1951-55; architect-designer firm Skidmore, Owings, Merrill, N.Y.C., 1955-59, LBC & W Asso., Columbia, S.C., 1959-65; dir. design firm J.N. Pease Assos., Charlotte, 1965—. Dir., sec. treas. Design World, Inc., Charlotte, 1968—; dir., pres. Space Planning Assos., Charlotte, 1966—. Editor Rev. Architecture, Columbia, 1962-65. Cons. Charlotte Planning Bd., 1954. Served with USAAF, 1943-46; PTO. Recipient various profl. awards, including Honor award S.C. chpt. A.I.A., 1964, 65, 66, N.C. chpt. A.I.A., 1956, 66, 68, 69. Fellow A.I.A. (bd. dirs. N.C.); mem. N.Y. Archtl. League, S.A., Phi Delta Theta. Episcopalian. Clubs: Charlotte Country; Piedmont. Home: 618 Museum Dr Charlotte NC 28207 Office: 2925 E Independence Blvd Charlotte NC 28205

BAETHKE, DOROTHY ELIZABETH, phys. therapist; b. Kewanee, Ill., June 15, 1905; d. John Henry and Louise (Nobling) Baethke; student Sargent Coll., 1926; phys. therapy certificate Mayo Clinic, 1927; postgrad. U. Minn., 1938-43; phys. therapy certificate Northwestern U., 1946; B.S., 1947. Phys. therapist Mayo Clinic, 1926-31; dir. phys. therapy Dowling Sch. Crippled Children, Mpls., 1931-45; teaching fellow Northwestern U., 1945-47; asst. prof. phys. therapy Grad. Sch. Medicine, U. Pa., 1947-50, dir. Sch. Phys. Therapy, Grad. Hosp., 1947-50, prof. dir. div. phys. therapy Sch. Allied Med. Professions, 1950-, also prof., chmn. dept. phys therapy. Mem. Am. Phys. Therapy Assn., P.E.O. Home: Garden Court Apt Philadelphia PA 19105 Office: Dept Phys Therapy U Pa Philadelphia PA 19104

BAETJER, ANNA MEDORA, scientist, educator; b. Balt., July 7, 1899; d. J. Frank and Katherine (Cook) Baetjer; B.A., Wellesley Coll., 1920; D.Sc., Johns Hopkins, 1924; D.P.H., Woman's Med. Coll. Pa., 1953; D.Sc., Wheaton Coll., 1966. Mem. faculty Johns Hopkins Sch. Hygiene and Pub. Health, Balt., 1923—, prof. environmental medicine 1961-70, prof. emeritus, 1970—. Cons. preventive medicine div. Office Surgeon Gen. U.S. Army, 1943—; mem. commn. environmental health Armed Forces Epidemiological Bd., 1954—; mem. com. on biol. effects of atmospheric pollutants NRC, 1970—; mem. radiation control adv. bd. Md. Health Dept., 1960—; cons. toxicology research div. Koppers Co., 1957—; mem. Permanent Commn. and Internat. Assn. Occupational Health, 1960—; mem. adv. com. on safety pesticide residues in foods FDA, 1966-70; safety and occupational health study sect. U.S. Dept. Health, Edn. and Welfare, 1968-70. Trustee Indsl. Hygiena Found., 1958—, vice chmn., 1964-68. Mem. Am. Physiol. Soc., Am. Pub. Health Assn., Am. Indsl. Hygiene Assn. (pres. 1951; Cummings Meml. award 1964), Nat. Conf. Gov. Indsl. Hygienists, Am. Acad. Occupational Medicine (hon.). Am. Acad. Indsl. Hygiene (bd. 1968—). Md. Acad. Scis. (trustee), Phi Beta Kappa, Sigma Xi. Author: Women in Industry-Their Health and Efficiency, 1946; also articles research papers, chpts, in books. Mem. editorial bd. Archives Environmental Health, 1960-70. Home: 4900 Roland Av Baltimore MD 21210

BAEUMER, MAX LORENZ, educator; b. Trier, Germany, May 19, 1917; s. Lorenz Max and Helene (Dahm) B.; Ph.L., Coll. Trier, 1939; postgrad. U. Frankfurt (Germany), 1947-49; Ph.D., Northwestern U., 1959; m. Helene Heine, Jan. 25, 1945. Came to U.S., 1952, naturalized, 1958. Instr., Northwestern U., 1958-59; asst. prof. Bowling Green State U., 1959-61; asso. prof. U. Kan., 1961- 63; faculty U. Wis., Madison, 1965—, prof. German lit., 1965—; dir. Northwestern U. Summer Inst., Germany, 1963; Fulbright vis. prof. U. Stuttgart (Germany), 1964-65. Evaluator Nat. Def. Edn. Act. Insts. in Germany, 1963; vis. prof. U. Wis. Inst. for Research in Humanities, 1968. Northwestern U. fellow, 1958; E.M. Watkins scholar, 1963; fellow Am. Philos. Soc., 1965. Mem. Modern Lang. Assn., Am. Assn. Tchrs. German, Internat. Germanist. Verband. Author: Das Dionysische i.d. Werken W. Heinses, 1964; Heinse-Studien, 1966; Editor: W. Heinse, Collected Works and Letters, 1970. Home: 6625 Wood Circle Middleton WI 53562 Office: Dept German University of Wis Madison WI 53706

BAEZ, JOAN, folk singer; b. S.I., N.Y., Jan. 9, 1941; d. Albert V. and Joan (Bridge) B.; student Boston U. Fine Arts Sch. Drama, 1958; m. David Victor Harris, Mar. 1968; 1 son, Gabriel Earl. Appeared in coffeehouses Ballad Room, Club 47, 1958-60, Gate of Horn, Chgo., 1958, Newport (R.I.) Folk Festival, 1959, 60; extended tour to colls. and concert halls, 1961—, Carnegie Hall, 1962; recording artist for Vanguard Records, 1960—; concert tours Europe, 1965-66, 70, Japan, 1966, U.S. and Europe, 1967-68; extensive TV appearances; speaking tour U.S. and Can. for draft resistance, 1967-68. Founder, v.p. Inst. for Study Nonviolence, Palo Alto, Cal., 1965. Author: Daybreak, 1968. Home: Los Altos CA 94022 Office: care Folklore Productions 176 Federal St Boston MA 02110

BAFFES, THOMAS GUS, heart surgeon; b. New Orleans, Apr. 3, 1923; s. Gus and Tina (Bores) B.; B.S., Tulane U., 1943. M.D., 1945; m. Mary Lou Amann, Feb. 23, 1958; children—Kathleen, Christine, Paul. Rotating intern Charity Hosp., New Orleans, 1945-46, residency tng. gen. surgery, 1948-51, residency tng. thoracic surgery, 1951-52; residency pediatric pathology Children's Meml. Hosp., Chgo., 1952, residency pediatric surgery, 1953, fellow cardiovascular research (surg.), 1954-56, now mem. staff; staff Swedish Covenant Hosp., head dept. surgery, 1960- 64; prof. surgery Chgo. Med. Sch.; staff Augustana Hosp., Lutheran Gen. Hosp., Ill. Central Hosp., Mt. Sinai Hosp. (all Chgo.). Served as capt. M.C., AUS, 1946-48; psychiatry and surgery VA hosps. Recipient Beta Mu award biology; Alpha Chi Sigma award chemistry; Isadore Dyer scholastic award Tulane U., 1945; chosen one of Ten Outstanding Young Men, 1957. Mem. Am. Acad. Pediatrics, A.M.A., A.C.S., Am. Coll. Chest Physicians, Chgo. Surg. Soc., Am. Soc. for Artificial Organs, Am. Assn. Thoracic Surgery, Soc. Thoracic Surgeons, Western Surg. Soc., Chicago Med. Soc., Phi Beta Kappa, Alpha Omega Alpha. Mem. Hellenic Orthodox Ch. Author med. articles. Home: 1701 Woodland Av Park Ridge IL 60068 Office: 4055 Main St Skokie IL 60076

BAGBY, FREDERICK LAIR, Jr., lab. dir.; b. Salt Lake City, Aug. 2, 1920; s. Frederick Lair and Marcia Fanny (Fitts) B.; B.S., U. Utah, 1942; m. Marilla Eudora Barlow, June 19, 1943; children—Dallas (Mrs. Fred E. Wells, Jr.), Marcia Norinne, Ross Frederick. Prodn. design engr. airplane div. Curtiss-Wright Corp., Columbus, O., 1942-46; with Battelle Meml. Inst., Columbus, 1946—, mgr. mech. engring. dept., 1966-70, asst. dir. Columbus Labs., 1970—. Asso. Fellow Am. Inst. Aeros. and Astronautics (v.p. sect. affairs); mem. Am. Soc. M.E., A.A.A.S. Contbr. articles to profl. jours. Research on smokeless combustion of bituminous coal, high temperature aerospace materials, tech. planning and forecasting. Home: 1714 Churchview Lane Columbus OH 43220 Office: 505 King Av Columbus OH 43201

BAGBY, JOHN ROSCOE, Jr., univ. inst. dir.; b. Aurora, Mo., Mar. 3, 1919; s. John R. and Grace (Seburn) B.; B.S., U. Ark., 1954. M.S., 1956; Ph.D., Emory U., 1962; m. Billie M. Hudson, Oct. 17, 1944; children—Caroline (Mrs. H. Turner Whitson), John Roscoe III, Charles Thomas. Pub. health biologist USPHS, 1946-66; dep. dir. Nat. Communicable Disease Center, 1966-69; dir. Inst. Rural Environmental Health, Colo. State U., 1969—. Chmn. interagy. commn. on back contamination NASA, 1966—; lectr., cons. in field, 1957—; mem. panel health effects of environmental pollution President's Sci. Adv. Com., 1965; U.S. del. Orgn. de Coorndination et de Coop. Pour la Lutte Contre les Grances Endemies, Bobo Dioulasso, Upper Volta, 1967—. Served with USAAF, 1942-45. Mem. Am. Soc. Tropical Medicine and Hygiene, Am. Mosquito control Assn., U.S.Mexico Border Pub. Health Assn., A.A.A.S., Sci. Research Soc. Am. Home: 5339 Jonathan Ct Fort Collins, CO 80521.

BAGBY, WESLEY ST. JOHN, ins. co. exec.; b. Los Angeles, Mar. 22, 1910; s. Wesley Abner and Ethel (Allan) B.; A.B., U. Cal. at Los Angeles, 1932, M.B.A., 1949; m. Evelyn Alice Hall, June 30, 1934; children—Linda Alice (Mrs. James M. McCue), Bonnie Ann (Mrs. Salvatore Spinella). Instr., U. Cal. at Los Angeles, 1932-34; clk. Pacific Mut. Life Ins. Co., Los Angeles, 1927-34, supr., 1934-42, mgr. underwriting dept., 1946-49, mgr. underwriting and issue depts., 1949-51, asst. treas., 1951-53, asst. v.p., 1953-54, comptroller, 1954-63, v.p., controller, 1963-70, v.p., treas., 1970—; v.p. Art Industries, Inc., Los Angeles, 1952-63. Bd. dirs. Honokeana Cove Apt. Owners Assn., Hawaii, 1968—, Los Angeles County br. and Cal. div. Am. Cancer Soc., 1959—. Served to comdr. USNR, 1942-46. Fellow Life Office Mgmt. Assn. (dir. 1966—, exec. com., chmn. bd. 1970—); mem. Los Angeles C. of C., Am. Cancer Soc., Financial Execs. Inst. (dir. 1966—), Navy League, Am. Mgmt. Assn., Med. Research Assn. Cal. (dir.) 1967—, treas. 1969—), Health Care Systems Adminstrs. (treas. Los Angeles), Phi Beta Kappa, Beta Gamma Sigma, Alpha Kappa Psi, Alpha Gamma Omega. Republican. Presbyn. Clubs: Crystalaire Country (Llano, Cal.); Deauville Country (Tarzana, Cal.); University (Los Angeles). Home: 11592 Sunshine Terrace Studio City CA 91604 Office: 523 W 6th St Los Angeles CA 90054

BAGDATOPOULOS, WILLIAM SPENCER, artist; b. Zante, Greece, July 23, 1888; s. Anastasius John and Amy Frederica (Sheath) B.; ed. Dulwich, Eng., Acad. van Beeldende Kunsten, Rotterdam, 1903-06, Athens Acad., 1906-07; m. Caralisa N. Nichols, 1938. Came to U.S., 1928, naturalized U.S. citizen. Chief artist Times of India publs., 1910-50; devel. advt. standards in India, affecting market for English and Am. goods; exhibited works Arlington Gallery, London, 1927, Kleeman Gallery, N.Y.C., 1928, Nat. Gallery, Washington, 1929, 30, 37, New Delhi, 1929, Los Angeles, 1931; rep. permanent collections Brit. Mus., London, Boyman's Mus., Rotterdam, Municipal Art Gallery, Amsterdam, Nat. Gallery Art, Washington, Nat. Pinakotec, Athens, Library Congress, Washington, Recipient bronze and silver medals South Kensington, London, 1913. Served with South African regt., British Army, World War I. Fellow Royal Soc. Arts, Imperial Art League (London); mem. Chgo. Soc. Etchers. Clubs: Column, London Sketch (London). Inventor folding boat puzzles. Home: San Maurice 801 Sutter St San Francisco CA 94109

BAGDIKIAN, BEN HAIG, writer; b. Marash, Turkey, Jan. 30, 1920; s. Aram Theodore and Daisy (Uvezian) B.; came to U.S., 1920, naturalized, 1926; A.B., Clark U., 1941, D.Litt., 1963; L.H.D., Brown U., 1961; m. Elizabeth Ogasapian, Oct. 2, 1942; children—Christopher Ben, Frederick Haig. Reporter, Springfield (Mass.) Morning Union, 1941-42; asso. editor Periodical House, Inc., N.Y.C., 1946; successively reporter, fgn. corr., chief Washington corr. Providence Jour., 1947-62; contbg. editor Sat. Eve. Post, 1963-67; project dir. study of future U.S. news media Rand, 1967-69; asst. mng. editor Fox Mut. News, The Washington Post, 1970—. Member board of trustees Clark U., 1964—; bd. directors National Capital Area Civil Liberties Union, 1964-66); president of the Lowell Mellett Fund for Free and Responsible Press, 1965—. Served with USAAF, 1942-45. Recipient George Foster Peabody award, 1951, Sidney Hillman Found. award, 1956; Ogden Reid Found. fellow, 1956; Guggenheim fellow, 1961-62. Mem. Overseas Writers, Authors League. Democrat. Unitarian. Club: Nat. Press (Washington). Author: In The Midst of Plenty: The Poor in America, 1964; The Information Machines: Their Impact on Men and the Media, 1971; also pamphlets. Contbr.: The Kennedy Circle, 1961. Editor: Man's Contracting World in an Expanding Universe, 1959. Office: 1515 L St NW Washington DC 20005

BAGEANT, KENNETH EDMOND, ret. ins. co. exec.; b. St. John, Wash., Oct. 3, 1903; s. Salem C. and Isabelle (Stover) B.; B.A., Wash. State U., 1927; m. Martha Faith Dyer, June 2, 1928; children—Susan Faith (Mrs. Harry C. Weiler), Judith Elaine (Mrs. David J. Driscoll). With Equitable Life Assurance Soc. U.S., N.Y.C., 1927-69, successively trainee, asst. cashier, Portland, Ore. and Omaha, cashier, Phoenix, then Louisville, asst. cashier home office, 1927-53, mgr. dept., 1953-60, v.p., 1960-69. Mem. N.Y.C. of C., Sigma Delta Chi, Phi Delta Theta, Phi Kappa Phi. Conglist. Mason (32, past dist. dep. grand master). Club: Marco Island Country. Home: 848 Chestnut Ct Marco Island FL 33937 Office: 1285 Av of Americas New York City NY 10019

BAGG, ROBERT ELY, poet; b. Orange, N.J., Sept. 21, 1935; s. Theodore Ely and Elma Hague (White) B.; A.B., Amherst Coll., 1957; postgrad. Harvard Grad. Sch., 1960; M.A., U. Conn., 1961, Ph.D., 1965; m. Sarah Frances Robinson, Aug. 24, 1957; children—Theodore Antibes Ariel, Christopher Augustus, Jonathan, Melissa, Robert. Asso. prof. English, U. Mass., Amherst, 1965—. Recipient Simpson Fellowship to study and write in France, 1957-58; Prix de Rome, Am. Acad. Arts and Letters, 1958-59; Nat. Def. fellow for study U. Conn., 1960, Ingram Merrill fellow, 1960; fellow Nat. Translation Center Austin, Tex., 1969; vis. prof. classics U. Tex., 1971. Recipient Armstrong Poetry prize, 1956, 57. Glascock Poetry prize, 1957; fellow Am. Acad. in Rome. Mem. Phi Kappa Phi, Phi Alpha Psi. Author: Poems, 1956-57, 1957; Madonna of the Cello, 1961; Liberations: Plays by Robert Bagg, 1969; also monographs. Translator: Euripides' Hippolytes, 1971. Home: 32 Barret Pl Northampton MA 01060 Office: Dept English U Mass Amherst MA 01002

BAGGE, CARL ELMER, lawyer, assn. exec.; b. Chgo., Jan. 12, 1927; s. Hjalmar and Adele (Elmquist) B.; B.A. summa cum laude, Augustana Coll., 1949; postgrad. Uppsala (Sweden) U., 1947, U. So. Cal., 1956; J.D., Northwestern U., 1952; m. Margaret Evelyn Carlson, June 27, 1953; children—Carol Eileen, Charles Edward, Barbara Ann, Beverly Jean. Admitted to Ill. bar, 1951; practiced in Chgo., 1951-52; atty. A., T. & S.F. Ry., Chgo., 1952-62, asst. gen. atty., 1962-63, spl. asst. exec. dept., 1963-64, gen. atty., 1964- 65; commr. FPC, Washington, 1965-70, vice chmn., 1966-67; pres., chief exec. officer, dir. Nat. Coal Assn., Washington, 1971—; dir. Bituminous Coal Research, Inc., 1971—. Mem. commn. ch. and econ. life Nat. Council Chs. Christ. Mem. Deerfield Zoning Bd. Appeals, 1955-58, Deerfield Plan Commn., 1958-62. Dir. Augustana Coll., Bituminous Coal Research; trustee Luth. Student Found. Met. Chgo. Served to ensign USNR, 1945-46. Mem. Nat. Assn. R.R. and Pub. Utility Commrs. (exec. com.), Am., Ill., Chgo. bar assns., ICC Practitioners Assn., Legal Club Chgo., Econ. Club Chgo., Assn. Western Ry. Counsel, Lexington Group Ry. Historians, Ill. Jr. C. of C., Am. Scandinavian Found., Ill. Hist. Soc., Ry. Systems and Mgmt. Assn., Phi Beta Kappa, Phi Alpha Delta, Pi Kappa Delta. Luthern. Republican. Clubs: Capitol Hill, Nat. Press, University, Congressional Country (Washington). Contbr. articles to legal and religious publs., contbr. to The Supreme Court, 1961. Home: 10019 Kendale Rd Potomac MD 20854 Office: 1130 17th St NW Washington DC 20036

BAGGENSTOSS, ARCHIE HERBERT, pathologist; b. Richardton, N.D., Apr. 13, 1908; s. Jacob R. and Louise (Kaiser) B.; B.A., U. N.D., 1930, B.S., 1931; M.D., U. Cin., 1933; M.S., Mayo Found., U. Minn., 1938; m. Mildred M. Burkhart, Feb. 25, 1934; children—Roger D., Janet L., Ruth A. Intern Deaconess Hosp., Cin., 1933- 34; practice medicine, Cin., 1934-35; fellow in pathology Mayo Found., 1935-38, 1st asst., 1938-40, cons., 1940; instr. pathology Mayo Found., Grad. Sch. U. Minn., 1939-43, asst. prof., 1943- 47, asso. prof., 1947-52, prof., 1952—; head sect. path. anatomy Mayo Clinic, 1955-68, sr. cons., 1968—. Served as lt. USNR, 1941-42. Diplomate Am. Bd. Pathology, Nat. Bd. Med. Examiners, Fellow A.M.A. (chmn. sect. pathology and physiology 1966-67); mem. Am. Assn. Pathologists and Bacteriologists, Am. (bd. censors), Minn. (pres. 1947) socs. clin. pathologists, Am. Gastroenterol. Assn., Am. Assn. for Study Liver Disease (pres. 1968-69), Internat. Acad. Pathology, Phi Beta Kappa, Sigma Xi, Phi Chi. Republican. Presbyn. Contbr. chpts. to books, articles to profl. jours. Mem. editorial bd. Gastroenterology, 1958-66, Archives of Pathology, 1964—. Home: 1166 Plummer Circle Rochester MN 55901 Office: 200 1st St SW Rochester MN 55901

BAGGETT, AGNES, state ofcl.; b. Columbus, Ga., d. John R. and Leila (Thomason) Beahn; student pub. schs., Columbus; m. George Lamar Baggett, Oct. 14, 1926 (dec. 1949). With L. & N. R.R., 1925-27; various positions sec. state's office, Montgomery, Ala., 1927-46, sec. state, 1951-55, 63-67, state auditor, 1955-58, state treas., 1959-63, 67-70, 71—; asst. clerk in Supreme Ct. Ala. 1946-50. Named Career Woman and One of Top 10 Women in Montgomery. Mem. Am. Legion Aux. (state legislative chmn.; chmn. Girls State, Ala.), Order Eastern Star. Clubs: Altrusa (corr. sec.), Bus. and Profl. Women's (past state pres). Home: 3202 Montezuma Rd Montgomery AL 36106 Office: State Capitol Montgomery AL 36104

BAGGETT, JACK P., union ofcl. Pres., United Allied Workers Internat. Union. Office: 5248 Hohman Av Hammond IN 47320*

BAGLEY, EDWARD N., investment co. exec.; b. Salt Lake City, 1912; ed. Utah State U., 1933. Resident partner Goodbody & Co., Los Angeles. Home: 616 S June St Los Angeles, CA 90005. Office: 507 W 6th St Los Angeles CA 90014*

BAGMAN,CHRISTOPHER BRUCEchemist, educator; b. Chicago, 1928; B.S. in Physics, Yale, 1950; Ph.D. in Chemistry, Harvard, 1956; m. Sally Ann Jones, July 5, 1957; children--Kenneth J., Nancy A. Chemist, Acme Chem. Co., Blue Island, Ill., 1950-51; director of Reseach Lab., Indsl. Chemicals Corp., Cambridge, Mass., 1956-60; project coordinator environmental sect. Steinmetz Assos., Chgo., 1960-61; v.p. for reseach Bauer Bros. Chem. Co., Inc., Memphis, 1961-64; asst. prof. chemistry Washington U., St. Louis, 1964-66, asso. prof., 1966-70, prof., 1970--, head of chemistry dept., 1970-71. Vis. prof. So. Ill. U., summer 1967, U. of Ore., 1969. Scoutmaster, Boy Scouts America, University City, Mo., 1968-70. Bd. dirs. Rest Haven Home for Elderly, 1960-61; trustee of the Lutheran Hosp., 1965-71. Served from lt. to capt., AUS, 1951-53. Mem. Am. Chem. Soc., Sci. Research Soc. Am. (chpt. treas. 1967), Sigma Xi. Author: (with others) Basic Inorganic Chemistry, 1971. Contbr. articles to profl. jours., encys., also chpts. to books. Home: Fairfax Apts 7291 Windermere Dr University City MO 63105 Office: Dept Chemistry Washington University St Louis MO 63130

BAGNOLD, ENID, (Lady Jones), novelist, playwright; b. Rochester, Kent, Eng., Oct. 27, 1889; d. Col. Arthur Henry and Ethel (Alger) Bagnold; student of schools in England, Paris, Lausanne, Marburg; m. Sir Roderick Jones, July 8, 1920, (dec. Feb. 1962); children—Laurian (wife of Comte Anne-Pierre d'Harcourt), Timothy, Richard, Dominick. Author: A Diary Without Dates, 1916; The Happy Foreigner, 1920; Sailing Ships (poems), 1917; Alice and Thomas and Jane (juvenile); Serena Blandish, 1924; National Velvet (prod. as movie, TV series), 1935; The Squire (The Door of Life) 1938; The Loved and Envied, 1951; (plays) Gertie, Lottie Dundas, Poor Judas (awarded Arts Theatre Prize in co. with John Whiting), The Chalk Garden (award of merit, Am. Acad. Arts and Letters); The Last Joke (play), 1960; The Chinese Prime Minister (produced in N.Y.C. and London), 1965; (3-act comedy) Call Me Jacky, 1966; Enid Bagnold's Autobiography, 1970; Four Plays, 1971. Home: North End House Rottingdean Sussex England

BAGRIT, LEON, automation co. exec.; b. Kieff, Russia, Mar. 13, 1902; s. Manuel and Rachel (Yusupovitch) B.; ed. Birkbeck Coll., U. (Eng.) London; D.Sc., U. Reading, 1968; hon. doctorate U. Surrey, 1966; m. Stella Feldman, August 1st 1926; children—Valerie Juliet (Mrs. R.S. Kahan), Patricia Fleur (Mrs. H. Bress). With W. & T. Avery Ltd., Birmingham; gen. mgr., designer new machinery Herbert & Sons Ltd., engrs., London; propr. B. & P. Swift Ltd., patented designs, London; company amalgamated with Elliott Bros., London, 1947, dep. chmn. Elliot-Automation Ltd., 1957-62, chmn., 1963—; dep. chmn. English Electric Co., Ltd., 1968—; Electronics Trust Ltd., Tech. Investments Ltd., Marconi Co. Ltd. Mem. adv. council Ministry of Tech.; council Dept. Edn. and Sci. Dir. Royal Opera House. Chmn. Friends Covent Garden. Created knight, 1962; recipient Gold Albert medal Royal Soc. Arts. Club: Devonshire (London). Pub. The Age of Automation, 1966. Home: Upper Terrace House London NW 3 England Office: 34 Portland Pl London W1 England

BAGSHAW, MALCOLM ARNOLD, medical educator; b. Adrian, Mich., June 24, 1925; s. Albert and Doris P. (Shutes) B.; B.A., Wesleyan U., Middletown, Conn., 1946; M.D., Yale, 1950; m. Muriel Frances Hanley, Mar. 15, 1948; children—Cassandra, David Paul, Sarah Maria. Intern, asst. resident surgery Grace-New Haven Hosp., 1950-53; resident, jr. clin. instr. radiology U. Mich. Univ. Hosp., 1953-56; practice medicine specializing in radiotherapy, San Francisco, 1956-59, Palo Alto, Cal., 1959—; mem. staff Stanford Med. Center, Palo Alto VA Hosp., Valley Med. Center, San Jose, Cal.; mem.faculty Stanford Med. Sch., 1956—, dir. div. radiation therapy, 1960—, prof. radiology, 1968—. Mem. steering com. combined irradiation and chemotherapy for cancers of head and neck Nat. Cancer Inst., NIH, 1964, now mem. com. radiation therapy studies; mem. ad hoc com. evaluation electron exposure for astronauts NASA,

USAF, 1967-69; mem. radiation study sect., div. research grants NIH, 1968—, chmn., 1971-72; mem. nat. adv. com. research Am. Cancer Soc., 1965-66, vice chmn., 1967, chmn., 1968; mem. adv. com. radiation therapy Los Alamos Meson Physics Facility; mem. Eleanor Roosevelt fellowship com. Union Internat. Contra Cancer, 1970—; mem. program com. X Internat. Cancer Congress, Houston, 1970. Bd. dirs. Santa Clara County Cancer Soc. Fellow Am. Coll. Radiology; mem. No. Cal. Radiotherapy Assn. (pres. 1967-68), Am. Soc. Therapeutic Radiologists, Am. Radium Soc., A.M.A., Assn. Univ. Radiologists, Cal. Med. Assn., Radiol. Soc. N. Am., Radiation Research Soc., Soaring Soc. Am., Pacific Soaring Council (pres. 1968). Home: 922 Lathrop Pl Stanford CA 94305

BAGUIDY, FERN D., Haitian diplomat; b. 1920; ed. Lycee Nord Alexis, Jeremie, Lycee Alexandre Petion, Law Sch. and Inst. Ethnology, Port-au-Prince. Asst. chief Immigration and Emigration Service, Govt. of Haiti, 1947-51; with Pan-Am. World Airways, 1951-57; 1st sec. Haitian delegation to OAS, 1957-58, minister-counselor, 1958-59, chargé d'affaires, 1961, ambassador to OAS, 1962—; minister, counselor Haitian embassy, Washington, 1961-62. Decorated grand cross Nat. Order of Honor and Merit (Haiti). Address: 4400 17th St NW Washington DC 20011*

BAGWELL, PAUL DOUGLAS, investment firm exec.; b. Hendersonville, N.C., Aug. 24, 1913; s. Vollie Vernon and Nancy Margaret (Brown) B.; B.S., U. Akron, 1937; M.A., U. Wis., 1938, student, summers 1939-40-41; Litt.D., Yankton Coll., 1960; m. Edith Harriet Clark, Feb. 1, 1938; children—Paul Timbrelle, Judith Naomi. Teacher, high sch., Akron, O., 1937; dir. religious edn. Congl. Ch., Stoughton, Wis., 1937-38; instr. speech, dramatics, radio Mich. State U., 1938-40, asst. prof., 1941-42, asso. prof., 1942-43, prof. and head dept. speech, radio and dramatics, 1942-47, head dept., prof. written and spoken English, 1944-52, head dept., prof. communication skills, 1952-59, dir. scholarships and financial aid, 1959-61; chmn. bd., pres., dir. K-S Funds, Inc., Detroit, 1961-67; pres., chmn. bd., dir. Royal Resources Exploration, Inc., Royal Resources Corp. 1967-68, chmn. bd., dir., 1968—. Mem. U.S. Commn. UNESCO, 1949-56; active in Community Chest, Boy Scouts Am.; pres. Ohio Assn. Physically Disabled; bd. dirs. Mich. Soc. Mental Health, 1957—, v.p., chmn. exec. com., pres., 1968-70; mem. President's Com. Employment Physically Handicapped, 1950-55; state chmn. March of Dimes, 1951-63; mem. Mich. Higher Edn. Assistance Authority, 1964-68; pres. Mich. State U. Friends of Library, 1959-60. Trustee Mich. State U., 1963-65, Cumberland U., Hampton Inst., Kirwood Gen. Hosp., 1965-70, Alvin M. Bentley Found., Mich. Jaycee Found. (chmn. bd. 1966-67), Detroit chpt. UN Assn. U.S., Nat. Found., N.Y.C. State chmn. Citizens for Eisenhower, 1952-56; Republican nominee for auditor gen. State of Mich., 1956, for gov., 1958, 60; mem. Nat. Rep. Com. on Program and Progress. Recipient Freed Forum award, 1951; Silver Beaver, Boy Scouts Am., 1959; Gallantry award Nat. Soc. Crippled Children and Adults, 1959. Fellow Internat. Inst. Arts and Letters; mem. Nat. Artists Found. (pres. 1956-60), Mich. Jr. C. of C. (pres. 1943-44; state v.p. 1944-45), U.S. Jr. C. of C. (nat. dir. 1945-46; v.p. 1947-48; pres. 1948-49), U.S. (nat. dir. 1949-50), Mich., Greater Detroit chambers commerce, Speech Assn. Am. (exec. v.p. 1951-54), Soc. Study Communication (pres. 1950-51), Atlantic Union Com. (nat. council 1948-52), Am. Assn. U. Profs., Ill. gas and oil assns., Ind. Petroleum Assn., Am. Petroleum Inst., Lambda Chi Alpha. Mason (K.T.), Elk. Clubs: Detroit, Detroit Athletic, Press, Economic (Detroit); Grosse Point; Lansing City. Home: 1051 Devonshire Rd Grosse Pointe Park MI 48230 Office: Penobscot Bldg Detroit MI 48226 ☆

BAGWELL, ROSS KENNEDY, advt. exec.; b. Madisonville, Tenn., Jan. 17, 1932; s. Charles H. and Jeanette (Kennedy) B.; student U. Tenn., 1956; B.A. in Broadcasting, N.Y.U., 1958; m. Sue Burchfield, Sept. 23, 1951; children—Ross Kennedy Jr., Susan Denise. Program prodn. and merchandising NBC, N.Y.C., 1957-63; salesman sta. WATE-TV, Knoxville, Tenn., 1963; with Lavidge & Assos., Inc., Knoxville, 1963—, pres., 1970—; pres. Lookout/Lavidge Advt., Chattanooga, 1970—. Served with USAF, 1950-53. Recipient award Best TV Nat. Campaign, Am. Fedn. Advertisers, 1964, 70. Mem. Alpha Delta Sigma. Republican. Presbyn. Contbr. articles mags. Home: 5312 Riverbriar Rd Knoxville TN 37919 Office: Lavidge & Assos Inc Bearden Park Circle Knoxville TN 37919

BAGWILL, JOHN WILLIAMS, indsl., pub. relations exec.; b. Neb. July 11, 1901; s. Clinton William and Stella (Williams) B.; B.A., U. Wash., 1924; student U. Chgo., Stanford; m. Amy Munday, June 8, 1929; children—John Williams, Molly Jane (Mrs. John B. Burnap), Phillips Franklin. With Pacific Steamship Co., 1925-26, Rayonier Corp., 1926-51; v.p. Fred Rudge, Inc., Mgmt. cons., 1951-57; v.p., dir. indsl. and pub. relations Cone Mills Corp., 1957-71; practice indsl. relations and personnel counseling to industry, 1971—. Mem. gov.'s commn. to establish minimum wages, women and children State of Wash.; past pres. Boy Scout council, Twin Harbors, Wash. Mem. Nat. Personnel Assn., Northwest Personnel Mgrs. Assn., Am. Pub. Relations Assn., Beta Theta Pi. Contbr. articles personnel, trade publs. Home: 4111 Dogwood Dr Greensboro CT 27410

BAHLKE, HAROLD O., educator; B.Ed., Wis. State U.; M.A., U. Minn., also Ph.D. Prof., area chmn. humanities Western Mich. U., Kalamazoo, 1962—. Office: Coll Arts and Scis Western Mich Univ Kalamazoo MI 49003*

BAHLMAN, DUDLEY WARD RHODES, educator; b. Cin., Mar. 19, 1923; s. William T. and Janet (Rhodes) B.; B.A., Yale, 1946, M.A., 1947, Ph.D., 1951; m. Jean Mitchell, Dec. 29, 1951; children—Dudley R., Anne M. Instr., asst. prof. Yale, 1951-59; asst. prof. Williams Coll., Williamstown, Mass., 1959-62, asso. prof., 1962-67, prof., 1967—, dean of faculty, 1968—. Served with Med. Dept., AUS, 1943-46. Morse fellow, 1957-58, Guggenheim fellow, 1965-66. Club: Elizabethan. Author: The Moral Revolution of 1688, 1957; The Diary of Sir Edward Hamilton, 1971. Home: Sabin Dr Williamstown MA 01267

BAHM, ARCHIE JOHN, educator; b. Imlay, Mich., Aug. 21, 1907; s. John Samuel and Lena (Kohn) B.; A.B., Albion Coll., 1929; M.A., U. Mich., 1930, Ph.D., 1933; m. Luna Parks Bachelor, Feb. 13, 1930; children—Raymond John, Elaine Lucia (Mrs. Arthur L. Fox). Instr. to asso. prof. Tex. Technol. Coll., 1934-46; asso. prof. philosophy U. Denver, 1946-48; prof. philosophy U. N.M., Albuquerque, 1948—. Fulbright research scholar U. Rangoon, 1955-56, Banaras Hindu U., 1962-63. Mem. Am. Philos. Assn., Am. Soc. for Aesthetics, Am. Humanist Assn., Metaphys. Soc. Am., Indian Congress Philosophy, Am. Assn. U. Profs., Soc. for Asian and Comparative Philosophy, Phi Beta Kappa, Phi Kappa Phi, Phi Sigma Tau. Author: Philosophy, An Introduction, 1953; Philosophy of the Buddha, 1958; What Makes Acts Right?, 1958; Tao Teh King by Lao Tzu, 1958; Logic for Beginners, 1960; Types of Intuition, 1961; Yoga: Union with the Ulitmate, 1961; The World's Living Religions, 1964; Yoga for Business Executives, 1965; The Heart of Confucius, 1969; Directory of American Philosophers I, 1962-63, II, 1964-65, III, 1966-67, IV, 1968-69, V, 1970-71; Bhagavad Gita, The Wisdom of Krishna, 1970; Polarity, Dialectic and Organicity, 1970. Contbr. articles to profl. jours. Home: 1915 Las Lomas Rd NE Albuquerque NM 87106.

BAHN, ROBERT CARLTON, medical educator; b. Newark, N.Y., July 24, 1925; s. Arlington Mott and Helen Esther (Houck) B.; student Albright Coll., 1942-43; M.D., U. Buffalo, 1947; Ph.D., U. Minn., 1953; m. Miriam Ruth Huer, July 30, 1949; children—David, Rebecca, Mark, Curtis. Intern, then resident patholgy E.J. Meyer Hosp., Buffalo, 1947-49; fellow pathology Mayo Found. and Clinic, Rochester, Minn., 1950-53; cons. pathology, 1956—; research fellow physiol. chemistry U. Minn., Mpls., 1952-53, prof. pathology, 1969—; sr. asst. surgeon USPHS, NIH, Bethesda, Md., 1954-55; mem. faculty Mayo Found., 1956-69, asso. prof. pathology, 1963-69. Diplomate in pathologic anatomy, clin. pathology and neuropathology Am. Bd. Pathology. Mem. Endocrine Soc., Biol. Stain Commn., Am. Physiol. Soc., Histochem. Soc., Assn. for Computing Machinery, Spl. Interest Group Biomed. Computing, Am. Assn. Pathologists and Bacteriologists, Internat. Acad. Pathologists, Soc. for Exptl. Biology and Medicine, Am. Assn. Neuropathologists, Sigma Xi. Research, numerous publs. in endocrine pathology, neuro-endocrine physiology and applications of digital computers to medicine. Home: 1650 NE 11th Av Rochester MN 55901

BAHNSON, HENRY THEODORE, surgeon, educator; b. Winston-Salem, N.C., Nov. 15, 1920; s. Frederick Fries and Bleeker Estelle (Reid) B.; B.S. summa cum laude, Davidson Coll., 1941; M.D. cum laude, Harvard, 1944; m. Louise Porter, Apr. 1, 1944; children—Henry Theodore, David Hastings, Alfred Blalock, Suzanne, Barbara Louise. Intern, then resident Johns Hopkins Hosp., 1944-51; research fellow physiology U. Rochester, 1949-50; faculty Johns Hopkins Sch. Medicine, 1951-62, prof. surgery, 1961-62; mem. staff Johns Hopkins Hosp., 1951-62; prof. surgery, chmn. dept. U. Pitts. Med. Sch., 1963—. Vis. prof. Royal Prince Alfred Hosp., Sydney, Australia, 1957, U. Vienna (Austria), 1962. Mem. Am. Assn. Thoracic Surgery (sec. 1961), Soc. Univ. Surgeons (pres. 1965), Am., So., Central surg. assns., A.M.A., Soc. Clin. Surgery, Peripatetic Club, Internat. Surg. Club, Halsted Soc. Author articles on surgery, cardiovascular disease, cardiovascular physiology. Home: 612 Dorseyville Rd Pittsburgh PA 15238.

BAHOLLI, SAMI, Albanian diplomat; b. Elbasan, Albania, Nov. 28, 1919; grad. as jurist, State U. Tirana, 1959; m. Efrosina Papamihali, Jan. 6, 1945; 4 daus. Sec., Presidium of Peoples Assembly, 1944-66; v.p. Supreme Ct., 1966-70; ambassador-permanent rep. of Albanian Peoples Republic to UN, N.Y.C., 1970—. Address: 250 E 87th St New York City NY 10028

BAHR, GUNTER F., pathologist; b. Altona, Germany, Oct. 10, 1922; s. Karl and Elfriede (Wedekind) B.; M.D., U. Wurzburg (Germany), 1952; M.D., Karolinska Inst., Stockholm, Sweden, 1957; m. Karina Edblad, Mar. 6, 1960; children—Josephine Karina, Nina Ingrid. Asst. Nobel Inst. Cell Research and Genetics, Stockholm, 1950-57, asst. prof., 1957-58; asst. prof. Karolinska Inst., 1957-58, asst. prof. Inst. Pathology, 1957-60; chief biophysics br. Armed Forces Inst. Pathology, 1960—; clin. prof. pathology Georgetown U., Washington, 1963—; vis. prof. pathology Northwestern U., 1958. Scandinavian rep. UNESCO com. on animal resources, 1955; Recipient award for meritorious civilian service, 1965, award for distinguished civilian service, 1967, Army research team award, 1967. Hon. fellow Internat. Acad. Reproductive Medicine; mem. Mil. Surgeons U.S. (hon.), Internat. Acad. Cytology (Maurice Goldblatt Cytological award 1966), Electron Microscopy Soc. Am., Soc. Exptl. Pathology and Biology, Histochem. Soc., Am. Soc. Cell Biology, Internat. Acad. Pathology, Scandinavian Soc. Electron Microscopy. Editorial bds. sci. jours. Research, publs. quantitative electron microscopy, malaria. chromosomes, pattern recognition. Home: 3206 Chestnut St NW Washington DC 20015

BAHR, WARREN ARTHUR, advt. exec.; b. N.Y.C., Nov. 5, 1924; s. Charles Walter and Elsie (Kauffmann) B.; B.A., Gettysburg Coll., 1949; student U. Va. Law Sch., 1950; m. Jeanne C. Walsh, June 23, 1951; children—Susan, Any, Lisa, Sarah, With Young & Rubicam, Inc., 1951—, sr. media dir., 1962-63, v.p., dir. media relations and planning, 1963-63, sr. v.p., dir. media relations and planning, 1964—, now executive senior vice president, Served with Army of U.S., 1942-45. Decorated Bronze Star. Purple Heart (2). Mem. Metro Advt. Golfers Assn., Tau Kappa Epsilon (past bd. govs. U. Va.). Presbyn. (trustee). Club: Waccabus Country. Home: Mead St Waccabuc NY 10597 Office: Young & Rubicam Inc 285 Madison Av New York City NY 10017

BAHRENBURG, FREDERIC EDWARD, ret. paper co. exec.; b. Bklyn., Aug. 14, 1907; s. Charles Claus and Anna (Willenbrock) B.; B.S. in Pulp and Paper, N.Y. State Coll. Forestry, 1930; m. Marian M. Minnes, Oct. 11, 1930; children—Robert M., Donall B. Asst. to pres. Strathmore Paper Co., 1930-48; dir. Hammermill Paper Co., 1957—, v.p., 1957-66, exec. v.p., 1966-70; exec. v.p., dir. Watervliet Paper Co., 1957-59; v.p., dir. Grays Harbor Paper Co., 1960-66; v.p. Beckett Paper Co., 1961-63. Mem. President's Com. and Gov. Pa. Com. Employment Handicapped; mem. Erie County United Fund. Bd. dirs. Hammermill Found., Erie YMCA, Syracuse Pulp and Paper Found.; trustee E. R. Behrend Trust. Clubs: Erie Kahkwa (past dir.). Home: Lake Shore Dr Chatham MA 02633 Office: Hammermill Paper Co Erie PA 16512

BAIARDI, JOHN CHARLES, sci. lab. adminstr.; b. Bklyn., Feb. 9, 1918; s. Joseph and Vivian (Oddo) B.; B.S., St. Francis Coll., 1940; M.A., Bklyn. Coll., 1943; Ph.D., N.Y. U., 1953; m. Rosalind Castaldi, May 15, 1943; children—Robert, Veronica. Instr., then asst. prof. biology St. Francis Coll., 1942-48; asso. prof. biology St. Johns U., 1948-54; prof. biology, chmn. dept. L.I. U., 1954-62, asso. dean Grad. Sch., 1960-62, v.p., provost, 1962-67, vice chancellor, 1967-70; pres., dir. N.Y. Ocean Sci. Lab., Montauk, 1970—. Vice chmn. med. adv. bd. Cooley's Anemia Found.; mem. Bi-County Marine Resources Council. Chmn. bd. trustees Affiliated Colls. and Univs., Inc.; trustee Verrazzano Coll., N.Y. Named to Bklyn. Hall of Fame for sci. activities, 1964. Fellow N.Y. Acad. Scis.; mem. Harvey Soc., Internat. Oceanographic Found., Sigma Xi, Phi Sigma. Home: 16 Thoedore Dr Plainview NY 11803 Office: New York Ocean Science Lab Drawer EE Montauk NY 11954

BAIER, KURT ERICH, educator; b. Vienna, Austria, Jan. 26, 1917; s. Emil and Maria (Hunna) B.; student law U. Vienna, 1935-38; B.A., U. Melbourne (Australia), 1942- 44, M.A., 1946; D.Phil., Oxford (Eng.) U., 1952; m. Annette Stoop, Dec. 28, 1958. Came to U.S., 1962. Lectr. philosophy U. Melbourne, 1948-56; prof. philosophy Australian Nat. U., 1956-62; prof. philosphy U. Pitts., 1962—, chmn. dept., 1962-67. Mem. Australian Humanities Research Council, Australian Assn. Philosophy (pres. 1961). Author: The Moral Point of View, 1958. Home: 100 Maple Heights Rd Pittsburgh PA 15232.

BAIER, MILTON LOUIS, ins. co. exec.; b. Buffalo, Apr. 5, 1903; s. Wendelin and Katherine (Berlet) B.; LL.B., U. Buffalo, 1924; m. Madonna Keller, June 30, 1932; 1 dau., Mary Katherine. Admitted to N.Y. State bar, 1925, practiced in Buffalo, Until 1955; with Mchts. Mut. Ins. Co., Buffalo, 1925—, pres., 1955—; chmn. bd. dirs. N.H. Mchts. Ins. Co.; pres. Mchts. Life Ins. Co.; dir. Liberty Nat. Bank & Trust Co. Dir. N.Y. State Citizens Council on Traffic Safety. Trustee, D'Youville Coll. Mem. Internat. Assn. Ins. Counsel, N.Y. State Bar Assn. Clubs: Buffalo. Wanakah Country, Lawyers, Buffalo Country (Buffalo). Home: 6129 Lake Shore Rd Hamburg NY 14075 Office: 250 Main St Buffalo NY 14202

BAIL, JOE PAUL, educator; b. Herold, W. Va., May 12, 1925; s. Alva Edward and Prudence (Wood) B.; B.S., W.Va. U., 1947, M.S., 1947; Ph.D., Mich State U., 1958; m. Nelma Louise Rapp, Oct. 20, 1945; 1 son, David Joe. Tchr. agr. Spencer (W. Va.) High Sch., 1947; head dept. agr. Glenville (W. Va.) State Coll., 1948-51; asst. prof., asso. prof. agrl. edn. W.Va. U., 1951-57; asso. prof. Cornell U., Ithaca, N.Y., 1957-64, prof. agrl. edn. div., 1964—. Cons. pub. schs., N.Y., Mass., W.Va., Ariz, Fla.; mem. com. Nat. Acad. Scis.; field review officer U.S. Office Edn. Dist. committeeman Boy Scouts Am., 1960-63; mem. Ch.-Community Action, Inc., 1968- Served to 1st lt. USAAF, 1943-45; ETO. Decorated Air medal with four oak leaf clusters; recipient 20 Year award in agrl. edn. N.Y. Assn. Tchrs. Agr., 1967. Mem. Am. Vocational Assn. (past nat. com. chmn.). Assn. Higher Edn., N.E.A., Alpha Zeta, Kappa Delta Pi, Delta Tau Delta. Democrat. Baptist (deacon). Rotarian. Contbg. author: Teacher Education in Agriculture. 1967. Contbr. articles to profl. jours. Home: 111 Winston Dr Ithaca, NY 14850.

BAIL, PHILIP MILO, ret. univ. pres.; b. Boonville, Mo., June 16, 1898; s. Philip Dunleavy and Mollie (Powell) B.; A.B., Mo. Valley Coll., 1920, LL.D., 1947; A.M. State U. Ia., 1928, Ph.D., 1931; LL.D., Creighton U., 1965; L.H.D., Omaha U., 1965; m. Josephine Scott Hayden, Dec. 18, 1920. Tchr. high sch., Redwood Falls, Minn., 1920-21, Keokuk, Ia., 1921-28; prin. U. Ia. High Sch., Iowa City, 1928-31; supr. high schs. Dist. 27, Hibbing, Minn., 1931-35; pres. Chevy Chase Jr. Coll., Washington, 1935-40; dean Coll. Edn., Butler U., Indpls., 1940-48; dir. Univ. Coll., 1945-48; pres. Municipal U., Omaha, 1948-65; pres. emeritus Omaha U., 1965—; vis. lectr., coll. edn. Ia. U., summers 1932-39; vice chmn. Omaha Planning Bd., 1965-68. Chmn. bd. trustees Cottey Coll., 1964-68; v.p. bd. trustees Mo. Valley Coll., Marshall, Mo.; trustee Coll. of St. Mary, Omaha, 1964-70; mem. exec. com., 1st v.p. Omaha Presbyn. Theol. Sem. Crowned King Ak-Sar-Ben LXI, 1955. Pres. North Central Assn. Colls. and Secondary Schs., 1952-53, mem. com. colls. and univs., 1952-62, chmn. com., 1960-61 mem. bd. rev. 1957-62, exc. bd., 1959-62. Trustee Joslyn Soc. Liberal Arts, Omaha. Named Exec. of Year, Ak-Sar-Ben chpt. Nat. Secs. Assn.; recipient Distinguished Service awards Neb. Wesleyan U., Kiwanis, Lions: Exceptional Service award USAF, 1965. Mem. Assn. Am. Colls., N.E.A., Nat. Assn. Secondary Sch. Prins., Dept. Supervisors, Am. Assn. Sch. Adminstrs., Omaha C. of C. (hon. life), Assn. Urban Univs. (pres. 1964), Rho Epsilon, Kappa Delta Pi, Phi Kappa Phi, Lambda Chi Alpha. Republican. Mason (33, Shriner). Clubs: Rotary (pres. 1958-59), Plaza. Milo Bail professorship and Milo Bail Student Center, Omaha U., named for him. Home: 1414 Marbee Dr Omaha NB 68124.

BAILAR, JOHN CHRISTIAN, Jr., chemist, educator; b. Golden, Colo., May 27, 1904; s. John Christian and Rachel Ella (Work) B.; B.A., U. Colo., 1924, M.A., 1925, D.Sc., 1959; Ph.D., U. Mich., 1928; D.Sc., U. Buffalo, 1959; m. Florence L. Catherwood, Aug. 8, 1931; children—John Christian III, Benjamin Franklin. Asst. in chemistry U. Mich., 1926-28; instr. chemistry U. Ill., Urbana, 1928-30, asso., 1930-35, asst. prof., 1935-39, asso. prof. 1939-43, prof., 1943—, sec. chem. dept., 1937-51. Vis. prof. chemistry U. Colo., summer 1962, U. Ariz., 1970, U. Wyo., 1970. Bd. dirs. Monmouth Coll., 1958—. Recipient Sci. Apparatus Makers award in chem. edn., 1961, John R. Kuebler award Alpha Chi Sigma, 1962, Priestley medal Am. Chem. Soc., 1964; Frank Dwyer medal Chem. Soc. New South Wales, 1965; Alfred Werner gold medal Swiss Chem. Soc., 1966; Teaching award Mfg. Chemists Assn., 1968; 1st recipient John C. Bailar Jr. medal U. Ill.; named Distinguished Alumnus, U. Mich., 1967, Ky. Col. Mem. Internat. Union Pure and Applied Chemistry (treas. 1963—). Am. Chem. Soc. (chmn. div. chem. edn., 1946-47, chmn. div. phys. and inorganic chemistry, 1949-50, chmn. div. inorganic chem., 1956-57, pres. 1959, dir. 1958-60), Phi Beta Kappa, Sigma Xi, Phi Lambda Upsilon, Alpha Chi Sigma. Presbyn. Author: (with B. S. Hopkins) General Chemistry for Colleges, Essentials of College Chemistry; (with Therald Moeller and Jacob Kleinberg) University Chemistry, 1965. Editor: The Chemistry of the Coordination Compounds, 1956; editor-in-chief; Vol. IV Inorganic Syntheses; mem. editorial bds. several chem. jours; also contbr. articles and revs. to chem. jours. Lectr. in field. Home: 304 W Pennsylvania Urbana IL 61801

BAILE, HAROLD SCOTT, ins. co. exec.; b. Phila., Dec. 31, 1912; s. Joseph Francis and Martha (Boyd) B.; LL.B., Temple U., 1938; m. Helen Bennett, Jan. 19, 1939; 1 dau., Pamela. Admitted to Pa. bar; asso., partner firm Pepper, Bodine, Stoke & Hamilton, Phila., 1930-51; gen. counsel Gen. Accident Fire and Life Assurance Corp., Ltd., Phila., 1951—, dep. gen. mgr., 1955-67, sr. dep. gen. mgr., 1967-68, gen. mgr. in U.S., 1968—; pres., dir. Potomac Ins. Co., Phila., Pa. Gen. Ins. Co., Camden Fire Ins. Assn. Bd. dirs. Phila. Crime Commn. Served to lt. comdr. USNR, 1942-46. Member Am., Pa., Phila. bar assns. Clubs: Down Town, Racquet (Phila.). Home: 2816 Hopkinson House Washington Sq Philadelphia PA 19106 Office: 414 Walnut St Philadelphia PA 19106

BAILEN, ELIOT, lawyer; b. Boston, Dec. 11, 1905; s. David and Anne (Gordon) B.; grad. Boston Latin Sch., 1922; A.B. summa cum laude, Harvard, 1926, LL.B., 1930; student in Rome, also U. Rome, 1926-27; m. Elise Elgin Thompson, Dec. 28, 1946; children—Ann Thompson, Emily Thompson, Eliot Thompson. Admitted to Mass. bar, 1930, N.Y. bar, 1933, D.C. bar, 1948, also U.S. Supreme Ct.; with firm Chadbourne, Wallace, Park & Whiteside, N.Y.C., 1930-42; spl. asst. to adminstr. FEA, 1945; practice in Washington. 1945- 51; organizer, partner firm Bailen & O'Sullivan, N.Y.C., 1951—, Holtzmann, Wise & Shepard, N.Y.C., 1964—. Dir. Onasis Corp., Victory Carriers, Inc., and subsidiaries, Improved Realty Corp., Boston. Served to lt. col. dir Transp. Command, 1942-45. Mem. Mass., N.Y. State D.C. bar assns., Phi Beta Kappa. Home: 1160 Park Av New York City NY 10028 also Sherman CT 06784 Office: 647 Fifth Av New York City NY 10022

BAILEY, ALAN RICHMOND, ret. utilities exec.; b.Boston, Jan. 1, 1901; s. William Henry and Florence (Murphy) B.; student U. So. Cal., 1925-30; m. Muriel A. Raymond, Sept. 3, 1938 (dec.); m. 2d, Marvel Williamson, Feb. 6, 1967. Part-time positions Cal. utilities, 1920-24; gen. foreman gas distbn. dept. Los Angeles Gas & Electric Corp., 1924-30; supt. all gas operations Coast Counties Gas & Electric Co., 1930-39, asst. to pres., 1939-42, dir., 1942-54, v.p., chief operating officer, 1948-54; mgr. orgn. planning and personnel dept. Pacific Pub. Service Co. and subsidiaries, 1945-49, dir., 1949-54, v.p., 1951-54; v.p., chief operating officer Arrowhead & Puritas Waters, Inc., 1948-51, dir., 1945-54; v.p., dir. Standard Pacific Gas Line, Inc., 1952-54; asst. to pres. Pacific Gas & Electric Co., 1954-56; sr. v.p., dir. So. Counties Gas Co. of Cal., Los Angeles, 1956-58, exec. v.p., dir. 1958-67; pres. Pacific Lighting Service & Supply Co., 1957-69. cons. on projects for pub. utilities, 1969—. Served from maj. to lt. col., AUS 1942-45. Mem. Soc. Advancement Mgmt. (nat. dir. 1954), Am., Pacific Coast (dir. 1953-54, 58-65, also past pres.), gas assns., Am. Mgmt. Assn. Mason (Shriner). Address: 5665 W 6th St Los Angeles CA 90036

BAILEY, ALBERT DAVID, elec. engr., educator; b. Waterloo, Ia., Feb. 16, 1915; s. Albert Oscar and Marie (Bunger) B.; B.A., Ia. State Tchrs. Coll., Cedar Falls, 1936; B.S., Ia. State Coll., Ames, 1938; M.S., U. Ill., Urbana, 1944, Ph.D., 1954; m. Madalin Webster, June 9, 1940; children-David Alan, James Hamilton. Field engr. K.R. Brown, Cons. Engr., Des Moines, 1938-41; faculty dept. elec. engring. U. Ill., Urbana, 1941—, now prof. elec. engring. Active Arrowhead council Boy Scouts Am., 1955—. Served from ensign to lt. (j.g.), USNR, 1944-46. Mem. I.E.E.E., Am. Assn. U. Profs., Sigma Xi, Eta Kappa Nu, Tau Beta Pi, Blue Key. Home: 307 S McKinley St Champaign IL 61820 Office: Elec Engring Research Lab U Ill Urbana IL 61801

BAILEY, ALFRED MARSHALL, mus. dir.; b. Iowa City, Feb. 18, 1894; s. William H. and Mary (Jelly) B.; A.B., U. Ia., 1916, D.Sc., Norwich U., 1944; Dr. Pub. Service, U. Denver, 1954; m. Muriel E. Eggenberg, June 16, 1917; children—Beth Elaine, Patricia Jean. Mem. U.S. Biol. Survey Expdn. to Hawaiian Islands, 1912-13; naturalist- curator of birds and mammals, La. State Mus., 1916-19; rep. U.S. Biol. Survey, Alaska, 1919-21; leader Arctic expdn. Colo. Mus. Natural History, 1921-22, curator of birds and mammals, 1922-26; dir. Chgo. Acad. Scis., 1926-36; zoologist Abyssinian expdn., Field Mus. Natural History; dir. Denver Mus. Natural History, 1936-69, dir. emeritus, 1970—. Expdns. to Labrador, Alaska, Mid-Pacific-Australia, also New Zealand, 1949-54, 57-58, Ecuador and Galapagos Islands, 1960, Botswana and South Africa, 1969. Fellow Am. Ornithologists Union, A.A.A.S. Author: Birds of Arctic Alaska, 1948; Birds of New Zealand, 1955; Birds of Colorado, 2 vols., 1965; Pictorial Checklist of Colorado Birds, 1967. Contbr. to Condor, Auk, Nat. Geog. Mag., Jour. Mammalogy, Natural Hist., Wilson Bull., Country Life in Am., Nature Mag., Am. Forests Life, Frontier. Address: Denver Museum of Natural History Denver CO 80206

BAILEY, AMOS PURNELL, clergyman; b. Grotons, Va., May 2, 1918; s. Louis William and Evelyn (Charnock) B.; B.A., Randolph-Macon Coll., 1942, D.D., 1956; B.D., Duke, 1948; Th.M., Union Theol. Sem., 1957; m. Ruth Martin Hill, Aug. 22, 1942; children—Eleanor Carol (Mrs. Thomas T. Harriman), Anne Ruth, Joyce Elizabeth, Jeanne Purpell. Ordained to ministry Meth. Ch., 1942; pastor, Emporia, Va., 1938, Richmond, Va., 1938-43, 54-61, New Kent circuit, 1943-44, Norfolk, 1948-50, Newport News, Va., 1950-54; supt. Richmond dist. Meth. Ch., 1961-67; sr. minister Reveille Ch., Richmond, 1967-70; exec. sec. Commn. on Chaplains United Meth. Ch., Washington, 1970—. Vice pres. Va. Conf. Bd. Missions, 1955-61, Meth. Commn. Town and Country Work, 1956-67; mem. Meth. Commn. on Higher Edn., 1960—, Meth. Interbd. Council, 1960-70; del. Southeastern Jurisdictional Conf., 1964, 68, Gen. Conf., 1964, 66, 68, 70, World Meth. Conf., London, 1966; mem. council, exec. com., pres. communications com. Southeastern Jurisdiction; mem. exec. com., rec. sec. Meth. Commn. on Chaplains; mem. exec. com. Va. Conf. Bd. Edn.; mem. World Meth. Council. Mem. Va. Commn. Aging; pres. adv. bd. Richmond Welfare Dept., 1956-68; group chmn. industry div. Richmond United Givers Fund, 1961; mem. Richmond Pub. Assistance Com., Richmond Council on Alcoholism; bd. mgrs. Richmond YMCA, 1961-69. Bd. dirs. Va. Meth. Advisers; exec. com., trustee Randolph-Macon Coll.; bd. visitors Duke Div. Sch.; trustee So. Sem. Served with Chaplains Corps, AUS, 1944-47. Mem. Meth. Hist. Soc., Duke Div. Alumni Assn. (pres.), Meth. Hist. Soc. Kiwanian. Writer syndicated column Bread of Life, syndicated radio devotional Daily Bread, 1945—; condr. weekly radio counseling program The Night Pastor, 1955—, Sunshine and Shadows, 1967—. Contbr. articles to profl. publs. Home: 7815 Falstaff Rd McLean VA 22101 Office: 3900 Wisconsin Av NW Washington DC 20016

BAILEY, CECIL CABANISS, lawyer; b. LaGrange, Ga., Oct. 29, 1901; s. Daniel B. and Maude (Layfield) B.; student Young Harris Coll., 1922, U. Ga., 1923; LL.B., Stetson U., 1927; m. Augusta Mann, Feb. 15, 1923; children—Dorothy (Mrs. C.G. McGehee, Jr.), Marilyn (Mrs. Hugh M. Evans), William C. High sch. prin., Byromville, Ga. and Madison, Fla., 1923-24; admitted to Fla. bar, 1929; asso. atty. firm Scarlett, Jordan, Futch & Fielding, DeLand, 1927- 29; clk. Judge's Ct. Volusia (Fla.) County, 1929-30; asso. firm Rogers & Towers, Jacksonville, 1930-37; sr. partner Rogers, Towers, Bailey, Jones & Gay, 1937—. Chmn. bd. gen. counsel Gulf Life Ins. Co.; sr. v.p., gen. counsel Gulf Life Holding Co.; chmn. bd. St. Johns River Bank; dir. Atlantic Discount Co., Cain & Bultman, Inc., Stonewall Ins. Co. Bd. overseers Stetson U. Coll. Law. Deland; bd. dirs. Stetson Law Center Found., Hope Haven Hosp.; pres., trustee Jacksonville Pub. Library System, 1957—. Mem. Am., Fla., Jacksonville bar assns. Methodist. Clubs: Civitan; Timuguana Country; San Jose Country. Home: 939 Arbor Lane Jacksonville FL 32207. Office: Fla Title Bldg Jacksonville FL 32202

BAILEY, CHARLES ELDON, Jr., banker; b. Hazlehurst, Miss., Nov. 11, 1931; s. Charles Eldon and Bessie Leonard (Tillman) B.; grad. La. State U. Sch. Banking, 1967; m. Ouida Ward, Feb. 22, 1958; children—Karen Leigh, Charles Eldon III. Vice pres., comptroller First Nat. Bank, Jackson, Miss., 1955—. Treas. Hinds County March of Dimes, 1965-66; treas., dir. Miss. div. Am. Cancer Soc., 1967-71. Served with USAF, 1951-55. Mem. Am. Inst. Banking (chpt. pres.), Nat. Assn. Bank Audit and Control, Jackson C. of C. Baptist. Lion. Club: Optimist (Jackson). Home: 115 Elms Ct Circle Jackson MS 39204 Office: PO Box 291 Jackson MS 39205

BAILEY, CHARLES LANNDON, educator; b. N.D., Aug. 2, 1918; s. Frank Hull and Olga Marie (Fischer) B.; B.A., Concordia Coll., Moorhead, Minn., 1940; Ph.D., U. Minn., 1947; m. Carol Helen Zank, July 11, 1942; children—Kathleen, Elizabeth. Asso. physicist Los Alamos Lab., 1942-46; prof. physics Concordia Coll., 1947-54, dean, 1954—. Concordinator with com. on liberal arts edn. North Central Assn. Colls. and Secondary Schs., 1954- 57; mem. adv. bd. U.S. Merchant Marine Acad., 1956-62. Mem. Am. Phys. Soc., Sigma Xi. Home: 1625 3d St S Moorhead MN 56560

BAILEY, CHARLES P., heart surgeon; b. Wanamasa, N.J., Sept. 8, 1910; student Rutgers U., 1926-28; M.D., Hahnemann Med. Coll., 1932, LL.D., 1953; M.S., U. Pa., 1943, D.Sc., 1955; m. Lillian Dann; children—Donald, Robert, Patricia. Rotating intern Fitkin Meml. Hosp., Neptune, N.J., 1932-33; gen. practice medicine and surgery, 1933-37, thoracic surgery, 1940—; resident Sea View Hosp., S.I., N.Y., 1938-40; hon. prof. thoracic surgery U. Monterrey (Mexico), 1949; formerly prof., head dept. thoracic surgery Hahnemann Med. Coll. and Hosp., Phila.; dir. dept. thoracic and cardiovascular surgery St. Barnabas Hosp., Bronx, N.Y., 1963—; cons. Jewish Hosp. Bklyn., 1971—. Recipient Man of Year Interfaith award B'nai B'rith, 1950; gold medal A.M.A., 1951, 71, bronze medal, 1967; Clarence E. Shaffrey award Med. Alumni St. Joseph's Coll., Phila., 1951, Humanitarian award B'rith Sholom, 1955, Page One award Newspaper Guild Am., 1955, George B. Kunkel award Harrisburg Hosp., 1956. Diplomate Am. Bd. Thoracic Surgery (founder group). Fellow A.C.S., Internat. Coll. Surgeons, Am. Coll. Chest Physicians, A.M.A.; hon. fellow Surg. Soc. Madrid; hon. mem. Bronx Surg. Soc.; mem. Phila. County Med. Soc., Phila. Acad. Surgery, Am. Heart Assn., Soc. Thoracic Surgeons (founder mem.), Laennee Soc., Hahnemann Alumni Soc., Am. Assn. Thoracic Surgery; hon. mem. Roman Med. Soc., Author: Surgery of the Heart, 1955. Pioneered several types heart surgery; developed several new techniques and instruments for heart surgery. Address: 4422 3d Av Bronx NY 10457

BAILEY, CHARLES WALDO, 2d, newspaper corr.; b. Boston, Apr. 28, 1929; s. David Washburn and Catherine Ruth (Smith) B.; grad. Phillips Exeter Acad., 1946; A.B. magna cum laude, Harvard, 1950; m. Ann Card Bushnell, Sept. 9, 1950; children—Victoria Britton, Sarah Tilden. With Mpls. Morning Tribune, 1950-54; corr. Washington bur. Cowles Publs., publs. Mpls. Star and Tribune, Des Moines Register and Tribune, Look mag., 1954-67; chief Washington bur. Mpls. Tribune, 1968—. Mem. Standing Com. Corr., Washington, 1962-63, sec., 1963. Mem. White House Corrs. Assn. (pres. 1969-70), Overseas Writers (sec. 1970-71), Asso. Harvard Alumni (dir. 1966-69). Clubs: Nat. Press, Gridiron, Federal City (Washington). Author: (with Fletcher Knebel) No High Ground, 1960; Seven Days in May, 1962; Convention, 1964. Contbr. to Candidates 1959, 1960; Exeter Remembered, 1965. Home: 3001 Albemarle St NW Washington DC 20008 Office: National Press Bldg Washington DC 20004

BAILEY, CONSUELO NORTHROP, lawyer, sec. Republican Nat. Com.; b. Fairfield, Vt. Oct. 10, 1899; d. Peter Bent Brigham and Katherine E. (Fletcher) Northrop; Ph.B., U. Vt., 1921, LL.D., 1952; LL.B., Boston U., 1925; LL.D., Cedar Crest Coll. 1956, Am. Internat. Coll. 1957; m. Henry A. Bailey, Sept. 2, 1940. Admitted to Vt. bar, 1926, Vt. Supreme Ct., 1926, U.S. Dist. Ct., 1927, U.S. Supreme Ct., 1933, U.S. Customs Ct., 1942; prosecutor City of Burlington, Vt., 1925; states atty., Chittenden County, Vt., 1927-31; elected state senator 1930; sec. to U.S. senator Ernest W. Gibson, 1931- 37; pvt. practice of law, 1937—; vice chmn. Vt. Rep. State Com., 1934-36; del. to Rep. Nat. Conv., 1936, 1944, delivered addresses for Rep. party, 1925—; Rep. nat. committeewoman for Vt., 1936—, sec. Rep. Nat. Com.; mem. Rep. Task Force, 1965; sec. Rep. Nat. Conv., 1968. Dir. Tuttle Law Print, Inc., Rutland, Vt. Mem. U.S. Civil War Centennial Commn., 1958, Vt. Civil War Centennial Commn., 1958; mem. nat women's adv. com. Fed. Civil Def. Adminstrn.; mem. White House Conf. World Refugee Year, 1959; mem. Vt. Historic Sites Commn., 1970—, Vt. Status of Women Commn., 1970—; mem. corp. Peter Bent Brigham Hosp., Boston; mem. nat. alumni council Boston U., 1963—; mem. alumni council U. Vt., pres. Class of 1921, 1971. Elected to Vt. Gen. Assembly, 1950, 52, elected speaker of Assembly, 1953; lt. gov. of Vt., 1954-57; chmn. com. on call Rep. Nat. Conv., 1960. Mem. U.S. Post Office Adv. Bd. Bd. Dirs. Womens Med. Coll., Phila.; mem. Calvin Coolidge Found. Recipient Distinguished Alumni Service awards Boston U., 1970, U. Vt., 1971; named Rep. Woman of Year, Nat. Fedn. Rep. Women, 1969, recipient Distinguished Service award, 1971. Vt. Bar Assn., Vt. Rose Soc. (pres.), Phi Beta Kappa, Sigma Gamma, Kappa Beta Pi. Club: Burlington Zonta Internat. (founder, first pres.). Author: Digest of Primary and Election Laws of Vt., 1928. Home: 1317 Spear St South Burlington VT 05401

BAILEY, DANIEL MILTON, gas co. exec.; b. Marshall, Ill., May 9, 1908; s. Clarence Grover and Edith (Bush) B.; A.B., U. Okla., 1931, LL.B., 1930; grad. Advanced Mgmt. Program, Harvard, 1948; m. Miriam Nicholas, Apr. 15, 1933; children—Daniel Nicholas, Lynne Bailey. Admitted to Okla. bar, 1930, Tex. bar, 1934; with Continental-Emsco Co., Dallas, 1931-61, gen. counsel, 1937-61, v.p., 1950-61; exec. v.p. So. Union Gas Co., Dallas, 1961—, also director. Served to maj. USAAF, 1942-45. Mem. Am. Bar Assn., American (member board of directors), Southern (dir.) gas assns., Mid-Continent Oil and Gas Assn., Delta Upsilon, Phi Delta Phi. Clubs: Petroleum (dir.), Dallas, Northwood Country (Dallas). Home: 3549 Marquette St Dallas TX 75225 Office: Fidelity Union Tower Dallas TX 75201

BAILEY, DUDLEY, educator; b. Lamoni, Ia., Feb. 7, 1918; s. Vaughn Corless and Lida (Hayer) B.; B.A., U. Kansas City, 1942, M.A., 1944; Ph.D., U. Ill., 1954; m. Sue Ogden, Apr. 27, 1945; children—Geoffrey Ogden, Paul Fletcher, Jane Barker. Instr., U. Neb., 1943-44, 45-46, Wentworth Mil. Acad., 1944-45, U. Kansas City, 1946-48; grad. asst. U. Ill., 1948-54; mem. faculty U. Neb., 1954—, prof. English, 1963—, chmn. dept., 1962- -. Mem. Nat. Council Accreditation Tchr. Edn., 1966-69. Mem. Coll. Conf. Composition and Communication (chmn. 1968), Nat. Council Tchrs. English (exec. com. 1967-68), Coll. English Assn. (bd. dirs. 1963-66), Am. Assn. U. Profs., Modern Lang. Assn., Assn. Depts. English. Democrat. Unitarian. Co-author: Form in Modern English, 1958. Editor: Essays on Rhetoric, 1963; Introductory Language Essays, 1963. Mem. editorial adv. bd. World Book Ency. Dictionary; editorial cons. Oxford Univ. Press. Home: 1800 S 22d St Lincoln NB 68502 Office: Andrews Hall Lincoln NB 68508

BAILEY, EDD HAMILTON, ret. r.r. ofcl.; b. Elmo. Mo., Sept. 13, 1904; s. Larkin A. and Iola (Hamilton) B.; grad. high sch.; m. Mabel Lavina Parker, May 24, 1926; children—Hugh Parker, Laura May (Mrs. Tedd Richardson). With U.P. R.R. Co., 1922—, successively car checker, mech. dept., Cheyenne, Wyo., transp. dept., brakeman, trainmaster, asst. supt., supt., gen. supt., gen. mgr. Northwestern dist., 1922-53, gen. mgr. Eastern dist., 1954-57, v.p. operations, 1957-64, pres., 1965-71, chief exec. officer, 1965-70, now dir. Mem. Omaha C. of C. Republican. Methodist. Mason (Shriner). Home: 206 S 95th St Omaha NB 68114 Office: 1416 Dodge St Omaha NB 68102

BAILEY, EDGAR L., treas. Gulf States Utilities Co. Address: 285 Liberty Av Beaumont TX 77701

BAILEY, EDWARD JAMES, editor; b. Klamath Falls, Ore., Sept. 18, 1932; s. Merrill Leon and Lillian (Smith) B.; B.S., Armstrong Coll., Berkeley, Cal., 1953; m. Joan Madeleine Henrion, Nov. 7, 1959; 1 son, Christopher Franklin. Asso. editor Daily Pacific Builder, San Francisco, 1954-59; exec. asst. Cal. Council, A.I.A., San Francisco, 1959-62, dir. Information Services, Washington, 1962-65; sr. editor Archtl. Forum mag., N.Y.C., 1965-69; dep. dir. editorial unit Nat. Urban Coalition (formerly Urban Am., Inc.), also mng. editor City, mag., Washington, 1969—. Home: 4317 Stanford St Chevy Chase MD 20015 Office: 2100 M St NW Washington DC 20037

BAILEY, EDWARD WELDON, ret. educator; b. Austin, Tex., Sept. 18, 1898; s. Osborne Lawrence and Leila (Hocutt) B.; B.A., U. Tex., 1920, LL.B., 1928; S.J.D., Harvard, 1942; m. Winifred Thorn, Jan. 30, 1933; 1 dau., Barbara Beth (Mrs. Charles F. Turrentine). Clk. retail store, Gunter, Tex., 1922-24; tchr. high sch., Greenville, Tex., 1924-27; admitted to Tex. bar, 1928; with firm Callaway & Reed, Dallas, 1928-30; asso. prof. law U. Tex., 1930-37, prof. law, 1937-60, Burleson prof. law, 1960-67, prof. law, 1967-70. Mem. bar com. which drafted Texas bus. corp. law, 1955. Served with U.S. Navy, 1918. Mem. Am. Bar Assn., State Bar Tex., Order of Coif, Phi Delta Phi. Contbr. articles legal revs. Author: Texas Law Wills, 2 vols., 1968. Home: 901 W 31st St Austin TX 78705

BAILEY, ERVIN GEORGE, mech. engr.; b. Damascus, O., Dec. 25, 1880; s. George W. and Ruthetta (Butler) B.; M.E., Ohio State U., 1903, D. Engring., 1941; Engring., Lehigh U., 1937; Sc. D., Lafayette Coll., 1942; m. Carrie Huntington, Aug. 23, 1904 (dec. March 1966); children—George Huntington (dec.), Mrs. Katharine Bailey Hoyt. Asst., chief testing dept. Consol. Coal Co., Fairmont, W.Va., 1903-07; in charge coal dept. Arthur D. Little, Boston, 1907-09; mech. engr., partner Fuel Testing Co., Boston, 1909-15; founder, pres. Bailey Meter Co., mfrs. fluid meters, automatic combustion control devices, Cleve., 1916-44; chmn. Bailey Meter Co., 1944-56; pres. Fuller Lehigh Co., mfrs. pulverized coal equipment, water cooled furnaces, 1926-36; v.p., dir. Babcock & Wilcox Co., N.Y.C., 1930-52, cons., dir., 1952-56; pres. Bailey Inventions, Inc., Easton, Pa., 1962—. Clayton lectr. Inst. Mech. Engrs., London, 1949. Life trustee Lafayette Coll., 1943-65, emeritus, 1965—. Recipient Longstreth medal Franklin Inst., 1930; Lamme medal Ohio State U., 1936, Distinguished Service award, 1952; Percy Nicholls award, fuels div. Am. Soc. M.E. and coal div. Am. Inst. Mining and Metall. Engrs., 1942; Fritz medal, 1952. Mem. Am. Inst. Mining, Metall. and Petroleum Engrs., Cleve. Engring. Soc. (meritorious mem.), Ohio State U. Assn. (life), Franklin Inst., Am. Soc. M.E. (hon., pres. 1948), Inst. Mech. Engrs. London (hon.), Am. Soc. C.E. (hon.), Instrument Soc. Am. (hon.), Sigma Xi, Pi Tau Sigma, Tau Beta Pi. Republican. Presbyn. Club: Northampton Country (Easton, Pa.); Engineers (N.Y.C., Lehigh Valley), Patentee, inventor in field. Address: 3502 Chipman Rd Easton PA 18042

BAILEY, FRANCIS LEE, lawyer; b. Waltham, Mass., 1933; student Harvard; LL.B., Boston U. m. Florence Gott (div. 1961); m. 2d, Froma; 1 son, Scott Frederic. Admitted to Mass. bar, 1960; partner firm Bailey, Alch & Gillis, Boston. Mem. Am. Bar Assn. Address: 40 Court Boston MA 08021*

BAILEY, FRANK HERNDON, lawyer; b. Herndon, Va., Apr. 3, 1902; s. Jesse Earle and Annie (Scott) B.; A.B., Coll. Charleston, 1925; LL.B., U.S.C., 1930; m. Anne Lee Johnston, Apr. 4, 1936; 1 dau., Anne Johnston. Tchr., Boys High 1930, since practiced in Charleston; member of the firm of Bailey & Buckley, Charleston; referee in Bankruptcy, 1941-42; spl. asst. U.S. dist. atty., 1942-45; asst. corp. counsel City of Charleston, 1948-52, corp. counsel, 1952-61; mem. Jud. Council of S.C., 1958; bar examiner State of S.C., 1958-61. Mem. commn. on uniform laws, 1946-50. Presdl., vice presidential elector for S.C., 1956. Fellow Am. Bar Assn.; mem. S.C. (pres. 1958-59), Charleston County (pres. 1950-51) bar assns., English Speaking Union (pres. 1956-59), Am. Judicature Soc., Hibernian Soc., St. Andrews Soc., Kappa Alpha. Democrat. Club: Carolina (S.C.) Yacht. Home: 12 Lamboll St Charleston SC 29401 Office: 17 Chalmers St Charleston SC 29401

BAILEY, FREDERICK WILLIAM, investor; b. Detroit, Oct. 14, 1926; s. Frederick W. and Myrtle E. (Wannemaker) B.; B.S., U. Cal. at Los Angeles, 1950; m. Mary Kathleen Call, July 10, 1948; children—Glenn R., Phillip W., Linda J., Anne Marie. Sec.-treas. Lambda Pacific Engring. Co., Van Nuys, Cal., 1953-56; pres. Am. Microwave Corp., North Hollywood, Cal., 1956-58, Electronic Wire & Cable Co., North Hollywood, 1957-58, Ling Systems, Inc., North Hollywood, 1958-59; pres., chmn. bd. Missile Systems Corp., Beverly Hills, 1959-63, Dalet Corp., 1959-64, Missile Systems Corp. of Tex., 1959-65; chmn. bd., treas., dir. Baifield Industries, Inc., 1964-67. Served with USNR, 1944-45. Adviser, Tahoe Inst. Mem. Esalen Inst., Kairos Inst., Topanga Human Devel. Center, U. Cal. at Los Angeles Alumnae Assn. Club: Ambassadors. Home: 30948 Broadbeach Rd Trancas Beach Malibu CA 90265

BAILEY, GEORGE GILBERT, lawyer; b. Wheeling, W.Va., Dec. 1, 1913; s. George Alfred and Anna Gibson (Rose) B.; A.B., W.Va. U., 1935, LL.B., 1937; m. Lucretia Anne Tucker, Aug. 5, 1944; children—Barbara Anne, Bruce Tucker, John Preston. Admitted to W.Va. bar, 1937, since practiced in Wheeling; partner firm Petroplus, Bailey, Byrum & Hesse, 1947—; city solicitor, Wheeling, 1955- -. Pres., dir. Central Union Co. Pres. Oglebay Inst., 1958-60; sec. Sandscrest Found., 1954—. Served with USCGR, 1942-45. Mem. Am. (ho. of dels. 1964—), W.Va. (pres. W.Va. 1962-63), Ohio County (pres. 1957) State Bar (pres. 1963-64), Am. Coll. Trial Lawyers, Am. Judicature Soc., Am. Legion, Symposiarchs, Theta Chi, Phi Delta Phi. Democrat. Episcopalian. Elk. Club: Fort Henry (Wheeling). Home: Dement Rd RD 2 Triadelphia WV 26059 Office: Central Union Bldg Wheeling WV 26003

BAILEY, GEORGE REILY, banker; b. Harrisburg, Pa., Mar. 16, 1899; s. Edward and Elizabeth (Reily) B.; grad. Harrisburg Acad., 1916, Phillips Andover Acad., 1919, B.S., Yale, 1923; D. Finance, Dickinson Coll., 1963; m. Elizabeth Lupton Scott, Jan. 8, 1931; children—Elizabeth Reily (Mrs. Othar Zaldastani), Anne King (Mrs. H. Hamilton Hackney, Jr.), Susan Elder (Mrs. S. Buford Scott, Jr.). With Commonwealth Nat. Bank, and predecessors, Harrisburg, 1923—, v.p., 1927-54, pres. 1954-64, chmn. bd., 1964-67, chmn. emeritus 1967—, also dir.; dir. Blue Cross, Harrisburg Hotel Co., United Gas Improvement Co., Magee Carpet Co., Bloomsburg, Pa. Chmn. finance com. Pa. Pub. Sch. Employees Retirement Fund. Trustee Homeland; bd. mgrs., finance com. Harrisburg Hosp. Mem. S.R., Newcomen Soc. Eng., Pa. Forestry Soc., Pa. Scotch-Irish Soc. (past pres.). Clubs: Yale (Phila.): Rolling Rock (Pitts.); St. Anthony (N.Y.C.); Gibson Island (Balt.); Country (Harrisburg). Home: 100 South St Harrisburg PA 17101 Office: 16 S Market Sq Harrisburg PA 17108

BAILEY, GEORGE WILLIAM, radio exec.; b. Quincy, Mass., May 14, 1887; s. Herbert Briggs and Alice (Brown) B.; grad. Adams Acad., 1903; A.B., Harvard, 1907; Sc.D. (hon.), Lawrence Coll., 1958; m. Alice Cooper, June 16, 1913; children—Mary Alice (Mrs. J.H. Montgomery), George William, Richard Briggs, Chmn. radio sect., office sci. personnel NRC, Washington, 1941-43; spl. asst. to chmn. NDRC, 1941-42; chmn. com. 1, mem. coms. 12, 13 War Communications Bd., 1942-45; asst. chief communications Mil. D.C., 1942-45; chmn. agy. com. Selective Service, 1942-45; mem. interagy. com. manpower shortages, 1945-47; chief sci. personnel office OSRD, 1944-46; exec. sec. I.R.E., N.Y.C., 1946-62; exec. cons. I.E.E.E., 1963—; owner, operator amateur radio sta. W2KH. N.Y.C., 1945—. Adviser to dir. SSS, 1948-58; cons. telecommunications to under-sec. Dept. State, 1957—; mem. nat. industry adv. FCC. Recipient Pres.'s certificate Merit; Edison citation N.Y. Acad. Scis. Fellow I.R.E., Radio Club Am.; mem. Armed Forces Communications, Electronics Assn. (dir., pres. 1954-56), Am. Radio Relay League (pres. 1940-52), Internat. Amateur Radio Union (pres. 1940-52), Vet. Wireless Operators Assn. (Marconi medal for service, hon.), Quarter Century Wireless Assn. (hon. life), Esperanto Assn. N.Am., Theta Delta Chi. Clubs: Harvard (N.Y.C., Boston); Cosmos (Washington). Office: IEEE 345 E 47th St New York City NY 10017

BAILEY, GLENN WALDEMAR, mfg. co. exec.; b. Cleve., May 8, 1925; s. Harry W. and Elizabeth Bailey; B.S., U. Wis., 1946; M.B.A., Harvard, 1951; m. Cornelia L. Tarrant, June 12, 1952. Project engr. Thompson Ramo Wooldridge, Cleve., 1946-49; finance staff Ford Motor Co., Dearborn, Mich., 1951-54; mgr. financial analysis Curtiss Wright Corp., 1954-57; asst. to v.p., gen. mgr. Overseas div. Chrysler Corp., Detroit, 1957-60; group gen. mgr. Internat. Tel. & Tel. Corp., N.Y.C., 1960-67; chmn. bd., pres. Keene Corp., N.Y.C., 1967—. Served to ensign USNR, 1943-46. Home: Contentment Island Darien CT 06820 Office: 345 Park Av New York City NY 10022

BAILEY, HAROLD STEVENS, Jr., coll. dean; b. Springfield, Mass., Apr. 18, 1922; s. Harold Stevens and Grace Evelyn (Anderson) B.; B.S., Mass. Coll. Pharmacy, 1944, M.S., 1948; Ph.D., Purdue U.,

1951; m. Barbara Ann Dewey, Sept. 8, 1946; children—Cynthia Ann, Lynda Jeanne, Gwen, Pamela, Harold Stevens III. Grad. asst. Mass. Coll. Pharmacy, 1946-48; instr. pharmacy Purdue U., 1950-51; faculty S.D. State U., Brookings, 1951—, prof. pharm. chemistry 1958—, head dept., 1960-61, dean acad. affairs, 1961—, dean Grad. Sch. 1965—, sec. inter-instutitional com. curriculum coordination S.D. Bd. Regents of Edn., 1963-; asso. leadership tng. project North Central Assn. Colls. and Secondary Schs., 1961—. Asso. dist. lay leader S.D. Conf. Methodist Ch., 1960-. Served with AUS, 1944-46. Fellow Am. Found. Pharm. Edn., 1948-50. Fellow A.A.A.S.; mem. Sigma Xi, Kappa Psi, Phi Kappa Phi, Rho Chi, Phi Lambda Upsilon. Mason, Kiwanian. Contbr. articles to profl. jours. Editor pharm. sect. S.D. Jour. Medicine and Pharmacy, 1953- 61. Home: 336 Eastern Av Brooking SD 57006

BAILEY, HAROLD WOOD, educator; b. Chgo., Oct. 16, 1901; s. John William and Celestine Marcella (Wood) B.; B.S., Ottawa U., 1921, LL.D., 1941; A.M., U. Ill., 1924, Ph.D., 1926; m. Marian A. Kinney, Aug. 31, 1926; children—Marjory Elizabeth, Mary Virginia. Instr. math. Ottawa U. 1921-22; asst. math. U. Ill., 1922-25, fellow, 1925-26, instr., 1926-28, asso., 1928-31, asst. prof., 1931-42, asso. prof., 1942- 49, prof. 1949—, exec. sec. dept. math., 1934-38, acting dir., 1938-39, dir., 1939-46, student counseling bur., asso. dean, liberal arts and scis. Chgo. Undergrad. Div., 1946-63, asst. v.p., 1963-66, asst. chancellor, 1966-67, asso. chancellor, 1967-71; vis. lectr. math. Va. Union U., 1971—; curriculum cons. Chgo. Bd. Edn., 1937-39. Civilian ednl. adv. Army Tng. Program, 1943-44; treas. Ill. League for Nursing, 1955-61. Fellow A.A.A.S.; mem. Am. Math. Soc., Math. Assn. Am., Am. Coll. Personnel Assn., Council of Guidance and Personnel Assns. (treas. 1948-50), Phi Eta Sigma. Pi Kappa Delta, Pi Mu Epsilon. Baptist. Home: 2827 Scarsborough Dr Richmond VA 23235

BAILEY, HARRY AUGUSTINE, Jr., educator; b. Ft. Pierce, Fla., Dec. 19, 1932; s. Harry Augustine and Ruth (Finlayson) B.; B.A. (Distinguished Mil. Grad.), Fla. A. and M. U., 1954, M.A., U. Kan., 1960, Ph.D., 1964; m. Mary L. Howard, Aug. 4, 1952; children—Harry Augustine III, Larry Berisford. Asst. dean men Fla. A. and M. U., 1958-59; asst. instr. polit. sci., Western civilization U. Kan., 1960-64, instr. sociology, summer 1964; asst. prof. polit. sci. Temple U., Phila., 1964-68, asso. prof., chmn. dept., 1968-70, prof., dept., 1970—. Cons. Phila. Antipoverty Action Com., 1965-67. Precinct committeeman Democratic party, Lawrence, Kan., 1961-63. Served to 1st lt., arty. AUS, 1954-57. Mem. Am. Polit. Sci. Assn., Am. Assn. U. Profs., Pi Sigma Alpha. Episcopalian. Contbr. articles to profl. jours. Editor: Negro Politics in America, 1967; co-editor; Ethnic Group Politics, 1969. Home: 11960 Dumont Rd Philadelphia PA 19116

BAILEY, HARRY PAUL, geographer, educator; b. Allentown, Pa., Feb. 12, 1913; s. Harry D. and Grace E. (Mader) B.; B.A., U. Cal. at Los Angeles, 1939, M.A., 1942, Ph.D., 1950; m. Shirley E. Pavlicek, May 22, 1942; children—Barbara R., Marian G., Ellen L. Asso. prof., head dept. Los Angeles State Coll., 1950-51; asso. prof. U. Cal. at Los Angeles, 1952-63; prof. U. Cal. at Riverside, 1963—, head dept. geography, 1963-70. Guggenheim fellow, 1958-59; Fulbright research scholar in New Zealand, 1959; guest prof. U. Aarhus (Denmark), 1966-67. Served to capt., Air Weather Service, USAAF, 1942- 46. Mem. Am. Geog. Soc., Assn. Am. Geographers, Am. Meteorol. Soc., Sigma Xi. Home: 1203 Monte Vista Dr Riverside CA 92507

BAILEY, HERBERT REEDER, educator; b. Denver, Nov. 2, 1925; s. Paul Shields and Anne Mildred (Baker) B.; B.S. in Elec. Engring., Rose Poly. Inst., 1945, B.S. in Chem. Engring., 1946; M.S. in Elec. Engring., U. Ill., 1947; Ph.D. in Math., Purdue U., 1955; m. Zelma L. Brown, June 23, 1951; children—John, Mark, Carol, Elizabeth, Rebecca. Mathematician, U.S. Naval Ordnance Plant, Indpls., 1948-51; sr. research mathematician Marathon Oil Co., Denver, 1956-61, Martin Co., Denver, 1961-62; asso. prof. math. Colo. State U., Fort Collins, 1962-66, dir. NIH research grant, 1963-66; prof. math. Rose-Hulman Inst. Tech., Terre Haute, Ind., 1966—, dir. NSF undergrad. research program, 1969—. Cons. applications math. to biology. Mem. Math. Assn. Am., Am. Math. Soc., Tau Beta Pi, Eta Kappa Nu, Pi Mu Epsilon. Contbr. articles to profl. jours. Home: 328 Potomac St Terre Haute IN 47803

BAILEY, HERBERT SMITH, Jr., publisher; b. N.Y.C., July 12, 1921; s. Herbert Smith and Viola (Howe) B.; A.B., Princeton, 1942; m. Elizabeth M. Brown, June 26, 1943; children—John R., James C., Robin Elizabeth, George W. Sci. editor Princeton U. Press, 1946-52, editor, 1952-54, dir., 1954—. Past mem. Princeton Twp. Bd. Edn., Princeton Regional Bd. Edn.; mem. adv. com. on tech. publs. AEC; chmn. sci. information council NSF, 1970, now mem.; vol. leader Boy Scouts Am. Served from ensign to lt. USNR, 1942-45. Mem. Am. U. Press Services, Am. Book Pubs. Council, Franklin Book Programs, Newcomen Soc. N.Am., Assn. Am. U. Presses, Sigma Xi. Clubs: Princeton (N.Y.C.); Nassau (Princeton). Author: The Art and Science of Book Publishing, 1970. Home: RD 1 Princeton NJ 08540 Office: Princeton U Press Princeton NJ 08540

BAILEY, HUGH COLEMAN, univ. adminstr.; b. Berry, Ala., July 2, 1929; s. Coleman Costello and Susie (Jenkins) B.; A.B. with honors, Samford U., 1950; M.A., U. Ala., 1951, Ph.D., 1954; m. Ahleida Joan Seever, Nov. 17, 1962; children—Debra Jane, Laura Joan. Instr. history and polit. sci. Samford U., 1953-54, asst. prof., 1954-56, asso. prof., 1956-59, prof., 1959—, chmn. dept., head div. social scis., 1967-70, dean Howard Coll. Arts and Scis., 1970—; editorial bd. Social Science, Alabama Rev. Guggenheim fellow, 1963-64; Am. Council Learned Socs. fellow, 1965-66; recipient award merit Am. Assn. State and Local History, 1967. Mem. Ala. Acad. Sci. (v.p. 1968-69), Pi Gamma Mu (nat. trustee-at-large 1969-71, nat. 2d v.p. 1971—). Author: John Williams Walker, 1964; Hinton Rowan Helper: Abolitionist-Racist, 1965; Edgar Gardner Murphy: Gentle Progressive, 1968; Liberalism in the New South, Southern Social Reformers and the Progressive Movement, 1969. Home: 1801 Windsor Blvd Birmingham AL 35209

BAILEY, JAMES F., union ofcl. Sec.-treas. Govt. Employee Council AFL-CIO. Office: 100 Indiana Av NW Washington DC 20001*

BAILEY, JAMES MARTIN, clergyman, editor; b. Emmetsburg, Ia., July 28, 1929; s. Allen Ransom and Kathryn (Ausland) B.; B.A. in Journalism, State U. Ia., 1951; B.D., Eden Theol. Sem., 1954, D.D., 1966; M.S. in Journalism, Northwestern U., 1956; D.D., Lakeland Coll., Sheboygan, Wis., 1967; m. Betty Jane Wenzel, June 5, 1954; children—Kristine Elizabeth, Susan Ruth. Ordained to ministry United Ch. Christ, 1954; mem. staff Nat. Council Chs., 1954-60, bus. mgr. Internat. Jour. Religious Edn., 1954-60; dir. circulation, advt. and promotion United Ch. Herald, 1960-63, editor, 1963—. Mem. interpretation com. N. Am. sect. World Council Chs., 1963—. Mem. Asso. Ch. Press (v.p.). Author: Windbreaks, 1959; Youth in the Town and Country Church, 1959; From Wrecks to Reconciliation, 1969; (with Mrs. Bailey) Worship with Youth, 1962; (with Douglas Gilbert) The Steps of Bonhoeffer, 1969. Editorial cons. The Lamp, Grassroots Jour. of Ecumenism; contbg. editor Reformed World, Geneva, Switzerland. Home: 45 Watchung Av Upper Montclair NJ 07043 Office: 297 Park Av S New York City NY 10010

BAILEY, JOEL FURNESS, educator; b. Pittsfield, Mass., Mar. 7, 1913; s. John Bowen and Clara (Cogswell) B.; B.S., Purdue U., 1935; M.S., Lehigh U., 1939, Ph.D., 1949; m. Arlene Sara Lynn, Mar. 29, 1940; children—Richard John, Betty Jo. Instr. mech. engring. Lehigh U., 1939-42; asst. prof. mech. engring. Ore. State Coll., 1942-43, Northwestern U., 1943-49; prof. mech. engring. U. Tenn., Knoxville, 1949—, head dept., 1952—. dir. Arnold Engring. Devel. Center, 1956-57, alumni distinguished service prof., 1967—. Cons. Union Carbide Nuclear Co., 1951-70. Mem. Am. Soc. M.E., Am. Soc. Engring. Edn., Sigma Xi, Tau Beta Pi, Pi Tau Sigma, Phi Kappa Phi. Methodist. Home: 1719 Maury St Alcoa TN 37701 Office: U Tenn Knoxville TN 37916

BAILEY, JOHN MILTON, educator; b. Memphis, June 3, 1925; s. John Milton and Ruth (Gregory) B.; B.S., Davidson Coll., 1949; M.S., U. Tenn., 1951; Ph.D., Ga. Inst. Tech., 1959; m. Agnes M. Johnston, July 8, 1949; children—Margaret Ruth (Mrs. Sidney Ray Hill, Jr.). Helen Patricia. Instrument engr. E.I. duPont de Nemours & Co., Orange, Tex., 1951-54; asst. prof. Ga. Inst. Tech., 1954-59; program mgr. Martin Marietta Corp., Orlando, Fla., 1959-63, tech. dir., 1963-68; head dept. elec. engring. Miss. State U., Starkville, 1963; Alcoa prof. indsl. engring. U. Tenn., Knoxville, 1968—; dir. Sci. Methods, Inc.; cons. Strategic Air Def., Martin Marietta Corp., Environmental Tech., Inc., Orlando. Served with USMCR, 1943-46. Decorated Purple Heart; recipient M. A. Ferst Sigma Xi award Ga. Inst. Tech., 1959. Publ. award Martin Marietta Corp., 1964. Mem. I.E.E.E., Sigma Alpha Epsilon. Republican. Episcopalian. Rotarian. Author: (with J.E. Alexander) Systems Engineering Mathematics, 1962. Home: 364 Seven Oaks Dr Concord TN 37920

BAILEY, JOHN MORAN, lawyer; b. Hartford, Conn., Nov. 23, 1904; s. Michael and Louise (Moran) B.; A.B. in Sci., Cath. U., 1926; LL.B., Harvard, 1929; m. Barbara Leary, Aug. 1, 1933; children—Louise (Mrs. Conrad Kronholm), Barbara (Mrs. James Kennelly), Judith (Mrs. Brewster B. Perkins) and John (twins). Admitted Conn. and Mass. bars, 1929, also U.S. Dist. Ct.; exec. sec. to mayor of Hartford, 1931-33; judge Hartford Municipal Ct., 1933-35, 39-41; law clk. judiciary com. U.S. Senate, 1937; commr. statute revision Conn., 1941-46; exec. sec. gov. Conn., 1946; sr. partner Bailey & Wechsler, Hartford. Mem. Democratic Party 1925—; mem. Conn. Central Com., 1932- -. chmn., 1946—; chmn. Dem. Nat. Com., 1961-68. Vice chmn. Met. Dist. Commn. within County of Hartford, 1951—, Greater Hartford Flood Commn., 1955—; mem. Conn. Fiscal Study Com., 1957; commr. Promotion Uniformity of Legislation in U.S. 1957—; mem. Conn. Econ. and Planning and Devel. Com., 1956—. Dir. New Amsterdam Casualty Co., South End Bank, Hartford. Bd. dirs. St. Francis Hosp., Hartford; mem. founders com. U. Hartford. Mem. Am. Bar Assn., Harvard U. Alumni Assn., Cath. U. Alumni Assn. (bd. govs.). Hartford C. of C. (dir.). Roman Catholic K.C. (4), Elk. Clubs: Wethersfield (Conn.) Country: Wampanoag Country (West Hartford Conn.); Burning Tree Country (Bethesda, Md.). Home: 150 Scarborough St Hartford CT 06105 Office: 266 Pearl St Hartford CT 06103

BAILEY, JOSEPH CANNON, educator; b. Danville, Ill., Dec. 5, 1899; s. Martin B. and Lucy (Payne) B.; A.B., U. Ill., 1924, M.A., 1934; Ph.D., Columbia, 1944; A.M. (hon.), Harvard, 1954; m. Wanda Wellner, Jan. 1, 1928 (div.); m. 2d. Mary Fuller, June 21, 1958; 1 dau., Hilary, Fuel insp. C.& N.W. R.R., 1916-18; fed. fuel adminstr. Moutain States, 1918; salesman, sales mgr. Schuman Pub. Co., Chgo., 1925-27; field sec. Fgn. Policy Assn., N.Y.C., 1926-27; cons., spl. asst. Resettlement Adminstrn., Washington, 1936-37; instr. Columbia, 1933-35; instr., asst. prof. Hunter Coll., 1937-46; lectr. human relations Harvard, 1947-49, asso. prof. human relations, 1948-52. prof., 1952—. Cons., trainer to govt. agys. and depts., armed forces, also pvt. corps., ednl. instns. Author: (with Jay Franklin) LaGuardia, A Political Biograhy, 1937; Seaman A. Knapp, 1945: (with others) Organizational Behavior and Administration, 1961, Administering Research and Development, 1964. Home: 232 Prospect St Belmont MA 02178 Office: Harvard Bus Sch Boston MA 02163

BAILEY, JOSEPH T., corp. exec.; b. 1914; B.S. in Mech. Engring., Newark Coll. Engring., 1937; m. With Gen. Electric Co., 1937; with Warner & Swasey Co., 1962—, exec. v.p., dir., 1967-69, pres., 1969—. Address: 11000 Cedar Av Cleveland OH 44106

BAILEY, MITCHELL MONTGOMERY, lawyer; b. Warsaw, Poland, May 25, 1921; s. Sol and Manya (Scheid) B.; came to U.S., 1923, naturalized, 1926; B.S., Coll. City N.Y., 1942; J.D., Columbia, 1947. Admitted to N.Y. bar, 1947, since practiced in N.Y.C.; asso. atty. Pross, Halpern, Lefevre, Raphael & Alter, 1947-53, partner, 1954—. Sec. Penn Yan Boats, Inc., Automated Environmental Systems, Inc.; dir. Wellington Overseas Corp., Camera Corp. Am., Electric Stapler Corp. Sec., counsel Citizens for Eisenhower, 1956, Citizens for Rockefeller, 1962, 66. Pres., bd. dirs. North Valley Stream Assn., N.Y.,; sec., counsel, trustee Nat. Pollution Control Found.; trustee Valley Stream Sch. Dist.; counsel, trustee Internat. Amateur Sports Devel. Fund. Served with USAAF, 1942-45; ETO. Recipient N.Y. Judge Adv. award, 1962. Air Force Res. Meritorious Service award, 1964. Mem. Bar Assn. City N.Y., Res. Officers Assn., Air Force Assn. Clubs: Lambs N.Y.C. Editor: The Jaguar, Air Force Res. monthly publ., 1962-69. Home: 230 Central Park South New York City NY 10019 Office: 530 Fifth Av New York City NY 10036

BAILEY, NATHAN LYNCH, clergyman; b. Wilmington, Del., Oct. 5, 1909; s. Nathan and Anita Marie (Lynch) B.; diploma Nyack (N.Y.) Missionary Coll., 1931; LL.D., Asbury Coll., Wilmore, Ky., 1960; m. Mary E. Dittmar, June 26, 1931; children—Marilyn Joyce (Mrs. Dahl B. Seckinger), Anita Carrol (Mrs. Fred Henry). Ordained to ministry Christian and Missionary Alliance Ch., 1932; pastor in Mattoon, Ill., 1931-34, Windsor, Ont., Can., 1934-40, Ottawa, Ont., 1940-46; dist. supt. Eastern Canadian Dist., Christian and Missionary Alliance, 1946-60, nat. v.p. 1954-60, nat. pres., 1960—. Pres. Christian Publs., Inc., Harrisburg, Pa., 1960—, William H. Dietz, Inc., Harrisburg, 1960—, World Relief Com., Inc., 1967—. Mem. Pres., Com. on Aging, 1961. Trustee Nyack Missionary Coll., 1954—. Mem. Nat. Assn. Evangelicals (exec. com. 1969—). Home: 24 Terrace Dr Nyack NY 10960 Office: 260 W 44th St New York City NY 10036

BAILEY, ORVILLE TAYLOR, neuropathologist; b. Jewett, N.Y., May 28, 1909; s. Milton O. and Ollie (Persons) B.; A.B., Syracuse U., 1928; M.D., Albany Med. Coll., 1932. Rotating intern Albany Hosp., 1932-33; house officer pathology Peter Bent Brigham Hosp., Boston, 1933-34, asso. pathologist, 1940-43; resident pathologist Children's Hosp., Boston, 1934-35; instr. pathology Harvard Med. Sch., 1935-40, asso. in pathology, 1940-46, asst. prof., 1946-51; prof. neuropathology Ind. U. Sch. Medicine, 1951-59; prof. neurology U. Ill. Med. Sch., 1959-70, prof. neurol. surgery, 1970—. Cons. Cook County Hosp., 1959—, Children's Meml. Hosp., Chgo., 1963-69. Mem. Harvard Soc. Fellows, 1937-40. Clubs: University, Literary (Chgo.). Editor: (with D.E. Smith) The Central Nervous System: Some Experimental Models of Neurologic Disease. Contbr. articles on radiation, vascular disease in childhood, brain tumors to med. jours. Home: 3000 N Sheridan Rd Chicago IL 60657 Office: 912 S Wood St Chicago IL 60612

BAILEY, PEARCE, physician; b. N.Y.C., July 22, 1902; s. Pearce and Edith Lawrence (Black) B.; diploma St. Paul's Sch., Concord, N.H., 1920; A.B., Princeton, 1924; A.M., Columbia, 1931; Ph.D., Sorbonne, U. Paris, 1933; honours course in chemistry U. London, 1936; M.D., Med. Coll. S.C., 1941; m. Georgette Dora Princess Mestchersky, July 3, 1936. Asso. dir. Psychol. Center (a founder), Paris, France, 1933-36; intern Roper Hosp., Charleston, S.C., 1941-42; resident neurology Bellevue Hosp., N.Y.C., 1942-44, vis. neuropsychiatrist, 1944-46; child neurology sect. VA Central Office, 1946-51, asst. chief psychiatry and neurology div., 1948-51, cons. regional office, Washington, 1950-51; dir. Nat. Inst. Neurol. Diseases and Blindness, 1951-60, dir. internat. neurol. research, 1960-63, spl. asst. to dir., 1963—; attending neurologist Georgetown U., D.C. Gen. hosps., 1947-60; faculty Georgetown U., 1947-60, prof. clin. neurology, 1950-60; adv. com. Psychiatry and Neurology Service, VA Central Office, 1952-60; hon. prof. clin. neurology U. P.R. Sch. Medicine, 1963-70. U.S. del. Internat. Poliomyelitis Congress, N.Y.C., 1948, 4th Internat. Neurol. Congress, Paris, 1949 (chmn. com. for advancement neurology 1949-53); asst. sec.-gen. N.Am., 6th Internat. Neurol. Congress, 1957. Served as comdr. M.C., USNR, 1944-46. Decorated Officer de la Sante Publique, 1949; commandador El Soldel Peru, 1963. Diplomate Am. Bd. Psychiatry and Neurology. Mem. Am. Acad. Neurology (editor Newsletter 1949-62, pres. 1951-53), A.M.A., Am. Neurol. Assn., Am. Psychiat. Assn., Nat. Epilepsy Soc. (pres. 1953-54), World Fedn. Neurology (sec.-treas. gen. 1957-65), Sociedad Neurologica Argentina (hon.), Sociedade de Neurologia do Rio de Janerio (hon.), Assn. Am. Med. Colls., Am. Acad. Cerebral Palsy, Nat. Soc. Crippled Children and Adults (profl. adv. council), Easter Seal Found. (trustee), Am. Med. Writers Assn., N.Y. Neurol. Soc. (hon.), Die Deutsche Gesellschaft Für Neurologie (hon.), Japanese Soc. Neurology (hon.), Sociedad de Neurologia y Neurocirugia (hon., Montevideo, Uruguay). Washington Acad. Medicine, N.Y. Acad. Scis., Harvey Cushing Soc., Assn. Mil. Surgeons, Nat. Multiple Sclerosis Soc. (adv. bd.), Société Francaise de Neurologie (hon.), Assn. for Research Nervous and Mental Diseases, S.C. Med. Assn., Med. Soc. D.C. Author: Neurologic Rehabilitation, Handbook of Neurology (with A.B. Baker, Joe R. Brown), 1952. Editor: World Neurology; mem. editorial bd. Neurology, 1951; editorial staff Internat. Jour. Neurol. Scis. Contbr. articles to med. jours. Home: 4000 Cathedral Av NW Washington DC 20016 Office: Bldg 31 NIH Bethesda MD 20014

BAILEY, PEARL (Mae), singer; b. Newport News, Va., Mar. 29, 1918; d. Joseph James Bailey; student pub. schs., Phila.; m. John Randolph Pinkett, Jr., Aug. 31, 1948 (div. Mar. 1952); m. 2d, Louis Bellson, Jr., Nov. 19, 1952. Singer, 1933- -; vocalist various popular bands; stage debut St. Louis Woman, N.Y.C., 1946; role Broadway musical House of Flowers; motion pictures include Variety Girl, Carmen Jones; contract artist Coral Records, Columbia Records, Decca; night club engagements N.Y.C., Boston, Hollywood, Las Vegas, Chgo., also London, 1950—; guest artist various TV programs. Recipient Donaldson award, 1956; Spl. Tony award for Hello, Dolly, 1967- 68. Author: Raw Pearl, 1969.

BAILEY, PHILIP SIGMON, educator; b. Chickasha, Okla., June 9, 1916; s. Thomas Leonard and Alma (Sigmon) B.; B.S., Okla. Bapt. U., 1937; M.S., U. Okla., 1940; Ph.D., U. Va., 1944; m. Marie Shultz, Feb. 2, 1941 (div. 1959); children—Philip Sigmon, Thomas F., Evalee F.; m. 2d, Frances Ming Tieman, Mar. 24, 1962; stepchildren—Rebecca Tieman (Mrs. Charles M. Gray), Terrell C. Tieman. Chemist, Halliburton Oil Well Cementing Co., Great Bend, Kan., 1940-41; research asso. U Va., 1944-45; asst. prof. chemistry U. Tex., 1945-49, asso. prof., 1949-57, prof., 1957—; cons. ozone chemistry, organic peroxides. Mem. Am. Chem. Soc., Sigma Xi, Alpha Chi Sigma, Phi Lambda Upsilon, Alpha Epsilon Delta. Episcopalian (vestryman). Contbr. articles profl. jours. Patentee in field. Home: Route 2 Box 390A Leander TX 78641 Office: Dept Chemistry Univ Texas Austin TX 78712

BAILEY, RALPH E., mining co. exec.; b. Pike County, Ind., Mar. 23, 1924; s. Enos M. and Gertie L. (Taylor) B.; B.S. in Mech. Engring., Purdue U., 1949; m. Bettye J. Holder, Sept. 2, 1945; children—Douglas G., Cinda C., Rhonda Y., Lisa A. With No. Ill. Coal Corp., 1949-50, Sinclair Coal Co., 1950- 55; with Peabody Coal Co., 1955-65, v.p. charge mining operations, 1963- 64, exec. v.p. operations, 1964-65; v.p. Consolidation Coal Co., Pitts., 1965-68, sr. v.p., 1968-70, exec. v.p., 1970—, also dir. Home: 3317 Ponoka Rd Pittsburgh PA 15241 Office: 1 Oliver Plaza Pittsburgh PA 15222

BAILEY, RALPH RUSSELL, lawyer; b. Washington City, Pa., May 5, 1902; s. Matthew McHenry and Eva Jane (Russell) B.; A.B., U. Ore., 1926, J.D., 1936; m. Eulalia Anita Butler, Oct. 5, 1923; 1 son, Stephen Michael. Tchr., Salem (Ore.) High Sch., 1926-27, Medford (Ore.) High Sch., 1927-34; admitted to Ore. bar, 1936; asst. atty. gen. Ore., 1936-41; practice in Portland, 1943—; partner firm Morrison & Bailey, 1966—. Mem. Phi Delta Pi, Tau Kappa Alpha. Clubs: Arlington: Waverly Country. Home: 267 SE 33d St Portland OR 97214 Office: Standard Plaza Portland OR 97204

BAILEY, RAYMOND VICTOR, chem. engr.; b. Strong, Ark., Nov. 22, 1923; s. Russel Victor and Zellie (Lewis) B.; B.S. cum laude, La. Poly. Inst., 1944; M.S., Louisiana State Univ., 1948, Ph.D., 1949; m. 2d. Amelia Shelby Weston, Sept. 5, 1959; 1 dau., Elizabeth; children by previous marriageJanet, Rachel, Raymond (dec.). Chemist Cities Service Refining Corporation, Lake Charles, La., 1944-45; grad. asst. chem. engring. La. State U., 1946-48; asso. prof. chem. engring. U. Miss., 1948-51; summer research participant Oak Ridge Nat. Lab., 1949-51, now development engr., cons.; prof., head sch. chem. engring. Tulane U., 1951-, also head Engring. Research Inst. Registered profl. engr., La. Mem. Am. Inst. Chem. Engrs., Am. Chem. Soc., Am. Soc. Engring. Edn., Phi Kappa Phi, Gamma Sigma Epsilon, Sigma Xi. Contbr. articles tech. publs. Home: 1118 Pine St New Orleans LA 70118

BAILEY, RICHARD EUGENE, ret. coll. prof.; b. Anson, Tex., Oct. 25, 1907; s. Claude Eugene and Lalla Ira (Davis) B.; A.B., Tex. Christian U., 1926, A.M., 1929; Litt.D., U. Dijon (France), 1936. Instr. Univ. Prep. Sch., Ft. Worth, 1926-27, summer 1928; instr. Tex. Christian U., 1927-30; instr. North Tex. State Coll., Denton summer 1929; instr. Okla. A. and M. Coll. (now Okla. State U.), Stillwater, 1930-36, asst. prof., 1936-37, asso. prof., 1937- 47, prof., 1947, prof. fgn. langs., chmn. humanities 1952-66, chmn. humanities, prof. French, 1966-70, prof. emeritus, 1970—. Lectr. U. Dijon, 1935-36, Lycée Marcel Roby Saint Germain-en-Laye, France, 1948-49. Decorated Palmes academiques (France). Mem. Pi Kappa Alpha. Episcopalian Author: La Culture (with René Tallard), 1948. Home: 1714 E 30th Pl Tulsa OK 74114

BAILEY, ROGER, architect, educator; b. Bradford, Pa., Oct. 3, 1897; s. Benjamin Milton and May (Andrews) B.; B.Arch., Cornell U., 1920; student L'Ecole des Beaux Arts, Paris, France, 1922-25; m. Elisabeth Lorch, Dec. 21, 1935. Engaged as practising and cons. architect, N.Y., 1929-32, Mich., 1932- 49, Utah, 1949—; prof. architecture U. Mich 1932-35, 38-49; vis. prof. Cornell U., 1936-38; head critic architecture Yale, 1936-38; prof. architecture U. Utah, 1949-66, emeritus prof., 1966—, head dept., 1949-64, mem. univ. campus design com., 1958-64; exec. dir. Salt Lake Art Center, 1971—, also trustee. Mem.

Citizens Adv. Com. Capital Improvements Salt Lake City, 1958; co-dir. program archtl. psychology Nat. Inst. Mental Health, 1961-68, prin. investigator research projects, 1964, 65, 69; project dir. State Rehab. Center, 1969-70; mem. State Adv. Com. on Rehab. Facilities, 1967; chmn. Com. on Archtl. Barriers, 1967; mem. tech. rev. com. Utah Div. on Aging, 1969—; Mem. adv. bd. YWCA, 1963-69. Bd. dirs. Utah Mental Health Assn., 1965—. Served to 2d lt., inf., U.S. Army, 1918. Recipient Paris prize, 1922; co-recipient Chgo. War Meml. Competition, 1930; recipient 1st Scarab Club water-color prize, Detroit, 1945; Architect of Year, Utah Producers Council, 1966. Fellow A.I.A. (bd. dirs. Detroit 1948, pres. Utah chpt. 1963), Assn. Collegiate Schs. Architecture (bd. dirs.), Am., Assn. U. Profs., U.S. Bldg. Research Inst., Nat. Soc. Applied Solar Energy. Episcopalian. Home: 1283 E South Temple St Salt Lake City UT 84103

BAILEY, SAMUEL HALL, educator, journalist; b. Wellsville, Utah, Aug. 21, 1922; s. Norval Bradshaw and Sarah (Hall) B.; B.S., Utah State U., 1942; M.S., U. Wis., 1947; m. Doris Louise Van Dam, Apr. 24, 1944; children—Linda Jean, Ann Louise, Sam Hall, Marilyn Sue, Steven David, Scott Alan. Staff mem. News Bur., Utah State U., 1942; sports editor Logan (Utah) Herald-Jour., 1946; prof. journalism Ore. State U., 1947-, dir. information, 1947—. Served to 1st lt., AUS, 1942-46; ETO; to capt. AUS, 1950-52. Decorated Purple Heart, Bronze Star. Mem. Am. Coll. Pub. Relations Assn. (past chmn. Pacific N.W. sect.), Sigma Delta Chi. Mem. Ch. of Jesus Christ of Latter-day Saints (pres. Corvallis stake 1965—). Home: 732 N 30th St Corvallis, OR 97330.

BAILEY, SCOTT FIELD, bishop; b. Houston, Oct. 7, 1916; s. William Stuart and Tallulah (Smith) B.; B.A., Rice U., 1938; postgrad. U. Tex. Law Sch., 1938-39; B.D., Va. Theol. Sem., 1942, D.D., 1965; S.T.M., U. of South, 1953, D.D., 1965; m. Evelyn Williams, Dec. 11, 1943; children—Louise (Mrs. Allen C. Taylor), Nicholas, Scott Field, Sarah. Ordained to ministry Episcopal Ch., 1942; pastor in Waco, Lampasas, San Augustine, Austin, Tex., 1942-51; asst. to bishop of Tex., 1961-64; suffragan bishop of Tex., 1964—. Sec. ho. of bishops Episcopal Ch., 1967—. Served as chaplain USNR, World War II. Fellow Coll. of Preachers; mem. Phi Delta Theta. Home: 5309 Mandell St Houston TX 77005 Office: 520 San Jacinto Houston TX 77002

BAILEY, STEPHEN KEMP, educator; b. Newton, Mass., May 14, 1916; s. Albert E. and Marion B. (Hall) B.; A.B., Hiram Coll., 1937; B.A. (Rhodes scholar), Oxford U., 1939, M.A., 1946; Harvard, 1943, Ph.D., 1948; LL.D., Reed Coll., 1963; m. Cornelia Wootton Brown, Aug. 31, 1940; children—Morris Edward, Lois Emerson. Research asso. Transcontinental Research, Inc., N.Y.C., 1939-40; dir. admissions Hiram Coll., 1941-42; asst. chief Am. Hemisphere div. Bd. Econ. Warfare, Washington, 1942; research fellow Social Sci. Research Council, Washington, 1946; asst. prof. govt. Wesleyan U., 1946-49, asso. prof., 1949-54, adminstrv. asst. Senator William Benton, 1951; William Church Osborn prof. pub. affairs Princeton, 1954-59, dir. grad. program Woodrow Wilson Sch. Pub. and Internat. Affairs, Princeton, 1954-58; prof. polit. sci. Maxwell Grad. Sch. Citizenship and Pub. affairs Syracuse (N.Y.) U., 1959—, dean Maxwell Grad. Sch., 1961-69; chmn. policy inst. Syracuse U. Research Corp., 1969—; sr. Fulbright lectr. Oxford U., 1957-58; staff asso. Pub. Adminstrn. Clearing House, Hoover Commn. on Orgn. Exec. Branch, Washington, 1948; mayor, Middletown, Conn., 1952-54. Bd. dirs. Woodrow Wilson Found., 1958-63; bd. regents State of N.Y., 1967—; trustee Hiram Coll., 1968—. Served as lt., OSS, USNR, 1942-45. Mem. Am. Polit. Sci. Assn. (v.p. 1968-69), Nat. Acad. Edn., Am. Acad. Arts and Scis., Am. Soc. Pub. Adminstrn. (pres. 1967-68), Am. Assn. U. Profs., Assn. Am. Rhodes Scholars. Conglist. Club: Cosmos. Author: Roosevelt and His New Deal, 1938; Congress Makes a Law, 1950; (with Howard Samuel) Congress at Work, 1951; (with H. Samuel and S. Baldwin) Government in America, 1957; (with Robert Wood, Richard Frost, Paul Marsh) Schoolmen and Politics, 1962; The New Congress, 1966; (with Edith Mosher) ESEA: The Office of Education Administraters at Law, 1968; Congress in the Seventies, 1970. Home: 770 Janus St Syracuse NY 13203

BAILEY, STUART L., cons. radio engr.; b. Mpls., Oct. 7, 1905; s. Orin P. and Emilie (Robinson) B.; B.S., U. Minn., 1927, M.S., 1928; m. Carol Linkenhelt, May 1, 1935. Radio engr. Dept. Commerce, 1928-30; partner Jansky & Bailey, cons. radio engrs., Washington, 1930-53; pres. Jansky & Bailey, Inc., 1953-60; pres. Jansky & Bailey div. Atlantic Research Corp., Alexandria, Va., 1960-65; v.p. Atlantic Research Corp., 1960-68; v.p. Susquehanna Corp., 1968-70, cons. Atlantic Research div., 1970—; dir. Gen. Communication Co., Boston, 1957-60, v.p., 1957-60; Mem. Small Bus. Industry Adv. Com., 1956-60; member Joint Tech. Adv. Council, 1969—. Recipient Outstanding Achievement award U. Minn., 1956. Fellow I.E.E.E. (treas. 1948, 61-62, pres. 1949); mem. Engrs. Joint Council (bd. 1964-67), Armed Forces Communications and Electronics Assn., Assn. FCC Cons. Engrs., Radio Pioneers, Sigma Xi, Tau Beta Pi, Eta Kappa Nu. Club: Cosmos (Washington), Contbr. articles to profl. jours. Home: 8502 Beech Tree Ct Bethesda MD 20034 Office: Shirley Hwy and Edsall Rd Alexandria VA 22314

BAILEY, STURGES WILLIAMS, geologist, educator; b. Waupaca, Wis., Feb. 11, 1919; s. Ralph Williams and Katharine (Simmons) B.; B.A., U. Wis., 1941, M.A., 1948; Ph.D., Cambridge (Eng.) U., 1955; m. Marilyn Lorraine Jones, Feb. 19, 1949, children—David S., Linda M. Faculty U. Wis., Madison, 1951—, prof. geology, 1961—, chmn. dept. geology and geophysics, 1968-71. Served with USNR, 1942-46. Fulbright scholar, 1949-51. Mem. Mineral Soc. Am. (council 1970—), Clay Minerals Soc. (exec. com. 1964—, v.p. 1970-71, pres. 1971-72), Phi Beta Kappa. Contbr. articles to profl. jours. Editor: Clays and Clay Minerals, 1964-69. Spl. research X-ray crystallography. Home: 5049 LaCrosse Lane Madison WI 53705

BAILEY, THOMAS ANDREW, historian, educator; b. San Jose, Cal., Dec. 14, 1902; s. James Andrew and Annie (Nelson) B.; A.B., (with great distinction), Stanford, 1924, A.M., 1925, Ph.D., 1927; m. Sylvia Dean, Aug. 28, 1928; 1 son, Arthur Dean. Teaching fellow in history, U. of Cal., 1925-26; acting instr. in citizenship Stanford, 1926-27, asst. prof. history, 1930-35, asso. prof., 1935-40, prof., 1940, Margaret Byrne prof. Am. History 1952-68, prof. emeritus, 1968—, exec. head history dept., 1952-55, 57-59; instr. history and polit. sci. U. Hawaii, 1927-28, asst. prof., 1928-30; asst. prof. history U. Wash., summer 1931; vis. prof. diplomatic history George Wash. U., 1936-37; vis. lectr. history Harvard U., 1943-44, Cornell, 1950. Fellow Rockefeller Found. Internat. Relations and mem. Inst. for Advanced Study, Princeton, N.J., 1939-40; Albert Shaw lectr. in diplomatic history, Johns Hopkins, 1941; observer in Europe and civilian mem. staff Nat. War Coll., 1947. Mem. bd. editors Pacific Hist. Rev., 1937-40. Mem. Am. Hist. Assn. (pres. Pacific Coast br. 1959-60), Orgn. Am. Historians (pres. 1968), Stanford Inst. Am. History (dir. 1952-53), Soc. for Historians of Am. Fgn. Relations (pres. 1968), Phi Beta Kappa. Delta Sigma Rho. Author: Theodore Roosevelt and the Japanese- American Crises, 1934; A Diplomatic History of the American People, 1940, 8th edit., 1969; The Policy of the United States Toward the Neutrals, 1917-18, 1942; America's Foreign Policies; Past and Present, 1943, rev. edit., 1945; Woodrow Wilson and the Lost Peace, 1944 (awarded Commonwealth Club gold medal); Woodrow Wilson and the Great Betrayal, 1945; Wilson and the Peacemakers, 1947; The Man in the Street, 1948; America Faces Russia, 1950 (Gold medal Commonwealth Club); The American Pageant, 1956, 4th edit., 1971; Presidential Greatness, 1966; The Art of Diplomacy, 1968; Democrats vs. Republicans, 1968; Essays Diplomatic and Undiplomatic, 1969. Editor: (with F. A. Golder and J. L. Smith) The March of the Mormon Battalion, 1928; The American Spirit, 1963. Contbr. articles to profl. jours. Home: 293 Santa Teresa St Stanford CA 94305

BAILEY, VIRGINIA LONG, educator; b. Mariposa, Cal., July 28, 1908; d. Charles William and Savilla Ann (Teague) Long; A.B., U. Cal. at Berkeley, 1930, M.A., 1932; Ph.D., U. Mich., 1959; m. Harold Edwards Bailey, Dec. 3, 1933. Teaching asst. botany U. Cal. at Berkeley, 1930-32, research asst., 1932-41; instr. biology Wayne State U., 1949-59; faculty Detroit Inst. Tech., 1959—, prof. biol. sci., chmn. dept., 1963—. Bd. dirs. Wesley Found., Wayne State U., 1959—, sec., 1960—. Recipient Edward L. Newcomb Meml. award for research papers Am. Found. Pharm. Edn., 1958, 60. Mem. Bot. Soc. Am., Am. Inst. Biol. Scis., A.A.A.S., Mich. Bot. Club (sec, 1957-59, v.p. 1962-67), Am. Soc. Plant Taxonomists, Am. Soc. Pharmacognosy, Nat. Assn. Biology tchrs., Mich. Acad. Scis., Arts and Letters. Author: (with H. E. Bailey) Forests and Trees of the Western National Parks, 1941, Woody Plants of the Western National Parks, 1949; A Guide to the Flowering Plants and Ferns of the Western National Parks, parts 1, 2, and 5, 1955, 57, 58; also articles. Home: 4727 2d Av Detroit MI 48201

BAILEY, WILFORD SHERRILL, educator; b. nr. Hartselle, Ala., Mar. 2, 1921; s. Ollis Wilford and Bessie (Widener) B.; D.V.M., Auburn U., 1942, M.S., 1946; Sc.D., Johns Hopkins U., 1950; m. Cratus Hester, May 30, 1942; children—Wilford Edward, Joe Sherrill, Margaret Ann, Sarah Jane. Instr. to head prof. dept. pathology and parasitology Sch. Vet Medicine, Auburn U., 1942-62, asso. dean Grad. Sch. and coordinator research, 1962-66, v.p. for academic affairs, 1966—; custodian Am. Soc. Parasitologists, 1952—. Mem. NRC, Council, 1962-68; mem. tng. grant com. Nat. Inst. Allergy and Infectious Diseases, 1964-69; mem. Nat. Adv. Allergy and Infectious Disease Council, 1971—. Recipient Research fellow Am. Vet. Med. Assn., Johns Hopkins Univ. scholar, NSF Sci. Faculty fellow. Mem. Am. Vet. Med. Assn., Am. Soc. Parasitologists (pres. 1971), Sigma Xi, Phi Kappa Phi, Phi Zeta, Omicron Delta Kappa. Mem. Ch. of Christ. Home: 778 Moore's Mill Rd Auburn AL 36830

BAILEY, WILLIAM JAMES, mfg. exec.; b. Los Angeles, Aug. 29, 1914; s. William James and Helen (Davis) B.; student U. So. Cal.; m. Miriam Kelley, November 4, 1944; children—Linda Ann (Mrs. John Stevens), Robin Ann (Mrs. Peter K. Barker), William James III. Assistant sales mgr. Day & Night Mfg. Company, 1939-42, asst. gen. mgr., 1942-44, pres., 1944-65; v.p., dir. Affiliated Gas Equipment, Inc., 1949- 55; v.p. Carrier Corp., 1955-71; pres. v.p., 1971—; pres. Carrier Air Conditioning Co., 1967-71; pres. Payne Company, 1949-65, also gen. mgr. Monrovia aviation div., Spectrol electronics div., 1955-58; chmn. bd. Spectrol Electronics Corp., 1954-65. Mem. Am. Soc. Heating, Refrigerating and Air Conditioning Engrs., Pacific Coast Gas Assn. (pres. 1962). Clubs: California (Los Angeles); Century (Syracuse); Onondaga Golf and Country (Fayetteville, N.Y.). Office: care Carrier Corp Syracuse NY 13201

BAILEY, WILLIAM JOHN, educator, chemist; b. East Grand Forks, Minn., Aug. 11, 1921; s. Admiral Ross and Erva (Stewart) B.; B.Chemistry, U. Minn., 1943; Ph.D., U. Ill., 1946; m. Mary Caroline Worsham, Aug. 27, 1949; children—Caroline Jane, John Robert, Barbara Ann. Arthur D. Little postdoctoral fellow Mass. Inst. Tech., 1946-47; asst. prof. chemistry Wayne State U., Detroit, 1947-49, asso. prof., 1949-51; research prof. organic chemistry U. Md., College Park, 1951—. Chmn. Gordon Resarch Conf. on Organic Reactions, 1960; mem. NSF postdoctoral selection com., 1963—; NRC adv. com. elastomers to U.S. Army Natick Labs., 1961—, chmn. com. macromolecular chemistry, 1967—; U.S. rep. macromolecular div. Internat. Union Pure and Applied Chemistry, 1967—. Recipient Fatty Acid Producers Research award, 1955. Mem. Chem. Soc. Washington (pres. 1961; Service award 1969), Am. Chem. Soc. (chmn. div. polymer chemistry, 1968, chmn. com. on nominations and elections council 1969-72, chmn. Middle Atlantic regional councilors 1970-72), A.A.A.S., Am. Oil Chemists Soc., Phi Beta Kappa, Sigma Xi, Phi Kappa Phi, Phi Lambda Upsilon, Pi Mu Epsilon, Alpha Chi Sigma. Mem. editorial bd. Jour. Organic Chemistry, 1957-63, Macromolecular Synthesis, 1960—, Record Chem. Progress, 1950-70, Jour. Macromolecular Science Chemistry, 1966—, Jour. Polymer Science,, 1967—, Macromolecules, 1967—. Developed several new methods for preparation of polymers; discovered several new polymers; produced a correlation between structure and properties in plastics and rubbers. Home: 6905 Pineway University Park MD 20782 Office: U Md Dept Chemistry College Park MD 20742

BAILEY, WILLIAM O. ins. co. exec.; b. Syracuse, N.Y., July 1, 1926; s. William E. and Kate (Oliver) B.; A.B. in Econs., Dartmouth, 1947; M.B.A. in Ins., Wharton Sch., U. Pa., 1949; m. Emily Wood, Oct. 7, 1950; children—George, Janet, Thomas, Carolyn. Asst. sect. Nat. Bur. Casualty Underwriters, 1952-54; with Aetna Life & Casualty Co., Hartford, Conn., 1954—, sr. v.p. casualty and surity div., 1968—. Corporator, mem. ins. com. Hartford Hosp.; trustee Hartford Rehab. Center; bd. corporators Hartford Sem. Found. Served with USNR, World War II. Mem. Nat. Ins. Actuarial and Statis. Assn. (chmn. N.Y.C.), Oil Ins. Assn. (past pres.), Soc. Chartered Property and Casualty Underwriters. Home: 29 Harvest Lane West Hartford CT 06117 Office: 151 Farmington Av Hartford CT 06115

BAILEY, WILLIAM RUFUS, steel co. exec.; b. N.Y.C., Nov. 16, 1916; s. Theodore L. and Gillian W. (Barr) B.; grad. Yale, 1939; grad. Law Sch. U. Va., 1947; m. Jeanne Maddux, Dec. 10, 1943; children-Louise Maddux, Rosalie Clifford, Chancey Greenleaf. Admitted to N.Y. bar, 1950, Ohio bar, 1952; atty. Breed, Abbott & Morgan, N.Y.C., 1948-51; asst. counsel Armco Steel Corp., Middletown, O., 1951-64, counsel, 1964-68, v.p., gen. counsel, 1968—. Served to lt. comdr., A.C., USNR, 1939-45. Home: 206 Alameda St Middletown OH 45042 Office: 703 Curtis St Middletown OH 45042

BAILEY, WILLIAM STUART, constrn. co. exec.; b. Calvert, Tex., Aug. 13, 1907; s. William Stuart and Tallulah (Smith) B.; B.A. Rice U., 1930; m. Jessie Jones, Oct. 1, 1931; children—William Stuart, Margaret Elizabeth. With Jesse H. Jones Interests, Ft. Worth, 1930-42; with Fischbach and Moore, Inc., Houston, 1946—, v.p., 1946-69, sr. v.p., 1969—, also dir.; dir. MacGregor Park Nat. Bank, Houston. Served with USAAF, 1942-46. Home: 5552 Tupper Lake St Houston TX 77027 Office: Fischbach and Moore Inc Houston TX 77002

BAILEY, WINSTON LEROY, banker; b. Eagle Bend, Minn., June 11, 1927; s. Walter N. and Clara (Eckroat) B.; A.B., San Diego State Coll., 1951; M.B.A., Stanford, 1953; m. June Teig, June 20, 1953; children—Chris, Lynn. With trust dept. bank of Am., Los Angeles, San Francisco, 1954-66, v.p., sec., San Francisco, 1966-68, v.p. mgmt. devel. and personnel adminstrn., 1968-71, v.p., asst. to pres., 1971—. Mem. adv. com. San Francisco Consortium. Served with AUS, 1945-47. Mem. Am. Soc. Personnel Adminstrn., Am., Cal. bankers assns., Stanford Bus. Sch. Assn., Kappa Alpha. Clubs: San Francisco Commercial, Bankers. Home: 124 Austin Av Atherton CA 94025 Office: World Hdqrs Bldg Bank of America Center San Francisco CA 94104

BAILIE, ARCHIE ALEXANDER, mfg. co. exec.; b. Ottawa, Ont., Can., Mar. 21, 1916; s. James Arthur and Stella Alvina (Lane) B.; grad. Lisgar Collegiate Sch., Ottawa, 1934; m. Eileen Gertrude Ross, Nov. 10, 1939; childrenJames Ross, Leslie Arthur, Ross Alexander. With Price, Waterhouse & Co., chartered accountants, Toronto, Ont., 1934-42, 45-48; treas. Davis Leather Co. Ltd., Ltd., Newmarket, Ont., 1948-52; with A. V. Roe Can. Ltd., Toronto, 1952-, treas., v.p. finance, 1953-, also dir.; chmn., pres. Dominion Coal Co. Ltd.; v.p., dir. Hawker Industries, Ltd.; dir. Canadian Steel Wheel, Ltd., Orenda Engines Ltd., Canadian Gen. Transit Co. Ltd.; sec.-treas. Racair Ltd., 1957-; v.p., dir. Hawker Siddeley Can. Ltd. Served to capt. Canadian Army, 1942-45. Mem. Inst. Chartered Accountants, Financial Financial Execs. Assn., Nat. Assn. Accountants. Clubs: Granite, Ontario (Toronto); St. Georges Golf and Country; Donalda Golf and Country. Home: 50 Sunnydene Crescent Toronto 12 Ontario Canada Office: 7 King St E Toronto Ontario Canada

BAILIE, ROBERT JAMES, business exec.; b. Ireland, 1911. Exec. v.p. operations, dir. Canron, Ltd.; dir. Tamper, Inc. Home: 5160 MacDonald Av Montreal 254 Quebec Canada Office: 1121 Pl Ville Marie Montreal 113 Quebec Canada

BAILIET, JOHN MASON, gen. ins. broker; b. Appleton, Wis., July 29, 1890; s. David Henry and Ellen (Cannon) B.; ed. pub. schs. of Appleton; m. Vivian Irene Brega, February 14, 1912; children—Richard S., Ellen, David (dec.), Bette (Mrs. Donald C. Grefe). Teacher Freedom, Wisconsin, 1907-08, Cedar Point, Illinois, 1908-09; staff engineering department, U.P. R.R., Omaha, 1909-14; gen. ins., surety bond agt. and broker Balliet Agy., Inc., 1914—, now chmn.; dir. Mich. Central R.R., Lake Erie and Eastern R.R., Pitts. & Lake Erie R.R.; mem. exec. com., dir. Detroit River Tunnel Co. Mem. Am. Arbitration Assn., Newcomen Soc. in N. Am. Elk, K.C. (4). Club: Butte des Morts Golf. Home: 2 Brokaw Pl Appleton WI 54911 Office: 123 South Appleton St Appleton WI 54911

BAILLE, JACK K., banker; b. Seattle, Mar. 26, 1911; s. John K. and Gertrude (Mellon) B.; B.S. in Bus. Adminstrn., U. So. Cal., 1934; m. Phyllis Dooley, Oct. 11, 1957; children—Brent K., Paige, Kathy Lyn. Chmn. bd., pres. Los Angeles Fed. Savs. Assn., 1950—; dir. King-Stanford Corp., First Los Angeles Corp. Mem. Commn. Los Angeles Harbor, 1957-59, Commn. Los Angeles Internat. Airport, 1959-60; del. Soc. Internat. Safety at Sea, 1958—. Trustee Los Angeles City Exhbn. Center. Served to comdr. USNR, 1943-46. Clubs: Los Angeles Yacht Transpacific Yacht (Los Angeles); Newport Harbor Yacht, Balboa (commodore) (Newport Beach, Cal.). Champion ocean racing fleet (sailing) So. Cal., 1970. Home: 1815 Bayadere Terrace Corona Del Mar CA 92625 Office: 1 Wilshire Blvd Los Angeles CA 90017

BAILLIE, CHARLES DOUGLAS, banker; b. Bklyn., Sept. 12, 1918; s. Charles Tupper and Nina (Vincent) B.; B.S. with distinction, Ind. U., 1940; certificate exec. program, U. Cal. at Los Angeles, 1956, m. Helen Elizabeth Kuehn, Feb. 15, 1941; children—Barbara Ann (Mrs. John Roland Obenchain), Charles Douglas, Nancy Helene (Mrs. John Michael King). Personnel and credit supervision Continental Ill. Nat. Bank, Chgo., 1940-52; v.p. treas., dir. Nat. Discount Corp., South Bend, Ind., 1952-54; with United Cal. Bank, Los Angeles, 1954—, asst. v.p., 1955-56, v.p., 1956-68, sr. v.p., 1968-70, exec. v.p., 1970—. Mem. adv. bd. Escalon, Inc., 1969—; mem. San Marino Community Council. Served from ensign to lt. Supply Corps, USNR, 1942-46. Mem. Am. Inst. Banking, Los Angeles C. of C., Stock Exchange Club Los Angeles, Rep. Assos., UCLA Exec. Program Alumni Assn., I Men's Assn., Robert Morris Assos., Delta Sigma Pi, Phi Gamma Delta, Beta Gamma Sigma. Clubs: San Marino City; San Gabriel (Cal.) Country; California. Home: 2155 Sherwood Rd San Marino CA 91108 Office: 600 S Spring St Los Angeles CA 90054

BAILLIE, STUART, librarian, educator; b. Pitts., Jan. 28, 1914; s. Alexander Stuart and Mary Olive (Stewart) B.; student Hiram Coll., 1931-34; A.B., Washington U., 1935, M.A., 1939, Ed.D., 1961; B.S. in L.S., George Peabody Coll., Tchrs., 1941; m. Sara Johnson, July 3, 1936; children—Grover Stuart, Susan Jane, Mary Nell. Librarian Festus (Mo.) High Sch., 1938-40; asst. Vanderbilt Med. Library, Nashville, 1940-41; reviser cataloging course Peabody Library Sch., 1941; social sci. librarian Stephens Coll., 1941- 42; asst. reference circulation dept. U. Mo., 1942-43; time study engr. Emerson Electric Co., St. Louis, 1943-45; librarian Ga. Tchrs. Coll., 1945-46, Luth. High Sch., St. Louis, 1946-47, Engring. Sch., Washington U., St. Louis, 1947-53; tchr. library sci. U. Coll., Washington U., 1947- 53; dir. libraries U. Denver, 1953-67, dir. Grad. Sch. Librarianship, 1955-67; librarian San Jose State Coll., since 1967—; chmn. exec. bd. Bibliog. Center for Research, 1953-54. Mem. Assn. Coll. and Ref. Libraries, Am. Mountain Plains (pres. 1961-63), Colo. (dist. pres. 1954- 55), Mo. (v.p. 1952-54) library assns., Spl. Libraries Assn., Kappa Delta Pi. Bus. mgr. Mo. Library Assn. Quar., 1947-51. Editor of Colo. Library Assn. Bull., 1955-58. Address: San Jose State College Library 125 S 7th St San Jose CA 95114

BAILY, NATHAN ARIEL, govt. ofcl., educator; b. N.Y.C., July 19, 1920; s. Saul and Eleanor (Mintz) B.; B.S.S., Coll. City N.Y., 1940; M.A., Columbia, 1941, Ph.D., 1946; m. Judith Bernstein, June 20, 1946; children—Alan Eric, Lawrence Joel. Economist OPA; sr. editor-econ. analyst Research Inst. Am.; moderator District Viewpoint, weekly TV program; faculty Advanced Sch. Retail Mgmt. Nat. Sales Execs., Stonier Grad. Sch. Banking at Rutgers U.; hon. faculty mem. U.S. Army Mgmt. Sch.; mem. nat. ednl. adv. com., instr., hon. dean faculty Washington chpt. Am. Inst. Banking; mem. history and econs. dept. Coll. City N.Y.; instr. Fashion Inst. Tech. and Design, N.Y.C.; faculty Am. U. Sch. Bus. Adminstrn., 1946-, prof. bus. adminstrn. and finance, 1953—, founding dean, 1955-70; now commr. U.S. Postal Rate Commn., Washington; dir. Washington Mut. Investors Fund, Carl M. Freeman & Assos., Carrols Devel. Corp., Am. Wholesalers, Inc.; mem. bd. advisers Columbia Realty Trust, Fed. Realty Investment Trust; ednl. cons. Nat. Appliance-Radio-TV Dealers Assn., Inst. Indsl. Launderers; editorial adv. bd. Internat. Classes Press; cons., participant tng. programs Brookings Instn., Milk Industry Found., Social Security Adminstrn., Electric Inst. of Washington, Internat. Bank for Reconstrn., IBM, Gen. Electric, Nat. Tire Dealers and Retreaders Assn. Mem. D.C. Small Bus. Adv. Council; mem. D.C. adv. council for State Tech. Services Act; mem. Commn. on Ch. Family Financial Planning. Trustee Council on Opportunities in Selling; bd. dirs. Friends of U.S. Latin America, Pioneer Found., Homer Hoyt Inst.; chmn. Invest-In-Am. nat. adv. council on econ. edn. Recipient fellowship E.I. duPont de Nemours, Swift & Co., Danforth Found. Harvard Bus. Sch., Volker Fund U. N.C. Mem. A.I.M., Am. Econ. Assn., Am. Assn. U. Profs., Middle Atlantic Assn. Colls. of Bus. Adminstrn. (pres. 1964-65), Am. Soc. Assn. Execs., Washington Soc. Investment Analysts, Washington

Sales Execs. Club (dir. 1962-63), Washington Bd. Trade, Washington Real Estate Bd. (affiliate mem.), Suburban Md. Builders Assn. (hon. mem., econ. cons.), Newcomen Soc. N.Am., Soc. for Religious Orgn. Mgmt., U.S. C. of C. (com. anti-trust and trade regulation, dir.), Phi Beta Kappa, Omicron Delta Kappa. Editor: Marketing Profitably Under the Robinson-Patman Act, 1963. Contbg. editor: Modern Security Services. Home: 5516 Greystone St Chevy Chase MD 20015 Office: Postal Rate Commn Washington DC 20268

BAILY, RICHARD OWEN, equipment mfg. co. exec.; b. Alexandria, S.D., Dec. 14, 1923; s. Owen R. and Ida Belle (James) B.; B.S. in Bus. Adminstrn., U. S.D., 1947; m. Elizabeth Ann Murry, Dec. 11, 1945; children—Thomas Owen, Diette Marie. With Burroughs Corp., 1947-71, asst. v.p. marketing, 1960-64, v.p. marketing, 1964-67, v.p., group exec. business machines group, Detroit, 1967-71; pres. Friden div. Singer Co., San Leandro, Cal., 1971—. Served with USAAF, World War II. Decorated. DF. C., Air medal, Presdl. citation. Mem. Sales/Marketing Execs. Internat. (v.p.), Sales/Marketing Execs. Internat. (chmn. bd.), Sales/Marketing Execs. Detroit (past president), Econ. Club C. of C. (U.S. council). Home: 3710 Rose Ct Lafayette CA 94549 Office: Singer-Friden Div 2350 Washington Av San Leandro CA 94577

BAILYN, BERNARD, historian, educator; b. Hartford, Conn., Sept. 10, 1922; s. Charles Manuel and Esther (Schloss) B.; A.B., Williams Coll., 1945, Litt.D., 1969; M.A., Harvard, 1947, Ph.D., 1953; L.H.D., Lawrence U., 1967, Bard Coll., 1968; m. Lotte Lazarsfeld June 18, 1952; children—Charles David, John Frederick. Faculty Harvard, Cambridge, Mass., 1953—, prof. history, 1961-66, Winthrop prof. history, 1966—; editor-in-chief John Harvard Library, 1962-70. Trevelyan lectr. Cambridge U., 1971. Trustee, Manhattanville Coll. Served with AUS, 1943-46. Recipient Robert H. Lord award Emmanuel Coll., 1967. Mem. Am. Acad. Arts and Scis. Nat. Acad. Edn., Am. Philos. Soc., Royal, Mass. hist. socs. Author: New England Merchants in the 17th Century, 1955; (with Mrs. Bailyn) Massachusetts Shipping, 1697-1714; A Statistical Study, 1959; Education in the Forming of American Society, 1960; Pamphlets of the American Revolution, 1750-1776, Vol. 1, 1965; The Ideological Origins of the American Revolution, 1967 (Pulitzer and Bancroft prizes 1968); The Origins of American Politics, 1968. Co- editor: Perspectives in American History, 1967—. Home: 3 Hurlbut St Cambridge MA 02138

BAIN, BARBARA (Mrs. Martin Landau), actress; B.A. in Sociology, U. Ill.; m. Martin Landau; children—Susan, Juliet. Formerly fashion model, N.Y.C.; appeared in TV series Mission Impossible. Recipient Emmy award. Address: care William Morris Agy Inc 151 El Camino St Beverly Hills CA 90212*

BAIN, CHARLES RANDALL, lawyer; b. Greeley, Colo., Feb. 1, 1934; s. Walter Lockwood and Harriet (Stewart) B.; B.A., Yale, 1955, LL.B., 1960; m. Joanne Berg. Aug. 4, 1956; children—Jennifer Harriet, Charles Alvin. Admitted to Ariz. bar, 1961, since practiced in Phoenix; asso. Jack E. Brown, 1961-63; partner Brown, Vlassis & Bain, 1963—. Dir. Scottsdale Pub., Inc. Pres., bd. dirs. Valley Big Bros. Mem. Am., Ariz., Maricopa County bar assns. Club: Yale (sec. Phoenix). Home: 824 E Hayward St Phoenix AZ 85020 Office: 222 N Central Av Phoenix AZ 85004

BAIN, CHESTER WARD, educator; b. Bradshaw, Va., Aug. 11, 1919; s. Hubert Ward and Nellie Mae (Gwynne) B.; student Roanoke Coll., 1937-38; B.A., U. Va., 1948, M.A., 1950, Ph.D., 1955; m. Sylvia Rubinowitz, Aug. 6, 1944; children—Eugene Ward, Charles Lynwood, Douglas Gwynne. Mem. faculty U. Va., 1951-60, asso. prof. polit. sci., 1957-60; vis. prof. W. Va. U., 1957-58; prof. polit. sci., head dept. U. S.C., 1960-63; prof. polit. science Emory U., 1963-66, chmn., 1964-66; Olin D. Johnston prof. polit. sci. U. S.C. Columbia, 1966—. Volunteer International Executive Service Corps. Served with AUS, 1941-45. Decorated Legion of Merit. Mem. Am. Polit. Sci. Assn., Phi Sigma Alpha. Methodist. Author: Annexation in Virginia, 1966. Contbr. articles profl. jours. Office: Dept Polit Sci U SC Columbia SC 29208

BAIN, JAMES ARTHUR, pharmacologist, educator; b. Langdon, N.D., May 22, 1918; s. James Hamilton and Mabel (Aldritt) B.; A.A., Wayland Jr. Coll., 1938; B.S., U. Wis., 1940, Ph.D., 1944; m. Eleanor Theo Hohaus, Dec. 5, 1947; children—Andrew J., Peter T. Research asst. McArdle Meml. Lab., U. Wis., 1940-44, Rockefeller fellow, 1946-47; research asso. U. Ill., 1947-50, asst. prof., then asso. prof., 1952-54; mem. faculty dept. pharmacology Emory U., 1954—, prof., 1954—, chmn. dept., 1957-62, dir. div. basic health scis., 1960—. Cons. to govt., nat. agys., industry, 1954—. Mem. Am. Chem. Soc., Soc. Exptl. Biology and Medicine, Am. Soc. Pharmacology and Exptl. Therapeutics, A.A.A.S., Am. Assn. Cancer Research, Sigma Xi. Contbr. articles profl. jours. Home: 2275 Tanglewood Rd Decatur GA 30033 Office: 209 Woodruff Meml Bldg Emory U Atlanta GA 30322

BAIN, JOHN CLINTON, constrn. co. exec.; b. Union Mills, Ind., Dec. 17, 1927; s. Robert Walker and Auddra (Rawles) B.; B.S., Ind. U., 1952; m. Mary Frances Snyder, Aug. 15, 1948; children—Jerri Beth, John William, Mark Edward. Sr. accountant Lybrand, Ross Bros. & Montgomery, Chgo., 1952-56; asst. treas., supr. costs and systems N.W. Paper Co., Cloquet, Minn., 1956-61; asst. to v.p. and treas. Blandin Paper Co., Grand Rapids, Minn., 1961-63; asst. controller Ind. Nat. Bank, Indpls., 1963-64; controller, treas. Huber, Hunt & Nichols, Inc., Indpls., 1965—; cons. mgmt. systems. Served with AUS, 1946-48. Mem. Nat. Assn. Accountants (nat. dir. 1962-63), Financial Execs. Inst. (treas., dir. Indpls. chpt. 1970-71), Am. Inst. C.P.A.'s, Ind. Soc. C.P.A.'s, Ind. C. of C., Stuart Cameron McLeod Soc. Club: Indianapolis Athletic. Home: 11511 Rolling Ct Carmel IN 46032 Office: 2450 S Tibbs Av Indianapolis IN 46241

BAIN, WILFRED CONWELL, coll. dean; b. Shawville, Que., Can., Jan. 20, 1908; s. James Alexander and Della Mary (Hawn) B.; A.B., Houghton Coll., 1929; B. Mus., Westminster Choir Coll., 1931; M.A., N.Y.U., 1936, Ed.D., 1938; Mus. D. (hon.), Am. Conservatory, 1951, Temple U., 1962, Westminster Choir Coll., 1965; m. Mary Freeman, July 1, 1929. Came to U.S., 1918, naturalized, 1940. Head music dept. Central Coll., S.C., 1929-30; head voice, choral music Houghton Coll., 1931-38; dean music N. Tex. State U., 1938-47; dean Sch. Music, Ind. U., Bloomington, 1947—. Chmn. music adv. panel USIA, 1967; music adviser, mem. bd. Coolidge Found.; mem. Nat. Council on Arts and Govt., 1966—; trustee Westminster Choir Coll., 1965—; mem. leadership tng. conf., examiners bd. N. Central Assoc.; mem. com. Central Opera Service; nat. council Met. Opera. Mem. Nat. A-sn. of Tchrs. of Singing., also mem. Nat. Assn. Schs. Music. (v.p.), Music Tchrs. Nat. Assn. (pres., sec.), Am. Musical Soc., Music Educators Nat. Conf., Am. Friends of Bayreuth (pres.), Phi Kappa Lambda, Phi Delta Kappa, Pi Sigma Kappa, Kappa Kappa Psi. Rotarian (hon.). Home: 2200 Convenanter Dr Bloomington IN 47401

BAIN, WILLIAM JAMES, architect; b. New Westminster, B.C., Can., Mar. 27, 1896; s. David and Annie Wilson (Forrester) B.; student U. of Pa., 1919-21; student in Europe, 1922; m. Mildred Worline Clark, May 29, 1924; children— Robert C., William James, Jr., Nancy Ann (Mrs. Edward George Lowry III). Employed in Boston, N.Y., Los Angeles, Seattle, 1922-24; practice architecture, Seattle, 1924—; mem. firm Naramore, Bain, Brady and Johanson, 1943—, also mem. Bain and Overturf. Mem. Nat. Pub. Adv. Panel for Archtl. Services, 1968-69; regional adv. bd. Small Bus. Adminstrn.; dir. Salvation Army. Served with 117th Field Signal Battalion, attached to 166th Inf., Rainbow Div., U.S. Army, 1917-18. Prin. works include Corregidor Bataan War Meml., Nat. FDA Bldg. (Washington), Washington Bldg. (Seattle); asso. architect U.S. Sci. Pavilion Century 21, 1st Nat. Bank of Missoula (Mont.), U. Wash. Med. Sch., Seattle, IBM Bldg., Seattle, Seattle 1st Nat. Bank, Seattle Post Intelligencer, Batelle Research Centers. Past mem. Seattle Housing Adv. Bd.; pres. Arthritis Found. Western Wash., 1968; trustee Seattle Urban Renewal. Fellow A.I.A. (jury of fellows 1950-55; mem. bd. past pres. Wash. chpt.; sec. coll. fellows 1966, Seattle pres. 1968); mem. English Speaking Union (mem. bd. 1964-70), C. of C. (mem. exec. com. 1968-69, mem. bd. dirs. 1960-70, treas. 1965, constrn. man of year 1966), Am. Arbitration Assn. Clubs: Harbor, Rainier (dir.), Rotary, Washington Athletic, Seattle Tennis. Home: 1540 Parkside Dr East Seattle WA 98102 Office: 904 7th Av Seattle WA 98104

BAINBRIDGE, FREDERICK FREEMAN III, architect; b. Charlottesville, Va., Sept. 15, 1927; s. Frederick Freeman and Cornelia Winston (Burnley) B.; B.Arch., U. Va., 1950; M. Indsl. Design, Kansas City Art Inst., 1952; m. Binki Baker, Jan. 6, 1948; children—Burnley, Susan Winifred, Meriwether, Robin. Asst. prof. Sch. Architecture Clemson (S.C.) U., 1952-55; asso. firm Toombs, Amisano & Wells, Architects, Atlanta, 1955-62; prin. firm Martin & Bainbridge, Atlanta, 1962-70, Bainbridge & Assos., 1970—; Southeastern project architect U. Ky. civil defense research project, 1964; vis. critic Ga. Inst. Tech., 1964-67. Chmn. archtl. rev. com. Atlanta Civic Design Commn., 1967—. Served with USNR, 1944-46. Recipient honor awards S. Atlantic Region A.I.A., 1964, 66, 68, 70; honor award prestressed Concrete Inst., 1967. Mem. A.I.A. Club: Fairington Golf and Tennis. Home: 2154 Monterey Dr NW Atlanta GA 30318 Office: 3290 Northside Parkway NW Atlanta GA 30327

BAINBRIDGE, JOHN, writer; b. Monticello, Minn., Mar. 12, 1913; s. William Dean and Bess (Lakin) B.; B.S., Northwestern U., 1935; m. Dorothy Alice Hazlewood, June 2, 1936; children—Jonathon, Janet. Mem. editorial staff The New Yorker since 1938. Mem-Athors Guild. Club: Coffee House (N.Y.C., N.Y.). Contbr. numerous "Profiles" to The New Yorker and articles to other nat. publs. Author: Little Wonder, or The Reader's Digest and How It Grew, 1946; The Wonderful World of Toots Shor, 1951; Biography of an Idea, 1952; Garbo, 1955; The Super-Americans, 1961; Like a Homesick Angel, 1964; Another Way of Living, 1968. Home: 51 Eaton Sq London SW England Office: care The New Yorker 25 W 43d St New York City NY 10036

BAINBRIDGE, KENNETH TOMPKINS, physicist; b. Cooperstown, N.Y., July 27, 1904; s. William Warin and Mae (Tompkins) B.; S.B., Mass. Inst. Tech., 1926, S.M., 1926; M.A., Princeton U., 1927, Ph.D., 1929; M.A. (hon.), Harvard, 1942; m. Margaret Pitkin Sept. 8, 1931; children—Martin Keeler, Joan, Margaret Tompkins; m. 2d, Helen Brinkley King, Oct. 11, 1969. Physicist, 1928-29; nat. research fellow Bartol Research Found., 1929-31, Bartol Research Found. fellow, 1931-33; Guggenheim Memorial Found. fellow at Cavendish Lab., Cambridge, Eng., 1933-34; asst. prof. physics, Harvard, 1934-38, asso. prof., 1938-46, prof., 1946—, chmn. dept. physics, 1953-55, George Vasmer Leverett prof. physics, 1961—; tech. cons. Nat. Def. Research Council, 1940-44, M.I.T. Radiation Lab., 1940-43, Los Alamos Lab., 1943-45; dir. Alamogordo Atomic bomb Test, Feb.-Sept. 1945. Trustee Associated Univs., Inc., 1957-59. Awarded Louis Edward Levy medal, Franklin Inst., 1933; Presdl. certificate of merit for work on radar, 1948. Mem. 7th Solvay Chemistry Congress, 1947. Mem. Am. Physical Soc., Nat. Academy Scis., Am. Acad. Arts and Sciences, Alpha Tau Omega, Tau Beta Pi. Contbr. tech. articles to Physical Review, Review of Scientific Instruments, Jour. of Franklin Inst. Holder of patents on photo electric cells, electronic multiplier and electro magnetic pumps. Address: Harvard University Cambridge MA 02138

BAINBRIDGE, THOMAS S., mfg. co. exec.; b. Scranton, Pa., 1919; ed. U. Scranton, 1940. Sr. finance and acquisitions, dir. Houdaille Industries, Inc.; treas., dir. Houdaille Industries, Ltd., Houdaille Machine Tools Can. Ltd., Houdaille Oshawa Ltd.; v.p., treas., dir. Logan Engring.; v.p. finance, dir. Houdaille Constrn. Materials, Inc.; adv. bd. Liberty Mut. Ins. Co. Bd. dirs. Psychiat. Clinic Buffalo. Home: Lancaster Lane Orchard Park NY 14127 Office: One M & T Plaza Buffalo NY 14203*

BAINE, JOHN C., utilities exec.; b. Arbroath, Scotland, 1905; grad. Tulane U., 1927. Pres., dir. Transit Service Corp. of Met. St. Louis; dir. Nat. City Lines, Inc., Balt. Transit Co., Gen. Bancshares, Inc., Bank of St. Louis. Home: 49 Log Cabin Dr St Louis MO 63124 Office: 3869 Park Av St Louis MO 63110*

BAINER, ROY, agrl. engr., educator; b. nr. Ottawa, Kan., Mar. 7, 1902; s. Harry M. and Clara Ellen (Nitcher) B.; B.S., Kan. State Coll., 1926, M.S., 1929; LL.D., U. Cal., 1969; m. Lena Mae Cook, May 29, 1926; 1 dau., La Nelle Marie. Instr. Kan. State Coll., 1926-27, asst. prof., 1927-29; asst. prof., asst. agrl. engr. U. Cal. at Davis, 1929-37, asso. prof., 1937-45, asso. agrl. engr., 1937-43, agrl. engr., 1943—, prof. agrl. engring., 1945—, chmn. div., 1947-61, asst. dean engring., 1952-61, asso. dean, 1961-62, dean, 1962-69, dean emeritus, 1969—. Cons. Brit. Ministry Agr., 1945, U.S. Army, Japan, 1948; asso. dir. mechanization center FAO of UN, Chile, 1958, cons. Peru, 1961, 62, 63-64, 65, 66, 69; cons. Dept. State in Laos, 1966, Kasetsart U., Thailand Thailand, 1966; cons. to minister agr., Brazil, 1969; hom. prof. Agrarian U. Peru, 1964; mem. agr. bd. Nat. Acad. Sci.-NRC 1957-62, mem. at large NRC. Recipient McCormick Gold Medal for outstanding achievement agrl. engring., Distinguished Service a award Am. Soc. Sugar Beet Technologists, 1960, Kan. State U., 1960, U. Mo., 1962. Mem. Am. Soc. Agrl. Engrs. (past pres.), Nat. Acad. Engring., Am. Soc. Engring. Edn. (Vincent Bendix gold medal 1962), Cal. Acad. Sci., Am. Soc. Sugar Beet Technologists, Sigma Xi, Phi Mu Alpha, Gamma Sigma Delta, Sigma Tau. Republican. Methodist. Clubs: Commonwealth, Faculty, Rotary (past pres. Davis). Co-author: Tractors and Their Power Units; Principles of Farm Machinery. Contbr. articles to profl. jours. Patentee in field. Home: 623 Miller Dr Davis CA 95616

BAINS, LEE EDMUNDSON, lawyer; b. Birmingham, Ala., June 18, 1912; s. Herman Lipsey and Myrtle (Edmundson) B.; student Birmingham So. Coll., 1930-31; B.S., U. Ala., 1934, J.D., 1936; m. Ruel Eneida Burton, Jan. 1, 1938; children-Sandra Anita (Mrs. Henry Barnard Hardegree), Myrtle Lee (Mrs. Dale Edward Trammell), Lee Edmundson. Admitted to Ala. bar, 1936, also U.S. Supreme Ct.; practiced in Bessemer, 1936—; instr. Birmingham Sch. Law, 1937-41; faculty Nat. War Coll., 1960; atty. for Ala. Power Co., S.Central Bell Telephone Co., Phillips Petroleum Co., First Nat. Bank of Birmingham. Pres. Bessemer Bd. Edn., 1955-58, Bessemer YMCA, 1961, Adv. Bd. Family Ct. Jefferson County, 1966—. Alternate del.Democratic Nat. Conv., 1941. Served to rear adm. USNR, 1941-46; ETO. PTO. Mem. Ala., Birmingham bar assns., Res. Officers Assn., Naval Res. Assn., Soc. Colonial Wars, S.A.R. (pres. Ala.), Phi Gamma Delta, Beta Gamma Sigma. Kiwanian. Club: Downtown (Birmingham). Home: 621 Melody Lane Bessemer AL 35020 Office: 1813 3d Av Bessemer AL 35020

BAIONE, LUKE, banker; b. N.Y.C., Aug. 23, 1921; s. Dominick and Mary (Marotta) B.; B.B.A., Coll. City N.Y., 1942; m. Juliet F. Bullard, Aug. 26, 1944; children—Mary, Dominick. With Brevoort Savings Bank (name changed to Metropolitan Savs. Bank after merger with Metropolitan in 1970), Bklyn., 1946—, pres., 1969—, dir., 1967—; di. Institutional Investors Mutual Fund. Served with USAAF, 1942-46. Decorated Bronze Star medal. Clubs: Richmond County Country Club, Brooklyn Club. Home: 4 Dalemere Rd Staten Island NY 10304 Office: 141 Livingston St Brooklyn NY 11202

BAIR, ALLAN EDWARD, ins. co. exec.; b. Bethlehem, Pa., Sept. 20, 1920; s. Eli F. and Emma (Billman) B.; grad. Girard College, 1938; student U. Cal. at Los Angeles, 1946-48; m. Marian McClure, Sept. 6, 1941; children—Kenda Mae (Mrs. Albert Logue), Lois Ann, Allan Edward. Underwriter, Am. Casualty Co., Phila., 1938-40; accountant Johnson and Higgins, Phila., 1940-42, Joseph Froggatt & Co., Inc., Los Angeles, 1948-61, Royal Ins. Co., Los Angeles, 1945-48; with Pacific Indemnity Co., Los Angeles, 1961—, comptroller, 1961—, sr. v.p., 1968—; v.p., comptroller Northwestern Pacific Indemnity Co.; v.p., comptroller, dir. Tex. Pacific Indemnity Co. Active Boy Scouts Am., Boys Clubs Am. Served with AUS, 1942-45. Mem. Ins. Accounting and Statis. Assn., Am. Legion. Baptist. Mason. Home: 1111 Chavez St Burbank CA 91506 Office: 3200 Wilshire Blvd Los Angeles CA 90005

BAIR, EDWARD JAY, educator; b. Ft. Collins, Colo., June 30, 1922; s. Jay Albert and Edith Hectos (Pegg) B.; B.S., Colo. State U., 1943; Ph.D. Brown U., 1949; m. Dorothy Helen Bimson, June 29, 1958; Chemist, Tenn. Eastman Corp., Oak Ridge, 1953-56; research asso. U. Wash., 1949-54; mem. faculty Ind. U., 1954—, prof. chemistry, 1965—. Mem. Am. Chem. Soc., Am. Phys. Soc., Faraday Soc., Am. Inst. Chemists. Home: 117 N Hillsdale Bloomington IN 47401

BAIR, HOWARD VERNON, psychiatrist, hosp. adminstr.; b. Robinson, Ill., May 2, 1918; s. Guy and Eva (Woods) B.; A.B., U. Kan., 1940, B.S. in medicine, 1940, M.D., 1943; m. Violet M. Grossardt, Dec. 31, 1941; children—Jeff, Jane, Julie, Jack. Intern St. Francis Hosp., Wichita, Kan., 1943-44; resident Cal. Dept. Mental Hygiene, Langley Porter Hosp., San Francisco, 1947-49; pvt. practice, Vallejo, Cal., 1946-47; sr. physician, surgeon Vets. Home, Cal., 1947; sr. psychiatrist Mendocino State Hosp., 1948-51; supt., med. dir. Parsons (Kan.) State Hosp. and Tng. Center, 1951—; lectr. psychiatry U. Kan. Sch. Med., 1954—. Cons. Labette County Med.; aviation med. examiner FAA, 1960—; cntr., Regional VA, Wichita. Bd. dirs. Joint Commn. Mental Health of Children, Joint Commn. for Accreditation Residential and Community Facilities for Mentally Retarded, 1969—. Served to maj. AUS, 1943-46. Fellow Am. Psychiat. Assn. (past pres. Kan., mem. com. on mental retardation 1969—, com. on diagnoses and nomenclature 1969—), Am. Assn. Mental Deficiency (past regional chmn., council 1969—), Am. Geriatric Soc.; mem. A.M.A., Western Inst. Epilepsy, Group Advancement Psychiatry, Western Soc. Electroencephalography. Home: Box 738 Parsons State Hosp and Tng Center Parsons KS 67357 Office: Parsons State Hosp and Tng Center Parsons KS 67357

BAIR, SCOTT SLAYBAUGH, real estate investment exec.; b. Westminster, Md., Feb. 27, 1901; s. Samuel Paul and Elizabeth (Slaybaugh) B.; student pub. schs.; m. Anita Bankard, June 8, 1930; children—Scott Slaybaugh, Harvey Bankard, Henry Neale, Emerson Francis, Elizabeth Anne, Glenn Spangler. Machinist apprentice, then bricklayer; sales work Eastern states, 1923-32; founder Nat. Advt. Co., 1932, propr., 1932-47, now operating subsidiary Minn. Mining & Mfg. Co.; devel. constrn. comml. and indsl. bldgs. for leasing on long-term basis, 1947-; chmn. Lincoln Mfg. Co.; pres. Devel. Co. Am.-Tenn., Inc., Devel. Co. Am.-Pa., Inc., Devel. Co. Am.-W.Va., Inc., Salisbury Shopping Center, Inc., Waynesboro Shopping Center, Inc., Westminster Shopping Center, Inc., Devel. Co. of Am., Inc.; v.p. Milford Shopping Center, Inc.; dir. Balt. Gas & Electric Co., Mut. Life Ins. Co. of Carroll County, Investors Loan Corp., Carroll County Bank & Trust Co., Westminster Hardware Co., Westminster Cemetery Co. Bd. dirs. Md. State Fair and Agrl. Soc. Mem. Carroll County Econ. Devel. Commn. Area dir. Salvation Army. Chmn. bd. Carroll County Gen. Hosp.; trustee Raymond I. Richardson Found., Hannah More Acad., Western Md. Coll. Named Ky. Col. Mem. Nat. Assn. Christians and Jews. Lutheran. Lion (life). Home: Westminster MD 21157

BAIR, WILLIAM J., radiation biologist; b. Jackson, Mich., July 14, 1924; s. William J. and Mona (Gamble) B.; B.A. in chemistry, Ohio Wesleyan U., 1949; Ph.D. in Radiation Biology, U. Rochester, 1954; m. Barbara Sites, Feb. 16, 1952; children—William J., Michael Braden, Andrew Emil. NRC-AEC fellow U. Rochester, 1949-50, research asso. radiation biology, 1950-54; biol. scientist Hanford Labs. of Gen. Electric Co., Richland, Wash., 1954-56, mgr. inhalation toxicology sect., biology dept., 1956-68; mgr. biology dept. Pacific Northwest Lab., Battelle Meml. Inst., Richland, Wash., 1968—; lectr. radiation biology Center Grad. Study, Richland, 1955—; cons. on reactor safeguards AEC, 1971—. Mem. subcom. inhalation hazards, com. pathologic effects atomic radiation Nat. Acad. Sci., 1957-64; chmn. internat. commn. on radiation protection task force on biol. effects of inhaled particles, 1970—; chmn. Hanford Symposium Inhaled Radioactive Particles and Gases, 1964; mem. Nat. Council Radiation Protection; U.S. participant and rep. numerous internat. confs. Recipient E.O. Lawrence Meml. award, 1970. Mem. Radiation Research Soc., Health Physics Soc. (bd. dirs. 1970-73), N.Y. Acad. Sci., Soc. Exptl. Biology and Medicine (vice chmn. N.W. sect. 1967-70), A.A.A.S., Reticuloendothelial Soc., Sigma Xi. Author numerous articles, reports. Home: 102 Somerset St Richland WA 99352 Office: Biology Dept Battelle PO Box 999 Richland WA 99352

BAIRD, ARCHIBALD W., ins. co. exec.; b. Schenectady, Aug. 5, 1912; A.B., Union Coll., 1933; LL.B., U. Conn., 1947. Admitted to Conn. bar, 1947; with Travelers Life Ins. Co., Hartford, Conn. 1937—, asst. sec., 1957-62, sec., 1962-63, 2d v.p. in charge personnel dept., 1963-66, v.p., 1966-68, sr. v.p. adminstrn., 1968—. Home: 19 Scarsdale Rd West Hartford CT Office: 1 Tower Sq Hartford CT 06115

BAIRD, CHARLES FITZ, bus. exec. b. Southampton, N.Y., Sept. 4, 1922; s. George White and Julia (Fitz) B.; A.B., Middlebury (Vt.) Coll., 1944; grad. Advanced Mgmt. Program, Harvard, 1960; m. Norma Adele White, Sept. 13, 1947; children—Susan Fitz, Stephen White, Charles Fitz, Nancy Williams. With Standard Oil Co. (N.J.) 1948-65, dep. European financial rep., London, 1955-58, asst. treas., 1958-62; dir. Esso Standard SA Francaise, 1962-65; asst. sec. of navy for financial mgmt., 1965-67, undersec. of navy for financial mgmt., 1967-69; v.p. finance Internat. Nickel Co. of Can. Ltd., 1969—. Mem. President's Commn. Marine Sci., Engring. and Resources, 1967-69. Trustee Bucknell U., 1969—; bd. advisers Naval War Coll., 1970—. Served as capt. USMCR, 1943- 46, 51-52. Mem. Council Fgn. Relations, Atlantic Council, Chi Psi. Conglist. (trustee 1960-62). Clubs: Chevy Chase (Md.); Metropolitan (Washington); India House

(N.Y.C.); Short Hills (N.J.); Links; Wequetonsing (Mich.) Golf. Home: 109 Forest Dr Short Hills NJ 07078 Office: 1 New York Plaza New York City NY 10005

BAIRD, DWIGHT CALVIN, coll. pres.; b. LaFollette, Tenn., Dec. 30, 1905; s. Ulysses S. and Melissa Belle (Mullins) B.; B.S., Colo. State U., 1928; M.S., U. Colo., 1936, Ed.D., 1958; m. Zoe Behrend, Aug. 1, 1929; children—Lowell David, Kenneth Lane, Marla Joan. High sch. tchr., prin., supt., Western and Northeastern Colo., 1928-39; asst. dir. student personnel Colo. State U., 1939-40; with Nat. Youth Adminstrn., 1940-42; state guidance dir., Colo., 1942-46; dir. placements U. Denver, 1946; pres. Trinidad (Colo.) State Jr. Coll., 1946-58, Clark Jr. Coll., Vancouver, Wash., 1958—. Local crusade com. Am. Cancer Soc. Mem. Am. Assn. Jr. Colls. (past pres.), Washington Assn. Jr. Colls. (pres.), N.W. Assn. Secondary and Higher Schs. (higher commn.), Vancouver C. of C. (pres. 1961), Phi Delta Kappa, Kappa Delta Pi, Methodist. Rotarian, Mason, Elk. Kiwanian (past lt. gov.). Home: 1301 W 43d St Vancouver WA 98660

BAIRD, EDWARD ROUZIE, ret. lawyer; b. Norfolk, Va., Nov. 20, 1909; s. Edward R. and Katherine (Michaux) B.; grad. Woodbery Forest Sch., Orange, Va.; LL.B., U. Va., 1933; m. Eleanor Gray Perry, Apr. 23, 1934, (div. 1958); children—Edward Rouzie, Eleanor Gray; m. 2d, Mary L. Riggan, Feb. 23, 1963. Admitted to Va. bar, 1933, practiced in Norfolk. Sec.-treas., mem. bd., gen. counsel Atlantic & Danville Ry. Former adviser to bd. Norfolk Seaman's Aid Soc. Past v.p., bd. mem. Tidewater Legal Aid Soc.; bd. dirs. Norfolk Zool. and Aquarium Soc.; pres. bd. trustees Norfolk Acad., Norfolk Soc. for Prevention Cruelty to Animals; trustee Ballantine Home. Served as lt. comdr. USNR, 1942-46. Mem. Am. Bar Assn. (mem. maritime law com., mem. ho. of dels.), Va. State (past pres., mem. council, chmn. com. legal ethics), Va., Norfolk, Portsmouth (pres. 1954) Cin. Soc., Va. Hist. Soc., Ducks Unltd. (past chmn. Norfolk chpt). Presbyn. Clubs: Virginia (pres. 1960), Norfolk Yacht and Country. Home: 6155 Westwood Terrace Norfolk VA 23508

BAIRD, EUGENE, consultant; b. Akron, O., Mar. 19, 1925; s. James Loyd and Lissie B. (Campbell) B.; B.S. in Bacteriology and Pub. Health, Wash. State U., 1950; M.S. in Econs. and Social Devel., U. Pitts., 1961; M.P.H. in Population Planning, U. Mich., 1970; m. Viola Dariene Lewis, Aug. 17, 1947 (div. 1965); children—Cynthia, Cheri; m. 2d, J. Kristin Peterson, Dec. 30, 1968. Associated with Seattle Public Health Departments, 1950-51; engaged in feasibility survey public health engineering program, Iran, 1952-54, implemented program, 1954-57, supervisor pilot public health in rural Chile, Joint Chilean-United States Technical Program, 1957-58; chief sanitary engring. adviser ICA, Chilean Nat. Health Service, 1958-60; acting chief ICA health program in Chile, 1960-61; with Peace Corps, 1961-68, dir. in Ecuador, 1964-66, Lima, Peru, 1966-68; Ford Found. grantee Govtl. Affairs Inst., Washington, 1969—. Served with USNR, 1942-46. Home: 2418 Hametown Rd Barberton OH 44203 Office: Governmental Affairs Institute 1776 Massachusetts Av NW Washington DC 20036

BAIRD, GEORGE HENRY, ednl. adminstr.; b. Rushville, Ill., Sept. 24, 1922; s. George H. and Rose (Cook) B.; B.E., Western Ill. U., 1943; M.A., U. Wyo., 1949; Ed.D., Columbia, 1954; m. Karole V. Litchfield, May 14, 1944; 1 dau., Cheryl Sue. Tchr., coach, Alexis, Ill., 1946-47, Dwight, Ill., 1947-48; asst. supt. elementary schs., Worland, Wyo., 1948-53; dir. research spl. services and guidance Shaker Heights, O., 1954-59; exec. dir. Ednl. Research Council of Am., Cleve., 1959-66, pres., exec. dir., 1966—; chmn. bd. Ramsey-Baird Enterprises. Ednl. cons. Jr. Achievement of Greater Cleve.; mem. regional interviewing com. U.S. Internat. Ednl. Exchange Program. Trustee Ednl. TV Assn. Met. Cleve.; mem. regional adv. council Western Ill. U. Served with Inf., AUS, 1944-46. Mem. Greater Cleve. Growth Assn. (mem. edn. com.), Am. Assn. Sch. Adminstrs., Phi Delta Kappa, Kappa Delta Pi. Mason (32, Shriner). Clubs: Union Rotary (Cleve.). Home: 3161 Huntington Rd Shaker Heights OH 44120 Office: Rockefeller Bldg Cleveland OH 44113

BAIRD, HAROLD LEONARD, ins. exec.; b. Stevensville, Mont., Jan. 10, 1901; s. Thomas and Annie (Fowler) B.; B.A., U. Mont., 1923; M.B.A., Harvard, 1925; m. Helen Newman, Oct. 23, 1926; childrenJames (dec.), William, Ritchie. Accountant, lumber firms; with United Pacific Ins. Co., Tacoma, 1930-, successively treas., exec. v.p., 1930-54, pres., 1954-62, chmn. bd., 1962-, dir. 1954-; dir. Puget Sound Nat. Bank. Bd. dirs. Tacoma Gen. Hosp. Republican. Kiwanian. Home: 7112 Interlaaken Dr S W Tacoma WA 98499 Office: 728 St Helens Av Tacoma WA 98402

BAIRD, J. N., savs. and loan exec. Exec. v.p., mgr. Honolulu Savs. and Loan and Co. Ltd. Office: PO Box 539 182 Merchant St Honolulu HI 96809*

BAIRD, JAMES ABINGTON, lawyer; b. Kirksville, Mo., Jan. 28, 1926; s. James Abington and Dorothy (LaGest) B.; B.S., U. Mich., 1949; J.D., U. Toledo, 1957; m. Georgia Jane Suliburk, Mar. 29, 1948; children—James Abington III, Mary Jacqueline. Sales rep. Fruehauf Trailer Co., Chgo., 1949-50; pres. Kaiser-Frazer dealership, Care, Mich., 1950-51; sales rep. Warren-Teed Products Co., Toledo, 1951-52, Dictaphone Corp., Toledo, 1952-53; claims adjuster Nationwide Ins. Co., Toledo, 1953-57; admitted to Ohio bar, 1957, since practiced in Toledo; judge Sylvania (O.) Municipal Ct., 1970- -. Chmn. Sch. Levy campaigns Sylvania Pub. Sch. System, 1968-69, candidate Sch. Bd., 1969. Served with USNR, 1944-46. Mem. Ohio, Toledo Bar assns., Am. Trial Lawyers Assn., U. Mich., U. Toledo alumni assns., Phi Delta Theta. Mason. Home: 4606 Wyndwood Dr Toledo OH 43623 Office: United Savs Bldg Toledo OH 43604

BAIRD, JAMES CATCHINGS, Jr., ch. ofcl., former fgn. service officer; b. Baird, Miss., Sept. 12, 1904; s. James Catchings and Mary Elizabeth (Long) B.; B.S., Va. Mil. Inst., 1924, student Harvard Law Sch., 1926- 28; LL.D., Temple U., 1940; m. Annie L. Sterrett, Jan. 6, 1931 (div. 1937); 1 dau., Anne (Mrs. Ben J. Chatoney, Jr.); m. 2d, Mary L. Hazel, Mar. 26, 1942; children—James Catchings III, Henry S. With Am. Tel. & Tel. Co., 1924, Chesapeake & Potomac Telephone Co. W. Va., 1924-26; store mgr. family plantation, Baird, 1928-30; cons. engr. Chase & Waring, N.Y.C., 1931-32; comml. engr. Pa. Power & Light Co., 1932-40; mgr., farmer, Baird, 1941-43, 44-54; sec.-treas., dir. Baird Gin Co., 1946-54, Baird Purchasing Assn., 1946-54; dep. dir. FOA mission to Karachi, Pakistan, 1954-56; dir. ICA mission to Djakarta, Indonesia, 1956-59, mission to Colombo, Ceylon, 1960-62; cons. MR ARD, AID, Dept. State, Washington, 1962-63; sec. Laymen relations Commn. on Ecumenical Mission and Relations, United Presbyn. Ch. U.S.A., 1963-70; sec. laymen relations Div. Overseas Ministries, Nat. Council Chs., N.Y.C., 1970—. Spl. farm labor adv. com. to sec. labor, 1948-54, mem. Mexican nat. subcom., 1948- 54; mem. S.E. Regional Labor Mgmt. Com., Atlanta, 1951-54, chmn. adv. com. Miss. Employment Security Commn., 1948-54. Mem. exec. and missions coms. Episcopal Diocese Miss., 1950-54; pres. Episcopal Laymen Miss., 1953-54. Recipient Distinguished Service award AUS, 1943-44, Distinguished Service award FOA, 1955. Home: 60 Riverside Dr New York City NY 10024 Office: Div Overseas Ministries Nat Council of Churches 475 Riverside Dr New York City NY 10027

BAIRD, JAMES RICHARD, educator; b. Jellico, Tenn., Nov. 2, 1910; s. Charles O'Connor and Nelle (Jones) B.; B.A., U. Tenn., 1931, M.A., 1935; M.A., Columbia, 1945; M.A., Yale, 1942, Ph.D., 1947, Asso. prof. English, U. Hawaii, 1949-50; faculty Conn. Coll., New London, 1950—, prof. English, 1962—, Brigida Pacchiani Ardenghi prof. English, 1967—. Vis. prof. Grad. Summer Sch. Tchrs., Wesleyan U., Middletown, Conn., 1963, 66, 67, 69, 71; vis. prof. Am. lit. Brown U., 1971—; chmn. Sch. and Coll. Conf. English, 1963-64; lectr. Am. lit. U.S. Ednl. Commn., Japan, 1970. Served to lt. USNR, 1943-46. Postwar fellow humanities Rockefeller Found., U. Paris, 1948-49; Ford fellow Yale, 1956-57. Mem. Modern Lang. Assn., Am. Assn. U. Profs., Am. Studies Assn., Pi Kappa Alpha, Phi Kappa Phi. Author: Ishmael: A Study of the Symbolic Mode in Primitivism, 2d edit., 1960; The Dome and The Rock: Structure in the Poetry of Wallace Stevens, 1968, also articles, revs. Asso. editor: American Literary Masters, 1965. Home: 147 Oswegatchie Rd Waterford CT 06385 Office: Connecticut Coll New London CT 06320

BAIRD, JOHN JULIUS, organist, composer; b. Washington, Pa., June 16, 1907; s. Joseph Clarke and Annie Kuhn (Lemoyne) B., B.S., Washington and Jefferson Coll., 1930, Mus. D., 1942; M.A., Carnegie Inst. Tech., 1938; m. Louise Leslie, Dec. 27, 1928; children—John Julius, Frederic Leslie; m. 2d, Barbara Ann Stouffer, July 30, 1954; children—Barbara, Katharine. Music director Bach Choir, Pittsburgh, 1934-54; organist, choirmaster, Calvary Episcopal Ch., Pitts., 1945-54; music dir. Pitts. Civic String Orchestra, 1946-54; dir. Greensburg (Pa.) Choral soc., 1946-49; dir. Pitts. Chamber Orchestra, 1949-51, Allegheny County Symphony Orch., 1949-54; instr. Duquesne U., 1948-52; tchr. organ and composition, Fillion Studios, Pitts., 1946-54; music dir., organist Episcopal Chs., Colorado Springs, Colo., 1954—; artistic and mus. dir. Colorado Springs Opera Assn., 1959—; coll. organist, instr. Colo. Coll., 1957—. Pres. Stannard Publishers, Inc., 1962—. Chmn. opera subcom. Colo. Council on Arts and Humanities, Mem. Am. Guild Organists, Am. Music Club, Colorado Springs Music Club, Beta Theta Pi. Composer, editor, choral and organ compositions. Home: 1623 N Cascade Av Colorado Springs CO 80907 Office: Grace Ch and St Stephens 631 N Tejon St Colorado Springs CO 80902

BAIRD, JOHN PIERSON, food co. exec., lawyer; b. St. Louis, Nov. 1, 1925; s. John Pierson and Janet (Harrison) B., student U. Ill., 1946-49; LL.B., St. Louis U., 1952; m. Virginia Marie Traeger, July 24, 1948; children—John Pierson, William Henry. Admitted to Mo. bar, 1952; asso. firm Fordyce, Mayne, Hartman, Renard & Stribling, St. Louis, 1952-57, partner firm 1956-57; dir. labor relations and prodn. personnel Ralston Purina Co., 1957-61, sec., gen. counsel 1961—, v.p., 1967—; dir. Bank of St. Louis. Bd. dirs. Asso. Industries of Mo.; mem. adv. board Southwestern Legal Found. Internat. and Comparative Law Center, 1967—. Served with inf., AUS, 1943-46; ETO. Mem. Am., Inter-Am., Mo., St. Louis bar assns., Am. Soc. Corporate Secs., Sigma Phi Epsilon, Phi Delta Phi. Home: 11 Bellerive Country Club Grounds St Louis MO 63141 Office: 835 S 8th St St Louis MO 63102

BAIRD, JOSEPH ARTHUR, educator; b. Boise, Ida., June 17, 1922; s. Jesse H. and Susanna (Bragstad) B.; B.A., Occidental Coll., 1943; B.D., San Francisco Theol. Sem., 1949; Ph.D., U. Edinburgh, 1953; student U. Basel (Switzerland), 1951, U. Marburg (Germany), 1962; m. Mary Harriet Chapman, June 10, 1947; children—Andrew Arthur, Paul Chapman. Ordained to ministry Presbyn. Ch., 1949; asst. pastor, San Francisco, 1946-47; Western field rep. Intersem. Movement, 1947-48; music tchr. Marin County (Cal.) scis., 1948-49; pastor, White Sulphur Springs, Mont., 1948-49; asst. pastor, Edinburgh, 1949-51; pastor, Burney, Cal., 1952-54; prof. religion Coll. Wooster (O.), 1954—, chmn. dept., 1967—; adj. prof. San Francisco Theol. Sem., 1964—. Rep. theol. edn. Am. Acad. Religion, 1956-66; chmn. Lilly Endowment study presem. edn., 1958-64, mem. internat. com. computer Bib. studies, 1968—; chmn. Pella Archaeol. Bd., 1965—; mem. dept. campus Christian life Synod Ohio, 1966—. Mem. Wooster Symphony Bd., 1960-64. Served to lt. (j.g.) USNR, 1943-46. Mem. Am. Acad. Religion, Soc. Bib. Lit., Studiorum Novi Testamenti Societas, Phi Beta Kappa. Rotarian (chmn. com. internat. service Wooster 196869). Author: Justice of God in the Teachings of Jesus, 1963; Audience Criticism and the Historical Jesus, 1969; also articles. Pioneer use computers for content research Greek N.T., devel. audience criticism for N.T. research. Home: 1435 Gasche St Wooster, OH 44691.

BAIRD, MICHAEL DAVID, educator; b. Portland, Ore., Apr. 19, 1931; s. David William and Mary (Alexander) B.; B.S., U. Ore., 1954, M.S., 1957, M.D., 1957; m. Gwendolyn Jane Spencer, June 22, 1954; children—Gwendolyn Anne, Jeffrey Hugh, Andrew Michael. Intern U. Ore. Med. Sch. Hosps. and Clinics, 1957-58, resident, 1958-61; instr. medicine U. Ore. Med. Sch., 1961-63, asst. prof., dir. out-patients psychiatry, 1963-65, asst. prof. medicine, asst. med. dir., 1965-68, asso. prof. medicine, asst. med. dir., 1968, prof. medicine, adminstr., med. dir. hosps. and clinics, 1968—; chmn. bd. dirs. Suicide Prevention Center Portland, 1968-69. Mem. joint com. Portland Council of Hosps. and Multnomah County Med. Soc.; mem. Tri-Community Health Council, 1968—. Mem. Am., Ore. med. assns., Multonomah County Med. Soc., A.C.P., Ore. Heart Assn. (mem. stroke and rehabilitation com. 1961-63), Nu Sigma Nu. Research synthesis of ascorbic acid in rats; double blind study of anticoagulent treatment of stroke victims; study of dietetic therapies in stroke victims. Office: U Ore Med Sch 3181 SW Sam Jackson Park Rd Portland OR 97201

BAIRD, ROGER ALLEN, corp. exec.; b. Canton, Ill., Mar. 14, 1914; s. Frederick R. and Ruth E. (Miller) B.; A.B., U. Chgo., 1936. J.D., 1938; m. Evelyn F. Rittenhouse, July 29, 1939; children—Jane E., Ann R. Admitted to Ill. bar, 1939, Wis. bar, 1956; asso. later partner Kirkland, Ellis, Hodson, Chaffetz & Masters, and predecessors, Chgo., 1939-56; asst. sec., gen. atty. Kimberly Clark Corp., Neenah, Wis., 1956-59, sec., 1959- -; also sec. U.S. and Canadian subsidiaries. Mem. Wis. Govt. Com. of 25, 1963-65. Trustee Appleton Meml. Hosp., 1961—, pres., 1966-68. Served with USNR, 1943-46. Mem. Am., Wis., Chgo. bar assns., Phi Gamma Delta, Presbyn. Clubs: Law, Legal (Chgo.); North Shore Golf (Menasha); Neenah Racquet, Neenah Yacht; Crystal Downs Country (Frankfort, Mich.). Home: Route 1 Menasha, WI 54952. Office: care Kimberly Clark Corp N Lake St Neenah WI 54956

BAIRD, RUSSELL MILLER, lawyer; b. Chgo., Aug. 4, 1916; s. Frederick Rogers and Ruth (Miller) B.; A.B., U. Chgo., 1938; LL.B., Harvard, 1941; m. Martha Steere, Mar. 28, 1942; childrenLindsay Ruth, Scott Rogers, Frederick Rogers II. Admitted to Ill. bar, 1941, since practiced in Chgo.; partner firm Leibman, Williams, Bennett, Baird & Minow, and predecessor, 1941—. Dir., Dir., sec. Chgo. Crime Commn., 1960—; mem. citizens bd. U. Chgo., 1958—; mem. vis. com. Div. Sch., U. Chgo., 1963—; pres. Mental Health Assn. Greater Chgo., 1962-64. Served to lt. USNR, 1942-46. Fellow Am. Bar Found. mem. Am. (chmn. standing com. publs., antitrust sect., patent, trademark and copyright sect.), Ill., Chgo. (author Christmas Spirits Gridiron shows 1954-64) bar assns., Legal Club Chgo. (pres. 1962-63), Law Club Chgo., Wine and Food Soc. Chgo. Clubs: University, Racquet, Executives, International House (gov.) (Chgo.); Nat. Lawyers (Washington); River Forest (Ill.) Tennis; Oak Park (Ill.) Country; Crystal Downs Country (Frankfort, Mich.). Home: 727 Keystone Av River Forest IL 60305 Office: 1 First Nat Plaza Chicago IL 60670

BAIRD, THEODORE coll. prof.; b. Warren, O., Feb. 28, 1901; s. Silas J. and Emma (Lane) B.; A.B., Hobart Coll., 1921; A.M., Harvard, 1922, Ph.D., 1929; m. Frances Haliburton Titchener, Aug. 24, 1928. Instr. English, Adelbert Coll., Western Res. U., 1922- 23, Union Coll., 1923-25; asst. in English, Harvard, 1926-27, Dexter traveling scholar, 1927; instr. English, Amherst (Mass.) Coll., 1927-29, asst. prof., 1929-32, asso. prof., 1932-39, Samuel Williston prof., 1939-70, emeritus, 1970—. Mem. Modern Lang. Assn. Am., Kappa Alpha. Editor: The First Years: Selections from Autobiography, 1931, rev. edit., 1935. Home: Shays St R D 1 Amherst MA 01002

BAIRD, VALLIANT CLINTON, physician; b. Gatesville, Tex., Sept. 28, 1904; s. Bythell Haines and Martha Viola (Rogers) B.; student So. Meth. U., 1921-22; B.S., Tulane, 1925, M.D., 1928; m. Mary Louise Burch, Aug. 3, 1938; children—Brenda Lea, Clinton, Mary Lou. Intern Mercy and Charity hosps., New Orleans, 1931; asso. prof. clin. medicine Baylor U., 1947—; med. dir. Humble Oil and Refining, 1946-70; prof. occupational medicine U. Tex., 1967—. Pres. Med. Research Found. of Texas, 1960-61. Diplomate Am. Bd. Preventive Medicine in Occupational Medicine. Fellow Am. Coll. Preventive Medicine; mem. Tex. Indsl. Med. Assn. (pres., 1956), A.M.A., (council indsl. health), Am. Assn. Indsl. Physicians Surgeons (counsellor S.W., 1946-50, dir., 1949-51), Harris County Med. Soc. (v.p., treas., 1948- 50), Houston Soc. Internal Medicine, Alpha Omega Alpha, Theta Kappa Psi. Episcopalian. Club: Houston Country. Contbr. articles to med. jours. Home: 506 506 Shadywood Houston TX 77027 Office: 6624 Fannin St Houston TX 77025

BAIRD, WALTER SCOTT, business exec.; b. Long Green, Md., Oct. 2, 1908; s. George William Curtis and Beulah (Dance) B.; A.B., St. John's Coll., 1930; Ph.D., Johns Hopkins, 1934; m. Mary Davis, Sept. 28, 1937; children—Brinna, Nancy, Douglas Scott, Davis. Instr. Harvard, 1934-35; physicist Watertown (Mass.) Arsenal, 1935-36; pres. Baird Assos., Inc., 1936-56, merged with Atomic Instrument Co., 1956, pres. merged corp. Baird Atomic, Inc., Cambridge, Mass., 1936-57, chmn., 1959-64, 67—, pres., 1964—; dir. Imtra Corp., Cambridge, W Inc., Washington, Burr-Brown Research Corp., Tucson. Vis. com. engring. Johns Hopkins; trustee St. John's College. Fellow Am. Acad. Arts and Scis.; mem. A.A.A.S., Am. Inst. Mining, Metall. and Petroleum Engrs., Optical Soc. Am., Am. Inst. Physics, Royal N.S. Yacht Squadron. Clubs: Cruising of Am., St. Botolph, Boston Yacht (Boston). Home: 14 Percy Rd Lexington MA 02173 Office: Baird Atomic Inc 125 Middlesex Turnpike Bedford MA 01730

BAIRD, WARNER GREEN, real estate exec.; b. Chgo., Mar. 26, 1885; s. Wyllys Warner and Olivia Pomeroy (Green) B.; M.E., Cornell U., 1908; m. Julia Dole, Jan. 14, 1913; childrenJohn Wyllys, Katharine (Mrs. Herbert Hansen), Warner Green, Olive (Mrs. Neil McKay). With Baird & Warner, Inc. (formerly Baird & Bradley), Chgo., 1911-, beginning as mgr. uptown office, successively treas., v.p., 1911-28, pres., 1928-64, chmn. bd., 1964-. Republican. Clubs: University, Commonwealth (Chgo.). Home: 926 Sunset Rd Geneva IL 60134 Office: 10 LaSalle St Chicago IL 60602

BAIRD, WILLIAM BRITTON (Bil), puppeteer; b. Grand Island, Neb., Aug. 15, 1904; s. William Hull and Louise (Hetzel) B.; A.B., U. Ia., 1926; m. Cora Burlar, Jan. 13, 1937 (dec. Dec. 1967); children—Peter Britton, Laura Jenne Baird; m. 2d, Patricia Courtleigh, June 1968. Began With Tony Sarg Marionettes, 1928-33; started Bil Baird's Marionettes at Chgo. World's Fair, 1934; appeared in vaudeville, nightclubs, Broadway shows including Ziegfeld Follies, 1943-44, Flahooley, 1951; produced Ali Baba and the Forty Thieves, 1956, Davy Jones' Locker, 1959, Man in the Moon, 1963, Chrysler Show Go Round, N.Y. World's Fair, 1964-65, Puppet sequence, Baker Street, 1965; produced govt. films, World War II; films Party Lines, 1946, Telezonia, 1949 for Am. Tel. & Tel.; produced TV series for CBS, Snarky Parker, 1950-51, Whistling Wizard, 1951-52, Bil Baird Show, 1953; appeared on Morning Show, 1954, Peter and the Wolf, 1958, Sorcerer's Apprentice, 1959, Winnie the Pooh, 1960, O'Halloran's Luck, 1961; film The Sound of Music, 1965; opened (with wife) Bil Baird Theater, N.Y.C., 1967; presented People Is, 1967, Winnie the Pooh, 1967-68, Wizard of Oz, 1968-69, Sultan of Tuffet, 1969-70, Ali Baba, 1970-71. Toured India, Nepal, Afghanistan for State Dept., 1962, Russia, 1963, India and Turkey, 1970. Bd. dirs. World Edn. Lt. O.R.C., 1926. Mem. Sigma Chi, Omicron Delta Kappa. Author: The Art of the Puppet, 1966. Address: 59 Barrow St New York City NY 10014

BAIRD, WILLIAM CAMERON, foundry exec.; b. Buffalo, Apr. 20, 1907; s. Frank B. and Flora (Cameron) B.; grad. Phillips Exeter Acad., 1925; B.A., Williams Coll., 1929; m. Marjorie B. Mitchell, July 19, 1930 (div. 1945); 1 dau., Barbara (Mrs. Joseph Jay Palladino). Treas., Buffalo Pipe & Foundry Corp., 1930-49, pres., 1949-67, chmn. bd., 1967—; pres., chief exec. officer Central Foundry Co., 1966-67; dir. Mfrs. & Traders Trust Co. Chmn., Peace Bridge Authority, 1958-60. Pres., Brent Manor, Inc., 1967- 70, Niagara Frontier Housing Devel. Corp., 1968-70, Boys' Clubs of Niagara Frontier, 1956-58, Boys' Clubs of Buffalo, 1962-63; chmn. council State U. Buffalo. Bd. Dirs. Buffalo chpt. A.R.C.; trustee Community Chest, Forest Lawn Cemetery; bd. dirs. Episcopal Ch. Home, Buffalo Fine Arts Acad., Millard Fillmore Hosp., Boys Clubs Am., Episcopal Ch. Found. Served to lt. comdr. USNR. Recipient Bishop's Cross, Diocese Western N.Y., 1963; Canisius Coll. Distinguished award, 1969; named Buffalo Evening News Man of Year, 1969. Mem. Soc. Alumni Williams Coll. (pres. 1955-56), C. of C. (past pres.), Delta Upsilon. Episcopalian (dep. gen. conv. 1937, 40, 49, 52, 61, 67, 69, 70, ch. warden). Clubs: Buffalo Yacht, Buffalo Canoe, Cherry Hill Country, Buffalo; Williams, Canadian (N.Y.C.). Home: Hotel Statler Hilton Buffalo NY 14202 Office: 91 Sawyer Av Tonawanda NY 14150

BAISLER, ALBERT WILFORD, edn. cons.; b. Youngstown, O., May 29, 1910; s. William Elmer and Mary Kathryn (Gault) B.; A.B., Muskingum Coll., 1935, LL.D., 1960; M.A., Ohio State U., 1941, Ph.D., 1950; m. Ruth Neeld, Aug. 31, 1937; children—Mary Alice, Patricia Ann, Linda Ruth. Asst. supt. Isaly Dairy Co., Akron, O., 1935; asst. prof. Muskingum Coll., 1936-43; instr. Ohio State U., 1946- 48; dean students State U. N.Y. at Cortland, 1948-57; pres. Jamestown (N.Y.) Community Coll., 1957-69; cons. Heald Hobson & Asso., 1969-70; edn. cons., 1970—; staff psychologist Mental Health Assn. Westchester County, 1971—. Dir. Jamestown Telephone Corp. Vocational cons. Dept. Health, Edn. and Welfare; cons. Middle States Assn. Colls. and Secondary Schs. Pres. Chautauqua County Heart Assn.; past chmn. Chautauqua County Red Cross, Chautauqua County Nat. Conf. Christians and Jews. Bd. dirs. YMCA, Jamestown Boys' Club. Served with AUS, 1945-46. Mem. N.E.A., Higher Edn. Assn., Am.. Psychol. Assn., Internat. Platform Assn. Clubs: Rotary (past pres.); University (past pres.). Home: 900 Palmer Rd Bronxville NY 10708

BAJ, ENRICO, artist; b. Milan, Italy, Oct. 31, 1924; s. Angelo and Maria Luisa (Rastelli) B.; degree in medicine, U. Geneva, 1943; degree in law U. Milan, 1948; student Acad. Fine Art, Milan, 1945-49; m. Roberta Cerini di Castegnate, July 15, 1965; children—Lucilla,

Angelo, Andrea, Pietro. One-man shows include N.Y.C., 1964, Paris, 1958, 60, 62, 65, 68, also Milan, Chgo. Arts Club, 1966, also museums Paris, Gand, Den Hag, Amsterdam, Stockholm, others. Bd. regents Patafisic's Coll., Paris. Illustrator for poets. Address: Via Privata Nino Bonnet 5 20154 Milan, Italy.

BAJPAI, KAYATYANI SHANKAR, diplomat of India; b. Jaipur, India, Mar. 30, 1928; s. Girja Shankar and M.D. (Misra) B.; B.A. (hons.) in History, Merton Coll., Oxford (Eng.) U., 1949; m. Meera Tewari, Apr. 30, 1955; children—Dharma Shankar, Javanti Shankar. Joined Indian Fgn. Service, 1952; consul gen. of India in San Francisco, 1967—. Office: 215 Market St San Francisco CA 94105

BAJUS, KENYON BROWNELL, pub. co. exec., b. Syracuse, N.Y., Nov. 8, 1928; s. Ernest and Edith (Rogers) B.; student Marion (Ind.) Coll., 1945; m. Roberta McCann, Nov. 9, 1946; childrenThomas, Judith, Stephen, Gary, Diane. With The Grolier Soc. Inc., N.Y.C., 1946-, exec. v.p., 1962-64, pres., 1964-, also dir.; chmn. bd. Met. Bank of Syracuse. Served with U.S. Navy, 1945- 46. Home: 4935 Bryn Mawr Pl Syracuse NY 13215 Office: 575 Lexington Av New York City NY 10022

BAKAL, CARL, author, pub. relations exec.; b. N.Y.C., Jan. 11, 1918; s. William and Esther (Tutelman) B.; B.S., City Coll. N.Y., 1939; postgrad. Columbia, 1949; m. Shirley Sesser, 1956; children—Stephanie, Emily, Amy, Wendy. Advt. mgr. Fotoshop, N.Y.C., 1939-41; editor Fotoshop Almanac, 1939-41; asso. editor, contbg. editor U.S. Camera, 1939-43; sales promotion mgr. Universal Camera Corp., 1941-43 editorial chief information control div. Mil. Govt., Germany, 1947-48; promotion writer N.Y. Mirror, 1948-50; asso. editor Coronet mag., N.Y.C., 1950-55; free-lance writer, photo-journalist, 1955-57, 58—; editor Real, See mags., 1957-58; pub. affairs cons. U.S. Dept. Commerce, 1961-62; sr. asso. Howard Chase Assos., N.Y.C., 1962-65; dir. mag. dept. Carl Byoir & Assos., 1966-68; account supr. Anna M. Rosenberg & Assos., 1968—. Guest lectr. photo-journalism U. Wis., 1953. Served to 1st lt. AUS, 1942-46, 51-52. Recipient 1st prize Popular Photograph $25,000 picture contest, 1956. Mem. Violioncello Soc., Soc. Mag. Writers (v.p. 1968). Club: Overseas Press (N.Y.C.). Author: Filter Manual, 1953; How To Shoot for Glamour, 1955; The Right To Bear Arms, 1966; No Right To Bear Arms, 1968. Contbr. articles and photographs to publs. including McCalls, Redbook, Life, Reader's Digest, Harper's, Saturday Rev., Esquire, Good Housekeeping; contbr. to Ency. Photography, 1942, Treasury of Tips for Writers, 1965. Photo-journalism columnist for Writers Digest. Home: 225 W 86th St New York City NY 10024 Office: 444 Madison Av New York City NY 10022

BAKALAR, DAVID, electronic components mfr.; b. Boston, Nov. 6, 1924; s. Joseph and Minnie (Lazar) B.; B.A. cum laude, Harvard, 1946, M.S., 1948; D. Metallurgy, Mass. Inst. Tech., 1951; m. June Gale Kaufman, May 1960; 1 son, Stephen David. Co-founder, 1952, since pres., dir., Transitron Electronic Corp., Wakefield, Mass.; co-owner Trancoa Chem. Co. Mem. Am. Soc. Metals. Inst. Radio Engrs., Am. Phys. Soc., Sigma Psi. Home: 330 Beacon St Boston MA 02116 Office: 168 Albion St Boston MA 02159

BAKALAR, LEO, electronic devices mfg. exec.; b. Boston, 1912; s. Joseph and Minnie (Lazar) B.; ed. high sch., Boston; m. Ann B. Lepie, 1939; children—John Stephen, Marjorie Jane. Various positions in industry, Boston, 1935-52; pres. Trancoa Chem. Corp., Reading, Mass., 1944—; founder with David Bakalar, Transitron Electronic Corp., Wakefield, Mass., chmn. bd. dirs., 1952—; pres. Maplewood Realty Co., 1955—. Mason. Home: 56 Galloupes Point Swampscott MA 01907 Office: 168 Albion St Wakefield MA 01880

BAKAN, DAVID, educator; b. N.Y.C., Apr. 23, 1921; s. Max and Rose (Rosenstrauch) B.; B.A., Bklyn. Coll., 1942; M.A., Ind. U., 1944; Ph.D., Ohio State U., 1948; m. Mildred Blynn, Dec. 24, 1942; children—Joseph, Deborah, Abigail, Jonathan, Daniel, Jacob. Psychologist, Ind. Dept. Pub. Welfare, 1942-43; dir. statis. dept. Coop. Test Service., U. Rochester, 1944, instr. and research asso., 1945-46; instr., then asst. prof. Ohio State U., 1946-49; asst. prof., then prof. U. Mo., 1949-61; vis. lectr. Harvard, 1956-58; prof. psychology U. Chgo., 1961—. Author: Sigmund Freud and the Jewish Mystical Tradition, 1958; The Duality of Human Existence; an essay on psychology and religion, 1966; On Method, 1967; Disease, Pain and Sacrifice, 1968. Office: Dept Psychology Univ Chgo Chicago IL 60637

BAKELESS, JOHN (Edwin) author, editor; b. Carlisle, Pa., Dec. 30, 1894; s. Oscar H. and Sara (Harvey) B.; State Normal Sch., Bloomsburg, Pa.; A.B., Williams Coll., 1918; A.M., Harvard, 1920, postgrad., 1919-26, Ph.D., 1936; m. Katherine Little, June 16, 1920. Lit. editor, Living Age, 1921-23, mng. editor 1923-25; lit. adviser to The Independent, 1925-26; mng. editor Forum, 1926-28; editor Living Age, 1928-29; lit. editor Lit. Digest, 1937-38. Lectr. journalism N.Y.U., 1927-29, instr., 1929-30, asst. prof., 1930-40, asso. prof., 1940-47, lectr. journalism, 1947-54, on grad. faculty, 1948-54; vis. instr. Harvard, summers, 1938, 39, U. Colo., summer 1962; Trumbull lectr. Yale, 1948, Adams lectr. U. Mich., 1960; Gray lectr. Yale, 1964; Sproul lectr. Dickinson, 1968; asst. comdt. 1031st O.R.C. Sch., New Haven, 1952-53. Guggenheim fellow, 1936-37, 46-47; Huntington Library fellow, 1968-69. Commd. 2d lt., inf., 1918, assigned as instr. Central Officers' Tng. Sch., Camp Lee; capt. Inf. Res., 1934; on active duty as capt., inf., 1940, maj., inf., 1941, maj., Gen. Staff Corps, 1942, lt. col., 1942; asst. mil. attache to Turkey, 1944; mem. Am. sect. Allied Control Commn. for Bulgaria, 1945, col., 1945. Fellow Company Mil. Historians; mem. P.E.N., Lepidopterists Soc., Res. Officers Assn., Conn. Entomol. Soc., Authors Guild, Phi Beta Kappa. Clubs: University, Harvard (N.Y.C.); Army and Navy (Washington); Graduates (New Haven). Author: The Economic Causes of Modern War, 1921; The Origin of the Next War, 1926; Magazine Making, 1931; Christopher Marlowe, The Man in His Time, 1937; Daniel Boone, Master of the Wilderness, 1939; The Tragicall History of Christopher Marlowe, 1942; Lewis and Clark, Partners in Discovery, 1947; Fighting Frontiersman, 1948; Eyes of Discovery, 1951; Background to Glory; Life of George Rogers Clark, 1957; Traitors, Turncoats and Heroes, 1959; The Adventures of Lewis and Clark, 1962; Spies of the Confederacy, 1970; (with Katherine Bakeless) They Saw America First, 1957, Spies of The American Revolution, 1962, Signers of the Declaration, 1969. Editor: Report of Round Tables and General Conferences of the Williamstown Institute of Politics, 1932; Journals of Lewis and Clark, 1964; Contbg. editor Current Literature, 1929-32; contbr. to Ency. Social Sciences, Dictionary American Biography. Dictionary Am. History, and to mags.; editorial bd. American Scholar (Phi Beta Kappa quar.). 1937-41. Home: Elbowroom Farm 179 Great Hill Rd Seymour CT 06483

BAKEMA, JACOB BEREND, educator, architect; b. Groningen, Germany, Mar. 8, 1914; s. Kiert and Tietsia (D'Jkhuis) B.; student Acad. Arch. Amsterdam, 1938-42, Tech. U. Delft, 1943; m. Silina Theodora Van Borssum Waalkes, Oct. 17, 1939; children—Brita Weber (Mrs. J. P. Weber), Eric, Nils. With archtl. offices Van Eesteren, 1937, Van Tgen, 1940; architect Municipal Housing Dept., Rotterdam, 1945-48; partner firm Van den Broek en Bakema, Rotterdam, Holland, 1948—; prof. archtl. design Tech. U. Delft, 1963—; prof. Townplanning acad. Hamburg, 1965—; vis. prof. Universities Am., Scotland, Poland, Norway, West-Germany, Italy, Yugoslavia, Spain, Can., Australia, Cameroun, Ghana, Bulgaria, France, Argentina. Decorated officer Order Orange-Nassau, 1958; officer Order of Crown (Belgium), 1958; Knight Order Nederlandsche Leeuw, 1971. Fellow A.I.A., Assn. Scottish Architects: mem. Zentral VereinigungArchitecten Osterreichs; Bund Deutscher Architekten. Home: 246 Westzeed'jk Rotterdam Holland Office: 12 B Posthoornstraat Rotterdam Holland

BAKER, A. B., neurologist; b. Mpls., Mar. 27, 1908; s. Solomon and Molly (Greenspan) B.; B.A., U. Minn., 1928, B.S., 1929, M.B., 1930, M.D., 1931, M.S., 1932, Ph.D., 1934; m. Rose Witzman, Aug. 6, 1933; children—Lowell Howard, Elaine Frances, Eleanor Jean, Judith Ann. Interne, Robert Packer Hosp., Sayre, Pa., 1930-31; clin. asst. in neuropsychiatry U. Minn., 1934-36, instr. in neuropsychiatry, 1936-37, asst. prof., 1937-40, asso. prof., 1940-47, prof. neurology, 1947—, dir. dept. neurology, 1946, head dept., 1968—; spl. cons. USPHS Neurol. Inst.; council Nat. Inst. Neurol. Diseases and Blindness. Diplomate Am. Bd. Psychiatry and Neurology. Fellow Am. Acad. Neurology (pres.); mem. A.M.A., Am. Neurol. Assn. (pres.), Epilepsy Found. Am. (pres.), Am. Assn. Neuropathologists, Am. Assn. Experimental Pathology, Minn. Soc. Neurology and Psychiatry, Minn. Pathol. Assn., Phi Beta Kappa, Alpha Omega Alpha, Sigma Xi. Editor: Clinical Neurology, 4 vols., 1962, 3d edit., 4 vols., 1971. Home: 2900 Douglas Dr Minneapolis MN 55422

BAKER, ALBERT A., business exec.; b. Erie, Pa., 1923; B.S. in Indsl. Engring., Pa. State U., 1948; married. With Zurn Industries, Inc., Erie, 1948—, group v.p. operations, 1966-69, exec. v.p., dir., 1969—; dir. Zurn Industries Can. Ltd. Home: 1316 Central Dr Erie PA 16505

BAKER, ALBERT ZACHARY, lawyer, former stock yards exec.; b. Whitesboro, Tex., Nov. 17, 1890; s. James Albert and Addie Isabella (Gilliland) B.; student U. Tenn., 1909-10; LL.B., Ohio No. U., 1924, John Marshall Law Sch., 1924; LL.D., Culver-Stockton Coll., 1956; L.H.D., California College Medicine, 1955; m. Grace D. Anderson, Feb. 21, 1914; children—Jane (Mrs. James J. Larson), Jean (Mrs. Hamilton W. Watt), Robert Gibson; m. 2d, Cornelia Anderson Thompson, Apr. 26, 1950; 1 stepson, Robert S. Thompson. With traffic dept. Morris & Co., Oklahoma City and Chgo., 1912-16; traffic mgr. Cleve. Provision Co., 1916-24; sec.-treas., commerce counsel Cleve. Union Stock Yards Co., 1924-25, pres., gen. mgr., 1925- 46, 63-67, chmn. bd., 1925-68; dir., dep. chmn. Fed. Res. Bank Cleve., 1942-50, Nat. City Bank of Cleve., 1925-40. Pres. emeritus Am. Stock Yards Assn. Trustee emeritus Baldwin-Wallace Coll., 1947—. Mem. Cleve. C. of C. (past dir.), Cleve. Bar Assn., Delta Theta Phi. Mason (Shriner, 33), Rotarian (past pres. Cleve.; pres. Internat. 1955-56). Home: Heritage Hill Farm Kinsman OH 44428 Office: 546 Washington NE Warren OH 44483

BAKER, ALTON WESLEY, educator; b. Chickasha, Okla., May 28, 1912; s. Charles Wesley and Frances Cornelia (Hennington) B.; B.B.A., U. Tex., 1936; A.M., George Washington U., 1947; Ph.D., Ohio State U., 1952; m. Mary Elizabeth Dill, June 4, 1938; children—Don Wesley, Viki Joan. Asso. prof. Ohio State U., 1947-54; prof., chmn. dept. mgmt. So. Meth. U., 1954—; div. head Fairchild Corp.; chmn. bd. Dill Mfg. Corp.; dir. research Ohio State U. Chmn. bd. regional postmaster selection U.S. Post Office Service, 1969—; cons. to Postmaster Gen. Chmn. bd. dirs. So. Meth. U. Retirement System, Inc. Mem. Acad. Mgmt., Soc. Advancement Mgmt., Indsl. Relations Research Assn., Nat. Vocational Guidance Assn., Am. Assn. Univ. Profs. Club: Rotary (Dallas). Author: Supervisor and His Job, 2d ed., 1971; Management: Small Manufacturing Plants, 1955. Home: 3809 Gillon Av Dallas TX 75205

BAKER, ARTHUR ALAN, geologist; b. New Britain, Conn., Oct. 31, 1897; s. Frank and Caroline (Goodbred) B.; Ph.B., Yale, 1919, Ph.D., 1931; m. Clara Edith Graves, Sept. 29, 1925; 1 dau. Carolyn (Mrs. Yelverton Cowherd, Jr.). With U.S. Geol. Survey, 1921—, geologic aide, adminstrv. geologist, 1953-56, asso. dir., 1956-69, spl. asst. to dir., 1969—. Dept. Interior mem. U.S. Bd. on Geog. Names, 1953—. Mem. Am. Assn. Petroleum Geologists, Geol. Soc. Am. (council 1952-55), Washington Geol. Soc. (pres. 1953), Washington Acad. Scis. (v.p. 1954). Utah Hist. Soc., Utah Geol. Assn. Club: Cosmos (Washington). Home: 5201 Westwood Dr Washington DC 20016 Office: U S Geol Survey Washington DC 20242

BAKER, ARTHUR LORENZ, machine tool mfr.; b. Toledo, Sept. 24, 1900; s. Arthur Earnest and Daisy (Lorenz) B.; Ph.B., Yale, 1921; m. Katharine Harrison, Apr. 26, 1926; childrenLucy (Mrs. R. J. Shutt), Joyce (Mrs. A. L. Patterson), Katharine (Mrs. R. Riordan). With Baker Bros., Inc., 1921-, successively draftsman, prodn. mgr., v.p., gen. mgr., pres., 1948-56, now chmn.; v.p. Woodlawn Cemetery. Bd. dirs. Toledo chpt. A.R.C.; life trustee Boys Club of Toledo. Clubs: Toledo, Toledo Country, Rotary. Home: 3912 Brookside Rd Toledo OH 43606 Office: 1000 Post St Toledo OH 43610

BAKER, BENJAMIN MAY, educator, physician; b. Norfolk, Va., Nov. 20, 1901; s. Benjamin May and Theodosia (Potts) B.; B.S., U. Va., 1922; M.A. with 1st class honours in Physiology (Rhodes scholar 1922-25), Oxford (Eng.) U., 1925; M.D., Johns Hopkins, 1927; m. Julia Scott Clayton, Feb. 20, 1939; childrenSusan Vaughan (Mrs. J. B. Powell), Julia May, Benjamin May III, William Clayton. Resident physician Johns Hopkins Hosp., 1930-31; prof. medicine Johns Hopkins Med. Sch. 1965-; vis. prof. medicine Guys Hosp., London, Eng., 1966; cons. medicine U.S. Army; spl. research ballistiocardiography, diet and coronary heart disease. Mem. exec. com., chief investigator Nat. Diet-Heart Study, 1961-. Dir. Anderson Clayton Co. Served to col., M.C., AUS, 1942-46; PTO. Decorated Legion of Merit; recipient research grants Nat. Heart Inst., 1948-62. Mem. A.M.A., Am. Heart Assn., Am. Clin. and Climatological Assn., Am. Soc. Clin. Investigation, Assn. Am. Physicians, Phi Beta Kappa, Delta Kappa Epsilon, Alpha Tau Omega. Home: Brightside Rd Baltimore, MD 21212.

BAKER, BENJAMIN OSWALD, Canadian diplomat; b. Portage LaPrairie, Man., Can., Jan. 10, 1917; s. Arthur B. and Emma (Chisem) B.; B.Sc., U. Man., 1940; m. Phyllis Ann Davidson, Nov. 2, 1963; children—Dennis B., Barry I., Jillian Elizabeth. Engr., Canadian Gen. Elctri., Peterborough, Ont., Can., 1940-46; supt. design, Armament Research and Devel. Establishment, Def. Research Bd., Valcartier, Que., 1945-59; dir. weapons and engring. research Def. Research Bd., Ottawa, 1959-66; dir. project formulation Canadian Forces Hdqrs., Ottawa, 1967-68; chief Canadian Def. Research Staff, Washington, 1968—. Mem. Engring. Inst. Can., Profl. Engrs. Ont., Delta Upsilon. Home: 5421 Albia Rd Westmoreland Hills Washington DC 20016 Office: 2450 Massachusetts Av Washington DC 20008

BAKER, BENTON, lawyer; b. Bismarck, N.D., Dec. 31, 1889; s. Isaac P. and Julia Franklin (Barnes) B.; grad. Smith Acad., St. Louis, 1906; Ph.B., Yale, 1910; LL.B., 1915; m. Cornelia Francis Pickett, Aug. 9, 1919; children—Jessica Pickett (Mrs. Robert Frederic Barnard) and Benton. Admitted to N.D. bar, 1915, and practiced at Bismarck, 1915-26; held various civic, state and federal offices, 1917-26; spl. atty. U.S. Govt., Washington, D.C., 1926-28; specialized in practice of law of patents, trade marks and unfair competition from 1928, in N.Y.C., 1928-29, in Chgo., 1929-68; mem. Zabel, Baker, York, Jones & Dithmar, 1953-69; of counsel Zabel, Baker, York & Jones, Chgo., 1969—; spl. lectr. on patent law John Marshall Law Sch., 1944-56. Recipient 50 Year award N.D. Bar Assn., 1965. Mem. Am., 7th Fed. Circuit, Chgo. bar assns., Yale Law Sch. Assn. (grad. bd. 1957-60), Patent Law Assn. Chgo., Chgo. Civic Study Forum. University (Chgo.); Filson (Louisville). Author various papers and pubis. Home: Santa Barbara CA 93102

BAKER, BERNARD ROBERT II, lawyer; b. Toledo, Nov. 19, 1915; s. Joseph Lee and Grace (Baker) O'Neil; A.B., Kenyon Coll., 1936; J.D., Harvard, 1941; m. Elinor Shutts, Oct. 16, 1943; children-Bernard Robert III, Lynn Agnes. Admitted to Ohio bar, 1946; practice in Toledo, 1947—; partner Boell, Bebout, Torbet & Baker, 1950—. Pres. B.R. Baker Co., 1946-60; dir. 1st Nat. Bank Toledo; sec., dir. Toledo Blade Co. Regional vice chmn. U.S. Com. for UN, 1955- 62. Past pres. Vincent Hosp. pres., Toledo United Appeal; trustee Med. Coll. Ohio at Toledo, Rutherford B. Hayes Found., Goodwill Industries Toledo, Salvation Army, Toledo, Boys Club Toledo, Blue Cross Assn. Toledo. Served from ensign to lt. comdr., USNR, 1940-45. Recipient Boys Club Bronze Keystone award, 1965; named Toledo Outstanding Man of Year, 1948. Mem. Am., Ohio, Toledo bar assns., Toledo C. of C., Chevalier du Tasstevin, Psi Upsilon. Roman Catholic. Clubs: Harvard (N.Y.C.); Toledo, Belmont Country, Belmont Gun (Toledo); Rockwell Trout (Castalia, O.). Home: 29829 E River Rd Perrysburg OH 43551 Office: Toledo Trust Bldg Toledo OH 43604

BAKER, BOB R., banker; b. Clarksville, Tenn., Aug. 7, 1936; s. Omer J. and Esther (Ward) B.; B.B.A., So. Meth. U.; M.B.A., Northwestern U. m. Arlyce Lou Ann Witt, June 26, 1965. Financial analyst Investors Dir. Diversified Services, Inc., 1962-65; with Columbia Savs. & Loan Assn., Denver, 1966—, exec. v.p., 1967-68, mng. officer, 1968, pres., 1968—, also dir. Mem. finance com. Central City Opera House Assn., 1968, bd. dirs., 1969-71, vice chmn. finance com., 1969; bd. dirs. Colo. Women of Achievement, 1967-69, Santa Claus Shop, 1967-68; bd. dirs., treas. Larry Tajiri Meml. Found., 1967-69. Served with USNR, 1958-61. Clubs: Denver, Denver Athletic; Brown Palace; Petroleum; Hiwan Country (Evergreen, Colo.). Home: 130 Vine St Denver CO 80209 Office: Columbia Savs & Loan Assn 16th and 120 Broadway Denver CO 80202

BAKER, BROUGHTON LEONARD, educator; b. Columbia, S.C., July 26, 1912; s. Andrew Charles and Lillian (Yarborough) B.; B.S. in Chem. Engring., U. S.C., 1933; Ph.D., N.C. State Coll., 1955; m. Margaret Smith, Nov. 12, 1932 (dec. 1946); children—Thomas, Julianne; m. 2d, Mary Rawls Gee, Oct. 22, 1952. Chem. engr. Gen. Chem. Co., 1935-40, Chem. Warfare 1940-42; plant mgr. Naylee Chem. Co., Phila., 1942-44; sec. Ellicott Labs., Inc., Lawrenceville, N.J., 1944-46; faculty U. S.C., Columbia, 1946—, prof. chem. engring., head dept., 1956—. Participant, Oak Ridge Inst. Nuclear Studies, 1951; cons. engr., 1947—; sec. S.C. State Bd. Engring. Examiners. Chmn. adv. com. sci., engring. and specialized personnel S.C. SSS. Registered profl. engr., S.C. Mem. Am. Soc. Engring. Edn. (pres. Southeastern sect. 1962-63), Nat. Soc. Profl. Engrs., Sigma Xi, Tau Beta Pi, Omicron Delta Kappa, Sigma Phi Epsilon. Baptist (deacon, Sunday sch. tchr.). Kiwanian. Contbr. articles to profl. jours. Home: 819 Burwell Lane Columbia SC 29205

BAKER, CARLOS HEARD, educator; b. Biddeford, Me., May 5, 1909; s. Arthur Erwin and Edna May (Heard) B.; A.B., Dartmouth, 1932, Litt.D., 1957; A.M., Harvard, 1933; Ph.D., Princeton, 1940; m. Dorothy Thomasson Scott, Aug. 22, 1932; childrenDiane, Elizabeth, Brian. Tchr. English Thornton Acad., Saco., Me., 1933-34. Nichols Sch., Buffalo, 1934-36; Princeton (N.J.), 1938—, became prof. English, 1951, Woodrow Wilson prof. lit., 1954-, dept. chmn., 1952-58; Fulbright lectr. Oxford U., 1957-58, Centre Universitaire, Nice, France, 1958; Guggenheim fellow., 1965-66. Mem. Am. Assn. U. Profs., Modern Lang. Assn. Am., Century Assn., mem. Phi Beta Kappa, Theta Delta Chi. Author: Shelley's Major Poetry, 1948; Hemingway, The Writer as Artist, 1952; (novels) A Friend in Power, 1958; The Land of Rumbelow, 1963; (poems) A Year and a Day, 1963; (biography) Ernest Hemingway: A Life Story, 1969. Editor: The American Looks at the World, 1943; Wordsworth's Prelude, etc., 1948; Shelley's Poetry and Prose, 1950; 1950; Fielding's Joseph Andrews, 1960; Hemingway and his Critics, 1961; Keats's Poetry and Letters, 1962; Hudson's Green Mansions, 1963; Coleridge"s Poetry and Prose, 1965; (with others) American Issues, 1941, Major English Romantic Poets, 1957, Masters of English Literature, 1958, Am. Lit. Record, 1961, Modern American Usage, 1966. Contbr. Dictionary Am. Biography, Lit. Hist. of U.S., various periodicals, newspapers. Home: 34 Allison Rd Princeton NJ 08540

BAKER, CARROLL, actress; b. Johnstown, Pa., May 28, 1935; d. William W. and Virginia (Duffy) Baker; student St. Petersburg (Fla.) Jr. Coll., 1953, Actors Studio, N.Y.C., 1954; m. Jack Garfein, Apr. 5, 1955; children—Blanche Joy, Herschel David. Broadway appearances include All Summer Long, 1954, Come On Strong, 1962; motion pictures include Giant, 1956, Baby Doll, 1957, The Big Country, 1958, But Not For Me, 1959, The Miracle, 1959, Bridge to The Sun, 1960, Something Wild, 1961, How The West Was Won, 1962, Station Six Sahara, 1962, Carpetbaggers, 1963, Cheyenne Autumn, 1963, Mr. Moses, 1964, Sylvia, 1964, Harlow, 1965, The Harem, 1967, Honeymoon, 1968, The Sweet Body of Deborah, Paranoia; made Vietnam tour with Bob Hope, 1966. Named as the Year's Best Supporting Actress, Nat. League Women's Clubs, 1956; nominated for best actress Acad. Motion Picture Arts and Scis., 1957; named Woman of Year, Hasty Pudding Club, Harvard, 1957; recipient Film Achievement award Look mag., 1957, Best Actress award San Francisco Critics, 1957, Best Dramatic Actress award Fgn. Press Club, 1957; named Ky. col., 1962. Mem. Acad. Motion Picture Arts and Scis., Actors Studio, Cheyenne Tribe (hon.). Home: 16 Via Armando Spadini Rome Italy Office: care Weisberger & Frosch 120 E 56th St New York City NY 10022

BAKER, CECIL, physician; b. Altamont, Ill., July 4, 1917; s. Cecil Herber and Mabel Thesesa (Graul) B.; B.S., St. Louis U., 1938, M.D., 1942; m. Nadine English, Aug. 21, 1943; children—Paul M., Kevin E., Craig D., Teresa AA., Peter J., Mary C., Barbara P., John F., Jane M. Sr. psychiatrist VA Hosp., Iowa., Iowa City, Ia., 195254; asst. supt. Ida. State Hosp. (South), 1954-56; supt. Yankton (S.D.) State Hosp., 1956-60; pvt. practice medicine, specializing in psychiatry, Bismarck, N.D., 1960-64; asst. supt. St. Louis State Hosp., 1964-67; supt. St. Louis State Sch. and Hosp., 1967-69; supt. State Hosp., Newberry, Mich., 1969—; asso. prof. clin. psychiatry St. Louis U. Served from 1st lt. to maj., M.C., AUS, 1943-46. Mem. Am. Psychiat. Assn., Pan Am. Med. Assn. Roman Catholic. K.C. Home: 91 Campbell St Newberry MI 49868 Office: State Hosp Newberry MI 49868

BAKER, CHARLES ALONZO, lawyer, banker; b. Clarendon, Tex., July 12, 1915; s. Charles P. and Susan (Baker) B.; student Tex. Christian U., 1932-34; LL.B., U. Tex., Austin, 1939; postgrad. Harvard, 1946; m. Mary Frances Hatfield, Jan. 30, 1944; children—C. Geoffrey, Alice Susan. Admitted to Tex. bar, 1939, Ohio bar, 1946; practiced in Ft. Worth, 1939-42, Cleve., 1946—; partner firm Burgess, Fullmer, Parker & Steck, 1946-61; sr. v.p., gen. counsel Union Commerce Bank, Cleve., 1961—; sec. Union Commerce Corp.,

1970—. Served to capt. USAAF, 1942-46. Mem. Ohio, Cleve. bar assns. Home: 84 Chillicothe Rd Aurora OH 44202 Office: 917 Euclid Av Cleveland OH 44114

BAKER, CHARLES DUANE, govt. ofcl.; b. Newburyport, Mass., June 21, 1928; s. Charles Duane and Eleanor (Little) B.; A.B., Harvard, 1951, M.B.A., 1955; m. Alice Elizabeth Ghormley, June 4, 1955; children—Charles Duane, Jonathan G., Alexander K. Buyer, Westinghouse Electric Corp., Elmira, N.Y., 1955-57, supr. purchasing sect., Jersey City, 1957-61, treas. United Research, Inc., Cambridge, Mass., 1961-62, v.p., treas., 1963-65; v.p., dir. transp. services Harbridge House, Inc., Boston, 1965-69; dep. under sec. U.S. Dept. Transp., Washington, 1969-70, asst. sec. policy and internat. affairs, 1970—. Served to lt. (j.g.) USNR, 1946-48, 51-53. Mem. Hasty Pudding, Pi Eta. Republican. Conglist. Clubs: Braeburn (Mass.) Country; Needham Pool and Racket; Harvard (Boston and Washington). Author: The Balance of Payments and the Merchant Marine, 1967; Intermodal Transport of the Far East Trade Through the Northwest Corridor, 1968. Home: 21 Cleveland Rd Needham MA 02192 Office: US Dept Transp Washington DC 20590

BAKER, CHESNEY H (Chet), trumpet player, singer; b. Yale, Okla., Dec. 23, 1929; student theory and harmony, El Camino Coll., Los Angeles, 1948-50. Played trumpet with marching and dance bands before 1948; played at Bop City, San Francisco, 1950-52, with Charlie Parker, 1952, with Gerry Mulligan, 1952-53; formed own group for clubs and records, 1953; toured Europe, Iceland and England, 1955-56, U.S. with Birdland All Stars, 1957, Scandinavia and Italy with own group, 1957; with quartet or quintet, 1957—; appeared in Italy, 1959-60. Served with AUS, 1946-48, 50-52; mem. 298th Army Band, Berlin, Germany, also Presidio Army Band, San Francisco. Recipient Down Beat Critics poll, 1953, 54, Met. poll, 1954-55, Melody Maker poll, 1955, German Jazz Echo poll, 1956, 58, Playboy poll, 1958. Address: care Verve Records 451 N Canon Dr Beverly Hills CA 90210 •

BAKER, CHESTER BIRD, educator; b. Mt. Union, Ia., Aug. 25, 1918; s. Herbert Victor and Florence Heston (Bird) B.; student Ia. Wesleyan Coll., 1934-35; B.S., Ia. State U., 1948; Ph.D., U. Cal. at Berkeley, 1950; m. Virginia Hall, Sept. 11, 1942; children—Edwin C., Barbara C. (Mrs. John F. Chaney), Thomas H. Asst. sec.-treas. Mt. Pleasant (Ia.) Prodn. Credit Assn., 1938-40; faculty Mont. State U., Bozeman, 1950-56, prof. agrl. econs., 1955-56; asso. prof. U. Ill., Urbana, 1957-58, prof. agrl. econs., 1958—; V.S. McLean vis. prof. Ont. Agrl. U., 1961. Cons. Western Agrl. Econs. Research Council, 1961, Midwest Research Inst., 1962, Nat. Assn. Food Chains, 1964-66, Ill. Bankers Assn., 1969, Canadian Task Force on Agr., 1967-69, U.S. Dept. Agr., 1963, Ford Found., 1971; vis. lectr. numerous univs., U.S., Eng., Asia, Australia. Served with AUS, 1941-46. Travelling fellow Social Sci. Research Council, India, 1958; Fulbright-Hays Sr. Research scholar U. Sydney, Australia, 1966-67. Mem. Am. Assn. Agrl. Economist, Australian Assn. Agrl. Economists, Internat. Assn. Agrl. Economists, Am. Econ. Assn., Gamma Sigma Delta, Alpha Gamma Rho. Presbyn. Author articles. Home: 601 E Pennsylvania Av Urbana IL 61801

BAKER, CHET, see Baker, Chesney H.

BAKER, CLARENCE R., food distbn. co. exec.; b. Freedom, Pa., Apr. 13, 1910; s. Scott W. and Clara (Wagner) B.; student Geneva Coll., Beaver Falls, Pa., 1932-33; m. L. Given Laymer, Feb. 4, 1933; children—John R., Barbara G. (Mrs. John S. Buno), William W. With S.M. Flickinger Co., Inc., 1961—, exec. v.p., 1966—. Home: 339 Maple St East Aurora, NY. Office: 45 Ayalea Dr Buffalo NY 14240

BAKER, CROWDUS, mail order exec.; b. Dallas, Feb. 27, 1906; s. Raymond Andrew and Alice Estella (Crowdus) B.; student Austin Coll., 1924-27; LL.D., Austin Coll., Villanova University; Dr. Comml. Science (hon.), Suffolk University; m. Lorena Ann Proctor, July 5, 1928; 1 dau., Julie Ann. With Sears, Roebuck & Co., Dallas, Boston, Phila. Seattle, 1929—, gen. mgr. Boston mail order store, 1945-51, treas. co., 1951-63, v.p., comptroller, 1954-60, pres., 1960-68, vice chmn. bd., 1968—, also dir.; dir. Continental Ill. Nat. Bank & Trust Co., Chgo., Allstate Ins. Co., Bethlehem Steel Corp., Archer-Daniels Midland Co., Chem. Bank, Sears Roebuck Acceptance Corp., Simpsons-Sears, Ltd., Homart Devel. Corp., Clark Equipment Co., Thompson Newspapers Inc., Conill Corp. Bd. dirs. Civic Fedn. Chgo., Sam Rayburn Found., Sears-Roebuck Found.; trustee, dir. Chicago Boys Clubs: trustee Ravenswood Hosp., Chgo., Jr. Achievement Chgo. Found.; v.p., dir. Jr. Achievement Chgo.; pres. dir. McGraw Wildlife Found. Mem. Northwestern U. Assos., Newcomen Soc. Clubs: Algonquin (Boston); Executives, Commercial, Chicago (Chgo.); Mid-Am. Home: 2298 Drury Lane Northfield IL 60093 Office: 925 S Homan Av Chicago IL 60607

BAKER, DANIEL CLIFTON, Jr., physician; b. Phila., Dec. 19, 1908; s. Daniel Clifton and Anna (Golden) B.; student U. Pa., 1929; M.D., Jefferson Med. Sch., 1933; Med. Sc.D. in Otolaryngology, Columbia, 1939; m. Geraldine Dieck, June 23, 1938; children—Geraldine, Daniel Clifton III, Judith, Marianne, Elizabeth. Intern, Jefferson Med. Coll. Hosp., 1933-35, fellow bronschoscopy and laryngeal surgery, 1935-37; fellow otolaryngology Columbia Coll. Physicians and Surgeons, 1937-39, mem. faculty, 1946—; dir. otolaryngol. service Presbyn. Hosp., N.Y.C., 1964—. Served to lt. comdr. USNR, 1942-46. Diplomate Am. Bd. Otolaryngology (dir.). Mem. A.C.S. (bd. govs.), Am. Acad. Ophthalmology and Otolaryngology (v.p.), Am. Laryngol. Soc., Am. Bronch-Esophagological Assn., Am. Triological Soc., Am. Coll. Chest Physicians, Am. Soc. for Study Headache. Home: 232 County Rd Demarest, NJ 07627. Office: 161 Fort Washington Av New York City NY 10032

BAKER, DAVID HODGE, govt. ofcl.; b. Paterson, N.J., Dec. 31, 1907; s. Frederick A. and Florence A. (Smith) B.; B.S., U.S. Mil. Acad., 1930; grad. Air Force Sch., 1932; M.B.A. with high distinction Harvard, 1941; student Nat. War Coll. Washington, 1947; m. Shirley Schrecongost, Oct. 17, 1969; 1 son, David Hodge. Commd. 2d lt. U.S. Army Air Force, 1930, advanced through grades to maj. gen.; chief plans div. 8th Air Force, Eng., 1942-44; dep. comdr. 9th A.S. Command, Europe, 1945, comdr., 1946; faculty Nat. War Coll., 1946-49; Office Joint Chiefs of Staff, 1948-50; comdr. Air Def. No. Alaska, 1951-52; dir. Command Support, A.M.C., 1952, comptroller, 1952-53, dir. prodn. and procurement, 1953-57; ret., 1957; pres., chief exec. officer Capital Airlines, Inc., Washington, 1957-61; v.p. Vickers Inc. div. Sperry Rand Corp., Detroit, also gen. mgr. Internat. div., 1961-65, v.p. Univac div., also gen. mgr. Internat. div., 1965-66, v.p. Internat., 1966-70; dir. Office Internat. Bus. Assistance, Bur. Inter Commerce, Dept. Commerce, Washington, 1970—. Decorated Legion of Merit with oak leaf cluster, Bronze Star medal; Croix de Guerre with Palm, Legion of Honor (France); Croix de Guerre (Luxembourg), Order of Merit (Nassau), Degree of Comdr. with Grand Cross, Leopold with Palm, Most Excellent Order of Britain, Order Polonia Restituta (Poland), Order of Leopold with Palm, Croix de Guerre with palm (Belgium). Clubs: University, Army-Navy. Home: 1600 S Eads St Arlington VA 22202 Office: Dept of Commerce 14th and Constitution Av NW Washington DC 20230

BAKER, DAVID KENNETH, univ. dean; b. Glasgow, Scotland, Oct. 2, 1923; s. David Thomas and Edith and (Horner) B.; came to U.S., 1946, naturalized, 1956; B.Sc., McMaster U., 1946; Ph.D., U. Pa., 1953; m. Vivian Christian Perry, Sept. 13, 1947; children—Paul D., Richard R. Prof. physics Union Coll., Schenectady, 1953-65; mgr. profl. personnel, research and devel. lab. Gen. Electric Co., 1965-67; v.p., dean St. Lawrence U., Canton, N.Y., 1967—; cons. NSF. Mem. Am. Inst. Physics, Am. Assn. U. Profs. Rotarian. Author: (with A.T. Goble) Elements of Modern Physics. Home: 16 Hillside Rd Canton NY 13617

BAKER, DEXTER FARRINGTON, air products co. exec.; b. Worcester, Mass., Apr. 16, 1927, s. Leland Dyer and Edith (Quimby) B.; B.S., Lehigh U., 1950, M.B.A., 1957; m. Dorothy Ellen Hess, June 23, 1951; children—Ellen L., Susan A., Leslie A., Carolyn J. Sales engr. Air Products & Chems., Inc., Allentown, Pa., 1952-56, gen. sales mgr., 1956-57, dir., 1964—, group v.p., 1967-68, exec. v.p., 1968—; mng. dir. Air Products, Ltd. 1957-67, dir., 1964—; dir. Air Products GmbH, Air Products S.A., Air Products (Nederland) N.V. Served with USNR, 1945-46; with U.S. Army, 1950-52. Mem. Theta Chi. Home: RD 2, Allentown, PA 18103.

BAKER, EARL DEWITT, coll. pres.; b. Hillsdale, Mich., Jan. 13, 1919; s. Horace DeWitt and Bessie (Dickey) B.; B.S., Huntington (Ind.) Coll., 1940; A.M., U. Mich., 1949, Ph.D., 1963; m. Evelyn Middaugh, Aug. 16, 1942; children—Marie, Ronald Paul, Joyce Evelyn, Annette. Pub. sch. sci. tchr., also high sch. prin., 1940-41, 45-49; ednl. missionary Sierra Leone, West Africa, 1949-65; pres. Huntington Coll., 1965—. Ge. sec. edn. Ch. United Brethren in Christ, 1965—. Served as pilot USNR, 1941-45. Mem. Christian Bus. Mem's Com. Rotarian. Home: 2145 College Av Huntington, IN 46750.

BAKER, EDGAR EUGENE, Jr., educator, microbiologist; b. Visalia, Cal., Oct. 13, 1913; s. Edgar Eugene and Annabelle (Byrd) B.; A.B., U. Cal. at Los Angeles, 1935, M.A., 1937, Ph.D., 1941; m. Marian Reed Logan, Sept. 3, 1938; 1 dau., Barbara Jean. Research asso. George Williams Hooper Found., U. Cal., 1941-46; asso. bacteriology and pathology Rockefeller Inst., 1946-49; asso. prof. Boston U. Sch. Medicine, 1949-52, prof. microbiology, 1952- -, now also chmn. dept. Fellow Am. Acad. Microbiology; mem. Am. Soc. Microbiology, Am. Assn. Immunologists, Soc. Exptl. Biology and Medicine. Home: Irvaan Rd Rockport MA 01966 Office: Boston Univ Sch Medicine Boston MA 02215

BAKER, EDGAR GATES STANLEY, educator, biologist; b. Peotone, Ill., June 7, 1909; s. Walter S. and Hallie E. (Gates) B.; A.B. (Rector scholar) DePauw U., 1931; postgrad. (Rector fellow) U. Chgo., 1931-33; Ph.D., Stanford, 1943; m. Julia E. Chapman, Dec. 29, 1935; children—Anne (Mrs Michael H. Siegel), Edgar C., James S. Faculty, Wabash Coll., 1932-39; asst. prof. biology Cath. U. Am., 1946-50; mem. faculty Drew U., Madison, N.J., 1950—, prof. zoology, 1951—, chmn. dept., 1951-70, Chief reader biology advanced placement program Coll. Entrance Exam. Bd., 1965-68. NSF Sci. Faculty fellow, 1957-58. Fellow A.A.A.S.; mem. Am. Soc. Zoologists, Soc. Protozoologists, N.Y. Acad. Scis., Am. Assn. U. Profs., Sigma Xi, Gamma Alpha, Beta Beta Beta (pres. 1967—). Home: 165 Green Village Rd Madison NJ 07940

BAKER, EDGAR PARK, lawyer; b. Bronxville, N.Y., Sept. 30, 1906; s. Vernon Pell and Mabel (Park) B.; A.B., Williams Coll., 1926; LL.B., Harvard, 1929; m. Katharine Jones, June 14, 1930; children—Donald Irwin, Gordon Park, Madge. Admitted to N.Y. bar, 1930, with firm of Milbank, Tweed, Hadley & McCloy, and predecessor firms, N.Y.C., 1929—; asst. works mgr. Clinton Engring. Works, Tenn. Eastman Corp., Oak Ridge, 1944-46. Trustee Vassar Coll., 1948-58. Mem. Am., N.Y. State, N.Y.C. bar assns., Phi Beta Kappa, Kappa Alpha. Clubs: Century Assn., University, India House, Wall Street, Williams (N.Y.C.). Home: 310 N Woodland St Englewood NJ 07631 Office: 1 Chase Manhattan Plaza New York City NY 10005

BAKER, EDWARD LAMAR, congressman; b. Chattanooga, Dec. 29, 1915; s. Rush Emmons and Sarah (Beall) B.; student David Lipscomb Coll., 1936-38; B.A., Harding Coll., 1940; m. Sue Jolly Batey, Aug. 21, 1945; children—Edward LaMar, Sarah Susan. Owner, Comml. Janitors, Inc., Chattanooga, 1962—; mem. Tenn. Ho. of Reps., 1966-68, Tenn. Senate, 1968-70; mem. 92d Congress 3d Tenn. dist.; mem. pub. works com. Chmn. Hamilton County Republican Party, 1964-65. Bd. dirs. Boyd-Buchanan Sch., Chattanooga. Served to maj. USAAF, 1941-46. Mem. C. of C., Am. Legion, Civitan. Home: 302 C St NE Washington DC 20002 Office: Longworth House Office Bldg Washington DC 20515

BAKER, ELBERT HALL, II, newspaper pub.; b. Quincy, Mass., July 18, 1910; s. Frank Smith and Gertrude (Vilas) B.; grad. Culver (Ind.) Mil. Acad., 1930; student Rensselaer Poly. Inst., 1932; m. Betye Martin, May 27, 1936; children—Suzanne (Mrs. Tephen F. Bethke), Martine (Mrs. Donald F. Prince). With Tribune Pub. Co., Tacoma, 1932—, pub., 1960, pres., 1969—, also dir. Bd. dirs. Tacoma Community Chest, United Good Neighbor Fund, Pierce County, Wash., Tacoma Gen. Hosp. Served with AUS, 1942-46. Mem. Sigma Delta Chi, Delta Kappa Epsilon. Home: 29 Forest Glen Lane SW Tacoma WA 98498 Office: Tribune Pub Co 711 St Helens Av Tacoma WA 98401

BAKER, ELMER ELIAS, Jr., educator; b. Hagerstown, Md., Apr. 15, 1922; s. Elmer Elias and Lena Rivers (Eichelberger) B.; student Emerson Coll., 1941-43, Littl.D., 1969; B.S. summa cum laude, N.Y.U., 1948, M.A., 1949, Ph.D., 1954; m. Keora Phyllis Kono, Aug. 17, 1945. Supr. speech therapy dept. phys. medicine and rehab. Bellevue Hosp., N.Y.C., 1948- 50; part-time instr. Pratt Inst. 1949-50; faculty N.Y.U., N.Y.C., 1950—, prof. speech edn. Sch. Edn., 1961—, chmn. dept. English and speech edn., Sch. Edn., 1960—, dir. summer sessions Sch. Edn., 1962-65, head div. English edn., speech and ednl. theatre, 1965—, acting vice dean Sch. Edn., 1966, 68, 69; clin. prof. Coll. Dentistry, 1961—; cons. St. Vincent's Hosp., N.Y.C., 1965—, VA Hosp., N.Y.C., 1967-68, Speech Rehab. Inst., N.Y.C., 1969—. Trustee Emerson Coll. Danforth Asso., 1964. Mem. Am. (clin. certificate speech 1955), N.Y. State (pres. 1965) speech and hearing assns., speech assns. Am., Eastern States, N.Y. State Speech Assn., Kappa Delta Phi, Phi Delta Kappa, Sigma Alpha Eta. Episcopalian. Club: Lotos (N.Y.C.). Co-author: Bibliography of Speech and Allied Areas, 1962; Listening and Speaking in the English Classroom, 1971; also chpts. in books. Contbr. articles to profl. jours. Home: 330 E 63d St New York City NY 10021

BAKER, FREDERICK SHERMAN, editor, author; b. Evanston, Ill., Sept. 15, 1902; s. Frederick S. and Josephine (Turck) B.; A.B., U. Wis., 1925; postgrad. Oxford U., 1928; m. Margaret Darlington, June 27, 1925; children—Penelope (Mrs. Frank E. Mee), Priscilla Darlington Griffin, Frederick Sherman. Advt. mgr. Appleton-Century-Crofts, 1942-45; sr. editor E. P. Dutton & Co., N.Y.C., 1946-54; v.p., editor, dir. St. Martin's Press, Inc., N.Y.C., 1955-63; adv. editor McGraw-Hill, N.Y.C., 1964-66; editor Funk & Wagnalls, N.Y.C., 1966-67. Club: Players (N.Y.C.). Author: Bradford Masters, 1949; Hidden Fire, 1955; The Making, 1966. F. Sherman Baker Collection, Mugar Meml. Library, Boston U. Home: Egypt Lane East Hampton NY 11937

BAKER, GEORGE, geol. research scientist; b. Coventry, Eng., Oct. 10, 1908; s. William James and Edith (Duggan) B.; B.Sc., Melbourne (Australia) U., 1933, M.Sc., 1934, D.Sc., 1956; m. Margaret Kathleen Mona Chisholm, June 3, 1950. Mem. staff geology dept. U. Melbourne, 1925-48; research scientist Commonwealth Sci. and Indsl. Research Orgn., Melbourne, 1948-68; hon. asso. mineralogy Nat. Mus. Victoria. Recipient David Syme Research medal, 1944; Nuffield spl. research grantee, 1964. Fellow Meteoritical Soc. Am., Am. Mineral. Soc.; life mem. Royal Soc. Victoria (Research medal 1961), Mineralogical Soc. (London), Melbourne U. Grad. Union; mem. Am. Geophys. Union, Australian Inst. Mining and Metallurgy, Geol. Soc. Australia, Australian and New Zealand Assn. Advancement Sci., Australian Marine Scis. Assn.; found. mem. Australia Sci. Club. Mem. Ch. of Eng. Spl. research mineralogy and mineragraphy, petrology, tektites, meteorites, phytoliths and zooliths, also sand drift relative to harbour installations. Home: 146 Wimbledon Av Mount Eliza Victoria 3930 Australia

BAKER, GEORGE CLAUDE, Jr., educator, clergyman; b. Atlanta, Aug. 23, 1904; s. George Claude and Willie Tallulah (Walters) B.; B.Ph., Emory U., 1925; B.D., 1938; B.D., Union Theol. Sem., N.Y., 1934, S.T.M., 1936; Ph.D., Columbia, 1941; D.D. (hon.), Southwestern U., Georgetown. Tex., 1946; m. Lovell Roena Wright, Feb. 2, 1948; children—George Leonard, George Claude III, Randolph Monroe, Lovell Jeannine, Merrimon Walters. Dir. student activities Wesley Found., U. Tex., 1928-31; ordained to ministry Meth. Ch., 1930; asst. minister Travis Park Meth. Ch., San Antonio, 1931-33; minister Asbury Community Meth. Ch., Mt. Vernon, N.Y., 1934-37, First Meth. Ch., Laredo, Tex., 1937-41, Harlingen, Tex., 1941-43, San Angelo, Tex., 1937- 41, Harlingen, Tex., 1941-43, San Angelo, Tex., 1943-46, Laurel Heights Meth. Ch., San Antonio, 1946-49; chaplain Southern Meth. U., also prof. homiletics, 1949-55, McCreless prof. evangelism Perkins Sch. Theology, 1955, also dir. Perkins Outreach; staff Lakewood United Methodist Church, 1968-70; asso. minister Kessler Park United Meth. Ch., 1970—; Decell lectr. Millsaps Coll., 1953; lectr. Methodist Mission Centers in Africa, 1960; lecture tour to Meth. Sems. in South Am., 1967. Fraternal del. Meth. Centennial Conf., Foochow, China, 1947; del. jurisdictional conf. South Central Jurisdiction Meth. Ch., 1948; fraternal del. Diamond Jubilee of Methodism in Mexico, 1949; mem. Inst. World Meth. Theol. Studies, Oxford U., 1958. Commnd. 2d lt., R,O.T.C., 1925; missioner to Air Force and Navy bases. Mem. Nat. Assn. Coll. Chaplains, Omicron Delta Kappa. Author: Early New England Methodism, 1941; Bible Lectures, 3 vols., 1944, 45, 46; Biography of Boldness, 1952. Editor The Ch. and Evangelism, 1960. Contbr. lessons Adult Student. Home: 2940 Daniels Av Dallas TX 75205

BAKER, GEORGE EMMETT, accountant; b. Chgo., Oct. 4, 1907; s. Addison Emmett and Hattie (Bray) B.; B.A., U. Wis., 1930; m. Jean Galloway Holmes, June 20, 1931; children—Shella Carrick (Mrs. Denslow E. Bolte), George Montgomery. With Ernst & Ernst, C.P.A.'s, 1936—, partner, 1954—, charge Louisville office, 1966—. Pres. Manor Country Club Community Assn., Rockville, Md., 1955-56, C.P.A., D.C., other states. Mem. Am., D.C., Ky. insts. C.P.A.'s, Nat Assn. Accountants, St. Andrews Soc. Washington (pres. 1957- 58). Clubs: Capitol Hill, University (Washington); Hunting Creek Country (Louisville). Home: 7400 Shadwell Lane Prospect KY 40059 Office: Commonwealth Bldg Louisville KY 40202

BAKER, GEORGE PIERCE, educator; b. Cambridge, Mass., Nov. 1, 1903; s. George Pierce and Christina (Hopkinson) B.; A.B. Harvard, 1925, A.M., 1930, Ph.D., 1934, LL.D., 1969; D.Sc., Clarkson Coll. Tech. 1955; D.B.A., Suffolk U., 1963, Allegheny Coll., 1965, C.Am. Inst. Bus. Adminstrn., 1970; D.Sc. in Bus. Adminstrn. Bowling Green State U., 1964; LL.D., Pace Coll., 1967, Harvard, 1969, Case Western Res. U., 1969; m. Ruth P. Bremer, Sept. 4, 1926; children—George Pierce, Sarah Uhle, Ruth Ursul, Elizabeth Fosket. Instr. econs., tutor div. history, govt. and econs. Harvard, 1928-36, asst. prof. transp., 1936-39, asso. prof., 1939-46 (on leave, 1940-46), James J. Hill prof. transp., 1946-63, emeritus, 1969—, George Fisher Baker prof. adminstrn., 1963-69, dir. Doctoral Program, 1953-58, dean Grad. Sch. Bus. Adminstrn., 1962-69; Transp. cons. N.Y. Central, Pa., C.B. & Q. r.r.'s 1939; apptd. mem. CAB 1940, vice chmn., 1942, resigned 1942 to become chief requirements div. Office of Q. M. Gen. War. Dept., 1942-43; col. War Dept. gen. staff, 1943-45; dir. Office Transport and Communications Policy, Dept. State, 1945- 46; vice chmn. President's Air Policy Commn., 1947; chmn. Com. on Aero. Research and Devel. Bd., Nat. Mil. Establishment, 1948-49 U.S. mem. Transport and Communications Commn., UN 1946-56; chmn. U.S. del. to Bermuda Civil Aviation Conf., 1946; mem. Pres.'s Commn. on Postal Orgn., 1967, Pres.' Council on Exec. Orgn., 1969-70. Dir. Am. Research & Devel. Corp., Jewel Cos., Inc.; trustee Penn Central Transp. Co. Decorated Legion of Merit; recipient Transp. Man of Yr. award Delta Nu Alpha, 1957; Harry E. Salzberg medal Syracuse U., 1958; Seley Transp. award, 1967. Fellow Am. Acad. Arts and Scis.; mem. Am. Soc. Traffic and Transp. (founder mem.), Transp. Assn. Am. (pres. 1954-62, chmn. bd. 1962-68), Soc. Cincinnati, Newcomen Soc., Phi Beta Kappa, Delta Nu Alpha. Clubs: Harvard (N.Y.C.); Chicago; Harvard, Brookline Country, Somerset (Boston); Chevy Chase, Metropolitan (Washington). Author: The Formation of the New England Railroad Systems, 1937, 49; (with Gayton E. Germane) Case Problems in Transportation, 1957; also articles in profl. jours. Address: Harvard Grad Sch Bus Adminstrn Soldiers Field Boston MA 02163

BAKER, GEORGE ROBERT, banker; b. Chgo., Nov. 5, 1929; s. George R. and Lucy (Kennelly) B.; B.A., Coe Coll., 1951; m. Maryanne Evans, Oct. 4, 1952; children—Anne Elizabeth, James Robert. Instl. trainee Continental Ill. Nat. Bank & Trust Co., Chgo., 1951-56, asst. cashier, 1956-60, 2d v.p., 1960-63, v.p., 1963-69, group v.p., 1967-69, sr. v.p. met. div., exec. officer bank, 1970—. Lectr., Marquette U., 1963-70. Pres., Chgo. Jr. C. of C., 1959-60; pres. Joint Civic Com. on Elections, Chgo., 1960-63; appointee Ill. Election Law Commn., 1961-63. Bd. dirs. Citizens Greater Chgo. Recipient One of Ten Outstanding Young Men in Chgo. award Jr. C. of C., 1963. Republican. Conglist. Clubs: Street, Bankers, Union League, Economics (Chgo.); Sunset Ridge Country. Home: 335 Shadowood Lane Northfield IL 60093 Office: 231 S LaSalle St Chicago IL 60690

BAKER, GLADDEN WHETSTONE, bus. exec.; b. Fall River, Mass., Jan 11, 1898; s. Marion Whetstone and Emma (James) B.; A.B., Washburn College, 1916, LL.D. (hon.), 1954; M.A., Yale, 1920, Ph.D., 1922; LL.D. (hon.), Trinity College, 1965; m. Marion Julia Williams, Oct. 11, 1923; children—Janet Williams (Mrs. J. Baker Tenney), Shepard Williams. Statistician N.Y. State Dept. Health, Albany, 1919; instr. econs. Yale, 1920-21; agts. dept. Fed. Res. Bank of N.Y., 1923-24; with Internat. Telephone Securities Corp., N.Y.C., 1925-26; joined Travelers Ins. Co., Hartford, Conn., 1926, asst. treas., 1930-34, treas., 1934-41, v.p., treas., 1941-55, director, mem. finance com., 1945-64, chmn. finance com., 1955-64; chmn. Broadcast-Plaza, Inc., 1964-68; spl. partner Wood, Struthers & Winthrop, 1965-69. Corporator St. Francis Hosp., Hartford Hosp., Mt. Sinai Hosp.;

trustee, treas. Kingswood Sch. West Hartford, 1943-58, Boys' Club; mem. Com. for Hartford. Trustee Washburn Coll., 1962-71. Recipient Distinguished Pub. Service award Conn. Bar Assn., 1963; Nathan Hale award, 1970; Yale medal, 1971; Wilbur Lucius Cross medal, 1971. Asso. fellow Silliman Coll.; mem. Yale Grad. Sch. Assn. (pres. 1965-70). Conglist. Clubs: Graduates (New Haven); Recess, Yale (N.Y.C.); Hartford (Hartford, Conn). Home: 31 Forest Rd West Hartford CT 06119 Office: 100 Constitution Plaza Hartford CT 06103

BAKER, GLADYS ELIZABETH, educator; b. Iowa City, July 22, 1908; d. Richard Phillip and Katherine (Riedelbauch) Baker; B.A., U. Ia., 1930, M.S., 1932; Ph.D., Washington U., St. Louis, 1935. Research asst. Washington U., 1935-36; instr. instr. biology dept. Hunter College, N.Y.C., 1936-40; instr. plant sci. dept. Vassar Coll., 1940-42, asst. prof., 1942-45, asso. prof., 1945-51, chmn. dept., 1948-60, prof., 1951-61, 62-63; vis. prof. botany dept. U. Hawaii, Honlulu, 1961-62, prof., 1963—. Summer Research Marine Biol. Lab., Woods Hole, Mass., 1941-48, Mont. Biol. Sta., 1951-62. Fellow A.A.A.S.; mem. Am. Soc. Microbiology, Brit. Mycol. Soc., Bot. Soc. Am., Mycol. Soc. Am., Soc. for Gen. Microbiology, Bot. Soc. Hawaii, Hawaiian Acad. Sci., Sigma Xi, Phi Sigma, Sigma Delta Epsilon. Home: 3687 Woodlawn Terrace Pl Honolulu HI 96822

BAKER, GORDON EDWARD, educator; b. Poughkeepsie, N.Y., Dec. 6, 1923; s. Gordon Denzil and Emma (Calhoun) B.; B.A., Reed Coll., 1948; M.A., U. Wash., 1949; postgrad. Brown U., 1950; Ph.D., Princeton, 1952; m. June LaVerne Sharpe, Sept. 2, 1947; children—Jeffery, Leslie Marie. Mem. faculty U. Cal. at Santa Barbara, 1952—, prof. polit. sci., 1965—, chmn. dept., 1965-71; cons. in field 1958—. Mem. 20th Century Fund Conf. Research Scholars and Polit. Scientists on Legislative Apportionment, 1962. Served with AUS, 1943-46. Guggenheim fellow, 1969; Social Sci. Research Council faculty research fellow, 1962. Mem. Am. Polit. Sci. Assn. (council 1968-70, exec. com. 1968-69), Nat. Municipal League. Author: Rural Versus Urban Political Power, 1955; The Reapportionment Revolution, 1966; also articles. Home: 1330 Orchid Dr Santa Barbara CA 93111

BAKER, HAROLD FRED, lawyer; b. Moriah, N.Y., Jan. 5, 1921; s. Maurice W. and Hattie I. 1949; m. Hazel Oliver, Dec. 13, 1943; children—Barbi S., Brant H., Randall O. Admitted to D.C. bar, 1949, also U.S. Supreme Ct.; asso. firm Sanders, Gravelle, Whitlock & Howrey, Washington, 1949-56; mem. firm Howrey, Simon, Baker & Murchison, Washington, 1956—. Cons. President's Conf. Adminstry. Procedure, 1953-54. Served with AUS, 1942-46. Mem. Am., D.C. bar assns., Nat. Lawyers Club, Order of Coif. Republican. Club: Congressional Country (Washington), Author: Buyer Liability Under Robinson-Patman Act, 1953; Federal Trade Commission Hearing Examiners: An Evaluation, 1962. Asst. editor: (Oppenheim) Unfair Trade Practices, 1950. Home: 9020 McDonald Dr Bethesda, MD 20034. Office: 1707 H St N W Washington DC 20006

BAKER, HARRY SUGG, business exec.; b. Dyersburg, Tenn., Mar. 1, 1904; s. John Franklin and Lalla Rookh (Sugg) B.; B.Sc., Ore. State Coll., 1927; m. Tina Amick, Apr. 2, 1927; children—Harriet Jane, David Franklin. With San Joaquin (Cal.) Cotton Oil Co., 1928-30; mgr. cotton gin Producers Cotton Oil Co. (Fresno). Helm, Cal., 1930-32, field mgr., 1933-37, pres., 1937-68, chmn. bd., 1968—; president Calflax Co., Fresno, 1937-68; past pres. Delta Cotton Co., Santa Rita Ginning Co.; chmn. bd. South Lake Farms; dir. Bangor Punta Corp., Bank Am. Nat. Trust & Savs. Assn. Mem. com., adv. bd. N.Y. Cotton Exchange. Adv. com. U.S. Dept. Agr. Exptl. Sta., Shafter, Cal. Past pres. Fresno Indsl. Site Devel. Found.; dir. Producers Cotton Oil Agrl. Foundation. Bd. dirs. Westlands Water Dist.; trustee St. Agnes Hosp. Member of National Cotton Council Am. (past pres.), Nat. Cottonseed Products Assn. (past pres.), Am. (dir.), Cal. (dir.) automobile assns., Cal. (agrl. com.), Fresno (past pres.) chambers commerce, 21st Dist. Agrl. Assn. (dir.). Clubs: Rotary Sunnyside Country (Fresno). Office: P O Box 1832 Fresno CA 93717

BAKER, HASTINGS WYMAN, lawyer and business exec.; b. Stovall, N.C., June 12, 1914; s. Hastings Wyman and Sallie (Younger) B.; student Harvard, 1932-33, Western Res. U., 1933-34, Wittenberg U., 1934-35, George Washington U., 1935-37, Coll. City N.Y., 1937, Columbia, 1937; LL.B., Fordham U., 1941; m. Beverly Higgins, July 7, 1938; childrenHastings Wyman III, Barry. Admitted to N.Y. bar, 1941; law clk., asso. atty. Chadbourne, Hunt, Jackel & Brown, N.Y.C., 1939-43; asst. to head legal dept. Mathieson Chem. Co., 1943-44; corp. counsel, asst. sec. Tubize Rayon Corp., 1944- 46; with Beaunit Mills, Inc., N.Y.C., 1947-, sec., treas., dir., 1959- , head legal dept., 1947-; various positions to sec.-treas. and head legal dept. Skenandoa Rayon Corp., Nat. Weaving Corp., North Am. Rayon Corp. (also dir.); mng. dir. Sta. Reps. Assn., Inc., 1964-; dir. Tyrex, Inc., subsidiaries 20th Century Fox Film Corp. Home: 220 W Norwalk Rd Darien CT 06820 Office: 366 Madison Av New York City NY 10017

BAKER, HERBERT, advt. co. exec.; b. Chgo., Aug. 14, 1924; s. Joseph David and Ida (Wilk) B.; student U. Ill., 1940, U. Chgo., 1941-42, Inst. Design, Chgo., 1946; m. Gwen Weber, Nov. 24, 1948 (div. 1969); children—Alison M., David A., Lauren B., Todd R.; m. 2d, Nadine Hess Spivack, Apr. 3, 1971. Dir. pub. relations Raymond Loewy Assos., Chgo., 1946-47; v.p. Burton Browne Advt., Chgo., 1947-48; creative coordinator Wetzel Bros., Milw., 1949-50; founder Herbert Baker Advt., Inc., Chgo., 1950, now chmn. bd. Pres. Found. Cancer Research, Chgo., 1960; mem. com. primitive art Art Inst. Chgo., 1960—; authority, collector African primitive art. Served with AUS, 1942-45. Address: John Hancock Center Chicago IL 60611

BAKER, HERBERT GEORGE, educator; b. Brighton, Eng., Feb. 23, 1920; s. Herbert Reginald and Alice (Bambridge) B.; B.S., U. London, 1941, Ph.D., 1945; m. Irene Williams, Apr. 4, 1945; 1 dau., Ruth Elaine. Came to U.S., 1957. Research chemist, asst. plant physiologist Hosa Research Labs., Sunbury- on-Thames, Eng., 1940-45; lectr. botany U. Leeds (Eng.), 1945-54; research fellow Carnegie Insn. Washington, 1948-49; prof. botany U. Coll. Ghana, 1954-57; faculty U. Cal. at Berkeley, 1957—, asso. prof. botany, 1957-60, prof. 1960—, dir. bot. garden, 1957-69. Fellow A.A.A.S.; mem. Orgn. Tropical Studies (dir.), Am. Inst. Biol. Sci., Internat. Assn. Botanic Gardens (v.p.), Internat. Orgn. Plant Biosystematists, Ecol. Soc. Am., Soc. for Study Evolution (past pres.), Bot. Soc. Am., Assn. Tropical Biology, Sigma Xi. Author: Plants and Civilization, 1965, 70. Editor: (with G.L. Stebbins) Genetics of Colonizing Species, 1965. Contbr. articles to sci. jours. Home: 635 Creston Rd Berkeley CA 94708

BAKER, HERMAN, publisher; b. Grand Rapids, Mich., Apr. 8, 1911; s. Richard and Jennie (Kregel) B.; m. Angeline Sterkenberg, May 13, 1932; childrenJean (Mrs. Charles D. Gardner, Jr.), Richard Lee, Ruthellen (Mrs. Donald Nyenhuis), Peter. Pres. Baker Book House Co., Grand Rapids, 1939-, also B.B.G. Corp., Allendale, Mich.; dir. Dickinson Printing Co., Grand Rapids. Vice pres. Christian Sch. Ednl. Found., Grand Rapids. Mem. Christian Reformed Ch. Home: 1030 Plymouth Rd Grand Rapids MI 49506. Office: 1019 Wealthy St Grand Rapids MI 49506

BAKER, HERSCHEL CLAY, educator; b. Cleburne, Tex., Nov. 8, 1914; s. Tyler Alexander and Mae (Deffebach) B.; A.B., So. Methodist U., 1935, Mus.B., 1935, LL.D., 1966; A.M. Harvard, 1936, Ph.D., 1939; LL.D., U. Vt., 1967; m. Barbara Morris, Sept. 6, 1939; children—Ann, William, Pamela. Instr. English, U. Tex., 1939-44, asst. prof. English, 1944-46; asst. prof. English, Harvard, Cambridge, Mass., 1946-49, asso. prof., 1949-56, prof., 1956—, chmn. dept., 1952-57, Higginson prof. English lit., 1967—. Guggenheim fellow 1957, 63. Mem. Phi Beta Kappa, Kappa Sigma. Author: John Philip Kemble, 1942; The Dignity of Man, 1947; The Wars of Truth, 1952; Hyder Edward Rollins: A Bibliography, 1960; William Hazlitt, 1962; The Race of Time, 1966. Editor: (with Hyder Rollins), 1954. The Renaissance in England, 1954. Contbr. articles to profl. jours. Home: 22 Clifton St Belmont MA 02178

BAKER, HOLLIS MACCLURE, furniture co. exec.; b. Allegan Mich., Apr. 27, 1916; s. Hollis Siebe and Ruth (MacClure) B.; student U. Va., 1935-37; m. Betty Jane Brown, Aug. 2, 1947; children—Tomelyn Ann, Susan MacClure. With Baker Furniture, Inc. Holland, Mich., 1938-40, 45—, v.p. treas., 1959-61, pres., 1961-70, chmn. bd., 1970—; v.p. gen. mgr. Grand Rapids Chair Co. (Mich.), 1959-61, pres. 1961-70; v.p., dir. Manor House, Inc., N.Y.C., 1958 , 70; pres. Boyne City R.R. Co. (Mich.); dir. Mich. Nat. Bank, Furniture Mfrs. Warehouse Co. (all Grand Rapids), Mich. Nat. Bank, Lansing. Pres., Exhibitors Bldg. Corp. Grand Rapids. Trustee Kendall Sch. Design, Grand Rapids; bd. dirs. Central Civic Auditorium, Grand Rapids. Served to lt. (s.g.) USNR, 1941-45. Mem. Nat. Assn. Furniture Mfrs. (dir.), Furniture Mfrs. Assn. Grand Rapids (dir., past pres.). Zeta Psi. Episcopalian. Clubs: Metropolitan, New York Yacht, Leash, (N.Y.C.); Chicago, Chicago Yacht; Kent Country, University, Indian, Peninsular (Grand Rapids); Bath and Tennis (Palm Beach, Fla.); Royal Yacht (Greece). Home: 2801 Lake Dr S E Grand Rapids MI 49506 Office: Exhibitors Bldg Grand Rapids MI 49502

BAKER, HORACE ROSS, Jr., life ins. co. exec.; b. Akron, O., Mar. 8, 1924; s. Horace Ross and Helen (Baldwin) B.; A.B. cum laude, Harvard, 1945; LL.B., 1951, postgrad. Advanced Mgmt. Program, 1962; m. Phyllis Laurence Green, Dec. 18, 1948; children—Robert Clarkson, Warren Ross, David Ware, Emily Laurence. Admitted to Mass. bar, 1951, to bar of U.S. Dist. Ct. for Dist. of Mass.; with John Hancock Mutual Life Insurance Co., Boston, 1951—, associate counsel, 1957-60, counsel, 1960-65, general solicitor, 1965-67, vice president and general solicitor, 1967—; director of Hingham Coop Bank (Mass.); instr. law exam. Soc. Actuaries, Life Office Mgmt. Assn. Mem. planning bd., Hingham, 1960-67, clk. of bd., 1961-62; chairman board of appeals, Hingham 1967—; mem. Mass. adv. com. U.S. Commn. Civil Rights, 1960-61. Served with AUS, 1943-46. Mem. Am., Mass., Boston bar assns., Assn. Life Ins. Counsel, Greater Boston C. of C., Am. Judicature Soc. Clubs: Algonquin (Boston); Hingham Yacht, Harvard (Hingham, Mass.). Home: 367 Main St Hingham MA 02043 Office: 200 Berkeley St Boston MA 02116

BAKER, HOWARD HENRY, Jr., U.S. senator, lawyer; b. Huntsville, Tenn., Nov. 15, 1925; s. Howard Henry and Dora (Ladd) B.; grad. McCallie Sch., 1943; student U. of South, Tulane U.; LL.B., U. Tenn., 1949; LL.D, Tusculum Coll.; D.C.L., Southwestern at Memphis. m. Joy Dirksen, Dec. 22, 1951; children—Darek Dirksen, Cynthia. Formerly sr. partner law firm Baker, Worthington, Barnett & Crossley, Knoxville; formerly chmn. bd. First Nat. Bank, Oneida, Tenn., pres. Colonial Natural Gas Co., Wytheville, Va.; U.S. senator from Tenn., 1966—. Presdl. elector, Tenn., 1956; chmn. Tenn. delegation to Republican Nat. Conv., 1968. Trustee Nat. Presbyn. Center, Washington. Served to lt. (j.g.) USNR, 1943-46. Mem. Am. Bar Assn., Bar Assn. Tenn. Home: Huntsville TN 37756 Office: Senate Office Bldg Washington DC 20510

BAKER, IVAN FRANKLIN, fgn. trade cons.; b. Cedar Rapids, Neb., Apr. 11, 1887; s. Frank N. and Etta I. (Bowers) I.; B.S. in Elec. Engring., U. Neb., 1909; m. Lucile Atkinson, 1911; 1 dau., Helen Merle (Mrs. Robert A. Cushman). Apprentice engr. Westinghouse Electric & Mfg. Co., Pitts. 1909-10, mgr. for Japan, later mng. dir. Westinghouse Electric Co. of Japan, and dir. Mitsubishi Electric & Engring. Co., 1919-27, mgr. far east Westinghouse Electric Internat. Co., N.Y.C., 1927-29, European sales mgr., European mgr., 1929-38, industry sales mgr., sales mgr., 1938-44, co. rep., Washington, 1942-43, asst. to pres., 1944-45, treas., 1945-57, v.p., treas., 1947-52, spl. rep. of the pres. on devel. electric power programs in Far East, 1953, dir. 1940—; dir. Constructora Nacional de Maguinaria Electrica, Spain, 1930-39; cons. War Dept., 1943; mem. adv. com. comml. activities fgn. service Dept. State and Dept. Commerce, 1946-53; cons. Fgn. Trade Fairs, Far Eastern Div. for U.S. Dept. Commerce. Del. from U.S. Govt. to ECAFE Conf. of UN, Manila, P.I., 1953. Mem. men's exec. com. Japan Internat. Christian U. Found., Inc. Mem. I.E.E.E Mason (32). Home: 266 E Dudley Av Westfield NJ 07090

BAKER, JAMES ANDREW, educator, animal virologist; b. Garland, La., Dec. 16, 1910; s. William Benjamin and Mary (Baldridge) B.; B.S., La. State U., 1932, M.A., 1934; Ph.D., Cornell U., 1938, D.V.M., 1940; m. Hallie Dudley Dodson, Nov. 27, 1934; 1 son, Andrew Lindsay. Fellow, Rockefeller Inst. Med. Research, Princeton, N.J., 1940, asst., 1941, asso., 1946; prof. virology Cornell U., 1947—, dir. Vet. Virus Research Inst., 1950—; cons. virology and immunology to hosps., govt., industry. Mem. adv. com. Office of Dir. Def. Research and Engring., Dept. Def., 1962—. Named Veterinarian of Year, 1951, Dogdom's Man of Year, 1956, Gaines Poll. Mem. Am. Vet. Med. Assn., N.Y. Acad. Scis., Soc. Exptl. Pathology, Soc. Exptl. Biology and Medicine, Soc. Microbiology, Acad. Microbiology, U.S. Livestock San. Assn., Conf. Research Workers. Contbr. articles profl. jours. and Ency. Brit. Research on viruses animals devel. into vaccines. Address: Vet Virus Research Inst Cornell U Ithaca NY 14850

BAKER, JAMES EDWARD, retail exec.; b. Tuckerman, Ark., Nov. 17, 1925; s. Eugene B. and Alma (Moon) B.; B.S. in Bus. Adminstrn. with honors, U. Ark., 1949, M.B.A., 1950; m. Ruth Lacko, Jan. 25, 1958; childrenMary Elizabeth, Donald Eugene, Robert James, Linda Ann. Exec. trainee Southwestern Bell Telephone Co., St. Louis, 1950-51; staff accountant Montgomery Ward & Co., Chgo., 1951-52; with No. Trust Co., Chgo, 1952-63, 2d v.p., 1961- 63; treas. Pet Inc., St. Louis, 1963-68; treas. Brown & Williamson Tobacco Corp., Louisville, 1968-69; v.p., treas. Kroger Co., Cin., 1969—. 1969—. Served with AUS, 1944-46. Mem. Financial Execs. Inst., Am. Mgmt. Assn.(mem. finance planning council). Home: 988 Chesterton Way Cincinnati OH 45230 Office: 1014 Vine St Cincinnati OH 45201

BAKER, JAMES GILBERT, scientist; b. Louisville, Ky., Nov. 11, 1914; s. Jesse Blanton and Hattie May (Stallard) B.; A.B., University of Louisville, 1935 Sc.D., 1948; A.M., Harvard University, 1936, Ph.D., 1942; m. Elizabeth Katherine Breitenstein, Jan. 1, 1938; children—Kirby Alan, Dennis Graham, Neal Kenton, Brenda Sue. Harvard U. scholarship, 1936-37, Soc. of Fellows, 1937-41, dir. Optical Research Lab., 1941-46, asso. prof., 1946-48; research asso. Lick Obs., 1949-60, Harvard Obs., 1949—; pres. of Spica, Inc., 1955-60; consultant in optical physics for Air Force; Lowell lecturer, 1940; research fellow Harvard Coll. Observatory, 1942-46. Chmn. U.S. Nat. Com. Internat. Commn. Optics, 1956-59, v.p. Internat. Commn. for Optics, 1959-62; scientific advisory board USAF, 1952-57. Awarded Adolph Lomb medal for contributions to optics, 1942, Medal of Merit for War Work, 1947; Magellanic Medal for Contbns. to Astron. Optics, 1953. Exceptional Civilian Service Award, USAF, 1957; Elliott Cresson medal Franklin Inst., 1962; Frederick Ives medal Optical Soc. Am., 1965. Mem. Nat. Acad. Scis., Am. Philos. Soc., Am. Astron. Soc., Am. Optical Soc. (pres. 1960), Am. Acad. Arts and Scis., Gamma Alpha (pres. Harvard Chpt., 1939), Am. Mathematical Society, Sigma Xi (sec.-treas. Harvard chapter, 1946-48). Author: Telescopes and Accessories (with George Z. Dimitroff), 1945. Home: 7 Grove St Winchester MA 01890 Office: Harvard College Observatory Cambridge MA 02139

BAKER, JAMES IRVIN, paper products mfr.; b. Detroit, Sept. 10, 1931; s. Irvin Frances and Loma B. (Mitchie) B.; B.A., Mich. State U., 1953; M.B.A., U. Detroit, 1959; m. Marion Jeanne Tracy, June 20, 1953; children—Teresa Ann, Scott Michael, Susan Jeanne, David James. Financial analyst Ford Motor Co., Dearborn, Mich., 1953-59; asso. Booz, Allen & Hamilton, Chgo., 1959-65; sr. v.p. planning and adminstrn. Avery Products Corp., San Marino, Cal., 1965—. Home: 1920 Lamp Post Lane La Canada CA 91011 Office: 415 Huntington Dr San Marino CA 91108

BAKER, JAMES KENDRICK, splty. metals mfg. co. exec.; b. Wabash, Ind., Dec. 21, 1931; s. Donald Dale and Edith (Swain) B.; A.B., DePauw U., 1953; M.B.A., Harvard, 1958; m. Beverly Baker, Apr. 11, 1959; childrenBetsy Ann, Dirk Emerson, Hugh Kendrick. Regional sales mgr. Arvinyl div. Arvin Industries, Inc., Columbus, Ind., 1958-60, gen. mgr. div., 1960-66, v.p., gen. mgr. div., 1966-68, exec. v.p., 1968-. Bd. dirs. Jr. Achievement, 1966; pres. DePauw U. Sigma Chi House Corp., 1965; pres. Columbus Found. for Youth, 1965; pres. Vinyl-Metal Laminators Inst. div. Soc. for Plastics Industry, 1963-64, dir., 1960-. Vice chmn. Ind. Republican Conv., 1966. Served with AUS. 1953-55. Named Outstanding Boss, C. of C., 1965; recipient Distinguished Service award Ind. Jr. Jr. C. of C., 1966; named One of 5 Outstanding Young Men of Ind., 1966. Mem. Mem. Columbus C. of C. (dir.). Rotarian. Clubs: DePauw University Alumni (pres. 1960): Harrison Lake Country; Columbia (Idpls.). Home: Rural Route 5 Deer Crossing Columbus IN 47201 Office: Gen Offices Arvin Industries Inc Columbus IN 47201

BAKER, JOEL WILSON, surgeon; b. Shenandoah. Va., Jan. 17, 1905; s. Martin Wharey and Ann (Hortenstine) B.; M.D., U. Va., 1928; LL.D., U. Alaska, 1969; m. Mary Elizabeth Russell, July 26, 1934; children—Joel Wilson, Samuel Russell, John Baillie, Martin Wharey. Extern, U. Va. Hosp., Charlottesville, 1927-28; intern Virginia Mason Hosp., Seattle, 1928-29, preceptor surgery, 1929-36, chief of surgery, 1936-70, emeritus chief of surgery, 1970—, pres. bd. trustees, 1960-66; mem. staff Mason Clinic, 1929-70, chmn., 1945-64; surg. cons. King County Harborview Hosp., Children's Orthodpedic Hosp.; courtesy staff King County, Doctors, Orthopedic hosps.; surg. cons. U.S. Army Madigan Hosp., Ft. Lewis, N.P. Ry. Co., Bremerton Naval Hosp., Seattle U.S. Pub. Health Hosp.; sr. cons. surgeon U. Wash. Sch. Medicine, 1949-67, clin. prof. surgery, 1967—. Adv. com. Cancer Control Program USPHS, 1966—. Trustee Lakeside Sch. Diplomate, emeritus mem. Am. Bd. Surgery (bd. mem. 1955-61). Fellow A.C.S. (v.p. 1952, exec. com. 1960-63, regent 1954-63, pres. 1969-70); mem. Pan-Pacific Surg. Assn., Pacific Coast (pres. 1970-71), So., Western, Seattle surg. assns., Wash., King County med. socs., Alaska Med. Assn. (hon.), Torii Med. Soc. (dir.; hon. Okinawa), James IV Assn. Surgeons, North Pacific Surg. Assn., A.M.A., Seattle Surg. Assn. (past pres.), Am. Thyroid Association, Am. Gastroenterol. Assn., Acad. Internat. Medicine, Societe Internationale de Chirurgie. Clubs: University (trustee), Surgeons Travel, Seattle Tennis, Seattle-Tacoma Civic of Soyps. Seattle Golf. Associate editor Western Journal Surgery, Obstetrics and Gynecology, 1951—; cons. editor Surgery. Gynecology and Obstetrics 1954-60; bd. editors Quar. Jour. Surg. Technique, 1968—. Home: 302 Maiden Lane E Seattle WA 98102 Office: 1118 9th Av Seattle WA 98101

BAKER, JOHN ALEXANDER, Jr., fgn. service officer; b. Bridgeport, Conn., Oct. 3, 1927; s. John A. and Adelaide (Nichols) B.; B.A., Yale, 1949; License Scis. Politiques, Geneva (Switzerland) U., 1950; m. Sarah K. Bragg, July 2, 1955 (dec. Sept. 1962); m. 2d, Katherine P. Gratwick, June 30, 1965; children—John Kendall, Andrew, Mitchell, Malcolm. Joined U.S. Fgn. Service, 1950; assigned Belgrade, 1951-52, Voice of Am., 1954-56, Munich, 1956-57, Moscow, 1957-58, Washington, 1958-60, Rome, 1960-63, U.S. mission to UN, 1963-67; fellow Harvard Center Internat. Affairs, 1967-68; counselor of embassy, dep. chief mission, Prague, 1968-70; dir. East Central European Affairs, Dept. State, Washington, 1970—. Served to 2d lt. AUS, 1946- 48. Recipient Meritorious Service award State Dept., 1960. Author articles. Home: 3610 Idaho Av NW Washington DC 20016 Office: EUR/CHP Dept State Washington DC 20525

BAKER, JOHN AUSTIN, cons.; b. Paris, Ark., Feb. 22, 1914; s. John I. and Eloise Austin (Weems) B.; B.S.A., U. Ark., 1935, M.S., U. Wis., 1937; postgrad. Princeton, Harvard, U.S. Dept. Agr. Grad. Sch.; m. Susan Reed Toepfer, July 4, 1939; children—Roger William, James Karl, Robert Charles, David Allan, Judith Ann, Gordon Reed. Staff instr. U. Wis., 1935-36, 36-38, grad. fellow, 1938-39; economist, exec. officer Dept. Agr., 1937-51, program analyst, regional dir. FSA, Ark., La., Miss., 1939-43, Bur. Agrl. Econs., 1937-39, 46-47, dir. land reform U.S. Mil. Govt., Korea, 1947-48, asst. to sec. agr., 1948-51, dir. legislative services Nat. Farmers Union, 1951-61, dir. agrl. credit Dept. Agr., 1961-62; asst. sec. of agr., mem. bd. CCC, 1962-69; pres. Community Devel. Services, 1969—; asso. James G. Patton Assos., 1970—. Mem. exec. com. Arlington Com. of 100. Bd. dirs. Nat. Capital Democratic Club; adviser Dem. Nat. Com., 1968-70. Served from ensign to lt. USNR, 1943-46. Mem. Am. Agrl. Econ. Assn., Am. Econ. Assn., Nat. Planning Assn. (agrl. policy com.), Blue Key, Alpha Zeta, Alpha Gamma Rho, Phi Eta Sigma. Democrat. Author: Guide to Federal Programs for Rural Development, 1971. Contbr. articles to profl. jours. Home and office: 6301 15th Rd N Arlington VA 22205

BAKER, JOHN D., invensment banker; b. Jacksonville Fla., May 16, 1903; s. John Daniel and Julia Simkins; B.S., Davidson Coll., 1925; m. Alice Bernice Yorke, Jan. 4, 1928; children—Barbara (Mrs. T. Down Mallory), Alice (Mrs. Irwin L. Brooks), Joan Brooks, Sr. partner Reynolds and Co., N.Y.C., 1958—. Mem. Assn. Stock Exchange Firms (past gov.), Sigma Alpha Epsilon. Presbyn. (trustee). Clubs: University, (bd. govs.), Bankers, Stock Exchange Luncheon, Clove Valley (bd. govs.), Trail Blazers (bd. govs.), Home: 1111 Park Av New York City NY 10028 Office: 120 Broadway New York City NY 10005

BAKER, JOHN EMERSON, educator; b. New Hebron, Ill., Feb. 25, 1910; s. Calvin Cornelius and Easter (Richart) B.; A.B. (Rector scholar), DePauw U., 1931; student Ind. U., 1931-32, Ind. State U., summer 1931-33; M.A., U. Minn., 1937; Ph.D. (fellow), U. Chgo., 1952; m. Helen U. Ditmars, May 22, 1937; children—Barbara Ann (Mrs. Richard Engle), Sue Ellen (Mrs. Peter Burns), John Garrett. Tchr., supr. Ind. pub. schs., 1932-39; prin. LaPorte County and Wendell Wilkie Jr.- Sr. High Sch., Elwood, Ind., 1939-44; supt. schs., Griffith, Ind., 1944- 48; asso. prof. edn. Ball State U., 1948-50, 53-55; vis. prof. U. Tex., 1950; asst. dir. Midwest Adminstrn. Center, U. Chgo., 1950-52; program dir. Bd. Fundamental Edn., Indpls., 1955-60; prof. edn. No. Ill. U., 1960-61; acad. dean Greensboro

(N.C.) Coll., 1960-63; prof. edn., chmn. dept. U. Vt., 1963—, acting dean Coll. Edn., 1968—; dir. adminstrn. and supervision Old Dominion U. Consultant to colleges, 1950—. Mem. Nat., Vt. edn. assns., Am. Assn. Sch. Adminstrn., Nat. Soc. Study Edn., Assn. Student Teaching, Nat. Conf. Profs. Ednl. Adminstrn., Phi Delta Kappa. Contbr. profl. jours, encys. Home: 4125 Cornwall Dr Virginia Beach VA 23452

BAKER, JOHN HERBERT, physician, fgn. service officer; b. Whitinsville, Mass., May 29, 1926; s. Hilka John and Cornelia Schultze (Wassenar) B; A.B., Calvin Coll., 1950; M.D., Tufts U., 1954; m. Marilyn Jean Orlebeke, Dec. 28, 1955; children—David John, Paul Alan, Ruth Ellen. Intern, St. Mary's Hosp., Grand Rapids, Mich., 1954-55; resident surgery St. Lukes Hosp., Chgo., 1955-59; post med. officer Am. embassy Taiz, Yemen, 1963-65; med. officer Am. embassy Baghdad, Iraq, 1965-67; with U.S. AID health program, VietNam, 1967-69; med. officer Am. embassy Kabul, Afghanistan, 1969-71; clin. dir. U.S. Dept. State, Washington, 1971—. Served with AUS, 1944-46. Recipient U.S. Dept. State honor award, 1965, U.S. AID Superior Honor award, 1969. Mem. Christian Ref. Ch. Mem. A.M.A. Home: 93 Cottage St Whitinsville MA 91588 Office: Dept State Washington DC 20525

BAKER, JOSEPHINE, singer; b. St. Louis, June 3, 1906; d. Louis Baker; ed. Phila. schs.; m. Pepito Abbitano (dec.); m. 2d, Jean Lion; m. 3d, Jo Bouillon (div.); 12 adopted children. Appeared as singer in Harlem nightclubs at age 8, later chorine in Broadway musical, Shuffle Along; appeared in Paris in Le Revue Negre, later starred in Folies Bergeres, Casino de Paris, L'Olympia de Paris, other French revues; stage appearances Carnegie Hall, also on Broadway's Brooks Atkinson Theater, N.Y.C.; star operattas, including La Creole; motion picture appearances include Zouzou, Princesse Tam-Tam, Fausse alerte. Decorated chevalier Legion of Honor, Croix de Guerre, Rosette de la Resistance (France). Mem. Internat. League Against Racism. Author: Les Memoires de Josephine Baker; La Tribu Arc-en-Ciel. Home: Chateau Milande 24 Castelnaud-Fayrac Dordogne France Office: care Bill Doll & Co 1700 Broadway New York City NY 10019

BAKER, J. STEWARD, Jr., cement co. exec.; b. Short Hills, N.J., 1918. With Bank of Manhattan Co., 1945-59, v.p., 1952-59; sr. v.p. Chase Manhattan Bank, 1959-63; dir. Alpha Portland Cement Co., 1958—, president, 1965-68, chairman board of directors, 1968—; director Grolier, Inc., North River Ins. Co. Pres. bd. trustees Miss Hall's Sch., Pittsfield, Mass.; trustee St. Luke's Hosp., N.Y.C., Grolier Found. Served with AUS. World War II. Office: Alpha Portland Cement Co 56 Water St Jersey City NJ 07304*

BAKER, JULIUS, musician; b. Cleve., Sept. 23, 1915; s. Max and Jeannette (Selznick) B.; student Eastman Sch., Music, Rochester, N.Y., 1932-33; diploma Curtis Inst. Music, Phila., 1937; m. Ruth Thorp, Mar. 28, 1961. Mem. Cleve. Orch., 1937-41; 1st flutist Pitts. Symphony, 1941-43, CBS Symphony, 1943- 51, Chgo. Symphony, 1951-53; mem. Bach Aria Group, 1947-65; solo flutist N.Y. Philharmonic Orch., 1965-; solo appearances throughout U.S., Europe and Japan; rec. artist for Decca, Oxford, Vanguard records; faculty Julliard Sch. Music, N.Y.C., 1954—. Home: Enoch Crosby Rd RFD 1 Brewster NY 10509

BAKER, LAWRENCE C., lawyer; b. Winnemucca, Nev., June 8, 1905; A.B., U. Nev., 1926; LL.B., Harvard, 1930. Now mem. firm Heller, Ehrman, White & McAuliffe. Mem. San Francisco Bar Assn. (pres. 1967). Address: 44 Montgomery St San Francisco CA 94104

BAKER, LENOX DIAL, orthopaedist; b. DeKalb, Tex., Nov. 10, 1902; s. James D. and Doda (Lenox) B.; student Pierce Sch. Bus. Adminstrn., Phila., 1920-21, U. Tenn., 1925-29, Sch. Medicine, U. N.C., 1929-30; M.D., Duke, 1934; m. Virginia Flowers, Aug. 22, 1933 (dec.); childrenRobert Flowers, Lenox Dial; m 2d, Margaret Copeland, Apr. 22, 1967. Athletic trainer U. Tenn., 1925-29, Duke, 1929-33; orthopaedic intern Johns Hopkins Hosp., 1933-34, surg. intern, 1934-35, asst. resident orthopaedics, 1935-36, resident orthopaedics, 1936-37; asst., instr. orthopaedic surgery, sch. med. Johns Hopkins, 1935-37; asst. orthopaedics Duke, Durham, N.C., 1937-38, asso., 1938- 39, asst. prof. orthopaedics, 1940-42, asso. prof., 1942-46, prof., 1947—; orthopaedist Duke Hosp., 1937—, dir. div. phys. therapy, 1943-62; co-op. orthopaedic surgeon crippled children's div. N.C. Bd. Health, also vocational rehab. div. N.C. Dept. Pub. Instrn., 1937—; orthopaedist Lincoln Hosp. 1937—, trustee, 1939—, exec. com., 1941-, chmn. exec. com. 1951-; vis. orthopaedist Watts Hosp., 1937—; faculty div. pub. health and soc. work U. NC., 1938-41; med. dir. N.C. Hosp. Cerebral Palsy, Durham, 1949—; orthopaedic cons. to several hosps., founds., sanitaria, govtl. agys.; active in cerebral palsy work; mem. N.C. Bd. Health, 1956—, pres., 1963-68, v.p., 1968—. Recipient U.S. President's Physician's award, 1958; Citizenship award Triangle chpt. Nat. Football Hall of Fame, 1969; Service to Athletics award Atlantic Coast Sportswriters, 1970. Diplomate Am. Bd. Orthopaedic Surgery. Mem. A.M.A. (chmn. orthopaedic sect. 1958-59), and other nat., regional, state, local profl. and sci. orgns., including Am. Acad. Cerebral Palsy (pres. 1954-55), Am. Orthopaedic Assn. (pres. 1963-64), So. Med. Assn. (editorial com. 1960—, past. chmn. orthopaedic sect.), Med. Soc. N.C. (pres. 1959), Tex. Orthopaedic Assn. (hon.), Internat. Cerebral Palsy Soc. (spl. mem.). Presbyn. Clubs: Tobac (Durham); Coral Bay (Atlantic Beach, N.C.); Barclay, Key (Chgo); Hope Valley Country; Sertoma (hon.). Author: Treatment of Minor Injuries of Baseball (with neous Bone Tumors, 1952. Mem. editorial com. Jour. Bone and Joints Surgery, 1960-61, trustee, 1967—. Contbr. articles to profl. publs. Home: 3106 Cornwall Rd Hope Valley Durham NC 27707 Office: Duke Hosp Durham NC 27710 ☆

BAKER, LISLE, JR. ret. newspaper exec.; b. Monticello, Ky., Apr. 11, 1902; s. Waller Lisle and Zona (Ramsey) B.; A.B., Centre Coll., 1922; m. Mary Elizabeth Turner, May 24, 1930; children—Elizabeth Maddox, Louis Ramsey, Robert Lisle, Mary Stuart. Asst. sec., later sec.-treas. Capital Trust Co., Frankfort, Ky., 1922-34; cashier, trust officer, dir. State Nat. Bank, Frankfort, 1934-36; past chairman finance com. and dir. Louisville Courier-Jour., Louisville Times Co., and affiliated Standard gravure Corp., WHAS, Inc., past pres. Bus. Devel. Corp. Ky.; dir. Photon, Inc. Mem. Ky. Council for Pub. Higher Edn. Past dir. Audit Bur. Circulations. Past trustee Centre Coll., (Danville, KY.); Ky.; past chmn. Louisville R.R. Planning Commn.; past pres. Louisville Fund, Am. Newspaper Pubs. Assn. Research Inst. Mem. So. Newspaper Pub. Assn., (pres., 1947-48), Louisville Philharmonic Soc. (past pres. and dir.), Louisville Com. on Fgn. Relations, English Speaking Union, Delta Kappa Epsilon, Omicron Delta Kappa. Clubs: Pendennis, Country (Louisville). Home: 330 Mockingbird Valley Rd Louisville KY 40207

BAKER, MELVIN C., food co. exec.; b. Sioux City, Ia., Nov. 9, 1920; s. Robert C. and Louise C. (Moran) B,; student U. S.D., 1939; B.S., Northwestern U., 1946; grad. Advanced Mgmt. Program Harvard, 1959; m. Ann Mead Payne, July 10, 1943; children—Michael, Deborah, Alison, Mark, John, Geoffrey, Courtney. Announcer, Aberdeen Broadcasting Co., 1939-41; advt. exec. Procter & Gamble Co., 1946-54; with Gen. Foods Corp., 1954-68, v.p., gen. mgr. Post div., 1964-67, v.p. marketing, 1968; dir., v.p. Thomas J. Lipton, Inc., 1968-69; v.p., pres. gen. edn. div. (N.Am.) FAS Internat., Inc., N.Y.C., 1969—. Served to lt. USNR, 1941-45. Home: Deacon's Way New Canaan, CT 06840. Office: 437 Madison Av New York City NY 10022

BAKER, MERL, univ. chancellor; b. Cadiz, Ky., July 11, 1924; s. Jesse F. and Argie (Coyle) B.; B.S. in Mech. Engring., U. Ky., 1945; M.S., Purdue U., 1948, Ph.D., 1952; m. Emily Wilson, Sept. 14, 1946; children—Merl Wilson, Marilyn Ruth. Graduate asst. Purdue U., 1946-48; mem. faculty U. Ky., 1948-63, prof. mech. engring., 1953-63, exec. dir. Ky. Research Found., 1957-63, exec. dir. research and relations with industry, 1957-63; dean U. Mo. Sch. Mines and Metallurgy, 1963; chancellor U. of Mo. Rolla, 1964- -. Vice pres. Blue Grass council Boy Scouts Am., 1960-62; chmn. adv. bd. U. Ky. YMCA, 1957-58. Named one of the 3 outstanding young men in Ky., Ky. Jr. C. of C., 1957; Pi Tau Sigma Gold medal award Am. Soc. M.E., 1953; Distinguished Engring. Alumnus award Purdue U., 1965. Mem. Am. Soc. M.E., American Institute Mining, Metallurgical and Petroleum Engineers, Am. Soc. Heating and Air Conditioning Engrs. (award of merit teaching 1959, vice chmn. edn. com. 1960-61), Am. Soc. Engring. Edn. (pres. S.E. sect. 1956-57, chmn. Internat. edn. com. 1961-63, exec. com.), American Association U. Profs., Mo., Ky. socs. profl. engrs., Ky. Acad. Sci., Newcomen Soc. N.A., Engring. Coll. Research Council (gen. chmn. com. research adminstrn. 1963-66), Lamp and Cross, Blue Key, Scabbard and Blade, Sigma Xi, Phi Kappa Phi, Phi Eta Sigma, also Tau Beta Pi, Pi Tau Sigma, Sigma Pi Sigma, Omicron Delta Kappa, Chi Epsilon. Rotarian (v.p. Lexington, Ky. 1962-63). Address: Chancellor's Office U Mo-Rolla Rolla MO 54301

BAKER, MICHAEL, Jr., cons. engr.; b. Beaver, Pa., Feb. 18, 1912; s. Michael and Anna (Thompson) B.; B.S. in Civil Engring., Pa. State U., 1936; D.Sc., Steubenville (O.) Coll., 1954; D. Engring., Ohio U., 1956, Tri-State Coll., 1965; L.H.D., Geneva Coll., 1960; m. Myrtle E. Pitzer, Mar. 23, 1932; children—Michael III, Carl Gene, Keith Joel (dec.). Boro engr. State Coll. Pa., 1936-38; contractor, 1938-40; pres. Michael Baker, Jr., Inc., Rochester, Pa., 1940—, Michael Baker, Jr., Air Maps, Inc., 1948—, Beaver Valley Engring. Supplies, 1955—; dir. Freedom Nat. Bank. Pres., Pa. Registration Bd. for Profl. Engrs.; cons. engr. Schuylkill Expressway, Pa. Turnpike, Squirrel Hill Tunnel, Ft. Pitt Tunnel, Pa.-Lincoln Pkwy., pub. works devel., Saudi Arabia, Peru, Ecuador, Hashemite Kingdom Jordan, Kingdom Yemen. Past mem. Brighton Twp. Sch. Bd.; mem. Salvation Army Bd.; mem. Nat. Hwy. Safety Adv. Com.; mem. exec. com. Boy Scouts Am.; mem. United Fund. Vice pres. bd. dirs. Rochester Hosp.; trustee Coll. of Steubenville, Pa. State U.; Pa. Better Hwys. Com. Recipient Horatio Alger award, 1954; Sons of Italy Service award; Am. Legion Distinguished award; Silver Beaver award Allegheny council Boy Scouts Am.; Distinguished Alumnus award Pa. State U., 1958; Man of Year, Rochester C. of C., Beaver Area C. of C. Registered profl. civil engr. 48 states, C.Z., D.C. Fellow Am. Soc. C.E.; mem. Nat., Pa. (Engr. of Year 1968, Beaver County chpt. 1954) socs. profl. engrs., Pi Kappa Alpha (hon.), Tau Beta Pi, Chi Epsilon, Triangle (hon.). Presbyn. Club: Duquesne (Pitts.). Home: 130 Evergreen Circle Mounted Route 9 Beaver PA 15009 Office: Penn-Beaver Hotel Rochester PA 15074

BAKER, MICHAEL HARRY, chem. engr.; b. Roanoke, Va., Oct. 25, 1916; s. Samuel A. and Freda (Herman) B.; B.Chem. Engring., Pratt Inst., 1938; postgrad. Va. Poly. Inst., 1939-40, U. Md., 1940-41; m. Margaret E. Zanger, 1940; children—Ellen, Martha, Zachary. Chem. engr. Norfolk (Va.) Waterworks, 1938-39, Seagram, Ltd., Balt., 1940-43, Davison Chem. Corp., 1943-47, Gen. Mills Research Labs., 1947-51; pres. M.H. Baker Co. div. Chem/Serv, Inc., 1952—. Mem. Minn. Fedn. Engring. Soc. (chmn. 1962-63, dir.), Am. Chem. Soc. (past chmn. Minn.), A.A.A.S., Minn. Acad. Scis. (pres. elect 1971, dir.), Am. Inst. Chem. Engr. (past chmn. Twin Cities), Mpls. Engrs. Club (program chmn., dir.), Minn. Indsl. Chemists Forum (past pres.), T.A.P.P.I., Inst. Food Technologists (nat. councillor 1964—, chmn. commn. on profl. relations and status), Fedn. Am. Scientists. Clubs: Campus (Mpls.); Chemists (N.Y.). Co-author: Successful Commercial Chemical Development Chemist, 1958-60, now book rev. editor; past editor, now editorial dir., columnist Minn. Chemist, Contbr. articles profl. jours. Home: 2012 Girard Av S Minneapolis MN 55405 Office: 606 Washington Av N Minneapolis MN 55401

BAKER, MILTON GRAFLY, mil. acad. adminstr.; b. Phila., Aug. 24, 1899; s. Frank Robertson and Sallie (Dimmock) B.; student Brown Prep. Sch., 1911-14; A.B., St. John's Coll., 1921; LL.D., Gettysburg Coll., 1939, Temple U., 1949, Norwich U., 1956; Pd.D., LaSalle Coll., 1955; LL.D., Villanova U., 1966; Ed.D., Suffolk U., 1966; D. Mil. Sci., PMC Colls., 1968; L.H.D., Hahnemann Med. Sch., 1969; m. May Porter Hagenbuch, Apr. 29, 1924 (dec. Mar. 1970); 1 dau., Ann Porter (Mrs. Winslow Martin); Pres., supt. Valley Forge Mil. Acad., Wayne, Pa., 1928—. Trustee Cabrini Coll., Radnor, Temple U., Gen. George Catlett Marshall Found., Lexington, Va., Gen. Douglas MacArthur Meml. Found., Norfolk, Va., Inf. Mus. Assn., Nat. Armed Forces Mus. Adv. Bd., Smithsonian Inst. Dir. Gettysburg Battle Centennial Commn.; chmn. U.S. nat. commn. UNESCO, 1953- 55, del.-at-large, 1953-58; chmn. Commonwealth of Pa. Mil. Commn., 1952- 58; chmn. Dept. Def. Res. Forces Policy Bd., 1955-57; mem. bd. Pa. Gen. State Authority, 1963-70. Chmn. inauguration Gov. of Pa., 1963, 67, Scott for Senate Com. (Pa.), 1964-70; del. Republican Nat. Conv., 1960, 64, 68. Served with U.S. Army, 1917-21; comdg. gen. Pa. N.G., 1943-46; gen. U.S. dir. Civil Def., Phila., 1941-42; commd. lt. gen., 1957. Decorated U.S.; Brazil, Nicaragua, Belgium, Ecuador, Bulgaria, France; Order Sword (Sweden); Spanish Naval Cross (Spain); Order of Merit Republic of Italy; comdr. Most Excellent Order Brit. Empire; recipient numerous awards, medals U.S. Dept. Army, Dept. Def., Dept. War; Pa. Distinguished Service medal with palm, Pa. Meritorious Service medal with palm, Pa. award for excellence in field edn., 1968; Silver medal Union League Phila., 1968. Fellow Co. Mil. Historians, Internat. Coll. Surgeons; mem. Navy League U.S. (Phila. council), Am. Ch. Union, Assn. U.S. Army (pres. 1960-63, chmn. council trustees 1964-70), Pa. Soc. S.R. (pres. 1966-67), Devon Horse Show Assn. (dir.), Mil. Colls. and Schs. U.S. (dir., past pres.), Mil. Order World Wars (past comdr. Pa. chpt., nat. comdr. 1950-51), Franklin Inst., Assn. Jr. Colls, Assn. Am. Colls., Old Guard City Phila., Mil. Order Loyal Legion, Saint Andrews Soc., Hist. Soc. Pa., Res. Officers Assn. U.S., Valley Forge Hist. Soc., Pa. Soc. N.Y., Nat. Assn. Secondary Sch. Prins., Mil. Order Fgn. Wars, Brotherhood St. Andrew, Confrerie des Chevaliers du Tastevin, English Speaking Union, Miniature Figure Collectors Am., Washington Crossing Found., World Affairs Council. Episcopalian. Mason (32). Clubs: Union League (N.Y.C., Phila.); Capitol Hill, F Street (Washington); Army Navy, Penn (Phila.); St. Davids Golf; British Officers; Rolling Rock, Ligonier (Pa.); Surf (Miami Beach); Bald Peak Colony (N.H.). Home: 14 Fariston Rd Wayne PA 19087

BAKER, PAUL, theatre dir., educator; b. Hereford, Tex., July 24, 1911; s. William Morgan and Retta (Chapman) B.; B.A., Trinity U., Waxachie, Tex., 1932, D.F.A. (hon.), 1958; student U. Wis., 1929; M.F.A. Yale, 1939; student of Elsie Fogarty, Central Sch. Speech, London, Eng., 1932; studied, observed theatre in Eng., Germany, Russia, Japan; m. Sallie Kathryn Cardwell, Dec. 21, 1936; children—Robyn Cardwell, Retta Chapman, Sallie Kathryn. Chief entertainment br. spl. services div., ETO, 1944-45; prof. drama, chmn. dept. Baylor U., 1934-63; dir. Dallas Theatre Center, 1959- -, prof. drama, chmn. dept. Trinity U., San Antonio, 1963—; organized S.W. Summer Theatre, Waco, 1939, also built theatre inside Waco Hall, Baylor U., 1939; designed Studio I, Baylor U., 1942; dir. exptl. prodn. Othello, 1953; co-designer Weston Theatre addition to Baylor Theatre, 1954; dir. A Different Drummer, Baylor U. and CBS-TV, 1955, Hamlet with Burgess Meredith and Charles Laughton, Baylor Theatre, 1956, Journey to Jefferson, Theatre des Nations, Paris, France, 1964 (recipient Spl. Jury Prize for season); promoted bldg., founding Frank Lloyd Theatre in Dallas, 1959, also establishment permanent sch. and repertory co. for Am. in Dallas, 1959; mem. Texas Fine Arts Commn., 1967-68; design cons. Taylor Theater, Trinity U. mem. Ad Hoc Com. on Profl.-Educational Theater Relationships. Bd. governors Am. Playwrights Theater. Served to maj. Army of U.S., 1943-45; ETO. Rockefeller Found. fellow, 1937-39, 41, 46, 59; recipient Rodgers and Hammerstein award for outstanding theatrical contbn. in S.W., 1961. Mem. Nat. Theatre Conf. (pres. 1958- 62), S.W. Theatre Conf. (pres. 1956), ANTA (dir. 1967-68), Am.Ednl. Theatre Assn., Tex. Inst. Letters. Presbyn. (past elder). Author chpts. in books. Home: 275 E Summit St San Antonio TX 78212. Office: Dallas Theatre Center 3636 Turtle Creek Dallas TX 75219

BAKER, PAUL, Jr., air force officer; b. Ashland, Ky., Feb. 10, 1921; s. Paul and Edna M. (Holbrook) B.; B.A., Washington and Lee U., 1942; B.S., U.S. Mil. Acad., 1945; M.S., N.C. State U., 1952; Ph.D. in Physics, U. Denver, 1966; m. Iantha Dunton, Mar. 14, 1948; children—Paul Mark, Miriam Anne, Jon Clark. Commd. 2d lt. U.S. Army, 1945, advanced through grades to col. U.S. Air Force, 1966; staff officer directorate requirements Hdqrs. USAF, 1952-56; chief tech. br. Hartford area office AEC, 1956-61; faculty USAF Acad., 1961-67, prof. physics, head dept., 1964-65, research asso., 1965, dir. research, 1966-67; chief tech. div. Directorate of Space, Hdqrs. USAF, 1967—. Mem. Am. Assn. Physics Tchrs., A.A.A.S., N.Y. Acad. Scis., Phi Beta Kappa, Sigma Xi, Beta Theta Pi. Conglist. Contbr. papers on cosmic ray physics. Home: 4404 Random Ct Annandale VA 22003 Office: Hdqrs USAF (AFRDSD) The Pentagon Washington DC 20330

BAKER, PAUL THORNELL, anthropologist, educator; b. Burlington, Ia., Feb. 28, 1927; s. Palmer Ward and Viola (Thornell) B.; student U. Miami, 1947-49; B.A., U. N.M., 1951; Ph.D., Harvard, 1956; m. Thelma M. Shoher, Feb. 22, 1948; children—Deborah, Amy, Joshua, Felicia. Phys. anthropologist research and devel. center Q.M.C., Natick, Mass., 1952-57; research asso. Pa. State U., 1957-58, asst. prof. anthropology, 1958-61, asso. prof., 1961-64, prof., 1964—, acting head dept. sociology and anthropology, 1964-65, head dept. anthropology, 1968-70. Dir. Andean Bio- Cultural Studies, 1964-68; coordinator high altitude research Internat. Biol. Program. Mem. Nat. Inst. Mental Health Fellowship Rev. Bd., 1966-69. Fulbright research scholar, Peru, 1962; NATO sr. sci. fellow, Eng., 1968. Pres. bd. dirs. Benner Twp. Sch. Served with M.C., AUS, 1945-47; ETO. Fellow Am. Anthrop. Assn.; mem. Am. Assn. Phys. Anthropologists (pres. 1969-71), Am. Ecology Soc. (asso.). Author: (with J.S. Weiner) The Biology of Human Adaptability. Asso. editor Am. Jour. Phys. Anthropology. Contbr. articles to tech. lit. Home: Box 115 E R D 1 Bellefonte PA 16823 Office: Pa State U University Park PA 16802

BAKER, PHILLP DOUGLAS, investment banker; b. Los Angeles, Mar. 19, 1922; s. J. Douglas and Alice (Brown) B.; B.S., U. Cal. at Los Angeles, 1947, M.B.A., at Berkeley, 1948; m. Cornelia Draves, July 16, 1955; children—Brinton, Todd, Claudia, and Samuel Baker. Associated with the Marshall Plan in Germany, from 1948-52; partner White, Weld & Co., N.Y.C., 1952—; adj. asso. prof. Grad. Sch. Bus. Adminstrn., N.Y.U., 1964-66. Served to capt. USMCR, 1943- 46. Decorated Purple Heart. Mem. Investment Bankers Assn. Am. (chmn. N.Y. group 1969-70), Bond Club of New York, Investment Bankers Association (1st v.p. 1970-71). Home: 293 Green Ridge Rd Franklin Lakes NJ 07417 Office: 20 Broad St New York City NY 10005

BAKER, RAYMOND CHARLES, savs. and loan exec.; b. Jermyn, Pa., Aug. 29, 1895; s. Charles F. and Mary L. (Robinson) B.; B.S., Wesleyan U., 1919; m. Mildred Louise Nicholson, Oct. 14, 1918; children—Aldine (Mrs. R.C. McCorkle), Phyllis (Mrs. John C. Wyckoff). With R.C. Baker, Inc., Winter Park, Fla., 1925-56; charter dir. Winter Park Fed. Savs. & Loan Assn., 1934—, pres., 1938-70, chmn. bd., 1970—; dir. First Nat. Bank of Winter Park, 1944—. Mem. Central Fla. Devel. Com., 1966—; pres. Winter Park C. of C., 1929, 47. Mayor Winter Park, 1934-35, 43-44; mem. Bd. Adjustments, Winter Park, 1954-67. Bd. dirs. Winter Park Country Club, 1948-69; trustee Winter Park Library, 1959—. Served to 1st lt., QM Corps, AUS, 1917-19. Mem. Beta Theta Pi. Republican. Methodist. Mason. Home: 965 Lakeview Dr Winter Park FL 32789 Office: 200 E New England Av Winter Park FL 32789

BAKER, RAYMOND EMERSON, paper co. exec.; b. Salem, Ind., Feb. 27, 1913; s. James Blaine and Mabel May (Miller) B.; A.B., DePauw U., 1935; M.S., Inst. Paper Chemistry, 1937, Ph.D. 1940; m. Jane E. Lesselyong, June 8, 1940; children—James Edward, Bonita Ann, John Clinton, David Blaine. Research chemist Brown Co., Berlin, N.H., 1940-41; pulp mill supt. Munising Paper Co. (Mich.), 1941-45; tech. dir. BFD div. Diamond Match Co., Plattsburg, N.Y., 1945-47; with pulp and paperboard div. Weyerhaeuser Co., 1947-60, v.p. mfg., 1955-60; exec. v.p. Southwest Forest Industries, Phoenix, 1960—; dir. Apache Ry. Co. Mem. T.A.P.P.I., Sigma Nu. Clubs: Arizona, Phoenix Country. Home: 5307 Questa Tierra Dr Phoenix AZ 85012 Office: P O Box 7548 Phoenix AZ 85011

BAKER, RAY PALMER, ret. educator, author; b. Fonthill, Can., Sept. 21, 1883; s. Jacob Johnson and Ida Emma (Fitch) B.; B.A., U. Western Ont., 1906; Ph.M., U. Chgo., 1910; M.A., Harvard, 1914, Ph.D., 1916; LL.D., U. Western Ont., 1928; m. Mary Irene Messenger, Sept. 1, 1914; children—Mary Elizabeth (dec.), Ray Palmer, Jr., David Wolverton. Modern lang. master Highfield Sch., Hamilton, Ont., 1906-09; prof. English, Okanagan Coll., 1910-11, asst. prin., 1911-13; prof. English, Rensselaer Poly. Inst., 1915-1940, head dept. arts. sci. and bus. adminstrn., 1925-40, asst. dir., 1930-49, v.p., 1949-54, dean students, 1944-49, v.p. emeritus, 1955. Gov. Union U. Trustee Albany Med. Coll. Dudley Obs. Pub. Library, Troy, Asso. Hosp. Service Capital Dist., Samaritan Hosp.; chmn. bd. Bus. History Found. Trustee Rensselaer County Hist. Soc. Mem Rensselaer Soc. Engrs., Newcomen Soc., Modern Lang. Assn. Am. Soc. Promotion Engring. Edn., Sigma Xi. Author: A History of English- Canadian Literature-Its Relation to the Literature of Great Britain and the United States, 1920, 68; Preparation of Reports, Engineering, Scientific, Administrative Business, 1923, 2d edit. (with A.C. Howell), 1937; A Chapter in American Education, 1924; Writing—A First Book for College Students (with William Haller), 1928. Editor: Engineering Education, 1919, 2d edit. 1928; Feathers with Yellow Gold, 1920; Sam Slick (by Thomas Chandler Haliburton), 1923; The Clockmaker (by Thomas Chandler Haliburton), 1927. Contbr. to ednl., lit. and hist. periodicals, to Dictionary Am. Biography, Columbia Course in Literature, etc. Club: Troy. Home: Hickory Hollow Averill Park NY 12018

BAKER, REX GAVIN, Jr., lawyer, savs. and loan exec.; b. Beaumont, Tex., Apr. 22, 1920; s. Rex Gavin and Edna (Heflin) B.; B.A., U. Tex., 1941, LL.B., J.D., 1947; m. Jeannette M. Russell, Sept. 6, 1947; children—Jeannette S., Bess Heflin, Ann Russell, Rex Gavin III. Admitted to Tex. bar, 1946; practice law, Houston, 1947—; partner Berry, Richards & Baker, 1947-57, Roberts, Baker, Richards, Elledge & Heard, 1957-62, Baker, Heart & Brunson, Houston, 1962—. Chmn. bd. Southwestern Savs. Assn.; pres., dir. Blanca Devel. Co., Baker Properties, Inc., Southwestern Group Investors, Inc.; past dir. Fed. Home Loan Bank Bd., Little Rock; dir., gen. counsel Western Nat. Bank; past trustee First Mortgage Investors Shares Beneficial Interest. Mem., sect. chmn. finance commn. State of Tex. Councilman, Bellaire, Tex., 1948-49; mem. Houston Juvenile Delinquency and Crime Commn., 1955-56; mem. Tex. Hi-Y Council, 1957-61. Bd. dirs. Holly Hall, Houston Housing Devel. Corp., Inst. Religion, Am. Cancer Soc. Served to lt. USNR, 1942-46. Mem. Am., Tex., Houston bar assns., Nat. League Insured Savs. Assns. (past pres., mem. exec. com.), Tex. Partners of Alliance with Peru (chmn. bd.), Inter-Am. Savs. and Loan Union (past pres., mem. exec. com.), Internat. Union Bldg. Socs. and Savs. Assns., Kappa Sigma. Baptist (bd. deacons). Home: 3747 Chevy Chase St Houston TX 77019 Office: 3300 Main St Houston TX 77002

BAKER, RICHARD SOUTHWORTH, lawyer; b. Lansing, Mich., Dec. 18, 1929; s. Paul Julius and Florence (Schmid) B.; student DePauw U., 1947-49; A.B. cum laude, Harvard, 1951; J.D., U. Mich., 1954; m. Marina Joy Vidoli, July 24, 1965; children—Garrick Richard, Lydia Joy. Admitted to Ohio bar, 1957, since practiced in Toledo; mem. firm Fuller, Seney, Henry & Hodge, 1956—, partner, 1961—. Chmn. nat. com. region IV, Mich. Law Sch. Fund, 1967- 69, mem.-at-large, 1970—. Bd. dirs. Asso. Harvard Alumni, 1970—. Served with AUS, 1954-56. Recipient award of merit Ohio Legal Center Inst., 1968. Mem. Am., Ohio (chmn. com.), Toledo bar assns., Phi Delta Theta, Phi Delta Phi. Clubs: Toledo, Harvard (pres. 1968—), Inverness (Toledo). Home: 2819 Falmouth Rd Toledo OH 43615 Office: 405 Madison Av Toledo OH 43604

BAKER, RICHARD T., accountant; b. Anderson, Ind., Sept. 4, 1917; s. Leslie and Rachel (Morgan) B.; B.S., Ohio State U., 1939; m. Martha Brown, Apr. 15, 1939; children—Ann, Laura, Jane, Richard. With Ernst & Ernst, C.P.A.'s, 1940- -, partner, 1952—, mng. partner, Cleve., 1964—. Mem. Greater Cleve. Growth Bd.; active Cleve. United Appeal, Cleve. chpt. Am. Cancer Soc. Chartered accountant, Ont.; registered in U.K. and S. Africa. Mem. Am. Inst. C.P.A.'s. Clubs: Cleveland Athletic, Clevelander, Skating, Union, Mid-Day (Cleve.); Pepper; Pike; Ottawa Shooting; Rockwell Springs Trout; Laurel Valley Golf; Chicago; Castalia Trout. Home: 2680 Chesterton Rd Shaker Heights OH 44122 Office: Union Commerce Bldg Cleveland OH 44115

BAKER, RICHARD TERRILL, educator; b. Coggon, Ia., Mar. 27, 1913; s. Earle Alonzo and Grace Eloise (Terrill) B.: A.B., Cornell Coll., Mt. Vernon, Ia., 1934, D.D., 1946; M.S., Columbia, 1937; B.D., Union Theol. Sem., N.Y.C., 1941; m. Marjorie Wilcox Coleman, Sept. 4, 1937; 1 son, Coleman E. Mem. editorial staff Christian Adv. and Epworth Herald, 1934-36; asso. editor World Outlook, 1939-47; ordained to ministry Methodist Ch., 1941; asso. prof., acting dean Postgrad. Sch. Journalism, Chungking, China, 1943-45; corr. in Orient, 1945-46; asso. prof. journalism Columbia Grad. Sch. Journalism, 1947-52, prof., 1952—, asso. dean sch., 1961-68, acting dean, 1968-70. Staff N.Y. Times, 1953-54; vis. prof. Nat. Chengchi U., Taipei, Taiwan, 1968. Cons. religious affairs br. Office High Commnr. for Germany, 1950. Trustee Glen Rock (N.J.) Pub. Library. Pulitzer traveling fellow, 1937- 38. Decorated Victory medal Republic of China, 1947; recipient Columbia Journalism Alumni award, 1967. Mem. Assn. Edn. Journalism, Phi Beta Kappa. Author: The Seed and the Soil, 1941; Trumpet of a Prophecy, 1943; Ten Thousand Years, 1947; Darkness of the Sun, 1947; The Graduate School of Journalism, 1954; The Christian as a Journalist, 1961. Mem. editorial bds. bds. Assn. Press, Christianity and Crisis, Columbia Journalism Rev. Home: 10 Boulevard Glen Rock NJ 07452 Office: Journalism Sch Columbia U New York City NY 10027

BAKER, RICHARD WHEELER, Jr., real estate exec.; b. Cambridge, Mass., May 13, 1916; s. Richard Wheeler and Doris (Newberry) B.; grad. Groton Sch., 1934; B.A., Yale, 1938; grad. Advanced Mgmt. Program, Harvard, 1957; m. Rachel Irvin Cooper, Dec. 23, 1940; children—Eileen Elizabeth (now Lady Strathnaver), Richard Wheeler III, John Cooper. Tchr., St. Paul's Sch., 1939-41; asst. to personnel dir. Mut. Life Ins. Co. of N.Y., 1946- 49, gen. asst. investments, 1949-54; real estate and mortgage loan dept., adminstrv. asst. N.Y. Life Ins. Co., 1954-55, exec. asst., 1955- 56, asst. v.p., 1956-58, 2d v.p., 1958-61, v.p., 1961-69; sr. v.p. finance, dir. Property Devel. Group, Inc., Ann Arbor, 1969—; trustee Bklyn. Savings Bank, First Pa. Mortgage Trust; exec. trustee Instnl. Investors Trust, Vice chmn. Stony Brook Dist. Com., Boy Scouts Am., 1959-61; mem. Presdl. Task Force on Low Income Housing, 1969. Mem. Republican County Com., Princeton Twp., 1953-59, capt., 1960-62; chmn. citizen's adv. com. Princeton Twp. Plan Bd., 1958-60. Chmn. bd. trustees Princeton Country Day Sch., 1958-62, vice chmn., 1962-63; trustee Princeton Hosp.; bd. dirs. Yale Alumni Fund, 1968—. Served to lt. comdr. USNR, 1941-46; capt. Res. Mem. Life Ins. Assn. Am., Am. Life Conv. (chmn. joint sub-coms. housing and mortgage lending policy of both 1965-68). Naval Order U.S., Mortgage Bankers Assn. (vice chmn. research com. 1964-67), Princeton Young Rep. Club (pres. 1954-56), Princeton Rep. Club (pres. 1956-59), Berzelius, Phi Beta Kappa. Episcopalian (vestry 1952-55). Clubs: Elizabethan (New Haven); Yale (N.Y.C.); Nassau, Pretty Brook (Princeton, N.J.). Address: 1 Armour Rd Princeton NJ 08540

BAKER, ROBERT CALHOUN, banker; b. Everett, Pa., May 22, 1902; s. Francis and Jennie (Calhoun) B.; B.S., U. Pa., 1927. Vice pres., dir. Central Nat. Bank, Richmond, Va., 1935-45; v.p. Columbia Nat. Bank, Washington, 1945-46; v.p. Am. Security & Trust Co., Washington, 1946-49, dir., 1948—, exec. v.p., 1949-59, pres., 1959-69, chmn. bd., 1962—; pres., dir. Am. Security Corp., 1959—; dir. Burlington Industries, Greensboro, N.C., Peoples Drug Stores, Inc., Washington Gas Light Co., Peoples Life Ins. Co., mem. adv. bd. Washington Mut. Investors Fund. Chmn., Nat. Capital Downtown Com. Bd. dirs. United Givers Fund; trustee Juniata Coll., Fed. City Council, George Washington U. Mem. Assn. Res. City Bankers (past dir.). Clubs: University (N.Y.C.); Chevy Chase, 1925 F St., Nat. Press, University, City Tavern, Capitol Hill, Metropolitan, Burning Tree (Washington); Everglades, Bath and Tennis (Palm Beach, Fla.), Lyford Cay (Nassau, Bahamas). Home: 2500 Calvert St NW Washington DC 20008 Office: 15th and Pennsylvania Av Washington DC 20013

BAKER, ROBERT ELLSWORTH, former naval officer; b. Mechanicsburg, O., Oct. 31, 1900; s. Lyman Ellsworth and Ada Opal (Taylor) B.; B.Sc., Ohio State U., 1922, M.D., 1924; certificate Naval Med. Sch., 1931-32; M.Sc., U. Pa., 1938; postgrad. George Washington U., 1951-52; m. Evelyn Ehrhardt, Mar. 15, 1930 (dec. Aug. 1968); children—Diana Joan, Robert Ellsworth. Commd. lt. (j.g.) M.C., USN, 1924, advanced through grades to capt., 1943; intern USN Hosp., San Diego, 1924-25; asst. chief surgery USN Hosp., Newport, R.I., 1929-31, chief surgery, 1946-48; chief surgery USN Hosp., Charleston, S.C., 1935-37, Coco Solo, C.Z., 1937-39, exec. officer, 1944, comdg. officer, 1945-46; chief surgery USN Hosp., Chelsea, Mass., 1939-41; exec. officer USN Hosp., Sampson, N.Y., 1943, USN Mobile Hosp. 12, 1943; exec. officer USN Hosp., Pensacola, Fla., 1948-50; comdg. officer hosp. U.S.S. Consolation, 1950; med. officer, Naval Training Sta. and Naval Base, Newport, R.I.; ship's med. officer U.S.S. Villalobos, Hart, Palos, Arctic, Henderson, ret. USN, 1954; dir. Newport, R.I. ship's med. Mass., Regional Blood Center, A.R.C., 1957-62. Recipient B.S.M., 1952. Fellow A.C.S.; mem. A.M.A., Mass. Med. Assn., Central Surg. Assn., Am. Legion, Order World Wars, Nat. Sojourners, Phi Rho Sigma. Methodist. K.T. Home: 33 Cranston Av Newport RI 02840

BAKER, ROBERT ERNEST, Jr., found. exec.; b. Tuscaloosa, Ala., Oct. 17, 1916; s. Robert Ernest and Faye (Whitson) B.; B.S. in Indsl. Engring., U. Ala., 1939; m. Billye Louise Driskell, June 25, 1947; 1 son, Brent Driskell. Engaged in indsl. engring., mgmt. and financial cons. 1939-62; exec. adminstr., sec. Moody Found., Galveston, Tex., 1962—. Bd. dirs. Bay Area council Boy Scouts Am., Moody House, Galveston Boys Club. C.P.A.; registered profl. engr., Tex. Mem. Houston Soc. Financial Analysts, Conf. of S.W. Founds. (pres.) Presbyn. Clubs: Country, Artillery (Galveston). Home: 6 Adler Circle Galveston TX 77550 Office: Moody National Bank Bldg Galveston TX 77550

BAKER, ROBERT HENRY, chemist, educator; b. Central City, Ky., June 14, 1908; s. Alfred T. and Mary (Henry) B.; A.A., Bethel Coll., Russellville, Ky., 1927; B.S., U. Ky., 1929, M.S., 1931, D.Sc., 1968; Ph.D. (Gen. Edn. Bd. fellow), U. Wis., 1940; m. Frances Holland, Mar. 25, 1932; children—Robert Henry, Peter Boyd. Instr. chemistry U. Ky., 1931-40, asst. prof., 1940-41; asst. prof. chemistry Northwestern U., Evanston, Ill., 1941-44, asso. prof., 1944-50, prof., 1950—, asst. dean Grad. Sch., 1949-61, asso. dean, 1961-63, dean, 1963—. Mem. nat. adv. com. Nat. Def. Grad. Fellowship Program, 1965-69; mem. exec. com. grad. deans African Am. Inst., 1964—; chmn. Midwest Conf. on Grad. Study and Research, 1967 -68. Mem. Am. Chem. Soc., Assn. Am. Univs. (pres. Assn. Grad. Schs. 1971-72), Sigma Xi, Alpha Chi Sigma, Phi Kappa Tau. Democrat. Presbyn. Contbr. articles to chem. jours. Home: 2420 Brown St Evanston IL 60432

BAKER, ROBERT LEWIS, educator; b. Taunton, Mass., Nov. 20, 1922; s. Winthrop Lewis and Miriam (Gregg) B.; A.B., Brown U., 1947; A.M., Princeton, 1949, Ph.D., 1955; student King's Coll., U. London, 1950-52; m. Virginia Clark, Mar. 14, 1964. Lectr., Rutgers U., 1954-55; instr., then asst. prof. Brown U., 1955-59; mem. faculty Kenyon Coll., Gambier, O., 1959—, prof. history, 1967—, chmn. dept., 1966—. Served with AUS, 1943-46. Mem. Am. Hist. Assn., Mediaeval Acad. Am., Conf. Brit. Studies, Inst. Hist. Research. Home: 101 E Wiggin St Gambier OH 43022

BAKER, ROBERT STEVENS, educator, organist; b. Pontiac, Ill., July 7, 1916; s. Stevens R. and Hattie (Thrasher) B.; B.Mus., Ill. Wesleyan U., 1938, Mus.D., 1960; Sacred Mus.M., Union Theol. Sem., 1940, Sacred Mus.D., 1944; L.H.D., Bradley U., 1964; D.F.I., Westminster Choir Coll., 1966; D. Mus. A., Susquehanna U., 1967; m. Mary F. Depler, June 24, 1943; children—James S., Martha Faye. Organist 1st Presbyn. Ch., Bklyn., 1941- 1941- 53, N.Y.C., 1946-51, Temple Emanu-El, N.Y.C., 1945-61; organist, choirmaster Fifth Av. Presbyn. Ch., N.Y.C., 1953-61; dean Sch. Sacred Music, Uion Theol. Sem., 1961—; concert organist, 1945—; recitalist Westminster Abbey, 900th Anniversary, 1966; organ bldg. cons. Bd. dirs. Union Theol. Sem., 1959-61; trustee Westminster Choir Coll., 1968—; chmn. organ award com. Inst. Internat. Edn., 1957-59, 63, 65, 66. Mem. Am. Guild Organists (dean N.Y.C. chpt. 1955-57, nat. councillor 1950-57, chmn. nat. conv. 1956, rep., opening recitalist 1st Internat. Congress Organists, London 1957, recitalist nat. convs. 1947, 56), Royal Coll. Organists, Hymn Soc. Am. (dir. 1961—), Bohemians, St. Wilfrid Soc., Oratorio Soc. N.Y. (dir.), Coll. Ch. Musicians (dir.). Home: 606 W 122d St New York City NY 10027. Office: 3041 Broadway New York City NY 10027

BAKER, ROBERT WILLIAM, educator; b. Brookline, Mass., July 30, 1924; s. Chauncey William and Marion (Power) B.; A.B., Hobart Coll., 1947; Ph.D., Clark U., 1953; m. Rita Agnes Knox, Dec. 29, 1951; children—Cheryl Alison, Jeffrey Clark, Susan Knox. Staff clin. psychologist VA Hosp., Northampton, Mass., 1953- 54; asst. prof. psychology Clark U., Worcester, Mass., 1954-57, asso. prof., 1957-66, prof., 1966—, dir. Psychol. Clinic, 1954-55, 56-65, 71—, dean students, 1965-68; asst. provost for student affairs, 1969-70. Field selection officer Peace Corps, 1964- 67. Pres. local chpt. Am. Humanist Assn., 1963-64; pres. local chpt. Med. Com. for Human Rights, 1965-66. Served with USNR, 1943-44. Diplomate Am. Bd. Examiners Profl. Psychology. Fellow Am. Psychol. Assn.; mem. Am. Civil Liberties Union (local exec. com. 1957—), Am. Assn. U. Profs. (com. on acad. freedom and tenure 1969—). Contbr. articles to profl. jours. Home: 398 May St Worcester MA 01602

BAKER, ROGER CARROLL, Jr., physician, educator; b. N.Y.C., June 18, 1919; s. Roger Carroll and Mary Berry (Lawrence) B.; student Seton Hall Coll., 1937-39; B.S., Boston Coll., 1941; M.D., Tufts U., 1944; Ph.D., U. Chgo., 1952; m. Genevieve Eremich, Jan. 4, 1946; children—Susan Lawrence, Leslie Greenberry, Abigail Kindley, Roger Carroll III, Alexander Cruise. Intern, St. Vincent's Hosp., N.Y.C., 1944-45, asst. resident gen. surgery, 1945-46; served as lt. (j.g.), resident urology USN, 1947-48; resident urology Mass. Meml. Hosp., Boston, 1948-49; fellow urology U. Chgo., 1949-50, head div. urology, 1949-53; prof., dir. urology Georgetown U. Sch. Medicine, 1953- -, now chief urologist hosp.; practice medicine, Washington, 1953—; chief urologist D.C. Gen., VA., Sibley hosps.; cons. VA, surgeon-gen. USPHS. chmn. bd., pres. Baker Research Corp., No-Load Selected Funds, Inc.; pres., dir. U.S. Physician Placement Agy., Inc. Recipient Research award Am. Assn. Urology, 1950, Research Exhibit awards Am. Assn. Urology, A.M.A., 1955. Fellow A.C.S., Am. Acad. Pediatrics; mem. A.A.A.S., Am. Urol. Assn., Am. Assn. Cancer Research, Soc. Exptl. Biology and Medicine, Nat. Assn. Security Dealers, Soc. Cin., S.A.R., Sigma Xi. Clubs: Cosmos, National Capitol Gun (Washington). Home: 1133 Chain Bridge Rd McLean, VA 22101. Office: 3800 Reservoir Rd Washington DC 20007

BAKER, ROGER DENLO, pathologist; b. East Lansing, Mich., April 10, 1902; s. Ray Stannard and Jessie Irene (Beal) B.; A.B., U. Wis., 1924; M.D. cum laude, Harvard, 1928; postgrad., Kiel, 1932, Tulane U., (tropical medicine), 1943; m. Eleanor Elizabeth Ussher, Sept. 3, 1929; children—David Remember, Douglas Ussher, Stephen Denio. Asst. resident pathologist Johns Hopkins Hosp.; asst., instr., Johns Hopkins Sch. Medicine, 1928- 30; instr. anatomy Duke U. Sch. Medicine, 1930-32, successively instr., asst. prof., asso. prof. pathology, 1932-44; asst. and asso. pathologist Duke Hosp., 1932-44; field work in tropical medicine, C.Am., 1944; prof. pathology, chmn. dept., Med. coll. Ala., 1944-52; pathologist Jefferson-Hillman Hosp., 1944-52; chief lab. service Durham VA Hosp., 1953-61; prof. pathology Duke Sch. Medicine, 1953-61; prof. pathology La. State U., New Orleans, 1961-70, Rutgers U. Med. Sch., New Brunswick, N.J., 1970—; on leave Facultad de Medicina, U. Antioquia, Medellin, Columbia, 1967- 68; vis. pathologist Charity Hosp., New Orleans; staff pathologist VA Hosp., New Orleans. Trustee Am. Bd. Pathology, 1948-61, pres. bd., 1960-61. Mem. Am. Soc. Clin. Pathologists, A.M.A. (chmn. sect. path. and physiology 1956-57), Am. Assn. Pathologists and Bacteriologists, Am. Soc. Exptl. Pathology, Coll. Am. Pathologists, A.A.A.S., Internat. Acad. Pathology, Am. Soc. Microbiology, Internat. Soc. Human and Animal Mycology, Sociedad Latinamericana de Anatomía Patológica, Alpha Omega Alpha, Med. Mycology Soc. Ams., Delta Chi, Nu Sigma Nu. Unitarian. Club: Cosmos (Washington). Author: Essential Pathology, 1961; Postmortem Pathology, 1967; sr. author Pathology of the Mycoses, 1971; co-author: Manual of Clinical Mycology, 1971. Contbr. chpt. on fungus diseases Anderson's Pathology, 1948, 57, 61, 66, 71; bd. Human Disease with Fungi, Actinomycetes and Algae, 1971. Bd. editors Am. Jour. Clin. Pathology. Contbr. articles on pathology, mycology, cardiovascular diseases, histochemistry and post-mortem exams. to med. jours. Home: 16 Ross Hall Blvd Piscataway NJ 08854 Office: Rutgers University Medical School New Brunswick NJ 08903

BAKER, ROLLIN HAROLD, biologist, educator; b. Cordova, Ill., Nov. 11, 1916; s. Charles Laurence and Minnie Louise (Perkins) B.; B.A., U. Tex., 1937; M.S., Tex. A. and M. U., 1938; Ph.D., U. Kan., 1948; m. Mary Elizabeth Waddell, Mar. 21, 1939; children—Elizabeth Alice, Bruce Rollin, Byron Laurence. Wildlife tech. Nat. Park Service, Texas Big Bend, summer 1937; field biologist Tex. Coop. Wildlife Research Unit, Coll. Sta., 1938-39; biologist Tex. Game and Fish Commn., 1939-43; asst. curator mammals Mus. Natural History, U. Kan., 1948-55, asst. instr., 1946-48, instr., 1948-49, asst. prof., 1949-54, asso. prof. zoology, 1954-55, acting dir. Mus. Natural History, U. Kan., 1950-51; dir. museum, prof. zoology and fisheries and wildlife Mich., State U., East Lansing, 1955—. Leader mus. expdns. western states and Mexico, for collection and observation animal life, 1949—. Served from ensign to lt. USNR, 1943-46; Naval Med. Research Unit, also vis. investigator Rockefeller Inst. Med. capt. Res. Fellow A.A.A.S.; mem. Mich. Audubon Soc., Am. Soc. Mammalogists (dir. 1956-70), Wildlife Soc., Am., Brit. ornithol. unions, Wilson Ornithol. Soc., Cooper Ornithol. Club, Am. Soc. Icthyologists and Herpetologists, Soc. Southwestern Naturalists, Soc. Study Evolution, Soc. Systematic Zoology (council 1958-61), Ecol. Soc. Am., Am. Mus. Assn., Soc. Study Animal Behaviour, Mich. Acad. Sci., Arts and Letters, Sigma Xi, Alpha Epsilon Delta, Beta Beta Beta. Phi Sigma, Tau Kappa Epsilon, Phi Kappa Phi. Author articles. Kiwanian. Clubs: Explorers; Mich. Polar-Equator (sec.- treas. 1965). Home: 420 W Grand River Av East Lansing MI 48823

BAKER, ROYAL NEWMAN, air force officer; b. Corsicana, Tex., Nov. 27, 1918; s. Morris John Whitney and Verna (McClure) B.; B.S. in Indsl. Arts, N. Tex. Tchrs. Coll., 1941; grad. Air Force Spl. Staff Sch., 1948, Air Command and Staff Sch., 1950, Nat. War Coll., 1961; m. Sarah Frances Hendricks, Apr. 14, 1942; childrenFrances, Robert, William, Sally. Commd. 2d lt. USAAF, 1942, advanced through grades to maj. gen. USAF, 1966; various assignments U.S. and ETO, 1941-44; asst. dir., then dir. tng. Peterson Field, Colo., Dalhart Field, Tex., Sumner Field, N.M., 1944-45; resigned 1945; oil operator, 1945-47; rejoined USAF, 1947; comdr. 115th Rev. Unit, Stewart AFB, N.Y., 1947-48, 2d Fighter Squadron, Mitchell AFB, N.Y., 1948-50; operations officer 52d Fighter Group, McGuire AFB, N.J., 1960; spl. project officer 52d Fighter Interceptor Group, McGuire AFB, 1950-51, dir. operations, 1951; dir. operations, exec. officer 52d Fighter Interceptor Wing, McGuire AFB, 1951; comdr. 52d Fighter Interceptor Group McGuire AFB, 1951-62; 116th Fighter Bomber Group, Japan 1952, 4th Fighter Interceptor Group Korea, 1952-53; liaison project officer Hdqrs. Air Def. Command, Wright-Patterson AFB, O., 1953; air def. command project officer Edwards AFB, Cal., 1953-57, dir. flight test Hdqrs. Air Force Flight Test Center, 1957-60; comdr. 20th Tactical Fighter Wing, Wethersfield, Eng., 1961-63; dep. comdr. 3d Air Force, S. Ruislip, Eng., 1963-64; chief regional plans div., I, J-5, Joint Chiefs Staff, 1964-66; comdr. comdr. 12th Air Force Hdqrs., Waco, Tex., 1966-68; asst. chief of staff for plans U.S. Mil. Assistance Command, Vietnam, 1968; vice comdr. 7th Air Force, Tan Son Nhut Air Base, Vietnam, 1968-69; Comdr. 17th Air Force, Ramstein Air Base, Germany, 1969-71; chief MAAG, Bonn, Germany, 1971—. Decorated D.S.C., D.S.M., Silver Star, Legion of Merit with 3 oak leaf clusters, D.F.C. with 3 oak leaf clusters, Air medal with 42 oak leaf clusters, Air Force Commendation medal; Croix de Guerre with palm (France); Mil. Order Ulchi (Republic Korea). Home: 1306 N Waddill McKinney TX 75069 Office: Chief MAAG Bonn Germany

BAKER, RUSSELL, lawyer; b. Portage County, Wis., Apr. 28, 1901; s. George W. and Mary (Day) B.; Ph.B., U. Chgo., 1923, J.D., 1955; m. Elizabeth Wallace, June 5, 1925; children—Wallace R., Donald, James A. Admitted to Ill. bar, James A. Admitted to Ill. bar, 1925, since practiced law, Chgo., with firm of Baker & McKenzie, specialist internat. law, 1928—, sr. partner, 1949-; adv. bd. World Tax Series, Harvard U. Law Sch. First v.p., chmn, research and law enforcement coms. Chgo. Crime Commn. Recipient citation U. Chgo. Alumni Assn., 1952. Mem. Chgo. Assn. Commerce and Industry (world trade com.), Internat., Inter-Am., Am. (chmn. com. on taxation sect. of criminal law), Ill., Chgo. bar assns., Chgo. Law Inst. (librarian). Author articles legal, internat., trade, tax subjects. Home: 232 Ravine Forest Dr Lake Bluff IL 60044 Office: Prudential Plaza Chicago IL 60601

BAKER, RUSSELL WAYNE, newspaperman; b. Loudoun County, Va., Aug. 14, 1925; s. Benjamin Rex and Lucy Elizabeth (Robinson) B.; B.A., Johns Hopkins, 1947; L.H.D., Hamilton Coll., Princeton U.; LL.D., Union Coll.; m. Miriam Emily Nash, Mar. 11, 1950; children—Kathleen Leland, Allen Nash, Michael Lee. With Balt. Sun, 1947-54; mem. Washington bur. N.Y. Times, 1954-62, author-columnist, Observer, editorial page, 1962—. Served with USNR, 1943-45. Author: An American in Washington, 1961; No Cause for Panic, 1964; All Things Considered, 1965; Our Next President, 1968. Home: 5211 39th St NW Washington DC 20015 Office: 1920 L St Washington DC 20036

BAKER, S. ORVILLE, educator; b. Chgo., Jan. 21, 1912; s. Max and Rae (Goldberg) B.; Ph.B., U. Chgo., 1934, M.A., 1935; Ph.D., Harvard, 1948; m. Adra Wollenweber, June 24, 1938; 1 dau., Patricia. Faculty, Carnegie Inst. Tech., 1937-40, Simmons College, 1946-47, Wellesley Coll. 1948-49, Carnegie Inst. Tech., 1949-50; faculty U. No. Ill., DeKalb, 1950—, prof., 1955—, also coordinator fgn. studies. Served from lt. (j.g.) to lt. comdr., USNR, 1942-46. Mem. Modern Lang. Assn., Am. Assn. U. Profs., N.E.A., Nat. Council Tchrs. English, Ill. Assn. Tchrs. of English (pres. 1965-66). Co- author: Horizon, 1963. Home: 715 Garden Rd DeKalb IL 60115

BAKER, SHERMAN N., shoe co. exec.; b. 1919; grad. Harvard, 1940; married. With J. Baker, Inc. (now subsidiary Nat. Shoes Inc.), 1939—, v.p. Nat. Shoes Inc., 1967-70, pres., treas., chief exec. officer, 1970—, also dir. Served to lt. USNR, 1942-45. Office: 595 Gerard Av Bronx NY 10451*

BAKER, SOLOMON REUBEN, alarm systems exec.; b. Fall River, Mass., July 4, 1902;; s. Nathan Nathan L. and Ida M. (Creamer) B.; student Bentley Sch. Accounting and Finance, Boston, 1924; m. Rebecca Darwin, Oct. 19, 1939; 1 son, Malcolm Frederic. Chmn. bd.

Baker Industries, Inc. Trustee Bentley Coll. Accounting and Finance. Home: 10375 Wilshire Blvd Los Angeles CA 90024. Office: 404 N Roxbury Dr Beverly Hills CA 90210

BAKER, STANNARD LUTHER, ins. co. exec.; b. Lansing, Mich., Mar. 2, 1900; s. Arthur Davis and Edith (Cooley) B.; student Mich. State U., 1918-19, Northwestern U., 1919-21; B.A., U. Mich., 1922; m. Gladys Kinney, July 26, 1924. With Mich. Millers Mut. Ins. Co., Lansing, 1922—, successively file clk., asst. sec., v.p., 1922-44, pres. dir., 1944-65, chmn. bd., 1965—; dir. Mich. Nat. Bank, Lansing. Mem. Sigma Nu. Mason. Club: Country of Lansing. Home: 121 Rampart Way East Lansing MI 48823 Office: Michigan Millers Mutual Insurance Co Lansing MI 48801

BAKER, STEPHEN, advt. co. exec.; b. Vienna, Austria, Apr. 17, 1923; s. Oscar and Renee (Lavesky) Bacher; B.A., William Jewell Coll., postgrad. N.Y.U., Art Students League; m. Oleda Baker, Oct. 1967; 1 son, Stephen Scott. Vice pres. Cunningham & Walsh, 1951-62; pres. Baker & Byrne, 1962-65; pres., dir. Mogul, Baker, Byrne & Weiss, N.Y.C., 1965-69, Baker Hartel, 1969—. Columnist Ad Age. Nominated as Art Dir. of Year, 1961, 63. Mem. N.Y. Art Dirs. Club. Clubs: N.Y. Athletic; Lords Valley Country. Author: How To Live With A Neurotic Dog; How to Play Golf in the Low 120's; How To Look Like Somebody in Business Without Being Anybody; Visual Persuasion; Advertising Layout and Art Direction; How To Live With A Neurotic Wife: How To Live With A Neurotic Husband; How to be Psychonalyzed by a Neurotic Psychoanalyst; (with wife) Models Beauty Dietbook. Home: 5 Tudor City Pl New York City NY 10017 also Lords Valley Mauley PA 18428 Office: 777 3d Av New York City NY 10017

BAKER, VERNON VENTRESS, lawyer; b. Jackson, Tenn., Oct. 7, 1904; s. Louis and Ellen Irene (Taylor) B.; LL.B., George Washington U., 1929; m. Alice Elizabeth Mandler, July 31, 1929; 1 son, Larry Vernon. Various positions Fed. Service, including VA, Bur. Mines, Geol. Survey. Fed. Emergency Adminstrn. Pub. Works, 1923-34; admitted to D.C. bar, 1929; practiced in D.C., 1935-38; examiner, ofcl. ICC, 1938-63, dir. bur. finance, 1957-63. Recipient trophy for outstanding civic achievement Washington Evening Star, 1951. Mem. D.C. Fedn. Citizens Assns. (chmn. pub. utilities com. 1949-51), Assn. ICC Practitioners, Motor Carrier Lawyers Assn., Phi Beta Gamma. Presbyn. Club: Argyle Country (Layhill, Md.). Home: 942 Dead Run Dr McLean VA 22101 Office: 1250 Connecticut Av Washington DC 20036

BAKER, VINCENT, govt. ofcl.; b. Amarillo, Tex., June 27, 1919; s. Horade and Hester (Morris) B.; A.B., So. Meth. U., 1940, M.A., 1941; A.M., Harvard, 1947, Ph.D., 1951. Instr. So. Meth. U., 1941-43; job analyst N. Am. Aviation, 1943-45; teaching fellow, tutor Harvard, 1945-51; fgn. affairs officer U.S. Dept. State, 1951-53, 55-62; asst. program dir. Carnegie Endowment Internat. Peace, 1953-55; supervising fgn. affairs officer Arms Control and Disarmament Agy., 1962-64; with U.S. Dept. State, 1964—, staff officer multilateral Force Negotiating Team, 1964-65, officer charge nuclear affairs Office Polit.-Mil. Affairs, 1965-66, officer charge internat. security affairs Office Atlantic Polit.-Mil. Affairs, 1967-69, counselor polit.-mil. affairs U.S. Mission to NATO, Brussels, 1970—. Mem. Am. Polit. Sci. Assn., Am. Soc. Internat. Law, Phi Beta Kappa. Home: 115 Av Moliere Brussels 1180 Belgium Office: N Atlantic Treaty Orgn Brussels 39 Belgium

BAKER, WAKEFIELD, JR., wholesale hardware co. exec.; b. San Francisco, July 2, 1922; s. Wakefield and Margaret (Madison) B.; grad. Phillips Exeter Acad., 1942; student U. Cal. at Berkeley, 1942-43. Pres. Baker & Hamilton Co. Mem. San Francisco, 1964—, also dir.; pres. 91 Land Co., 1960—,, Bollibokka Land Co., 1965—. San Francisco Distbrs. Assn. (dir.), Strybing Arboretum Soc. (dir., treas.). Club: Pacific Union (San Francisco). Home: 32Julius St San Francisco CA 94133 (summer) White Horse Ranch St Helena CA 96042 Office: 700 7th St P O Box 3199 San Francisco CA 94119

BAKER, WALLACE RUSSELL, lawyer; b. Chgo., June 11, 1927; s. Russell and Elizabeth (Wallace) B.; A.B., Harvard, 1948, LL.B., 1952; m. Miriam Nye Loomis, Apr. 10, 1964; children—Ann Graham, Christopher Loomis, Charles Russell. Admitted to Ill. bar, 1952; partner firm Baker and McKenzie, Chgo., 1954-59, partner in Brussels, Belgium, 1959-62, resident partner, Paris, France, 1963—; hon. consul of Honduras, Chgo., 1954-56. Served to 1st lt. AUS, 1944-46. Mem. Am. Bar Assn. Clubs: Mid-Day, University (Chgo.); Lincolns Inn (Cambridge, Mass.); Union Interalliée, Travelers (Paris, France). Author, lectr. in field. Home: 29 rue des Graviers Neuilly France Office: 94 rue du Faubourg St Honore Paris France

BAKER, WILLIAM AVERY, naval architect; b. New Britain, Conn., Oct. 21, 1911; s. William Elisha and Margaret MacDonald (Sanderson) B.; S.B., Mass. Inst. Tech., 1934; m. Ruth Stuart, May 2, 1936. With shipbldg. div. Bethlehem Steel Co., 1934-64; curator Francis Russell Hart Nautical Mus., Mass. Inst. Tech., 1963—; compiler plans, specifications for hist. ships Gjoa, 1946-48, Mayflower II, 1951-57, others. Mem. constrn. com. revision, 1948, Safety of Life at Sea Conv., 1957-60, USCG working com. on stability and subdiv., 1961—, com. on revision 1930, load line conv. Trustee Pilgrim Soc. Registered profl. engr., Cal., Mass. Mem. Soc. Naval Architects and Marine Engrs. (co-founder New Eng. sect. 1943, sec.-treas. 1943-44, chmn. 1957-58, sec.-treas. No. Cal. sect. 1949), Soc. Nautical Research, Hakluyt Soc., Marine Hist. Assn., Boston Marine Soc., Harvard Musical Assn., Delta Upsilon. Author: The New Mayflower, Her Design and Construction, 1958; Colonial Vessels, 1962; The Engine Powered Vessel, 1965; Sloops and Shallops, 1966; A History of the Boston Marine Society, 1968; C.J.A. Wilson's Ships, 1971; also numerous articles, chpts. in books. Mem. editorial adv. bd. Am. Neptune, 1952—. Address; 10 Rice Rd Hingham, MA 02043.

BAKER, WILLIAM CHARLES, real estate exec., lawyer; b. Port Arthur, Tex., May 14, 1933; s. Harry Winters and Martha (Newby) B.; LL.B., U. Tex., 1957; m. Janice Yeteva Haskin, Jan. 14, 1965; children—William Charles, Cynthia Carol, Lisa Lanette, Stacy Allison, Katharine Suzanne. Admitted to Tex. bar, 1957, N.Y. bar, 1959; trial atty. U.S. Dept. Justice, Washington, 1957-59; practiced in N.Y.C., 1959-62, Dallas, 1962-64; gen. mgr. N.Y. World Fair, Tex. Pavilion, N.Y.C., 1964; gen. counsel Gt. S.W. Corp., Dallas, 1964-67, pres., dir., 1968-70; pres. Macco Corp., Newport Beach, Cal., 1967-70, also dir.; partner Baker & Caldwell, Newport Beach, 1970—. Home: 2 Harbor Island Newport Beach CA 92660 Office: 500 Newport Center Dr Newport Beach CA 92660

BAKER, WILLIAM DUNLAP, lawyer; b. St. Louis, June 17, 1932; s. Harold Griffith and Bernice (Kraft) B.; A.B., Colgate U., 1954; LL.B., U. Cal. at Berkeley, 1960, J.D., 1969; m. Kay Stokes, May 23, 1955; children—Mark William, Kathryne X., Beth Kristie, Frederick Martin. Admitted to Cal. bar 1961, Ariz. bar, 1961, U.S. Supreme Ct. bar, 1970; practice in Coolidge, 1961, Florence, 1961-63. Phoenix, 1963—; law clk. Stokes & Moring, 1960; spl. investigator Office Pinal County Atty., 1960-61, dep. county atty., 1961- 63; partner McBryde, Vincent, Brumage & Baker, 1961-63; asso. atty. Rawlins, Ellis, Burrus & Kiewit, 1963-65, partner, 1965—; referre Juvenile Ct. Maricopa County Supreme Ct., 1966—. Mem. Gov.'s Adv. Council, Phoenix, 1969—. Spl. legal counsel Ariz. Com. Republican Party, 1964; legal counsel Ariz. Com. Rep. Party, 1965-69; vice-chmn. Maricopa County Rep. Com., 1968-69, chmn., 1969—. Pres., bd. dirs. San Pablo Home for Youth; bd. dirs. Maricopa County chpt. Nat. Found. March of Dimes. Served to 1st lt. USAF, 1954-57. Mem. Am., Ariz., Cal., Pinal County (past v.p.) bar assns., Sigma Chi, Phi Delta Phi. Episcopalian. Mason (Shriner). Home: 5309 N 34th St Phoenix AZ 85018 Office: Security Bldg Phoenix AZ 85004

BAKER, WILLIAM F., business exec.; b. Waterford, N.Y., 1913; B.S., Manhattan Coll., 1933; married. With Cluett, Peabody & Co., Inc., N.Y.C., 1933—, asst. controller, 1949-51, controller, 1951—; dir. Alatex, Inc. K.C. Home: 19 Knollwood Rd Eastchester NY 10707 Office: 510 Fifth Av New York City NY 10036*

BAKER, WILLIAM HUDSON, educator, botanist; b. Portland, Ore., Dec. 16, 1911; s. William T. and T. and Helen T. (Hudson) B.; diploma Ore. Coll. Edn., 1933; B.S., Ore. State Coll., 1935, M.S., 1942, Ph.D., 1949; m. Molly A. Cochran, Nov. 17, 1934; 1 son, James William. Pub. sch. adminstr., Ore., 1935-42; asst. botany Ore. State Coll., 1946-49; asst. prof. botany U. Ida., Moscow, 1948-53, asso. prof., 1953-58, prof., 1958-, acting chmn. dept., 1953-54, chmn. dept., 1954-, acting head dept. biol. scis., 1955-56, head div., 1956- 67. Park ranger naturalist Crater Lake Nat. Park, summers 1949, 50. Served to lt. USNR, World War II. Fellow A.A.A.S.: mem. Bot. Soc. Am., Am. Fen Soc., Am. Soc. Plant Taxonomists, Internat. Soc. Plant Taxonomists, Am. Assn. U. Profs., N.E. Bot. Club, Cal. Bot. Soc., Ida. Acad. Scis. (pres. 1958-60), N.W. Sci. Assn. (hon. life program chmn. 1953-56, trustee 1956-59, pres. 1963), Cal. Acad. Scis., Naval Res. Assn., Navy League, Sigma Xi (pres. Ida. 1955-56), Phi Sigma, Alpha Tau Omega. Kiwanian, Elk. Author (with others) Wildlife of the Northern Rocky Mountains. Home: 1041 W A St Moscow ID 83843

BAKER, WILLIAM KAUFMAN, geneticist; b. Portland, Ind., Dec. 2, 1919; s. Frank K. and Jennie (Schaeffer) B.; B.A., Coll. of Wooster, 1941; M.A., U. Tex., 1943, Ph.D. (NRC fellow 1946-48), 1948; sr. postdoctoral fellow NSF, U. Rome, 1963-64; m. Margaret Stewart, Mar. 4, 1944; childrenBruce, Ann, Brian. Asst. prof. U. Tenn., 1948-51; sr. biologist Oak Ridge Nat. Lab., 1951-55; asso. prof. U. Chgo., 1955-59, prof. zoology, 1959—, chmn. dept. biology, 1968-. Served to 1st lt. USAAF, 1943-46. Mem. Am. Soc. Naturalists (sec.). Co-editor American Naturalist, 1965-70. Author Articles on genetics. Home: 5505 Kenwood Av Chicago IL 60637.

BAKER, WILLIAM OLIVER, research chemist; b. Chestertown Md., July 15, 1915; s. Harold May and Helen (Stokes) B.; B.S., Washington Coll., 1935, Sc.D., 1957; Ph.D., Princeton, 1938; Sc.D., Georgetown U., 1962, U. Pitts., 1963, Seton Hall U., 1965, U. Akron, 1968, U. Mich., 1970; D.Eng., Stevens Inst. Tech., 1962; LL.D., U. Glasgow, 1965; m. Frances Burrill, Nov. 15, 1941; 1 son, Joseph Burrill. With Bell Telephone Labs., 1939—, in charge polymer research and devel., 1948-51, asst. dir. chem. and metall. research, 1951-54, dir. research, phys. scis., 1954-55, v.p. research, 1955—; trustee Aerospace Corp.; dir. Babcock & Wilcox Corp., Ann. Revs., Inc., Summit and Elizabeth Trust Co. Vis. lectr. Northwestern U., Princeton, Duke U.; Schmitt lectr. U. Notre Dame, 1968; Harrelson lectr. N.C. State U., 1971; NIH lectr., 1958. Mem. Princeton grad. council, 1956-64; bd. visitors Tulane U., 1963—; mem. div. engring. NRC, also chmn. adv. bd. on mil. personnel supplies, 1964—, mem. com. on phys. chemistry of div. chemistry and chem. tech., 1963-70; mem. panel on phsy. chemistry Office Naval Research, 1948-51; past mem. Pres.'s Sci. Adv. Com., 1957-60, nat. sci. bd. NSF, 1960-66; past chmn. Nat. Sci. Information Council, 1959-61; cons. Dept. Def., 1958-71, to spl. asst. for sci. and tech., 1963—, to Panel of Operations Evaluation Group, USN, 1960-62; mem. N.J. Bd. Higher Edn., 1967—, vice chmn., 1970; mem. liaison com. for sci. and tech. Library of Congress, 1963—; mem. Pres.'s Fgn. Intelligence Adv. Bd., 1959—; bd. regents Nat. Library Medicine; bd. visitors Air Force Systems Command, 1962—; mem. mgmt. adv. council Oak Ridge Nat. Lab., 1970—; mem. Nat. Commn. on Libraries and Information Scis., 1971—; chmn. tech. panels adv. to Nat. Bur. Standards, Nat. Acad. Scis.-NRC, 1969—; mem. sci. adv. bd. Robert A. Welch Found., 1968—; vis. com. Harvard, 1959—; vis. com., div. chemistry and chem. engring. Cal. Inst. Tech., 1969—; vis. com. on scis. and math. Drew U., 1969—; asso. in univ. seminar on tech. and social change Columbia, 1969—. Bd. dirs. Council on Library Resources; trustee Urban Studies, Inc., Carnegie-Mellon U., Rockefeller U., Princeton U., Andrew W. Mellon Found. Named 1 of 10 top scientists in U.S. industry, 1954; recipient Perkin medal, 1963; Priestley medal, 1966; Honor scroll Am. Inst. Chemists, 1962; award to execs. Am. Soc. Testing and Materials, 1967; Edward Marburg award, 1967; Indsl. Research Inst. medal, 1970. Harvard fellow 1937-38, Procter fellow, 1938-39. Fellow Am. Phys. Soc., Am. Inst. Chemists, Am. Acad. Arts and Scis.; mem. Dirs. of Indsl. Research, Am. Chem. Soc. (past mem. com. nat. def., mem. com. chemistry and pub. affairs), Am. Philos. Soc., Nat. Acad. Scis. (council 1969—, com. sci. and pub. policy 1966-69), Indsl. Research Inst. (dir. 1960-63, medal 1970), U.S. C.of C. (council on trends and perspective 1966—), Sigma Xi, Phi Lambda Upsilon, Omicron Delta Kappa. Clubs: Cosmos, Princeton of Northwestern N.J. Contbr.: High Polymers, 1945, Svmposium on Basic Research, A.A.A.S., 1959, Rheology, Vol. III, 1960, Technology and Social Change, 1964. Science: The Achievement and the Promise, 1968; various other books. Also numerous articles to tech. jours. Mem. editorial adv. bd.Jour. Polymer Sci.; past mem. adv. editorial bd. Research Mgmt., Chem. and Engring. News; hon. editorial adv. bd. Carbon. Holder 13 patents. Home: Spring Valley Rd Morristown NJ 07960 Office: 600 Mountain Av Murray Hill NJ 07974

BAKER, WILLIAM WALLACE, newspaperman; b. Kansas City, Mo., July 2, 1921; s. William Reaune and Grace (Wallace) B.; A.B., U. Mich., 1947; m. Virginia Elizabeth Graham, Dec. 21, 1941; 1 son, William Wallace (dec.). U. Mich. corr. for Detroit Times, 1940-41; with SSS, 1945; with Kansas City Star, 1947—, editorial writer, 1954-63, asso. editor, 1963-67, editor, 1967-71, exec. v.p., 1971—, also dir. Served with AUS, World War II; PTO. Decorated Bronze Star medal. Mem. Am. Soc. Newspaper Editors, Am. Newspaper Pub. Assn., Nat. Conf. Editorial Writers, Sphinx, Phi Beta Kappa, Phi Kappa Phi, Phi Eta Sigma, Sigma Delta Chi. Episcopalian. Clubs: Kansas City Press, Kansas City. Home: 4900 W 64th St Shawnee Mission KS 66208 Office: 1729 Grand Av Kansas City MO 64108

BAKER, WILLIE ARTHUR, Jr., educator; b. San Antonio, Nov. 7, 1933; s. Willie Arthur and Rosa (Hornsby) B.; B.S., Tex. Arts and Industries U., 1955; Ph.D., U. Tex., 1959; m. Cynthia Ann Henderson, Nov. 19, 1954; children—Richard Kent, Cheryl Denise. Faculty Syracuse (N.Y.) U., prof. chemistry, chmn. dept., 1965-71; prof. chemistry U. Tex. at Arlington, 1971—, dean grad. sch., 1971—. Mem. Am. Chem. Soc., Chem. Soc. (London), Am. Assn. U. Profs., Sigma Xi, Phi Lambda Upsilon, Alpha Chi Sigma. Club: Torch. Author numerous research articles. Home: 1809 Hillvalley Dr Arlington TX 76013

BAKER, WINTHROP PATTERSON, Jr., broadcasting exec.; b. N.Y.C., July 12, 1931; s. Winthrop Patterson and Josie Lou (Kendrick) B.; student Vanderbilt U., 1952; B.S. in Bus. Adminstrn., La. State U., 1953; m. Elizabeth Muriel Allegret, July 30, 1955; children—Winthrop Patterson III, John Adams, Michael Kendrick. TV dir sta. WJMR-TV, New Orleans, 1954-55; producer-dir. sta. WBRZ-TV, Baton Rouge, 1955-56; TV program dir. sta. KLFY-TV, Lafayette, La., 1956-57; program dir. sta. WMBD-TV, Peoria, Ill., 1957-60; asst. program mgr. sta. WBZ-TV, Boston, 1960-61; program mgr. sta. WJZ-TV, Balt., 1962-65; program mgr. sta. KYW-TV, Phila., 1965-67; asst. gen. mgr. sta. KDKA-TV, Pitts., 1967; gen. mgr. WBZ-TV, Boston, 1968—, v.p., 1970—; dir. TV Advt. Reps., N.Y.C., 1969—, Mem. Boston Youth Activities Commn., Boston, 1970—, Adv. Com. U.S. Youth Games, 1971. Bd. dirs., vice-chmn. Boston Community Media Com., 1970—; bd. dirs. Intercom, Boston, 1970—, Consumer-care Council, Boston, 1970-71. Mem. New Eng. Broadcast Execs. Club, Mass. Broadcasters Assn. (treas., dir. 1970-71), Freedom House, Inc., Mass. Audubon Soc., De Cordova Museum, Phi Kappa Phi, Mu Sigma Rho, Phi Eta Sigma, Pi Tau Pi, Beta Gamma Sigma. Home: Lindsay Pond Rd Concord MA 01742 Office: WBZ TV 1170 Soldiers Field Rd Boston MA 02134

BAKEWELL, HENRY PALMER, lawyer; b. New Haven, June 1, 1907; s. Charles Montague and Madeline (Palmer) B.; Ph.B., Yale, 1929; LL.B., Harvard, 1932; m. Hester Livingstone Adams, Nov. 16, 1934; children—Henry Palmer, Charles Adams, Hester Livingstone, Sarah Ferris. Admitted to Conn. bar, 1932, since practiced in Hartford; mem. Alcorn, BakeWell & Smith. Bd. dirs. Hartford Sch. Music; bd. dirs. Symphony Soc. of Greater Hartford, pres., 1953-55. Trustee Hartford (Conn.) Coll. for Women, Hobart and William Smith Colleges. Served from lt. (j.g.) to comdr., USNR, World War II, 1952. Mem. Am., Conn., Hartford County bar assns., Am. Legion, Beta Theta Pi. Republican. Episcopalian (treas. Christ Ch. Cathedral, 1946-55; mem. exec. council Diocese of Conn., treas., 1960-65, chancellor, 1965—, lay dep. Gen. Conv. P.E. Ch., 1949, 52, 58, 61, 64, 67, 69, 70). Clubs: Hartford, University. Home: 63 Foxcroft Rd West Hartford CT 06119 Office: 1 American Row Hartford CT 06103

BAKKALI, AHMAD ABDESLAM, diplomat of Morocco; b. Assilah, Morocco, Dec. 22, 1932; s. Abdesslam Ahmad and Fattouma (Gailan) B.; B.A., Cairo U., 1959; M.A., Columbia, 1962; m. Assia Benali, Jan. 3, 1970. Head dept. Ministry Information, Morocco, 1961-62; with Ministry Fgn. Affairs, Morocco, 1962; cultural attache Moroccan embassy, Washington, 1962-65; press attache Moroccan embassy, London, 1965-67; cultural counsellor Moroccan embassy, Washington, 1967—; columnist Al-Alam, 1961-65. Recipient Nat. Day Poem award, 1951-53, short story award, 1952-54, Independence Anthem award, 1956. Author: Stories From Morocco, 1957; The False Dawn, 1966; The Blue Deluge, 1969. Contbr. Morocco Nat. Radio. Home: 5500 Prospect Pl Chevy Chase MD 20015 Office: 1601 21st St NW Washington DC 20009

BAKKE, E. WIGHT, educator; b. Onawa, Ia., Nov. 13, 1903; s. Oscar C. and Harriet (Wight) B.; B.A., Northwestern U., 1926, LL.D., 1964; Ph.D., Yale, 1932; m. Mary Sterling, Sept. 1, 1926; children—Karl E., Carolyn S. (Mrs. Albert S. Bacdayan), William W. Instr. sociology Yale, 1932-34, asst. prof. econs., 1934-38, dir. unemployment studies, Inst. Human Relations, 1932-39, dir. studies in trade unionism, 1939—, prof. econs., 1938—, Sterling prof., 1940—, dir. grad. studies in econs., 1940-50, dir. Labor and Mgmt. Center, 1944—; Fulbright prof. to Denmark, 1953. Prin. cons. social economist Social Security Bd., 1936-39; dir. Nat. Bur. Econ. Research; chmn. appeals com. Nat. War Labor Board; cons. Dept. Labor, Navy Dept.; mem. several Presdl. emergency bds.; mem. adv. council Cornell Sch. Indsl. and Labor Relations; mem. Nat. Manpower Policy Task Force. Bd. overseers Amos Tuck Sch.; trustee Quinnipiac Coll., New Haven. Mem. Am. Econ. Assn., Indsl. Relations Research Assn. (pres. 1958), A.A.A.S., Internat. Indsl. Relations Assn., Am. Arbitration Assn., Conn. Acad. Arts and Scis., Corp. of Haverford, Delta Sigma Rho. Mem. Soc. of Friends. Author numerous publications on orgn., labor, unemployment, social security. Home: 55 Rimmon Rd Woodbridge CT Office: 2 Hillhouse Av New Haven CT 60520 ☆

BAKKE, OSCAR, govt. ofcl.; b. Bergen, Norway, June 8, 1919 (parents U.S. citizens); s. Olaf E. and Karen N. (Knutsen) B.; B.A., Wagner Coll., 1941; postgrad. Bklyn. Law Sch., 1941, Agrl. and Tech. Coll. Tex., 1944, Columbia Law Sch., 1946; m. Astrid J. Josephsen, Oct. 2, 1943; children—Stephen H., Kenneth A., Robert O., Daniel B. With CAB, 1946—, reports editor accident investigation div., 1946-47, flight operations specialist internat. standards div., Bur. Safety Regulation, 1947-50, chief air carrier div. Bur. Safety Regulation, 1950-54, dep. dir. Bur. Safety Regulation, 1954-56, dir., 1956-57, dir. Bur. Safety, 1957-60; dir. Bur. Flight Standards, FAA, 1960-61, asst. adminstr. Eastern region, 1961-67, asso. adminstr. plans, 1967-68, acting dep. adminstr., 1968-71, asst. adminstr. for Europe, Africa and Middle East, 1971—. Pres. Gateway Park Corp., Prince Georges Co., Md. Served as officer (pilot), USAAF, 1941-46; maj. Res. Asso. fellow Am. Inst. Aeros. and Astronautics; mem. Air Force Assn. Lutheran. Home: 7009 Berkshire Dr Camp Springs MD 20031 Office: 800 Independence Av Washington DC 20003

BAKKEN, GLENN P., mfg. exec.; b. Mpls., Jan. 12, 1919; s. Luther G. and Ida (Skappel) B.; B.S. in Mech. Engring., U. Minn., 1942; m. Jean E. Luce, June 6, 1942; children—Laurie, Leslie, Richard. Pres., dir. Chase Brass & Copper Co., Waterbury, Conn., 1957—; dir. Kennecott Copper Corp. Home: 1062 Canyon View Rd Northfield OH 44067 Office: 20600 Chagrin Blvd Cleveland OH 44122

BAKKO, ORVILLE EDWIN, hosp. adminstr.; b. Kenyon, Minn., Oct. 10, 1919; s. Marcus and Caroline (Leding) B.; B.A., St. Olaf Coll., Northfield, Minn., 1941; M.Hosp. Adminstrn., Northwestern U., 1948; m. Norma Evelyn Cronquist, Sept. 25, 1951; children—Sandra Karen, Kristi Camille. Adminstv. intern, resident U. Ia. Hosps., 1947-49; adminstrv. asst. Kadlec Hosp., Richland, Wash., 1949-50, asst. adminstr., then adminstr., 1950-56; asst. supt. Arroyo Del Valle Sanatorium, Livermore, Cal., 1956-58, Highland-Alameda County Hosp. and Arroyo Del Valle Sanatorium, 1958-60; adminstr. Fairmont Hosp., San Leandro, Cal., 1960—. Mem. Alameda County Work Safety Com., 1959—; mem. med. services adv. com. Chabot Coll., San Leandro, 1962—. Served to capt., Med. Adminstrv. Corps, AUS, 1942-46; N. Africa. Decorated officer Ordre du Nichan-Iftikhar (Tunisia). Fellow Am. Coll. Hosp. Adminstrs.; mem. Am. (governing council rehab. and chronic disease hosp. sect.), Cal. (mem. com. on continuing care and rehab. 1967-70) hosp. assns., Assn. Western Hosps., Health Care Execs. No. Cal., East Bay Hosp. Council (exec. com.). Presbyn. Home: 345 Marlow Dr Oakland CA 94605 Office: 15400 Foothill Blvd San Leandro CA 94578

BAKLANOFF, ERIC NICOLAS, univ. dean; b. Gaz, Austria, Dec. 9, 1925; s. Nicolas W. and Lucille (King) B.; came to U.S., 1937, naturalized, 1943; student Antioch Coll., 1943-44; A.B., Ohio State U., 1949, M.A., 1950, Ph.D., 1958; postgrad. (Fulbright scholar), U. Chile, 1957, Harvard Grad. Sch. Bus. Adminstrn., 1959, (Nat. Def. Edn. Act postdoctoral fellow), U. Tex., summer 1963; m. H. Christina Janes, June 17, 1956; children—Nicholas, Tanya. Instr. econs. Ohio State U., 1957-58; asst. prof. La. State U., 1958-61, asso. prof., 1961-62, prof. econs., dir. Latin Am. Studies Inst., 1965-69; asso. prof. econs., dir. Grad. Center for Latin Am. Studies, Vanderbilt U., 1962-65; prof. econs., dean for internat. programs U. Ala., 1969—.

Cons., Am. Council on Edn., USAF Inst., Pres.'s Southeastern Conf. on Latin Am. Studies, 1963-64. Active Boy Scouts Am. Served with USNR, 1944-46: PTO. Fellow Center Advanced Study Behavioral Scis., 1964-65. Mem. Nat. Honor Soc., Delta Chi, Beta Gamma Sigma, Omicron Delta Epsilon. Episcopalian. Editor, contbr. The Shaping of Modern Brazil, 1969; New Perspectives of Brazil, 1966; also contbr. articles to profl. jours. Home: Box 114 B Route 2 Northport AL 35476 Office: Box 6186 University AL 35486

BAKST, HENRY JACOB, physician; b. Providence, May 19, 1906; s. Adolph and Sophie (Himowitz) B.; Ph.B., Brown U., 1927; M.D., Harvard, 1931; m. Ruth Elene Miller, June 23, 1933; 1 son, David Allan. Intern, resident physician Boston City Hosp., 1931-34, asst. vis. physician, 1935—, teaching fellow histology and embryology Harvard, 1928-31; instr. medicine Boston U., 1935-45, asst. prof. medicine, 1946-48, asso. prof., preventive medicine, 1948-51, prof. preventive medicine, 1952-71, prof. emeritus, 1971—; chmn. dept., 1952-66, asso. dean Sch. Medicine, 1965-69, dean, 1969-71; dir. rehab. tng. Boston U., 1955-63; vis. physician Univ. Hosp., 1956-71, dir. ambulatory services, 1959-65, dir. div. health conservation, 1961-71, chief rehab. and phys. medicine. Chmn. health council United Community Services, Boston, 1953-57; mem. nat. adv. com. on pub. health tng. USPHS, 1965-69. Former trustee Univ. Hosp. Served as comdr. MC., USNR, World War II. Fellow A.C.P., Am. Pub. Health Assn.; mem. A.M.A., Mass. Assn. Mental Health (pres. 1956-57), Mass. Med. Soc., Assn. Tchrs. Preventive Medicine (sec.-treas. 1960-63, pres. 1963-64), Sigma Xi, Alpha Omega Alpha. Democrat. Jewish religion. Contbr. articles to med. jours. Home: 285 Clinton Rd Brookline MA 02146 Office: 80 E Concord St Boston MA 02118

BAKUTIS, FRED EDWARD, ret. naval officer; b. Brockton, Mass., Nov. 4, 1912; s. Francis and Anna (Ptak) B.; B.S., U.S. Naval Acad., 1935; grad. Naval War Coll., 1950; m. Helen Marie Flucker, July 17, 1937; children—Suzanne (Mrs. Joseph Ganem), Barbara (Mrs. Robert Syvenson), Robert E. Commissioned as ensign U.S. Navy, 1935, advanced through grades to rear adm., 1963; designated naval aviator, 1939; various assignments in ships, 1935-43; exec. officer Fighter Squadron VF-16 on U.S.S. Lexington and comdg. officer VF-20 on U.S.S. Enterprise, 1943-44; assigned Office Chief Naval Operations and Bur. Aero., 1945-46; group comdr. Carrier Air Group One on U.S.S. Tarawa, 1947; comdr. Carrier Air Group Five on U.S.S. Valley Forge, 1948; exec. officer U.S.S. Valley Forge, 1952; mem. staff comdr. Air Force Pacific Fleet, 1953-54; assigned Office Dep. Chief Naval Operations, 1955; comdg. officer U.S.S. Gardiners Bay, 1956-57; operations officer on staff comdr.-in-chief U.S. Pacific Fleet, 1957-59; comdg. officer U.S.S. Hancock, 1960; asst. dir. fleet operation div. Office Chief Naval Operations, also dep. chief Joint Alternate Command Element, Joint Chiefs Staff, 1961; comdr. Alaskan Sea Frontier, also commandant 17th Naval Dist., Kodiak, 1962-63; comdr. Antisubmarine Warfare Group One, 1964, U.S. Naval Support Force, Antarctica, 1965-66, Fleet Air Alameda, 1967-68; comdr. Hawaiian Sea Frontier, 14th Naval Dist., Naval Bases Pearl Harbor, Fleet Air Hawaii, 1968-69; ret., 1969. Decorated Navy Cross, Legion of Merit with combat V and gold star, D.F.C. with silver and gold star, Bronze Star with combat V. Home: 87659 Farrington Hwy Waianae HI 96792

BAKWIN, EDWARD MORRIS, banker; b. N.Y.C., May 13, 1928; s. Harry and Ruth (Morris) B.; B.A., Hamilton Coll., 1950, M.B.A., U. Chgo., 1961. With Nat. Stock Yards Nat. Bank of National City, Nat. Stock Yards, Ill., 1953-55; with Mid-City Nat. Bank Chgo., 1955—, asst. cashier, 1957-60, v.p., 1960-62, pres., 1962—; dir. Darling-Del. Corp., Chgo. Mem. Chgo. Crime Commn.; adv. bd. U. Chgo., 1967—; citizens bd. George Williams Coll., 1968—. Bd. dirs. Duncan-Med. YMCA, W. Central Assn., pres. 1962-65. Served with AUS, 1951-52. Named one of Ten Outstanding Young Men Jr. Assn. Commerce and Industry, 1962. Mem. Am., Ill. (bd. govs. 1966-69) bankers assns., Young Presidents' Orgn. Clubs: Chicago Yacht, Chicago Press. Home: 900 Lake Shore Dr Chicago IL 60611 Office: Mid-City National Bank of Chicago Chicago IL 60607

BAKWIN, HARRY, pediatrist; b. Utica, N.Y., Nov. 19, 1894; s. Simon and Emma (Nadele) B.; B.S., Columbia, 1915, M.D., 1917; postgrad. Berlin and Vienna univs., 1924-25; m. Ruth Morris, 1925; children—Edward Morris, Barbara Swift (Mrs. W. S. Rosenthal), Patricia Anne (Mrs. F. R. Selch), Michael. Interne Bellevue Hosp., 1917-18, asst. vis. phys., 1925-30, asso. attending phys., 1930-43, vis. phys. children's med. service, 1943—; research asst., N.Y. Nursery and Childs, 1919-24; asst. instr. pediatrics Cornell Med. Coll., N.Y.C., 1919-24; instr. pediatrics Columbia, 1925-30; asst. prof. pediatrics N.Y.U., 1939-40, asso. prof., 1940-49; asso. prof. pediatrics N.Y.U.-Bellevue Med. Center, 1940-50, prof. clin. pediatrics, 1950—; courtesy staff Univ. Hosp., N.Y.C.; cons. Norwalk (Conn.) Hosp., Elizabeth A. Horton Meml. Hosp., Middletown, N.Y. Infirmary, N.Y.C., Bayonne (N.J.) Hosp. and Dispensary, Newark, Beth Israel Hosp., Mt. Vernon (N.Y.) Hosp.; Phelps Meml. Hosp., Tarrytown, N.Y. Served as 1st lt., M.C., AUS, 1918-19. Fellow Am. Pub. Health Assn.; hon. mem. N.J. Soc. Dentistry Children; mem. Am., World med. assns., Am. Soc. Human Genetics, Am. Acad. Pediatrics (pres. 1955-56), Am. Pediatric Soc., N.Y. Acad. Medicine, Soc. Exptl. Biology and Medicine, N.Y. State, N.Y. County med. societies, Soc. for Research in Child Devel., Brit. Pediatric Assn. (corr.), Sociedad Antioqueña de Pedjatria (hon.), Sociedad Ecuadorana de Pediatria (hon.), AssociacioE Pediatrica de Guatemala (hon.), Sociedad Peruana de Pediatria (hon.), Sociedad de Puericultura y Pediatria (hon.), Sociedad Argentina de Pediatria (hon.), Brazilian Pediatric Soc. (hon.), South African Pediatric Assn. (hon.), Alpha Omega Alpha. Author: Psychologic Care during Infancy and Childhood, 1942; Clinical Management of Behavior Disorders in Children, 1953, 60, 66. Contbr. numerous articles on growth and devel. of children. Address: 132 E 71st St New York City NY 10021

BAKWIN, RUTH MORRIS, pediatrician; b. Chgo., June , 1898; d. Edward Morris and Helen (Swift) Neilson; B.A., Wellesley Coll., 1919; M.D., Cornell U., 1923; M.A., Columbia U., 1929; postgrad. grad. sch., Vienna and Berlin, 1924-25; m. Harry Bakwin, Feb. 2, 1925; children—Edward Morris, Patricia Anne (Mrs. F. R. Selch), Barbara Swift (Mrs. W. S. Rosenthal), Michael. Interne, Fifth Avenue Hosp., 1923-24; instr. pediatrics Columbia, 1927-30; instr. pediatrics N.Y. U., 1930-40, asst. clin. prof. pediatrics, 1940-49, asso. prof. clin. pediatrics, 1949-60, prof. clin. pediatrics, 1961—; asst. pediatrician, Bellevue Hosp., 1927-43, asst. vis. physician, 1943-48; asso. vis. physician children's medical service, 1948-55, vis. phsyician, 1955—; asst. pediatrician Fifth Avenue Hosp., 1925-35, asso. pediatrician N.Y. Infirmary for Women and Children, 1929-31; dir. pediatrics, 1936-54; cons. dir. pediatrics N.Y. Infirmary, 1954, dir. emeritus, 1955-, also trustee, 1962-, co-director dept. pediatrics, 1966-67; courtesy staff pediatrics Univ. Hosp. Mem. com. on child health White House Conf., 1960. Recipient Elizabeth Blackwell award, 1950, N.Y. Infirmary award of merit, 1960. Diplomate Am. Bd. Pediatrics. Mem. Pan Am. Med. Women's Alliance, World Med. Assn., A.A.A.S., Am. Acad. Pediatrics (state chmn. 1965-67), Med. Women's Internat. Assn., A.M.A, N.Y. Acad. Medicine, Child Study Assn. Am., N.Y. Sch. for Mental Hygiene, Soc. Research Child Devel., Am. Med. Women's Assn., Women's Med. Soc. N.Y. State, Women's Med. Soc. N.Y.C., Nat. Assn. for Mental Health, Inc. (adv. council on childhood mental illnesses 1962—, dir. 1962-66), Alpha Phi (award 1952). Clubs: Cornell Women's of N.Y.; Cosmopolitan, Wellesley. Author: Psychologic Care During Infancy and Childhood, 1942; Clinical Management of Behavior Disorders in Children, 1953, 60, 66. Address: 132 E 71st St New York City NY 10021

BALABAN, EMANUEL, condr., educator; b. Bklyn., Jan. 27, 1895; s. Joseph and Olga (Liebman) B.; student Inst. Mus. Art, N.Y.C., 1912-14, also pvt. study; m. Nina de Witt, Aug. 1923 (div. July 1942); m. 2d, Priscilla Sanford Brown, July 27, 1942. Accompanist for Zimbalist, Morini, Elman, others, 1915-22; asst. condr., Dresden (Germany) Opera, 1922-25; guest condr. Berlin Philharmonic, Nat. Symphony, Washington, N.Y. Philharmonic, others; dir. opera dept. Eastman Sch. Music, 1929-44; condr. Ballet Russe de Monte Carlo, 1944-45; condr. N.Y.C. Ballet, Eng., 1950; faculty Juilliard Sch. Music, 1947—; condr., coach opera theatre and dept. vocal lit., 1963—; faculty Tanglewood-Berkshire Music Center, 1953-56. Mem. Beethoven Assn., The Bohemians, AGMA. Home: 235 W 76th St New York City NY 10023 Office: Juilliard School Lincoln Center Plaza New York City NY 10027

BALABANIAN, NORMAN, educator, elec. engr.; b. New London, Conn., Aug. 13, 1922; s. Adam and Elizabeth (Seklemian) B.; Sci. Diploma, Aleppo (Syria) Jr. Coll., 1942; B.E.E., Syracuse U., 1949, M.S., 1951, Ph.D., 1954; m. Jean Tajerian, Aug. 16, 1947; children—Karen J., Doris R., Gary N., Linda C. Instr. elec. engring. Syracuse U., 1949-54, asst. prof., 1954-57, asso. prof., 1957-61, prof., 1961—. vis. prof. U. Colo., summer 1965, U. Cal. at Berkeley, 1965-66; UNESCO specialist in engring. edn. Nat. Poly. Inst., Mexico City, 1969-70. Mem. tech. staff Bell Telephone Labs., Murray Hill, N.J., summer 1956, IBM Devel. Lab., Poughkeepsie, N.Y., summer 1962. Dir. Syracuse Electronics Corp., 1963-65; cons. Electro Networks, Caledonia, N.Y., 1963; cons. editor Elec. Engring. series Allyn & Bacon, Inc. Mem. Onondaga County Democratic Com., 1960-62; candidate for U.S. Ho. of Reps., 1966. Bd. dirs. UN Assn. Central N.Y., Syracuse Peace Council. Recipient of Ann. Sci. award Armenian Students Assn. Am., annual merit award Sword of Damocles, 1965; Ann. Peace award Syracuse Peace Council, 1967; Ann. award Central N.Y. chpt. Am. Civil Liberties Union, 1968. Fellow I.E.E.E. (chmn. Syracuse circuit theory group 1955-56; editor Trans. on Circuit Theory (1963-66); mem. Am. Civil Liberties Union (pres. Central N.Y. chpt. 1963-64, mem. bd. Upstate N.Y. div. 1964-65, 66-68), Am. Soc. Engring. Edn. (sec. elec. engring. div. 1964-65, vice chmn. 1965-66, chmn. 1966-67), Am. Assn. U. Profs. (pres. Syracuse U. chpt. 1964-65), A.A.A.S., Inst. Cybercultural Research, Am. Humanist Assn. (pres. Syracuse chpt. 1959-60), Sigma Xi. Author: Network Synthesis, 1958 (trans. Russian and Czech.); (with S. Seshu) Linear Network Analysis, 1959 (trans. Russian, Spanish); Fundamentals of Circuit Theory, 1961; The Method of Images, 1963; Electrostatic Boundary Value Problems, 1965; (with T.A. Bickart) Electrical Network Theory, 1969 (translated Spanish); (with W.R. LePage) Introduction to Electrical Science, 1970 (translated Spanish). Contbr. articles to tech. publs., also to Ency. Electronics, Ency. Americana, Britannica Revs. in Engring. Edn., 1970. Home: 134 Clarke St Syracuse NY 13210

BALABANIS, HOMER PAUL educator; b. Brussa, Asia Minor. Turkey, Aug. 25, 1897; s. Paul and Maria (Psomas) B. (Greek parentage); came to U.S., 1913, naturalized, 1918; Ph.B., U. Chgo., 1920, A.M., 1923; Ph.D., Stanford, 1931; m. Frances Deane Fechter, June 16, 1928; children—Nancy Maria, Gordon Paul. Social worker Immigrants Protective League, Hull House, Chgo., 1919-20; financial research Continental Comml. Bank, 1920-22; asst. Sch. Bus., U. Chgo., 1922-23; asst. in econs., Stanford, 1928-29; instr. Humboldt State Col., Arcata, Cal., 1923-30, prof. econs., 1930, now prof. econs. emeritus, became v.p., 1931, v.p. for acad. affairs emeritus, 1964—, dean arts and scis., from 1964, dean of instr. 1951, dir. Humboldt summer session 1936-41. Vis. prof. San Jose State Coll., Fresno State Coll., Miami U., Oxford, O.; mem. staff, Am. Inst. Banking, from 1930. Sr. economist OPA, Washington,1943; prin. divisional asst. Dept. State, Washington, 1943-44. Dir., Calif. Conf. on Social Work; mem. Cal. Arts Commn., 1963-67; founding dir. Humboldt Arts Council. Mem. Am. Pacific Coast econ. assns., Am. Acad. Polit. and Social Scis., A.A.A.S., N.E.A. Rotarian. Author: American Discount Market, 1934; Travel Sketches of Europe, 1938; The Life and Death of a Greek Village, 1970; contbr. to Ency. Americana and Americana Ann. on Greece and Bulgaria. Home: 45 California Av Arcata CA 95521

BALAGUER, JOAQUIN, pres. Dominican Republic; b. 1906; ed. U. Santo Domingo, also U. Paris (Sorbonne). Served in Madrid, 1932-35; undersec. fgn. affairs, 1936-40; minister to Colombia, 1940-46; alternate rep. to UN, 1947; ambassador to Mexico, 1948-50; minister of fgn. affairs, 1954-55, of edn. and arts, 1951-57; v.p. Dominican Republic, 1957-60, pres., 1960, 66—; vol. exile in U.S., 1962-65. Founder, 1962, since leader Reformist Party. Address: Office of The President Santo Domingo Dominican Republic

BALAKRISHNAN, ALAMPALLAM VENKATACHALAIYER, educator; b. India, Dec. 4, 1922; s. Alampallam S. and Ammukutty (Ammal) B; B.Sc. with honors, U. Madras (India), 1945; A.M., M.S., U. So. Cal., 1950, Ph.D., 1954; m. Kay Moulton, Sept. 2, 1952; children—David, Sarala, Robert, Jerald, Kenneth. Came to U.S., 1947, naturalized, 1959. With RCA, 1954-56; asst. prof. U. So. Cal., 1956-57; vis asst. prof. U. Cal. at Los Angeles, 1957-59, prof. engring., 1963—, chmn. dept. system sci., 1969—; with Space Tech. Labs., 1959-61. Cons. NASA, chmn. Symposium Information Theory, 1966-67; cons. Rand Corp.; chmn. tech. com. optimisation Internat. Fedn. Internat. Processing; mem. rev. com. AROD. Fellow I.E.E.E.; mem. N.Y. Acad. Scis. Author: Communication Theory, 1967; Introduction to Optimization Theory in Hilbert Space, 1971. Editor: Advances in Communications Systems, 1964; Computing Methods in Optimization Problem, 1964; Jour. Computer and Systems Scis., 1967—; cons. editor McGraw-Hill Book Co. series System Sciences, 1964- -. Home: 7609 W 91st St Los Angeles CA 90045

BALAMUTH, WILLIAM, educator; b. N.Y.C., Jan. 16, 1914; s. Maurice and Elizabeth (George) B.; B.S., Coll. City N.Y., 1935; Ph.D. (Univ. fellow), U. Cal. at Berkeley, 1939; m. Mollie Elizabeth Anderton, June 15, 1938; childrenWilliam Barry, Barbara Louise. Instr. zoology U. Mo., 1939-40; from instr. to asso. prof. zoology Northwestern U., 1940-53; mem. faculty U. Cal. at Berkeley, 1953—, prof. zoology, 1955—, asso. dean Coll. Letters and Sci., 1968-; cons. commn. enteric infections Armed Forces Epidemiological Bd., 1956-. Bonnie Wallace LeClair fellow U. Freiburg (Germany), 1933-34. Fellow A.A.A.S.; mem. Am. Soc. Zoologists, Soc. Protozoologists, Am. Soc. Parasitologists, Am. Soc. Tropical Medicine and Hygiene, Phi Beta Kappa, Sigma Xi. Mem. editorial bds. jours. in field. Spl. research nutrition and differentiation free-living protozoa, human parasitic amoebae. Home: 1725 Sonoma Av Berkeley, CA 94707.

BALANCHINE, GEORGE, choreographer; b. Petrograd, Russia, Jan. 9, 1904; s. Meliton and Marie Balinchinvadze; student Imperial Ballet and Conservatory of Music, Petrograd; m. Tanaquil Le Clerq, Dec. 31, 1952 (div. 1969). Came to the U.S., 1933. Danced in state theatres of opera and ballet, Russia, 1921-24; toured Germany, then joined Ballets Russcs de Sergei Diaghileff; became director Royal Theater of Copenhagen, 1929; helped organize Ballets Russes de Monte Carlo, 1932; with Metropolitan Opera House, N.Y.City, 1934-37; helped organize Sch. of Am. Ballet, 1934, now dir.; dir. N.Y. City Ballet (toured Europe, USSR 1962); choreography for motion pictures, plays, "On Your Toes." "Goldwyn Follies," "Boys from Syracuse," "Cabin in the Sky," "I Married an Angel." Ballets: The Nightingale, 1925; Barabau, 1925; Pastorale, 1927; Triumph of Neptune, 1927; Jack-in-the-Box, 1927; Apollon, 1928; Bal, 1929; Prodigal Son, 1929; Cotillion, 1932; Mozartina, Errante, Seven Capital Sins 1933 Song of Norway, 1944, numerous others; staged revisions; On Your Toes, House of Flowers, 1954. Mem. Greek Orthdox Ch. Author: Ballanchine's Book of Ballet. Office: 144 W 66th New York City NY 10023

BALANCY, PIERRE GUY GIRALD, ambassador of Mauritius; b. Mauritius, Apr. 8, 1924; s. Pierre Rene and Marie Alix (Herse) B.; student Royal Coll., 1939-42, Bhujoharry Coll., 1943-44; m. Therese Louis, July 14, 1947; children—Pierre Gervais Gerard, Anne-Marie Jacqueline Clairette, Marie-France Janine Josianne, Marie Thérèse Rènèe Ginette, Philippe Gaetan Gilles. Local govt. officer, 1946-63; founder, chief editor daily newspaper l'Express, 1963-64; joined Diplomatic Service, 1968; ambassador of Mauritius to U.S., also high commr. to Can., 1968—. Mem. Mauritius Legislative Council, 1963-68; municipal councillor, 1963-64; parliamentary sec. Ministry Edn. and Cultural Affairs, 1963-65; minister of information, posts and telegraphs, 1965-67, of works, 1967-68. Sec. Cercle Litteraire de Port Louis, 1962, Cercle Remy Ollier, 1955-59, Action Sociale, 1959-60; mem. com. direction Centre Cultural Francais, 1967-68. Recipient Cercle Litteraire de Port Louis award, 1956. Mem. Internat. Platform Assn. Mem. Labour Party (exec. com. 1961-68). Roman Cath. Club: Internat. (Washington). Author: Human Brotherhood in a Modern Multi-Racial Society, 1956. Home: 2308 Wyoming Av NW Washington DC 20008

BALAS, EGON, educator; b. Cluj, Rumania, June 7, 1922; s. Ignat and Boriska Balas; D.L., Bolyai U., Cluj, 1949; D.Sc.Ec. summa cum laude, U. Brussels; D.Sc., U. Paris; m. Edith Loui 1948; children—Ann, Vera. Came to U.S., 1967. Asso. prof. econs. Inst. Econ. Sci., Bucharest, 1949-58, also research economist Inst. Econ. Research of Rumanian Acad., 1956-58; econ. analyst Designing Inst. for Forestry and Timber Industry, Bucharest, 1959-61, head math. programming group, 1962-64; head math. programming sector Center of Math. Statistics of Rumanian Acad., 1964-66; research mathematician Internat. Computation Centre, Rome, 1966; vis. prof. operations research U. Toronto, 1967, Stanford U., 1967; Ford distinguished research prof. Carnegie-Mellon U., 1967-68, prof. indsl. adminstrn. and applied mathematics, 1968—; cons. Mem. Operations Research Soc. Am., Inst. Mgmt. Scis., Econometric Soc., Soc. Indsl. and Applied Mathematics, Am. Math. Soc. Asso. editor of Operations Research, 1967—. Research on math. programming, especially integer programming, networks and scheduling. Home: 104 Maple Heights Rd Pittsburg PA 15232

BALASSA, BELA, educator; b. Budapest, Hungary, Apr. 6, 1928; s. George and Charlotte (Andreics) B.; Diplomkaufmann, Acad. Fgn. Trade, Budapest, 1948; Dr. iuris rerumque Politicarum, U. Budapest, 1951; Ph.D. in Econs., Yale, 1959; m. Carol Ann Levy, June 12, 1960. Came to U.S., 1957, naturalized, 1962. Asst., later asso. prof. Yale, 1959-67; adviser, later cons. econs. dept. Internat. Bank Reconstrn. and Devel., 1966—; prof. polit. economy Johns Hopkins, 1967—; vis. prof. U. Cal. at Berkeley, 1961-62, Columbia, 1963-64; cons. to govt. and industry, 1963—. Rockefeller fellow, 1957-58; Relm Found. grantee, 1958; Ford Found. dissertation fellow, 1958-59; Social Sci. Research Council grantee, 1963; NSF grantee, 1970-72. Mem. Am. Econ. Assn., Econometric Soc., Royal Econ. Soc. Author: The Hungarian Experience in Economic Planning, 1959; The Theory of Economic Integration, 1961; Trade Prospects for Developing Countries, 1964; Economic Development and Integration, 1965; Trade Liberalization among Industrial Countries: Objectives and Alternatives, 1967; The Structure of Protection in Developing Countries, 1971. Home: 2139 Wyoming Av NW Washington DC 20008 Office: 1818 H St N W Washington DC 20433

BALBACH, STANLEY BYRON, lawyer; b. Normal, Ill., Dec. 26, 1919; s. Nyle Jacob and Gertrude (Cory) B.; B.S., U. Ill., 1940, LL.B., 1942; m. Sarah Troutt Witherspoon. May 22, 1944; children—Stanley Byron, Nancy Ann (Fehr), Barbara, Edith, Jacob. Admitted to Ill. bar, 1942, U.S. Supreme Ct. bar, 1950; practiced in Hoopeston, 1945-47, Urbana, 1948—. Nat. chmn. Jr. Bar Conf., 1955. Served as capt. USAAF, 1942-45. Mem. Am. Bar Assn. (ho. of dels. 1956, 65, chmn. spl. com. lawyers title guaranty funds 1962-70), Am. Judicature Soc., Phi Delta Phi, Alpha Kappa Lambda. Home: 1005 S Douglas St Urbana IL 61801 Office: Lincoln Sq Urbana IL 61801

BALCER, CHARLES LOUIS, coll. pres.; b. McGregor, Ia., May 23, 1921; s. Ludwig Frank and Iva (Vaughan) B.; B.S., Winona (Minn.) State Tchrs. Coll., 1942; M.A., State U. Ia., 1949, Ph.D., 1954; m. Martha Elizabeth Belgum, Jan. 6, 1944; children—Mary Elizabeth, Mark Lewis, Beth Louise, Brian Charles. Tchr., Minn. and Ia. high schs., 1942-43, 46-47; instr. State U. Ia., 1947-50; high sch. prin., Detroit Lakes, Minn., 1950-54; asso. prof. speech St. Cloud (Minn.) State Coll., 1954-56, prof., acad. dean, 1958-64; prof. speech State U. N.Y., Oswego, 1956-57; pres. Augustana Coll., Sioux Falls, S.D., 1965—. Mem. Nat. Lutheran League, Nat. Luth. Council. Bd. dirs. Family Life Service, also Sioux Falls Symphony Assn. Served with AUS, 1943-46. Mem. Speech Assn. Am., Central States Speech Assn. (pres. 1954), N.E.A., Assn. Higher Edn., Delta Sigma Rho, Kappa Delta Pi, Phi Delta Kappa. Republican. Author: (with H. F. Seabury) Teaching Speech Address: Augustana College Sioux Falls SD 57102

BALCH, CLYDE WILKINSON, chem. engr., educator; b. Winterset, Ia., June 11, 1917; s. Harry C. and Beulah (Wilkinson) B.; B.S., U. Md., 1937, M.S., 1938; M.S. in Engring. Sci., U. Toledo, 1958; m. Mary Jo Mitchell, Apr. 13, 1940; children—Charles M., Thomas S., John R. Phys. chemist U.S. Naval Research Labs., 1938-39; chem. engr. E.I. duPont de Nemours & Co., Inc., 1939-46; v.p. Maumee Chem. Co., 1946-65, dir., 1946-66; prof. chem. engring., chmn. dept. U. Toledo, 1964-68, dean adult and continuing edn., dir. evening sessions, 1967—; cons. in field 1960—. Dir. Dolphin Paint & Chem. Co. Bd. dirs. Toledo Goodwill Industries, 1967—. Named Toledo Engr. of Year, 1962. Mem. Am. Inst. Chem. Engrs., Am. Chem. Soc., Nat. Soc. Profl. Engrs., Am. Assn. U. Profs., Am. Soc. Engring. Edn., Tau Beta Pi, Sigma Rho Tau, Sigma Alpha Epsilon, Alpha Chi Sigma, Alpha Phi Omega. Home: 2114 Bridlewood Dr Toledo OH 43614

BALCH, GLENN, author; b. Venus, Tex., Dec. 11, 1902; s. Glenn Olin and Edith (Garrison) B.; student North Tex. State Tchrs. Coll., Denton, 1921-23, U. Tex., 1923-24; A.B., Baylor U., 1924; postgrad. Columbia, 1937; m. Faula Mashburn (div. 1935); 1 dau., Betty Lou; m. 2d. Elise Kendall, May 15, 1937; children—Lynne Kendall, Mary, Olin. Newspaper reporter Ida. Daily Statesman, Boise, 1925-29; bank clerk, 1923-24; forest ranger, 1925; free-lance mag. writer and publicity, 1929—. Served to lt. col. USAAF, 1943-45; CBI. Recipient George Washington Meml. awards Freedoms Found., 1954, 56, 57. Author: Riders of the Rio Grande, 1937; Tiger Roan, 1938; Hide-rack

Kidnapped, 1939; Indian Paint, 1942; Wild Horse, Viking Dog, 1948; Christmas Horse, 1949; Lost Horse, 1950 (Boys' Club Book award 1951); Winter Horse, Squaw Boy, Midnight Colt; Indian Saddle-Up, 1953; Little Hawk and The Free Horses, 1956; The Brave Riders, 1958; White Ruff, Horses, 1959; Horse in Danger 1960; The Stallion King, 1960; Spotted Horse, 1961; Stallion's Foe, 1962; The Runaways, 1963; Guide to Western Horseback Riding, 1965; The Book of Horses, 1966; Keeping Horse, 1966; The Flaxy Mare, 1967; Horse of Two Colors, 1968. Contbr. to periodicals. Home: Route 2 Meridian ID 83642

BALCH, JOHN NETHERCOT, supermarket co. exec.; b. Evanston, Ill., June 27, 1927; s. John Harold and Elizabeth (Nethercot) B.; B.S. in Bus. Adminstrn., Northwestern U., 1950; m. Olga Goy, Nov. 26, 1952; children—Clifton, Kathy, Karen. Accountant, Touche, Ross, Bailey & Smart, Chgo., 1950-52; accountant Jewel Cos., Inc., Chgo., 1952-64, controller, 1964-68, treas., 1968—. Served with USNR, 1945-46. C.P.A., Ill. Mem. Am. Ist. C.P.A.'s, Alpha Delta Phi. Club: Economic (Chgo.). Home: 3227 Park Pl Evanston IL 60201 Office: 5725 E River Rd Chicago IL 60631

BALCH, MARSTON STEVENS, educator, dramatic director, author; b. Detroit, Nov. 21, 1901; s. Ernest Alanson and Bertha Lou (Stevens) B.; B.A., Kalamazoo Coll., 1923, L.H.D. (hon.), 1960; A.M., Harvard, 1925, Ph.D. 1931; m. Germaine Cornier, Sept. 6, 1927 (dec. July 1969); 1 dau., Gabrielle (Mrs. Anthony Mazza). Instr. English, Williams Coll., 1925-27; instr. English and tutor in div. of modern langs., Harvard, 1928-33; instr. English, Phillips Exeter Acad., 1933-34; asso. prof. English, Tufts Coll., 1934-37, dir. u. theater, 1935-66, prof. drama, Fletcher prof. oratory, 1937-71, prof. emeritus, 1971—, head dept. drama and speech 1940-66. Vice pres. Boston chpt. France Forever, 1941-43. Field rep. overseas branch OWI, 1943-46; Algiers corr. for UN radio; chief cable desk, Physchol. Warfare Branch, Allied Force Hdqrs., 1943-44; chief French press and radio analysis sect. USIS, Paris, 1944-45, chief cultural relations sect., 1945-46. Trustee French Library in Boston, Inc., also ednl. religious, cultural societies. Decorated Medaille de la Reconnaissance; Chevalier Legion d'Honneur; recipient Margo Jones U. award, 1966. Mem. National Council of Arts in Edn. (mem. bd.), Am. Assn. Univ. Profs., Dramatists Guild, Nat. Theatre Conf. (exec. soc. 1960-68), Am. Soc. Theatre Research, Am. Ednl. Theatre Assos. Assn., ANTA, New Eng. Theater Conf. Episcopalian. Club: Boston Authors. Author: The Dramatic Legacy of Thomas Middleton, 1930; co-author You and College, 1936; Theater in America: Appraisal and Challenge, 1968. Editor Modern Short Biographies, 1935; Modern Short Biographies and Autobiographies, 1940; (with others): The College Omnibus, 1936. Transl. The Steamship Tenacity (by Charles Vildrac), 1948; Beggars in Paradise (by G. M. Martens), 1949; The Chief Thing (by N.N. Evreinoff), 1952; Dr. Knock (by Jules Romains), 1957; The Would-be Gentleman (by Moliere), 1960. Contbr. to Dictionary Am. Biography, World Book Ency., Ency. Britannica, also U.S., French and Brit. periodicals. Home: 50 Sawyer Av Medford MA 02155 ☆

BALCH, RICHARD HORROCKS, ret. mfg. exec.; b. Bklyn., Mar. 2, 1901; s. Burton M. and Mary J. (Horrocks) B.; A.B., Williams Coll., 1921; LL.D., Hartwick Coll., 1955; m. Elizabeth S. Prescott, Sept. 15, 1928; children—Cynthia, James P., Barbara, Richard H. Vice pres. Horrocks Ibbotson Co., Utica, N.Y., 1927-42, pres., 1942-67, chmn. bd., 1967-69; dir. Divine Bros. Mfg. Co., Utica Fire Ins. Co. Pub. Service Commr., N.Y. State, 1955-60. Pres. Community Chest, Utica, 1949, mem. bd. edn. Del., Democratic Nat. Conv. 1944, 48; Dem. candidate for lt. gov. N.Y., 1950; chmn. N.Y. State Dem. Com. 1952-55. Presbyn. Mason. Clubs: Ft. Schuyler (Utica); Williams, Manhattan (N.Y.C.). Contbr. articles to sporting goods publs. Home: 1202 Pkwy Utica NY 13501 Office: 258 Genesee St Utica NY 13502

BALCH, SAMUEL EASON, lawyer; b. Madison, Ala., Sept. 5, 1919; s. Joseph Austin and Clara Irene (Vaughn) B.; B.S. in Commerce and Bus. Adminstrn., U. Ala., 1940; LL.B., U. Va., 1948; m. Elizabeth Gordon Brock, Apr. 17, 1943; children—Samuel Eason, Elizabeth Gordon, Gene Austin, Ann Warwick. Admitted to Ala., bar, 1948, since practiced in Birmingham; mem. firm Martin, Balch, Bingham & Hawthorne (now Balch, Bingham, Baker, Hawthorne & Williams), 1953—. Dir. Ala. Power Co. Sec., Gorgas Scholarship Found., 1955-64; mem. legal com. Edison Electric Inst. Trustee Birmingham Civic Opera Assn. Served with AUS, 1941-46. Mem. Am., Ala., Birmingham bar assns., Newcomen Soc., Am. Judicature Soc., Kappa Sigma. Episcopalian. Clubs: Mountain Brook (Ala.); Downtown, Relay House (Birmingham). Home: 4229 Old Leeds Rd Birmingham AL 35213 Office: 600 N 18th St Birmingham AL 35203

BALCHEN, BERNT (balken), ret. air force officer; b. Tveit, Topdal, Norway, Oct. 12, 1899, s. s. Lauritz and Dagny (Dietrichson) B.; ed. Norway, arty. and air force line, War Acad., Oslo and Horten, 1918-21; D.Sc., Tufts Coll., 1953 U. Alaska, 1954; m. Emmy Soerlie, Oct. 18, 1930 (separated 1941); 1 son, Bernt; m. 2d. Inger Engelbrethsen, Feb. 26, 1948; 1 son, Lauritz; m. 3d. Audrey Schipper, Nov. 30, 1966. Came to U.S., 1926, naturalized 1931. Pilot engr. Roald Amundsen, Svalbard, 1925-26: test pilot Fokker, Northrop aircraft corps., 1926-33; piloted Adm. Byrd across Atlantic, 1927; pilot of Bremen relief expdn. to Greenly Island, Laborador, 1928; chief pilot Adm. Byrd's Antarctic Expdn. (piloted first flight over South Pole Nov. 29 1929), 1928-30; pilot Viking Rescue Expdn. to Newfoundland. 1931; chief pilot Ellsworth Antarctic Expd., 1933-35; chief insp. Norwegian Airlines, Oslo, 1935-40, mng. dir., 1946-48; served with RAF Ferry command as pilot-navigator, assigned Air Forde Hdqrs., 1951056. Cons. Gen. Precision airbase Bluie West 8 on Greenland, cmdg. officer of sta., 1941-43; chief Allied A.T.C. for Norway, Sweden, Denmark, Finland, USSR in Stockholm, Sweden, 1943-45; also support Norwegian underground resistance against German occupation forces, comdg. officer air operations against German forces in no. Norway, 1944-45, evacuation of 70,000 Russians from slave labor camp no. Norway; spl. missions 8th Air Force U.S.S.T.A.F.-O.S.S. (Scandinavia), 1943-45; stationed Ft. Richardson, Alaska, 1948-50; assigned Head Quarters, Air Force, 1951-56. Consultant Gen. Precision Labs., Inc., Tarrytown, N.Y., Gen. Dynamics Corp., N.Y.C. Decorated Congressional medal, Legion of Merit, D.F. C., Air medal with silver oak leaf cluster, D.S.M., 2 medals of Valor, City of N.Y., King Albert's Flying Cross, City of Paris Gold medal, Leiv Erickson medal, Medaille de Merit, King Christian X medal of freedom, comdr. 1st class Order of St. Olav with Swords and Stars; recipient Explorers Club's medal, Harmon Trophy, 1953; comdr. 1st class Royal Order of Sword, Sweden. Mem. Quiet Birdmen, Norwegian Geog. Soc. Am., Norwegian Polar Soc. Mason. Clubs: Explorers (hon.) N.Y.C.); Aero (Norway); Adventurers. Author: Next Fifty Years of Flight, 1954; Come North With Me. Exhibited paintings, 3d watercolor show Grand Central Galleries, 1955. Home: 159 Campfire Rd Chappaqua NY 10514

BALDANZI, GEORGE, trade union ofcl.; b. Black Diamond, Pa., Jan. 23, 1907; s. Natale and Clelia (Rutille) B.; m. Lena Parenti, Feb. 25, 1932; 1 son, George M. An organizer, 1st pres. Dyers Fedn. Am., 1933; merged with Textile Works Union Am. CIO, 1939, exec. v.p., 1939-52; dir. orgn. United Textile Workers Am., AFL, 1952-53; on leave as regional dir. Eastern Conf. Teamsters, Internat. Brotherhood Teamsters, 1953-55; internat. pres. United Textile Works Am., AFL-CIO, 1958—. Vice pres. United-Italian Am. Labor Council, 1958—; mem. Sec. Commerce Textile Adv. Com., 1959—. Chmn. Passaic County (N.J.) Area Redevel. Bd., 1963—. Named Outstanding Citizen of Italian Descent in Passiac Area, Unity, Neighborliness, Integrity, Charity and Opportunity, 1956; recipient Star Solidarity, 1949, Order Merit, 1964 (Italy). Home: 224 Washington Av Hawthorne NJ 07506 Office: 44 E 23d St New York City NY 10010

BALDASSARE, ERNEST WILLIAM, tobacco co. exec.; b. Paterson, N.J., Sept. 2, 1921; s. Adolf and Catherine (Lisi) B.; B.S. cum laude, N.Y.U., 1942, M.B.A., 1948; m. Roslyn Komack, Oct. 28, 1943. Prin. Haskins & Sells, N.Y.C., 1945-63; treas. Liggett & Myers Inc., N.Y.C., 1963—. Bd. dirs. 12 Beekman Pl., N.Y.C. Served with AUS, 1942-44. C.P.A., N.Y. Mem. Financial Execs. Inst., Am. Inst. C.P.A.'s, N.Y. State Soc. C.P.A.'s, N.Y.U. Alumni Assn. Contbr. articles profl. jours. Home: 12 Beekman Pl New York City NY 10022 Office: 630 Fifth Av New York City NY 10020

BALDERSTON, C. CANBY, business exec.; b. Kennett Square, Pa., Feb. 1, 1897; s. John L. and Anna E. (Marshall) B.; ed. Westtown Sch., 1912-14; student Pa. State Coll., 1915-17; B.S. in Econs., U. Pa., 1921 A.M., 1923, Ph.D., 1928, LL.D., 1955; LL.D., Swarthmore, 1965; m. Gertrude Emery, July 18, 1922 (dec.); children—Frederick E., Robert W.; m. 2d, Ida Roberts Smedley, Nov. 21, 1942; stepchildren—Walter, Henry, Alice. Asst. prof. industry U. Pa., 1925-31, prof., 1931-54, dean Wharton Sch. Finance and Commerce, 1941-54; gov. Fed. Res. System, 1954-66, vice chmn. bd. governors, 1955-66; pres. Leeds & Lippincott Co. (Chalfonte-Haddon Hall hotels), 1951—; adj. prof. finance American Univ., 1966—; dir. Fed. Res. Bank of Phila., 1943-53, dep. chmn., 1949-53; dir. Security Nat. Bank, Washington. Chief War Dept. Wage Adminstrn. Agy., and wage adminstrn. sect. Hdqrs. Army Service Forces, 1942-45. Emeritus trustee Bryn Mawr Coll.; bd. advisers Indsl. Coll. Armed Forces, 1964-66; formerly trustee Indsl. Relations Counselors; chmn. pres., dir. Nat. Bur. Econ. Research; pres. Am. Assn. Collegiate Sch. of Bus. Chmn. investment com. Westtown School; bd. mgrs. Friends Hosp. Frankford; bd. dirs. Sidwell Friends Sch., Elwyn Inst. Recipient War Dept. Exceptional Civilian Service award, 1944. Formerly v.p., dir. Phila. C. of C. Mem. Am. Econ. Assn., Theta Xi, Beta Gamma Sigma (nat. pres. 1952-55). Republican. Mem. Soc. of Friends. Clubs: Varsity (U. Pa.); Franklin Inn (Philadelphia); Cosmos (past pres.) (Wash.); Rolling Green Golf and the Ozone. Author: Managerial Profit Sharing, 1928; Profit-Sharing for Wage Earners, 1937; Group Incentives, 1930; Executive Guidance of Industrial Relations, 1935; Wage Setting Based on Job Analysis and Evaluation, 1940. Co-author: Wages—A Means of Testing Their Adequacy, 1931; Management of an Enterprise, 1935; Management of a Textile Business, 1938. Home: Penngrant 749 W Rosetree Rd Media PA 19063 also 3337 P St NW Washington DC 20007 Office: Chalfonte-Haddon Hall Atlantic City NJ 08404

BALDERSTON, FREDERICK EMERY, educator; b. Phila., Aug. 15, 1923; s. C. Canby and Gertrude (Emery) B.; student Deep Springs Jr. Coll., 1940-42; A.B., Cornell U., 1948; M.A., Princeton, 1950, Ph.D., 1953; m. Judith S. Braude, June 20, 1949; children—Daniel E., Sara C., Thomas M., Jonathan B. Research Asso. Mass. Inst. Tech., 1950-53; asst. prof. bus. adminstrn. U. Cal. Berkeley, 1953- 57, asso. prof., 1957-61, prof., chmn. Center For Research in Mgmt. Sci., 1961-66, 70—, v.p. bus. and finance, 1966-67, v.p. planning and analysis, 1967-70; vis. asso. prof. indsl. adminstrn. Carnegie Inst. Tech., 1955-56; Cal. savs. and loan commr., 1963-65. Trustee Am. Field Service Internat. Scholarships, Inc. Served with Am. Field Service, 1943-45. Mem. Am. Econ. Assn., Inst. Mgmt. Scis., Am. Marketing Assn., Soc. Mgmt. Scis. Mem. Soc. of Friends. Clubs: Sierra; Commonwealth; Berkeley Tennis. Author: (with A.C. Hoggatt) Simulation of Market Processes, 1962. Editor: (with Hoggatt) Symposium on Simulation Models, 1963. Home: 641 Alvarado Rd Berkeley CA 94705

BALDES, EDWARD JAMES, biophysicist; b. Fairfield, Neb., July 5, 1898; s. Joseph James and Margaret (Lenzen) B.; B.A., U. Sask., 1918, LL.D., 1955; M.A., Harvard, 1920, Whiting Fellow, 1922, Ph.D., 1924; Ph.D., Univ. Coll., London U. (Eng.), 1936; m. Mary Cooney, June 27, 1934; children—Joseph James, Mary Margaret, Honora, Elizabeth Louise. Asst. physics U. Sask., 1918-19, Radcliffe Coll., Cambridge, Mass., 1921-24; instr. physics Harvard, 1923-24; asso. div. physics and biophys. research Mayo Clinic, 1924-63, sr. cons. sect. biophysics, 1948-58; vice chmn. Mayo Aero Med. Unit, 1942-63; prof. biophysics Mayo Found. Grad Sch., U. Minn., 1943-63; with sci. analysis br., life sci. div. U.S. Army Research Office, 1963-67, sci. adviser U.S. Army Aeromed. Research Lab., Fort Rucker, Ala., 1967—. Cons. council on phys. medicine and rehab. A.M.A., 1946-56; mem. council Am. Electroencephalographic Soc., 1947-51; chmn. panel on aviation medicine Research and Devel. Bd., Nat. Mil. Establishment, 1946-53; mem. panel on aero. medicine Sci. Adv. Bd., Chief Staff USAF, 1948-54; alternate mem. Aero Space Med. Panel Adv. Group, Aero. Research and Devel.-NATO, 1960-64, mem. com. biodynamics; adv. panel sci. and technology Ho. Reps. com. sci and astronautics, 1960-69; mem. subcom. acceleration NRC, 1942-46, com. aviation medicine 1946-49, com. hearing, bioacoustics and biomechanics; spl. cons. Aero Med. Lab., Wright-Patterson AFB, 1942-49; mem. adv. panel physiology Office Naval Research, 1947-51. Decorated chevalier Legion of Honor (France); knight St. Gregory the Great; recipient of War Dept. Commendation and Medal for Exceptional Civilian Service in aviation medicine to USAF, 1945; predl. citation for work in aviation medicine, 1948; Eric LilJencrantz award Aerospace Med. Assn., 1968. Fellow Aerospace Med. Assn. (exec. council 1953-56), Am. Phys. Soc.; mem. Am. Inst. Aero. and Astronautics, Am. Physiol. Soc., A.A.A.S., Biophys. Soc., Minn. Acad. Sci. (pres. 1956-57), Am. Minn. heart assns., Air Force Assn., Sigma Xi (hon.). Author of over 100 sci. papers in field of biophysics, physiology, aviation medicine. Editorial bd. Internat. Jour. EEG and Clin. Neurophysiology, 1947-54, Jour. Physiology, Jour. Applied Physiology, 1956-63; adv. editorial bd. Aerospace Medicine, Aerospace Med. Assn., 1957—. Home: 24 Goff St Daleville AL 36322

BALDESCHWIELER, JOHN DICKSON, chemist, educator; b. Elizabeth, N.J., Nov. 14, 1933; s. Emile L. and Isobel (Dickson) B.; B. Chem. Engring., Cornell U., 1956; Ph.D., U. Cal. at Berkeley, 1959; m. Marcia Ewing, June 20, 1959; children—John Eric, Karen. From instr. to asso. prof. chemistry Harvard, 1960-65; faculty Stanford (Cal.), 1965—, prof. chemistry, 1967—. Mem. President's Sci. Adv. Com., 1968—, vice chmn., 1970—. Served to 1st lt. AUS, 1959-60. Sloan Found. fellow, 1962-64, 64-65; recipient Frensenius award Phi Lambda Upsilon, 1968. Mem. Nat. Acad. Scis., Am. Chem. Soc. (award in pure chemistry 1967). Home: 221 Durazno Way Portola Valley CA 94026 Office: Dept Chemistry Stanford Univ Stanford CA 94305

BALDIN, LIONEL SILUAN, engring. co. exec.; b. St. Petersburg, Russia, May 28, 1907; s. Siluan F. and Augusta J. (Malkoff) B.; came to U.S., 1919, naturalized, 1939; B.S. in Elec. Engring., Columbia, 1927, M.S., 1928; m. Jane M. Campbell, June 21, 1934. Engr., N.Y. Telephone Co., 1928-29; indsl. engr. Arthur Andersen & Co., N.Y.C., 1929-30; with Ford, Bacon & Davis, Inc., N.Y.C., 1935—, mgr. valuation, report and indsl. dept., 1954-63, v.p. 1957—, also dir.; dir. Ford, Bacon & Davis Constrn. Corp., Monroe, La., Ford, Bacon & Davis, Tex., Inc., Dallas, Ford, Bacon & Davis, Can. Ltd., Calgary, Alta. Mem. adv. ednl. com. Russian Student Fund N.Y.C., 1961—. Registered profl. engr., N.Y., Conn. Mem. Am. Indsl. Devel. Council, Nat., N.Y. State socs. profl. engrs., N.A.M., Am. Mgmt. Assn., A.A.A.S., Newcomen Soc. N.Am., Sigma Alpha Epsilon, Theta Tau, Epsilon Chi. Club: Downtown Athletic (N.Y.C.). Home: 27 Cannon St Norwalk CT 06851 Office: 2 Broadway New York City NY 10004

BALDINGER, WALLACE SPENCER, art educator; b. Springdale, Pa., Apr. 19, 1905; s. Albert Henry and Mary Estelle (Spencer) B.; student Westminister Coll., 1924-25; A.B., Oberlin Coll., 1928, M.A., 1932; postgrad. Pa. Acad. Fine Arts, 1928-30; summer study U. Paris, 1932-33; Ph.D., U. Chgo., 1937; m. Ellen Nichols, June 12, 1933; children—Richard Nichols, Marna Louise. Dir. dept. art, also dir. Mulvane Art Mus., asso. prof. history and appreciation art Washburn Coll., Topeka, 1932-40; asso. prof. art Lawrence Coll., 1940-44; asso. prof. history of art U. Ore., 1944-56, prof., 1956—, curator Mus. of Art, 1953-55, dir., 1955-70; vis. lectr. Doshisha U., Japan, 1952-53, 67-68; chmn. Parliament of World Religions, 1952, East Meets West Festival of Arts, 1957. Mem. Kan. adv. com. Fed. Art Project, 1937-40; mem. Gov.'s Adv. Com. for Arts and Humanities; mem. hon. bd. advisers Chanoyu Quar., Kyoto, Japan. Fulbright lectr. Nat. Coll. Arts, Lahore, 1960-61. Mem. Coll. Art Assn., Asia Soc., Assn. Asian Studies, Soc. Archtl. Historians. Conglist. Author: The Visual Arts, 1960; The Dance in Art (catalogue of exhbn.), 1963; Morris Graves: A Reprospective (exhbn. catalogue), 1966; A University Collects: Oregon Pacific Northwest Heritage (exhbn. catalogue), 1966. Home: 1790 Walnut St Eugene OR 97403

BALDINI, MARIO GIULIO, educator; b. Santareangelo, Italy, Jan. 15, 1917; s. Antonio and Giulia (Cecchi) B.; student U. Vienna, 1936-38; M.D., U. Rome, 1942; m. Dorothy Lucie Hovey, Feb. 22, 1958; children—Daniel, Julia, Edward. Came to U.S., 1954, naturalized, 1960. Intern, Polyclinic, U. Rome, 1942-43; resident U. Pavia (Italy) Med. Sch. Hosp., 1945-49; asso. prof. medicine Tufts U., 1958-65; clin. prof. medicine Brown U., 1966-68, prof. medicine, 1968-70, prof. med. scis., 1970—; dir. div. hematologic research Meml. Hosp. and Brown U., 1965—. Served with Italian Air Force, World War II. Contbr. articles hematology to med. jours. Home: 246 Dudley St Brookline MA 02146 Office: Memorial Hosp Pawtucket RI 02860

BALDINO, JOHN FRANK, govt. ofcl.; b. Portland., Ore., Mar. 23, 1919; s. Philip and Catherine (Maino) B.; student U. Ore. Extension Center, Multnomah Coll., m. Betty Jean Hayes, Aug. 19, 1950; 1 dau., Gloria Jean. With Dept. Interior, 1938—, dep. adminstr. Bonneville Power Adminstrn., Portland, Ore., 1967-71. Served with USAAF, 1942-45. Recipient Distinguished Service medal Dept. Interior, 1968. Home: 1810 NE Schuyler Portland OR 97220 Office: 1001 NE Lloyd Blvd Portland OR 97208

BALDRIDGE, B. BRUCE, gas co exec.; b. 1929; Gas Co., 1954-64; with Petrolane Inc., 1964—, became treas., 1965, now pres. C.P.A., Tex. Address: 1600 E Hill St Long Beach CA 90806*

BALDRIDGE, CARL, banker. Vice chmn. bd., chmn. exec. com. Am. Bank & Trust Co., Baton Rouge. Office: 2531 Plank Rd Baton Rouge LA 70805*

BALDRIDGE, EDGAR EARL, oil co. exec.; b. Ft. Worth, Nov. 19, 1904; s. Edgar Earl and Florence (Gibson) B.; student Kemper Mil. Acad., Bonneville; m. Hazel Gorman, Nov. 18, 1934; children—Martha (Mrs. John W. McMackin), Edgar Earl. Partner Baldridge, King & Nichols, McAllen, Tex., 1941-48, Baldridge & King, Inc., 1948-54; pres. Champlin Oil & Refining Co., Ft. Worth, 1954-61, chmn. bd., pres., 1961-64; chmn. exec. com. Champlin Petroleum Co.; dir. Union Pacific Corp., 1st Nat. Bank of Ft. Worth. Mem. Am. Petroleum Inst. (dir.), Mid-Continent Oil and Gas Assn. (dir.). Episcopalian. Clubs: Chicago; Fort Worth. Home: 1424 Indian Creek Dr Fort Worth TX 76107 Office: Commerce Bldg Fort Worth TX 76102

BALDRIDGE, HOLMES, lawyer; b. Connersville, Okla., Sept. 27, 1902; s. Albert S. and Ripple (Holmes) B.; A.B., U. Okla., 1925; LL.B. cum laude, U. Neb., 1931; m. Anna Marie Dolan, September 3, 1955; 1 son, Albert Sidney Cates. Employed as a reporter Scripps Howard Newspaper, 1926; instr. English and pub. speaking U. Ore., 1927-29; admitted to Neb. bar, 1931, Okla. bar, 1932, D.C. bar, 1947, Ill. bar, 1955, Colorado bar, 1967; engaged as general counsel with Corp. Commn. of Okla., 1933-36; counsel in charge nationwide telephone investigation F.C.C., 1937-38; spl. asst. to Atty. Gen. in charge gen. litigation sect., antitrust div. Dept. of Justice, 1938-50; asst. atty. gen. of U.S. in charge civil div. Dept. of Justice, 1951-53; now mem. firm McNichols, Nigro & Baldridge, Denver. Mem. Okla., Ill., Chgo. bar assns., Phi Beta Kappa, Order of Coif, Delta Sigma Rho, Alpha Kappa Psi. Home: 5530 E 6th Av Pkwy Denver CO 80220 Office: Denver-Hilton Office Bldg Denver CO 80202

BALDRIDGE, HOWARD DAVIS, apparel mfr. exec.; b. Carbondale, Ill., May 17, 1915; s. P.B. and Pearle Mae (Davis) B.; A.B., Union U., Jackson, Tenn., 1936; m. Betty Claypoole, Oct. 12, 1938; children—Kay, Beverly, Howard Davis (dec.). with Genesco, Inc., Nashville, 1940—, former v.p., also dir.; v.p., div. mgr., dir. Dominion Shoe Co. Mem. Nat. Shoe Mfrs. Assn., Nat. Shoe Inst. Kiwanian. Club: Richland Country (past pres.). Home: Belle Meade Tower Apts 105 Leake Av Nashville TN 37202 Office: Geneseo Park Nashville TN 37202

BALDRIGE, MALCOLM, Jr., mfg. exec.; b. Omaha, Neb., Oct. 4, 1922; s. Howard Malcolm and Regina (Connell) B.; grad. Hotchkiss Sch., 1940; B.A., Yale, 1944; m. Margaret Trowbridge Murray, Mar. 31, 1951; children—Megan Brewster, Mary Trowbridge. With Eastern Co. (formerly Eastern Malleable Iron Co.), 1947- 62, mng. dir. Frazer & Jones div., 1951-57, v.p. co., 1957-60, pres. 1960-62, now dir.; exec. v.p. Scovill Mfg. Co., 1962-63, pres., chief exec. officer, 1963-69, chmn. bd., 1969—, also dir.; dir. Cooper Devel. Assn., Inc., Conn. Mut. Life Ins. Co., Lewis Engring. Co., Naugatuck, Conn., Am. Chain & Cable Co., Bridgeport, Conn., N.E. Utilities, Hartford, Torin Corp., Rodeo Cowboys Assn., Inc., Denver; trustee Swiss Re-Ins. Co. Mem. Conn. Republican Finance Com.; mem. Woodbury Rep. Town Com. Bd. dirs., past chmn. Waterbury A.R.C.; Trustee U.S. council Internat. C. of C. Served to capt., F.A., AUS, 1943-46. Home: RFD 2 Woodbury CT 06798 Office: Scovill Mfg Co 99 Mill St Waterbury CT 06720

BALDT, CARL BORNER, banker; b. New Castle, Del., Feb. 18 1907; s. Frederick and Lulu (Jackson) B.; grad. Am. Inst. Banking, 1925; m. Josephine Maginnis, May 2, 1934; children—Leonard M., William R., Jane. With N. Phila. Trust Co. 1922-30, nat. bank examiner, 1930-34; examiner Fed. Res. Bank, Phila., 1934-36; with Wilmington Trust Co. (Del.), 1936-71, v.p., 1954-71. Tchr., Am. Inst. Banking, 1940—. Vice chmn. Del. Chpt. A.R.C., 1965-68, chmn., 1968—; mem. New Castle Adv. Bd. Pensions, 1967-68. Trustee Del. Found. Retarded Children, 1963-68. Mem. Am. (v.p. Del. chpt.

1967-68), Del. (pres. 1966-67) bankers assns. Home: 716 Greenwood Rd Wilmington DE 19807 Office: Wilmington Trust Bldg Wilmington DE 19801

BALDWIN, ALFRED LEE, educator; b. Winfield, Kan., Oct. 5, 1914; s. Onias Barber and Jennie Waldena (Martindale) B.; A.B., U. Kan., 1935, M.A., 1936; Ph.D., Harvard, Harvard, 1941; m. Margery Frances Cole, July 14, 1939; childrenLawrence, Eldon, Constance; m. 2d, Clara P. Melville, July 5, 1963. Research asso. Fels Research Inst., Antioch Coll., 1941-49; prof. psychology U. Kan., 1949-53, chmn. dept., 1951-53; prof., chmn. dept. child devel. and family relationships, Cornell U., 1953-64; now dir. Center for Research in in Edn.; prof. psychology N.Y.U., fr9m 1964. Mem. Am. Psychol. Assn., Soc. Research Child Devel. Author: Behavior and Development in Childhood, 1955; Theories of Child Development, 1967. Home: 201 Hunt Hill Rd Ithaca, NY 14850.

BALDWIN, BENJAMIN HARRISON, educator; b. St. Louis, Mar. 1, 1919; s.Benjamin H. and Ella (Conley) B.; B.Ed., So. Ill. U., 1940; M.S. in Journalism, Northwestern U., 1946; m. Jeanne Helen Holliger, June 25, 1955; children—Mark Frederick, Claudia Eloise. News editor radio sta. WGN, Chgo., 1946-48, WOR-MBS, N.Y.C., 1948-56; mem. faculty Medill Sch. Journalism, Northwestern U., 1956—, prof. journalism, chmn. editorial dept., 1965—, dir. Nat. High Sch. Journalism Inst., 1958-67. Served to 1st lt. AUS, World War 11; PTO. Mem. Assn. Edn. Journalism, Nat. Assn. Sci. Writers, Sigma Delta Chi, Phi Kappa Tau. Lutheran (mem. commn. on ch. papers Luth. Ch. Am. 1967—). Home: 1000 Rolling Pass Glenview IL 60025 Office: Medill Sch Journalism Northwestern U Evanston IL 60201

BALDWIN, BERNARD COLEMAN, Jr., lawyer; b. Lynchburg, Va., June 17, 1911; s. Bernard Coleman and Mary (Bell) B.; B.S., U. Va., 1934, LL.B., 1935; m. Ida Reeder Davidson, Feb. 26, 1938; children—Mary Lyons (Mrs. William C. Scott), Bernard Coleman III. Admitted to Va. bar, 1935, since practiced in Lynchburg; partner Edmunds, Williams, Robertson, Sackett, Baldwin & Graves, 1940—. Sec., dir. Baldwin Stores, Inc., Rulon-Maynard Corp.; dir. Fidelity Nat. Bank, Fidelity Am. Bankshares, Old Dominion Box Co., Montague-Betts Co., Strother Drug Co., J.P. Bell Co., Royal Crown Bottling Co. Trustee Randolph-Macon Woman's Coll., Denney Found., Dillard Found., Plymale Found. Mem. Am., Va., Lycchburg (pres. 1955) bar assns., Bob White Lodge (pres. 1966). Episcopalian. Kiwanian. Clubs: Boonsboro Country; James River (sec. 1960-70) (Lynchburg); Princess Anne Country Virginia Beach, Va.). Mem. editorial bd. Va. Law Rev., 1934-35. Home: 920 Old Trents Ferry Rd Lynchburg VA 24503 Office: 916 Main St Lynchburg VA 24503

BALDWIN, CHARLES EDWARD, Jr., ret. ins. exec.; b. Staten Island, N.Y., Apr. 6, 1905; s. Charles Edward and Marianne Moseley (Perry) B.; student Morristown Sch., 1919-22; A.B., Harvard, 1926, M.B.A., 1928; m. Gwendolyn Maddocks, June 14, 1930; children—Charles Edward III, Beverley, John M. With State Mut. Life Assurance Co., Worchester, Mass., 1928-51, asst. treas., mgr. mortgage loans, 1950-51; treas. N.Y. Life Ins. Co., N.Y.C., 1951-58, v.p., treas., 1958-70; mem. adv. bd. 34th St. office Chem. Bank N.Y. Trust Co., 1951-70. Treas. Worchester Children's Friend Soc., 10 years; former chmn. City Loan Conf. Clubs: Harvard (N.Y.C.); Boothbay Harbor (Me.) Yacht; Treasurers (N.Y.C.); Ponte Vedra (Fla.). Home: 507B Heritage Village Southbury CT 06488

BALDWIN, CHARLES FRANKLIN, former ambassador; b. Zanesville, O., Jan. 21, 1902; s. Charles Scott and Harriet (Templeton) B.; B.S., Georgetown U., 1926; m. Helen Rosenbaum, Mar. 27, 1938; children—Nancy (Mrs. Michael Taylor) (dec.), Charles Stephen. Joined U.S. Fgn. Commerce Service, 1927; asst. trade commr., then trade commr., Sydney, Australia, 1927-30; counselor of embassy for econ. affairs, Oslo, Norway, 1946-48; U.S. polit. adviser, Trieste, 1948-49; counselor of embassy for econ. affairs, London, Eng., 1950-51; consul gen. in Singapore, 1952-53; dep. asst. sec. of state for Far East econ. affairs, 1954-55; ret., 1955, lived in Europe and Washington until 1961; U.S. ambassador to Malaya, 1961-64; diplomat in residence U. Va., 1964-69; exec. dir. Va. Asian Studies Consortium, 1966—. Dep. chmn. Fgn. Student Service Council, Washington, 1959- 60, 64. Trustee Meridian House Found., Washington, 1959-60. Clubs: Cosmos (Washington); Torch, Colonnade, Keswick (Charlottesville). Home: 113 Falcon Dr Charlottesville VA 22901

BALDWIN, DAVID MERRILL, civil engr.; b. Urbana, Ill, July 31, 1912; s. Edward C. and Mabel (Merrill) B.; B.C.E., U. Ill., 1933, M.S., 1934; m. Frances Beals, June 25, 1935; 1 dau., Elizabeth (Mrs. Donald A. Kettlestrings). City traffic engr., Evanston, Ill, 1934-37; safety engr. Va. State Police, 1937-42; traffic engr., dir. traffic div. Nat. Safety Council, Chgo., 1942-56; exec. sec. Inst. Traffic Engrs., Washington, 1956-62; chief traffic operations div. Office Hwy. Safety, U.S. Bur. Pub. Roads, Washington, 1962-67, chief operations div., dep. dir. Office of Traffic Operations, 1967-70; chief traffic performance and analysis div. Office Traffic Operations, Fed. Hwy. Adminstrn., 1970—. Vice-chmn. Nat. Com. Uniform Traffic Laws and Ordinances, 1971—; guest lectr. Central U., Caracas, Venezuela. Pres. Rock Creek Hills Citizens Assn., Montgomery County, Md., 1964-65. Mem. Inst. Traffic Engrs. (pres. 1968), Pan-Am. Hwy. Com. (alternate U.S. del. com. traffic and safety), Am. Soc. C.E., Tau Beta Pi, Sigma Xi, Alpha Sigma Phi, Chi Epsilon. Presbyn. Club: University (Washington). Author: (with G.E. Miller) State Traffic Law Enforcement. 1944. Home: 3609 Littledale Rd Kensington MD 20795 Office: Federal Highway Adminstrn US Dept Transp Washington DC 20591

BALDWIN, DENNIS ANDERSON,chemist, educator; b. Chicago, 1928; B.S. in Physics, Yale, 1950; Ph.D. in Chemistry, Harvard, 1956; m. Sally Ann Jones, July 5, 1957; children--Kenneth J., Nancy A. Chemist, Acme Chem. Co., Blue Island, Ill., 1950-51; director of Reseach Lab., Indsl. Chemicals Corp., Cambridge, Mass., 1956-60; project coordinator environmental sect. Steinmetz Assos., Chgo., 1960-61; v.p. for reseach Bauer Bros. Chem. Co., Inc., Memphis, 1961-64; asst. prof. chemistry Washington U., St. Louis, 1964-66, asso. prof., 1966-70, prof., 1970--, head of chemistry dept., 1970-71. Vis. prof. So. Ill. U., summer 1967, U. of Ore., 1969. Scoutmaster, Boy Scouts America, University City, Mo., 1968-70. Bd. dirs. Rest Haven Home for Elderly, 1960-61; trustee of the Lutheran Hosp., 1965-71. Served from lt. to capt., AUS, 1951-53. Mem. Am. Chem. Soc., Sci. Research Soc. Am. (chpt. treas. 1967), Sigma Xi. Author: (with others) Basic Inorganic Chemistry, 1971. Contbr. articles to profl. jours., encys., also chpts. to books. Home: Fairfax Apts 7291 Windermere Dr University City MO 63105 Office: Dept Chemistry Washington University St Louis MO 63130

BALDWIN, DEWITT CLAIR, educator, clergyman; b. Verona, N.J., Apr. 12, 1898; s. Clinton Dodd and Carrie Sophia (Cook) B.; student Foxcroft Acad., 1912-15; A.B., Wesleyan U., Middletown, Conn., 1919; B.D., Garrett Bibl. Inst., Evanston, Ill., 1921; M.A., Northwestern U., 1922; postgrad. U. Chgo., 1929-30; L.H.D., Ia. Wesleyan Coll., 1967; m. Edna Frances Aikin, Aug. 3, 1921; 1 son, DeWitt Clair. Ordained to ministry Methodist Ch., 1921; pastor St. Luke's Meth. Ch., Chgo., 1920- 22, Meth. Ch., Corinth, Me., 1922-23; ednl. missionary under Methodist Ch., Rangoon, Burma, 1923-33, dist. missionary for Pegu Dist., 1923-24, supt. Indian Dist., 1924-33, supt. English Dist. 1926-33; pastor Meth. Ch. in Rangoon, also chaplain for all non- conformist troops in Rangoon and So. Burma, 1925-33; sec. student work Bd. Missions and Ch. Extension of Meth. Ch., 1933-45; founder, exec. dir. Lisle Fellowship, Inc., 1936—; dir. Lane Hall and Student Religious Assn., U. Mich., 1948-54, coordinator religious affairs, 1954-68; dean students, dir. internat. edn. Ia. Wesleyan Coll., Mt. Pleasant, 1968-70; exec. dir. Religious Centennial Program, U. Mich., 1957-58. Mem. No. N.J. Conf. of Methodist Ch., 1936—. Exec. com. Council on Student Travel, 1957-59; gen. chmn. Ann Arbor chpt. Nat. Conf. Christians and Jews, 1960-63. Pres. Assn. for Coordination Univ. Religious Affairs, 1959-61. Served with S.A.T.C., U.S. Army, 1917-18. Recipient Nat. Brotherhood award, 1968. Mem. Alpha Chi Rho. Mason, Rotarian. Contbr. articles to mags. and ch. publs. Home: 511 Meadow Hill Dr Rockville MD 20851

BALDWIN, DONALD KRING, editor; b. Vermilion, S.D., Dec. 10, 1917; s. Ernest Joy and Madge (Kring) B.; student Ida. So. U., 1939; m. Madalyn Leah Cope, May 3, 1940; children—Steven Worth, Lori Ann. Reporter, Pocatello (Ida.) Tribune, 1939-40; city editor Idaho Falls (Ida.) Post-Register, 1940-41; copy editor Santa Barbara (Cal.) News-Press, 1941-42; with A.P., 1942- 58, news editor, Tokyo, Japan, 1955-58; mng. editor St. Petersburg (Fla.) Times, 1958-61, exec. editor, 1961-69; pres., editor Times Pub. Co., 1969—. Mem. Am. Soc. Newspaper Editors, Sigma Delta Chi. Home: 1000 Brightwaters Blvd St Petersburg FL 33704 Office: 440 1st Av S St Petersburg FL 33731

BALDWIN, DONALD R., lawyer; b. Minewaska, N.Y., Aug. 1895; s. Arthur J. and Frances (Smiley) B.; A.B., Cornell U., 1916; B.L., Columbia, 1920; m. Winifred Barrett, June 1922; children—Patricia Whipple, Joan Baldwin, Diana Dunnan. Admitted to N.Y. State bar; with Griggs, Baldwin & Baldwin, 1924—. Pres. Grosvenor, Inc.; Trustee Drew U., YMCA of Oranges. Served as 2d lt. F.A., Am. Field Service, Ambulance Corps, French Army, World War I. Home: South Orange NJ 07079 Office: 225 Broadway New York City NY 10007

BALDWIN, ERNEST COLIN, paint co. exec.; b. Amityville, N.Y., Feb. 9, 1908; s. Peter Arthur and Nellie (McDonald) B.; A.B., Williams Coll., 1930; M.B.A., Harvard, 1932; m. Jean Corcoran, Mar. 24, 1934; children—Gordon C., Gail C. (Mrs. Ronald S. Rosenstock). With Sherwin-Williams Co., 1934- -, successively mem. exec. sales dept. Sherwin-Williams Co., Cleve., positions in marketing research, sales promotion, advt. and br. operations, gen mgr. stock distbn., pres.'s aide, dir., 1957, pres., 1960—, chief exec. officer, 1966—, also chmn. exec. com., exec. v.p. Sherwin-Williams Co. Can., Ltd., 1956, v.p., mng. dir., 1957, pres., mng. dir., 1958-59; dir. Nat. City Bank, Republic Steel Corp., Cleve. Elec. Cliffs Iron Co. Served as maj. Med. Supply Corps, AUS, 1942-45. Mem. Nat. Paint, Varnish and Lacquer Assn. (dir., mem. exec. com.). Clubs: Union (Cleve.); Pepper Pike Country; Kirtland Country (Willoughby, O.). Home: 2705 Wadsworth Rd Shaker Heights OH 44122 Office: 101 Prospect Av NW Cleveland OH 44115

BALDWIN, FAITH, writer; b. New Rochelle, N.Y., Oct. 1, 1893; d. Stephen Charles and Edith Hervey (Finch) Baldwin; ed. Briarcliff, Mrs. Dow's Sch., Briarcliff Manor., N.Y.; m. Hugh H. Cuthrell, Nov. 6, 1920 (dec. Aug. 1953); children—Hugh, Hervey, Stephen, Ann. Mem. guiding faculty Famous Writers Sch. Nat. sponsor, dir. Conn. Save the Children Fedn. Bd. mem. Silver Hill Found. Mem. Women's Nat. Book Assn. Author: Mavis of Green Hill, 1921; Laurel of Stoney Stream, 1923; Magic and Mary Rose, 1924; Signposts (verse), 1924; Thresholds, 1925; Those Difficult Years, 1925; Three Women, 1926; Departing Wings, 1927; Alimony, 1928; Garden Oats, 1929; The Incredible Year, 1929; Broadway Interlude (with Achmed Abdullah), 1929; Office Wife, 1930; Make Believe, 1930; Judy (juvenile), 1931; Skyscraper, 1931; Babs and Mary Lou (juveniles), 1931; Myra (juvenile), 1932; Week-End Marriage, 1932; District Nurse, 1932; Self- Made Woman, 1932; Girl-on-the-Make (with Achmed Abdullah), 1932; Beauty, 1933; White Collar Girl, 1933; Love's a Puzzle, 1933; Innocent Bystander, 1934; Honor Bound, 1934; Within a Year, 1934; American Family, 1935; The Puritan Strain, 1935; The Moon's Our Home, 1935; This Man Is Mine, 1936; Men Are Such Fools, 1936; The Heart Has Wings, 1937; Twenty-Four Hours a Day, 1937; Manhattan Nights. 1937; Enchanted Oasis, 1938; Rich Girl, Poor Girl, 1938; Hotel Hostess, 1938; The High Road, 1939; Career By Proxy, 1939; White Magic, 1939; Station Wagon, 1939; Rehearsed for Love, 1939; Something Special, 1939; Letty and the Law, 1940; Medical Centre, 1940; And New Stars Burn, 1941; Temporary Address: Reno, 1941; The Heart Remembers, 1941; Blue Horizons, 1942; Breath of Life, 1942; Five Women in Three Novels, 1942; Rest of My Life with You, 1942; Washington, U.S.A., 1943; You Can't Escape, 1943; He Married a Doctor, 1943; Change of Heart, 1944; Arizona Star, 1945; A Job for Jenny, 1945; No Private Heaven, 1946; Woman on Her Way, 1946; Sleeping Beauty, 1947; Give Love the Air, 1947; Marry for Money, 1948; They Who Love, 1948; Golden Shoestring, 1949; Lookout for Liza, 1950; The Whole Armor, 1951; Face Toward the Spring, 1956; (poems) Widow's Walk, 1954; Three Faces of Love, 1957; Many Windows, 1958; Blaze of Sunlight, 1958; Testament of Trust, 1960; The West Wind, 1962; (non-fiction) Harvest of Hope, 1962; The Lonely Man, 1964; Living by Faith, 1964; There is a Season, 1966; Evening Star, 1966, The Velvet Hammer, 1969; Take What You Want, 1970; Any Village, 1971; also serials, short stories, and verse Radio and motion pictures from books and stories; Apt. for Peggy, 1948; Second Chance, 1950; The Juniper Tree, 1952. Republican. Home: RD 2 Weed Av Norwalk CT 06850

BALDWIN, FRANK BRUCE, JR., business exec.; b. Phila., Aug. 28 1907; s. Frank B. and Julia (Reynolds) B.; B.S., Pa. State Coll., 1930, Ph.D., 1934; M.S., U. Minn., 1932; D.Sc., Drexel U., 1966, LL.D., St. Joseph's Coll., 1967; m. Eleanor Dutton, June 23, 1934; children Frank Bruce, Nancy E. Vice pres. Baldwin Dairies, Inc., 1936-50; v.p., asst. to pres. Abbotts Dairies, Phila., 1950-60, exec. v.p., 1960-62, pres., 1963-67, v.p. Fairmont Foods Co., Omaha, 1963-67, also dir.; past chmn. bd. and chief exec. officer Horn & Hardart baking Co., now dir.; dir. Phila. Port Corp., Cloverlay, Inc., Polychorme Corp., B.M.C. Services, Inc., Provident Nat. Corp. Ritter Financial Corp., Provident Nat. Bank, Phila. Dir. courses applied dairy procedure Temple U., 1936-68; past dir. Nat. Dairy Council. Council. Mem. Phila. council Boy Scouts Am.; chmn. Phila. Redevel. Aut Authority; mem. SSS; pres., dir Crime Commn. Phila., Inc. Chmn. bd. dirs. Phila. Heart Assn.; bd. dirs. Phila. Indsl. Devel. Corp., Blue Cross Phila., bd. govs. Acad. Food Mdsg., St. Joseph's Coll.; trustee Beaver Coll., Phila. Coll. Osteopathy, Pa. State U. Mem. Pa. Assn. Milk Dealers (past pres., dir.), Milk Distbrs. Assn. Phila. Area (past pres., dir.), Milk Industry Found. (past pres., dir.), Sigma Xi, Alpha Gamma Rho, Alpha Zeta, Gamma Sigma Delta. Clubs: Union League (Phila.); Seaview Country Center Hills Country; Atlantic City Country. Home: 4141 Orchard Lane Philadelphia PA 19154. Office: Western Savings Bldg Philadelphia PA 19107

BALDWIN, GEORGE CURRIDEN, educator, physicist; b. Denver, May 5, 1917; s. Harry Lewis and Elizabeth (Watson) B.; B.A., Kalamazoo Coll., 1939; M.A., U. Ill., 1941, Ph.D., 1943; m. Winifred M. Gould, Apr. 27, 1952; children—George T., John E., Celia M. Instr. physics U. Ill., Urbana, 1943-44; research asso. Gen. Electric Co., Schenectady, 1944-55, nuclear engr., Cin., 1955-57, reactor mgr. Argonne (Ill.) Nat. Lab., 1957-58, physicist, Schenectady, 1958-67; adj. prof. nuclear engring. and sci. Rensselaer Poly. Inst., 1964-67, prof., 1967—. Councilman Niskayu ña, N.Y., 1965-69. Fellow Am. Phys. Soc.; mem. A.A.A.S., mem. Phi Beta Kappa, Sigma Xi, Phi Kappa Phi, Gamma Alpha. Author: An Introduction to Nonlinear Optics, 1969. Contbr. articles profl. jours. Home: 1046 Merlin Dr Schenectady NY 12309 Office: Rensselaer Poly Inst Troy NY 12181

BALDWIN, HANSON WEIGHTMAN, author, editor; b. Balt., Mar. 22, 1903; s. Oliver Perry and Caroline (Sutton) B.; prep. edn. Boys' Latin School, Balt.; B.S., U.S. Naval Acad., 1924; m. Helen Bruce, June 8, 1931; children— Barbara, Bruce, Elizabeth. Commd. ensign U.S. Navy, 1924, advanced through ranks to lt. (j.g.); served aboard battleships and a destroyer on East Coast, Caribbean and European Squadron; resigned, 1927; police reporter Balt. Sun, later gen. assignment reporter, 1928-29; with N.Y. Times, 1929—, mil. and naval corr., 1937-42, mil. editor, 1942—. Recipient Pulitzer Prize, 1942. Author: Men and Ships of Steel (with W.F. Palmer), 1935; The Caissons Roll-A Military Survey of Europe, 1938; Admiral Dealth, 1939; What the Citizen Should Know About the Navy, 1941; United We Stand!, 1941; Strategy for Victory, 1942; The Price of Power, 1948; Great Mistakes of the War, 1950; Sea Fights and Shipwrecks, 1955; The Great Arms Race, 1958; World War I: An Outline History, 1962; Battles Lost and Won: Great Campaigns of World War II, 1966; Strategy for Tomorrow, 1970. Editor: We Saw It Happen (with Shepard Stone), 1938. Contbr. N.Y. Times mag., U.S. Naval Inst. Proc., Harpers, Atlantic Monthly, Sat. Eve. Post. Office: New York Times New York City NY 10036

BALDWIN, HENRY FURLONG, banker; b. Balt., Jan. 15, 1932; s. Henry du Pont and Margaret (Taylor) B.; A.B., Princeton, 1954; m. Mary Carolyn Hammond, Oct. 13, 1956; children—Mary Stevenson, Severn Eyre. With Merc.-Safe Deposit & Trust Co., Balt., 1956, v.p., 1963-65, sr. v.p., 1965 exec. v.p., 1965-70, pres., 1970—; pres. dir. Merc. Bankshares Corp., 1970—; dir. J. S. Young Co., Merc. Safe Deposit & Trust Co., U.S. Fidelity & Guarantee Co. Trustee Hannah More Acad., Gilman Sch. Served with USMCR, 1954-56. Home: 4408 Atwick Rd Baltimore MD 21210 Office: Mercantile-Safe Deposit & Trust Co Baltimore MD 21203

BALDWIN, HORACE STROW, physician; b. Englewood, N.J., Oct. 14, 1895; s.John Hall and Annie (Strow) B.; B.S., Wesleyan U., 1917; M.D., Cornell, 1921; m. Florence V. Reed, Sept. 3, 1924; children—Judith Ann Hutcheson, Horace (dec.). Intern N.Y. Hosp., 1921-23, dir. allergy clinic, 1935-61, asso. attending physician, 1947-61, consultant in med., 1961—; pneumonia research Bellevue Hosp., 1923-27; practice medicine, specializing in allergy diseases, N.Y.C., 1927-68; asso. prof. clin. medicine Cornell, 1947-61. Cons. in medicine Nassau Hosp., Mineola, N.Y., North Country Community Hosp., Glen Cove, N.Y., Dobbs Ferry (N.Y.) Hosp., until 1968. Bd. dirs., v.p. Sunden Forest Preserve, Inc., 1955-65; v.p. Point O'Woods Assn., 1953-55. Trustee Wesleyan U., 1952-60; pres. Allergy Found. Am., 1953-57, chmn., 1957-66, v.p., 1966—. Served as hosp. apprentice U.S. Navy, World War I. Diplomate in allergy Am. Bd. Internal Medicine. Fellow N.Y. Acad. Medicine (chmn. sect. internat medicine 1943), Am. Acad. Allergy (treas., pres. 1951-52); Sociedade Brasileria de Alergia (hon.), mem. Harvey Soc., N.Y. Acad. Scis., Delta Tau Delta. Episcopalian. Club: Field. Author sci. papers. Address: 7372 Melaieuga Way Sarasota FL 33581

BALDWIN, IRA LAWRENCE, bacteriologist, educator; b. Oxford, Ind., Aug. 20, 1895; s. Thomas Atkinson and Eva (Mock) B.; B.S.A., Purdue U., 1919, M.A., 1921, D.Sc., 1945; Ph.D., U. Wis., 1926; m. Mary Eliza Lesh, Dec. 29, 1920 (dec.); children—Helen Lucile (Mrs. Maurice Guptill), Frances Mary (dec.), Robert Lesh; m. 2d, Ineva R. Meyer, Apr. 17, 1954. Tchr. bacteriology, Purdue U., 1919-23, asst. prof., 1924-25, asso. physiology, exptl. station, 1926; asst. prof. agrl. bacteriology. Coll. Agr., U. Wis., Madison, 1927-29, asso. prof., 1929-32, prof., 1932—, head dept., 1941-44, asst. dean, 1932-42, dean Grad. Sch., 1944- 45, dean Coll. Agr. and dir. Agr. Expt. Station and Agr. Extension Service, 1945-48, v.p. acad. affairs, 1948-58, spl. asst. to pres. 1958-66, emeritus v.p., 1966—. Mem. Natural Resources Com. of State Agys. Wis., 1952-66; cons. North Central Assn. Colls. and Secondary Schs., bd. dirs., 1961-65; dir. internat. rural devel. office, Nat. Assn. State Univs. and Land-Grant Colls., 1963-64; mem. NSF panel on regulatory biology, 1963-66; dir. rural devel. research project CIC-AID, 1964-68; adminstr. Indonesian agrl. higher edn. project AID, 1968-71. Served as 2d lt., F.A., U.S. Army, 1918; cons. U.S. Army, 1945, WPB, 1942-43, FSA, 1943-44, Research & Devel. Bd., 1946-53, USPHS, 1946-48, Dept. Army; mem. Chem. Corps Adv. Bd., 1953-65, chmn., 1958-65; mem. Munitions Command Adv. Group, 1965-69. Fellow Royal Soc. Arts; mem. Am. Acad. Microbiology (mem. bd. 1956-61, 62-68, chmn. bd. 1957-60), Am. Soc. Bacteriologists (pres. 1944, hon. mem.), Am. Soc. Agronomy, Am. Podiatry Assn. (spl. commn. on status of podiatry edn. 1961), Wis., Ind. acads. sci., A.A.A.S., Am. Phytopathol. Soc., Am. Soc. Plant Physiologists, Sigma Xi, Alpha Zeta, Phi Lambda Upsilon, Phi Sigma. Home: 1111 Dartmouth Rd Madison WI 53705

BALDWIN, JAMES, writer; b. N.Y.C., Aug. 2, 1924; s. David and Berdis Emma (Jones) B.; ed. high sch. Mem. nat. adv. bd. Congress Racial Equality, Nat. Com. for Sane Nuclear Policy; lectr. civil rights. Saxton fellow, 1945; Rosenwald fellow, 1948; Guggenheim fellow, 1954; Partisan Rev. fellow, 1956; recipient Nat. Inst. Arts and Letters award, 1956; Ford Found. grant-in-aid, 1959. Mem. Actors Studio, Nat. Inst. Arts and Letters. Author: Go Tell It on the Mountain, 1953; (essays) Notes of a Native Son. 1955; Giovanni's Room, 1958; (essays) Nobody Knows My Name, 1960; Another Country, 1962; (essays) The Fire Next Time, 1963; Blues for Mr. Charlie (play), 1964; Going to Meet the Man, 1966; Tell Me How Long the Train's Been Gone, 1968. Contbr. numerous articles to nat. mags.

BALDWIN, JAMES G., chem. co. exec.; b. Seattle, Mar. 17, 1925; s. Harry G. and Eleanor (Mullinix) B.; B.S., U. Wash., 1945; M.B.A., Harvard, 1948; children— Leslie, James G., Michael R., Richard B.; m. 2d, Gale Hartung, Apr. 10, 1965; 1 dau., Stasse Gale. Dist. sales mgr. Los Angeles, Pennsalt Chems. Corp., 1948-54; mgr. chem. sales Collier Carbon & Chem. Corp., Los Angeles, 1954-60; gen. mgr. Western div. Hooker Chem. Corp., 1960-62, v.p., 1962-65, group v.p., 1965-68, exec. v.p., 1968—; pres. Hooker Chems. & Plastics Group, Occidental Petroleum Corp., 1970—. Served with USNR, 1943-46. Home: 9 Old Parish Rd Darien CT 06820 Office: 1515 Summer St Stamford CT 06905

BALDWIN, JAMES G., ret. banker; b. Bklyn., Oct. 7, 1905; s. James R. and Kathryn (Donohue) B.; student Am. Inst. Banking, Stonier Grad. Sch. Banking; m. Margaret Gallagher, Nov. 11, 1943; children—Gerald, Richard, William. With Marine Midland Grace Trust Co. N.Y., N.Y.C., 1921-70, exec. v.p., 1964-70, sec., dir., 1955-70; dir., treas. Internat. Center, N.Y.C. Mem. exec. bd. Greater N.Y. councils Boy Scouts Am. Clubs: Bankers of Am.; Hempstead (L.I., N.Y.) Country. Home: 42 Vassar Pl Rockville Centre NY 11570

BALDWIN, JAMES LEON, army officer; b. Omaha, Feb. 28, 1921; s. William Henry and Lotus (Bruce) B.; student Kan. State Tchrs. Coll., 1938-40; B.A., George Washington U., 1954; student Columbia, 1957-58; m. Margaret Mary Albright, Dec. 6, 1945; children—Robert

J., Timothy B., Margaret Ann, John W. Enlisted U.S. Army, 1940, commd. 2d lt., 1942, advanced through grades to maj. gen., 1969; with 99th Inf., World War II; comdr. 1st Battalion, 21st Inf., 1955-56; grad. Nat. War Coll., 1962; exec. officer to sec. army, 1962-64; comdr. 3d Brigade, 4th Armored Div., 1964-66, U.S. Berlin Brigade, 1966-67; dep. comdr. XXIV Corps, Vietnam, 1970—, comdg. gen. 23d Inf. Div., Vietnam, 1970—. Decorated D.S.M., Legion of Merit, Bronze Star, Purple Heart, Combat Inf. badge. Home: 5743 N 18th St Arlington VA 22205 Office: Hdqrs 23d Inf Div APO San Francisco CA 96374

BALDWIN, JOHN, airline exec.; b. Toronto, Can., July 8, 1912; s. John R. and Florence (Byers) B.; B.A., McMaster U., 1933; M.A., U. Toronto, 1934; B. Litt., Oxford (Eng.) U., 1936; D.C.L. (hon.), Acadia U., 1971; m. Dorothy Perason, June 24, 1944; children—John R., Richard, Blair. Lectr. history McMaster U., 1937-38; nat. sec. Canadian Inst. Internat. Affairs, 1938-41; with Canadian Dept. External Affairs, 1941-42; asst. sec. to Canadian Cabinet, 1942-48; chmn. Canadian Air Transp. Bd., 1949-54, dep. minister transp., 1954-58; pres. Air Canada, 1968—. Home: 1382 McGregor Av Montreal 109 Quebec Canada Office: Air Canada Pl Ville Marie Montreal 109 Quebec Canada

BALDWIN, JOHN C., banker; b. Osceola, Ia., May 13, 1920; s. John C. and Jessie (Boulware) B.; student Phoenix Coll., 1939-41; m. Doris M. McLellan, Nov. 2, 1944; children—John C. III, Mary Elizabeth. With Valley Nat. Bank Phoenix, 1939—, from messenger to br. mgr., 1939-48, v.p., mgr. Indian-Central office, 1958-61, v.p., head bus. devel. dept., home office, 1961-63, sr. v.p., 1963—, mgr. home office, 1963-70, mgr. corporate services div., 1970-71, sr. v.p. customer relations and indsl. accounts, 1971—. Served as officer USAAF, 1942-45, USAF, 1951-52. Mem. Phoenix C. of C. (dir.), Thunderbirds. Clubs: Phoenix Rotary, North Phoenix Rotary (past pres., charter mem.), Phoenix Country (dir., mem. membership com., pres.), Kiva Cloud (charter mem.), Valley Field Riding and Polo (Phoenix); Arizona. Home: 6635 N 36th St Phoenix AZ 85018 Office: PO Box 71 Phoenix AZ 85001

BALDWIN, JOHN EDWIN, educator; b. Berwyn, Ill., Sept. 10, 1937; s. Francis Miller and Irville (Miller) B.; A.B. summa cum laude, Dartmouth, 1959; Ph.D., Cal. Inst. Tech., 1963; m. Anne Kruesi Nordlander, Sept. 23, 1961; children—Claire Miller, John Nordlander, Wesley Hale. Mem. chemistry faculty U. Ill., 1962-68; prof. chemistry U. Ore., Eugene, 1968—, cons. Stauffer Chem. Co., Office Sci. and Tech., NIH. Guggenheim fellow, 1967; Sloan fellow, 1966-68. Author: Experimental Organic Chemistry, 1965; also articles. Home: 2550 Fairmount Blvd Eugene OR 97403

BALDWIN, JOHN THOMAS, botanist; b. Chase City, Va., Sept. 5, 1910; s. John Thomas and Lona Earle (Price) B.; A.B., Coll. William and Mary, 1932; Ph.D., U. Va., 1937; Gen. Edn. Bd. fellow Cornell U., 1937-38. Asst. prof. biology Coll. William and Mary, 1937-39; instr. in botany U. Mich., 1939- 42; agt. (asso. cytologist) Rubber Plant Investigations, U.S. Dept. Agr., Amazon Valley, 1942-44; mgr. Blandy Exptl. Farm, also asst. prof. U. Va., 1944-46; prof. biology Coll. William and Mary, 1946—, chmn. dept. biology, 1952-62. Horticulturist U.S. Econ. Mission to Liberia, U.S. Dept. of State, 1947-48; prin. botanist Div. Plant Exploration and Introduction, U.S. Dept. of Agr., in Africa and Mexico, 1949-50. Mem. Va. State Parks Study Com. Exec. dir. William and Mary participation in Va. 350th Anniversary Year; mem. adv. com. Orland E. White Research Arboretum, Blandy Exptl. Farm, Boyce, Va. Recipient Alumni medallion Coll. William and Mary, 1971; award Council Williamsburg Garden Clubs, 1971. Fellow A.A.A.S.; mem. Boxwood Soc. Am. (dir. 1960-64, 1st v.p. 1964—), Am. Soc. Naturalists, Am. Assn. Bot. Gardens and Arboretums (dir.), Am. Genetic Assn., Am., New Eng., Cal. bot. socs., Association pour l'Etude Taxonomique de la Flore d'Afrique Tropicale, Am. Soc. Plant Taxonomists, Soc. Study Evolution, Soc. Venezolana de Ciencias Naturales, Torrey, South Appalacian bot. clubs, Phi Beta Kappa (v.p. Alpha of Va. 1960-62), Phi Kappa Phi, Sigma Xi, Phi Sigma. Club: Cosmos (Washington). Contbr. papers to tech. jours. Mem. editorial bd. Brittonia, 1957-61, Jour. Heredity, Am. Hort. Mag. Home: Box 1588 Williamsburg VA 23185

BALDWIN, JOHN WESLEY, educator; b. Chgo., July 13, 1929; s. Edward N. and H. Gladys (McDaniel) B.; B.A., Wheaton Coll., 1950; M.A., Pa. State U., 1951; Ph.D., Johns Hopkins, 1956; m. Jenny Jochens, Dec. 24, 1954; children—Peter, Ian, Birgit, Christopher. Instr., then asst. prof. U. Mich., 1956-61; mem. faculty Johns Hopkins, 1961—, prof. history, 1966—. Guggenheim fellow, 1960-61; Howard fellow, 1960-61; Fulbright fellow, 1965-66; grantee Am. Council Learned Socs., 1965-66. Mem. Am. Hist. Assn., Medieval Acad. Am. Author: The Medieval Theories of the Just Price, 1959; Masters, Princes and Merchants, 2 vols., 1970; The Scholastic Culture of the Middle Ages, 1971. Home: 4828 Roland Av Baltimore MD 21210

BALDWIN, LUDLOW HOPKINS, educator; b. Balt., Dec. 25, 1905; s. Rignal Woodward and Augusta (Hopkins) B.; A.B., Johns Hopkins, 1926, M.A. in Archaeology, 1948; LL.B., Harvard, 1929; m. Anne Gordon Boyce, June 19, 1946. Mem. statis. dept. Gillet & Co., investment bankers, Balt., 1929-33; with Terminal Warehouse Co., Balt., 1933-42, pres., 1937-42; mem. faculty Gilman Sch., Balt., 1946-69, dean, 1951-63, headmaster, 1963-69; lectr. archaeology Community Coll. Balt., 1969—. Pres., Balt. Soc. Archaeol. Inst. Served to comdr. USNR, 1942-46. Home: 1115 Bryn Mawr Rd Baltimore MD 21210

BALDWIN, LYTTLETON MATHERS, ret. ins. co. exec.; b. Springfield, O., Oct. 1, 1904; s. Henry and Lucretia (Mathers) B.; student Mercersburg (Pa.) Acad., 1922-24; Ph.B., Yale, 1928; m. Dorothy Norton, June 28, 1930; children—Henry Norton, Lucretia Ann. Marine spl. agt. Fireman's Fund Ins. Co., offices in N.Y.C. and Chgo., 1928-30; marine underwriter Travelers Fire Ins. Co., Hartford, Conn., 1930-42, marine asst. sec., 1942-45, marine sec., 1945; ret. sr. v.p. exec. dept. Travelers Ins. Cos. Treas. Conn. Tb Assn.; mem. steering com. Hartford Vol. Action Program. Corporator St. Francis Hosp., Hartford Hosp.; mem. bd. Hartford Pub. Library, pres. Greater Hartford Community Chest; bd. dirs. Mt. Sinai Hosp., Greater Hartford Tb and Pub. Health Soc.; bd. regents Mercersburg Acad. Mem. Conn. Hist. Soc., S.A.R., Beta Theta Pi. Episcopalian (sr. warden). Mason. Clubs: Yale (N.Y.C.); Hartford, Hartford Golf; Mid-ocean (Bermuda); Highland Park (Lake Wales, Fla.). Contbr. articles trade publs. Home: 25 Hunter Dr West Hartford CT 06107

BALDWIN, MARCIA, mezzo soprano; b. Milford, Neb., Nov. 5, 1936; d. George W. and Edna (Carlson) Baldwin; student Northwestern U. Music Sch. Debut in recital Carnegie Hall, N.Y.C., 1959; apprentice Santa Fe Opera Co., 1960-61, Balt. Symphony Orch., 1961; West Coast tour of Rigoletto with Goldovsky Opera Theatre, 1962; appearances with San Francisco Spring Opera, 1962, Cin. Zoo Opera, 1963, Met. Opera Co., 1963—, Phila. Lyric Opera, 1964, 65, Central City (Colo.) Opera Festival, 1964, 66, Am. Opera Soc., 1966, Grant Park Concerts, Chgo., 1971. Ford Found. fellow, 1962; recipient award Internat. Music Competition, Munich, Germany, 1962. Mem. Alpha Phi. Home: 155 W 68th St New York City NY 10023 Office: Metropolitan Opera Co Lincoln Center Plaza New York City NY 10023

BALDWIN, OLIVER HAZARD PERRY, banker; b. Lansdowne, Pa., Feb. 26, 1904; s. Charles Edward and Marianne Moseley (Perry) B.; A.B., Harvard, 1927; grad. Rutgers U. Grad. Sch. Banking, 1943; m. Elizabeth S. Webb, Nov. 27, 1929; children—Oliver Hazard Perry, Roger Conant, Jean (Mrs. T.M. Ritchie, Jr.), Mgr., T. Hogan & Sons, Inc., port stevedores, N.Y.C., 1928-30; asst. cashier Nat. Shawmut Bank, Boston, 1930-44; v.p. First Nat. Bank of Akron, O., 1944-46; sr. v.p., Dir. Farmers Bank of State of Del., Wilmington, 1946-59, chmn. bd., pres., 1959-71, hon. chmn., 1971—; pres. Mulco Products, Inc., 1953-55, dir., 1953—; pres., dir. Kent Real Estate Corp., 1959-66; dir. Rollins Leasing Corp., Dover Builders, Inc., Newark Realestate & Ins. Co., Benjamin F. Shaw Co., Chesapeake Utilities Corp., Continental Am. Life Ins. Budd Chem Co., Del. News. Pres., Wilmington Clearing House Assn., 1950- 52, 62-64, mem. exec. com., 1948-71; rep. Del. Savs. Bond div. U.S. Treasury, 1952-70. Bd. dirs., mem. exec. com. United Community Fund No. Del., 1948-66, chmn. campaign, 1951, pres., 1957-59; chmn. for Del. nat. U.S.O. campaign, 1955-63; bd. dirs., mem. exec. com. Wilmington Gen. Hosp., 1947-64, vice chmn., 1951, chmn. 1952-55, pres., 1955-58; mem. finance com., trustee Wesley Jr. Coll., 1959—, vice chmn., 1964-68, chmn., 1968—; trustee Bd. State Employees Pension Trustees, 1965-70, mem. fed. agy. relations com., 1965-67, fed. legislative com., 1967-70; bd. dirs. finance com. Wilmington Med. Center, 1965—; chmn. trustees State Judiciary Retirement Fund, 1962-70. Mem. Am. (exec. council 1960-65. mem. fed. agy. relations com. 1965-67, fed. legislative com. 1967-70), Del. (exec. com. 1953-59, pres. 1958-59) bankers assn., Del. Econ. Devel. Bd., Del. C. of C. (exec. finance com. 1955-65, pres. 1962-64), Bank Pub. Relations and Marketing Assn., Robert Morris Assos., Assn. Mil. Banks (pres. 1963-64), Newcomen Soc. Rotarian. Clubs: Harvard (N.Y.C.); Wilmington, Wilmington Country; Thursday (Boston); Ponte Vedra (Fla.). Home: 1002 Berkeley Rd Wilmington DE 19807 also Canaan St Canaan NH 03741 Office: 10th and Market Sts Wilmington DE 19899

BALDWIN, PAUL CLAY, business exec.; b. Tully, N.Y., May 19, 1914; s. Fred Lynn and Grace Ann (Clay) B.; B.S., Syracuse U., 1936; M.S., Inst. Chemistry, 1938, Ph.D., 1940; m. Margaret Mary Fargo, Nov. 2, 1940 (dec. July 1970); children—Barbara F., Paul Clay, Robert F. With Scott Paper Co., 1940—, tech. dir., prodn. supr., 1940-46, gen. plant mgr., 1946-51, asst. v.p., 1951-53, v.p., 1953-57, v.p. mfg., engring. and research, 1957-60, exec. v.p. mfg., engring. and research, 1960-62, exec. v.p., 1962-68, vice chmn., 1968—, also dir.; dir. Brunswick Pulp & Paper Co.; chmn. bd., dir. Scott Maritimes Pulp & Paper Co., Ltd., Burgo Scott S.p.A. Compania Indsl. de San Cristobal, Sanyo Scott Co. Bd. dirs. Syracuse U., chmn. Research Corp.; bd. dirs. Am. Paper Inst.; chmn. bd. trustees Inst. Paper Chemistry. Mem. Nat. Council Paper Industry for Air and Stream Improvement (vice chmn. bd. govs.), Nat. Indsl. Pollution Control Council (paper subcom.), T.A.P.P.I, Tau Beta Xi, Phi Kappa Psi, Alpha Chi Sigma, Phi Kappa Phi. Clubs: Corinthian Yacht; Union League (Phila.). Home: PO Box 9 Westtown PA 19395 Office: Scott Plaza Philadelphia PA 19113

BALDWIN, PETER ARTHUR, educator, psychologist, clergyman; b. Andover, Mass., Apr. 7, 1932; s. Alfred Graham and Katherine (Ashworth) B.; grad. Phillips Andover Acad., 1951; B.A., Middlebury Coll., 1955; S.T.B., Boston U., 1959, Ph.D., 1964; student New Coll. U. London (Eng.), 1957-58; m. Carolyn Whitmore, Sept 3, 1955; children—Sarah MacDonald, Robert Henry, Judith Helen. Ordained to ministry Unitarian Ch., 1959; pastor 2d Ch., Boston, 1955-57, in Dighton, Mass., 1958-62; religious counselor Mass. Inst. Tech., 1959-63; exec. dir. Liberal Religious Youth, Unitarian Universalist Assn., 1963-66; asst. prof. Crane Theol. Sch., Tufts U., 1965-67, Meadville Theol. Sch., U. Chgo. 1967—. Chaplain supr. clin. pastoral tng. insts. at Univ. Hosp., Boston, summer 1963, Boston City Hosp., summer 1964; chief trainer Inter- Generations Workshops, Unitarian Universalist Assn., 1963—; trainer Leadership Devel. Inst., Lake Geneva, Wis., 1966; dir. Sr. High and Family Insts., Rowe, Mass., 1967-71; Nat. Edn. Conf. lectr. Williston Acad., 1967; Judy lectr., Omaha, 1970. Mem. Liberal Religious Youth (life), Assn. Clin. Pastoral Edn. (bd. dirs. North Central region), Liberal Religious Edn. Dirs. Assn., Am. Assn. U. Profs., Assn. Theol. Profs. in Practical Field, Unitarian Universalists Ministers Assn. Democrat. Author pamphlets. Home: 7431 S Oglesby Av Chicago IL 60649

BALDWIN, PHILLIP BENJAMIN, U.S. judge; b. Marshall, Tex., Dec. 23, 1924; s. Jack B. and Lucille (Jones) B.; student U. Tex., 1942-43; B.A. in Biology, N. Tex. State Tchrs. Coll., 1949; student E. Tex. Bapt. Coll., 1949, Baylor U. Law Sch., 1950-51, S. Tex. Sch. Law, 1951-52; m. Mertie Bellamy, July 2, 1948; children—Rebecca, Nancy, Jane, Phillip Benjamin. Admitted to Tex. bar, 1952; asst. dist. atty., Marshall, 1953-54; criminal dist. atty. Harrison County, Tex., 1954-58; practice in Marshall, 1958-68; U.S. asso. judge Ct. Customs and Patent Appeals, 1968—. Served with USAAF, 1943-46; PTO. Mem. Am., Tex., N.E. Tex., Harrison County (sec. 1957, pres. 1958-60) bar assns., Tex. Trial Lawyers Assn., Nat. Assn. Def. Lawyers in Criminal Cases, Am. Legion, V.F.W., Alpha Tau Omega, Phi Delta Phi. Episcopalian. Elk. Home: 6439 Walters Wood Dr Falls Church VA 22044 Office: 717 Madison Pl NW Washington DC 20439

BALDWIN, RALPH BELKNAP, mfg. exec., astronomer; b. Grand Rapids, Mich., June 6, 1912; s. Melvin D. and Julie (Belknap) B.; B.S., U. Mich., 1934, M.S., 1935, Ph.D., 1937; m. Lois Virginia Johnston, Aug. 3, 1940, children—Melvin Dana, II, Pamela, Bruce Belknap. Asst. dept. astronomy U. Mich., 1935-36, U. Pa., 1937-38; instr. dept. astronomy Northwestern U., 1938-42; lectr. Adler Planetarium, Chgo., 1940-42; sr. physicist applied physics lab. Johns Hopkins, Silver Spring, Md., 1942-46, cons., East Grand Rapids, Mich., 1946-47; acting supt. schs., East Grand Rapids, 1947; prodn. mgr. Oliver Machinery Co., Grand Rapids, 1947—, dir., 1948—, successively personnel dir., prodn. mgr., sec., 1949-56, v.p., 1956-70, pres., 1970. Chmn. bd. Internat. Woodworking Machinery and Furniture Supply Fair- U.S.A., 1969-70. Recipient Presdl. Certificate of Merit, 1947; U.S. Naval Bur. Ordnance award, U.S. Army Chief of Ordnance award; Distinguished Alumnus award U. Mich., 1967. Fellow A.A.A.S., Am. Geophys. Union; mem. Am. Astron. Soc., Grand Rapids Museum Assn., N.A.M. (dir.), Employers Assn. Grand Rapids (pres. 1960-64), Woodworking Machinery Mfrs. Assn. (pres. 1964-68). Clubs: Rotary, Peninsular, University; Grand Rapids Yacht; Kent Country. Author: The Face of the Moon, 1949; The Measure of the Moon, 1963; The Moon—A Fundamental Survey, 1966. Contbr. tech. articles profl. Home: 3110 Manhattan Lane SE East Grand Rapids MI 49506 Office: 445 6th St NW Grand Rapids MI 49504

BALDWIN, RAYMOND PEACOCK, lawyer; b. Brookline, Mass., Nov. 3, 1894; s. Alvi Twing and Margaret Isabelle (Peacock) B.; A.B., Harvard, 1916; LL.B., 1921; m. Joan Waddy, July 28, 1920; children—Stephen Peacock, Rosemary Honor (Mrs. David Douglas Coffin). Admitted to Mass. bar, 1921, U.S. Supreme Ct., 1938, N.Y. bar, 1946, D.C. bar, 1947; asst. gen cousel Bd. Econ. Warfare, 1943, Fgn. Econ. Adminstrn., 1943-44; spl. asst. to U.S. Atty. Gen., 1944-45; mem. appeal bd. Office of Contract Settlement, 1945-53, chmn., 1951-53; regional counsel Renegotiation Bd., Boston, 1952-55. Cmdg. officer 140th Aero Squadron, 1918-19; chmn. N.E. Aviation Cadet Com., 1941-42. Clubs: Harvard (N.Y.C.); Cosmos (Washington). Author: (with Joan Baldwin) The Fun of Acting, 1951; (with David Dempsey) The Triumphs and Trials of Lotte Crabtree, 1968. Home: 29 Lexington Rd Concord MA 01742

BALDWIN, RIGNAL WOODWARD, lawyer; b. Balt., Sept. 12, 1902; s. Rignal Woodward and Augusta (Hopkins) B.; grad. Balt. City Coll., 1919; A.B., Johns Hopkins, 1923; LL.B., U. Md., 1927; m. Ann Elizabeth Williams, Apr. 18, 1933; children—Ann Williams (Mrs. Harry L. Smith), Rignal Woodward IV. Admitted to Md. bar, 1927, since practiced in Balt.; mem. firm Semmes, Bowen & Semmes. Served as capt. Combat Intelligence, with 3d Bombardment Group USAAF, 1942-45. Decorated Air medal. Fellow Am. Bar Found., Am. Coll. Trial Lawyers; mem. Am., Md. (pres. 1967-68), Balt. (pres. 1959-60) bar assns., Johns Hopkins Alumni Assn. (pres. 1962-64), U. Md. Law Sch. Alumni Assn. (v.p.), Phi Beta Kappa, Beta Theta Pi, Omicron Delta Kappa. Methodist (trustee, ofcl. bd.). Home: 1100 W Lake Av Baltimore MD 21210 Office: 10 Light St Baltimore MD 21202

BALDWIN, ROBERT BEMUS, naval officer; b. Mpls., Apr. 24, 1923; s. William Prendergast and Nell (Pickard) B.; B.S., U.S. Naval Acad., 1944; postgrad. U.S. Naval Test Pilot Sch., 1952; m. Rowena June Wilson, Mar. 24, 1950; children—Scott W., Jared M., Sylvia. Commd. ensign USN, 1944, advanced through grades to rear adm., 1968; naval test pilot Patuxent River, Md., 1952-54; comdg. officer Fighter Squadron 51, U.S.S. Ticonderoga, 1961-62; comdr. Carrier Air Wing 16, U.S.S. Oriskany, 1963-64; comdg. officer U.S.S. Forrestal, 1967-68; comdr. Carrier Div. 6, U.S.S. Saratoga, 1971—. Decorated Legion of Merit, Bronze Star medal, Purple Heart. Home: 547 Ozbourn Naval Sta Jacksonville FL 32227 Office: Comdr Carrier Div 6 FPO New York City NY 09501

BALDWIN, ROBERT CHESTER, educator; b. Seymour, Conn., June 21, 1905; s. Herbert York and Ida Mae (Fisher) B.; A.B., Wesleyan U., Middletown, Conn., 1929, M.A., 1930; Ph.D., Yale, 1932; m. Catherine A. Roche, June 23, 1932; children—Mary (Mrs. Mary E. Spector), James York, Robert Chester. Faculty U. Conn., 1932-61, prof. philosophy, 1950-61, chmn. dept., 1932-61; prof. philosophy, chmn. dept. Am. Internat. Coll., Springfield, Mass., 1961—; vis. prof. Wesleyan U., 1946-47, Conn. Coll. Women, 1947, Springfield Coll., 1964-65. Mem. Am. Philos. Assn., Metaphys. Soc. Am. Internat. Platform Assn., Conn. Acad. Arts and Scis., Assn. Realistic Philosophy, Delta Sigma Rho, Phi Kappa Phi. Editor: (with James A. S. McPeek) An Introduction to Philosophy Through Literature, 1950. Home: Route 3 Box 5 Storrs CT 06268 Office: Am Internat Coll Springfield MA 01109

BALDWIN, ROBERT EDWARD, educator; b. Niagara Falls, N.Y., July 12, 1924; s. Gilbert and Margaret (Ostman) B.; B.S., U. Buffalo, 1945; M.A., Harvard, 1947, Ph.D., 1950; m. Janice Murphy, July 31, 1954; children—Jean, Robert, Richard, Nancy. Instr., then asst. prof. econs. Harvard, 1950-57; asso. prof., then prof. econs. U. Cal. at Los Angeles, 1957-64; prof. econs. U. Wis. at Madison, 1964—; chief economist Office Spl. Trade Rep., Exec. Office of President, 1963-64; vis. prof. Brookings Instn., Washington, 1967-68. Mem. Am. Econ. Assn. Author: (with G.M. Meier) Economic Development, 1957; Economic Development and Export Technology, 1965; Economic Development and Growth, 1966; Nontariff Distortions of International Trade, 1970. Home: 125 Nautilus Dr Madison WI 53705

BALDWIN, ROBERT HAYES BURNS, bus. exec.; b. E. Orange, N.J., July 9, 1920; s. John Frank and Anna (Burns) B.; grad. Phillips Exeter Acad., 1938; A.B., Princeton, 1942; m. Geraldine Gay Williams, May 28, 1949; children—Janet Kimball, Deborah Gay, Robert Hayes Burns, Whitney Hayes, Elizabeth Brooks. With Morgan Stanley & Co., N.Y.C., 1946—, gen. partner, 1958-65, 67—, ltd. partner, 1965-67; mng. dir. Morgan Stanley & Co., Inc., N.Y.C., served as under sec. of navy, 1965-67; chmn. bd. Brooks, Harvey & Co., Inc., N.Y.C.; dir. Urban Innovations, Inc. Trustee Seeing Eye, Inc., Indsl. Relations Counselors, Inc. Served to lt. USNR, 1942-46. Mem. Assn. Stock Exchange Firms (gov.), Council Fgn. Relations, Phi Beta Kappa. Republican. Presbyn. Clubs: Links, Down Town Assn., Bond of N.Y., Bankers (gov.) (N.Y.C.); Chevy Chase (Md.); Metropolitan (Washington); Morris County Golf (Convent, N.J.); Morristown (N.Y.) Field; Bridgehampton (N.Y.). Home: Village Rd New Vernon NJ 07976 Office: 140 Broadway New York City NY 10005

BALDWIN, ROBERT JAMES, aircraft mfg. co. exec.; b. East Lansing, Mich., Aug. 11, 1917; s. Robert James and Bertha Lillian (Van Orden) B.; B.S. with honors in Chem. Engring., Mich. State U., 1940; m. Margaret Eloise Burlington, Oct. 19, 1941; children—Bonnie Lee (Mrs. Jon MacDonald), Steven Robert. With McDonnell Douglas Corp., St. Louis, 1940—, chief systems engr., 1955-60, asst. chief engr., 1960-61, dir. aircraft engring., 1961-64, v.p. avionics engring., 1964—. Mem. Am. Inst. Aero. and Astronautics, Navy League, Assn. U.S. Army, Phi Kappa Phi, Tau Beta Pi, Phi Delta Theta. Club: University (Washington). Home: 60 Calverton Park Lane St Louis MO 63135 Office: Box 516 St Louis MO 63166

BALDWIN, ROBERT LESH, educator, biochemist; b. Madison Wis., Sept. 30, 1927; s. Ira Lawrence and Mary (Lesh) B.; B.A., U. Wis., 1950; D.Phil. (Rhodes scholar 1950- 53), Oxford (Eng.) U., 1954; m. Anne Theodora Norris, Aug. 28, 1965; children—David Norris, Eric Lawrence. Asst. prof., then asso. prof. biochemistry U. Wis., 1955-59; mem. faculty Stanford, 1959—, prof. biochemistry, 1964-. Served with AUS, 1946-47. Guggenheim fellow, 1958-59. Mem. Am. Soc. Biol. Chemists, Am. Chem. Soc. Asso. editor Jour. Molecular Biology, 1964-68. Home: 1243 Los Trancos Rd Portola Valley CA 94025. Office: Dept Biochemistry Stanford Univ Stanford CA 94305

BALDWIN, ROGER NASH, polit. reformer; b. Wellesley, Mass., Jan 21, 1884; s. Frank Fenno and Lucy Cushing (Nash) B.; A.B., Harvard, 1904, A.M., 1905; LL.D., Washington U., 1968; Yale, 1969, Brandeis U., 1969; m. Madeleine Zabriskie Doty, Aug. 9, 1919 (div.); m. 2d, Evelyn Preston, Mar. 7, 1936 (dec. June 1962); 1 dau., Helen T. Instr. sociology Washington U., St. Louis 1906-09; chief probation officer Juvenile Court, St. Louis, 1907-10; sec. Nat. Probation Assn., 1908-10; sec. St. Louis Civic League, 1910-17, St. Louis Children's Commn., 1913-14; dir. Am. Civil Liberties Union, N.Y.C., 1917-50, nat. chmn., 1950-55, adviser internat. work, 1950—; law faculty U. P.R., 1966—. Cons. civil liberties U.S. occupation of Japan and Korea, 1947, Germany and Austria, 1948, 50, Govt. P.R., V.I., 1954-64; former chmn., hon. pres. Internat. League Rights Man, 1946—; bd. dirs. Nat. Audubon Soc., 1934-46; faculty New Sch. for Social Research, 1938-42; mem. Harvard Overseers' Com. on Econs. Dept., 1938- 50. Recipient Am. Vets. Com. award, 1950; Florina Lasker civil liberties award, 1957; Order of Rising Sun (2d class), Emperor Japan; medal City of N.Y., 1966. Fellow Am. Acad. Arts and Scis. Author: (with Bernard Flexner) Juvenile Courts and Probation, 1912; Liberty under the Soviets, 1928. Editor: Kropotkin's Freedom Pamphlets, 1928; Civil Liberties and Industrial Conflict (Harvard Godkin lectures), 1938; A New Slavery, Forced Labor, 1953. Home: Dell Brook Oakland NJ 07436 Office: 156 Fifth Av New York City NY 10010

BALDWIN, ROSECRANS, accountant; b. Chgo., Jan. 20, 1914; s. A. Rosecrans and Helen (Poole) B.; grad. St. Mark's Sch., Southboro, Mass., 1931; B.S. with highest honors, Yale, 1935; m. Sarah S. Griffin, May 21, 1949; children—Rosecrans, Sarah Sherburne, Elizabeth Langdon. With Arthur Young & Co., Chgo., 1935—, audit mgr., 1946-49, partner, 1950—. Trustee, sec. Chgo. Symphony Orch.; trustee Chgo. Sunday Evening Club; past dir., pres. Chgo. Hearing Soc.; bd. dirs. Chgo. Area Project; past pres., trustee Latin Sch., Chgo. Served to comdr. USNR, 1941-46. C.P.A., Ill. Mem. Am. Inst. C.P.A.'s (council), Ill. Soc. C.P.A.'s (past treas., v.p., dir.). Episcopalian. Contbr. articles profl. jours. Home: 1224 Astor St Chicago IL 60610 Office: 111 W Monroe St Chicago IL 60603

BALDWIN, VINCENT JOHN, bishop; b. Bklyn., July 13, 1907; s. John O. and Josepha (Haefelein) B.; student Inst. Philosophy, Huntington, N.Y., 1926-28; J.C.B., Gregorian U., Rome, Italy, 1929, S.T.D., 1932. Ordained priest Roman Catholic Ch., 1931; mem. matrimonial tribunal Diocese Bklyn., 1934-49, vice chancellor diocese, 1949-53; apptd. papal chamberlain, 1948; chancellor, diocesan consultor Diocese Rockville Center, N.Y., 1957, vicar gen. diocese, 1957- 62, aux. bishop, 1962—; apptd. domestic prelate, 1959. Home: 130 5th St Garden City NY 11530 Office: 253 Sunrise Hwy Rockville Centre NY 11570

BALDWIN, WALTER DOUARIN, mfg. exec.; b. Korbel, Cal., Jan. 16, 1910; s. Hubert A. and Helouise (Douarin) B.; B.S. U. Cal., 1931; m. Ann Wagner, May 17, 1935; 1 dau. Judith Anne. With U.S. Rubber Co., 1935-, successively tire salesman, sales mgr. U.S. Tires div., dir. mfrs. sales tire div., asst. gen. mgr. tire div., v.p. charge automotive sales, 1935-62, v.p. charge corporate sales, 1962-64, v.p. adminstrn., 1967—, dir., 1968—, co. name now Uniroyal, Inc.; dir. Uniroyal Ltd. (Gt. Britain), Uniroyal, Ltd. (Can.). Bd. dirs. Detroit Met. Bldg. Fund, United Found., Detroit Citizens Research Inst.; trustee Automotive Safety Found. Detroit Inst., Automotive Safety Found. Mem. Detroit Traffic Safety Assn. (dir.), Detroit Bd. Commerce Rubber Mfrs. Assn. (dir.), Newcomen Soc., Alpha Tau Omega, Delta Sigma Pi. Clubs: Economic (N.Y., Detroit); Detroit Athletic, Detroit, Country, Recess (Detroit); Bloomfield Hills (Mich.) Country; Greenwich (Conn.) Country; Twenty Nine (N.Y.C.). Home: 27 Oxford Rd Grosse Point Shores MI 48236 Office: 1230 Av Americas New York City NY 10020 also 4500 Enterprise Dr Allen Park NY 48101.

BALDWIN, WILLIAM LEE, educator; b. N.Y.C., Apr. 12, 1928; s. William Lee and Mildred (Karnes) B.; B.A., Duke, 1951; M.A., Princeton, 1953, Ph.D., 1958; m. Marcia Diane Hurt, Aug. 18, 1956; children—Douglas Lee, Ellen Parker. Asst. in instrn., instr. Princeton, 1952-56, vis. asst. prof., 1961-62; instr., asst. prof., asso. prof., prof. Dartmouth, Hanover, N.H., 1956—, chmn. social scis. div., 1970—; vis. prof. Thammasat U., Bangkok, Thailand, 1968-70. Served with AUS, 1946-47. Brookings research prof., 1963-64. Mem. Am. Econ. Assn., Am. Assn. U. Profs., Phi Beta Kappa, Omicron Delta Kappa. Author: Antitrust and the Changing Corporation, 1961; The Structure of the Defense Market, 1955-64, 1967. Contbr. articles profl. jours. Home: 8 Rayton Rd Hanover NH 03755

BALENCIAGA, CRISTOBAL, ret. couturier; b. Guetaria, Prov. Guipuzcoa, Spain, 1895. Opened his first fashion house, San Sebastian, Spain, 1916, Madrid, 1932, Barcelona, 1938, Paris, 1937-68. Decorated Cross of Knight of Order of Isabella La Catolica (Spain). Home: 28 Av Marceau Paris 8 France Office: 10 Av George V Paris 8 France

BALENTINE, CONRAD JAMES, electric mfg. co. exec.; b. Easton, Pa., May 24, 1917; s. Howard M. and Eulalie (Brunner) B.; grad. Blair Acad., 1936; B.S. in Elec. Engring., Princeton, 1940; m. Margaret Anne Hollohan, June 7, 1947; children—Catherine Eulalie, Anne Margaret. Mgr. power circuit breaker engring. Gen. Electric Co., Phila., 1940-42, test engr., head circuit breaker testing lab., 1942-50, design and product engr., mgr. power circuit breaker engring., 1950-61; exec. v.p., then pres., chief exec. officer Franklin Electric Co., Inc., Bluffton, Ind., 1961—, also dir.; pres. Franklin Electric Co. of Can., Ltd., Strathray, Ont., Franklin Electric Europa GmbH, Wittlich, Germany, 1965—, Exact Weight Scale Co., Columbus, O.; chmn. bd. Battle Creek Packaging Machines, Inc. (Mich.), J.B. Dove, Inc., Fallsington, Pa. Mem. industry-coll. adv. com., fellow Ind. Inst. Tech. Registered profl. engr., Pa. Mem. I.E.E.E. (asso.), Am. Mgmt. Assn., Princeton Engring. Assn., Nat. Elec. Mfrs. Assn., Am. Gear Mfrs. Assn., Ind. Mfrs. Assn. (bd. dirs.), Newcomen Soc. N.Am., Am. Standards Assn. Clubs: Parlor City Country; Fort Wayne Country. Contbr. articles on switchgear to profl. publs. Patentee switchgear field. Home: R R 4 Fackler Rd Bluffton IN 46714 Office: 400 E Spring St Bluffton IN 46714

BALES, ALLEN, educator; b. Birmingham, Ala., July 9, 1920; s. John Wesley and Blanche Laura (Muckenfuss) B.; A.B., U. Ala., 1943, M.A., 1947; Ph.D., Northwestern U., 1959; m. Carolyn Baldwin Carpenter, Feb. 15, 1944; 1 son, Allen Wheeler. Mem. faculty U. Ala., 1947—, prof. speech, 1963—, chmn. dept. 1969—; dir., actor in first prodn. Dylan Thomas' Under Milk Wood, 1961-62; adapted, staged Robert Frost on Stage, 1965; guest artist theatre prodns. with Birmingham Festival of Arts, 1955, 57, 59. Co-chmn. Arts and Humanities Council, Tuscaloosa County, Ala., 1970—. Served with AUS, 1943-46; ETO. Mem. Ala. Speech Assn. (past pres.), Southeastern (mem. exec. council), Ala. theatre assns., Speech Assn. Am., Ala. Ednl. Assn., Nat. Forensics League, Nat. Collegiate Players, Tau Kappa Alpha, Omicron Delta Kappa, Alpha Psi Omega. Author: Point of View in the Novels of Nathaniel Hawthorne, 1959; Oral Interpretation: An Extension of Literary Study, 1969. Asso. editor: Speech Monographs, 1963-65. Home: 224 The Highlands Tuscaloosa AL 35401 Office: U Ala Box 1965 University AL 35486

BALES, RICHARD HENRY HORNER, condr., composer; b. Alexandria, Va., Feb. 3, 1915; s. Henry Ahijah and Henrietta Wyeth (Horner) B.; Mus.B., Easman Sch. Music, U. Rochester, 1936; student Julliard Grad. Sch., 1938-41; pvt. pupil Serge Koussevitzky, 1940; m. Mary Elizabeth Starley, Nov. 7, 1942; 1 dau., Mary Starley. Debut as condr. with Nat. Symphony Orch., 1935; condr. Va.-N.C. Symphony, 1936-38; music dir. Nat. Gallery Art and condr. Nat. Gallery Orch., Washington, 1943—; condr. Washington Cathedral Choral Soc., 1945-46; music dir. Nat. Symphony Orch., summer 1947; guest condr. orchs. of several cities in U.S. including Phila., N.Y.C., St. Louis, San Antonio, Cleve. summer, Nat. Symphony Orch., Am. Little Symphony, Naumburg Orch., tchr. Mass. State Tchrs. Coll., summer 1941, George Washington U., 1953; lectr. music. Recipient first prize string composition, Arts Club Washington, 1940; award Merit, Nat. Assn. Composers and Condrs., 1959, Alice M. Ditson award Columbia U., 1960, Acad. of Achievement, Monterey, Cal., 1961. Life fellow Internat. Inst. Arts and Letters, 1961. Mem. Nat. Assn. Am. Composers and Condrs. (dir.), Am. Fedn. Musicians, Soc. Cincinnati, Civil War Round Table D.C. (Gold medal 1960, pres. 1960- 61). U.S. Navy Band (hon. life), Bruckner Soc. in Am. (hon.), Md. Hist. Soc., Kindler Found. (pres. 1959-62), Alexandria Library Co. (life mem., pres. 1962-63), S.C.V. (hon. life mem.; 1st lt. comdr. 1963-64). Episcopalian. Clubs: Internat. (Washington); Cosmos. Composer various works, orchestral instrumental, choral selections. Home: 6022 Pike Branch Dr Alexandria VA 22310 Office: Nat Gallery of Art Washington DC 20565

BALES, ROBERT FREED, educator; b. Ellington, Mo., Mar. 9, 1916; s. Columbus Lee and Ada Lois (Sloan) B.; B.A., U. Ore., 1938, M.S., 1940; M.A., Harvard, 1943, Ph.D., 1945; m. Dorothy Louise Johnson, Sept. 14, 1941. Research asso. sect. on alcohol studies, Yale, 1944-45; instr. sociology Harvard, Cambridge Mass., 1945-57, asst. prof. sociology, research asso. Lab. Social Relations, 1947-51, lectr. sociology, research asso. 1951-55, asso. prof., 1955-57, prof. social relations, 1957—, dir. Lab. Social Relations, 1960-67, cons. psychology Univ. Health Services, 1970—. Vis. lect. sociology and social psychology U. Mich., summer 1949, Columbia, summer 1950; lectr. Salzberg Austria Seminar of Am. Studies, summer 1952, 56. Mem. bd. sci. counsellors Nat. Inst. Mental Health, 1957-60. Trustee Ella L. Cabot Trust. Mem. Am., Eastern (pres. 1962-63) sociol. socs., Am. Acad. Arts and Scis., Boston Psychoanalytic Soc. (affiliate). Author: Interaction Process Analysis: A Method for the Study of Small Groups, 1950; Personality and Interpersonal Behavior, 1970; (with Talcott Parsons, Edward A. Shils) Working Papers in the Theory of Action, 1953; (with Talcott Parsons, et al) Family, Socialization, and Interaction Process, 1955. Contbr. to Group Dynamics, Research and Theory, 1953, and several other compilations. Editor: (with A. Paul Hare and Edgar F. Borgatta) Small Groups, Studies in Social Interaction, 1955. Home: 61 Scotch Pine Rd Weston MA 02193 Office: Harvard University Cambridge MA 02138

BALET, JOHN WILLIAM, ret. utility exec.; b. N.Y.C., Nov. 13, 1904; s. Joseph William and Margaret Agnes (Ryan) B.; A.B., Columbia, 1925, B.S., 1926. E.E., 1927; m. Kathleen Ethridge Giblin, Sept. 19, 1936; children—William John, Kathleen Carmody, Mary Margaret, Jane Giblin. Constrn. engr. E.L. Phillips & Co., 1927-33; with Consol. Edison Co., N.Y.C., 1933-69, gen. mgr. data processing dept., 1957-58, asst. v.p., 1958-62, v.p., 1962-69; cons. to Police Dept. City N.Y., 1969—. Mem. I.E.E.E. (life), Tau Beta Pi, Theta Tau. Club: University (N.Y.C.). Home: 122 Loring Av Pelham NY 10803

BALEY, JAMES MAJOR, JR., lawyer, b. Greensboro, N.C. Jan. 23, 1912; s.James Major and Mary Mary Katherine (Redmond) B.; grad. Mars Hill (N.C.) Jr. Coll., 1929; A.B., U. N.C., 1932, LL.B., 1933; m. Diana Chandley, Mar. 27, 1943; children—James Major, Kathy Deane. Admitted to N.C. bar, 1933, since practiced in Marshall; U.S. atty. for Western Dist. N.C., 1953-61; mem. law firm McGuire, Baley and Woods, Asheville, 1961-. Mem. Ho. Reps. N.C. General Assembly, 1937, 39. Chairman Madison County chapter A.R.C., 1946-48. Attorney Madison County, 1937-42. Served from lieutenant (j.g.) to lieutenant comdr., USNR, 1942-46. Named Alumnus of Year, Mars Hill Colleg ˝, 1959. Member North Carolina State Bar, Am., N.C. Boncombe County bar assns., Am. Judicature Society, Am. Legion. Republican (state com. field organizer, 1940, asst. state chmn. 1946-50, state chmn. 1950- 53). Baptist. Mason. Club: Civitan. Home: Asheville NC 28801 Office: 1st Union Nat Bank Bldg Ashville, NC

BALFOUR, LLOYD G., jewelry mfg. co. exec.; b. Wauseon, O., Jan. 6, 1886; s. Claude and Elizabeth (Lloyd) B.; LL.B., U. Ind., 1907, LL.D., 1966; grad. U. Louisville, 1904, A.B. (hon.), 1948; m. Mildred McCann, Feb. 5, 1923. Pres., treas. L. G. Balfour, Attleboro, Mass., mfrs. jewelry, now chmn. bd. Chmn. Nat. Interfrat. Conf., 1940-41, Interfrat. Research and Adv. Council, 1946-54. Life mem. council Friends Library Wash. State U. Bd. dirs. Sturdy Meml. Hosp., Attleboro. Recipient Significant Sig award Sigma Chi, 1941, Semi-Century Sig award, 1956; Gold medal Nat. Interfrat. Conf., 1946; Distinguished Service Alumni award Ind. U., 1959; Distinguished Service award Theta Chi; award for interfrat. leadership Lambda Chi Alpha, 1960; Zora G. Clevenger Service award I Men's Assn. Ind. U., 1963. Mem. New Eng. Mfg. Jewelers Assn., Newcomen Soc., Tau Kappa Alpha, Sigma Upsilon, Phi Mu Alpha, Kappa Pi, Gamma Lambda Epsilon, Theta Alpha Phi, Alpha Phi Omega, Alpha Chi Alpha, Chi Delta Phi, Sigma Chi (past grand consul), Phi Delta Phi. Republican. Mason (32, Shriner), Elk. Clubs: Highland Balfour Country (Attleboro, Mass.); Porcupine (Nassau, Bahamas); Triton Fish and Game (Que., Can.); Royal and Ancient Golf of Saint Andrews (Fife, Scotland). Home: Pine St Norton MA 02766 Office: County St Attleboro MA 02703

BALFOUR, MAXWELL W., corp. exec.; b. Traer, Ia., June 22, 1895; s. William and Rachel (Coulter) B.; B.A., Northwestern U., 1916; m. Marie Louise Petot, Dec. 30, 1919 (div.); 1 dau., Claude (Mrs. E. Kenneth Hadden). Aviation cadet, 1917; commd. 1st lt. AC, U.S. Army, 1918, ret. as capt., 1931; dir. aviation div. Spartan Aircraft, 1939-61, v.p. Spartan Aircraft Co., 1941-61, pres., 1961-68; pres. Minnehoma Ins. Co., Minnehoma Life Ins. Co., Minnehoma Finance Co., 1961-71, chmn. bd., 1971—. Decorated Order Brit. Empire. Mem. Quiet Birdmen, Order Daedalians, Aero. Tng. Soc. (past pres.), Newcomen Soc., Delta Tau Delta. Clubs: University; John Evans; Army-Navy. Home: 3701 S Birmingham Av Tulsa OK 74105 Office: Minnehoma Financial Co PO Box 51168 Tulsa OK 74151

BALFOUR, REGINALD JAMES, lawyer; b. Regina, Sask., Can., May 22, 1928; s. Reginald Mcleod and Martha (McElmoyle) B.; student Luther Coll., 1946-48; LL.B., U. Saskatchewan, 1950; m. Beverly Jane Davidson, June 6, 1951; children—John Alan, James Roberts, Reginald William, Beverly Ann. Admitted to Sask. province bar, 1952; sr. partner firm Balfour, MacLeod, McDonald, Moss, Laschuk & Kyle, Regina, 1952—; appointed Queen's Counsel, 1969. Dir. The Royal Trust Co., Duval Corp. Can. Chmn. Alcoholism Comms. Sask., 1968; hon. Swedish consul for Sask. Bd. dirs. Can. Petroleum Law Found. Served to lt. Royal Can. Arty., 1950-54. Mem. Can., Regina (pres. 1956-57) bar assns., Law Soc. Sask., United Services Inst. Home: 51 Academy Park Rd Regina Saskatchewan Canada Office: 1850 Cornwall St Regina Saskatchewan Canada

BALFOUR, ST. CLAIR, communications exec.; b. Hamilton, Ont., Can., Apr. 30, 1910; s. St. Clair and Ethel May (Southam) B.; grad. Trinity Coll. Sch., 1927; B.A., Trinity Coll., U. Toronto, 1931; m. Helen Gifford Staunton, Jan 21, 1933; children—Elizabeth S., St. Clair. With Southam Press, Ltd., Toronto, Can., 1931—, mng. dir., 1955-69, pres., 1961—; v.p., pub. Hamilton Spectator, 1951; dir. several Canadian mass communications cos. Trustee Am. Newspaper Pubs. Found.; v.p. Can. Heart Found. Decorated Distinguished Service Cross. Mem. Canadian Daily Newspaper Pubs. Assn.; hon. life mem. Canadian Press. Home: 17 Ardwold Gate Toronto Ontario Canada Office: Southam Press Ltd 321 Bloor St E Toronto Ontario Canada

BALFOUR, WILLIAM MAYO, educator, physician; b. Pasadena, Cal., Nov. 26, 1914; s. Donald Church and Carrie (Mayo) B.; B.S., U. Minn., 1936, M.D., 1939; M.S., Mayo Grad. Sch., 1948; m. Oane McQuarrie, Jan. 7, 1939; children—James, Barbara, Laurie (Mrs. Dale Tremain), Wendy. Intern. resident Strong Meml. Hosp., Rochester, N.Y., 1939-42; resident Mayo Found., Rochester, Minn. 1942-48: cons. sects. metabolism and endocrinology Mayo Clinic, 1948-57; instr. Mayo Found., 1949-57; USPHS postdoctoral fellow U. Kan., Lawrence, 1957-59, research asso., 1959-62, asso. prof., 1962-66. prof., 1966—, dir. Pearson Coll., 1967, vice chancellor student affairs, 1968—; dir. In-Service Inst. for High Sch. Tchrs. Biol. Scis., 1962-63. Served to maj., M.C., AUS, 1942-45. Mem. Am. Diabetes Assn., Am. Physiol. Soc., A.M.A., Nat. Assn. Student Personnel Adminstrs., N.Y. Acad. Scis., Soc. Exptl. Biology and Medicine, Sigma Xi. Unitarian. Contbr. articles profl. jours. Home: 1505 University Dr Lawrence KS 66044

BALGOOYEN, HENRY WARREN, economist; b. Hadley, Mich., May 16, 1906; s. Albert and Wilhelmina (Seegmiller) B.; A.B., U. Mich., 1928, M.B.A., 1929; m. Violet M. Linden, Sept. 5, 1930; children—Carol Arden, Warren Prentis, Bruce Willard, Marjorie Ellen. With fgn. dept. Chase Nat. Bank, 1930-36; staff Ebasco Services, Inc., 1936-42, economist, 1944—, asst. comptroller, 1945-46, sec., 1946-56, v.p., 1952, exec. v.p., 1955-57; sec. Am. and Fgn. Power Co., Inc., 1946-51, v.p., sec., 1952-55, exec. v.p., sec., 1955- 67, pres., chief exec. officer, 1967, dir., 1962-67; sr. v.p. Ebasco Industries, Inc., N.Y.C., 1968, dir., 1968-69; dir. First Fed. Savs. & Loan Assn., Internat. Mining Corp., Selective Capital Fund, Selective Am. Realty Fund; mem. adv. bd. Marine Midland Trust Co. Mem. U.S. delegation Internat. Trade Orgn. Conf. UN, Havana, 1947-48, Rio de Janeiro Econ. Conf., 1954; v.p. Inter- Am. Council Commerce and Prodn., Montivideo, Uruguay, 1958-60. Bd. dirs. Americas Found., 1967—, pres., 1969—; mem. nat. council Inst. Internat. Edn., 1970—. Recipient Capt. Robert Dollar Meml. award, 1960; Outstanding Achievement award U. Mich., 1964. Mem. Am. Enterprise Inst. (trustee), Council for Latin Am. (vice chmn. 1964-68), U.S. Inter-Am. Council (trustee, chmn. bd. 1958- 60), Pan Am. Soc. U.S. (pres. 1964-67), N.Y.C. C. of C. (exec. com. 1965-68), Argentine-Am., Ecuadorian-Am. Assn. (pres. 1964-65), Alpha Kappa Psi. Methodist. Club: Metropolitan (N.Y.C.). Home: The Crossways Katonah NY 10536

BALIN, MARTY singer, musician with Jefferson Airplane, pop-rock group; recordings include After Bathing, Bless Its Pointed Little Head, Crown of Creation, Surrealistic Pillow, Somebody to Love, Fat Angel, Plastic Fantastic Lover, Turn Out the Lights. Address: care RCA Victor Records 155 E 24th St New York City NY 10010*

BALINT, DENNIS MARTIN, lawyer; b. Cleve., Apr. 5, 1933; s. Denes M. and Julia, (Czaban) B.; B.S., U. Ariz., 1955; LL.B., Western Res. U., 1958; m. Betty Sue Rogers, Oct. 17, 1964; children—Tamara, Dennis Martin, Brady, Tiffany. Admitted to Ariz. bar, 1959, Ohio bar, 1958; practice in Phoenix, 1959; partner firm Rawlins, Ellis, Burrus & Kiewit, 1963—; lectr. Ariz. Inst. Banking 1967—. Pres. Valley Big Bros., 1968; chmn. Phoenix YMCA bd. mgmt., 1971—. Mem. Ariz. Acad., Phoenix Execs. Club, Phoenix Jr. C. of C., Scottsdale 20-30. Kiwanian (pres. Aurora club, Phoenix 1967). Home: 1809 Palmcroft Dr N E Phoenix AZ 85007 Office: Security Bldg Phoenix AZ 85007

BALIS, MOSES EARL, educator, biochemist; b. Phila., June 19, 1921; s. Harry and Frances (Spector) B.; B.A., Temple U., 1943; M.S., U. Pa., 1947, Ph.D., 1949; m. Bernice M. Lamborg, Dec. 30, 1945; children—Frances Andrea, Ellen Joyce. With Sloan-Kettering Inst., 1949—, head nucleoprotein metabolism sect., 1957—, asso. mem., 1960-65, mem., 1965—, chief div. cell metabolism, 1970—; asso. prof. Med. Coll. Cornell U., 1954-66, prof. biochemistry, 1966—, chmn. biochemistry unit, 1969—; vis. lectr. Adelphi U., 1963-64. Served to lt. (j.g.) USNR, 1944-46. Recipient Research Career award USPHS, 1963. Mem. Am. Chem. Soc. (past sect. chmn.), A.A.A.S., Am. Cancer Soc., Am. Soc. Biol. Chemists, Harvey Soc., Am. Assn. Cancer Research, Sigma Xi. Editorial bd. Cancer Research, 1969—. Research, numerous publs. on metabolism of purines in normal and malignant tissues; determined biochem. action of anti-cancer drugs. Home: 450 E 63d St New York City NY 10021 Office: 425 E 68th St New York City NY 10021

BALK, EUGENE NORMAN, lawyer; b. Toledo, Oct. 11, 1929; s. Harold H. and Mamie (Glow) B.; B.S. cum laude, Ohio State U., 1950; J.D. magna cum laude, U. Toledo, 1959; m. Beverly Christine Spino, June 24, 1967; children-Angela J., Christine M., Mark D., Lance C., Adele M. Admitted to Ohio Bar, 1959, since practiced in Maumee; partner, gen. counsel The Andersons, 1967—. Trustee Community Planning Council Northwestern Ohio. Anderson Found. Served to 1st lt., inf., U.S. Army, 1950-53. Mem. Am., Ohio, Toledo (com. chmn.) bar assns., Am. Judicature Soc., N.A.A.C.P., Gamma Sigma Delta, Phi Kappa Phi. Lutheran. Rotarian. Home: 1902 Perrysburg-Holland Rd Holland OH 43528 Office: 127 E Dudley St Maumee OH 43537

BALKE, BRUNO A., educator; b. Braunschweig, Germany, Sept. 6, 1907; s. Albert and Therese (Karnath) B.; student Deutsche Hoshschule f. Leibesuebungen, Berlin, 1927-31; M.D., U. Berlin, 1935; postgrad., U. Leipzig, 1945; m. Annemarie Anacker, Sept. 17, 1935; children—Horst Z., Frank H., Hedda A. (Mrs. Klaus Marg), Per Olof. Came to U.S., 1950, naturalized, 1959. Research asst. in sports medicine U. Berlin, 1937-42; free med. practice, 1946-49; research scientist USAF Sch. Aviation (Aerospace) Medicine, 1950-60; br. chief Civil Aeromed. Research Inst., Oklahoma City, 1960-64; prof. physiology and phys. edn. U. Wis.-Madison, 1964—; research prof. U. Okla., 1960-64; asso. prof. Air U., 1956-60. Served with German Army, 1939-45. Fellow Am. Coll. Sports Medicine (pres. 1966). Editor Jour. Medicine and Science in Sports, 1969—; contbr. articles profl. jours., textbooks. Home: 906 Swarthmore Ct Madison WI 53705

BALL, BENJAMIN WALKER, electric co. exec.; b. Middlesex County, Ont., Can., Mar. 14, 1912; s. Robert Tudor and Blanche Elizabeth Ball; B.A., U. Toronto, 1934; m. Rhoda Elizabeth Darnbough, Dec., 1937 (dec. 1959); children—John Michael, Benjamin Walker, Mark Andrew, Mary Elizabeth, Sarah Margaret; m. 2d, Margaret Jean Wilkinson, July 29, 1961. Trainee, Hudson's Bay Co., Winnipeg, 1934; dept. mgr., Vancouver, B.C., 1935-42; prodn. mgr. Cemco Elec. Mfg. Co., Vancouver, 1942-45, sales mfg., 1945-52, pres., 1952-58; pres., FPE Can. Ltd., Toronto, 1958, FPE Pioneer Electric Ltd., Toronto, 1963—; CoFed Ltd.; dir. Fed. pacific Electric Co., E.C.C. Ltd., Fed. Electric Ltd. Mem. Canadian Mfrs. Assn., Can. Elec. Mfrs. Assn. (dir.). Home: 222 Blythwood Rd Toronto 12 Ontario Canada Office: FPE-Pioneer Electric Ltd 19 Waterman Av Toronto Ontario Canada*

BALL, BILLY JOE, mathematician, educator; b. Crowell, Tex., Nov. 29, 1925; s. Clement Earnest and Cora (Layton) B.; B.A., U. Tex. at Austin, 1948, Ph.D., 1952; m. Emma Gayle Kissinger, Jan. 29, 1947; 1 dau., Margaret Elizabeth. Instr., U. Tex., 1949-52; asst. prof. U. Va., 1952-59; asso. prof. U. Ga., Athens, 1959-63, prof., 1963—, head dept. math., 1963-69. Served with USNR, 1944-46. Mem. Am. Math. Soc., Math. Assn. Am. Contbr. articles profl. jours. Home: Route 1 Box 250 Watkinsville GA 30677 Office: Dept Math U Ga Athens GA 30601

BALL, BURNETT, publisher; b. Canton, Ill., Nov. 3, 1903; s. Cullen Bert and Edna (Kessler) B.; student Lake Forest (Ill.) Coll., 1921-22; B.Ed., Western U., Macomb, Ill., 1927; m. Vera M. Cass, Jan. 20, 1924; 1 dau., Karen (Mrs. James C. Goar). Tchr. English and Social studies, Centralia, Ill., 1927-31; with Harcourt, Brace & World, Inc., and predecessor, N.Y.C., 1931-70, gen. sales mgr., 1955-70, sr. v.p. 1962-70, dir. state adoption sales, 1967-70, also dir. Mason, Kiwanian. Home: 60 W Morris Rd Norris TN 37828

BALL, CHARLES STANDISH, clergyman; b. Delaware County, Ohio, Jan. 10, 1914; s. Stephen C. and Phoebe T. (Standish) B.; B.Th., Marion Coll., 1937; A.B., Friends U., 1950; A.M., Winona Lake Sch. Theology, 1941; postgrad. Garrett Bibl. Inst., Asbury Theol. Sem., State U. Ia., summers; D.D., William Penn Coll., 1959; m. Maxine E. Scott, August 16, 1938; 1 dau., Jacqueline Marie. Ordained to ministry Friends Ch., 1938; pastor, Ohio, 1937-42; pres. Friends Bible Coll., Haviland, Kan. 1942-46; asst. prof. Friends U., Wichita, 1946-50; pres. William Penn Coll., Oskaloosa, Ia., 1950-58; pastor East Whittier Friends Ch., Whittier, Cal., 1958-64, Newberg (Ore.) Friends Ch., 1964-68, Alamitos Friends Ch., Garden Grove, Cal., 1968-70; asso. prof. Azusa- Pacific Coll., Azusa, Cal., 1970—. Prof., Western Evangelical Sem., Portland, 1965-67; lectr. to ministers, students in colls. Bd. dirs. Christian Freedom Found. Mem. Nat. Assn. Evang. Friends, Nat. Assn. Evangs. Author: Remembering Our Heritage, 1964; Commentary on I and II Peter, 1966. Contbr. articles to regigious publs. Office: Azusa-Pacific Coll Azusa CA 91702

BALL, EBERHARD ERICH, lawyer; b. Peenemünde, Germany, Aug. 24, 1942; s. Erich and Elisabeth (Blassman) B.; came to U.S., 1947, naturalized, 1955; A.B., U. Ala., 1964, LL.B., 1966; m. Barbara Jane Harris, Sept. 5, 1964. Admitted to Ala. bar, 1966; practice in Bay Minette, 1969—; mem. firm Chason, Stone & Chason, 1969—. Leader, Mobile council Boy Scouts Am., 1970—. Bd. dirs. Bay Minette Little Theater Guild. Served from 2d lt. to capt., C.E., U.S. Army, 1967-69. Decorated Bronze Star medal. Mem. Ala., Baldwin County bar assns., Soc. Am. Mil. Engrs., Phi Alpha Delta. Democrat. Presbyn. Kiwanian. Home: 605 Armstrong Av Bay Minette AL 36507 Office: P O Box 120 Bay Minette AL 36507

BALL, EDMUND FERDINAND, business exec.; b. Muncie, Ind., Jan. 8, 1905; s. Edmund Burke and Bertha (Crosley) B.; student Asheville (N.C.) Sch., 1920-23, Wabash Coll., 1923-25; Ph.B., Yale, 1928; LL.D., Ball State U., DePauw U., Ind. U.; Dr. Humanities, Wabash Coll.; m. Isabel Urban, Jan. 11, 1936 (dec. Mar. 1949); children—Frank Edmund, Marilyn Bertha (Mrs. Shanahan), Frederick Crosley; m. 2d, Virginia Beall Stewart, June 28, 1952; children—Robert Burke, Nancy Lee. Asso. Ball Corp., 1928—, asst. sec., 1931, v.p., 1938, dir., exec. v.p., 1945, pres., 1948-63, 68-70, chmn. bd., 1956-69, chmn. exec. com., 1970—; pres. Ball Bros. Found.; chmn. Muncie Aviation Corp.; pres. Muncie Airport, Inc.; dir. Am. Nat. Bank & Trust Co., Muncie, Borg-Warner Corp., Tomlinson Fleet Corp., Cleve., Indiana Bell Telephone Co. Indpls., Mchts. Nat. Bank, Muncie, Am. Fletcher Corp., Indpls. Trustee Wabash Coll., Muncie YMCA; former trustee Asheville (N.C.) Sch. for Boys; bd. dirs., pres. Ball Meml. Hosp.; council U. Chgo. Sch. Bus., S.W. Research Inst.; mem. bd. Nat. Assn. Ednl. Broadcasters, Eastern Ind. Ednl. TV Bd. Served as maj. USAAF, 1941-45. Mem. Glass Container Mfrs. Inst. (past pres., trustee), Nat. Council Humanities, Phi Gamma Delta. Republican. Unversalist. Mason (K.T., nat. treas. K.T., trustee K.T. Eve Found., 33). Clubs: Yale, Explorers (N.Y.C.); Columbia (Indpls.). Home: 1707 Riverside Av Muncie IN 47303 Office: Ball Corp Muncie IN 47302

BALL, EDWARD, railroad co. exec. Pres., dir. Jacksonville Properties, Inc., St. Joseph Tel. & Tel. Co., Wakulla Silver Springs Co., Apalachicola No. R.R., Almours Securities, Inc. of Va., St. Joseph Land and Devel. Co., Fla. Nat. Realty Co., Keystone Sand Co., Silver Glenn Springs Co., Ballynahinch Castle, Inc.; chmn. exec. com., vice chmn. bd. dir. St. Joe Paper Co., Jacksonville; dir. Fla. Nat. Bank of Jacksonville, Fla. Nat. Bank & Trust Co. at Miami, Fla. Nat. Bank at Orlando; chmn. Fla. E. Coast Ry. Sec., treas., bd. dirs. Nemours Found.; bd. dirs. Alfred I. duPount Found. Office: Florida East Coast Ry Co 1 Malago St St Augustine FL 32084*

BALL, ERIC GLENDINNING, biol. chemist; b. Coventry, Eng., July 12, 1904; s. C. Sturges and Nellie (Glendinning) B.; brought to U.S., 1905, naturalized, 1919; B.S. Haverford Coll., 1925, M.A., 1926, D.Sc. (hon.), 1949; Ph.D., U. Pa., 1930; M.A. (hon.) Harvard, 1942; m. Grace L. Snavely, Sept. 10, 1927. Nat. Research fellow in medicine Johns Hopkins Med. Sch., 1929-30, instr. physiol. chemistry, 1930-33, asso., 1933-40; Internat. Physiol. Congress fellow, Rome, Italy, 1932; Guggenheim fellow Kaiser Wilhelm Inst., Berlin, Germany, 1937-38; asst. prof. biol. chemistry Harvard Med. Sch., 1940- 41, asso. prof., 1941-46, prof., 1946-71, prof. emeritus, 1971—, chmn. div. med. scis., 1951-68; vis. prof. U. Brazil, 1945; Guggenheim fellow, vis. investigator Scripps Clinic and Research Found., La Jolla, Cal., 1963. Trustee Woods Hole Oceanographic Inst., 1953-57, Marine Biol. Lab., Woods Hole. Recipient Eli Lilly award in biochemistry, 1940, Cruzeiro do Sol, 1945. Fellow A.A.A.S.; mem. Am. Chem. Soc., Am. Soc. Biol. Chemistry, Biochem. Soc. Gt. Britain, Am. Acad. Arts and Scis., Nat. Acad. Sci., Soc. Gen. Physiologists, Endocrine Soc., Sigma Xi, Alpha Omega Alpha. Mem. editorial bd. Jour. Biol. Chem., 1950-60, Biochemistry, 1961-70, Biochemical Prep, 1948-56, editor-in-chief vol. 2, 1952. Contbr. sci. and tech. jours. Home: 234 Oyster Pond Rd PO Box 406 Falmouth MA 02541 Office: Marine Biol Lab Woods Hole MA 02543

BALL, F.W., mem. for Canada Joint Bd. Def. Can.-U.S. Address: Canadian Sect State Dept Washington DC 20525*

BALL, GEORGE HUDSON, educator; b. Junee, Australia, May 23, 1915; s. Frederick Joseph and Anna (Schultes) B.; came to U.S., 1926, naturalized, 1936; A.B., Cornell U., 1936, LL.B., 1938; B.D., Yale, 1941, S.T.M., 1946, Ph.D., 1950; m. Nancy Ann Cronon, Sept, 24, 1949; childrenAlan Mills, Sarah Anna, Larry Frederick, Eric Martin. Ordained to ministry Methodist Ch., 1941; pastor, Shelburne, Vt., 1941-42; chaplain Alfred U., 1946-47, U. Denver, 1950; dir. religious activities Oberlin Coll., 1951-55; chaplain Hamline U., 1955-60; Weyerhauser prof. Bib. lit. Whitman Coll., 1960-; mem. philosophy faculty U. Md., summer 1962, U. N.M., summer of 1967; admitted to N.Y. bar. 1939. Bd. dirs. Walla Walla YMCA, 1962-; mem. adv. council Danforth Found., 1960-63. Served as chaplain, inf., AUS, 1942-46. Decorated Bronze Star; Croix de Guerre (France). Mem. N.Y. State Bar Assn., Walla Walla Archaeol. Soc., Soc. Religion Higher Edn., Phi Beta Kappa. Home: 217 Fulton St Walla Walla, WA 99362.

BALL, GEORGE WILDMAN, lawyer, investment banker; b. Des Moines, Dec. 21, 1909; s. Amos and Edna (Wildman) B.; B.A., Northwestern U., 1930, J.D., 1933; m. Ruth Murdoch, Sept. 16, 1932; children—John Colin, Douglas Bleakly. Admitted to Ill. bar. 1934. D.C. bar, 1946; with Gen. Counsel's Office, Treasury Dept., Washington, 1933-35; practice of law, Chgo., 1935-42, Washington, 1946-61, mem. firm Cleary, Gottlieb, Steen & Ball; asso. gen. counsel Lend-Lease Adminstrn., then Fgn. Econ. Adminstrn., 1942-44; dir. U.S. Strategic Bombing Survey, London, 1944- 45; gen. counsel French Supply Council, Washington, 1945-46. undersec. of state for econ. affairs, 1961; undersec. state, 1961- 66; of counsel Cleary, Gottlieb, Steen & Hamilton, attys., 1966-68, 69- -; chmn. Lehman Bros. Internat., Ltd., 1966-68; U.S. permanent rep. to UN, 1968; sr. partner Lehman Bros., Jan-May 1968, 69—. Trustee Am. Assembly, Columbia. Decorated Legion of Honor (France); Grand Cross Order of Crown (Belgium); Medal of Freedom (U.S.). Author: The Discipline of Power, 1968. Home: 860 United Nations Plaza New York City, NY 10017. Office: 1 William St New York City NY 10004

BALL, HERBERT MORTON, lawyer, business exec.; b. Syracuse, N.Y., June 9, 1908; s. Charles and Freda (Rosenson) B.; grad. Mercersburg, (Pa.) Acad., 1925; A.B., Dartmouth, 1929; postgrad. Cornell, summer 1927; LL.B., Harvard, 1932; grad. Berlitz Sch., 1941; m. Joan Florence Cameron, June 9, 1950; children—Charles Cameron, Herbert Morton, Craig Douglas. Newspaper corr., 1923-29; admitted to Pa. bar, 1932, D.C. bar, 1942, N.Y. bar, 1947, Supreme Ct. U.S., 1941; pvt. law practice, Scranton, Pa., 1932-40; v.p., gen. mgr. Blue Ribbon Co., Wilkes-Barre, Pa., 1939- 40; atty.-negotiator R.F.C., Washington, 1940-42; spl. asst. to pres. Fansteel Metall. Corp., North Chicago, Ill., 1942; counsel, asst. to chmn. bd. Pal-Personna Blade Co;, 1946-47; asst. gen. atty. Am. Home Products Corp., N.Y.C. 1947-51; asst. sec. to asst. gen. atty. Johns- Manville Corp., Johns-Manville Sales Corp., Johns-Manville Products, Canadian Johns-Manville Co., Ltd., 1951-52, sec., gen. atty., now v.p., gen. counsel, sec. Johns Manville Corp., also officer or dir. numerous subsidiaries; sec. Asbestos & Danville Ry. Co., Johns-Manville Dutch Brand Products Corp.; sec., dir. Johns-Manville (Overseas) Ltd. Served as lt. comdr. USNR, 1942-46: PTO. Mem. Res. Officers Assn. (v.p., dir. N.Y. Navy chpt.), Naval Order U.S., Am., N.Y. State, Lackawanna County bar assns., Assn. Bar City N.Y. Club: Dartmouth Coll. (bd. govs.) (N.Y.C.) Home: 28 Pasadena Rd Bronxville NY 10708 Office: 22 E 40th St New York City NY 10016

BALL, JOHN DUDLEY, Jr., author; b. Schenectady, N.Y., July 8, 1911; s. John Dudley and Alena (Wiles) B.; B.A., Carroll Coll., Waukesha, Wis., 1934; m. Patricia Hamilton, Aug. 22, 1942; 1 son, John David. With Montgomery Ward & Co., 1935-37; mem. editorial staff Fortune mag., 1937-40; asst. curator Hayden Planetarium, N.Y.C., 1940-41; with Columbia Recording Corp., 1945-47; music editor Bklyn. Eagle, 1946-51; columnist music and recordings N.Y. World Telegram, 1951-52; dir. pub. relations Inst. Aero. Scis., 1958-61; editor-in-chief DMS, Inc., 1961-62; full time writing, 1963—. Served with Air Transport Command, 1942-45. Mem. Aviation and Space Writers Assn., Mystery Writers Am., Baker St. Irregulars, All Am. Karate Fedn., Japanese-Am. Citizens League, Japan America Soc., Ox-5 Club, Mensa, Civil Air Patrol. Mem. Lutheran Church. Author: Records for Pleasure, 1947; Operation Springboard, 1958; Spacemaster I, 1960; Edwards: USAF Flight Test Center, 1962; Judo Boy (Jr. Lit. Guild selection), 1964; In the Heat of the Night (Edgar award 1966, Critics' award, London; Acad. award Best Picture of Year 1968), 1965; Arctic Showdown, 1966; Rescue Mission, 1966; The Cool Cottontail (Mystery Guild selection), 1966; Dragon Hotel, 1968; Miss 1000 Spring Blossoms, 1968; Johnny Get Your Gun, 1969; Last Plane Out, 1969; The First Team, 1971. Address: 16401 Otsego St Encino CA 91316

BALL, JOHN WILLIS, lawyer; b. Jacksonville, Fla., Jan. 22, 1910; s. Philip Manville and Anna McNeill (Bullock) B.; A.B. magna cum laude, Washington and Lee U., 1932, LL.B., 1935; m. Margaret Ann Moreland, Apr. 11, 1936; children—Haywood Moreland, John Willis, Margaret Ann. Admitted to Fla. bar, 1935, since practiced in Jacksonville; mem. law firm Ulmer, Murchison, Ashby & Ball, 1947—; spl. atty. lands div. Dept. Justice, 1937-54. Mem. 5th Circuit Fed. Jud. Com., Am. Bar Assn., 1963-69. Bd. dirs. Family Consultation Service, Jacksonville. Fellow Am. Bar Found. (chmn. Fla.), Am. Coll. Probate Counsel; mem. Am. (com. jud. selection, compensation and tenure 1959-63, 69—, ho. dels. 1964-67), Inst. Jud. Adminstrn., Jacksonville bar assns., Am. Judicature Soc., Am. Law Inst., Fla. Bar, Phi Beta Kappa, Order Coif, Phi Gamma Delta, Omicron Delta Kappa, Phi Delta Phi. Office: PO Box 479 Jacksonville FL 32201

BALL, JOSEPH A., lawyer; b. Styart, Ia., Dec. 16, 1902; s. Joseph A. and Ellen (Ryan) B.; A.B., Creighton U., 1925; LL.B., U. So. Cal., 1927; m. Elinor Thon, Apr. 23, 1931; children—Mary Patricia, Jo Ellen (Mrs. C. Wayne Smith). Admitted to Cal. bar., 1927, since practiced in Long Beach; mem. firm Ball, Hunt, Hart and Brown. Cons., sr. trial counsel Presdl. Commn. to Investigate Assassination of John F. Kennedy, 1964; tchr. criminal la and proc. U. So. Cal.; mem. Cal. Law Revision Commn., 1960—, Commn. Revise Cal. Constrn., 1963—, Adv. Com. Fed. Criminal Laws, 1960- -. Fellow Am. Coll. Trial Lawyers; mem. Am. (chmn. Nat. Conf. Bar Presidents 1960-61), Los Angeles County, Long Beach (pres. 1951-52) bar assns., State Bar Cal. (pres. 1956-57), Am. Judicature Soc. (dir. 1963-64). Home: 4281 Country Club Dr Long Beach CA 90807 Office: 120 Linden Av Long Beach CA 90802

BALL, LUCILLE, actress; b. Jamestown, N.Y., Aug. 6; d. Henry D. and Desiree (Hunt) Ball; ed. high sch., dramatic sch.; studied with John Murray Anderson; m. Desi Arnaz, Nov. 30, 1940 (div.); children—Lucie Desiree, Desiderio Alberto IV; m. 2d, Gary Morton, Nov. 19, 1961. Motion picture actress, 1934—; pictures include Roberta, Chatterbox, Follow the Fleet, Stage Door, Having Wonderful Time, Affairs of Annabell, Room Service, Valley of the Sun, Seven Days Leave, DuBarry Was a Lady, Best Foot Forward, Meet the People, Thousands Cheer, Without Love, Love from a Stranger, Her Husband's Affairs, Long, Long, Trailer, Forever Darling, Facts of Life, Critic's Choice; Yours, Mine and Ours; star TV shows I Love Lucy, The Lucy Show; starred on Broadway in Wildcat; now starring in TV show Here's Lucy; pres. Desilu Prodns., Inc., 1962-67, Lucille Ball Prodns., 1967—. Recipient Emmy award for best comedienne, 1952, 55, 67, 68. Presbyn. Home: Beverly Hills CA 90213

BALL, LYLE EDWIN, lawyer; b. Mankato, Minn., Aug. 1, 1925; s. Byron David and Helen Mae (Bohn) B.; B.S., Ill. State U., 1949; M.S., U. Ill., 1950; J.D. with distinction, U. N.D., 1956; m. Norma Lee Reeser, June 13, 1948; children—Jeffrey D., Stacy L., Todd S. Tchr. ghigh schs., also jr. colls., Ill. and Ia., 1950-53; mem. mgmt. faculty U. N.D., 1953-56, bus. adminstrn. faculty Ferris State Coll., 1956-57; admitted to Mich. Bar, 1957, Minn. bar, Neb. bar, 1970; practiced in Big Rapids, Mich., 1957, St. Cloud, Minn., 1958—, Omaha, 1969-70, St. Peter, Minn., 1970—; faculty St. Cloud State Coll., 1958-69, prof. bus., 1948-69, dean Sch. Bus. and Industry, 1962-66; prof. bus. U. Neb., Omaha, 1969-70. Served with USNR, 1943- 46. Decorated Air medal. Mem. Minn., Neb. bar assns., Midwest Econ. Assn., Midwest Bus. Law Assn., Assn., St. Peter C. of C., Delta Sigma Pi, Pi Omega Pi, Phi Delta Kappa, Gamma Phi. Contbr. articles to profl. jours. Home: 1029 Willow Dr St Peter MN 56082

BALL, MARY MARGARET, educator; b. Los Angeles, Aug. 29, 1909; d. Jesse W. and Mary Elizabeth (Messerly) Ball; student Vassar Coll., 1928-29; A.B., Stanford, 1931, A.M., 1931, Ph.D., 1935; D.J., U. Cologne, 1933. Instr. polit. sci. Vassar Coll., 1935-36; instr. to asso. prof. Wellesley Coll., 1936-47, prof. polit. sci., 1947-56, Ralph Emerson prof. 1956-63; dean women's coll., asso. dean arts and scis., Duke U., Durham, 1963-69, prof. polit. sci., 1963—, dir. grad. studies in political sci., 1969-70; specialist internat. orgn. affairs Dept. State, 1943-44, 46. Trustee Wellesley Coll., 1967-70. Carnegie fellow internat. law, 1932-33; German-Am. Student Exchange fellow, 1932-33; Social Sci. Research Council fellow, 1940-41; Guggenheim fellow, 1949-50; NATO fellow and awards Harbison Fund and Mayling Soong Found. of Wellesley Coll., 1956-57. Fellow Am. Acad. Arts and Scis.; mem. Am. Polit. Sci. Assn. (mem. council 1966-68), Phi Beta Kappa. Author: Post- War German-Austrian Relations, 1918-36, 1937; The Problem of Inter- American Organization, 1944; (with Hugh B. Killough) International Relations, 1956, NATO and the European Union Movement, 1959; The OAS in Transition, 1969. Mem. bd. editors Internat. Orgn., 1947-56. Home: 2305 Elmwood Av Durham NC 27707

BALL, NORMAN TOWER, lawyer; b. Toledo, Feb. 14, 1905; s. John Stanley and Nina Belle (Frary) B.; student U.S. Naval Acad., 1924-27, Universite de Poitiers, 1927; B.S., U. Toledo, 1928; B.F.S., Georgetown U., 1929; J.D., George Washington U., 1934; student Harvard, 1943, Mass. Inst. Tech., 1943; m. Margaret Herrmann, Oct. 24, 1936. Examiner, U.S. Patent Office, 1928-47; exec. dir., com. on tech. information, Research and Devel. Bd., 1947-50; econ. commr. European Recovery Program, Am. embassy, London, Eng., 1950-51; cons. microwave lab. Stanford U., 1952-53, NSF, 1953-54, exec. sec. interdeptl. com. on sci. research and devel., 1954-59, U.S. del. OEEC, Paris, 1956-59; counsel Nat. Council Patent Law Assns., 1960-61. Trustee Fla. Ocean Scis. Inst., 1966—. Served from lt. to comdr. USN, 1940-46. Mem. I.E.E.E., Am. Patent Law Assn. Mason. Author sects. of books, also articles in profl. jours. Home: 245 NE 8th Av Delray Beach FL 33444

BALL, PETER, investment banker; b. Highland Park, Ill., July 9, 1894; s.Joseph and Elizabeth (Hawkins) B.; B.A., Yale, 1917; m. Julia M. Dangler, Aug. 8, 1924; 1 dau., Janet (Mrs. A.H. Stoddard). Vice pres. Union Cleve. Corp., 1928-32; pres. Ball, Coons & Co., Cleve, 1932-44; sr. partner Ball Burge & Kraus, Cleve., 1944-70; mem. N.Y. Stock Exchange, 1944-70, gov., 1959-62; dir. Cuyahoga Mgmt., Ingram-Richardson Mfg. Co., Forest City Products Co. Mem. adv. bd. St. Vincents Charity Hosp., Cleve., 1967-70, also chmn. endowment fund. Trustee Cleve. Council on World Affairs, 1960-66, exec. com., 1963-66, treas., chmn. investment com., chmn. financial devel. com., 1960-63; trustee Corporate Partnership Investment Fund; mem. investment com. Superannuates Fund of Meth. Ch., 1957-64. Mem. Nat. Assn Security Dealers (gov. 1944-46, mem. spl. research com. 1946-55, mem. nat. bus. conduct com. 1944-46), Investment Bankers Assn. (scholarship fund No. Ohio 1961—). Clubs: Union, Cleveland Athletic, Chagrin Valley Hunt, Mid- Day (Cleve.).; Pepper Pike Golf. Home: Deerfield Rd Gates Mills OH 44040 Office: Union Commerce Bldg Cleveland OH 44115

BALL, RICHARD EDWARD, educator; b. Buffalo, Aug. 22, 1919; s. Edward Theodore and Edith Anne (Richter) B.; B.C.S., U. Notre Dame, 1941, Ph.D., 1955; A.M., Ind. U., 1942; m. Maragret Nunn, Mar. 20, 1943; children—Richard, Cynthia (Mrs. Francis Bellini), Robert, William. Asso. prof. bus. adminstrn. U. Notre Dame, 1946-56, Mich. State U., 1956-59; prof., head, dept. finance U. Cin., 1959—, Briggs Swift Cunningham prof. finance, 1969—. Served to lt. USNR, 1942-45; PTO. Mem. Am., Midwest (past pres.), Ohio finance assns. Author: (with Simonds and Kelley) Principles of Business Administration, 1962. Editor: Readings in Investment, 1965. Home: 8928 Sandymar Dr Cincinnati OH 45242

BALL, RICHARD STUART, coll. dean; b. Buffalo, May 30, 1914; s. Stewart F. and Nellie (Erdle) B.; A.B., U. Buffalo, 1935; M.A., Ind. U., 1937, Ph.D., 1952. Clin. psychologist VA, 1946-55; exec. sec. Nat. Inst. Mental Health, 1956-58; pvt. cons. practice, 1959-61; dean student Cooper Union, 1961-68, Albert Einstein Coll. Medicine, 1968-, also asst. prof. psychology. Served to 1st lt. AUS, 1942-46. Diplomate Am. Bd. Examiners in Profl. Psychology. Mem. Am. Psychol. Assn., Nat. Assn. Student Personnel Adminstrs. Home: 230 E 79th St New York City NY 10021. Office: 1300 Morris Park Av Bronx NY 10469

BALL, ROBERT F., utility exec.; b. Red Lodge, Mont., May 12, 1917; s. William C. and Agnes (Spencer) B.; B.A. in Bus. Adminstrn., U. Mont., 1939; m. Sophie Jo Papez, July 6, 1940; children—Robert S., Brian F. Salesman, Asso. Mchts. Mont., 1939-40, mgr., 1940; mgr. La Grande (Ore.) C. of C., 1942-44, Baker County (Ore.) C. of C., 1946-49; with Ida. Power Co., becoming exec. v.p., dir., 1949-68; exec. v.p. Grand Bahama Port Authority, Ltd., Freeport, also dir.; pres., dir. Freeport Power Co. Ltd., Grand Bahama Island, 1968—, Freeport Homes Ltd., Grand Bahama Utility Co., Freeport Oil Co.; chief adminstrv. officer Grand Bahama Airport Co., Freeport Harbour Div.; dir. Northwest Electric Light & Power Assn. Bd. dirs. Booth Meml. Hosp., Boise. Served with AUS, 1944-46. Kiwanian (pres. Boise). Home: Lucayan Towers Freeport Grand Bahama Island Office: P O Box F 2666 Freeport Grand Bahama Island

BALL, ROBERT HAMILTON, educator, theatre historian; b. N.Y.C., May 21, 1902; s. George Martin and Flora Cristene (Hill) B.; A.B., Princeton, 1923, A.M., 1924, Ph.D. (Charlotte Elizabeth Proctor fellow 1926-27), 1928; m. Esther Marshall Smith, June 26, 1928; 1 dau., Marcia Merrill (Mrs. Benjamin R. Carson). Instr. English and dramatic art Princeton, 1927-31, asst. prof., 1931- 39, curator William Seymour Theatre Collection, 1936-39; asst. prof. English, Queen's Coll., Flushing, N.Y., 1939-43, chmn. dept., 1941-47, 60-64, asso. prof., 1944-51, prof., 1951-71, emeritus, 1971—, chmn. arts div., 1949-55; 1st prof. Am. lit. U. Ankara, Turkey, 1955-56; occasional vis. prof. U. Colo., N.Y. U., U. Cal. at Los Angeles. Mem. art adv. council Port Washington Pub. Library; adv. council Folger Shakespeare Library; past dir. pub. relations Port Washington Civil Def. Past mem. exec. bd. Port Washington br. A.R.C. Guggenheim fellow 1946-47; Rockefeller Found. grantee, 1955- 56. Mem. Modern Lang. Assn. Am., Shakespeare Assn. Am., Modern Humanities Research Assn., Theatre Library Assn. (past chmn. theatre documents bd., past mem. exec. bd.), Am. Assn. U. Profs. (past chpt. pres.), Am. Soc. Theatre Research (exec. com.), Internat. Fedn. Theatre Research. Author: The Amazing Career of Sir Giles Overreach, 1939; (with T. M. Parrott) A Short View of Elizabethan Drama, rev. edit., 1960; (with W. P. Bowman) Theatre Language, 1961; Shakespeare on Silent Film, 1968. Editor: The Plays of Henry C. DeMille, 1941; adv. bd. editors America's Lost Plays, 20 vols., 1939-42. Contbr. Collier's Ency., Ency. Americana, also jours. Cons. theatre terms Random House Dictionary of English Language. Home: 11 N Washington St Port Washington NY 11050 Office: Queens College Flushing NY 11367

BALL, ROBERT M., social security specialist; b. N.Y.C., Mar. 28, 1914; s. Archey Decatur and Laura Elizabeth (Crump) B.; A.B., Wesleyan U., 1935. M.A., 1936; m. Doris Jacqueline McCord, June 30, 1936; children—Robert Jonathan, Jacqueline Elizabeth. With Bur. Old Age and Survivors Ins., Social Security Bd., 1939-46, asst. dir., 1949-52, dep. dir., 1953-62, commr. of social security, 1962—; asst. dir. com. on edn. and social security Am. Council on Edn., 1946-49; staff dir. adv. council on social security to U.S. Senate Finance Com., 1947-48; staff dir. pension study Nat. Planning Assn., 1950-52. Bd. govs. Internat. Social Security Assn.; mem. com. social ins. experts ILO. Recipient Distinguished Service award Nat. Civil Service League, 1958; Rockefeller pub. Service award, 1961. Mem. Am. Pub. Welfare Assn. (dir.), Nat. Acad. Pub Adminstrn., Am. Soc. Pub. Adminstrn., Nat. Conf. Social Welfare (dir.), Phi Beta Kappa, Delta Kappa Epsilon. Club: International (Washington). Author: Pensions in the United States, 1952; also articles on social security. Home: 4009 Villa Nova Rd Baltimore MD 21207 Office: Social Security Adminstration Washington DC 20201

BALL, ROBERT PEARL, physician; b. Harlan, Ky., July 14, 1902; s. Robert Lee and Sarah Margaret (Carter) B.; student Centre Coll., Danville, Ky., 1918-19, D.Sc. (hon.), 1948; M.D., U. Louisville, 1924; m. Grace Baggerly, Aug. 13, 1927; children—Robert P., Elizabeth Castleman. Intern, Louisville City Hosp., 1924-26; fellow in surgery Cleve. Clinic, 1926-28; surg. pathologist U. Louisville Sch. Medicine, 1928- 30; gen surg. practice, Louisville, 1928-32; radiologist, Chattanooga, 1932-36, Presbyn. Hosp. and Coll. Phys. and Surgs., Columbia U., 1936-49; prof. radiology. Coll. Phys. and Surg., 1947, Cornell U. Med. Coll., 1949-51; radiologist-in-chief N.Y. Hosp., 1949-51; pvt. practice radiology, Baton Rouge, 1951-52; radiologist-in-chief Oak Ridge Hosp., 1952—. Served to lt. col. M.C., AUS, 1942-45. Mem. A.M.A., Am. Coll. Radiology (chancellor 1945-50, v.p.), Am. Roentgen Ray Soc. (rep. on NRC 1949-51), Radiol. Soc. N.Am., N.Y. Roentgen Soc. (pres. 1950- 51), N.Y. State Med. Soc., N.Y. Acad. Medicine, Harvey Soc., Brit. Inst. Radiology, Soc. Medico-Quirurgica del Guayas, Ecuador, S.A. Home: 112 Orchard Circle Oak Ridge TN 37830 Office: Oak Ridge Hosp Oak Ridge TN 37830

BALL, STUART SCOBLE, lawyer; b. Marshalltown, Ia., Sept. 5, 1904; s. Amos and Jessie Edna (Wildman) B.; B.A., Northwestern U., 1924, M.A. 1927, J.D., 1927; m. Marion Wolcott Watrous, Sept. 5, 1930 (dec.); children—Marion Watrous (Mrs. Wilmot Tramel), Eleanor (Mrs. Robert Hausheer), Stuart; m. 2d, Bernice Beckman Wilson, June 2, 1969. Admitted to Ill., Ia. bars, 1927; mem. firm Parrish, Cohen, Guthrie and Watters, Des Moines, 1927-32; asst. sec. Montgomery Ward & Co., Chgo., 1932-33, sec., 1933-49, v.p., 1949, pres., 1949-52, dir., 1950-52; partner Sidley & Austin, Chgo., 1953—. Chmn. selection com. Cook County Hosps. Governing Commn., 1969—. Bd. dirs., v.p. Cook County Sch. Nursing; trustee, v.p. Orchestral Assn. Chgo.; trustee Wesley Meml. Hosp. Fellow Am. Coll. Trial Lawyers; mem. Am. Ill., Chgo. bar assns. Chgo. Assn. Commerce and Industry (dir. 1946-70), Asso. Stationers (dir. 1956-64, chmn. bd. 1957-58), Order Coif, Delta Sigma Rho. Republican. Methodist. Clubs: Economic (past pres.), Law, Legal, Chicago, Glen View, Commercial, University. Home: 1419 Sheridan Rd Wilmette IL 60091 Office: 1 First National Plaza Chicago IL 60670

BALL, WILLIAM, producer, director; b. 1931; A.B., Fordham U.; M.A. (NBC/RCA fellow) Carnegie Inst. Tech. Appearances with Ore. Shakespeare Festival, 1950-53, Antioch Shakespeare Festival, 1954, Group 20 Players, 1955, San Diego Shakespeare Festival, 1956, Arena Stage, Washington, 1957-58; in Back to Methuselah, Broadway and on tour, 1958; Six Characters in Search of An Author, 1959; Cosi Fan Tutte, 1959; The Inspector General, 1960; Porgy and Bess, 1961; Midsummer Night's Dream, 1963; with off-Broadway N.Y.C. Center Opera Co. in The Misanthrope, The Lady's Not for Burning, The Country Wife, Ivanov, A Month in the Country, 1956-58, Under Milkwood, 1956-61, Six Characters in Search of An Author, 1963; in The Tempest, Stratford (Conn.) Festival, 1964; in Yeoman of the Guard, Stratford, Can., 1964; librettist, dir. Natalia Petrovna, N.Y.C. Center Opera Co., 1964, Tartuffe for Lincoln Center Repertory Co., 1965. Founder, Gen. dir. Am. Conservatory Theater, 1966- -. Fulbright scholar to Eng., 1953-54; recipient Ford Found. Director's grant, 1959, commn. for Natalia Petrovna, 1964. Address: 450 Geary St San Francisco CA 94102

BALL, WILLIAM HENRY, food co. exec.; b. Farco., N.D., Dec. 25, 1909; s. Frederick Eugene and Laura (Loomis) B.; student U. Minn., 1927-30, Babson Inst., 1932; m. Mae Louise Eichler, Jan. 26, 1945; children—Frederick Eugene II, Betty Louise. With Harris Trust & Savs. Bank, Chgo., 1932-40; with Quaker Oats Co., 1940—, asst. treas., 1945-49, became treas. 1949; dir. Quaker Oats Co. Can., Ltd., Quaker Oats, Ltd., Bank of Arlington Heights, Productos Quaker de Mexico, Productos Quaker Oats Co., 1940-66; account exec. Walston & Co., Inc., Phoenix, 1967—. Served as lt. comdr. USNR, 1942- 46: PTO. Mem. Psi Upsilon. Club: Cloud (Phoenix). Home: 501 Wakonda Lane Phoenix AZ 85023 Office: 3800 N Central Phoenix AZ 85012

BALL, WILLIAM KENNETH, lawyer; b. DeQueen, Ark., Jan. 15, 1927; s. William P. and Lucille (Jeter) B.; LL.B., U. Ark., 1953; m. Ella Hubbard Scaife, Dec. 28, 1950; children—Lucy Jane, William Ramsay, Charles Scaife. Admitted to Ark. bar 1953; law clk. George Rose Smith, asso. justice Ark. Supreme Ct., 1953-54; practice in Monticello, 1954—; partner firm Williamson, Williamson & Ball, 1958—; city atty., Monticello, 1961—. Served with AUS, 1945-47, 50-52. Mem. Am., Ark., S.E. Ark. (pres. 1957-58) bar assns., Kappa Sigma, Delta Theta Phi. Presbyn. Rotarian (pres. 1962-63). Home: Westwood Dr Monticello AR 71655 Office: Union Bank Bldg Monticello AR 71655

BALLAINE, HORACE D., lawyer; b. Cleveland, Okla., Jan. 22, 1908; ed. Baylor U., Okla. A. and M. Coll.; LL.B., U. Okla., 1931. Admitted to Okla. bar, 1930; county atty., 1936-42, legal asst. Okla. Supreme Ct., 1943; dist. judge, 1946-51; mem. firm Conner, Witners, Randolph and Ballaine, Tulsa. Mem. Am., Okla., Tulsa County bar assns., Order of Coif, Phi Alpha Delta. Office: 711 First Nat Bldg Tulsa OK 74103*

BALLAINE, JERROLD C., artist, educator; b. Seattle, Feb. 16, 1934; s. Jerrold Felch and Elizabeth (Maxson) B.; student U. Wash., 1952-54; B. F.A., Cal. Sch. Fine Art, 1959; M.F.A., San Francisco Art Inst., 1961; m. Jo Ann Heinbaugh, Dec. 3, 1961; children—Anna Theresa, Peter Alexander. Artist, Zabriskie Gallery, N.Y.C., 1961-62, Schoelkopf Gallery, N.Y.C., 1962-63; instr., chmn. dept. art Cornish Sch. Allied Art, Seattle, Wash., 1963-65; mem. faculty U. Cal. At Berkeley, 1966—, asst. prof. art, 1967—; one man exhbn. Mills Coll., 1967, Vandervoort Gallery, San Francisco, 1968; two man exhbn. Worth Ryder Gallery. U. Cal. at Berkeley, 1966; group exhbns. include San Francisco Mus., 1960, 63, Henry Gallery, U. Wash., 1960, Richmond, Cal., 1960, 66, Zabriski Gallery, 1960, Gump Gallery, San Francisco, 1961, Palace Legion of Honor, 1961, 62, Schoelkopf Gallery, 1963, Scott Gallery, Seattle, 1964, 65, Slan Step Show, Berkeley, 1966, 4th Internat. Young Artists Exhbn., Tokyo, Japan, 1967, Mus. Contemporary Crafts, N.Y., 1968, Ithaca (N.Y.) Coll. Mus. Art, 1968, Kranert Mus. at U. Ill., Champaigne, Whitney Mus. Am. Art, 1968; represented permanent collections Joseph Hirschorn, San Francisco Mus. Recipient awards San Francisco Mus., 1960, 4th Internat. Young Artists, 1967. Served with AUS, 1954-56.

BALLAM, JOSEPH, physicist, educator; b. Boston, Jan. 2, 1917; s. John Joseph and Sarah (Roosov) B.; B.S. in Physics, U. Mich., 1939; Ph.D., U. Cal. at Berkeley, 1951; m. Ethel Ada Hirsh, Dec. 28, 1938; children—John Joseph, Elysa Denise. Physicist, Navy Dept., 1940-45; instr., research asso. Princeton, 1951-56; prof. physics Mich. State U., 1956-60; asso. dir., head research div. Stanford Linear Accelerator Center, 1961—, prof. physics, 1963—. Research collaborator, guest physicist Brookhaven Nat. Lab., 1955. Ford Found. fellow, Geneva, Switzerland, 1960-61; Guggenheim fellow, 1971-72. Fellow Am. Phys. Soc. Author articles on cosmic rays, high energy exptl. physics. Editor proc. VI, Internat. Conf. High Energy Physics, 1956. Home: 840 Lathrop Dr Stanford CA 94305

BALLAM, ORAL, univ. dean; b. Hyde Park, Utah, Sept. 12, 1925; s. Oral Lynn and Delis (Lamb) B.; B.S., Utah State U., 1949, M.S., 1955; Ed.D., U. Cal. at Los Angeles, 1961; m. Tacy Chambers, Dec. 27, 1948; children—Gary, Debra, Pamela, Julie, Craig George. Tchr. English and speech Cache County Sch. Dist., Logan, Utah, 1949-55, supt. schs., 1959-63: prof. ednl. adminstrn. Utah State U., Logan, 1963-65, asst. dean edn., 1965-69, dean Coll. Edn., 1969—. Mem. exec. com. Boy Scouts Am. Served with USNR, 1943-46. Mem. N.E.A., Utah Edn. Assn., Phi Delta Kappa, Pi Kappa Alpha. Lion. Home: 135 S 1st St W Smithfield UT 84335 Office: 179 N Main St Logan UT 84321

BALLAM, SAMUEL HUMES, Jr., banker; b. Phila., Apr. 12, 1919; s. Samuel H. and Mary (McGarvey) B.; A.B., U. Pa., 1950; grad. Grad. Sch. Banking, 1955, Advanced Mgmt. Program, Harvard, 1959; m. Dorothy Meadowcroft, May 1, 1943; children— Barbara, Samuel Humes III. With Fidelity Bank, Phila., 1936—, financial analyst, 1938-41, 46-48, asst. to v.p. investments, 1948-51, asst. trust investment officer, 1952-55, asst. to pres., 1955-56, v.p. charge br. system, 1956-60, sr. v.p. charge personal trust dept., 1960-64, charge comml. loan div., 1964-66, exec. v.p. charge corp. dept., 1966-71, pres., 1971—, also dir.; pres. Fidelity Corp. Pa., 1971—; dir. Westmoreland Coal Co., Reliance Ins. Co., Reliance Standard Life Ins. Co., Wentz Corp., Leasco Corp., Fidelco Growth Investors, Smith, Kline & French Labs. Dir. Crime Commn. Phila., 1965—; bd. dirs., N.E. Boys Club; active in United Fund; v.p. Internat. House, Phila. Served to capt. AUS, 1941-46; as capt. USAF, 1951-52. Mem. Gen. Alumni Soc. U. Pa. (pres. 1970-71). Episcopalian. Clubs: Merion Cricket; Rittenhouse, Union League (Phila.). Home: 270 Kent Rd Wynnewood PA 19096 Office: Broad and Walnut Sts Philadelphia PA 19109

BALLANCE, PAUL SALEN, librarian; b. Maple, N.C., Sept. 7, 1906; s. Frank and Laura (Griggs) B.; B.S., N.C. State U., 1929; B.L.S., Columbia, 1932; m. Susan Covington, Sept. 24, 1932; 1 son, Frank Covington. Reference asst. N.Y. Pub. Library, 1929-36; head sci. and tech. div. Rochester (N.Y.) Pub. Library, 1936-42 librarian Tex. Engrs. Library, 1943-49; librarian Tex. A. and M. Coll., 1944-49, Greensboro (N.C.) Pub. Library, 1949-51, Winston-Salem (N.C.) Pub. Library, 1951—; cons. in field, 1948—. Mem. N.C. Library Commn., 1953-56; mem. N.C. Library Bd., 1956—, acting chmn. 1969-70; mem. Library Certification Bd., 1965-67, chmn., 1967-69. Mem. Am. (chmn. coms.) N.C. (chmn. coms. 1958-63, v.p. 1963-65, pres. 1965-67), Southeastern (chmn. coms.), Tex. (past treas.) library assns., Winston- Salem C. of C. Contbr. profl. jours. Editor; North Carolina Index, 1955—. Compiler: First Fifty Years of Public Library Service in Winston-Salem, 1906-56, 1956; List of Books in Texas Engrs. Library, of Periodicals in Selected North Carolina Libraries, 1959. Home: Route 8 Winston-Salem, NC 27106. Office: 660 W 5th St Winston-Salem NC 27101

BALLANTINE, IAN, publisher; b. N.Y.C., Feb. 15, 1916; s. Edward James and Stella (Commins) B.; A.B., Columbia, 1938; student London Sch. Econs., 1938-39; m. Elizabeth Jones, June 22, 1939; 1 son, Richard. Gen. mgr. Penguin Books, Inc., N.Y.C., 1939-45; pres., dir. Bantam Books, Inc., N.Y.C., 1945-52; pres., dir. Ballantine Books, Inc., N.Y.C., 1952—; instr. sociology Columbia. Mem. Phi Beta Kappa. Home: 60 E 9th St New York City NY 10003 Office: 101 Fifth Av New York City NY 10003

BALLARD, CLAUDE KAY, chem. co. exec.; b. Mineral, Tex., July 16, 1912; s. Chester E. and Lela A. (Smith) B.; B. Chem. Engring., Tex. Coll. Arts and Industries, 1934; m. Dorothy Lee Wells, May 6, 1940; children—Douglas Alan, Charles Lee. With chem. div. Pitts. Plate Glass Co., 1934-42, 46-52, dist. sales mgr., Houston, 1955-62; pres., dir. Columbia Nitrogen Corp., Augusta, Ga., 1962-70, Columbia Nipro Corp. subsidiary DSM-Netherlands, Augusta, 1970—. Served to capt. Chem. Corps, AUS, 1942-46. Mem. Am. Inst. Chem. Engrs. Methodist. Home: 2281 Overton Rd Augusta GA GA 30904 Office: P O Box 1483 Augusta GA 30903

BALLARD, EATON WALLING, dept. store exec.; b. Seattle, June 27, 1911; s. Roy Page and Olive (Murphy) B.; A.B., Stanford, 1932; M.B.A., Havard, 1937; m. Beverly Holtenhouse, Dec. 28, 1933; children—Sarah Eaton (Mrs. Nicholas Pileggi), Gretchen Walling (Mrs. Donald D. Guard), Jonathan Roy. With Marshall Field & Co., Chgo., 1937-38, May Co., Los Angeles, 1939-46; with Broadway Hale Stores, Inc., Los Angeles, 1947—, treas., 1956-63, v.p., 1959-67, exec. v.p., 1967—, also dir.; dir. Airhorne Freight Corp., Pacific Ins. Co., Am. Mut. Fund, Inc., Music Center Operating Co. Bd. dirs. Am. Retail Fedn. Council; trustee Cal. Council for Econ. Edn.; bd. govs. Town Hall of Cal. Mem. Nat. Planning Assn. Served to lt. USNR, 1943-45. Clubs: California, Harvard, Stock Exchange (Los Angeles). Home: 635 Rockwood Rd Pasadena CA 91105 Office: 600 S Spring St Los Angeles CA 90014

BALLARD, EDWARD GOODWIN, educator, author; b. Fairfax, Va., Jan. 3, 1910; s. James W. and Margaret (Lewis) G.; B.A., Coll. of William and Mary, 1931; diploma U. Montpelier (France), 1933; M.A., U. Va., 1936, Ph.D., 1946; postgrad. U. Sorbonne, (Paris, France), 1951, Harvard, 1931-32; m. Lucy McIver Watson, Nov. 22, 1938; children—Susanne (Mrs. M. Dowouis), Lucy (Mrs. D. Armentrout), Edward Marshall. Asst. prof. English, Va. Mil. Inst., 1939-41; asst. in philosophy U. Va., 1941-42, asst. prof. philosophy Tulane U., 1946-56, prof., 1956—; vis. prof. Yale, 1963-64, La. State U. at Baton Rouge, 1969. Mem. selection com. Woodrow Wilson fellowship, 1966-69, selection panel Nat. Endowment for Humanities, 1970. Served to comdr. USNR, 1942-46; PTO. Decorated three battlestars. Grantee Tulane U., 1959-60, 68-69. Mem. So. Soc. Philosophy and Psychology (pres. 1967), Am. Philos. Assn., A.A.A.S., Am. Metaphys. Soc. Author: Art and Analysis, 1957, Socratic Ignorance, 1965, Philosophy at The Cross Roads, 1971. Editorial Bd. So. Jour. of Philosophy, 1963—, Yearbook in Phenomenology, 1969—. Contbr. articles philos. jours. Office: Dept of Philosophy Tulane U New Orleans LA 70118

BALLARD, EMERALD GARRETT, educator; b. East Fork, Miss., Feb. 18, 1912; s. Kirby Smith and Velma (Lilly) B.; B.A., M.A., U. Miss., 1931; M.A., U. Ill., 1935, Ph.D., 1939; m. Laura Louise Hutchins, Aug. 3, 1935; children-Laura Leah (Mrs. Kevin J. Kennelly), Mary Ann, Evelyn Claire (Mrs. Frank LaRosa). Asst. prof. English, Delta State Coll., Cleveland, Miss., 1931-34; asst. English, U. Ill., 1935-39; mem. faculty N. Tex. State U., Denton, 1939—, prof. English, 1949—, chmn. div. humanities, 1965-69; dir. insts. Nat. Def. Edn. Act., also English workshop coordinator; cons. in field, 1954—. Chmn. civic fund com. N. Tex. State U., 1948-67; mem. budget com. Denton United Fund, 1960-62; mem. standing com. Episcopal Diocese Dallas, 1962-65, sr. ch. warden, 1950-53, 61-63. Served to comdr. USNR, 1942-46, Mem. S. Central Coll. English Assn. (pres. 1959-60), Tex. Assn. Coll. Tchrs. (pres. N. Tex. U. br. 1952), Modern Lang. Assn., Phi Beta Kappa, Sigma Upsilon. Home: 2044 W Oak St Denton, TX 76201.

BALLARD, FREDERICK ARMSTRONG, lawyer; b. Penn Yan, N.Y., July 13, 1907; s. Hiram C. and Agnes R. (Armstrong) B.; A.B., Hamilton Coll., 1928; LL.B., Harvard, 1931; m. Mary Elizabeth Brackett, Apr. 22, 1933; children—Sally Welles, Mary Elizabeth. Kimberly. Admitted to D.C. bar, 1931, since practiced in Washington; mem. firm Ballard & Beasley, 1948—; prof. law Washington Coll. Law, 1935-40. Vis. lectr. Aviation law U. Va. Law Sch., 1948; adj. prof. law Georgetown U. Law Sch., Washington, 1959-61; mem. President's Commn. on Crime in D.C., 1965-66. Served as capt. USNR, 1942-45. Decorated Commendation ribbon with combat device. Fellow Am. Bar Found.; mem. Am. Bar Assn. (state del. D.C. 1964- -), Bar Assn. D.C. (pres. 1959-60), Am. Law Inst. (council 1966—), Am. Arbitration Assn. (mem. nat. panel), Harvard Law Sch. Assn. D.C. (pres, 1948), Am. Legion, Phi Beta Kappa, Chi Psi, Sigma Delta Kappa (hon.). Episcopalian (sr. warden 1956-57). Home: 6060 Woodmount Rd Alexandria VA 22307 Office: American Security Bldg Washington DC 20005

BALLARD, FREDERIC LYMAN, lawyer; b. Phila., Sept. 29, 1917; s. Frederic Lyman and Frances (Stoughton) B.; grad. St. George's Sch., 1935; A.B., U. Pa., 1939, LL.B., 1942; m. Ernesta Drinker, Dec. 22, 1939; children—Frederic Lyman, Sophie, Ernesta, Alice Walker. Admitted to Pa. bar, 1942, since practiced in Phila.; partner firm Ballard, Spahr, Andrews & Ingersoll. Bd. mgrs. Western Savs. Fund Soc. Phila.; dir. ESB Inc. Mem. Pa. Bd. Pub. Welfare, 1963-70, chmn. adv. com. pub. assistance, 1965-66; mem. Pa. Adv. Com. for Comprehensive Health Planning, 1970-71. Bd. dirs. Health and Welfare Council, 1957-70, Greater Phila. Movement; trustee, mem. exec. com. United Fund Phila., 1959-70; trustee Radcliffe Coll., Thomas Jefferson U.; mem. bd. law U. Pa. Law Sch. Served with USNR, 1943-46. Rhodes scholar elect, 1939. Mem. Am., Pa., Phila. bar assns., Phi Beta Kappa, Zeta Psi. Club: Philadelphia. Home: 9120 Crefeld St Philadelphia PA 19118 Office: Land Title Bldg Philadelphia PA 19110

BALLARD, JOHN HENRY, business cons.; b. Bklyn., June 23, 1893; s. John and Mary (Maguire) B.; with Bulova Watch Co., N.Y.C., 1909-59, beginning as office boy, becoming pres., dir.; former chmn. bd., dir. Gruen Industries, Inc.; now cons. several companies; dir. Standard Financial Corp., Standard Prudential United Corp. Clubs: Metropolitan, N.Y. Athletic (N.Y.C.). Home: Sherry-Netherland Hotel Fifth Av and 59th St New York City NY 10022 Office: 630 Fifth Av New York City NY 10022

BALLARD, JOHN STUART, mayor; b. Akron, O. Sept. 30 1922; s.Irby S. and Sarah (McCormick) B.; A.B. U. Akron, 1943; LL.B., U. Mich., 1948; m. Ruth Frances Holden, Oct. 22, 1949; children—Susan, Karen, John H., Mark, Ward. Admitted to Mich. bar, 1948, Ohio bar, 1949; spl. agt. FBI, 1949-52; practice law, Akron, O., 1952-56; pros. atty. Summit County, O., 1957-64; practice law, Akron, 1964-65; mayor of Akron, 1966-. Mem. Summit County Republican Exec. Com., 1956—; candidate for U.S. senator from Ohio, 1962. Served with inf. AUS, 1943-46. Recipient Distinguished Service award Akron Jr. C. of C., 1957. Mem. Am., Ohio, Akron bar assns., Am. Judicature Soc. Episcopalian. Home: 107 Kenilworth Dr Akron, OH 44313. Office: Municipal Bldg High St AKron OH 44308

BALLARD, JOHN WILLIAM, Jr., banker; b. Kingston, Ont., Can., Mar. 8, 1922; s. John William and Evelyn Mary (Toohill) B.; came to U.S. 1922; B.S., U. Kan., 1947; m. Imogen Dean Billings, Dec. 29, 1947; children—John William III, Paul Billings, Jenny Evelyn. With Safety Fed. Savs. and Loan Assn., Kansas City, Mo., 1947—, asst. v.p., 1949-58, treas., 1958-62, pres., 1962—, chmn. bd., 1968—; trustee Kansas City Blue Cross, sec., 1960-61, treas., 1961-71, chmn. bd., 1971—; pres. Safety Ins. Agy., 1962—. Vice pres. Jr. C. of C., 1950, C. of C., dir. Downtown Inc., 1967—. Trustee Savings and Loan Found., Inc., 1966-70. Served with AUS, 1942-45. Mem. Am. Royal Assn. (bd. gov. 1962—), Real Estate Board (dir. 1964-65), Mo. (pres. 1964-65), Kansas City (pres. 1966-67) savs. and loan leagues, Ind. Ins. Agents, Sigma Alpha Epsilon. Episcopalian. Clubs: Mission Hills Country (Shawnee Mission, Kan.); Saddle and Sirloin (Leawood, Kan.); Kansas City. Home: 9311 Buena Vista Prairie Village KS 66207 Office: 910 Grand Av Kansas City MO 64106

BALLARD, KAYE, actress; b. Cleve., Nov. 1926; d. Vincent and Lena (Nararata) Balotta. Broadway appearances include Touch and Go, Golden Apple, Ziegfeld Follies, Carnival; TV appearances include Jack Paar, Johnny Carson and Perry Como shows, The Mothers-in-Law, Hollywood Squares, The Jerry Lewis Show, The Steve Allen Show; nightclub appearances include Plaza Hotel and Bon Soir, N.Y.C., Palmer House, Chgo. Recipient Italian-Am. award. Mem. Actors Equity Assn., A.F.T.R.A., Screen Actors Guild, Am. Guild Variety Artists. Home: 7250 Franklin Av Los Angeles CA 90046

BALLARD, LUCINDA, (Mrs. Howard Dietz), stage designer, mural painter; b. New Orleans, Apr. 3, 1906; d. Richard and Anna (Farrar) Goldsborough; student Art Students' League, N.Y.C., Am. Sch., Fontainebleau, France, 1927, 29, 32, Sorbonne U., Paris, 1929; m. W. F. R. Ballard, Feb. 6, 1930; children—Robert Fitz Randolph, Jenifer Farrar; m. 2d, Howard Dietz, July 31, 1951. Painted church ceiling, Kalamazoo, Mich., 1929; murals, Princeton; designer scenery, costumes including Peter and the Wolf, Giselle; costumes for I Remember Mama, Annie Get Your Gun, Show Boat, Fourposter, play and movie A Streetcar Named Desire (Oscar nomination), Cat on a Hot Tin Roof, Silk Stockings, Clearing in the Woods, J.B., The Sound of Music, Invitation to a Waltz, Dark at the Top of the Stairs, Girls in 509, The Gay Life, Romulus, Lord Pengo, Tiger, Tiger, Portrait of Jennie. Recipient Donaldson award; 2 Antoinette Perry awards, Critics prize. Mem. Art League, ANTA, United Scenic Artists. Lectr., author articles on costume and theatre experiences and personalities. Home: Cow Neck House Sands Point NY 10050

BALLARD, RUSSELL WARD, social worker; b. Donnellson, Ill., Nov. 25, 1893; s. Elbert Suveyor and Mary (Lee) B.; Ph.B., U. Chgo., 1922, postgrad., 1922-24; m. Ethel Horn, Sept. 1, 1921; children—John Horn, William Lee. Teacher, 1921-24; dir. community recreation, 1924-25; prin. elementary sch., 1925-36; county dir. pub. welfare, 1936-41; supt. Ill. State Tng. Sch. for Delinquent Boys, 1941-43; dir. Hull House, 1943-62; part-time tchr. Roosevelt U., Chgo., 1962-70; dir. community relations Midway Tech. Inst., Chgo., 1965-70. Bd. dirs. Kobe Coll., Hyde Parke YMCA, Citizens Sch. Com. Served as capt., inf. U.S. Army, 1917-18. Mem. Nat. Fedn. Settlements, Nat. Conf. Social Welfare, U.S. Assn. of UN, Japan-Am. Soc. (dir.), Nat. Assn. Social Workers, Phi Delta Kappa, Kappa Sigma. Methodist. Democrat. Home: 5462 S Blackstone Av Chicago IL 60615

BALLARD, STANLEY, labor ofcl.; Valentine, Neb., Mar. 30, 1905; s. Henry and Minnie (Roan) B.; B.S., U. Minn., 1934, LL.B., 1945 m. Lorraine Gentry, June 22, 1925; 1 son, Edgar. Sec., Mpls. local Am. Fedn. Musicians, 1936—, internat. exec. bd., 1950—, internat. sec.-treas., 1959—, editor mag., Internat. Musicians, 1959—; treas. Interam. Fedn. Musicians; dir. Union Labor Life Ins. Co. Admitted to Minn. bar, 1947. Unitarian. Mason (Shriner). Home: 700 B Plymouth Dr Lakewood NJ 08701 Office: Mount Pleasant St Newark NJ 07104

BALLARD, STANLEY SUMNER, educator, physicist; b. Los Angeles, Oct. 1, 1908; s. John Hudson and Myrtle (Stanley) B.; A.B., Pomona Coll., 1928; M.A., U. Cal. at Berkeley, 1932, Ph.D., 1934; m. Mary Elizabeth Miller, Sept. 13, 1935; children—Mary Susan, John

Stanley. Asst. physics Dartmouth Coll., 1928-30; teaching fellow physics U. Cal. at Berkeley, 1930-34, research fellow, 1934-35; instr. physics, U. Hawaii, 1935- 37, asst. prof. physics, 1937-41; research asso. geophysics Hawaii Nat. Park, 1936-41; cons. spectroscopy exptl. sta. Hawaiian Sugar Planters' Assn., 1937-40; collaborator in soil chemistry Hawaii Agrl. Expt. Sta., 1939-41; prof. physics, chmn. dept. Tufts Coll., 1946-54; research physicist U. Cal. Scripps Instn. Oceanography, 1954-58; prof. physics U. Fla., Gainesville, 1958—, chmn. dept. physics, 1958-71, dir. div. phys. and math. scis., 1968—. Cons. physicist Polaroid Corp., 1946-54, Baird Assos., Inc., 1946-51, Planning Research Corp., 1956-58; cons. Rand Corp., 1952—, physicist electronics dept., 1953-54; cons. Willow Run Labs., U. Mich., 1957-65; infrared cons. USAF Atlantic Missile Range, 1960-63; cons. astrionics div. Aerojet Gen. Corp., 1961-66; cons. Douglas Advanced Research Labs., 1966-70; prof. physics U. of Cal. at Berkeley, summer 1949; U.S. del. Internat. Commn. of Optics (Internat. Union of Pure and Applied Physics), Delft, Holland, 1948, London, 1950, Madrid, Spain, 1953, Boston, 1956, Stockholm, Sweden, 1959, Munich, 1962, Paris, 1966, Reading, Eng., 1969; chmn. U.S. Nat. Com. Internat. Commn. Optics, 1948-57; mem. Armed Forces NRC vision com., exec. sec., 1956-59; v.p. Internat. Commn. Optics, 1948-56, pres., 1956-59. Served as lt. to comdr. USNR, 1941-46; officer-in-charge research and development in optics and infrared instruments Bur. Ordnance, Navy Dept., and of radiometry sect. tech. staff Joint Task Force One (atom bomb tests). Fellow Am. Phys. Soc., A.A.A.S. (sec. sect. B (physics) 1960-67, v.p. 1968), Phys. Soc. London, Optical Soc. Am. (sec. local sects. 1947-53, asso. editor jour. 1950—, v.p. for meetings 1955-59, pres. 1963); mem. Am. Inst. Physics (governing bd. 1962-65, 67—), Japan Soc. Applied Physics (hon.), Fla. Acad. Scis., Netherlands Phys. Soc., Am. Assn. Physics Tchrs. (pres. elect 1967-68, pres. 1968-69), German Soc. Applied Optics, Western Spectroscopy Assn. (chmn. 1956-57), Hawaiian Acad. Sci., Am. Assn. U. Profs., Am. Geophys. Union, Phi Beta Kappa, Sigma Xi, Gamma Alpha, Sigma Pi Sigma (nat. pres. 1959-62), Sigma Alpha Epsilon. Co-author: Physics Principles 1954; Polarized Light, 1964. Contbr. to Ency. Brit., Ency. Americana, jours. physics, geophysics, and optica. Home: 1615 N W 14th Av Gainesville FL 32601

BALLARD, WALTER EUGENE, Jr., lawyer; b. Prattville, Ala., June 15 1908; s. Walter Eugene and Laura Adele (McGaugh) B.; student Va. Mil. Inst., 1926, Emory U., 1927-28, U. Ala., 1929-30; LL.B., J.D., George Washington U., 1933; m. Eleanor Farrel Bowen, May 11, 1935; children—Almon Bowen, Adele Armistead (Mrs. Oscar Rollie Chester). Admitted to Ala. bar, 1933, since practiced in Montgomery; partner Ballard & Ballard. Pres. Ballard Mortgage Co.; gen. partner Ballard Realty Co. Pres. Montgomery Real Estate Bd., 1952. Mem. Bd. Adjustment, Montgomery, 1949-53; chmn. U.S.O., 1956-58. Bd. dirs. Montgomery Bapt. Hosp. Served to lt. USNR, 1943-46. Mem. Am., Fed., Ala. bar assns., Montgomery Bapt. Assn. (trustee), Nat. Assn. Real Estate Bds. Home: 3473 Bankhead Av Montgomery AL 36111 Office: First Nat Bank Bldg Montgomery AL 36104

BALLARD, WALTER LANGFORD, oil co. exec.; b. Fort Myers, Fla., Dec. 30, 1919; s. Elmo M. and Fay (Langford) B.; student U. Fla., 1938-41; m. Jean V. Banks. Mar. 29, 1946; children—James, Barbara, Walter L., Douglas. With Petroleum Heat & Power Co., since 1947—, div. mgr., White Plains, N.Y., 1956-67, v.p., Stamford, Conn., 1967, pres., 1967—; dir. Bklyn. Eastern District Terminal, 1967—, Petroleum Heat & Power Co., Inc., 1967—, Signal Oil & Gas Co. Mem. town council, N. Castle, N.Y., 1967—. Served with USCG, 1941-46. Republican. Methodist. Mason. Home: 26 Old Parish Rd Darien CT 06820 Office: Petroleum Heat & Power Co Davenport St Stamford CT 06904

BALLARD, WILLIAM FITZ RANDOLPH, architect; b. Morristown, N.J., Apr. 1, 1905; s. William Robert and Elizabeth Fitz (Randolph) B.; grad. Kent Sch., 1923; A.B., Princeton, 1927, M.F.A., 1932; student Fontainbleau Sch., 1931; postgrad. Columbia, 1931; m. Pamela M.D. Clarke Silvertop, June 13, 1962; children by previous marriage— Robert F.R., Jenifer (Mrs. Walter P. Ramberg), Wendy. Draftsman, 1928-31; pvt. archtl. practice, N.Y.C., 1932-63; partner Harrison, Ballard & Allen, 1945-50, Ballard, Todd & Snibbe, 1952-58, Ballard-Todd Assos., 1958-63; ret., 1969; inaugurated master plan City of New York, 1965-66; initiated Lower Manhattan Plan, 1966; works include housing projects, schs. and coll. bldgs. Conductor Lauanburg Found. symposium on planning, 1964; chmn. N.Y.C. Planning Commn., 1963-66; cons. architect U. City N.Y., 1967-69; pres., chmn. bd. dirs. Citizens Housing and Planning Council N.Y., 1959-63; chmn. adv. com. Princeton Archtl. Sch., 1950-55. Served from 1st lt. to lt. col., USAAF, 1942-45; ETO. Decorated Bronze Star; mem. Order Brit. Empire; recipient Woodrow Wilson award Princeton, 1966. Clubs: Tiger Inn (Princeton); Bucks (London). ‡

BALLARD, WILLIAM WHITNEY, educator, biologist; b. Colrain, Mass., Apr. 4, 1906; s. Joseph William and Mary Ellen (Whelpley) B.; B.S., Dartmouth, 1928; Ph.D., Yale, 1933; m. Helen Elizabeth Flanders, June 9, 1938; children—Nancy Jean (Mrs. Lester Seigel), David Josiah, Helen Hartness (Mrs. Jervis), William. Mem. faculty Dartmouth, 1930—, prof. biology, 1942-62, Sydney E. Junkins prof. biology, 1962—. An organizer 1st interstate sch. dist., Hanover and Norwich, 1962; mem. Dresden and Norwich sch. bds., 1958-64. Mem. corp. Marine Biol. Lab., Woods Hole, Mass. Mem. Soc. Devel. Biology, Am. Soc. Zoology, Soc. Study Evolution, Phi Beta Kappa, Sigma Xi. Author: Comparative Anatomy and Embryology, 1964; also articles vertebrate embryology, anatomy. Home: Beaver Meadow Rd Norwich VT 05055 Office: Gilman Lab Dartmouth Coll Hanover NH 03755

BALLENGER, FELIX PETTEY, naval med. officer; b. Lubbock, Tex., June 4, 1914; s. Curtis Murray and Vivian Lee (White) B.; B.A. in Chemistry, Tex. Tech. Coll., 1934; M.D., U. Tex., 1938; m. Mayme Benton, Apr. 19, 1940; children—Ann (Mrs. David L. Steffen), Charles Curtis, Jane. Commd. lt. (j.g.) USN, 1942, advanced through grades to rear adm., 1967; intern John Sealy Hosp., Galveston, Tex., 1938-39; resident surgery med. center Ind. U., 1939-42; various assignments naval hosps., ships, 1942-57; resident thoracic surgery U.S. Naval Hosp., San Diego, 1957-60; chief surgery U.S. Naval Hosp., Great Lakes, Ill., 1960-64, exec. officer, 1964-65; comdg. offiicer U.S. Naval Hosp., Yokosuka, Japan, 1966-67; insp. gen. medicine USN, 1967-69; comdg. officer Nat. Naval Med. Center, Bethesda, Md., 1969—. Active Boy Scouts Am. Diplomate Am. Bd. Surgery, Am. Bd. Thoracic Surgery. Fellow Am. Coll. Chest Physicians, A.C.S.; privileged fellow Chgo. Sur. Soc.; mem. Assn. Mil. Surgeons, A.M.A., Phi Beta Phi. Office: Nat Naval Med Center Bethesda MD 20014

BALLENGER, WILLIAM SYLVESTER, Jr., banker; b. Flint, Mich., Jan. 28, 1908; s. William Sylvester and Minnie I. (Wheeler) B.; A.B., Princeton, 1929; m. Marie Elizabeth Daley, Oct. 25, 1930; children—William Sylvester III, Robert D., Irene E. (Mrs. Richard H. Pierpont), Marie Elizabeth. With Citizens Comml. & Savs. Bank, Flint, Mich., 1934—, trust officer, 1947—, v.p., 1951-68, sr. v.p., 1968—, dir., 1951—; pres. Miller Rd. Center, Flint; dir. 1st Fed. Savs. & Loan Assn. Flint. Adv. bd., chmn. Flint YWCA; trustee, vice chmn. McLaren Gen. Hosp. Mem. Mich. Bankers Assn. (truste div.). Elk. Clubs: Golf, City (Flint). Home: 1801 Woodburn Dr Flint MI 48503 Office: Citizens Comml & Savs Bank 328 S Saginaw St Flint MI 48502

BALLER, STUART TAYLOR, ednl. adminstr.; b. De Witt, Nebr., July 19, 1903 s. Albert H. and Mary (Taylor) B.; A.B., Neb. Wesleyan U., 1924; A.M., U. Nebr., 1932, Ph.D., 1950; student George Peabody Coll., 1937; m. Mabel B. Lake, July 25, 1926; children—Richard H., Robert S. Coach, tchr. Exeter (Neb.) High Sch., 1924-25; head coach Univ. Place High Sch., Lincoln, Neb., 1925-30; head coach Lincoln High Sch., 1930-1936; coach, asst. dir. phys. edn. Peru (Neb.) State Tchrs. Coll., 1936-38; coach, dir. phys. edn. U. Omaha, 1938-44; dir. recreation Martin Aircraft Co., 1944-1945; supt. schs., Wayne, Neb., 1945-49; dean Carthage (Ill.) Coll., 1949-61, acad. v.p., 1961-64; dean acad. affairs Robert Morris Jr. Coll. of Carthage, 1965- 66; prof. edn. and psychology, asso. dean for research and grants William Penn Coll., Oskaloosa, Ia., 1966-67, asso. dean, 1967—. Named Ark. Traveler, 1967, adm. Neb. Navy, 1969. Mem. N. Central Academic Deans Assn. (pres. 1956- 57), Phi Delta Kappa. Mason; mem. Order of Eastern Star (worthy patron 1962); Kiwanian. Contbr. articles to ednl. publs. Home: 210 Rosenberger Av Oskaloosa IA 52577

BALLER, WARREN ROBERT, ednl. psychologist; b. Trenton, Neb., June 19, 1900; s. Albert Ernest and Mary Louise (Taylor) B.; A.B., York Coll., 1923; M.A., U. Neb., 1927, Ph.D., 1935; student Columbia, 1930, U. Minn., 1932; LL.D., George Williams Coll., 1961; m. Dorothy Gwendolyn Jensen, Feb. 15, 1941; children—William Warren, John Timothy, Elizabeth Claire, Prin. Callaway (Neb.) High Sch., 1923-24; supt. schs., Cheney, Neb., 1925-28; tchr. York Coll., 1928-34, dean, 1933-34; asst. prof. ednl. psychology U. Neb., 1936-38, asso. prof., 1938- 43, prof., 1943-67, also chmn., 1961-67, dir. jr. div., 1948-50; vis. prof. edn. U. Cal. at Los Angeles, 1955-57; prof. ednl. psychology Cal. Western U., 1967-68, U.S. Internat. U., San Diego, 1968—. Fellow gen. edn. bd. U. Chgo., 1940-41; vis. prof. (summers) George Peabody Coll., 1941, Northwestern U., 1941, U. Fla., 1950, U. Cal., 1951, U. Tex., spring 1949; cons. on child behavior and devel., Lincoln, 1938—. Mem. N.E.A., Am. Psychol. Assn., Am. Assn. U. Profs., Nat. Soc. for Study Edn., Midwestern Psychol. Assn., A.A.A.S., Am. Ednl. Research Assn., Western Psychol. Assn., Nat. Soc. Coll. Tchrs. Edn. (past pres.), Phi Delta Kappa, Sigma Xi. Democrat. Presbyn. Author: Psychology of Human Growth and Development, 1961; 2d edit., 1968; Readings in the Psychology of Human Growth and Development, 1962, 2d edit., 1969. Home: 3275 Loma Riviera Dr San Diego CA 92110

BALLESTEROS, CRESCENCIO, constrn. co. exce.; b. Guadalajara, Jalisco, Mexico, Mar. 5, 1914; s. Luis P. and Carlota (Ybarra) B.; Civil Engr., State of Jalisco Coll.; student U. State Jalisco; m. Josefina Franco, June 16, 1941; childrenJose Luis, Susana (Mrs. Miguel Icaza), Jorge Eduardo, Carlos, Josefina. With Mexican Ministry Hydraulic Resources, 1935-42; dir. gen. Constructora Aztlan, 1943-58, Constructore Cuauhtemoc, 1943-58, Constructora Moderna, 1943-48, Constructora Anahuac, 1943-58; chmn. Promotora Immoviliaria, S.A., 1958—, Elementos Electronicos Mexicanos, S.A., 1958-, Anticorrosivos, S.A., 1959-68, Proyectos, Estructuras Acabados, 1965-, Compania Mexicana de Aviacion, S.A., 1968-; dir. gen. Constructora Ballesteros, 1958-; pres. John Deere de Mexico; exec. v.p. Reliance Universal de Mexico, S.A., 1958-; v.p. Compania Mexicana de Aviacion, S.A., 1961-67; dir., mem. exec. com. Negromex, S.A., Kimberly Clark de Mexico, Hotel Camino Real Puerto Vallarta, S.A.; dir. Las Estacas, S.A., Camino Real de Mexico, S.A., Banco Nacional de Mexico, S.A., Union Carbide Mexicana, S.A., Sherman Aditivos Mexicanos, S.A., Derivados Macroquímicos, S.A., Tele Radio Nacional, S.A. Bd. dirs. Centro de Adiestramiento de Operadores, A.C., Universidad Iberoamericana, A.C., Assn. Mexicana de Caminos, A.C. Rotarian. Clubs: Jockey (Lomas de Barnilaco); Club de Industriales (Mexico City). Home: 520 Alpes Mexico D F 10 Mexico Office: 36 Balderas Mexico D F 1 Mexico

BALLEW, LEIGHTON MILTON, educator, theatre dir.; b. Des Arc, Ark., Feb. 17, 1916; s. Lawrence Durant and Allie (Schnebly) B.; B.S., Memphis State Coll., 1937; M.A. (grad. fellow), Western Res. U., 1941; Ph.D., U. Ill., 1955; m. Despy Karlas, Mar. 19, 1949; 1 son, Christopher Durant. Founder, Memphis Civic Theatre, 1936; mng. dir. Jacksonville (Fla.) Little Theatre, 1941; profl. actor, dir., 1937-42; prof., chmn. dept. drama and theatre U. Ga., Athens, 1946—, dir. univ. theatre, 1946—, founder Jr. Artist Fellowship Program, 1950, vis. dir. program, 1965. Chmn. Harry Davis Meml. Scholarship Fund, 1969, Leighton Ballew Scholarship Fund, 1969. Served with USAAF, 1942-46. Mem. Ga. Speech Assn. (past pres.), Southeastern Theatre Conf. (past pres.), Am. Ednl. Theatre Assn. (past dir.), Ga. Theatre Conf. (past pres.), Nat. Theatre Conf. Author articles, revs., plays. Home: 175 Duncan Springs Road Athens GA 30601

BALLHAUS, WILLIAM FRANCIS, engring. exec.; b. San Francisco, Aug. 15, 1918; s. William Frederick and Eva Rose Callero (O'Connor) B.; B.S., Stanford, 1940, M.E. (Switzer research fellow, Rosenberg research fellow 1940-42), 1942; Ph.D., Cal. Inst. Tech., 1947; m. Edna Dooley, Feb. 13, 1944; children—William Francis, Katherine Louise, Martin Dennis, Mary Susan. Mem. tech. adv. panel on aeros. Office Sec. Def., 1954-60; mem. NACA, 1954-57; chief engr. Northrop Aircraft, 1953-57, v.p. engring., 1957; v.p., gen. mgr. Nortronics, 1957-61; exec. v.p., dir. Northrop Corp., Beverly Hills, Cal., 1961-64, now dir.; pres. Beckman Instruments, Inc., Fullerton, Cal., 1965—; dir. Bank of Long Beach, Beckman-Toshiba Ltd., Cal. Bankers Trust Co. Cons., Office of Critical Tables, Nat. Acad. Scis. Active Boy Scouts Am. Trustee Northrop Inst. Tech., Harvey Mudd Coll.; fellow Claremont U. Center; adv. council Sch. Engineering, Stanford. Registered profl. engr. Fellow Am. Inst. Aeros. and Astronautics; mem. Electronic Industry Assn. (past dir.), Aircraft Industries Assn. (past chmn. guided missile com. 1956-57), Soc. Automotive Engrs., Am. Ordnance Assn., Assn. U.S. Army (pres. Greater Los Angeles chpt. 1963-65, council of trustees 1965-69). Home: 21 Portuguese Bend Rd Rolling Hills CA 90274 Office: Beckman Instruments Inc Fullerton CA 92634

BALLIETT, WHITNEY, writer, critic; b. N.Y.C., Apr. 17, 1926; s. Fargo and Dorothy (Lyon) B.; student Phillips Exeter Acad.; B.A. with honors, Cornell U., 1951; m. Elizabeth Hurley King, 1951; children—Julia, Elizabeth, William; m. 2d, Nancy Kraemer, 1965; children—Whitney, James. Mem. editorial staff New Yorker mag., N.Y.C. 1951—, successively collator, proofreader, reporter, 1951-57, staff writer, 1957—, columnist on jazz recordings, concerts, book reviewer, reporter, contbr. poetry, also to Sat. Rev., Atlantic Monthly; also movie, theatre reviewer New Yorker, 1960-62; originated plan CBS- TV show Sound of Jazz, 1957; wrote scripts, appeared on ednl. TV program Trio, 1962. Served as sgt. USAAF, 1946-47. Mem. Delta Phi. Author: The Sound of Suprise; 46 pieces on Jazz, 1959; Dinosaurs in the Morning; 41 Pieces of Jazz, 1962; Such Sweet Thunder; 49 Pieces on Jazz, 1966; Super-Drummer; A Profile of Buddy Rich, 1968; Ecstasy at the Onion: 29 Pieces on Jazz, 1971. Office: New Yorker Mag 25 West 43d St New York City NY 10036

BALLIF, ARLEL SMITH, Sr., educator; b. Logan, Utah, Dec. 9, 1901; s. John Lyman and Emma (Smith) B., Sr.; Jr. Coll. certificate, Ricks Coll., Rexburg, Ida., 1922; B.S., Brigham Young U., 1925; M.A., U. So. Cal., 1937, Ph.D., 1945; m. Arta Romney, Aug. 28, 1925; children—Ariel Smith, Moana, Maralyn, Jae Romney, Bonnie Lauris. Social sci. instr. Jr. High Sch., Parker, Ida., 1922-23, Madison High Sch., Rexsburg, 1925; athletic dir., Ricks Coll., 1926; prin. Maori Agrl. Coll., Hastings, New Zealand, also missionary for Ch. of Jesus Christ of Latter-Day Saints to New Zealand, 1927-30; instr. in social science, Midway High Sch., Menan, Ida., 1930; prin. Midway Latter-Day Saints Sem., Menan, 1931-36; instr. of sociology, Brigham Young U., 1938, asst. prof., 1939-43, asso. prof., 1943-44, prof. sociology, 1944—, chmn. dept. sociology, 1948-54, acting dean summer school, 1950-54, dean summer sch., 1954-58, fgn. student adviser, 1958—. Community adjustment adviser for War Relocation Authority, 1944-46 (on leave from Brigham Young U.). Mem. and chmn. Provo City Planning Commn. and Bd. Adjustment, 1942-47; commr. Utah County Planning Bd., 1959-61; mem. Provo City Council, mayor of Provo City, 1961-62. Fellow Am. Sociol. Soc.; mem. Pacific Sociol. Soc., A.A.A.S., Nat. Conf. Social Work, Utah State Conf. Social Work (exec. council 1944-50), Alpha Kappa Delta, Phi Kappa Phi. Mem. Ch. Jesus Christ of Latter-Day Saints (bishop Provo Ninth ward 1942-47, pres. East Provo State 1950-55; pres. New Zealand Mission 1955-58). Home: 2181 North 1220 East Provo UT 84601

BALLINGER, HARRY RUSSELL, artist; b. Port Townsend, Wash., Sept. 4, 1892; s. James Guy and Lourena (Russell) B.; student U. Cal. at San Francisco, 1910-11, Art Student's League, 1912-13, Acad. Colorossi, Paris, France, 1927; pupil of Harvey Dunn, Paris, 1915-16; m. Madeline Waters, Feb. 19, 1922; m. 2d, Kay Mollison, Oct. 12, 1951. Illustrator nat. mags. 1916-17, 19-35; instr. Grand Central Art Sch., 1930-36, Central Conn. Coll., New Britain, 1945- 58, marine painting chasses, Rickport, Mass., 1952-60, U. Hawaii, 1960; rep. permanent collections New Haven Paint and Clay Club, New Britain Mus. Am. Art, Wadsworth Atheneum, Hartford, Conn., Springfield (Mass.) Art Mus., Central Conn. State Coll., Meriden (Conn.) Arts and Crafts Soc., also mural Plant High Sch., W. Hartford, Conn.; ann. exhbns. Allied Artists, Audubon Artists, Nat. Acad. Design, Am. Watercolor Soc., Salmagundi Club: one man shows include New Britain Mus. Am. Art, 1947, Ward Eggleston Gallery, N.Y.C., 1948, Rockport Art Assn., 1951, Marblehead (Mass.) Art Assn., 1954, Choate Sch., 1959, Guild Boston Artists, 1960, Woodmere Art Gallery, Phila., 1962, Central Conn. Coll., 1965, Cayuga Mus. Art, Auburn, N.Y., 1955, U. Conn., 1966. Recipient watercolor prizes Salmagundi Club, 1944, 52, 54, 58, 70, oil prizes., 1958, 59 60, 61, 63, 65, 66, 69, 70; prizes Conn. Acad., 1944, 36, Conn. Watercolor Soc., 1944, 45, Meriden Arts and Crafts Soc., 1944, 52, 57, 61, 65, 68, Springfield Art Assn.,Assn., 1952, 53, 55, 62, 64, 65, 70, Hudson Valley Art Assn., 1958, 60, 64, 70, Jordan Marsh Co., Boston, 1953, 56, 60, Am. Artists Profl. League, 1961, Rockport Art Assn., 1953, 55, 60 (2), 63, 65, 68, N. Shore Art Assn., 1963, 64, 70, Audubon Artists Annual Exhbn., 1968, 71. Asso. Nat. Academician. Mem. Allied Artists, Audubon Artists, Salmagundi Club, New Haven Paint and Clay Club, Conn. Acad., Kent (Conn.) Art Assn., Springfield Acad. Art, N. Shore Art Assn., Rockport Art Assn., Guild Boston Artists. Author: Painting Surf and Sea, 1957; Painting Boats and Harbors, 1959; Painting Landscapes, 1965; Painting Sea and Shore, 1966; also articles. Address: R F D 2 New Hartford CT 06057

BALLINGER, ROBERT IRVING, Jr., architect; b. Phila., Feb. 8, 1918; s. Robert Irving and Francis (Taylor) B.; B.Arch., Cornell U., 1940; m. Elizabeth S. Mulford, 1942 (dec.); children—Robert Irving III, Elizabeth M., Nadya, Stuart, David, Ashley; m. 2d, Dorothy C. Coon, 1958 (div.); m. 3d, Wynne Shaiples, Oct. 21, 1967. With The Ballinger Co., Phila., 1945—, partner, 1955-69, chmn. bd. dirs., 1969—; works include Phila. Food Distbn. Center, Montgomery Hosp., City Hall, Atlantic City, N.J. Mem. exec. bd. Com. of 70; past pres. Neighborhood League Upper Main Line. Served with USNR, 1942-45. Mem. A.I.A., Nat. Council Archtl. Registration Bds., Pa. Soc. Architects, Am. Hosp. Assn. Clubs: Racquet, Cornell (Phila.). Home: 454 S Ithan Av Villanova PA 19085 Office: 1625 Race St Philadelphia PA 19103

BALLINGER, WALTER FRANCIS, educator, surgeon; b. Phila., May 16, 1925; s. Robert I. and Frances (Taylor) B.; student Cornell U., 1942-44; M.D., U. Pa., 1948; m. Ellen Fezandie, June 26, 1953; children—Walter Francis III, Christopher Bardin, David Gordon. Intern 1st Surg. Div., Bellevue Hosp., N.Y.C., 1948-49, asst. resident surgery, 1949-50, chief resident surgery, 1955- 56; asst. resident surgery Columbia-Presbyn. Med. Center, 1953-55; from instr. to asso. prof. Jefferson Med. Coll., Phila., 1956-63; asso. prof. surgery Johns Hopkins Sch. Medicine, 1964-67; Bixby prof. surgery, head dept. Washington U. Sch. Medicine, St. Louis, 1967—. Served to capt. U.S. Army, 1950-52. Markle scholar med. sci., 1961-66. Mem. Am. Surg. Assn., Soc. Clin. Surgery, Soc. Univ. Surgeons, A.C.S., James IV Assn., Halsted Soc. Editor: (with others) Research Methods in Surgery, 1964, The Management of Trauma, 1968. Home: 1 Warson Lane St Louis MO 63124 Office: 4960 Audubon Av St Louis MO 63110

BALLIS, WILLIAM BELCHER, educator; b. Portland, Ore., June 8, 1908; s. William and Bertha (Belcher) B.; A.B., Stanford, 1929; fellow polit. sci., U. Chgo., 1931- 32, Ph.D., 1936; postgrad. Columbia, 1935, U. Cal., 1936; fellow Russian studies Rockefeller Found., 1937-39, 1948-49; m. Eunice Minette Schuster, Nov. 20, 1933; children—Nancy Eunice, William Albert, Instr. polit. sci. U. Chgo., 1932-37; asst. prof. polit. sci. Ohio State U., 1939-41; Russian analyst Nat. Def. and War Agys., Washington, 1941- 42; chief polit. sect., later chief Eastern European br., div. research for Europe, Dept. State, 1946-48; prof. polit. sci. U. Wash., 1948-57, prof. Russian govt. and politics Far Eastern and Russian Inst., 1948-57, prof. polit. sci. U. Mich., Ann Arbor, 1957—, dir. Center for Russian Studies, 1961-65; Chester W. Nimitz prof. social and polit. philosophy Naval War Coll., 1964-65; acting dir. Inst. Internat. Affairs, U. Wash., 1954-55; dir. internat. studies Nat. War Coll., 1949; cons. Army War Coll., 1961, 62; lectr. Air War Coll. Am. advisor Inst. Study History and Instns. of USSR, Munich, Germany, 1953-54 Rackham Sr. Faculty Research fellow, summer 1960; research in Middle East under Rackham grant, 1966. Del. Sino-Am. Conf. Intellectual Coop., Seattle, 1960, XXV Internat. Congress of Orientalists, Moscow, USSR, 1960, XIII World Congress Hist. Scis., Moscow 1970, participant Internat. Conf. on World Politics, West Berlin, 1967. Recipient Inter-Univ. Com. Travel award to USSR, Europe, 1957. Served as comdr. USNR, 1942-46, asst. U.S. naval attache Am. embassy, Moscow, 1945-46. Mem. Am. Polit. Sci. Assn., Inst. Study USSR (hon.), Mich. Acad. Scis. (pres. Russian studies sect. 1959-60), Am. Assn. Advancement Slavic Studies (chmn. Mid-West conf. 1963), Detroit Com. Fgn. Relations (chmn.), Phi Beta Kappa. Presbyn. (elder). Author: The Legal Position of War, 1937. Editor, co-author: Mongolian Peoples Republic, 1956. Cons., World Book Ency., 1965—. Contbr. articles to profl. jours. Home: 3011 Geddes Av Ann Arbor MI 48104

BALLMAN, DONALD KARL, chem. co. exec.; b. Indpls., Apr. 18, 1910; s. Frank E. and Fern (Armstrong) B.; student Butler U., 1926-28; A.B. in Chemistry, U. Ind., 1931, M.S. in Chemistry, 1935; m. Elizabeth Margaret Jerome, Nov. 19, 1938; children—Donald Karl, Brenda Katherine. Salesman Dow Chem. Co., Midland, Mich., 1935-43, mgr. Dowicide sales, 1943, mgr. tech. service and devel., 1943-45, asst. gen. sales mgr., 1945-49, gen. sales mgr., 1949- 57, dir. sales, 1957-61, v.p., 1959-68, v.p. charge marketing, purchasing and distbn., 1961-68, sr. v.p., 1968—, mem. exec. com., 1962- -, mem.

finance com., 1968—, also dir.; pres. Ventures Investment and Finance Co. div. Dow, 1969—; dir. Dorco Packaging Corp., Dow Chem. Can. Ltd., Dow Chem. Financial Corp. Recipient award Comml. Chem. and Devel. Assn., 1956. Mem. Am. Chem. Soc., Comml. Chem. and Devel. Assn., Soc. Chem. Industry (Am. sect.). Clubs: Union League, Canadian (N.Y.C.). Home: 209 Revere St Midland MI 48640 Office: Dow Chem Company 2030 Dow Center Midland MI 48640

BALLMANN, DONALD LAWRENCE, educator; b. Dayton, O., Apr. 25, 1927; s. Adam Ignatius and Martha (Barhorst) B.; A.B. in Philosophy, St. Joseph's Coll., Rensselaer, Ind., 1954; B.S. in Geology, U. Ill., 1955, M.S., 1956, Ph.D., 1959. Ordained priest Roman Cath. Ch., 1953; mem. faculty St. Joseph's Coll., 1956—, acad. dean, 1963-68, asso. prof. geology, 1963—, dir. devel. for founds., govt. relations, 1968—; field party chief Ind. Geol. Survey, summers 1962, 63. Mem. Geol. Soc. Am., Am. Assn. Petroleum Geologists, Soc. Econ. Paleontologists and Mineralogists, Nat. Assn. Geology Tchrs., A.A.A.S., Sigma Xi. Author bulls. Address: St. Joseph's Coll., Rensselaer, IN 47978.

BALLOCH, ANTHONY EDWARD, paper co. exec.; b. Woking, Eng., Mar. 29, 1916; s. Gideon and Kitty (Mort) B.; B.A. with honours, Oxford (Eng.) U., 1937; grad. Advanced Mgmt. Program, Harvard, 1958; D.C.L., Acadia U., 1967; LL.D., St. Francis Xavier U., 1968; m. Mary Chase Howard, Feb. 23, 1946; children—Patricia Ann (Mrs. S.D. McLellan), Josephine Mary Chase (Mrs. P.F.W. Ahrens III), Howard Robert, Hugh McCauley. Trainee, Bowater Paper Corp., 1937-39, dir., 1967—; with Bowater's Nfld. Ltd., 1946-48, asst. gen. mgr., 1956-61, chmn. bd., 1967-70; with Bowaters Paper Mills, Eng., 1948-52; pres., gen. mgr. Bowaters Mersey Paper Co., 1962-66, chmn. bd., 1967—; pres. Bowaters Canadian Corp., 1967-70; dep. chmn. Bulkley Valley Forest Industries Ltd., 1967—; v.p. adminstrn. and planning Bowater Inc., 1970—. Mem. exec. com. N.S. Vol. Planning Bd., 1963-66. Mem. grants com. N.S. U., 1964-66. Served with Brit. and U.S. armies, 1939-45. Decorated Order Brit. Empire; Legion of Merit, Bronze Star. Home: 7 Glen Hill Lane Wilton CT 06897 Office: Bowater Inc 1500 E Putnam Av Old Greenwich CT 06870

BALLOU, CLINTON EDWARD, educator, biochemist; b. King Hill, Ida., June 18, 1923; s. William C. and Molly (Bernt) B.; B.S. in Chemistry, Ore. State Coll., 1944; Ph.D. in Biochemistry, U. Wis., 1950; m. Dorothy Lun Wu, Dec. 21, 1949; children—Linda, Philip. USPHS fellow U. Edinburgh (Scotland), 1950-51; USPHS fellow U. Cal. at Berkeley, 1951-52, research asso., 1952-55, mem. faculty, 1955—, prof. biochemistry, 1961—, chmn. dept., 1964-68. Cons. com. biol. chemistry USPHS, Nat. Acad. Sci.-NRC, 1965—. Served to lt. (j.g.) USNR, 1944-46. NSF fellow, Paris, France, 1961-62; Guggenheim fellow, Kyoto, Japan, 1968-69. Mem. Am. Soc. Biol. Chemists, Am. Chem. Soc., Chem. Soc. (London, Eng.). Author papers related to biochemistry of carbohydrates, sugar phosphates, complex lipids. Home: 1081 Creston Rd Berkeley CA 94708

BALLOU, DONALD HENRY, educator; b. Chester, Vt., Mar. 28, 1908; s. Henry Lincoln and Carrie (Hubbard) B.; grad. Phillips Acad., Andover, Mass., 1924; B.A., Yale, 1928; M.A., Harvard, 1931, Ph.D., 1934; m. Dorothy Edith Pollard, Sept. 14, 1933; 1 son, Donald Pollard. Instr., Harvard, 1933-34; instr., then asst. prof. Ga. Inst. Tech., 1934-42; mem. faculty Middlebury (Vt.) Coll., 1942—, prof. math., 1956—, chmn. dept., 1954-68, Beman prof. math., 1964-71, Charles A. Dana prof. math., 1971—; Carnegie fellow gen. edn. Yale, 1951-52. Mem. Am. Math. Soc., Math. Assn. Am., Am. Assn. U. Profs., Phi Beta Kappa. Author: (with F. H. Steen) Plane and Spherical Trigonometry, 2d edit., 1953, Analytic Geometry, 3d edit., 1955. Home: 27 Weybridge St Middlebury VT 05753

BALLOU, LOUIS WATKINS, architect; b. Halifax, Va., Oct. 12, 1904; s. Dr. Nathaniel Talley and Annie John (Ballou) B.; student architecture, U. Va., 1923-27; m. Ellen Frances Patterson, June 23, 1930; children—Richard Patterson and Frances (Mrs. Richard A. Ledford). Draftsman, 1927-33; designer Lee, Smith & VanDervoort, 1933-36; pvt. archtl. practice, 1943-45; partner Ballou & Justice, architects and engrs., Richmond, Va., 1945—; guest lectr. Va. Commonwealth U.; dir. So. Bank & Trust Co., So. Bankshares, Natural Gas Co. Va.; works include restoration Va. State Capitol and Rotunda of U.Va., Blue Cross bldg., Richmond City Hall, Bank of Va. Bldg., Supreme Ct. Bldg. for Commonwealth of Va. Mem. Art Commn. Commonwealth Va., 1952—. Pres. U. Va. Student Aid Found., 1960-61. Served with AUS, 1942-43. Recipient Bronze medal Beaux Inst. Design, N.Y.C., 1926, Meritorious Service citation Va. N.G. Assn., 1968. Fellow A.I.A.; mem. U.Va. Alumni Assn. (pres. 1961-63), Alpha Rho Chi, Omicron Delta Kappa. Presbyn. Club: Richmond Commonwealth (pres. 1965-66). Home: 1509 Palmyra Av Richmond VA 23227 Office: 530 E Main St Richmond VA 23219

BALLOU, W. FRED, ins. co. exec.; b. N.Y.C., 1908. Former exec. v.p., now dir. Phoenix Assurance Co., N.Y.C.; former dep. U.S. mgr. London Guarantee & Accident Co., Ltd. Home: Clapboard Ridge Road Greenwich CT 06830 Office: 80 Maiden Lane New York City NY 10038*

BALLWEG, JOHN MICHAEL, educator; b. Elizabeth, N.J., May 2, 1930; s. Henry G. and Loretta (O'Donnell) B.; A.B., Seton Hall U., 1952; degree in Classical langs. Immaculate Conception Sem., Darlington, N.J., 1956. Ordained priest Roman Cath. Ch., 1956; engaged in parish work, 1956-63; tchr. religion, sociology St. Mary's High Sch., Elizabeth, N.J., 1959-62; mem. faculty Seton Hall U., South Orange, N.J., 1963—, dean men, 1965-70, part-time instr. theology, 1965—. Mem. Personnel Bd. for Assignment Priest Personnel, Archdiocese Newark, 1968- -; mem. Concerned Community Conf. Greater Newark Area, 1967—. Mem. Cath. Theol. Soc., Religious Edn. Assn., Coll. Theology Tchrs. Assn., N.J. Coll. Personnel Conf., Am. Teilhard de Chardin Assn. Address: Seton Hall Univ South Orange NJ 07079

BALMAIN, PIERRE, dress designer; b. St. Jean de Maurienne, Savoie, France, May 18, 1914; s. Maurice and Francoise (Ballinari) B.; student Lycee de Chambery, 1926- 32; B.S. and B.L., U. Grenoble, 1932; studied architecture Ecole des Beaux Arts, Paris, 1932-34. Dress designer with Paris couturiers, 12 yrs.; continued designing while in service at front with the army, 1939- 40; established in 1945 and since operated own business, Paris. Conseiller du Commerce Extérieur, 1953—. Served with French Army, 1939- 40. Decorated cross Legion of Honor (France); knight Order of Danebrog (Denmark); cavaliere Ufficiale dell'Ordine Al Merito della Repubblica Italiana. Home: 6 Blvd Suchet 75 Paris 16 France Office: 44 rue Francois Ier Paris 8 France

BALMER, JOHN BEVERLEY, mfg. co. exec.; b. Toronto, Ont., Can., July 4, 1906; s. John Lancelot and Leila Elspeth (Stewart) B.; St. Andrew's Coll., Toronto, 1925; children—John Ellsworth, Anthony Stewart, Diane Carroll. Came to U.S., 1946, naturalized, 1950. Pres., chief exec. officer The Murray Corp. Am., N.Y.C., 1961-66, also dir., merged to form Wallace-Murray Corp., 1966, exec. v.p., 1966-67, pres., chief exec., 1967-69, chmn. exec. com., 1969—. Club: Union League (N.Y.C.). Home: 620 Park Av New York City NY 10021 Office: 299 Park Av New York City NY 10017

BALMER, THOMAS JAMES, metal products co. exec.; b. Chgo., Sept. 9, 1913; s. Edwin and Katharine (MacHarg) B.; grad. Choate Sch., 1931; A.B., Harvard, 1935; postgrad. Mass. Inst. Tech., 1942-43, N.Y.U., 1946-48; m. Eleanor Eliza Hamant, Oct. 19, 1935. Mem. pub. relations staff N.Y. Stock Exchange, 1939-57; account exec. Fiscal Information Service, 1957-61; account supr. Dudley-Anderson-Yutzy, 1961-68 (all N.Y.C.); corporate sec., dir. pub. relations MSL Industries, Inc., Beverly Hills, Cal., 1968—; cons. pub. relations Pacific Am. Industries, Cal. Shopping Centers, Inc., Exeter Oil Co., Ltd. Dir. fund raising Dobbs Ferry (N.Y.) Hosp., 1964. Served with AUS, 1942-46. Recipient Oscar award Financial World Nat. Contest, 1970. Mem. Nat. Investor Relations Inst., Am. Soc. Corporate Secretaries, New Eng. Soc. City N.Y., Sigma Alpha Epsilon. Club: Harvard (N.Y.C.). Author: Investment Facts about Common Stocks and Cash Dividends, 1947; Do Electronics Companies Need a New Kind of Public Relations?, 1967. Home: 124 S Oakhurst Dr Beverly Hills CA 90212 Office: MSL Industries Inc 212 S Gale Dr Beverly Hills CA 90211

BALOGH, JOSEPH KENNETH, educator, sociologist; b. Donora, Pa., July 8, 1914; s. Daniel and Julia (Nagy) B.; B.S., Pa. State Coll., 1937; Litt.M., U. Pitts., 1939, Ph.D., 1945; m. Virginia Lillian Macko, Sept. 6, 1947; children—Merlin J., Randy J., Kevin M. Tchr., Donora Pub. Schs., 1937-43; asst. prof. sociology Hillsdale (Mich.) Coll., 1945-46, St. Lawrence U., Canton, N.Y., 1946-48; faculty Bowling State (O.) U., 1949—, prof. sociology, 1959—, chmn. dept., 1965—. Cons., lectr., demonstrator in field, 1950—. U.S. Brewery Found. fellow Yale, 1956; Danforth Found. fellow, 1959. Fellow Ohio Acad. Sci. (membership v.p. sect. sociology and anthropology 1961-62, exec. com. 1961-62, exec. v.p. sect. 1962-63, chmn. research com. 1966, exec. com. 1966, pres. 1967), Am. Sociol. Assn., A.A.A.S.; mem. Ohio Valley Sociol. Assn. (chmn. sect. juvenile delinquency and criminology 1962, 63), Internat. Soc. Criminology, Am. Correctional Assn., Nat. Probation and Parole Assn., Am., Internat. socs. criminology, Nat. Jail Assn., N.Y. Acad. Scis., Am. Acad. Polit. and Social Sci., Phi Delta Kappa, Phi Alpha Theta, Pi Gamma Mu, Alpha Kappa Delta, Phi Eta Sigma, Phi Kappa Phi, Omicron Delta Kappa. Author: (with Charles Rumage) Juvenile Delinquency Proneness: A Study of the Kvaraceus Scale, 1956; (with others) Milieu Therapy with Chronic Regressed Female Schizophrenics, 1961; A Critical Evaluation of the In Service Training Program at State Penitentiary, San Quentin, California, 1953; A Survey of Juvenile Delinquency in Hillsdale County, Michigan for the Years 1935-50, 1952; A Critical Evaluation of the Semantic Training Program at State Penitentiary, San Quentin, California, 1953; others. Contbr. numerous articles to profl. jours. Home: Cherry Hill Drive Bowling Green, OH 43402.

BALOPOLE, WILLIAM, savs. and loan assn. exec. Pres., Empire Savs. and Loan Assn. Office: PO Box 3308 6750 Van Nuys Bldg Van Nuys CA 91407*

BALOUN, JOHN CHARLES, distbn. co. exec.; b. Chgo., May 1, 1934; s. John Nicholas and Anne (Giera) B.; B.S.C., DePaul U., 1956; m. Lynette Anne Jehs, July 27, 1963; children—John Christopher, Michael Warren. Mem. audit staff Arthur Andersen & Co., C.P.A.'s, Chgo., 1956-63; controller, asst. sec. Super Food Services, Inc., Chgo., 1963-67, treas., 1967-68; treas. Dog'N Suds, Inc., Champaign, Ill., 1968-69; dir. planning and control Distbn. div. U.S. Plywood-Champion Papers, Inc., Chgo., 1969—. Served as 2d lt. AUS, 1957, C.P.A. Ill. Mem. Ill. Soc. C.P.A.'s, Republican. Home: 610 Western Av Glen Ellyn IL 60137 Office: 1 E Wacker Dr Chicago IL 60601

BALOW, IRVING HENRY, educator; b. Wabasha, Minn., Jan. 19, 1927; s. Laurence Christian and Katherine (Yost) B.; B.S., U. Minn., 1951, M.A., 1957, Ph.D., 1959; m. Joyce Elizabeth Binner, June 8, 1950; children—Mary, Thomas, Michael, Robert, Ann. Elementary sch. tchr., Theilmam, Minn., 1951-53, Wabasha, 1953-54, 56-57; instr. U. Minn., 1957-59; mem. faculty U. Cal. at Riverside, 1959—, prof. edn., 1968—, chmn. dept., 1963-70, asso. dean, 1970-71, acting dean, 1971—; reading cons., 1959—. Served with USAAF, 1945-47. Mem. Am. Ednl. Research Assn., Nat. Council Tchrs. English. Contbr. profl. jours. Home: 138 Green Oak Dr Riverside CA 92507

BALSA, CESAR, hotel exec.; b. Barcelona, Spain, June 21, 1923; s. Antonio and Elisa (Carralero) B.; ed. in Spain; m. Carmen Cruz, July 16, 1948; children—Carmen Cesar, Elena, Elisa, Christina, Monica, Antonineta. Bell boy Oriental Hotel, Barcelona, Spain, 1938; mgr. food services Palace Hotel, Madrid, 1945; mgr. Tampico Club, Mexico City, 1949; opened Focolare Restaurant, beginning of Balsa Chain, Mexico City, 1952; pres. Nacional Hotelera, S.A., Mexico City, 1956—; dir. Eastern Airlines, Inc. Bd. dirs. Mexican Council Businessmen of Mexico. Mem. Young Pres. Orgn. Catholic. Home: Calzada del Desierto 24 San Angel Inn Mexico DF Mexico Office: Hamburgo 135 Mexico 6 D F Mexico

BALSAM, ARTHUR, pianist; b. Warsaw, Poland, 1906; ed. in Berlin; m. Ruth R. Balsam. Debut, 1918; appearances in concerts and recitals throughout U.S.; has accompanied Menuhin, Milstein and Morini; now mem. Balsam-Kroll-Heifetz Trio. Address: care Decca Recording Co 445 Park Av New York City NY 10022*

BALSAM, MARTIN HENRY, actor; b. N.Y.C., Nov. 4, 1919; s. Albert and Lillian (Weinstein) B.; ed. New Sch. Social Research 1946-48; m. Pearl L. Somner, Oct. 1952 (div. 1954); m. 2d, Joyce Van Patten, Aug. 1959 (div. 1962); 1 dau.; m. 3d, Irene Miller, Nov. 1963. Profl. acting debut in The Play's the Thing, Locust Valley, N.Y., 1941, N.Y.C. debut in Ghost for Sale, 1941; stage appearances include Lamp at Midnight, N.Y.C., 1947, The Wanhope Building, N.Y.C., High Tor, A Sound of Hunting, Macbeth, N.Y.C., 1948, Sundown Beach, 1948, The Closing Door 1949, You Know I Can't Hear You When the Water's Running (Tony award), 1967; appeared in summer stock, 1949—, appearances include Three Men on a Horse, The Rose Tattoo, Camino Real, Detective Story, Middle of the Night, A View from the Bridge, The Iceman Cometh; motion pictures include On the Waterfront, 1954, 12 Angry Men, 1957, Marjorie Morningstar, 1957, Al Capone, 1959, Middle of the Night, 1959, Psycho, 1960, All at Home, 1960, Breakfast at Tiffany's, 1961, Ada, 1961, Cape Fear, 1962, The Captive City, 1962, Who's Sleeping in My Bed, 1963, Seven Days in May, 1963, The Carpetbaggers, 1963, 1000 Clowns (Acad. award), 1964, Bedford Incident, Harlow, After the Fox, 1965, Hombre, 1966, Among the Paths to Eden, 1967, Me, Natalie, Good Guys and Bad Guys, 1968, Catch 22, Tora Tora Tora, Little Big Man, 1969, The Anderson Tapes, The Commissioner, 1970; numerous nightclub, TV appearances. Served with AUS, 1941-45. Mem. Actor's Equity Assn., A.F.T.R.A., Screen Actor's Guild, Actor's Studio. Home: 300 Central Park W New York City NY 10024 Office: care Lazarow 119 West 57th St New York City NY 10019

BALSEIRO, JOSE AGUSTIN, educator, cons. Hispanic affairs; b. Barceloneta, P.R., Aug. 23, 1900 s. Rafael and Dolores (Ramos-Casellas) Balseiro; LL.B., U. P.R., 1921; Litt., Inter-Am. U. P.R., 1950; Sc.D., Catholic U. Chile, 1954; L.H.D., Belmont Abbey, 1962; m. Mercedes Pedreira, Mar. 3, 1924; children—Yolanda (Mrs. George Buchmann), Liliana (Mrs. Frank Mees). Prof. Romance langs. U. Ill., 1930-33; 36-38, U. P.R., 1933- 36, Northwestern U., summer 1937, Duke, summers 1947, 49, 50, Inter-Am. U. P.R., summer 1957-63; prof. Hispanic lit. U. Miami, Coral Gables, Fla., 1946-67; vis. prof. Spanish lit. U. Ariz., Tucson, 1967—; lectr. U. Mexico, summer 1959, also State Dept. Internat. Ednl. Exchange Program, Guatemala, Panama, Ecuador, Bolivia, Paraguay, Chile, Argentina, Uruguay, Brazil, summer 1954, Spain and Eng., 1955-56, Spain, 1964; U.S. del. 1st Internat. Congress Ibero-Am. Lit., Mexico, 1938; v.p. 4th Congress Acads. Spanish Lang., 1964. Mem. Internat. Inst. Ibero-Am. Lit. (pres. 1955-57); corr. mem. Spanish Royal Acad., Colombian Acad. Letters, Instituto Sarmiento of Argentina. Author: Cuatro Individualistas de Espanã, 1949; En Vela Mientras el Mundo Duerme, 1953; Saudades de Puerto Rico, 1957; Visperas de Sombra, 1959; Expresion de Hispanomérica, 1960, vol. 2, 1963, 70; Seis Estudios sobre Rubén Dario, 1967; The Americas Look at Each Other, 1969; La Gratitud Humana, 1969. Home: 7740 SW 142d St Miami FL 33158

BALSLEY, GERARD EARL, steel co. exec.; b. Fresno, Cal., Oct. 25, 1916; s. Lorin and Elberta Elizabeth (Heath) B.; A.B., U. Cal. at Berkeley, 1939; student Golden Gate Law Sch., 1947-48, Indsl. Coll. Armed Forces, 1952; div.; children—Susan Elizabeth, Wendy Lora, Gerard Earl, Lynne Ellen. With Pacific Can Co., 1939-42, Schenley Industries, 1946-50, Kaiser Frazer Corp., 1950-52, Chase Aircraft Co., 1952-53; with Kaiser Steel Corp., 1953—, v.p., 1961—; v.p., gen. mgr. Kaiser Resources Ltd., Can., Westshore Terminals Ltd. Served with USNR, 1942-46. Mem. Am. Mgmt. Assn., Am. Soc. Personnel Adminstrn. Am. Iron and Steel Inst. Home: 265 Scenic Av Piedmont CA 94611 Office: Box 940 Fernie British Columbia Canada

BALSLEY, JAMES ROBINSON, Jr., educator; b. Pitts., Dec. 27, 1916; B.S., Cal. Inst. Tech., 1938; A.M., Harvard, 1941, Ph.D., 1960; married, 1943; two children. Geologist, U.S. Geol. Survey, 1941-47, airborne geophysicist, 1947-53, chief geophys. br., 1953-59, asst. chief geologist, 1959-62; prof. geology Wesleyan U., Middletown, Conn., 1962—; Am. Geol. Inst. lectr., 1959—, Am. Geophys. Union lectr., 1963. Served with USAAF, 1944. Recipient Distinguished Service award U.S. Dept. Interior, 1962. Mem. Geol. Soc., Soc. Exploratory Geophysics, Geophys. Union. Office: Wesleyan U Middletown CT 06457*

BALTHROP, WILLIAM PLUMMER, air conditioning co. exec.; b. Clarksville, Tenn., July 27, 1920; s. Gus Henry and Ruby (Moss) B.; B.S., U. Tenn., 1944; M.S., Chrysler Inst. Engring., 1946; m. Thlema Butts, Mar. 7, 1941; children—Michael W., Brian D. With Chrysler Corp., 1944—, mfg. mgr. Mound Rd. engine plant, Warren, Mich., 1957-59, Trenton (Mich.) engine plant, 1959-60, pres. Amplex div., 1960-61, pres. Air-temp div., Dayton, O., 1961—. Trustee Engring. and Sci. Inst., Dayton Art Inst., Dayton Boys Club, Jr. Achievement, Air Force Mus. Found., Dayton Philharmonic Orch., One Hundred Club. Trustee St. Elizabeth Med. Center, Kettering Med. Center. Recipient Community Service award Nat. Electronic Mfgs. Assn., 1966. Mem. Air Conditioning and Refrigeration Inst. (pres. 1970-71), Dayton Area C. of C. (pres. 1958-59), Newcomen Soc. Club: Dayton Kiwanis (pres. 1969-70), Moraine Country, Dayton Country, Dayton Racquet. Home: 3849 Ridgeway Rd Dayton OH 45429 Office: 1600 Webster St PO Box 1205 Dayton OH 45401

BALTHUS, (Balthus, Klossowski de Rola), artist; b. Paris, France, Feb. 29, 1908; s. Erich and Baladine Klossowski; married 1937. Painted frescoes, Ch. of Beatenberg Bernese Oberland, 1928; exhibited Galerie Pierre, Paris, France, 1934, Pierre Matisse Gallery, N.Y.C., 1938, 39, 49, 57, 62, 67, Moos Gallery, Geneva, Switzerland, 1943, Wildenstein Galleries, Paris, 1946, 56, Galerie des Beaux Arts, Paris, 1956; exhibited retrospective exhbns. Mus. Modern Art, 1956, E.V. Thaw & Co., N.Y.C., 1963, B.C. Holland Gallery, Chgo, 1966, Musee des Arts Decoratifs, Paris, 1966, Casino Knokke le Toute, Belgium, 1966, Tate Gallery, London, 1968; designer costumes, sets for Antonin Artaud's The Cenci, 1935; executed costumes, sets for Cosi Fan Tutte, Festival at Aix-en-Provence, 1950. Dir. French Acad., Villa Medici, Rome, Italy. Military service, Morocco. Composer: (picture-book) Mitsou, 1921. Office: care Pierre Matisse Gallery 41 E 57th St New York City NY 10022

BALTZ, EDWARD F., advt. agy. exec. Sr. v.p. Compton Advt. Inc., N.Y.C. Office: 625 Madison Av New York City NY 10022*

BALTZ, FLORENCE LUCILLE, nurse, instn. exec.; b. White Pigeon, Mich., Nov. 23, 1910; d. T. Avery and Magdalena (Ingold) Weaver; R.N., Mennonite Hosp. Sch. Nursing, Bloomington, Ill.; m. Max H. Baltz, May 25, 1945. Gen. pvt. duty nurse, 1934-37; hosp. adminstr., Ill., Ia., 1937-45; partner, nursing home adminstr., Washington and Baltz Nursing Homes, 1951-62; v.p. operations Americana Nursing Homes, Inc., 1961-66; adminstr. Baltz Nursing Home, 1956-62; pres. Washington (Ill.) Nursing Center, Inc., 1962—. Mem. adv. council Ill. Dept. Pub. Health, 1952-65; cons. com. long term facilities Am. Hosp. Assn., 1963; mem. Ill. Com. Improvement Econ. and Social Status Older Persons; mem. U.S. Surgeon Gen.'s Adv. Com on Community Health Services, 1963-64; chmn. Joint Council Health Care Aged, Chgo., 1959; mem. nat. adv. com., Ill. com. White House Conf. Aging, 1961; mem. adv. com. Nat. Conf. Med. Cost, 1967; mem. Ill. Council on Health Aging, 1965-; participant Sec. Health, Edn. and Welfare Conf. on Health Care Cost, Cleve., 1968. Mem. Am. (v.p. 1957, 58, pres. 1959-60, Nat. Better Life Award 1968), Ill. (pres. 1954, 55, Better Life award 1968, pres. dist. 6, 1969), nursing home assns., Am. Hosp. Assn., Nat., Ill. (steering com. div. nursing services) leagues for nursing, Am., Ill., Dist. nurses assns., Ill. Hosp. Assn. (hon.), Am. Assn. of Consultants Inc. (dir. mgmt., nursing homes 1961), Washington Bus. and Profl. Womens Club. Mennonite. Club: Woman's (Washington, Ill.). Home: 104 E Holland St Washington IL 61571 Office: 1110 New Castle Road Washington IL 61571

BALTZ, WILLIAM STANLEY, lawyer, mfg. exec.; b. Lansing, Mich., Feb. 16, 1918; s. William D. and Ethel Belle (Cassidy) B.; B.A., Yale, 1940; LL.B., Harvard, 1943; m. Phyllis Ruth Snyder, Jan. 3, 1948; children—Stephen Lambert, Randee Elizabeth, William Allan. Admitted to Ill. bar, 1948; with firm Scott, MacLeish & Falk, Chgo., 1947-49; gen. counsel Ency. Britannica Films, Inc., Wilmette, Ill., 1949-53; with Admiral Corp., Chgo., 1953—, gen. counsel, v.p., 1960-66, v.p. govt. electronics div., 1966—. Pres. Fed. Excise Tax Council, Washington. Home: 98 Woodley Rd Winnetka IL 60093 Office: 3800 Cortland St Chicago IL 60647

BALYO, JOHN GABRIEL, clergyman; b. Greenville, S.C., Jan. 18, 1920; s. John Gabor and Etta (Groce) B.; student Atlanta Law Sch., 1937-40; LL.B., Valparaiso U., 1945; student Goshen Coll., 1945-46; A.B., Grace Theol. Sem., 1944, B.D. magna cum laude, 1946; D.D., Grand Rapids Theol. Sem., 1960; m. Betty Louise Lindstrand, Oct. 14, 1945; 1 son, John Michael. Ordained to ministry Bible Baptist Ch., 1950; pastor in Three Oaks, Mich., 1942-45, Elkhart, Ind., 1945-46, Kokomo, Ind., 1946-53, Cedar Hill Bapt. Ch., Cleve., 1953—. Mem. Gen. council Bapt. Mid-Mission, 1954—, adminstrv. com., 1962—, trustee, 1963—, chmn. bd. trustees, 1968—, chmn. council, 1966-68; mem. council 14, Gen. Assn. Regular Bapt. Chs., 1955- 59, 60-64, sec. council, 1957-58, chmn. publs. com., 1956-60, 63-66, chmn. council 14, 1966-68, mem. finance com., 1968-69, publs. com., 1968- 69, chmn. program com., 1968-69, chmn. edn. com., 1960-62, vice chmn. council, 1962-64, chmn., 1970—; exec. bd. dirs. Grand Rapids Bapt.

Bible Coll. and Sem., 1961—, chmn. curriculum com., 1963-66; missionary survey trips to Europe and Africa, 1957-58, Ecuador, 1962, Peru, 1969. Bd. dirs. Hebrew Christian Soc., 1956-64. Asso. mem. Am. Sci. Affiliation. Author Sunday sch. material for Regular Bapt. Press, also booklet Creation and Evolution. Home: 1104 Brandon Rd Cleveland Heights OH 44112 Office: 12601 Cedar Rd Cleveland OH 44106

BALZHISER, RICHARD EARL, educator; b. Wheaton, Ill., May 27, 1932; s. F. Earl and Esther (Merrill) B.; B.S., U. Mich., 1955, M.S., 1956, Ph.D., 1961; m. Christine R. Karnuth, Sept. 15, 1951; children—Gary R., Robert M., Patricia C., Cheryl M. Asst. prof. chem. engring. U. Mich., Ann Arbor, 1960-64, asso. prof., 1964-67, spl. asst. to v.p. planning and state relations, 1968-69, prof. chem. engring., 1967—, chmn. chem. engring. dept., 1970—; White House fellow Dept. Def., 1967-68. Editor chem. engring. series Holt, Rinehart & Winston, 1964-69; dir. Chemotronics, 1965—; cons. E.I. duPont de Nemours & Co., 1966—. City councilman, Ann Arbor, 1965-67, mayor pro tem, 1966-67; mayoral candidate, Ann Arbor, 1969; chmn. Republican State Conv., 1969. Recipient Oustanding Prof. award, 1962, Outstanding Young Man in Mich. award Jr. C. of C., 1967. Mem. Am. Inst. Chem. Engrs., Am. Soc. Engring. Edn., Sigma Xi, Sigma Chi. Rotarian. Author: Chemical Engineering Thermodynamics, 1970. Home: 3930 Waldenwood St Ann Arbor MI 48105

BAM, FOSTER, lawyer; b. Bridgeport, Conn., Jan. 11, 1927; s. Frederick and Alma (Foster) B.; grad. Loomis Sch., 1944; A.B., LL.B., Yale, 1950; m. Edith Taylor Schultz, Mar. 3, 1964; children—Sylvia Carol, Sheila Catherine, Eric Foster. With Charles Hecht & Co., C.P.A.'s N.Y.C., 1950; faculty accounting Yale, 1952-53; admitted to N.Y. bar, 1954; with firm Spence & Hotchkiss, N.Y.C., 1954-55; asst. U.S. dist. atty. So. Dist. N.Y., 1955-58; partner firm Feldman, Kramer, Bam Nessen, N.Y.C., 1958-67; admitted to Conn. bar, now partner Cummings & Lockwood. Dir. Brookline Instrument Co., Fidelity Trust Co., Stamford, Conn.; sec. Am. Natural Gas Co. Recipient Johny Foyle Meml. award, 1969. Mem. Am., N.Y. State, Greenwich bar assns., Assn. Bar City N.Y., N.Y. County Lawyers Assn., N.Y. State Dist. Attys. Assn., Phi Beta Kappa. Home: 51 Londonderry Dr Greenwich CT 06830 Office: 2 Greenwich Plaza Greenwich CT 06830

BAMBERGER, BERNARD JACOB, rabbi; b. Balt., May 30, 1904; s. William Burk and Gussie (Erlanger) B.; A.B., Johns Hopkins, 1923; Rabbi, Hebrew Union Coll., Cin., 1926, D.D., 1929, D.H.L., 1950; m. Ethel Ruth Kraus, June 14, 1932; children—Henry, David. Rabbi, Temple Israel, Lafayette, Ind., 1926-29, Congregation Beth Emeth, Albany, N.Y., 1929-44, Temple Shaaray Tefila, N.Y.C., 1944-70, rabbi emeritus, 1970—. Mem. com. preparing new translation of Bible, Jewish Publ. Soc. Am.; pres. Central Conf. Am. Rabbis, 1959-61; pres. Synogogue Council Am., 1950-51; pres. World Union for Progressive Judaism, 1970—. Mem. Soc. Bibl. Lit. and Exegesis, Am. Acad. Jewish Research. Author: Proselytism in the Talmudic Period, 1939; Fallen Angels, 1952; The Bible: A Modern Jewish Approach, 1955; The Story of Judaism, 1957. Editor: Reform Judaism: Essays by Hebrew Union College Alumni, 1949; Studies in Jewish Law, Custom and Folklore (Jacob Z. Lauterbach), 1970. Contbr. essays learned and popular jours. Contbg edg. editor The Universal Jewish Ency. Home: 225 West 86th Street New York City NY 10024

BAMBERGER, FRITZ, coll. adminstr.; b. Frankfurt-am-Main, Germany, Jan. 7, 1902; s. Max and Amalie (Wolf) B.; Ph.D., U. Berlin, 1923; m. Kate Schwabe, Mar. 21, 1933 (dec.); children—Michael Albert, Gay; m. 2d, Maria E. Nussbaum, Sept. 29, 1963. Came to U.S., 1939, naturalized, 1944. Research prof. Acad. for Jewish Research, Berlin, 1926-33; prof. philosophy Coll. Jewish Studies, Berlin, 1933-34; dir. Bd. Edn. for Jews, Berlin, 1934-38; also pres. Jewish Tchrs. Coll. of Prussia; mem. Bd. Jewish Edn. Chgo., faculty mem. Coll. Jewish Studies 1939-44; dir. research Coronet and Esquire mags., 1942-48; editorial dir. Coronet, 1948-52, editor, 1952-56; exec. dir. Esquire and Coronet. 1956-61; cons. Esquire, 1962—; prof. intellectual history, asst. to pres. Hebrew Union Coll., N.Y.C., 1962—; mem. exec. com. scholars Inst. Advanced Studies in Religion and Humanities; v.p. Leo Baeck Inst. Mem. Am. Acad. Polit. and Social Sci., Overseas Press Club. Author: Entstehung des Wertproblems, 1924; Moses Mendelssohn, 1929; Das System des Maimonides, 1935; Das neunte Schuljahr, 1937 (all pub. Germany); Zunz's Conception of History, 1941; Leo Baeck-The Man and the Idea, 1958; The Philosophy of Julius Guttmann, 1960; Books Are the Best Things, 1962. Editor or compiler: Lehren des Judentums, 1928-30; new edit., 1971; Moses Mendelssohn's Gesammelte Schriften, 1929-32; Denkmal der Freundschaft, 1929; Das Buch Zunz, 1932; Herder's Blaetter der Vorzeit, 1936 (all pub. Germany). Contbr. articles to various publs. Home: 415 East 52d Street New York City NY 10022 Office: 40 West 68th Street New York City NY 10023

BAMBERGER, JULIAN, lawyer; b. Indpls., 1905; student Ohio State U.; LL.B., Ind. Law Sch., 1934. Admitted to Ind. bar, 1934, since practiced in Indpls.; mem. firm Bamberger & Feibleman. Instr. bus. agencies Ind. Law Sch., 1942-44. Mem. Am., Indpls. bar assns., Lawyers Assn. Indpls. Author: Legal Aspects of Group Insurance. Office: Union Federal Bldg Indianapolis IN 46204

BAMPTON, JAMES WILLIAM, rubber and plastic products mfg. co. exec.; b. Lakewood, O., Aug. 15, 1909; s. Samuel Wesley and Henrietta Frances (Hunt) B.; A.B., Hobart Coll., 1932, LL.D., 1968; M.B.A., Harvard, 1934; m. Lois Irene Thomasson, June 23, 1937; children—Robin Ann, James William, Barbara. Sales executive for Goodyear Tire & Rubber Co., Akron, O., 1934-44; spl. rep. U.S. Bd. Econ. Welfare, Australia and New Zealand, 1943-44; dir. advt. promotion and comml. research James Lees & Sons Co., Bridgeport, Pa., 1944-48; pres. Theodore Presser Co., Bryn Mawr, Pa., 1948-51; asst. to pres. Charles Lachman Co., Phoenixville, Pa., 1951-53; pres. Krylon, Inc., 1953-67; pres., dir. Thomasson of Pa., Inc., 1956- 61; pres., chief exec. officer Globe Rubber Products Corp., Norristown, Pa., 1970—. Cons. to Borden, Inc., 1967—. Trustee Hobart and William Smith Colls. Clubs: Harvard (N.Y.C. and Phila.); Union League (Phila.). Home: 602 Old Eagle Sch Rd Strafford PA 19087 Office: 9401 Bluegrass Rd Philadelphia PA 19114

BANAUGH, ROBERT PETER, educator, computer applications scientist; b. Los Angeles, Oct. 27, 1922; s. Rudolf Otto and Elizabeth (Mantz) B.; A.B., U. Cal. at Berkeley, 1946, M.A., 1952, Ph.D., 1962; m. Catherine M. Haun, July 6, 1946; childrenElizabeth, Catherine, Robert, Mary Louise, Laura, Marjorie, John, Peter, Secondary sch. tchr. Richmond (Cal.) Union High Sch. Dist., 1947-50; applied mathematician Cal. Research and Devel. Corp., Livermore, 1952-54; research engr. Pioneer Indus., Reno, 1954-55; theoretical physicist Lawrence Radiation Lab., Livermore, Cal., 1955-62; head applied math. group Northrop-Venture Corp., 1962-64; prof. computer sci., chmn. dept., dir. Computer Center, U. Mont., 1964- ; extension instr. U. Cal. at Berkeley, 1949-; cons. in field, 1965-. Served with USAAF, 1943-45. Decorated Air medal with 3 oak leaf clusters. Mem. Seismological Soc. Am., Am. Geophys. Soc., Sigma Xi, Phi Kappa Psi. Catholic. Contbr. profl. jours. Home: Route 5 Miller Creek Missoula, MT 59801.

BANBURY, THOMAS JOHN, lawyer, state govt. ofcl.; b. Aurora, Ill., Feb. 4, 1920; s. George A. and Catherine (Biever) B.; student Aurora Coll., 1941-46; LL.B., John Marshall Law Sch., 1946, J.D., 1948; m. Anita M. Amoni, Apr. 25, 1942; children—John C., Carol M. (Mrs. Michael Brown), Linda A. (Mrs. William Hagel). Admitted to Ill. bar, 1948, since practiced in Aurora; atty. Ill. Div. Hwys., 1956-62; clk. Ill. Supreme Ct. Judge Solfisburg, 1962- 65; spl. asst. Ill. Atty. Gen. William J. Scott, 1969—; atty. Nat. Accelerator Labs., Ill. Dept. Pub. Works and Bldgs. Mem. Kane County Bar Assn., Am. Legion, Delta Theta Phi. Moose, Elk. Clubs: Aurora Country; Phoenix Country. Home: 3050 E Northern St Phoenix AZ 85028 also 64 N Buell St Aurora IL Office: 122 W Downer Pl Aurora IL 60507

BANCHERO, JULIUS THOMAS, educator; b. N.Y.C., June 18, 1914; s. John Battista and Mary (Ponte) B.; A.B., Columbia, 1933, B.S., 1935, Chem.E., 1936; Ph.D., U. Mich., 1950; m. Faye L. Mambourg, June 11, 1938; childrenJulia Ann, Mary Gainor, Barbara Aileen. Chem. engr. Carbide & Carbon Chem. Corp., South Charleston, W.Va., 1936-38; instr. chem. engring. U. Detroit, 1938-41; instr. chem. engring. U. Mich., 1943-49, asst. prof., 1949-55, asso. prof., 1955-58, prof., 1958-59; prof., head dept. chem. engring. U. Notre Dame, South Bend, Ind., 1959—. Mem. Adv. bd. Chem. Abstracts Service, 1968-70. Mem. Am. Chem. Soc., Am. Inst. Chem. Engrs., Am. Soc. M.E., Am. Soc. Engring. Edn., N.Y. Acad. Scis. Author: (with others) Unit Operations, 1950; (with W.L. Badger) Introduction to Chemical Engineering, 1955. Home: 202 South Jacob Street South Bend, IN 46615.

BANCROFT, ANNE, actress; b. N.Y.C., Sept. 17, 1931; d. Michael and Mildred (DiNapoli) Italiano; grad. Christopher Columbus High Sch., N.Y.C.; m. 2d, Mel Brooks, 1964. Broadway debut in Two for the Seesaw, 1958; starred as Anne Sullivan in The Miracle Worker, Broadway, 1959-60, also in movie version; motion pictures include Don't Bother to Knock, Tonight We Sing, Demetrius and The Gladiators, The Pumpkin Eater, 1964, The Graduate; TV appearances include Bob Hope Show, Perry Como Show, The Goldbergs, Danger, Suspense, Philco-Goodyear Playhouse, Kraft Music Hall, Anne Bancroft Spl., Tom Jones Show; plays include Mother Courage and Children. Recipient Acad. Award for performance in The Miracle Worker, 1962; Golden Globe award,1968; spl. Annie, The Woman in the Life of Men, 1970. Address: care David Cogan 350 Fifth Av New York City NY 10001

BANCROFT, HARDING FOSTER, newspaper exec.; b. N.Y.C., Dec. 29, 1910; s. Francis Sidney and Beatrice F. (Jordan) B.; ed. Lawrenceville Sch., 1925-29; A.B., Williams Coll., 1933; LL.B., Harvard, 1936; LL.D., Wilmington Coll., 1968; m. Jane Northrop, July 2, 1936; children—Alexander, Mary Jane, Harding F., Catherine. Lawyer with Searle James & Crawford, N.Y.C., 1936-41; OPA, Washington, 1941-43; office of Lend Lease Adminstrn., Washington, 1943; chief, div. UN Polit. Affairs, Dept. State, 1945, later dir. Office UN Polit. and Security Affairs, U.S. dep. rep. UN Collective Measures Com., with personal rank of minister, 1950- 53; legal adviser ILO, Geneva, 1953-56; sec. New York Times Co., 1956-63, exec. v.p., 1963-, dir., 1961-; dir. Gaspesia Pulp & Paper Co., Ltd., Interstate Broadcasting Co., Spruce Falls Power & Paper Co., Ltd. Mem. U.S. delegation to 21st UN Gen. Assembly with rank of ambassador. Bd. dirs. Greer Children's Community; trustee Williams Coll., Coll., Carnegie Corp. N.Y., Sarah Lawrence Coll., 1960-70, Carnegie Endowment Internat. Peace, Clark Art I Inst.; mem. mem. internat. council Mus. Modern Art; adv. council Columbia U. Sch. Internat. Fgn. Relations. Mem. Fgn. Policy Assn. (dir.), Overseas Devel. Council (dir.). Club: Century Assn. Home: 180 E 9 St New York City NY 10021 Office: New York Times 229 W 43d St New York City NY 10036

BANCROFT, JAMES RAMSEY, lawyer; b. Ponca City, Okla., Nov. 13, 1919; s. Charles Ramsey and Maude (Viersen) B.; A.B., U. Cal. at Berkeley, 1940, M.S. in Bus. Adminstrn., 1941; J.D., Hastings Coll. Law, 1949; m. Jane Marguerite Oberfell, May 28, 1944; children—John Ramsey, Paul Marshall, Sara Jane. Admitted to Cal. bar, 1950; with McLaren, Goode, West & Co., C.P.A.'s, San Francisco, 1946-50; partner firm Bancroft, Avery & McAlister, San Francisco, 1950—. Pres. Madison Properties, Inc., San Francisco, 1967- -, Adams Properties, Inc., 1969—, Adams-Western Inc., 1969—; chmn. bd. dirs. Uniline Corp., Union City, Cal.; dir. Recortec Inc., Mountain View, Cal., United Nuclear Corp., Elmsford, N.Y. Pres. Suisun Conservation Fund, 1963—; dir. Suisun Soil Conservation dist., 1963—. Trustee Dean Witter Found., Harvey L. Sorensen Found. Served to lt. USNR, 1942-46. C.P.A., Cal. Mem. Am. Bar Assn., Phi Beta Kappa. Clubs: Bohemian, Olympic (San Francisco). Office: 240 Stockton St San Francisco CA 94108

BANCROFT, RICHARD HUNTER, former ins. co. exec.; b. St. Paul, Nov. 3, 1902; s. Franck Churchill and Alice Hunter (Rhodes) B.; student U. Minn., 1925; m. Pauline Griggs Spindler, Sept. 16, 1926; children—Richard Hunter, Elizabeth (Mrs. Malcom S. Cammack), Polly (Mrs. Charles M. Hebble), Mary (Mrs. Charles F. Field). With St. Paul Fire & Marine Ins. Co., 1924-70, corp. sec., 1948-55, v.p., 1955-70; dir. St. Paul Mercury Ins. Co. Mem. Chi Psi. Clubs: Minnesota, Somerset Country (St. Paul). Home: 715 Linwood Av Saint Paul MN 55105

BANCROFT, THEODORE ALFONSO, educator, statistician; b. Columbus, Miss., Jan. 2, 1907; s. Frank Hammond and Laura Louise (Cox) B.; B.A., U. Fla., 1927; M.A., U. Mich., 1934; Ph.D., Ia. State U., 1943; m. Lenore Springer, Dec. 1, 1933; children—Alice Muriel, Lenore Louise. Teaching asst. math. Vanderbilt U., 1937-38; head math. dept. Mercer U., 1938-41; asso. prof. math. U. Ga., 1946-47; dir. statis. lab. Auburn U., 1947-49; asso. prof. Ia. State U., Ames, 1949, dir., prof., head statis. lab., dept. statistics, 1950—. UN assignment Middle East, India, 1954, Mexico, 1955. Univ. tng. command, Italy, 1945. Fellow Am. Statis. Assn. (pres. 1970), A.A.A.S.; mem. Internat. Statis. Inst., Econometric Soc., Inter-Am. Statis. Inst. (asso.). Inst. Math. Statistics, Biometric Soc. (mem. council, past pres.), NRC, Sigma Xi, Phi Kappa Phi, Nu Sigma Rho (bd. dirs.). Author: (with R.L. Anderson) Statistical Theory in Research, 1952; Topics in Intermediate Statistical Methods, vol. 1, 1968. Editor: (with Kempthorne, Gowen, Lush) Statistics and Mathematics in Biology, 1954, 64; statistical papers in Honor of George W. Snedecor, 1971. Contbr. articles to profl. jours. Home: 3515 Woodland Av Ames IA 50010

BAND, MAX, artist; b. Naumestis, Lithuania, Aug. 21, 1900; s. Abraham and Anna (Tumpowsky) B.; student Art Acad., Berlin, Germany, 1920-22; m. Bertha Finkelstein, Apr. 19, 1921; 1 son, Albert A. Came to U.S., 1940, naturalized, 1948. One man shows at Heller, Casper, Flechtheim galleries, Berlin, 1924-31, Quatre Chemins, Girard, Marcel Bernheim galleries, Paris, Wildenstein, N.Y., 1948, Galerie de l'Elysee, Paris, 1949, Vigevano Galleries, Los Angeles, 1950; Cal. Palace Legion of Honor, 1956, Raymond and Raymond Galleries, Beverly Hills, Cal., 1957, Michel Thomas Gallery, Beverly Hills, 1963; participated exhbns. in Salon d. Salon de Tuileries, 1924-39, J. B. Neuman, Balzac, J. Seligman galleries, French Art Gallery, Wildenstein Gallery, 1926-48, Stendahl Gallery, County Mus., James Vigveno Galleries, Los Angeles, 1952, San Diego Fine Arts Mus., 1941, Maxwell Galleries, San Francisco, 1946, Va. Mus., Richmond, 1950, Dayton (O.) Art Inst., 1945, Durand Ruel Gallery, N.Y.C., Malboro Gallery, London, 1950, A Century of French Art (1850-1950), Paris, 1953, Musee du Petit Palais, Paris, Art Inst. Chgo., 1954, Jewish Mus., N.Y.C., 1953, exhbn. French, art Amsterdam, Bruxelles, Tokyo, Osaka, Los Angeles, 1958, Acosta Gallery, Beverly Hills, 1959; paintings in permanent collections Musee de Jeu de Paume, Parliament of Israel, Musee de l'Art Moderne, Petit Palais. Paris, Musee de Ville de Paris, Musee de Ceret, France, Riverside Mus., N.Y.C., Philips Meml. Mus., White House, Washington, French Art Inst., Phila., Mus. Rome, Jerusalem, Tel Aviv, Israel, Lithuania, and throughout U.S., also numerous pvt. collections. Painted portrait of Pres. Franklin Roosevelt in the White House, 1934, also sculptor bust Pres. Roosevelt presented to Pres. Kennedy for White House, 1961; artist in residence U. Judaism, Los Angeles; one of founders Original Sch. Paris. Fellow Internat. Inst. Arts and Letters; hon. mem. Cal. Art Club. Paintings and sculptures reproduced in book Themes from the Bible, 1964. Home: 6401 Ivarene Av Hollywood CA 90028

BAND, WILLIAM, educator; b. Eng., Aug. 27, 1906; s. William David and Amy Louisa (Cooke) B.; B.Sc. (hon.), Liverpool (Eng.) U., 1925, M.Sc., 1927, D.Sc., 1946; m. Claire M. Edwards, Aug. 12, 1931. Came to U.S., 1946, naturalized, 1953. Tchr. physics Yenching U., Peking, China, 1929-41; mem. Brit. Council, Chungking, China, 1943; mem. staff Nuclear Studies Inst., U. Chgo., 1946, Metals Inst., 1947-48; prof. physics faculty Wash. State U., Pullman, 1949-71, prof. emeritus, 1971—, chmn. dept., 1961-67. Fellow Am. Phys. Soc., Inst. Physics (London); mem. Sigma Xi. Author: (with wife) Dragon Fangs, 1947, Two Years with Chinese Communists, 1947; Introduction to Quantum Statistics, 1955; Introduction to Mathematical Physics, 1959. Asso. editor Am. Jour. Physics, 1962-68. Home: 1609 Fisk St Pullman WA 99163

BANDA, HASTINGS KAMUZU, president of Malawi; b. Kasungu district, Nyasaland, 1906; studied Livingstonia Mission Ch. of Scotland, later night sch., Johannesburg; grad. (scholar) Wilberforce Inst., Xenia, O., 1928; student U. Ind., 1928; Ph.B., U. Chgo., 1931; M.D., Meharry Med. Coll., 1937; student univs. Glasgow and Edinburgh, tropical medicine U. Liverpool, (Eng.). Practice medicine, Liverpool, also North Shields, Eng., 1942-44, Mission for Colored Seamen, 1944-45, Kilburn Dist. of London, 1945-53, Gold Coast (became ind. nation of Ghana 1957), 1953-58; leader opposition to fedn. Rhodesia and Nyasaland, 1949-53; assisted establishment Nyasaland African Congress, 1950, elected pres.-gen., 1958; imprisoned for polit. activities, 1959-60; apptd. minister natural resources and local govt. Malawi, 1961, prime minister, 1963-66, pres., 1966—. Chancellor, U. Malawi, 1965—. Address: Office of Pres Zomba Malawi*

BANDO, SAL, third baseman for Oakland Athletics Profl. Baseball Team. Address: care OaklandAlameda County Colliseum, Oakland, CA 94621.*

BANDY, ORVILLE LEE, geologist, educator; b. Linden, Ia., Mar. 31, 1917; s. Alfred Lee and Blanche (Meacham) B.; B.S., Ore. State U., 1940, M.S., 1941; Ph.D. (Shell Oil fellow), Ind. U., 1948; m. Alda Ann Umbras, June 10, 1943; children—Janet Lee, Donald Craig. Mem. faculty geology U. So. Cal., Los Angeles, 1948—, prof., 1954-67, chmn. dept. geol. scis., 1967—. Bd. dirs. Cushman Found. for Foraminiferal Research. Fellow Geol. Soc. Am.; mem. A.A.A.S., Soc. Econ. Paleontologists and Mineralogists (counselor 1963-64, v.p. 1969-70, pres. 1971-72), Am. Assn. Petroleum Geologists (trustee research fund 1960-64, distinguished lectr. 1963-64), Am. Soc. Limnology and Oceanography, Ecol. Soc. Am., Schweiz. Geologische Gesellschaft, Sigma Xi. Contbr. articles profl. jours. Home: 6536 Holt Av Los Angeles CA 90056

BANDY, WILLIAM THOMAS, Jr., educator; b. Nashville, May 11, 1903; s. William Thomas and Margaret (Villines) B.; B.A., Vanderbilt U., 1923, M.A., 1926; Ph.D., Peabody Coll. Tchrs., 1931; postgrad. U. Ill., 1927-28, U. Grenoble (France), 1924, U. Strasbourg (France), 1928; student U. Paris (France), 1925, 26-27, Am. Field Service fellow, 1928-30; m. Alice Scudder Burghardt, Nov. 5, 1929 (dec. Mar. 2, 1970); children—Jane (Mrs. Burr McWilliams), William Thomas III, Peter Burghardt, Helen Margaret (Mrs. George Boole Spiegelman), Carol Villines (Mrs. Michael Oberdorfer), Cynthia Palmer (Mrs. T.J.P. O'Brien); m. 2d, Carol Dieckman Poggenburg, Oct. 20, 1970. Professor French, chmn. dept. modern langs. Stephens (Mo.) Coll., 1931-36; faculty U. Wis., 1936—, prof. French, 1949-68, emeritus, 1968—, chmn. dept. French and Italian 1959—, chmn. div. humanities, 1958-61, mem. Inst. for Research in Humanities, 1962-63; distinguished prof. French, dir. Center for Baudelaire Studies, Vanderbilt U., 1968—. Fulbright research scholar, 1955-56. Served to lt. comdr. USNR, 1942-46; comdr. Res. Mem. Modern Lang. Assn. (exec. council), Am., Am. Assn. Tchrs. French, Sociéte histoire littéraire de la France. Author: Baudelaire Judged by His Contemporaries, 1933; Baudelaire en 1848, 1946; Baudelaire Devant Ses Contemporains, 1957. Compiler; A Word-Index of Baudelaire's Poems, 1939. Home: 3415 West End Av Nashville TN 37203

BANE, CHARLES ARTHUR, lawyer; b. Springfield, Ill., May 1, 1913; s. Fred Weller and Frances (Tilley) B.; A.B., U. Chgo., 1935; LL.M., Harvard, 1938; B.A. in Jurisprudence (Rhodes scholar), Oxford U., 1937; m. Eileen Blackwell, Jan. 17, 1942; children—Susan Magary, Janet, Peter, Charles. Admitted to N.Y. bar, 1939, Ill. bar, 1949; asso. Sullivan & Cromwell, N.Y.C., 1939-42, 46-48; mem. firm Bishop, Mitchell & Burdett, Chgo., 1949-50, Mitchell, Conway & Bane, 1950-52, Isham, Lincoln & Beale, 1953—. Sr. atty. Office Lend Lease Adminstrn., 1942-43; chief counsel Emergency Crime Com., Chgo. City Council, 1952; sec. Crime Detection Inst., 1957-60; chmn. Ill. adv. com. Fed. Civil Rights Commn., 1958-61. Mem. Rhodes Scholarship Selection Com. Pres. United Charities Chgo., 1961-63. Lectr. in law U. Chgo. Law Sch., 1954, 58. Nat. chmn. plaintiff's counsel steering com. Elec. Equipment Antitrust Litigation. Bd. dirs. Community Fund Chgo.; bd. dirs., exec. com. United Cerebral Palsy of Chgo.; mem. cancer research bd. U. Chgo. Served as lt. USNR, 1943-45. Fellow Am. Bar Found. (Ill. chmn.); mem. Am. (council mem. pub. utility sect. 1958-61), Ill., Chgo. (bd. mgrs.) bar assns., Am. Law Inst., Council Fgn. Relations (pres. 1956-58), Family Service Assn. Am. (v.p. 1966—, dir.), English-Speaking Union (pres. Chgo. br. 1964-66), Phi Beta Kappa, Phi Kappa Sigma. Clubs: Economic, Commercial, Saddle and Cycle (pres. 1965-67), Tavern, Casino (Chgo.); Internat. House (pres. 1967-69); Harvard (N.Y.C.); Everglades (Palm Beach, Fla.). Contbr. articles profl. pubs. Editor-in-chief Chgo. Bar Record, 1966-68; mem. bd. editors Am. Bar Assn. Jour., 1968-70, chmn., 1970—. Home: 219 E Lake Shore Dr Chicago IL 60611 Office: 1 First National Plaza Chicago IL 60670

BANE, DAVID MORGAN, fgn. service officer; b. Uniontown, Pa., Sept. 12, 1915; s. David Emulous and Nellie Ray (Ramage) B.; A.B. magna cum laude, Duke U., 1938; LL.B., U. Pa., 1941; m. Patricia Huston Miller, May 12, 1945; 1 dau., Patricia Huston (Mrs. Allen I. Price). Apptd. to U.S. Fgn. Service, 1947; 2d sec., Tokyo, 1947-49, Seoul, 1949-50; consul, Bordeaux, 1950-53, first sec., Paris, 1953-56; fgn. affairs office Dept. of State, 1956—, assigned Nat. War Coll., 1957-58; dep. dir. Office N.E. Asian Affairs, 1958-59, dir., 1959-61; U.S. consul gen., Lahore, Pakistan, 1961-64; univs. exchange program

State U. Ia., Iowa City, 1964-65; ambassador to Gabon, Libreville, 1965-69; polit. adviser CINC U.S. Strike Command, 1969-71; Am. consul gen., Bombay, India, 1971—. Served with AUS, 1941-46; PTO; col. Res. Decorated Soldier's medal, Bronze Star (U.S.); grand officer Order Equatorial Star (Gabon). Mem. Pa. Bar Assn., Phi Beta Kappa, Pi Gamma Mu, Alpha Kappa Psi. Office: care Dept of State Washington DC 20520

BANE, FRANK, pub. welfare ofcl.; b. Smithfield, Va., Apr. 7, 1893 s. Charles Lee and Carrie Howard (Buckner) B.; A.B., Randolph-Macon Coll., 1914; student Columbia, 1914-15; m. Lillian Greyson Hoofnagle, Aug. 14, 1918; children—Mary Clark, Frank. Prin. high sch., Nansemond County, Va., 1914, supt. schs., 1916-17; sec. Va. Bd. Charities and Corrections, 1920- 23; dir. pub. welfare, Knoxville, 1923-26; asso. prof. sociology U. Va., 1926-28; commr. pub. welfare Va., 1926-32; mem. President's Emergency Employment Com., 1930-31; dir. Am. Pub. Welfare Assn., 1932-35; lectr. pub. welfare adminstrn. U. Chgo., 1932—. Cons., Fed. Emergency Relief Adminstrn., 1933, pub. welfare adminstrn. Nat. Inst. Pub. Adminstrn., 1930, Brookings Instn., 1931-35; exec. dir. Fed. Social Security Bd., 1935-38; dir. div. state and local coop., adv. commn. Council Nat. Def., 1940-41; mem. civilian protection bd. Office Civilian Def., 1941; dir. field operations OPA, 1941-42; mem. homes utilization div. Nat. Housing Authority, 1942; sec. Gov.'s Conf., 1938-59; exec. dir. Council State Govts., 1938-59; mem. adv. council Social Security, U.S. Senate Com. on Finance, 1947; dir. research fed.-state relations Com. on Orgn. exec. br. govt., 1948; chmn. cons. group med. edn. office Surg. Gen. USPHS, 1959; chmn. Adv. Commn. Intergovtl. Relations, 1959—. Served with A.C., U.S. Army, World War I. Mem. Am. Polit. Sci. Assn., Phi Kappa Sigma. Democrat. Club: Quadrangle. Contbr. to mags. Home: 2701 Connecticut Av NW Washington DC 20008 Office: Exec Office Building 17th and H Sts NW Washington DC 20009

BANE, JOHN CURRY, Jr., forging co. exec., lawyer; b. Pitts., July 23, 1904; s. John Curry and Kate Gertrude (Miller) B.; A.B., Princeton, 1925; B.A., LL.B., U. Cambridge (Eng.), 1927; LL.D., Thiel Coll., 1962; m. Sally Rawstorne, July 5, 1928. Admitted to Pa. bar, 1928, since practiced in Pitts.; partner Reed, Smith, Shaw & McClay; sec., dir. Pitts. Forgings Co. (Pa., Mich.), 1933- -, v.p., 1951—; v.p., sec., dir. Greenville Steel Car Co., 1936—; sec., counsel Neville Chem. Co., Pitts., 1944—, dir., 1951—; dir. Nat. Ben Franklin Ins. Co. Cons. in basic steel and iron ore disputes, WSB, 1952. Trustee Thiel Coll. Presbyn. Mason. Clubs: Duquesne, Pittsburgh; Capitol Hill, Metropolitan (Washington); Princeton (N.Y.C.). Home: 1204 Malvern Av Pittsburgh PA 15217 Office: Union Trust Building Pittsburgh PA 15230

BANEN, DAVID MERTON, physician; b. Kiev, USSR, June 1, 1904; s. Harry and Lena (Hecht) B.; came to U.S., 1906, naturalized, 1935; B.S., U. Ill., 1926, M.D., 1930; m. Ruth N. Schwartz, May 7, 1939; 1 dau., Elsa Harriet (Mrs. Revan A.F. Tranter). Intern, Cook County Hosp., Chgo., 1930-32; served as col., M.C., U.S. Army, 1935-38, 41-47, USPHS, 1938-41; chief of staff VA, Brockton, Mass., 1947-66; supt. Cushing Hosp., Mass. Dept. Mental Health, Framingham, 1966—; cons. Jewish Vocational Service. Mem. Mass. Commn. on Aging, 1968. Decorated Purple Heart, Bronze Star medal. Diplomate Am. Bd. Psychiatry and Nuerology. Fellow Am. Geriatric Soc., N.E. Soc. Gerontologic Psychiatry, Am. Psychiat. Assn. Jewish religion (pres., chmn. bd. temple). Contbr. articles profl. jours. Home: 41 Stanley Rd Waban MA 02168 Office: Cushing Hosp Framingham MA 01201

BANERJEE, PURNENDU KUMAR, Indian diplomat; b. Calcutta, India, Dec. 1917; s. Pramatha Nath and Amala (Mookerju) B.; student U. Calcutta, 1933-42, N.Y.U., 1952-54, Harvard, 1957-58; LL.D., W.Va. State Coll., 1965; D.C.L., Luther Coll. (Ia.), 1966; D.Litt., Whitman Coll., 1967; D.H.L., Wesleyan U. (Kan.), 1967; LL.D., Elmira Coll. 1968; D.Sc., San Fernando Valley. U., 1968. Prof. law U. Calcutta (India), 1944-48, also faculty arts, mem. Senate; v.p. Bengal Nagpur Ry. Employees Union, 1942- 46; chief editor Ry. Union Jour., 1942-46; v.p. Press Workers Union, 1942-43; bd. editors Calcutta Rev., 1945-46; with Indian Fgn. Service, 1948—, acting high commr. for India in Can., 1948-51, mem. Permanent Mission of India to UN, N.Y.C., 1951-54, dep. high commr. from India in East Pakistan, 1958-59, counsellor, charge d'affaires from India in Japan, 1959-61, minister, charge d'affaires, Peking, 1961-64; became minister Indian embassy, Washington, also ambassador from India to Costa Rica, 1964. Mem. numerous internat. confs. including UN Gen. Assembly Sessions, 1951-54, Peace Observation Commn., 1951-52, Security Council, 1951-52, UNICEF, 1953-54, Social Commn., 1953, Commn. on Information from Non-Self-Governing Ters., 1953, Econ. and Social Council, 1952-53, Human Rights Commn., 1954, Trusteeship Council, 1954, Internat. Commn. for Supervision and Control in Laos, 1954-55, UNESCO, 1956, ECAFE, 1957, Asian-African Legal Consultative Confs., 1957, 61 GATT Conf., 1959, Colombo Plan Conf., 1961, World Bank and Internat. Monetary Fund Conf., 1965, Internat. Conf. on Social Work, 1966. Recipient Padma Shri award Pres. India for meritorious work in China, 1963. Author: Pages from History, 1948; Disarmament-A Review, 1956; Certain Aspects of United Nations, 1955; Trust and Non-Self-Governing Territories, 1954; Peaceful Settlement of International Disputes, 1956. Office: Embassy of India 2107 Massachusetts Av NW Washington DC 20008

BANERJI, RANAN BIHARI, educator; b. Calcutta, India, May 5, 1928; s. Bijan Bihari and Setabja (Chaterji) B.; B.S., Patna U., 1947; M.S., Calcutta U., 1949, D.Phil., 1956; m. Purnima Purkayastha, July 8, 1954; children—Anindita, Sunandita. Came to U.S., 1961, naturalized, 1969. Research scholar Calcutta U., 1950-53, lectr., 1956; vist. asst. prof. Pa. State U., 1953- 55; maintenance engr. Indian Statis. Inst., 1956-58; mem. faculty Case Western Res. U., 1958—. prof. computer sci., 1968—; asst. prof. engring. U. New Brunswick (Can.), 1959-61; cons. in field. Patron, mem. E. Cleveland Fine Arts Assn., 1967—; mem. Heights Council Human Rights, 1967—. Gold medalist univs. Patna and Calcutta. Sr. mem. I.E.E.E.; asso. mem. Brit. Inst. Electronics and Radio Engrs.; mem. Assn. Computing Machinery, Assn. Computational Linguistics. Author: Theory of Problem Solving, 1969; also articles. Home: 965 Brunswick Rd Cleveland Heights OH 44112 Office: Case Western Reserve Univ Cleveland OH 44106

BANES, DANIEL, govt. ofcl., chemist; b. Chgo., Apr. 19, 1918; s. David and Fanny (Bornstein) B.; B.S., U. Chgo., 1938, M.S., 1940; Ph.D., Georgetown U., 1950; m. Helen Mae Richter, Apr. 6, 1941; childrenSusan Penny (Mrs. Laurence E. Harris), Elisabeth Ann (Mrs. Joseph R. Bell, Jr.), Sally Rachel. With FDA, 1939—, asso. commr. for sci., 1968-69, dir. pharm. research and testing, 1969—; adj. prof. chemistry Am. U., 1951-. Served with USAAF, 1942-46. Recipient Distinguished Service award Dept. Health, Edn. and Welfare, 1964. Mem. Am. Chem. Soc. Author: Principles of Regulatory Drug Analysis, 1968. Home: 805 Malcolm Dr Silver Spring MD 20901 Office: 200 C St SW Washington DC 20204

BANET, CHARLES HENRY, coll. pres., clergyman; b. Ft. Wayne, Ind., Dec. 8, 1922; s. Henry Alexander and Cecilia Marie (Henry) B.; A.B., St. Joseph's Coll., Renssalaer, Ind., 1950; M.A. in L.S., U. Mich., 1952; D.Litt., St. Joseph's Coll., East Chicago, Ind., 1969. Joined Soc. of Precious Blood, 1937, ordained priest Roman Cath. Ch., 1949; with Notre Dame Convent, Milw., 1949. St. Joseph's Ch., Colfax, La., 1949. St. Stephen's Ch., Toledo, 1952; librarian, dir. audio-visual instrn. St. Joseph's Coll., 1952-65, dir. libraries, 1952-65, v.p., 1964-65, pres., 1965—. Trustee St. Joseph's Coll. Bd. dirs. coll. sect. Cath. Library Assn., 1954-56, vice chmn. 1956-57, v.p., 1964-65. Mem. Am. Council Edn., Assn. Am. Colls., Nat. Cath. Edn. Assn. (dir.), N. Central Assn., Ind. Council Higher Edn., Ind. Colls. and Univs. Ind. (exec. com. 1967-69), Ind. Conf. Higher Edn. (exec. com. 1969—), Indiana Cath. Conf. (mem. edn. com. 1967—), Blue Key, Asso. Colls. Ind. (dir.), Soc. Precious Blood (dir.), Phi Kappa Phi, Beta Pi Mu. Author: Our Lady and the Precious Blood, 1962. Asso. editor Philosophy Today. Home: Saint Joseph's College Rensselaer IN 47978

BANFIELD, ARMINE FREDERICK, cons. geologist; b. Winnipeg, Man., Can., Jan. 27, 1909; s. Armine Frederick and Sarah (Boyd) B.; grad. St. John's Coll. (Can.); B.S., McGill U., 1930; M.S., Northwestern U., 1933, Ph.D. in Geology, 1940; m. Cordelia May Dunkin, Nov. 1, 1941; children—Armine Frederick, Susan Del, James Andrew, Robert Hugh. Instr. geology U. Man., 1930-31, Northwestern U., 1931-33; with Geol. Survey Can., summers 1930-32; geologist Island Lake Gold Mines, Man., 1933-35; chief geologist Beattie Gold Mines, Que., 1935-41; geologist Ventures, Ltd. and subsidiaries, 1935-41, 45; cons. geologist, Noranda, Que., 1945-46; mgr. Aruba Gold Mines, Netherlands W.I., 1947, Equatorial Mining Corp., French Guiana, 1948; cons. geologist, N.Y.C., 1948—; partner Behre Dolbear & Co.; head geol. expdn. to Galapagos Islands and Ecuador, 1953; head field group for mineral reconnaissance for Iran Govt., 1958. Mem. library bd. Engring. Socs. Library, N.Y.C., 1956-60, 60-64. Served as lt. RCAF, 1941-45. Mem. Am. Inst. Mining, Metall. and Petroleum Engrs. (exec. com. N.Y. sect. 1959-61), Am. Assn. Petroleum Geologists, Canadian Inst. Mining and Metallurgy, Soc. Econ. Geologists, Mining and Metall. Soc. Am., Am. Inst. Profl. Geologists (v.p. N.Y. sect. 1970—), Geol. Soc. Am., Instn. Mining and Metallurgy (London) (councillor, treas. 1968—), Sigma Xi. Conglist. Mason. Clubs: Mining, Explorers (N.Y.C.); Nutmeg Curling (sec., gov. 1966-70) (Darien, Conn.). Home: Westview Lane S Norwalk CT 06854 Office: 11 Broadway New York City NY 10004*

BANFIELD, EDWARD CHRISTIE, educator; b. Bloomfield, Conn., Nov. 19, 1916; s. Edward Christie and Helen (Adams) B.; A.B., Conn. State Coll., 1938; Ph.D., U. Chgo., 1951; m. Laura Fasano, Sept. 24, 1938; children—Laura, Elliott. Jr. adminstrv. asst. U.S. Forest Service, Boston, 1939-40; sec. N.H. Farm Bur. Fedn., Concord, 1940-41; successively information specialist U.S. Farm Security Adminstrn. in Upper Darby, Pa., Indpls., Washington and San Francisco, 1941-47; from instr. to asso. prof. polit. sci., U. Chgo., 1948-59; Henry Lee Shattuck prof. urban govt. Harvard, 1959—. Author: Government Project, 1951; The Moral Basis of a Backward Society, 1958; Political Influence, 1961; Big City Politics, 1965; Unheavenly City: The Nature and the Future of Our Urban Crisis, 1970 (with Martin Meyerson) Politics, Planning and the Public Interest, 1955; (with Morton Grodzins) Government and Housing in Metropolitan Areas, 1958; (with James Q. Wilson) City Politics, 1963. Editor: Urban Government: Reader in Administration and Politics, 1961, 2d edit., 1969.‡

BANG, FREDERIK BARRY, educator, physician; b. Phila., Nov. 5, 1916; s. A.F. and Carol (Klee) B.; A.B., Johns Hopkins, 1935, M.D., 1939; m. Betsy Garrett, June 1, 1940; children—Caroline Moyer, Molly Garrett, Axel Frederik. Intern U.S. Marine Hosp., Balt., 1939-40; fellow NRC, 1940-41; asst. Rockefeller Inst., Princeton, 1941-46; asst. prof. medicine Johns Hopkins, 1946-49, asso. prof., 1949—, prof. pathobiology, 1953- -. Dir. Johns Hopkins Internat. Center Med Research and Tng., Calcutta. Fulbright fellow Nat. Inst. for Med. Research, London, Eng., 1955-56; Guggenheim fellow, 1961, 64. Served with M.C., AUS, 1943-46. Mem. Am. Soc. Tropical Medicine, Interurban Clin. Club, Am. Soc. Immunologists, Am. Soc. Clin. Investigation, Am. Soc. Exptl. Pathology, Soc. Exptl. Biology and Medicine, Sigma Xi. Editor: Adv. in Virus Research. Home: 3956 Cloverhill Rd Baltimore MD 21218

BANGDIWALA, ISHVER SURCHAND, educator, statistician; b. Surat Gujarat State, India, Jan. 9, 1922; s. Surchand D. and Kamala (Jariwala) B.; B.S., U. Bombay, 1943, M.S., 1946, LL.B., 1946; M.S., U. N.C., 1950, Ph.D., 1958; m. Pushpa Sukhadia, May 2, 1947; children—Dweepkumar I., Shrikant I. Came to U.S., 1948, naturalized, 1960. Head statistics sect. and legal adviser K.A. Pandit, cons. actuary. Bombay, India, 1944-48; statistician in charge statistics sec. Agrl. Expt. Sta., U. P.R., 1952-58, subdir. research Superior Ednl. Council, U. P.R., Rio Piedras, 1958-66, lectr. statistics Inst. of Statistics, part-time, 1953-67; prof. U. P.R., 1966—; cons. statistics and research to govt., other agys. Trustee El Hogar del Nino, Cupey Alto, 1963—. Fellow Am. Statis. Assn., Inter-continental Biograph. Assn.; mem. Inst. Math. Statistics, P.R. Statis. Assn., Biometric Soc., A.A.A.S., P.R. Econ. and Statis. Assn., Am. Soc. Agrl. Sci., P.R. Tchrs. Assn., P.R. Assn. Ex-alumnae U. N.C., N.Y. Acad. Sci., Internat. Platform Assn., P.R. Statis. Soc. (founder, pres. 1968-70), Am. Acad. Polit. and Social Scis., Sigma Xi, Pi Mu Epsilon, Gamma Sigma Delta. Lion. Contbr. articles profl. jours. Address: PO Box 21648 U PR Rio Piedras PR 00931

BANGOURA, KARIM, diplomat of Guinea; b. Wonkifong, Dubreka, Guinea, July 17, 1922; ed. normal sch., Guinea. Dep. to Territorial Assembly Guinea, 1946-57; counselor to Assembly French Union, 1954-58; dir. i'Agence Guineennee de Presse, 1960; dir. cabinet ministry information and tourism, Republic Guinea, 1961-62; ambassador from Guinea to U.S., Mexico and Can., 1963-69, also to U.K., 1968-69. Served with EOR, 1942-45. Decorated cross Companions Nat. Ind. Republic Guinea. Home: 2940 Edgevale Terrace NW Washington DC 20008

BANGS, JOHN KENDRICK, lawyer, toiletries co. exec.; b. Fairfield, Ia., Nov. 7, 1920; s. William Henry and Edna (Weller) B.; A.B., U. Ia., 1942; LL.B., Columbia, 1948; m. Elizabeth Harlow, Dec. 16, 1944; childrenJohn Harlow, Amy Elizabeth, Gregory William. Admitted to N.J. bar, 1948; asso. firm Crummy & Consodine, Newark, 1948-52; atty. W.R. Grace & Co., N.Y.C., 1952-59, asst. sec., 1956-59; atty. Shulton, Inc., Clifton, N.J., 1959- -, sec., gen. counsel, 1963—, v.p., 1967—, also dir. 1969—. Served to lt. USNR, 1942-45. Mem. Sigma Nu. Republican. Lutheran. Home: 42 Hawthorne Pl Summit NJ 07901 Office: 697 Route 46 Clifton NJ 07015

BANGS, JOHN R., educator; b. Balt., Sept. 13, 1892; s. John Robert and Maria (Rippel) B.; grad. Balt. Poly. Inst., 1914; M.E., Cornell U., 1921; postgrad. Columbia and N.Y.U., 1929-30; m. Clara Margaretta Zeigler, Dec. 22, 1925; 1 dau., Mary Emilie (Mrs. Donald W. Richler). Asst. dept. shop practice Balt. Poly. Inst., 1914-15, instr. elec. engring., 1916-17; draftsman, designer, engr. Henry Smith & Son, Balt., 1918; instr. machine design Cornell U., 1919-20 instr. indsl. engring, 1921-26, asst. prof., 1926-29, prof., head dept. adminstrv. engring., 1930-43; dir. indsl., personnel relations Budd Co., Phila., 1943-57; prof. mgmt. U. Fla., 1958-63, prof. indsl. and personnel relations, 1946—, now instr. courses courses mgmt. and personnel Div. Continuing Edn., asst. coach Fla. track team. Arbitrator Fed. Mediation and Conciliation Service, currently arbitrating cases in south; cons. labor relations and edn. Detroit Edison Co. Mem. editorial and cons. staff Alexander Hamilton Inst.; tech. cons. War Manpower Commn. Mem. Am. Soc. M.E., So. Econ. Assn., Am. Mgmt. Assn., Am. Arbitration Assn. (nat. palel), Atmos, Phinx Head, Spike Shoe, Tau Beta Pi, Phi Kappa Phi, Kappa Tau Chi. Club: Gainsville Golf and Country. Author: Factory Management, 1929; Industrial Accounting for Executives, 1930; Business and Industrial Management, 1934, rev. edit., 1941; (with G.R. Hanselman) Accounting for Engineers, 1941; (with James W. Townsend) The Implications for Executives in the 1947 Labor-Management Relations Act, 1947; Plant Management, 1955; (with William V. Wilmot) Plant Management, 1963, Collective Bargaining, 1964; The Future of Collective Bargaining in the U.S., 1963; Labor's Goal for 64-more money, 1963; also author of booklets, privately printed. Editor: (with L.P. Alford): Prodn. Handbook, 1944; cons. and contbg. editor Personnel Handbook 1955, 58. Contbr. articles to profl. jours. Home: 1839 N W 31st Terrace Gainsville FL 32601

BANISTER, JOHN ROBERT, librarian; b. Saginaw, Mich., Feb. 5, 1912; s. John Lansing and Agnes (Bell) B.; A.A., Bay City (Mich.) Jr. Coll., 1934; A.B., U. Mich., 1936; B.S. in L.S., U. Ill., 1937; m. Nancy Simpson, Sept. 9, 1944; 1 dau., Nancy Anne (Mrs. Edmund Alan Attebury, Jr.). Asst. reference librarian Mich. State Library, Lansing 1936- 41; order librarian, tech. library TVA, 1942-44; extension librarian Lansing Pub. Library, 1944-46; regional librarian Ill. State Library, Mt. Carmel, 1946-48; pub. library cons. gen. extension div. U. Fla., 1948-50; dir. libraries Chattahooches Valley Regional Library, Columbus, Ga., 1951—; cons. in field, 1960—. Del. Assembly Libraries of Ams., 1946; chmn. jr. mems. round table Mich. Library Assn., 1941, Ill. Library Assn., 1946. Chmn. Muscogee County (Ga.) chpt. Am. Heart Assn., 1952, Community Services Assn. Columbus, 1956-58; bd. dirs. Columbus Symphony Guild, 1962—, Columbus United Givers, 1957-59. Mem. Am. (council 1940-41, chmn. jr. mems. round table 1946), Ga. (v.p. 1960), Southeastern (chmn. pub. libraries sect, 1948) library assns. Presbyn. Rotarian (dir. Columbus 1963—), Club: Columbus Country. Editor: The Junior Librarian, 1939-41; The Florida Public Library News-Letter, 1948-50. Contbr. articles to profl. jours. Home: 2952 Roswell Lane Columbus GA 31906 Office: W C Bradley Mem Library Columbus GA 31906

BANK, MERRILL LEE, paper products co. exec.; b. Balt., Feb. 5, 1915 s. Simon P. and Rose (Fox) B.; student Balt. City Coll., 1932; m. Helen Shapiro, Nov. 29, 1936; children—Herbert, Phyllis, Marjorie. With Md. Cup Corp., Owings Mills, Md., 1949—, exec. v.p., 1961—, vice chmn. bd., 1961—; dir. Union Trust Co. of Md., Sweetheart Plastics Ltd., Fareham, Eng.; Strike-Rite Matches, Ltd., London, Ont., Can., Hygienic Drinking Straws Co., Ltd., Bristol, Eng. Bd. dirs. Sinai Hosp., Balt. Mem. Chief Exec. Forum. Home: 6701 Park Heights Av Baltimore MD 21215 Office: Maryland Cup Corp Owings Mills MD 21117

BANK, THEODORE PAUL, Jr., anthropologist; b. Patterson, La., Aug. 31, 1923; s. Theodore Paul and Madlyn (Huber) B.; student (Harvard Club scholar) Harvard, 1941-43; B.S. in Forestry, U. Mich., 1947, M.S. in Ethnobotany, 1950, postgrad. anthropology, 1947-53; m. Janet Fowler, Sept. 1948 (div. Oct. 1953); 1 son, Theodore Paul; m. 2d, Shirley Waterman, May 1954 (div. Oct. 1962); m. 3d, Trina Paula Lindenstein, Apr. 10, 1963; 1 dau., Kristin Kara. Field dir. Aleutian-Bering Sea Expdns., U. Mich. and U.S. Office Naval Research, 1949-55; research asso. Mus. Anthropology, U. Mich., 1956- 57; exec. dir. Am. Inst. Exploration, Inc., Ann Arbor, Mich., Chgo., San Francisco, 1954—; asst. prof. anthropology Chgo. Tchrs. Coll. N., 1961- 63; social research analyst Agnews State Hosp., San Jose, Cal., 1964-65; vis. lectr. anthropology Coll. San Mateo, Cal., 1965-66; asst. prof. anthropology Seven Seas div. Chapman Coll., 1967; asst. prof. social sci. Western Mich U., Kalamazoo, 1967—, exec. producer ednl. TV series on non-Western World, 1968-69; conducted anthrop. expeditions to Argentina and West Africa, 1967; expdns. to Aleutian Islands, 1969-71; dir. Aleutian Insts. Program, 1969—; lectr. various univs. U.S. and abroad. Chmn. U.S. Com. for Clark Meml. Student Center, Hokkaido U., 1958-60. Asso., Current Anthropology, 1968—. Served with USNR, 1945-46. Fulbright research scholar, vis. lectr. anthropology Hokkaido (Japan) U., 1955-56. Trustee Am. Inst. for Exploration, Inc. Fellow A.A.A.S., Am. Anthrop. Assn.; mem. Pacific Sci. Assn. (chmn. sub- com. ethnobotany 1954-57), Soc. Am. Archaeology, Am. Ecol. Soc., Polar Soc., Asia Soc., Japan Soc., Nature Conservancy, Japan- Am. Soc. Sapporo, Internat. Platform Assn., Sigma Xi, Phi Sigma. Club: Explorers (N.Y.C.). Author: Birthplace of the Winds, 1956; Student Manual for Cultural Anthropology, 1966; Readings in Anthropology, 1971. Contbg. editor: Explorers Journal, 1959- -. Contbr. articles Alaska, Aleutian Islands, Japan and others to various pubs. Home: 1809 Nichols Road Kalamazoo MI 49007

BANKART, HENRY REGINALD, ret. advt. exec.; b. Schenectady, Apr. 6, 1913; s. Henry and Marjorie (Hickok) B.; A.B., Dartmouth, 1935; student Mass. Sch. Art, 1936-37; m. Barbara Ganteaume, Aug. 27, 1938; children—Beverly, Marilyn, Henry Reginald III. Prodn. foreman, designer Hood Rubber Co., 1937-39; salesman Wearever Aluminum Cooking Utensil Co., 1940-41; advt., sales promotion Liberty Mut. Ins. Co., 1941-42; staff art dept. Compton Advt., N.Y.C., 1946-47, account exec., 1947-65, v.p., 1952-65, dir., 1955-65, sr. v.p., 1960-65, chmn. marketing plans bd., mgmt. supr., 1963-65; sr. v.p. Sullivan, Stauffer, Colwell & Bayles, Inc., N.Y.C., 1965-71, also dir. Served as lt. USNR, 1942-45. Clubs: Dartmouth (pres. 1956-57) (N.Y.C.); Scarsdale. (N.Y.) Golf. Home: 29 Walworth Av Scarsdale NY 10583

BANKER, BROOKS, financial co. exec.; b. N.Y.C., Oct. 28, 1929; s. Leslie Avery and Frances Almyra (Klingemann) B.; A.B., Yale, 1952; LL.B., Harvard, 1957; m. Carol Billings, May 7, 1954; children—Brooks, Carol, Derek, Laurens. With Chem. Bank N.Y. Trust Co., 1947-60, Am. Express Co., 1960—, treas., 1964-66, v.p., 1966-68, exec. v.p., treas., 1968-; pres. Uni- Serv Corp., 1966-69; chmn. Am. Express Credit Corp., N.Y.C., 1969—. Served to 1st lt. USAF, 1952-54. Home: 104 Silverside Av Little Silver NJ 07739 Office: 65 Broadway New York City NY 10006

BANKER, GILBERT STEPHEN, educator; b. Tuxedo Park, N.Y., Sept. 12, 1931; s. Gilbert Miller and Mary Edna (Gladstone) B.; B.S. in Pharmacy, Union U., 1953; M.S., Purdue U., 1955, Ph.D., 1957; m. Gwenivere May Hughes, Mar. 31, 1956; children—Stephen Robert, Susan Renae, David Wayne, William Gilbert. Research Found. fellow Purdue U., 1956-57, mem. faculty, 1957—, prof. pharmacy, 1964—, head dept. indsl. and phys. pharmacy, 1966—; cons. Eli Lilly Lab., 1963-70, Rowell Labs., 1962-63. Coop. Sci. Program fellow Upjohn Co., 1958; recipient 1st Lederle Pharmacy Faculty award research, 1961; award advancement indsl. pharmacy Searle Co., 1971. Fellow Acad. Pharm. Scis.; mem. Am. (1st v.p. 1964, chmn. indsl. pharm. tech. sect. 1968, vice chmn. acad. 1970-71), Ind. pharm. assns., Am. Chem. Soc., A.A.A.S., Sigma Xi, Rho Chi (exec. council 1964-66), Kappa Psi, Phi Lambda Upsilon. Rotarian, Elk. Co-author: Advances in Pharmaceutical Sciences, 1964. Contbr. articles profl. jours. Patentee in field. Home: 1210 Western Dr Lafayette IN 47906

BANKER, PAUL ALBERT, newspaper editor; b. Middletown, O., Jan. 30, 1921; s. Paul Jacob and Alfretta (Wilcox) B.; B.A., Yale, 1942; m. Martha Carey, Sept. 5, 1942; childrenNancy Carey, Carol Anne. Mem. staff Balt. Sun, 1945-48, asst. city editor, 1948-54, city editor, 1954-66, chief Rome (Italy) bur., 1960-62, mng. editor, 1966—; v.p. A.S. Abell Co., 1969—. Served to lt. USNR, 1942-45. Mem. Alpha Sigma Phi. Home: 1116 Bellemore Rd Baltimore MD 21210 Office: AS Abell Co Calvert and Centre Sts Baltimore MD 21202

BANKHEAD, WALTER WILL, lawyer; b. Jasper, Ala., July 21, 1897; s. John H., Jr. and Musa (Harkins) B.; A.B., U. Ala., 1919, LL.B., 1920; m. Emelil Crumpton, June 5, 1920; children—Blossom B. (Mrs. Olen A. Dill), Marion B. (Mrs. W.A. Grant), Barbara B. (Mrs. John T. Oliver, Jr.), John H. Admitted to Ala. bar, 1920, since practiced in Jasper. Chmn. bd. Bankhead Mining Co., Inc., Bankhead Devel. Co., Inc., TRI W Broadcasting, Inc., Franklin Broadcasting, Inc., Bankhead Broadcasting Co., Inc.; vice chmn. bd. First Nat. Bank, Jasper. Mem. U.S. Ho. of Reps., 1941. Mem. Sigma Alpha EpsilonÂMethodist. Mason (Shriner). Clubs: Musgrove Country (Jasper), Downtown (Birmingham, Ala.). Home: 811 8th Av Jasper AL 35501 Office: PO Box 1629 Jasper AL 35501

BANKS, ELOISE HARDISON, (Mrs. Edward Banks), publisher, editor; b. Indpls., July 24, 1926; d. Otho and Hattie (Yateman) Hardison; B.A., Ind. Central Coll., 1947; M.A., Ariz. State U., 1953; m. Edward Banks, Dec. 27, 1957 (dec. Oct. 1969). Tchr. English, Julian Elementary Sch., Alhambra High Sch. Phoenix, 1950-70; co-pub., asso. editor weekly Ariz. Tribune, Phoenix, 1958-69, pub., editor, 1969—. Del. S.W. regional implementation council White House Conf. Children; mem. pub. information and pub. affairs unit White House Conf. Aging; mem. adult task force delegation White House Conf. Youth; mem. Phoenix Citizens Commn., Valley Forward Com. Sec. Republican Women in Black Affairs, 1970-71; mem. Cactus Wrens Rep. Women, 1970—, pub. relations officer, 1971—. Bd. dirs. Ariz. Tb and Respiratory Disease Assn.; mem. Phoenix aux. Heard Museum. Mem. Ariz. Mental Health Assn., Phoenix Urban League, N.A.A.C.P., Phoenix C. of C., Nat. Newspaper Pubs. Assn. (bd. dirs. 1970-71), Ariz. Newspaper Assn., League Bus. and Profl. Women, Nat., Ariz. edn. assns., Nat. Media Women, Theta Sigma Phi. Club: University (Phoenix). Home: 2137 E Broadway Rd Phoenix AZ 85040 Office: PO Box 8248 Phoenix AZ 85040

BANKS, EPHRAIM, educator; b. Norfolk, Va., Apr. 21, 1918; s. Israel and Ada (Gesunsky) B.; B.S., Coll. City N.Y., 1937; Ph.D., Bklyn. Poly. Inst., 1949; m. Libby Kohl, Mar. 17, 1945; children—Thomas Israel, Jay Lewis. Various positions to jr. metallurgist U.S. Naval Shipyard, Bklyn., 1938-46; with Poly. Inst. Bklyn., 1946—, prof., 1958—. Head dept. chemistry, 1968—; cons. chemistry and electronics to corps. Served with USNR, 1944-46. Weizmann fellow, 1963-64; Nat. Sci. Found. faculty fellow, 1971-72. Fellow A.A.A.S.; mem. Am. Chem. Soc., Am. Phys. Soc., Am. Crystallog. Assn., Mineralog. Soc., Electrochem. Soc., N.Y. Acad. Sci. Editor: (with others) Structure Reports, 1963; asso. editor of Jour. Electrochem. Soc., 1957—; editorial bd. of Jour. Solid State Chemistry, 1969—. Research on solid state chemistry, crystal growth, magnetic materials, luminescence. Home: 2307 Stuart St Brooklyn NY 11229

BANKS, ERNEST, baseball athlete; b. Dallas, Jan. 31, 1931; s. Eddie Banks; grad. high sch.; m. Mollye Louise Ector, Apr. 6, 1953. Player with Kansas City Monarchs, Negro Am. League, 1950-51, 53; shortstop, then 1st baseman Chgo. Cubs, 1953—; formerly co-owner, v.p. Bob Nelson-Ernie Banks Ford, Inc., Chgo. Mem. bd. Chgo. Transit Authority, 1969—. Active Boy Scouts Am., YMCA. Served with AUS, 1951-53; Europe. Named most valuable player Nat. League, 1958, 59; played in 13 All Star Games; holds nat. record for Grand Slam home runs; recipient awards from Fans, 1969, Press Club, 1969, Jr. C. of C., 1971; named to Tex. Sports Hall Fame, 1971. Republican. Author: Mr. Cub. Address: 8159 S Rhodes Chicago IL 60619*

BANKS, FRANK ARTHUR hotel mgr.; b. Bronx, N.Y., Aug. 12, 1932; s. Arthur and Francis (Calter) B.; B.A., Mich. State U., 1961, M.B.A., 1962; m. Claire Loveland, June 10, 1957; children—Laura, Diane, Suzanne. Food and beverage controller Sheraton Motor Inn, N.Y.C., 1962-63; exec. asst. mgr. Sheraton Biltmore, Providence, 1963-66; resident mgr. St. Regis Sheraton, N.Y.C., 1966-68; v.p., mgr. Waldorf-Astoria, N.Y.C., 1968—. Treas. Hotel and Motel Expn., 1970. Served with USNR, 1950-54. Named hotelman of the year, Mich. State U., 1961, alumnus of the year, 1970. Mem. Chain de Rotesserie, Hotel Execs. Club N.Y., Culinary Inst. Am. (dir.), Mich. State U. Alumni Assn., Sigma Pi Eta. Mason. Address: Waldorf-Astoria Hotel 301 Park Av New York City NY 10022

BANKS, HARLAN PARKER, educator; b. Cambridge, Mass., Sept. 1, 1913; s. Carl T. and Hazel (Cummings) B.; A.B., Dartmouth, 1934; Ph.D., Cornell U., 1940; m. Rosamond L. Shurtleff, Dec. 23, 1939; children—Jane Ann, Susan Elizabeth. Instr. botany Dartmouth, 1934-36; asst. botany Cornell U., 1937-39; instr., 1939-40, asso. prof., 1949-50, prof., 1950—, head dept. botany, 1952-61; instr. biology Acadia U., Wolfville, N.S., 1940- 41, asst. prof., 1941-43, asso. prof., 1943-47; asst. prof. botany U. Minn., 1947-49; dir. Summer Inst. Botany, Cornell, 1956, 57; lectr. A.I.B.S. Vis. Biologists program, 1969-70, 71—. Fulbright research scholar U. Liege, 1957-58; Guggenheim fellow, 1963-64; fellow Clare Hall, Cambridge U., 1968—. Fellow A.A.A.S.; mem. Bot. Soc. Am. (treas. 1964-67, pres. 1969), Internat. Soc. Plant Morphology, Torrey Bot. Club, Internat. Assn. Plant Taxonomists, Internat. Orgn. Paleobotany (v.p. 1964-69, pres. 1969—), Societe Geologique de Belgique, Phi Kappa Phi, Sigma Xi. Mem. editorial bd. Plant Sci. Bull., 1953—, Rev. Paleobotany and Palynology, 1968—. Home: 1005 Highland Rd Ithaca NY 14850

BANKS, HAROLD, newspaper columnist. Columnist Boston Record Am. and Advertiser. Office: Hearst Corp 5 Winthrop Sq Boston MA 02106*

BANKS, JOHN HOUSTON, educator; b. Ripley, Tenn., Feb. 9, 1911; s. Roderick Stanton and Ella Celestine (Sinclair) B.; B.S., Tenn. Poly. Inst., 1935; M.A., George Peabody Coll. Tchrs., 1938, Ph.D., 1949; m. Mary Rhea Fowler, Mar. 11, 1933; children—John Fowler, Betty Rhea. Tchr., Tenn. pub. schs., 1934- 42; instr. 133d Army Tng. Detachment, 1942-44; dean East Central Jr. Coll., Decatur, Miss., 1944-46; prof. math. Florence (Ala.) State Coll., 1946-49; asso. prof. math. George Peabody Coll. Tchrs., Nashville, 1949-58, prof. math., 1958—, chmn. dept., 1959—; vis. prof. edn. Auburn U., 1956, New Brunswick (Can.) U., 1960. Adviser Am. Council Edn., 1960—; cons. AID/ROCAP Textbook Project in C.Am., 1964-70. Mem. Tenn. Math. Tchrs. Assn. (pres. 1954), Nat. Council Tchrs. Math. (dir. 1960-63), Tenn. Acad. Scis., Nat. Tenn. edn. assns., Math. Assn. Am., Sigma Xi, Kappa Delta Pi, Phi Delta Kappa, Pi Mu Epsilon. Author: Elements of Mathematics, 3d edit., 1969; Learning and Teaching Arithmetic, 2d edit., 1964; (with A. Wheeler) Teachers Question and Answer Book on Arithmetic, 1960; (with F.L. Wren) Elements of Algebra, 1962; (with Sobel and Walsh) Algebra: Its Elements and Structure, 1965, 2d edit., 1971; (with Butler and Wren) The Teaching of Secondary Mathematics, 5th edit., 1970. Home: 3708 Lealand Lane Nashville TN 37204

BANKS, JOHN VALLERY, mfg. exec.; b. Boise, Ida., Jan. 17, 1917; s. Frank Arthur and Theodora (Drummond) B.; B.C.E., U. Ida., 1938; m. Beatrice Jane Fisher, Feb. 7, 1938; children—Jan T., T., Catherine K., Becky J., Elisabeth V. Constrn. engr. Pacific Constructors, Inc., Shasta Dam, Cal., 1938-40; profl. structural engr., asso. Donald Stewart, Vancouver, Wash., 1945-46; various engring., mfg. positions Kaiser Motors Corp., Willow Run, since 1946, v.p. charge mfg.; prodn. mgr. Kaiser Steel Fabricating div., Los Angeles; now exec. v.p. Nat. Steel & Shipbldg. Co., San Diego. Served as capt. C.E., U.S. Army, 1940-45. Mem. Soc. Naval Architects and Marine Engrs., Structural Engrs. Assn. of Cal., Am. Bureau of Shipping. Club: Propeller of U.S. Contbr. articles to profl. publs. Home: 6041 Camino de la Costa La Jolla CA 92037 Office: Nat Steel & Shipbuilding Co 28th St and Harbor Dr San Diego CA 92113

BANKS, JOSEPH EUGENE, investment economist; b. Kirksville, Mo., Jan. 26, 1908; s. Charles and Etta May (Dille) B.; B.S. Washington U., 1930; m. Ruth Henckier, Oct. 1, 1932; m. 2d, Barbara H. Vietor, Apr. 21, 1956; 1 foster dau., Diana. Investment analyst Boatmen's Nat. Bank, St. Louis, 1930-31; mgr. pvt. investment funds, St. Louis, 1932-37; market analyst Merrill Lynch, Pierce, Fenner & Beane, N.Y.C., 1938-42; investment economist Brown Bros. Harriman & Co., N.Y.C., 1942, 45—, asst. mgr., 1950-57, mgr., 1957-61, partner, 1962—, head instnl. brokerage div., 1950—. Trustee, Tchrs. Coll. Columbia U., Trinity Ch. Assn. Served to lt. comdr. USCGR, 1942-45. Mem. Am. Econ. Assn., Soc. Security Analysts, Mil. Order World Wars, Theta Xi. Episcopalian (vestry). Clubs: University, Downtown Assn. (N.Y.C.). Author: Guides to Stock Market Policy, 1949; Institutional Investment Guides, 1955, Guides to Growth Stock Investing, 1959; also articles in field. Home: 880 Fifth Av New York City NY 10021 also Long Beach Rd Saint James NY 11780 Office: Brown Bros Harriman & Company 59 Wall Street New York City NY 10005

BANKS, LAWRENCE HAMILTON, chemist, educator; b. Chicago, 1928; B.S. in Physics, Yale, 1950; Ph.D. in Chemistry, Harvard, 1956; m. Sally Ann Jones, July 5, 1957; children--Kenneth J., Nancy A. Chemist, Acme Chem. Co., Blue Island, Ill., 1950-51; director of Reseach Lab., Indsl. Chemicals Corp., Cambridge, Mass., 1956-60; project coordinator environmental sect. Steinmetz Assos., Chgo., 1960-61; v.p. for reseach Bauer Bros. Chem. Co., Inc., Memphis, 1961-64; asst. prof. chemistry Washington U., St. Louis, 1964-66, asso. prof., 1966-70, prof., 1970--, head of chemistry dept., 1970-71. Vis. prof. So. Ill. U., summer 1967, U. of Ore., 1969. Scoutmaster, Boy Scouts America, University City, Mo., 1968-70. Bd. dirs. Rest Haven Home for Elderly, 1960-61; trustee of the Lutheran Hosp., 1965-71. Served from lt. to capt., AUS, 1951-53. Mem. Am. Chem. Soc., Sci. Research Soc. Am. (chpt. treas. 1967), Sigma Xi. Author: (with others) Basic Inorganic Chemistry, 1971. Contbr. articles to profl. jours., encys., also chpts. to books. Home: Fairfax Apts 7291 Windermere Dr University City MO 63105 Office: Dept Chemistry Washington University St Louis MO 63130

BANKS, LOUIS LAYTON, editor; b. Pitts., June 17, 1916; s. Louis Layton and Laura S. (Shrom) B.; A.B., U. Cal. at Los Angeles, 1937, postgrad., 1938-40; Nieman fellow Harvard, 1969-70; m. Mary Margaret Campbell, Apr. 21, 1945; children—Robert, William, Theodore, Margaret. Contbg. and asso. editor Time mag., 1950-54, nat. affairs editor, 1955-61; asst. mng. editor Fortune mag., 1961-64, exec. editor, 1964-65, mng. editor, 1965-70; editorial dir. Time Inc., 1970—. Served as naval aviator, USNR, 1941-45. Clubs: University (N.Y.C.); Larchmont (N.Y.) Yacht. Home: Mamaroneck NY 10543 Office: Time and Life Building New York City NY 10020

BANKS, ROBERT BLACKBURN, found. ofcl.; b. Wichita, Kan., Oct. 12, 1922; s. Bernard T. and Georgia (Corley) B.; B.S., Northwestern U., 1947, M.S., 1948; Ph.D. (Hilp fellow), U. Cal., 1951; D.I.C., U. London, 1952; m. Gunta Matisons, December 25, 1960; children—Steven, Erik. Research engr. U. Cal., 1949- 51, Infilco, Inc., Tucson, 1952-54; asso. prof. civil engring. Northwestern Univ., 1954-59, chmn. sci.-engring. com., 1955-57, chmn. dept. civil engring., 1956-59, asst. dean research and grad. studies, prof. engring. sci., 1959-61; dean engring. U. Ill., Chgo., 1963-67; adviser sci. and engring. Ford Found., Mexico and C.Am., 1967—; vis. prof. Grad. Sch. Engring., Nat. Univ. of Mexico, 1967—; dir. of research SEATO Grad. Sch. Engring., Bangkok, Thailand, 1961-63. Cons., McDonnell Aircraft Corp., 1958, Space Tech. Labs, Inc., 1960. Served from ensign to lt. (j.g.), USNR, 1943-46. Fulbright fellow, 1951- 52. Mem. Am. Inst. Aeros. and Astronautics, Am. Soc. C.E., Internat. Hydraulics Research Assn., A.A.A.S., Am. Geophys. Union, Am. Soc. Engring. Edn., Sigma Xi, Tau Beta Pi, Pi Mu Epsilon, Delta Nu Alpha, Sigma Chi. Home: Meseta 111 Pedregal Mexico 20 DF Mexico Office: Ford Found Reforma 243 Mexico 5 D F Mexico

BANKS, RUSSELL, chem. corp. exec.; b. N.Y.C., Aug. 2, 1919; s. Thomas and Fay (Cowen) B.; B.B.A., Coll. City N.Y., 1936-40; LL.B., N.Y. Law Sch., 1960; m. Janice Reed, July 19, 1949; children—Gordon, L. Banks. Sr. accountant Selverne, Davis Co., N.Y.C., 1940-45; pvt. practice as C.P.A., N.Y.C., 1945-61; admitted to N.Y. bar, 1961, since practiced law, N.Y.C.; exec. v.p. Met. Telecommunications Corp., Plainview, N.Y., 1961-62; pres. Grow Chem. Corp., N.Y.C., 1962—, also dir. Trustee Am. Place Theatre, Inc., N.Y.C. C.P.A., N.Y. Mem. Am. Bar Assn., N.Y. Soc. C.P.A.'s, Am. Mgmt. Assn. (gen. mgmt. planning council 1966—), Phi Delta Phi. Home: 1000 Park Avenue New York City NY 10028 also Pawling NY Office: 345 Park Avenue New York City NY 10022

BANKS, SAM WALLACE, physician; b. Salisbury, N.C., June 10, 1905; s. Louis and Hannah (Spiegel) B.; B.S., U. Chgo., 1930, M.D., 1934; m. May Pope Thompson, Dec. 24, 1930 (dec.); m. 2d, Ruth G. Ohlin July 11, 1964. Intern Michael Reese Hosp., Chgo., 1935-36; resident orthopaedic surgery U. Chgo., 1937-41; practice medicine, specializing orthopaedic surgery, Chgo., 1941-71, Sun City, Ariz., 1971—; staff Chgo. Wesley Meml. Hosp.; asso. prof. orthopaedic surgery Northwestern U., 1952-71. Past pres. adv. bd. Med. Specialties, Inc. Served from capt. to lt. col. AUS, 1942-46. Diplomate Am. Bd. Orthopaedic Surgery (sec.- treas. 1956-62). Fellow A.C.S.; mem. A.M.A., Chgo. Med. Soc., Am. Orthopaedic Assn. (sec. 1963-66), Am. Acad. Orthopaedic Surgeons, Clin. Orthopaedic Soc., Chgo. Orthopaedic Soc. (pres. 1952-53), Chgo. Surg. Soc., Chgo. Com. Trauma (chmn. 1954-66). Author: (with Dr. Harold Laufman) An Atlas of Surgical Exposure of the Extremities, 1954; (with others) Pictorial Handbook of Fracture Treatment, rev. edit., 1963. Home: 10705 Buccaneer Way Sun City AZ 85351 Office: care Lakeview Medical Arts Bldg 13200 N 103d Av Sun City AZ 85351

BANKS, SEYMOUR, advt. exec.; b. Chgo., Oct. 3, 1917; s. Louis and Dorothy (Hass) B.; student No. Ill. State Tchrs. Coll., 1934-36; B.S. in Chem. Engring., Ia. State Coll., 1939; M.B.A., U. Chgo., 1940, Ph.D. Swift Consumer Preference Measurement and Laminated Paperboard fellows), 1949; m. Miriam Gollub, Jan. 30, 1949; children—Hannah L., Joel A., David E. Elec. testing asst. Prest-O-Lite Storage Battery, Speedway, Ind., 1939-40; metall. observer Gary Works, Carnegie-Ill. Steel Corp., 1940-42; asso. prof. De Paul U. Coll. Commerce, Chgo., 1946-51; with research and media depts. Leo Burnett Co., Inc., Chgo., 1951—, v.p., 1955—; lectr. U. Chgo., 1960—; vis. prof. advt. Mich. State U., U. Ill., 1970. Vice chmn. Hyde Park-Kenwood Community Conf., 1962-65; pres. Ray Sch. P.T.A., Chgo., 1965-67; mem. citizens' com. U. Ill., 1970—. Bd. dirs. Citizens Schs. Com., Chgo. Served with AUS, 1942-46. Mem. Am. Marketing Assn. (pres. Chgo. chpt. 1954-55, v.p. marketing research div. 1964-65, chmn. ethics com. 1969—), Am. Statis. Assn., Am. Psychol. Assn., Advt. Research Found. (chmn. tech. com.). Author: Experimentation in Marketing, 1965; also articles. Home: 5625 S Blackstone Av Chicago IL 60637 Office: Prudential Plaza Chicago IL 60601

BANKS, TALCOTT MINER, lawyer; b. Englewood, N.J., June 23, 1905; s. Talcott M. and Olive H.S. (Dawes) B.; grad. Hotchkiss Sch., Lakeville, Conn., 1924; A.B., Williams Coll., 1928; LL.B., Harvard, 1931; LL.D., Northeastern U., 1971; m. Kathleen Macy Hall, July 23, 1935 (dec. 1966); children—Ridgway, Oliver, Helen M.; m. 2d, Ann Smith Monks, June 23, 1967 (dec. 1969). Pres. Nat. Intercollegiate Lawn Tennis Assn., 1927-28; editorial staff Time mag., 1930; admitted to Mass. bar, 1931; asso. firm Palmer & Dodge, and predecessors, Boston, 1931-41, mem., 1944—; gen. counsel Bd. Investigation and Research, Washington. 1941-44; dir. Comstock & Wescott, Inc. Pres. Sterling and Francine Clark Art Inst.; trustee The Fessenden Sch., Cultural Found. Boston, Williams Coll., New Eng. Conservatory Music, WGBH Ednl. Found.; hon. pres. Boston Opera Assn., Inc.; pres. Boston Symphony Orch. Mem. Am. (chmn. spl. com. on securities laws and regulations 1940-42), Mass., Boston bar assns., Am. Law Inst., Am. Judicature Soc., Boston Legal Aid Soc. (dir.); Phi Beta Kappa, Kappa Alpha. Unitarian. Clubs: University (N.Y.C.); Boston Yacht, Badminton and Tennis, St. Botolph (pres. 1949-53) (Boston); Cruising of Am.; Am. Alpine; Somerset. Contbr. articles legal periodicals, mags. Home: Bedford Road Lincoln MA 01773 Office: 28 State St Boston MA 02109

BANKS, VIRGINIA, artist; b. Norwood, Mass., Jan. 12, 1920; d. Henry Lewis and Ottilie (Rietzel) Banks; A.B., Smith Coll., 1941; M.A., State U. Ia., 1944; m. Arthur W. Freidinger, Jan. 1, 1946. One man shows include Grand Central Moderns, N.Y.C., 1950, 52, 56, 59, 65, Dusanne Gallery, Seattle, 1952, 58, Collectors Gallery, Bellevue, Wash., 1965; exhbt. nat. and internat. shows, 1946-; rep. permanent collections U. Ill., Seattle Art Mus., IBM Coll., U. Ore., San Francisco Mus. Art, Springfield (Mo.) Art Mus., Davenport (Ia.) Municipal Art Gallery, Plattsburg (N.Y.) State Tchrs. Coll., State U. Ia., Univ. of Notre Dame, Cornell U.; instr. art State U. Iowa, 1942-47, Albright Art Sch., 1947-48, U. Buffalo, 1947-48, N.Y. State Tchrs. Coll., 1947-48, U. Wash., 1949, Cornish Art Sch., Seattle, 1951-52. Area chmn. capital campaign Smith Coll., 1968-70. Recipient award Pepsi-Cola Competition, 1948, Hallmark Internat. Art award, 1949. Mem. Alpha Phi Kappa Psi, Pi Lambda Theta. Clubs: Smith College (pres. 1960-61, hon. bd. mem. 1967-68) (Seattle). Address: 3879 51st Avenue N E Seattle, WA 98105.

BANKS, WILLIAM VENOID, broadcasting co. exec.; b. Geneva, Ky., May 6, 1903; s. Richard Dentis and Clara Ann (Barnett) B.; LL.B., Detroit Coll. Law, 1929, D.D., 1966, LL.D., 1968; m. Ivy Burt, June 24, 1964; children—Tenicia Gregory, Harumi, Altereo. Admitted to Mich. bar, 1931; since practiced in Detroit; pres. radio sta. WGPR, Detroit, 1962—. Mem. Republican State Central Com., 1970—. Mem. N.A.A.C.P. Baptist. Mason (supreme grand master 1950—). Home: 17220 Ponchatrain Dr Detroit MI 48204 Office: 2101 Gratiot Detroit MI 48207

BANNAN, THOMAS JOSEPH, machinery mfr.; b. San Francisco, May 22, 1901; s. Philip Laurence and Teresa (Kelley) B.; B.S., U. Santa Clara, 1923; m. Arline F. Spaulding, Sept. 24, 1938; 1 dau., Adele Kathleen. With Pacific Gear & Tool Works, San Francisco, 1919-29, pres., 1945—; mgr. Western Gear Works, Seattle, 1929-45; pres. Western Gear Corp. (formerly Western Gear Works), 1945-63, chmn. 1963-71, hon. chmn., 1971—; dir. Pacific Nat. Bank, Seattle. Bd. regents Seattle U. Mem. Am. Gear Mfrs. Assn. (past pres.), Wash. Metal Trades Assn. (pres. 1935-39), C. of C. (dir.), Assn. Washington Industries (past dir.), N.A.M. Clubs: Washington Athletic, Rainier, Seattle Tennis (Seattle): California (Los Angeles); Eldorado Country, Committee of Twentyfive (Palm Springs, Cal.). Home: 875 Comstock Av Los Angeles CA 90024 Office: Post Office Box 182 Lynwood CA 90262

BANNARD, WILLIAM NEWELL III, investment banker; b. Hazelton, Pa., June 12 1918; s. William Newell, Jr. and Emily (Markle) B.; grad. Hill Sch., 1937; B.A., Yale, 1941; m. Marion H. Sutphen, Oct. 22, 1942; children—Marie S. (Mrs. William Carter), David N., Barbara M. With Graham, Parsons & Co., N.Y.C., 1946-50; v.p., chmn. exec. com. Am. Securities Corp., 1950—, now exec. v.p., dir. Trustee Huntington Hosp. Served with USNR, 1942-46. Decorated Silver Star. Mem. Investment Bankers Assn. Am., Nat. Assn. Dealers (vice chmn. dist. bd.), N.Y. Soc. Security Analysts, Kappa Beta (mem. council), Chi Psi. Clubs: Huntington Country (dir.); Bond (gov.) (N.Y.C.); Mid-Ocean. Home: White Hill Rd Cold Spring Harbor NY 11724 Office: 25 Broad St New York City NY 10004

BANNER, BOB, television producer-dir.; b. Ennis, Tex., Aug. 15, 1921; s. Robert James and Viola (Culbertson) B.; B.B.A., So. Meth. U., 1943; M.A., Northwestern U., 1948; m. Alice Jane Baird, Jan. 14, 1946; children—Baird Allen, Robert James, Charles Moore. Faculty, Northwestern U., 1947-49; dir. Garroway-at-Large, NBC-TV, 1949-50, producer, dir. Nothing but the Best, 1953, Dinah Shore Chevy Show, 1954-58, Fred Waring Show, CBS-TV, 1950-52; dir. Omnibus, 1953-54; TV producer, pres. Bob Banner Assos.; TV shows include Garry Moore Show, Candid Camera, Carol Burnett Show, Carnegie Hall Salutes Jack Benny, Julie and Carol at Carnegie Hall, Carol and Company, Jimmy Dean Show, The Entertainers, Here's Peggy Fleming, The Kraft Music Hall, John Davidson Specials, Features-Warning Shot; movie for TV, My Sweet Charlie. Recipient Emmy award for best direction TV, 1957. Mem. of Acad. of TV Arts and Scis. Presbyn. Home: Roland Rd Irvington-on-Hudson NY 10533 Office: 545 Madison Av New York City NY 10022

BANNER, FRANKLIN COLEMAN, ret. educator, journalist; b. Unionville, Mo., Aug. 10, 1895; s. Winfield Scott and Rebecca (Roberts) B.; A.B., B.J., U. Mo., 1919, A.M., 1920; D. Journalism, U. London (Eng.), 1925. Reporter, Kansas City Jour., 1920-22; on editorial staffs Chgo. Jour., Chgo. Daily News, 1922-24, London Chronicle, 1925; fgn. corr. Am. newspapers, 1925; head dept. journalism Pa. State U., 1926, now prof. emeritus, former head journalism. Traveled throughout So. Hemisphere, 1949-50, pub. studies Australian, S. African press others; organizer 1st nat. joint Com. of editors, pubs. and dirs. journalism for raising standards of schs.; past exec. sec. Pa. Council on Edn. in Journalism. Mem. pubs. com. Nat. Pub. Recipient award for distinguished service Pa. pubs. and editors. Mem. Royal Inst. Journalists Eng., Press Congress World, Am. Assn. Schs. and Depts. Journalism (past v.p.), Am. Assn. Tchrs. Journalism (past v.p.), Nat. Com. on Research in Journalism, Sch. Adv. Com. Pa., Newspaper Pubs. Pubs. Assn., Pa. Press Conf. (dir.), Am. Press Soc., Sigma Delta Chi (award for advisers), Pi Delta Epsilon. Methodist. Clubs: London Press; Brisbane (Australia) Johnsonian; University (State College). Writer feature stories on travel. Home: 4145 Iowa Street San Diego CA 92104

BANNER, JAMES WORTH, educator; b. Mt. Airy, N.C., Dec. 22, 1909; s. John Edward and Elizabeth (Fulton) B.; B.S., Roanoke Coll., 1930; M.A., U. N.C., 1942, Ph.D., 1948; m. Elizabeth Jane Durham, Dec. 29, 1941; 1 son, Worth Dunham. With U.S. Fgn. Service, 1934-40; asso. prof. Spanish, U. Ga., 1949-59; chmn. dept. modern langs. Coll. William amd Mary, 1959-63, prof. Spanish, studies Rollins Coll., 1963-64; prof. Spanish, N.C. Wesleyan Coll., Served as officer USNR, 1942-45. Mem. Modern Lang. Assn., S. Atlantic Modern Lang. Assn., Am. Assn. Tchrs. Spanish and Portuguese, Am. Assn. U. Profs., Pi Kappa Phi. Author: (with others) Spanish: A Brief Introduction, 1957. Office: Coll William and Mary Williamsburg, VA 23185.

BANNER, JOHN, actor; b. Stanislaw, Poland, Jan. 28, 1910; s. David and Mina (Treiber) B.; came to U.S., 1938; m. Christine Gemenne, June 19, 1965. Actor plays Zurich, Switzerland, Vienna, Austria, N.Y.C., also films, TV. Served with USAF. Home: 3820 Glenridge Dr Sherman Oaks CA 91403 Office: care Robert Raison Agy 9000 Sunset Blvd Los Angeles CA 90069

BANNER, WILLIAM AUGUSTUS, educator; b. Phila., Sept. 18, 1915; s. Zacharias and Nannie Beatrice (Perry) B.; B.A., Pa. State U., 1935; B.D., Yale, 1938; M.A., Harvard, 1944, Ph.D. (Sheldon traveling fellow), 1947; m. Beatrice Vera Suggs, June 7, 1941; children—Beatrice Anne, William Perry. Instr. philosophy Bennett Coll., Greensboro, N.C., 1938-43; asst. to asso. prof. Sch. Religion, Howard U., Washington, 1945-55, asso. prof. philosophy, 1955-58, prof., 1958—; vis. prof. philosophy Yale, 1964-65; distinguished vis. prof. U. Rochester, 1970. Fellow Soc. Religion in Higher Edn.; mem. Am. Philos. Assn. Club: Harvard (Washington). Author: Ethics: An Introduction to Moral Philosophy, 1968. Home: 5719 1st St NW Washington DC 20011

BANNERMAN, ARTHUR MARLING, ret. coll. pres.; b. Juneau, Alaska, May 26, 1900; s. William S. and Grace (Mitchell) B.; A.B., Lafayette Coll., 1922, L.H.D., 1945; A.M., U. N.C., 1940; LL.D., Berea Coll., Johnson C. Smith U.; student U. Wis., Middlebury Coll.; m. D. Lucile Patton, Nov. 27, 1930; children—Janet Patton, Mary Mitchell. Instr. Asheville (N.C.) Farm Sch., 1928-42, prin., 1930-38, supt., 1940-42; pres. Warren Wilson Coll., Swannanoa, N.C., 1942-71. Dir. Swannanoa Bank & Trust Co. Mem. adv. bd. Asheville Country Day Sch. Trustee James G. K. McClure Devel. and Ednl. Fund. Pres. Swannanoa Community Council, Greater Asheville Council; pres. bd. dirs. United Fund of Asheville and Buncombe County, 1957-58; mem. Buncombe County Planning Council; treas. N.C. Found. Ch. Related Colls., 1959-60; pres. N.C. Council Ch. Related Colls., 1959-60; trustee Asheville City Libraries. Mem. So. Mountain Workers (past pres. council), United Church Men (bd. mgrs.), Nat. Council Presbyn. Men (pres.), Sigma Alpha Epsilon. Presbyn. Clubs: Civitan of Asheville (past pres.); Biltomore Forest Country. Address: Warren Wilson College Swannanoa NC 28778

BANNERMAN, CHARLES S., lawyer; b. Bklyn., Apr. 12, 1905; s. David Boyce and Alice (Scott) B.; B.S. Princeton, 1926; LL.B., Harvard, 1929; m. Jane H. Campbell, Sept. 17, 1938; 1 dau., Ann McDonald. Admitted to N.Y. bar, 1931, since practiced in N.Y.C.; mng. partner Clark, Carr & Ellis, 1943-69, Casey, Tyre, Wallace & Bannerman, 1969—; partner Francis Bannerman Sons, 1946- 58, pres., 1958-68. Author: The Story of Bannerman Island, 1962; The Bannerman Catalog, 1966. Home: 1088 Park Av New York City NY 10028 Office: 345 Park Av New York City NY 10022

BANNERMAN, GRAEME CAMPBELL, univ. ofcl.; b. Washington, Apr. 1, 1910; s. William Thackeray and Mary Louise (Tufts) B.; B.S., Hamilton Coll., 1931; J.D., George Washington U., 1936, LL.M., 1938; m. Ruth Elinor Shauck, Nov. 23, 1935; children—Susan Campbell (Mrs. Donovan Thesenga), Martha Graeme. partner Mayer, Bannerman & Rigby, Washington, 1946-47; staff U.S. Govt. agys., including Treasury Dept., RFC, Navy Dept., Dept. Def., 1935-46, 48-58, dir. procurement policy Dept. Def., 1957-61, dep. asst. sec. of def., 1961-65; asst. sec. of navy, 1965-68; v.p. for bus. and finance U. Cal., 1968—. Served to lt. USNR, 1942-44. Recipient Career Service award Nat. Civil Service League, 1963; Navy Distinguished Pub. Service award, 1968. Mem. Gryphon, Phi Delta Phi. Home: 6110 Ocean View Dr Oakland CA 94618 Office: 2200 University Av Berkeley CA 94720

BANNEROT, FREDERICK GEORGE, refinery exec.; b. Pitts., May 29, 1908; s. Frederick G. and Margaret R. (Long) B.; B.S., Yale, 1929; m. Mary Frances Palmer, Feb. 17, 1931; children—Frederick George III, Oroon Palmer. With Elk Refining Co., Charleston, W.Va., 1930—, successively refinery chemist, sec., v.p., exec. v.p., 1930-51, pres., 1951-69, chmn. bd., 1969—; dir. Kanawha Valley Bank, Chesapeake & Potomac Telephone Co. W.Va. Bd. dirs. Meml. Hosp.; trustee Morris Harvey Coll. Mem. C. of C. Mem. Episcopal Ch. Clubs: Edgewood Country, Berry Hills Country (Charleston); Duquesne (Pitts.). Amateur golf champion, W.Va., 1932, 33, 41. Home: 1230 Upper Rideway Rd Charleston WV 25314 Office: Kanawha Valley Bldg Charleston WV 25301

BANNING, ELIZABETH, (Mrs. Charles Perry Davies), color cons.; b. Waterloo, Ia., Sept. 11, 1908; d. Evert Alonzo and Odessa Rebecca (Fogleman) Hollenbeck; student Chgo. Art Inst., 1928- 29, Northwestern, 1930; research in color in Germany, 1932-35; m. William Clyde Morehead, Aug. 15, 1942; m. 2d, Charles Perry Davies, July 17, 1956. As color technician and archtl. color cons. established office and lab. under name Elizabeth Banning, San Francisco, 1936; color cons. for many orgns., including A.T. & S.F. R.R., W.P. Fuller & Co., Mannings, Inc., Petroleum Exhibitors, Spreckles Sugar Co., Standard Oil of Cal., Fred Harvey, and architects for Ford Motor Co. Republican. Protestant. Gertrude Atherton, 1946. Collector Modern French and Am. Fine Art. Mem. Marin County Park Commn. Mem. Am. Inst. Decorators. Home: Indian Valley Ranch 501 Old Ranch Rd Novato CA 94947 also Captain Cook HI Office: 1709 Indian Valley Rd Novato CA 94947

BANNING, MARGARET CULKIN, author; b. Buffalo, Minn., Mar. 18, 1891; d. William Edgar and Hannah Alice (Young) Culkin; A.B., Vassar Coll., 1912; certificate Chgo. Sch. Civics and Philanthropy, 1913; m. Archibald Tanner Banning, Oct. 13, 1914; children—Mary Margaret, Archibald Tanner, William Culkin (dec.), Margaret Brigid (dec.); m. 2d, LeRoy Salsich, Nov. 15, 1944. Russell Sage Found. fellow for research, 1913. Trustee Duluth (Minn.). Pub. Library, Nat. Fund for Med. Edn., Nat. Health and Welfare Retirement Fund: bd. dirs. Alworth Meml. Scholarship Fund. Hon. mem. Jr. League (Duluth); mem. Am. Assn. U. Women (ex-pres. Duluth), League Women Voters, Authors League Am. (mem. council 1948-50), League Am. Penwomen, P.E.N., Phi Beta Kappa. Republican. Roman Catholic. Clubs: Cordon (Chgo.); Duluth Woman's Northland Country; Tryon Country, Tryon Riding and Hunt, Business and Professional Women's; Pen and Brush, Cosmopolitan (N.Y.C.). Author: This Marrying, 1920; Half Loaves, 1921; Spellbinders, 1922; Country Club People, 1923; A Handmaid of the Lord, 1924; The Women of the Family, 1926; Pressure, 1927; Money of Her Own, 1928; Prelude to Love, 1929; Mixed Marriage, 1930; The Town's Too Small, 1931; Path of True Love, 1932; The Third Son, 1933; The First Woman, 1934; The Iron Will, 1935; Letters to Susan, 1936; The Case for Chastity, 1937; Too Young to Marry, 1938; Enough to Live On, 1939; Out in Society, 1940; Salud: A South American Journal, 1941; Letters from England, 1942; Conduct Yourself Accordingly, 1944; The Clever Sister, 1947: Give Us Our Years, 1949; Fallen Away, 1951; The Dowry, 1955; The Convert, 1957; Echo Answers, 1960; The Quality of Mercy, 1963; The Vine and the Olive, 1964; I Took My Love to the Country, 1966; Mesabi, 1969; Lifeboat Number Two, 1971. Contbr. short stories to mags.; writer essays on phases Am. life and activities. Address: 740 East Superior St Duluth MN 55802

BANNISTER, CONSTANCE, (Mrs. Joseph Holmes Hatcher), photographer; b. Ashland City, Tenn., Feb. 11, 1919; d. Arthur Thomas and Bessie Lorraine (Jackson) Gibbs; student N.Y. Sch. Applied Design, N.Y. Sch. of Modern Photography, N.Y. Inst. of Photography; m. Stephen Arthur Bannister, Jan. 28, 1937; m. 2d, Charles G. Fredericks (div. 1953); m. 3d, Joseph H. Hatcher, Dec. 28, 1956; children—Lynda Jo, Lisa Jo. Photographer A.P., 1938-39; photographs appearing on graphic cover Chgo. Tribune 1946—; strip Baby Banters by Bannister syndicated in numerous newspapers twice weekly, 1946—; producer movie shorts Bannister's Babies for Harold Young Prodns., 1947, Bantering with Bannister's Babies for Warner Bros., 1948; inc. under name Constance Bannister, Inc. (known as Bannister Enterprises). 1948, pres. Constance Bannister Enterprises, Inc.; photographed stars in Three's A Family, for R.K.O.; covers appeared continuously on nat. mags. U.S., Can., S. Am. Europe; photographs appear in advertisements for Clapp's Baby Food, Heinz, Bordens, Hood's Milk, Gerber's Beechnut, and Johnson & Johnson; now with Music Corp. Am.; syndicated Columbia Features, Inc., N.Y.C., 1971—; personal appearances U.S. and abroad, radio and TV appearances in U.S. Assisted on posters to sell War Bonds, contbr. U.S.O. doing photographic stories, World War II. Republican. Episcopalian. Clubs: Atlantic Beach (Long Beach, L.I.): The Sea Spray (Palm Beach, Fla.). Won mixed tennis doubles The Bath and Tennis Club, Palm Beach, Fla., 1946, silver trophy for tennis, several prizes for ballroom dancing. Pub. 58 books, 1951—, including: The Baby, Senator, I'm Glad You Asked Me That; Puppy and Me; How I Photograph Babies and Pets; International Date Book; Calendar Date Book, 1950; Appointment Calendar, 1964; What to Expect When You're Expecting, It's a Riot to Diet, Organization Baby, Visiting Hours Are Over, Infernal Revenue, From the Back of the Incubator, Astrotots, I Love You Truly, Members of the PTA, Jr. Executive, Gal Friday, If You're Selling Baby, I'm Buying, Home Is Where the Heart Burns, Holy Deadlock, What's Cookin' Baby. Movie editor baby films on TV show Home. Patentee. Address: Cold Spring Rd Box 8 Syosset NY 11791

BANNISTER, DAN WESLEY, ins. co. exec.; b. Erie, Pa., May 13, 1921; s. Earl F. and Hortense (Ashley) B.; B.S., Ind. U., 1942; J.D. cum laude, Albany (N.Y.) Law Sch., 1946; m. Audrey M. Shell, May 20, 1944; children-Dan Wesley, Shelley, James E. Admitted to N.Y. bar, 1947; practiced in Rochester, 1946-49; controller Vaisey Bristol Shoe Co., Rochester, 1949-51; financial control dir. Allstate Ins. Co., Skokie, Ill., 1951-61; v.p. Security Ins. Group, New Haven, 1961-62; exec. v.p., gen. mgr. Horace Mann Educators Group, Horace Mann Fund, Inc., Horace Mann Investors, Inc., Springfield, Ill., 1962-66, pres., chief exec. officer dir. Horace Mann Educators Corp., 1968—; pres., chief exec. officer other Horace Mann cos., 1966—; dir. Ill. Nat. Bank Springfield. Gen. chmn. United Fund Campaign of Springfield and Sangamon County, 1965-66; v.p. Springfield Central Area Devel. Assn., 1966, pres., 1967; v.p. United Community Services Springfield, 1967-68, pres., 1968-69, bd. dirs., 1967- 70; chmn. Capital City R.R. Relocation Authority, 1967—. Bd. dirs. N.E.A. Mut. Fund, Tchrs. Services Corp. div. N.E.A.; mem. adv. bd. Salvation Army Springfield. Served with USAAF, 1942-45. Mem. Soc. Chartered Property and Casualty Underwriters, Casualty Actuarial Soc. Episcopalian. Home: 2005 Willemoore St Springfield IL 62704 Office: 216 E Monroe St Springfield IL 62701

BANNISTER, THOMAS TURPIN, educator; b. Orange, N.J., Apr. 20, 1930; s. Turpin Chambers and Charlotte (Thomas) B.; B.S., Duke, 1951; M.S. in Botany, U. Ill., 1953, Ph.D. in Biophysics, 1958; m. Mary Jeanne Hoggard, Dec. 29, 1953; children—Nathan C.T., Horatio T.B. Mem. faculty biology dept. U. Rochester (N.Y.), 1958—, asso. prof., 1964-69, prof., 1969—, chmn., 1969—, prof. radiation biology and biophysics, 1969—; vis. prof. botany U. Ill., 1968. Served with Chem. Corps, AUS, 1953-55. NIH Postdoctoral fellow Centre Nationale de Recherche Scientifique, France, 1962-63. Mem. Am. Soc. Plant Physiologists, Biophys. Soc., Limnological and Oceanographic Soc., Sigma Xi. Research and publs. in mechanism of photosynthesis, algal ecology. Home: 223 Rockingham St Rochester NY 14620

BANNISTER, TURPIN CHAMBERS, architect; b. Lima, O., Oct. 1, 1904; s. John Kirtley and Willie (Chambers) B.; B.S., Denison U. 1925, Phi D. in Fine Arts, 1949; B.Arch., Columbia, 1928; Ph.D., Harvard, 1944; m. Laura Charlotte Thomas, Dec. 20, 1926; children—Thomas Turpin, Christopher Freeman. Archtl. draftsman, 1918-32; Perkins-Boring fellow Columbia, 1928-29; instr. to asso. prof. Rensselaer Poly. Inst., 1932-44; Henry Adams fellow for research in medieval architecture A.I.A., 1937; archtl. editor N.Y. State Guide, Fed. Writers Project, 1939-41; research grants A.I.A., Rensselaer Poly. Inst. and Am. Iron Steel Inst., 1943-44; dean Sch. Architecture and Arts, Ala. Poly. Inst., 1944-48; prof. architecture U. Ill., 1948-57; head dept., 1948-54; cons. Art Inst., Chgo., 1948-49; dean Coll. Architecture and Fine Arts, U. Fla., 1957-67. Mem. Ala. Bd. for Registration Architects, 1944-48, chmn. 1947- 48; mem. Commn. for Survey of Archtl. Edn. and Registration, 1949- 54, editor report The Architect at Mid-Century, 1954; mem. adv. bd. Nat. Parks Service, 1951-57, chmn. adv. bd. Historic Am. Bldgs. Survey, 1961-63. Recipient Kemper award A.I.A., 1955. Fellow A.I.A. (mem. com. on preservation historic bldgs. 1945-54, sec. Albany chpt. 1940-41, pres. Ala. chpt., 1945-46), Soc. Archtl. Historians (pres. 1940-42, dir. 1942-50), Assn. Collegiate Schs. Architecture (sec.-trea. 1947), Coll. Art Assn., Medieval Acad. (mem. council 1963—), New York Hist. Assn., Thornton Soc. Phi Beta Kappa, Phi Kappa Phi, Omicron Delta Kappa, Sigma Chi, Phi Mu Alpha. Baptist. Editor Jour. Archtl. Edn., 1946-48. Author: New York State Architecture, 1941; (under K.J. Conant) Public Restoration Drawings: Third Abbey Church, Cluny, France and Villa Papa Giulio, Rome (with J. P. Coolidge); also contbr. numerous articles and revs. to profl. jours. Home: 229 S W 42d Street Gainesville FL 32601

BANNON, JOHN FRANCIS, clergyman, educator; b. St. Joseph, Mo., Apr. 28, 1905; s. William Joseph and Clara (Shortle) B.; A.B., St. Louis U., 1928, A.M., 1929, S.T.L., 1936; Ph.D., U. of Calif., 1939. Entered Soc. of Jesus, 1922; ordained priest, Roman Cath. Ch., 1935; instr. history, St. Louis U., 1939-41, asst. prof., 1941-44, asso. prof., 1944-49, prof. history, 1949—, chmn. dept. of history, 1943-71; vis. lectr. in history, Marquette U., summer 1936, U. San Francisco, Summer 1939, 47, Mount Saint Mary's Coll., Cal., summer 1964, U. Colo., Boulder, summer 1965, U. Cal. at Santa Barbara, 1967-68, U. N.M., 1971-72. Pres. Jesuit Hist. Conf., 1947-48; chmn. Conf. on Latin Am. History, 1955; dir. Inst. on Fgn. Trade of the Export Mgrs. Club of St. Louis. Mem. Am. Hist. Assn., Am. Cath. Hist. Assn., Orgn. of Am. Historians, Cath. Commn. on Intellectual and Cultural Affairs, Acad. of Am. Franciscan History (corr. mem.), St. Louis Council on World Affairs (chmn. inter-Am. div. 1949-62), Western History Assn. (mem. exec. council 1962-69, pres. 1965-66), Alpha Sigma Nu, Phi Alpha Theta, Gamma Theta Upsilon, Phi Kappa Theta. Author: Epitome of Western Civilization, 1942; Colonial North America, 1946; Latin America-An Historical Survey (with P.M. Dunne), 1947, rev. 1958, 63; History of the Americas, 2 vols., 1952, rev. edit., 1963; The Mission Frontier in Sonora, 1955; Nat. ETV series: The U.S.A., 1955; The Spanish Conquistadores, Men or Devils?, 1960; Bolton and the Spanish Borderlands, 1964; Indian Labor in the Spanish Indies, 1966; The Spanish Borderlands Frontier, 1970. Editor: The Historical Bulletin, 1943-50; The American West series and reprint series, 1962—. Mem. editorial bd. Hispanic Am. Hist. Rev., 1954-60; Manuscripta, 1957—, Arizona and the West, 1959—, Saint Louis Archdiocesan Bicentennial Series, 1964-65. Studied and traveled in Europe and Latin Am. Address: St Louis University St Louis MO 63103

BANOS, ALFREDO, Jr., educator, physicist; b. Mexico City, Mexico, Nov. 14, 1905; s. Alfredo and Martha (Garcia) B.; student U. Tex., 1923-26; B.E., Johns Hopkins, 1928. Dr. Engring., 1932; Ph.D., Mass. Inst. Tech., 1938; m. Alice Sousikian; children—Alfredo (dec.), Margarita. Came to U.S., 1943, naturalized, 1949. Dir. Inst. Physics, Nat. U. Mexico, 1938-43; prof. physics, head dept. faculty of scis. Nat. U. Mexico, 1938-43; staff mem. theory group Mass. Inst. Tech. Radiation Lab., Cambridge, 1943-46; asso. prof. physics U. Cal. at Los Angeles, 1946-49, prof. physics, 1949—; cons. Air Force Office Sci. Research, 1952-57, AEC, 1956-61, Aerospace Corp., 1962—; with Office Naval Research, London, Eng., 1967-68, 70-71. Fulbright fellow, 1958, Guggenheim fellow, 1935-38, 58. Author: Dipole Radiation in the Presence of a Conducting Half-Space, 1966. Address: Physics Dept Univ Cal Los Angeles CA 90024

BANSER, HENRY P., machine mfr.; b. Chgo., Oct. 5, 1914; s. Henry P. and Mary (DeBore) B.; m. Alma Watkins, Oct. 20, 1940 (dec. Oct. 1951); 1 son, Henry P. III (dec. July 1967); m. 2d, Tracie Falduto, Mar. 7, 1969; children—Valerie, Joanne, Dennise. Factory foreman Ross Mfg. Co., 1940; purchasing agt. E. I. Guthman & Co., 1940-44; sec.-treas. Electronic Comptometer Corp., Chgo., 1944-46, pres., chmn. 1946—; gen. mgr. Henald Mfg. Co., 1952; pres. Electronics Components Corp., 1947—; chmn. bd. Atlas Cable Corp., Chgo., 1970—. Mem. Ill. Adv. Com. on Pub. Health. Bd. dirs. Kidney Found. Ill. Home: 411 Cardinal Av Addison IL 60101 Office: 520 Interstate Rd Addison IL 60101

BANTA, CHARLES URBAN, investment banker; b. Buffalo, Oct. 26, 1916; s. Charles Woodbury and Clara (Urban) B.; grad. Hotchkiss Sch., 1935; B.A., Yale, 1939; M.B.A., Harvard, 1941; m. Melissa Wickser, Dec. 7, 1946; children—Charles Wickser, Philip Livingston, Melissa Winspear. Mgr. mil. contracts Curtiss Wright Co., Buffalo, 1942-43; indsl. cons. Rath & Strong, Boston, 1946-50; v.p. First Nat. Bank Buffalo, 1950-54; with S. D. Lunt & Co., Buffalo, 1954—, partner, 1958—; dir. Roblin Steel Corp., Bison Mfg. Co., Consol. Bowling, Albright Knox Gallery, Bisonite Corp., Tree Pickle Company, Chemtrol Pollution Services, Inc., Buffalo. Served to lieutenant USNR, 1943-46; PTO. Clubs: Buffalo Country, Buffalo Tennis and Squash, Saturn, Mid-Day (Buffalo; Yale (N.Y.C.). Home: 4985 Sheridan Drive Williamsville, NY 14221. Office: Marine Trust Building Buffalo NY 14203

BANTA, GEORGE, III, printing co. exec.; b. Neenah, Wis., June 19, 1923; s. George and Margaret (Killen) B.; student Lawrence Coll., 1941-43; m. Virginia Jensen, Dec. 28, 1943; children—Robert Mason, David Demaree, Virginia Lee. Dir. George Banta Co., Inc., Menasha, Wis., 1951—, sec., 1955-61, v.p., 1961-65, pres., 1965-71, chmn., 1971—; dir. First Nat. Bank of Menasha (Wis.), First Wis. Nat. Bank of Oshkosh (Wis.); pres., dir. Daniels Packaging Co., 1969—, Hart Press, Inc., 1970—; v.p., dir. Northwestern Engraving Co. Mem. Menasha Sch. Bd., 1961-62. Bd. dirs. Theda Clark Meml. Hosp., Neenah, Wis., 1000 Yard Found. Served with AUS, World War II. Recipient Boy Scouts Am. Silver Beaver award. Mem. Phi Delta Theta. Presbyterian. Clubs: Menasha Rotary, Oshkosh Power Boat Club. Home: 1520 Palisades Dr Appleton WI 54911 Office: Curtis Reed Plaza Menasha WI 54952

BANTA, GEORGE, Jr., editor, publisher; b. Menasha, Wis., Mar. 25, 1893; s. George and Ellen Lee (Pleasants) B.; ed. Lawrence Acad., 1906-10, Wabash Coll., 1910-11, LL.D., (hon.), 1968; M.A. (hon.), Lawrence Coll., 1951; L.H.D., (hon.) Franklin Coll., Ind., 1960; m. Margaret Killen, Oct. 10, 1916; children—Margaret M., George R. With George Banta Co., Menasha, 1911—, v.p., 1916-51, pres., 1951, 54-61, chmn., 1951-54, 61-70; editor Banta's Greek Exchange, 1935—; v.p. First Nat. Bank, Menasha, Northwestern Engraving Co. Mem. exec. com. Nat. Interfrat. Conf., 1936-39, vice chmn., 1938-39; pres. Coll. Frat. Editors' Assn., 1929-30; pres. Menasha Park Bd., 1930-35. Trustee Lawrence Coll., 1930-38, pres., 1939-43, 54-59, v.p., 1960-66; trustee Milwaukee-Downer Sem., 1935-39; bd. dirs. Valley Council Boy Scouts Am., 1928—, pres., 1939-40, mem. Nat. Council, 1949—; bd. dirs. Wis. Hist. Found., 1962—. Mem. Wis. Hist. Soc. (curator 1944-68, exec. com., 1946, v.p., 1947, pres 1949-52, hon. v.p. 1968—), Holland Soc. N.Y., Ry. and Locomotive Hist. Soc., Phi Delta Theta (nat. editor 1923-32, nat. pres. 1932-34; chmn. survey commn. 1940-50). Clubs: North Shore Golf; Ormond (Fla.) Country. Author: Typographical Tips, 1912. Assisted in editing and compiling 5 edits. Baird's Manual of Am. College Fraternities; asst. editor History of the Wisconsin Central. Contbr. to jours. Home: Riverlea Menasha WI 54952 Office: 450 Ahnaip St Menasha WI 54952

BANTLE, LOUIS A., business exec.; b. Danbury, Conn., Oct. 14, 1906; s. Louis F. and May L. (White) B.; ed. pub. schs. Bridgeport, Conn.; m. Marie Daisenberger, Dec. 28, 1927; 1 son, Louis F. With sales dept. R. J. Reynolds Tobacco Co., 1927, U.S. Tobacco Co., 1929—, div. mgr. N.J., 1931, dept. mgr. N.Y.C., 1938, West Coast mgr., 1942, v.p., dir., 1945-59, pres., 1959—; pres. House Windsor Cigar Co., 1965—; chmn. bd. Tucker-Sharp Pen Co., 1964—, B.A. Barnard Co., 1966—. Republican. Home: 791 Weaver St Larchmont NY 10538 Office: 630 Fifth Avenue New York City NY 10020

BANYARD, ALFRED LOTHIAN, bishop; b. Merchantville, N.J., July 31, 1908; s. Lothian Rupert and Emma May (Irwin) B.; A.B., U. Pa., 1929; student Gen. Theol. Sem., 1929-31, S.T.B., 1933, S.T.D., 1946; postgrad. Phila. Div. Sch., 1932, D.D., 1947: m. Sarah Alice Hammer, Sept. 1, 1938; 1 son, Richard David. Ordained to ministry Episcopal Ch., N.J., 1931; pastor St. Lukes Ch., Westville, N.J., 1932-36; rector Christ Ch., Bordentown, N.J., 1936-43; archdeacon Episcopal Diocese N.J., 1943-55; suffragan bishop, 1945-55, bishop of N.J., 1955—. Mem. Bd. Examining Chaplains, 1938-55, chmn., 1941-55; dep. to provincial synod, 1940-46, sec. Ho. of Bishops, 2d Province, 1945-48; trustee Diocesan Found., 1941-43, ex-officio, 1945—, pres., 1955—; pres. Procter Found., 1955—; master of Young Men's Conf., 1936-37, dean, 41; mem. Bd. Religious Edn., 1939-41, 1943-46, Bd. of Social Service, 1940-42, 44-46; field, publicity dept., 1943-45; trustee Burlington Coll., 1945-53, v.p., 1946-53. Bd. mgrs. St. Martins Ho. of Retreats, Bernardsville, N.J., 1948—; trustee Evergreens, Moorestown; v.p. Corp. for Relief Widows and Orphans of Clergymen, 1945-; pres. Mission Advancement, 1955-; trustee Phila. Div. Sch. Mem. Newcomen Soc., Philomathean Soc. of U. Pa.

(scriba 1929), Phi Beta Kappa, Eta Sigma Phi. Republican. Home: 13 Perdicaris Pl Trenton NJ 08618 Office: 808 West State Street Trenton NJ 08618

BANZHAF, JOHN F., III, lawyer, orgn. exec.; b. N.Y.C., July 2, 1940; s. John F. and Olga (Mischenko) B.; B.S. in Elec. Engring., Mass. Inst. Tech., 1962; J.D. magna cum laude, Columbia, 1965. Civilian research asst. Signal Corps Engring. Labs., 1957; research engr., cons. Lear Siegler Corp., 1959-62; editor Columbia Law Rev., 1964-65; research fellow Nat. Municipal League, 1965; law clk. to U.S. Dist. Judge Spottswood W. Robinson III, 1965-66; asso. firm Watson, Leavonworth, Kelton & Taggart, N.Y.C., 1967; exec. dir. Action on Smoking and Health, Washington, 1968—; asso. prof. law Nat. Law Center, George Washington U., 1968—; exec. trustee Legislative Action on Smoking and Health, 1969—. Recipient 17th ann. Sat. Rev. award distinguished TV programming in pub. interest, 1969; Advt. Age award, 1967, 68, those who made advt. news, 1967, 68. Mem. Sigma Xi, Eta Kappa Nu, Tau Beta Pi. Home: S-908 Harbour Sq 530 N St SW Washington DC 20024 Office: 2000 H St NW Washington DC 20006

BANZHAF, MAX, corp. exec.; b. Marshalltown, Ia., May 26, 1915; s. Michael F. and Florence (Ball) B.; B.S., Ia. State Coll., 1937 m. Mary Louise De Pugh, May 12, 1940; children—Judith Louise (Mrs. T.L. Kruse), and Michael Allen. With Armstrong Cork Co., 1938—, successively salesman bldg. materials div., mgr. bldg. materials advt., 1938-52, dir. co. advt., promotion, pub. relations, 1952-63, staff v.p., 1963-68, v.p., treas., 1968—, also dir. Active charitable orgns.; past mem. bd. Phila. Mus. Sch. Art. Recipient Advt. Man of Year award Indsl. Marketing Soc., 1955. Mem. Assn. Nat. Advertisers (bd. dirs. 1958-62, vice chmn.), C. of C. U.S. Home: 310 Eshelman Rd Lancaster PA 17601 Office: Armstrong Cork Co Lancaster PA 17604

BAPTISTA, FEDERICO GUILLERMO, petroleum co. exec.; b. Coro, Venezuela, May 9, 1914; s. Federico Baptista-Galindo and Manuela (Hernandez) de Baptista; B.S. in Civil Engring., Cooper Union, 1936; Dr. Civil Engring., U. Central de Venezuela, 1936; M.S. in Bus. Adminstrn. (Sloan fellow 1950-51), Mass. Inst. Tech., 1951; m. Mercedes Guevara, Dec. 1943; children—Federico Jose, Mercedes Maria. Engr., Creole Petroleum Corp., 1936-52, adminstr., 1952-60, dir., 1960—. Mem. Colegio Ingenieros de Venezuela, Association Venezuela de Ejecutivos. Home: Caracas Venezuela Office: Apartado 889 Caracas Venezuela

BARAB, SEYMOUR, musician; b. Chgo., Jan. 9, 1921; s. Leo and Leah (Yale) B.; m. Mary A. Fretz, Dec. 28, 1953; children—Miriam, Jesse, Cellist, Indpls. Symphony Orch., 1939-41; pianist All-Am. Youth Orch. summer 1940; cellist Cleve. Symphony Orch., 1941-42; mem. staff CBS, 1945-47, also Galimir String Quartet and N.Y. Trio; solo cellist Portland (Ore.) Symphony Orch., 1947-48, San Francisco Symphony Orch., summer 1948; mem. staff ABC, also Concert-Masters, string orchestra; viola de gambist with N.Y. Pro Musica Antiqua, 1957- -; free-lance TV, radio, comml. orchs. 1948-51, 53-57; concert tours, composing, rec. dir. Am. rec. firms, France, 1951-53; composer TV and films, 1955—; vis. asst. prof. Rutgers U. Served with USNR, 1942-45. Composer; A Child's Garden of Verses (songs with instruments), 1954; Four Songs (voice and piano); Songs of Perfect Propriety (songs with instruments); Six Pieces for Recorder Trio, 1957; The Silver Swan (chorus a cappela), 1956; Chanticleer (comic opera), 1954; The Rajah's Ruby (musical farce), 1954 A Game of Chance (comic opera), 1956; Reba (fantasy with music), 1956; Four Songs (voice and piano), 1953; An Angel-Chorus (chorus a cappela) 1956. Address: 2308 Broad St Yorktown Heights NY 10598

BARACH, ALVAN LEROY, physician; b. Newcastle, Pa., Feb. 22, 1895; s. Nathan L. and Jennie C. (Silman) B.; student Coll. City N.Y., 1912-15; M.D., Coll. Physicians and Surgeons (Columbia), 1919; m. Frederica P. Pisek, Apr. 24, 1933; children—Jeffrey Alvan, John Paul. Intern, Presbyn. Hosp., N.Y.C., 1919-20; asst. in medicine Harvard (research at Mass. Gen. Hosp.), 1920-21; asst. in medicine Presbyn. Hosp., 1922-31; asst. in medicine. Coll. Phys. and Surg., 1922-25, instr. in medicine, 1925-28, asso. in medicine, 1928-35; cons. medicine Woman's Hosp., 1928-34, also asso. prof. clin. medicine Columbia Coll. Phys. and Surgeons, 1936, cons. in medicine, 1960—; clin. prof. Presbyn. Hosp., 1952-65, now cons. in medicine. Mem. Nat. Inventors Council, Dept. of Commerce. Mem. Med. R.C., World War. Awarded bronze medal, Class I, for original investigation helium and oxygen in various types of dyspnea, A.M.A., 1936; scroll of honour for meritorious research in clin. med. and gas therapy Internat. Anesthesia Research Soc., 1936, Townsend-Harris medal Coll. City of N.Y., 1940, award of merit Am. Assn. Inhalational Therapists, 1960; Redway medal N.Y.C. Med. Soc., 1964; Henderson medal Am. Soc. Geriatrics, 1971. Fellow Am. Coll. Chest Physicians (Coll. gold medal 1961), A.M.A., N.Y. Acad. of Med.; mem. Am. Soc. Clin. Investigation, Assn. Am. Physicians, Soc. Exptl. Biol. and Med., N.Y. County Med. Soc., Am. Acad. Allergy, Trudeau Society, Alumni Assn. Presbyn. Hosp., Alpha Omega Alpha, Omega Pi Alpha. Democrat. Jewish religion. Author: (with Hylan A. Bickerman) Pulmonary Emphysema, 1956; A Treatment Manual For Patients With Pulmonary Emphysema, 1969. Contbr. articles to profl. jours. Devised oxygen tent generally adopted for use in treatment of pneumonia, cardiac disease and other cardio-respiratory conditions; introduced helium as a new therapeutic gas in treatment of asthma and obstructive lesions in larynx and trachea. Address: 72 E 91st St New York City NY 10028 ☆

BARACH, FREDERICA PISEK (Mrs. Alvan L. Barach), ret. editor, educator; b. Lake Honatcong, N.J., Aug. 1, 1904; d. Godfrey R. and Rosalie (Paul) Pisek; A.B., Vassar Coll., 1925; m. Alvan L. Barach, Apr. 24, 1933; children—Jeffrey Alvan, John Paul. Asst. editor Review of Reviews, 1925-28; lit. editor Golden Book mag., 1928-29, editor-in- chief, 1930-34; tchr. creative writing Sarah Lawrence Coll., 1929-31; liaison officer OWI, 1941-45; exec. sec. Writers War Bd., 1941-46; asst. prof. English, Barnard Coll., 1948-56. Pres. Elizabeth N. Arnstein Fund; chmn. bd. trustees Vassar Coll., 1957-61; vice chmn. bd. trustees Bank St. Coll. Edn. Mem. Pub. Edn. Assn. (chmn. bd. trustees) 1962-70), Phi Beta Kappa. Clubs: Cosmopolitan, Women's City (N.Y.C.) Home: 72 E 91st St New York City NY 10028

BARACH, PHILIP G., shoe co. exec.; b. Boston, 1930; ed. Boston U., 1951, Harvard Grad. Sch. Bus. Adminstrn., 1955; m.; 3 children. Pres., chief exec. officer, dir. U.S. Shoe Corp.; dir. Fifth Third Union Trust Co., Cin. Enquirer. Bd. visitors Boston U. Home: 7600 Willow Brook Lane Cincinnati OH 45237 Office: 1658 Herald Av Cincinnati OH 45207

BARAHAL, HYMAN SAMUEL, psychiatrist, hosp. adminstr.; b. Berezniezа, Russia, May 21, 1905; s. Oscar and Pearl (Rothman) B.; brought to U.S., 1914, naturalized, 1923; M.B., Wayne State U., 1930, M.D., 1931; m. Irene Jaffe, Dec. 24, 1939; children—Paul, Susan. Gen. intern Gorgas Hosp., C.Z., 1930-31; staff psychiatrist Kings Park (N.Y.) State Hosp., 1931, then supervising psychiatrist; clin. dir. Pilgrim State Hosp., West Brentwood, N.Y., 1946- 53, asso. dir., 1953-58, acting dir., 1958-64; prof. psychiatry N.Y. Sch. Psychiatry, 1955—; dir. Hoch Psychiat. Hosp., 1968- -. Served to maj., M.C., AUS, 1942-46. Diplomate Am. Bd. Psychiatry and Neurology. Fellow Am. Psychiat. Assn. (life), Acad. Psychoanalysis; mem. Suffolk County Med. Soc. (chmn. com. on mental health, alcoholism and drug addiction). Contbr. numerous articles profl. jours., chpts. to books. Home: 130 S Bay Av Brightwaters NY 11718 Office: Hoch Psychiatric Hospital West Brentwood NY 11717

BARALL, MILTON, fgn. service officer; b. N.Y.C., Oct. 28, 1911; s. Louis and Rose (Barall) B.; B.S.S., Coll. City N.Y., 1932, M.S., 1933; certificate U. Grenoble, France, 1932; Ph.D., N.Y.U., 1948; grad. Nat. War Coll., 1957; m. Grace Glaberson, Oct. 28, 1940; 1 son, James David. Tchr. high schs., N.Y.C., 1934-41, 46-48; 2d sec., vice consul Am. embassy, Santiago, Chile, 1948-50; Chilean desk officer, officer charge West Coast affairs, Dept. State, 1950-54; 1st sec., then counselor embassy, Port-au- Prince, Haiti, 1954-56; counselor for econ. affairs, dep. dir. econ. mission Am. embassy, Madrid, Spain, 1957-60; dep. asst. sec. of state Bur. Inter-Am. Affairs, 1960-62; v.p., supr. overseas operations Am. Machine & Foundry Internat., Geneva, Switzerland, 1962-64; dep. U.S. rep. Inter-Am. Com. on Alliance for Progress, 1964-67, dep. asst. adminstr. AID, 1966-67; head Caribbean Study Group with rank ambassador, 1967-69; minister Am. embassy, Buenos Aires, Argentina, 1969—. Served from capt. to col., AUS, 1941-45. Decorated Croix de Guerre. Medaille de la Reconnassance (France). Mem. Am. Fgn. Service Assn., Diplomatic and Consular Officers Ret. Contbr. articles polit. sci. to profl. publs. Home: American Embassy Buenos Aires Argentina Office: Bur Inter-Am Affairs State Dept Washington DC 20525

BARANANO, EDUARDO, univ. adminstr.; b. Montevideo, Uruguay, June 2, 1914; s. Ildefonso Francisco and Sara (Da Costa) B.; prof. music Sch. Music, Montevideo, 1934; B.A., U. Uruguay, 1933, M.A., 1935, Ph.D. in Architecture, 1941; M. City Planning (univ. scholar, Emerson fellow), Mass. Inst. Tech., 1943; univ scholar Princeton, 1943-44; postgrad., Brit. Council, London, Eng., 1944-46; m. Marie Louise Fernandez, Aug. 31, 1947; children—Eduardo Carlos, Mariá Teresa, Sara, Susana, Gerardo. Came to P.R., 1941, naturalized, 1959. Asst. prof. U. Montevideo, 1940-41; research planner N.J. State Planning Bd., Trenton, 1943-44; regional planner Regional Assn. Cleve., 1946-47; planning cons. P.R. Housing Authority, Rio Piedras, 1947-48; vis. prof. U. Tex., Austin, 1948-50; cons. Govt. Commonwealth of P.R., also mem. P.R. Planning Bd., 1950-60; dir. urban affairs Pan Am. Union-coordinator with Interam. Devel. Bank, also dir. Tech. Mission to Chile; adviser Housing Center, Colombia, 1960-62; pres. Internat. Finance and Devel. Corp., Ltd., Washington, 1962-63; regional dir. Am. Inst. Free Labor Devel., AFL-CIO, AID, 1963-65; dir. planning programs D.R.C. Devel. Corp., Santa Barbara, Cal., 1965-67; v.p. planning Wilsey & Ham, San Mateo, Cal., 1967-70; dir. planning and devel. U. P.R., San Juan, 1970—; lectr. univs., U.S., Latin Am., Europe; cons., adviser on planning. Recipient 1st Planning prize Planning Conv., N.Y., 1958, II Hispanoamericana de Arte, 1954, Emerson Prize medal Mass. Inst. Tech., 1943. Edward Langley scholar A.I.A., Washington, 1949; State Dept. grantee, 1944; Pan Am. scholar Inst. Internat. Edn., N.Y., 1941-42; Roosevelt scholar, 1942-43. Fellow Am. Geog. Soc.; mem. Am. Acad. Polit. and Social Sci., Am. Inst. Planners, Am. Soc. Planning Ofcls., Soc. Architects, A.I.A., Inst. Higher Learning (Montevideo), Internat. Fedn. Housing and Town Planning, Assn. for Planning and Regional Reconstrn., Town and Country Planning Assn., Am. Planning and Civic Assn., Inst. Nazionale di Urbanistica (Torino, Italy), Soc. for Internat. Devel. Clubs: Massachusetts Institute for Technology (San Juan and San Francisco). Contbr. articles to planning jours. Home: 106 Betances Hato Rey PR 00919

BARANIK, RUDOLF, painter; b. Lithuania, Sept. 10, 1920; student Art Inst. Chgo., Art Students League, Academie Julien, Paris, Academie Fernand Leger, Paris; m. May Stevens; 1 son, Steven Baranik. Exhibited Pa. Acad. Fine Arts, 1954, 64, Brandeis U., 1954, U. Neb., 1954, 60, Mus. Modern Art circulating exhbn., 1954-55, Ill. Wesleyan U., 1954, Art U.S.A., 1958, Provincetown Art Festival, 1958, Whitney Mus. Am. Art, 1958, 60, Critics Choice, 1960, Butler Inst. Am. Art, 1959-61, Silvermine Guild, 1957, 58, Nat. Inst. Arts and Letters, Sch. Visual Arts Gallery, N.Y.C., 1967, Am. Fedn. Arts, 1967, Lacarda Gallery, N.Y.C., 1968, Nihon Gallery, Tokyo, Japan, 1968; exhibited one-man shows including: Galerie 8, Paris, France, 1951, RoKo Gallery, 1958, 61, Miami, Fla., 1958, Rena Gallery, Princeton, N.J., 1961, Katonah (N.Y.) Gallery, 1961, Ball State Tchrs. Coll., 1963; represented in permanent collections Living Arts Found., Whitney Mus. Am. Art, U. Mass., N.Y. U., Ball State U., Jacksonville Mus. Art, Peabody Mus., Nashville, Mus. Modern Art, N.Y.C., Nat. Mus. Stockholm, U. Miami, Hampton Coll. Mus., State U. N.Y. Binghamton, pvt. collections. Instr. Art Students League, N.Y., Pratt Inst., Art Students League. Recipient Joseph W. Beatman and Charles Shipmen Payson awards Silvermine Guild Artists, 1958; Raymond Speiser Meml. award Pa. Acad. Fine Arts. 1964; Childe Hassam Purchase prize Am. Acad. Arts and Letters, 1968. Mem. Artists Equity Assn. Address: 97 Wooster St New York City NY 10012

BARANOWSKI, FRANK PAUL, govt. ofcl.; b. Bayonne, N.J., Nov. 1, 1921; s. John G. and Leona (Besser) B.; B.Chem. Engring., N.Y.U., 1943; M. Chem. Engring., U. Tenn., 1954; m. Alma J. Anders, Oct. 12, 1946; children—Jan Teresa, Susan Leona, Michael Paul, Carol Ann, Krystyn Marie. Exec. asst. Union Carbide Co., Oak Ridge, 1948-51; with AEC, 1950—, chief isotope separation br., div. prodn., 1954-57, chief chem. processing br., div. prodn., 1957-59, dep. dir. div. prodn., 1959-61, dir., 1961—. Served with C.E., AUS, 1943-46. Home: 9206 Laurel Oak Dr Bethesda MD 20034 Office: Atomic Energy Commn Washington DC 20545

BARANSKY, CARLOTTA ORDASSY, soprano; b. Budapest, Hungary; d. Janos and Margarite (Jungwirth) Ordassy; student, pianist, later singer, Ferenc Liszt Music Acad., Budapest, 1939-47, La Scuola della Scala, Milan, Italy, 1948-49; m. Wolodimir Baransky, Oct. 7, 1950; children—Wolodimir, Yurij-Andrew. Naturalized U.S. citizen, 1955. Semi-finalist Internat. Music Competition, Geneva, Switzerland, 1947; operatic debut at La Scala in Magic Flute, 1950; winner Met. Audition of Air, 1956; Met. Opera debut in Die Walküre, 1957; concerts in Hungary, Switzerland, Italy, 1947, U.S., 1952—. Ford Found. fellow, 1962. Address: 6103 Liebig Av Riverdale NY 10471

BARATI, GEORGE, musician; b. Györ, Hungary, Apr. 3, 1913; s. Miksa B. and Regina (Schreiber) B.; grad. Royal Hungarian Franz Liszt Conservatory of Music, Budapest, 1935; diploma State Tchrs. Coll., 1938, state artist diploma in cello, 1938; postgrad. study with Georges Couvreur and Henry Switten, 1938-40, Roger Sessions, 1940-43, Princeton U.; m. Ruth Carroll, Oct. 31, 1948; children—Stephen George (by previous marriage), Lorna, Donna. Mem. Budapest Concert Orchestra, 1933-36; first cellist Budapest Symphony and Municipal Opera House Orchestra, 1936-38; cellist, founder Pro Ideale String Quartet, 1935-40; instr. Westminster Choir Coll., Princeton, N.J., 1938-40, Lawrenceville Sch., Princeton, also N.J. State Tchrs. Coll., 1939-43; condr., founder Princeton Ensemble, 1940-43, condr. Princeton Choral Union, 1942-43; mem., guest condr. San Francisco Symphony, mem. Cal. String Quartet, 1946-50; musical dir. Barati Chamber Orch. of San Francisco (formation of Barati Chamber Orch. Soc. 1950), 1948-52; musical dir. Honolulu Symphony Orchestra, lectr. U. Hawaii, 1950-68, world tours 1955, annually, 1958-66; exec. dir. Montalvo Center for the Arts; New York debut conducting Madame Butterfly, Bklyn. Opera Co., 1961. Guggenheim fellowship, 1965- 66. Bd. govs. Pacific and Asian Affairs Council. Served AUS, 1943-46. Naumburg award, composition, 1959. Mem. Am. Musicol. Soc., Composers Forum, MacDowell Colony, Am. Composers Alliance, Berlioz Soc. Am. (founding mem.), Bruckner Soc. (hon.). Compositions: (orchestral) Chamber Concerto (recorded Columbia Records), Configuration, Scherzo, Cello Concerto (recorded by the London Philharmonic), Tribute, Lamentoso, Symphony, Polarization, The Dragon and the Phoenix, Festival Hula, The Waters of Kane, Noelani; (chamber music) String Quartet, Woodwind Quintet, Violin Sonata, String Quartet No. 2, Oboe Quintet, Harpsichord Quartet, Octet with Harpsichord; (solo instruments) Two Dances for violin, Prisma for harp Cantabile E Ritmico for viola, others. Recording artist Lyrichord, Decca, Columbia, CRI. Home: Villa Montalvo PO Box 158 Saratoga CA 95070 Office: Montalvo Assn PO Box 158 Saratoga CA 95070

BARATZ, MORTON SACHS, educator; b. New London, Conn., Nov. 18, 1923; s. Moss and Lydia (Sachs) B.; B.A., U. Conn., 1947; M.A., Yale, 1949, Ph.D., 1952; m. Marleigh Morland, Aug. 24, 1952; children—Cynthia Leigh, Mark Everett, Matthew Anatole. Asst. instr., then instr. econs. U. Conn., 1947-48; asst. instr., then instr. Yale, 1948-55; asst. prof. econs. Haverford Coll., 1955-57; asso. prof., then prof. Bryn Mawr Coll., 1957-69, chmn. dept. econs., 1964-69; prof., chmn. dept. econs. Boston U., 1969—, dir. Urban Inst., 1970—; vis. research prof. U. Pa., 1965-70. Research cons. Inst. Urban Studies, U. Pa., 1956-58, Office of Mayor, Phila., 1957-60; dir. Franklin Custodian Funds, N.Y.C., 1958-62; nat. research prof. Brookings Instn., 1960-61. Chmn. Housing Authority, City of New London, 1949-54; chmn. Willistown Twp. (Pa.) Democratic Com., 1956-61; adv. bd. Chester County (Pa.) Bd. Pub. Assistance, 1959-61. Mem. Am. Econ. Assn., Nigerian Econ. Soc. Author: The Union and the Coal Industry, 1955; The Economics of the Postal Service, 1962; (with others) Economies of the World Today, 1965; (with W.G. Grigsby) Meaning and Measurement of Poverty, 1968; The American Business System in Transition, 1970; (with P. Bachrach) Power and Poverty, 1970. Contbr. articles profl. jours. Home: 89 Thornberry Rd Winchester MA 01890 Office: Dept of Economics Boston Univ Boston MA 02215

BARBA, LOUIS ROBERT, constrn. exec.; b. Harrison, N.J., May 9, 1915; s. John and Rose (Letterie) B.; B.A., U. N.C., 1939; m. Jean D. Schill, Oct. 18, 1941; children—Jean Louise (Mrs. Robert Strickler), Douglas, Lee, Joan, Susan. Pres. The Barba Co., 1946-56, Barcon Assos., Inc., Chatham, N.J., 1956—; sec. Hickory Tree Properties, Inc., Regional Realty and Mortgage Corp. Mem. adv. bd. Fed. Nat. Mortgage Assn., 1970, Govt. Nat. Mortgage Assn., 1971, Fed. Home Loan Bank, 1969; bd. dirs. Fed. Nat. Mortgage Assn., 1971—. Dir. State Bank of Chatham; adviser to U.S. delegation UN Econ. Com. Europe on Housing and Planning, Geneva, 1970; trustee Nat. Housing Center, 1970-71. Trustee, treas. Millburn Library, 1970-71; dir. Nat. Assn. Home Builders Research Found., 1964, treas., 1968; mem. nat. adv. council Peace Corps, 1970-71. Named N.J. Builder of Year for Industry and Community, N.J. Home Builders Assn., 1964; mem. N.J. Home Builder Assn. Hall of Fame, 1966; recipient distinguished service award to home building industry, Nat. Assn. Home Builders, 1965-66. Mem. Nat. Assn. Home Builders (pres. 1970, exec. com. 1967-71), Met. Assn. Home Builders (pres. 1959-60), N.J. Home Builders Assn. (pres. 1963), Chi Psi. Republican. Roman Catholic. Home: 22 Taylor Rd Short Hills NJ 07078 Office: 159 Main St Chatham NJ 07928

BARBASH, JACK, educator, economist; b. Bklyn., Aug. 1, 1910; s. Louis and Rose (Titel) B.; B.S., N.Y.U., 1932, M.A., 1937; m. Kate Hubbelbank, May 27, 1934; children—Louis, Fred, Mark. Investigator, N.Y. State Dept. Labor, 1937- 39; economist NLRB, 1939-40, U.S. Office Edn., 1940-45, WPB, 1943-45, Dept. Labor, 1945-48; research and edn. dir. Amalgamated Meat Cutters Union, 1948-49; economist, staff dir. subcom. labor and labor mgmt. relations U.S. Senate, 1949-53; economist legal dept. CIO, 1953-55; research and edn. dir., indsl. union dept. AFL-CIO, 1955-57; mem. faculty U. Wis., 1957—, prof. econs., 1959—. Mem. Salzburg Seminar on Am. Studies, 1962; lectr. U.S. Dept. State on Cultural affairs, Europe, Asia, 1966. Mem. Wis. Commn. Status of Women, 1959-62. Recipient Teaching Excellence award U. Wis., 1968. Mem. Am. Econ. Assn., Indsl. Relations Research Assn. (exec. bd. 1963-68), Am. Assn. U. Profs. (pres. U. Wis. chpt. 1970-71), Phi Kappa Phi (hon.). Democrat. Author: Labor Unions in Action, 1948; Practice of Unionism, 1956; Labor's Grass Roots, 1961; American Unions, Structure, Government, Politics, 1967; Trade Unions and National Economic Policy in Western Europe and the United States, 1971. Home: 1836 Keyes Av Madison WI 53711

BARBE, WALTER BURKE, educator; b. Miami, Fla., Oct. 30, 1926; s. Victor Elza and Edith (Burris) B.; B.S., Northwestern U., 1949, M.A., 1950, Ph.D., 1953; m. Marilyn E. Wood, Feb. 7, 1967; 1 son, Frederick Walter. Teacher, Dade County Bd. Pub. Instrn., 1947; asst. Psycho-Ednl. Clinic, Northwestern U., 1949-50; instr. psychology, dir. reading clinic Baylor U., 1950; asst. prof. elementary edn. Kent State U., 1952-53, prof., head spl. edn. dept., 1960-64; adj. prof. U. Pitts., 1964—; editor Highlights for Children; prof. edn., dir. Jr. League Reading Center, U. Chattanooga, 1953-59. Served with AUS, 1944-46. Mem. Am. Psychol. Assn., Nat. Assn. Gifted Children (pres. 1958). Presbyn. Clubs: Rotary, Lookout Mountain Fairyland. Author: Reading Clinic Directory, 1955; (with Ralph Roberts) Teenage Tales, 1957; (with Dorothy Hinman) We Build Our Words, 1957; Educators Guide to Personalized Reading, 1961; Exceptional Children, 1963. Editor: Psychology and Education of the Gifted: Readings, 1965; Teaching of Reading; Selections, 1965; (with Edward Frierson) Educating Children with Learning Disabilities, 1967; Compass Points in Literature, Searchlights in Literature, 1969. Home: RD 1 Narrowsburg NY 12764 Office: Highlights for Children Honesdale PA 18431

BARBEE, JAMES DORRIS, textile co. exec.; b. Carthage, Tenn., Oct. 2, 1912; s. Joe Dorman and Willie (Smith) B.; B.S. in Elec. Engring., U. Tenn., 1933; m. Lois Beatrice Dunn, Nov. 10, 1935; children—James Dorris, Linda Bruce. With Brookside Mills, Knoxville, Tenn., 1933-40, 42-45, Dan River Mills, Danville, Va., 1940-41, Borden Mills, Kingsport, Tenn., 1945-46; with Burlington Industries, Inc., 1946—, exec. v.p., 1963—, also mem. exec. com., mem. mgmt. com., dir. Dir. So. States Indsl. Council. Bd. advisers N.C. Vocational Textile Sch., 1954-60, Belmont Abbey Coll., 1958—; chmn. devel. bd. Lenoir Rhyne Coll.; vice chmn. devel. bd. U. Tenn. Mem. Yarn Spinners Assn. (past dir.), Gastonia (N.C.) C. of C. (past 1st v.p.). Presbyn. Clubs: Charlotte (N.C.) Textile (past pres., dir.); Greensboro Country; Kiwanis (past pres. Cramerton, N.C.); University (N.Y.C.). Home: 105 Elmwood Terrace Greensboro NC 27408 Office: 3330 Friendly Av Greensboro NC 27401

BARBER, ALBERT ALCIDE, educator, zoologist; b. Providence, July 13, 1929; s. Benjamin Arthur and Alice (Proulx) B.; B.S., U. R.I., 1950, M.S., 1952; Ph.D., Duke, 1958; m. Mary Lee Sparling, Sept. 1, 1956; children—Bonnie, Bradley. Mem. faculty U. Cal. at Los Angeles, 1958—, prof. zoology, 1968—, chmn. dept., 1968-70, asst. vice chancellor research, 1970—. Recipient Phi Sigma Grad. award U. R.I., 1952; Purkyne medal Czechoslovakian Med. Soc., 1969. Mem.

A.A.A.S., Am. Inst. Biol. Scientists, Am. Soc. Zoology, Am. Physiol. Soc., Sigma Xi. Research biology cell membranes. Home: 2100 Eric Dr Los Angeles CA 90049

BARBER, ALDEN G., chief exec. Boy Scouts Am. Address: 123 Penwood Rd Basking Ridge NJ 07920*

BARBER, ANTHONY PERRINOTT LYSBERG, British politician; b. Hull, Eng., July 4, 1920; s. John and Katy (Lysberg) B.; M.A., Oriel Coll., Oxford U., 1947; m. Jean Patricia Asquith, Sept. 5, 1950; children—Louise, Josephine. Barrister-at-law, Inner Temple, 1948; Parliamentary pvt. sec. to air minister, 1952-54; asst. govt. whip, 1955-57; lord commr. of Treasury, 1957-58; Parliamentary pvt. sec. to prime minister, 1958-59; econ. sec. to Treasury, 1959-62, financial sec., 1962-63; minister of health, mem. Privy Council and Cabinet, 1963-64, M.P., 1951—; mem. Opposition Shadow Cabinet; prin. Opposition Spokesmen on trade, industry and power; chmn. Brit. Conservative Party, 1967-70; chancellor of Duchy of Lancaster, 1970; chancellor of the Exchequer, 1970—. Served with Brit. Army and RAF, 1939-45; prisoner of war, 1942-45. Home: 11 Downing St London SW 1 England Office: Treasury Great George St London SW 1 England

BARBER, ARTHUR WHITING, govt. ofcl.; b. Meriden, Conn., July 4, 1926; s. Arthur Leslie and Winifred (Whiting) B.; B.A. in Physics, Harvard, 1950; m. Margaret Shorey, Aug. 27, 1949; children—Jeffrey, Christopher, Jonathan Scott, Kimberley Susan, Cynthia. Physicist, Air Force Cambridge (Mass.) Research Center, 1950-61, Mitre Corp., 1961-62; dep. asst. sec. internat. security affairs Dept. Def., 1962-67; pres. Inst. Politics and Planning, 1967—. Home: 7600 Hemlock St Bethesda MD 20034 Office: 1411 K St Washington DC 20005

BARBER, BERNARD, educator; b. Boston, Jan. 29, 1918; s. Albert and Jennie (Lieberman) B.; A.B., Harvard, 1939, A.M., 1942, Ph.D., 1949; m. Elinor Gellert, Sept. 25, 1948; children—Leslie Marianne, Christine Ruth, Philip Gellert, John Robert. Tutor, teaching fellow Harvard, 1946-48; instr., then asst. prof. Smith Coll., 1948-52; mem. faculty Barnard Coll., 1952—, prof. sociology, 1961—, chmn. dept., 1962-65, 68—. Pres. trustees Dobbs Ferry Pub. Library, 1960—. Served to lt. USNR, 1942-46. Author: Science and Social Order, 1952; Social Stratification, 1957; Drugs and Society, 1967. Editor; (with Walter Hirsch) Sociology of Science, 1962; (with Elinor G. Barber) European Social Class, 1965; L.J. Henderson on the Social System, 1970; (with Alex Inkeles) Stability and Social Change, 1971. Home: Braeside Lane Dobbs Ferry NY 10522 Office: Dept Sociology Barnard Coll New York City NY 10027

BARBER, CESAR LOMBARDI, educator; b. Berkeley, Cal., June 3, 1913; s. Alvin Barton and Lucy (Lombardi) B.; grad. Phillips Exeter Acad., 1929-31; B.A., Harvard, 1935, Jr. fellow, 1936-39; Henry fellow Cambridge (Eng.) U., 1935-36; M.A. (hon.), Amherst Coll., 1956; m. Elizabeth Putnam, Oct. 10, 1936; children—George Putnam, Lucy Lombardi, Robert Ennis. Instr., Harvard, 1939-42; from asst. prof. to prof. English, Amherst Coll., 1942-62; prof. English, Ind. U., 196267, chmn. dept., 1962-66; prof. English, State U. N.Y., Buffalo, 1967-70; vice chancellor humanities U. Cal., Santa Cruz, 1970—, also prof. lit., 1970—; vis. prof. Yale Sch. Music, summers 1942, 48, 49, Harvard, 1950; vis. prof., sr. fellow Council Humanities, Princeton, 1961-62; vis. prof. Smith Coll., 1966-67. Fellow Center for Advanced Study in Behavioral Scis., 1969-70. Rep. mem. Amherst Town Meeting, 1955-62; mem. Amherst Town Democratic Com., 1952-62. Trustee Cummington Sch. Arts, 1958—, Bennington Coll., 1960-64, Sarah Lawrence Coll., Bronxville, N.Y., 1965-70. Served to lt. (s.g.) USNR, 1943-46; PTO. Decorated Bronze Star; fellow Folger Shakespeare Library, 1951, 54-55; Ford fellow, 1954-55; recipient George Jean Nathan prize for drama criticism, 1960. Mem. Coll. English Assn. (pres. New Eng. 1960 61), Modern Lang. Assn., Am. Assn. U. Profs. Author: Shakespeare's Festive Comedy, 1959; More Power to Them, a Report on . . . Encouraging Student Initiative, 1962; (with others) The New College Plan, 1958. Address: 1025 Laurent St Santa Cruz CA 95060

BARBER, CHARLES FINCH, lawyer, metals co. exec.; b. Chgo., Feb. 26, 1917; s. Henri Newton and Lillian (Wanner) B.; B.S., Northwestern U., 1939; LL.B., Harvard, 1942; B.Phil., Oxford U., 1948; m. Lois Helen LaCroix, Aug. 30, 1947; children—Charles Bradford, Ann McDonald, Robin Goodhue, Elizabeth Louise. Admitted to D.C. bar, 1942; asso. Covington & Burling, Washington, 1948-54; asst. Solicitor Gen. U.S., 1954-56; gen. counsel Am. Smelting & Refining Co., N.Y.C., 1956-63, v.p., 1959-63, exec. v.p., 1963-69, pres., 1969-71, chmn., 1971—, also dir.; dir. So. Peru Copper Corp., Asarco Mexicana, S.A. Mem. Nat. Indsl. Conf. Bd. Bd. mgrs. Swarthmore Coll., 1966—; trustee Council of Americas. Served to lt. comdr. USNR, 1941-46. Decorated Legion of Merit. Mem. Am. Bar Assn., Am. Inst. Mining, Metall., and Petroleum Engrs. (asso.), Council Fgn. Relations, Phi Beta Kappa. Clubs: Bankers, Down Town Assn., Mining (N.Y.C.); Metropolitan (Washington); Belle Haven (Greenwich). Home: 66 Glenwood Dr Greenwich CT 06830 Office: 120 Broadway New York City NY 10005

BARBER, EDWARD JOHN, shipping exec.; b. Englewood, N.J., Oct. 4, 1916; s. Edward John and Gladys (Lemmel) B.; student Manlius Sch., 1929-34; m. Jane Rose, July 3, 1940 (div. 1946); 1 dau., Ray; m. 2d, Eleanor Ogden, Apr. 19, 1952; children—Edward John, Catherine, James. Pres., dir. Barber S.S. Lines, Inc., Am.-West African Line, Inc.; dir. Barber S.S. Lines. Ltd. Maritime Assn., Pouch Terminal, Inc. Hurum Shipping Corp., Geo. W. Rogers Constrn. Corp; trustee Dollar Savs. Bank. Trustee Manlius (N.Y.) Sch. Served as lt. USAAF, World War II. Home: lt. USAAF, World War II. Home: Heywood Rd Pelham Manor NY 10803 Office: 17 Battery Pl New York City NY 10004

BARBER, EVERETT MCMULLIN, mech. engr.; b. Oil City, Pa., July 14, 1909; s. Everett J. and Mary Chaplin (McMullin) B.; B.Sc. in Mech. Engring., Pa. State U., 1931, M.S. in Mech. Engring. (Elliott fellow), 1933; Gordon McKay fellow, Harvard, 1935-36; m. Emily Elizabeth Porter, Nov. 3, 1934; children—Everett McMullin, Mary Frances. With Texaco Research Center, Beacon, N.Y., 1934- -, supr. engring. research, 1942-59, sr. research technologist, 1959-60, dir. process devel., 1960-68, dir. planning, 1968—. Mem. NRC, 1956-58; mem. NACA com. aircraft fire prevention. Bd. dirs. Engring. Found., 1950-63, chmn. bd. 1956-58. Recipient student prize Am. Soc. Refrigeration Engrs., 1932; Levy medal Franklin Inst., 1946. Registered profl. engr., N.Y. Fellow Am. Soc. M.E. (dir. 1958- 63, recipient Richards Meml. award 1957); mem. Engrs. Joint Council, Combustion Research Inst., Research Soc. Am., Solar Energy Soc., Sigma Xi, Pi Tau Sigma, Pi Mu Epsilon. Episcopalian (warden). Home: RFD 1 Box 340 Wappingers Falls NY 12590 Office: Texaco Inc Beacon NY 12508

BARBER, FRANK ELLIOTT, Jr., lawyer; b. Brattlesboro, Vt., June 8, 1912; s. Frank Elliott and Elsie (Haskell) B.; B.S., Norwich U., 1934; LL.B., Harvard, 1937; m. Jeanne Freund, Jan. 20, 1938; children—Susan E., Frank Elliott; m. 2d, Frances Fairbrother, Aug. 27, 1949; children—Hugh W., Allison Frances. Admitted to Vt. bar, 1937; propr. Barber & Barber law offices; town counsel, Brattleboro, 1941-43, 45-47, moderator, 1950-62, judge Municipal Ct., 1947-49; mem. Vt. Senate, 1947-49, rep. Vt. Gen. Assembly, 1951-53; atty. gen. State of Vt., 1953-55. Chmn. Vt. Liquor Control Bd., 1959-63; legislative counsel Vt. Bankers Assn., 1969—. Mem. Am. Legion, V.F.W., Am., Vt. (bd. mgrs. 1959-65), Windham County (pres. 1966) bar assns., Theta Chi. Mason, Elk. Club: Brattleboro Country (pres.). Home: 16 Linden St Brattlesboro VT 05301 Office: 114 Main St Brattlesboro VT 05301

BARBER, HARRY ASHLEY, mfg. co. exec.; b. Aurora, Ill., May 30, 1911; s. Harry Haughey and Blanche (Capron) B.; B.S., U. Ill., 1933; m. Ruth Reid, May 29, 1937; children—Ann (Mrs. Alvin Kaltofen), Joan (Mrs. Terrance Hewitt), Susan Peter. Engr. Barber-Greene Co., Aurora, Ill., 1933-38, v.p., dir., 1938-54, pres., 1954—, chmn. bd., 1966—, dir. subsidiaries; dir. No. Council Community Services, 1955-58; bd. dirs. Copley Hosp., Aurora. Mem. Phi Delta Theta. Conglist. Inventor heavy constrn. equipment. Home: 1445 Garfield Av Aurora IL 60506 Office: 400 N Highland Av Aurora IL 60506

BARBER, HENRY P. C. W., lawyer; b. Evanston, Ill., May 28, 1907; s. Charles S. and Alicia B. (Wilson) B.; A.B., Princeton, 1928; J.D., Northwestern U., 1931; m. Mary McElwain, Sept. 8, 1934; children—Charles, Mary Stewart. Admitted to Ill. bar, 1931, since practiced in Chgo.; asso. Peterson, Ross, Rall, Barber & Seidel and predecessor firms, 1931—, partner, 1944—. Chmn. Zoning Amendment Com., Evanston, 1964-71. Alderman, Evanston, 1945-53. Asso., Nat. Coll. Edn. Republican. Episcopalian. Clubs: Attic (Chgo.); Glen View (Ill.). Home: 927 Michigan Av Evanston IL 60202 Office: 135 S La Salle Chicago IL 60603

BARBER, HOLLIS WILLIAM, educator; b. Cin., Apr. 2, 1910; s. George Franklin and Mabel (Potter) B.; A.B., Oberlin Coll., 1930; A.M., Am. U., 1931; postgrad. U. Berlin (Germany), 1932-33; Ph.D., U. Wis., 1935; m. Dorothy Lillian Grosser, Sept. 3, 1937; children—Hollis William, Frederick Allan. Instr. polit. sci. U. Ala., 1935-36. U. Cin., 1936-39; asst. prof., then asso. prof. Tulane U., 1939-47; mem. faculty U. Ill. at Chgo. Circle, 1947—, prof. polit. sci., 1953—, head dept., 1964-69. Served to lt. USNR, 1942-45. Author: Foreign Policies of the United States, 1953; United States in World Affairs, 1955, 1957. Home: 211 Thatcher Av River Forest IL 60305 Office: 1108 BSB Box 4348 Chicago IL 60680

BARBER, JAMES DAVID, polit. scientist, educator; b. Charleston, W.Va., July 31, 1930; s. Daniel Newman and Edith (Naismith) B.; B.A., U. Chgo., 1950, M.A., 1955; Ph.D. (Samuel S. Fels fellow), Yale, 1960; m. Ann Goodridge Sale, Dec. 27, 1951; children—Sara Naismith, Jane Lewis. Research staff U. Chgo. Indsl. Relations Center, 1951-53, 55; asst. prof. polit. sci. Stetson U., DeLand, Fla., 1955-57; instr., asst. prof., asso. prof. Yale, New Haven, 1960-68, prof. polit. sci., 1968—, dir. grad. studies in polit. sci., 1965-67, dir. Office for Advanced Polit. Studies, 1967-68; dir. Harvard-Yale-Columbia Intensive Summer Studies Program, 1966-67; series editor Harcourt Brace Jovanovich, 1970—; cons. Nat. Indsl. Conf. Bd., Com. on Econ. Devel., Center for Information on Am., Commn. on Year 2000. Mem. Charter Commn., Wallingford, Conn., 1959-61, Bd. Finance, 1960-61; chmn. Nat. Coalition for a Responsible Congress, 1970, Bd. Univs. Nat. Anti-war Fund, 1970. Served with U.S. Army, 1953-55. NSF fellow, 1961-63; guest scholar Brookings Instn., 1964-65; fellow Center for Advanced Study in Behavioral Scis., 1968-69. Mem. Am. Polit. Sci. Assn., Am. Assn. U. Profs. Democrat. Author: The Lawmakers: Recruitment and Adaptation to Legislative Life, 1965; Power in Committees: An Experiment in the Governmental Process, 1966; Citizen Politics, 1969. Editor: Political Leadership in American Government, 1964; chmn. editorial bd. Polit. Sci., 1969-71. Contbr. articles profl. jours. Home: 99 Garfield Av North Haven CT 06517 Office: Dept Polit Sci Yale New Haven CT 06520

BARBER, JOHN BARRON, steel co. exec.; b. Sault Ste. Marie, Ont., Can., June 4, 1912; s. Roland and Helena Alice (Moorehouse) B.; B.Commerce, Queen's U., 1935; m. Hilda Elaine Crawford, Oct. 11, 1946; childrenLeslie Dalton, Susan Elizabeth. Vice chmn., sr. v.p., dir. the Algoma Steel Corp., Ltd., Sault Ste. Marie; dir. Dominion Bridge Co. Ltd., Can. S.S. Lines Cannelton Coal Co., Yankanuck Steamships Ltd. Bd. govs. Ont. Research (dir.), Internat. Iron and Steel Inst. (dir.), Am. Iron and Steel Inst. Clubs: Sault Ste. Marie Golf (dir.), Algoma Steel Mens (Sault Ste. Marie); National (Toronto, Ont.). Home: Summit Av Sault Ste Marie Ontario Canada Office: The Algoma Steel Corp Ltd Sault Ste Marie Ontario Canada

BARBER, JOSEPH, editor, b. Lowell, Mass., June 20, 1909; s. Joseph and Grace Greenleaf (Harris) B.; student Phillips Acad., Andover, Mass., 1925-27; A.B., Harvard, 1931; student U. Munich (Germany), 1931-32; Columbia, 1933; m. Eileen Paradis, Feb. 15, 1936. Berlin corr. Hearst Newspapers, 1933-34; dir. publs. Am. Council, Inst. Pacific Relations, 1934-35; mng. editor Atlantic Monthly, 1935-38; pub. relations counsel, Honolulu, 1938-40; asso. editor Washington Post, 1941-43; dir. Com. on Fgn. Relations in 33 cities, affiliate Council on Fgn. Relations, Inc., N.Y.C., 1946-63. Served from lt. (j.g.) to lt. comdr. USNR, 1943-46. Awarded Pulitzer traveling scholarship, 1933. Mem. Council Fgn. Relations, Grand Jury Assn. N.Y.C., Sigma Delta Chi. Clubs: Century, Harvard (N.Y.C.); St. Botolph (Boston). Author: Hawaii: Restless Rampart, 1941: Good Fences Make Good Neighbors, 1958; These Are The Committees, 1964; co-author: Political Handbook of the World, 1953. Editor: American Policy Toward Germany, 1947; The Marshall Plan as American Policy, 1948; Military Cooperation with Western Europe, 1949; American Policy Toward China, 1950; The Containment of Soviet Expansion, 1951; Foreign Aid and the National Interest, 1952; Foreign Trade and U.S. Tariff Policy, 1953; Diplomacy and the Communist Challenge, 1954; Alliances and American Security, 1960; Red China and Our U.N. Policy, 1961; Atlantic Unity and the American Interest, 1963. Home: 16 E 84th St New York City NY 10028 also Fortunes Rocks Biddeford ME 04005

BARBER, RICHARD LESLIE, coll. dean; b. N. East, Pa., Apr. 22, 1920; s. Chester Clifford and Agnes (Leslie) B.; A.B. in Philosophy and Math., Ohio U., 1940; postgrad. student, U.S. Naval Acad., 1944-45; M.A. in Philosophy, Ind. U., 1948; Ph.D., Yale, 1950; m. Frances Pardue McCutchon, Aug. 1, 1944; children—Richard Leslie, Frances Edith. Successively grad. asst., all univ. fellow, teaching asst. Ind. U., 1941, 46-48; asst. instr. Yale, 1948-50; successively asst. prof., asso. prof. philosophy, coordinator ednl. TV prodn. Tulane U., 1950-59; prof. philosophy, dean Coll. of Arts and Scis., U. Louisville, 1959—. Bd. dirs. Ky. Youth Devel. Found. Served to lt. (S.G.) USNR, 1941-45; ETO. PTO; capt. Res. Mem. Am. Assn. U. Profs. (pres. Tulane 1954), Am. (mem. exec. com. 1965-70), Ky. confs. acad. deans, Assn. Higher Edn., Nat. Soc. Study Edn., Assn. Am. Colls., Am. Assn. Colls. Tchr. Edn., Metaphys. Soc. Am. (charter), So. Soc. Philosophy and Psychology, Assn. Realistic Philosophy, Southwestern, Ky. (pres. 1965) philos. assns., Conf. Acad. Deans So. States (pres.), English-Speaking Union (mem. bd. Ky. br.), Navy League, Naval Res. Assn., Res. Officers Assn., Louisville Com. Fgn. Relations, Phi Kappa Phi, Delta Tau Delta, Omicron Delta Kappa, Phi Eta Sigma, Alpha Phi Omega, Kappa Delta Pi, Phi Mu Alpha. Methodist. Kiwanian. Clubs: Filson, Conversation, Helium (Louisville). Author numerous articles. reviews. Home: 2431 Top Hill Rd Louisville KY 40206

BARBER, SAMUEL, composer; b. West Chester, Pa., Mar. 9, 1910; s. Samuel Leroy and Marquerite McLeod (Beatty) B.; student Curtis Inst. Music. Phila., 1923-32. student piano with Isabelle Vengerova, singing with Emilio de Gogorza, composition with Rosario Scalero; grad. Curtis inst. Music, 1932, Dr. Mus., 1945; hon. doctorate Harvard, 1959. Compositions; Serenade for String Quartet, 1929; Dover Beach (for voice and string quartet, 1931; String Quartet in B minor, 1936; Sonata (for cello and piano), 1932; Overture to "School for Scandal" (for orch.), 1932; Music for A Scene from Shelley (for orch.), 1933; Symphony in One Movement (for orch., 1936 Adagio for Strings (recorded by Toscanini), 1936; Essay for Orchestra, 1937; The Virgin Martyrs (choral), 1935; Concerto for Violin and Orchestra, 1940; Second Essay, 1942; Second Symphony, 1944; Capricorn Concerto, 1944; Four Excursions (for piano, introduced by Horowitz), 1944; Cello Concerto, 1945; Ballet for Martha Graham, 1946; Medea, 1946; Knoxville, Summer of 1915 (for voice and orchestra), 1947; Piano Sonata, 1948; Souvenirs (ballet-suite for orchestra), 1953; Prayers of Kierkegaard (for chorus, soprano solo and orch.), 1954; A Stopwatch and an Ordnance Map (men's chorus and drums); Reincarnations (mixed chorus); Let Down the Bars, O Death (chorus); numerous songs including Hermit Songs, 1953; opera Vanessa, Salzburg festival, 1958, Met. Opera House, 1958; Toccata Festival for Organ and Orchestra, 1950; Die Natali; Chorale Preludes for Christmas (for orch.), 1960; Piano Concerto, 1962; Andromache's Farewell (for soprano and orch.), 1963; Antony and Cleopatra (opera), 1966; Despite and Still (song cycle), 1968; a cappella choruses Twelfth Night, To be Sung on the Water, 1969. Compositions performed in U.S., also in Europe and USSR. Recipient Prix de Rome, 1935; Pulitzer prize music for opera Vanessa, 1958, piano concerto, 1963; Guggenheim award, 1945; N.Y. Music Critics award, 1946. Served with AUS, 1943. Mem. A.S.C.A.P. (dir. 1969—), Nat. Acad. of Arts and Letters. Home: Mt Kisco NY 10549 Address: care G Schinmer Inc 609 Fifth Av New York City NY 10017

BARBER, SAUL BENJAMIN, educator; b. Somerville, Mass., Sept. 3, 1920; s. Samuel and Ida (Polashuk) B.; B.S., R.I. State Coll., 1941; Ph.D., Yale, 1954; m. Ellen M. Brown, Dec. 25, 1955; children—Lisa Ruth, Lowell Brown, David Joshua. Instr. zoology R.I. State Coll., 1946-48; instr. biology Williams Coll., 1952-54; instr. zoology Smith Coll., 1954-55; research asso. Narragansett Marine Lab., U. R.I., 1955-56; asst. prof. biology Lehigh U., Bethlehem, Pa., 1956-59, asso. prof., 1959-64, prof., head dept., 1964—; NIH Spl. fellow as research asso. zoology dept. Oxford (Eng.) U., 1963-64. Past 2d v.p. Lehigh Valley chpt. Pa. Assn. Brain Injured Children. Past bd. dirs. Lehigh Valley chpt. Am. Heart Assn. Served to capt. USAAF, 1943-46; PTO. Mem. A.A.A.S., Am. Inst. Biol. Scis., Am. Soc. Zoologists, Am. Assn. U. Profs. (past pres. Lehigh chpt.), Sigma Xi (past pres. Lehigh). Contbr. chpts. to Ency. Biol. Scis., 1960; also articles to profl. jours. Home: 1954 Sycamore St Bethlehem PA 18017

BARBER, SHERBURNE F., coll. dean; b. Nunda N.Y., Oct. 25, 1907; s. George F. and Ethelwyn (Clark) B.; A.B., U. Rochester, 1929, A.M., 1930; Ph.D., U. Ill., 1933; m. Virginia L. Roy, Apr. 8, 1944; children—John, David, Andrew. NRC fellow math. Johns Hopkins, 1933-34, Princeton, 1934-35; instr. math. State U. Ia., 1935-37; mem. faculty City Coll. N.Y., 1937—, prof. math., 1956—, dean Coll. Liberal Arts and Scis., 1967—. Mem. Phi Beta Kappa, Sigma Xi. Research on Cremona and birational transformations, algebraic geometry. Home: Setalcott Pl Setauket NY 11733 Office: City Coll NY New York City NY 10031

BARBER, WILLIAM JOSEPH, educator, economist; b. Abilene, Kan., Jan. 13, 1925; s. Ward Seymour Henry and Esther (Roop) B.; A.B., Harvard, 1949; B.A., Oxford (Eng.) U., 1951, M.A., 1955. D.Phil., 1957; M.A. (hon.). Wesleyan U., Middletown, Conn., 1965; m. Sheila Mary Marr, Apr. 16, 1955; children—Thomas, John, Charles. Asst. prof. Kan. State U., 1951-52; lectr. Balliol Coll., Oxford U., 1956; mem. faculty Wesleyan U., Middletown, Conn., 1957—, prof. econs., 1965- -. Am. sec. Rhodes Scholarship Trust, 1970—; bd. electors Eastman professorship Oxford U., 1970—. Served with AUS, 1943-46; ETO. Rhodes scholar, 1949-51; Ford Found. Fgn. Area fellow Africa, 1955-56. Mem. Am. Econ. Assn., Royal Econ. Soc., African Studies Assn., Am. Assn. Rhodes Scholars, Phi Beta Kappa. Author: The Economy of British Central Africa, 1961; A History of Economic Thought, 1967. Contbr. to Asian Drama: An Inquiry into the Poverty of Nations, 1968. Home: 306 Pine St Middletown CT 06457

BARBER, WILLIAM WYATT, headmaster; b. Southborough, Mass., Dec. 13, 1909; s. William Wyatt and Florence (Harmon) B.; grad. St. Mark's Sch., 1928; A.B., Princeton, 1932; Carnegie fellow, Yale, 1936-37; m. Margaret Hazlehurst Patton, June 21, 1933; children—Louise Eustis (Mrs. Lewis M. Cowardin), William Wyatt III. With St. Marks Sch., Southborough, Mass., 1932—, successively tchr. English, tchr. Greek, asst. headmaster, acting headmaster, 1932-48, headmaster, 1948—, hockey coach 1936—. Treas. Ind. Schools Found. of Mass. Mem. Ind. Sch. Assn. Mass. (past pres). Address: St Mark's Sch Southborough MA 01772

BARBERA, JOE, TV cartoonist; b. N.Y.C.; grad. Am. Inst. Banking. Formerly accountant trust co.; free-lance mag. cartoonist; story man MGM, 1937 co-producer (with Bill Hanna) Tom and Jerry, animated cartoon series; partner Hanna and Barbera Prodn., N.Y.C., 1957—; cartoon series include Ruff and Reddy, -, Huckleberry Hound, 1958—, Quick Draw McGraw, 1959—, The Flintstones, cartoon series for adults. Recipient numerous Acad. awards for animated cartoons. Office: 235 Elizabeth St New York City NY 10012

BARBIERI, CHRISTOPHER GEORGE, c. of c. exec.; b. Bklyn., Jan. 9, 1941; s. Nicholas Joseph and Marie Anne (Bacigalupo) B.; B.S. in Econs., Cornell U., 1962; M.S. in Econs., U. Vt., 1964; m. Joanne Lee Barnett, Jan. 30, 1965; children—Matthew, Deborah, Lisa. Asst. new product mgr. H.P. Hood & Sons, Boston, 1965-68, new product mgr., 1968-69, sales mgr., Burlington, Vt., 1969-70; exec. v.p. Vt. C. of C., Montpelier, 1970—. Served with Vt. Air N.G., 1964-70. Mem. Vt. Soc. Assn. Execs. (v.p.), Vt. Assn. Chamber Execs. (pres.). Author: (service bull.) Pure Maple Marketing in Urban Areas, 1964. Home: RFD Underhill VT 05489 Office: 7 Langdon Montpelier VT 05602

BARBIERI, FEDORA, mezzo-soprano; b. Trieste, Italy, June 4, 1919; d. Rafaele and Ida Barbieri; studied voice with Maestro Bugamelli, Luigi Toffolo; scholarship student Centro Amiamento-Teatro-Lirico, Florence, Italy; m. Luigi Barlozzetti, 1943; children—Franco, Ugo. First pub. appearance as soloist Ch. of San Giusto, Trieste; Italy; opera debut Teatro Comunale, Florence, Italy, 1940, also appeared, 1949; singer opera co. Teatro Real, Rome, Italy, 1941-42; debut La Scala, Milan, Italy, 1943; appeared in opera Teatro Verdi, Florence, 1945; toured Eng. with La Scala Co., 1950; debut Met. Opera, N.Y.C., 1950, mem., 1950—; tours U.S., S.A., Europe; operatic repertoire includes Il Trovatore, Aida, Norma, Cavalleria Rusticana, Carmen. Address: care Metropolitan Opera Co Lincoln Center Plaza New York City NY 10023*

BARBIERI, LEANDRO, (Gato), tenor saxophonist; b. Rosario, Argentina, Nov. 28, 1933. Played in Europe with Jim Hall, Lalo Schifrin, Ted Curson; with Don Cherry Quintet, 1966— ; recording artist for Blue Note Records. Address: via F. Crispi 90 Rome, Italy.*

BARBIERI, PIERRE M., Jr., diversified mfg. co. exec.; b. Cin., May 21, 1910; grad. Phillips Acad., Andover, Mass., 1927; B.S., Princeton, 1931; postgrad. Mass. Inst. Tech., 1931-33; m. Jean R. Holland, June 16, 1935; children--Lois A., Andrew M., James. Salesman, Brown Mfg. Co., Boston, 1932-33; jr. engr. Ball Metals Co., Carson City, Nev., 1933-36, engr., 1936-37, sr. engr., 1937-40; project engr. Kingston Engring. Co., Los Angeles, 1940-43; with dept. engring. City of Denver, 1946-50, dep. head, 1950-52; 2d v.p. Johnson Mfg. Co., Kansas City, Kansas, 1952-54, v.p. for engring., 1954-57; v.p. research Consol. Industries, Inc., South Bend, Ind., 1957-60, exec. v.p., 1960-65, pres., 1965-70, chmn. bd., chief exec. officer, 1970--, also dir.; dir. ABC Chem. Co., 2d Nat. Bank, Country Food Storage Co., Providence Indsl. Corp. Pres., Dewey High Sch., Kansas City, Mo., 1953-54; fund chmn. local div. Salvation Army, 1959-60. Mem. South Bend Republican Com., 1964-68. Bd. dirs. Ind. council Boy Scouts Am., 1969-71; trustee Lovell Found. Served to lt., Corps Engrs., AUS, 1943-45. Decorated Bronze Star medal. Member N.A.M., South Bend C. of C. (v.p. 1963-65, dir. 1965-70), Am. Mgmt. Assn., Ind. Engrs. Soc. (program com. 1961-63), Princeton Alumni Assn. Episcopalian. Home: 6823 Broad Terrace Av South Bend IN 46505

BARBIERI, SANTE UBERTO, bishop; b. Dueville, Italy, Aug. 2, 1902 (naturalized Brazilian 1928); s. Sante and Maria Luisa (Zanzotto) B.; B.D., Little So. Meth. U., Brazil, 1926; A.B., B.D., M.A., So. Meth. U., Dallas, 1932, LL.D., 1956; M.A., Emory U., L. H. D., 1956; m. Odette de Oliveira, Oct. 4, 1924; children—Laura, Stelvio, Livio Uberto, Flavio Ennio. Became naturalized Argentine citizen, 1956. Ordained to ministry Meth. Ch., 1925; pastor, pres. So. Sem. Meth. Ch. of Brazil, 1923-28, 1934-39; pastor, exec. sec. bd. evangelism River Plate Ann. Conf., 1940-47; pres. Union Theol. Sem., Buenos Aires, Argentina, 1948, prof., bd. dirs., 1940-49; bishop Meth. Ch. in Argentina, Uruguay, Bolivia; chmn. exec. com. Latin Am. Central Conf.; chmn. First Latin Am. Conf. Evang. Chs., Buenos Aires, 1949; dir. El Predicador Evangelico mag. Latin Am. preachers, 1943-66; exec. sec. Council Evang. Meth. Chs. in Latin Am., 1970—. Del. 6th Ecumenical Meth. Conf., 1931, 8th Conf., Oxford, Eng., 1951; del. Internat. Fellowship of Reconciliation Council, Dortmund, Germany, 1953; ofcl. World Council Chs., New Delhi, India, 1961. Named Distinguished Alumnus, So. Meth. U., 1955. Mem. World Council Chs. (pres. 1954-64. mem. exec. and Central coms), Internat. Meth. Hist. Soc., World Christian Edn. and Sunday Sch. Assn. (v.p., dean inst. 1962, dir.), Acad. Letters Rio Grande do Sul Brasil, Eta Sigma Phi. Mason (past master). Author: Spirtual Currents in Latin America, 1950, The Land of Eldorado, 1961; author numerous religious novels, sermons, biographies in Portuguese and Spanish. Contbr. articles Latin Am. mags. Home: Los Celbos 56 El Palomar Prov Buenos Aires Argentina Office: Casilla 5296 Correo Central Buenos Aires Argentina

BARBOUR, IAN GRAEME, educator; b. Peking, China, Oct. 5, 1923; s. George Brown and Dorothy (Dickinson) B.; B.A., Swarthmore Coll., 1943; M.A., Duke, 1946; Ph.D., U. Chgo., 1950; B.D., Yale, 1956; m. Deane Kern, Nov. 29, 1947; children—John Dickinson, Blair Winn, David Freeland, Heather Deane. Asst. prof. physics Kalamazoo Coll., 1949-51, asso. prof., chmn. dept., 1951-53; mem. faculty Carleton Coll., Northfield, Minn., 1955—, chmn. dept. religion, 1956—, prof. religion and physics, 1965—. Ford Faculty fellow, 1953; recipient Harbison award distinguished teaching Danforth Found., 1963; fellow Am. Council Learned Socs., 1963-64; Guggenheim and Fulbright fellow, 1967-68. Mem. Phi Beta Kappa, Sigma Xi. Author: Christianity and the Scientist, 1960; Issues in Science and Religion, 1966; Science and Religion: New Perspectives on the Dialogue, 1968; Science and Secularity; The Ethics of Technology, 1970; Earth Might Be Fair, 1971. Mem. editorial bd. Process Studies, Zygon, Jour. Sci. and Religion. Author numerous articles. Home: 106 Winona St Northfield MN 55057

BARBOUR, ROSS, singer; b. Columbus, Ind., Dec. 31, 1928; s. Harold L. and Maude (Fodrea) B.; student Arthur Jordan Conservatory, Indpls., 1947; m. Nancy Sue Carson, Dec. 31, 1948; children—Kent, Gary, Kathy. Mem. singing group Four Freshmen, 1948—; world tours; pres. Rossdon Music Pub. Co., Kenbob Music Pub. Co.; sec. Viscount Internat. Prodns.; recording artist Liberty, Capitol, Stylist labels. Hon. mem. Tau Kappa Epsilon. Composer: Tears in Our Eyes, 1963; Love Lost, 1959; And So It's Over, 1963; Crazy Bones, 1955; First Affair, 1960. Home: 16200 Keeler Dr Granada Hills CA 91344 Office: 8720 Woodley Av Sepulveda CA 91343

BARBOUR, WALWORTH, U.S. ambassador; b. Cambridge, Mass., June 4, 1908; s. Samuel Lewis and Clara (Hammond) B.; grad. Phillips Exeter Acad., 1926; A.B., Harvard, 1930. Foreign service officer, 1931—; vice consul, Naples, Italy, 1932, Athens, Greece, 1933-36; vice consul, 3d sec., Baghdad, Iraq, 1936-39; vice consul, 3d sec., Sofia, Bulgaria, 1939-41, 2d sec., vice consul, Dec. 1941; 2d sec., vice consul, Cairo, Egypt, 1942-44; 2d sec., vice consul, Athens, Greece, Nov.-Dec. 1944, consul, Dec. 1944; assigned Dept. of State, 1945-49; assigned minister-counselor, Moscow, U.S.S.R., 1949; dir. office Eastern European affairs State Dept., 1951-54; dep. asst. sec. of state for European affairs, 1954-55; U.S. minister London, Eng., 1955-61; ambassador to Israel, 1961—. Clubs: University (Washington); Chevy Chase (Md.). Office: Tel Aviv Dept of State Washington DC 20521

BARBOUR, WILLIAM ERNEST, Jr., co. exec.; b. Evanston, Ill., Nov. 1909; s. William Ernest and Mabel Ridgeway (Hair) B.; B.S., Mass. Inst. Tech., m. Georgiana Whitney, Dec. 16, 1950; children—Alicia Barbour, Gigi. Cons. in field indsl. instrumentation, 1933-36; with Raytheon Mfg. Corp., 1936-39, Boston Edison Co., 1939-41; pres. Tracerlab, Inc., Boston, 1946-57; pres. Controls for Radiation, Inc., 1957-58; cons. nuclear and magnetic fields, 1965—; pres. Magnion, Inc., 1960-65; exec. sec. Assn. Nuclear Instrument Mfrs., 1966—. Dir. QSC Industries, Cons. tech. utilization NASA. Mem. New Eng. Govs.' Com. on Atomic Energy, also Atomic Indsl. Forum. Mem. alumni council Mass. Inst. Tech. Mem. council atomic energy Nat. Indsl. Conf. Bd., 1955—; mem. So. Regional Edn. Bd. Nuclear Energy Devel. Project, 1955-56. Bd. corporators Emerson Hosp., 1968—. Served with USAAF, 1941-46. Mem. Nat. Aviation Assn. (dir. 1970—), Am. Standards Assn. (mem. nuclear standards bd.), Am. Inst. E.E. (mem. standards com., Geneva observer, 1956 chmn. com. nucleonics 1954-57), Am. Nuclear Soc. (dir. 1954-56), Nat. Pilots Assn., Aircraft Owners and Pilots Assn., Nuclear Instrument Mfrs. (exec. sec. 1965—), I.E.E.E. (adminstrv. com. group on nuclear sci.), Delta Kappa Epsilon. Clubs: Aero of New England (dir., pres. 1971—), Concord Country. Address: Barbour Assos Box 460 Concord MA 01742

BARBOUR, WILLIAM RINEHART Jr., book publisher; b. N.Y.C., Mar. 2, 1922; s. William Rinehart and Mary (McKelvey) B.; student Mich. State Coll., 1941-42; m. Mary Munsell, Nov. 17, 1951; children—Bruce R., Elizabeth M., Alan W. With Fleming H. Revell Co., 1944—, pres., 1968—, also dir. Advisory bd. Walter Hoving Home. Served with USAAF, 1942-44. Methodist. Home: 11 Black Oak Lane Mahwah NJ 07430 Office: 184 Central Av Old Tappan NJ 07675

BARCELLA, ERNEST LAWRENCE, auto co. exec.; b. Hamden, Conn., June 7, 1910; s. Battista J. and Ernesta R. (Casella) B.; A.B., Dartmouth, 1934; m. Louise Marian Berniere, June 18, 1935; children—Andrea Louise (Mrs. Bruce M. Kelleher), Ernest Lawrence. Engaged as reporter, sports writer New Haven Register, New Haven Times, 1928-30; with United Press Assn., 1930—, successively staff New Haven, Hanover, N.H., Phila., Albany, N.Y., New Eng. sports editor and night mgr., Boston, central div. night mgr., Chgo., 1930-40, staff Washington bur., 1940, Pacific War Theater, 1945, bur. mgr. U.P.I, Washington, 1953-61; pub. relations exec. Gen. Motors Corp., 1961-65, dir. communications, public relations, 1963-65, Washington mgr., 1965—. Washington trustee Fed. City council Dartmouth Alumni Council. Recipient Nat. Headliners award for fgn. coverage, 1960. Mem. White House Corrs. Assn., Am. Baseball Writers Assn., Sigma Chi, Sigma Delta Chi. Club: Nat. Press (Washington); Kenwood Country (Bethesda, Md.); Gridiron. Contbr. articles nat. mags. Home: 7113 Millwood Rd Bethesda MD 20034 Office: 1660 L St NW Washington DC 20036

BARCHOFF, HERBERT, business exec.; b. N.Y.C., Apr. 3, 1915; s. Abraham and Mollie (Berkowitz) B.; B.S., N.Y. U., 1935, J.D., 1938; m. Lilyan Blum; children—Michael, Jared Blum. Vice pres. Eastern Brass & Copper Co., 1938-45, exec. v.p., sec., 1945-54, pres., 1954—, name co. changed to Eastern Rolling Mills, Inc.; pres. Tubotron, Inc., 1959. Guest lectr. Columbia, Farleigh Dickinson Coll., Pace Coll.; seminar leader conference, program Alliance for Progress, Bogota, Colombia. Mem. Pres.'s Council Econ. Advisers, 1952; mem. exec. com. Action Com. for Internat. Devel.; dir. United Cerebral Palsy, 1959; adv. bd., nat. commn., nat. chmn. trades and industry, also vice chmn. N.Y. exec. com. Anti-Defamation League. Cons. Copper Recovery Corp, 1942; mem. industry adv. com. NPA, 1951-53; survey small plants NATO area Europe, Mut. Security Agy., 1952; mem. citizens adv. com. on fgn. trade Senate Banking and Currency Com.; nat. adviser Small Bus. Adminstrn.; mem. bd. govs. Joint Def. Appeal, 1956; mem. adv. com. to Small Bus. of Nat. Dem. Com., 1956; chmn. mgmt. of smaller co. Am. Mgmt. Assn.; mem. Canadian Am. Nuclear Proliferation Conf., 1967, Am. Assembly Arden House Conf.-Uses of Sea, 1968. Mem. Nat. Assn. Ind. Bus. (pres.) Copper and Brass Warehouse Assn. (treas., dir. 1951-54, v.p. 1954, pres. 1955), Young Presidents Orgn. (vice chmn. N.Y. chpt. 1959, dir. 1961), Conf. to Plan Strategy for Peace, Am. Assembly Arms Control, Am. Baseball Acad. (exec. bd. dirs.), Nat. Planning Assn. (nat. council), Theta Sigma Lambda. Club: Copper (dir.). Contbr. articles trade publs. Home: 50 Sutton Pl S New York City NY 10022 Office: 1122 E 180th St New York City NY 10460

BARCK, OSCAR THEODORE, Jr., ret. educator; b. Bklyn., Oct. 11, 1902; s. Oscar T. and Viola G. (Silence) B.; A.B., Hamilton Coll., 1923; student Cornell U., 1925; Ph.D., Columbia, 1931; m. Olive Marie Aschenbach, Jan. 31, 1929; children—Barbara Jean, William Brewster. With Met. Life Ins. Co., 1923-24; prof. Am. history Syracuse (N.Y.) U., 1928-63, 65-68, history dept.; prof. Am. history Sacramento State Coll., 1963-65; prof. Am. history Cornell U., 1949-50. Mem. Am. Hist. Assn., Am. Assn. U. Profs., Miss. Valley Hist. Assn., S.R., Phi Beta Kappa, Psi Upsilon. Republican. Presbyn. Author: New York City During The American Lefler), 1950; Colonial America, World, 1961; America in the World, 1962; The United States since 1945, 1965. Home: 2450 Canadian Way Clearwater FL 33515

BARCKLEY, ROBERT EUGENE, educator, economist; b. Page, N.D., Sept. 14, 1922; s. Adelbert Eugene and Frona (McClure) B.; B.S., U. N.D., 1948; M.A., Columbia, 1950; Ph.D., U. Ill., 1957; m. Claire M. Petterson, Aug. 22, 1948; children—Thomas Eugene, Maureen Frona. Instr. econs. N.D. State U., 1950-51; economist Dist. Office OPS. Fargo, N.D., 1951-53; prof. econs. San Diego State Coll., 1955—, chmn. econs. dept., 1970—. Served with AUS, 1943-46. Mem. Am., Western econ. assns. Home: 6884 50th St San Diego CA 92120

BARCLAY, ELTON WILLIAM, hosp. adminstr.; b. Camden, N.J., Nov. 11, 1915; s. William Henry and Anna (Knox) B.; student U. Fla., 1943; m. Laura Fenton, Feb. 14, 1941; children—Bonnie Susan (Mrs. Merwyn Delano Rimel), Leslie Benton (Mrs. Crawford Raymond Lord). Commd. 2d lt., Med. Service Corps, U.S. Army, 1943, advanced through grades to maj., 1953; company officer, ETO, 1943-45; exec. officer Army Hosp., Carlisle, Pa., 1945-48; dir. personnel 22d Gen. Hosp., Guam, 1948-50; liaison officer Navy Hosp., Phila., 1950-52; comdg. officer detachment of patients Valley Force (Pa.) Army Hosp., 1952-54; registrar Army Hosp., Ft. Hood, Tex., 1954-56; ret., 1956; adminstr. Stetson Hosp., Phila., 1956-60, Croxer Hosp., Chester, Pa., 1960-63, Crozer-Chester Med. Center, 1963-68; exec. dir. Phila. Gen. Hosp., 1968—. Dist. commr. Boy Scouts Am., 1963-67. Bd. dirs. Delaware County Health and Welfare Council, 1962-65, Delaware Valley Hosp. Council, 1967—, Inter-County Hosp. Plan, 1966-68. Recipient Achievement award Olney High Sch. Alumni Assn., 1968. Fellow Am. Coll. Hosp. Adminstrs.; mem. Am. Hosp. Assn., Hosp. Assn. Pa. Home: 1801 Kennedy Blvd Philadelphia PA 19103 Office: Phila Gen Hosp 34th St and Civic Center Blvd Philadelphia PA 19104

BARCLAY, HARRIET GEORGE, educator, botonist; b. Mpls., Aug. 31, 1901; d. Arthur Abbott and May Hammond (Stewart) George; B.A., U. Minn., 1923, M.A., 1924; Ph.D., U. Chgo., 1928; B.A., U. Tulsa, 1945; m. Betram Donald Barclay, Sept. 4, 1928 (dec. 1953); children—Bertram Donald, Arthur Stewart. Asst. botany U. Minn., 1923-25; research fellow U. Chgo., 1925- 28, asst. botany, 1927-28; acting instr. U. Tulsa, 1929-30, acting asso. prof., 1931-35, 1936-39, 1942-46, prof. botany, 1949—, head dept., 1953-58. Mem. teaching staff Rocky Mountain Biol. Lab., Crested Butte, Colo., 1936-58, Summer Sci. Inst., U. Wyo. and U. Ark., 1955-56; N.S.F. grant research Andes, S.A., 20 months, supplemental grant Creole Found., 1958-60; research staff Inst. Ciencias Naturales, U. Nac. de Colombia, 1959; vis. prof. U. So. Ill., summer 1960, U. Okla., summers 1964-68; pub. lectr. on Latin Am.; exhibited one-man state and local art shows. Trustee Philbrook Art Center, Rocky Mountain Biol. Lab., 1954—, v.p., 1954. Recipient Willie S. Wright medal for watercolor painting Assn. Okla. Artists, 1949; named Woman Yr., Sooner chpt. Am. Women Radio TV, 1959. Fellow A.A.A.S., Okla. Acad. Sci. (exec. council 1953-55, v.p. 1961, pres. 1962); mem. Ecol. Soc. Am., Southwestern Assn. Naturalists (gov. 1954-56), Tulsa Artists Guild (pres. 1955-56), Internat. Assn. Plant Taxonomists, Mortarbd., Sigma Xi, Phi Beta Kappa, Phi Sigma, Delta Kappa Gamma, Pi Gamma Mu, Sigma Kappa, Sigma Delta Epsilon. Republican. Presbyn. Club: Altrusa (Woman of Year award Tulsa chpt. 1966). Contbr. articles profl. jour. Home: 302 N Lynn Lane Rd Tulsa OK 74138

BARCLAY, HARTLEY WADE, editor, pub.; born Gladbrook, Ia., Dec. 3, 1903; s. Wade Crawford and May (Hartley) B.; A.B., Ohio Wesleyan U., 1924; m. Marjorie Kathleen Whitley, Feb. 16, 1924 (dec.); children—Jean Marrie (dec.), Hartley Wade, James Crawford; m. Lois Beveridge Wilson, Oct. 28, 1967. Indsl. advt. mgr. N.Y. Times, 1952-56; pub. Tide mag., 1956-59; editor, pub. Automotive Industries, 1959-70; v.p., dir. Chilton Co.; exec. sec. Mgmt. Research Inst.; cons. research dir. Analysis & Programming Corp., Taft-Pierce Mfg. Co., Marine Products Co., Henry G. Thompson & Son Co.; cons. Gen. Motors Corp.; indsl. edn. cons. Copper and Brass Research Assn.; editor Mill and Factory Mag., N.Y.; editorial dir., sec. Conover-Mast Corp., 1931-42; research dir. elec. trades div. McGraw Hill Pub. Co., 1930-31; editor, pub. Automotive Industries mag., 1959-70; editor, pub. Found. Survey of Corporate and Indsl. Systems Communications, 1970—. Lectr. U.S. Army Indsl. Coll., Washington, 1937, 38, 39, 40, 41 aviation pilot; C.A.A. instr. aero navigation, meteorology and regulations; lectr. before ednl., governmental, engring, and bus. groups; arbitrator Am. Arbitration Assn.; sec. Am. Conf. Nat. Def. Mem. Pres.'s Com. Employment Physically Handicapped, 1957-71. Trustee Polyclinic Med. Coll. and Hosp. Mem. Civil Air Patrol, Am. Ordnance Assn., Assn. U.S. Army, Am. Acad. Consultants, Tech. Soc. Council N.Y., Inst. Mgmt. Scis., Edison Pioneers (asso.), Newcomen Soc., Am. Soc. Tool Engrs., Am. Soc. for Metals, Society Automotive Engrs., Am. Soc. Quality Control, Am. Inst. Indsl. Engrs., Sigma Delta Chi, Phi Gamma Delta, Pi Delta Epsilon. Republican. Member Protestant Episcopal Church (perpetual deacon). Clubs: Tri-State Yacht (Phila.); Nat. Press (Wash.); Bahamas Auto. Author: Survey of Industrial Distribution, 1931; Ford Production Methods, 1936; Labor's Stake in The American Way, 1938; The Timetable of Dictatorship, 1940; Industrial News Subjects; Public Relations Methods Manual. Editor: How Your Business Can Help Win the War, 1942; The Foundation Survey of Production and Sales Planning; Business News; The First Standard Manual of Public Information Procedures. Contbr. articles to Atlantic Monthly, N.Y. Times and other jours. Home: King St Port Chester NY 10573 Office: PO Box 811 Port Chester NY 10573

BARCLAY, IAN A., forest products co. exec.; b. Montreal, Que., Can., 1921; grad. McGill U., 1948, Harvard, 1959. Pres., dir. B.C. Forest Products Ltd. Home: 5925 Chancellor Blvd Vancouver 8 British Columbia Canada Office: 1190 Melville St Vancouver 5 British Columbia Canada*

BARCLAY, JOHN DONNELLY, transport equipment mfg. co. exec.; b. Mpls., Sept. 27, 1914; s. Samuel A. and Sallie (James) B.; B.S., Northwestern U., 1939; m. Edith Domine, Nov. 20, 1940; children—Margaret Anne (Mrs. Robert A. Ittner), Donnelly James Barclay. Sec., Cargill, Inc., Mpls., 1932-35; salesman Pure Oil Products Co., Evanston, Ill., 1935-39; with Heil Co., 1939—, v.p. sales, 1954-58, v.p. body and hoist div., 1958-62, v.p. exec., 1962-69, marketing, 1969—, also dir.; dir. Schetky Equipment Corp., Portland, Ore., Mem. Sales Execs. Club Milw. (bd. dirs. 1956-59), Delta Upsilon. Episcopalian. Mason (Shriner), Rotarian. Club: Rancho Santa Fe Golf. Home: Rancho Sante Fe CA Office: 3000 W Montana St Milwaukee WI 53201

BARCLAY, THOMAS SWAIN, polit. scientist; b. St. Louis, Jan. 26, 1892; s. George Reppert and Lillie (Swain) B.; A.B., U. Mo. 1915, Gregory scholar, 1915-16, A.M., 1916, LL.D. (hon.), 1962; Ph.D., Columbia, 1924; fellow U. Chgo., 1916-17; scholar in pub. law Columbia, 1920-21; cons. fellow Brookings Instn., 1931-33. Instr. polit. sci. U. Mo., 1920, asst. prof., 1922-26, asso. prof., 1926-27; asso. prof. polit. sci. Stanford U., 1928-37, prof. 1937-57. vis. prof. summers, U. N.C., 1921, U. Mo., 1930, Syracuse U., 1931, U. Wash., 1935, 40, Cornell U., 1936, 41, U. Minn., spring 1936; acting prof. U. Mich., first semester, 1949-50, Columbia, summer 1950. Leader Des Moines Public Forums, 1936; vis. prof., U. of Idaho, summer 1946, U. Wash., 1957; acting prof. U. Ill., first semester 1947-48; mem. com. on award Bancroft Prizes, Columbia, 1955-56; with internat. law div. Am. Commn. to Negotiate Peace, Paris, and sec. to Henry White, 1919; mem. council Cal. Congl. Recognition Plan, 1958-70. Bd. dirs. George D. Hart Found. Del. Dem. Nat. Conv., 1936, 44, 48; presdl. elector for Cal., 1944; mem. Dem. county and state coms., 1932-50. Mem. Am. Polit. Sci., Assn. (exec. council 1932-35, v.p. 1939-40), Am. Acad. Polit. Sci., Nat. Municipal League, Am. Assn. U. Profs., State Hist. Soc. Mo., Am. Hist. Assn., Soc. Cal. Pioneers, Phi Beta Kappa (senator 1949-61, vis. scholar 1958-59), Beta Theta Pi. Democrat. Episcopalian. Clubs: Bohemian, Commonwealth (San Francisco, California), Cosmos Club (Washington). Author: Liberal Republican Movement in Missouri, 1926; The Movement for Municipal Home Rule, 1943; A Home Rule Charter of 1876, 1962. Contbr. to mags. including Am. Political Sci. Rev., mem. bd. editors, 1941-44, 1947-50, Nat. Municipal Rev., Cal. Law Rev., Mo. Hist. Rev., Dictionary Am. Biography, Dictionary Am. History, Western Polit. Quarterly. Mem. Alien Enemy Hearing Bd., Cal., 1942-45, Nat. Alien Enemy Hearing Bd., 1943-45. Contbr. Ency. Brit. Home: Stanford U Stanford CA 94305

BARCO, JAMES WILLIAM, govt. ofcl., lawyer, b. Benton Harbor, Mich., Apr. 5, 1916; s. William John and Maude (Bryan) B.; A.B., U. Mich., 1938; LL.B., Harvard, 1941; Doctor of Laws, Missouri Valley Coll., 1967. Admitted to Md. bar, 1942; asst. to legislative counsel HOLC, Fed. Home Loan Bank Bd., and Fed. Savs. & Loan Ins. Corp., Washington, 1941-42; with Dept. State, 1946-61, mem. U.S. delegation UN Good Offices Com. for Indonesia, 1948, U.S. delegation UN Conciliation Commn. for Palestine, 1948-49, acting dep. rep. from U.S., 1949, 1954-61, dep. counselor mission, 1954, counselor mission with rank of minister, 1955-60, dep. rep. U.S. on UN Security Council, 1956-60, alternate rep. UN Com. Peaceful Uses Outer Space, 1959-61, dep. permanent rep. UN and UN Security Council, with rank of ambassador extraordinary and plenipotentiary, 1960-61; spl. asst. to pres. Time, Inc., 1961-62; exec. vice chmn. Atlantic council U.S., Inc., 1961-62; admitted to D.C. bar, 1962; sr. partner Barco, Cook and Patton, Washington, N.Y.C. Mem. UN Adminstrv. Tribunal, 1962-66. Trustee, vice chmn. bd. Am. U. in Cairo, also vice chmn. exec. com. Served AUS, 1942, USNR, 1942-46; defense counsel Gen. Ct. Martial, 5th Naval Dist., Norfolk, Va., 1943, staff officer Allied Naval Comdr.-in-Chief Expdn. Force, 1944, Comdr. U.S. Naval Forces Europe, 1944-46, Judge Adv. Gen. Navy, Washington, 1946. Mem. France-Am. Soc., Am. Bar Assn., Council Fgn. Relations, Pilgrims of U.S., Delta Upsilon. Episcopalian. Clubs: River, The Brook (N.Y.C.); 1925 F Street (Washington). Home: Hare Forest Orange VA 22960 also 2712 N St NW Washington 20007 Office: 1066 31st St NW Washington DC 20007 also 866 UN Plaza New York City NY 10017

BARCO, VIRGILIO, economist; b. Cucuta, Colombia, Sept. 17, 1921; s. Jorge E. and Julieta (Vargas-Duran) B.; B.S. in Civil. Engring., Mass. Inst. Tech., 1943, postgrad., 1951-54; M.A., Boston U., 1950; m. Mary Carolina Isakson, July 1, 1950; children—Carolina, Julia, Diana, Virgilio. Colombian govt. ofcl., 1943-69; sec. pub. works and finance Norte de Santander, 1943-45; Sec. Gen., acting minister communications, 1945-46; mem. Colombian Ho. of Reps., 1949-51; mem. Colombia Senate, 1958-66; minister of pub. works, 1958-61; ambassador to Ct. of St. James, 1961-62; minister of agr., acting minister of finance, 1963-64; mayor City of Nogota, 1966-69; exec. dir. for Brazil, Colombia, Dominican Rep., Ecuador and Philippines to Internat. Bank for Reconstrn. and Devel., Washington, 1968—. Pres. 8th Pan Am. Hwy. Congress, 1960; Presdl. rep. for formation of Andean Group, 1966. Trustee Mass. Inst. Tech., 1970-75, chmn. vis. com. econs., 1970-71, mem. vis. com. Center Internat. Studies, 1970-71; trustee Internat. Inst. Improvement Corn and Wheat, Mexico City, 1966-73. Home: 4770 Reservoir Rd NW Washington DC 20007 Office: 1818 H St NW Washington DC 20433

BARCOME, DONALD FRANCIS, educator, physician; b. Oconto Falls, Wis., Mar. 13, 1928; s. Earl William and Eleanor (Neumann) B.; B.S., U. Wis., 1950, M.D., 1954; m. Lilas Shirley Shepard, Apr. 26, 1957; children—Donald Francis Jr., Shirley Johanna, Earl William. Intern St. Joseph's Hosp., Marshfield, Wis., 1954-55; resident, Baylor Affiliated Hosps., Houston, 1960-65; pvt. practice medicine, Gillette, Wis., 1957-60; med. dir. Med. Center Rehabilitation Hosp., Grand Forks, N.D., 1965—; prof., chmn. dept. phys. medicine and rehabilitation U. N.D. Sch. Medicine, 1965—. Served with USNR, 1955-57. Diplomate Am. Bd. Phys. Medicine and Rehab. Fellow Am. Acad. Phys. Medicine and Rehab. A.C.P. Home: 2424 Olson Dr Grand Forks ND 58201

BARD, ALLEN JOSEPH, educator, chemist; b. N.Y.C., Dec. 18, 1933; s. John J. and Dora (Rosenberg) B.; B.S. summa cum laude, Coll. City N.Y., 1955; A.M., Harvard, 1956, Ph.D. (NSF fellow), 1958; m. Frances Joan Segal, June 15, 1957; children—Edward David, Sara Lynn. Research chemist Gen. Chem. Co., Morristown, N.J., 1955; faculty U. Tex., Austin, 1958—, prof. chemistry, 1967—; cons. Phillips Petroleum Co., Bartlesville, Okla., E.I. duPont de Nemours & Co., Wilmington, Del. Recipient Ward medal, 1955. Mem. Am. Chem. Soc., Electrochem. Soc., A.A.A.S., Sigma Xi. Author: Chemical Equilibrium, 1966. Editor: Electroanalytical Chemistry-A Series of Monographs on Recent Advances, 1966, 67, 69, 70, 71. Contbr. articles profl. jours. Devised (with H.B. Herman) technique cyclic chronopotentiometry; originated use coulometric techniques to study rates of reactions. Home: 6202 Mountainclimb St Austin TX 78731

BARD, HARRY, educator; b. Balt., Dec. 24, 1906; s. Rubin and Fannye (Rothenberg) B.; B.S., Johns Hopkins, 1929; M.S., Columbia, 1938; Ed.D., U. Md., 1950; LL.D., Morgan Coll., 1959, Loyola U., Balt., 1963; m. Eleanor Ruth Blumberg, Aug. 19, 1934; children—Fane, Robert. Tchr. pub. schs., Balt., 1926-35; supr. social studies, 1935-46; part-time instr. history, polit. sci., edn. several colls., 1939—; asst. dir. Secondary Curriculum Bur., Balt., 1946-56; dir. instructional services Gen. Secondary Edn., Balt., 1956-59; pres. Balt. Community Coll., 1959—. Chmn. aviation commn. Am. Council Edn., 1946-56; pres. Middle States Council Social Studies. Mem. exec. bd. Balt. Council Social Agys.; active Balt. Jr. Red Cross; mem. Nat. Conf. Christians and Jews; chmn. Mayor-City Council Commn. on Redistricting City of Balt., 1965; mem. Md. Adv. Com. on Fed. Appropriation Higher Edn. Facilities. U.S. del. to internat. seminar UNESCO, Lake Success, 1948. Mem. Md. Constl. Conv. Commn., 1966-67; del. Md. Constl. Conv., 1967-68. Recipient Balt. YMCA Ann. Service to Youth award, 1960, Fellowship House citation in human relations, 1958, Md. State Senate citation for writings on Md. govt., 1957, Ann. Alumni award Md. State Tchrs. Coll., 1959, Balt. YMCA Youth and Govt. medal, 1949. Mem. Citizen's Planning and Housing Assn., Md. Hist. Soc. (mem. edn. com.), UN Assn. Md. (pres. 1957-59), Assn. for Supervision and Curriculum Devel. (dir.), Nat. Council Social Studies, Am. Assn. Jr. Colls., Flag House Soc. Balt., Phi Delta Kappa. Author: Maryland, The State and Its Government, rev., 1952; Maryland Today, rev., 1961; Homework: A Guide for Secondary School Teachers, 1958; Teachers and the Community, 1952; (with H. Manakee) Active Citizenship, 1951; (with others) Citizenship and Government in Modern America, 1965. Home: 5705 Rubin Av Baltimore MD 21215

BARD, PHILIP, physiologist, educator; b. Hueneme, Cal., Oct. 25, 1898; s. Thomas Robert and Mary Beatrice (Gerberding) B.; student Thacher Sch., Ojai, Cal., 1913-17; A.B., Princeton, 1923; A.M., Harvard, 1925, Ph.D., 1927; Sc.D. (hon.), Princeton, 1947, Washington and Lee U., 1949; Dr. honoris causa U. Catolica de Chile, 1951, U. Mayor de San Marcos de Lima, 1951; LL.D., Johns Hopkins, 1968; m. Harriet Hunt, June 29, 1922 (dec. Apr. 1964); children—Virginia Hunt (Mrs. M.K. Johnson, Jr), Elizabeth Stanton (Mrs. John P. Stephens); m. 2d, Janet Mackenzie Rioch, Jan. 25, 1965. Teaching fellow in physiology Harvard Med. Sch., 1925-26, instr. physiology, 1925-28, asst. prof. physiology, 1931-33; asst. prof. biology Princeton U., 1928-31; prof. physiology and dir. dept. Johnhns Hopkins U. Sch. Medicine, 1933-64, prof. emeritus physiology, 1964—, dean med. faculty, 1953-57; Harvey Soc. lectr., 1938; Hughlings Jackson lectr. Montreal Neurol. Inst., 1943; George Cyril Graves lectr. Ind. U., 1948. Pres., trustee Internat. Found.; trustee Rockefeller U., Thacher Sch. Served as pvt. Ambulance Service, U.S. Army, Section 578, A.E.F., 1917-19. Recipient Jacoby award Am. Neurol. Assn., 1959; Achievement award A.C.P., 1968. Fellow A.A.A.S., Am. Acad. Arts and Scis.; hon. mem. facultad de Biologia y Ciencias Medicas, U. de Chile, Sociedad Medica de Santiago, Sociedad Argentina de Biologia; mem. Nat. Acad. Scis., Am. Physiol. Soc. (councilor 1936-39; sec. 1939-41, pres. 1942-46, chmn. bd. publ. trustees 1959-62), Am. Neurol. Assn. (hon.), Am. Philos. Soc. (Lashley award in neurobiology 1962), Harvey Soc., Soc. for Exptl. Biology and Medicine (pres. 1959-61), NRC (3 com. on mil. medicine, World War II), Nat. Bd. Med. Examiners, 1935-46, Assn. for Research in Nervous and Mental Disease (pres. 1950), Assn. Am. Physicians, Phi Beta Kappa, Sigma Xi. Clubs: 14 W. Hamilton St., Tower (Princeton); Elkridge (Balt.). Editorial bd. Am. Jour. Physiology, 1939-46; chmn. editorial bd. Physiol. Revs., 1950-53. Contbr. to physiol. and med. jours., especially on neuro-physiology; editor, contbr. Macleod's Physiology in Modern Medicine, 8th edit., 1938, 9th edit., 1941; Medical Physiology, 10th edit., 1956, 11th edit., 1962. Home: 6 Meadow Rd Baltimore, MD 21212.

BARDACH, JOHN EUGENE, educator, ecologist; b. Vienna, Austria, Mar. 6, 1915; s. Frederick and Anna (Jerusalem) B.; student U. Berlin, 1936-37; B.A., Queens U., Kingston, Ont., Can., 1946; M.Sc., U. Wis., 1949, Ph.D., 1949; m. Josephine Handler, Nov. 7, 1947. Came to U.S., 1946, naturalized, 1953. Mem. faculty Ia. State Tchrs. Coll., 1949-53; mem. faculty U. Mich., 1953—, prof. ecology, 1953—. Dir. Bermuda Fisheries Research Program, 1955-58; fisheries adviser to Cambodia, ICA, 1958-59, Internat. Indian Ocean Expdn., 1964, Pacific Sci. Bd. of U.S. Nat. Acad., 1968-69; cons. AID, 1967—, hon. cons. Meking com. UN, 1969. Sr. vis. fellow sci. Orgn. European Econ. Coop., 1961. Fellow A.A.A.S., Internat. Acad. Zoology; mem. Mich. Assn. Conservation Ecologists (pres. 1963-64). Author: Downstream, 1964; Harvest of the Sea, 1968; co-author: Ichthyology, 1962; Status and Potential of Aquaculture, 1968. Home: 4858 Grandview Dr Ypsilanti MI 48197 Office: Univ Mich Ann Arbor MI 48104

BARDEEN, JOHN, physicist; b. Madison, Wis., May 23, 1908; s. Charles Russell and Althea (Harmer) B.; B.S., U. Wis., 1928, M.S., 1929; Ph.D., Princeton, 1936; D.Sc. (hon.), Union Coll., 1955, U. Wis., 1960; m. Jane Maxwell, July 18, 1938; children—James Maxwell, William Allen, Elizabeth Ann (Mrs. Greytak). Geophysicist, Gulf Research & Devel. Corp., Pitts., 1930-33; asst. prof. physics U. Minn., 1938-41; with Naval Ordnance Lab., Washington, 1941-45; research physicist Bell Telephone Labs., Murray Hill, N.J., 1945-51; prof. physics, elec. engring. U. Ill., 1951—. Mem. Pres.'s Sci. Adv. Com., 1959-62. Recipient Ballantine medal Franklin Inst., 1952; John Scott medal, Phila., 1955; Fritz London award, 1962; Vincent Bendix award, 1964; Nat. Medal Sci., 1966; -Morley award, 1968; medal of honor I.E.E.E., 1971; co-recipient Nobel prize in physics, 1956. Fellow Am. Phys. Soc. (Buckley prize 1954, pres. 1968-69); mem. Am. Acad. Arts and Sci., Am. Philos. Soc. Home: 55 Greencroft Champaign IL 61820 Office: Dept of Physics Univ of Ill Urbana IL 61801

BARDELLI, CESARE MASSIMO, baritone; b. San Pier da Rena, Italy, Jan. 2, 1916; s. Alfredo and Vera (Dal Sarto) B.; grad. with honors Liceo Politti, Milan, Italy, 1942; m. Lina Pierina Novali, June 23, 1943; 1 dau., Vera. Came to U.S., 1955, naturalized, 1964. Debut as Amonasro in Aida, Allessandra, Piemonte, Italy, 1942; appearances include opera cos. in San Francisco, Chgo., Miami, Fla., Phila., Dallas, Tulsa, Hollywood, Cal., Tampa, Fla., New Orleans, Hartford, Conn., St. Louis, Dayton, O., Washington, Indpls. also in Ireland, Switzerland, Yugoslavia, Italy, Mexico, S. Am.; mem. Met. Opera Co., 1957—; radio and TV appearances, 1947—. Served with Italian Air Force, 1941-45. Recipient Gold hon. cup Israel Philharmonic, 1958; hon. mem. Boys Town Italy, 1963—. Mem. Am. Guild Mus. Artists, A.F.T.R.A. Republician. Mem. Christian Ch. Home: Lincoln Towers 142 West End Av New York City NY 10023 Office: Metropolitan Opera Lincoln Center Plaza New York City NY 10023

BARDEN, HORACE GEORGE, accountant; b. Kenosha, Wis., Jan. 30, 1906; s. John T. and Eva (Holcomb) B.; B.S. in Accounting and Bus. Adminstrn., U. Wis., 1931; m. Laura Stauffacher, Sept. 21, 1929; children—Thomas P., Martha J. With Ernst & Ernst, C.P.A.'s, 1931-68, various exec. capacities, Indpls. and Chgo., partner, 1951-68, mem. mng. com., 1956-68; speaker, writer profl. accounting and mgmt. cons. Mem. Am. Inst. Accountants (council, v.p.), Ill. Soc. C.P.A.'s, Ind. Assn. C.P.A.'s (past pres.), Nat. Assn. Cost Accountants (past pres. Indpls.), Phi Kappa Sigma, Beta Gamma Sigma, Beta Alpha Psi (hon.). Clubs: Chicago, University, Chicago (Chgo.); Bob- O'Link Country (Highland Park, Ill.); Westmoreland Country. Home: 615 Park Dr PO Box 153 Kenilworth IL 60043

BARDEWYCK, LORETTA A., coll. dean; b. Glencoe, Ill., Sept. 3, 1915; d. Theodore L. and Ellen Natalie (Johnson) Anderson, R.N., Michael Reese Hosp. Sch. Nursing, Chgo., 1936; B.S. in Pub. Health Nursing, U. Minn., 1940; M.S. in Child Guidance, 1948; m. Guy M. Hanner, July 27, 1957 (dec. Oct. 1960); m. 2d, Arthur H. Bardewyck, Mar. 25, 1970. Chief nurse Internat. Grenfell Assn., St. Anthony, Newfoundland and St. Mary's River, Labrador, 1940-41; pub. health nurse Community Service Soc., N.Y.C., 1941-42; asso. pub. health nurse cons. Pan-Am. San. Bur., Prince, Haiti, Inst. Inter-Am. Affairs, Port-Au-Prince, 1944-47; mental health nurse Nat. Inst. Mental Health, Phoenix, 1948-52; pub. health nurse Alameda County (Cal.) Health Dept., 1952-53; asso. dir. nursing Good Samaritan Hosp., Phoenix, 1953-54, dir. of nursing, 1954-57; dir., asso. prof. Sch. Nursing, Ariz. State U., 1957-64, now dean, prof.; asso. dir. on leave Peace Corps project, Cuiaba, Mato Grosso, Brazil, 1964-66. Leader skills workshops, div. Indian health, Ariz., 1959; mem. sub-com. nursing, mental health tng. com., Nat. Inst. Mental Health, 1961-65; mem. expert adv. com., profl. nurse tng. USPHS, 1961-64; cons. conf. nursing edn., AID, Teheran, Iran, 1964; mem. Ariz. staff devel. com. Western Interstate Council Higher Edn., 1966; mem. spl. project grants rev. com. div. nursing Pub. Health Service, Health, Edn. and Welfare, 1967-71. Bd. dirs. Vis. Nurse Service, 1961-62; mem. legislative com. Ariz. Tb and Health Assn., 1958- bd. dirs., 1961-62. Decorated officer d'Honneur et Merite (Haiti), 1947. Fellow Am. Pub. Health Assn.; mem. Ariz. Mental Health Assn., Nat., Ariz. (chmn. careers com.) leagues nursing, Ariz. Nurses Assn., Am. Assn. U. Profs., Western Council Higher Edn. in Nursing (exec. com. 1961-62), Pi Lambda Theta, Phi Kappa Phi, Alpha Phi (asso.). Author paps in field. Home: 6722 N 21st St Phoenix AZ 85016 Office: Coll Nursing Ariz State U Tempe AZ 85281

BARDI, PIETRO MARIA, museum dir., writer; b. La Spezia, Italy, Feb. 2, 1900; s. Pasquale and Elisa (Viggiani) B.; m. Bo Lina, Aug. 24, 1946. Dir. Museum of Art of Saõ Paulo (Brazil), 1947—; redactor Il Secolo, Milan; editor art mags. Belvedere, Quadrante. Author: Carrà e Soffici, Rapporto Jull' Architectura, Ciorgio Morandi, Lasar Segall, The Arts in Brazil, Profile of the New Brazilian Art, The Tropical Gardens; L'Opera completa di Velazquez. Address; Sao Paulo Mus Caixa postal 6789 Sao Paulo Brazil

BARDINI, GAETANO, tenor; b. Riparbella, Pisa, Italy, Oct. 8, 1929; s. Giuseppe and Orfea (Panicacci) B.; ed. Liceo Classico, Livorno, Italy; student voice with Galliano Masini, also Prof. Ettore Lattes. Debut in Iris, Livorno, Italy, 1957; appeared at Teatro Massimo Bellini as Caturia in Iris as substitute of Di Stefano, 1958, then sang throughout Europe, S. Africa, S. and C. Am.; debut Met. Opera Co. in Fanciulla del West, 1966. Recipient First prize Internat. Contest, Rome, Italy, 1956. Mem. Am. Guild Mus. Artists. Home: Riparbella Pisa, Italy. Office: Metropolitan Opera Assn Lincoln Center Plaza New York City NY 10023

BARDIS, PANOS DEMETRIOS, sociologist, educator; b. Lefcohorion, Arcadia, Greece, Sept. 24, 1924; s. Demetrios George and Kali (Christopoulos) B.; came to U.S., 1948, naturalized, 1958; student Panteios Sch., Athens, Greece, 1945-47; B.A. magna cum laude, Bethany (W.Va.) Coll., 1950; M.A., Notre Dame U., 1953; Ph.D., Purdue U., 1955; m. Donna Jean Decker, Dec. 26, 1964; children— Byron Galen, Jocson Dante. Mem. faculty Albion Coll., 1955-59; faculty U. Toledo, 1959- -, prof. sociology, 1963—. Sec.-treas. World Student Relief, Athens, Athens, 1946-48; U.S. rep. Internat. Congress Social Scis., Spain, 1965, 66; participant World Congress Sociology, 1966, 70, Inst. Internat. de Sociologie, 1969. Trustee Marriage Mus., N.Y.C. Recipient Couphos prize Anglo-Am.-Hellenic Bur. Edn., 1949. Fellow Am. Sociol. Assn., A.A.A.S., Internat. Inst. Arts and Letters (life); mem. Am. Assn. U. Profs., Nat. Council Family Relations, Internat. Sociol. Assn., Conférence Internationale de Sociologie de la Religion, Institut International de Sociologie, Internat. Sci. Commn. on Family, Am. Soc. for Neo-Hellenic Studies (bd. advisers 1969—), Group for Study Sociolinguistics, Nat. Council on Family Relations, N.Y. Acad. Scis., Nat. Acad. Econs. and Polit. Sci. (dir.), Nat. Writers Club, Nat. Assn. Standard Med. Vocabulary (cons. 1963—), Alpha Kappa Delta, Pi Gamma Mu. Author: (novel) Ivan and Artemis, 1957; The Family in Changing Civilizations, 1967, 69; Encyclopedia of Campus Unrest, 1971. Editor-in-chief Social Sci., 1959—, book rev. editor, 1963—; asso. editor Indian Sociol. Bull., Indian Psychol. Bull., Revista del Instituto de Ciencias Sociales (Spain), 1965—, Internat. Jour. Sociology of Family, 1970—; book rev. editor Internat. Rev. History and Polit. Sci. (India), 1966—; asst. Am. editor Indian Jour. Social Research, 1965—; Am. editor Sociology Internat. (India), 1967—; editorial bd. Darshana Internat. (India), Jour. Edn. (India), 1965—, Sociologia Religiosa (Italy), 1966—; co- editor Internat. Rev. Sociology, 1970—. Contbr. poems, articles to profl. jours. Home: 2833 Goddard Rd Toledo OH 43606

BARDOLPH, RICHARD, historian, educator; b. Chgo., Feb. 18, 1915; s. Mark and Anna (Veldman) B.; B.A., U. Ill., 1940, M.A., 1941, Ph.D., 1944; Litt.D., Concordia Coll., 1968; m. Dorothy Corlett, July 28, 1945; children—Virginia Ann (Mrs. George Haskett), Mark III, Richard. Mem. faculty dept. history U. N.C. at Greensboro, 1944—, head dept., 1960—, Jefferson Standard prof., 1970—; Fulbright lectr., Denmark, 1953-54. Mem. regional selection com. Woodrow Wilson Nat. Fellowship Found.; mem. commn. theology and church relations Luth. Ch.-Mo. Synod; mem. exec. com. Luth. Council in U.S. Active Am. Civil Liberties Union, N.A.A.C.P. Ford Found. fellow, Harvard, 1952-53; Guggenheim fellow, 1956-57; sr. fellow Nat. Endowment for Humanities, 1971-72. Mem. Am. Hist. Assn., Orgn. Am. Historians, So. Hist. Assn., Phi Beta Kappa. Author: Agricultural Literature and Illinois Farmer, 1948; Negro Vanguard, 1959; Civil Rights Record, 1948-1970, 1970. Mem. bd. editors of Jour. Negro History. Contbr. articles profl. jours. and encys. Home: 207 Tate St Greensboro NC 27403

BARDOT, BRIGITTE, actress; b. Paris, France, Sept. 28, 1934; d. Louis and Ann Marie Bardot; m. Roger Vadim, Dec. 12, 1952; (div.); m. 2d, Jacques Charries, June 18, 1959 (div.); 1 son, Nicolas; m. 3d, Gunther Saches, July 14, 1966 (dissolved). Films include Manina, Helen of Troy, Doctor at Sea, Futures, Vendettes, Clair de Lune, Parisienne, Very Private, Celebrated Lovers, Jamais, History of the Plague, And God Created Woman, The Bride is Much Too Beautiful; Love is My Profession, Babbette Goes to War, La Verite, A Very Private Affair, Two Weeks in September, Viva Maria, Shalako, Spirits of the Dead, Les Femmes. Address: 71 Av Paul-Doumer Paris 16 France also La Madrague Saint-Tropez France*

BARDSHAR, FREDERIC ABSHIRE, naval officer; b. Seattle, Oct. 20, 1915; s. Deyo Edward and Sybil (Abshire) B.; B.S., U.S. Naval Acad., 1938; postgrad. Naval War Coll., 1948; m. Phyllis Elizabeth Plant, Oct. 17, 1940; children—Nan Louise (Mrs. Michael Conroy Dillon), Lucy Elizabeth (Mrs. Harry Prescott Beighley). Commd. ensign USN, 1938, advanced through grades to vice. adm., 1970; test pilot Naval Air Test Center, 1950-53; staff duty SHAPE, 1958-60, 6th Fleet, 1961-63, Joint Staff, 1965-67; comdg. officer U.S.S. Constellation during Tonkin Gulf incident, 1964, comdr. Carrier Task Group, 1969-71, comdr. attack carriers 7th Fleet, 1971—. Decorated Silver Star medal, Legion of Merit with three gold stars, D.F.C. with two gold stars, Air medal with five gold stars. Mem. Soc. Exptl. Test Pilots, Am. Fighter Aces Assn. Clubs: New York Yacht; Nat. Avation. Home: Naval Station Subic Philippines Office: Attack Carrier Striking Force 7th Fleet FPO San Francisco CA 96601

BARDWELL, ROBERT FOWLER, investment banker; b. Mpls., Apr. 29, 1933; s. Robert Lewis and Eileen (Fowler) B.; grad. Lawrenceville Sch., 1951; B.A., U. Minn., 1955; m. Sheila Smith, June 18, 1955; children—Robert Fowler, Bryan Field. With Bardwell-Robinson Co., Fargo, N.D., 1959-61; with Boettcher & Co., Denver, 1961—, gen. partner, 1971—. Mem. bd. mgrs. Jefferson County YMCA, 1963-66. Served from ensign to lt., USN, 1955-59. Mem. Investment Bankers Assn. Am. (nat. gov.). Clubs: Hiwan Golf, Twenty Six (Denver). Episcopalian. Home: Rt 5 Box 755 Golden CO 80401 Office: 828 17th St Denver CO 80202

BARE, JOHN KIRBY, educator; b. Lexington, Mo., Dec. 10, 1917; s. John Winchell and Olive (Moore) B.; A.B, Oberlin Coll., 1940; M.Sc., Brown U., 1942, Ph.D., 1947; m. Lota Pauline Brandt, May 27, 1944; 1 dau., Lota Theresa. Instr., then asst. prof. Brown U., 1947-49; asst. prof., then asso. prof. Coll. William and Mary, 1949-58; prof. psychology, co-chmn. dept. psychology and edn. Carleton Coll., Northfield, Minn., 1958-; cons. NSF, 1963-. Served to 2d lt. AUS, 1942-46. Decorated Bronze Star. Fellow A.A.A.S.; mem. Am., Midwestern, Eastern psychol. assns., Psychonomic Soc., Phi Beta Kappa, Sigma Xi. Home: 613 E 5th St Northfield, MN 55057.

BAREFOOT, JOHN ROY, Jr., mfg. co. exec.; b. Braddock, Pa., Oct. 20, 1918; s. J. Roy and N.B. (Thompson) B.; student Carnegie Inst. Tech.; grad. Pa. State Coll., 1941; m. Margorie L. Miller, Nov. 28, 1951; childrenBrian M., Bruce L., Sallie L. Staff research and exptl. dept. Fed. Machine & Welder Co., Warren, O., 1941-46, asst. to exec. v.p., 1946-47, dir. personnel, 1947- 48, asst. to pres. charge personnel and pub. relations, 1948-49, mgr. operations, 1949-52, v.p., 1952-57, pres., 1957-60, merged with McKay Machine Co., 1960; exec. v.p. McKay Machine Co., Youngstown, O., 1960- 67, pres., 1967-70, merged into Wean Industries, Inc., Youngstown, 1970, Berkeley-Davis, Inc., Am. Welding & Mfg. Co., Wean-McKay of Can., Ltd., McKay-Mannesmann-Meer Co., United Engring & Foundry Co., Vickers-McKay, Ltd., London, Eng. Past pres. Trumbull County Tb and Health Assn. Served to lt. (j.g.) USNR, 1944-46. Mem. Am. Welding Soc., Resistance Welders Mfrs. Assn. (past pres.), S.A.R. Mason. Clubs: University (Pitts.); Youngstown; Question, Trumbull Country, Buckeye (Warren). Home: 556 Fairway Dr NE Warren OH 44483 Office: 3805 Henricks Rd Youngstown OH 44501

BARELARE, BRUNO, urol. surgeon; b. Scranton, Pa., July 9, 1913; s. Bruno and Teresa (Villone) B.; A.B., Johns Hopkins, 1934, M.D., 1938; m. Helen Dorner, Feb. 24, 1939; children—Judith, Joseph, Joan, John, Helen Elizabeth. Research asst. Johns Hopkins Hosp., 1938-39, intern urology, 1939-40; resident staff, dept. urology U. Va. Hosp., Charlottesville, 1940-43; asst. prof. urology U. Va., 1943-46; asso. prof. urology Med. Coll. Ala., Birmingham, 1946-48, prof. and chmn. dept. urology, 1948-62, clin. prof. urology, 191962—; pvt. practice urol. surgery. Mem. Am. Urol. Assn., A.M.A., So. Med. Assn., Alpha Omega Alpha (charter), Alpha Kappa Kappa. Home: 216 Beech Circle Birmingham AL 35205 Office: 2701 S 10th Av Birmingham AL 35205

BARENBOIM, DANIEL, pianist, condr.; b. Buenos Aires, Argentina, Nov. 15, 1942; s. Enrique and Aida (Schuster) B.; grad. Santa Cecilia Acad., Rome, Italy, 1956; student piano with father; m. Jacqueline de Prè, 1967. Piano soloist, condr. with Berlin Philharmonic Orch., Royal Philharmonic Orch., N.Y. Philharmonic Orch., Israel Philharmonic Orch.; mus. tours major cities Australia, 1958, 62, S.Am., 1960, Far East, 1962; appearances as pianist, condr. all music capitals in recitals and with orchs.; condr. English Chamber Orch., 1967—. Recipient Beethoven medal, 1958, Paderewski medal, 1963. Home: PO Box 39050 Tel Aviv Israel Office: c/o Hurok 730 5th Av New York City NY 10019

BARES, RUDOLPH, Jr., hotel exec.; b. Chgo., Feb. 1, 1915; s. Rudolph and Pauline (Stepanik) B.; B.S.C., Northwestern U., 1937; postgrad. Cornell U., 1955; m. Elizabeth Houston Raymond, May 15, 1943; children—Robert Edward, Barbara Houston, David Raymond. Sales research dir. Ditto, Inc., Chgo., 1937-40, br. mgr., Norfolk, Va., 1940-45; dir. mgmt. engring. sect. Bur. Ships, Navy Dept., 1945-51; asso. Cresap, McCormick and Paget, mgmt. cons., N.Y.C., 1951-53; asst. dir. hotel operations Williamsburg Restoration, Inc. (Va.), 1953-56; v.p., sec. Colonial Williamsburg, Inc. and Williamsburg Restoration, Inc., 1956-63, v.p., exec. dir. visitor accomodation services, 1963—. Mem. Williamsburg Sch. Bd. Served to lt. comdr. USNR, 1942-45. Mem. Am. (chmn. quality environment com. 1967-70, vice chmn. resort com. 1971), Va. (pres., 1968) hotel and motel assns., Williamsburg C. of C. (v.p., dir. 1965-67, chmn. quality environment com. 1969—), Delta Sigma Pi. Episcopalian. Contbr. articles in field. Home: Ludwell-Paradise House Williamsburg VA 23185 Office: Colonial Williamsburg Found Williamsburg VA 23185

BAREUTHER, ERNST ELLIS, financial exec.; b. Aurora, Ill., June 24, 1910; s. Ernst and Lucy (Ellis) B.; B.S. in Accountancy, U. Ill., 1933; m. Eleanor Geiler, Apr. 1934; children—Richard, Jean. Treas. home appliance div. Fairbanks Morse, 1934-39; chief accountant refrigerating div. Philco Corp., 1940- 44, then of radio div., 1944-47, budget dir., 1947-48, asst. treas., 1948-52, controller, 1952-62, treas., asst. controller, 1962; controller Air Products & Chems. Inc., Allentown, Pa., 1963-65; v.p. finance McCall Corp., N.Y.C., 1965-69; financial cons., 1969—; v.p., treas. Patagonia Corp., Tucson, 1970—, Slick Corp., N.Y.C., 1971—. Mem. Financial Execs. Inst., Planning Execs. Inst., Nat. Assn. Accountants, Beta Gamma Sigma, Beta Alpha Psi, Sigma Phi Epsilon. Clubs: Huntingdon Valley Country (Abington, Pa.); Seaview Country (Absecon, N.J.); Union League (N.Y.C.); Skytop (Pa.); Old Pueblo (Tucson). Home: 100 Hunt Dr Princeton NJ 08540 Office: Patagonia Corp Box 1470 Tucson AZ 85702

BARFIELD, THOMAS HARWELL, army officer; b. Lineville, Ala., Jan. 20, 1917; s. Jesse Morton and Janie Isobel (Davis) B.; grad. Marion Mil. Inst., 1935; A.B., U. Ala., 1937; M.S., George Washington U., 1962; grad. Nat. War Coll., 1960; m. Beri Harrison Young, Aug. 16, 1941; children—Thomas H., Jane Young. Commd. 2d lt. U.S. Army, 1938, advanced through grades to maj. gen., 1969; assigned U.S. Forces in S. Pacific, World War II, Gen. Hdqrs. Far East Command in Occupation of Japan, then UN Command in Korea; assigned Army Gen. Staff, 1945-48, 60-62, U.S. Army Air Def. Command, 1952-53, 62-64, 68-71, Joint Chiefs Staff, 1967-68, U.S. Army Air Def. Center, 1953-56, 65-66, 8th U.S. Army, Korea, 1966-67, N. Am. Air Def. Command, 1969—. Decorated Army Commendation medal with oak leaf cluster, Bronze Star, Meritorious Service medal, Legion of Merit with 3 oak leaf clusters. Mem. Phi Gamma Delta. Home: Lineville AL 36266 Office: Hdqrs 23 NORAD Region Duluth MN 55814

BARFORD, RALPH MACKENZIE, elec. machinery and supplies co. exec.; b. Toronto, Ont., Can., July 6, 1929; s. Ralph Alexander and Geraldine Edna (MacKenzie) B.; B.Comm., U. Toronto, 1950; M.B.A., Harvard U., 1952; m. Elizabeth June Stevens, June 9, 1951; children—Ralph, Anne, John, Patricia, Elizabeth, Jane. Analyst, Am. Research & Devel. Corp., Boston, 1952-54; pres. Nat. Merchandising Corp., Boston, 1954-60, Beatty Bros. Ltd., Fergus, Ont., 1960-62, GSW Ltd., Toronto, Ont., Can., 1962—; dir. Sovereign Life Assurance Co. ITE (Can.) Ltd., Thiokol Chem. Corp. Gov. Trinity Coll. Schs. Mem. Can. Elec. Mfg. Assn. (pres. 1967-68), Young Presidents Orgn., Phi Gamma Delta. Mem. United Ch. Can. Clubs: Granite, Rosedale Golf (Toronto). Home: 11 Valleyanna Dr Toronto Ontario Canada Office: 45 St Clair Av W Toronto Ontario Canada

BARG, BERNARD B., diversified industry exec.; b. 1926; B.S., Temple U., 1948; postgrad. U. Pa., 1948-49; married. With Aldon Industries, Inc., Lenni, Pa., 1949—, exec. v.p., 1963-69, pres., chief operating officer, 1969—, also dir. Home: 1712 Josie Lane Havertown PA 19083 Office: Aldon Industries Inc Lenni PA 19481*

BARG, HERBERT, diversified industry exec.; b. Phila., 1923; student Phila. Textile Coll., 1945, U. Pa., 1943. With Aldon Industries, Inc., Lenni, Pa., 1939—, pres., 1963-69, chmn. bd., chief exec. officer, 1969—. Mason. Home: 1453 Colton Rd Gladwyne PA 19035 Office: Aldon Industries Inc Lenni PA 19052*

BARG, JANKIEL, psychiatrist, mental health adminstr.; b. Miedzyrzec, Poland, Aug. 8, 1913; s. Meyer and Szeina (Szejn) B.; M.D. cum laude, U. Rome, Italy, 1942; postgrad. N.Y. Sch. Psychiatry, 1960-61; m. Sylvia Josty, Nov. 9, 1945; 1 dau., Anna. Came to U.S., 1951, naturalized, 1957. Pvt. practice medicine and pediatrics, Rome and Milan, Italy, 1942-47, Cleve., 1955-58; staff psychiatrist Fairhill Psychiat. Hosp., Cleve., 1961-63, clin. dir., 1963-68; supt. Toledo State and Receiving Hosp., 1968—; clin. asso. prof. Med. Coll. Ohio at Toledo; cons. psychiatrist Juvenile Ct. Cleve., 1967-69, Putnam County Mental Health Center. Diplomate Am. Bd. Psychiatry and Neurology. Mem. Assn. Physicians of Ohio (pres. 1968), A.M.A., Ohio Med. Assn., Cleve., Lucas County acads. medicine, Am., Ohio psychiat. assns., World Fedn. Mental Health, Am. Med. Soc. Vienna, Ind. Mezricher Assn. Cleve. (pres. 1965-67). Home: 46 Riverside Dr Rossford OH 43460 Office: 930 S Detroit Av Toledo OH 43614

BARGEN, J. ARNOLD physician; b. Mountain Lake, Minn., Oct. 25, 1894; s. Jacob I. and Anna J. (Balzer) B.; student Carleton Coll., 1915-17; B.S., U. Chgo., 1918; M.D., Rush Med. Coll., 1921; M.S. in Medicine, Mayo Found., 1927; m. C. Ruth Burns, Aug. 27, 1921; childrenRobert Burns, Terese Ann, Loretta Mae, Cornelia Marie, Ruth Jacqueline (dec.). Borland fellow medicine St. Luke's Hosp., Chgo., 1922-23; 1st asst. in medicine Mayo Found., 1923-27, asst. prof. 1927-29, asso. prof. 1929-48, prof., 1948—; cons. medicine Mayo Clinic, chmn. dept. gastroenterology, 1942-60, pres. staff, 1956-60, head sect. gastroenterology Scott-White Clinic, Temple, Tex., also chmn. postgrad, tng. program in gastroenterology; dir. med. edn. Scott-White Meml. Hosp., Scott-Sherwood-Brindly Found.; med. cons. M.D. Anderson Cancer Inst., Houston; cons. gastroenterology Lackland AFB, San Antonio; clin. prof. medicine U. Cal. at Irvine, 1968- -. Med. adv. bd. Sears Roebuck Med. Found.; judge Nat. Sci. Fair, 1961, 63-65; mem. Library Bd. Rochester, Minn. Bd. Med. Examiners (pres. 1954-55). Mem. Med. Enlisted Res. Corps, World War I. Recipient J. Arnold Bargen award inaugurated by Mayo Found., 1960; Caldwell medal, 1966; Friedenwald medal, 1967. Fellow A.C.P.; mem. A.M.A. (Minn. del. ho. dels. 1948-59, mem. council on sci. assembly 1957—, chmn. council 1962-64, Distinguished Service award 1969), Interstate Postgrad. Med. Assn. N.Am. (pres. 1964-65), Am. Gastroent. Assn. (sec. 1941-45, pres. 1950), Central Clin. Research Club, Minn. Med. Assn. (Distinguished Service medal 1959, pres. 1957) , Tex. Acad. Medicine, Sigma Xi, Phi Chi. Kiwanian. Author: Chronic Recurative Colitis, 1968; 5 other books, numerous articles. Home: 28640 Snead Dr Sun City CA 92381 Office: Riverside Med Clinic 3660 Arlington Av Riverside CA 92506

BARGER, A. CLIFFORD, educator, physiologist; b. Greenfield, Mass., Feb. 1, 1917; s. Paul and Rose (Solomon) B.; A.B., Harvard, 1939. M.D., 1943; m. Claire Basch, June 6, 1943; children—Craig, Cheryl, Curtis. Research asst. Harvard Fatigue Lab., 1938-41; intern Peter Bent Brigham Hosp., Boston, 1943-44, med. house officer, 1945, cons. medicine, 1959—; mem. faculty Harvard Med. Sch., 1946—, prof. physiology, 1961—, Robert Henry Pfeiffer prof. physiology, 1963—; cons. physiology Childrens Med. Center, 1966—. Bd. sci. counselors Nat. Cancer Inst., 1969—. Pres., Elbanobscot Found., 1964, bd. dirs., 1965—, pres. Harvard Apparatus Found., 1970—. Served with AUS, 1944-45. Commonwealth Fund travelling fellow, 1959-60. Fellow Am. Acad. Arts and Scis.; mem. Am. Physiol. Soc. (chmn. publs. com. 1962-63, 66-69, councilor 1968—, pres. 1970-71), Asso. editor Circulation Research, Am. Heart Assn., 1962-66. Home: 14 Orchard Rd Brookline MA 02146 Office: 25 Shattuck St Boston MA 02115

BARGER, FLOYD, newspaper editor; b. Boardman, O., Oct. 26, 1906; s. Emery and Susan (Nelson) B.; B.A., Wittenberg U., 1927, LL.D., 1969; m. Elizabeth Chick, Dec. 28, 1928; 1 son, Bruce. With Flushing (N.Y.) Jour., 1927-28, Bklyn. Eagle, 1928-40; with N.Y. Daily News, 1941—, mng. editor, 1966-68, asso. editor, 1968-69, exec. editor, 1969—. Mem. Silurians, Lutheran. Clubs: Nat. Press (Washington); Garden City (N.Y.); Dutch Treat. Home: 22 Roosevelt Rd Garden City NY 11530 Office: 220 E 42d St New York City NY 10017

BARGER, HAROLD, educator, economist; b. London, Eng., Apr. 27, 1907; s. George and Florence E. (Thomas) B.; B.A., Kings Coll., Cambridge (Eng.) U., 1930; Ph.D., London Sch. Econs., 1937; m. Anne Macdonald Walls, July 8, 1937; m. 2d, Gwyneth Evans Kahn, Dec. 10, 1955. Came to U.S., 1939, naturalized, 1944. Lectr., Univ. Coll., London, 1931-36, 38-39; Garton traveling fellow, 1936-37; instr. Columbia, 1939-43, asst. prof., 1943- 47, asso. prof., 1947-54, prof. econs. 1954—, chmn. dept., 1961-64; staff Nat. Bur. Econ. Research, 1940-54. Served to 1st lt. OSS, AUS, 1943-45. Mem. Am. Econ. Assn., Econometric Soc., Am. Assn. U. Profs. Author: Money, Banking and Public Policy, 1962; The Management of Money, 1964; others. Home: 54 Morningside Dr New York City NY 10025

BARGER, HERMAN H., fgn. service officer; b. Springfield, Mass., Nov. 28, 1915; s. Paul and Rose (Barger) B.; B.A. cum laude, Harvard, 1937; J.D., George Washington U., 1955; m. Dolly King, May 3, 1943; children—Lesli Kristine, Brian King. Fgn. corr. for newspapers and news agys., Japan, China, Argentina, 1937-42; with U.S. Dept. of State, 1942—, successively econ. analyst fgn. service aux., Buenos Aires, LaPaz, Bolivia, acting asst. chief fgn. activity correlation div., internat. trade economist, chief comml. policy br. trade agreements and treaties div., 1942-55, acting asst. chief trade agreements and treaties div., consul, sec. in diplomatic service, 1956-58; assigned Naval War Coll., Newport, R.I., 1957; counsellor of embassy econ. affairs Am. embassy, Djarkata, Indonesia, 1958-60; dep. spl. asst. to undersec. of state for econ. affairs Dept. State, Washington, 1960-61, dep. dir. office Internat. Trade and Finance, 1961-63; counselor of embassy for econ. affairs Am. embassy, 1963-66, coordinator AID, Mexico City, 1964-66, alternate dir. Asian Devel. Bank, Manila, 1966-68; minister-counselor econ. affairs, Tokyo, 1968-70; dep. asst. sec. state for East Asian and Pacific affairs, 1970—; partner Buddie Products Co., Greenfield, Mass., 1947-48; admitted to D.C. bar, 1955. Served as ensign USNR, 1944-46; ETO, PTO; lt. (j.g.) USNR, ret. Recipient commendable service award U.S. Dept. State, 1950. Mem. Fgn. Service Assn., Am. C. of C. of Japan (hon.). Office: Fgn Service Mail Room Dept State Washington DC 20525

BARGER, JAMES WILLARD, educator; B.S., U. N.C., 1956; M.B.A., U. Ala., 1960, Ph.D., 1963. Prof., head dept. accounting U. Alaska. C.P.A., Tenn. Office: Dept Accounting U Alaska College AK 72476*

BARGER, RICHARD HUGH, food processing co. exec.; b. Woodland, Cal., Jan. 25, 1923; s. Edgar Hugh and Ada (Weiss) B.; B.A., Stanford U., 1944; m. Doris Jean Murphy, Oct. 10, 1943; children—Walter Murphy, Stephen Richard. Purchasing agt. Arabian Am. Oil Co., San Francisco, 1944-45; head canned goods div. Wilbur-Ellis Co., San Francisco, 1945-58; asst. mgr. Blue Lake Packers Inc., Salem, Ore., 1958-67, pres., gen. mgr., 1967—; dir. Salem Fed. Savs. & Loan Assn. Served with AUS, 1943. Mem. Nat. Canners Assn. (dir. 1969—), Nat. Council Farmer Cooperatives (dir. 1968—), Northwest Packers and Growers (dir. 1966—), Merchants Exchange Club. Republican. Episcopalian. Clubs: Arlington (Portland, Ore.); Illahe Ills Country Home: 3235 Crestview Dr S Salem OR 97302 Office: 325 Patterson NW Salem OR 97308

BARGER, RICHARD WILSON, hotel exec.; b. Cleve., Aug. 16, 1934; s. Harold Wilson and Blanche (Smith) B.; B.S., Cornell U., Ithaca, N.Y., 1956; m. Barbara K. Schroeder, July 20, 1963; children—Scott Wilson, Chriostpher Armon. Resident mgr. Sheraton Cleve. Hotel, 1964-67, gen. mgr. Sheraton Biltmore Hotel, Providence, 1967-68, Sheraton Peabody Hotel, Memphis, 1968-69, Sheraton Boston Hotel, 1969—. Cons., lectr. hotel adminstrs. Active local United Fund, Youth Service, Inc., Jr. Achievement. Mem. council Cornell U. Ithaca, N.Y. Mem. Boston C. of C., Boston Conv. Bus., Cornell U. Alumni Fund, Sigma Chi. Republican. Mem. P.E. Ch. Home: Sheraton Boston Hotel Prudential Center Boston MA 02199

BARGER, THOMAS CHARLES, former petroleum co. exec.; b. Mpls., Aug. 30, 1909; s. Michael Thomas and Mary (Donohue) B.; student St. Mary's Coll., 1926-28; B.S., U. N.D., 1931; Doctor of Laws (hon.), 1966; m. Kathleen Elizabeth Ray, Nov. 18, 1937; children—Ann, Michael, Timothy, Mary, Norah, Teresa. Engr. Lake Shore Mines. Ltd., Kirkland Lake, Ont., 1931-34, Bear Exploration & Radium, Contact Lake, N.W. Ty., 1934-35; asso. prof. mining U. N.D., 1935-37; with Arabian Am. Oil Co., N.Y.C., 1937-69, geologist, govt. relations mgr., 1954-69, chief exec. officer, 1961-69, v.p., dir. Aramco, 1958-69, pres., 1959-68, chmn., 1968-69; cons. to Bd. Nat. Estimates, pvt. corps.; dir. Offshore Tech. Corp., Diebold Internat. Decorated knight comdr. Order St. Gregory the Great; Knight Holy Sepulchre. Mem. Am. Inst. M.E., Council Fgn. Relations, Sigma Xi, Sigma Tau, Kappa Sigma. Roman Catholic. Clubs: Explorers, University (N.Y.C.); University (San Diego). Home: 2685 Calle Del Oro La Jolla CA 92037

BARGER, VERNON DUANE, educator, physicist; b. Curllsville, Pa., June 5, 1938; s. Joseph F. and Olive (McCall) B.; B.S., Pa. State U., 1960, Ph.D., 1963; m. Annetta McLeod, 1967; children—Victor A., Amy J. Research asso. U. Wis., Madison, 1963-65, asst. prof., then asso. prof. physics, 1965-68, prof. physics, 1968—; vis. prof. U. Hawaii, 1970. Guggenheim fellow, 1972. Mem. Am. Phys. Soc., Phi Kappa Phi, Tau Beta Pi. Research in phenomenological description of high energy scattering processes; classification of fundamental particles as Regge recurrences. Home: Route 2 River Rd Box 208 Waunakee WI 53597 Office: U Wis Dept Physics Madison WI 53706

BARGHOORN, ELSO STERRENBERG, educator; b. N.Y.C., June 30, 1915; s. Elso S. and Elizabeth (Brust) B.; A.B., Miami (O.) U., 1937; M.A., Harvard, 1938, Ph.D., 1941; m. Margaret Alden MacLeod, Aug. 16, 1941 (div. 1951); children—Jonathan (dec.), Steven Frederick; m. 2d, Teresa Joan La Croix, July 21, 1953 (div. 1963); m. 3d, Dorothy Dellmer Osgood, Oct. 31, 1964. Instr. biology Amherst (Mass.) Coll., 1941-43, asst. prof., 1944-46; asst. prof. botany Harvard, 1946-49, asso. prof., 1949-55, prof., 1955—, curator paleobot. collections, 1949—. Field service cons. to War Dept., OSRD, 1944-48. Recipient Hayden Meml. award Phila. Acad. Natural Scis. Fellow Linnaean Soc. London; mem. Nat. Acad. Scis., Geol. Soc. Am., Am. Acad. Arts and Scis., Bot. Soc. Am., Geochem. Soc., Phi Beta Kappa, Sigma Xi. Contbr. articles to sci. jours. Home: RD 1 Carlisle MA 01741 Office: Harvard University Herbarium Cambridge MA 02138

BARGHOORN, FREDERICK CHARLES, polit. scientist, historian; b. N.Y.C., July 4, 1911; s. Elso Sterrenberg and Elizabeth (Brust) B.; A.B., Amherst Coll., 1934; A.M., Harvard, 1935. Ph.D., 1941. Staff, Am. embassy, Moscow, USSR, 1942-47; staff dept. polit. sci. Yale, 1947-, prof., 1957-; with Dept. of State, Germany, 1949-51; lectr., staff history and polit. sci. depts. U. Chgo., Columbia, others; cons. various govt. agencies, also Ford Found., 1955-56. Mem. Am. Polit. Sci. Assn., Am. Hist. Assn., Council on Fgn. Relations. Phi Beta Kappa. Author: The Soviet Image of the United States, 1950; Soviet Russian Nationalism, 1956; The Soviet Cultural Offensive, 1960; Politics in the U.S.S.R., 1966; Soviet Foreign Contbr. articles profl. jours., periodicals. Office: Dept Political Science Yale Univ New Haven CT 06520

BARGMANN, VALENTINE, educator; b. Berlin, Germany, Apr. 6, 1908; s. Abram and Rosa (Rosenblatt) B.; student U. Berlin, 1926-32; Ph.D., U. Zurich, Switzerland, 1936; m. Sophie Goldberg, July 21, 1941. Came to U.S., 1937, naturalized, 1943. Mem. Inst. for Advanced Study, Princeton, N.J., 1937-46; vis. lectr. Princeton, 1946-47, asso. prof. math. physics, 1948- 57, prof., 1957—; asso. prof. U. Pitts., 1948. Mem. Am. Phys. Soc., Am. Math. Soc., Sigma Xi. Home: 50 Western Way Princeton NJ 08540

BARICH, DEWEY FREDERICK, educator; b. Chisholm, Minn., Feb. 19, 1911; s. Eli and Angelia (Erro) B.; student Jr. Coll., Hibbing, Minn., 1929-31; B.S. in Indsl. Edn., Stout Inst., Menomonie, Wis., 1933; A.M. in Edn., U. Mich., 1939; Ed.D., Wayne State U., Detroit, 1961; LL.D., Western New Eng. Coll.; m. Verna Arling Eddy, Dec. 29, 1934; children—Judy, Dewey, Barbara, Wendy. Tchr. indsl. arts, pub. schs., Flint, Mich., also dept. chmn. Long-fellow Jr. High Sch.; chmn. Indsl. Survey Com. on Flint Industries, and mem. Indsl. Arts. Supr.'s Council, 1936-38; grad. asst. in edn. U. Mich., summer 1939; instr. metal trades Trenton (Mich.) High Sch., 1938-39; instr. indsl. arts Central Mich. Coll. of Edn., Mt. Pleasant, 1939-40; state supr. Nat. Defense (later War Prodn.) Tng., Mich. State Bd. of Control for Vocational Edn., 1940-42; prof. and head of indsl. arts dept. Kent State U., 1942 (on mil. leave 1943-45), univ. coordinator of vets. affairs, 1945-51; mgr. ednl. affairs dept. Ford Motor Co., 1951- 58; pres. Detroit Inst. Tech., 1958—. Mem. Pres. Truman's Conf. Occupational Safety, Pres. Eisenhower's Conf. Occupational Safety, Vice chmn. bd. dirs., schs. and colls. Nat. Safety Council; chmn. occupational safety standards commn. Mich. Dept. Labor, 1969-70; State Dept. cons. Internat. Adv. Com. on Medium Level Manpower, Ibadan, Nigeria, 1969. Served as lt. (j.g.), U.S.N.R.; engring. officer LCI, (L) Flotilla 24 Staff, 1943-45, 21 mos.; South Pacific and Philippine Islands theaters of operation. Awarded commendation for service by flotilla comdr.; recipient Indsl. Vocational Edn. Laureate Award. Mem. State Bd. Control Vocational Edn. Mem. N.E.A. (div. higher edn.), Am. Vocational Assn. (speaker; mem. nat. policies and planning com. for indsl. arts edn.), Am., Ohio indsl. arts assns., Soc. Automotive Engrs., Mich. Indsl. Edn. Assn. (speaker), Nat. Assn. Indsl. Tchrs. Educators, Engring. Soc. Detroit, Am. Soc. for Engring. Edn., Miss. Valley Indsl. Arts Consf., Epsilon Pi Tau, Phi Delta Kappa, Iota Lambda Sigma. Episcopalian. Clubs: Economic, Detroit Athletic, Rotary. Co- author of Applied Drawing and Sketching; Metal Work for Industrial Arts Shops. Contbr. articles to profl. jours. Home: 714 Cambridge Rd Ypsilanti MI 48197 Office: 2300 Park Av Detroit MI 48201

BARICH, RUSSELL WILLIAM, publisher; b. S. Range, Mich., June 4, 1913; s. John and Margaret (Schwegel) B.; B.A. in Edn., Coll. St. Thomas, St. Paul, 1935; m. Lois R. Peterson, June 1, 1940; children-Russell William, David, Christine. Traveller, Macfadden Publns., 1937-49, v.p. sales, 1953-59; circulation mgr. Pubs. Distbg. Corp., N.Y.C., 1949-53; pres., pub. Ace News Corp. Inc., N.Y.C., 1959—; v.p., dir. Charter Communications, Inc., 1969—. Chmn. bd. Bur. Ind. Pubs. and Distbrs. Served with AUS, 943-46. Home: 71 Mellow Lane Westbury NY 11590 Office: 1120 Av Americas New York NY 11590

BARING, WALTER STEPHAN, congressman; b. Goldfield, Nev., Sept. 9, 1911; s. Walter Stephen and Emilie Louise (Froehlich) B.; grad. (Gold medal hon. student) Reno High Sch., 1929; B.S., B.A., U. Nev., 1934; high sch. tchrs. certificate; m. Alma Geraldine Buchanan, Jan. 31, 1942; children—Walter Stephan III, William Robert, John Buchanan, Thomas Jefferson. Elected chmn. Dem. Central Com. of Washoe County, 1936; assemblyman from Washoe County to Nev. Legislature, 1936, 1942; councilman 6th Ward, Reno City Council 1947; asso. with father in Sierra Furniture Co., Reno, 1945-48; mem. 81st-82d Congress, 85th-92d Congresses, Nev. at large, chmn. pub. lands subcom. of interior com., mem. vets. affairs com. Served with USNR, 1942-45. Mem. Am. Legion. Mason (34, Shriner), Eagle; mem. Order Eastern Star. Democrat. Club: Sertoma. Home: 580 Casazza Dr Reno NV 89502 Office: Rayburn Bldg Washington DC 20515

BARIONI, DANIELE, tenor; b. Milan, Italy, Sept. 6, 1933; s. Umberto and Fedora (Chendi) B.; grad. Giuseppe Verdi Conservatory Music, Milan; m. Vera Franceschi, Oct. 28, 1957; 1 son, Giulio. Debut in Cavalleria Rusticana, Milano Theatre, 1954; toured Africa, Italy, Switzerland, Egypt, 1955; appeared with Met. Opera Co., N.Y.C., 1956-60, now with Phila. Grand Opera Co.; appeared Italian motion picture Carosello di Canzoni, 1958; debut Rome Opera in Tosca, 1959. Home: 168 W 86th St Philadelphia PA 19153 Office: Phila Grand Opera Co 1422 Chestnut Philadelphia PA 19102

BARISH, NORMAN NORTON, educator, indsl. engr.; b. N.Y.C., July 29, 1920; s. Meyer and Sayde (Spiro) B.; B.S magna cum laude, Coll. City N.Y., 1940; student Georgetown U., 1941-42; B.S., U. Mich., 1943; M.S., U. Pa., 1945; postgrad. Columbia, 1946-47; m. Esther Florence Braverman, Oct. 11, 1947; children—Michael Edward, Jean Ellen. Statis. bus., econ. analyst U.S. Govt., 1940-42; indsl. engring. supr. RCA, 1943-45; indsl. engr., mgmt. cons., 1945—; instr. indsl. engring. Newark Coll. Engring, 1946-47; asst. prof. adminstrv. engring. N.Y. U., 1947-50, asso. prof. mgmt. engring, 1950-55, prof., 1955—, chmn. dept. indsl. engring. and operations research, 1955—, statis. officer Coll. Engring, 1947-48, sec., 1948-58, acting dean, 1957-58, asso. dean, 1958-59; cons. editor, 1959—; tech. cons. indsl. engring. to Austrian govt., 1960-62. Registered profl. engr., Pa. Mem. Econometric Soc., Am. Soc. M.E., Am. Soc. Engring Edn. (gen. council 1962-64, chmn. engring. economy div. 1960-62, exec. com. 1956-64), Coll. Managerial Econs. (chmn. 1964-68), Internat. Univ. Contact for Mgmt. Edn. (mem. council 1963—), Am. Econ. Assn., Operations Research Soc. Am., Inst. Mgmt. Scis., Am. Inst. Indsl. Engrs. (pres. N.Y. chpt. 1953-54), Acad. Mgmt., Am. Assn. U. Profs., Sigma Xi, Phi Beta Kappa, Alpha Pi Mu, Pi Tau Sigma, Tau Beta Pi. Clubs: Engineers, University, Michigan (N.Y.C.). Author: Break Even Analyses, 1950; Systems Analysis for Effective Administration, 1951; (with J.M. Juran) Case Studies in Industrial Management, 1955; Engineering Enrollment in the United States, 1957; Economic Analysis for Engineering and Managerial Decision-Making, 1962; (with M. Verhulst) Management Sciences in the Emerging Countries: New Tools for Economic Development, 1964. Co-editor: Long Range Planning, 1967. Asso. editor Engring. Economist, 1955-59, editor Mgmt. Sci., 1965-69, asso. editor, 1969-70. Mem. editorial bd. Jour. Indsl. Engring., 1966-70; cons. editor Engring. Economist, 1959—; publ. com. Jour. Engring. Edn., 1962-63. Contbr. articles indsl. engring., operations research and mgmt. to mags., jours. Home: 7 Carthage Rd Scarsdale, NY 10583. Office: New York U University Heights New York City NY 10453

BARITZ, LOREN, educator; b. Chgo., Dec. 26, 1928; s. Joseph Harry and Helen (Garland) B.; B.A., Roosevelt U., 1953; M.A., U. Wis., 1954, Ph.D., 1956; m. Phyllis L. Handelsman, Dec. 26, 1948; children—Tony, Joseph. Asst. prof. history Wesleyan U., Middletown, Conn., 1956-62; asso. prof. Roosevelt U., Chgo., 1962-63; prof. U. Rochester, 1963-69, chmn. dept., 1963-65; prof. State U. N.Y. at Albany, 1969—; vis. lectr. U. Wis.-Madison, 1959-60. Rep. for U.S. to UNESCO Conf. on Film, Locarno, Italy, 1970; co-chmn. policy council research and service Assembly Univ. Goals, Am. Acad. Arts and Scis., 1969-70. Del. Democratic Nat. Conv.,

1968. Research tng. fellow Social Sci. Research Council, 1955-56, grantee, 1960; grantee Am. Council Learned Socs., 1963. Mem. Am. Hist. Assn., Am. Assn. U. Profs. Author: City on a Hill, 1964; Servants of Power, 1960; Sources of the American Mind, 2 vols., 1966; The Culture of the Twenties, 1970. Home: RD 2 Hawes Rd Altamont NY 12009 Office: History Dept State Univ NY Albany NY 12223

BARK, WILLIAM CARROLL, educator, historian; b. Tacoma, Dec. 10, 1908; s. Nelson and Daisy (Shea) B.; B.A. with great distinction, Stanford, 1931, M.A., 1932; Ph.D., Cornell U., 1936; m. Eleanor Carlton, Aug. 12, 1937; children—Dennis Laistner, Jared Carlton. Instr. history Stanford, 1936- 40; asso. prof. Lawrence Coll., 1940-45; asst. prof. U. Chgo., 1945-47; mem. faculty Stanford, 1947—, prof. history 1957—; sr. fellow Hoover Instn., 1968—; cons. in field. Co-chmn. San Francisco Curriculum Survey Com., 1959-60; mem. Cal. Coordinating Council Higher Edn., 1967-71, Carnegie Commn. Ednl. Inquiry, 1951-56. Region 9 Archives Adv. Council, Gen. Services Adminstrn., 1971—; mem. Am. br. internat. com. for revision of August Potthast, Bibliotheca historica medii aevi, 1956-58. Boldt fellow Cornell U., 1935; Sterling fellow Yale, 1944-45; Bollingen fellow Europe, 1962-63; Relm Found. fellow, 1968-69. Mem. Am. Hist. Assn., Assn. Cal. Ind. Colls. and Univs. (trustee at large 1967-71), Phi Beta Kappa, Sigma Alpha Epsilon. Episcopalian. Club: Bohemian (San Francisco). Author: Origins of the Medieval World, 1958; co-author: A History of World Civilization, 1957. Home: 721 Alvarado Row Stanford CA 94305

BARKA, TIBOR, med. educator; b. Debrecen, Hungary, Mar. 31, 1926; s. Imre and Hajnal (Szekely) B.; M.D., Debrecen U., 1950; m. Katalin Szalay, Mar. 3, 1957. Came to U.S., 1958, naturalized, 1963. First research asso. dept. morphology Inst. Exptl. Medicine, Hungarian Acad. Sci., Budapest, 1954-56; research asso. Inst. Cell Research and Genetics, Karolinska Institutet, Stockholm, Sweden, 1956-58; research asso. Mt. Sinai Hosp., N.Y.C., 1958-62, asst. attending pathologist, 1962-64, asso. attending pathologist, 1964—; prof. dept. pathology Mt. Sinai Sch. Medicine, 1966—, prof., chmn. dept. anatomy, 1967—. Mem. Histochem. Soc., Am. Soc. Exptl. Pathology, Council Biol. Editors, Am. Soc. Cell Biology. Author: (with G. Kiszely) Practical Microtechnique and Histochemistry, 1958; Histochemistry, Methods of the Experimental Medicine, 1959; (with P. J. Anderson) Histochemistry: Theory, Practice and Bibliography, 1963. Editor-in-chief Jour. Histochemistry and Cytochemistry, 1965—. Contbr. numerous articles profl. jours. Research in devel. and application of histochem. methods, studies on regulation of cell div. Home: 5700 Arlington Av New York City NY 10471

BARKALOW, FREDERICK SCHENCK, Jr., educator, zoologist; b. Marietta, Ga., Feb. 23, 1914; s. Frederick Schenck and Katherine Aurelia (White) B.; B.S. in Chemistry, Ga. Inst. Tech., 1936; student Auburn U., 1936-38; M.S. in Zoology, U. Mich., 1939, Ph.D. (Rosenwald fellow 1946-47), 1948; m. Joan Metzger, Nov. 23, 1937; 1 dau., Joanna. Instr. zoology Auburn U., 1936-39, instr. botany and plant pathology, 1946; chief biologist Ala. Dept. Conservation, 1939-41; mem. faculty N.C. State U. of N.C., Raleigh, 1947—, prof. zoology, 1950-67, prof. zoology and forestry, 1967—, head dept., 1950-63; cons. wildlife, 1939—. Mem. Sec. Agr. Adv. Com. Multiple Use Nat. Forests, 1963-68; del. White House Conf. Conservation, 1962; panelist NSF, 1959—. mem. tropical biology panel U. Costa Rica, 1962; sr. vis. fellow to Great Britain for OEEC, 1960; cons. disease vector study in Alaska for Dept. Def., 1951. Chmn. edn. div. United Fund Raleigh, 1954, bd. dirs., 1955-58. Served to lt. col. AUS, 1941-46. Recipient Am. Motors Conservation award, 1967; Gov.'s award for Conservationist of Year, 1968. Mem. Archaeol. Soc. N.C. (pres. 1959-60), N.C. Acad. Sci. (v.p. 1962, pres. 1971), N.C. Wildlife Fedn. (sec. 1948, trustee 1960—, pres. 1965-66), Am. Soc. Mammalogists (dir. 1961—, chmn. land mammals com. 1961-66), Soc. Am. Foresters, A.A.A.S., Am. Inst. Biol. Sci., Am. Ornithol. Union, Assn. Tropical Biology, Biol. Soc. Washington, Ecol. Soc. Am., Am. Soc. Systematic Zoology, Wildlife Soc., Phi Beta Kappa (pres. Wake County assn. 1954-55), Sigma Xi, Phi Kappa Phi (pres. N.C. State chpt. 1960- 61), Phi Sigma. Contbr. numerous articles in field. Home: 3439 Bradley Pl Raleigh NC 27607

BARKAN, ADOLPH WILLIAM, banker; b. San Francisco, Oct. 24, 1917; s. Hans and Phoebe (Bunker) B.; B.A., Stanford, 1939, student Law Sch., 1945-47; m. Joan M. Robbins, June 27, 1942; children—Constance J. (Mrs. John C. Kerr), John. San Francisco Call-Bull., 1939-41; with Wells Fargo Bank, San Francisco, 1947-, sr. v.p., 1966-. Chmn. exec. com. San Francisco Planning for Urban Renewel; mem. Market St. Adv. Com. Bd. dirs. San Francisco YMCA. Served to lt. comdr. USNR, 1941-45. Mem. Am. Bankers Inst. (chmn. adv. bd. San Francisco). Clubs: Pacific-Union, St. Francis Yacht (San Francisco); Burlingame Country (Hillsborough). Home: 611 Devon Dr Hillsborough, CA 94010. Office: 44 Montgomery St San Francisco CA 94120

BARKAN, ALEXANDER ELIAS, labor ofcl.; b. Bayonne, N.J., Aug. 9, 1909; s. Jacob and Rachel (Perelmen) B.; Ph.B., U. Chgo., 1933; m. Helen Stickno, May 10, 1942 children—Lois, Carol. With Textile Workers Organizing Com., 1937; organizer Textile Workers Union Am., 1938, sub-regional dir., 1938-42, polit. action dir., 1947-55; vets. dir. CIO community services dir., 1945; exec. dir. N.J. CIO Council, 1946; asst. dir. com. polit. edn. AFL- CIO, Washington, 1955-57, dep. dir. com. polit. edn., 1957-63, dir., 1963—. Served with USNR, 1942-45. Home: 6515 E Halbert Rd Bethesda MD 20034 Office: 815 16th St NW Washington DC 20006

BARKAN, JOSEPH GEORGE, shipping co. exec.; b. N.Y.C., Feb. 22, 1915; s. Asher and Rose (Solomon) B.; B.S., N.Y.U., 1946; grad. Indsl. Coll. Armed Forces, 1955; m. Helen Grossman, Nov. 6, 1938; children—Barbara G., Steven L. Accountant for various firms, 1931-34; finance officer War Dept., also Fed. Works Agy., 1935-42; auditor-in-charge Gen. Accounting Office, N.Y. area, 1943-51; comptroller Atlantic coast dist. Maritime Adminstrn., 1952-60; exec. v.p. Prudential Lines, Inc., N.Y.C., 1961-69; pres. Am. Export Isbransten Lines Inc., N.Y.C., 1970-71, Universal Stevedoring & Terminal Corp., 1971—. Mem. N.Y.C. Bd. Edn., 1963-69; exec. bd. Anti-Defamation League, 1961—. Mem. Fed. Govt. Accountants Assn. (v.p. 1959). Mem. B'nai B'rith (gov.). Clubs: Downtown, Athletic, Whitehall, Produce Exchange (N.Y.C.). Home: 70-20 108th St Forest Hills NY 11375 Office: 26 Broadway New York City NY 10004

BARKAN, LEONARD, mfg. co. exec.; b. N.Y.C., Nov. 15, 1928; s. Isadora Nathan and Sadie (Levine) B.; student Coll. City N.Y.; m. Mae Sara Solomon, Nov. 19, 1960; children—Andrew, Donna Rene. Trader, A. C. Israel Commodity Co., N.Y.C., 1947-57; with Fulton Industries, Inc., Atlanta, 1957-68; v.p. Allied Products Corp., 1968-70; exec. v.p., dir. Continental Moss Gorden, Inc., Prattville, 1959-70; chmn. bd. Thomas Pride Mills, Inc. Home: 665 Londonberry Rd NW Atlanta GA 30327 Office: 170 Boulevard SE Atlanta GA 30312

BARKER, ARTHUR EDWARD, educator; b. Toronto, Can., Jan. 21, 1911; s. Frank Harold and Gertrude Arthur (Hendra) B.; B.A., Trinity Coll. U. Toronto, 1933, M.A., 1934; Ph.D., U. Coll., U. London (Eng.), 1937; m. Dorothy May Riley, June 4, 1938; children—Jane Gertrude Gale (Mrs. Robert G.J. Couchman), Arthur Frank Kynaston. Came to U.S., 1961. Mem. faculty Trinity Coll., U. Toronto, 1937-61, prof. English, 1942-61; prof. English U. Ill. at Urbana, 1961-70, asso. mem. Center Advanced Study, 1964. Vis. prof. Columbia, 1945, 46, 60, 61, U. Wis., 1949, U. Toronto, 1962, U. Cal. at Los Angeles, 1965. Mem. bishop's com. Episcopal Chapel St. John the Divine, Champaign, Ill., 1962—. Overseas War Meml. scholar, 1935-37; Guggenheim fellow, 1945; fellow Folger Library, 1957, 58. Mem. Modern Lang. Assn., Renaissance Soc. Am. Author: Milton and the Puritan Dilemma, 3d edit., 1964; John Milton: Samson Agonistes and Early Poems, 2d edit., 1965; John Milton; Modern Essays in Criticism, 1965. Mem. editorial bd. Jour. English and Germanic Philology, Studies English Lit. Home: 310 W Delaware Av Urbana IL 61801

BARKER, BURT BROWN, lawyer; b. Waitsburg, Wash., Nov. 3, 1873; s. William Clement and Elvira Chadwick (Brown) B.; student Willamette U., Salem, Ore., 1889-93; A.B., U. of Chicago, 1897; LL.B., Harvard, 1901; LL.D., Linfield Coll., Ore., 1935; Litt.D., Pacific Univ., Forest Grove, Ore., 1964; m. Ella Starr Merrill, June 15, 1904; 1 dau., Barbara (Mrs. John A. Sprouse). Began practice of law, Chicago, 1901; mem. Wolseley & Barker, 1902-15; practiced alone in Chicago, 1915-17; practiced in N.Y. City, 1917-29; vice-pres. University Oregon, 1928—; member of the board of directors First Nat. Bank (Portland). Mem. Legal Advisory Bd. N.Y. City during period of World War, also sec. War Work Com. of Chicago Bar Assn. during same period. Trustee, dir. Salem Art Assn.; trustee Catlin Sch.; dir. Multnomah Co. Chpt. A.R.C., McLoughlin Meml. Assn.; chmn. liaison com. Ore. Hist. Soc. for Ore. history and mem. exec. com. Oregon Territorial Centennial Commission; president Herbert Hoover Foundation. Pres. Doernbecker Children's Hosp. Guild; chancellor Columbia Basin Session of Inst. of Internat. Relations, 1932; president dir. Ore. Hist. Soc.; chmn. Northwest Regional Committee of Advisory Committee to Treasury Dept. on Fine Arts; regional art dir. Federal Works of Art Projects, Ore., Wash., Idaho and Mont., 1935-36; state dir. for Ore. and regional advisor Fed. Art Project since 1936; chmn. Ore. Com. to place statues in Nat. Statuary Hall, Washington; chmn. Ore. Lewis and Clark Sequicentennial Celebration. Mem. Am. Bar Assn. com. of Am. Inst. for Endowments; chmn. Portland Advisory com. of 2d Am.-Japan Student Conf., 1935, 4th Conf., 1937, 6th Conf., 1939. Recipient of U. Chgo. Alumni Assn. citation for pub. service as useful citizen, Edith Knight Hill Meml. award for distinguished service in field of edn. and hist. research, award of distinction for services in scholarly fields and contbn. hist. materials American Association for State and Local History. Member American, New York State and Illinois State bar assns., U. of Chicago Alumni Assn., Delta Sigma Rho (charter mem.); life mem. Chicago Bar Assn., sec. 2 terms; pres. Henckel Family Assn.; mem. S.A.R. (vice president general 1954-56), Sons and Daughters Ore. Pioneers, Native Sons and Daughters of Ore., Patrons and Friends of the U. of Ore. Library (pres.). Republican. Baptist. Clubs: University, City (Portland); Montclair (N.J.) Art Assn.; Nantucket (Mass.) Yacht. Author: Letters of Dr. John McLoughlin; Financial Papers of Dr. John McLoughlin; The Dr. John McLoughlin House; Ore., Prize of Discovery, Exploration and Settlement; Introduction—Ogden's Snake Country Journals; Vol. 13 Hudson's Bay Record Society Publications; Oregon and Statuary Hall; Oregon Territorial Centennial (chpt. IV); Nation Claims in Old Oregon; McLoughlin Empire and Its Rulers; The Henckel Geneology; other hist. and geneal. publs. Donor bronze statue Pioneer Mother to University of Oregon, 1935. Home: 3438 SW Brentwood Dr Portland OR 97201

BARKER, CHARLES ALBRO, educator; b. Washington, Sept. 15, 1904; s. Charles A. and Alice H. (Albro) B.; B. A., Yale, 1926, Ph.D., 1932; m. Louise C. Cottle, July 23, 1932; children—John Gaylord, Louise Albro (Mrs. David S. Cannell). Instr. history Smith Coll., 1928-31; asst. prof. history Mills. Coll., 1932-33; instr., asst. prof., asso. prof. history, Stanford U., 1933-45; prof. Am. history Johns Hopkins U., 1945—, chmn. dept., 1961-66. Smith-Mundt vis. prof. Am. U., Beirut, Lebanon, 1953-54; vis. prof. history U. Wis., 1956; Fulbright-Hays lectr. Panjab U., India, U. Melbourne (Australia), 1970-71. Social Sci. Research Council research fellow, 1962-63; Guggenheim fellow, 1965. Recipient A. J. Beveridge prize Am. Hist. Assn., 1941. Mem. Am. Studies Assn. (pres. 1953), Am., Miss. Valley, Md. hist. socs., Am. Assn. Univ. Profs., Phi Beta Kappa. Club: Hamilton Street (Baltimore). Author: Backgroud of the Revolution in Maryland, 1940; Biography of Henry George, 1955; American Convictions, 1600-1850, 1970. Editor: The Memoirs of E.B. Crosby, 1945; Problems of World Disarmament, 1963; Power and Law, 1971. Contbr. articles, revs. for hist. jours., books. Home: 3913 Canterbury Rd Baltimore MD 21218 also Wonalancet NH 03897

BARKER, CLARENCE AUSTIN, finance exec., economist; b. Centralia, Wash., Dec. 2, 1911; s. Clarence G. and Susan (McElroy) B.; A.B., Stanford, 1934; postgrad. Columbia U. Grad. Sch. Bus., 1935-36; M.B.A., N.Y.U., 1937-39; m. Mary Ellen Brown, Mar. 29, 1941; children—Beverly Jean, Stephen Warner. Accountant, regulatory analyst Pub. Service Electric & Gas Co. of N.J., Newark, 1936-44; sr. economist charge financial and econ. research Cleve. Electric Illuminating Co., 1944-59, sec. to finance com. bd. dirs., 1954-59; dir. research Hornblower & Weeks-Hemphill, Noyes, investment bankers, N.Y.C., 1959-65, general partner, 1962—, economist, pub. utility cons., 1965—, adv. bd. affilate, 1965—; charter financial analyst, 1964—. Lectr. corp. finance and investment analysis Case-Western Res. U. Grad. div., 1955-59; lectr. pub. utility seminars Irving Trust Co., 1959—; prepared testimony on stock splits SEC. Bd. dirs. Rye Conservation Soc., 1965—, pres., 1965-68. Mem. nat. adv. council Stanford Alumni, 1952-57. Mem. Am. Econ. Assn., Am. Statis. Assn., Nat. Economists Club (charter mem.), Acad. Polit. Sci. (life), Economists Nat. Com. on Monetary Policy, Am. Finance Assn., Nat. Assn. Bus. Economists (charter mem.), N.Y. Soc. Security Analysts, S.A.R., Founders and Patriots (treas. 1965-68, councillor 1970- -), Rye Hist. Soc. Republican. Episcopalian. Clubs: Broad Street, Stanford, (N.Y.C.); Rowfant (Cleve.); Apawamis. Asso. editor Financial Analysts Jour., 1969-70. Contbr. articles to profl. jours. Home: 2 Hickory Dr Rye NY 10580 Office: 8 Hanover St New York City NY 10004

BARKER, GEORGE GRANVILLE, writer; b. Essex, Eng., Feb. 26, 1913; s. George and Marion Frances (Taafe) B.; student Regents Street Poly. Inst., London, 1926-29; m. Jessica Woodward, Nov. 1933; children—Anthony and Anastasia (twins). Chair, English lit. Tohoku U., Japan, 1939; lectr. Oxford, Cambridge univs. Mem. Soc. Authors of London, Poetry Soc. Oxford U. (elected patron 1953). Arts fellow York U., 1966-67. Author: 30 Preliminary Poems, 1933; Alanna Autumnal, 1933; Poems, 1935; Calamiterror, 1937; Lament and Triumph, 1940; Janus, 1940; Sacred and Secular Elegies, 1943; Eros in Dogma, 1944; News of the World, 1950; The Dead Seagull, 1950; A Vision of Beasts and Gods, 1954; The True Confession George Barker, 1957; The View from Blind 1, 1962; Dreams of a Summer Night, 1966; The Golden Chains, 1968; Runes and Rimes and Tunes and Chimes, 1970; To Aylsham Fair, 1970; Essays, 1970; Poems of Places and People, 1971. Home: Bintry House Itteringham Aylsham Norfolk England Office: care Faber & Faber Ltd 24 Russell Sq London WC 1 England

BARKER, GREGSON LEARD, corp. exec.; b. Chgo., Jan. 19, 1918; s. Walter R. and Margaret (Gregson) B.; m. Mary Louise Nichols, Sept. 8, 1939 (div.); children-Margaret Louise (Mrs. William A. Boyd), John Leard, Eric Walter, William Jordan; m. 2d Betty McPherson King, Apr. 27, 1968. With UARCO, Inc., Barrington, Ill., designers, printer bus. forms, 1937—, pres., 1955—; dir. LaSalle Nat. Bank, Hammond Corp., Chgo. Profl. Basketball Assn. Mem. citizens bd. U. Chgo.; bd. dirs., v.p. Jr. Achievement Chgo.; bd. dirs. Infant Welfare Soc. Chgo. Mem. Ill. Mfrs. Assn. (pres., dir.), Chgo. Assn. Commerce and Industry (bd. dirs.), Employers Assn. Chgo. (bd. dirs. 1956-59), Chgo. Pres. Orgn., Northwestern U. Assos. Republican. Episcopalian. Clubs: Economic, Executive, Commonwealth, Chicago, Racquet (Chgo.); Barrington Hills Country. Home: 81 Meadow Hill Rd Barrington IL 60010 Office: UARCO Inc Barrington IL 60010

BARKER, HAROLD GRANT, surgeon; b. Salt Lake City, June 10, 1917; s. Frederick George and Jennetta (Stephens) B.; A.B., U. Utah, 1939, postgrad., 1939-41; M.D., U. Pa., 1943; m. Kathleen Butler, July 29, 1949; children—Janet Stephens, Douglas Reid. Intern. Hosp. U. Pa., 1943-44, asst. resident in surgery, 1947-51, sr. resident in surgery, 1951-52, asst. attending surgeon, 1952-53, also asst. instr., research fellow U. Pa., 1946-51, instr., research fellow, 1951-52, asso. in surgery, 1952-53; asst. prof. clin. surgery Columbia, 1953-57, asso. prof., 1957-68, prof., 1968—; asst. attending surgeon Presbyn. Hosp., 1953-57, asso. attending surgeon, 1957-69, attending surgeon, 1969—; pvt. practice, Phila., 1952-53, N.Y.C., 1953—. Served from 1st lt. to capt., M.C., AUS, 1944- 46; ETO Diplomate Am. Bd. Surgery. Fellow A.C.S.; mem. Soc. U. Surgeons, N.Y. Surg. Soc. Am. Physiol. Soc., Soc. Exptl. Biology and Medicine, Am. Fedn. Clin Research, A.M.A., Halsted Soc., N.Y. State (chmn. surg. sect. 1961-62), N.Y. County med. socs., N.Y. Acad. Sci., Am. Surg. Assn., N.Y. Gastroent. Assn., Societe Internationale de Chirurgie, Soc. Surgery Alimentary Tract, Allen O. Whipple Surg. Soc., Am. Assn. History Medicine, Sigma Xi. Republican. Presbyn. Clubs: Charaka; Century Assn. Contbr. articles med. jours. Home: 1 Forest Av Rye NY 10580 Office: 630 W 168th St New York City NY 10032

BARKER, HAROLD KENNETH, univ. dean; b. Louisville, Apr. 14, 1922; s. J.M. and Fannie Mae (Elliott) B.; A.B., U. Louisville, 1948, M.A., 1949; Ph.D., U. Mich., 1959; m. Elizabeth Johns, Mar. 11, 1948; children—Leslie Ann, Glen Lewis. Instr. Gunfire Prep. Sch., Hanau, Germany, 1946; sch. psychologist, vis. tchr. Bay City (Mich.) pub. schs., 1949-52, also instr. Bay City Jr. Coll.; sch. psychologist Ypsilanti (Mich.) pub. schs., 1952-53; instr. Eastern Mich. U., 1954-58, asst. dir. Bur. Appointments and Occupational Information, 1954-59; asso. exec. sec. Am. Assn. Colls. Tchr. Edn., Washington, 1959-66; dean Coll. Edn., dean internat. programs U. Akron, 1966—. Bd. dirs. World U., San Juan, P.R., 1966—. Served with USAAF, 1942-46. Recipient award outstanding profl. service Am. Assn. Colls. Tchr. Edn., 1966. Mem. Am. Assn. Higher Edn., Regional Council Internat, Edn., Phi Delta Kappa (internat. commn. 1962-69). Editor: AACTE Handbook of International Education Programs, 1963. Contbr. articles profl. jours. and periodicals. Home: 570 Tamiami Trail Akron OH 44303

BARKER, HORACE ALBERT, biochemist; b. Oakland, Cal., Nov. 29, 1907; s. Albert C. and Nettie (Hindry) B.; A.B., Stanford, 1929, Ph.D., 1933; m. Margaret McDowell, Aug. 29, 1933; children—Barbara, Elizabeth, Robert. Instr. soil microbiology U. Cal., Berkeley, 1936-40, asst. prof., 1940-45, asso. prof., 1945-46, prof., 1946-50, chmn. div. plant nutrition, 1949-50, prof. plant biochemistry and microbiologist agrl. expt. sta., 1950-59, prof. biochemistry, 1959—, chmn. dept., 1962-64, chmn. dept. plant biochemistry, 1950-53; asso. editor Ann. Rev. Microbiology, 1946-53; editor Archives of Biochemistry, 1951-54; mem. editorial bd. Jour. Bacteriology, 1955-60, jour. Biochemistry, 1960-65. Recipient Sugar Research award Nat. Acad. Sci., 1945; Neuberg medal Am. Soc. European Chemists, 1959, Borden award in nutrition, 1962; Cal. Scientist Year award Cal. Mus. Sci. and Industry, 1965; Nat. Medal Sci., U.S. govt., 1968. Mem. Am. Chem. Soc., Soc. Am. Bacteriology, Am. Soc. Biol. Chemists, Biochem. Soc. (Hopkins medal 1967), Nat. Acad. Sci. Author: Bacterial Fermentations, 1956; also tech. articles sci. jours. Home: 561 Santa Clara Av Berkeley CA 94707

BARKER, HUGH ALTON, electric utility co. exec.; b. Stillwater, Minn., Nov. 26, 1925; s. George Clarence and Minerva (Register) B.; B.B.A. with distinction, U. Minn., 1949; m. Janet M. Breitenbucher, Mar. 18, 1949; 1 dau., Pamela J. Prin., Haskins & Sells, C.P.A.'s Mpls., 1949-58; asst. to exec. v.p. Pub. Service Ind., Plainfield, 1958-60, financial v.p., 1960-68, exec. v.p., dir., 1968—; dir. 1st Nat. Bank & Trust Co., Plainfield. Pres. Guilford Sch. Bldg. Corp., Plainfield; mem. Ind. State Commn. on Tax and Financing Policy. Pres., bd. dirs. Hendricks County United Fund; treas., bd. dirs. Hendricks County Hosp. Fund. Served with AUS, 1944-45; ETO. C.P.A., Minn. Mem. Am. Inst. C.P.A.'s, Minn. Soc. C.P.A.'s, Sigma Alpha Epsilon, Beta Gamma Sigma. Home: Plainfield IN Office: 1000 E Main St Plainfield IN 46168

BARKER, JAMES FRANCIS, brewing co. exec.; b. Romney, Ind., May 26, 1912; s. Grover Cleveland and Edna Doris (Allman) B.; B.S., Purdue U., 1934, M.S., 1936; m. Phyllis Kathleen Hollis, June 14, 1932; children—Patricia (Mrs. B. Michael Strunk), James Hollis, Kathi Ann. Asst. plant supt. Terre Haute Brewing Co. (Ind.), 1936-47; asst. brewmaster Drewrys Ltd. U.S.A. Inc., S. Bend, Ind., 1947-48; brewmaster Storz Brewing Co., Omaha, 1949-51, George Wiedemann Co., Newport, Ky., 1951-52; v.p. prodn. Drewrys Ltd., S. Bend, 1952—, also dir.; dir. Sterling Brewers. Served with USNR, 1943-46. Mem. Master Brewers Assn. Am., Am. Soc. Brewing Chemists, Sigma Xi. Presbyn. Mason (Shriner), Elk. Club: South Bend Country. Home: 1721 E Wayne St South Bend IN 46615 Office: 1408 Elwood St South Bend IN 46624

BARKER, JAMES MADISON, b. Pittsfield, Mass., Mar. 13, 1886; s. Charles T. and Emma J. (Burke) B.; S.B., Mass. Inst. Tech., 1907; D.Sc., Middlebury Coll., 1939; LL.D., Westminister Coll., 1964; m. Margaret Clark Rankin, April 13, 1914; children—Robert Rankin, Hugh, Cecily Helen (Mrs. R.W. Finley), Ralph. Asst., Mass. Inst. Tech., 1907; draftsman, designer Am. Bridge Co., 1909-10; engr. Canadian Pacific Ry., Montreal, Can., and Bur. Engring. Statistics, N.Y., 1910-12; with E.A. Tucker Co., Boston, 1912-13; instr. Harvard, 1914-15; instr., asst. prof. structural engring., cons. structural engr. Mass. Inst. Tech., 1914-19; cons. engr. Navy Dept. Div. Constrn. and Repair, 1918; with 1st Nat. Bank, Boston, 1919-20, mgr., Buenos Aires, Argentina, br., 1920-28; with Sears, Roebuck & Co., 1928—, regional mgr., Phila., eastern v.p., retail adminstr. v.p., v.p. and treas. v.p., treas., controller, dir., 1930-68, hon. dir., 1968—. Mem. Price Adjustment Bd., Chgo. Ordnance Dist., War Dept., 1942-47; mem. reorgn. com. C.M.S.P. & P. Ry. Co., 1945-46, voting trustee, 1946-50, mem. finance com., dir., 1946-69; chmn. Savs. and Profit Sharing Pension Fund Sears Roebuck & Co. Employees, 1956-60, trustee, chmn. investment com., 1956-66; dir. Allstate Ins. Co., 1935-68, chmn. finance com. 1956-60, chmn. bd., 1943-60; hon. dir. Allstate Fire Insurance Co. Life trustee Northwestern U.; hon. trustee Newberry Library, Mus. Sci. and Industry (Chgo.). Participant missions to Iran, 1948, 49; chief econ. mission to Turkey, Internat. Bank for Reconstrn. and Devel., 1949-51; mem. Real Property Task Force Hoover Commn. on Orgn. Exec. Br. Govt.; governing life mem.

Art Inst. Chgo. Clubs: Chicago, University, Commercial, Wayfarers (Chgo.); Century, University, Brook (N.Y.C.); Jockey (Buenos Aires, Argentina). Home: 1430 N Lake Shore Dr Chicago, IL 60610. Office: 221 N LaSalle St Chicago IL 60601

BARKER, LEBARON R., Jr., editor; b. Plymouth, Mass., Jan. 13, 1904; s. LeBaron Russell and (Hutchins) B.; A.B., Harvard, 1926; m. Mary Pope, June 28, 1926 (div. Apr. 1933); children—LeBaron Russell, III, Randolph; m. 2d, Leslie Greenough, Sept. 14, 1934 (dec. Aug. 1939); 1 dau., Leslie Lindsay; m. 3d, Eileen Lange, Apr. 10, 1941 (div. 1950); children—Jeffery, Stephanie; m. 4th, Adeline Crankshaw, Jan. 17, 1952. Worked in advt., sales, editorial departments Houghton Mifflin & Co., 1927-43; New York editor, 1937-43; trade advt. mgr. Doubleday Doran, 1943, editor-in-chief, 1943-45, exec. editor, 1945-69, sr. editor, 1969—. Pres. Publishers Ad Club, 1941-43; chmn. radio com., Council on Books in Wartime, 1942; v.p. Am. Inst. Graphic Arts, 1947-52. Club: Dutch Treat (N.Y.C.). Co-author: (pseud. Admiral Jettison) Addelgrams, 1934. Home: 222 E 71st St New York City NY 10021 Office: 277 Park Av New York City NY 10017

BARKER, LESLIE PAXTON, physician; b. Elba, Ida., 1901; s. A.J. and Elizabeth (Stauffer) B.; M.D., Columbia; m. Katherine Buckhout Bonnell, Jan. 28, 1953. Dir. dermatology St. Luke's Hosp., also St. Barnabas Hosp., N.Y.C., 1942-67, now cons. dermatologist; cons. dermatologist Presbyn. Hosp., Columbia Med. Center (both N.Y.C.); clin. prof. dermatology Columbia Coll. Phys. and Surg., 1955-67, now spl. lectr. Mem. Am., N.Y. dermatol. socs., Soc. Investigative Dermatology, Acad. Dermatology, N.Y. Acad. Medicine, A.M.A. Contbr. med. jours. Home: East Woods Rd Pound Ridge NY 10576 Office: 120 E 75th St New York City NY 10021

BARKER, NORMAN, Jr., banker; b. San Diego, July 30, 1922; s. Norman and Grace (Bolger) N.; B.A., U. Chgo., 1947, M.B.A., 1953; m. Sue Keefe, June 27, 1947; children—Peter, Timothy, Michael, Beth. Asst. cashier Harris Trust & Savs. Bank, Chgo., 1947-55; credit mgr. Am. Can Co., 1955-57; with United Cal. Bank, Los Angeles, 1957—, pres., 1968—, also dir.; dir. ACSC Mgmt. Co., Western Bancorp. Treas. United Way, Los Angeles, 1968. Trustee Occidental Coll., Los Angeles Orthopaedic Found. and Orthopaedic Hosp. Served to lt. USNR, 1944-46, 50-52. Mem. Delta Kappa Epsilon. Home: 1301 Rancho Rd Arcadia CA 91006 Office: 600 S Spring St Los Angeles CA 90054

BARKER, RALPH HOLLENBACK, pub. utility exec.; b. Hillsdale, Kan., Feb. 9, 1912; s. Edgar Rusell and Edna (Morrison) B.; certificate proficiency in accounting U. Kan., 1944; m. Eunice Katherine Miller, May 27, 1931; 1 dau., Delores Marie (Mrs. Jess O. Ewing). With Gas Service Co., Kansas City, 1929-71, dir., 1962-71, sec., 1962-71, treas., 1964-71. Mem. Nat. Assn. Accountants (past dir.), Financial Execs. Inst. (past dir.), Inst. Internal Auditors (past treas., dir.). Presby. (ruling elder, treas.), Mason (Shriner); mem. Order Eastern Star. Club: Kansas City. Home: PO Box 126 Hilldale KS 66036 Office: Scarritt Bldg PO Box 2119 Kansas City MO 64142

BARKER, RICHARD L., clothing mfr.; b. Myrtle Point, Ore., May 26, 1934; s. Joel L. and Vida E. (Hoffman) B.; B.B.A., U. Ore., 1956; m. Louann (Cowan), Oct. 10, 1954; children—Steven Lynn, Douglas Allan, Cheryl Kay. Audit mgr. Price Waterhouse & Co., Portland, Ore., 1956-64, Chgo., 1964-66; asst. controller Household Finance Corp., 1966-69; v.p., comptroller Hart Schaffner & Marx, Chgo., 1969—. C.P.A., Ill. Mem. Am. Inst. C.P.A.'s, Ill. Soc. C.P.A.'s, Financial Execs. Inst., Execs. club. Club: University (Chgo.). Home: 156 S Maple Ct Palatine IL 60067 Office: 36 S Franklin St Chicago IL 60606

BARKER, ROBERT RAY, publishing co. exec.; b. Boswell, Okla., Dec. 16, 1917; s. Robert O. and Pearl (Spencer) B.; student Southeastern Okla. Coll., 1935-36, Baylor U., 1937-38; m. Christie Matthews, Oct. 12, 1940; children—Robert Ray, Constance Ann (Mrs. Steven Griffin), Joan Lee. With Field Enterprises Ednl. Corp., Chgo., 1939—, pres., 1966—, chief exec. officer, 1968—, also dir.; dir. Field Enterprises, Inc., also subsidiaries. Mem. bd. benevolence Evangel. Convenant Ch. Am. Trustee Chgo. Endl. TV Assn., Avery Coonley Sch., Downers Grove, Ill. Served with USAAF, 1943-45. Mem. Sigma Tau Delta. Democrat. Clubs: Executives, Chicago Athletic Assn., Mid- American, Tavern (Chgo.); Post and Paddock (Arlington, Ill.); La Grange (Ill.) Country. Home: 441 E 8th St Hinsdale IL 60521 Office: Field Enterprises Ednl Corp Merchandise Mart Chicago IL 60654

BARKER, ROBERT WHITNEY, lawyer, ch. ofcl.; b. Ogden, Utah, July 9, 1919; s. George Simon and Florence Emily (Dee) B.; B.S. with honors, U. Utah, 1941; J.D., Georgetown Law Center, 1947, postgrad. 1949-50; m. Amy Vera Thomas, June 30, 1942; children-Amy Ann, Robert Whitney, Paul Thomas, Philip Dee, Jeffrey Cutler, Brian Thomas. Admitted to Utah bar, 1948, D.C. bar, 1949, also U.S. Supreme Ct.; partner firm Barker & Barker, Ogden, Utah, 1948; asso. Ernest L. Wilkinson, Washington, 1948-50; adminstrv. asst. to Senator Wallace F. Bennett, 1951-53; partner firm Wilkinson, Cragun & Barker, Washington, 1953—. Dir., sec. Barlow Corp., 1969—; sec., gen. counsel, dir. Bonneville Internat. Corp., 1965—; v.p., sec., gen-counsel Radio N.Y. Worldwide, Inc., 1964—, Radio Skokie Valley, Inc., 1970—. Gen. counsel presdl. inaugural com., 1969. Pres. Weber County (Utah) Young Republican Club, 1948. Served to maj., F.A., AUS, 1941-46; MTO, ETO. Decorated Bronze Star with two oak leaf clusters. Mem. Am. (chmn. Indian matters com. Adminstrv. Law sect., 1957-59), Fed. (dep. chmn. Indian law com., 1966—), D.C. (chmn. U.S. Ct. of Claims com., 1965-67), Utah, Fed. Communications bar assns., U. Utah Nat. Adv. Council. Mem. Ch. of Jesus Christ of Latter-day Saints (bishop 1953-57, first counselor Washington stake presidency, 1959-67, regional rep. Council of Twelve, 1967—). Editorial bd. Georgetown Law Jour., 1947-48. Home: 9913 Hillridge Dr Kensington MD 20795 Office: 1616 H St N W Washington DC 20006

BARKER, ROBINSON FRANKLIN, glass co. exec.; b. Boston, Dec. 20, 1913; s. Williston Wright and Gertrude (Sherman) B.; A.B., Harvard, 1935; grad. Advanced Mgmt. Program, 1956; LL.D., Thiel Coll., 1966; D.Sc., Seton Hall Coll., 1968; L.H.D., Westminster Coll., 1970; m. Mary Lucinda Haskins, July 8, 1938; children—Christopher Haskins, Susan. With Pitts. Plate Glass Co., 1935—, successively mgr. Nashville br., asst. mgr. plate glass sales, asst. gen. mgr. merchandising branches, asst. to pres., gen. mgr. planning, glass div., 1955-57, v.p., gen. mgr., glass div., 1957-62, v.p. glass and fiber glass group, 1962-66, pres. 1966-67, chmn. bd. dirs., chief exec., 1967— (co. name changed to PPG Industries, Inc.); pres., dir. PPG Industries (Europe) S.A.; dir. Columbia Nitrogen Corp., Pitts. br. Fed. Res. Bank of Cleve., Mellon Nat. Bank & Trust Co., Pitts. Corning Corp., Carrier Corp., Smith & Stone, Ltd., Societe Anonyme des Glaces de Courcelles, Canadian Pitts. Industries, Ltd., Duplate Canada, Ltd.; mem. sr. execs. adv. council Conf. Bd.; pres., mem.. exec. com. Allegheny Conf. Community Devel.; finance com. Com. for Econ. Devel.; mem. adv. council Nat. 4-H Found.; chmn. Pitts. area U.S. Savs. Bond campaign; mem. Western Pa. adv. com. Radio Free Europe; exec. com. program for sci. Harvard Coll.; overseers com. on univ. resources Harvard; bus. adv. council Grad. Sch. Indsl. Adminstrn., Carnegie-Mellon U.; v.p., dir. United Fund Allegheny County; exec. com. Pa. Economy League. Bd. dirs. Regional Indsl. Devel. Corp. Western Pa., Pitts.-Allegheny County chpt. A.R.C., Hosp. Planning Assn. Allegheny County, Action-Housing, Inc., Pitts. Symphony Soc., Pitts. Urban Transit Council, Western Pa. Safety Council, Internat. Exec. Service Corps. Trustee Sewickley Valley Hospital, Health, Research and Services Found., Automotive Safety Found., Roxbury Latin Sc. Nat. Safety Council; trustee U. Pitts., mem. bd. visitors Grad. Sch. Pub. and Internat. Affairs; chmn. bd. directors PPG Industries Found. Served from ensign to lt. with USNR, 1942-45. Mem. C. of C. Pitts., Am. Ordnance Assn. (dir. Pitts. chpt.), Harvard Bus. Sch. Assn. (dir.), Nat. Indsl. Pollution Control Council, Soc. Automotive Engrs., Newcomen Soc., Pa. Soc. Episcopalian (diocesan council Pitts.). Clubs: Duquesne (Pitts.); Harvard of Western Pa.; Edgeworth; Allegheny Country, Sewickley Heights Gun (Sewickley, Pa.); Laurel Valley Golf; Rolling Rock; Stonedale Guns; Fifth Avenue, Harvard (N.Y.C.); Allegheny (dir.). Home: 8 Woodland Rd Sewickley PA 15143 Office: One Gateway Center Pittsburgh PA 15220

BARKER, SAMUEL BOOTH, univ. adminstr., educator; b. Montclair, N.J., Mar. 3, 1912; s. Harry and Marion (Booth) B.; B.S. cum laude, U. Vt, 1932; student Yale, 1932-34; Ph.D., Cornell, 1936; medicine fellow, 1936-41; m. Justine Rogers, July 31, 1934. Mem. faculty U. Tenn. Coll. Medicine, 1941-44; asst. prof. State U. Ia. Coll. of Medicine, 1944-46, asso. prof. physiology, 1946-52; prof. pharmacology U. Ala. in Birmingham, 1952-62, prof. physiology-biophysics, 1965—, dir. grad. studies, asso. dean Med. Coll and Sch. Dentistry, 1965-70, dean Grad. Sch. 1970—; prof. pharmacology Coll. Medicine, U. Vt., 1962-65. Cons. NIH, NSF, 1944—. Krichesky fellow, 1951; recipient Career Research award USPHS, 1962-65. Fellow A.A.A.S., Am. Inst. Chemists; mem. Am. Physiol. Soc., Soc. Exptl. Biology and Medicine, Harvey Soc., Am. Assn. U. Profs. (pres. Ia. chpt. 1950), Ala. Acad. Scis. (pres. 1959-60), Am. Fedn. Clin. Research, Endocrine Soc., Am. Chem. Soc. (chmn. Ala. sect. 1957-58), Biochem. Soc. London, N.Y. Acad. Scis., Am. Thyroid Assn. (pres. 1970-71), Phi Beta Kappa, Sigma Xi. Author: (with J.H.U. Brown) Basic Endocrinology, 2d edit., 1966; also research and publs. in endocrinology and metabolism. Home: 1812 Woodcrest Rd Birmingham AL 35209

BARKER, STEPHEN FRANCIS, educator; b. Ann Arbor, Mich., 1927; s. Ernest F. and Emma (Swigart) B.; B.A., Swarthmore Coll., 1949; M.A., Harvard, 1951, Ph.D., 1954; m. Evelyn Masi, Aug. 28, 1961; childrenCharles, George. Instr., U. So. Cal., 1954-55; asst. prof. U. Va., 1956-58, asso. prof., 1958-61; prof. Ohio State U., 1961-64; prof. Johns Hopkins, Balt., 1964-; Santayana fellow Harvard, 1955-56; Guggenheim fellow, 1964-65. Served with USNR, 1945-46. Mem. Am. Philos. Assn. Author: Induction and Hypothesis, 1957; Philosophy of Mathematics, 1964: The Elements of Logic, 1965. Home: 4003 Keswick Rd Baltimore, MD 21211.

BARKER, WILEY FRANKLIN, surgeon, educator; b. Sante Fe, Oct. 16, 1919; s. Charles Burton and Bertha (Steed) B.; B.S., Harvard, 1941, M.D., 1944; m. Nancy Ann Kerber, June 8, 1943; children—Robert Lawrence, Jonathan Steed, Christina Lee. Intern, then resident Peter Bent Brigham Hosp., Boston, 1944-46; Arthur Tracy Cabot fellow Harvard Med. Sch., 1948-49; asst. chief surg. service, then chief surg. sect. Wadsworth VA Hosp., Los Angeles, 1951- 54, attending physician, 1951—; mem. faculty U. Cal. at Los Angeles Med. Sch., 1954—, prof. surgery, 1964—, also chief div. gen. surgery; cons. Sepulveda VA Hosp., 1966—. Mem. com. trauma NRC, 1964—. Served as lt. (j.g.) M.C., USNR, 1946- 47. Harvard Nat. scholar, 1937-44. Diplomate Am. Bd. Surgery (bd. dirs. 1964—). Fellow A.C.S.; mem. Am. Surg. Assn., Soc. Clin. Surgery, Soc. Univ. Surgeons, Soc. Vascular Surgery, Internat. Cardiovascular Soc. (v.p. N.Am. chpt. 1964-65), Pacific Coast Surg. Assn., Am., Cal., Los Angeles County med. assns., Phi Beta Kappa, Sigma Xi, Alpha Omega Alpha. Republican. Episcopalian. Author: Surgical Treatment of Peripheral Vascular Disease, 1962; Peripheral Arterial Disease, 1966; also papers, chpts. in books. Mailing Address: Office: Dept Surgery Univ Cal Sch Medicine Los Angeles CA 90024

BARKER, WILLIAM ALFRED, educator; b. Los Angeles, May 9, 1919; s. Lawrence and Natalie (Cole) B.; B.A., Yale, 1941; M.S., Cal. Inst. Tech., 1949; Ph.D., St. Louis U., 1952; m. Mary Louise Miller, June 25, 1941; children—Gail (Mrs. Michael Kahle), Patrick Cole, Claire (Mrs. Jeffrey Stewart), Louisa Lawrene, Michael Lawrence. Mem. faculty St. Louis U., 1949-64, Swiss Fed. Inst. Tech., 1953-55; prof. physics U. Santa Clara, 1964—; cons. Argonne Nat. Lab., 1958-64, industry. Served with USNR, 1941-45; PTO. Mem. Am. Phys. Soc., Am. Assn. Physics Tchrs., Phi Beta Kappa, Sigma Xi, Pi Mu Epsilon, Alpha Sigma Nu. Roman Catholic. Contbr. articles profl. jours. Research on quantum mechs., relativity, statis. physics, nuclear orientation, planetary atmospheres, quantum electronics, cosmology, exclusive interaction. Home: 26444 Taaffe Rd Los Altos Hills CA 94022 Office: Univ Santa Clara Santa Clara CA 95053

BARKER, WILLIAM GARDNER, food co. exec.; b. Brookline, Mass., May 27, 1913; s. Charles Miller and Lila Brookhouse (Rice) B.; A.B., Harvard 1935; student Stanford, 1936; M.S., Mass. Inst. Tech., 1937; m. Milda Allen, June 20, 1935; children—Sue Brookhouse, William Gardner, Elizabeth H., Bruce Allen. Successively market research analyst, asst. to advt. mgmt., market exploration mgr. Lever Bros. Co., 1937-48, dir. new products Pepsodent div., 1948-50; exec. v.p., dir. Simonize Co., Chgo., 1950-56; v.p. new products Thomas J. Lipton, Inc., Englewood Cliffs, N.J., 1956- 57, exec. v.p., dir., 1957-58, pres., chief exec. officer, dir., 1959—; chmn. bd. Thomas J. Lipton, Ltd., Can., Lipton Pet Foods, Inc., Good Humor Corp.; dir. Constn. Exchange Fund, Inc. Served to lt. (j.g.) USNR, 1943-46. Mem. Am. Marketing Assn., Consumer Research Inst. (dir.), Tea Assn. U.S.A., (dir. 1958-63, pres. 1960-62), Tea Council U.S.A. (dir. 1961—; chmn. 1963-65, 67-69, 71-73). Episcopalian. Clubs: N.Y. Yacht, Brook, Sales Executives (N.Y.C.); University (Chgo.); Indian Harbor Yacht, Pleon Yacht (Marblehead, Mass.); Eastern Yacht (Boston); Blind Brook (Port Chester, N.Y.). Home: Andrews Rd Greenwich CT 06830 Office: 800 Sylvan Av Englewood Cliffs NJ 07632

BARKES, CURTIS, retired air line exec.; b. Alledonia, O., Oct. 4, 1905; s. Cornelius Ellsworth and Elizabeth Jane (Bright) B.; student pub. schs. Springfield, O., also advanced mgmt. tng. Harvard Bus. Sch., 1945; m. Martha Wadsworth, June 11, 1929; children—Elizabeth Jean (Mrs. James P. Griffith), Mary Carolyn (Mrs. Donald M. Smith). With United Air Line, Inc., and predecessor co., Chgo., 1926-70, v.p. finance and property, 1949-60, exec. v.p. finance and property, 1960-70, dir., 1956—, also dir. subsidiaries; pres., dir. United Air Lines Found., 1950-70; dir. Curtis Pub. Co., Phila., 1956-68. Bd. dirs., v.p. finance Nat. Safety Council, 1959-61. Mem. Newcomen Soc. Clubs: Chicago, Chicago Athletic Assn.; Hinsdale (Ill.) Golf. Home: Rancho Santa Fe CA

BARKEY, PATRICK TERRENCE, librarian; b. Flint, Mich., Feb. 11, 1922; s. James Daniel and Damie Ann (Terwilliger) B.; B.A., Pomona Coll., 1948; A.M. in L.S., U. Mich., 1949; m. Mary Ann Schutte, Nov. 18, 1960; children—Susan, Brian, Leslie, Daniel. Audio-visual librarian Flint Pub. Library, 1949-57; head circulation dept. U. Notre Dame Library, 1957-60, Eastern Ill. U. Library, 1960-64; head librarian Tex. A and I Univ., Kingsville, 1964-67; dir. univ. libraries U. Toledo, 1967—. Served with USNR, 1942-44. Mem. Am., Ohio library assns., Am. Assn. U. Profs. Democrat. Catholic. Elk. Contbr. library jours. Home: 2303 Goddard Rd Toledo OH 43606

BARKHORN, HENRY CHARLES, life ins. co. exec.; b. Newark, Aug. 25, 1915; s. Henry Charles and Mariette (Gless) B.; A.B., Princeton, 1936; m. Helen Butler, Jan. 16, 1943 (dec. 1967); children—Joan Alexandra (Mrs. Hass), Henry Charles, William Butler; m. 2d, Jean Davis Cook, May 14, 1971. With Prudential Ins. Co. Am., 1936-56; with Mut. Life Ins. Co. N.Y., 1956—, 2d v.p. securities investment, 1957-63, v.p. securities investment, treas., 1963—; pres., dir. Mony Advisers, Inc.; dir. Mony Fund; West Side adv. bd. Chem. Bank. Served to lt. (j.g.) USNR, 1944-46, Mem. Phi Beta Kappa. Clubs: Princeton (N.Y.C.); Nassau (Princeton, N.J.). Home: 36 E 72d St New York City NY 10021 Office: 1740 Broadway New York City NY 10019

BARKIN, BEN, pub. relations cons.; b. Milw., June 4, 1915; s. Adolph and Rose Dora (Schumann) B.; student pub. schs.; m. Shirley Hinda Axel, Oct. 19, 1941; 1 son, Coleman. Nat. field dir. Jr. B'nai B'rith, 1937-41; cons. war finance dept. U.S. Treasury Dept., 1941-45; pub. relations cons. Ben Barkin & Asso., 1945-52; partner Barkin, Herman & Asso., Milw., N.Y.C., pub. relations counsel, 1952—. Sec. bd. dirs. Wis. Coll. Medicine; nat. trustee Archives Am. Art; bd. mem. Cenco Instruments Corp., Chgo. Mem. Gov's Econ. and Research Devel. Bd., 1965—; bd. dirs. Mt. Sinai Hosp. Named man of yr., Milw., 1945. Mem. Pub. Relations Soc. Am., Nat. Conf. Christians and Jews. Mem. B'nai B'rith (nat. chmn. youth commn. 1966-68). Home: 1610 N Prospect Av Milwaukee WI 53202 Office: 735 N Water St Milwaukee WI 53202

BARKIN, SOLOMON, economist; b. N.Y.C., Dec. 2, 1907; s. Julius and Lillian (Kroll) B.; B.S., Coll. City N.Y., 1928; M.A., Columbia, 1929, univ. fellow, 1932-33; m. Elaine N. Rappaport, Apr. 21, 1940; children—David Peter, Roger Michael, Amy Claire. Instr., Coll. City N.Y., 1928-31; asst. dir. N.Y. State Commn. on Old Age Security, 1929-33; NRA, 1933-36; chief labor sect., div. indsl. econs., U.S. Dept. Commerce, 1936-37; dir. research Textile Workers Union Am., 1937-63; dep. dir. manpower and social affairs directorate OECD, 1963-68; prof. economics U. Mass., Amherst, 1968—; adj. prof. indsl. relations, Columbia, 1959-63; labor cons. WPB. Mem. Am. standard textile safety code, standing adv. com. U.S. Bur. Labor Statistics; vice chmn. com. on research Pres.'s Conf. on Indsl. Safety chmn. bd. Interunion Inst., Inc.; textile cons. U.K. Mission of ECA. Specialist Internat. Information Service, U.S. Dept. State; mem. Sec. Labor's Com. on Automation; chmn. com. on redesign, Nat. Com. on the Aging; v.p., Joint Council on Econ. Edn.; mem. AFL-CIO Standing Com. on Research; Am. del. Inter-Am. Statis. Congress, to European Productivity Agy. Conf. on Human Relations, Rome, 1956, OEEC Internat. Textile Conf., Milan, 1957; del. ILO, 1961; econ. adviser Internat. Fedn. Textile and Clothing Workers Assns. Fellow div. psychol. and social scis. Gerontological Soc., Inc.; mem. Indsl. Relations Research Assn. (past pres.), Am. Statis. Assn., Am. Econ. Assn., Nat. Planning Assn. (trustee), Phi Beta Kappa Assos., Phi Beta Kappa. Author: Toward Fairer Labor Standards, 1948. Co-author: Air Conditioning in Textile Mills; Work Duty Charts for Textile Operations, 1951; Textile Workers' Job Primer, 1953; Forms for Calculating the Frequency of Periodic Work Duties; Manpower Policies and Problems in the Netherlands, 1967; co-editor The Decline of the Labor Movement, 1961, International Labor, 1968; editor Technical Change and Manpower Planning, 1967. Home: Long Hill Rd Leverett MA 01054 Office: U Mass Amherst MA 01003

BARKSDALE, CLARENCE CAULFIELD, banker; b. St. Louis, June 4, 1932; s. Clarence M. and Elizabeth (Caulfield) B.; A.B., Brown U., 1954; m. Emily Catlin Keyes, Apr. 4, 1959; children—John Keyes, Emily. With 1st Nat. Bank, St. Louis, 1958—, asst. cashier, 1960-62, asst. v.p., 1962-64, v.p., 1964, exec. v.p., 1968-70, pres., 1970—, also dir., dir. 1st Union, Inc., Credit Systems Inc., UMC Industries, Inc., K-V Pharm. Co. Vice chmn. Midland dist. Boy Scouts Am. Trustee Mo. Bot. Gardens; bd. dirs. Family and Children's Service Greater St. Louis, Asso. Industries Am., Arts and Edn. Council Greater St. Louis. Served with M.I., AUS, 1954-57. Mem. Am. Bankers Assn., Assn. Res. City Bankers, St. Louis Country Day Sch. Alumni Assn. (pres.), Alpha Delta Phi. Clubs: St. Louis Country, Noonday, Brown University (pres. 1963—), Bogey (St. Louis); University (N.Y.C., St. Louis); Links (N.Y.C.). Office: First Nat Bank St Louis MO 63166

BARKSDALE, ETHELBERT COURTLAND, ret. educator; b. Athens, La., Oct. 24, 1905; s. Ethelbert Courtland and Eliza (Wellborn) B.; B.A., U. Tex., 1928, M.A., 1931, Ph.D., 1941; m. Marjorie Miller, June 12, 1937; children—Ethelbert Courtland, Stephen Webb. Tchrs., Tex. Pub. Schs., 1926-39; tchr. U. Tex., Austin, 1940-41, prof. history, Arlington, 1942—, head dept. history, govt., sociology, philosophy, 1954-71. Mem. adv. com. Civil War, 1961-65. Kennedy U.S. Senate com. selection outstanding U.S. Senators, 1958. Pres. San Antonio Young Democrats, 1934, Baytown (Tex.) Young Democrats, 1937. Mem. Orgn. Am. Historians, Acad. Am. Polit. Social Sci., Am., So., Western, Tex. hist. assns., Southwestern Social Sci. Assn. (gen. program chmn. 1964-65, mem. exec. bd. 1965-67). Methodist. Author: Financing a System of State Highways, 1935; The Art and Science of Speech, 1937; Genesis of Texas Aviation, 1957; The Meatpackers Come to Texas, 1959; The Power Structure and Southern Gukernatorial Conservatism, 1969. Editor: History as High Adventure, 1969. Mem. editorial bd. Texana, 1967; mem. adv. editorial bd., contbr. articles Ency. Brit. Home: 1333 S Pecan St Arlington TX 76010

BARKSDALE, HIRAM COLLIER, educator; b. Sandersville, Ga., Dec. 4, 1921; s. William Henry and Maude (Smith) B.; B.B.A., U. Ga., 1948; M.S., N.Y.U., 1949, Ph.D., 1955; m. Jeanne Epp, July 22, 1950; children—Hiram Collier, Beverly Jeanne, Sally Braswell, and Addison Andrew. Instr., Washburn Municipal U., 1949-51; projects mgr. Advt. Research Found., 1952-56, asst. to pres., 1956-60; mem. faculty N.Y.U., 1956-65, asso. prof. Sch. Commerce and Grad. Sch. Bus., 1956-60, prof., chmn. dept. marketing Sch. Commerce, 1960-65; prof. Coll. Bus. Adminstrn., U. Ga., Athens, 1965—, chmn. marketing dept., 1968—. Served with AUS, 1943-46. Grantee Ford Found., Harvard Bus. Sch., summer 1957, Carnegie Inst. Tech., summer 1962. Mem. Am. Marketing Assn., Inst. Mgmt. Scis., A.A.A.S., Soc. for History of Tech., Phi Beta Kappa, Beta Gamma Sigma. Author: The Use of Survey Research Findings as Legal Evidence, 1957; Problems in Marketing Research: In-Basket Simulation, 1963; co-author: Marketing Research, 1966. Editor: Marketing in ProgressPatterns and Potentials, 1964; MarketingChange and Exchange, 1964. Book rev. editor: Media/scope mag., 1964-69. Mem. editorial bd. Jour. of Marketing, 1965—. So. Jour. of Bus., 1968—. Home: 340 Cedar Creek Dr Athens GA 30601

BARKSDALE, JAMES ALTON, educator; b. McKenzie, Tenn., Nov. 29, 1904; s. James Monroe and Judith Ada (Esch) B.; A.B., Bethel Coll., McKenzie, Tenn., 1925, D.Litt., 1959; A.M., U. Colo., 1936; student Peabody Coll., 1927; Ed.D., U. Tenn., 1954; m. Eleanor Herrin, May 18, 1928. Tchr., prin., Charlotte (Tenn.) High Sch., 1925-35; prin. Central High Schs., Ashland City, Tenn., 1935-41,

E.W. Grove High Sch., Paris, Tenn., 1941-43, Tenn. High Sch., Bristol, 1943-46; supt. pub. schs., Union City, 1946-49; dir. Tenn. Dept. Personnel, 1949-50; Tenn. commr. edn., 1950-53; pres. Cumberland Presbyn. Bd. Edn., 1951-57; acting assoc. prof. edn. U. Tenn. Coll. Edn., Knoxville, 1953-55; dean Tenn. Poly. Inst., 1955-60; adviser higher edn. U.S. Overseas Mission ICA, Ankara, Turkey, 1961-62; chief edn. adviser AID, Am. embassy, Amman, Jordan, 1963-65; prof. history Bethel Coll., McKenzie, Tenn., 1965—, interim pres., 1969. Vis. prof. Memphis State U., summer 1967; cons. Henry County Bd. Edn. 1967-68. Del., Tenn. Ltd. Constl. Conv., 1971. Mem. Am. Assn. Sch. Adminstrs., Tenn. Edn. Assn. (pres. 1959), Tenn. Coll. Assn. (pres. 1959). Mason, Rotarian. Home: Highland Dr McKenzie TN 38201

BARKSDALE, RICHARD KENNETH, educator; b. Winchester, Mass., Oct. 31, 1915; s. Simon Daniel and Sarah Irene (Brooks) B.; A.B., Bowdoin Coll., 1937; A.M., Syracuse U., 1938; A.M., Harvard, 1947, Ph.D., 1951; m. Mildred Alois White, Apr. 15, 1960; children—Adrienne Maxine, James Austin, Richard Kenneth, Calvin Philip. Instr. English, So. U., 1938-39; chmn. dept. English, Tougaloo Coll., 1939-42; prof. English, dean Grad. Sch. of N.C. Coll., Durham, 1949-58; chmn. dept. English Morehouse Coll., 1958-62; prof. English, dean Grad. Sch. of Atlanta U., 1962-71; prof. English, U. Ill., Urbana, 1971—. Cons. United Negro Coll. Fund, Nat. Endowment for Humanities; dir. So. Consortium on Internat. Edn. Served to 2d lt. F.A., AUS, 1943-46. Named outstanding educator of Am., 1971. Mem. Modern Lang. Assn., Assn. Negro Life and History, Phi Beta Kappa. Editor: (with Keneth Kinnamon) Black Writers of America: a Comprehensive Anthology, 1971. Home: 3786 Wisteria Lane SW Atlanta GA 30331

BARKSDALE, WALTER LANE, educator, biologist; b. Emporia, Va., Nov. 23, 1914; s. Wallace and Helen (Weaver) B.; A.B., U. N.C., 1938, M.A., 1940; Ph.D. William H. Park fellow 1949-53), N.Y.U., 1953; m. Alma Joslyn Whiffen, June 29, 1952. NSF postdoctoral fellow with André Lwoff, Pasteur Inst., 1953-54; mem. faculty N.Y.U. Med. Sch., 1954—, prof. microbiology, 1966—; vis. prof. Osaka and Kyoto U., 1960-61. Mem. bacteriology and mycology study sect. USPHS adv. groups, 1961-65. Served to capt., San. Corps, AUS, 1941-46. Mem. Am. Acad. Microbiology, Soc. Internat. de la Lepre, Harvey Soc., N.Y. Acad. Medicine. Author papers in field. Mem. editorial bd. Jour. Bacteriology, 1964—. Home: 37 W 12th St New York City NY 10011

BARLASS, JACK S., publishing co. exec.; b. Des Moines, May 14, 1915; s. Herbert L. and Grace (Sloan) B.; student Drake U., 1933-34, U. Ia., 1934-37; m. Florelle L. Copeland, June 4, 1938; children—Robert C., Barbara Ann. Account exec. Direct Advt., Inc., Des Moines, 1937; mgr. book sales Meredith Pub. Co., Des Moines, 1937-41, book and newsstand sales mgr., 1941-45, gen. promotion mgr., 1945-51, asst. dir. circulation, 1948-51, dir. book and promotion div., 1951-59, corporate v.p., 1959—. Mem. Assn. Am. Pubs. (dir.), Newcomen Soc., Sigma Nu. Presbyn. Clubs: Des Moines; Embassy; Cornell 60 East, N.Y. Athletic (N.Y.C.); Westhampton Country. Home: 530 Park Av New York City NY 10021

BARLOON, MARVIN JOHN, educator, economist; b. Carroll, Ia., Dec. 11, 1906; s. William and Mary Ellen (Ryan) B.; B.S. in Commerce, State U. Ia., 1931; M.B.A., Harvard, 1935; m. Blanche Eynon Davies, Sept. 3, 1938; childrenJonathan Peter, Anne Stuart. With sales dept. Firestone Tire and Rubber Co., 1931-33; instr. Case Western Res. U., Cleve., 1935-38, prof., 1938-40, prof. econs., 1946—; asst. prof. Tulane U. of La., 1940-41; asst. prof. Harvard, 1941-46. Mem. Am. Assn. U. Profs., Am. Econ. Assn., Am. Statis. Assn., A.I.M., Delta Sigma Pi, Beta Gamma Sigma. Contbr. articles to Jour. Accountancy, Harvard Bus. Rev., Harpers Mag., Iron Age, Business History Rev. Home: 3064 Edgehill Rd Cleveland Heights OH 44118 Office: Case Western Reserve University Cleveland OH 44106

BARLOW, CHARLES FRANKLIN, educator, physician; b. Mason City, Ia., Nov. 10, 1923; s. Frank Richard and Marie Gertrude (McCabe) B.; student Coe Coll., 1941-43; S.B., U. Chgo., 1945, M.D., 1947; A.M. (hon.), Harvard, 1963; m. Patricia Keith, June 30, 1953; childrenEllen, John Keith, Margaret Katherine. Intern Johns Hopkins Hosp., 1947-48; jr. asst. resident Boston Children's Hosp., 1948-49; resident neurology, then instr. neurology U. Chgo. Sch. Medicine, 1951-55; asst. prof., then asso. prof. U. Chgo., 1960-63; Bronson Crothers prof. neurology Harvard Med. Sch., 1963-; neurologist-in-chief Children's Hosp. Med. Center, Boston, 1963—; cons. Peter Bent Brigham Hosp., Boston, 1963—, Beth Israel Hosp., Boston, 1966—. Served Recipient McClintock Teaching award U. Chgo., 1963. Mem. Am. Neurol. Assn., Am. Assn. Neuropathologists, Am. Acad. Neurology. Home: 482 Jerusalem Rd Cohasset, MA 02025. Office: 300 Longwood Av Boston MA 02115

BARLOW, JOEL, lawyer; b. Deckerville, Mich., May 15, 1908; s. Luther Stanley and Jae (McKown) B.; A.B., Alma (Mich.) Coll., 1929; LL.B., George Washington U., 1935; LL.D., Norwich U.; m. Eleanor Livingston Poe, Feb. 19, 1936; children—Eleanor Poe, Jae (Roosevelt), Grace M. (Schneider). Admitted to Washington bar, 1934; partner Covington & Burling, 1934—; prof. law Columbus U., 1937; lectr. George Washington Law Sch. Trustee Madeira Sch., Greenway, Va.; bd. dirs. Historic Figures Va. Mem. Tax Inst. (pres. 1959, dir.), Am., D.C., N.Y. bar assns., Am. Bar Found., Am. Law Inst., U.S. C. of C. (treas., dir.) Order of Coif, Sigma Alpha Epsilon, Phi Delta Phi. Episcopalian. Clubs: Metropolitan; International; Chevy Chase; Burning Tree; Country of Fla. Author articles on fed. taxation. Home: 2500 Virginia Av NW Washington, DC 20037. Office: 888 16th St NW Washington DC 20006

BARLOW, MARK, Jr., univ. ofcl.; b. Utica, N.Y., June 15, 1925; s. Mark and Henrietta S. (Siegenthaler) B.; A.B., Wesleyan U., Middletown, Conn., 1947; M.A., Colgate U., 1952; Ed.D., Cornell U., 1961; m. Jane N. Atwood, Nov. 27, 1954; children—Mark Andrew, Sarah Endicott, Elizabeth Atwood. Tchr. N.Y. State pub. schs., 1947-49; asst. to dean, asst. dir. preceptorial studies, also instr. math. Colgate U., 1949-51; asst. dean. men Cornell U., Ithaca, N.Y., 1951-57, v.p. student affairs, 1965—; dean students Wesleyan U., 1957-63, dean coll., 1963-65. Pres. Middletown Council Community Services, 1961-63; vice chmn. com. ind. schs. Episcopal Diocese Conn., 1962—, chmn. com. on coll. work. Trustee Wesleyan U. Served with USNR, 1943-46. Mem. Nat. Assn. Student Personnel Adminstrs., New Eng. Assn. Colls. and Secondary Schs., New Eng. Assn. Deans. Home: 106 Midway Rd Ithaca NY 14850

BARLOW, MELVIN LEWIS, educator; b. Edmond, Okla., Mar. 13, 1910; s. Ralph Rewel and Hazel (Garey) B.; A.B., U. So. Cal., 1933, M.S., 1934; Ed.D., U. Cal. at Los Angeles, 1949; m. Alice Marion Demaree, Oct. 12, 1935; 1 son, Ralph Robert. Research physicist oil companies in Cal., 1933-39; instr. sci. and math. San Juan Capistrano (Cal.) High Sch., 1939-40; instr. petroleum tech. Taft (Cal.) Jr. Coll., 1940-42; supr. ind. tchr. edn. Cal. Dept. Edn., 1942-57; dir. div. vocational edn. U. Cal. at Los Angeles, 1953-, prof. edn., 1957-; indsl. cons. in edn., 1946-. Mem. Pacific region manpower adv. com. Dept. Labor, 1964-67; chief cons. AID project, Turkey, 1965-68; mem. Cal. Gov.'s Adv. Council on Vocational outstanding service Cal. Indsl. Edn. Assn., 1966; Outstanding Educator Assn. (historian, editor tech. edn. for jour.). Methodist. Author: History of Industrial Education in the United States, 1967. Editor Nat. Soc. Study Edn. Yearbook, 1965. Home: 3264 Mountain View Av Los Angeles, CA 90066.

BARLOW, MILTON ALLAN, bldg. devel. exec.; b. Clearfield, Utah, Dec. 3, 1911; s. Ianthus H. and Alice (Willey) B.; A.B., George Washington U., 1938; M.B.A., Harvard, 1940; m. Gloria Gregerson, Oct. 9, 1942; children—Milton Allan, Gregory, Alice, Kathleen, Nancy, Jeannette, Gloria. With Reconstrn. Finance Corp., 1933-38, Cleve. Trust Co., 1940-41; sec.-treas. Marriott-Hot Shoppes, Inc., Washington, 1941-48, v.p., treas., 1948-56, exec. v.p., 1956-64, dir., 1945-67; pres. Barlow Corp., Inc., Chevy Chase, Md., 1964—. Mem. Washington Bd. Trade. Trustee, mem. exec. com. Washington Hosp. Center, pres., 1965-67; trustee Boys Club; bd. dirs. Washington chpt. A.R.C., 1964-68; mem. Nat. Capital council Boy Scouts Am., 1962—, exec. com., 1965—. Mem. Ch. of Jesus Christ of Latter-day Saints (dist. pres. 1933-35, counselor Del.-Md. mission 1970—, bishop ward 1962-66). Rotarian. Clubs: Harvard Business (Washington); Columbia Country. Home: 6416 Elmwood Rd Chevy Chase MD 20015 Office: 5454 Wisconsin Av Chevy Chase MD 20015

BARLOW, ROBERT FRANCIS, univ. ofcl., economist; b. Cambridge, Mass., May 6, 1927; s. Thomas F. and Ellen Agnes (O'Mahoney) B.; B.A., Colby Coll., 1950; student London (Eng.) Sch. Econs. and Polit. Sci., 1951-52; M.A., Fletcher Sch. Law and Diplomacy, 1951, Ph.D., 1960; m. Priscilla M. Potier, Sept. 19, 1953; children—Ian C., Paul M., Elizabeth A., Mark P. Mem. faculty Colby Coll., 1952-55, 56-62, asso. prof., asst. to pres., 1961-62; instr. U. Del., 1955-56; prof. econs., dean Whittemore Sch. Bus. and Econs., U. N.H., 1962-66, acad. v.p., 1966-70, prof. econs. and adminstrn., 1970—. Chmn. Gov. N.H. Indsl. Adv. Council, 1963-69, N.H. Fgn. Trade Council, 1963-69, Council on Econ. Edn. in N.H., 1969—; mem. voluntary labor dispute tribunal Am. Arbitration Assn.; mem. natural resources, econ. adv. coms. New Eng. Council. Bd. dirs. N.H. Heart Assn., 1968-69; trustee Theatre-by-the Sea, Portsmouth, N.H. Fulbright grantee, 1951-52. Mem. Am. Econ. Assn., Am. Assn. U. Profs., Phi Beta Kappa, Phi Kappa Phi. Home: Colony Cove Rd Durham NH 03824

BARLOW, SAMUEL LATHAM MITCHILL, composer; b. N.Y.C., June 1, 1892; s. Peter Townsend and Louise (Matthews) B.; student Groton Sch., 1904-10, Harvard, 1910-14; studied piano with Philipp, Paris, orchestration with Respighi, Rome; m. Ernesta Drinker, Mar. 10, 1928; 1 dau., Audrey Townsend (Mrs. W.R. Orndorff). Composer, lectr., writer. Composer: Mon Ami Peirrot (1st performance, Opera Comique Paris), 1934; Ballo Sardo (ballet), symphonic works played by Stokowsky, Goossens, Reiner, Paray, others; lectr. U. P.R., 1944. Pres., Citizens Com. for Govt. Art Projects; sec. and trustee Asia. Inst.; gov. Am. Composers Alliance; moderator of Forum for Democracy. Fellow Carnegie Found., 1943; mission to S.A. Trustee F.H. Beebe Fund, Boston; dir. Composers Forum, Hour of Music Concerts, Castle Hill Found.; pres. Am. Opera Soc. Served as 1st lt. A.E.F., 1917. Decorated Legion of Honor; Bundesverdienst-Kreuze 1st class (Bonn Govt.). Fellow Internat. Acad. Arts and Letters. Democrat. Club: Union (N.Y.C.). Author: The Astonished Muse, 1961. Contbr. various publs. Address: 11 Gramercy Park New York City NY 10003

BARLOW, THOMAS JAMES, indsl. corp. exec.; b. Houston, June 22, 1922; s. Thomas Jefferson and Dorothy (James) B.; B.S., Tex. A. and M. Coll., 1943; postgrad. Harvard, 1962; m. Billye Louise Sears, May 31, 1944; children—Lance, Lynne. Trainee, Western Cottonoil Co., Abilene, Tex., 1946-47, asst. gen. mgr., 1958-59; constrn. engr. San Joaquin Cottonoil Co., Bakersfield, Cal., 1948; supt. Western Cotton Products Co., Phoenix, 1949-50; prodn. mgr. Nile Ginning Co., Minia, Egypt, 1951-55; process engr. Anderson, Clayton & Co., Houston, 1956-57, v.p., 1960-66, pres., chief exec. officer, 1966—, also dir.; dir. Ranger Ins. Co., Pan Am. Ins. Cos., Anderson, Clayton & Hunt (Pty.) Ltd., 1st Nat. Bank Abilene (Tex.), Central & S.W. Corp. Mem. Chgo. Bd. Trade, Memphis Bd. Trade, Internat. Comml. Exchange. Trustee United Fund Houston and Harris County. Served from ensign to lt. USNR, World War II; PTO. Mem. Houston C. of C. (dir. at large 1940—), Tex. A. and M. U. Assn. Former Students (council), Newcomen Soc., Tex. Research League. Clubs: River Oaks Country, University (Houston). Home: 35 Willowend St Houston TX 77024 Office: Box 2538 Houston TX 77001

BARLOW, WALTER GREENWOOD, pub. opinion analyst; b. Liverpool, Eng., Sept. 10, 1917; s. Walter and Sarah Ellen Greenwood; brought to U.S., 1920, naturalized, 1928; B.A., Cornell U., 1939; m. Hanna Hansen, June 30, 1951; children—Eric, Francine, Deborah, Alison. Reporter, Washington Daily News, 1940; mem. editorial staff Time mag., 1941; with Opinion Research Corp., 1946-65, pres., 1960-65; pres. Howard Chase Assos., Inc., N.Y.C., 1965-68, Research Strategies Corp., N.Y.C., 1966—; sr. partner, dir. Partners for Growth, Inc., 1968—; dir. Popular Printing, Inc., N.Y.C. Mem. N.J. Bd. Pub. Welfare, 1966—. Trustee Cornell U., 1968—; mem. bd. Presbyn. Life Mag., 1968—, pres., 1970; mem. bd. Family Service Assn. Am., 1958-69, v.p., 1964-67, pres., 1967-69; mem. bd. Center for Ind. Action, Inc., 1964—. Served with AUS, 1941-46. Mem. Pub. Relations Soc. Am., Am. Statis. Assn., Am. Marketing Assn., Am. Mgmt. Assn., Phi Beta Kappa, Phi Kappa Phi. Sigma Delta Chi. Presbyn. (trustee 1967—). Club: Cornell of N.Y. Home: Poor Farm Rd RD 1 Pennington NJ 08534 Office: FAIM Information Services 6 E 43d St New York City NY 10017

BARLOW, WAYNE BREWSTER, composer, organist; b. Elyria, O., Sept. 6, 1912; s. Edmund Brewster and Josephine (Muenscher) B.; B.M., Eastman Sch. Music, 1934, M.M., 1935, Ph.D. in Composition 1937; m. Helen Hutzen, Aug. 7, 1937; children—Robert Wayne, Joan Helen. Prof. music composition theory and acoustics, asso. dean grad. research studies, head dept. composition, dir. electronic music studio Eastman Sch. Music. Organist, choir dir. St. Thomas Episcopal Ch. Fulbright sr. lectr. Royal U., Conservatory Copenhagen, U. Aarhus, Denmark, 1955-56. Awarded Lillian Fairchild Meml. award for outstanding achievement in arts, 1936; Fulbright research grant for work in electronic music, 1964-65. Mem. A.S.C.A.P., Phi Mu Alpha Sinfonia. Episcopalian. Rotarian. Composer: Lyrical Piece for clarinet and strings, 1945; Nocturne for chamber orchestral (commd. for radio, 1946; Sinfonietta in C, 1948; Mass in G, 1951; Sinfonia de Camera, 1959; Images for harp and orchestra, 1961; Concerto for saxophone and band, 1970; also church, chamber, electronic music. Author: Foundations of Music, 1953. Contbr. to Music Jour. Lectr. Home: 95 Elmcroft Rd Rochester NY 14609 Office: Eastman School of Music Rochester NY 14604

BARLOWE, RALEIGH, economist; b. Lincoln, Ida., Nov. 10, 1914; s. George Edward and Charlotte (Campbell) B.; B.S., Utah State Agrl. Coll., 1936; M.A., Am. U., 1939; student U.S. Dept. Agr. Grad. Sch., 1938-40; Ph.D., U. Wis., 1946; m. Jeannette Topp, Oct. 4, 1941; 1 son, Raleigh R.B. Instr., Am. U., 1937-38; asst. Library of Congress, 1937-40; grad. asst. U. Wis., 1940-42; land economist Southwestern Land Tenure Research Project, Fayetteville, Ark., 1942-43; agrl. economist U.S. Dept. Agr., Milw., 1943-47; economist FAO, Washington, 1947; from lectr. to prof. agrl. econs. Mich. State U., 1948-59, prof., 1959—, chmn. dept. resource devel., 1959-71; economist Robert R. Nathan Assn., Bogota, Colombia, 1959; cons. U. P.R., 1958, Govt. Colombia, 1959, Pub. Land Law Rev. Commn., 1969, Korea, 1971—. Mem. Gov.'s Water Com., 1955-56; staff Mich. Tax Study, 1957-58; chmn. tech. com. Lansing Water Adv. Com., 1961-63; staff Mich. Constl. Convention Prep. Commn., 1961; treas. Mich. Natural Resources Council, 1961-63, chmn., 1963-65; mem. Gov.'s Task Force on Water Rights, Use and Pollution Control, 1964-66. Mem. Soil Conservation Soc. Am., Am. Agrl. Econs. Assn., Am. Econ. Assn., Econ. History Assn., Agrl. History Soc., Regional Sci. Assn. Author: Land Resource Economics, 1958, rev. 1972; (with V. Webster Johnson) Land Problems and Policies, 1954; also numerous article, bulls. Home: 907 Southlawn East Lansing MI 48823

BARMACK, JOSEPH EPHRAIM, educator; b. N.Y.C., Sept. 20, 1910; s. Louis and Pauline (Sigman) B.; B.S., City Coll. N.Y., 1930; Ph.D., Columbia, 1937; research student N.Y. Psychoanalytic Inst., 1950-55; m. Therese Mayer, 1935 (dec. 1965); m. 2d, Edna Beilenson, June 19, 1966; children—Anthony Beilenson, Roger Beilenson, Elizabeth Schildkraut, John A. Barmack, Neal H. Barmack. Mem. faculty City Coll. N.Y., 1938—, prof. psychology, 1955—, chmn. dept., 1962-70; asst. project dir. Psychol. Corp, 1948-49; project dir. to asst. v.p. Dunlap & Assos., 1949-60; research asso. Inst. Def. Analyses, 1962-63; cons., 1963—. Served to lt. col. USAAF, 1942-46. Diplomate indsl. psychology Am. Bd. Examiners Profl. Psychology. Mem. Am., Eastern, N.Y. State psychol. assns., Am. Assn. Pub. Opinion Researchers, Am. Gerontological Assn. Research on physiol. effects of antihypnotic drugs on boredom, accident causation and prevention, methods of classifying behavioral sci. research, social sci. research, research planning to Dept. Def. Home: 720 Claflin Av Mamaroneck NY 10543 Office: City Coll NY 138th St and Amsterdam Av New York City NY 10031

BARNARD, CHARLES NELSON, editor; b. Arlington, Mass., Oct. 5, 1921; s. Charles Nelson and Mae E. (Johnson) B.; B.J., U. Mo., 1949; m. Diana Lee Pattison, Aug. 6, 1949 (div. Aug. 1970); children—Jennifer Lee, Rebecca, Charles Nelson IV, Patrick; m. 2d, Karen Louis Zakrison, Apr. 18, 1971. Editor Dell Pub. Co., N.Y.C., 1949; asso. editor True mag., Fawcett Publs., N.Y.C., 1949-54, mng. editor, 1954-63; sr. editor Sat. Eve. Post, N.Y.C., 1964-65; exec. editor True Mag., 1965-67, editor, 1968-70; editorial cons., freelance writer, 1971—. Served from pvt. to sgt. AUS, 1944-46, war corr. Mem. Alpha Tau Omega, Sigma Delta Chi, Kappa Tau Alpha. Editor: A Treasury of True, 1957; Official Automobile Handbook, 1959; Anthology of True, 1962. Contbr. motor racing to Ency. Brit. Home: 311 E 75th St New York City NY 10021

BARNARD, CHRISTIAAN NEETHLING, surgeon; b. Beaufort West, Cape Province, S. Africa, Nov. 8, 1922; M.B., Ch.B., U. Capetown, 1946, M.D., 1953; M.Surgery, U. Minn., 1958, Ph.D., 1958; D.Sc. (hon. causa), U. Capetown, 1967, Hope Coll., 1968, Fla. So. Coll., Collegii Spei, Holland, Mich.; M.D. (hon.) Pahlavi U., Shiraz, Iran. Formerly engaged as gen. practitioner, Ceres, S. Africa; fellowship to Russia to Study transplants of heads of dogs, 1960; now mem. staff Groote Schuur Hosp., Capetown, also asso. prof. U. Capetown Med. Sch.; transplanted heart of accident victim into diseased heart patient, Dec. 1967. Decorated Order of Sun (Peru); Order Hipolito U nanue (Peru); Order of Merit (Ecuador); recipient Dag Hammerskjoeld Internat. prize, Dag Hammarskjoeld Peace prize; gold medal Med. Assn. S. Africa; Henrietta Sxold award Hadassah, Women's Zionist Orgn., 1969, many others. Fellow A.C.S., Am. Coll. Cardiology, N.Y. Cardiol Soc. (hon.); mem. Venezuelan Soc. Cardiology (hon.), Montreal Clin. Soc. (hon.). Address: care Dept Cardio-Thoracic Surgery Med Sch Observatory Cape Town South Africa

BARNARD, GEORGE BOSLER, advt. exec.; b. Phila., Jan. 30, 1916; s. Everett P. and Eliza (Bosler) B.; grad. Phillip Exeter Acad., 1934; A.B., Williams Coll., 1938; m. Frances Fleming, Jan. 17, 1942; children—George Bosler, Henry Whittlesey, Samuel Fleming. With Aitkin-Kynett Co., Phila., 1938-, v.p., sec., 1958-61, sr. v.p., sec. 1961-66, exec. v.p., 1966-67, pres., 1968—. Trustee Gladwyne Free Library; bd. dirs. Pa. Economy League, St. Christopher's Hosp. Children, Phila., Americans Competitive Enterprise System, Southeastern Pa. chpt. A.R.C.; mem. Phila. Com. 70. Served to maj., cav., AUS, 1941-46: ETO. Mem. Am. Assn. Advt. Agys. (bd. govs. Atlantic council). Presbyn. (trustee). Clubs: Racquet, Fourth Street (Phila.); Gulph Mills (Pa.) Golf; Pine Valley (N.J.) Golf; Merion (Pa.) Cricket; Edgartown (Mass.) Yacht; Williams (N.Y.C.). Home: 636 Black Rock Rd Bryn Mawr, PA 19010. Office: 4 Penn Center Philadelphia PA 19103

BARNARD, HARRY, biographer, journalist; b. Pueblo, Colo., Sept. 5, 1906; s. David and Paula (Halpern) Kletzky; student U. Denver, 1923-25; Ph.B. cum laude, U. Chgo., 1928; student John Marshall Law Sch., Chgo., 1937-38; m. Miriam Helstein, June 20, 1929; 1 dau., Karen; m. 2d, Ruth Eisenstat, Oct. 23, 1943; children—Judith (Mrs. Jerre Papier), Ronald L., Harry David. Mem. editorial staff Chgo. Herald-Examiner, 1928-34; research staff Ill. Tax Commn., 1934-35; dir. research Chgo. Law Dept., 1935-42; dir. press relations U. Chgo., 1943; chief editorial writer Chgo. Times, 1944; mem. staff Chgo. Sun, 1945-47; engaged in pub. relations and advt., 1948-58; biog. writer, lectr., tchr., writer other works, 1958—; writer editorial page column, Liberal at Large, Chgo. Daily News and Des Moines Register Syndicate, 1958-60; mem. faculty Am. politics Columbia Coll., Chgo., 1964-66; dept. pub. relations Northwestern U., 1966-68; writer-in-residence, instr. biography and journalism Roosevelt U., Chgo., 1968-69. Chmn. Altgeld Centennial Com., 1947; v.p. Nat. Com. to Abolish House Un-Am. Activities Com., 1962-64. Publicist, Henry Horner for Gov. Ill., 1932, E.J. Kelly for Mayor Chgo., 1935, 39; chmn. W. O. Douglas for Democratic presdl. nomination, 1952. Mem. bd. Chgo. Civil Liberties Com., 1940-42, Onward Neighborhood House Settlement, Chgo., 1962-69. Recipient Cooper Ohioana Library award, 1955; two selections in White House Library Am. Lit., 1962; Pontifical medal Pope John XXIII, 1963. Mem. Soc. Midwest Authors, Chgo. Press Vets, Phi Sigma Delta. Democrat. Jewish religion. Author: Eagle Forgotten, the Life of John Peter Altgeld, 1938; Rutherford B. Hayes and His America, 1954; Independent Man, the Life of Senator James Couzens, 1958. Editor: (Pope John) Mater et Magistra, 1962; (with Preston Bradley) Along the Way, 1962. Contbr. encys., mags.; author privately distributed studies. Address: 801 Lavergne Av Wilmette IL 60091

BARNARD, HARRY ELIOT, lawyer; b. Denver, July 11, 1893; s. Henry F. and Eugenia (Buffum) B.; A.B., Oberlin Coll., 1915; LL.B., U. Mich., 1920; m. Helen L. Coleman, December 6, 1922 (died 1945); children— Robert C., Margaret A. (Mrs. Robert Edgar Maxwell), Mary L. (Mrs. George Yannopoulos); m. 2d, Mrs. Erma S. Boulton, April 10, 1948. Admitted to Michigan bar, 1920, and since practiced in that state; former prosecuting atty., Jackson County; formerly member Mich. State Legislature. Trustee Oberlin College. Served with U.S. Army, World War I. Mem. Am., Mich. State, Detroit bar assns., Baronial Order Magna Charta. Presbyn. Clubs: Circumnavigators, Detroit, Grosse Pointe Yacht. Home: 181 Merriweather Rd Grosse Pointe Farms MI 48236 Office: Penobscot Bldg Detroit MI 48226

BARNARD, HERBERT ELEROY, lawyer; b. St. Louis, May 28, 1902; s. William L. and Katherine Anna (Knight) B.; student Mo. Sch. Mines; LL.B., Washington U., St. Louis, 1925; m. Jane McCoy, Oct. 20, 1928; childrenJohn, Lawrence. Admitted to Mo. bar, 1925-, since practiced in St. Louis; mem. Barnard, Timm & McDaniel and predecessor firms. Mem. Bar Assn. St. Louis (pres. 1959- 60), Am., Mo. bar assns., Internat. Assn. Ins. Counsel, Delta Theta Phi, Kappa Alpha. Home: 520 East Dr University City MO 63130 Office: 611 Olive St St Louis MO 63101

BARNARD, JOHN, Jr., lawyer; b. Cleve., Aug. 13, 1917; s. John and Mildred (Safford) B.; A.B., Harvard, 1939, LL.B., 1947; m. Cornelia Bridge, Sept. 4, 1943; children—Felicity, Jeremy. Admitted to Mass. bar, 1947, since practiced in Boston, partner Gaston, Snow, Motley & Holt, 1951-63; mng. trustee Mass. Investors Trust; v.p., dir. Mass. Investors Growth Stock Fund, Inc., 1969—; sr. v.p., dir. Mass. Financial Services, Inc.; dir. Mass. Income Devel. Fund, Mass. Capital Devel. Fund, Inc., Suffolk Franklin Savs. Bank, Digital Equipment Corp., Maynard, Mass. Trustee New Eng. Deaconess Hosp., Boston; bd. dirs. Rogerson House, Boston. Mem. Investment Co. Inst. (chmn. bd. 1970—). Clubs: Somerset (Boston); Metropolitan (Washington); Harvard (N.Y.C.). Co-author: Federal Regulation of Investment Companies, 1940-50. Home: 5 Clapp Rd Scituate MA 02066 Office: 200 Berkley St Boston MA 02116

BARNARD, JOHN DARRELL, educator; b. Johnstown, Colo., Apr. 20, 1906; s. Jahu Kimbo and Mary Ann (Mooney) B.; A.B., Colo. State Coll., 1932, M.A., 1935; Ph.D., N.Y. U., 1941; m. Genevieve Bess Noble, May 7, 1926; 1 dau., Patsy Jean (Mrs. George R. Christie, Jr.). Sch. tchr., rural schs., Windsor, Colo., 1933- 36; supt. schs., Galeton, Colo., 1932-34, Ault, Colo., 1934-37; prof. biology Colo. State Coll. Edn., 1937-41; ednl. cons. Kellogg Found., 1946-47; prof. edn. N.Y. U., 1947—, also chmn. dept. sci. edn., until 1971. Asso. dir. COPES. Served as capt. USAAF, 1942-46; officer in charge planning programs for re-edn. Japanese tchrs., 1945-46. Mem. Nat. Sci. Tchrs. Assn. (pres. 1961-62, citation Distinguished Service to Sci. Edn. 1970), Nat. Assn. Research in Sci. Teaching (pres. 1953—, Am. Assn. U. Profs., A.A.A.S., Phi Delta Kappa, Kappa Delta Pi. Mem. Community Ch. Author book series on science. Home: 16 Links Dr Great Neck NY 11020 Office: Washington Sq New York City NY 10003

BARNARD, JOHN LAWRENCE banker; b. N.Y.C., Jan. 28, 1912; s. John Augustus and Margaret Ruth Lawrence (Walsh) B.; grad. St. Paul's Sch., 1930; A.B., Yale, 1934; m. Diana Kissel, June 3, 1938; childrenDaphne, Sylvia, Pamela. Officer, State Dept., 1945-54; Am. consul, Antwerp, Belgium, 1955-59; Am. consul, Aruba, Dutch West Indies, 1960; Am. consul gen., Nassau, Bahamas, 1960-66; mgr. Nassau br. Pitts. Nat. Bank, 1968—. Served to maj. AUS, 1942-45. Mem. Soc. Colonial Lords Manors, Soc. Colonial Wars. Clubs: Union (N.Y.C.); Metropolitan (Washington). Author: Revelry by Night, 1940; Land of Promise, 1941. Home: Red Brook Stonington CT 06378

BARNARD, NILES HUTTON, ret. educator, mech. engr.; b. Chgo., Sept. 2, 1903; s. J.T. Allen and Bernice Edna (Hutton) B.; B.S., in Ry. M.E., U. Ill., 1928, M.S., 1930, M.E., 1934; m. Rhoda Eleanor Hall, June 23, 1928; children—Roger H., Allen R., Kenneth N., Ann J. (Mrs. David M. Rau). With Ill. Steel Co., South Works, Chgo., 1920-21, I.C. R.R., Chgo., 1921-24, summers 1925- 28; asso. prof. Tenn. Poly. Inst., 1930-35; instr. dept. mech. engring. U. Neb., Lincoln, 1935-36, asst. prof., 1936-40, asso. prof., 1940-48, acting chmn., 1947-48, prof., 1948-70, emeritus, 1970—, chmn. dept., 1948-66; vis. prof. indsl. engring. State U. Ia., summers 1950-58. Pres. Lincoln Council Christian Edn., 1940-44, Lincoln Goodwill Industries, 1944-46. Registered profl. engr., Neb. Fellow Am. Soc. Quality Control (Brumbaugh award com. 1954-66), Am. Soc. M.E. (life fellow, regional v.p. 1962-66); mem. Am. Assn. U. Profs., Am. Soc. Engring. Edn., Am. Interprofl. Inst. (pres. 1961-62), Tau Beta Pi, Pi Tau Sigma (regional v.p. 1963), Sigma Tau. Methodist (asso. sec. gen. bd. lay activities 1946-47, lay leader Neb. Conf. 1945-59). Mason. Home: 1130 H St Lincoln NB 68508

BARNARD, ROLLIN DWIGHT, savs. and loan exec.; b. Denver, Apr. 14, 1922; s. George Cooper and Emma (Riggs) B.; B.A., Pomona Coll., 1943; m. Patricia Reynolds Bierkamp, Sept. 15, 1943; children—Michael Dana, Rebecca Susan, Laurie Beth. Clk., Morey Merc. Co., Denver, 1939-40; partner George C. Barnard & Co., gen. real estate and ins., Denver, 1946-47; v.p. Foster & Barnard, Inc., 1947-53; instr. Denver U., 1949-53; dir. real estate U.S. P.O. Dept., Washington, 1953-55, dep. asst. postmaster gen., bur. facilities, 1955-59, asst. postmaster gen., 1959-61; pres., dir. Midland Fed. Savs. & Loan Assn., Denver, 1962—. Pres., Denver Area council Boy Scouts Am., 1970-71; chmn. Planning and Zoning Commn. Greenwood Village, Colo., 1969—; mem. nat. council Pomona Coll., 1963—; adv. panel Denver Research Inst., U. Denver, 1963-66, mem. pub. affairs adv. bd., 1965—; nat. adv. council Urban Am., 1967—; v.p. Denver organizing com. 1976 Winter Olympics; bd. Colo. Bus. Devel. Corp., 1967—; Bd. dirs. Downtown Denver Improvement Assn., pres., 1965; bd. dirs. Pitts. Theol. Sem. (Presbyn.), YMCA Met. Denver; trustee Mile High United Fund; trustee, treas. Morris Animal Found., 1969—. Served to capt. AUS, World War II. Nominated One of Ten Outstanding Young Men in Am., U.S. Jr. C. of C. 1955, 57; recipient Distinguished Service award Postmaster Gen. U.S., 1960. Mem. Denver C. of C. (pres. 1966-67), U.S. Savs. and Loan League (mem. nat. legislative com., 1962-69, chmn. br. operations com. 1967-68), Savs. League Colo. (v.p. 1970-71), Assn. U.S. Army (trustee Denver centennial chpt.), Fellowship Christian Athletes (Denver area dir.), Nu Alpha Phi. Republican. Presbyn. Clubs: 26 (pres. Denver 1970); Mountain and Plains Appaloosa Horse (pres. 1970-71). Home: 101 Long Rd Littleton CO 80121 Office: 444 17th St Denver CO 80202

BARNARD, WILLIAM CALVERT, news service exec.; b. Corpus Christi, Tex., Feb. 25, 1914; s. W.C. and Eleanor (Erb) B.; student Tex. Coll. Arts and Industries, Kingsville, 1933-35; m. Julia Lacy Salter, Mar. 25, 1961; children—William Cornell, Diana Eugenia. Reporter-columnist Corpus Christi Caller-Times, 1935-40; feature editor San Antonio Express-News, 1941-42; writer, state editor A.P., Dallas Bur., 1942-50; A.P. war corr. Korean War, Far East news editor, 1950-54; chief of bur. A.P., Dallas, 1954-62, gen. exec., N.Y.C., 1962-71, gen. exec. for seven Western states, San Francisco, 1971—. Recipient Journalism Forum award for coverage Korean War, So. Meth. U., 1954. Presbyn. Office: 318 Fox Plaza San Francisco CA 94119

BARNATHAN, JULIUS, broadcasting co. exec.; b. N.Y.C., Jan. 22, 1927; s. Elias L. and Julia (Amado) B.; A.B., Bklyn. Coll., 1951; A.M. in Math. Statistics, Columbia, 1955; m. Lorraine Glogower, Jan. 13, 1952; children—Joyce Linda, Daniel Elias, and Jacqueline Frances. Actuarial asst. Nat. Council for Compensation Ins., 1951-52; dir. media research, statis. analyst Kenyon & Eckhardt, 1952-54; with ABC, 1954—, dir. research, 1957-59, v.p., 1959, v.p. affiliated stas., 1959-62, v.p., gen. mgr., 1962-65, v.p. charge broadcast operations and engring., 1965—; pres. O. & O. TV Stas., 1962. Pres. Bklyn. Coll. Bur. Econ. Research, 1949-50. Served with USNR, 1944-46. Mem. Advt. Research Found. (tech. com.), Radio-TV Research Council (past pres.), Internat. Radio-TV Soc., Acad. Radio and TV Arts and Scis., Am. Statis. Assn., Phi Beta Kappa, Pi Mu Epsilon. Home: 59 Harbor Lane Roslyn Harbor NY 11576 Office: 1330 Av Americas New York City NY 10019

BARNDS, WILLIAM PAUL, bishop; b. Sweet Springs, Mo., Aug. 5, 1904; s. William Tyson and Virginia (Larsen) B.; B.A., Mo. Valley Coll., 1925, D.D. (hon.), 1947; M.A., U. Mo., 1927; Ph.D., U. Neb., 1949; B.D., U. Chgo., 1940; S.T.M., Seabury-Western Sem., 1944, S.T.D. (hon.), 1967; D.D., U. of South, 1967; m. Ida Lou Sterrett, June 30, 1930; children—William Joseph, Mary Ida (Mrs. James W. Garrard), Virginia Lou (Mrs. Nicholas George Albanese, Jr.). Ordained deacon Episcopal Ch., 1932, priest, 1933, bishop, 1966; rector in Mo., Kan., Neb. and Ind., 1933-56; lectr. philosophy and lit. Ind. U. extension at South Bend, 1954-56; rector Trinity Ch., Ft. Worth, 1956-66; suffragan bishop Diocese Dallas, 1966- -; adj. prof. philosophy Tex. Christian U., 1956—. Chmn. dept. Christian edn. Diocese Kan., 1939-44, dept. Christian social relations Diocese Neb., 1945-48, dep. promotion, also mem. bishop and council Diocese No. Ind., 1954-56; mem. exec. council depts. Christian edn., promotion and div. missions Diocese Dallas, 1956-66, mem. standing com., 1958-61; dep. to gen. convs., 1937, 43, 46, 49, 52, 55, 58, 61, 64. Club: Torch. Author articles. Home: 6800 Woodstock Rd Fort Worth TX 76116 Office: 1630 N Garrett Dallas TX 75206

BARNDT, WILLIAM HENRY, banker; b. Perkasie, Pa., Oct. 11, 1919; s. Elmer Cressman and Elizabeth Hockman (Roberts) B.; student U. Pa., 1948-50, 52-54; diploma Stonier Grad. Sch. Banking, Rutgers U., 1965; m. Marjorie Dawn Duke, Apr. 14, 1944; children—Stephen Duke, Douglas Ray, Suzanne Duke. With First Nat. Bank of Phila., 1936-55, asst. treas., 1948-55; with First Pa. Banking & Trust Co., Phila., 1955—, asst. v.p., 1957-61, v.p., 1961-69, sr. v.p., 1969—. Pres. Jr. C. of C. Phila., 1955; v.p. Bucks County Indsl. Devel. Corp., 1970—. Mem. exec. com. Grandview Hosp., Sellersville, Pa., 1968—. Served to maj. AUS, World War II; PTO; to lt. col. U.S. Army, Korean War; col. Res. Club: Huntingdon Valley (Pa.) Country. Home: M R Box 164 Telford PA 18969 Office: 555 City Line Av Bala-Cynwyd PA 19004

BARNEBY, MALCOLM R., dep. chief U.S. mission to La Paz, Bolivia. Address: APO New York City NY 09867*

BARNES, BEN F., lt. gov. Tex.; b. Gorman, Tex., Apr. 17, 1938; s. B.F. Barnes; B.B.A., U. Tex., 1960; LL.D., McMurry Coll.; m. Martha Jane Morgan, Feb. 22, 1957; children—Greg, Amy. Mem. Tex. Ho. of Reps., from 1960, chmn. rules com., 1963, speaker, 1965, now lt. gov. Tex., Austin. Vice chmn. Tex. legislative council and legislative budget bd.; mem. nat. legislative conf. com. fed.-state relations, 1965-66. Mem. Tex. Jr. C. of C. (one of 5 outstanding young Texans 1965), S.W. Cattle Growers Assn. Methodist. Elk. Home: De Leon TX Office: State Capitol Bldg Austin TX

BARNES, BENJAMIN SHIELDS, Jr., banker; b. Dothan, Ala., Jan. 26, 1919; s. Benjamin Shields and Ruth Graham (Blue) B.; B.S., U. Ga., 1941; postgrad. Rutgers U., 1950-52, Harvard, 1968; m. Bettye Osborne Withers, Apr. 2, 1948; children—Julia Lee (Mrs. Richard A. Reid), Elizabeth Randylyn (Mrs. Terry L. Miller), Carole Osborne, Bettye Graham. With Atlantic Refining Co., 1941; with First Nat. Bank of Atlanta, 1946—, asst. v.p., 1950-54, v.p., 1954-67, exec. v.p., dir., 1967—; exec. v.p., dir. First Nat. Holding Corp., 1967—; pres., dir. First Atlanta Tri-South, Inc., 1st Atlanta Internat. Corp., First Nat.-Heller Factors, Inc.; dir. London Interstate Bank, Ltd., Tharpe & Brooks, Inc., Munich Am. Reassurance Co. Bd. dirs. Downtown Atlanta YMCA, Community Chest Met. Atlanta. Served to lt. USNR, 1941-46; PTO. Recipient Distinguished Service award Alumni Assn. Baylor Sch., Chattanooga, 1968. Mem. Res. City Bankers Assn., Atlanta C. of C. (dir.), Chi Phi. Presbyn. Clubs: Capital City, Commerce (Atlanta). Home: 671 Andover Dr NW Atlanta GA 30327 Office: 2 Peachtree St NW Atlanta GA 30303

BARNES, BERNARD, magazine cons.; b. Phila., Mar. 21, 1909; s. Earl and Anna (Kohler) B.; A.B., Harvard, 1930; m. Carolyn H. Payne, Dec. 3, 1936; children—Timothy E., Mary P., Peter G., Frederick P. Advt. promotion Time, Inc., 1931-37; promotion dir. Ladies Home Jour., 1937-41, Life mag., 1941-43; dept. dir. No. European Operations, OWI, London, Eng., 1944-45; asst. to exec. v.p. Time, Inc., 1945-53, v.p., 1953-60, v.p., sec., 1960-68, cons., 1968—. Sec.-treas. Catalyst. Bd. dirs. Morningside Heights, Inc.; trustee Internat. House. Clubs: Harvard, University (N.Y.C.); Washington (Conn.) Country. Home: 54 Morningside Dr New York City NY 10025

BARNES, BILLY LEE, educator; b. Sherman, Tex., Nov. 26, 1922; s. Lee Thomas and Ruby Regina (Williams) B.; B.S., Austin Coll., 1947; M.B.A., Tex. Christian U., 1949; Ph.D., U. Ill., 1957; m. Melba Jo Gathright, Dec. 21, 1924; children—Janice Kay, Cynthia Jeanne, Tracy Ann. Mem. faculty U. Ia., 1955—, prof. accounting, dean Coll. Bus. Adminstrn., 1963—; sec.- treas., chief adminstrv. officer Am. Accounting Assn., 1964-65. Served with AUS, 1942-45; ETO. C.P.A., Tex. Mem. Am. Inst. C.P.A.'s, Am. Accounting Assn., Beta Gamma Sigma, Alpha Kappa Psi (past nat. dir.), Beta Alpha Psi. Rotarian. Author: Development and Significance of the Independent Auditor's Certificate, 1948; Development and Present Status of the Accounting Concept of Surplus, 1957. Home: 1805 Glendale Rd Iowa City IA 52240

BARNES, CARL BELTON, former govt. ofcl.; b. Embree, S.C., Dec. 13, 1915; s. Guy and Mattie (Beard) B.; student Cocoran Sch. Art, 1935-37, George Washington U., 1937, Am. U., 1943; m. Helen Fischer, Sept. 13, 1941; children—Diane, Linda, Bruce, Nancy. With Library of Congress, 1936-42, Bd. Econ. Warfare, 1942; with Dept. Agr., 1942-71, dir. personnel, 1961-71, ret., 1971; asso. Inst. Pub. Adminstrn., 1971—. Mem. Civil Service Commn., Fairfax County, Va. Recipient Certificate of Merit award Dept. Agr., 1957, 67, 69, 71, Superior Service award, 1957, 63, Distinguished Service award, 1969. Mem. Soc. Personnel Adminstrn. (pres. 1956-57, Stockberger award 1969), Pub. Personnel Assn. (Charles Cushman award 1966). Home: 1923 Martha's Rd Hollin Hills Alexandria VA 22307 Office: Dept of Agr Washington DC 20251

BARNES, CARLYLE FULLER, mfg. exec.; b. Bristol, Conn., Feb. 16, 1924; s. Fuller Forbes and Myrtle (Ives) B.; A.B., Wesleyan U., 1948; m. Elizabeth Anne May, Oct. 1, 1949; children—Lynne Elizabeth, Janis Lee, Joan Wells, Fuller Forbes. Staff asst. Wallace Barnes Co. (div. Asso. Spring Corp.), 1948-50, gen. mgr., 1951-53; dir. Asso. Spring Corp., 1951—, pres., 1953-64, chmn. bd., 1964—; dir., mem. exec. com. United Bank & Trust Co., N.E. Utilities Co., Stanadyne, Inc.; dir. Travelers Ins. Cos. Pres. Bristol Hosp. Trustee MacDuffie Sch. for Girls, Springfield, Mass. Young Pres.'s Orgn. Club: Economic (N.Y.C.). Home: Peacedale St Bristol CT 06010 Office: 18 Main St Bristol CT 06010

BARNES, CHARLES ANDREW, elec. mfg. co. exec.; b. York, Pa., Apr. 3, 1919; s. Charles Wm. (Evans) B.; A.B., Ursinus Coll., 1940; m. Dorothy Krusen, June 29, 1940; childrenBeverley Ann (Mrs. John Hederick), C. Jeffrey, Nancy Krusen. Controller's staff York Corp. (Pa.), 1940-44, asst. sec., asst. treas., 1946-56; asst. treas. Borg Warner Corp., Chgo., 1956-57; v.p., controller P.R. Mallory & Co., Inc., Indpls., 1958-59, v.p. finance, 1959-61, adminstrv. v.p., 1961-63, v.p. operations, 1963-67, exec. v.p., 1967-68, pres., chief exec. officer, 1968—, dir., mem. exec. com., mem. adv. bd. Liberty Mut. Ins. Co.; dir. Mallory Batteries (Australia) Inc., Mallory Battery Co. of Can., Ltd., Ind. Nat. Bank, State Life Ins. Co., Johnson Matthey & Mallory, Ltd., Methodist Hosp. Found., Mallory Metall. Products, Ltd., Industries P.R. Mallory, S.A., Mallory Baterias Mallory de Argentina S.A., Contractos y Electrodos Mallory S.A., Nat. Mallory Denchi K.K., Mallory Batteries, Ltd. N.V. Mallory exec. com. Meth. Hosp. Served as lt. USNR, 1944-46. Mem. Ind. C. of C. (dir.). Methodist. Home: 7951 Morningside Dr Indianapolis, IN 46240. Office: 3029 E Washington St Indianapolis IN 46206

BARNES, CHARLES ANDREW, educator, physicist; b. Toronto, Ont., Can., Dec. 12, 1921; s. Adella (Davidson) B.; B.A., McMaster U., 1943; M.A., U. Toronto, 1944; Ph.D., Cambridge (Eng.) U., 1950; m. Phyllis Malcolm, Sept. 15, 1950; childrenNancy E., Steven. A. Came to U.S., 1953, naturalized, 1961. Physicist, Joint Brit.-Canadian Atomic Energy Project, 1944-46; asst. prof. physics U. B.C., 1950-53, 55-56; mem. faculty Cal. Inst. Tech., 1953-55, 56—, prof. physics, 1962—. NSF sr. fellow, Denmark, 1962-63. Fellow Am. Phys. Soc. Contbr. profl. jours. Home: 1546 Rose Villa Pasadena, CA 91106.

BARNES, CHARLES BENJAMIN, lawyer; b. Hingham, Mass., July 18, 1900; s. Charles Benjamin and Josephine Lea (Low) B.; B.S., Harvard, 1924, LL.B., 1927; m. Phoebe Washburn, June 15, 1929; children—Phoebe (Mrs. John E.Z. Caner), Josephine Lea (Mrs. John Jay Iselin), Charles Benjamin, Cornelia Bradford. Admitted to Mass. bar, 1927; asso. firm Hemenway & Barnes, Boston, 1927—, partner, 1929—. Pres., dir. Washburn Investment Co., Worcester, Mass.; dir. Allied Stores Corp., N.Y.C., Jordan Marsh Co., Boston; mem. dirs. adv. com. State St. Bank & Trust Co. Alternate del. Republican Nat. Conv., Kansas City, 1928, Chgo., 1932. Hon. chmn. bd. trustees Peter Bent Brigham Hosp. Mem. Am. Bar Assn., Bar Assn. City of Boston. Clubs: Somerset, Curtis, Knockers, Lawyers (Boston); Harvard, Anglers (N.Y.C.); Country Polo (Dedham, Mass.); Republican of Mass. (past dir.). Home: 267 Fox Hill St Westwood MA 02090 Office: 73 Tremont St Boston MA 02108

BARNES, CLIVE ALEXANDER, drama and dance critic; b. London, Eng., May 13, 1927; s. Arthur Lionel and Freda Marguerite (Garratt) B.; B.A., U. Oxford (Eng.), 1951; m. Patricia Amy Evelyn Winckley, June 26, 1958; children—Christopher John Clive, Joanna Rosemary Maya. Came to U.S., 1965. Co-editor Oxford dance mag. Arabesque, 1950; asst. editor Dance and Dancers, 1950-58, asso. editor, 1958-61, exec. editor, 1961-65, editor, N.Y.C., 1965—; writer music, dance, drama, films Daily Express, London, 1956-65; dance critic The Spectator, London, 1959-65, N.Y. Times, N.Y.C., 1965—, drama critic, 1967—; adj. asso. prof. dept. journalism. N.Y. U., 1968—. Served with R.A.F., 1946-48. Mem. Critics Circle London (past sec., chmn. ballet sect.), N.Y. Drama Critics Circle. Mem. Ch. of Eng. Author: Ballet in Britain Since the War, 1953; Frederick Ashton and His Ballets, 1961; (with others) Ballet Here and Now, 1961; Dance Scene, U.S.A., 1967. Home: 344 W 72d St New York City NY 10023 Office: NY Times 229 W 43d St New York City NY 10036

BARNES, DJUNA, author, artist; b. Cornwall-on-Hudson, June 12, 1892; d. Wald and Elizabeth (Chappell) Barnes; student art Pratt Inst., Art Students League. Reporter, illustrator, spl. feature writer for newspapers, mags., 1913-31; short stories appeared in All-story mag., Smart Set, Morning Telegraph, Little Rev., Dial, Vanity Fair, Transatlantic Rev. (psaud. Lydia Steptoe); one act plays prod. by Provincetown Players, 1919-20, The Studio Theatre of Manhattan, 1926. Trustee N.Y. com. Dag Hammarskjold Found. Mem. Nat. Inst. Arts and Letters. Author: (illustrator) A Book, 1923; (novel, also illustrator) Ryder, 1928; (also illustrator) The Ladies Almanack, 1928; Night Among the Horses, 1929; (novel) Nightwood, 1936; (play in verse) The Antiphon, 1958 (transl. into Swedish 1961); Spillway (short stories), 1962; The Selected Works of Djuna Barnes, 1962; represented in The Present Age (Edwin Muir), Vol. 5, The Widening Gyre, 1963, The Personal Voice, 1964, The World of Love, 1964, Modern Poetry, Little Treasury of American Prose, Modern Women in Love (transl. 8 langs.), Dial Anthology. Large oil painting, Alice, exhibited Art of this Century Gallery, N.Y.C., 1946. Address: 5 Patchin Pl New York City NY 10011

BARNES, DONALD LEE, Jr., finance co. exec.; b. Springfield, Ill., July 11, 1917; s. Donald Lewis and Dorothy (Ide) B.; B.S.C., St. Louis U., 1939; m. Leslie Jane Newell, Nov. 8, 1939; children—Donald Leslie III (dec.), James D., Barbara Ann, Dennis N., L. Neil, Donna Lynn. With Am. Investment Co., St. Louis, exec. v.p., 1959-64, pres., 1964—, chmn. bd., 1967—, also dir.; pres., dir. Charter Nat. Life Ins. Co., 1962-67, chmn. bd., 1967-; pres., dir. Barwell Devel. Corp., 1952-, Clarkson Valley Estates, Inc., 1962—, Charter Nat. Ins. Co., 1964; chmn. bd. Am. Nat. Stores; dir. St. Louis County Nat. Bank, Mo. Portland Cement Co. Trustee, St. Louis U., Cardinal Glennon Meml. Hosp. Children, Boys Town, Mo., Calvary Cemetery Assn., Govt. Research Inst., chmn. adv. bd. Mo. Colls. Fund, St. Louis. Served to lt. (j.g.) USNR, 1944-46; PTO. Recipient Alumni Merit award St. Louis U., 1962. Mem. St. Louis C. of C. (bd. dirs.), Alpha Sigma Nu (hon.), Clubs: Forest Hills Golf and Country, St. Louis (charter), Mo. Athletic, Old Warson Country, St. Louis Stadium (founding mem., dir.)(St. Louis). Home: 19 Woodcrest Dr Ladue, MO 63124. Office: 8251 Maryland St St Louis MO 63105

BARNES, EDWARD LARRABEE, architect; b. Chgo., Apr. 22, 1915; s. Cecil and Margaret Helen (Aver) B.; grad. Milton Acad. 1934; B.S. cum laude, Harvard, 1938; B. Arch., Sheldon Travelling Fellowship, Harvard Grad. Sch. Design, 1942; m. Mary Elizabeth Coss, Mar. 4, 1944; 1 son, John Cecil. Prefabricated (with Henry Dreyfuss) house of aluminus for Consol. Vultee Aircraft Corp., 1948; architect, N.Y.C., 1949—, practice includes design pvt. houses, apts., low-cost housing, camps, campus planning, art museums, jet plane interiors, visual identification program for Pan Am. World Airways; archtl. design critic Pratt Inst., Bklyn., 1953-54; urban renewal projects in Sacramento, Cal., San Juan P.R.; design critic Yale Univ., 1957-59, cons. on physical planning, 1964. Work exhibited Mus. Modern Art. Trustee Am. Acad., Rome; bd. dirs. Municipal Art Soc. N.Y. Modern Art. Recipient award for distinction in arts Yale, 1959; Arnold Brunner prize Nat. Inst. Arts and Letters, 1959; Progressive Architecture Top-Design award, 1959; silver medal Archtl. League N.Y., 1960; co-recipient Ford Found. grant for devel. theatre project; Progressive Arch. Design award, 1963; 1st Honor award FHA, 1963. Fellow A.I.A. (medal of honor N.Y. chpt. 1971); mem. Westchester Council Arts, Century Assn.; asso. N.A.D. Work pub. in various house and archtl. mags. Home: Wood Rd Mount Kisco NY 10549 Office: 410 E 62d St New York City NY 10021

BARNES, EDWIN, banker. Exec. v.p. Grand Rapids office Mich. Nat. Bank. Office: 77 Monroe St NW Grand Rapids MI 49502*

BARNES, FRANCIS MERRIMAN, III, paper mfg. co. exec.; b. St. Louis, July 19, 1918; s. Francis Merriman and Carlotta M. (Kimlin) B.; A.B., U. Mo., 1941; LL.B., Washington U., St. Louis, 1948; m. Mary Shore Johnson, Oct. 16, 1948; children—Elizabeth Johnson, Francis Merriman IV, Barbara Anne. Admitted to Mo. bar, 1947; asst.

city counselor, St. Louis, 1948-49; atty. Southwestern Bell Telephone Co., 1949-51; gen. counsel Gaylord Container Corp., St. Louis, 1951-59; asst. v.p. Crown Zellerbach Corp., San Francisco, 1959-62, v.p. corp. adminstrn., 1962-69, sr. v.p., 1969—. Bd. dirs. Mgmt. Council for Bay Area Employment Opportunity, Met. YMCA, San Francisco, Opportunity Enterprise Corp.; chmn. bd. trustees San Francisco Art Inst.; trustee Mechanics Inst. Served to 1st lt. F.A., AUS, 1941-46. Mem. Greater San Francisco C. of C. (dir.). Clubs: University (San Francisco); Peninsula Golf and Country (San Mateo, Cal.). Home: 546 W Santa Inez Av Hillsborough CA 94010 Office: 1 Bush St San Francisco CA 94119

BARNES, FRANK STEPHENSON, elec. engr., educator; b. Pasadena, Cal., July 31, 1932; s. Donald Porter and Thedia (Schellenberg) B.; B.S., Princeton, 1954; M.S., Stanford, 1955, Ph.D., 1958; m. Gay Dirstine, Dec. 17, 1955; children-Stephen, Amy. Fulbright prof. Coll. Engring., Baghdad, Iraq, 1957-58; research asso. Colo. Research Corp., Broomfield, 1958-59; prof. dept. elec. engring. U. Colo., Boulder, 1959—, chmn. dept., 1964—; mem. G-Ed Adcom, I.E.E.E., 1970—. Dir. World Foods Corp. Recipient Curtis W. McGraw Research award, 1965. Faculty Research lectr. U. Colo., 1965. Fellow I.E.E.E. Editor: I.E.E.E. Student Jour., 1967-70; regional editor I.E.E. Letters, 1970—; editorial bd. I.E.E.E., 1967—. Home: 225 Continental View Dr Boulder CO 80302

BARNES, FREDERICK WALTER, Jr., educator, physician; b. Cleve., Mar. 3, 1909; s. Frederick Walter and Susan (Anderson) B.; A.B., Yale U., 1930; M.D., Johns Hopkins Med. Sch., 1934; Ph.D., Columbia U., 1943; m. Catherine Gardner Bowden, Apr. 6, 1940; children—William Anderson, Susan Hammond. Intern Johns Hopkins Hosp., 1934-36; resident Childen's Hosp., Boston, 1936-38; asst. prof. medicine and biochemistry Cin. Med. Sch., 1942-46; asso. prof. medicine and biochemistry Johns Hopkins Med. Sch., 1946-62; prof. med. sci. Brown U., 1962—. Vice-pres. Urban League R.I., 1965; mem. Urban Coalition, 1969—; mem. Progress for Providence 1970, Bd. dirs. R.I. Tb Assn., 1966—. Mem. Am. Assn. Biochemists, Pediatric Research Soc., Am. Coll. Physicians, N.Y. Acad. Sci., Assn. Am. Med. Colls. (chmn. group student affairs Northeast 1970-71). Home: 21 George St Providence RI 02906

BARNES, FREDERIC PAGE, stockbroker; b. Grand Forks, N.D., Nov. 27, 1904; s. Orville J. and Dorothy (Crain) B.; student U. N.D., 1922-24; A.B., Dartmouth, 1926; m. Margaret Louise Ott, Nov. 24, 1932; children—Peter Crain, Bryant Page. With Lamson Bros. & Co., 1926-43, resident partner, Kansas City, Mo., 1939-43; gen. partner H.O. Peet & Co., Kansas City, Mo., 1943—. Mem. N.Y. (gov. 1970—), Midwest stock exchanges. Trustee Pembroke-Country Day Sch., Midwest Research Inst., U. Mo. at Kansas City. Episcopalian. Home: 3109 W 69th St Shawnee Mission KS 66208 Office: 23 W 10th St Kansas City MO 66102

BARNES, GEORGE BUTLER, lawyer; b. Norway, Me., Oct. 17, 1904; s. Charles Putnam and Annie (M. Richardson) B.; A.B., Ricker Classical Inst., 1922; A.B., Colby Coll., 1926, M.A. (hon.), 1946; LL.B., Harvard, 1929; LL.D., Ricker Coll., 1961; m. Ada Flora Wheeler, June 27, 1931; children—Forrest Wheeler, Ann Butler, George Butler. Admitted to Me. bar, 1929; states atty. for Aroostook Co., Me., 1933-39; mem. Ho. of Reps., 1943-47, speaker, 1945; state senator, 1947-53; mem. Me. Jud. Council, 1953-70. Pres. bd. trustees Ricker Classical Inst. and Ricker Coll., 1952-62; chmn. vis. com. on govt., history and econs. Colby Coll., 1950-58. Asst. appeal agt., co. draft bd., 1943-46. Fellow Am. Coll. Probate Lawyers; mem. Am. (com. on credentials and admissions ho. of dels.), Me. (pres. 1954) bar assns., Am. Arbitration Assn. (nat. panel arbitrators), Delta Kappa Epsilon. Republican (del. to. nat. conv. 1952). Baptist. Mason, Elk. Home: 6 Madigan St Houlton ME 04730 Office: Houlton Trust Co Bldg Houlton ME 04730

BARNES, GEORGE ELTON, stock broker; b. Garner, Iowa, Mar. 17, 1900; s. Charles M. and Cora (Staver) B.; student Hamilton U., Mason City, Ia., 1916-18; m. Florence Herrcke, Oct. 5, 1922; 1 dau., Ruth Adele. With LaSalle Nat. Bank (Ill.), 1918-30; partner A.C. Baur & Co., 1930-31; partner Wayne Hummer & Co., 1931—; mem. N.Y. Stock Exchange; gov., chmn. exec. com. Chgo. Stock Exchange, 1946; chmn. bd. Midwest Stock Exchange, 1956-58; dir. LaSalle Extension U., 1952-60, Suburban Trust & Savs. Bank. Chmn. budget finance com. Oak Park and River Forest Community Chest, 1941-49, pres., 1950-51; mem. nat. budget com. Community Chests Councils of Am., 1956-60; bd. dirs. Infant Welfare Soc. Chgo., 1956-60; chmn. corporate large gifts div., Chicago Community Fund, 1946; v.p., gov. Nat. Assn. Stock Exchange Firms, 1942-46; pres. Chicago Tennis Assn., 1947-48, U.S. Lawn Tennis Assn., 1960-61; mem. com. on mgmt. 1955 Davis Cup championships; nat. chmn. sponsors com. 1955 Davis Cup; pres. Nat. Tennis Ednl. Found., Inc., 1958-66; founder, past pres. Chgo. Tennis Patrons, Inc. Named Sportsman of Year, Chgo. Press Club, 1961; recipient Hardy award for contbn. to tennis edn. U.S. Lawn Tennis Assn., 1962, 68. Mem. Ill. C. of C. (dir.). Clubs: Oak Park Country, River Forest-Tennis, Tavern, Bankers, Executives, Midday, Ft. Lauderdale Country. Author: Pay-as-you-go and Corporate Fed. Tax Plans. Home: 1400 Jackson Av River Forest IL 60305 Office: Wayne Hummer & Co 105 W Adams St Chicago IL 60603

BARNES, HARRY GEORGE, Jr., fgn. service officer; b. St. Paul, June 5, 1926; s. Harry George and Bertha Pauline (Blaul) B.; A.B., Amherst Coll., 1949; student Russian Inst., Columbia, 1949-50; M.A., 1968; m. Elizabeth Ann Sibley, June 19, 1948; children—Pauline, Adrienne, Douglas, Sibley. Joined U.S. Fgn. Service, 1950; vice consul, Bombay, India, 1951-53; vice consul, 2d sec., Prague, Czechoslovakia, 1953-55; Russian area and lang. trainee, Obermmergau, Germany, 1955-56; 2d sec., consul, Moscow, USSR, 1957-59; internat. relations officer Office Soviet Union Affairs, State Dept., 1959-62; student Nat. War Coll., 1962-63; counselor Kathmandu, Nepal, 1963-67, Bucharest, Romania 1968—. Served with AUS, 1944-46. Mem. Phi Alpha Psi. 7019 Armart Dr Bethesda, MD 20034. Office: Am Embassy Bucharest Romania

BARNES, HAZEL ESTELLA, educator; b. Wilkes-Barre, Pa., Dec. 16, 1915; d. Olin James and May (Petersen) Barnes; B.A., Wilson Coll., 1937; Ph.D., Yale, 1941; D.Litt., Wilson Coll., 1965; summer study Columbia, U. Hawaii. Instr. classics Womans Coll. U. N.C., 1941- 43; asso. prof. classics Queens Coll., Charlotte, N.C., 1943-45; tchr. and asst. to pres. Pierce Coll., Elleniko, Athens, Greece, 1945-48; asst. prof. classics and philosophy U. Toledo, 1948-51; asst. prof. philosophy Ohio State U., 1951-53; asst. prof. classics U. Colo., 1953- 56, asso. prof., 1956-61, prof. classics, 1961—, also chmn. dept. classics, 1965-69. Mem. Am. Philos. Assn., Rocky Mountain and Plains States Philos. Inst., Am. Soc. for Aesthetics, Classical Assn. Middle West and South, Am. Civil Liberties Union, United World Federalists. Author intro. and translator: (Jean-Paul Sartre) Existential Psychoanalysis, 1953, Being and Nothingness, 1956, Search For a Method, 1963. Author: The Literature of Possibility: A Study in Humanistic Existentialism, 1959; (with D. Sutherland) Hippolytus in Drama and Myth, 1960; An Existentialist Ethics, 1967; The University as the New Church, 1970; also articles in field. Preparer series Self Encounter, Nat. Ednl. TV, 1962. Home: 896 17th St Boulder CO 80302

BARNES, HOWARD G., film exec.; b. N.Y.C., Dec. 27, 1913; A.B., U. Mich., 1935; m. Joan Lesavoy, Jan. 9, 1949 (div. Nov. 1957); children—(foster children) Marshall Alan (dec.), Denis Joy; m. 2d, Mary Ellena Mock, Dec. 7, 1958 (div.); children—Christie Ann, Paul Louis Lloyd; m. 3d, Partricia Lee Sills, August 4, 1965; children—Paxton Louise, Gillian Leigh. Radio announcer WIP, Phila., 1935, KYW, WHN, N.Y. C., 1936; producer WOR Mut., 1936-38; exec. producer MCA, 1938; producer, writer, exec. CBS, N.Y.C., 1938-46, v.p. in charge network programs CBS Radio, 1955-60; dir. programs CBS-TV, Hollywood, 1960-63; producing independently, 1946-48; v.p. in charge radio and TV, Dorland, Inc., N.Y.C., 1948-51; pres. Gen. Entertainment Corp., 1949—; TV exec. Ashley Famous Agy., Inc., 1963-66; dir. film prodn. Westinghouse Broadcasting Co., N.Y.C., 1966-67, exec. v.p. Group W Films, 1967—, also dir. parent co.; dir. Trio Films, Ltd., London, Eng. Served as lt. USNR, motion picture producer-writer, 1942-45. Home: 135 E 74th St New York City NY 10021 Office: 90 Park Av New York City NY 10016

BARNES, IRSTON ROBERTS, educator, economist; b. New Haven, Feb. 14, 1904; s. Niar and Mabel Jane (Roberts) B.; Ph.B., Yale, 1926, Ph.D. in Econs., 1928; m. Lidorra Holt Putney, June 30, 1936; 1 son, Chapliplin Bradford. Faculty, Yale, 1928-41, 1928-41, asst. prof. polit. economy, 1932-41, fellow Pierson Coll., 1935-41; cons. economist antitrust div. Dept. Justice, 1941-44; dir. econ. bur. CAB, 1944-45, econ. adviser to bd., 1945-48; economist FTC, 1948-52, 54- 60, chief div. econ. evidence, 1952-54; professorial lectr. George Washington U., 1954-55; vis. lectr. Columbia Grad. Sch. Bus., 1949-50, prof. polit. economy, 1960-63; econ. cons. antitrust and Am. govt. regulation, 1963—. Mem. Am. Econ. Assn., Am. Ornithologists Union, Audubon Soc. Central Atlantic States (pres. 1946-61, chmn. bd. 1961-68), Phi Beta Kappa. Clubs: Faculty Club (New Haven); Cosmos (Washington); Yale (N.Y.C.). Author: Public Utility Control in Massachusetts, 1930; Cases on Public Utility Regulation, 1938; The Economics of Public Utility Regulation, 1942. Contbr. articles to profl. jours., weekly column The Naturalist in Washington Post, 1951—. Home: 58 N Branford Rd Wallingford CT 06492 Office: 80 Broad St New York City NY 10004

BARNES, JAMES WOODROW, educator, musician; b. Winslow, Ind., Jan. 14, 1918; s. George W. and Bernice (Gatton) B.; B.A., Oakland City (Ind.) Coll., 1941; M.A., Ind. State U., 1949; student U. Cal. at Los Angeles, 1946; Ph.D., Ind. U., 1960; m. Elizabeth J. Woodruff, Nov. 20, 1941; childrenRebecca Ann (Mrs. Byron L. Elmendorf), Susan Lynn (Mrs. Donald R. Adams), James Mark. Tchr. music and math. Winslow High Sch., 1941-42; music dir. Oakland City High Sch., 1946-48; mem. faculty Ind. State U., 1948-; prof. music, 1960—, head music dept., 1964—; condr. Terre Haute Symphony, 1949—; guest condr., adjucator, string clinician, music cons. Served to capt. USAAF, 1942-46. Recipient Mid-West East honor award for outstanding service to music Duquesne U., 1968. Mem. Am. String Tchrs. Assn. (pres. Ind. 1960-61), Ind. Music Educators Assn. (exec. sec. 1953-56), Music Educators Nat. Conf., Am. Fedn. Musicians, Pi Kappa Lambda, Phi Mu Alpha. Home: 1232 S Center St Terre Haute, IN 47802.

BARNES, JOHN LANDES, mathematical engr.; b. Haddonfield, N.J., Oct. 16, 1906; s. Eugene Howard and Naomi Grace (Landes) B.; grad. William Penn Charter Sch., 1924; S.B., Mass. Inst. Tech., 1928, S.M. in E.E., 1929; A.M., Princeton, 1930, Ph. D. in Math., 1934; m. Mabel F. Schmeiser, July 3, 1935; children—George Gared, Lynne Ries. Asst. instr., research asst. math. and elec. engring. Princeton, 1932-34; instr. elec. engring. Mass. Inst. Tech., 1934-35; asst. prof. math. Tufts U., 1935-39, acting chmn. elec. engring. dept., asso. prof., chmn. dept. applied math., 1940-41, prof., chmn. dept., 1941-42, 45-47; research engr. RCA Mfg. Co., 1939-40; cons. Hazeltine Service Corp., 1941-42; mem. tech. staff Bell Telephone Labs., 1942-45; cons. Raytheon Mfg. Co., 1945-47, N.Am. Rockwell Corp., 1947-53, chief Guidance Aerophysics Lab., 1948-51, asso. tech. dir. electromech. dept., 1951-53; cons. Ramo-Wooldridge Corp., 1953-54; dir. control and computer lab. Missile Systems div. Lockheed Aircraft Corp., 1955; v.p. Systems Research Corp., 1955-56; founder, pres. Systems Labs. Corp., Sherman Oaks, Cal., 1956-57; pres. Systems Corp. of Am., 1957—. Prof. engring., applied sci. U. Cal., Los Angeles, 1947—. Fellow A.A.A.S., Am. Acad. Arts and Scis., Am. Inst. Aeros. and Astronautics (asso.), I.E.E.E., Brit. Interplanetary Soc.; mem. Am. Math. Soc., Am. Phys. Soc., Inst. Math. Statistics, Sigma Xi, Sigma Nu. Co-author: Transients in Linear Systems, 1942. Co-editor, contbr. to math. sect. Handbook of Engineering Fundamentals, 1936, 52. Home: 14710 Mulholland Dr Los Angeles CA 90024 Office: Sch Engring and Applied Sci U Cal Los Angeles CA 90024 also 1007 Broxton Av Los Angeles CA 90024

BARNES, JOHN WINTHROP, army officer; b. El Paso, Tex., Mar. 6, 1921; s. Elmer Ellsworth and Dorothy (Risk) B.; B.S., U.S. Mil. Acad., 1942; M.S., Cal. Inst. Tech., 1946; student U.S. Army Engring. Sch., 1947-48, U.S. Army Armor Sch., 1950-51, Comd. and Gen. Staff Coll., 1952-53, Armed Forces Indsl. Coll., 1955, Armed Forces Staff Coll., 1957, U.S. Naval War Coll., 1962-63; m. Mary Jess Schafhirt, May 30, 1942; children—John Winthrop Jr., Katharine Dorothy (Mrs. Dennis E. Aubrey), Brian MacLean. Commd. 2d lt. U.S. Army, 1942, advanced through grades to maj. gen., 1971—; staff officer Far East Command, 1955-56, exec. officer, 1957; dep. comdr. 502d Airborne Battle Group, 1958; staff officer Office Chief Research and Devel., 1959-62; comdr. 3d Brigade, 7th Div., Korea, 1963-64; staff officer Office Dir. Def. Research and Engring. 1966-67; dep. sr. adv. II Corps Tactical Zone, Vietnam, 1967-68; comdg. gen. 173d Airborne Brigade, Vietnam, 1968-69, dir. devel. Office Chief of Research and Devel., 1969-70, dir. plans, programs and internat., 1971—. Decorated D.S.M., Legion of Merit; Soldiers medal, Bronze Star, Air medal with 9 oak leaf clusters, Commendation medal. Mem. Assn. U.S. Army, Phi Gamma Delta. Episcopalian. Home: 4218 47th St Washington DC 20016 Office: OCRD DA Washington DC 20310

BARNES, KENNETH KIRTLAND, educator, agrl. engr.; b. San Jose, Cal., Nov. 16, 1921; s. Roy Merrill and Helen (Kirtland) B.; student Cal. State Poly. Coll., 1939-41; B.S. in Agrl. Engring., Ia. State U., 1947, M.S. in Agrl. Engring., 1948, Ph.D., 1951; m. Elizabeth Anderson, Aug. 24, 1946; children—Ricky Sue, Roy Merrill II. Instr., Ia. State U., 1948-50, prof., 1952-59; asst. prof. Purdue U., 1950-52; mem. faculty U. Ariz., 1959—, prof. agrl. engring., head dept., 1960—; spl. research mgmt. agrl. machines, machines for vegetable harvesting. Served with AUS, 1943-46. Registered profl. engr., Ia., Ariz. Fellow Am. Soc. Agrl. Engrs. (chmn. power and machinery div. 1960-61, Pacific Coast region 1963-64, chmn. edn. and research div. 1968-69, dir. edn. and research div. 1969-71, v.p. 1971—); mem. Am. Soc. Engring. Edn., Nat. Soc. Profl. Engrs., A.A.A.S., Sigma Xi, Phi Kappa Phi, Tau Beta Pi, Pi Mu Epsilon, Gamma Sigma Delta, Alpha Zeta. Co-author: Soil and Water Conservation Engineering, 2d edit., 1966; Elementary Soil and Water Engineering, 1957, 2d edit., 1971. Home: 7562 N San Lorenzo Dr Tucson AZ 85704

BARNES, LAWSON, lawyer; b. Syracuse, N.Y., May 12, 1907; s. George M. and Agnes (Rafferty) B.; LL.B., Syracuse U., 1931; m. Elizabeth M. Devine, July 30, 1938; children—George L., Joan (Mrs. C. Robert Miller), Gary M. (dec.), Barbara E. (Mrs. Peter G. Duryea). Admitted to N.Y. bar, 1932, since practiced in Syracuse; partner firm Melvin & Melvin, 1938-70. Pres., dir. Wrecking & Salvage Corp., 1948-52, Lodi Iron Works, Inc., 1950-54, Onondaga Hotel, Inc., 1950-61, On-Co Realty & Personalty, Inc., 1933-70, Fayette Warren Parking Corp., 1960-69; partner Griffin Sq. Co., 1964-70. Active local March of Dimes, Community Chest; organizer Onnodaga County chpt. Nat. Found. Infantile Paralysis, 1940. Sec. Onondaga County Democratic Com., 1942-62; Dem. candidate for U.S. Congress, 1946. Served to lt. (s.g.) USNR, World War II. Mem. Fed., Am., N.Y. State, Onondaga County bar assns., Fed. Bar Council, Am. Judicature Soc., Ret. Officers Assn., Am. Legion, Navy League U.S., Psi Upsilon, Phi Delta Phi. Catholic. Home and office: 4900 Longacre Dr Syracuse NY 13215 also Round Island Frontenac NY 13624

BARNES, LESLIE O., airline exec.; b. Canisteo, N.Y., 1917; ed. Buffalo Tech. Inst., U. Chgo. Pres., dir. Allegheny Airlines, Inc., Washington Nat. Airport; pres., dir. Allegheny Ventura Corp.; dir. Allegheny Services Corp., Bradford Fairway Sales & Leasing, Inc. Vice chmn. Pres.'s Adv. Commn. on Aviation. Mem. Air Transport Assn. (dir.). Address: 4625 Holly Rd Rockville MD 20853

BARNES, MAURICE EVERETT, packing co. exec.; b. Richmond, Ky., May 16, 1906; s. Clarence and Dove (McCoy) B.; LL.B., Kansas City Sch. Law, 1933; m. Lillian Katharine Lane. With Armour & Co., 1928-68, v.p., regional mgr., South St. Paul, Minn., 1963-67, v.p. mfg. all foods, Chgo., 1967-68; v.p. mfg. world-wide operations IPL, Inc., Chgo., 1968-70; v.p. mfg. Delec Internat. Ltd., Chgo., 1971—; dir. Stock Yards Nat. Bank, South St. Paul. Pres. Commn. San. Dirst. S. St. Paul, 1964—. Pres. bd. St. Paul Winter Carnival Assn., 1960; bd. dirs. Divine Redeemer Hosp., S. St. Paul, 1962. Served with USAAF, 1925-26. Recipient certificate of merit St. Paul Area C. of C., 1965. Mem. S. St. Paul C. of C. (dir. 1962—). Rotarian (charter pres. S. St. Paul). Clubs: St. Paul Athletic, Minnesota (St. Paul). Home: 1550 N Lake Shore Dr Chicago IL 60611 Office: 401 N Michigan Av Chicago IL 60611

BARNES, MELVIN WALLACE, pub. exec.; b. Milanville, Pa., Jan. 21, 1910; s. Earl O. and Anna M. (Seifried) B.; A.B., Greenville (Ill.) Coll., 1932; M.S., U. Ill., 1934, Ph.D., 1941; m. Florence Alice Joy, Aug. 6, 1935; children—Melvin Wallace, Walter Earl, James Richards. Prin., Damascus (Pa.) High Sch., 1934-36; instr. U. Ill., 1936-40, examining technician, 1940-43; dir. tng. Dept. Justice, 1943-46; dir. adult and extension edn. San Diego pub. sch., 1946-50; dep. supt. Oklahoma City pub. schs., 1950-56, supt., 1957-61; supt. Portland (Ore.) pub. schs., 1961-69; v.p., dir. Scholastic Mags., Inc., N.Y.C., 1969—. Mem. Gov. Ore. Adv. Com. Edn., 1962-66; mem. Commn. Presdl. Scholars, 1964-65; mem. Exploratory Com. Assessing Progress Edn., 1964- 65. Trustee Ednl. Testing Service, 1967-71, Nat. Assn. for Social Policy and Devel.; mem. bd. overseers Lewis and Clark Coll. Mem. N.E.A. (chmn. nat. project instrn. 1959-61), Ednl. Policies Commn., Am. Assn. Sch. Adminstrs., Am. Psychol. Assn. Presbyn. Rotarian. Home: 9 Hathaway Rd Bronxville NY 10708 Office: 50 W 44th New York City NY 10036

BARNES, MICHAEL FOWLER, ins. co. exec.; b. Salt Lake City, June 10, 1918; s. Frank H. and Margaret (Fowler) B.; student pub. schs., Salt Lake City, Los Angeles; m. Barbara Mahanna, Nov. 8, 1953; children—George, SharyLee, Kellie, Patrick, Kaly Erin. With Occidental Life Ins. Co. Cal., 1945—, gen. mgr. Can., 1958—, sr. v.p., 1969—. Served to maj. Royal Canadian Dragoons, Canadian Army, 1939-45. Home: Route 1 Schomberg Ontario Canada Office: 2200 Yonge St Toronto Ontario Canada

BARNES, NATHAN, Liberian diplomat; b. Cape Palmas, Liberia, Apr. 14, 1914; s. Nathan and Elizabeth (Knight) B.; ed. Cape Palmas Sem.; m. 2d, Josephine Brewer, Nov. 15, 1950. With Liberian Revenue Service, 1937-44; admitted to bar; county atty. Maryland County, Liberia, 1944; circuit judge 4th Jud. Circuit Liberia, 1945-56; Liberian minister to Italy, 1956, Liberian ambassador, 1956-60; permanent rep. from Liberia to UN, N.Y.C., 1960—. Chmn. Liberian delegation to 1st UN Conf. on Law of Sea, Geneva, 1958, 2d conf., 1960, UN Conf. Diplomatic Intercourse and Immunities, Vienna, 1961; pres. UN trusteeship council, 1963; chmn. 1st com. UN Conf. on Consular Relations; chmn. UN com. defining aggression; rubber-planter in Liberia. Decorated knight Grand Band Humane Order African Redemption; grand condr. Star Africa (Liberia); cavalier Order Merit (Italy). Mem. Am. Soc. Internat. Law. Mason, Odd Fellow. Mem. United Bros. of Friendship. Address: Printing St Cape Palmas Liberia also Mission of Liberia to UN 235 E 42d St New York City NY 10017

BARNES, PAUL HOWARD, banker; b. Hazlewood, Ind., Aug. 28, 1916; s. Conrad Wilson and Emma (Turner) B.; grad. U. Wis. Banking Sch., 1958; m. Marilou Muir, Aug. 30, 1945; children—Sandra, Emilou, Paula. With Albuquerque Nat. Bank, 1935—, asst. cashier, auditor, 1948-53, asst. v.p., auditor, 1953-56, v.p., auditor, 1956-63, v.p., controller, 1963-65, sr. v.p., controller, 1965—. Pres., N.M. Conf. Meth. Found. Trustee McMurry Coll., Manzana Day Sch. Served with AUS, 1941-45; ETO, PTO. Mem. Assn. for Bank Audit, Control and Operation (past state v.p.). Clubs: Four Hills Country, Albuquerque Petroleum. Home: 6918 Shoshone Rd NE Albuquerque NM 87110 Office: 123 Central Av NW Albuquerque NM 87101

BARNES, RALPH M., educator, indsl. engr.; b. Clifton Mills, W.Va., Oct. 17, 1900 s. John J. and Martha (Mosser) B.; B.S. in Mech. Engring., U. of W.Va., 1923, M.E., 1928; M.S., Cornell U., 1924, Ph.D., 1933; m. Mary Goodykoontz, June 13, 1931; children—Elizabeth, Carolyn Martha. Asst. to chief engr., U.S. Window Glass Co., Morgantown, W.Va., June-Sept., 1923; asst. engr. on product devel. Bausch & Lomb Optical Co., Rochester, N.Y., 1924-25; indsl. engr. The Gleason Works, Rochester, N.Y., 1925-26; instr. in indsl. mgmt. dept. of bus. orgn. and operation Coll. of Commerce, U. Ill., 1926-28; indsl. engr. Eastman Kodak Co., Kodak Park Works and Camera Works, Rochester, N.Y., summers, 1927-28-29, 30, 34, 35; cons. indsl. engr. Kodak Ltd., London, Eng., summer 1936, Dow Chem. Co., summer 1942; asst. prof. indsl. engring. mech. engring. dept. Coll. of Engring. U. Ia., 1928-30, asso. prof., 1930-34, prof., 1934-49, dir. of personnel, 1936-49, also dir. summer mgmt. course, 1939-48; now emeritus prof. engring. and prodn. mgmt. U. Cal. at Los Angeles. Served as cons. engr. during World War II. Cons. Fedn. Norwegian Industries, Swedish Industries, 1950; cons. to F.U.N.S.A., Montevideo, Uruguay, 1958, Spain, Mexico, Costa Rica, Japan, Peru, 1958-63. Recipient U. Mo. Honor award for distinguished service in engring., 1967. Fellow Internat. Acad. Mgmt., Soc. Advancement Mgmt. (Gilbreth Medal, 1941; Indsl. Incentive Award, 1951), Am. Soc. M.E., Am. Inst. Indsl. Engrs. (Frank & Lillian Gilbretis Indsl. Engring. award 1969), A.A.A.S.; mem. Indsl. Mgmt. Soc., Am. Mgmt. Assn., Am. Soc. Engring. Edn., Tau Beta Pi, Sigma Xi, Sigma Iota Epsilon, Pi Tau Sigma, Alpha Pi Mu, Beta Gamma Sigma. Author: Work Measurement Manual, 1951; Motion and Time Study; Design and Measurement of Work, 6th edit., 1968; Work Sampling, 2d edit., 1957. Home: 12304 Fifth Helena Dr Los Angeles CA 90049

BARNES, REID BOYLSTON, lawyer; b. Opelika, Ala., Aug. 4, 1903; s. Reid Boylston and Lillie (Barnet) B.; B.S., Auburn U., 1923; LL.B., U. Ala., 1926; m. Nell Woodall, Jan. 29, 1940; children—Celeta (Mrs. Duncan Young Manley), Lyndall (Mrs.

Joseph Byrns Hutchison, Jr.), Reid Boylston. Admitted to Ala. bar, 1926; practice in Opelika, 1926-29, Birmingham, 1929—; partner Barnes, Walker & Barnes, 1926-27; partner Walker & Barnes, 1927; pvt. practice, 1928-29; asso. W.H. McGowen, 1929-30; asso. Lange, Simpson & Brantley, 1930-35; mem. firm Lange, Simpson, Robinson & Somerville, 1935—; atty. Birmingham Sch. Bd., 1958—; tchr. Birmingham Sch. Law, 1935-41. Rep. State of Ala. in Voting Rights Act case, State Dept. Pensions and Securities before Dept. Health, Edn. and Welfare in U.S. Dist. Ct., U.S. Ct. of Appeals, Supreme Ct. U.S. against charges of violation civil rights act. Vice pres. Baggett Transp. Co. Served to lt. col., Judge Adv. Gen. Dept., AUS, 1942-46. Decorated Legion of Merit. Mem. Am. Legion (past post vice comdr., adjutant), Phi Beta Kappa, Phi Delta Theta, Phi Delta Phi, Omicron Delta Kappa. Elk. Clubs: Mountain Brook (Ala.) Exchange; Birmingham Country. Home: 2524 Aberdeen Rd Birmingham AL 35223 Office: City Fed Bldg Birmingham AL 35203

BARNES, RICHARD GEORGE, educator, physicist; b. Milw., Dec. 19, 1922; s. George Richard and Irma (Ott) B.; B.A., U. Wis., 1948; M.A., Dartmouth Coll., 1949; Ph.D., Harvard U., 1952; m. Mildred A. Jachens, Sept. 9, 1950; children—Jeffrey R., David G., Christina E., Douglas A. Teaching fellow Harvard, 1950-52; asst. prof. U. Del., 1952-55, asso. prof., 1955-56; asso. prof. Ia. State U., 1956-60, prof., 1960—, chmn. dept. physics, 1971—; sr. physicist Ames Lab., AEC, 1960—, chief physics div., 1971—; vis. research prof. Cal. Inst. Tech., 1962-63. Served with USAAF, 1942-43, C.E., AUS, 1944-46. Fellow Am. Phys. Soc.; mem. Am. Assn. Physics Tchrs., Phys. Soc. Japan, Sigma Xi. Home: 1221 Michigan Av Ames IA 50010

BARNES, RICHARD HENRY, dean; b. San Diego, Cal., June 29, 1911; s. Willard Gray and Nell (Tribby) B.; B.A., San Diego State Coll., 1933; Ph.D., U. Minn., 1940; m. Marjorie Ironside, Mar. 24, 1942; children—Kyle, Marjorie Anne, Lisa. Research chemist Scripps Metabolic Clinic, La Jolla, Cal., 1933-37; teaching asst., then instr., asst. prof. U. Minn., 1937-44; dir. biochem. research, asso. dir. research Sharp & Dohme Research Labs., 1944-56; dean Grad. Sch. Nutrition, Cornell U., 1956—; hon. prof. biochemistry Rutgers U., 1948-56. Adv. council Masonic Med. Research Labs., Utica, N.Y. Mem. com. on nutrition-adv. bd. on mil. personnel supplies Nat. Acad. Scis.-NRC, chmn. com., 1964-68, mem. Food and Nutrition Bd., 1969—, chmn. com. on food standards and fortification policy, 1970—; mem. U.S. Nat. Com. of Internat. Union Nutritional Scis., NRC-Nat. Acad. Scis., 1970—. Fellow A.A.A.S., N.Y. Acad. Scis.; mem. Am. Chem. Soc. (chmn. div. biol. chemistry 1951-53), Am. Soc. Biol. Chemists, Am. Inst. Nutrition (pres. 1968-69), Soc. Exptl. Biology and Medicine, Nutrition Soc. (Britain), Group European Nutritionists, Sigma Xi. Editorial bd. Jour. Nutrition, 1948-51, editor, 1959-69. Contbr. profl. jours. Home: 140 N Sunset Dr Ithaca NY 14850

BARNES, ROBERT BOWLING, scientist, corp. exec.; b. Montgomery, Ala., June 9, 1906; s. Elly Ruff and Ula (Bowling) B.; A.B., Birmingham-So. Coll., 1925; Ph.D., Johns Hopkins, 1929; m. Eva Hoffman, Aug. 8, 1933; children—Robert Bowling, George McIlwaine. Instr. Birmingham-So. Coll., 1924-25; high sch. tchr. The Barnes Sch., Montgomery, 1925-26; Nat. Research fellow U. Berlin and Breslau, Germany, 1930-32; tchr. physics Johns Hopkins, 1932-33, Princeton, 1933-36; joined staff Am. Cyanamid Co., 1936, organized div. for application phys. tools, and methods to indsl. chem. problems, dir. physics div. Stamford Research labs., 1936-48; v.p. charge research and devel. Am. Optical Co., 1948-51; pres., dir. Barnes Engring. Co., 1952-71, chmn. bd., dir., 1971—; dir. Union Trust Co. Mem. adv. com. to research and devel. br. Office Q.M., Nat. Research Council; mem. optics adv. com. Inst. Optics, U. Rochester. Fellow Am. Phys. Soc., N.Y. Acad. Scis.; mem. Phi Beta Kappa, Sigma Xi, Gamma Alpha, Omicron Delta Kappa. Clubs: Woodway Country, Stamford Yacht. Author sci. publs. Inventor, patentee. Home: Westover Rd Stamford CT 06902 Office: 30 Commerce Rd Stamford CT 06904

BARNES, ROBERT DRANE, educator; b. New Orleans, Apr. 3, 1927; s. Henry Drane and Katharine (Talmage) B.; B.S., Davidson Coll., 1949; Ph.D., Duke, 1953; m. Betty Jean Martin, Jan. 17, 1953; children—Katherine Elizabeth, Edward Martin, David Talmage. Research asso. Rice U., 1954-55; mem. faculty Gettysburg Coll., 1955—, prof. biology, 1963—, chmn. dept., 1965-70; vis. prof. zoology Duke Marine Lab., 1965-67, 71. Mem. Air Pollution Control Assn. Pa., 1968—. Served with USNR, 1945-46. Mem. A.A.A.S., Marine Biol. Assn. U.K., Am. Soc. Zoologists (chmn. invertebrate div. 1966-67), Soc. Systematic Zoology, Phi Beta Kappa, Sigma Xi. Author articles in field. Author: Invertebrate Zoology, 2d edit., 1968. Home: 309 Ridge Av Gettysburg PA 17325

BARNES, ROBERT GAYLORD, corp. exec.; b. Battle Creek, Mich., Oct. 18, 1914; s. George Emerson and Myrtle Kendall (Montague) B.; grad. Haverford Sch., 1933; A.B., Princeton, 1937, postgrad., 1938-39; Yen-ching U., 1937-38; M.A., Yale, 1942; m. Natalie Jane Stirling, Apr. 10, 1942; children—George Emerson, Jane Stirling. Instr. Yale, part-time 1940-42; spl. asst. to dir. European Affairs Dept. State, 1945-47, chief policy reports staff, 1948-51, dep. dir. Exec. Secretariat, 1951-52; apptd. to permanent internat. staff N. Atlantic Treaty Orgn., 1952; adviser to Sec. State various internat. confs., 1949-52; dep. exec. sec. NATO, 1953-55; sec. Four Power and Nine Power confs. in Paris, 1954; dir., exec. secretariat Dept. State, 1955-56, spl. asst. mut. security affairs, 1956-59; counselor embassy, Ankara, Turkey, 1959-62, minister-counselor, dep. chief mission, 1962-64; ambassador to Jordan, 1964-66; internat. affairs adviser Mobil Oil Corp., N.Y.C., 1966-67, mgr. internat. govt. relations, 1967—. Bd. dirs. Middle East Inst. Served AUS, 1942-45. Mem. Council Fgn. Relations, Fgn. Policy Assn., Phi Beta Kappa. Presbyn. Club: Princeton (N.Y.C.). Home: 58 Colonial Av Dobbs Ferry NY 10522 Office: 150 E 42d St New York City NY 10017

BARNES, ROBERT GOODWIN, publishing co. exec.; b. Augusta, Ga., Sept. 1, 1914; s. John Andrew and Charlotte R. (Jones) B.; A.B., Columbia, 1937; m. Helen Z. Jeffries, June 21, 1941; children—Susan Jeffries, John Andrew II, Frances Goodwin. With Procter & Gamble, 1937-42, B. Heller & Co., 1946-47; with Doubleday & Co., Inc., N.Y.C., 1947-51, 52-69, v.p., 1964-69; pres., dir. Columbia U. Press, 1969—. Served to lt. comdr. USNR, 1942-46, 51-52. Home: 40 E 83d St New York City NY 10028 Office: 562 W 113th St New York City NY 10025

BARNES, ROBERT MERTON, artist; b. Washington, Sept. 24, 1934; s. Mahlon Willis and Marjorie (Bain) B.; B.F.A., Art Inst. Chgo., 1956; B.F.A., U. Chgo., 1956; postgrad. Columbia, 1956, Hunter Coll., 1957-60, U. London Slade Sch., 1961-63; m. Lia Sayers, Sept. 22, 1956; children—Catlin Sayers, Forrest MacKay. Exhibited in one man shows at Allan Frumkin Gallery, N.Y.C., 1963, 65, 66-67, Chgo., 1961, 64, Gallerie Du Dragon, Paris, 1966-67; exhibited in group shows Art Inst. Chgo., 1955, 58, 60, 61, 63. Exhbn. Momentum, 1952-55, Cliff Dwellers Print Exhbn., Chgo., 1955, U. Chgo., 1956, Rockford Coll., 1956, Boston Arts Festival, 1958, U. Ia., 1960, U. Colo., 1961, Am. Fedn. Arts Traveling Exhbn., 1961, 65, David Herbert Gallery, N.Y.C., 1961 Ravinia Exhbn., 1961, U. Ind., 1961, Galerie Du Dragon, Paris, 1962, Whitney Mus. Am. Art, 1962-65, Yale, 1962, Kansas City Art Inst., 1962-63, Allan Frumkin Gallery, Chgo. N.Y.C., 1960, 63, San Francisco Mus. Fine Arts, 1963, Mus. Modern Art, N.Y.C., 1963, 65, Exhbn. Palazzo D'Accursio, Bologna, 1965, Ind. U. Mus., 1965, Larry Aldrich Mus., 1965, Pa. Acad. Fine Art, 1965, 66, Va. Mus. Fine Arts, 1966, Burpee Art Gallery, 1965, R.I. Sch. Design, 1965, 1966, Parrish Art Mus., 1965; represented in permanent collections Mus. Modern Art, Whitney Mus. Am. Art, Chgo. Art Inst., Pasadena Mus. Art; faculty Ind. U., summers 1960-61; vis. artist Kansas City Art Inst., 1963-64; asso. prof. Ind. U. 1965—. Recipient award Copleyy Found., 1961; Fulbright grant, 1961-62, 1962-63. Home: 501 N Washington St Bloomington IN 47401 Office: care Allan Frumkin Gallery 41 E 57th St New York City NY 10022

BARNES, ROGER WILLIAM, physician; b. Littleton, Colo., Sept. 22, 18O7; s. William Jull and Ada (Jull) B.; A.B., Pacific Union Coll., 1922; M.D., Coll. Med. 1922; M.S., U. So. Cal., 1939; D.Sc., U. Okayama, Japan, 1954; m. Oca Davis, Mar. 23, 1923; children—Bonnie Rae (Mrs. H. Hadley). Joanne (Mrs. C. Fisher), Joelle (Mrs. D. Emery), Richard (dec.), Duane, Dwight (dec.). Intern Los Angeles County Hosp., 1922-23, resident in urology, 1923-25; pvt. practice medicine specializing in urology, Los Angeles, 1925—; instr. urology Loma Linda U. Sch. Medicine, 1925-30, asst. prof., 1930-36, asso. prof., 1936-44, prof. surgery, 1944-65, distinguished service prof. urology, 1965—, chmn. sect. surgery, 1948-63; chief dept. urology White Meml. Hosp., 1928-65; sr. attending surgeon, urology Los Angeles County Hosp., 1935-64, chmn. urology staff, 1957-60; sr. surgeon (resident) USPHS, 1942-61. Diplomate Am. Bd. Urology. Fellow A.C.S., Internat. Coll. Surgeons; mem. A.M.A. (chmn. urology sect. 1958), Am. Urol. Assn., Cal., Los Angeles County (v.p. 1961, sec.-treas. 1963) med. assns. Republican. Seventh-day Adventist. Author: Endoscopic Prostatic Surgery, 1943; Urological Practice, 1954; Endoscopy, 1958; Urology Review, 1967; also articles med. jours. Home: 4804 Hillard Av La Canada, CA 91011. Office: 1700 Brooklyn Av Los Angeles CA 90033

BARNES, RUSSELL, fgn. news analyst; b. Huntington, Ind., Aug. 31, 1897; s. James F. and Lucy A. (Stewart) B.; A.B., U. Mich., 1920; m. Constance Ingalls, Oct. 1, 1927; chhildren—Lucie J. (Mrs. T.T. Seymour), John J. Fgn. corr. Detroit News, 1925-31, 41-53, Washington corr., 1931-32, fgn. news columnist, radio commentator Detroit News Sta. WWJ, 1932-41, London corr., 1941, fgn. news analyst, 1953-70, contbr. articles, 1970—. Lectr. fgn., domestic politics Oakland U., Oakland Community Coll. Staff radio div. OWI, 1942, dir. Cairo Bur., 1943; asst. to Am. ambassador to Egypt, 1943; Am. press officer Cairo and Tehran confs., 1943; dir. psychol. warfare bur. Allied Force Hdqrs., Algiers and Caserta, 1944-45. Recipient exceptional Civilian Service medal War Dept. Mem. Phi Delta Theta. Home: 788 Randall Ct Birmingham MI 48009 Office: Detroit News Detroit MI 48226

BARNES, STANLEY NELSON, judge; b. Baraboo, Wis., May 1, 1900; s. Charles Luling and Janet (Rankin) B.; A.B., U. Cal., 1922, J.D., 1925, LL.D., 1961; student Harvard Law Sch., 1923-24; m. Anne Fisk, Oct. 18, 1929; children—Janet Anne Hansen, Judith Fisk Melkesian, Joyce Rankin Robinson. Admitted to Cal. bar, 1925; practiced in San Francisco, 1925-28, Los Angeles, 1928-46; lectr. law U. So. Cal., 1947-52, forensic medicine, 1950-59; judge superior ct., Los Angeles, 1947-53, presiding judge Los Angeles County, 1952-53; asst. atty. gen., anti-trust div. Dept. Justice, 1953-56; judge U.S. 9th Circuit Ct. Appeals, 1956-70, sr. judge, 1970—. Mem. President's Conf. Adminstrv. Proc., 1953; co-chmn. Atty. Gen.'s Nat. Com. Study Antitrust Laws, 1953-55; adv. council appellate rules jud. Conf. U.S., 1956-66; adv. council Practising Law Inst. Bd. dirs. S.W. Mus., Los Angeles, Regent U. Cal., 1946-48. Named Alumnus of Year, U. Cal., 1966, Boalt Hall Sch. Law, U. Cal., 1967. Berkeley fellow, 1969. Fellow Am. Bar Found., Am. Coll. Trial Lawyers, Am. Acad. Forensic sci.; mem. Fed. (nat. pres. 1954-55), Am. (chmn. sect. jud. adminstrn. 1966-67), Cal., San Francisco, Los Angeles, (Shattuck-Price distinguished service award 1971), N.Y.C. bar assns., Am. Judicature Soc., Inst. Jud. Adminstrn., Cal. Alumni Assn. (pres. 1946-48), Phi Delta Phi. Sigma Chi (nat. pres. 1952-55, nat. trustee 1950-52). Episcopalian. Adv. bd. Anti-Trust. Bull. Mem. Foothall Hall of Fame. Home: 747 S Orange Grove Av Pasadena CA 91105 Office: U S Courthouse Los Angeles CA 90012

BARNES, WALLACE, lawyer, mfg. exec.; b. Bristol, Conn., Mar. 22, 1926; s. Harry Clarke and Lillian (Houbertz) B.; grad. Deerfield Acad.; B.A., Williams Coll., 1949; LL.B., Yale, 1952; m. Audrey Kent, June 14, 1947 (div. Aug. 1962); children—Thomas Oliver, Jarre Ann; m. 2d, Mrs. Frederick B. Hollister, Jr.; 1 son (adopted), Frederick Hollister. Admitted to Conn. bar, 1952; asso. firm Beach, Calder & Barnes, and predecessor, Bristol, 1953-55, partner, 1956-62; exec. v.p. Asso. Spring Corp., 1962-64, pres., 1964—, asst. to treas. Northeast Airlines, Inc., Boston, 1951; dir. mem. trust com. Northside Bank & Trust Co.; dir. Bristol Savs. Bank, Planned Investment Fund, Boston, Wallace Barnes, Ltd., Broadbent & Co., Rochdale, Eng., Tevema Co., Amsterdam, Aetna Life & Casualty Co., Resortes Argentina S.A., Cordoba. Pres. Bristol Community Chest, New Eng. Council, 1956; dir., mem. exec. com. Bristol Boys Club, pres., 1965—. Nominee for Congress, 1st Congl. Dist. Conn., 1954; town chmn., Bristol, 1954; mem. Conn. Senate from 5th Dist., 1958-62, from 8th Dist., 1967-70, minority leader, 1969. Bd. dirs. Westledge Sch., Simsbury, Conn. Served as aviation cadet USAAF, 1944-45. Recipient distinguished service award Bristol Jr. C. of C. Mem. Am. Bar Assn., Hartford County Mfrs. Assn. (pres. 1965-68), Am. Legion. Republican. Episcopalian. Elk. Clubs: Economic, Yale, Williams (N.Y.C.); N.Y. Amateur Ski. Home: 50 High St Farmington CT 06032 Office: 18 Main St Bristol CT 06010

BARNES, WILFRED EATON, educator, mathematician; b. Oak Park, Ill., June 3, 1924; s. Guy Leslie and Nellie (Straw) B.; S.B., U. Chgo., 1949, S.M., 1950; Ph.D., U. B.C., 1954; m. Bernice Elizabeth Michaels, Aug. 24, 1946; children—Julia Kathryn, Karen Wanda. From instr. to prof. math. Wash. State U., 1954- 66; prof. math., head dept. Ia. State U., 1966—. Served to 2d lt. USAAF, 1943- 46. Mem. Am Math. Soc., Math. Assn. Am., Soc. Indsl. and Applied Math., Nat. Council Tchrs. Math., A.A.A.S., Sigma Xi, Phi Kappa Phi. Mem. United Ch. Christ. Author: Introduction Abstract Algebra, 1963; (with others) Fundamental Concepts of Arithmetic, 1963; also articles. Home: 511 Oliver Circle Ames IA 50010

BARNES, WILLIAM ALEXANDER, physician; b. N.Y.C., Jan 7, 1912; s. William E. and Jessie (Milne) B.; B.A., Coll. City N.Y., 1933; M.D., Cornell, 1937; m. Shirley Mayer, July 1945; childrenWilliam Christopher, Esme Alexandra, Robin Bruce, George Evan. Intern surgery N.Y. Hosp., 1937-38, asst. resident surgeon, 1938-41, 42-43, resident surgeon, 1943-44, asst. attending surgeon, 1946- 51, asso. attending surgeon, 1951-57, attending surgeon, 1957—; instr. surgery Cornell U. Med. Coll., 1943-44, asst. prof. clin. surgery, 1944-46, clin. asso. prof. surgery, 1946-67, clin. prof. surgery, 1967—; asst. resident surgeon Bellevue Hosp., 1941-42; cons. surgery Valley Hosp., Ridgewood, N.J.; cons. thoracic surgery Vets. Hosp., Montrose, N.Y. Fellow N.Y. Acad. Medicine; mem. Soc. Univ. Surgeons, N.Y. County, N.Y. State med. socs., A.M.A., Am. Assn. Cancer Research, N.Y. Surg. Soc. Contbr. articles profl. jours. Home: 303 E Franklin Turnpike Ho-Ho-Kus NJ 07423 Office: 862 Fifth Av New York City NY 10021

BARNES, WILLIAM OLIVER, Jr., lawyer; b. Balt., Mar. 18, 1922; s. William Oliver and Jane Ann (Krug) B.; A.B., Hamilton Coll., 1943; J.D., Rutgers U., 1948; m. Marilyn Louise Isenberg, July 13, 1945; children—William Oliver 3d, Patrick Douglas, Timothy Lee, Jefferson Todd. Admitted to N.J. bar, 1949; asso. Judge R. J. Wortendyke, Jr., Newark, 1949-52; pvt. practice specializing trial work, Newark, 1952—. Chmn. Rutgers U. Bond Com., 1959, pres. Rutgers Sch. Law Alumni Assn., 1960-61, Alumni Fedn., 1962-63, Univ., 1962—; v.p., asso. counsel N.J. Cancer Soc., 1963-65, pres., asso. counsel, 1965-68, counsel, 1968—, dir., del., 1971; mem. West Branch (N.J.) Bd. Edn., 1961-64; chmn. South Orange March of Dimes, 1959; pres. Monmouth Players, 1961-62. Mem. N.J. Assembly from Essex County, 1952-55, majority leader, 1955; Republican candidate for Congress, 1952; chmn. South Orange Rep. County Com., 1954-58, N.J. Young Reps., 1954-56. Served to lt. (j.g.) USNR, 1943-46. Recipient Gold medal Rutgers U., 1960. Fellow Am. Coll. Trial Lawyers; mem. Am., N.J., Essex County, Monmouth County bar assns., Trial Attys. N.J. (pres. 1971-72), Delta Kappa Epsilon, Delta Sigma Rho. Methodist. Mason (Shriner). Clubs: Orange Lawn Tennis; Monmouth Beach Bath and Tennis, Channel (Monmouth Beach); Downtown (Newark). Home: 23 Arlene Dr West Long Branch NJ 07764 Office: 1180 Raymond Blvd Newark NJ 07102

BARNES, WILLIAM P., oil co. exec.; b. Marlin, Tex., May 31, 1920; s. William P. and Katharine E. (Horne) B.; B.A., So. Meth. U., 1947, LL.B., 1949; m. Sally Temple, Oct. 20, 1950; children—William P., Joseph L., James H., and Thomas L. Admitted to Tex. bar, 1949, practiced Dallas, 1949-53; atty. Gen. Am. Oil Co. of Tex., 1953-54, v.p., 1955-60, exec. v.p., gen. counsel, 1960-66, dir., 1960—, pres., 1966—; chmn. bd. Meadows Bldg. Corp., 1966—; dir. Premier Petrochem. Co., Stockton, Whatley, Davin & Co. Served from pvt. to maj. AUS, 1942-46. Mem. Am., Tex., Dallas bar assns., Kappa Sigma, Phi Alpha Delta, Blue Key. Clubs: Petroleum, Texas, City (Dallas); Deerwood, Ponte Vedra (Jacksonville, Fla.). Editor in chief Southwestern Law Jour., 1948. Home: 3629 Princeton Av Dallas TX 75205 Office: Meadows Bldg Dallas TX 75206

BARNES, WILLIAM P., educator; B.S. in Mech. Engring., U. Ida.; M. Mech. Engring., Yale. Prof. mech. engring., chmn. dept. nuclear engring., U. Ida., Moscow. Office: Dept Engring U Ida Moscow ID 83843*

BARNES, ZANE EDISON, communications co. exec.; b. Marietta, O., Dec. 2, 1921; s. Emmet A. and Frances (Canfield) B.; B.S., Marietta Coll., 1947; m. Virginia Harris, May 29, 1948; children-Frances Lynn, Zane Edison, Shelley. With Ohio Bell Telephone Co., 1941-59, asst. v.p. operations, Cleve., 1961-63, gen. plant mgr., 1963-64, v.p. personnel, 1965-67; with engring. dept. Am. Tel. & Tel. Co., N.Y.C., 1960-61; v.p., gen. mgr. Ore. area Pacific N.W. Bell Telephone Co., Portland, Ore., 1964-65, v.p. operations, 1967- 70, pres., Seattle, 1970—; dir. Nat. Bank Commerce, Seattle. Mem. Gov.'s Adv. Com. Wash. Dept. Commerce and Econ. Devel., 1970—. Mem. adv. nd. Grad. Sch. Bus. Adminstrn., U. Wash., 1970—; bd. dirs. United Good Neighbors; trustee Pacific Sci. Center, Seattle Symphony Orch. Served to lt. (j.g.) USNR, 1942-46. Mem. Seattle C. of C. (trustee), Seattle Area Indsl. Council (dir.), Kappa Mu Epsilon. Clubs: Rainer, Wash. Athletic, Harbor, Mercerwood Shore (Seattle); Overlake Golf and Country (Bellevue, Wash.); Arlington (Portland). Home: 4245 Mercerwood Dr Mercer Island WA 98040 Office: 821 2d Av Seattle WA 98104

BARNESS, AMNON, corp. exec.; b. Tel Aviv, Israel, Oct. 16, 1924; s. Nahum R. and Lea (Muhlmann) B.; certificate, Hebrew U., Jerusalem, 1942; B.A., Am. U., Cairo, 1947; M.A., Syracuse U., 1950; m. Lillian Sarkin, June 20, 1947; children—Rena Tamar, Dalia Ruth, Daniel Isaac, Jordan Gerson. Came to U.S., 1947, naturalized, 1951. Vice pres. ISECO Securities Corp. subsidiary Ampal Corp., Chgo., 1950-52, Los Angeles, 1952-57; dir. devel. Fed. Mart Corp., San Diego, 1957-60; chmn. bd. Daylin, Inc., Beverly Hills, Cal., 1960—; pres. Internat. Merc. Corp., Los Angeles, 1960-65; chmn. finance com., dir. A & E Plastik Pak Co., Inc.; sr. partner Adam Assos. Chmn. Guardian div. Israel Bonds, Los Angeles, 1966, So. Cal. chmn., 1968-70; pres. Fund for Job Corps Grad. Fund, 1966; pres. Barness, Candiotty and Finkle Found.; v.p. Brandeis (Cal.) Inst.; pres. So. region Am. Friends Hebrew U.; chmn. bd. trustees Israel Publ. Soc.; trustee U.S. Capitol Hist. Soc. Decorated knight comdr. Equestrian Order, Ch. Holy Sepulchre of Jerusalem. Jewish religion (dir. temple). Author: History of the Israel Press, 1961. Home: 628 N Arden Dr Beverly Hills CA 90210 Office: 9606 Santa Monica Blvd Beverly Hills CA 90210

BARNET, EDWARD MALCOLM, educator; b. Brookline, Mass., May 29, 1912; s. Lucius Jean and Stella (Kohn) B.; grad. Phillips Exeter Acad., Andover, Mass., 1930; A.B. cum laude, Harvard, 1934, M.B.A., 1936; Ph.D., Columbia, 1954; m. Orpah Rice Paul, Nov. 26, 1936; 1 dau., Holly Jane (Mrs. Clifford A. Frohlich). Mem. marketing faculty Mich. State U., Buffalo U., U. Toronto, Northwestern U., 1947-63; prof. marketing, dir. Mgmt. Inst., Northwestern U., 1954-59; prof. marketing, also dir. programs mass marketing mgmt. Mich. State U., 1959-63; former asst. dean, co-ordinator exec. program Columbia; v.p. planning Sara Lee Kitchens, Inc., 1963-65; asso. dean Coll. Bus. Adminstrn., dir. Sch. Travel Industry Mgmt., U. Hawaii, 1965-68, acting dean of Coll., 1968-69, dean Sch. Travel Industry Mgmt., 1967—, prof. marketing and mgmt., 1969—; dir. AMP program Creole Petroleum Corp., Caracas, Venezuela, 1956-57. Cons. in field; dir. Hawaiian Life Ins. Co., Pacific Basin Travel Systems, Marshall Field & Co., Chgo. Served to maj. Office Mil. Govt. for Germany, AUS, World War II. Decorated Bronze Star medal. Mem. Hawaii Vis. Bur., Pacific Area Travel Assn., Am. Mgmt. Assn., Am. Marketing Assn., Beta Gamma Sigma, Pi Sigma Epsilon, Alpha Kappa Psi. Rotarian. Author: Innovate or Perish, 1954; also articles. Home: 2115 Atherton Rd Honolulu HI 96822

BARNET, SYLVAN, educator; b. Bklyn., Dec. 11, 1926; s. Philip and Esther (Katz) B.; A.B., N.Y. U., 1948; A.M., Harvard, 1950, Ph.D., 1954. Teaching fellow Harvard, 1951-54; mem. faculty Tufts U., 1954—, chmn. dept. English, 1962-67, Fletcher prof. English, 1963-; editorial cons. Little, Brown and Co. Served with AUS, 1945-46. Mem. Modern Lang. Assn., Shakespeare Assn., Renaissance Soc. Author: (with M. Berman and W. Burto) The Study of Literature, 1960, An Introduction to Literature, 4d edit., 1971; also essays. Editor: (with M. Berman and W. Burto) Tragedy and Comedy, 1967; also other anthologies; gen. editor Signet Shakespeare, 1963-69. Home: 29 Ash St Cambridge, MA 02138. Office: East Hall Tufts Univ Medford MA 02155

BARNET, WILL, artist, art educator; b. Beverly, Mass., May 25, 1911; s. Noah and Sarah (Toahnich) B.; student Boston Mus. Fine Arts Sch., 1927-30, Art Students League, N.Y. City 1930-33; m. Mary Sinclair, Feb., 1935 (div.); children—Peter George, Richard Sinclair, Todd Williams; m. 2d, Elean Ona Ciurlys, Mar. 4, 1953; 1 dau., Ona Willa. Instr. painting Art Students League, N.Y.C., 1946—; faculty Cooper Union, N.Y.C., 1945—, prof., 1965—; instr., critic Pa. Acad., Phila., 1967—; faculty Famous Artists Painting Course, Westport, Conn., 1954—, Mont. State Coll., summer 1951, Summer Artists Workshop, Regina Coll., U. Saskatchewan (Can.), 1957; instr.

advanced painting U. Minn. at Duluth, summer 1959, Wash. State U., Spokane, summer 1963, Pa. State U., summer 1965, Des Moines Art Center, summer 1965; distinguished vis. prof. Pa. State U., 1965-66; vis. critic Yale, 1952-53; vis. prof. Cornell U., 1968-69; condr. grand art tour of Europe, April, 1959; Ford Found. artist in residence program, 1964. One-man show at Hudson D. Walker Gallery, 1938, Galerie St. Etienne, 1943; Berthe Schaefer Gallery, Arthur Harlow & Co., Inc. (all N.Y.C.), 1946; U.S. Nat. Museum, Washington, 1946; Bertha Schaefer Gallery, N.Y.C., 1947, 48, Krasner Gallery, N.Y.C., Gallery Trastevere, Rome, Italy, 1960, Retrospective Inst. of Contemporary Art, Boston, 1961, Mary Harriman Gallery, Boston, 1963, 64, Va. Mus., Richmond, 1964, Waddell Gallery, N.Y.C., 1965, 66, 68, 70, Des Moines Art Center, 1965, retrospective, Pa. Acad. Phila., 1969; exhibited in Art U.S.A., 1959. Work represented in permanent collections of Minn. Inst. of Arts, Metropolitan (N.Y.C.), Fogg Art Museum, Library of Congress, Art Gallery, U.N.D., Univ. Art Gallery, Berkeley, Cal., Cin. Art Mus., Duncan Phillip Memorial Museum (Washington, D.C.), Philadelphia Art Mus., Honolulu Acad. (Hawaii), Mus. Modern Art, Bklyn. Mus., Mont. State Coll., Whitney Mus. Am. Art, Mus. Fine Arts (Boston), Guggenheim Museum (N.Y.C.). Exhibited in museums throughtout U. S., including Art Inst. Chgo., Los Angeles Museum, Portland Museum, John Herron Inst., Carnegie Inst., Virginia Mus. Fine Arts, Columbia (S.C.), Mus. Art (1st Biennial). Recipient bronze medal, 3d prize, Corcoran Biennial, 1961. Life mem. Art Students League (N.Y. City), Phila. Print Club. Mem. Am. Abstract Artists, Soc. Am. Graphic Artists, Inc., Fedn. Modern Painters and Sculptors, Inc. Liberal. Unitarian. Contbr. Art Students League Mag. Home: 43 W 90th ST New York City NY 10024 Office: 215 W 57th St New York City NY 10019

BARNETSON, WILLIAM DENHOLM, publisher; b. Edinburgh, Scotland, Mar. 21, 1917; s. William and Ella (Moir) B.; M.A., Edinburgh U., 1940; m. Joan Fairley Davidson, July 6, 1940; children—Astraea (Mrs. J.R.D. Moore), Louise, Denholm, Julia. Mng. editor Edinburgh (Scotland) Ev. News, 1954-61; joint mng. dir. United Newspapers, London, Eng., 1961—, chmn., 1965—; chmn. Reuters, London, 1968—. Chmn. Press Assn. London, 1967-68; mem. Press Council London, 1968—; dir. publns. N.W. Germany, 1945-48. Served to maj. Brit. Army, 1940-44. Fellow Inst. Dirs. (London). Home: Broom Chillies Lane Crowborough Sussex England Office: 23 27 Tudor St London EC 4 England

BARNETT, ARTHUR DOAK, educator, polit. scientist; b. Shanghai, China, Oct. 8, 1921 (parents U.S. Citizens); s. Eugene Epperson and Bertha Mae (Smith) B.; B.A., Yale, 1942, M.A., 1947, certificate Chinese, 1947; Doctor of Laws, Franklin and Marshall Coll., 1967; m. Jeanne Hathaway Badeau, Mar. 22, 1954; children—Katherine Hathaway, Stewart Doak, Martha Jeanne. Fellow Inst. Current World Affairs in China and S.E. Asia, 1947-50, 52-53; corr. Chgo. Daily News, 1947-50, 52-53, 53-55; cons. ECA, 1950-51; consul, pub. affairs officer Am. consulate-gen., Hong Kong, 1951-52; asso. Am. Univs. Field Staff, 1953-55; head dept. fgn. area studies Fgn. Service Inst., State Dept., 1956-57; research fellow Council Fgn. Relations, 1958-59; program asso. Ford Found., 1959-61; prof. polit. sci. Columbia, 1961-69; senior fellow Brookings Instn., 1969—. Mem. joint com. contemporary China. Social Sci. Research Council and Am. Council Learned Socs., 1963-64, 65-67, chmn., 1963-64, sub-com. Chinese govt., 1965—; exec. com. Internat. Com. Chinese Studies, 1963-65; bd. dirs. Nat. Com. on U.S.-China Relations, 1966—, chmn. bd. dirs., 1968-69; mem. adv. panel on China, Dept. State, 1966-69; vis. com. E. Asian civilizations Harvard, 1962-64; chmn. contemporary China studies com. Columbia, 1961-67; mem. Inst. Current World Affairs, 1958-60, 66—, bd. govs., 1960-66, liaison com. study contemporary China, 1965-70; mem. com. on scholarly communication with mainland China, Nat. Acad. Scis.-Am. Council Learned Socs.-Social Sci. Research Council, 1970—. Served to capt. USMCR, 1942-46. Mem. Am. Polit. Sci. Assn. (chmn. Conf. on Communist Studies 1965-66), Assn. Asian Studies (dir. 1962-65), Asia Soc. (council on Chinese affairs), Council on Fgn. Relations (steering com. Project on U.S. and China in World Affairs 1962-66), UN Assn. (China panel 1966-67), Phi Beta Kappa. Author: Communist Economic Strategy: The Rise of Mainland China, 1959; Communist China and Asia: Challenge to American Policy, 1960; Communist China in Perspective, 1962; China on the Eve of Communist Takeover, 1963; Communist China: The Early Years, 1964; Cadres, Bureaucracy and Political Power in Communist China, 1967; China after Mao, 1967; A New U.S. Policy Toward China, 1970. Editor: Communist Strategies in Asia: A Comparative Analysis of Governments and Parties, 1963; United States and China in World Affairs, 1966; Chinese Communist Politics in Action, 1969; (with Edwin O. Reischauer) The United and China: The Next Decade, 1970. Home: 1023 Shipman Lane McLean VA 22101 Office: Brookings Instn 1775 Massachusetts Av NW Washington DC 20036

BARNETT, BURLEIGH FRANCIS, banker; b. Osceola, Mo., Jan. 6, 1896; s. John Carter and Mary Jane (Rothgeb) B.; student pub. schs., Osceola; m. Mary Nanon Linney, June 24, 1916; children—Leigh Frances (Mrs. G.M. Baccash), George C. Clk., Farmers & Mchts. Bank, Osceola, 1915-16, Internat. State Bank, Trinidad, Colo., 1917; v.p. First Nat. Bank of Tulsa, 1918-49; pres. Comml. Nat. Bank of Shreveport (La.), 1949-52; pres. Citizens First Nat. Bank of Tyler (Tex.), 1952-67, chmn. bd., 1967-69; dir. Coop. Savs. & Loan Assn., Tyler. Mem. Robert Morris Assos., C. of C. (pres. 1957-58). Mason. Home: 1521 S College Tyler TX 75701 Office: Citizens First Nat Bank Tyler TX 75701

BARNETT, CHARLES CONDITT, utilities exec.; b. Dermott, Ark., Aug. 14, 1915; s. Uzal Conditt and Alam (Daniels) B.; B.S. in Civil Engring., U. Ark., 1937; m. Mary Lee Mitchell, Feb. 7, 1942. With United Gas Pipe Line Co., Shreveport, La., 1937—, engr., 1937-41, gas engr., 1946-55, v.p., dir., 1955-69, sr. v.p., 1969—. Served as maj. C.E., AUS, 1941-46. Mem. Am. Gas Assn., Am, Petroleum Inst. Presbyn. Home: 6009 Dillingham St Shreveport LA 71106 Office: Box 1407 Shreveport LA 71104

BARNETT, CHARLES WENTWORTH, ret. physician, educator; b. Santa Rosa, Cal., Sept. 27, 1903; s. Charles Dwight and Emma (Fryer) B.; A.B., Stanford, 1923; M.D., Harvard, 1927; m. Helen Fairclough, June 11, 1927 (dec.); children—Charles George, James Wentworth; m. 2d, Barbara Connolly, Dec. 31, 1953. Intern Stanford Hosp., 1927-28, asst. resident, 1928-29, resident in medicine, 1929-31; instr. medicine Stanford, 1931-35, asst. prof., 1935-40, asso. prof., 1940-51, prof. medicine, 1951-69, emeritus, 1969—. Fellow A.C.P.; mem. Am., Cal. med. assns., Santa Clara County Med. Soc., Cal. Acad. Medicine. Author reports in med. jours. Home: 1835 Doris Dr Menlo Park CA 94025

BARNETT, CLAUDE C., educator; B.S., Walla Walla Coll., 1952; M.S., State Coll. Wash., 1956; Ph.D., Wash. State U., 1960. Prof., chmn. dept. physics Walla Walla Coll., College Place, Wash. Office: Dept Physics Walla Walla Coll College Place WA 99342*

BARNETT, DAS KELLEY, sociologist; b. Heber Springs, Ark., Dec. 16, 1914; s. Monroe Washington and Grace (Birdsong) B.; A.B., Hardin-Simmons U., 1936; Th.M., So. Bapt. Theol. Sem., 1941, Th.D., 1943; M.A., Yale, 1957; spl. study U. N.C., 1945, Columbia, 1948; m. Virginia Anne Craver, June 10, 1942; children—Martha Anne, David Kelley, Mary Elizabeth. Rosenwald fellow U. N.C., 1946-47; Columbus Roberts prof. sociology Mercer U., 1947-52; adjunct prof. sociology Weslayan Coll., Macon, Ga., 1947-52; prof. social ethics Episcopal Theol. Sem. of S.W., Austin, Tex., 1952-61; vis. prof. U. of South, summers 1956-57; dir., founder Research Centre in Christian Theology and Culture, Episcopal Theol. Sem. S.W., 1957-61; asso. prof. social philosophy N.Tex. State U., Denton, 1966-68, acting chmn. sociology dept. Stetson U., DeLand, Fla., 1968-69, asso. prof. sociology, 1969—; vis. prof. sociology Loyola U., Chgo., 1970, U. No. Ill., 1971; dir. Protestant Research Center, Houston, 1961-66. Past pres. Austin Commn. Human Relations. Mem. Am. Soc. Christian Social Ethics (past pres.), Am. Assn. of U. Profs., Alpha Chi, Pi Kappa Delta. Author: History of Philosophy, Ancient and Medieval, 1951; contbg. author: Christianity and Communism, 1958. Editor: Disciples of DissentTexas Style, Apostles of DiscordOperation Texas, The Church Faces the Community, The Church and the Urban Ministry, The Mission of the Anglican Communion to Mexico and Central America, Mission de la Comunion Anglicana en Mexico y Centro America, La Familia en la Sociedad Contemporanea. Editor, co-founder Christian publs., popular mags. Home: 431 S Stone St DeLand FL 32720

BARNETT, DAVID LEON, editor; b. Savannah, Ga., Jan. 21, 1922; s. Jack and Ida (Levy) B.; B.S. with honors in Govt., Harvard, 1943; M.S., Columbia, 1947; m. Jeanne Kahn, Dec. 29, 1946; children—Randel, Megan, Jane. Mem. staff Richmond (Va.) News Leader, 1947-54, chief statehouse bur. and polit. corr., 1950-51, asst. city editor, 1951-54; regional corr. Business Week mag., 1951-54; Washington corr. N.Am. Newspaper Alliance, 1954-55, chief Washington bur., columnist, 1955-65; Washington news editor Hearst Newspapers, 1966—. Served with USAAF, 1943-46. Mem. White House Corr. Assn. Clubs: Harvard, Nat. Press, Internat., Federal City (Washington). Contbr. articles to mags. Home: 7218 Beechwood Rd Alexandria VA 22307 Office: 1701 Pennsylvania Av NW Washington DC 20006

BARNETT, FRANK EUGENE, corp. exec.; b. Fairport Harbor, O., July 14, 1912; s. George Forrest and Hazel (Roberts) B.; A.B., Duke, 1933, LL.B., Western Res. U., 1936; m. Virginia Severens Russ, Sept. 24, 1936 (div. 1953); 1 son, John Severns; m. 2d, Wana Allison, Dec. 31, 1954; 1 stepdau., Pamela Allison. Admitted to Ohio bar, 1936, N.Y. bar, 1943; tax lawyer Lybrand, Ross Bros. & Montgomery, 1936-41; asso. Clark, Carr & Ellis, 1942-44, partner, 1945- 68; Eastern gen. counsel U.P. R.R., 1951-60, v.p., 1955-60, v.p., gen. counsel, 1961-66, chmn. exec. com., 1967-69, chmn. bd., chief exec. officer Union Pacific Corp., U.P. R.R., 1969—, O.S.L. R.R. Co., O. W. R.R. & N. Co., L.A. & L.S. R. R. Co., 1969—, Spokane Internat. R.R. Co., 1971—, Union Pacific Land Resources Corp., 1971—, Union Pacific Mining Corp., 1971—, Upland Industries Corp., 1971—; chmn. bd. Champlin Petroleum Co., 1970—; v.p., dir. St. Joseph & Grand Island Ry. Co., Utah Parks Co., 1969—; mem. trust bd. 1st Nat. City Bank; trustee Seamen's Bank of Savs. Trustee, chmn. exec. com. Union Pacific R.R. Found. Mem. Am. Bar Assn., Assn. Bar City N.Y., Transp. Assn. Am. (dir.), Phi Delta Phi. Clubs: Whippoorwill (Armonk, N.Y.); Downtown Association, Economic of N.Y., University, River (N.Y.C.); Preston Mountain (Kent, Conn.); Metropolitan (Washington); Union League (Chgo.). Home: 1185 Park Av New York City NY 10028 Office: 345 Park Av New York City NY 10022

BARNETT, GWEN HUGHES, polit. worker; b. Dallas, Oct. 8, 1925; d. Palmer and Marian Taylor (Rogers) Huges; student Stanford, 1942-43, U. Tulsa, 1943-44, Stanford, 1943-44; m. Steele Barnett, Aug. 24, 1946; children—Carol Jean, Susan Kay, Lawrence Steele. Rep. precinct committeewoman, Boise, Ida., 1956—, committeewoman for Ada County, 1958-60; became mem. Rep. Nat. Com. for Ida., 1960; mem. Young Reps. Ida., 1959—. Mem. Delta Delta Delta. Episcopalian. Home: 6525 Robertson Boise ID 83705

BARNETT, HAROLD JOSEPH, educator; b. Paterson, N.J., May 10, 1917; s. Abraham and Lena (Schiff) B.; B.S., U. Ark., 1939; M.S., U. Cal. at Berkeley, 1940; M.A. (Social Sci. Research Council fellow), Harvard, 1948, Ph.D., 1952; m. Mildred Denn, Aug. 4, 1940; children—Peter, Alexander, Katherine. Teaching asst. U. Cal. at Berkeley, 1939-40; economist Treasury Dept., 1941-42, Dept. State, also Dept. Interior, 1946-52; economist Rand Corp., Washington, 1952-55; economist, dir. econ. growth studies Resources For Future, Washington, 1955-59, cons., 1959—; prof. econs., chmn. dept. Wayne State U., 1959-63; prof. econs. Washington U., St. Louis, 1963—, chmn. dept., 1963-66; cons. White House Task Force on Communication Policy, NSF, U.S. Office Edn., Com. for Econ. Devel., Nat Acad. Scis.-NRC. Served to maj. AUS, 1943-46. Mem. Am. Econ. Assn., Regional Sci. Assn., Assn. Am. Geographers, Am. Assn. U. Profs. Author: Energy Uses and Supplies, 1950; Malthusianism and Conservation, 1959; (with C. Morse) Scarcity and Growth, 1963; Wired City monographs, 1968-71; Population Problems—Myths and Realities, 1971. Contbr. articles profl. jours. 51 Crestwood Dr Clayton MO 63105

BARNETT, HENRY LEWIS, med. educator, pediatrician; b. Detroit, June 25, 1914; s. Lewis and Florence (Marx) B.; student Dartmouth, 1931-32; B.S., Washington U., St. Louis, 1934, M.D., 1938; m. Shirley Blanchard, Oct. 19, 1940; children—Judith Florence, Martin David. Instr. dept. pediatrics Washington U. Sch. Medicine, 1941-43; asst. prof. dept. pediatrics Cornell U. Med. Coll., 1946-50. asso. prof., 1950-55; prof., chmn. dept. pediatrics Albert Einstein Coll. Medicine, 1955—, asso. dean clin. affairs, 1970—; dir. pediatric service Bronx Municipal Hosp. Center, 1955—. Mem. WHO Infant Metabolism Team to Netherlands and Sweden, 1950; adv. bd. Internat. Pediatric Assn., 1969-71. Served to capt., M.C., AUS, 1943-46. Mem. A.A.A.S., Am. Acad. Pediatrics, (E. Mead Johnson award 1949), Soc. Pediatric Research, Soc. Exptl. Biology and Medicine, Harvey Soc., Am. Pediatric Soc., Am. Soc. Clin. Investigation, Assn. Am. Physicians, Brit. Pediatric Soc. (hon.), Am. Physiol. Soc., N.Y. Acad. Sci., N.Y. Acad. Medicine, Sigma Xi, Alpha Omega Alpha. Contbr. articles profl. jours. Editor Pediatrics, 15th edit. Home: 118 W 79th St New York City NY 10024 Office: 1300 Morris Park Av Bronx NY 10461

BARNETT, HERBERT CHESTER, educator, med. scientist; b. N.Y.C., Nov. 19, 1917; s. Joseph Van Buren and Bessie Avery (Rennick) B.; B.S., Cornell U., 1939; M.S., U. Minn., 1946; M.P.H., U. Pitts., 1953, Ph.D., 1954; m. Lisa Margaret Brandt, May 29, 1943; children—Ralph Michael, Ronald Evan. Commd. 2d lt. U.S. Army, 1941, advanced through grades to lt. col., 1960; served in New Guinea and Philippines, World War II, Korea and Japan during Korean War, also service in Malaya, Pakistan; dir. div. Walter Reed Army Inst. Research, Washington, 1954-62; ret., 1962; prof., div. dir. U. Md. Sch. Medicine, Balt., 1962—, dir. Inst. Internat. Medicine, 1965, dir. Pakistan Med. Research Center, 1966-68, dir. Brazilian-Am. Biomed. Program, Brazil, 1971; cons. NIH, Armed Forces Epidemiology Bd. Decorated Silver Star, Bronze Star, Commendation medal. Recipient grants NIH, 1962—, Nat. Communicable Disease Center, 1970. Fellow Royal Soc. Tropical Medicine and Hygiene; mem. Am. Inst. Biol. Scis., A.A.A.S., Am. Soc. Tropical Medicine and Hygiene, Entomol. Soc. Am. Clubs: Punjab (Lahore); Yacht (Bahia, Brazil). Contbr. articles profl. jours. Home: 6612 Greyswood Rd Bethesda MD 20034 Office: 660 W Redwood St Baltimore MD 21201

BARNETT, HERBERT PHILLIP, artist educator; b. Providence, July 8, 1910; s. Phillip Herbert and Elizabeth (Feldt) B.; grad. Sch. Mus. Fine Arts, Boston, 1931; European study and travel, 1931-33; m. Elizabeth Lewellyn Lettinger, Aug. 7, 1940; 1 son, Peter Herbert. Instr. painting U. Vt., 1943; instr. painting Norfolk Art Sch., Yale, 1948, dir. sch., 1949; head Sch. Worcester (Mass.) Art Mus., 1940-51; affiliate prof. art Clark U., 1946- 51; dean Art Acad. Cin., 1951—; adj. prof. art U. Cin., 1958—; one man exhbns. include Robert Hall Fleming Mus., Manchester, Vt., Phila. Art Alliance, Fitchburg (Mass.) Art Center, Worcester Art Mus., Cin. Art Mus., Grace Horne Gallery, Boston, Marie Harriman Gallery, N.Y.C., Contemporary Arts, N.Y.C., Mortimer Levitt Gallery, N.Y.C., Wittenberg (O.) Coll., Miami (O.) U., Dayton (O.) Art Inst., rep. permanent collections Cin., Worcester art museums, Pa. Acad. Fine Arts, Amherst Coll. Mus. Art, Randolph-Macon Womans Coll. Art Gallery, U. Ariz. Gallery Art, Hallmark Co., Hallmark Internat. Gallery; works included in numerous invitational exhbns.; juror nat. and regional arts exhbns.; frequent lectr. Instl. rep. Nat. Assn. Schs. Art; mem. diocesan com. fine arts Episcopal Diocese So. Ohio. Recipient Lambert purchase prize Pa. Acad., 1938; Hallmark Internat. award, 1950. Mem. McDowell Soc., Art Dirs. Club, Print and Drawing Circle, Mens Art Club Cin., Profl. Artists Assn., Allied Artists Am. Home: 3 Moyer Pl Cincinnati OH 45226

BARNETT, HERMAN L., lawyer b. San Antonio, Dec. 12, 1893; s. Walter Michael and Fannie Edit (Lyon) B.; A.B. summa cum laude, Tulane U., 1914, LL.B., 1916; m. Irma Samson, Sept. 30, 1920; children—Marilyn, William Michael. Admitted to La. bar, 1916; since practiced law, New Orleans; sr. partner, Guste, Barnett & Colomb, New Orleans, 1957—; dir. Continental Savs. & Loan Assn., 1922-70, dir. emeritus, 1970—. Instr. pub. speaking Am. Inst. Banking, 1921, lectr. comml. law, 1930-43; spl. lectr. comml. law Tulane U. Sch. Commerce, 1922-29. Chmn., New Orleans Civil Service Commn., 1942-51; mem. exec. com. La. Civil Service League, 1950—, chmn. legal com., 1963-66. Bd. dirs. Lighthouse for Blind, New Orleans. Served from 2d lt. to capt. U.S. Army, 1917-19; AEF. Recipient certificate of merit and key City of New Orleans, 1951, 66. Mem. Confrerie des Chevaliers du Tastevin (France), La. Law Inst., La. Civil Service League (gov. 1954—), Am., La., New Orleans (1st v.p. 1936) bar assns., Mil. Order World Wars (comdr. 1942-43), Am. Legion, La Coalition Patriotic Socs. (past pres.), New Orleans C. of C. (past chmn. nat. legislation com.), Order of Lafayette (charter), Phi Beta Kappa. Kiwanian. Former mem. bd. editors So. Law Quar. (Tulane Law Review). Home: 579 Broadway New Orleans LA 70118 Office: National Bank of Commerce Bldg New Orleans LA 70112

BARNETT, HOMER GARNER, educator; b. Bisbee, Ariz., Apr. 25, 1906; s. Lee and Lottie L. (McEuen) B.; A.B., Stanford, 1927; Ph.D., U. Cal., 1938; m., Judith H. Skaggs, Apr. 12, 1941; children—Linda Ann, Susan Marie. Research asso. anthropology, U. Cal., 1937-38; instr. anthropology U. N.M., 1938-39; anthropologist bur. Am. ethnology Smithsonian Inst., 1944-46; asst. prof. anthropology U. Ore., 1939-44, asso. prof., 1946-50, prof. since 1950; staff anthropologist Trust Ter. Pacific Islands, 1951-53; mem. Research Council South Pacific Commn., 1952-53; cons. Netherlands New Guinea Govt., 1955. Sr. fellow NSF, 1956-57; fellow Center for Advanced Study in Behavorial Scis., 1964-65. Mem. Pacific sci. bd. Coast Adv. Com. Mem. A.A.A.S., Am. Ethnol. Soc., Soc. Applied Anthropology (pres.), Sigma Xi, Phi Beta Kappa. Author: Innovation: The Basis of Cultural Change, 1953; Palauan Society, 1949; Anthropology in Administration, 1956; Coast Salish of British Columbia, 1955; Indian Shakers, 1957; Being a Palauan, 1959; The Nature and Function of the Potlatch, 1968; also articles on anthropology. Home: 2610 Tyler St Eugene OR 97405

BARNETT, HOWARD ALBERT, educator; b. Dallas, June 14, 1920; s. Carl Harry and Jennie Bess (McHatton) B.; student Butler U., also Arthur Jordan Conservatory, 1938- 41; B.A., Ind. U., 1947, M.A., 1948, Ph.D., 1959; student U. Chgo., summers 1950, 51; m. Barbara Joan Brandenberg, Sept. 2, 1947; children—Victoria Joan, Gregory Howard. Asst. prof. English, Bridgewater (Va.) Coll., 1948-50, Washington (Md.) Coll., 1950-52, Wis. State Coll., Whitewater, 1957-59; Marshall Evans prof. lit. Morris Harvey Coll., Charleston, W.Va., 1959-65, chmn. dept. English, 1963-65; chmn. dept. English, Lindenwood Colls., St. Charles, Mo., 1965-69, Alice Parker prof. English, 1965-69, v.p., dean, 1969—. Served with USNR, 1941-45. Mem. Am. Conf. Acad. Deans, Am. Assn. for Higher Edn., Mo. Com. for Humanities, St. Louis Council on World Affairs, Modern Lang. Assn., Nat. Council Tchrs. English, Am. Conf. Acad. Deans, Am. Assn. for Higher Edn., Theta Xi, Tau Kappa Alpha. Episcopalian. Author articles, revs. Home: 816 Elmwood Dr St Charles MO 63301

BARNETT, JAMES ALLEN, corp. exec.; b. New Orleans, Sept. 1, 1908; s. Jacob Allen and Grace (Dunlap) B.; student Taft Sch., Watertown, Conn., 1923-27; A.B., Princeton, 1931; m. Jane Dodge, June 23, 1933; children—Fayal, Lucy Jane; m. 2d, Harriet Brownell Pope, Sept. 18, 1949. With N.Y. Herald Tribune, 1931-38; account exec. Benton & Bowles Advt. Agy., 1938-40; v.p. Sherman & Marquette Advt., Chicago, 1940-43; v.p. charge advt. Pepsodent Co., 1943-46, v.p. and gen. mgr., 1946-49; v.p. charge advt. and promotion Lever Bros. Co., 1949-55, v. p. and asst. to the pres. 1955-56, dir., 1952-56; v.p. Rexall Drug Co., Los Angeles, 1956-59; dir. Purex Corp., Ltd., Southgate, 1957—, officer in charge product planning and market research, 1959-61, v.p. also pres. Wrisley-Potter div., 1961-62, sr. v.p., 1962-68, pres. Drug and Toiletries div., 1962-68, dir., exec. com., chmn. corporate devel. com., 1965—; dir. Pope & Talbot Lumber Co., Portland, Ore., 1971—. Advt. council vol. coordinator advt. and fund raising material Nat. A.R.C. Clubs: Princeton (N.Y.C.); Cottage (Princeton U.); Bel Air Country. Home: 800 Tortuoso Way Bel Air Los Angeles CA 90024 Office: Purex Corp Ltd Lakewood CA 90714

BARNETT, JOHN VINCENT, assn. exec.; b. Lapel, Ind., July 23, 1912; s. Harley E. and Vayne (Castor) B.; student Ind. U., 1930-33; m. Jane Callane, Feb. 10, 1940; children—Bonnie (Mrs. Larry Burdick), John Jr. Statistician, Ind. Dept. Pub. Welfare, 1934-42; asst. research dir. Ind. C. of C., Indpls., 1942-52, dir. taxation dept., 1952-61, dir. research, 1962, exec. v.p., 1962—. Past pres. Council of State Chambers of Commerce; mem. indsl. adv. com. Ind.-Purdue U.; sec., treas. Ind. Tax Study Com.; mem. econ. growth adv. bd. Ind. U.; mem. adv. council Ind. Dept. Commerce. Trustee Ind. Traffic Safety Council, Ind. Ednl. Services Found., Ind. Vocational Tech. Coll. Mem. C. of C. of U.S., Ind. Commerce Execs. Assn. (past pres.), Ind. Soc. of Chgo. Republican. Presbyn. Mason, Elk. Clubs: Columbia, Press, Meridian Hills Country (Indpls.); Ulen Country (Lebanon). Home: 8750 Washington Blvd W Dr Indianapolis IN 46240 Office: Bd Trade Bldg 2d Floor Indianapolis IN 46204

BARNETT, JONATHAN, architect, city planner; b. Boston, Jan. 6, 1937; s. David and Josephine (Wolff) B.; B.A. Magna cum laude, Yale, 1958, B. Arch., 1963; M.A. (Mellon fellow), U. Cambridge (Eng.), 1960. Designer, Haines, Lundberg & Waehler, architects, N.Y.C., 1963, 64; asso. editor Archtl. Record, N.Y.C., 1964-67; planning cons.

N.Y.C., also New City Exhbn. at Mus. Modern Art, 1966, 67; prin. urban designer N.Y.C. Planning Dept., 1967- 68, dir. urban design group, 1969-71; prof., dir. grad. program in urban design Coll. City N.Y., 1971—. Corporate mem. A.I.A.; mem. Archtl. League N.Y. (v.p. 1968-70), Municipal Art Soc. (dir. 1970—), Berzelius Soc. Clubs: Yale (N.Y.C.); Elizabethan (Yale). Unitarian. Contbr. profl. jours. Editor: Perspecta 8, 1962. Contbr. New Zoning, 1970. Contbg. editor Archtl. Record, 1968—; mem. adv. bd. Environment and Behavior, 1968—. Home: 440 W 24th St New York City NY 10011 Office: Sch Architecture City Coll New York City NY 10031

BARNETT, JOSEPH H. lawyer; b. Equality, Ill., Aug. 6, 1927; s. Reuben and Nora (Elliott) B.; student So. Ill. U., 1946-48; B.S., U. Ill., 1949, J.D., 1951; m. Regina M. Reynolds, Nov. 1, 1958; children-Rebecca M., Benetta E. Admitted to Ill. bar, 1951, since practiced in Aurora; atty. O'Brien, Burnell, Puckett & Barnett and predecessor firm, 1951—. Pres. Fox Valley Montessori Sch., Kane County Fair; bd. dirs. Aurora Mental Health, Inc. Candidate for Kane County states atty., 1964. Served with USNR, 1945-46. Mem. Ill., Kane County bar assns. Elk. Home: 741 Leigh St Aurora IL 60538 Office: 220 E Galena St Aurora IL 60507

BARNETT, LINCOLN KINNEAR, author; b. N.Y.C., Feb. 12, 1909; s. Leon H. and Jessie (Kinnear) B.;A.B., Princeton, 1929; B. Litt., Columbia, 1931, M.S., 1932; m. Hildegarde Harris, Oct. 10, 1935; children—Timothy Lincoln, Robert Morgan. Reporter, N.Y. Herald Tribune, 1932-37; staff writer, war corr., asso. editor Life mag., 1937-47; contbr. leading magazines, 1947—. Trustee Westport (N.Y.) Library Assn., 1953—. Guggenheim fellow, 1950; recipient journalism Alumni award Columbia, 1960. Mem. S.A.R., Sigma Delta Chi. Club: Princeton (N.Y.C.). Author: The Universe and Dr. Einstein (Nat. Book award spl. citation 1950), 1949; Writing on Life, 1952; The World We Live In (Benjamin Franklin mag. award 1953, George Westinghouse Sci. Writing award, 1953, Christopher award 1953), 1955; The Epic of Man (Benjamin Franklin mag. award 1956), 1956; The Wonders of Life on Earth, 1960; The Treasure of Our Tongue, 1964. Address: Old Arsenal Rd Westport NY 12993

BARNETT, MAX GEORGE, univ. exec.; b. Sioux Falls, S.D., Feb. 22, 1909; s. Frank J. and Anne (Collins) B.; A.B., St. Louis U., 1932, A.M., 1933, postgrad. 1937-42. Instr. classical langs. and asst. dean, Rockhurst Coll., Kansas City. Mo., 1935-37; asst. dean, Coll. Liberal Arts, Marquette U., 1943-45, dean, 1945-48; became v.p. Marquette U., 1948, exec. asst. to pres., 1954-55, exec. v.p., 1955-58, v.p. pub. relations and devel., 1958-59, asso. dean, 1959—. Mem. Catholic Edn. Assn., Jesuit Edn. Assn., N. Central Assn. Colls. and Secondary Schs. Mem. Society of Jesus. Home: 1131 W Wisconsin Av Milwaukee WI 53233

BARNETT, M. ROBERT, orgn. exec.; b. Jacksonville, Fla., Oct. 31, 1916; s. Marvin Robert and Bessie Grace (Groves) B.; student Fla. Sch. for the Blind, 1935-36; A.B. cum laude, John B. Stetson U., 1940; L.H.D. (honorary), Pfeiffer Coll. 1958; H.H.D. (honorary), Stetson U., 1964; m. Sara Ellen Buttorff, Nov. 10, 1941 (div.): children—Alice Sylvia, Robert Ira; m. 2d, Marian Weller, May 22, 1965. Pub. relations, instr. in journalism Stetson U., 1940-42; reporter, br. mgr. Daytona Beach News Jour., 1943-44; rehab. specialist for the blind Fla. Council for the Blind, Tampa, 1944-45, exec. dir., 1945-49; exec. dir. Am. Found. for the Blind, Am. Found. for Overseas Blind, 1949—. Chmn. Am. delegation, v.p. for N.Am. and S.Am., mem. exec. com. World Council Welfare of the Blind; advisor Blinded Vets. Assn.; mem. President's Com. on Employment of the Handicapped. Repeated and/or continuous service with spl. study groups, research coms. concerned with social ednl., econ. facilities for the visually handicapped, nationwide, regional, 1944—. Mem. Nat. Rehab. Assn., Am. Assn. Workers for the Blind (legislative com.), Canadian Council for Blind, Pi Gamma Mu, Phi Sigma Mu. Democrat. Unitarian. Lion. Home: 16 W 16th St New York City NY 10011 Office: 15 West 16th St New York City NY 10011

BARNETT, PROCTOR HAWTHORNE, ins. co. exec.; b. Birmingham, Ala., Dec. 11, 1906; s. Frank Willis and Maude (Proctor) B.; student Sanford U.; 1924-26, U.S. Mil. Acad., 1927-28, Columbia, 1953; m. Mary Reeder, Dec. 11, 1929; 1 dau., Mary Frances. Sec., dir. Jackson Securities & Investment Co., Birmingham, 1929-33; with Prudential Ins. Co. Am., 1933—, successively mortgage loan insp., mortgage loan appraiser, Birmingham, asst. mgr. prodn., Dallas, asst. gen. mgr., gen. mgr., exec. dir., Newark, 1933-56, exec. gen. mgr. western region, 1956-63, v.p., Newark, 1963-65, sr. v.p. mortgage loans and real estate investment dept., 1965—, pres. PIC Realty Corp. (subsidiary). Mem. governing com. urban renewal div., dir. Action Council for Better Cities; mem. nat. action council, mem. governing com. urban redevel. div. Urban Am., Inc.; mem. adv. bd. Real Estate Inst., N.Y. U., 1970—. Served to col. USAAF, 1941-46. Mem. Exec. Assn. (chmn. exec. com.), Regional Plan Assn. N.Y., N.J. and Conn. (dir., mem. N.J. com.), Navy League U.S. (life), Am. Legion, Am. Life Conv., Life Ins. Assn. Am. (chmn. housing and mortgage sub-com, 1969). C. of C. U.S., Nat. Assn. Home Builders (mem. redevelopers and spl. programs council), Urban Land Inst., Pi Kappa Alpha. Club: Essex County Country (W. Orange, N.J.). Home: 19 Kings Hill Ct Summit, NJ 07901. Office: Prudential Plaza Newark NJ 07101

BARNETT, ROBERT WARREN, assn. exec.; b. Shanghai, China, Nov. 6, 1911 (parents Am. citizens); s. Eugene Epperson and Bertha Mae (Smith) B.; A.B., U. N.C., 1933, M.A., 1934; B.A. (Rhodes scholar), Oxford U., 1936, B.Litt., 1937; postgrad. (Gen. Edn. Bd. fellow) Yale, 1937-39, U. Mich., 1938, Universita per Stranieri, Perugia, Italy, 1935; m. Patricia Robertson Glover, Apr. 26, 1940; children—Dickson Glover, Robert Warren, Clare, Eugenia. Mem. staff Inst. Pacific Relations. exec. sec. program com. United China Relief, 1941-42; U.S. mem. econs. and reparations coms. Far Eastern Commn. representing U.S. Dept. State, Japan, 1945-49, officer charge China econ. affairs, 1949-51, charge Western European econ. affairs, 1951-54, charge European econ. orgns., 1954-56, econ. counselor U.S. embassy, The Hague, Netherlands, 1956-60; counselor U.S. Mission European Communities, Brussels, Belgium, 1960-61; dep. dir. fgn. econ. adv. staff. Dept. State, Washington, 1961-62, dep. asst. sec. state for East Asian and Pacific affairs, 1963-70; dir. Washington Center, Asia Soc., also v.p., 1970—. Rockefeller Found. fellow, 1940-41; Center Internat. Affairs Fellow Harvard, 1959-60. Served from 1st lt. to maj., USAAF, 1943-45: PTO. Decorated Legion of Merit. Mem. Council Fgn. Relations, Assn. Asian Studies, Am. Polit. Sci. Assn., Am. Rhodes Scholar Assn., Phi Beta Kappa, Beta Theta Pi. Methodist. Clubs: Internat., Chevy Chase (Washington). Author: Economic Shanghai: Hostage to Politics, 1941; Orientation Booklet for U.S. Military Personnel in China, 1945. Contbr. to U.S. Economic Foreign Policy, 1948. Home: 5205 Abingdon Rd Washington DC 20016 Office: 1785 Massachusetts Av NW Washington DC 20036

BARNETT, THOMAS JAMES, adminstr. mental health center; b. Barberton, O., Aug. 22, 1932; s. Thomas J. and Mildred (Ellis) B.; m. Beverly Ann Marrs, Nov. 9, 1962; children—Carla Rachell, Mark Lane. Buyer, Ric Wil Co., Barberton, 1950-55; collection mgr. Securities Acceptance Corp., Carlsbad, N.M., 1955-57; loan mgr. Southwestern Investment Co., Carlsbad, 1957-59; collection mgr. Guy Chevrolet Co., Artesia, N.M., 1959-60; asst. adminstr. St. Francis Hosp., Carlsbad, 1960-65, Ft. Bayard (N.M.) Hosp., 1965-66; adminstr. Meadows Hosp., Las Vegas, N.M., 1966-68, Las Vegas Med. Center, 1968-69; coordinator Regional Mental Health Center, Oxford, Miss., 1970-71, dir., Clarksdale, Miss., 1971—. Vice pres. Carlsbad Consumer Credit Assn., 1958-60. Mem. Assn. Mental Health Adminstrs. Elk. Clubs: Toastmasters, Clarksdale Chess. Address: PO Box 1046 Clarksdale MS 38614

BARNETT, VINCENT MACDOWELL, Jr., educator; b. Whittier, Cal., Sept. 1, 1913; s. Vincent MacDowell and Ethel (Roper) B.; A.B., U. Cal. at Los Angeles, 1935, M.A., 1936; Ph.D., Harvard, 1938; LL.D., Syracuse U., 1963, Williams, 1963; Litt.D., Union Coll., 1965; L.H.D., Carnegie Inst. Tech., 1965, Hamilton Coll., 1968; D.C.L., Colgate U.; 1969; m. Barbara Brown, June 24, 1939; children—Peter, Deborah (Mrs. Robert Venman), Stephen, Mary, Wendy. Resident tutor Leverett House and instr. hist. govt. and econs., Harvard, 1937-39; instr. polit. sci. Williams Coll., 1939-42, asst. to asso. prof., 1942-48, prof., chmn. dept. polit. sci., 1948-50, David A. Wells prof. polit. sci., 1950-51, A. Barton Hepburn prof. govt., chmn. dept. polit. sci., 1953-62, chmn. grad. center for devel. econs., 1960-62, dean coll., 1957-58; pres. Colgate U., 1963-69; James P. Baxter III prof. pub. affairs Williams Coll. Williamstown, Mass., 1969-71; dir. Harvard U. Devel. Adv. Service, Malaysia Project, Kuala Lumpur, 1971—; counselor for econ. affairs, U.S. Embassy, Rome, 1958-59; vis. prof. U. Cal. at Los Angeles, summer 1948, Stanford, summer 1954; exec. dir. Williams Coll. Inst. Am. Studies, 1956-58; tech. dir. 9th Am. Assembly Columbia, 1956. Spl. asst. to dir. retail trade div. O.P.A., 1942-43; vice chmn. requirements com. W. P.B., 1943-45; chief program div. Spl. Mission to Italy, E.C.A., 1948-50; chief econ. affairs Am. embassy, Rome, 1951-53; U.S. mem. FAO (UN) Council, 1959-60, alternate del. conf., 1959, U.S. liaison officer, 1958-60; mem. numerous adv. coms. and commns. Trustee Bookings Instn., Edn. and World Affairs. Recipient U. Cal. at Los Angeles Alumni Profl. Achievement award, 1968; Superior Service medal U.S. State Dept., 1960. Mem. Am. Polit. Sci. Assn., Phi Beta Kappa, Pi Gamma Mu, Pi Sigma Alpha. Contbr. to books. Author articles. Editor: The Representation of the U.S. Abroad, 1956, rev. edit., 1965. Address: PO Box 2255 Kuala Lumpur Malaysia

BARNETT, WALTER MICHAEL, lawyer; b. New Orleans, Apr. 12, 1903; s. Walter Michael and Fannie Edith (Lion) B.; A.B., Tulane U., 1923, M.A., J.D., 1925; m. Virginia Mae Fuerst, Sept. 24, 1930; children—Linda (Mrs. Albert Mintz), Walda (Mrs. Sydney J. Besthoff III). Admitted to La. bar, 1925, since practiced in New Orleans; mem. firm Montgomery, Barnett, Brown & Read, 1950—; asst. city atty., New Orleans, 1935-46; atty. Dept. Pub. Welfare, 1935-46 Bd. dirs. Community Chest; pres. United Fund Greater New Orleans Area; chmn., Mayor's Adv. Com. on Community Improvement, Urban Renewal Commn. pres. Family Service Soc., Council Social Agencies, Citizens Housing Council Greater New Orleans Area; treas. Mental Health Soc.; pres. Touro Infirmary, 1960-64; bd. dirs. Eye, Ear, Nose and Throat Hosp.; chmn. New Orleans War Recreation Com.; bd. dirs. officers Town House. Served as lt. (j.g.) USCGTR. Mem. Am., La., New Orleans (pres. 1965-66) bar assns., Internat. Assn. Ins. Counsel, Am. Law Inst., Am. Judicature Soc., Tulane U. Alumni Assn. (nat. pres. 1939-40), Phi Beta Kappa. Clubs: Internat. House, Plimsoll New Orleans). Home: 124 Audubon Blvd New Orleans LA 70118 Office: Nat Bank of Commerce Bldg New Orleans LA 70112

BARNETT, WAYNE G., educator. Prof. law Stanford. Office: Stanford U Law Sch Stanford CA 94304*

BARNETTE, JOSEPH D., investment co. exec.; b. Rochester, Ind., 1908; student South Bend Coll. Commerce. Pres., dir. Assos. Corp. N.Am., South Bend, Ind., Assos. Financial Services Co.; chmn. exec. com., dir. Capitol Life Ins. Co., Emco Ins. Cos. South Bend; chmn. First Bank & Trust Co.; Discount dir. Gulf & Western Industries, Inc. Home: 874 East Shore Dr Culver IN 46511 Office: 1700 Mishawaka Av South Bend IN 46615*

BARNETTE, NEWTON HALL, engr.; educator; b. Magnolia, Ark., July 18, 1917; s. Andrew Lacy and Eunice (Newton) B.; student La. State Normal Coll., 1935-37; B.S., La. Poly. Inst., 1941; M.E.E., Va. Poly. Inst., 1946; Ph.D., Cornell, 1958; m. Ella Mae McMahon, Sept. 1, 1937; children—Jon Hall, Lynne, Andra. Engr. U.S. Army, New Orleans dist., 1941-42, Ft. Belvoir, Va., 1944-45; asst. prof. elec. engring. La. Poly. Inst., 1942-44; instr. Va. Poly. Inst., 1945-46; head engring., math. depts. U. Tenn., Martin br. 1946- 48; asso. prof. elec. engring. U. Ark., Fayetteville, 1948-49, prof. elec. engring., head dept. elec. engring., 1951- 61; asso. dir., Westinghouse prof. Ga. Inst. Tech. Sch. Elec. Engring., 1961-64; chmn. dept. engring. U. N.C., Charlotte, 1964-68, chmn. div. engring., 1968-70, dean Coll. Engring., 1970—; cons. engr. electric power systems. Mem. I.E.E.E. (past chmn. Northwest Ark. Sect.) Am. Soc. for Engring. Edn., Am. Assn. U. Profs. (past pres. U. Ark. chpt.), Tau Beta Pi, Phi Kappa Phi, Sigma Xi. Home: Route 10 Box 362K Charlotte NC 28213

BARNETTE, STUART MOFFETT, educator, architect; b. Dover, Del., Mar. 20, 1905; s. John Stuart and Daisy (Moffett) B.; student U.S. Naval Acad., 1923-26; B.S. in Architecture, Mass. Inst. Tech., 1929; diploma architecture Ecole des Beaux Arts Americaine, Fontainbleau, France, 1930; m. Stella Norma Dorsey, Sept. 15, 1961; children—Stuart Moffett, Mark. Joined USNR, 1930, advanced through grades to comdr., 1956; retired, 1956; pvt. practice architecture, specializing preservation-restoration Early Am. architecture, 1933—; asst. chief architect Nat. Park Service, 1946; chief Hist. Am. Bldg. Survey, 1946; archtl. adviser Nat. Adv. Bd. Selection-Designation Nat. Hist. Sites Bldgs., 1938-46; prof. Ala. Poly. Inst., 1946-47; mem. faculty Cornell U., 1947—, prof. architecture, 1952-70, prof. emeritus architecture, 1970—. Fulbright fellow, 1954; grantee Thomas and Helen Hastings Found., 1954. Mem. Newcomen Soc., Freize and Cornice, L'Oglve, Scarab, Gargolye. Author surveys and reports. Home: 6 Lodge Way Ithaca NY 14850 also Sentry Hill York Harbor ME 03911

BARNEY, ALBERT WILKINS, Jr., judge; b. St. Johnsbury, Vt., Oct. 23, 1920; s. Albert Wilkins and Marion A. (Bisbee) B.; A.B., Yale, 1942; LL.B., Harvard, 1945; m. Helen Elizabeth Rondeau, Oct. 16, 1948; children—Marianne Elizabeth, Joan Shirley, Kathleen Arletta. Admitted to Vt. bar, 1949; judge Caledonia County Municipal Ct., 1951-52; mem. Vt. Superior Bench, 1952- 59, chief judges, 1958-59; asso. justice Supreme Ct. Vt., 1959—. Mem. town planning commn., St. Johnsbury, Vt., 1960. Mem. Vt. Ho. of Reps. from St. Johnsbury, 1951-52, mem. ct. rules revision commn., 1958. Trustee St. Johnsbury Acad. Served to lt. (s.g.) USNR, 1942-46. Mem. Am., Vt. bar assns. Rotarian. Home: 8 Western Av St Johnsbury VT 05819

BARNEY, WILLIAM JOSHUA, Jr., gen. contractor; b. N.Y.C., Aug. 17, 1911; s. William Joshua and Lilian C. (Warner) B.; grad. Choate Sch., 1929; B.S., Yale, 1933; m. Priscilla S. Payne, Feb. 10, 1940. With W. J. Barney Corp., gen. contractors, N.Y.C., 1933—, sec.-treas., 1948—, exec. v.p., 1952-71, chmn. bd., 1971—; pres., treas., dir. W. J. Barney Corp of Conn., 1957—; pres., sec., trustee W. J. Barney Found., Inc., 1958—; dir. Am. Mutual Liability Ins., Co., 1959—, Am. Policyholders Ins. Co. Bd. dirs. Nat. Horse Show Assn. Am., Ltd., 1956—; dir. U.S. Equestrian Team, Inc., 1956—. Bd. mgrs. Am. Soc. Prevention Cruelty to Animals, 1959—; dir. N.Y. Heart Assn., Inc., 1959-70, adv. dir., 1970—. Served from lt. (j.g.) to comdr., USNR, 1940-45. Registered profl. engr., N.Y. Fellow Am. Soc. C.E.; mem. Soc. Cin., Soc. Colonial Wars, Am. Horse Shows Assn. Clubs: Yale, Pinnacle, University, Madison Square Garden (N.Y.C.); Country of Fairfield, Fairfield County Hunt (Fairfield, Conn.); Church (N.Y.C.); Half Moon-Rose Hall Golf (Jamaica, W.I.). Home: 209 Southport Woods Dr Southport CT 06490 Office: 360 Lexington Av New York City NY 10017

BARNHARDT, WILLIAM HORACE, textile mfr.; b. Harrisburg, N.C., Feb. 3, 1903; s. John Addison and Sarah E. (McClellan) B.; B.S., N.C. State Coll. Sch. Textiles, Raleigh, 1923; m. Margaret McLaughlin, Oct. 8, 1927; children—William M., Nancy (Mrs. William D. Thomas), Charles, John. Pres., treas., dir. Barnhardt Bros. Co., Charlotte, 1938—, Barnhardt Elastic Corp., 1945—, Barnhardt Internat. Corp., 1945—, Am. Textile Corp., Tryon Processing Co. (N.C.), Am. Realty Corp., Novelty Yarns Corp.; pres., dir. So. Webbing Mills, Inc., Greensboro, N.C.; v.p., dir. Gotswold Homes, Inc., Providence Corp., Sharon Corp., Charlotte; treas., dir. Providence Acres, Inc., Riverview Acres Corp., Thomas Constrn. Corp., Univ. Heights, Inc., Carolinas Corp., Univ. Plantation, Inc., (all Charlotte, N.C.); dir. Standard Bonded Warehouse Co., Charlotte, N.C. Nat. Bank, Charlotte, N.C., Arlie, Inc., Spartanburg, Dan River Mills, Inc., Danville, Va., Am. Credit Corp., Jackson Engring. Corp., Cedar Hills, Inc., Met. Savs. & Loan Assn. Pres., treas., dir. Barnhardt Found., Inc.; past pres., dir. N.C. Textile Found.; bd. trustees, exec. com., chmn. finance com. Queen's Coll., Charlotte, 1946-68; bd. trustees, chmn. finance com. Crossnore (N.C.) Sch., Johnson C. Smith U., Charlotte; trustee, nat. chmn. patrons fund Protestant Radio and Television Center, Atlanta; bd. trustees Charlotte Country Day Sch.; trustee, treas. Greater Charlotte Found., dir. Found. U. N.C.-Charlotte, 1963-66; regional com. Boy Scouts Am., adv. council Mecklenburg council; past v.p., chmn. capital funds bd. United Community Services; past chmn. exec. bldg. coms. Hist. Found., Montreat, N.C. Recipient Silver Beaver award Boy Scouts Am., 1947, Silver Antelope, 1949; Algernon Sydney Sullivan award Queens Coll., 1953, Service Youth award Charlotte YMCA, 1954; Nat. Conf. Christians and Jews award, 1966. Mem. N.C. Textile Mfrs. Assn. (past dir.), Royal Soc. Knights Carrousel (governing council, king, 1955), Carolina Yarn Assn. (pres. 1946), Newcomen Soc., Phi Kappa Phi, Pi Kappa Alpha. Presbyn. (vice moderator 1965, elder). Clubs: Charlotte Textile, Quail Hollow Country (pres. 1963, 64, 65, gov.), Executives (pres. 1956), Charlotte City (past v.p.), Charlotte Country (past v.p.) Metropolitan, New York Athletic (N.Y.C.). Home: 1512 Queens Rd W Charlotte NC 28207 Office: NC Nat Bank Bldg Charlotte NC 28202

BARNHART, CLARENCE LEWIS, ret. lexicographer, editor; b. nr. Plattsburg, Mo., Dec. 30, 1900; s. Franklin Chester and Frances Nora (Eliot) B.; Ph.B., U. Chgo., 1930, postgrad., 1934-37; m. Frances Knox, Feb. 21, 1931; children—Robert, David. Editor, Scott, Foresman & Co., 1929-45, War Dept., 1943, Random House, 1945-48. Hon. research asso. Inst. Psychol. Research, Columbia, 1945, 46. Recipient War Dept. certificate appreciation, 1946. Mem. Am. Dialect Soc., Linguistic Soc., Modern Lang. Assn., Nat. Council Tchrs. English, Am. Name Soc. (3d v.p.), Phi Beta Kappa. Clubs: University (N.Y.C.); Century Association; Authors' (London). Author: (with Leonard Bloomfield) Let's Read: A Linguistic Approach, 1961; co-author, pub.; Let's Read 1, 2, 3, 1963, 4, 5, 6, 1964, 7, 8, 1965, 9, 1966. Editor: Thorndike Century Junior Dictionary, 1935, 42; Thorndike Century Senior Dictionary, 1941; Dictionary of United States Army Terms, 1943; American College Dictionary, 1948; Thorndike-Barnhart Comprehensive Desk Dictionary, 1951; Thorndike-Barnhart Junior Dictionary, 1952; Thorndike- Barnhart High School Dictionary, 1952; New Century Cyclopedia of Names, 1954; New Century Handbook of English Literature, 1956; Thorndike- Barnhart Advanced Junior Dictionary, 1957; World Book Encyclopedia Dictionary, 1963; Thorndike-Barnhart Beginning Dictionary, 1964. Home: 19 Ridge Rd Bronxville NY 10708

BARNHART, DONALD STANFORD, educator; b. St. Louis, July 18, 1925; s. Kenneth Edwin and Katherine (Stanford) B.; A.B., San Diego State Coll., 1949; M.A., U. Chgo., 1950, Ph.D., 1953; postgrad. (Rotary Found. fellow), Nat. U. Colombia, 1951; m. Janice Evelyn Stanley, Dec. 31, 1950; children—Frederick Stanford, Rebecca Jane, Julia Ann. Asst. prof., dean of men Simpson Coll., Indianola, Ia., 1953-56; asso. prof. U. W.Va., Morgantown, 1956-59; lectr. econs. U. Pa. Wharton Sch. Finance, Phila., 1959-60; prof. social sci. San Francisco State Coll., 1960—. Served with USNR, 1943-46. Fulbright lectr., Colombia, 1965, Peru, 1970-71. Mem. Soc. for Internat. Devel., Latin Am. Studies Assn. Unitarian. Home: San Bruno CA 94066 Office: San Francisco State Coll San Francisco CA 94132

BARNHART, HUGH ARTHUR, telephone co. exec., newspaper pub.; b. Rochester, Ind., July 14, 1892; s. Henry A. and Louretta (Leffel) B.; student Notre Dame U., 1911; A.B., Ind. U., 1915; m. Martha Anspaugh, June 25, 1928. Pres. Rochester Sentinel Corp., 1919—; pres. Rochester Telephone Co., 1932-67, chmn. bd., bd., 1967—; dir. Midwestern Companies, Inc. Dir. Ind. Excise Dept., 1937- 41, Ind. Dept. Conservation, 1945-51, Ind. Hwy. Dept., 1932-33; dir. Bus. and Def. Services Adminstrn., Dept. Communications, Dept. Commerce, 1955. Democratic nominee 2d Congl. Dist. Ind., 1936. Adv. bd. Ind. U., 1950-53. Served to 1st. lt., F.A., U.S. Army, 1917-19. Mem. U.S. Independent Telephone Assn. (pres. 1959, bd. dirs.), Ind. (bd. dirs.), Rochester (pres. 1942-44) chambers commerce, Am. Legion (past post comdr.), Fulton County Hist. Soc. (pres. 1967-69). Delta Tau Delta. Baptist. Mason, Elk, Moose, Odd Fellow, Kiwanian (pres. Rochester 1929). Home: RR2 Rochester IN 46975 Office: 117 W 8th St Rochester IN 46975

BARNHART, RALPH CLAYTON, univ. dean; b. nr. Springfield, O., Oct. 18, 1905 s. Charles Anthony and Adell (Patterson) B.; student Battle Creek Coll., 1927-30; A.B., Simpson Coll., 1931; LL.B., U. Cin., 1934; m. Mary Elizabeth Gerber, Aug. 26, 1930; children—Lloyd, Daniel, Clayton. Admitted to Ohio bar, 1934, Ark. bar, 1958; practiced in Cin., 1934-37; mem. editorial staff Lawyers Coop. Pub. Co., Rochester, N.Y., 1937-42; atty. War Relocation Authority, Dept. Interior, 1942-46; prof. law U. Ark., 1946—, dean Sch. Law, 1958—. Chmn. Ark. Statue Revision Commn. Mem. Am., Ark. bar assns., Nat. Acad. Arbitrators. Unitarian. Home: 634 Oliver Av Fayetteville AR 72701

BARNHART, ROBERT D., corp. exec.; b. 1912; B.S. in Econs., Wharton Sch., U. Pa., 1935. m. With Phelps Dodge Corp., 1935—, treas., asst. sec., 1963—. Home: 80 Winton Rd Fairfield CT 06430* Office: 300 Park Av New York City NY 10022

BARNHART, WILLIAM RUPP, coll. prof., clergyman; b. Saegerstown, Pa., Feb. 7, 1903; s. John L. and Emma A. (Rupp) B.; A.B., Johns Hopkins U., 1923; A.M., Columbia, 1924; student Union Theol. Sem., 1923-25, 1926-27; D.D., Pacific U., 1938; m. Eleanor Welch Lyles, Sept. 1, 1927; children—Eleanor Hoyle, Joanne Sanford. Student asst. Madison Av. Presbyn. Ch., N.Y.C., 1926- 27; prof. philosophy and religion Pacific U., Ore., 1927-30; head dept. of religion Hood Coll., Frederick, Md., 1930-47, head dept. of religion and philosophy, 1947-58; minister cicular Congl. Ch., Charleston, S.C., 1958-68, minister emeritus, 1968—; exec. sec. Fedn. of

Churches, Washington, 1940-41; ordained to ministry Congl. Ch., 1930; mem. Potomoc Synod of Evang. and Reformed Ch., 1930-58. Past mem. Edn. and Research of Fed. Council of Churches of Christ in America; mem. Inter-Faith com. on Religious Life in Nation's Capital, 1940-42; lectr. religious emphasis weeks at various univs. and colls.; weekly religious broadcaster, 1958—; bd. dirs. Community Chest, Washington, 1940-42; mem. Md.-Del. Council Chs., 1942-58; mem. Univ. Christian Mission Team sent out by Fed. Council Chs. of Christ, 1946-49. Mem. preaching mission teams. Mem. Am. Philos. Assn., Nat. Assn. Bibl. Instrs., Charleston Ministerial Assn. (pres. 1964). Clubs: University (Balt.); Interchurch (pres. 1948-49) (Washington); Rotary, Charleston Country (Charleston, S.C.). Contbr. articles to religious jours. Home: 16 Broughton Rd Charleston SC 29407

BARNHILL, JOHN HENRY, univ. athletic dir.; b. Savannah, Tenn., Feb. 21, 1903; s. James Monroe and Alice (Bryan) B.; B.S.A. in Agr., U. Tenn., 1928; m. Katherine Peeler, Aug. 28, 1930; 1 dau., Nancy (Mrs. Ellis Trumbo). Coach all sports Bristol (Tenn.) High Sch., 1928-31; asst. coach U. Tenn., 1931- 41; head football coach, athletic dir., 1941-45; athletic dir., head football coach U. Ark., Fayetteville, 1946-49, athletic dir., 1949—. Mem. Alpha Tau Omega. Methodist. Mason (Shriner), Rotarian. Home: 1425 Markham Rd Fayetteville AR 72702

BARNO, PETER SANDEN, mfg. co. exec.; b. Wolf Run, O., May 24, 1912; s. John and Rose (Sanden) B.; B.A., Baldwin-Wallace Coll., 1935; postgrad. Western Res. U., 1936-37, U. N.C., 1938-40; m. Janet Campbell, Sept. 25, 1937; children—Douglas, Margaret, Cathleen, Peter. Athletic coach, instr. Baldwin-Wallace Coll., 1935-41; personnel adminstr. Thompson Products, 1941-51; dir. indsl. relations Studebaker-Packard, 1952-57; v.p., dir. Chase Brass & Copper Co., Waterbury, Conn., 1957-61; v.p., Worthington Corp., Harrison N.J., 1961-68; pres. P.S.B. Assos. Inc., Bernardsville, N.J., 1968—; chmn. bd., chief exec. officer Transmarine Merc. Corp., N.Y.C. Active Boy Scouts Am. Trustee Baldwin-Wallace Coll., 1954-57. Mem. N.A.M., Nat. Metal Trades Assn., United Community Funds and Councils Am. Presbyn. Home: 59 Fieldstone Dr Basking Ridge NJ 07920 Office: PSB Associates Inc Bernardsville NJ

BARNOTHY, MADELEINE FORRO, (Mrs. Jeno Michael Barnothy), educator, physicist; b. Zsambok, Hungary. Aug. 21, 1904; d. Robert and Margaret (Somlo) Forro; Ph.D. in Physics, Royal Hungarian U., Budapest, 1927; m. Jeno Michael Barnothy, Dec. 24, 1938. Came to U.S., 1948, naturalized, 1953. Postdoctoral fellow U. Gottingen (Germany). 1928-29; asst. prof. Royal Hungarian U., 1929-43, asso. prof., 1943-48; prof. Barat Coll., Lake Forest, Ill., 1948-53; research asso. Northwestern U., Evanston, Ill., 1953-63; asso. prof. physics U. Ill. Coll. Pharmacy, Chgo., 1955-64, prof., 1964—. Vice pres. Biomagnetic Research Found. Recipient medal Hungarian Acad. Sci., 1937, Eotvos prize, 1947. Am. Assn. U. Women nat. fellow, 1956. Mem. Am. Phys. Soc., Biophys. Soc. Am., Astron. Soc. Am. Editor: Biological Effects of Magnetic Fields, Vol. I, 1964, Vol. II, 1969. Contbr. articles profl. jours. Home: 833 Lincoln St Evanston IL 60201 Office: 833 S Wood St Chicago IL 60612

BARNOUW, ERIK, educator, writer; b. The Hague, Holland, June 23, 1908; s. Adriaan Jacob and Anne Eliza (Midgley) B.; came to U.S., 1919, naturalized, 1928; A.B., Princeton, 1929; m. Dorothy Maybelle Beach, June 3, 1939; children—Jeffrey, Susanna, Karen. Radio writer and dir. Erwin Wasey & Co., advt., 1931-35, Arthur Kudner, advt., 1935-37; writer, editor CBS, 1939-40; script editor NBC, 1942-44; commentator overseas br. OWI, 1943-44; supr. edn. unit Armed Forces Radio Service, War Dept., 1944- 45; mem. faculty Columbia, 1946—, prof. dramatic arts charge film, radio and TV, 1964-69; editor Center for Mass Communication, Columbia U. Press, 1948—; occasional writer, adapter Theater Guild radio and TV series, 1945-61; writer, producer Decision series for Nat. Ednl. TV, 1957-59. Cons. communications USPHS, 1947-50. Recipient Gavel award for Decision films Am. Bar Assn., 1959; Fulbright Research fellow, India, 1961-62; Guggenheim fellow, in 1969. Mem. Authors League Am. (sec. 1949- 53), Radio Writers Guild (pres. 1947-49), Writers Guild Am. (chmn. 1957- 59). Acad. TV Arts and Scis. (bd. govs. 1966-68), Am. Civil Liberties Union, PEN Club, Pub. Affairs Com. (mem. bd.,), Internat. Film Seminars (pres. 1960-68), Phi Beta Kappa. Author: (3 act play) Open Collars, 1928; Handbook of Radio Writing, 2d edit., 1947; Handbook of Radio Production, 1949; Mass Communication, 1956; The Television Writer, 1962; (with S. Krishnaswamy) Indian Film, 1963; A History of Broadcasting in The U.S.: A Tower in Babel, vol. 1, 1966, The Golden Web, vol. 2, 1968, The Image Empire, vol. 3, 1970 (Bancroft prize 1971). Editor: Radio Drama in Action, 1945. Home: 16 Center Av Larchmont NY 10538 Office: Columbia U New York City NY 10027

BARNOUW, VICTOR, educator; b. The Hague, Netherlands, May 25, 1915; s. Adriaan Jacob and Anne E. (Midgley) B.; student Princeton, 1933-35; A.B., Columbia, 1940, Ph.D. in Anthropology, 1948; m. Sachiko Miyagawa, Jan. 7, 1964. Instr. anthropology Bklyn. Coll., eves. 1945-48; vis. asst. prof. U. Buffalo, 1948-51; tchr. Verde Valley (Ariz.) Sch., 1953-54; research asso. U. Ill., 1955-56, vis. asst. prof., 1956-57; mem. faculty U. Wis. Milw., 1957—, prof. anthropology, 1965—. Recipient Stirling award in culture-personality studies, 1968. Fellow Am. Anthrop. Assn.; mem. Am. Ethnological Soc. Author: Acculturation and Personality Among the Wisconsin Chippewa, 1950; Culture and Personality, 1963; (novel) Dream of the Blue Heron, 1966; An Introduction to Anthropology, 2 vols., 1971. Home: 2518 N Terrace Av Milwaukee WI 53211

BARNSTONE, HOWARD, architect, educator; b. Auburn, Me., Mar. 27, 1923; s. Robert C. and Dora (Lempert) B.; student Amherst Coll., 1942; A.B., Yale, 1944, B.Arch., 1946; children—Dora Lempert, Lily Elizabeth Gisella, George Arthur. Pvt. practice architecture, Houston, 1948-52, 61-66; partner firm Bolton and Barnstone, Houston, 1952-61, Barnstone and Aubry, Houston, 1961-68; pvt. practice architecture, Houston, 1968—; mem. faculty U. Houston, 1948—, prof. architecture, 1958—; vis. prof. Yale, 1964, U. St. Thomas, Houston, 1965; prin. works include Harris County Center for Retarded, 1967, John F. Maher residence, 1967, Vassar Pl Apts., 1966, office bldg., Houston, 1966, Rothko Chapel, 1971. Bd. dirs. Contemporary Arts Assn., 1960-66, Houston Council Human Relations, 1958-62, 67—, Cystic Fibrosis Assn., 1965—, Tex. Bill of Rights Found., 1967—. Served to lt. (j.g.) USNR, 1944-46. Recipient award of excellence Am. Inst. Steel Constrn., 1961. Fellow A.I.A. (award of merit 1966); mem. Tex. Soc. Architects (award of merit), Tex. Soc. Archtl. Historians. Author: The Galveston That Was, 1966. Home: 4040 San Felipe Houston TX 77027 Office: 1222 Barkdull Houston TX 77006 also U Houston Houston TX 77004

BARNUM, ROBERT HUDSON, ret. naval officer; b. Bklyn., Oct. 6, 1910; s. Clifford Starr and Lucy (Redall) B.; B.S. in Naval Engring., U.S. Naval Acad., 1933; grad. Naval War Coll., 1958; m. Audrey Watson, Oct. 19, 1934; children—Sandra (Mrs. Richard B. Nygaard), Patricia (Mrs. Harry Rich). Operating mgr. Tidewater Oil Co., 1934-39; pres., gen. mgr. William Hunt & Co., N.Y.C. and Far East, 1939-49; asst. to pres. U.S. Steel Corp., 1949-68; mem. USNR-Ready, 1934—; asst. naval attache embassy, Santiago, Chile, 1942-45; rear adm., dep. dir. naval intelligence 1962-70. Bd. dirs., mem. exec. com. Nat. Security Indsl. Assn., 1961-68, N.Y. Def. Supply Assn., 1962-64. Bd. dirs. N.Y. USO, 1961—; bd. govs., exec. and finance com. U.S. Naval Acad. Found., 1961- -. Recipient commendation exceptionally meritorious performance duty Chief Naval Operations, 1957, sec. navy commendation outstanding performance duty, 1958, meritorious pub. service citation, 1960, scroll of honor Navy League, 1962; Al Merito (Republic Chile), 1945; Conspicious Service cross N.Y. State, 1946; Navy Intelligence commendation, 1955; Distinguished Pub. Service award Navy Dept., 1964. Mem. Mil. Order World Wars (comdr. N.Y. 1963-64, nat. jr. vice comdr.), Navy League U.S. (nat. dir., mem. exec. com. 1959—, nat. pres. 1963-65, chmn. nat. adv. council 1965-67). Clubs: Scarsdale Golf (Hartsdale, N.Y.); Wall Street, Metropolitan (gov., chmn. exec. com.) (N.Y.C.); Army- Navy Town (Washington). Address: Flag Quarters St Michaells MD 21663

BARNWELL, DAVID KITZMILLER, clergyman; b. Los Angeles, Oct. 7, 1900; s. Allen Yost and Julia (Kitzmiller) B.; A.B., U. Cal. at Berkeley, 1923; B.D., Union Theol. Sem., N.Y.C., 1928; student U. Edinburgh, 1928-29; D.D., Hillsdale Coll., 1946; m. Madeline Buzzell, July 1960. Ordained to ministry of the Baptist Church, 1928; asso. sec. YMCA, U. Cal., 1923-24; pastor First Bapt. Ch., successor Christ Ch., Summit, N.J., 1929-68, minister emeritus, 1969—; summer chaplain Hamilton Coll., Clinton, N.Y., summers, 1943-45; Nat. Council Chs. interchange preacher to Britain, 1959, chmn. interchange com.; lectr. Bapt. polity Union Theol. Sem., 1959-70. Bd. dirs. Union Theol. Sem., 1953-57, 58-70, dir. emeritus, 1970—. Mem. Union Theol. Sem. Alumni Assn. (pres. 1953-55), Athenaeum of Summit (pres. 1939-68), English-Speaking Union Kappa Chi. Home: 44 Hilltop Rd Millington NJ 07946

BARON, ALBERT ROBERT, fgn. service officer; b. Boston, Mar. 16, 1926; s. Albert and Lennea (Nystrom) B.; B.A., Harvard, 1948; postgrad. Sorbonne, Paris, 1968-69, Nat. War Coll., 1969-70; M.A., George Washington U., 1970; m. Yvette Genevieve Buvat, Oct. 20, 1952; 1 dau., Danielle. With U.S. Fgn. Service, 1949—; posts in Paris and Marshall Plan, 1949-57, Vienna, 1957-60, Washington, 1960-61, Niger, 1962-65, Turkey, 1965-67, Vietnam, 1967-69, Washington, 1969-70; asst. dir. U.S. AID Mission to Afghanistan in charge Helmand Valley Devel. Program, 1970—. Served with USNR, 1944-46. Recipient Govt. of S. Vietnam Revolutionary Devel. award, 1969, AID Meritorious Service award, 1965. Mem. Am. Fgn. Service Assn., Com. Internat. Devel. Address: Kabul (ID) Dept State Washington DC 20521

BARON, HANS, educator, historian; b. Berlin, Germany, June 22, 1900; s. Theodor and Marta (Mecklenburg) B.; grad. Leibniz Gymnasium, Berlin, 1917; student U. Leipzig; Ph.D., U. Berlin 1922; L.H.D., Lawrence U., 1957; m. Edith Alexander, Mar. 31, 1929; children—Rinehart, Renate. Came to U.S., 1938, naturalized, 1945. Research asso. hist. com. Munich Acad. Scis., 1928-33; privatdozent history U. Berlin, 1929-33; asst. prof. history Queens Coll., 1939-42; mem. Inst. Advanced Study, 1944-48; lectr. history Johns Hopkins, 1946-47; research fellow, bibliographer Newberry Library, 1949-65, distinguished research fellow, 1965-70, distinguished research fellow emeritus, 1970—; Mershon vis. prof. history Ohio State U., 1958-59; F. J. Whiton lectr. Cornell U., 1961; professorial lectr. Renaissance studies U. Chgo., 1963-68; vis. prof. history Dartmouth, spring 1964, Harvard, spring 1970. Guggenheim Meml. fellow, 1942-43; recipient Rockefeller Found. grant for 1961-63; Premio Internazionale Forte dei Marmi for Italian history, 1965; fellow Center Advanced Study Behavioral Scis., Stanford, Cal., 1967-68. Fellow Am. Acad. Arts and Scis., Tuscan Acad. Scis. and Letters La Colombaria (corr.); mem. Am. Soc. for Reformation Research (v.p., pres. 1955-57), Am. Hist. Assn., Renaissance Soc. Am., Dante Soc. Am., Mediaeval Acad. Am., Soc. Italian Hist. Studies, Am. Assn. Tchrs. Italian. Author: The Crisis of the Early Italian Renaissance, 1955, rev. 1966; Humanistic and Political Literature in Florence and Venice, 1955; from Petrarch to Leonardo Bruni, 1968. Contbg. author: New Cambridge Modern History. Co-editor: Bibliothèque d'Humanisme et Renaissance (Geneva), 1956—, Studies in Medieval and Renaissance History, 1962—. Contbr. to jours. Home: 28 Huron Av Cambridge MA 02138 also North Pomfret VT 05053 Office: Radcliffe College Library Harvard U Cambridge MA 02138

BARON, HARRY, educator, biochemist; b. N.Y.C., Dec. 31, 1908; s. Myer Max and Rose (Shapiro) B.; B.S., Bates Coll., 1931; M.S., N.Y. U., 1933; Podiatric Medicine, N.Y. Coll. Podiatry, 1947; Ph.D., Rutgers U., 1954; m. Laura Baelen, June 16, 1938; children—Cora Sue, Eric Mark. Instr. biology N.Y.U., 1931-34; museum curator N.Y. State Psychiat Inst., 1939-41; from instr. to asso. prof. biochemistry N.Y. Med. Coll., 1941-60; prof. biol. scis. M.J. Lewi Coll. Podiatry, N.Y.C., 1944-60; prof. chemistry Bklyn. Coll. Pharmacy of L.I. U., 1960-68; lectr. Bklyn. Coll., 1962-67; dean, prof. basic scis. M.J. Lewi Coll. Podiatry, N.Y.C., 1968—; spl. research intermediary metabolism, nutrition, amino acids, protein. Fellow Am. Inst. Chemists; mem. Am. Assn. Clin. Chemists, Am. Chem. Soc., N.Y. Acad. Scis., A.A.A.S., Harvey Soc., Sigma Xi. Home: 268 E 7th St New York City NY 10009

BARON, JUDSON RICHARD, educator; b. N.Y.C., July 28, 1924; s. Louis and Leah (Berzin) B.; B.Aero. Engring., N.Y. U., 1947; S.M., Mass. Inst. Tech., 1948, Sc.D., 1956; m. Selma Francine Wasserman, Sept. 4, 1949; children—Jason Roberts, Jeffrey Scott. Stress analyst Change Vought Aircraft Co., 1947; mem. research staff Mass. Inst. Tech., 1948-54, research asst., 1954-56, mem. faculty, 1957—, prof. aero. and astronautics, 1957—; cons. in Field, 1957—. Served with AUS, 1943-46. Decorated Bronze Star, Mem. Am. Inst. Aero. and Astronautics, Sigma Xi, Tau Beta Pi. Home: 7 Gould Rd Lexington MA 02173 Office: 77 Massachusetts Av Cambridge MA 02139

BARON, MELVIN LEON, cons. engr.; b. Bklyn., Feb. 27, 1927; s. Frank and Esther (Hirskowitz) B.; B.C.E., Coll. City N.Y., 1948; M.S., Columbia, 1949, Ph.D., 1953; m. Muriel Wicker, Dec. 24, 1950; children—Jaclyn Adele, Susan Gail. Structural designer Corbett-Tinghir Co., N.Y.C., 1949-50; research asso. civil engring. Columbia, 1951-53, asst. prof., 1953-57, adjunct asso. prof., 1958-61, adjunct prof., 1961—; chief engr. Paul Weidlinger, N.Y.C., 1957-60, asso., 1960-64, partner, dir. research, 1964—, also v.p. Advanced Computer Techniques Corp., N.Y.C., 1962-66. Recipient Spirit of St. Louis Jr. award Am. Soc. M.E., 1958; J. James R. Cross medal Am. Soc. C.E., 1963, Walter L. Huber Research prize, 1966, Arthur M. Wellington prize, 1969. Licensed profl. engr., N.Y., Mass. Fellow Am. Soc. C.E. (exec. com. engring. mechanics div. 1966-69); mem. Am. Soc. M.E., N.Y. Acad. Scis., A.A.A.S., Sigma Xi. Author: (with M.G. Salvadori) Numerical Methods in Engineering, 1952. Editor Jour. Engring. Mechs. Div. Am. Soc. C.E., 1970—. Contbr. articles profl. jours. Home: 3801 Hudson Manor Terrace Riverdale Bronx NY 10463 Office: 110 E 59th St New York City NY 10022

BARON, RICHARD WARREN, publisher; b. N.Y.C., Apr. 4, 1923; s. Samuel T. and Mabel Baron; student U. N.C., 1940-42, N.Y. U., 1943; m. Pamela Stearns, Sept. 4, 1946; children—Susan, Wendy, Vicki; m. 2d, Virginia Olsen, Feb. 15, 1963; children—Jonathan, Geoffrey, Lee, Amy, Richard Thomas. Vice pres., dir. Royal Paper Corp., 1947-59, Prodn. Research Corp., 1951-53; pres., chmn. Dial Press, Inc., 1958-68; pres., pub. Richard W. Baron Pub. Co., Inc., N.Y.C., 1969—. Served to 1st lt., inf., AUS, World War II. Clubs: Players (N.Y.C.); P.E.N. Home: 188 Orchard Ridge Rd Chappaqua NY 10514 Office: 201 Park Av S New York City NY 10003

BARON, SALO W., educator; b. Tarnow, Austria, May 26, 1895; s. Elias and Minna (Wittmayer) B.; Ph.D., U. Vienna, 1917, Polit. Sc.D., 1922, Jur.D., 1923; M.H.L., Jewish Theol. Sem., Vienna, 1920; D.H.L., Hebrew Union Coll., Cin., 1944; LL.D., Dropsie Coll., 1962; Litt. D., Rutgers U., 1963; Litt. D., Columbia, 1963; golden doctorate Vienna, 1969; Ph.D., U. Tel-Aviv, 1970; m. Jeannette G. Meisel, June 12, 1934; children—Shoshana Baron Tancer, Tobey Baron Gitelle. Came to U.S., 1926. Lectr. history Juedisches Paedagogium, Vienna, 1919-25; vis. lectr. Jewish Inst. Religion, N.Y.C., 1926, prof. history, acting librarian, 1927-30, dir. dept. advanced studies, 1928-30; prof. Jewish history, lit. and instns. Columbia, 1930-63, prof. emeritus, 1963—, dir. Center of Israel and Jewish Studies, 1950-68, dir. emeritus, 1968—; Rauschenbusch lectr. Colgate-Rochester Div. Sch., 1944; vis. prof. history Jewish Theol. Sem., 1954-71, Hebrew U., Jerusalem, 1958, Rutgers U., 1964-69; vis. prof. dept. religious studies Brown U., 1966-68. Pres. Conf. Jewish Social Studies, 1941-55, 59-68, hon. pres., 1955-59, 68—; pres. Jewish Cultural Reconstrn., Inc., 1947—; chmn. commn. survey Nat. Jewish Welfare Bd., 1947-49; chmn. library information Am. Jewish Com.; chmn. cultural adv. com. Conf. Jewish Material Claims against Germany, 1953-55; corr. mem. internat. com. for sci. history mankind UNESCO, 1953—. Trustee Jewish Inst. Religion, 1937-55; pres. acad. council Hebrew U., 1940-50; bd. govs. U. Tel-Aviv, 1968—, U. Haifa, 1971—. Fellow Am. Acad. Jewish Research (pres. 1940-43, 58-63, 67, 69—), Am. Acad. Arts and Scis.; mem. Am. Jewish Hist. Soc. (pres. 1953-55), Am. Hist. Assn., Soc. Bibl. Lit. Jewish religion. Author: Die Judenfrage auf dem Wiener Kongress, 1920; Die Politische Theorie Ferdinand Lasalle's, 1923; Azariah de Rossi'e Attitude to Life, 1927; The Israelitic Population under the Kings (Hebrew), 1933; A Social and Religious History of the Jews, 3 vols., 1937, rev. edit. vols. I-XIV, 1952-69; Bibliography of Jewish Social Studies, 1938-39, 1941; The Jewish Community, 3 vols., 1942; Modern Nationalism and Religion, 1947; The Jews of the United States 1790-1840 (with Joseph L. Blau), 3 vols., 1963; The Russian Jew under Tsars and Soviets, 1964; History and Jewish Historians, 1964; Ancient and Medieval Jewish History: Essays, 1971; Steeled by Adversity: Essays and Addresses on American Jewish Life, 1971. Editor: Jewish Studies in Memory of G.A. Kohut, 1935; Jewish Social Studies, quar., 1939—; Essays on Maimonides, 1941. Contbr. articles various publs. Home: Honey Hill Rd Canaan CT 06018 Office: 420 W 118th St New York City NY 10027

BARON, SAMUEL, flutist; b. Bklyn., Apr. 27, 1925; s. Jacob and Bella (Deutsch) B.; student Bklyn. Coll., 1940-44; B.S., Juilliard Sch. Music, 1948; m. Carol Lynn Kitzes, Dec. 21, 1963; children—Pamela Rachel, David Lazar. Flutist, N.Y. Woodwind Quintet, 1948-69, N.Y. Chamber Soloists, 1958-65, Contemporary Chamber Ensemble, 1962-65, Bach Aria Group, 1965—; lectr. flute Yale, 1965-67; instr. chamber music U. Milw., summers 1955-67; cons. N.Y. State Arts Council, 1964; asst. prof. flute and chamber music State U. of N.Y., Stony Brook, 1966-67, lectr. in flute, 1966—, also performing artist in residence Harpur College, 1967-69; prof. chamber music Juilliard Sch., 1971—. Recipient award distinguished in performing arts Sch. Fine Arts, U. Milw., 1964; officer Order Merit Monisaraphon (Cambodia), 1962. Internat. concert tours auspices State Dept. to S.Am., 1956, S.E. Asia and Orient, 1962, Central and South Am., 1969. Transcribed for chamber music; (J. S. Bach) The Art of the Fugue, 1958. Address: 317 W 89th St New York City NY 10024

BARON, SHIRLEY HAROLD, physician; b. Salt Lake City, Oct. 22, 1904; s. Henry Albert and Bertha (Lewis) B.; student U. Cal., 1920-23; A.B., U. Ore., 1924; M.D., Cornell U., 1927; m. Gene Doris Camp, Nov. 22, 1942; children—Barry, Joan, Herbert Marcus III (foster son). Intern Mt. Sinai Hosp., N.Y.C., 1928-30; resident ear, nose and throat Presbyn. Hosp., N.Y.C., 1930-32; pvt. practice, specializing ear, nose and throat, New London, Conn., 1932-41; staff Lawrence Meml. Hosp., New London, 1932-42; pvt. practice, San Francisco, 1946—; staff Mt. Zion Hosp., 1946—, chief ear, nose and throat, 1948-65; staff French Hosp., 1946—, chief ear, nose and throat, 1964—; cons. ear, nose and throat Children's Hospital; cons. U.S. Naval Hosp., Oakland; staff Presbyn. Hosp.; vis. chief otolaryngology Mt. Sinai Hosp., N.Y.C., 1964; expert cons. Letterman Army Hosp., 1947—; cons. Surg. Gen. Army, hosps. in Germany and Austria, 1949; faculty Stanford U. Med. Sch., 1946—, asst. to asso. clin. prof. surgery, div. otolaryngology; clin. prof. otolaryngology U. Cal. at San Francisco Medical Center. Bd. dirs. Harry Camp Co. Pres. Centurion Club of the Deafness Research Found., 1968-69; dir. San Francisco Hearing and Speech Center, pres., 1962-63. Served from lt. to comdr., USNR, 1941-45. Recipient Honor award Am. Acad. Ophthalmology ant Otolaryngology, 1964; Outstanding Civilian Service medal dept. Army, 1967; spl. citation Am. Soc. Mil. Otolaryngologists, 1970. Diplomate Am. Bd. Otolaryngology. Fellow A.C.S. (bd. govs. 1956-58, 59-64, adv. council otolaryngology 1960-64, chmn. 1964); mem. A.M.A. (chmn. sect. laryngology, otology, rhinology 1966-67), Am. Laryng., Rhinol., Otol. Soc. (pres. 1966-67), Am. Otol. Soc., Am. Acad. Ophthalmology and Otolaryngology, Otosclerosis Study Group, Am. Broncho-Esophagol. Assn. (council 1959), Pacific Coast Oto-Ophthal. Soc. (president 1967-68, council 1959-69), Am. Rhinologic Soc., San Francisco County Med. Soc. (bd. dirs. 1966-69). Clubs: Olympic, Lake Merced Golf. Contbr. papers med. publs. Home: 7 Presidio Av San Francisco CA 94115 Office: 516 Sutter St San Francisco CA 94102

BARON, STUART T., fgn. service officer; b. N.Y.C., Nov. 14, 1910; s. Alfred E. and Louise May (Tenney) B.; A.B., U. Cal at Los Angeles, 1933; J.D., U. So. Cal., 1937; postgrad. U. Chgo., 1944-45; m. Ruth Barlow Cooke, Dec. 24, 1935; 1 dau., Elizabeth Woodhull (Mrs. Oakley J. Dollard). Admitted to Cal. bar; practiced in Los Angeles, 1937-42; civilian adviser problems pub. finance and finance internat. trade Supreme Comdr. Allied Powers, Tokyo, Japan, 1946-51; dir. econs. and finance U.S. Civil Adminstrn., Ryukyu Islands, Naha, Okinawa, 1951-57; asst. dir. econ. policy U.S. operations mission to P.I., ICA, 1957-59; dir. USOM, Cambodia, Phonom-Penh, 1959-62; dir. AID mission to Ivory Coast, 1962-63, Republic of Congo, also counselor of embassy for econ. affairs, Leopoldville, 1963-65; dir. AID mission to Tunisia, Tunis 1965-70; dir. Central West African affairs AID, Dept. State, Washington, 1970—. Served to maj. AUS, 1942-46. Mem. State Bar Cal., Beta Theta Pi. Address: AID Dept of State Washington DC 20520

BARON, SYDNEY STUART, pub. relations co. exec.; b. N.Y.C., May 30, 1920; s. Hyman C. and Anne (Stuart) B.; B.S., St. John's U., 1942; m. Sylvia Schreibman, Oct. 23, 1938; children—Barbara Joyce (Mrs. Barbara Balsam), Eric, Richard, Daniel Henry. Practice as publicist, 1940-50; chmn. bd. Sydney S. Baron Pub. Relations Corp., N.Y.C., 1952—; dir. Allied Products Corp., United Aricraft Products, Inc., Daitch Shopwell Supermarkets, Inc., Nan-Flower Corp. Instr. polit. sci. N.Y. U., N.Y.C., 1954-58; pub. relations cons. Beth Jacob Schs., N.Y.C., 1956—, Aluminum Co. Am., 1956—, Am. Can Co., 1966—, Asso. Hosp. Service N.Y., 1965—, Cerro Corp., 1957- -, Columbia, 1967—, Tishman Realty & Constrn. Co., Inc., 1955—, Atlantic Cement Co., Inc., 1965—, Martin Marietta Corp., 1970—,

Pitts. Urban Transit Council, 1970—, Franklin Nat. Bank, 1971—; dep. commr. N.Y.C. Dept. Marine and Aviation, 1950; dep. commr., dir. promotion N.Y.C. Dept. Commerce, 1951. Dir. N.Y.C. bd. dirs. Nat. Assn. Retarded Children, N.Y.C. Big Bros. Movement; trustee Maimonides Hosp., N.Y.C. Recipient Civic Merit award N.Y.C., 1951; certificate commendation Jewish War Vets. U.S.A., 1960. Mem. A.I.M. (pres.'s council), Pub. Relations Soc. Am., U.S. C. of C., Am. Mgmt. Assn., Soc. of Silurians. Democrat. Mason. Clubs: Lone Star Boat, Friars (N.Y.C.); Fenway Golf (White Plains, N.Y.). Author: One Whirl, 1942; Men without Humor, 1944; The Bells Ring Loudly, 1946. Contbr. numerous articles to popular mags. Producer other Broadway stage shows including Tambourines to Glory. Home: Scarsdale NY 10583 Office: 540 Madison Av New York City NY 10022

BARONE, JOHN ANTHONY, univ. provost; b. Dunkirk, N.Y., Aug. 30, 1924; s. John A. and Josephine (Audino) B.; B.A., U. Buffalo, 1944; M.S., Purdue U., 1948, Ph.D., 1950; m. Rose Marie Pace, Aug. 23, 1947. Grad. asst. Purdue U., Lafayette, Ind., 1947-48, research fellow, 1948-50; instr. Fairfield (Conn.) U., 1950-51, asst. prof., 1951-56, asso. prof., 1956-62, prof. chemistry, 1962—, dir. research and grad. sci., 1963-66, v.p. planning, 1966-70, provost, 1970—. Mem. sci. adv. com. Conn. Dept. Edn., 1965-66; mem. review and evaluation com. Conn. Regional Med. Program, 1970—; dir. NSF In-Service Inst., 1961-69. Pres. UN Assn. Conn., 1970—. Trustee Conn. Council for Sci. Edn.; bd. dirs. Jesuit Research Council Am., chmn., 1968-70; bd. dirs. Higher Edn. Center for Urban Studies. Served with AUS, 1944-46. NIH cancer research grantee NSF Undergrad. Research Program, 1961-67. Fellow A.A.A.S.; mem. Am. Chem. Soc. (chmn. western Conn. sect. 1966), Am. Assn. U. Profs. (1st pres. Fairfield U. chpt.), Newcomen Soc., Phi Beta Kappa, Sigma Xi, Phi Lambda Upsilon. Democrat. Roman Catholic. Contbr. articles profl. jours. Home: 1283 Round Hill Rd Fairfield CT 06430

BARONE, PAUL LOUIS, hosp. adminstr.; b. Paterson, N.J., Oct. 11, 1902; s. Joseph and Jennie (Iozia) B.; B.S., Alfred U., 1926; M.D., Royal U., Naples, Italy, 1936; m. Martha Watkins, Jan. 20, 1940; children—Joe A., Jean Ann. Intern, St. Joseph (Mo.) Hosp., 1937, resident, 1938-39; practice medicine, specializing in psychiatry, Nevada, Mo., 1939—; staff physician Mo. State Hosp., 1939—, asst. supt., 1943-48, supt., 1948-70; clin. dir. Nevada (Mo.) State Hosp., 1970—. Fellow Am. Geriatric Soc., Am. Psychiat. Assn.; mem. A.M.A., Mo., West Central Mo. Counties med. assns., Am. Soc. Med. Psychiatry, Western Mo. Psychiat. Assn. (counsellor, past pres.). K.C., Elk, Rotarian. Home: 716 S Main St Nevada MO 64772 Office: State Hosp No 3 PO Box 308 Nevada MO 64772

BARONE, SAM, educator. Prof., chmn. dept. mgmt. scis. St. Louis U. Office: Dept Mgmt Scis St Louis U St Louis MO 63103*

BAROODY, JAMIL MURAD, diplomat; b. Souk el Gharb, Lebanon, Aug. 8, 1905; s. Murad H. and Edma H. (Daoun) B.; B.A., Am. U., Berut, 1926; postgrad. in Eng., France; m. Lorraine Fischer; children—Robert J., Lloyd J., Leila J., Nancy J. Arab polit. and econ. observer, London, Eng., 1929, 35-39; sec.-gen., acting commr. gen. Republic of Lebanon at N.Y. World's Fair, 1939-40; tchr. Arabic, lectr. Princeton, 1943; adviser Reader's Digest Arabic edit., other mags., also free lance writer Middle East internat. affairs, 1944-47; adviser to Syrian delegation Internat. Bus. Conf., Rye, N.Y., 1944; with Royal Delegation from Saudi Arabia on 3d Com. of UN Gen. Assembly, also alternate permanent rep. Saudi Arabia to UN, 1947—, now ambassador, dep. permanent rep. from Saudi Arabia to UN. Named hon. citizen N.Y.C., 1939; decorated Gold medal Order of Merit (Republic of Lebanon), 1940. Author: Poems, 1936. Contbr. articles mags. Address: care of Permanent Delegation of Saudi Arabia to UN New York City NY 10017

BAROODY, WILLIAM JOSEPH, research inst. exec., b. Manchester N.H., Jan. 29, 1916; s. Joseph Assad and Helen (Hasney) B.; B.A., St. Anselm's Coll., Manchester, N.H., 1936; postgrad U. N.H., 1937-38, Am. U., 1938; m. Nabeeha Marion Ashooh, Oct. 15, 1935; children—Anne Mary (Mrs. John G. Gallagher), William Joseph, Joseph D., Helene (Mrs. Michael Payne), Michael E., Mary Frances, Kathryn Jane. Asst. statistician N.H. Unemployment Compensation Div., 1937-40, supr. fiscal, research and legislative planning sects., 1941-44; dir. statis. div. N.H. War Finance Com., 1943-44; research asso. N.H. Legislative Commn. on Disability Benefits, 1940-44; chief research and statistics div., readjustment allowance service VA, Washington, 1946-49; exec. sec. com. on econ. security U.S. C. of C., asso. editor Am. Econ. Security, 1950- 53; exec. v.p. Am. Enterprise Assn. (now Am. Enterprise Inst. for Pub. Policy Research), 1954-62, pres., 1962-; adv. bd. Hoover Instn. Stanford U. 1960—. Dir. Melkite Assn. N.Am.; founding mem. exe. bd. Georgetown Center for Strategic Studies; mem. adv. bd. DeSales Sch. Theology; mem. bishop's liturgical commn. Diocese Richmond (Va.); bd. dirs. Cambridge Center for Social Studies, Herbert Hoover Birthplace Found.; mem. bd. Near East Found. treas., trustee Inst. for Social Sci. Research, Washington, 1957—; trustee St. Anselm's Coll., 1957—; bd. dirs. Catholic Virginian. Served to lt. (j.g.) USNR, 1944-45. Mem. Acad. Polit. Sci., John Carroll Soc., Newcomen Soc., K.C. Clubs: Army-Navy, Carlton (Washington). Author articles on employment security, ecumenism, Eastern rites. Home: 1111 Francis Hammond Pkwy Alexandria VA 22302 Office: 1200 17th St NW Washington DC 20036

BARR, ALFRED HAMILTON, Jr., art historian; b. Detroit, Jan. 28, 1902; s. Alfred Hamilton and Annie Elizabeth (Wilson) B.; student Boys Latin Sch., Balt., 1911- 18; A.B., Princeton, 1922, A.M., 1923, Litt.D., 1949, Ph.D., Harvard, 1946; Ph.D. (hon.), U. Bonn (Germany), 1958; Dr. Fine Arts, U. Buffalo, 1962, Yale, 1967; L.H.D., Columbia, 1969; m. Margaret Scolari-Fitzmaurice, May 27, 1930; 1 dau., Victoria Fitzmaurice. Instr. history of art Vassar Coll., 1923-24; asst. in fine arts Harvard, 1924-25; instr. art and archeol., Princeton, 1925-26; asso. prof. art, Wellesley Coll., 1926-29; dir. Mus. Modern Art, N.Y. City, 1929-43, dir. research in painting and sculpture, 1944-46, dir. collections, 1947-67, counselor to bd. of trustees, 1967—, v.p. bd., 1939-43, trustee, 1939—. Mem. advisory com. on art Office of Coordinator of Inter-Am. Affairs, 1940- 43; mem. adv. coms. Inst. of Modern Art, Boston, Cincinnati Modern Art Soc.; adv. council, dept. art and archaeol., Princeton, 1946; vis. com. fine arts Fogg Art Mus., Harvard, 1958-60, chmn., 1965—, bd. overseers Harvard, 1964-70. Recipient Cross, Chevalier, Legion of Honor, 1959; Grand Cross Order of Merit, West Germany, 1959; spl. merti award for notable creative achievement Brandeis U., 1964; N.Y. State award, 1968; award for distinguished service to arts Nat. Inst. Arts and Letters, 1968. Trustee Am. Fedn. Arts, 1948-55; pres. Found. for Arts, Religion and Culture, 1962-65. Mem. Assn. of Art Museum Dirs. (v.p. 1940-41), College Art Assn. (dir. 1943-48), Am. Assn. of Museums (councilor). Presbyn. Editor (with Holger Cahill): Art in America, 1936; American Painters Series, Penguin Books (Londonn), 1944-45. Author: Cubism and Abstract Art, 1936; What is Modern Painting?, 1943; Picasso; Fifty Years of His Art, 1946; 20th Century Italian Art (with J. T. Soby), 1949; Matisse: His Art and His Public, 1951. Editor of 31 museum exhibition catalogs; Masters of Modern Art, 1954. Mem. editorial bd. Art Bulletin, 1939—, Gazette des Beaux-Arts, 1940—, Mag.. of Art, 1942-52, Art Quar., 1953-, Art in Am., 1957-. Mary Flexner lectures, Bryn Mawr Coll., 1946. Home: 49 E 96th St New York City NY 10028 Office: 11 W 53d St New York City NY 10019

BARR, ANDREW, govt. ofcl.; b. Urbana, Ill., May 6, 1901; s. Andrew and Hortense (Call) B.; B.S., U. Ill., 1923, M.S., 1924; grad. student econs., Yale, 1926- 28. Pub. accountant Reckitt, Benington & LeClear, C.P.A.'s, Chgo., 1924- 26; instr., then asst. prof. accounting Yale, 1926-38; staff accountant SEC, 1936-56, chief accountant, 1956-. Served with AUS, 1941-46. Recipient Career Service award Nat. Civil Service League, 1955; Pres. U.S. award for distinguished fed. civilian service, 1960; elected to Ohio State U. Accounting Hall Fame, 1963; Alpha Kappa Psi Found. award, 1963. C.P.A., Ill. Mem. Am. Inst. C.P.A.'s (gold medal 1964), Am. Accounting Assn. (v.p. 1956), Fed. Govt. Accountants Assn. (pres. 1954- 55), Ill. Soc. C.P.A.'s, D.C. Inst. C.P.A.'s, Nat. Assn. Accountants, Beta Gamma Sigma, Beta Alpha Psi, Phi Kappa Phi, Phi Gamma Delta. Club: University (bd. govs. 1956-64) (Washington). Home: University Club Washington DC 20036 Office: Securities and Exchange Commn Washington DC 20549

BARR, CLYDE THOMAS, educator; b. Amanda, O., June 29, 1918; s. Clyde Alva and Mayme (Griffith) B.; B.S., Miami U. (Oxford, O.), 1940; M.M., U. Mich., 1947; Ed.D., Columbia, 1956; m. Helen Catherine Sterling, June 1947; children—Karen Louise, Dane Barton. Instr. Metamora (O.) pub. schs., 1940-42, Hays (Kan.) Jr.-Sr. High Sch., 1947-49; chmn. music dept. Fort Hays Kan. State Coll., 1950-56; asso. prof. music Ohio State U., 1956-64; chmn. dept. music, prof. State U. N.Y. at New Paltz, 1964—. Served with USCGR, 1942-47. Mem. Phi Kappa Phi, Pi Kappa Lambda, Phi Mu Alpha, Phi Delta Kappa. Home: 3 Old Mill Rd New Paltz NY 12561

BARR, ERNEST SCOTT, physicist; b. Lincolnton, N.C. Nov. 27, 1905; s. Peyton Arthur and Ida Beatrice (Brindle) B.; A.B., U. N.C., 1926, A.M., 1933; Ph.D., 1936; m. Phoebe E.S. Baughan, May 9, 1931. Public sch. tchr. in Honolulu, 1926-28; fgn. rep. Vick Chem. Co., Nfld., Mexico, and countries around Mediterranean, 1928-32; instr., Tulane Univ., 1936-37, asst. prof. of physics, 1937-40, asso. prof. 1940-47; sr. physicist research work on naval ordnance, Applied Physics Lab., Johns Hopkins Univ., 1945-46; prof. physics U. Ala., 1947—; cons. to Redstone Arsenal, 1952-65. Fellow A.A.A.S., Am. Phys. Soc., Optical Soc. Am.; mem. Am. Assn. Physics Tchrs., Am. Inst. Physics, Southeastern sect. Am. Phys. Soc. (sec. 1940-45; chmn. 1948-49), Sigma Xi, Sigma Pi Sigma, Delta Upsilon, Pi Mu Epsilon, Alpha Epsilon Delta. Episcopalian. Contbr. tech. articles chiefly in history of physics in Am. Jour. Physics, Applied Optics, Infrared Physics, Physics Teacher, others. Home: 926 25th Av E Tuscaloosa AL 35401 Office: Box 714 University AL 35486

BARR, HARRY FORRESTER, former automobile co. exec.; b. Enid, Okla., Aug. 28, 1904; s. Alexander F. and Retta (Gaitskill) B.; B.S. in Auto Engring., U. Detroit, 1929; Dr. of Sci. (honorary), U. Mo., 1966; m. Helen Spayd, December 25, 1929; children—Bradford F., Gaitskill S., Elyse (Mrs. Edward B. Bragg). With Gen. Motors Corp., 1929-69, chief engr. Chevrolet div., 1956-63, v.p. corp. engring. staff, 1963-69. Chmn. bd. trustees Detroit Inst. Tech. Mem. Nat. Acad. Engring. (dir. chmn. finance com.), Soc. Automotive Engrs. (pres. 1970, dir.), Am. Ordnance Assn., Detroit Board of Commerce. Mem. Franklin Community Ch. Clubs: Detroit Economic, Detroit Athletic, Recess (Detroit); Bloomfield Hills Country. Home: 25620 Meadowdale Franklin MI 48025

BARR, HOWARD RAYMOND, architect; b. Pitts., Feb. 15, 1910; s. Robert Wesley and Myrtle (Hockensmith) B.; B.Arch., U. Tex., 1934; m. Margaret Claire Pressler, Apr. 30, 1938; children—Richard Stuart, Alan Robert. Gen. practice architecture, Austin, Tex., 1939-42, 46; asso. Giesecke, Kuehne & Brooks, Architects, 1946-50; partner Kuehne, Brooks & Barr, 1950-60, Brooks & Barr, 1960-64, Brooks, Barr, Graeber & White, 1964—; dir. First Fed. Savs. of Austin. Sec., Tex. Bd. Plumbing Examiners, 1961-67; mem. City of Austin Parks and Recreation Bd., 1966-70; commnr. Tex. Urban Devel. Commn., 1970—. Served to lt. comdr. USNR, 1942-46. Fellow A.I.A.; mem. Tex. Soc. Architects (pres. 1969), Tex. Ex-Students Assn., Tau Sigma Delta, Phi Kappa Psi, Sphinx. Methodist. Clubs: Forty Acres, Citadel, Headliners. Works include: U.S. Embassy Bldg., Mexico; Manned Spacecraft Center, Houston; Lyndon B. Johnson Library and Sid Richardson Hall, Austin; U.S. Dept. Labor Bldg., Washington; S.W. Tex. Med. Sch., U. Tex., San Antonio; FAA Communication Bldgs., San Juan, P.R. and Balboa, C.Z. Home: 4602 Ridge Oak Dr Austin TX 78731 Office: Perry-Brooks Bldg Austin TX 78701

BARR, J. MCFERRAN, ret. banker; b. Louisville, Oct. 17, 1892; s. John W. and Margaret (McFerran) B.; student, The Hill School, Pottstown, Pa., 1909-12; A.B., Princeton, 1916; LL.D., Centre Coll. Ky., 1967; m. Anita Lawton Carrington, Aug. 31, 1918; children—Anita B. Watkins, John W., III, Margaret B. Matton. Employed by Ky. Wagon Mfg. Co., 1916-21; v.p. E. D. Morton Co., Louisville, Ky., 1921-26, Ky. Title Co., 1927-36, First Nat. Bank and Ky. Trust Co., 1928; v.p. Kentucky Trust Co.; pres. First Nat. Bank, 1944-57; pres., dir. Cave Hill Investment Co., 1941—; dir. Louisville Gas & Electric Co., Louisville Cement Co., Cave Hill Cementery Co., Mengel Co. Trustee The Hill Sch., 1943-66; trustee Louisville Presbyterian Theol. Sem., 1959-60, hon. life dir., 1970; trustee Centre Coll., 1958-64; alumni trustee, Princeton, 1936-40; dir. Am. Printing House for Blind, 1941—, pres., 1963-69. Chmn. finance com. Community Chest of Louisville and Jefferson County, 1927-67. Bd. overseers U. Louisville; pres.'s council Bellarmine Coll.; bd. dirs. Louisville Collegiate Sch. Served as capt. U.S. Res., 1917-18. Presbyn. (chmn. bd. trustees, deacon). Clubs: Ivy, Nassau (Princeton, N.J.); Louisville Country, Pendennis (Louisville). Home: 424 Mockingbird Valley Rd Louisville KY 40207 Office: 305 W Broadway Louisville KY 40202

BARR, JOHN ANDREW, univ. dean, lawyer; b. Akron, Ind., Sept. 10, 1908; s. Earl Ray and Bertha (Mattix) B.; student DePauw U., Greencastle, Ind., 1925-27; LL.B., Ind. U., 1930; LL.D., Ill. Coll., 1962; m. Louise Steniz, Oct. 28, 1933; children—John Robert, George Louis, Richard Allen, Barbara Ann. Admitted to Ind. bar, 1930, Ill. bar, 1933; in practice of law, Gary, Ind., 1930-33 and 1935- 38, Chicago, 1933-35; with Montgomery Ward & Co., Chgo., 1938-65, v.p., sec., dir. and gen. counsel, 1949-55, pres., chmn. bd., dir., mem. exec. com., 1955-61, chmn. bd., prin. policy making officer, 1961-65; dean Grad. Sch. Mgmt., Northwestern U., 1965—; dir. Northern Trust Co., Swift & Co., Commonwealth Edison Co., S.C. Johnson & Son, Inc., Stewart-Warner Corp., Marlennan Inc. Chmn. com. on hosp. effectiveness Dept. Health, Edn. and Welfare, 1967-68. Bd. dirs. Chgo. chpt. A.R.C., 1956-71, Evanston Hosp. Assn. Distinguished Alumni service award Ind. U.; Horatio Alger Award, Robins award. Mem. Nat. Indsl. Conf. Bd., Chgo. Assn. Commerce and Industry (bd. dirs.), Sigma Nu, Phi Delta Phi, Order of Coif. Episcopalian. Clubs: Economic, Chicago, Commercial, Law, Mid-America (Chicago); Old Elm; Indian Hill Country. Home: 670 Midfield Lane Northbrook IL 60062 Office: 339 E Chicago Av Chicago IL 60611

BARR, JOSEPH MORAN, former mayor; b. Pitts., May 28, 1906; s. James P. and Blanche (Moran) B.; grad. U. Pitts. Sch. Bus. Adminstrn., 1928; m. Alice White, June 4, 1949; children—Alice Elizabeth, Joseph Moran. Salesman, United Motors Service div. Gen. Motors, Pitts., 1924-29, George S. Dougherty Co., Pitts., 1929-36; mem. Pa. Senate, 1940-60; mayor, Pitts., 1959-70. Sec., Allegheny County Democratic Com., 1936; Bd. dirs. Pitts. chpt. A.R.C., Roselia Foundling Home: trustee U. Pitts., Mercy Hosp., Carnegie Inst. Tech., Carnegie Mus. Mem. Young Democrats of Pa. (pres. 1939) Young Democratic Clubs Am. (v.p. conv. assn.). Home: 6839 Juniata Pl Pittsburgh PA 15208

BARR, JOSEPH WALKER, banker; b. Vincennes, Ind., Jan. 17, 1918; s. Oscar Lynn and Stella Florence (Walker) B.; A.B., DePauw U., 1939; M.A., Harvard University, 1941; LL.D., Vincennes U., 1966, DePauw U., 1967; m. Beth Williston. September 3, 1939; children—Bonnie (Mrs. Michael Gilliom), Cherry (Mrs. Donald N. Briggs), Joseph Williston, Elizabeth Eugenia, Lynn Hamilton. Treas., O.L. Barr Grain Co., 1946—; mem. 86th Congress, 11th Indiana Dist.; asst. to sec. of treasury, 1961-64; chmn. FDIC, 1964-65; under sec. of treasury, 1965-68; sec. of treasury, 1968-69; pres. Am. Security & Trust Co., Washington, 1969—; dir. 3M Co., Comml. Credit co.; chmn. Washington Redskins. Mem. fed. adv. council Fed. Res. Bd. Trustee DePauw U. Served to lt. comdr. U.S. Navy, 1942- 45. Decorated Bronze Star. Mem. Phi Beta Kappa. Democrat. Home: 2554 Massachusetts Av Washington DC 20008 Office: 15th and Pennsylvania Av Washington DC 20013

BARR, MARTIN, univ. dean; b. Phila., Nov. 11, 1925; s. Louis and Bella (Moskowitz) B.; B.Sc. in Pharmacy, Temple U., 1946; M.Sc. in Pharmacy, Phila. Coll. Pharmacy and Scis., 1947; Ph.D., Ohio State U., 1950; m. Nancy Lipschutz, July 15, 1951; children—Lawrence Allen, Richard Andrew, Debra Ann, Steven Bruce. Grad. Asst., then instr. Ohio State U. Coll. Pharmacy, 1947-50; from asst. prof. pharmacy to prof. phys. pharmacy and pharm. research Phila. Coll. Pharmacy and Sci., 1950-61; prof. pharmaceutics Wayne State U. Coll. Pharmacy, 1961—, chmn. dept., 1961- 63, dean, 1963—; cons. Dept. Health, Edn. and Welfare, 1964—. chmn., Mayor's Com. for Narcotics Rehab., Detroit, 1971—; pres. Oakland County unit Mich. Heart Assn., 1970-72. Recipient Distinguished Service award Alumni Assn. Coll. Pharmacy, Temple U., 1957; named Distinguished Alumnus, Temple U., 1964. Fellow Am. Coll. Apothecaries, A.A.A.S.; mem. Am. Pharm. Assn. (pres. Phila. 1954-55, chmn. sci. sect. 1959-60; Ebert medal 1956), Am. Soc. Hosp. Pharmacists, Mich. State Pharm. Assn. (named Mich. Pharmacist of Yr., 1971), Am. Assn. Colls. Pharmacy (chmn. sect. tchrs. pharmacy 1959-60, chmn. conf. tchrs. pharmacy 1961-62), Sigma Xi, Rho Chi. Contbg. author: Pharmacy, Compounding and Dispensing, 2d edit., 1956; Remington's Practice of Pharmacy, 11th edit., 1956, 12th edit., 1965. Profl. editor: Mid-Atlantic Apothecary, 1953-64, Apothecary, 1953-64, Central Pharm. Jour., 1961-64. Home: 20285 Beechaven Drive Southfield MI 48076 Office: Wayne State Univ Detroit MI 48202

BARR, RICHARD DAVID, theatre producer; b. Washington, Sept. 6, 1917; s. David Alphonse and Ruth Nanette (Israel) Baer; A.B., Princeton, 1938. Appeared with Orson Welles Mercury Theatre War of the Worlds Program, exec. asst. to Orson Welles, asso. Citizen Kane, 1938-41; dir. City Center, dir. Volpone, 1948; dir. Richard III Booth Theatre, N.Y.C., 1949; producer Broadway plays At Home With Ethel Water, Ruth Draper, All In One, Trouble In Tahiti, Paul Draper Dance, 27 Wagons Full of Cotton, Fallen Angels, Hotel Paradiso; nat. companies Auntie Mame, 1952-49; producer, director of Theatre 1960-67; producer off Broadway shows The Zoo Story, Krapp's Last Tape, The Killer, The American Dream, The Death of Bessie Smith, Happy Days, Mrs. Dally Has A Lover, Whisper Into My Good Ear, 1959-64; producer Broadway show Who's Afraid of Virginia Woolf, 1962-63, Nat. Co., London Co., 1963-64; producer off Broadway shows Corruption in the Palace of Justice, Play, The Lover, Funnyhouse of a Negro, The Two Executioners, Dutchman, 1963-64; producer Paris Co., Bus & Truck Co. Who's Afraid of Virginia Woolf, 1964-65; producer New Playwrights series Cherry Lane Theatre, Paul Taylor Dance Co. Ambassador Theatre, Do Not Pass Go, That Thing at the Cherry Lane, The Giant's Dance at Cherry Lane Theatre, Playwrights Unit at Village South Theatre, On Broadway Tiny Alice, 1964—; on Broadway-Malcolm, 1966, A Delicate Balance, 1966-67; off Broadway-Good Day, The Exhaustion of Our Son's Love, The Butter and Egg Man, Match Play, A Party for Divorce, The Night of the Dunce; producer on Broadway-Johnny No-Trump, Everything in the Garden, 1968, Theater 1969 Playwrights Repertory, Theater 1969 Dance Repertory, revival The Front Page, 1969, off Broadway-The Boys in the Band, 1968, also London, Los Angeles, Boston cos., 1966-71. Pres. League N.Y. Theatres, 1967-69, Cultural League N.Y., 1969. Pres., N.Y. Cultural Found., Inc. Served to capt. USAAF, 1941-46. Mem. ANTA (dir. 1969-71, pres. 1971). Home: 26 W 8th St New York City NY 10011 Office: 165 W 46th St New York City NY 10036

BARR, ROBERT ALFRED, Jr., ednl. adminstr.; b. Cleve., Feb. 14, 1934; s. Robert Alfred and Adelaide Sutphen (Polhemus) B.; A.B., Swarthmore Coll., 1956; M.A., U. Pa., 1961; m. Eleanor Mary Moore, June 17, 1961; children—Richard Andrew, Jeffrey Robert. With Esso Standard Oil Co., 1956-57; asst. dean admissions Swarthmore Coll., 1957-62, dean men, 1962-70; asst. to pres. Chatham Coll., Pitts., 1970—. Mem. bd. Model Cities Program, Pitts.; mem. Pitts. Council on Higher Edn.; adv. com. Inst. for Higher Edn. Mem. Am. Studies Assn., Pa. Hist. Soc., Pitts. Council Higher Edn., Phi Kappa Psi. Home: 1167 Murray Hill Av Pittsburgh PA 15217

BARR, STRINGFELLOW, author, lectr.; b. Suffolk, Va., Jan. 15, 1897; s. William Alexander and Ida (Stringfellow) B.; student Tulane, 1912-13; B.A., U. of Va., 1916, M.A., 1917; Rhodes scholar, Oxford U., 1919-21, B.A., M.A.; diplome U. Paris, 1922; studied U. Ghent, Belgium, 1922-23; m. Gladys Baldwin, Aug. 13, 1921. Asst. prof. modern European history U. Va., 1924-27, asso. prof., 1927-30, prof., 1930-37; vis. prof. liberal arts U. Chgo., 1936-37; pres., mem. bd. of visitors and gov. St. John's Coll., 1937-46; pres. Found. for World Govt., 1948-58; vis. prof. polit. sci. U. Va., 1951-53; prof. humanities Newark Coll., Rutgers U., 1955-64; fellow Center for Study Democratic Instns., 1966-69; adv. editor Va. Quar. Review, 1926-30, 34-37, editor, 1930-34; adv. editor Britannica edit. of Great Books, 1944-46. Served with ambulance service, U.S. Army, 1917; trans. to Surgeon General's Office, 1918; discharged, 1919. Mem. Phi Beta Kappa, Raven Soc. Democrat. Episcopalian. Author: Mazzini-Portrait of an Exile, 1935; Pilgrimage of Western Man, 1949; Let's Join the Human Race, 1950; Citizens of the World, 1952; Copydog in India, 1955; The Kitchen Garden Book, 1956; Purely Academic (a novel), 1958; The Will of Zeus, 1962; The Three Worlds of Man, 1963; The Mask of Jove, 1966; Voices that Endured, 1971. Contbr. articles to various mags. Address: Kingston NJ 08528

BARRACLOUGH, SOLON LOVETT, educator, UN ofcl.; b. Beverly, Mass., Aug. 17, 1922; s. Kenneth E. and Esther (Lovett) B.; B.S., U. N.H., 1944; M.A., Harvard, 1949, Ph.D., 1950; m. Frances Horning, July 18, 1952; children—Ann, Esther, Kenneth. Research asso. Harvard, 1950; economist U.S. Forest Service, 1951-53; asso. forester U. Tenn. Agrl. Expt. Sta., 1954-58; agrl. econ. adviser USO, Beirut, Lebanon, 1958-59; UN regional officer land tenure and colonization FAO, Santiago, Chile, 1960-63; project mgr. Chilean Agrarian Reform Tng. and Research Inst., 1964—; prof. agrl. econs. Cornell U., Ithaca, N.Y., 1963—. vis. prof. U. Chile, 1962—; dir. studies land tenure and agrl. devel. in Argentina, Brazil, Colombia, Chile, Ecuador, Guatemala and Peru, InterAm. Com. Agrl. Devel., 1962-67; sec. Gov. N.H. Forest Policy Com., 1952. Served with AUS, 1943-46; PTO. Mem. Am. Farm Econ. Assn., Am. Econ. Assn., A.A.A.S., Soc. Am. Foresters, Internat. Assn. Agrl. Economists. Author: Notas Sobre Tenencia de la Tierra er America Latina, 1968; (with E.M. Gould) Economic Analysis for Farm Forest Operating Units, 1952; also articles. Home: Mast Rd Durham NH 03824 Office: Warren Hall Cornell Univ Ithaca NY 14850 also FAO UN Casilla 1949 Santiago Chile

BARRAN, ALFRED JOSEPH, utilities exec.; b. Newport, R.I., Oct. 13, 1919; s. Anthony Joseph and Elsie M. (Gross) B.; B.A., Denison U., 1941; m. Jean Lois Bunje, Apr. 18, 1942; children—Linda (Mrs. Frank Stull), Sally (Mrs. John P. Fiske), Melissa, Laura. With Gen. Telephone Co. of Cal., Santa Monica, 1946-53, pub. relations dir., 1953-58; pres. Gen. Telephone Co. N.W., Spokane, 1958-64, Gen. Telephone Co. of Ind., Ft. Wayne, 1964-67, Gen. Telephone Co. N.W., Inc., Everett, Wash., 1967—; chmn. bd. Gt. Columbia Corp.; mem. adv. bd. Everett br. Seattle-First Nat. Bank. Met. chmn. Nat. Alliance of Businessmen, 1970—; mem. Gov.'s Task Force on Rural Affairs, 1970—. Bd. dirs. Everett YMCA, Seattle Jr. Achievement; trustee Denison U., Everett Gen. Hosp. Served to lt. comdr. USNR, 1941-46. Recipient Denison U. citation for outstanding achievements, 1966; named to Sports-Illustrated Silver Anniversary All-Am. Football Team, 1964. Mem. Assn. Wash. Bus. (chmn. bd.), Seattle C. of C. (trustee), Sigma Alpha Epsilon. Republican. Elk. Clubs: Seattle Rainer; Edmonds Yacht; Everett Country, Everett Cascade, Everett Yacht. Home: 22819 Woodway Park Rd Edmonds WA 98020 Office: 1800 41st St Everett WA 98201

BARRAN, DAVID HAVEN, oil co. exec.; b. London, Eng., May 23, 1912; s. John Nicholson and Alice Margarita (Parks) B.; B.A., Trinity Coll., Cambridge U., 1934; m. Jane Lechmere Macaskie, Mar. 29, 1944; children—Tristram C., Julian M., Marius P., Francesca, Lalage, Adrian, Calista. With Shell Petroleum Co., 1934—, dir. Shell Transp. and Trading Co., 1961—, dep. chmn., 1966-67, mng. dir., 1964—, chmn., 1967—; dir. Shell Oil Co., 1964—, chmn., 1970—. Mem. gov. body London Bus. Sch. Knighted, 1971. Home: 36 Kensington Sq London W England Office: Shell Center London SE 1 England

BARRAND, HARRY PERCIVAL, Jr., banker; b. London, Eng., Nov. 13, 1922 (parents Am. citizens); s. Harry Percival and Helen (Drayton) B.; grad. Westminster Sch., 1940; B.A., Yale, 1944; m. Helen A.D. Stukenborg, Apr. 3, 1948; childrenKeith Frederick, Katherine Drayton, Stephen Ayers, David Charles. With Hanover Bank, N.Y.C., 1946—, asst. mgr. fgn. dept., 1951-53, European rep., 1953-56, v.p., 1956-58, sr. v.p. charge fgn. dept., 1958-61; sr. v.p. fgn. dept. Mfrs. Hanover Trust, 1961-63, exec. v.p. fgn. dept., 1963-66, exec. v.p. banking dept., 1966—. Pres. bd. trustees Westminster Sch., Simsbury, Conn.; bd. dirs. Musa Alami Found. Served with USNR, 1942-43; from 2d lt. to 1st lt. USMCR, 1943-46; Mem. U.S., Austrian (pres.), Internat. (trustee U.S. council) chambers commerce, Internat. Center in N.Y., Inc. (pres.). Clubs: Bankers of America (gov.); Yale, Economics, Church (N.Y.C.); American (London). Home: 227 Fairmount Rd Ridgewood NJ 10022 Office: 350 Park Av New York City NY 10022

BARRATT, DALE W., transp. co. exec.; b. Salt Lake City, 1912; children—John, Kent. Pres., dir. Union Street Ry., Union Street Inc.; pres. Salt Lake City Lines, Union St. Ry. Co., Greater Portland Transp. Co.; dir. Nat. City Lines. Office: 935 Purchase St New Bedford MA 01730*

BARRATT, RAYMOND WILLIAM, educator, biologist; b. Holyoke, Mass., May 4, 1920; s. George A. and Elizabeth (Bretschneider) B.; B.Sc., Rutgers U., 1941; M.Sc., U. N.H., 1943; Ph.D., Yale, 1948; M.A. (hon.), Dartmouth, 1958; m. Helen Ruggles. July 1943 (div. 1968); children—Marguerite E., William R. Asst. plant pathology and horticulture U. N.H., 1943-44; research asso., asst. plant pathologist Conn. Agrl. Expt. Sta., 1944-45; research asso. biology Stanford, 1948-53, research biologist, acting asst. prof., 1953-54; mem. faculty Dartmouth, 1954-70, prof. botany, 1958-62, prof. biology, 1962-70, chmn. dept., 1965-69, lectr. microbiology Med. Sch., 1962-70; prof. biology, dean of sci. Humboldt State Coll., 1970—; mem. vis. staff Vt. Environmental Center, Ripton, summers 1970, 71. Mem. Hanover Sch. Bd., 1964-68, Dresden (N.H.) Sch. Bd., 1964-68, chmn., 1968. Mem. No. New Eng. Acad. Scis., A.A.A.S., Am. Inst. Biol. Scis., Genetics Soc. Am. (chmn. com. maintenance genetic stocks 1964-68), Sigma Xi, Alpha Zeta, Phi Sigma, Kappa Sigma. Research microbial genetics. Home: 1696 Ocean Dr McKinleyville CA 95521

BARRAULT, JEAN-LOUIS, actor, producer; b. Sept. 8, 1910; ed. Coll. Chaptal. Made stage debut in Volpone, 1931; producer, actor numerous plays including Autour d'une Mére, 1937, Hemlet, Tandis que J'agonise, Namance, 1937, La Faim, Rabelais, 1970; with Comédie-Française, 1940-47; founder Compagnie M. Renaud J. L. Baurrault, 1947; dir. Thétre de France, 1959, Thétre des Nations, 1965—; films include Hélène, 1936, Le Puritain, 1937, L'Or dans la Montaigne, 1939, La Symphonie Fantastique, 1942, Les Enfants du Paradis, 1944, Le Cocu Magnifique, 1946, La Ronde, 1950, Versailles, 1955. Decorated officer Legion of Honor. Author: Rélexions sur le Thétre, 1959; (with Andre Gide) Trial: A Dramatization Based on Kafka's Novel, 1963. Editor: Cahiers de la Compagnie M. Renaude-J.-L. Barrault. Address: 18 ave du President Wilson Paris 16e France

BARRECA, VINCENT, mfg. co. exec.; b. Oct. 30, 1916; children—Stephen, Susan, Vincent, Laura Jane. With Admiral Corp., 1934—, established Canadian Admiral Corp., Toronto, Ont., 1946, pres., 1946-55, v.p. operations, Chgo., 1955- 57, exec. v.p., 1957-62, pres. 1962-69, also dir.; chmn., pres. Admiral Internat. Enterprises Corp., 1969—. Address: 9575 Higgins Rd Rosemont IL 60018

BARRELL, CHARLES ALDEN, educator; b. Buckingham, Va., Mar. 21, 1909; s. Charles Martin and Fannie Stuart (Hall) B.; A.B., Hampden Sydney Coll., 1931; A.M., U. Va., 1932; Ph.D., Ohio State U., 1938. Instr. polit. sci. Washington and Lee U., 1936-38, Ohio State U., 1938-39, Oberlin Coll., 1939-40; mem. faculty Bowling Green (O.) State U, 1940—, chmn. dept. polit. sci., 1946-65, prof., 1949—. Served as pvt. to 2d lt. AUS., 1942-46, M.I. officer, M.I. Service, War Dept. Gen. Staff, Washington. Mem. N.E.A., Am., Midwest polit. sci. assns., Am. Assn. U. Profs., Pi Sigma Alpha, Sigma Nu, Phi Alpha Theta, Sigma Upsilon, Tau Kappa Alpha. Club: Kiwanis. Author: RepresentationAn Analysis of Its Numerical and Functional Forms, Abstracts of Doctoral Dissertations, 1938; chpt. in An Introduction to American Government, 1954. Home: 722 N Grove St Bowling Green OH 43402

BARRETT, ALAN HILDRETH, educator; b. Springfield, Mass., June 7, 1927; s. Raymond L. and Sibyl (Jesseman) B.; B.S., Purdue U., 1950; M.S., Columbia, 1953; Ph.D. in Physics, 1956; m. Virginia McCulloch, Sept. 3, 1949; children—Richard Alan, Bonnie Jean. Postdoctoral research fellow U.S. Naval Research Lab., Washington, 1956-57; lectr., research asso. U. Mich., 1957-61; asso. prof. Mass. Inst. Tech., Cambridge, 1961-65, prof. elec. engring., 1965-67, prof. physics, 1967—. Served with USNR, 1944-46. Co-recipient Count Rumford award Am. Acad. Scis., 1971. Mem. Am. Astron. Soc., Internat. Astron. Union, Internat. Sci. Radio Union, Am. Geophys. Union. Mem. editorial bd. Astrophys. Jour., 1971—. Home: 3 Dane Rd Lexington MA 02173 Office: Mass Inst Tech 77 Massachusetts Ave Cambridge MA 02130

BARRETT, ASHTON CHICHESTER, govt. ofcl., laundry, and real estate exec.; b. nr. Edwards, Miss., Mar. 4, 1901; s. Thomas Hickman and Minnie (Chichester) B.; B.S., U. Miss., 1923; m. Virginia Anderson, June 7, 1926; children—Ann (Mrs. Joe M. Hancock), Patricia (Mrs. Jay E. Milam). Owner Barrett's Laundry & Cleaning, Biloxi, Miss., 1923—, A.C. Barrett & Assos., 1923—; pres. A.C. Barrett & Assos., Birmingham, Ala., 1960—; commr. Fed. Maritime Commn., Washington, 1961—. Bd. dirs. Nat. Soc. Crippled Chrildren and Adults; v.p. Miss. Soc. Crippled Children and Adults. Mem. Navy League Am. Mason (Shriner). Clubs: Great Southern Golf (past pres.), Sunkist Country (past pres.), Young Mens Business (past pres.), Propeller of United States. Home: 2400 Virginia Av Washington DC 20037 Office: Fed Maritime Commn Washington DC 20573

BARRETT, CHARLES CLAYTON, comml. banker; b. Milton, Ore., Mar. 8, 1918; s. Lawrence Clayton and Capitola (Scott) B.; student U. Ore., 1936-39; J.D., John Marshall Law Sch., Chgo., 1949; m. Dorothy Grace Smith, Oct. 6, 1942; children—Barbara Lynn, Jeffrey Scott, Pamela Jean, Bradley Clayton, Mark Douglas. With Percy Wilson Mortgage & Finance Corp., Chgo., 1940-53, v.p., 1948-53; v.p. Greenbaum Mortgage Co., Chgo., 1953-55; with Franklin Life Ins. Co., Springfield, Ill., 1955-65, v.p. charge real estate dept., 1965; v.p. charge real estate dept. Continental Ill. Bank and Trust Co., Chicago, 1965—; dir., mem. exec. com. Republic Realty Mortgage Corp.; dir. Marina Mgmt. Corp., Royal-Conith Corp., Continental Ill. Realty Advisors Co., Builders Capital Ltd. (Can.), N. Marina Bldg. Corp. Adv. com. Central Bus. Dist. Assn.; capital funds com. United Community Services. Served to maj., ordnance dept., AUS, 1942-46. Mem. Springfield Assn. Commerce and Industry (dir.), Am., Chgo. (dir.) mortgage bankers assns., Am. Inst. Banking. Presbyn. (deacon). Clubs: Bankers; Illini Country (Springfield). Home: 117 Tennyson Rd Wheaton IL 60187 Office: 231 S LaSalle St Chicago IL 60690

BARRETT, CHARLES SANBORN, metallurgist; b. Vermillion, S.D., Sept. 28, 1902; s. Charles H. and Laura (Dunham) B.; B.S., U. S.D., 1925; fellow U. Chgo., 1927-28, Ph.D., 1928; m. Dorothy A. Adams, Aug. 2, 1928; 1 dau., Marjorie A. With metallurgy dept. Naval Research Lab., 1928-32; metals research lab., dept. metall. engring. Carnegie Inst. Tech., 1932-46; prof. James Franck Inst., U. Chgo., 1946-71, emeritus, 1971—; prof., sr. research engr. U. Denver, 1970—; exchange prof. U. Birmingham, Eng., 1951-52; vis. prof. U. Denver, 1961, Stanford, 1963, U. Va., 1968, 69; Eastman prof. Oxford U., Eng., 1965-66. Mem. nat. com. on crystallography, 1950-54. Recipient Mathewson medal Am. Inst. Mining and Metall. Engrs., 1934, 44, 51; Howe medal Am. Soc. Metals, 1939; Clamer medal Franklin Inst., 1950; Heyn medal Deutsches Gesellschaft für Metallkunde, 1966; Sauveur medal Am. Soc. Metals, 1966. Fellow Am. Phys. Soc., Am. Soc. Metals (hon. mem.), Am. Inst. Mining and Metall. Engrs. (chmn. Inst. Metals div. 1956); mem. Am. Crystallographic Assn., Nat. Acad. Scis., Inst. Metals (London), Internat. Union Crystallography (editor metals sect. Structure Reports, 1949-51), Phi Beta Kappa, Sigma Xi, Delta Tau Delta, Sigma Pi Sigma, Alpha Sigma Mu. Author: Structure of Metals, 1943, rev. edits., 1952, (with T.B. Massalski,) 1966. Author tech. papers, phys. metallurgy, crystallography. Office: Metallurgy Dept U Denver Denver CO 80210

BARRETT, CLIFFORD LESLIE, educator; b. Conn., Dec. 3, 1894; s. Charles Leslie and Catherine Luella (Gibson) B.; A.B., Occidental Coll., 1917; A.M., Princeton, 1920; student U. Cal., 1921-23; Ph.D., Syracuse U., 1926; research in Eng., France, 1939, Harvard, 1950; m. Nancy Whitton, May 17, 1923; 1 son, Norman Whitton. Instr., asst. prof., chmn. philosophy dept. U. Cal., at Los Angeles, 1923-25, 1926-31; asst. prof., deptl. rep. Princeton, 1931-40; honors examiner Swarthmore Coll., 1935, 37, 39; prof. philosophy Scripps Coll. and Claremont Grad. Coll., 1944-66, prof. emeritus, 1966—; Alexander prof. Scripps Coll., 1961, acting dean, 1962—; chmn. Intercollegiate Program Grad. Study; regional asso. Am. Council of Learned Socs., 1957—; vis. prof. (summers) U. Cal. at Los Angeles, 1932, Coll. William and Mary, 1946; Harvard, 1948. Mem. Am. Philos. Assn., Mind Assn. (Gt. Britain) Phi Beta Kappa. Republican. Club: Princeton (N.Y.). Editor, contbr. Contemporary Idealism in America, 1932. Author: Ethics, 1933; Philosophy, 1935; What Makes Anything Important?, 1949; Norms of Law, 1971. Contbr. Am. Philosophy, 1954; Insight and Vision, also articles to jours. Home: 233 S Orange Grove Blvd Pasadena, CA 91105.

BARRETT, CLIFTON WALLER, author, lectr., bibliophile; b. Alexandria, Va., June 1, 1901; s. Robert S. and Annie Viola (Tupper) B.; student U. Va., 1917-20; Litt.D., Clark U., 1966; L.H.D., Brown U., 1966; m. Cornelia C. Hughes, Apr. 24, 1924; children—Clifton Waller, William Hughes, Jon Sherwood, Robert Paul, Richard Tupper, Kate Waller. Asst. to v.p. Munson S.S. Line, N.Y.C., 1920-32; co-founder, v.p., dir. North Atlantic & Gulf S.S. Co., Inc., N.Y.C., 1932-52, pres., 1952-54; pres., chmn. Norgulf Corp.; dir. Eastern Broadcasting Corp., Alexandria Improvement Corp., 620 Park Avenue Corp., Henry Holt & Co. Pres. bd. edn. Garden City, N.Y., 1945-46; mem. N.Y.C. Art Commn.; regent's lectr. Am. lit. U. Cal., 1959; chmn. fellows Pierpont Morgan Library. Bd. dirs. Barrett Found., Beekman Downtown Hosp.; trustee exec. com., pres. Lake Placid Edn. Found.; trustee McGregor Library, U. Va., U. Va. Alumni Fund; chmn. Friends of Columbia Libraries; mem. council Princeton Library Assos.; trustee N.Y. Pub. Library, Sweet Briar Coll., Clark U., Thomas Jefferson Found., John Carter Brown Library, Mt. Vernon Jr. Coll.; adv. bd. Mt. Vernon (Washington Homestead); chmn., bd. regents James Monroe Meml. Library; bd. visitors U. Va. Decorated comdr. Order Cespedes (Cuba). Mem. Poetry Soc. Am. (trustee), Cuban C. of C. U.S. (pres. 1949-55), Am. Antiquarian Soc. (pres.), Fgn. Policy Assn. N.Y. (dir., exec. com.), Bibliographical Soc. Am. (pres. 1962-64), Am.- Italy Soc. (dir.), Century Assn., Mass., Va. (exec. com.) hist. socs., Phi Beta Kappa. Episcopalian (vestryman). Clubs: Downtown Assn., Grolier (pres. 1957-61), Union (library com.) (N.Y.C.); Lake Placid (pres. 1960-63); Cosmos (Washington); Corinthian Yacht (Oyster Bay, L.I.); Rowfant (Cleve.); Southampton (L.I.); Odd Volumes (Boston). Author: Bibliographical Adventures in Americana, 1950; Henry Adams, 1951; American Fiction, The First Seventy-Five Years, 1954; John Greenleaf WhittierPolitician, Antiquarian. Poet: Henry Adams and The Making of a History; Italian Influence on American Literature, 1962; The American Writer in England; also author govtl. monographs on sugar transp. Editor: The Anatony of Freedom by Judge Medina, 1959. Founder Clifton Waller Barrett Library Am. Lit., U. Va. Home: Arcadia Farmington Charlottesville VA 22901

BARRETT, EDWARD LOUIS, Jr., educator; b. Wellington, Kan., Aug. 11, 1917; s. Edward Lewis and Jeannette (Ostlund) B.; B.S., Utah State U., 1938; J.D., U. Cal. at Berkeley, 1941; m. Beth Lockhart, Jan. 1, 1942; children—Douglas James, Susan Marie, Kent Edward. Admitted to Cal. bar, 1941; research asst. Cal. Jud. Council, 1941-42; mem. faculty U. Cal. at Berkeley, 1946-64, prof. law and criminology, 1962-64; prof. law, dean Sch. Law, U. Cal. at Davis, 1964-71, prof. law, 1971—; spl. asst. atty. gen. U.S., 1957. Mem. adv. com. criminal rules Jud. Conf. U.S., 1966-71; asso. reporter prearraignment project Am. Law Inst., 1963-66. Served to lt. USNR, 1942-45. Guggenheim fellow, 1964. Mem. Am. Bar Assn., State Bar Cal., Am. Judicature Soc., Order of Coif, Phi Kappa Phi. Democrat. Mem. Ch. of Jesus Christ of Latter Day Saints. Author: The Tenney Committee, 1950; (with others) Constitutional Law-Cases and Materials, 3d edit., 1968. Home: 518 Antioch Dr Davis CA 95616

BARRETT, EDWARD MITCHELL, lawyer; b. N.Y.C., July 18, 1920; s. Edward F. and Elizabeth (Schoder) B.; grad. Phillips Exeter Acad., 1938; B.S. in Engring., Princeton, 1942; LL.B., Bklyn. Law Sch., 1949; m. Rita E. Ferris, Mar. 20, 1921; children—Edward Mitchell, James F. Admitted to N.Y. State bar, 1949; engr. L.I. Lighting Co., Mineola, N.Y., 1945-48, atty., 1950-53, gen. atty., 1953-66, sec., gen. atty., 1966-70, gen. counsel, 1970—; asso. firm Bernard, Remsen, Millham & Bowdish attys., N.Y.C., 1949-50. Served with AUS, 1942-45. Home: 332 Southdown Rd Lloyd Harbor NY 11743 Office: 250 Old Country Rd Mineola NY 11501

BARRETT, FRED DENNETT, educator; b. Sheboygan, Wis., Sept. 19, 1906; s. Edward Jenner and Julia (Dennett) B.; B.A., U. Wis., 1928, M.A., 1931, Ph.D., 1953; m. Eileen Gertrude Meyer, Feb. 15, 1936; 1 dau., Cynthia Julia (Mrs. Bruce B. Wilson). Asst. psychology U. Wis., 1929-31; commd. 2d lt. U.S. Army, 1928, advanced through grades to col., 1960; retired, 1966; supt. schs., Grand View, Ida., 1948-50, Melba, Ida., 1950-52; dir. extension div. Ida. State Coll., 1953-55; prof. edn., chmn. dept. coll. Wooster (O.), 1955-70. Research comparative edn. U. London, 1960-61, Ministero della Pubblica Istruzione, Rome, 1966-67. Mem. Am. Assn. U. Profs., Nat., Ohio edn. assns., Phi Delta Kappa, Tau Kappa Epsilon. Rotarian, Kiwanian, Elk. Home: 4929 Whitcomb Dr Madison WI 53711

BARRETT, FREDERICK THORNTON, lawyer, corp. exec.; b. Chgo., Oct. 31, 1909; s. Fred Thornton and Marion (Irving) B.; Ph.B. in Econs., U. Wis., 1930; J.D., U. Chgo., 1934; m. Blanche Smith, Feb. 7, 1942. Admitted to Ill. bar, 1934; practice in Chgo., 1934-36; with law dept. Montgomery Ward & Co., 1936- 43; with firm Nicholson, Snyder, Chadwell & Fagerburg, Chgo., 1943-44; partner firm Nicholson, Barrett, Nisen & Keyes, Chgo., 1945-47; with the Cudahy Company, 1947—, gen. counsel, 1958—, v.p., 1960-70, sr. v.p., 1965-67, exec. v.p., 1970, pres., chief exec. officer, 1970—, also dir. Mem. Am. Bar Assn., Phi Kappa Psi, Phi Delta Phi. Republican. Episcopalian. Home: 3021 W Manor Dr Phoenix AZ 85014 Office: 100 W Clarendon St Phoenix AZ 80213

BARRETT, GEORGE FRANCIS, lawyer; b. Chgo., Nov. 17, 1907; s. George Francis and Mary Frances (Sullivan) R.; B.A., U. Ill., 1929; J.D., Northwestern U., 1932; m. Marcia Bates, Feb. 11, 1937. Admitted to Ill. bar, 1932, since practiced in Chgo.; master in chancery Superior Ct. Cook County, Chgo., 1936-38; atty. gen. Ill., 1941-49. Mem. Cook County Rep. Central Com., 1937-45; del. Rep. Nat. Conv., 1944, 48, 56. Mem. Am., Ill., Chgo. bar assns., Am. Judicature Soc., Chgo. Law Inst., Zeta Psi, Phi Alpha Delta. Republican. Clubs: Tavern (Chgo.); Bel Air Country (Los Angeles); Racquet, Thunderbird Country (Palm Springs, Cal.). Home: 70 E Walton St Chicago IL 60611

BARRETT, GEORGE WEST, clergyman; b. Iowa City, Ia., May 10, 1908; s. Edward Cecil and Mary Parsons (West) B.; student Pasadena Jr. Coll., 1926-28; A.B., U. Cal. at Los Angeles, 1930; B.D., Episcopal Theol. Sch., 1933; D.D., Occidental Coll., 1952; m. Emma Dee Hanford, Oct. 6, 1936; children—Myra Dee, Richard Newell, Margaret Anne; m. 2d, Bettina Trede Durland, Apr. 25, 1970. Dir. religious edn. St. Paul's Ch., Upland, Cal., 1936-42; Episcopal chaplain Pomona, Scripps and Claremont colls., 1940-42; rector St. Luke's Ch., Monrovia, 1942-47, St. James' Ch., Los Angeles, 1947-52; prof. pastoral theology Gen. Theol. Sem., N.Y.C., 1952-55; rector Christ Church, Bronxville, N.Y., 1955-63; bishop Episcopal Diocese of Rochester, 1963-70, cons., 1970—. Sec. Diocese of Los Angeles, 1947-50, chmn. com. on strategy and policy, 1949-52, chmn. bd. mgrs. Ch. Welfare Bur. of Ch. Fedn. Los Angeles, 1950-52; chmn. dept. of promotion Diocese of N.Y., 1960-62. Author: (with J. V. L. Casserley) Dialogue on Destiny, 1955; Key Words for Lent, 1963; Demands on Ministry Today, 1969; Christ's Keys to Happiness, 1970. Home: 431 44th Av San Francisco CA 94121 Office: 2185 Pacific Av San Francisco CA 94115

BARRETT, JAMES E., atty. gen. Wyo. Address: State Capitol Bldg Cheyenne WY 82001*

BARRETT, JAMES EMMETT, ins. co. exec.; b. Omaha, May 30, 1923; s. John C. and Elizabeth M. (Wilson) B.; LL.B., Creighton U., 1948; m. Mary Ann Forsyth, Oct. 20, 1944; children—Mary Margaret (Mrs. Richard Slye), Susan Elizabeth, Joanne, James Emmett. With Mut. of Omaha Ins. Co., 1948—, v.p., 1959- 65, exec. v.p., 1965—; vice chmn. bd. dirs. Tele-Trip Co., Inc., Omaha, 1964—, also dir.; dir. Companion Life Ins. Co., N.Y.C., 1960—. Admitted to Neb. bar, 1948. Mem. Met. Washington Bd. Trade. Mem. pres.'s council Creighton U., Omaha, 1969—. Served with AUS, World War II; ETO. Mem. Health Ins. Assn. Am. (bd. dirs. 1966-69); Am., Fed., Neb. bar assns., Neb. Soc. Washington (pres. 1962), Delta Theta Phi, Alpha Sigma Nu. Club: Kenwood Golf and Country (Washington). Home: 5002 Rockmere Ct Washington DC 20016 Office: 1700 Pennsylvania Av NW Washington DC 20006

BARRETT, JAMES MADISON, Jr., lawyer; b. Fort Wayne, Ind., Jan. 14, 1895; s. James Madison and Marian Anna (Bond) B.; A.B., U. Mich., 1916, LL.B., U. Mich., 1918; m. Edna H. Fee, Feb. 18, 1922; children—James Madison, Joan F. Cahalan (stepdau.). Admitted to Ind. bar, 1919; mem. Barrett, Barrett & McNagny, 1920—; dir. Fort Wayne Nat. Bank, Paul Pumps, Inc. Hon. dir. Fort Wayne Philharmonic Orch.; bd. dirs. Ft. Wayne Found. Served as 2d lt. with 26th Inf., 1st Div., AEF, 1917-19. Decorated Purple Heart. Mem. Am., Ind., Allen County bar assns.; mem. Am. Acad. Polit. and Social Sci., Psi Upsilon, Phi Delta Phi. Republican. Episcopalian. Mason (Scottish Rite). Clubs: Quest, Summit, Fort Wayne Country. Home: 1725 Hawthorne Rd Fort Wayne IN 46804 Office: Lincoln Bank Tower Fort Wayne IN 46802

BARRETT, JEAN, nurse educator; b. San Francisco, Oct. 4, 1903; d. Eugene Thompson and Eva Maria (Benton) Barrett; A.B., Upper Ia. U., 1924; diploma Ia. Meth. Hosp. Sch. Nursing, 1926; M.A., Columbia Tchrs. Coll., 1931; M.A. (hon.), Yale, 1969. Instr. nursing arts Washington County (Ia.) Hosp. Sch. Nursing, 1927-29, Decatur-Macon County (Ill.) Hosp. Sch. Nursing, 1929-30; adminstrv. supr. New Haven Hosp., also instr. nursing adminstrn. Yale Sch. Nursing, 1931-36; from asst. to asso. prof. nursing arts Yale Sch. Nursing, 1936- 48; chmn. dept. nursing edn., prof. nursing edn. Syracuse U. Sch. Nursing, 1948-63; Annie W. Goodrich vis. prof. nursing Yale, 1963-64, prof. nursing, 1964-71, asst. dean School of Nursing, 1968-71, emeritus, 1971—. Nurse cons. workshop in Formosa for nurse tchrs. Western Pacific region, WHO, 1952, mem.

expert adv. panel nursing, 1953-60; nurse cons. WHO projects, Tehran, Alexandria, summer 1965. Woman of Achievement award in health Syracuse Post Standard, 1954. Mem. Nat., Conn. leagues nursing, Am. Nurses Assn., Nat. Citizens Com. for UN, P.E.O. Methodist (mem. adminstrv. bd.). Author: Ward Management and Teaching, rev. edit., 1954; The Head Nurse, 1962, rev. edit., 1968. Editor: Contribution of Physical Therapy to Nursing Education, 1948. Contbr. articles profl. jours. Home: 1080 Patterson St Eugene OR 97401

BARRETT, JOE CLIFFORD, lawyer; b. Jonesboro, Ark., Mar. 29, 1897; s. William F. and Catherine (Siniard) B.; A.B., U. Ark., 1920; LL.B., George Washington U., 1924; LL.D., U. Ark., 1953; m. Bertha Campbell, Dec. 30, 1923; 1 dau., Dorine (Mrs. J.C. Deacon). Admitted to Ark. bar, 1922, since practiced in Jonesboro; sr. partner Barrett, Wheatley, Smith & Deacon, 1943—; city atty., 1926-30; dist. atty. St. Louis S.W. Ry. Lines, 1935-62; dir. 1st Ark. Devel. Finance Corp., Merc. Bank (Jonesboro). Del., pres. nat. exec. comm. Nat. Conf. Commrs. on Uniform State Laws, 1956, 59; mem. U.S. observer delegation 8th, 9th sessions Hague Conf. Pvt. Internat. Law, 1956, 60, U.S. delegation 10th session, 1964; U.S. delegation Diplomatic Conf. Uniform Law on Internat. Sale of Goods, 1964. Bd. mgrs. Council State Govs., 1959, Adv. Com. on Water Conservation and Use; adv. com. Commn. on Internat. Rules Jud. Procedure, 1959; mem. adv. panel U.S. Dept. State. Chmn. trustee Jonesboro Pub. Library, 1948-59. Recipient Outstanding Lawyer award Ark. Bar Assn. and Ark. Bar Found., 1960. Mem. Am. Bar Assn. (ho. of dels. 1947-55, chmn. scope and correlation 1958, spl. com. on internat. unification of pvt. law 1957-61, sect. internat. and comparative law 1967-68, council), Am. Judicature Soc., Am. bar Internat. Law Assn., Am. Law Inst., Internat. Assn. Ins. Counsel, Bar Assn. Ark. (past pres.). Democrat. Baptist. Rotarian, Mason. Club: Country (Little Rock). Home: 923 W Washington Jonesboro AR 72401 Office: Citizen's Bank Bldg Jonesboro AR 72401

BARRETT, JOHN DAVID, Jr., former found. exec.; b. N.Y.C., Dec. 8, 1903; s. John David and Nellie Redington (Adams) B.; grad. Hotchkiss Sch., Lakeville, Conn., 1922; Ph.B., Yale, 1926. Engaged in travel, also resident abroad, 1927-40; engaged in war relief, 1940-44; with Bollingen Found., N.Y.C., 1945—, pres., 1956-69, also trustee; v.p., trustee Old Dominion Found., N.Y.C., 1956-69; Nat. Trust Historic Preservation, 1958-63. Mem. bd. advisers Dumbarton Oaks Research Library and Collection. Fellow Jonathan Edwards Coll., Yale. Clubs: Century Assn., Union (N.Y.C.). Home: Belle Haven Greenwich CT 06830

BARRETT, JOHN J., lawyer; b. N.Y.C., Mar. 23, 1904; grad. Georgetown U., 1924; LL.B., Fordham U., 1928. Admitted to N.Y. bar, 1929; now mem. firm Barrett, Knapp, Smith & Schapiro, N.Y.C. Mem. Am., N.Y. State bar assns., Assn. Bar City N.Y. Office: 26 Broadway New York City NY 10004*

BARRETT, JOHN LAFAYETTE, govt. ofcl.; b. Kansas City, Mo., Nov. 29, 1917; s. John George and Lillian (Moran) B.; student U. Mo., 1937-41, George Washington U., 1958-60, U. Tex., 1945-46, 69; m. Carol Liggett, July 15, 1941; children—Carol Ellen (Mrs. Roger T. Baker), John Edward. Entered U.S. Fgn. Service, 1947, presently fgn. service officer class 2, 1st sec. Diplomatic Service, also consul; assigned to Lisbon, Portugal, 1947-49, Mexico City, 1949-52, Bonn, Germany, 1952-55, Berlin, 1955-57, Washington, 1958-62, Madrid, Spain, 1962-64, Lima, Peru, 1964-69, Hamburg, Germany, 1969—. Served with AUS, 1941-45. Decorated Silver Star, Purple Heart; recipient Meritorious Honor award State Dept., 1970. Club: Ruder Favorite Hammonia (Hamburg). Home: 532 S Chilton St Tyler TX 75701 Office: American Consulate General Hamburg Germany

BARRETT, JOHN TOWNSEND, educator; b. Peoria, Ill., Dec. 19, 1924; s. George F. and Julia (Zimmerman) B.; B.S., Northwestern U., 1952; M.F.A., Columbia, 1955; Ph.D., U. Mich., 1968; m. Wyllis Maurine Wiegman, June 3, 1949. Instr. Marietta Coll., 1955-59; teaching fellow U. Mich., 1959-62; asst. prof. Western Mich. U., 1962-65; asst. prof. theatre State U. N.Y. at Binghamton, 1965-69; vis. prof. Brock U. St. Catharines, Ont., Can., 1969-70; prof., chmn. dramatic arts State U. N.Y. Coll. at Geneseo, 1969—. Mem. Am. Ednl. Theatre Assn., Speech Assn. Am. Home: 12 2d St Geneseo NY 14454

BARRETT, J. WILSON, banker; b. Paducah, Ky., May 18, 1919; s. William G. and Lena (Threlkeld) B.; grad. Tucson Sr. High Sch., 1939; m. Frances Perry, June 27, 1942; children—James Wilson, Linda Lee, Thomas P. With Valley Nat. Bank, Phoenix, 1939—, now exec. v.p. Home: 524 W Kaler St Phoenix AZ 85021 Office: PO Box 71 Phoenix AZ 85001

BARRETT, LINTON LOMAS, educator; b. Lanett, Ala., Sept. 1, 1904; s. Linton Stephens and Carrie Elizabeth (Lomas) B.; B.A. magna cum laude, Mercer U., 1928; duPont fellow, U. Va., 1930-31; Ph.D., U. N.C., 1938; m. Elizabeth Elliott, June 1929 (dec. 1932); 1 son, Arthur Lomas; m. 2d, Marie Hamilton McDavid, May 26, 1937; 1 dau., Ellen Marie. From instr. to prof. Mercer U., U. Ala., Furman U., U. N.C., Princeton, U. Kan., 1928-48; prof. Romance langs. Washington and Lee U., head dept., 1960-70; vis. prof. Spanish, U. N.C., summers; pub. affairs officer Am. embassy, Bogota, Colombia, 1951, Quito, Ecuador, 1951-53; fellow Southeastern Inst. Medieval and Renaissance Studies, Duke U., summer 1966; lectr. Universidad Central, 1952; bd. examiners Coll. Entrance Exam. Bd., 1954- 57; dir. NDEA Lang. Inst., 1965; research fellow coop. program in the humanities Duke-N.C., 1965-66. Mem. Modern Lang. Assn. (sec., chmn. various groups), Am. Assn. Tchrs. Spanish and Portuguese, Phi Beta Kappa. Episcopalian. Author: The Supernatural in the Spanish Non- Religious Comedia of the Golden Age, 1938; A Simplified Approach to Don Quixote, 1970. Editor: A Mediaeval Italian Anthology, 1938; Five Centuries of Spanish Literature: From the Cid to the Golden Age, 1962. Translator 10 novels, other books from the Portuguese. Asso. editor: Hispania, 1950-64. Contbr. articles to profl. jours., U.S., Mexico, Ecuador, Spain. Address: Box 741 Lexington VA 24450

BARRETT, NESTOR, planning cons., journalist; b. Republic, Wash., Sept. 2, 1907; s. Thomas Francis and Catherine Elizabeth (Nestor) B.; student San Jose State Coll.; m. Margaret Mary Rose, Sept. 7, 1939; 1 stepson Charles C. Folks. Dep. county surveyor Santa Clara County, Cal., 1927-40; planning dir. Santa Clara County Plan Commn., 1940-52; v.p. Hodges, Pierce & Co., Inc., San Francisco; partner Pierce & Co., 1952-54; photographer, columnist San Jose Mercury-News, 1941—; instr. photography San Jose Jr. Coll., Los Gatos and Campbell, 1940-42. Mem. San Francisco Bay Area Rapid Transit Commn., 1951-57; 1st chmn. San Francisco Bay Area Council Planning Dirs. Fellow Photog. Soc. Am. (hon.; exec. v.p. 1959-63, pres. 1963-67); mem. Am. Inst. Planners (pres. Cal. chpt. 1951), Soc. Motion Picture and TV Engrs., Am. Soc. Planning Ofcls., Royal Photog. Soc. Gt. Britain (asso.), Urban Land Inst., Internat. Fedn. Housing and Town Planning. Clubs: Commonwealth, University. Home: 1625 Sweetbriar Dr San Jose CA 95125 Office: 675 N First St San Jose CA 95112

BARRETT, PATRICK J., chain store co. exec.; b. Chgo., 1928; grad. U. Notre Dame, 1951. Vice pres., treas. Aldens, Inc. Home: 9345 S Millard St Evergreen Park, IL 60642. Office: 5000 Roosevelt Rd Chicago IL 60650*

BARRETT, PHILIP S., banker; b. 1922; student Atlanta Law Sch.; married. With Mut. of N.Y., 1946-51; exec. v.p. Spratlin, Harrington & Thomas Inc., 1951-65; with Barrett & Knight Inc., 1965-66; v.p. Citizens & So. Nat. Bank, Savannah, Ga., 1966-69, exec. v.p., 1969—. Office: 300 Bull St Box 9586 Savannah GA 31402*

BARRETT, RICHARD HENRY, medical educator; b. Worcester, Vt., Feb. 4, 1910; s. Henry Howard and Eula (Conner) B.; A.B., Bowdoin Coll., 1932; postgrad. Dartmouth Med. Sch., 1932- 33; M.D., Vt. Coll. Medicine, 1937; M.S. in Anesthesiology, U. Minn., 1941; m. Marguerite Louise Carley, June 24, 1934; children—Richard Henry II, Katherine Eula (Mrs. Charles Adams Tillinghast). Intern, Mary Hitchcock Meml. Hosp., Hanover, N.H., 1937-38; resident May Found., Rochester, Minn., 1938-41; practice medicine, specializing in anesthesiology, Hanover, N.H., 1941—; chmn. anesthesiology sect. Hitchcock Clinic, Mary Hitchcock Meml. Hosp., 1941—; clin. prof. anesthesiology Dartmouth Med. Sch., Hanover, 1970—; con. anesthesiology VA Hosp., White River Junction, Vt., 1964—. Diplomate Am. Bd. Anesthesiologists (pres. 1969-70, dir. 1959-71). Fellow Am. Coll. Anesthesiologists (chmn. 1955- 56); mem. A.M.A. (vice chmn. anesthesiology sect. 1957), Acad. Anesthesiology, Am. (dir. 1948-56), New Eng. (pres. 1955-56) socs. anesthesiologists, N.H., Grafton County (pres. 1968) med. socs. Contbr. articles profl. jours. Home: Elm St Norwich VT 05055 Office: 2 Maynard St Hanover NH 03755

BARRETT, RICHARD WICHGAR, lawyer; b. Cin., Jan. 8, 1913; s. Glenn F. and Helen (Wichgar) B.; A.B., Dartmouth, 1934; J.D., U. Mich., 1937; m. Kathryn Louise Ferson, Sept. 3, 1935; children—Joan Bidwell, Richard Ferson. Admitted to Ohio bar, 1937; Supreme Ct. Ohio, U.S. Supreme Ct.; practiced in Cin., 1937—; asso. Dinsmore, Shohl, Sawyer & Dinsmore, 1937-44, partner, 1946-60; sr. partner Dinsmore, Shohl, Barrett, Coates & Deupree, 1960-67; sec. and gen. counsel Procter & Gamble Co., 1968—, v.p., 1971—. Pres. Cincinnatus Assn.; trustee Cin. Art Mus. Served with USNR, 1944-46. Mem. Am., Ohio, Cin. (past chmn. antitrust law com.) bar assns., Phi Delta Phi, Phi Gamma Delta. Clubs: Commonwealth, Camargo, Queen City. Home: 8575 Kugler Mill Rd Cincinnati OH 45243 Office: PO Box 599 Cincinnati OH 45201

BARRETT, RICHARD WILLIAM, mgmt. cons.; b. N.Y.C., July 8, 1922; s. Joseph and Gladys (Stocum) B.; B.A. with honors and distinction, U. N.M., 1949; m. Shirley Patterson, Nov. 20, 1943; children—Christopher Joseph, Patterson Hall, Robert William. Teller, Union Sq. Savs. Bank, N.Y.C., 1941-43; reporter Louisville Times, 1943; personnel investigator Dun & Bradstreet, Inc., N.Y.C., 1943-45; personnel placement officer UNRRA, 1945-46; orgn. and methods examiner Dept. Interior, 1949-50; budget examiner, div. natural resources Bur. of Budget, then mgmt. analyst Office Mgmt. and Orgn., 1950-61; mem. President's Task Force on Fgn. Aid, 1961; asst. dir. personnel for plans and programs AID, 1961; exec. recruitment officer White House staff, 1961-62; spl. asst. to dep. undersec. state for adminstrn. State Dept., 1962-63; dir. Office Mgmt. Planning, 1963-68; dir. mgmt, systems staff Bur. Budget, 1968-69; exec. dir. Am. Revolution Bicentennial Commn., 1969; pres. Barrett & Bonham, mgmt. cons., 1969—; pres. Bicentennial Services Corp.; pub. USA 200. Mem. John D. Rockefeller III Task Force on Youth. Bd. dirs. Greenbelt Consumers Services, 1956-60, Urban Home Ownership Corp., 1969—; cons. Md. Library Assn., 1961. Recipient Superior Honor award State Dept., 1964. Home: 19 E 88th St New York City NY 10028 Office: 3 E 54th St New York City NY 10022

BARRETT, ROBERT JOHN, Jr., aerospace exec.; b. Bayonne, N.J., Dec. 20, 1917; s. Robert John and Neta (Clark) B.; B.S., Ohio U., 1940; postgrad. U. Cal. at Los Angeles, 1961-62; m. Jane Sponseller, Jan. 24, 1942; children—Betsy Stanton, Robin. Staff mem. Price Waterhouse & Co., Cleve., 1940-42; exec. v.p. dir. Leach Relay Co., Los Angeles, 1947-54; dir. adminstrn. Ramo- Wooldridge Corp., Los Angeles, 1954-62; dir. adminstrn. and finance Northrop Corp., Anaheim, Cal., 1962-65; treas., chief finance officer Aeronca, Inc., Torrance, Cal., 1965—, v.p., treas., 1969—; dir. Aeronca Internat. Ltd., Aeronca Indsl. Products, Inc. Bd. dirs., v.p. Palos Verdes (Cal.) Homes Assn. Served from 2d lt. to maj., AUS, 1942- 46. Mem. Financial Execs. Inst. (past Western area v.p., chpt. pres., nat. dir.). Clubs: Jonathan (Los Angeles); N.Y. Athletic; Charlotte (N.C.) City; Breakfast (past pres.) (Palos Verdes). Home: 376 Via Almar Palos Verdes Estates CA 90274 Office: 24751 S Crenshaw Blvd Torrance CA 90505

BARRETT, SAMUEL, gas co. exec.; b. Norman, Okla., Feb. 3, 1911; s. Stephen Melvil and Dolly Susan (Cassell) B.; B.S., U. Mo., 1933, M.S., 1939; m. Lucille Miriam Shoop, June 8, 1934; children—Miriam Joan (Mrs. Gibson Hazard, Jr.), Margaret Dianne (Mrs. Timothy N. Tinnes). Tchr., Independence (Mo.) Pub. Schs., 1934-41; engr. Stanolind Oil & Gas Co., Tex.-Okla., 1941-44, supt. gas sales, Tulsa, 1934-53; mgr. gas sales and supply Colo. Interstate Gas Co., Colorado Springs, 1953-54, v.p., 1954-62, sr. v.p., 1962—; sr. v.p. Colo. Interstate Corp.; v.p. Trans-Colo. Pipeline Co.; dir. Colo. Oil & Gas Corp. Nat. chmn. Future Requirements Com., 1960-70; chmn. liaison com. Fed. Power Commn. Future Requirements Com., 1969—. Scoutmaster, Kansas City and Tulsa councils Boy Scouts Am., 1937-48; pres. Sch. Bd., 1959-63. Bd. dirs. YW-YMCA; trustee Iliff Sch. Theology, Denver. Mem. Am., Ind. Natural, So. gas assns., State Gas Mens Assn. Tex., Okla., Colo. Methodist. Home: 58 Cheyenne Mountain Blvd Colorado Springs CO 80906 Office: PO Box 1087 Colorado Springs CO 80901

BARRETT, SIDNEY RAY, architect; b. Albany, Ga., Nov. 15, 1933; s. James Samuel and Effie Cleo (Touchton) B.; B.S. in Architecture, Ga. Inst. Tech., 1956, B.A. in Architecture, 1961; postgrad., E'cole de Beaux-Arts, Paris, France, 1961-62; m. Alberta Consuelo Coldwell, Jan. 26, 1957; children—Sidney Ray, Steven Craig, Ashley Helene. With Stevens & Wilkinson, Architects, Atlanta, 1960-65; owner firm Sidney R. Barrett, architect, and assos., Atlanta, 1966—; asso. prof. Ga. Inst. Tech., 1969—. Coach, Clairmont Youth Football League, 1969, 70; sponsor Barrett Scholarship Fund, Ga. Inst. Tech., 1969—. Served to capt. USAF, 1957-60. Recipient Paris prize, 1961, Design award A.I.A., 1961. Ga. Inst. Tech. Sch. Architecture grantee, 1961. Mem. Atlanta, DeKalb chambers commerce, A.I.A., Tau Sigma Delta (faculty adviser), Kappa Alpha. Club: Atlanta Athletic. Designer Exec. Park, Atlanta, Perimeter Center, Coastal States Bldg. (both Atlanta). Home: 1220 Tynecastle Way NE Atlanta GA 30338 Office: 8 Perimeter Center E Atlanta GA 30346

BARRETT, SISTER MARY OLIVIA, educator; b., Chgo., Oct. 3, 1920; d. Thomas F. and Mary E. (Murphy) Barrett; B.S., St. Xavier Coll., 1942; M.S., U. Notre Dame, 1953, Ph.D., 1957. Joined Order of Religious Sisters of Mercy, Roman Cath. Ch., 1943; mem. faculty St. Xavier Coll., Chgo., 1956—, prof. chemistry, 1961—, chmn. div. natural scis., 1961-63, pres. coll., 1963-69. Mem. Am. Chem. Soc., Nat. Cath. Ednl. Assn., Sigma Xi, Kappa Gamma Pi. Address: St Xavier Coll 103d and Central Park Av Chicago IL 60655

BARRETT, WILLIAM A., legislator; grad. Brown Prep. Sch. and St. Joseph's Coll., Phila.; 3 children. Engaged as real estate broker; mem. 79th, 81st, 89-91st congresses from 1st Pa. Dist. Democrat. Address: House of Representatives Washington DC 20515

BARRETT, WILLIAM C., educator, author; b. N.Y.C., Dec. 30, 1913; s. John Patrick and Delia (Connolly) B.; A.B. (fellow 1929-33), Coll. City N.Y., 1933; M.A., Columbia, 1934, Ph.D., 1938. Instr. philosophy U. Ill., 1938-40, Brown U., 1940-42; vice consul, Rome, Italy, 1944-45; mem. faculty N.Y. U., 1948—, prof. philosophy, 1950—. Editor, Partisan Rev., 1946-53; lit. reviewer Atlantic Monthly, 1961-65. Fellow U. Chgo., 1936-38; Rockefeller Found. fellow, 1946-47. Mem. Am. Philos. Assn., Authors' Guild, Phi Beta Kappa. Author: What is Existentialism?, 1947, 64; Irrational Man, 1958; Wine and the Music (later pub. as Pieces of Dreams 1970); (with Theodore Besterman) Divining-Rod, 1967; (with Daniel Yankelovich) Ego and Instinct, 1969. Editor: Zen Buddhism, 1956; co-editor Philosophy in the Twentieth Century, 1961; adv. bd. Jour. Existential Psychoanalysis. Home: 34 Harwood Av North Tarrytown NY 10591 Office: New York Univ New York City NY 10003

BARRETT, WILLIAM EDMUND, author; b. N.Y.C., Nov. 16, 1900; s. John Joseph and Eleanor Margaret (Flannery) B.; student Manhattan Coll., N.Y.C.; Litt.D. (hon.), Creighton U., 1961; m. Christine m. Rollman, Feb. 15, 1925; children—Marjorie Christine, William Edmund. Cons. in aeros. Denver Pub. Library, 1941—; civilian lectr. for Army Air Forces, 1942. Recipient citation Regis Coll., 1956. Fellow Internat. Inst. Arts and Letters; mem. P.E.W., Authors League Am. Roman Catholic. Clubs: The Players (N.Y.C.); Nat. Press (Washington); Denver Press, Denver Athletic; Colo. Authors League (pres. 1943-44). Author: Woman on Horseback, 1938 (translated into German, Swedish, Spanish and Portuguese); Flight from Youth, 1939 (bought by MGM); The Last Man, 1946; The Evil Heart, 1946; The Number of My Days, 1946; Man From Rome (motion picture, Mgm), 1949; The Left Hand of God, 1951 (choice Fiction Book Club 1951; translated into 13 langs. motion picture 1955); Shadows of the Images, 1953 (translated into 5 langs.); Sudden Strangers, 1956 (translated into 5 langs.); The Empty Shrine, 1958 (translated 9 langs.; 5 Acad. award the Field, 1962 (motion picture 1963, translated 3 langs.; 5 Acad. Award nominations, 1 award); The Fools of Time (translated 3 langs.), 1963; Shepherd of Mankind (biography of Pope Paul VI), 1964; The Red Lacquered Gate, 1967; Best Am. Short Stories, 1944; Son-of-a-Gun Stew, 1945; Denver Murders, 1946; The Sudden Strangers, 1956 (translated into Dutch, Spanish, Italian); The Edge of Things, 1960; The First War Planes, 1960; The Glory Tent, 1967; The Wine and the Music (Lit. Guild choice, Readers Digest Book Club choice, translated 5 langs.; made into movie Pieces of Dreams), 1968; A Woman in the House, 1971, book reviews in Boston Transcript and Boston Post, 1941-; novels and serials, Red Book, Cosmopolitan, etc. Home: 1282 Detroit St Denver CO 80206

BARRETT, WILLIAM GROUT, physician; b. San Francisco, Cal., July 9, 1902; s. Charles Leland and Olga (Block) B.; B.S., U. Cal., 1924; M.D., Harvard Med. Sch., 1929; m. Anne Dorothea Nagel, June 9, 1928; childrenCharles N., Sarah S., Elizabeth; m. 2d Dorothy Pratt Register, Aug. 18, 1941; 1 son, Eliot Steven; m. 3d, Emmy Sylvester, M.D., Feb. 14, 1957; m. 4th, Estelle Caen Weymouth, Sept. 9, 1961. Intern, Barnes Hosp., St. Louis, 1930-31, pvt. practice medicine specializing in psychiatry, N.Y. Psychiatric Inst. and Hosp., 1931-32, Boston, 1932-41; mem. staff Mass. Gen. Hosp.; cons. to Mass. Eye & Ear Infirmary, 1934-41; pvt. practice San Francisco, 1941-. Lt. col. USAAF, 1942-46. Mem. A.M.A., Am. Psychiat. Assn., Am. Psychoanalytic Assn. (past pres.), San Francisco Psychoanalytic Soc. and Inst. (past pres.). Address: 17 Commonwealth Av San Francisco CA 94118

BARRETT, WILLIAM R., chem. co. exec.; b. Allegan, Mich., 1918; ed. Mich. State U., 1939. Exec. v.p., dir. Interchem. Corp. Home: 70 Dunning Rd New Canaan, CT 06480. Office: 67 W 44th St New York City NY 10036*

BARRETT, WILLIAM RIKER, engraving and printing co. exec.; b. East Orange, N.J., Dec. 13, 1915; s. Hugh Campbell and Eleanor (Riker) B.; grad. Choate Sch., 1934; A.B., Princeton, 1938; m. Margery Welles, July 13, 1940; children—William Riker, Eleanor, Bruce, Paul Welles, Anthony. With Am. Bank Note Co., N.Y.C., 1945—, 1st v.p. 1961-65, president, 1965—, also dir. Served to capt., pilot USAAF, World War II. Clubs: University Cottage (Princeton); Plainfield Country. Home: 1341 Prospect Av Plainfield NJ 08861 Office: 70 Broad St New York City NY 10004

BARRICK, NOLAN ELLMORE, educator, architect; b. Pearland, Tex., Oct. 30, 1913; s. Charles Emery and Hester (Harris) B.; B.A., Rice Inst., 1935, B.S., 1936, M.A., 1937, traveling fellow, 1937-38; m. Rosemary Watkin, Oct. 17, 1938; children—Bruce Watkin, Anne Hester. Gen. practice of architecture, 1940- 1940- -; asst. prof., asso. prof. architecture and archtl. engring. Ia. State Coll., 1945-49; asso. prof. Sch. Architecture, U. Tex., 1949-53, prof., head dept. architecture and allied arts, 1953-, supervising architect Tex. Technol. Coll., 1953-65. Pres. Res: Con, Inc., 1969—. Archtl. adv. com. to State Bldg. Com., 1958—. Mem. Lubbock Zoning and Planning Commn. 1967—; mem. Lubbock Urban Renewal Bd. Commrs., 1971—. Dir. regional meetings, sec. Assn. Collegiate Schs. Architecturee, 1963-65; sec.- treasurer Texas Architectural Found., 1964; archtl. TV project com. So. Regional Edn. Bd.; dir. Tex. Technol. Coll. Art Inst.; asso. trustee S. Plains Mus. Assn. Served as lt. USNR, World War II. Decorated Bronze Star medal. Registered architect, Tex. Mem. A.I.A. (pres. Lubbock chpt. 1964, scholarship com. 1968), Tex. Archtl. Found. (sec. 1964), Am. Soc. Planning Ofcls., Tex. Soc. Architects (v.p. 1968, chmn. edn. com. 1969), Theta Xi, Tau Sigma Delta (nat. pres. 1950-58). Mem. publs. bds. Tex. Architect, Jour. Archtl. Edn. Home: 4521 22d St Lubbock TX 79407

BARRIE, ERWIN SEAVER, artist, art dealer; b. Canton, O., June 3, 1886; s. Evan and Jennis Josephine (Erwin) B.; student Cornell U., 1906-10; studied landscape painting Art Inst. Chgo., 1914; m. Grace Belle Beeny, Apr. 17, 1913. Dealer Am. art, 1917—; co-founder, dir., mgr. Grand Central Art Galleries, Inc., N.Y.C., 1923—; exhbns. Art Inst. of Chgo., Grand Central Art Galleries, N.Y.C., Joslyn Art Mus., Omaha, Neb., others; works in pvt. collections The White House, Bobby Jones, Atlanta, others. Created collection Famous Golf Holes I Have Played. Dir. Am. sect. Biennial Internat. Exhbn., Venice, 1937. Recipient citation Am. Artist Profl. League. Mem. U.S. (committeeman), Am., Westchester seniors' golf assns., Greenwich Artists, Greenwich Archers, Sigma Nu. Clubs: Business Men's Art in Am. (co- founder Chgo., 1917); Royal and Ancient Golf (St. Andrews, Scotland); Tin Whistles, Pinehurst Country (Pinehurst, N.C.); Greenwich Country (gov.); Boca Raton (Fla.). Home: West Brother Dr Greenwich CT 06830 Office: 40 Vanderbilt Av New York City NY 10017

BARRIGER, JOHN WALKER, ry. exec. b. Dallas, Dec. 3, 1899; s. John Walker, Jr. and Edith (Beck) B.; B.S., Mass. Inst. Tech., 1921; m. Elizabeth Chambers Thatcher, Sept. 25, 1926; children—John Walker, IV, Elizabeth Thatcher, Ann Biddle (Mrs. Robert R. Salyard), Stanley Huntington. With the Pa. R.R., serving principally in maintenance of way and transp. depts., 1917- 27; with Kuhn, Loeb & Co., N.Y., 1927-29, Calvin Bullock & Co., N Y., 1930-33; asso. with F. H. Prince of Boston in preparation of Prince Plan of R.R. Consolidation, 1933; chief, R.R. div., R.F.C., Washington, 1933-41; reorgn. mgr. Chgo. & Eastern Ill. R.R. Co., 1940, dir. and mem. exec. com., 1941-42; asso. dir. Div. Ry. Transport., Office Def. Transp., Washington, and Fed. mfg., Toledo, Peoria & Western R.R., 1942; v.p. Union Stockyard & Transit Co. Chgo., 1943-44; mgr. Diesel Locomotive Div., Fairbanks, Morse & Co., 1944-45, reorg. mgr., 1946; pres. C., I & L. Ry., 1946-52; v.p. N.Y., N.H. & H.R.R. Co., 1953, Rock Island R.R., Chgo., 1953-56; pres. P. & L.E. R.R. 1956-64; pres. M.-K.-T. R.R. Co., 1965-70, chief exec. officer Boston & Me. Corp., 1971—. Trustee Thomas Alva Edison Found. Pvt. U.S. Army, 1918. Mem. S.R., Am. Ry. Engring. Assn., Am. Soc. C.E., Am. Soc. M.E., Newcomen Soc. (trustee). Rep. Presbyn. Clubs: Chicago, Racquet (Chgo.); Noonday, University, Racquet (St. Louis); Duquesne (Pitts.); Pendennis (Louisville); Indianapolis Athletic (Indpls.); St. Botolph's (Boston). Author: Super-Railroads, 1956. Contbr. articles to jours. Home: 15 Washington Terrace St Louis MO 63112 Office: 420 Gimblin Rd St Louis MO 63147

BARRINGER, BRANDON, investment adviser; b. Capt May, N.J., June 11,, 1899; s. Daniel Moreau and Margaret (Bennett) B.; A.B., Princeton, 1921; D.Sc., Jefferson Medical Coll., 1968; m. Sonia Converse, June 9, 1945 (dec.); children—Carla (Mrs. Philip W. Robinowitz), Elizabeth Brandon (Mrs. James W. Fentress), Felicity A.; m. 2d, Diana Johnson Richardson, Jan. 19, 1967. Joined Pa. Co. for Banking & Trusts, 1921, statistician, 1928-33, v.p. trust investments, 1933-49; treas. Curtis Pub. Co., 1949-62, dir., 1941-42, 48-62; pvt. practice as investment adviser, Phila., 1962—; pres., dir. E. Texas Iron Co., Barringer Crater Co., 1963—; dir. Bryn Mawr Group, Inc., Germantown Labs., Inc. Spl. cons. to acting sec. of State, 1947; econ. cons. ECA, U. K., 1948. Mem. finance com. Wellington Fund, 1929-60; trustee Thomas Jefferson U., Phila., 1936—; asso. trustee U. Pa., mgr. U. Mus., 1937—, Franklin Inst., 1957—; treas., trustee Acad. Natural Scis., 1947—; mem. Corp. for Relief of Widows, Phila., 1939—, also sec.; bd. govs. Nature Conservancy, 1968—; Eastern Pennsylvania Psychiatric Inst.; dir. Research Inst. Temple U.; bd. dirs. Phila. div. Am. Cancer Soc., 1947-50, Community Chest, 1948-51, 1948-51, United Fund, 1966—; dir., sec. Nat. Mental Health Assn., 1949-61; bd. dirs., sec. Hospital Council, 1951-61, bd. dirs., 1968—; mem. grad. council Princeton, 1951-53. Served as pvt., U.S. Army, 1918; capt. to col. A.A.C., dept. chief, office statis control Hdgrs. A.A.F., 1942-45. Decorated Legion of Merit. Fellow A.A.A.S., Meteroritical Soc. (v.p. 1966—). Clubs: Philadelphia, Racquet, Princeton, Mill Dam, Wilderness (Phila.); Army and Navy (Washington); Princeton (N.Y.C.); Nassau (Princeton). Author: The Wethered Book; also articles on meteoriteics and archeology. Home: Villanova PA 19085 Office: 2 Girard Pl Philadelphia PA 19102

BARRINGER, LEWIS TRANTHAM, cotton merchant; b. Spencer, N.C., June 30, 900; s. John N. and Lela (Dauvault) B.; LL.B., U. Memphis, 1939; m. Josephine D. Davenport, Jan. 18, 1928; childrenLewis Tranthan, John William. Pres. L.T. Barringer and Co., Memphis, 1930—; v.p. Cannon Mills Co., N.Y.C., 1960—. Dir. Nat. Cotton Council Am., 1940. Methodist. Clubs: Summit, Tennessee (Memphis); University (Washington). Home: 2877 Central Av Memphis TN Office: 1195 Union Av Memphis TN 38104

BARRINGER, PAUL BRANDON, Jr., lawyer; b. Davidson, N.C., Aug. 28, 1887; s. Paul Brandon and Nannie (Hannah) B.; B.A., U. Va., 1907; LL.B. U. Mich., 1914; m. Lucy Landon Minor, Nov. 28, 1917; children—Charles Minor, Rufus. Engaged in bus., N.C., 1907-10, Tex., 1912-13; admitted to N.Y. bar, 1915, also U.S. Supreme Ct.; asst. counsel Nat. Biscuit Co., 1914-15, Am. Sugar Refining Co., 1916-17; asso., then partner firm Jackson, Nash, Brophy, Barringer & Brooks, and predecessors, N.Y.C., 1919—. Trustee, mayor Village of Matinecock, L.I., N.Y., 1928-38. Trustee Soc. St. Johnland, 1940-63, Locust Valley Pub. Library, 1937—. Served to capt. U.S. Army, 1917-19; AEF in France. Mem. Am., N.Y. State bar assns., Assn. Bar City N.Y., Am. Law Inst., Phi Beta Kappa, Order of Coif, Zeta Psi, Phi Delta Phi. Democrat. Episcopalian (vestry). Clubs: Century Assn., Pilgrims, Down Town Assn. (N.Y.C.); Piping Rock (Locust Valley). Home: Town Cocks Rd Locust Valley NY 10017 Office: 330 Madison Av New York City NY 10017

BARRINGER, PHILIP E., govt. ofcl.; b. Haverford, Pa., Oct. 2, 1916; s. D. Moreau and Margaret (Bennett) B.; grad. Episcopal Acad., Overbrook, Pa., 1933; student Heidelberg (Germany) Coll., 1934; A.B. cum laude in European History, Princeton, 1938; LL.B., U. Pa., 1948; grad. Nat. War Coll., 1952; m. Sophia F. Hazard, Aug. 10, 1946; children—Thomas H., C. Frances, Paul M. Staff aide Phila. City charter Com., 1938-39; research asst. Am. Inst. Pub. Opinion, 1939-40; admitted to Pa. bar, 1949; with Office Sec. Def., 1949-64, dep. dir. European region Office Asst. Sec. (internat. security affairs), 1956-64; attaché, politico-mil. affairs Am. embassy, London, Eng., 1964-66; dep. dir. Near East and South Asia region Office Asst. Sec. Def. for Internat. Security Affairs, Washington, 1966-67, dir. fgn. mil. rights Dept. of Def., 1967—; mem. of numerous U.S. delegations. Dir. Barringer Crater Co., Phila., 1947-63. Pres. Alexandria (Va.) Civic Orch., 1950-52; pres., chmn. legislative com. Phoebe Hearst Sch. P.T.A., Washington, 1959-61; exec. com. N. W. Com. Transp. Planning, Washington, 1959-64; trustee All Souls Unitarian Ch., Washington, 1956-54, 1964, 67-70, chmn., 1969-70; del. to Unitarian-Universalist Gen. Assemblies, 1968-71. Mem. Pa. N.G., 1937-40; served to lt. col., arty., AUS, 1941-46; ETO. Decorated Army Commendation ribbon. Mem. Am. Soc. Internat. Law, Inst. Strategic Studies (London), Coop. Forum Washington, Washington Urban League. Clubs: Princeton, Cleveland Park (Washington); Landsowne (London). Home: 3711 Idaho Av Washington DC 20016 Office: Office of Asst Secretary of Defense ISA Washington DC 20301

BARRIO, RAYMOND, author, artist; b. W. Orange, N.J., Aug. 27, 1921; s. Saturnino and Angelita (Santos) B.; student Coll. City N.Y., 1940, U. So. Cal., 1941 43, Yale, 1943; B.A., U. Cal. at Berkeley, 1947; B.F.A., Los Angeles Art Center Coll. Design, 1952; m. Yolanda Sanchez, Feb. 2, 1957; children—Angelita, Gabriel, Raymond, Andrea, Margarita. Artist, 1950—; exhibited Oakland (Cal.) Art Mus., 1955-60, San Francisco Museum Art, 1956-58, Am. Color Print, Phila., 1956-60, numerous others; art tchr., Los Angeles, Burbank, Cal., 1961, Ventura (Cal.) Coll., 1961-63, U. Cal. at Santa Barbara, 1963-64; tchr. adult edn. San Francisco area, 1965—. Served with arty. AUS, 1943-46. Creative Arts Inst. Faculty grantee U. Cal., 196465. Author: The Big Picture, 1967; Experiments in Modern Art, 1968; Selections from Walden, 1968; The Plum Plum Pickers, 1969; others. Contbr. articles, fiction to publs. Office: Ventura Press PO Box 2268 Sunnyvale CA 94087

BARRITT, CARLYLE WESTBROOK, educator; b. Greensboro, N.C., Mar. 31, 1921; s. Carlyle and Sinclaire (Westbrook) B.; B.A., Washington and Lee U., 1943; student Harvard, 1948; M.A., U. Va., 1950, Ph.D., 1952; m. Mabel Cunningham Sites, Aug. 24, 1949; childrenWinifred C., Julia W. Mem. faculty Emory U., 1946, Muhlenberg Coll., 1946-47; mem. faculty Washington and Lee U., 1947-48, 52-, prof. Spanish and linguistics, 1962-; linguist Nat. Def. Edn. Act lang. insts. 1961-. Mem. local council Total Action Against Poverty Program. Served with AUS, 1943-45. Mem. Linguistic Soc. Am., Am. AAssn. Tchrs. Spanish and Portuguese, Soc. Advancement Scandinavian Studies, Phi Phi Beta Kappa. Presbyn. (elder). Home: 6 Wallace St Lexington VA 24450.

BARRNETT, RUSSELL JOFFREE, medical educator; b. Boston, July 27, 1920; s. Thomas Warren and Dora G. (Shopwick) B.; A.B., Ind. U., 1943; M.D., Yale, 1948; children—Russell J., William T., Elissa. Intern Beth Israel Hosp., Boston, 1948-49; fellow Harvard Med. Sch., Boston, 1949-51, instr., 1951-53, asso., 1953-55, asst. prof. anatomy, 1955-59; asso. prof. Yale Med. Sch., New Haven, 1959-62, prof. anatomy, 1962—, dir. grad. studies, 1967—, chmn. dept., 1968—. Mem. com. on growth NRC, 1954-56, mem. div. biology and agr., 1967—; vis. investigator Rockefeller Inst.; adviser div. biology and medicine AEC, med. edn. and research WHO. Bd. dirs. Am. Child Guidance Found. Served with AUS, 1943. Mem. Histochem. Soc. (pres. 1962), Am. Assn. Anatomy, Cell Biology Soc., Biophys. Soc., Am. Assn. Electron Microscopy, A.A.A.S., Sigma Xi. Asso. editor Anat. Record, 1962-67, Jour. Histochemists, 1963—, Jour. Ultrastructure Research, 1965—, Annales D'Histochemie, 1963—. Home: 23 Eld St New Haven CT 06511

BARROMI, JOEL, Israeli diplomat; b. Rome, Italy, Feb. 26, 1920; s. Carlo and Emma (Zevi) B.; Ph.D., U. Rome Law Sch., 1945; M.A., Hebrew U. Jerusalem 1951; m. Hedva Katz, Aug. 26, 1953; children—Gad, Orna, Edna. Immigrated to Israel, 1939. Tchr., Jewish Agy.'s Inst. Youth Leaders 1949-51; joined Israeli Diplomatic Service, 1951; successively with research dept., Western European and Latin Am. divs. Ministry Fgn. Affairs, 1951-55; 1st sec., later counsellor embassy, Buenos Aires, Argentina, 1955-61, also charge d'affaires ad interim, Montevideo, Uruguay and Havana, Cuba; dept. dir. Western European div. Ministry Fgn. Affairs, 1961, dir. Latin Am. div., 1962-63; mem. Israeli delegation gen. assemblies UN, 1961, 63- 68, ambassador and alternate permanent rep. Israel to UN, 1963—; ambassador to Republic of Haiti, 1963—. Home: 300 Central Park W New York City NY 10024 Office: Israeli Delegation to UN 11 E 70th St New York City NY 10021

BARRON, ALEXANDER JOHNSTON, lawyer; b. Connellsville, Pa., July 16, 1880; s. John and Margaret Clark (Johnston) B.; s student Lawrenceville (N.J.) Prep. Sch., 1898; A.B., Princeton, 1902; student Harvard Law Sch., 1903-04; LL.B., U. Pittsburgh, 1905; m. Elizabeth Congdon, Sept. 26, 1907. Admitted to Pa. Admitted to Pa. bar, 1905 and since practiced in Pittsburgh; now of counsel Alter, Wright & Barron; mem. bar Supreme Ct. U.S., 1909-. Sec., mem. board of directors Leechburg Mining Company, Leechburn Supply Company.Past mem., pres. Osborne Borough Council; trustee, past dir., pres. Sewickley YMCA. Served with A.E.F., France, 1918- 19, in YMCA as sec. in Savoie Leave Area, as bus. mgr. Britany and Dauphine Leave Areas, div. sec. Rivera Leave Area. Mem. Am. Law Inst., Am., Pa. and Allegheny County bar assns., Am. Judicature Soc., Harvard Law Sch. Assn. Republican. Presbyn. (elder). Clubs: Law, Duquesne, H-Y-P (Pitts.); Allegheny Country, (Sewickley, Pa.); Cap and Gown (Princeton). Home: Glen Osborne Sewickley PA Office: Union Bank Bldg Pittsburgh PA 15222

BARRON, BRYTON, writer, lectr.; b. Doon, Ia., Dec. 6, 1898; s. Hiram H. and Emma J. Barron (grandparents); A.B., Sioux Falls Coll., 1922; B.Litt. (Rhodes scholar at Pembroke Coll. 1920-23), Oxford U. (Eng.), 1923, diploma in econ. and polit. sci., 1922; m. Ella Rosalie Lillibridge, Dec. 31, 1922; childrenBebe (Mrs. Edgar Carl Seward, Jr.), Roger L. Editorial writer Daily Argus-Leader, Sioux Falls, S.D., 1923-25; ednl. work, P.I., 1925- 28; asst. editor Dept. State, Washington, 1929, chief pub. sect., 1929- 40, asst. chief div. research and publ., 1940-44, chief of treaty staff, adv. on treaty affairs, 1944-50, research historian, 1950-56; pub. Crestwood Books, 1962-66, sr. editor, 1966-; lectr. on fgn. affairs throughout the U.S., 1956—. Founder, treas., gen. mgr. Dept. of State Fed. Credit Union, 1935-42; founder, pres. Dept. of State Recreation Assn., 1935. Active Conservative causes. Recipient award Am. Acad. Pub. Affairs of Los Angeles, 1964, Liberty award Congress Freedom, 1959; award Young Americans Against Communism, 1964. Mem. Acad. Model Aeros. (nat. sec. 1952). Fla. Modelers Assn. (sec.-treas. 1969—). Author: Inside the State Department, 1956; The Untouchable State Department, 1962, rev. as State Department: Blunders or Treason?, 1965. Co-author: Dream Becomes a Nightmare: The UN Today, 1964; The Inhumanity of Urban Renewal, 1965. Compiler: Trouble Abroad: An Independent Survey of World Affairs, 1965. Contbr. articles to mags. and newspapers. Co-author (with wife) series of grammar textbooks. Barron papers in Library U. Ore. Address: 7710 NW 8th St Pembroke Pines Hollywood FL 33024

BARRON, CHARLES IRWIN, physician; b. Chgo., July 21, 1916; s. Joseph and Jennie (Buyer) B.; B.S., U. Ill., 1940, M.D., 1942; m. Iris Louisa Barklow, July 24, 1945; childrenMichael Craig, Suzanne Lee, Scott Walter, Cherie Ann. Rotating intern Los Angeles County Gen. Hosp., 1942-43; resident internal medicine Portland (Ore.) VA Hosp., 1946-48; surgeon Q.M. depot, U.S. Army Chgo., 1948-50; with Lockheed-Cal. Co., Burbank, 1950—, med. dir., 1953—; spl. work coordinating aerospace and indsl. med. and human engring.; lectr. aviation safety div. U. So. Cal., 1954—, U. So. Cal. Med. Sch., 1956—; clin. prof. of aerospace pathology U. So. Cal.; lectr. postgrad. avaiation medicine U. Cal. at Los Angeles, 1955, asso. clin. prof. occupational medicine; lectr. postgrad. avaiation medicine, Ohio State U., 1960. Mem. com. hearing and bioacoustics NRC, 1955-57; med. adv. council civil air surgeon FAA, 1960-; chmn. research adv. com. biotech. and human research NASA, 1963—; chmn. med. adv. council, fed. air surgeons, 1964-; mem. rehabilitation com. Los Angeles County Heart Assn., 1955—. Trustee Los Angeles Com. Alcoholism, 1955-59, 1955-59, Sheltered Workshops, 1955-. Served to maj., flight surgeon, USAAF, 1943- 46. Diplomate Am. Board of Preventive Medicine. Fellow Indsl. Med. Assn., Assn., Aerospace Med. Assn. (exec. council, pres. 1963); mem. Am., Cal., Los Angeles County med. assns., Inst. Aero. Scis., Aeromed. Engring. Assn., Am. Rocket Soc., Civil Aviation Med. Assn. (past v.p.), Airlines Med. Dirs. Assn. (past pres.). Presbyn. (elder). Author articles in field. Home: 19303 Itasca Av Northridge CA 91324 Office: 2555 N Hollywood Way Burbank CA 91502

BARRON, DEAN JAMES, govt. ofcl.; b. Peoria, Ill., Dec. 21, 1919; s. James and Alberta (Sprague) B.; student Bradley U.; J.D., Am. U., 1959; C.P.A., Ill.; m. Anna Belle Bristol, July 27, 1940; children—Deanna A., Stephanie G. Admitted to Va. bar, 1960, Pa. Supreme Ct. bar, 1969, U.S. Supreme Ct., 1970; asso. with Internal Service Treasury Dept., 1942—, dir. audit div., Washington, 1960-62, regional commnr., Phila., 1962-70, asst. commr. accounts, collection and taxpayer service, Washington, 1970—. Chmn. Phila. Fed. Exec. Bd., 1964. Mem. Am., Fed., Pa. bar assns., Va. State Bar, Ill. Soc. C.P.A.'s. Author article. Home: 2615 Child's Lane Alexandria VA 22308 Office: 12th and Constitution Av Washington DC 20036

BARRON, DEMPSEY J., state senator; b. Andalusia, Ala., Mar. 5, 1922; s. Jessie Carl Dempsey and Minnie (Brown) B.; B.S., Fla. State U.; LL.B., U. Fla.; m. Louverne Hall, Jan. 27, 1952; children—Stephen C., Stuart J. Atty. firm Barron & Hilton, 1954—; owner A-Bar-H ranch, Gulf Asphalt Corp.; mem. Fla. Ho. of Reps., 1956-60; mem. Fla. senate, 1960—, pres. pro tem, 1967—. Dir. Panama City and Bay Co. Chmn. Panama City (Fla.) Heart Fund Drive, United Fund. Bd. dirs. Boys Club Am., Farm Bur. Served with USNR, 1942-47; PTO, ETO. Named one of 10 outstanding mems. Fla. legislature by press, 1957—, one of 2 outstanding mems. Fla. senate, 1965. Mem. Panama City C. of C. (bd. dirs.) Methodist. Home: 224 Woodlawn Dr Panama City FL 32406 Office: Box 1638 Panama City FL 32402*

BARRON, DONALD H., educator; b. Flandreau, S. D., Apr. 9, 1905; s. George E. and Mae Louella (Reed) B.: A.B., Carleton Coll., 1928; M.S., Ia. State Coll. of Agr. and Mechanic Arts, 1929; Ph.D. Yale, 1932; M.A. (hon.), Cambridge, 1936; m. Marie Annette La Courciere, Oct. 22, 1932; children—Marie Annette (Mrs. Stephen G. McCarthy), Donna Marie (Mrs. Robert Gomez). Asst. plant physiology Ia. State Coll., 1928-29; asst. biology Yale U., 1929-31, anatomy, 1931-32; instr. anatomy Albany Med. Coll., 1932-33, asst. prof. anatomy, 1934-35; NRC fellow univs. of Berne and Cambridge, 1933-34; demonstrator anatomy U. of Cambridge, 1935- 36, lecturer, 1936-40, fellow St. John's Coll. and dir. med. studies, 1937-40; asst. prof. zoology U. of Mo., 1940-42, asso. prof., 1942-43; asso. prof. physiology Yale Sch. of Medicine, 1943-47, prof., 1947-69, prof. emeritus, 1969—, asst. dean sch. medicine, 1945-48; J. Wayne Reitz prof. reproductive biology and medicine U. Fla., Sch. Medicine, Gainesville, 1969—; head expdn. to study pregnancy at high altitudes in Peru, 1958; Linacre lectr. St. John's Coll. Cambridge, Eng., 1966. Hon. fellow Am. Gynecol. Soc.; asso. fellow Am. Coll. Obstetrics and Gynecology; mem. Am. Assn. Anatomists, Physiol. Soc. (Gt. Britain and Ireland), Anatomical Soc. (Great Britain and Ireland), Cambridge (Eng.) Philos. Soc., Am. Physiol. Soc., Am. Acad. Arts and Scis., Soc. for Gynecologie Investigation (hon.), Blair-Bell Soc. (hon.), Phi Beta Kappa, Gamma Sigma Delta, Sigma Xi. Contbr. articles to sci. publs. Mem. editorial bd. Jour. Comparative Neurology 1948-69, mng. editor, 1956-69. Home: 2892 NW 4th Lane Gainesville FL 32601 Office: University Florida College Medicine Gainesville FL 32601

BARRON, FRANK WALTER, metal products mfr.; b. Hastings, Mich., May 20, 1907; s. Walter Scott and Verna Elizabeth (Denyes) B.; grad. Am. Inst. Banking, 1928; m. Jean Mary Scott, June 7, 1930; children—Georgina (Mrs. Richard James Durham). Asst. sec. Nat.-Standard Co., Niles, Mich., 1956-69, sec., 1969—. Chmn. Niles Bd. Pub. Works, 1963, 67. Mem. Am. Soc. Ins. Buyers (charter). Mason, Elk. Club: Pickwick (Niles). Home: 745 Colony Court Niles MI 49120 Office: 601 N 8th St Niles MI 49120

BARRON, GEORGE FRANCIS, univ. dean, choral condr., singer; b. Ashland, Ore., Apr. 14, 1908; s. Homer Walker and Minnie (Ross) B.; Mus. B., U. Ore., 1929, A.B., 1931, M.F.A., 1933; pvt. studies music, Vienna, N.Y.C.; m. Mary Frances Schaeuble, June 10, 1940; 1 dau., Beverly Anne. Ranger, Crater Lake Nat. Park, summers 1929-33; grad. asst. U. Ore.. 1931-33; church and radio soloist, N.Y.C., 1935-36; faculty Miami U., 1936-, asst. prof. music, 1936-47, asso. prof. music, 1947-53, prof. music 1953-, acting dean Sch. Fine Arts, 1952-54, dean, 1954—, chmn. artists series com., 1961—; assisted in preparing Miami U. Choruses for performances with Cin. Symphony Orch. 1947—; dir. Miami U. A Capella Singers. Pres., Ohio Regional Assn. Concert & Lect. Enterprises, 1967-69. Served as 1st lt. AUS, 1943-46. Mem. Nat. Assn. Tchrs. Singing, Music Educators Nat. Conf., Phi Mu Alpha, Phi Sigma Kappa. Presbyn. Kiwanian. Address: Miami U Sch of Fine Arts Oxford OH 45056

BARRON, HAROLD SHELDON, lawyer, b. Detroit, July 4, 1936; s. George Leslie and Rose (Weinstein) B.; A.B., U. Mich., 1958, J.D., 1961; m. Roberta Yellin, Nov. 17, 1963; children—Lawrence Ira, Jean Louise. Admitted to N.Y. bar, 1963, Mich. bar, 1961; practice in N.Y.C., 1962-68, Southfield, Mich., 1968—; atty. Hughes, Hubbard & Reed, 1962-68; corp. counsel Bendix Corp., 1968-69, sec., asso. gen. counsel, 1969—. Served with U.S. Army, 1961-62. Mem. Am., Mich., N.Y. bar assns., Am. Arbitration Assn. Clubs: Economic, Torch (Detroit). Home: 23909 Reading Rd Southfield MI 48075 Office: Bendix Center Southfield MI 48076

BARRON, JOHN W., lawyer; b. St. Louis, Apr. 2, 1904; LL.B., Washington U., St. Louis. Admitted to Ark. bar, 1927; now mem. firm Rose, Barron, Nash, Williamson, Carroll & Clay, Little Rock. Mem. Am., Ark., Pulaski County bar assns. Office: 720 W 3d St Little Rock AR 72201*

BARRON, MILTON LEON, sociologist; b. Derby, Conn., Feb. 25, 1918; s. Harry Bernard and Anne (Tevlin) B.; A.B., Yale, 1939, A.M., 1942; Ph.D., 1945; m. to Matilda Cogan, June 1, 1947; one son, Benjamin. Instr. in sociology, Jr. Coll. Phys. Therapy, New Haven, Conn., 1942; orgns. and propaganda analyst, Dept. of Justice, Washington, 1943; instr. in sociology, St. Lawrence U., 1943-44; asst. prof. of sociology, Syracuse U., 1944-48; asst. prof. of sociology and anthropology, Cornell U., 1948-54; asso. prof. sociology Coll. of City N.Y., 1954-61, prof., chmn. sociology dept., 1961-65, exec. officer Ph.D. program in sociology, 1965-69; dir. study of occupational retirement Social Sci. Research Center, Cornell U.; vis. lectr. (part time), Wells Coll., 1949-50; Fulbright lectr. Bar-Ilan U., Israel, 1962-63. Mem. Am. Assn. Univ. Profs., Am. Sociol. Soc., Alpha Kappa Delta. Author: People Who Intermarry, 1946; The Juvenile in Delinquent Society, 1954; American Minorities, 1957; The Aging American, 1961. Co-author: Delinquent Behavior, 1959. Editor: Contemporary Sociology, 1964; Minorities in Changing World, 1967. Home: 51 Appleton Pl Dobbs Ferry NY 10522 Office: College City of N Y New York City NY 10031

BARRON, NORMAN MACDONALD, lawyer; b. Highland Falls, N.Y., Nov. 1, 1900; s. Alexander Robertson and Emma (Wyant) B.; A.B., Hamilton Coll., 1921; LL.B., Harvard, 1924; m. Frances Clifton Byers, Oct. 24, 1930; children—Fraser, Mortimer Byers, Timothy House and Norman Alexander (twins). Admitted to N.Y. bar, 1924, since practiced in N.Y.C.; asso. Burlingham, Veeder, Masten & Fearey, 1924-29; asso. Burlingham, Veeder, Fearey, Clark & Hupper, 1929- 34; asso. Burlingham, Veeder, Clark & Hupper, 1934-43, partner, 1943-52; partner Burlingham, Hupper & Kennedy, 1952-61; sr. partner Burlingham, Underwood, Barron, Wright & White, 1961-68; counsel Burlingham, Underwood, Wright, White & Lord, 1968—. Dir. Lissone-Lindeman U.S.A., Inc., Olson Travel Orgn., Inc., Olson's Royal Coach Tours, Inc., Olson's Campus Tours, Inc. Vice pres., trustee YWCA of Oranges and Maplewood. Mem. Am. Bar Assn., Maritime Law Assn. U.S., Hamilton Coll. Alumni Assn., Alpha Delta Phi. Presbyn. Clubs: University (N.Y.C.); Rock Spring (West Orange). Home: 240 Irving Av South Orange NJ 07079 Office: 25 Broadway New York City NY 10004

BARRON, TILTON MARSHALL, librarian; b. Phillipsburg, Kan., Jan. 19, 1916; s. James Walter and Minnie (Livermore) B.; A.B., Colo. Coll., 1937; B.L.S., Columbia, 1940; m. Sue Clark, Dec. 28, 1946; childrenJames Tilton, William Clark, John Marshall. Library asst. N.Y.U. Libraries, 1937-40; evening supr. Bklyn. Coll. Library, 1940-41; circulation librarian Pa. State Coll., 1945-46; reference asst. Coll. City N.Y., 1947-48; librarian Ursinus Coll., 1948- 54, Clark U., 1954-. Served to tech. sgt. USAAF, 1942-45. Mem. Am., Mass., New Eng. library assns., Bibliog. Soc. Am. Club: Bohemians. Home: 120 Amherst St Worcester MA 01602.

BARRON, WILLIAM WALLACE, lawyer, former gov. W.Va.; b. Elkins, W.Va., Dec. 8, 1911; s. Frederick H. and Mary Cuthbert (Butler) B.; A.B., Washington and Lee U., 1934; LL.B., W. Va. U., 1941; LL.D., W. Va. U., Marshall U., W.Va. State, Glenville State, Concord Coll.; m. Opal Wilcox, Feb. 15, 1936; children—Cuthbert (Mrs. Terry Penn), Nancy (Mrs. Ron Smith), Jane Fair (Mrs. Philip Stroup, Jr.). Admitted to W. Va. bar, 1941, practiced in Elkins; atty. gen W.Va., 1957-61; gov. W. Va., 1961-64; now with firm Barron & Davis, Charleston, W.Va. Co-chmn. W.Va. Cleanup, Inc.: crusade chmn. W.Va. div. Am. Cancer Soc., 1967. Served as mayor Elkins, W.Va., 1949-51; dep. land commr., commr. accounts, commr. chancery Randolph County; mem. W.Va. Ho. of Dels. from Randolph County, 1950, 52. Served with AUS, World War II. Mem., Am. Legion, 40 and 8. Am., W.Va., Randolph County bar assns., W.Va. State Bar, Am. Judicature Soc. Democrat. Presbyn. Mason (Shriner), Elk, Moose, Odd Fellow. Clubs: Civitan, Rotary, Press, Kanawha Country. Home: 1800 Roundhill Rd Charleston WV 25314 Office: Nelson Bldg Charleston WV 25314

BARROW, ALLEN EDWARD, U.S. judge; b. Okemah, Okla., Jan 22, 1914; s. Alfred E. and Minnie Lee (Coffelt) B.; student Okla. A. and M. Coll. 1935-36; B.A., U. Okla., 1936; postgrad. U. Tulsa; LL.B., Southeastern Coll., 1942; m. Dorothy Elaine Dalton, Oct. 2, 1942; children—Allen Edward, Karla Elaine, Mary Celeste. With FBI, 1940-42; admitted to Okla. bar, 1942, also Supreme Ct. U.S.; pvt. practice, Tulsa, 1946-50, 54-62; counsel Southwestern Power Adminstrn., Dept. Interior, Tulsa, 1950-54; chief judge U.S. Dist. Ct. No. Dist. Okla., 1962—. Adv. bd. Tulsa Salvation Army, 1956—. Mem. bd. A.R.C. Served to maj. AUS, 1942-46. Mem. Am. Okla., (Outstanding Service award 1959) bar assns., S.A.R. (pres. Okla. 1954), Delta Theta Phi, Phi Eta Sigma, Sigma Chi (pres. alumni assn. 1950). Democrat. Mem. Christian Ch. Home: 2142 E 25th Pl Tulsa OK 74103 Office: U S Courthouse Tulsa OK 74103

BARROW, CHARLES HERBERT, banker; b. Evanston, Ill., July 23, 1930; s. Franklin and Arda (Mozingo) B.; A.B., Princeton, 1952; M.B.A., U. Chgo., 1956; m. Patricia Wandelt, Dec. 27, 1952; children—Paula, Carla, Barbara. Asst. cashier No. Trust Co., Chgo., 1955-59, 2d v.p., 1959-62, v.p., 1962-68, sr. v.p., 1968—. Treas. Planned Parenthood Assn., Chgo., 1968-71. Presbyn. Clubs: Chicago, Economic, Bankers (Chgo.); Michigan Shores (Wilmette, Ill.). Home: 2735.Colfax St Evanston IL 60201 Office: 50 S LaSalle St Chicago IL 60690

BARROW ERROL WALTON, prime minister Barbados; b. Barbados, W.I., Jan. 21, 1920; s. Reginald Grant and Ruth (O'Neal) B.; student Harrison Coll., Barbados, 1934-39; barrister Lincoln's Inn, London, 1949; B.Sc., U. London, 1950; LL.D., McGill U., 1966; m. Carolyn Plaskett, Nov. 18, 1945; children—Lesley, David O'Neal. Practiced law, Barbados, Eastern Carribbean, 1951-61; mem. Barbados Legislature, 1951—, premier, 1961-66, prime minister, 1966—. Chmn. Democratic Labour Party Barbados, 1959—. Served with R.A.F., 1940- 47. Home: Culloden Farm St Michael Barbados Office: Bay St St Michael Barbados

BARROW, GEORGE TERRELL, lawyer; b. Wichita Falls, Tex., July 23, 1909; s. George W. and Jena (Magee) B.; LL.B., U. Tex., 1932; m. Margaret Forrest, Nov. 5, 1954; children—David G., Blake W. Admitted to Tex. bar, 1932, since practiced in Houston; partner firm Barrow, Bland & Rehmet and predecessor, 1956—; mem. Bd. Law Examiners Tex. Dir. Fed. Home Loan Bank, Litt Rock, 1965-69. Served to lt. comdr. USNR, 1942-45. Fellow Am. Bar Found., Tex. Bar Found., Am. Coll. Probate Counsel, Am. Bar Assn; mem. Houston Bar Assn. (pres. 1963- 64), State Bar Tex. (bd. dirs. 1959-62), Am. Judicature Soc., Am. Arbitration Assn., Sons Republic of Tex., English Speaking Union (pres. 1970—), Navy League U.S., Big Bros. of Houston (pres. 1959), Alpha Tau Omega. Kiwanian. Clubs: Petroleum, Knife and Fork (Houston); Forest; Champions Golf. Home: 6151 Bordley Dr Houston TX 77027 Office: Main Bldg 1212 Main St Houston TX 77002

BARROW, GORDON MILNE, chemist, educator; b. Vancouver, B.C., Can., Nov. 13, 1923: s. Edward and Kathleen (Love) B.; B.A.Sc., U. B.C., 1946, M.A.Sc., 1947; Ph.D., U. Cal. at Berkeley, 1950; m. Harriet Heuser, Sept. 8, 1957; children—Andrew G., Elizabeth A., Peter J. NRC fellow Oxford (Eng.) U., 1950-51; from instr. to asso. prof. chemistry Northwestern U., 1951-59; Guggenheim fellow Eidignosiche Technische Hochschule, Zurich, Switzerland, 1957-58; prof. chemistry, head dept. Case Inst. Tech., 1959- 67; exec. dir. Adv. Council Coll. Chemistry, 1967-69; adj. prof. Dartmouth Coll., 1970-71. Author: Physical Chemistry, 1961; An Introdroduction to Molecular Spectroscopy, 1962. Home: Middle Canyon Rd Carmel Valley CA 93924

BARROW, HENRY, newspaper cartoonist. Editorial cartoonist Omaha World-Herald. Office: 14th and Dodge Sts Omaha NB 68102*

BARROW, J. GORDON, med. educator; b. Sept. 8, 1919; B.S., Emory U., 1940, M.D., 1943; m. Janie Cook, June 2, 1944. Clin. prof. medicine Emory U. Sch. Medicine, Atlanta. Diplomate Am. Bd. Internal Medicine. Office: Emory U Sch Medicine Atlanta GA 30322*

BARROW, JOHN RALPH, fgn. service officer; b. Washington, Mar. 9, 1921; s. John Ralph and Marie Theresa (Carroll) B.; student Los Angeles City Coll., 1938-41; student U. Cal. at Los Angeles, 1947, Am. U., Washington, 1948-49; m. Mary Jean Wolf, May 10, 1952; childrenGuy Hamilton, Paul Gordon. Mem. Diplomatic Service, Dept. State, 1945—, chief polit. sect. Am. embassies, Bagdad and Damascus, 1951-54, 56-58, polit. officer Am. embassy, Cairo, Egypt, 1958-60, officer charge UAR affairs, Dept. of State, 1960-65, Am. consul gen., Aleppo, Syrian Arab Republic, from 1965, now dept. supr. internal relations office. Home: 2304 Clayburn Dr Laurel MD 20810 Office: Dept United Arab Republic Affairs Dept of State Washingron DC 20525

BARROW, ROBERT GEORGE, educator; b. Washington, July 9, 1911; s. Frank Harding and Edith Mary (Bond) B.; B.A., Yale, 1932, M.A. 1933 Mus.M., 1934; pupil of Ralph Vaughan Williams and Paul Hindemith, 1934-35; m. Esther Elizabeth Jones, 1938; 1 son, Arthur H. Orgainst, choir dir. Nat. Episcopal Cathedral, Washington, 1935-39; asst. prof., then asso. prof. music Williams Coll., 1939-49, prof. music, chmn. dept. 1949—. Founder, dir. Benkshire Choral Soc., 1947-58; conductor Williams Coll. Glee Club, 1940-49, 60-66. Mem. Coll. Music Assn. (sec. 1947-55), Am. Guild Organists. Composer: (cantata) The Risen Christ, 1956; (cantata) Emmanuel, 1965; (suite for organ) (Christus Natus Est), 1956; Sonata for Organ, 1967; Suite for Small Orchestra, 1958; Two Chorale-Preludes for Organ, 1966; Partita for Orchestra, 1968; Suite for String Orchestra, 1945. Editor, contbr. Williams Series of Music for Men's Voice. Home: Jerome Dr Williamstown MA 01267

BARROW, ROSCOE LINDLEY, educator; b. La Grange, N.C., Oct. 17, 1913: s. Zebulon Vance and Ada Elizabeth (Mewborn) B.; B.S. A.S., Lewis Inst. (now Ill. Inst. Tech.), Chgo., 1935; J.D., Northwestern U., 1938; m. Ruth Elizabeth Coberly, June 4,1941; children—Beverly Ruth, Elizabeth Rose, Lucy Vivian, Roscoe Lindley II. Admitted to Ill. bar, 1938, Ohio bar, 1951; spl. asst. to the Atty. Gen. U.S., 1951, N.L.R.B., 1939-40, Dept. Agr., 1940-42, O.P.A., 1942, Dept. Justice, 1945-49, 1951; staff contract termination Bur. Aero., 1944-45; prof. law U. Cin., 1949—, acting dean, 1952-53, dean, 1953-65, Wald prof. law, 1965—, chmn. faculty, 1970—. Dir. broadcast network study, FCC, 1955-57, cons., 1961-63: moderator hearings on Fairness Doctrine, Spl. House Subcom. on Investigations, 1968; consultant Fed. agys.; trial examiner Ohio Civil Rights Commn., 1961- 62; vis. prof. law U. N.C., summer 1962, U. Va. Law Sch., 1965-66. Served with USNR, 1942-45. Mem. Cin. Bar Assn. (pres. 1961-63). Club: Literary Club (Cincinnati). Author: (with Howard D. Fabing, M.D.) Epilepsy and the Law, 1956, rev. edit. 1966; (with others) Network Broadcasting, 1957. Contbr. articles profl. publs. Home: 230 Linden Dr Wyoming OH 45215

BARROW, THOMAS DAVIES, oil co. exec.; b. San Antonio, Dec. 27, 1924; s. Leonidas Theodore and Laura Editha (Thomson) B.; B.S., U. Tex., 1945 M.A., 1948; Ph.D., Stanford, 1953; grad. Advanced Mgmt. Program, Harvard, 1963; m. Janice Meredith Hood, Sept. 16, 1950; children—Theodore Hood, Kenneth Thomson, Barbara Loyd, Elizabeth Ann. With Humble Oil & Refining Co., 1951—, regional exploration mgr., New Orleans, 1962-64, sr. v.p., 1967-70, pres., 1970—; dir., 1965—; exec. v.p., dir. Esso Exploration, Inc., 1964-65. Mem. adv. council Geology Found., U. Tex. Trustee Kinkaid Sch. Served to ensign USNR, 1943-46. Mem. Am. Assn. Petroleum Geologists, Geol. Soc. Am., A.A.A.S., Nat. Oceanography assn. (dir., pres. 1969—), Am. Geophy. Union, Am. Soc. for Oceanography (pres. 1970—), Sigma Xi, Tau Beta Pi, Sigma Gamma Epsilon, Phi Eta Sigma, Alpha Tau Omega. Episcopalian. Home: 307 Shadywood St Houston TX 77001 Office: Box 2180 Houston TX 77001

BARROW, WILLIAM RUSSELL, investment banker; b. Dallas, May 2, 1902; s. William Hill and Addie (Johnson) B.; student U. Tex., 1918-21; m. Bess Harman, June 25, 1931; 1 dau., Sidney Harman (Mrs. John W. Peacock). With Comml. Nat. Com., Shreveport, 1923-33, pres., 1930-33; organizer, 1934, since partner Barrow, Leary & Co., Shreveport; pres. Lamtex Equipment Corp., Ft. Worth 1938-67, Ind. Ice & Cold Storage Co., Shreveport, 1947—. Pres., mem. Nat. Budget Com., 1953-55; pres. Shreveport Community Chest, 1947, Shreveport Council Social Agys., 1948, Shreveport Pub. Solicitations Rev. Council, 1950-55. Trustee Pub. Affairs Research Council, Council For A Better La., Centenary Coll. Shreveport, Gulf South Research Inst. Recipient Medallion award Shreveport United Fund, 1957. Mem. Investment Bankers Assn. Am. (bd. govs. 1945-48), Shreveport C. of C. (v.p., dir.), Pi Kappa Alpha. Democrat. Baptist. Clubs: Shreveport, Shreveport Country; Boston, Rotary. Mason. Home: 412 Sherwood Rd Shreveport LA 71106 Office: 575 Market St Shreveport LA 71102

BARROWS, LELAND JUDD, corp. exec.; b. Hutchinson, Kan., Oct. 27, 1906; s. Eugene and Forence Emma (Judd) B.; A.B., U. of Kan., 1928, A.M. 1932; m. Mabel Irene Conley, Mar. 21, 1935; childrenLeland Conley, Jennifer Irene. High Sch. prin., Glen Elder Kan. 1928-30; newspaper reporter, univ. teacher, grad. student, radio broadcaster, Lawrence, Kan., 1930-34; exec. asst. to chief, Soil Conservation Service, U.S. Dept. Agr., 1934-38, chief of personnel mgmt., 1938-42; spl. asst. to adminstr. Agrl. Marketing Adminstrn., 1942; asst. dir. War Relocation Authority, 1942-44; dir. Office of Budget and Planning, O.P.A., 1945-46; spl. asst. to commr., asst. commr. for adminstrn., Fed. Pub. Housing Authority, 1946-47; dept. dir. Office of Information and Ednl. Exchange, Dept. State, 1947-48; exec. asst. to spl. rep. in Europe, Econ. Coop. Adminstrn., 1948-53; dir. mission to Greece, Fgn. Operations Agy., 1952- 54, dir. mission to Vietnam, 1949-58; regional dir. Near East and South Asia Operations ICA, 1958-60: U.S. ambassador to Togo, 1960-61, Cameroun, 1960-66; prof., head dept. econ. and social devel. Grad. Sch. Pub. and Internat. Affairs, U. Pitts., 1966-68; mem. exploratory devel. group Research Analysis Corp., McLean, Va., 1968-. Served as lt. USCG Res., 1944-45. Mem. Beta Kappa. Office: Research Analysis Corp McLean VA 22101

BARROWS MARJORIE, editor, author; b. Chgo.; d. Dr. Ranson Moore and Caroline (Dixon) Barrows; student Northwestern U., U. Chgo. Asso. editor Child Life, 1922- 31, editor, 1931-38; co-editor Consol. Books, 1943-48; editor-in-chief Children's Hour, 1952-62; editor Treasure Trails, 1954-56, Jr. Treasure Chest, Family Weekly, 1954-62. Hon. mem. bd. govs. Heckscher Found., Nat. Council Radio Listeners. Recipient scroll for contbn. lit. heritage of Chgo., Chgo. Found. for Lit.; hon. scroll Rand McNally. Mem. Internat. P.E.N., Inst. Am. Geneology, Chgo. Drama League (past dir.), Soc. Midland Authors (mem. bd.), Theta Sigma Phi, Zeta Phi Eta. Presbyn. Clubs: Cordon (past v.p., sec.); Evanston Drama, University Guild; Arts (Chgo.). Author: Muggins, 1931; Fraidy Cat, 1941; Four Little Kittens, Tut!Tut! Tales, 1950; Muggins Takes Off, 1964; Muggins' Big Balloon, 1965; Muggins Becomes a Hero, 1965; Favorite Stores of Muggins, 1966; that Parade, 1967; Little Red Boot, 1968; and other books. Also compiler: 100 Best Poems, 1931; 200 Best Poems, 1939; Organ Grinder's Garden, 1939; The Children's Treasury, 1947; 1000 Beautiful Things, 1947, 56; 1000 American Things, 1948, 56; Read Aloud Poems, 1957-60; Treasure Trail Parade, 1957; (with Bennett Cerf) A Treasury of Humor, 1955; A Treasury of Beauty and Romance 1959; The Family Reader, 1956, 61. Home: 1615 Hinman Av Evanston IL 60201.

BARRY, ALLEN GIFFORD, business exec.; b. N. Troy, N.Y., Aug. 22, 1907; s. Henry Willis and Sarah Theresa (Horan) B.; A.B., Harvard, 1928; m. Margaret E. Sachs, Aug. 29, 1931; children—Allen Gifford, Richard S., John H. Student engr. N.Y. Telephone Co., N.Y.C., 1928, traffic mgr., Binghamton, 1929, Elmira, 1930, Schenectady, 1933-34, dist. traffic supt., Kingston, 1934, Elmira, 1935-37, Syracuse, 1938, gen. traffic supr., Albany, 1935- 40, div. traffic supt. Buffalo, 1940-44, gen. traffic supr. N.Y. City, 1944, asst. v.p., 1944, gen. traffic mgr. Albany, 1945, gen. comml. mgr., 1945-48; v.p. operations and dir. Wis. Tel. Co., Milw., 1948-56; v.p. gen. mgr., dir. Mich. Bell Telephone Co., Detroit, 1956-61; v.p., sec. Am. Tel. & Tel. Co., 1961-63; pres., dir., mem. exec. com. New Eng. Tel. & Tel. Co., 1963—; dir. 1st Nat. Bank of Boston, New Eng. Mut. Life Ins. Co., Boston, Boston Old Colony Ins. Co.; trustee Suffolk Savs. Bank, Boston. Served as orgn. div. chief Office Civil Def. Planning, Washington, 1948. Mem. corp. Wentworth Inst.; bd. dirs. Mass. Bay United Fund; mem. corp. Northeastern U., Peter Bent Brigham Hosp., Mus. Sci.; trustee Boston Symphony Orch. Mem. Greater Boston C. of C. (dir.). Clubs: Union, Algonquin, Commerical (Boston). Home: 23 Plymouth Rd Wellesley Hills MA 02181 Office: 185 Franklin St Boston MA 02107

BARRY, CHARLES C., radio, TV exec.; b. Newton Mass., July 1, 1911; s. M. John and Julia (Meehan) B.; Radio announcer NBC, Washington; Eastern program mgr., 1942- 44; nat. dir. programs ABC, N. Y.C., 1944-47, v.p. charge programming- radio and TV, 1947-50; v.p. NBC radio-TV programs, 1952-54; v.p. Wm. Morris Agy., 1955-56; v.p. Loew's Inc., charge TV, 1956-59; v.p. Young & Rubicam. Inc., N.Y.C., 1959-61, exec. v.p., dir. radio-TV dept., 1961-71. Home: 215 E 68th St New York City NY 10021 Office: 285 Madison Av New York City NY 10017

BARRY, COLMAN JAMES, coll. pres.; b. Lake City, Minn., May 29, 1921; s. John and Frances (O'Brien) B.; B.A., St. John's U., 1942; M.A., Cath. U. Am., 1950, Ph.D., 1953. Joined Order St. Benedict, 1942, ordained priest Roman Cath. Ch., 1947; sec. Am. Benedictine Rev.; mem. faculty St. John's U., 1953-, prof. history, 1953-64, pres., 1964-; summer tchr. San Raphael (Cal.) Coll., 1956-59, Cath. U. Am., 1959-64. Sec. Commn. Jours. Acad. and Profl., 1958; chmn. Nat. Com. Edn. for Ecumenism, 1965; commnr. N. Central Assn. Colls., 1966; pres. Assn. Minn. Colls., 1967. Penfield fellow in Germany, 1950. Author: The Catholic Church and German Americans, 1953; The Catholic University of America, IV, 1950; Worship and Work, 1956; Catholic Minnesota, 1958; Readings in Church History, 3 vols., 1959-65; American Nuncio: Cardinal Aloisius Muench, 1969; also numerous articles. Editor Benedictine Studies, 1958-. Home: St. John's Abbey Collegeville MN 56321.

BARRY, DAVID JOSEPH, banker; b. N.Y.C., Oct. 4, 1917; s. Dennis E. and Elizabeth (Marsh) B.; grad. Stonier Sch. Banking, Rutgers U., 1955; Advanced Mgmt. Program, Harvard, 1967; m. Elizabeth A. Jopp, Jan. 31, 1942; children—Barbara Ann, David Joseph, Maureen. With Mfrs. Hanover Trust Co., N.Y.C., 1936—, asst. v.p., 1954-60, v.p. 1960-67; v.p.-treas., 1967-71, sr. v.p., 1971—. Mem. Investment Bankers Assn., N.Y. Soc. Security Analysts, Municipal Forum. Republican. Clubs: Garden City (N.Y.) Country; Bond, Broad Street (N.Y.C.). Home: 74 Princeton St Garden City NY 11530 Office: 40 Wall St New York City NY 10002

BARRY, DAVID W., clergyman, assn. exec.; b. Minneapolis, Kan., Nov. 7, 1917; s. Frank Touzian and Sarah (MacArthur) B.; B.A., Oberlin Coll., 1938; B.D., Chgo. Theol. Sem., 1941, D.D., 1955; postgrad. U. Chgo., 1941-44; m. Marion Virginia McAlister, July 5, 1942; children—Mary Katharine, David McAlister, Philip Monte, Samuel MacArthur. Ordained to ministry Presbyn. Ch.; dir. urban research Presbyn Bd. Nat. Missions, 1944-47; dir. Pathfinding Service N.Y.C. Mission Soc., 1947-50, exec. dir., 1955—; dir. research Nat. Council Chs., 1950-54. Mem. Com. Religious Leaders of City N.Y. Bd. dirs. Union Theol. Sem., North Side Center For Child Devel., N.Y. Theol. Sem., Council Chs. N.Y., Opportunities Industrialization Center N.Y.C., Interfaith City-Wide Co-ordinating Com. Against Poverty, Met. Urban Service Tng. (N.Y.C.), Citizens Com. for Children City N.Y., Met. Applied Research Corp., Inst. for Juvenile Justice. Home: 148 Elizabeth Pl Armonk NY 10504 Office: 105 E 22d St New York City NY 10010

BARRY, FRANK JOSEPH, lawyer, govt. ofcl., educator; b. Nogales, Ariz., Feb. 5, 1913; s. Frank and Mollie (Dunne) B.; A.B., U. Cal. at Los Angeles, 1934; LL.B., Loyola U., Los Angeles, 1941; m. Juanita Martha Procter, Nov. 25, 1949; children—Michael Procter, Francis Patrick, William Dunne. Admitted to Ariz. bar, 1946, D.C. bar, 1961; pvt. practice, Nogales, 1946-51, Tucson, 1951-61; county atty. Santa Cruz County, Ariz., 1949-50; asso. Udall, Udall & Barry, Cole & Barry, 1951-57, Goddard & Barry, and predecessor, 1957-61; solicitor Dept. of Interior, 1961—; program adviser Ford Found., 1968-69; prof. law U. Ore., Eugene, 1969—. Mem. Pima County Democratic Central Com., 1952-61; del. Dem. Nat. Conv., 1956. Served to lt. (s.g.) USNR, 1942-45. Mem. Am., D.C. bar assns., Ariz. State Bar, Am. Judicature Soc., Am. Legion, Vets. Fgn. Wars, Am. Civil Liberties Union. Lion, Elk. Home: 2085 University St Eugene OR 97403

BARRY, FRED, Jr., lawyer; b. Mt. Vernon, O., Mar. 2, 1920; s. Fred and Ruth (Gebhardt) B.; B.A., Kenyon Coll., 1942; LL.B., Harvard, 1949, J.D., 1969; m. Virginia Ruth Motherall, June 5, 1948; children—Douglas Alan, Barbara Anne. Admitted to Ohio bar, 1949, since practiced in Mt. Vernon; acting judge Mt. Vernon Municipal Ct., 1954-59. Vice pres., dir. First-Knox Nat. Bank Mt. Vernon; adv. bd. Lumbermen's Mut. Casualty Co.; dir. J.S. Ringwalt Co., Worley's, Inc. Trustee Kenyon Coll. Served with USAAF, 1942-45. Recipient Distinguished Service award Mt. Vernon Jr. C. of C., 1956, Outstanding Pres. award, Ohio Jr. C. of C., 1955. Mem. Am., Ohio (mem. exec. com.), Knox County (past pres.) bar assns., Mt. Vernon Area C. of C. (past pres.), Kenyon Coll. Alumni Assn. (past pres.), Phi Kappa Sigma. Rotarian. Home: 207 Coshocton Av Mount Vernon OH 43050 Office: 111 S Mulberry St Mount Vernon OH 43050

BARRY, GENE, actor; b. N.Y.C., June 4, 1922; s. Martin and Eva (Conn) Klass; student pub. schs., N.Y.C.; m. Betty Claire Kalb, Oct. 22, 1944; children—Michael Lewis, Fredric James, Liza. Actor on Broadway, 1942—; plays include Rosalinda, Merry Widow, Catherine Was Great, They Would be Gentle Men, Bless You All, The Perfect Setup, 1962; nightclub performer; motion pictures include Atomic City, War of the Worlds, Sisters form Seattle, Red Garters, Alaska Seas, Soldier of Fortune, Naked Alibi, Back from Eternity, China Gate, Forty Guns, Thunder Road; star TV series Bat Masterson, NBC, 1958—, Burke's Law, 1963—; Name of the Game, 1969—. Active Boy Scouts Am. Office: care Gilbert & Levine 9601 Wilshire Blvd Beverly Hills CA 90210

BARRY, JEFF, composer; b. Bklyn., Apr. 3, 1939; s. Alan H. and Ruth (Hartman) Adelberg; student Coll. City N.Y., 1956-60; m. Nancy Calcagno, Jan. 23, 1967; children—Lisa Andi, Jon Colton. Staff writer E.B. Marks Music, 1960-62, T.M. Music, 1963-64, Trio Music, 1964-67, Unart Music, 1968-70, Heiress Music, 1970—; owner Jeff Barry Enterprises, N.Y.C.; producer Off Broadway show The Dirtiest Show in Town. Lectr. in grade and high schs. on hazards of drugs and importance of edn. Served with AUS, 1955. Composer Shoot 'Em Up Baby, Skooby-Doo, Solitary Man, Sugar, Sugar, Tell Laura I Love Her, Thank the Lord For the Nighttime, Then He Kissed Me, Wait Till My Bobby Gets Home, What A Guy, Who's Your Baby. Home: 2320 Surrey Lane Baldwin NY 11510 Office: 137 W 52d St New York City NY 10019

BARRY, JOHN, composer; b. York, Eng., Nov. 3, 1933; s. John and Doris (Wilkinson) Prendergast; ed. St. Peter's Pub. Sch.; m. Jane Birkin, Oct. 16, 1965; 1 dau., Kate; children by previous marriage—Suzanne, Sian. Leader J. Barry 7 Pop Group; film credits include Beat Girl, Never Let Go, Mix Me a Person, The Amorous Prawn, Doctor No, From Russia with Love, The Man in the Middle, Zulu, Goldfinger (Gold Disc award), Seance in a Wet Afternoon, Four in the Morning, The Ipcress File, The Knack, Mr. Moses, Thunderball, King Rat, Born Free (Oscar award), The Chase, The Wrong Box, The Quiller Memorandum, You Only Live Twice, 1967, Deadfall, The Lion in Winter (Oscar award winner 1968): theatre credits include Passion Flower Hotel; TV credits include Elizabeth Taylor in London, Sophia Loren in Rome. Recipient Clio award, 1968. Home: 74 Cadogan Sq London SW 1 England Office: 69 Cadogan Sq London SW 1 England

BARRY, SISTER MARY DAVID, coll. pres.; b. N.Y.C., May 31, 1915; d. David R. and Mary (Creagh) Barry; A.B., Coll. Mount Saint Vincent, N.Y.C., 1937; A.M., Columbia, 1946; postgrad. Cath. U. Am., Nat. U. Ireland, Dublin; D.H.L., Manhattan Coll., 1966. Joined Order of Sisters of Charity, 1938; tchr. English, Cathedral High Sch., N.Y.C., 1940-55; mem. faculty English, Coll. Mount Saint Vincent, 1955-56, dean student, 1956-63, pres., 1963—. Co-founder Cath. Forensic League N.Y., 1944; bd. dirs. Commn. on Ind. Colls. and Univs. N.Y.; pres. Race Relations Council N.Y.C., 1937. Past trustee Elizabeth Seton Coll., Yonkers, N.Y. Mem. Council Higher Ednl.

Instns. N.Y.C. (dir., sec.), Nat. Cath. Ednl. Assn., Am. Assn. U. Women, Conf. Cath. Colls. and Univs. N.Y. (v.p.), Nat. Assn. Women Deans and Counsellors. Author articles, monograph. Address: Coll Mount Saint Vincent Riverdale NY 10471

BARRY, PETER, banker; b. Rochester, N.Y., Mar. 22, 1912; s. William C. and Grace (Goodloe) B.; student Mass. Inst. Tech., 1934. With Rochester Gas & Electric Corp., 1936-65; with Monroe Savs. Bank, 1965—, exec. v.p., 1965-67, pres., 1968—, also trustee; pres. Ellwanger & Barry Realty Co., 1964-66; dir. Lae Ont. Cement Co., Ltd., Livonia, Avon & Lakeville R.R., Instl. Securities Corp., Rochester & Genesee Valley R.R. Pres. Soc. Genesee and the Lakes, 1967-70; v.p. Otetiana council Boy Scouts Am., 1962—, chmn. finance com., 1966-69; chmn. Rochester regional Red Cross Blood Program, 1951-56; exec. com. bd. advisers Salvation Army; mem. ad hoc com. Greater Rochester Transp. Authority, 1967; pres. Rochester Clearing House Assn., 1967-70; mem. Genesee Area Regional Planning Bd., 1967—. Councilman, Rochester, 1950-65, mayor, 1955-62; commr. Rochester-Monroe Civic Center Commn., 1956—. Trustee Rochester C. of C.; chmn. bd. regents Nazareth Coll. 1967—; bd. dirs. Rochester Gen. Hosp., Genesee River Basin Regional Water Resources Planning Bd., Rochester Bus. Opportunity Corp., Vis. Nurse Service of Rochester and Monroe County. Better Rochester Living, Inc., Council Social Agys., Rochester Community Chest. Served with U.S. Merchant Marine, 1934-36; from ensign to comdr. USNR, 1941-46. Recipient Civic medal Rochester Mus. Arts and Scis., 1958; Lester P. Slade award Real Estate Bd. Rochester, 1961; named Man of Year, Rochester Rotary Club, 1964, Citizen of Year, Rochester Kiwwanis Club, 1965; recipient Civic award Rochester Fire Fighters Assn., 1965. Mem. Nat. Assn. Mut. Savs. Banks. Home: 630 Mt Hope Av Rochester NY 14620 Office: 300 Main St E Rochester NY 14604

BARRY, ROBERT RAYMOND, business exec., former congressman; b. Omaha, May 15, 1915; s. Ralph and Ethel (Thomas) B.; student Hamilton Coll., 1933-36, Dartmouth, 1936-37, Sch. Finance, N.Y.U., 1938, Law Sch., 1946-47; m. Anne Rogers Benjamin, July 19, 1945; children—Cynthia Herndon, Henry Huttleston Rogers. Investment banker Kidder Peabody & Co., 1937-38; with Mfrs. Trust Co., 1938-40; mgr. exec. Bendix Aviation Corp., 1940-44; asst. to pres. Yale & Towne Mfg. Co., 1945-50; pres. Plumas Mining Co., 1945—, Calicopia Corp., 1965—; engaged in ranching and land devel., Coachella Valley, Cal., also in mining, Quincy, Cal.; mem. 86th-87th Congresses, 27th Dist. N.Y., 88th Congress, 25th Dist. N.Y., mem. coms. govt. operations, 1959-61, post office and civil service, 1959-65, fgn. affairs, 1961-65. Mem. Nat. council Boy Scouts Am. Active campaign Dewey for dist. atty., 1937, Willkie presdl. campaign; mem. N.Y. Republican County Com., 1945; del. coordinator, statistician for Dewey, Rep. Nat. Conv., mem. Rep. Nat. Campaign Com., Washington, 1948; personal staff Eisenhower campaign tour, Denver, Chgo., 1952; chmn. finance com. N.Y. State Congl. Campaign Com., Citizens for Eisenhower, 1954; chmn. Yonkers Citizens Eisenhower Com., 1956; U.S. del. NATO Parliamentarian Conf., 1959, 60, UNESCO Conf., 1963; Rep. nominee for congress 38th Cal. Dist., mem. Nixon-Agnew Nat. Staff, 1968; dir. Cal. Rep. Central Com., 1966-68. Former mem. bd. dirs. Greater N.Y. YMCA; active community, civic affairs. Mem. Acad. Polit. Sci., Citizens Union, Internat. Seaman's Union, Cal. Farm Bur., Alpha Delta Phi. Presbyn. Clubs: Eldorado Country (Palm Springs, Cal.): St. Andrews Golf (Hastings, N.Y.); Sierra; Economic, Blue Hill Troupe, Dartmouth College (N.Y.C.); Metropolitan, Capitol Hill (Washington). Home: 155 Wildwood Way Woodside CA 94026 also Thunderbird Country Club Palm Springs CA 92262 also 3001 Normanstone Dr NW Washington DC 20008 Office: 8500 Wilshire Blvd Beverly Hills CA 90211

BARSANTI, JOHN RICHARD, Jr., mfg. co. exec., lawyer; b. Davenport, Ia., July 1, 1928; s. John Richard and Lucille (Canks) B.; B.S. in Indsl. Engring., Washington U., St. Louis, 1949, LL.B., 1952; m. Nancy Lee Anne Nansen, Oct. 22, 1955; children—Lisa Anne, William B., Lori Anne, Lucy Anne. Admitted to Mo. bar, 1952; asso. firm Greensfelder, Hemker & Weise, St. Louis, 1952-54; partner firm Husch, Eppenberge, Donohue, Elson & Cornfield, St. Louis, 1954-67; gen. counsel, sec. Kellwood Co., St. Louis, 1967—; atty., Kirkwood, Mo., 1960-67. Bd. dirs. Kirkwood R-7 Sch. Dist., 1965-70, sec., 1967-68, pres., 1968-70. Bd. dirs. Mo. Assn. Retarded Children, 1963-67, St. Louis Assn. Retarded Children, 1957-60; bd. dirs. Washington U. Alumni Fedn., 1965—, pres., 1968-69. Mem. Bar Assn. Met. St. Louis (pres. 1966-67), Am. Bar Assn., Mo. Bar, Nat. Conf. Bar Presidents, Kirkwood C. of C. (pres. 1959-60), Order of Coif, Phi Delta Phi, Omicron Delta Kappa. Club: Washington Univ. (pres. 1969-70, gov. 1969-71. Home: 28 Hurtland Dr Jackson TN 38301 Office: 9909 Clayton Rd St Louis MO 63124

BARSANTI, OLINTO MARK, army officer; b. Tonopah, Nev., Nov. 11, 1917; s. Silvio and Agatha (Vangeliste) B.; B.A., U. Nev., 1940; M.A. in Internat. Affairs, George Washington U., 1962; grad. Nat. War Coll., 1958, Command and Gen. Staff Coll., 1946; m. Aletha Imogene Howell, Oct. 22, 1942; 1 dau., Bette (Mrs. Harvey Daniels). Commd. 2d lt. U.S. Army, 1940, advanced through grades to maj. gen., 1967; assigned Europe, 1943-45. Korea, 1950-52; chief staff, Berlin, Germany, 1955-57; assigned Army Staff, 1958-60, Joint Chiefs Staff, 1961-62; comptroller U.S. Army, Europe, 1963-65, Army Material Command, 1966; comdg. gen. 101st Airborne Div., Vietnam, 1967-68; chief staff 5th U.S. Army, 1968—; mem. faculty Command Gen. Staff Coll., 1946-49. Decorated D.S.C., D.S.M., Silver Star (5), Purple Heart (7), Legion of Merit (2), Bronze Star (8), D.F.C. Mem. Assn. U.S. Army, Sigma Nu. Lion, Kiwanian. Home: 93 Scott Loop Fort Sheridan IL 60037 Office: Fifth US Army Fort Sheridan IL 60037

BARSCHALL, HENRY HERMAN, educator; b. Berlin Germany, Apr. 29, 1915: A.M., Princeton, 1939, Ph.D., 1940; m. Eleanor A. Folsom; two children. Instr. Princeton, 1940-41, U. Kan., 1941-43; mem. staff Los Alamos Sci. Lab., 1943-46, asst. div. leader, 1951-52: mem. faculty U. Wis., 1946-71, prof. physics 1950-71, chmn. dept., 1951, 54, 56-57, 63-64; with Lawrence Livermore Labs., 1971—. Fellow Am. Phys. Soc. (chmn. div. nuclear physics 1968-69; Bonner prize 1965). Asso. editor Revs. Modern Physics. 1951-53, Nuclear Physics, 1959—. Home: 3900 Princeton Way Livermore CA 94550

BARSHAI, RUDOLF, conductor; b. Krasnodar City, USSR, Sept. 28, 1924; s. Borsi and Mari (Alekseeva) B.; ed. Moscow Conservatory, also Leningrad Conservatory. Solo viola player, 1949-52; founder, 1953, since condr. Moscow Chamber Orch. Instrumentation, editing: (Bach) Die Kunst Der Fuge, 1959, Das Musikalische Opfer, 1957; several concerts of Vivaldi, also Prokofiev's Visions Fugitives, others. Address: 20 Mayakovsky Sq Moscow USSR

BARSKY, ARTHUR JOSEPH, educator, plastic surgeon; b. N.Y.C., Dec. 7, 1899; s. Joseph and Rebecca (Koengisen) B.; D.D.S., U. Pa., 1922; M.D., N.Y. Med. Coll., 1926; tng. plastic surgery, N.Y. Postgrad. Med. Sch. and Hosp., 1927-34; postgrad. student of Sir Harold Gillies, London, Eng., 1934; m. Hannah Kahn, June 12, 1941; 1 son, Arthur Joseph III. Prof. surgery Albert Einstein Coll. Medicine 1955—; attending surgeon, chief plastic surgery Bronx Municipal Hosp. Center, 1955—; cons. surgeon Beth Israel Hosp., Mt. Sinai Hosp., Bronx-Lebanon Hosp., U.S. Naval Hosp., St. Albans, N.Y. Mem. tech. adv. com. cleft palate N.Y.C. Dept. Health, 1960—; sec.-gen. Internat. Fedn. Socs. Surgery Hand, 1965—. Pres. Children's Med. Relief Internat. Served to lt. col., M.C., AUS, 1943- 46. Recipient Health medal Govt. South Vietnam, 1969. Diplomate Am. Bd. Plastic Surgery (chmn. residency rev. com. 1964-66). Fellow N.Y. Acad. Medicine; mem. Am. Soc. Surgery Hand (founder mem., pres. 1965), Am. Assn. Plastic Surgeons, Am. Soc. Plastic and Reconstructive Surgeons, N.Y. Regional Soc. Plastic and Reconstructive Surgery (pres. 1963-64), Assn. Mil Surgeons U.S., Am. Soc. Maxillofacial Surgeons, Am. Cleft Palate Assn., German Assn. Plastic Surgeons, Brazilian Coll. Surgeons, Tissue Culture Assn., Hiroshima Soc. Medicine (adviser), A.M.A., N.Y.C., N.Y. State med. socs.; asso. mem. British Assn. Plastic Surgeons; hon. mem. Peruvian Soc. Pediatric Surgery, Israel, Argentine socs. plastics surgeons, Japan Soc. Plastic Surgery, Plastic Surgery Soc. Colombia (S.Am.), Miss. Valley Med. Soc., Peruvian- N. Am. Med. Assn. Author: Plastic Surgery, 1938; Principles and Practice of Plastic Surgery, 1950; Congenital Anomalies of the Hand and Their Surgical Treatment. 1958; (in Spanish) Anomalias Congenitas de la Mano, 1962: Principles and Practice of Plastic Surgery (with Drs. S. Kahn and B. E. Simon), 1964; also numerous articles, chpts. in books. Home: 174 E 72d St New York City NY 10021 Office: 1825 Eastchester Rd Bronx NY 10461

BARSTOW RICHARD, choreographer, prod., director; born Ashtabula, Ohio; son of Thomas Arthur and Ada Mary (Hatton) B.; studied with pvt. tutors. Began show bus. career, 1916; danced, appeared stock companies on tour, Mont., Okla., Tex., 1918-21; appeared Midnight Frolic, Chgo., 1924-25, The Palace, N.Y.C., also on tour U.S.; featured musical comedies, Australia, then movie housesU.S., to London and on tour Europe. 1928-30; appeared with sister The Palace, N.Y.C., 1930-39; single dancing act Radio City Music Hall, N.Y.C., Palmer House, Chgo., 1939; choreographer motion pictures Buck Benny Rides Again, Love Thy Neighbor, Swing Fever, also road company musical Helzapoppin'; prod. Olsen and Johnson show Carnival High Club, 1946; choreographer, prod. shows including Barefoot Boy with Cheek, Tonight at 8:3O, New Faces of 1952, revival of Sally, others; choreographer Municipal Opera, St. Louis, 1948; choreographer Greatest Show on Earth, Ringling Bros. Barnum and Bailey Circus, 1949-51, full director, 1952-57; director 3 summer tent theatres simultaneously, 1957; special writer, Choreographer, stager Colgate Comedy Hour, numerous other TV shows; prod., choreographer, dir. revues Shooting High, What's My Act, Toast of the Town; motion pictures include Girl Next Door, New Faces, Greatest Show on Earth, A Star is Born; staged, prod., dir. choreographed with sister Champagne on Ice, London Hippodrome, 1953; prod., wrote, dir., staged with sister Motorama shows Gen. Motors, N.Y.C. and on tour, also Powerama, Chgo., 1955; dir. Theater-in-the Round, mus. tent show, Westbury, L.I., summer 1956. 57; author, producer, dir. March of Dimes show Waldorf Astoria, N.Y.C., 1958; dir., choreographer appearances of Judy Garland, N.Y.C. Chgo., San Francisco, 1959; staged, directed Song of Norway, N.Y.C., 1959; prod., staged directed (with sister) Am. Youth Expn., N.Y.C., 1959; dir. summer theatres. Originated toe skate, with sister tap toe dancing on a staircase.

BART, LIONEL, author, composer; b. London, Eng., Aug. 1, 1930; s. Maurice Begleiter; student St. Martin's Sch. Art, London, 1943-49. Writer popular songs, 1959—; writer score and lyrics for movies Tommy Steele Story, 1957, The Duke Wore Jeans, 1958, Tommy the Toreador, 1959, also Serious Charge, In the Nick; writer score and lyrics for Fings Ain't Wot They Used T'Be, Theatre Workshop, 1959, Garrick Theatre, London, 1960-62, book music, lyrics for Oliver, London, 1960, Broadway, 1963, book, music, lyrics, dir. Blitz Adelphi Theatre, London, 1962-64, music and lyrics Maggie May, Adelphi Theatre, 1964; composer theme and lyrics for films Man in the Middle, 1964, From Russia with Love, 1963. Recipient Ivor Novello awards for Handful of Songs, Water, Water, The Tommy Steel Story, 1937, Maggie May, 1965, Living Doll, Little White Bull, Lock Up Your Daughters. Outstanding Personal Services to Brit. Music, 1959, As Long As He Needs Me (2 awards), Oliver, 1960, Blitz, 1962; Silver Heart award as show bus. personality of year Variety Club, 1962, Tony award for Oliver, 1963, Broadcast Music award for Oliver, 1963. Office: Apollo Music Ltd 37 Soho Sq London W 1 England

BARTA, FRANK RUDOLPH, psychiatrist, neurologist; b. Omaha, Nov. 3, 1913; s. Rudolph J. and Anna (Smejkal) B.; A.B., Creighton U., 1935; M.D., Johns Hopkins, 1939; m. Mildred K. Ware, Aug. 12, 1939; children—Frank B., Nancy and Carol (twins), Richard J., Matthew, Michael. Intern Harper Hosp., Detroit, 1939-40; asst. psychiatry Yale Sch. Medicine, 1942-43; resident neurology U. Chgo. Clinics, 1942-43; pvt. practice psychiatry and neurology, 1946—; instr. psychiatry and neurology Creighton U. Sch. Medicine, 1946-49, dir. dept., 1949-56, prof. psychiatry and neurology, 1956—; clin. prof. psychiatry Chgo. Med. Sch.; attending psychiatrist St. Joseph's Hosp., St. Catherine's Hosp., 1949-67; cons. in psychiatry A.R.C., VA Hosp., Cath. Charities, SAC, 1949-67; med. dir. Mental Health Center LaSalle County, Ottawa, Ill., 1968—. Chmn. personnel bd., City of Omaha, 1959—. Dir. mental hygiene unit, U.S. Army, Fort Bliss, Tex., 1943-46. Diplomate Am. Bd. Psychiatry and Neurology. Fellow A.C.P. (life), Am. Geriatrics Soc., Am. Psychiat. Assn; mem. A.M.A., Ill., LaSalle County med. socs., Ill. Psychiat. Soc., Assn. Mil. Surgeons, Am. Psychosomatic Soc., Guild Cath. Physicians, Guild Cath. Psychiatrists, Nat. Acad. Religion and Mental Health (charter, life mem.), Omaha Midwest Clin. Soc. Roman Catholic. Clubs: Omaha Athletic, Omaha Clin. Author: The Moral Theory of Behavior—A New Answer to the Enigma of Mental Illness, 1952. Contbr. articles med. jours. Home: 609 Illinois Av Ottawa IL 61350 Office: 305 W Jefferson St Ottawa IL 61350

BARTA, WESLEY JAMES, mfg. co. exec.; b. Finley, N.D., Apr. 26, 1913; s. James John and Anne Marie (Lieske) B.; B.S. in Elec. Engring., Mich. Coll. Mining and Tech.; student naval architecture U. Mich.; grad. student bus. Northwestern U.; m. Rita Bebber, Nov. 19, 1938; children—Thomas J. Carole J. Formerly naval architect Great Lakes Engring. Works; marine engr. Pitts. Steamship Co.; machinery surveyor Am. Bur. of Shipping; successively supt. maintenance Miss. Valley Barge Line Co., gen. traffic mgr., v.p., then pres., dir. until 1969; vice chmn. bd. transit/marine Chromalloy Am. Corp., 1969-70, vice chmn. bd. adminstrv., 1970—, also dir.; dir. Coyle Lines, Inc., Island Terminal Co. Mem. Nat. Def. Transp. Assn., Soc. Naval Architects and Marine Engrs., Nat. Nat. Indsl. Pollution Control Council, Marine Transp. Council, Water Resources Resources Associated, Ohio Valley Improvement Assn., Upper Miss. Gulf Valley Assn., Gulf Intracoastal Canal Assn., Sigma Alpha Epsilon. Clubs: Mo. Athletic Sunset Country, Noonday (St. Louis). Home: 10 Lindworth Lane (Ladue) St Louis MO 63124 Office: 120 S Central Av (Clayton) St Louis MO 63105

BARTALINI, C. RICHARD, lawyer; b. Kincaid, Ill., Sept. 25, 1931; s. Chester Richard and Florinda (Galli) B.; A.B., U. Cal., Berkeley, 1954; J.D., Hastings Coll. Law, San Francisco, 1957; m. Anne M. Evanoff, June 4, 1955; children-Robert Charles, Denise Anne, David Chester. Admitted to Cal. bar, 1957; practice in Oakland, 1957-66, Alameda, 1966—; dep. dist. atty. Alameda County, 1957-59; chief def. counsel Transit Casualty Co., 1959-60; chief trial atty. Alameda/Contra Costa Transit Co., 1960-61; asso. Nichols, Williams, Morga & Digardi, 1961-66; partner Davis, Craig & Bartalini, 1966—; atty., counselor Supreme Ct. U.S.; del. Cal. Bar Conf., 1963-68. Chmn. Alameda Youth Activities Com., 1958-63, Nat. Council on Mental Health and Retardation, 1965-69; mem. President's Council on Youth Opportunity, 1965-70. Pres. Alameda Bd. Edn.; v.p., bd. dirs. Alameda Boys Club; mem. exec. com. Nat. Found. March of Dimes. Named Alameda's Young Man of Year, 1965, Oustanding Young Man of Am., 1966, Outstanding Young Man of Cal., 1966, Outstanding civic Leader of Am., 1967. Mem. Am., Cal., Alameda County (dir.), Criminal Cts. bar assns., Am. Trial Lawyers Assn., Alameda County Lawyers Club (past pres.), Cal. (past dir.), Alameda Jr. (past pres.) U.S. (past legal counsel) jr. chambers commerce, Phi Alpha Delta. Elk, Eagle, Kiwanian. Clubs: Alameda Rod and Gun; Commonwealth. Home: 1224 Bay St Alameda CA 94501 Office: Times Star Bldg 1516 Oak St Alameda CA 94501

BARTEL, HERBERT HERMAN, educator; b. Dallas, Mar. 31, 1924; s. Herbert Herman and Freda (Metzger) B.; B.S. in Civil Engring., So. Meth. U., 1944; M.S., U. Tex., 1950; Ph.D., Tex. A. and M. U., 1962; m. Dorothy Jean Angus, July 19, 1950; children—Peggy Jean and Kathy Jean (twins). From instr. to prof., chmn. dept. civil and environmental engring. So. Meth. U., 1946—; design engr. Tex. Hwy. Dept., summer 1953, Forrest & Cotton, Inc., summers 1967-68. Commr. Boy Scouts Am., 1952-55. Served as ensign, C.E.C., USNR, 1943-46; PTO. NSF faculty fellow, 1960-61; Automotive Safety Found. fellow, 1958-59; recipient Excellence in Engring. Teaching award Gen. Dynamics Corp., 1969. Mem. Am. Soc. C.E., Am. Soc. Engring. Edn., Am. Road Builders Assn., Hwy. Research Bd. Lutheran (elder). Clubs: Town North Lions (v.p. 1969-70), Dallas (dir.), Dan Rogers Volleyball (Dallas). Home: 6144 Annapolis Lane Dallas TX 75214

BARTEL, WILLIAM A., corp. exec.; b. Newark, Feb. 9, 1915; s. Frederick William and Augusta Mathilda (Clarenbach) B.; student Dartmouth, Oberlin Coll.; m. Jesse King Feland, Feb. 18, 1936; children—Paul, Lucy, Peter, Wendy. Formerly copy chief v.p., dir. John A. Cairns Co., exec. v.p., dir. Ellington & Co. (merger West. Weir & Bartel, Inc.), N.Y.C., 1949-60, pres., dir., 1960-65, chmn. bd., 1965—; now v.p. communications Celanese Corp. Home: 197 Midland Av Montclair NJ 07042 Office: 522 Fifth Av New York City NY 10036

BARTELL, GERALD AARON, corp. exec.; b. Chgo., May 20, 1914; s. Benjamin and Lena (Tartakowsky) Beznor; B.A., U. Wis., 1937., 1937, M.A., 1939, postgrad. Law Sch., 1939-40; m. Joyce Jaeger, Nov. 2, 1941; children—Jeffrey, Denis, Laura, Jane, Thad and Thomas, (twins). Radio actor, dir., producer, 1932-37; faculty U. Wis. Dept. Radio Edn., 1937-47, asso. prof. 1946; founder Bartell Broadcasting Corp., Milw., 1947, pres., 1947-66; pres. Bartell Media Corp., N.Y.C., 1961-63, chmn. bd., 1963-69, chief exec. officer, pub., 1961-68; pres. Emerald Realty Co., Milw.; founder, former pres. Netherlands Antilles Broadcasting Corp., Curacao and Aruba; chmn. bd. Am. Med. Bldg. Guild Inc., Madison, Wis.; dir. Capital Indemnity Corp., Madison, Milw. Equity Fund, Inc., Off-Network Prodn., Inc., N.Y.C., Continental Mortgage Ins., Inc.; producer, performer children's radio programs, records, TV movies. Served to lt. (j.g.) USNR, 1942-45. Rockefeller fellow, 1937. Unitarian. Home: 3959 Plymouth Circle Madison WI 53705 Office: 2525 University Av Madison WI 53705

BARTELL, LEE, corp. exec.; b. Milw., 1910: s. Benjamin and Lena Bartell; student Milw. State Tchrs. Coll., 1932; student Marquette U., 1933; LL.B., U. Wis., 1936; m. Ina Berginn, Jan 13, 1934; children—Michael, Rusti, Richard. Admitted to Wis. bar, 1936, Cal. bar, 1960; with Wis. Atty. Gen.'s Office; counsel Wis. Devel. Authority; trial atty. U.S. Govt.; founder Bartell Broadcasting Corp.; mng. dir. Bartell Radio Sta.; former pres. Bartell Media Corp., KCBQ, Inc.; sec., dir. Bartell Broadcasters, Inc., Bartell Broadcasters N.Y., Inc. Served to lt. (j.g.) USNR, 1943-44. Mem. State Bar Wis., State Bar Cal., Fed. Bar Assn., Fed. Communications Bar Assn., Am Legion (past post comdr.), Order of Coif. Mason. Editor Wis. Law Rev. Office: 205 E 42d St New York City NY 10017

BARTELS, JOHN RIES, fed. judge; b. Balt., Nov. 8, 1897; s. William Nicholas and Louise (Reuter) B.; A.B. cum laude, Johns Hopkins, 1920; LL.B, Harvard, 1923; m. Anne Bell Willson, May 3, 1930; children—John Ries, William Gilpin. Admitted to N.Y. Bar, 1924; praticed in N.Y.C., 1924—, mem. firm Bartels & Hartung, 1951-59; justice N.Y. Supreme Ct., 1950-51; mem. N.Y. State Law Revision Commn., 1945-50, 52-57; Fed. Dist. judge, 1959—; spl referee Appellate div. N.Y. State Supreme Ct.; former counsel Govt. of Ecuador fgn. debt readjustment; former gen. counsel Gen. Acceptance Corp. and subsidiaries, The Fyr Fyter Co. and subsidiaries, Brilhard Plastics Corp., Dir. Bklyn. Council for Social Planning, 1953-58; mem. Mayor's Com. on Puerto Rican Affairs, N.Y.C., 1955-57. Alumni trustee Johns Hopkins, 1953-54; sec. bd. regents L. I. Coll. Hosp.; chmn. Kings County Hosp. Center Lay Adv. Bd. Bd. dirs. Nat. Conf. Christians and Jews, Brotherhood-In- Action, Bklyn div. Protestant Council. Vice pres. Navy Yard Boy's Club. Fellow Am. Coll. Trial Lawyers; mem. Am. N.Y. State, Bklyn. bar assns., Assn. Bar City of N.Y., N.Y. Co. Lawyers Assn., Fundacion Internacional Eloy Alfaro, Am. Law Inst. Am. Judicature Soc., Squadron A Ex-Mems. Assn., Omicron Delta Kappa, Delta Upsilon. Republican (former treas. Kings Co. exec. com.). Conglist. (ch. trustee). Clubs: Harvard, Down Town Assn., Nat. Lawyers, Inc. (hon.), Brooklyn. Home: 24 Monroe Pl Brooklyn NY 11201 Office: 225 Cadman Plaza E Brooklyn NY 11201

BARTELS, MILLARD, lawyer; b. Syracuse, N.Y., Feb. 24, 1905; s. Herman and Jane Agnes (Millard) B.; A.B., Cornell, 1927, LL.B., 1929; m. Eulalia Stevens; children—Millard Stevens, Chester Bruce, Jane Lee. Admitted to Conn. bar, 1930, since practiced in Hartford; gen. counsel Travelers Ins. Cos., Hartford, 1945- 69, chmn. ins. exec. com., 1955-70; trustee Soc. for Savs.; dir. Corporation, The Travelers Insurance Company, also The Travelers Indemnity Company, Charter Oak Fire Ins. Co., Broadcast Plaza, Conn. Bank and Trust Co., Hosp. Corp. Am. Mem. Parole Bd., Conn. State Prison, 1953-55. Mem. Town Council of West Hartford, 1939-45, pres., 1943-45. Dir. Health Ins. Inst., chmn., 1966- 67; pres. Health Planning Council Hartford; mem. Cornell U. Council; adv. adv. bd. Cornell Law Sch.; trustee Bishop's Fund, Diocese of Conn. Wadsworth Atheneum, Bushnell Meml. Hall Corp. Mem. Am., Conn., Hartford County bar assns., Assn. Life Ins. Counsel (pres. 1957-58), Conn. C. of C. (dir.), Health Ins. Assn. Am. (pres. 1960-61), Inst. for Living (dir.). Clubs: Tunxis (pres. 1966, 67), Hartford (pres. 1956-57), Hartford Golf; Metropolitan (Washington). Home: 29 Westwood Rd West Hartford CT 06007 Office: 1 American Row Hartford CT 06103

BARTELS, STANLEY LEONARD, financial co. exec.; b. N.Y.C., Sept. 1, 1927; s. Abraham and Anna (Schultz) B.; B.S., N.Y.U., 1954, M.S.A., 1956; grad. N.Y. State Maritime Acad., 1947; m. Estelle Grossman, Nov. 28, 1948; children—Jonathan Scott, Nancy Merrill, Diane Brooke. Examiner, Hanover Bank, N.Y.C., 1948-50; security analyst Standard & Poor's Corp., N.Y.C., 1950-53; sr. financial analyst Internat. div. Ford Motor Co., N.Y.C., 1953-56; asst. to treas. Grace Line, Inc., N.Y.C., 1956-57; v.p. Tex. McCrary, Inc. also controller, asst. to pres., N.Y.C., 1957-60; gen. partner J.R. Williston & Beane, N.Y.C., 1960-62, ltd. partner, 1962- 63; vice chmn., treas. Bogue Electric Mfg. Co., Paterson, N.J., 1962-63; pres., dir. Electrocopy Corp., 1963-66; v.p., dir. Shaskan & Co., Inc., mem. N.Y. Stock Exchange, 1966—; dir. Patrician Paper Co. Trustee Rubens-Filligree Foods Found. Served to lt. USNR. 1945-47, 51-53. Mem. Bankers Club Am., N.Y. Soc. Security Analysts, Phi Alpha Kappa. Clubs: New York University, Netherland of N.Y. Home: 48 Bertrand Dr Princeton NJ 08540 Office: 67 Broad St New York City NY 10004

BARTELSMEYER, RALPH R., dep. adminstr. Fed. Hwy. Commn. Home: 4201 Cathedral Av Washington DC 20016 Office: 400 7th St SW Washington DC 20591

BARTELT, LOUIS FRANKLIN, Jr., educator; b. Milw., Nov. 22, 1922; s. Louis Franklin and Viola (Steffen) B.; student Marquette U., 1940-43; A.B., Valparaiso U., 1944, LL.B., 1946; LL.M., Yale 1954; postgrad. U. Wis., 1959-60; m. Carlene Ruth Heidbrink, Aug. 31, 1946; children—Mark Louis, Dan Jonathan. Admitted to Wis. bar, 1947; with firm Affeldt & Lichtsinn, Milw., 1947-48: mem. faculty Valparaiso U., 1948—, prof. law, 1962—, also dean Sch. Law. Sterling fellow, 1953; Rockefeller Research fellow, 1959. Mem. Am., Ind. bar assns., Am. Judicature Soc., State Bar Wis., Ind. Jud. Council. Lutheran. Home: 608 Washington St Valparaiso IN 46383

BARTEMEIER, LEE HENRY, psychiatrist; b. Muscatine, Ia Sept. 12, 1895; s. John Albert and Katherine (Schaab) B.; A.B., Catholic U. Am., 1914, A.M., 1916, Doctor of Science (honoris causa), 1964; M.D., Georgetown Med. Coll., 1920; m. Elizabeth Haltigan, Nov. 23, 1921; children—Mary Elizabeth, (Mrs. William L. Hurley), John Albert (dec.), Katharine Schaab (Mrs. Thomas J. Roney). Served internship and also as resident Henry Ford Hosp., Detroit, 1920-24; research student Henry Phipps psychiat. clinic Johns Hopkins Hosp., 1924-26; vol. asst. instr. neurol. anatomy Johns Hopkins Hosp., 1925-26; pvt. practice psychiatry, Detroit, 1926-54; research student Harper Hosp. phychiat. clinic, Detroit, 1926-30, instr. mental hygiene Dept. of Nursing, Harper Hosp., 1926-33, asso. staff Harper Hosp., 1926-47; dir. Vets Psychiat. Clinic, Detroit, 1946-50; v.p. Chgo. Inst. for Psychoanalysis, 1930-31, instr., 1938-39; dir. profl. staff Haven Sanitarium, Rochester, Mich., 1942-54; asso. prof. psychiatry Wayne U. Med. Sch., Detroit, 1944-54; cons. in psychiatry, U.S. Army, Detroit, 1942-45; mem. vis. staff Henry Ford Hosp., Detroit, 1924-54; lectr. in psychiatry U. of Mich., 1950-54; med. dir. The Seton Pychiat. Inst., 1954-71; chmn. council on mental health A.M.A., Chgo., 1952-61; chmn. bd. trustees Joint Commn. on Mental Illness and Health, Inc.; clin. prof. psychiatry Georgetown U. Med. Sch., 1954—; tng. analyst Detroit Psychoanalytic Inst., 1940-45, Washington Psychoanalytic Inst., 1954-57, Balt. Psychoanalytic Inst., 1958—; clin. prof. psychiatry U. Md., 1961—. Trustee Menninger Found., 1947—, Salk Inst. Biol. Studies, 1961—. Mem. Md. Commn. on Alcoholism, 1961-62. Recipient John Carroll medal of merit George Washington U., 1970; named Knight St. Gregory, 1970. Fellow A.C.P., Am. Psychiat. Assn. (pres. 1951-52); mem. Group Advancement Psychiatry (pres. 1963-65), A.M.A., Am. Orthopsychiat. Assn., Am. Psychoanalytic Assn., Internat. Psychoanalytic Assn. (pres. 1949-50), World Health Orgn., World Med. Assn. Republican. Roman Catholic. Clubs: Cosmos (Washington). Address: 4203 N Charles St Baltimore MD 21218

BARTENSTEIN, FREDERICK, Jr., lawyer, pharm. mfr.; b. Warrenton, Va., Oct. 28, 1917; s. Frederick and Anna (Curtis) B.; A.B., Washington and Lee U., 1939, LL.B., 1941: m. Isabel Burnham Anderson, May 31, 1947; children—Frederick III, Arthur Anderson, John Curtis, Thomas Webster. Admitted to Va. bar, 1941; atty. Merck & Co., Inc., Rahway, N.J., 1942-47, asso. gen. atty., 1947-49, gen. atty., 1949-53, gen. counsel, 1953-61, adminstrv. v.p., 1961—. Trustee Pingry Sch., Elizabeth, N.J. Mem. N.J. Hist. Soc. (trustee), Phi Beta Kappa, Order of Coif, Omicron Delta Kappa. Presbyn. Home: R D 1 Mendham NJ 07945 Office: 126 Lincoln Av Rahway NJ 07067

BARTER, ROBERT HENRY, physician; b. Harvard, Ill., Mar. 15, 1913; s. Francis Albert and Lula Mae (Rowbottom) B.; B.S., U. Wis., 1937, M.D. 1940; m. Joanne Rae Blied, Dec. 29, 1948; children—Robert Raymond, James Francis, Mary Joanne. Intern Cleve. City Hosp., 1940-41; resident Chgo. Lying-In Hosp., 1941- 42, Wis. Gen. Hosp., Madison 1946-48; chief med. officer obstetrics and gynecology Galinger Municipal Hosp., Washington, 1948-50; faculty George Washington U. Sch. Medicine, 1950—, prof. 1958—, chmn. dept. obstetrics and gynecology. 1958-67; cons. surgeon gen. USAF, Walter Reed Army Med. Center, NIH. Served to maj., M.C., AUS 1942- 46. Mem. Am. Gynecol. Soc., Am. Assn. Obstetricians and Gynecologists, A.C.S., Am. Coll. Obstetricians and Gynecologists, A.M.A., Sigma Xi, Alpha Omega Alpha, Nu Sigma Nu, Kappa Sigma. Clubs: Burning Tree, Columbia Country. Home: 6211 Garnett Dr Chevy Chase MD 20015 Office: 2141 K St NW Washington DC 20037

BARTH, ALAN, editorial writer; b. N.Y.C., Oct. 21, 1906; s. Jacob and Flora (Barth) Lauchheimer; Ph.B., Yale, 1929; Nieman fellow, Harvard, 1948-49; m. Adrienne Mayer, July 1, 1939; children—Flora, Andrew. Reporter Beaumont (Tex.) Enterprise, 1936; editorial writer Beaumont Jour., 1937-38; Washington corr. McClure Newspaper Syndicate, 1938-41; editorial asst. Sec. Treasury, 1941-42; editor reports O.W.I., 1942-43; editorial writer Washington Post, 1943—; vis. prof. govtl. affairs U. Cal, at Berkeley, 1958-59. Recipient Sigma Delta Chi award, distinguished service Am. journalism. 1947; Am. Newspaper Guild award, distinguished editorial writing, 1948, Sidney Hillman Found., 1952; Oliver Wendell Holmes Bill of Rights award, 1964; Lasker Civil Liberties award, 1967. Mem. Am. Acad. Arts and Scis. Author: The Loyalty of Free Men, 1951; Government By Investigation, 1955; The Price of Liberty, 1961; Heritage of Liberty, 1965. Contbr. articles to popular mags. Home: 3520 Rodman St NW Washington DC 20008 Office: Washington Post Washington DC 20005

BARTH, EARL E., physician; b. Olivet, S.D., May 1, 1901; s. Albert and Matilda (Boegler) B.; A.B., North Central Coll., Naperville, Ill., 1922, hon. D. Sc. 1968; M.D., Northwestern U., 1928; m. Elia M. Jensen, Feb. 26, 1927; 1 dau., Barbara B. Myers. Practice medicine and surgery, 1928—; faculty Northwestern U., 1931—, dir. x-ray dept., 1936—, asso. prof. radiology, 1948-53, prof., 1953-69, emeritus prof., 1969—, chmn. dept. of radiology, 1957-69, acting chmn., 1969—; radiologist Passavant Meml. Hosp., Chgo., 1936—; chief cons. radiology VA Research Hosp.; cons. radiology Commonwealth Edison Co., Peoples Gas, Light and Coke Co., Ill. Bell Telephone Co.; vis. prof. radiology Mayo Clinic, 1960. Me. radiation com. NRC-Nat. Acad. Scis. Treas. 5th Inter-Am. Congress Radiology; del., chmn. U.S. delegations to Internat. Congresses Radiology, Montreal, 1962, Rome, 1965, Tokyo, 1969. Grubbe gold medalist Chgo. Med. Soc., 1967. Served as comdr. M.C. USNR, World War II. Diplomate Am. Bd. Radiology (mem. bd. 1958-64). Fellow Acad. Internat. Medicine; mem. A.M.A., Chgo., Ill. med. socs., Inst. Medicine of Chgo., Societa Italiana di Radiologia Medica and Medicina Nucleare (hon. mem.), Am. Roentgen Ray Soc. (past v.p. and chmn. exec. council, pres. 1962-63), Radiol. Soc. N.Am., Am. Coll. Radiology (chmn. bd. of chancellors, 1957-60, pres. 1960-61, gold medalist 1962), Chgo. Roentgen Soc. (past pres.), Am. Assn. Ry. Surgeons, Inter-Am. Coll. Radiology, Nipon Radiol. Soc. (hon.), Phi Chi, Alpha Omega Alpha. Presbyn. Clubs: Rotary, Lake Shore (Chgo.). Contbr. articles med. jours. Home: 2258 Lincoln Park W Chicago IL 60614 Office: 670 N Michigan Av Chicago IL 60611

BARTH, ELMER ERNEST, wire and cable co. exec.; b. Phila., May 15, 1922; s. Paul Adolph and Anna (Miller) B.; student Bentley Sch. Accounting, 1947-51; B.B.A., Northeastern U., 1956; m. Ruth Bradstreet Stone, Sept. 18, 1943; 1 dau., Rebecca Ordway. Asst. treas. Hayward Hosiery Co., Ipswich, Mass., 1945- 56; treas. Cerro Wire & Cable Co. div. Cerro Corp., New Haven, 1956—; sec., treas., dir. Computer Databanks, Inc., New Haven, 1961—; trustee Ipswich Savs. Bank, 1947-56. Bd. govs., vice chmn. finance com. Childrens Center, Hamden, Conn., 1965-68. Served with USNR, 1942-45. Home: 3 Sandra Dr Branford CT 06405 Office: 285 Nicoll St New Haven CT 06510

BARTH, FRANK R., coll. pres.; b. Chgo., Mar. 19, 1918; s. Frank Phillip and Esther (Pedersen) B.; A.B., Luther Coll., 1940, LL.D., 1969; M.B.A., Northwestern U., 1947; C.P.A., 1947; m. Marjorie V. Hove, Sept. 28, 1940; children—Eugene F., Kathryn L., Frank P. II, James A. Prof., head dept. econs. Luther Coll., 1946-53; partner Barth & Hayes, C.P.A.'s, Decorah, Ia., 1947-54, Alexander Grant & Co., Washington and Chgo., 1953 59; financial v.p. Pettibone Corp., Chgo., 1959-69; pres. Westrac Corp., Ft. Worth, 1967-69; pres. Gustavus Adolphus Coll., St. Peter, Minn., 1969—; financial cons. Post Office Dept., 1953-55. Mem. Lake Forest (Ill.) Bd. Edn., 1964-69, pres., 1966-69; mem. Gov's Commn. on Salaries, 1970. Alternate del. Republican Nat. Conv., 1952. Bd. dir. Minn. Pvt. Coll. Fund, Luth. Ednl. Conf. N. Am.; bd. dirs., Sec. Central States Coll. Assn. Served as navigator USNR, 1943-46. Named Outstanding Young Man Ia., 1952. Mem. Am. Inst. Accountants, Ia. (chmn. com. taxation 1950-51, com. coop. with bankers 1951-52), Ill. (com. bankers and creditors 1965- 66), Minn. socs. C.P.A.'s, Beta Alpha Psi, Alpha Kappa Psi. Lutheran. Club: Lake Forest (bd. dirs., treas. 1957-61). Home: Gustavus Adolphus Guest House St Peter MN 56082

BARTH, FREDERIC H., osteopathic coll. pres.; grad. Phila. Textile Inst.; LL.D. (hon.). Pres. Phila. Coll. Osteopathic Medicine, 1957—. Propr. Indsl. Rubber Co., also Fifer and Beatty, hardware supplies. Mem. Phila. Bd. Pub. Edn., 1957; postmaster of Phila., 1959. Trustee Phila. Textile Inst. Clubs: Union League Engineers (Phila.); Capitol Hill (Wachington). Patentee textile and chem. equipment. Address: Front and Lehigh Av Philadelphia PA 19125*

BARTH, JOHN ANDREW, tool and die co. exec.; b. Lakewood, O., May 3, 1910; s. John Joseph and Minnie (Andrew) B.; B.S. in Mech. Engring., Case Inst. Tech., 1932; m. Katherine E. Wagenhals, Oct. 27, 1934; children—Jon E., Donald D., Theodore A., Timothy D. With Barth Corp., Cleve. 1932—, v.p. gen. mgr., 1953-60, exec. v.p., 1960-63, pres., chief exec. officer, 1964—, now chmn. bd. Bd. mgrs. West Park, Fairview Park YMCA. Registered profl. engr., Ohio. Mem. Cleve. Tool, Die and Machine Shops Assn. (past pres.), Nat. Tool and Die Mfrs. Assn. (pres., past v.p., trustee). Lutheran. Mason (Shriner). Home: 18501 Hilliard Rd Rocky River OH 44116 Office: 12665 Brook Park Rd Cleveland OH 44130

BARTH, JOHN C., distillery co. exec.; b. Louisville, Mar. 29, 1924; s. Paul C. and Lilliam (Hinzen) B.; B.A., Miami U., Oxford, O., 1948; m. Mary Helen Reed, June 8, 1948; children—Linda Sue, Gregg Paul. With Joseph E. Seagrams & Sons, Inc., 1948—, v.p. adminstrn., 1967—. Served with USMCR, 1942-46. Elk. Home: 1315 Colonial Ct Mamaroneck NY 10543 Office: 375 Park Av New York City NY 10022

BARTH, JOHN SIMMONS, author, educator; b. Cambridge, Md., May 27, 1930; s. John Jacob and Georgia (Simmons) B.; B.A., Johns Hopkins, 1951, M.A., 1952; m. Harriette Anne Strickland, Jan. 11, 1950; children—Christine Anne, John Strickland, Daniel Stephen; m. 2d, Shelly I. Rosenberg, Dec. 27, 1970. From instr. to asso. prof. English, Pa. State U., 1953- 65; prof. English. State U. N.Y. at Buffalo, 1965—. Recipient Nat. Inst. grant, 1968. Author: The Floating Opera, 1956; The End of the Road, 1958; The Sot-Weed Factor, 1960; Giles Goat-Boy, 1966; Lost in the Funhouse, 1968. Home: RD 1 Mayville NY 14757

BARTH LESTER GEORGE, biologist; b. Detroit, June 29, 1905; s. Charles and Mary (Schroeder) B.; B.A., Wayne U., 1926; M.A., U. Mich., 1928; Ph.D., U. Chgo., 1930; m. m. Lucena Jaeger, June 9, 1948. NCR fellow, Naples, Italy, Berlin, Germany, 1930-31; Nat. Edn. fellow U. Cal., 1941; prof. biology Columbia, 1950-; mem. staff, also trustee Marine Biol. Lab., Woods Hole, Mass. Mem. Internat. Inst. Embryology (Amsterdam), Soc. Growth and Devel., Am. Soc. Zoologists. Author: Embryology, 1950, 54; The Energetics of Development, 1954. Translator: (French) Chemical Embryology, 1950. Asso. editor Physiol. Zoology, 1945-55. Home: 26 Quissett Av Woods Hole MA 02543 02543 Office: Marine Biological Lab Woods Hole MA 02543

BARTH, MAX, architect; b. Manchester, N.H., Aug. 15, 1907; s. Abraham and Frieda (Kagan) B.; B.Arch., U. Pa, 1928, M.Arch., 1930; m. Sarah Laster, Aug. 17, 1930; children—Richard Carl, Paul Edward, Linda Claire (Mrs. George S. Newman). Instr. archtl. design, graphics and archtl. history Wash. State U., 1930-34; architect Treasury Dept., 1934-37, architect Dept. Army Corps Engrs., 1938-53; sr. cons. architect, staff dir. tech. div., installations and logistics, Office Sec. Def., 1953-69; pvt. practice architecture, Washington, 1969—; cons. to govt.; cons. architect Pa. Gen. State Authority. Mem. bldg. research adv. bd. Nat. Acad. Scis.; exhbtd. water colors group shows Smithsonian Inst., Corcoran Gallery, Arts Club Washington, Am. Art League Shows. Registered architect, D.C., Md., Pa. Fellow A.I.A.; mem. Am. Nat. Standards Inst. (chmn. com. A-42), Washington Water Color Soc., Landscape Club Washington. Address: 5535-41st St NW Washington DC 20015

BARTH, RICHARD, corp. counsel; b. N.Y.C., May 23, 1931; s. Alexander Haddon and Georgina (Grant) B.; grad. Hill Sch.; A.B. cum laude, Wesleyan U., Middletown, Conn., 1952; LL.B., Columbia, 1955; student N.Y.U. Grad. Sch. Law, 1959-62; m. Mary Elizabeth McAnaney, June 13, 1959; children—Leanore, Jennifer, Richard, Michele. Admitted to N.Y. bar, 1958, N.J. bar, 1966; asso. firm Burke & Burke, 1957-65; gen. counsel, sec., mem. mgmt. com. CIBA, 1965-70; v.p., gen. counsel, mem. mng. com. CIBA-GEIGY Corp., 1971—; dir. Radio Shack Corp., 1964-65. Mem. substandard housing bd., Summit, N.J., 1968-70. Served with AUS, 1955-57. Mem. Am., N.Y., N.J. bar assns., Phi Delta Phi, Psi Upsilon. Club: Beacon Hill (Summit). Author articles. Home: 431 Grace Church St Rye NY 10580 Office: 444 Saw Mill River Rd Ardsley NY 10502

BARTH, WILLIAM PHILLIP, orgn. exec.; b. Bismarck, Mo., June 2, 1923; s. Phillip Henry and Elma (Keathley) B.; B.S. in Social Sci., Washington U., St. Louis, 1950. Cons. adult edn. U. Mich., 1956-59; mng. editor, mem. editorial bd. Jour. Conflict Resolution, 1957—; exec. sec., asst. dir. Center for Research on Conflict Resolution, U. Mich., 1959-68, asso. dir., 1968—, asso. prof. dept. arch., 1969—. Cons. Mich. State Library, 1956-57, Office Econ. Opportunity, 1964-65, World Inst. for World Peace, 1963- 66; pres. Independent Research and Devel. Corp., 1963—; sec.-treas. Univ. Research Corp., 1963—; coordinator U. Mich.-Tuskegee Inst. Program Race Relations Research, 1963—; mem. organizing com., staff mem. Internat. Conf. Social Psychol. Research in Developing Countries, 1966; mem. organizing com. Nat. Conf. Race Relations Research, 1967. Served with USAAF, 1943-46; CBI. Decorated Air medal with oak leaf cluster. Mem. Soc. Study Psychol. Issues, Internat. Studies Assn. Mem. founding com. Jour. Conflict Resolution, 1955-57. Home: 1206 Henry St Ann Arbor MI 48104 Office: Center for Research on Conflict Resolution 529 Thompson St Univ of Mich Ann Arbor MI 48104

BARTHA, DENNIS RICHARD, educator: b. Budapest, Hungary, Oct. 2, 1908: s. Richard and Paula (Imling) B.; ed. Budapest Acad. Music, Ph.D. in Musicology, U. Berlin (Germany), 1930; m. Susanna Barta, Dec. 2, 1939; children—Imre, Maria, Francis. Librarian music dept. Nat. Museum, Budapest, 1930-42; privat. docent U. Budapest, 1935; extraordinary prof. music Budapest Acad. Music, 1935-42, ordinary prof. music, 1942-71, chmn. dept. musicology, 1951-69; W.A. Nielson vis. prof. Smith Coll., 1964; lectr. Harvard, Yale, Princeton, Cornell U., Columbia, Ann Arbor (Mich.) U., 1961; vis. prof. Harvard, summers 1964-65, Cornell U., 1965-66; A. Mellon vis. prof. U. Pitts., 1966-67, permanent Mellon prof., 1969—. Directorium mem. Internat. Musicol. Soc., 1961—. Recipient Dent medal, 1963. Mem. Am. Musicol. Soc. (council 1969—). Author books on Liszt, Beethoven, Mozart, Bach, Haydn, others. Editor musicol. periodicals Zenei Szemle, Zenetudom, Tanulmanyok, Studia Musicologica, others. Office: Music Dept Univ of Pitts Pittsburgh PA 15213

BARTHE, RICHMOND, sculptor; b. Bay St. Louis, Miss., Jan. 28, 1901; s. Richmond and Marie Clementine (Roboteau) B.; student Art Inst. Chgo., 1924-28; pvt. study under Charles Schroeder; Dr. Fine Arts (hon.), St. Francis Coll. 1947; M.A. (hon.), Xavier U., New Orleans, 1934. Began as painter; sculptor since 1928. Exhibited Whitney Mus., Mus. Modern Art, Met. Mus., N.Y.C.; Century of Progress, Chgo; Dallas Mus.; Balt. Mus., Phila. Mus., Bklyn. Mus., Sculptors Guild. Received $500 prize, Artists for Victory Exhbn., N.Y.C., 1942. Awarded Julius Rosenwald fellowships, 1931, 1932; Guggenheim fellowships, 1940, 41; recipient James J. Hoey award for Interracial Justice, 1945, citation and $1000 grant Am. Acad. Arts and Letters and Nat. Soc. Arts and Letters, Audubon Gold Medal of Honor, 1945. Did bust of Booker T. Washington for Hall of Fame, N.Y.U.; heroic figure Toussaint L'Ouverture, Haiti; figure of Gen. Dessalines, Haiti; Haitian coins, mem. Nat. Sculpture Soc. Democrat. Roman Catholic. Home: Cole Gate PO St Ann Jamaica British West Indies ☆

BARTHELMAS, NED KELTON, stock broker; b. Circleville, O., Oct. 22, 1927; s. Arthur and Mary Bernice (Riffel) B.; B.S. in Bus. Adminstrn., Ohio State U., 1950; m. Marjorie Jane Livezey, May 23, 1953; children—Brooke Ann, Richard Thomas. Stock broker Ohio Co., Columbus, 1953-58; pres. First Columbus Corp., stock brokers and investment bankers, 1958—; pres., dir. Ohio Financial Corp., Columbis, 1960—; trustee, chmn. Am. Guardian Financial, Republic Financial; dir. Worthington Steel Co., Nat. Foods, Midwest Capital Corp., Lancaster Colony Corp., United Capital Corp., Republic-Franklin Life Ins. Co., Aircraft Acceptance Corp., Mid-Continent Capital Corp., 1st Nat. Equity Corp., Union Nat. Corp., Franklin Nat. Corp., Midwest Nat. Corp., Gen. Nat. Corp., Am. Nat. Realty Corp., 1st Columbus Realty Corp., Court Realty Co., Flight Lease, Inc., Aircredit Publs., Inc. (all Columbus), Eastern Bancorp. (Washington), Annual Enterprises (Chgo.). Served with Adj. Gen.'s Dept., AUS, 1945-47. Mem. N.Y., Am. midwest stock exchanges, Nat. Assn. Securities Dealers (past vice chmn. dist. bd. govs.), Investment Bankers Assn. Am. (exec. com.), Investment Dealers Ohio (sec., treas.), Nat. Stock Traders Assn., Young Pres. Orgn. (pres. 1971), Columbus Jr. (pres. 1956), Ohio Jr. (trustee 1957-58), Columbus Area (dir. 1956, named an outstanding young man of Columbus, 1962) chambers commerce, Newcomen Soc., Phi Delta Theta. Kiwanian. Clubs: Executives, Stock and Bond, Columbus Athletic, Columbus, Scioto Country (all Columbus), Crystal Downs Country (Frankfort, Mich.). Home: 1998 Cambridge Blvd Columbus OH 43221 Office: 58 E Gay St Columbus OH 43215

BARTHELME, DONALD, author; m. Birgit Barthelme; 1 dau., Anne. Author: Snow White; (short stories) Come Back, Dr. Caligari; Unspeakable Practices, Unnatural Acts; City Life, 1970. Guggenheim fellow, 1966. Address: care New Yorker Magazine 25 W 43d St New York City NY 10036

BARTHELME, DONALD, educator, architect; b. Galveston, Tex., Aug. 4, 1907; s. Fred and Mary A. (Anderson) B.; student Rice Inst., 1924-26; B. Arch., U. Pa., 1930; m. Helen Bechtold, June 23, 1930; children—Donald, Joan, Peter, Frederic, Steven. Prof. archtl. design U. Houston, 1946-58; William Ward Watkin prof. Rice U., 1959-61; vis. prof. U. Pennsylvania School Architecture, 1956, Rice Institute, 1958, Tulane, 1962; prof. U. Houston, 1962—; work exhibited Mus. Modern Art, Nat. Gallery Art, Washington, 1952, Sao Paulo, Brazil, Switzerland; work pub. numerous profl. mags. Recipient 1st award for schs., Sao Paulo biennial, 1954, Sch. Exec. mag., 1952. Fellow A.I.A.; mem. Tex. Soc. Architects, Tau Sigma Delta. Roman Catholic. Home: 11 Wynden Dr Houston TX 77027

BARTHES, ROLAND, author; b. Cherbourg, France, Nov. 12, 1915; s. Louis and Henriette (Binger) B.; Licencie es Lettres, Diplome d'Etudes Superieures Paris, Sorbonne. Prof. letters, fellow Nat. Center Sci. Research, Paris 1952-59; dir. d'Etudes a l'Ecole des Hautes Etudes, Sorbonne, 1962, vis. prof. Johns Hopkins, 1967. Author: On Racine, 1964: Elements of Semiology, 1967; Writing Degree Zero, 1967. Address: 11 Rue Servandoni Paris 6 France

BARTHOLD, ALLEN JENNINGS, educator; b. Phila., Aug. 6, 1900; s. Allen Henry and Emma Agnes (Gregory) B.; B.A., Lehigh U., 1921; Ph.D., Yale, 1931; m. Mildred Jane Cleavelane, June 30, 1927; 1 son, Gregory Bradford, Lecteur Américain, U. of Clermont-Ferrand, France, 1922-23; instr. French and Spanish, Lehigh U., Bethlehem, Pa., 1921-22 and 1923-24, prof. and head dept. of Romance langs., 1939—, leave of absence, 1951-53; dir. Instituto Cultural Dominico-Americano, 1951-53; instructor French, Yale, 1924-36, assistant prof., 1936-39; dir. adult education program at Lehigh U., 1966-67, prof. emeritus, 1967—; prof. emeritus East Stroudsburg State Coll., 1967-70. Mem. Alpha Chi Rho, Pi Delta Epsilon. Republican. Home: 1438 Glenbrook Rd Stroudsburg PA 18360 Office: East Stroudsburg State Coll East Stroudsburg PA 18301

BARTHOLOMAY, ANTHONY FRANCIS, educator; b. Utica, N.Y., Aug. 11, 1919; s. James A. and Grace D. (Abbate) B.; A.B., Hamilton Coll., 1940; M.A., Syracuse U., 1942; S.D., Harvard, 1957; m. Priscilla Millicent Upham, Jan. 3, 1944; children—Alan L., Marsha L., James A., Andrea F. Instr. math. Syracuse U., 1940-42, Brown U., 1942-45; asst. prof., chmn. depts. maths. and physics, Keuka Coll., 1945-46; instr. math. Rensselaer Poly. Inst., 1946-47; instr. math. Rutgers U., 1947-51; mathematician Lab. Electronics, Boston, 1951-52; mathematician Lincoln Lab., Mass. Inst. Tech., 1952-54; staff Biophysics Research Lab., Peter Bent Brigham Hosp., Harvard Med. Sch., Boston, 1954-62, asso. staff medicine, 1954-67, asst. prof.

math. biology, 1960-67, dir. div. math. biology and biomath. lab., 1962-67; prof. asst. prof. math. biology, dept. biostatistics Harvard Sch. Pub. Health 1957-60; biomath. N.C. State U., Sch. Medicine and Pub. Health U.N.C., 1967-69; prof., chmn. dept. math. medicine Med. Coll. Ohio, Toledo, 1969—; ind. investigator Howard Hughes Med. Inst., 1957-67; dir. research and tng. grants biomath. NIH, 1962-67; mem. Pres. Adv. Bd. Biometric Soc., 1966-69; lectr. in field. Mem. A. Math. Soc., Am. Statis. Assn., Soc. Indsl. and Applied Math., Soc. Gen. Systems Research, Biometric Soc., Am. Inst. Biol. Scis., A.A.A.S., Assn. Am. Med. Colls., Am. Pub. Health Assn., Math. Assn. Am., Ohio Pub. Health Assn. Contbr. articles profl. jours., books. Home: 1724 Mount Vernon St Toledo OH 43607

BARTHOLOMAY, WILLIAM CONRAD, ins. co. exec., baseball club ofcl.; b. Evanston, Ill., Aug. 11, 1928; s. Henry C. and Virginia (Graves) B.; student Oberlin Coll., 1946-49, Northwestern U., 1949-50; B.A., Lake Forest Coll., 1950; m. Gail Dillingham, May 25th, 1968; 1 dau., Karen; children (by previous marriage)—Virginia, William T., Jamie, Elizabeth, Sara. Asso. with Batholomay & Clarkson, Chgo., 1950-57; partner Bartholomay Bros., Chgo., 1957—; v.p. Bartholomay & Clarkson div. Alexander & Alexander, 1965; v.p., dir. Frank B. Hall & Co., Inc., also pres., dir. Olson & Bartholomay div.; v.p. Atlanta/LaSalle Corp.; pres. Atlanta Chiefs soccer team, Stadium Club, Braves Prodns. Inc., Surprise, Inc.; chmn., pres. Atlanta Braves, Inc.; dir. Pacific Coast Corp., Seeburg Corp., United Trust Life Ins., Parker & Co. (Ga.). Dir. United Republican Citizens League Ill., 1961. Bd. dirs. Chgo. Maternity Center, Atlanta Boys Club; trustee Lake Forest Coll., Oglethorpe Coll.; chmn. Tb Christmas Seal Assn. Ga., 1968, sch. savs. program U.S. Savs. Bond Com. of Ga. Served with USNR, 1951-54. Mem. Young Republican Orgn. (pres. 1959-61, chmn. bd. 1961—, treas. 1961), Delta Kappa Epsilon. Episcopalian. Clubs: Racquet (dir. 1957—), Saddle and Cycle, University, Chicago, Commonwealth (Chgo.); Shoreacres, Bath and Tennis (Lake Bluff, Ill.); Onwentsia (Lake Forest); Peachtree, Piedmont Driving, Commerce, Atlanta Country, Capital City (Atlanta). Home: 1500 N Lake Shore Dr Chicago IL 60610

BARTHOLOMEW, ARTHUR PECK, Jr., accountant; b. Rochester, N.Y., Nov. 20, 1918; s. Arthur Peck and Abbie West (Dawson) B.; A.B., U. Mich., 1939, M.B.A., 1940; m. Mary Elizabeth Meyer, Oct. 4, 1941; children—Susan (Mrs. William Hoyt Krebs), Arthur Peck III, James M., Virginia L. With Ernst & Ernst, 1940—, successively jr. accountant, partner charge Eastern dist., Detroit office, 1940-64, nat. office, Cleve., 1964-65; N.Y. office, 1965—, also mem. mng. com.; instr. accounting U. Mich., 1940, George Washington U., 1945-46. Mem. Mich. Gov.'s Task Force for Expenditure Mgmt., 1963-64; mem. 2d Regional Plan Commn. N.Y. Bd. dirs. Detroit League for Handicapped, 1952-64; treas. Grosse Pointe War Meml. Assn., 1961; mem. exec. bd., treas. Greater N.Y. council Boy Scouts Am. Served from pvt. to capt., AUS, 1942-46. Mem. N.A.M., Nat. Assn. Accountants (pres. Detroit 1963-64, nat. v.p. 1968-69), The Conf. Bd., Mich., N.Y., Ohio socs. C.P.A.'s, Am. Inst. C.P.A.'s, Phi Beta Kappa, Phi Kappa Phi, Beta Gamma Sigma, Phi Eta Sigma, Beta Alpha Psi, Phi Kappa Sigma. Republican. Presbyn. Clubs: Country (Detroit); Grosse Pointe Yacht (treas. 1964); Greenwich Country; Clevelander: Wall Street (treas., gov.); Union League. Home: 103 Doubling Rd Greenwich CT 06830 Office: 140 Broadway New York City NY 10005

BARTHOLOMEW, FRANK H., press assn. exec.; b. San Francisco, Oct. 5, 1898; s. John William and Kate Leigh (Schuck) B.; LL.D., Ore. State U.; m. Antonia Luise Patzelt, May 18, 1922. Joined U.P., Portland, 1921, v.p. in charge Pacific Area, 1930, later becoming 1st v.p., dir. U.P. Assns., pres., gen. mgr., 1955-62, chmn. bd., 1962—(became U.P.I. 1958); chmn., dir. Brit. U.P., Ltd., United Feature Syndicate, Inc., Planet News, Ltd., U.P. Assns. Co., Wire Service Supply Co., Inc.; pres., dir. United Radio Shows, Inc., U.P. Wireless, Inc., Met. Newspaper Feature Service, Inc.: war corr. covering New Guinea, Aleutian campaign, 1943, Okinawa (10th Army), Luzon (38th Div.), 1945; covered Japanese surrender aboard U.S.S. Missouri, Tokyo Bay, 1945; atomic bomb tests, Bikini, 1946; war in China, Fall of Shanghai, 1949, Korean War, 1950, Indo China 1954. Owner of Buena Vista Vineyards, Sonoma, Cal.; v.p. Widmer Vineyards Inc.; dir. San Francisco Fed. Savs. & Loan Assn., San Francisco; adv. dir. Security Pacific Nat. Bank, Los Angeles. Served as 1st lt. Inf., U.S. Army, 1918. Recipient citations V.F.W., Gen. MacArthur, 1945, Gen. Omar N. Bradley award. Fellow Sigma Delta Chi; mem. Am. Legion, Kappa Tau Alpha. Mason (Shriner). Clubs: Bohemian, Press, World Trade (San Francisco); Foreign Correspondents (Tokyo); Metropolitan, Pinnacle (N.Y.C.); Balboa (gov.) (Mazatlan, Mexico). Home: Glenbrook NV 89413 Office: 220 E 42d St New York City NY 10017 also Fox Plaza San Francisco CA 94102

BARTHOLOMEW, GEORGE ADEL zoologist; b. Independence, Mo., June 1, 1919; s. George A. and Esther (Carstensen) B.; A.B., U. Cal. at Berkeley, 1940. M.A., 1941; Ph.D., Harvard. 1947; m. Elizabeth Burnham, Nov. 7, 1942; childrenKaren Elizabeth, Bruce Monroe. Faculty, U. Cal. at Los Angeles, 1947-, prof. zoology, 1959—; research on physiology and behavior desert vertebrates and marine birds and mammals. Mem. Am. Soc. Zoologists, Am. Soc. Mammalogy, Ecol. Soc. Am., Am. Ornithologists Union. Home: 551 W Rustic Rd Santa Monica CA 90402 Office: University of California Los Angeles CA 90024

BARTHOLOMEW, HARLAND, city planner; b. Stoneham, Mass., Sept. 14, 1889; s. Aden Luther and Harriet Mary (Lewin) B.; civ. engring. course, Rutgers Coll., hon. C.E., 1921, D.Sc., 1952; m. Gladys B. Funsten, May 15, 1968. Formerly cons. engr. City Plan Commn., St. Louis; formerly Cons. Mo. State Planning Bd.; prof. civic design U. Ill. ret.; former chmn. Nat. Capital Planning Commn.; cons. Harland Bartholomew & Assos., civil engrs., city planners and landscape architects, St. Louis. Adv. preparation city plans and zoning ordinances numerous Am. cities, including St. Louis, Washington, Williamsburg, Va., Pitts., Louisville, Ky., Memphis, New Orleans, Omaha, Neb., Mpls., Dallas, Los Angeles, Portland, Vancouver, B.C. Former pres. Am. City Planning Inst., Nat. Conf. on City Planning. Mem. Am. Soc. C.E. (hon.), Am. Inst. Cons. Engrs., Am. Soc. Landscape Architects (hon.), American Soc. Planning Officials, Zeta Psi, Tau Beta Pi. Republican. Clubs: Engineers, St. Louis, Bellerive Country, University (St. Louis); Metropolitan, Cosmos (Washington). Author: Urban Land Uses; Land Uses in American Cities, 1955. Home: 19 Wydown Terrace St Louis MO 63105 Office: 165 N Meramec St St Louis MO 63105

BARTHOLOMEW, LLOYD GIBSON, physician; b. Whitehall, N.Y., Sept. 15, 1921; s. Emerson F. and Minnie (Swinton) B.; A.A., Green Mountain Jr. Coll., 1939; B.A., Union Coll., Schenectady, 1941; M.D., U. Vt., 1944; M.S. in Internal Medicine (fellow), U. Minn., 1952; m. Elisabeth Thrall, Dec. 17, 1943; children—Suzanne, Lynne, Lloyd Gibson, Deborah, Douglass Thrall. Intern Mary Hitchcock Meml. Hosp., Hanover, N.H., 1944-45, resident, 1945-46, 48-49; asst. internal medicine Dartmouth, 1948-49; 1st asst. div. internal medicine Mayo Clinic, Rochester, Minn., 1949-52, asst. to staff div. internal medicine, 1952-53; practice medicine, specializing in gastroenterology, Rochester, 1952—; instr. internal medicine Mayo Found., U. Minn., 1952-58, asst. prof., 1958-63, asso. prof. internat. medicine, 1963-67, prof. medicine, 1967—; attending physician St. Mary's, Meth. hosps., Rochester, 1952, Worrall Hosp., Rochester. Served to capt., M.C., AUS, 1946-47; lt. col. Res. Recipient Woodbury prize in medicine, 1944, Carbee prize in obstetrics, 1944. Diplomate Am. Bd. Internal Medicine. Mem. A.M.A. (sec. gastroenterology sect. 1962-68, vice chmn. gastroenterlogy sect. 1968-69, chmn. 1969-70; mem. council on scientific assembly 1969, chmn. program planning com. 1970—), Minn. (del Ho. Dels. 1964—), So. Minn. (pres. 1963-64) med. assns., Zumbro Valley Med. Soc. (sec.-treas. 1969-70, v.p. 1970-71), Am. Gastroent. Assn. (com. on procedures 1970—), Soc. Study Liver Diseases, Minn. Soc. Internal Medicine, Sigma Xi. Contbr. articles profl. publs. Home: 1201 6th St SW Rochester MN 55901 Office: 200 1st St SW Rochester MN 55901

BARTHOLOMEW, PAUL CHARLES, educator; b. Salem, O., July 15, 1907; s. Charles Edward and Laura Frances (Doyle) B.; A.B., U. Notre Dame, 1929, A.M., 1931; postgrad. Northwestern U., summers 1931-33; Ph.D., U. Ky., 1938; m. Mary Agnes Carey, June 13, 1933; children—Thomas Charles, Robert Paul. Grad. asst. in polit. sci. U. Notre Dame, 1929-30, instr., 1930-33, asst. prof., 1933-36, asso. prof., 1936-42, prof., 1942—, head dept. polit. sci., 1938-47; sometime vis. prof. polit. sci. St. Mary's Coll., Northwestern U., Mich. State U., Loyola U., Chgo., U. Chgo., U. Tenn., Nat. U. Ireland, Queen's U., Belfast, Trinity Coll., Dublin, Univ. Cobl., Galway, Chulalongkorn U., Bangkok, Thailand. Cons. Urban Renewal, Chgo., 1959, Dept. of Navy, State of Indiana. Coordinator, prin. lectr. Philippine Constn. Conf., Manila, 1970. Political Commentator, radio station WSBT, 1938. Originator and dir. Wasington tours of dept. of polit. sci., 1932—; orginator and adviser quadrennial Model Nat. Polit. Conv. of dept. of polit. sci. Republican. Club: Faculty (pres. 1944). Author: American Government Under the Constitution, 1947, rev. 49, 56; Summaries of Leading Cases on the Constitution, 1954, rev. edits. 1956, 58, 62, 65, 67, 70; Public Administration, 1959,62; Profile of a Precinct Committeeman, 1968; The Third Indiana Congressional District, A Political History, 1970; Ruling American Constitutional Law, 2 vols., 1970; The Irish Judiciary, 1971. Contbr. to jours. Home: 415 E Pokagon St South Bend IN 46617 ☆

BARTHOLOMEW ROBERT H., mining co. exec.; b. Cleve., Nov. 2, 1918; s. Rob bO. and Elizabeth (Lee) B.; B.A., Amherst Coll., 1940; m. Margaret Johnson, Mar. 12, 1945: childrenSuzanne, Janet. With Hanna Mining Co., Cleve., 1940-, comptroller, 1958-60, dir. planning and spl. projects, 1960-62, asst. to pres., 1962-; comptroller M.A. Hanna Co., Cleve., 1958-60. Mem. Am. Inst. Mining Engrs., Soc. Mining Engrs., Canadian Inst. Mining and Metallurgy. Office: 100 Erieview Plaza Cleveland OH 44114

BARTILUCCI, ANDREW JOSEPH, coll. dean; b. N.Y.C., Nov. 29, 1922; s. Rocco and Philomena (Innello) B.; B.S., St. John's U., 1944; M.S. Rutgers U., 1949; Ph.D., U. Md., 1953: m. Lucy Ann Fulvio, June 10, 1950; childrenMary Ann, Phyllis, Eugenie, Andrew. Asso. research pharmacist, research and devel. div. Merck & Co., 1949-50; prof. pharmacy. asst. dean St. John's U. Coll. Pharmacy, 1952-56, dean, 1956-. Mem. adv. council N.Y. State Senate Com. on Health. Fellow Am. Found. Pharm. Edn., 1950-52. Served as pharmacist's mate USNR, 1944-46; ensign, 1949-57. Pharmacist USPHS(R), 1957—. Fellow A.A.A.S.; mem. Am. Coll. Apothecaries, N.Y. Acad. Scis., N.Y. Acad. Pharmacy, Am. Pharm. Assn., Sigma Xi, Rho Chi, Phi Delta Chi. Home: 115 Roosevelt St Garden City NY 11530 Office: Grand Central and Utopia Parkways Jamaica NY 11432

BARTKY, ADOLPH JOHN, educator; b. Chgo., Apr. 10, 1899; s. Adloph and Louise (Schaar) B.; student Ill. Inst. Tech., 1915-17; M.S., U. Chgo., 1923; A.M., Northwestern U., 1933, Ph.D., 1935; LL.D., Golden Gate Coll., 1965; m. Ruth Ashworth, Dec. 21, 1929; childrenJohanna Louise, Judith, Joyce, Janet, Jill. Asst. prof. engring. mathematics, Ill. Inst. Tech. (then Lewis Inst.), 1921; prin. elementary schs., Chgo., 1925- 33, Calumet High Sch., Chgo., 1933-37; dist. supt. of schs., Chgo., 1938-39; pres. Chgo. Teachers Coll., 1939-42; also dean Woodrow Wilson Jr. Coll.; prof. emeritus Stanford U. Sch. Edn., dean, 1946-53; distinguished prof. Golden Gate Coll., San Francisco. Trustee Golden Gate College, San Francisco. Served with U.S. Army, World War I; in tng. as officer in charge, instr. training and asst. dir. Standards and Curriculum Div., with rank of capt., U.S.N.R., during World War II. Awarded Legion of Merit. Mem. Phi Delta Kappa. Author: Supervision as Human Relations; Adminstration as Educational Leadership Social Issues in Education. Co-Author: The High School Teacher and His Job. Contbr. to Saturday Evening Post, and ednl. jours. Home: 50 Chumasero Dr San Francisco CA 94132

BARTLE, RUSSELL C., electric co. exec.; b. Kingston, Pa., 1928; B.S., Susquehanna U., 1952; married. Staff auditor Lybrand, Ross Bros. & Montgomery, C.P.A.'s, 1952-56; arena mgr. Cambria County War Meml., 1956-60; auditor, mgr. tax dept. Air Products and Chems. Inc., 1960-64; sr. accountant Pa. Electric Co., Johnstown, 1964-65, asst. comptroller, 1965-69, comptroller, 1969—; comptroller Nineveh Water Co., Waverly Electric Light & Power Co. Served with USNR, 1946-48. C.P.A., Pa. Home: 1449 Paulton St Johnstown PA 15905 Office: 1001 Broad St Johnstown PA 15907*

BARTLETT, ALBERT ALLEN, educator, physicist, b. Shanghai, China, Mar. 21, 1923 (parents Am. citizens); s. Willard William and Marguerite (Allen) B.; student Otterbein Coll., 1940-42; B.A., Colgate U., 1944; M.A., Harvard, 1948, Ph.D., 1950; m. Eleanor Frances Roberts, Aug. 24, 1946; children—Carol Louise, Jane Elizabeth, Lois Jeanne, Nancy Marie. Research asst. Los Alamos Sci. Lab., 1944-46; faculty U. Colo., Boulder, 1950—, prof. physics, 1962—; faculty Harvard Summer Sch., 1952, 53, 55, 56; vis. research worker Nobel Inst. Physics Stockholm, Sweden, 1963-64. Mem. Boulder City Parks and Recreation Adv. Bd., 1967—, vice chmn., 1969-70, chmn., 1970. Mem. Am. Phys. Soc., Am. Assn. Physics Tchrs. (recipient Distinguished Service citation 1970), Sigma Xi. Contbr. articles profl. jours. Home: 2935 19th St Boulder CO 80302

BARTLETT, CALVIN PAGE, lawyer; b. Portsmouth, N.H., Oct. 8, 1901; s. John H. and Agnes (Page) B.; grad. Phillips Acad., Andover, Mass., 1920; A.B., Yale, 1924, LL.B., 1927; m. Nancy White, June 21, 1947; children by previous marriage—John H., Faith (Mrs. Alan O. Hickok). Admitted to Mass. bar, 1927, since practiced in Boston; partner firm Hill & Barlow, and predecessor, 1944—; spl. asst. atty. gen. Mass., 1964-66. Chmn. bd. Portsmouth Trust Co., 1965—. Pres., later chmn. bd. N.H. Soc. Prevention Cruelty to Animals, 1952—, Thompson Acad., Boston, 1953—. Fellow Am. Coll. Trial Lawyers; mem. Am. Law Inst., Am., Mass., Boston (past mem. council) bar assns., Yale Law Sch. Assn. Boston (past pres.). Unitarian. Clubs: Yale, Union (Boston). Home: 32 Martin Rd Concord MA 01742 Office: 225 Franklin St Boston MA 02110

BARTLETT, CHARLES LEFFINGWELL, newspaperman; b. Chgo., Aug. 14, 1921; s. Valentine C. and Marie (Frost) B.; student St. Mark's Sch., Southboro, Mass., 1934-39; A.B., Yale, 1943; m. Josephine Martha Buck, Dec. 16, 1950; children—Peter B., Michael V., Robert S., Helen B. Reporter Chattanooga Times, 1946-63, Washington corr., 1948-63; editor News Focus Service, 1958-63; columnist Chgo. Sun-Times, 1963—. Served as lt. USNR, 1943-46. Recipient Pulitizer prize for nat. reporting, 1955. Roman Catholic. Clubs: National Press, Gridiron, Federal City. Author: (with Edward Weintal) Facing the Brink, 1957. Home: 4615 W St N W Washington DC 20007 Office: Nat Press Bldg Washington DC 20004

BARTLETT, CHARLES WILLIAM, lawyer; b. Quincy, Mass., June 21, 1905; s. Joseph Warren and Susan (Brown) B.; A.B., Dartmouth, 1927; LL.B., Harvard 1930; m. Barbara A. Hastings, June 20, 1931; children—Joseph W., Samuel B., Albert A. H. Admitted to Mass. bar, 1930, since practiced in Boston; partner Ely, Bartlett, Brown & Proctor. 1946—; asst. U.S. atty. Dist. Mass., 1933- 37. Dir. Nat. Shawmut Bank Boston, Union Freight R.R.; trustee Dedham Instn. for Savs., Boston & Providence R.R., Boston and Me. R.R. Mem. bd. trustees Plimoth Plantation, 1963—; sec., trustee Faulkner Hosp.; chmn. exec. com. Mass. Heart Assn. Served to lt. comdr. USNR, 1942-45. Mem. Am., Mass., Boston (past pres.) bar assns., Am. Coll. Trial Lawyers. Democrat. Episcopalian. Editor, pub. Cruising Guide to the Nova Scotia Coast, 1952—; Cruising Directions-Newfoundland With Some Material on The Labrador, 1955—. Home: 51 Common St Dedham MA 02026 Office: 225 Franklin St Boston MA 02110

BARTLETT, CHRIS HAMMOND, mfg. exec.; b. Bessemer, Ala., June 23, 1907; s. John Wesley and Dora Ella (Christopher) B.; B.S., U. Colo., 1928; student advanced mgmt. program, Harvard, 1953; m. Marie Powers, Nov. 22, 1930; 1 son, Peter Barry. Grad. student tng. Westinghouse Electric Corp., 1928-30, transformer sales, 1930-33, 42-46, mgr. specialty transformer dept., sales mgr., div. mgr. transformer div., Sharon, Pa., 1946-53, mgr. mfg. and repair div. Westinghouse Electric Corp., Pitts., 1954-64, v.p., 1955- -, v.p. S.E. region, Atlanta, 1964—. Bd. dirs. Southeastern Elec. Exchange. Mem. I.E.E.E., Beta Theta Pi. Home: 53 Chaumont Sq NW Atlanta GA 30327 Office: 1299 Northside Dr N W Atlanta GA 30302

BARTLETT, CLAUDE JACKSON, psychologist, educator; b. Columbus, O., Oct. 1, 1931; s. Claude Jay and Cecil (Richmond) B.; B.S., Denison U., 1954; M.A., Ohio State U., 1956, Ph.D., 1958; m. Gloria Kuechenberg, Aug. 29, 1953; children-Andrew William, Scott Jackson. Asst. prof. psychology George Peabody Coll. for Tchrs., 1958-61; asst. prof. psychology U. Md., College Park, 1961-64, asso. prof., 1964-68, prof., chmn. dept. psychology, 1968—; cons. indsl. psychologist Performance Research, Inc., Am. Insts. for Research. Recipient James McKeen Cattell awards, 1966, 68. Diplomate Am. Bd. Examiners in Profl. Psychology. Mem. Am., Md. (past treas.) psychol. assns. Home: 3521 Duke St College Park MD 20740

BARTLETT, COSAM JULIAN, clergyman; b. New Orleans, July 1, 1913; s. Aubrey and Nellie May (Munson) B.; B.E., Tulane U., 1935; student Robert Morris Sch. Bus., Pitts., 1935-36, Am. U., Washington, 1952-54: D.D., Ch. Div. Sch. of Pacific, 1961; m. Jeannette B. Limerick, Dec. 2, 1939 (dec. Nov. 1959); children—Jeannette, Aubrey, Olivia; m. 2d, Marjorie Craig Merrell, Apr. 29, 1961. Accountant tech. sales dept. Diamond Alkali Co., Pitts., 1935-39; pres. Bartlett Chems. Inc., New Orleans, 1939-50, now dir.; ordained deacon Protestant Episcopal Ch., 1948, priest, 1949; asst. minister St. Paul's Episcopal Ch., New Orleans, 1948-50; rector St. Paul's Ch., Rock Creek Parish, Washington. 1950-55; dean Grace Cathedral, San Francisco, 1956—. Chmn. exec. com. Overseas Mission Soc. Episcopal Ch., 1953-55, 67-70, v.p., 1967-70; bd. dirs. San Francisco Council Chs., 1958-68, v.p. bd., 1959-60, pres., 1961-63; mem. strategy adv. com. Protestant Episcopal Ch., 1961-64. Mem. Human Rights Commn. San Francisco. Bd. dirs. Gaudet Sch., New Orleans, 1948-50, Nat. Cathedral Sch., Washington, 1955, Edgewood Protestant Orphanage, 1957-65; v.p. St. Margaret's House, Berkeley, Cal., 1960-62. Bd. visitors Tulane U., 1968—. Served with USCG, 1943-45. Mem. Newcomen Soc., Brotherhood of St. Andrew, Kappa Delta Phi, Delta Kappa Epsilon, Omicron Delta Kappa, Phi Phi. Clubs: Boston, (New Orleans): Delta Kappa Epsilon (N.Y.C.); University (San Francisco). Home: 207 Maple St San Francisco CA 94118 Office: 1051 Taylor St San Francisco CA 94108

BARTLETT, DEWEY FOLLETT, former gov. Okla.; b. Marietta, O., Mar. 28, 1919; s. David A. and Jessie (Follett) B.; grad. Lawrenceville (N.J.) Sch., 1938; B.S. in Geol. Engring., Princeton, 1942; m. Ann C. Smith, Apr. 2, 1945; children—Dewey Follett, Joan, Mike. Partner, Keener Oil Co., Tulsa, 1951- -; pres. Dewey Supply Co. (Okla.), 1953-56; owner-operator ranch in Wagoner Co., Okla., 1958-64, in Tulsa County, 1958—, in Delaware County, 1968—; mem. Okla. Senate from Tulsa County, 1962-66; gov. of Okla., 1967-71. Bd. dirs. Tulsa County chpt. A.R.C. Served as pilot USMCR, World War II. Decorated Air medal. Mem. Ind. Petroleum Assn. Am. (bd. dirs.), Okla. Ind. Producers Assn. (bd. dirs.). Republican. Roman Catholic. Home: 2462 E 30th St Tulsa OK 74114 Office: Keener Oil Co NBT Bldg Tulsa OK

BARTLETT, EDWARD TOTTERSON II, banker; b. Phila., Apr. 2, 1908; s. George Griffith and Cecilia (Neall) B.; student William Penn Charter Sch., 1921-24; grad. Phillips Acad., 1925; A.B., Harvard, 1929; D.C.S. (hon.), Cleve. State U., 1968; m. Florence Creech, Sept. 10, 1929, (dec. May 1964); children-Elizabeth (Mrs. Donald R. Saunders), Cecilia B. (Mrs. Richard C. Distad), Edward T. III; m. 2d, Sarah G. White, Feb. 13, 1965. Accountant, Firestone Tire & Rubber Co., 1929-33; investment analyst Hornblower & Weeks, Cleve., 1933-34; with Cleve. Trust Co., 1934—, sr. v.p., mem. exec. officers com., head personal trust div., 1969—; dir., v.p. Payne-Bingham Co.; dir. Lake Erie Mgmt. Co., Ajax Mfg. Co. Chmn. met. div. United Appeal Greater Cleve., 1939-40; trustee Family Service Assn. Cleve., mem. exec. com., 1939-62, pres. 1947-50. Trustee Holden Arboretum, treas., 1952—, Shaker Lakes Regional Nature Center, treas., 1966—, Cleve. Council of Independent Schs., treas., 1967—, Norweb Found., sec.-treas., 1952—, The Bishop Fund, sec.-treas., 1969—, Cleve. chpt. Arthritis, Rheumatism Found., Hawken Sch. (life). Served to lt. col. AUS, 1942-45; ETO. Decorated Bronze Star, Legion of Merit; Croix de Guerre (France). Clubs: Tavern, Union, Kirtland Country, Harvard (pres. 1941-42) (Cleve.). Home: 31700 Fairmount Blvd Cleveland OH 44124 Office: 916 Euclid Av Cleveland OH 44101

BARTLETT, FORD, engring. exec.; b. Bklyn., Aug. 28, 1905; s. Frederick Lorenzo and Isabelle Louise (Whitbeck) B.; student Bklyn. Poly. Inst., 1925; m. Anna Louise Shields, Aug. 28, 1926; 1 dau., Judith (Mrs. Harvey T. Harrison). Civil engineer with the firm of Frederick L. Bartlett, 1923- 32; partner Howard T. Lockwood and Cletus Kessler, 1932-34; pres. Lockwood, Kessler & Bartlett. Inc., Syosset, N.Y., 1934—; pres., dir. Viatech, Inc.; trustee Lincoln Savings Bank; dir. First Nat. City Bank. Trustee United Fund Long Island, Inc. Del. UN Scientific Conf. Conservation and Utilization Resources, 1949. Trustee Hofstra U. Recipient Certificate of Distinction, Bklyn. Polytech. Registered profl. engr., Tenn., land surveyor, N.Y., Mich., Conn Fellow Am. Congress Surveying and Mapping, Am. Soc. C.E.; mem. N.Y. State Soc. Profl. Engrs., Am. Soc. Photogrammetry, Soc. Am. Mil. Engrs., L.I. Assn. Commerce and Industry (pres.), Chi Epsilon, Tau Beta Pi. Clubs: Creek, Union League, Economic (N.Y.C.); Island (Nassau Bahamas). Home: Dock Lane Great Neck NY 11024 Office: 1 Aerial Way Syosset NY 11791

BARTLETT, FRED STEWART, ret. museum dir.; b. Brush, Colo., May 15, 1905; s. Arthur Frank and Vera (Stewart) B.; A.B., U. Colo., 1928; art student U. Denver, 1932-34; Carnegie fellow Harvard, 1937. Ednl. dir., asst. to dir., curator fine arts, acting dir. Denver Art Mus.,

1932-43; curator painting Colorado Springs Fine Arts Center, 1943-54, asst. dir., 1954-55; dir., 1955-71. Mem. Am. Assn. Mus., Assn. Art Mus. Dirs., Air Force Acad. Fine Arts Com. (chmn.), Phi Kappa Tau, Sigma Delta Chi. Clubs: El Paso; Cheyenne Mountain Country. Home: 5440 Manitou Rd Littleton CO 80120

BARTLETT, GENE EBERT, div. sch. pres.; b. Elkins, W. Va., Apr. 18, 1910; s. Genus Ebert and Susan Jessie (Lyon) B.; A.B., Denison U., 1931, D.D., 1952; B.D., Colgate-Rochester Div. Sch., 1935; LL.D., U. So. Cal., 1962; L.H.D., Kenyon Coll., 1968; D.D., Colgate U., 1969; m. Jean Kenyon, June 30, 1937; children—David Lyon, Marion Elizabeth, Randall Kenyon, Stephen James, Sarah Margaret. Ordained to ministry Baptist Ch., 1934; pastor, Syracuse, N.Y., 1937-42, Columbia, Mo., 1942-47, Evanston, Ill., 1947-53, 1st Bapt. Ch., Los Angeles, 1953-60: pres. Colgate-Rochester Div. Sch., 1960—; Beecher lectr. Yale, 1961; speaker Chgo. Sunday Evening Club, 1959—; univ. preacher Rockefeller Chapel, U. Chgo., 1947- -; preaching missions to Korea and Japan for USAF, 1954. Mem. bd. edn. Am. Bapt. Conv., 1943-52, gen. council, 1959—; mem. univ. Christian mission Nat. Council of Chs., 1942-52. Bd. dirs. Ch. Fedn. Los Angeles; trustee Berkeley (Cal.) Bapt. Div. Sch.; trustee Stephens Coll. Mem. Kappa Sigma. Club: University (Rochester). Author: The News in Religion, 1947; The Audacity of Preaching, 1962; also chpt. on preaching in book. Home: 1122 S Goodman St Rochester NY 14620

BARTLETT, GEORGE L., investment banker; b. 1908; ed. U. N.C., 1932. Vice pres. Thompson & Mc Kinnon Auchincloss, N.Y.C.; v.p. Thompson & McKinnon Corp. Mem. N.Y. Soc. Security Analyst, Pub. Relations Soc. Am., Bd. Trade Chgo. Mason (Shriner). Clubs: Southampton Yacht, Union League, Harbour View, N.Y. Stock Exchange, Luncheon, Tuxedo. Contbr. financial articles to jours. Home: 781 Fifth Av New York City NY 10022 Office: 2 Broadway New York City NY 10004

BARTLETT, GEORGE ROBERT, univ. prof.; b. Chicago, June 26, 1909; s. George Robert and Adelaide Margaret (Scott) B.; Ph. B., U. of Chicago, 1931, Ph.D., 1942; student McCormick Sem., 1937-38; m. Helena Virginia Porter, Apr.16, 1937; children—Cornelia (Mrs. E.J. Whitley, Jr.), George Robert IV. Instr. humanities Chicago Municipal Coll., Chicago; dean of men. head philosophy dept., chmn. div. social sciences, Boise Jr. Coll., Ida.: prof. humanities U. of Fla. 1947- 49, prof. logic, 1949-50, prof. philosophy. 1950—, head dept. of philosophy, 1953-63, chairman 1964, counselor office of dean U. Coll., 1948-50, grad. faculty, 1949—, mem. U. personnel com., 1951-52, mem. curriculum comm. Coll. arts and Scis., 1952-62, mem. petitions com., 1954-64; ednl. work in field of business, 1931-37. Field work A.R.C. counselling, liaison social agencies armed forces, 1942-46. Recipient Ford Found. grant, 1953-54. Mem. Am., Fla. philos. assns., A.A.A.S., Am. Assn. U. Profs., Fla. Psychol. Assn. (hon.), So. Soc. for Philos. and Psychol. Home: 2610 S W 3d Pl Gainesville FL 32601

BARTLETT, HARLAND BURTON, mfg. exec.; b. Swan Creek O., Apr. 24, 1908; s. David C. and Elizabeth (Wiley) B.; student Mich. State U., 1926-28; m. Viola D. Johnson, June 30, 1940; childrenStephen David, Rebecca Sue. Advanced through various positions with Dana Corp., RReading, Pa., v.p., pres. parish divs.; chmn. chmn. bd. Brentwood Plastic Co., Dana-Whitney Corp.; dir. Hayes-Dana Corp. (Canadian Dana affiliate), Mardigian Corp., C & M Spring Co., Berks County Trust Co., Am. Bank & Trust Co. Bd. dirs. Becks County United Fund Mem. Pa. State C. of C. (dir.), Soc. Automotive Engrs., Am. Soc. Tool Engrs., Am. Ordnance Assn. Home: 1575 Argonne Reading PA 19601 Office: care Robeson & Weiser Reading PA 19603

BARTLETT, HOWARD RUSSELL, ret. univ. prof.; b. Auburn, Me., Oct. 1, 1901; s. Frank L. and Annie (Young) B.; B.S., Dartmouth Coll., 1923; A.M., Harvard, 1928; m. Helen Root, Sept. 18, 1926; 1 dau., Linda Ann. Instr. history Haverhill (Mass.) High Sch., 1927-28; instr. history Mass. Inst. Tech., 1929-35, asst. prof. and acting head dept. English and history, 1938-40, prof. and head dept., 1940-63, head dept. humanities, 1953-63, prof. history dept. humanities, 1963-67, sr. lectr., 1967-70. Ford Found. cons., Pilani, India, 1963; Am. specialist to India; Am. specialist Br. of Div. Leaders and Specialists Internat. Ednl. Exchange Service, U.S. State Dept. 1957. Vice pres. Winchester Community Chest, 1948. Mem. Winchester Sch. Com., 1948-54. Mem. Kappa Sigma. Republican. Conglist. Author articles on indsl. research in U.S. Home: Basin Point South Harpowell ME 04079

BARTLETT, IRVING HENRY, educator, historian; b. Springfield, Mass., Feb. 2, 1923; s. Lewis Irving and Carrie Elisabeth (Jones) B.; B.A., Ohio Wesleyan U., 1948; M.A., Brown U., 1949, Ph.D., 1952; m. Virginia Kostulski, Nov. 30, 1944. With U.S. Govt. in Hawaii, 1946-47; lectr. USIS, Pakistan, 1952; asst. prof. history R.I. Coll. Edn., 1953-54, Mass. Inst. Tech., 1954-60; pres. Cape Cod Community Coll., 1960-64; prof. history, head dept. Carnegie Inst. Tech., 1964—; Guggenheim fellow, 1966-67. Vice chmn. board of trustees Community Coll. of Allegheny County. Served to capt. C.E., AUS, 1943- 46. Mem. Am. Hist. Assn., Am. Studies Assn., Am. Acad. Polit. and Social Sci., Am. Arbitration Assn. (edn. arbitration panel), Phi Beta Kappa. Author: From Slave to Citizen, 1953; Wendell Phillips; Brahmin Radical, 1961; The American Mind in the Mid- Nineteenth Century, 1967; A New History of the United States, 1969. Editor: Channing; Unitarian Christianity and Other Essays, 1958. Home: 5816 Howe Pittsburgh PA 15232

BARTLETT, JAMES VINCENT, naval officer; b. Point Pleasant, W.Va., Oct. 28, 1917; s. Ira Stump and Blanche (Mitchell) B.; B.Sc., U.S. Naval Acad., 1941; B.C.E., Rensselaer Poly. Inst., 1944, M.C.E., 1945; m. Betty Vars Baker, Dec. 27, 1941; (dec. June 1961) children—James Vincent, David Mitchell; m. 2d, Margaret Herrin Turkington, Aug. 3, 1962; stepchildren—John Edward Turkington, Timothy Turkington, Michael Turkington. Commd. ensign U.S. Navy, 1942, advanced through grades to rear adm., 1968; comdg. officer Mobile Constrn. Bn. 4, 1953-55, Chesapeake div. Bur. Yards and Docks, 1965-67; comdr. 3d Naval Constrn. Brigade, Vietnam, 1967-69; vice comdr. Naval Facilities Engring. Command, 1969—; dep. chief Civil Engrs., 1969- -. Decorated D.S.M. Mem. Soc. Am. Mil. Engrs., Am. Soc. C.E., Am. Soc. Profl. Engrs., Sigma Xi, Chi Epsilon, Tau Beta Pi, Sigma Xi. Home: 5100 Colebrook Pl Alexandria VA 22312 Office: Naval Facilities Engring Command Washington DC 20390

BARTLETT, JOHN CANNON, lawyer; b. Tuolumne, Cal., Dec. 2, 1910; s. George Francis and Ellen Jane (Wilson) B.; B.A., Stanford, 1933; LL.B., U. Cal. at Berkeley, 1937; m. Jean Frances Wheeler, June 26, 1940; 1 dau., Joyce Ellen. Admitted to Nev., Cal. bars; practice of law, Reno; partner Vargas, Bartlett & Dixon Ltd.; asst. dist. atty. Washoe Co., 1947- 52; Bd. dirs. Reno Little Theatre, 1953. Served with USAAF, 1942-43, USNR, 1943-45. Mem. State Bar Nev. (pres. 1963, bd. govs. 1954-64), Am. Coll. Trial Lawyers, Am. Judicature Soc. (dir.), Am. (ho. dels. 1964-67, 71—, gov. 1967-70), Washoe Co.)pres. 1956) bar assns., State Bar Cal., V.F.W., Delta Tau Delta. Home: 1400 Granite Dr Reno NV 89502 Office: Vargas Bartlett & Dixon Ltd 195 S Sierra St Reno NV 89501

BARTLETT, KENNETH GILL, educator; b. Plymouth, Mich., Mar. 13, 1906; s. Wyman J. and Alta (Gill) B.; B.A., Albion (Michigan) Coll., 1927, LL.D., 1955; A.M., Syracuse Univ., 1931; m. Bernice Kleinhans, Sept. 6, 1930; children—Elizabeth Anne, John Gill. Instr. sch. of speech, Syracuse Univ., 1929-35, asst. prof. of radio edn., 1935-41, asso. prof., 1941-45, prof. radio and TV since 1945, dean univ. coll., 1946-52, v.p., dean pub. affairs, 1953-70, spl. asst. to chancellor, 1970-71. Mem. N.Y. State Assembly, 1967-70; mem. State Commn. on Powers of Local Govt., 1970—. Dir. Onondaga Savings Bank. Mem. Hosp. Rev. and Planning Council Central N.Y., 1971—. Bd. dirs. Met. Devel. Assn., Sta WCNY-TV, trustee Crouse-Irving Meml. Hosp. Mem. Sigma Nu. Rep. Presbyn. Clubs: Century, University, Onondaga Country. Home: 11 Bradford Dr Syracuse NY 13224

BARTLETT, MARSHALL KINNE, surgeon; b. New Haven, Jan. 18, 1904; s. Charles Joseph and Genevieve (Kinne) B.; B.A., Yale, 1924; M.D., Harvard, 1928; m. Barbara Frazier Hume, Dec. 21, 1935; childrenCharles Joseph II, Barbara Hume, Susan Kinne. Intern Mass. Gen. Hosp. 1928-31; pvt. practice surgery, Boston, 1932—; clin. prof. surgery emeritus Harvard; bd. consultation Mass. Gen. Gen. Hosp.; cons. Mass. Eye and Ear Infirmary, Free Hosp. for Women, Boston Lying- In, Faulkner, Mt. Auburn, Leominster hosps. Served as lt. col. M.C., AUS, 1942-46. Decorated Bronze Star. Diplomate Am. Bd. Surgery. Mem. Boston, New Eng. surg. socs., Mass. Med. Soc., A.M.A., A.C.S., Am. Surg. Assn. Contbr. articles profl. jours. Home: 43 Chestnut St Dedham, MA 02026 Office: 275 Charles St Boston MA 02114

BARTLETT, NEIL, educator, chemist; b. Newcastle-upon-Tyne, Eng., Sept. 15, 1932; s. Norman and Ann Willins (Voak) B.; B.Sc., Kings Coll., U. Durham (Eng.), 1954, Ph.D. in Inorganic Chemistry, 1957; D.Sc. (hon.), U. Waterloo (Can.), 1968; m. Christina Isabel Cross, Dec. 26, 1957; children—Jeremy John, Jane Anne, Christopher, Robin. Lectr. chemistry U. B.C., 1958-63, prof., 1963-66; prof. chemistry Princeton, 1966-69, U. Cal., Berkeley, 1969—; spl. research synthesis 1st true compound of xenon; E.W.R. Steacie Meml. fellow NRC, Can., 1964-66; Alfred P. Sloan fellow, 1964—; Miller vis. prof. U. Cal., Berkeley, 1967-68. Recipient Research Corp. award, E.W.R. Steacie prize, 1965, Elliott Cresson medal Franklin Inst., 1968; Kirkwood medal Yale U. and New Haven sect. Am. Chem. Soc., 1969; award in inorganic chemistry Am. Chem. Soc., 1970. Fellow Chem. Soc. London (Corday Morgan medal 1962); Royal Inst. Chemistry, Chem. Inst. Can. (1st Noranda lectr. 1963); mem. Am. Chem. Soc. (exec. divs. fluorine chemistry and inorganic chemistry). Bd. editors Inorganic Chemistry; adv. bd. McGraw-Hill Ency. Sci. and Tech. Home: 6 Oak Dr Orinda CA 94563 Office: Latimer Hall Univ of Cal Berkeley CA 94720

BARTLETT, NEIL RILEY, educator, psychologist; b. Underhill, Vt., Aug. 10 1917; s. Arthur Neil and Elizabeth (Wall) B.; B.S., U. Vt., 1937; M.Sc., Brown U., 1939, Ph.D., 1941; m. Susan Carson, Aug. 22, 1942; children—David C., Robert W. (dec.), William, Thomas. Research psychologist Brown U., 1941-43; asst. prof., research asso. Johns Hopkins, 1946-48; prof. psychology Hobart and William Smith Colls., Geneva, N.Y., 1948-58; prof. psychology, head dept. U. Ariz., 1958-. Asso. vision com. Armed Forces-NRC, 1947-54, mem. panel tng. com. undersea warfare, 1952-56; cons. human factors office Rome Air Devel. Center, USAF, 1951-58; physiol. psychologist U.S. Navy Electronics Labs., summers 1959—; bd. govs. So. Ariz. Mental Health Center, 1961-62; mem. Ariz. Com. Staff Devel. Mental Health, 1962-67, Nat. Inst. Mental Health fellow U. Paris, 1965-66. Served with USNR, 1943-46. Mem. Am. Psychol. Assn. (chmn. policy and planning bd. 1962-63, pres. div. 2 1966-67), Optical Soc. Am., A.A.A.S., Phi Beta Kappa, Sigma Xi. Home: 6761 Topke Pl Tucson AZ 85715

BARTLETT, PAUL DANA, Jr., grain co. exec.; b. Kansas City, Mo., Sept. 16, 1919; s. Paul Dana and Alice Mae (Hiestand) B.; B.A., Yale, 1941; m. Joan Jenkins, May 14, 1949; children—Joan Alison, Marilyn, Paul Dana III, Frederick Jenkins. With Bartlett & Co., grain merchants, Kansas City, Mo., 1947—, exec. v.p., 1955-62, pres., 1962—; dir. Employers Reins. Corp., City Nat. Bank & Trust Co. Trustee Linda Hall Sci. and Tech. Library, Kansas City, Mo. Home: 5353 Sunset Dr Kansas City MO 64112 Office: Board of Trade Bldg Kansas City MO 64112

BARTLETT, PAUL DOUGHTY, chemist; b. Ann Arbor, Mich., Aug. 14, 1907; s. George Miller and Mary Louise (Doughty) B.; A.B., Amherst Coll., 1928, Sc.D. (hon.), 1953; M.A., Harvard, 1929, Ph.D., 1931; Sc.D. (hon.), U. Chgo., 1954; Dr. honoris causa, U. Montpellier, 1967, U. Paris, 1969; m. Mary Lula Court, June 24, 1931; children—Joanna Court (Mrs. Stephen D. Kennedy), Geoffrey McSwain, Sarah Webster. NRC fellow Rockefeller Inst., 1931-32; instr. chemistry U. Minn., 1932-34; mem. faculty Harvard, 1934—, prof. chemistry, 1946—, Erving prof. chemistry, 1948—. chmn. dept., 1950-53; George Fisher Baker lectr. Cornell U., spring 1949; vis. prof. U. Cal. at Los Angeles, 1950; Walker-Ames lectr. U. Wash., 1952; guest lectr. U. Munich (Germany); speaker 15th Internat. Congress Pure and Applied Chemistry, Paris, France, 1957; Karl Folkers lectr. U. Ill., 1960; Spl. Univ. lectr. U. London (Eng.), 1961. Mem. div. com. math., phys. and engring. scis. NSF, 1957-61. Recipient award in pure chemistry Am. Chem. Soc., 1938; August Wilhelm von Hofmann gold medal German Chem. Soc., 1962; Roger Adams award organic chemistry, 1963, Willard Gibbs medal, 1963, Theodore William Richards medal, 1966; Nat. Medal of Sci., 1968; James Flack Norris award in phys. organic chemistry Am. Chem. Soc., 1969; John Price Wetherill medal, 1970; Guggenheim and Fulbright fellow, spring 1957. Hon. fellow Chem. Soc. (London); mem. Nat. Acad. Scis., Am. Acad. Arts and Scis., Am. Chem. Soc. (chmn. Northeastern sect. 1953-54), Internat. Union Pure and Applied Chemistry (pres. organic div. 1967-69, program chmn. 23d internat. congress 1971), Deutsche Akademie der Naturforscher Leopoldina, Phi Beta Kappa, Sigma Xi. Clubs: Skating (Boston); Duroboros. Research kinetics and mechanism organic reactions. Author: Nonclassical Ions, 1965; also chpts. in textbooks, research papers. Mem. editorial bd. Jour. Am. Chem. Soc., 1945-55, Jour. Organic Chemistry, 1954-57, Tetrahedron. Home: Westeston MA 02193 Office: Dept Chemistry Harvard U Cambridge MA 02138

BARTLETT, ROBERT CARRICK, pub. exec.; b. Worchester, Mass., Aug. 15, 1915; s. Elwin Irving and Rena Pearl (Carrick) B.; B.A., Williams Coll., 1936; LL.B., Chgo. Kent Coll. Law, 1944, LL.M., 1945; m. Rita Evelyn Fitzgerald, July 24, 1937; children—Beverly A., Robert W., Jeffrey W. Admitted to Ill. bar, 1944; with Commerce Clearing House, Inc., Chgo., 1939—, pres., 1959—, also dir. subsidiary cos. Mem. Am. Bar Assn., Atomic Indsl. Forum, Nat. Tax Assn., Beta Theta Pi. Clubs: University (Chgo.); Williams (N.Y.); Nat. Lawyers (Washington). Office: 4025 W Peterson Av Chicago IL 60646

BARTLETT, ROBERT MERRILL, clergyman; b. Kingston, Ind., Dec. 23, 1899; s. Robert Alexander and Minnie Lou (Dobson) B.; A.B., Oberlin Coll., 1921; B.D., Yale Div. Sch., 1924; D.D., Yankton Coll., 1940; m. Theresa Sue Nuckols, Aug. 9, 1923; children—Susan Jane (Mrs. Seward Weber), Mary Warren (Mrs. Joseph R. Engle), Robert Hill. Ordained ministry of Congl. Church, 1924; minister First Congl. Ch., Lyme, Conn., 1922-23; asst. minister Dwight Pl. Congl. Ch., New Haven, 1923-24; prof. lit. Yenching U., Peking (China) U., 1924-27; minister First Congl. Ch., Norwood, Mass., 1927-32, First Ch. of Christ, Longmeadow, Mass., 1932-42, Plymouth Congl. Ch. Lansing, Mich., 1942-51, First Congl. Ch., Shrewsbury, Mass., 1951-64; mem. faculty Springfield Coll., 1937-39; lectr. social ethics and biography Boston U., 1940-41, ethics and philosophy Mich. State U., 1944-48. Attended F.A. Officers Tng. Camp, World War I. Mem. Goodwill Pilgrimage to Eng., 1930, representing Council for Exchange of Speakers between Gt. Britain and U.S., 1933; del. World Council of Chs., (Evanston, Ill.), 1954, seminar to Middle East, 1954, USSR, 1960, Caribbean, 1961. Scandinavian Countries, 1963, South Am., 1964; mem. lecture staff Plimoth Plantation, 1963-69; lectr. Chautaugua, 1964, 66, Pilgrim Mayflower Cruise, 1970, Rotterdam and Dutch cities, 1970; chmn. Mass. Cong. Com. on Ch. Unity, Mass. Council Chs. Com. on Ch. Unity; lectr. confs. on lit., world affairs; radio speaker on ednl. and religious programs. Vice chmn. Plymouth 350th Anniversary Com., 1969-71; dir. Gen. Theol. Library Boston; Mass. UNICEF. Trustee Bartlett Hall, Manomet, Plymouth. Mem. Soc. Mayflower Descs. (elder Mass. soc., editor Quar. of Gen. Soc. 1963-66), Soc. Descs. Robert Bartlett (pres.), Am. Legion, Yale Div. Sch. Alumni Assn. (pres., 1937-39), Conn. Valley Oberlin Assn. (pres., 1937-42); Mich. Cancer Prevention Soc. (dir.), Mich. Planned Parenthood Fedn., Phi Beta Kappa. Clubs: Fortnightly, Monday (Boston); Connecticut Valley Theological, Boston Authors, Mich. State Univ. Faculty, Kiwanis, Eel River Beach. Mason (K.T.). Author of books, 1929—, including They Dare to Believe, 1952; Fighters for Freedom, 1958, They Stand Invincible-Mem Who Are Transforming Our World, 1959; With One Voice—Prayers From Around the World, 1961; The Huguenots and Their Cross, 1964; Thanksgiving Day, 1965; Pilgrim Robert Bartlett, 1603-1676, and Some of His Descendants, 1966; The Pilgrim Way, 1971. Contbr. to mags. Research on Pilgrim History, Eng. and Holland. Home: Bartlett House Brook Rd Plymouth RFD 1 MA 02360

BARTLETT, RUHL JACOB, educator; b. Webster, W.Va., Jan. 24, 1897; s. Adolphus J. and Mary Anne (Shroyer) B.; A.B., Ohio U., 1920; A.M., U. Cin., 1923; student Columbia U., summer, 1926; Ph.D., Ohio State U., 1927; m. Lela May Work, Aug. 30, 1924. Tchr. history, high sch., Piqua, O., 1920- 21, high sch., Norwood, O., 1921-23, U. of Iowa, 1925-26, Ohio State U., 1927; asst. prof. history, Tufts U., 1927-32, prof. and head dept. of history, 1932-56, dean Grad. Sch., 1938-39; dean Fletcher Sch. of Law and Diplomacy, Tufts University, 1944-45; prof. Fletcher Sch., 1944—; taught summers La. State U., Ill. State Tchrs. Coll., Hyannis State Teachers Coll., University Wyo., Ohio State University, U. Wash. Served in USN, 1918. Mem. Orgn. Am. Historians, Am., So. hist. assns., Phi Kappa Tau, Phi Beta Kappa. Mason. Author: John C. Frémont and the Republican Party; The League to Enforce Peace; The Record of American Diplomacy; People and Politics of Latin America; Policy and Power; Two Centuries of American Foreign Policy. Contbr. to hist. publs. Home: 40 Lake St Winchester MA 01890 Office: Fletcher Sch Law and Diplomacy Tufts U Medford MA 02155

BARTLETT, THOMAS ALVA, univ. pres.; b. Salem, Ore., Aug. 20, 1930; s. Cleave Wines and Alma (Hanson) B.; student Willamette U., 1947-49; A.B.,Stanford U., 1951; M.A., Oxford U., 1953; Ph.D., Stanford U., 1959; m. Mary Louise Bixby, Mar. 20, 1954; children—Thomas Glenn, Richard A., Paul H. Instr. U. Santa Clara, 1955-56; mem. U.S. Permanent Mission to UN, 1956-63; pres. Am. U. in Cairo, 1963-69, Colgate U., 1969—. Mem. UAR-U.S. Ednl. Exchange Commn. Mem. Am. Polit. Sci. Assn., Internat. Assn. Univ. Pres.'s, Council Fgn. Relations, Commn. Ind. Colls. N.Y., Am. Acad. Polit. and Social Sci. Phi Beta Kappa. Club: University (N.Y.C.). Home: Watson House College Hill Hamilton NY 13346

BARTLETT, WES H., lodge exec.; b. New Sharon, Ia., July 11, 1915; s. George Elton and Grace (Ballinger) B.; B.S., Parsons Coll., 1938; student U. Ia., 1941-42; m. Mary Elizabeth Foster, June 20, 1940; children—Barbara Ann (Mrs. Jerold Seiler), William George, Donald Brett. Operator Fed. License Bird Banding Sta. and Lab., asst. dept. biology Parsons Coll., 1936-38; tchr., coach Primghar Pub. Sch., 1938-41; instr. biology and chemistry, athletic mgr. Eagle Grove (Ia.) pub. schs., 1941-43; instr. Ia. State Coll., 1943-44; tchr. biology and chemistry Ames (Ia.) pub. schs., 1944-45; owner Foster Furniture Co., Algona, Ia., 1945—. Trustee Kiwanis Internat., 1964-68, v.p., 1968-69, treas., 1969-70, pres. elect, 1970-71, pres., 1971-72; trustee Kiwanis Internat. Found., 1968—, mem. exec. com., 1969—, treas., 1969-70. Mem. Kossuth County Bd. Edn., 1946-68, pres., 1954-68; pres. Kossuth Community Concert Assn., 1957-59, Algona Indsl. Devel. Corp., 1961; chmn. North Ia. Seven County Study Council on Pub. Schs., 1960-62. Recipient Boy Scouts Am. Silver Beaver award, 1954. Mem. Ia. Ornithol. Union. Methodist (lay del. ann. conf. 1957—, chmn. bldg. com. 1966—, chmn. trustees 1959-66). Home: 122 Ridgley St Algona IA 50511 Office: PO Box 473 Algona IA 50511

BARTLEY, HUGH J., army officer. Commd. 2d lt. U.S. Army, advanced through grades to col.; now exec. Office Asst. Sec. Army for financial mgmt. Address: 2111 Jefferson Davis Hwy Arlington VA 22202*

BARTLEY, ROBERT TAYLOR, govt. ofcl.; b. Ladonia, Tex., May 20, 1909; s. Samuel Edward and Meddie Bell (Rayburn) B.; student So. Meth. U., 1927-29; m. Ruth Adams, 1936; children—Robert Taylor, Jane, Thomas Rayburn. Exec. sec. investigation pub. utility holding cos. House Com. Interstate and Fgn. Commerce, Washington, 1932-34; dir. telegraph div. in charge regulation telegraph land line, cable and radio carriers F.C.C., 1934-37; sr. securities analyst Securities and Exchange Commn., 1937-39; asst. to pres., v.p. Yankee Network, Inc., 1939-43; sec.-treas. FM Broadcasters, Inc., 1939- 43; dir. war activities and govt. relations Nat. Assn. Broadcasters, 1943-47; adminstrv. asst. to Speaker of House Sam Rayburn, 1948-52; apptd. commr. F.C.C., by President Truman, 1952, reapptd. by President Eisenhower, 1958, reapptd. by President Johnson 1965. Chmn. U.S. delegation World Adminstrv. Radio Conf. for Maritime Mobile Matters, 1967. Marconi Meml. Gold Medal Vet. Wireless Operators Assn., 1965. Democrat. Home: Ladonia TX also: 2111 Jefferson Davis Hwy Arlington VA 22202 Office: Fed Communications Comm Washington DC 20554

BARTLEY, WILLIAM WARREN, III, educator; b. Pitts., Oct. 2, 1934; s. William Warren and Elvina (Henry) B.; A.B., Harvard, 1956, A.M., 1958; Ph.D., London (Eng.) Sch. Econs. and Polit. Sci., 1962. Lectr. logic London Sch. Econs., 1960-63; lectr. history of philosophy of sci. Warburg Inst. U. London 1961-64; vis. asso. prof. philosophy U. Cal. at Berkeley, 1963-64; asso. prof. U. Cal. at San Diego, 1964-67, co.-dir. humanities program, 1965-66; asso. prof. philosophy U. Pitts., 1967-69, asso. prof. Population Div., 1967-69, prof. philosophy sr. research asso. Philosophy of Sci. Center, 1969—; prof. philosophy, Cal. State Coll. at Hayward, 1970—; seminar leader Austrian Coll., 1961, 65; spl. lectr. Royal Inst. Philosophy, London, 1961, 68, Institut für Wissenschaftstheorie U. Salzburg (Austria), 1964; vis. asso. prof. U. Ill., 1964; spl. lectr. U. Karlsruhe, 1965; adj. prof. philosophy L.I.U., 1966. Danforth Found. fellow, 1956-60, 66-67; S.A. Cook Bye fellow Gonville and Caius Coll., Cambridge U., 1966-67; Fulbright award, 1958-60. Mem. Oxford and Cambridge Soc., Signet Soc.,

Aristotelian Soc., Brit. Soc. Philosophy of Sci. (mem. exec. com. 1964), Am. Philos. Assn., Am. Assn. U. Profs., Phi Beta Kappa. Author: The Retreat to Commitment, 1962, 64; Flucht ins Engagement, 1964; Morality and Religion, 1971; Wittgenstein, 1972; Die Notwendigkeit des Engagements, 1972. Asso. editor History and Theory, 1958-65. Editorial bd. History and Theory, 1960-65, Soundings, 1967-69, Philos. Forum, 1967—. Contbr. articles profl. jours. Office: care Dept Philosophy U Pitts Pittsburgh PA 15213

BARTLING, MARTIN LUTHER, Jr., builder; b. Carrollton, Mo., Jan. 14, 1917; s. Martin Luther and Frances M. (Lewis) B.; student Kan. State Tchrs. Coll., Pittsburg, 1934-35; m. Catherine E. Hines, Mar. 8, 1937; children—Martin Luther III, Harrison Hines. Dep. regional priorities WPB, Atlanta, 1942-45; v.p. Homes, Inc., Knoxville, Tenn., 1946-52, Fonde-Bartling, Knoxville, 1946-51, Ceilheat, Inc., Knoxville, 1950-57; pres. Componenets, Inc., Knoxville, 1956—; owner Bartling Constrn. Co., Knoxville, 1951—; v.p. research and product devel. U.S. Gypsum Co., 1962-65, v.p. trade and govt. relations, 1965—. Mem. Knoxville Met. Planning Commn., 1956-60; mem. Russian housing tour of Nat. Assn. Home Builders, 1956, chmn. Czechoslovakian housing tour, 1956, builder research house for assn., 1958. Served with AUS, 1945-46. Mem. Nat. Assn. Home Builders (chmn. numerous coms., dir. 1951—, pres. 1960-61), Knoxville Home Builders Assn. (past pres), Bldg. Research Inst., Urban Am., U.S. C. of C. Lutheran (vice chmn.). Clubs: City (Knoxville); Capital Hill (Washington). Home: 300 N State St Chicago IL 60610 Office: 101 S Wacker Dr Chicago IL 60606

BARTLING, THEODORE CHARLES, oil co. exec.; b. St. Louis, Feb. 19, 1922; s. George Reynard and Dorothy (Adams) B.; B.S. in Geology, Ohio State U., 1947; m. Phyllis McGinness, Aug. 2, 1946; children—Eric C., Pamela A., Theodore A. Staff geologist Pitts. Plate Glass Co., 1947-49; exploration mgr. W. C. McBride Inc., 1949-55; founder, pres., dir. Apache Oil Corp., Mpls., 1955-67; pres. Ada Oil Exploration, 1967-70, Bartling Oil Corp., 1971—; founder, 1st pres. Oil Investment Inst. Mem. Assn. Petroleum Geologists, Houston Geol. Soc., Ind. Producer's Assn. Am. (dir.) Home: 11 Inwood Oaks Houston TX 77024 Office: 720 Executive Plaza Houston TX 77035

BARTLOME, ROBERT ERNEST, ship bldg. co. exec.; b. Lorain, O., Nov. 7, 1922; s. Ernest and Clara Ann (Graber) B.; B.A., Spencerian Coll., 1943; m. Juanita Ann Marsac, Nov. 27, 1942; children—Robert E., Judith Ann (Mrs. Glenn A. Thompson), Marilyn L. (Mrs. Gary R. Hendershot). Mgr. planning and prodn. control, systems analyst, programmer Lorain div. Koehring Co., 1945-65; mgr. systems and procedures, asst. sec., sec. Am. Ship Building Co., Lorain, 1965—; v.p., dir. Lorain-Elyria Sand Co.; sec., dir. Cin. Sheet Metal & Roofing Co., Nashville Bridge Co., Kinsman Marine Transit Co., Gt. Lakes Internat. Corp., Gt. Lakes Assos., Inc., Biogest Corp. Mem. Ch. of Christ (elder). Mason, K.P. Home: 274 Sunrise Dr Amherst OH 44001 Office: 400 Colorado Av Lorain OH 44052

BARTOLANZO, LEO JOSEPH, financial exec.; b. Somerville, N.J., June 3, 1926; s. Dante J. and Ida (Manara) B.; B.S., Rutgers U., 1956; postgrad. Harvard, 1967; m. Gabrielle M. Morin, Oct. 18, 1958; children—Gabrielle D., Leo Joseph, Richard M. Financial analyst Johns-Manville Corp., N.Y.C., 1959-62, chief analytical sect., 1962-64, controller research and devel., 1964-66, asst. treas., 1967, treas., 1968—, controller, 1971—. Served with USNR, 1944-46, 50-52. Mem. Financial Exec. Inst. Office: 22 E 40th St New York City NY 10016

BARTOLETTI, BRUNO, conductor, Conductor in Italy; a prin. conductor Teatro Comunale di Firenze; also conductor opera houses in Copenhagen, Lisbon, Wiesbaden, Teatro Colon in Buenos Aires; Am. debut with Lyric Opera of Chgo. with Il Travatore, 1956, then conducted La Traviata, Tosca and Il Barbiere di Siviglia; conducted Otello, also premier performance Mabucco, Lyric Opera, 1963; prin. conductor Lyric Opera, 1964-65. Address: care Lyric Opera 20 N Michigan Av Chicago IL 60602*

BARTOLONE, JOSEPH, advt. exec.; b. N.Y.C., Aug. 1, 1929; s. Sebastian Paul and Lucia Nancy (Rischio) B.; B.S., Fordham U., 1950; postgrad. Rutgers U., 1956-57; m. Loretta Dziemianowska, Jan. 16, 1954; children—Joseph, John Brian, Cynthia Ann, Mark Christopher. Account exec. Benton & Bowles, Inc., 1950- 57, Robert E. Wilson, Inc., 1957-60, Burdick & Becker, Inc., 1960-62; pres. Joseph F. Bartolone, Inc., N.Y.C., 1962—, Med. Directions, Inc., 1969—; chmn. bd. Llewelyn Consultants, Ltd., 1970—. Served with AUS, 1951-53. Mem. A.I.M. (pres.'s council 1966—), Internat. Platform Assn. Home: City, NY 10036. 10 Cardinal Ct., West Nyack, NY 10994. Office: 500 Fifth Av New York City NY 10036

BARTON, ALAN RAYMOND, utility exec.; b. West Haven, Conn., Feb. 6, 1925; s. Alan Raymond and Edith Beatrice (Mulcahy) B.; student Ga. Inst. Tech., 1944; B.Mech. Engring., Tulane U., 1946; B.Elec. Engring., Auburn U., 1948; m. Peggy Finneran, Feb. 11, 1952; children—Alan, Mary Rae, Elizabeth, William. With Ala. Power Co., Birmingham, 1948—, v.p., 1964-69, sr. v.p., 1969—, also dir.; dir. Ala. Property Co., So. Elec. Generating Co., Birmingham. Served to ensign USNR, 1943-47. Mem. I.E.E.E. Roman Catholic. Kiwanian. Home: 3541 Victoria Rd Birmingham AL 35223 Office: 600 N 18th St Birmingham AL 35203

BARTON, BLAYNEY JONES, labor rel. exec.; b. Beaver City, Utah, Oct. 22, 1910; s. Ray Hunter and Emma Jay (Jones) B.; student U. Utah, 1929, 30, 33; LL.B., George Washington U., 1938; m. Hazel Lavina Whitaker, July 31, 1937; 1 son, John Whitaker. Spl. agt. FBI, 1940-44; dir. indsl. and pub. relations Bayer Aspirin, Winthrop-Stearns Pharm. Co., Sterling-Winthrop Research Inst., Rensselaer, N.Y., 1945-51; dir. employee relations M & M Woodworking Co., Portland, Ore., 1952- 53; dir. labor relations Acme Markets, Inc., Phila., 1954-56, v.p., 1957-68; labor relations cons. to asst. sec. labor U.S. Dept. Labor, Washington, 1970—. Mem. arbitration panel Fed. Mediation and Conciliation Service. Mem. bd. commrs. Ft. Orange council, Boy Scouts Am., Albany, N.Y., former nat. committeeman; asst. dir. Albany Community Chest; dir. Albany Chamber of Commerce, 1952-53; v.p. Albany YMCA. Mem. D.C. Bar Assn., State Bar Utah, Am. Arbitration Assn. (mem. panel), Sigma Pi. Mem. Ch. of Jesus Christ of Latter-day Saints (missionary to Brit. Isles). Rotarian, Kiwanian (v.p., Albany). Home: Signal Hill Lane and Newtown Rd Berwyn PA 19312 Office: Main Labor Bldg 14th and Constitution Av Washington DC 20210

BARTON, CARL P., ins. co. exec.; b. Haverhill, Mass., Dec. 31, 1916. With N.H. Ins. Co., Manchester, 1936—, asst. sec., 1953-56, sec., 1956-60, sec., comptroller, 1960-63, v.p., comptroller, then exec. v.p., 1963—; dir. Granite State Ins. Co., Ill. Nat. Inst. Co. Office: 1750 Elm St Manchester NH 03104*

BARTON, CLIFF SMITH, educator, civil engr.; b. Preston, Ida., July 18, 1919; s. Walter K. and Jennie (Smith) B.; B.S. in Civil Engring., Utah State U., 1947; M.Civil Engring., Rensselaer Poly. Inst., 1953, Ph.D., 1959; m. Emma Whitehead, Feb. 1, 1942; children—Joan (Mrs. John Cross, Jr.), Cliff Bruce, Anne Marie, Clyde Walter, John K. Design engr. Lockheed Aircraft Co., Los Angeles, 1941-45; asst. prof. Rensselaer Poly. Inst., Troy, N.Y., 1947-59; mech. engr. Watervliet Arsenal (N.Y.), 1957-59; prof. civil engring. Brigham Young U., Provo, Utah, 1959—, chmn. dept., 1962-69, asst. dean Coll. Phys. and Engring. Scis., 1969—. cons exptl. mechanics. Served with USAAF, 1945-47. Recipient U.S. Army award for sci. and engring. achievements, 1959. Mem. Am. Soc. E.E., Am. Soc. C.E., Soc. for Exptl. Stress Analysis (pres. 1969-70), Am. Soc. Metals, Sigma Xi. Contbr. articles profl. jours. Home: 1101 Elm Av Provo UT 84601

BARTON, DEREK HAROLD RICHARD, organic chemist; b. Gravesend, Eng., Sept. 8, 1918; s. William Thomas and Maude (Lukes) B.; B.Sc. with 1st Class Honors, Imperial Coll., Eng., 1940, Ph.D. in Organic Chemistry, 1942; D.Sc., U. London, 1949; D.Sc. (hon.), U. Montpellier (France), 1962, U. Dublin (Ireland), 1964, St. Andrew's U., 1970, Columbia, 1970 1 son, William Godfrey Lukes. Research chemist on govt. project, 194244, Messrs. Albright and Wilson, Birmingham, Eng., 194445; asst. lectr. dept. chemistry Imperial Coll., 194546, Imperial Chem. Industries research fellow, 194649, prof., organic chemistry, 1957; vis. lectr. chemistry of natural products Harvard, 1949-50; faculty Birbeck Coll., 1950-55, prof. organic chemistry, 1953-55; Regius prof. chemistry U. Glasgow (Scotland), 1955-57; Max Tishler lectr. Harvard, 1956; Arthur D. Little vis. prof. Mass. Inst. Tech., 1958; Karl Folkers vis. prof. U. Ill., also U. Wis., 1959. Mem. Council for Sci. Policy U.K., 1965; pres. organic chemistry div. Internat. Union of Pure and Applied Chemistry, 1969 Recipient Hofmann prize Imperial Coll., 1940, Harrison Meml. prize Chem. Soc., 1948; Fritzsche medal Am. Chem. Soc., 1956, 1st Roger Adams medal, 1959; corecipient Nobel prize in chemistry, 1969. Fellow Royal Soc., 1954 (Davy medal 1961), Royal Soc. Edinburgh; mem. Brit. Assn. Advancement of Sci. (pres. sect. 1969), Belgian Chem. Soc. (hon.), Nat. Acad. Scis. (fgn. asso.), Chilean Che. Soc. (hon.), Argentinian Chem. Soc. (corr. mem.), Polish Chem. Soc. (hon.), Pharm. Soc. Japan (hon.), Am. Acad. Arts and Scis. (fgn. hon.). Contbr. numerous articles to Jour. Chem. Soc. Research in steroid and terpene fields led to opening of field of conformational analysis in organic chemistry, 1949; stated theory that structures of many phenols and alkaloids could be predicted which aided in understanding biosynthesis of many complex alkaloids, 1956; contbr. to pyrolysis of organic chlorides, 1945-52, devel. and application of carbanion autoxidations, after 1960; pioneer in study of relationship of molecular rotation to structure in complex organic molecules. Home: 1A Grove R D Northwood, Middlesex, England. Office: Chemistry Dept Imperial Coll London SW 7 England

BARTON, DONALD WILBER, educator; b. Fresno, Cal., June 12, 1921; s. Harold Dwight and Esther Eliza (McBride) B.; B.S., U. Cal. at Berkeley, 1947, Ph.D., 1949; m. Virginia Adams Winston, Jan. 10, 1944; children—Richard Paul, Kenneth Allen, Donna Kathleen, Alan Roy. AEC postdoctoral fellow U. Mo., 1949-50; asst. prof. genetics, 1950-51; asso. prof. vegetable crops N.Y. State Agrl. Expt. Sta., 1951-59, prof., head dept. vegetable crops, 1959-60; dir. expt. sta. Cornell U. Coll. Agr., 1960—, asst. dir. research, 1960-68, asso. dir. research, 1968—. Dir. Geneva Savs. Bank. Bd. dirs. YMCA. Mem. Internat. Soc. Hort. Sci., Am. Soc. Hort. Sci., Genetic Soc. Am., Sigma Xi, Alpha Zeta. Home: 597 W North St Geneva NY 14456

BARTON, ELEANOR DODGE, educator; b. Willsborough, N.Y., Jan. 23, 1918; d. Lyman Guy and Aethel (Dodge) Barton; A.B., Vassar Coll., 1938; A.M., Inst. Fine Arts, N.Y.U., 1942; Ph.D., Radcliffe Coll., 1952. Staff asst. Yale, 1940-42; teaching fellow Smith Coll., 1942-43, instr., 1943-48, asst. prof., 1948- 52; prof., chmn. dept. art Sweet Briar (Va.) Coll., 1952-71; vis. lectr. Wellesley Coll., 1956-57; vis. prof. art Vassar Coll., 1971; prof., chmn. dept. art history U. Hartford, 1972—. Shirley Farr fellow, 1960-61. Mem. Coll. Art Assn. Am. (dir. 1958-59), Am. Assn. U. Women, Archeol. Inst. Am., Renaissance Soc., Phi Beta Kappa. Democrat. Episcopalian. Address: Univ Hartford West Hartford CT 06117

BARTON, EVAN MANSFIELD, physician; b. Chgo., Nov. 7, 1903; s. Enos Melancthon and Mary C. (Rust) B.; grad. Choate Sch., 1920; A.B., Williams Coll., 1924; M.D., Johns Hopkins, 1929; m. Jane Purvis High, Oct. 16, 1937; children—Cynthia, Eric McMillan. intern, Presbyn. Hosp., Chgo., 1929-30, resident pathology, Presbyn. Hosp., 1931-34; practice medicine, specializing internal medicine, Chgo., 1935—; attending physician Presbyn.-St. Lukes Hosp.; clin. prof. medicine Rush. Med. Coll.; cons. rheumatology VA Hosp. (Hines, Ill.). Chmn. med., sci. com. Ill. chpt. Arthritis Found. Served from maj. to col., M.C., AUS, 1942-46. Fellow A.C.P.; mem. A.M.A., Am. Rheumatism Assn., Chgo. Rheumatism Soc., Chgo. Soc. Internal Medicine (pres. 1969), Chgo. Pathol. Soc., Phi Beta Kappa, Phi Gamma Delta, Nu Sigma Nu. Republican. Baptist. Clubs: Ruth Lake Country; Quadrangle. Home: 5817 S Blackstone Av Chicago IL 60637 Office: 1725 W Harrison St Chicago IL 60612

BARTON, FRED JACKSON, coll. dean; b. Lynn, Ala., Oct. 7, 1911; s. James Garfield and Jessie Josephine (Gravlee) B.; student Ala. Poly. Inst. (Auburn U.), 1929-30, Freed-Hardeman Coll., Henderson, Tenn., 1932-33; B.A. in Speech, Abilene Christian Coll., 1937; M.A., State U. Ia., 1939, Ph.D., 1949; m. Eleanor Creel Brockman, Dec. 10, 1941; children—James Brockman, Fredda Grey. Tchr. pub. schs. in Ala. and Tex., 1933-38; mem. faculty Abilene Christian Coll., 1938—, prof. speech and homiletics, 1949—, dean of Grad. Sch., 1957—, also dir. research. Vice chmn., bd. dirs. Tex. System Natural Labs.; mem. environmental panel Tex. Water Conservation Assn. Served to capt. USAAF, 1941-46; lt. col. USAF Res. Mem. Assn. Higher Edn., Speech Assn. Am., So., Tex. (past pres.) speech assns., Am. Acad. Religion, Assn. Tex. Grad. Schs. (pres. 1965-66). Mem. Ch. of Christ. Author articles, chpts. in books. Home: 681 College Dr Abilene TX 79601.

BARTON, GEORGE ESTES, educator; Ph.D., Ohio State U.; LL.D., St. Edward's U. Prof. philosophy Tulane U., New Orleans. Office: Dept Philosophy Tulane U New Orleans LA 70118*

BARTON, JACKSON MOUNCE, petroleum co. exec.; b. Shawnee, Okla., Jan. 12, 1917; s. Jesse Downy and Elizabeth (Mounce) B.; student Phillips U., 1934-36; B.S., U. Okla., 1938; postgrad. Yale, 1939-41; m. Dorothy King, May 9, 1942; children—Jackson M., Charles D., Elizabeth B. Geologist Magnolia Petroleum Co., 1938-47; div. geologist Coop. Refinery Assn., Kansas City, Mo., 1947-49, chief geologist, 1949-50, exploration mgr., 1950; mgr. geol. dept. Deep Rock Oil Corp., Tulsa, 1950-53; exploration mgr. to v.p., gen. mgr., dir. No. Natural Gas Producing Co., 1953-65; gen. mgr. Glover Hefner Kennedy Oil Co., Oklahoma City, 1965-68; exec. v.p., dir. Royal Resources Corp., also exec. v.p. Royal Resources Exploration, Inc., 1968-70; exec. v.p., dir. Champlin Petroleum Co., Ft. Worth, 1970—; dir. Union Pacific Resources Corp. Bd. dirs. Omaha Planned Parenthood, 1963-65. Mem. Westside Community Schs. Bd. Edn., 1955-65, pres., 1962-65. Mem. alumni adv. council Sch. Geology of U. Okla., 1968-72. Fellow Geol. Soc. Am., A.A.A.S.; mem. Am. Assn. Petroleum Geologists, Am. Inst. Mining and Metall. Engrs., Soc. Exploration Geophysicists, Am. Geol. Inst., Am. Geophys. Union, Am. Inst. Profl. Geologists, Rocky Mountain Oil and Gas Assn. (past pres. Neb. sect.), Ind. Petroleum Assn. Am., Am. Petroleum Inst., Am. Gas Assn., Ind. Natural Gas Assn., Mid-Continent Oil and Gas Assn., Omaha C. of C. Unitarian (pres. bd. trustees). Contbr. articles profl. jours. Home: 6451 Crestmore Rd Ft Worth TX 76116 Office: PO Box 9365 Ft Worth TX 76107

BARTON, JAMES DON, Jr., univ. adminstr.; b. Anna, Ill., Oct. 25, 1929; s. James Don and Allie (Harrelson) B.; B.S., No. Ill. U., 1952, M.S., 1953; Ph.D., Purdue U., 1956; m. Grace E. Valentine, June 30, 1967; children—Robert J., Mark C., Peter V., Maral J., Jayne Dee, Diana J. Instr. sci. Boston U., 1956-58, asst. prof. sci. Coll. Basic Studies, 1958-63, dir. NSF Summer Insts., 1960- 64; asso. prof. Southampton (N.Y.) Coll., 1963-68, dir. div. natural scis., 1963-66, dean of Coll., 1966-68, acting dir. Marine Sta., 1963-64; provost, v.p. acad. affairs, prof. biology Alfred (N.Y.) U., 1968—. Radiol. officer Norfolk (Mass.) Civil Def., 1956-63. Trustee L.I. chpt. Nature Conservancy. Recipient Purdue Research Found. grant, 1955. Mem. Ecol. Soc. Am., Ind., Ill. acads. sci., Sigma Xi, Phi Kappa Phi. Author: Forest Phytosociological Techniques, 1958; Land Use and Vegetation Map, Southampton Town, N.Y., 1969. Cons. to conservation commn. Instructional Sound Film on Ecology, 1961. Home: 15 Reynolds St Alfred NY 14802 Office: PO Box 1106 Alfred NY 14802

BARTON, JAY, II, univ. adminstr., biologist; b. Chgo., June 22, 1922; s. Jay and Agnes (Heisler) B.; A.B., U. Mo., 1947, M.A., 1948, Ph.D. in Zoology, 1951; m. Ann Taylor, Aug. 1, 1946; children—Sarah (Mrs. Ronald Feigin), Elizabeth, Peter, Rachel, Matthew, Mary, Judith. Instr. zoology, then asst. prof. Columbia, 1950-55; from asst. prof. to prof. biology St. Joseph's Coll., Rensselaer, Ind., 1955-65, staff biologist commn. undergrad. edn. in biol. scis., 1965-67; prof. biology, chmn. dept. W.Va. U., 1967-69, provost for instrn., 1968—. Cons. NSF; mem. Commn. on Instns. of Higher Edn. at N. Central Assn. Colls. and Secondary Schs., 1970—. Served with AUS, 1943-46. AEC fellow, 1949-50; Lalor fellow, 1951-52; NSF fellow and Fulbright scholar, Copenhagen, Denmark, 1961-62. Asso. investigator Argonne Nat. Lab., 1958; cons. biol. scis. curriculum scis., sci. edn. program A.A.A.S., 1965—. Mem. Nat. Assn. Biology Tchrs. (bd. dirs., exec. com.), Nat. Sci. Tchrs. Assn., Am. Inst. Biol. Scis., A.A.A.S., Am. Assn. U. Profs., Soc. Protozoologists, W. Va. Acad. Scis., Assn. So. Biologists, Sigma Xi. Home: 604 Grand St Morgantown WV 26505

BARTON, JOHN CLIB, lawyer; b. Antoine, Ark., July 9, 1903; s. Clib and Etta (Hardin) B.; student Hendrix Coll., 1922-23, U. Ark., 1923-24, George Peabody Coll., 1924-25, Vanderbilt U., 1925-26; LL.B., Cumberland Law Sch., 1927; m. Wilma Stone, Feb. 14, 1929; children-Patsy (Mrs. Ralph McDonald), John Club, James Grover. Admitted to Ark. bar, 1927, since practiced in Ft. Smith; partner firm Hardin, Barton, Jesson & Dawson. Vice Pres. Alma Canning Co., Ft. Smith, 1942-62, Good Canning Co., Ft. Smith, 1945-52, Charleston Canning Co., Ft. Smith, 1945-52; chmn. bd. Superior Fed. Savs. & Loan Assn., Ft. Smith, 1932—; organizer, pres., dir. Harbor House, Inc., Western, Ark., 1965—. Mem. Sebastian County Welfare Bd., 1952—; pres, Ark, area council Boy Scouts Am., 1948-51, Chmn. Young Democrats Orgn., 1927-34. Bd. dirs. Sebastian County chpt. A.R.C., 1942- 49; chmn. Doss T. Sutton Charitable Found.; pres. Tabitha Godrey and Maude J. Thomas Charitable Found. Recipient Silver Beaver award Westark council Boy Scouts Am., 1955. Mem. Ft. Smith C. of C., Sigma Chi. Methodist (ofcl. bd.). Clubs: Town, Hardscrabble Country (Ft. Smith). Author: (pamphlet) How to Dismantle a Corporation, 1946. Home: 3001 Beverly Dr Fort Smith AR 72901 Office: Superior Fed Bldg Fort Smith AR 72901

BARTON, LOREN ROBERTA, artist, designer, illustrator; b. Oxford, Mass.; d. Loren Chandler and Jessie (Woodbury) Barton; student U. So. Cal; m. Perez Rogers Babcock, June 24, 1930 (dec. 1947); m. 2d, Jervis R. Miller, Aug. 3, 1951. Instr., Chouinard Inst., Los Angeles. Represented in Chgo. Art Inst., Cal. State Library, Los Angeles Pub. (Smithsonian Instn.), Bklyn. Mus., San Diego Fine Arts Gallery, Los Angeles Mus., Library of Congress, Met. Mus., Nat. Library of France, Pomona Coll., Wesleyan Coll., Tex. Tech. Inst., Municipal Collection (Phoenix), Los Angeles County Collections, Va. Mus. Fine Arts, collection Ency. Brit., others. Award 1st prize for etching, 1920; 1st prize for etching, figure painting, 1922; 1st prize for etching, water color prize, 1923; 2 hon. mentions, 1926; 1 prize for water color (all from Ariz. Art Exhbns.), 1927; silver cup for best work and 1st prize for water color Arcadia (Cal.) Exhbn., 1924; Joan of Arc medal Nat. Assn. Women Painters and Sculptors, 1928; water color prize Pacific Southwest Expn., 1928; water color prize, 1927, and hon. mention for etching and water color prize Pomona Fair, 1928; 1st prize for etching Los Angeles County Exhbn., 1937; George A. Zabriski prize in ann. exhibit Am. Water Color Soc., Purchase prize Santa Paula, Aug. 1941; 1st prize for water color Laguna Beach Art Assn., 1941; 1st prize oil, Santa Cruz, 1946; Purchase prizes Clearwater, 1946, Gardena, San Fernando, Santa Paula, 1947, Gardena, 1950. . Fellow Royal Soc. Arts (London); mem. Am. Water Color Soc., Cal. Water Color Soc. (Purchase prize 1945). Illustrator numerous books. Home: Mt San Antonio Gardens 900 E Harrison Av Pomona CA 91767 also Address: care Dalzeli Hatfield Gallery Ambassador Hotel Los Angeles CA 90005

BARTON, MILLARD VERNON, research engineer; b. Weiser, Ida., April 16, 1910; s. John W. and Cressa (Reigleman) B.; B.S., Calif. Inst. Tech., 1932; M.S., U. of Colo., 1937; Ph.D., Cornell U., 1940; m. Gladys J. Ingoldt, June 21, 1935; children—Kathryn Margo, Dana Westwood. Jr. engr. U.S. Bureau of Reclamation, 1934-37; instr. machine design and asst. prof. engring. mechanics, Cornell U., 1937-40; asst. prof. mech. engring., in charge aeronautic labs., U. of Md., 1940-41; stress analyst Bell Aircraft Co., 1940-41; prof. aero. engring. in charge of structures U. of Tex., 1942-51, prof. engring. mechanics, 1950-54, chmn. dept. engring., mechanics, 1952-54; research engr. defense research lab., 1945- 54; sr. tech. staff. mgr. engring. mechanics Ramo-Wooldridge Corp. (name later changed to TRW Systems), Los Angeles, 1954, sr. state engr. for engring. mechanics operation, 1966—; engineer Douglas Aircraft Co. summer 1944; research engr. applied physics lab. Johns Hopkins, summer 1945; cons. Sandia Corp. Mem. NASA com. on missile and space vehicle structures, 1961-62. Recipient Snoopy Award (Apollo), 1969. Registered professional engr., Texas. Fellow Inst. Aero. Sci. (asso.), Am. Soc. M.E. (chmn. applied mechanics div. 1965-66); mem. Tex. Soc. Profl. Engrs., Am. Soc. Engring. Edn., Sigma Xi, Phi Kappa Phi, Pi Tau Sigma, Tau Beta Pi. Author: Fundamentals of Aircraft Structures, 1948; Elementary Aircraft Structures, 1943; (co-author) Space Technology, 1959. Editor, co-author: Shock and Structural Response, 1960; also articles on structures, elasticity, dynamics. Office: TRW Systems 1 Space Park Redondo Beach CA

BARTON, NELDA ANN, (Mrs. Harold Bryan Barton), Rep. nat. committeewoman; b. Providence, Ky., May 12, 1929; d. Eulis Grant and Ruble (West) Lambert; student Western Ky. U., 1947-49; grad. Norton Meml. Infirmary Sch. Med. Tech., Louisville, 1950; m. Harold Bryan Barton, May 11, 1951; children—Barbara Lynn, Harold Bryan, Stephen Lambert, Suzanne. Med. technologist, 1950-53; v.p. Newcomers Club, Ind., 1953; dist. chmn. P.T.A., 1958-59; vice-gov. 9th Dist. Ky. Fedn. Woman's Club, 1962-64; gov. 5th Dist. Ky. Fedn. Rep. Women, 1963-67; Ky. councilor Woman's Aux. So. Med. Assn., 1965-66, Southeastern councilor, 1966-67; health career chmn. Woman's Aux. Ky. Med. Assn., 1965-68; chairwoman 5th Dist. Rep. Campaign, 1967; Whitley County Rep. chairwoman, 1968—; 2d v.p. Ky. Fedn. Rep. Women, 1968-70; conf. chmn. for Ky., Nat. Rep. Women's Conf., 1969; Rep. Nat. Committeewoman for Ky., 1968—, mem. DO com., 1969—; mem. Gov.'s Commn. on Women, Ky., 1968—; co-chmn. Corbin Urban

Renewal and Devel. Agy., 1970—; mem. Corbin Adv. Council, 1969-70. Pres. Woman's Aux. Whitley County Med. Soc., 1959- 60, Ossoli Woman's Club, 1961-62, Corbin Central Elementary P.T.A., 1963- 65, Corbin Rep. Woman's Club, 1968; charter mem. Fine Arts Assn. Southeastern Ky. Recipient life membership award P.T.A., 1964; named Ky. col.; Ky. Republican Woman of Year, 1969. Mem. Christian Ch. (circle chmn. 1964-65, youth fellowship leader 1965-68). Home: 1311 7th St Rd Corbin KY 40701

BARTON, RICHARD FLEMING, educator, univ. adminstr.; b. Oshkosh, Wis., Sept. 29, 1924; s. Dan Wiley and Margaret (Freeman) B.; B.S., Northwestern U., 1948; Ph.D., U. Cal. at Berkeley, 1961; m. Nancy Ann Schalk, Oct. 25, 1952; children—Ted Steven, Dan Richard, Jean Nancy. With Procter & Gamble, 1948-50, Travelers Ins. Co., 1952-58; asst. prof. bus. orgn. and mgmt. U. Neb., 1961-64; asso. prof. bus. adminstrn. U. Kan., 1964-67; prof. mgmt. and cocomputer sci. Tex. Tech U., Lubbock, 1967—, dir. planning and analyses, 1968-71, acting computer center dir., 1970-71; lectr., cons. in field, 1961—. Served with USAAF, World War II. Ford Found. fellow, 1959-61. Mem. Operations Research Soc. Am., Inst. Mgmt. Scis., Am. Econ. Assn., Acad. Mgmt., Southwestern Social Sci. Assn., Assn. Computing Machinery, Assn. Instl. Research, Interuniv. Communications Council (instl. rep.), Am. Assn. for Higher Edn., Simulation Councils, Inc., Soc. for Coll. and Univ. Planning, Beta Gamma Sigma, Sigma Iota Epsilon. Author: A Primer on Simulation and Gaming, 1970; The Imaginit Management Game, 1971; also numerous articles, papers on policy, oligopoly, simulation, mgmt. sci., amdinstrn. of higher edn. Home: 5409 8th Pl Lubbock TX 79416

BARTON, ROBERT A., book pub; b. Bklyn., Oct. 28, 1924; s. Arthur Frederick and Violet M. (Youngson) B.; B.B.A., Pace Coll., 1952; M.S., L.I.U., 1955; m. Virginia M. Teodor, Aug. 25, 1946; children—Robert A., Ronald J. Controller, Dun & Bradstreet, Inc., 1946-65; v.p. finance Crowell Collier & Macmillan, Inc., 1966-70, exec. v.p., 1970—, also dir. Active local Cub Scouts Am. Bd. dirs. Berlitz Schs. Langs. Am., LaSalle Extension U. Served with AUS, 1943-45; ETO. Mem. Financial Execs. Inst. Home: 116 Guston Rd Garden City NY 11530 Office: 866 3d Av New York City NY 10022

BARTON, ROBERT BROWN MORISON, ret. bus. exec.; b. Pikesville, Md., Aug. 19, 1903; s. Randolph and Eleanor (Morison) B.; student Phillips Exeter Acad.; A.B., Harvard, 1926, LL.B., 1929; m. Sally Parker, Oct. 3, 1931; children—Randolph Parker, Sally B. King, Richard Morison. Admitted to Md. bar, 1929. Mass. bar, 1932; engaged in practice of law, 1929-32; asst. treas. Parker Bros., Inc., mfrs. games and kindergarten supplies, Salem, Mass., 1932-33; pres., dir. Parker Bros., 1933-68, chmn. bd., 1968-70. Trustee Salem Hosp. Served as lt., U.S. Naval Res. 1942-44. Clubs: Harvard (New York and Boston); Eastern Yacht (Marblehead, Mass.); Tedesco Country (Salem); Metropolitan (Washington); Tennis and Racquet (Boston). Home: 329 Ocean Av Marblehead Neck MA 01945 Office: PO Box 97 Marblehead MA 01945

BARTON, ROBERT DURRIE, fgn. service officer; b. London, Eng., Aug. 29, 1920; s. Robert Shawmut and Agnes (Durrie) B.; (parents U.S. citizens); A.B., Bowdoin Coll., 1941; M.A., U. Okla., 1971; m. Nancy Hemenway Whitten, Sept. 26, 1942; children—Robert Bradford, William Emerson, Frederick Durrie. Dir. Inter-Am. dept. Inst. Internat. Edn., N.Y.C., 1957-61; dir. East Campus devel. Columbia, 1961-64; dir. human resources devel. A.I.D., Santo Domingo and Washington, 1964-66; cultural attache, LaPaz, Bolivia, 1966-68; pub. affairs officer, Guadalajara, Mexico, 1968—. Asso. dir. Internat. Fellows Program of Columbia, 1961-64. Dir. Spanish Inst. and Tinker Found., 1958-65. Served to capt. USMCR, 1942-46. Mem. Pan-Am. Soc., Assn. Latin Am. Studies, S.A.R., Am. Fgn. Service Assn., Alpha Delta Phi. Conglist. Clubs: Southern Cross, Coffee House (N.Y.C.); Boothbay Harbor (Me.) Yacht; Dacor (Washington); Guadalajara Country. Author: A Short History of Bolivia, 1968. Contbr. articles profl. jours., chpts. in books. Home: Milestone Juniper Point West Boothbay Harbor ME 04575 Office: USIS-American Consulate General Guadalajara Jal Mexico

BARTON, ROBERT THOMAS, R., lawyer; b. Winchester, Va., Oct. 15, 1891; s. R. T. and Gertrude W. (Baker) B.; student Shenandoah Valley Acad., 1901-08; B.S., U. of Va., 1914, LL.B., 1914; m. Eleanor W. Parrish, Oct. 21, 1926; children—Robert T., III, Edith P., Eleanor R. Admitted to Va. bar, 1913; mem. Barton & Barton, Winchester, Va., 1914-16, Christian, and Barton (now Christian, Barton, Parker, Epps & Brent), Richmond, Va., 1926—. Served as 2d lt., Inf., Mexican Border Service, capt. F.A., 1918-19; col., AC, World War II. Decorated Legion of Merit. Former chmn. bd. visitors Med. Coll. Va. Mem. Am. (ho. dels., former chmn. exec. com. nat. conf. uniform state laws of bd. govs.), Va. (former chmn. exec. com.) bar assns., Va. State Bar (pres. 1950-51), Am. Coll. Trial Lawyers, Am. Legion (former state dept. comdr. and nat. exec. com.). Clubs: Soc. of Cincinnati, Richmond Country, Deep Run Hunt, Richmond German, Commonwealth. Author: Barton's Chancery Practice, 3d edit. 1926. Mem. bd. editors Am. Bar. jour. Home: 4238 Southampton Rd Richmond VA 23220 Office: Mutual Bldg Richmond VA

BARTON, ROGER, author, editor; b. N.Y.C., Dec. 27, 1903; s. Joseph Jewett and Olive (Pettipierre) B.; B.S. cum laude, Harvard, 1925; A.M., Columbia, 1932; m. Priscilla M. Sargent, Sept. 10, 1932; children—Seth Sargent, Deborah Ann (Mrs. R. J. Miller). News editor Daily Herald, Passaic, N.J., 1925-27; reporter Newark Evening News, 1927-30; account exec. Daniel Starch & Staff, N.Y.C., 1930-38; advt. agy. Barton & Goold, Inc., N.Y.C., 1939-40, pres., chmn., 1939-40; editor Advt. Agy. (formerly Advt. & Selling), 1946-55, The Am. Printer, 1950-55; project and pub. relations dir. Alfred Politz Research, Inc., N.Y.C., 1955-57; editor Media-Scope mag., N.Y.C. 1957-65; lectr. advt., grad. sch. business Columbia, 1947-65. Editorial writer nature subjects, author column on outdoors Newark Eve. News, 1946—; Am. corr. Advt. and Marketing Review, London, 1948-51, Advt. Review, London, 1953- 59. Mem. Pres.'s Com. Employment Handicapped. Served as lt. col. AUS, 1940-46. Decorated Legion of Merit (U.S.); Conspicuous Service Cross (N.Y.); Armed Forces Res. medal. Mem. S.R., Soc. Colonial Wars, Marine Corps League (hon.), Am. Marketing Assn., Nat. Conf. Bus. Paper Editors (pres.) N.J. Audubon Soc. (pres.), Am. Assn. U. Profs. Copy Research Council N.Y. (sec.-treas. 1966-67). Episcopalian. Club: Harvard (N.Y.C.). Author: (with O. D. Keep) The Quiz Book, 1927; (with Daniel Starch) Faith, Fear and Fortunes, 1934; Advertising Agency Operations and Management, 1954; How to Watch Birds, 1955; Media in Advertising, 1964. Editor: Advertising Handbook, 1950; Handbook of Advertising Management, 1970. Contbr. articles on advt. Ency. Brit., 1948-59. Home: Mt Salem Farm R D 1 Pittstown NJ 08867

BARTON, THOMAS FRANK, geographer, educator, writer; b. Cornell, Ill., Dec. 3, 1905; s. Frank Douglas and Martha (Gamblin) B; diploma Ill. State U., 1929, B.Ed., 1930; Ph.M., U. Wis., 1931; Ph.D., U. Neb., 1935; m. Erselia M.A. Monticello, Sept. 26, 1931; 1 son, Thomas Frank Monticello. Rural sch. tchr., 1925-27; grad. teaching asst., dept. geography U. Wis., 1930-32, U. Neb., 1932-34; asst. prof. geography Memphis State Coll., summers 1933, 34; asso. prof. social studies Neb. State Tchrs. Coll., 1934-35; prof. geography, head geography-geology dept. So. Ill. U., 1935-47; prof. vis. prof. geography U. Neb., summer 1947; asso. prof. Ind. U., 1947-51, prof. geography, 1951—, on leave, 1955-57; vis. prof. geography and social studies Coll. Edn., Bangkok, Thailand, 1955-57; supr. U.S. Airway Weather Sta., So. Ill. U., 1941-47. One of 4 dels. representing U.S. at 6 week UNESCO seminar McDonald Coll., St. Anne de Bellevue, Que., Can., July-Aug. 1950; sec. Internat. Geog. Union Commn. on Teaching of Geography in Schs., 1952-55; ednl. motion picture collaborator and adviser. Mem. Ill. Reserve Militia, ground instr. meterology Civilian Pilot Tng. Program; geography instr. Army A.C. Tng. Program (all 1942-43). Recipient Distinguished Service award Nat. Council for Geog. Edn., 1965. Fellow A.A.A.S., Ind. Sci., Nat. Council Geog. Edn. (recipient distinguished service award 1965), Nat. Council Geography Teachers (pres. 1948); mem. Am. Geog. Soc., Neb. (pres. 1935), Ill. (pres. 1939-40), Indiana (pres. 1961-62) councils geography tchrs., Ill., Ind. acads. sci., Ill. Edn. Assn., Ind. State Tchrs. Assn., Assn. Am. Geographers, Am. Assn. U. Profs., Sigma Xi, Phi Delta Kappa, Kappa Phi Kappa, Pi Kappa Delta, Kappa Delta Pi. Author: Living in Illinois, 1941; Patrick Henry; Boy Spokesman, 1960; Jamestown Boy, 1966; (with others) Southeast Asia In Maps, 1970; also (with Sidman P. Poole and Clara Belle Baker) Through The Day, 1947, From Season to Season, 1947, In Country and City, 1947; (with Sedman P. Poole and Irving Robert Melbo) The World About Us, 1948. Co-author; Geography of the North American Midwest; Cirriculum Guide for Geographic Education, 1963; Methods of Geographic Instructions, 1968; An Overall Economic Development Study of Southeastern Indiana, 1970. Senior Author: An Economic Geography of Thailand, 1958. Asso. editor Jour. of Geography, 1940-45, asst. editor, 1948-50, editor, 1950-65; editor land surface wall map series, including world, U.S., Europe, 1952, S.A., Africa, Eurasia, N.A. Editor series maps and globes Pictorial Relief with Emerging Color. Contbr. chpts. tech. publs., articles profl. jours. Home: 940 S Jourdan Av Bloomington IN 47401

BARTON, WALTER EARL, physician, psychiatrist; b. Oak Park, Ill., July 29, 1906; s. Alfred J. and Bertha (Kalish) B.; B.S., U. Ill., 1928, M.D., 1931; m. Elsa Benson, July 2, 1932; children—John, Gail, Paul. Rotating intern West Suburban Hosp., Oak Park, Ill., 1930-31; asst. physician med. and surg. services Worchester State Hosp., 1931, women's reception service, 1932-34, sr. physician men's reception service, 1934-38, asst. supt., 1938-42; acting supt., 1939-40; clin. clerk Nat. Hosp., London, Eng., 1938; supt. Boston State Hosp., 1945-63; med. dir. Am. Psychiat. Assn., Washington, 1963—; cons. physician medicine, rehab. div. Brockton, Bedford VA hosps.; lectr., staff Worcester State Hosp., Simmons Coll. Sch. Social Work, Smith Coll. Sch. Social Work, Clark U., Tufts U. Med. Sch.; faculty adult edn. Worcester YMCA; asso. prof. psychiatry Boston U. Med. Sch., 1952-62, clin. prof. psychiatry, 1962—; professorial lectr. George Washington U., 1967-71; cons. Sibley Hosp., Washington, 1966. Trustee Joint Commn. Mental Illness and Health; cons. in hosp. adminstrn. VA Wash.; mem. study com. Nat. Inst. Mental Health; dir. Joint Commn. Mental Health Careers, 1966-69; asst. Sec. Am. Psychiat. Mus. Assn., Inc. Mem. Mass. N.G., 1936-42; served to lt. col. M.C., AUS, 1942-46. Decorated Legion of Merit; recipient Nolan D.C. Lewis award for distinguished services to psychiatry, 1962; Bowis award for distinguished service, 1970. Diplomate Am. Bd. Psychiatry and Neurology (dir.) Fellow Am. Psychiat. Assn. (pres. 1961-62), Am. Coll. Psychiatrists, A.C.P. (life), Royal Coll. Psychiatrists, Australian and New Zealand Coll. Psychiatrists (hon.); mem. A.M.A., Mass. Psychiatry Assn. (past pres.), Group for the Advancement of Psychiatry (past pres.), Mass. Assn. for Research Psychiatry, Mass. Occupational Therapy Assn., Indian Psychiat. Soc. (corr. mem.), Am. Acad. Child Psychiatry (hon.), New Eng. Psychiat. Assn., Mass. Med. Assn. Methodist. Clubs: Cosmos, Kiwanis. Author: (with others) Observations on European Psychiatry, 1961 Administration in Psychiatry, 1962; Training the Psychiatrist to Meet Changing Needs, 1964; The Role and Methodology of Classification in Psychiatry and Psychopharmacology, 1968; also numerous sci. papers. Home: 3254 Arcadia Pl N W Washington DC 20015 Office: 1700 18th St NW Washington DC 20009

BARTON, WILLIAM BLACKBURN, lawyer, indsl. relations specialist; b. Pratt, Kan., Aug. 4, 1899; s. William Burnston and Frances (Blackburn) B.; A.B., Northwestern U., 1921; A.M., Columbia, 1924, LL.M., 1938; LL.B., Yale, 1927; m. Marian Ruth Humphreys, Sept. 25, 1926; children—Sara Ellen, William Blackburn. Tchr. pub. speaking Danville (Ill.) High Sch., Maywood, Ill., 1924-26; admitted to Cal. bar, 1928, D.C. bar; practiced in Cal., 1928-37; tchr. pub. speaking U. Cal. at Los Angeles, 1927-29, bus. law Los Angeles City Coll., 1932-37; atty., trial examiner NLRB, 1938-44; in charge employer-employee relations C. of C. U.S., 1944-64, mgr. labor relations dept., 1951-53, mgr. labor relations and legal dept., gen. counsel, 1953-64, editor Labor Relations Letter, 1945-53; lectr. labor relations C. of C. insts. Northwestern U., 1954, Mich. State, Houston univs., 1958; now in pvt. practice law, Washington. Del., Pres.'s Indsl. Safety Conf., 1949; rep. Pres.'s Conf., Minn. and Ore. Govs.' Indsl. Safety Confs., 1950; mem. U.S. employer delegation Internat. Labor Conf., 1947-53; faculty Silver Bay Conf. Human Relations in Industry, 1956; mem. dept. labor mgmt. adv. com. Labor-Mgmt. Reporting and Disclosure Act of 1959; mem. Pres.'s Com. for Dept. Labor 50th Anniversary Year; mem. Regional Law Com. for D.C., 1966-68. Mem. prep. com. 4th nat. study conf. Nat. Council of Chs. Trustee Sibley Meml. Hosp. Mem. Am. Bar Assn. (past co-chmn. regional labor law com. for D.C.), Nat. Safety Council (chmn. Marcus A. Dow Meml. award com. 1955-64), Delta Sigma Rho, Delta Theta Phi. Methodist. Mason. Clubs: Cleveland Park (pres. 1955-56), Yale, Cosmos Club (bd. mgmt.). Speaker, writer on labor relations. Author: (pamphlets) Management-Labor Relations and Management Attitudes, Labor in Politics. Home: 5035 Rockwood Pkwy Washington DC 20016 Office: Shoreham Bldg Washington DC 20005

BARTON, WILLIAM LOUIS, banker; b. N.Y.C., Apr. 28, 1908; s. A. Harry and Betty (Brown) B.; student Carnegie Inst. Tech., 1929-32; B.S., Columbia, 1934; Stonier Grad. Sch. Banking, Rutgers U., 1956, mgmt. program, Dartmouth, 1965; m. Helen Bazzle, Feb. 15, 1946; 1 son, Jeffrey Preston. With City N.Y. Dept. Purchase, 1934-41; mgmt. cons. Office Quartermaster Gen., Washington, 1940-42; v.p. East River Savs. Bank, N.Y.C., 1941—, adminstrv. v.p. mgmt., 1962—. Mem. Gov. Rockefeller's Bus. Adv. Commn. on Mgmt. Improvement, 1966-69. Served to lt. comdr. USNR, 1942-46. Mem. Am. Inst. Banking (past pres., trustee N.Y. chpt.), Adminstrv. Mgmt. Assn., Res. Officers Assn., Am. Legion, Mil. Order World Wars, N.Y. C. of C., Commerce and Industry Assn. N.Y., Savs. Banks Assn. N.Y. State, Nat. Assn. Mut. Savs. Banks. Clubs: Commissioned Officers (West Point, Bklyn.); New York Athletic. Author: How They Handle Personnel, 1956; Present Day Banking, 1956. Contbr. articles profl. jours. Office: 26 Cortlandt St New York City NY 10007

BARTOO, JAMES BREESE, educator, mathematician; b. Swanton, Vt., July 2, 1921; s. DeForest and Lina Martha (Douglass) B.; B.S. in Edn., Edinboro (Pa.) State Coll., 1947; M.S., State U., Ia., 1949, Ph.D., 1952; m. Mary Viola Mead, Oct. 5, 1943; children—Janice, Jill, Kim, Scott, Brenda. Tchr. math., Erie, Pa., 1947; mem. faculty Pa. State U., 1952—, prof. math., head dept., 1960-68, prof. math. statistics, head dept. statistics, 1968-69, dean Grad. Sch., 1969—, acting v.p. for research, 1970—. Served AUS, 1943-46; ETO. Mem. Inst. Math. Statistics, Am. Math. Soc., Math. Assn. Am., Am. Statis. Assn. Home: 706 Windsor Ct State College PA 16801 Office: Graduate Bldg Penn State U University Park PA 16802

BARTOS, JOSEPH T., govt. ofcl.; b. N.J., Apr. 30, 1918; married. Teller, clk. various banks, 1937-42; with U.S. Dept. of State, 1949—, counsel adminstrv. affairs, Lagos, Nigeria, 1965-67, Cairo, UAR, 1967, exec. dir. Bur. Intelligence Research, 1967—. Recipient Superior Honor award Dept. of State, 1969. Address: 4709 Windom Pl Washington DC 20016*

BARTOSH, HENRY, union ofcl. Sec.-treas. Internat. Union Am. Bakery and Confectionery Workers. Office: 1000 16th St NW Washington DC 20036*

BARTOW, CLARENCE W., retired investment banker; b. South Orange, N.J., Apr. 13, 1907; s. Francis D. and Sabina Redmond (Martin) B.; grad. Phillips Exeter Acad., 1927; B.A., Williams Coll., 1931; m. Elizabeth Vaux Woolston, Nov. 11, 1949; 1 son, Clarence W.; stepdaus., Josephine, Beulah, Jeannie. With Drexel & Co., Phila., 1931-38, partner, 1947-66; v.p., dir. Drexel Harriman Ripley, Inc., N.Y.C., 1966-70; with J.P. Mogan & Co., 1938-41. Past gov. Am. Stock Exchange. Served to capt. AUS, 1941-47. Clubs: Links, Tuxedo (N.Y.C.). Home: Tuxedo Park NY 10987

BARTSCHT, HERI BERT, sculptor, educator; b. Breslau, Germany, Aug. 30, 1919; s. Richard and Emma (Philipp) B.; student Acad. Fine Arts, Munich, Germany, 1946-52; m. Waltraud Erika Gutensohn, Mar. 31, 1950; 1 son, Martin Donald. Came to U.S., 1952, naturalized, 1959. Prof. sculpture, U. Dallas, 1961—, head div. art, music, speech and drama, 1965—. One-man shows, including Dallas, Oklahoma City, Austin, Tex.; exhibited in group shows, 1951—, including Ball State Tchrs. Coll., Muncie, Ind., 1959, U. Ill., 1961, Cranbrook Acad. Art, Mich., 1969; important works include Pieta, Ch. in Munich, 1952, Stas. of Cross, Jesuit High Sch., Dallas, 1963, library sculpture The Graduate, Tex. A. and M. U., 1968, sanctuary embellishment First Meth. Ch., Alexandria, La. Mem. Council for German Day in Tex., 1963; mem. condrs. com. Dallas Symphony, 1963; 2d v.p. Dallas Goethe Center. Served with German Army, 1939-45. Mem. Am. Soc. Ch. Architecture, Nat. Art Edn. Assn., Ch. Archtl. Guild, Dallas Fine Arts Assn., Dallas Soc. Contemporary Arts (founder, dir., trustee 1955-61), Guild Religious Architecture. Author: Twenty Years of My Sculpture, 1969, Research on Bronze Casting. Home and studio: 1125 N Canterbury Ct Dallas TX 75208

BARUCH, EDUARD, mgmt. cons. exec.; b. Bklyn., Dec. 19, 1907; s. Emile and Grace (Willis) B.; student Rhenania Coll. (Switzerland), 1924-26; A.B., Columbia, 1930, postgrad. Law Sch., 1933; m. Dorothy Hurd, Sept. 8, 1934; 1 son, Hurd. Trust adminstr. spl. loan div. Irving Trust Co., N.Y.C., 1933-39; sales exec. Bankers Life Co., Des Moines 1939-42; v.p. charge sales James H. Rhodes & Co., 1942-47; nat. sales mgr. vending div. Pepsi Cola Co., 1947-49; v.p. Heli-Coil Corp., Danbury, Conn., 1949-55, exec. v.p., 1955-56, pres., 1956-70; corp. cons., 1970—; dir., chmn. exec. com. John L. Schwab Assos., Fairfield, Conn.; dir. Fairfield Med. & Surg. Co., Southport, Conn., Timpte, Inc., Denver, Union Trust Co., Stamford, Conn., Savs. Bank of Danbury, Risdon Mfg. Co., Naugatuck, Conn. Chmn. bd. dirs. Conn. council New Eng. Council; dir., mem. bd. mgrs. Danbury Hosp. Mem. Soc. Automotive Engrs., Sales Execs., Psi Upsilon, Phi Delta Phi. Conglist. Mason (K.T., Shriner, Jester). Clubs: Union League (Chgo.); Shadow Mountain (Palm Springs, Cal.); Columbia University, Wings (N.Y.C.); Ridgewood Country (Danbury); Coral Ridge Yacht, Lago Mar Beach and Tennis (Ft. Lauderdale, Fla.). Home: Candlewood Point New Milford CT 06776 also Harbor Beach Fort Lauderdale FL 33316 Office: City Trust Bldg Danbury CT 06810

BARUCHELLO, GIANFRANCE, painter; b. Livorno, Italy, 1924. Collaborated with Alberto Grifi on film La Verifica Incerta, 1965, with Edoardo Sanguineti on visual continuum titled Traumdeutung Cancellato, 1967; writer TV scripts; one man shows Galleria La Tartaruga, Rome, 1963, Cordier & Ekstrom, N.Y., 1964, 66, Galleria Schwarz, Milan, 1965, 66, Galleria Il Punto; group shows including Galerie de Cercle, Paris, 1962, Sidney Janis Gallery, N.Y.C., 1962, Mus. Modern Art, N.Y.C., 1965, Guggenheim Mus., N.Y.C., 1966, Galleria Schwarz, Milan, 1966, 67, Civico Padiglinoe d'Arte Contemporanea, Milan, 1966, Salon Valentino, Turin, 1966, Il Biennale dell'Arte Giovanne, Museo Civico, Bologna, 1967, Pitts. Internat., Carnegie Inst., 1967, Chgo. Mus. Contemporary Art, 1967. Home: Rome Italy

BARVOETS, ERNEST FRANCIS, printing co. exec.; b. Albany, N.Y., July 6, 1903; s. Ernest Alexander and Edna (Dennison) B.; B.S., Dartmouth, 1922; grad. printing engring., Carnegie Inst. Tech., 1924; m. Patricia Brooks, Dec. 1, 1924; children—Brooks, Ernest Francis, Donald. With Williams Press, Inc., Albany, 1924—, pres., 1939—; dir. Nat. Comml. Bank, Albany. Bd. dirs. Printing Industry Assn.; United Typographers Am. Clubs: Rotary, Albany Country, Schuyler Meadows, Fort Orange, Wolfert Roost (Albany); New York Athletic, Union League, Dartmouth (N.Y.C.). Home: Spring St Loudonville NY 12211 Office: Williams Press Inc 99 N Broadway Albany NY 12207

BARWELL, BASIL B., tobacco co. exec.; b. Eng., 1915; student Harvard Bus. Sch. Advanced Mgmt. Program; married. With Gen. Cigar Co., Inc., N.Y.C., 1932—, sr. v.p. tobacco div., 1961—, also dir. Home: 197 Brewster Rd Scarsdale NY 10583 Office: 605 3d Av New York City NY 10016*

BARWICK, EUGENE THOMAS, mfg. exec.; b. Lake City, Fla., Dec. 23, 1913; s. T. J. and Etta (Revels) B.; B.S., U. N.C., 1936; m. Ann McDougall, Aug. 19, 1944; children—Nancy Jean, Avis Ann, Eugene T., Beverly Allison. Buyer floor covering Sears, Roebuck & Co., 1936-48; founder, now pres., chmn. bd., chief exec. officer E. T. Barwick Mills, 1949—; chmn. Monarch Rug Mills, Inc., Morrill Mfg. Co., 1954—, E. T. Barwick Mills, Ltd., Bolton, Eng.; dir. Walter E. Heller & Co. Presbyn. Clubs: Cat Cay (Bahamas); Peachtree Golf, Capital City, Cherokee Town and Country (Atlanta); Detroit Yacht; Lyford Cay, Coral Harbor Yacht, Porcupine (Nassau, Bahamas). Home: 50 Valley Road Atlanta GA 30305 Office: E T Barwick Industries Inc 5025 New Peachtree Rd Chamblee GA 30341

BARZILAY, ISAAC, educator; b. Vilkovishky, Lithuania, Mar. 15, 1915; s. Simon Asher Eisenstein and Taube (Rosenthal) B.; grad. Hebrew Gymnasium Tarbut, Biaystock, Poland, 1934; M.A., Hebrew U., Jerusalem, 1939; Ph.D., Columbia, 1955; m. Helly Frost, Sept. 20, 1949; children—Joshua, Sharona. Came to U.S., 1946, naturalized, 1951. Instr. Herzliyah Hebrew Tchrs. Inst., N.Y.C., 1946-57; asst. prof. Wayne State U., 1958-60; asso. prof. Columbia, 1960—, prof. Hebrew lang. and lit., 1966—; vis. prof. history Jewish Theol. Sem., N.Y.C., 1967—. Bd. dirs. Matz Found., Friends Hebrew U., Hebrew Pen Club Am. Mem. Am. Acad. Jewish Research. Author: Between Reason and Faith, 2d edit., 1969; Shlomo Yehudah Rapoport (Shir) and His Contemporaries, 1969; also articles. Home: 258 Riverside Dr New York City NY 10025

BARZIN, LEON EUGENE, condr.; b. Brussels, Belgium, Nov. 27, 1900; s. Leon and Marie (Debacher) B.; came to U.S., 1902, naturalized, 1924; father was first music teacher; studied under Pierre Henotte, Edoward Deru, Alfred Meergerlin, Eugene Isaye; composition under Lienthal; m. Marie Antoinette Vandeputte, Dec. 15, 1928; children—Richard Lambert, Lora Gene; m. 2d, Janet Stanley (div. Aug. 1948); m. 3d, Mina Quevli, 1949; 1 son, Leon; m. 4th, Eleanore Close, Sept. 2, 1954. Violinist with Astor Hotel Salon orch., 1917-18; leader Alps Restaurant orch., N.Y., 1919-20; solo violist N.Y. Philharmonic Orch. under Mengelberg, Furtwangler, Toscanini, 1919-30; an organizer Nat. Orchestral Assn., 1930, mus. dir., 1930-58; orch. dir. Interstate Broadcasting Co., WQXR-WQXQ, N.Y.C., 1944-48; guest condr. Nat. Orch., Washington, Lamoureux, Cologne orchs., Paris, N.Y. Philharmonic, Mpls. Symphony, St. Louis Symphony, Buffalo Philharmonic Orchs.; mus. dir. Ballet Soc. and N.Y.C. Ballet, 1948-58; 1st condr. Assn. des Concerts Pasdeloup, Paris, France, also prof. Scola Cantorium in Paris, France, 1958- 60; prof. Académie Marguerite Long, 1961—; mus. dir. L'Orchestra Philharmonique de Paris, 1960—; mus. cons. New Eng. Conservatory, Boston, 1968, head orchestral dept., 1969-70; orchestral dir., tchr. condrs.' program Tanglewood, summer 1969; dir. Nat. Orchestral Assn., 1970-71; mus. cons. sta. WQXR. Recipient Alice Ditson award for outstanding efforts in presenting Am. music and ednl. approach throughout country, 1946; decorated Gold medal, Lebanon, 1956, Legion Honor, France, 1960. Mem. Nat. Assn. Am. Composers and Conductors. Club: Lotos (bd. govs). Address: 53 Rue de Monceau Paris VIII France

BARZINI, LUIGI, author, journalist; b. Milan, Italy, Dec., 21, 1908 s. Luigi and Mantica (Pesavento) B.; B. Lit., Columbia, 1930; m. Giannalisa Gianzana, Apr. 12, 1940; m. 2d, Paola Gadola, Sept. 12, 1949; children—Giovanna Ludovica, Benedetta, Luigi, Andrea, Francesca. Travelling corr. for Corriere della Sera, Milan, 1931-40; editor Il Globo, Rome, 1944-47; contbr. Italian and fgn. magazines, 1954- 65; mem. Italian Parliament for Liberal Party from Milan-Pavia 1958—. Author: Americans are Alone in the World, 1953; Mosca Mosca, 1961; L'Europa Domani Mattina, 1964; The Italians, 1964; (play) I Disarmati, 1957. Address: 1055 Via Cassia Rome 00189 Italy

BARZUN, JACQUES, educator; b. Creteil, France, Nov. 30, 1907; s. Henri Martin and Anna Rosa B.; came to U.S., 1920, naturalized, 1933; ed. Lycee Janson de Sailly, Paris; A.B., Columbia, 1927, M.A., 1928, Ph.D., 1932; m. Mariana Lowell, Aug. 1936; children—James Lowell, Roger Martin, Isabel. Lectr. history Columbia, 1927, instr., 1929, asst. prof., 1938, asso. prof., 1942, prof., 1945, dean grad. faculties, 1955-58, dean faculties and provost, 1958-67, Univ. prof., 1967—, also spl. adviser on arts. Dir. Crowell-Collier, Inc. Trustee N.Y. Soc. Library; bd. dirs. Council for Basic Edn. Little Orch. Soc., Inc. Decorated Legion of Honor. Extraordinary fellow Churchill Coll., U. Cambridge (Eng.). Fellow Royal Soc. Arts; mem. Am. Hist. Assn., Mass. Hist. Soc. (corr.), Council Fgn. Relations, Am. Acad. Arts and Letters, Inst. Arts and Letters, Friends Columbia Libraries, Phi Beta Kappa. Clubs: Authors, Athenaeum (London, Eng.); Century (N.Y.C.). Author: Teacher in America, 1945; Berlioz and the Romantic Century, 3d edit., 1969; Pleasures of Music, 1951; God's Country and Mine, 1954; Music in American Life, 1956; The Energies of Art, 1956; The Modern Researcher, 2d edit., 1970; The House of Intellect, 1959; Classic, Romantic and Modern, 1961; Science: The Glorious Entertainment, 1964; The American University, 1968; A Catalogue of Crime, 1971. Editorial bd. The American Scholar. Editor: Selected Letters of Lord Bryon, 1953; Nouvelles Lettres de Berlioz, 1954; The Selected Writings of John Jay Chapman, 1957; Follett's Modern American Usage, 1966. Address: Columbia U New York City NY 10027

BASALDELLA, AFRO, artist; b. Udine, Italy, Mar. 14, 1912; s. Leo and Virginia Basaldella; Diploma Belle Arti, Lyceum of Venice; student art, Rome and Florence. Artist from early years, working and receiving tng. with family's decorating firm, later became painter (first of traditional school, now abstract); executed mural, Rodi, Greece, 1937, had first one-man show, Milan, Italy, 1932; one-man show, Rome, 1936; first one-man show in U.S., Viviano Gallery, N.Y.C., 1950; in group shows Mus. Modern Art (N.Y.C.), City Art Mus. (St. Louis), 1955; represented in collections numerous museums in U.S. and abroad, including Mus. Modern Art, City Art Mus. St. Louis, Solomon R. Guggenheim Mus. (N.Y.C.), Cin. Art Mus.; one of artists of internat. fame commd. to execute murals (or sculptures) for UNESCO hdqrs., Paris, 1958; prof. painting Florence Acad. Fine Arts. Mem. jury of awards Pitts. Internat. Exhbn. of Contemporary Italian painters Venice Biennale, 1956. Recipient 2d prize Pitts. Internat. Exhbn. Contemporary Painting, 1959. Served with Italian Resistance, World War II. Home: Via Nicolo Tartaglia 3 Rome Italy also Viale Parioli 76 Rome Italy Office: care Catherine Viviano Gallery 42 E 57th St New York City NY 10022

BASCHET, BERNARD, sculptor; b. Paris, 1917; student engring., Ecole Centrale. Formerly chief musical research French Broadcasting System; first to use wave potential of metal and glass for acoustical purposes; built three dozen prototypes of unique sculptured musical instruments; exptl. orch. formed with Jacques Lasry, 1955; applications mainly to musical sculpture. Address: care Arts Club 109 E Ontario St Chicago IL 60611*

BASCHET, FRANCOIS, sculptor; b. Paris, 1920; pupil of Emmanuel Auricoste and Hubert Yencesse. Applications mainly to musical sculpture. Address: care Arts Club 109 E Ontario St Chicago IL 60611*

BASCOM, DAVID F., newspaper exec.; b. Oil City, Pa., Jan. 29, 1912; s. Frank and Mabel (Rathbun) B.; student Acad. Advt. Art, San Francisco, 1931-32; m. Mary C. Smith, Oct. 23, 1937; 1 son, Dickens. With circulation dept. Curtis Publs., San Francisco, 1932-34, San Francisco Chronicle, 1934-36, McCloud Lumber Co., 1936: package designer, later advt. mgr. Awful Fresh MacFarlane Candy Co., Oakland, Cal., MacFarlane Candy Co., Oakland, Cal., 1937-42; copywriter, later copy chief Garfield & Guild, San Francisco, 1942-49; partner Guild, Bascom & Bonfigli, San Francisco, 1949-65; sr. v.p. West Coast operations Dancer-Fitzgerald-Sample, Inc. (merger with Guild, Bascom & Bonfigli 1965), 1965-68; pres. Wretched Mess News, Inc., Oakland, Cal. and West Yellowstone, Mont., 1968—. Recipient award of merit Am. Graphic Arts Soc., 1950, Sylvania TV award, 1954, Art Directors Club medal, 1955, citation Assn. Advt. Men and Women N.Y.C., 1947, Ryder award, 1957. Home: 8 Aztec Way Oakland CA 94611 Office: Box 13268 Oakland CA 94611

BASCOM, NATHAN TUFTS, banker; b. Lancaster, Mass., Nov. 1, 1906; s. Frank Preston and Lucy (Tufts) B.; B.S. with honors, Norwich U., 1927; M.B.A., Harvard, 1929; m. Ellen Seguine, Sept. 10, 1932 (dec.); children—Faith (Mrs. James T. Fifer), Preston Tufts; m. 2d, Priscilla Adams, Sept. 17, 1966. With Irving Trust Co., N.Y.C., 1929-34, State Mut. Life Assurance Co., Worcester, Mass., 1934-51; pres. Worcester Mechanics Savs. Bank, 1951-70; chmn. bd. dirs., chief exec. officer Peoples Mechanics Savs. Bank, Worcester, 1970—; dir. Mechanics Nat. Bank, Worcester Gas Light Co., Mechanics Bancorp.; v.p., dir. Savs. Bank Investment Fund; trustee Tri-South Mortgage Investors. Pres. Worcester Bus. Devel. Corp., 1970—. Mem. Nat. Assn. Mut. Savs. Banks (past dir., exec. com.), Mortgage Bankers Assn. Am. (gov.), Savs. Banks Assn. Mass. (past pres.), Worcester C. of C. (exec. com.). Home: 136 Flagg St Worcester MA 01609 Office: 450 Main St Worcester MA 01608

BASCOM, WILLIAM RICHARDSON, lawyer; b. St. Louis, Sept. 12, 1910; s. Calvin P. and Virginia (Clarke) B.; B.A., Yale, 1932; LL.B., Harvard, 1935; m. Jean A. Hall, Sept. 7, 1935; children—C. Perry, William A., Harriet E. A., Thomas O. Admitted to Mass. bar. 1935, and practiced in Boston until 1938; admitted to Mo. bar, 1938; partner firm Nagel, Kirby, Orrick & Shepley, and successor firms, St. Louis, 1942-54, Bryan, Cave, McPheerers & Roberts, St. Louis, 1954-57; v.p. Granite City Steel Co. (Ill.), 1957-63; partner Bryan, Cave, McPheeter & McRoberts, St. Louis, 1963—. Member St. Louis Social Planning Council, 1954-55; mem. budget com. St. Louis Community Chest, 1949-52. Mayor City of Ladue (Mo.), 1957-59; chancellor Episcopal Diocese of Mo. Trustee John Burroughs Sch., St. Louis County, 1948- 55; pres. Grace Hill House, St. Louis, 1946, 63-65. Mem. Am. Law Inst., Am., St. Louis bar assns. Clubs: St. Louis, Yale (past pres.), Noonday, St. Louis Country (St. Louis); Yale (N.Y.C.). Home: 9725 Litzinger Rd St Louis MO 63124 Office: 314 N Broadway St Louis MO 63102

BASCOM, WILLIAM RUSSEL, anthropologist; b. Princeton, Ill., May 23, 1912; s. George Rockwell and Litta Celia (Banschbach) B.; B.A., U. Wis., 1933, M.A., 1936; Ph.D., Northwestern U., 1939; m. Berta Maria Montero-Sanchez. Mem. U. Chgo. archeol. field party, 1934; fellow Santa Fe Lab. Anthropology, 1935; asst. U. Wis., 1935-36; mem. U. Wis.-Milw. Pub. Museum Archeol. Party, 1936; asst. Northwestern U., 1938-39, instr. 1939-42, asst. asso., 1949-54, prof., 1954-57, acting chmn. dept. anthropology, 1942, 53, chmn. 1956-57; acting dir. program Afican studies, 1953,57; spl. asst. OSS, 1942; sr. analyst Bd. Econ. Warfare, 1942-43; asst. spl. rep. Brit. West Africa, 1943-44; spl. rep. Brit. West Africa, spl. asst. Am. consul, spl. agt. U.S.C.C., 1944-46; chief economist U.S.C.C., 1946; Fulbright research scholar, 1950-51; prof. U. Cal. at Berkeley, summer 1955, now prof. dept. anthropology, dir. Lowie Mus. Anthropology. Bd. dirs. Cal. League Am. Indians, 1964-65, Am. Indian Films, 1965-67, Oakland Mus. Assn., 1964-66, 67—. NSF senior fellow, Cambridge, Eng., 1958; Ethnol. field research, Kiowa, Okla., 1935, Yoruba, Nigeria, 1937-38, 1950-51, 60, 65, Gullah, Ga. and S.C., 1939, Caroline Islands, 1946; Lucumi (Yoruba) Cuba on grant from Wenner-Gren Found., 1948. Fellow Am. Folklore Soc. (v.p. 1951-52, pres. 1952-54; pres. fellows of soc. 1969-70), Am. Anthrop. Assn. (exec. bd. 1961-64), Royal Anthrop. Inst., Royal African Soc., Nigerian Field Soc.; mem. Central States Anthrop. Soc. (v.p. 1947-50, pres. 1950-51), Am. Assn. Museums (council 1962-67), Soc. Internat. Ethnologie et Folklore, Internat. Council Museums, Am. Ethnol. Soc., Internat. African Inst., Cal. Folklore Soc. (v.p. 1962-68), A.A.A.S., Am. Assn. U. Profs., Phi Beta Kappa, Sigma Xi, Phi Eta Sigma, Alpha Kappa Delta. Clubs: Faculty, Cal. Sailing (Berkeley). Author: Continuity and Change in African Cultures, 1959; Ponape: A Pacific Economy in Transition, 1965; African Arts, 1967; Ifa Divination, 1969; The Yoruba of Southwestern Nigeria, 1969. Home: 624 Beloit Av Berkeley CA 94708

BASEHART, RICHARD, actor; b. Zanesville, O.; s. Harry T. and Mae (Wetherald) B.; student pub. schs. Columbus and Zanesville. O.; m. Stephanie Klein, Jan. 14, 1940 (dec.); m. 2d, Valentia Cortesa, Mar. 24, 1951; 1 son, John. Appeared Hedgerow Theatre. Moylan. Pa., 1938-42, on Broadway in Counterattack, 1943, Othello, 1944, Take It as It Comes, 1944, The Hasty Heart (N.Y. Drama Critics award), 1945, The Survivors, 1948; The Day the Money Stopped; motion pictures include: He Walked by Night; The House on Telegraph Hill, 1950; Decision before Dawn, 1950; Fixed Bayonets 1951; Portrait in Black, 1960, The Good Die Young, Il Dibone, The Brothers Karamozov, Moby Dick, Time Limit; TV show Voyage to the Bottom of the Sea, 1964- 68; (movies) The Satan Bug, Four Days in November, La Strada, Five Branded Women. Named best actor in Fourteen Hours, Nat. Bd. Review, 1951.

BASERGA, RENATO LUIGI, educator, scientist; b. Meda, Italy, Apr. 11, 1925; s. Alessandro and Giuseppina (Annoni) B.; M.D., U. Milan, 1949; m. Jane Ellen Conrad, Dec. 27, 1953; children—Susan Jane, Janice Renee. Came to U.S., 1952, naturalized, 1958. Intern Columbus Hosp., Chgo., 1952-53, Inst. Pathol. Anatomy, U. Milan, 1949-51; resident pathology St. Luke's Hosp., Chgo., 1955-58; asso. oncology Chgo. Med. Sch., 1953-54; instr. to asso. prof. pathology Northwestern U., 1958-65; research prof. Temple U., 1965-67, prof., chmn. dept. pathology, 1968—; sr. investigator Fels Research Inst. to Temple U., 1965—. Mem. Damon Runyon Sci. Adv. Com., 1969, pathology B study sect. Nat. Insts. Health, 1966-70. Served with Italian Army, 1943-45. Mem. Am. Assn. Cancer Research, A.A.A.S., Am. Assn. Pathologists and Bacteriologists, Am. Soc. Exptl. Pathology, Radiation Research Soc., Am. Soc. Cell Biology, Am. Soc. Biol. Chemists. Author: Autoradiography: Techniques and Applications (with D. Malarmd), 1969. Editor: Biochemistry of Cell Division, 1969; The Cell Cycle and Cancer (Marcel Dekker), 1971; asso. editor of Cancer Research; editorial bd. of Lab. Investigation, Cell and Tissue Kinetics, Exptl. and Molecular Pathology. Contbr. articles profl. jours. Home: 562 Manor Rd Wynnewood PA 19096 Office: 3420 N Broad St Philadelphia PA 19140

BASH, PHILIP EDWIN, advt. exec.; b. Huntington, Ind., Aug. 13, 1921; s. Philip Purviance and Nell (Johnson) B.; B.A., DePauw U., 1943; m. Flora Wilev Oberg, Mar. 11, 1944; children—Barbara, Kingsley, Roger, Amy. Account exec. Leo Burnett Co., Inc., Chgo., 1947-54; account supr., v.p., sr. v.p. marketing services Clinton E. Frank Inc., Chgo., 1954-64, pres., 1964—, also dir.; dir. Market Measurements, Inc. Vice chmn. bd. Barrington Consol. High Sch. Bd., 1957-65. Trustee Shimer Coll. Served to lt. (j.g.) USNR, 1943-46; PTO. Mem. Am. Assn. Advt. Agys. (bd. govs. Chgo. council), Am. Marketing Assn., Sigma Chi. Methodist (trustee). Clubs: University, Economics (Chgo.); Barrington Hills Country. Home: Oakdene Rd Barrington IL 60010 Office: 120 S Riverside Plaza Chicago IL 60606

BASHEV, IVAN HRISTOV, Bulgarian diplomat; b. 1916. Mem. Workers Youth Union, 1934—, also Gen. Union Students Bulgaria; mem. staff newspaper Akademik; editor Narodna Mladej (People's Youth) newspaper, 1944-46-51; mem. Bulgarian Communist Party, 1946—, now mem. central com; mem. exec. com., sec. propaganda work World Fedn. Democratic Youth, Paris, France, 1948-51; sec. central com. Dimitrov Union of People's Youth, 1951; chief bd. Ministry Edn. and Culture, 1954-56; dep. minister edn. and culture, 1956; dep. minister fgn. affairs, 1962, also mem. Parliament. Office: Minister Fgn Affairs Sofia Bulgaria

BASHKIN, STANLEY, educator, physicist; b. Bklyn., June 20, 1923; s. Max and Bessie (Kovalik) B.; B.A. cum laude, Bklyn. Coll., 1944; Ph.D., U. Wis., 1950; m. Margaret Mary Turnbull, Aug. 22, 1957; children—James K., Margaret J., John S. Faculty, State U. Ia., 1953-62; asst. prof. La. State U., 1950-53; prof. physics U. Ariz., Tucson, 1962—, also dir. Van de Graaf Lab.; research fellow Cal. Inst. Tech., 1959, Australian Nat. U.; cons. in optics. Fulbright Research scholar Australian Nat. U., 1959-60. Mem. Am. Phys. Soc., Am. Astron. Soc., A.A.A.S., Royal Soc. Arts (London, Eng.); Royal Soc. (Gotenberg, Sweden). Contbg. author: Stars and Stellar Systems. Contbr. articles tech. jours. Invented method of studying atomic systems using nuclear apparatus. Home: 4152 E 6th St Tucson AZ 85711

BASHKOW, THEODORE ROBERT, engring. educator; b. St. Louis, Nov. 16, 1921; s. Maurice Louis and Caroline (Davidson) B.; B.S., Washington U., St. Louis, 1943; M.S., Stanford, 1947, Ph.D., 1950; m. Delphina Brownlee, Sept. 12, 1960; 1 stepdau., Lynn Michele. Mem. tech. staff David Sarnoff Research Labs., RCA, 1950-52, Bell Telephone Labs., 1952-58; mem. faculty Columbia, 1958- -, prof. elec. engring., 1967—, chmn. dept., 1968-71, mgr. Sch. Engring. Computing Center, 1961-64; cons. to industry, 1959—. Dir. MSI Inc., Woodside, N.Y., 1961—. Chmn. tech. program 1968 Spring Joint Computer Conf.; chmn. sci. sec. Internat. Fedn. Information Processing Congress, 1965. Served to 1st lt. USAAF, 1943-45. Mem. Assn. Computing Machinery, I.E.E.E., Profl. Group Circuit Theory and Electronic Computers. Author articles, chpts. in books. Home: Jay St Katonah NY 10536 Office: SW Mudd Bldg Columbia U New York City NY 10027

BASIE, WILLIAM COUNT, composer, band leader; b. Red Bank, N.J., Aug. 21, 1904; s. Harvey Lee and Lillian (Child) B.; student pub. schs., Red Bank; m. Catherine Morgan, July 12, 1942; 1 dau., Diane. Musician, theatres, hotels, night clubs; pianist Benny Moten Band, Kansas City, 1929-36, band leader, 1936- -; bookings Music Corp. Am., managed by Maceo Birch, 1937-40, bookings William Morris Agy., mgr. Milt Ebbins, 1941-46, bookings Willard Alexander, mgr. Catherine Basie, 1946—; Broadway debut Roseland Ballroom, 1938; jazz concert Carnegie Hall, 1939; participated in jam session Apollo Theatre, N.Y.C., 1940; motion picture debut Reveille with Beverly, 1942, later roles in Stage Door Canteen, Mister Big, Crazy House, 1943; theatre tours various cities U.S., guest star appearances radio show, TV spls.; toured with Frank Sinatra, 1965, with Tony Bennett in Europe; performed at Kennedy Inaugural Ball; command performance Queen of Eng. Named most popular band Musicians Am., 1933; named Top Band, Pitts. Courier ann. popularity poll, 1941; recipient All- Am. Band award Esquire, 1945, Jazz Merit award The Lamplighter, 1945, Down Beat internat. critics' poll winner, 1952-56, numerous other awards, U.S. and Europe. Mem. A.S.C.A.P., Dance Orch. Leaders Assn. (exec. bd. dirs.), N.A.A.C.P. Home: 174-27 Adelaide Lane St Albans NY 11412

BASILE, C.M., mfg. co. exec.; b. Toluca, Ill., Aug. 9, 1910; s. Mariano and Domenica (Germano) B.; m. Genevieve Bucci, Sept. 3, 1931; children—Marian (Mrs. Glenn W. Stello), Christine (Mrs. Richard Schmity). With Sears, Roebuck & Co., 1939-42; with Link-Belt Co., 1960—, exec. v.p., 1959, pres. 1959—, also dir.; pres. dir. Link-Belt Speeder (Can.) Ltd., Link-Belt S.p.A., Milan, Italy; now sr. v.p. FMC Corp.; dir. Mchts. Nat. Bank Cedar Rapids. Mem. Cedar Rapids C. of C. Rep. Roman Catholic. Elk. Office: FMC Corp 1700 Prudential Plaza Chicago IL 60611

BASILE, WILLIAM BASIL, mfg. exec.; b. Chicago, Mar. 17, 1911; s. Ralph and Carmella (D'Urso) B.; Ph.B., U. Chgo., 1931, J.D., 1933; research asso. Northwestern U. Law Sch., 1933-34; m. Ruth Rutledge, July 25, 1935; children—Bette Claire, William Basil, Ralph Rutledge. Admitted to Ill. bar, 1933; practice in Chgo., 1934-43; v.p., dir. indsl. relations Richardson Co., 1943-52, dir., 1944—, exec. v.p., 1952-53, pres., 1953—; atty. price adjustment bd. A.A.F., 1943. Mem. Am., Ill. bar assns., Chgo. Mus. Natural History, Art Inst. Chgo., Phi Alpha Delta, Alpha Sigma Phi. Clubs: Skokie Country (Glencoe); Columbia (Indpls.); University, Economic (Chgo.). Home: 501 Monroe Av Glencoe IL 60022 Office: Richardson Co Melrose Park IL 60161

BASILIUS, HAROLD A., ret. educator; b. Toledo, Jan. 15, 1905; s. William and Louise (Gerson) B.; student Concordia Coll., Ft. Wayne, Ind., 1919-25, B.D., Concordia Theol. Sem. St. Louis, 1928; A.M., Ohio State U., 1929, Ph.D., 1935; m. Imogene Ferris, Nov. 27, 1929. Instr. German, Capital U., Columbus, O., 1929- 31; univ. fellow Ohio State U., 1930-31; instr. German, U. Chgo., 1931-36, adviser in coll., 1933-36; prof., chmn. dept. German, Wayne U., Detroit, 1936-50; dir. Wayne State U. Press, 1956-70, Franklin Meml. chair in human relations, 1953-54. Mem. Am. Fedn. Tchrs., Modern Lang. Assn. Am., Nat. Fedn. Modern Lang. Tchrs. Author: A Workbook for Reading German, 1939, rev. edit., 1942; Contemporary Problems in Religion, 1956; College Graduates in Industry, 1957. Home: Oliver Lake A-27 LaGrange IN 46761

BASKA, JOHN WILSON, air force officer; b. Kansas City, Kan., Jan. 28, 1917; s. John J. and Stella M. (Wilson) B.; B.S. in Engring., Kan. State Coll., 1939; grad. Nat. War Coll., 1960; J.D., George Washington U., 1955; grad. USAF Spl. Investigations Sch., 1966; m. Edna Mildred Benke, Aug. 23, 1944; children—Karen Ann (Mrs. Robert E. McMahon), John Kevin and Peter Michael (twins), Patrick Martin (dec.), David Francis, Douglas Thomas. Commd. 2d lt. USAAF, 1942, advanced through grades to brig. gen., 1968; pilot for RAF, 1943, in CBI, 1943-44; air attache, Tehran, Iran, 1957-59; with operations div. Joint Chiefs Staff, Washington, 1960-62; exec. officer Directorate of Operations. Hdqrs. USAF, 1962-64; asst. chief staff Hdqrs. Pacific Hdqrs. USAF, 1962-64; dep. dir. Directorate Spl. Investigations, Hdqrs. USAF, 1966-68; dir. insp., dep. insp. gen. for insp. and safety Hdqrs. USAF, Norton AFB, Cal., 1968—. Admitted to D.C. bar, 1956—. Decorated Legion of Merit with oak leaf cluster, numerous units and area ribbons. Mem. Air Force Assn., Phi Delta Phi, Sigma Alpha Epsilon. Home: Quarters 79 G St Norton AFB CA 92409 Office: 1002d Insp Gen Group Norton AFB CA 92409

BASKERVILLE, CHARLES, artist; b. Raleigh, N.C., Apr. 16, 1896; s. Charles and Mary Boylan (Snow) B.; student Tome Sch., 1912-15; student Cornell U., Coll. of Architecture (class of 1919), Art Student League, Acad. Julien (Paris). Illus. mags. and advt., 1921-30; mural and screen specialist, 1930-34; became portrait painter, 1934, now doing murals and portraits; murals in many Am. homes and in lounge of S.S. Am., also Grace Line S.S. Santa Magdalena, 1963. Exhibited 60 portraits of A.A.F. heroes at Nat. Gallery of Art, Wash., D.C., Oct. 1944; represented portraits at Nat. Fine Arts Collection, Nat. Portrait Collection, U. Hosp., Phila., Nat. Coll. Surgeons, Chgo., Palm Springs Desert Mus., Nat. Mus. Racing. Served as portraits at Nat. Fine Arts Collection, Nat. Portrait Collection, U. Hosp., Phila., Nat. Coll. Surgeons, Chgo., Palm Springs Desert Mus., Nat. Mus. Racing. Served as 1st lt. 166th Inf., 42d Div., W.W. I Decorated with Silver Star, Order of the Purple Heart with Oak Leaf Cluster, Victory Medal with four bronze battle clasps, and Legion of Merit, 1945. Commd. capt. Air Corps U.S. Army, Aug. 1942; promoted to maj., May 1, 1943, lt. col. June 18, 1945—; assigned as ofcl. artist to paint Air Corps heroes and generals; selected artists and assigned subjects for Chrysler Corp. War Art Project; first Western artist to visit Nepal. Mem. Am. Artists Profl. League, Nat. Soc. of Mural Painters (sec. 1953-55, v.p. 1956, pres. 1957, 58, 59), Delta Kappa Epsilon. Episcopalian. Address: 130 W 57th St New York City NY 10019 ☆

BASKERVILLE, JACK H., banker; b. Virginia, 1907; ed. U. Richmond, 1928; m. Josephine A.; children—Susan B., George T., III. Exec. v.p., sr. trust officer First & Merchants Nat. Bank, Richmond; dir. Richmond Block, Inc., Arvonia Buckingham Slate Co. Trustee Crippled Children's Hosp.; bd. dirs. Richmond Area Tb Assn. Clubs:

Kiwanis (dir.), Country of Va., Downtown of Richmond (pres.). Home: 4308 Cutshaw Av Richmond VA 23230 Office: 827 E Main St Richmond VA 23219

BASKETT, THOMAS SEBREE, biologist; b. Liberty, Mo., Jan. 23, 1916; s. William Denny and Maybelle (Grigsby) B.; A.B., Central Meth. Coll. (Mo.), 1937; M.S., U. Okla., 1939; Ph.D., Ia. State U., 1942; m. Marjorie Kenison, Feb. 14, 1967; children—Thomas Sebree, Richard K., Jann D. Extension specialist in wildlife conservation Ia. State U., Ames, 1941-42, asst. prof. zoology, 1946-47; asst. prof. wildlife mgmt. U. Conn., Storrs, 1947-48; biologist U.S. Bur. Sport Fish and Wildlife, leader Mo. Coop. Wildlife Research Unit, asst. prof., asso. prof., prof. zoology U. Mo., Columbia, 1948-68; chief div. wildlife research Bur. Sport Fish and Wildlife, U.S. Dept. Interior, Washington, 1968—. Served from ensign to lt., USNR, 1942-46; PTO. Mem. Am. Ornithologists Union, Am. Soc. Ichthyologists and Herpetologists, Wildlife Soc. (pres.), Council Biology Editors. Editor: Jour. Wildlife Mgmt., 1966-68. Contbr. articles profl. jours. Home: 14001 Drake Dr Rockville MD 20853 Office: Div Wildlife Research Bur Sport Fish and Wildlife Dept of Interior Washington DC 20240

BASKIN, LEONARD, sculptor, graphic artist, educator; b. New Brunswick, N.J., Aug. 15, 1922; s. Samuel and May (Guss) B.; student Yale Sch. Art, 1941-43; A.B., New Sch., N.Y.C., 1949, D.F.A., 1966; L.H.D., Clark U., 1966; D.F.A., U. Mass., 1968; student Paris and Florence; m. Estherhane, Nov. 26, 1946; 1 son, Tobias Isaac; m. 2d, Lisa Unger, Oct. 1957; one son, Hosea Thomas. One man shows in N.Y.C., 1954, 56, 57, 60- 62, Boston, 1952, 55, 59, also London, Rotterdam, Paris; rep. perm. colls. Met. Mus. Art, Mus. Modern Art, Library of Congress, Nat. Gallery Art, Art Inst. Chgo., museums Phila., Boston and Worchester, Fogg Mus. at Harvard, others; prof. graphics Smith Coll., 1953—. Tiffany fellow, 1947; Guggenheim fellow 1953; grantee Nat. Inst. Arts and Letters, 1961; recipient 1st prize engraving Sao Paulo Biennial, 1962; medal Am. Inst. Graphic Arts, 1965. Served with USNR, 1943-46. Mem. Nat. Inst. Arts and Letters (medal of Merit for Graphic Arts 1969), William Morris Soc., Am. Inst. Graphic Artists. Club: Grolier (N.Y.C.). Address: Fort Hill Northampton MA 01060

BASKIN, ROBERT EDWARD, newspaperman; b. Seymour, Tex., Sept. 30, 1917; s. Robert Edward and Alma Elizabeth (Hood) B.; B. J., U. Tex., 1938; m. Caludia Jo Clark, Dec. 14, 1946; children—Courtenay Elizabeth, Martha Melinda, Mary Caroline. Reporter, editor Wichita Falls (Tex.) Record News, 1938-41; news editor Ft. Worth Star-Telegram, 1946-47; mem. staff Dallas Morning News, 1947—, chief news Washington bur., 1960—. Served to lt. col., inf., AUS, 1941-46; ETO; maj. Tex. N.G., 1953-56. Recipient Delta Chi award, Dallas Press Club award. Mem. Sigma Delta Chi. Episcopalian. Clubs: International National Press (Washington); Dallas Press (charter); Headliners (Austin, Tex.). Home: 6231 Lakeview Dr Falls Church VA 22041 Office: Nat Press Bldg Washington DC 20004

BASLER, ROY PRENTICE, educator, writer, librarian; b. St. Louis, Nov. 19, 1906; s. Roy Prentice and Mary Dorothea (Olsen) B.; A.B., Central Coll., Fayette, Mo., 1927; A.M., Duke, 1930, Ph.D., 1931; hon. Litt.D., Blackburn Coll., 1952; m. Virginia Pearl Anderson, Aug. 31, 1929; children—Mary Rose, Roy Prentice, Andrine Anderson, Chris Olsen, Virginia Carolyn. Tchr. English, Caruthersville (Mo.) High Sch., 1926-28; grad. asst., fellow in English, Duke, 1928-30; head dept. English, Ringling Coll., Sarasota, Fla., 1931-34, State Tchrs. Coll., Florence, Ala., 1934-43; prof. English, U. Ark., 1943-46; head dept. English, George Peabody Coll., 1946-50; chief div. gen. reference and bibliography div. Library of Congress, 1952-54, asso. dir. reference dept., 1954-58, dir. reference dept., 1958-68, chief manuscript div., chair Am. history, 1968—. Mem. Modern Lang. Assn., So. Atlantic Modern Lang. Assn., Abraham Lincoln Assn. (exec. sec. 1947-52), Phi Beta Kappa, Sigma Tau Delta, Pi Gamma Mu. Methodist. Club: Cosmos (Washington). Editor: The Abraham Lincoln Quarterly, 1947-52; Abraham Lincoln: His Speeches and Writings, 1946; The Collected Works of Abraham Lincoln (9 vols.), 1953; A Short History of the American Civil War, 1967. Home: 3030 Lake Av Cheverly MD 20785 Office: Library of Congress Washington DC 20540 ☆

BASNIGHT, ARVIN ODELL, govt. ofcl.; b. Manteo, N.C., Sept. 14, 1915; s. Thomas A. and Mary (Meekins) B.; student N.C. State Coll., 1932-35, Am. U., 1935-38, George Washington U., 1940-41; m. Marjorie Jane Gauthier, Dec. 6, 1941; children—Mary Ann, William Gaylord, Michael Andre. Park ranger U.S. Park Service, Mesa Verde, Colo., also Kitty Hawk, N.C., 1935-40; personnel mgr. CAA, Washington, 1940-42, budget officer, 1945-59; dep. asst. adminstr. mgmt. services FAA, Washington, 1959-61, dir., Atlanta, 1961- 65, asso. adminstr. programs, Washington, from 1965, now dir. Western region, Los Angeles. Served with USAAF, World War II. Decorated D.F.C., Air medal. Elk. Home: 30033 Avenida Celestial Palos Verdes Peninsula CA 90274 Office: FAA 5651 W Manchester P O Box 9007 Los Angeles CA 90009

BASOLO, FRED, chemist, educator; b. Coello, Ill., Feb. 11, 1920; s. John and Catherine (Marino) B.; B.E., So. Ill. U., 1940; M.S., U. Ill., 1942, Ph.D., 1943; m. Mary P. Nutley, June 14, 1947; children-Mary Catherine, Freddie, Margaret-Ann, Elizabeth Rose. Research chemist Rohm & Haas Chem. Co., Phila., 1943-46; mem. faculty Northwestern U., Evanston, Ill., 1946—, prof. chemistry, 1958—, chmn. dept. chemistry, 1969—. Guggenheim fellow, 1954-55, NSF fellow, 1961-62. Mem. Am. Chem. Soc. (asst. editor jour. 1961-64), A.A.A.S., Chem. Soc., Sigma Xi, Phi Lambda Upsilon, Alpha Chi Sigma, Phi Kappa Phi. Author: (with R.G. Pearson) Mechanisms of Inorganic Reactions, 1958. Contbr. to Chemistry of the Coordination Compounds, 1956. Asso. editor Chem. Revs., 1960—; editorial bd. Jour. Inorganic and Nuclear Chemistry, 1959—. Contbr. articles profl. jours. Home: 1125 Colfax St Evanston IL 60201

BASOV, NIKOIAI GENNADIEVICH, physicist; b. Voronerh, Russia, Dec. 14, 1922; s. Gennadii Fedorovich and Zinaida Andreevna (Molchanova) B.; grad. Moscow Inst. Phys. Engrs., 1950, postgrad., 1953; m. Ksenia Tikhonovna, July 18, 1950; children—Gennadii, Dmitrii. Mem. staff P. N. Lebedev Phys. Inst., Moscow, 1948—, vice dir., 1958—, head lab. quantum radio physics, 1963- -; prof. solid state physics Moscow Inst. Phys. Engrs., 1963—; spl. research molecular oscillators, quantum oscillators, lasers. Recipient Lenin prize, 1959, Nobel prize for physics, 1964. Mem. Acad. Scis. USSR, Acad. Scis. German Dem. Republic (hon.), German Acad. Leopoldina. Address. P N Lebedev Phys Institute Leninsky Prospect 53 Moscow USSR

BASS, ALLAN DELMAGE, educator, physician; b. Marcus, Ia., Feb. 12, 1910; s. John Charles and Ethel Alice (Delmage) B.; B.S., Simpson Coll., 1931; M.S., Vanderbilt U., 1932, M.D., 1939; m. Sara Augusta Thompson, July 28, 1944; children—Allan Delmage, Sara Jean. A.C.P. fellow, Yale Med. Sch., 1941- 42, instr. pharmacology, 1942-43; instr. medicine, resident physician, Vanderbilt U. Med. Sch., 1943-44, prof. pharmacology, chmn. dept., 1952—, dir. univ. neuroscis. program, 1971—; prof. pharmacology, med. sch. Syracuse U., 1945-52. Mem. Nashville C. of C. Drug Abuse Council, 1971—; med. adv. bd. FDA, 1967-70; mem. research adv. com. Nat. Inst. Mental Health, 1968-70; cons. research analysis and evaluation NIH, 1968. Chmn. bd. Tenn. Neuropsychiat. Inst. Served with M.C., AUS, 1944-45. Fellow A.C.P., A.A.A.S. (sec. med. scis. sect. 1952-60, v.p. med. sci. sec. 1969), N.Y. Acad. Scis.; mem. Am. Soc. Pharmacology, Exptl. Therapeutics (council 1951-54, treas. 1958-60, pres. 1967-68), A.M.A. (council on drugs), Fedn. Am. Socs. Exptl. Biology (exec. com. 1966-69), Am. Soc. for Cancer Research, Soc. for Exptl. Biology and Medicine, Nashville Acad. Medicine (chmn. alcoholism and drug abuse com. 1969—). Author research papers, reviews, chpts. in textbooks. Editorial bd. Ann. Rev. Pharmacology. Home: 4521 Price Circle Rd Nashville TN 37205

BASS, BOYLSTON B., retired mortgage banker; b. Yukon, Okla., Apr. 7, 1905; s. Harry B. and Etheyln (Bowlby) B.; B.S., Okla. U., 1928; grad. Oklahoma City Law Sch., 1939; m. Nancy J. Bacon, Apr. 28, 1934; children—Philip B., David A. Engaged in real estate and property mgmt., Oklahoma City, 1928-40; admitted to Okla. bar, 1939; mortgage banker, Oklahoma City, 1946-71; v.p. Am.-First Title & Trust Co., 1946-53; 1st v.p. Am. Mortgage and Investment Co., 1953-54, pres., 1954-70; dir. First Nat. Bank & Trust Co. Oklahoma City, 1969—. Served to col. AUS, World War II; Australia, New Guinea, Philippines, Japan. Decorated Legion of Merit, Bronze Star, Okla. Meritorious Service award Okla. N.G. Mem. Mortgage Bankers Assn. Am. (pres. 1959-60), Sigma Nu. Home: 1706 Pennington Way Oklahoma City OK 73116

BASS, GEORGE HENRY, II, leather products exec.; b. Wilton, Me., Aug. 30, 1914; s. John Russell and Alice Mary (Ness) B.; grad. Deerfield Acad., 1933; A.B., Bowdoin Coll., 1937; m. Catherine Forbush, Nov. 26, 1938; children—Nancy (Mrs. Charles Wolfram), Joanne (Mrs. Richard O'Connor). With G.H. Bass & Co., Wilton, 1937—, pres., 1956—, chmn. bd. dirs., 1968—; farmer, lumberman, 1954-68. Dir. Me. div. Am. Cancer Soc., 1967—, chmn. exec. com., 1969—. Trustee Kents Hill Sch., 1963—. Served with USNR, 1943-45. Mem. Am. (dir.), New Eng. (pres., dir.) footwear assns. Conglist. Home: RFD 3 Farmington ME 04938 Office: GH Bass and Co Wilton ME 04294

BASS, HYMAN, mathematician, educator; b. Houston, Oct. 5, 1932; s. Isador and Fanny (Weiss) B.; B.A., Princeton, 1955; M.S., U. Chgo., 1956, Ph.D., 1959; m. Mary Ellen Popkin, June 9, 1957; children—Anne Ruth, Ivan Philip. Ritt instr. mathematics Columbia, 1959-62, asst. prof., 1963-64, asso. prof., chmn. at Barnard Coll., 1964-65, prof., 1965—; vis. mem. Inst. Advanced Study, Princeton, 1964, 65-66, Inst. de Hautes Etudes Scientifiques, Paris, 1968-69; vis. prof. Universidad Nacional Autonoma de Mexico, 1965, Tata Inst. Fundamental Research, Bombay, 1965-66, 69, U. Paris, 1968. Chmn. com. pure mathematics Nat. Research Council, 1970-71. NSF fellow Coll. de France, 1962-63; Slaon fellow, 1964-66; Guggenheim fellow, 1968-69; recipient Van Amridge book prize Columbia, 1969. Mem. Am. Math. Soc. (council 1969-72), Societe Mathematique de France, Math. Assn. Am., A.A.A.S. Editorial bd. Jour. Indian Math. Soc., 1968—, Cambridge Tacts in Pure and Applied Mathematics, 1968—, Jour. Pure and Applied Algebra, 1970—, Am. Jour. Mathematics, 1971-73. Home: 435 Riverside Dr New York City NY 10025

BASS, JAMES ORIN, lawyer; b. Summer County, Tenn., July 12, 1910; s. Francis Marion and Sadi (Dunn) B.; B.A., U. of South, 1931; LL.B., Harvard, 1934; m. Susanne Warner, June 9, 1937; children—James Orin, Edwin Warner, Francis Marion II, Susan Richardson. Admitted to Tenn. bar, 1934, since practiced in Nashville; partner firm Bass, Berry & Sims, 1937—. Dir. First Am. Nat. Bank Nashville, Tenn. Natural Gas Lines, Inc. Mem. Tenn. Ho. of Reps. from Davidson County, 1936-38, Tenn. Senate, 1940-42. Served to lt. col. AUS, 1942-45. Mem. Am., Tenn., Nashville bar assns., Am. Coll. Trial Lawyers. Democrat. Presbyn. Home: 4400 Chickering Lane Nashville TN 37215 Office: American Trust Bldg Nashville TN 37201

BASS, LAWRENCE WADE, chem. engr.; b. Streator, Ill., June 18, 1898; s. John Hiram and Sara (Leek) B.; Ph.B., Yale, 1919, Ph.D., 1922; student Tulane U., U. Lille, Sorbonne, Pasteur Inst., N.Y.U. Sch. Law, 1923- 27; m. Edna Maria Becker, Nov. 23, 1935. Mem. sci. staff, Rockefeller Inst., N.Y.C., 1925-28; exec. asst. Mellon Inst. Indsl. Research, Pitts., 1929-31; dir. research Borden Co., N.Y.C., 1932-36; asst. dir. Mellon Inst., 1937-42; dir. New Eng. Indsl. Research Found., Boston, 1942-44; dir. chem. research Air Reduction Co., 1944-48 dir. research and devel. U.S. Indsl. Chems., Inc., N.Y.C., 1944-48, v.p., 1948-52; exec. staff Arthur D. Little, Inc., Cambridge, Mass., 1952-54, v.p., 1954-64, cons., 1964—; project dir. industrialization studies, Egypt, Iraq, 1953-55; mem. bd. Inveresk Research Internat., Musselburgh, Scotland, 1957—; cons. UN Indsl. Devel. Orgn., 1965—. Chmn. com. equipment and supplies Research and Devel. Bd., Dept. Def., 1951- 53. Recipient President's Certificate of Merit, 1947. Mem. A.A.A.S., Am. Inst. Chemists, Inst. Food Technologists, Am. Chem. Soc. (dir. 1946-49), Am. Inst. Chem. Engrs. (pres. 1945), Soc. Chem. Industry, Engrs. Joint Council (1946-49, chmn. 1948), Yale Engring. Assn. (pres. 1950-52), Sigma Xi, Sigma Nu, Tau Beta Pi, Sigma Tau, Alpha Chi Sigma. Phi Lambda Upsilon. Clubs: Chemists (N.Y.C.); Cosmos (Washington). Author: Inorganic Complex Compounds, 1923; Nucleic Acids, 1931; Management of Technical Programs, 1965; numerous articles profl. jours. Editor: Formulation of Reserach Policies, 1967. Home: 2000 N St NW Washington DC 20036 Office: 1735 I St NW Washington DC 20006

BASS, MARY CARSON, editor, writer; b. Chgo.; d. James S. and May (Emerson) Carson; A.B., Columbia; m. Joseph P. Cookman, 1926 (dec. 1944); m. 2d, Basil N. Bass, Dec. 25, 1945 (dec. Nov. 1956); 1 son, Richardson Carson; m. 3d, George Rollings Gibson, May 16, 1964. Asst. curator publs. Hispanic Soc. Am.; exec. editor Ladies' Home Jour., N.Y.C., 1945-62; editor Seventeen mag., N.Y.C., 1962-65; TV producer R.F.T. Inc., 1967-68; asso. dir. MacDowell Colony, 1967—; roving editor Family Circle mag., 1968—; also lectr. Mem. Authors Guild. Clubs: Women's Nat. Press Club (Washington); Cosmopolitan, Overseas Press (N. Y.C.). Home: 850 Park Av New York City NY 10021 Office: 1083 Fifth Av New York City NY 10022

BASS, PERKINS, lawyer; b. East Walpole, Mass., Oct. 6, 1912; s. Robert Perkins and Edith (Bird) B.; A.B., Dartmouth, 1934; LL.B., Harvard, 1938; m. Katharine Jackson, June 6, 1941; children—Alexander, Katharine, William J., Charles F., Roberta. Admitted to N.H. bar, 1938; practiced Manchester, Peterborough; mem. firm Sheehan, Phinney, Bass and Green, 1946—; bd. dirs., mem. exec. com. Bird & Son, Inc., East Walpole; dir. Bird Machine Co., Walpole; trustee N.H. Savs. Bank, Concord, N.H. Mem. N.H. Ho. of Reps., 1939-43, 47-49; pres. N.H. State Senate, 1949-51; mem. 84th-87th Congresses, 2d N.H. Dist. Rep. Nat. Committeeman from N.H., 1964-68. Home: Peterborough NH Office: 875 Elm St Manchester NH 03101 also: Peterborough NH 03458

BASS, PERRY RICHARDSON, oil producer; b. Wichita Falls, Tex., Nov. 11, 1914; s. E. Perry and Annie (Richardson) B.; grad. Hill Sch., 1933; B.S., Yale, 1937; m. Nancy L. Muse, June 28, 1941; children—Sid R., Edward P., Robert M., Lee M. Engaged in oil exploration, drilling and prodn., 1937—; pres., dir. Perry R. Bass Inc., 1963—, Sid Richardson Carbon Co., Bass Bros. Enterprises, Inc.; chmn. bd., dir. Bass Bros. Telecasters, Inc.; chmn. bd. Western Telecasters, Inc., Corsicana TV Cable Co., Hammar Petroleum Co., Bass Broadcasting Co.; dir. Bass Explorations, Inc., Bass Enterprises Prodn. Co., D'Amores, Inc., Delhi-Australian Petroleum, Ltd., Allegheny Airlines, Inc., Dugue, S.A., Fomento de Inversiones, S.A., Ins. Securities, Inc., Sid W. Richardson Found., Delbasin Corp., S.W. Expn. and Fat Stock Show; designer, builder fire boats for U.S. Navy, World War II. Mem. adv. com. Tex. Mid-Continent Oil and Gas Assn. of Interstate Oil Compace Commn. Vice-pres. Longhorn council, mem. exec. bd. Boy Scouts Am.; mem. adv. council Stanford Grad. Sch. Bus. Bd. dirs. Texas Research Found. chmn. bd. dirs. Ft. Worth Country Day School; bd. govs. Ochsner Found. Hosp.; chmn. bd. dirs. Internat. Sci. Fair, 1969; trustee S.W. Research Inst.; mem. devel. bd. Yale. Mem. Am. Petroleum Inst. (dir.). Clubs: Ft. Worth (gov.), Rivercrest Country, Ridglea Country (Ft. Worth); Petroleum (Ft. Worth, Dallas, Houston and New Orleans). Office: Ft Worth Nat Bank Bldg Fort Worth TX 76102

BASS, ROBERT NESS, leather products co. exec.; b. Wilton, Me., Aug. 23, 1917; s. John Russell and Alice Mary (Ness) B.; A.B., Bowdoin Coll., 1940; M.B.A., Harvard, 1942; m. Martha Wheeler Lord, Aug. 6, 1948; children—John Russell II, Peter L., Ann Elisabeth, Robert Ness, Mary L. With G.H. Bass & Co., Wilton, 1946—, treas., 1963-69, pres., 1969—, dir., 1946—; dir. Union Mut. Life Ins. Co., Portland, Me., Depositors Trust Co., Augusta, Me.; chmn. bd. dirs. Sugarloaf Mountain Corp., Kingfield, Me.; pres. Ski Industries Am.; treas. Nat. Ski Credit Assn.; mem. adv. bd. Liberty Mut. Life Ins. Co., Boston. Bd. dirs. Me. Publicity Bur.; pres. Franklin County Meml. Hosp.; overseer Bowdoin Coll. Served as lt. USNR, 1941-46. Mem. Me. C. of C. (dir.), Newcomen Soc., Delta Kappa Epsilon. Republican. Conglist. (deacon). Clubs: Wilson Lake, Lions (Wilton); Boothbay Harbor (Me.) Yacht; Megantic (Me.) Fish and Game. Address: Wilton ME 04294

BASS, ROBERT OLIN, mfg. co. exec.; b. Denver, July 22, 1917; s. Olin R. and Cora (Durham) B.; B.S. in Bus. Adminstrn., U. Denver, 1941; m. Isabelle Cantrell, Mar. 22, 1941; 1 dau., Susan. Pres. Eberhardt-Denver Co., 1956; exec. v.p., asst. gen. mgr. Morse Chain Co., Ithaca, N.Y., 1956-58, pres., 1958-66; group v.p. indsl. Borg-Warner Corp., 1966-68, exec. v.p., 1968—. Chmn. metals and machinery sect. Chgo. Met. Crusade of Mercy, 1968. Mem. adv. council Grad. Sch. Bus. and Pub. Adminstrn., Cornell U., 1961—. Home: 1242 Lake Shore Dr Chicago IL 60610 Office: 200 S Michigan Av Chicago IL 60604

BASS, ROSS, former U. S. senator, corp. exec., cons.; b. Pulaski, Tenn., Mar. 17, 1918; s. Rev. William Arch and Ethel (Shook) B.; student Martin Coll., Pulaski, 1939-41; m. Avanell Keith, June 1946 (div.). Owner-operator soft drink bottling plant, Pulaski, 1946- 48; postmaster, Pulaski, 1947-54; mem. 84th to 88th Congresses, 6th Tenn. Dist., mem. ways and means com.; U.S. senator from Tenn., 1964-66, mem. commerce com., mem. agr. and forestry com.; head Ross Bass Assos., Washington. Past pres. Tenn. Postmasters Assn., Tenn. Assn. Pub. Housing Ofcls. Served to capt. USAAF, 1942-46. Democrat. Clubs: Burning Tree (Washington); La Gorce (Miami Beach, Fla.) Home: E Jefferson St Pulaski TN 38478 Office: 4000 Massachusetts Av Washington DC 20036

BASS, S. Z., savs. and loan assn. exec. Pres., Unity Savs. Assn. Office: 4242 N Harlem Av Norridge IL 60634*

BASS, SAUL, designer; b. N.Y.C., May 8, 1920; s. Aaron and Pauline (Feldman) B.; student of Howard Trafton at Art Students League, 1936-39, Gyorgy Kepes at Bklyn. Coll., 1944-45; hon. doctorates Phila. Mus. Coll. Art, also Los Angeles Art Center College of Design; m. Elaine Makatura, Sept. 30, 1961. Free-lance designer, N.Y.C., 1936-46; propr. Saul Bass & Assos., Inc., Los Angeles, 1946—; dir. short films, motion picture titles, prologues, epilogues, spl. sequences for films (Psycho, Spartacus, Grand Prix), TV openings and commls.; live action epilogue for West Side Story; animated epilogue for Around the World in Eighty Days, 1956, also designs for Man With the Golden Arm, 1955, Anatomy of a Murder, 1960, Exodus, 1961, others; rep. permanent collections Library of Congress, Smithsonian Instn., Prague Museum, Stedelijk Museum, Amsterdam, also Mus. Modern Art; numerous one man shows, group exhbns. U.S., Europe. Mem. exec. bd Internat. Design Conference, Aspen, Colo., 1955—; honorary member of faculty of Royal Designers for Industry, Royal Society Arts, England, 1965. Recipient of award for high artistic value in all work, Mus. de Arte Moderna, Rio de Janiero, 1959; citation for distinction to profession Phila. Mus. Art, 1960; awards for films The Searching Eye, Venice Film Festival, From Here to There, Chgo. Film Festival; Oscar for documentary short Why Man Creates, 1969. Mem. Acad. Motion Picture Arts and Scis., Soc. Typographic Arts, Am. Inst. Graphic Arts, Nat. Soc. Art Dirs. (designated art dir. of year 1957), Assn. Graphic Designers Sweden, Package Designers Council, Alliance Graphique Internationale. Author numerous articles in field. Address: 7039 Sunset Blvd Los Angeles CA 90028

BASS, SHAILER LINWOOD, chem. co. exec.; b. Paducah, Ky., Apr. 5, 1906; s. Bernard W. and Olivia C. (Sledd) B.; B.A., Butler U., 1926, LL.D. (hon.), 1967; Ph.D. in Chemistry, Yale, 1929; m. Elizabeth Alberti, Oct. 3, 1931; children—Jon Dolf, Arlen Linwood, Jeralyn Joan (Mrs. Hans Friedli), Heather Elizabeth, Derwin Hartley, Walden Rockwell. With Dow Chem. Co., 1929-44, dir. research cellulose ethers and organosilicon compounds, cellulose products div., 1936-44; with Dow Corning Corp. 1944— , v.p., asst. gen. mgr., 1954-60, exec. v.p., 1960-62, pres., 1962-67, chmn. bd., 1967-71, now dir. Mem. Am. Chem. Soc., Sigma Xi, Phi Kappa Phi. Home: 1805 W Sugnet Rd Midland MI 48640 Office: Dow Corning Corp Midland MI 48640

BASS, WESLEY EDWARD, Jr., title ins. trust co. exec.; b. Milledgeville, Ga., Aug 21, 1931; s. Wesley Edward and Florence (Cole) B.; B.B.A. in Accounting, U. Ga., 1952; M.B.A., Northwestern U., 1958; m. Helen Eves Long, July 2, 1955; children—Elizabeth Lanier, Catherine Randolph. Registered rep. Paine, Webber, Jackson & Curtis, 1959-60; with Chgo. Title & Trust Co., 1960—, treas., 1964—, treas., 1965—, sr. v.p., 1967—, also dir.; dir. Chas. A. Stevens & Co., Chgo. Title & Trust Bldg. Corp. Bd. dirs. Better Bus. Bur. Met. Chgo., Inc. Mem. United Charities Council of Chgo.; mem. guaranty fund com. Ravinia Festival Assn. Served to 1st lt. AUS, 1952-55; Korea. Mem. Investment Analyst Soc., Pub. Utilities Security Club, Grad. Bus. Alumni Assn. Northwestern U. (pres. 1965-66, chmn. bd. 1966-67), S.A.R., Nat. Planning Assn. (nat. council), Corporate Fiduciaries Assn. Chgo. (sec.- treas.), Sigma Alpha Epsilon. Episcopalian. Clubs: Executives, Economic, Northwestern (dir.), University (Chgo.). Home: 560 Sheridan Rd Winnetka IL 60093 Office: 111 W Washington St Chicago IL 60602

BASSET, GENE, editorial cartoonist; b. Bklyn., July 24, 1927; student U. Mo., 1946-47, Cooper Union, 1947-50; B.A., Bklyn. Coll., 1950; student Pratt Inst., 1954, Art Students League N.Y., 1953-54; m. Charlotte Goldenberg, July 8, 1951; children—Darien, Roger, Brian. Sketch artist Indpls. Times, 1951-53; theatrical and sports cartoonist Bklyn. Eagle, 1953-54; sports cartoonist Boston Post, 1955-56; tchr. Famous Artists Sch., Westport, Conn., 1957-62; editorial cartoonist Honolulu Star- Bull., 1962, Scripps-Howard Newspapers, 1962—. Served with USCGR, 1944- 46. Mem. Nat.

Cartoonist Soc., Assn. Am. Editorial Cartoonists. Home: 8106 Birnam Wood Dr McLean, VA 22101 Office: 1013 13th St NW Washington DC 20005

BASSETT, ANGELO JOHN, hotel exec.; b. Athens, Greece, Apr. 21, 1915; s. John Nicholas and Stella (Georgantas) B.; student Law Sch., U. Athens, 1935; student Boston U., 1936; m. Aliki H. Galanis, Mar. 2, 1941; children—Stephan Anton, Peter John. Came to U.S., 1935, naturalized, 1940; tchr., Dorchester, Mass., 1935-36; accountant restaurant, Boston 1936-38, asst. mgr., 1938-41, owner, 1941-45; partner Marine Transp. Co., Boston, 1945- 47; function mgr. Somerset Hotel, Boston, 1947-60; mgr. Samoset (Me.) Hotel, summers 1961, 62; mgr. Palm Beach (Fla.) Hotel, winters 1961, 62; gen. mgr. Charter House Hotel, Cambridge, Mass., 1962-64; v.p., gen. mgr. Somerset Hotel, 1964—. Sec., pres. Greek Demetrios Ch., Newton Wellesley, Mass., 1959; div. chmn. Boston chpt. Am. Cancer Soc., 1966. Mem. Newton Republican Com., 1964—. Trustee Holy Cross Theol. Sem. Mem. Mass. Hotel Assn. (bd. dirs.), Greater Boston (treas.) Hotel-Motel Assn., Les Amis d'Escoffier. Mason. Home: 5 Agawam Rd Waban MA 02168 Office: Somerset Hotel 400 Commonwealth Boston MA 02122

BASSETT, BEN, fgn. news editor; b. Topeka, Kan., Oct. 30, 1909; s. William T. and Sophia (Hoffman) B.; m. Eileen Ewing; children—Elizabeth E., Jonathan, W. Brian. Reporter, Topeka State Jour., 1925- 27; copy editor New Bedford (Mass.) Standard, 1928-30; wire editor Asso. Press, Kansas City, Mo., 1930-35; news editor New Bedford Standard- Times, 1935-36; with A.P., 1936—, successively assigned Cleve., Washington, N.Y.C., fgn. news editor, N.Y.C., 1948—. Clubs: Deadline (N.Y.C.); Nat. Press (Washington). Home: 16 Fernwood Rd Larchmont NY 10538 Office: 50 Rockefeller Plaza New York City NY 10020

BASSETT, CHARLES ANDREW LOOCKERMAN, surgeon, educator; b. Crisfield, Md., Aug. 4, 1924; s. Harold Reuben and Vesta (Loockerman) B.; student Princeton, 1941-43; M.D., Columbia, 1948, Sc.D., 1955; m. Nancy Taylor Clark, June 15, 1946; children—Susan, David Clark, Lee Sterling. Intern, resident St. Lukes Hosp., N.Y.C., 1948-50; asst. resident orthopedic surgery N.Y. Orthopaedic Hosp., 1950, Annie C. Kane fellow, 1953-55; asst. attending orthopedic surgeon Presbyn. Hosp., 1955-60, asso. attending, 1960-63, attending orthopedic surgeon, 1963—; instr. orthopedic surgery Columbia, 1955-59, dir. orthopedic research labs., 1957—, asst. prof., 1959-61, asso. prof., 1961-67, prof., 1967- -; cons. Naval Med. Research Inst., Bethesda, Md., 1952-54; spl. cons. NIH, Nat. Inst. Neurol. Diseases and Blindness, Bethesda, 1959-62; career scientists N.Y.C. Health Research Council, 1961-71; vis. scientist Strangeway, Research Lab., Cambridge, Eng., 1965-66; cons. div. med. scis., cons., exec. sec. com. on skeletal system NRC-Nat. Acad. Scis., 1963-71; pres. Patronage Assembly, Inst. Calot, Berck-Plage, France, 1969—; cons. N.Y. State Rehab. Hosp., West Haverstraw, 1968—; cons. on med. devel. FDA, Dept. Health, Edn. and Welfare, 1970—. Served to lt. (j.g.) USNR, 1950-54. Recipient Nat. award Paralyzed Vet. Am., 1959, Max Weinstein award United Cerebral Palsy, 1960; James Mather Smith prize Columbia Coll. Phys. and Surg., 1971. Diplomate Am. Bd. Orthopedic Surgery. Fellow A.C.S., N.Y. Acad. Scis.; mem. Am. Acad. Orthopaedic Surgeons, A.M.A., Am. Orthopaedic Assn., Am. Soc. Cell Biology, Internat. Soc. Orthopedic Surgery and Traumatology, N.Y. State, N.Y. County med. socs., Orthopaedic Research Soc. (pres.), Royal Coll. Medicine (Eng.), Royal Micros. Soc., Tissue Culture Assn., Soc. Exptl. Biology and Medicine, Harvey Soc., Sigma Xi, Alpha Omega Alpha. Contbr. articles profl. jours., books. Home: 108 Midland Av Bronxville NY 10708 Office: 630 W 168th St New York City NY 10032

BASSETT, EDWARD CHARLES, architect; b. Port Huron, Mich., Sept. 12, 1921; B. Arch., U. Mich., 1949; M. Arch., Cranbrook Acad. Art, 1951. Designer, Saarinen & Saarinen, 1950-51, Eero Saarinen & Assos., 1951-55; with Skidmore, Owings & Merrill, 1955—, partner in charge of design, San Francisco, 1960—. Served with AUS, 1943-46; PTO. Recipient Arnold W. Brunner Meml. prize in architecture Nat. Inst. Arts and Letters. Mem. A.I.A., Phi Kappa Phi, Tau Sigma Delta. Office: Skidmore Owings & Merrill One Maritime Plaza San Francisco CA 94111

BASSETT, EDWARD LEWIS, educator. Prof. classical langs. and lit. U. Chgo. Home: 5550 S Dorchester Av Chicago IL 60637 Office: Dept Classical Langs and Lit U Chgo 5801 Ellis Av Chicago IL 60637*

BASSETT, EDWARD POWERS, univ. dean; b. Boston, Feb. 27, 1929; s. Fraser W. and Fanny (Powers) B.; A.B., Washington and Lee U., 1951; student law U. Va., 1951-52; M.A., U. Mich., 1955; Ph.D., U. Ia., 1967; m. Karen Elizabeth Jack, Dec. 21, 1954; children—Sarah Jack, Laura Powers, Lisa Wightman. Acting chmn. U. Mich. Dept. Journalism, 1969-70; instr., pub. U. Ia., 1960-67; editorial writer Longview (Wash.) Daily News, 1958-60; lectr. Lower Columbia Jr. Coll., 1959-60; city editor Anderson (Ind.) Herald, 1957-58; asst. editor Falmouth (Mass.) Enterprise, 1956-57; court reporter Louisville Courier- Jour., 1955-56; dean Sch. Journalism, U. Kan., 1970—. Mem. accreditation com. Am. Council on Edn. Journalism, 1970—. Recipient citation for excellence in state and local reporting Am. Polit. Sci. Assn., 1960. Mem. Assn. Edn. in Journalism, Sigma Delta Chi, Kappa Tau Alpha. Republican. Presbyn. Rotarian. Home: 2614 Orchard Lane Lawrence KS 66044

BASSETT, GLENN COTTRELL, Jr., banker; b. Rochester, N.Y., Jan. 22, 1922; s. Glenn Cottrell and Rebea (White) B.; B.S. in Indsl. Engring., U. Rochester, 1948; m. Linaford Kershner, July 3, 1949; children—Sarah Llewellyn, Abigail White, Glenn C. III. With William Wrigley, Jr. Co., Chgo., 1948-49; with Chase Manhattan Bank, and predecessors, 1949-66, v.p. internat. div., 1959-66; sr. v.p. Wells Fargo Bank, San Francisco, 1966—; pres. Wells Fargo Internat. Investment Corp.; pres. Wells Fargo Interam. Bank, Miami, Wells Fargo Internat. Ltd., London, Wells Fargo Bank Internat. Corp., N.Y.; dir. Western Am. Bank (Europe) Ltd., London, Martin Corp., Sydney, Australia. Bd. dirs. Save the Children Fedn., Community Devel. Found., N.Y.C.; pres. San Francisco World Affairs Council; trustee Council of Americas. Served as pilot USAAF, 1941-45; CBI. Mem. U.S. (chmn. com., bd. dirs.), Internat. (mem. U.S. council) chambers commerce, Pan Am. Soc. (pres.), San Francisco World Trade Assn., Psi Upsilon. Rep. Home: 17 Tanfield Rd Tiburon CA 94920 Office: 464 California St San Francisco CA 94120

BASSETT, HARRY HOOD, banker; b. Flint, Mich., May 6, 1917; s. Harry Hoxie and Jessie Marie (Hood) B.; B.S., Yale, 1940; children—Harry Hood, George Rodney, Patrick Glenn; m. 2d, Florence Schust Knoll, June 22, 1958. Asst. trust officer First Nat. Bank, Palm Beach, Fla., 1940-42, chmn. bd., 1965—, also dir.; asst. v.p. First Nat. Bank, Miami, 1947-48, dir., 1947-48, v.p., 1948-56, asst. to pres., 1951—, chmn. exec. com., 1959—, pres., 1962-66, chmn. bd., 1966—. dir. Wometco Enterprises, Gen. Devel. Corp., Eastern Airlines, Inc., Maule Industries, chmn. bd. S.E. Banking Corp., Inc. Mem. Orange Bowl Com. Chmn. Bd. trustees U. Miami. Served as pilot Civil Coastal Patrol (anti-submarine), 1941-42; 1st lt. USAAF, 1944-46. Decorated Air medal. Mem. Fla. Bankers Assn., Am. Inst. Banking, Assn. Res. City Bankers, Assn. Registered Bank Holding Co. Episcopalian. Clubs: Bath, LaGorce Country (Miami Beach); Miami, Palm Bay (Miami); Yale, River, Sky (N.Y.C.); Lyford Cay, East Hill Club (Nassau, Bahamas); Everglades (Palm Beach, Fla.); Biscayne Bay (Fla.) Yacht; Bohemian (San Francisco); Metropolitan (Washington). Home: 1801 W 27th St Sunset Island 2 Miami Beach FL 33139 Office: 100 S Biscayne Blvd Miami FL 33131

BASSETT, JAMES ELIAS, newspaper editor, author; b. Glendale, Cal., Oct. 18, 1912; s. James Elias and Lucille (Emerton) B.; B.A. cum laude, Bowdoin Coll., 1934; m. Wilma Moreland, June 13, 1936; 1 dau. Cynthia Ann. Reporter, Los Angeles Times, 1934-37, aviation editor, 1937-41, sci. editor, 1947-48, polit. analyst, editor, 1961, dir. editorial pages, 1963-71, asso. editor, 1971—; polit. editor Los Angeles Mirror, 1948, city editor, 1954, asst. mng. editor, 1957. Pres sec. Nixon presdl. campaign, 1952; pub. relations dir. Republican Nat. Com., 1954; campaign mgr. Vice Pres. Nixon, 1956; campaign planning activities dir. Nixon presdl. campaign, 1960. Served to capt. USNR, 1941-45. Decorated Bronze Star with combat clasp. Mem. Am. Soc. Newspaper Editors, Nat. Conf. Editorial Writers, Authors League Am., Phi Beta Kappa, Psi Upsilon, Kappa Tau Alpha. Clubs: Los Angeles Press, Los Angeles Athletic. Author: Harm's Way, 1962; The Sky Suspended, 1968; Commander Prince, USN, 1971. Home: 15 Malibu Cove Colony Malibu CA 90265 Office: Los Angeles Times Editorial Dept Times Mirror Square Los Angeles CA 90053

BASSETT, JOHN EDWIN, furniture co. exec. b. Bassett, Va., Sept. 16, 1901; s. Charles C. and Roxie (Hundley) B.; student Randolph Macon Coll., 1917-20, U. Va., 1920- 21, Nat. Bus. Coll., 1921-22; m. Ruby Williams, May 19, 1927; children—John Edwin, Roxanne (Mrs. D.L. Dillon), Charles C. III. Former pres., now chmn. bd., chief exec. officer, treas. Bassett Furniture Industries (Va.); chmn. Bassett Mirror Co.; chmn., pres. First Nat. Bank; dir. Blue Ridge Hardware & Supply Co.; dir. Hooker Furniture Corp., Burkenville Veneer Co., Ray Stone Trucking Co. Trustee Ferrum Jr. Coll. Recipient Silver Beaver award Boy Scouts Am. Methodist. Mason (32#55, Shriner), Kiwanian. Home: Box 191 Bassett VA 24055 Office: Bassett Furniture Industries Bassett VA 24055

BASSETT, JOHN JEWETT, mfg. exec.; b. Aberdeen, S.D., June 5, 1919; s. Wilfred W. and Angela (Jewett) B.; LL.B., U. S.D., 1941; m. Helen Gibbs, Jan. 23, 1942; children—John, Peter, Judith, Stephen. Admitted to S.D. bar, 1941; legal dept. Internat. Tel. & Tel. Corp., 1946-54; with Internat. Standard Electric Corp., N.Y.C., 1954-61, v.p., dir. 1957- 61; v.p., dir. Internat. Standard Engring., Inc.; vice chmn. Internat. Tel. & Tel. Corp. Espana, Madrid until 1961; regional dir. Latin Am., Cyanamid Internat.; vice pres., dir. Cyanamid International; regional dir. Europe Cyanamid Internat. Corp.; dir. Formica Internat. Ltd., London, Cyanamid of Great Britain, Ltd., Cyanamid GmbH, Munich, Cyanamid Italia, Rome, Cyanenka S.A., Barcelona, Titaandioxydefabrick Hague, Cyanamire SpA Milan, Cyanamid Ketjen Amsterdam, Lederle Belge Brussels, Laboratories Reunidos, Laboratoires Lederle-Novalis, Lyon, France until 1970; corp. v.p., pres. internat. div. Carter-Wallace, Inc.; v.p., dir. Carter-Wallace N.S., Carter-Wallace O.S.; dir. Carter-Wallace, Ltd., U.K., Carter-Wallace (Hong Kong) Ltd. Served from 2d lt. to lt. col., Signal Corps, AUS, 1941-46. Mem. Beta Theta Pi. Phi Delta Phi. Catholic. Clubs: Seabright (N.J.) Beach, Seabright Lawn Tennis; American (Buenos Aires, Argentina). Home: 72 Navesink Av Rumson NJ 07760 Office: 767 Fifth Av New York City NY 10022

BASSETT, JOHN WHITE HUGHES, newspaper pub.; b. Ottawa, Can., Aug. 25, 1915; s. John and Marion (Avery) B.; B.A., U. Bishop's Coll., Lennoxville, Que., 1936; m. Isabel Glenthorne Macdonald, July 17, 1967. Mem. staff The Telegram, Toronto, Can., 1948—, chmn. bd., pub., 1952—; chmn. bd. Baton Broadcasting Co., 1960—, Toronto Argonaut Football Club, 1958—, CKLW-TV, Windsor, Ont., 1970—; dir. CTV TV Network Ltd., 1966—. Served to maj., Seaforth Highlanders, Royal Canadian Army, World War II. Home: 76 Binscarth Rd Toronto Ontario Canada Office: 440 Front St W Toronto Ontario Canada

BASSETT, LESLIE RAYMOND, educator, composer; b. Hanford, Cal., Jan. 22, 1923; s. Archibald Leslie and Vera (Starr) B.; B.A. in Music, Fresno State Coll., 1947; M.Music in Composition, U. Mich., 1949, A.Mus.D., 1956; student Ecole Normale de Musique, Paris, France, 1950-51; m. Anita Elizabeth Denniston, Aug. 21, 1949; children—Wendy Lynn, Noel Leslie, Ralph (dec.). Tchr. music Fresno pub. schs., 1951-52; mem. faculty U. Mich., 1952—, prof. music, 1965—, chmn. composition dept. U. Mich., 1970; guest composer Interlochen Arts Acad., 1966, Fresno State Coll., 1966, Eastern Ill. U., 1967, East Carolina Coll., 1967. Served with AUS, 1942- 46. Fulbright fellow, 1950-51; recipient Rome prize Am. Acad. in Rome, 1961-63; grantee Soc. Pub. Am. Music, 1960, Nat. Inst. Arts and Letters, 1964, Nat. Council Arts, 1966; recipient Pulitzer prize in music for Variations for Orch., 1966; citation U. Mich. regents, 1966. Mem. Am. Composers Alliance, Pi Kappa Lambda, Phi Kappa Phi, Phi Mu Alpha. Methodist. Home: 1618 Harbal Dr Ann Arbor, MI 48105.

BASSETT, ROBERT COCHEM, lawyer, publisher; b. Sturgeon Bay, Wis., Mar. 2, 1911; s. Clark Patterson and Lillian Catherine (Cochem) B.; B.A., U. Wis., 1932; LL.B., Harvard, 1935; m. Frances E. Whiting, Feb. 28, 1942 (dec. Jan. 1945); m. Mary Catherine Holmes, Mar. 28, 1946; children—Robert Andrew, Jane, Pamela, Karen. Admitted to Wis. bar, 1935, U.S. Supreme Ct. bar, 1942; partner Minahan & Bassett, lawyers, Green Bay, Wis., 1935-46; gen. counsel Wis. Daily Newspaper League, 1936-43; spl. counsel Inland Daily Press Assn., Chgo., 1937-43; labor counsel Hearst Corp., 1946-54, also dir., v.p., 1954-56; pub. Milw. Sentinel, 1954-56; v.p. Jos. Schlitz Brewing Co., Milw., 1956-61; pres., dir. Haywood Pub. Co. of Ill., 1961-63; exec. v.p., dir. Haywood Pub. Co., 1961-63; v.p., dir. Haywood Tag Co., 1961-63; pres., dir. Visual Communications, Inc., 1963-65; chmn., pres. Bassett Pub. Co., 1965—; marketing dir. Grant/Jacoby, Inc., 1968-70; exec. v.p., dir., editorial dir. Omnibus Mag., 1965-67; pub. Boxboard Containers Mag., 1963-65. Pub. mem. shipbldg. stablzn. com. WPB, 1943-46, shipbldg. commn. Nat. War Labor Bd., 1943; mem. nat. Wage Stblzn. Bd., 1952-53; industry del. Internat. Labor Conf., Switzerland, 1953; mem. Sec. Labor's Mgmt. Adv. Com. Regent, U. Wis., 1958-61. Trustee Nat. Small Bus. Assn.; bd. dirs. Better Bus. Chgo., chmn. pub. relations. Served as lt. comdr. USNR, 1942-46. Mem. U.S. C. of C., N.A.M., Artus, Phi Kappa Phi, Phi Eta Sigma, Delta Sigma Rho, Delta Upsilon, Sigma Delta Chi. Clubs: Racquet, Bob O'Link (Chicago); Burning Tree (Washington). Author: Wisconsin Laws Affecting Newspapers, 1938; Labor Guide for Italy. 1944. Contbr. articles to profl. jours. Home: 1500 Lake Shore Dr Chicago IL 60610 Office: 203 N Wabash Av Chicago IL 60601

BASSETT, WOODSON WILLIAM, Jr., lawyer; b. Okmulgee, Okla., Nov. 7, 1926; s. Woodson William and Bee Irene (Knerr) B.; J.D., U. Ark., 1949; m. Marynm Shaw, Dec. 16, 1950; children—Woodson William III, Beverly M., Tod Corbett. Admitted to Ark. bar, 1949; employed in New Orleans and Monroe, La., 1949-51; claims examiner Employers Group Ins. Cos., 1949-51; mgr. Light Adjustment Co., 1951-56; v.p. legal dept. Preferred Ins. Cos., 1957-62; partner Putman, Davis & Bassett, 1962—. Pres. Sherman Lollar Boys Baseball League, 1962; v.p. Babe Ruth Baseball Assn., 1968. Served with AUS, 1950-51. Mem. Am., Ark., Washington County bar assns., Am., Ark. trial lawyers assns., Delta Theta Phi, Kappa Sigma. Elk. Club: Fayetteville Country. Mem. editorial staff Ark. Law Review, 1949. Home: 2210 Manor Dr Fayetteville AR 72701 Office: 28 S College Av Fayetteville AR 72701

BASSETTI, FREDERICK FORDE, architect; b. Seattle, Jan. 31, 1917; s. Frederick Michael and Sophia (Fórde) B.; B.Arch., U. Wash., 1942; M.Arch., Harvard U., 1946; m. Mary Stuart Wilson, July 26, 1944; children—Ann, Catherine, Margaret. Designer Alvar Aalto, Cambridge, Mass., 1945-46; partner firm Bassetti & Morse, Seattle, 1947-62; partner firm Fred Bassetti & Co., Seattle, 1962—; cons. Govt. Italy on exptl. housing, 1956-57; vis. prof. Columbia, U. Wash., Rice U.; mem. jury Sunset mag., A.I.A. honor awards jury, Progressive Architecture jury. Pres. Allied Arts of Seattle, 1970—, designer Seattle Fed. Bldg. Trustee Virginia Mason Research Center. Fellow Am. Inst. Architects (pres. Seattle chpt. 1967), Tau Sigma Delta. Author: Solid Shapes Laboratory. Home: 3146A Portage Bay Pl E Seattle WA 98102 Office: 2027 5th Av Seattle WA 98121

BASSFORD, CHARLES A., lawyer; b. St. Paul, Oct. 29, 1914; A.A., U. Minn., 1935; LL.B. magna cum laude St. Paul Coll. Law, 1939. Admitted to Minn. bar, 1939; now mem. firm Richards, Montgomery, Cobb & Bassford, Mpls. Mem. Internat., Am., Minn., Hennepin County bar assns., Am. Judicature Soc., Internat. Assn. Ins. Counsel, Internat. Soc. Barristers, Delta Theta Phi. Office: Richards Montgomery Cobb & Bassford Dain Tower Minneapolis MN 55402*

BASSIE, V. LEWIS, educator, economist; b. Chgo., Dec. 22, 1907; s. William Jones and Mathilda Candida (Rush) B.; Ph.B., U. Chgo., 1931, postgrad, 1931-35; m. Janet Montgomery Hooks, Oct. 2, 1937; children—Carol Montgomery, William Chester. Economist Fed. Reserve Bd., 1937-39; chief civilian requirements div. Nat. Defense Advisory Commn. and OPM, 1940-41; chief prodn. analyst WPB, 1942-44; adviser on U.S. fgn. trade Fgn. Econ. Adminstrn., 1944-45; asst. to Sec. of Commerce, 1945-48; prof. econs., dir. bur. of econ. and business research U. Ill., 1948—. Fellow Am. Statis. Assn.; mem. Am. Econs. Assn., Conf. on Income and Wealth, Nat. Bur. Econ. Research, Econometric Soc. Author: Economic Forecasting, 1958; (with H.H. Afifi) Water Pricing Theory and Practice in Illinois, 1969. Home: 708 La Sell Drive Champaign IL 61820 Office: Coll of Commerce and Business Adminstrn U of Ill Urbana IL 61801

BASSIN, JULES, fgn. service officer; b. N.Y.C., Apr. 16, 1914; s. Abe and Bessie (Brooks) B.; B.S., Coll. City N.Y., 1936; J.D., N.Y.U., 1938; student Criminal Investigation Sch., U.S. Army, 1943, Security Intelligence Sch., 1944, Mil. Govt. Sch., U. Va., 1944, Far East Civil Affairs, Harvard, 1945; grad. Armed Forces Staff Coll., 1960; m. Beatrice M. Kellner, Dec. 25, 1938; children—Arthur Jay, Nelson Jay. Admitted to N.Y. bar, 1939; dir. law div. Gen. Hdqrs., Supreme Comdr. Allied Powers, Tokyo, Japan, 1945-51; legal attache Am. embassy, Tokyo, 1951-56, also spl. asst. to ambassador for politico-mil. affairs; spl. asst. to ambassador for mut. security affairs Am. embassy, Karachi, 1956-59; State Dept. faculty adviser Armed Forces Staff Coll., Norfolk, Va., 1960-62; chief titles and rank br. Dept. State, 1962-63, chief functional assignments br., 1963-65, dir. functional personnel program, 1965-67, spl. asst. to dep. undersec. state for adminstrn., 1967-69; dep. rep. of U.S. to European office UN and other internat. orgns., also dep. chief U.S. mission with personal rank of minister, Geneva, Switzerland, 1969—. Served from 2d lt. to maj., Judge Adv. Gen. Corps. AUS, 1942-46; col. Res. Club: American Internat. (exec. com.) (Geneva). Home: 2891 Audubon Terrace NW Washington DC 20008 Office: Dept of State Washington DC 20520

BAST, WILLIAM HERBERT, corp. exec., lawyer; b. Mpls., May 12, 1937; s. William E. and Esther (Brahs) B.; student Holy Cross Coll., 1955-57; B.A., U. Minn., 1959, LL.B., 1965; m. Karin Anderson, Aug. 19, 1967. Admitted to Minn. bar, 1965, Wis. bar, 1969; atty. Doherty, Rumble & Butler, St. Paul, 1965-69; sec., gen. counsel Trane Co., LaCrosse, Wis., 1969—. Served with USNR, 1959-62. Home: 2407 Vine St LaCrosse WI 54601 Office: 3600 Pamell Creek Rd LaCrosse WI 54601

BASTABLE, CHARLES WILLIAM, Jr., educator, cons.; b. Buffalo, Sept. 24, 1917; s. Charles William and Elsie (Fischer) B.; B.S., Columbia, 1938, M.S., 1939, Ph.D., 1952; m. Joan Talbot Reynolds, Aug. 24, 1956; children—Catherine Stewart, William Talbot, Caroline Cory. Accountant, Haskins & Sells, C.P.A.'s N.Y.C., 1939-41; mem. faculty Columbia, 1946—, dir. Office Facts and Figures, 1961-63, spl. asst. to pres., 1963-64, prof. bus., 1964—; controller Am. Geog. Soc., 1952-65, sec., 1961-65; bus. cons., 1952—. Served to lt. comdr. USNR, 1941-46. Decorated Commendation medal. C.P.A., N.Y. Mem. Am. Accounting Assn. (v.p. 1961), Am. Inst. C.P.A.'s, Financial Execs. Inst. Contbr. profl. jours. Contbg. editor: Accountants' Cost Handbook, 1960. Home: 11 Cedar Lane Closter, NJ 07624. Office: Columbia Univ New York City NY 10027

BASTEDO, PHILIP, lawyer; b. N.Y.C., Dec. 13, 1908; s. Walter A. and Helen Russell Kip (Priest) B.; A.B., Princeton, 1929; J.D., Harvard, 1932; m. Helen C. Wilmerding, Feb. 4, 1937; children—Philip R., W. Bayard, Cecily, Christopher. Admitted to N.Y. bar, 1933, since practiced in N.Y.C.; mem. firm Wickes, Riddell, Bloomer, Jacobi & McGuire, 1941-69, counsel, 1970—. Dep. dir. Office Civilian Def., Washington, 1942-43. Pres., trustee Hosp. Spl. Surgery; v.p., trustee United Hosp. Fund. Served with USNR, OSS, 1943-45. Mem. Council Fgn. Relations, Bar Assn. City N.Y. Episcopalian. Clubs: Pilgrims, River, University, Down Town, Century (Washington). Home: 925 Park Av New York City NY 10028 also Dublin NH 03444 Office: 59 Maiden Lane New York City NY 10038

BASTEN, RAY FRANK, banker; b. Camp Point, Ill., Sept. 23, 1911; s. Frank A. and Clara (Peters) B.; student Gem City Coll., 1928-30; M.B.A., Northwestern U., 1936; m. Margaret Gunderson, May 24, 1937; children—Barbara (Mrs. Dale K. Jensen), Margaret Jean (Mrs. H. Carl Vandervoort, Jr.), Elizabeth, Nanci (now Mrs. R. Gary Mitchell), Robert, Richard. With Harris Trust & Savings Bank, Chicago, Ill., 1930-49; with 1st Nat. Bank of Miami (Fla.), 1949-68, dir., 1962—; dir. Southeast Bancorp., Inc.; pres., dir. Southeast Data Processing, Inc.; dir. Southeast Nat. Bank Orlando, Southeast Nat. Bank Coral Way. Pres. Children's Home Soc., Fla. 1967-68; bd. dirs. Child Welfare League Am. Mem. Am. Inst. Banking (past pres. Miami chpt.), Bank Adminstrn. Inst. (past pres. Fla. chpt.), Financial Execs. Inst. (past pres. Fla. chpt., past nat. dir.). Home: 425 Aledo Av Coral Gables FL 33134 Office: 1001 NW 7th St Miami FL 33136

BASTERT, RUSSELL HENRY, educator; b. Quincy, Ill., Oct. 1, 1920; s. Henry William and Helen (Rottman) R.; B.A., Knox Coll., Galesburg, Ill., 1941; M.A., Yale, 1943, Ph.D., 1952; Lillian M. Mancini, Aug. 17, 1955; 1 dau., Carol Maria. Mem. faculty Loomis Inst., 1944-46; mem. faculty Williams Coll., 1948—, prof. history, 1965—, Stanfield prof. history, 1968—. Chmn. Am. history and social studies achievement test com. Coll. Entrance Exam. Bd., 1966-70. Recipient James A. Robertson Meml. prize Hispanic Am. Hist. Assn., 1959. Mem. Am. Hist. Assn., Orgn. Am. Historians, Phi Beta Kappa,

Beta Theta Pi, Delta Sigma Rho. Democrat. Author: (booklet) American Foreign Policy to 1880, 1967; also articles. Home: 124 Park St Williamstown MA 01267

BASTIAN, JAMES HAROLD, lawyer; b. Hannibal, Mo., Nov. 26, 1927; s. Ira Russell and Opal (Maddox) B.; B.S., U. Mo., 1950; J.D., George Washington U., 1956; m. Mary Jean Zugel, Feb. 5, 1955; children—Raphael Maria, Marquette Maria, Bartholomew Barnabus, Boniface Benedict. Admitted to D.C. bar, 1956, since practiced in Washington; asso. Adair, Ulmer, Murchison, Kent & Ashby, 1956-61; v.p., sec. Pacific Corp., 1961—; sec. Air Am., Inc., 1961—; partner Howard, Poe & Bastian, 1965—. Served with USNR, 1945-46. Mem. Am., Va., D.C. bar assns. Clubs: Nat. Aviation (Washington); Congressional Country (Potomac, Md.). Home: 1728 P St NW Washington DC 20036 Office: 1701 Pennsylvania Av NW Washington DC 20006

BASTIAN, WALTER MAXIMILLIAN, judge; b. Washington, D.C., Nov. 16, 1891; s. Charles Sandal and Katherine (Draeger) B.; LL.B., Georgetown U., 1913; LL.D., Nat. U., 1953, George Washington U., 1958; m. Eva E. Alger, July 3, 1914; children—Walter M., David C. Admitted to D.C. bar, 1913, practiced in D.C., 1915-50; U.S. Dist. Judge, U.S. Dist. Ct. for D.C., 1950-54; Circuit Judge, U.S. Ct. of Appeals, D.C. Circuit, 1954- 68, sr. judge U.S. Ct. of Appeals for D.C., 1968—; lectr. Nat. U. Sch. of Law, 1918-48. Served as 1st lt. chem. warfare service, World War I. Trustee George Washington U. Mem. Bar Assn. D.C. (treas., past pres.), Am. Bar Assn. (treas. 1945-50; ho. of dels. 1936-53, 56—), Order of Coif. Republican. Methodist. Mason (past master). Clubs: Metropolitan, Columbia Country, Lawyers, Alfalfa (Washington); University (Winter Park, Fla.). Author legal articles. Home: 1533 4th Av W Bradenton FL 33505 Office: US Court House Washington DC 20543

BASTIAN, WALTER MAXIMILLIAN, Jr., fgn. service officer; b. Washington, Mar. 27, 1918; s. Walter Maximillian and Eva Emmeline (Alger) B.; B.A. summa cum laude, Am. U., 1939; M.A., Yale, 1941; m. Carolyn Louise Sorenson, Dec. 18, 1939; 1 son, Walter Maximillian III. Tchr. English, George Washington U., 1941-42; asst. prof. U.S. Naval Acad., 1946-48; exchange prof. Autonomous U., El Salvador, 1948-50; joined U.S. Fgn. Service, 1950; cultural attache embassy, Havana, Cuba, 1950-54; pub. affairs officer embassy, Quito, Ecuador, 1954-56; cultural attache embassy, Buenos Aires, Argentina, 1956-58; cultural attache embassy, Ankara, Turkey, 1963-64, mem. Sr. Seminar Fgn. Policy, State Dept., 1965, pub. affairs officer embassy, Bogota, Colombia, 1968—. Tchr. history Am. theatre U. Havana, 1951, U. Villaneuva, Marianao, Cuba, 1953-54. Served to lt. USNR, 1942-46. Recipient spl. award for introduction theatre-in-round Nat. Theatre Assn. Havana, 1952. Mem. Am. Fgn. Service Assn., Omicron Delta Kappa. Office: USIA Washington DC 20547

BASYE, PAUL EDMOND, lawyer, educator; b. Nappanee, Ind., Oct. 2, 1901; s. Otto and Carrie C. (Wynekoop) B.; A.B., U. Mo., 1923; J.D., U. Chgo., 1926; LL.M., U. Mich., 1943, S.J.D., 1946; m. Margaret Louise deClercq, June 13, 1931; children—Charles E., John P. Admitted to Mo. bar, 1926, Cal. bar, 1945; practiced in Kansas City, Mo., 1926-42, San Francisco, 1944-48, Burlingame, Cal., 1948-70, San Mateo, Cal., 1970—; asst. prof. law U. Kansas City, 1938-42; prof. law Hastings Coll. Law, U. Cal. at San Francisco, 1948—; prof. law summer sessions Stanford, 1950, U. Tex., 1956, U. So. Cal., 1963, 65. Mem. Am. Bar Assn. (chmn. sect. real property, probate and trust law 1965-66), State Bar Cal. (lectr. continuing edn. program), Order of Coif, Phi Beta Kappa. Author: Clearing Land Titles, 1953, 2d edit., 1970; (with Lewis M. Simes) Problems in Probate Law Including a Model Probate Code, 1946. Contbr. articles legal jours. Home: 471 Cumberland Rd Burlingame CA 94010 Office: 630 N San Mateo Dr San Mateo CA 94401

BATA, THOMAS JOHN, footwear mfr.; b. Prague, Czechoslovakia, Sept. 17, 1914; s. Thomas and Marie (Mencik) B.; ed. pvt. schs., Eng. and Switzerland; grad. Acad. Commerce, Uherske Hradiste, Czechoslovakia; m. Sonja Ingrid Wettstein, Oct. 26, 1946; children—Thomas George, Christine Patricia, Monica Mary Ann, Rosemarie Caroline. Chief exec. Bata Shoe Orgn.; pres. Bata, Ltd.; chmn. Bata Shoe Co. Can., Ltd., Batawa, Ont., 1939—; dir., officer cos. connected with Bata group. Bd. govs. Trent U. Mem. Can. council Nat. Indsl. Conf. Bd.; chmn. Can. Bus. and Industry Adv. Com. to OECD; v.p. Chief Execs. Forum. Bd. dirs. Nat. Ballet Can. Mem. Young Pres.'s Orgn., Am. Mgmt. Assn. Rotarian. Address: 44 Park Lane Circle Don Mills Toronto Ontario Canada also Batawa Ontario Canada

BATASTINI, RALPH CHARLES, transp. co. exec.; b. Chgo., Aug. 30, 1929; s. Charles and Catherine (Tognotti) B.; B.S. in Bus. Edn., Ill. State U., 1951; M.B.A., U. Chgo., 1957; m. Catherine V. Belt, Sept. 3, 1960; children—Brian J., Lynn Ann. Associated with Joseph T. Ryerson & Son, Inc., Chgo., 1956-57; with Greyhound Corp., 1957—, treas., 1961-66, v.p. finance, 1966-71, exec. v.p. finance, dir., 1971—; treas. Greyhound Lines Can. Ltd., 1961-66, now dir.; dir. Eastern Canadian Greyhound Lines Ltd., Travelers Express Co., Inc., Gen. Fire & Casualty Co., Greyhound Brokerage Corp., Compass Ins. Co., Armour & Co. Served to 1st lt. USAF, 1951-55. Decorated D.F.C., Air medal with oak leaf cluster. Office: 111 E Wacker Dr Chicago IL 60601

BATAULT, CLAUDE, French diplomat; b. Paris, Jan. 2, 1918; m. Deborah Martin Richards, May 10, 1954; children—Sylvie, Jean-Claude, Philippe. With French Diplomatic Service, 1945—; head div. Commissary for German Affairs, 1945-46; assigned Ministry Fgn. Affairs, Paris, 1946, tech. assistance econ. affairs, 1954-55, dep. dir. internat. unions div., 1956-58, head Information Service, 1963-65; sec. French embassy, Lisbon, 1952-54; mission of liaison and assistance to Allied Forces, 1955-56; consul gen. of France in Denver, 1958-62, in San Francisco, 1965—; head information div. Ministry Fgn. Affairs, Paris, 1962-65. Served to capt. Free French Forces, 1941-45. Decorated officer Legion of Honor, Croix de Guerre with palms, Medaille de la Resistance, officer d'Orange Nassau, officer Christ of Portugal. Mem. Cercle de l'Union San Francisco Truite, Ombre Saumon, Trout Unlimited, Steamboaters. Clubs: Burlingame Country; Fario, Fly Fishers of Oregon; Club des Pilotes des 24 heures du Mans; Bohemian. Home: 12 Rue Leconte de Lisle Paris XVI France Office: 2570 Jackson St San Francisco CA 94115

BATCHELDER, ANNE STUART (Mrs. Clifton Brooks Batchelder), former mem. Republican Nat. Com.; b. Lake Forest, Ill., Jan. 11, 1920; d. Robert Douglas and Harriet (McClure) Stuart; student Lake Forest Coll., 1941-43; m. Clifton Brooks Batchelder, May 26, 1945; children—Edward, Anne Stuart, Mary Clifton, Lucia Brooks. Clubmobile driver A.R.C., Eng., Belgium, France, Holland and Germany, 1943-45; pub., editor Douglas County Gazette, 1970—; v.p. U.S. Check Book Co., 1971—; dir. Ralph Printing Co., Omaha. Mem. Republican Central Com. Neb., 1955-62, 70—, vice chmn. Central Com., 1959-64, mem. finance com., 1957-64; chmn. women's sect. Douglas County Rep. Finance Com., 1955, vice chmn. com., 1958-60; v.p. Omaha Woman's Rep. Club, 1957-58, pres., 1959-60; alternate del. Nat. Conv., 1956; mem. Rep. Nat. Com. for Neb., 1964-70; asst. chmn. Douglas County Rep. Central Com., 1971—; 1st v.p. Neb. Fedn. Rep. Women, 1971—. Sr. v.p. Neb. Founders Day, 1958; past trustee Brownell Hall, Vis. Nurse Assn. Mem. Mayflower Soc., Colonial Dames, P.E.O. Presbyn. Clubs: Omaha Country, Omaha. Home: 6875 State St Omaha NB 68152

BATCHELDER, ARDERN R., dept. store exec.; b. San Mateo, Cal., Dec. 7, 1910; s. Edgar B. and Edna M. (Hillebrand) B.; B.S., U. Cal. at Berkeley, 1933; m. Marjorie Lee Bowles, July 20, 1935; children—Ardern R., Gabrielle Ann. Gen. mgr. H.C. Capwell Co., Oakland, Cal.; formerly exec. vice pres., chief operating officer, dir. Emporium Capwell Co., Oakland, Cal., now pres., chief exec. officer, dir.; v.p., dir. Broadway Hale Stores; dir. Asso. Merchandising Corp. Active United Crusade. Bd. dirs. Bay Area Council, San Francisco Symphony Assn. Mem. San Francisco C. of C. (bd. dirs.), Sons Pioneers. Club: Orinda. Home: 10 El Sueno Orinda CA 94563 Office: 835 Market Sts San Francisco CA 94103

BATCHELDER, AUGUSTUS HUGH, chemist; b. San Francisco, Dec. 7, 1903; s. John Hugh and Mary (Leech) B.; B.S., U. Cal., 1927; children—George, Paul, James, Ann, John. With research dept. Cal. Ink Co., 1927-30; with petroleum prods. research and devel. Standard Oil of Cal. and Cal. Research Corp., also Chevron Research Co., 1930—, v.p., gen. mgr. labs., 1953-63, pres., 1963-67; v.p. research Standard Oil of Cal., 1968-70. Tech. advisor Cal. Air Resources Bd. Mem. Atomic Indsl. Forum, Coordinating Research Council (bd.), Am. Chem. Soc. (chmn. petroleum div. 1963-64), Am. Ordnance Soc., Faraday Soc., Gordon Research Conf., A.A.A.S., Soc. Automotive Engrs., Am. Petroleum Inst., Soc. Naval Engrs., Sigma Xi, Phi Lambda Upsilon, Alpha Chi Sigma, Tau Beta Pi. Clubs: Commonwealth, Stock Exchange, Engineers. Home: 5557 Yerba Buena Rd Santa Rosa CA 95405 Office: 225 Bush St San Francisco CA 94104

BATCHELDER, EARLE CLAYTON, headmaster; b. Braintree, Mass., Apr. 13, 1928; s. Chester S. and Olive V. (Jones) B.; A.B., McGill U., 1951; M.Ed., Harvard, 1961; m. Nancy Ober, Dec. 19, 1959; children—Mark Edward, Peter Ober, Douglas Nason, Peter Hill. Asst. to headmaster Proctor Acad., Andover, N.H., 1955-59; dir. admissions Bradford (Mass.) Jr. Coll., 1959-62; headmaster Walnut Hill Sch., Natick, Mass., 1962—. Corporator Natick 5 Savs. Bank. Trustee Pingree Sch., Hamilton, Mass., Chapel Hill Sch., Waltham, Mass. Served with AUS, 1945-47. Mem. Nat. Assn. Prins. Schs. Girls (v.p. 1967-69). Rotarian Rotarian (past pres. Natick). Home: 24 Highland St Natick MA 01760

BATCHELDER, ESTHER LORD, home econs. cons.; b. Hartford, Conn., May 19, 1897; d. Joseph W. and Margaret J. (Odell) Batchelder; B.S., Conn. Coll., 1919; M.A., Columbia, 1925, Ph.D., 1929. Chemist, H. Souther Engring. Co., Hartford, 1920-24; research asst. Columbia, 1924-29; nutrition editor Butterick Pub. Co., 1929-32; asst. prof. nutrition Wash. State Coll., 1932-34, U. Ariz., 1934-36; prof., dir. home econs. U. R.I., 1936-42; asst. dir. human nutrition research U.S. Dept. Agr., Washington, 1942-56, dir. clothing and housing research, 1956-65; home economics cons., 1965—. Trustee Conn. Coll. for Women. Recipient Distinguished Service award Dept. Agr., 1954; Alumnae award Conn. Coll., 1969. Mem. Am. Inst. Nutrition, Am. Dietetic Assn., Am. Home Econs. Assn., Am. Women's Assn. Rome (pres. 1971—), Phi Beta Kappa, Sigma Xi, Phi Kappa Phi. Club: Corinthian Yacht (Washington). Address: Viale della Piramide Cestia 1c Rome 00153 Italy

BATCHELDER, HOWARD TIMOTHY, educator; b. Greensboro Bend, Vt., Nov. 24, 1909; s. Charleton Harvey and Marcia Abigail (Fayer) B.; B.S., West Tex. State Coll., 1936; A.M., U. Mich., 1938, Ph.D., 1942; m. Mary Lockwood Sternenberg. Aug. 27, 1931; children—William Howard, Robert Wesley. Prin. Wildorado (Tex.) Pub. Sch., 1931-34, Lakeview Sch., Claude, Tex., 1934-35; high sch. prin., Dimmitt, Tex., 1935-37; prof. social sci. and edn. Miss. State Coll. for Women, 1939-41, prof. edn., head dept., 1942-43; asso. dean Sch. Edn., Ind. U., 1954-68, prof. edn., 1947—; ednl. cons., editor films in tchr. edn. McGraw-Hill Book Co., Inc., 1947-57; adviser AID with U.S. Mission to Pakistan, 1960-67. Served from lt. (j.g.) to lt. comdr., USNR, 1943-46. Mem. N.E.A., Ind. Tchrs. Assn., Am. Assn. U. Profs., Phi Delta Kappa, Phi Kappa Phi, Pi Gamma Mu. Methodist. Author: (with McGlasson and Schorling) Student Teaching in Secondary Schools, 1965. Contbr. articles profl. jours. Home: 1213 Pickwick Pl Bloomington IN 47401

BATCHELDER, LAURENCE, acoustical engr.; b. Cambridge, Mass., Oct. 26, 1906; s. Charles Foster and Laura Poor (Stone) B.; A.B., Harvard, 1928, M.S., 1929; m. Nancy Thayer, Nov. 22, 1929; 1 son, David (dec.). With Submarine Signal Co., Boston, 1929—, merged with Raytheon Co., 1946, now cons. engr. submarine signal div. Mem. U.S. Naval Tech. Mission in Europe, 1945. Chmn. electroacoustics com. Internat. Electrotech. Commn., 1963—. Mem. NRC com. on conservation of hearing, bioacoustics. Trustee Goddard Coll. Fellow A.A.A.S., I.E.E.E., Acoustical Soc. Am. (exec. councilor 1952-54, pres. 1961-62, chmn. acoustical tech. adv. bd.); mem. Am. Nat. Standards Inst. (chmn. sect. com. Z24, acoustics, vibration and mech. shock 1953-57, mem. acoustical standards bd., chmn. com. on standards), Marine Tech. Soc., Am. Inst. Physics (gov. 1963-66). Clubs: Harvard Faculty (Cambridge); Cosmos (Washington). Home and office: 983 Memorial Dr Cambridge MA 02138

BATCHELDER, RICHARD DAVID, edn. assn. exec.; b. Canton, Mass., Mar. 19, 1925; s. Nelson David and Marjorie E. (Curra) B.; student Northeastern U., 1942; A.B., Boston U., 1949; M.Ed., Bridgewater (Mass.) State Tchrs. Coll., 1952; LL.D., Ind. State U., 1966, Elmhurst (Ill.) Coll., 1966; m. Martha Cook, Dec. 23, 1955; children—Anne Elizabeth, Amy Sinclair, Richard David. Tchr. social studies Chatham (Mass.) High Sch., 1949-57; tchr. psychology and U.S. history Newton (Mass.) High Sch., 1957-66, housemaster, 1960-66; exec. sec. so. sect. Cal. Tchrs. Assn., 1967—. Dir. Tchrs. Ins. Co., Edn. Life Ins. Co., Horace Mann Edn. Corp.; chmn. bd. Tchr. Services Corp. Mem. exec. com. N.E.A., 1961-65, v.p., 1964-65, pres., 1965-66; pres. Barnstable Co. Edn. Assn., 1954-55, Chatham Tchrs. Assn., 1952-53, Monomauset Tchrs. Assn., 1950-51, Newton Tchrs. Assn., 1961-63; bd. dirs. Mass. Tchrs. Assn., 1965-66; N.E. Regional dir. Dept. Classroom Tchrs., N.E.A., 1956-59, pres., 1959-60; bd. dirs. N.E.A. Mut. Fund, 1965—; chmn. bd. Educators Fund Mgmt. Corp., 1965—. Served with A.C. USNR, 1942-46. Recipient Nicholas I. Tillinghast award Bridgewater State Coll., 1966. Mem. P.T.A., Sigma Alpha Epsilon. Episcopalian. Home: 1160 S Oakland Pasadena CA 91106 Office: 1125 W 6th St Los Angeles CA 90017

BATCHELDER, WILLIAM GEORGE, Jr., lawyer; b. Cleve., July 30, 1914; s. William George and Mary (Hutchins) B.; B.A., Ohio Wesleyan U., 1936; LL.B., U. Cin., 1939, J.D., 1967; m. Eleanor Dice, Feb. 22, 1941; children-William, Barbara (Mrs. Donald H. Adams, Jr.), Marvin, Kathryn, John. Admitted to Ohio bar, 1939, since practiced in Medina; prosecuting atty., Medina County, 1941-53; asso. Thompson, Hine & Flory, Cleve., 1953-58; partner Williams & Batchelder, 1958—. Sec. Medina County Properties. Mem. Bd. Edn. Medina City Sch. Dist., 1960-64. Chmn. Medina County Republican Exec. Com., 1952-54. Trustee Medina County Hist. Soc.; mem. Berks County, Montgomery County (Pa.) hist. socs., Geneal. Soc. Pa., Ohio Family Historians. Served with AUS, 1942-45. Fellow Coll. Am. Probate Counsel; mem. Am., Ohio, Medina County, Cleve, bar assns., Internat. Assn. Ins. Counsel., S.A.R., V.F.W., Phi Beta Kappa, Omicron Delta Kappa, Delta Sigma Rho, Delta Tau Delta. Episcopalian. Mason (32, K.T., Shriner). Home: 513 E Washington St Medina OH 44256 Office: 120 W Washington St Medina OH 44256

BATCHELLER, EDGAR HADLEY, ret. naval officer; b. Mattapoisett, Mass., May 2, 1910; s. James Hervey and Elizabeth Towne (Field) B.; B.S., U.S. Naval Acad., 1934; M.S., Mass. Inst. Tech., 1939; grad. Naval War Coll., 1954; m. Anne Gordon King, June 14, 1936; children—Edgar Hadley, Gordon Douglass, James. Commd. ensign U.S. Navy, 1934, advanced through grades to rear adm., 1961; assigned Boston Naval Shipyard, 1939-44, Western Pacific, 1944-46, Navy Dept., 1946-50, maintenance office Pacific Fleet, 1950-53, Naval Shipyard, Portsmouth, N.H., 1954-56; comptroller Bur. Ships, 1956-59; supr. shipbldg. Quincy (Mass.) Shipyard, 1959-61; asst. chief plans adminstrn., inspr. gen. Bur. Ships, 1961-63; comdr. Charleston Naval Shipyard, S.C., 1963-68; inspr. gen. Naval Ship Systems Command, 1968-69; retired, 1969. Decorated Bronze Star, Legion of Merit, Commendation ribbon. Mem. Am. Soc. Naval Engrs., Soc. Naval Architects and Marine Engrs., Mil. Order Carebao, Master Mechanics and Foremans Assn. (hon.), Sigma Xi. Home: 3806 Kanawha St NW Washington DC 20015

BATCHELLER, WILLIS TRYON, cons. engr.,; b. Joliet, Ill., Dec. 23, 1889; s. Willis Watson and Leonore (Tryon) B.; B.S. in Elec. Engring., U. Wash., 1911, E.E., 1915; m. Alice Louise Rapp, Mar. 25, 1914. Testing engr. Puget Sound Power & Light Co., 1910-11; with Seattle Light & Power System, 1912-21; pres. and chief engr. Canadian Alaska Ry. Co.; pres. and dir. Willis T. Batcheller Internat., Inc., Seattle, also N.Y.C., Washintton, La Paz, Bolivia, Manila, Philippines, Saigon, Vietnam; cons. engr. hydro-electric, hydraulic and power projects or systems; served as engr. design and constrn. three 10,000 kilowatt units of Lake Union steam electric plant; 18,000 h.p. hydro- electric devel. at Cedar Falls; preliminary work and design Skagit River power project; report and survey 2,800,000 h.p. hydro-electric devel. on Columbia River, at Grand Coulee, 1,600,000 h.p. Chief Joseph power project, with 1,800,000-acre Columbia Basin irrigation project; engr. Nimpkish River pulp, paper and power project of Internat. Harvester Co. on n. end Vancouver Island; engr. Quincy Valley Irrigation Dist.; engr. Columbia Basin Project; engr. Richland Atomic Energy Project, including research upgrading Hanford nuclear reactor and steam turbine plant, Bolsa Island nuclear power and desalting plant, Los Angeles; pioneered WEST Four Corners (N.M.) coal and power plant 632,000 kw turbines to be followed by several 750,000 kw turbines, similar Centralia (Wash.) plant with two 750,000 kw Turbines along with coal processing facilities for by-products; planning 2,000,000 kw nuclear power plants to supply power shortage in Northwest Power Pool; also engr. many power, irrigation and water supply and indsl. projects; cons. govt. war indsl. projects. Cons. Washington Toll Bridge Authority and State Hwy. Commn. Pres., chief engr. Canadian Alaska Ry. Co. involving 3300 mi. transcontinental system from Seattle, and Vancouver, B.C. to Fairbanks, Alaska. Mem. state devel. com. and indsl. com. Seattle C. of C., former chmn. Reclamation Com. Chmn. Northwest Br. Y.M.C.A., Seattle. Registered profl. engr., Wash., Ore., B.C. Mem. Am. Concrete Inst., I.E.E.E., Am. Soc. M.E. (profl. practice com., dir. Western Wash. sect. divs. on fuels, heat transfer, power, nuclear engring., energetics), S.A.R., Seattle Municipal League, Engrs. Club, Nat. Soc. Profl. Engrs. Christian Scientist. Mason (32, K.T., Shriner). Contbr. engring. and financial subjects. Home: 1848 N 51st St Seattle WA 98103 Office: Alaska Bldg 618 2d Av Seattle WA 98104 also 17 Park Av New York City NY 10016

BATCHELOR, CLARENCE DANIEL, cartoonist; b. Osage City, Kan.; s. Daniel L. and Lillian Eugenia (James) B.; ed. Osage City Pub. sch. and Salina High Sch., 1894-1907, Chicago Art Inst., 1907-10; m. Hazel Deyo, 1918 (dec.); m. 2d, Julie Margaret Forsyth, June 19, 1948 (dec.); m. 3rd, Allegra Summers Taylor, 1959. Staff artist Kansas City Star, 1911; free lance mag. drawings, 1914-18; cartoonist Ledger Syndicate, N.Y. Post, 1923-31; N.Y. News editorial cartoonist, 1930-69. Bronze bust J. M. Patterson; oil murals Infinity and History of Printed Word in News Bldg. Awarded $200 prize for 6 best cartoons on pub. health by A.M.A., 1912; Pulitzer prize, 1937; Nat. Headliners Plaque, 1938; Page One award, 1965. Mem. Nat. Assn. Editorial Cartoonists. Clubs: Dutch Treat, Silurian, Mile Creek; Nat. Arts, Originator automobile safety series, Inviting the Undertaker. Home and studio: Deep River CT 06417

BATCHELOR, HAROLD WALTER, librarian; b. Vancouver, Wash., May 28, 1910; s. Harry Job and Emma (Jost) B.; student Reed Coll., Portland, Ore., 1927-29; A.B., U. Ore., 1932; B.L.S., U. Ill., 1933, M.S., 1937; m. Alberta Kern, Aug. 11, 1936; children—Eric Brian, Brenda Louise, Bret Alan. Cataloger, U. Ill., 1934-39; head librarian, asso. prof. Baldwin-Wallace Coll., Berea, O., 1939-43; librarian, head dept. library sci. Arizona State Univ., Tempe, 1943-59, u. librarian, 1959-62, prof., 1956, chmn., prof. dept. library sci., 1962-69; bookseller, propr. The Bookshelf, Tempe, 1969—. Mem. A.L.A., Assn. Coll. and Reference Libraries, S.W., Ariz. (editor of quar. bull.) library assns., Am. Assn. U. Profs., Bibliog. Soc. Am. Phoenix Exec. Club, Newcomen Soc., Beta Phi Mu, Alpha Beta Alpha. Republican. Home: 111 W 7th St Tempe AZ 85281 Office: 21 E 7th St Tempe AZ 85281

BATDORFF, EMERSON, newspaperman. Motion picture editor Cleve. Plain Dealer. Office: 1801 Superior Av Cleveland OH 44114*

BATE, ROGER REDMOND, air force officer; b. Denver, Jan. 17, 1923; s. Harold Thomas and Eunice (Redmond) B.; student Cal. Inst. Tech., 1941-43; B.S., U.S. Mil. Acad., 1947; B.A. (Rhodes scholar 1947-50), Oxford (Eng.) U., 1949, B.S., 1950, M.A., 1955; Ph.D., Stanford, 1966; m. Jeannette Stevens Hockman, June 3, 1947; children—Kathryn, Anne, Donald, Gordon, Carol, Constance. Commd. 2d lt. U.S. Army, 1947, advanced through grades to maj., 1960; trans. to USAF, 1962, advanced through grades to col.; with reactor theory group Oak Ridge Nat. Lab., 1953-56; various Army assignments, 1950-53, 56-59; faculty dept. astronautics USAF Acad., 1959—, prof., 1962—, head dept., 1963—, chmn. engring. scis. div., 1966—, vice dean faculty, 1970—. Decorated Bronze Star medal. Mem. Assn. Computing Machinery, Assn. U.S. Army, Am. Inst. Aeros. and Astronautics, Sigma Xi. Home: Quarters 4186 USAF Acad CO 80840

BATE, WALTER JACKSON, educator; b. Mankato, Minn., May 23, 1918; s. William G. and Isabel (Melick) B.; A.B., Harvard, 1939, M.A., 1940, Ph.D., 1942; L.H.D., Ind. U., 1969; Litt.D., Merrimack Coll., 1970. Mem. faculty English. Harvard, 1946—, prof., 1956—, prof., 1956—, chmn. dept. history and lit., 1955-56, chmn. dept. English, 1956-63, 66-68; Abbott Lawrence Lowell prof. humanities, 1962—. Guggenheim fellow, 1956. Member American Philosophical Society, American Academy of Arts and Scis., Phi Beta Kappa (Christian Gauss award lit. history and criticism 1956, 64, 70). Author: Negative Capability, 1939; The Stylistic Development of Keats, 1945; From Classic to Romantic, 1946; Criticism: the Major Texts, 1952; The Achievement of Samuel Johnson, 1955; Prefaces to Criticism, 1959; John Keats, 1963 (Pulitzer Prize 1964); Coleridge,

1968; The Burden of the Past and the English Poet, 1970. Contbr. editor Yale edit. of Works of Samuel Johnson. Home: Eliot House Harvard U Cambridge MA 02138 Office: 3 Warren House Cambridge MA 02138

BATEMAN, DUPUY, Jr., indsl. exec.; b. Henderson, Tex., Dec. 19, 1904; s. Dupuy and Lola Bell (Harris) B.; student Rice Inst., 1922-25; m. Nancy Gay, Apr. 15, 1945; children—Sally, Elizabeth, George, Dupuy III. With Anderson, Clayton & Co. (or subsidiaries), Houston, 1927-64, v.p., dir. 1945-59, exec. v.p., dir., 1959-64; partner Anderson, Clayton & Fleming, N.Y.C., 1945-64; partner Golightly & Bateman, mgmt. cons., 1964-65; v.p., asst. to pres. for corporate devel. N.Am. Rockwell Corp., 1965-68, sr. v.p., dir., 1968—. Mem. standing liturgical commn. and exec. council P.E. Ch. Episcopalian. Home: 418 Emerson St Pittsburgh PA 15206 Office: 2300 E Imperial Hwy El Segundo CA 90245 also N Am Rockwell Bldg Pittsburgh PA 15222

BATEMAN, DURWARD FRANKLIN, plant pathologist, educator; b. Tyner, N.C., May 28, 1934; s. Benny Franklin and Grace (Cale) B.; B.S., N.C. State Coll., 1956; M.S., Cornell U., 1958, Ph.D., 1960; m. Shirley Eugenia Byrum, June 23, 1953; children—Cynthia Anne, Brenda Sue, Diane Mia. Asst. prof. dept. plant pathology Cornell U., Ithaca, N.Y., 1960-65, asso. prof., 1965-69, prof., 1969-70, prof., chmn. dept., 1970—, tchr. grad. course in area of disease and pathogen physiology, 1963—, field rep. dept. plant pathology Grad. Sch., 1966-69; cons. NIH, 1968. Spl. NIH fellow U. Cal., Davis, 1967. Fellow Am. Soc.; mem. Am. Soc. Plant Physiologists, A.A.A.S., Internat. Soc. Plant Pathology, Sigma Xi, Phi Kappa Phi, Kappa Phi Kappa, Gamma Sigma Delta. Contbr. articles profl. jours. Home: 7 Bean Hill Lane Ithaca NY 14850

BATEMAN, FRANK BRACE, investment banker; b. Grenloch, N.J., Nov. 20, 1897; s. Frederic Harlan and Ellen (Brace) B.; war diploma, Cornell, 1919; m. Dorothy Hawkins, June 29, 1932; children—Barbara Ellen, Brace John. Sales mgr. Bateman Mfg. Co. and successor cos., 1919-30; with Blair & Co., Inc., N.Y.C. as dir., v.p., vice chmn., 1930-55; pres., dir. Fla. Growth Co., Fla. Growth Fund, Inc.; mng. partner Frank B. Bateman, Ltd., investment co., Palm Beach, Fla.; financial v.p., dir. Ocean Measurements, Inc.; dir. Gulf States Devel. Corp., Corpus Christi, Jupiter Oils Ltd., Toronto, Ont., Can. Served as cpl. C.A.C., U.S. Army, 1918. Mem. Inter-Frat. Council Cornell U., Zeta Psi. Presbyn. Clubs: Bond, City Midday (N.Y.C.); Cornell; Everglades, Bath and Tennis, Beach (Palm Beach, Fla.). Home: 209 Banyan Rd Palm Beach FL 33480 Office: 243 S County Rd Palm Beach FL 33480

BATEMAN, FRED WILLOM, lawyer; b. Roper, N.C., Sept. 18, 1916; s. N.D. and Eloise (Tarkenton) B.; B.A., Wake Forest Coll., 1939; postgrad. Law Sch., U. N.C., 1939-42; m. Frances M. Sondag, June 12, 1944; 1 son, Michael Stuart. Admitted to Ill. bar, 1947, Va. bar, 1950, also U.S. Supreme Ct.; pvt. practice, Newport News, Va., 1952—; sr. partner Bateman, West & Beale. Mem. Va. Senate from Newport News, 1960-68; permanent mem. Fed. Jud. Conf. for 4th circuit. Dir. Guaranteed Foods Inc.; chmn. bd. First Va. Bank of Peninsula. Mem. Warwick (Va.) Electorial Bd., 1955; mgr. Congl. and Senatorial Democratic campaigns, 1955—; chmn. Jefferson Jackson Dinner, 1965. Served as officer USNR, World War II; PTO. Mem. Va. State Bar (pres. 1964-65), Va. Bar Assn. (jud. inquiry and rev. commn.), Magna Carta Commn., Nat. Conf. Bar Pres. Rotarian, Elk, Mason. Home: 23 Cedar Lane Newport News VA 23601 Office: 11048 Warwick Blvd Newport News VA 23601

BATEMAN, GEORGE MONROE, retired educator; b. Bloominton, Ida., Sept. 12, 1897; s. Alfred John and Clara (Hess) B.; B.S., Utah State U., 1921; M.S. in Chemistry, Cornell U., 1926, Ph.D., 1927; m. Florence Harris, May 24, 1922; children—Cornella (dec.), Flora Mae, Georgia Rose, Harold Harris. Instr. sci. and math. Grace (Ida.) High Sch., 1921-22; prin. sch., Arimo, Ida., 1922-24; instr. dairy chemistry Cornell U., 1925-27, prof. chemistry, head sci. dept., 1927-51; prof. chemistry Ariz. State Univ., Tempe, 1936-69, emeritus prof., 1969—, head phys. sci. div., 1951-64. Bishop, Tempe Ward, Church of Jesus Christ of Latter-day Saints, 1944-48. Served as pvt. U.S. Army, 1918; O.R.C., 1932-42; capt., C.W.S., 1941-42. Recipient Silver Beaver award Boy Scouts Am. Fellow A.A.A.S., Am. Inst. Chemists, Ariz. Acad. Sci., Phi Kappa Phi, Sigma Xi. Author scientific articles. Home: 515 E Bradmor Dr Tempe AZ 85282

BATEMAN, JOHN JAY, educator; b. Elmira, N.Y., Feb. 17, 1930; s. Joseph Earl and Etha M. (Edwards) B.; B.A., U. Toronto, 1953; M.A., Cornell U., 1954; Ph.D., 1958; m. Patricia Ann Hageman, July 5, 1952; children—Kristine M., Kathleen A., John Eric. Lectr., Univ. Coll., U. Toronto, 1956-57; lectr., then asst. prof. U. Ottawa, 1957-60; mem. Faculty U. Ill., Urbana, 1960—, prof. Classics, 1968—, head dept., 1966-71. Democratic precinct committeeman, 1964-68; sec. Champaign Dem. Central Com., 1965- 66. Mem. Am. Philol. Assn. (sec.-treas. 1968-72), Am. Classical League, Classical Assn. Middle West and South, Renaissance Soc. Am., Am. Civil Liberties Union. K.C. Author articles. Home: 706 W Healey St Champaign IL 61820 Office: Fgn Lang Bldg Univ Ill Urbana IL 61801

BATEMAN, JUSTUS CARROLL, pub. relations exec.; b. Norwood, Pa., July 13, 1917; s. Thomas Birkhead and Louise (Mueller) B.; B.S., Johns Hopkins, 1952; M.A., N.Y.U., 1963; m. Marguerite Helen Foerster, Aug. 11, 1940; children—Carol Anne (Mrs. James S. Hannum), Walter Raymond. Reporter, rewriteman, also spl. assignments Balt. Eve. Sun, 1934-41; asst. editor B. & O. mag., B. & O. R.R., Balt., 1942, pub. relations rep., 1946-51, asst. dir. pub. relations, 1951-53; asst. chmn. Eastern R.R. Presidents' Conf., N.Y.C., 1953-55; dir. pub. relations Milk Industry Fund, Washington, 1955-60; gen. mgr. Ins. Information Inst., N.Y.C., 1960, pres., 1967—. Mem. bd. edn. Kinnelson Borough, N.J., 1964-67. Bd. dirs. Greater N.Y. Safety Council, N.Y.C., 1963—; trustee Found. Pub. Relations Research and Edn., N.Y.C., 1963-67. Served to capt. AUS, 1943-46. Mem. Pub. Relations Soc. Am. (pres. 1967), Am. Council Edn. for Journalism, Newcomen Soc. Clubs: Bankers (N.Y.C.); Army-Navy, Nat. Press. (Washington); Johns Hopkins (Balt.). Contbr. profl. jours. Home: 101 Fox Ledge Rd Smoke Rise NJ 07405 Office: 110 William St New York City NY 10038

BATEMAN, PAUL TREVIER, educator, mathematician; b. Phila., June 6, 1919; s. Harold John and Anna (Yeager) B.; A.B., U. Pa., 1939, A.M., 1940, Ph.D., 1946; m. Felice Hilda Davidson, June 25, 1948; 1 dau., Sarah Elizabeth. Lectr., Bryn Mawr Coll., 1945-46; instr. Yale, 1946-48; mem. Inst. Advanced Study, Princeton, 1948-50; mem. faculty U. Ill. at Urbana, 1950—, prof. math., 1958—, head dept., 1965—; vis. prof. U. Pa., 1961-62, City U. N.Y., 1964-65. Sr. Postdoctoral fellow NSF, 1956-57. Mem. Math. Assn. Am., London, Indian, Am. (asso. sec. 1966—, trustee 1971—, mem.-at-large council 1961-63) math. socs., Am. Assn. U. Profs. Home: 108 Meadows St Urbana IL 61801

BATEMAN, RICHARD MARION, coll. pres.; b. Cin., July 2, 1910; s. Ralph Gray and Viola Ellen (Stoltz) B.; B.S., Purdue U., 1933, M.S., 1934; Ph.D., U. Chgo., 1948; m. Maxine Elnora Fogleman, Aug. 8, 1936. Asst. freshman football coach Purdue U., 1933-34; instr. social studies, asst. football and basketball coach Peru (Ind.) High Sch., 1934-36, dean boys, dir. guidance, instr. social sci., 1936-38, prin., 1938-42; research asst. to Dr. Leonard Koos, U. Chgo., 1946, asst. edn. to Dr. William C. Reavis, 1946-47, ednl. dir. Internat. Harvester Co. research project at univ., 1946-47, asst. dir. project, 1947, dean students Univ. Coll., 1947; dist. mgr., asso. prof. adminstrn. Purdue U. Center, Ft. Wayne, 1947-50, dir., asso. prof., 1950-59, prof., dir., 1959-60, mgr., N.W. Ind. Dist. of center, 1960; pres. Tri-State Coll., Angola, Ind., 1960—. Mem. adv. bd. 2668th Air Res., Ft. Wayne, 1955-57; mem. Ind. Gov.'s Youth Council, 1960-61. Bd. Bd. dirs. Ft. Wayne Art Sch. and Mus., 1958-61, 2d v.p., 1955-60; edn. adv. com. Parkview Meth. Hosp. Sch. Nursing, Ft. Wayne, 1957-61; pres. bd. trustees Cameron Hosp., 1965-67, mem. Ind. State Bd. Vocational and Tech. Edn., 1965-69, exec. com. Independent Colls. and Univs. Indiana, 1969—; bd. dirs. N.E. Ind. Heart Found., 1956- 57; adv. bd. Sr. Citizens Ft. Wayne,1957-59. Served to lt. comdr. USNR, 1942-46; capt. Res. Mem. Am. Assn. Adult Edn. (Ind. del. 1956-58), Ind. Assn. Adult Ed., Am. Soc. Engring. Edn., Am. Ednl. Research Assn., N.E.A., Purdue Alumni Assn., Naval Res. Assn., Nat. U. Ednl. Assn., Nat., Ind. leagues nursing, Phi Delta Kappa, Angola C. of C., Navy League U.S. (nat. dir., pres. Ind. 1968—). Methodist. Rotarian, Kiwanian. Contbr. articles profl. jours. Home: 520 Gale St Angola IN 46703

BATEMAN, WILLIAM BAILEY, banker; b. Peace Dale, R.I., Mar. 11, 1924; s. Everett J. and Hortense (Bailey) B.; B.A., Brown U., 1945; M.B.A., Harvard, 1947; m. Nancy Greene Sherman, Feb. 7, 1948; children—Pamela Ann, Robert William, Carol Jean, Alison Susan. With Chase Manhattan Bank, 1947—, sr. v.p., 1969-71, exec. v.p., 1971—. Republican. Conglist. (deacon). Home: 20 Beach Dr Noroton CT 06820 Office: 1 Chase Manhattan Plaza New York City NY 10015

BATEMAN, WILLIAM H., III, business exec.; b. Balt., Feb. 10, 1907; s. W.H. and E. Lois (Coates) B.; m. Annabelle Phillips, Apr. 20, 1951; children—William Phillips, Sally Ann, Judith Coates, Jennifer Davis. Devel. engr. Atlantic Refining Co., 1929-33; pres. Solgas, Inc.-Sun Oil Co., 1933-49, Martin & Schwartz, 1937-51; pres. Wayne Pump Co., 1951-58, co. merged with Symington-Gould Corp., now pres., dir. Symington Wayne Corp., also chmn. exec. com.; dir. Farmers & Merchants Bank. Office: West College Av Salisbury MD 21780

BATES, A. ALLAN, physical sci. adminstr.; b. Elyria, O., July 28, 1901; s. Adram Peterman and Evalyn (Sipes) B.; B.A., Ohio Wesleyan U., 1923, D.Litt., 1970; B.S., Case Inst. Tech., 1925, M.S., 1927; D.Sc., U. Nancy (France); D.Eng. (hon.), Stevens Inst. Tech., 1944; D.Sc. (hon.), Rose Poly. Inst., 1948; m. Ruth Nanette Barnes, Sept. 1, 1926; children—Allan Charles, Richard Robert. Prof. metallurgy Case Inst., 1926-36; mgr. materials research Westinghouse Electric Corp., 1936-46; v.p. Portland Cement Assn., 1947-60; dir. N.Y.U., 1960-62; chief bldg. research div. Nat. Bur. Standards, 1962-70, dir. Office Standards Policy, Dept. Commerce, 1968-70; prof. metallurgy Escola Politechnica, Sao Paulo, Brazil, 1943. Chmn. exchange delegation on constrn. U.S.A.-USSR, 1960, 65, 70. Mem. Alsos Mission, spl. intelligence, ETO, 1944-45. Recipient Award of Merit, Dept. Def., World War II. Mem. Am. Soc. Testing and Materials (nat. pres. 1960), Am. Concrete Inst. (nat. pres. 1965-66), Internat. Council Bldg. Research (exec. com.), Internat. Union Materials Testing Labs. (exec. com.), Nat. Acad. Scis. (vice chmn. bldg. research adv. bd. 1961), Am. Soc. C.E., Am. Inst. M.E., Am. Soc. Metals, Am. Chem. Soc., Sigma Xi, Phi Delta Theta, Tau Beta Pi. Mem. Soc. Friends. Clubs: Cosmos (Washington); Racquet (Phila.); University (Chgo.). Home: 3342 Stephenson Pl NW Washington DC 20015 Office: Bldg Research Div Nat bureau of Standards Washington DC 20234

BATES, ALAN, actor; b. Allestree, Derbyshire, Eng., Feb. 17, 1934; s. Harold Arthur and Florence Mary (Wheatcroft) B.; student Royal Acad. Dramatic Arts, London; pupil of acting with Claude W. Gibson, of voice with Gladys Lea; m. Victoria Ward; 2 sons (twins). Theatrical appearances include You and Your Wife, 1955; The Mulberry Bush, 1956; The Crucible, 1956; Look Back in Anger, 1956; Cards of Identity, 1956; The Country Wife, 1956; The Apollo de Bellac, 1957; Yes and After, 1957; Long Day's Journey Into Night, 1958; The Caretaker, 1960, others; films include The Entertainer, 1960; Whistle Down the Wind, 1962; A Kind of Loving, 1962; The Running Man; The Caretaker; Nothing But the Best, 1963, Georgie Girl, King of Hearts, The Fixer (Oscar nomination), others; numerous TV appearances in Eng. and U.S. Served with RAF two years. Recipient Forbes Robertson award Royal Acad. Dramatic Art; Clarence Derwent award. Mem. Actors Equity Assn., Brit. Actors Equity Assn. Address: care William Morris Agy Melrose House Savile Row London W 1 England

BATES, ALAN P., educator; b. Chgo., June 5, 1915; s. Lewis George and Grace Bates; B.A., U. Wash., 1938; M.A., 1940, Ph.D., 1950; student U. Minn.; m. Elsie Alvene Buckman, Sept. 1, 1939; children—Eugene Paul, Thomas Philip. Labor market analyst War Manpower Commn., 1942-44; asst. to regional adminstr. Nat. Housing Agy., 1946-47; asso. dept. sociology U. Wash., 1947-49; from instr. to asso. prof. dept. sociology U. Neb., chmn. dept. sociology, 1956-69, now prof. Served with AUS, 1944-46. Fellow Am. Sociol. Assn.; mem. Midwest Sociol. Soc., Am. Assn. U. Profs., Alpha Kappa Delta. Author: (with Julius Cohen, R.A.H. Robson) Parental Authority: The Community and the Law; The Sociological Enterprise, also articles in profl. jours. Home: 6446 Westshore Dr Lincoln NB 68516

BATES, BLANCHARD WESLEY, educator; b. Portland, Me., June 19, 1908; s. Wesley Wilmore and Edith (Littlefield) B.; B.A., Bowdoin Coll., 1931; M.A., Harvard, 1933; Ph.D., Princeton, 1941; m. Margaret Thayer Andrews, June 22, 1935; children—Leila Thayer (Mrs. Cevat Erder), Barbara Edith (Mrs. F. William Marshall, Jr.), George Wesley. Tchr. Ecole Normale, LaRochelle, France, 1931-32, Fresnal Ranch Sch., Tucson, 1934-37, Princeton, 1937-39, 46—, prof. Romance langs. 1965—. Served with OSS, AUS, 1943-45. Mem. Modern Lang. Assn., Renaissance Soc., Soc. French Hist. Studies. Author: Loys LeRoy: De la vicissitude ou variete des choses on l'univers, 1944; Literary Portraiture in the Historical Narrative of the French Renaissance, 1945; Selected Essays of Michel de Montaigne, 1949. Home: 10 College Rd Princeton NJ 08540

BATES, CHARLES CARPENTER, oceanographer; b. nr. Harrison, Ill., 1918; s. Carl Albert and Vera Elizabeth (Carpenter) B.; grad. (Rector scholar 1936-39) DePauw U., 1939; M.A., U. Cal. at Los Angeles, 1944; Ph.D. in Geol. Oceanography, Tex. A. and M. Coll., 1953; student Cath. U., 1947-48, Johns Hopkins, 1951, George Washington U., 1954; m. Pauline Barta; children—Nancy Ann, Priscilla Jane, Sally Jean. Geophys. trainee Carter Oil Co., 1939-41; spl. asst. to pres. Am. Meteorol. Soc., 1945-46; mem. survey phys. and geol. environment Marshall Is. relative to pending Bikini atomic bomb tests, 1946; with div. oceanography U.S. Navy Hydrographic Office, 1946- 57, dept. dir. div., 1953-57; part-time cons. in field to govt. and industry, 1946-52; environmental surveillance coordinator Office Devel. Coordinator, Office Naval Research, 1957-60; chief VELA uniform br. Advanced Research Projects Agy., Office Sec. Def., 1960-64; sci. and tech. dir. U.S. Naval Oceanographic Office, 1964-68; sci. adviser to comdt., also dep. and chief scientist Office Research and Devel., USCG, 1968—. Mem. bd. experts Civil Service Examiners, 1954-60; mem. adv. com. postdoctoral awards for Fulbright grants NRC, 1957-60, chmn., 1959-60; vis. geoscientist Am. Geol. Inst., 1959-60; mem. meteorology panel, space sci. bd. Nat. Acad. Sci., 1959-61; mem. Mcht. Marine Council, 1968- 71, Nat. Transp. Research Bd., 1968—; mem. sea grant adv. council La. State U. System, 1968—; co-chmn. U.S.-Japan panel in air facilities U.S.-Japan Natural Resource Program, 1969-71. Served to capt. USAAF, 1941-45. Decorated Bronze Star; recipient U.S. Navy Meritorious Civilian award, 1962; U.S. Navy Superior Civilian Service award, 1969. Mem. Am. Geophys. Union (chmn. com. interaction sea and atmosphere 1950, mem. council 1964-67), Soc. Exploration Geophysicists (council 1963- 67, v. p. 1965-66), Am. Meteorol. Soc. (chmn. com. indsl. bus. and agrl. meteorology 1946-48), Am. Assn. Petroleum Geologists (President's award 1954), Geol. Soc. Washington, Sigma Xi. Author numerous articles, reports in field. Editor meteorol. terms Glossary of Geology and Related Items, 1957. Home: 5807 Massachusetts Av NW Washington DC 20016 Office: Hdqrs U S Coast Guard Washington DC 20591

BATES, CORNELIUS JOHN LIGHTHALL, Jr., clergyman; b. Karulzawa, Japan, July 25, 1911 (parents Can. citizens); s. Cornelius John Lighthall and Harriet Edna (Philp) B.; B.A., Victoria U., Toronto, Can., 1933; diploma Emmanuel Coll., Toronto, 1936; S.T.M., Union Theol. Sem., N.Y.C., 1940; D.D., Coll. Wooster, 1952; student New Coll., Edinburgh, Scotland, summer 1961; m. Jean Hardie Welford, July 6, 1936: children—Madelaine Anne, Margaret Elizabeth (Mrs. Roger K. Fawcett), Cornelius John Lighthall III. Ordained to ministry United Ch. Can.; pastor in Hornepayne, Ont., Can., 1937-39, Pitts., 1940-42, Saltsburg, Pa., 1942-45, Wooster, O., 1945-51. 1st Presbyn. Ch., Greenwich, Conn., 1951-65, Westminster Presbyn. Ch., Mpls., 1965—. Former pastoral asso. Union Theol. Sem.; past moderator synods New Eng. and Minn.; chmn. brotherhood com. Greenwich Clergy; former mem. United Presbyn. Found.; former mem. Gen. Assembly Dept. Ministerial Relations. Active local A.R.C., Community Chest, Boy Scouts Am., UN Council. Bd. dirs. McCormick Theol. Sem., Chgo., United Theol. Sem., Mpls., Macalester Coll., St. Paul. Abbott-Northwestern Hosp., Mpls., Presbyn. Homes St. Paul. Clubs: Minikahda, Minneapolis, Rotary. Office: Westminster Presbyn Ch Minneapolis MN 55440

BATES, DAVID EDWARD, mfg. co. exec.; b. Montreal, Que., Can., Mar. 4, 1919; s. Charles Wesley and Florence (Wilcox) B.; came to U.S., 1930, naturalized, 1943; grad. Am. Inst. Banking, 1946; student Golden Gate Coll., San Francisco, 1946-49; m. Colette Bowers, July 4, 1941; children—Bonnie Bonita, Robert Charles; m. 2d, Marie Catherine Holmes, May 28, 1967. Asst. casher Bank of Am., San Francisco, 1936-51; asst. sec. Hewlett Packard Co., Palo Alto, Cal., 1951-62; sr. financial analyst Electronics Capital Corp., San Diego, 1962-63; treas., controller Lynch Communications Systems, Inc., San Francisco, 1963-66; treas. Omark Industries, Inc., Portland, Ore., 1966—. Served with USNR, 1943-45. Mem. Financial Execs. Inst., Tax Execs. Inst., Nat. Tax Assn., Am. Mgmt. Assn. Home: 1864 Campus Way Lake Oswego OR 97034 Office: 2100 SE Milport Portland OR 97222

BATES, DAVID VINCENT, educator, physician; b. Kent, Eng., May 20, 1922; s. John Vincent and Alice (Dickins) B.; M.B., B.Ch., Cambridge (Eng.) U., 1945, M.D., 1954; m. Margaret Sutton, Mar. 24, 1948; children—Anne Elizabeth, Joanna Margaret, Andrew Vincent. Intern, resident St. Bartholomew Hosp. 1944- 45; sr. lectr. medicine, U. London Sch. Medicine, 1953-56; research fellow U. Pa., 1952; physician Royal Victoria Hosp., Montreal, Can., 1967—; asst. prof. medicine McGill U. Sch. Medicine, 1956—, prof. exptl. medicine, 1965—, asso. dean grad. studies and research, 1964-67, chmn. dept. physiology, 1967—; dir. respiratory div., joint cardiorespiratory service Royal Victoria, Montreal Childrens hosps., 1957-67. Fellow Royal Coll. Physicians (London), Royal Coll. Physicians (Can.); mem. Am., Canadian socs. clin. investigation, Am., Canadian physiol. socs., Physiol. Soc. London. Author: (with Christie) Respiratory Function in Disease, 1965; also articles. Home: 470 Portland Av Montreal 305 Quebec Canada

BATES, EDWARD BRILL, ins. co. exec.; b. Lexington, Mo., May 14, 1919 s. Worth and Faye Marvin (Brill) B.; B.A. in Bus. Adminstrn., U. Chgo., 1940; m. Mary Louise Van Sickle; children—Lynn Louise, Russell, Stephen Worth. With Conn. Mut. Life Ins. Co., 1946—, gen. agt., Kansas City, 1949-53, gen. agt., Los Angeles, 1953-59, 2d agy. v.p., Hartford, 1960-61, v.p., 1961-62, exec. v.p., 1962-67, pres., 1967—; dir. Cushman Industries, Inc., Coca-Cola Bottling Co. So. New Eng., Stanley Works, Hartford Courant; asso. dir. Conn. Bank & Trust Co.; trustee N.E. Utilities Bd. dirs.; Hartford Hosp.; trustee Am. Coll. Life Underwriters. C.L.U., 1957. Clubs: Hartford; Hartford Golf (West Hartford); Country of Florida (Delray Beach). Home: 75 Bloomfield Av Hartford CT 06105 Office: 140 Garden St Hartford CT 06115

BATES, EMMERT WARREN, pub.; b. Detroit, May 14, 1910; s. Royal Teele and Helen (Emmert) B.; A.B., Yale, 1932; m. Louise George, July 20, 1935; children—Richard Emmert, Barbara (Mrs. Charles R. Stevens). Sec. Am. Book Co., N.Y.C. 1942-49, 1st v.p., 1946-67, dir., 1944-67, mgr. coll. div., 1953-57; sr. v.p. Litton Ednl. Pub., Inc., 1967—. Dir. American Textbook Pubs. Institute, 1951-54, 60-61, pres., 1953-54. Mem. N.Y. State Citizens Com. for the Public Schools, Inc., 1959-68. Bd. dirs. Nat. Center for Citizens in Edn., 1965-68. Mem. Am. Ednl. Pubs. Inst., Met. Assn. United Ch. of Christ, Phi Beta Kappa Assos., Phi Beta Kappa, Alpha Delta Phi. Clubs: Grolier (N.Y.C.); Riverdale Yacht. Home: 2501 Palisade Av New York City, NY 10463 Office: 450 W 33d St New York City NY 10001

BATES, FREDERICK LEROY, educator; b. Washington, Dec. 2, 1924; s. Alvaro R. and Ruth C. (King) B.; B.A., George Washington U., 1949, M.A., 1950; Ph.D. with spl. commendation, U. N.C., 1954; m. Hettie Dowtin, July 13, 1946; children—James Frederick, Robert Mark. Asst. prof. rural sociology N.C. State Coll., 1954-56; asst. prof. hosp. adminstrn., acting dir. research Sloan Inst. Hosp. Adminstrn., Cornell U., 1956-57; prof. sociology La. State U., 1957-63; prof., head dept. sociology and anthropology U. Ga., 1963—, dir. Social Sci. Research Inst., 1963-64. Served with USAAF, 1943-45, USAF, 1951-54. Fellow Inst. Research Social Sci., 1951-54. Mem. Ga. Sociol. and Anthrop. Assn., Am., So., Rural sociol. assns., Alpha Kappa Delta, Pi Gamma Mu. Author: (with others) And the Wind Blew, 1964; also articles. Home: 200 Pine Valley Dr Athens GA 30611

BATES, GEORGE WALLACE, corp. exec., lawyer; b. Battle Lake, Minn., May 17, 1908; s. George Wilson and Anna (Burke) B.; A.B., U. Minn., 1928, LL.B., 1930; LL.M., Columbia 1931; m. Frances E. Trump, June 25, 1932; children—Elizabeth B. (Mrs. Robert Zenowich), Anne W. Admitted to Minn. bar, 1930, N.Y. bar, 1936, Mo. bar, 1950; asso. Root, Clark, Buckner & Ballantine, N.Y.C., 1931-43; atty. Am. Tel. & Tel. Co., N.Y.C., 1943-50, gen. atty., 1953-57; gen. counsel Southwestern Bell Telephone Co., St. Louis, 1950- 53; v.p., gen. counsel, dir. N.Y. Telephone Co. and Empire City Subway Co., Ltd., 1958—. Bd. dirs. Police Athletic League, State Traffic Safety Council N.Y. Mem. Am. Law Inst., N.Y. C. of C. (exec. com., pres. 1970-71) Am., N.Y. State (exec. com., chmn. com. law in changing society) bar assns., Assn. Bar City N.Y., N.Y. Law Inst.,

N.Y. County Lawyers Assn. Clubs: Fort Orange (Albany, N.Y.); Indian Harbor Yacht (Greenwich); Down Town Assn., Pinnacle (N.Y.C.). Home: Glenville Rd Greenwich CT 06830 Office: 140 West St New York City NY 10007

BATES, GRACE ELIZABETH, educator, mathematician; b. Albany, N.Y., Aug. 13, 1914; d. Walter M. and Julia (Dexter) Bates; B.S., Middlebury (Vt.) Coll., 1935; Sc.N., Brown U., 1938; Ph.D., U. Ill., 1946. Instr. math. George (Pa.) Sch., 1938-44, Sweet Briar Coll., 1944-45; mem. faculty Mt. Holyoke Coll., 1946—, prof. math., 1956—; vis. asst. prof., then vis. asso. prof. U. Cal. at Berkeley, summers 1951, 52, 54, 55; vis. prof. Dartmouth, 1959- 60. Trustee Tchrs. Ins. and Annuity Assn., 1965-69. Mem. Math. Assn. Am. (chmn. Northeastern sect. 1964-65, mem. commn. on undergrad. program in math), Assn. Tchrs. Math. New Eng. (pres. Conn. Valley sect. 1965-66), Am. Math. Soc., Phi Beta Kappa, Sigma Xi. Author: (with F. Kiokemeister) The Real Number System, 1960; (with others) Modern Algebra, Second Course, 1962; Probability, 1965; also articles. Home: 16 College View Heights South Hadley MA 01075

BATES, HERBERT ERNEST, author; b. Rushden, Eng., May 16, 1905; s. Albert Ernest and Elizabeth (Lucas) B.; m. Marjorie Cox, July 18, 1931; children—Ann, Judith, Richard, Jonathan. Novelist, short story writer, playwright and critic, 1926—. Served with RAF, 1941-46. Fellow Royal Soc. Lit. Author: Country of White Clover; Face of England; Fair Stood the Wind for France; The Nature of Love; The Purple Plain, 1947; The Jacaranda Tree, 1949; Scarlet Sword, 1951; Love for Lydia, 1952; The Feast of July, 1954; The Sleepless Moon, Death of a Huntsman; The Darling Buds of May, 1958; The Cruise of the Breadwinner; Two Sisters; Daffodil Sky, Country Heart; A Breath of French Air, 1959; An Aspidistra in Babylon, 1960; When the Green Woods Laugh, 1960; The Day of the Tortoise; Hark, Hark the Lark, 1960; The Grapes of Paradise, 1960; The Golden Oriole, 1962; A Crown of Wild Myrtle, 1962; Oh! to be in England, 1963; Seven by Five, 1963; A Moment in Time, 1964; The Wedding Party, 1965; The Distant Horns of Summer, 1967; The Four Beauties, 1968; The Triple Echo (novella), 1969; The Vanished World (autobiography), 1969; A Little of What You Fancy, 1970; also short stories, essays, criticism. Address: Little Chart Kent England

BATES, HUBERT BISSELL, banker; b. Lansing, Mich., Dec. 29, 1909; s. Donald E. and Mary E. (Bissell) B.; student Deerfield (Mass.) Acad., Kenyon Coll., 1932; m. Jane M. Kessel, June 30, 1934; 1 dau., Lucy Jane (Mrs. David. L. Knappen). With Am. Bank & Trust Co., Lansing, 1946—, pres., 1957, now chmn. bd. Pres. United Community Chest Ingham Co., 1954; mem. nat. adv. council Community Chests and Councils U.S., 1955-56. Served to capt. USAAF, 1942-46. Episcopalian (sr. warden). Clubs: City, Lansing Country, Press (Lansing); Detroit; Rotary. Home: 3118 S Cambridge Rd Lansing MI 48910 Office: 101 S Washington Av Lansing MI 48933

BATES, J. W., Sr., offshore drilling co. exec.; b. 1889; grad. Dartmouth Coll., 1910; married. With Reading & Bates Co., 1937—, now vice chmn. bd., dir. Reading & Bates Offshore Drilling Co., Tulsa. Served with USAAF, World War II. Office: Philtower Bldg Tulsa OK 74103

BATES, JAMES WARTH, banker; b. Steubenville, O., July 5, 1928; s. James Hawkins and Ethel (Warth) B.; B.A. cum laude, Kenyon Coll., 1950; grad. Stonier Grad. Sch. Banking, Rutgers U., 1965; m. Ellen Miller, May 13, 1950; children—Peter, James, Patricia. With Cleve. Trust Co., 1950—, sec., 1966—, also mem. exec. officers com. Active YMCA. Served to 1st lt. AUS, 1952-56. Mem. Am. Soc. Corporate Secs., Am. Inst. Banking (instr. Cleve. chpt. 1960-61), Assn. U.S. Army, Greater Cleve. Growth Assn., Res. Officers Assn., Sigma Pi. Episcopalian. Club: City (Cleve.). Office: Cleve Trust Co 900 Euclid Av Cleveland OH 44101

BATES, JOHN LOREN, pub. utilities exec.; b. Beeville, Tex., Dec. 24, 1898; s. Mark Warren and Myra (Wilder) B.; student Tex. A. and M. Coll., 1916-17; LL.D., U. Corpus Christi, 1958; m. Alline Ellison, June 12, 1929. Engaged in silver mining and contracting; with Central Power & Light Co., 1923—, successively mgr., McAllen and Mission, Tex., distbn. engr., asst. dist. mgr., San Benito, Valley dist. mgr., San Benito, v.p., div. mgr., Victoria, Tex., v.p., 1923-54, gen. mgr. 1940—, now chmn.; dir. United Savs. Assn., Corpus Christi, Tex., Central and South West Corp., Chgo., Wilmington, Del. Bd. dirs. Tex. Atomic Energy Research Found., Dallas; adv. bd. Tex. Indsl. Commn. Mem. Navy League U.S., C. of C. Clubs: Rotary; Corpus Christi Country, Corpus Christi Town; Harlingen (Tex.) Country. Home: 318 Doddrige St Corpus Christi TX 78411 Office: 120 N Chapparral St Corpus Christi TX 78401

BATES, JOHN W., Jr., offshore drilling co. exec.; b. 1919; grad. Dartmouth Coll., 1941; married. With Reading & Bates Co., 1946—, now chmn. bd., chief exec. officer, dir. Reading & Bates Offshore Drilling Co., Tulsa. Served with USNR, 1941-46. Office: Philtower Bldg Tulsa OK 74103*

BATES, KENNETH, artist; b. Haverhill, Mass., Oct. 28, 1895; s. Welcome Elliott and Sarah Frances (Hester) B.; grad. Westerly (R.I.) High Sch., 1912; student Art Students League, 1914-15, Pa. Acad. Fine Arts, 1916-21; m. Gladys Edgerly, July 12, 1923; children—Kenneth, David Dunlop, Thomas Edgerly. Represented in permanent collections, Pa. Acad. Fine Arts, Woodmere Art Gallery, Phila., Slater Meml. Mus., Internat. Bus. Machines collection, Beach Meml. collection U. Conn. numerous pvt. collections. Awarded Cresson traveling scholarship, 1920; Toppan prize, 1921; hon. mention Art Inst. Chgo., 1926; Charles Noel Flagg prize, 1927; Jennie Sesnan gold medal, 1928; John I.H. Downes prize, 1929; hon. mention Conn. Acad. Fine Arts, 1931, 1946; 1st prize Conn. Acad., 1950; New Haven Paint and Clay Club prize, 1953; 1st prize, Meriden Arts Crafts Assn., 1956; Famous Artists Sch. prize Mystic Art Assn., 1965. Served as corporal Q.M.C., U.S. Army, Camp Devens, 1918-19. Elected A.N.A., 1942, N.A., 1960. Author: Brackman, His Art and Teaching, 1951. Home: Stonecroft Mystic CT 06355

BATES, MARSTON, naturalist; b. Grand Rapids, Mich., July 23, 1906; s. Glenn Freeman and Amy Mabel (Button) B.; B.S., U. Fla., 1927; A.M., Harvard, 1933, Ph.D., 1934; D.Sc., Kalamazoo Coll., 1956; m. Nancy Bell Fairchild, Jan. 11, 1939; children—Marian Hubbard, Sally Norton, Barbara Fairchild, Glenn Peregrine. Entomologist, advancing to dir. Servicio Tecnico de Cooperacion Agricola, United Fruit Co., 1928-31; Sheldon traveling fellow Harvard, 1934-35; research asst. Mus. Comparative Zoology, 1935-37; staff internat. health div. Rockefeller Found., 1937-50, spl. asst. to pres., 1950-52; prof. zoology U. Mich., 1952-71 (on leave 1956-57, 70); dir. research U. Puerto Rico, 1956-57; Timothy Hopkins lectr. Hopkins Marine Sta., Stanford U., 1954. Mem. div. com. biol. and med. scis. Nat. Sci. Found., 1952-58, chmn., 1956-58; adv. bd. Guggenheim Found., 1955-58; fellow Center for Advanced Studies, Weleyan U., Spring 1961; Phi Beta Kappa vis. scholar, 1962-63, 68-69. Trustee Cranbrook Inst. Sci., 1955-62; Recipient Daly medal Am. Geog. Soc., 1967. Mem. Pacific Sci. Bd., Am. Society Naturalists (pres. 1961), Council Fgn. Relations, Am. Acad. Arts and Scis., many sci. socs. Club: Cosmos (Washington). Author: The Natural History of Mosquitoes, 1949; The Nature of Natural History, 1950; Where Winter Never Comes, 1952; The Prevalence of People, 1955; The Darwin Reader, 1957; Coral Island, 1958; The Forest and the Sea, 1960; Man in Nature, 1960; Animal Worlds, 1963; The Land and Wildlife of South America, 1964; Gluttons and Libertines, 1968; A Jungle in the House, 1970. Editorial bd. Am. Scholar, 1955-58. Contbr. to publs. Home: 630 Oxford Rd Ann Arbor MI 48104

BATES, MAURICE EDWARD, educator; b. Romeo, Mich., Sept. 2, 1911; s. Lafayette H. and Alice (Crissman) B.; B.S., U. Mich., 1934; S.M., Mass. Inst. Tech., 1935; Ph.D., U. Mich., 1937; m. Margaret Crozer Smith, June 8, 1943; children—Laurence Russell, Marilyn Crozer. Asso. prof. mech. engring. Trinity Coll., 1941-43; research engr. Arma Corp., Bklyn., 1943-45; asst. prof. mech. engring. Princeton, 1945-46; prof. mech. engring. U. Mass., 1946—; cons. Registered profl. engr., Mass. Mem. Am. Soc. M.E. Republican. Conglist. Patentee stable element for navigation. Home: 86 Cowls Rd North Amherst MA 01059 Office: Univ Massachusetts Amherst MA 01003

BATES, MERLE BANKER, univ. ofcl.; b. Green Island, N.Y., 1892; s. William Watson and Altha Louise (Soyer) B.; Syracuse U., ex 1912; m. Marguerite Louise Eberwein, July 3, 1923; 1 son, Bruce Banker. Pres., dir. Life Savers, Ltd., Hamilton, Ont., Can., Beech-Nut Co. of Can., Ltd., Life Savers & Beech- Nut Sales Co., Ltd., 1934-58; v.p., dir. Life Savers Corp., Port Chester, N.Y., 1934-56. Chmn. bd. govs. Art Gallery, Hamilton, 1960-61; past pres. Community Chest Hamilton, Air Cadet League of Can.; mem. Nat. War Finance Com., Hamilton, 1942-43; vice chmn. bd. trustees Hamilton United Appeal, 1956-63; bd. govs., mem. exec. com. McMaster U., 1954-69, chmn. devel. fund council, 1960-63, vice chmn. finance com. (growth fund), 1964-69, assistant to pres. (fund-raising), 1969—; past pres., dir. The Hamilton Foundation, 1960-63. Served as 2d lt. Ordnance Dept., U.S. Army, 1917-19. Awarded Royal Canadian Air Force Scroll, 1946. Mem. Assn. Nat. Advertisers (chmn. bd. U.S.A. 1926). Clubs: Hamilton Golf and Country, (Hamilton). Home: 240 Rossmore Blvd Burlington Ontario Canada Office: McMaster University Hamilton Ontario Canada

BATES, OSCAR KENNETH, educator; b. Boston, Dec. 23, 1900; s. Oscar Francis and Flora Louise (Creber) B.; S.B., Mass. Inst. Tech., 1921, S.M., 1922, Sc.D., 1932; m. Frances Guest Westbrook, Sept. 2, 1925; children—Margaret Westbrook, Carolyn Ardis (Mrs. Walter Monteith), Sarah Seymour (Mrs. John Arvid Eckberg), Westbrook. Tchr. indsl. research dept. physics Mass. Inst. Tech., 1921-33; Cummings prof. math., head dept. St. Lawrence U., Canton, N.Y., 1933-67, Cummings prof. math. emeritus, 1967—, charge engineering program, 1936-67, on leave, 1949-51; asst. head science sect., br. office Office Naval Research, Boston, 1949-51. Coordinator civilian pilot tng. program Civilian Aero. Authority, 1941-42; coordinator C.A.A. War Tng. Service, U.S. Naval Aviation Unit, St. Lawrence U., 1942-43. Fellow A.A.A.S.; mem. Am. Soc. Engring. Edn., Nat. Council Tchrs. Math., Assn. Math. Tchrs. N.Y. State, Soc. Indsl. and Applied Math., Am. Assn. U. Profs., Math. Assn. Am., A.A.A.S., Sigma Xi, Omicron Delta Kappa, Sigma Pi Sigma, Pi Mu Epsilon, Phi Gamma Delta. Episcopalian (vestryman, warden). Mason. Contbr. tech. jours. Home: 44 E Main St Canton NY 13617

BATES, RICHARD OLIVER, banker, lawyer; b. Painesville, O., Oct. 20, 1933; s. Oliver White and Eleanor (Dick) B.; B.A., Bethany (W.Va.) Coll., 1955; LL.B., J.D., Case Western Res. U., 1958; m. Joanne Blackburn, July 21, 1956; children—Karen Jo, William Delos. Admitted to Ohio bar, 1958; law clk. for Oliver W. Bates, Madison, O., 1958; partner firm Bates and Bates, Madison, 1962-65; asst. v.p. N. Madison Banking Co., 1966—; v.p. Western Res. Bank Lake County, Painesville, 1966—. Co-chmn. Madison Citizens for Schs. Com. Bd. dirs. Madison YMCA, Lake County YMCA, Lake County Bd. Mental Retardation, United Fund Central and Eastern Lake County; v.p., trustee Northeastern Ohio Gen. Hosp.; v.p. Lake County Mental Health Assn. Served to 1st lt. AUS, 1959-62. Mem. Am., Ohio, Lake County bar assns, Madison Area C. of C. (bd. dirs.), Northeastern Ohio Bankers Assn. (pres.), Am. Mensa Ltd. Kiwanian (pres.). Club: Lake County Garfield Men's (treas.) (Painesville). Home: 149 Square Dr Madison OH 44057 Office: 70 N St Clair St Painesville OH 44057

BATES, RICHARD WALLER, ret. naval officer; b. San Francisco, Jan. 16, 1892; s. Henry Lesley Alexander and Rebecca Helen (Rixon) F.; B.S., U.S. Naval Acad., 1915, postgrad., 1920-21; M.S., Columbia, 1922; postgrad. Naval War Coll., 1940-41; Litt.D., L.I.U., 1958. Commd. ensign U.S. Navy, 1915, advanced through grades to rear adm., 1949; exec. officer U.S.S. Cincinnati, 1918-19; comdg. officer U.S.S. Buchanan, 1932-33, U.S.S. Ramapo, 1933, U.S.S. Long, 1934-35, U.S.S. Clark, 1938-40, U.S.S. Minneapolis, Pacific, 1943-44; on staff comdr. in chief Pacific Fleet, 1944; chief staff Bombardment and Fire Support Group, 3d Fleet, Palau, 1944, and 7th Fleet, 1944-45, participating in battles Leyte Gulf and Surigao Strait; chief staff Battleship Squadron 1, Lingayen and Okinawa, 1945; comdr. motor torpedo boats Pacific Fleet, 1945; chief staff Philippine Sea Frontier, 1945-46; mem. staff Naval War Coll., 1941-42, chief of strategy, 1942-43, head dept. analysis, 1946-49, now lectr.; ret. for phys. disability, 1949; recalled and served on active duty as head of World War II Battle Evaluation Group, 1949-58. Decorated Navy Cross, Legion Merit with 2 gold stars, Navy Unit citation, Victory Medal World War I (with star), Mexican Campaign, Yangtze Service, Am. Def., Am. Area Campaign, Asiatic- Pacific Area Campaign (with 10 bronze stars), Philippine Liberation, Nat. Def. medals, Victory Medal World War II. Episcopalian. Clubs: N.Y. Yacht (N.Y.C.); Army-Navy Country, University (Washington); Bohemian (San Francisco); Reading Room, Clambake, Ida Lewis Yacht (Newport, R.I.); Army-Navy (Manila, P.I.). Author numerous analyses of major naval battles of World War II. Contbr. to Colliers Ency. Home: 12 Mt Vernon St Newport RI 02840

BATES, ROBERT CALDWELL, found. exec.; b. Great Falls, Mont., June 13, 1914; s. George Martin and Emma Elizabeth (Caldwell) B.; B.A., Univ. of Mont., 1936; LL.B., 1949; B.A., M.A. (Rhodes scholar 1937-39, 46-47), Oxford (Eng.) U., 1947; LL.D. (honorary), Rocky Mountain College, 1967; m. Marcia Hartley, Sept. 29, 1951; children—Jonathan Hartley, Peter Caldwell, Douglas William. Instr. econs. Univ. of Mont., 1936-37, asst. prof. law and polit. sci., 1947-50; intern Nat. Inst. Pub. Affairs, 1940-41; analyst Adminstrv. Office U.S. Cts., Washington, 1941; vice consul, Georgetown, British Guiana, 1941-43; admitted to Mont. bar, 1949; mem. staff Rockefeller Brothers Fund, 1950—, sec., 1952—, v.p., 1969—; trustee, vice president of Sealantic Fund, 1952-57, sec., 1952—; trustee, v.p. Martha Baird Rockefeller Fund Music, 1962—; trustee Foundation Center, 1963-69. Served to lt. (j.g.) USNR, 1944-46. Mem. Assn. of Am. Rhodes Scholars (treas. 1965—, trustee 1966—). Home: 100 Marshall Ridge Rd New Canaan, CT 06840 Office: 30 Rockefeller Plaza New York City NY 10020

BATES, ROGER GORDON, educator, chemist; b. Cummington, Mass., May 20, 1912; s. Rollin Elder and Nellie (Robbins) B.; B.S., U. Mass., 1934; A.M., Duke, 1936, Ph.D., 1937; Sterling fellow, Yale, 1937-39; m. Jo Jones, Sept. 9, 1941; 1 dau., May Joan (Mrs. Carl P. Daw, Jr.). Chemist, Nat. Bur. Standards, Washington, 1939-57, chief electro-chem. analysis sect., 1957-69, asst. chief analytical chemistry div., 1958-68; prof. chemistry U. Fla., Gainesville, 1969—; lectr. phys. chemistry Trinity Coll., Washington, 1947- 49. Chmn. commn. electrochem. data analytical sect. Internat. Union Pure and Applied Chemistry, 1953-58. USPHS fellow, Zurich, Switzerland, 1953- 54; recipient Hillebrand prize Washington sect. Am. Chem. Soc., 1955; Dept. Commerce exceptional service award, 1957; award in analytical chemistry Am. Chem. Soc., 1969. Fellow Am. Inst. Chemists; mem. A.A.A.S., Electrochem. Soc., Am. Chem. Soc., Phi Beta Kappa, Sigma Xi, Phi Kappa Phi, Alpha Chi Sigma. Club: Cosmos (Washington). Author: Electrometric pH Determinations, Theory and Practice, 1954; Determination of pH, 1964. Home: 2210 NW 21st St Gainesville FL 32601

BATES, SANFORD, lawyer, penologist, educator; b. Boston, July 17, 1884; s. Samuel W. and Nellie G. (Sanford) B.; LL.B. cum laude, Northeastern U., 1906, LL.D., 1937; L.H.D. (hon.), Rutgers U., 1954; m. Helen S. Williams, Oct. 3, 1908; children—Mary Elizabeth, Sanford Loring. Admitted to Mass. bar, 1906, U.S. Supreme Ct. bar, 1933, N.Y. bar, 1940; mem. firm Achorn & Bates, Boston, 1906-21; commr. Mass. Dept. Correction, 1919-29; supt. fed. prisons, 1929-30; dir. U.S. Bur. Prisons, 1930, 33-37; exec. dir. Boys Clubs Am., 1939-40; faculty N.Y. Sch. Social Work, 1937—; instr. div. handicapped Columbia Tchrs. Coll., 1938—; parole commr. N.Y. State, 1940-45; commr. Instns. and Agys., N.J., 1945-54; cons. pub. adminstrn. to states, municipalities, also Fed. Prison Bur., 1954—; pres. Fed. Prison Industries, Inc., 1940—; hearing officer U.S. Dept. Justice. Ofcl. U.S. del. Internat. Prison Congress, London, 1925, Prague, 1930, v.p. congress, 1930-31; chmn. delegation Internat. Penal and Penitentiary Congress, Berlin, 1935, presided over congresses, 1950, 55; pres. Internat. Panel and Penitentiary Commn., 1946, 55; v.p. Inst. Criminal Law and Criminology; mem. Commn. Investigate Criminal Law; chmn. nat. adv. com. prisoners and parolees SSS, 1944—; cons. restoration mil. prisoners War Dept., 1944—, Am. Law Inst., 1955-62, Am. Bar Survey on Criminal Justice, 1957-59; mem. UN Commn. Crime Prevention, 1951; adv. council dept. econ. and social instns. Princeton; Parole Compact adminstr., 1945; chmn. council Compact Adminstrs., 1946; mem.-at-large Nat. Social Welfare Assembly; mem. N.J. Rehab. Com.; cons. penology Am. Bar. Found.; cons. President's Committee on Crime, 1966, Com. on Correctional Manpower, 1966; U.S. corr. to UN; ofcl. del. UN Conf. Crime, London, 1960; spl. cons. N.J. Dept. Instns. and Agys., 1969—. Mem. George Washington council Boy Scouts Am. Bd. dirs. N.J. Welfare Council, Nat. Boys Tng. Sch., Citizenship Edn. Service, N.J. Tb League, Nat. Com. Mental Hygiene, Correctional Services Fedn.; trustee Vineland Tng. Sch. Mem. Mass. Ho. of Reps., 1912, 14. Mass. Senate, 1915, 16. Decorated Order Orange Nassau. Fellow Am. Assn. Mental Deficiency; mem. Nat. Probation Assn. (trustee), Assn. Pub. Welfare Ofcls. (dir.), Nat. Conf. Social Agys., Nat. Conf. Juvenile Agys., Nat. Probation and Parole Assn. (trustee), Am. Pub. Welfare Assn., Am. Hosp. Assn., Morrow Assn. Correction (v.p.), Royal Arcanum, Am. Bar Assn., Am. Prison Assn. (pres. 1926), Am. Parole Assn. (pres.), Am. Crime Study Commn. (exec. com. 1927), Nat. Acad. Arts and Sci., Am. Pub. Health Assn., Am. Sociol. Assn., Am. Assn. Parole Compact Adminstrs. (pres. 1949), Acad. Polit. Sci., Morrow Assn. on Correction (N.J.), Nat. Jail Assn., Nat. Council Crime and Delinquency, Inst. Criminology Republic Argentina (hon.). Unitarian (moderator 1938-39). Rotarian. Author: Prison and Beyond, 1938; also numerous articles. Home: 12 Baldwin St Pennington NJ 08534 ☆

BATES, THEODORE LEWIS, advt. exec.; b. New Haven, Sept. 11, 1901; s. Vernal Warner and Elizabeth B. (Hailes) B.; student Andover Acad., 1916-20; B.S., Yale, 1924; m. Evelyn Turull, Aug. 4, 1934; children—Evelyn B. Owen and Patricia B. Johnson (twins). Advt. mgr. Chase Nat. Bank, N.Y.C., 1924-25; with George Batten & Co. and Batten Barton Durstine & Osborn, Inc., N.Y.C., 1925-35, v.p., 1929-35; v.p., dir. Benton & Bowles, Inc., 1935-40; pres., treas., founder Ted Bates, Inc., also mem. exec. com.; hon. chmn. bd. Ted Bates & Co. Bd. dirs. Advt. Council. Knight Malta (comdr.). Clubs: Moisle Salmon; Yale (N.Y.C.); Lawrence Beach (N.Y.); Cedarhurst (N.Y.) Yacht; Rockaway (N.Y.) Hunting; Lyford Cay (Nassau). Home: 1120 Park Av New York City NY 10028 also Breezy Way Lawrence NY 11559 Office: 666 Fifth Av New York City NY 10019

BATES, THOMAS FULCHER, univ. ofcl.; b. Evanston, Ill., Jan. 2, 1917; s. Alfred Ricker and Eleanor (Fulcher) B.; B.A., Denison U., 1939; M.A., Columbia, 1940, Ph.D. (Nathaniel Lord Britton and Univ. fellow), 1944; D.Sc., Denison U., 1968; m. Virginia Scott, July 4, 1942; children—Thomas Scott, James Gordon, Barbara Anne. Mem. faculty Pa. State U., 1942—, prof. mineralogy, 1953—, asst. to v.p. research, 1961-65, dir. Inst. Sci. and Engring., 1963-65, asst. dean Grad. Sch., 1964-65, v.p. planning, 1967—; asst., also sci. adviser to sec. Dept. Interior, 1965-67; mineral. cons., 1945—. Dir. Tem-Pres Research, Inc., 1961-66. Mem. Fed. Council Sci. and Tech., 1965- 67. Sr. Postdoctoral fellow NSF, 1958-59. Fellow Mineral. Soc. Am., Geol. Soc. Am., A.A.A.S.; mem. Mineral. Soc. London, Clay Minerals Soc., Phi Beta Kappa, Sigma Xi, Omicron Delta Kappa, Phi Mu Alpha, Sigma Alpha Epsilon. Asso. editor Clays and Clay Minerals, 1957-65. Home: 903 Outer Dr State College PA 16801 Office: 405 Old Main University Park PA 16802

BATES, WILLIAM, Jr., banker; b. Phila., Aug. 1, 1921; s. William and Marie (Bergstresser) B.; student Wm. Penn Charter Sch., 1939; B.A., Duke, 1943; postgrad. Rutgers U., 1956; m. Elizabeth Anne Martin, June 9, 1945; children—William III, Jeffrey Lloyd. With Phila. Nat. Bank, 1947—, v.p., 1958-68, sr. v.p., 1968-70, exec. v.p., 1970—; thesis adviser, examiner Grad. Sch. Banking, Rutgers U., 1963-70. Dist. chmn. Philenape Dist., Boy Scouts Am., 1966-69. Served to capt. USAAF, 1942-46. Recipient Distinguished Service award Boy Scouts Am., 1969. Mem. Bank Officers Club Phila. (pres.), Newcomen Soc., Royal Arcanum, Robert Morris Assos., Sigma Phi Epsilon. Presbyn. (deacon). Home: 329 Mill Rd Havertown PA 19083 Office: Phila Nat Bank Philadelphia PA 19101

BATES, WILLIAM BARTHOLEMEW, lawyer; b. Nacogdoches County, Tex., Aug. 16, 1890; s. James Madison and Mary Frances (Cook) B.; grad. Sam Houston State Teachers Coll., 1911; LL.B., Univ. of Texas, 1915; LL.D., conferred by the 7 state teachers colleges of Tex., 1944; LL.D., Baylor U., 1950; D.H.L., Trinity U., 1952; m. Mary Estill Dorsey, February 21, 1921; children—Juan (Mrs. Reagan Cartwright), Mary Dorsey. Practiced law, Bay City, Texas, 1915-17, Nacogdoches, Texas, 1919-21; district attorney, 2d Judicial District of Texas, 1921-22; partner Fullbright & Crooker, and successor firm, Fullbright, Crooker, Freeman, Bates & Jaworski, Houston, 1923—; dir. Gulf Atlantic Warehouse Co.; chmn. bd. Bank of the Southwest (formerly Second Nat. Bank) of Houston. Commd. 2d lt., U.S. Army; served with 358th Inf., 90th Div., overseas; in Army of Occupation, Germany, 1918-19; twice wounded and promoted for gallantry in action. Mem. bd. edn. Houston Pub. Schs., 1927-35 (pres., 1932-35). Mem. bd. regents Tex. State Teachers Colls., 1937-43; pres., trustee M. D. Anderson Foundation (charitable orgn.); vice pres. Clayton Foundation for Research; trustee San Jacinto Mus. of History Assn.; gov., trustee S.W. Research Inst., San Antonio, Texas; chmn. bd. of regents U. of Houston; dir. Tex. Med. Center. Presbyterian. Mason (32, Scottish Rite). Clubs: Houston, River Oaks Country (Houston), Piney Woods Country (Nacogdoches, Tex.). Home: 210 Pine Hollow Dr Houston TX 77027 Office: Bank of SW Bldg Houston TX 77002

BATHO, EDWARD HUBERT, educator, mathematician; b. West Hoboken, N.J., Apr. 13, 1925; s. Edward and Catherine (Kiely) B.; B.S., Fordham U., 1950; M.S., U. Wis., 1952, Ph.D., 1956. Instr. U. Rochester, 1955-57, asst. prof., 1957-60; mem. Inst. for Advanced Studies, 1958-59; asso. prof. mathematics U. N.H., 1960-66, prof., 1966—; vis. fellow Harvard, 1959, U. Sheffield Eng., 1960; vis. prof. Am. U. of Beirut, 1966-67. Served with AUS, 1943-46. Nat. Sci. Found. fellow, 1958-60. Mem. Am. Math. Soc., Math. Assn. Am. Home: 7 Austin Dr Dover NH 03824

BATLEY, HARRY A., chem. co. exec.; b. Clayville, N.Y., Sept. 21, 1909; s. John Armitage and Mary Gertrude (Foley) B.; B.S., Newark Coll. Engring., 1932, Chem. Engr., 1935; student Bklyn. Poly. Inst., 1936; m. Doretha Katherine Todd, Oct. 5, 1935; 1 dau., Ann Alexis. With Nopco Chem. Co., Newark, 1931—, v.p., dir., 1958-60, exec. v.p., dir., 1960—; now pres. Nopco Chem. Div., v.p. Diamond Shamrock Chem. Co.; pres., dir. Jacques Wolf & Co., 1960—, Nopco Chem. Can., Ltd., 1961—, Canadian Aniline & Extract Co., Ltd., 1961—, Nopco Chem. Co. Pa., Superior Zinc Co.; dir. Adamas Carbide Corp. Bd. dirs. Employers Assn. N.J.; mem. adv. council Research Found., Newark Coll. Engring. Mem. Am. Inst. Chemists, Am. Chem. Soc., Am. Oil Chemists Soc. Clubs: Morris County (N.J.) Engineers; Down Town (Newark). Home: Franklin Rd Denville NJ 07834 Office: 60 Park Pl Newark NJ 07102

BATON, CHARLES BICKLEY, mining engr.; b. Pitts., July 22, 1908; s. George S. and Mary (Brickley) B.; B.S., Princeton, 1930; m. Caroline Wilson Murray, June 24, 1933; children—George S., Louise Coleman, Linda. Propr., George S. Baton & Co., Pitts., 1935—; pres., dir. Baton Coal Co., Pitts., 1945—; v.p., dir. Carpentertown Coal & Coke Co., Pitts., 1946—; pres. Greensburg- Connellsville Coal & Coke Co., Pitts., 1948-50; v.p. Joanne Coal Co., Pitts., 1950—; pres., dir. Farm Coal Co.; dir. Joy Mfg. Co., H.K. Porter Co., Old Republic Ins. Co., Vulcan, Inc., Peoples Union Bank; trustee Dollar Savs. Bank. Bd. dirs. Shadyside Acad., Pitts. Mem. Am. Inst. Mining Engrs. Home: 126 Penham Lane Pittsburgh PA 15208 Office: Union Trust Bldg Pittsburgh PA 15219

BATOR, FRANCIS MICHEL, educator, economist; b. Budapest, Hungary, Aug. 10, 1925; s. Victor and Franciska Elisabeth (Sichermann) B.; came to U.S., 1939, naturalized, 1944; grad. Groton Sch., 1943; B.S., Mass. Inst. Tech., 1949, Ph.D., 1956; M.A. (hon.), Harvard, 1967; m. Micheline Charlotte Martin, June 30, 1949; children—Nina, Christopher Francis. Exec. asst. to dir. Center Internat. Studies, Mass. Inst. Tech., 1951-54, sr. research staff, 1954-63, asst. prof. econs., 1957-60, asso. prof., 1960-63; sr. econ. adviser AID, Dept. State, 1963-64; sr. staff Nat. Security Council, White House, 1964- 65; dep. spl. asst. to pres. for nat. security affairs White House, 1965- 67; prof. polit. economy John F. Kennedy Sch. Govt., Harvard, 1967—; cons. Rand Corp., Inst. Def. Analysis, Office Sec. Treasury, 1961-63, under sec. state for econ. affairs, 1961. U.S. mem. consultative group on econ. projections UN, 1962, on internat. monetary arrangements, 1969; spl. cons. sec. treasury, 1967-69; mem. Pres'. Adv. Com. Internat. Monetary Arrangements, 1967-69; adviser Internat. Affairs Subcom. CED, 1970—. Dir. Natvar Corp., Rahway, N.J. Mem. com. econ. affairs and fgn. relations Democratic Policy Council 1970—. Trustee Bela Bartok Archives, N.Y.C.; bd. dirs. Atlantic Council U.S.; Served to 1st lt., inf., AUS, 1944-46. Recipient Distinguished Service award Treasury Dept., 1968; Guggenheim fellow, 1959. Fellow Am. Acad. Arts and Scis.; mem. Council on Fgn. Relations, Am. Econ. Assn., Inst. Strategic Studies, Econometric Soc., Royal Econ. Soc. Clubs: Century Assn. (N.Y.C.). Author: The Question of Government Spending, 1960; also articles. Home: 17 Farrar St Cambridge MA 02138

BATOR, PAUL MICHAEL, educator, lawyer; b. Budapest, Hungary, July 2, 1929; s. Victor and Franciska Elisabeth (Sichermann) B.; came to U.S., 1939, naturalized, 1945; grad. Groton Sch., 1947; A.B., Princeton, 1951; M.A. in History, Harvard, 1953, LL.B., 1956; m. Alice Garrett Hoag, June 2, 1956; children—Thomas Ewing, Michael G., Julia. Admitted to N.Y. bar, 1958; law clk. to Supreme Ct. Justice Harlan, 1956-57; with firm Debevoise, Plimpton & McLean, N.Y.C., 1957-59; asst. prof. law Harvard Law Sch., 1959-62, prof., 1962—; vis. prof. law U. Cal. at Berkeley, 1966, Stanford, 1971-72. Dir. Natvar Corp., Rahway, N.J., Abacus Fund, N.Y.C. Mem. Am. Law Inst. Home: 11 Garden Terrace Cambridge MA 02138

BATRUS, FREDERICK EDWARD, govt. ofcl.; b. Altoona, Pa., May 28, 1915; s. Elias and Elizabeth (Hallow) B.; B.S. in Econs., U. Pa., 1937; LL.B., Dickinson Sch. Law, 1940; m. Eleanor Louise Harlan, Feb. 28, 1948; children—Harlan, Carol, Elizabeth. Admitted to Pa. bar, 1940; practice in Altoona, 1940-42; atty. Post Office Dept., 1946-52, asso. gen. counsel transp., 1952-55, spl. asst. bur. transp., 1955-61, dep. asst. postmaster gen., bur. transp., 1961-68, asst. postmaster general, bureau transp., 1968-69, exec. asst. to dept. postmaster gen., 1969-71, asst. postmaster gen. logistics and engring., 1971—. U.S. del. Congress Universal Postal Union, Paris, France, 1947, Ottawa, Can., 1957, Vienna, Austria, 1964. Served with inf. AUS, 1942-45; ETO. Decorated Silver Star, Bronze Star, Purple Heart. Mem. Am., Fed. bar assns., Kappa Sigma. Club: Nat. Lawyers. Home: 7124 Fairfax Rd Bethesda MD 20014 Office: US Postal Service Washington DC 20260

BATSCHELET, EDWARD, educator, mathematician; b. Biel, Switzerland, Apr. 6, 1914; s. Ernst and Anna (Kohler) B.; Ph.D., U. Basel, 1942; m. Hedwig E. Mader, Mar. 23, 1942; 1 dau., Elizabeth (Mrs. Paul Bloesch). Came to U.S., 1960, naturalized, 1967. Privatdozent, U. Basel, 1951-57, asso. prof., 1958-60; prof. math. Cath. U., Washington, 1960-71; prof. Math. Inst. U. Zurich (Switzerland), 1971—. Mem. Inst. Math. Statistics, Biometric Soc., A.A.A.S., Am. Inst. Biol. Sci. Contbr. articles profl. jours. Address: Math Inst U Zurich Freiestrasse 36 Zurich Switzerland

BATSON, BLAIR EVERETT, physician, educator; b. Hattiesburg, Miss., Oct. 24, 1920; s. Claud L. and Mary Eaton (Bryan) B.; B.A., Vanderbilt U., 1941, M.D., 1944; M.P.H., Johns Hopkins, 1954; m. Margaret Donovan Bailly, Oct. 2, 1954. Intern dept. pediatrics Vanderbilt U. Hosp., 1944-45, asst. resident, 1948-49, resident pediatrician, 1949-50; instr. pediatrics Vanderbilt U. Sch. Medicine, 1949-52; asst. resident dept. pediatrics Johns Hopkins Hosp., 1945-46; instr. pediatrics Johns Hopkins Sch. Medicine, 1952-54, asst. prof., 1954-55, instr. pub. health adminstrn., div. maternal and child health Sch. Hygiene and Pub. Health, 1952-54, asst. prof. pub. health adminstrn., 1954-55; prof. pediatrics, chmn. dept. U. Miss. Sch. Medicine, 1955—. Chmn. health com., adv. council Miss. Children's Code Commn., 1958-61; chmn. Miss. Conf. on Handicapped Children, 1960-61; nat. adviser children, pub. children's bur. Dept. Health Edn. and Welfare; ofcl. exam. Am. Bd. Pediatrics, 1963—. Trustee Easter Seal Research Found., 1969—. Served to captain M.C., AUS, 1946-48. Mem. Am. Acad. Pediatrics (Mead Johnson awards com. 1958-61; exec. com. child devel. sect. 1964-67; charter mem. sect. on community pediatrics 1968, hosp. car com. 1970), A.M.A., So. Soc. Pediatric Research, Am. Assn. Med. Colls., So. Med. Assn. (sec. pediatric sec. 1956-58, pres. 1959), Vanderbilt Alumni Club (pres. Jackson, Miss. 1960-64), Am. Pediatric Soc., Sigma Chi, Phi Chi. Home: 4157 Crane Blvd Jackson MS 39216

BATSON, CHARLES ALVIN, broadcasting exec.; b. Greenville, S.C., Aug. 14, 1916; s. Charles Austell and Bessie (McCauley) B.; B.A., Furman U., 1938; 1 son, Reginald Fleming. Program dir. sta. WFBC, Greenville, 1938-41; dir. information, dir. tv Nat. Assn. Broadcasters, Washington, 1946-51; dir. TV Broadcasting Co. of South, Columbia, S.C., 1951-53; gen. mgr. sta. WIS-TV, Columbia, 1953-66; gen. mgr. sta. WTOL-TV, Toledo, 1966-68; pres. Cosmos Broadcasting Corp., Columbia, 1968—, chmn. exec. com., 1969—, also dir.; dir. Liberty Corp., TV Stas., Inc.; mem. adv. bd. C&S Nat. Bank, Columbia. Mem. Nat. Assn. Broadcasters adv. com. Corp. for Pub. Broadcasting, 1969—, TV Code Rev. Bd., 1970—. Dir., chmn. pub. information com. United Community Services, Columbia, 1961, trustee, 1969-71; mem. adv. bd. Aurora Center of Blind, 1971—. Bd. dirs. S.C. Bd. Easter Seal Soc. Crippled Children and Adults. Served with AUS, 1941-46. Recipient Abe Lincoln award So. Bapt. Radio and TV Commn., 1971. Mem. S.C. Broadcasters Assn. (pres. 1957). Presbyn. (deacon, chmn. finance com.). Rotarian. Clubs: Pallmetto, Forest Lake (Columbia). Author series television: A Report on the Visual Broadcasting Art, 1948-49. Home: 1623 Milford Rd Columbia SC 29206 Office: PO Box 367 Columbia SC 29202

BATSON, DOUGLAS NORMAN, fgn. service officer; b. Kansas City, Mo., Feb. 3, 1918; s. Col. Roscoe Conkling and Getty (Norman) B.; A.B., Johns Hopkins, 1939; postgrad. Georgetown U., 1940-41; grad. Nat. War Coll., Washington, 1957. Ednl. exchange service Dept. State, 1950-56, fgn. service officer, 1954—; chief cultural presentations staff Dept. State, 1954-56, organizer program to assist Am. performing artists to tour fgn. countries auspices Pres.'s spl. fund and ANTA; 1st sec. Am. embassy, Bangkok, Thailand, 1957-61, counselor embassy, 1961-62; dep. chief of mission Am. embassy, Monrovia, Liberia, 1962-64; office dir. Bur. Ednl. and Cultural Affairs, Dept. State, 1964-66, dep. asst. sec. state, 1966-69; exec. dir. Thailand-U.S. Ednl. Found., Bangkok, 1969—. Served from pvt. to maj. AUS, 1941-50. Recipient Dept. State Superior Honor award, 1969. Mem. Am. Fgn. Service Assn. Episcopalian. Club: Royal Bangkok Sports. Home: 98 Soi Rajakru Paholyothin Rd Bangkok Thailand Office: care Am Embassy APO San Francisco CA 96346

BATSON, PHILIP DORR, govt. ofcl.; b. Seattle, Mar. 13, 1911; s. Philip and Vesta Ellen (Brown) B.; student accounting Met. Coll., 1930, traffic police adminstrn. Traffic Inst. Northwestern U., 1943, FBI Nat. Acad., 1945; m. Melba E. Muir, 1933 (div. 1963); children—Joan (Mrs. Ralph Seamens), Randall Goodwin, Alan Goodwin; m. 2d, Mozelle Leavitt Goatwin, May 4, 1963. Accountant, Continental Casualty Co., Seattle, 1931-36; mem. Seattle Police Dept., 1936-51, advanced through grades to dep. chief, 1946-51; police adviser Def. Dept., Washington, 1949; Wash. dir. civil def., Olympia, 1950; dir. pub. safety div. Fed. CDA, Washington, then regional dir. Fed. OCDM, Santa Rosa, Cal., 1954-59, Everett, Wash., 1959-61; police expert, Cal., 1962; research analyst Stanford Research Inst., Menlo Park, Cal., 1963; chief pub. safety adviser AID, State Dept., 1963-71, Indonesia, 1963-65, Vietnam, 1966-68, Thailand, 1968—. Mem. Alumni Assn. Northwestern U. Traffic Inst., Internat. Assn. Chiefs Police. Mason (32, Shriner). Home: 5847 Monte Verde Santa Rosa CA 95405 Office: USOm-AD/PS APO San Francisco CA 96346

BATSON, RANDOLPH, univ. dean, physician; b. Hattiesburg, Miss., Oct. 26, 1916; s. John O. and Nellie (Nicholson) B.; B.A., Vanderbilt U., 1938, M.D., 1942; m. Bennie Wells Shaw, Nov. 18, 1950; children—Bennie Barbara, Nellie Wells, Randolph, Alicia Bond. Intern pediatrics Vanderbilt U. Hosp., 1942- 43, asst. resident, fellow, then resident, 1943-47, dir. polio clin. study center, 1959-63; mem. faculty Vanderbilt U. Sch. Medicine, 1947—, prof. pediatrics, 1959—, acting dean Sch. Medicine, 1962-63, dean, also dir. med. affairs, 1963—. Mem. Tenn. Commn. Youth Guidance; chmn. Tenn. Subcom. Handicapped Child, nat. adv. com. Tenn. Crippled Childrens Service; adv. com. emotionally disturbed children Nashville Mental Heath Assn.; mem. spl. med. adv. group VA; pres. Assn. for Acad. Health Centers, 1970-71; mem. exec. com. Assn. Am. Med. Colls. Served with AUS, 1944-46. Diplomate Am. Bd. Pediatrics. Mem. Am. Acad. Pediatrics (chmn. Tenn. chpt.), Am., So. med. assns., Am., Nashville pediatric socs., Am. Acad. Cerebral Palsy, A.A.A.S., Assn. Am. Med. Colls., Am. Coll. Chest Physicians, Nashville Acad. Medicine, Nashville C. of C., Sigma Chi, Omicron Delta Kappa, Alpha Omega Alpha. Rotarian. Home: 4406 Chickering Lane Nashville TN 37205

BATT, GEORGE KENNETH, former industrialist; b. New Albany, Ind., Oct. 18, 1894; s. George George McClelland and Hettie (Markland) B.; student Purdue U., 1913-15; LL.D., Bloomfield Coll. and Sem.; m. Margaret Robinson Dugan, Oct. 11, 1921; children—Peggy (Mrs. Solon Palmer, Jr.), Mary (Mrs. Arnett B. Taylor). Mem. exec. staff R.H. Macy Co., N.Y.C., 1919-25, becoming 1st asst. controller; v.p., treas., mem. firm Dugan Bros., 1925-62, now ret. dir.; ret. dir. N.J. Bell Telephone Co.; mem. exec. com. Montclair Nat. Bank & Trust Co. Industry mem. Nat. War Labor Bd., Washington, 1943-44; mem. Pres.'s Cost of Living Com., 1943-44; vice chmn. Gov. N.J. War Transp. Commn., Gov. N.J. Human Resources Commn.; chmn. Ann. Rutgers Bus. Forum, 1950; chmn. citizens council N.J. Jet Port Assn., 1960-61. Mayor, Montclair, N.J., 1944-48; chmn. N.J. Republican Finance Com., 1945-48. Retired dir. Morristown (N.J.) Meml. Hosp., Bloomfield Coll.; ret. trustee Vineland (N.J.) Tng. Sch. Served to 1st lt. F.A., U.S. Army, 1917-19; AEF. Recipient Man of Year award Notre Dame Alumni Assn., N.J., 1946; named Man of Year in N.J. Agr. and Industry, 1962. Mem. N.J. C. of C. (pres. 1941-43), Beta Gamma Sigma, Theta Xi, Presbyn. Address: 7711 Hillside Dr PO Box 1623 La Jolla CA 92037

BATTAGLIA, JOSEPH, headmaster Marmion Mil. Acad. Address: Marmion Military Academy Aurora IL 60507

BATTAN, LOUIS JOSEPH, educator, scientist; b. N.Y.C., Feb. 9, 1923; s. Anibale and Louise (Webber) B.; student City Coll. N.Y., 1941-43; B.S., N.Y.U., 1946; student Harvard, 1944, Mass. Inst. Tech., 1944; M.S., U. Chgo., 1949, Ph.D., 1953; m. Jeannette A. Waitches, June 8, 1952; children—Suzette, Paul. Research meteorologist U.S. Weather Bur., 1947-51; research meteorologist, lectr. U. Chgo., 1951-58; prof. meteorology, asso. dir. Inst. Atmospheric Physics, U. Ariz., 1958—. Cons. NSF, 1964—, U.S. Weather Bur., 1957-59, USAF, 1963-65, U.S. Army, 1954, NIH, 1965; Served to capt. USAAF, 1943-46. Fellow Am. (pres. 1966-68, councilor 1959-61; Meisinger award 1962, Brooks award 1971), Royal meteorol. socs., Am. Geophys. Union, Ariz. Acad. Sci., A.A.A.S. (sec. sect. on atmospheric and hydrospheric scis.), Mem. Nat. Assn. Sci. Writers, Sigma Xi. Roman Catholic. Author: Radar Meteorology, 1959; The Nature of Violent Storms, 1961; Radar Observes the Weather, 1962; Cloud Physics and Cloud Seeding, 1962; The Unclean Sky, 1966; The Thunderstorm, 1964; (with others) Earth and Space Sciences, 1966, 71; (with others) Laboratory Manual for Earth and Space Science, 1966, 71; Harvesting the Clouds, 1969; also numerous articles. Asso. editor Jour. Meteorology, 1961, Jour. Atmospheric Sciences, 1962-66. Home: 5141 E Rosewood Av Tucson AZ 85711

BATTE, GEORGE ALBERT, Jr., textile co. exec.; b. Greensville County, Va., Sept. 12, 1906; s. George Albert and Fannie (Mallory) B.; A.B., Davidson Coll., 1927; m. Cynthia Louise Thompson, May 6, 1939; children—Cynthia Anne, Frances Mallory. With Cannon Mills Co., Kannapolis, N.C., 1927—, v.p., 1959-63, treas., 1962—, exec. v.p., 1963—, also dir.; sec., treas., dir. Imperial Cotton Mills., 1960—; sec., treas., dir. Social Circle Cotton Mills Co., 1960—; v.p., dir. Brown Mfg. Co., 1956—, Roberta Mfg. Co., 1956—;asst. sec. Cannon Mills Inc., 1962-66, sec., 1966—; also dir.; asst. sec., dir. Wiscassett Mills Co.; dir. Cabarrus Bank & Trust Co. Chmn. trustees, chmn. exec. com. Cabarrus Meml. Hosp.; treas., dir. Cannon Meml. YMCA. Mem. Kappa Alpha, Knights of York Cross of Honour. Methodist (trustee). Mason. Home: 70 Spring St NW Concord NC 28025 Office: Cannon Mills Co Kannapolis NC 28081

BATTELLE, PHYLLIS MARIE, columnist; b. Dayton, O., Jan. 4, 1922; d. Gordon S. and Marie (Sides) Battelle; B.A., Ohio Wesleyan U., 1944; m. Arthur Van Horn, Dec. 6, 1957; 1 son, Jonathan Gordon. Police reporter, feature writer, teen-age columnist, Dayton Herald, 1944-47; women's editor, fashion editor Internat. News Service, 1947-54, writer three-times weekly syndicated column Assignment: America, 1955—. Free-lance contbr. to nat. mags. Recipient ann. award for best domestic news coverage N.Y. Newspaperwomen's, 1951; prizes ann. Ohio Newspaper Women's Assn., 1944-47. Mem. Delta Gamma. Methodist. Club: New York Newspaperwomen's. Home: 310 E 70th St New York City NY 10021 and Estate Carlton St Croix VI 00840 Office: King Features Syndicate 235 E 45th St New York City NY 10017

BATTELSTEIN, JERRY EDWIN, metal products co. exec.; b. Houston, May 1, 1932; s. Abraham Moses and Betty (Harris) B.; student U. Tex., 1950-53, U. Houston, 1956; m. Anna Winnicki, June 6, 1962; children—Elizabeth, Adam, Ania. Mdse. mgr. women's div. Battelstein's, Houston, 1957-65, mdse. mgr. men's div., 1965-67; v.p. Mortgage Co. Am., Houston, 1967; chmn. bd. Oak Forest Bank, Houston, 1968-69; chmn. bd. Peden Industries, Inc., Houston, 1969—, also dir.; dir. Am. Mchts. Life, MCA Financial Corp., Mortgage Co. Am., Oak Forest Bank. Served as lt. AUS, 1956. Clubs: Petroleum, University, Westwood Country, Racquet (Houston). Home: 9201 Memorial Houston TX 77024 Office: care Peden Industries Inc PO Box 1891 Houston TX 77001

BATTEN, FRANK newspaper publisher; b. Norfolk, Va., Feb. 11, 1927; s. Frank and Dorothy (Martin) B.; A.B., U. Va., 1950; M.B.A., Harvard, 1952; m. Jane Neal Parke; children—Frank, Mary, Dorothy. Asst. sec., treas., v.p., dir., Norfolk Newspapers, Inc., 1952-54; pub. Norfolk Virginian-Pilot, Norfolk Ledger-Dispatch, and The Portsmouth Star, 1954—; chmn. Greensboro (N.C.) Daily News, Greensboro Record and WFMY-TV, Greensboro, 1965—, WTAR Radio-TV Corp., Landmark Communications Inc., 1966—, Roanoke Times and World-News, Tele Cable Corp.; dir. Va. Nat. Bank. Chmn. 1957 Internat. Naval Rev., Hampton Roads, Va. Pres. Norfolk Area United Fund, 1964. Dir. Norfolk Gen. Hosp., 1954—; chmn. of bd. Old Dominion U., 1962-70; trustee Norfolk Acad., Hollins Coll. Recipient Norfolk's First Citizen award, 1966. Mem. Asso. Press, Norfolk C. of C. (pres. 1961), Delta Kappa Epsilon. Episcopalian. Clubs: Princess Anne Country, Norfolk Yacht (Norfolk). Home: Holly Lane North Shore Point Norfolk VA 23505 Office: 150 W Brambleton Av Norfolk VA 23501

BATTEN, FRED WILLIAM, gas co. exec.; b. Detroit, Nov. 29, 1912; s. John W. and Maude (McCutcheon) B.; B.S. in Engring., U. Mich., 1935, M.S., 1936; m. Barbara Anne Beckjord, Dec. 16, 1939; children—Mary McCutcheon, Barbara Anne, Kathryn Holly. Engr., Binghamton Gas Works, 1936-47; v.p., gen. mgr. Mfrs. Light and Heat Co., 1952-57; sr. v.p., chief operations officer, dir. Columbia Gas System, Inc., 1961—; pres., dir. Columbia Gas Transmission Corp., Wilmington, Del., 1970—; dir. Columbia Hydrocarbon Corp., Wilmington. Home: 155 Lucky Hill Rd West Chester PA 19380 Office: 20 Montchanin Rd Wilmington DE 19807

BATTEN, JAMES KNOX, newspaperman; b. Suffolk, Va., Jan. 11, 1936; s. Eugene Taylor and Josephine (Winslow) B.; B.S., Davidson Coll., 1957; M. Pub. Affairs, Princeton, 1962; m. Jean Elaine Trueworthy. Feb. 22, 1958; children—Mark Winslow, Laura Taylor, Taylor Edison. Reporter, Charlotte (N.C.) Observer, 1957-58, 62-65; corr. Washington bur. Knight Newspapers, 1965- 70; editorial staff Detroit Free Press, 1970—. Served with AUS, 1958- 60. Recipient George Polk Meml. award for regional reporting, 1968; Sidney Hillman Found. award, 1968. Presbyn. (deacon 1967-70). Home: 4220 Arlington Dr Royal Oak MI 48072 Office: 321 Lafayette Blvd Detroit MI 48231

BATTEN, JOHN HENRY, III, mfg. exec.; b. Chicago, Jan. 16, 1912; s. Percy Haight and Lisa (Stockton) B.; grad. Phillips (Andover) Acad., 1931; A.B., Yale, 1935; Cert. M.E., U. Wis. Extension, 1949; m. Katherine Vernet Smith, June 30, 1938; children—Edmund Peter Smith, Michael Ellsworth, Linda Vernet. With Twin Disc, Inc., Racine, Wis., 1935—, dir., 1937—, asst. treas., 1942-43, v.p., asst. gen. mgr., 1943-45, exec. v.p., 1945-48, now pres., chief exec. officer; chmn., dir. Twin Disc Clutch AG, Vaduz Liechtenstein, Paragon Gears, Inc., Taunton, Mass.; dir. LEM Instrument Corp., Farmingdale, N.Y., Twin Disc Internat. S.A., Nivelles, Belgium, British Twin Disc Ltd., Rochester, Kent, Eng., Twin Disc (Pacific) Pty., Ltd., Sydney, Australia, Niigata Converter Co., Tokyo, Japan, Harris Metals, Inc., Racine, Wis., Racine Comml. Airport Corp., Am. Bank & Trust Co., Racine, Walker Forge, Racine, Employers Ins. of Wausau, Giddings & Lewis, Inc., Fond du Lac. Mem. bd. edn., Racine, 1936-46. Mem. N.A.M. (Midwest v.p., dir.), Wis. Mfrs. Assn. (past dir.), Soc. Automotive Engrs., Chief Execs. Forum, S.A.R., Phi Beta Kappa. Episcopalian. Home: 3030 Michigan Blvd Racine WI 53402 Office: 1328 Racine St Racine WI 53403

BATTEN, ROGER LYMAN, educator, curator; b. Hammond, Ind., June 22, 1932; s. Verne Lyman and Mae I. (Anuta) B.; B.A., U. Wyo., 1948; Ph.D., Columbia, 1955; m. Loretta Elizabeth Lepeska, Jan. 29, 1965. Geologist U.S. Geol. Survey, Washington, 1954; prof. geology U. Wis., 1955-62, Columbia, 1962—, also curator Am. Mus. Natural History, N.Y.C., 1962—; cons. McGraw-Hill Book Co. Served with inf., AUS, 1943-45. Decorated Purple Heart. Mem. Paleontol. Soc., Soc. Systematic Zoology, Paleontog. Soc. Great Britain, Malacol. Soc. London, Sigma Xi. Author: (with R.H. Dott, Jr.), The Evolution of the Earth, 1971. Home: 1575 Center Av Ft Lee NJ 07024 Office: Am Museum Natural History New York City NY 10024

BATTEN, W. ARTHUR, pipe line co. exec.; b. Detroit, 1915; grad. U. Mich., 1936, LL.B., 1939. Vice pres., gen. atty. Mich. Wis. Pipe Line Co. Home: 184 Hillcrest Lane Grosse Point, MI 48236. Office: 1 Woodward Av Detroit MI 48226*

BATTEN, WILLIAM MILFRED, retail co. exec.; b. Reedy, W.Va., June 4, 1909; s. Lewis Allen and Gurry Frances (Goff) B.; B.S. Ohio State U., 1932; LL.D., Morris Harvey Coll., 1960, W.Va., U., 1966, Alderson-Broaddus Coll., 1970; L.H.D. (hon.), Marietta Coll., 1965; m. Kathryn P. Clark, Aug. 10, 1935; children—David Clark, Jane Louise. Formerly sales promotion rep. Kellogg Co., Battle Creek, Mich.; with J. C. Penney Co., Inc., 1935—, asst. store mgr., 1937-40, tng. dir., 1940- 46, zone personnel rep., 1946—, asst. to pres., 1951-58, v.p., 1953-58, pres., chief exec. officer, 1958-64, chmn. bd., chief exec. officer, dir., 1964—; dir. The Boeing Co., AT&T Co., First Nat. City

Bank N.Y., First Nat. City Corp. Chmn. Bus. Council, 1971. Served to lt. col. AUS, 1942-45. Mem. Econ. Club N.Y. (pres. 1967-68). Home: Heather Lane Mill Neck NY 11765 Office: 1301 Av of Americas New York City NY 10019

BATTERMAN, BORIS WILLIAM, educator; b. N.Y.C., Aug. 25, 1930; s. Herman and Dora (Zimney) B.; student Cooper Union Coll., 1949-50, Technische Hochschule, Stuttgart, Germany (Fulbright scholar), 1953-54; S.B., Mass. Inst. Tech., 1952, Ph.D., 1956; m. Elfriede Vollrath, June 24, 1953; children—Robert W., William E., Thomas A. Mem. tech. staff Bell Telephone Labs., Murray Hill, N.J., 1956-58, 59-65; research physicist IBM, 1958-59; asso. prof. Cornell U., 1965-67, prof. material sci. and applied physics, 1967—; cons. x-ray diffraction. Mem. U.S.A. Nat. Com. Crystallography, NSF, 1969—. Guggenheim fellow, 1971. Fellow Am. Phys. Soc. Asso. editor Jour. Crystal Growth. Home: 11 Knoll Tree Rd Ithaca NY 14850

BATTIN, JAMES FRANKLIN, U.S. dist. judge; b. Wichita, Kan., Feb. 13, 1925; student Eastern Mont. Coll., Billings; J.D., George Washington Univ., 1951; m. Barbara Choate; children—Loyce, Patricia, James Franklin. Admitted to D.C. and Mont. bars; practice in Washington, 1951-52; now in Billings; past dep. county atty.; past sec.-counsel City-County Planning Bd.; past asst. city atty., Billings, then city atty.; mem. Mont. Ho. of Reps., 1958-59; mem. 87th-91st congresses 2d Dist. Mont.; resigned when apptd. U.S. dist. judge, 1969. Served with USNR, World War II; PTO. Mem. Am. Legion. DeMolay Legion of Honor. Presbyn. Mason (Shriner). Elk. Office: Federal Bldg Billings MT 59101

BATTISTI, FRANK JOSEPH, U.S. judge; b. Youngstown, O., Oct. 4, 1922; s. Eugene and Jennie (Dalesandro) B.; B.A., Ohio U., 1947; LL.B., Harvard, 1950. Admitted to Ohio bar, 1950; asst. atty. gen. Ohio, 1950; atty. adviser C.E., U.S. Army, 1951-52; instr. law Youngstown U., 1952-54; 1st asst. dir. law, Youngstown, 1954-59; judge Common Pleas Ct., Mahoning County, O., 1959-61; U.S. judge No. Dist. Ohio, 1961- 69, chief judge, 1969—. Served with C.E., AUS, 1943-45; ETO. Mem. Am., Mahoning County bar assns., Am. Judicature Soc. Roman Catholic. Home: 13900 Shaker Blvd Cleveland OH 44120 Office: US Court Cleveland OH 44114

BATTISTI, PAUL ORESTE, hosp. adminstr.; b. Herkimer, N.Y., Mar. 16, 1922; s. Oreste and Ida (Fiore) B.; student Cornell U., 1947-48, U. Neb., 1951-52; m. Donna Marie Johannes, Nov. 2, 1945; children—Paul J., Cathy (Mrs. D. Capage), Deborah, Thomas, Daniel, Melora, Stephen. With VA, 1946—, dir. VA Hosp., Martinez, Cal., 1969—. Mem. Contra Costa County Comprehensive Health Planning, Health Facilities Task Force; mem. adv. com. East Bay Med. Program. Bd. dirs. Easter Seals Contra Costa County. Served with AUS, 1942-46. Fellow Am. Coll. Hosp. Adminstrs. Rotarian (bd. dirs. Martinez). Home: 120 Arlene Dr Walnut Creek CA 94595 Office: 150 Muir Rd Martinez CA 94553

BATTLE, HAWTHORNE DILL, lawyer; b. Petersburg, Va., Dec. 15, 1901; s. Henry Wilson and Margaret (Stewart) B.; LL.B., U. Va., 1924; m. Martha Julia Thomas, Mar. 27, 1929; children—Hawthorne Dill, George Thomas, Henry Wilson III, Martha Julia. Admitted to Va. bar, 1924; asso. Price, Smith & Spilman, Charleston, 1924-29; partner Spilman, Thomas, Battle & Klostermeyer, Charleston, 1929—. Dir. Kanawha Banking & Trust Co., and others. Pres. Kanawha Charleston Bd. Health, 1946-54. Served as lt. USNR., 1942-45. Mem. Am., W.Va. (pres. 1958), Charleston (pres. 1938) bar assns., Phi Beta Kappa, Phi Delta Phi, Alpha Tau Omega. Episcopalian (sr. warden). Clubs: Charleston Rotary (pres. 1955); Press; Edgewood Country. Home: 1426 Connell Rd Charleston WV 25314 Office: Kanawha Banking & Trust Co Charleston WV 25301

BATTLE, HYMAN LLEWELLYN, textile mfr.; b. Rocky Mount, N.C., Aug. 11, 1896; s. Thomas Hall and and Sallie Dorch (Hyman) B.; student U. N.C., 1915-16; m. Mamie Louise Braswell, June 22, 1921; children—Hyman Llewellyn, Thomas Braswell. With Rocky Mount (N.C.) Mills 1919—, treas., mgr., dir. 1933—, pres., 1954—; v.p. Rocky Mount Cord Co., 1937—; dir. Sterling Cotton Mills, Coastal Plain Life Ins. Co., Planters Nat. Bank & Trust Co., Rocky Mount Investment Co., A.C.L. R.R., Waltzinger, Inc. State, Bus. Found. Adviser to employer del. Internat. Labor Conf., Washington, 1937; expert yarn cons. O.Q.M.G., AUS, 1945; mem. carded yarn adv. com. OPA and Civilian Prodn. Adminstrn., Washington, 1942-51. Chmn. Housing Authority. Pres. bd. trustees Rectory Sch., Pomfret, Conn., 1937-41; trustee St. Marys Sch. and Jr. Coll., Raleigh, N.C., 1954-57. Served with U.S. Army, 1917-19. Recipient Distinguished Service award U. N.C. Sch. Medicine, 1957. Mem. Rocky Mount C. of C., S.A.R., Soc. Colonial Wars, N.Y. So. Soc., Newcomen Soc. Democrat. Episcopalian. Clubs: Princess Anne Country (Virginia Beach, Va.); Benvenue Country (Rocky Mount, N.C.). Home: 226 Sunset Av Rocky Mount NC 27801 also 5902 Ocean Virginia Beach VA 23451 Office: Rocky Mount NC 27801

BATTLE, HYMAN LLEWELLYN, Jr., lawyer; b. Rocky Mt., N.C., Jan. 19, 1925; s. Hyman Llewellyn and Mamie (Braswell) B.; grad. Choate Sch., 1942; B.A., Princeton, 1946; LL.B., U. Pa., 1949; m. Margaretta S. Harrison, June 22, 1945 (div.); children—Craig L., David H., John M., Kemp P. Admitted to N.Y. bar, 1949, since practiced in N.Y.C.; partner Battle, Fowler, Stokes & Kheel, 1957—. Dir. Chase Bag Co. Trustee Rectory Sch., Pomfret, Conn., 1967—. Served with USMCR, 1943-46, 51-52. Mem. Zeta Psi. Home: 860 United Nations Plaza, New York City, NY 10017 Office: 280 Park Av New York City NY 10017

BATTLE, JEAN ALLEN, educator; b. Talladega, Ala., June 15, 1914; s. William Raines and and Lemerle McLemore (Allen) B.; student Birmingham So. Coll., 1932-33; B.S., Middle Tenn. State Coll., 1937; M.A., U. Alta., 1941; Ed.D., U. Fla., 1952; m. Lucy Troxell, Aug. 25, 1940; 1 dau., Helen Carol. Dept. chmn., dean students Fla. So. Coll., 1940-55, dean coll., 1956-59; dean coll. edn. U. S. Fla., Tampa, 1959-71, prof. higher edn., 1971—; editor, pub. Tenn. Valley News. Mem. Fla. Tchrs. Edn. Adv. Council, Fla. Continuing Edn. Council; mem. courses study com. Fla. Bd. Edn. Adv. com. Hillsborough County Hosp. Bd. dirs. Fla. Univ. System Honduras Program, World Trade Council, Tampa, Poynter Found., St. Petersburg, Fla.; bd. dirs., v.p. Southeastern Edn. Lab., Atlanta. Served from pvt. to capt. USAAF, 1942-46. Recipient Distinguished Service awards Fla. So. Coll., 1952, Fla. Citizenship Clearing House, 1957; Outstanding Alumnus award Middle Tenn. State U. Mem. S.A.R., Fla. Hist. Soc., N.E.A., Fla. Edn. Assn. (co-chmn. tchr. recruitment com.), Tampa C. of C. (edn. com.), Acad. Polit. Sci., Omicron Delta Kappa, Pi Gamma Mu, Kappa Delta Pi, Phi Delta Kappa, Sigma Alpha Epsilon. Methodist. Rotarian. Co- author: The New Idea in Education; author: Culture and Education for the Contemporary World, 1969. Contbr. papers tech. lit. Home: 11011 Carrollwood Dr Tampa FL 33618

BATTLE, KEMP DAVIS, lawyer; b. Rocky Mount, N.C., Oct. 9, 1888; s. Thomas Hall and Elizabeth (Mershon) B.; A.B., U. N.C., 1909, LL.D., 1960; LL.B., U. Denver, 1914; m. Laura Maud Bunn, Oct. 30, 1917; children—Elizabeth Mershon (Mrs. Irving Grossberg), Laura (Mrs. Emerson C. Winstead, Jr.). Admitted to N.C. bar, 1910, since practiced in Rocky Mount; mem. firm Battle, Winslow, Merrell, Scott & Wiley, 1911—; judge municipal ct., Rocky Mount, 1918-20. Vice pres., dir. Rocky Mount Mills; dir. Carolina Tel. & Tel. Co. Pres. N.C. Tb Assn., 1949; del. triennial con. Episcopal Ch., mem. exec. council, chancellor Diocese N.C., 1954-57. Bd. dirs., sec. Nat. Tb Assn., 1952-55; trustee Rocky Mount pub. schs., 1923-44, Braswell Meml. Library, Rocky Mount, 1925-40, U. N.C., 1927-59, Park View Hosp., Rocky Mount, 1927—. Recipient Will Ross medal Nat. Tb Assn., 1956. Mem. Am., N.C. (pres. 1932-33) bar assns., N.C. State Bar (council 1933-41). Democrat. Kiwanian. Club: Benvenue Country (Rocky Mount). Contbr. N.C. Law Rev. Home: RFD 3 Rocky Mount NC 27801 Office: Planters Nat Bank Bldg Rocky Mount NC 27801

BATTLE, LUCIUS DURHAM, business exec. b. Dawson, Ga., June 1, 1918; s. Warren Lazarus and Jewel Beatrice (Durham) B.; A.B., U. Fla., 1939, LL.B., 1946, LL.D.; L.H.D., Fla. State U.; m. Betty Jane Davis, Oct. 1, 1949; children—Lynne, John, Laura, Thomas. Mgr. student staff U. Fla. Library, 1940-42; asso. adminstrv. analyst War Dept., 1942-43; fgn. affairs specialist Dept. State, Washington, 1946-49, spl. asst. to sec. of state, 1949-53, 61-64, also exec. sec. Dept. State. 1961-62; asst. sec. of state for ednl. and cultural affairs, 1962-64; 1st sec. Am. embassy, Copenhagen, 1953-55; dep. exec. sec. NATO, Paris, France, 1955-56; ambassador to UAR, 1964-67; asst. sec. state for Near Eastern and South Asian affairs, Washington, 1967-68; v.p. corporate relations Communications Satellite Corp., 1968- -. Chmn. UNESCO Gen Conf. Paris, 1962. Vice pres. Colonial Williamsburg, Inc., Williamsburg Restoration, Inc., 1956-61; dir. Franklin Book Programs: trustee Meridian House Found. Served to lt. (s.g.) USNR, 1943-46. Mem. Am. Fgn. Service Assn. (pres. 1962-63), Phi Beta Kappa, Alpha Tau Omega, Phi Delta Phi. Home: 3200 Garfield St NW Washington DC 20008 Office: Communications Satellite Corp Washington DC 20024

BATTLE, MARK GARVEY, assn. exec.; b. Brighton, N.J., July 28, 1924; s. Edward M. and Mary (Noble) B.; B.A., U. Rochester, 1948; M.S. in Social Adminstrn., Western Res. U., 1950; m. Dolores Tierney, June 6, 1946; children-Erica Lynn, Kenana Caroline, Marcus Edward. Group worker Baden St. Settlement, Rochester, N.Y., 1947-48; indsl. field sec. Cleve. Urban League, 1949- 51; dir. youth activities Friendly Inn Settlement, Cleve., 1950-52; exec. dir. Lower N. Community Center, Chgo., 1952-60; exec. dir. Franklin Settlement, Detroit, 1960-64; dep. asst. manpower adminstr. Dept. Labor, 1964-65; dep. dir. Neighborhood Youth Corps, 1965-67, adminstr. Bur. Work Tng. Programs, 1967-69; pres. Mark Battle Assn., Washington, 1969—. Served with USNR, 1943-46. Recipient Cowan award Nat. Council Christians and Jews, 1969; Group award Dept. Labor, 1966; Service award City of Patterson, N.J., 1967. Mem. Am. Assn. Social Workers, N.A.A.C.P., Nat. Urban League, Acad. Certified Social Workers, Am. Soc. Pub. Adminstrn., Alpha Phi Alpha. Home: 1269 Delaware Av S W Washington DC 20024 Office: 1025 Connecticut Av N W Washington DC 20036

BATTLE, WILLIAM CULLEN, textile co. exec., lawyer; b. Charlottesville, Va., Oct. 9, 1920; s. John Stewart and Mary Jane (Lipscomb) B.; B.A., U. Va., 1941, LL.B., 1947; m. Frances Barry Webb, Nov. 14, 1953; children—William Cullen, Robert Webb, Jane Tavernor. Admitted to Va. bar, 1947; atty. Charleston group companies Columbia Gas System, 1947-51; partner firm Battle, Neal, Harris, Minor & Williams, and predecessor, Charlottesville and Richmond, 1951-62; U.S. ambassador to Australia, 1962-64; partner firm McGuire, Woods & Battle, Charlottesville and Richmond, Va., 1964-71; pres. Field Crest Mills, Inc., Eden, N.C., 1971—; dir., exec. com. Va. Nat. Bank, Mem. adv. panel internat. law and fgn. policy State Dept. Chmn. budget commn. Charlottesville-Albemarle County Community Chest; Democratic nominee for gov. Va., 1969. Dir. Va. Assn. Mental Health; chmn. Va. adv. bd. Salvation Army. Served to lt. (s.g.) USNR, 1941-45. Decorated Silver Star. Mem. Am., Va., W.Va. bar assns. Democrat. Baptist. Home: Charlottesville VA 22901

BATTLE, WILLIAM ROBERT, newspaper exec.; b. Nolensville, Tenn., Dec. 25, 1927; s. William Robert and Cleo (Smith) B.; student George Peabody Coll., 1946-49; m. Elizabeth Ogilvie, Dec. 23, 1948; children—Valerie Elizabeth, William Robert III. With Nashville Banner, 1943—, police beat, county polit. beat, 1943-53, city editor, 1953-64, mng. editor, 1964-71, exec. editor, 1971—, movie columnist, 1955—; editor Hurst Constrn. News; corr. Nat. Enquirer, N.Y.C.; Tenn. rep. Screen Daily. Supt. gates and admissions, Tenn. State Fair, 1953-64; pub. relations chmn. Davidson County chpt. Nat. Found., 1958—; bd. dirs. Goodwill Industries, 1960—. Chmn. publicity Davison County Council for Retarded Children, 1961—; publicity chmn. Davidson County Cancer Soc.; mem. exec. bd. Middle Tenn. council Boy Scouts Am.; col. Gov.'s staff. Recipient Big Story award NBC TV, 1956, Silver trophy for outstanding service Cerebral Palsy Telethon, 1967. Appeared in movie as a newspaperman in Teacher's Pet, 1957; appeared in movie Country Music on Broadway, 1963. Mem. Nashville Area C. of C., Tenn. Press Assn., A.P. Mng. Editors Assn., Nat. Screen Council, Sigma Delta Chi. Methodist. Mason (32, Shriner, Jester), Elk (chmn. scholarship com.). Clubs: Nashville City, Executive of Nashville; Colemere Country; Admiral's. Contbr. numerous articles nat. publs. Home: 4108 Crestridge Dr Nashville TN 37202 Office: 1100 Broadway St Nashville TN 37202

BATTLEY, JOSEPH F., ret. army officer; b. Norfolk, Va., Dec. 19, 1896; s. Joseph Franklin and Effie Ada (Sadler) B.; student Norfolk (Va.) Acad.; M.B.A., Harvard, 1926; grad. Army Indsl. Coll., 1933, Chem. Warfare Sch., 1938, Army War Coll., 1946; m. Joyce Russell Zappia. With Va. N.G., 1917; commd. 2d lt., Engrs. Res. Corps, U.S. Army, 1918, advanced through grades to brig. gen., 1944; served with Chem. Warfare Service, France, 1918; exec. officer Chem. Warfare Service Arsenal, Edgewood, Md., 1920-23; with Office Under Sec. War, 1932-36, on loan to NRA as adminstr. chem. div., 1933-36, later asst. to adminstr. WPA N.Y.C.; assigned to Edgewood Arsenal, 1936-39, chief protective devel. div., developing and perfecting fully molded gas mask and plastic lenses, also chief war plans div. to 1939; mem. joint Army and Navy Munitions Bd. for indsl. and manpower phases of plans for emergency, 1939-41; asst. constrn. Q.M.C., 1940-41; chief manpower and liaison div. Office Under Sec. War, 1941-42, also cons. labor div. OPM (later WPB), 1942; nat. occupational adviser SSS, 1940-42; chief, adminstrv. mgmt. br., control div. Army Service Forces, 1942; exec. for service commands Office Chief Adminstrv. Services, 1942- 1943; exec. officer dept. chief of staff for service commands, 1943-44, dep. chief of staff, 1944-46; asst. Office Comdg. Gen., Army Service Forces, charge Army Service Forces pub. relations, 1946; spl. around world mission Aug.-Sept. 1945; exec. chief pub. information Office Gen. Eisenhower, 1946; ret. 1947; exec. asst. pres. Sands, Las Vegas, Nev.; partner Labor-Mgmt. Sales Cons. Pres. Nat. Clean-Up Paint- up Bur.; mem. Nat. Planning Council; sponsor Atlantic Council U.S. Decorated Army Commendation ribbon with two clusters, D.S.M., Legion of Merit. Mem. Nat. Paint Varnish and Lacquer Assn. (pres. 1947-61). Clubs: Nat. Press; Harvard; Harvard Business School of S.C., SKAL, Internat.; Army Navy. Home: 4680 Rubidoux Av Riverside CA 92506

BATTS, HENRY LEWIS, educator; b. nr. Damascus, Ga., Oct. 23, 1894; s. Henry and Iola (Free) B.; A.B., Mercer U., 1914; postgrad. Harvard, 1915-16; M.R.E., Hartford Sem. Found., 1927, Ph.D., 1935; D.D., Mercer U., 1968; m. Ferris Sherwood, Aug. 8, 1918; children—Henry Lewis, Juliette Ferris (Mrs. G. Watson Turk). State sec. Ga. Bapt. Young People's Union, Atlanta 1919-24; instr. English, religious edn. Mercer U., 1924-29, Curry prof. religious edn., 1945-63, emeritus Curry prof., 1963—, chmn. dept. Christianity, 1957-63, dean of chapel, 1958-62, tchr. Mercer Extension Dept. 1960-68; pastor East Granby (Conn.) Congl. Ch., 1929-30; dir. edn. Lake Av. Bapt. Ch., Rochester, N.Y., 1930-35; dir. inter-ch. student council, Kalamazoo, 1935-45; ordained to ministry Bapt. Ch., 1937; pastor Bradley Ch., 1951-65. Pres., Ministerial Alliance, 1944-45; chmn. program com. Religious Edn. Assn. Mich., 1942; chmn. com. on character edn. Mich. Congress Parents and Teachers, 1943-45. Democrat. Baptist. Author: History of First Baptist Church, Macon, Georgia, 1968. Writer Sunday School lessons Christian Index, 1956. Contbr. articles to religious jours. Home: 187 W Ridge Circle Macon GA 31204

BATZER, R. KIRK, accountant; b. Bismarck, N.D., Nov. 28, 1915; s. Reinhold K. and Edna (MacLachlan) B.; student Macalester Coll., 1931-34; A.B., Cornell U., 1935; M.S., Syracuse U., 1940; m. Marjorie M. White, May 5, 1945; children—John L., Barbara W., Susan M., Kirk W., Laura M. With Lybrand, Ross Bros. & Montgomery, C.P.A.'s, N.Y.C., 1940—, partner, 1953—, dir. internat. services, 1964—. Bd. dirs. Essex County (N.J.) Girl Scout Council, 1961-68. Commr., housing authority City of Summit, 1968-. Served to lt. USNR, 1941-45. C.P.A., N.Y., N.J., Ill., Okla., Mo. Mem. Am. Inst. C.P.A.'s, N.Y. Soc. C.P.A.'s (bd. dirs. 1955-58). Episcopalian. Home: 55 Silver Lake Dr Summit, NJ 07901 Office: 2 Broadway New York City NY 10004

BAUBE, JEAN CAMILLE, French diplomat; b. Paris, France, Mar. 25, 1907; s. Gaston and Marie (Janvier) B.; B.A., U. Paris, 1926; m. Lilian Whaley, July 2, 1932; children—Anne Francoise, Ian Gaston. Prodn. engr. Renault Works, Paris, 1929-31; newspaperman AP, Paris, 1931-32, Havas Newsagency, London, 1932-36, head, Washington, 1936-41; press officer Gen. de Gaulle's Hdqrs., London, 1941; mem. Free French Delegation, Washington, 1942-45; counselor French embassy, Washington, 1945—. Decorated officer Legion Honor, cross Free France Order. Home: Boca Grande FL 33921 Office: French Embassy Washington DC 20008

BAUCHAT, JAMES L., real estate devel. co. exec.; b. Detroit, Jan. 21, 1914; s. George A. and Casmira (Smolinski) B.; B.A., U. Mich., 1935, M.B.A., 1939; m. Margaret Snow Biddle, Nov. 29, 1941; children—James L., David. A., C. Geoffrey, L. Renee. With Ford Motor Co., 1943-60, gen. mgr. Ypsilanti (Mich.) plant, 1957-60; v.p., controller Bankers Trust Co., N.Y.C., 1960-66; controller, dir. Am. Tobacco Co., 1966-69; pres., dir.. Sunshine Biscuit Inc., 1969—; sr. v.p., treas. Kassuba Co., Kassuba Corp.; pres., dir. Kassuba Inns, Inc., Briggs Mfg. Co.; Bd. dirs. Washtenaw County chpt. A.R.C., 1957-60, chmn. for Mich. nat. fund drive, 1960; bd. dirs. Washtenaw County United Fund, 1956-60; mem. adv. bd. Washtenaw County Salvation Army, 1957-60. Recipient Community Service award Ypsilanti C. of C., 1960. Mem. Financial Execs. Inst. (bd. dirs. N.Y. chpt. 1965- 66), Nat. Assn. Bank Audit, Control and Operations (pres. N.Y. chpt. 1965-66), Theta Chi. Republican. Episcopalian. Clubs: Overlake Golf and Country (Medina, Wash.); Cypress Lake Golf (Ft. Myers, Fla.); Union League, Pinnâcle (N.Y.C.); Morris County Golf (Convent, N.J.). Home: 1849 77th Av NE Bellevue WA 98004 Office: 350 Royal Palm Way Palm Beach FL 33480

BAUCUM, A.W., petroleum co. exec.; b. 1917; B.S., Tex. A. & M. Coll., 1934; m. With Texaco, Inc., 1934—, v.p., 1958-61, exec. v.p., 1961—, chief exec. officer So. operations, Houston, 1964—; dir. Texaco Can. Ltd. Home: 5949 Stone's Throw Houston TX 77027 Office: 1111 Rusk Av Houston TX 77002*

BAUDER, DARIO G., Venezuelan diplomat; b. Caracas, Venezuela, Mar. 9, 1939; s. Dario M. and Enriqueta (Fonturvel) B.; D. in Econs., U. Rome, 1963; diploma social scis. U. Stockholm, 1965; m. Neyita Mantellini, Dec. 10, 1967; 1 son, Guillermo Henrique. Economist, dept. econ. research Ministry Mines and Hydrocarbons, Caracas, 1965-67; 1st sec. petroleum affairs, Washington, 1968-70, counselor, 1971—. Dir. Scamerica, Caracas. Mem. Am. Econ. Assn., Soc. Internat. Devel., Societa di Economia Internazionale. Home: 12000 Old Georgetown Rd Rockville MD 20852 Office: 2445 Massachusetts Av Washington DC 20008 also: PO Box 5028 Caracas Venezuela

BAUDER, FRANK EDWARD, banker; b. Elgin, Ia., July 30, 1920; s. Edward Emmet and Irene (Bakeman) B.; B.A. summa cum laude, Coe Coll., 1941; m. Marijane Waitley, Nov. 6, 1943; children—Barbra Jane, Elizabeth Ann. With Continental Ill. Nat. Bank and Trust Co., Chgo., 1946-63, v.p. comml. lending div., 1956-63; exec. v.p. Central Nat. Bank in Chgo., 1963-64, pres., 1964-68, chmn. bd., 1968—, also dir.; dir. Rapistan, Inc., Unarco Industries, Inc. Asso. bd. assos. Presbyn.-St. Luke's Hosp., Chgo.; trustee Coe Coll., Cedar Rapids, Ia.; bd. dirs. Am. Found. for Agr. Mem. Am. Bankers Assn. (mem. fed. legislative com.), Ill. Bankers Assn. (Chgo. treas.), Assn. Res. City Bankers. Clubs: Union League, Mid-Am., Executives, Economic, Bankers, Chicago, Commercial (Chgo.). Home: 51 Coventry Rd Northfield IL 60093 Office: 120 S LaSalle St Chicago IL 60603

BAUDER, RUSSELL STICKNEY, educator, economist; b. Elburn, Ill., Aug. 20, 1902; s. George Stickney and Anna (Taylor) B.; B.S., Knox Coll., Galesburg, Ill., 1924; A.M., U. Wis., 1925, Ph.D., 1933; m. Hazel Mikkelsen, Mar. 5, 1929; children—Martha Anne, Susan Stickney. Instr. econs. U. Mo., 1927-30, asst. prof., 1930-34, asso. prof., 1934-40, prof., 1940-71, chmn. dept. econs. and bus., 1947-52, emeritus, 1971—. Asso. dir. Mo. Employment Service, 1934-35; subject matter cons. Mo. Merit System Council, 1937-42; dir. div. wage stblzn. region VII, Nat. War Labor Bd., 1942- 44, vice chmn. region VII, 1944-45, pub. mem. region VII, Nat. Wage Stblzn. Bd., 1945-46; chmn. regional labor mgmt. adv. com. U.S. Conciliation Service, 1945-47; mem. Nat. Panel Arbitrators, 1946- 47; mem. arbitration panel Fed. Mediation and Conciliation Service, 1947—; labor arbibrator, 1946—; mem. wage stblzn. bd. panel on agrl. wages, 1951; vice chmn. to chmn. region IX, Wage Stblzn. Bd., 1951- 52. Mem. Am., Midwest econ. assns., Indsl. Relations Research Assn., Nat. Acad. Arbitrators, Phi Beta Kappa, Beta Gamma Sigma, Alpha Pi Zeta, Lambda Chi Alpha. Democrat. Home: 13813 Sahara Dr Sun City AZ 85351 ☆

BAUDER, WARD W., educator, sociologist; b. Pauline, Neb., May 31, 1913; s. Clarence Wesley and Ellen Ann (Jones) B.; B.Sc., U. Neb., 1936, M.Sc., 1938; Ph.D., Cornell U., 1948; m. Dorothy Charlotte Nelson, Apr. 18, 1941; children—Mary Ellen (Mrs. Frank Risler), Thomas Ward, Richard Scott. Asst. prof., then prof. U. Ky., 1948-53; prof. U. Ill., 1953-56; social sci. anaylst Agr. Marketing Service, 1956-62; sociologist Econ. Research Service, 1962—; prof. rural sociology Cornell U., 1968—. Served with USAAF, 1942-45. Mem. Am. Sociol. Assn., Rural Sociol. Soc. (sec.-treas. 1954-56), FarmHouse, Alpha Zeta, Gamma Sigma Delta, Phi Kappa Phi, Phi Delta Kappa, Alpha Kappa Delta. Democrat. Methodist. Author chpts. in books, bulls., monographs, articles. Home: Cedar Lane Ithaca NY 14850

BAUDHUIN, FRANCIS J., paint and varnish mfg. co. exec.; b. 1915. With Rockcote Paint Co., Rockford, Ill., and predecessor, 1940-60; with Valspar Corp., Chgo., 1960—, now v.p., dir., Mpls. Address: care Valspar Corp 1101 Third St S Minneapolis MN 55415

BAUDHUIN, RALPH JULIAN, paint mgr.; b. Brussels, Wis., Dec. 6, 1902; s. William and Alice (Chaudoir) B.; m. Bernice Roche, Feb. 22, 1936; children—Edward, Barbara. Pres. Rockcote Paint Co. (formerly Rockford Paint Mfg. Co.), Rockford, Ill., 1927—, Custom Colors Corp., Rockford, 1952—; also pres. Midwest Synthetics Co., Rockcote Colour Ltd., London, Wood-Davis Co., Chgo.; now chmn. Valspar Corp.; sec. Color Corp. of Am., Rockford; treas. Verland, Inc.; dir. Central Ill. Electric & Gas Co., Ill. Nat. Bank & Trust Co. (both Rockford). Trustee Rockford Coll.; bd. dirs. Holy Cross Hosp., Ft. Lauderdale, Fla. Mem. Rockford C. of C., Nat. Paint, Varnish and Lacquer Assn. (treas.). K.C. Clubs: Union League (Chgo.); Rockford Country (Rockford). Home: 2315 Rock Terrace Rockford IL 61103 Office: 200 Sayre St Rockford IL 61101

BAUDOUIN, KING, (Baudouin Albert Charles Leopold Axel Marie Gustave), King of the Belgians; b. Brussels, Sept. 7, 1930; s. King Leopold III and Queen Astrid, Princess of Sweden; m. Doña Fabiola de Mora y Aragon, Dec. 15, 1960. During invasion of Belgium by Germany, 1940, went to France, later to Spain returning to Belgium, 1940; was removed to Germany, 1944; after Allied invasion of Normandy; liberated, May 1945; lived in Switzerland until Leopold returned to Belgium as king, 1950; Prince Royal, Aug. 1950; held office as Chief of State until accession to throne; became king upon abdication of Leopold, July 1951. Address: Royal Palace Brussels Belgium

BAUDOUX, MAURICE, archbishop; b. La Louvière, Belgium, July 10, 1902; s. Norbert and Marie (Moreau) B.; student College de Saint-Boniface, Manitoba, 1919-23, St. Joseph's Sem., Edmonton, Alberta, 1923-27; S.T.D., Grand Seminaire et U. Laval, Que., 1929. D.ès L. (hon.), 1952; Ph.D., U. Montreal, 1957; D.D., United Coll., Winnipeg, Man., 1967; L.L.D., U. of Manitoba, 1967; Ordained priest, 1929; asst. Prud'homme, Saskatchewan, 1929-31, pastor, 1931-48, domestic prelate, 1944; bishop of Saint-Paul, Alberta, 1948-52; archbishop coadjutor Saint-Boniface, 1952-55, archbishop of Saint-Boniface, 1955—. Home: 151 Avenue de la Cathédrale Saint Boniface Manitoba Canada Office: Archevché Saint-Boniface Manitoba Canada

BAUE, ARTHUR EDWARD, surgeon; b. St. Louis, Oct. 7, 1929; s. Arthur Christian and Viola (Wegener) B.; A.B. summa cum laude, Westminster Coll., 1950; M.D. cum laude, Harvard, 1954; m. Rosemary Dysart, Nov. 24, 1956; children—Patricia Sage, Arthur Christian II, William Dysart. Successively intern, resident, chief resident surgery Mass. Gen. Hosp., Boston, 1954-61; asst. prof. surgery U. Mo. Sch. Medicine, 1962-64; asst. prof., then asso. prof. surgery U. Pa. Sch. Medicine, 1964-67; Harry Edison prof. surgery Washington U. Sch. Medicine, St. Louis, 1967; surgeon-in-chief, dir. dept. surgery Jewish Hosp., St. Louis, 1967—. Cons. surgery Nat. Bd. Med. Examiners. Mem. alumni council Westminster Coll. Served to capt. USAF, 1959. John and Mary R. Markle scholar acad. medicine, 1963; recipient Research Career Devel. award USPHS, 1964. Diplomate Am. Bd. Surgery (thoracic surgery). Mem. Am. Assn. Thoracic Surgery, Am. Coll. Cardiology, Am. Coll. Chest Physicians, A.C.S., Assn. Acad. Surgery, Internat. Cardiovascular Soc., Soc. Thoracic Surgeons, Soc. U. Surgeons, Soc. Vascular Surgery, Internat. Soc. Surgery, Am. Assn. Surgery Trauma, Am. Assn. Artificial Internal Organs, Am. Physiol. Soc., A.M.A., Am., Central, Western surg. assns., Soc. Surgery Alimentary Tract, Alpha Omega Alpha. Home: 6420 Cecil Av Clayton MO 63105 Office: 216 S Kingshighway St Louis MO 63110

BAUER, CHARLES THEODORE, ins. exec.; b. Boston, Mar. 3, 1919; s. Louis Hopewell and Helena (Meredith) B.; A.B., Harvard, 1942; M.B.A., N.Y. U., 1953; m. Dorothy A. Coffin, June 8, 1946; children—Janet, Theodore. Asst. financial v.p. U.S. Fidelity & Guaranty Co., Balt., 1954-69; sr. v.p., chief investment officer Am. Gen. Ins. Co., Houston, 1969—, also dir.; vice chmn., dir. Channing Funds; vice chmn., dir. Van Strum & Towne, Inc.; pres., dir. Am. Gen. Bond Fund, Inc.; v.p., treas., dir. Am. Gen. Life Ins. Cos.; v.p., dir. Variable Annuity Life Ins. Co., Md. Casualty Co., Me. Bonding and Casualty Co., No. Ins. Co. N.Y., Assurance Co., Am., Patriot Life Ins. Co., Am. Gen. Mgmt. Co., Knickerbocker Corp.; v.p. Life and Casualty Ins. Co. Tenn., Md. Am. Gen. Ins. Co., Md. Life Ins. Co. Balt., Nat. Standard Ins. Co. Gen. bldg. campaign chmn. Union Meml. Hosp., 1968. Dir. Houston Grand Opera Assn., 1970—. Served to lt. (s.g.), USNR, 1942-45. Mem. Houston Soc. Financial Analysts, Balt. Security Analysts Soc. (past pres.), N.Y. Soc. Security Analysts, Inst. Chartered Financial Analysts (past trustee), Financial Analysts Fedn. (past v.p., dir.). Home: 33 Broad Oaks Dr E Houston TX 77027 Office: 2727 Allen Pkwy Houston TX 77019

BAUER, GEORGE W., banker; b. Linden, N.J., 1885; ed. Rutgers U., 1905. Chmn. bd., chmn. exec. com., dir. Union County Trust Co.; pres. dir. C.H. Winans Co. Home: 350 Westminster Av Elizabeth NJ 07207 Office: 142 Broad St PO Box 680 Elizabeth NJ 07207*

BAUER, HARRY CHARLES, librarian; b. St. Louis, July 22, 1902; s. Emile George and Jennie Theresa (Cannan) B.; A.B., Washington U., 1927, M.S., 1929; grad. St. Louis Library Sch., 1931. Chief circulation div. library, U. Mo., 1931-34; chief tech. library TVA, Knoxville, 1934- 42; asst. librarian U. Wash., 1945-46, asso. librarian, 1946-47, dir. libraries and prof. librarianship, 1947-59, prof. librarianship, 1959-67, emeritus, 1967—, sec. faculty U. Wash., 1962-66; pres. Bibliog. Dowsers America, 1959—; specialist in bibliog. dowsing, 1966—. Pres. Tenn. Credit Union League, 1941-42. Sec. Allied Arts Seattle, Inc., People's Meml. Assn., Seattle Creative Activities Center; pres. Pacific N.W. Internat. Writers Conf., 1958. Mayor, Norris, Tenn., 1940. Served to maj. USAAF, 1942-45; group intelligence officer, 98th Bombardment Group, 1942-54. Awarded Bronze Star, Air medal, Purple Heart. Mem. Retired Officers Assn. (affiliate pres. 1953), Am., Pacific N.W., Wash. library assns., Assn. Coll. and Reference Libraries, Spl. Libraries Assn., Sigma Xi, Pi Mu Epsilon, Phi Kappa Tau, Scabbard & Blade, Oval Club. Baptist. Mason, Kiwanian (pres. 1951). Clubs: Rainier, Faculty Men's (pres. 1948) Author: Seasoned to Taste, 1961. Joint editor: Public Administration Libraries, 1941; Columnist, "Seasoned to Taste," for Wilson Library Bull., 1951-61. Editor, pub. Prose Bowl. Contbr. articles profl. jours. Home: 4203 Brooklyn Av NE Seattle WA 98105

BAUER, LEO D., brewery exec.; b. 1924; B.Mech. Engring., U. Louisville, 1947; married. With Brown-Forman Distillers Corp., Louisville, 1946—, sr. v.p., exec. dir. prodn. and engring., 1968-69, sr. v.p., exec. dir. operations, 1969—, also dir. Office: 850 Dixie Hwy Louisville KY 40210*

BAUER, LUDWIG, educator; b. Forchheim, Bavaria, Germany, July 27, 1926; s. Anton and Paula (Sommerich) B.; B.Sc., U. Sydney (Australia), 1949, B.Sc. with 1st class honors, 1950; Ph.D., Northwestern U., 1952; m. Ella Bamberger, Oct. 15, 1957; children—Phillip M., Alan J. Came to U.S., 1950, naturalized, 1961. Research asso. Harvard U., Cambridge, Mass., 1952, Columbia, N.Y.C., 1953, U. Sydney, 1954; mem. faculty Coll. Pharmacy, Med. Center, U. Ill., Chgo., 1955—, prof., 1966—. Mem. Am. Chem. Soc., Chem. Soc. (London). Home: 504 Maple St Wilmette IL 60091 Office: 833 S Wood St Chicago IL 60612

BAUER, MALCOLM CLAIR, newspaper editor; b. Enterprise, Ore., Mar. 19, 1914; s. John Jacob and Lucile (Corkins) B.; B.S., U. Ore., 1935; Nieman fellow, Harvard, 1950- 51; Journalism fellow Stanford U., 1968; m. Roberta Moody, July 11, 1937; children—Bette B., Mary, Kent, Roberta Jean. News editor Eugene (Ore.) Register Guard, 1935-36; news editor Pendleton East- Oregonian, 1936; with The Oregonian, Portland, 1936—, city editor, 1941- 51, asso. editor, 1951—, book editor, 1951—; lectr. journalism Portland State Coll., 1956—. Ore. commr. Edn. Commn. States, since 1966—. Bd. dirs. Reed Coll.; trustee Mills Coll. Served from 1st lt. to col, AUS, World War II. Decorated Bronze Star medal, Legion of Merit with oak leaf cluster; Order Brit. Empire. Mem. Ore. Hist. Soc. (past pres.), Phi Delta Phi, Phi Beta Kappa, Phi Delta Theta. Author: Profile of Oregon, 1971. Oregon corr. for Christian Science Monitor, also London (Eng.) Economist. Home: 1641 SW Englewood Dr Lake Oswego OR 97034 Office: 1320 SW Broadway Portland OR 97201

BAUER, NORMAN JAMES, educator; b. Milw., June 13, 1929; s. Hugo Andrew and Erna (Cocker) B.; student Wis. State U., La Crosse, 1947-49; B.S., Wis. State U., Oshkosh, 1953; M.A., Northwestern U., 1956; postgrad. U. Ill., 1958-60; Ed.D., Ind. U., 1964; m. Betty Jane Zwicky, Dec. 26, 1953; children—Michael, Barbara. Tchrs., Ripon (Wis.) sch. system, 1953, W. Allis (Wis.) pub. sch. system, 1954-57; asst. prof. Eastern Ill. U., 1957-62; teaching asso. Ind. U., 1962-64; asso. prof. Wis. State U., Oshkosh, 1964-67; prof. edn., chmn. dept. State Univ. Coll., Geneseo, N.Y., 1967—; dir. Wis. State U., Oshkosh, Lab. Sch., 1964-67. Mem. Nat. Soc. Study Edn., Assn. Supervision and Curriculum Devel., John Dewey Soc., Center for Study Democratic Instns. (asso.), Kappa Delta Pi, Phi Delta Kappa. Contbr. articles to ednl. jours. Home: 28 Westview Crescent Geneseo NY 14454

BAUER, RAYMOND AUGUSTINE, educator; b. Chgo., Sept. 7, 1916; s. William Henry and Anna Barbara (Diedrich) B.; student Ill. Inst. Tech., 1936-38; B.S. with highest distinction, Northwestern U., 1943; M.A., Harvard, 1948, Ph.D., 1950; m. Alice Haugh, June 12, 1941 (dec.); 1 dau., Linda Carol (Mrs. Donald H. Sibley); m. 2d, Katharine Goldthwaite Dorr Clar, Apr. 30, 1966. Chem. analyst Crane Co., 1936-44; research asst. Harvard, 1947-48, fellow Russian Research Center, 1948-50, lectr. social psychology, research asso. Russian Research Center, 1950-55, Ford Found. vis. prof. Grad. Sch. of Bus. Adminstrn., 1957-60, prof., 1960—; research asso. Center for Internat. Studies, 1953-57; fellow Center for Advanced Studies in the Behavioral Scis., 1955-56; asso. prof. social psychology Mass. Inst. Tech., 1955-57; cons. Nat. Goals Research Staff, The White House, 1969-70. Served as lt. (j.g.), USNR, 1944-46; Russian lang. officer. Fellow Am. Acad. Arts and Scis.; mem. Am., Eastern, Mass. (pres. 1964-66) psychol. assns., Am. Sociol. Soc., Am. Marketing Assn., Am. Assn. Pub. Opinion Research (pres. 1965-66), Phi Beta Kappa. Author: The New Man in Soviet Psychology, 1952; Nine Soviet Portraits, 1955; (with Alex Inkeles, Clyde Kluckhohn) How the Soviet System Works, 1956; (with Alex Inkeles) The Soviet Citizen, 1959; (with Ithiel Pool) American Businessmen and International Trade, 1960; (with Pool and Dexter) American Business and Public Policy, 1963; (with Gross, Biderman, and others) Social Indicators, 1966; (with S.A. Greyser) Advertising in America, 1968; (with others) Second Order Consequences, 1969; (with Scott M. Cunningham) Studies in the Negro Market, 1970. Editor: (with K. Gergen) The Study of Policy Formation, 1968. Home: 16 Highland St Cambridge MA 02138 Office: Harvard Grad Sch Bus Adminstrn Boston MA 02163

BAUER, RICHARD H., clergyman; b. Cin., May 19, 1913; s. Samuel B. and Alice (Helck) B.; Comml. Engr., U. Cin., 1936; B.D., Garrett Theol. Sem., 1947; D.D., Ohio No. U., 1962; m. Eleanor Nye, July 3, 1941. With Proctor & Gamble Co., 1932-44; ordained to ministry Methodist Ch., 1948; pastor in Cin., 1942- 44, N. College Hill, 1947-53, Ashley, Ind., 1944-47, Bellefontaine, O., 1953-56; supt. Portsmouth (O.) dist. Meth. Ch., 1956-60; exec. sec. interboard com. enlistment for ch. occupations Meth. Ch., 1960—. Del. World Meth. Conf., 1961, 66, 71; mem. World Meth. Council, 1966-71; mem. assembly Nat. Council Chs., 1963-66, 66-69, 70—, chmn. commn. vocation and enlistment, 1963—, vice chmn. dept. ministry, 1966—; sec. Meth. Council Secretaries, 1964-68. Trustee Meth. Home Aged, 1956-60. Mem. Am. Personnel and Guidance Assn., Sigma Chi, Omicron Delta Kappa. Contbr. articles ch. publs. Home: 3809 Brighton St Nashville TN 37205 Office: 1001 19th Av S Nashville TN 37202

BAUER, ROBERT F., business exec.; b. Declo, Ida., 1918; B.S., U. So. Cal., 1942; married. With Union Oil Co., 1942-53, CUSS Group, 1953-59; with Global Marine, Inc., 1959—, now chmn. bd., chief exec. officer, dir. Home: 8602 Via Santa Cruz Whittier CA 90605 Office: 811 W 7th St Los Angeles CA 90017*

BAUER, ROBERT PAUL, indsl. exec.; b. Cin., Oct. 19, 1920; s. Elmer John and Ione (Koehne) B.; B.B.A., U. Cin., 1949; m. Alice M. Miller, Sept. 23, 1944; children—Barbara Jo, Peggy Lou, Robert M. Pub. accountant Haskins & Sells, C.P.A.'s, Cin., 1947-51; div. controller Baldwin-Lima-Hamilton Corp., Lima, O., 1951-57, gen. controller exec. office, Phila., 1957-61; treas., controller Cessna Aircraft Co., 1961-67, v.p., treas., 1967-69, sr. v.p., 1969—; chmn., dir. Cessna Finance Co., Reims Aviation, France; pres., chmn. Cessna Internat. Finance Corp. Bd. dirs. Wichita United Fund. Named outstanding young man of the year, Lima, 1956. C.P.A., Ohio. Mem. Am. Inst. C.P.A.'s. Home: 642 Longford Lane Wichita KS 67206 Office: Cessna Aircraft Co 5800 Pawnee St Wichita KS 67218

BAUER, SIMON HARVEY, chemist, educator; b. Kaunas, Lithuania, Oct. 12, 1911; s. Benzion and Goldie (Betten) B.; came to U.S., 1921, naturalized, 1927; B.S., U. Chgo., 1931, Ph.D., 1935; postgrad. Cal. Inst. Tech., 1935-37; m. Miriam L. Rosoff, June 25, 1938; children—Frederick, Deborah, Ross. Instr., Pa. State U., 1937-39; mem. faculty Cornell U., 1939—, prof. chemistry, 1950—. Guggenheim fellow, 1949, Sr. NFS postdoctoral fellow, 1962. Fellow Am. Phys. Soc., A.A.A.S., Am. Inst. Chemists; mem. Am. Chem. Soc., Faraday Soc., Am. Acad. Polit. and Social Sci., Am. Fedn. Scientists. Asst. editor Jour. Am. Chem. Soc., 1964. Home: 312 Comstock Rd Ithaca NY 14850

BAUER, THEODORE JAMES, physician; b. Iowa City, Ia., Nov. 18, 1909; s. Charles A. and Anna (Braun) B.; B.S., U. Ia.; M.D., U. of Ia., 1933; m. Helen Mattes, Sept. 1, 1938; children—Jane Helen, Virginia, Mary, Martha. Intern, U.S. Marine Hosp., L.I., N.Y., 1933-34; spl. tng. USPHS, 1934-38, regional cons. venereal disease control Dist. 5, San Francisco, 1938-41, veneral disease control officer, Kansas City, Mo., 1941-42, chief, div. venereal disease Washington, 1948-52, med. officer in charge Communicable Disease Center, Altanta, 1953-56, asst. surgeon gen., dep. chief Bur. State Services, Washington, 1956-60, chief Bur. State Services, 1960-62; veneral disease control officer Chgo. Health Dept., and med. officer charge Chgo. Intensive Treatment Center, 1942-48; med. dir. Becton, Dickinson and Co., 1962—, sr. v.p. research and med. affairs, 1967—; asso. prof. bacteriology and immunology Emory U., 1952-57; spl. lectr. on veneral diseases Georgetown U. Sch. Medicine, Washington. Mem. expert com. on venereal infections, trepinematoses WHO; mem. Surgeon Gen.'s Adv. Com. on Community Health Services; mem. Adv. Council on the Chronic Sick of N.J. Recipient Distinguished Service award USPHS, 1962. Diplomate Am. Bd. Preventive Medicine and Pub. Health. Fellow A.C.P., Am. Pub. Health Assn. (chmn. evaluation and standards com.); mem. U.S. Mexico Border Pub. Health Assn., Am. Med. Assn., Am. Social Hygiene Assn., Sci. Research Soc. Am., Am. Venereal Disease Assn. (mem. exec. bd.), Sigma Xi. Editor: Journal Venereal Disease Information; mem. editorial bd. Am. Jour. of Syphilis, Gonorrhea and Other Venereal Diseases. Home: 451 Weymouth Dr Wyckoff NJ 07481 Office: Becton Dickinson & Co Rutherford NJ 07070

BAUER, WALTER EMIL, univ. dean; b. Chicago, July 22, 1897; s. Anton Ernst and Anna Teresa (Schwotzer) B.; student Concordia Coll., Ft. Wayne, Ind., 1915-17, Concordia Theol. Sem., St. Louis, 1917-21; A.M., Columbia, 1922; student Harvard, 1922-23; Ph.D., Cornell U., 1932; m. Clara Hedwig Brauer, Feb. 14, 1925 (dec. Mar. 12, 1956); children—Walter Richard, Johanna Emily, Sharon Elizabeth, Susan Marie; m. 2d, Della Marie Krentz, Dec. 14, 1957. Ordained to ministry of the Lutheran Ch., 1923, and served as pastor, Trinity Lutheran Ch., Scarsdale, N.Y.,1923- 26; instr. in history, Valparaiso (Ind.) U., 1926-29, asst. prof. history, 1929-33, asso. prof., 1933-40, prof., 1940—, head dept. history, 1946-67, dean college of Arts and Scis., 1946-57, dean of faculty, 1946-62, dean emeritus of faculty, 1962—. Mem. Am. Soc. Ch. History, N.E.A., Am. Hist. Soc., Pi Gamma Mu. Author: In Thy Light, 1944; God and Caesar, 1959. Home: 601 Indiana Av Valparaiso IN 46383

BAUER, WALTER HERMAN, polytech. inst. dean; b. Red Oak, Ia., Sept. 9, 1907; s. Philip J. and Emma M. (Herold) B.; B.S. in Chem. Engring., Ore. State Coll., 1929; Ph.D. in Phys. Chem., U. Wis., 1933; m. Ingeborg Marie Midelfart, Dec. 26, 1933 (dec. June 1, 1963); children—Karen Ingeborg (Mrs. Barry A. Taylor), Hans Philip, Dagny Marie (Mrs. Richard Wilcox). Asst. instr. U. Wis., 1929-33, research asst., 1933-34; faculty Rensselaer Polytech. Inst., 1934—, prof. phys. chem., 1948-60, dean Sch. Sci., 1960—; cons. industrials; spl. research fuels rocket launching, chem. and structure aluminum soap-hydrocarbon systems, explosive oxidation boranes and borane derivatives, rheology non-Newtonian systems. Served to capt. AUS, 1942-45. Fellow Am. Inst. Chemists, Am. Soc. Testing and Materials; mem. Am. Chem. Soc., Soc. Rheology, A.A.A.S., Am. Soc. Engring. Edn., Sigma Xi, Phi Lambda Upsilon, Alpha Chi Rho, Alpha Chi Sigma. Author: (with Davison and van Klooster) Laboratory Manual of Physical Chemistry, rev edit., 1956. Home: 1625 Tibbits Av Troy NY 12180

BAUER, WILLIAM CECIL, communications co. exec.; b. Baton Rouge, Nov. 12, 1916; s. Charles Edward and Harriet (Dunn) B.; B.S. in Elec. Engring., La. State U., 1937; m. Jean Claire Roberts, Nov. 10, 1946. With So. Bell Tel. & Tel. Co., Birmingham, Ala., 1937-68, exec. v.p., 1967—; pres. S. Central Bell Telephone Co., 1968—; dir. Liberty Nat. Life Ins. Co., Birmingham, Am. Air Filter Co., Inc., Louisville, Ala. br. Fed. Res. Bank, Birmingham. Pres., Birmingham Festival Arts Assn., 1971; mem. exec. com. region V, Boy Scouts Am., 1968—, dir., 1969—. Bd. dirs., mem. exec. com. Operation New Birmingham, 1968—; mng. mem. bd. dirs. Birmingham Centennial Corp., 1968; bd. dirs. Lurleen B. Wallace Meml. Cancer Hosp. Fund, Nat. Conf. Christians and Jews; trustee Eye Found. Birmingham, Birmingham Symphony Assn.; bd. Ala. div. Am. Cancer Soc., Greater Birmingham Arts Alliance. Served to capt. AUS, 1942-46. Named Boss of Year, Nashville Jr. C. of C., 1963; recipient Silver Antelope award Boy Scouts Am., 1970. Mem. U.S. C. of C., Armed Forces Communications and Electronics Assn., Ala. C. of C. (dir.). Episcopalian. Rotarian. Clubs: Mountain Brook, Club, Downtown, Relay House (Birmingham). Home: 3227 E Briarcliff Rd Birmingham AL 35223 Office: 600 N 19th St Birmingham AL 35203

BAUER, WILLIAM JOSEPH, dist. atty.; b. Chgo., Sept. 15, 1926; s. William Francis and Lucille (Gleason) B.; A.B., Elmhurst Coll., 1949; J.D., DePaul U., 1952; m. Mary Nicol, Jan. 28, 1950; children—Patricia, Linda. Admitted to Ill. bar, 1951; partner law firm Erlenborn, Bauer & Hotte, Elmhurst, 1953-64; asst. state's atty., Du Page County, Ill., 1952-56. 1st asst. state's atty., 1956-58, state's atty., 1959-64; judge Jud. Circuit Ct., 1964-70; U.S. dist. atty. No. Ill., Chgo., 1970—; instr. bus. law Elmhurst Coll., 1952-59. Vice pres. Ill. Fed. Savs. & Loan Assn. Pres. Elmhurst Young Republicans, 1958-59. Bd. govs. Du Page Meml. Hosp. Served with AUS, 1945-47. Mem. Am., Ill., Du Page County (pres.) bar assns., Ill. State's Attys. Assn. (dir.). Roman Catholic. Clubs: Union League (Chgo.); Glen Oak Country (Glen Ellyn, Ill.) Home: 188 Rex Blvd Elmhurst IL 60126 Office: 219 S Dearborn St Chicago IL 60604

BAUERMEISTER, MARY, painter, sculptor; b. Frankfurt, Germany, Sept. 7, 1934; d. Wolf and Laura (Ranzi) B.; self taught; m. Karlheinz Stockhausen, Apr. 3, 1967; children—Julika, Simon. One-man shows include Stedelijk Mus., Amsterdam, Holland, 1962, Mus. von Stadt en Ommelanden, Groningen, Holland, 1962, Stedelijk Mus., Schiedam, Holland, 1962, Haags Gemeentemus., Den Haag, Holland, 1963, Stedelijk van Abbe-Mus., Eindhoven, Holland, 1963, Galeria Bonino, N.Y.C., 1964, 65, 67, 70; group shows include Galerie Parnass, Wuppertal, Germany, 1961, Atelier Neufert, Köln, Germany, 1961, Ars Viva, Kunstverein. Oldenburg, also Kunsthalle, Bremen, Germany, 1962, L'Art et l'Ecriture, Stedelijk Mus., also Kunstalle, Baden Baden, Germany, 1962-63, Internat. Artists Summer Seminar, Fairleigh Dickinson U., Riverside Mus., N.Y.C., 1963, 2 Sculptors, 4 Painters, Galeria Bonino, 1963-64, Mus. Art, Sci. and Industry, Bridgeport, Conn., 1964, Concert-Exhbn., MacMillan Theatre, Toronto, Can., 1964, Old Hundred, Larry Aldrich Mus., Ridgefield, Conn., 1962, annual exhbn. Am. sculpture Whitney Mus., 1964-65, Stone and Crystal, Staempfli Gallery, N.Y.C., 1965, Box shows Byron Gallery, N.Y.C., 1965, Art Today Albright-Knox Gallery, Buffalo, 1965, 113 (retinal art) Mus. U. Tex., 1965, Norfolk (Va.) Mus. Arts and Scis., 1966, Guggenheim Mus., N.Y.C., 1966, Nat. Collection Fine Arts, Smithsonian Instn., 1966, Pitts. Internat., Carnegie Inst., 1967, Akron (O.) Art Inst., 1967, Ohio State U., Columbus, 1967, Mus. Contemporary Art, Chgo., 1967, Hemis Fair '68, San Antonio, 1968, Albright-Knox Gallery, Buffalo, 1968, Whitney Mus. Am. Art, N.Y.C., 1968, Art Inst. Chgo., 1969, Balt. Mus. Art, 1969, San Francisco Mus. Art, 1970, N.J. State Mus., 1970, Art Inst. Chgo., 1971, Birmingham (Ala.) Mus. Art, 1971, Minn. Mus. Art, St. Paul, 1971; represented in permanent collections Guggenheim Mus., Whitney Mus., Mus. Modern Art, Bklyn. Mus., Larry Aldrich Mus., Stedelijk Mus., Albright-Knox Art Gallery, Minn. Mus. Art, also pvt. and corporate collections. Address: care Galeria Bonino 7 W 57th St New York City NY 10019

BAUERNFEIND, HOWARD K., book pub.; b. Council Bluffs, Ia., Apr. 12, 1900; s. James Harrison and Matilda (Koenig) B.; A.B., N. Central Coll., Naperville, Ill., 1921; A.M., U. Chgo., 1929; m. Lorraine Shrook, Aug. 9, 1922; children—Robert Howard, Dorothy B. Ring. Supt. city schs., Polo, Ill., 1921-27, Monmouth, Ill., 1927-30; editor J.B. Lippincott Co., Phila., 1930-33, mng. editor, ednl. dept., 1933-36, v.p., 1936-40, exec. v.p., 1940-49, pres., 1949-58, chmn. bd.,

1958—, dir., 1936—; chmn. bd. A.J. Holman Co., Phila. Mem. A.I.M., Acad. Polit. Sci., Am. Hist. Assn., Pi Beta Alpha. Republican. Presbyn. Mason. Clubs: Down Town, Franklin Inn (Philadelphia). Home: Wyndon Av and Kennedy Lane Bryn Mawr PA 19010 Office: East Washington Sq Philadelphia PA 19106

BAUERS, ELOI, lawyer, assn. exec.; b. Osseo, Minn., Aug. 5, 1890; s. Casper and Anna Frances (Jacomet) B.; LL.B., U. Minn., 1913; m. Mary F. O'Malley, July 27, 1911 (dec. May 31, 1966); children—Catherine A. (Mrs. Richard W. Kimball), Helen M. (Mrs. Richard P. Mahoney), Mary J. (Mrs. J. Austin Boulay). Admitted to Minn. bar, 1913, since practiced in Mpls.; mem. firm Bauers & Kelly, 1959—. Exec. v.p. Am. Coll. Allergistis, 1953—; field v.p. sales Loew's Hotels, 1966—. Dir. Gen. Securities, Inc., Hubert W. White, Inc. (both Mpls.). Served as 2d lt., F.A., U.S. Army, World War I. Named Knight Equestrian Order Holy Sepulchre Jerusalem. Mem. Am., Minn., Hennepin County bar assns., Am. Legion, Phi Delta Phi. Delta Sigma Rho. Republican. Roman Catholic. Clubs: Interlachen Country (Edina. Minn.); Mpls. Athletic. Home: Edina MN 55424 Office: Dain Tower Minneapolis MN 55402

BAUGH, ALBERT CROLL, educator; b. Phila., Feb. 26, 1891; s. Horace L. and Margaret (Croll) Baugh; A.B., U. Pa., 1912, A.M., 1914, Ph.D., 1915; L.H.D., 1961; LL.D., Ursinus Coll., 1939; Litt.D., Franklin and Marshall Coll., 1956; m. Nita Emeline Scudder, June 20, 1925; children—William Scudder, Daniel. With U. Pa., 1912—, beginning as asst. instr. English, prof. English, 1928—; holds Felix E. Schelling Meml. professorship emeritus; vis. prof., summers, Stanford U., 1928, Duke U., 1935, 37, 39, 41, Northwestern U., 1940, U. So. Cal., 1949. Mem. Modern Lang. Assn. Am. (editorial bd., 1930-41, 1946-51, exec. council 1943-46, 2d v.p., 1950, pres. 1952), Modern Humanities Research Assn. (pres. 1949-50); fellow Medieval Acad. Am. (adv. bd., 1939-41, clerk 1948-51, pres. fellows 1960- 63, pres. 1963—), Internat. Arthurian Soc., Am. Dialect Soc. (v.p. 1951), Linguistic Soc., (exec. com., 1940-42, 46-48), Internat Fedn. for Modern Langs. and Lits. (pres. 1960-63), Am. Philos. Soc., Pa. Hist. Soc., Phi Beta Kappa. Clubs: The Franklin Inn, The Collectors. Author: (with P.C. Kitchen and M.W. Black) Writing by Types, 1924; History of the English Language, 1935, rev. edit., 1957; Literary History of England (with others), 1948, rev. edit., 1967; Chaucer, 1968. Editor: William Haughton's Englishmen for My Money, 1917; Schelling Anniversary Papers, 1923; (with G. W. McClelland) Century Types of English Literature, 1925; (with P.C. Kitchen) Synonymns, Antonyms and Discriminations (in New Century Dictionary), 1927; Thomas Hardy's Return of the Native, 1928; (with A.H. Quinn and W.D. Howe) The Literature of America (2 vols.), 1929; (with N.E. McClure) Essays Toward Living, 1929; English Literature; A Period Anthology (with G.W. McClelland), 1954; Chaucer's Major Poetry, 1963. Contbr. articles in mags. Asso. editor Philol. Quar., 1934- 50; Word, 1945-49. Home: 4220 Spruce St Philadelphia PA 19104

BAUGHAN, ROBERT LOUIS, Jr., naval officer; b. Huntington, W.Va., Sept. 6, 1919; s. Robert L. and Elsie (Martin) B.; E.E., U.S. Naval Acad., 1941; postgrad., Naval Postgrad. Sch., 1946-47; M.S., Mass. Inst. Tech., 1949; postgrad., Indsl. Coll. Armed Forces, 1966; m. Eleanor Yount, June 26, 1942; children—George Robert, David Martin, Thomas Howard. Commd. ensign USN, 1941, advanced through grades to rear adm., 1969; comdg. officer USS Leacy, 1962-64; comdr. destroyer Squadron 6, 1964-65; joint staff Orgn. Joint Chiefs of Staff, Washington, 1966-68; dep. dir. operations Nat. Mil. Command Center, 1968-69; comdr. Cruiser-Destroyer Flotilla 9, 1969-70, also serving overseas as comdr. Cruiser Destroyer Group 7th Fleet; vice comdr. Naval Ordnance Systems Command, Washington, 1970—. Decorated Legion of Merit with gold star, Bronze Star with gold stars. Mem. Officers' Christian Union U.S. Lutheran. Home: 5803 Folkstone Rd Bethesda MD 20034 Office: Naval Ordnance Systems Command Dept of Navy Washington DC 20360

BAUGHMAN, ERNEST THEODORE, banker; b. Ackworth, Ia., Dec. 27, 1915; s. Lawrence E. and Nellie (Booth) B.; B.S. in Econs., U. Minn., 1939, M.S., 1941; m. Esther M. Bajari, Aug. 28, 1940; children—Carol Mae (Mrs. John Dudzik), Verna Lee, Francine Lou. Instr., U. Minn., 1939-43; with Fed. Res. Bank Chgo., 1946—, 1st v.p., 1970—; mem. editorial bd. Am. Farm Econ. Assn., lectr. Sch. Banking, U. Wis. Bd. dirs. Farm Found. Served with USNR, 1943-45. Mem. Am. Farm Econ. Assn., Am. Econ. Assn., Am. Finance Assn., Chgo. Assn. Commerce and Industry. Kiwanian (pres. Franklin Park, Ill. 1957). Clubs: Executives, Bankers (Chgo.). Home: 240 Silver Lane Melrose Park IL 60160 Office: 230 S LaSalle St Chicago IL 60690

BAUGHMAN, GENE KNOX, chem. co. exec.; b. Perrysville, O., Apr. 24, 1918; s. Charles Clayton and Emma (Knox) B.; B.S., Miami U., Oxford O., 1944; student U. Cin., 1946; m. Naomi Jean Volz, Dec. 30, 1942; children—Barbara (Mrs. Frank Killey), Carol Joan (Mrs. David Smith), Linda E. (Mrs. Albert Beety). With Isaly Dairy, Loudonville, O., 1936, Gardner Motors, Loudonville, 1936-38, Queen City Flying Service, Inc., Cin., 1942-44, Streitmann Biscuit Co., Cin., 1945-47; with Montgomery Ward & Co., 1947-53, head accounts payable dept., 1953; with Norge div. Borg-Warner Corp., 1953-62, plants controller, 1958-62; controller DeSoto, Inc., Des Plaines, Ill., 1962—; controller Sonneborn Bldg. Products, Inc., 1962-69. Capt. Mont Clare-Lyden YMCA Fishers of Men campaign, 1955. Asso. mem. United Republican Fund Ill. Served with USNR, 1944-45. Mem. Nat. Assn. Accountants, Nat. Assn. Credit Men, Sigma Nu, Delta Sigma Pi. Presbyn. (elder, clk. session 1967-69). Home: 15 N Forrest Av Arlington Heights IL 60004 Office: 1700 S Mt Prospect Rd Des Plaines IL 60018

BAUGHMAN, GEORGE FECHTIG, found. exec.; b. Tampa, Fla., July 19, 1915; s. G. Norman and Mary (Dodds) B.; B.S., U. Fla., 1937, J.D., 1939, grad. student, 1949-53; student Am. Inst. of Banking, 1941; M.A., George Washington U., 1944; D.Sc., New England Coll. Pharmacy, Boston, D.C.S., New York University, 1962; m. Hazel Ruth Zoerner, Apr. 27, 1940; children—Sharon Ruth, Mary Gaye. With Nat. Met. Bank, Washington, summers, 1932-39, 39-41; with Phifer State Bank, Gainesville, 1936-38; admitted Fla. bar 1939, D.C., 1940-41; United States Supreme Court bar, 1968; practiced Washington, D.C., 1940-41; faculty Coll. Bus. Adminstrn., U. Fla., 1941-42, asst. bus mgr., 1945-48, v.p. bus. affairs, 1954-55; bus. mgr. N.Y.U. 1955-56, v.p. bus. affairs, treas. N.Y. U., 1956-61; pres. New Coll., Sarasota, Fla., 1961-65; pres. The College Found., Sarasota, 1966—, also mem. bd. Pres., chmn. bd. Sarasota Jungle Gardens, Inc.; dir. First Fed. Savs. & Loan Assn. of Manatee County, Plymouth Harbor Center, Inc., Sarasota Jungle Gardens, Inc., Lehigh Acres Devel., Inc., Watergate Center, Sarasota Bank & Trust Co., USLIFE Corp., Environmental Devel. Inc., Gen. Telephone Co. Fla., U.S. Life Ins. Co., Land Resources Corp., Longboat Key Bank, Sarasota, First Manatee Corp., Bradenton, Fla., Land Resources Corp., Phila. Exec. com., chmn. finance com. Ednl. Testing Service, Inc., Princeton, N.J.; dir., past v.p. N.E. Coll. Pharmacy, Boston; past pres. N.Y.U. Press. Bd. dirs. U.S. Navy Supply Corps Found., Athens, Ga.; trustee U. Fla. Found., Gainesville. Served to comdr. Supply Corps, USNR, 1942-46; rear admiral Res. Honorary fellow of New College. Decorated Legion of Honor (France); Military Order Brit. Empire. Mem. Bar State Fla., D.C. Bar Assn., Nat., So. (past pres.) assns. colls. and bus. ofcls., Supply Officers Assn. (past pres.), Hon. Order Ky. Colls., N.Y.U. Hon. Soc., George Washington U. Alumni Assn., U. Fla. Alumni Association, Sarasota County Chamber of Commerce (pres.), United States Squash Racquet Association, also Beta Theta Pi, Phi Kappa Phi, Beta Gamma Sigma, Phi Delta Phi, Pi Gamma Mu, Alpha Kappa Psi. Methodist. Clubs: University, University Faculty (New York City); Field, Sara Bay Country, Bird Key Yacht, Ivy League, University (chmn. bd. govs.) (Sarasota). Contbr. mgmt., edn. publs. Home: 460 Pheasant Dr Sarasota FL 33577 Office: 333 N Tamiani Trail Sarasota FL 33577

BAUGHMAN, GEORGE W., engring. exec.; b. Gilboa, O., Feb. 11, 1900; s. George W. and Mertle Bell (Peckinpaugh) B.; B.S., Ohio State U., 1920, E.E., 1924; m. Cecile M. Lytel, June 30, 1928; children—George, John. With labs. Bell Telephone System, 1920-23; with Union Switch & Signal div. Westinghouse Air Brake Co., 1923-67 asst. chief engr. in charge electronics,1944-45, chief engr., 1945-50, asst. v.p. engring., 1950-51, exec. engring. officer, 1951-55, v.p., 1951-60; asst. to pres. Westinghouse Air Brake Co., 1961-65, cons., 1965-67; cons. U.S. Dept. transp., 1968. Mem. r.r. panel Radio Technical Planning Bd., 1945, Radio Tech. Commn. Aviation, 1950-54; mem. organizing com. VIII Pan Am. Railway Congress. Mem. 4 man team representing ICA of State Dept., Mexico, 1956; tech. adviser U.S. delegation IX Pan American Railway Congress, Buenos Aires, 1957; mem. Elmer A. Sperry Bd. Award. Fellow I.E.E.E.; mem. Assn. of Am. R.R.'s (signal communication sects.), Inst. Railway Signal Engrs. Gt. Britain, Sigma Xi, Phi Kappa Tau, Eta Kappa Nu, Tau Beta Pi. Holds over 100 patents on automatic and cab signaling, train control, automatic braking, others; maj. contbr. field of centralized traffic control, and remote control and automatic operation vehicles and trains. Home: 4601 5th Av Pittsburgh PA 15213

BAUGHMAN, HARRY W., Jr., union ofcl. Pres., Window Glass Cutters League Am. AFL-CIO. Office: 1078 S High St Columbus OH 43206*

BAUGHMAN, JOHN JOSEPH, educator; b. Evansville, Ind., May 31, 1925; s. Cavins and Blanche (Coker) B.; A.B., DePauw U., 1948; M.A., Harvard, 1949; postgrad. U. Paris, 1951-52; Ph.D., U. Mich., 1953; m. Elizabeth Bowden, Aug. 26, 1961; 1 son, John Cavins. Teaching fellow U. Mich., 1950-51, 52-53; with dept. history DePauw U., Greencastle, Ind., 1953—, instr., 1953-56, asst. prof., 1956-60, asso. prof., 1960-65, prof., 1965—, head dept. history, 1966-69. Served with AUS, 1943-45. Mem. Am., Ind. hist. assns., Societe d'Histoire Moderne (Paris), Soc. French Hist. Studies, Soc. Italian Hist. Studies, Soc. Ind. Pioneers, Alpha Tau Omega, Phi Beta Kappa, Phi Kappa Phi. Kiwanian. Home: 704 Highwood Av Greencastle IN 46135

BAUGHMAN, LEWIS EDWIN, banker; b. Warren, O., Nov. 15, 1923; s. Milton Day and Katherine (Boone) B.; B.Sc. in Bus. Adminstrn., Ohio State U., 1947; grad. Stonier Grad. Sch. Banking, Rutgers U., 1955; m. Ann Hawkins Buker, Sept. 7, 1946; children—Milton Day, James Lewis. With Second Nat. Bank of Warren, 1948—, pres. 1962—, also dir.; dir. Rappold Co., Oakes Bronze and Aluminum Co., Sommer Electric Co., Gus Orwell, Inc. Chmn. Warren United Appeal campaign, 1959, Warren YMCA bldg. campaign, 1963. Past pres. Warren Bd. Edn. Trustee Ohio div. Am. Cancer Soc. Served with AUS, 1943- 46. Named Young Man of Year, Warren Jaycees, 1954. Man of Year, 1964. Mem. Ohio Bankers Assn. (chmn. bank operations com., exec. com. group 9), Phi Kappa Psi, Beta Alpha Psi. Home: 662 Wildwood Dr NE Warren OH 44483 Office: 108 Main Av S W Warren OH 44482

BAUGHMAN, MILO RAY, Jr., furniture designer; b. Goodland, Kan., Oct. 7, 1923; s. Milo Ray and Lila (Dilling) B.; student Art Center Design Sch., Los Angeles, 1946, Chouinard Design Sch., 1947, U. Me., 1958, Bangor (Me.) Theol. Sch., 1961; m. Caroline Fotheringham, Sept. 5, 1956; children—Gary Scott, Debra Leigh, Tracy Leigh, Mark. Freelance furniture designer in Cal., 1948-51; with Drexel Co., also Winchendon Furniture Co., (Mass.), 1951-53; with Thayer Coggin, Inc., High Point, N.C., 1953—; designer case goods Directional Industries, N.Y.C., 1961-67; pres., treas. Milo Baughman Design, Inc. Wellesley, 1961—; tchr. Chouinard Design Sch., also U. Cal. at Los Angeles, 1951-53; chmn. environmental design Brigham Young U., 1969—; lectr. Eastern univs. Active chaplain's programs Norfolk (Mass.) Correctional Inst., 1963-69; mem. Provo (Utah) Planning Commn. Served with USAAF, 1942-46. Recipient award Am. Inst. Interior Designers, 1962, 64, 65. Mem. Ch. of Jesus Christ of Latter Day Saints (seventy). Home: 115 Mountain Ridge Rd Provo UT 84601 Office: 381 East Center Provo UT 84601

BAUGHN, WILLIAM HUBERT, ednl. adminstr.; b. Marshall County, Ala., Aug. 27, 1918; s. J.W. and Beatrice (Jackson) B.; B.S., U. Ala., 1940; M.A., U. Va, 1941, Ph.D, 1948; m. Mary Madiera Morris, Feb. 20, 1945; children—Charles Madiera, William Marsteller. Instr., U. Va., 1942-43. asst. prof., 1946-48; asso. prof., then prof. econs. and bus. adminstrn. La. State U., 1948-56; prof. U. Tex., 1956-62, chmn. finance dept., 1958-60, asso. dean Coll. Bus. Adminstrn., 1959-62, asso. dir. Sch. of Banking of the South, 1952-66; dean U. Mo. Coll. Bus. and Pub. Adminstrn., 1962-64; dean Sch. of Bus., U. Colo., 1964—. Project dir. Am. Bankers Assn. project to study banker edn. programs, 1959-61. Dir. Stonier Grad. Sch. of Banking, Rutgers U., 1966—. Served to 1st lt., USAAF, World War II; lt. col., Res. Mem. Am. Finance Assn. Home: 555 Baseline Rd Boulder CO 80302

BAUHENS, GEORGE JULIUS, printing co. exec.; b. Galveston, Tex., Dec. 22, 1902; s. William and Wilhelmina (Lobenstein) B.; student spl. courses in bus. mgmt. and selling; m. Salome Slagle, Mar. 10, 1938. With Clarke & Courts, Houston, 1920—, gen. mgr., 1946—, pres., 1954—. Mem. Bank Stationers Assn., Graphic Arts Assn., Houston C. of C. Lutheran. Home: 2919 Albans St Houston TX 77005 Office: 1210 W Clay St Houston TX 77019

BAUHOF, RUDOLF, accountant; b. Canton, O., Jan. 6, 1902; s. Ralph Addison and Florence (Smith) B.; A.B., Mt. Union Coll., 1924; m. Adelaide Cash, July 7, 1965; children—Barbara Sue (Mrs. James L. Barth), Robert Hamilton. Entered bus. as indsl. accountant with two cos. now part of Republic Steel Corp., 1924-28; asso. Ernst & Ernst. C.P.A.'s Cleve., 1928—, partner, 1946—. C.P.A., Ohio. Mem. Am. Inst. C.P.A.'s, Am. Accounting Assn., Ohio Soc. C.P.A.'s, Sigma Nu, Psi Kappa Omega, Beta Alpha Psi. Clubs: Union, Country, Mid-day. Home: 19101 Van Aken Blvd Shaker Heights OH 44122 Office: Union Commerce Bldg 925 Euclid Av Cleveland OH 44115

BAUKE, JOSEPH PADUR, educator; b. Briesen, Germany, May 18, 1932; s. Joseph and Maria (Padur) B.; came to U.S., 1950, naturalized, 1957; B.A., U. Cin., 1956, M.A. (Taft fellow), 1957; Ph.D. (Carl Schurz fellow), Columbia, 1963. Instr. German, Columbia, N.Y.C., 1960-63, asst. prof., 1963-65, asso. prof., 1965-69, prof., 1969—, chmn. dept. Germanic langs., 1967—. Mem. Am. Assn. Tchrs. German, Schiller-Gesellschaft, Soc. for 18th Century Studies, Germanistic Soc. Am. (pres. 1970), Phi Beta Kappa, Delta Phi Alpha. Editor: Germanic Rev., 1966—. Contbr. articles profl. jours. Home: 423 W 120th St New York City NY 10027

BAUKHAGE, HILMAR ROBERT, radio commentator, writer, lectr., newspaperman; b. LaSalle, Ill., Jan. 7, 1889; s. Frederick Robert and Alice (Blood) B.; Ph.B. in Lit., U. Chgo., 1911; student Univs. of Bonn, 1933, Kiel, 1912, Jena, 1912, Freiburg, 1913, Sorbonne, 1913; m. Marjorie Collins, Nov. 8, 1922. With Chautauqua Daily, 1908; with Paris bur. London Pall Mall Gazette, 1913, Washington bur. Asso. Press, 1914; asst. mng. editor Leslie's, 1916; with Consol. Press, 1919-32, as supt. Washington and San Francisco, and supt. and bus. mgr., Chgo.; with U.S. News, 1932-37, N.Am. Newspaper Alliance, 1937; Washington corr. Western Newspaper Union, 1940-45; news commentator Farm and Home Hour NBC, 1934-42; broadcast outbreak of World War II from Berlin for NBC, 1939; cons. editor Army Times Pub. Co.; columnist Army Navy Air Forces Register, 1955- 62; spl. writer U.S. News and World Report, 1963. First person to give news broadcast from White House (Pearl Harbor attack, 1941); Washington commentator ABC Network, 1942-51; commentator MBS 1951-54. Enlisted as pvt. CAC, AUS, 1918, commd. 2d lt., F.A., and served with A.E.F.; covered Peace Conf., Paris, for Stars and Stripes after Armistice. Recipient Nat. Headliners Club Award, 1945, for best domestic broadcast of the year, award for Pub. Service by U. Chgo. Alumni Assn., 1946, Poor Richard Citation for Merit. Mem. Overseas Writers, Radio Corrs. (pres. 1941-42), Radio News Analysts Assn., S.A.R., Am. Legion, Owl and Serpent, Mil. Order World Wars, Delta Upsilon. Mason. Clubs: National Press, Cosmos (Washington). Author: (with C.L. Baldridge) I Was There, 1919; also several translations from German and French. Co-author, editor: American Military Leaders WWI: American Military Leaders WWII; Tangled Web; Yanks Are Coming (Pershing biography; MacArthur (biography).

BAUKHAGES, FREDERICK EDWIN, lawyer; b. Balt., Feb. 6, 1910; s. Frederick Edwin, Jr. and Elizabeth Wallace (Cartwright) B.; LL.B., U. Va., 1933; m. Dorothy Meier Freeman, Oct. 26, 1935; children—Frederick Edwin IV, Frederick William, Dorothy Elizabeth, Frederick Hilmar Robert. With So. Ry., 1925- 28; admitted to Va. bar, 1932; pvt. practice, Mathews, Va., 1933-34; atty., counsel RFC, Washington, 1935-40; personnel asst. to v.p. operations U.P. R.R., 1941-44; exec. asst. to v.p. finance B.O. R.R., 1944-46, gen. solicitor, 1946-61, v.p. finance, 1961-63; counsel law firm Hunton, Williams, Gay, Powell and Gibson, Richmond, Va., 1963-65, Mathews, Va., 1965—; partner Blair & Baukhages, Washington, 1965—. Dir. Balt. Union Stock Yards, Inc. Mem. Newcomen Soc. N.Am., Alpha Chi Rho. Episcopalian. Clubs: Wall Street (N.Y.C.); University (Balt.). Home: Arach Landing Mathews VA 23109 Office: Mathews VA 23109 also 1156 15th St NW Washington 20005

BAUKNIGHT, WILLIAM COOPER, lawyer; b. Jacksonville, Fla., July 29, 1921; s. William Cooper and Nellie (Martin) B.; B.S. in Commerce, U. Va., 1942; LL.B., George Washington U., 1950; m. Margaret Bowen Watts, Jan. 24, 1956; children—Lynn Ann, Linda Leigh, Rebecca Sue. Admitted to D.C. bar, 1947, Va. bar, 1952; asso. W. Edwin Cumberland, Washington, 1948-50; asst. city atty., Alexandria, 1952-53; practiced law, Fairfax, 1953—; partner Bauknight, Prichard, McCandlish & Williams, 1960—. Dir. Suburban Savs. & Loan Assn., Bird Engring. Research Assos., Inc. Counsel, Cts. of Justice com. Va. Ho. of Dels., 1954. Served to lt. comdr. USNR, 1942-46, 50-52. Mem. Raven Soc. U. Va., Omicron Delta Kappa. Episcopalian. Home: 9607 Verveille Dr Vienna VA 22180 Office: 3976 Chain Bridge Rd Fairfax VA 22030

BAUM, HARRY A., stock broker; b. Chgo., Oct. 4, 1902; s. Joseph and Mary (Silhovy) B.; student Northwestern U., 1918-22, LaSalle Extension U., 1923-26; m. Bessie Flagg, 1923 (dec. 1952); children—Jeane (Mrs. William C. Alston), Harry Flagg; m. 2d, Odella Labounty, Mar. 7, 1954; children—Barbara Tera, Ralph Lemley. Floor mgr. Charles Sincere & Co., 1919-22; securities salesman Paul H. Davis & Co., Chgo., 1922-28; partner Benjamin E. Minturn & Co., stock brokers, Chgo., 1929-31, Wayne Hummer & Co., 1932—. Mem. Midwest Stock Exchange, 1932—, gov., 1954-57, 58-61, 63-66, chmn. finance com., 1958-61, chmn. exec. com., 1963-66; allied mem. N.Y. Stock Exchange, gov., 1959—; chmn. Chgo. Assn. Stock Exchange Firms, 1952-54. Bd. dirs. LaSalle Extension U., 1947-62; chmn. bd. Pres. Council Marmion Mil. Acad., 1960-63, chmn. exec. com., 1964—. Mem. Chgo. Assn. Commerce and Industry. Clubs: Executives (Chgo.); Chgo. Athletic Assn., Marmion Mil. Acad. Dads (pres. 1959-60). Home: 1366 N Dearborn Parkway Chicago IL 60610 Office: 105 W Adams St Chicago IL 60603

BAUM, JOHN HARRY, publisher; b. Lemoyne, Pa., Sept. 21, 1917; s. Harvey Emanuel and Cora Anna (Donkel) B.; A.B., Gettysburg Coll., 1939; m. Virginia Marie Hale, Mar. 23, 1940; children—J. Robert, Diane Marie, Deborah Mae, James A. With the Patriot-News Co., Harrisburg, Pa., 1939—, retail advt. mgr., 1953-59, advt. dir., 1959-63, gen. mgr., 1963-67, v.p., 1967, pub., 1968- -; v.p. Harrisburg Area Indsl. Corp., 1956—; dir. Dauphin Deposit Trust Co., Lemoyne Trust Div., Harris Savings Assn., Community Consumer Discount Co. Bd. fellows, Gettysburg Coll. Served with USNR, 1944-47. Mem. Newspaper Advt. Execs. Assn., Harrisburg Area C. of C. (pres. 1959), Sigma Alpha Epsilon. Lutheran. Kiwanian, Mason (Shriner, K.T., Jester). Club: Executives (Harrisburg). Home: 809 Riverview Rd Lemoyne PA 17043 Office: P O Box 2265 Harrisburg PA 17105

BAUM, JOHN PINSON, ret. textile exec.; b. Rome, Ga., Jan. 5, 1902; s. Firley and Anna Cornelia (Pinson) B.; student Boys High Sch., Atlanta, 1920; B.S. Ga. Inst. Tech., 1924; B.S., Ga. Tech. Eve. Sch. Commerce, 1927; m. Martha Miller Bowen, Oct. 14, 1936; children—Martha L., John Pinson, Mary Anna, Marjorie B. Mem. engring. dept. Ga. Marble Co., Tate, Ga., 1924-25; asst. mgr., textile engring. dept. Robert & Co., Atlanta, 1925-31; sales engr. Gen. Elec. Vapor Lamp Co., 1931-32; asst. mgr. Pepperell Mfg. Co., Opekika, Ala., 1932-40; v.p. and dir. J.P. Stevens & Co., Inc., Milledgeville, Ga., 1945-67, former chmn. bd. dirs.; v.p. Derby Co., Nyanza, Inc. Chmn. Baldwin County Bd. Edn. Pres. Ga. Tech. Found., 1959, Textile Edn. Found., 1958; trustee Ga. State Coll. for Women Found. Served with U.S. Army, Q.M. Gen. Office, Washington, 1940-45; disch. as col. Decorated Legion of Merit; recipient Ga. Tech. Alumni Distinguished Service award, 1962; Distinguished Service award Woman's Coll. Ga., 1967. Mem. Ga. Textile Mfrs. Assn. (pres. 1961), ANAK Sr. Soc., Delta Tau Delta. Phi Kappa Phi. Presbyn. Mason. Address: Milledgeville GA 31061

BAUM, JOST J., mfg. co. exec.; b. 1928; J.D., U. Chgo., 1953. Sec. and gen. counsel Nationwide Industries, Inc. Home: 925 Sheridan Rd Evanston IL 60202 Office: 1603 Orrington Av Evanston IL 60201

BAUM, KURT, operatic tenor; b. Cologne, Germany, Mar. 15, 1908; naturalized; s. Simon and Frieda (Baum-Marcus) B.; student U. Prague Med. Sch.; Mus. Acad., Berlin, 1930; studied in Munich, Milan, Rome, Vienna; m. Debut in La Boheme, Zurich, 1933; has sung opera in Prague, Vienna, Salzburg, Budapest, Paris, Antwerp, Brussels, Amsterdam, Rotterdam, Monte Carlo, Cannes, Nice, Ostend, Copenhagen, Stockholm, under dirs. Walter Kleiber, Busch, George Szell, Gaubert, Alwin; U.S. debut as Rhadames in "Aida," Chgo. Civic Opera, 1939; has sung in opera houses in Phila., Boston, St. Louis, Buenos Aires, Rio de Janeiro, Caracas, Mexico, Italy, London; debut with Met. Opera, N.Y.C., 1941-42, now leading tenor and voice tchr. Met. Opera; concerts North Central and S.Am.,

Named "Kammersaenger," hon. award for most beautiful voice, in competition with 700 vocalists, Vienna, 1932. Home: 220 Central Park South New York City NY 10019 Office: Metropolitan Opera Co New York City NY 10023

BAUM, MAURICE, educator; b. Ft. Wayne, Ind., May 9, 1901; s. James and Pearl (Pritzsky) B.; B.A. summa cum laude, Princeton, 1923; M.A., U. Chgo., 1926, Ph.D., 1928; m. Cecil Heilweil, June 10, 1923 (dec. 1965); 1 son, James Robert. Instr. philosophy Univ. Coll., U. Chgo., 1928-30; instr. U. Cin., 1931-32; prof., chmn. dept. philosophy Kent State U., 1932-69; retired, 1969. Mem. Am., Ohio (pres. 1968-69) philosophy assns. Home: 17020 Sunset Blvd Pacific Palisades CA 90272

BAUM, ROLLAND O., mfg. exec.; b. Cleveland, Jan. 31, 1915; s. Percival G. and Decora D. (Honsberg) B.; student Case Inst. Tech., 1933-34, Western Res. U., 1935- 36, N.Y. U., 1949-51; m. Beatrice M. Blackmur, Jan. 9, 1937; children—Nicholas R., Gregory C. Purchasing agt. Tampa Shipbldg. Corp., 1938-49; exec. v.p. Merritt-Chapman & Scott Corp., N.Y.C., 1949-58; pres., dir., mem. exec. com. Tenn. Products & Chem. Corp., Nashville, 1958-63; pres., dir. Tenn-Tex Alloy & Chem. Corp., Houston, 1958-63; v.p. Standard Kollsman Industries, Inc., 1963-65; pres., dir. Applied Devices Corporation, College Point, N.Y., 1965-68; asst. pres. B.T.B. Inc., N.Y.C., 1968-69; pres., chief exec. officer, dir. Ecology Industries, Inc., Little Ferry, N.J., 1969—; pres., dir. mem. exec. com. Environmental Services, Inc., Little Ferry, 1970—; pres., dir. Carco, Inc., Denver, 1970—, Fed. Hydronics, Inc., Midland Park, N.J., 1970—. Mem. Air Force Assn., Mfg. Chemists Assn., Process Equipment Mfrs. Assn. Am. Inst. Mining, Metall. and Petroleum Engrs., Electrochem. Soc., Am. Iron and Steel Inst., Am. Mgmt. Assn., Am. Ordnance Assn., U.S. C. of C., Case Inst. Tech. Alumni Assn., Jr. Achievement Am. (past pres., dir.), Coke and Coal Chem. Inst., Nat. Export Expansion Council, Phi Kappa Tau. Club: Advertising (N.Y.C.). Home: 9 Bayeau Rd New Rochelle NY 10804 Office: Granite and West Sts Midland Park NJ 07432

BAUM, STEFAN HELMUTH, chem. exec.; b. Berlin, Germany, June 20, 1902; s. Hermann and Clara (Meyer) B.; M.E., Tech. Inst., Berlin-Charlottenburg, 1925; Ph.D., U. Berlin, 1927; m. Gertrud Goette, Feb. 14, 1928; 1 son, Axel H. Came to U.S., 1932, naturalized, 1939. Asst. instr. Tech. Inst., 1925-27; plant mgr. Ultraphone Corp., 1928-31; pres Sealerine, Inc., Detroit, 1934-36; exec. v.p., dir. Reichhold Chems., Inc., White Plains, N.Y., 1938-63, pres., dir., 1963—; dir. Japan Reichhold Chems., Inc. (Tokyo), Reichold Chems., Ltd. (Liverpool, Eng.), Reichhold Chems. (Can.) Ltd. (Toronto). Clubs: Rockefeller Center Luncheon (N.Y.C.); Riverside Yacht (Conn.). Home: Skyridge Rd Greenwich CT 06830 Office: 525 N Broadway White Plains NY 10603

BAUM, WERNER A., meteorologist, univ. pres.; b. Giessen, Germany, Apr. 10, 1923; s. Theodor and Beatrice (Klee) B.; brought to U.S., 1933, naturalized, 1934; B.S., U. Chicago, 1943, M.S., 1944, Ph.D., 1948; grad. study U. Colo., 1945-46; m. Shirley Bowman, Jan. 20, 1945; children—Janice Michelle, Sandra Roslyn. Teaching asst. U. Chicago, 1943, instr., 1943- 44, 1947, research asst., 1946; research asso., asst. prof. U. Md., 1947- 49; asso. prof., head dept. meteorology Fla. State U., 1949-51, professor, head dept., 1951-58, director univ. research, 1957-58, dean grad. sch. and dir. research, 1958-60, dean of the faculties, 1960-63; v.p. academic affairs U. Miami, 1963-65; v.p. scientific affairs N.Y.U., N.Y.C., 1965-67; dep. adminstr. Environmental Sci. Services Adminstrn., 1967-68; president University of Rhode Island, 1968—. Cons. climatologist USAF, summer 1953; mem. exec. res. U.S. Weather Bur., 1958- 62; councilor Oak Ridge Inst. Nuclear Studies, 1958-62; cons. Nat. Acad. Scis., 1962-64; mem. NRC com. on climatology, adv. to U.S. Weather Bur., 1955-57; trustee mem. exec. com. U. Corp. Atmospheric Research, 1959-63, 65-67, corporate sec., 1963-67; chmn. adv. com. edn. and manpower U.S. Weather Bur., chmn. adv. panel atmospheric scis. program NSF, 1965-67; dir. Fund Overseas Research Grants and Edn., 1965—; traveling fellow in higher edn. Carnegie Corp. of N.Y., 1964-65. Served with USNR, 1944-46. Certified Consulting Meteorologist. Fellow A.A.A.S. (councilor 1955-56), Am. Geophys. Union; mem. Am. Meteorol. Soc. (councilor 1956-59, 63-66, editor-in-chief periodicals 1957-61, spl. award for distinguished service 1962), Phi Beta Kappa, Sigma Xi, Delta Sigma Pi, Chi Epsilon Pi, Phi Sigma Delta. Club: Cosmos (Washington). Author: Russian-English Dictionary of Meteorological Terms and Expressions, 1950. Contbr. sci. jours. Home: 4600 Connecticut Av washington DC 20008 Office: Environmental Science Services Adminstrn Rockville MD 20852

BAUM, WILLIAM WAKEFIELD, bishop; b. Dallas, Nov. 21, 1926; s. Harold E. and Mary Leona (Hayes) W.; student Kenrick Sem., St. Louis, 1947-51, U. St. Thomas Aquinas, Rome, Italy, 1956-58; S.T.L., Muhlenberg Coll., Allentown, Pa., 1957, S.T.D., 1958, D.D., 1967. Ordained priest Roman Cath. Ch., 1951; asso. pastor St. Aloysius Parish, St. Therese's Parish and St. Peter's Parish, Kansas City, Mo., 1951-56, 61-64, 67-68; adminstr. St. Cyril's Parish, Sugar Creek, Mo., 1960-61; pastor St. James Parish, Kansas City, Mo., 1968-70; chancellor Diocese Kansas City-St. Joseph, 1967-70; bishop of Springfield-Cape Girardeau, Mo., 1970—; instr., then prof. Avila Coll., Kansas City, Mo., 1954-56, 58-63. Hon. chaplain of the Pope, 1961; peritus 2d Vatican Council, 1962-65; hon. prelate of the Pope, 1968; 1st exec. dir. Bishops' Commn. Ecumenical and Inter-religious Affairs, 1964- 67; mem. Joint Working Group, reps. Cath. Ch. and World Council Chs., 1965-69; mem. Mixed Commn., reps. Cath. Ch. and Lutheran World Fedn., 1965-66. Trustee Cath. U. Am. Author: The Teaching of Cardinal Cajetan on the Sacrifice of the Mass, 1958; Considerations Toward the Theology on the Presbyterate, 1961. Home: 1320 E Walnut St Springfield MO 65802 Office: Landers Bldg Public Sq Springfield MO 65806

BAUMAN, GEORGE DUNCAN, publisher; b. Humboldt, Ia., Apr. 12, 1912; s. Peter William and Mae (Duncan) B.; student Loyola U., Chgo., 1930-35; LL.B., Washington U., St. Louis, 1948; m. Nora Kathleen Kelly, May 21, 1938. Reporter, Chgo. Herald Examiner, 1931-39; archtl. rep. Pratt & Lambert, Inc., Chgo. and St. Louis, 1939-43; with St. Louis Globe-Democrat, 1943—, publisher, 1967—; dir. City Bank St. Louis. Mem. Mo. Child Welfare Adv. Com., 1967—, St. Louis Welfare Commn., 1967—; mem. lay adv. bd. St. Vincent's Hosp., 1952—, chmn., 1957-58; mem. lay adv. bd. St. Mary's Hosp., St. Louis, 1968-69; mem. exec. bd. St. Louis council Boy Scouts Am., 1967—, Mo. Baptist Hosp. Assn., 1967—, Blue Shield Voting Membership Bd., 1968—, St. Louis Municipal Theatre Assn., 1968—, United Service Orgns. Council St. Louis, 1968—; mem. adv. bd. Newman Chapel, 1964-68, pres., 196 —; sec. Policemen and Firemen Fund St. Louis, 1963-69; bd. dirs. Herbert Hoover Boy Club, St. Louis, 1966—, pres., 1968; active United Fund Greater St. Louis, 1963—, now mem. exec. com., v.p., bd. dirs.; pres. Health and Welfare Council Met. St. Louis, 1965-67; bd. dirs. Sec. Bd. Election Commnrs., St. Louis, 1957-61. Bd. dirs. Catholic Charities, Child Center Our Lady of Grace, Jr. Achievement Miss. Valley, Salvation Army Midland Divisional Hdqrs., Conv. and Tours Bd. Greater St. Louis, St. Louis Symphony Soc., Better Bus. Bur., St. Louis YMCA, Jefferson Nat. Expansion Meml. Assn., Freedoms Found. at Valley Forge; trustee Govtl. Research Inst. Mem. Am. Newspaper Pubs. Assn., Am. Soc. Newspaper Editors, Japan-Am. Soc. St. Louis, Mo. C. of C., Newspaper Personnel Relations Assn. (past pres.), St. Louis C. of C. (chmn. nat. affairs com.), Bar Assn. St. Louis, Am., Mo. bar assns. Home: 6233 Northwood St St Louis MO 63105 Office: St Louis Globe-Democrat 12th Blvd at Dilmer St Louis MO 63101

BAUMAN, HAROLD ERNEST, clergyman; b. Iron Springs, Pa., May 16, 1922; s. Norman G. and Ella (Shoup) B.; B.A., Goshen (Ind.) Coll., 1946; Th.B., Goshen Bib. Sem., 1947, B.D., 1956; Th.M., So. Bapt. Theol. Sem., 1962; student Columbia Tchrs. Coll., 1964-66; m. Elizabeth Hershberger, June 10, 1947; children—Philip, John, David, Rebecca. Ordained to ministry Mennonite Ch., 1947; minister in Orville, O., 1947-54, bishop, 1954-58; campus pastor Goshen Coll., 1958—; moderator Mennonite Gen. Conf., 1965- 67. Danforth fellow, 1964-66. Mem. Nat. Assn. Coll. and Univ. Chaplains (sec. 1967-70, pres., 1970-71). Author: Grief's Slow Work, 1960; The Price of Church Unity, 1962. Home: 427 Westwood Rd Goshen IN 46526

BAUMAN, HELEN WOOD, C.S. practitioner, tchr.; b. St. Joseph, Mo., Nov. 17, 1891; d. Horace W. and Mary (Vance) Wood; mus. edn. with Arthur Foote, Boston; student Tobias Mattay Sch., London, Eng., 1928; master classes, Thomas Whitney Surette Sch., Concord, Mass., 1927; m. Oscar George Bauman, Jan. 1, 1922. C.S. practioner, 1932—; C.S. tchr., 1946—; asso. editor publs. C.S. Pub. Soc., 1948-59, editor in chief, 1959-70; tchr. normal class Mother Ch., 1958, pres. Mother Ch., 1963—; editor C.S. Jour., 1959-70, C.S. Sentinel, 1959-70, C.S. Herald (in 12 langs. in Braille), 1959-70. Mem. D.A.R. Home: 274 Beacon St Boston MA 02116

BAUMAN, JOHN ANDREW, legal educator; b. Eau Claire, Wis., Jan. 28, 1921; s. John William and Agnes (Prueher) B.; B.S.L., U. Minn., 1942, LL.B., 1947; LL.M., Columbia, 1952, Jur. Sc.D., 1958; m. Mary Regina Heggie, June 21, 1952; 1 son, John Heggie. Admitted to Wis. bar, 1947, Minn. bar, 1948; asso. prof. law U. N.M. Law Sch., 1947-54; prof. law Ind. U. Law Sch., 1954-60, University of California at Los Angeles Law Sch., since 1960—, associate dean, since 1969—. Served with USAAF, 1942-45. Mem. Wis. Bar Assn., Am. Assn. U. Profs., Order of Coif, Phi Delta Phi. Roman Cath. Author: (with K.H. York) Cases on Remedies, 1967. Home: 1138 Chautauqua Blvd Pacific Palisades CA 90272 Office: 405 Hilgard Av Los Angeles CA 90024

BAUMAN, JOHN DUANE, lawyer; b. Kaskaskia, Ill., Aug. 22, 1930; s. Louis W. and Veronica (Schmerbauch) B.; B.A., S.E. Mo. State Coll., 1952; LL.B., Washington U., St. Louis, 1957, J.D., 1968; m. Avis C. Moore, Sept. 15, 1956; children—Mark Duane, Jeffery Paul, Thomas Jon. Admitted to Mo. bar, 1967, Ill. bar, 1967; practice in St. Louis, 1967-68, Belleville, 1967- -; chmn. Legal Aid Bd. St. Clair County, Ill. Sec. Metal Services Corp. Served with U.S. Army, 1952-54. Mem. Ill. Bar Assn. (com. chmn.). Roman Catholic. Elk. Club: St. Clair Country. Home: 409 Southgate St Belleville IL 62223 Office: St Clair Nat Bank Belleville IL 62220

BAUMAN, JOHN NEVIN, motor mfg. exec.; b. Jeannette, Pa., Mar. 11, 1899; s. John Nevin and Ada (Barnhart) B.; B.S., Bucknell U., 1920; M.S., U. Mich., 1922; m. Lucille Pattern. Oct. 8, 1925; children—Robert, Susan. With automotive engine plant Standard Steel Car Co., Pitts., 1921; with White Motor Co., 1922—, successively apprentice transp. engr., retail salesman White br., Balt., transp. engr. fleet operations, mgr. sales promotion dept., asst. to v.p. in charge sales, v.p., 1936-56, pres., 1956-69, became chief exec. officer, 1960, chmn. bd., 1969—, also chmn. exec. com., dir. Mem. Soc. Automotive Engrs., Cleve. C. of C., Sales Execs. Clubs: Union, Shaker Heights Country, Pepper Pike Country, Mid-Day. Home: 2701 Park Driveway Shaker Heights OH 44120 Office: 100 Erieview Plaza Cleveland OH 44114

BAUMANN, CARL A., biochemist (nutrition, cancer research, vitamins); b. Milw., Aug. 10, 1906; s. Edward Carl and Minna (Einwaldt) B.; B.S., U. of Wis., 1929; Ph.D., agrl. chemistry, 1933. Asst. in agrl. chemistry, U. of Wis., 1929-34, instr. and research asso., 1936-39, asst. prof. biochemistry and cancer research, 1939-46, prof. biochemistry, 1946—. Mem. Alsos Mission, 1945; chief party Midwest Universities Consortium for International Activities mission U. Agraria-La Molina, Lima, Peru, 1966-69. Mem. Gen. Edn. Bd. Decorated Medal of Freedom, M.B.E. Fellow, Heidelberg, Cambridge, Copenhagen, 1934-36. Mem. Am. Chem. Soc., Am. Soc. Biol. Chemists, Am. Inst. Nutrition, Am. Assn. Cancer Research, A.A.A.S., Soc. Exptl. Biology and Medicine, Sigma Xi, Phi Beta Kappa. Contbr. articles in field to scientific journals. Editorial bd. Jour. of Nutrition. Office: Biochemistry Bldg University of Wisconsin Madison WI 53706

BAUMANN, DONALD JOSEPH, educator, chemist; b. Mecosta, Mich., Nov. 16, 1915; s. Joseph S. and Mary (Lehnert) B.; B.S., U. Detroit, 1943; M.S. Creighton U., 1944; Ph.D., Ia. State U., 1952; m. Betty A. Boyer, Dec. 28, 1945; children—Thomas, Theresa, James, Mary, John, Margaret, Barbara, Paul, William, Jean. Teaching fellow, then instr. Creighton U., 1943-46, mem. faculty, 1951—, prof. chemistry, chmn. dept., 1960—; instr. Ia. State U., 1946-51. Mem. Am. Chem. Soc. (sec.-treas. Omaha 1952-57, chmn. 1957- 58). Home: 520 N 38th St Omaha NB 68131

BAUMANN, EDWARD ROBERT, educator; b. Rochester, N.Y., May 12, 1921; s. John Carl and Lillie Minnie (Roth) B.; B.S., U. Mich., 1944; B.S. in San. Engring., U. Ill., 1945, M.S., 1947, Ph.D., 1954; NSF faculty fellow U. Durham, Eng., 1959-60; m. Mary A. Massey, June 15, 1946; children—Betsy Louise, Philip Robert. Research asso. U. Ill., 1947-53; asso. prof. civil engring. Ia. State U., 1953-56, prof., 1956—; cons. Water Quality Office of Environmental Protection Agy., Engring.-Sci., Inc., Lakeside Engring. Co., many cities and industries. Vice pres. research Nat. Water Purification Found., 1960—. Served with Corps of Engrs., AUS, 1944-46. Recipient gold medal Filtration Soc., Eng., 1970; George B. Gascoigne medal, Water Pollution Control Fedn., 1962, Publns. award, 1963, Purification div. award, Am. Water Works Assn., 1965, Anson Marston medal Ia. Engring. Soc., 1966, Distinguished Service award, 1968. Fellow Am. Soc. C.E.; mem. Am. Assn. Profs. in San. Engring. (pres. 1967-70), Nat. Soc. Profl. Engrs. (nat. dir.), Am. Assn. U. Profs., Am. Soc. Engring. Edn., Sigma Xi, Phi Kappa Phi. Rotarian. Author: Sewerage and Sewage Treatment, 1958. Mem. editorial bd. Internat. Jour. Air and Water Pollution, London, 1960-67; asst. editor San. Engr. Newsletter of Am. Soc. C.E., 1962—. Contbr. articles profl. jours. Home: 1627 Crestwood Circle Ames IA 50010

BAUMANN, HANS, author; b. Amberg, Bavaria, Apr. 22, 1914; s. Johann and Elisabeth (Kraus) B.; student German Gymnasium, Amberg, also U. Berlin; m. Elisabeth Zoglmann, Dec. 17, 1942, 1 dau., Veronica Eva. Tchr., Bavaria; writer poems, some with music, 1931—; plays produced, State Theatre, Berlin, also Burg Theatre, Vienna; writer juvenile books, 1946—. Served as lt., Germany Army, Russian Front, also France, World War II. Recipient Gerstäcker prize Braunschweig, 1956, award for best book for youngsters N.Y. Herald Tribune, 1958. Author: The Caves of the great Hunters, Son of Columbus, Sons of the Steppe, The Barque of the Brothers, Jackie the Pit Pony, The Crotchety Crocodile, Angelina and the Birds, The Lion and the Unicorn, The Dragon Next Door, The World of the Pharoahs, I Marched with Hannibal, The Roudabout on the Roof, The Bear and the Brothers, Gold and Gods of Peru, Tina and Nina, Alexander's Great March, Casper and His Friends.

BAUMANN, VICTOR G., accountant; b. Toledo, Feb. 22, 1927; s. Perry Herman and Ella (Becker) B.; B.B.A., U. Toledo, 1954; m. Marcella Ann Fisher, Mar. 22, 1952; children—Karen, Richard, James, David. Office mgr. Oscar Joseph Stores, Inc., Toledo, 1954-58; partner I.R. Miller & Co., C.P.A.'s, Toledo, 1958- 71; prin. J.K. Lasser & Co., C.P.A.'s, Toledo, 1970-71; individual practice, 1971—. Served with USNR, 1945-46, with AUS, 1950-52. C.P.A., Ohio. Mem. Am. Inst. C.P.A.'s, Ohio Soc. C.P.A.'s, Nat. Assn. Accountants. Mem. United Ch. Christ (elder). Home: 1742 Fallbrook Rd Toledo OH 43624

BAUMBACH, EUGENE ANDREW, brewing co. exec.; b. Balt., Oct. 22, 1918; s. Andrew Charles and Louise Elizabeth (Shuman) B.; B.B.A., Balt. Coll. Commerce, 1948; m. Carol Lenora Vroom, Nov. 24, 1945; children—Eugene Andrew, Sheila Ann Chuchel. Internal auditor Continental Can Co., N.Y.C., 1948-52; asst. sec. Gunther Brewing Co., Balt., 1952-60; office mgr. Theodore Hamm Brewing Co., Balt., 1960-63, office mgr., Houston, 1963-67, treas., St. Paul, 1967—. Served with USCGR, 1942-45. Mem. Tax Execs. Inst. Rotarian. Home: 1960 Asbury St St Paul MN 55113 Office: 720 Payne Av St Paul MN 55165

BAUMBERGER, JAMES PERCY, physiologist; b. San Leandro, Calif., Sept. 17, 1892; s. James and Elise Marie-Louise (Deprez) B.; B.S. U. Cal., 1914; M.S., Harvard, 1916, Sc.D., 1918; m. Alberta Loraine Jackson, Dec. 22, 1914. Asst. or teaching fellow in entomology, zoology, botany, or physiology at Harvard or Radcliffe, 1914-18; instr. natural scis. Lowthorpe Hort. Sch., Groton, Mass., 1915-18; mem. faculty, dept. physiology Stanford Medical School, 1919—; professor physiology, 1935-58, professor emeritus, 1958- -; senior research associate with the Palo Alto Medical Research Foundation, since 1961—; research associate, department of medicine Collis P. Huntington Cancer Hosp., Harvard Med. Sch., 1932-33; vis. prof. anatomy dept. Washington U., 1941, also research asso. Barnard Free Skin and Cancer Hosp., St. Louis; vis. prof. aviation physiology U. So. Cal. Sch. Medicine, 1943 (working on O.S.R.D. project on explosive decompression); spl. consultant. Aero. Med. Lab., Army Air Force, Wright Field, Dayton, O., 1944; responsible investigator Office Naval Research project on field physiology, 1952-53, on bird migration, 1953-55; prin. investigator project oxygen delivery rate of erythrocytes, other projects for Air Force. Served with M.C., AUS, AEF, in traumatic shock lab., 1918. Held Commn. for Relief in Belgium Ednl. Found. Fellowship, Bruxelles, 1925-26; Am. Scandinavian Fellowship, Lund, Sweden, and Copenhagen, Denmark, 1926; Rockefeller Table, Naples Biol. Sta., 1926. Fellow A.A.A.S.; mem. Am. Physiol. Soc., Am. Assn. U. Profs., Soc. Exptl. Biology and Medicine (chmn. Pacific coast section 1956-58), Am. Association Cancer Research, Soc. Gen. Physiol., Western Soc. Naturalists, Sigma Xi, Cercle des Alumni de la Foundation Universitaire. Club: Commonwealth of Cal. (San Francisco). Asso. editor Physiol. Revs., 1945-52; Ann. Reviews Physiology, 1952-58. Contbr. to sci. jours. Home: 850 Webster St Palo Alto CA 94301 Office: Palo Alto Medical Research Foundation 860 Bryant St Palo Alto CA 94301

BAUMEISTER, THEODORE, engr.; b. N.Y.C., July 19, 1897; s. Theodore and Mary L. (Wilson) B.; B.S., City Coll., 1918; M.E., Columbia, 1922; m. Margaret Kilpatrick, January 23, 1925; children—Theodore III, Heard Kilpatrick, Mary Berrein Baumeister (Mrs. Murray B. Parker). Asst. Columbia, 1922, instr., 1924-31, asst. prof., 1931-38, asso. prof., 1938-41, prof. in charge of power, thermo-dynamic courses since 1941, exec. officer, dept. mech. engring., 1941-48, Stevens prof. mech. engring., 1950-64, emeritus, 1964—; adj. prof. mech. engring. U. S.C., 1965-70; cons. engr. Stevens & Wood, 1926-38, Am. Gas & Electric System, 1936-52, Sociéte Edison de Milano, 1950. Gen. Pub. Utilities Corp., 1950-64, Babcock & Wilcox Co., 1950—, S.C. Electric & Gas Co., 1952-65. Mayor's Com. on Transit Power Plant, N.Y.C., 1957-58, Consol. Coal Co., 1959- 64; asso. on power plant valuation M.R. Scharff, 1937-41; E.I. Dupont de Nemours & Co., 1945-55, Duke Power Co., 1948-49, Brookhaven Nat. Lab., AEC, 1940-58, central Hudson Gas & Electric Corp., 1953-64, Worthington Corp., 1955-57, others. Trustee Engring. Socs. Library, 1947- 55, N.Y. P.E. City Mission Soc., 1954-64. Licensed profl. engr., N.Y.; chartered mech. engr., Gt. Britain. Mem. Am. Soc. M.E. (chmn. met. sect., 1936-38; chmn. power div., 1943; mem. standing com. on power test codes), Inst. Mech. Engrs. (Gt. Britain), Am. Nuclear Soc., A.A.A.S., Am. Soc. Engring. Edn., Carolina Plantation Soc., St. George's Soc., Am. Assn. U. Profs., Newcomen Soc., Am. Soc. Naval Engrs., Nat. Soc. Profl. Engrs., Agrl. Soc. S.C., Navy League, Air Force Assn., Am. Ordnance Assn., Sigma Xi, Tau Beta Pi, Phi Gamma Delta, Theta Tau. Episcopalian (vestryman). Clubs: University, Riverdale Yacht (N.Y.C.); Onteora; Carolina Yacht, Country of Charleston. Contbr. sects. to Peele's Mining Engineers Handbook, 1941; Fans, 1935; Perry's Chemical Engineers Handbook, 1949; (with Sporn and Ambrose) Heat Pumps, 1947; Kent's Mechanical Handbook, 1948; Knowlton's Standard Handbook for Electrical Engineers, 1968; Bonilla's Nuclear Engineering, 1957; also tech., sci. jours., Ency. Brit., Streeter's Fluid Dynamics Handbook, 1961; Perry's Engineering Manual, 1967. Editor-in-chief Standard Handbook for Mechanical Engineers (Marks'); cons. editor McGraw-Hill Ency. of Sci. and Tech. Home: Parsonage Willtown Bluff Yonges Island SC 29494 summer Laghet Onteora Park Tannersville NY 12485

BAUMER, FRANKLIN L., educator; b. Johnstown, Pa., May 10, 1913; s. Herman E. and Anna (Dibert) B.; A.B., Yale, 1934, Ph.D., 1938; student London (Eng.) U., 1935-36; m. Margarita Thieler, June 22, 1936; children—Constance, Joanna. Prof. history Yale, 1954—, Randolph W. Townsend prof. of history, 1963—, dir. grad. studies in history, 1951-60. Guggenheim fellow, 1945-46; faculty fellow Fund for Advancement Edn., 1953-54. Mem. Am. Hist. Assn., Hist. Sci. Soc. Episcopalian. Author: The Early Todor Theory of Kingship, 1940, 2d edit., 1966; Main Currents of Western Thought, 1952, 3d rev. edit., 1970; Religion and the Rise of Scepticism, 1960, 69. Contbr. articles profl. jours. Home: 9 Hawley Rd Hamden CT 06517 Office: 1525 Yale Station New Haven CT 06520

BAUMER, WILLIAM HENRY, mfg. co. exec.; b. Omaha, Nov. 27, 1909; s. William H. and Winifred (Mitchell) B.; student Creighton U., 1927-29; B.S., U.S. Mil. Acad., 1933; M.S., Columbia, 1941; m. Alice Hull Brough, Aug. 29, 1936 (dec.); children—Winifred Joan, Natalie Brough, Marjorie Ann, William Henry, Carolyn Jean; m. 2d, Peggy O'Neill Bruen, Sept. 3, 1970. Commd. 2d lt. U.S. Army, 1933, advanced through grades to col., active duty, 1933-50, brig. gen. Res., 1961, maj. gen., 1966, ret., 1969; served with Supreme Hdqrs. AEF, Brit. War Cabinet, U.S. Mission to Moscow; mil. adviser Paris Peace Conf., 1942-46; asst. to pres. and chmn. exec. com. Johnson & Johnson, New Brunswick, N.J., 1950-62; exec. v.p. Atlas Gen. Industries, N.Y.C., 1962-63; pres., mem. bd. Internat. Gen. Industries (formerly Bradford Speed Packaging & Devel. Corp.), 1963—, IB Industries, Inc., Washington, 1963—; v.p. Internat. Bank; dir. Kliklok Corp., Foster Wheeler Corp., Pierce Governor Co., Woodman Co., Globe Industries, Avis Indsl. Corp., Phila. Fund. Mem. adv. com. Nat. Capital area Boy Scouts Am.; adv. bd. Blinded Vets. Assn. Decorated

Legion of Merit with 2 clusters (U.S.); Order of Leopold, Croix de Guerre (Belgium). Mem. West Point Soc. D.C. (past pres.). Council on Fgn. Relations. Republican. Roman Catholic. Clubs: Army- Navy (Washington); Kenwood Golf and Country (D.C.); LaJolla (Cal.) Golf and Country. Author: Sports as Taught and Played at West Point, 1939; How to Be An Army Officer, 1940; 18-35, The Draft and You, 1940; He's in the Army Now, 1941; Not All Warriors, 1941; West Point—Moulder of Men, 1942; Politics is Your Business, 1960; Little Wars of the United States, 1969; Buy, Sell, Merge: How to Do It, 1971. Contbr. to Ency. Brit., also articles to mags. Home: 6338 Muirlands Dr La Jolla CA 92037 Office: 1701 Pennsylvania Av NW Washington DC 20006

BAUMGARDNER, ROBERT LORAIN, advt. exec.; b. Cleve., Nov. 2, 1913; s. Jacob Lorain and Florence (Reynolds) B.; B.A., Kent State U., 1936; m. Margaret Urban, Apr. 3, 1943; children—Robert Lorain (dec.), Lorraine. Reporter, Akron (O.) Times Press, 1936-38; sales promotion mgr. Seiberling Rubber Co., Akron, 1938-42; adv. mgr. Gen. Tire & Rubber Co., Akron, 1945-50; account exec. Fuller & Smith, Cleve., 1950-52; vice chmn. Griswold-Eshleman Co., Cleve., 1968—, also dir. Chmn. citizens adv. com. Westlake (O.) Bd. Edn. Trustee Lake Erie Opera Theatre; bd. govs. Cleve. YMCA; v.p. trustees Kent State U. Served to capt. USAAF, 1942-45. Decorated Bronze Star. Mem. Cleve. Advt. Club (past trustee), Newcomen soc. N.Am., Blue Key. Clubs: Portgage Country (Akron); Westwood Country (Rocky River, O.). Office: 55 Public Sq Cleveland OH 44113

BAUMGART, NORBERT K., coll. pres.; b. Kampsville, Ill., Sept. 4, 1931; s. Karl J. and Esther (Hvelskoetter) B.; B.A., U. No. Ia., 1954, M.A., 1958; Ed.D, Ind. U., 1960; m. Bernita Y. Riedemann, July 24, 1955; children-Timothy, Susan, Jean. Pub. sch. relations counselor, Cedar Falls, Ia., 1956-58; counselor Ind. U., 1958-60; dean students Wilmington (O.) Coll., 1960- 63, Mankato (Minn.) State Coll., 1963-68; pres. No. State Coll., Aberdeen, S.D., 1968—. Dir. Aberdeen Nat. Bank. Bd. dirs. St. Luke's Hosp., Aberdeen YMCA. Served with AUS, 1954-56. Mem. Aberdeen C. of C. (bd. dirs.), Assn. State Colls. and Univs., Sigma Tau Gamma, Phi Delta Kappa. Contbr. articles. Home: 1314 N Main St Aberdeen SD 57401 Office: No State College Aberdeen SD 27401

BAUMGARTNER, LEONA, (Mrs. Alexander D. Langmuir), physician, educator; b. Chgo., Aug. 18, 1902; d. William J. and Olga (Leisy) Baumgartner; A.B., U. Kan., 1923, M.S., 1925; grad. work Kaiser Wilhelm Inst., Munich, 1928-29; Ph.D. (univ. fellow, 1930-31, Sterling fellow, 1931-32), Yale, 1932, M.D., 1934, LL.D., 1970; D.Sc. Women's Med. Coll., 1950, N.Y.U., 1954, Russell Sage Coll., 1955, Smith Coll., 1956, Western Coll. Women, 1960, U. Mass., 1963, U. Mich., 1967, McMurray Coll., 1967, N.Y. Med. Coll., 1968, Clark U., 1969; L.H.D., Keuka Coll., 1963; LL.D., Skidmore Coll., 1959, Oberlin Coll., 1965; m. Nathaniel M. Elais, 1942 (dec. 1964); m. 2d, Alexander D. Langmuir, 1970. Mem. faculty Colby (Kan.) Community High Sch., 1923-24; Kansas City Jr. Coll., 1925-26; U. Mont., 1923-28; intern, asst. resident and asst. in pediatrics N.Y. Hosp. and Cornell Med. Coll., 1934-36; acting asst. surg. USPHS, 1936-37; lectr. nursing edn. Columbia, 1939-42; with N.Y. City Dept. Health, 1937-62, commr. health, 1954-62; exec. director N.Y. Found., 1953-54; asso. chief U.S. Children's Bur., Fed. Security Agy., 1949-50, cons., 1950-56; mem. faculty Med. Coll., Cornell, 1939-66, pediatrics and pub. health faculty, 1957-66; vis. lectr. maternal and child health Harvard Sch. Pub. Health, 1948-62; vis. prof. social medicine Harvard Medical Sch., Boston, 1966—; asst. adminstr. Office Tech. Coop. and Research, AID, Dept. State, 1962-65; exec. dir. Med. Care and Edn. Found., Inc., Boston, 1968—. Adviser Indian minister health, 1955, French Ministry Health, 1945; mem. ofcl. exchange mission to USSR, 1958; lectr. for Tokyo Met. Govt., 1961; mem. nat. adv. council Peace Corps., 1961-63. Mem. bd. N.Y. Fund for Children. Recipient many awards including Albert Lasker award, Am. Pub. Health Assn., 1954, Elizabeth Blackwell award Hobart and William Smith Colls., 1961, Samuel J. Crumbine award Kan. Pub. Health Assn., 1961, Albert Einstein award 1964, Herman M. Biggs award N.Y. State Pub. Health Assn., 1968, Wilbur Lucius Cross medal Grad. Sch. Assn., Yale U., 1970; numerous others. Licentiate Am. Bd. Pediatrics, 1942, Am. Bd. Preventive Med. and Pub. Health, 1949. Mem. Harvey Soc., HIstory Sci. Soc., Am. Assn. History Medicine, Oxford Bibliographies Soc., Am. Pub. Health Assn. (pres. 1958-59), Am. Acad. Pediatrics, Am. Pediatric Soc., N.Y. Acad. Medicine, Child Welfare League Am. (bd.), Nat. Social Welfare Assembly (v.p.), Nat. Conf. Social Work (exec. com.), Nat. Health Council (pres. 1956), Mortar Bd., Phi Beta Kappa, Sigma Xi, Pi Beta Phi, Phi Sigma. Club: Cosmopolitan. Contbr. med. and sci. articles profl. jours. Home: 1010 Memorial Dr Cambridge MA 02138 Office: Med Care and Edn Fond Inc 1 Boston Place Boston MA 02108

BAUMGARTNER, WILFRID, financier; b. Paris, France, May 21, 1902; s. Dr. A. And Mrs. Baumgartner-Clamageran B.; student Lycee Buffon, Ecole des Sciences Politiques; LL.D., Law U. of Paris; m. Christiane Mercier, Feb. 5, 1930; children—Sylvie, Eric, Florence. Insp. finance, France, 1925; chief Cabinet of Minister of Finances, 1930; sub-mgr. of Treasury, 1930- 34, asst. mgr., 1934-35, mgr., 1935-37; pres. gen. mgr. Crédit National, 1937-49; mem. bd. Banque de France, 1936-49, gov., 1949-60; minister of finance, 1960-62; chmn. bd. Rhode-Poulenc, S.A., 1963—. Decorated grand officer Legion of Honor, 1953. Mem. Inst. de France. Club: Automobile of France. Home: 98 rue de Grenelle Paris (7ème) France Office: 22 Avenue Montaigne Paris (8e) France

BAUMHART, RAYMOND CHARLES, univ. pres.; b. Chgo., Dec. 22, 1923; s. Emil and Florence (Weidner) B.; B.S., Northwestern U., 1945; Ph.L., Loyola U., 1952, S.T.L., 1958; M.B.A., Harvard, 1953, D.B.A., 1963. Ordained priest Roman Catholic Ch., 1957; asst. prof. mgmt. Loyola U., Chgo., 1962-64, dean Sch. Bus. Adminstrn., 1964-66, exec. v.p., acting v.p. Med. Center, 1968-70, pres., 1970—; research fellow Cambridge Center for Social Studies, 1966- 68. Trustee Boston Coll., St. Louis U. Served to lt. (j.g.) USNR, 1944- 46. John W. Hill fellow Harvard, 1961-62. Mem. Acad. Mgmt., Assn. Chgo. Priests. Author: An Honest Profit, 1968; (with Thomas Garrett) Cases in Business Ethics, 1968; (with Thomas McMahon) THe Brewer-Wholesaler Relationship, 1969. Corr. editor: America, 1965-70. Home: 6525 N Sheridan Rd Chicago IL 60626 Office: 820 N Michigan Av Chicago IL 60611

BAUMHEFNER, CLARENCE HERMAN, banker; b. Lester Prairie, Minn., Apr. 1, 1912; s. Walter P. and Clare A. (Jacobs) B.; grad. Am. Inst. Banking, 1940; student Grad. Sch. Banking, Rutgers U., 1951; m. Virginia Haight, May 11, 1941; children—Robert, Bonnie. With Bank of Am., 1940—, inspection dept., 1940-43, insp., 1943-47, asst. chief insp., 1947-50, asst. to cashier, 1950-56, cashier and v.p., 1956-65, sr. v.p., cashier, 1965-66, exec. v.p., 1966-70, vice chmn. bd., 1970—. Clubs: Villa Taverna, Commonwealth, Merchants Exchange, Commercial, Family, Bankers (San Francisco); Town (Los Angeles). Home: 40 McLaren Av San Francisco CA 94121 Office: 555 California St San Francisco CA 94120

BAUMHOF, HEINRICH WILHELM, German diplomat; b. Hannover, Germany, July 27, 1929; s. Anton and Katharina (Oelrich) B.; Baccalaureate, Inst. Higher Edn. of Blind, Marburg, Germany, 1951; Ph.D., Ruprecht-Karl U., Heidelberg, Germany, 1958; m. Hannelore Krahner, Oct. 6, 1951; children—Annette, Christopher. Journalist, German radio stas., 1956-61; with cultural sect. Fgn. Office, Bonn, 1961-65; 1st sec. cultural sect. German embassy, Washington, 1966—. Home: 1405 Cola Dr McLean VA 22101 Office: 4645 Reservoir Rd NW Washington DC 20007

BAUML, FRANZ HEINRICH, educator; b. Vienna, Austria, June 12, 1926; s. Gustav Heinrich and Josefa (Sam) B.; came to U.S., 1942, naturalized, 1945; B.S., Armstrong Coll., 1950; B.A., U. Cal., Berkeley, 1953, M.A., 1955, Ph.D., 1957; m. Betty Zeidner, Aug. 28, 1958; children—Carolyn, Mark, Deborah. Prof. German, U. Cal., Los Angeles, 1957—. Served with AUS, 1944-46, U.S. Army, 1950-51. Mem. Medieval Acad. Am., Modern Lang. Assn. Am., Internationaler Germanistenverein. Author: Rhetorical Devices and Structure in the Ackermann aus Bohmen, 1960; Kudrun: Die Handschrift, 1969; Medieval Civilization in Germany, 800-1273, 1969. Home: 12400 Marva Av Granada Hills CA 91344 Office: Germanic Langs U Cal Los Angeles CA 90024

BAUMOL, WILLIAM JACK, educator; b. N.Y.C. Feb. 26, 1922; s. Solomon and Lillian (Itzkowitz) B.; B.S.S. Coll. City N.Y., 1942; Ph.D., London U., 1949; LL.D. (hon.), Rider Coll., 1965; hon. doctorate, Stockholm Sch. Econs. (Sweden), 1971; m. Hilda Missel, Dec. 27, 1941; children—Ellen Frances, Daniel Aaron. With U.S. Dept. Agr., 1942-43, 46; asst. lectr. London Sch. Econs., 1947-49; asst. prof. Princeton, 1949-52, asso. prof., 1952-54, prof., 1954—; prof. N.Y.U., 1971—; cons. Mathematica, Inc., Princeton. Chmn. Econ. Policy Council of N.J. Trustee Rider Coll., Lawrenceville, 1960-70. Guggenheim fellow, 1957-58; Ford Faculty Fellowship, 1965-66. Fellow Econometric Soc.; mem. Am. Assn. U. Profs. (v.p., chairman com. on econ. status of the profession 1968-70), Am. Econ. Assn. (mem. exec. com., v.p. 1966-67), Econ. Policy Council N.J. (chmn.). Author: Economic Dynamics: An Introduction, 1951; Welfare Economics and the Theory of The State, 1952; Business Behavior, Value and Growth, 1959; Economic Theory and Operations Analysis, 1960; (with L.V. Chandler) Economic Processes and Policies, 1954; The Stock Market and Economic Efficiency, 1965; (with W.G. Bowen) Performing Arts: The Economic Dilemma, 1966; (with S.M. Goldfeld) Precursors in Mathematical Economics, 1969. Editor: (with Klaus Knorr) What Price Economic Growth?, 1961. Home: 61 Jefferson Rd Princeton NJ 08540

BAUMUNK, GEORGE PETER, steel co. exec.; b. St. Louis, Jan. 1, 1913; s. John and Gertrude (Klein) B.; B.S., Washington U., St. Louis, 1949; m. Beverly Houston Mayhall, Aug. 24, 1940; 1 son, Creston Neal. With Joseph T. Ryerson & Sons, 1929-30; with Metal Goods Corp., 1936-61, v.p., dir., 1947-61; with Washington Steel Corp. (Pa.), 1963—, pres., 1968—, also chief exec. officer, dir.; pres. Calstrip Steel Corp., 1968—, also dir. Bd. dirs. Steel Service Center Inst., 1957-58, pres. St. Louis chpt., 1958. Mem. Am. Soc. Metals, Nat. Assn. Corrosion Engrs., Am. Iron and Steel Inst. Presbyn. (elder). Home: 230 Old Mill Rd Pittsburgh PA 15238 Office: Washington Steel Corp Washington PA 15301

BAUR, JOHN IRELAND HOWE, mus. dir.; b. Woodbridge, Conn., Aug. 9, 1909; s. Paul V.C. and Susan (Whiting) B.; B.A., Yale, 1932, M.A., 1934; m. Louise Weld Chase, Jan. 7, 1938; children—Susan W., Arthur M., Jean E. Supr. edn. Bklyn. Mus., 1934-36, curator painting and sculpture, 1936-52; curator Whitney Mus. Am. Art, N.Y.C., 1952-58; asso. dir. museum, 1958-68, director of the museum, 1968—; visiting lecturer of history of art Yale, 1950-51. Trustee Council of the Arts, Westchester, 1968-69. Served as sgt. AUS, 1944-45. Author: Eastman Johnson, 1946; John Quidor, 1942; Theodore Robinson, 1946; Revolution and Tradition in Modern American Art, 1951 (also Italian and Japanese editions); Loren MacIver and I. Rice Pereira, 1953; George Grosz, 1954; Charles Burchfield, 1956; Bradley Walker Tomlin, 1957; Nature in Abstraction, 1958. Editor: The New Decade, 1955, New Art in America, 1957; Four American Expressionists, 1959; William Zorach, 1959; Philip Evergood, 1960; Balcomb Greene, 1961; (with Lloyd Goodrich) American Art of Our Century, 1961; Bernard Reder, 1961. Editorial bd. Mag. of Art, Art in America. Home: Mount Holly Rd Katonah NY 10536 Office: 945 Madison Av New York City NY 10019

BAUR, WERNER HEINZ, educator, mineralogist; b. Warsaw, Poland, Aug. 2, 1931; s. Heinrich Ernst and Melanie (Borkowski) B.; Dr.rer.nat., U. Gottingen, Germany, 1956, privat-dozent, 1961; m. Renate Grossmann, June 22, 1962; children—Wolfgang, Brigitte. Came to U.S., 1962. Sci. officer U. Gottingen, 1956-63; asst. to asso. prof. U. Pitts., 1963-65; asso. prof. to prof. U. Ill. at Chgo. Circle, 1965—, head dept. geol. scis., 1967—; postdoctoral fellow U. Berne (Switzerland), 1957; vis. asso. chemist Brookhaven Nat. Lab., 1962-63; vis. prof. U. Karlsruhe (Germany), 1971-71. Fellow Mineralog. Soc. Am., mem. Am. Crystallog. Assn., German Mineralog. Soc. Contbr. articles sci. jours. Research on crystal chemistry of minerals and inorganic compounds, crystal structure determination, hydrogen bonding, lattice energy calculations, computer programming. Office: Box 4348 Univ Illinois at Chicago Circle Chicago IL 60680

BAUTZ, EDWARD, Jr., army officer; b. Union City, N.J., Apr. 2, 1920; s. Edward and Marie (Onimus) B.; B.Sc., Rutgers U., 1941; grad. Advanced Mgmt. Program, Harvard, 1963; grad. Army War Coll., 1958; m. Marjorie Ellen Quirk, Nov. 10, 1945; children—Edward W., Patricia Anne. Commd. 2d lt. U.S. Army, 1941, advanced through grades to maj. gen., 1969; armor officer, World War II and Vietnam; comdg. gen. 25th Inf. Div., 1970; dep. chief staff mil. operations and res. forces Hdqrs. USCONARC, 1970—. Decorated D.S.M. with oak leaf cluster, Silver Star, Legion of Merit with oak leaf cluster, Bronze Star with 2 oak leaf clusters, Air Medal with 11 oak leaf clusters, Purple Heart with 2 oak leaf clusters, Joint Service Commendation medal (U.S.); Croix de Guerre (Luxembourg); War Cross (Czechoslovakia); Order Mil. Merit (Korea); Nat. Order Merit, Gallantry Cross with palm, Armed Forces Honor Medal (Vietnam). Home: 51 Fenwick Rd Ft Monroe VA 23351 Office: DCSOPS Hdqrs USCONARC Ft Monroe VA 23351

BAVASI, EMIL JOSEPH, baseball co. exec.; b. N.Y.C., Dec. 12, 1915; s. Joseph Peter and Sue (Maggio) B.; B.A. in Polit. Sci., De Pauw U., 1938; m. Evit Rice, May 25, 1940; children—Peter, Chris, Bobby, Billy. Gen. mgr. Voldosta Baseball Club (Ga.), 194143, Dunham Baseball Club (N.C.), 194347, Nashua Baseball Club (N.H.), 1947-48, Montreal Baseball Club (Can.), 1947-50; exec. v.p., gen. mgr. Los Angeles Dodgers Baseball Club, and predecessor, 1951-68; pres. San Diego Padres, Nat. League Profl. Baseball Club, 1969—. Chmn. La Canada (Cal.) Community Chest. Served with AUS, World War II; ETO. Decorated Bronze Star; named No. 1 Exec. in Baseball in 1959. Sporting News. Mem. Los Angeles C. of C. Home: 620 Georgian Rd La Canada, CA. Office: care San Diego Padres San Diego CA

BAVETTA, LUCIEN ANDREW, educator; b. Italy, June 4, 1907; s. Andrew and Bertha (Giovinco) B.; came to U.S., 1915, naturalized, 1926; B.S., N.Y. U., 1930; M.S., U. So. Cal., 1933, Ph.D., 1942; m. Mildren Pomeroy, Nov. 9, 1933; children—Ruth (Mrs. Charles Reeman), Andrew. Mem. faculty U. So. Cal., 1943—, prof. biochemistry and nutrition Sch. Dentistry, 1948—, prof. biochemistry and nutrition Grad. Sch., 1954—; vis. scientist NIH, 1955-56. Cons. dental study sect. USPHS. Recipient USPHS sr. research fellowship, 1964. Mem. Inst. Food Technologists, Internat. Assn. Dental Research, Soc. Exptl. Biology and Medicine, Greater Los Angeles Nutrition Council, Am. Inst. Nutrition, A.A.A.S., Gerontological Soc., N.Y. Acad. Scis., So. Cal. Biochemistry Soc., Am. Soc. Biol. Chemists, Sigma Xi, Phi Sigma, Omicron Kappa Upsilon. Author papers nutrition, connective tissue metabolism, developmental biology. Home: Box 245 Meadow Vista CA 95722

BAVIER, FRANCEO, actress; b. N.Y.C., 1905; d. Charles Samuel and Mary Loretta (Birmingham) Bavier; grad. Am. Acad. Dramatic Art, 1925. Made 1st Broadway appearance in the Poor Nut, 1925; other Broadway appearances include On Borrowed Time, Morning at Seven, Kiss and Tell, Point of No Return, The Strings are False; TV appearances in It's a Great Life, Andy Griffith, Mayberry R.F.D.; motion pictures include Bend of the River, Sally and Saint Anne, My Best Friend. Entertained troops in Europe and Pacific Islands, 1945-57. Mem. Screen Actors Guild, Actors Equity. Address: 332 1/2 N Sycamore St Los Angeles CA 90036

BAWDEN, JAMES WYATT, univ. dean; b. St. Louis, Apr. 23, 1930; s. Leland M. and Rose (Wyatt) B.; D.D.S., State U. Ia., 1954, M.S. in Pedodontics, 1960, Ph.D. in Physiology (USPHS fellow), 1961; m. Shirley Suzanne Stevens, June 10, 1951; children—Steven L., Michael J., Timothy C., David W., Becky Sue. Pvt. practice Glenwood Springs, Colo., 1956-58; mem. faculty Sch. Dentistry, U. N.C., 1961—, prof. pedondontics, 1965—, asst., dean, coordinator research, 1963-66, dean, 1966—. Served with USNR, 1954-56. Fellow Am. Coll. Dentists, Internat. Coll. Dentists; mem. So. Conf. Dental Deans and Examiners (pres. 1968), Am. Acad. Pedodontics (chmn. research com. 1968-70), Am. Dental Assn., Internat. Assn. Dental Research, Am. Assn. Dental Schs. (chmn. council deans 1970), Omicron Kappa Upsilon. Research in Maternal-fetal calcium metabolism. Home: 600 Lake Shore Lane Chapel Hill NC 27514

BAXTER, ANNE, actress; b. Michigan City, Ind., May 7, 1923; d. Kenneth Stuart and Catherine (Wright) B.; ed. pub. schs. White Plains, Chappaqua and Bronxville, N.Y., Theodora Irvine's Sch. of the Theater, 1934-36, The Lenox Sch., 1937, The Brearley Sch., 1938-39, Studio Sch. Twentieth Century Fox, 1940; m. John Hodiak, July 7, 1946; 1 dau., Katrina Baxter; m. 2d, Randolph Galt, Feb. 18, 1960; children—Melissa, Maginel. Studied with Ouspenskava for 3 years; played in Seen But Not Heard, 1936; There's Always A Breeze; Madame Caped (with La Gaiiene), 1937; Susan and God, Summer Playhouse, Dennis, Mass., 1938; Spring Meeting (first ingenue role) Cape Playhouse, 1939; (Broadway play) Square Root of Wonderful; (London play) The Joshua Tree; moving pictures: 20 Mule Team (with Wallace Beery) M.G.M.; Great Profile (with John Barrymore), Twentieth Century Fox; Charley's Aunt (with Jack Benny), Fox; Swampwater, Fox; Magnificent Ambersons (Orson Welles), R.K.O.; Pied Piper (with Monty Wooley), Fox; Crash Dive (with Tyrone Power), Fox; Five Graves To Cairo (with Franchot Tone), Paramount; North Star, Samuel Goldwyn; The Sullivans; Guest in the House; Angel on My Shoulder; Royal Scanda; Outcasts of Poker Flat, My Wife's Best Friend, Blue Gardenia, I Confess, Carnival, All About Eve, Yellow Sky, You're My Everything, Fool's Parade, Stranger on the Run, The Glass Hammer, Lapin 360, The Late Liz, Ten Commandments, One Desire, The Spoilers, Three Violent People, Chase a Crooked Shadow, Summer of the 17th Doll; Cimarron, 1960, Walk on the Wild Side, 1961; Mix Me a Person, 1962, The Tall Women; The Busy Body; 5 mos. tour John Browns Body, 1955-56; appeared on Broadway in Applause. Received Acad. Award and Fgn. Press award as best supporting actress in The Razor's Edge, 1947. Presbyn. Office: care Park-Citron Agy 10889 Wilshire Blvd West Los Angeles CA 90024

BAXTER, BATSELL BARRETT, educator, minister; b. Cordell, Okla., Sept. 23, 1916; s. Batsell and Frances Fay (Scott) B.; B.A., Abilene Christian Coll., 1937; M.A., U. So. Cal., 1938, Ph.D., 1944; B.D., Vanderbilt U., 1957; m. Mavis Wanda Roberts, Dec. 22, 1938; children—Barrett Scott, Richard Alan, John Douglas. Prof. speech George Pepperdine Coll., 1938-45; prof. speech, chmn. dept. David Lipscomb Coll., 1945-54, chmn. Bible dept. 1957—; minister Hillsboro Ch., Nashville, 1951-70; speaker on nat. Herald of Truth, radio and TV religious programs, 1960—. Named Alumnus of Year, Abilene Christian Coll., 1962. Mem. So. Speech Assn. (pres. 1951), Soc. Bib. Lit. and Exegesis. Author: Heart of the Yale Lectures, 1947; Speaking for the Master, 1954; If I Be Lifted Up, 1956, Great Preachers of Today, Vol. I, 1960; Making God's Way Our Way, 1964; I Believe Beacause.., 1971, Staff writer Gospel Advocate, 1950—, 20th Century Christian, 1938—. Home: 3703 Mayfair Av Nashville TN 37215

BAXTER, BERNICE, cons.; b. Oakland, Cal., May 24, 1896; d. James McIntyre and Mary Elizabeth (Smith) B.; A.B., San Francisco State Teachers Coll., San Francisco, 1928; Ph.D., Yale 1935; student U. Cal., 1919-20. Began as sch. tchr. and prin., 1917; tchr., later counselor, junior high sch., Oakland, Cal., 1919-24; prin. elementary sch., Oakland, 1924- 31, 33-34; vice prin., sr. high sch., Oakland, 1934, teaching fellow Yale, 1931-32; coordinator of instruction, Oakland, 1938-42; became adminstrv. asst. to supt. schs., Oakland 1942 (on leave 1947-49); dir. edn. in human relations Oakland pub. schs., 1949-59; instr. summer schs., Mills Coll., San Francisco State Coll., U. Cal.; lectr. edn. Mills Coll., 1959-65, U. B.C., Vancouver, Can., 1962-63; cons. pre-sch. and kindergarten edn., early childhood edn. Nat. pres. Camp Fire Girls, Inc., 1944-46. Dir. planning 1950 White House Conf. on Children, U.S. Children's Bur., 1947-49. U.S. del. UNESCO Conf., Florence, Italy, 1950. Mem. N.E.A. (life), P.T.A. (life), Assn. Childhood Edn. Internat., Am. Assn. U. Women, Pi Lambda Theta (past nat. pres.), Delta Kappa Gamma (hon.). Club: Soroptomist (hon.). Author: Teacher-Pupil Relationships, 1951; Education in Human Relations, 1952; Growth in Human Relations, 1952. Co-author: Group Experience, the Democratic Way, 1943; Overview of Elementary Education, 1945; Global Geography, 1945; The Role of Elementary Education, 1952. Home: 25 Blair Av Piedmont CA 94611 ☆

BAXTER, C. KENNETH, business exec.; b. Lafayette, Ind., Aug. 17, 1903; s. Charles A. and Aetna Melissa (Byers) B.; Ph.B., Yale Univ., 1926; Milford Sch., 1920- 22; m. Laura B. Hopkins, July 15, 1946. Pres., Va. Industries, Inc., Phila., now ret.; former dir. AVC Corp., Wilmington, Del., Gen.-Gilbert Corp., N.Y.C., Utilities & Indsl. Corp., N.Y.C.; past mem. adv. com. Bank of New York. Served as lieutenant colonel gen. staff corps, budget div., War Dept. Gen. Staff, 1942-44. Republican. Presbyn. Clubs: Merion Cricket, Merion Golf, Union League (Phila.); Everglades, Bath and Tennis (Palm Beach, Fla.); Pine Valley Golf; Gulf Stream Golf; Seminole Golf. Home: 450 Garden Lane Bryn Mawr PA 19010 also 624 Island Dr Palm Beach FL 33480

BAXTER, DANA FRANKLIN, investment banker; b. Lynn, Mass., Dec. 5, 1908; s. Leon H. and Mildred (Briggs) B.; B.S. in Bus. Adminstrn., Miami U., 1930; student John Marshall Law Sch., 1934; m. Jean Winsper, Apr. 12, 1949; children—Dana Franklin II, William T. With Hayden, Miller & Co., Cleve., 1930-71, beginning as salesman, trader, 1934-41, partner, 1947-64, v.p., 1965-71; with Allen & Co., Winter Haven, Fla., 1971—. Served as lt. comdr. USNR,

1942-46. Mem. Investment Bankers Assn. Am. (gov.). Home: 1030 W Lake Hamilton Dr Winter Haven FL 33880 Office: 250 2d St SW Winter Haven FL 33880

BAXTER, DENVER FORREST, assn. exec.; b. Cosby, Tenn., Sept. 23, 1918; s. Walter Carroll and Nora Esther (Valentine) B.; B.S. in Sci. and Math., Middle Tenn. State Coll., 1940; B.S. in Bus. Adminstrn. With honours in accounting, U. Fla., 1947; m. Ann Blount, Nov. 7, 1942; children—Anne Forrest, Denver Forrest. Tchr., Lawrence Co. (Tenn.) pub. schs., 1940-41; gen. staff Price Waterhouse & Co., C.P.A.'s, N.Y.C., 1947-52; chief accountant Lavoie Labs., Inc., Morganville, N.J., 1952-53; asst. treas. Melchoir, Armstrong, Dessau Co. Del., Inc., Ridgefield, N.J., 1953-55; with Courtaulds, Inc., N.Y.C., also Courtaulds (Ala.) Inc., Mobile, 1955- 59, asst. treas., 1957-59; controller Am. Mgmt. Assn., 1959—, v.p. treas., 1961—, v.p. finance, 1966—, also dir., chmn. retirement com., 1967—. Bd. dirs., treas. Haworth Community Chest; treas. President's Profl. Assn., Inc. (name changed to President's Assn., Inc.), Hamilton, N.Y., 1959—, also dir.; treas. Internat. Mgmt. Assn., Inc., N.Y.C., 1959—, also dir.; treas. Am. Found. Mgmt. Research, Inc., N.Y.C., 1959—, also trustee Bd. mgrs. N.J. Baptist Conv., 1962-68, mem. finance commn., also com. wills, 1962-68, vice chmn. finance com., 1966; chmn. bd. trustees Demarest (N. J.) Bapt. Ch., 1967-69, gen. chmn. new bldg. exec. com., 1961-67. Served to lt. comdr., A.C., USNR, 1941-45. Decorated D.F.C. Mem. C.P.A., N.Y. Am. Inst. C.P.A.'s, Phi Kappa Phi, Beta Gamma Sigma, Beta Alpha Psi. Republican. Clubs: Haworth Men's (gov., treas.), Haworth Golf. Home: 33 Owatonna St Haworth NJ 07304 Office: American Management Assn 135 W 50 St New York City NY 10020

BAXTER, DUNCAN MCCUNN, ret. steel co. exec.; b. Scotland, July 31, 1912; s. Thomas and Janet (McCunn) B.; student Detroit Inst. Tech., 1931-32, Walsh Inst., 1935-38; m. Ruth Reagin, Oct. 2, 1937; children—Dale Keith, Martha Ruth. With Detroit Steel Corp., 1933-71, v.p., 1951-71, gen. mgr., v.p., dir. Portsmouth div., 1964-67, v.p. spl. services, exec. offices, Detroit, 1967-71. Chmn. bd. trustees Ohio U. Mem. Am. Iron and Steel Inst., Am. Mgmt. Assn., Ohio C. of C. Clubs: Economic of Detroit, Rotary. Home: 1100 Noel Dr Portsmouth OH 45662

BAXTER, EDMUND, mgmt. cons.; b. Richmond, Ky., June 5, 1913; s. June Gaines and Harriet (Baldwin) B.; B.A., U. Louisville, 1939; Litt.D. (hon.), Gallaudet Coll., 1964; m. Margaret Kennedy Dewberry, Nov. 6, 1935; 1 dau., Margaret Ann (Mrs. Henry Alansin Gardner, III). Served as a reporter, editor small newspapers, 1933-35; asst. for pub. relations and asst. to state adminstr. Nat. Youth Adminstrn., Ky., 1936-39, asst. dir. student work program, nat. hdqrs., 1940, dep. adminstr., Ky., 1941, dir. property and procurement, nat. hdqrs., 1942; chief pub. interest br. War Assets Adminstrn., 1946-49; dir. surplus property utilization, FSA, 1950-51, dir. office material requirements, 1952-53; cons. on spl. instrns., representing Dept. Health, Edn. and Welfare in responsibilities connected with Howard U., Gallaudet Coll., Am. Printing House for Blind, Freedmens Hosp., St. Elizabeth's Hosp., 1953-56; regional dir. Dept. Health, Edn. and Welfare, for region III (Ky., Md., N.C., Va., W.Va., D.C., P.R. and Virgin Islands) Charlottesville, Va., 1956-66, dir. field coordination, Washington, 1966-68; now cattle breeder, Madison, Va.; also mgmt. counsel; cons. to Gov. Virgin Islands, 1968. Dir. Remote Console Information Corp., Washington. Bd. dirs. Gallaudet Coll. Served from ensign to lt. USNR, 1942-46; PTO; lt. comdr. Res. Recipient of Superior Service award Department of Health, Education, and Welfare, 1961. Mem. Virginia-Carolinas Charolais Assn. (bd. dirs.), Keys, Kappa Alpha. Ky. Colonel. Clubs: University (Washington); Farmington Country, Keswick Country (Charlottesville, Va.); Greene Hills Country (Standardsville, Va.). Home: Branchwater Farm Box 90-A Route 1 Madison VA 22727

BAXTER, FRANK CONDIE, educator; b. Newbold, N.J., May 4, 1896; s. Frank C. and Lilliam Douglas (Murdoch) B.; A.B., U. Pa., 1923, A.M., 1925; Ph.D., U. Cambridge, 1932; grad. study, U. Cal., 1929-30; Litt.D. (hon.), U. So. Cal., 1955, Ripon Coll., 1957, Elmira Coll., 1959, La Salle Coll., Phila., 1963; D.F.A., Cal. Coll. Medicine, 1956; m. Lydia Spencer Morris, May 28, 1927; children—Lydia Morris, Francis Condie. With (Phila.) Pa. Salt Mfg. Co., 1912-17; mus. asst. U. Pa., 1921, asst. instr. zoology, 1922-23, instr. English, 1923-27; part time instr. English, Swarthmore Coll., 1925-27, U. Cal., 1929-30; asst. prof. U. So. Cal., 1930-33, asso. prof., 1934-36, prof. English, 1937-61, prof. English emeritus, 1961—, Chairman univ. senate, 1947; asst. to Dr. Harold S. Colton, scientific work in Painted Desert area, summers, 1920, 21, 24. Recipient Peabody award, Sylvania, Ohio State U. awards; 7 Emmys from Acad. TV Arts and Sciences. Member Am. Assn. U. Profs., Phi Beta Kappa, Phi Kappa Phi, Beta Sigma Tau. Baptist. Author: Days in the Painted Desert (with Dr. Harold S. Colton), 1932. Maker original charts, models illustrating history printing, paper, history of alphabet, etc. Lectr. Pioneer Ednl. TV Programs; Shakespeare on TV; Now and Then; Harvest; The Written Word; The Bell System Science Series. Home: 775 Winthrop Rd San Marino CA 91108

BAXTER, J. F., savs. and loan assn. exec. Pres., mgr. Western Fed. Savs. and Loan Assn., Denver. Office: 700 17th St Denver CO 80202*

BAXTER, JAMES PHINNEY, 3d, educator; b. Portland, Me., Feb., 15, 1893; s. James Phinney, Jr., and Nelly Furbish (Carpenter) B.; A.B., William Coll., 1914, A.M., 1921; A.M., Harvard, 1923, Ph.D., 1926; LL.D., Harvard and Amherst, 1938, U. of Me. and Wesleyan U., 1939, Hobart Coll., 1942; Bowdoin College, 1944; Litt.D., Syracuse University, 1945, L.H.D., Case Institute of Technology, 1948, American International College, 1954; LL.D., Williams College, 1947, Kenyon College, 1949, Columbia Univ., 1954, Brown U., 1956, U. Rochester, 1960; D.Sc., Union Coll., 1949; m. Anne Holden Strang, June 21, 1919 (dec. May 1962); children—James Phinney IV, Arthur Brown, Stephen Bartow. With Indsl. Finance Corp., New York City, 1914- 15; instructor history, Colo. College, 1921-22; Harvard traveling fellow, 1924-25; instr. history, Harvard, 1925-27, asst. prof., 1927-31, asso. prof., 1931-36, prof., 1936-37, master of Adams House, 1931-37; president of Williams Coll.,1937-61, pres. emeritus, 1961—; educational adviser U.S. Military Academy; lecturer, Lowell Inst., Boston, 1931, Naval War Coll., since 1932, Cambridge U., 1936. Dir. research and analysis for Coordinator of Information, Washington, D.C., August 1941- June 1942; deputy director, Office of Strategic Services, June 1942-43; historian Office of Scientific Research and development, Washington, D.C., 1943-46. Pres. Assn. of American Colls., 1945. Trustee Williams Coll., 1934-37, World Peace Found., Phillips Acad.; member board of overseers Harvard University; dir. State Mutual Life Ins. Co. (Worcester, Mass.). Term trustee Mass. Inst. Tech., 1956-61; trustee Tchrs. Ins. and Annuity Assn., 1955-59. Presdl. Certificate of Merit. Fellow A.A.A.S., Council on Foreign Relations (Senior); mem. American Council Education (1st vice chmn. 1954-55), Am. Historical Association (executive committee, 1937-38), Am. Antiquarian Soc., Am. Soc. Internat. Law, Am. Polit. Science Assn., Council on Foreign Relations, Colonial Soc. of Mass., Mass. Hist. Soc., Soc. of Am. Historians (pres., 1945- 46), Gargoyle Soc., Phi Beta Kappa, Kappa Alpha. Republican. Episcopalian. Clubs: Harvard, Tavern (Boston, Mass.); Century, Williams (New York City, New York). Author of the Introduction of the Ironclad Warship, 1933 (translation, Naissance du Cuirassé, Paris, 1935); Scientists Against Time, 1946 (translation, Secrets de la Science Americaine, Paris, 1947). Winner 1947 Pulitzer prize in history. Contbr. to hist. and law jours. Home: Union Club 701 Park Av New York City, NY 10021. Office: 58 E 68th St New York City NY 10021

BAXTER, JAMES PHINNEY, 4th, banker; b. Colorado Springs, Colo., June 4, 1920; s. James Phinney 3d and Anna (Strang) B.; A.B. cum laude, Harvard, 1941; m. Cornelia Baker, May 24, 1941; 1 dau., Edith Prescott. With First Nat. Bank Chgo., 1941—, sr. v.p., 1969—, head trust dept., 1970—; dir. Am. Rubber & Plastics Corp., Rothschild Enterprises, Inc., Rothschild Properties. Mem. gov. bd. Passavant Meml. Hosp., Chgo.; bd. dirs. Chgo. Urban League; trustee Inst. Psychoanalysis, Chgo.; mem. adv. bd. Chgo. YMCA. Served to lt. USNR, 1942-45. Decorated Bronze Star. Mem. Corp. Fiduciaries Assn. Chgo. (exec. com., sec.-treas.), Corp. Fiduciaries Assn. Ill. (v.p.), Am., Ill. (pres. trust div.) bankers assns. Clubs: University, Commonwealth, Harvard, Bankers (Chgo.), Dunham Woods Riding (Wayne, Ill.). Home: Box 107 Route 4 St Charles IL 60174 Office: 1 First Nat Plaza Chicago IL 60670

BAXTER, JOHN LINCOLN, food processing exec.; b. Brunswick, Me., May 28, 1896; s. Hartley Cone and Mary (Lincoln) B.; A.B. cum laude, Bowdoin Coll., 1916, M.A. (hon.), 1961, LL.D. (hon.), 1970; m. Constance French, June 10, 1919 (dec. 1945); children—John L., Hartley Cone 2d; m. 2d, Beatrice Hennessey Dec. 1953 (dec. July 1968). Tchr., Bowdoin Coll., 1916; mem. firm H.C. Baxter & Brother, food processors, Brunswick, 1917—; pres. Snow Flake Canning Co., Brunswick, 1955—, Puritan Sales Corp, 1935—; v.p. Maine Canned Foods, Inc., Portland, Me., 1930—; dir. First Nat. Bank of Portland, Union Mutual Life Ins. Co., Rockland Rockport Lime Corp.; adv. council Liberty Mutual Life Ins. Co. Dir. New Eng. Council, 1924-25, sec., 1934-36, state chmn., 1936-40; chmn. Me. Joint Tax Conf., 1937; regional chmn. Com. Econ. Development, 1943; mem. Me. Development Commn., 1943-53; cons. canned foods Dept. Agr., 1944. Trustee Bowdoin Coll. Served as 2d lt. U.S. Army, 1918; mem. Nat. Def. Adv. Council, 1940-41; chief processed foods sect., govt. presiding officer canned foods adv. com. OPM, WPB, 1941-43. Mem. Nat. Assn. Frozen Food Packers (v.p. 1953, pres. 1954), Me. Canners Assn. (pres. 1924-25), Phi Beta Kappa, Delta Kappa Epsilon. Contbr. mag. articles. Home: Topsham ME 04086 Office: PO Box 69 Brunswick ME 04011

BAXTER, JOHN WALLACE, educator; b. Grover, Colo., Feb. 4, 1918; s. John Haskins and Edna (Cole) B.; B.S., U. Wyo., 1948; M.S., Purdue U., 1950, Ph.D., 1952; m. Elizabeth Jane Collins, Feb. 4, 1950; children—John Robert, Carol Elizabeth. Forage crops pathologist Ia. State U., 1952-56; prof. botany U. Wis.-Milw., 1956—. Served with USAAF, 1941-45. Mem. Mycol. Soc. Am., Am. Inst. Biol. Sci., Sigma Xi. Home: 7617 N Bell Rd Milwaukee WI 53217

BAXTER, L.C., hosp. adminstr.; b. Sherman, Tex., Mar. 22, 1917; s. Thomas Andrew and Ethel (Hartwig) B.; grad. Dallas Inst. Mortuary Sci., 1946; m. Caromae Reese, Apr. 10, 1937; children—Thomas Reese, L.C. Embalmer, funeral dir. Guardian Funeral Home, Ft. Worth, 1934-48; adminstr. Ft. Worth Osteopathic Hosp., 1948-53, Okla. Osteopathic Hosp., Tulsa, 1953—. Med. adv. com. Dept. Pub. Welfare, Okla., vice chmn., 1964—; adv. council for nursing homes, Okla. Dept. Health; mem. Tulsa Hosp. Council, pres., 1946-66; mem. exec. com., trustee Okla. Blue Cross-Blue Shield; mem. Okla. Regional Med. Program's Adv. Group Com. on Hosps. and Med. Services; mem. health facilities adv. council. Okla. State Dept. Health; treas. Tulsa area Health and Hosp. Planning Council. Served with AUS, World War II. Mem. Okla. Hosp. Assn. (trustee 1967—), Am. Osteopathic Hosp. Assn. (bd. trustees 1955—, pres. 1963-64, merit award), Am. Coll. Osteopathic Hosp. Adminstrn., C. of C., Osteo. Hosp. Founders Assn. (treas.). Mem. Christian Ch. Clubs: Tulsa, University, Petroleum. Home: 1722 S Carson Tulsa OK 74119 Office: 9th and Jackson Sts Tulsa OK 74127

BAXTER, LEONARD LADELL, utilities exec.; b. Ashland, Tex., June 26, 1902; s. William Wilson and Lisa (Peteet) B.; student Coll. of Marshall, 1918-20, U. Tex., 1922-24; m. Laura Hill, June 9, 1926; 1 dau., Laura (Mrs. W.J. Smith). Dist. mgr. ark. Western Gas Co., Fayetteville, 1932-39, later v.p., pres., now chmn.; dir. McIlroy Bank, Arkla Air Conditioning Corp., First Ark. Devel. Finance Corp. Pres. Fayetteville Indsl. Found. Bd. dirs. Cotton Bowl Athletic Assn. Mem. Am. (dir.), So. gas assns., Mid-Continent Oil and Gas Assn. (exec com. La.-Ark. div. 1964), Ark. C. of C., Acacia, Beta Gamma Sigma. Methodist. Mason. Rotarian. Home: 318 Ila St Fayetteville AR 72701 Office: PO Box 4275 Fayetteville AR 72701 2FA

BAXTER, LEONE, (Leone Baxter Whitaker), pub. relations exec.; b. Kelso, Wash., Nov. 20, 1906; d. Leon and Grace P. (Hayes) Smith; student Stanford, 1928; m. Alexander D. Baxter, June 16, 1927 (dec. 1931); m. 2d, Clem S. Whitaker, Apr. 15, 1938 (dec. 1961); stepchildren—Clem Sherman, Milton O., Patricia (Mrs. Joseph Morse), Burdette (dec.). Co-founder with Clement Whitaker, 1930, since v.p. Campaigns, Inc., profl. mgmt. ballot issues and candidates, San Francisco; v.p. Whitaker & Baxter pub. relations counselors, San Francisco, 1930—; pres. Whitaker & Baxter, Internat.; editor-pub. Cal. Feature Service, San Francisco, 1936—; partner Whitaker & Baxter, advt., San Francisco, 1933—; mng. editor San Francisco Neighborhood Newspapers, 1940-45. Mgr. Earl Warren's campaign for gov. Cal., 1942, nat. campaign against compulsory health ins. for A.M.A., 1942-52, campaign of Nat. Profl. Com. for Eisenhower and Nixon, 1952, Goodwin J. Knight's campaign for gov. Cal., 1954; polit. adviser Gov. Goodwin Knight, 1946—; gen. mgr. Cal. host com. to Republican Nat. Conv., 1956. Sec.-mgr. No. Cal. Mining Assn., 1928-30, Redding (Cal.) C. of C., 1928-30; mgr. Cal. campaign to create Central Valley Water Project, 1933. Mem. pub. relations com. U.S. People-to-People Program; mem. U.S. com. World Med. Assn. Mem. internat. adv. bd. Dooley Found.; trustee Presbyn. Med. Center, San Francisco; trustee Merola Fund Pub. Relations Soc. Am. (nat. chmn. com. profl. standards), Am. Newspaper Pubs. Assn., Nat. Council Women U.S., Internat. Council Women, Nat. Editorial Assn., San Francisco Opera Guild, DeYoung Mus. Soc., San Francisco Mus. Art Soc. Club: Lake Shore (Chgo.). Author articles in field. Home: Canary canyon 22 S Ridgewood Rd Kentfield CA 94904 Office: The Fairmount Nob Hill San Francisco CA 94108

BAXTER, MORRIS RICHARD, gas co. exec.; b. Hobbs, N.M., May 21, 1936; s. Russel and Ruby (Loftis) B.; student Navarro Jr. Coll., 1953-55; B.B.A., So. Meth. U., 1961, M.B.A., 1966; m. Frances Ann Sullivan, Jan. 1, 1958; children—Julie Annette, Brett Richard. Various positions So. Union Gas Co., Dallas, 1957-61, budget accountant, 1962—, gen. ledger supr., 1962-64, dir. budgets and statistics, 1964-67, controller, 1967—; gen. ledger accountant Oil Well Div., U.S. Steel, Dallas, 1961-62; adj. prof. accounting Braniff Grad. Sch. Mgmt., U. Dallas, 1969—. Mem. Am. Inst. C.P.A.'s, Tex. Soc. C.P.A.'s, Am., So. gas assns. Home: 1861 Meadow Valley Lane Dallas TX 75232 Office: Fidelity Union Tower Dallas TX 75201

BAXTER, NEAL EDWARD, physician; b. Bluffton, Ind., Sept. 13, 1908; s. Roy Earl and Josephine (Yaeger) B.; A.B. in Chemistry (Balfour Outstanding Sr. award), 1932, M.D., 1935; m. Patricia Anne Casey; children—Patsy, Beth,Sean, Kathy, Neal Edward. Intern, City Hosp., Indpls., 1935-36; gen. practice, Bloomington, Ind., 1936-54, specializing internal and aerospace medicine, 1954—; postgrad. work in field at Ind. U., Ford Hosp., Detroit, Harvard, also Aerospace Research Center, Brooks Field, San Antonio; mem. staff Bloomington Hosp., 1936—; coroner Monroe County, 1955-64; med. dir. Westinghouse Elec. Co., Bloomington, 1957—. Cons., mem. adv. bd. Aerospace Research Center in Aerospace Medicine, Ind. U., 1964-68; chmn. Gov. Ind. Commn. Handicapped, 1967-68, Gov. Ind. Long Range Planning Com. Mental Health, 1964-68; bd. dirs. Found. for Ind. U. Sch. Bus., 1969—. Served to comdr., M.C., USNR, 1942- 46; PTO. Recipient award Aerospace Medical Assn., 1965. Fellow Aerospace Med. assn. (pres. 1965-66), mem. A.M.A. (chmn. com. aerospace medicine 1967-69, mem. council on occupational health 1969—), Flying Physicians Assn. (a founder), Am. Acad. Gen. Practice, Am. Diabetic Assn. Am., Ind., Monroe County (chmn.) heart assns., Pub. Health Nursing Assn. (past pres.), Ind. Soc. Chgo., Beta Theta Pi, Nu Sigma Nu. Mason (32, Shriner). Clubs: Columbia (Indpls.); Sycamore of the Wabash, Bloomington Country (past pres.). Author articles in field. Home: 515 Hawthorne Lane Bloomington IN 47401 Office: 306 E Kirkwood Av Bloomington IN 47401

BAXTER, RALPH FELIX, indsl. co. exec.; b. Hamburg, Germany, Aug. 31, 1925; s. Felix and Irmy (Münden) B.; came to U.S., 1941, naturalized, 1944; student Rensselaer Polytech. Inst., 1943-44, U. Cal. at Los Angeles, 1946-48; B.S. in Mech. Engring., U. Cal. at Berkeley, 1949; m. Janice Phillips, 1960; children—David P., Eric F., Robert. Asso. General Air Conditioning Corp., 1949-50; group project mgr. Rheem Mfg. Co., 1950-56; asst. to pres., dir. mfg. Revell, Inc., 1956-59; with Hunt Foods & Industries, Inc., 1959-67, dir. corp. planning. gen. mgr. operations, v.p. operations, 1959-64, vice president corporate planning and analysis, 1964-67; sr. v.p. Avery Products corp., 1967—; instructor with division extension Univ. Cal. at Los Angeles, 1959-60. Served with AUS, 1943-46. Mem. Am. Soc. M.E. (asso. chmn. So. Cal. sect.), Inst. Mgmt. Scis. (national chairman college on planning 1966-68), Operations Research Soc. Am., Am. Arbitration Assn., Nat. Panel Arbitrators, Am. Ordnance Assn. (Walsh Meml. award 1953). Home; 1263 N Citrus Dr La Habra CA 90631 Office: 415 Huntington Dr San Marino CA 91108

BAXTER, RAYMOND CARLOS, chem. co. exec.; b. Granville, Pa., Sept. 21, 1922; s. Myron I. and Dorothy L. (Gilliland) B.; B.S. in Chem. Engring., Cornell U., 1944; m. Martha A. Edson, June 26, 1944; children—Frederick E., Bruce A., Susan L., Andrew T. Chem. engr. Standard Oil Co., Whiting, Ind., 1944-46; project engr. to chief engr. Solvay div. Allied Chem., Syracuse, N.Y., 1941-59, asst. dir. operations, 1959-61, v.p. engr. and constrn. nat. aniline div., 1961-63, v.p. mfg., 1963-66; asst. to exec. v.p. Allied Chem. Corp., 1966-67, v.p. tech. plastics div., 1967, exec. v.p., 1967- 68, pres. plastics div., 1968—. Mem. Cornell Soc. Engrs. (dir.), Am. Inst. Chem. Engrs., Tau Beta Phi. Home: 9 Keats Rd Short Hills NJ 07078 Office: PO 2 Box 365 R Morristown NJ 07960

BAXTER, REGINALD ROBERT, plant food co. exec.; b. Cushman, Ark., May 14, 1925; s. Remmel M. and Mary (Wilson) B.; B.S. in Chem. Engring., U. Ark., 1948; M.S., Ia. State U., 1949; m. Jeanne Estes, Nov. 14, 1953; 1 son, Sean Lee. Plant mgr. Anioniaco del Caribe, Columbia, S.A., 1961-63; project mgr. Esso Research and Engring Co., 1963-65; gen. mgr. First Nitrogen Corp., Donaldsville, La., 1965-67; with CF Industries, Inc., and predecessor, Chgo., 1967—, exec. v.p., 1969-71, pres., 1971—; pres. CF Chems., Inc., Bartow, Fla., First Nitrogen Corp.; v.p. CF Chems., Ltd., Ont., Can.; dir. Central Can. Potash Co. Ltd. Bd. dirs. Fertilizer Inst. Served with AUS, 1944-46. Mem. Am. Inst. Chem. Engring., Am. Mgmt. Assn. Methodist. Mason. Club: Union League (Chgo.). Home: 254 Windy Hill Dr Barrington Hills IL 60010 Office: 100 S Wacker Dr Chicago IL 60606

BAXTER, RICHARD REEVE, educator; b. N.Y.C., Feb. 14, 1921; s. Charles Minturn and Gladys (Van Deventer) B.; A.B., Brown U., 1942; LL.B., Harvard, 1948; diploma internat. law, Cambridge (Eng.) U., 1951; LL.M., Georgetown U., 1952; m. Harriet Nell Latson, May 29, 1943; children—Alison Lawrence, Prudence Oliver. Admitted to Mass. bar, 1948; atty. Office Gen. Counsel, Office Sec. Def., 1954; research asso. Harvard Law Sch., 1954-55, mem. faculty, 1955—, prof. law, 1959—; head of South House, Radcliffe Coll., 1968-70; vis. prof. Cambridge (Eng.) U., 1966-67. Cons. to govt., 1955—; counselor on internat. law Office Legal Adviser, U.S. Dept. State, Washington, 1971-72; mem. adv. com. Internat. Law Reports, 1962—; adv. com. Inst. Air and Space Law, McGill U., 1965—. Mem. Permanent Ct. Arbitration, The Hague, 1968—; mem. Mass. Commn. on Ocean Mgmt., 1968-71, Commn. on Marine Boundaries and Resources, 1969-71; bd. advisers law and population programme Fletcher Sch. Law and Diplomacy, 1971—. Served to maj. AUS, 1942-46, U.S. Army, 1947-54. Decorated Bronze Star medal, also Legion of Merit; recipient hon. mention Harvard Univ. Press Faculty prize, 1964. Mem. Am. Law Inst., Am. Bar Assn., Am. (v.p. 1968-70, mem. exec. council), Egyptian, Indian (hon.). socs. internat. law, Internat. Law Assn. (v.p. Am. br. 1963—), Brit. Inst. Internat. and Comparative Law, Am. Acad. Arts and Scis., Phi Beta Kappa. Editor: Documents on the St. Lawrence Seaway, 1960; The Law of International Waterways, 1964; (with Doris Carroll) The Panama Canal, 1965; (with Louis B. Sohn) Convention on the International Responsibility of States for Injuries to Aliens, 1961. Editor-in-chief Am. Jour. Internat. Law, 1970—. Home: 25 Brewster St Cambridge MA 02138

BAXTER, ROBERT DONALD, banker; b. Syracuse, N.Y., Aug. 15, 1927; s. Donald Dewitt and Matilda (Steier) B.; student Syracuse U., 1945-55, Stonier Grad. Sch. Banking, Rutgers, 1960, Nat. Ass. Mut. Savs. Banks Mgmt. Devel. Program, 1970; m. Dolores Marie LaTreillé, Sept. 12, 1953; children—Steven, Edward, Donald, Douglas. Teller, Onondaga Savs. Bank, Syracuse, 1944-54, head bookkeeper, 1954-61, asst. comptroller, 1961-66, comptroller, 1966—. Mem. Am. Inst. Banking (past pres. Syracuse chpt.), Nat. Assn. Accountants, Financial Execs. Inst. Republican. Roman Catholic. Home: 239 Homecroft Rd Syracuse NY 13206 Office: 101 S Salina St Syracuse NY 13202

BAXTER, ROBERT HAMPTON, III, ins. exec.; b. Glasspost, Pa., Mar. 27, 1931; s. Robert Hampton, Jr. and Charlotte (Biddlestone) B.; student Carnegie Inst. Tech., 1949-50; A.B., U.S.C., 1954, LL.B., 1958; m. Barbara Miller, Aug. 4, 1956. Trust officer Citizens & So. Nat. Bank, Charleston, S.C., 1958-60, First Citizens Bank & Trust Co., Charlotte, N.C., 1960-68; with Participating Annuity Life Ins. Co., McLean, Va., 1968-70, Aetna Life & Casualty Co., Atlanta, Ga., 1971—; admitted to S.C. bar, 1959. Served to lt. (j.g.) USNR, 1954-57; comdr. USNR. Mem. Am. Bar Assn., N.C. Bankers Assn. (pres. trust div. 1966-67), Navy League U.S. (pres. Charlotte 1966-67), Phi Delta Phi. Republican. Presbyn. Home: 4526 Club Valley Dr NE Atlanta GA 30319 Office: Suite 1938 Fulton Nat Bank Bldg Atlanta GA 30303

BAXTER, ROBERT REGAN, hotel exec.; b. Collingston, Utah, Apr. 11, 1920; s. Valton B. and Cecelia (Regan) B.; student Golden Gate Coll., 1939-42; B.S. U. Santa Clara, 1952, grad. Advanced Mgmt. Program, 1954; m. Lorraine C. Bidia, Aug. 11, 1946; children—Laurel E., Elizabeth. Controller, asst. sec. Matson Lines, Hawaii, 1953-60, budget dir., San Francisco, 1961-62; div. mgr. Sheraton Hotels,

Omaha, 1963—; v.p., gen. mgr. Sheraton-Fontenelle, Omaha, 1965—. Mem. exec. com. Omaha Sister City Assn., 1964—. Bd. dirs. Omaha Urban League, 1965—, Neb. Centennial Commn., 1964—, Keep Omaha Beautiful, 1965—. C.P.A., Cal. Mem. Am. Inst. C.P.A.'s, Am. Hotel and Motel Assn. (bd. dirs., exec. com.), Northwestern Hotel and Motel Assn. (pres.), Neb. Hotel Assn. (bd. dirs.). Address: Sheraton-Fontenelle Hotel 1806 Douglas St Omaha NB 68102

BAXTER, SAMUEL NEWMAN, Jr., clergyman; b. Phila., Aug. 14, 1913; s. Samuel Newman and Lucy A. (Bolton) B.; B.A., Pa. State U., 1935; S.T.B., Gen. Theol. Sem., 1939, S.T.D., 1970; m. Catharine D. Fagan, June 8, 1949; children—C. Dallas Dixon, Lucy A. Bolton. Ordained deacon P.E. Ch., 1939, priest, 1940; pastor in N.C., 1939-41, Pa., 1941-48; archdeacon Diocese Western N.Y., 1948-54; rector Ch. of Good Shephard, Austin, Tex., 1954—. Former sec. Ho. of Deputies and Gen. Conv. P.E. Church; secretary of Diocese of Texas, 1965—. Member Theta Chi. Rotarian. Home: 1405 Kent Lane Austin TX 78703 Office: Church of Good Shepherd Box 5176 Austin TX 78703

BAXTER, SAMUEL SERSON, city ofcl.; b. Phila., Feb. 6, 1905; s. Matthew and Elizabeth (Serson) B.; student Drexel Inst. Tech. Evening Coll., 1921-25, D.Eng. (hon.), Drexel Inst. Tech., 1966; m. Norma Ruth Winter, Oct. 8, 1932; children— Richard A., Linda C. Various engrng. positions Bur. Engrng., Phila., 1923-39, asst. chief engr., chief engr., 1946-52; asst. dir. Pub. Works, Phila., 1939-42; commr., chief engr. Water Dept., Phila., 1952—; chmn. bd. East Girard Savs. Assn., Phila., 1962—. Vice pres. Phila. council Boy Scouts Am., 1963-68, pres., 1968-69. Trustee Drexel U., 1971. Served to maj., C.E., AUS, 1942-46. Named Engr. of Year, Phila. chpt. Pa. Soc. Profl. Engrs., 1959. Registered profl. engr., Pa. Fellow Am. Soc. C.E. (dir. 1959-62, pres. 1971); mem. Am. Pub. Works Assn. (pres. 1947; chmn. research found. 1965—), Am. Water Works Assn. (dir. 1959-62, pres. 1965-66), Engrs. Club Phila. (pres. 1963), Nat. Acad. Engring., Drexel U. Alumni Assn. (pres. 1969—). Methodist. Home: 14035 Kelvin Av Philadelphia PA 19116 Office: Municipal Service Bldg Philadelphia PA 19107

BAXTER, STEPHEN BARTOW, educator; b. Boston, Mar. 8, 1929; s. James Phinney 3d and Anne (Strang) B.; B.A., Harvard, 1950; Ph.D., Cambridge (Eng.) U., 1955; m. Ann Sweeney, Aug. 22, 1953; children—Clare, Persis, James Phinney 5th, Nicholas Holden, Stephen Padraic, Michael Philip. Instr., Dartmouth, 1954-57; vis. asst. prof. U. Mo., 1957-58; mem. faculty U. N.C., 1958—, prof. history, 1966—, Alumni Distinguished prof., 1968-69. Charles Henry Fiske III scholar Trinity Coll., Cambridge U., 1950-51; Guggenheim fellow, 1959-60. Fellow Royal Hist. Soc.; mem. Am., So. hist. assns., Conf. British Studies, Mediaeval Acad. Am. Democrat. Author: The Development of the Treasury, 1660-1702, 1957; William III, 1966; also articles. Editor: Basic Documents of English History, 1968. Home: 608 Morgan Creek Rd Chapel Hill, NC 27514.

BAXTER, WILLIAM FRANCIS, educator; b. N.Y.C., July 13, 1929; s. William Francis and Ruth (Cummings) B.; B.A., Stanford, 1951, J.D., 1956; m. Barbara Metzger, Nov. 11, 1951; children—William Francis III, Marcia, Stuart. Asst. prof. Stanford Sch. Law, 1956-59, asso. prof. 1959-64, prof., 1964—; admitted to Cal. bar, 1956; practice in Washington, 1958-60; asso. Covington & Burling, 1958-60; cons. FAA, 1967-68, Brookings Instn., 1968—, Fed. Res. Bd., 1969—. Mem. White House Task Force on Communications Policy, 1968-69, White House Task Force on Antitrust Policy, 1969. Served with USNR, 1951-54. Mem. Phi Beta Kappa. Contbr. articles profl. jours. Home: 749 Mayfield Av Stanford CA 94305

BAXTER, WILLIAM MACNEIL, clergyman; b. Halifax, N.S., Can., Oct. 5, 1923; s. William John and Mary Ellen (MacNeil) B.; B.A., Amherst Coll., 1946; M.Div., Va. Theol. Sem., 1951; m. Jean Marlin Taylor, Oct. 25, 1946; children—Nancy Graeme, Gary MacNeil, Rebecca Roberts, Anne Marlin. Advt. salesman Reuben H. Donnelley, Inc., 1947-49; ordained to ministry Episcopal Ch., 1951; curate, asst. minister, St. Louis, 1951-54; rector, Washington, 1954-66; dir. career information service, also dir. pub. affairs Peace Corps, 1966-68; pres. Baxter Assos., cons. edn. and tng., 1969-70; v.p. Marriage and Family Inst., counselling and ednl. center, Washington, 1971—; spl. cons. to State Dept. on refugee problems in Vietnam; vis. lectr. pastoral theology Va. Theol. Sem., 1960-66; Luccock lectr. Yale Div. Sch., 1965; mem. faculty field tng. coloquium Chgo. Div. Sch., 1960-64. P.E. del. Nat. Conf. Radiation and Social Ethics, 1963; pres. Diocese of Washington Clergy, 1960-62; candidate for suffragen bishop, Washington, 1963. Mem. planning com. White House Conf. to secure These Rights, 1964. Bd. dirs. Capital Hill Community Council, Friendship Settlement House, Washington Area Council on Alcoholism, Neighborhood Service Com., Health and Welfare Council. Served with Merchant Marine, 1946. Mem. Chi Psi. Democrat. Club: University (Washington). Contbr. articles. Home: 3915 Military Rd NW Washington DC 20015 Office: 500 Massachusetts Av NW Washington DC 20005

BAY, ALFRED PAUL, physician, hosp. supt.; b. Chgo., Feb. 2, 1910; s. Jens Christian and Dora (Detjen) B.; B.S., U. Ill., 1932, M.D., 1934; m. Gerda Constance Pearson, July 2, 1935; children—John, Dorothy. Intern Ill. Research and Ednl. Hosp., 1934-35; resident Chgo. State Hosp., 1935-36; practice medicine, specializing in psychiatry, Chgo., 1936-40, Alton, Ill., 1940- 47, Manteno, Ill., 1947-54, Topeka, 1954—; physician Chgo. State Hosp., 1935-42; supt. Alton State Hosp., 1942-47, Manteno State Hosp., 1947-53, Topeka State Hosp., 1954-70, Jacksonville (Ill.) State Hosp., 1970—; cons. Nat. Insts. Mental Health, USPHS, VA Hosp., Topeka; cons. in psychiat. hosp. architecture. Mem. Mid-Continent Psychiat. Soc., Am. Psychiat. Assn., Golden Belt, Kan. psychiat. socs., Central Neuropsychiat. Assn., A.A.A.S., Chgo. Inst. Medicine, Group Advancement Psychiatry. Author: (with others) Therapy by Design, 1965. Contbr. articles profl. jours. Address: Caucus Hill Route 8 Topeka KS 66604

BAY, EMMET BLACKBURN, physician; b. Aurora, Ill., Feb. 20, 1901; s. Emmet L. and Martha (McQuade) B.; B.S., U. Chgo.,1920; M.D., Rush Med. Coll., 1923; m. Margaret Seymour, Oct. 23, 1925; children—Margaret (Mrs. Richard J. Dinning), Martha (Mrs. John H. Mathis). Intern, Presbyn. Hosp., Chgo., 1922-23, resident in medicine, 1923-25; pvt. practice medicine, Chgo., 1925-27; prof. medicine U. Chgo., 1934-70, prof. emeritus, 1970—, dean Rush Med. Coll., 1936-39. Mem. com. on med. research Nat. Def. Research Council, 1943-46. Mem. Assn. Am. Physicians, Am., Chgo. (v.p. 1948-58) heart assns., Central Soc. Clin. Research. Club: Central Interurban. Editor; Modern Concepts of Cardiovascular Disease, 1949-51. Med. adviser for Ency. Brit., 1951—. Home: 1321 E 56th St Chicago IL 60637 Office: 950 E 59th St Chicago IL 60637

BAY, HOWARD, stage and film designer; b. Centralia, Wash., May 3, 1912; s. William D. and Bertha A. (Henkins) B.; student U. Wash., 1928, U. Colo., 1929, Marshall Coll., 1929-30, Carnegie Inst. Tech., 1930-31, Westminster Coll., 1931-32, Chappell Sch. of Art, Denver, 1928-29; study in Europe, 1939; m. Ruth Jonas, Nov. 23, 1932; children—Ellen, Timothy. Designed Food Pavillion, St. Louis Mid-Am. Jubilee, 1956; designer settings for many stage shows, including The Wall, Pal Joey, Toys in the Attic, Milk and Honey, The Music Man, Romanoff & Juliet, The Night of the Auk; Red Rose for Me; The Desperate Hours; Sand Hog; Carmen Jones; Show Boat; One Touch of Venus; The Children's Hour; The Shrike; The Little Foxes; One Third of a Nation; Interlock; Regina; also designer for TV shows; staged and designed As the Girls Go, 1948; puppets and settings for Pete Roleum, 1939; resident designer Bucks Co. Playhouse, 1941; designer-dir. to Universal-Internat. Pictures, 1946-48; designer My Mother, My Father and Me, 1963; (opera) Natalia Petrovna, 1964; Man of La Mancha, Chu Chem for Broadway; art dir. film Balanchine's Midsummer Night's Dream; art dir. television series Mr. Broadway, 1964. Vis. instr. Purdue U., 1962; instr. Circle-in-the-Square Theatre Sch., 1962- 63; guest designer, dir., instr. Ohio U., 1964; designer setting and lighting for prodn. Fire: Andrew W. Mellon guest dir. Carnegie-Mellon U., 1963; dir. theatre, prof. theatre arts Brandeis U., 1965—, also chmn. theatre arts dept.; vis. prof. Yale, 1966—. Recipient Guggenheim fellowship, 1940-41; cited for year's best setting by Donaldson Awards for best designs for musicals, N.Y. stage, 1943-44, 44-45 seasons; Antoinete Perry award for best setting, 1960, 66. Mem. United Scenic Artists Am. (pres.), Nat. Soc. Interior Designers (nat. bd. mem.). Author U.S. Navy Handbook, Navy on Stage, 1944. Home: 236 Marlborough St Boston MA 02116

BAYER, BRUCE MARTIN, engrng. educator; b. Nashville, Sept. 20, 1912; s. David Martin and Lilliam (Scott) B.; B.E. in Mech. Engrng., Vanderbilt U., 1935, M.S. in Physics, 1952; m. Nancy Tucker, Dec. 29, 1936; children—Carolyn Shadwell, William Tucker. With IBM Corp., 1935-46, project engr., plant engrng., 1939-46; mem. faculty Vanderbilt U., 1946—, prof. mech. engrng., 1956—, chmn. dept., 1964—. Mem. Am. Soc. Engrng. Edn., Am. Soc. Heating, Refrigeration and Airconditioning Engrs., Am. Soc. M.E., Tau Beta Pi, Omicron Delta Kappa. Methodist. Home: 6957 Highland Park Dr Nashville TN 37205

BAYER, HERBERT, artist, architect, designer; b. Haag, Austria, Apr. 5, 1900; s. Maximillian and Rosa (Shimmer) B.; studied design Schmidthammer, Linz, Austria, 1919, Emanuel Margold, Darmstadt, Germany, 1920, Bauhaus, Weimar, 1921-23, wall-painting with Kandinsky, 1921. Came to U.S., 1938, naturalized, 1943. Tchr. advt., layout, typography Bauhaus, Dessau, 1925-28; advt., typography, painting, photography, exhbn. planning, dir. Dorland Studio, Berlin, 1928-38; chmn. dept. design Container Corp. Am., 1956-65; cons. Atlantic Richfield Co., 1965- -; as artist, represented in museums throughout U.S., Europe; one- man exhbns. in Berlin, Paris, London, Munich, Milan, Salzburg, Los Angeles, Cleve., N.Y.C., Chgo., San Francisco; retrospective exhibit 33 years of Herbert Bayer's work in Nürnberg, Munich, Zürich, Amsterdam, Brussels, Berlin; designed articulated wall constrn. for 1968 Olympics, Mexico City; archtl. works include bldgs. of Aspen (Colo.) Inst. for Humanistic Studies, indsl. bldgs. for Container Corp. Am.; has done fundamental work in modern typography and new alphabets; designed many posters, exhbn. installations including Bauhaus Exhibit, Mus. Modern Art, 1938, traveling shows for coordinator Inter-Am. Affairs, 1942, traveling Bauhaus Exhbn., Stuttgart, London, Amsterdam, Paris, Chgo., Toronto, Pasadena, Tokyo, 1968-71. Edited and designed World Geo-Graphic Atlas, 1953; Herbert Bayer Book of Drawings, 1961; portifolio "bayer", 1965; suite of lithographs, 8 monochromes, 1965; portfolio of 6 silk screens, 1968. Books of his work: The Way Beyond Art, The Work of Herbert Bayer, 1947; Herbert Bayer-Visual Communication, Architecture, Painting, 1967. Address: Box B Aspen CO 81611

BAYER, KENNETH HOWARD, army officer; b. N.Y. C., Apr. 16, 1918; s. Charles H. and Emily M. (Fiechtelman) B.; B.S., U. Ala., 1940; M.S., U. Pa., 1949; postgrad. Armed Forces Staff Coll., 1958, Nat. War Coll., 1963; m. Meryl L. Tatje, Feb. 2, 1941; 1 dau., Kimberley H. Commd. 2d lt. U.S. Army, 1940, advanced through grades to maj. gen., 1966; mil. operations staff officer, amphibious groups, Saipan, Philippines, Iwo Jima, Okinawa in World War II; asst. dir. gunnery dept. Antiaircraft and Guided Missile Sch., Ft. Bliss, Tex., 1949-52; staff officer, Europe, 1952-54; comdr. officer 60th Antiaircraft Arty. Bn., Eng., 1954-55; chief weapons system sect. Antiaircraft and Guided Missile Sch., Ft. Bliss, 1955-56; dep. chief staff operations Air Def. Center, Ft. Bliss, 1956-58; office chief research and devel. Dept. Army, Washington, 1958-60; asst. exec. to Sec. Army, 1960-62; asst. div. comdr. 7th Div., Korea, 1963-64; comdg. gen. III Corps. Arty., Ft. Chaffee, Ark., 1964; dep. dir., research and devel. U.S. Army Materiel Command, Washington, 1964-66; dir. research and devel. M.C., 1966, dir. devel., 1966-67; comdg. gen. 32d Army Air Def. Command, Europe, 1967—. Decorated D.S.M., Bronze Star medal, Army Commendation medal with two clusters, Navy Commendation medal with pendant (U.S.); Order of Orange Nassau (Netherlands). Mem. Tau Beta Pi, Theta Tau. Home: New York City NY 10001 Office: c/o Adj Gen Dept Army Washington DC 20310

BAYER, MERWIN, specialty store exec. With Arnold Constable Corp., N.Y.C., 1933—, formerly v.p. and gen. mdse. mgr., now pres., chief exec. officer. Address: 543 Fifth Av New York City NY 10016

BAYER, MILDRED V.N. BRANT, univ. trustee; b. East Orange, N.J., Oct. 10, 1903; d. Robert R. and Luella R. (Van Ness) Brant; student Centenary Jr. Coll., Hackettstown, N.J., 1922, Nat. Park Sem., Forest Glen, Md., 1922-24, U. Madrid (Spain), 1957; m. John H. Bayer, May 9, 1927; 1 son, Ross Van Ness. With Nat. Recreation Assn.,1925; dir. Spring Lake (N.J.) Community House, 1925-28; dist. v.p. N.J. Fedn. Women's Clubs, 1947-50, state v.p., 1950- 53, state chmn. civil def., 1953-54; with Ednl. Testing Service, Princeton, N.J., 1949—, Coll.Scholarship Service, Princeton, 1959—. Trustee Spring Lake Pub. Library, 1934-46, Rutgers U., 1957—, also Columbus Boys Choir, Princeton, N.J.; chairman of Coll. Nursing Newark, Douglass Coll.; com. Rutgers U. Library. Republican. Presbyn. Clubs: Town Hall (N.Y.C.); Nassau, Present Day (president) (Princeton). Home: 2 Pardoe Rd Princeton NJ 08540 Office: Ednl Testing Service 20 Nassau St Princeton NJ 08540

BAYERSCHMIDT, CARL FRANK, educator; b. Providence, Feb. 18, 1905; s. Edward and Elsie (Korsmier) B.; A.B., Brown U., 1926; M.A., Columbia, 1928, Ph.D., 1934; student U. Frankfurt, Germany, 1929-30, U. Hamburg, 1930-31; m. Dorothy J. Gutgsell, June 17, 1935; children—Carol Dorothy, Janet Virginia. Instr. German Rutgers U., 1934-37, asst. prof., 1937-40; asst. prof. Germanic philology U. Chgo., 1940-41; asst. prof. Germanic philology Columbia, 1941-46, asso. prof., 1946-50, prof., 1950-71, exec. chmn. dept. Germanics, 1948-61, Villard prof. emeritus Germanic philology, 1971—; chmn. com. on publs. Am.-Scandinavian Found., 1961- -. Decorated knight Order of Falcon (Iceland); Royal Order of North Star 1st class (Sweden). Mem. Modern Lang. Assn. Am., Medieval Acad. Am., Am. Assn. Tchrs. German, Germanistic Soc. Am. (pres.). Baptist. Author: A Middle Low German Book of Kings, 1934; The Njal's Saga (translated from Old Icelandic), 1955. Co-editor: Scandinavian Studies, 1965; Sigrid Undset, 1970. Home: 14 Franklin Av Yonkers NY 10705 Office: Columbia U New York City NY 10027

BAYH, BIRCH EVANS, Jr., U.S. senator; b. Terre Haute, Ind., Jan. 22, 1928; s. Birch Evans and Leah (Hollingsworth) B.; B.S., Purdue U., 1951; J.D., Ind. U., 1960; student Ind. State U., 1953-60; m. Marvella Hern, Aug. 24, 1952; 1 son, Evan. Engaged in farming, Terre Haute, 1952-57; admitted to Ind. bar, 1961; mem. Ind. Ho. of Reps. from Vigo County, 1954-62, minority leader, 1957-58, 61-62, speaker, 1959-60; U.S. senator from Ind., 1962—, chmn. senate subcom. constl. amendments, senate subcom. to investigate juvenile delinquency. Named Outstanding Young Man in Ind., Ind. Jr. C. of C., 1959; one of 10 outstanding Reps. in Ind. Gen. Assembly, Ind. Newspaper Men and Women Vets., 1961. Democrat. Office: Senate Office Bldg Washington DC 20510

BAYLEN, JOSEPH OSCAR, educator; b. Chgo., Feb. 12, 1920; s. Leo and Mary (Lakin) B.; A.A., Wright Coll., 1939; B.E., No. Ill. U., 1941; M.A., Emory U., 1947; Ph.D., U. N.M., 1949; m. Martha Louis Pharr, Mar. 27, 1943; 1 son, James Leo. Instr. history U. N.M., 1948-49; asst. prof. history N.M. Highlands U., Las Vegas, 1950-52, asso. prof., 1952-54; prof. history, chmn. div. social sci. Delta State Tchrs. Coll., 1954-57; prof. history Miss. State U., 1957-61; prof. history U. Miss., 1961-66, chmn., 1963-66; Regents' prof., chmn. dept. history Ga. State U., 1966—; vis. asst. prof. U. Md. Overseas Program. Europe, 1952-53; vis. asso. prof. Agnes Scott Coll., 1953; vis. prof. summers, Emory U., 1952, U. Ala., 1960, Georgetown U., 1964, 1965, Tulane U., 1966, 1968; Fulbright-Hays lectr. University Coll. of Wales, 1961-62. Mem. Miss. Hist. Commn., 1954- 57, 63-66; vice chmn. So. Humanities Conf., 1964-65, chmn., 1965-66; mem. Nat. Fulbright Adv. Screening Com., 1962-64, chmn., 1964-65; cons. Nat. Endowment for Humanities, 1969—. Served from pvt. to capt., AUS, 1941-45. Guggenheim fellow, 1958-59; Fulbright lectr. U.K., 1961-62; research fellow Inst. Advanced Studies, Princeton, 1966; summer fellowships and awards include So. Fellowship Found., 1955, Am. Philos. Soc., 1956, 65, Am. Council Learned Socs., 1961-62. Fellow Royal Hist. Soc.; mem. Am., So. hist. assns., Conf. Brit. Studies, So. Humanities Conf., Am. Assn. U. Profs., Phi Kappa Phi, Omicron Delta Kappa, Phi Alpha Theta, Pi Gamma Nu, Kappa Delta Pi, Phi Kappa Tau. Author monographs: Mme. Juliette Adam, Gambetta, and the Idea of a Franco-Russian Alliance, 1960; Lord Kitchener and the Viceroyalty of India, 1910, 1965; Soldier-Surgeon; The Crimean War Letters of Dr. D.A. Reid, 1855-1856, 1968; W.T. Stead And The Russian Revolution of 1905, 1969. Bd. editors So. Humanities Rev., Miss. Quar. Contbr. articles profl. jours. Home: 916 Barton Woods Rd NE Atlanta GA 30307

BAYLES, ROGERS, ins. co. exec.; b. Nutley, N.J., June 19, 1914; s. James M. and Althea (Rogers) B.; A.B., Dartmouth, 1936; m. Lois Brown, Dec. 28, 1940; children—Richard, David, James. Vice pres., sec. Home Ins. Co., N.Y.C., 1960-68, exec. v.p. finance, 1968—, also dir.; v.p., sec. Home Indemnity Co., N.Y.C., 1960-68, exec. v.p. finance, 1968—; dir. Seaboard Surety Co., Peoples-Home Life Ins. Co., Fed. Life and Casualty Co., Westamerica Securities Inc., C.I. Mgmt. Co., C.I. Spl. Fund; City Ins. Co., Spectra Fund, Inc., Investors Mgmt. & Research Corp., Thico Plan, Inc.; trustee Prudential Savs. Bank. Mem. N.Y. Soc. Security Analysts, Ins. Soc. N.Y., Bond Club N.Y.C., Municipal Forum N.Y.C., Am. Fgn. Ins. Assn. (chmn. finance com.). Home: Indian Rock Rd New Canaan CT 06840 Office: 59 Maiden Lane New York City NY 10008

BAYLES, SAMUEL HEAGAN, advt. exec.; b. Port Jefferson, L.I., N.Y., Nov. 10, 1910; s. Edward Post and Mary Jane (Lerch) B.; student Stony Brook Prep. Sch., 1928; B.A., Dartmouth, 1933; m. Gladys Grinnell, Sept. 25, 1933; children— Elizabeth Jane (Mrs. Frederick Joseph Wheeler), Samuel Heagen, Christina Mary (Mrs. William Francis Callahan, III). With Ruthrauff & Ryan, Inc., 1933-46, v.p., dir., co- dir. radio and television, 1940-46; a prin., chief exec. officer, chmn. bd. SSC & B, Inc. (formerly Sullivan, Stauffer, Colwell & Bayles, Inc.), N.Y.C., 1946—; mem. policy, operations coms. SSC & B Lintas Internat., Ltd. Chmn. Bd. overseers Hanover Inn, Dartmouth Coll.; vice chmn. bd. dirs. Advt. Research Found. Mem. Phi Beta Kappa, Psi Upsilon. Clubs: Cloud, Dartmouth (N.Y.C.); North Hempstead Country (Port Washington, N.Y.); North Fork Country (Cutchogue, L.I., N.Y.). Author and pub.: F/F The Power of Intersensory Selling; The Golden Book on Writing; Modern Man's Quest for Identity. Home: Sands Light Sands Point NY 12123

BAYLESS, NEVILLE, advt. exec.; b. Toledo, Mar. 6, 1912; s. William Niven and Bertha (Snyder) B.; A.B. cum laude, Western Res. U., 1933, M.A., 1934; m. Margaret Falke, Apr. 3, 1937; children—William, Ronald, Robert, Thomas, David. Prodn. mgr. Bayless-Kerr Advt. Agy., Cleve., 1934-38, account exec., 1938-56, pres., 1956—. Mem. Indsl. Marketers Cleve., Am. Assn. Advt. Agys., Delta Upsilon. Clubs: City, Hermit, Advertising, Cheshire-Cheese (Cleve.). Home: 310 Morewood Pkwy Rocky River OH 44116 Office: Hanna Bldg Cleveland OH 44115

BAYLEY, FRANK SAWYER, lawyer; b. Seattle, June 7, 1910; s. Frank S. and Mary (Bass) B.; B.A., Harvard, 1932; J.D., U. Wash., 1936; m. Frances A. Stimson, June 24, 1938 (div. 1958); children—Frank Sawyer III, Thomas S., Douglas C.; m. 2d, Margaret M. Hayes, Nov. 28, 1958; children—Margaret A., Colby J. Admitted to Wash., bar, 1936, since practiced in Seattle; mem. firm Jones, Grey, Bayley & Olson, 1966—; cons. ECA, 1948; regional counsel NPA, 1951. Dir., v.p. Tally Corp. Bd. dirs. Ryther Child Center, 1947—, pres., 1952-54. Served to capt., USNR, 1941-45. Decorated Navy Cross. Mem. Am., Wash. bar assns. Clubs: Seattle Yacht, Seattle Golf, Rainier, Harbor, University. Home: 16725 15th Av NW Seattle WA 98177 Office: Norton Bldg Seattle WA 98104

BAYLEY, NED DUANE, govt. ofcl.; b. Battle Creek, Mich., Dec. 29, 1918; s. Howard G. and Beulah (Sperry) B.; B.S., Mich. State U., 1940; student U. Minn., 1940- 41; Ph.D., U. Wis., 1950; student pub. adminstrn., Harvard, 1963-64; m. Lillian Joyce Safstrom, June 5, 1943; children—Gwen Ellen, Will Douglas, Fred Wallace. Asst. prof. U. Wis., 1948-53; asso. prof. U. Minn., 1953- 55; with Dept. Agr., 1955—, dir. sci. and edn. Office of Sec., 1968—. Del. 4th Food and Agr. Orgn. Far East Regional Conf. Animal Prodn. and Health, Ceylon, 1966. Recipient Outstanding Performance award Dept. Agr., 1965; Nat. Civil Service League Career Service award, 1970. Mem. Am. Dairy Sci. Assn., Am. Soc. Animal Prodn., A.A.A.S. (sec. sect. O, 1966-67). Author papers. Home: 13907 Overton Lane Silver Spring MD 20904 Office: Sci and Edn Office of Secretary Dept Agr Washington DC 20250

BAYLIS, ARTHUR EUGENE, mgmt. cons.; b. Colorado Springs, Colo., Apr. 9, 1910; s. Richard Arthur and Viola (Hardin) B.; A.B., Colo. Coll., 1932; M.A., Tufts Coll., 1934; m. Dorcas Billings, July 11, 1936 (dec. Apr. 1952); 1 dau., Bonnie Alayne (now Mrs. Derwin H. Stevens); m. 2nd, E. Elizabeth Colwell, May 27, 1955. Instr. transp. and econs. Tufts Coll., 1932-34; staff asst. Fed. Coordinator Trans., Washington, 1934-35; asst. to v.p. in charge traffic N.Y.C. R.R., chief clk. office of v.p. in charge traffic, asst. v.p., 1935-42, fgn. freight traffic mgr., 1944-46, asst. gen. freight traffic mgr., 1946-50, gen. freight traffic mgr., 1950-51, asst. v.p. in charge freight traffic, 1952, v.p. in charge freight traffic, 1953-60, v.p. marketing, 1960-65, v.p. staff, 1965-66; pres. Arthur E. Baylis & Co., Inc., cons., Scarsdale, N.Y., 1966—. Dir. Nat. Com. on Internat. Trade Documentation. Asst. dir. ry. transp. div. Office Def. Transp., Washington, 1942-44. Mem. Phi Beta Kappa, Kappa Sigma. Presbyn. Clubs: N.Y. Traffic; Chicago (Chgo.); Golf, Town (Scarsdale). Home: 18 Cohawney Rd Scarsdale NY 10583

BAYLIS, CHARLES AUGUSTUS, educator; b. Portland, Ore., Apr. 2, 1902; s. Thomas Farrow and Hermine Antoinette (Weber) B.; A.B., U. Wash., 1923, A.M., 1924; Ph.D., Harvard, 1926; m. Ruth Woodruff Weage, Aug. 21, 1925; children—Thomas Aurthur, William Eric. Mem. philosophy dept. Brown U., 1927-48, asso. prof., 1937-48; dir. N.Y.C. Freshman Coll., Providence, 1935-37; sec. Univs. Com. on Post-War Internat. Problems, Boston, 1943-45; prof. philosophy and dept. head U. Md., 1949-52; prof. philosophy Duke, 1952-70, dir. grad. studies, 1952-56, dept. chmn., 1956- 68. Mem. summer sch. faculty U. Wash., 1924, 25, 48, 62, Stanford, 1936, 60, Harvard, 1947, Pacific Philosophy Inst., 1956, 60, 64, San Jose (Cal.) State Coll., 1964. Sheldon traveling fellowship Harvard, with study in England, France and Germany, 1926-27; Guggenheim fellow and Senior Fulbright scholar Univ. Coll. Oxford, Eng., 1958-59. Mem. Am. Philos. Assn. (Eastern div., mem. exec. com., 1940, v.p. 1954, chmn. com. on publ., 1961-64, chmn. nat. bd. 1965-67), Assn. for Symbolic Logic (sec.-treas., 1936-42, v.p., 1942-46), So. Soc. for Philosophy and Psychology (pres. 1955). Author: (with A.A. Bennett), Formal Logic, 1939; Ethics, 1958; Metaphysics, 1965. Mng. editor Symbolic Logic, 1936-42, cons. editor, 1942—; editorial cons. The Philos. Rev., 1950-53; editorial staff Philosophy and Phenomenological Research. Mem. editorial bd. Cornell Publs. in Contemporary Philosophy, 1956-60. Research in epistemology, metaphysics, ethics and perception. Home: 2610 Sevier St Durham NC 27705

BAYLIS, CHESTER, Jr., banker; b. N.Y.C., Aug. 28, 1908; s. Chester and Evelyn Muir (Hoagland) B.; B.S., Princeton, 1929; m. Dorothy M. Smith, Oct. 6, 1934; 1 son, Robert M. With Bankers Trust Co., N.Y.C., 1929—, 1st v.p. charge Eastern div., 1954-65, sr. v.p. N.Y. div., 1965-66, sr. v.p. internat. banking dept., 1966-68, exec. v.p., dir., 1968-70, chmn. exec. com., 1970—; dir. Baylis Industries, Melville Shoe Corp., Huyck Corp., Nat. Union Bank, Dover, N.J., Balt. Gas & Electric Co., Internat. Minerals & Chem. Corp. Bd. dirs. Riverview Hosp. Served with USNR, 1942-45. Clubs: University (N.Y.C.); Princeton, Maryland (Balt.); Rumson (N.J.) Country. Home: PO Box 91 Locust NJ 07760 Office: 280 Park Av New York City NY 10017

BAYLIS, JAMES ROBERT, cigar co. exec.; b. Cranford, N.J., July 13, 1910; s. Albert Wilbur and Ellen Grubb (Cleland) B.; B.A., Williams Coll., 1932; m. Sarah Adams Whiting, June 10, 1938; children—Butler Whiting, James Edgar, Linda. Engaged in textile bus., 1932-36; with Shields & Co., investments, 1936- 42, Lazard Freres & Co., Investments, 1946-49; with Consol. Cigar Corp., N.Y.C., 1949—, sr. v.p., 1959-65, exec. v.p., 1965-66, pres., chief operating officer, 1967-, chmn. bd., 1969—; trustee American Savs. Bank. Served to lt. (s.g.) USCGR, 1942-45. Clubs: N.Y. Yacht, Madison (Conn.) Beach. Home: 46 Lawrence Rd Scarsdale NY 10583 Office: 529 Fifth Av New York City NY 10017

BAYLOR, HUGH MURRAY, educator; b. What Cheer, Ia., Apr. 8, 1913; s. John Thomas and Elizabeth (Murray) B.; B.A., U. Ia., 1934, M.A. 1936, Ph.D., 1950; diplome d'exécution, Conservatoire Americain, Fontainebleau, France, 1938; m. Elisabeth A. Barbou, Sept. 1, 1937; children—Denis A., Michael G., Stephen M. Asst. U. Ia., 1934-37; prof. music chmn. dept., William Penn Coll., Oskaloosa, Ia., 1937-42; prof. music Knox Coll., Galesburg, Ill., 1942—, Distinguished Service prof., 1959—, chmn. music dept., 1969—. Mem. Phi Beta Kappa, Pi Kappa Lambda. Composer chamber music, songs and comic opera. Contbr. jours in field. Home: 1187 N Cherry St Galesburg IL 61401

BAYMAN, BENJAMIN FRANK, educator; b. N.Y.C., Dec. 12, 1930; s. Leo and Jennie (Sandhaus) B.; B.Chem. Engring., Cooper Union, 1951; Ph.D. in Physics, U. Edinburgh, 1956; m. Aroti Gupta, July 18, 1957; children—Paul, Samuel. Postdoctoral research fellow Niels Bohr Inst., Copenhagen, 1956-60; asst. prof. Princeton, 1960-65; prof. U. Minn., 1965—, asso. head Sch. Physics and Astronomy, dir. grad studies, 1969—; cons. in field. Fulbright scholar, 1951-52, Ford fellow, 1956-60; recipient Distinguished Tchr. award Inst. Tech., 1969. Mem. Am. Phys. Soc., Am. Assn. U. Profs., Zero Population Growth, Isaac Walton League, Wilderness Soc. Author papers on structure atomic nuclei. Home: 3611 Abbott Av S Minneapolis MN 55410

BAYNE, DAVID COWAN, educator, lawyer; b. Detroit, Jan. 11, 1918; s. David Cowan and Myrtle (Murray) B.; A.B., U. Detroit, 1939; LL.B., Georgetown U., 1947, LL.M., 1948; M.A., Loyola U., Chgo., 1947; S.T.L., West Baden (Ind.) Coll., 1953; Scientiae Juris Dr. (grad. fellow), Yale, 1949. Joined Soc. of Jesus, 1941, ordained priest Roman Cath. Ch., 1952; admitted to Fed. and D.C. bars, 1948, Mich. bar, 1960; asst. prof. law U. Detroit, 1954-60, acting dean Law Sch., 1955-59, dean, 1959-60; research asso. Nat. Jesuit Research Orgn., Inst. Social Order, St. Louis, 1960-63; vis. lectr. St. Louis U. Law Sch., 1960-63, prof. law, 1963-67; vis. prof. Mich. Law Sch., 1967, Inst. fur Auslandisches und Internationales Wirtschaftrecht, Frankfurt, 1967; prof. Coll. Law, U. Ia., Iowa City, 1967—; vis. prof. U. Koln, Germany, 1970. Mem. Bar State Mich., Am., Fed., D.C. bar assns., Mo. Bar, Delta Theta Phi. Research corp. law. Author: Conscience, Obligation and the Law, 1966. Contbr. articles profl. jours. Office: Coll of Law U Ia Iowa City IA 52240

BAYNE, STEPHEN FIELDING, Jr., bishop; b. N.Y.C., May 21, 1908; s. Stephen Fielding and Edna Mabel (Ashley) B.; A.B., Amherst Coll., 1929, honorary D.D., 1948; S.T.B., Gen. Theological Sem., 1933, S.T.M., 1934, S.T.D., 1947; LL.D., Mills Coll., 1951; D.D., Whitman Coll., 1952, Anglican Theol. Coll., 1954; S.T.D., Columbia, 1952; D.Litt., Hobart Coll., 1957, Kenyon Coll., 1960; L.H.D., U. Puget Sound, 1959; D.D., St. Paul's (Rikkyo) Tokyo, 1960, Harvard, 1961, Australian Coll. Theology, 1962, Huron Coll., 1963, Cuttington Coll., 1967, Trinity Coll., 1969; m. Lucie Culver Gound, June 19, 1934; children—Stephen Fielding, Maurice Philip Gould, Duncan A., Lydia L., Bruce G.C. Fellow and tutor Gen. Theol. Sem., 1932- 34; ordained diaconate, 1932, priesthood, 1933, Protestant Episcopal Ch.; rector Trinity Ch., St. Louis, 1934-39, St. John's Ch., Northampton, Mass., 1939-42; chaplain Columbia U., 1942-47 (on leave serving as chaplain USNR, 1944-45); bishop Diocese of Olympia, 1947- 59; Anglican exec. officer, 1960-64; 1st v.p. exec. council Protestant Episcopal Ch. U.S.A., 1964-70, dir. overseas dept., 1964-68, dep. for program, 1968-70; prof. Christian mission Gen. Theol. Sem., 1970—. Chmn. com. on the family Lambeth Conf., 1958. Mem. Theta Delta Chi. Clubs: Century (N.Y.C.); University Seattle); Athenaeum (London, England). Author: The Optional God, 1953; Christian Living, 1957; In The Sight of the Lord, 1958; Enter with Joy, 1961; Mindful of the Love, 1962; An Anglican Turning Point, 1964. Home: Chelsea Square New York City NY 10011 Office: 175 9th Av New York City NY 10011

BAYNES, HAROLD LOSEY, banker; b. Elmira, N.Y., May 24, 1935; s. Harold Edgar and Helen Brown (Losey) B.; B.A. in English with distinction, U. Va., 1956; grad. Va.-Md. Sch. Banking, 1967; m. Patricia Ann Dent, June 26, 1956; children—Jennifer Shannon, James Patrick, Megan Elizabeth. With United Va. Bank, Richmond, 1959—, v.p., cashier, head operations div., 1968—; dir., mem. exec. com. UVB Service Corp. Vice pres., treas. Richmond Area Arthritis Found., 1966-68; vice chmn. Richmond com. Nat. Council Crime and Delinquency, 1967—; chmn., treas. Northside FISH, 1969—. Bd. dirs., treas., team capt. Youth Emergency Service, Lewis Ginter Community Bldg.; bd. dirs. Vol. Service Bur. Served with USN, 1956-59. Mem. Soc. Advancement Mgmt., Bank Adminstrn. Inst., Am. Inst. Banking, MENSA, Richmond 1st Club, Omicron Delta Kappa, Phi Gamma Delta, Raven Soc. Republican. Methodist. Home: 3310 Gloucester Rd Richmond VA 23227 Office: PO Box 6 E Richmond VA 23214

BAYOUMI, MOHAMED M. EL, banker. Mng. dir. Bank Alexandria SAE. Office: 6 Salab Salem St Alexandria Egypt*

BAYRD, EDWIN DORRANCE, physician; b. Chgo., Nov. 12, 1917; s. George Oliver and Helen (Dorrance) B.; A.B. magna cum laude, Dartmouth, 1939; M.D., Harvard, 1942; M.S. in Med., U. Minn., 1947; m. Muriel Helen Burns, Oct. 17, 1942; children—Edwin Dorrance, Garrett Thomas, Deborah, George Oliver, Linda. Practice medicine, specializing in internal medicine. Rochester, Minn., faculty U. Minn., Grad. Sch., 1947—, prof. medicine, 1967—, chmn. hematology sect., 1967—; Norman Paul vis. prof. medicine Sydney (Australia) Hosp., 1963. Pres. staff Mayo Clinic, 1969. Diplomate Nat. Bd. Med. Examiners, Am. Bd. Internal Medicine. Mem. A.M.A., Minn. So. Minn. med. assns., Am. Fedn. for Clin. Research, Internat., Am. (chmn. membership com. 1965) socs. hematology, Central Clin. Research Club (pres. 1964). Minn. Soc. Internal Medicine. Central Soc. for Clin. Research, Hematology Club, A.C.P., Phi Beta Kappa. Editor-in-chief Mayo Clinic Proc., 1963—; editorial bd. Minn. Medicine, 1964—, Year Book Cancer, 1964-68. Research, numerous publs. on understanding and distinguishing plasmocytic diseases, their natural course and their treatment. Home: 1116 10th St SW Rochester MN 55901 Office: Mayo Clinic Rochester MN 55901

BAYS, KARL DEAN, hosp. supply co. exec.; b. Loyall, Ky., Dec. 23, 1933; s. James K. and Myrtle (Criscillis) B.; B.S., Eastern Ky. U., 1955; M.B.A., Ind. U., 1958; m. Billie Joan White, June 4, 1955; children—Robert D., Karla. With Am. Hosp. Supply Corp., 1958—, pres., dir., 1970, chief exec. officer, 1971—. Dir. Northern Trust Co., Chgo. Mem. adv. council Northwestern U. Grad. Sch. Mgmt. Served with USMCR, 1955-57. Named One of Outstanding Young Men in Am., U.S. Jr. C. of C., 1964. Mem. Northwestern U. Assos. Clubs: Executives, Economic, Chicago (Chgo.). Home: 1521 Tara Lane Lake Forest IL 60045 Office: 1740 Ridge Av Evanston IL 60204

BAYTON, JAMES ARTHUR, educator, psychologist; b. Whitestone, Va., Apr. 5, 1912; s. George L. and Helen (Stevens) B.; B.S., Howard U., 1935, M.S., 1936; Ph.D., U. Pa., 1943; m. Daisy Armstrong, Oct. 1, 1948. Asso. prof. Va. State Coll., Petersburg, 1939-43; social sci. analyst Dept. Agr., 1943-45; prof. psychology So. U., Baton Rouge, 1945-46, Morgan State Coll., Balt., 1946-47, Howard U., 1947—; mem. sr. staff Brookings Instn., 1967- 68; cons. in field, 1950—; v.p. Nat. Analysts, Inc., Phila., 1953-62, 66-67, Universal Marketing Research, Inc., N.Y.C., 1962-66; sr. staff psychologist Chilton Research Services, 1968—; cons. Nat. Acad. Pub. Adminstrn., 1969—. Mem. research adv. com. social security Adminstrn., 1962-64; com. on agrl. sci. Dept. Agr., 1965—. Recipient Superior Service award Dept. Agr., 1954. Fellow Am. Psychol. Assn.; mem. Am. Marketing Assn. (Alpha Kappa Psi award 1958), Eastern, D.C. psychol. assns., Phi Beta Kappa, Sigma Xi. Club: Cosmos. Author: Tension in the Cities, 1969. Home: 5908 17th St NW Washington DC 20011

BAYULKEN, UMIT HALUK, Turkish diplomat; b. Istanbul, Turkey, July 7, 1921; s. Hüsnü H. and Melek B. (Sabri) B.; student Lycée of Haydarpasa, Istanbul, 1938-39, U. Ankara, 1942-43; m. Valihe Salci, Oct. 11, 1952; children—Orhan, Handan. Served in numerous diplomatic posts in Europe and U.S., 1944-64; sec. gen. with rank of ambassador, 1964-66; leader Turkish delegation at Meeting Fgn. Ministers for 2d Afro-Asian Conf., Algiers, 1965, Delegation with paid ofcl. visit to UAR, 1966; Turkish ambassador to Ct. of St. James, 1966-69, to Malta, 1968-69; permanent rep. to UN, 1969—; mem. Turkish Delegation to UN Gen. Assembly Meetings, 1952-65; lectr. Faculty Polit. Sci., U. Ankara, 1963-66. Hon. pres. Pendik Hosp. Found., Istanbul; hon. gov. Sch. Oriental and African Studies, London. Decorated Spanish Isabel la Catolica, German Grand Cross of Merit, Grand Cross Victoria Order. Club: St. James (London). Contbr. articles profl. jours. Home: 10 Gracie Sq New York City NY 10028 Office: UN Plaza New York City NY 10017

BAZAINE, JEAN, French Painter; b. 1904. Executed stained glass windows for ch. at Assy. 1946, at Audincourt, 195154, ceramic mural UNESCO, 1960, also Maison de la Radio, Paris, 1963, St. Severin, Paris, 1963-69; exhbn. Galerie Carre, also Galerie Maeght. Paris; retrospective exhbns. at Berne, 1958, Eindhoven, 1959, Amsterdam, 1959, Hanover, 1961, Zurich, 1963, Oslo, 1963, Paris, 1965; rep. biennali of Venice, Sao Paulo and Carnegie; represented in main mus. Europe and U.S.A. Recipient Grand Prix Nat. des Arts, 1964. Author: Notes Sur la Peinture d'Aujourd'hui, 1948. Address: 36 Rue Pierre Brossolette 92 Clamart, France.*

BAZAN, JOSE, corp. exec.; b. Colon, Panama, 1924; grad. Canal Zone Jr. Coll., 1934. Mem. Nat. Assembly as rep. from Colon, then mayor of Colon for 2 terms, 2d v.p. Panama, and now minister govt. and justice; now also pres. Colon Free Zone Transp. Address: P.O. Box 835, Colon, Panama.*

BAZELON, DAVID LIONEL, judge; b. Superior, Wis., Sept. 3, 1909; s. Israel and Lena (Krasnovsky) B.; student U. of Ill., 1928-29; B.S. in Law, Northwestern U., 1931; LL.D. (honorary), Colby Coll., 1966; LL.D., Boston U. Law School, 1969; m. Miriam M. Kellner, June 7, 1936; children—James A., Richard Lee. Admitted to practice in Ill., 1932, private practice until 1935; asst. U.S. atty. No. Dist. Ill., 1935-40; sr. mem. firm of Gottlieb and Schwartz, 1940-46; asst. atty. gen. U.S. Lands Div., 1946-47, Office of Alien Property, 1947-49; judge U.S. Ct. of Appeals for D.C. Circuit, 1949—, chief judge, 1962; lectr. law and psychiatry U. Pa. Law Sch., 1957-58, 58-59; Sloan vis. prof. Menninger Found., Topeka, 1960-61; lectr. psychiatry Johns Hopkins U. Sch. Medicine, 1964—; Lowell Inst. lectr. Harvard Med. Sch., 1964; Regent's lectr. U. Cal. at Los Angeles, 1964; clin. prof. socio-legal aspects of psychiatry George Washington U., 1966—; David K. Niles Meml. lectr. Hebrew U., 1966. Chmn. task force on law President's Panel on Mental Retardation, 1961- 62; mem. adv. council Nat. Assn. Mental Health Program Dirs., 1963- -; chmn. steering com. Model Sch. Subsystem, Washington, 1964-66; mem. adv. com. program on tech. and soc. Harvard, 1966—; mem. nat. adv. mental health council USPHS, 1967—; mem. 20th Century Fund Task Force on Working Women, 1970; mem. U.S. mission on mental health USSR, 1967; chmn. adv. bd. Boston U. Center for Law and Health Scis., 1970; nat. adv. com. J.F. Kennedy Center for Research on Edn. and Human Devel., 1968—; Bd. dirs. Citizens Bd. Inquiry into Health Services, Joint Commn. on Mental Health of Children, Inc., Washington Sch. Psychiatry; trustee Salk Inst. for Biol. Studies, William Alanson White Found., Washington; mem. spl. com. procedures in hospitalization and discharge of mentally ill Am. Bar. Found., 1958—. Recipient Isaac Ray Award Am. Psychiat. Assn., 1960. Hon. fellow Am. Psychiat. Assn.; fellow Am. Acad. Arts and Scis.; mem. Am., Fed., D.C. bar assns., Am. Orthopsychiat. Assn. (pres. 1969—, dir.). Jewish religion. Democrat. Club: Cosmos. Home: 2700 Virginia Av NW Washington DC 20037 Office: Court of Appeals Washington DC 20001

BAZELON, DAVID THOMAS, writer, lawyer, educator; b. Shreveport, La., Mar. 2, 1923; s. Jacob Louis and Florence Ethel (Groner) B.; student U. Ill., 1940-41, U. Va., 1941-42, U. Chgo., 1942-43; B.S., Columbia, 1949; LL.B., Yale, 1953; m. Mary Loretto Coleman, Jan. 25, 1963 (div. Feb. 1969); 1 son, Coleman David Bazelon. Free-lance writer and editor, 1943—; instr. lit. Bard Coll., 1949-50; admitted to N.Y. bar, 1953; asso. atty. firm Hays, Podell, Algase, Crum & Feuer, N.Y.C., 1953-56, Paul, Weiss, Rifkind, Wharton & Garrison, N.Y.C., 1956-58; prof. policy scis. State U. N.Y. at Buffalo, 1969—; vis. fellow Inst. for Policy Studies, Washington, 1963-65, now asso. fellow; vis. prof. Sch. Law, Rutgers-The State U., Newark, 1966-67. Trustee A. Phillip Randolph Inst. Guggenheim fellow, 1967-68. Mem. P.E.N., Authors Guild, League for Indsl. Democracy. Author: The Paper Economy, 1963; Power in America; The Politics of the New Class, 1967; Nothing But a Fine Tooth Comb: Essays in Social Criticism, 1944-69, 1970. Home: 849 Delaware Av Buffalo NY 14209

BAZIN, GERMAIN RENE MICHEL, writer, lectr.; b. Paris, France; s. Charles and Laurence (Mounier-Poutht) B.; student Ste Croix d'Orléans, Ste Croix Neuilly, Coll. de Pontlevoy, Sorbonne; Docteur ès Lettres; hon. degress U. Rio de Janeiro (Brazil), Villanova U.; m. Countess Heller Bielotzerkowka, 1947. Univ. prof., curator paintings and drawings Louvre Mus., 1937-50, chief curator paintings and drawings, 1951-65; dir. restoration paintings Museums of France, 1965; prof. museology dept. Louvre Sch., 1941, also dir. writing lab., lectr.; now research prof. York U., Toronto, Ont., Can. Served as capt., inf., French Army, 1939-44. Decorated officer Légion d'Honneur, commandeur Arts et Lettres (France); Order of Leopold, grand officier Couronne Belge (Belgium); Order of Santiago (Portugal); Order Merit Republic of Italy; officer Cruzeiro do Sul (Brazil), Pole-Star (Sweden), others. Mem. Latin-Am. Union, Inter-Allied Circle Paris, Cercle Union, also numerous acads. Roman Catholic. Author: Mont Saint- Michel, 1932; Fra Angelico, 1941, 1948; Crépusle des Images, 1946; Corot, 1942, 51; l'Epoque Impressioniste, 1949; l'Architecture religieuse baroque au Brésil, 1957; Histoire générale de l'Art, 1951, 58, 63; Chefs d'oeuvres au Louvre, 1958; French Impressionists in the Louvre, 1959; Ermitage Écoles èstrangères, 1958; Gallery of Flowers, 1960; Aleijadinho, 1963; The Loom of Art, 1961; The Museum Age, 1967; World Sculpture, 1968; The Baroque Age, 1968; La Peinture d'avant Garde, 1969; others; articles French and fgn. mags. Home: 29 Avenue Georges Mandel Paris XVIe France

BAZZINI, ALLEN B., film co. exec.; b. N.Y.C., May 16, 1939. Exec. producer Aquarian Prodns. Ltd., N.Y.C., producer films That Fatal Winter, Seeds, Twisted Vines. Mem. Motion Picture Assn. Am., Ind. Film Importers and Distbrs. Am. Inc. Office: 55 W 42d St New York City NY 10036*

BEABER, JAMES DUANE, educator; b. Fowler, Colo., Sept. 12, 1927; s. William Garner and Hazel (Fullerton) B.; B.A., Denver U., 1951; Ed. D., Syracuse U., 1959; m. Shirley Harding, Mar. 2, 1952; children—James Garner, Thomas Norvan, Liane Margaret, William Douglas. Tchr., Derby (Colo.) Elementary Sch., 1951-52; tchr. mentally retarded Evanston (Ill.) Twp. High Sch., 1952- 54; tchr. mentally retarded, sch. psychologist, Geneva, N.Y., 1954- 55; prin. Roosevelt (L.I.) Cerebral Palsy Sch., 1955-57; research asso. spl. edn., Syracuse, N.Y., 1957-59; prof. edn., chmn. dept. spl. edn. U. Va., 1959-68; prof. edn., dir. program spl. edn. La. State U., 1968-70; prof. spl. edn. Ohio State U., 1970—. Pres. La. Assn. Mental Deficiency, 1969-70. Served with USNR, 1944-45. Fellow Am. Assn. Mental Deficiency. Home: 1789 Willoway Ct Columbus OH 43220

BEACH, CECIL PRENTICE, librarian; b. Knoxville, Tenn., July 12, 1927; s. Frank Alfred and Lillie Maude (Sims) B.; A.B., U. Chattanooga, 1950; M.A., Fla. State U., 1952; m. Doris Jean Pardue, Apr. 17, 1949; children—Steven Prentice, Rex Arthur, Keven Sanders, Kyle Alfred, Quentin Anthony; m. 2d, Marcia Gibson Buckley, June 20, 1969; children—Stephanie Lynn, Shannon, Sue. Bookmobile librarian Chattanooga Pub. Library, 1948-51; extension librarian Decatur-de-Kalb Regional Library, Decatur, Ga., 1952-54; dir. Piedmont Regional Library, Winder, Ga., 1954- 60, Gadsden (Ala.) Pub. Library, 1960-64, Tampa-Hillsborough Library System, Tampa, Fla., 1965—; cons. library bldgs. and service. Pres. Gadsden Community Council, 1963. Served with USNR, 1944-46. Mem. Am., Southeastern Ala., Ga., Fla. (president 1969) library assns., Adult Edn. Assn., Tampa C. of C., Fla. State U. Alumni Assn. (pres. 1967). Democrat. Baptist. Mason. Home: 1312 Ivywood Dr Brandon FL 33511 Office: 900 Ashley St Tampa FL 33602

BEACH, EARL EDWARD, educator, musician; b. Crestline, O., May 22, 1909; s. Carl Theodore and Arzona (Zellner) B.; B.S., Capital U., 1931; student Ohio State U., 1931, U. Pitts., 1935, U. Mich., 1936, U. Ga., 1951; M.A., Western Res. U., 1948; m. Vivian Frances Stout, Apr. 28, 1945; children—Theodore Wayne, Marcia Rae. Supervising instr. music, Bellaire, O., 1931-40. Alliance, O., 1940-43; dir. bands, instr. music Mt. Union Coll., 1941- 43; dir. sch. and community music, Charlevoix, Mich., 1943-44; dir. instrumental music South High Sch., Cleve., 1944-45; chmn. music edn., dir. bands and symphonette Ohio Wesleyan U., 1945-50; chmn. grad. and undergrad. divs. music edn. U. Ga., 1950-58; dir. dept. music East Caroline Coll., Greenville, N.C., 1958-62, dean School of Music, 1962—; organizing dir. Ogelby Park High Sch., Music Camp, 1937, Ohio Wesleyan Summer Music Camp, 1946-50, U. Ga. Music Festival, also U. Ga. Summer Youth Camp, 1951—. Named Outstanding Music Educator, N.C. Music Educators Assn., 1970. Fellow Inst. Arts and Letters; mem. Nat. Council Coop. Tchrs. Edn. (rep. Music Educators Nat. Conf. 1961-63), N.C. Music Educators Conf. (life mem.; pres. 1967-69), Music Educators Nat. Conf. (research council 1952-58, nat. chmn. music in higher edn. 1952-54, pres. So. div. 1957-59, mem. exec. com. 1958-60; nat. chmn. Go Project 16; mem. commn. on reorgn. and devel. 1970—), Ga. Music Assn. (dir.), Phi Mu Alpha, Pi Kappa Lambda, Phi Beta Mu (pres. N.C. chpt., nat. bd. dirs.), Beta Theta Pi, Phi Delta Kappa. Editorial bd. Music Educators Jour., 1950-58, 70—, Jour. Research Music Edn., 1952-58; chmn. editorial bd. Ga. Music mag., 1950-56; editor Triad pub. Ohio Music Edn. Assn., 1947-49. Editor Bibliography of Music Edn. Materials, 1958. Home: 1603 Beaumont Dr Greenville NC 27834

BEACH, EDWARD RITCHIE, investment banker; b. Delphi, Ind., July 2, 1906 s. Edward and Irene (Ritchie) Beach; A.B., U. Cal., 1926; M.B.A., Harvard, 1932; m. Josephine Gray, Mar. 19, 1936; children—Sarah Josephine, Edward Gray, Advt., merchandising exec. Procter & Gamble Co., 1932-43; v.p., sec., dir. Benton & Bowles, Inc., 1943-55; v.p., chmn. marketing plans bd. McCann-Erickson, Inc., 1955; pres. McCann-Erickson Corp. (Internat.), N.Y.C., 1956-58, v.p. McCann-Erickson, Inc., 1958-62; mgr. advt. and pub. relations Reynolds & Co., N.Y.C., 1963-69. Rep. Presbyn. Home: 285 Lake Av Greenwich CT 06830

BEACH, FRANK AMBROSE, psychobiologist; b. Emporia, Kan., Apr. 13, 1911; s. Frank Ambrose and Bertha (Robinson) B.; B.S., Kan. State Tchrs. Coll., 1932, M.S., 1934; Ph.D., U. Chgo., 1940; Sc.D., McGill U., 1966, Williams Coll., 1968; m. Anna Beth Odenweller, Mar. 1935; children—Frank Ambrose, Susan Elizabeth. Research asst. to Dr. K. S. Lashley, dept. of psychology, Harvard, 1937-38; asst. curator, dept. exptl. biology, Am. Museum Natural History, 1938-41, asst. curator in charge, 1941-42, asso. curator in charge, dept. of animal behavior, 1942, chmn. and curator, dept. animal behavior, 1942-46; prof. psychology Yale U., 1946—, Sterling prof., 1951-58; prof. psychology U. Cal. at Berkeley, 1959—; research asso. Am. Mus. Natural History; asso. Wash. Sch. Psychiatry. Fellow New York Zool. Soc., A.A.A.S., Am. Psychol. Assn.; mem. Am. Soc. Naturalists, Nat. Acad. Sci., Soc. Exptl. Psychologists, Am. Philos. Soc., Western Psychol. Assn., Sigma Xi, Phi Beta Kappa (hon.). Office: Dept of Psychology U Cal Berkeley CA 94720

BEACH, JAMES WEBSTER, TV exec.; b. Chgo., Dec. 21, 1912; s. Frederick Woodward and Louise Louise (Hicks) B.; student Northwestern U., 1930-31; m. Anne McDonald McKay, 1949; childrenValerie Mildred (Mrs. Ralph Eugene Boger), Jeffrey Herbert, James Webster III. Newspaperman Hearst Orgn., 1931-40; radio sta. exec., 1940-45; pres. B & W Corp., Chgo., 1945-49; v.p. Westfield Corp., Chgo., 1945-46, Crawfordsville Brick Mfg. Co., Ind., 1949; TV exec. WBKB, Chgo., 1949-53; nat. network TV exec., v.p. ABC-Paramount Theaters, 1953-61; v.p. ABC, 1955-61; v.p. Foote, Cone & Belding, Chgo., 1962-. Vice pres., nat. trustee Nat. Acad. TV Arts and Scis., 1958-65. Mem. Broadcast Pioneers (pres. Chgo. chpt., nat. dir.), Chgo. Advt. Club (pres. 1966-67). Clubs: Broadcast Advertising (pres. 1958-59). Chicago Press. Ill. Athletic (dir.) (Chgo.). Home: Lake Forest, IL Office: 401 N Michigan Av Chicago, IL

BEACH, JOSEPH WATSON, ins. exec.; b. Hartford, Conn., Mar. 26, 1888; s. Charles Coffin and Mary Elizabeth (Batterson) B.; student U. Va., 1910, Williams Coll., 1911; m. Jessie Anderson, Apr. 25, 1912; m. 2d, Caroline Zezzette, Apr. 26, 1964. With Travelers Ins. Co. 1910-12; with Hartford Accident & Indemnity Co., 1914-17; with J. Watson Beach, Inc., 1917—, chmn. dir., 1925—; dir. Riverside Trust Co., United Bank & Trust Co. Pres. Bd. Edn. City Hartford, 1929-31; mayor, Hartford, 1933-35. Bd. dirs. St. Anthony Ednl. Found., Hartford Art Sch. Served as gunner's mate USN, World War I; lt. col. AUS. World War II. Mason. Clubs: St. Anthony (N.Y.C.); Hartford, Hartford Golf. Home: 41 Mountain Rd Farmington CT 06032 Office: 21 Central Row Hartford CT 06103

BEACH, LEONARD BROTHWELL, educator; b. Bridgeport, Conn., Jan. 14, 1905; s. William D. and Edith (Waldo) B.; A.B., Wesleyan U., Middletown, Conn., 1925; A.M., Yale, 1930. Ph.D., 1933; Doctor of Laws, U. Chattanooga, 1964; m. Cicely Cone, Aug. 18, 1936; children—Beatrice, Caroline, Anne. Instr. Latin Tilton Sch., N.H., 1925-28; asst. English Yale, 1930-33; instr. English, Northwestern, 1934-38; asst. prof. English, Ohio State U., 1939-44; prof. English, U. Okla., 1945-51, chmn. English dept., 1945-51; dean grad. sch., Vanderbilt U., Nashville, 1951-65, dean of univ. for instnl. relations, 1965—, also prof. English; vis. prof. English, U. Mo., summer 1945, U. Cal., 1947. Received Rockefeller Grant, 1948. Mem. Modern Lang. Assn. Am., Am. Assn. U. Profs., South-Central Modern Lang. Assn. (pres. 1950), Assn. Am. Univs. (pres. assn. grad. schs. 1957-58), Conf. Deans So. Grad. Schs. (pres. 1957-58), Phi Beta Kappa, Phi Nu Theta. Methodist. Club: Belle Meade. Editor: The Journal of Emily Foster, 1938; The Journals of Peter Irving, 1943. Contbr. articles on Washington Irving in learned jours. Home: 412 Ellendale Dr Nashville TN 37205

BEACH, MORRISON H., ins. co. exec.; b. Winsted, Conn., Jan. 10, 1917; s. Howard Edmund and Edith (Morrison) B.; B.A., Williams Coll., 1939; postgrad. Mass. Inst. Tech., 1942; LL.B., U. Conn., 1954; m. Evelyn R. Harris, Sept. 6, 1942; children—Howard, Linda, Deborah. With Travelers Ins. Co., Hartfod, Conn., 1939—, with exec. dept., 1962—, exec. v.p., 1970—; dir. Travelers Corp., 1970—, pres., 1971—; dir. Broadcast-Plaza, Inc., Hartford Nat. Corp., Hartford Nat. Bank & Trust Co. Mem. Regional Council for Greater Hartford Community Coll., Greater Hartford Community Council. Bd. dirs. Combined Health Appeal; bd. dirs., mem. exec. com. Greater Hartford chpt. A.R.C.; trustee Rensselaer Poly. Inst. Conn., Health Planning Council, Am. Inst. for Property and Liability Underwriters/Ins. Inst. Am.; corporator Hartford Hosp., Hartford Sem. Found. Served to maj. USAAF; ETO. Fellow Soc. Actuaries; mem. Conn. Bar Assn., Am. Acad. Actuaries, Conn. Williams Alumni Assn., Greater Hartford C. of C. (dir., mem. exec. com). Home: 100 Uplands Dr West Hartford CT 06107 Office: 1 Tower Sq Hartford CT 06115

BEACH, NORMAN FREDERICK, photographic mfg. co. exec.; b. Morristown, N.J., Dec. 23, 1909; s. William Norman and Minnie Catherine (Blanchard) B.; A.B., Princeton, 1930; m. Irene M. Gerstner; 1 dau., Deborah. With Eastman Kodak Co., 1930—, asst. gen. manager Kodak Park Div., 1961-67, gen. mgr. Kodak Park div., 1967—, v.p. co., 1962—, also mem. exec. com.; dir. Page Airways, Inc., Buffalo br. Fed. Res. Bank of N.Y. Trustee Rochester Gen. Hosp., Clarkson Coll. Mem. Phi Beta Kappa. Clubs: St. George's (Toronto, Can.); Genesee Valley (Rochester); Princeton (N.Y.C.), Denver; Nantucket (Mass.) Yacht. Home: 820 East Av Rochester NY 14607 Office: Kodak Park Rochester NY 14601

BEACH, P. GOFF, food co. exec.; born Chgo., Dec. 25, 1914; s. Pierre Goff and Barbara S. (Young) B.; student U. Ill., 1933-36; B.S. in Bus. Adminstrn. Northwestern U., 1940; m. Mary Ellen Thompson, Sept. 12, 1942; children—Robert T., Thomas G., Nancy L., Sally A. With Oscar Mayer & Co., Chgo., 1936—, plant mgr., Madison, 1952-53, v.p. operations, 1953- 60, exec. v.p., 1960-66, pres., 1966—, also dir.; dir. First Wis. Nat. Bank, Madison, First Wis. Bankshares Corp., A.O. Smith Corp., Western Pub. Co., Inc. Past dir. Nat. Livestock and Meat Bd., Livestock Conservation, Inc. Past pres. Madison Community Chest; mem. adv. com. St. Mary's Sch. Nursing. Trustee Nutrition Found., Inc. Served to lt. (s.g.) USNR, 1943- 46. Mem. Am. Meat Inst. (past chmn. membership com., past chmn. packing house practice and research com., dir., mem. exec. com.), Madison C. of C. (past v.p.), Wis. C. of C. (past dir.). Presbyn. Clubs: Chicago; Madison, Maple Bluff Country (past pres.) (Madison). Home: 41 Fuller Dr Madison WI 53704 Office: 910 Mayer Av Madison WI 53701

BEACH, ROBERT EDGAR, aircraft co. exec.; b. New Britain, Conn., Sept. 12, 1911; s. Clarence Clark and Marion (McNary) B.; B.S. in Econs., Wharton Sch., U. Pa., 1933; LL.B., Yale, 1937; m. Ruth Powell Meyer, 1941 (div.); children—Mary Anne B. Chew, Margaret B. Bye, Robert Edgar; m. 2d, Dorothy Case Jacobson, May 1, 1968. Admitted to Conn. bar, 1937; asso. and partner Shipman and Goodwin (Hartford) 1937-42; with United Aircraft Corp., 1942—, corp. counsel, 1952-69, v.p., 1960—, head Washington office, 1969—; dir. Superior Electric Co. Mem. Nat. Security Indsl. Assn. (pres. 1962-64, chmn. bd. 1964-65), Am. Bar Assn., Am. Arbitration Assn. (dir. 1967-69). Home: 2810 29th St NW Washington DC 20008 Office: 1725 DeSales St NW Washington DC 20036

BEACH, ROBERT FULLERTON, librarian; b. Bklyn., July 14, 1911; s. William DeVerne and Edith (Waldo) B.; B.A., Wesleyan U., 1932; B.L.S., Columbia, 1933, M.L.S., 1940; m. Eva Ripley, Aug. 29, 1936; 1 dau., Judith Ripley. Reference, circulation asst. Yale U. Library, 1933-36; supr. reserves Berea Coll. Library, 1936-43; librarian Garrett Bibl. Inst. Library, Evanston, Ill., 1946-51, Union Theol. Sem., N.Y.C., 1951—. Mem. A.L.A. (council 1952- 54), Am. Theol. Library Assn. (sec. 1947-50, v.p. 1953-54, pres. 1954- 56). Contbr. religious, library jours. Home: 99 Claremont Av New York City NY 10027

BEACH, WALTER RAYMOND, former ch. adminstr.; b. St. John, N.D., Jan. 18, 1902; s. Herbert Cooke and Margaret (Milliken) B.; B.A., B.Th., Walla Walla Coll., 1923, LL.D., 1954; M.A., Sorbonne div., U. Paris, 1927; m. Gladys Iola Corley, Aug. 9, 1923; children—Bert Beverly, Joyce Raymond (Mrs. David Cotton). Colette Cecile (Mrs. Charles B. Witt). Ordained to ministry Ch. of Seventhday Adventists, 1926; tchr., 1922-26; church adminstr., France and Belgium, 1928-36, so. Europe and European Colonial Territories in Africa, 1936-54; sec. Gen. Conf. Seventh-day Adventists, Takoma Park, Wash., 1954-70. Mem. Livre d'Or (Sorbonne U.). Author: (in S. European langs.) South to the Mascareignes, 1938; Eventide or Morning Glory, 1946; We and Our Children, 1948. Home: 7410 Aspen Av Takoma Park WA Office: 6840 Eastern Av Takoma Park WA 98499

BEACH, WARREN, artist; b. Mpls., May 21, 1914; s. Joseph Warren and Elizabeth (Northrop) B.; B.F.A., Yale, 1939; A.M., U. Ia., 1940, Harvard, 1947; m. Eleanor Gilmore Denham, Jan. 4, 1941; children—David Warren, Margaret Elizabeth, Richard Denham. Dir. extension services Walker Art Center, Mpls., 1940-41; asst. art mus. Addison Gallery Am., Andover, Mass., 1946- 47; asst. dir. Columbus Gallery, 1947-55; dean Columbus Art Sch., 1947- 49; dir. Fine Arts Gallery of San Diego, 1955-69. Exhibited paintings Minn., Mass., Ia., Ohio. Served as 1st lt. AUS, Alaskan Theatre, 1941- 45. Mem. Am. Assn. Mus., Addison Gallery Am. Arts, Nat., Western assns. art mus. dirs., Friends Fogg Art Museum, Yale Gallery Assos. Rotarian. Home: 3740 Pio Pico San Diego CA 92106

BEACH, WILLIAM WALDO, educator; b. Middletown, Conn., Aug. 2, 1916; s. William D. and Edith (Waldo) B.; B.A., Wesleyan U., Middletown, 1937; B.D., Yale, 1940, Ph.D., 1944; m. Mary Heckman, Jan. 2, 1943; children—Richard Waldo, Margaret Ann, Elizabeth Ann. Ordained to ministry Methodist Ch., 1940; prof. religion, coll. pastor Antioch Coll., 1942-46; prof. Christian Ethics Duke Div. Sch., also Duke Grad. Sch. Arts and Scis., 1946—, dir. grad. studies in religion at univ., 1959-69. Chmn. Council Grad. Studies in Religion, 1962-65. Trustee Wesleyan U., Middletown. Del. N. Am. Conf. Faith and Order, World Council Ch., Oberlin, O., 1956. Mem. Soc. Religion Higher Edn. (dir.), Am. Theol. Soc., Phi Beta Kappa. Author: (with Richard Niebuhr) Christian Ethics, 1955; Conscience on Campus, 1958; The Christian Life, 1967; Christian Community and American Society, 1969. Bd. editors Christianity and Crisis. Home: 130 Pinecrest Rd Durham NC 27705

BEACHBOARD, WALTER WILLIAM, pharm. co. exec.; b. Berkeley, Cal., Oct. 14, 1907; s. Walter William and Louise (Lehman) B.; A.B., U. Pa., 1929, LL.B., 1932; m. Harriet Colby, Dec. 17, 1938; 1 dau., Louise, Admitted to Pa. bar, 1932, N.J. bar, 1937, N.Y. bar, 1940, U. S. Supreme Ct. bar, 1968; atty. Prudential Ins. Co. Am., 1932-40; asso. firm Hughes, Hubbard & Ewing. N.Y.C., 1940-43; contract negotiator USAAF, 1943-45; atty. R. H. Macy & Co., Inc., N.Y.C., 1945-47; gen. atty. Smith Kline & French Labs., 1947-65, sec., gen. counsel, 1965-70, v.p., 1971—. Pres. Main Line Center of Arts, 1965-66; mem. Gov.'s Rev. of Govt. Mgmt. Commn., 1971. Bd. dirs. Haverford Civic Assn. Mem. Am., Phila. bar assns., Pa. Economy League (bd. dirs.). Republican. Unitarian. Clubs: Racquet (Phila.); Merion Cricket (Haverford). Home: 120 Orchard Lane Haverford PA 19041 Office: 1500 Spring Garden St Philadelphia PA 19101

BEADLE, GEORGE WELLS, biologist and educator; b. Wahoo, Neb., Oct. 22, 1903; s. Chauncey Elmer and Hattie (Albro) B.; B.S., U. Neb., 1926, M.S., 1927; Ph.D., Cornell U., 1931, M.A., Oxford, 1958, D.Sc. (hon.), 1959; D.Sc., Yale, 1947, U. Neb., 1949, Northwestern, 1952, Rutgers U., 1954, Kenyon Coll., 1955, Wesleyan U., 1956, D.Sc., Birmingham U., 1959, Pomona Coll., 1961, Lake Forest Coll., 1962, Rochester, 1963, U. Ill., 1963, Brown U., 1964, Kan. State U., 1964, U. Pa., 1964, Wabash Coll., 1966. Syracuse U., 1967, Loyola U., Chgo., 1970, Hanover Coll., 1971; LL.D., U. Cal. at Los Angeles, 1962, Miami, 1963, Brandeis U., 1963, Johns Hopkins, 1966, Beloit Coll., 1966, U. Mich., 1969; D.H.L., Jewish Theol. Sem. Am., 1966, DePaul U., 1969, U. Chgo., 1969, Canisius Coll., 1969, Knox Coll., 1969, Carroll Coll., 1971, Roosevelt U., 1971; D. Pub. Service, Ohio No. U., 1970; m. Marion Cecile Hill, Aug. 22, 1928 (div. 1953); 1 son, David; m. 2d, Muriel Barnett, Aug. 12, 1953; stepson, Redmond James Barnett. Teaching asst. Cornell U., 1926-27, experimentalist, 1927-31; NRC fellow, Cal. Inst. Tech., 1931-33, instr., 1933-35; guest investigator, Institut of Biologie, physico-chimique, Paris, 1935; asst. prof. genetics Harvard, 1936-37; prof. biology (genetics) Stanford, 1937-47; prof. biology and chmn. div. of biology Cal. Inst. Tech., 1946-60, acting dean faculty, 1960-61; pres., trustee prof. biology U. Chgo., 1961-68, pres. emeritus, William E. Wrather Distinguished Service prof., 1969—; dir. Inst. for Biomed. Research, A.M.A., Chgo., 1968-70; Eastman vis. prof. Oxford U., 1958-59. Mem. President's Sci. Adv. Council, 1960; hon. pres. 12th Internat. Congress Genetics, 1968. Hon. trustee Mus. Sci. and Industry, Chgo.; trustee Cal. Inst. Tech. Recipient Lasker award, 1950, Dyer award, 1951, Emil C. Hansen prize (Denmark), 1953; Albert Einstein Commemorative award in sci., 1958; Nobel Prize in medicine and physiology (with Edward L. Tatum and Joshua Lederberg), 1958; Am. Cancer Soc. award, 1959; Kimber Genetics award, 1960; Priestley Meml. award, 1967. Mem. Nat. Acad. Scis. (mem. council 1969-71), Am. Philos. Soc., Royal Soc., Japan Acad. (hon.), Inst. Lombardo, Scienze e Lettre (Milan), A.A.A.S. (pres. 1946), Am. Acad. Arts and Scis., Genetics Soc. Am. (pres. 1955), Genetics Soc. Gt. Britain, Indian Soc. Genetics and Plant Breeding, Indian Nat. Sci. Acad., Chgo. Hort. Soc. (pres. 1968-71, trustee) Danish Royal Acad. Scis., Phi Beta Kappa (hon.), Sigma Xi. Clubs: Cosmos, Chicago; Tavern; University (N.Y.C.). Author: (with Alfred H. Sturtevant) An Introduction to Genetics, 1939; Genetics and Modern Biology, 1963; (with Muriel B. Beadle) The Language of Life, 1966 (Edison award best sci. book for youth 1967). Home: 5533 Dorchester Av Chicago IL 60637 Office: Dept Biology U Chgo Chicago IL 60637

BEADLE, MURIEL MCCLURE BARNETT, (Mrs. George Wells Beadle), civic worker, writer; b. Alhambra, Cal., Sept. 14, 1915; d. Richard and Eunice L. (Bothwell) McClure; B.A., Pomona Coll., 1936; Dr. of Humane Letters, Mundelein Coll., 1966; m. Joseph Y. Barnett, July 3, 1941 (dec. Feb. 1951); 1 son, Redmond James; m. 2d. George Wells Beadle, Aug. 12, 1953. Advt. copywriter Carson Pirie Scott & Co., Chgo., 1936-40, Bullock's Pasadena (Cal.), 1946-48; fashion editor, women's editor Los Angeles Mirror-News, 1948-59; freelance writer newspapers and mags., 1958—. Lectr. on edn. and social welfare, cons. various educator groups, 1957—; v.p. Pasadena Com. on Pub. Edn., 1957-60; mem. Pasadena Library Bd., 1959-61; chmn. Harper Ct. Found., 1962—. Recipient citation City of Pasadena, 1960, citation for service to pub. edn. Pasadena Edn. Assn., 1959, award Chgo. Friends of Lit., 1962, Thomas Alva Edison Found. award, 1966. Mem. Phi Beta Kappa, Delta Kappa Gamma. Democrat. Clubs: Fortnightly, Friday (Chgo.). Author: These Ruins are Inhabited, 1961; (with husband) The Language of Life, 1966; A Child's Mind, 1970. Address: 5533 Dorchester Av Chicago IL 60637

BEADLE, ROY JAMES, newspaper editor; b. Gresham, Ore., May 9, 1912; s. Richard and Erdine (Brooks) B.; A.B., Linfield Coll., McMinnville, Ore., 1934, L.H.D. (hon.), 1966; m. Ruth Genevieve Gustafson, Sept. 23, 1939; 1 son, Charles R. Reporter, Gresham Outlook, 1936-37; mem. staff Ore. Jour., Portland, 1937—, asso. editor editorial page, 1967—. Sec. bd. trustees Linfield Coll., 1962—; mem. bd. Ore. Colls. Found., 1961—; mem. adv. com. Lewis and Clark Trail, 1967—; adv. council Mt. Hood Nat. Forest, 1959—; br. bd. chmn. Portland YMCA, 1962-64; mem. bd. Ore. Tb and Respiratory Disease Assn., 1971—. Served with USNR, 1943-45. Recipient Beaver award Izaak Walton League Ore., 1959; citation Ore. com. Am. Forest Products Industry, 1961; award Portland Traffic Safety Commn., 1969. Mem. Linfield Alumni Assn. (pres. 1952-53), Portland C. of C. (com. chmn. 1960-62). Republican. Baptist (moderator 1969—, adv. com. nat. mag. Crusader 1962-65). Rotarian. Author newspaper series on Israel, 1959, on Republic of S. Africa, 1966. Home: 1626 N Willamette Blvd Portland OR 97217 Office: 1320 SW Broadway Portland OR 97201

BEADLES, JACK ANDREWS, banker; b. Union City, Tenn., Oct. 20, 1914; s. Arleigh Joe and Mary (Stephens) B.; grad. Am. Inst. Banking, 1942; m. Jenny Eunice Jones, Nov. 20, 1951. With First Am. Nat. Bank, Nashville, 1937—, auditor, 1952—, v.p. 1962—, v.p. and controller, 1968—. Served with USAAF, 1942-45. Mem. Bank Adminstrn. Inst. (pres. Nashville 1953-54). Presbyn. Mason (32). Home: 4210 Hillcrest Av Nashville TN 37204 Office: 326 Union St Nashville TN 37202

BEAGLE, PETER SOYER, writer; b. N.Y.C., Apr. 20, 1939; s. Simon and Rebecca (Soyer) B.; B.A., U. Pitts., 1959; student Stanford, 1960-61; m. Enid Nordeen, May 8, 1964; children—Vicki Lynn, Kalisa, Daniel Nordeen. Author: A Fine and Private Place, 1960; I See By My Outfit, 1965; The Last Unicorn, 1968; The California Feeling, 1969; screenwriter; free-lance writer for Holiday, Sat. Eve. Post, Venture, West, Atlantic Monthly, Ladies Home Jour., others. Vice chmn. Santa Cruz chpt. Am. Civil Liberties Union, 1968-69. Address: 311 E Rianda Rd Watsonville CA 95076

BEAHRS, OLIVER HOWARD, surgeon; b. Eufaula, Ala., Sept. 19, 1914; s. Elmer Charles and Elsa Kathryn (Smith) B.; B.A., U. Cal. at Berkeley, 1937; M.D., Northwestern U., 1942; M.S. in Surgery, Mayo Grad. Sch. Medicine, 1949; m. Helen Edith Taylor, July 27, 1947; children—John Randolf, David Howard, Nancy Ann. Fellow surgery Mayo Grad. Sch. Medicine, 1942, 46-49; prof. surgery, 1966—; asst. surgeon Mayo Clinic, 1949-50, head sect. gen. Surgery, 1950—, vice chmn. bd. govs., 1964—. Bd. trustees Mayo Found. Served to lt. comdr. USNR, 1942-46; capt. Res. Diplomate Am. Bd. Surgery. Mem. A.C.S., Minn. Surg. Soc. (pres. 1960- 61), A.M.A., Am. Thyroid Assn., James IV Assn. Surgeons, Am., So., Central, Western surg. assns., Soc. Head and Neck Surgeons (pres. 1966-67), Soc. Surgery Alimentary Tract, Soc. Pelvic Surgeons, Sigma Xi, Phi Kappa Epsilon, Phi Beta Pi, Theta Delta Chi. Republican. Methodist. Author articles in field. Home: Route 1 Rochester MN 55901 Office: 200 First St SW Rochester MN 55901

BEAIRD, BETTY JO, actress; b. El Paso, Tex.; d. Benjamin Jessup and George Bell (Rowell) Beaird; B.B.A., U. Tex., 1956; postgrad. U. Hawaii, 1956, Columbia, 1960-61, Pepperdine Coll., 1970-71. Radio writer KTBC-TV, Austin, Tex., 1956-58; prodn. estimator NBC-TV, N.Y.C., 1958-62; prodn. asst. Arthur Murray Show, N.Y.C., 1962-65; comml. producer Edward H. Weiss Advt., N.Y.C., 1965-67; prodn. asst.-writer Goodson Todman, N.Y.C., 1967-69; appeared in N.Y. performance Upstairs at the Downstairs, Julia NBC-TV role Marie Waggedorn, 1969-71; owner Deux Bes Fashion Boutique, Malibu, Cal., 1971—. Named Outstanding Young Woman of Am., 1970. Mem. Kappa Alpha Theta. Comedy writer, creater TV scripts and ideas. Home: 24942 Malibu Rd Malibu CA 90265 Office: 22237 Pacific Coast Hwy Malibu CA 90265

BEAKES, KENDALL DOUGLAS, govt. ofcl.; b. Washington, Pa., Nov. 17, 1923; s. Edwin Augist and Elsie (Hauck) B.; B.A., Western Mid. Coll., 1948; student U.Paris, 1948 49, U. Aix Marselle, 1949, U. Strasbourg, 1949-50; Docteur es Lettres, U. Besancon (France), 1964; m. Maria M. Haas, Aug. 16, 1954; children—Douglas Edwin, Christine Maria. Edn. adviser U.S. Army, Austria, 1950-54, edn. cons., Morocco, 1954-56; liaison officer for edn. USAF, Germany, 1956-58; dep. dir. U.S. Armed Forces Inst., Germany, 1958- 61; dir. edn. USAF, Europe, 1961—. Active Boy Scouts Am. Served with AUS, 194345. Recipient Meritorious Civilian Service award, Air Force Outstanding award (3), Air Force Sustained Superior award. Mem. European Programmed Instrn. Assn. (v.p. 196265), Beta Beta Beta, Gamma Beta Chi. Author: Moroccan Arabic Simplified, 1955; Skiing in Austria, 1953; East and West at Stalingrad, 1969. Home: 2 Heilengenbornstrasse Wiesbaden 62 Federal Republic of Germany Office: Hdqrs USAFE (DPBTE) APO NY 09633

BEAL, GEORGE MELVIN, univ. adminstr.; b. Parkdale, Ore., May 21, 1917; B.S., Ia. State U., 1943, M.S., 1947, Ph.D., 1953; m. Evelyn Frances Miller, June 6, 1944; children—Carolee, Linda, Dirk, David. Mem. faculty Ia. State U., Ames, 1946—, now chmn. dept. sociology and anthropology. With Ford Found., India, 1958; mem. evaluation com. on health, edn. and communications Dept. Health, Edn. and Welfare, 1964-65; mem. surgeon gen.'s Task Force on Smoking and Health, 1967-68; research Agrl. Devel. Council (Rockefeller), Guatemala, 1964; U.S. rep. to UNESCO com. to develop evaluation plan for literacy programs, 1966. Served to capt. AUS, 1943-46. Mem. Internat. (rep. on council), Am. sociol. assns., Midwest, Rural sociol. socs., Sigma Delta Chi, Alpha Kappa Delta, Gamma Sigma Delta, Phi Kappa Phi. Co-author: Leadership and Dynamic Group Action, 1962; Social Action and Integration in program planning, 1966. Co-editor: Sociological Perspective of Domestic Development, 1971. Contbr. chpts. books, articles profl. jours. Home: 2022 McCarthy Rd Ames IA 50010

BEAL, JAMES HARVEY, lawyer; b. Pitts., Aug. 28, 1898; s. James H. and Beatrice (Littell) B.; A.B., Princeton, 1920; LL.B., U. Pitts., 1923; LL.D., Waynesburg (Pa.) Coll., 1959; m. Rebecca Jones, July 21, 1923. Partner Reed, Smith, Shaw & McClay; dir. Allegheny Trust Co., 1942-69, Pitts. Gage & Supply Co. 1935-70. Trustee Carnegie Inst., Carnegie-Mellon U.; Carnegie Library, Pitts. Assn. for Improvement of Poor (v.p.), Hist. Soc. W.Pa. (v.p.), Pitts. Zool. Soc. (v.p.). Mem. Allegheny Co., Pa., Am. bar assns., Am. Law Inst. Presbyn. (trustee). Home: Park Plaza Apts Craig St Pittsburgh PA 15213 Office: Union Trust Bldg Pittsburgh PA 15219

BEAL, JOHN M., physician; b. Starkville, Miss., 1915; M.D., U. Chgo., 1941. Intern N.Y. Hosp., N.Y.C., 1941-42, asst. resident surgery, 1942-44, 46-47, surgeon, 1947-48, asst. attending surgeon, 1953-63; chmn. tumor bd. and staff surgeon Wadsworth Gen. Hosp., West Los Angeles, Cal., 1949-50, chief surg. service, 1950-53; cons.

staff St. John's Hosp., Santa Monica, Cal., 1950-53; instr. surgery Cornell U., 1948-49, asso. prof. clin. surgery, 1953-63; instr. surgery U. Cal. at Los Angeles, 1949-50, asst. prof., 1950-53; now prof., chmn. dept. surgery Northwestern U.; chmn. dept. surgery Chgo. Wesley Meml. Hosp., 1963-69; chief of surgery Passavant Meml. Hosp., Chgo. Served to capt. M.C., AUS, 1944-46. Diplomate Am. Bd. Surgery (chmn. 1970-71). Fellow A.C.S.; mem. Soc. U. Surgeons, Soc. Clin. Surgery, A.M.A., Am. Surg. Assn. Address: Northwestern U Medical School Chicago IL 60611

BEAL, KENNETH MALCOLM, educator; b. Salem, Mass., July 4, 1906; s. Kenneth and Annie May (Lopaus) B.; B.A., Dartmouth, 1928; A.M., Harvard, 1935; m. Rachel Weston Palmateer, Sept. 8, 1931; 1 dau., Nancy May (Mrs. James M. Keech, Jr.). Instr. English, preparatory dept. Am. U., Beirut, Lebanon, 1928-31; instr. French and English, Jr. High Sch., Wellesley, Mass., 1932-39; mem. faculty U. Miami (Fla.). 1939—, prof. English, 1952—, chmn. dept., 1959-61, chmn. div. humanities, 1960-62. Mem. Am. Assn. U. Profs., S. Atlantic Modern Lang. Assn., Hist. Assn. So. Fla. Home: 3615 Poinciana Av Coconut Grove, FL 33133. Office: Univ Miami Coral Gables FL 33124

BEAL, ORVILLE ELLSWORTH, ins. exec.; b. Monvue, Pa., Mar. 11, 1909; s. John Dinsmore and Viola Pearl (Grimm) B.; A.B., Rutgers U., 1937, M.B.A., 1954; m. Jean Doris Vivers, Oct. 1, 1938; children—Bruce, Beverly. With Prudential Ins. Co. of Am., Newark, 1926-69, sr. v.p. dist. agys. 1947-51; sr. v.p. pub. relations, 1951-53, sr. v.p. charge north central operation, 1953-57, exec. v.p., 1957-62, sr. exec. v.p., 1962, pres., 1962-69, now dir.; chmn. bd. Engelhard Enterprises; dir. R.H. Macy, Engelhard Minerals & Chems. Corp., Servomation, Howard Savs. Instn. Mem. Nat. council Boy Scouts Am. Trustee past pres. Life Underwriters Tng. Council, Newark YM-YWCA; trustee Rutgers U., Symphony Hall, Inc., Newark Mus. Assn., Greater Newark Hosp. Devel Fund. C.L.U., Am. Coll. Life Underwriters, 1941 (trustee). Mem. Am. Soc. C.L.U.'s, Phi Beta Kappa, Beta Gamma Sigma. Conglist. Clubs: Baltusrol, Lost Tree, Essex. Home: Short Hills NJ 07078 Office: 10 Oaklawn Rd Short Hills NJ 07078

BEAL, THADDEUS REYNOLDS, lawyer, govt. ofcl.; b. N.Y.C., Mar. 22, 1917; s. Thaddeus Reynolds and Alice (Dresel) B.; A.B., Yale, 1939; LL.B., Harvard, 1947; m. Katharine Putnam, June 4, 1944; children—Katharine, Thadeus Reynolds. Alice, George P. Admitted to Mass. bar, 1947; asso. Herrick, Smith, Donald, Farley & Ketchum, Boston, 1947-55, partner, 1956-57; pres., dir. Harvard Trust Co.; under sec. of army, 1969—. Home: 3500 Lowell St Washington DC 20016

BEAL, THOMAS PRINCE, banker; b. Boston, Apr. 12, 1883; s. Thomas P. and Ida (DeFord) B.; grad. Noble and Greenough Sch., Boston, 1900; A.B., Harvard, 1904; m. May Lefferts Morgan, Aug. 11, 1921; children—Judith Drew (Mrs. Herbert T. Nadal), Thomas Prince. Asst. cashier 2d Nat. Bank of Boston, 1908, v.p., 1910, pres., 1923, chmn. bd., 1950- -, now chmn. adv. com. State Street Bank and Trust Co., merger of 2d Nat. Bank and State St. Trust Co.; hon. trustee Suffolk Franklin Savs. Bank; incorporator Charlestown Savs. Bank, Boston. Trustee Mt. Auburn Cemetery. Pres. Boston Clearing House, 1943, 45, 48, 52. Republican. Episcopalian. Clubs: Somerset, Union (Boston); Country (Brookline). Home: 47 Lawrence Rd Chestnut Hill MA 02167 Office: 225 Franklin St Boston MA 02110

BEAL, WALTER HUBERT, mgmt. cons.; b. Toledo, Ia.; s. Albert M. (M.D.) and Carrie (Middlekauff) B.; grad. U. of Ill., 1916; m. Dorothy Barratt, June 2, 1920; children—Walter Hubert, Richard Barratt. Began with Lycoming Mfg. Co., Williamsport, Pa., 1919, sales mgr., 1919-27, v.p., 1927-30, gen. mgr., 1930-31, became pres., 1931; pres. Auburn (Ind.) Automobile Co., 1932-34; chmn. bd. N.Y. Shipbuilding Corp., 1935-38; pres. Aviation Mfg. Corp., N.Y.C., 1938- 40; now mgmt. cons. Riker-Maxson Corp.; dir. Somat Corp., Pomeroy, Pa.; chmn. bd. Penn-Jersey Shipbldg. Corp., 1941-46, pres. 1942-46. Served to capt. Ordnance Dept., U.S. Army, World War I. Mem. Delta Kappa Epsilon. Presbyterian. Clubs: Merion Cricket, Merion Golf (Haverford, Pa.); Racquet (Philadelphia). Home: Quarry Hill Righter's Mill Rd Gladwynne PA 19035 Office: 225 S 15th St Philadelphia PA 19102

BEALE, BETTY (Mrs. George K. Graeber), columnist; b. Washington; d. William Lewis and Edna (Sims) Beale; A.B., Smith Coll.; m. George Kenneth Graeber, Feb. 15, 1969. Columnist Washington Post, 1937-40; reporter and columnist Washington Evening Star, 1945—; weekly columnist Publishers Hall Syndicate, 1953—; lectr. Named Am. Woman of Accomplishment, Multiple Sclerosis Soc.; Assn. Fed. Investigator Spl. Act award, 1968; Freedom Found. award, 1969. Clubs: Washington Press, 1925 F Street (Washington). Address: 2926 Garfield St NW Washington DC 20008

BEALE, FRANKLIN AMBROSE, sugar co. exec.; b. Enfield, N.H., Feb. 14, 1914; s. Arthur W. and Bernice (Follansbee) B.; B.S., U. N.H., 1935; grad. Advanced Mgmt. Program, Harvard, 1958; exec. control certificate, Syracuse U., 1960; m. Anita C. Reilly, Apr. 6, 1938; children—Bernice E., Carolyn B. Research agronomist Luce and Co., SenC, Aguire, P.R., 1935-40, asst. div. supt., 1941-46, div. supt., 1947-58, gen. mgr., 1949-56, gen. mng. partner, 1956-57; exec. v.p. Central Aguirre Sugar Co., 1957-68; exec. v.p., dir. Central Machete Co., 1965-68, Coddea, Inc., 1968; v.p. Ponce Guayana R. R., 1965-68, also dir.; v.p. Casco Sales Corp. Inc.; adminstr. Sucesion J. Serralles, 1969-70; gen. mgr. The New Central Aguirre 1970—. dir. Equipment Services, Inc., Casco Sales Inc., Banco Crédito y Ahorre Ponceño. Mem. adv. com. sugar research and marketing U.S. Dept. Agr. Mem. Sugar Products Assn. P.R. (dir.), Sugar Technologists P.R. (pres. 1965), Alpha Zeta. Clubs: Bankers (San Juan, P.R.); Aguirre Country; Ponce Yacht and Fishing, Depontivo (Ponce, P.R.). Address: The New Central Aguirre Aguirre PR 00608

BEALE, HOWARD, former Australian diplomat; b. Tamworth, Australia, Dec. 10, 1898; s. Rev. Joseph and Clara Elizabeth (Vickery) B.; B.A., U. Sydney, 1921, LL.B., 1925; LL.D., Kent U., 1959, Marquette U., 1969; Marquette U., 1969; L.H.D., Neb. Wesleyan U., 1963; m. Margery E. Wood, Dec. 19, 1927; 1 son, Julian Howard. Called to bar, 1925, created King's counsel, 1950; minister information and transport Australian Govt., 1949-50, minister supply, 1950-58, minister def. prodn., 1956-58; minister charge of the Australian Aluminum Prodn. Com., 1950-58, minister in charge Australian Atomic Energy Com. and Rum Jungle uranium project, 1950-58; acting minister immigration, 1951-52, 53, 54, for nat. devel., 1952-53, for air, 1952, for def., 1957; Australian ambassador to U.S., 1958-64; Regents vis. prof. U. Cal., 1966; Distinguished vis. prof. Marguette U., Milw., 1967, 69. Chmn. bd. Pye Industries Ltd., Munduna Investments Ltd., Offshore Royalties, Inc. (U.S.); v.p. Occidental Mining & Petroleum Corp. (U.S.); dir. Selcast Exploration Ltd., Engelhard Industries Ltd. Mem. Commonwealth Parliamentary Pub. Works Com., 1947-49; chmn. Australian Transport Adv. Council, 1949-50; mem. Australian Def. Council, 1950-58, Cabinet Com. Def. Preparations and Com. Uranium and Atomic Energy, 1950-58. Australian del. Internat. Bar Congress. The Hague, 1948; Australian rep. Anzus Council, Washington, 1958-59, Canberra, Australia, 1962; dep. leader Australian delegation to UN, N.Y., 1959; dep. leader, later leader Australian delegation to Antarctic Conf., Washington, 1959, Australian del. SEATO Confs., Washington, 1959, 60; leader Australian delegation Colombo Plan Conf., Seattle, 1958, World Food Congress, Washington, 1963; alternate gov. IMF, 1960, 62. Woodward lectr. Yale, 1960. Liberal mem. Australian Parliament, 1946-58. Served with Royal Australian Navy, 1942-45. Created knight comdr. Order Brit. Empire, 1961, Queen's Counsel, 1961. Dean Brit. Commonwealth diplomatic corps, Washington, 1961-64. Clubs: Union, Pioneers, Am. Nat. (Sydney, Australia); Elanora Country. Address: 21 Cranbrook Lane Bellevue Hill Sydney Australia

BEALL, ARTHUR CHARLES, Jr., educator, physician; b. Atlanta, Aug. 17, 1929; s. Arthur Charles and Clare (Scott) B.; B.S., Emory U., 1950, M.D., 1953; m. Cornelia Louise Williams, Aug. 22, 1949; children—Arthur Charles III, Vincent Lane, Intern Barnes Hosp., St. Louis, 1953-54; resident Baylor U. Coll. Medicine Affiliated Hosps., 1954-61; mem. faculty Baylor U. Coll. Medicine, 1959—, prof.. surgery, 1971—; mem. active staff Methodist, Ben Taub Gen., Jefferson Davis and VA hosps., Houston; cons. Tex. Inst. Rehab. and Research, Tex. Research Inst. Mental Scis. Served with USNR, 1956-58. Diplomate Am. Bd. Surgery, Am. Bd. Thoracic Surgery. Mem. Am., So., Pan Am., Tex. med. assns., Harris County Med. Soc., Am., Tex., Houston, (dir. 1965-68) heart assns., Am. Fedn. Clin. Research, So. Soc. Clin. Investigation, Tex., Houston surg. socs., Southwestern Surg. Congress, So., Western, and Pan Pacific surgical assns., Internat. Cardiovascular Soc., Soc. Vascular Surgery, Soc. Univ. Surgeons, Soc. Thoracic Surgeons, Am. Gerontol. Soc., Am. Assn. Surgery Trauma, Am. Assn. Thoracic Surgery, A.C.S., Am. Coll. Cardiology (v.p. 1971—), So. Thoracic Surgery Assn., Am. Coll. Chest Physicians (chmn. bd. regents 1970—), Alliance for Engring. in Medicine and Biology (v.p. 1969-71), Assn. Advancement of Medical instrumentation (president 1967-69). Author numerous articles published in field. Research, devel. techniques open heart surgery, particularly areas pulmonary embolectomy and heart vale replacement. Home: 3218 Ella Lee Lane Houston TX 77019

BEALL, CARLTON G., govt. ofcl.; b. Ritchie, Md., May 4, 1918; s. James Bernard and Mildred (Ritchie) B.; ed. pub. schs., Md.; m. Jean Gordon Tranband, July 10, 1940; children—Carlton G., Richard T. Spl. asst. Md. Racing Commn., 1947- 49; Sheriff prince George's Co., Md., 1950-54; U.S. Marshall for D.C., 1954-58; postmaster, Washington, 1958—; owner, operator tobacco firm so. Md.; pres. Carlton Manor Realty Corp. Chmn. Republican Central Com. Prince George's County. Served with USNR, 1943-46. Mem. Am. Legion. Nat. Assn. Postmasters U.S. Methodist. Mason, Lion. Club: Circle. Home: 2806 West Av SE Washington DC 20028 Office: Post Office N Capitol and Massachusetts Av Washington DC 20002

BEALL, CHARLES CLYDE, Jr., banker; b. Oxford, Miss., Mar. 28, 1935; s. Charles Clyde and Jennie Dale (Buford) B.; B.B.A., U. Miss., 1957, M.B.A., 1961; m. Ines Anne Watts, July 21, 1961; 1 son, Charles Clyde III. With Tex. Commerce Bank, Houston, 1961—, sr. v.p., 1969—. Served to capt. USAF, 1958-60. Home: 7910 Burgoyne St Houston TX 77042 Office: 712 Main St Houston TX 77001

BEALL, CHARLES ROBERT, paper co. exec.; b. Philadelphia, Miss., Nov. 4, 1918; s. Joshua Henry and Annie Laura (Byars) B.; grad. high sch.; m. Jessie Margaret Culver, Jan. 20, 1940; children—Mary Tina, Charles Robert, Marcia Ellen, James Henry. With McKesson & Robbins, Inc., 1937-68, S.W. dist. sales mgr., 1951-56. v.p., retail trade promotion mgr., N.Y.C., 1956-60, v.p. charge drug sales and promotion, 1960-63, v.p. marketing, 1963-66, v.p. corporate planning, 1966-67; exec. v.p. devel. Foremost-McKesson, 1967; asst. to pres. Internat. Paper Co., 1968, v.p. devel., 1969; chmn. bd. Davol Internat. Ltd., 1969—; dir. Davol, Inc., Providence. Mem. Nat. Wholesale Druggists Assn., Disposables Assn. (bd. govs.). Clubs: American (London); Scarsdale (N.Y.) Golf; Sky (N.Y.C.). Home: 17 Church Lane S Scarsdale NY 10583 Office: 220 E 42d St New York City NY 10017

BEALL, FRANKLIN MELVIN, aerospace co. exec.; b. Washington, Oct. 3, 1912; s. John Franklin and Hester (Melvin) B.; B.A., Balt. Coll. Commerce, 1935; m. Margaret Ashton, Sept. 18, 1940 (dec. 1967); children—Anne Ashton, Jane Marshall (Mrs. Van T. Hoffmann), Barbara Hyde (Mrs. Steven L. Mixter). Accountant, Haskins & Sells, C.P.A.'s, Balt., 1936-40; accounting machine rep. Nat. Cash Register Co., Balt., 1940-42; mem. comptroller's staff Pitts. Plate Glass Co., 1942-43; div. controller Martin Marietta Corp., Balt., 1943-66; comptroller Fairchild Hiller Corp., 1967—. Trustee Balt. Coll. Commerce. C.P.A., Md. Mem. Am. Inst. C.P.A.'s, Financial Execs. Inst., Nat. Assn. Accountants, Md. Assn. C.P.A.'s. Club: Balt. Country. Home: 5418 St Albans Way Baltimore, MD 21212. Office: Sherman Fairchild Tech Center Germantown MD 20767

BEALL, GEORGE BROOKE, lawyer; b. Dallas, Nov. 1, 1926; s. George Brooke and Alta (Phillips) B.; student So. Meth. U., 1946-47; A.B., U. Chgo., 1949, J.D., 1953; student U. Paris (France) Law Sch., 1963-65; m. Ingrid Ingeborg Lillehei, Dec. 20, 1950. Admitted to Ill. bar, 1953; with firm Kennedy & Kennedy, Chgo., 1952-55, Isham, Lincoln & Beale, Chgo., 1955-63, Baker & McKenzie, Paris and Chgo., 1964—. Served with USNR, 1944-46. Home: 175 E Delaware Pl Chicago IL 60611 Office: Baker & McKenzie Prudential Bldg Chicago IL 60601

BEALL, JOHN ALLEN, Jr., army officer; b. Tex., May 23, 1912; grad. Tex. Mil. Acad.; B.S., U.S. Mil. Acad., 1935; grad. Air War Coll., 1951. Commd. 2d lt. U.S. Army, advanced through grades to maj. gen., 1966. Decorated Silver Star, Legion of Merit with 2 oak leaf clusters, Bronze Star. Address: care Office Adj Gen US Army Washington, DC 20310.*

BEALL, PAUL RENSSELAER, communications cons.; b. Des Moines, Aug. 28, 1909; s. Ollie Monroe and Helen May (Paul) B.; A.B., Grinnell Coll., 1932; student law Harvard, 1935-36; A.M., U. Mich., 1940; Ph.D., Pa. State U., 1948, spl. courses indsl. engring., 1948-50; m. Helen Minerva Wadsworth, Sept. 18, 1937; children—Helen Wadsworth, Sarah Evarts, Christopher Wadsworth Paul, Nancy Patch. Eastern states sales mgr. Morrison-Shults Mfg. Co., leather products, 1932-39; teaching fellow speech U. Mich., 1939-41; from instr. to asso. prof. speech and rhetoric Pa. State U., 1941-50, lectr. indsl. engring. extension, 1941-50, summer sch. lectr. in communications problems in mgmt., 1951-57; dir. information, research and devel. bd. Dept. of Def., 1950-51; sci. adviser to comdg. gen. Air Research and Devel. Command, 1952, to comdg. gen. for operations USAF, 1953, to comdg. gen. USAF-Far East, 1955, 57; lectr. Joint U.S.-NATO commands in Europe, intermittently, 1955-58, cons. to founding faculty USAF Acad.; communications cons. in indsl. and mil. mgmt., 1953—; pres. Oglethorpe Coll., Atlanta, 1964-67. Trustee Aerospace Edn. Found. Cons. Community Welfare Dr., Greater Balt., 1955-57; mem. bd. Annapolis Roads (Md.) Property Owners Assn., 1958, 62; mem. visitors adv. council Grinnell Coll., 1962—; mem. pres.'s council Rollins Coll., 1968—; mem. tech. adv. com. Atlanta-Fulton County Econ. Opportunity Authority, 1965- 68. Bd. dirs. Atlanta chpt. UN Assn. U.S., 1964-67. Mem. Speech Assn. Am., Am. Arbitration Assn., Nat. Conf. Adminstrn. Research (pres. 1961), U.S. Air Force Assn. Episcopalian. Mason. Clubs: Cosmos (Washington); Racquet. Contbr. tech. mags. Home: Randall House 323 Trismen Terrace Winter Park FL 32789

BEALL, WELLWOOD E., airplane designer and engring. exec.; b. Cañon City, Colo., Oct. 28, 1906 s. Robert Stevens and Narcissa Mary (Wellwood) B.; student U. Colo., 1924-28, Aeronautical Engr. (profl. degree), 1948; B.S., N.Y.U., 1929, graduate engr.'s degree, 1930; m. Jean S. Cory. Aug. 18, 1934; children—Alan Cory, Cory Wellwood, Barbara Jean; m. 2d, Martha Evelyn Paulding, July 3, 1970. Asst. chief aero. engineer Walter M. Murphy Co., Pasadena, Cal., 1929-30; aero. engr. instr., Boeing Sch., of Aero., Oakland, 1930-34; sales engr., Boeing Co., Seattle, 1934, Far Eastern Mgr., Shanghai, China, 1934-35, chief comml. projects engr., 1936-39, chief engr., 1939-43, v.p. engring., 1943-45; v.p. engring. and sales, 1946-51, sr. v.p. 1952-64, also dir. charge design Boeing Model 314 Flying Boats, Stratoliners, Boeing Super-Fortresses, Stratocruisers, Stratofreighters, Stratojets, guided missiles and attendant engring. research; exec. v.p. operations Douglas Aircraft Co., 1964-68; v.p. McDonnell Douglas Corp., 1967—, also dir.; Dir. Pacific Sci. Found., 1964-68, exec. v.p., 1968—. Served as Lt. (j.g.) USNR, 1931-39. Fellow Am. Inst. Aeros. and Astronautics; mem. Soc. Automotive Engrs., Conquistadores del Cielo, Am. Ordnance Assn., Sigma Chi. Clubs: Los Angeles Country, California, Bel Air Bay, Explorers, Bohemian. Author articles various sci. and engring. mags. Home: 234 S Beverly Glen Blvd Los Angeles CA 90024 Office: 3855 Lakewood Blvd Long Beach CA 90801

BEALL, WILLIAM CHARLES, photographer; b. Washington, Feb. 6, 1911; s. Frank and Zula (Walters) B.; student pub. schs., Washington; m. Mildred Watson, May 30, 1929 (div. 1939); 1 dau., Betty Jane; m. 2d, Anna Mahoney Norman, Aug. 2, 1941; children—Dennis Wade, March Ann, Louise Mahoney and Janet Evelyn (twins). Photog. printer Underwood & Underwood. 1927-32; photographer Washington Post, 1933-35; photographer Washington Daily News, 1935-39, chief photographer, 1939-. Served as combat photographer, corr., cpl. USMC, 1944-46. Decorated Air medal; recipient Pulitzer prize for news photography, 1957. Mem. Nat. Press Photographers Assn., White House Photographers Assn. Home: 2221 Sweet Briar Dr Alexandria VA 22307 Office: 1013 13th St NW Washington DC 20005

BEALS, CARLETON, author, lectr.; b. Medicine Lodge, Kan., Nov. 13, 1893; s. Leon Elverson and Elvina Sybila (Blickensderfer) B.; B.A. cum laude, U. of Cal., 1916; M.A., Columbia, 1917; student U. of Madrid, 1920, U. of Rome, 1922, U. of Mexico, 1923; m. Carolyn Kennedy, 1956. Dir. of the English Prep. Institute, Mexico City, 1919; prin. Am. High Sch., Mexico City, 1919-20; instr. personal staff President Carranza, 1920; lecturer New York Bd. of Edn., 1924; asso. editor Mexican Folkways, 1925-37; asso. editor Latin-Am. Press Syndicate, 1933-34; pres. editorial bd. Latin-Am. Digest, 1934-36; contbg. editor, Common Sense, 1933-41, Modern Monthly, 1935-37, Current History, 1939; mem. adv. bd. Living Age, 1933-35; advisory editor Controversy, 1935. Correspondent in Italy, 1920-22, Mexico, 1923, 1925-28, 1930-32, 1937, 46, 61. in Central Am., 1927-28, (with Gen. Sandino in Nicaragua, 1928), Spain, North Africa, Italy, Turkey, Russia and Germany, 1929, Cuba, 1932-33, 1935, 57, 59-61, Panama, Colombia, Ecuador, Peru, 1934, 46, 61; researcher Housing Authority New Haven, 1959-60; spl. corr. N. Am. Newspaper Alliance, 1935; spl. corr. New York Post, Scottsboro Trial, Ala., 1936; mem. expdns. to Indian regions, Mexico, 1930-31; spl. corr. Argentina, Chile, Bolivia, Peru, 1946, Haiti, 1957, 59, 60, Colombia, Brazil, Paraguay, Venezuela, B.C., Uruguay, 1961; lectr. Latin-Am. Univs., 1961, Mexican-Am. relations, Conf. Cause and Cure of War (Washington), 1927, Seminar on Relations with Mexico, 1925-28 and 1930-31; lecturer on Central America, Nat. U. of Mexico, 1928; faculty lecturer on Modern Mexico and Caribbean, U. of Calif., summer, 1933, New Sch. of Soc. Research, 1935; chmn. Com. Jacques Romain, 1935, mem. adv. bd. Better Understanding Found.; mem. bd. govs. Acad. Fgn. Relations. Mem. roundtable Harris Found., U. Chgo., 1951. Research Fuller F. Barnes Fund, 1952-53. Received Bonnheim Award, 1916, 1917; The Bryce History Prize, 1917; Best Article prize Arizona Quarterly, 1961; Nat. Acad. of Recording Arts and Scis. award, 1965. Fellow John Simon Guggenheim Found., 1931-32. Fellow Am. Geog. Soc., Soc. of Am. Historians; mem. P.E.N., Foreign Press Club (Mexico City), Pi Gamma Mu. Sponsor Nat. Gallery of the Am. Indian; hon. mem. Eugene Field Society. Author: Rio Grande to Cape Horn, 1947; Lands of the Dawning Morrow, 1948; The Long Land Chile, 1948; Our Yankee Heritage (series), The Making of Greater New Haven, 1951, The Making of Bristol, 1954, New England's Contributions to American Civilization, 1955; Stephen Austin; Father of Texas, 1953; American Earth, 1939; Rome or Death, 1923; Taste of Glory, 1956; Adventure of the Western Sea, The Story of Robert Gray, 1956; John Eliot: The Man Who Loved the Indians, 1958; House in Mexico, 1958; The Brass Knuckle Crusade: The Great Know-Nothing Conspiracy, 1959; Nomads and Empire Builders, 1961; Cyclone Carry, The Story of Carry Nation, 1962; Latin America: World in Revolution, 1963; Eagles of the Andes, 1963; War Within a War, 1965; Under the Fifth Sun, Mexico Past and Present, 1965; Land of the Mayas, Past and Present, 1966; The Great Crusade and its Leaders, 1968; Stories Told by the Aztecs, 1968; Great Guerilla Warriors, 1969; Politics U.S.A., 1961; Bits of Silver, 1961. Contributor Ency. of Social Sciences, Ency. Brit., Book of Knowledge Ency.; World Book Ency.; Land and Peoples Ency.; Ency. of Sexual Behavior; also to mags. Address: Firetower Rd Kellingworth Rd 2 Box 25 Deep River CT 06417

BEALS, CARLYLE SMITH, astronomer; b. Canso, N.S., Can., June 29, 1899; s. Francis Harris Parker and Annie (Smith) B.; B.A., Acadia U., 1919, D.Sc., 1948; M.A., U. Toronto, 1923; Ph.D., London U., 1926, D.Sc., 1934; D.Sc., U. N.B., 1956, Queens U., 1960, U. Pitts., 1963; m. Miriam Bancroft, Sept. 13, 1931. Asso. prof. physics Acadia U., 1926-27; astronomer Dominion Astrophys. Obs., Victoria, B.C., 1927-40, asst. dir., 1940-46; dominion astronomer Dominion Obs., Nat. Obs., Can., Ottawa, 1946-64; pvt. sci. consultant, Manotick, Ont., 1964—. Recipient Gold medal Profl. Inst. Pub. Services Can., 1958; Tory gold medal Royal Soc. Can., 1957; Leonard medal Meteoritical Soc., 1966; service medal Order of Can., 1969. Fellow Royal Soc., Royal Astron. Soc., Royal Soc. Can.; mem. Am. Astron. Soc. (pres. 1962). Author papers astrophysics, lunar and terrestrial craters. Address: Manotick Ontario Canada

BEALS, FRANK LEE, retired army officer, educator, author; b. Morganton, Tenn., Sept. 2, 1881; s. Francis (M.D.) and Sadie Louisiana (Dawson) B.; ed. Reidville (S.C.) High Sch., George Washington U., U. Chgo.; B.S., De Paul U., 1930. A.M., 1932; m. Alice Alexandra Barnes, Apr. 17, 1909; children—Elena Louise (dec.), Bettina Byrd; m. Ida Catherine Dusbek, May 1, 1941. Enlisted in U.S. Army, 1898; commd. 2d lt., Oct. 9, 1903; retired for disability in line of duty, May 1, 1908; 1st lt. retired, Oct. 30, 1916; capt. retired, Jan. 1918; maj. retired, Jan. 6, 1922. Served in Philippines, 1899-1900, 1905-06; San Francisco earthquake and fire; mil. attaché, Brazil, 1909-10; comdt. Northwestern Mil. and Naval Acad., 1911-17, examining officer for Wis. state O.T.C., 1917; prof. mil. science and tactics; supr. phys. edn., high schs. Chgo., 1917-32; est. Camp Roosevelt (summer tng. camp for boys), 1919; pres. Racine (Wis.) Mil. Acad., 1930-33; asst. supt. schs., Chgo., 1935-46, supt. compulsory Edn., 1946-48. Wounded at the Battle of Big Bend, P.I., 1899.

Awarded Purple Heart, 1932. Author: Topographical Primer, 1914; Squad Leaders' Note Book, 1917; Beal (e,l,s) the Ancient Name, 1929; Look Away Dixieland, 1937; Kit Carson, David Crocket, 1941; Chief Black Hawk, Buffalo Bill, 1943; The Story of Robinson Crusoe; The Story of Lemuel Gulliver in Lilliput Land; Rush for Gold, 1945; The Story of the Three Musketeers, Boswell in Chicago, 1946; The Story of Treasure Island, 1947; The Story of Moby Dick, 1949; The Patriot Silversmith, 1949; The Story of Deerslayer, 1950; Backwoods Baron, The Life Story of Claude Albert Fuller, 1951; The Story of Two Years Before the Mast, 1952; The Story of the Prince and The Pauper, 1953; American Heroes Series, 1954; Spanish Adventure Trails, 1960. Home: Eureka Springs AR 72632

BEALS, HAROLD, univ. adminstr.; B.S., Wis. State U.; M.S., Ph.D., U. Wis. mem. faculty Wis. State U. Platteville, dean students, now v.p. for student affairs. Office: Dept Agr Wis State U Platteville WI 53818

BEALS, JOHN DAVID, Jr., lawyer; b. N.Y.C., Jan. 19, 1896; s. John D. and Mary Helen (Nicholson) B.; student Collegiate Sch., 1905-13; A.B., Columbia, 1917, LL.B., 1921; m. Anna E. Lohman, Jan. 26, 1924; 1 dau., Julia B. Lewis. Admitted to N.Y. bar, 1921, since practiced in N.Y.C.; partner firm Beals & Nicholson, 1921-53, Towsend & Lewis, 1958—; dir. 1220 Park Av. Corp.; sec., dir. A. W. McDonald. Inc. Pres. Am. Soc. Prevention Cruelty to Animals, 1948-52; past pres. Collegiate Sch., Inc. Asso. govt. appeal agt. S.S.S., World War II. Mem. Assn. Bar City of N.Y., Am., N.Y. State bar assns., N.Y. County Lawyers Assn., Soc. Colonial Wars, Soc. War of 1812, Soc. Mayflower Descs. (past gov.), Sigma Alpha Epsilon, Phi Alpha Delta. Presbyn. Clubs: Country (Fairfield, Conn.); Union (N.Y.C.); Downtown Assn.; Bankers of Am. Home: 1220 Park Av New York City NY 10028 Office: 120 Broadway New York City NY 10005

BEALS, LAWRENCE WILSON, educator; b. Mt. Vernon, N.Y., May 10, 1907; s. Hallock Wilson and Gertrude (Starr) B.; B.A., Williams Coll., 1929; M.A., Harvard, 1931, Ph.D., 1933; m. Elizabeth Ohl, Mar. 28, 1964. Mem. faculty Williams Coll., 1933—, prof. philosophy, 1951—; chmn. dept., 1955-60; mem. faculty Columbia, summer 1948, Harvard, summer 1950, Emory U., spring 1968, U.S. Fla., spring 1967. Mem. Am. Philos. Assn., Phi Beta Kappa, Kappa Alpha. Democrat. Home: Jerome Dr Williamstown MA 01267

BEALS, RALPH LEON, anthropologist, educator; b. Pasadena, Cal., July 19, 1901; s. Leon Eli and Elvina (Blickensderfer) B.; A.B., Univ. Cal., 1926, Ph.D., 1930; LL.D., 1970 NRC fellow biol. sci., 1930-32, S.W. Soc. fellow, 1932- 33; m. Dorothy Manchester, June 13, 1923; children—Ralph Carleton, Alan Robin, Mariana. Technician, field div. edn. Nat. Park Service, 1933-35; lectr. U. Cal. at Berkeley, 1935, instr., Los Angeles, 1936-38, asst. prof., 1938-41, asso. prof., 1941-47, prof., 1947-69, prof. emeritus, 1969—, chmn. dept. anthropology and sociology, 1941-42, 44-48, faculty research lectr., 1953; dir. Latin Am. ethnic studies Smithsonian Instn., 1942-43. Tech. adviser U.S. delegations 1st Inter-Am. Indianist Conf., Patzcuaro, Mexico, 1939, 4th Assembly Pan-Am, Inst. History and Geography, Caracas, Venzuela, 1947. Hon. mem. faculty medicine U. Concepcion. Chile. Fellow Center Advanced Studies Behavioral Scis., 1955-56, Guggenheim Found., 1958. Fellow A.A.A.S., Am. Anthrop. Assn. (exec. bd. 1947-49, pres. 1950), Am. Sociol. Soc.; mem. Sociedad Mexicana de Antropologia, Soc. Am. Archeology (exec. com), Am. Folklore Soc., NRC (div. anthropology and psychology 1944-47, com. Latin Am. anthropology 1943- 52, internat. coop. anthropology 1949-52), Soc. Applied Anthropology, Am. Ethnological Soc., Social Sci. Research Council (dir. 1946- 52, com. on world area research, 1947-52, com. on personnel 1953-55), Latin Am. Studies Assn. (exec. com. 1969-71), Sigma Xi, Phi Beta Kappa Pi Gamma Mu. Author: Archeological Studies in Northeastern Arizona (with George W. Brainerd, Watson Smith), 1945; Ethnology of the Western Mixe Indians, 1945; The Contemporary Culture of the Cahita Indians, 1945; Cheran; A Sierra Tarascan Village, 1946; Introduction to Anthropology (with Harry Hoijer), 1953, 4th edit, 1971; No Frontier to Learning, 1957; Community in Transition; Nayon Ecuador, 1966; Politics of Social Research, 1969. Editor of Notes on Latin American Studies, 1942-43, Acta America, 1943-47; contbg. editor Handbook of Latin American Studies, 1943-47; asso. editor Jour. Am. Folklore, 1947-51; adv. editor Am. Anthropologist, 1952-53, 55-59. Contbr. articles profl. jours. Home: 16016 Anoka Dr Pacific Palisades CA 90272 Office: U of California Los Angeles CA 90024

BEALS, ROBERT DIGGS, mgmt. cons.; b. Winchester, Ind., Aug. 11, 1914; s. John H. and Nellie Edger (Diggs) B.; A.B., Colgate U., 1936; M.B.A., Harvard, 1938; m. Joanna Huttenlocher, Dec. 11, 1946; children—Joanna Jane, Diggs Huttenlocher. Asst. to v.p. Met. Life Ins. Co., N.Y.C., 1938-41, asst. to pres. Am. Express Co., N.Y.C., 1946-49; pres., dir. Film Strip-of the-Month Clubs, Inc., N.Y.C., 1949- 63; treas., bus. mgr. Popular Sci. Pub. Co., Inc., N.Y.C., 1949-63; pres. Wells Fargo & Co., N.Y.C., 1963-64, chmn. bd., exec. com., 1964-67; pres., dir. Wells Fargo Armored Service Corp., N.Y.C., 1963-64; 64; v.p. Am. Express Co., Am. Express Co., Inc. (N.Y.C.), 1964-67. also gen. mgr. credit card div. world-wide, 1964-67; pres., dir. Computicket Corp. subsidiary Computer Scis. Corp., El Segundo, Cal., 1967-68; cons., 1968- -. Mem. Greater N.Y. councils Boy Scouts Am., 1958—; mem. com. univ.. relations, Maroon council Colgate U., 1961—, also dir. Alumni Corp. Nat. dir. spl. orgns. and mailings Citizens for Eisenhower and Nixon, 1952. Served to comdr. USNR, 1940-46. Recipient commendation Sec. Navy. Mem. Harvard Bus. Sch. Assn. (exec. council 1963-66), Phi Beta Kappa, Alpha Tau Omega. Republican Presbyn. (elder, mem. planning bd., bus. devel. com. 1970—.). Clubs: Harvard, Wall Street (N.Y.C.). Home: 15 Old Sleepy Hollow Rd Briarcliff Manor NY 10510 Office: Box 26 Scarborough NY 10510

BEAM, ALVIN WESLEY, book editor, columnist; b. Erie, Pa., Aug. 2, 1912; s. Josiah and Olea (Ohlson) B.; B.A., Hiram (O.) Coll., 1949; postgrad. Syracuse U., 1950- 52; m. Arline Mildred Fellow, Oct. 4, 1941; 1 son, Larry R. Reporter, Ravenna (O.) Record, 1952-54, Youngstown (O.) Vindicator, 1954-56; reporter, TV-radio columnist, editorial writer, asst. book editor Cleve. Plain Dealer, 1956-68, book editor, columnist, 1968—; instr. English, Hiram Coll., 1949-50. Served with AUS, 1942-46. Mem. Rowfant Club, Sigma Delta Chi. Home: 5670 Cumberland Dr Garfield Heights OH 44125 Office: 1801 Superior Av Cleveland OH 44114

BEAM, CHARLES GRIER, motor transp. exec.; b. Cherryville, N.C., Jan. 15, 1906; s. Charles Lefter and Nancy (Carpenter) B.; student Brevard Coll., 1927-29; B.S., N.C. State U., 1931; m. Lena Sue Brawley, June 14, 1936; children—Joel V., Linda Sue. Owner, Beam Trucking Co., Cherryville, 1933-37; pres., dir., chief exec. officer, mem. exec. com. Carolina Freight Carriers Corp., Cherryville, 1937—, now chmn. bd., chief exec. officer; dir. Cablevision, Inc.; v.p. City Sales, Inc. Mem. Gaston County Bd. Commrs., 1951—, chmn. bd., 1960—. Trustee Brevard Coll., Childrens Home Soc. of N.C., Inc. Mem. N.C. Motor Carriers Assn. (past pres., dir.), Am. Trucking Assn. (bd. govs. 1965- -), N.C. Jersey Breeders Assn. (mem. exec. com. 1964), Am. Jersey Cattle Club (past dir.). Democrat. Methodist. Mason (Shriner), Lion. Home: 207 S Elm St Cherryville NC 28021 Office: Hwy No 150 E Cherryville NC 28021

BEAM, JACOB D., U.S. ambassador; born Princeton, N.J., Mar. 24, 1908; s. Jacob Newton and Mary (Prince) B.; attended Kent Sch., 1920-24; B.A., Princeton, 1929; student Cambridge U., England, 1929-30; married Margaret Glassford; one son, Jacob Alexander. Vice consul, U.S. Consulate, Geneva, 1931-34; sec. U.S. Embassy, Berlin, 1934-40; divisional asst., dept. State, 1940-41; sec. U.S. Embassy, London, 1941-45; political officer Hdqrs. U.S. Forces in Germany, 1945-47; chief central European Division, State Department; counselor U.S. Embassy 1952-53; dep. dir. policy planning staff Dept. State 1953; U.S. ambassador to Poland, 1957- 61; asst. dir. Internatl. Relations Bur., Arms Control and Disarmament Agy. U.S., 1962-66; U.S. ambassador to Czechoslovakia, 1966-69; United States Ambassador to USSR, 1969—. Former U.S. rep. U.S.A.-Communist Chinese Talks. Warsaw. Clubs: Metropolitan, University (Washington). Address: Am Embassy Moscow, USSR.

BEAM, JOHN GREER, mfg. co. exec.; b. Louisville, May 15, 1920; s. John B. and Flora (Greer) B.; B.A., U. Louisville, 1942; m. Jeanne Driver, July 11, 1942; children—Holly, John Greer, Bradley, Laurie. Asst. to pres., treas. Am. Elevator & Machinery Co., Louisville, 1942-48; exec. v.p. Am. Saw & Tool Co., Louisville, 1948-58, dir., 1948—; exec. v.p., dir. Thomas Industries, Inc., Louisville, 1958-61, pres., 1961—, also dir. Bd. dirs. Louisville Indsl. Found. Home: 25 Southwind Rd Louisville KY 40207 Office: 207 E Broadway Louisville KY 40202

BEAM, PHILIP CONWAY, educator; b. Dallas, Oct. 7, 1910; s. Millard Filmore and Georgia Bettye (Avera) B.A.B. cum laude, Harvard, 1933, M.A., 1943, Ph.D., 1944; certificate Courtauld 1st., U. London (Eng.), 1936; m. Frances Merriman, Aug. 8, 1939; children—Christopher Merrimah, Rebecca Randall. Asst. to dir. William Rockhill Nelson Gallery Art, Kansas City, Mo., 1933-36; dir. Bowdoin Coll. Museum of Art, 1939-64, curator Homer collection, 1967—; mem. Kansas City, (Mo.) Art Inst., 1934-35; curator Bowdoin Coll., Mus. Art, 1936—, dir., 1939-64; faculty Bowdoin Coll., 1937—, prof. art, 1949—, chmn. dept., 1958—, Henry Johnson prof. art and archaeology, 1958—; vis. summer prof. Wesleyan U., Middletown, Conn., 1960, 69; vis. prof. art U. Vt., lectr. Shelburne (Vt.) Mus., summer 1967, 70. Mem. Me. Art Commn., 1946-52, chmn, 1951-52. Chmn. ct. honor Bunswick chpt. Boy Scouts Am., 1939-42; campaign chmn. Brunswick United Fund, 1960, dir., 1960-62. Bd. govs. Portland Art Mus. 1945-50; bd. corporators Ogunquit (Me.) Art Festival, 1960, 61. Mem. Coll. Art Mus., 1956—; patron Me. Art Festival, 1960, 61. Mem. Coll. Art Assn., New Eng. Council Am. Assn. Mus. Dirs.; Am. Assn. Museums. Episcopalian (past treas., vestryman). Author: The Language of Art, 1958; The Art of John Sloan, 1962; Winslow Homer at Prout's Neck, 1966; also articles, mus. catalogues, Contbg. editor Dictionary of the Arts, 1944, Am. Peoples Ency., 1968. Cons. editor The World of Homer Winslow, 1966; The World of John Singleton Copley. Home: 41 Spring St Brunswick ME 04011

BEAM, WALTER RALEIGH, educator; b. Richmond, Va., Aug. 27, 1928; s. Walter Raleigh and Rose Emma (Evans) B.; B.S. in Elec. Engring., U. Md., 1947, M.S. in Elec. Engring., 1950, Ph.D., 1953; m. Emma Victoria Reese, Mar. 22, 1951; children—David, James. Instr. elec. engring. U. Md., 1947-52; tech. staff RCA Labs., 1952-56; mgr. microwave advanced development RCA, 1956- 59; head elec. engring. dept. 1959-62, prof. elec. engring. Rensselaer Poly. Inst., 1959-64; with research div. IBM, Yorktown Heights, N.Y., 1964-67, dir. engring. tech., systems devel. div., White Plains, 1967-69; ind. cons., 1969—. Fellow I.E.E.E.; mem. Assn. for Computing Machinery, Am. Arbitration Assn. (nat. panel), Sigma Xi, Tau Beta Pi, Eta Kappa Nu (hon. mention Outstanding Young Elec. Engr. award 1957), Phi Kappa Phi, Omicron Delta Kappa, Phi Kappa Sigma. Author: Electronics of Solids, 1965. Contbr. to handbook, author articles. Patentee microwave devices and systems. Home: 24 Hilltop Dr Chappaqua NY 10514 Office: PO Box 172 Chappaqua NY 10514

BEAMAN, BERRY NELSON, tool mfg. exec.; b. Jackson, Mich., Aug. 15, 1890; s. Fred J. and Grace A. (Berry) B.; student George Washington U., 1910-12; Dr. Bus. Adminstrn., Cleary (Mich.) Coll., 1953, m. Lucretia C. Comstock, Aug. 24, 1915; children—Nelson, James. chmn. bd. Universal Vise & Tool Co., Parma, Mich., 1942—. Mem. Mich. State Corrections Commn., 1942-45; mem. Fed. Prison Industries Bd., 1953—; mem. Mich. Racing Commn., 1963-66. Del., Mich. Constl. Convention, 1961-62. Finance chmn. Mich. of Rep. Nat. Com., 1948-54. Mem. Sigma Chi. Elk. Clubs: Jackson Country, Jackson Town, Burr Oak Golf. Home: 808 S Thompson St Jackson MI 49203 Office: Parker St Parma MI 49269

BEAMAN, CHESTER EARL, fgn. service officer; b. Kokomo, Ind., Jan. 16, 1916; s. Court Franklin and Gladys Ruth (Pierce) B.; A.B., DePauw U., 1938; A.M., U. Mich., 1939; student Am. Inst. Fgn. Trade, 1948; m. Mary Ruth Tyler, Nov. 8, 1947; children—Bruce Tyler, Mary Anina Ruth. With U.S. Civil Service Commn., 1940-41, FSA., 1941-42, O.Q.M.G., 1942-43; chief salary and wage adminstrn. Hdqrs. European Command, 1946-47, chief employee utilization, 1948-49; with Am. Fgn. Service, 1949—; personnel specialist U.S. High Commn., Germany, 1949-52; attache Am. embassy, London, Eng., 1952-54; consul, Cardiff, Wales, 1954-55, Cairo, Egypt. 1957-59, Port Said, Egypt, 1960-61; faculty Fgn. Service Inst., Washington, 1961-63; supervisory adminstrv. officer Dept. of State, Washington, 1963-64, internat. relations officer, 1967; supervisory econ. officer Am. embassy, Manila, P.I., 1964-67; dep. chief of mission Am. embassy, Damascus, Syria, 1967, Valletta, Malta, 1968-70; chief position and pay mgmt. Dept. State, Washington, 1971—. Served with AUS, 1943-46. Mem. Am. Fgn. Service Assn., Phi Beta Kappa, Phi Kappa Phi. Lion. Home: 6122 Beech Tree Dr Alexandria VA 22310 Office: Dept of State (PER/PMS/PPM) Washington DC 20520

BEAMAN, J. FRANK, editor, pub.; b. Pueblo, Colo., Oct. 26, 1897; s. James Lincoln and Jeannette (Bowman) B.; m. Louise Loughner; 1 dau., Mrs. J. J. Cordes. With United Press, Chgo., 1917, becoming bur. mgr., St. Louis, Mo. and Columbus, O., then div. mgr., Kansas City, Mo. and Atlanta, Ga.; city editor, San Francisco News, 1929-30; financial editor and columnist, Pitts. Press, 1930-36, Phila. (Pa.) Record, 1936- 37; pub. relations dir. and asst. to pres. Curtis Pub. Co., Phila., 1937-45; creator, 1st editor Holiday, Jan. 1945-July 1946; editor Daily Comml. News, San Francisco. Mem. Sigma Delta Chi. Club: San Francisco Press. Author: The Dotmakers. Home: 1900 Jackson St San Francisco CA 94109 Office: 125 12th St San Francisco CA 94103

BEAME, ABRAHAM DAVID, banker, cons.; b. London, Eng., Mar. 20, 1906; s. Philip and Esther (Goldfarb) B.; came to U.S., 1906, naturalized. 1914; B.B.A., City Coll. N.Y., 1928; m. Mary Ingerman, Feb. 18, 1928; children—Edmond M., Bernard W. Tchr., N.Y.C. high schs., 1929-45; partner Beame-Greidinger, C.P.A.'s, N.Y.C., 1925-45; instr. accounting and auditing Rutgers U., 1944-45; asst. budget dir., N.Y.C., 1946-52, budget dir., 1952-61, comptroller, 1962-65; chmn. finance com. Am. Bank & Trust Co., N.Y.C., 1966—, also dir.; propr. Abraham D. Beame Assos., 1966—; chmn. bd. Arrow-Lock Corp., 1966—. Mem. N.Y.C. Citizens Com. Pub. Higher Edn., Park Slope N. Improvement Corp.; chmn. nat. edn. program Religious Zionists Am. Mem. lecture and forum com. Nat. Democratic Club: chmn. polit. affairs and legislation Kings County Dem. Exec. Com.; bd. dirs. Affiliated Young Democrats, Inc.; Dem. candidate for mayor N.Y.C., 1965; del. Dem. nat. convs., 1956, 60, 64. Bd. dirs. Bklyn. regional Nat. Conf. Christians and Jews, N.Y. State com. America's Conscience Fund, City Coll. Fund, Brownsville Boys Club, United Jewish Appeal, Gil Hodges Found., Am.-Israel Cultural Found., Internat. Synagogue, Bklyn. Jewish Community Council, Kyle Rote Met. Football Conf., Countee Cullen Scholarship Found., Coordinating Council Edn. Disadvantaged, Bklyn., Hebrew Home and Hosp. for Aged, Grand St. Boys Assn., Israel Bond Com.; mem. Hillel Bldg. Fund, Bklyn. Coll.; trustee-at-large Fedn. Jewish Philanthropies; mem. Friends of Univ. Settlement; mem. regional adv. Anti-Defamation League; mem. grad. adv. bd. Baruch Sch., City Coll. N.Y.; mem. nat. legacies com. Yeshiva U.; bd. sponsors art festival for N.A.A.C.P. legal def. Recipient Townsend Harris medal, 1957; decorated knight comdr. Order St. Dennis of Zante (Greece); recipient Man of Year awards numerous charitable, religious and civic orgns. Mem. Zionist Orgn. Am., City Coll. Alumni Assn. (mem. bd. 1952- 58), Beta Gamma Sigma Epsilon. Mem. B'nai B'rith (past trustee). Clubs: Brookboro (Bklyn.). Home: 60 Plaza St Brooklyn NY 11238 Office: 70 Wall St Brooklyn NY 10005

BEAMER, ELMER GEORGE, accountant; b. Cin., May 10, 1909; s. Roy Arlington and Lulu (Niederhelman) B.; student U. Cin.; m. Esther Kihn, Nov. 30, 1933; 1 dau., Linda (Mrs. David Bender). Staff accountant Haskins & Sells, C.P.A.'s 1931-46, resident partner, Cleve., 1946-52, mng. partner, 1952- -. Chmn. bd. nominations Ohio State U. Accounting Hall of Fame, 1962-64; chmn. Commn. on Study Common Body of Knowledge, sponsored Am. Inst. C.P.A.'s and Carnegie Corp., 1963-67. Mem. council City Shaker Heights, 1963-64, 66-70; trustee Shaker One Hundred, Inc., 1965-68. Chmn. speaker's bur. Cleve. Growth Bd., 1960-67; treas., bd. trustees Cleve. Hearing and Speech Center, 1964-66; mem. exec. com. Council on World Affairs, 1960- 62, trustee, 1962-66. Mem. Ohio Soc. C.P.A.'s (pres. Cleve. chpt. 1955- 56, v.p. Ohio 1961-62, pres. 1965-66), Am. Inst. C.P.A.'s (chmn. bd. mgrs. profl. devel. div. 1960-66, mem. exec. com. 1960-61, mem. council 1963-68, v.p. 1968-69 Gold medal for distinguished service 1970, chmn. edn. exec. com. 1970—), Am. Accounting Assn. (v.p. 1956-57), N.Y. Soc. C.P.A.'s, Citizens League Greater Cleve., Alpha Kappa Psi, Beta Alpha Psi, Beta Gamma Sigma. Episcopalian (lay reader, warden, mem. diocesan council, dep. Gen. Conv. 1964—, sec. standing com., diocese 1969-70), Clubs: Union, Shaker Heights Country, Rowfant, Forth, Clevelander. Home: 22149 Westchester Rd Shaker Heights OH 44122 Office: 1717 E 9th St Cleveland OH 44114

BEAMER, GEORGE CHARLES, educator; b. Holden, Mo., Mar. 4, 1907; s. Charles and Lucy (Smith) B.; A.B., William Jewel Coll., 1929; M.A., U. Mo., 1940, Ph.D., 1947; m. Mary Susan Walker, Dec. 23, 1934; 1 son, George Charles. Asst. mgr. William Jewell Press, Liberty, Mo., 1929-36, mgr., 1936-43, asso. prof. psychology, 1936-43; asso. prof. edn., psychology N. Tex. State Coll. (name changed to N. Tex. State U. 1961), Denton, 1947-49, prof. edn., 1949—, chmn. div. counselor edn., 1968—; cons. to industry. Mem. Denton Welfare Assn.; chmn. City Parks Bd. Served with USNR, 1943-46. Mem. Am. Personnel and Guidance Assn., Am. Psychol. Assn., Tex. (past pres.), Am. personnel and guidance assns., Student Personnel Assn. Tchr. Edn. (past sec. treas.). Nat. Vocational Guidance Assn. (del to Senate 1964-65), Sigma Psi, Phi Delta Kappa, Lambda Chi Alpha. Baptist. Kiwanian. Home: 2233 W Oak St Denton TX 76201

BEAMER, GEORGE H., U.S. judge; b. Bowling Green, Ind., Oct. 9, 1904; s. Jasper F. and Frances M. (Roush) B.; LL.B., Notre Dame U., 1929; LL.D., Ashland Coll., 1971; m. Charlotte L. Hoover, May 14, 1932; children—George N., Judith Ann. Admitted to Ind. bar, 1929, began practice in South Bend; city judge, 1933-35; pros. atty. St. Joseph County, 1937-39, city atty., 1939-41; atty. gen. of Ind., 1941-43; chmn. Pub. Service Commn. of Ind., 1943-44; mem. firm Crumpacker, May, Beamer, Levy & Searer, South Bend, 1944-62; judge U.S. Dist. Ct., No. Dist. Ind., Hammond, 1962—. Mem. Am., Ind., St. Joseph County bar assns. Mason. Club: Optimist (pres. 1948-49). Home: 1043 Elliott Dr Munster IN 46321 Office: Federal Bldg Hammond IN 46325

BEAMER, PARKER REYNOLDS, pathologist, educator; b. Centralia, Ill., July 27, 1914; s. Powhatan Reynolds and Bessie Louise (Poole) B.; student U. Louisville, 1931-32; A.B., U. Ill., 1935, M.S., 1937, Ph.D., 1940; M.D., Washington U., 1943; m. Mary Jo Scovill, 1939; children—Jo Ellen, Ellen, Mary Susan, Grant Scovill. Asst. bacteriology U. Ill., 1935-39; Jackson Johnson fellow med. sci. Washington U., 1939-41, lectr. bacteriology Sch. Dentistry, 1941-42, asst. pathol. Sch. Medicine, 1942-44, asst. prof. pathology, 1946-49; asst. pathologist Barnes, St. Louis Children's, St. Louis Maternity and McMillan hosps., 1946-49; attending physician pathology Jefferson Barracks Vets. Hosp., 1947-49; prof. microbiology and immunology, dir. dept., asso. prof. pathology Bowman Gray Sch. Med., 1949-53, asso. dean, 1951-53; bacteriologist, asso. pathologist N.C. Bapt. Hosp., 1949-53; prof. pathology Ind. U. Med. Center, 1953-64, chmn. dept., 1962-64; dir. labs. and pathology, prof. pathology Los Angeles County- U. So. Cal. Med. Center, 1965—; vis. prof. pathology Washington Hosp. Center, 1961. Mem. chancellor's com. of 500, Washington U., 1969- -. Served from 1st lt. to maj. M.C., AUS, 1943-46; comdg. officer, chief med. bacteriology and parasitology divs. Antilles Gen. Med. Lab., San Juan, P.R., 1945-46. Diplomate Am. Bd. Pathology (trustee 1950—, bd. dirs., 1964—). Fellow Am. Soc. Clin. Pathologists, Coll. Am. Pathologists; mem. Am. Assn. Pathologists, Bacteriologists, Am. Pub. Health Assn., Soc. Am. Bacteriologists, A.M.A., Am. Soc. Exptl. Biology and Medicine, A.A.A.S., Assn. Am. Med. Colls., Sigma Xi, Phi Chi, Alpha Omega Alpha, Gamma Alpha. Republican. Baptist. Kiwanian. Author: (with others) Principles of Human Pathology, 1959; Microscopic Pathology, 1964; Damage to the Brain During Birth, 1970. Editor-in-chief Am. Jour. Clin. Pathology, 1956-64; founding editor Survey of Pathology in Medicine and Surgery, 1964; cons. editor (pathology) Stedman's Med. Dictionary, 1958— (clin. pathology) Current Med. Digest, 1959—. Contbr. articles profl. jours. Home: 607 Coventry Valparaiso IN 46383

BEAMESDERFER, JOHN WILLIAM, chemist, educator; b. Schaefferstown, Pa., Aug. 24, 1910; s. David Newman and Catherine Sophia (Mann) B.; B.S., Gettysburg Coll., 1932; M.S., U. Mich., 1939, Ph.D., 1948; m. Maurine A. Smith. Feb. 7, 1940; children—J. Newman, Betty Ann. Chemist Gen. Chem. Co., Marcus Hook, Pa., 1932-34; instr. chemistry, physics Fredericksburg High Sch., 1934-38; teaching fellow, research fellow U. Mich., 1938-43; chief chemist engring. and research dept. Argus, Inc., Ann Arbor, Mich., 1943-47; asst. prof. chemistry U. Me., 1947-52, asso. prof., head chemistry dept., 1952-55, prof., head chemistry dept., 1955-67, prof., 1967—. Fellow A.A.A.S., Am. Inst. Chemists; mem. Am. Chem. Soc., Am. Assn. U. Profs., Am. Assn. Engring. Edn., Sigma Xi, Phi Lambda Upsilon, Gamma Alpha, Phi Kappa Phi. Home: 3 Chanel Rd Orono ME 04473.

BEAMLER, WILLIAM JOSEPH, educator; b. Atlanta, Mo., Sept. 9, 1919; s. L. and Beulah (Dabney) B.; B.S., N.E. Mo. State Tchrs. Coll., 1940; M.F.A., U. Colo., 1946; m. Lucille Paulls, Aug. 19, 1956; children—Alison, Kara. Tchr. art Moline (Ill.) High Sch., 1940-46; faculty Drake U., Des Moines, 1946-49; dir. art edn., River Forest, Ill.,

1949-53; instr. art Art Inst., Chgo.; dir. art edn. State of Ill., Springfield, 1953-69, asst. supt. instrn., 1960-69; asso. prof. art, chmn. art edn. No. Ill. U., DeKalb, 1969—; cons., reader U.S. Office Edn. Mem. adv. bd. CEMREL. Mem. Nat. (pres.), Ill. art edn. assns., N.E.A., Art Inst. Chgo., Art Club Chgo. Bd. mem. Art and Activities mag. Home: 612 S Main St Sycamore IL 62107 Office: Art Bldg No Ill U DeKalb IL 60115

BEAMS, GEORGE W., utility exec.; b. Campbellsville, Ky., 1907; ed. Tex. A. and M. Coll., 1929. Sr. v.p. Tex. Power & Light Co. Home: 5837 Lupton Dr Dallas TX 75225 Office: 1511 Bryan St Dallas TX 75201

BEAMS, HAROLD WILLIAM, educator; b. Belle Plaine, Kan., Aug. 3, 1903; s. Jesse W. and Katherine (Wylie) B.; A.B., Fairmount Coll., 1925; A.M., Northwestern U., 1926; Ph.D., U. Wis., 1929; m. Mona Murphy, July 6, 1935; children—David W., Marilyn. Teaching asst. U. Wis., 1926-29; Gen. Edn. Bd. fgn. fellowship, 1934-35; prof. zoology U. Ia., 1940—; acting chmn. dept. zoology State U. Ia., summer 1958. Cons. Argonne Nat. Lab.; mem. corp. Marine Biol. Lab.; mem. fellowship panel USPHS, 1962-64. Fellow A.A.A.S., Royal Micros. Soc. (London); mem. Am. Assn. Anatomists, Am. Micros. Soc., Am. Soc. Naturalists, Am. Soc. Zoologists (treas. 1941-44), Electron Micros. Soc. Am. (com. standardization biol. stains), Soc. Exptl. Biology and Medicine (councilor 1953-54), Soc. Protozoologists (v.p. 1956-57), Ia., Wis., N.Y. acads. scis., Internat., Am. socs. cell biology, (Am. com. 1950), Am. Assn. U. Profs., Sigma Xi, Gamma Alpha, Phi Sigma, Phi Beta Pi. Co-editor of Lee, The Microtomists Vade-Mecum. Contbr. articles profl. publs. Home: 110 Lusk Av Iowa City IA 52240

BEAMS, JESSE WAKEFIELD, educator; b. Belle Plaine, Kan., Dec. 25, 1898; s. Jesse Wakefield and Kathryn (Wylie) B.; A.B., Fairmount (Kan.) Coll., 1921; M.A., U. Wis., 1922; Ph.D., U. Va., 1925; Sc.D., William and Mary Coll., 1941; Sc.D., U. N. C., 1946; Sc.D., Washington and Lee U. 1949; m. Maxine Sutherland, June 16, 1931. Instr. physics and math. Ala. Poly. Inst., 1922-23; Nat. Research fellow U. Va., 1925-26, Yale, 1926- 27; instr. physics, Yale, 1927-28; asso. prof. physics, U. Va., 1928- 30, prof., 1930—, Francis H. Smith prof. physics, chmn. dept. of physics, 1948-63. Bd. dirs. Oak Ridge Inst. Nuclear Studies, Va. Inst. Sci. Research; mem. Nat. Research Fellowship com. NRC, 1949; mem. gen. adv. com. AEC, 1954-60. Recipient Potts medal Franklin Inst., 1942; John Scott award, 1956; Lewis award Am. Philos. Soc., 1958; Nat. Medal of Science, 1968. Fellow Am. Phys. Soc. (pres. 1938-39, 1958-59, 68) A.A.A.S. (chmn. sect. B, 1943); mem. Am. Acad. Arts and Scis., Am. Philos. Soc. (v.p. 1960-63), Am. Optical Soc., Va. Acad. Sci. (pres. 1947), Am. Physics Teachers Assn., Am. Assn. U. Profs., Nat. Research Council (physics div. 1933-36, 37-40), Nat. Acad. Scis., Phi Beta Kappa, Sigma Xi, Sigma Pi Sigma (hon.), Raven Soc. Club: Colonnade. Contbr. numerous articles. Home: 1705 Kenwood Lane Charlottesville VA 22901

BEAN, ALAN L., astronaut; b. Wheeler, Tex., Mar. 15, 1932; s. Arnold H. Bean; B.S. in Aero. Engring., U. Tex., 1955; grad. USN Test Pilot Sch.; m. Sue Ragsdale; children—Clay, Amy. Commd. ensign USN, 1955, advanced through grades to capt.; project officer various aircraft for preliminary evaluation, initial trials, final bd. inspection and survey trials, Patuxent, Md., 1960-63; replacement pilot Attack Squadron 44, Cecil Field, Fla., 1963; now astronaut with Manned Spacecraft Center, NASA, 1963—, lunar module pilot Apollo XII, 1969. Decorated D.S.M. Fellow Am. Astron. Soc.; mem. Soc. Exptl. Test Pilots, Delta Kappa Epsilon. Home: 18706 Point Lookout Dr Houston TX 77058 Office: Manned Spacecraft Center NASA Houston TX 77058

BEAN, ATHERTON, business exec.; b. New Prague, Minn., Sept. 14, 1910; s. Francis Atherton and Bertha Juniata (Boynton) B.; student Blake Sch.; A.B. summa cum laude, Carleton Coll., 1931; B.A., Oxford U. (Rhodes Scholar), 1934; grad. study Harvard Bus. Adminstrn. Sch., 1931-32; m. Winifred E. Wollaeger, June 26, 1934; children—Douglas Atherton, Bruce William. With Upjohn Co., Dallas, 1934-36, duPont Co., Wilmington, Del., 1936-37; price exec. O.P.A., Washington, 1942-43; joined Internat. Milling Co. (co. name changed to Internat. Multifoods), Mpls., 1937, exec. v.p., 1938-55, pres., 1955-64, chmn., chief exec., 1964-68, chmn. exec. com., 1968—; chmn. bd. 9th dist. Fed. Reserve Bank, 1961-65; dir. 1st Nat. Bank Mpls., Bus. Internat. Trustee Mpls. Inst. Arts; trustee Mayo Found., Rochester, chmn. bd., 1969—; trustee Carleton Coll., Northfield, Minn., chmn. bd., 1961-68. Served as civilian, spl. br. M.I., 1943-44. Home: 2525 E Lake of Isles Blvd Minneapolis MN 55405 Office: Investors Bldg Minneapolis MN 55402

BEAN, GEORGE CLARKE, banker; b. Peoria, Ill., Mar. 16, 1918; s. George Tinney and Elizabeth (Clarke) B.; A.B. cum laude, Princeton, 1939; m. Pamela Phyllis Dodwell, Aug. 19, 1939; children—Wendy W. (Mrs. Laurence E. Barker), Elizabeth C. (Mrs. Timothy Piatt), Patricia B. (Mrs. Douglas McConnell). With auditing dept. Bankers Trust Co., N.Y.C., 1939-47; asst. mgr. credit dept. Valley Nat. Bank, Phoenix, 1947-51, asst. v.p., Tucson, 1951-53; v.p., area supr. Ariz. Bank, Tucson, 1953-59, sr. v.p. charge earning asset div., Phoenix, 1960-64, exec. v.p., 1965-67, pres., 1967—, also chief exec. officer, 1969—, also dir.; pres., dir. BODCO Bldg. Corp., Phoenix, 1968—; dir. Signal Equities Inc., Exchange Finance Co., Gen. Leasing Co. (all Phoenix). Mem. Ariz. Gov.'s Adv. Commn. on Manpower. Pres. Phoenix United Fund, 1964. Bd. dirs. Central Ariz. Project, Planned Parenthood Assn. Phoenix; trustee Phoenix Art Mus. Named Tucson Outstanding Young Man of Year, Jr. C. of C., 1954. Mem. Ariz. (pres. 1966-67), Am. (chmn. recodification com. 1968, chmn. exec. com. state bank div. 1968-69, mem. steering com. on state bank legislation; mem. exec. council, 1967—) bankers assns., Robert Morris Assos., Phoenix C. of C. (dir. 1964-66), Nat. Alliance Businessmen (dir.). Club: Paradise Valley Country. Office: 44 W Monroe St Phoenix AZ 85002 also Round Hill Greenwich NY 12834

BEAN, JACOB, museum curator; b. Stillwater, Minn., Nov. 22, 1923; s. William Bronson and Lurain (Eichten) B.; student Harvard, 1941-45. Chargé de mission Cabinet des Dessins. Musée du Louvre, Paris, 1957-60; asst. curator charge drawings Met. Mus. Art, 1960-62, asso. curator, 1962, curator, 1963—; adj. prof. fine arts N.Y.U., 1967—. Clubs: Turf, Athenaeum (London). Author: Les Dessins Italiens de la Collection Bonnat, 1960: 100 European Drawings in the Metropolitan Museum of Art, 1964; Italian Drawings in the Art Museum, Princeton University, 1966. Co- author. Drawings from New York Collections I, The Italian Renaissance, 1965, II, The Seventeenth Century in Italy, 1967, III, The Eighteenth Century in Italy, 1971. Asso. editor Master Drawings mag., 1962—. Office: Met Mus of Art Fifth Av and 82d St New York City NY 10028

BEAN, JOHN WILLIAM, univ. prof.; b. Attercliffe, Oct., Can., Sept. 8, 1901; s. Rev. Eusebius Hailer and Anna Gazina (Gieske) B.; came to U.S., 1921, naturalized, 1945; student Stratford (Ont.) Collegiate, 1920, Northwestern Coll., 1921-23; A.B., U. of Mich., 1924, M.S. 1925. Ph.D., 1930, M.D., 1936. Mem. faculty Med. Sch., U. Mich., 1929—, prof. physiology, 1944—, acting chmn. dept. physiology, 1954-56, 62-63. Research, Instituto de Fisiologia, Facultad de Ciencias Medics de Buenos Aires, 1941. Mem. med. com. on compressed air code Dept. of Labor, N.Y. State, 1950-53 Mem. Mich. Acad. Arts and Letters, Am. Physiol. Soc., A.A.A.S., Soc. Exptl. Biology and Medicine, Undersea Med. Soc., Barton Boat Club, Sigma Xi, Phi Kappa Phi, Alpha Kappa Kappa. Contbr. numerous articles on circulation, hypertension, effects of oxygen at high pressure, respiration, etc. in med. publs. Editor respiration sect. Biol. Abstracts, 1954—. Home: 810 W Davis St Ann Arbor MI 48103

BEAN, MAURICE DARROW, govt. ofcl.; b. Gary, Ind., Sept. 9, 1928; s. Everett Thomas and Vera Mae (Curry) B.; B.A. in Govt., Howard U., 1950; M.A. in Social and Tech. Assistance, Haverford Coll., 1953; postgrad., certificate Sch. Advanced Internat. Studies, Johns Hopkins, 1959; m. Ruth C. Lancaster, May 13, 1951; children—Linda D., Karen M. With U.S. Bur. Census, 1950-51, AID, 1951-61; with Peace Corps, 1961-66, operations officer for Malaysia and Indonesia, 1961-62, regional program officer for Far East, 1962-63, dep. regional dir., 1963-64, dir. Peace Corps/Phillipines, 1964-66; dir. Malaysia and Singapore affairs Bur. East Asian and Pacific Affairs, Dept. of State, 1966-70; mem. Sr. Seminar in Fgn. Policy, 1970-71; Am. consul, Ibadan, Nigeria, 1971—. Active Neighbors, Inc., Washington, Christopher Reynolds Found. fellow, 1953; William E. Mosher Meml. scholar, 1961. Mem. Am. Fgn. Service Assn., Am. Sch. Assn., Manila Urban League, Omega Psi Phi. Club: Royal Bangkok (Thailand) Sports (life). Home: 5261 Nebraska Av NW Washington DC 20015 Office: Am Consulate Ibadan Nigeria

BEAN, ORSON, (Dallas Frederick Burrows), actor, comedian; b. Burlington, Vt., July 22, 1928; s. George and Marian (Pollard) Burrows; ed. Cambridge, Mass.; m. Jacqueline De Sibour, July 2, 1956 (div. 1962); 1 dau.; m. 2d, Carolyn Maxwell, Oct. 3, 1965. Started as night club performer, Blue Angel, N.Y.C., 1952; stage debut in The Spider, summer stock, 1945; later appeared in Goodbye Again, 1948, Josephine, 1953, The School of Scandal, 1953, The Scarecrow, 1953, Men of Distinction, 1953, Almanac, 1953, Will Success Spoil Rock Hunter?, 1955, Mr. Roberts, 1956, Nature's Way, 1957, Say, Darling, 1959, Subways Are for Sleeping, 1961, Never Too Late, 1962; film debut in How To Be Very, Very Popular, 1955, later appeared in Anatomy of a Murder, 1959; TV appearances, 1953—; former regular panelist on To Tell the Truth; also appears other panel shows. Founder, adminstrv. dir. Fifteenth St. Sch., sch. for children based on Summerhill model, N.Y.C., 1964—. Served with AUS, 1946-47; Japan. Mem. Actors Equity Assn., A.F.T.R.A., Screen Actors Guild. Address: Australia

BEAN, RICHARD BRADLEY, physician; b. Schenectady, Dec. 4, 1907; s. Berten B. and Ethel (Karr) B.; M.D., U. Buffalo, 1931; m. Mary E. Craig, Sept. 23, 1933; children—Bradley Craig, Carolyn Ann. Intern Buffalo Childrens Hosp., 1931-32, resident, 1932-33; practice medicine, specializing in internal medicine, Castile, N.Y., 1933-42, Buffalo, 1946-51, Boston, 1955-58, Albany, N.Y., 1958—; physician specialist adminstrv. medicine and hosp. adminstrn. dept. medicine. surgery U.S. VA, Buffalo, Boston, Albany, 1946—; dir. VA Hosp., Albany, 1958-70; asso. Albany Med. Coll., 1958—. Mem. Northeastern N.Y. Hosp. Rev. and Planning Council. Bd. dirs. Albany area chpt. A.R.C., Workshop, Incorporated, Albany, N.Y. Served to comdr. USNR, 1942-46. Mem. Assn. Am. Med. Colls., A.M.A., N.Y., Wyoming County med. socs., Am. Coll. Hosp. Adminstrs., Am., N.Y., Northeastern N.Y. hosp. assns., A.A.A.S.

BEAN, WILLIAM BENNETT, physician; b. Manila, P. I., Nov. 8, 1909; s. Robert Bennett and Adelaide Leiper (Martin) B.; B.A., U. Va., 1932, M.D., 1935; m. Abigail Shepard, June 17, 1939; children—Robert Bennett, Margaret Harvey, John Perrin. Intern Johns Hopkins Hosp., 1935-36; asst. resident physician Boston City Hosp., 1936-37; sr. med. resident Cin. Gen. Hosp., 1937-38, asst. attending physician, 1941-46, clinician out-patient dept., 1946-48, attending physician, 1946-48; asst. prof. medicine U. Cin. Med. Coll., 1940-47, asso. prof., 1947-48; prof. medicine, head dept. internal medicine U. Ia. Coll. Medicine, 1948-70, physician-in- chief Univ. Hosps., 1948-70,; Sir. William Osler prof. medicine, 1970—; vis. prof. medicine and history of medicine U. Va., 1968. Sr. med. cons. VA, 1947—. Served from capt. to lt. col. M.C., AUS, 1942-46. Recipient John Horsley Meml. prize U. Va., 1944; Groedel medal, 1961; named Ky. col. Diplomate Am. Bd. Internal Medicine, Am. Bd. Nutrition. Fellow Am. Coll. Chest Physicians (past gov. Ia.), Am. Med. Writers Assn., A.A.A.S., A.C.P. (past gov. Ia.); mem. Am. Coll. Cardiology (past gov. Ia.), Nat. Assn. Standard Med. Vocabulary (dir.), Nockian Soc., A.M.A., Soc. Exptl. Biology & Medicine, Am. Med. Residents Assn., Soc. Med. Cons. to Armed Forces, Am. Coll. Sports Medicine (charter), N.Y. Acad. Scis., Am. Acad. Polit Sci., Archeology Inst. Am. (pres. Iowa 1956-58), Am. Clin. and Climatol. Assn. (pres. 1967-68), Am. Assn. Study Liver Diseases (charter), Am. Assn. Med. History, Am. Soc. Tropical Medicine, Am. (exec. com., sci. council), Ia. (pres. 1950) heart assns., Ohio, Ia. med. socs., Assn. Mil. Surgeons, Med. and Jockey Soc. Interior Valley N. Am., Tb and Health Assn., Central Interurban Clin. Club (pres. 1959-61), Am. Soc. Clin. Nutrition, John Fulton Soc. (charter mem.), Ia. Clin. Soc., World Med. Assn., Am. Osler Soc. (charter, 1st pres. 1970—), Assn. Am. Phys. Central (councillor 1946-49), Am. (pres. 1951) socs. clin. research, Sigma Xi, Alpha Omega Alpha, Episcopalian. Clubs: Cosmos (Washington); Stuart and Tudor (Johns Hopkins); Triangle (Iowa City). Author: Sir William Osler: From His Bedside Teachings and Writings, 3d edit., 1968; Vascular Spiders and Related Lesions of the Skin, 1958; Aphorisms from Latham, 1962; Rare Diseases and Lesions: Their Contribution to Clinical Medicine, 1967. Editor: Monographs in Medicine, 1951-52; book review editor of Archives of Internal Medicine, 1954-62, editor in chief, 1962-67; editorial cons. Modern Medicine, Stedman's Med. Dictionary, Familiar Medical Quotations; editor Current Med. Digest, 1967—. Home: 723 Bayard St Iowa City IA 52240

BEANE, ALPHEUS C., investment banker; b. Augusta, Ga., July 10, 1910; s. Alpheus C. and Marian E. (Bignon) B.; B.S., Yale, 1931; m. Jean A. Tegder, Feb. 26, 1938; children—Alpheus C., Mary C., Marian; m. 2d, Elizabeth Geren Souchon. Aug. 21, 1956. Clk. Fenner & Beane, N.Y.C., 1931, gen. partner 1935; gen. partner Merrill Lynch, Pierce, Fenner & Beane, 1941- 58; directing partner J. R. Williston and Beane, N.Y.C., 1958-63; v.p., dir. Walston & Co., 1963-64; partner Reynolds & Co., 1965-71; v.p., mem. exec. com. Reynolds Securities Inc., N.Y.C., 1971—. Served with AAF, 1942-45, disch. as maj. Mem. bd. covs. N.Y. Curb Exchange, 1938-42. Club: Yale. Home: 10 Pinecroft Rd Greenwich CT 06830 Office: 120 Broadway New York City NY 10005

BEANE, FRANK EASTMAN, mfg. exec.; b. Augusta, Ga., June 16, 1912; s. Alpheus Crosby and Marian Elizabeth (Bignon) B.; B.S., Yale, 1933; m. Mary Holton, June 20, 1942; children—Frank Eastman, George Holton, Anne C., Susan. With Underwood Corp., N.Y.C., 1956-59, chmn., 1957-59, chief exec. officer, 1957- 59, pres., 1958-59; v.p. finance, dir., mem. exec. com. McCall Corp., 1960-65; pres., dir. John P. Maguire & Co., subsidiary of Fieldcrest Mills, Inc., 1965—, with Gen. Chem. div. Allied Chem. & Dye, 1949-55, asst. to pres., 1952-55; pres., dir. Equitable Bearing Co., 1943-49; gen. partner Fenner & Beane. Past dir. Brunswick Sch., Greenwich, Conn.; past pres., trustees Greenwich Acad. Clubs: St. Anthony; Round Hill (Greenwich). Home: 8 Grahampton Lane Greenwich CT 06830 Office: 1290 Av of Americas New York City NY 10019

BEANEY, WILLIAM MERRITT, educator; b. Wilkes-Barre, Pa., Nov. 27, 1918; s. William Merritt and Mildred (Hill) B.; A.B., Harvard, 1940; LL.B., U. Mich., 1947, Ph.D., 1951; m. Patricia Daniels, June 7, 1947; children—Barbara, Carol. Teaching fellow polit. sci. U. Mich., 1946-49; instr. politics Princeton, 1949-52, asst. prof., 1952-56, asso. prof., 1956-59, prof., 1959-64, chmn. dept., 1959-61, William Nelson Cromwell prof. law, 1964-69; prof. Coll. of Law, U. Denver, 1969—. Served to maj. AUS, 1942-46. Mem. Am. Polit. Sci. Assn., Am. Assn. U. Profs. Author: The Right to Counsel in American Courts, 1955; (with Alpheus T. Mason) American Constitutional Law, 4th edit., 1968; The Supreme Court in a Free Society, 1959, rev. edit, 1968. Home: 2555 Holly Pl Denver CO 80222

BEANSTOCK, SAM, hosp. adminstr.; b. London, Eng., Dec. 4, 1907; s. Morris and Bluma (Piasetzki) B.; came to U.S., 1920, naturalized, 1923; B.S., N.Y.U., 1929; M.D., U. Md., 1933; m. Winifred Teresa Glennon, Sept. 25, 1937. Intern Cumberland Hosp., Bklyn., 1933- 35; resident Tb Sea View Hosp., S.I., N.Y., 1935-37; resident neurology Jewish Hosp. Chronic Diseases, Bklyn., 1937, psychiatrist, 1937-42; with VA, 1945—, dir. profl. services VA Hosp., Lebanon, Pa., 1955-58, dir. VA Hosp., Chillicothe, O., 1958-70. Served to capt., M.C., AUS, 1942-45. Diplomate Am. Bd. Psychiatry and Neurology. Fellow Am. Psychiat. Assn. (life); mem. D.A.V., Ret. Officers Assn. (life). Home: 431 E Hathaway Dr San Antonio, TX 78209.

BEAR, CHARLES BENSON, mag. publisher; b. Washington, Ia., Mar. 12, 1919; s. Charles H. and Grace (Benson) B.; B.A., Grinnell Coll., 1939; M.A., Fletcher Sch. Law and Diplomacy, 1940. With Gallup Poll, Am. Inst. Pub. Opinion, Princeton, N.J., 1940-41; adminstrv. asst. Office Govt. Reports, Chgo., 1940-42; bus. mgr. Time-Life Internat., 1945-49, dep. mng. dir., 1960-64, mng. dir., 1965-68; v.p. internat. Time Inc., 1965-69, adminstrv. v.p., 1969—; bus. mgr. Fortune mag., 1949-53, asso. pub., 1953-60, gen. mgr. Archtl. Forum, 1954-60. Former chmn., now mem. exec. com. Am. Viewpoint, Inc.; mem. bd. mem. Internat. Marketing Inst.; trustee Grinnell Coll. Served from pvt. to capt. USAAF, 1942-45. Home: 127 E 71st St New York City, NY 10021. also E Mountain Rd N Cold Spring-on-Hudson NY 11724 Office: Time-Life Bldg Rockefeller Center New York City NY 10020

BEAR, FRED BERNARD, mfr. archery equipment, hunter; b. Waynesboro, Pa., Mar. 5, 1902; s. Harry Leon and Florence (Drawbaugh) B.; student Detroit Inst. Tech., 1923-25; m. Henrietta Oleson Thomas, Sept. 8, 1947; children—Julia Thomas Kroll, Michael John Steger. Patternmaker, Packard Motor Car Co., Chrysler Motor Car Co., 1923-26, 27-28; supt. Zahrndt Mfg. Co., Jansen Mfg. Co., 1929- 30, 30-33; founder Bear Archery Co., 1933, became Bear Archery Co., Inc., pres., treas., dir.; author motion picture films on big game hunting with bow and arrow. Mem. Archery Mfrs. and Dealers Assn. (1st pres., dir.). Holder patents on mfr. archery equipment; holder world records Pope and Young regulations for bow and arrow trophies in woodland and Mountain Caribou, Elk, Stone Sheep and Canada Moose. Home: Au Sable River Grayling MI 49738 Office: W Lake St Grayling MI 49738

BEAR, HENRY CHARLES, corp. exec.; b. Chgo., Nov. 18, 1906; s. Robert Guy and Bessie (Hornbeck) B.; B.S., U. Ill., 1928; m. Florence M. Starn, 1930; 1 dau., Barbara L. Alseth, Sales promotion, advt., sales B. F. Goodrich Co., Akron, O., 1928-35; with U.S. Gypsum Co., Chgo., 1936—, sales and sales mgmt., 1936-52, v.p. charge purchasing, 1953-59, v.p. merchandising, 1959-62, v.p. adminstrn., 1962-65, v.p. acquisitions, 1966—. Presbyn. Clubs: Tower (Chgo.); Sunset Ridge Country (Winnetka, Ill.). Home: 1350 N Western Av Lake Forest IL 60045 Office: 101 S Wacker Dr Chicago IL 60606

BEAR, HERBERT STANLEY, Jr., educator, mathematician; b. Phila., Mar. 13, 1929; s. Herbert Stanley and Katharine (Schaeffer) B.; student Cal. Inst. Tech., 1946-48, Read Coll., 1948-49; B.A., U. Cal. at Berkeley, 1950, Ph.D., 1957; m. Jean Isobel Munro, May 30, 1951; children—Katharine Ann, John Stanley. Instr., U. Ore., 1955-56; asso. U. Cal. at Berkeley, 1956-57; instr. U. Wash., 1957-58, asst. prof., 1958-59, 60-62; vis. asst. prof. Princeton, 1959-60; asso. prof. U. Cal. at Santa Barbara, 1962-67; prof. N.M. State U., 1967-69; Gastprof. U. Erlangen-Nürnberg W. Germany, 1967; prof., chmn. math. dept. U. Hawaii, Honolulu, 1967—. Mem. Am. Math. Soc., Math. Assn. Am., A.A.A.S. Home: 550 Portlock Rd Honolulu HI 96821

BEAR, RICHARD SCOTT, educator; b. Miamisburg, O., June 8, 1908; s. Harris V. and Georgianna (Scott) B.; B.S., Princeton, 1930, Ph.D., U. of Calif., 1933; m. Madelaine Borncamp, Aug. 7, 1931 (dec.); children—Andrea Scott, Janet Foster; m. 2d, Josephine Hoyt, Sept. 4, 1942 (dec. 1967). NRC fellow in chemistry, Princeton, 1933-34; research asso., zoology dept., Washington U., 1934-38; asst. prof. chemistry Ia. State Coll., 1938-41; asso. prof. biology Mass. Inst. of Tech., 1941-46, prof., 1946-57; dean Coll. Scis. and Humanities, Ia. State U., 1957-61; dean Grad. Sch., Boston U., 1961-66, prof. biology, 1961-69; prof. anatomy Sch. Medicine, U. N. C., Chapel Hill, 1969—. Fellow Am. Acad. Arts and Scis. (v.p. Class II, 1967-69); mem. Am. Chem. Soc., Biophys. Soc. (council mem. 1961-64, chmn. edni. affairs com. 1962-64), A.A.A.S., Phi Beta Kappa, Sigma Xi. Contbr. sci. publs. Office: Dept of Anatomy Univ of NC Chapel Hill NC 27514

BEARD, CHARLES LEONARD, state govt. ofcl.; b. Cochran, Va., May 11, 1905; s. Charles Spivey and Isla (Edge) B.; A.B., U. N.C., 1928; m. Therese Augusta Schmidt, June 21, 1928; 1 son, Charles Leonard. Owner Royal Crown Bottling Co., Sheffield, Ala., 1934—; mayor of Sheffield, 1950-63. Pres. Ala. Planning and Indsl. Devel. Bd., 1963-68, also dir. Pres. Ala. League Municipalities, 1953-56, Tenn. River Tributaries Assn., 1961-63, So. Assn. State Planning and Devel. Agencies, 1966-67, Ala. Indsl. Devel. Authority, 1965—, Citizens for TVA, 1955-63; rep. Ala. on resources adv. bd. S.E. River Basins Commn., 1964—; chmn. Ala. Commn. Inter-govtl. Coop., 1967—. Mem. Sheffield City Bd. Edn., 1938- 48. Past chmn. Colbert-Lauderdale Salvation Army, Colbert County United Fund; nat. vice chmn. Ala. chpt. A.R.C., 1959-60; adv. bd. Methodist Children's Home, Selma, Ala.; dist. chmn. Tenn. Valley council Boy Scouts Am. Vice chmn. Colbert County Democratic Com., 1960—; Dem. elector of Ala., 1960. Mem. Ala. Bottlers Assn. (past pres.). Methodist (past sch. supt., past chmn. ofcl. bd.). Kiwanian (past pres., lt. gov.), Elk. Home: 1000 Montgomery Av Sheffield AL 35660 Office: 3000 30th St Sheffield AL 35660

BEARD, CHRIS, TV producer/writer; b. Richmond, Eng., June 18, 1936; s. Donald Frederick and Gladys (Messer) B.; grad. E. Sydney (Australia) Tech. Sch.; m. Diana Jean Norris, July 4, 1958; children—Amanda, Samantha, Emma, Barnaby. Came to U.S., 1967. Master of ceremonies childrens TV show, Sydney, Australia, 1959; TV writer and producer, 1961-62; writer Canadian Broadcasting Co., 1962-67; writer Laugh In series, TV, 1967-69; producer Andy William TV series, 1969-71; v.p. United Cons. Services; v.p. Chris Beard Prodns., Toronto, 1967—; co-producer Sonny and Cher Show, 1971. Served with Australian Army, 1953-55. Recipient Emmy award for TV writing, 1968. Mem. Writers Guild Am. (West), A.F.T.R.A., Australian Writers Guild (hon.). Author TV mus. specials: Elvis Presley show, 1968; Andy Williams spl., 1969; Dinah Shore spl., 1969:

Grammy Awards show, 1969; Arte Johnson pilot show, 1969. Address: CBS Studio Center 4024 Radford Av North Hollywood CA 91604*

BEARD, DAVID BREED, physicist, educator; b. Needham, Mass., Feb. 1, 1922; s. Daniel Breed and Anne (Curran) B.; B.S., Hamilton Coll., 1943; postgrad. Cal. Inst. Tech., 1943-44; Ph.D., Cornell U., 1951; m. Eileen Mona Hersey, Mar. 5, 1945; children—Lawrence Bennett, Jonathan Breckenridge, Valerie Curran, Rosemary Diane. Instr., Cath. U. Am., Washington, 1950-51, U. Conn., Storrs, 1951-53; asst. prof. U. Cal., Davis, 1953-56, 58-59, asso. prof., 1959-62, prof., 1962-64; staff scientist Lockheed Missiles & Space Co., Palo Alto, Cal., 1956-58; chmn. dept. physics and astronomy U. Kan., Lawrence, 1964—, prof. physics, 1964—; cons. to pvt. cos., govt. agys. Nat. Acad. Sci.-NRC fellow, 1962, 63, 68; Fulbright scholar, Guggenheim fellow, U.K., 1965-66. Fellow Am. Phys. Soc., A.A.A.S.; mem. Am. Assn. U. Profs., Am. Geophys. Union, Am. Assn. Physics Tchrs., Am. Assn. Engring. Scientists, Fedn. Am. Scientists, Sigma Xi, Sigma Pi Sigma. Author: Quantum Mechanics, 1963; Quantum Mechanics With Applications, 1970. Contbr. articles profl. jours. Home: 1200 Mississippi St Lawrence KS 66044

BEARD, FRANK, profl. golfer; b. Dallas, May 1, 1939; s. Ralph and Pauline (Sheeran) B.; B.A. in Accounting, U. Fla., 1961; m. Pat Roberts, Oct. 30, 1965; 3 children. Winner, Ky. Amateur title, 1961, 62, Frank Sinatra Open, Palm Springs, Cal., 1963; 3d place U.S. Open, Hawaiian Open, 1963; 1st place Tex. Open, San Antonio, Greater New Orleans Open, 1966, Houston Invitational tournament, 1967, Indpls. 500 Festival; 2d place Tournament of Champions, Las Vegas, 1967, Greater New Orleans Open, 1969; 1st place Minn. Golf Classic, Mpls., Westchester Golf Classic, Harrison, N.Y., 1969. Author: Pro: Frank Beard on Gulf Tour, 1970; also series Shaving Strokes. Address: 2209 Wiston Av Louisville KY 40205*

BEARD, GEOFFREY G., business exec.; b. Scotland, July 4, 1904; s. Herbert and Agnes (Macdonald) B.; grad. Merchiston Castle Sch., Edinburgh, 1917-21; B.Sc. with honors, U. Strathclyde, Glasgow, 1926; m. Gwendoline Amy Love, June 18, 1930; children—Marjorie Mary, Marcia May, Madeline Macdonald. Came to U.S., 1927, naturalized, 1934. Research engr., safety in mines underground workings, Royal Sch. of Mines, London, 1926; draftsman, United Engring & Foundry Co., Pitts., 1927-30, engr., 1930-35, mgr. proposal dept. 1935-43, vice pres. sales engr., 1943-46, v.p. and exec. asst., 1946-49, exec. v.p. 1949-52, pres., gen. mgr., 1952-64 chmn., chief exec. officer, 1964-69, chmn., 1969-70; chmn. Stedmans Foundry & Machine Co., Aurora, Ind., Unefcan, Ltd., Toronto; dir. Pitts. Internat. Finance Corp.; chmn. Adamson United Co., Akron; chmn. Wean United, Inc., Warren, O., 1968-70; dir. Pitts. Bank, Continental Steel Co., Kokomo, Ind., 1950-55, Sunstrand Corp., Rockford, Ill., 1965-69. Bd. dirs. Pitts. Regional Planning Com., Allegheny council Boy Scouts Am.; mem. Pitts. Pub. Schs. Community Resource and Adv. Committee. Trustee Episcopal Diocese of Pitts., Episcopal Ch. Home. Recipient Montgomery Neilson Medal and James Riley Medal (Britain) for original research. Mem. Assn. Iron and Steel Engrs., Am. Soc. M.E., Machinery and Allied Products Inst. (v.p. 1960-69). Republican. Episcopalian. Home: Old Salt Works Rd RFD 1 Chatham MA 02633

BEARD, JAMES ANDREWS, food cons.; b. Portland, Ore., May 5, 1903; s. Jonathan A. and Mary Elizabeth (Jones) B.; student Reed Coll., Portland, 1920-21, U. Wash., 1931. Carnegie Inst. Tech., 1931-32. Active amateur theatrical group, Portland; appeared to stage in revivals (with Walter Hampden) of Cyrano de Bergerac, 1924, 25, Othelo, 1925; appeared on radio in San Francisco and Portland, 1927-32, then as announcer for food comms.; pvt. tchr. cooking, Portland, 1932-37; tchr. country day sch. in N.J., 1938; co- propr. Hors d'Oeuvre, Inc., N.Y.C., 1938-44; asso. dairy and vegetable farm, Reading, Pa., 1943; established clubs for United Seamen's Service throughout world, 1943-46; featured on TV food program Elsie Presents, 1946-47; guest on TV shows in U.S., France and Eng., 1947-55; lectr., demonstrator before groups, 1949—; food cons., 1956—; propr. James Beard Cooking classes. N.Y.C., 1955—. Served with AUS, 1942-43. Author: Hors d'Oeuvre Canapes, 1940; Cook it Outdoors, 1941; Fowl and Game Cookery, 1944; Fireside Cookbook, 1949; James Beard's Fish Cookery, 1954; The Complete Book of Barbecue and Rotisserie Cooking, 1954; The Complete Cookbook for Entertaining, 1954; Jim Beard's New Barbecue Cookbook, 1958; James Beard's Treasury of Outdoor Cooking, 1960; The James Beard Cookbook, 1961; (autobiography) Delights and Prejudices, 1964; (with Alexander Watt) Paris Cuisine, 1952; (with Helen E. Brown) The Complete Book of Outdoor Cookery, 1955; (with Sam Aaron) How to Eat Better for Less Money, 1956, rev. edit., 1971; James Beard Cook Book, 1959, rev. edit., 1971; James Beard's Menus for Entertaining, 1965. Writer Gourmet mag.; columnist Beard on Food, Washington Star Syndicate. Contbr. numerous mags. Address: 119 W 10th St New York City NY 10011

BEARD, JOHN ROBERT, librarian; b. Milk River, Alta., Can., Dec. 29, 1918; s. Henry Fred and Ora May (Cheesman) B.; B.A., U. B.C., 1952; B.S. in L.S., U. Toronto, 1954; D. in L.S., Columbia, 1965; m. Patricia Dawn Hehir, Aug. 19, 1955; children—John Robin, Janet Suzanne. Came to U.S., 1964. Tchr., Alta. elementary schs., 1939-42; technician Consol. Mining & Smelting Co., 1942-50, 52-53; reference librarian Windsor (Ont.) Pub. Library, 1954- 56; circulation librarian Bus. Library, Columbia, 1956-58, teaching asst. Sch. Library Service, 1958-59; head acquisitions Vancouver (B.C.) Pub. Library, 1959-61; chief libraries devel. sect. UNESCO, Paris, France, 1962-64; mem. faculty Montclair (N.J.) State Coll. Library 1965- -, prof., head librarian, 1966—. Mem. library use com. N.Y. Met. Reference and Research Library Agy., 1967-70. Can. Council fellow, 1960, 61; recipient Distinguished Service award, coll. and univ. sect. N.J. Library Assn., 1970. Mem. Am., Canadian, N.J. (chmn. coll and univ. library resources com. 1967—, pres. coll. and univ. sect. 1970-71) library assns., Nat., N.J. edn. assns., Am. Assn. U. Profs., Am. Soc. Information Sci. Author: Canadian Provincial Libraries, 1967. Home: 501 W 123d St New York City NY 10027 Office: Montclair State Coll Normal Av and Valley Rd Upper Montclair NJ 07043

BEARD, JOSEPH WILLS, surgeon; b. Athens, La., Nov. 5, 1901; s. Jasper N. and Martha (Bridges) B.; B.S., U. Chgo., 1926; M.D., Vanderbilt U. 1929; m. Dorothy Lowe Waters, June 18, 1932. Intern, asst. resident, resident, instr. in surgery. Vanderbilt Hosp., Nashville, 1929-32; asst. pathologist Rockefeller Inst. Med. Research, 1932-35, asso. pathologist, 1935-37; asst. prof. surgery, in charge exptl. surgery Duke U., 1937-42, asso. prof. surgery, 1943-46, prof. surgery, 1946—, James B. Duke prof. surgery, 1965—, prof. virology, 1965—; cancer research 1949—. Recipient G.H.A. Clowes award in cancer research, 1966. Mem. Soc. Am. Bacteriologists, So. Soc. Clin. Investigation, A.A.A.S., Am. Assn. Immunologists, Am. Soc. Exptl. Pathology, Soc. Exptl. Biology and Medicine, Harvey Soc., Soc. Univ. Surgeons, Am. Assn. Cancer Research, Electron Microscope Soc., Sigma Xi, Lambda Chi Alpha, Phi Chi, Alpha Omega Alpha. Research on surg. shock, chick embryo vaccine against equine encephalomyletis, purfication of animal viruses influenza vaccines, virus induced cancer. Home: Hillsboro NC 27278 Office: Duke Hosp Durham NC 27706

BEARD, RICHARD LEONARD, educator; b. Findlay, O., Dec. 10, 1909; s. Jesse William and Mae (Leonard) B.; A.B., Findlay Coll., 1936; M.A., Bowling Green State U., 1936; Ph.D., Ohio State U., 1943; m. Reva Leona Coleman, July 3, 1937; children—Elaine Louise (Mrs. A. W. Pinkerton, Jr.), John Coleman. Tchr. English, Elida (O.) Pub. Schs., 1936-37; head English dept. Whitmer High Sch., Toledo, 1937-42; asst., then instr. Ohio State U., 1942-43; asst. prof. edn. Ia. State Tchrs. Coll., 1946-48; prof. edn. Marshall U., Huntington, W.Va., 1948-52; asso. prof. edn. U.N.C. 1952-57; head counselor tng. N.C. Coll. at Durham, 1952-56; chmn., prof. edn., counselor edn. dept. U. Va., Charlottsville, 1957—. Lectr. radio sta. KXEL, Waterloo, Ia., 1947-48; TV instr. WUNC, Chapel Hill, N.C., 1954-57; ednl. cons. Served to 1st lt. AUS and USAAF, 1943-46; CBI. Recipient Distinguished Service award Va. chpt. Phi Delta Kappa, 1966; Career Service award Va. Personnel and Guidance Assn., 1967. Mem. Am. Personnel and Guidance Assn., Am. Assn. Counselor Edn. and Supervision, Nat. Vocational Guidance Assn., Am. Assn. U. Profs., N.E.A., Va. Edn. Assn., Phi Delta Kappa. Home: 1812 Meadowbrook Heights Rd Charlottesville, VA 22901.

BEARD, RODNEY RAU, physician, educator; b. Guinda, Cal., Dec. 27, 1911; s. Aiton Holmes and Mathilda Anne (Rau) B.; A.B., Stanford, 1932, M.D., 1938; M.P.H., Harvard, 1940; m. Marion Lucile Harper, July 3, 1938; children—Anne, Philip, Marian, Edin. Intern Gorgas Hosp., Panama Canal, 1937-38; asst. resident Stanford U. Hosps., 1938-39; Rockefeller fellow in med. sci., 1939-40; med. officer Pacific-Alaska div. Pan Am. Airways, 1940-49; instr. med. sch. Stanford, 1940-42, asst. prof., 1942-45, asso. prof., 1945-49, prof., chmn. dept. preventive medicine, 1949-69, prof. community and preventive medicine, 1969—. dir. rehab., 1955-60; medical cons. W. P. Fuller & Co., 1952-63; clin. prof. occupational health U. Cal. at Berkeley, 1952-63, lectr., 1963—; cons. Surgeon General, U.S. Army, 1941-45, 54—, Cal. Dept. Public Health, 1948—, VA, 1954-64. Vis. prof. Clinica del Lavoro, U. di Milano, 1960-61. Chmn. health council San Francisco Community Chest, 1941-44, pub. health com. San Francisco C. of C., 1951-54, San Francisco Bd. Health, 1954-59; mem. com. aviation medicine NRC, 1942-45; mem. comm. environmental hygiene Armed Forces Epidemiological Bd., 1954-55, dir., 1955-67; mem. nat. adv. heart council NIH, Dept. Health. Edn., and Welfare, 1957-61, mem. nat. adv. council pub. health tng., 1965- 69, mem. nat. adv. com. Nat. Inst. Environmental Health Scis., 1971—; cons. Surgeon Gen., USAF, 1966-69. Diplomate Am. Bd. Preventive Medicine (trustee 1961-70), Am. Bd. Indsl. Hygiene. Fellow Am. Coll. Preventive Medicine (v.p. 1967), Am. Public Health Assn., Indsl. Med. Assn. (sec. Western sect. 1945-46, pres. 1949), A.A.A.S.; mem. A.M.A. (sec. sect. preventive medicine, 1964-69, chmn. 1971—, mem. com. on occupational toxicology), Internat. Assn. Occupational Health, Am. Indsl. Hygiene Assn. (dir. 1956-60), Assn. Tchrs. Preventive Medicine (pres. 1958- 59), Am. Heart Assn., Cal. Acad. Medicine, Am. Civil Liberties Union, Airline Med. Dirs. Assn. (hon.), Cal. Acad. Preventive Medicine, Sigma Xi, Delta Omega. Unitarian. Author: Essentials of Public Health (with W.P. Shepard et al), 2d edit. 1952. Author papers. Home: 542 Alvarado Row Stanford CA 94305 Office: Stanford Medical Center Stanford CA 94305

BEARD, SAMUEL SHERWOOD, pub. service exec.; b. N.Y.C., June 24, 1939; s. Anson McCook and Rosanne (Hoar) B.; B.A., Yale U., 1961; M.S., Columbia U., 1966; m. Patricia Dranow, Jan. 18, 1968; 1 son, Alexander. Staff asso. Office of Sen. Robert F. Kennedy, Washington, 1966-67; staff asst. Bedford-Stuyvesant D & S Corp., N.Y.C., 1967-68; chmn. Capital Formation, Inc., N.Y.C., 1968—; dir. J.P. M. Assos.; gen. partner First Horizon Assos.; pres. N.Y.C. Comml. Devel. Corp. Finance chmn. Lowenstein for Congress, 1970. Bd. dirs. Lenox Hill Neighborhood Assn. Democrat. Episcopalian. Author: Ready or Not, 1969; Commitment is a Red Herring, 1970. Home: 16 E 84th St New York City NY 10017 Office: 5 Beekman St New York City NY 10038

BEARD, THEODORE HEMINGWAY, office equipment mfr.; b. Bethel, Conn., June 9, 1895; s. George Edwards and Cora Augusta (Barnum) B.; B.S., M.E. M.S., N.Y.U., 1917; m. Margaret Durant Shepard, Dec. 7, 1929; children—Constance Shepard (Mrs. Willard I. Emerson, Jr.), John Edwards, Betsy Ann (Mrs. Peter B. Salisbury). Staff engr. Columbia Graphophone Mfg. Co., N.Y.C., 1920-23, cons. mech. engr., 1923-29; with Dictaphone Corp., N.Y.C., 1929—. successively supervising eng., v.p., 1936-53, vice chmn. exec. com., dir., 1953—; dir. Bullard Corp., United Illuminating Co., Conn. Nat. Bank Co., Bridgeport Hydraulic Co.; trustee Bridgeport Peoples Savs. Bank. Served as maj. U.S. Army, 1917- 20. Mem. Am. Soc. M.E., Newcomen Soc., S.A.R., Nat. Rifle Assn., Army Ordnance Assn. Republican. Conglist. Mason, Rotarian. Clubs: University Brooklawn Country (Bridgeport); Army and Navy (Washington). Home and Office: 29 Ridgeway St Easton CT 06612

BEARD, THOMAS REX, educator; b. Baton Rouge, Aug. 12, 1934; s. Rex and Gertrude Louise (Hampton) B.; B.S., La. State U., 1956, M.A., 1958; Ph.D., Duke, 1963; m. Sharon Virginia Petty, Dec. 21, 1957; children—Thomas Randolph, Sharon Elizabeth. Asst. prof. La. State U., Baton Rouge, 1961-64, asso. prof., head econs. dept., 1965-68, prof., head econs. dept., 1969—; economist Fed. Res. Bd. of Govs., Washington, 1964-65; 4th Nat. Bank Distinguished prof. Wichita State U., 1968-69; cons. La. Coordinating Council for Higher Edn., 1970, also various fed. govt. agys. Earhart Found. fellow, 1957-58, Ford Found. fellow, 1960, James B. Duke fellow, 1958-60. Mem. Am., So. (mem. exec. com. 1967-69), Southwestern (pres. 1969-70) econ. assns., Am. Finance Assn., Nat. Tax Assn., Phi Beta Kappa, Kappa Alpha, Omicron Delta Kappa, Phi Kappa Phi. Methodist. Author: U.S. Treasury Advance Refunding, 1966. Editor: The Louisiana Economy, 1969; asso. editor Social Science Quarterly, 1966-70. Contbr. articles profl. jours. Home: 5952 Hibiscus Dr Baton Rouge LA 70808

BEARD, WILLIAM, author; b. N.Y.C., May 18, 1907; s. Charles Austin and Mary (Ritter) E.; B.S., Mass. Inst. of Tech., 1928; A.M., U. Cal. at Los Angeles, 1938; Ph.D., Columbia, 1941; m. Melba Gorby, Oct. 5, 1933; children—Wayne, Arlene. Research asst. N.Y. State Joint Legislative Com. on Texation and Retrenchment, 1928-29; wrote with father, 1929-30; instr. Cal. Inst. Tech., 1931-34; chief publs. sect. TVA, 1936; asst. prof. U. Wis., 1940-42; civilian instr. USAAF, 1942-43; radio operator, 1943-44. Served with U.S. Army, 1945. Author or co-author more than a dozen books and numerous mag. articles on history and polit. sci. Address: PO Box 728 Scottsdale AZ 85252

BEARD, WINSTON CLINGAN, economist; b. Camden, Ark., Apr. 17, 1930; s. Cleburne M. and Ruby (Bullock) B.; B.A., Ouachita Bapt. U., 1953; M.B.A., U. Ark., 1954; Ph.D., U. Ill., 1961; m. Mildred Shaffer, June 25, 1955; children—Jon Winston, Kevin David, Research economist Indsl. Research Center. U. Ark., 1958-62; asst. prof. finance U. Tex., 1962-65; prof. econs., chmn. dept. Baylor U., 1965-67; exec. dir. Ark. Planning Commn., 1967-69; prof., chmn. dept. finance U. Ark., Little Rock, 1969—. Mem. Am. Econ. Assn., Am. Finance Assn., Financial Analysis Fedn., Inst. Chartered Financial Analysts, Beta Gamma Sigma, Omicron Delta Epsilon. Home: 11112 Yosemite Valley Dr Little Rock AR 72207

BEARDEN, JAMES HUDSON, univ. dean; b. Marion, Ala., Sept. 25, 1933; s. Joseph N. and Lula (Worrell) B.; B.S., Centenary Coll. La., 1956; M.A., E. Carolina Coll., 1959; Ph.D., U. Ala., 1966; m. Pauline Larkins, Mar. 31, 1961; children—James Hudson, Pauline Larkins. Bus. mgr. Marion Inst., 1959-60; mem. faculty E. Carolina U., Greenville, N.C., 1960—, prof. bus. adminstrn., 1964—, dir. bur. bus. research, 1964, dean, 1968—. Dir. Planters Nat. Bank & Trust Co., Mem. Tar River Basin Devel. Assn., Greenville Bd. Edn., N.C. Emergency Indsl. Prodn. Task Group. Bd. dirs. Pitt County United Fund; trustee N.C. Council Econ. Edn. Served with AUS, 1956-58. Grad. fellow U. Ala., 1961; grantee Nat. Assn. Purchasing Agts., 1962; fellow Birmingham Sales Execs., 1961. Mem. Am. Assn. U. Profs., Am. Marketing Assn., Assn. Edn. Internat. Bus., N.C. World Trade Assn., So. Econ. Assn., So. Marketing Assn., Beta Gamma Sigma. Rotarian (bd. dirs. Greenville). Author articles in field. Home: 106 Crown Point Rd Greenville NC 27834

BEARDEN, JOYCE ALVIN, educator; b. Greenville, S.C., Oct. 19, 1903; s. Joseph Sylvester and Annie (Haley) B.; A.B., Furman U., 1923; Ph.D., U. Chgo., 1926; D.Sc., Furman U., 1951; m. Lillian S. Singleton, June 6, 1923; 1 son, Alan Joyce. Fellow, U. of Chgo., 1925, asst., 1926, instr. physics, 1926-29; asso. physics, Johns Hopkins U., 1929-32, asso. prof., 1932-39, prof. 1939—, chmn. dept. physics, 1947. Physicist Applied Physics Lab., Washington, D.C., 1942-46; dir. Radiation Lab., Johns Hopkins U., 1943- 55; physicist Carnegie Instn., Washington, 1941-42. Cons. Nat. Def. Research Com., 1940-42. Col. U.S. Army on tech. mission to European Theater, 1944-45. Fellow Am. Physics. Soc., A.A.A.S.; mem. Am. Physical Soc. (mem. council, 1946-50), Phi Beta Kappa Sigma Xi, Research in X-rays, physical constants, solid state. Home: 214 Lambeth Rd Baltimore MD 21218 Office: Johns Hopkins University Baltimore MD 21218

BEARDEN, ROMARE HOWARD, artist; b. Charlotte, N.C., Sept. 2, 1914; s. Howard R. and Bessye (Johnson) B.; B.S., N.Y. U., 1935; postgrad. Art Students League, 1937; m. Nanette Rohan, Sept. 4, 1954. Exhibited in one man shows at Kootz Gallery, N.Y.C., 1945-47, Niveau Gallery, N.Y.C., 1949, Barone Gallery, N.Y.C., 1955, Michel Warren Gallery, N.Y.C., 1960, Cordier-Eckstrom, N.Y.C., 1961, 64, 67, 69, Corcoran Gallery, Washington, 1965, Carnegie Inst. Tech., 1966, Bundy Mus., Vt., 1966, Mus. Modern Art, 1971; exhibited in two-man show Phila. Art Alliance, 1971; exhibited numerous group shows in Europe, S.Am. Art dir. Harlem Cultural Council. Served with AUS, 1942-45. Recipient award Nat. Inst. Arts. and Letters, 1966, purchase award Am. Acad. Arts and Letters, 1970; Guggenheim fellow, 1970-71. Author: (with Carl Holty) The Painter's Mind, 1969. Home: 351 W 114th St New York City NY 10026 Studio: 357 Canal St New York City NY 10013

BEARDEN, WALTER SCOTT, Jr., life ins. co. exec.; b. Nashville, Sept. 4, 1910; s. Walter Scott and Elizabeth (Thomas) B.; B.A., Vanderbilt U., 1932; m. Frances Bevington, May 10, 1934; children—Walter Scott III, Julie Elaine, John Bevington, With Nat. Life & Accident Ins. Co., Nashville, 1932—; dir., 1962—, v.p., sec., 1962-63, sr. v.p., sec.-personnel, 1963-65, exec. v.p., sec., 1965-69, vice chmn. bd., sec., 1969—, also mem. exec. com. Trustee Nashville United Givers Fund, pres., 1966. Mem. Life Office Mgmt. Assn. (pres. 1965, dir.), Nashville Area C. of C. (exec. com., gov.), Vanderbilt U. Alumni Assn. (past dir.), Phi Delta Theta. Clubs: Rotary, Belle Meade Country (past dir.) (Nashville). Home: 636 Timber Lane Nashville, TN 37215. Office: 301 7th Av N Nashville TN 37219

BEARDMORE, GEORGE WOLCOTT, timber co. exec.; b. Priest River, Ida., Apr. 29, 1908; s. Charles W. and Lucy E. (Gumaer) B.; B.A., U. Ida., 1930, LL.B., 1933; m. Edith M. Eklund, June 22, 1935; children—Nancy J. (Mrs. Ronald G. Osborn), Ann M. (Mrs. Richard D. LaCourse), Lucy E. (Mrs. David P. Mulalley), and Nelda L. Beardmore (now Mrs. Gary D. Drage). Admitted to Ida. bar, 1933; pvt. practice law, Sandpoint, Ida., 1933-40; with Potlatch Forests, Inc., Lewiston, Ida., 1940—, now v.p. Mem. Ida. Coop. Bd. Forestry, 1947-55; alternate mem. W. Coast lumber commn. War Labor Bd. Mem. N. Ida. Forestry Assn. (sec. 1945-66), Potlatch Timber Protective Assns., Lewiston, Lewiston Jr., N. Ida. (past pres.) chambers commerce, Soc. Am. Foresters, Sigma Alpha Epsilon, Phi Alpha Delta. Elk. Home: 620 19th Av Lewiston ID 83501 Office: PO Box 1016 Lewiston ID 83501

BEARDSLEE, BETHANY, soprano; b. Lansing, Mich., Dec. 25, 1927; d. Walter and Ella (Simpson) Beardslee; B.Mus., Mich. State U.; student Juilliard Inst.; m. Godfrey Winham, July, 1957; children—Baird, Christopher. Singer modern Music, contemporary vocal music, 1951—; appearances maj. contemporary festivals U.S. and Can., also Internat. Soc. Contemporary Music. League Composers, Composers Forum, B. de Rothschild Found., Fromm Found., Camera Concerts, Chgo. Contemporary Concerts, Caramor Festival, Tanglewood, Library of Congress; singer in resident seminar advanced mus. studies Princeton, 1960; mem. N.Y. Pro Musica Antiqua, 1958-60; premier singer numerous young Am. composers; recordings for Am. Recording Soc., Dial Records, Epic Records, Columbia Records, Son-Nova Records; soloist with Boston, Chgo., Mpls., Detroit, St. Louis Symphonies, N.Y., Buffalo philharmonic orchs. Recipient Laurel Leaf award Am. Composers Alliance, 1962, Concert Soloists award Ford Found. 1962. Address: River Rd Belle Mead NJ 08502

BEARDSLEE, WILLIAM ARMITAGE, educator, clergyman; b. Holland, Mich., Mar. 25, 1916; s. John Walter, Jr., and Frances Eunice (Davis) B.; A.B., Harvard, 1937; B.D., New Brunswick Theol. Sem., 1941; M.A., Columbia, 1948; Ph.D., U. Chgo., 1951; m. Kathryn Quinby Walker, June 11, 1941; children—Joy Walker (Mrs. Richard L. Huffman), William Rigby. Became ordained to the ministry, Reformed Church in America, 1941, minister, Queens Village, N.Y., 1941- 45; asst. prof. Bible, Emory U., 1947-52, asso. prof., 1952-56, prof. religion, 1956—, dir. Grad. Inst. Liberal Arts, 1957-61. acting dean Coll. Arts and Scis., 1958; Fulbright Sr. Research grant, U. Bonn. Germany, 1961- 62; vis. prof. Pomona Coll., spring 1969. Mem. Am. Acad. Religion (asso. editor 1961-69), Soc. Bibl. Lit. (pres. So. sect. 1957-58), Archeol. Inst. Am., Am. Assn. U. Profs., Phi Beta Kappa. Author: (with E. H. Rece) Reading Bible: A Guide, 1952, 2d edit., 1964; Human Achievement and Divine Vocation in The Message of Paul, 1961; (with J. Boozer) Faith to Act, 1967; Literary Criticism of the New Testament, 1970. Editor: American and the Future of Theology, 1967. Home: 1728 Vickers Circle Decatur GA 30030

BEARDSLEY, CHARLES EDWARD, lawyer; b. Des Moines, Apr. 21, 1904; s. John and Anna (Wyman) B.; A.B., Stanford, 1925, J.D., 1927; m. Marian Gower, Aug. 12, 1926; children—Frances (Mrs. John L. Dee), Anna (Mrs. Thomas J. McHugh), Jane Margery (Mrs. C. A. Lemeland). Admitted to Cal. bar, 1927, since practiced in Los Angeles: mem. Beardsley, Hufstedler & Kemble. Mem. Am., Los Angeles (1st chmn. jr. barristers, past chmn. constnl. rights com., juvenile court com.) bar assns., State Bar Cal. (chmn. com. bar examiners, bd. govs. 1950-53, pres., 1952-53), Am. Coll. Trial Lawyers, Los Angeles Jr. C. of C. (past dir.), Am. Law Inst. Clubs: Chancery, University (Los Angeles); San Marino City (past pres.),

Oneonta (past pres.) (South Pasadena, Cal.). Home: 2390 Ridgeway Rd San Marino CA 91108 Office: Crocker-Citizens Bldg 611 W 6th St Los Angeles CA 90017

BEARDSLEY, ELIZABETH LANE (Mrs. Monroe Curtis Beardsley), philosopher, educator; b. Ann Arbor, Mich.; d. Robert Porter and Bess (Edwards) Lane; A.B., Swarthmore Coll., 1935; M.A., Columbia, 1937; Ph.D., Yale, 1940; m. Monroe Curtis Beardsley, June 29, 1940; children-Philip Lane, Mark Monroe. Lectr. philosophy U. Del., 1949-52; prof., chmn. philosophy dept. Lincoln U., 1953-60; asso. prof. Temple U., Phila., 1962-64., 1965—; judge Melcher Book Award Contest, 1963-68. Bd. dirs. Housing Assn. Delaware Valley, Fellowship of Religious Humanists. Recipient Lindback award for distinguished teaching Temple U., 1969. Mem. Am. Philos. Assn., Am. Soc. for Polit. and Legal Philosophy, Am. Assn. U. Profs. (chpt. pres.), Am. Civil Liberties Union. Democrat. Unitarian. Author: (with M.C. Beardsley) Philosophical Thinking, 1965. Editor: (with M.C. Beardsley) Foundations of Philosophy series, 1963—. Contbr. articles profl. jours. Home: 1916 Delancey Pl Philadelphia PA 19103

BEARDSLEY, JAMES HARTNESS, utility corp. exec.; b. Springfield, Mass., Mar. 20, 1914; s. William Henry (M.D.) and Anna (Hartness) B.; A.B., Dartmouth, 1937; m. Margaret Harriet Whitcomb. Aug. 28, 1937; children—Christopher, William Henry, Anthony Whitcomb, Anna Katherine. Prodn. mgr. Jones & Lamson Machine Co., Springfield, Vt., 1941-48, clk., 1943-58, dir., 1943-58, 61-64; dir., clk., asst. to pres. Bryant Chucking Grinder Co., Springfield, Vt., 1948-49, dir., clk., v.p. and gen. mgr., 1949-54, exec. v.p., 1954-58, pres., 1958-59; pres., gen. mgr., dir. Twin Falls Power Corp., Ltd., Montreal, Can., 1959-66; v.p., pres., dir. Ascutney Fund. Inc., 1964-67; pres., gen. mgr., dir. Bowater Power Co., Ltd., Deer Lake, Newfoundland, 1966—. Bd. overseers Thayer Sch. Engring., Dartmouth, 1954-62; v.p., treas., dir. Early Sites Found., 1955-67. Mem. Thayer Soc. Engrs., Engring. Inst. of Can. Home: Poplar Rd Deer Lake Newfoundland Canada

BEARDSLEY, MONROE CURTIS, educator, author; b. Bridgeport, Conn., Dec. 10, 1915; s. Samuel Birdsey and Esther (Carney) B.; A.B., Yale, 1936, Ph.D., 1939; m. Elizabeth Bobette Lane, June 29, 1940; children—Philip, Mark. Instr. Yale, 1940- 44, asst. prof., 1946-47; asst. prof. Mt. Holyoke Coll., 1944-46; mem. faculty Swarthmore Coll., 1947-69, prof. philosophy, 1959-69; faculty Temple U., Phila., 1969—. Pres. Greater Phila. Am. Civil Liberties Union, 1967- 70; sec. Chester br. N.A.A.C.P., 1965-69. Guggenheim fellow, 1950-51. Mem. Am. Assn. U. Profs., Am. Soc. Aesthetics (trustee; pres. 1967-68), Am. Philos. Assn. (past bd. dirs. Eastern div., v.p. div. 1970-71), Am. Soc. Legal and Polit. Philosophy, Unitarian-Universalist. Author: Practical Logic, 1950; (with Elizabeth Beardsley) Philosophical Thinking, 1965; Aesthetics: Problems in the Philosophy of Criticism, 1958; Aesthetics from Classical Greece to the Present: A Short History, 1966; Thinking Straight, 3d edit., 1966; The Possibility of Criticism. 1970. Editor: (with Elizabeth Beardsley) Foundations of Philosophy series. Mem. bd. adviser, contbr. Ency. Philsoophy; mem. editorial bd. The Monist, Am. Philps. Quar., Jour. Aesthetic Edn., Jour. History of Ideas, Metaphilosophy. Home: 1916 Delancey Pl Philadelphia PA 19103 Office: Dept Philosophy Temple U Philadelphia PA 19122

BEARDSLEY, ROBERT EUGENE, educator, microbiologist; b. Walton, N.Y., June 11, 1923; s. Harrison R. and Margaret (Sliter) B.; B.S., Manhattan Coll., 1950; A.M., Columbia, 1951, Ph.D., 1960; m. Philomena E. Pecora, Aug. 28, 1948; children—Luisa M., Margaret R., Robert E. Instr. Manhattan Coll., 1951-54, asst. prof., 1954-58, asso. prof., 1958-68, prof., 1968—, dir. Lab. Plant Morphogenesis, 1962-69, head dept. biology, 1969—; vis. investigator Inst. Pasteur, Paris, 1966-67. Co-chmn. Scientists Com. Radiation Information, 1960. Served with AUS, 1943-46. Guggenheim fellow, 1966. Mem. Am. Inst. Biol. Scis., Am. Soc. Microbiologists, A.A.A.S., Sigma Xi, Epsilon Sigma Pi. Contbr. articles profl. jours. Home: 242 Mountaindale Rd Yonkers NY 10710 Office: Manhattan Coll Bronx NY 10471

BEARDSLEY, WALTER RAPER, drug co. exec.; b. Elkhart, Ind., Oct. 23, 1905; s. Andrew Hubble and Helen (Brown) B.; student Phillips Andover Acad., 1921-24; B.S. in Politics with honors, Princeton, 1928; m. Marjory Buchanan, Nov. 20, 1929; 1 son, Robert. Asst. to pres. Miles Labs., Inc., medicines, Elkhart, 1929-33, v.p., 1933-47, pres., 1947-61, chmn. bd., 1961—; dir. TV Communications Corp., N.Y.C., First Nat. Bank, Truth Pub. Co. Mem. Ind. Senate, 1936-40; chmn. Elkhart County Republican Com., 1930-34; del. Rep. Nat. Conv., 1948, 52, 56, 60, 68; mem. Nat. Rep. Com. from Ind., 1961-68; nat. chmn. Rep. Congl. Boosters Club, Washington. Pres. bd. trustees Elkhart Gen. Hosp.; mem. art adv. council U. Notre Dame. Served as lt. col., USAAF, 1942-45. Benjamin Franklin fellow Royal Soc. Arts, London, Eng. Mem. Nat. Indsl. Conf. Bd., Proprietary Assn. Am. (pres. 1948-50), Nat., Ind. socs. of S.A.R., Am. Legion. Presbyn. Elk. Clubs: Princeton of N.Y.; Elcona Country, City (Elkhart, Ind.); Columbia (Indpls.); University, Sky (N.Y.C.); Capital Hill (Washington); Princeton (Chgo.). Home: 2233 Greenleaf Blvd Elkhart IN 46514 Office: Miles Laboratories Inc 1127 Myrtle St Elkhart IN 46514

BEARE, GENE KERWIN, electrical equipment mfr.; b. Chester, Ill., July 14, 1915; s. Nicholas Eugene and Minnie Cole (St. Vrain) B.; B.S. in Mech. Engring., Washington U., 1937; M.B.A., Harvard, 1939; m. Doris Margaret Alt, Dec. 11, 1943 (dec.); children—Gail Kathryn, Joanne St. Vrain; m. 2d, Patricia Pfau Cade, Sept. 12, 1964. With Automatic Electric Co., Chgo., 1939-58, successively asst. to v.p. and gen. mgr., asst. to pres., mgr. affiliated cos., gen. comml. mgr., prodn. mgr., 1939-54, v.p. charge prodn., 1954-58, dir., 1956-61; pres. dir., Automatic Electric Internat., Inc., 1958-61; chmn., dir. Automatic Electric (Can.), Ltd., Automatic Electric Sales (Can.), Ltd., 1958-61; pres. Sylvania Internat., 1959-60; pres. Gen. Telephone & Electronics Internat., Inc., 1960-61, dir., 1960—; pres., dir. Sylvania Electric Products, Inc., 1961-69, dir., 1961—; exec. v.p. mfg. Gen. Telephone & Electronics Corp., 1969—, dir., 1969—; dir. Am. Research and Devel. Corp., Arkwright-Boston Mut. Ins. Co., Westvaco Corp., Gen. Telephone & Electronics Labs. Inc., GT & E Service Corp. Served from ensign to lt. USNR, 1942-45. Registered profl. engr., Ill. Mem. Nat. Elec. Mfrs. Assn. (bd. govs. 1963—, pres. 1965- 66), Armed Forces Communications and Electronics Assn., Nat. Security Indsl. Assn. (trustee), Pan Am. Soc. Clubs: Wee Burn (gov. 1963-68) (Darien, Conn.); Union League, Economic. Home: 5 Salem Straits Darien CT 06820 Office: Gen Telephone & Electronics Corp 730 3d Av New York City NY 10017

BEARMAN, RICHARD JOHN, educator; b. N.Y.C., June 23, 1929; s. William J. and Sonia (Ginsberg) B.; A.B., Cornell U., 1951; Ph.D., Stanford, 1956; m. Mirion Yang, Aug. 5, 1961; children—Michael, Margaret Lynn. NSF postdoctoral fellow Yale, 1955-56, research asst., 1956-57, asst. prof. U. Kan., Lawrence, 1957-62, asso. prof., 1962-67, prof. chemistry, 1967—; vis. reader U. New Eng., New S. Wales, Australia, 1968-69. Guggenheim fellow, 1962-63; hon. fellow diffusion research unit Australian Nat. U., 1968-69. Fellow Am. Inst. Chemists; mem. N.Y., Kan. acads. scis., Am. Chem. Soc., Am. Phys. Soc., Sigma Xi. Author: (with B. Chu) Problems in Chemical Thermodynamics, 1967. Contbr. numerous articles profl. jours. Home: 125 E 17th St Lawrence KS 66044

BEARN, ALEXANDER GORDON, physician, scientist; b. Surrey, Eng., Mar. 29, 1923; s. Edward Gordon and Rose (Kay) B.; ed. Epsom Coll.; M.B., B.S., Guy's Hosp., U. London (Eng.), 1946, M.D., 1951; m. Margaret Slocum, Dec. 20, 1952; children—Helen Elliot, Gordon Clarence Frederic. Came to U.S., 1951. House physician Guy's Hosp., 1946-47; house physician, registrar Postgrad. Med. Sch., London, 1948-51; mem. staff Rockefeller Inst., N.Y.C., 1951-64, asso. prof., 1957-64, prof., sr. physician, 1964-66; prof., chmn. dept. medicine Cornell U., 1966—; physician-in-chief N.Y. Hospital, 1966—; med. dir., bd. dirs., sec.-treas. Russell Sage Inst. of Pathology, 1967—. Bd. sci. cons. Sloan Kettering Inst., 1967—; cons. genetics tng. com., div. gen. med. scis. USPHS, 1961-65, cons. genetics study sect., 1966-70; sec., mem. bd. sci. cons. Royal Soc. Medicine Found., Inc. Mem. bd. scientific overseers Jackson Lab., Bar Harbor; mem. Inst. Medicine, Nat. Acad. Scis. Trustee Rockefeller U., Helen Hay Whitney Found. Served as med. officer RAF, 1947-49. Fellow A.A.A.S., Royal Coll. Physicians (Edinburgh, Scotland), Royal Coll. Physicians (London, Eng.); mem. Assn. Am. Physicians, Am. Soc. Clin. Investigation, Am. Soc. Human Genetics (pres. 1971), Genetics Soc. Am., Am. Soc. Biol. Chemists, Soc. Exptl. Biology and Medicine, Harvey Soc. (sec. 1960-64), Harveian Soc. London (Council 1959), Assn. Physicians Great Britain and Ireland, Med. Research Soc. Great Britain, Am. Assn. History Medicine, Sigma Xi (pres. Rockefeller chpt. 1962-63); hon. mem. Sociedad Medica de Santiago, Sociedad de Biologia de Santiago. Presbyterian. Clubs: The Bath (London, England): Century Association, Grolier (N.Y.C.), Co-editor; Progress in Medical Genetics, 1962—; asso. editor Cecil-Loeb Textbook of Medicine. Contbr. profl. jours. Home: 1225 Park Av New York City NY 10028 Office: 525 E 68th St New York City NY 10028

BEASLEY, DELMAR OTIS, lawyer; b. Rockport, Miss., Oct. 13, 1907; s. James Bascom and Floyd Catherine (Fox) B.; A.B., George Washington U., 1934, LL.B., 1941; m. Virginia Macklin Shell, June 20, 1934; children—Elizabeth, Nancy. Office boy W. P. Brown & Sons Lumber Co., Zama, Miss., 1927-28; clk.-typist War Dept., 1928-30; clk., bookkeeper, asst. chief div. accts., U.S. Dept. Interior, 1930-41, budget officer geol. survey, 1941-42, asst. budget officer, asst. dir. Div. Budget and Adminstrv. Mgmt. and dir. Div. Budget and Finance, 1942-52, asst. sec. admistrn., 1952-65; admitted to D.C. bar, 1937; in law practice, 1966—; chmn. Oil Import Appeals Bd., 1961-62. Mem. adv. bd. Marine Heart Research Found. mem. marine fisheries adv. com. Dept. Commerce, 1971—. Recipient Interior Dept. Distinguished Service award. Mem. Internat. Light Tackle Tournament Assn. (dir., pres. 1966-67), Inter-Am., Am., Fed. bar assns., Phi Sig Sigma Kappa. Clubs: Touchdown, University, George Washington University (Washington). Home: 4716 44th St NW Washington DC 20016 Office: 1000 16th St NW Washington DC 20036

BEASLEY, JERE LOCKE, lt. gov. Ala.; b. Tyler, Tex., Dec. 12, 1935; s. Browder L. and Florence (Camp) B.; B.S., Auburn U., 1959; LL.B., U. Ala., 1962; m. Sara Baker, Mar. 15, 1958; children—Jere Locke, Julia Anne, Linda Lee. Admitted to Ala. bar, 1962; practice in Tuscaloosa, 1962-64, Clayton, 1964-71; mem. firm Beasley, Williams & Robertson, 1969-71; dir., legal counsel Bank of Commerce, Clayton; lt. gov., Ala., 1971—. Mem. Am., Ala., Barbour County (past pres.) bar assns., Am. Trial Lawyers Assns., Clayton C. of C. (past pres.). Lion (past pres. Clayton). Home: 301 N Midway St Clayton AL 36016 Office: 104 Court Sq Clayton AL 36016 also 125 S Orange St Eufaula AL 36027

BEASLEY, JOHN MICHAEL, profl. basketball player; b. Texarkana, Ark., Feb. 5, 1944; s. Russell Sage and Grace Aileen (Rambo) B.; B.B.A., Tex. A. and M. U., 1966; m. Janice Mae Mills, June 8, 1962; children—Kimberly Ann, Michael Barton. Sales trainee Phillips Petroleum Co., Bartlesville, Okla., 1966-67; profl. basketball player, mem. Chaparrals of Am. Basketball Assn., Dallas, 1967—. Named Sophomore of Year S.W. Conf., 1964, to All Conf. Team, 1964, 65, 66, Most Valuable Player S.W. Conf., 1966, Helms Found. All-Am., 1966, Distinguished Student, Tex. A. and M. U., 1966, Amateur Athletic Union All-Am., 1967, All Profl. Am. Basketball Assn. 1968, 69, Am. Basketball Assn. All-Star Team, 1968, 69, 70, Most Valuable Player Am. Basketball Assn. All-Star Game, 1969.

BEASLEY, KENNETH EPHRAIM, educator; b. Terre Haute, Ind., Aug. 27, 1925; s. Kenneth and Gladys O. (Cordrey) B.; B.A. in Polit. Sci., U. Kan., 1948, M.A., 1949, Ph.D., 1955; m. Rachel K. Martin, Dec. 23, 1945; children—Kenneth Ephraim II, Ronald Wilson, Russell Wilbur. Asst. prof. polit. sci. U. Kan., 1955-61; asso. prof. Pa. State U., 1961-63; dir. research Kan. Legislative Council, prof. polit. sci. U. Kan., 1964-67; prof. polit. sci., head dept. U. Tex., El Paso, 1967-69, dean Grad. Sch., dir. Bur. Pub. Affairs, 1969—. Cons. pub. library adminstrn., 1962—. Exec. sec. senate ways and means com. Kan. Legislature, 1956-57; budget analyst Kan. Budget Div., 1956; exec. sec. Kan. Legislative Com. Econ. and Efficiency, 1957-59. Bd. dirs. El Paso County Mental Health and Mental Retardation Bd., El Paso County Jr. Coll. Bd. Served with AUS, 1943-45. Recipient award of merit Pa. Library Assn., 1965. Mem. Am. Polit. Sci. Assn., Am. Soc. Pub. Adminstrn., A.L.A. Contbr. monographs, articles to profl. lit. Home: 4010 Santa Ana El Paso TX 79968

BEASLEY, L.R., corp. exec.; b. Warren, Ark., 1909. Treas. Murphy Oil Corp., Deltic Farm & Timber Co., Sipsey Valley Lumber Co., Murco Libya Oil Co., Murphy Oil Trading Co., Murphy Spain Oil Co., Ocean Drilling & Exploration Co., Compagnie Murphy Des Petroles Au Sahara, El Dorado Exploration S.A., Murphy- Australia Oil Co., Murphy North Sea Co., Murphy Exploration Co., Murphy Middle East Oil Co., Murphy Oil Venezolano C.A., Norske Murphy Oil Co., Ark. Oil Co., Murphy Netherlands Oil Co., Murphy Eastern Can. Oil Co., Murphy Eastern Oil Co., Murphy New Zealand Oil Co.; treas., dir. Murco Stations, Inc., El Dorado Investments, Inc., Murphy Oil Internat. Finance Corp. Home: 1015 W 5th St El Dorado AR 71730 Office: Murphy Bldg El Dorado AR 71730

BEASLEY, ROBERT POWER, rubber co. exec.; b. Nashville, Feb. 26, 1914; s. Wilson H. and Lucy H. (Bridgewater) B.; grad. Webb Sch., 1932; student Duke, 1933-33; B.A., Vanderbilt U., 1936, M.A., 1937; LL.B., U. Akron, 1953; m. Emily F. Taggart, Mar. 7, 1938. With Firestone Tire & Rubber Co., 1938—, asst. comptroller, 1955-60, asst. treas., 1960-62, treas., 1962-65, v.p., treas., 1965-66, v.p. finance, 1966-68, exec. v.p., 1968—, also dir.; dir. Firestone Bank. Admitted to Ohio bar, 1954. Trustee U. Akron. Served with USNR, 1943-46. Mem. Am., Ohio, Akron bar assns., Kappa Sigma, Omicron Delta Kappa. Clubs: Portage Country, City. Home: 2253 Tinkham Rd Akron OH 44313 Office: 1200 Firestone Pkwy Akron OH 44301

BEASLEY, THEODORE PRENTIS, life ins. exec.; b. Mt. Ayr, Ia., June 29, 1900; s. Clarence H. and Ada (Prentis) B.; student pub. schs., Ia., Kan.; LL.D., Tex. Christian U., 1968; m. Beulah F. Porter, June 21, 1921; children—Ronald Rex, Betty Jean (Mrs. Howard D. McElroy). Organized Joplin Life Ins. Co. (Mo.), 1928; sec., gen. mgr. Public Nat. Life Ins. Co., Little Rock, 1935-37; pres. Republic Nat. Life Ins. Co., Dallas, 1937-61, chmn. bd., chief exec. officer, 1961—; dir. Merc. Nat. Bank Dallas, Oak Cliff Savings & Loan Assn., Southwest Title Ins. Co., S.W. Abstract Co. Trustee Tex. Christian U.; mem., v.p. bd. Nat. City Christian Ch. Corp., Washington; mem. Greater Dallas Council Chs.; life dir. Dallas met. bd. YMCA, former U.S. mem. World's Council, mem. nat. com. U.S. and Can.; past mem. and chmn. adv. bd. Salvation Army, Dallas Citizens Council, Greater Dallas Planning Council; past dir. Dallas Community Chest. Trustee, vice chmn. George Williams Coll. Served from pvt. to sgt. U.S. Army, 1918-20. Recipient Lay Churchman of Year award, 1952; Nat. Brotherhood citation Nat. Conf. Christians and Jews, 1965. Mem. Oak Cliff (past pres.), Dallas (past dir.) Chambers commerce, Am., Tex. life convs., Ins. Econ. Soc. Am. (past v.p.), Health Ins. Assn. Am., Life Insurers Conf. Mem. Christian Ch. Mason (32, Shriner), Kiwanian. Clubs: Dallas Country, Dallas Athletic, Dallas. Home: 4260 Bordeaux St Dallas TX 75205 Office: 3988 N Central Expressway Dallas TX 75204

BEASLEY, WALLIS, ednl. adminstr.; b. Red Bay, Ala., Oct. 8, 1915; s. Joseph Thomas and Emma Elizabeth (Shamblin) B.; B.A., Harding Coll., 1938; M.A., George Peabody Coll., 1941, Ph.D., 1948; m. Totsie Orriebelle Smith, Nov. 20, 1943. Faculty social sci. Middle Tenn. State Coll., 1942-43, George Pepperdine Coll., 1945-47; faculty sociology and anthroplogy Wash. State U., 1948- -, prof., 1955—, chmn. dept., 1949-64 acad. v.p., 1965-68, acting pres., 1966-67, exec. v.p., 1968—. Chmn. Wash. State Census Bd., 1965; mem. State Wash. Planning Adv. Council, 1966—, Athletic Assn. of Western Univs. Council, 1962-66 (chmn. 1965-66); mem. exec. com. council for acad. affairs Nat. Assn. State Univs. and Land Grant Colls., 1967—, mem. exec. com., 1968—. Home: 510 Derby St Pullman WA 99163

BEASON, ROBERT GAYLE, magazine editor; b. Prescott, Kan., May 21, 1927; s. Henry M. and Ruth (Herman) B.; student U. Neb., 1945-46; B. Journalism, U. Mo., 1949, B.A., 1950; m. Sylvia Elizabeth Toulouse, Nov. 18, 1950; 1 son, Drew. News editor Rolla (Mo.) Daily Herald, 1950; sports editor Moberly (Mo.) Monitor-Index, 1950-51; reporter, then copy editor Kansas City (Mo.) Star, 1951-54; promotion editor, then asst. editor Mechanix Illus. mag., 1955-60; editor Electronics Illus. mag., 1960-63, Mechanix Illus. amd Electronics Illus. mags., 1963—. Served with USNR, 1945-46. Mem. Electronics Press Club (pres. 1965-67), Inst. High Fidelity (pubs. com.), Am. Soc. Mag. Editors, Tau Kappa Epsilon, Sigma Delta Chi. Democrat. Conglist. Club: Madison Avenue Sports Car Driving and Chowder Soc. Home: Chestnut Hill Rd Stamford CT 06903 Office: 1515 Broadway New York City NY 10036

BEATIE, BRUCE ALAN, educator; b. Oakland, Cal., Mar. 4, 1935; s. Charles B. and M. Berenice (Putnam) B.; B.A., U. Cal. at Berkeley, 1959; M.A., U. Colo., 1960; Ph.D., Harvard U., 1963; m. Rita Virginia Nicklos, May 11, 1956; 1 son, Robert Bruce. Tchr. German U. Colo., 1960; part-time tchr. English, Harvard, 1960-63; asst. prof. German and comparative lit. U. Colo., 1964-68; asso. prof. German and comparative lit. U. Rochester, 1968-70; prof. German and comparative lit. Cleve. State U., 1970—, chmn. dept. modern Langs., 1970—. Served with USAF, 1953-57. Mem. Medieval Acad. Am., Modern Lang. Assn., Phi Beta Kappa. Home: 2924 Edgehill Rd Cleveland Heights OH 44118 Office: Dept Modern Languages Cleve State U Cleveland OH 44115

BEATLES, [(see **Harrison, George; Lennon, John Winston;** McCartney, James Paul; Starr, Ringo),] musi. quartet. James Paul; Starr, Ringo

BEATON, CECIL WALTER HARDY, photographer, artist, stage and film designer, author; b. London, Eng., Jan. 14, 1904; s. Ernest Walter Hardy and Etty (Sisson) B.; ed. Harrow and Cambridge U. Portrait photographer; stage designer since 1936; designer scenery and costumes for theatrical prodns. and ballet; has exhibited photographs, paintings, stage designs; ballet decors for the N.Y.C. Ballet Co., Les Illuminations, Swan Lake, Picnic at Tintagel. Conservative. Mem. Ch. of Eng. Author: the Book of Beauty, 1930; Cecil Beaton's Scrapbook, 1937; My Royal Past, 1939; Time Exposure (photographs with commentary by Peter Quennell), 1941; Winged Squadrons, 1942; Near East, 1943; British Photographers, 1944; Far East, 1945; Chinese Album, 1946; Time Exposure, 1946; Ashcombe, 1949; Ballet, 1951; Photobiography, 1951; The Glass of Fashion, 1954; I Take Great Pleasure, 1956; The Face of the World, 1958; Japanese, 1959; Cecil Beaton's Diaries; The Wandering Years, 1961; Quail in Aspic, 1962; Images, 1963; Cecil Beaton's Fair Lady, 1964; Cecil Beaton's Diaries: The Years Between, 1964; The Best of Beaton, 1968; My Bolivian Aunt, 1971. Designed Vanessa, Turandot, La Traviata for N.Y. Met. Opera. Photographic illustrator: History Under Fire (James Pope Hennessey), 1941. Recipient Antoinette Perry award for costume design My Fair Lady, 1956; Motion Picture Academy Award for costume design Gigi, 1958, for set and costume design of My Fair Lady, 1965, Coco, 1970. Home: 8 Pelham Pl London SW 7 England also Reddish House Broadchalke Salisbury Wiltshire England

BEATON, RODERICK WHITNEY, journalist; b. Escalon, Cal., Apr. 26, 1923; s. Philip C. and Wilma (Whitney) B.; student Coll. of Pacific, 1942-43, Cal. Poly., 1943, St. Mary's Coll., 1944; B.A., U. Cal., 1948; m. Evelyn Miller, Oct. 7, 1945; children—Anne Whitney, Roderick Miller. Copyboy, part-time corr. Stockton (Cal.) Jour., 1947; staff corr. San Francisco bur. United Press, 1948-50, mgr. Fresno bur., 1950-54, regional bus. rep., Los Angeles, 1954, bus. mgr. So. div., 1956, mgr. So. div., 1957-59, central div., 1959-62, gen. bus. mgr. U.P.I., N.Y.C., 1962-63, v.p., 1963-65, v.p., gen. mgr. Europe, Middle East Africa, 1965-69, N.Y.C., 1969—; dir. U.P.I. (U.N.) Ltd., UPITN, Inc. Served as enlisted corr., USNR, 1944-45. Mem. Fgn. Press Assn. (London), Sigma Delta Chi. Clubs: Overseas Press (N.Y.C.). Home: 37 Kingston House North Prince's Gate London SW 7 England Office: 220 E 42d St New York City NY 10017

BEATTIE, DONALD SHERMAN, labor union exec.; b. Canisteo, N.Y., May 20, 1921; s. Leo Milton and Catherine (Cornish) B.; B.S., Cornell U., 1951; m. Virginia Anna Maguire, May 6, 1943; children—James Milton, Thomas Michael, Donald Sherman. Dir. research Brotherhood Locomotive Engrs., 1951-62; exec. sec.-treas. Ry. Labor Execs. Assn., 1962-70; exec. sec. Congress Ry. Unions, 1970—. Chmn. labor union research com. Presdl. R.R. Commn., 1960-62; mem. exec. bd. and mgmt. com. Internat. Transport Workers Fedn.; mem. U.S. nat. com. Pan Am. Ry. Congress; mem. Nat. Labor-Mgmt. Manpower Policy Com., U.S. Dept. Labor; labor adv. Served with AUS, 1942-46. Mem. Brotherhood Locomotive Engrs., United Transp. Union. Mason. Home: 827 Empress Ct Alexandria VA 22308 Office: 400 1st St NW Washington DC 20001

BEATTIE, EDWARD JAMES, physician; b. Phila., June 30, 1918; B.A., Princeton, 1939; M.D., Harvard, 1943; m. Joan Booth; one son, Bruce Stewart. Intern, surg. resident Peter Bent Brigham Hosp., Boston, 1942-46; Mosely traveling fellow (Harvard) to U. London (Eng.), 1946-47; surg. fellow, Markle scholar George Washington U., 1947-52; chief thoracic surgery Presbyn. Hosp., 1952-58, chmn. dept. surgery, 1954-58; chmn. dept. surgery Presbyb.-St. Luke's Hosp., 1958-66; cons. thoracic surgery Hines VA Hosp., 1953-65, Chgo. Tb San., 1954-65, Ill. Research and Edn. Hosp., 1956-65; prof. surgery U. Ill., 1955-65, Cornell U., 1965—; chief thoracic surgery Meml. Hosp.,

N.Y.C., 1965—, chmn. dept. surgery chief med. officer, 1966—. Mem. Sloan Kettering Inst. Adv. bd. Medical Specialties, Inc. Diplomate Am. Bd. Surgery, Am. Bd. Thoracic Surgery (mem. bd. 1960—, chmn. of the board 1967-69), Fellow A.C.S.; mem. Am. Assn. Thoracic Surgery, Am. Surg. Assn., Soc. Vascular Surgery, A.M.A., Chgo. Surg. Soc., Central Surg. Assn., Western Surg. Assn., Soc. Clin. Surgery. Republican. Editorial bd. Jour. Thoracic and Cardiovascular Surgery, 1962—, Pediatric Digest, 1962—. Home: 430 E 67 St New York City NY 10021 Office: 444 E 68th St New York City NY 10021

BEATTIE, EDWARD JAMES, physician; b. Phila., June 30, 1918; B.A., Princeton, 1939; M.D., Harvard, 1943; m. Joan Booth; one son, Bruce Stewart. Intern, surg. resident Peter Bent Brigham Hosp., Boston, 1942-46; Mosely traveling fellow (Harvard) to U. London (Eng.), 1946-47; surg. fellow, Markle scholar George Washington U., 1947-52; chief thoracic surgery Presbyn. Hosp., 1952-58, chmn. dept. surgery, 1954-58; chmn. dept. surgery Presbyn.-St. Luke's Hosp., 1958-65; cons. thoracic surgery Hines VA Hosp., 1953-65, Chgo. Tb San., 1954-65, Ill. Research and Edn. Hosp., 1956-65; prof. surgery U. Ill., 1955-65, Cornell U., 1965—; chief thoracic surgery Meml. Hosp., N.Y.C., 1965—, chmn. dept. surgery chief med. officer, 1966—. Mem. Sloan Kettering Inst. Am. Bd. Med. Specialties, Inc. Diplomate Am. Bd. Surgery, Am. Bd. Thoracic Surgery (bd. dirs. 1960-69, chmn. bd. 1967-69). Fellow A.C.S.; mem. Am. Assn. Thoracic Surgery, Am. Surg. Assn., Soc. Vascular Surgery, A.M.A., Chgo. Surg. Soc., Central, Western surg. assns., Am. Acad. Pediatrics, Internat. Soc. Surgery, Soc. Clin. Surgery. Republican. Editorial bd. Jour. Thoracic and Cardiovascular Surgery, 1962—, Pediatric Digest, 1962—. Home: 430 E 67 St New York City NY 10021 Office: 444 E 68th St New York City NY 10021

BEATTIE, JOHN ROBERT, banker; b. Greenwood, B.C., May 30, 1910; s. John Thomas and Maude (Minkler) B.; B.A., U. Man., 1930; B.A., Oxford U., 1933; m. Katharine McIntyre, Jan. 16, 1937 (dec., Sept. 1960); childrenPeggy, Joan, Barbara, Elisabeth; m. 2d, Mary Angus Rogers, Jan. 3, 1964. With actuarial dept. Mfrs. Life Ins. Co., Ltd., 1933-35; with Bank of Can., 1935-, successively dep. chief research dept., chief, exec. asst. to govs., 1940-55, dep. gov., 1955-. Clubs: Royal Ottawa Golf, Five Lakes Tishing, Country. Home: 252 Buena Vista Rd Rockcliffe Park, Ontario, Canada. Office: 234 Wellington St Ottawa, Ontario, Canada.

BEATTIE, RICHARD IRWIN, advt. photographer; b. N.Y.C., Mar. 15, 1914; s. Richard I. and Evelyn (Nagle) B.; m. Ruth Fischer, May 1937 (div. 1948); children—Richard Irwin, Evelyn L. (Mrs. Donald Lewis); m. 2d, Crystal Cooper, Feb. 24, 1954. Mem. guiding faculty Famous Photographer Sch., Westport, Conn., 1964—. Served to 1st lt. USMCR, 1943-46. Home: Martin Rd Rye NY 10580 Office: 155 E 35th St New York City NY 10016

BEATTIE, ROSEMARY HELEN HAMILTON, prodn. stage mgr. and dir.; b. Edinburgh, Aug. 17, 1942; d. Malcolm Hamilton and Margaret (Spence) Beattie; certificate English lang. and lit., also French history, London U., 1958. State mgr., actress Wimbledon Repertory Co., London, 1959-61; stage mgr. BBC TV Co., London, 1961, Royal Shakespear Co., 1962-67; dir. Am. company the Homecoming, N.Y.C. and U.S. tour. 1967-68; tchr. ballet Asso. Arts Sch., London, 1958—. Home: 141 Copse Hill Wimbledon London England Office: care Alexander H Cohen Shubert Theatre 225 W 44th St New York City NY 10036

BEATTIE, WALTER MATTHEW, Jr., univ. dean; b. Roselle, N.J., Feb. 9, 1923; s. Walter Matthew and Mary (Jennings) B.; B.S., U.S. Mcht. Marine Acad., 1944; B.A., Rutgers U., 1948; M.A., U. Chgo., 1950; m. Elisabeth Morton Watts, June 21, 1952; children—Linda Elisabeth, Robert Watts. Instr. sociology Westminster Coll., Fulton, Mo., 1950-51, U. Wis., 1951-53; prof. sociology, chmn. dept. Lindenwood Coll., St. Charles, Mo., 1956-59; lectr. community orgn. Washington U., St. Louis, 1960-62; dir. Services to Aging, Community Welfare Council, Madison, Wis., 1953-56; dir. planning Services to Aging, Health and Welfare Council Met. St. Louis, 1959-63; dir. Nat. Task Forces Project, Nat. Commn. Community Health Services, Bethesda, Md., 1963-66; dean, prof. Syracuse (N.Y.) U. Sch. Social Work, 1966—. Chmn., U.S. com. applied social gerontology 7th Internat. Congress gerontology, Vienna, Austria, 1966; cons. program of aging, mem. nat. adv. Nat. Inst. Child Health and Human Devel., NIH, Bethesda; mem. steering com. Exptl. City, U. Minn.; mem. adv. council to spl. com. on aging U.S. Senate; mem. White House Conf. on Aging, 1971; mem. tech. rev. com. N.Y. State Office for Aging. Bd. dirs. Consol. Industries Greater Syracuse. Fellow Gerontological Soc. (asso. editor jour. 1959-63; pres. 1962-63); mem. Acad. Certified Social Workers, Assn. U. Profs., Am. Pub. Health Assn., Am. Pub. Welfare Assn., Nat. Assn. Social Workers, Internat. Assn. Gerontology (council), Nat. Council Aging (bd. dirs.). Presbyn. Asso. editor for welfare research Jour. Gerontology, 1961-63, 69—. Contbr. profl. jours. Home: 7 Erregger Terrace Syracuse NY 13224

BEATTY, FLOY WARD (Mrs. Richmond Croom Beatty), book editor; b. Birmingham, Ala., Apr. 25, 1908; d. Walter Rowland and Monica (Morris) Ward; A.B., Birmingham So.-Coll., 1928; m. Richmond Croom Beatty. May 7, 1927 (dec. Oct. 1961). Asso. book editor and youth columnist Nashville Tennessean, 1959-61, book editor, 1961-. Mem. Theta Sigma Phi. Home: 1808 Lombardy Lane Nashville, TN37215. Office: Nashville Tennessean 1100 Broadway Nashville, TN 37201.

BEATTY, GEORGE EDWARD, architect; b. Bklyn., Apr. 15, 1902; s. John Joseph and Mary T. (Gerety) B.; student Cath. U. Am., 1922-24; B.Arch., George Washington U., 1927; postgrad. U. Rome (Italy), 1929-31, Columbia, 1938; m. Eloise Magdalen Conahan, June 29, 1936; children—George Edward, Christopher James, David John deMontfort. With Beatty & Berlenbach, and successor firm, Beatty & Beatty, Bklyn., 1927—, partner, 1933—, in leave as designer Il Foro Mussolini, 1929-31; works include schools, churches, hosps., pub. bldgs., jails, Holloy Coll., Loyola Coll. (Balt.). Pres. Brookhaven Indsl. Commn., 1957-71; mayor, Shoreham, N.Y., 1954-66; pres. Dist. 10 Bd. Edn., Brookhaven, 1945-57. Trustee St. Charles, Good Samaritan hosps.; vice chmn. bd. trustees Brookhaven Campus of L.I. U.; trustee Molloy Coll.; dir. Maryhaven Sch. Served as ensign, USCG, 1942-45. Decorated Order of Merit (Italy); knight comdr. Order Holy Sepulchre (Vatican). Fellow A.I.A. (pres. Bklyn. chpt. 1965), Accademia degl. Illusi (Italy). Clubs: Brooklyn, Shoreham Boat (commodore 1944-60), Smithtown Hunt. Home: 10 Sturgis Rd Shoreham NY 11786 Office: 32 Court St Brooklyn NY 11201

BEATTY, GEORGE SAMUEL, Jr., army officer; b. Clinton, N.C., Oct. 26, 1917; s. George Samuel and Elsie (Barker) B.; A.B., Presbyn. Coll., 1938; student law, U. N.C., 1938-40; m. Helen Ann Jacobs, May 3, 1941; children—Anne Elizabeth (Mrs. Charles P. Cole, Jr.), Helen McLaurin (Mrs. Alfred S. Callahan III). Commd. 2d lt., U.S. Army, 1938, advanced through grades to maj. gen., 1969; bn. comdr. 187th Airborne Regtl. Combat Team, Korea; brigade comdr., chief of staff 1st Air Cavalry Div., Vietnam, 1965-66; comdg. gen. U.S. Army Flight Tng. Center, Hunter Army Airfield, Ga., 1969-70; chmn. Joint Brazil-U.S. Mil. Commn., Rio de Janeiro, 1970—. Decorated D.S.M., Legion of Merit with 2 oak leaf clusters, Bronze Star, Air Medal with 7 oak leaf clusters, Army Commendation Medal. Mem. Am. Helicopter Soc., Army Aviation Assn. Am., Assn. U.S. Army, Mil. Order World Wars, Kappa Alpha. Rotarian. Home: 3621 Colgate Av Dallas TX 75225 Office: Joint Brazil-US Military Commission APO New York City NY 09676

BEATTY, HENRY RUSSELL, coll. pres., machine mfg. exec., cons. mgmt. engr.; b. Eastport, Me., May 14, 1906; s. Harry Hamilton and Susan (Ferguson) B.; B.S., U. Me., 1927; M. Adminstrv. Engring., N.Y.U., 1945; D. Engring., Stevens Tech., Northeastern U., 1962; Doctor Engring. University of Maine, 1963; m. Alice C. Van Schagen, Feb. 14, 1934; 1 son, Robert C. Supr. indsl. engring. Gen. Electric Co., 1927-33; salesman Remington Rand, 1933-34; prodn. supt. Holtzer Cabot Electric Co., 1934-37; prof., asst. to pres., dean engring. Pratt Inst., 1937-53; pres., trustee Wentworth Inst., Boston, 1953-71; pres., trustee Wentworth Coll. Tech., 1970—; cons. mgmt. engr., 1944—; cons. Coll. Petroleum Minerals, Saudi Arabia, 1968—. Dir. Reed & Barton Co., N.J. Machine Corp. of N.H., N.J. Packaging Corp. Mem. Mass. Health and Ednl. Facilities Authority; mem. adv. bd. Greater Boston Salvation Army. Mem. sci. edn. adv. com. NSF; bd. trustees Gordon Coll. Chmn. Corp. Open Ch. Found. Registered profl. engr., N.Y., N.J., Mass., Me. Fellow Am. Soc. M.E., Assn. Ind. Colls. and Univs. Mass. (sec.-treas. 1967-71); mem. Nat. Soc. Profl. Engrs., Engring. Soc. New Eng. (past pres.), Mass. Schoolmasters Club (past pres.), Am. Soc. Engring. Edn., Project Bd., A.A.A.S., Am. Nuclear Soc., Boston C. of C. Conglist. (trustee). Mason. Clubs: Congregational (pres.), Executives (Boston). Revised: Principles of Industrial Management (L.P. Alford), 1951. Home: 43 Bishop Rd Quincy MA 02170 Office: 550 Huntington Av Boston MA 02115

BEATTY, JOHN CABEEN, Jr., judge; b. Washington, Apr. 13, 1919; s. John Cabeen and Jean (Morrison) B.; A.B., Princeton, 1941; J.D., Columbia, 1948; m. Clarissa Hager, Feb. 8, 1943; children—John Cabeen III, Clarissa Jean. Admitted to Ore. bar, 1948, practiced in Portland, 1948-70; partner Dusenbery, Martin, Beatty, Bischoff & Templeton, 1956-70; judge circuit ct., 1970—. Mem. Ore. Bd. Bar Examiners, 1953-54. Mem. Ore. Civil Service Commn., 1962-64; mem. legislative com. Nat. Sch. Bds. Assn., 1966-68; chmn. Council Large City Sch. Bds., Nat. Sch. Bds. Assn., 1967-68; Counsel, Democratic Party Ore., 1956-58; co-chmn. Ore. for Kennedy Com., 1968. Chmn. bd. dirs. Portland Pub. Schs., 1967, 69. Served to capt. AUS, 1941-46; ETO. Decorated Bronze Star medal; recipient City Club of Portland award, 1967. Mem. Am., Ore., Multnomah County bar assns., Am. Judicature Soc., Maritime Law Assn. Clubs: City (past pres., bd. govs.) Yacht, University, Racquet (Portland). Home: 2958 SW Dosch Rd Portland OR 97201 Office: 1107 Standard Plaza Portland OR 97204

BEATTY, JOHN MATTHEW, educator; b. Meriden, Conn., May 30, 1906; s. John Norton and Margaret (Lawton) B., C.E., Rensselaer Poly. Inst., 1929, M. Civil Engring., 1934; m. Grace Virginia Bernardine, Sept. 3, 1930. Mem. faculty Rensselaer Poly. Inst., 1929—, prof. civil engring., 1953—, exec. officer civil engring. dept., 1961-67, exec. officer machines and structures div., 1967-71; pvt. engring. practice, 1935—; cons. in field 1935—. Registered profl. engr., N.Y. Fellow Am. Soc. C.E.; mem. Am. Concrete Inst., Internat. Assn. Bridge and Structural Engring., Am. Soc. Engring. Edn., Sigma Xi. Chi Epsilon. Roman Cath. Club: Troy Country. Home: East Acres Troy NY 12180

BEATTY, LLOYD EDWARD, banker, lawyer; b. Plymouth, Ind., Mar. 11, 1925; s. Lloyd and Esther (Steinebach) B.; B.S., Ind. U., 1947 J.D., 1951; m. Jean McKinney, Oct. 25, 1947; children—Amanda, Amy, Marshall, Angela, Grant. Admitted to Ind. bar, 1952; with Lincoln Nat. Bank and Trust Co., Ft. Wayne, Ind., 1954—, v.p. comml. loan dept., 1960-68, pres., 1968—, also dir. Past chmn. budget com. United Chest Council of Allen County, 1959, dir., 1960; gen. chmn., United Fund, 1963; bd. dirs. Ft. Wayne chpt. A.R.C Served to lt. (j.g.) USNR, 1943-46, 51-53. Named Outstanding Young Man, Ft. Wayne Jr. C. of C., 1959. Mem. Am., Ind., Allen County bar assns., Am. Soc. Judicature. Presbyn. Clubs: Rotary (bd. dirs. 1960), Quest, Ft. Wayne Country (Ft. Wayne). Home: 1712 Hawthorne Rd Fort Wayne IN 46806 Office: 116 E Berry St Fort Wayne IN 46802

BEATTY, MORGAN, news analyst; b. Little Rock, Sept. 6, 1902; s. Hugh Mercer and Caroline Sarah (Morgan) B.; ed. pub. and high schs., Ft. Smith, Ark., also Centre Coll., Danville, Ky., and Washington U., St. Louis, Mo.; m. Mary Virginia Garwood, Oct. 15, 1928 (dec. May 1957); children—Hugh (dec.), Morgan Mercer, Stephen Garwood; m. 2d, Kathryn Josephine Ring, Apr. 13, 1958. Reporter, Ft. Smith Southwest Am., 1920; news editor Ft. Smith Southwest Times-Record, 1922-23; telegraph editor Little Rock Gazette, 1923-27; wire editor A.P., Atlanta, 1927-28, N.Y.C., 1928-31, asst. news supr., N.Y.C., 1931-32, fgn. cable editor, 1932-33, bur. chief, Cleve., 1933-34, asst. feature editor, N.Y.C., 1934-35, bur. chief, Albany, N.Y., 1935-36, chief feature editor, Washington, 1936-42; NBC fgn. corr., London, 1942-43, news analyst, Washington, 1941-56, Chgo., 1959, N.Y.C., 1958-61; war corr. ETO, London, 1943; radio corr. representing all Am. networks, Berlin Big Three Conf., 1945. Recipient Dupont award, 1949, Headliner's award, 1948, Dell radio Excellence award, 1959, American Legion award, 1961. Mem. Overseas Writers' Assn., Kappa Alpha. Clubs: Nat. Press (Washington); London Press (hon.); Overseas Press (N.Y.C.). Author: Our Nation's Capital. Address: 24 E 73d St New York City NY

BEATTY, ROBERT OWEN, writer, corp. exec., conservationist, editor; b. Chicago, Nov. 12, 1924; s. Vernon David and Elizabeth (Rubinkam) B.; student Shattuck Sch., 1937-41, Dartmouth, 1941-42; B.S., U. Mich., 1945, M.S., 1946; m. Louise Forbush, Feb. 23, 1946; children—Deborah, David Clarke, II, Barbara. Timber stand improvement U.S. Forest Service, 1941; research asst. fish div. U. Mich. Mus. Zoology, 1942-43; staff asst. Izaak Walton League Am., 1946-47, conservation dir., 1948-53; sec.- treas. Izaak Walton League Am. Endowment Inc., 1950-53; editor Outdoor America, 1946-53, N.W. public relations officer of Crown Zellerbach Corporation, 1953-56; assistant to president Western Kraft Corp., 1956-62, mgr. product devel., advt., pub. relations, 1958-62; asst. to pres. Electro-Sci. Industries, 1962-64; mgr. Sunset Sci. Park, Inc., 1962-65; director of public relations and advt. Boise Cascade Corp., 1965-70, dir. communications, 1970-71; asst. sec. for pub. affairs U.S. Dept. Health, Edn. and Welfare, 1971—; free-lance writer outdoor conservation and bus. subjects, 1945—. Exec. bd. Ore.-Ida. council Boy Scouts Am. Pres. Ore. Mus. Sci. and Industry, 1961, chmn. bd., 1962. Served as pvt., USMC Res., 1942-45. Mem. Pub. Relations Soc. Am., (dir., former chmn.), Am. Forest Inst. (chmn. pub. relations com.), Outdoor Writers Assn. Am., Phi Sigma (hon.), Psi Upsilon. Republican. Presbyn. Clubs: University (Portland, Ore.); Hillcrest Country, Rotary; San Francisco Press. Flyfishers of Oregon (founding mem.); New York Athletic; Fed. City; Arid. Office: Boise Cascade Corp Box 200 Boise ID 83701 also Dept Health Edn and Welfare Washington DC 20014

BEATTY, ROSS JAMES, realtor; b. Chgo., Mar. 16, 1905; s. Ross James and Mildred (Ryan) B.; grad. Lawrenceville Sch., 1925; student Princeton, 1929; m. Janet Ayer, Sept. 16, 1936; children—Phoebe Lord, Susan Day, Ross James, Jr., Peter Ayer. Engaged in real estate bus., Chgo., 1940—; mgr. Estate of Leander J. McCormick, Chgo., 1945—; partner McCormick-Beatty Co., Chgo., 1956—; gen. partner Union Tank Car Bldg.; dir. Ill. State Bank Chgo., Met. Housing and Devel. Corp.; dir., past pres. Bldg. Mgrs. Assn. Chgo.; dir. Met. Housing and Planning Council Chgo.; past pres. Real Estate Bd.; trustee Bradley Real Estate Investment, Boston, Chgo. Real Estate Trust. Bd. dirs. Planned Parenthood Assn. Chgo. Mem. Lambda Alpha (past pres.). Clubs: Realty, Digest, Princeton, Chicago, University, Casino (Chgo.); Onwentsia (Lake Forest). Home: 111 Onwentsia Rd Lake Forest IL 60045 Office: 332 S Michigan Av Chicago IL 60604

BEATTY, WARREN, actor; b. Richmond, Va., Mar. 30, 1938; s. Ira O. and Kathlyn (MacLean) B.; student Northwestern U., 1956, Stella Adler Theatre School, N.Y.C., 1957. Film appearances include Splendor in the Grass, 1961, The Roman Spring of Mrs. Stone, 1962, All Fall Down, 1962, Lilith, 1963, Mickey One, 1965, Promise Her Anything, 1965, Kaleidoscope, 1966, Bonnie and Clyde, 1967, The Only Game in Town, 1969, McCabe and Mrs. Miller, 1971, "$", 1971; made appearance on Broadway in play A Loss of Roses, 1960; TV appearances in Suspicion, Studio One, Kraft Playhouse, Playhouse 90, U.S. Steel Hour. Office: care John Springer Assos Inc 667 Madison Av New York City NY 10021

BEATY, JACK, govt. ofcl.; b. Huntington, Ark., July 19, 1917; s. Zack T. and Margaret (Jack) B.; grad. Albuquerque Bus. Coll., 1936; m. Lucille T. Thursby, Aug. 14, 1940; 1 dau., Patricia Rae (Mrs. Joe Patterson). Accountant, Valley Gold Dairies, Inc., Albuquerque, 1937-39; mgr. Frosted Foods Distbg. Co., Inc., Albuquerque, 1939-42; pres. Rocky Mountain Wholesale Co., Inc., Albuquerque, 1942-61, chmn. bd., 1961-63; mem. U.S. Renegotiation Bd., 1963-70. Bd. dirs. Nat. Candy Wholesalers Assn., 1946-52; bd. dirs. Nat. Assn. Tobacco Distbrs., Inc., 1954-60, v.p., 1960-63, 1st hon. life mem., 1963. Western states coordinator Democratic campaign, 1959. Recipient Tobacco Man of Year award, Nat. Assn. Tobacco Distbrs. Mason (Shriner, Jester), Elk. Clubs: Albuquerque Petroleum; Fez. Home: 805 McDuffie Circle NE Albuquerque NM Office: 1101 New Hampshire Av NW Washington DC 20446

BEATY, JOHN RICHARD, dancer; b. Gorgetown, S.C., Apr. 20, 1932; s. John Paul and Hilda A. (Antilla) B.; student ballet, 1952-56. Mem. Am. Ballet Theatre, 1956-64; prin. guest soloist with Het Nat. Ballet of Holland, 196465; prin. dancer Pa. Ballet Co., 1966; prin. male dancer Les Grands Ballets Canadiens, 1966—; numerous TV appearances, U.S. and Can. Home: 3610 McTavish St Montreal 112 Quebec Canada Office: 5415 Queen Mary Rd Montreal Quebec Canada

BEATY, ORREN, Jr., govt. ofcl.; b. Clayton, N.M., June 13, 1919; s. Orren and Edith (Mason) B.; A.B., N.M. State U., 1941; postgrad. U. Houston, 1951-52; m. Mary Ethel Turner, Dec. 30, 1944; children—Orren III, Laura Leigh, Susan Ray. Mng. editor Las Cruces (N.M.) Sun-News, 1946-47; reporter, polit. writer, columnist Ariz. Republic, Phoenix, 1948-55; adminstrv. asst. to Rep. Stewart L. Udall, 1956-61; asst. to Sec. Dept. Interior, 1961-67; fed. co-chmn. Four Corners Planning Commn., Econ. Devel. Adminstrn., Dept. Commerce, 1967-69; editor Congl. Quar., 1969-70; legislative asst. to Rep. Mike McCormack, Washington, 1971—. Democratic candidate for Ho. of Reps. from 3d Ariz. dist., 1970. Served to 1st lt. AUS, 1942-46, USAF, 1950-52; maj. Res. Home: 1784 Proffitt Rd Vienna VA 22180 Office: Longworth House Office Bldg Washington DC 20525

BEAUBIEN, CLAUDE PANET, aluminum co. exec.; b. Montreal, Can. Mar. 2, 1908; s. Joseph and Josephine (Larue) B.; B.A., Loyola Coll., Montreal, 1930; B.Sc., Mass. Inst. Tech., 1934; m. Jeannine Charbonneau, Oct. 18, 1941; childrenClaude, Jeannine, Andrew, Luc. With Aluminum Co. Can., Ltd., 1935-, v.p. pub. relations and advt., 1958-; dir. Roberval & Saguenay Roberval & Saguenay Ry. Co., Saguenay Transmission Company Limited. President Montreal Bd. Trade, 1957-58; bd. dirs. Better Bus. Bur Montreal. Pres. Montreal Citizens Com., 1959-60; mem. Royal Commn. Publs., 1956-; chmn. bd. dirs. National Theatre School of Canada, 1963. Alderman, City of Westmount, 1964-65. Exec. com. Montreal Symphony Orch., 1967-; mem. bd. dirs. Montreal Museum Fine Arts. Montreal Citizenship Council. Concerts Symphoniques. Mem., Canadian Indsl. Preparedness Assn. (vice chmn.), Internat., dir. 1950-60), Canadian (v.p. exec. com.), Que. Provincial (pres. 1961-62), chambers com. Roman Cath. Clubs: St. James, St. Denis, Denis, Mount Bruno, Montreal. Royal St. Lawrence Yacht (Montreal); Quebe Garrison. Winter (Quebec). Home: PO Box 6090 Montreal, Que. Canada. Office: PO Box 6090 Montreal 101 Quebec Canada

BEAUBIEN, DE GASPE, cons. engr.; b. Outremont, Can., May 18, 1881; s. Honr. Louis and Lauretta (Stuart) B.; B.Sc., McGill U., 1906; D.Sc., U. Man., 1945; m. Gabrielle Dandurand, Oct. 1910 (dec.); children—Jacques, Claire, Andrée; m. 2d, Angeline Rodier, May 10, 1934. Asst. to constrn. engr. Montreal Light, Heat & Power, 1903; demonstrator McGill U., 1907; apprentice Westinghouse Electric & Mfg. Co., Pittsburgh, 1908; ind. cons. engr., 1908-22; cons. engr. Beaubien, Busfield & Co., 1922-27, De Gaspe, Beaubien & Co., 1927—; pres. Beaubien, Ltd.; dir. W. Can. Collieries, Ltd., Dominion Ltd. Formerly nat. joint chmn. War Savs. Com.; mem. Nat. War Finance Com. Decorated comdr. Order Brit. Empire. Mem. Canadian Standards Assn., Engring. Inst. Can. (past pres.), Assn. Cons. Engrs. (hon.), Am. Inst. E.E., Corp. Profl. Engrs. of Que. Roman Catholic. Clubs: Canadian (past pres.); Rotary (past pres.); Montreal, University: Cercle Universitaire (past pres.); Royal Automobile of Can. (past pres.) (Mt. Royal): Laval sur-lelac Golf. Home: 462 Saint Catherine Rd Outremont Quebec Canada Office: De Gaspe Beaubien & Co 462 St Catherine Rd Montreal Quebec Canada

BEAUCHAMP, ROBERT, artist; b. Denver, Nov. 19, 1923; s. John Rilla (Beavans) B.; student Colorado Springs Fine Arts Center, 1946; B.F.A., Cranbrook Art Acad., 1950; student Hans Hoffmann Sch. Art, Denver, 1950-53. One-man shows Tanager Gallery, N.Y.C., 1954, March Gallery, N.Y.C., 1954, Great Jones Gallery, N.Y.C., 1961, Green Gallery, N.Y.C., 1962, 64, Graham Gallery, N.Y.C., 1966; represented in permanent collections Carnegie Inst., Mus. Modern Art, Whitney Mus. Served with USNR, 1943-46. Fulbright fellow, Italy, 1959-60; grantee Walter K. Gutman Found., 1961. Address: 168 1/2 Delancey St New York City NY 10002

BEAUCHAMP, WILLIAM ELLSWORTH, fgn. service officer; b. Bklyn., Aug. 30, 1912; s. William Ellsworth and Mary (Klingmann) B.; student Bklyn. Poly. Inst., 1929-31, U. Md., 1953-56, George Washington U., 1956-57; m. Kathryn Goodman, June 11, 1933; 1 son, William Edward; m. 2d, Veronica Ellen Klimek, July 14, 1943; children—Danielle Marie, Mary Anne. With N.Y. Telephone Co., 1928-42; chief tripartite mil. permit officer for Germany, Prague, 1946, Berne, 1946-49, Paris, 1949-50; attache Am. embassy, Paris, 1951-54; mem. U.S. delegation NATO meeting, 1953; 2d sec., consul, Paris, 1954, polit. officer, 1955-56; prof. Fgn. Service Inst., 1956-58, past mgmt. officer European affairs, 1958-61; 1st sec., consul, Belgrade, Yugoslavia, 1961-64; 1st sec. and consul, chief of adminstrv. sect. Am. embassy, Algiers, Algeria, 1964-66; fgn. service insp. Dept. State, 1966-69; adminstrv. counselor Am. embassy, Taipei, Taiwan, 1969—. Sec. local No. 7 Telephone Employees Union, 1938-40;

sub-area chmn. United Givers Fund, Washington, 1958-61; co-founder, v.p. Alexandria (Va.) Soc. Retarded Children, 1958- 61; chmn. instl. com. Va. Assn. Retarded Children, 1958-60; liaison officer Alexandria Sch. Bd., 1959; v.p. Minnie Howard PTA, Alexandria, 1959. Bd. dirs. No. Va. Sheltered Occupational Tng. Center; chmn. bd. Embassy Shop, Embassy Civilian Fund (both Taipei). Served to capt. AUS, 1942-47; ETO. Mem. Am. Fgn. Service Assn., Am. Acad. Polit. and Social Sci., Internat. Platform Assn. Clubs: Cosmos, Maag Officers (Taipei). Office: American Embassy Taipei Taiwan Republic of China

BEAUDOIN, ADRES, bus. exec.; b. Saint-Denis-de-'Hote, France; m. Renee Gilles, Jan. 15, 1922; 1 dau., Martine (Mrs. Gerard Martin). Dir., then hon. dir. Crédit Industrial et Commercial; past pres. Crédit Natais; v.p. Crédit Indsl. de l'Quest, Banque Regionale de l'Quest adminstr. Galeries Modernes. Decorated knight Legion of Honor. Addres: 5 rue Isabey Paris 16 France.

BEAUDRY, ROBERT MANN, fgn. service officer; b. Lewiston, Me., May 12, 1923; s. Altheode A. and Elsie (Mann) B.; A.B. in Econs., Cath. U. Am., 1943; m. Jacqueline Chouinard, Sept. 7, 1946; children-Paul S., John J., Catherine A., Mary E. Joined U.S. Fgn. Service, 1946; assigned Ireland, Morocco, Germany, Surinam, Switzerland; internat. economist State Dept., 1956-64; counselor for polit. affairs Am. embassy, Brussels, Belgium, 1964-66; assigned Canadian Def. Coll., 1966-67; country dir. Italy, Austria, Switzerland, State Dept., 1967—. Served with AUS, 1943-46. Home: 120 Granite St Auburn ME 04210 Office: Bur European Affairs Dept of State Washington DC 20520

BEAULIEU, ROGER LOUIS, lawyer; b. Montreal, Que., Can., Sept. 26, 1924; s. Guillaume A. and Eulalie (Galibert) B.; B.A., Brébeuf Coll., 1944; B.C.L., McGill U., 1947; M.B.A., Harvard Bus. Sch., 1949; m. Andrée Prieur, Mar. 5, 1955; children—Marc, Nicole, Michèle. Called to bar, 1947, Queen's counsel, 1959; partner firm Martineau, Walker, Allison, Beaulieu, Phelan & Mackell, 1949—. Dir. Provident Group of Ins. Lectr. corp. law U. Montreal, 1960-70. Pres. Montreal Citizen's Com., 1959-60. Bd. advisers Can. Permanent Trust. Mem. Can. Bar Assn. Clubs: University; St. Denis. Home: 3044 St Sulpice Rd Montreal Quebec Canada Office: Stock Exchange Tower Place Victoria Montreal Quebec Canada

BEAULINE, JOSEPH CHARLES LEONARD YVON, Canadian diplomat; b. Ottawa, Ont., Can., Feb. 22, 1919; s. Leonard and Yvonne (Baoust) B.; B.A., L.Ph., Ottawa U.; student Am. U., 1966-67; m. Therese Pratte, Feb. 7, 1946; children—Francois, Pierre, Louise, Leonard, Gilles. With Canadian Post Office Dept., 1939-40, Dept. Sec. State, 1940- 42; Parliamentary translator. 1947-48; joined Dept. External Affairs. 1948; 2d sec., Rome. 1949-52; with CBC. 1952-53; with Dept. External Affairs, 1953-56; 1st sec., Buenos Aires. 1956-59; assigned Ottawa, 1959- 60; counsellor, Havana, 1960; head Latin Am. div., Ottawa, 1960-61; ambassador to Venezuela, 1961-64, to Dominican Republic, 1963-64; minister Washington, 1964-67; ambassador to Brazil, 1967-69; ambassador, permanent rep. Can. to UN. 1969—. Served to capt. Canadian Army. 1942- 46. Address: Permanent Mission Canada to UN 866 United Nations Plaza New York City NY 10017

BEAUMONT, ROBERT GEORGE, banker; b. New Orleans July 16, 1930; s. George Perry and Rita (Zansler) B.; B.C.S., Loyola U. of South, 1963; grad. Nat. Trust Sch., 1968; m. Helen Ann Usner, Jan. 5, 1951; children-Phyllis, Robert George, Michael, Susan, Greg, Jennifer, Steven, Christine. With Whitney Nat. Bank New Orleans, 1954—, asst. trust officer, 1966-70, v.p., trust officer, 1970- -. Served AUS, 1952-54. Mem. New Orleans C. of C., New Orleans Estate Planning Council, Financial Analyst Assn., Stock Transfer Assn. Home: 884 Matador Dr Gretna LA 70053 Office: 228 St Charles Av New Orleans LA 70130

BEAUPRE, ROBERT SHOWERS, banker; b. Anaconda, Mont., Feb. 14, 1911; s. John P. and Mable (Showers) B.; grad. Pacific Coast Banking Sch., U. Wash., 1949; m. Dorothy Fiala, Jan. 27, 1940; children—John Joseph, Linda Fiala. With Seattle First Nat. Bank, 1929—, v.p., 1948-61, pres., 1961—, also dir. Mem. finance com. Overlake Meml. Hosp.; mem. men's finance com. Planned Parenthood; mem. adv. com. Pub. Defender Demonstration Project, mem. adv. com. of exec. bd. Boy Scouts Am. Treas., trustee Pacific Northwest Research Found., 1955—; mem. bldg. and grounds com. Whitman Coll.; bd. dirs. Jr. Achievement of Seattle (pres. bd.); trustee Northwest Council for Econ. Edn., N.W. Kidney Center. Mem. Am. (mem. savs. bond com., state coordinator and regional vice chmn. for savs. bonds), Wash. bankers assns., Am. Mgmt. Assn., Clearing House Assn. (pres.), Am. Inst. Banking, U.S. C. of C. (dir., mem. Can.-U.S. com., accredited banking and monetary policy), Seattle C. of C. (trustee), Assn. Res. City Bankers. Episcopalian. Mason (Shriner). Clubs: Variety, Overlake Golf and Country, Harbor, Rainier, Wash. Athletic. Home: 1837 Evergreen Point Rd Bellevue WA 98004 Office: PO Box 3586 Seattle WA 98124

BEAUPRE, THOMAS NORBERT, forest industry exec.; b. Montreal, Can., Aug. 17, 1917; s. George Norbert and Johanna (McDonnell) B.; B.Sc., McGill U., 1939, M.Sc., 1940; m. Hazel Elizabeth Genereaux, Apr. 25, 1945; children—Carolyn Ann, Robert George. With Dept. Trade and Commerce, Ottawa, Ont., 1946-51; asst. dep. minister, dir. aircraft prodn. Dept. Def. Prodn., Ottawa, 1951-53; v.p., sec. Canadian Chem. & Cellulose Co., Ltd., Montreal, 1953-57; exec. v.p. Columbia Cellulose Co., Ltd., also Celgar Ltd., Vancouver, B.C., 1957, pres., 1958-61; pres., dir. B. C. Forest Products, Ltd., Vancouver, 1961-67, chmn. bd., 1964-69; chmn. bd. Domtar, Ltd., 1966—, pres., 1966—; dir. United Corps., Ltd., Standard Broadcasting Corp., Royal Bank of Can., Argus Corp., Hudson's Bay Co., Hudson's Bay Oil & Gas Co., Ltd. Mem. Canadian-American Com.; hon. v.p. Que. council St. John's Ambulance, 1969-71; bd. govs. Canadian Export Assn.; chmn. bd. dir. Pulp and Paper Research Inst. Can., 1968-70. Served lt. to capt., Royal Canadian Army Service Corps, 1940-45. Mem. Newcomen Soc. N. Am., Inst. Dirs. (London, Eng.), Canadian Council Christians and Jews. Clubs: Vancouver; Rideau (Ottawa); Mount Royal, Saint-Denis, Royal Montreal Golf, St. James's (Montreal); Toronto. Home: 3207 The Boulevard Westmount Quebec Canada Office: 395 de Maissoneuve Blvd W Montreal 111 Quebec Canada

BEAUVOIR, SIMONE BERTRAND DE, author; b. Paris, France, Jan. 8, 1908; d. George Bertrand and Francoise (Brasseur) deB.; ed. U. of Paris, degree in philosophy, 1929. Taught philosophy girls' schs. Marseilles, Rouen, Paris, 1931-43; editor (with J.-P. Sartre) rev. Les Temps Modernes, 1946—. Author: L'Invitée, 1943; The Blood of Others, 1945; (play) Les Bouches Inutiles, 1945; Tous les Hommes sont Mortels, 1947; Ethics of Ambiguity, 1947; The Second Sex, 1949; The Mandarins, 1954; The Long March, 1957; Memoirs of a Dutiful Daughter, 1958; Force of Circumstance, 1960; (with G. Halimi) Djamala Boupacha, 1962; A Very Easy Death, 1964; Les Belles Images, 1966; Woman Destroyed, 1969. Recipient Prix de Goncourt, 1954. Address: 11 bis Rue Schoelcher Paris 14e France*

BEAVER, PAUL CHESTER, educator; b. Glenwood, Ind., Mar. 10, 1905; s. John Chester and Blanche Emma (Murphy) B.; A.B., Wabash Coll., 1928, D.Sc., 1963; M.S. U. Ill., 1929, Ph.D., 1953; m. Lela E. West, Oct. 16, 1931; 1 dau., Paula Jean (Mrs. David Ross Chipman). Asst. zoology U. Ill., 1928-29. 31-34; instr. zoology U. Wyo., 1929-31; instr. biology Oak Park Jr. Coll., 1934-37; asst. prof. biology Lawrence Coll., 1937-42; biologist Ga. Dept. Pub. Health, 1942-45; asst. prof. parasitology Tulane U. Med. Sch., 1945-47, asso. prof., 1947-52, prof., 1952—, head dept. parasitology, 1956—, William Vincent prof. tropical diseases and hygiene, 1958—; vis. prof. Eastern Mont. Normal Sch., summers 1935-37, Colo. State Coll., 1940, U. Mich., 1954-56, 58, U. Natal Med. Sch., Durban, South Africa, 1957, hon. vis. prof. Universidad del Valle, Cali, Colombia, 1970—. Cons. Ga. Dept. Pub. Health, 1946-53, USPHS Hosp., New Orleans, 1949—, WHO, 1960—; mem. com. standards and exams. Am. Bd. Microbiology, 1960-67; mem. commn. parasitic diseases Armed Forces Epidemiological Bd., 1953—, director commission on parasitic diseases, 1967—; mem. Am. Found. for Tropical Medicine, 1960-66; microbiology fellowships rev. panel NIH, 1960-63; mem. WHO expert com. on intestinal helminths, 1963, also WHO expert panel on parasitic diseases, 1963—; bd. sci. counselors Nat. Inst. Allergy and Infectious Diseases, NIH, 1966-68; mem. parasitic diseases panel U.S.-Japan Coop. Med. Sci. Program, Nat. Insts. of Health, 1965-69; adv. sci. bd. Gorgas Meml. Inst. Tropical and Preventive Medicine, 1970—. Diplomate of the Am. Bd. of Microbiology. Fellow Am. Acad. Microbiology (bd. govs.), A.A.A.S.; mem. Internat. Filariasis Assn., Am. Soc. Tropical Medicine and Hygiene (fellow, councilor, 1956-57, pres. 1969), Royal Soc. Tropical medicine and Hygiene, Am. Soc. Parasitologists (past councilor, 1952-54, 56-59, pres. 1968), Am. Micros. Soc. (v.p. 1953, exec. com. 1955-59, 61-62), Am. Pub. Health Assn., Soc. Exptl. Biology and Medicine, Societe Belge de Medecine Tropicale de Parasitologie et de Mycologie Societe de Pathologie Exotique (France; hon.), Sociedad Mexicana de Parasitologia (hon.), New Orleans Acad. Sci., Sigma Xi, Delta Omega, also Alpha Omega Alpha (honorary member). Clubs: International House, Round Table (New Orleans). Co-author: Animal Agents and Vectors of Human Disease, rev. edit. Contbg. author: Mitchell-Nelson's Pediatrics, Meakins' Practice of Medicine, Diagnostic Procedures and Reagents. Editorial bd.; Am. Jour. Tropical Medicine and Hygiene, 1958-60, 67-70, editor-in-chief, 1960-66. Asso. editor: Am. Jour. Hygiene, 1961-64, Jour. Parasitology, 1965—. Am. Jour. Epidemiology, 1966—, editorial bd. Transactions of Am. Micros. Soc., 1966—, Ceskoslovenska Parasitologie, 1966—. Author sci. papers. Home: 1416 Cadiz St New Orleans LA 70115 Office: 1430 Tulane Av New Orleans LA 70112

BEAVER, ROBERT PIERCE, clergyman, educator; b. Hamilton, O., May 26, 1906; s. Joseph Earl and Caroline (Neusch) B.; A.B., A.M., Oberlin Coll., 1928; Ph.D., Cornell U., 1933; student U. Munich, Yale U. Div. Sch., Coll. Chinese Studies at Peking, Union Theol. Sem., Columbia; m. Wilma Manessier, Aug. 22, 1927; children—Ellen (dec.), David Pierce, Stephen Robert. Ordained to ministry Evang. and Ref. Ch. (now United Ch. Christ), 1932; pastor Evang. Ref. Ch. of Oakley, Cin., 1932-36, Huber Meml. Ch., Balt., 1936-38; mem. China Mission, Evang. and Ref. Ch., 1938-47; prof. Central China Union Theol. Sem., 1940-42; prof. missions and ecumenics Theol. Sem. of Evang. and Ref. Ch., Lancaster, Pa., 1944-48; dir. Missionary Research Library, N.Y.C., research sec. div. fgn. missions Nat. Council Chs., 1948-55; lectr. Union Theol. Sem., 1949-55; prof. missions Bibl. Sem., N.Y.C., 1950-55; professor of missions. Divinity School U. Chgo., 1955-71, now prof. emeritus. Bd. trustees Found. for Theol. Edn. in S.E. Asia; mem. program bd., div. overseas ministries Nat. Council Ch. Mem. Am. Soc. Ch. History, Am. Hist. Assn., S.E. Asia Soc. Ch. History and Ecumenics (hon. pres. 1968—). N. Am. Academy of Ecumenics, Association of Professors of Missions (president 1956-58), Deutsche Gesellschaft für Missions Wissenschaft, Phi Beta Kappa, Phi Kappa Phi. Author: House of God: Year of Grace: Below the Great Wall; The Christian World Mission: A Reconsideration; Ecumenical Beginnings: The History of Comity; Envoys of Peace; From Missions to Mission: Christianity and African Education; Pioneers in Missions; Church, State and the American Indians; To Advance the Gospel; Selections from the Writings of Rufus Anderson; All Loves Excelling: American Protestant Women in World Mission; The Missionary Between the Times. Editoral bd. Church History, Jour. Ch. and State; editor World Christian Mission Books. Contbr. articles profl. publs. Home: PO Box 59 Sherman CT 06784

BEAVERS, CHARLES ALFRED JONES lawyer; b. Birmingham, Ala., Nov. 3, 1921; s. Frank Austin and Flora (Jones) B.; student Birmingham So. Coll., 1940-42, 45-46; LL.B., U. Ala., 1948; m. Gillian Lucille Branscomb, Oct. 6, 1949; children-Charles Alfred Jones, Anita Louise, Rebecca Lucille. Admitted to Ala. bar, 1948; practice in Birmingham, 1955—; v.p., title officer Ala. Title Co., 1949-55, also dir., gen. counsel; mem. firm Beavers, Shannon, Harrison & Odom and predecessor firms, 1955—; faculty U. Ala., Birmingham. Pres. Goodwill Industries Ala. Served to 1st lt. USAAF, 1942-45. Decorated D.F.C., Air medal with oak leaf cluster. Mem. Am., Ala., Birmingham (com. chmn.) bar assns., Am. Judicature Soc., Kappa Alpha, Phi Alpha Delta. Home: 4340 Old Brook Trail Birmingham AL 35203 Office: 620 N 22d St Birmingham AL 35243

BEAVERS, WILEY IAEGER, utility exec.; b. Raven, Va., Mar. 31, 1923; s. Wiley Iaeger and Mary (Hammond) B.; student Washington & Lee U., 1941-42, U. Vienna, 1945-46; B.A., U. Wyo., 1948; M.S., U. Utah, 1966; m. Margaret Jean Thompson, Apr. 25, 1946; 1 dau., Margaret Lynn. Truck driver, coal miner Drumheller Coal Co., Odd, W.Va., 1939-41; ranch hand William D. Thompson, Rock Springs, Wyo., 1946, Thomas Dodds, Bosler, Wyo., 1947-48; garage roustabout, clk., accountant, landman Mountain Fuel Supply Co., Rock Springs, Wyo., 1948-56; personnel dir., indsl. relations mgr. Mountain Fuel Supply Co., Salt Lake City, Utah, 1956-66, asst. to pres., 1967-68, v.p. adminstrn., 1968—; guest lectr. indsl. relations Cal. State Coll. at Long Beach, U. Utah, U. Wis. Mem. Citizens' Adv. Com. Salt Lake City, 1967, 1970-71; chmn. budget com. United Fund, 1971-72; mem. Gov. Utah Com. Employment Handicapped, 1967-71. Bd. dirs. Community Services Council, Research Found. of Am. Soc. Personnel Adminstrn. Served with AUS, 1942-46. Mem. Utah Personnel Assn. (pres. 1965), Am. Soc. Personnel Adminstrn. (nat. pres. 1967), Acad. Mgmt., Sigma Nu, Phi Sigma Iota, Beta Gamma Sigma. Mason, Rotarian. Home: 3425 Millcreek Salt Lake City UT 84109 Office: PO Box 11368 Salt Lake City UT 84111

BEAZLEY, GEORGE GRIMES, JR., clergyman, ch. orgn. ofcl.; b. Danville, Ky., Feb. 13, 1914; s. George Grimes and Hettie Page (Miller) B.; B.A., Centre Coll. of Ky., 1935, D.D., 1965; B.D., Coll. of Bible, 1938; postgrad. U. Chgo., U. Mo., Union Theol. Sem.; D.D., Culver-Stockton Coll., 1964; m. Charlotte Strother Holman, June 24, 1939. Ordained to ministry Christian Ch., 1938; pastor in Richmond, Mo., 19238-47, Bartlesville, Okla., 1947-60; pres. Council on Christian Unity, Christian Church (Disciples of Christ), Indpls., 1960-. Del. 3d assembly World Council Chs., 1961, del. 4th assembly, 1968, mem. faith and order commn., 1962-; secretary com., 1968—; del. 4th World Conf. Faith and Order, 1963; mem. gen. bd. Nat. Council Chs., 1961—, adv. com. faith and order, 1962—; sec. Unity Commn. Christian Ch., 1961—, mem. central com. on restructure Disciples, 1961—; sec. Consultation on Church Union, 1966-68, vice chairman, since 1968-; elder Central Christian Ch., Indianapolis, Ind. Board dirs. Ecumenical Inst., Chateau de Bossey, 1961-. Mem. Soc. Bibl. Lit. and Exegesis, Am. Sch. Oriental Research (asso.), N. Am. Acad. Ecumenists, Soc. Ky. Cols., Theta Phi, Omicron Delta Kappa. Home: 5364 N Kenwood St Indianapolis, IN 46208. Office: 222 S Downey St Indianapolis, IN 46219.

BEBAN, GARY JOSEPH, athlete; b. San Francisco, Aug. 8, 1946; s. Frank and Anna (Consani) B.; B.A. in History, U. Cal. at Los Angeles, 1968; m. Kathy Hanson, June 14, 1968; 1 son, Paul Frank. Quarterback Washington Redskins, 1968-70, Denver Broncos, 1970—; salesman real estate, Los Angeles, 1971—; TV color commentary Bruins, 1964-68, U. Cal. at Los Angeles, 1964-68. Served with N.G., 1968—. Recipient Heisman trophy, 1967. Home: 1827 Veteran St Los Angeles CA 90025

BEBER, MEYER, educator, physician, hosp. adminstr.; b. Minsk, Russia, Dec. 27, 1899; s. Israel and Rose (Greenglass) B.; B.Sc., U. Neb., 1920, Ph.D., 1925, M.D., 1933; m. Lillian Rubenstein, Nov. 25, 1926; children—Charles Robert, Bernard Arthur. Instr., then asst. prof. biochemistry U. Neb. Sch. Medicine, 1923-33, asso. prof., 1955-70, asso. prof. emeritus, 1970—; intern St. Elizabeth Hosp., Washington. 1933-35; mem. faculty U. Neb. Coll. Medicine, 1935—, prof. internal medicine, 1963-70, prof. emeritus, 1970—; chief staff Douglas County Hosp., Omaha. 1947-55; med. dir. Douglas County Hosp. and County Instns., Omaha. 1956-71, ret.; asso. prof. internal medicine Creighton U., 1958—; dir. med. services, adminstr. Douglas County Hosps., 1963—; cons. staff internal medicine Immanuel Hosp., 1954—; staff internal medicine Bishop Clarkson Hosp., 1947—, mem. exec. com., 1970—. Served with U.S. Army, World War I. Fellow A.C.P., Am. Geriatrics Soc., Gerontol. Soc.; mem. Am., Neb. (chmn. council profl. practice 1964-68), Omaha (pres. 1968) hosp. assns., A.M.A., Neb. Med. Soc., Omaha MidWest Clin. Soc., Am. Coll. Hosp. Adminstrs., Phi Beta Kappa, Sigma Xi, Zeta Beta Tau, Alpha Omega Alpha. Jewish religion Contbr. med. jours. Home: 20 Island Av Apt 214 Miami Beach FL 33139

BEBOUT, JOHN WILLIAM, lawyer; b. Newark, O., Apr. 10, 1898; s. Edmund and Bessie (Hobbs) B.; A.B., Ohio State U., 1921, J.D., 1923; m. Vonda F. Eley, Sept. 15 , 1924; childrenBonnie Lou (Mrs. Richard Wening), Barbara Ann (Mrs. Roger Farley). Admitted to Ohio bar, since practiced in Toledo; sr. mem. firm Boxell, Bebout, Torbet & Potter, 1950-; instr. Coll. Law, U. City Toledo, 1926-45; lectr. on fed. estate taxes at bar insts., 1945-. Dir. and-or sec. numerous indsl. corps.; exec. sec. Funeral Dirs. Assn. Northwestern Ohio, 1935-. Active local United Appeal, Lutheran Orphans and Old Folks Home. Fellow Am., Ohio bar assns. founds., Am. Coll. Probate Counsel; mem. Am. (ho. of dels. 1958-), Ohio (chmn. probate and trust law com. 1940-52 exec. com. 1952-58, council dels, 1958-60) bar assns., Am. Trial Lawyers Assn., Toledo C. of C., Delta Theta Phi. Lutheran (mem. council, pres. of council). Mason (Shriner). Clubs: Toledo, Inverness (Toledo). Author: (with J. W. Yager) Ohio Inheritance Tax, 1950; also articles. Home: 4030 W Bancroft St Toledo, OH 43606. Office: Toledo Trust Bldg Toledo, OH 42604.

BECHERER, ROBERT CHARLES machinery mfg. exec.; b. Indpls., June 25, 1902; s. Constantine H. and Lillie (Otte) R.; B.S., Purdue U., 1923, D. Eng. (hon.), 1955; D. Eng. (honorary) Rose Polytechnic Institute, 1965; married Nell R. Norton, June 21, 1930; childrenNell J. (Mrs. Roger C. Smith), Marjorie E. (Mrs. David B. Sterrett, Junior). With Link-Belt Co., 1923-, v.p., gen. mgr. Ewart Plant, Indpls., 1949-51, exec. v.p., 1951O52, pres., dir., Chicago, Ill., 1952-65, chmn. bd., 1965-67; cons., dir. FMC Corp.; dir. dir. Powers Regulator Co., Bastian Blessing Corp., Am. Fletcher Nat. Bank. Nat. Bank, Indpls., 1951-60, Continental Ill. Nat. Bank & Trust Co., Chgo., 1959-. Chgo., 1959-70. Trustee Tudor Hall, Indpls., 1949-51; mem. exec. com. trustee Ill. Inst. Tech.; mem. citizens com. U. Ill., 1958-. Member Ill. State C. of C. (director 1952-58). Machinery and Allied Products Inst., (executive committee, 1953-67), Illinoise. Mfrs. Association (director 1961-67), Chicago Association of Commerce and Industry (vice president), Tau Beta Pi fraternity, also mem. Phi Lambda Upsilon, Delta Tau Delta. Republican. Evangelical. Mason. Clubs: Westmoreland Country, University, Chicago, Economic (dir. 1957-), Mid-America (Chgo.). Home: 750 Sheridan Rd Winnetka, IL60093. Office: Prudential Plaza Chicago 1, IL

BECHERT, CHARLES, liquor co. exec.; b. Bklyn., July 14, 1910; s. Charles H. and Anne (Ehrgott) B.; student Pace Coll., 1937; m. Gertrude Usher, Sept. 11, 1937; children—Charles R., Richard T. Accountant, Am. Water Works & Electric Co., Inc., N.Y.C., 1929-32, Jaburg Bros., Inc., N.Y.C., 1932-36; Jaburg Bros., Inc., N.Y.C., 1936—. Mem. Nat. Assn. Alcoholic Beverage Importers (bd. dirs.). Home: 6708 183d St Flushing NY 11365 Office: 620 Fifth Av New York City NY 10020

BECHHOFER, ROBERT ERIC, statistician; b. N.Y.C., Mar. 11, 1919; s. Julius and Lillian (Meyer) B.; A.B., Columbia, 1941, Ph.D. in Math. Statistics, 1951; m. Joan Edith Lebrecht, Oct. 4, 1952; children—Robin Ann, David Jay, Ellen Ruth, Laurie Jean. Asst. prof. dept. indsl. engring. Columbia, 1951-52; faculty Cornell U., Ithaca, N.Y., 1953—, prof., 1957—, chmn. dept. operations research, 1967—. Fellow Inst. Math. Statistics, Am. Statis. Assn. (dir. 1964-65, chmn. sect. phys. and engring. scis. 1962). Author: (with others) Sequential Identification and Ranking Procedures, 1968. Research in statis. multiple-decision ranking procedures; developed new procedures for ranking means, variances. Home: 36 Cornell St Ithaca NY 14850

BECHHOLD, BENNO MANN, banker, corp. exec.; b. Feuchtwangen, Bavaria, Germany, Feb. 18, 1902; s. Abraham and Pauline (Mann) B.; student U. Frankfurt A/Main, Germany, 1920-22, U. Berlin, Germany, 1922-24; m. Georgiana B. Snyder, Feb. 4, 1951. Came to U.S., 1937, naturalized, 1944. Prin. partner pvt. banking firms, Bechhold & Co. K.G., Berlin, 1927-35, Bechhold & Co., Ltd., London, Eng., 1935-39; v.p., dir. Savoy-Plaza, Inc., N.Y.C., 1942-43, exec. v.p., pres., dir., 1943-58; pres., dir. Cockshutt Farm Equipment, Inc., Ltd., Can., 1959-61, Hilton Credit Corp., 1961-64; dir. Cockshutt Farm Equipment, Inc., Ponder and Best, Inc.; pres. Woodland Savs. & Loan Assn., 1963-67, also dir.; pres., dir., mem. exec. com. Am.-Hawaiian S.S. Co., 1962-65. Mem. Berlin Stock Exchange. Berlin Metal Exchange, 1927-35. Home: 1131 Wallace Ridge Beverly Hills CA 90210

BECHILL, WILLIAM DANIEL, educator; b. Grosse Pointe Park, Mich., Apr. 26, 1928; s. George and Eluned (Jones) B.; A.B., Beloit (Wis.) Coll., 1949; M.S.W., U. Mich., 1952; m. Lucy Ann Purnell, Jan. 27, 1951; children—Richard William, Robert David, John Edward. County adminstr. Mich. Dept. Social Welfare, 1952-55; lectr. Sch. Social Work, U. Mich., 1955-60; exec. sec. Cal. Citizens Adv. Com. Aging, 1960-65; U.S. commr. on aging, 1965-69; asso. prof., chmn. social policy sequence U. Md. Sch. Social Work, 1969—; vis. prof. U. So. Cal., 1969, 70; cons. in field, 1958—. Pres. Mich. Rehab. Assn., 1959, Western Gerontological Soc., 1965; mem. Montgomery County Commn. Aging, 1968; del. White House Conf. Aging, 1961; chmn. Adv. Com. Older Americans, 1965-69, chmn. social policy com. Nat. Parks and Recreation Assn., 1968; mem. consumer adv. com. U.S. Dept. Transp., 1969—; cons. Md. Commn. on Aging, 1969—. Recipient Sesquicentennial medal U. Mich., 1967; Distinguished service citation Beloit Coll., 1969. Mem. Am. Pub. Welfare Assn., Gerontological Soc., Md. Conf. Social Welfare, Phi Kappa Phi. Democrat. Presbyn. Home: 11505 Rokeby Av Kensington MD 20795

BECHT, ARNO CUMMING, educator, lawyer; b. E. Peoria, Ill., Feb. 17, 1910; s. Frank Christian and Ruby (Cumming) B.; B.A., Colgate U., 1931; J.D., U. Chgo., 1936; LL. M., Columbia, 1938, J. Sc.D., 1951; m. LaVerne Ruth Galley, Aug. 20, 1938. Admitted to N.Y. bar, 1939, Mo. bar, 1942; with firm Miller, Owen, Otis & Bailey, N.Y.C., 1937-39, Igoe, Carroll, Keefe & Coburn, St. Louis, 1942; asst. prof. law U. Ga., 1939-40; mem. faculty Washington U., St. Louis, 1940—, prof. law, 1950—, Madill prof., 1962—. Served with AUS, 1943-45. Mem. Order of Coif, Phi Beta Kappa. Unitarian. Author: (with Frank W. Miller) The Test of Factual Causation in Negligence and Strict Liability Cases, 1961; also column, The Flag, Mo. Bar Jour., 1960-65. Contbr. articles legal jours. Home: 211 Linden Av Clayton MO 63105 Office: Washington U St Louis MO 63130

BECHT, GEORGE H., banker; b. 1908; grad. Rutgers U. Sch. Banking, 1949; married. With Mfrs. Trust Co., N.Y.C., 1927-43; with Franklin Nat. Bank, 1943—, exec. v.p., cashier, 1968—. Mem. U.S. Assay Commn.; chmn. Nassau County Clearing House Assn., 1961. Fellow Am. Numis. Soc.; mem. N.Y. State Bankers Assn. (past chmn. group VII). Address: 199 2d St Mineola NY 13116

BECHTEL, JOHN FREDERICK, equipment co. exec.; b. Milw., Aug. 19, 1914; s. John H. and Hatti (Schmitt) B.; B.S. in Mech. Engring. with honors, U. Wis., 1935, J.D., 1937; m. Frances A. Bechtel, Jan. 24, 1970; 1 dau., Julia C. Admitted to bar, Wis., 1937, N.Y., 1947, Mich., 1952; patent atty. Gen. Electric Co., 1937-41, project mgr. Army Ground Radar, 1942-45; asst. counsel Internat. Gen. Electric Co., 1945-50, exec. responsible for fgn. licensing activities, 1950-51; v.p. Clark Equipment Co., Buchanan, Mich., 1956—, gen. counsel, sec., 1952-61, pres. internat. div., 1970—, now pres., dir. Clark Internat. Marketing S.A.; chmn. bd. adminstrs., exec. v.p. Clark Equipment A.G.; v.p., dir. Clark Equipment Overseas Finance Corp.; dir., 1st v.p. Eximia, S.A. (Argentina); dir. Clark Equipment Credit Corp., Clark Equipment Australia Pty. Ltd., Clark Equipment Ltd. (Eng.), Premier Metal Co. South Africa Ltd., Productos Industriales Metallcos S.A. (Mexico), Macmor (Spain). Mem. Am. Bar Assn., Am. Judicature Soc., Nat. Planning Assn., Phi Delta Phi, Pi Tau Sigma, Phi Eta Sigma, Kappa Sigma. Clubs: Union League, University (Chgo.); Pickwick (Niles, Mich.); Economic of Southwestern Mich.; Point O'Woods Country (Benton Harbor, Mich.); Sarasota Yacht. Home: 2205 Mount Curve E St Joseph MI 49085 Office: Clark Equipment Co Buchanan MI 49107

BECHTEL, KENNETH KARL, ins. exec.; b. Oakland, Cal., July 4, 1904; s. Warren A. and Clara (West) B.; student U. of Cal., 1922-23; m. Nancy Foote, Nov. 2, 1961; children (by previous marriage)—Peter Bechtel, Jon. Began career with W. A. Bechtel Co. (est. 1895), constrn. engrs., San Francisco, 1921, v.p., dir. 1935-45; chairman exec. com., sr. dir. Industrial Indemnity Co., pres. 1931-55, chmn. bd., 1955-70; pres., dir. Marinship Corp., 1942—; dir. Wells Fargo Bank. Mem. nat. exec. bd. Boy Scouts Am., 1947—, pres. nat. council, 1956-59. Trustee, pres. Belvedere Sci. Fund, Indsl. Indemnity Found.; dir. World Wildlife Fund. Trustees for Conservation. Mem. Cal. Acad. Scis. (trustee), Cal. Hist. Soc., Nat. Audubon Soc., Beta Theta Pi frat. Rep. Mason (Shriner). Clubs: San Francisco Yacht (Belvedere); Commonwealth, Bohemian, Stock Exchange, Marin Yacht (San Rafael); Pacific Union, Cal. (Los Angeles); Sierra; Meadow (Fairfax). Home: Kentfield CA 94904 Office: 255 California St San Francisco CA 94111

BECHTEL, PAUL MOYER, educator; b. Phila., Dec. 13, 1909; s. Henry M. and Eva (Reid) B.; A.B., Juniata Coll., 1932; M.A., Cornell U., 1936; Ph.D., Northwestern U., 1957; m. Mary Krom, Aug. 25, 1948; children—Lawrence, Stephen, Susan, Pamela. Prin., Waynesboro (Pa.) High Sch., 1944-46; prof. English, Wheaton (Ill.) Coll., 1946—, chmn. div. lang. and lit., 1957-65, chmn. dept. English, 1965—; Fulbright lectr. in Am. lit. Istanbul U., Turkey, 1968-69. Chmn. Danforth Ill.-Ind.-Mich. Assos., 1960-63. Chmn. A.R.C., Waynesboro, 1945-46. Mem. Nat. Council Tchrs. English, Modern Lang. Assn., Chgo. Coll. English Assn. (dir. 1963-66), Juniata Coll. Nat. Alumni Assn. (pres. 1962-63). Republican. Club: Caxton (Chgo.). Book editor: Christian Life mag., 1963-70, Christian Bookseller, 1963-70. Home: 707 University Pl Wheaton IL 60187

BECHTEL, STEPHEN DAVISON, engr., constructor; b. Aurora, Ind., Sept. 24, 1900; s. Warren A. and Clara (West) B.; student engring. U. Cal., LL.D., 1954; LL.D., Loyola U., 1958; D.Engring., U. of Pacific, 1966; m. Laura Adaline Peart, Sept. 7, 1923; children—Stephen Davison, Barbara (Mrs. Paul L. Davies, Jr.). Gen. constrn. bus. with father, 1919; with W.A. Bechtel Co., v.p., 1925-36, pres. 1936; 1st v.p., dir. Six Cos., Inc., builders Hoover Dam, 1931-35; co-organizer, dir. Bechtel-McCone Corp., 1937-46; during World War II, chmn. Cal. Shipbldg. Corp., Wilmington, Cal., dir. Marinship Corp. (Sausalito, Cal.); now sr. dir. Bechtel Corp.; pres., dir. Lakeside Corp.; dir. Indsl. Indemnity Co., Canadian Bechtel Ltd., S.P. Co.; adv. com. Export-Import Bank U.S.; mem. dirs. adv. council, internat. council Morgan Guaranty Trust Co. N.Y. Mem. Bus. Adv. Council, U.S. Dept. Commerce, 1950-60, chmn., 1958-59, mem. bus. council, 1961—; mem. Pres.'s Adv. Com. on Nat. Hwy. Program, 1954-55; sr. mem. Nat. Indsl. Conf. Bd. Bd. dirs. Stanford Research Inst.; trustee Ford Found., San Francisco Bay Area Council. Served with 20th Engrs., U.S. Army, World War I; AEF. Decorated Order of Cedar (Lebanon), 1956; knight Order of St. Sylvester, Pope (Holy See); knight Comdr. Ct. Honor; recipient John Fritz gold medal, certificate, 1961, Nat. Def. Transp. award, 1960, achievement award Bldg. Industry Conf. Bd., San Francisco, 1951; Moles award for outstanding achievement in constrn. 1952; Alumni Assn. award, 1951, Alumnus of year, U. Cal., 1952; 1st Internat. Achievement award World Trade Club, 1970; 1st Outstanding Alumnus award U. Cal. Bus. Adminstrn. Alumni Assn., 1970. Registered profl. engr., Cal. Mem. Am. Petroleum Inst., Am. Soc. C.E., Soc. Naval Architects and Marine Engrs., Cons. Constructors Council Am., Soc. Am. Mil. Engrs., Bus. Council, World Affairs Council No. Cal., Cal. Inst. Assos., Moles, Beavers, Beta Theta Pi. Republican. Methodist. Mason (32, Shriner). Clubs: Pacific Union, Commonwealth, Press and Union League, Engineers, Stock Exchange, Bohemian (San Francisco); California (Los Angeles); Claremont Country (Oakland, Cal.); Cypress Point (Monterey Peninsula, Cal.); Links, River, Pinnacle, Sky, Cloud (N.Y.C.); Blind Brook (Port Chester, N.Y.). Home: 244 Lakeside Dr Oakland, CA 94612. Office: 155 Sansome St San Francisco CA 94104

BECHTEL, STEPHEN DAVISON, Jr., engr., exec.; b. Oakland, Cal., May 10, 1925, s. Stephen Davison and Laura (Peart) B.; student U. Colo., 1943-44; B.S., Purdue U., 1946; M.B.A., Stanford, 1948; m. Elizabeth Mead Hogan, June 5, 1946; children—Shana (Mrs. R.C. Johnstone, Jr.), Lauren, Gary, Riley, Nonie. Engring. and mgmt. positions Bechtel Corporation, San Francisco, 1948-60, president 1961—; dir. Gen. Motors Corp., Hanna Mining Co., Crocker Nat. Bank, So. Pacific Co. Mem. Bus. Council; life councillor Conf. Bd. Trustee Cal. Inst. Tech.; adv. council Stanford Grad. Sch. Bus. Served with USMC, 1943-46. Registered engr., N.Y., Mich., Cal., Md., Hawaii, D.C., Va. Mem. Am. Soc. C.E., Am. Inst. Metall. Engrs., Cal. Acad. Scis. (hon. trustee), Beta Theta Pi. Clubs: Pacific Union Stock Exchange (San Francisco); Claremont County (Oakland, Cal.); Cypress Point (Monterey Peninsula, Cal.); Vancouver (B.C.); Ramada (Houston); Bohemian, San Francisco Golf (San Francisco); Fifth Ave, Links, Blind Brook (N.Y.C.); Augusta (Ga.) National Golf; York (Toronto). Home: Piedmont CA Office: 50 Beale St San Francisco CA 94104

BECK, ABE JACK, air force officer; b. Dallas, May 24, 1914; s. Jacob S. and Mollie (Pollock) B.; LL.B., So. Methodist U., 1939; m. Anne Gilaire Michlin, Oct. 21, 1945; children—Stephanie Jo, Melanie Gilaire, Darcy Jane, John Dallas. Admitted to Tex. bar, 1939; pvt. practice law, Dallas, 1939-40; joined USAAF, 1940; grad. Flying Sch., 1941; commd. 2d lt. USAAF, 1941, advanced through grades to maj. gen., USAF, 1963; tactical officer, engring. officer, also pilot instr. Air Cadet Advanced Flying Sch., Luke Field, Ariz., 1941-42; aide Hdqrs. 5th Air Force, later operation officer 374th Troop Carrier Group, New Guinea, 1942-43; asst. chief staff A-3, 54th Tractical Wing, New Guinea, also operations officer Hdqrs. 5th Air Force, New Guinea, and later asst. chief staff A-3, 310th Bomb Wing and Chief staff 310th Bomb Wing, S.W. Pacific, 1943-45; student Command and Gen. Staff Sch., 1945; officer charge classification and assignment br. A-1, Office Records Br., 400th AAFBU, San Francisco, 1946; resigned, and returned to civilian life, 1946-47; rejoined USAF, 1947; staff legal officer, later asst. staff judge adv. Hdqrs. 8th Air Force, Ft. Worth, 1947-48; chief air judge adv. sect., personnel and adminstrn. SAC. Andrews AFB, Md., 1948; chief air judge adv. sect., personnel and adminstrn., also project officer, command sect. Hdqrs. SAC, Offutt AFB, Omaha, 1948-52; dep. comdr., then comdr. 3902d Air Base Wing, Offutt AFB, 1952-54; comdr. 340th Bomb Wing, Sedalia AFB, Mo., 1954-57, 4082d Strategic Wing, Goose AFB, Labrador, 1957-59; chief staff, command sect. Hdqrs. 8th Air Force, SAC, Westover AFB, Mass., 1959-61; comdr. 817th Air Div., Pease AFB, N.H., 1961-63; insp. gen. Hdqrs. SAC, Offutt AFB, 1964, dir. materiel 1964-66; sr. air force mem. weapon systems evaluation group, directorate def. research and engring. Office Sec. Def., 1966-68; comdr. Warner Robins Air Materiel Area, 1968—. Decorated Legion of Merit with 2 oak leaf clusters. D.F.C., Air medal with 3 oak leaf clusters, Air Force Commendation medal; British Mil. Cross (Australia). Home: 400 Officers Circle Robins AFB GA 31093 Office: Warner Robins Air Materiel Area Robins AFB GA 31093

BECK, ANATOLE, educator, mathematician; b. N.Y.C., Mar. 19, 1930; s. Morris and Minnie (Rosenblum) B.; B.A., Bklyn. Coll., 1951; M.A., Yale, 1953, Ph.D., 1956; m. Evelyn Torton, Apr. 10, 1954; children—Nina Rachel, Micah Daniel. Instr., Williams Coll., 1955-56; research asso. Tulane U., 1956-57; traveling postdoctoral fellow Yale, 1957-58; mem. faculty U. Wis., 1958- -, prof. math., 1966—; vis. scholar Cornell U., 1960, Hebrew U. Jerusalem (Israel), 1964-65, U. Göttingen (Germany), 1965, U. Warwick (Eng.), 1968, Imperial Coll., London, 1969, U. Erlangen (Germany), 1969, U. Md., 1971. NSF sr. postdoctoral fellow, 1968-69. Mem. Math. Assn. Am., Am. Math. Soc., Am. Fedn. Tchrs. (pres. U. Wis. United Faculty and local 223 1971-72), Phi Beta Kappa, Sigma Xi, Pi Mu Epsilon. Co-author several books, contbr. profl. jours. Home: 4221 Wanetah Trail Madison WI 53711

BECK, AXEL JOHN, lawyer; b. Sweden, May 6, 1894; s. C. M. and Anna (Jonson) B.; came to U.S., 1906, naturalized, 1916; A.B., Morningside Coll., 1920; J.D., U. Chgo., 1922; m. Georgia C. Clark, Sept. 10, 1930; children—Byron John, Craig Allen. Admitted to Ill. bar, 1923, S.D. bar, 1924; practiced in Chgo., 1923-24, Union County, S.D., 1924—; organizer Bank of Union County, Elk Point, 1943, pres., chmn. bd., 1947-58; pres. Thermoflector Corp., North Sioux City, S.D. Republican Nat. Committeeman of S.D., 1948-57, also mem. exec. com. Mem. and officer Commn. on Uniform Laws for S.D.; mem. Nat. Conf. on Uniform Legislation, 1938-57. Mem. Elk Point Bd. of Edn., 1945-50, pres. 1949. Served as 2d lt., U.S. Army, World War I. Recipient Distinguished Service award Morningside Coll., 1966. Mem. Am. Legion (judge adv. Dept. of S.D.), State Bar of S.D., Am. Bar Assn., Pi Kappa Delta, Gamma Eta Gamma. Republican. Conglist. Mason (32, Shriner). Home: Aberdeen SD 57401

BECK, BURT, editor; b. Phila., June 12, 1918; s. Nathan G. and Betty (Solomon) B.; B.A.; U. Pa. 1938; postgrad. Price Sch. Journalism, 1939; m. Dora Torch, Jan. 5, 1952; children—Nora Evelyn, Thomas Nathaniel. With Phila. and N.Y.C. newspapers, 1938-46; pub. relations dir. Seafarers Internat. Union, 1946-49; mem. pub. relations staff Internat. Union Elec. Workers, 1950-55, Hotel Workers Union, 1955-57; mng. editor Textile Workers Union, 1957-63; editor, pub. relations dir. Amalgamated Clothing Workers Am., AFL-CIO, 1963—; lectr. journalism Rand Sch. Social Scis., N.Y.C., 1946-51. Exec. v.p. Atlantic Labor Press Conf., AFL-CIO, 1964-67; v.p. Internat. Labor Press Assn., 1967—. Served as officer, F.A., AUS, 1942-45. Recipient awards and citations Internat. Labor Press Assn. Author: (motion picture scripts) Battle of Wall Street, 1948, Armored Attack, 1957. Home: 15 Park Pl Suffern Park Suffern NY 10901 Office: 15 Union Sq New York City NY 10003

BECK, BURTON EARL, pharm. mfg. co. exec.; b. Indpls., Jan. 31, 1918; s. Earl and Vera (Torbet) B.; A.B., in Psychology, Cornell U., 1939; m. Bettie Ann Putnam, Apr. 6, 1940; children—Elizabeth Ann, Sarah (dec.), Cynthia Lee. With Eli Lilly & Co., Indpls., 1939—, successively chief placement and wage studies, chief incentives and job evaluation, asst. mgr. methods and standards, staff asst. to v.p. charge prodn., chmn. organizational planning staff, exec. dir. personnel and pub. relations, v.p. indsl. relations, 1958-59, pres. Eli Lilly Internat. Corp., 1959-64, group v.p. marketing and domestic subsidiary operations, 1964-65, exec. v.p., 1965- 69; pres. Eli Lilly & Co., 1969—, also mem. exec. com., mem. bd. dirs.; director Eli Lilly Internat. Corp., Merchants Nat. Bank & Trust Co., Lilly Endowment, Inc., Indpls. Power & Light Co., Am. United Life Ins. Co., R.R. Donnelley & Sons Company; chmn. bd. mgmt. Elanco Products Company. Mem. development council Butler University. Mem. bd. trustees Tudor Hall Sch., Inc., Indpls.; trustee YMCA of Greater Indpls. Served to maj. AUS, 1942-46. Mem. Indpls. C. of C., Am. Legion. Episcopalian. Club: Meridian Hills Country. Home: 7525 Marsh Rd Indianapolis, IN 46278. Office: 307 E McCarty Indianapolis IN 46206

BECK, CHARLES ELMORE, mfg. co. exec.; b. Stanford, Ky., Apr. 5, 1921; s. Charles Elmore and Lena Elizabeth (Lindholm) B.; B.S., Berea Coll., 1941; postgrad. U. Detroit, 1941-42; B.S. in Bus. Adminstrn., Wayne State U., 1951, M.A. in Indsl. Engring. and Mgmt., 1953; LL.D., La Salle U., 1963, Eastern Ky. State Coll., 1965; m. Ruth Sintay, Sept. 17, 1949; children—Bobby, Susan, David. With Murray Corp., Detroit, 1946-49; with Ford Motor Co., 1949-61, asst. treas., 1959-60, dir. bus. planning office of finance staff, 1960-61, group exec. gen. products group, 1964; pres., chief exec. officer, dir. Philco Corp., 1961-64; pres., chief exec. Ambac Industries, 1964—, also dir.; dir. 3d Nat. Bank of Hampden County, Springfield, Mass., Anchor Savs. Bank. Trustee Adelphi U., Berea Coll. Served with USAAF, 1942-45. Clubs: Garden City Golf, Valley (Garden City, N.Y.); Cherry Racquet (Phila.). Home: 91 3d St Garden City NY 11530 Office: Ambac Industries Garden City NY 11530

BECK, CLIFFORD KEITH, physicist; b. nr. Salisbury, N.C., Apr. 12, 1913; s. Arthur Bradley and Zelma Pauline (Weant) B.; A.B. cum laude, Catawba Coll., 1933, D.Sc. (hon.), 1951; M.S., Vanderbilt U., 1940; Ph.D., University of North Carolina, 1943; m. Mary Elizabeth Lassetter, May 28, 1943; children—Mary, Clifford K., Barbara, Jon. Research scientist Manhattan project, Columbia, 1943-45; tech. aide to mgr. of Gaseous Diffusion Project, Oak Ridge, Tenn., 1945-46, dir. of research, 1946-49; head physics dept., N.C. state Coll., Raleigh, 1949-56; on leave to AEC, 1957- 58, sci. adviser to dir. Div. Civilian Applications; chief reactor safety evaluation and coordinator for safety research AEC, 1957-60; asst. dir. Div. Licensing and Regulation, 1960-61, dep. dir. regulation, 1961—; dir. v.p. Oak Ridge Inst. Nuclear Studies, 1953-55; mem. nuclear standards bd. Am. Nuclear Standards Inst., 1966—; U.S. mem. Com. Reactor Safety Tech., European Nuclear Energy Assn., 1966—; mem. standards com. U.S.A. Standards Inst., 1960-66. Mem. bd. trustees, Montgomery Jr. Coll., 1960-69, pres., 1966-68; mem., pres. bd. edn., Montgomery County, Md., 1960-69; pres. Md. Bd. for Community Colls., 1969—. Bd. mgrs. Ministers and Missionaries Retirement Fund, Am. Bapt. Conv., 1970—. Fellow Am. Phys. Soc.; mem. Am. Nuclear Soc. (dir. 1955-56). Home: RD 1 Shiloh Church Rd Boyds MD 20720 Office: USAEC Washington DC 20545

BECK, CURT WERNER, chemist, educator; b. Halle/Saale, Germany, Sept. 10, 1927; s. Curt Paul and Clara (Fischer) B.; student U. Munich, 1946-48; B.S., Tufts U., 1951; Ph.D., Mass. Inst. Tech., 1955; m. Lily Yallourakis, Feb. 10, 1953; children—Curt Peter, Christopher Paul. Came to U.S., 1950, naturalized, 1955. Instr., Franklin Tech. Inst., Boston, 1955-56; asst. prof. Roberts Coll., Istanbul, Turkey, 1956-57; lectr. Vassar Coll., Poughkeepsie, N.Y., 1957-59, asst. prof., 1959-62, asso. prof., 1962-66, prof. chemistry, 1966—, Matthew Vassar Jr. prof., 1970—. Mem. Zoning Bd. Appeals, La Grange, N.Y., 1965- -; mem. Dutchess County council Boy Scouts Am., 1965-67. Candidate supr., La Grange, 1967. Recipient Research award Mid-Hudson sect. Am. Chem. Soc., 1965. Fellow Internat. Inst. for Conservation Historic and Artistic Works (London); mem. Am. Chem. Soc. (past sect. chmn.), Chem. Soc. (London), Gesellschaft Deutscher Chemiker, Archeol. Inst. Am., Internat. Inst. for Conservation Historic and Artistic Works (London), Sigma Xi. Co-editor: Art and Archaeology Tech. Abstracts, 1966—. Sect. editor Chem. Abstracts, 1967—. Home: Skidmore Rd La Grange Pleasant Valley NY 12569 Office: Vassar Coll Poughkeepsie NY 12601

BECK, EARL RAY, educator; b. Junction City, O., Sept. 8, 1916; s. Ernest Ray and Mary Frances (Helser) B.; A.B., Capital U., 1937; M.A., Ohio State U., 1939, Ph.D., 1942; m. Marjorie Culbertson, Nov. 7, 1944; children—Ann, Mary Sue. Instr., Capital U., 1942-43, Ohio State U., 1946-49; asst. prof. Fla. State U., Tallahassee, 1949-52, asso. prof., 1952-60, prof. history, 1960—, chmn. dept. history, 1967—; summer vis. prof. La. State U., 1955, Tulane U., 1959, Duke, 1966. Mem. com. on library research sources European history sect. So. Hist. Soc., 1959-67, chmn., 1963-64. Served with AUS, 1946-49. Mem. Am., So. hist. assns., Conf. Group for Central European History. Presbyn. Author: Verdict on Schacht, 1956; The Death of the Prussian Republic, 1959; Contemporary Civilization I, 1959; On Teaching History in Colleges and Universities, 1966; Germany Rediscovers America, 1968. Home: 2514 Killarney Way Tallahassee FL 32303

BECK, FRED JOHN, educator; b. N.Y.C., Jan. 4, 1904; s. Frederick and Caroline (Weber) B.; E.E., Poly. Inst. Bklyn., 1925; Ph.D., Yale, 1932; m. Edna Eccles, June 4, 1932; children—Frederick Herbert, Phyllis Caroline, Richard Russell. Grad. tng. program Westinghouse Elec. & Mfg. Co., 1925-26; research engr. Bell Telephone Labs., 1926-29; instr. Yale, 1929-35, asst. prof., 1935-40, asso. prof., 1940-53, prof. elec. engring., 1953—. Mem. Am. Phys. Soc., I.E.E.E., Sigma Xi, Tau Beta Pi, Lambda Chi Alpha. Republican. Mem. Christian Ch. Author articles tech. publs. Home: 4044 92d St SE Mercer Island WA 98040

BECK, GLENN HANS, univ. adminstr.; b. Chester, Utah, July 27, 1915; s. Andrew Marinus and Christie (Monsen) B.; B.S., U. Ida., 1936; M.S., Kan. State Coll., 1938; Ph.D., Cornell U., 1950; m. Genevieve Spalding, Dec. 28, 1936; children—Ferol Doreen, Thelma Suzanne. Mem. faculty Kan. State Coll., 1936-53, prof. dairy husbandry, 1946-53; dir. agrl. expt. sta. Kan. State U., Manhattan, 1956-60, dean agr., 1960-65, v.p., 1965—; on leave as provost for agr. and vet. medicine Ahmadu Bello U., Zaria, Nigeria, 1969-70. Chmn. bd. dirs. 1st Nat. Bank Manhattan. Pres., Agrl. Hall of Fame and Nat. Center. Served with AUS, 1943-46; PTO. Mem. Am. Dairy Sci. Assn., Am. Soc. Animal Prodn., Sigma Xi, Phi Kappa Phi, Alpha Zeta, Gamma Sigma Delta, Farm House. Home: 1405 Skyline Dr Manhattan KS 66502

BECK, HENRY CONSTABLE, Jr., bldg. contractor; b. Shreveport, La., Dec. 18, 1917; s. Henry Constable and Elizabeth (Brown) B.; A.B., Dartmouth, 1938; postgrad. Harvard Sch. Bus. Adminstrn., Mass. Inst. Tech.; m. Patricia Davis, June 22, 1946; children—Patricia Hardin, Pamela Constable, Henry Constable, Kalita Hardin. With Henry C. Beck Co., Dallas, 1939—, pres., 1948—; dir. First Nat. Bank Dallas, Dallas Power & Light Co. Bd. dirs. Gaston Episcopal Hosp.; mem. bd. overseers Thayer Sch. Engring., Dartmouth Coll. Served with USNR, 1942-45. Mem. Dallas Citizens Council. Episcopalian (past warden). Clubs: Brook Hollow Golf, Northwood Country (Dallas). Home: 10210 Strait Lane Dallas TX 75229 Office: First Nat Bank Bldg Dallas TX 75202

BECK, JOHN MATTHEW, orgn. exec.; b. Rogoznig, Austria, Apr. 10, 1913; s. Matthias and Antoinette (Bukowski) B.; came to U.S., 1914, naturalized, 1942; B.S., Indiana (Pa.) State Coll., 1936; M.A., U. Chgo., 1947, Ph.D., 1953; m. Frances Josephine Mottey, Aug. 23, 1941. Tchr., Clymer (Pa.) High Sch., 1937-41; instr. history and philosophy of edn. De Paul U., 1948-53; instr. Chgo. Tchrs. Coll., 1953-56, chmn. dept. edn., 1956-60, asst. dean, prof. edn., 1960; dean Chgo. State Coll., 1966-67; dir. Chgo. Tchr. Corps., 1967-70; exec. dir. Chgo. Consortium Colls. and Univs., 1968—. Mem. Ill. Adv. Com., on Guidance, 1963—, Citizens Schs. Com. Chgo., 1953—; cons. U.S. Office Edn., 1968-70. Bd. govs. Chgo. City Club, 1961—, v.p., 1962-63, 64-65. Served with AUS, 1941-46. Decorated Bronze star. Fellow A.A.A.S., Philosophy of Edn. Soc.; mem. Am. Hist. Assn., Am. Edn. Research Assn., Ill. Edn. Assn. (pres. Chgo. div. 1960-62). Editor: Chgo. Sch. Jour., 1964-65; co-editor Teaching the Culturally Disadvantaged Child, 1966. Contbr. articles profl. jours. and encys. Office: 410 S Michigan Av Chicago IL 60605

BECK, JULIAN, dir., scenic designer, actor, producer; b. N.Y.C., May 31, 1925; s. Irbing and Mabel (Blum) B.; student Yale, 1942-43, City Coll., N.Y., 1946- 49; m. Judith Malina, Oct. 30, 1948; 1 son. A founder with wife of Living Theatre Prodns., Inc., 1947, now pres., treas.; designer The Thirteenth God, 1951; producer, designer Doctor Faustus Lights the Lights, 1951; producer, designer, dir. Beyond the Mountains, 1951, An Evening of Bohemian Theatre, 1952, Faustina, 1952, The Heroes (also acted in) and Ubi Roi, 1952; designer R.U.R., 1953, Ticklish Acrobat. 1954: producer, designer, actor The Age of Anxiety, 1954, The Spook Sonata, 1954, Orpheus' 1954. The Idiot King, 1954, Tonight We Improvise, 1954, Phaedra, 1955; dir. The Young Disciple, 1955; designer operas Voices for a Mirror and the

Curious Fern, 1957, Dances Before a Wall, 1958; designer, producer, dir. Many Loves, 1959, The Cave at Machpelah, 1959. The Connection, 1959, Tonight We Improvise (also acted in), 1959, Madrigal of War, 1959, triple bill All that Fall, Embers and Act Without Words, I and III, 1959, triple bill Bertha, Theory of Comedy, Love's Labour, 1959, The Devil's Mother, 1960, Faust Foutu, 1960, double bill The Marrying Maiden and The Women of Trachis, 1960, triple bill The Herne's Egg, Purgatory and A Full Moon in March, 1960, The Election (also acted in), 1960, In The Jungle of the Cities, 1960, The Mountain Giants, 1961, The Apple (also acted in). 1961, Man is Man, 1962, The Brig, 1963; European tour of some prodns., 1961, 62. Living Theatre has received Lola D'Annunzio award, 1959, Page One award Newspaper Guild N.Y., 1960, Obie award. 1960. 64, Brandeis U. Creative Arts Award, 1961, Grand Prix de Theatre de Nations, Paris, 1961, medallion Paris Theatre Critics Circle, 1961, Prix de 'lUniversite. Paris, 1961, New Eng. Theatre Conf. award. 1962. Mem. Actors quity Assn., N.Y. Com. for Gen Strike for Peace. Address: 789 West End Av New York City NY 10225

BECK, LEON L., business exec.; b. 1926; grad. U. So. Cal.; married. Formerly partner Candiotty & Beck; treas. Daylin Inc., Beverly Hills, Cal., 1968—, now also sr. v.p. C.P.A., Cal. Office: 9606 Santa Monica Blvd Beverly Hills CA 90210*

BECK, LESTER E., educator; B.S. in Elec. Engring., Pa. State U., 1926; M.S. in Elec. Engring., Purdue U., 1932. Now prof. elec. engring. Purdue U. Registered profl. engr. Address: Dept Elec Engring Purdue U Lafayette IN 47907*

BECK, LEWIS WHITE, educator; b. Griffin, Ga., Sept. 26, 1913; s. Erasmus Williams and Inez Deane (Hammond) B.; A.B., Emory U., 1934; M.A., Duke U., 1935, Ph.D., 1937; fellow U. Berlin, 1937-38; m. Caroline Hagy, Sept. 5, 1939; children—Brandon Hagy, Hamilton Hammond Hagy. Instr. philosophy Emory U., 1938-41; asst. prof. philosophy U. Del., 1941-46, asso. prof., 1946- 48; prof. philosophy Lehigh University, 1948-49, prof. philosophy University of Rochester, N.Y., 1949—, chairman department of philosophy, 1949-66, Burbank prof. intellectual and moral philosophy, 1962—, associate dean of the Graduate School, 1952-56, dean Grad. Sch., 1956-57; vis. prof. philosophy George Washington U., 1947, 48, Columbia, 1951, U. Minn., 1953, U. Western Ontario, 1967-68, Sir George Williams University, 1969. Bd. dirs. Am. Council Learned Socs. Rosenwald fellow, 1937-38; Guggenheim fellow, 1957-58. Fellow Am. Council Learned Socs., 1964-65. Fellow Am. Acad. Arts and Scis.; mem. Council Nat. Endowment for Humanities, Am. Assn. U. Profs. (mem. council 1954-56), Am. Philos. Assn. (chmn. com. information service 1946-50, exec. com. 1949-51, v.p. Eastern division 1964, pres. 1971, chmn. com. on publication 1964-68, del. American Council of Learned Societes, 1968-70, chmn. com. on lectures, research and publ. 1969-70), Phi Beta Kappa. Author: Philosophic Inquiry, 1952, 2d edit., 1968 Six Secular Philosophers, 1960; Commentary on Kant's Critique of Practical Reason, 1960; Studies in the Philosophy of Kant, 1965; Early German Philosophy, 1969. Editor: Philosophy of the Eighteenth Century, 1965; The Macmillan Sources in Philosophy, 1965; Kant Studies Today, 1969; Proceedings of The Third International Kant Congress, 1971. Member of the bd. editors Kantstudien, 1954—, The Monist, 1962—, Encyclopedia of Philosophy, 1962-67, American Philosophical Quar., 1964-68. Translator, editor Kant's Critique of Practical Reason and Other Writings in Moral Philosophy, 1949, other Kant works. Contbr. articles profl. jours. Home: 110 Highland Parkway Rochester 20 NY

BECK, LLOYD, educator; b. Chatham, Ont., Can., Nov. 1, 1922; s. Isaac P. and May (Moore) B.; B.Sc., U. Western Ont., 1948, M.Sc., 1950, Ph.D., 1953; m. Dorothy Rosamond Sweet, Aug. 26, 1950; children—Joan Marie, John Warren, Barbara Jean, Catherine Anne. Came to U.S., 1953. Research asso. pharmacology U. Mich., 1953-54, instr., 1954-58, asst. prof., 1958-63, asso. prof., 1963-67, prof., 1967-69; prof., chmn. dept. pharmacology U. N.M., 1969—. Mem. exec. com. Gov. N.M. Drug Abuse Adv. Com., 1969-70. Served with R.C.A.F., 1944, Canadian Army, 1945. Mem. Council High Blood Pressure Research, Am. Heart Assn., Internat. Soc. Biochem. Pharmacology, Am. Soc. Pharmacology and Exptl. Therapeutics, Canadian Pharm. Soc. Contbr. articles profl. jours. Home: 7708 Osuna Rd NE Albuquerque NM 87109

BECK, MARGIT, artist; b. Tokay, Hungary; d. Samuel and Johanna (Blau) Beck; student Art Inst. of Oradeamare, Rumania, 1929-32, Art Student League, N.Y.C., 1945-46; m. Sidney Schwartz, Feb. 15, 1935; children—Joan, John. Came to U.S., 1932, naturalized, 1938. Theatrical scenic designer, 1934-36; formerly mem. art faculty Hofstra U.; now mem. art faculty N.Y.U.; exhibited works in one man shows Contemporary Arts, N.Y.C., 1955, 58, 59, San Joquin Mus., Stockton, Cal., 1956, Hofstra Coll., L.I., 1958, Lincoln High Sch., N.Y.C., 1959, Mus. Fine Arts, Greenville, S.C., 1959, Babcock Gallery, N.Y.C., 1962, 64, 66, 68, 71, Phila. Art Alliance, 1968, Mansfield (Pa.) State Coll., 1965; exhibited in group shows Whitney Mus. Ann., Corcoran Biennial, Chgo. Inst. Ann., Pa. Acad. Ann., Bklyn Mus. Internat. W.C. Biennial, Nat. Acad. Design Ann., Butler Inst. Ann., U. Neb. Ann., Springfield (Mass.) Mus., Art U.S.A., Ringling Mus., Davenport (Ia.) Municipal Gallery, Sao Paulo Mus., N.Y. World's Fair, Am. Fedn. Arts Internat. Travelling Exhbns., State Dept. sponsored exhbns., Am. Embassies and museums abroad, and others; represented in permanent collections Peabody Mus., Cambridge, Mass., Speed Mus., Louisville, Morse Mus., Rawlins Coll., Hofstra Coll., Hunter Coll., N.Y.C., Miami U., Oxford, O., Norfolk (Va.) Mus., Glichtenstein Mus., Safaad, Israel, Mansfield (Pa.) State Coll., Whitney Mus., others, also many pvt. collections and pub. bldgs. Recipient Gold medal oil Hofstra Coll., 1954, Purchase prize watercolor, 1955, Silver medal, 1956, Gold medal, 1957; medal of honor Nat. Assn. Women Artists, 1956, watercolor award, 1957, 63, oil award, 1958, 64, Winsor and Newton oil award, 1959, others; MacDowell Found. Residence fellowship, 1957, 59, 60; Walker award oil Audubon Artists, 1965, medal honor, 1968; Henry Ward Ranger Fund Purchase award, N.A.D., 1965; Child Hassam award Am. Acad. Arts and Letters, 1968, 69. Mem. Artists Equity Assn., Audubon Artists (v.p. 1968-71). Am. Soc. Contemporary Artists. Address: 22 Florence St Great Neck NY 11023

BECK, MARTIN LUTHER, architect; b. Budapest, Hungary, Sept. 24, 1900; s. Michael and Theresa (Bodan) B.; came to U.S., 1920, naturalized, 1926; student Royal Inst. Tech., Budapest, 1918-20, Beaux Arts Inst. Design, N.Y.C., 1923-27, Sch. Architecture, Grad. Coll. Princeton (Princeton prize architecture 1927), 1927-28; m. Ruth Dorf, June 16, 1934; 1 dau., Terry Ann (Mrs. Dryden P. Morse). Practice architecture, 1928—; major works include homes, schs., sci. labs., univ. plans and bldgs.; mem. faculty Sch. Architecture, Princeton, 1929-42; exec. officer OSRD, Princeton Sta., 1943-44; dir. planning and supervising architect N.Y.U., 1961-65, cons. architect, 1966—, lectr. Sch. Edn., 1966—. Bd. rev. Nat. Council Archtl. Registration Bds., 1958-61; cons. edn. and world affairs study Nigerian univs., 1963; pres. N.J. State Bd. Architects, 1961-62; chmn. Princeton Borough Planning Bd., 1960-61. Trustee Nat. Inst. Archtl. Education, 1961-67. Fellow A.I.A.; mem. N.J. Soc. Architects (chpt. pres. 1968), Archtl. League N.Y. Council Ednl. Facility Planners. Clubs: Princeton (N.Y.C.); Faculty (N.Y. U.). Home: 30 Westcott Rd Princeton NJ 08540 Office: Washington Sq Center NYU New York City NY 10003

BECK, PAUL ADAMS, metallurgist, educator; b. Budapest, Hungary, Feb. 5, 1908; s. Philip O. and Laura (Bardos) B.; brought to U.S., 1928, naturalized, 1944; M.S., Mich. Coll. Mining and Tech., 1929; M.E. Royal Hungarian U. Tech. Scis., 1931; children—Paul John, Philip Odon. Metallurgist, Am. Smelting & Refining Co., Perth Amboy, New Jersey, 1937-41; chief metallurgist Beryllium Corp., Reading, Pa., 1941-42; supt. metall. lab. Cleveland Graphite Bronze Co., 1942-45; faculty U. of Notre Dame since 1945, prof. metallurgy since 1949, head dept. metallurgy, 1950-51; research prof. phys. metallurgy U. Ill., 1951—. Fellow Metall. Soc. of Am. Institute Mining, Metallurgical and Petroleum Engineers (Mathewson Gold Medal award 1952), Am. Soc. Metals, Am. Phys. Soc. Co-author: The Physics of Powder Metallurgy, 1951; Metal Interfaces, 1952; Recrystallization, Grain Growth and Textures, 1966. Editor: Theory of Alloy Phases, 1956; Electronic Structure and Alloy Chemistry of Transition Elements, 1963; co-editor: Magnetic and Inelastic Scattering of Neutrons by Metals, 1968. Home: PO Box 2130 Station A Champaign IL 61820 Office: Metallurgy Bldg U Ill Urbana IL 61803

BECK, ROBERT ALFRED, univ. dean; b. Boston, Nov. 1, 1920; s. Alfred and Laura Martha (Reissman) B.; B.S., Cornell U., 1942, M.S. in edn., 1952, Ph.D., 1954; m. Mary Kathryn Murray, Nov. 5, 1944; children—Susan Jane, Janice Barbara, Robin Maria. Food technologist, personnel mgr. Quincy Market Cold Storage and Warehouse Co., Boston, 1945-50; mem. faculty Sch. Hotel Adminstrn., Cornell U., 1954—, prof., 1960—, dean, 1961—; vis. lectr. USAF in PTO and ETO, also U.S. Army in Europe. Served to 1st lt., F.A., AUS, 1942-45; ETO. Decorated Purple Heart. Mem. Am. Assn. U. Profs., Phi Kappa Phi, Phi Delta Kappa. Home: 2498 Slaterville Rd Slaterville Springs NY 14881 Office: Statler Hall Cornell Univ Ithaca NY 14850

BECK, ROBERT ARTHUR, ins. co. exec.; b. N.Y.C., Oct. 6, 1925; s. Arthur C. and Alma (Wickware) B.; B.S. summa cum laude, Syracuse U., 1950; m. Frances Theresa Kenny, Aug. 7, 1948; children—Robert Arthur, Arthur Francis, Kathleen Ann; Stephen Duncan, Theresa Frances. Financial analyst Ford Motor Co., Detroit, 1950-51; with Prudential Ins. Co. of Am., 1951—, v.p., Newark, 1965-66, sr. v.p., 1966-70, exec. v.p., 1970—. Trustee Coll. of Ins., N.Y.C.; mem. exec. bd. Christian Bros. Acad. Served as 1st lt., inf., AUS, World War II. Mem. Life Ins. Agy. Mgmt. Assn. (chmn. bd. Hartford), Life Underwriters Tng. Council (trustee), Million Dollar Round Table Found. Bd. Home: 4 Somerset Dr Rumson NJ 07760 Office: Prudential Plaza Newark NJ 07101

BECK, ROBERT GEORGE, mfg. co. exec.; b. Winnipeg, Man., Can., Mar. 30, 1904; s. Arthur and Lucina (Blow) B.; B.Sc. with honours, McGill U., 1927; m. Marian Courtice, Nov. 1, 1933; children—Sybil, Jennifer, Arthur. With Miehle Printing Press and Mfg. Co., Chgo., 1927-30, Direct Control Valve Co., Milw., 1930-31, Dominion Engring. Co. Ltd., Montreal, 1931; with Canadian Industries Ltd., 1931-54, v.p., 1948-54, dir., 1949-54; v.p. DuPont of Can. Ltd., 1954-60, exec. v.p., 1950-65, pres., chief exec. officer, 1965-69, dir., 1954—. Clubs: St. James's, Mount Royal (Montreal). Home: Tandalla Farm RR 1 Inverary Ontario Canada Office: Du Pont of Can Ltd Box 660 Montreal 101 Quebec Canada

BECK, ROBERT NELSON, educator, author; b. Ft. Dodge, Ia., Sept. 27, 1924; s. Victor E. and Elizabeth (Nelson) D.; B.A., Clark U., 1947; A.M., Boston U., 1948, Ph.D., 1950; m. Gladys E. Johnson, Mar. 28, 1942; children—Margaret E. (Mrs. Richard B. Knowlton), JoAnne M. (Mrs. John H. Gottcent), Ronald N. Prof. philosophy Clark U., 1948—, chmn. dept., 1957—, Carnegie intern Yale, 1955-56; prof. philosophy U. So. Cal., 1967-68. Moderator, Town of Leicester, Mass., 1953-67. Trustee Leicester Jr. Coll., 1966-68. Served with AUS, 1943-46. Mem. Am. Philos. Assn., Metaphys. Soc. Am. (sec.-treas. 1965-68), Phi Beta Kappa. Lutheran (exec. bd. New Eng. Synod). Author: The Meaning of Americanism, 1956; Perspectives in Philosophy, 1961; American Ideas, 1963; C.J. Bostrom's Philosophy of Religion, 1962; Perspectives in Social Philosophy, 1967; Ethical Choice, 1970. Founder, editor Idealistic Studies. Home: 25 Brentwood Dr Holden MA 01520 Office: Clark Univ Worcester MA 01610

BECK, ROSEMARIE, painter; b. N.Y.C., July 8, 1924; d. Samuel and Margit (Weisz) Beck; A.B., Oberlin Coll., 1944; student Inst. Fine Arts, N.Y.U., 1944-45, Columbia, 1945, Atelier of Robert Motherwell, 1950; m. Robert Phelps, Sept. 14, 1945; 1 son, Roger. One man shows include Peridot Gallery, N.Y.C., 1953, 55, 56, 59, 60, 63, 65, 66, 68-70, Vassar Coll., 1957, 61, Wesleyan U., Middletown, Conn., 1960, State U. N.Y. at New Paltz, 1962, Zachary Waller Gallery, Los Angeles, 1971, Duke, 1971; exhibited group shows including Chicago Art Institute, 1962, Pa. Acad. Fine Arts, 1954, 66. Whitney Mus., 1955-57, 58, Tate Gallery, London, Eng., 1958, Butler Inst., Indpls., 1962, Kootz Gallery, N.Y.C., 1951, Felix Landau Gallery, Los Angeles, 1962. Tchr., Vassar Coll., 1957-55, 61-62, 63-64, Middlebury (Vt.) Coll., 1958, 60, 63, Queens Coll., 1968—. Grantee Ingram Merrill Found., 1966. Address: 6 E 12th St New York City NY 10003

BECK, SAMUEL JACOB, psychologist; b. Tecuciu, Roumania, July 19, 1896; s. Abraham and Beatrice (Ciora) B.; brought to U.S., 1903; A.B. cum laude, Harvard, 1926 (as of 1916); M.A., Columbia, 1927, Ph.D., 1932; m. Anne Goldman, Sept. 14, 1926; children—James Ciora, Ruth Louise. Fellow psychology Inst. for Child Guidance, N.Y.C., 1927-28; fellow psychiatry Harvard Med. Sch., 1932-33, 35-36, Rockefeller Found., 1933-35; psychologist Jewish Bd. Guardians, 1928-29; sr. resident psychologist Boston Psychopathic Hosp., 1929-32; head psychology lab. Psychosomatic and Psychiat. Inst., Michael Reese Hosp., Chgo., 1936-50, staff asso., 1950—, now dir. emeritus psychology lab.; professorial lectr. depts. psychology, Sch. Medicine, U. Chgo., 1957-64, emeritus, 1964—; v.p. Internat. Congress Mental Health, London, Eng., 1948. Recipient Distinguished Contbn. award, clin. sect. Am. Psychol. Assn., 1961, also 1st Ann. Distinguished Psychologist award, 1969. Fellow Am. Orthopsychiat. Assn. (v.p. 1943- 44, pres. 1948-49); mem. Am. Psychol. Assn. (pres. div. clin. and abnormal psychology 1951-52), Nat. Com. Mental Hygiene (council 1947- 48), Soc. Rorschach Internationale (v.p. 1952—), Soc. for Projective Techniques (pres. 1954-55, first ann. hon. award 1965), Sigma Xi. Democrat. Jewish religion. Clubs: Quadrangle, Harvard. Author: Introduction to the Rorschach Method, 1937; Personality Structure in Schizophrenia, 1938; Rorschach's Test, Vol. 1, 1944, Vol. II, 1945 (rev. 1949), Vol. III, 1952; The Six Schizophrenias, 1952; (with H. B. Molish) From Reflex to Intelligence, 1959; The Rorschach Experiment, 1960; Phychological Processes in the Schizophrenic Adaptation, 1965; also numerous scientific articles. Asso. editor Am. Jour. Orthopsychiatry to 1956, 62-69, mem. editorial bd., until 1971; mem. editorial bd. Zeitschrift for Diagnostische Psychologie und Personlichkeitsforschung (Bern and Stuttgart). Home: 5236 Greenwood Av Chicago IL 60648 Office: Univ of Chgo Chicago IL 60637

BECK, WARREN, prof., author; b. Richmond, Ind.; s. Wilbur H. and Lillian (Kemper) B.; A.B., Earlham Coll., D.Litt. (hon.), 1955; A.M., Columbia; m. Carmen Haberman, July 31, 1930 (div. 1956); 1 son, James Peter. Prof. English, tutor in literary composition, Lawrence U., Appleton, Wis., 1926-68, prof. emeritus, 1968—; interim teaching appts.: U.S. Army Univ., Shrivenham, Eng., 1945, Conn. Coll., summer 1946, Bread Loaf Sch. of English, Middlebury Coll., summers, 1947-55, U. Minn., 1956, U. Colo., 1957; on grant Rockefeller Found. to write fiction, criticism, 1948-49; Ford fellowship, 1952-53; Am. Council of Learned Societies fellow, 1963; staff writers' confs. Midwestern, Bread Loaf, Mo., U. Pitts., U. Colo., Univ. of Notre Dame, Vanderbilt Univ. Am. Council Learned Societies grantee, 1968. Member Phi Beta Kappa. Author: (collections short stories) The Blue Sash, 1941, The First Fish, 1947, The Far Whistle, 1951, The Rest Is Silence, 1963; (novels) Final Score (winner 1945 Friends Am. Writers award), 1944; Pause Under the Sky, 1947, Into Thin Air, 1951, Man in Motion: Faulkner's Trilogy, 1961, Joyce's Dubliners: Substance, Vision, and Art, 1969. Contbr. critical articles and essays, reviewer. Home: 207 N Park Av Appleton WI ☆

BECKEL, CHARLES LEROY, univ. dean; b. Phila., Feb. 7, 1928; s. Samuel Mercer and Katherine (Linskey) B.; B.S., U. Scranton, 1948; Ph.D., Johns Hopkins, 1954; m. Josephine Ann Beck, June 27, 1958; children—Amanda S., Sarah K., Timothy C., Andrea C. Asst. prof. physics Georgetown U., 1953-59, asso. prof., 1959-64; research staff mem. Inst. for Defense Analyses, Arlington, Va., 1964-66; asso. prof. physics U. N.M., 1966-69, prof., 1969—, asst. dean Grad. Sch., 1971—; Fulbright Lectr. U. Peshawar (Pakistan), 1957-58, Cheng Kung U., Tainan, Taiwan, 1963-64; cons. Ballistics Research Lab. Aberdeen Proving Ground, Md., 1955-57, Dikewood Corp., Albuquerque, 1967—, Albuquerque Urban Observatory, 1969—. Pres. Kidney Found. of N.M. Inc., 1968—. Bd. dirs. Nat. Capitol area Nat. Kidney Found., 1965-66. Mem. Am. Phys. Soc., Am. Assn. Physics Tchrs., Sigma Xi. Home: 7212 Dellwood Rd NE Albuquerque NM 87110

BECKENBACH, EDWIN FORD, educator, mathematician; b. Dallas, July 18, 1906; s. Charlie Geiger and Lucy Emma (Richardson) B.; B.A., Rice U., 1928, M.A., 1929, Ph.D., 1931; m. Madelene Shelby Simons, Aug. 30, 1933 (div. June 1960); children—Edwin Simons, Madelene Lenann, Sonya Suzann; m. 2d, Alice Judson Curtiss, June 24, 1960. Nat. research fellow Princeton, Ohio State U., U. Chgo., 1931-33; instr. Rice U., 1933-40; asst. prof. U. Mich., 1940-42; asso. prof. U. Tex., Austin, 1942-45; prof. math. U. Cal. at Los Angeles, 1945—; cons. Rand Corp., Santa Monica, Cal., 1949—. Mem. Inst. for Numerical Analysis, Nat. Bur. Standards, 1948-50, Inst. for Advanced Study, Princeton, 1951-52; vis. scholar Swiss Fed. Inst. Tech., Zurich, Switzerland, 1958-59; mem. Sch. Math. Study Group, NSF, 1958-60. Guggenheim fellow, 1958-59. Fellow A.A.A.S.; mem. Am. Math. Soc., Math. Assn. Am., Soc. for Indsl. and Applied Math., Indian Math. Soc., Societe Mathematique de France, Circolo Mathematico di Palermo, Phi Beta Kappa, Sigma Xi, Pi Mu Epsilon. Author: Construction and Applications of Conformal Maps, 1952; Modern Math. for the Engineer, 1st series, 1956, 2d series, 1961; An Introduction to Inequalities, 1961; Inequalities, 1961; College Algebra, 1964; Modern Introductory Analysis, 1964; Applied Combinatorial Analysis, 1964; Essentials of College Algebra, 1965; Integrated College Algebra and Trigonometry, 1966; Modern School Mathematics, Course 1, 1967, Course 2, 1967, Algebra I, 1965, Algebra 2 and Trigonometry, 1968, Pre-Algebra, 1970; Modern College Algebra and Trigonometry, 1969; Analysis of Elementary Functions, 1970; Intermediate Algebra for College Students, 1971; Modern Analytre Geometry, 1972; Concepts of Communications: Interpersonal, Intrapersonal and Mathematical, 1972. Founder editor Pacific Jour. Math. Contbr. articles profl. jours. Home: 13478 Bayliss Rd Los Angeles CA 90049

BECKENBACH, JOSEPH RILEY, research adminstr.; b. Cleve., May 3, 1918; s. Edward and Jennie S. (Hatch) B.; A.B., Antioch Coll., 1932; M.Sc., Ohio State U., 1933; Ph.D., Rutgers U., 1937; m. Ruth Dickerson, Sept. 12, 1936; children—John E., Susan M. Wehlburg, Joseph Riley, Andrew T. Asso. horticulturist Everglades Expt. Sta., Belle Glade, Fla., 1937-39; horticulturist charge Gulf Coast Expt. Sta., 1939-50; asso. dir. Fla. Agrl. Expt. Stas., 1950-55, dir., 1955-68, dir. emeritus, 1968—. Chmn. Fla. Tech. Com. Fertilizers and Pesticides; chmn. Com. of Nine, U.S. Dept. Agr. Mem. Am. Soc. Hort. Sci., Am. Soc. Plant Physiologists, So. Expt. Sta. Dirs. Assn. (past chmn.), Fla. Hort. Soc. (pres. 1968). Sigma Xi, Gamma Sigma Delta, Phi Epsilon Phi. Unitarian. Rotarian (past pres. Bradenton). Home: 2126 NW 11th Av Gainesville FL 32601

BECKENBAUGH, DON A., mfg. exec.; b. Polo, Ill., Mar. 13, 1910; s. Walter K. and Camilla (Geary) B.; student Moore's Bus. Coll., Racine, Wis., 1927-28, Ind. U. extension, 1933-35; m. Virginia Lloyd, June 21, 1932; children—Sue Ann (Mrs. R. L. Duesler), Judy (Mrs. Jerry Hardman), Robert D. With J. I. Case Co., Racine, 1928-62, v.p. marketing services, 1959-62; pres. equipment div. Young Spring & Wire Corp., 1962-64, gen. mgr. truck and constrn. equipment div., 1964-65; v.p. Paul Hardeman, Inc., Stanton, Cal., 1964-65; asst. to pres. Gar Wood Industries, Inc., Wayne, Mich., 1965-66, became v.p., 1966 (co. merged into G.W. Holding, Inc. 1970). Pres., Rockford (Ill.) YMCA, 1955; v.p. Rockford Meml. Hosp., 1955. Methodist. Home: 16048 Fairlane Dr Livonia MI 48154 Office: 32500 Van Born Rd Wayne MI 48184

BECKENSTEIN, MYRON, journalist; b. Cleve., Mar. 11, 1938; s. Irwin and Rachel (Miller) B.; B.S., Northwestern U., 1959, M.S., 1960; m. Charlotte Hunt, Oct. 17, 1970. Mem. staff Chgo. Daily News, 1959—, editor, editorial writer, 1967—. Served with AUS, 1961-64. Mem. Sigma Delta Chi. Home: 2630 Hampden Ct Chicago IL 60614 Office: 401 N Wabash Av Chicago IL 60611

BECKER, ARTHUR PETER, economist, educator; b. Milw., Apr. 28, 1918; s. Peter Joseph and Theresa (Hanacek) B.; student U. Wis., Milw., 1935-37; B.A., U. Wis., Madison, 1939, M.A., 1940, Ph.D., 1943; m. Bernita Mae Thompson, Nov. 20, 1941; children—Bonita (Mrs. Mathew J. Wielgosz), Jan Peter, Lee Arthur, Nancy, Arthur Earnest, Karen. Instr. econs. U. Conn., 1942-44; instr. econs. U. Kansas City, Mo., summer 1944; prof. econs., chmn. dept. Eastern N.M. U., Portales, 1944-45; prof., chmn. dept. econs. Morningside Coll., Sioux City, Ia., 1945-46; asst. prof. econs. Ohio State U., 1946-48; asso. prof. econs. U. Wis.-Milw., 1948-57, prof., 1957—, chmn. dept. econs., 1948-63; chmn. Com. on Taxation, Resources and Econ. Devel., 1962—. Commr. Redevel. Authority City of Milw., 1963—. Pres. U. Wis.-Milw. Credit Union; bd. dirs. Robert Schalkenbach Found., N.Y.C., Tax Inst. Am. Recipient Research grants U. Wis.-Milw., 1965, Com. Econ. Devel., 1965, Robert Schalkenbach Found., 1969; Fulbright-Hays faculty scholar, 1968. Mem. Nat. Tax Assn. (com. chmn.), Nat. Assn. Housing and Redevel. Ofcls., Am. Econ. Assn., Internat. Assn. Assessing Officers. Co-author, editor: Land and Building Taxes: Their Effect on Economic Development, 1969. Contbr. articles profl. jours. Home: 2612 E Kenwood Blvd Milwaukee WI 53211

BECKER, CHARLES, Jr., life ins. co. exec.; b. Hutchinson, Kan., June 5, 1923; s. Charles Everett and Winifred (Crouch) B.; grad. Hill Sch., Pottstown, Pa., 1941; student Northwestern U., 1941; m. Mary

Elizabeth McLain, June 14, 1952; children—Mary Elizabeth, Charles Everett II, Bruce McLain. Vice pres., dir. Great Am. Life Underwriters, Inc., San Antonio, 1946-62; with Franklin Life Ins. Co., Springfield, Ill., 1946—, v.p., 1953-61, 1st v.p., 1961-64, exec. v.p., 1964—, also mem. bd. dirs., dir. Ill. Nat. Bank, Springfield. Vice chmn. Ill. Spl. Events Comm., 1970—. Served with USAAF, 1943-45. Home: 1900 W Lawrence St Springfield IL 62704 Office: 800 S 6th St Springfield IL 62703

BECKER, CHARLES HENRY, educator; b. Chgo., May 26, 1914; s. Stanley Frank and Katherine (Kwiatkowska) B.; B.S. in Pharmacy, U. Ill., 1937; M.S., U. Fla., 1939, Ph.D., 1940; m. Katherine E. Tomkies, July 27, 1940; children—Nancy K. (Mrs. Carlos Hope), Ann T. From asst. prof. to prof. Sch. Pharmacy, Duquesne U., 1940-47; dir. research Balch Flavor Co., Pitts., 1942-47; mem. faculty U. Fla., 1947—, prof. pharmacy, 1954—, chmn. dept., 1961- -; cons. in field, 1941—. Mem. Am., Fla. pharm. assns., Sigma Xi, Sigma Phi Epsilon, Phi Kappa Phi, Rho Chi, Rho Pi Phi, Kappa Psi. Author, patentee in field. Home: 2235 NW 5th Pl Gainesville FL 32601

BECKER, CHARLES LEE, supermarket exec.; b. Cheyenne, Wyo., Oct. 1, 1919; s. A. L. and Adele (Moussier) B.; student U. Tex.; m. Peggy Friedrich, Dec. 2, 1950; 1 dau., Peggy Lee; 1 stepson, George Karutz. With Handy-Andy, Inc., 1937- -, v.p., 1950-54, pres., chmn. bd., 1964—, also dir.; gen. partner Community Realty Co.; dir. San Antonio Savs. Assn., San Antonio Belt & Terminal Ry. Co., Great So. Life Ins. Co. Trustee Handy-Andy Found. Tex., Handy-Andy Employees Profit Sharing Trust. Served to 1st lt. USAAF, 1941-45. Mem. San Antonio C. of C. (bd. dirs. 1967-69), Tex. Cavaliers, Order of Alamo. Club: San Antonio German. Home: 8715 Starcrest San Antonio TX 78219 Office: 3000 E Houston St San Antonio TX 78206

BECKER, CHARLES STEVE, transp. co. exec.; b. Webster Grove, Mo., Feb. 9, 1921; s. Edwin Dillman and Barbala (Magos) B.; student Ind. Bus. Coll., 1946, Rubicam Sch. Bus., 1947; m. Irene Evelyn Killough, Apr. 28, 1944; 1 dau., Ruth Evelyn. Vice pres. Central Truckaway System, Inc., Louisville, 1947-59; v.p. Jaguar Distbg. Co., Inc., Indpls., 1959-60, Wolfe Distbg. Co., Inc., Tampa, 1960-64; v.p., treas. Nat. City Lines, Inc., Denver, 1964—; dir., v.p., treas. Beaumont City Lines, Inc., Canton City Lines, Inc., Davenport City Lines Inc., Decatur City Lines, Inc., El Paso City Lines, Inc., El Paso & Juarez Traction Co., Houston, Joliet, Lincoln, Mobile, Montgomery, Spokane, Wichita City Lines, Inc., Southwest Wheel & Mfg. Co., Nat. Seating Co., Nat. City Truck Rental Co.; v.p., treas. FWL, Inc., Fort Wayne Leasing Co., Inc.; dir. Janesville Auto Transport Co., Automobile Carriers, Inc., Dealers Transit, Inc. Served with USN, 1942-45. Named Ky. col. Mem. Am. Trucking Assn., Nat. Accounting and Finance Council, Am. Legion, V.F.W., Sons Am. Legion (charter). Home: 3440 70th Dr Lubbock TX 79413

BECKER, CLARENCE FREDERICK, educator; b. Dozey, N.D., Mar. 27, 1920; s. Henry Ludwig and Ermie (Svenningson) B.; B.S., N.D. State U., 1943, M.S., 1949; certificate in meteorology, U. Cal., Los Angeles, 1944; Ph.D., Mich. State U., 1956; m. Irene Harriet Sad, Jan. 10, 1944; children-Bradford Clarence, Rodney Richard. Dist. rep. Food Machinery & Chem. Corp., Lansing, Mich., 1946- 48; asst. prof. agrl. engring. U. Wyo., Laramie, 1949-56, prof., 1957—, chief of party U. Wyo. Team in Afghanistan, 1968-70; cons. FAO of UN, Iran, 1964, 66. Served with USAAF, 1943-46. Mem. Blue Key, Sigma Xi, Phi Kappa Phi, Alpha Zeta, Sigma Tau. Contbr. articles profl. jours. Home: 2010 Thronburg Dr Laramie WY 82070

BECKER, DONALD EUGENE, Sr., educator; b. Delavan, Ill., Feb. 2, 1923; s. George Edwin and Esther (Peters) B.; B.S., U. Ill., 1945, M.S., 1947; Ph.D., Cornell U., 1949; m. Elsie Jo Hendrickson, Dec. 28, 1949; children—Esther Adeline, Phyllis Elsie, Donald Eugene, William Edwin, Beth Ann. Asst., U. Ill., 1945-47, Cornell U., 1947-49; asso. prof. nutrition U. Tenn., 1949-50; prof. nutrition U. Ill., 1950—, head dept., 1967—. Chmn. Animal Nutrition Research Council, 1959. Recipient award outstanding nutrition research Am. Feed Mfrs., 1957. Mem. Am. Inst. Nutrition, Am. Soc. Animal Sci., (pres. 1970-71), Poultry Sci. Assn. Editor in chief Jour. Animal Sci., 1966-69. Home: 2209 Combes St Urbana IL 61801

BECKER, EDMUND FRANCIS, Sr., fgn. service officer; b. Evansville, Ind., Nov. 1, 1908; s. Val and Johanna (Niehaus) B.; student Georgetown U., 1928-31; A.B., George Washington U., 1940; grad. Nat. War Coll., 1953; m. Ann Ebbeson, Nov. 25, 1932; children—Edmund Francis, Robert W., Stephan M., Donald R. Various positions govt. agencies, assigned successively U.S. Patent Office, Dept. State, Dept. Commerce, FCA: dir. comml. intelligence div. Dept. Commerce, 1946-56, dep. dir. office trade promotion, 1956-58; comml. attache Am. embassy, Bonn, 1958-61; dir. Office Comml. Services, Dept. Commerce, 1961-62; dir. U.S. Trade Center, Frankfurt, Germany, 1962-65; chief comml. affairs Am. Consulate Gen., Frankfurt, 1965-66; comml. counselor Am. embassy, Bonn, 1966-71. U.S. del. Econ. Com. for Asia and Far East, UN regional commn., Manila, Bangkok; head U.S. Dept Commerce trade mission to Italy, 1954, Syria, 1956; chief U.S. delegation Internat. Conf. Comml. Arbitration, UN, 1958. Served with USMC, 1931-33. Mem. Delta Phi Epsilon. Author articles on fgn. trade. Home: 55 Turmstrasse Bad Godesberg Germany

BECKER, EDWARD D., pub.; b. Balt., May 23, 1901; s. John Lerp and Elizabeth (Toal) B.; A.B., Loyola Coll., Balt., 1923; LL.B., U. Md., 1927; m. Catherine Mary Dolan, July 23, 1938; children—Edward Francis, John Francis. Admitted to Md. bar, 1928; with circulation and bus. depts. Balt. News-Post, 1915-37, bus. mgr., 1934-37; became bus. mgr. Pitts. Sun-Telegraph, also sec. Pitts. Pub. Co., Pitts., 1937, v.p. dir., 1943; asst. pub. Pitts. Sun- Telegraph, 1944, pub., 1945-57; v.p., dir. sta. WCAE, Pitts., 1942-57; pres., dir. Hearst Pub. Co., Inc., 1960; v.p., dir. Hearst Consol. Publs., Inc., 1948; gen. mgr. Los Angeles Examiner, Los Angeles Herald-Express and Hilbro Newspaper Printing Co. div. Hearst Pub. Co., Inc., 1957-66; gen. v.p. Hearst Corp.; asst. gen. mgr. Hearst Newspapers. Club: South Hills Country. Home: 1431 Navahoe Dr Pittsburgh PA 15228 Office: 959 8th Av New York City NY 10019

BECKER, EDWARD ROY, U.S. judge; b. Phila., May 4, 1933; s. Herman A. and Jeannette (Levit) B.; B.A., U. Pa., 1954; LL.B., Yale, 1957; m. Flora Lyman, Aug. 11, 1957; children—James Daniel (dec. 1969), Jonathan Robert, Susan Rose, Charles Lyman. Admitted to Pa. bar, 1957, also all state and fed. cts.; partner Becker, Becker & Fryman, Phila., 1957-70; U.S. dist. judge, 1970—. Asso. gen. counsel Phila. Republican City Com., 1965-70. Bd. dirs. N.E. Community Mental Health Center, 1969—, Phila. chpt. Am. Jewish Com., 1970—. Treas. Pa. Lawyers for Nixon, 1960; candidate Phila. City Council, 1963, Pa. Senate, 1966; mem. exec. com. Phila. Rep. Policy Com., 1965-70. Mem. Am., Pa., Phila. bar assns., Am. Judicature Soc., Phi Beta Kappa. Jewish religion (dir. congregation). Mem. B'nai B'rith. Club: Yale (Phila.). Home: 936 Herbert St Philadelphia PA 19124 Office: US Court House 9th and Chestnut Sts Philadelphia PA 19107

BECKER, ERNEST I., educator, chemist; b. Cleve., Aug. 18, 1918; s. Harry and Esther (Cohen) B.; B.S. in Pharmacy, Western Res. U., 1941. M.S. in Chemistry, 1943, Ph.D., 1946; m. Marion Ferris, Dec. 20, 1947; children—Jonathan David, Kenneth Alan, Mark Edward, Robert Neal, Paula Sarah. From instr. to prof. chemistry Poly. Inst. Bklyn., 1946-65; prof. chemistry, chmn. dept. U. Mass., 1965—; cons. to industry, 1951—. Fellow N.Y. Acad. Scis., mem. Am. Chem. Soc., Chem. Soc. London, Am. Assn. U. Profs., A.A.A.S., Sigma Xi, Phi Lambda Upsilon, Rho Chi. Co-editor: Organometallic Reactions, 1971. Home: 32 Oxford Rd Newton MA 02159 Office: 100 Arlington St Boston MA 02116

BECKER, EUGENE MATTHEW, govt. ofcl., banker; b. St. Paul, Sept. 1, 1930; s. John Joseph and Evelyn (Patterson) B.; B.A., Colgate U., 1952; M.A., U. Chgo., 1953; Fulbright scholar, U. Paris, 1953-54; M.F.A., Princeton, 1958, Ph.D., 1959. Research asst. lectr. Frick Collection, N.Y.C., 1959-60; dir. information municipal securities Investment Bankers Assn. Am., 1960-61; asst. v.p. First Nat. City Bank, N.Y.C., 1962-65; dir. budget N.Y.C., 1966; asst. sec. army (financial mgmt.), Washington, 1967—. Trustee Carnegie Hall Corp., Carnegie Hall Soc., 1966—; v.p., exec. com. Carnegie Hall Corp., 1968—; v.p. Carnegie Hall Soc., 1968—. Served with AUS, 1954-56. Hon. pres. Army Finance Assn., 1967. Mem. Phi Beta Kappa. Clubs: Army and Navy (Washington); Princeton (N.Y.). Home: 2440 Virginia Av NW Washington DC 20037 Office: The Pentagon Washington DC 20310

BECKER, GARY STANLEY, educator; b. Pottsville, Pa., Dec. 2, 1930; s. Louis William and Anna (Siskind) B.; A.B., Princeton, 1951; A.M., U. Chgo., 1953; Ph.D., 1955; m. Doria Slote, Sept. 19, 1954; children—Judith Sarah, Catherine Jean. Asst. prof. econs. U. Chgo., 1955-57; men. faculty Columbia, 1957-70, prof. econs., 1960-70, Arthur Lehman professor of economics, 1968-70; Univ. prof. econs. U. Chgo., 1970—; mem. research staff Nat. Bur. Econs. Research, 1957—; Ford Found. visiting prof. U. of Chgo., 1969-70. Recipient W. S. Woytinsky award U. Mich., 1965, John Bates Clark medal Am. Economic Assn., 1967; Profl. Achievement award University of Chicago, 1968. Fellow Econometric Society. Am. Statis. Assn.; mem. Nat. Acad. Edn. (founding mem.; v.p. 1965-67). Author: The Economics of Discrimination, 1957, 2d edit., 1971; Human Capital, 1964; Human Capital and the Personal Distribution of Income, 1967; Economic Theory, 1971; also numerous articles in profl. jours. Home: 5811 S Dorchester Av Chicago IL 60637 Office: Dept Economics U Chgo Chicago IL 60637

BECKER, GEORGE HENRY, Jr., ret. corp. exec.; b. Orange, N.J., June 6, 1926; s. George Henry and Margaret (Rogge) B.; student Cranwell Prep. Sch., Lenox, Mass., 1940-43; B.S., U.S. Merchant Marine Acad., 1946; B.S. in Fgn. Service, Georgetown U., 1949; Dr. Polit. Sci., Inst. Internat. Studies, U. Geneva, 1952; m. Patricia Anne FitzGerald, Aug. 9, 1950; children—Leslie Anne, Stacey Marie, Margaret Dean. Fgn. service staff officer, 1952-56, press and information officer Am. Consulate, Salzburg, Austria, 1952-55, spl. asst. to pub. affairs officer Am. Embassy, Vienna, 1955-56; cons. U.S. Commn. on Govt. Security, 1956-57; spl. asst. to Sec. Commerce, 1957-60; dep. asst. Sec. Commerce for Internat. Affairs, 1960-61; with Gen. Dynamics Corp., N.Y.C., 1961; organizer, pres. Interser, Inc., internat. trade and investment services, N.Y.C., 1961-64; president Kysor International division Kysor Industrial Corporation, 1964-71, cons., 1971—; vis. prof. Rutgers Grad. Sch. Bus. Adminstrn., Newark, 1971—. Member of National Defense Exec. Res. Served as ensign, USNR, World War II. Mem. U.S. C. of C. Clubs: Navesink Country (Middletown, N.J.); Seabright Lawn Tennis and Cricket; Seabright Beach; Belle Haven Country (Alexandria). Home: Black Point Horseshoe Rumson NJ 07760

BECKER, GEORGE JOSEPH, educator; b. Aberdeen, Wash., Apr. 19, 1908; s. George Joseph and Ella (Fox) B.; B.A., U. Wash., 1929, M.A., 1930, Ph.D., 1937; m. Marion Kelleher, Aug. 25, 1932; children—John, Dennis, Michael. Faculty, Immaculate Heart Coll., Los Angeles, 1934-39, Los Angeles City Coll., 1939-42; translator War Dept., 1942-45; faculty Swarthmore Coll., 1945- 70, chmn. dept. English, 1953-70, Alexander Griswold Cummins prof. English, 1961-70; faculty Western Wash. State Coll., Bellingham, 1970—; Fulbright lectr. Am. lit. and civilization, univs. Bordeaux and Lille, 1956-57; Fulbright lectr. in Am. lit., Pau, summer 1963; Fulbright research grant to Spain, 1963-64. Chmn. selection com. pre-doctoral Fulbright grants to Gt. Britain, 1958. Mem. Modern Lang. Assn., Phi Beta Kappa. Translator Jean-Paul Sartre, Anti-Semite and Jew, 1948; editor translator: Documents of Modern Literary Realism, 1963. Author articles on Am. novelists of social criticism. Editor, translator Paris Under Siege, 1870-1871, 1969; Paris and The Arts 1851-1896, 1971. Home: 2225 Niagara Dr Bellingham WA 98225

BECKER, GEORGE ROTH, security broker; b. LaSalle, Ill., Nov. 17, 1915; s. Godhard T. O. and Eda (Roth) B.; student Phillips Exeter Acad., 1931-33, Milford (Conn.) Prep. Sch., 1933-35, Williams Coll., 1935-36; m. Carol V. Rinehimer, June 28, 1937; children—Richard O., Randall B., George T., Steven R. Clk., Wayne Hummer & Co., Chgo., 1936-42, various positions, 1945-54, partner, 1954—; salesman Bankers Life Ins. Co., Des Moines, Ia., 1942- 44. Bd. govs., mem. and chmn. exec. com. Midwest Stock Exchange, 1965—, chmn. bd. govs., 1972—; bd. dirs. Midwest Stock Exchange Service Corp., 1962-71, chmn. bd., 1964-71; bd. dirs. Midwest Stock Exchange Clearing Corp., 1962-67, chmn. bd., 1963-64; bd. dirs. accounting div. Assn. Stock Exchange Firms, 1964-67. Trustee, Village of Glen Ellyn, Ill., 1953-61, pres., 1957-61. Served with AUS, 1944-45. Club: Glen Oak Country (Glen Ellyn) (bd. dirs. 1961-69, pres. 1966-67). Home: 470 Rain Tree Ct Glen Ellyn IL 60137 Office: 105 W Adams St Chicago IL 60690

BECKER, HARRY J., hosp. ins. cons.; b. Lincoln, Neb., Oct. 3, 1909; s. Harry J. and Julia (Hotaling) B.; A.B., U. Neb., 1933, A.M., 1941; student Columbia, 1940, N.Y. Sch. Social Work, 1937, Yale, 1940; children(by previous marriage)— Harry J., Ruth M., Martha Jane. Spl. asst. to state dir. Kan. Emergency Relief Adminstrn., hdqrs. Topeka, 1935-37; state dir. Neb. State Child Health and Welfare Services, Lincoln, 1937-41; cons. med. care administrn. N.Y. City Dept. Health, 1940-41, USPHS, 1941-42; dir. adminstrv. methods, med. care adminstrn. cons. Fed. Security Agy., Washington, 1942-48; dir. social security dept. United Automobile Workers-C.I.O., Detroit, 1948-57; also dir. Commn. on Financing Hosp. Care; now hosp.-med. program cons.; tchr. hosp. econs. and prepayment plan adminstrn., program in hosp. adminstrn. Northwestern U.; exec. sec. com. on spl. studies N.Y. Acad. Med.; v.p. Nat. Blue Cross Assn., also mem. faculty Sch. Adminstrv. Medicine Columbia, 1957—; prof. community medicine Albert Einstein Medical Coll.; prof. New Sch. for Social Research; cons. Health Services Adminstrn., N.Y.C. Mem. pension research council Wharton School of Finance. Dir. United Automobile Workers-C.I.O. Health Inst.; labor rep. bd. trustees Mich. Hosp. Service (Blue Cross), Mich. Med. Service (Blue Shield); mem. com. pensions 20th Century Fund. Author: Financing Hospital Care in the U.S.; Prepayment and the Community; Financing Care for Non-Wage and Low Income Groups; also contbr. various publs. Editor: Expanding Ambulatory Services, others. Home: Brookfield Center CT 06805 also 445 E 80th St New York City NY 10021 Office: Dept of Community Health Albert Einstein College of Medicine Bronx NY 10461

BECKER, HOWARD S., educator, sociologist; b. Chgo., Apr. 18, 1928; s. Allan S. and Donna (Goldberg) B.; Ph.B., U. Chgo., 1946, A.M., 1949, Ph.D., 1951; m. Nan Harris, June 21, 1949; 1 dau., Alison. Instr., U. Chgo., 1951-53; research fellow U. Ill., 1953-55; research sociologist Community Studies, Inc., Kansas City, Mo., 1955-62; research asso. Stanford, 1963- 65; prof. sociology Northwestern U., 1965—. Mem. Soc. Study Social Problems (pres. 1965-66). Author: Boys in White, 1961; Outsiders, 1963. Editor: The Other Side, 1964. Editor Social Problems, 1961-64. Home: 37 E Schiller Chicago IL 60610 Office: Dept Sociology Northwestern U Evanston IL 60201

BECKER, ISIDORE A., corp. exec.; b. N.Y.C., May 10, 1926; s. Max and Eva (Chester) B.; B.A., Bklyn. Coll., 1949; m. Adele Sandler, Dec. 20, 1947; children—Steven Richard, Carol Ann. Partner, Herbert D. Silver & Co., N.Y.C., 1956-63; vice chmn. bd., financial v.p., chmn. financial com., dir. Rapid-Am. Corp., N.Y.C., 1964- -; chief financial officer, treas., dir. McCrory Corp., N.Y.C., 1964—, vice chmn., 1967-70, vice chmn. exec. com., 1970—; vice chmn. bd., dir. Glen Alden Corp., N.Y.C., 1964- -; chmn. bd., dir. Schenley Industries, Inc., 1968—; dir. North Shore Nat. Bank, Chgo. Vice chmn. Boys Town Jerusalem, Nat. Jewish Hosp., Denver; founder Albert Einstein Coll. Medicine; asso. chmn., bd. govs. Anti Defamation League B'nai B'rith; chmn. bd. trustees Columbia Grammar Sch. Treas. Radip-Am. Found., 1961. Served with USMCR, 1944-46. Home: 215 E 68th St New York City NY 10021 Office: 711 Fifth Av New York City NY 10022

BECKER, JOSEPH, information scientist; b. N.Y.C., Apr. 15, 1923; s. Julius and Bella (Mazer) B.; B.Aero. Engring., Poly. Inst. Bklyn., 1944; M.S. in L.S., Cath. U. Am., 1955; research fellow computer sci., U. Cal. at Los Angeles, 1960; m. Arlene Berlin, Apr. 17, 1945; children—Jane C., Wendy L., William S., Sara E. Library asst. N.Y. Pub. Library, 1939-44; electronic data processing with Fed. Govt., 1946-66; lectr. Cath. U. Am., 1960—; v.p. Interuniv. Communications Council, 1966-70; adj. prof. U. Pitts., 1966-69; now pres. Becker and Hayes, Inc. subsidiary John Wiley and Sons sci. and tech. pub.; cons. in field, 1955—, tech. dir. computerized World's Fair library exhibits. Mem. Nat. Commn. Libraries and Information Sci., 1971—. Served to capt. AUS, 1944-46. Mem. Assn. Computing Machinery, Am. Cybernetics Soc., Am. Soc. Information Sci. (pres. 1969). A.L.A. (pres. information sci. and automation div. 1968). Clubs: Army-Navy, George Town, Cosmos (Washington). Author: (with R. M. Hayes) Information Storage and Retrieval, 1963; Handbook of Data Processing for Libraries, 1970. Editor: Information Sciences Series, 1963—, Data Processing Equipment in Libraries Series, 1964-65. Home: 5805 Marbury Rd Bethesda MD 20034 Office: 6400 Goldsboro Rd Bethesda MD 20034

BECKER, LOFTUS EUGENE, lawyer; b. Buffalo, Apr. 29, 1911; s. Rueben Ezra and Helen Mary (Gilmartin) B.; A.B. magna cum laude, Harvard, 1932, LL.B. magna cum laude, 1936; student U. Vienna, 1932-33; m. Ellen Vander Voort, Dec. 25, 1933; children—Susan B. Hussein, Gretchen E., Loftus Eugene, and Kathleen Elizabeth. Admitted to the Hawaii bar, 1936, also New York State bar, 1940; asso. Anderson, Marx Wrenn & Jenks, Honolulu, T.H., 1936-38, Wright, Gordon, Zachry, Parlin & Cahill, N.Y.C., 1938-42; partner Cahill, Gordon Zachry & Reindel, N.Y.C., 1946-51; mil. advisor delegations Nuremberg War Trials; dep. dir. C.I.A., Washington, 1951-53; Washington partner Cahill, Gordon, Reidnel & Ohl, 1953-56, resident partner European office, 1959-67; legal adviser Dept. of State, 1957-59; partner Cahill, Gordon, Sonnett, Reindel & Ohl, N.Y.C., 1959—. Served U.S. Army, 1942-45. Member American, Fed., D.C., N.Y. State, Hawaii, N.Y.C. bar assns. Clubs: University, Brook, Metropolitan (Washington); Orenta Beach and Yacht. Home: 554 Claflin Av Mamaroneck NY 10543 Office: 80 Pine St New York City NY

BECKER, MAURICE, artist; b. Nizhni Novgorod, now Gorki, Russia, Jan. 4, 1889; s. Isor and Rose (Simonoff) B.; brought to U.S. at age of 3; student Comml. High Sch., N.Y.C., 1 year; studied art with Robt. Henri and Homer Boss, N.Y.C.; m. Dorothy Baldwin, Sept. 28, 1918. Exhibited at Armory Show, 1913; contbg. art editor Masses (mag.), 1913-17; mem. art staff N.Y. Call and N.Y. Tribune, 1915; artist corr., West Indies, for Scripps N.E.A. Syndicate, 1917; painted in Mexico, 1921-23; exhibited with Orozco and Rivera in Mexico, 1922. Exhibited 1-man shows Whitney Studio, 1924, J.B. Neumann Gallery, Delphic Studio, 1930, Dorothy Paris Gallery, 1935, Artists Gallery, 1940, Macbeth Gallery, 1942, 45, A.F.I. Gallery, 1952, Hartert Galleries, 1954, 55, 57, Art of Today Gallery, 1955, Mansfield 1st Nat. Bank (Pa.). Exhibited maj. galleries, museums, U.S., Europe. Retrospective exhbn. oils, water colors and black and white, Berkshire Mus., Pittsfield, Mass., 1948, C.C.C. Gallery, Brighton Beach, N.Y.C.; included Met. Mus. Water Color Show, 1952-53, also in the 53 Contemporaries show Greenwich Gallery, N.Y.C., 1957, Armory Show's 50th Ann., N.Y.C., 1963, art exhbn. commemorating Warsaw Ghetto Uprising and founding State of Israel, N.Y.C., 1963. Represented in N.Y. Hist. Soc., Phila. Hist. Soc., Nicholas Gallery, N.Y.C., Chrysler Mus., Provincetown, Mass., Ringling Mus., Sarasota, Fla., U. Mich., Norfolk Mus. Arts and Scis., Local 65, AFL-CIO (mural), Chapellier Gallery, Bernhardt Crystal Gallery. Recipient Am. Fedn. Arts award, 1950. Mem. Fedn. Modern Painters and Sculptors, An American Group, Artists Equity Assn., Audubon Artists, N.C. Acad. of Arts and Scis. and Professions, N.Y. Hist. Soc. Address: Box 17 Tioga PA 16946 ☆

BECKER, MURRY CHARLES, lawyer, co. exec.; b. Hamilton, Ont., Can., Mar. 10, 1895 (parents Am. citizens); s. Louis and Rachel (Herschler) B.; LL.B., N.Y. U., 1916, LL.D., 1960; m. Ida Verowitz, Dec. 6, 1916; children—Lois A. (Mrs. Samuel B. Lawrence), Alan D. Admitted to N.Y. bar, 1917, since practiced in N.Y.C.; sr. partner Becker, Ross & Stone, 1942—. Gen. counsel, dir. Asso. Products, Inc., Rival Dog Food, Tootsie Roll Industries, Inc.; asso. counsel, dir. Bankers Securities Corp.; v.p., gen. counsel, chmn. bd. Nestle- Le-Mur Co., Citizens Life Ins. Co.; dir. City Stores Co., Colorado Springs Transit Co., Loft Candy Corp., Sterling Nat. Bank & Trust Co. Chmn. bd. N.Y. U. Club, 1968-69; alumni trustee N.Y. U.; bd. dirs., v.p. Bklyn. YMHA. Served as lt. U.S. Army, World War I. Recipient medal of honor for alumni service N.Y.U., 1954. Mem. N.Y.U. Law Alumni Assn. (past pres., dir.), Assn. Bar City N.Y., N.Y. County Lawyers Assn., Am. Bar Assn. Home: 36 E 36th St New York City NY 10016 Office: 41 E 42d St New York City NY 10017

BECKER, NATHAN MAURICE, coll. dean; b. Cin., Jan. 8, 1914; s. Joseph and Fannie (Saxe) B.; A.B., U. Cin., 1935, A.M., 1936, Ph.D., 1938; m. Carolyn R. Strasburger, July 6, 1938; childrenMichael L., Stephen F., Judith S. (Mrs. Harold M. Troper). Taft fellow econs. U. Cin., 1936-37; instr., then asst. prof. U. Toledo, 1937-41; econ. adviser, coordinator information, Bd. Econ. Warfare, State Dept., 1941-47; lectr. Baruch Sch., City Coll. N.Y., 1947- 63; econ. adviser Gen. Staff U.S.-UN Forces, Korea, 1952-53; prof econs. Pace Coll. 1963-, dean Sch. Bus., 1966-; cons. to industry, 1947-. Mem. Am. Econ. Assn., Am. Assn. U. Profs., Tau Kappa Alpha, Pi Sigma Epsilon, Sigma Alpha Mu, Jewish religion. Author: (with others) Towards World Prosperity, 1947; Liquidity and the Dollar, 1963. Home: 44 Overlook Rd West Orange, NJ 07052. Office: 41 Park Row New York City, NY 10038.

BECKER, PAUL ALFRED, educator; b. Jersey City, N.J., Aug. 2, 1932; s. Paul Alfred and Dorothy (Ryer) B.; B.A., Loyola U., 1954, M.A., 1958; Ph.L., West Baden Coll., 1956; S.T.L., Woodstock Coll., 1963; Ph.D., U. Mich., 1968. Instr. Latin, English, Am. history St. Peter's Prep Sch., Jersey City, 1956-59; instr. edn. U. Mich., 1966; adj. asso. prof. urban studies St. Peter's Coll., 1968-70, dean Coll. Arts and Scis. day session, 1967-68, acad. dean, 1968—, dean Coll. Arts and Scis., Sch. Bus. Adminstrn., 1968—. Mem. Am. Conf. Acad. Deans, Eastern Assn. Coll. Deans and Advisers Students, Am. Assn. Higher Edn., Delta Sigma Pi. Address: St Peter's Coll 2641 Kennedy Blvd Jersey City NJ 07306

BECKER, RALPH ELIHU, lawyer; b. N.Y.C., Jan. 29, 1907; s. Max Joseph and Rose (Becker) B.; LL.B., St. John's U., 1928; m. Ann Marie Watters; children—William Watters, Donald Lee, Pamela Rose, Ralph Elihu. Admitted to N.Y. bar, 1929, D.C. bar, 1949; practice in Washington, 1948—. Gen. counsel, trustee John F. Kennedy Center for Performing Arts, 1958—; gen. counsel Am. Thrift Assembly, 1957—, Met. Washington Bd. of Trade, 1964—; gen. counsel, sec. Albert Schweitzer Fund, 1955; gen. counsel, dir. Reconstrn. & Devel. Corp. D.C., Save a Voice Found., Nat. Capital Area Found.; gen. counsel, trustee Belford Towers Found.; gen. counsel, adv. com. Filene Center at Wolf Trap Farm Park for Performing Arts, Vienna, Va., minority counsel privileges and election com. U.S. Senate, 1951; participant workshops legal problems atomic energy U. Mich., 1956; del. drafting com. World Sugar Conf., Geneva, Switzerland, 1958. Treas., D.C. chpt. Am. Nat. Theater Acad.; mem. Arctic Expdn. for polar bears Washington Zoo, 1962, Antarctic-S. Pole Operation Deepfreeze, 1963; chmn. arrangements com. Lincoln Inaugural Centennial Com., 1961, 65. Nat. chmn. Young Republicans, 1946-49; mem. Rep. Nat. Exec. Com., 1948—; mem. exec. com. Rep. Nat. Com., 1958-59; mem. Pres.'s Inaugural Com., 1953, 57, 69. Bd. dirs. Friends of Nat. Zoo, Inst. Contemporary Arts. Donor collection polit. American to Smithsonian Instn., 1960, Dartmouth, St. Albans Sch., L.B.J. Library-U. Tex., Austin. Served to capt. AUS, 1942-45; ETO. Decorated Bronze Star medal (U.S.); chevalier Legion of Honor, Croix de Guerre with palm (France); Belgian Fourragere; chevalier, officer So. Cross of Brazil; Order Homayoun, Order of Taj (Iran); Knight's Cross, Order of Dannebrog (Denmark); Gt. Cross for Meritorious Services to Austrian Republic; Antarctic Service medal; honored by OAS, 1968. Presdl. appt. rank spl. ambassador Independence Ceremonies Switzerland, 1965. Fellow Corcoran Gallery Art, Aspen Inst. Humanistic Studies; mem. Am. (mem. com. on presdl. inability, legislation, pensions and retirement, space laws coms., del. Internat. Bar Assn. com., meeting Monte Carlo 1954, Oslo, 1956, chmn. Vienna post conv. Am. Bar Assn. meeting London 1957), D.C., N.Y. State, Internat., Fed., Inter-Am. bar assns., Fedn. Ins. Counsel (v.p. 1958, sec.-treas. 1956), Am. Law Inst., Fgn. Law Assn., Judge Adv. Gen. Assn., Soc. Internat. Law, Am. Judicature Soc., Am. Legion, Jud. Conf. D.C., Am. Soc. French Legion of Honor, Am. Fedn. Arts, Am. Polit. Items Collectors Assn., Nat. Trust Historic Preservation, Manuscript Soc., Co. Mil. Historians, Am. Inst. Aeros. and Astronautics, 30th Inf. Div. Assn. (pres. 1958), U.S. C. of C. (pub. affairs com.), Smithsonian Assos., Brazilian-Am. Cultural Inst., U.S. Capitol Hist. Soc. (dir.), N.Y. State Soc. (pres. 1963-64), Iran-Am. Soc. (pres.), Soc. More Beautiful Nat. Capital (trustee), Arctic Polar Inst. (hon.). Republican. Mason (32, Shriner), Elk (past exalted ruler, past dist. dep.). Clubs: National Press, Capitol Hill, International of Washington, National Lawyers, Explorers; City Tavern, Washington Athletic. Author numerous booklets, articles. Home: 2916 32d St NW Washington, DC 20008. Office: 1819 H St NW Washington DC 20006

BECKER, RALPH SHERMAN, educator; b. Benton Harbor, Mich., Mar. 14, 1925; s. Ralph S. and Rose Mary (Koranda) B.; B.S., U. Vt., 1949; M.S., U. N.H., 1951; grad. student Mass. Inst. Tech., 1950-52; Ph.D., Fla. State U., 1955; m. JoAnn Cowles, June 7, 1952; children—Mark K., Sherryl D., Janet C., Scott M. Mem. faculty U. Houston, 1955, prof. chemistry, 1963—, chmn. dept., 1961-66; Fulbright vis. prof. U. Barcelona (Spain), 1962-63; vis. lectr. Weizmann Inst. Sci., Israel, 1963. Scientific cons. in field. Served with USAAF, 1943-45. Decorated Air medal. Mem. A.A.A.S., Am. Chem. Soc., Am. Phys. Soc., Sigma Xi, Alpha Chi Sigma, Phi Kappa Phi, Phi Delta Theta. Mason. Author articles, books, chpts. in books. Home: 518 Knipp Rd Houston TX 77024

BECKER, RAYMOND CARL, former assn. exec.; b. Worcester, Mass., Oct. 20, 1906; s. Carl Theiphillus and Alma Pauline (Johnson) B.; A.B., Clark U., 1928; student Johns Hopkins, 1930-31, 33-34; m. Elizabeth Wellshear, July 17, 1961. Bus. mgr. 16th Internat. Geol. Congress, Washington, 1932-33; geologist Soil Erosion Service, Washington, 1934, Union Packing Co., Shreveport, La., 1935-44; with U.S. Geol. Survey, 1944-62, tech. adviser to dir. Geol. Survey Indonesia, 1956-57, div. geologist, geol. div. Denver Fed. Center, 1950- 62; exec. sec. Geol. Soc. Am., N.Y.C., 1965-71. Chmn. subcom. Gulf Coast, Natural Gas and Condensate Res., 1943-44. Home: 850 Willowbrook Rd Boulder CO 80302

BECKER, REX LOUIS, architect; b. St. Louis, May 20, 1913; s. Louis Henry and Elsie (Schroeder) B.; B.Arch., Washington U., St. Louis, 1934, M.Arch., 1935; m. Ada Sylva Schmidt, Nov. 20, 1937; children—Susan (Mrs. Robert L. Barley), Kathryn (Mrs. Russell Kisling), Rex Louis, Roger G. With Johnson & Maack, architects, St. Louis, 1935-42; employee C.E., U.S. Army, 1942-45; partner Froese, Maack & Becker, architects, St. Louis, 1946—. Pres. Council Lutheran Chs. Greater St. Louis, 1960-61. Fellow A.I.A. (president St. Louis 1956, regional dir. 1966-69, treasurer, 1969- -). also Missouri Assn. Registered Architects (pres. 1955), Guild Religious Architecture, Scarab. Clubs: Missouri Athletic, Engineers (St. Louis). Works include: Luthern Hosp., St. Louis; Civil Engring. Bldg., U. Mo. Rolla. Home: 9 Wakefield St Louis MO 63124 Office: 705 Olive St St Louis MO 63101

BECKER, ROBERT A., advt. exec.; b. Mar. 3, 1920; s. William and Eva (Kats) B.; B.S. in Marketing, N.Y.U., 1941; B.S. in Pharmacy, L.I.U., 1949; m. Pearl Pehr, Aug. 22, 1948; 1 son, David Jonathan. Copywriter, Plough Inc., Memphis, 1940-42, Murray Breese Assos., N.Y.C., 1944-48; copywriter, product mgr. E.R. Squibb & Sons, N.Y.C., 1949-52, profl. adv. mgr., 1955-57; advt. dir. Nepera Pharm. Co., Yonkers, N.Y., 1953-54; v.p. Burdick & Becker Inc., N.Y.C., 1957-61; pres. Robert A. Becker, Inc., N.Y.C., 1961—, D. J. Publs., Inc., 1962—. Hosp. Publs., Inc., 1963—, RAB Publs., Inc., 1936—. Mem. A.A.A.S., N.Y. Acad. Sci., Med. Writers Assn. Club: Nat. Arts. Home: 4 E 66th St New York City NY 10021 Office: 299 Park Av New York City NY 10017

BECKER, SAMUEL LEO, educator; b. Quincy, Ill., Jan. 5, 1923; s. Nathan and Rose (Dicker) B.; B.A., U. Ia., 1947, M.A., 1949, Ph.D., 1953; postgrad. Columbia, 1958- 59; m. Ruth Henrietta Salzmann, June 14, 1953; children—Judith Ann, Harold Craig, Anne Louise. Instr., U. Wyo., 1949-50; from instr. to prof. U. Ia., 1950—, chmn. dept. speech and dramatic art, 1968—; vis. prof. U. Wis., 1956; Fulbright prof. U. Nottingham (Eng.), 1963-64. Bd. dirs. Goodwill Industries S.E. Ia. Served with inf. AUS, 1942-45. Decorated Bronze Star. Mass Media fellow Fund for Adult Edn., 1958-59. Mem. Speech Assn. Am. (mem. exec. com., adminstrv. council). Nat. Assn. Ednl. Broadcasters (past dir.), Central States Speech Assn., Nat. Soc. for Study Communication, Am. Ednl. Theatre Assn., Am. Assn. U. Profs., Am. Civil Liberties Union, UN Assn. Author: (with H.C. Harshbarger) Television, 1958; (with others) A Bibliographical Guide to Research in Speech and Dramatic Art, 1963, General Speech Communication, 1971. Editor: Speech Monographs, 1969-71. Contbr. articles profl. jours. Home: 521 W Park Rd Iowa City IA 52240

BECKER, STEPHEN, writer; b. Mt. Vernon, N.Y., Mar. 31, 1927; s. David and Lillian (Kevitz) B.; B.A., Harvard, 1947; student Yenching U. (Peking, China), 1947-48; m. Mary Elizabeth Freeburg, Dec. 24, 1947; children—Keir, Julia, David. Free-lance writer, 1948—; tchr. Tsing Hua U., Peking, China, 1947-48; faculty Brandeis U., 1951-52. Paul Harris Found. fellow, 1947-48; Guggenheim fellow, 1954. Author: The Season of the Stranger, 1951; Shanghai Incident, 1955; Juice, 1959; Comic Art in America, 1959; Marshall Field III, 1964; A Covenant with Death, 1965; The Outcasts, 1967; When the War Is Over, 1969. Home: Katonah NY 10536

BECKER, WESLEY CLEMENCE, educator; b. Rochester, N.Y., Mar. 17, 1928; s. William Henry and Alcey (Cole) B.; A.B., Stanford, 1951, M.A., 1953, Ph.D., 1955; m. Barbara Ann Beckel, June 15, 1950 (div. Sept. 1968); children—Jill, Jeffrey, Linda, James; m. 2d, Janis Lynn Wetherell, Oct. 14, 1969; 1 dau., Karen. Instr., U. Ill., Urbana, 1955-56, asst. prof., 1956-60, asso. prof., 1960-63, prof., 1963- 70; prof. U. Ore., Eugene, 1970—; cons. U.S. Office Edn., 1968—. Served with AUS, 1946-49. Mem. Am. Psychol. Assn., Am. Ednl. Research Assn., Phi Beta Kappa, Sigma Xi. Research in behavior modification, edn. of disadvantaged children. Home: Route 3 Box 379 Eugene OR 97405

BECKER, WILLIAM ALBERT army officer; b. Kaufman, Tex., Apr. 2, 1919; s. George and Florence (Nash) B.; B.S., Tex. A. and M. Coll., 1941; postgrad. F.A. Sch., 1941, Command and Gen. Staff Coll., 1952-53, Army War Coll., 1956-57, Army Lang. Sch., 1958-59; m. Frances Louise Carlyle, Dec. 2, 1949; children-William George, Anne Ellen, Christopher Carlyle, Kimberly. Commd. 2d lt. U.S. Army, 1941, advanced through grades to maj. gen., 1968; battery officer, F.A. Bn. staff officer, bn. comdr. 1st Cav. Div., Ft. Bliss, Tex. and S.W. PTO, 1941-46; instr. tactics Tex. A. and M. Coll., 1946-49; F.A. adviser to Army of Venezuela, 1949-52; staff officer Dept. Army, Washington, 1953-56; U.S. Army attache to Yugoslavia, 1959-61; exec. officer 2d Inf. Div. Arty., Ft. Benning, Ga., 1961; dir. combat devel. and doctrine Arty. and Missile Sch., 1961; comdg. officer Combat Devel. Command Arty. Agy., 1962-63; comdg. officer 1st F.A. Brigade, Ft. Sill, Okla., 1963-64; comdg. officer 11th Air Assault Div. Arty., redesignated 1st Cav. Div. Arty. (Airmobile), 1964- 66, and asst. div. comdr. (in Vietnam), 1966-67; dep. dir. research and labs. U.S. Army Materiel Command, Washington, 1967-68; dep. comdg. gen., chief of staff U.S. Army Combat Devel. Command, Ft. Belvoir, Va., 1968; chief legislative liaison Dept. Army, Washington, 1968—. Vice pres., bd. govs. United Services Benefit Assn.; bd. govs. U.S. Pony Clubs. Decorated D.S.M., Legion of Merit with three oak leaf clusters, Bronze Star medal with oak leaf cluster, Air medal with ten oak leaf clusters, Venezuela Army Cross, Republic of Vietnam Gallantry Cross with palm, with silver star and bronze star. Mem. Assn. U.S. Army, 1st Cav. Div. assn. (v.p., trustee 1st Cav. Div. Found.), Assn. Former Students Tex. A. and M. U. Methodist. Mason. Club: National Capital Texas A. and M. Home: Route 1 Kaufman TX 75142 Office: The Pentagon Washington DC 20310

BECKER, WILLIAM HENRY, judge; b. Brookhaven, Miss., Aug. 26, 1909; s. William Henry and Verna (Lilly) B. student La. State U., 1927-28; LL.B., Mo. U., 1932; m. Geneva Moreton, June 9, 1932; children—Frances (Mrs. Robert A. Mills), Patricia (Mrs. Richard H. Hawkins), Nancy (Mrs. George Lemual Hewes), Geneva (Mrs. Edwin J. Jacks), William Henry III. Admitted to Miss. bar, 1930, Mo. bar, 1932, U.S. Supreme Ct., 1937; asso. Clark & Becker, Columbia, Mo., 1932-36, mem. firm, 1936-61; judge, now chief judge U.S. Dist. Ct. Western Mo., 1961—. Counsel to Gov. Lloyd Stark in Kansas City Criminal Investigation, 1938-39; spl. asst. to dir. Econ. Stblzn., 1945-46; spl. commr. Mo. Supreme Ct., 1954-58; spl. counsel Mo. Ins. Dept., 1936-44; chmn. Mo. Supreme Court Com. Drafting Rules of Civil Procedure for Mo., 1952-59, vice chmn. coordinating com. for multiple litigation, 1967-68; mem. jud. panel on multidist. litigation jud. Conf. U.S., 1968—; faculty Seminars for New U.S. Dist. judges, 1968—. Served to lt. (j.g.) USNR, 1944-45. Mem. Am. Bar Assn., Am. Bar Found., Am. Judicature Soc., Mo. Bar, Am. Coll. Trial Lawyers, Am. Coll. Probate Counsel, Order of Coif. Home: 1026 W 63rd St Kansas City MO 64113 Office: US Courthouse Kansas City MO 64106

BECKERMAN, BERNARD, educator; b. N.Y.C., Sept. 24, 1921; s. Morris and Elizabeth (Scheftel) B.; B.S.S., Coll. city N.Y., 1942; M.F.A., Yale, 1943; Ph.D., Columbia, 1956; m. Gloria Brim, Aug. 21, 1940; children—Jonathan, Michael. Mem. faculty Hofstra Coll., 1947-65, organizer, dir. Annual Hofstra Shakespeare Festival, 1950-64, chmn. dept. drama and speech, 1957-65; mem. faculty Columbia, 1957-60, 65—, prof., chmn. dept. theatre arts, 1965—; Fulbright lectr. U. Tel-Aviv (Israel), 1960-61. Bd. dirs. L.I. Arts Center, 1963-64. Served with inf. AUS, 1943-45; ETO. Decorated Bronze Star; recipient 7th Annual award Am. Shakespeare Festival Theatre and Acad., 1962. Mem. L.I. Speech Assn. (v.p. 1953-54). N.Y. Dist. Theatre Conf. (pres. 1961-62), ANTA (bd. dirs. 1963-68), Am. Ednl. Theatre Assn., Am. Soc. Theatre Research, Nat. Theatre Conf. Club: Columbia (N.Y.C.). Author: Shakespeare at the Globe, 1599-1609, 1962; Dynamics of Drama, 1970; also articles, revs. Home: 27 W 67th St New York City NY 10023 Office: 632 W 125th St New York City NY 10027

BECKERS, WILLIAM KURT, investment banker; b. Elberfeld, Germany, May 2, 1900; s. William Gerard and Antoinette (Pothen) B.; came to U.S., 1902, naturalized, 1914; B.A., Yale, 1924; student Columbia Grad. Sch. Econs., 1925; m. Annadel Kelly, Apr. 20, 1929; children—Antoinette (Mrs. Robert W. Macnamara), Annadel (Mrs. James Timpson). Sr. v.p. Spencer Trask & Co., Inc., N.Y.C., 1929—. Bd. govs. N.Y. Stock Exchange, 1938-42, 44-47, vice chmn. bd., 1947-50. Dir. Church & Dwight Co., Inc., W & T Investing Co., Inc. Rep. Episcopalian. Clubs: Yale, University, Stock Exchange Lunch, Recess Maidstone, Devon Yacht. Home: E Dune Lane East Hampton NY 11937 Office: 60 Broad St New York City NY 10004

BECKET, MACDONALD GEORGE, architect; b. Seattle, Nov. 2, 1928; s. Hugh M. and Muriel N. Becket; student San Jose (Cal.) Coll., 1947, U. Wash., 1948; B.A. in Architecture, U. So. Cal., 1952, certificate bus. economics, 1956; m. Marjorie Lesnett, Sept. 25, 1949; children—MacDonald George, Thomas Lane, Michael Newcomb, David Malcolm. With Welton Becket and Assos., Los Angeles, 1948—, pres., 1969—; coordinating architect master planning Century City, Los Angeles, 1959-65; projects include Xerox Sq., Rochester, N.Y., 1969, Mut. Benefit Life bldg., San Francisco, 1969, Equitable Life bldg., Los Angeles, 1969, Aetna Life bldg., San Francisco, 1969, Manila (P.I.) Hilton Hotel, 1968, Center Plaza, Boston, 1969, Intercontinental Hotel, Auckland, New Zealand, 1968, Gulf Life Tower, Jacksonville, Fla., 1967, Hartford (Conn.) Nat. Bank, 1967, Willowbrook Shopping Center, Wayne Twp., N.J., 1969. Mem. A.I.A. Office: 10000 Santa Monica Blvd Los Angeles CA 90045

BECKETT, JOHN ANGUS, educator; b. Portland, Ore., Apr. 27, 1916; s. John Wallace and Agnes Peacock (Scott) B.; B.S., U. Ore., 1949; M.B.A., Harvard, 1946; m. Elizabeth Ann DeBusk, June 15, 1940; children—Ann Meredith (now Mrs. Martin S. Wasserman), Kathleen Scott, John Thomas. Assistant prof. bus. adminsr. Alfred P. Sloan Sch. Indsl. Mgmt., Mass. Inst. Tech., 1946-52; cons. McKinsey & Co., San Francisco, 1952-54; treas. Spreckels Sugar Co., also Spreckels Companies, Inc., San Francisco, 1954-56; prin., regional dir. mgmt. services Arthur Young & Co., Chgo., 1956-59; asst. dir. Bur. of Budget, 1959-61; adminstrv. mgr. Smith, Barney & Co., 1961- 62; Forbes prof. mgmt. U. N.H., Durham, 1962—; vis. prof. bus. policies Sch. Bus., U. Chgo., 1967; vis. prof. Grad. Sch. Bus., Columbia, 1968, 70, Grad. School of Business, U. Washington, 1969. Dir., Dalton Foundries, Inc., Warsaw, Ind.; cons. to govt. and industrial organizations. Rep. to gen. ct. (legislature) N.H., 1970-72. Mem. bd. dirs. No. Cal.-Nev. Council Chs., 1952-54, C.P.A., N.H., Wash. Mass., Ill. Mem. Am. Inst. C.P.A.'s, Financial Execs. Inst., Nat. Assn. Accountants, Armed Forces Mgmt. Assn., Fed. Govt. Accountants Assn., Am. Mgmt. Assn., Am. Assn. U. Profs., Beta Alpha Psi. Conglist. Clubs: Harvard (N.Y.C.); Chicago. Co-author: Accounting: A Management Approach, 1950; author: Management Dynamics: The New Synthesis, 1970. Editor: Industrial Accountants Handbook, 1953. Contbr. articles profl. jours. Research on impact of systems on bus. orgn. and mgmt. Home: Mill Pond Rd Durham NH 03824

BECKETT, JOHN RAYMOND, bus. executive; b. San Francisco, Feb. 26, 1918; s. Ernest J. and Hilda (Hansen) B.; A.B., Stanford, 1939, M.A., 1940; m. C. Dian Calkin, Nov. 27, 1947 (dec.); children—Brenda Jean, Belinda Dian; m. 2d, Marjorie D. Abenheim, July 1969. Valuator, Pacific Gas & Electric Co., 1941-42; utility financial analyst Duff & Phelps, 1942-43; utility financial expert SEC, 1943-44; asst. to pres. Seattle Gas Co., 1944-45; investment banker Blyth & Co., San Francisco, 1945-60, v.p., 1955-60, also dir.; pres., dir. Transamerica Corp., 1960-68, chmn. bd., 1968-70, chmn. bd., pres., dir., 1970—; dir. Occidental Life Ins. Co., also dir. various other subsidiary cos. of Transam. Corp., dir. Trans Internat. Airlines, United Artists Corp., Bank of Am. N.Y., Tex. Eastern Transmission Corp. Chmn., State Dept. Adv. Com. Internat. Bus. Problems, 1971. Episcopalian. Clubs: Pacific Union, San Francisco Golf, Bohemian (San Francisco); Cypress Point (Pebble Beach, Cal.); Menlo Circus; California (Los Angeles); Links (N.Y.C.). Home: 45 Prado Secoya Atherton CA 94025 Office: 701 Montgomery St San Francisco CA 94111

BECKETT, PAUL LOUIS, educator; b. Warren County, Ill., Oct. 18, 1913; s. Henry Lewis and Anna Rebecca (Simonson) B.; student U. Ia., 1934; B.A., Monmouth Coll., 1935; M.A., U. Ill., 1938; student La. State U., 1938-39; Ph.D., U. Cal., Los Angeles, 1949; m. Harriett Marie Hamilton, Oct. 19, 1935; children—Paul A. H., Linda K. Teaching and research asst. La. State U., also U. Cal., Los Angeles, 1938-41; exec. sec. Town Hall, Los Angeles, 1941-42; asso. adminstrv. analyst Bur. budget, 1942-43; research technician Haynes Found., Los Angeles, 1943-44, Los Angeles County Bur. Adminstrv. Research, 1944-45; asst. prof. govt., asst. dir. div. govt. research U. N. Mex., 1945-47; asst. prof. pub. adminstrn. Wash. State Univ., 1947- 49, asso. prof., 1949-54 (on leave 1951-53), prof. political sci., 1954- -, chmn. dept. polit. sci., 1956-64; prof. pub. adminstrn., chmn. dept. Am. U. of Beirut, 1951-53; consultant public adminstration Planning Board of Pakistan, 1957. Mem. Am., Western (council 1959-61), Pacific N.W. (council 1955-57, pres. 1957-58) polit. sci. assns., Western Govtl. Research Assn. (council 1959-61), Am. Soc. Pub. Adminstrn. (ed. Nat. Conf. Proc. 1959, comparative adminstrn. group), Soc. Internat. Devel., Pub. Personnel Assn., Am. Civil Liberties Union, Pi Sigma Alpha, Phi Kappa Phi. Editor: Research Studies of the State College of Wash. (Quar.), 1951-55. Bd. editors Western Polit. Quar., 1964-66. Author: From Wilderness to Enabling Act: The Evolution of a State of Washington, 1968; also pamphlets, articles and profl. reports. Home: 1305 Upper Dr Pullman WA 99163

BECKETT, SAMUEL, writer; b. Dublin, Ireland, Apr. 13, 1906; s. William Frank and Mary (Roe) B.; B.A., Trinity Coll., Dublin, 1927, M.A., 1931, D.Litt. (hon.), 1959. Author: (poems) Whoroscope, 1930, Echo's Bones, 1935; (essay) Proust, 1930; (short stories) More Pricks Than Kicks, 1933; (novels) Murphy, 1937, Watt, 1942-45; (novels in French) Molloy, 1946, Malone Dies, 1947, The Unnamable, 1949, How It Is, 1961; (plays in French) Waiting for Godot, 1948, Endgame, 1956; (plays for radio) All That Fall, 1956, Embers, 1958; (plays) Krapp's Last Tape, 1958, Happy Days, 1961; (short stories in French) Texts for Nothing, 1951; Poems in English, 1961; Cascando and Other Short Dramatic Pieces, 1969. Address: care Grove Press 53 E 11th St New York City NY 10003

BECKETT, THEODORE CHARLES, lawyer; b. Boonville, Mo., May 6, 1929; s. Theodore Cooper and Gladys (Watson) B.; B.S., U. Mo., Columbia, 1950, J.D., 1957; m. Daysie Margaret Cornwall, 1950; children-Elizabeth, Theodore Cornwall, Margaret Lynn, William, Anne Marie. Admitted to Mo. bar, 1957, since practiced in Kansas City; mem. firm Morris, Foust, Moudy & Beckett, 1969—. Bd. dirs. Kansas City Civic Ballet. Served to 1st lt. U.S. Army, 1950-53; ETO. Mem. Am., Mo., Kansas City bar assns., Lawyers Assn. Kansas City, Newcomen Soc. N.Am., Order of Coif, Sigma Nu, Phi Alpha Delta. Clubs: Kansas City, Blue Hills Country (Kansas City, Mo.), Home: 11337 Wornall Rd Kansas City MO 64114 Office: 1006 Grand Av Kansas City MO 64106

BECKETT, WHEELER MARTIN ALFRED, conductor-composer; b. San Francisco, Mar. 7, 1898; s. Frederick Arthur and Frances Mason (Bowen) B.; grad. optimus, Grace Ch. (N.Y.) Choir Sch., 1913; student Columbia, 1917-19; B.S., U. Calif., 1921; mem. master class for conductors and pvt. pupil, Felix Weingartner, Basel, Switzerland, 1928-30; m. Jane Wintermute, June 15, 1922. Organist and choirmaster Grace Cathedral, San Francisco, 1921-25; instr. English, Mills Coll., Oakland, 1926; dir. Children's Choral Club, Berkeley, 1924- 30; condr. Young People's Concerts, San Francisco Symphony Orch., 1927-30; guest condr. Berlin (Germany) and Vienna (Austria) philharmonic orchs., Vienna Symphony and Straram (Paris) orchs., 1930; condr. Richmond Symphony Orch., 1932-1936; guest condr. summer concerts Nat. Symphony, Washington, 1936; guest condr. Boston Pops and Esplanade concerts, 1938-47, others; founder, condr. Boston Symphony Youth Concerts, 1938-48; founder, now pres., condr. New York Youth Concerts Assn., Inc., and Wheeler Beckett Orch. and Opera Co. at Philharmonic Hall, Lincoln Center, N.Y.C.; pres. Music Edn. Record Corp., 1957—. Head music cons. WPB, Washington, 1942-43; specialist in music for Dept. State to develop and/or conduct symphony orchs. Japan, Taiwan, S. Vietnam, Philippines, Indonesia, 1959-62. Fellow Internat. Inst. Arts and Letters (life); mem. A.S.C.A.P., Delta Epsilon. Republican. Episcopalian. Composer: incidental music to plays, Asses Ears, 1922, Rajvara, 1924; Cinderella Fantasy, Mystic Trumpeter, (opera) Snow White, Symphony C Minor. Concerto for Organ; ch. music, songs: Dedication to Indonesia, 1960. Author: Music in War Plants; (ednl. albums) The Complete Orchestra and Essential Musical Knowledge. Home: 277 Walnut St Englewood NJ 07631

BECKHAM, CLIFFORD MYRON, entomologist; b. nr. Mobile, Aug. 4, 1915; s. Charles Edward and Cornelia Edith (Campbell) B.; B.S., Auburn U., 1941; M.S., Ohio State U., 1947, Ph.D., 1951; m.

Marie Calderaro, May 30, 1942; children—Linda, Stephen, Bruce. Head dept. entomology Ga. Expt. Sta., Coll. Agr., U. Ga. Expt., 1948—, chmn. div. entomology, 1950—. Served with USAAF, 1942-46. Mem. Entolmol. Soc. Am., Ga. Entomol. Soc. Office: Ga Expt Sta Experiment GA 30212

BECKHAM, WALTER HULL, Jr., lawyer; b. Albany, Ga., Apr. 18, 1920; s. Walter Hull and Clara Octavia (Marshall) B.; A.B., Emory U., 1941; LL.B. cum laude, Harvard, 1948, J.D. cum laude, 1969; m. Ethel Brooks Koger, Mar. 13, 1943; children—Barbara Elaine, Walter Hull III, James Koger. Admitted to Fla. bar, 1949, U.S. Supreme Ct. bar; practiced in Miami, 1949—; asso. prof. law Law Sch., U. Miami, 1948-50; prof., 1967—, dir. Med. Inst. for Attys., Law Center, 1969—; asso. firm Dixon, DeJarnette & Bradford, 1949-50, Nichols, Gaither & Green, 1950-52; partner firm Nichols, Gaither, Green, Fates & Beckham, 1952-62, Nichols, Gaither, Beckham, Colson & Spence, 1962-67; counsel Podhurst & Orseck & Parks, and predecessor firm, 1967—. Treas., dir. Sea View Realty Co.; dir. Fisher Island, Inc. Past pres. Greater Miami YMCA; past mem. Internat. Com., Nat. Councils YMCA's in U.S. and Can.; past pres., mem. bd. dirs. Dade County Crippled Childrens Soc. Served to capt. USNR, 1941-46. Mem. Am. (council ins., negligence and compensation sect., mem. liaison com. to Am. Med. Assn., Dade County bar assns., Fla. Bar, Am. Trial Lawyers Assn. (past chmn. aviation sect.), Am. Judicature Soc., Internat. Acad. Law and Sci., Internat. Acad. Trial Lawyers, Law-Sci. Acad. Am., Phi Beta Kappa, Omicron Delta Kappa, Chi Phi, Phi Alpha Delta. Democrat. Methodist. Clubs: Miami, Kiwanis (Miami); Riviera Country, Century (past pres.) (Coral Gables). Editor: Harvard Law Review, Vol. 61, 1947-48; aviation editor Nat. Assn. Claimants Compensation Attys. Law Jour., 1957—. Home: 4209 Santa Maria St Coral Gables FL 33146 Office: Concord Bldg 66 W Flagler St Miami FL 33130

BECKHART, BENJAMIN HAGGOTT, economist; b. Denver, Nov. 9, 1897; s. William Edmund and Jessica (Haggott) B.; A.B., Princeton U., 1919, M.A., Columbia, 1920, Ph.D., 1925; m. Margaret Good Myers, June 18, 1921; 1 son, Gordon Haggott. Instr. in economics and social instns., Princeton, 1920-21; instr. banking, Columbia, 1921-24, asst. prof., 1924-31, asso. prof., 1931-39, prof., 1939-63. Ednl. supr. N.Y. chpt. Am. Inst. of Banking, 1927-36; sec. bd. trustees Banking Research Fund of Assn. of Reserve City Bankers, 1938-45; dir. research The Chase Nat. Bank, 1939-49, econ. cons., 1949-54; econ. cons. Equitable Life Assurance Soc., 1954-61. Dir. research Am. Assembly's project on inflation, 1951- 52; del. Internat. Credit Conf. Rome, 1951; del. Internat. Conf. Bank Economists, 1947, 50, 53, 56; vis. prof. univs. Melbourne and Sydney, 1957, Australian Adminstrv. Staff Coll., 1960; vis. prof. Kobe U., Japan, 1967. Pres. Dutchess Sr. Citizens Housing Corp., 1968—. Japanese banking research fund named in his honor, 1956. Recipient distinguished citizens' award Denver, 1959. Mem. Am. Finance Assn. (pres. 1948), Conf. Bus. Econ. (chmn. 1953), Am. Assn. U. Profs., Am. Econ. Assn., Phi Beta Kappa, Delta Sigma Rho, Beta Gamma Sigma. Clubs: Men's Faculty (Columbia U.); Nassau (Princeton); Princeton (N.Y.); Amrita (Poughkeepsie). Author: The Discount Policy of the Federal Reserve System, 1924. Co-author: Foreign Banking Systems, 1929. Co-author and editor: The New York Money Market, 4 vols. 1931-32. Editor: Banking Systems, 1954 (trans. into Japanese 2 vols.), 1956, 57, Spanish edit. 1958, Indian edit., 1967. Co-author and editor: Business Loans of American Commercial Banks, 1959. Contbr. profl. jours. Home: 24 Thelberg Rd Poughkeepsie NY 12601

BECKLER, DAVID ZANDER, govt. ofcl., chem. engr.; b. Detroit, June 29, 1918; s. William J. and Thekla (Levy) B.; B.S. in Chem. Engring., U. Rochester, 1939; J.D., George Washington University, 1943; m. Harriet Levy, Aug. 1, 1943; children—Stephen, Paul, Rochelle. Admitted to Washington bar, 1942; patent attorney, Pennie, Davis, Marvin & Edmonds, Washington, 1939-42; tech. aide Fgn. Liaison Office, Office Sci. Research and Development, 1942-44, chief tech. intelligence group, 1945; patent atty. Eastman Kodak Co., Rochester, N.Y., 1946; dep. tech. historian Joint Task Force One (Operation Crossroads), Joint Chiefs of Staff, 1946; chief of the technical intelligence branch Research and Development Board, Office Sec. of Def., 1947-49; mem. internat. sci. policy survey group Dept. of State (on leave from Research and Development Bd.), 1949-50; exec. dir. com. atomic energy Research and Devel. Bd. 1950-52; asst. dir., Office Indsl. Devel., AEC, 1952-53; exec. officer Pres.'s Sci. Adv. Com., 1954- spl. asst. dir. Office Def. Moblzn., 1954-57; asst. to spl. asst. Pres. for sci., technology, 1957-62; asst. to dir. Office Sci. and Tech., Exec. Office Pres., 1962-70, asst. dir., 1970—. Recipient Certificate of Appreciation for services rendered during World War II (War and Navy depts.). Registered patent atty. U.S. Patent Office. Home: 8709 Duvall St Fairfax VA 22030 Office: Exec Office Bldg Washington DC 20506

BECKLEY, DONALD KAUFFMAN, cons.; b. Washington, Mar. 27, 1916; s. Frank Ross and Lila Strock (Kauffman) B.; A.B., Columbia, 1936, M.S., 1937; Ph.D., U. Chgo., 1948; m. Eugenie E. Smith, Nov. 14, 1942. Dept. store work, 1936-39; instr. retailing Rochester (N.Y.) Inst. Tech., 1939-42; prof. retailing and dir. Prince Sch. Retailing, Simmons Coll., Boston, 1946-58; exec. dir. Boston Center for Adult Edn., 1958-62; dir. Devel. Operations and Donor Relations, N.Y.U., 1962-68; cons. Frantzreb & Pray Assos., Inc., 1968—. Served USAAF, 1944-45; staff U.S. Armed Forces Inst., U. Chgo., 1942-43; tchr. naval flight prep. Sch., Monmouth (Ill.) Coll., 1943-44. Author: Merchandising Techniques (with Edwina B. Hogadone), 1942; The Retail Salesperson at Work (with W. B. Logan), 1948; Modern Retailing (with John W. Ernest), 1950; The Retailer (with Wenzil K. Dolva), 1950. Home: 29 Harvard Av Staten Island NY 10301 Office: 60 E 42d St New York City NY 10017

BECKLEY, THOMAS MALLOY, railroad ofcl.; b. Mpls., Mar. 2, 1922; s. Miles E. and Rosemary (Malloy) B.; B.S., Yale, 1942; LL.B., Harvard, 1948; m. Nancy M. Arntsen, 1950; children—Rosemary, Margaret, Nancy, Kathryn. Admitted to Minn. bar, 1948, Mich. bar, 1955; practiced in Mpls., 1948-60; atty. Stinchfield, Mackall, Crounse & Moore, 1948-52; gen. counsel, sec. Duluth, South Shore & Atlantic R.R., Mpls., 1953-60; asst. to pres., sec. Soo Line R.R., Mpls., 1961-68, v.p., sec., 1968—. Served to 1st lt., Adj. Gen. Dept., AUS, 1943-46. Clubs: Athletic, Minikahda (Mpls.). Home: 15 Park Lane Minneapolis MN 55416 Office: Soo Line Bldg Minneapolis MN 55440

BECKMAN, ALFRED ROSS, TV exec.; b. E. Orange, N.J., Sept. 11, 1911; s. Robert R. and Constance I. (Harrison) B.; A.B., Rutgers U., 1933; m. Esther B. Glasson, Feb. 23, 1935; childrenNancy C., Bruce O. Sales positions Rensello Co., N.Y.C., 1933-39; customer relations Pub. Service Electric & Gas Co., Newark, 1939-42; asst. sales service mgr. ABC, 1943-46, sales service mgr., 1946; bus. mgr. radio dept. Buchanan & Co., advt., 1946-47; regional mgr. sta. relations ABC, 1947-50, dir. sales and sta. traffic operations, 1950-52, nat. dir. sta. relations, 1952-57, v.p. charge TV sta. relations, 1957-60, v.p. charge Washington office, 1960-. Member Radio Television Executives Society, also Chi Psi. Clubs: Capitol Hill, Broadcasters, International (Washington); Congressional Country (Bethesda, Md.). Home: 7606 Marbury Rd Bethesda, MD 20034. Office: 1124 Connecticut Av NW Washington, DC 20036.

BECKMAN, ARNOLD ORVILLE, chemist; b. Cullom, Ill., Apr. 10, 1900; s. George W. and Elizabeth E. (Jewkes) B.; B.S., U. Ill., 1922, M.S., 1923; Ph.D., Cal. Inst. Tech., 1928; m. Mabel S. Meinzer, June 10, 1925; children—Gloria Patricia, Arnold Stone. Research asso. Bell Telephone Labs., N.Y.C., 1924-26; chem. staff Cal. Inst. Tech., 1926-39; v.p. Nat. Tech. Lab., Pasadena, 1935- 39, pres., 1939-40; pres. Helipot Corp., 1944-58, Arnold O. Beckman, Inc., S. Pasadena, 1946-58, Beckman Instruments, Inc., Fullerton, 1940- 65, chmn. bd., 1965—; mem. bd. dirs. Continental Airlines, Inc., Security Pacific Nat. Bank, So. Cal. Edison Co., Chmn. bd. trustees System Development Found.; member bd. of trustees Cal. Museum Found., Cal. Inst. Tech. (chmn. board), California Institute Research Foundation. Served as private USMC, 1918-19. Member Stanford Research Inst. Council, Los Angeles C. of C. (dir. 1954-58, pres. 1956), California C. of C. (dir., pres. 1967-68), Nat. Academy of Engineering, National Assn. Mfrs., American Inst. Chemists, Instrument Soc. Am. (pres. 1952), Am. Chem. Soc., A.A.A.S., Sigma Xi, Delta Upsilon, Alpha Chi Sigma, Phi Lambda Upsilon Clubs: Jonathan, California, Newport Harbor Yacht. Author articles in field. Patentee in field. Home: 107 Shorecliff Rd Corona del Mar CA 92625 Office: 2500 Harbor Blvd Fullerton CA 92632

BECKMAN, MILLARD WARREN, investment securities co. exec.; b. Lodi, Cal., Jan. 8, 1926; s. Sherwood W. and Christine (Koenig) B.; student Am. Inst. Banking, also Stockton Jr. Coll., Sacramento Jr. Coll., 1949- 60; m. Lucille Stark, May 23, 1948; children—Bruce, Don, Joan. Founder Beckman & Co., 1954, pres., chmn. bd., 1961—; sec., treas., dir. Insulation Tech., Inc. Home: 135 S Fairmont Av Lodi CA 95240 Office: 212 W Pine St Lodi CA 95240

BECKMAN, NORMAN, govt. ofcl.; b. Bklyn., May 16, 1927; s. William and Jean (Seigerman) B.; B.A., Bklyn. Coll., 1949; M.Pub. Adminstrn., Syracuse U., 1952; Ph.D., Columbia, 1957; m. Harriet Rosenzweig, Jan. 21, 1951; children—Diane, Robin, Amy, Steven. Program mgmt. officer USPHS, Washington, 1952-57; orgn. examiner Bur. of Budget, Washington, 1957-62; asst. dir. Adv. Com. on Intergovernmental Relations, Washington, 1962- 66; dir. Urban Mgmt. Assistance Adminstrn., Dept. Housing and Urban Devel., Washington, 1966-70; dep. dir. Congl. Research Service, Library Congress, Washington, 1970—; prof. George Washington U., Va. Poly. Inst.; mem. dept. urban transp. planning Hwy. Research Bd. Served with USNR, 1945-46. Recipient Louis Brownlow award Am. Soc. Pub. Adminstrn., 1966. Mem. Am. Soc. Pub. Adminstrn., Nat. Acad. Pub. Adminstrn., Am. Inst. Planners (affiliate; mem. editorial adv. bd.). Contbr. articles profl. jours. Home: 6849 Strata St McLean VA 22101 Office: 10 1st St SE Washington DC 20540

BECKMAN, THEODORE N., educator, cons. economist; b. Russia, Sept. 3, 1895; s. Nahum and Pearl (Treistman) B.; B.Sc. in Bus. Adminstrn., Ohio State U., 1922, Ph.D., 1924; m. Esther G. Baker, July 27, 1920 (dec. Sept. 1961); children—Gloria June, Marilyn Adelle, Joanne; m. 2d, Sarah Martin Langue, Mar. 15, 1962. Instr. econs. and sociology Ohio State U., 1921-22, instr. bus. orgn., 1922-24, asst. prof., 1924-27, asst. prof. marketing, 1927-29, asso. prof., 1929-32, prof., 1932-66, prof. emeritus, 1966—. Instr., Columbus chpt. Nat. Inst. Credit of Nat. Assn. Credit Men, 1921-25; dir. wholesale application program Allied Food Com., Louisville, 1929; in charge wholesale census of distbn. Bur. of Census, 1929-32; cons. expert in charge wholesale census of Am. bus., 1933-35; adviser to com. on elimination of waste in distbn. Dept. of Commerce, 1934-36; cons., Atty. Gen.'s Office, State of Fla., 1935; dir. Washington Indsl. Loan Corp., 1931-37; vis. prof. U. Colo., summers 1939-40; cons. Wage and Hour div. U.S. Dept. Labor, 1940, Nat. Def. Adv. Commn., 1940; chief cons. Office Civilian Supply, War Prodn. Bd., 1942; cons. Atty. Gen.'s Office, State of Ohio, 1954-55; served as 2d lt. AUS, World War II. Named Marketing Exec. of Year, Sales and Marketing Execs. Internat., 1962; recipient Distinguished Teaching award Ohio State U., 1962. Fellow Internat. Inst. Arts and Letters; mem. Am. Econ. Assn., Am. Assn. U. Profs., Am. Marketing Assn. (past v.p., past dir., Paul D. Converse award 1959, central Ohio chpt. award 1960), Am. Statis. Assn., Newcomen Soc., Ohio State U. Alumni Assn., Distbn. Research and Edn. Founds. (hon. chmn. 1968—), Beta Gamma Sigma, Tau Delta Phi, Mu Beta Chi. Jewish religion. Clubs: Cosmos (Washington); Winding Hollow Country; Faculty (Columbus). Author: (with W. R. Davidson) Marketing, 8th edit., 1967; (with N.H. Engle and R.D. Buzell) Wholesaling, 3d edit., 1959; (with R.S. Foster) Credits and Collections: Management and Theory, 8th edit., 1969; (with S.F. Otteson) Cases in Credits and Collections, 1949. Contbr. articles to encys. and profl. jours. Spl. cons. G. and C. Merriam Co. on Webster's Dictionaries. Home: 2158 N Parkway Columbus OH

BECKMAN, VERNON EARL, educator; b. Appleton, Wis., June 4, 1915; s. John Frederick and Ella Louise (Hintz) B.; B.A., Lawrence Coll., 1936; M.S., U. Wis., 1949; Ph.D., U. Minn., 1956; m. Alice Lydia Rotzoll, Mar. 23, 1940; children—Barry, Sue, Ronald, Marsha. High sch. tchr., Niagara, Wis., 1937-43, Two Rivers, Wis., 1943-49; mem. faculty Mankato (Minn.) State Coll., 1949—, prof. speech, 1959—, chmn. dept., 1964—. Mem. Central States, Minn. speech assns., Speech Communication Assn. Am., Minn. Assn. Coll. Dept. Chmn. (past pres.). Home: 116 Porter St Mankata MN 56001

BECKMANN, HERBERT W.K., educator; Dipl. Ing., U. Hanover (Germany), 1944, Dr.Ing., 1957. Now prof. mech. engring. Rice U. Address: Dept Mech Engring Rice U Houston TX 77001

BECKMANN, MARTIN JOSEPH, economist, educator; b. Ratingen, Germany, July 5, 1924; s. Josef and Katharina (Linnartz) B.; B.A. in Math., U. Göttingen, 1945-48; Dipl.- Volksw., U. Freiburg, 1948, Dr.rer.pol., 1950; m. Gloria Gronna Rice, Dec. 31, 1956; children—Sybilla, Carl-Josef, Chantal, Gwendolyn. Postdoctoral fellow in econs. U. Chgo., 1950-1951, research asso. Cowles Commn. for Research in Econs., 1951-55; fellow Center for Advanced Study in Behavioral Scis., Stanford, Cal., 1955-56; asst. prof. Cowles Found. for Research in Econs., Yale, 1956-59; asso. prof. dept. econs. Brown U., Providence, prof., 1959—; prof. econometrics, operations research and econs., dir. Inst. Econometrics and Operations and Research, U. Bonn (Germany), 1962-69; prof. applied math. Technische Hochschule, Munich, Germany, 1969—. Cons., Generalverkehrsplan Northrhine-Westfalia, 1965—, transp. dept. GM Research Labs., 1967—. Served with German Army, 1942-45. Fellow Econometric Soc.; mem. Internat. Inst. Statistics, Mont Pelerin Soc., Operations Research Soc. Am., Inst. Mgmt. Scis. (council), Regional Sci. Assn. (founder), Am. Econ. Assn., List Gesellschaft, Verein Für Socialpolitik. Author: (with others) Studies in the Economics of Transportation, 1956; Linear Programming, 1959; Location Theory, 1968; Dynamic Programming of Economic Decisions, 1969; (with H. Künzi) Mathematik für Oekonomen, 1969. Co-editor Ökonometrie und Unternehmensforschung series; Lecture Notes in Mathematical Economics and Operations Research. Contbr. numerous articles to prof. jours. Home: 77 Arlington Av Providence RI 02906 also 8032 Lochham Lochhamerstr 38 Germany Office: Dept of Economics Brown University Providence RI 02912 also Institute for Applied Mathematics and Oekonometrie Technische Hochschule Munich Germany

BECKMAN, MARVIN ROCKNELL, diversified mfg. co. exec.; b. Cin., May 21, 1910; grad. Phillips Acad., Andover, Mass., 1927; B.S., Princeton, 1931; postgrad. Mass. Inst. Tech., 1931-33; m. Jean R. Holland, June 16, 1935; children--Lois A., Andrew M., James. Salesman, Brown Mfg. Co., Boston, 1932-33; jr. engr. Ball Metals Co., Carson City, Nev., 1933-36, engr., 1936-37, sr. engr., 1937-40; project engr. Kingston Engring. Co., Los Angeles, 1940-43; with dept. engring. City of Denver, 1946-50, dep. head, 1950-52; 2d v.p. Johnson Mfg. Co., Kansas City, Kansas, 1952-54, v.p. for engring., 1954-57; v.p. research Consol. Industries, Inc., South Bend, Ind., 1957-60, exec. v.p., 1960-65, pres., 1965-70, chmn. bd., chief exec. officer, 1970--, also dir.; dir. ABC Chem. Co., 2d Nat. Bank, Country Food Storage Co., Providence Indsl. Corp. (Ind.), Wilson Investment Co., Inc., Hammond Life Ins. Co., Inc. (Ind.), Prudential Ins. Co., Haverford Mfg. Co., Leader Pub. Co. Pres., Dewey High Sch., Kansas City, Mo., 1953-54; fund chmn. local div. Salvation Army, 1959-60. Mem. South Bend Republican Com., 1964-68. Bd. dirs. Ind. council Boy Scouts Am., 1969-71; trustee Lovell Found. Served to lt., Corps Engrs., AUS, 1943-45. Decorated Bronze Star medal. Member N.A.M., South Bend C. of C. (v.p. 1963-65, dir. 1965-70), Am. Mgmt. Assn., Ind. Engrs. Soc. (program com. 1961-62), Princeton Alumni Assn. Episcopalian. Rotarian, Optimist. Clubs: South Bend Golf; Links (N.Y.C.). Home: 6823 Broad Terrace Av South Bend IN 46505 Office: PO Box 1019 South Bend IN 46501

BECKMANN, ROBERT BADER, coll. dean, chem. engr.; b. St. Louis, Sept. 15, 1918; s. Harry Frederick and Lydia Meta (Bader) B.; student U. Okla., 1936-37; B.S. in Chem. Engring., U. Ill., 1940; Ph.D. in Chem. Engring., U. Wis., 1944; m. Barbara Jane Lee, Sept. 5, 1942; children—Robert Lee, Mary Lee; m. 2d, Grace Hope Todd, July 30, 1957. Research chem. engr. Humble Oil & Refining Co., 1944-46; tchr., research chem. engring. dept. Carnegie Inst. Tech., 1946-61; prof., head dept. chem. engring. U. Md., 1961-66, dean College of Engineering, 1966—; consultant, 1946—; spl. research process engring. and design, kinetics and catalysis, solvent extration and liquid phase mass transfer. Fellow Am. Inst. Chemists; member American Chemical Society, A.A.A.S., American Institute of Chemical Engineers, American Soc. Engring. Edn., Phi Kappa Phi, Omicron Delta Kappa, Sigma Xi, Phi Eta Sigma, Phi Lambda Upsilon, Tau Beta Pi, Sigma Pi, Phi Kappa Phi. Club: Rotary Internat. Contbr. profl. jours. Home: 10201 Grosvenor Pl Rockville MD 20852 Office: Coll Engring U Md College Park MD 20742

BECKNER, HARRY GENE, retail food co. exec.; b. Oak Park, Ill., Dec. 6, 1928; s. Harry Keyser and Rose Ida (Doornbosch) B.; B.S. cum laude in Bus. Adminstrn., Northwestern U., 1950; M.A. in Food Distbn., Mich. State U., 1951; m. Anne Louise Storms, June 15, 1954; children—James David, Paul Norman, Laura Lee, Meredith Anne. With Jewel Cos., Inc., 1949—, v.p. food stores sales, 1963-66, vice pres., gen. mgr. Jewell Food Stores, 1966- 67, pres., 1967—, dir. parent co., 1969—. Bd. dirs. Better Bus. Bur., Super Market Inst., Chgo. Alliance Businessmen, Chgo. Bus. Opportunity Fair; adv. com. Chgo. Civic Fedn.; bus. adv. council U. Ill., Circle Campus. Mem. Supermarket Inst. (dir.), Chgo. Alliance of Businessman (dir.), Chgo. Assn. Commerce and Industry (dir.), Beta Gamma Sigma. Mem. Union Ch. Clubs: Hinsdale Golf; Economic (Chgo.). Home: 408 Pamela Circle Hinsdale IL 60521 Office: 1955 W North Av Melrose Park IL 60160

BECKWITH, CHARLES EMILIO, educator; b. Oberlin, O., June 8, 1917; s. Charles Clifton and Anna (Wilkinson) B.; A.B., U. Cal. at Berkeley, 1948, M.A., 1950; Ph.D., Yale, 1956; m. Elizabeth Ungar, Sept. 8, 1951; children—Constance Anne, James Allan, Margaret Andrea. Instr. English, Cornell U., 1956-57; mem. faculty Cal. State Coll. at Los Angeles, 1957—, prof. English, 1964—, chmn. div. lang. arts, 1963-64, chmn. dept. English, 1964-67. Served to 2d lt. AUS, 1942-45. Mem. Modern Lang. Assn., Cal. State Employees Assn., United Profs. Cal., Am. Assn. U. Profs. Democrat. Unitarian. Home: 410 Raymondale Dr South Pasadena CA 91030 Office: 5151 State College Dr Los Angeles CA 90032

BECKWITH, CHARLES GATES, architect; b. Allentown, Pa., Dec. 28, 1921; s. Charles Leach and Fannie Lincoln (Kirkman) B.; B.Arch., Cornell U., 1949; m. Mary Ann Davis, Mar. 31, 1951; children—Thomas G., Kirkman D., Spencer E. Designer LaFarge, Knox & Murphy, N.Y.C., 1948-49; designer, renderer Eggers & Higgins, N.Y.C., 1949-57, asso., 1957-63, partner, 1963-71; sr. partner The Eggers Partnership, N.Y.C., 1971—; pub. speaker, panelist, prin. works include Seamen's Church Inst. of N.Y., Pace Civic Center Campus. Trustee Darien (Conn.) Pub. Library. Served to capt. AUS, World War II. Mem. A.I.A., School Facilities Council for Architecture, Edn. and Industry, N.Y. State Assn. Architects, N.Y. Bldg. Congress, Am. Assn. Arbitrators, Assn. Ednl. Communications and Tech.-School Plant Design, Zeta Psi. Episcopalian. (vestryman). Club: Wee Burn Country (dir.) (Darien). Contbr. articles profl. jours. Home: 68 Greenleaf Av Darien CT 06820 Office: 100 Park Av New York City NY 10017

BECKWITH, HERBERT LYNES, architect; b. Midland, Mich., Feb. 4, 1903; s. Herbert W. and Antoinette (Lynes) B.; M.Arch., Mass. Inst. Tech., 1927; 1 dau., Suzanne. Draftsman Mus. Fine Arts, Boston, 1927-28; pvt. practice architecture, Boston, 1930—, partner firm Anderson & Beckwith, 1938—; co- designer, swimming pool and radiation lab., John Thompson Dorrance Lab., asso. architect Kresge Auditorium and Chapel, Mass. Institute Tech.; also bldgs. designed for Burma, Philippines, P.R., Taiwan; faculty Mass. Inst. Tech., 1927—, prof. architecture, 1947—, dir. exhibits, 1945-66, acting chmn. dept. architecture, 1956- 57; cons. architect George Mason Coll., U. Va., Copley Hill Devel., Charlottesville, others; works include exec. office bldg. Raytheon Mfg. Co., office bldgs. Town of Brookline, Mass., New Eng. Electric Service Co., Lab. for Life Scis. and Dormitory for Women, Mass. Inst. Tech., U.Va. bldgs., A.I.U. building, Tokyo. Co-designer Sci. Complex at U. Rochester. Mem. corp. vis. com. Case Inst. Tech. Served asst. to chmn. dept. physics, Princeton and exec. officer, Princeton Sta., Div. 2, Nat. Defense Research Com., 1943-45. Cons. Mass. Civil Def. Agy. Sec. Nat. Archtl. Accrediting Bd., 1949-54, pres. 1954-56. Recipient College of Fellows Citation, A.I.A., 1955. Registered architect, Del., Me., Md., Mass., Mich., N.J., N.Y., O., Va. Fellow A.I.A. (nat. com. on edn. 1953-60, vice chmn. 1959-60; nat. com. on profession 1958—); mem. Boston Soc. Architects, Mass. Assn. Architects, Mus. Modern Art N.Y., Mus. Fine Arts Boston. Marine Hist. Assn. Mystic, Phi Kappa Psi. Scarab. Episcopalian. Clubs: Century Assn., N.Y. Yacht (N.Y.C.); Royal Bermuda Yacht; New Bedford Yacht; St. Botolph. Home: Indian Pond Rd Kingston MA 02360

BECKWITH, JONATHAN ROGER, educator, physician. Prof. bacteriology and immunology Harvard Med. Sch. Office: Harvard Med Sch 25 Shattuck St Boston MA 02115*

BECKWITH, WILLIAM HUNTER, clergyman; b. Noank, Conn., Oct. 8, 1896; s. Walter Howard and Annie Elizabeth (Keddy) B.; Mus.B. magna cum laude, N.Y. U., 1929, A.M., 1931, Ph.D., 1936; studies at Universite de Politiers, France; fellow of Am. Guild of Organists; unmarried. Organist and choir master Ch. of the Transiguration, N.Y.C., 1917-18, Trinity Ch., Lenox, Mass., 1918-19, Trinity Chapel, Trinity Parish, N.Y.C., 1919-43; instr. French,

Washington Sq. Coll., N.Y. U., 1931-36; instr. French, Hofstra Coll., 1936-38, asst. prof., 1938-39, asso. prof., 1939-40; prof. French and dean of Coll., 1941-48; prof., past dir. div. gen. studies Coll. Agr. and Mechanic Arts, Mayaguez, P.R.; ordained priest Protestant Episcopal Ch. of U.S., 1954; asst. San Andrés Episcopal Mission, Mayaguez. Served in U.S. Navy, 1918. Mem. Modern Lang. Assn., Am. Assn. U. Profs., Eastern Assn. Dean, Phi Beta Kappa. Republican. Episcopalian. Author: The Formation of the Esthetic of Romain Rolland, 1935. Home: 1201 Taylor Av Dunedin FL 33528

BECKWORTH, LINDLEY, lawyer; b. Kaufman County, Tex., June 30, 1913; s. Otis Jefferson and Josie (Slaughter) B.; ed. Tex. U., Baylor U., Southern Meth. U., E. Tex. State Tchrs. Coll., Sam Houston State Tchrs. Coll., Nadodoches, Tex.; m. Taught school 3 years; admitted to Tex. bar, 1937; mem. Tex. Legislature, 1936-38; mem. 76th-82d, 85th-89th U.S. Congresses, 3d Tex. Dist.; former judge U.S. Customs Ct.; now in practice law, Longview, Tex., also mem. Tex. Senate. Baptist. Mason, Odd Fellow. Home: RFD Gladewater TX 75647 Office: 503 N Green St Longview TX 75601

BECTON, HENRY P., bus. exec.; b. 1914; B.S., Yale; married. With Becton, Dickinson & Co., 1937—, now chmn. exec. com., dir.; v.p., dir. Nat. Community Bank, Rutherford, N.J. Trustee Fairleigh Dickinson U. Served with AUS, World War II. Address: Beckton Dickinson & Co East Rutherford NJ 07073

BEDARD, BERNARD JOHN, educator; b. Detroit, May 27, 1928; s. Treffley Anthony and Veronica (Brynes) B.; A.B., U. Notre Dame, 1949; M.A., U. Mich., 1950, Ph.D., 1959; m. Beatrice Irene Weber, Nov. 24, 1962; children—Véronique Céline, Maria Thérèse, Treffley Anthony II, Aimée Jeanne d'Arc. Instr., U. Notre Dame, 1950-51; teaching fellow U. Mich., 1951-55; asst. prof. Villanova U., 1955-62; asso. prof. U. Dayton, 1962-67, prof., 1967—, chmn. dept. English, 1962—. Del. Miami Valley Arts Council, 1963-68. Bd. dirs. Dayton Civic Ballet. Mem. Modern Lang. Assn., Nat. Council Tchrs. English, Milton Soc. Am. Home: 5535 Knollcrest Ct Dayton OH 45429

BEDAU, HUGO ADAM, educator; b. Portland, Ore., Sept. 23, 1926; s. Hugo Adam and Laura (Romeis) B.; student U. So. Cal., 1944-45; B.A., summa cum laude, U. Redlands, 1949; M.A., Boston U., 1951; M.A., Harvard, 1953, Ph.D., 1961; m. Jan Lisbeth Peterson Mastin, Jan. 19, 1952; children—Lauren, Mark Adam, Paul Hugo, Guy Antony. Instr., Dartmouth, 1953-54; instr. Princeton, 1954-57. lectr., 1958-61; asso. prof. Reed Coll., 1962-66; prof. philosophy Tufts U., 1966—. Bd. dirs. Am. League to Abolish Capital Punishment, 1959—, pres., 1969—. Served with USNR, 1944-46. Danforth fellow, 1957-58; Carnegie fellow law and philosophy, 1961-62. Mem. Am. Philos. Assn., Am. Assn. U. Profs., Am. Soc. Polit. and Legal Philosophy. Editor: Death Penalty in America, rev., edit. 1967; Civil Disobedience, 1969; Justice and Equality, 1971. Contbr. articles and essays on social, polit. and legal philosophy to profl. jours. Home: 172 Annursnac Hill Rd Concord MA 01742 Office: Dept Philosophy Tufts U Medford MA 02155

BEDDALL, THOMAS HENRY, lawyer; b. Pottsville, Pa., Apr. 24, 1922; s. Thomas and Martha Roberta (Gallagher) B.; grad. Phillips Acad., Andover, Mass., 1940; A.B., Yale, 1943; LL.B., U. Va., 1950; m. Priscilla Kimball, July 26, 1956; children—Laurence, Frederic, Margaret, and Katherine. Admitted to N.Y. bar, 1951, D.C. bar, 1968; asso. firm of Sullivan & Cromwell, N.Y.C., 1950-57; asso. Paul Mellon Interests, Pitts., 1957—; dir. Carborundum Co., Niagara Falls, N.Y. Served to 1st lt., inf., AUS, 1944-46. Mem. Am. Bar Assn., Bar Assn. City N.Y., Mil. Order World Wars, Order of Coif, Raven Soc., Phi Delta Phi, Omicron Delta Kappa, Pi Delta Epsilon, Chi Psi. Club: Metropolitan (Washington); Rolling Rock (Ligonier, Pa.); Yale (N.Y.C.). Office: 1729 H St NW Washington DC 20006

BEDE, JEAN-ALBERT, educator; b. Caussade, France, Apr. 2, 1903; s. Honore and Heloise (Aillet) B.; Agrege des Lettres, Ecole Normale Superieure, Paris, 1927; dipl., Ecole des Sciences Politiques, Paris, 1929; m. Lise Sittner, May 23, 1953 (dec. Feb. 1969). Came to U.S., 1929, naturalized, 1939. Instr., Princeton, 1929-30, asst. prof., 1930-35; asso. prof. Brown U., 1935-37; asso. prof. Columbia, 1937-45, prof., 1945-69; Blanche W. Knof professor of French, 1969-71, emeritus, 1971—; Guggenheim fellow, 1948-49; Fulbright teaching fellow U. London, 1964-65; vice dean Faculty Letters, Ecole Libre des Hautes Etudes, French U. N.Y., 1950—. Dir. French translations Office War Information, N.Y.C., 1944-45. Decorated chevalier Legion D'Honneur, 1959, chevalier Palmes Academiques, 1961. Mem. Modern Lang. Assn. Am., Societe des Professeurs Francais en Amerique (past pres.). Editor: The Romanic Review, 1967-71. Contbr. sect. to Ency. Americana, 1957—; contbr. Columbia Dictionary of Modern European Lit., 1947, gen. editor rev. edit., 1971—; gen. editor for 19th century Critical Bibliography of French Lit., 1971—. Contbr. articles profl. jours. Home: 400 W 119th St New York City NY 10027

BEDELIA, BONNIE, actress; b. N.Y.C., Mar. 25, 1948; d. Philip Harley and Marian (Wagner) Culkin; student Hunter Coll., 1965-66; m. 1 son, Uri Luber. Appeared in Broadway shows Isle of Children, 1962, Enter Laughing, 1963, The Playroom, 1965, My Sweet Charlie, 1966; appeared in motion pictures The Gypsy Moths, 1968, They Shoot Horses, Don't They?, 1969, Lovers and Other Strangers, 1969; appeared with Inner City Repertory Co., Los Angeles, in The Glass Menagerie, 1967, The Sea Gull, 1968, Midsummer Night's Dream, 1968. Recipient Theater World award, 1966-67. Mem. Actors Equity Assn., A.F.T.R.A., Screen Actors Guild. Address: c/o Lew Sherrell 8961 Sunset Blvd Los Angeles CA 90069

BEDELL, RALPH CLAIRON, psychologist, educator; b. Hale, Mo., June 4, 1904; s. Charles E. and Jennie (Eaton) B.; B.S. in Edn., Central Mo. State Coll., 1926; A.M., U. Mo., 1929, Ph.D., 1932; m. Stella Virginia Bales, Aug. 19, 1929; m. 2d, Ann Barclay Sorency, Dec. 21, 1968. Tchr., Hale (Mo.) Pub. Schs., 1922-24; tchr. sci. and math. S.W. High Sch., Kansas City, Mo., 1926-30, 32-33; asst. prof. ednl. psychology N.E. Mo. State Coll., 1933-34, prof. ednl. psychology, 1934-37, dir. Bur. Guidance, 1934-37; dean, faculty and student personnel Central Mo. State Coll., 1937-38; Tchrs. Coll., freshman counselor, dir. reading labs., asso. prof. ednl. psychology and measurements U. Neb., 1938-46, prof. 1946-50; chmn. dept., prof. psychology and edn. Sch. Social Scis. and Pub. Affairs, Am. U., Washington, 1950-52; dir. program planning and review br. internat. div. U.S. Office Edn., Fed. Security Agency, Dept. Health, Edn., and Welfare 1952- 55; sec.-gen. South Pacific Commn. Noumea, New Caledonia, 1955-58; dir. counseling and guidance insts. br. U.S. Office of Edn., Washington, 1959-66; prof. edn., dir. nat. edn. studies U. Mo., Columbia, 1967—. Mem. study group to Surinam, 1954. Advisor, U.S. delegation UN, 1953, 62, U.S. delegation Caribbean Commn., and West Indian Conf., 1952, 53. Served as comdr. USNR, 1943-46. Diplomate Am. Bd. Profl. Psychology. Fellow Am. Psychol. Assn.; mem. N.E.A., Nat. Soc. for Study Edn., Mil. Order of World Wars, Am. Personnel and Guidance Assn., Am. Assn. for Higher Edn., Mo. Tchrs. Assn., Mo. Guidance Assn. Clubs: Explorers (N.Y.C., Washington); Army and Navy (Washington). Author several books in field; also numerous textbooks and standardized achievement exams., articles profl. publs. Home: 300 Brandon Rd E Columbia MO 65201

BEDFORD, CLAY PATRICK, aircraft, electronics industry exec.; b. Benjamin, Texas, Aug. 25, 1903; grad. Rensslaer Poly. Inst., D.Engring. (hon.), 1971; m. Catherine Ann Bermingham; children—Clay P. II, Peter, Ann. With Kaiser and affiliates in heavy constrn., shipbuilding, automobiles, aircraft, 1925—; former pres. Kaiser Aerospace & Electronics Corp.; dir. Kaiser Industries Corp. Served as asst. to dir. def. moblzn., 1951- 52, asst. to sec. of def., 1952. Hon. trustee Rensselaer Poly. Inst.; dir. Ednl. Facilities Laboratories, Inc., Thunderbird Grad. Sch. Internat. Mgmt.; regent St. Mary's Coll. Cal. Mem. Civil Engrs. Soc., Am. Ordnance Assn., Alpha Tau Omega. Clubs: Paradise Valley Country; Claremont Country; Athenian-Nile; Royal and Ancient Golf (St. Andrews, Scotland). Home: 5223 E Palo Verde Pl Scottsdale AZ 85253 Office: 300 Lakeside Dr Oakland CA 94612

BEDFORD, NORTON MOORE, educator; b. Mercer, Mo., Nov. 11, 1916; s. Cornelius David and Mary (Moore) B.; B.B.A., Tulane U., 1940, M.B.A., 1947; Ph.D., Ohio State U., 1950; m. Helen Grace Horn, Mar. 19, 1943; children—Norton Mark, Martha Ann. Faculty, Ohio State U., 1947-50, Washington U., St. Louis, 1950- 53; prof. U. Ill., Urbana, 1954—; mgmt. cons., C.P.A., 1950—. Trustee Wesley Found. Served with AUS, 1942-46. Named Sch. Bus. Outstanding Alumnus, Tulane U., 1963. Weldon Powell prof., 1969. Mem. Am. Accounting Assn. (pres.), Am. Inst. C.P.A.'s (mem. council), Inst. Mgmt. Sci. Rotarian. Author: Income Determination Theory, 1965; Advanced Accounting, 1967; Introduction to Modern Accounting, 1968; Future of Accounting in a Changing Society, 1970. Contbr. articles profl. jours. Home: 1208 Belmeade St Champaign IL 61820 Office: 302 Commerce W U Ill Urbana IL 61801

BEDFORD, THOMAS ARCHIBALD, corp. exec.; b. San Diego, Cal., Feb. 7, 1909; A.B., Stanford, 1931; m. Adela Shipley Tyler, Dec. 24, 1935; children—Michael, Barbara, Elizabeth. With Kaiser Corp. in engring. and constrn., shipbldg., aircraft and automotive mfg., research and engring., 1932—; v.p. Kaiser Co., 1946; pres., dir. Kaiser (Can.), 1961-68; now v.p. Kaiser Engrs., Kaiser Engr. Internat. Trustee Darling Found. Fellow Am. Soc. C.E.; mem. Am. Fisheries Soc, Am. Mgmt. Assn. Clubs: Trout Unlimited; Ore. Flyfishers; United Fly Tyers, L'Alliance Francaise. Home: 5701 Country Club Dr Oakland CA 94618 Office: Kaiser Center Oakland CA 94604

BEDINI, SILVIO A., museum dir., historian; b. Ridgefield, Conn., Jan. 17, 1917; s. Vincent and Cesira (Stefanelli) B.; student Columbia, 1942; LL.D. (hon.), U. Bridgeport, 1970; m. Gerda Hintz, Oct. 20, 1951; children—Leandra, Peter. Self-employed in Ridgefield, 1945-61; spl. research history of horology, 1950—; curator div. mech. and civil engring. U.S. Nat. Mus., Smithsonian Instn., 1961-65, asst. dir. Mus. History and Tech., 1965-71, dep. dir., 1971—. Dir., mem. exec. com. Ridgefield Library and Hist. Assn., 1959—; mem. exec. council Soc. History Tech., 1963—. Chmn. U.S. nat. com. UNESCO world inventory scientific instruments. Served with AUS, 1942-45. Fellow Washington Acad. Scis.; mem. Am. Hist. Assn., Soc. Am. Historians, Soc. History Discoveries, Astrolabe Soc., Internat. Council Museums, Am. Assn. Mus. History Sci. Soc., A.A.A.S. Roman Catholic. Club: Cosmos (Washington). Author: Ridgefield in Review, 1958; The Scent of Time, 1963; Early American Scientific Instruments and Their Makers, 1964; (with F.R. Madison) Mechanical Universe, 1966; (with W. Von Braun and F.L. Whipple) Moon, Man's Greatest Adventure, 1970. Home: 4303 47th St NW Washington DC 20016 Office: Smithsonian Instn Washington DC 20560

BEDNAR, CHARLES SOKOL, coll. dean; b. N.Y.C., Nov. 3, 1930; s. Karel and Anna (Tomcala) B.; A.B., Rutgers U., 1951, M.A., 1952; Ph.D., Columbia, 1960; m. Beluse Alzbeta Pokorny, Aug. 31, 1959. Asso. prof. Lynchburg Coll., 1958-62; prof., chmn. dept. polit. sci., asso. dean of coll. Muhlenberg Coll., 1962—, also adjunct prof. gen. edn. program for tchrs., chmn. social sci. panel Temple U., 1963—. Chmn. natural resources com. Lehigh Valley Citizens for Progress, 1967. Recipient award Lindback Found., 1965. Mem. Czechoslovak Acad. Arts and Scis., Am. Assn. Univ. Profs., Acad. Polit. Sci., Am. Polit. Sci. Assn., Phi Beta Kappa, Delta Phi Alpha, Tau Kappa Alpha, Omicron Delta Kappa. Contbr. articles profl. jours. Home: RD 2 Coopersburg PA 18036 Office: Muhlenberg Coll 2400 Chew St Allentown PA 18104

BEDNAREK, ALEXANDER ROBERT, Educator; b. Buffalo, July 15, 1933; s. Alexander G. and Bertha (Wlodarz) B.; B.S., State U. N.Y., Albany, 1957, M.A., Buffalo, 1959, Ph.D., 1961; m. Rosemary Anderson, Aug. 29, 1954; children- Robert A., Andrew R., Thomas C., Eugene P. Sr. mathematician Goodyear Aerospace Corp., Akron, O., 1961-62, cons. inforamation scis. dept., 1963-65; asst. prof. math. U. Akron, 1962-63; asst. prof. math. U. Fla., Gainesville, 1963-66, asso. prof., 1967-69, prof., chmn. dept. math., 1969—; mem. adv. bd. CRC Handbook Math. Tables. Served with U.S. Army, 1952-54. Mem. Am. Math. Soc., Math. Assn. Am. (past chmn. Fla. sect.), Sigma Xi. Contbr. to Ency. of Library and Information Sci., Vol. 3, 1970. Contbr. articles profl. jours. Home: 530 NE 7th Av Gainesville FL 32601

BEDNAREK, DAVID ISADORE, journalist; b. Berlin, Wis., Jan. 18, 1936; s. Isadore S. and Bridget (Drover) B.; student Northwestern U., 1953-54; B.A., U. Wis., 1960, M.A., 1967; m. Jane Margaret Gillette, July 30, 1960; children—Adam, David, Ellen. Edn. writer, reporter Wis. State Jour., Madison, 1960-66; edn. writer Milw. Jour., 1966-70, asst. city editor, 1970—. Lectr. journalism Marquette U., 1970—. Served with AUS, 1955-58. Mem. Theta Delta Chi, Sigma Delta Chi. Home: 2050 Ludington Av Wauwatosa WI 53226 Office: 333 W State St Milwaukee WI 53226

BEDSOLE, JOSEPH LINYER, dry goods co. exec.; b. Clarke County, Ala., Aug. 7, 1881; s. Travis L. and Martha (Goodman) B.; ed. pub. schs.; m. Phala Bradford, Aug. 10, 1910; 1 son, Joseph Linyer (dec.). With Bedsole Dry Goods Co., Thomasville, Ala., 1902—, chmn. bd., 1946—; pres. Bedsole-Colvin Drug Co., Mobile, 1919-28; v.p., dir. McKesson & Robbins, Inc., 1928-46; v.p. S. B. Adams Lumber Co., Inc., Mobile, 1927-39, pres., 1939-51, chmn. bd., 1951-68; pres. Bedsole Surg. Supply Co., Inc., Mobile, 1957—, Mobile Fixture & Equipment Co., Inc., 1927—, Bedsole Trading Co., Mobile, 1952—; pres. Alco Land & Timber Co., Mobile, 1951-68, chmn. bd., 1968—; pres. Bedsole Investment Co., Mobile, 1928—. Vice-pres. Ala. War Chest, 1942. Chmn. bd. Mobile Coll., 1962-67, hon. chmn., 1967—; trustee Mobile Infirmary, Mobile United Fund, So. Research Inst. Mem. Newcomen Soc. Baptist. Mason (Shriner). Clubs: Athelstan, Bienville (Mobile). Home: 2151 Venetia Rd Mobile AL 36605 Office: First Nat Bank Bldg Mobile AL 36602

BEDWELL, THEODORE CLEVELAND, Jr., govt. ofcl.; b. Caddo Mills, Tex., Mar. 31, 1909; s. Theodore Cleveland and Mary Rebecca (Gary) B.; B.S., So Meth. U., 1931; M.D., Baylor U., 1933; certificate indsl. medicine, Harvard Sch. Pub. Health, 1941; M.P.H., Johns Hopkins U., 1951; m. Blanche Elizabeth Harper, June 1, 1935; 1 dau., Beverly Anne. Intern Baylor Hosp., Dallas, 1933-34; gen. practice medicine and surgery, Longview, Tex., 1934-35; commd. 1st lt. M.C., U.S. Army, 1935, advanced through grades to maj. gen. USAF, 1963; staff duties various army hosp., 1935-40; grad. Army Med. Field Service Sch., 1940; chief indsl. medicine Army Surgeon Gen. Office, 1940-42; grad. USAAF Sch. Aviation Medicine, 1942; base surgeon, comdg. officer USAAF hosps., 1942-46; dep. surgeon Air Material Command, 1946-47, surgeon, 1947-48; staff surgeon 5th Air Force, Nagoya, Japan, 1948-50; grad. Air War Coll., 1951-52; assigned Office Asst. Sec. Def. Health and Medicine, 1952-53; chief preventive medicine USAF Surgeon Gen.'s Office, 1953-56; dep. surgeon SAC, 1956-59, surgeon, 1959- 61; comdr. USAF Aero. Med. Center, 1961, Aerospace med. div. Air Force Systems Command, 1961-66; dir. staff Office Dep. Asst. Sec. Def., health and dep. asst. sec. of def., health and med., Washington, 1966-68; ret., 1968; chief med. officer Bur. Health Ins., Social Security Adminstrn., Balt., 1968—. Decorated D.S.M., Air Force medal with oak leaf cluster; Republic Korea Presdl. citation; recipient Distinguished Alumnus award So. Meth. U., 1966. Diplomate Am. Bd. Preventive Medicine (founders group aviation medicine 1953, occupational medicine 1956). Fellow Am. Coll. Preventive Medicine (v.p. aviation medicine 1960-61), Aerospace Med. Aesn. (pres. 1964-65), Royal Soc. Health (Eng.); mem. Soc. USAF Flight Surgeons (pres. 1961-62), Am. Pub. Health Assn., Assn. Mil. Surgeons, Internat. Acad. Aviation and Space Medicine, Phi Chi, Alpha Omega Alpha. Home: 6218 Hardy Dr McLean VA 22101 Office: Adminstrn Bldg Social Security Adminstrn 6401 Security Blvd Baltimore MD 21235

BEE, AUGUST JOHN, mfg. co. exec.; b. Chgo., June 10, 1914; s. August and Anna (Neiss) B.; diploma in commerce, Northwestern U., 1939; m. Marie Rheinschmidt, Feb. 4, 1950; children—Barbare Ann, Patricia Susan, John August. Cost Accountant Armour & Co., 1939-42; chief cost accountant S. C. Johnson & Son, 1946-47; chief cost accountant Johnson Suture Corp., 1945-46, plant controller, 1947; asst. treas., controller Ethicon Suture Labs., 1949; with Ethicon, Inc., 1949-69, exec. v.p., 1956-57, pres., 1957-69, also dir.; dir. Johnson & Johnson, 1958-69; corp. group v.p. Becton, Dickinson and Co., Rutherford, N.J., 1969—. Trustee Somerset Hosp., Somerville, N.J. Served to lt. (j.g.) USCGR, 1942-45. Club: Raritan (N.J.) Valley Country. Home: Childs Rd Basking Ridge NJ 07920 Office: Becton Dickinson and Co Rutherford NJ 07073

BEE, DANIEL HAROLD, physician; b. Summit Station, O., Dec. 18, 1909; s. Charles Howard and Clare (Poorman) B.; B.S., U. Pitts., 1933; M.D., Temple U., 1937; m. Gladys Overholt, Sept. 7, 1940; 1 dau., Mary Susan (Mrs. Stine). Intern Windber (Pa.) Hosp., 1936, Columbia Hosp., Pitts., 1937-38; gen. practitioner, Indiana, Pa., 1938—; mem. staff Indiana Hosp., 1939—, pres., 1948, chief med. dept., 1955-69; med. dir. Indiana County, 1948-63; clinician Tb Clinic, Indiana County, 1948—; chief med. examiner Indiana pub. schs., 1946-66; physician in charge Indiana County Instl. Dist., 1942—. Mem. com. health, med. care and transp. of injured, adv. council President's Com. Traffic Safety, 1963-64; mem. Adv. Health Bd. Pa., 1952- 55; profl. adv. com. div. pub. health nursing Dept. of Health, Commonwealth of Pennsylvania, 1966—. Bd. dirs. Indiana County unit Am. Cancer Soc., Indiana County Tb and Health Soc. Mem. Am. (del. from Pa. 1956-67, chmn. com. med. aspects automotive safety 1962-64), World med. assns., Pa. (trustee, councilor 1950-60, chmn. bd. trustees 1958-60, pres. 1961-62), Indiana County (past editor, sec., pres.) med. socs., Am., Pa. acads. gen. practice, Pa. Trudeau Soc., Pa. Pub. Health Assn. (hon.), Pa. Med. Polit. Action Com. (hon.), Ind. C. of C. Methodist. Mason (Shriner). Home: 555 Water St Indiana PA 15701 Office: 561 Water St Indiana PA 15701

BEEBE, FREDERICK SESSIONS, pub. co. exec.; b. Utica, N.Y., Feb. 20, 1914; s. Henry R. and Dora Mertice (Sessions) B.; A.B., Dartmouth, 1935; LL.B., Yale, 1938; m. Liane Petzl-Basny, Aug. 5, 1939; children—Walter H., Michael. Admitted to N.Y. bar, 1938; partner firm Cravath, Swaine & Moore, N.Y.C., 1950- 61; chmn. bd. Washington Post Co., owners Washington Post, Newsweek mag., TV and radio stas., 1961—; dir. Allied Chem. Corp., Bowaters Mersey Paper Co., Ltd., S.E. Bancorp., Inc., Tri-Continental Corp. Mem. Council Fgn. Relations; trustee Com. Econ. Devel. Mem. Am. Bar Assn., Bar Assn. City of N.Y. Clubs: Metropolitan, University (N.Y.C.). Home: 210 E 62nd St New York City NY 10021 Office: 444 Madison Av New York City NY 10022

BEEBE, GEORGE HOLLIS, newspaper editor; b. Pittsfield, Mass., Mar. 1, 1910; s. Dr. George Hatch and Lila (Brainard) B.; B.S., Boston U., 1932; m. Helen Plato Lewis, Aug. 14, 1938. With Billings (Mont.) Gazette, 1933- 43; joined Miami (Fla.) Herald, 1944, mng. editor, 1951-66, sr. mng. editor, 1966—. Mem. Inter-Am. Press Assn. (dir. 1963—), Am. Assn. Sunday and Feature Editors (pres. 1950), Asso. Press Mng. Editors Assn. (dir. 1958-64, pres. 1965), Asso. Press. Assn. Fla. (pres. 1958-59), Am. Soc. Newspaper Editors, Sigma Delta Chi. Home: 650 NE 52d St Miami FL 33137 Office: Miami Herald Miami FL 33101

BEEBE, HAMILTON KELLER, lawyer; b. Chicago, Sept. 1, 1902; s. Walter Eugene and Katherine (Krausgrill) B.; A.B., U. Ill., 1923; J.D., Northwestern U., 1926; m. Helen McCullough, Oct. 9, 1926; childrenBarbara Anne (Mrs. John G. Parrish, Jr.), James, Jane (Mrs. A. Richard Turner). Admitted Ill. bar, 1926; partner Lord, Bissell & Brook. Mem. Hinsdale Grade and Twp. High sch. bds., 6 yrs. Mem. Am., Ill. and Chgo. bar assns., Lambda Chi Alpha, Delta Theta Phi. Republican. Episcopalian. Clubs: Law, Union League, Chicago Yacht (Chgo.). Home: 1881 7th St S Naples, FL 33940. Office: 135 S LaSalle St Chicago, IL 60603.

BEEBE, HIRAM KEITH, educator; b. Anaheim, Cal., Mar. 16, 1921; s. Marshall Earl and Anna (Ullrich) B.; B.A., Occidental Coll., 1943; B.D., Princeton Theol. Sem., 1945; Ph.D., Columbia, 1951; m. Wilma Kerr, Jan. 31, 1943; children—Sara Kerr, Lawrence Keith. Instr. marine, navy and army phys. edn. Princeton, 1943-45; player with N.Y. Profl. Football Team Football Giants, 1944; ordained to ministry Presbyn. Ch., 1946; minister to youth Pasadena (Cal.) Presbyn. Ch., 1946-48; instr. field work dept. Union Theol. Sem., N.Y.C., 1948-49; asst. football coach Columbia, 1948; asst. dean chapel Princeton, 1949-54; asst. prof. religion Occidental Coll., 1954-57, asso. prof., 1957-67, David B. and Mary H. Gamble prof. religion, 1967—; vis. prof. religion Beirut Coll. Women, 1963-64; field supr. Am. Sch. Oriental Research-Concordia Theol. Sem. Archaeol. excavation, Taanach, 1963, 68. Jerusalem excavation British Sch. Archaeology, 1965; ann. prof. Albright Inst. Archaeol. Research, Jerusalem, 1970-71; supr. joint archaeol. expdn. to Caesarea Maritima, 1971. Chmn. com. candidates for ministry Presbytery San Gabriel, Cal., 1966-70. Bd. dirs. Princeton Yenching Found., 1949-54. Mem. Am. Acad. Religion (pres. Pacific coast sect. 1958), Soc. Bib. Lit., Am. Schs. Oriental Research. Home: 1843 Campus Rd Los Angeles CA 90041

BEEBE, RICHARD TOWNSEND, physician; b. Great Barrington, Mass., Jan. 22, 1902; s. John and Louise (Taylor) B.; B.S., Princeton, 1924; M.D., John Hopkins, 1928; m. Jean Wickersham, Aug. 10, 1932; children—Nancy Taylor, John Wickersham, Louise Townsend. Intern Johns Hopkins Hosp., 1928-29, asst. resident physician, 1930-32; residency tng. Thorndike Meml. Lab., Harvard, 1929- 30; asso. medicine Albany Med. Coll., 1932-37, asst. prof. medicine, 1937-48, prof. medicine, dir. of dept., 1948-67, now professor of medicine, 1967—; asst. physician Albany Hosp., 1932-34, clin. asst. medicine, 1934-37, attending physician, 1937-48, dispensary physician in charge, 1941-48, physician in chief, 1948-67, sr.

physician, 1967—; consultant in internal medicine Albany VA Hospital. Diplomate Am. Bd. of Internal Medicine 1948. Fellow A.C.P.; mem. A.M.A., N.Y. State, Albany Co. med. socs., Am. Soc. Clin. Investigation, Am. Clin. and Climatol. Assn., Alpha Omega Alpha. Home: Schuyler Rd Loudonville NY 12211 Office: Albany Med Coll Albany NY 12208

BEEBE, ROBERT PARK, yacht designer; b. Ft. McKinley, P.I., Nov. 21, 1909; s. Royden Eugene and Sara Reid (Park) B.; B.S., U.S. Naval Acad., 1931; M.A., Boston U., 1957; grad. Naval War Coll., 1958; m. Lucy Maude Ord, Oct. 21, 1933 (dec. Dec. 1960); 1 dau., Lucy Gresap Ord (Mrs. J.A. Tobias); m. 2d, Linford B. Donovan, on July 6th, 1963. Commd. ensign U.S. Navy, 1931, advanced through grades to capt., 1950; comdr. U.S.S. Sitkoh Bay, 1953, Bombing Squadron 12, 1942; assigned Office Naval Intelligence, 1952; dept. chief staff, J-2 staff comdr. in chief Alaska, 1954-56; chmn. naval warfare Naval War Coll., 1957-58, head advanced study group, 1957; dir. Gen. Line and Naval Sci. Sch., U.C. Naval Postgrad. Sch., 1958-61; ret. 1961. Designer yachts. Mem. U.S. Naval Inst. Club: N.Y. Yacht. Author articles on yachts and yacht design, also politico-mil. affairs. Address: Box 1452 Carmel CA 93921

BEEBE, WILLIAM THOMAS, airline exec.; b. Los Angeles, Jan. 26, 1915; s. Dewey Sheldon and Elsie (Thomas) B.; B.B.A., U. Minn., 1937; m. Nancy Lee Gragg, Feb. 3, 1951; children—Marshall J., Linda Lee, Deborah Susan. Coll. trainee Gen. Electric Co., 1938-40; personnel mgr. United Aircraft Corp., Hartford, Conn., 1940-46; v.p. Delta Air Lines, Inc., Atlanta, 1947-67, sr. v.p. adminstrn., 1967-70, pres., 1970—, also dir. Regional chmn. Nat. Alliance Businessmen; former mem. Atlanta Bd. Edn. Bd. dirs. Ga. Motor Club. Episcopalian. Kiwanian. Office: Atlanta Airport Atlanta GA 30320

BEEBY, ARTHUR EDWARD GERALD, business exec.; b. Canada, Sept. 18, 1915; s. Henry Arthur and Jennie (Davie) B.; student Nutana Collegiate Sch., Saskatoon, 1932; student bus. adminstrn., U. Western Ont., 1960; m. Margaret Ann Morrow, Sept. 2, 1939; children—Janice Margaret (Mrs. Chester Chatman), Catherine Dorothy. With Salada Foods, Ltd., 1936-68, former pres., dir., gen. mgr., 1964-68; pres., dir. Canadian Food Products Ltd., 1967-68; mng. dir. Place Bonaventure, Inc., Montreal, Que., Can., 1968—, pres., gen. mgr., dir., 1968—. Mem. Montreal Bd. Trade. Club: Donalda (Toronto, Ont., Can.). Office: Place Bonaventure Inc Montreal Quebec Canada

BEEBY, ROBERT HALL, food co. exec.; b. Chgo., June 17, 1914; s. Frank F. and Ethel L. (Hall) B.; M.E., Ill. Inst. Tech., 1941; m. Emma Jane McLallen, Nov. 24, 1937; children-John E., Thomas H., Ruthann. With Campbell Soup Co., 1933-57, plant mgr., Camden, N.J.s 1954-57; mng. dir. Campbell Soup, Ltd., Kings Lynn, Norfolk, Eng. and Campbell Soup S.P.A., Parma, Italy, 1957-62; dir. prodn. devel. Campbell Soups Internat., Camden, 1962-63; mgmt. cons., Phila., 1963-64; exec. v.p. Chun King Corp., Duluth, Minn., 1964- 66; v.p. R.J. Reynolds Foods, Inc., 1966-68; exec. v.p. Rogers Bros. Co., Idaho Falls, Ida., 1968-69; pres. Pacific Vegetable Oil Corp., San Francisco, 1969—. Mem. Am. Mgmt. Assn. Club: World Trade (San Francisco). Home: 550 Battery Pl San Francisco CA 94111 Office: World Trade Center San Francisco CA 94111

BEECH, KEYES, fgn. corr.; b. Pulaski, Tenn., Aug. 13, 1913; s. Walter and Leona (Carden) B.; fellow Harvard, 1952-53; m. Linda Corley Mangelsdorf, June 15, 1951; children—Walter, Keyes, Barnaby. Copy boy Eve. Ind., St. Petersburg, Fla., 1930-37; reporter Akron (O.) Beacon Jour., 1937-42, Honolulu Star-Bull., 1945-47; Far East corr. Chgo. Daily News, 1947—. Served with USMC, 1942-45. Awarded Pulitzer prize, Sigma Delta Chi award for coverage Korean war, 1950. Author: (with Marine Combat corrs.) U.S. Marines on Iwo Jima, 1945; (with Marine Combat Corrs.) Uncommon Valor, 1946; Tokyo and Points East. Contbr. Sat. Eve. Post and other mags. Home: 18 Date-machi Shibuya-ku Tokyo Japan Office: Fgn Correspondents Club Number 14 2 Chome Marunouchi Chiyoda-Ku Tokyo Japan

BEECH, OLIVE ANN MELLOR, aircraft exec.; b. Waverly, Kan., Sept. 25, 1903; d. Frank B. and Suzannah (Miller) Mellor; ed. pub. schs., Paola; student pvt. schs. and night courses; D.Sc. (hon.), Southwestern Coll.; m. Walter H. Beech, Feb. 24, 1930; children—Suzanne Mellor (Mrs. Thomas N. Warner), Mary Lynn (Mrs. John E. H. Pitt.). Gen. office asst. and bookkeeper Staley Elec. Co., Augusta, Kan., 1920-24; office mgr. and sec. to Walter H. Beech, pres. Travel Air Mfg. Co., Wichita, Kan., 1925-29; asst. in founding Beech Aircraft Corp., Wichita, 1932, sec., treas., dir. to 1950, pres., dir., 1950-68, chmn. bd., chief exec. officer, 1968—, also subsidiary orgn.; dir. Fourth Nat. Bank; adv. bd. Marine Midland Internat. & Overseas Corp. Chosen by N.Y. Times as one of 12 most distinguished women U.S., 1943; speaker at 1943 conf.; awarded Lady Hay Drummond Hay Trophy for 1952, as woman having done most for aviation; named Kansan of Year by Native Sons and Daughters of Kan., 1958; recipient directors' medal Freedoms Found., Valley Forge, 1953. Adv. bd. Nat. Air and Space Mus. of Smithsonian Instn.; adv. council Air Force Mus. Found.; adv. bd. Assn. U.S. Army, Inst. Fiscal and Polit. Edn., exec. council Med. Coll. Pa.; adv. com. YWCA; adv. council Nat. 4-H Found.; mem. adv. com. Central Christian Coll., Friends Univ.; bd. dirs. Wichita Symphony; nat. exec. com. Jr. Achievement; adv. com. Gov.'s Commn. Status of Women; trustee Southwestern Coll., Winfield, Nat. Safety Council, Wichita State U. Edn. Assn., Wesley Med. Center; chmn. bd. trustees Wichita Art Assn.; council St. Francis Hosp. Sch. Nursing; bd. dirs. Met. Wichita Council, Wichita Area Devel. Bd., Nat. Corp. Commn. of Freedoms Found., Found. Econ. Edn., YMCA, United Fund of Wichita and Sedgwick County, Salvation Army, A.R.C., Wichita council Girl Scouts U.S. Participated in Am. Bankers Assn. Forum in panel discussion on Women's Part in War Effort, N.Y.C. 1943. Mem. Women's Aero. Assn., Nat. Aero. Assn., U.S. (dir.), Kan., Wichita Chambers of Commerce, Am. Inst. Aeros. and Astronautics, Nat. Aviation Hall of Fame (bd. nominations) Nat. Fedn. Bus. and Profl. Women (dir.), Methodist (trustee). Clubs: Soroptimist (hon. life dir. Wichita), Wichita Country, Wichita, Wings. Home: 48 Mission Rd Eastborough Wichita KS 67207 Office: Beech Aircraft Corp Wichita KS 67201

BEECHAM, CLAYTON TREMAIN, gynecologist; b. Ladd, Ill., Mar. 1, 1907; s. Horace King and Bessie (File) B.; B.S., U. Minn., 1930, M.D., 1932; m. Nina Milner Bowers, Aug. 23, 1941; children—Richard K., Jackson B., Nina B. (Mrs. Robert Stratton). Intern U. Minn. Hosp., 1932-33; resident U. Kan. Hosp., 1933- 34, Kensington Hosp. Women, Phila., 1934-36; instr. obstetrics and gynecology U. Pa. Sch. Medicine, 1936-40; prof. obstetrics and gynecology Temple U. Med. Sch., 1940-64, dir. tumor clinic, 1940-64; dir. gynecology and obstetrics Gelsinger Med. Center, Danville, Pa., 1965—, editor bull. Examiner, Am. Bd. Obstetrics and Gynecology. Pres., Am. Assn. Obstetricians and Gynecologists Found., Inc., 1969—. Bd. dirs. Solebury Sch., New Hope, Pa., 1951-53, Chestnut Hill Acad., Phila., 1955-57. Hon. fellow Kansas City (Mo.), N.J., Pitts., Seattle obstet., and gynecol. socs.; fellow A.C.S., Am. Assn. Obstetricians and Gynecologists (exec. bd. 1960—, pres. 1968); mem. Am. Coll. Obstetricians and Gynecologists (exec. bd. 1965-68), Obstet. Soc. Phila. (exec. bd. 1963-66, pres. 1964-65), Soc. Pelvic Surgeons, Am. Cancer Soc. (dir. Phila. 1964). Author: (with others) Obstetrics and Gynecology, 3d edit., 1966. Mem. editorial bd. Obstetrics and Gynecology, 1968-71; cons. surgery Year Book Cancer, 1965-. Home: Mile Post Rd RD 1 Sunbury PA 17801 Office: Geisinger Med Center Danville PA 17821

BEECHER, HENRY KNOWLES, physician, educator; b. Wichita, Kan., Feb. 4, 1904; s. Mary Julia (Kerley) B.; A.B., U. Kan., 1926, A.M., 1927; M.D., Harvard, 1932; M.D. (hon.) U. Lund, Sweden, 1961; children—Jonathan French, Harriet, Mary Knowles. Intern, Mass. Gen. Hosp., 1932-34, asst. resident in surgery, 1936, dir. dept. anesthesia, 1936—; research (as Moseley Traveling fellow Harvard) lab. of Prof. August Krogh, Copenhagen, 1935; Henry Isaiah Dorr prof. research in anesthesia Harvard, 1941—; Hodgen lectr., St. Louis, 1940, Calhoun lectr., Atlanta, 1948, Kellogg lectr., Washington, 1948, Lowell lectr., Boston, 1948, Judd lectr., Mpls., 1950; exchange lectr. on anesthesia Nat. U., Colombia, 1941; Holme lectr., London, 1954, Macarthur lectr., Edinburgh, 1954, Eastman Meml. lectr., Rochester, 1954, State lectr., Turin, Italy, 1954; Alpha Omega Alpha lectr., Louisville, 1955; in 1956, lectr. Oxford, Hartman Meml. Switzerland, Royal Acad. Medicine, Ireland, Gross Meml., Can., Acad. Sci., Leningrad, others. Mem. com. on Shock NRC, 1940, mem. subcom. on anesthesia, 1942-43, chmn. subcom. on anesthesia, 1946—. Served as maj. AUS, 1943; cons. resuscitation and anesthesia MTO, 1943-45; disch. rank of lt. col., 1945; cons. to surgeon gen. U.S. Army, 1946—, USAF, 1952-54, USN (hon.), 1953-56, USPHS, 1947-52, 57-58; mem. pharmaceology tng. com. NIH, 1958-61. Decorated Legion of Merit, Chevalier de la Legion d'Honneur (France); recipient Warren Triennial prize Mass. Gen. Hosp., 1931, 1937, plaque by Forum of Anesthetists, 1939. Diplomate Am. Bd. Anesthesiology. Fellow Royal Coll. Surgeons, A.A.A.S.; mem. Internat. Soc. for Research in Anesthesia and Analgesia, A.M.A. (mem. therapeutic trials com., 1949-50, council on pharmacy and chemistry 1949, com. on med. research 1950—), Am. Soc. Pharmacology and Exptl. Therapeutics, Soc. Clin. Investigation, Am. Soc. Anesthesiology, Mass. Med. Soc., N.Y. Acad. Sci. (life mem.), St. Louis Med. Soc. (hon. mem.), Royal Soc. Medicine London, hon., Argentina Soc. for Thoracic Surgery (hon. mem.), Am. Acad. Arts and Scis., Assn. Anaesthetists of Gt. Britain and Ireland (corr. fellow), Sociedad Nacional de Anestesiologic (fgn. corr. mem.), Swedish Soc. Anesthesiologists (hon.), Assn. Univ. Anesthetists, Am. Surg. Assn., Sigma Xi, Alpha Omega Alpha. Author: Resuscitation and Anesthesia for Wounded Men, 1949; Experimentation in Man, 1959; Measurements of Subjective Responses: Quantitative Effects of Drugs, 1959; Disease and the Advancement of Basic Science (editor H. K. Beecher), 1959; also articles. Editor: Physiological Effects of Wounds, 1951. Home: 101 Chestnut St Boston MA 02108 Office: Countway Library Medicine 10 Shattuck St Boston MA 02115 ☆

BEECHER, JOHN, poet; b. N.Y.C., Jan. 22, 1904; s. Leonard Thurlow and Isabel (Garghill) B.; A.B., U. Ala., 1925; M.A., U. Wis., 1930; L.H.D., Ill. Coll., Jacksonville, 1948; m. Barbara Marie Scholz, Aug. 16, 1955; children (by previous marriage)—David, Leonard, Joan (Mrs. J. Eichrodt), Michael, Thomas Edward. Steel worker, Birmingham, Ala., 1918-19, 20-21, 23-24, 28- 29; instr. English, Dartmouth, 1927, U. Wis., 1929-33; adminstr. fed. govt. agencies in South, 1934-42; staff writer N.Y. Post, 1943; chief editor Nat. Inst. Social Relations, 1946-47; asst. prof. sociology San Francisco State Coll., 1948-50; lectr. English, Ariz. State U., 1959-61; poet in residence U. Santa Clara (Cal.), 1963-65; vis. prof. Miles Coll., 1966-67; poet in residence North Shore Community Coll., Beverly, Mass., 1969-71, St. John's U., Collegeville, Minn., 1969-71; nationwide poetry readings, 1963—; operator Rampart Press, 1959-63. Served as officer U.S. Mcht. Marine, 1943-45. Recipient Western Books Exhbn. award, 1960, 61, 63. Fellow Fund Advancement Edn., 1951-52; fellow arts program Assn. Am. Colls., 1969—. Author: And I Will Be Heard, 1940; Here I Stand, 1941; All Brave Sailors, 1945; Land of the Free, 1956; Observe the Time, 1956; In Egypt Land, 1960; Phantom City, 1961; Report to the Stockholders and Other Poems, 1962; To Live and Die in Dixie and Other Poems, 1966; Hear the Wind Blow, 1968. Home: care Scholz 1322 31st Av San Francisco CA 94122 Office: PO Box 341 Newburyport MA 01950

BEECHER, WILLIAM JOHN, zoologist, museum dir.; b. Chgo., May 23, 1914; s. Edward J. and Anna (Lawlor) B.; Ph.B., B.S., U. Chgo., 1947, M.S., 1949, Ph.D., 1954. Zoology asst. Chgo. Natural History Mus., 1937-54; sr. naturalist Conservation Dept., Cook County Forest Preserve Dist., 1955-57; dir. Chgo. Acad. Scis., 1958—. Chmn. Chgo. Conservation Council, 1964—; mem. open lands project Welfare Council Met. Chgo., mem. policy com.; Chgo. com. Ill. Sesequicentennial; mem. Ill. Nature Preserves Commn., 1971—; mem. biology com. Ill. Bd. Higher Edn., 1970—; mem. environmental aspects com. Northeastern Ill. Planning Commn. Bd. dirs. Girl Scouts Chgo. Served with AUS, 1942-45; PTO. Recipient citation Who's Who in Midwest, 1963; Annual Science award Adult Edn. Society Greater Chicago, 1963; Ecology award Chgo. Outdoor Art League, 1970. Fellow A.A.A.S., Am. Ornithol. Union; mem. Nature Conservancy (vice chmn. Ill. chpt., Green Leaf award 1969), Ecol. Soc. Am., Wilson, Cooper ornithol. socs., Geog. Soc. Chgo. (v.p. 1971—), Am. Soc. Zoologists, Ill. Audubon Soc. (bd. dirs.), Sigma Xi. Clubs: Garden of America (member of the conservation committee); Kennicott; Bandar Log; Adventurers. Author: Nesting Birds and the Vegetation Substrate, 1942; Attracting Birds to your Backyard, 1954; also articles. Spl. research anatomy and classification birds of world, ecologist, conservationist. Home: 1960 N Lincoln Park W Chicago IL 60614 Office: 2001 N Clark St Chicago IL 60614

BEECHING, RICHARD, co. dir.; b. Sheerness, Kent, Eng., Apr. 21, 1913; s. Hubert J. and Annie Beeching; B.Sc. with 1st Class Honours, Imperial Coll. Sci. and Tech., London, 1933, diploma, 1934, Ph.D., 1936; LL.D., U. London; D.Sc., Nat. U. Ireland; m. Ella Margaret Tiley, Aug. 8, 1938. With Fuel Research Sta., Greenwich, 1936-37, Mond Nickel Co. Ltd., 1937-43; with armaments design dept. Ministry Supply, 1943-48, dep. chief engr., 1946-48; with Imperial Chem. Industries, 1948-61, 65-68, chmn. metals div., 1955-57, dir., 1957-61; dep. chmn., 1966-68; v.p. Imperial Chem. Industries Can., 1953-55, chmn. Redland Ltd., 1970—; dir. Lloyds Bank, Ltd., Rolls-Royce Ltd. Mem. spl. adv. group Brit. Transp. Commn., 1960-61, chmn. commn., 1961-63; mem. Nat. Econ. Devel. Council, 1962-64; chmn. British Rys. Bd., 1963-65, Royal Commn. on Adminstrn. Justice, 1966; pres. Royal Soc. for Prevention of Accidents, 1968—. Created Knight, 1965. Fellow Imperial Coll. Sci., Inst. of Physics, Inst. of Mgmt.; Companion Inst. Mech. Engrs.; asso. Royal Coll. Sci. Author: Electron Diffraction, 1936; also papers. Home: Little Manor East Grinstead Sussex England

BEECROFT, ERIC ARMOUR, economist; b. Toronto, Can., Sept. 7, 1903; s. Frank Lloyd and Eva (Armour) B.; A.B., U. Toronto, 1925, A.M., 1927; student Brookings Grad. Sch. (fellow), 1926-27; Ph.D., Yale (Cowles fellow in govt.), 1934; m. Ann Granger, 1952; 1 son, Douglas Armour. Asst. prof. econs. Hamline U., 1927-29; lectr. U. Cal., 1931-36, asst. prof. polit. sci., 1936-41; exec. sec. for internat. econ. studies Nat. Planning Assn., Washington, 1941-42; mem. Fgn. Econ. Adminstrn., U.S. Govt. Service, 1942-46, chief Far Eastern sect. Bd. Econ. Warfare, 1942-43, econ. adviser to spl. rep. in India, 1943-44, spl. rep. in India, Ceylon, Afghanistan, 1944-46, spl. asst. to sec. of interior, Dept. of Interior, 1946, chief Pacific br., 1947; loan officer Internat. Bank Reconstrn. and Development, 1947-54; on bank missions to Philippines, 1948, 49, India, 1949, Ceylon, 1949, 51, Pakistan, 1951, Ethiopia, 1950, 52; nat. dir. Community Planning Assn. of Can., 1954-60; dir. urban planning, Ottawa rep. Canadian Fedn. Mayors and Municipalities, 1960-65; prof. polit. sci., dir. urban and regional devel. studies U. Western Ont., 1965—. Mem. Canadian Council Urban and Regional Research (chmn. 1966-69), Sci. Council Can. (urban devel. com.), Inst. Pub. Adminstrn. of Canada, Soc. Internat. Devel., Internat. Union Local Authorities (exec. com.), Canadian Polit. Sci. Assn., Canadian Economic Assn., Am. Econ. Assn. Clubs: Rideau (Ottawa); Cosmos (Washington). Editor: Community Planning Review, 1954-60. Home: 727 Old Hunt Rd London Ontario Canada

BEEDER, RUDOLPH HENRI, civil engr.; b. Mobile, Ala., Aug. 26, 1905; s. Charles R. and Mary J. (Bressingham) B.; student U. Mich.; m. Ruth Ann Fleming, July 24, 1926; children—David C., John R. With A.T.&S.F. Ry., 1920-70, asst. chief engr. system, Chgo., 1953-58, chief engr. system, 1958-70; cons. engr., Colorado Springs, Colo., 1970—. Mem. Am. Ry. Engring. Assn. (pres. 1961-62), Am. Soc. C.E., Roadmasters and Maintenance of Way Assn., Ry. Bridge and Bldg. Assn., Am. Wood Preservers Assn., Newcomen Soc., Kan., Ill. acads. sci., Western Ry. Club (pres. 1967-68), Ry. Tie Assn., Hist. Soc. Colo., No. Ariz. Soc. Sci. and Art, Field Mus. Natural History, Tex. Folklore Soc., Evanston Hist. Soc., Western History Assn., Denver Posse of Westerners C.M., Assn. Am. R.R.s (gen. com. data system div.), Chgo. (pres. 1956-57), Miss. Valley maintenance of way clubs, Tau Beta Pi. Address: 1616 Mesa Av Colorado Springs CO 80906

BEEDLE, LYNN SIMPSON, educator; b. Orland, Cal., Dec. 7, 1917; s. Graville L. and Carol (Simpson) B.; B.S., U. Cal., 1941; M.S., Lehigh U., 1949, Ph.D., 1952; m. Ella Marie Grimes, Oct. 20, 1946; children—Lynn, Helen, Jonathan, David, Edward. With Todd-Cal. Shipbldg. Corp., Richmond, Cal., 1941; dir. Fritz Engring. Lab. of Lehigh U., 1960—. Served with USNR, 1941-47. Recipient Robinson award Lehigh U., 1952; E.E. Howard award Am. Soc. C.E., 1963, Research prize, 1956; Silver medal Am. Welding Soc., 1957; Constrn. award Engring. News Record, 1965; Regional Tech. Meeting award Am. Iron and Steel Inst., 1958. Fellow Am. Soc. C.E.; mem. Column Research Council (chmn. 1966-70, dir.), Welding Research Council, Am. Inst. Steel Constrn., Am. Ry. Engring. Assn., Nat. Acad. Engring., Internat. Joint Com. Planning and Design Tall Bldgs. (chmn. 1970—), Nat. Acad. Scis. (adv. panel). Author: Plastic Design of Steel Frames, 1958; (with others) Structural Steel Design, 2d edit., 1972. Contbr. articles profl. jours. Home: 102 Cedar Rd Hellertown PA 18055 Office: Fritz Engring Lab Lehigh Univ Bethlehem PA 18015

BEEGHLY, CHARLES MILTON, ret. steel co. exec.; b. Bloomville, O., Oct. 6, 1908; s. Leon A. and Mabel (Snyder) B.; A.B., Ohio Wesleyan Univ., 1930; LL.D., Juniata Coll., 1964, Thiel College, 1965; m. Janet Turner, May 12, 1934; children—Judith (Mrs. Richard C. Wallis), Margaret (Mrs. J.D. Hogan), Charles Milton. Employed as clerk Metal Carbides Company, Newark, N.J., 1931; clerk trainee sales Goff-Kirby Co., Cleve., 1932-33; sales trainee Buffalo Slag Co., 1934; salesman The Cold Metal Products Co., Youngstown, O., 1935-38, prodn. mgr., 1939-42, sales mgr., 1939-50, v.p., dir., 1946—, gen. mgr., 1952—; pres. strip steel div. Jones & Laughlin Steel Corp., Pitts., 1957—, exec. v.p. corp., 1958-60, pres., 1960-63, chmn. bd., chief exec. officer, 1963-69, chmn. exec. com., 1969- 71; v.p., gov. T. Mellon & Sons, 1969—; dir. Dollar Savs. & Trust Co., Youngstown, Columbia Gas Systems Inc., Cleve. Cliffs Iron Co., Pitts., PPG Industries, Pitts. br. Fed. Res. Bank of Cleve. Trustee Carnegie-Mellon U., Ohio Wesleyan U. Served as maj. USAAF, 1942-45. Mem. Am. Iron and Steel Inst. Office: 3 Gateway Center Pittsburgh PA 15222

BEEK, BARTON, lawyer; b. Pasadena, Cal., Jan. 24, 1924; s. Joseph Allan and Carroll Brewster (Guillou) B.; B.A., Cal. Inst. Tech., 1942; M.B.A., Stanford, 1948; LL.B., Loyola U., Los Angeles, 1955; m. Dorothy May Martens, July 18, 1949; childrenCharles Frederick, Carroll Brewster, Barton Brewster, Barbara, Joseph Allan. Admitted to Cal. ba., 1955; with firm O'Melveny & Myers, Beverly Hills, Cal., 1955-, partner, 1960-. Dir. Sierracin. Thrifty Drugs, Balboa Savs. & Loan Assn. Served with USNR, World War II. Clubs: Lincoln, Newport Harbor Yacht (Newport, Cal.); California (Los Angeles). Home: 620 W Ocean Front Balboa, CA 92661. Office: 9601 Wilshire Blvd Beverley Hills, CA 90210.

BEEKEY, CYRUS EZRA, retired coll. pres.; b. Myerstown, Pa., Mar. 29, 1906; s. Samuel Peter and Elvy (Kilmer) B.; B.S., Albright Coll., 1927, LL.D., 1968; M.S., Cornell U., 1934, Ph.D., 1940; postgrad. Temple U., 1929-30; m. Viola B. Sweigart, June 25, 1932; children—Lois Elva, Sara Ann, Cyrus Ezra. Tchr. math. pub. schs., Reading, Pa., 1927-29, tchr. biology, 1931-43; instr. physics Commonwealth Pa. State Tchrs. Coll., 1943-44, prof., dept. head biology, 1944-56, dean instrn., 1956-64, dean acad. affairs, 1964-67; pres. Kutztown (Pa.) State Coll., 1967-69. Mem. Pa. Acad. Sci. (pres. 1954-55), Phi Kappa Phi, Kappa Delta Pi, Phi Delta Kappa, Kappa Mu Epsilon. Home: 301 Pennsylvania Av Kutztown PA 19530

BEEKMAN, EMILE, airline exec.; b. Amsterdam, Holland, Dec. 2, 1917; s. Valk E. and Clara (Hamburger) B.; degree Netherlands Inst. Chartered Accountants, 1946; m. Truus E. Benjamins, Aug. 9, 1945; children—Valk E., Philibert R., Eline C.M. Asst. auditor, 1934-35; research bur. asst., asst. gen. mgr. De Bijenkorf, dept. store, 1935-42, Nat. orgn. bur., 1942-46, internal auditor, 1946-50; controller variety chain HEMA. 1950-60; finance mgr., controller De Bijenkorf, 1960-65; retail system's mgr. Europe Nat. Cash Register Corp., 1965-67; sr. v.p. finance KLM, 1967—; mem. bd. tow real estate companies. Treas. Child Guidance Clinic. Amsterdam. Bd. dirs. Stichting Het Nederlands Studiecentrum voor Informatica. Mem. Subversive Forces, 1944-45. Mem. Netherlands Inst. Chartered Accountants. Author two books, also articles. Home: 81 Weerdestein Amsterdam The Netherlands Office: Amsterdamseweg 55 Amstelueen The Netherlands

BEEKS, WILLIAM TRULOCK, U.S. judge; b. El Reno, Okla., May 5, 1906; s. William Tecumseh and Elsie Jane (Rawles) B.; LL.B., U. Wash., 1932; m. Florence Carlson, Jan. 4, 1929; 1 son, William Trulock. Admitted to Wash. bar, 1932; practice in Seattle, 1932-61; U.S. judge Western Dist. Wash., 1961—. Served to col. AUS, 1942-46; col. Res. Mem. Am., Wash., Seattle-King County bar assns., Maritime Law Assn. U.S., Delta Tau Delta, Order of Coif. Mason (32, Shriner). Clubs: Rainier, Harbor, Washington Athletic (Seattle). Home: 6437 Hampton Rd S Seattle WA 98118 Office: US Court House Seattle WA 98104

BEEL, JOHN ADDIS, educator, chemist; b. Butte, Mont., Sept. 20, 1921; s. John Addis and Minnie (Johnson) B.; B.S., Mont. State U., 1942; Ph.D., Ia. State U., 1949; student Mont. Sch. Mines, 1938-40; m. Martha Marijean Menard, Aug. 19, 1944; children—John Addis III, Jeffrey Alan. Instr. Ia. State U., 1945-49; mem. faculty U. No. Colo., 1949—, prof. chemistry, 1954—, acting asso. dean Coll. Arts and Scis., summer 1969, acting chmn. sci. div., 1957, 64, 65. Cons. NSF, 1965; dir. NSF Inst., summers 1960-61, 65-67, 70-71; cons. law enforcement agencies on problems involving chemistry. Mem. Am. Chem. Soc. (chmn. Colo. sect. 1967, councilor Colo. sect. 1970—), Colo.-Wyo. Acad. Sci. (chmn. chemistry sect. 1963-66, pres. 1968-69), Phi Lambda Upsilon, Sigma Xi. Home: 2524 14th Av Ct Greeley CO 80631

BEEL, LOUIS JOSEPH MARIA, Dutch govt. ofcl.; b. Roermond, Netherlands, Apr. 12, 1902; s. T. A.L. and A.M. (Rutten) B.; D.Juridical Sci., U. Nijmegen; m. H.G.M.J. van der Meulen, Aug. 1, 1926; children—Joseph, Louis, Margareth, Maria Theresa. With Ofcl. Town Clk.'s Officer, Roermond and Eindhoven, Netherlands, 1925-42; barrister, 1942-44; minister interior, 1945-47, prime minister, 1946-48; Queen's commr. for Indonesia, 1948-49; prof. U. Nijmegen and Tilburg, 1949-51; minster interior, 1951-56, vice prime minister, 1952-56, minister of state, 1956-58, prime minister, 1958-59, minister state, v.p. Privy Council, 1959—; vice chmn. Nationale Nederlanden N.V. Mem. Catholic party. Address: 596 Rijksstraatweg Wassenaar Netherlands*

BEELAR, DONALD CASPER, lawyer; b. Sand Point, Ida., June 10, 1903; s. John W. and Cora (King) B.; A.B., U. Ore., 1928; LL.B., George Washington U., 1932; J.D., Georgetown U., 1936; m. Helen Webster, 1930; 1 dau., Betty Coe (Mrs. James R. Ekstrom); m. 2d, Virginia Patterson, Dec. 23, 1939 (dec. June 1970); 1 dau., Barbara Ann; m. 3d, Priscilla Martin Cragun, Sept. 18, 1970. Admitted to D.C. bar, 1931; law clk. Dept. Justice, 1929-30; atty. RFC, 1931-33; with Kirkland, Ellis, Hodson, Chaffetz & Masters, Washington, 1933—. President, Potomac Plaza Terraces, Inc., 1962-64. Served as col. USAAF, 1942-46. Decorated Legion of Merit. Mem. Am. Bar Assn. (chmn. sect. adminstrv. law 1957-58, chmn. spl. com. on fed. adminstrn. practice act 1957-62, ho. of dels. 1960-64), Bar Assn. D.C. (dir. 1954-55), Fed. Communications Bar Assn. (pres. 1963). Home: Watergate South 700 New Hampshire Av NW Washington DC 20037 Office: 1776 K St NW Washington DC 20036

BEELER, DEELROY, govt. ofcl.; b. Lyndon, Kan., Aug. 3, 1915; s. Charles Elroy and Freda (Rogers) B.; student Kan. State U., Manhattan, 1941; m. Florence De Crensento, Sept. 25, 1952; children—Susan Dee, DeElroy II, Jr. scientist Wright Aero. Corp., Paterson, N.J., 1941; with NACA, 1941-59; with NASA, 1959—, dep. dir. Flight Research Center, Edwards, Cal., 1962—, member aerodynamics com., 1959—, supersonic transp. com., 1961—, chmn. hypersonic research com., 1962—, also member of the aeronautics committee, 1967—. Recipient Outstanding Leadership medal NASA, 1963. Asso. mem. Inst. Aero. and Space Sci., Am. Inst. Astronautics and Aero.; mem. Am. Rocket Soc. Home: 1813 W Av J Lancaster CA 93534 Office: PO box 273 Edwards CA 93523

BEELER, JOHN WATSON, physician; b. Indpls., July 2, 1921; s. Raymond Cole and Myra (Watson) B.; student Wesleyan U., Middletown, Conn., 1939-41; B.S., Ind. U., 1942, M.D., 1944; M.S. in Radiology, U. Minn., 1950; m. Marcella Thorson, Jan. 13, 1951; children—John Cole, Richard Thorson, Thomas Watson. Intern Phila. Gen. Hosp., 1945; fellow radiology Mayo Found., 1947-51; pvt. practice radiology, Indpls., 1950-64, 66—; chmn. dept., radiology Methodist Hosp., Indpls., 1963-66, dir. dept., 1964-66; asst. prof. radiology Ind. U. Sch. Medicine, 1960—; mem. courtesy staff Community Hosp., Indpls., 1957—; radiologist Hancock Meml. Hosp., Greenfield, Ind., 1954—; sec. exec. staff Marion County Gen. Hosp., Indpls., 1956-58; dir. dept. radiology Winona Meml. Hosp., 1970—. Bd. dirs. Ind. Blue Shield, 1958—, sec., 1969—. Served with M.C., USAAF, 1945-47; with med. dept. AUS, 1953-54. Diplomate Am. Bd. Radiology. Fellow Am. Coll. Radiology (councilor for Ind. 1961-66, mem. bd. chancellors 1969—); mem. Am., Ind. (del. 1958-66, 69—) med. assns., Radiol. Soc. N.Am. (counselor for Ind. 1961-66, 1st v.p. 1969-70, dir.), Ind. Roentgen Soc. (chmn. exec. council 1958, pres. 1961), Marion County Med. Soc. (mem. bd. dirs. 1956-58, 68-70, chmn. 1969-70), Am. Roentgen Ray Soc., Eastern Radiol. Soc. Rotarian. Club: Indianapolis Athletic. Home: 7974 N Illinois St Indianapolis IN 46260 Office: Hume Mansur Bldg Indianapolis IN 46204

BEELER, MADISON SCOTT, educator; b. Seattle, Apr. 24, 1910; s. Adam M. and Florence L. (Scott) B.; A.B., Harvard, 1931, A.M., 1935, Ph.D., 1936; student U. Munich (Germany), 1936-37, U. Paris (France), 1937-38, U. Berlin (Germany), 1938; m. Florence C. Rosene, Dec. 29, 1955; children—Peter Gordon, Roxane Catherine. Instr. German, tutor comparative philology Harvard, 1938-41; mem. faculty U. Cal. at Berkeley, 1941—; prof. German and linguistics, 1958-66, professor of linguistics, 1966—, acting chmn. dept. Near Eastern langs., 1958-60, chmn. dept. German, 1962-65; visiting professor Stanford, 1953, 61, U. Mich., 1957, U. Colo., 1959, Princeton, 1962, Ind. U., 1964, Ohio State U., 1970. Served to lt. (j.g.) USNR, 1942-44. Mem. Philol. Assn. Pacific Coast (pres. 1961), Modern Lang. Assn., Linguistic Soc. Am., Soc. de linguistique de Paris, Am. Name Soc. (editor jour. 1957-60). Club: Sierra. Author: The Venetic Language, 1949; also articles. Home: 1060 Contra Costa Dr El Cerrito, CA 94530.

BEELEY, ARTHUR LAWTON, educator; b. Manchester, Eng., Aug. 28, 1890; s. John William and Elizabeth Ann (Lawton) B.; came to U.S., 1908; A.B., Brigham Young U., 1913; A.M., U. Chgo., 1918, Ph.D., 1925; LL.D., U. Utah, 1955; m. Glenn Johnson, June 6, 1916; children—Mary (Christensen), Stephen. Prin. Emery Acad., Castle Dale, Utah, 1917-18; asst. professor psychology U. Utah, 1919-21; research asso. Ill. state criminologist, 1924-25; asst. prof. social economy U. Chgo., 1925-26; prof. sociology, dir. Bur. Student Counsel, U. Utah, 1927-47, dean Grad. Sch. Social Work, 1937-56, dean, prof. emeritus, 1956—; dir. Inst. World Affairs, 1946-56; vis. prof. U. Chgo., summers 1928, 29, 31, U. So. Cal., 1936, U. Minn., 1938, San Francisco State Coll., 1954; lectr. Nat. Police Acad., 1943-45; adviser War Relocation Authority 1943; educational cons. 9th Service Command, 1943-46. Mem. Utah Council Criminal Justice Adminstrn., 1961- -; del. Internat. Congress Mental Hygiene, London, 1948; mem. White House Conf. Child Health and Protection, 1929-30. Criminol. research in England, 1932-33, under grant from Am. Social Sci. Research Council; recipient award distinguished service to social science Utah Acad. Scis. Arts and Letters, 1954. Fellow Am. Ortho-Psychiatric Assn., A.A.A.S.; mem. Am. Sociol. Soc., Nat. Assn. Social Workers, Am. Correctional Assn., Am. Soc. Criminology (August Vollmer award 1965), Am. Judicature Soc., Nat. Conf. Bail and Criminal Justice Adminstrn. (exec. bd. 1964—), English-Speaking Union U.S., Utah Soc. Mental Hygiene (pres. 1928-29), Utah Conf. Social Work (pres. 1929-30), Phi Beta Kappa, Phi Kappa Phi. Author: An Experimental Study of Left-Handedness, 1918; The Bail System in Chicago, 1927; Boys and Girls in Salt Lake City, 1929; Community Health and Hygiene (with L. L. Daines), 1935; Outlines of Social Psychology, 1949; also articles. Home: 263 S 12th St E Salt Lake City UT 84102

BEELKE, RALPH GILBERT, educator; b. Buffalo, Dec. 16, 1917; s. William and Elizabeth (Toy) B.; diploma, Buffalo Sch. Fine Arts, 1937; Ed.B., U. Buffalo, 1939; M.A., Columbia Tchrs. Coll., 1947, Ed.D., 1952; m. Hazel Hart, May 20, 1944; children—Christine, John, Ralph Alan. Fabric designer, 1939-41; supr. art, Frankfort, N.Y., 1940-42; instr. art, Washingtonville, N.Y., 1947- 49; deptl. asst. Columbia Tchrs. Coll., 1949-50; instr. art Md. State Coll., 1950-51; prof. art, chmn. dept. State U. N.Y. Coll., Fredonia, N.Y., 1951-56; specialist edn. in arts U.S. Office Edn., 1956-58; exec. sec. Nat. Art Edn. Assn., 1958-62; head dept. of creative arts Purdue U., 1962-69, prof. art and design, 1969—; paintings and prints in pvt. collections; exhibited regional and internat. shows. Mem. arts edn. delegation to Soviet Union, 1960. Named Nat. Art Edn. Assn. Art Educator of Year 1963. Mem. N.E.A., Coll. Art Assn., Am. Soc. Aesthetics, Am. Assn. U. Profs. Kappa Delta Pi, Phi Delta Kappa. Author: Curriculum Materials in Art Education, 1962. Editor Art Edn. Bull., 1952-56, Art Edn., 1958-62; mem. good practices bd. Arts and Activities mag., 1956-66; adv. editorial bd. Sch. Arts mag., 1957-69; author monthly column, New Teaching Aids, 1954-62. Home: 304 Hollowood Dr West Lafayette IN 47906 Office: Purdue U Lafayette IN 47907

BEEM, JACK D., lawyer; b. Chgo., Nov. 17, 1931; s. J. Darrel and Margie (Jacks) B.; A.B., U. Chgo., 1952; J.D., 1955. With firm Wilson & McIlvaine, Chgo., 1958-63; partner firm Baker & McKenzie. Chgo. and Tokyo 1963—. Mem. Am. Chgo. bar assns., Phi Beta Kappa. Home: 175 E Delaware Pl Chicago IL 60611 Office: Baker & McKenzie Prudential Plaza Chicago IL 60611

BEEM, MARC, pediatrician; b. Chgo., June 25, 1923; B.A., Williams Coll., 1945; M.D., U. Chgo., 1948. Intern Bobs Roberts Meml. Hosp. for Children, Chgo., 1948-49, asst. resident, 1949-50, 53-54; research fellow Children's Med. Center Boston, 1950-51; from asst. prof. pediatrics to prof. U. Chgo., 1954—. Served with AUS, 1943-46, USPHS, 1951-53. Home: 327 E 3d St Hinsdale IL 60521 Office: Dept Pediatrics U Chgo 5801 Ellis Av Chicago IL 60637*

BEEMAN, ELIZABETH ANN, educator; b. Barre, Vt., Aug. 12, 1916; A.B., Grinnell Coll., 1938; M.S., U. Chgo., 1939, Ph.D. in Behavior, 1947; M.A., Mt. Holyoke Coll., 1941. Asst. U. Chgo., 1941-44, asst. in biol. sci., 1944-45, instr., 1945-49, asst. prof., 1949-51; mem. sci. faculty Sarah Lawrence Coll., 1951-60; asso. prof. Mt. Holyoke Coll., 1960-70, prof. biol. scis., 1970—. NSF faculty fellow, 1959-60. Mem. A.A.A.S., Am. Soc. Zoology, Am. Ecol. Soc., N.Y. Acad. Scis. Office: Dept Biology Mt Holyoke Coll South Hadley MA 01075*

BEEMAN, WILLIAM WALDRON, educator, physicist; b. Detroit, Oct. 21, 1911; s. Joseph John and Mary E. (Waldron) B.; student Wayne U., 1929-35; B.S. in Math., U. Mich., 1937; Ph.D. in Physics, Johns Hopkins, 1940; m. Eleanor Mildred Coswell, June 22, 1940; children—Ann Margaret, Richard William, John Michael and David Kevin (twins). Research physicist Gen. Motors Research Labs., Detroit, 1940-41; instr. physics U. Wis.-Madison, 1941-44, asst. prof., 1944-47, asso. prof., 1947-52, prof., 1952—, chmn. dept., 1951-52, chmn. grad. com. biophysics, 1956—, dir. biophysics lab., 1963-70. Vice pres., dir. Design, Inc., Madison, 1954—. Sci. adviser to gov. Wis., 1963-64; adv. com. Wis. Dept. Resource Devel., 1963-64; cons. Argonne Nat. Lab., Lemont, Ill., Los Alamos Nat. Lab., 1947-52. Citizen mem. Madison Plan Com., 1957-63. Alderman, Madison, 1955-57. Trustee Madison Gen. Hosp., 1955-57. Fellow Am. Phys. Soc.; mem. Am. Crystallographic Assn., Biophys. Soc., Phi Beta Kappa, Sigma Xi. Democrat. Unitarian. Editorial bd. Rev. Sci. Instruments, 1958- 61. Author numberous research papers in field. Home: 5010 Tomahawk Trail Madison WI 53705

BEENE, GEOFFREY, designer; b. Haynesville, La., Aug. 30, 1927; s. Albert and Lorene (Waller) B.; student Tulane U., 1941-45, Traphagen Sch. Fashion, 1949, Acad. Julien, Paris, France, 1949. Designer for Samuel Winston, 1949-50, Harmay, 1950-57, Teal Traina, 1958-62; pres., designer Geoffrey Beene, Inc., N.Y.C., 1962-. Recipient Nat. Cotton award, 1965, Coty award, 1964, 66, Nieman Marcus award, 1965, Ethel Traphagen award, 1966. Mem. Fashion Designers Council Am. Home: 333 E. 69th St. Office: 530 7th Av New York City, NY

BEER, FERDINAND PIERRE, educator; b. Binic, France, Aug. 8, 1915; s. Max and Marthe (Le Gouaille) B.; maturité, Coll. Geneva (Switzerland), 1933; licence ès scis. math., U. Geneva, 1935, doctorat ès scis. math., 1937; licence ès scis., U. Paris (France), 1938; postgrad. fellow Brown U., summer 1942; m. Vivienne Clara Chappuis, Jan. 22, 1940; children—Michelle C.M., Marguerite V. Came to U.S., 1941, naturalized, 1947. Instr. math. Goddard Coll., Plainfield, Vt., 1941-42, U. Kansas City (Mo.), 1942-43; asst. prof. physics William Coll., 1943-47; mem. faculty Lehigh U., 1947- -, professor mechanics, 1951—, chairman dept. of mechanical engineering and mechanics, 1968—; cons. to industry and govt., 1942—. Served with French Army, 1939-40. Mem. Am. Soc. Engring. Edn. (chmn. mechanics div. 1962-63), Am. Soc. M.E., Am. Inst. Aero. and Astronautics, Am. Assn. U. Profs., Sigma Xi, Tau Beta Pi, Pi Tau Sigma. Author: Pour continuer le Calcul Différentiel, 1940; (with E. R. Johnston, Jr.) Mechanics for Engineers, 1956; (with E. R. Johnston, Jr.) Vector Mechanics for Engineers, 1962; also articles. Home: RD 1 Coopersburg, PA 18036. Office: Dept of Mechanical Engineering and Mechanics Lehigh Univ Bethlehem PA 18015

BEER, IRVING, cosmetic co. exec.; b. Perth Amboy, N.J., June 21, 1920; s. Elias and Minnie (Friedberg) B.; B.S. cum laude, N.Y.U., 1940; m. Silvea Mandresh, Aug. 1, 1942; children—Lawrence A., Arlene S. Accountant, then partner Jablow & Jablow, N.Y.C., 1940-60; v.p., treas., then exec. v.p. finance and adminstrn. Charles of the Ritz, Inc., N.Y.C., 1960-64; exec. v.p. finance and adminstrn. Lavin-Charles of the Ritz, N.Y.C., 1964-66, pres., 1966-71, also past chmn. exec. com., dir.; dir. Alexandra de Markoff Inc., Yves Saint Laurent S.A. (France), Imperial Toiletries Ltd., Gilbert Merrill Ind., Inc. Bd. dirs. Lanvin-Charles of the Ritz Found., Inc., Richard and Edna Salomon Found., Inc.; trustee Bklyn. Coll. Pharmacy. Served with USAAF, 1943-46. C.P.A., N.Y. Mem. N.Y. State Soc. C.P.A.'s, Beta Gamma Sigma. Home: 4 Melbourne Rd Great Neck NY 11021 Office: 730 Fifth Av New York City NY 10019

BEER, MICHAEL, educator, biophysicist; b. Budapest, Hungary, Feb. 20, 1926; s. Paul and Lidia (Pap-Kovacs) B.; came to U.S., 1958, naturalized, 1965; M.A., U. Toronto, 1950; Ph.D., U. Manchester (Eng.), 1953; m. Margaret Terry Peters, Jan. 22, 1954; children—Nicholas, Suzanne, Wendy. Research asso. U. Mich., 1953-56; research fellow Nat. Research Council Can., 1956-58; mem. faculty Johns Hopkins, 1958—, prof. biophysics, 1964—. Home: 4623 Wilmslov Rd Baltimore MD 21210

BEER, SAMUEL HUTCHISON, educator; b. Bucyrus, O., July 28, 1911; s. William Cameron and Jesse Blanche (Hutchison) B.; grad. Staunton Mil. Acad.; A.B., U. Mich., 1932; B.A. (Rhodes Scholar 1932-35), Oxford U., Eng., 1935; Ph.D., Harvard, 1943; m. Roberta Frances Reed, June 22, 1935; children—Katherine, Frances, William. Writer, Resettlement Adminstrn. and Dem. Nat. Com., 1935-36; reporter N.Y. Post, 1936-37; writing, research Fortune mag., 1937-38; instr. govt. Harvard, 1938-42, asst. prof., 1946-48, asso. prof., 1948-53, prof. govt., 1953—, Eaton prof. sci. of govt., 1971—, chmn. dept. govt., 1954-58; Messenger lectr. Cornell U., 1969. Nat. chmn. Ams. for Democratic Action, 1959-62, chmn. Mass. chpt. 1955-57. Served from pvt. to capt. AUS, 1942-45. Deocrated Bronze Star; Fulbright and Guggenheim fellow, 1953-54; Mem. Am. Polit. Sci. Assn., Phi Beta Kappa. Democrat. Presbyn. Author: The City of Reason, 1949; Treasury Control: The Coordination of Financial and Economic Policy in Great Britain, 1956; co-author: Patterns of Government: The Major Political Systems of Europe, 1958; British Politics in the Collectivist Age, 1965 (Woodrow Wilson Found. award 1966); The State and the Poor, 1970. Home: 87 Lakeview Av Cambridge MA 02138

BEER, WALTER EUGENE, Jr., lawyer; b. N.Y.C., Nov. 17, 1904; s. Walter Eugene and Bella (Nathan) B.; student The Choate Sch., Wallingford, Conn., 1918-22; A.B., Harvard Coll., 1926, LL.B., 1929; m. Florence Louise Fay, Sept. 2, 1930; children—John Walter, David Wells. Admitted to N.Y. bar, 1929, and practiced as asso. Simpson Thacher & Bartlett, N.Y.C., 1929-41, Beer, Richards & Haller, 1945-49, Beer, Richards, Lane & Haller, 1949-52, Beer, Richards, Lane, Haller & Buttenweiser, 1952-59, Beer, Richards & Haller, 1960-68, Beer, Richards, Haller and O'Neil, 1968—; mem. legal staff General Counsel to United States OPM and WPB, 1941-44. Dir. Group Health Hosp. Ins., Inc., Group Health Ins., Inc., Group Health Dental Ins., Inc. Bd. dirs. Assn. for Crippled Children and Adults N.Y. State; trustee Montefiore Hosp., N.Y.C. Mem. Assn. Bar City N.Y. Clubs: Harvard (N.Y. City); Brooklyn Heights (New York) Casino (v.p. 1969—); Keene Valley (N.Y.) Country; West Side Tennis (Forest Hills, N.Y.); Ausable (N.Y.) Club. Home: 2 Montague Terrace Brooklyn NY 11201 Office: 26 Broadway New York City NY 10004

BEERITS, HENRY CHRISTOPHER, lawyer, orgn. exec.; b. Somerset, Pa., Jan. 12, 1912; s. John H. and Florence (Knepper) B.; A.B., Princeton, 1933; LL.B., Harvard, 1938, postgrad. Grad. Sch. Bus. Adminstrn., 1935-36; m. Janet Penrose Robinson, Aug. 14, 1943; children-Chrisopher, Susan, Peter. Research asst. to Chief Justice Charles E. Hughes, 1933-34; admitted to Pa. bar, 1939, since practiced in Phila.; mem. firm Morgan, Lewis & Bockius, 1954- -; atty. Girard Trust Bank, Phila., 1951; adminstrv. sec. Am. Friends Service Com., 1948-50, asso. exec. sec., 1952-53, vice chmn. bd., 1964- 69, chmn., 1969—. Chmn. Phila. Com. City Policy, 1944-47; mem. exec. bd. Com. Seventy, Phila., 1945-49; pres. Citizens Council City Planning, 1949-52; pres. Phila. Housing Assn., 1955-58; mem. bd. Pa. Economy League, 1965—; sec. Pa.-N.J.-Del. Met. Project. Inc., 1963—. Mem. Am., Pa., Phila. bar assns. Clubs: Princeton, Harvard, Midday (Phila.). Home: 235 Upper Gulph Rd Radnor PA 19087 Office: Fidelity Bldg Philadelphia PA 19109

BEERMAN, HERMAN, physician; b. Johnstown, Pa., Oct. 13, 1901; s. Morris and Fannie (Toby) B.; A.B., U. Pa., 1923, M.D., 1927, Sc.D. (Med.), 1935; m. Emma N. Segal, May 13, 1924. Asst. Dept. Agr., Phila., 1925-26; intern Mt. Sinai Hosp., Phila., 1927-28; resident Hosp. U. Pa., 1929-33, asst. chief dermatology clinic, 1938-65, Abbott fellow in chemotherapeutic research, 1932-46; with U. Pa. Sch. Medicine, 1929—, prof. dermatology, 1951-70, prof. emeritus, 1970—, prof. Grad. Sch. of Medicine, 1947-67, chmn., 1949-67; asso. serology Pepper Laboratory, 1949—, asst. dir. Inst. Study Venereal Disease, 1939- 54; physician out patient dept. Pa. Hosp., 1929-36, hosp. dermatologist, chief Out-Patient Service B, 1935-45, asso. dermatologist, 1946-47, dermatologist, head dept., 1947-67, consultant dermatologist, 1967- -; asst. dermatologist radium clinic Phila. Gen. Hosp., 1938-40, dermatologist, 1940-53, active cons. dermatology, 1953-68, honorary consultant in dermatology, 1968—; cons. lab. Children's Hosp., Phila., 1949—; cons. VA Hosp., Phila., 1953-66; cons. pathology U.S. Naval Hosp., Phila., 1954—; cons. dermatology VA Hosp., Coatesville, Pa., 1967—, USPHS, 1937—; pvt. practice, Phila., 1933—. Mem. panel venereal diseases subcom. infectious disease, chemotherapy NRC, 1954—. Sigmund Pollitzer lectr. N.Y. U., 1963; Irving Wershaw Meml. lectr., Israel, 1967; Pusey Meml. speaker Chgo. Dermatol. Soc., 1968; Ruben Nomland Meml. lectr. U. Ia., 1968. Treas., trustee Inst. Dermatologic Communication & Education, 1963—. Diplomate Am. Bd. Dermatology, 1935. Fellow A.C.P., A.A.A.S., Phila. Coll. Physicians; mem. N.Y. Acad. Scis., Tissue Culture Assn., Med. Club Phila., Am. Acad. Dermatology (bd. dirs. 1941-48, 62-67, pres. 1965-67), Am. Soc. Dermatopathology (pres. 1965-66), Assn. Professors Dermatology (dir. 1963-68, pres. 1967-68), Dermatology Foundation (past trustee), Am. (dir. 1960-65, pres. 1967-68), Pacific (honorary), Phila. dermatol. assns., Brit. Assn. Dermatology (hon. fgn. member), Swedish Dermatol. Soc., Soc. Francaise de Dermatologie et Syphiligraphie (fgn. corr.), Finnish Dermatologic Soc. (hon.), Greek Dermatol. and Venereological Union (hon.), Deutsche Dermatologische Gesellschaft (hon.), Med. Soc. Study Venereal Disease (hon.; Eng.), Soc. Investigative Dermatology (ann. Herman Beerman lecture 1960—, past pres., bd. dirs., sec.-treas. 1950-65), A.M.A., Med. Soc. State Pa., Am. Assn. U. Profs., Soc. Investigation Psychosomatic Problems, John Morgan Soc., La Societe Dermatol. Danoise (corr.), Am. Venereal Disease Assn., Solomon Solis-Cohen Med. Lit. Soc. (pres. 1961), Iranian Soc. Dermatology and Venereology (hon.), Sociedad Venezolana De Dermatologie, Venereologia y Leprologia Carcaras (hon.), Phila. County Med. Soc. (chmn. com. on infectious diseases 1968—), Israeli Dermatol. Soc. (hon.), La Academia Mexicana de Dermatologia (hon.), Academia Espanola de Dermatolgie y Sifilografia, Dermatol. Assn. Poland, Internat. Coll. Exptl. Dermatology, Laboratorio de Investigaceione's Leprologicas, Societati Dermatologicae Danicae, Ia. Dermatol. Soc., Asociacion Argentina de Dermatologia (corr.), Am. Acad. Vet. Medicine (hon. asso.), Royal Soc. Medicine London (hon.; sect. dermatology), Pa. Acad. Dermatology (hon.), Physiol. Soc. Phila., Phila. Art Alliance, Pub. Health Soc. U. Pa., Phila. Rheumatism Soc., Am. Med. Writers Assn., Sigma Xi, Phi Lambda Kappa. Editorial bd. Jour. Investigative Dermatology, 1948-53, Am. Jour. Med. Scis. Bd. editors sect. XIII-Dermatology and Syphilology, Excerpta Medica, 1950—. Author articles in field. Home: 2422 Pine St Philadelphia PA 19103 Office: 255 S 17th St Philadelphia PA 19103

BEERMAN, RALPH F., ex-congressman; b. Dakota City, Neb., Aug. 13, 1912; s. Fred W. and Agnes Ellen (Ralph) B.; student Morningside Coll., Sioux City, Ia.; m. Marjorie Smythe, March 1, 1938. Partner, Beerman Brothers, farming, cattle feeding, alfalfa dehydrating, Dakota City; mem. 87th Congress 3d Dist. Neb., 88th Congress 1st Dist. Neb. Organizer, dist. chmn. central com. Dakota County Young Republicans. Served with AUS, World War II. Mem. Am. Legion, V.F.W., Am. (past pres.), Neb. alfalfa dehydrators assns., Neb. Grain and Feed Dealers Assn., Midwest Feed Mfrs. Assn., U.S., South Sioux City (past pres.) chambers commerce, Nat., Neb. flying farmers. Lutheran. Kiwanian. Home: Dakota City NB

BEERS, HENRY SAMUEL, former ins. co. exec.; b. New Haven, Conn., June 22, 1898; s. George Emerson and Margaret (Lowry) B.; student Guilford (Conn.) High Sch., 1911-15; A.B., Trinity Coll., 1918, recipient honorary Doctor of Laws, 1968; m. Dorothy Carpenter, Apr. 28, 1926; children—Henry Samuel, Elizabeth (Raymond), John William. Pres., Aetna Life Ins. Co., Hartford, Aetna Casualty and Surety Co., Standard Fire Ins. Co., 1956- 62, chmn. bd., 1962-63, also dir.; chmn. bd. Excelsior Life Ins. Co., Toronto, Ont., Can., 1960-63; chmn. bd. N.Am. Reins. Corp., also N.Am. Reassurance Co., 1964-70. Chmn. of Gov.'s Commn. on Unemployment Compensation, 1936; mem. Conn. State Employees' Retirement Commn., 1939-64; Chmn. bd. trustees S.S. Huebner Found. for Ins. Edn., 1958-61; trustee Trinity Coll., Hartford College for Women. Fellow Soc. Acturaries; mem. Phi Beta Kappa, Delta Psi. Episcopalian. Clubs: Hartford, Hartford Golf, Appalachian Mountain. Home: 10 Newell Lane Glastonbury CT 06033

BEERS, ROLAND FRANK, geologist, geophysicist; b. Owego, N.Y., June 6, 1899; s. Archibald Stephen and Jessie Bevans (Creveling) B.; E.E., Rensselaer Poly. Inst., 1921; S.M., Mass. Inst. Tech., 1928, Ph.D., 1943; postgrad. Harvard Grad. Sch. Arts and Scis., 1940-41; m. Helen Elizabeth Clark, Oct. 29, 1921; children—Roland F., Barbara Helen. Instr. physics and elec. engring. Rensselaer Poly. Inst., Troy, N.Y., 1921-22; devel. engr. Western Electric Co., N.Y.C., 1922-23; mgr. A.S. Beers, Binghamton, N.Y., 1925; devel. engr. Raytheon Mfg. Co., Cambridge, Mass., 1925-26; physicist Submarine Signal Corp., Boston, 1927-28; party chief Geophys. Research Corp., Houston, 1928-31; party chief Geophys. Service, Inc., Dallas, 1931-34, v.p., 1934-36; pres., dir. The Geotechnical Corp., Dallas, 1936—; chmn. bd. and dir., 1947-56; pres., dir., Geotech. Corp. of Can., Ltd. (Montreal), 1944-56; partner Beers and Heroy, Dallas 1946-56; pres., dir. Roland F. Beers, Inc., 1955—; cons. U.S. AEC, 1957—; pres. Geodynamics, Inc., Alexandria, Va., 1963—; chmn. bd. Beers & Rodemann, Inc., Alexandria, 1964—; pres. Knox Mining Corp., 1964—; research asso., dept. geol. Mass. Inst. Tech., Cambridge, 1943-46; geophys. cons. U.S. Geol. Survey, Washington, 1943-46; mem. NRC Com. on Measurement of Geologic Time, 1945—; mem. NRC Com. on Seismic Effects of Detonations, 1945-46, com. on sedimentation, 1947—; head dept. fuel resources, prof. geophysics Rensselaer Polytech. Inst., 1948- 52; permanent adv. com. geol. dept. So. Meth. U., 1947; lectr. geophysics Rensselaer Poly. Inst., Troy, N.Y., 1947; mem. adv. com. on geophysics Office of Naval Research; mem. com. on rock mechanics Nat. Acad. Scis. Trustee Russell Sage Coll., Albany Med. Coll., Vt. Acad. Mem. Internat. Geologic Year nat. com. seismology and gravity. Fellow Geol. Soc. Am., A.A.A.S., Am. Acad. Arts and Scis.; mem. Am. Assn. Petroleum Geologists, Soc. Exploration Geophysicists (chmn. best paper award com. 1946-47), Am. Inst. Mining Metall. and Petroleum Engrs., I.E.E.E., Am. Geophys. Union, Seismol. Soc. Am., Photog. Soc. Am., Royal Photog. Soc. (London), Am. Soc. for Testing Materials, Sigma Xi, Eta Kappa Nu, Tau Beta Pi, Alpha Tau Omega. Presbyn. Clubs: Cosmos (Washington); Harvard (Boston); Mass. Institute Technology (N.Y.C.); Petroleum, Brook Hollow (Dallas). Contbr. tech. publs. Home: West Rd Manchester VT 05254 Office: 813 N Royal St PO Box 1061 Alexandria VT 22313

BEERS, THOMAS MOULDING, orgn. exec.; b. Chgo., Sept. 11, 1912; s. Sylvester Piper and Sarah Pearl (Moulding) B.; B.A., Dartmouth, 1934; grad. student, Northwestern U., 1934-35; m. Mary Ella Waidner, Sept. 16, 1939; children—Susan Elizabeth (Mrs. Peter R. Betzer), Thomas Moulding, Nancy Waidner, Richard William. With R. R. Donnelley & Sons Co., Chgo., 1934-58, v.p., 1957-58; with Nat. Geog. Soc., Washington, 1959—, asso. sec., 1961-62, v.p., 1962—. Bd. dirs. Wildfowl Fund. Served to lt. comdr. USNR, 1942-46. Mem. Phi Kappa Psi. Republican. Methodist. Clubs: University (Washington); Chicago Yacht; Chevy Chase (Md.). Home: 10801 Admirals Way Potomac Rockville MD 20854 Office: Nat Geog Soc 17th and M Sts Washington DC 20036

BEERS, WILLIAM O., food co. exec.; b. Lena, Ill., May 26, 1914; s. Ernest and Rose (Binz) B.; student U. Ill., 1933-37, LL.D., 1970; m. Mary Elizabeth Holmes (dec.); m. 2d, Frances Lemaux Miller, Feb. 17, 1954; children—Barbara Ann, Mary Elizabeth (Mrs. Daniel L. Commes), Richard W.; stepchildren—Duncan R. Miller, Marila Miller (Mrs. John T. Beatty, Jr.). With Kraftco Corp., 1937—, dir., 1965—, pres., 1968—, pres. Kraft Foods div., 1965-68; dir. Mfrs. Hanover Trust Co., Mfrs. Hanover Corp., Sears Roebuck and Co., Sperry and Hutchinson Co., Nat. Blvd. Bank Chgo., A.O. Smith Corp. Trustee Consumer Research Inst., Nutrition Found. Inc., Food and Drug Law Inst., Wis. Alumni Research Found.; bd. dirs. U. Wis. Alumni Found. Mem. Internat. C. of C. (trustee U.S. council), Agribus. Industry Adv. Com., Am. Acad. Polit. and Social Sci., Grocery Mfrs. Am.-IDA Council, President's Club of U. Wis. Alumni Found. Clubs: Economic, Union League (N.Y.C.); Blind Brook (Portchester, N.Y.); Greenwich (Conn.) Country, Indian Harbor Yacht, Indian Hill (Greenwich); Chicago, Tavern (Chgo.); Monroe Country (Wis.); Westmoreland Country (Wilmette, Ill.). Home: 45 Woodley Rd Winnetka IL 60093 Office: 260 Madison Av New York City NY 10016

BEERY, JOHN REPLOGLE, educator; b. Tyrone, Pa., Mar. 4, 1909; s. Rev. Charles O. and Louella (Replogle) B.; A.B., Juniata Coll., 1930, LL.D., 1951; A.M., U. Chgo., 1934; Ph.D., Columbia, 1942; m. Anna Florence Stayer, June 18, 1943; 1 dau., Linda Althea. Instr. math. Martinsburg (Pa.) High Sch., 1930-32, Merchantville (N.J.) High Sch., 1932-35, Princeton (N.J.) High Sch., 1935-38; asst. secondary edn. Columbia Tchrs. Coll., summers 1938-39; asst. dir. occupational adjustment study Nat. Assn. Secondary-Sch. Prins., 1939-40, asso. dir., 1940-41; asso. prof. edn. U. Miami, Fla., 1941-46, prof. edn., 1946—, coordinator univ. guidance center, 1946-47, dean Sch. Edn., 1947—, dir. of instrn., 1948-64. Served as capt. USAAF, 1942-45. Mem. A.A.A.S., Am. Assn. U. Profs., Am. Coll. Personnel Assn., Am. Ednl. Research Assn., Am. Psychol. Assn., Fla. Acad. Sci., Fla. Edn. Assn., Fla. Teacher Edn. Adv. Council, Nat. Assn. Secondary Sch. Prins., N.E.A., Nat. Vocational Guidance Assn., Phi Delta Kappa, Kappa Delta Pi. Ch. Brethren. Author: Current Conceptions of Democracy, 1943; co-author: The School Follows Through, 1941; Occupational Adjustment and the School 1940; Professional Preparation and Effectiveness of Beginning Teachers, 1960. Contbr. articles to ednl. jours. Home: 7921 SW 50 Ct Miami, FL 33143.

BEESLEY, EDWARD MAURICE, educator; b. Belvidere, N.J., Jan. 11, 1915; s. Maurice Edward and Eva Lena (Bair) B.; A.B. magna cum laude, Lafayette Coll., 1936; Sc.M., Brown U., 1938, Ph.D., 1943; m. Audrey Champlin Maymon, July 11, 1940; children—Barbara (Mrs. Donald Wayne Heath), Maurice Edward, Norman Ernest. Faculty, U. Nev., Reno, 1940—, prof. math., 1955—, chmn. dept., 1944—. Mem. Math. Assn. Am., Am. Math. Soc., Am. Fedn. Musicians, Phi Beta Kappa, Sigma Xi, Phi Kappa Phi, Pi Mu Epsilon. Home: 2338 Westfield Av Reno NV 89502

BEESLEY, EUGENE NEVIN, pharm. exec.; b. Thorntown, Ind., Jan. 29, 1909; s. Ralph N. and Della Mae (Rinehart) B.; A.B., Wabash Coll., 1929; LL.B., Ind. U., 1943; LL.D., DePauw U., 1956, Wabash College, 1959; D.Sc., U. Toledo, 1957; Doctor of Humanities, Ind. Central Coll., 1964; D.H.L., Butler U., 1966; LL.D., Ind. U., 1966; m. Marian L. Crehore, Oct. 23, 1931; children—Mary Louise (Mrs. Needham S. Hurst), Mark Crehore. Econ. research dept. Eli Lilly & Co., Indpls., 1929, salesman, 1929-37, dist. sales mgr., 1937-41; mgr. trade relations, 1941-44, dir. personnel relations, 1944-49, asso. dir. sales, 1949-51, v.p. 1951, became dir. and exec. v.p., 1952, pres., 1953-69, chairman of the board, 1969—; chmn. bd. dirs. Eli Lilly Internat. Corp.; dir. Eli Lilly Interam., Inc., Eli Lilly & Co. of India, Inc., Lilly Industries Ltd., Eli Lilly & Co. (Can.) Ltd., Eli Lilly Industries Pty. Ltd., Eli Lilly y Compania de Mexico, S.A. de C.V., Procter & Gamble Co., Am. Fletcher Corp., Gen. Motors Corp., Pub. Service Ind. Admitted to Ind. bar, 1943. Mem. Bus. Council. Bd. govs. Asso. Colls. Ind.; bd. dirs. Radio Free Europe Fund, Inc., Am. Found. for Pharm. Edn., Ind. U. Found., United Fund Greater Indpls., Inc.; bd. mem. Nat. Indsl. Conf. Bd.; v.p., dir. Lilly Endowment, Inc.; v.p. bd. trustees Wabash Coll. Mem. Pharm. Mfrs. Assn. (dir.), Am., Ind. bar assns., Newcomen Soc. N.Am., James Whitcomb Riley Meml. Assn., Beta Theta Pi. Presbyn. (elder). Mason (Shriner). Clubs: Indpls. Athletic, Meridian Hills Country, Columbia (Indpls.); Links (N.Y.). Home: 6099 Sunset Lane Indianapolis IN 46208 Office: 307 E McCarty St Indianapolis IN 46206

BEESLEY, JOSEPH L., ins. exec.; b. Alert, Ind., Aug. 24, 1904; s. John W. and Mary (Stephenson) B.; A.B., DePauw U., 1926; m. Alta M. Biddinger, June 27, 1924; children—Lester, John E. With Equitable Life Assurance Soc. U.S., 1926—, beginning as trainee, successively cashier, Denver, Phoenix, Syracuse, asst. cashier, N.Y.C., cashier, Chgo., agy. mgr., Syracuse, field v.p. charge N.Y. area agencies, 1953, sr. v.p. charge sales, 1955-61, sr. v.p., asst. to chmn. 1961-69, spl. rep., 1969—. Commr., treas. Nat. Commn. Community Health Services, 1962-66; mem. regional health adv. com. USPHS. Trustee Am. Fund for Dental Education, 1961-69, DePauw U. C.L.U. Mem. Equitable Group Millionaires, Nat. Assn. Life Underwriters (chmn. edn. com. Chgo.; dist. dir. Syracuse 1947-48), Life Agy. Mgrs. Assn., Syracuse Life Trust Council, Life Ins. Agy. Mgmt. Assn. (dir. 1961-63), Am. Coll. Life Underwriters (pub. relations com.), Am. Life Conv. (chmn. agy. sect. 1960), Agy. Officers Round Table (chmn. 1959-60), Phi Beta Kappa, Delta Chi. Methodist. Mason. Clubs: Rotary; Garden City Country, Union League. Home: 63 Osborne Rd Garden City NY 11530 Office: 98 Cutter Mill Rd Great Neck NY 11021

BEESLEY, KENNETH HORACE, educator; b. Salt Lake City, Nov. 14, 1926; s. Alvin Douglas and Theresa (McAllister) B.; student Brigham U., 1948-49; B.A. with honors, U. Utah, 1952; M.A., Columbia Tchrs. Coll., 1954, Ed.D., 1957; m. Donna Deem, Dec. 2, 1950; children—Kenneth Reid, Rulon Deem, Diane, Tamara, Ellen Christine. Lectr. health edn. Columbia, 1954-55, research asso. coop. study tchr. recruitment Tchrs. Coll., 1955-56, coordinator student tours, 1956; asst. coordinator student activities Bklyn. Coll., 1955-57; mem. faculty and staff Columbia Tchrs. Coll., 1957-67, asst. provost, registrar, asst. prof. edn., 1958-66, asst. provost, asst. prof. edn., 1966-67; exec. dean, dir. instl. studies, Fresno State Coll., 1967-68, exec. dean, 1968-70; asso. commr. edn. coll. and schs. Ch. Jesus Christ Latter-Day Saints, Salt Lake City, 1970—. Mem. Morningside Renewal Council, 1964-67; mem. coordinating council and adv. com. Fresno Interagy. Planning for Urban Edn. Needs, 1968-69. Trustee Eastchester (N.Y.) Library, 1961-63. Served with USNR, 1944-46. Mem. Assn. Higher Edn. Mem. Ch. of Jesus Christ of Latter Day Saints (bishop Fresno 1st ward Fresno E. stake 1967-70). Home: 1457 Wilton Way Salt Lake City UT 84108

BEESON, CARROL MENEFEE, educator, cons.; b. Jacksonville, Ala., Dec. 13, 1903; s. William James and Auline (Moore) B.; A.B., U. Cal. at Los Angeles, 1935; PH.D., Cal. Inst. Tech., 1939; m. Helen Elizabeth Booher, Jan. 1, 1924; children—Barbara (Mrs. Mersini), Virginia (Mrs. Ruffolo). Propr. Beeson Bros. Ice Cream Distbrs., Los Angeles, Beverley Hills, Cal., 1924-42; chem. engr. Gen. Petroleum Corp., Los Angeles, 1938-40; supr. prodn. research div. Lab. Dept., Gen. Petroleum Corp., 1940-48; asso. prof. petroleum engring. U. So. Cal., 1948-52, prof., 1952-65, head dept. petroleum engring., 1954-65; prof. engring. and chmn. div. engring Cal. State Coll. at Los Angeles, 1965-67; pres. Oilwell Research, Inc., 1949-50. Mem. Registration Bd. Civil, Prof. Engrs., 1959-67, v.p., 1962, pres., 1963-64, chmn. petroleum engring. com., 1959-67; chmn. com optimum edn. requirements to profl. engrs. for Nat. Council of State Bds. Engring. Examiners, 1963-64. Registered petroleum chem. engr., Cal. Mem. Am. Petroleum Inst. (nat. chmn. com. core analysis and well-logging 1947-49, chmn. Pacific Coast dist. study com. prodn. tech. 1952-53), Am. Inst. Mining, Metall. and Petroleum Engrs. (organizer, 1st chmn. com. lab. methods prodn. research So. Cal. petroleum sect. 1946; nat. chmn. Carll award com. 1962), Am. Chem. Soc. (asso. editor Scalacs, So. Cal. sect.), Am. Soc. Engring. Edn., Nat., Cal., Los Angeles socs. profl. engrs., Phi Beta Kappa, Sigma Xi, Tau Beta Pi, Phi Kappa Phi, Pi Epsilon Tau. Author numerous tech. articles. Home: 2818 Haddington Dr Los Angeles CA 90064

BEESON, JACK HAMILTON, educator, composer; b. Muncie, Ind., July 15, 1921; ed. Eastman Sch. Music, U. Rochester, Columbia; studied with Bela Bartok; m. Nora Beate Sigerist; children—Christopher Sigerist, Miranda. Tchr., Juilliard Sch. Music; asso. dir. opera workshop, MacDowell prof. music, chmn. dept. and div. music Columbia. Sec. Alice Ditson Fund; v.p. Composers Recordings, Inc.; vice chmn. bd. Composers Forum. Mem. bd. Am. Music Center. Recipient Rome prize, City of Rochester prize, Marc Blitstein Mus. Theatre award Nat. Inst. Arts and Letters; Guggenheim fellow; Fulbright fellow to Italy. Mem. A.S.C.A.P., League Composers (bd.). Composer: Symphony in A, other works for orch. and band; (operas) Jonah, Hello Out There, The Sweet Bye and Bye, Lizzie Bordon, My Heart's in The Highlands; also choral, chamber and vocal works. Home: 445 Riverside Dr New York City NY also Hightowers Shelter Island Heights NY Office: Dept Music Columbia Univ New York City NY 10027

BEESON, PAUL BRUCE, physician; b. Livingston, Mont., Oct. 18, 1908; s. John Bradley and Martha Gerard (Ash) B.; student U. Wash., 1925-28; M.D., C.M., McGill U., 1933, D.Sc., 1971; D.Sc., Emory U., 1968; m. Barbara Neal, July 10, 1942; children—John, Peter, Judith. Asst. Rockefeller Inst., 1937-39, Harvard Med. Sch., 1939-40; asst. prof. medicine Emory U. Med. Sch., 1942-46; prof., chmn. dept., 1946-52; Ensign prof. medicine, chmn. dept. internal medicine Yale Med. Sch., 1952-65; physician-in-chief univ. service Grace-New Haven Community Hosp., 1952-65; vis. investigator Wright-Fleming Inst., London, 1958-59; Nuffield prof. clin. medicine Oxford (Eng.) U., 1965—. Named Alumnus Summa Laude Dignatus, U. Wash., 1968; recipient Fiftieth Anniversary Gold medal Peter Bent Brigham Hosp., 1962. Fellow Berkeley Coll., Yale, also Magdalen Coll., Oxford U. Fellow Royal Coll. Physicians (London); Mem. Nat. Acad. Scis., Am. Acad. Arts and Scis., A.C.P. (master), Soc. Exptl. Biology and Medicine, Am. Soc. Clin. Investigation, Assn. Am. Physicians (pres. 1967), Assn. Physicians Gt. Britain and Ireland. Episcopalian. Club: Athenaeum. Co-editor: Cecil Loeb Textbook of Medicine. Home: Woodbridge House Old Boars Hill Oxford England Office: Radcliffe Infirmary Oxford England

BEESON, RICHARD CALVIN, consumer products co. exec.; b. Muncie, Ind., Sept. 10, 1928; s. Ronald Louis and Margaret (Taylor) B.; B.A., Johns Hopkins, 1949; m. Ellen Emery, Aug. 21, 1950; children—Gayle, Cathy, Scott. With Colgate- Palmolive Co., 1951-68, Caribbean area mgr., San Juan, P.R., 1968; pres. Salada Foods Ltd., Toronto, Can., 1968-71, Canadian Food Products Ltd., Toronto, 1968-71, Erindale Foods Ltd., Toronto, 1968-71; exec. v.p., dir., mem. exec. com. Ky. Fried Chicken Corp., 1971—; dir. Coffee Co. Jamaica Ltd. Club: Toronto Cricket Skating and Curling. Office: PO Box 13331 Louisville KY 40213

BEETLE, DAVID HAROLD, editorial writer, author, columnist; born Edgartown, Martha's Vineyard Island, Mass., June 5, 1908; s. Frank Wasson and Susan (Phillips) B.; A.B., Hamilton Coll., 1930; m. Gladys Elizabeth Small, July 8, 1937 (div. Oct. 1955); 1 son, David H.; m. 2d, Patricia Gibson, Jan. 2, 1958; children—Christopher G., Karen A. Reporter Utica Daily Press, 1930-33, state editor, 1933-36, columnist, 1936-39; dir. public relations, editor Alumni Review, Hamilton Coll., Clinton, N.Y., 1939-54, instr. English, 1941-43, cons. pub. relations, 1954-55; legislative corr. N.Y. State, Gannett Newspapers, Inc., 1944-55; editor editorial page Albany (N.Y.) Knickerbocker News, 1955-56, editor, 1956-60; special correspondent, editorial writer Gannett Newspapers, Albany, 1961—. Cons. N.Y. State Dept. Edn., 1964- -; mem. N.Y. State Commn. History, 1959, Recipient Order Orange-Nassau (Netherlands). Mem. N.Y. State Legislative Corr.'s Assn., N.Y. State Soc. Newspaper Editors, Phi Beta Kappa. Conglist. Clubs: National Press (Wash.); Torch. Adirondack Mountain, University (Albany, N.Y.). Author: West Canada Creek, 1946; Along the Oriskany, 1947; Up Old Forge Way, 1948; The New York State Citizen, 1955. Contbr. articles nat. mags. Home: Sunset Rd RFD 1 Castleton-on-Hudson NY 12033 Office: State Capitol Albany NY

BEETON, ALFRED MERLE, educator, limnologist; b. Denver, Aug. 15, 1927; s. Charles Frederick and Edna (Smith) B.; B.S., U. Mich., 1952, M.S., 1954, Ph.D., 1958; m. Mary Eileen Wilcox, July 20, 1945; children—Maureen Ann, Heather Ann, Celeste Nadine; m. 2d, Ruth Elizabeth Holland, June 4, 1966. Fishery biologist U.S. Bur. Comml. Fisheries, Ann Arbor, Mich., 1957-65, chief environmental research, 1960-65; prof. zoology, asst. dir. Center for Gt. Lakes Studies, U. Wis.-Milw., 1965-69, prof., asso. dir., 1969—; lectr. biology Wayne State U., 1957-61; lectr. civil engring. U. Mich., 1961-65; mem. research adv. council Wis. Dept. Natural Resources; cons. U.S. Army C.E., 1967—. Mem. Internat. Assn. Theoretical and Applied Limnology, Am. Soc. Limnology and Oceanography (treas. 1962—), Am. Soc. Zoologists, Internat. Assn. Gt. Lakes Research, Sigma Xi. Contbr. chpts. to books, articles Ency. Brit. Home: 340 Park Circle Cedarburg WI 53012 Office: U Wis Milwaukee WI 53201

BEETON, RALPH ALBERT, banker; b. Alexandria, Va., May 30, 1927; s. Frank Emerson and Anna (Vetter) B.; B.A., U. Va., 1950, LL.B., 1954; m. Virginia Elizabeth Holland, Apr. 30, 1955; children—Thomas McHarg, Sarah Elizabeth, William Trammell, Charlotte Ames. Admitted to Va. bar; pvt. practice law, Waynesboro, Va. and Arlington County, 1954-60; exec. v.p., gen. counsel First Va. Bankshares Corp., Arlington, 1960-62, pres., gen. counsel, 1962-67, pres., chief exec. officer, 1967—, dir., 1957—; dir. First Va. Bank, Larchmont Realty Mgmt., Inc. Mem. Va. Gov.'s Bus. Adv. Bd., 1967, 69, 70, Va. Ports Study Commn., 1969. Bd. visitors Longwood Coll., Farmville, Va. Served with USNR, 1945-46. DuPont scholar U. Va., 1952-54, Marcuse scholar, 1953-54, Bennett scholar, 1953-54. Mem. Newcomen Soc., Va., Arlington County bar assns. Methodist. Clubs: Washington Golf and Country (Arlington); Farmington Country, University of Va. (Charlottesville). Home: 4524 35th Rd N Arlington VA 22207 Office: 2924 Columbia Pike Arlington VA 22204

BEETS, FREEMAN HALEY, govt. ofcl.; b. Chickasha, Okla., Apr. 17, 1919; s. Daniel Walter and Ida Belle (Alverson) B.; B.A. in Journalism, U. Okla., 1946, M.A., 1948, Ed.D., 1954; m. Margaret Elizabeth Edwards, Dec. 25, 1941; 1 dau., Susan Belle. Instr. journalism Okla. Bapt. U., 1948, asst. prof. journalism and bus., 1950, dir. night sch., chmn. div. applied arts and sci., 1951-53; asst. exec. sec. edn. commn. So. Bapt. Conv., Nashville, 1953-55; dir. admissions, registrar Hardin-Simmons U., 1955-56; asst. to pres., prof. journalism Okla. Coll. Liberal Arts, 1956-58, pres., 1958-61; regional rep. div. coll. and unvi. assistance U.S. Office of Edn., 1961-66, regional asst. commnr. edn., Kansas City, Mo., 1966-70; dir. higher edn. U.S. Office Edn., Kansas City (Mo.), regional office, 1970—. Served to 1st lt. AUS, 1941-45. Decorated Bronze Star. Mem. Am. Assn. Sch. Adminstrs., Assn. Higher Edn. Home: 7900 Roe Av Shawnee Mission KS Office: Fed Office Bldg 601 E 12th St Kansas City MO 64106

BEEVERS, HARRY, educator, plant physiologist; b. England, Jan. 10, 1924; s. Norman and Olive (Ayre) B.; B.Sc. with honours, Durham (Eng.) U., 1945, Ph.D., 1947; m. Jean Sykes, Nov. 19, 1949; 1 son, Michael Harry. Came to U.S., 1950, naturalized, 1958. Postdoctoral research asst. botany Oxford (Eng.) U., 1946-50; mem. faculty Purdue U., 1950-69, prof. plant physiology, 1958-69; prof. biology U. Cal. at Santa Cruz, 1969—; cons. NSF, 1958-60, 63-65. Sr. postdoctoral fellow NSF, Cambridg, Eng., 1963- 64. Mem. Nat. Acad. Scis., Soc. Exptl. Biology, Assn. Biol. Chemists, Soc. Plant Physiology (pres. 1960, trustee 1964-67; Stephen Hales award 1970). Author: Respiratory Metabolism in Plants, 1961. Home: 46 S Circle Dr Pasatiempo Santa Cruz CA 95060

BEEVOR, JOHN GROSVENOR, banker; b. Newark, Eng., Mar. 1905; s. Henry and Alice Mary (Bryant) B.; student Winchester Coll., Eng., 1917-24, New Coll., Oxford (Eng.) U., 1924- 28; m. Carinthia Waterfield, 1933; m. 2d, Mary Christine Grepe, Feb. 1957. Practice law, London, Eng., 1931-53, partner Slaughter & May, solicitors, company law; mng. dir. Commonwealth Devel. Finance Co., London, 1954-56; v.p. Internat. Finance Corp., Washington, 1956-64; chmn. Doulton & Co. (U.K.), Lafarge Organisation (U.K.), Tilburg Contracting; dir. Ciments Lafarge (France); Glaxo Group, Williams & Glyns Bank (U.K.). Adviser Brit. delegation Marshall Plan Conf., Paris, 1947. Served to lt. col. Brit. Army, 1939-45. Club: Brooks (London). Home: 51 Eaton Sq London SW 1 England

BEFFA, HARVEY ARTHUR, brewery exec.; b. St. Louis, June 19, 1900; s. Anton and Mary (Degan) B.; student pub. schs. St. Louis; m. Henrietta Stahl, June 24, 1922; children—Harvey Arthur, Helen, Mary Etta, Daniel. Clk. Anton Beffa & Son Wrecking & Supply Co., St. Louis, 1915-20, gen. mgr., 1920-32; sec. Falstaff Brewing Corp., St. Louis, 1933-35, v.p., dir. 1935, later exec. v.p., gen. mgr., then chmn. bd., 1962-69, now chmn. exec. com.; dir. Mercantile Commerce Nat. Bank. Dir. Midwest Polio Assn.; vice chmn. bd. trustees Shriners Hosps. for Crippled Children, also chmn. emeritus St. Louis unit. Recipient St. Louis Humanistics award, 1964; named Big Brother of Year, St. Louis, 1966. Mem. Master Brewers Assn. Am. Republican. Presbyn. Mason (32, Shriner; past imperial potentate). Clubs: Missouri Athletic, Advertising, Glen Echo Country, St. Louis, University. Home: 5 Lucas Lane Normandy MO 63121 Office: 5050 Oakland Av St Louis MO 63110

BEG, MIRZA ABDUL BAQI, theoretical physicist; b. Etawah, India, Sept. 20, 1934; s. Mirza Abdul Hai and Sarah (Khan) B.; B.Sc. with honours, D.J.S. Govt. Sci. Coll., Karachi, Pakistan, 1951; M.Sc., Karachi U., 1954; Ph.D., U. Pitts., 1958; m. Nancie Stager Kress, Nov. 7, 1958. Came to U.S., 1966. Research fellow U. Birmingham (Eng.), 1958-60; research asso. Brookhaven Nat. Lab., 1960-62, cons., 1965—; mem. Inst. Advanced Study, Princeton, 1962-64; mem. faculty Rockefeller U., 1964—, prof. physics, 1968—; vis. positions at U. Cal. at Berkeley, Argonne Nat. Lab., Niels Bohr Inst., U. Wash., Scuola Normale Superiore, Pisa. Italy, Stanford. Mem. Am. Phys. Soc. Contbr. profl. jours. Home: 444 E 82d St New York City NY 10028

BEGANDO, JOSEPH SHERIDAN, ednl. adminstr.; b. Roseland, Kan., Jan. 7, 1921; s. James and Bessie (Barcus) B.; B.S., Kan. State Coll., Pittsburg, 1942; M.S., U. Ill., 1947, Ph.D., 1951; m. Virginia DeVillo Suttee, Aug. 6, 1943; children—DeVillo, Dana, Darcy. Asst. in marketing U. Ill., 1946-47, instr., 1948-51; instr. commerce Kan. State Coll., Pittsburg, 1947-48, asst. prof. econs., summer 1951; asst. prof. marketing U. Kan., 1951-53; asst. dean, asso. prof. pharmacy adminstn. U. Ill., 1953-58, asst. to pres., 1958-61; v.p. U. Ill. at Chgo.

Med. Center, 1961-66, chancellor, 1966—. Acad. fellow Inst. Medicine Chgo., 1964-70. Mem. nat. adv. council on nurse training USPHS; mem. Illinois League Nursing; mem. Orgn. Univ. Health Center Adminstrs.; Bd. dirs. Med. Center YMCA, Ill. Soc. Med. Research. Served to lt. (s.g.) USCGR, 1942-45. Recipient Meritorious Achievement award Kan. State Coll., 1959. Mem. Assn. Am. Med. Colls., Pi Omega Pi, Beta Gamma Sigma, Alpha Kappa Psi, Rho Chi, Delta Kappa Sigma, Phi Delta Chi. Clubs: Chicago, City, Executives (Chgo.). Home: 842 Washington St Elmhurst IL 60126 Office: 1737 W Polk St Chicago IL 60612

BEGG, JOHN ALFRED, artist, book designer; b. New Smyrna, Fla., June 23, 1903; s. John Alfrd and Rose (Gradick) B.; student U. Fla., 1920-21; B.S., Columbia, 1924; m. Miriam Mendelsohn, Mar. 3, 1934; children—John Alfred, Barbara Jane. Free lance artist, Fla., 1924-25; advt. mgr. Taylor- Alexander Properties, Inc., Winter Haven, Fla., 1925-26; art dir. Anderson Advt. Agency Tampa, 1926-27, Madison Square Press, N.Y.C., 1927-31, Union Lithogrpah Co., San Francisco, 1931-32; art editor, book designer, Am. Book Co., N.Y.C., 1932-37; free lance book designing, N.Y.C., 1937-39; prodn. mgr. Oxford U. Press, N.Y.C., 1939—, asst. sec., 1956-60, v.p., 1960-68; instr. typography and design N.Y.U., 1950-57. Exhbn. book work Am. Trade Book Designers, 1945; books designed rep. annual textbook exhbns. sponsored by Am. Inst. Graphic Arts, in the Fifty Books of the Year and in Artes del libros los Estados Unidos; one-man show, sculpture, water colors, Wakefield Gallery, N.Y.C., 1942, Friedman Gallery, 1947, Feist Gallery; 1969. exhbtd. group shows Whitney, Worcester, Bklyn., Riverside, Albany museums; retrospective exhbn. (with wife) Hudson River Mus., 1962, sculpture show 1967; rep. Addison Gallery Am. Art, N.Y. Pub. Library, pvt. collections. Bd. dirs. Am. Inst. Graphic Arts, 1942-44, 51-54. Recipient 1st prize in sculpture Hudson River Mus., 1958, 59, 64, purchase award, 1970. Club: Typophiles. Address: 137 S Broadway Hastings-on-Hudson NY 10706

BEGG, JOHN MURRAY, investment co. executive; b. San Jose, Costa Rica, Jan. 5, 1903; s. John William and Blanche Eugenie (Bowns) B.; student Clifton Coll., 1916-19; A.B., Harvard, 1924; A.B., Magdalen Coll., U. Oxford, Eng., 1925; Master of Arts, Oxford University, 1965; m. Jeanne Frederique van den Bosch, June 27, 1940. Pub. relations writer Internat. Tel. & Tel. Co., 1926-27; producer ednl. films, Cal., 1927-28; asst. editor and Far Eastern dir. Fox Movietone News, 1928-30; editor Newsreel Theatres, Radio News and Newsreels, Pathe, 1930-36; v.p. Motion Picture Merchandising Corp., 1936- 40; asst. to pres. Phillips Lord, Inc., radio program producers, 1940- 41; with Dept. of State 1941-53; asst. chief cultural relations, 1941, acting chief motion picture and radio div., 1944, chief internat. information div., 1944-46, chief internat. motion pictures div., 1946, asst. dir. office internat. information and cultural affairs, 1947, dir. pvt. enterprise coop. staff internat. inform. adminstrn. 1948-53; alternate U.S. rep. sucom. on edn., Com. for Strengthening Democratic Processes, Far Eastern Commn., 1946; cons. U.S. Delegation, London Preparatory Commn. UNESCO, 1946; v. chmn. U. S. Delegation to Internat. High Frequency Broadcasting Conf., Atlantic City, N.J., 1947; spl. asst. to U.S. Ambassador to The Netherlands, 1949; dep. examiner for Bd. of Examiners for the Fgn. Service 1952-53; became dep. dir. Office of Private Corp., USIA, 1953-60; president Islands Investment Corp., Washington, 1960—, Begg Disher Associates Inc., Washington, 1966- -. Recipient Merit Citation, Nat. Civil Service League, 1956; Superior Service Award. U.S. Information Agy., 1956. Member United States Foreign Service Association, Washington, Virgin Islands, National, and International real estate boards. Episcopalian. Clubs: Harvard (N.Y. City); Metropolitan (Washington); Gibson Island (Md.); Sprat Bay (V.I.). Home: Roedown Farm Davidsonville MD 21035 Office: 1714 Connecticut Av NW Washington DC 20009

BEGGS, ELMORE DIXIE, lawyer; b. Pensacola, Fla., Apr. 3, 1908; s. Elmore Dixie and Lily (Clubbs) B.; A.B., J.D., U. Fla., 1931; m. Margaret Ridley, Oct. 18, 1947 (dec. Mar. 1966); children—Caroline Cornelia, Elmore Dixie III; m. 2d, Leonora Risher, Sept. 26, 1970. Admitted to Fla. bar, 1931; state atty. 1st Jud. Circuit of Fla., 1933-41; partner Beggs, Lane, Daniel, Gaines & Davis, Pensacola, 1937; dir. Barnett Banks Fla. 1st Bank & Trust Co. Pensacola. Mem. Fla. Jud. Council, 1953-59. Past pres. Fla. Bapt. Found.; pres. Bapt. Hosp. Pensacola. Served as lt. col. AUS, 1942-46. Decorated Legion of Merit, Bronze Star; Order Brit. Empire; Croix de Guerre (France); Medal for Merit (Czechoslovakia); Crown of Italy medla. Fellow Am. Bar Found. (chmn. 1968), Am. Coll. Trial Lawyers; mem. Am. Coll. Probate Counsel (regent), Am. (state del. Ho. Dels. 1949-58, bd. govs. 1958-61), Fla. (pres. 1947-48) bar assns., Am. Judicature Soc., Internat. Assn. Ins. Counsel, Am. Counsel Assn., Fedn. Ins. Counsel, Phi Beta Kappa, Phi Delta Phi, Omicron Delta Kappa, Phi Kappa Phi, Scabbard and Blade, Blue Key. Mason (32), Rotarian. Home: 510 N 20th Av Pensacola FL 32501 Office: 700 Brent Annex Pensacola FL 32503

BEGGS, GEORGE ERLE, Jr., mfg. exec.; b. Princeton, Aug. 6, 1916; s. George Erle and Frances May (Ingalls) B.; grad. Lawrenceville Sch., 1934; B.A. in Physics, Princeton, 1938; m. Margaret Mueller, Mar. 19, 1940; children—Barbara Anne, Robert Eric. Research dept. John A. Roebling's Sons & Co., Trenton, N.J., 1938-40; with Leeds & Northrup Co., Phila., 1940—, now pres., dir.; dir. Leeds & Northrup, Ltd. (Eng.), Leeds & Northrup Italiana S.p.A., Leeds & Northrup, Can., Leeds & Northrup, Mexicana, S.A., Leeds & Northrup Australia Pty. Ltd., Provident Mut. Life Ins. Co. Phila., 1st Pa. Banking & Trust Co., Carpenter Tech. Corp., NARCO Sci. Industries Inc., Phila. Port Corp., Cin. Milacron Inc., Computer Hardware Consultants and Services, Inc. Bd. mgrs. North Pen Hosp., Franklin Inst. With nat. def. research com. OSRD, 1942-45. Recipient President's Certificate of Merit. Fellow I.E.E.E.; mem. Sci. Apparatus Makers Assn., Franklin Inst., Machinery and Allied Products Inst. (exec. com.). Rotarian. Home: Warrington PA 18976 Office: Sumneytown Pike North Wales PA 19454

BEGGS, JAMES MONTGOMERY, govt. ofcl.; b. Pitts., Jan. 9, 1926; s. James Andrew and Elizabeth (Mikulen) B.; student So. Meth. U., 1942-44; B.S. in Engring., U.S. Naval Acad., 1948; M.B.A., Harvard Grad. Sch. Bus. Adminstrn., 1955; m. Mary Elizabeth Harrison, Oct. 3, 1953; children—Maureen Elizabeth, Kathleen Louise, Teresa Lynn, James Harrison, Charles Montgomery. Commd. ensign U.S. Navy, 1947, advanced through grades to lt. comdr., 1954; resigned, 1954; gen. mgr. Westinghouse Electric Corp. underseas div., 1955-61, systems operations, 1960-63; v.p. surface div. Westinghouse Def. and Space Center, 1965-67; dir. purchases and traffic Westinghouse Corp., 1968; asso. adminstr. advanced research and tech. NASA, 1968-69; undersec. Dept. Transp., 1969—; dir. Comml. and Farmers Bank, Ellicott City, Md. Vice chmn. Howard County (Md.) Charter Bd., 1966-67; mem. Md. Bd. Natural Resources, 1966-67. Mem. Nat. Acad. Pub. Adminstrn., Am. Soc. Pub. Adminstrn., Am. Inst. Aero. and Astronautics, Am. Soc. Naval Engrs. Home: 10000 Carmelita Dr Potomac MD 20854 Office: 400 7th St SW Washington DC 20590

BEGGS, LYALL T., lawyer; b. Plainfield, Wis., Nov. 9, 1899; s. Charles A. and Mavorite (Booth) B.; student Eau Claire State Teachers Coll., 1922, U. Wis., 1925; m. Christine C. Kaether, June 25, 1927; children—Geraldine Ann. Robert Kaether, Nancy Belle. Admitted to Wis. bar, 1926; mem. firms Lowry, Beggs and Dawson, Beggs and Lawton, 1928—. Elected dist. atty. Dane County, 1936, 1940; elected mem. legislature 1940, 42, 44, 46; now serving as county pub. adminstr. Recipient Distinguished Service award Eau Claire State Tchrs. Coll., 1965. Mem. V.F.W. (comdr. post 1918, 1939; Wis. dept. comdr., 1941; nat. legislative com., 1942-46; nat. judge adv. gen., 1945; nat. jr. vice-comdr. in chief, 1946; nat. comdr.-in- chief, 1948); mem. Am., Wis. (gov., pres. 1964), Dane County (pres. 1957) bar assns., Am. Legion, Gamma Eta Gamma. Republican. Lutheran. Eagle, Elk. Mason (32 Shriner). Home: RD 1 Oregon WI 53575 Office: 119 Monona Av Madison WI 53703

BEGGS, THOMAS MONTAGUE, fine arts cons.; b. Bklyn., Apr. 22, 1899; s. Thomas P. and Alice M. (Darby) B.; G.A., Pratt Inst., 1920; Bachelor of Fine Arts, Yale, 1924; diplomé Ecole Americaine des Beaux Arts, Fontainebleau, France, summer 1924, Harvard, summers 1928, 29; m. Alice E. Powers, June 18, 1929; children—Robert T. (dec.), Patricia L. (Mrs. John A. Westberg), Malcolm L. Instr. Pomona Coll., Claremont, Cal., 1926-30, chmn. art dept., 1926-47, asst. prof., 1930-36, asso. prof., 1936-44, prof. art, 1944-47; asst. dir. Nat. Collection of Fine Arts, Smithsonian Instn., Washington, 1947-48, dir., 1948-64; spl. asst. to Sec. for Fine Arts, 1964-65. Mem. O.C.B. Cultural Presentations Com., 1957-61, Com. for Preservation Am. Art, 1958-62. Trustee Barney Neighborhood House. Recipient travel grant Fed. Republic of Germany, 1954. Mem. Internat. Inst. for Conservation Historic and Artistic Works, Am. Assn. Mus., Coll. Art Assn. Episcopalian. Club: Cosmos (Washington). Contbr. articles on art subjects to art and ednl. mags. Home: 6540 Hitt Av McLean VA 22101

BEGGS, WALTER KENTON, educator; b. Coin, Ia., May 16, 1905; s. Henry Clark and Lena Jane (Amick) B.; A.B., Tarkio Coll., 1928; M.A., U. Neb., 1936, Ph.D., 1939; m. Ruth Bernice Tice, Dec. 20, 1936; children—Kathryn, Margaret, Karen. Supt. schs., Summerfield, Kan., 1928-36; grad. asst. U. Neb., 1936-39, instr., 1939-40, asst. prof., 1940-42, asso. prof., 1942-48, prof., chmn. dept. history and prin. edn., 1948-58, dean Tchrs. Coll., 1958-71, prof. ednl. adminstrn., 1971—. Mem. Neb. Coop. Sch. Study Council; mem. U.S. commn. for UNESCO, 1968—. Mem. Neb. Edn. Assn., N.E.A., Am. Assn. Sch. Adminstrs., Phi Delta Kappa. Presbyn. (elder). Rotarian. Home: 2225 S 24 St Lincoln NB 68502

BEGHE, RENATO, lawyer; b. Chgo., Mar. 12, 1933; s. Bruno and Emmavve (Frymire) B.; B.A., Coll. U. Chgo., 1951, J.D., 1954; m. Bina House, July 10, 1954; children—Eliza Ashley, Francesca Forbes, Adam House, Jason Deneen. Mng. editor U. Chgo. Law Review, 1953-54; admitted to N.Y. bar, 1955, since practiced in N.Y.C.; asso. Carter, Ledyard & Milburn, 1954-65, partner, 1965—; lectr. N.Y. U. Fed. Tax Inst., 1967. Mem. Am., N.Y. State (chmn. com. on corporate taxation 1970—) bar assns., Assn. Bar City N.Y., Bankers Club Am., Phi Beta Kappa, Order of Coif, Phi Gamma Delta. Home: 300 West End Av New York City NY 10023 Office: 2 Wall St New York City NY 10005

BEGHIAN, LEON EDWARD, educator; b. Istanbul, Turkey, July 25, 1919; s. Edward and Nouvart (Beshiktashlian) B.; B.A., Oxford (Eng.) U., 1947, Ph.D., 1951, postdoctoral sci. scholarship, Magdalen Coll., 1948-50; m. Iris Lucas, Apr. 18, 1964. Came to U.S., 1956, naturalized, 1967. Mem. staff Clarendon Lab., Oxford U., 1950-56; lectr. nuclear engring. Mass. Inst. Tech., 1962; prof. nuclear sci. and Engring. Lowell (Mass.) Tech. Inst., 1965—, head dept. nuclear engring., 1967—, head dept. physics, 1968—. Mem. Gov. Mass. Sci. and Tech. Adv. Com.; chmn. activational analysis panel Gov. Mass. Com. Law Enforcement; mem. goals and aims com. Mass. Bd. Higher Edn. Life mem. Magdalen Coll., Oxford U. Mem. Am. Phys. Soc. Author articles in field. Home: 6 Sentry Hill Pl Boston MA 02114 Office: 1 Textile Av Lowell MA 01854

BEGICH, NICHOLAS JOSEPH, congressman; b. Eveleth, Minn., Apr. 6, 1932; s. John and Anne (Martinich) B.; student Eveleth Jr. Coll., 1950; B.A., St. Cloud State Coll., 1952; M.A. in Ednl. Adminstrn. and Polit. Sci., U. Minn., 1954; postgrad. U. N.D.; m. Pegge Jendro, Dec. 29, 1956; children—Nichelle, Nicholas J., Thomas, Mark, Stephanie, Paul. Tchr., St. Cloud (Minn.) High Sch., 1952-56; boys' counselor West Anchorage High Sch., Anchorage, 1956-57; dir. student personnel Anchorage Sch. Dist., 1957-59; prin. Ursa Minor Sch., Ft. Richardson, Alaska, 1959-63; supt. schs., Ft. Richardson Sch. System, 1963-68; mem. Alaska Senate, 1963-71, minority whip, 1967-71; mem. 92d Congress from Alaska at large, 1971—. Mem. Nat. Compact of Edn., 1967; instr. Am. govt., U.S. history U. Alaska, Anchorage, 1956-68. Life mem. P.T.A. Chmn., Kennedy-Johnson campaign, Anchorage, 1960. Recipient Community Service award V.F.W., 1964; Human Rights award N.A.A.C.P., 1965. Mem. N.E.A. (life), Alaska, Ft. Richardson (past pres.) edn. assns. Home: 1303 Forestwood Dr McLean VA 22101 also 5232 E 24th Av Anchorage AK 99501 Office: 1210 Longworth Bldg Washington DC 20515

BEGIFORE, LAWRENCE STONER, mfg. exec.; b. Lima, O., Apr. 1, 1932; B.S., U. San Francisco, 1954; M.S., Stanford University, 1956; m. Rosemarie Lois Brown, May 15, 1955; 1 son, Anthony Robinson. Sales rep. Ames-Brockton Fabricated Products, Akron, O., 1956-58, sales mgr. Coshocton, Ohio, 1959-61, gen. manager plant, 1961-68, v.p. sales, 1968--. Instr. bus. Coshocton Jr. College, 1968-69. Named Man of Year, Coshocton Junior Chamber of Commerce, 1968. Mem. Coshocton C. of C. (vice president 1967-68, pres. 1969-70), English Speaking Union, Coshocton Sertoma Club, Nat. Assn. Mfrs., Sales Executives Institute, Phi Beta Kappa, Sigma Chi, Phi Mu. Democrat. Mem. Christian Ch. (lay leader). Mason (32, Shriner). Clubs: Coshocton Country, Coshocton City, Running Deer Country. Home: 2d Av Coshocton OH Office: 3d Av Coshocton OH

BEGIN, FLOYD LAWRENCE, bishop; b. Cleve., Feb. 5, 1902; s. Peter H. and Stella (McFarland) B.; Ph.D., U. Propaganda, Rome, Italy, 1924, S.T.D., 1928; J.C.D., U. Apollinaris, Rome, 1930. Ordained priest Roman Catholic Ch., 1927; asst. rector North Am. Coll., Rome, 1928-30; diocesan sec., vice chancellor Diocese of Cleve., 1930; apptd. monsignor, 1934, domestic prelate, 1935, officialis, diocesan tribunal, 1938; diocesan dir. Nat. Council of Cath. Men, Eucharistic Congresses, 1934; vicar gen., women in religious communities; consecrate bishop of Sala and aux. bishop, Cleve., 1947; vicar gen. of Cleve., 1948; pastor St. Agnes Parish, Cleve., 1949-62; bishop Oakland, Cal., 1962—. Mem. adminstrv. tribunal 2d Vatican Council, 1963; mem. papal commn. revision code of canon law, 1967—. Home: 65 Sea View Piedmont CA 94611 Office: 2900 Lakeshore Av Oakland CA 94610

BEGLE, EDWARD GRIFFITH, mathematician; b. Saginaw, Mich., Nov. 27, 1914; s. Ned G. and Cornelia (Campbell) B.; B.A., U. Mich., 1936, M.A., 1937; Ph.D., Princeton, 1940; m. Elise Alkin Pierce, Aug. 14, 1937; children—Cornelia, Sarah, James, Emily, Elsie, Edward, Douglas. NRC fellow, 1941-42; instr. Yale, 1942- 44, asst. prof., 1944-49, asso. prof. 1949-61, dir. sch. mathematics study group, 1958—; prof. mathematics edn. Stanford, 1961—. Mem. Am. Math. Soc. (sec. 1951-56), Math. Assn. Am. (recipient award for distinguished service 1969), A.A.A.S., Sigma Xi, Phi Delta Theta. Home: 1445 Bryant St Palo Alto CA 94301 Office: SMSG-Cedar Hall Stanford Univ Stanford CA 94305

BEGLEY, JOHN PATRICK, educator; b. Omaha, Feb. 11, 1894; s. Michael James and Catherine (Lafferty) B.; B.S.C., Creighton U., 1926, M.A., 1928; Ph.D., U. Ia., 1933; student U. Chgo., summers 1927-30. Accountant, Swift & Co., 1911- 24; admitted to Ia. bar, 1940; mem. faculty Creighton U., 1924—, prof. accounting, 1947, head dept., 1947-65; cons., pub. accountant, 1924-62; sr. partner Begley, Herbert, Graham & Waring, C.P.A.s, 1962—. Dir. Begley Realty, Heafey & Heafey, Andersen Fire Equipment Co., Begley Investment Co. Mem. Neb. Bd. C.P.A. Examiners, 1942-61. Served with U.S. Army, World War I. Recipient Bene Merenti medal Pope John XXIII, 1959; decorated knight of St. Gregory, 1966. C.P.A., Neb., Ia. Mem. Neb. Soc. C.P.A.'s, Am. Inst. C.P.A.'s, Am. Accounting Assn., Nat. Assn. Accountants, Holy Name Soc. (pres. Met. council 1956), Delta Sigma Pi, Omicron Delta Epsilon, Beta Gamma Sigma, Alpha Sigma Nu, Beta Alpha Psi. Democrat. Roman Catholic. K.C. Home: 515 N 26th St Omaha NB 68131 Office: Creighton Univ Omaha NB 68131

BEGOVICH, NICHOLAS ANTHONY, physicist, mfg. co. exec.; b. Oakland, Ca., Nov. 29, 1921; s. Dinko and Anna (Juka) B.; B.S. in Elec. Engring. (Francis J. Cole scholar 1946), Cal. Inst. Tech., 1943, M.S., 1944, Ph.D., 1948; m. Joan Munson Deopker, Apr. 14, 1944. Research physicist Hughes Aircraft Co., Culver City, Cal., 1948-61, corporate v.p., 1961, asst. group exec. ground systems group, 1961-67, group exec., 1967-70; corporate v.p., pres. Data Systems div. Litton Industries, 1970—; cons. weapons system evaluation group Dept. Def., 1952-57; spl. work devel. electronic-scan radar, Frescan family three dimensional radars. Fellow I.E.E.E.; mem. Am. Phys. Soc., Operations Research Soc. Am., Sigma Xi. Home: 136 Miramonte Dr Fullerton CA 92632 Office: 8000 Woodley Av Van Nuys CA 91409

BEGUE, LOUISE, educator; licence diplome, d'et Sup., U. Aix (France); student Columbia Grad. Sch., 1947-48, City Coll. N.Y., 1949-53, Sch. Gen. Studies, Columbia, 1949-51. Mem. faculty Sarah Lawrence Coll., 1953—, now prof. French; interpreter State Dept., 1947-53; recorded textbooks for schs. and colls. Author: Au pays de Soleil; Choix de Poesies; Au fil de l'eau; Poesie la vie entiere; co-author: Speak and Read French; La France Moderne. Editor novelette by Andre Dhotel. Address: care Dept of French Sarah Lawrence Coll Bronxville NY 10708*

BEHA, JAMES JOSEPH, lawyer; b. N.Y.C., Oct. 15, 1916; s. James A. and Katharine E. (McMorrough) B.; A.B., Williams Coll., 1937; LL.B., Harvard, 1940; m. Macy Anne Reilly, Aug. 14, 1948; children—James A. II, Ann Macy. Admitted to N.Y. bar, 1941; practiced in N.Y.C., 1941—, mem. firm Gasser & Hayes, 1949—. Pres., Capital Investment Corp. Montreal Ltd. (Que., Can.); dir. Skil Corp., Chgo., Western & So. Life Ins. Co., Cin., Stuart-Dean, Inc. Mem. N.Y. State Commn. Correction. Trustee St. Joseph's Day Nursery, Mt. St. Mary Coll., Newburgh, N.Y. Mem. Am., N.Y. State bar assns., N.Y. County Lawyers Assn., Internat. Assn. Ins. Counsel. Home: 222 E 48th St New York City NY 10017 Office: 1 Chase Manhattan Plaza New York City NY 10005

BEHAN, EDMUND JOSEPH, banker; b. New Haven, Oct. 18, 1929; s. Edmund Joseph and Marie (Ridinger) B.; B.A., Yale, 1951, M.B.A., Columbia, 1956; m. Ellen Patricia Leary, Apr. 8, 1953; children—Edmund Joseph, Bruce Robert, John David. Agt., State Mut. Life Assurance Co., Worcester, Mass., 1953-54; auditor Price Waterhouse & Co., Hartford, Conn., 1956-59; asst. controller Fafnir Bearing Co. div. Textron, Inc., New Britain, Conn., 1959-69; v.p., controller Colonial Bank & Trust Co., Waterbury, Conn., 1969—; adj. asst. prof. mgmt. Rensselaer Poly. Inst., Hartford Grad. Center, 1970—. Served to 2d lt., USAF, 1951-53. Recipient auditing prize, Columbia U., 1956, C.P.A., Conn. Mem. Am. Mgmt. Assn. Home: 20 Jensen Rd West Hartford CT 06117 Office: 81 W Main St Waterbury CT 06702

BEHAN, LAWRENCE GERARD, physician; b. St. Louis, Aug. 17, 1917; s. Lawrence and Mary (Leonard) B.; M.D., St. Louis U., 1942; postgrd. psychiatry Menninger Sch., 1950- 51; m. Helen Landess, Feb. 12, 1942; children—Nancy, Patricia, Larry, Kevin, Deborah. Intern St. Louis U. Hosp., 1942-43; resident St. Louis City Sanitarium, 1946; gen. practice medicine, O'Fallon, Mo., 1947-50; chief mental hygiene clinics VA Hosp., Dallas, 1951-53, Pensacola, Fla., 1954-57, Gulfport, Miss., 1957-59; cons. La. State U., 1958-59; supt. Yankton (S.D.) State Hosp., 1960—; mem. staff Sacred Heart Hosp., Yankton, 1960—; prof. psychiatry S.D. U. Sch. Medicine, 1960—. Served to maj., M.C., AUS, 1943-46; lt. col. Res. Mem. A.M.A., Am. Psychiat. Assn. (pres. dist. br. 1961-62), Am. Legion, V.F.W., Yankton C. of C. Elk. Address: Box 76 Yankton, SD 57078.

BEHAN, ROBERT F., banker; b. New Haven, May 16, 1933; s. Edmund Joseph and Marie (Ridinger) B.; grad. Phillips Andover Acad., 1951; B.A., Yale, 1955; M.B.A., Columbia, 1959; m. Patricia Sanders Behan, Dec. 27, 1958; children—Carolyn Ann, Katherine Louise. With Conn. Bank & Trust Co., 1959-71, mgr. Conn. Charge Card, 1966-68, dir. marketing, 1968-69, mgr. West Hartford Office, 1969, liason, zone mgr. New Haven, Wallingford, Meridan, 1970—. Conn. treas., United Negro Coll. Fund. Served with AUS, 1955-57. Mem. Robert Morris Assos., Alpha Kappa Psi. Clubs: Quinnipiack, Yale (New Haven). Home: 101 Five Fields Rd Madison CT 06443 Office: 1 Columbus Plaza New Haven CT 06510

BEHAR, MOISES, physician; b. Huehuetenango, Guatemala, Aug. 28, 1922; s. Elias and Eugenia (Alcahé) B.; M.D., U. San Carlos (Guatemala), 1949; postgrad. Sch. Medicine, U. Paris, Hosp. des Enfants Malades, Paris, Vanderbilt U.; M.PH., Harvard, 1960; m. Beatriz Aldana, Aug. 14, 1954; children—Michelle, Jacqueline, Henri. Chief nutrition div. Guatemala Pub. Health Service, 1951-53; asso. prof. hematology U. San Carlos Sch. Medicine, 1951-55; spl. cons. WHO in Kwashiorkor Studies, 1951; cons. pediatrics Inst. Nutrition Central Am. and Panama, 1953-55; asso. dir., chief div. clin. investigation INCAP, 1957-61, dir., 1961—; asso. prof. nutrition in pub. health Columbia, 1962—; vis. prof. nutrition Tulane U., 1962—; related dir. Gorgas Meml. Lab., Panama, 1965—. Mem. commn. operations programs, chmn. com. nutritional surveys IUNS, 1967—. Recipient Bonfman award pub. health, 1968. Mem. Am. Pub. Health Assn. (v.p. 1966-67), Pediatric Assn. Guatemala (past pres.), Pediatric Assn. Costa Rica (corr.), Soc. Belge de Medicine Tropicale (corr.), Pediatric Soc. Panama (hon.), Am. Inst. Nutrition, Am. Soc. Pediatric Research, Fedn. Am. Soc. Exptl. Biology, Am. Soc. Clin. Nutrition. Research, articles characteristics, epidemiology, treatment and prevention protein- calorie malnutriton in children. Home: Av Hincapie 25-10 Zone 13 Guatemala City Office: INCAP Carretera Roosevelt Zone 11 Guatemala City Guatemala

BEHEN, DAVID MARION, educator; b. Cloverport, Ky., Dec. 9, 1909; s. Ira DeHaven and Grace Mae (Plank) B.; Ph.B., U. Chgo., 1932, Ph.D., 1953; m. Dorothy Margaret Forbis, Oct. 17, 1947; children—John David, William Ira. Asst. Am. history U. Chgo., 1948-49, lectr. history Univ. Coll., 1948-49, 50-52; instr. Knox Coll.,

1953-54; mem. faculty Youngstown U., 1954—, chmn. dept. history, 1957-67, prof. history, 1958—. Served with USAAF, 1942-45. Home: 3898 Ascot Ct Youngstown OH 44511

BEHLE, CALVIN AUGUSTUS, lawyer; b. Salt Lake City, Mar. 16, 1907; s. Augustus Calvin and Daisy (Harroun) B.; A.B., Stanford, 1928; LL.B., U. Utah, 1931; m. Grace Clayton, Aug. 18, 1934; children—Marilyn (Mrs. Peter Hugh Graham), Marcia (Mrs. Donald L. Goobin); m. 2d, Hope F. Eccles, June 26, 1968. Admitted to Utah bar, 1931, since practiced in Salt Lake City; mem. firm Parsons, Behle & Latimer, 1947—. Vice pres., dir. Carbon County Ry., Tracy Collins Bank & Trust Co. Pres. Rocky Mountain Mineral Law Found., 1964-65 Utah State Bar Found. Chmn. Salt Lake City Civil Service Commn., 1952-58; pres. Utah State Civil Service Commn., 1957; vice chmn. Utah Bd. Corrections, 1958-63; mem. Salt Lake City Adv. Commn., 1961—; dir. Utah Council Econ. Edn., 1960—. Vice chmn. YMCA Found.; chmn. Mt. Olivet Cemetery; bd. dirs. Rowland Hall Sch. for Girls; chmn. bd. trustees Gt. Salt Lake council Boy Scouts Am.; trustee Westminster Coll., Ballet West U.S.A. Served with AUS, 1942-46. Decorated Bronze Star; Order White Lion (Czechoslovakia). Fellow Am. Coll. Trial Lawyers, Am. Bar Found.; mem. Am. (ho. dels.), Inter-Am., Salt Lake County (past pres.) bar assns., Utah State Bar, Selden Soc., Order of Coif, Phi Kappa Phi, Phi Alpha Delta, Alpha Tau Omega. Republican. Episcopalian. Mason, Kiwanian (pres. 1963). Clubs: University (pres. 1959); Alta (pres. 1971). Home: The Stansbury 710 E 2d South St Salt Lake City UT 84102 also 1855 27th St Ogden UT 84403 Office: Kearns Bldg 136 S Main St Salt Lake City UT 84101

BEHLE, WILLIAM HARROUN educator; b. Salt Lake City, May 13, 1909; s. Augustus C. and Daisy (Harroun) B.; A.B., U. Utah, 1932, A.M., 1933; Ph.D., U. Cal. at Berkeley, 1937; m. Dorothy M. Davis, July 11, 1934; children—Howard William, Raymond David. Research asst. Cal. Mus. Vertebrate Zoölogy, U. Cal. at Berkeley, 1933-37; instr. U. Utah, 1937-41, asst. prof. zoölogy, 1941-46, asso. prof., 1946-51, prof., 1951—, head dept. gen. biology, 1948-54, dir. biology gen. edn., 1954-63; naturalist Grand Canyon Nat. Park 1935, 39, 40, 42. Fellow Am. Ornithol. Union, A.A.A.S., Western Found. Vertebrate Zoology; mem. Wildlife Soc., Soc. Study Evolution, Am. Soc. Mammalogists, Cooper (hon.), Wilson ornithol. socs., Western Bird-banding Assn., Soc. Systematic Zool., Am. Assn. U. Profs., Utah Acad. Scis. (pres. 1959-60), Nat. Utah Audubon socs., Am. Inst. Biol. Scis., Utah Hist. Soc., S.A.R., Sigma Xi, Phi Kappa Phi, Phi Sigma, Alpha Epsilon Delta. Episcopalian. Contbr. numerous articles on birds, mammals of Utah and Western U.S. to various publs. Home: 1233 E Eighth South St Salt Lake City UT 84102

BEHLEN, HERBERT PETER, mfg. co. exec.; b. Columbus, Neb., Oct. 15, 1909; s. Frederick Arthur and Ella Sarah (Benthack) B.; student U. Neb., 1934-35; m. Ethel Minnie Russell, Apr. 13, 1940 (dec. Aug. 1946); children—James William, Karen Jean (Mrs. David Senften) (foster children), Donna Lee (Mrs Kenneth Kalkowski); m. 2d, Lois Viola Hickey, Jan. 24, 1948; 1 son, Frederick Michael. Co-founder, Behlen Mfg. Co., Columbus, 1936, now pres., dir.; pres. Behlen-Wickes Co. Ltd., Brandon, Man., Can. Dir. Industries Neb. Pres. Columbus YMCA, 1960, St. Mary's Hosp. Adv. Bd., 1961. Trustee Platte Coll., Columbus, Neb.; mem. bd. Doane Coll., Crete, Neb. Served with USAAF, World War II. Recipient Legion of Merit award Sec. War for design of aircraft tng. aids, 1945. Mem. Columbus C. of C. (past pres.), Am. Legion. Republican. Conglist. Elk. Club: Wayside Country. Home: RFD 2 Columbus NB 68601 Office: Behlen Mfg Co Columbus NB 68601

BEHLEN, WALTER DIETRICH, metal products mfr., b. Columbus, Neb., Oct. 16, 1905; s. Fred Arthur and Ella (Benthack) B.; student pub. schs., Columbus; D.Engring., U. Neb., 1959; Sc.D., Midland Coll., 1959; m. Ruby Mae Cumming, Apr. 13, 1940; children—Mary Ann (Mrs. Roman Hruska), Kent Walter. Asso., Ry. Express Agy., Columbus, Neb., 1925-41; pres. Behlen Mfg. Co., Columbus, 1941-63, chmn. bd., 1963—; dir. Columbus Savs. & Loan Assn., First Nat. Bank of Columbus, Wickes Corp., Saginaw, Mich.; past dir. Loup River Pub. Power Dist.; dir. Asso. Industries Neb. Vice chmn., dir. Neb. Indsl. Research Inst. Trustee U. Neb. Found., Neb. Independent Coll. Found., 1959—; adv. com. U. Neb. Coll. Agr. Recipient Horatio Alger award, 1968. Mem. Columbus Community Concert Assn. (past pres.), Columbus YMCA (dir., past pres.), Mississippi Valley Assn. (v.p. Neb.-Iowa div.), Columbus C. of C. (past dir.), Metal Bldg. Mfrs. Assn. (dir. 1956-66), N.A.M. (nuclear energy com.). Elk. Clubs: Rotary, Wayside Country. Patentee hydraulic presses; inventions relating to stressed skin structures. Home: 2555 Pershing Rd Columbus NB 68601 Office: Behlen Mfg Co E Hwy 30 Columbus NB 68601

BEHLKE, CHARLES EDWARD, univ. dean; b. Butte, Mont., Jan. 12, 1926; s. Herman E. and Estelle (Mondloch) B.; B.S. in Mech. Engring., Wash. State Coll., 1948, M.S. in Hydraulic Engring., Ph.D. in Civil Engring., Stanford, 1957; diploma in Coastal Engring., Tech. U. Delft (The Netherlands), 1960; m. Jane H. McMullen, Nov. 25,1953; children—Susan, Carol, James. Instr., then asst. prof. civil engring. U. Alaska, 1950-54; asso. prof., then prof. civil engring. Ore. State U., 1956-65; acting dean, then dean Coll. Math., Phys. Scis. and Engring., dir. Arctic Environmental Engring. Lab., U. Alaska, 1966—, dir. Inst. Water Resources, 1965-68; cons. in field, 1957—. Recipient Carter award for outstanding teaching Sch. Engring., Ore. State U., 1961. Mem. Am. Soc. Engring. Edn., Am. Water Resources Assn., Am. Soc. C.E., Marine Tech. Soc. Home: Box 8-0257 College AK 99701

BEHN, CLARENCE HENRY, food co. exec.; b. Chgo., Apr. 3, 1915; s. Clarence J. and Anna (Ihde) B.; student U. Ill., Champaign, 1934-36; m. Marion Gertrude Scott, Feb. 15, 1941; children—Norman Scott, Carol Louise (Mrs. Richard Maes), Patti Ann. With Armour & Co., Chgo., 1938—, asst. sec., 1958-64, asst. controller, 1964-70, v.p., controller, 1970—. Mem. caucus com. Sch. Bd., Palos-Orland, Ill., 1960-62; mgr. Little League Baseball, 1951-55. Pres. bd. trustees Fire Dept., Palos Heights. Mem. Machinery and Allied Products Inst. (accounting council), Delta Chi. Lutheran. Club: Midlothian (Ill.) Country. Home: 7648 Sequoia Dr Palos Heights IL 60463 Office: 111 E Wacker Dr Chicago IL 60601

BEHNKE, ALBERT RICHARD, Jr., physician; b. Chgo., Aug. 8, 1903; s. Albert Richard and Clara (Weertz) B.; B.A., Whittier Coll., 1925; M.D., Stanford, 1930; postgrad, Harvard, 1932-35; M.A., Yale, 1942; m. Ruth Elizabeth Rue, July 27, 1957; 1 dau., Alice Ann. Commd. lt. (j.g.) USN, 1929, advanced through grades to capt., 1944; intern Naval Hosp., Mare Island, Cal., 1929-30; research Dr. Drinkers Lab. Harvard, 1932-35; instr. U.S. Naval Med. Sch., Washington, 1937-42; sci. dir. U.S. Naval Med. Research Inst., Bethesda, Md., 1943-50, asst. naval attache for med. research, London, 1946; coordinator European Area World Atlas Epidemiology, 1950-52; med. dir., head biol. and med. scis. div. U.S. Naval Radiol. Def. Lab., San Francisco, 1953-59; ret., 1959; cons. research div. Lankenau Hosp., Phila., 1960-61; lectr. dept. nutrition Sch. Pub. Health U. Cal., San Francisco, 1961-71, clin. prof. preventive medicine, 1963-71; cons. Hyperbaric Oxygenation Program, Duke, 1963—. Recipient Sir Henry Wellcome prize for mil. research, 1940, A. Cressy Morrison prize N.Y. Acad. Scis., 1952, Mil. certificate for exceptional service, 1959; Albert R. Behnke, Jr. award Undersea Med. Soc., 1969, Poseidon award, 1970. Nathalie G. Bernard lectr. Bowman Gray Sch. Medicine, 1942, 67, John Wycoff lectr. N.Y.U., 1944, Harvey lectr., 1942. Fellow N.Y. Acad. Scis., Am. Coll. Preventive Medicine; mem. Am. Physiol. Soc., Am. Soc. Clin. Investigation, Gerontology Soc., Cal. Acad. Medicine, Cal. Acad. Sci., Western Assn. Physicians, Sigma Xi. Address: 2241 Sacramento St San Francisco CA 94115

BEHNKE, ROY HERBERT, medical educator; b. Chgo., Feb. 24, 1921; s. Harry and Florence Alice (MacArthur) B.; A.B., Hanover Coll., 1943; M.D., Ind. U., 1946; m. Ruth Gretchen Zinszer, June 3, 1944; children—Roy, Michael, Donald, Elise. Intern Ind. U. Med. Center, 1946-47, resident, 1949-51, chief resident medicine, 1951-52; instr. medicine Ind. U. Sch. Medicine, 1952-55, asst. prof. medicine, 1955-58, asso. prof., 1958-61, prof., 1961—; chief medicine VA Hosp., Indpls., 1957—. A.M.A. rep. to residency rev. com. in internal medicine, 1970—; mem. exec. and adv. com. Inter-Soc. Commn. Heart Disease Resources, 1969—, chmn. pulmonary study sect., 1969—. Mem. Met. Sch. Bd. Washington Twp., 1968—, pres., 1971. Bd. dirs. Southside Community Health Center. Served with AUS, 1943-45, 47-49. Recipient Clin. Tchr. of Year award Ind. U. Sch. Medicine, 1968, 69, 70, Distinguished Tchr., Standard Oil Found. award, 1971, Alumni Achievement award Hanover Coll., 1971; John and Mary Markle scholar, 1952-57. Diplomate Am. Bd. Internal Medicine. Fellow A.C.P., Am. Coll. Chest Physicians. Home: 6249 Graham Rd Indianapolis IN 46220

BEHR, JOHN HENRY, metal products mfr.; b. Bklyn., Feb. 26, 1912; s. John Henry and Charlotte Catherine (Reuper) B.; B.A., Hamilton Coll., 1934. With Wilson Jones Co., Chgo., 1934-70, v.p., gen. sales mgr., 1958-66, exec. v.p., 1966-70; pres., chief exec. officer; Swingline, Inc., subsidary Am. Brands, Inc., Long Island City, N.Y., 1970—. Mem. Bus.-Industry Polit. Action Com. Served to 1st lt., inf., AUS, 1943-46. Mem. Nat. Alliance Businessmen, Nat. Office Producta Assn., Wholesale Stationers Assn. (dir. 1967-69), Lambda Chi Alpha. Republican. Christian Scientist. Mason (Shriner). Home: 6150 W Touhy Av Chicago IL 60648 Office: 32-00 Skillman Av Long Island City NY 11101

BEHR, LYELL CHRISTIAN, educator; b. Mpls., May 4, 1916; s. Christian and Elsie Alma (Schissler) B.; B.Chemistry, U. Minn., 1937; Ph.D., U. Ill., 1941; m. Patricia Ekander, June 5, 1954; children—Christopher, Barbara. Hormel postgrad. fellow U. Minn., 1941-42; chemist Chem. Warfare Service, Columbia, 1942-43, E. I. duPont de Nemours & Co., Inc., 1943-47; mem. faculty Miss. State U., 1947—, prof. chemistry, 1954—, head dept., 1963-64, dean Coll. Arts and Scis., 1964—; vis. lectr. U. Ill., summers 1951-54, 59-60. Mem. region VII selection com. Woodrow Wilson Fellowship Found., 1964- . Fellow A.A.A.S., Chem. Soc. (London, Eng.); mem. Am. Chem. Soc. (councilor), Sigma Xi, Blue Key, Alpha Chi Sigma, Phi Lambda Upsilon, Alpha Epsilon Delta, Omicron Delta Kappa, Phi Kappa Phi. Home: Box 644 State College MS 39762

BEHRE, CHARLES HENRY, Jr. geologist; b. Atlanta, Mar. 16, 1896; s. Charles H. and Emilie (Schumann) B.; student U. Wis., 1914-16; B.S., U. Chgo., 1918, Ph.D., 1925; D.Sci. (hon.), Franklin and Marshall Coll., 1949; m. Jeanette Allen, June 25, 1921. Geologist, tchr., 1915; field geologist Wis. Geol. Survey, 1916-17; part time asst., asso., sr. geologist U.S. Geol. Survey, 1921-45; asst. zoölogy and geology U. Chgo., 1917, 19-20; instr. geology Lehigh U., 1921-23; co-operating geologist Pa. Geol. Survey, 1922—; asst. prof. geology U. Cin., 1924-30; asso. prof. geology Northwestern U., 1930-35, prof., 1935-41, chmn. dept. geology and geography, 1933-37; prof. geology Columbia, 1941-64, professor emeritus, 1964—, exec. officer geology dept. 1956-59; cons. Behre Dolbear & Co., 1946—, pres., 1961-68, v.p., sr. geologist, 1968—; distinguished lectr. Assn. Petroleum Geologists, 1950; John A. Bownocker lectr. Ohio State U., 1962; distinguished lectr. Am. Geol. Inst., 1962. Gen. cons., tech. adviser metals Govt. Union Burma, 1949, Govt. Haiti, 1951; chmn. com. geog. exploration Joint Research and Devel. Bd., 1946-47; mem. U.S. Nat. Com. on Geology, 1968-69. recipient Miner citation Guggenheim fellow, 1937-38; Nat. Assn. Geology Tchrs., 1958; Posepny medal Czechoslovak Acad. Scis., 1969. Served with M.C., U.S. Army, World War I. Fellow A.A.A.S., Mineral. Soc. Am.; mem. Am. Inst. Mining and Metall. Engrs. (past chmn. div. indsl. mining and mineral econs.), Geol. Soc. Am. (mem. council 1940-42), Am. Assn. Geographers, Ill. Acad. Sci. (v.p 1933, pres. 1934), Ohio Acad. Sci. (past v.p.), Assn. Petroleum Geologists, Nat. Assn. Geology Tchrs., Soc. Econ. Geologist (councillor 1936-39, sec. 1942-46, chmn. com. on research, v.p. 1963, pres. 1967-68), Assn. Am. Geography, Am. Geog. Soc. (hon.), Assn. Des Ingenieurs Sortis de Liege (hon.), Soc. Geologique de Belgique (corr.), Chgo. Acad. Sci., Deutsch A.K. Leopoldina (Halle), Sigma Xi (pres. Columbia chpt. 1960-61). Home: 330 Christie Heights St Leonia NJ 07605 Office: care Behre Dolbear & Co Inc 11 Broadway New York City NY 10004

BEHRENDS, RALPH EUGENE, educator; b. Chgo., May 20, 1926; s. Oluf and Marie-Thérèse (Ichtertz) B.; B.S., U.S. Naval Acad., 1947; Ph.D., U. Cal. at Los Angeles, 1956; m. Marlene I. Bowman, Oct. 7, 1961; children—Jon Carlo, Kendra Ralene. Instr., U. Cal. at Los Angeles, 1956-57; asst. physicist Brookhaven Nat. Lab., 1957-59; NSF fellow Inst. for Advanced Study, Princeton, N.J., 1959-60; research asso. U. Pa., Phila., 1960-61; asst. prof. physics Belfer Grad. Sch. Sci., Yeshiva U., N.Y.C., 1961-62, asso. prof., 1962-66, prof., 1966—. Served as ensign USNR, 1947-50. NSF research grantee, 1962-70. Mem. Am. Phys. Soc. Democrat. Contbr. articles on theory elementary particles to tech. jours., books. Home: 100 W 92 St New York City NY 10025

BEHRENDT, DAVID FROGNER, journalist; b. Stevens Point, Wis., May 25, 1935; s. Allen Charles and Vivian (Frogner) B.; B.S., U. Wis., 1957, M.S., 1960; m. Mary Ann Weber, Feb. 4, 1961; children—Lynne, Liza, Sarah. Reporter, Decatur (Ill.) Review, 1957-58; reporter Milw. Jour., 1960-70, copy editor, 1970-71, editorial writer, 1971—. Recipient Am. Polit. Sci. Assn. award for distinguished reporting pub. affairs, 1963, Nat. Council for Advancement Edn. Writing award for best newspaper series on edn., 1968. Home: 1928 Hillside Ct Delafield WI 53018 Office: 333 W State St Milwaukee WI 53201

BEHRENDT, FRITZ, polit. cartoonist; b. Berlin, Germany, Feb. 17, 1925; s. Paul and Agnes (Schonfelder) B.; student Sch. Applied Arts, Amsterdam, Holland, 1943-45, Acad. Arts, Zagreb, Yugoslvia, 1948; m. Renate Müller, May 16, 1958; 1 son, Stefan. Free-lance polit. cartoonist, 1952—; exhbns. in Amsterdam, Zurich, Vienna, Copenhagen, Berlin, Bonn, The Hague. Decorated Yugoslav Order of Labour and shock-worker medal for reconstrn. work in Yugoslavia, 1947. Author: No Jokes Please, 1956; Strickly Forbidden, 1957; Nevertheless, 1961; Behrendt's Omnibus, 1964; It Could Be Nice, 1967; Keep Smiling, 1968; To The Moon and Back, 1969; Next Please, 1971. Address: 57 Parmentierlaan Amstelveen Holland

BEHRENS, ALFRED J., beverage co. exec.; b. Des Plaines, Ill., May 13, 1915; B.A. in Bus. Adminstrn., Lake Forest Coll., 1938; m. Margaret Rigge; children—Elisabeth, Barbara, A. John, Stephen. With Pepsi-Cola Gen. Bottlers, Inc., Chgo., 1940—, sec., 1949—, exec. v.p., 1954—, also dir. Past mem. bd. edn. Oak Park-River Forest High Sch. Presbyn. (elder). Home: 1123 Lathrop Av River Forest IL 60305 Office: 1745 N Kolmar Av Chicago IL 60639

BEHRENS, CHARLES FREDERICK, radiologist; b. Phila., Mar. 18, 1896; s. Charles William and Augusta Emelia (Hulsman) B.; M.D., U. Pa., 1920; postgrad. radiology Cornell U. Med. Center, 1936-37; m. Emma G. Spencer, May 30, 1920 (dec. May 1964); children—Eleanor (Mrs. John E. Parker), Diana E. (Mrs. M.J. Swann), Charles Frederick, Sylvia M. (Mrs. Richard P. Ellison). Served with S.A.T.C., Army Med. Res., World War I; entered U.S.N. as lt. (j.g.), 1920, advanced through grades to rear adm., 1951; specialist radiology, 1925—; dir. atomic def. div. Bur. Medicine and Surgery, also comdg. officer Naval Med. Research Inst., 1948-51; med. officer staff Eastern Sea Frontier, N.Y.C., 1951-53; dist. med. officer 6th Naval Dist., 1953-56; ret., 1956; radiologist Yater Clinic, Washington, 1956-66; cons. in radiology Naval Hosp., Bethesda, 1957-67. Mem. Baruch Com. Phys. Medicine, 1943-51. Diplomate Am. Bd. Radiology, Am. Bd. Internal Medicine. Fellow Am. Coll. Radiology. Mem. Radiol. Soc. N.A., Assn. Mil. Surgeons, N.Y. Acad. Scis., A.M.A., Radiation Research Soc. Editor: Atomic Medicine, 5th edit., 1969; After the A Bomb, 1951. Contbr. articles profl. jours. Aided in establishing photofluorographic chest survey procedure, U.S.N., World War II. Home: 8514 Rayburn Rd Bethesda MD 20034

BEHRENS, EGBERT FREDERICK, govt. ofcl.; b. Bryant, S.D., Apr. 8, 1923; s. Ernest H. and Catherine (Kaucher) B.; B.S., S.D. State U., 1955; m. Wanda Deviney, July 1, 1949; 1 son, Christopher F. Exec. sec. to U.S. Senator Karl E. Mundt, 1949-58; mgr. gen. operations, Nat. Forest Products Assn., Washington, 1958-67; minority cons. exec. reorgn. subcom. U.S. Senate, 1967-69; exec. asst. to sec. agr., 1969—. Served with AUS, 1943-46. Republican. Episcopalian (vestry). Mason. Home: 1910 Shannon Ct Alexandria, VA 22306. Office: Dept Agr Washington DC 20250

BEHRENS, ROBERT HERMAN, fgn. service officer; b. Jersey City, N.J., Oct. 8, 1923; s. Herman H. and Pearl Reynolds (Rhodes) B.; B.A., Haverford Coll., 1946, M.A., 1947; Ph.D., U. Tuebingen (Germany), 1951; m. Helen Yvonne Kindler, May 5, 1945; children—Christine (Mrs. Bartlett L. Grahl), Eric, Yvonne, Diane, Peter. With N.W. Ayer, Phila., 1947; pub. relations Campbell Soup Co., 1948; fgn. service officer HICOG, German, 1950-52, USIA, 1952-68; counselor embassy pub. affairs Am. embassy, Vienna, 1968-71. Rabat, Morocco, 1971—; adviser U.S. delegation Strategic Arms Limitation Talks, 1970—. Served with USNR, 1943-45. Contbr. articles in field to mags. Home: Culver Lane Branchville NJ 07826 Office: Am Embassy Rabat Dept of State Washington DC 20521

BEHRENS, ROLAND CONRAD, banker; b. St. Louis, June 29, 1898; s. Charles Henry and Emma (Windhorst) B.; grad. St. Louis U. Sch. Law, 1927, extension div. Washington U.; m. Ruth Gertrude Barrett, Aug. 7, 1928; 1 dau., Jeanne Elizabeth (Mrs. Michael Melvin McCarthy). With St. Louis Union Trust Co., 1917-24, asst. sec., 1924-30, v.p., 1930-56, sr. v.p., 1956-65, now asso. dir.; dir. Griesedieck Co., Mo. Natural Gas Co., H.C. Cole Milling Co., Chester, Ill., Laclede Steel Co., Pilot Knob Ore Co., St. Louis, Wis. Electric Power Co., Milw. Trustee Govtl. Research Inst., St. Louis. Mem. Mo. Bar Assn., Newcomen Soc. N.Am. Clubs: Media, Old Warson Country (St. Louis). Home: 9 Devondale Lane Frontenac St Louis MO 63131 Office: 510 Locust St St Louis MO 63101

BEHRMAN, JACK NEWTON, educator; b. Waco, Tex., Mar. 5, 1922; s. Mayes and Marguerite (Newton) B.; student U. Cal. at Los Angeles, 1939-40; B.S., Davidson Coll., 1943; M.A., U.N.C., 1945; M.A., Princeton, 1950, Ph.D., 1952; m. Louise Sims, Sept. 6, 1945; children—Douglas, Gayle, Andrea. Research asst. ILO, 1945-46; asst. prof. econs. Davidson Coll., 1946-48; research asst. internat. finance sect. Princeton, 1950-52; asso. prof. econs. and polit. sci. Washington and Lee U.,1952-57; prof. econs. and bus. adminstrn. U. Del., 1957-61; asst. sec. commerce for internat. affairs, 1961-62, asst. sec. for domestic and internat. bus., 1962-64; prof. internat. bus. Sch. Bus., U.N.C., 1964—, Drexel research prof., 1970-71; vis. prof. Harvard Bus. Sch., 1967, chmn. M.B.A. Program, 1971—. Cons. U.S. Dept. of State, Pan Am. Union, Com. Econ. Devel., Econ. Council Can., OAS, Nat. Fgn. Trade Council, Nat. Planning Assn., Nat. Acad. Sci., U.S. C. of C., also pvt. bus.; cons. Patent, Trademark and Copyright Research Inst., George Washington U., Presdl. Commn. on Internat. Trade and Investments; lectr. Am. Mgmt. Assn., Columbia, Salzburg Seminar. Mem. Council Fgn. Relations, Regional Export Expansion Council, Assn. for Edn. in Internat. Bus. (pres. 1966-68), mem. N.C. World Trade Assn. (dir.), Sigma Phi Epsilon, Pi Gamma Mu, Alpha Phi Omega, Beta Gamma Sigma. Presbyn. (elder). Co-Author: Survey of United States International Finance, 1950-53; International Economics, 1957; Financing Free World Trade with the Sino-Soviet Bloc, 1958; U.S. Private and Government Investment Abroad, 1962. Author: Rise of the Multinational Enterprise, 1969; National Interests and the Multinational Enterprise, 1970; U.S. International Business and Governments, 1971; Multinational Production Consortia, 1971. Contbr. profl. jours. Home: 1702 Audubon Rd Chapel Hill NC 27514

BEHRMAN, SAMUEL JAN, educator, obstetrician and gynecologist; b. S. Africa, Sept. 10, 1920; s. Louis and Betty (Danemann) B.; M.B., Ch.B., U. Cape Town (S.Africa); M.Sc., U. Mich., 1949; m. Patrisha Ann McManus, Oct. 14, 1956; children—Michael, Andrea. Rotating intern Johannesburg (S.Africa) Hosp., 1945; surg. resident Brad-Royal Infirmary, Yorkshire, Eng., 1946; resident obstetrics and gynecology Royal Maternity Hosp., Belfast, Ireland, 1946-48; postgrad. Postgrad. Sch. Medicine, London, Eng., 1948; research fellow U. Mich., 1948-49; asso. dir. clin. research Ortho Research Found., 1949-50; mem. faculty U. Mich. Med. Sch., 1949—, prof. obstetrics and gynecology, 1960—, dir. Center Research and Tng. in Reproductive Biology, 1956, resident lectr. family planning Sch. Pub. Health, 1956, coordinator obstetrics and gynecology to dept. postgrad. medicine, 1958—; cons. Sinai Hosp., Detroit, 1956, Ypsilanti (Mich.) Hosp., 1954. Wayne County Gen. Hosp., 1962, com. maternal care A.M.A., 1954, spl. com. Nat. Inst. Child health and Devel., 1965. conf. immunological aspects of human reprodn. WHO, 1965—, population service AID, 1969—, sci. adv. com. Human Life Found., 1970—; vis. prof. U. London, 1965, U. Cape Town, 1969. Recipient numerous research grants, 1948—; recipient Ortho medal for research, 1967; recipient Galen Sr. award for teaching U. Mich., 1956, Galen Shovel award for teaching, 1963. Diplomate Am. Bd. Obstetrics and Gynecology. Fellow A.C.S., Am., Royal colls. obstetrics and gynecologists, Royal Soc. Medicine; founding fellow Coll. Physicians and Surgeons S. Africa; mem. Internat. Fertility Assn., Internat. Soc. Research Biology Reprodn. (founder, trustee 1967—). Central Assn. Obstetricians and Gynecologists, A.M.A., Am. (bd. dirs.), Pacific Coast fertility socs., Am. Pub. Health Assn., Population Assn. Am., Mid-Eastern Obst. and Gynecol. Travel Soc., Norman F. Miller Gynecol. Soc., Mich. Obstetrics and Gynecology Soc., Washtenaw County Med. Soc., Phi Delta Epsilon. Author 3 textbooks, numerous articles in field. Editor Internat. Jour. Fertility, 1960—; asso. editor Fertility and Sterility, 1970—. Home: 2866 Provincial Dr Ann Arbor MI 48104

BEHRMAN, SAMUEL NATHANIEL, playwright; b. Worcester, Mass., June 9, 1893; s. Joseph and Zelda (Feingold) B.; student Clark Coll., 1912-14, LL.D., 1949; A.B., Harvard, 1916; A.M., Columbia, 1918; m. Elza Heifetz, 1936; one son, Arthur David. Trustee Clark Coll. Author: (plays) Lord Pengo, 1962, But For Whom Charlie, 1964; The Memoirs of S.N. Behrman, 1972. Mem. Nat. Inst. Arts and Letters. Contbr. The New Yorker. Has done many films in Hollywood including "Queen Christina" for Greta Garbo and Tale of Two Cities for Ronald Colman; also Me and the Colonel for Danny Kaye, 1958. Author: (plays) The Second Man, 1927; Serena Blandish, 1928; Meteor, 1929; Brief Moment, 1932; Biography, 1933; Love Story, 1934; Rain from Heaven, 1935; End of Summer, 1936; Amphitryon 38 (adapted from French), 1937; Wine of Choice, 1938; No Time for Comedy, 1939; The Talley Method, 1941; The Pirate, 1942; Jacobowsky and the Colonel (with Franz Werfel), 1944; Dunnigan's Daughter, 1945; Jane (from Somerset Maugham), 1946; I Know My Love (from Achard), 1949; Fanny (with Joshua Logan). 1954; The Cold Wind and The Warm, 1958; Lord Pengo, 1962; But For Whom Charlie, 1964; (books) Duveen (biography), 1952; The Worcester Account, 1954; Portrait of Max, 1960; The Suspended Drawing Room, 1965; The Burning Glass, 1968. Recipient Brandeis U. Creative Arts award-Theatre medal, 1962. Address: 1185 Park Av New York City NY 10028

BEHYMER, EDGAR HUGH, univ. dean; b. Liberty, Ind., Aug. 3, 1907; s. Forney L. and Hallie Moore (Hughes) B.; A.B., Ind. U., 1934; A.B., in L.S., U. Mich., 1938; M.A., U. Chgo., 1940; postgrad. Univ. Coll., London, England, 1949-50. Librarian, Law Library Ind. U., 1928-34, U. Mich., 1934-36, La. State U., 1936-38, Ala. U., 1940-41, Bethany (W.Va.) Coll. Library, 1941-55; dir. libraries, prof. library sci., dean Grad. Library School of Long Island U., Brookville, N.Y., 1955-71, prof., dean emeritus Grad. Library Sch., C.W. Post Center, 1971—; lectr. Library Sch. Peabody Coll., summer 1945; Fulbright lectr. Australian Library Assn., 1952; asso. prof. State U. N.Y. at Albany, summers 1953-58. Mem. Am., W.Va., N.Y. library assns., Assn. Coll. and Reference Librarians (past pres. Tri-State chpt.). Democrat. Episcopalian. Contbr. articles library publs. Home: CW Post Center Greenvale NY 11548

BEICHNER, PAUL EDWARD, educator; b. Franklin, Pa., July 23, 1912; s. Edward Louis and Mable (Piper) B.; A.B., U. Notre Dame, 1935, M.A., 1941; theol. studies, Holy Cross Coll., 1935-39; Ph.D., Yale, 1944, postdoctoral research fellow, 1944-45. Ordained priest Roman Cath. Ch., 1939; asst. head dept. English, U. Notre Dame, 1947-49, asst. dean Coll. Arts and Letters, 1949- 50, asst. to academic v.p., 1950-52, dean Grad. Sch., 1952-71, prof. med. studies, 1971—. Mem. nat. selection com. Fulbright awards for study in U.K., 1955, Woodrow Wilson Fellowship Program, 1958-67. Mem. Mediaeval Acad. Am., Modern Lang. Assn. Editor: Aurora, Petri Rigae Biblia Versificata, 2 vols., 1965. Contbr. articles profl. jours. Home: U of Notre Dame Notre Dame IN 46556

BEIDLER, JOHN KAUFMAN, corp. exec.; b. Oakville, Pa., May 21, 1911; s. Earl J. and Chloe (Reed) B.; B.S., Lehigh U., 1934; m. Grace Alma Lark, Jan. 2, 1937; children—Elizabeth C. Schwartz, Susan L. Malarkey, Reed L., Sarah K., John Kaufman. With Dravo Corp., Pitts., 1935—, v.p., 1953- -, sr. v.p., 1962—, also dir.; v.p. Dravo for Can. Ltd., Dravo Constrn. Ltd.; dir. Gibbs & Hill Inc., Potomac Sand & Gravel Co., So. Transfer Co., Union Barge Line Corp., Zeni-McKinney-Williams Corp., Dravo-Doyle Co. Served to maj., ordnance dept. AUS, 1942-45. Decorated Croix de Guerre (France). Mem. Am. Ordnance Assn., Nat. Transp. Assn., Pitts. C. of C., Newcomen Soc. N. Am., Pa. Soc., Engrs. Soc. Western Pa., Am. Iron and Steel Inst., Am. Nuclear Soc. (adv. council Pitts. sect.). Presbyn. Clubs: Pittsburgh, Duquesne; Longue Vue; Saucon Valley Country, Allegheny Country. Home: 118 Youngwood Rd Pittsburgh PA 15228 Office: 1 Olive Plaza Pittsburgh PA 15222

BEIDUK, FELIX M., educator; b. N.Y.C., Dec. 13, 1923; s. Michael and Melania (Schulhann) B.; B.S., Coll. City N.Y., 1944; M.S., Ind. U., 1947; Ph.D. (AEC fellow), 1949; m. Norma Ethel Skinner, Aug. 17, 1947; children—Lisa Michele, Lilli Suzanne. Physicist, NACA, Langley Field, Va., 1944-46; instr. physics Villanova U., 1950-53, asst. prof., 1953-55, asso. prof., 1955-60, prof., 1960—, acting chmn. dept., 1970-71, chmn., 1971—; vis. lectr. physics Bryn Mawr Coll., 1956-57, 58-59, 62-63, 63-64; cons. physics Bryn Mawr Hosp., 1957-60. Mem. Am. Phys. Soc., A.A.A.S., Am. Assn. Physics Tchrs., Franklin Inst., Sigma Xi. Research in aerodynamics, electrodynamics, nuclear physics. Home: 2221 Dickens Lane Broomall PA 19008

BEIERSDORF, KENNETH EUGENE, mutual fund exec.; b. Chgo., May 6, 1925; s. Robert C. and Eva (Johnson) B.; B.S., U. Minn., 1949; m. Sally Jean Sandborg, Dec. 29, 1949; children—Susan, Kenneth, Roland, Lisa. With Van San Co Services, Inc., 1970—, exec. v.p., 1971—. Home: 6541 Navaho Trail Minneapolis MN 55435

BEIERWALTES, WILLIAM HENRY, educator, physician; b. Saginaw, Mich., Nov. 23, 1916; s. John Andrew and Fanny (Aris) B.; A.B., U. Mich., 1938, M.D., 1941; m. Mary Martha Nichols, Jan. 1, 1942; children—Andrew George, William Howard, Martha Louise. From intern to asst. resident medicine Cleve. City Hosp., 1941- 43; mem. faculty U. Mich. Med. Center, 1944—, prof. medicine, 1959—, dir. nuclear medicine, also dir. Thyroid Research Lab., 1952—, mem. exec. com. Inst. Sci. and Tech., 1963-64; lectr. Nat. Naval Med. Center, 1964—. Diplomate Am. Bd. Internal Medicine. Mem. Am. Fedn. Clin. Research (pres. 1954-55), Soc. Nuclear Medicine (pres. 1965-66), Central Clin. Research Club (pres. 1958-59), Am. Thyroid Assn. (v.p. 1964-65, 66- 67), Central Soc. Clin. Research (councillor 1964-67, 67-71), Galens Med. Soc. (prefect 1950-51), Am. Cancer Soc., A.M.A., Assn. Am. Physicians, A.C.S., Mich. Med. Soc., Am. Endocrine Soc. Author: Clinical Use of Radioisotopes, 1957; also numerous articles. Asso. editor Jour. Lab. and Clin. Medicine, 1954-60; editorial bd. Jour. Nuclear Medicine, 1959-64, Jour. Clin. Endocrinology and Metabolism, 1963. Home: 1025 Forest Rd Ann Arbor MI 48105

BEIGHTLER, CHARLES SPRAGUE, educator; b. Cin., Mar. 18, 1924; s. Donald Sprague and Elizabeth (Bainer) B.; B.S., U. Mich., 1950, M.S., 1954; Ph.D., Northwestern U., 1961; m. Patricia Ann Thompson, Mar. 3, 1957; children-William John, Judith Ann, Susan Jeanne, Carole Lynn, Barbara Gail. Design engr. Aeronca Mfg. Co., Middletown, O., 1950-51; research engr. Gen. Motors Research Lab., Detroit, 1954-55; operations research analyst Caywood- Schiller Assos., Chgo., 1956-57; dir. operations research Ernst & Ernst, Chgo., 1957-58; asst. prof. mech. engring. U. Tex., Austin, 1961-65, asso. prof., 1965-68, prof., 1968—; cons. Tracor Computing Corp., Austin, Humble Oil Co., Houston. Served with inf. AUS, 1943-45; to 1st lt., arty., U.S. Army, 1951-52. Decorated Bronze Star medal, Combat Inf. Badge; recipient Lanchester prize Operations Research Soc. Am., 1967. Book of the Year award Am. Inst. Indsl. Engrs., 1969. Mem. Operations Research Soc. Am., Inst. Mgmt. Scis., N.Y. Acad. Scis., Sigma Xi, Pi Tau Sigma, Kappa Sigma. Author: (with Douglass J. Wilde) Foundations of Optimization, 1967. Home: 7007 Edgefield Dr Austin TX 78731

BEIK, PAUL HAROLD, educator; b. Olivet, Mich., Jan. 23, 1915; s. Arthur Kennedy and Katie (Larson) B.; A.B., Union Coll., 1935; M.A., N.Y. State Coll. Tchrs., 1938; M.A., Columbia, 1939, Ph.D., 1943; m. Doris Humphrey, Sept. 1, 1939; children—William Humphrey, Stephen Wright. Tchr. social studies Bethlehem Central High Sch., 1935-38; instr. history Columbia, 1941-45; asst. prof., asso. prof. Swarthmore (Pa.) Coll., 1945-57, prof. history, 1957—, Centennial professor history, 1968—; dir. advanced studies group Free Europe U. in Exile, Paris, France, 1956-57. Guggenheim fellow, 1948-49; Fund for Advancement Edn. fellow, 1952-53; Social Sci. Research Council fellow, 1953; Fulbright Research fellow, France, 1968-69. Mem. Am. Hist. Assn., Soc. French Hist. Studies, Am. Assn. U. Profs., Phi Beta Kappa, Delta Upsilon. Author: A Judgement of the Old Regime, 1944; The French Revolution Seen from the Right, 1956; (with Barzun, Crothers and Golob) Introduction to Naval History, 1944; (with Laurence Lafore) Modern Europe: A History Since 1500, 1959; Louis Philippe and the July Monarchy, 1965. Editor: The French Revolution, 1971. Home: 4 Whittler Pl Swarthmore PA 19081

BEILE, H.M., lumber products co. exec. Controller, Alton Box Board Co. (Ill.). Office: PO Box 276 Alton IL 62002*

BEILENSON, EDNA, book publisher, designer; b. N.Y.C., June 16, 1909; d. John and Anna (Beilenson) Rudolph; B.A., Hunter Coll., 1928; m. Peter Beilenson, July 20, 1930; children—Anthony C., Roger N., Elizabeth R.; m. 2d, Joseph E. Barmack, June 19, 1966. Owner, Peter Pauper Press, Mt. Vernon, N.Y., 1930—; pres. Walpole Printing Office, Mt. Vernon, N.Y.; free-lance designer children's books; books exhibited Fifty Books of the Year, Best Children's Books of the Year; dir., v.p. Am. Inst. Graphic Arts, 1953- 57, pres., 1958-60; dir. The Goudy Soc., 1967-68, chmn. bd. 1968—. Author: Festive Cookery, 1951; Recipes Mother Used to Make 1952; ABC of Casseroles, Canapes, others (series), Holiday Cook Book Series, Simple French Cookery, Simple Italian Cookery, others. Editor: Little Riddle Book, Little Quiz Book, Little Joke Book; (as Elisabeth Deane) Gift of Friendship, Gentle Thoughts, Words of Love, Gift of Prayer. Fellow Royal Soc. Arts, London. Home: 1035 Fifth Av New York City NY 10028 Office: Peter Pauper Press 629 N McQuesten Pkwy Mount Vernon NY 10552

BEILHARZ, EDWIN ALANSON, educator; b. Phillipsburg, Kan., June 18, 1907; s. William Tobias and Lavara (Lowe) B.; A.B., Creighton U., 1931; M.A., U. Neb., 1934; Ph.D., U. Cal. at Berkeley, 1951; m. Frances Marion Fuller, June 19, 1937; children—Frieda Marie (Mrs. Donald K. Rosenberg), Ann Elizabeth (Mrs. Philip Pflager), Alan Francis, Claire Genevieve, Prin., Roseland (Neb.) High Sch., 1931-33; faculty U. Santa Clara (Cal.), 1936—, prof. history, 1941—, chmn. dept., 1941-68, dir. div. social studies, 1951-63. Mem. Am. Hist. Assn., Am. Catholic Hist. Assn. (chmn. program com. 1965), Pacific Coast Council Latin Am. Studies (sec.-treas. 1965-66), Cal. Hist. Soc. Author: The New Frontiers and The Old, 1962. Home: 16021 Wood Acres Rd Los Gatos, CA 95030. Office: History Dept University of Santa Clara Santa Clara CA 95053

BEIMFOHR, EDWARD GEORGE, lawyer; b. Marissa, Ill., Dec. 31, 1932; s. Edwin Erdmann and Alvina (Knecht) B.; A.B., Washington U., St. Louis, 1953, LL.B., 1956; m. Joella Jane White, March 26, 1951; children—Catherine Jane, Laurence Edward, Douglas Alan. Admitted to Mo. and N.Y. bars; legal asso. firm Thompson, Mitchell, Thompson & Douglas, St. Louis, 1956-57, Sullivan and Cromwell, N.Y.C., 1957-65; partner firm Casey, Lane & Mittendorf, N.Y.C., 1965—; lectr. in field. Mem. Am. N.Y. State bar assns., Bar Assn. City N.Y., Phi Beta Kappa, Order of Coif, Omicron Delta Kappa,Delta Theta Phi. Conglist. Author articles in field. Editor-in- chief Washington U. Law Quar., 1955-56. Home: 48 Kenilworth Dr Short Hills, NJ 07078. Office: 26 Broadway New York City NY 10004

BEIMFORD, LOUIS ARMSTEAD, lawyer; b. Hamilton, O., Oct. 9, 1924; s. William B. and Katheryn (Armstead) B.; B.S., Miami U., Oxford, O., 1948; LL.B., George Washington U., 1950; m. Barbara Hepting, Aug. 13, 1952; children—Peter, James. Admitted to Ohio bar, 1950, since practiced in Hamilton; asst. pros. atty., Butler County, 1953-56; partner Parrish, Beeler, Bartels, Beimford, Fryman & Smith, 1956—; tchr. seminars in bus. Miami U. Chpt. chmn. A.R.C., 1965-67. Trustee Butler County Welfare Adv. Bd., Sr. Citizens, Inc. Served to 1st lt., inf., AUS, 1943-46; ETO. Decorated Combat Inf. Badge, Mem. Am., Ohio, Butler County (trustee) bar assns., Air Group, Phi Delta Theta. Elk. Clubs: New London Hills, City (Hamilton City). Home: 673 S Washington Blvd Hamilton OH 45013 Office: First Nat Bank Hamilton OH 45011

BEIN, JOHANAN, Israeli diplomat; b. Berlin, Germany, Aug. 7, 1929; immigrated to Israel, 1933; s. Alex and Betty (Bildstein) B.; B.A., Hebrew U. Jerusalem, 1953; m. Meira Weidenfeld, Apr. 14, 1954; 1 dau., Liat. Joined Ministry Fgn. Affairs, Jerusalem, 1953; 2d sec., vice consul, Helsinki, Finland, 1958-60; 1st sec., consul, Oslo, Norway, 1960-63; 1st sec., Dar es Salaam, Tanzania, also consul, Zanzibar, 1963-66; councellor, Washington, 1969—. Mem. Soc. Internat. Devel. (council Washington chpt.). Home: 4515 Willard Av Chevy Chase MD 20015 Office: 1621 22d Av NW Washington DC 20008

BEINECKE, WILLIAM S., bus. exec.; b. N.Y.C., May 22, 1914; s. Frederick William and Carrie (Sperry) B.; student Phillips Acad., Andover, Mass., Westminster Sch., Simsbury, Conn.; A.B., Yale, 1936; LL.B., Columbia, 1940; LL.D. (hon.), Southwestern U., 1967; m. Elizabeth Barrett Gillespie, May 24, 1941; children—Frederick W. II, John B., Sarah S., Frances G. Formerly asso. law firm Chadbourne, Wallace, Parke & Whiteside; co-founder law firm Casey, Beinecke & Chase; became gen. counsel the Sperry and Hutchinson Co., N.Y.C., 1952, v.p., 1954- 60, pres., 1960-67, now chmn. bd., chief exec. officer, also dir.; dir. Mfrs. Hanover Trust Co., Tex. Gulf Sulphur Co., Inc., N.Y.C. Trustee Pingry Sch., Elizabeth, N.J., Roosevelt Hosp., N.Y.C., Yale Corp.; chmn. Yale Devel. Bd. Served with USNR, World War II. Mem. Am., N.Y. State bar assns., Assn. Bar City N.Y., Council on Fgn. Relations. Clubs: Yale, Union League, Fifth Avenue, The Links (N.Y.C.); Baltusrol Golf (Springfield, N.J.); Eastward Ho! Country (Chatham, Mass.); Cotton Bay (Eleuthra); Country of Florida (Delray). Home: 20 Prospect Hill Av Summit NJ 07901 Office: Sperry and Hutchins Bldg 330 Madison Av New York City NY 10017

BEIRNE, JOSEPH ANTHONY, labor union ofcl.; b. Jersey City, Feb. 16, 1911; s. Michael Joseph and Annie T. (Giblin) B.; evening student Hudson Coll., St. Peter, Jersey City, 1933-37, N.Y.U., 1937-39; m. Anne M. Abahaze, July 2, 1933; children—Carole Anne (Mrs. James McDonald III), Maureen Anne (Mrs. Clifford Houston), Bren Anne (Mrs. Robert Leiss). Utilities and instrument repairman Western Electric Co., N.J. and N.Y., 1928-39; pres. Western Electric Employees, N.Y.C., 1937-38; organized Nat. Assn. Telephone Equipment Workers, 1937, nat. pres., 1938-45; v.p. Nat. Fedn. Telephone Workers, 1940- 43, pres., 1943-47, pres. Communications Workers Am. (successor union), 1947—; v.p. CIO, 1949-55, AFL-CIO, 1955—. Vice pres., dir. United Community Funds and Councils of Am., Inc., 1956—; mem. adv. council, career planning bd. Peace Corps; mem. WSB, 1951-52; bd. dirs. Religion and Labor Council Am., 1949—; mem. labor com. Am. Heart Assn., 1955—. Councilman, Fairview, N.J., 1941-46. Mem. bd. visitors U.S. Mil. Acad., West Point. Named one of 10 outstanding men of year Jr. C. of C., 1946; recipient Guadregisimo Anno medal Assn. Cath. Trade Unionists, 1950; Bicentennial medal Columbia U. N.Y. Sch. Social Work, 1955. Mem. Am. Arbitration Assn. (dir.). Democrat. Roman Catholic. Elk. Author: New Horizons for American Labor, 1962. Home: 3103 Cummings Lane Chevy Chase MD 20015 Office: 1925 K St NW Washington DC 20006

BEISEL, DANIEL CUNNINGHAM, newspaper publisher; b. Phila., June 30, 1916; s. Frederick C. and Margaret S. (Cunningham) B.; student U. Mich.; m. Catherine E. Turnbull, Nov. 6, 1941; children—Jane Ellen (Mrs. Edward Quinn), Catherine E. (Mrs. Eldon Arden), Sarah T. (Mrs. Dennis Thulin), Margaret A. With Green Bay & Western R.R. Co. (Wis.), 1936-42, 45-46; with Green Bay Press Gazette, 1946—, exec. v.p., mgr., 1962-63, pres., pub., 1963—, also dir.; dir. Peoples Bank of Green Bay, Green Bay Packers; past chmn. Gregby Com. for Greater Green Bay. Bd. dirs. Green Bay YMCA, Green Bay chpt. Am. Found. Religion and Psychiatry, Mem. Am., Newspaper Publs. Assn., Inland Daily Press Assn. (dir.), Green Bay Area C. of C. (past pres.). Mason. Home: 3418 Langlade Rd Green Bay WI 54301 Office: PO Box 430 Green Bay WI 54305

BEISEL, ERVIN EUGENE, beverage co. exec.; b. Frankfort, Ind., Sept. 22, 1913; s. Ervin N. and Nellie (Miller) B.; student N.M. Mil. Inst., 1930-31; Ph.B., U. Chgo., 1933; m. Mary Martha Raaba. With F.S. Yantis & Co., 1933- 34; from credit mgr. to pres. Old Poindexter Distillery, and predecessor companies, 1934-41. 46-48; pres. Pepsi-Cola Louisville Bottlers, 1949- 50; pres. Pepsi-Cola Gen. Bottlers, Inc., Chgo., 1951—, also dir.; sec. Beisel Veneer Co., Helena, Ark. Served from pvt. to maj., F.A., AUS, 1942-46. Decorated Bronze Star medal. Mem. Nat. Soft Drink Assn. (dir.), Pepsi Cola Bottlers Assn. (pres. 1956-57, dir.). Home: 99 Woodley Rd Winnetka, IL 60093. Office: 1745 N Kolmar Av Chicago IL 60639

BEISER, JOSEPH RYAN, educator; b. Alton, Ill., Mar. 20, 1909; s. Frank Landolin and Teresa Elizabeth (Ryan) B.; A.B., St. Ambrose Coll., Davenport, Ia., 1931; A.M., Georgetown U. (fellow in history 1931-33), 1932; Ph.D., Catholic U. Am (K C. fellow in history, 1935-36, 1941); student St. Mary of the Lake Sem., Mundelein, Ill., 1941-43, Kenrick Seminary, St. Louis, 1943-44; m. Betty I. Lane; 1 dau., Theresa Ryan. Ordained priest Roman Cath. Ch., 1944; instr. Springfield (Ill.) Jr. Coll., 1933-34; instr. St. Ambrose Coll., 1934-36, asst. prof., 1937-40; instr. Georgetown U., 1936-37; vis. lectr. Cath. U. Am., summer 1942; asso. prof. Sch. Religion, State U. Ia., 1944-47, prof., 1947-49; prof., chmn. history dept. St. Ambrose Coll., 1949-52; asso. prof. history Fla. So. Coll., Lakeland, 1952-53; prof. history and polit. sci., head dept. U. Tampa (Fla.), 1953-. Bd. dirs. Florida Council for Social Studies. Served as auxiliary chaplain, attached to Ia. Pre-Flight Sch., USN, 1944- 46. Mem. State Hist. Soc. Ia., So. Hist. Assn., Fla. Hist. Soc. (dir.). Am. Assn. UN (v.p. Tampa), Am. Assn. U. Profs., Fla. Council for Econ. Edn., Nat. Council Social Studies, Am. Studies Assn., Sigma Phi Epsilon. Mason. Author: The Vatican Council and The American Secular Newspapers, 1869-70, 1941. Home: 106 Huron Av Tampa FL 33606

BEISHLINE, MILES GAYLORD, mfg. co. exec.; b. Berwick, Pa., Apr. 17, 1910; s. Guy Clem and Erma (Smith) B.; student So. Ill. Normal U., U. Ill.; m. Delores Headley, Apr. 16, 1938; children—Judith (Mrs. B. S. Koles), Carol (Mrs. F. K. Holtzman), Mary Lou. Engaged in ry. car building, 1930-31; with Owens-Illinois Glass Co., Toledo, 1931—, successively engring., plant mgmt. positions, 1931-53, v.p. mfg., 1953—. Home: 3645 Brookside Rd Toledo OH 43606 Office: Owens-Illinois Bldg Toledo OH 43604

BEISSNER, HENRY MARTIN, investment banker; b. Galveston, Tex., July 21, 1907; s. Henry and Minnie (Martin) B.; B.A., Rice Y., 1929; M.B.A., Harvard, 1931; m. Dorothy Louise Brown, Aug. 31, 1938; children-Henry Martin, Sally Sue. Mgr. bond dept. Am. Nat. Ins. Co., Galveston, Tex., 1931-37; mgr. municipal dept. Milton R. Underwood & Co., Houston, 1937-40; partner Moroney, Beissner & Co., Galveston, 1940—; pres. Beissner & Co., Moroney, Beissner Mortgage Co.; dir. River Oaks Bank & Trust Co., Hycel, Inc., Hinshaw's Dept. Store. Served to comdr. USNR, 1942-45. Decorated Purple Heart, Sec. Navy commendation. Mem. Municipal Adv. Council (past trustee), Houston Soc. Financial Analysts (past pres.), Financial Analysts Fedn. (past bd. dirs.), Investment Bankers Assn. Am. (bd. govs.). Home: 3727 Willowwick Rd Houston TX 77019 Office: Bank of Southwest Bldg Houston TX 77002

BEISTLINE, EARL HOOVER, coll. dean; b. Juneau, Alaska, Nov. 24, 1916; s. Ralph H. and Katherine (Krinach) B.; B. Mining Engring., U. Alaska, 1939, E.M., 1947, LL.D., 1969; m. Dorothy Ann Hering, Aug. 24, 1946; children—Ralph Robert, William Calvin, Katherine Noreen, Lynda Marie. Mem. faculty U. Alaska, 1946—, dean Sch. Mines, 1949-61, dean Coll. Earth Sci. and Mineral Industry, 1961—, provost, exec. officer, 1970—. Served to maj. AUS, 1941-46. Fellow A.A.A.S.; mem. Am. Inst. Mining and Metall. Engrs., Arctic Institute N. Am., Pioneers of Alaska. Home: Box 5148 College AK 99701.

BEITH, ROBERT BRUCE, newspaper exec.; b. Camden, N.J., Dec. 15, 1904; s. Alexander and Charlotte (Schooley) B.; B.S. in Econs., U. Pa., 1926; m. Brina P. Hutchinson, Apr. 23, 1927; children—Brucine (Mrs. John E. Wilbur), Marla (Mrs. Amory M. Houghton III), Robert Bruce. Reporter Camden (N.J.) Courier Post, 1926-27; reporter Portland (Me.) Evening Express, 1927-34, city editor, 1937, asst. mng. editor, 1940-41, mng. editor, 1945-47, exec. editor, 1948-59; editorial writer Portland Press Herald, 1938-39, asst. mng. editor, 1940-41, mng. editor, 1945-47, exec. editor, 1948-59; exec. editor Sunday Telegram, Portland, 1948-59; reporter Asso. Press, Newark, 1934-36; with Guy Gannett Pub. Co., Portland, 1927—, exec. editor, dir., 1948—, v.p., pub., 1959—; dir. Guy Gannett Broadcasting Co.; corporator Me. Savs. Bank. Corporator Maine Med. Center. Trustee Westbrook Coll.; bd. dirs., past pres. Portland YMCA; dir. Area Devel. Council. Served from lt. (j.g.) to comdr., USNR, 1941-45. Mem. N.E. Soc. Newspaper Editors, Me. Daily Newspaper Assn., Maine (chmn. activities com.), Greater Portland (dir.) chambers commerce, Am. (dir.), Me. (pres.) automobile assns. Conglist. Office: 390 Congress St Portland ME 04111

BEITLER, SAMUEL REID cons. engineer; b. Carey, O., Mar. 19, 1899; s. Samuel Bennet and Clara (Myers) B.; B.M.E., Ohio State U., 1920, M.E., 1932; m. Katherine Lathouse, Sept. 16, 1924; 1 son, Richard Samuel. Apprentice engr. Whiting Corp., 1920-21; draftsman Kilbourne & Jacobs Mfg. Co., 1921; mem. faculty Ohio State U., 1921—, successively asst. in mech. engring., instr., asst. prof., asso. prof. hydraulic engring., prof. mech. engring., 1944-62, emeritus, 1962—, dir. personnel budget, 1954- 57, budget dir., 1957-59; sr. research cons. Am. Soc. M.E., 1962-66, director of research, 1966-72; cons. engr. Bailey Meter Co., Columbia Engring, Corp. and affiliates, 1931—, Daniels Industries, 1963—. Mem. engring. adv. com. Nat. Bureau Standards, 1955- 61, chmn. adv. panel to mechanics div., 1961-69; chmn. Ohio com. guidance Engring. Council Profl. Devel.; exec. sec. Internat. Conf. Properties of Steam, 1963-72; pres. Columbus Tech. Council, 1956-57. Fellow Am. Soc. M.E. (v.p. 1946-47, dir. 1942-47, chmn. research exec. com. 1961-62); mem. Am. Soc. Engring. Edn. (chmn. Ohio sect. 1949-50), Internat. Standards Orgn., A.A.A.S., Nat. Soc. Profl. Engrs., Nat. Assn. Power

Engrs. (hon.) Texnikoi, Sigma Xi, Tau Beta Pi, Pi Tau Sigma, Pi Mu Epsilon. Methodist (pres. trustees 1944—; bd. trustees Ohio Conf., 1961-69; mem. Ohio area commn. higher edn. 1962-70, mem. West Ohio conf. bd. pensions 1970—). Mason. Author: Hydraulic Machinery, 1948; also articles. Home: 71 W Beaumont Rd Columbus OH 43214 Offices: 206 W 18th Av Columbus OH 43210 also 345 W 47th St New York City NY 10017

BEITZEL, GEORGE BREUNINGER, bus. exec.; b. Phila., July 23, 1893; s. William Henry and Hester Jacoby (Brenner) B.; grad. U. Pa., 1916; m. Mary Elizabeth Bickley, Sept. 10, 1918; children—George Bickley, Anna Margaret. Joined Pa. Salt Mfg. Co., Phila., 1930, pres., dir., 1949-55, later spl. rep. fgn. operations; dir. Fidelity-Phila. Trust Co., Pensalt Chems. Corp., Globe Ticket Co., asst. dir. for prodn. ODM, Washington 1957-65; v.p. market operations data processing div. IBM, 1965-67, pres. div., 1967—, v.p. corp. Cons. to ICA. Pres. bd. Delaware County Hosp.; bd. dirs. Meth. Hosp. Republican. Methodist. Mason. Clubs: Union League (Phila.); Rolling Green Golf. Office: IBM Corp Armonk NY 10504

BEJART (pseudonym of Maurice Jean Berger), dancer, choreographer; b. Marseille, France, Jan. 1, 1927; s. Gaston and Germaine (Capeilleres) Berger; ed. Lycee Marseille. Dancer, 1955—; dir. Ballets de l'Etoile, 1955, ballet au Theatre de Paris, 1957, Ballet du XXe Siecle, Brussels, Belgium, 1960. Works include Symphonie pour un homme seul; Orphee; Haut-Voltage; Promethe; Bolero; Sacre du Printemps; l'Etranger; la Reine verte (spoken opera), 1963; la Damnation de Faust (staged at opera), 1964; Mathilde on le temps perdu (novel), 1963. Address: Theatre royal de la Monnaie Brussels Belgium*

BEKEFI, GEORGE, educator; b. Prague, Czechoslovakia, Mar. 14, 1925; s. Emerich and Klara (Braun) B.; B.Sc., U. Coll., London, 1948; M.Sc., McGill U., 1950, Ph.D., 1952. Asst. prof. McGill U., Montreal, Can., 1952-57; asso. prof. physics Mass. Inst. Tech., 1958-66, prof., 1966—. Home: 16 Marie Av Cambridge MA 02139

BEKINS, MILO W., business exec.; b. Sioux City, Ia., Dec. 21, 1891; s. Martin and Katherine (Cole) B.; ed. pub. schs.; m. Dorothy E. Watson, Feb. 24, 1917; children—Barbara, Virginia, June, Milo. With automobile agy. Berkins Speers Motor Co., Los Angeles, 1909-16; chmn., dir. Bekins Van & Storage Co. of Cal., Los Angeles, Bekins Van & Storage Co. of Ariz., Phoenix, 1948—, Bekins Van and Storage Co. of N.M., 1954—; officer Bekins Van Lines Co., Omaha, 1939—; dir., mem. finance com. Douglas Aviation Co.; dir. Citizens Nat. Bank. Mem. adv. bd., nat. council Boy Scouts Am., 1949—. Mem. Nat. Furniture Warehouse Assn. (past pres.), Cal. Van and Storage Assn. (past pres.), Beverly Hills C. of C. (past pres.). Mason (Shriner). Clubs: California, Los Angeles Country, Bel Air Bay (Los Angeles). Home: 811 N Alpine Dr Beverly Hills CA 90210 Office: 1335 S Figueroa St Los Angeles CA 90015

BEKKEDAHL, NORMAN, chemist; b. Shelly, Minn., Mar. 16, 1903; s. Ole and Martha (Ueland) B.; B.S., U. Minn., 1925; M.S., George Washington U., 1929; Ph.D., Am. U., 1931; m. Katherine Andrick, Sept. 2, 1943; 1 dau., Bonnie. With Nat. Bur. Standards, 1928-68, dep. chief polymers div., 1964-68, cons., 1968—. Recipient Meritorious Service award Dept. of Commerce, 1954. Fellow Washington Acad. Scis.; mem. Am. Chem. Soc. (counciler 1945-49, chmn. membership com. 1953, dir. div. rubber chemistry 1951, chmn. editorial bd. Rubber Revs. 1957-59; Charles Goodyear medal rubber div. 1967), Chem. Soc. Washington (pres. 1942), Sigma Xi. Club: Cosmos (Washington). Home: 405 N Ocean Blvd Pompano Beach FL 33062 Office: PO Box 3003 Pompano Beach FL 33062

BEKKUM, OWEN D., gas co. exec.; 1924; B.B.A., U. Wis., 1950; postgrad. Northwestern U.; married. Auditor, Arthur Andersen & Co., 1951-57; acquisition auditor Hertz Corp., 1957-62, asst. treas., 1960-62; gen. staff accountant No. Ill. Gas Co., Aurora, 1963-64, mgr. tech. accounting, 1964-66, asst. comptroller, 1966-68, comptroller, 1968—. Served with AUS, 1943-46. C.P.A. Office: PO Box 190 Aurora IL 60507

BELAFONTE, HARRY singer, actor; b. N.Y.C., Mar. 1, 1927; s. Harold George and Melvine (Love) B.; student pub. schs.; D.H.L. (hon.), Park Coll., Mo., 1968; hon. doctorate liberal arts, New Sch. Social Research; children by previous marriage—Adrienne, Shari; m. 2d, Julie Robinson, Mar. 8, 1957; children—David, Gina. Singer, actor in Broadway shows Almanac, 1953, Three for Tonight, 1955; motion pictures including Bright Road, 1952, Carmen Jones, 1954, The World, the Flesh and the Devil, 1958, Odds Against Tomorrow, 1959, Buck and the Preacher, 1971; producer, co-star The Angel Levine (motion picture), 1970; pres. Belafonte Enterprises, Inc.; producer TV specials: Belafonte: New York 19; The Strollin' Twenties; A Time for Laughter, 1967; Harry and Lena, 1969; concert attractions in U.S., nat. tours, 1957—, also Far East, Australia, Israel, Canada. Spl. adviser to Peace Corps. Served with USNR, 1943-46. Recipient Antoinette Perry award for best feature act in a musical, 1953, Donaldson award for outstanding achievement in the Theatre, 1953- 54, U.S. Dept. State award, 1958, TV Acad. award for musical Tonite with Belafonte, 1960, also other profl. and pub. service awards. Mem. CORE, Equity, Am. Guild Variety Artists, A.F.T.R.A. Recording artist RCA Victor. Office: care The Mike Merrick Co 9000 Sunset Blvd Los Angeles CA 90069

BELANGER, GUY, bishop; b. Valleyfield, Que., Can., Jan. 24, 1928; s. Raphael and Blanche (Gauthier) B.; B.A., Valleyfield Coll., 1943-47; B.Th., St. Paul Sem., Ottawa, 1949, M.A. Th., 1951; Ph.D., Angelicum U., Rome, 1953. Ordained priest Roman Cath. Ch., 1951; tchr. Valleyfield High sch., 1953-54, Valleyfield Coll., 1954-62; chaplain Montreal U., 1962-65; rector Valleyfield Coll., 1965-67; dir. gen. Valleyfield Pub. Coll., 1967-69; bishop of Valleyfield, 1969—. Address: 31 Fabrique Valleyfield Quebec Canada

BELANGER, VALERIEN, Cath. aux. bishop Montreal. Address: 2000 Sherbrooke St W Montreal 25 Quebec Canada*

BELASCO, LEON, actor; b. Odessa, Russia, Oct. 11, 1902; s. Simeon Yakovlevich and Seraphima Isaevna (Lev) Berladsky; student High Sch. of Commerce, Harbin, Manchuria, St. Joseph's Coll., Yokohama, Japan; m. Laureine Back, Apr. 12, 1949. Came to U.S., 1921, naturalized, 1927. Concert violinist and radio appearances in Hawaii and Hollywood, 1921-28; orch. leader N.Y. Embassy Club, Ambassador Hotel, St. Moritz Hotel, Casino de Paree, Palace Theater, 1929-36; toured U.S.A., 1936-39; appeared in numerous motion pictures since 1939—, including Nothing But the Truth, 1940, Everybody Does It, 1949, The Golden Horde, 1951,Loves of Don Juan, 1946, Love Happy, 1949, The Son of Ali Baba, 1952, The Flame and the Arrow, 1950, Call Me Madam, 1957, Geraldine, 1954, Can-Can, 1961, The Art of Love, 1964; appeared on numerous radio shows including The Man Called X, 1949, Screen Guild, 1950, Lux Theatre, 1947; appeared in N.Y. Broadway musicals Silk Stockings, 1955, Happy Hunting, 1957, play Once More With Feeling, 1958; appeared on TV in Hollywood and N.Y., 1960. Home: 4048 Ventura Canyon Av Sherman Oaks CA 91403

BELAVAL, EMILIO S., Puerto Rican justice; b. Fajardo, P.R., Nov. 8, 1903; s. Ricardo S. and Emilia (Maldonado) B.; LL.B., U. P.R., 1927; m. Josefina Gonzalez Sicardo, June 15, 1929; children—Emilio, Jose E., Joaquin, Maria I. Admitted to P.R. bar, 1927; comml. supt., head legal dept. P.R. Telephone Co., 1928-30; pvt. law practice, 1930-41; judge dist. ct. Bayamon. P.R., 1942-44, San Juan, 1945-53; asso. justice Supreme Ct. P.R.; v.p. Superior Ednl. Council P.R. Mem. Ateneo Puertorriqueno (pres. 1937-38), Sociedad Puertorriqueña de Periodistas, Colegio de Abogados de P.R. Author essays, short stories, biographies, play, travel articles. Home: 562 Cuevillas St San Juan PR Office: Supreme Ct Bldg San Juan PR

BELCHER, ALGERNON SHEFTALL, coll. dean; b. Savannah, Ga., Aug. 18, 1915; s. Fannin Saffore and Mamie (Sheftall) B.; A.B., Ga. State Coll., 1937; M.A., Cath. U. Am., 1949, Ph.D., 1954; m. Eloise Usher, Aug. 27, 1955. Analyst, Wage Stblzn. Bd., Washington, 1951-53; prof. econs. S.C. State Coll., 1953-55, prof. social scis., chmn. dept., 1955-58, dean Sch. Arts and Scis., 1959-63, dean of faculty, 1963-67, v.p. academic affairs, 1967—. Served to capt. AUS. World War II. Mem. Am. Econ. Assn., Am. Acad. Polit. and Social Sci., Am. Assn. U. Profs., Pi Gamma Mu, Alpha Phi Alpha, Sigma Pi Phi. Address: South Carolina State Coll Orangeburg SC 29115

BELCHER, BENJAMIN MOORE, paint mfr.; b. Montclair, N.J., June 30, 1912; s. Ward C. and Ella (Moore) B.; grad. Taft Sch., Watertown, Conn., 1932; student U. Va.; m. Nancy Knapp, May 19, 1934; 3 sons, 2 daus. With Benjamin Moore & Co., 1934—, pres., 1952-70, chmn. bd., chief exec. officer, 1955—; staff Chem. Bur., WPB, 1942-45, chief paint sect., 1942-45; cons. NPA. Mem. Nat. Paint Varnish and Lacquer Assn. (chmn., 1958, 65, dir., mem. exec. com. 1958, 65, 69—). Home: Lakeville CT 06039 Office: 548 Fifth Av New York City NY 10036

BELCHER, DONALD JENKS, engr., educator; b. Chicago, Feb. 11, 1911; s. Ova Clifford and Helen (Edson) B.; B.S., Purdue U., 1934, M.S., 1940, Ph.D., 1942; m. Nancy Foote Davies, July 1, 1954, children—Mrs. Gerald D. Whisman, Mrs. J. Peter Brann, Mark, Neil, Helen Stacey (deceased). Drainage engineer, U.S. Bureau Agricultural Engineering., 1935-36; research engineer, assistant professor civil engineering, Purdue University, 1937-46; civilian consultant, chief engr., Southwest Pacific area, 1943-44; consultant, Alaska Permafrost Investigations, 1945-46; prin. investigator Canadian Arctic Research (Permafrost), 1947; asso. prof. civil engring., Cornell, 1947-49, prof. since 1949, director, research and development in measurement of soil moisture and density by neutron and gamma ray scattering, since 1949, director of the Cornell Center of Aerial Photography since, 1950, head, dept. transportation engring., 1948-57; vis. lectr. Grad. Sch. Design, Harvard, 1963—, spl. lectr. Grad. Sch. Engring. and Applied Physics, 1965—; pres. Donald J. Belcher & Assos., Inc., 1952—; cons. specializing in engring. geology 1938—. Chief of UN Mission to Iran, 1950; selected site for new capital city, Brasilia; cons. to govts. Burma, India, Spain, Colombia, Brazil. Recipient National Research Council award, 1944; Sigma Xi award, 1945; UN medal for civilian duty with Armed Forces in combat areas, Korea. Mem. Am. Soc. C.E., Chi Epsilon, Sigma Xi, Tau Beta Pi, Pyramid. Prin. author: Formation, Distribution and Engineering Characteristics of Soils, 1943; The Formation, Distribution and Airphoto Identification of U.S. Soils, 1945. Home: 1044 Cayuga Heights Rd Ithaca NY 14850

BELCHER, DONALD RAY, financial cons.; b. Albion, Mich., Nov. 4, 1887; s. Sylvester H. and Margaret (Donald) B.; A.B., Kalamazoo Coll., 1909. LL.D., 1944; A.M., Columbia, 1915; student Sorbonne U., Paris, 1919; m. Mary Carver Williams, August 9, 1921; children—Donald William, Mary (Mrs. Robert Dello-Russo), Jonathan. Math. teacher pub. schs., 1909-10; prof. math., Hanover (Ind.) Coll., 1910-14; instr. math. Columbia, 1914-18; asst. chief statistician Am. Telephone and Telegraph Co., 1919-43; asst. comptroller, 1943-44, treas., 1944-52; cons. bd. trustees U. Pa., 1957-59, Case Inst. Tech., 1961, Winterthur Corp., 1961, Lake Erie Coll., 1964, Cornell U., 1964-65; dir. Group Securities, Inc., Bowen Engring., Inc., Botany Industries, Inc. Asst. chief Office Procurement and Material, Navy Dept., 1942-43; asst. dir. U.S. Bur. Bud., 1953-55; regents prof. U. Cal., 1955-57. Cons., Cleve. Mus. Natural History Recipient medal for distinguished Civilian Service by sec. of navy. 1944, Presidential Certificate of Merit, 1947. With A.E.F., France, World War I. Mem. N.J. Pension Survey Commn., 1930-32; mem. and approval officer N.J. Commn. for Blind, 1932-39; pres. Westfield Bd. Edn., 1939-42 and 1945-1947. Trustee Nat. Music Camp, Interlochen Arts Acad. Fellow A.A.A.S., Am. Statis. Assn.; mem. Am. Math. Soc., Am. Econ. Assn., Acad. Polit. Sci. Republican. Clubs: Century Assn.; Cosmos (Washington). Author: The Board of Trustees. Home: 550 Prospect St Westfield, NJ 07090.

BELCHER, EDWIN NEWTON, oil co. exec.; b. Miami, Fla., Aug. 10, 1913; s. Edwin Newton and Margaret (Cannon) B.; student U. Fla., 1937; m. Virginia Groos, June 29, 1936; children—Edwin Newton III, Gary Lee. Mgr. Belcher Constrn. Co., Miami, 1937—, Belcher Towing Co., Miami, 1940—; pres. Belcher Oil Co., Miami, 1948—; dir. First Nat. Bank Miami, Fla. East Coast Ry.; operating partner Oolite Rock Co. Bd. dirs. So. States Indsl. Council. Mem. Sigma Alpha Epsilon. Home: 1041 Coral Way Coral Gables FL 33134 Office: PO Box 1751 Miami FL 33101

BELCHER, FRANK BAKER, lawyer; b. Carrolton, Mo., Oct. 6, 1891; s. George L. and William A. (Beazley) B.; A.B., Stanford, 1913; postgrad. U. So. Cal. Law Sch. 1913-14; m. Ruth B. Reynolds, May 29, 1917; children—Dorothy J. (Mrs. J. Addison Sawyer), Frank Baker II, Nancy B. (Mrs. Philip Watson). Admitted to Cal. bar, 1914; mem. firm Jennings & Belcher, Los Angeles. 1914-48. Belcher, Kearney & Fargo, 1948-57, Belcher, Henzie & Fargo, 1957-63, Belcher, Henzie & Bregenzahn, Los Angeles, Cal., 1963—. Vice pres. Bank of Los Angeles; dir. Bell Petroleum Co. Mem. Cal. Bd. Bar Examiners, 1943-48. Exec. officer Sheriff's Aero Squadron, Los Angeles County. Served from pvt. to maj., inf., U.S. Army, 1917-19; AEF in France. Fellow Am. Coll. Trial Lawyers; mem. Am. (ho. of delegates 1941- 43). Cal. (pres. 1943), Los Angeles County (pres. 1938) bar assns., Am. Bar Found., Res. Officers Assn. (pres. Los Angeles chpt. 1928). Home: 163 S Plymouth Blvd Los Angeles CA 90004 Office: Security Bldg 510 S Spring St Los Angeles CA 90013

BELCHER, PAGE, congressman; b. Jefferson, Okla., Apr. 21, 1899; s. George Harvey and Jessie (Ray) B.; student Friends U., U. Okla.; LL.D., Oklahoma City U.; m. Gladys Collins, June 16, 1922; children—Page, Carol Jean (Mrs. Clyde V. Collins). Admitted to Okla. bar, 1936, also U.S. Supreme Court, other fed. courts; ct. clk. Garfield Co., Okla., 1934-38; municipal judge, Enid, Okla., 1938; sec. to Congressman Ross Rizley, eighth dist., Okla., 1941; pvt. practice, Enid, Oklahoma. Mem. 82d to 92d Congresses from 1st Okla. dist., mem. com. on agr., ho. Republican policy com. Mem. Great Salt Plains council Boy Scouts Am. Recipient Silver Beaver award Boy Scouts Am., 1948; named to Okla. Hall of Fame, 1965. Mem. Okla. Bar Assn., Tulsa County Bar, Tulsa C. of C., Am. Legion (comdr. 1947). Methodist. Odd Fellow, Kiwanian. Club: Varsity O. Home: Tulsa OK Office: House Office Bldg Washington DC 20515

BELCHER, PAUL EUGENE, banker; b. Gallipolis, O., Jan. 13, 1901; s. James P. and Frances (Schneeberger) B.; A.B., Ohio U., 1922; LL.B., Am. Extension U., 1929; J.S.D., Lake Erie Sch. Law, 1931; m. Thelma Massie, Dec. 24, 1947; 1 dau., Jacqueline (Mrs. Paul D. Miller). Admitted to Ohio bar, 1929; vice chmn. bd. First Nat. Bank, Akron, O., 1967—. Mem. Ohio Devel. Financing Commn. Chmn. bd. Edwin Shaw Hosp., Akron Met. Housing Authority; mem. Ohio Bd. Regents. Named Ohio Commodore, 1966. Mem. Am., Ohio, Akron bar assns., Akron Marketing Assn. Columnist Akron Beacon Jour., 1955—. Home: 21 Hampshire Rd Akron OH 44313 Office: 106 S Main St Akron OH 44308

BELCHER, TAYLOR GARRISON, U.S. ambassador; b. Staten Island, N.Y., July 1, 1920; s. Taylor and Miriam (Frazee) B.; B.A., Brown U., 1941; m. Edith Anthony, Oct. 22, 1942; children—Anthony, Taylor III. Joined U.S. Fgn. Service, 1946; diplomatic sec., Mexico City, 1947-50; consul, Glasgow, Scotland, 1950-54; internat. affairs officer Dept. of State, 1954-57; consul, Nicosia, Cyprus, 1957-58, consul gen., 1958-60; assigned Canadian Nat. Defence Coll., Kingston, Ont., 1960-61; dir. West Coast Affairs, Bur. Inter-Am. Affairs, State Dept. 1961-64; U.S. ambassador to Cyprus, 1964-69, to Peru, 1969—. Served to lt. USNR, 1942-45. Mem. Fgn. Service Assn. Office: care Dept of State Washington DC 20525

BELDA, BERTRAND JOHN, public accounting co. exec.; b. Chgo., Feb. 7, 1916; s. Albert George and Elizabeth (Ploger) B.; student Loyola U., Chgo., 1938-40, Northwestern U., 1941; m. Catherine T. Tuite, July 1, 1939; children—Elizabeth Marium (Mrs. William M. Bauer), David Tuite, Daniel Phillip. With Ernst & Ernst, C.P.A.'s, 1941—, staff accountant, Chgo., 1941-47, asst. mgr., 1947-51, asst. mgr., Pitts., 1951-53, partner, 1953- -, partner charge mgmt. services, Central Dist., Cleve., 1957-64, nat. dir. mgmt. services, mem. operating com., 1964—. Mem. nat. adv. council Nat. Multiple Sclerosis Soc., 1970—, vice chmn. Cleve. chpt. Recipient Silver Medal award Ill. Soc. C.P.A.'s, 1940, C.P.A., Ill., Pa., Ohio, Cal., Mich., others. Mem. Am. Inst. C.P.A.'s, Ohio Soc. C.P.A.'s, Nat. Assn. Accountants, N.A.M., Am. Mgmt. Assn., Budget Execs. Inst., Cleve. C. of C. (fed. budget com.). Clubs: Cleveland Athletic, Union (Cleve.); Hill 'N Dale Rod and Gun (Medina, O.); Pine Lake Trout (Chagrin Falls, O.); Wings (N.Y.C.). Home: 33 Lyman Circle Shaker Heights OH 44122 Office: Ernst & Ernst Union Commerce Bldg Cleveland OH 44115

BELDEN, CLARK, ret. business assn. exec., writer, speaker; b. Falls Village, Conn., Apr. 4, 1896; s. John H. and Frances M. (Clark) B.; grad. high sch., Hartford, Conn., 1914; student Brown U., 1914-15, 1916-17 (asso. editor Brunonian), Cornell U., summer 1914, Northwestern U., summers 1926, 27; m. Alice Bradford Chapman, 1931; 1 dau., Constance Chapman (dec.). Reporter, Hartford Courant, 1914; spl. reporter Providence Jour., 1916-17; in advt. and publicity dept. Travelers Ins. Co., 1919-23, Aetna Life Ins. Co., 1923- 24, Hartford Fire Ins. Co., 1924; mgr. legislative bureau Conn. C. of C., 1924-25, asst. sec., 1925-26, acting sec., later sec., 1926- 27, exec. v.p., sec., dir., 1927-29; dir. pub. relations and employee edn., Nat. Electric Power Co., N.Y.C., 1929-32; exec. sec., later mng. dir. New Eng. Gas Assn., Boston, 1932-65. Lectr. pub. relations Mass. Inst. Tech., Boston U. Sch. Pub. Relations and Communications, Harvard Bus. Sch., Harvard Sch. Edn.; lectr. Mass. Dept. Edn., Boston. Mem. bd. mgrs. Northeastern Inst., Yale, 1951-54. Corp. mem. New Eng. Bapt. Hosp., Boston, 1955- 62. Army paper work, F. A. Replacement Camp, Le Courneau, France, 1918- 19. Has served as mem. numerous advt. and pub. relations groups for pvt. and govtl. purposes, N.E. and nat. areas. Mem. faculty for trade assn. insts. at Northwestern U., 1944, 46, Yale, 1949, 1955. Mem. Pub. Relations Soc. Am. (dir. 1950-52, 1954-57, exec. com. 1952, eastern v.p. 1954, pres. N.E. chpt. 1953), Am. Soc. Assn. Execs. (dir. 1939-42; pres. Boston chpt. 1940-41), and other nat., state, local profl. orgns. and trade assns. Mason. Author several books, 1935-49. Contbr. mags. and profl. jours. Home: 2500 Virginia Av NW Washington DC 20037

BELDEN, GAIL CHESTER, ret. bus. adv. service dir.; b. Vicksburg, Miss., Jan. 18, 1903; s. William S. and Lillian C. (Elliott) B.; B.S., Northwestern U., 1925; M.B.A., Harvard, 1927; m. Louise Reynolds Conway, June 27, 1936; children—Gail Chester, Elizabeth Conway, Louise Elliiott. With Middle West Utilities Co., Chgo., 1927-32, 32-36; sec. Middle West Corp., pres., dir. Central & S.W. Utilities Co. (name changed to Central and S.W. Corporation 1947), 1938-46, v.p., 1946-68, treas., 1950-68; dir. Delmarva Bus. Adv. Service, U. Del., 1968-71; pres., dir. Am. Pub. Service Co., 1938-47; pres., dir. North West Utilities Co., 1938-51; dir. Sigma Ventura Shares, Inc., 1971—; lectr. econs. and corp. finance Northwestern U. Evening Sch. Commerce, 1927-38; instr. corp. finance, U. Pa. Evening Sch. of Accounts and Finance, 1939-41. Mem. Bd. Pub. Edn., Wilmington 1951-65, pres., 1953-65; mem. bd. mgrs., Wilmington Savs. Fund Soc., 1955—. Sigma Chi. Republican. Episcopalian. Clubs: Greenville Country, Rotary. Home: 700 Coverdale Rd Wilmington DE 19805

BELEN, FREDERICK CHRISTOPHER, lawyer; b. Lansing, Mich., Dec. 25, 1913; s. Christopher Frederick and Elizabeth (Lehman) B.; A.B. Mich. State U., 1937, recipient of honorary Doctor of Laws, 1967; LL.B., George Washington U., 1942; m. Opal Marie Sheets, Feb. 7, 1943; 1 son, Frederick Christopher. Admitted to Mich. and D.C. bars, 1945, also U.S. Supreme Ct. bar; sec. to Hon. Andrew Transue, 75th Congress, Hon. George D. O'Brien, 77th-79th Congresses; counsel, chief counsel Post Office and Civil Service Com., Ho. of Reps., 1946-61; asst. postmaster gen. charge bur. operations Post Office Department, 1961-64, deputy postmaster general, 1964-69. Director special investigations personnel mgmt.; dir. spl. studies U.S. Postal Service; mem. U.S. delegations, various subcoms. of Universal Postal Union. Trustee Multiple Sclerosis Soc., Washington. Served from 1st lt. to lt. col., AUS, 1941-46; dep. chief intelligence and security div. Army Transp. Corps. Recipient Benjamin Franklin award, 1963; Alumni Achievement award George Wash. U., 1968. Mem. Am. Soc. Pub. Adminstrn., Delta Chi. Presbyn. (elder). Author Congl. com. reports and studies. Home: 626 W Kalamazoo St Lansing MI 48933 also 2658 N Upshur St Arlington VA 22207 Office: Pennsylvania Bldg 425 13th St NW Washington DC 20004

BELES, JOSEF, banker; b. Mosty, Czechoslovakia, Dec. 3, 1932; s. Josef and Helen (Kokotek) B.; student U. Brno (Czechoslovakia), 1950-52; Diplom- Volkswirt, U. Innsbruck (Austria), 1956; m. Judith G. King, June 4, 1960; children—Karen, Audrey, Jennifer. Came to U.S., 1956, naturalized, 1962. Deleque tchechoslovaque, Innsbruck, 1954-56; with First Western Bank, Los Angeles. 1956-69, v.p., 1966-67, sr. v.p., 1967-69; dir. gen. Capital Internat. S.A., Switzerland, 1969—. Served wth AUS, 1957-59. Mem. Financial Execs. Inst., Am. Econ. Assn., Am. Statis. Assn., Czechoslovak Soc. Arts and Scis. (U.S.) (v.p., treas. W. coast chpt. 1966-68). Club: Los Angeles Athletic. Author: Concentration of Capital in Russia, 1956. Office: 15 Rue du Cendrier 1201 Genève Switzerland

BELEW, HOWARD H., oil co. exec.; b. Buffalo, Kan., Nov. 8, 1916; s. Howard Franklin and Mary Kathryn (Dulany) B.; B.S. in Chem. Engring., Kan. State U., 1938; m. Janet Courtright; children—Janet

Ann, Cynthia Sue; m. 2d, Ina M. Cox, Oct. 8, 1955; With Skelly Oil Co., 1938—, gen. mgr. mfg., 1961-62, v.p. mfg., 1963—. Mem. com. mgmt. Tulsa YMCA. Mem. Nat. Petroleum Refiners Assn., Soc. Automotive Engrs., Am. Petroleum Inst., Tulsa C. of C. Home: 2955 E 57th Pl Tulsa OK 74105 Office: Box 1650 Tulsa OK 74102

BELEW, JOHN SEYMOUR, educator, chemist; b. Waco, Tex., Nov. 3, 1920; s. George H. and Mary (Seymour) B.; B.S., Baylor U., 1941; M.S., Wichita State U., 1947; Ph.D., U. Wis., 1951; m. Ruth Edna McAtee, June 3, 1944; children—James Seymour, Janet Elizabeth. Instr. USAF Tech. Tng. Command, 1941-43; research asso. Brown U., 1951-53; acting asst. prof. U. Va., 1953-56; asst. prof. to prof. chemistry Baylor U., 1956—; prof. Paul Quinn Coll., Waco, Tex., 1964-69. Dir. Waco Heart Assn. Trustee Midway Ind. Sch. Dist., Waco, 1962-73. Served with USAAF, 1943-46. Mem. Am. Chem. Soc. (chmn. sect. 1965), Am. Inst. Chemists, Chem. Soc. London, Sigma Xi. Home: Box 16 Rt 2 McGregor TX 76657 Office: Baylor Univ Waco TX 76703

BELFER, ARTHUR B., petroleum co. exec.; b. Vodzislow, Poland, May 30, 1907; s. Benjamin and Linda (Plapla) B.; LL.D., U. Wyo.; L.H.D., Yeshiva U.; m. Rochelle Anisfeld, Feb. 22, 1931 (dec. 1961); children—Selma (Mrs. Lawrence Ruben), Anita (Mrs. Jack Saltz), Robert A. Pres. Belfer Corp., 1941-59; engaged in mfr. sleeping bags for armed forces, 1942-52; engaged in mfr. foamrubber pillows and mattresses, 1949- 51; founder, mng. partner Belfer Natural Gas Co., 1954-59; founder, chmn. bd., pres. Belco Petroleum Corp., N.Y.C., 1953-65, chmn. bd., 1962—; pres., dir. Fundamental Building Corp., 1951—; gen. partner 630 3d Av. Assos., 1957—. Pres. Belfer Found.; bd. overseers Albert Einstein Coll. of Medicine of Yeshiva U.; trustee Am. Jewish Com.; mem. bd. Am. Friends Hebrew U.; trustee Yeshiva U., also sponsor Belfer Grad. Sch. Sci. of univ. Clubs: Elwood Country; Town (N.Y.C.). Jewish religion (v.p. synagogue). Office: 630 3d Av New York City NY 10017

BELFER, ROBERT ALEXANDER, petroleum co. exec.; b. Chorzow, Poland, Mar. 27, 1935; s. Arthur B. and Rachelle (Anisfeld) B.; came to U.S., 1942, naturalized, 1947; A.B., Columbia, 1955; J.D., Harvard, 1958; m. Renee Elissa Kones, Dec. 3, 1960; children—Rachelle Lisa, Laurence David. Admitted to N.Y. bar, 1959; partner Belfer Natural Gas Co., N.Y.C., 1958-59; v.p. Belco Petroleum Corp., N.Y.C., 1958-64, exec. v.p., 1964-65, pres., 1965—, also dir.; dir. Smith, Miller & Patch, Inc. Founder Hebrew U. Jerusalem. Trustee Fedn. Jewish Philanthropies, 1964—; sec., bd. dirs. Belfer Found., 1958—; bd. dirs. Columbia Coll. Fund, 1965-68; mem. adv. bd. Odyssey House; patron Brandeis U.; founder Albert Einstein Coll. Medicine; sponsor Belfer Grad. Sch. Sci., Yeshiva U., 1962. Mem. Am. Judicature Soc., Oil Investment Inst. (dir.), Ind. Petroleum Assn. Am. (dir.), Sigma Alpha Mu. Jewish religion (trustee synagogue). Club: Old Oaks Country. Office: 630 3d Av New York City NY 10017

BELFIELD, JOHN COTTON, advt. exec.; b. Phila., Apr. 2, 1906; s. Percy C. and Harriet (Coffin) B.; B.A., Pa. State U., 1928; m. Lillian F. Baker, Dec. 27, 1930; 1 dau., Nancy C. (Mrs. James Robert Bower). Account exec. N. W. Ayer & Son, advt., 1928-40; advt. mgr. Gelatin Products Corp., 1941-44; Detroit mgr. Good Housekeeping mag., 1944-45; joined Lewis & Gilman, Inc., advt., Phila., 1945, became pres. and chmn. bd. Mem. Delta Upsilon. Clubs: Merion Golf (Ardmore, Pa.); Racquet (Phila.). Home: 903 Weldon Lane Bryn Mawr PA 19010 Office: 1700 Market St Philadelphia PA 19103

BELFORD, JOHN STUART, lawyer; b. Denver, May 29, 1898; s. Samuel W. and Helen (Thomas) B.; A.B., U. Nev., 1920; LL.B., Harvard, 1923; m. Marion E. Bishop, May 31, 1934; children—Frances B. (Mrs. Frederick E. Bickle), Susanah, Samuel W. Admitted to Nev. bar, 1922; practiced in Reno, 1923—; mem. firm Belford and O'Mara and predecessor firms, 1958—; dist. judge 2d Jud. Dist., 1952-54. Mem. adv. com. on rules of civil procedure Supreme Ct. Nev., 1951—. Mem. Am., Washoe County bar assns., State Bar Nev. (bd. govs. 1951-52), Sigma Alpha Epsilon. Republican. Mason. Club: Prospectors (Reno). Home: Belford Rd Reno NV 89502 Office: 43 N Sierra St Reno NV 89501

BELFORD, LEE ARCHER, clergyman, educator; b. Savannah, Ga., Oct. 14, 1913; s. William Thomas and Minnie (Archer) B.; B.A., U. of South, 1935, B.D., 1938; S.T.M., Union Theol. Sem., N.Y.C., 1947; Ph.D, Columbia, 1953; m. Cora Louise McGee, Apr. 12, 1939; children—Fontaine Maury, Mildred Humphreys. Ordained to ministry Episcopal Ch., 1938; vicar in Douglas and Fitzgerald, Ga., 1938-41; rector, Brunswick, Ga., 1941-43; asso. Ch. of Epiphany, N.Y.C., 1948—; lectr.-prof. Sch. Edn., N.Y.U., 1949—, chmn. dept. religious edn., 1954—. Served as chaplain USNR, 1943-46. Mem. Religious Edn. Assn., Nat. Council Chs., Protestant Council N.Y.C., Nat. Assn. Bible Instrs., Soc. Sci. Study Religion, Delta Tau Delta, Sigma Upsilon. Club: Torch. Author: The Christian and His Jewish Neighbor, 1959; Introduction to Judaism, 1961. Editor: Religious Dimensions in Literature. Contbr. to Philosophy and History, Advances in Sex Research, Dictionary of Christian Education, The Episcopal Church and Education, also articles to publs. Editor: The Church in Georgia, 1949-53. Contbg. editor The Churchman, 1958—; editorial bd. The Witness, 1961—. Home: 55 Bank St New York City NY 10014

BELFORD, WILLIAM WIESS, pediatrician; b. Georgetown, Tex., Nov. 24, 1897; s. Charles Sanford and Mary Emily (Carothers) B.; A.B., Southwestern U., 1918; M.D., Johns Hopkins, 1922; m. Elizabeth Russell, Oct. 8, 1925; children—Mary (Mrs. Martin R. Engler, Jr.), Martha (Mrs. Donald E. Root). Intern New Haven Hosp., 1922-23; intern, then resident St. Louis Childrens Hosp., 1923- 26; instr. pediatrics Washington U. Med. Sch., St. Louis, 1924-25; pvt. practice pediatrics, San Diego, 1926—; attending pediatrician San Diego County, Mercy, Childrens, Grossmont, Sharp Meml., Scripps Meml., Chula Vista Community hosps.; cons. Cal. Crippled Childrens Services, U.S. Navy Hosp., San Diego. Del. White House Conf. Children and Youth, 1960, 6th Pan Am. Congress Pediatrics, 1960. Fellow Am. Acad. Pediatrics (chmn. Cal. 1954-58, nat. pres. 1959-60); mem. Am., Cal. med. socs., San Diego County Med. Soc., Am. Heart Assn., Am. Cancer Soc., San Diego Tb Assn., Southwestern Pediatric Soc., San Diego Acad. Medicine (pres. 1957), Phi Delta Theta, Phi Chi. Episcopalian. Home: 3245 Front St San Diego CA 92103

BEL GEDDES, BARBARA, (see Geddes, Barbara Bel), actress.

BELHORN, LEROY WILLIAM, ret. banker; b. Lancaster, O., June 26, 1906; s. John N. and Maude Mae (Wilson) B.; student Franklin U.; grad. Am. Inst. Banking, 1937, Grad. Sch. Banking, Rutgers U., 1944; m. Louise M. Thissen, Sept. 5, 1936; children—Paul C., Stephen L., Leanne L., William J. Asst. cashier City Nat. Bank & Trust Co., Columbus, O., 1944-52, cashier, 1952-60, v.p., cashier, 1960-67, exec. v.p., 1967-70. Past pres. Berwick Civic Assn., Jr. Achievement Columbus. Mem. Nat. Assn. Bank Auditors and Comptrollers (past pres. Central Ohio chpt.), Am. Inst. Banking (past pres. Columbus chpt.), Columbus Controllers Club (past pres.), Am. Radio Relay League. Clubs: Athletic, Lions, Columbus Maennerchor, Columbus V.I.P., Walnut Hills Country, Swiss (Columbus); Buckeye Lake Yacht (Hebron, O.), Home: 1115 Kingslea Rd Columbus, OH 43209.

BELIEU, KENNETH EUGENE, govt. ofcl.; b. Portland, Ore., Feb. 10, 1914; s. Perry Gordon and Ilia Jean (Rood) BeL.; B.A., U. Ore., 1937; grad. Advanced Mgmt. Program, Harvard, 1955; m. Margaret Katherine Waldhoff, Dec. 22, 1951; children—Kenneth Eugene, Christopher Michael. Business exec., Portland, Ore., 1937-40; staff Senate Armed Services Com., 1955-58; staff dir. Preparedness Sub-Com., staff dir. Senate Com. on Aero. and Space Sci., 1958-61; asst. sec. for installations and logistics Navy Dept., Washington, 1961-65, undersec. navy, 1965; bd. advisers Ryan Aero. Co., 1965-69; dep. asst. to Pres. U.S., 1969-71; under-sec. Dept. of Army, 1971—. Mem. Def. Sci. Bd., 1966-68. Served to col. U.S. Army, 1940-55. Home: 1214 Westgrove Blvd Alexandria VA 22307 Office: The White House Washington DC 20500

BELIN, DAVID WILLIAM, lawyer; b. Washington, June 20, 1928; s. Louis I. and Esther (Klass) B.; B.A., U. Mich., 1951, M.B.A., 1953, J.D., 1954; m. Constance Newman, Sept. 14, 1952; children—Jonathan L., James M., Joy E., Thomas R., Laura R. Admitted to Ia. bar, 1954, since practiced in Des Moines; sr. partner firm Herrick, Langdon, Belin & Harris, 1966—; counsel President's Commn. on Assassination of President Kennedy, 1964. Dir. Alodex Corp., Berkley and Co., Inc., Delavan Mfg. Co., Dial Financial Corp., Northwest Growth Fund, Inc. Chmn. Lawyers for Nixon-Agnew, 1968. Bd. dirs. Des Moines Civic Music Assn., 1959-61, Des Moines Community Drama Assn., 1961-64, Des Moines Symphony, 1968-70, U. Mich. Alumni Assn., 1963-66. Served with AUS, 1946-47. Recipient Henry M. Bates Meml. award U. Mich. Law Sch.; hon. orator U. Mich., 1950. Mem. Phi Beta Kappa, Order of Coif, Phi Kappa Phi, Delta Sigma Rho, Beta Alpha Psi. Michigamua. Home: 1705 Plaza Circle Des Moines IA 50322 Office: Home Federal Bldg Des Moines IA 50309

BELIN, GASPARD D'ANDELOT, lawyer; b. Scranton, Pa., May 30, 1918; s. Gaspard d'Andelot and Margery (Jenks) B.; grad. Hotchkiss Sch., Lakeville, Conn., 1935; B.A., Yale, 1939, LL.B., 1946; m. Harriet Lowell Bundy, Oct. 11, 1941; children—Harriet Lowell (Mrs. Joseph Winkelman), Constance (Mrs. Allan P. Gibb), Richard, Margaretta, Alletta. Admitted to Mass. bar, 1947; with firm Choate, Hall & Stewart, Boston, 1947-62, partner, 1955-62, 65—; gen. counsel Dept. Treasury, 1962-65. Dir. New Eng. Mchts. Nat. Bank of Boston. Bd. dirs. past pres. Cambridge Civic Assn.; trustee Mus. Sci., Boston Athenaeum, Peter Bent Brigham Hosp.; v.p. Yale Devel. Bd.; mem. Yale Univ. Council. Past city councillor, Cambridge. Served to capt. AUS, 1942-45; ETO. Fellow Am. Acad. Arts and Scis.; mem. Am., Fed., Mass., Boston bar assns. Episcopalian. Home: 4 Willard St Cambridge MA 02138 Office: 28 State St Boston MA 02109

BELIN, JACOB CHAPMAN, paper co. exec.; b. DeFuniak Springs, Fla., Oct. 28, 1914; s. William Jacob and Addie (Leonard) B.; student George Washington U., 1935-38; m. Myrle Fillingim, Nov. 28, 1940; children—Jacob Chapman, Stephen Andrew. Dir. sales St. Joe Paper Co., Jacksonville, Fla., 1949-56, v.p., 1956-68, pres., dir., 1968—; mng. dir. Toymaster Products, Ltd., M. Duan & Co., Irish Paper Products, Killeen Paper Mill, Ltd. (all Dublin), Nat. Bd. and Paper Mills, Ltd., Nat. Waste Paper Co., Ltd. (both Waterford, Ireland); v.p., dir. Fla. 1st Nat. Bank at Port St. Joe, St. Joseph Land & Devel. Co.; dir. Apalachicola No. R.R. Co., St. Joseph T. & T. Co., Fla. East Coast Ry. Co., Ulster Paper Products, Ltd. (Craigavon, No. Ireland), Anglia Paper Products, Ltd. (Slough, Eng.), Holiday Inns of No. Ireland, Ltd. (Craigavon), Holiday Motels of Ireland, Ltd. (Dublin). Mem. Fla. Dem. Exec. Com., 1938-42; mayor, commr. Port St. Joe, Fla., 1949-55. Trustee Alfred I. duPont Estate; dir. Alfred I duPont Inst., Alfred I. duPont Found., Nemours Found., Edward Ball Wildlife Found., Fourdrinier Kraft Bd. Inst. Mem. Kappa Alpha Order. Baptist (trustee). Elk, Rotarian. Home: 1601 Garrison Av Port St Joe FL 32456 Office: PO Box 190 Port St Joe FL 32456

BELINGER, HARRY ROBERT, newspaper editor; b. Phila., Sept. 16, 1927; s. Harry and Florence (McGovern) B.; B.S., Temple U., 1957; m. Jean Marie O'Neill, Nov. 30, 1957; 1 dau., Lizanne. Reporter, Phila. bur. U.P.I., 1957-61; reporter Phila. Daily News, 1961-63, asst. city editor, 1963-66, city editor, 1966-68, 70—; city editor Phila. Inquirer, 1968-70. Served with inf. AUS, 1950-52. Mem. Phila. Press Assn. (dir. 1964-66). Home: 829 Anderson Av Drexel Hill PA 19026 Office: Philadelphia Daily News 400 N Broad St Philadelphia PA 19101

BELITT, BEN, author, educator; b. N.Y.C., May 2, 1911; s. Lewis and Ida (Lewitt) B.; B.A., U. Va., 1932, M.A., 1934, postgrad., 1934-36. Asst. lit. editor Nation, 1936-37; prof. English, Bennington (Vt.) Coll., 1938—; mem. faculty dance summer schs., Bennington Coll., Mills Coll., 1939, Conn. Coll., 1948-49. Served with AUS, 1942-44. Recipient Shelley Meml. award in poetry, 1936, Oscar Blumenthal award, 1956, Chgo. Civic Arts award, 1957, Brandeis Creative Arts award in poetry, 1962, Nat. Inst. Arts and Letters award in poetry, 1965; Guggenheim fellow, 1946; Nat. Endowment for the Arts grantee, 1967-68. Member P.E.N., Authors Guild, Phi Beta Kappa. Author: (poems) The Five-Fold Mesh, 1938, Wilderness Stair, 1955, The Enemy Joy (New and Selected Poems), 1964, Nowhere But Light: Poems 1964-1969; (prose.) School of the Soldier, 1949. Editor and translator; Four Poems by Rimbaud: The Problem of Translation, 1947; Poet in New York (Federico García Lorca), 1955; Selected Poems of Pablo Neruda, 1961; Juan de Mairena and Poems from the Apocryphal Songbooks (Antonio Machado), 1963: The Selected Poems of Rafael Alberti, 1965; Pablo Neruda: A New Decade: Poems 1958-67, 1969; Poems from Canto General, 1969; To Painting (Rafael Alberti), 1972. Contbr. to Cántico; Selections (Jorge Guillén), 1965. Address: Bennington College Bennington VT 05201

BELK, HENRY, newspaper columnist, coll. trustee; b. Monroe, N.C., May 8, 1898; s. Robert Lee and Lula (Rape) B.; A.B., Duke, 1923; m. Lucile Marie Bullard, Oct. 7, 1923; 1 dau., Marie (Mrs. Edgar L. Lipton) (dec.). Publicity dir. Trinity Coll. of Duke, 1920-23; instr. English, publicity dir. Wake Forest Coll., 1923-25; lectr. journalism New Rochelle (N.Y.) Coll., 1924- 25; editor Goldsboro (N.C.) News, 1926-29; mng. editor Goldsboro News- Argus, 1929-55, editor, 1949-68; editor emeritus, columnist editorial page, 1968—; columnist Greensboro Daily News, 1956—. Mem. President's Com. Employment Physically Handicapped, 1960—, N.C. Citizens Commn. Better Schs., 1957—, vice chmn., 1962—; trustee E. Carolina Univ., 1947—, chmn. 1963-64; mem. N.C. Gov.'s Study Com. Vocational Rehab. Sec. N.C. R.R. Bd., 1942; mem. Commn. Monument 3 Native N.C. U.S. Presidents, 1945-48; mem. Gov. Aycock Meml. Commn., 1949-67; life member of adv. bd. Goldsboro Salvation Army. Bd. dirs. Bib. Recorder, 1959-62, North Carolina Baptist Homes for the Aging, 1963-67, Wayne County (N.C.) Coll. Aid, Inc., 1954—. Named Foremost Handicapped Man of Year in N.C., Gov. Com. Employment Handicapped, 1960; recipient Citizenship award Goldsboro Rotary Club, 1956. Mem. N.C. (pres. 1950-51), Eastern N.C. (pres. 1944) press assns., Goldsboro Jr. C. of C. (hon. life mem. 1957), A.P. Council N.C. (pres. 1953; hon. plaque 1964), Am. Soc. Newspaper Editors, N.C. Lit. and Hist. Assn. (hon. life mem.; pres. 1962-63), Sigma Delta Chi, Alpha Phi Gamma. Baptist. Mason, Elk. Home: 1409 E Walnut St Goldsboro NC 27530 Office: 310 N Berkeley Blvd Goldsboro NC 27530

BELK, IRWIN, corp. exec., Democratic nat. committeeman for N.C.; b. Charlotte, N.C., Apr. 4, 1922; s. William Henry and Mary Leonora (Irwin) B.; student McCallie Sch., Davidson Coll.; grad. U. N.C., 1946, Student Exec. Group; m. Carol Grotnes, Sept. 11, 1948; children—William Irwin, Irene Grotnes, Marilyn, Carl Grotnes. Pres. Belk Enterprises, Inc., Bros. Investment Co., Charlotte; v.p., dir. Belk Group Stores, Charlotte, Randolph Mills, Franklinville, N.C., Pilot Mills, Raleigh, N.C.; exec.v.p. finance, treas. Belk Stores Services, Inc., Charlotte; pres. Monroe Hardware Co.; dir. Adams- Millis Corp., High Point, N.C., Fidelity Bankers Life Ins. Co., Richmond, Va., First Union Nat. Bank, Charlotte, Henry River Mills Co. (N.C.), Highland Park Mfg. Co., Park Yarn Mill, Kings Mountain, N.C., Pilot Realty Co., Raleigh, Stonecutter Mills, Spindale, N.C. Former legislative rep. So. Regional Edn. Bd., Atlanta; former pres. men's council N.C. Synod, Presbyn. Ch.; finance com. N.C. Council Chs.; chmn. businessmen for heart N.C. Heart Assn.; v.p. 8th congl. dist. N.C. Soc. Preservation Antiquities, Inc.; chmn. World Service Com. YMCA. Rep. Mecklenberg County to N.C. Ho. Reps., 1959-60, 61-62, senator, 1963-66; past mem. State Legislative Council; Democratic nat. committeeman for N.C., 1969—. Mem. Nat. Council Crime and Delinquency, Bd. dirs. Am. Heart Assn., Charlotte and Mecklenburg, Carolinas Carrousel, Charlotte; bd. dirs. Charlotte and Mecklenburg chpt. Am. Cancer Soc., past pres. N.C. div.; chmn. bd. Belk Found.; adv. chmn. exec. com. Hist. Found. Presbyn. and Reformed Chs., Montreat, N.C.; bd. dirs. Charlotte and Mecklenburg Mental Health Assn., Nat. Amateur Athletic Union Adv. Council, N.C. State Coll. Found., Bus. Found. N.C., Home Econs. Found. N.C., Ednl. Found., Inc., Chapel Hill, N.C. Ednl. Council Nat. Purposes, Med. Adv. Council U. N.C., N.C. chpt. Nat. Assn. Prevention Blindness; bd. dirs., finance bd. Charlotte Opera Assn. Mecklenburg Assn., Mecklenburg Opportunity Sch.; trustee U. N.C.; trustee past pres., dir., St. Andrews Presbyn. Coll.; trustee Queens Coll; chmn. bd. advisors Chowan Coll.; chmn. vis. com. U. N.C., Charlotte; bd. visitors Wingate Coll., Appalachian State U., Western Carolina U.; bd. assos. Meredith Coll.; bd. counselors Erskine Coll. Served with USAAF, World War II. Recipient Outstanding Young Man award Charlotte, 1954-57. Mem. N.C. (past pres., dir.), Charlotte mchts. assns., Charlotte C. of C. (past dir.), N.C. Presbyn. Hist. Soc. (2d v.p.), Kappa Alpha, Delta Sigma Pi. Democrat. Presbyn. Mason, Lion (dir., past pres. Charlotte, dep. dist. gov.). Clubs: Charlotte City, Charlotte Country, Charlotte Executives (past pres.), Myers Park Country (Charlotte): Sphinx (Raleigh, N.C.). Home: 400 Eastover Rd Charlotte NC 28207 Office: 308 E 5th St Charlotte NC 28202

BELKIN, JOHN NICHOLAS, educator, zoologist; b. Petrograd, Russia, Oct. 24, 1913; s. Nicholas Paul and Ina (Tardent) B.; came to U.S., 1928, naturalized, 1938; student Harvard, 1931-33; B.S., Cornell U., 1938, Ph.D., 1946; m. Natalie Yantsin (div.); children—Nicholas J., Tanya, Natasha J.; m. 2d, Lorraine Lyla Marvin (dec. 1967); children—Laura T., Michael J., Elisabeth J.; m. 3d, Sharon Lee Shannon. Asst. then instr. entomology Cornell U., 1938-42, 46; asst. research specialist entomology Rutgers U., 1946; asso. prof. biology Asso. Colls. Upper N.Y., 1946-49; resident head biology dept. Mohawk Coll., Utica, N.Y., 1946-48, Sampson Coll., also Champlain Coll., 1948- 49; mem. faculty U. Cal. at Los Angeles, 1949—, prof. zoology, 1958—. Served to capt. AUS, 1942-46; PTO. NSF grantee, 1955-66, USPHS grantee, 1962—, Med. Research and Devel. Command. U.S. Army, 1963—. Fellow A.A.A.S., Entomol. Soc. Am.; mem. Soc. Systematic Zoology (council), Sigma Xi, Phi Kappa Phi. Author: The Mosquitos of the South Pacific, 2 vols., 1962; also numerous research papers. Home: 3631 Tilden Av Los Angeles CA 90034

BELKIN, SAMUEL, univ. pres.; b. Swislicz, Poland, Dec. 12, 1911; s. Solomon and Mina (Sattir) B.; rabbi, Radun Theol. Sem., 1929; Ph.D. (hon. fellow), Brown U., 1935, D.D. (hon.), 1959, student Harvard, 1934; L.H.D. (hon.), Dropsie U., 1964; m. Selma Ehrlich, Nov. 10, 1935; children—Linda Rose Schuchalter, Salo Maurice; m. 2d, Abby Polesie, Jan. 3, 1963. Came to U.S. 1929, naturalized, 1941. Instr. Greek, Yeshiva Coll. (now Yeshiva U.), N.Y.C., 1935-40, prof. Hellenistic lit., 1940-43, pres., Yeshiva U., 1943—, instr. Talmud, 1936-40, dean of Rabbi Isaac Elchanan Theol. Sem., 1940—; publ. com. Jewish Publ. Soc. Am. Mem. Nat. Jewish Welfare Bd.; adv. bd. Am. Friends Hebrew U.; nat. adv. bd. United World Federalists; trustee World Acad. in Jerusalem; bd. dirs. Soc. Friends Touro Synagogue Nat. Hist. Shrine, Youth Aid, Inc., Council of Higher Ednl. Instns. in N.Y.C. Mem. Union Orthodox Rabbis U.S. and Can., Jewish Book Council Am., Jewish Acad., Arts and Scis., N.Y. Acad. Pub. Edn., Am. Acad. Polit. and Social Sci., Acad. Religion and Mental Health, Am. Assn. Jewish Edn., Am. Acad. Jewish Research (bd. fellows), Phi Beta Kappa. Author: The Alexandrian Halakhah in Apologetic Literature, 1936; Philo and Oral Law, 1940; Essays in Traditional Jewish Thought, 1956; In His Image, 1961. Contbr. to various learned publs. including Jour. of Bibl. Lit., Jewish Quar. Rev., Hapardes, Talpioth, Horeb, Sura. Home: 101 Central Park W New York City NY 10023

BELKNAP, CHAUNCEY, lawyer; b. Roselle, N.J., Jan. 26, 1891; s. Chauncey and Emma Louise (McClave) B.; Litt.B., Princeton, 1912; LL.B., Harvard, 1915; m. Dorothy Lamont, June 26, 1926; children—Louise (Mrs. David G. Carter), Robert Lamont, Barbara. Legal sec. to Justice Oliver Wendell Holmes, U.S. Supreme Court, 1915-16; admitted to N.Y. bar, 1916, D.C. bar, 1966; mem. firm Patterson, Belknap & Webb, and predecessor firms, N.Y.C., 1920—; past dir. Am. Steel Foundries, Lehn & Fink Products Corp. Commd. 2d lt., inf., U.S. Army, 1917; overseas with A.E.F., 1st Div. and G.H.Q., 1917-19; promoted capt.; demobilized with rank maj. O.R.C. Decorated Legion of Honor (France), cited by G.H.Q. (U.S.). Past mem. visitors com. Harvard Law Sch. Trustee emeritus Princeton U., Internat. House. N.Y.C. Pres. Nat. Alumni Assn. Princeton U., 1938-41. Fellow Am. Bar Found.; mem. Am. Law Inst., Am., N.Y. State (pres. 1960) bar assns., Bar Assn. City N.Y. (v.p. 1966), Harvard Law Sch. Assn. N.Y.C. (pres. 1957), N.Y. County Lawyers Assn., Phi Beta Kappa Assos., Phi Beta Kappa. Clubs: University, Century, Princeton, Down Town Assn. (N.Y.C.). Author chpt. The Alumni in Volume, The Modern Princeton. Home: 575 Park Av New York City NY 10021. Office: One Wall St New York City NY 10005

BELKNAP, PAUL EDWARD, bus. exec.; b. Bay City, Mich., Mar. 17, 1910; s. Joseph Howard and Ida (Dell) B.; B.S., Northwestern U., 1936; m. Mary Elizabeth Gibb, July 28, 1936; children—Gail (Mrs. Robert A. Nelson), Michael Howard Paul. Writer, Bauer & Black, Chgo., 1936-37; advt. mgr. Gibb Mfg. Co., Chgo., 1937-38; asst. advt. mgr. Standard Oil Co. (Ind.), 1938-43; advt. mgr. Atlas Supply Co., Newark, 1943-51; dir. marketing, account exec. McCann-Erickson, N.Y.C. and Chgo., 1951-54; exec. v.p., mng. dir. NY div. Needham, Harper & Steers, Inc., 1954-67, also dir., mem. exec. com.; partner Gibb Groves, Clermont, Fla., 1955-70, Group Six Assos., citrus groves, Winter Park, Fla., 1969—; dir. Financial Data Scis., Inc., Winter Park, 1970—. Mem. Am. Assn. Advt. Agys. (dir. Chgo. 1953), Fla. Citrus Mut., Sigma Delta Chi. Republican. Episcopalian. Mason.

Clubs: Union League (N.Y.C.); University (Chgo.); University (Winter Park). Home: 691 Greene Dr Winter Park FL 32789 Office: Financial Data Sciences Inc PO Box 1300 Winter Park FL 32789

BELL, AL, rec. co. exec.; b. Little Rock, Mar. 15, 1940; s. Albert and Viola Isbell; B.S. in Polit. Sci., Philander Smith Coll., Little Rock; m. Lydia Mae Purify, Dec. 25, 1964; 1 son, Gregory Isbell. Radio announcer Stas. KOKY, Little Rock, WUST, Washington; exec. v.p. Stax Records, Memphis, 1967—; bd. dirs. Bell Gavins Radio Program Conf. and Nat. Bus. League. Chmn. fund raising drive Goodwill Boys Club of Memphis. Recipient N.A.A.C.P. Service award, Smoty award Stax Records, Ark. Travellers award, C. of C. Recognition award; named Man of Year, Nat. Assn. TV and Radio Announcers, Exec. of Year, Bill Gavin. Hon. sgt. at arms Tenn., Hon. page Tenn. Senate. Mem. Nat. Assn. TV and Radio Announcers, N.A.A.C.P., Memphis Heart Assn., Memphis Music Assn., So. Christian Leadership Conf. Alpha Phi Alpha. Home: 2143 S Pkwy E Memphis TN 38114 Office: 98 N Avalon St Memphis TN 38114

BELL, ALBERT LAVERNE, educator; b. Hop Botton, Pa., June 15, 1914; s. Clarence Duane and Grace May (Williams) B.; B.S. Franklin and Marshall Coll., 1935; M.A., Pa. State U., 1940; Ph.D., U. Pa., 1951; m. Ethel Heisey, June 10, 1939; children—Linda (Mrs. Lawrence Wittle), Robert Duane, Richard Leigh. Head comml. dept. Hummelstown (Pa.) High Sch., 1935-36, Manheim Twp. High Sch., Neffsville, Pa., 1936-42; prof. bus. adminstrn. Hershey (Pa.) Jr. Coll., 1942-46, chmn. dept., 1944-46; from asst. prof. to prof. econs. and bus. adminstrn. Franklin and Marshall Coll., 1946—, chmn. dept. bus. adminstrn., 1952-66, 68—. Mem. Nat. Assn. Accountants (asso. dir. manuscripts), Am. Econ. Assn., Am. Accounting Assn., Am. Assn. Univ. Profs., Pi Gamma Mu. Contbr. articles profl. jours. Home: 1545 Hollywood Dr Lancaster PA 17601

BELL, ALBERT RICHARD, corp exec.; b. Chgo. 1911; ed. Northwestern U., 1932, J.D., 1935. Exec. v.p., sec. Spiegel Inc., Chgo. Home: 1223 Fairfield Rd Glencoe IL 60022 Office: 2511 W 23d St Chicago IL 60608

BELL, ALDEN JOHN, clergyman; b. Peterborough, Ont., Can., July 11, 1904; s. Henry Harold and Catherine Marie (Galvin) B.; B. Th., St. Patrick's Sem., 1932; M.S., Cath. U. Am., 1939. Ordained priest Roman Cath. Ch., 1932; asst. pastor St. Elizabeth's, Altadena, Cal., 1932-36, Cathedral Chapel, Los Angeles, 1936-37, Catholic U. Am. 1937; asst. dir. Cath. Welfare Bur., 1939-42, 46-53; adminstr. St. Bibiana's Cathedral, 1953—; archdiocesan dir. charities, Los Angeles, 1954-56; titular bishop of Rhodopolis and aux. to Los Angeles, 1956; chancellor Archdiocese of Los Angeles, bishop of Sacramento, 1962—. Mem. standing com. Nat. Conf. Cath. Charities, 1954-56. Served from 1st lt. to lt. col., chaplain, USAAF, World War II; PTO. Mem. Am. Legion. Home: 4300 Fair Oaks Blvd Sacramento CA 95826 Office: 1119 K St Sacramento CA 95814

BELL, ALEX W., mfg. co. exec.; b. Anniston, Ala., 1909; grad. Ga. Sch. Tech., 1932. Formerly exec. v.p., chmn. Am. & Efird Mills, Inc., how pres.; v.p., dir. Guild Mills, Inc.; dir. Am. & Efird Mills, Inc. (Mich.). Office: American & Efird Mills Inc Mount Holly NC 28120*

BELL, ALPHONZO, congressman; b. Los Angeles, Sept. 19, 1914; s. Alphonzo Edward and Minnewa (Shoemaker) B.; grad. Occidental Coll., Los Angeles, 1938; m. Marian McCargo, Nov. 7, 1970; children by previous marriage—Stephen Helms, Fonze Helms, Mattew Temple, Robert Louis, Anthony Edward. Chmn. bd. Bell Petroleum Co.; mem. 89th Congress from 16th Dist. Cal., mem. 88th-92d Congresses from 28th Dist. Cal. Mem. Phi Gamma Delta. Presbyn. Clubs: Jonathans California (Los Angeles). Office: Cannon Office Bldg Washington DC 20515

BELL, ARTHUR DONALD, author, psychologist; b. Vancouver, Wash., July 17, 1920; s. Arthur and Lois Myrtle (Cox) B.; B.A. William Jewell Coll., 1942; M.R.E., Southwestern Bapt. Theol. Sem., 1945, Ed.D. with honors, 1949; postgrad. U. London, Menninger Found. Clinic, Miss. State Hosp., Central Baptist Theological Seminary, Asia Grad. Sch.; m. Evelyn Brantley, June 2, 1944; 1 dau., Judy. State sec. coll. work Missouri Baptists, 1944-46; dean, prof. religious edn. and psychology Bapt. Found., So. Ill. U., 1946-48; asst. to pres. chmn. dept. psychology Mississippi Coll., 1948-51; dir. grad. studies, prof. psychology, sch. religious edn. Southwestern Bapt. Theol. Sem., 1951-60, prof. psychology and human relations, 1963—; exec. v.p. Howard Payne Coll., 1960-63; adj. prof. psychology Tex. Christian U., 1970—; vis. prof., lectr. U. Tex., Baylor U., Golden Gate Bapt. Theol. Sem., Philippine Bapt. Theol. Sem., Hong Kong Coll., Hong Kong Bapt. Theol. Sem.; Southwestern writing grantee, 1967, 70. Adviser Baguio com. for AID grant to pres. Philippines, 1968. Past pres. Tarrant County Mental Health Assn.; mem. Miss., Tex. mental health bds. Named Achiever, Alumnus of Year, William Jewell Coll., 1971. Mem. Southwestern Religious Edn. Assn. (past pres.), Am. Assn. U. Profs., Old Santa Fe Assn., Sigma Nu. Club: River Crest Country. Author: Creative Arts, 1939; The Arts in Our Churches, 1948; How to Get Along with People in the Church, 1960, Spanish edit., 1972; The Changing Family and the Unchanging Word, 1967; In Christian Love, 1968; co-author: Introduction to Pastoral Counseling, 1958; The Family in Dialogue, 1968; Dimensions of Christian Writing, 1970, others; (4 nat. book-of-month club selections); also articles in nat. publs. Area editor: Ency. of So. Bapts. Papers and memoirs deposited in Southwest Collection Tex. Tech. Biog. Hall, U. Manchester (Eng.). Home: Taos Hwy Santa Fe NM 87501 also Box 33 Glorieta NM 87535

BELL, CAROLYN SHAW, educator, economist; b. Framingham, Mass., June 21, 1920; d. Clarence Edward and Grace (Wellington) Shaw; A.B. magna cum laude, Mount Holyoke Coll., 1941; Ph.D., London (Eng.) Sch. Econs., 1949; m. Nelson S. Bell, Aug. 26, 1953; 1 dau. by previous marriage, Tova Marie. Economist, OPA, 1941-45; research economist London Sch. Econs., 1946-47, Social Sci. Research Council, Harvard, 1950-53; mem. faculty Wellesley Coll., 1950- -, prof. econs., 1962—, chmn. dept., 1962-65, Katharine Coman prof. econs., 1970—. Mem. Am. Econs. Assn., Am. Assn. U. Profs. (pres. Wellesley chpt. 1965-66), Am. Assn. U. Women (Shirley Farr fellow 1961-62), Assn. Evolutionary Econs., Council Consumer Information, Phi Beta Kappa. Author: (with W. W. Cochrane) Economics of Consumption, 1956; Consumer Choice in the U.S. Economy, 1967; The Economics of the Ghetto, 1970; also articles. Home: Clay Brook Rd Dover MA 02030 Office: Wellesley Coll Wellesley MA 02181

BELL, CHARLES ALBERT, ins. co. exec.; b. E. Orange, N.J., Aug. 20, 1911; s. George E. and Florence (Butler) B.; A.B., Colgate U., 1933; student U. Ia., 1933-34; m. Winifred Cross, Nov. 30, 1935; children—John C., Richard J. With Bankers Nat. Life Ins. Co., 1946—, adminstry. v.p., 1963-67, exec. v.p., 1967—; dir. Palisades Life Ins. Co. Bd. dirs. N.J. Council Econ. Devel. Mem. bd. Passaic Valley Regional High Sch., 1963-69, v.p., 1967. Home: 144 2d A Little Falls, NJ 07424. Office: Littleton Rd Parsippany NJ 07054

BELL, CHARLES ANDERSON, hotel exec.; b. New Brighton, Pa., Aug. 30, 1925; s. Charles Anderson and Elizabeth (Pollock) B.; B.S., Cornell U., 1949; m. Claire Naughton, Oct. 1, 1949; children—Charles Anderson III, Jane Canning. Food and beverage controller Caribe Hilton Hotel, San Juan, P.R., 1949, purchasing agt., 1950; food cons. Harris, Kerr, Forster, N.Y.C., 1952-53; chief steward Hotel Plaza, 1953; mgr. coffee house Hotel New Yorker, 1954, food and beverage mgr., 1955-56; asst. dir. food and beverage operations Eastern div. Hilton Hotels Corp., 1957; dir. food and beverage operations Hilton Internat. Co., 1958-61, v.p. adminstrn., 1962-70, sr. v.p. adminstrn., 1970—. Served with USAAF, 1943-46. Mem. Am. Hotel Assn., Cornell Soc. Hotelmen, Les Amis d'Escoffier Soc., Chevaliers du Tastevin Soc., Commanderie du Bontemps du Medoc et des Graves (grand councilor), Alpha Sigma Phi. Republican. Clubs: Quaker Hill Country (Pawling, N.Y.); Marco Polo (N.Y.C.). Mem. editorial rev. bd. Hotel Mgmt. and World Rev. Mag. Home: 29 Washington Sq W New York City NY 10011 Office: Waldorf Astoria Hotel 301 Park Av New York City NY 10022

BELL, CHARLES HEFFELFINGER, business exec.; b. Minneapolis, Sept. 24, 1907; s.James Ford and Louise (Heffelfinger) B.; student Blake Sch., Hopkins, Minn., 1923, Hotchkiss Sch., Lakeville, Conn., 1923-26, Yale, 1926-29; m. Lucy Winton, Jan. 4, 1930; children—David Winton (dec.), Lucy Bell Hartwell. With General Mills Incorporated, 1930-42; administrative assistant for War Production Board Tools Div., Jan.-Mar. 1942; research-production coordinator Gen. Mills, 1946, v.p., 1947-50, exec. v.p., 1950-52, pres., 1952-61, chmn. bd., 1961-67; dir. Gen. Mills, Incorporated, Northwestern Nat. Bank of Mpls., N.O. Ry. Burlington No., Inc. Trustee N.Am. Wildlife Found., Mpls. Soc. Fine Arts. Served as maj., A.A.F., 1942-45. Mem. Am. Legion, Minn. Wing Air Force Assn. Conglist. Clubs: Woodhill Country (Wayzata, Minn.); Minneapolis; The Links (N.Y.C.), Minnetonka Yacht. Home: 501 Bushaway Rd Wayzata, MN 55391. Office: 9200 Wayzata Blvd Minneapolis MN 55440

BELL, CHARLES HOEY, airline exec.; b. Parkersburg, W.Va., Mar. 24, 1927; s. Charles H. and Helen Lea (Cramer) B.; B.S., U.S. Mil. Acad., 1950; m. Lea Maria Mortensen, Sept. 16, 1966; 1 son, Charles Edward. Commd. 2d lt. U.S. Army, 1950, advanced through grades to capt., 1955; ret., 1955; with Polan Industries, Huntington, W.Va., 1955-56; with Propulsion Research Corp., Santa Monica, Cal., 1957-58; dir. marketing Am. Machine & Foundry Co., Dayton, O. and Greenwich, Conn., 1958-64; v.p. marketing Dortech, Inc., Stamford, Conn., 1963-66; sr. v.p. operations Seaboard World Airlines, JFK Internat. Airport, Jamaica, N.Y., 1966—. Mem. Assn. Grads. U.S. Mil. Acad., Order Ky. Cols. Home: 491 Den Rd Stamford CT 06903 Office: JFK Internat Airport Jamaica NY 11430

BELL, CLARENCE EDWIN, Jr., naval officer; b. Hamlet, N.C. July 25, 1916; s. Clarence Edwin and and Mabel (Haines) B.; B.S. in Elec. Engring., U.S. Naval Acad.; m. Ellen Muller, June 28, 1941; children—Cynthia A. (Mrs. Alexis Doster), Susan H., Gail E. Commd. ensign U.S. Navy, advanced through grades to vice. adm.; served in submarines PTO, World War II; successively comdr. submarine div., guided missile cruiser, amphibious ships; exec. asst. to vice chief naval operations; insp. gen. Office Sec. Def.; dir. gen. plans and programs naval operations; dir. navy program planning; now comdr. amphibious force U.S. Atlantic Fleet. Decorated D.S.M., Legion of Merit, Silver Star (2). Clubs: Columbia Country (Washington); Army-Navy Country (Arlington, Va.); Norfolk (Va.) Yacht and Country. Home: Quarters A Naval Amphibious Base Norfolk VA 23520 Office: Naval Amphibious Base Norfolk VA 23520

BELL, CLARENCE S., grain milling exec.; b. Flemingsburg, Ky., July 30, 1931; s. C. Stanley and Margaret (Campbell) B.; B.S. in Agr., U. Ky., 1936; m. Virginia Hunter, Dec. 22, 1934. Agrl. extension work with U. Ky., 1936-48; grain milling exec. Pillsbury Co., 1948-63; pres. Honegger & Co., Fairbury, Ill., 1963-70, dir., mem. exec. com., 1970—; chmn. bd. Central Farms Credit Co., Fairbury, 1964—, Keystone Mills (Ia.), 1964—. Mem. Am. Feed Mfrs. Assn., Am. Guernsey Cattle Club, Am. Dairy Sci. Assn. Presbyn. Mason, Moose, Elk, Rotarian (past pres., sec. Lawrenceburg, Ky.). Home: 2856 Middlesex Way Lexington KY 40503 Office: 206 W Locust St Fairbury IL 61739

BELL, COLIN WEDDERBURN, ednl. exec.; b. Liverpool, Eng., Apr. 10, 1903; s. Douglas Wedderburn and Jessie (Russell) B.; student Liverpool Coll., 1915-21; LL.D., Haverford Coll., 1965, Swarthmore Coll., 1966, Earlham Coll., 1971; m. Elaine Conyers, Sept. 28, 1946; children—Jennifer Conyers, Alister Wedderburn, Graham Wedderburn. Salesman, Liverpool Produce Exchange and London Mincing Lane Sugar Exchange, Eng., 1922-28; buyer, then personnel dir. British Home Stores, Ltd., London, 1928-42; driver Friends Ambulance Unit, London, 1942-43; chmn. Friends Ambulance Unit China Convoy, Chungking, China, 1943-46; dir. Asian activities Am. Friends Service Com., Phila., 1946-49; adminstr. Quaker relief for Palestine refugees in Gaza Strip under UN auspices, 1948-49; dir. Friends Internat. Center, Geneva, Switzerland, rep. Friends World Com. to ECOSOC, 1950-55; asso. exec. sec. Am. Friends Service Com., Phila., 1955-59; exec. sec. Am. Friends Service Com., 1959-68; dir. Davis House, Washington, 1968-71, Pendle Hill Study Center, Wallingford, Pa., 1971—. Home and office: Pendle Hill Wallingford PA 19086

BELL, DANIEL, educator; b. N.Y.C., May 10, 1919; s.Benjamin and Anna (Kaplan) B.; B.S., Coll. City N.Y., 1938; Ph.D., Columbia; m. Nora Potashnick, Sept. 20, 1943; 1 dau., Jordy; m. 2d, Elaine Graham, Apr. 3, 1949 (div.); m. 3d, Pearl Kazin, Dec. 18, 1960; 1 son, David. Staff writer The New Leader, 1939-41, mng. editor, 1941-44; mng. editor Common Sense, 1945; instr. to asst. prof. social scis. U. Chgo., 1945-48; lectr. sociology Columbia, 1952-58, prof. sociology, 1958-69; prof. sociology Harvard Univ., 1969—; labor editor Fortune mag., 1948-58. Mem. Pres.'s Commn. on Tech., Automation and Econ. Progress. Recipient Center for Advanced Studies in Behavioral Sciences fellowship; Am. Council on Edn. prize, 1966. Fellow Am. Acad. Arts and Sci. (v.p.); mem. Council on Fgn. Relations, Century Assn., Am. Sociol. Soc. Author: History of Marxian Socialism in the U.S., 1952; The New American Right, 1955; The End of Ideology, 1960; The Radical Right, 1963; The Reforming of General Education, 1966; Towards the Year 2000, 1968; Confrontation, 1969; Capitalism Today, 1971. Mem. editorial board Daedalus, The American Scholar; co-editor The Public Interest. Contbr. to acad., tech. jours. Home: 65 Francis Av Cambridge MA 02138

BELL, DAVID BONAR, ret. naval officer; b. Fargo, N.D., Nov. 16, 1913; s. William Bonar and Clara (Preston) B.; student George Washington U., 1933; B.S., U.S. Naval Acad., 1937; M.S. in Mech. Engring., U.S. Navy Postgrad. Sch., 1949; grad. Nat. War Coll., 1961; m. Mary Elizabeth Walsh, Dec. 30, 1946; children—Ann C., William B. Commd. ensign U.S. Navy, 1937, advanced through grades to rear adm., 1964; duty in battleships and submarines prior to World War II; comdr. submarines U.S.S. Pargo, 1944-45, U.S.S. Trumpetfish, 1946, U.S.S.S. Dogfish, 1949-50; comdr. submarine div., 1955, submarine squadron, 1957-58, 62-64, fleet oiler, 1961-62; assigned Navy Dept., 1952-54, 66-68; dep. chief staff Supreme Allied Comdr. Atlantic (NATO), Norfolk, Va., 1964-66; dep. commandant Nat. War Coll., Washington, 1968-70. Decorated Navy Cross with gold star, D.S.M., Legion of Merit, Silver Star with gold star, Bronze Star with 2 gold stars. Mem. Sigma Alpha Epsilon. Episcopalian. Club: Army-Navy Country (Washington). Home: 127 Glenwood Av New London CT 06320

BELL, DAVID ELLIOTT, found. exec.; b. Jamestown, N.D., Jan. 20, 1919; s. Reginald and Florence (Boise) B.; B.A., Pomona (Cal.) Coll., 1939, LL.D., 1961; M.A. in Econs., Harvard, 1941, LL.D., 1965; LL.D., U. Vt., 1965, Notre Dame, 1966, U. N.D., 1967; m. Mary Louise Barry, Nov. 17, 1943; children—Susan, Peter. Mem. staff Bur. Budget, 1942, 45-47, 48-49; spl. asst. White House, 1947-48, 49-51; adminstrv. asst. to Pres. Truman, 1951-53; adviser gen. econs. Govt. Pakistan Planning Bd., also project field supr. Harvard Adv. Group, 1954-57; lectr. econs. Harvard Grad. Sch. Arts and Scis., 1957-61, sec. Grad. Sch. Pub. Adminstrn., 1959-61; dir. Bur. Budget, 1961-62; adminstr. AID, Washington, 1962-66; v.p. Ford Found., N.Y.C., 1966-69, exec. v.p., 1969—. Served to 1st lt. USMCR, 1942-45. Recipient Rockefeller Pub. Service award, 1953. Mem. Am. Econ. Assn., Am. Soc. Pub. Adminstrn., Phi Beta Kappa. Author: Allocating Development Resources: Some Observations Based on Pakistan Experience, 1959. Home: 444 E 52d St New York City NY 10022 Office: 320 E 43d St New York City NY 10017

BELL, DAVITT STRANAHAN, steel mfr.; b. Maywood, Ill., Nov. 27, 1905; s. Frank Breckenridge and Mary Ewing (Stranahan) B.; M.E., Lehigh U., 1926; m. Marian Whieldon, June 27, 1931; children—Margaret W. (Mrs. William H. Woodwell), Frank B. II, Michael, Susan (Mrs. DeCourcy E. McIntosh). Engr., Weirton (W.Va.) Steel Co., 1926-28, Edgewater Corp., Pitts., 1928-37, asst. to pres., 1937-42, pres., 1942-67, chmn. bd. dirs., 1967—; dir. Dravo Corp. Bd. dirs., pres. Tb League; bd. dirs. Pa. Tb and Health Soc., WQED Ednl. Television; first v.p., bd. trustees Children's Hosp., Pitts. Mem. Am. Soc. M.E. Republican. Presbyn. Clubs: Duquesne, Oakmont Country, Rolling Rock (Ligonier); Pittsburgh Golf. Home: B311 Woodland Manor Apts 5903 Fifth Av Pittsburgh PA 15232 Office: Edgewater Corp Oakmont PA 15139

BELL, DONALD LISLE, utility co. exec.; b. San Francisco, Aug. 25, 1916; s. William L. and Annabelle (Wheeler) B.; A.B. in Econs., U. Cal. at Berkeley, 1938; student Harvard, 1943; m. Barbara Newell, July 25, 1970; children—Pamela, Peter, children—Pamela, Peter, Bonnie, James, Carolyn, Christopher, Beverly. Bonnie, James, Carolyn, Christopher, Beverly. With Pacific Gas and Electric Co., San Francisco, 1946—, treas., 1962—, v.p. finance, 1970—. Served to 1942— 45. Mem. Delta Kappa lt. (s.g.) USNR, 1942-45. Mem. Delta Kappa Epsilon. Home: 1165 Bay Laurel Dr Menlo Park CA 94025 Office: 245 Market St San Francisco CA 94105

BELL, EDWARD FRANK, judge; b. Grand Rapids, Mich., Apr. 22, 1929; s. William McKinley and Mentie (Moore) B.; B.A., U. Mich., 1951; J.D. Detroit Coll. Law, 1954; m. Marilyn Alma Morton, Mar. 12, 1960; children—Celeste Darling, Whitney April. Admitted to Mich. bar, 1959; social worker Children's Aid Soc., Detroit, 1956-59; pvt. practice law, Detroit, 1959-69; Wayne County Circuit Judge, Detroit, 1969—. Mem. Nat. Transp. Adv. Council, 1970-73, Mich. Housing Authority, 1967-70. Bd. dirs. Holy Cross Hosp.; bd. dirs. Homes for Black Children. Served with AUS, 1954-56. Mem. Nat. (pres. 1962-64), Detroit, Wolverine bar assns., State Bar of Mich., Mich. Assn. Trial Judges, Mich. Judges Assn. Home: 19675 Stratford St Detroit MI 48221 Office: City-County Bldg Detroit MI 48226

BELL, ELLIOTT VALLANCE, ret. publishing exec.; b. N.Y.C., Sept. 25, 1902; s. William and Harriett (Elliott) B.; A.B., Columbia, 1925; LL.D., Bard Coll., 1950, St. Lawrence U., 1954; m. Amelia Lange, Nov. 23, 1927; 1 dau., Nancy Melissa (Mrs. Thomas P. F. Hoving). Financial writer N.Y. Herald Tribune, 1929, N.Y. Times, 1929-39; 1st pres. N.Y. Financial Writers Assn., 1938-39; econ. adviser Thomas E. Dewey, 1939-40; research cons. Wendell Wilkie, 1940; mem. editorial bd. N.Y. Times, 1941-42; supt. banks N.Y. State, 1943-49; chmn. exec. com. McGraw-Hill, Inc., 1950-68; editor, pub. Bus. Week mag., 1950-67; dir. N.Y. Life Ins. Co. Carrier Corp., N.Y. Telephone Co. Trustee Com. Econ. Devel., John Simon Guggenheim Meml. Found., Roger Williams Straus Meml. Found. Mem. Council Fgn. Relations. Republican. Clubs: Anglers, University, Century Association (N.Y.C.). Author: We Saw It Happen (with other corrs. N.Y. Times), 1938. Home: 200 E 66th St New York City NY 10021

BELL, EUGENE GIBBS, pipeline co. exec., lawyer; b. Charleston, W.Va., Nov. 13, 1921; s. Hollie Paige and Lorena (Gibbs) B.; LL.B., W.Va. U., 1948; m. Jane Constance McClintock, Jan. 13, 1946; children—Patricia Jane (Mrs. Harry E. Niles, Jr.), Betty Gene, Robert McClintock. Admitted to W.Va. bar, 1948, Okla. and Tex. bars, 1960, also I.C.C., Fed. Power Bar Assn.; adviser to tax commr. W.Va., 1948, dir. motor carrier dept., 1949-50; div. mgr. tax., ins. and claims dept. Phillips Petroleum Co., Midland, Tex., 1950-56; asso. Kirkwood & Darby, Ft. Worth, 1956-58; partner Hall, Bell & Walker, Houston, 1958-60; with MAPCO, Inc., Tulsa, 1960—, sec., 1962—, gen. counsel, 1966—; sec., gen. counsel all subsidiaries MAPCO, Inc.; dir. 107 subsidiaries. Served with USAAF, 1942-46; PTO. Decorated D.F.C. Mem. Am., Tex., W.Va., Okla. Tulsa County bar assns., Am. Judicature Soc., Commodity Exchange, Cotton Exchange, Kappa Alpha. Presbyn. Mason. Home: 5514 S Toledo Pl Tulsa OK 74135 Office: 1437 S Boulder Av Tulsa OK 74119

BELL, GORDON HUMPHREY, fgn. service officer; b. Boston, Sept. 25, 1920; s. Harold Ingersoll and Ellen Morrell (Foster) B.; student Ia. State U., 1939-42, Am. U., 1969; m. Theodora M. Clarke, June 26, 1944; children—Ellen, Laramie, Allyson, Gordon C. Divisional head for govt. sales John Morell & Co., Sioux Falls, S.D., 1950-53; v.p. Foster-Bell Co., Sioux Falls, 1953-66; asst. dir. for pvt. cooperation USIA, 1967-68, chief cultural affairs div. JCS, 1968-69, pub. affairs officer, Sydney, Australia, 1969—. Dir. Raven Industries, Inc., Sioux Falls. Pres. Zool. Soc. Sioux Falls, 1958-66. Bd. dirs. Sioux Valley Hosp., 1953-64, v.p., 1960, pres., 1961. Served with USNR, 1942-45. Recipient outstanding achievement award pub. service S.D. Sch. Mines, 1965. Club: Explorers (N.Y.C.). Address: Am Consulate Gen APO San Francisco CA 96209

BELL, GRIFFIN B., U.S. judge; b. Americus, Ga., Oct. 31, 1918; s. A.C. and Thelma (Pilcher) B.; student Ga. Southwestern Coll.; LL.B. cum laude, Mercer U., 1948, LL.D., 1967; m. Mary Foy Powell, Feb. 20, 1943; 1 son, Griffin B. Admitted to Ga. bar, 1947; practice in Savannah and Rome, 1947-53; partner firm King and Spalding, Atlanta, 1953-59, mng. partner, 1959-61; U.S. judge 5th Circuit, 1961—. Chief of staff Gov. Vandiver of Ga., 1959-61; chmn. Atlanta Commn. on Crime and Delinquency, 1965-66. Mem. vis. com. Law Sch., Vanderbilt U.; trustee Inst. Continuing Legal Edn. in Ga. Served to maj. AUS, 1941-46. Mem. Am. Law Inst., Order of Coif. Baptist. Home: 3100 Habersham Rd NW Atlanta GA 30305 Office: Old Post Office Bldg Atlanta GA 30303

BELL, HAROLD K., lawyer; b. Lima O., Apr. 4, 1895; s. Frank M. and Lelia (Kelly) B.; A.B., Case Western Res. U., 1916, LL.B. 1919; m. Margaret Mohler, Feb. 24, 1922; children—Martha Bell (Mrs. Hartmann), Jol..than C. Admitted to Ohio bar, 1919, since practiced in Cleve.; partner firm Spieth, Bell, McCurdy & Newell. Trustee Hudson Library and Hist. Soc. Served to 1st lt. U.S. Army, 1917-19. Mem. Am., Ohio, Cleve. bar assns., Delta Tau Delta, Phi Delta Phi.

Episcopalian (past vestryman, jr. and sr. warden). Home: 69 College St Hudson OH 44236 Office: Union Commerce Bldg Cleveland OH 44115

BELL, HAROLD W., Jr., airline exec. Sr. v.p. Continental Air Lines, Inc., Los Angeles. Office: Continental Air Lines Inc Los Angeles Internat Airport Los Angeles CA 90009*

BELL, HARRY HAINES, internat. econ. cons.; b. Haddonfield, N.J., Jan. 2, 1917; s. Ezra Comfort and May Thornton (Haines) B.; B.S., Haverford Coll., 1938; student Grad. Inst. Internat. Studies, Geneva, Switzerland, 1938-39; M.A., U. Cal. at Berkeley, 1957; m. Mildred Harriet Post, Dec. 7, 1941; 1 dau., Jane Matlack. Econ. research analyst Fed. Res. Bank of N.Y., 1939-41; fgn. service officer, 1945-69; 3d sec., vice consul, then 2d sec. and consul, Paris, 1946-48; assigned Dept. of State, Washington, 1949-50, 56-61, 68-69; 1st sec. and financial adviser U.S. Mission to European Communities, Brussels, Belgium, 1961-65; dir research div. UN Conf. Trade and Devel., 1965-68; adviser on financial policy Treasury Dept., 1968-69; staff ECA, Rome, Italy, 1950-51; chief econ. sect., 2d sec., consul, Djakarta, Indonesia, 1952-54; 2d sec., consul, Paris, 1954-56; detailed to Air War Coll. Maxwell AFB, Montgomery, Ala., 1960-61; cons. on internat. finance and comml. policy, 1969—, cons. for Dept. State, UN Conf. on Trade and Devel., Pres., Commn. on Internat. Trade and Investment, AID. Served from pvt. to capt., AUS, 1941-46. Mem. Fgn. Service Assn., Am. Econ. Assn., Am. Statis. Assn., Soc. for Internat. Devel. A.A.A.S., Phi Beta Kappa. Contbr. articles profl. periodicals. Home: 2820 38th St NW Washington DC 20007 Office: 1028 Connecticut Av NW Washington DC 20036

BELL, HENRY MARSH, Jr., banker; b. Tyler, Tex., Jan. 23, 1928; s. Henry Marsh and Elizabeth (Loftin) B.; B.S. in Indsl. Adminstrn., Yale, 1948; m. Dorothy N. Allen, Dec. 8, 1951; children—Henry Marsh III, John Allen. With Citizens First Nat. Bank of Tyler, 1948—, v.p. and trust officer, 1955-62, sr. v.p., 1962-65, exec. v.p., 1965-68, pres., 1968—, also dir. Regional chmn. A.R.C.; exec. bd. Episcopal Discese Tex.; bd. dirs. Tyler YMCA; trustee Tex. Tchr. Retirement System. Mem. E. Tex. (dir.), Tyler (pres. 1966-67) chambers commerce, Newcomen Soc. N.A. Episcopalian (vestry, finance com. Diocese Tex.). Mason (32, Shriner, Jester). Clubs: Tyler, Willow Brook Country, Tyler Petroleum. Home: 2725 Pecan Dr Tyler TX 75701 Office: 100 E Ferguson St Tyler TX 75701

BELL, HERBERT HAUGHTON, lawyer; b. Cincinnati, Oct. 11, 1895; s.Dr. William Herbert and Agnes Elizabeth (Haughton) B.; A.B. magna cum laude, Harvard,1917, LL.B. cum laude, 1922; m. Helen Frances Locke, July 30, 1927; children—Malcolm Haughton, David Procter, Richard Locke. Admitted to Ohio Bar, 1923, N.Y. Bar, 1924; asso. Paxton, Warrington & Seasongood, Cincinnati, 1922-23, Root, Clark, Buckner & Howland, N.Y. City, 1923-33; dir., v.p. North Va. Corp., 1929-33; asst. financial mgr. Mutual Life Ins. Co. of N.Y., 1933- 38. asst. gen. counsel, 1938-50, v.p., gen. counsel, 1950-60; dir., treas. life Ins. Guaranty Corp., N.Y.C., 1950-60, executive committee, 1955-60; consultant on law to the International Finance Corporation, Washington, assistant general counsel, 1961-65; dir. Kanawha & Hocking Coal & Coke Co., Charleston, W. Va., 1932-51. Mem. adv. com. Valuation Requirements Research Project, U. Wis. Dir. Bklyn. Legal Services Corp. A; trustee Bklyn. YWCA; hon. trustee Poly. Preparatory Country Day Sch., Brooklyn. Served as lt. inf. U.S. Army, 1917-19. Member Bar Association New York City, American Bar Association, Assn. Life Ins. Counsel, Acad. Polit. Sci., Phi Beta Kappa. Epsicopalian. Republican. Clubs: Harvard, Rembrandt, Ihpetonga, Heights Casino (Bklyn). Episcopalian (vestryman). Contbr. ins., law financial publs. Home: 38 Grace Ct Brooklyn, NY 11201; also RFD 1 West Redding CT 06875

BELL, HOWARD HOLMAN, historian; b. Morland, Kan., Mar. 13, 1913; s. Ernest Paul and Irene Lucy (Stiles) B.; B.A., U. Cal. at Berkeley, 1941, M.A., 1947; Ph.D., Northwestern U., 1953; grad. student Cath. U. Am., 1955, 64; m. Pauline Margaret Perrine, Jan. 12, 1942. Tchr. country grade schs., 1932- 35; instr. history Dillard U., 1949-51; manuscript specialist Am. lit. and social devel. Library of Congress, 1952-54, asst. head gift sect., 1954-56; mem. faculty and staff Tex. So. U., 1956-67, prof. history, 1962-67, librarian, 1963-66; prof. history Morgan State Coll., Balt., 1967—. Mem. faculty senate State Colls. Md., 1969—. Served with USNR, 1942-45. Mem. Tex. Assn. Coll. Tchrs. (pres. 1965-66), A.L.A., Am. Hist. Assn., Orgn. Am. Historians, Assn. Study Negro Life and History, Am. Assn. U. Profs. Author: A Survey of the Negro Convention Movement, 1830-1861, 1969. Editor: Minutes of the Proceedings of the National Negro Conventions, 1969; Black Separatism and the Caribbean (James Theodore Holly and J. Dennis Harris), 1970. Contbr. profl. jours. Home: 4528 Northwood Dr Baltimore MD 21239

BELL, JACK L., newspaperman; b. Yates Center, Kan., July 24, 1904; s. John H. and Anna J. (Peterson) B.; A.B., U. Okla., 1925; m. Helen Morey, Aug. 21, 1926; 1 son, Stratton Morey. City editor Daily Oklahoman and Times, 1929-37; chief polit. writer, head Senate staff Asso. press, 1937-69; columnist for Gannett Newspapers. Mem. Phi Beta Kappa, Pi Kappa Alpha. Clubs: Nat. Press, Gridiron, Internat., Chevy Chase. Author: the Splendid Misery; Mr. Conservative: Barry Goldwater; The Johnson Treatment; The Presidency: Office of Power. Home: 4000 Cathedral Av NW Washington DC 20016 Office: National Press Building Washington DC 20004

BELL, JAMES ADRIAN, journalist; b. Altoona, Kan., Nov. 12, 1917; s. George Andrew and Fay (Commons) B.; grad. Brent Sch., Baguio P.I., 1936; A.B., U. Kan., 1940; m. Virginia Gray, July 8, 1941; children—Jane Gray, George Edward. Reporter, Topeka Daily Capital, 1940-42; corr. Chgo. bur. Time, Inc., 1942-48, White House corr. Washington bur. 1948-50, chief N.Y. bur., 1950, war corr. Tokyo bur., 1950, Middle East bur. chief, 1951-54, Central European bur. chief, 1954-56, chief China and Southeast Asia bur. Hong Kong, 1956-59, chief Africa bur., 1959-61, chief Central European bur., Bonn, Germany, 1961-66, chief N.Y. Bur., 1966-68, chief London bur., 1968, chief Rome bur., 1968—. Served from pvt. to 2d lt., AUS Signal Corps, 1942-45. Decorated VerdienstKruez Fed. Rep. Germany; recipient Distinguished Service citation U. Kan. Mem. Delta Tau Delta, Sigma Delta Chi. Club: Players (N.Y.C.), Home: Via del Foraggi 78 Rome Italy Office: Via Sardegna 14 Rome Italy

BELL, JAMES DUNBAR, former U.S. ambassador; b. Lebanon, N.H., July 1, 1911; s. Frank Upham and Louise (Dunbar) B.; A.B., U. N.M., 1934; A.M., U. Chicago, 1936, Ph.D., 1941; m. Helen Foy Johnstone, Dec. 4, 1934 (div. May 1960); children—James Dunbar, Diane Elizabeth, Christopher Johnstone; m. 2d, Stephanie Ann Mathews, June, 1961; children—Stephanie Susan, Jefferson Matuzic. Reporter Alburquerque Journal, 1933-34; chief statistician N. M. Dept. Public Welfare, 1936-37; instr. Gary (Indiana) College, 1939-41; analyst Office Coordinator Inter-American Affairs, 1941-42; spl. asst., Dept. Justice, 1943-44; asst. prof. Hamilton Coll., 1946-47; labor attache, consul Am. embassy, Bogota, Colombia, 1944-46; consul Am. embassy, Santiago, Chile, 1947, Manila, P.I., 1950; 1st sec. and consul, Am. embassy, Manila, 1951; assigned to Dept. State, Washington, 1953-55, dep. dir. Philippine and Southeast Asian Affairs, 1955, dir. Office Southwest Pacific Affairs, 1956, 1960-64; dep. chief of mission Am. embassy, Djarkarta, 1957-60; U.S. ambassador to Malaysia, 1964-69; diplomat in residence U. Cal. at Santa Cruz, 1969-70, fellow Merrill Coll., 1969—. Adviser U.S. delegation to UN Gen. Assembly, 1961. Mem. Am. delegation ILO Regional Conf., Montevideo, Uruguay, 1949. Mem. Cal. State Democratic Com., 1971—; dist. dir. Cal. Dem. Council, 1971—. Mem. Soc. Cin., UN Assn. (pres. Santa Cruz chpt. 1971). Club: Internat. (Washington). Office: care Dept of State Washington DC 20520

BELL, JAMES DUNCAN, food co. exec.; b. Kansas City, Mo., Feb. 25, 1937; s. Carl A. and Mary (Duncan) B.; student DePauw U., 1955-56; B.S., U. Ill., 1959; m. Nancy Grant, Jan. 25, 1959; children—Michael, Pamela, John. With J.M. Jones Co., Champaign, Ill., 1959—, beginning as asst. advt. mgr., successively advt. mgr., dir. merchandising, v.p. merchandising, exec. v.p., gen. mgr., 1959-69, pres., dir., 1969—; dir., mem. exec. com. Ind. Grocers Alliance Distbn. Co., Inc.; trustee IGA, Inc.; dir. Am. Nat. Bank Bd. dirs. Champaign County United Fund, 1966-69; 71-74; mem. exec. bd. Arrowhead council Boy Scouts Am., 1970-72. Mem. Champaign-Urbana Advt. and Sales Club (pres. 1964), Beta Theta Pi, Alpha Delta Chi. Republican. Methodist (adminstrv. bd.). Home: 1608 S Mayfair St Champaign IL 61820 Office: 2611 N Lincoln Av Urbana IL 61801

BELL, JAMES FINLEY, lawyer; b. London, O., Jan. 12, 1915; s. James Finley and Rowena (Moore) B.; A.B., DePauw U., 1936; LL.B., Ohio State U., 1939; m. Charlotte Engard, Feb. 17, 1940; children—Stephen Ross, Betsey Ann. Admitted to Ohio bar, 1939; practice in London, O., 1939-42; spl. agt. FBI 1942- 46; judge Ct. Common Pleas, Madison County, O., 1947-54; judge Supreme Ct. Ohio, 1955-62; practice in Columbus, O., 1962-70; gen. counsel Gen. Telephone of Fla., Tampa, 1971—. Active Boy Scouts Am.; pres. Ohio Conf. Tb Workers, 1954-55. Mem. London Bd. Edn., 1940-52. Dem. candidate Ohio Gen. Assembly, 1946. Mem. Am., Madison County, Ohio bar assns., London Jr. C. of C. (past pres.), Sigma Chi, Phi Delta Phi. Presbyn. (elder). Club: London Rotary (past dist. gov.). Home: 304 66th St Holmes Beach FL 33509 Office: PO Box 110 Tampa FL 33601

BELL, JAMES FREDERICK, educator; b. Melrose, Mass., Apr. 21, 1914; s. John Joseph and Hester (Walsh) B.; B.A., N.Y. U., 1940; m. Perra Somers, Aug. 30, 1940; children—Jane Elizabeth, Christopher James. Design engr. Arma Corp., 1940- 45, prof. solid mechanics Johns Hopkins, Balt., 1945—; vis. prof. U. Va., summers 1951, 52; sr. visitor dept. applied math., theoretical physics U. Cambridge, Eng., 1962-63; Ricercatore associato Instituto Matematico Università di Bologna, Italia, 1970-71. Cons. U.S. Govt. Mem. Chamber Music Soc. (bd. govs. 1957), Soc. Natural Philosophy, Soc. Exptl. Stress Analysis. Am. Assn. U. Profs. Author: The Physics of Large Deformation of Crystalline Solids, 1968; Experimental Foundations of Solid Mechanics, Handbuch der Physik, vol. VI, 1971; also numerous sci. papers. Home: 606 W 40th St Baltimore, MD 21211.

BELL, JAMES IRVING, petroleum co. exec.; b. Glasgow, Scotland, Jan. 27, 1924; s. John Kidd and Georgina Drummond (Summers) B.; Chartered Accountant, U. Man., 1949; m. Geraldine Joan Fonseca, Jan. 8, 1949; children—Sydney Kathryn, David Irving, Ian Thomas. With Glendinning, Jarret, Gray & Roberts, chartered accountants, Winnipeg, Man., 1940-41, 45-49, Calgary, 1950-52; resident mgr. Union Oil Co. of Cal., Calgary, 1952-61; treas., comptroller Union Oil Co. of Can., Ltd., Calgary, Alta., 1961—. Served with RCAF, 1942-45. Mem. Financial Execs. Inst., Inst. Chartered Accountants of Alta. and Man., Calgary Petroleum Club. Club: Glencoe. Home: 1914 11th St SW Calgary 3 Alberta Canada Office: PO Box 999 335 8th Av SW Calgary 2 Alberta Canada

BELL, JOHN CROMWELL, Jr., judge; b. Phila., Oct. 25, 1892; s. John Cromwell and Fleurette deBenneville (Myers) B.; grad. Episcopal Acad., 1910; A.B., U. Pa., 1914, LL.B., 1917; m. Sarah Andrews Baker, June 29, 1918; children—John Cromwell, Louis Baker, George deBenneville, Sarah (Mrs. Lyman Greenleaf Bullard), Sophie Shepley. Admitted to Pa. bar, 1917; asst. city solicitor, Phila., 1919-22, asst. dist. atty., 1922-25; sec. banking Commonwealth of Pa., 1939-43; lt. gov. Pa., pres. State Senate, chmn. Pa. Bd. Pardons, 1943-47; gov. Pa., Jan. 2-21, 1947; justice Supreme Ct. Pa., 1950—, now chief. Mem. Am., Pa., Phila. bar. assns., Colonial Soc. Pa., Soc. S.R., Cursaders Pa. (past comdr.), Delta Psi. Clubs: Racquet (past pres.), Rittenhouse, Gulph Mills Golf, Merion Cricket (Phila.) Ranked In 1st 10 Am. Lawn Tennis Doubles, 1920; finalist U.S. Ct. Tennis Doubles Championship, 1926, 29, 31, 32, 34. Home: 283 Hathaway Lane Wynnewood PA 19096 Office: City Hall Philadelphia PA 19107

BELL, JOHN FRED, educator; b. Cambridge, O., Feb. 21, 1898; s. Walter R. and Nancy (McCulloch) B.; A.B., Muskingum College, New Concord, O., 1923; M.A., U. of Ill., 1924; Ph.D., 1928; LL.D., Muskingum College, 1957; m. Ruth B. Sinclair, June 22, 1929; children—Barbara Bell Thomson, Elizabeth (Mrs. Pierson), John Sinclair. Instr. U. of Ill., 1923-28; asst. prof. Syracuse U., 1928- 29; asso. prof. Cleve. Coll. of Western Res. U., 1929-31; prof. econs., chmn. dept., Sch. of Commerce, Temple U., 1931-41; prin. economist, Chief Wool and Woolens Unit, Office of Price Adminstrn., 1941, asso. price exec. in charge of Textiles, 1942; prof. economics U. Ill., 1941-57, prof., chmn. dept., 1957-63, prof. emeritus, 1966—; dir. bur. econ. bus. research, 1942-45; prof. econs. Cal. State Coll. at Los Angeles, 1966-67, Cal. State Coll., Fullerton, 1967-69; Chicago War Labor Bd., 1942-44; fellow Harvard, summer 1927; vis. prof. U. W. Va., summers 1932, 33. Served in R. O. T. C., 1918. Mem. Ill. Postwar Planning Commission, 1944- 45. Mem. Am. Econ. Assn., Delta Sigma Phi, Beta Gamma Sigma. Kiwanian. Clubs: Artus, University. Republican. Presbyn. Author: A History of Economic Thought, 1953, 2d edit., 1967. Contbr. econ. financial and hist. mags. Home: 18072 Gillman St Irvine CA 92664

BELL, JOHN HOWARD, air force officer; b. Lewistown, Pa., Aug. 3, 1916; s. William Herbert and Sara (Seiber) B.; B. Sc., Temple U., 1939; grad. Air Command Staff Coll., 1947, Air War Coll., 1954, Advanced Mgmt. Program, Harvard, 1953; m. Marjorie A. Gorsuch, Feb. 20, 1943. Commd. 2d lt. USAAF, 1940, advanced through grades to maj. gen. USAF, 1964; dep. chief staff plans Hdqrs. Air Def. Command, 1960-61; dir. plans NORAD Hdqrs., Colorado Springs, Colo., 1961-63; chief USAF sec. JBUSMC, Rio de Janeiro, Brazil, 1963-65; dir. tng. and edn. Hdqrs. USAF, 1965-66, dir. personnel plans and programs, 1966-68, asst. dep. chief of staff for personnel, 1968-69; comdr. 3d Air Force, London, Eng., 1969-71; chief MAAG, Rome, Italy, 1971—. Bd. dirs. Nat. Rifle Assn., 1965—. Decorated D.S.M. with oak leaf cluster, Legion of Merit, Air medal, Air Force Commendation with 2 oak leaf clusters, Army Commendation with 2 oak leaf clusters; Order So. Cross (Brazil). Home: 1415 Via Cassia Rome Italy Office: 62 Via Veneto Rome Italy

BELL, JOHN OSCAR, educator; b. Manila, Philippines, Oct. 4, 1912 (parents Am. citizens); s. John Oscar and Frances Earl (Cooley) B.; B.S., George Washington U., 1934, J.D., 1939; grad. Nat. War Coll., 1948; m. Jeannette Shahan, July 5, 1934; children—John Shahan, Patricia, Kathleen. Admitted D.C. bar, 1938; joined U.S. Dept. of State, 1931, exec. officer Passport Div., 1939-41, chief Air Priorities Sect., 1943-46, chief Air Transport Sect., 1946, asst. chief Aviation Div., 1946-47, asso. chief, 1947-48, chief 1948, asso. chief Div. of Northern European Affairs, 1948; dep. coordinator Mut. Security, 1949; asst. dir. Mut. Defense Assistance Program, 1949; asst. dir. Internat. Security Affairs, 1951; apptd. fgn. service officer, 1951, econ. counselor U.S. Embassy, Copenhagen, also dep. chief Mut. Security Agy. Mission to Denmark, 1952; dep. chief U.S. Embassy, Copenhagen and dir. U.S. Operations Mission, Denmark, 1954; dir. U.S. Operations Mission, Karachi, Pakistan, 1955; regional director Near East and South Asia, ICA, 1957; dep. coordinator fgn. assistance, 1958-61; U.S. ambassador to Guatemala, 1962-65; polit. adviser to comdr.-in-chief U.S. Strike Command, 1965-69; lectr. U. South Fla., Tampa, 1969—. Sec. for documentation Internat. Civil Aviation Conference, Chicago, 1944; conference registration officer United Nations Conf., San Francisco, 1945; spl. rep. of U.S. State Dept., Aviation Negotiations in Peru, Ecuador, Chile, Argentina, Uraguay, 1946-47; alternate mem. U.S. Dept. of State Loyalty and Security Bd. 1948-50; vice chmn. President's Task Force for Fgn. Aid, 1962. Mem. D.C. Am. Foreign Service Assn., George Washington U. Law Assn., Alpha Chi Sigma. Democrat. Home: 956 39th Av N St Petersburg FL 33703 Office: U of South Fla Tampa FL 33620

BELL, JOSEPH MILLIGAN, Jr., utilities exec.; b. Columbia, S.C., June 17, 1903; s.Joseph Milligan and Helen Iredell (Jones) B.; B.S., U. S.C., 1924; D. Sc., Hartwick Coll., 1961; LL.D., Alfred U., 1964; m. Evangeline Bell, Sept. 15, 1933; children—Evangeline I., Judith M. Engr. W.S. Barstow & Co., Inc. 1924- 28; with Harris, Forbes & Co., 1928-31, Chase Nat. Bank, 1931-35; mgr. pub. utility investments Equitable Life Assurance Soc. U.S., 1935-49; pres., dir. N.Y. State Elec. & Gas Corp., 1949-66, chmn. bd., dir. 1966—; dir. Security Mut. Life Ins. Co., First City Nat. Bank, Binghamton, N.Y., Utilities Mut. Ins. Co., N.Y. Erie-Lackawanna R.R., Midland Capital Corp., Lincoln First Group Inc., Rochester. Clubs: University, The Recess, Binghamton, Binghamton Country. Home: 22 Stratford Pl Binghamton, NY 13905. Office: 4500 Vestal Parkway E Binghamton NY 13902

BELL, L. NELSON, surgeon, editor; b. Longdale, Va., July 30, 1894; s. James Harvey and Ruth Lee (McCue) B.; student Washington and Lee U., 1911-12; M.D., Med. Coll. Va., 1916; LL.D., King Coll., Bristol, Tenn., 1964; m. Virginia Myers Leftwich, June 30, 1916; children—Rosa (Mrs. C. Donald Montgomery), Ruth (Mrs. Billy Graham), Virginia (Mrs. John N. Somerville), Benjamin Clayton. Chief surgeon Tsingkiangpu (China) Gen. Hosp., 1916-41; surg. fellowship grant Rockefeller Found., 1922-23; practice surgery, Asheville, N.C., 1941-56; sec. staff Meml.-Mission Hosp., Asheville, 1942-46, asst. chief staff, 1947-48; retired from surgery, 1956; a founder Christianity Today, 1955, exec. editor, 1955—, also dir.; founder, dir. Presbyn. Jour.; dir. Blue Ridge Broadcasting Corp., Christian Broadcasting Assn., Honolulu. Del. meeting Royal Coll. Surgeons, Geneva, Switzerland, 1956. Bd. dirs. Billy Graham Evangelistic Assn., Mountain Retreat Devel. Corp.; trustee King Coll., Bristol, Tenn. Recipient Editorial award Freedoms Found., 1954, 57, 58, 59, 60, 65, 67; subject of biography A Foreign Devil in China, 1971. Fellow A.C.S.; mem. A.M.A., N.C. Med. Soc. Author: Convictions to Live By, 1966; While Men Slept, 1970. Contbr. numerous articles, editorials to med., secular, religious mags. Home: 100 Assembly Dr Montreat NC 28757 Office: Washington Bldg Washington DC 20005

BELL, MALCOLM, Jr., banker; b. Savannah, Ga., 1913; grad. U. N.C., 1935. Pres., dir. Savannah Bank & Trust Co.; dir. Atlanta Gas Light Co. Home: 105 E Oglethorpe Av Savannah GA 31401 Office: 2 E Bryan St Box 9947 Savannah GA 31402*

BELL, MAURICE EVAN, educator, physicist; b. New Castle, O., Sept. 10, 1910; s. Samuel Evan and Della Geneva (Hagans) B.; Sc.B., Kenyon Coll., 1932; research student Trinity Coll. of Cambridge U., 1935-36; Ph.D., Mass. Inst. Tech., 1937; m. Joan Mary Ridley, June 18, 1943; 1 son, Alan George Ridley. Research engr. Westinghouse Elec. & Mfg. Co., Pitts. and Bloomfield, N.J., 1937-41; operations researcher USN, Washington, 1942-47; sci. liaison officer Am. Embassy, London, 1948-53; research mgr. Sylvania Elec. Products, Inc., Bayside, N.Y., 1954-55; asst. dean research Coll. Earth and Mineral Scis., prof. geophysics Pa. State U., 1956—. Recipient Presdl. certificate of merit for civilian service, USN, 1947. Mem. Operations Research Soc. Am., Am. Phys. Soc., A.A.A.S., Research Soc. Am., Phi Beta Kappa. Episcopalian. Elk. Contbr. articles profl. jours. Patentee in field. Home: 1008 Glenn Circle N State College PA 16801 Office: Mineral Science Bldg University Park PA 16802

BELL, MAX SIBBALD, life ins. co. exec.; b. Ont., Can., Feb. 12, 1902; s. Michael C. and Mary A. (Mayberry) B.; B.A., U. Toronto, 1923; m. Clare M. Jackson, Aug. 16, 1927; children—Barbara Helen, Max Sibbald. Came to U.S., 1924, naturalized, 1934. With State Mut. Life Assurance Co., Worcester, Mass., 1923-26; with Continental Am. Life Ins. Co., Wilmington, Del., from 1926, became pres. and chmn. bd., now dir.; dir., mem. trust com. Bank of Del. Fellow Soc. Actuaries. Home: 4303 Whittier Rd Brandywine Hills Wilmington DE 19802

BELL, NORMAN HENRY, truck sales co. exec.; b. Brantford, Ont., Can., Nov. 21, 1911; s. Frederic Wallace and Mary (Tunnicliffe) B.; student Barntford Collegiate Inst. and Vocational Sch., 1925-31, U. Toronto, 1931-32, mgmt. tng. course U. Western Ont., 1955; m. Winnifred Miller, July 26, 1941; 1 dau., Kathryn Joanne. Sales rep. George Weston, Ltd., 1932-38; sales rep. Brantford Coach & Body, Ltd., 1938-41, personnel mgr., 1941-42, br. mgr., Winnipeg, Man., 1947-48, Western sales mgr. Calgary, Atla., 1948- 49, gen. sales mgr., 1949-55, gen. mgr., 1955-57, dir., 1954-57; exec. asst. to pres. White Trucks div. White Motor Corp. of Can., Toronto, Ont., 1957-58, pres., 1958—; dir. Sterling Trusts Corp. Past pres. Canada Safety Council; bd, diirs. Mississauga Hosp. Served from pvt. to flying officer, Canadian Army, RCAF, 1942-46. Mem. Canadian C. of C. (dir. Ont. regional com.), Soc. Automotive Engrs., Lambda Chi Alpha. Mem. Angelican Ch. Mason. Clubs: Empire, Mississaugua Golf and Country (dir.), National Club, Metropolitan, Board of Trade (Toronto): Scottish Rite (Hamilton); The Brantford. Home: 1560 Staveband Rd N Port Credit Ontario Canada 6205 Airport Rd Malton Ontario Canada

BELL, PHILIP WILKES, univ. adminstr.; b. N.Y.C., Oct. 24, 1924; s. Samuel Dennis and Miriam (Wilkes) B.; B.A., Princeton, 1947, Ph.D., 1954; M.A., U. Cal., Berkeley, 1949; m. Katharine Elizabeth Hubbard, June 16, 1945; children—Susan E., Geoffrey H., Mary Eilen W., James C. IV. Corr., N.Y. Times, 1946-47; research asst. Council on Fgn. Relations, 1949-50; instr. Princeton, 1950-51, research asso. Inst. for Advanced Study, 1951-52; asst. prof. econs. Haverford Coll., 1952-56, asso. prof., 1956-57, 60-62, prof., 1962; asso. prof. econs. U. Cal., Berkeley, 1957-60, Ford Found. prof., 1959; vis. prof. U. Pa., 1963-64; prof., head, dept. econs. Markerere U. Coll., Uganda, 1963-65, dean social sci. faculty, 1964-65; prof., acting head econs. Fisk U., 1965-66; prof., chmn. dept. econs. Lincoln U., 1966-68; provost Merrill Coll., U. Cal., Santa Cruz, 1968—. Lectr., Salzburg Seminar in Am. Studies, Austria, 1955; East and Central African rep. Rockefeller Found., 1963-65, asso. dir. humanities and social sci., 1965-67; cons. Treasury Dept., 1961-63, 65-67, AID, 1962-63, State

Dept. on African Affairs, 1966—. Mem. tech. asst. panel Pres.'s Sci. Adv. Bd., 1966—. Author: The Sterling Area in the Postwar World, 1956; (with E.O. Edwards) The Theory and Measurement of Business Income, 1961; (with Michael P. Todaro) Economic Theory, 1960; editor, author 8 vol. series African Economic Problems, 1965. Contbr. articles to textbooks, profl. jours. Home: Merill Provost's House U Cal Santa Cruz CA 95060

BELL, RICHARD WILLIAM, educator; b. Elyria, O., Mar. 9, 1918; s.William Frederick and Lois (Dickinson) B.; A.B., Oberlin Coll., 1939; Aero. Engr., Cal. Inst. Tech., 1941, Ph.D., 1958; m. Sarah Elizabeth Reid, Aug. 20, 1948; children—Victoria Gay, William Frederick II, Sarah Elizabeth, Richard Reid Supr., then chief wind tunnel testing Cal. Inst. Tech., 1941-51; mem. faculty U.S. Naval Postgrad. Sch., 1951-, asso. prof. aero. Naval Postgrad. Sch., 1951-53, prof. aero., 1953—, chmn. dept. 1962—; lectr., cons. in field; dir. scis. div. U.S. Office Naval Research, London, 1961-62. Mem. Am. Inst. Aero. and Astronautics, Sigma Xi. Republican. Presbyn. Kiwanian. Home: 2658 15th Av Carmel CA 93921 Office Dept Aero US Naval Postgrad Sch Monterey CA 93940

BELL, ROBERT EDWARD, univ. chancellor; b. New Malden, Eng., Nov. 29, 1918; s. Edward R. and Edith (Rich) B.; B.A., U. B.C., 1939, M.A., 1941; Ph.D., McGill U., 1948; m. Jeanne Atkinson, July 5, 1947; 1 dau., Alison Ann. Radar devel. Nat. Research Council, Ottawa, Can., 1941-45; nuclear research Chalk River Nuclear Labs., 1946-52; prof. physics McGill U., Montreal, Que., 1956—, Rutherford prof., 1960—, dir. Foster Radiation Lab., 1960-69, vice dean arts and sci., 1964-67, dean Faculty Grad. Studies and Research, 1969-70, prin., vice chancellor, 1970—. Fellow Am. Phys. Soc., Royal Soc. (London), Royal Soc. (Can.); mem. Canadian Assn. Physicists (pres. 1965-66). Home: 363 Olivier Av Montreal 215 Quebec Canada

BELL, ROBERT EUGENE, educator; b. Marion, O., June 16, 1914; s. Harry Thew and Clara (Stouffer) B.; student Ohio State U., 1936-38; B.A. with honors, U. N.M., 1940; M.A., U. Chgo., 1943, Ph.D., 1947; m. Emily Virginia Merz, Aug. 31, 1938; children—Patricia (Mrs. Paul Lindsey), David Eugene. Asst. prof. anthropology Okla. U., 1947-51, asso. prof., 1951-55, prof., 1955-69, George L. Cross Research prof., 1969—, chmn. dept., 1947-55, 61-64, head curator Stovall Mus. of U. Okla., 1947—. Dir. Miss. Valley Dendochronology Lab. of U. Chgo., 1942-43, 46-47, Okla. River Basin Salvage Lab., 1962—. Served with M.C., AUS, 1943-46. Mem. Am. Anthropol. Assn., Am. Assn. Phys. Anthropology, A.A.A.S., Far Eastern Prehist. Assn., Okla. Hist. Soc., Am. Ethnol. Soc., Tree Ring Soc., Soc. Am. Archaeology, Sigma Xi. Author: Oklahoma Archaeology: an Annotated Bibliography, 1969. Editor of Am. Antiquity, 1966-70, Bull. Okla. Anthropol. Soc., 1963-66. Archaeol. investigations at site of El Inga, Ecuador. Home: 1120 Berry Circle Norman OK 73069

BELL, ROBERT KINSLOE, lawyer; b. Mt. Union, Pa., Jan. 6, 1900; s. William T. and Francina (Shaver) B.; B.S., Bucknell U., 1920; LL.B., U. Pa., 1924; m. Elizabeth Kress, June 10, 1926. Admitted to Pa. bar, 1924, N.J. bar, 1925, U.S. Supreme Ct., 1932; practice of law, Phila., 1924-25, Ocean City, N.J., 1925—; county counsel, Cape May County, N.J., 1930-61; counsel Cape May County Bridge Commn., 1936—. Dir. Atlantic City Electric Co., Econ. ambassador State of N.J. Past trustee Bucknell U. Sec., dir., chmn. exec. com. Am. Bar Found. Recipient citation for activities medico-legal problems Lovelace Found., 1958. Fellow Am. Coll. Probate Counsel; mem. Am. Law Inst., Internat. Bar Association (patron), N.J. C. of C. (dir.), Nat. Legal Aid Assn. (past dir.), Nat. Conf. Commrs. on Uniform State Laws, Am. Judicature Soc. (dir.), Am. (ho. of dels. 1948-59, bd. govs. 1959-61), N.J. (pres. 1949-50) bar assns., S.A.R. Clubs: Union League (Phila.); Seaview Country (Absecon, N.J.); Hillsboro (Pompano Beach, Fla.). Home: 359 Seabright Rd Ocean City NJ 08226 Office: 801 Asbury Av Ocean City NJ 08226

BELL, ROBERT PAUL, coll. dean; b. Charlottesville, Ind., Sept. 28, 1918; s. Paul H. and Emma Adaline (Overman) B.; B.S., Ball State Tchrs. Coll., Munice, Ind., 1940; M.C.S., Ind. U., 1942, Ed.D., 1952; m. Margaret Cora Strattan, Apr. 3, 1942; children—Paul Strattan, Barbara Ann. Tchr. bus. Pendleton (Ind.) High Sch., 1940-41; grad. asst. Sch. Bus., Ind. U., 1941-42, instr. U.S. Naval Tng. Sch., 1942-44; instr. Lab. Sch., Sch. Edn., Ind. U., 1944-47; mem. faculty Ball State Univ., Muncie, 1947—, prof. head dept. bus. 1954-61, prof. bus. edn., dean div. fine and applied arts, 1961-65, dean Coll. of Business, 1964—. Dir. Muncie Fed. Savings & Loan Assn. Div. chmn. Muncie United Fund, 1962-63. Bd. dirs. Delaware County Soc. Crippled, 1963—. Mem. Nat. Bus. Tchrs. Assn. (1st v.p. 1960), N. Central (pres. 1963), Nat. (bd. dirs. 1963) bus. edn. assns., Future Bus. Leaders Am. (Ind. adviser 1954- 61), N.E.A., Ind. Tchrs Assn., Nat. Thrift Com., Blue Key, Delta Pi Epsilon, Pi Omega Pi, Sigma Tau Gamma. Club: Exchange (pres. Muncie 1962- 1962- 63). Author: Instructional Materials in Accounting, 1948; Instructional Materials in Typewriting, 1963; also articles. Editor Ball State Commerce Jour., 1954—. Home: 76 Eucalyptus Dr Rural Route 2 Muncie IN 47302

BELL, ROBERT SAMUEL, electronics co. exec.; b. Milw., May 29, 1915; s. Arthur Zwebell and Nina Louise (Jacobsen) B.; A.B., U. Cal., 1936; LL.B., Harvard, 1940; D.Sc., Heald Engring. Coll., 1957; m. Carolyn Crowell, Jan. 2, 1943; 1 son, Robert McKim. Admitted to Cal. bar, 1940; with Dept. of Justice, 1931- 43; pvt. practice, 1946-48; owner, mgr. Burnham Mfg. Co., 1947-48, now merged into Packard-Bell; asst. to pres. Packard-Bell Electronics Corp., 1948, v.p., 1949-51, exec. v.p., 1951-56, pres. 1956-61, pres., chmn. bd. 1961-64, chmn. bd., 1964—; asst. to pres. Teledyne, Inc., 1968—; dir. Gen. Telephone Co. of Cal. Chmn. dir. Western Space Age Conf., Los Angeles C. of C., 1958. Vice pres., finance chmn., mem. exec. bd. Crescent Bay area council Boy Scouts; bd. regents St. John's Hosp., Santa Monica; vis com. Grad. Sch. Bus. Adminstrn., U. Cal. Los Angeles, Mchts. and Mfrs. Assn. Served from pvt. to maj., USAAF, World War II; judge adv. 20th Air Force. Recipient Silver Beaver award Boy Scouts, 1958. Mem. Fed., Cal. bar assns., Electronic Industries Assn. (sr. v.p., dir., exec. com. consumer products div.), Am. Ordnance Assn., Los Angeles C. of C., Navy League, Def. Orientation Conf. Assn., Town Hall, Jr. Radio Pioneers So. Cal., Hist. Soc. So. Cal., Beverly Hills Wine and Food Soc., Judge Advs. Assn., Confrerie des Chevaliers du Tastevin, Commanderie de Bordeaux, Chaine des Rotisseurs, Phi Kappa Sigma (dir.). Clubs: Harvard, Army-Navy, Jonathan, Bel Air Bay, Los Angeles Country (Los Angeles). Home: 10428 Sunset Blvd Los Angeles CA 90024 Office: 12333 W Olympic Blvd Los Angeles CA 90064

BELL, RONALD D., lawyer; b. Deloraine, Man., Can., Feb. 12, 1932; B.A., Brandon Coll., U. Man., 1951; LL.B., Man. Law Sch., 1955. Admitted to Man. bar, 1955, Alta. bar, 1959; partner firm Fenerty, McGillivray, Robertson, Prowse, Brennan, Fraser, Bell & Code, Calgary, Alta. Mem. Calgary, Man., Canadian bar assns., Law Soc. Alta. Office: 1500 Guinness House Calgary 2 Alberta Canada*

BELL, ROSCOE E., natural resources cons.; b. Payette, Ida., Mar. 11, 1905; s. Harry Miller and Cornelia Lucy (Smith) B.; B.S. State Coll. Wash., 1927, M.S., 1930; grad. study State Coll. Wash., U. Ida., 1930-35, U. Wis., 1956; m. Gladys Viola Kerns, Jan. 30, 1927; children—Paul Eugene, Earnest Roy, Winifred Viola, Gordon Kenneth. Instr. soils State Coll. Wash., 1926-31; asst. prof. agronomy U. Ida., 1931-35; land classification, land use planning work in western states Dept. Agr., 1935-42; chief agr., asst. dir. Central Utah War Relocation Project, War Relocation Authority, 1942-45; indsl. analyst Bonneville Power Administrn., also coordinator Western phosphate program Dept. Interior, 1945-48; successively asst. dir., asso. dir. Bur. Land Mgmt., 1948-51, Pacific N.W. regional adminstr., 1951-53, bus. economist, 1953-54; chief natural resources adviser Fgn. Operations Agy., Cairo, Egypt, 1954- 56, 56-57; program coordination officer, area 2, Bur. Land Mgmt., Salt Lake City, 1957-59, dir. Alaska div. lands, Anchorage, 1959-67; lectr. Sch. Natural Resources, research asso. natural resources policy center U. Wis.-Madison, 1968; natural resources cons., 1969—. Program coordinator Nat. Phosphorus Research Work Group, 1948-52; mem . Pacific N.W. field com. Dept. Interior; chmn. phosphate fertilizer task force Columbia Basin Interagy. Com.; mem. Ore. World Affairs Council; adv. council Fed. Pub. Land Law Rev. Commn.; mem. Portland Council Chs. Adv. bd. Salvation Army. Mem. A.A.A.S., Am. Soil Conservation Soc., Soc. Internat. Devel., Anchorage C. of C., Sigma Xi (asso.), Phi Sigma, Alpha Zeta. Methodist. Club: City (Portland). Contbr. articles sci. jours. Address: 4241 NE 81st Av Portland OR 97218

BELL, TERREL HOWARD, educator; b. Lava Hot Springs, Ida., Nov. 11, 1922; s. Willard Dewain and Alta (Martin) B.; B.A., So. Ida. Coll. Edn., 1946; M.S., U. Ida., 1953; Ed.D. (Ford fellow 1954-55), U. Utah, 1961; m. Betty Ruth Fitzgerald, Aug. 1, 1957; children—Mark Fitzgerald, Warren Terrel, Glenn Martin. Tchr. high sch. chemistry and phys. edn., Eden, Ida., 1946-47; supt. schs. Rockland (Ida.) Valley schs., 1947-54, Star Valley Sch. Dist., Afton, Wyo., 1955-57, Weber County Sch. Dist., Ogden, Utah, 1957-62; prof. sch. adminstrn. Utah State U., 1962-63; supt. pub. instrn. Utah, 1963-70; dep. for sch. systems U.S. Office Edn., 1970—. Chmn. Utah Textbook Commn., Utah Course of Study Commn.; mem. Utah Land Bd.; exec. officer Utah Bd. Edn. Served with USMCR, 1942-45; PTO. Mem. Am. Assn. Sch. Adminstrs., Council Chief State Sch. Officers, Phi Delta Kappa. Mem. Ch. of Jesus Christ of Latter Day Saints. Kiwanian. Club: Salt Lake. Author: (novel) The Prodigal Pedagogue, 1956; Effective Teaching: How to Recognize and Reward Competence, 1962; A Philosophy of Education for the Space Age, 1963. Office: US Office Edn Washington DC 20202

BELL, THOMAS J., paper co. exec.; b. Southampton, Can., 1914; ed. Ridley Coll., also U. Toronto. Pres., chief exec. officer, dir. Abitibi Paper Co., Ltd.; dir. Can. Lafarg'e Ltd., Royal Bank Can., Fiberglas Can. Ltd., Simpsons, Ltd. Home: 175 Teddington Park Toronto Ontario Canada Office: Abitibi Paper Co Ltd Toronto-Dominion Centre Toronto 1 Ontario Canada

BELL, WALTER DOUGLAS, ins. co. exec.; b. Elma, Ia., July 24, 1921; s. William J. and Vera (Shelhamer) B.; B.S., Drake U., 1943, J.D., 1949; m. Sophia Marianna Mihailina, Mar. 25, 1946; children—Tala, Douglas W., David, Scott. Field rep. Paul Revere Life Ins. Co., Worcester, Mass., 1949-50, atty., 1950-51, asst. counsel, 1951-53, gen. mgr., Can., 1953-56, v.p., gen. mgr., Can., 1956-59; mng. dir. Canadian Health Ins. Assn., Toronto, 1959-61; v.p. State Mut. Life Assurance Co. Am., Worcester, 1961-62, v.p., gen. counsel, 1962-68, sr. v.p., 1968-69, pres., 1969—, also dir.; chmn. bd. pres., dir. Am. Variable Annuity Life Assurance Co.; chmn. bd., pres. SMA Equities, Inc.; pres., dir., mem. exec. com. Hanover Life Ins. Co.; v.p., dir. State Mut. Broadcasting Corp., Worcester Mut. Fire Ins. Co., Guarantee Mut. Assurance Co.; dir., mem. exec. com. Colonial Distbrs., Inc.; dir. Citizens Mut. Ins. Co., Beacon Mut. Indemnity, Worcester Gas Light Co., Guaranty Bank & Trust Co., Am. Group Cos. Fund, Hannover Ins. Co., Mass. Bay Ins. Co., Colonial Mgmt. Assos., Inc.; bd. mgrs., exec. com. Am. Variable Annuity Fund. Trustee Memorial Hosp. Worcester; incorporator Worcester Hahnemann Hosp.; bd. dirs. Community Services Greater Worcester; mem. pres. council Leicester Jr. Coll. Served with USNR, 1942-46. Emeritus mem. Ins. Hall Fame Bd. Electors. Mem. Am. Bar Assn., Assn. Life Ins. Counsel, Newcomen Soc. N.Am. Republican. Mason. Clubs: Worcester, Worcester Country; Tatnuck Country. Home: 50 Wyndhurst Dr Holden MA 01520 Office: 440 Lincoln St Worcester MA 01605

BELL, WENDELL, educator, sociologist; b. Chgo., Sept. 27, 1924; s. Wendell and Blanche (Leiferman) B.; B.A. with highest honors, Fresno (Cal.) State Coll., 1948; M.A., U. Cal. at Los Angeles, 1951, Ph.D., 1952; M.A. (hon.), Yale, 1963; m. Lora-Lee Edwards, June 15, 1947; children—Sharon Lee, David Howard. Asst. prof. sociology, acting dir. survey research facility Stanford, 1952-54; asso. prof. sociology Northwestern U., 1954- 57; from asso. prof. to prof. sociology, dir. West Indies study program U. Cal. at Los Angeles, 1957-63; prof. sociology Yale, 1963—, chmn. dept., 1965-69, dir. comparative sociology tng. program, 1969—; editor Internat. Studies in polit. and Social Change, Schenkman Publishing Company, 1966—. Mem. exec. com. div. behavioral scis. NRC, 1968-69. Served with USNR, 1943-46; Philippines. Research Tng. predoctoral fellow Social Sci. Research Council, 1951-52, Faculty fellow, 1956-59; fellow Center Advanced Study Behavioral Scis., 1963-64; NSF grantee, 1969-70. Mem. Am., Eastern sociol. assns., Soc. Study Social Problems, Am. Polit. Sci. Assn., Acad. Polit. Sci., Am. Assn. U. Profs., Internat. Studies Assn. (v.p. 1970-71), Bethany Horsemen's Assn. Author: (with E. Shevky) Social Area Analysis, 1955; (with R. J. Hill and C. R. Wright) Public Leadership, 1961; (with I. Oxaal) Decisions of Nationhood, 1964; Jamaican Leaders, 1964; (with James A. Mau) The Sociology of the Future, 1971. Editor, contbr.; The Democratic Revolution in the West Indies, 1967; asso. editor Am. Sociol. Rev., 1958-61. Home: Sperry Rd Bethany CT 06525 Office: Dept Sociology Yale Univ New Haven CT 06520

BELL, WHITFIELD JENKS, Jr., historian; b. Newburgh, N.Y., Dec. 3, 1914; s. Whitfield Jenks and Lillian Victoria (Hengstler) B.; A.B., Dickinson Coll., 1935, LL.D., 1964; A.M., U. Pa., 1938, Ph.D., 1947; Litt.D., Franklin College, 1960. Instructor history Dickinson College, 1937, 38-39, 41-43, asso. prof.. 1945-50, prof., 1950-54; vis. prof. Coll. William and Mary, 1953-54; asst. editor Papers of Benjamin Franklin, 1954-56, asso. editor, 1956-61; asso. librarian Am. Philos. Soc., 1961-66, librarian, 1966—. Vol. American Field Service, Italy, Germany, 1943-45. Hon. fellow Coll. Physicians Phila.; mem. Am., Pa. hist. assns., Am. Philos. Soc., Soc. Am. Studies, Phi Beta Kappa. Club: Cosmos (Washington); Franklin Inn (Phila.). Author: Needs and Opportunities for Research in the History of Early American Science, 1955; John Morgan, 1965. Editor: Bibliography of the History of Medicine in the U.S. and Canada, 1948-53. Vis. editor: William and Mary Quarterly, 1953-54. Edited (with L. W. Labaree), Mr. Franklin, 1956. Office: Am Philos Soc Library 105 S Fifth St Philadelphia PA 19106

BELL, WILLIAM HENRY, Jr., banker; b. Schenectady, Oct. 15, 1918; s.William Henry and Elizabeth (Lambert) B.; B.A., Princeton, 1939; m. Alice Creedon, Sept. 13, 1947; children—Susan, Martha, Patricia, Barbara, Alexandra, Madeline. With J. P. Morgan & Co., N.Y.C., 1939-49; officer First Nat. Bank, Jersey City, 1950-52; exec. v.p., dir. South Jersey Nat. Bank (formerly First Camden Nat. Bank & Trust Co.), 1953-64, pres., dir., 1964—; chmn., dir. Heritage Bancorp., 1971—. Treas. Burlington County council Girl Scouts U.S., 1957-59; pres. Moorestown (N.J.) Community Fund, 1962; mem. exec. com. Camden County United Fund, 1965—; pres. Camden Housing Improvement Projects, 1967—; mem. Gov.'s Commn. to Evaluate Capital Needs of N.J., 1968; chmn. South Jersey Port Corp., 1969. Trustee Camden Home For Children. Mem. N.J. Bankers Assn. (exec. com. 1964), Phi Beta Kappa. Roman Catholic. Clubs: Princeton of West Jersey (pres. 1968-69); Tavistock (N.J.) Country; Pine Valley (N.J.) Golf. Home: 711 Lippincott Av Moorestown NJ 08057 Office: Broadway and Cooper Sts Camden NJ 08101

BELL, WILSON B., veterinarian; b. Surry County, Va., May 16, 1913; s. John Franklin and Lelia Estelle (Stallings) B.; B.S., Va. Poly. Inst., 1934, M.S., 1935, Ph.D., 1952; D.V.M., Cornell U., 1939; postgrad. U. Cal., 1939-41; m. Marian Lucille Wormuth, June 14, 1940; children—Julia Ann, Virginia Stallings. Asst. bacteriology N.Y. State Vet. Coll., Cornell U., 1935- 39; asso. vet. sci. Coll. Agr. and Agr. Expt. Sta., U. Cal., 1939-46; asso. prof. vet. medicine Va. Poly Inst., 1946-47, prof., 1947- 54, coll. veterinarian, 1946-54, dean agr., 1962-68, dir. univ. devel., 1968—, bd. dirs. ednl. found.; dir. diagnostic lab. Va. Agrl. Expt. Sta., 1946-54, asso. dir. exptl. sta., 1954-62. Dir. Farmers & Merchants Nat. Bank, Blacksburg. Mem. Gov. Va. Commn. on Industry and Agr., Va. Agrl. Found., 1966—, Gov. Va. Cost Study Subcom. Programs and Units. Commd. 2d lt., U.S. Army Coast Arty., O.R.C., 1934, advanced through grades to lt. col., 1953; active duty as comdr. antiaircraft arty. battery and bn., Am. and European theaters of operations, 1941-46, in European campaigns of 3d Army and 7th Army. Named Man of Year in Va. Agr., 1961. Mem. A.A.A.S., Va. Acad. Sci., (pres. 1960). Am., Va. (v.p. 1960, pres. 1962), So. (dir. 1958) vet. med. assn., Am. Inst. Biol. Scis., Conf. Research Workers Animal Diseases, So. Regional Research Workers, Va. Tech. Athletic Assn. (pres. 1966—), Sigma Xi, Phi Sigma, Phi Kappa Phi, Omicron Delta Kappa, Phi Zeta, Alpha Zeta. Democrat. Baptist. Rotarian. Club: University (Blacksburg). Asso. editor Cornell Veterinarian; contbr. articles agrl. and vet. jours. Home: Blacksburg VA 24060

BELLA, SALVATORE JOSEPH, educator; b. Lawrence Mass., Dec. 21, 1919; s. Joseph and Theresa (Zinno) B.; B.S., Boston U., 1947, M.A., 1948; Ph.D. (Danforth Found. scholar 1955-56), Cornell U., 1962; m. Dantina Quartaroli, Dec. 30, 1946; children—Theresa, Joseph, Jennifer. Asst. prof. Alfred U., 1948-55; asst. prof. U. Notre Dame, 1958-63, asso. prof., 1968—, dir. supervisory devel. program, 1962—, head dept. bus. orgn. and mgmt., 1964—, Jesse Jones prof. mgmt., 1965—. Mem. Am. Econ. Assn., Am. Assn. U. Profs., Indsl. Relations Research Assn., Phi Kappa Phi. Beta Gamma Sigma. Contbr. articles profl. jours. Home: 1029 Clermont Dr South Bend IN 46617 Office: U of Notre Dame Notre Dame IN 46556

BELLAGAMBA, LAURENCE, coll. dean; b. East Paterson, N.J., Feb. 13, 1926; s. Lorenzo and Olympia (Pierantozzi) B.; student Drew U., 1944-45, Princeton, 1945-46; B.S., N.Y.U., 1947, M.A., 1950; Ed.D., Columbia, 1963; m. Anne Darian, Aug. 7, 1948; children—Larry, Marc, Richard. Tchr. math. Fair Lawn (N.J.) High Sch., 1947-51, vice prin., 1951-52; vice prin. Thomas Jefferson Jr. High Sch., Fair Lawn, 1954-56; vice prin. Meml. Jr. High Sch., Fair Lawn, 1956-59, prin., 1959-63; from asso. prof. to prof. edn. Montclair State Coll., 1963-65, asso. dean coll., 1965-68, dir. instnl. devel., 1968-69, dean Sch. Edn., 1969—; ednl. cons. sch. dists. in N.J., N.Y., Pa., Conn., Me.; vis. prof. U. Neb., summer 1964. Served with USNR, 1944-46, 52-54. Mem. N.J. Edn. Assn., N.E.A., Am. Assn. Sch. Adminstrs., N.J., Nat. assns. secondary sch. prins., Assn. Supervision and Curriculum Devel., N.J. Assn. Coll. and U. Profs., Phi Delta Kappa. Home: 163 Hiawatha Blvd Oakland NJ 07436 Office: Montclair State Coll Upper Montclair NJ 07043

BELLAH, JAMES WARNER, author; b. New York City, Sept. 14, 1899; s. James Warner and Harriette Louise (Johnson) B.; A.B., Columbia U., 1923; M.A. (history), Georgetown U., 1945; student Grad. Sch. Polit. Science U. of Pa., 1946; m. Helen Lasater Hopkins, Oct. 22, 1942; children—James, Ann (1st. m.), John Stephen. Advt. writer, 1923-25; instr. Eng., Columbia, 1923-26, and 1936-37; foreign corr. Aero Digest, Europe and Far East, 1927-28; story writer and novelist since 1923; vice president of Lancaster and Chester Railroad; lecture tour of United States and Can., 1947-49; mem. 9th Global Strategy Conf., Naval War Coll., 1957; Dance Meml. lectr. Va. Mil. Inst., 1957. Mem. Cal. Civil War Centennial Commn.; nat. adv. com. Civil War Centennial Commission. Corporal Company E, 1st Provisional Training Regt., Fort Terrry, N.Y., 1916; served as 2d lt., pilot, 117th Squadron, Royal Air Force and Royal Flying Corps, 1917-19. World War. First reserve officer called for General Staff duty with 1st Div., Oct. 7, 1940; grad. command and General Staff School, Ft. Leavenworth, Kansas, April 1940; detailed to General Staff Corps as first lieutenant; G-2, 80th Infantry Division, 1942-43, headquarters Southeast Asia Command, 1943-44, hdqrs. Army Ground Forces, 1944. Member Crew on first regular mail plane, Pan- American Airways, Miami to Havana, Central America, and Panama, February 19, 1929. Received pilot's license Federation Aeronautique Internationale, July 15, 1918. Companion Military Order of World Wars, Companion Mil. Order of Loyal Legion of U.S., Mil. Knight of Holy Order of St. John of Jerusalem, Legion of Merit, Bronze Star Medal, Air Medal Army Commendation Pendant; 175th Anniversary medal of Honor, Georgetown U. Chmn. Conn. div. Amateur Fencers League of America (Conn. open champion Epee 1934, vice-pres. of League, 1936-37 and 1937-38); mem. exec. com. Intercollegiate Aerial Assn., 1919-20. Mem. Am. Legion, Soc. Colonial Wars (governor of California state society 1969), S.R., Quiet Birdmen. Republican. Episcopalian. Clubs: Royal Air Force (London); Chesapeake Bay Yacht; Author twenty books, later ones including, among others; Irregular Gentleman, 1947; Land Actions, 1812-14, A Reconsideration, 1947; Rear Guard, and Soldier's Battle: Gettyburg; (screen plays) She Wore a Yellow Ribbon, Ten Tall Men; also dialogue for This Is Korea (John Ford), Sergeant Rutledge, A Thunder of Drums; The Journal of Colonel DeLancey, 1967. Contributor Holiday Mag., Saturday Evening Post, 1926—. Donor James Warner Bellah collection books and papers to Boston U. Library. Address: Goldman Kagon 356 Camden Dr Beverly Hills CA 90210

BELLAH, MILDRED MARIE, editor; b. N.Y.C.; d. Harry Bolton and Teresa V. (Lynch) Finn; student Speyer Sch., Brentwood Acad., Columbia Sch. Journalism. With promotion dept. N.Y. Am., 1926-28; with McNaught Syndicate, Inc., N.Y.C., 1928—, exec. editor, 1942—, sec. corp., 1938—. Clubs: Women's Nat. Press; Advertising (N.Y.C.) Author articles trade mags., newspapers. Home: 630 Gramatan Av Mount Vernon NY 10552 Office: 60 E 42d St New York City NY 10017

BELLAH, ROBERT NEELLY, educator, sociologist; b. Altus, Okla., Feb. 23, 1927; s. Luther Hutton and Lillian (Neelly) B.; B.A., Harvard, 1950, Ph.D., 1955; m. Melanie Claire Hyman, Aug. 17, 1949; children—Thomasin, Jennifer, Abigail, Harriet. Research asso. Inst. Islamic Studies, McGill U., 1955-57; successively research asso., lectr., asso. prof., prof. Harvard, 1957-67; Ford prof. sociology and comparative studies U. Cal. at Berkeley, 1967—, chmn. Center Japanese and Korean Studies, 1968—; fellow Center Advanced Study Behavioral Scis. Stanford, Cal., 1964-65. Served with AUS, 1945-46. Mem. Am. Acad. Arts and Scis., Am. Sociol. Assn., Am. Soc. Study Religion, Assn. Asian Studies. Author: Apache Kinship Systems,

1952; Tokugawa Religion, 1957; Religion and Progress in Modern Asia, 1965; Beyond Belief, 1970. Home: 10 Mosswood Rd Berkeley CA 94704

BELLAMY, FRANCIS RUFUS, author, editor; b. New Rochelle, N.Y., Dec. 24, 1886; s. Rufus W. and Charella (Tappen) B.; Williams Coll., 1904-05; Cornell Univ., 1906; m. Virginia Mackall (nee Woods); children—Rufus, Jane; m. 2d, Ruth Fletcher. Engaged in farming, 1907-11; salesman for Grosset and Dunlap, New York, 1912-15; Washington editor Red Cross Mag., 1917-18; European corr., 1918-19; editor and pub. Outlook Mag., 1927-32; exec. editor New Yorker, 1933; editor and pub. relations, Scribner's Commentator, 1939-40; pub. relations, pub. cons.; spl. Washington corr. Reader's Digest, 1941-55; pres. University Publishers, Inc., 1958—; director Asso. Coll. Presses, N.Y.U., 1955-58. Member Sigma Phi. Democrat. Mem. Unitarian Ch. Author: The Balance, 1917; A Flash of Gold, 1922; March Winds, 1924; Spanish Faith, 1926; We Hold These Truths, 1942; Blood Money, 1947; The Strange Blooming, 1948; Private Life of George Washington, 1951; Atta, 1953; What About Maisie? (a play, with Ruth Bellamy), 1953; Pledge of Allegiance; A Promise to Our Country, 1961; How to Keep Out of Jail, 1966; also short stories, plays and articles; editor Conversations across the Nation, 1954.

BELLAMY, PETER, drama critic, lectr.; b. Cleve., Nov. 9, 1914; s. Paul and Marguerite Scott (Stark) B.; student Harvard, 1932-36; m. Jean Margaret Dessel, Mar. 11, 1939; children—Sheila Bellamy Lebenson, Stephon Paul, John Stark II, Christopher Aladdin, Nicole Marie. Comml. editor Des Moines Register, 1936-37; mem. staff Cleve. News, 1938-60, gossip columnist, soc. editor, until 1960; mem. staff Cleve. Plain Dealer, 1960—, entertainment editor, drama critic, 1962—; lectr. Shakespeare and criticism Western Res. U., 1963-64. Trustee Neighborhood Settlement Assn., 1952-64; pres. bd. Glenville Community Center, 1952-54; bd. dirs. Nationalities Service Center, 1961-65, Elinor T. Rainey Inst., 1958-60, Golden Age Center, 1961-64. Served with USNR, 1945-46. Hon. mem. Nat. Council Tchrs. English. Episcopalian (mem. com. 100). Club: Cleveland Press (pres. 1960-62). Home: 2476 Kenilworth Rd Cleveland Heights OH 44106 Office: 1801 Superior Av Cleveland OH 44114

BELLAMY, RALPH, actor; b. Chgo., June 17, 1904; s. Charles Rexford and Lilla Louise (Smith) B.; ed. high sch.; m. Alice Delbridge, 1922 (div. 1930); m. 2d, Catherine Willard, 1931 (div. 1945); children—Lynn, Willard; m. 3d, Ethel Smith, 1945 (div. 1947); m. 4th, Alice Murphy, 1949. With William Owen in Shakespeare and the classics, 1921; appeared in Shepherd of the Hills, Old Matt and Wash Gibbs road company, 1922; with stock company, Madison, Wis., Evansville, Ind., 1922-23; traveling repertoire Beach & Jones Co., 1924; with John Wininger Co., 1925; with stock company in other cities, 1923-28, 30; played leading parts, dir. own co., Des Moines, Nashville, Evanston, Ill. 1928-1930; appeared in N.Y.C. prodns. Town Boy, Roadside, 1930; also appeared in plays, Oh, Men Oh, Women 1934; starred in play Sunrise at Campobello, on Broadway, 1958-59, on tour, 1959, 60, in movie based on play, 1960; and has appeared in about 92 motion pictures, 1930—; appeared in Tomorrow the World, 1943-44, State of the Union, 1943-47, Detective Story, 1949-50; producer, dir. Pretty Little Parolor, N.Y.C., 1944; weekly TV series Man Against Crime, 1949-54; guest star appearances TV dramatic programs, 1954—; radio guest maj. programs; narrator Victor Record Album, Rubaiyat of Omar Khayam and Leaves of Grass by Walt Whitman; starred in Eleventh House TV series, 1963-64; NBC documentary Hope-Ship, Saigon, South Vietnam, 1962; 13 week TV series for Episcopal Ch., 1965-66; co-star The Deadly Game series, ABC-TV, 1970—; appeared motion pictures The Professionals, 1966, Rosemary's Baby, 1968. Mem. nat. bd. U.S.O., 1958-60; mem. Pres.'s Com. on 50th Anniv. Dept. Labor, 1962; vice chmn. nat. campaign. A.R.C., 1963; chmn. N.Y. Regional Nat. Conf. Christians and Jews Brotherhood Week 1963; past mem. Cal. Arts Commn.; bd. dirs. Person to Person Project Hope. Recipient 1st ann. Best Actor award Acad. Radio and TV Arts and Scis., 1950; Antoinette Perry award, 1958; award of merit State of Israel. Mem. Actors Equity Assn. (pres. 1952-64), Am. Arbitration Assn. (dir. 1962-64). Clubs: Players (bd. 1958-64), Dutch Treat, Lambs (council 1952-56) (N.Y.C.). Home: 1258 Devon Av Los Angeles CA 90024 Office: 116 E 27th St New York City NY 10016

BELLAMY, WALTER, profl. basketball player; b. New Bern, N.C., July 24, 1939; s. Walter A. and Theo (Jones) B.; B.S., Ind. U., 1961; m. Helen Ragland, June 11, 1960; 1 son, Derrin. Mem. Chuck Taylor's All Am. Coll. Basketball Team, 1959-61; with Asso. Life Ins. Co., Chgo., 1961-64; basketball player Chgo. Packers, 1961-62, Chgo. Zephyrs., 1962-63, Balt. Bullets, 1963-65, N.Y. Knickerbockers, 1965-69, Atlanta Hawks, 1969—. Adv. bd. Md. Old Line Corp.; pres., founder Men of Tomorrow Inc., Balt.; dir. S.T. Wilson Enterprises, Toll, Inc. Mem. sports com. Am. Negro Emancipation-Centennial Authority, 1963; mem. sports com. So. Christian Leadership Conf. Basketball Benefit Games, also bd. dirs., 1971—; mem. Better Bus. Found. Chgo. Bd. mgrs. Woodlawn Chgo. Boys Club, 1963; mem. Big Bros. Balt., Drurd Hill YMCA, Balt., Mem. Olympic Basketball Team, 1960; named Rookie of Year, Nat. Basketball Assn., 1961-62. Mem. N.A.A.C.P., Alpha Tau Omega, Ind. Alumni Club, Phi Alpha. Home: 3709 Egerton Rd Baltimore MD 21215 Office: 1913 W Baltimore St Baltimore MD 21223

BELLAMY, WILLIAM BUTLER, newspaper editor; b. Little Rock; Nov. 28, 1920; s. William B. and Eva (Lee) B.; student Tulane U., 1939-41; m. Carolyn Wright, May 12, 1943; children—William B. III, Linda Carol, Russell Wright. With Express Publishing Co. 1946; sports editor San Antonio News, 1947-49, sports dir., 1949-52, Express mng. editor, 1952. News mng. editor, 1953-56; exec. adminstr. news, Express Publishing Co., KENS, television and radio, 1956-57; asst. to pres., 1957-62; asst. mng. editor San Antonio Light, 1962-67, mng. editor, 1967—. Commnr. Fiesta San Antonio Assn. Bd. dirs. San Antonio 200, San Antonio Boy Scout Council, San Antonio Livestock Show, Mental Health Assn., 1962, Council on Alcoholism, 1963; bd. govs. S.W. Found. for Research and Edn. Served as test pilot USAAF, 1941-45. Named San Antonian of Year, Jr. C. of C., 1950; recipient Latin-Am. Good Neighbor award, 1950, San Antonio Bar Assn. award, 1969; named most outstanding young Texan, Texas Jr. C. of C., 1956. Mem. San Antonio Air Force Assn. (squadron commander), Am. Athletic Union (1st v.p. S. Tex.), Express-News Athletic Assn. (pres. 1948-62), Sigma Delta Chi. Christian Ch. (elder 1961-64). Clubs: Kiwanis (dir.), San Antonio Breakfast (pres. 1955); San Antonio Exchange (pres. 1961, dist. gov. 1962), San Antonio Press (trustee 1963). Home: 185 Terrell Rd San Antonio TX 78209 Office: Light Pub Co San Antonio TX 78209

BELLANO, WILLIAM, petroleum co. exec.; b. Phila., Nov. 2, 1912; s. Adolph and Mary (D'Alfonso) B.; B.S. in Mining Engring., Pa. State U., 1936; m. Daisy M. Eyrich, Nov. 21, 1945; children—Robert William, Barbara Anne. Chmn., Island Creek Coal Co., Cleve., 1965—; pres., dir. Occidental Petroleum Corp.; dir. Canadian Occidental Petroleum Ltd. Trustee Pike Coll. Served to 1st lt. USMCR, 1942-46; PTO. Decorated Silver Star, Bronze Star (2). Mem. Am. Inst. Mining, Metall. and Petroleum Engrs., Canadian Inst. Mining and Metall. Engrs., Am. Acad. Polit. Sci. Mining and Metall. Soc. Am., Mining Club N.Y.C. Home: 435 N Oakhurst Dr Beverly Hills CA 90210 Office: 10889 Wilshire Blvd Los Angeles CA 90024

BELLAVIA, JOSEPH VINCENT, cosmetics co. exec.; b. Palermo, Italy, Jan. 14, 1915; G. s. Joseph G. and Frances (Scarpulla) B.; came to U.S., 1921, naturalized 1921; grad. high sch.; m. Madeline C Rooney, Feb. 8, 1941; children—Wayne J., Jolynn. With Coty, Inc., N.Y.C., 1933-62, Eastern sales mgr., 1956-62, v.p. sales and marketing Lanvin Parfums, Inc., N.Y.C., 1962-63; v.p., dir. sales Faberge, Inc., N.Y.C., 1963-65, v.p. marketing, 1965-66, exec. v.p., 1966; exec. v.p. Rayette-Faberge, Inc., N.Y.C.; sr. v.p. Yardley of London, Inc., 1968-70; pres. Hawaiian Surf Industries Internat. Corp., Deer Park, N.Y., 1970—. Mem. Sales Exec. Club of N.Y. Home: Deer Park, N.Y., 1970—. Mem. Sales Exec. Club of N.Y. Home: 69 Barkers Point Rd Sands Point NY 12123 Office: 715 Grand Blvd Deer Park NY 11729

BELLI, MELVIN MOURON, lawyer, writer; b. Sonora, Cal., July 29, 1907; s. Caesar Arthur and Leonie (Mouron) B.; A.B., U. Cal. at Berkeley, 1929, LL.B., Boalt Hall, 1933; J.D. (hon.), New Eng. Sch. Law; m. Betty Ballantine, 1933; children—Richard R., Melvin Mouron, Jean, Susan; m. 2d, Joy Maybelle Turney, May 3, 1956; 1 son, Caesar Melvin. Admitted to Cal. bar, 1933; sr. partner firms, Belli, Ashe, Ellison, Choulos & Lieff, and predecessor firms, San Francisco, 1940—, Los Angeles, 1958—; condr. Belli Seminars in Law, 1953—; pres. Belli Found. Lecturers, 1960—. Mem. Cal. Bldg. Standards Commn. Bd. dirs. Disability & Casualty Inter-Ins. Exchange, N.W. Affairs Council. Named dean emeritus Coll. Law, Riverside U.; grand ofcl. St. Brigidian Order. Fellow Internat. Acad. Trial Lawyers (dir., past dean); mem. Authors Guild, Am. Acad. Forensic Scis., Tuolumne County Hist. Soc., Inter-American, Am., Cal., San Francisco, Fed., Internat. (patron) bar assns., Internat. Legal Aid Assn., San Diego, Hollywood, Beverly Hills bars, Am. Trial Lawyers Assn. (past president chmn. torts sect. 1959), Barristers Club San Francisco (past dir.), La Asociacion Nacional de Abogados, Mexico (hon. mem.), Societe Driot (pres.), Phi Delta Phi, Delta Tau Delta. Mason (Shriner). Clubs: Olympic, The Commonwealth, Lawyers (San Francisco). Author: Modern Trials and Modern Damages, 6 volumes, 1954, abridged edition, 1962; Ready for the Plaintiff, 1956; Trial and Tort Trends, 14 volumes, 1954-62; The Adequate Award, 1953; Demonstracrative Evidence and The Adequate Award, 1955; Malpractice, 1955; Modern Trials (student edition); (with Danny Jones) Life and Law in Russia; (with Maurice Carroll) Dallas Justice, 1964; The Law Revolt, two volumes, 1968; author numerous articles, also syndicated column, So That's The Law, Asso. editor Am. Trial Lawyers Assn. Law Jour., 1950—; adv. editor Negligence and Compensation Service, 1955—; legal adv. bd. Traumatic Medicine and Surgery for the Atty., 1958—. Home: San Francisco CA Office: 1228 Montgomery St San Francisco CA 94133 also 8447 Wilshire Blvd Beverly Hills CA 90211

BELLINGER, FREDERICK, educator, chem. engr.; b. New Orleans, Aug. 14, 1904; s. Lyle Frederick and Annie Beall (Dobbs) B.; B.S., Ga. Inst. Tech., 1926; M.S. Emory U., 1935; D. Eng., Yale, 1940; m. Emma Marie Parker, July 6, 1937; 1 dau., Barbara Lynn. Chem. engr. C.W.S., U.S. Army, 1926-28; chief plants design, then chief chem. engr. Huntsville Arsenal, 1941- 43; chem engr. R & H., Chem. Co., 1928-32; self-employed, 1932-33; chem. engr. Mfrs. Cons. Engrs., 1933; market devel. Robert & Co., 1933-34; instr. chem. engring. Yale, 1935-37; research chem. engr. cellulose plastics Hercules Powder Co., 1937-40; from asso. prof. to prof. chem. engring. Ga. Inst. Tech., 1945—, head chem. scis. div. engring. expt. sta., 1953-56, asst. dir. for industry, Engring. Exptl. Sta., 1956-58, chief material sci. div., 1958- 61, chief chem. sci. and materials div., 1961—; cons. Chem. Corps, 1952- 66. UNESCO adviser Nat. Research Center, Egypt, 1955-56; spl. cons. to Under Sec. of War on German chem. industry, 1948; dir. Civil Def. Preliminary Operation Survival Project of Ga., 1957; mem. Gov.'s Commn. Sci. Research and Devel., 1963-64. Trustee Ocean Sci. Center, Atlantic, 1969—. Served from maj. to lt. col., C.W.S., AUS, 1943-45, 51-52; col. Res., 1952—. Decorated Legion of Merit, 1956. Registered profl. engr., Ga. Fellow Ga. Acad. Sci. (treas. 1958-61, pres. 1962); mem. Inst. Am. Strategy, Am. Inst. Chem. Engrs. (past chmn. Atlanta sect.), Am. Chem. Soc., Ga. Engrng. Soc., Sigma Xi, Tau Beta Pi, Alpha Chi Sigma. Presbyn. (elder). Club: Atlanta Athletic. Contbr. Ency. Chemistry, 1958, 65. Home: 1275 The-By Way NE Atlanta GA

BELLINGER, JOHN DOOLEY, banker; b. Honolulu, May 13, 1923; s. Eustace L. and Lei (Williams) B.; grad. Roosevelt High Sch., Honolulu; m. Joan Simms, Apr. 7, 1945; children—Dona, Jan. Neil. With First Hawaiian Bank, and predecessor, Honolulu, 1942—, pres., 1969—, also dir.; dir. Alexander & Baldwin, Honolulu, Allied Bank Internat., Lillie Continental Mech. Corp. Hawaii chmn. U.S. Savs. Bonds. Mem. U.S. Army Adv. Com. Trustee Franics Brown Scholarship Fund; bd. govs. Kamehameha schs., Hawaii Employers Councils. Served with AUS, 1946-47. Mem. Honolulu C. of C., Assn. U.S. Army, Navy League, Am. Bankers Assn. (adv. com. state legislation 1965-66, state v.p. exec. council). Clubs: Civic, Oahu Country, Waialae Country (past pres.) (Honolulu); 200 (asst. treas.). Home: 1057 Waiholo St Honolulu HI 96821 Office: First Hawaiian Bank King and Bishop Sts Honolulu HI 96801

BELLINO, CARMINE SALVATORE, accountant; b. Elizabeth, N.J., July 26, 1903; s. Frank and Frances (Lafaso) B.; B.C.S. in Accounting with honors, N.Y. U., 1928; m. Santina I. Novello, June 6, 1936; children—Francis, Robert, Joseph, Mary Catherine, Mary Joan, Mary Sandra, Maryan Joyce. Accountant, Mills & Co., N.Y.C., 1927-34; spl. agt. accountant, also adminstrv. asst. to dir. FBI, 1934-45; asst. dir. RFC, 1945-46, War Assets Adminstrn., 1946-47; pvt. practice as accountant, Washington, N.Y.C., 1947-62, resident agt. Wright Long & Co., N.Y.C., 1951-60, resident partner, 1964-70; spl. cons. Pres. John F. Kennedy, 1961-64. Mem. bd. contact appeals AEC, 1964-70; accountant cons. to U.S. Permanent Sub Com. on Investigations. Served to lt. col. USAAF Res. C.P.A., N.J., D.C., N.Y. Mem. Am. Inst. C.P.A.'s, D.C. Soc. C.P.A's, Soc. Former Spl. Agts. FBI, K.C. (4). Clubs: Dowd Boys, Don Bosco (Elizabeth). Home: 9200 Burning Tree Rd Bethesda MD 20034

BELLIS, CARROLL JOSEPH, surgeon; b. Shreveport, La.; s. Joseph and Rose (Bloome) B.; B.S., U. Minn., 1930, M.S. in Physiology, 1932, Ph.D., 1934, M.D., 1936, Ph.D. in Surgery, 1941; m. Mildred Darmody, Dec. 26, 1939; children—Joseph, David. Resident surgery U. Minn. hosps., 1937-41; mem. staff St. Mary's, Seaside, Community hosps., Long Beach, Cal.; cons. surgery Long Beach Gen. Hosp., San Pedro Community Hosp.; pvt. practice surgery, Long Beach, 1945—; prof. chmn. dept. surgery Cal. Coll. Medicine; lectures in med. physiology. Served to col. M.C., AUS, 1941- 46. Nat. Cancer Inst. fellow, 1934; recipient Charles Lyman Green prize in physiology, 1934; prize Mpls. Surg. Soc., 1938; ann. award Mississippi Valley Med. Soc., 1955. Diplomate, regent, gov. Internat. Bd. Proctology; diplomate Am. Bd. Surgery. Fellow A.C.S., Internat. Coll. Surgeons, Internat. Acad. Proctology, Am. Coll. Gastroenterology, Am. Med. Writers Assn., Internat. Coll. Angiology (sci. council), Am. Soc. Abdominal Surgeons; mem. Med. Research Assn. Cal. (bd. dirs.), Am. Assn. Study Neoplastic Diseases, Mississippi Valley Med. Soc., N.Y. Acad. Sci., Hollywood Acad. Medicine, Am. Geriatrics Soc., Gerontol. Soc., Irish Med. Soc., A.A.A.S., Am. Assn. History Medicine, Phi Beta Kappa, Sigma Xi, Alpha Omega Alpha. Author: Fundamentals of Human Physiology, 1935; A Critique of Reason, 1938; Lectures in Medical Physiology, also numerous articles in field of surgery, physiology. Home: Quail Ridge Rd Rolling Hills CA 90274 Office: 117 E 8th St Long Beach CA 90813

BELLIS, LEON ROBERT, profl. diamond jewelry appraiser; b. Elizavetgrad, Russia, Mar. 25, 1910; s. Harry J. and Rachel (Levinsky) B.; came to U.S., 1923, naturalized, 1928; student U. Pa., 1928-30; m. Bobbye Aronowitz, Oct. 23, 1943; children—Jac, Marlene. Salesman, Pitts. Triangle Co., 1930-42; owner Leon R. Bellis & Co., Wholesale Jewelers, New Orleans, 1945-59; owner Central Appraisal Bur., Chgo., 1959; pres. Central File and Identification Bur., Chgo. Served to 1st lt. AUS, 1942-45. Recipient Gavel for outstanding profl. achievement Am. Soc. Appraisers, 1960, Appreciation award, 1962. Sr. mem. Am. Soc. Appraisers (dir. Ill., past pres. Greater Chgo. chpt.). Mason (Shriner); mem. B'nai B'rith. Author: Too Much for Too Little, Tech. Valuation Mag. Lectr. on secrets of diamond expert; inventor system fingerprinting and indentification diamonds. Home: 3172 N Sheridan Rd Chicago IL 60657 Office: 55 E Washington St Chicago IL 60602

BELLM, CHARLES NEWTON, Sr., indsl. mfg. exec.; b. Denver, Nov. 9, 1912; s. Charles Louis and Mary Ann (Wade) B.; E.M., Colo. Sch. Mines, 1934; student George Washington Sch. of Law, 1942-45; m. Cecilia Catherine Condon, Dec. 9, 1933; children—Charles Newton, Carol Nanette (Mrs. Thomas Huntington). Various positions mineral industry, southwestern U.S. and Mexico; with Sterling Precision Corp., N.Y.C., 1957-59, pres., dir. 1958-59; with Real Estate Equities, Inc., 1949-59, exec. v.p., 1950-59; with Atlas Gen. Industries, Inc., N.Y.C., 1959-64, pres., dir., 1959-64; v.p. N.Am. Philips Corp., N.Y.C., 1964—; dir. Atlas Valley Inc., Ionic, Inc., Sci. Industries, Inc., Newmont Resources Corp., Carolina Coach Corp., Broad Arrow Investment Corp. Expert cons. Dept. Army, 1946, 50. Trustee Prescott Coll. Served from capt. to col., AUS, 1940-46. Decorated Legion of Merit. Mem. A.I.M. (fellow presidents council), Pilgrims, Am. Friends Middle East, Newcomen Soc., Alpha Tau Omega. Roman Catholic. Clubs: Marco Polo; Sales Executives (N.Y.C.). Home: Post House Rd Morristown NJ 07960 Office: 100 E 42d St New York City NY 10017

BELLMAN, RUSSELL, retail furniture exec.; b. Louisville, June 29, 1896; s. John Hutchins and Mary (Theobald) B.; M.E., Lehigh U., 1920; m. Katharine Haverty, May 1, 1926; children—John, Ann. Sales engr., asst. dist. mgr. Elliott Co., 1920-28; sec. Haverty Furniture Cos., 1928-38, sec.-treas., 1938-46, v.p., treas., 1946-48, exec. v.p., 1948-55, vice chmn., 1955-61, chmn. bd., 1961—, also dir.; dir. Fulton Nat. Bank Atlanta. Bd. dirs. YMCA, Atlanta Symphony Guild; chmn., trustee St. Joseph's Infirmary. Served as ensign USN, World War I. Mem. Atlanta Art Assn. (exec. chmn. exec. com.) U.S. C. of C., Kappa Sigma, Tau Beta Pi. Club: Atlanta Civitan (dir., past pres.). Home: 2575 Peachtree Rd NE Atlanta 5 GA Office: 22 Edgewood Av Atlanta 3 GA

BELLMON, HENRY, U.S. senator; b. Tonkawa, Okla., Sept. 3, 1921; s. George and Edith (Caskey) B.; B.S. in Agr., Okla. State U., Stillwater, 1942; m. Shirley Osborn, Jan. 24, 1947; children—Patricia, Gail, Ann. Engaged in farming, Billings, Okla., 1946; mem. Okla. Ho. of Reps., from Noble County, 1946- 48; gov. Okla., 1962-66; member of U.S. Senate from Okla., 1968—. Chmn. Okla. Republican Com., 1960-62. Served with USMCR, 1942-46. Presbyn. Home: Route 1 Red Rock OK Office: New Senate Office Bldg Washington DC 20510

BELLO, FRANCIS CESARE, editor; b. Newark, Dec. 19, 1917; s. Cesare and Marianna (Fielding) B.; A.B., Drew U., 1939; m. Ann Elizabeth Walker, Oct. 3,1942; children—Stephen, Christopher. Asst. unit head Carbide & Carbon Chem. Corp., Institute, W.Va., 1942-45; mem. staff Fortune mag., N.Y.C., 1940-42, 45-60, sci. editor, 1953-60, bd. editors, 1959-60; bd. editors Scientific Am., N.Y.C., 1960—, asso. editor, 1964—. Recipient Albert Lasker Medical Journalism award for article, The Murderous Riddle of Coronary Disease, 1958; A.A.A.S. writing award, 1959; Blakeslee award Am. Heart Assn., 1960. Mem. Fellowship of Reconciliation, Society Social Responsibility in Sci. Home: 377 S Harrison St East Orange NJ 07018 Office: 415 Madison Av New York City NY 10017

BELLONI, ROBERT CLINTON, judge; b. Riverton, Ore., Apr. 4, 1919; s. John Edward and Della (Clinton) B.; B.A., U. Ore., 1941, LL.B., 1951; m. Doris A. Adams, Jan. 27, 1946; children—James L., Susan K. Admitted to Ore. bar, 1951; practiced in Coquille, Ore., 1951-52, Myrtle Point, Ore., 1952-57; judge Ore. Circuit Ct., Coos and Curry Counties, Coquille, 1957-67; U.S. dist. judge Dist. Ore., 1967-71, chief judge, 1971—. Councilman, Myrtle Point, 1953-57, mayor, 1957; chmn. Coos County Democratic Central Com., 1957. Served to 1st lt. AUS, 1942-46. Mem. Am., Ore. bar assns., Am. Judicature Soc., Ore. Juvenile Ct. Judges Assn. (pres. 1963), Circuit Ct. Judges Assn., Ore (pres. 1966), Sigma Alpha Epsilon, Delta Theta Phi. Episcopalian. Mason, Elk, Rotarian; mem. Order Eastern Star. Home: 5055 Summit St West Linn OR 97068 Office: US Dist Ct Portland OR 97207

BELLOW, EVERETT HOLLIS, corp. exec.; b. Toledo, July 13, 1913; s. Sidney F. and Bessie (Brittingham) B.; A.B., George Washington U., 1939, M.A., 1941; m. Edna Walter, Apr. 8, 1939; 1 dau., Joanna Christine (Mrs. Rush Taylor, Jr.). Placement officer Fed. Security Agy., 1939-41; personnel dir. Office for Emergency Management, 1941-43; exec. officer Office of Fgn. Service, State Dept., 1946-48; dep. exec. asst. Office of U.S. Spl. Rep. Europe, Paris, France, E.C.A., 1948-50, spl. asst. to adminstr. ECA/MSA, 1950-51; dir. productivity and tech. assistance div. Office of U.S. Spl. Rep. in Europe, Paris, Mutual Security Agency, 1951-54, asst. to v.p. for operations Olin Corp., 1954-56, asst. to exec. v.p., 1956-59, dir. personnel, 1959-61, v.p., 1962—. Served lt. (j.g.) USNR, 1943-46. Mem. Soc. Advancement Mgmt., Phi Beta Kappa, Omicron Delta Kappa. Episcopalian. Club: Washington Golf and Country, Cosmos (Washington). Home: 3701 N 27th St Arlington VA 22207 Office: Olin Corp 1730 K St NW Washington DC 20006

BELLOW, SAUL, writer; b. Lachine, Quebec, Can., July 10, 1915; s. Abraham and Liza (Gordon) B.; student U. Chgo., 1933-35; B.S., Northwestern U., 1937, Litt.D., 1962; D.Litt., N.Y.C., 1970; m. Anita Goshkin, Dec. 31, 1937; 1 son, Gregory; m. 2d, Alexandra Tschacbasov, Feb. 1, 1956; 1 son, Adam; m. 3d, Susan Glassman, Dec. 10, 1961; 1 son, Daniel. Tchr., Pestalozzi-Froebel Tchrs. Coll., Chgo., 1938-42; first work as writer pub. 1940; mem. editorial dept. Ency. Brit., 1943-46; tchr. English, U. Minn., 1946, asst. prof. English, Guggenheim fellow, 1948-49; prof. com. social thought U. Chgo. Fellow Branford Coll., Yale, Bard Coll., 1953-54; Creative Writing fellow Princeton, 1952-53; fellow Acad. Policy Study, 1966; recipient Nat. Inst. Arts and Letters award, 1952; Nat. Book Award in Fiction for Herzog, 1965, for Mr. Sammler's Planet, 1970; Guggenheim fellow, 1955-56; Ford Found. grantee, 1959-61; recipient Friends of Lit. Fiction award, 1960; Internat. Lit. prize, 1965. Mem. Am. Inst. Arts and Letters. Author: Dangling Man, 1944; The Victim, 1947; Best Stores of 1950; Treasury of American Prose; The Adventures of

Augie March, 1953; Seize the Day, 1956; Henderson the Rain King, 1959; Herzog, 1964 (Internat. Lit. prize 1965, James L. Dow award, 1964), Last Analysis (play), 1964; Mosby's Memoirs, 1968; Mr. Sammler's Planet, 1969. Address: Univ Chicago Chicago IL 60637

BELLOWS, CHARLES SANGER, lawyer; b. Mpls., Oct. 20, 1915; s. Henry Adams and Mary (Sanger) B.; grad. Milton (Mass.) Acad., 1933; A.B. cum laude, Harvard, 1937; LL.B., Yale, 1940; m. Eunice Boggs, Feb. 5, 1944 (div. 1966); children—Mary (Mrs. Michael B. Ayoub), Eleanor (Mrs. Douglas G. Cochrane, Jr.), Charles S., Henry Adams; m. 2d, Barbara Waldron Earling, Mar. 18, 1967; stepchildren—John P., Nina D., George P. Admitted to N.Y. bar, 1941, Minn. bar, 1945; with firm Simpson, Thacher & Bartlett, N.Y.C., 1940-41; partner firm Best, Flanagan, Lewis, Simonet & Bellows, Mpls., 1946—. Pres. Mpls. Citizens League, 1952, Minn. Orch. Assn., 1959-62; chmn. bd. dirs. Abbott Northwest Hosp., 1971—. Bd. dirs. N.W. Hosp., 1966—, Mpls. Med. Center, 1967—, Minn. Orch. Assn., 1959—; trustee Northrop Sch., 1962-65. Served to maj. AUS, 1941-46; PTO. Decorated Bronze Star. Mem. Am., N.Y. State, Minn., Hennepin County bar assns. Club: Woodhill Country (trustee) (Wayzata). Home: 170 Ferndale Av Wayzata MN 55391 Office: First Nat Bank Bldg Minneapolis MN 55402

BELLOWS, JAMES GILBERT, newspaper editor; b. Detroit, Nov. 12, 1922; s. Lyman Hubbard and Dorothy (Gilbert) B.; A.B., Kenyon Coll., 1946, L.H.D., 1965; m. Keven Ryan; children—Amelia, Priscilla, Felicia. Mng. editor Miami (Fla.) News, 1958-61; editor N.Y. Herald Tribune, N.Y.C., 1963-66; asso. editor Los Angeles Times, 1966—. Trustee Kenyon Coll.; bd. dirs. Constitutional Rights Found. Served to lt. (j.g.) USNR, World War II. Mem. Psi Upsilon, Sigma Delta Chi. Home: 2270 Betty Lane Beverly Hills CA Office: Los Angeles Times Times-Mirror Sq Los Angeles CA

BELLOWS, KENDRICK FITZROY, Jr., banker; b. N.Y.C., Oct. 3, 1936; s. Kendrick Fitzroy and Sylvia (Miller) B.; grad. Kent Sch., 1953; A.B. in English, Princeton, 1957; m. Patricia Morgan, Sept. 10, 1960; children—Kendrick Fitzroy III, Catherine Morgan. With Conn. Bank and Trust Co., Hartford, 1961—, treas., 1968—, now chief financial officer, investment portfolio mgr. Mem. Republican Key Man Com., 1969—. Trustee Conn. Forest and Park Assn.; bd. dirs. Conn. Pub. TV. Served to 1st lt. USMCR, 1957-60. Republican. Presbyn. Home: 121 East St North Granby CT 06060 Office: 1 Constitution Plaza Hartford CT 06115

BELLPORT, BERNARD PHILIP, govt. ofcl.; b. LaCrosse, Kan., May 25, 1907; s. Bernard P. and Louise H. (Groves) B.; B.S. in Mining Engring., Poly. Coll. Engring., Oakland, Cal., 1927; m. Elsy V. Johnson, June 11, 1931 (dec. Mar. 1954); children—Louise (Mrs. L. B. Garcia), Bernard Philip III; m. 2d, Mabelle W. Kandolin, Sept. 26, 1955. Mining engr. Western U.S., 1927-28; engr.- geologist St. Joseph Lead Co., 1928-31; with Phoenix Utility Co., 1931- 32, Mont. Hwy. Commn., 1932-35; with Bur. Reclamation, 1936—, regional dir. region 2, Cal., 1957-59, asso. chief engr., Denver, 1959-63 chief engr., 1963-70, dir. design and constrn., 1970—. Mem. Denver Fed. Exec. Bd. Recipient distinguished service award Dept. Interior; Golden Beaver for engring.; named Man of Yr., Am. Pub. Works Assn., 1970. Registered profl. engr., Colo. Mem. Nat. Acad. Engring., Internat. Commn. Large Dams (chmn.), Internat. Commn. Irrigation and Drainage, Am. Soc. C.E. (pres. Colo. 1966), Chi Epsilon (hon.). Episcopalian. Mason (32). Clubs: Aviation, Mt. Vernon, Executives (Denver). Home: 1900 Zinnia St Golden CO 80401 Office: Bldg 67 Denver Fedn Center Denver CO 80225

BELLUSCHI, PIETRO, architect, educator; b. Ancona, Italy, Aug. 18, 1899; s.Guido and Camilla (Dogliani) B.; student U. Rome Sch. Engring., 1919-22 (doctor's degree in civil engring.); C.E., Cornell U. (Italian scholarship) 1924; LL.D., Reed Coll., Portland, Ore., 1950; Sc.D., Christian Brothers Coll., Memphis, 1957; D.F.A. (hon.), U. R.I., 1963, U. Mass., 1967; D.Arch. (hon.), U. Mich., 1967; L.H.D. (hon.), Oklahoma City U., 1968; m. Helen Hemmila, Dec. 1, 1934 (dec. Mar. 1962); children—Peter, Anthony; m. 2d, Marjorie Bruckner, June 25, 1965. Naturalized U.S. citizen, 1929. Insp. housing devel., Rome, 1923; elec. engr. work Bunker Hill and Sullivan Mining Co., Kellogg, Ida., 1924-25; draftsman A.E. Doyle, architect, Portland, 1925-27; chief designer A. E. Doyle & Asso., architects, 1927-42, mem. firm, 1932-42; practice architecture under own name, Portland, 1943—; dean Mass. Inst. Tech. Sch. Architecture and Planning, 1951-53. Mem. Nt. Fine Arts Commn. 1950; adviser State Dept. on design fgn. bldgs.; Am. del. conv. Inst. Intellectual Coop. of League of Nations, Madrid, 1934. Past pres. bd. trustees Portland Art Mus. N.A. Fellow A.I.A., Danish Royal Acad. Fine Arts, Am. Acad. Arts and Scis., Nat. Inst. Arts and Letters (v.p.). Address: 1 Fairfield St Boston MA 02116

BELLVILLE, JOHN WELDON, physician, educator; b. Wauseon, O., Aug. 7, 1926; s. John Francis and Sarah (Brose) B.; B.A., Cornell U., 1948; M.D., 1952; student Vanderbilt U., 1945-46; m. Lynette Frances Brandstater, Nov. 6, 1969; children by previous marriage—Jon P., David George, Steven René, Paul André. Intern, Mpls. Gen. Hosp., 1952-53; resident anesthesiology N.Y. Hosp., 1953-55; research fellow Sloan-Kettering Inst., 1955-56, asso., 1960; asst. prof. Cornell U. Med. Coll., 1959-60; asso. prof. Stanford Med. Sch., 1960-65, prof., 1965—; cons. Arthur D. Little, Inc., 1970—, nat. halothane study NRC, 1963-68. Served with USNR, 1944-46. Recipient Borden Undergrad. Research award in medicine Cornell U., 1952; Bowen-Harlow Brooks scholar N.Y. Acad. Medicine, 1955. Mem. Assn. U. Anesthetists, A.A.A.S., Am. Soc. Pharmacology and Exptl. Therapeutics, Am. Chem. Soc., Am. Soc. Anesthesiologists, Biomed. Engring. Soc. Author: Techniques in Clinical Physiology, 1969; also numerous articles. Patentee servo-medicator. Home: 793 Mayfield Av Stanford CA 94305

BELLWOOD, SHERMAN J., judge; b. Sugar City, Ida., June 13, 1917; s. Ollie J. and Myrtle J. (Polson) B.; A.B., U. Ida., 1938; J.D., U. Mich., 1941; m. Eleanor Jane Lee, May 14, 1938; 1 son. Sherman Lee. Admitted to Ida. bar, 1942; pvt. practice, Hailey, 1942-47, Rupert, 1947- 57, 60-66; pros. atty., Minidoka County, 1951-57; judge 11th Jud. Dist., Ida., 1957-60, 5th Jud. Dist., 1966—. Commr. Ida. State Bar, 60, pres., 1960. Served as capt., CAC, AUS, World War II. Recipient 1st annual Chase A. Clark Meml. award, 1971. Mem. Am. (ho. dels. 1958-59, 61-66), 5th Jud. Dist. (past pres.), Ida. bar assns., Am. Judicature Soc., Nat. Conf. Conciliation Cts., Nat. Conf. State Trial Judges, Beta Theta Pi. Mason (32, Shriner), Elk. Office: Court House Rupert ID

BELMONDO, JEAN-PAUL, actor; b. Neuilly-sur-Seine, France, Apr. 9, 1933; s. Paul and Madeleine (Reinaud-Richard) B.; ed. Ecole Alsacienne à Paris; m. Renee Constant, Jan. 27, 1959; children—Patricia, Florence, Paul. Started acting career touring with Comedie-Francaise; appeared in motion pictures, 1957—, including Cartouche, 1962, The Man from Rio, 1964. Pres., Syndicat francais des acteurs, 1963—. Home: 16 rue de Savoie Paris 6e France Office: 22 rue de Chaillot Paris 16e France*

BELMONT, ALAN HARNDEN, orgn. exec.; b. N.Y.C., Jan. 22, 1907; s. Arthur B. and Teresa Annie (Harnden) B.; student San Diego State Coll., 1927-30; A.B., Stanford, 1931; m. Loretta Agnes Drzyeimski, May 14, 1938; children—Barbara Lenore, Alan Nicholas. Acct., Cal., 1931-36; spl. agt. F.B.I., 1936, assigned Birmingham, Ala., Chgo. and N.Y.C., 1936-43, in charge field office, Cin., 1943-44, asst. dir. domestic intelligence div., 1951-62, asst. to dir. charge investigations, 1961-65; exec. asst. to dir. Hoover Instn. on War, Revolution and Peace, Stanford U., 1966-69, dir. for adminstrn., 1969—. asso. dir. for adminstrn., 1969—. Episcopalian. Home: 240 Chatham Way Mountain View CA 94040 Office: Hoover Instn Stanford U Stanford CA 94305

BELMONT, AUGUST, investment banker; b. N.Y.C., Dec. 30, 1908; s. August and Alice Wall (de Goicouria) B., Jr.; student St. Mark's School, Southboro, Mass., 1922-27; A.B., Harvard, 1931; m. Elizabeth Lee Saltonstall, June 16, 1931; children—Alice Lee, August, John Saltonstall, Priscilla; m. 2d, Louise Victor Winston, Feb. 8, 1946. With Bonbright & Co., Inc., investment bankers, N.Y.C., 1932-42, v.p., dir., 1939-42; v.p. Dillon, Read & Co. Inc., 1946-62, pres., 1962-70, chmn., 1971—, dir., 1952—; pres. Nassau Assos., Inc., 1958-70, chmn., 1971—, also dir.; dir. U.S. & Fgn. Securities Corp., Am. Kennel Club, Cameron Iron Works, Inc., Rouse Co.; trustee Provident Loan Soc. Spl. asst. to under sec. Navy, 1940. Vice chmn. finance com., mem. exec. com., trustee Presbyn. Hosp., N.Y.C.; v.p., trustee Green-Wood Cemetery. Served to lt. comdr. USNR, 1942-45; served under comdr. Air Force, Pacific Fleet. Decorated Bronze Star. Mem. Bond Club. Clubs: Links, Lunch (N.Y.C.). Home: Route 1 Box 564 Easton MD 21601 Office: 46 William St New York City NY 10005

BELMORE, FREDERICK MARTIN, chem. co. exec.; b. Schnyler, Va., Apr. 9, 1915; s.Albert Joseph and and Florence Mabel (Johnson) B.; B.S., U. Va., 1936, B.S. in Chem. Engring., 1937; m. Charlotte Lee Munn, Nov. 6, 1937; children—Frederick Martin, Page Randolph, Charlette Lee. With E. I. du Pont de Nemours & Co., Inc., 1937-43, asst. tech. dir. tetra ethyl lead plant, 1939-43; chief metals prodn. sect. Manhattan project, 1943-47; metals dir. prodn. div. AEC, 1947-53, dep. mgr. N.Y. office, 1953-54; asst. to chmn. bd. Singmaster and Breyer Co., N.Y.C., 1954-55; asst. to pres. Mallinckrodt Chem. Works, St. Louis, 1955-60, v.p., gen. mgr. indsl. chems. div., 1960-63; pres., chief exec. officer Matheson Co., Inc. E. Rutherford,N.J., 1963-67, chmn. bd., 1966-67, past dir.; chmn. bd., dir. Matheson Sci., Inc. Chgo., 1963-67; chmn. bd., sr. v.p., dir. Will Ross, Inc., Milw., 1967-68, pres., chief chief operation officer, dir., 1968—; dir. York Research Corp., Marine Corp., Milw. Bd. dirs. Va. Engring. Found. of U. Va., 1963—. Recipient Exceptional Civilian Service award War Dept., 1946. Mem. Am. Chem. Soc., Am. Inst. Chem. Engrs., Am. Nuclear Soc., Phi Beta Kappa, Tau Beta Phi, Alpha Chi Sigma. Clubs: Milwaukee Hunnt, Milwaukee Country, Milwaukee. Home: 7275 N River Rd Milwaukee WI 53217 Office: 2727 W Good Hope Rd Milwaukee WI 53201

BELOOF, ROBERT LAWRENCE, author, educator; b. Wichita, Kan., Dec. 30, 1923; s. Ida P. A. and Ida (Dungan) B.; student Haverford Coll., 1944, Swarthmore Coll., 1945; B.A., Friends U., 1946; M.A., Northwestern U., 1948; M.A., Bread Loaf Sch. English, Middlebury Coll., 1948; Ph.D., Northwestern U., 1954; m. Ruth Madeleine LaBarre, June 14, 1946; children—Marshall H., Laird D., Douglas E., Grant L. Faculty, U. Cal., 1948—, lectr., asst. prof., then asso. prof., 1948-64, prof., 1964—, chmn. dept. speech, 1964-68; author poetry and articles. Fellow Inst. Advancement Edn., 1951-52, Inst. Creative Arts, 1963-64; Fulbright prof., Italy, 1959-60. Mem. Speech Assn. Am. Author: The One-Eyed Gunner, 1956; The Performing Voice in Literature, 1966. Editor, record performer of hist. anthology of Am. poetry, 2 vol. LP, 1965. Office: Dept Rhetoric U Cal Berkeley CA 94720

BELOTTI, MARIO LORENZO, educator; b. Bergamo, Italy, Oct. 15, 1926; s. Lorenzo A. and Rosa (Savoldi) B.; came to U.S., 1951, naturalized 1962; B.S., Midwestern U., 1954, M.A., 1955; Ph.D., U. Tex., 1960. Mem. faculty U. Santa Clara (Cal.), 1959—, prof. econs., 1967—, chmn. dept., 1964—. Home: 19401 San Marcos Rd Saratoga, CA 95070. Office: Univ Santa Clara Santa Clara CA 95053

BELSHE, FRANCIS BLAND, univ. dean; b. Richland, Mo., Apr. 24, 1920; s. Ovid Harvey and Autie Bland (Gibson) B.; B.A., B.S. in Edn., Southwest Mo. State Coll., 1941; M.A., Yale, 1943, Ph.D., 1946; m. Bonnie Taylor, Apr. 13, 1941; children—Robert Bland, Ann Taylor. Tchr. Social Scis. Springfield (Mo.) Jr. High Sch., 1941-42; teaching asst. Yale 1942-46; tchr. English, New Haven Jr. Coll., 1942-43, tchr. Hopkins Grammar Sch., New Haven, 1943- 46; asst. prof. Central Conn. State Coll., 1946-48; mem. faculty Ill. State University, 1948—, dean undergraduate school, 1957-66, associate dean of faculty, 1966—, also dean the summer session, 1966—; Fulbright lecturer at Kwansei Gakuin U., Nishinomiya, Japan, 1953-54. Mem. Nat. Philosophy of Edn. Soc., Chgo. Regional Philosophy of Edn. Soc., Phi Delta Kappa, Kappa Delta Pi. Mem. editorial bd. Ednl. Theory, 1953-54. Home: 402 N School St Normal IL 61761

BELSHEIM, EDMUND OLAF, educator, lawyer; b. Grand Meadow, Minn., Jan. 14, 1905; s. Ole G. and Eda Mabel (Blacklin) B.; A.B., U. N.D., 1927, LL.D., 1952; B.A. in Jurisprudence, U. Oxford (Eng.), 1929, B.C.L., 1930; J.S.D., U. Chgo., 1931: m. Elizaveth Ann Ducey, Sept. 2, 1933; children—Karen Elizabeth, Helen Blacklin, Edmund Olaf, Jr. Admitted to Ill. bar, 1931, N.Y. bar, 1944. Neb. bar. 1953; with firm Foreman, Bluford, Krinsley & Schultz, Chgo., 1931-33, Rosenthal, Hamill & Wormser, Chgo., 1933- 37; asst. prof. law U. Tenn., 1937-38, asso. prof., 1938-39; asst. counsel Office Comptroller Currency, Treas. Dept., Washington, 1939-40; asso. prof. law U. Va., 1940-43; head atty. Bd. Econ. Warfare, Washington, 1943; with Root Clark, Buckner & Ballantine, N.Y.C., 1943-45; prof. law U. Neb., 1946—, dean Coll. Law, 1949-60; vis. prof. law George Washington U., 1947, U. Tex., 1948, U. Okla., 1949, N.Y.U., 1954-55, U. So. Cal., 1965-66; Dir. Lincoln (Neb.) Legal Aid Bur., 1947-59. Rhodes Scholar, 1927-30. Mem. Neb. Bar Assn., Phi Beta Kappa, Order of Coif, Sigma Alpha Epsilon, Phi Alpha Delta. Author: Modern Legal Forms (16 vols.); Materials on Property Taxation in Nebraska, 1947; Bigelow's Cases on Rights in Land, 1945. Contbr. legal jours. Home: 3838 Sheridan Blvd Lincoln NB

BELSKIE, ABRAM, sculptor; b. London, Eng., Mar. 24, 1907; s. Mark and Sarah (Itovich) B.; student Glasgow (Scotland) Sch. Art, 1923-27, also London, Paris and Rome, 1927-29; studied with John Gregory and Malvina Hoffman; m. Helen Atkinson, Mar. 19, 1930; children—Albert Alexander, Victor Maxbert. Came to U.S., 1929, naturalized, 1939. Asso. with N.Y. Acad. Medicine; mem. faculty, combining sculpture and med. teachings aids N.Y. Med. Coll.; provided with Dr. Robert Latou Dickinson, models series in Hall of Man, N.Y. Worlds Fair, 1939; provides sculptured med. teaching models to med. univs., colls., and hosps. throughout U.S.; works rep. Am. Mus. Natural History, Chgo. Nat. History Mus., Cleve. Health Mus., Maternity Center Assn., N.Y. Acad. Medicine, N.Y. Med. Coll., Am. Heart Assn., N.Y. Heart Series; works include Christ Child, Moonbeam, Strock Meml., War Meml., Surgeon at Ethicon Bldg., Raritan, N.J., 1962, others; portraits and small sculptures in pvt. collections; designer medals and medallions various commemorative occasions, including 1954 issue Society of Medallists, Flag Pole Meml., Battery Park, N.Y.C., 1955, Space Award, 1968, Three Astronauts, 1967, Stone Mountain Confederate Meml. Medal, 1970. Recipient Sir John Edward Burnett prize, also Lindsey Morris prize, 1951, Golden Anniversary prize Allied Artists Am., 1963. N.A. Fellow Nat. Sculpture Soc., Am. Numis. Soc. (J. Sandford Saltus award 1959). Author: (with Robert Latou Dickinson) Birth Atlas. Home: 38 Brook St Closter NJ 07624

BELT, ELMER, physician; b. Chgo., Apr. 10, 1893; s. Charles Elmer and Minnie (Drier) B.; A.B., U. Cal., 1916; M.S., Hooper Inst. for Med. Research, San Francisco, 1918; M.D., U. Cal. Med. Sch., San Francisco, 1920; LL.D., Pacific Coll. Law, 1930, U. Cal. at Los Angeles, 1962; m. Mary Ruth Smart, June 9, 1918; children—Charles Elmer, Bruce Gregory. Student fellow in med. research Hooper Inst., 1917-18, fellow in med. research, 1920, 1921; asso. and clin. instr. urology U. Cal. at San Francisco, 1920, 1921, research in urology, 1921, 1922, clin. prof. surgery (urology) Sch. Med., 1951—; asst. resident in gen. surgery Peter Bent Brigham Hosp., Boston, 1922-23; asso. prof. urology Coll. of Med. Evangelists, Los Angeles, 1924-40; chief urologic service Harbor Gen. Hosp. (div. Los Angeles County Gen. Hosp., 1953-58; chief cons. urology VA Facility, West Los Angeles, 1924-47, 56—; cons., mem. urology staff, hosps. Los Angeles area; guest speaker fgn. med. soc. meetings and internat. confs. Asso. Calif. Inst. Tech.; commonwealth prof. urology, Louisville U., 1946; pres. Los Angeles Co. Med. Research Found., 1948, now dir.; mem. Cal. State Bd. Health, 1940-56, chmn., 1940-44; trustee Los Angeles County Med. Soc., 1945—. Mem. WHO. Trustee Cal. Arboretum Found., Inc., 1958; dir. Pilgrimage Theatre Found., 1958; founding mem. bd. trustees U. Cal. at Los Angeles Found. Awarded Italy's Silver Star Solidarity, 1952; Bronze Minerva, 1954; v.p., Societe Leonard de Vinci, Amboise, France, 1959. Diplomate Am. Bd. Urology. Fellow A.C.S., U.S. chpt. Internat. Coll. Surgeons; mem. Pan-A.M.A. (pres. So. Cal. div., 1935), Internat. Urol. Soc., Nat. Conf. of Christians and Jews (bd. mem. So. Cal. region, 1957-58), Dante Alighieri Soc. (pres. Los Angeles chpt. 1958), Soc. for History Tech. (pres. 1966-68), Phi Beta Kappa, also several nat. and local med. and sci. socs. Clubs: Los Angeles Country, University (Los Angeles). Co-author: Cabot's Modern Urology, The Cystoscope and Its Uses, Modern Tests of Renal Function, 1940; (with G. C. Schausfler) Pediatric Gynecology, 1944; The Manuscripts of Leonardo da Vinci, 1949. Contbr. to med. and surg. jours. Home: 2201 Fern Dell Pl Los Angeles CA 90028 Office: 1893 Wilshire Blvd Los Angeles CA 90057

BELT, ROBERT MCCOLL, cons. engr; b. Troutdale, Ore., June 5, 1907; s. Dr. Walter Cayley and Nina (McColl) B.; B.S., Ore. State Coll., 1928; m. Dorothy I. Roendahl, June 29, 1933; children—Alice Cayley Belt Faust, Louise Roendahl Belt Summers. With Ore. Hwy. Dept., 1926- 27, 30; newspaper work in Olympia, Wash., 1929; with U.S. Bur. Pub. Rds., Hawaii 1931, engr. Dept. Pub. Works, 1931, asst. supt., 1946-47, supt., 1947-53; gen. mgr. Belt, Collins & Assos., 1953—; exec. v.p. Belt, Lemmon & Lo, 1953—; chmn. bd. Harbor Commn., 1947-53. Trustee Leahi Hosp. Commd. lt. (j.g.) C.E., USNR, 1941, advanced through grades to comdr., 1945. Mem. Am. Soc. C.E. (pres. Hawaii sect. 1952, nat. dir. 1964-66), Honolulu C. of C. (dir.), Am. Inst. Cons. Engrs., Nat. Soc. Profl. Engrs., Soc. Am. Mil. Engrs., Tau Kappa Epsilon, Sigma Delta Chi. Episcopalian. Home: 2542 Olopua St Honolulu HI 96822 Office: 1402 Kapiolani Blvd Honolulu HI 96814

BELT, WILLIAM ALVIN, lawyer; b. Kenton, O., July 13, 1903; s. William A. and Barbara (Garst) B., A.B., Ohio Wesleyan U., 1924; J.D., U. Mich. 1927; m. Virginia Gordon, June 25, 1930; children—Stephen G., Susan L., William A. III, Thomas G. Admitted to Ohio bar, 1928, since practiced in Toledo; partner Marshall, Melhorn, Bloch & Belt. Gen. counsel, dir. Champion Spark Plug Co.; dir. Toledo Trust Co., Ia. Industries, Inc., Hellertown Mfg. Co. Fellow Am. Bar Assn.; mem. Ohio, Toledo bar assns., Phi Delta Phi. Mason (32). Clubs: Castalia Trout, Toledo Country, Toledo (pres., dir. 1949-52); Ottawa Skeet; Belmont Country; Explorers. Home: 5602 Ryan Rd Toledo, OH 43614. Office: Nat Bank Bldg Toledo OH 43604

BELTAIRE, MARK ANTHONY, III, journalist; b, Detroit, Apr. 9, 1914; s. Mark Anthony and Marion (Waters) B.; A.B., Princeton, 1937; m. Beverly Anne Strauss, Nov. 7, 1947; children—Mark Anthony IV, Jeffrey Allan, Barbara Marion, Suzanne Michele. Sports writer Detroit News, 1937-42; comml. slide film writer Jam Handy Orgn., Detroit, 1942-44; daily columnist Detroit Free Press 1945—; commentator on Detroit radio stas. WJR, WXYZ, WKMH at various times; tchr. creative writing U. Detroit, 1946-47. Mem. Detroit Press Club, Players, Box 12, Sigma Delta Chi. Presbyn. Club: Grosse Pointe Hunt. Home: 1227 Yorkshire Rd Grosse Pointe MI 48230 Office: 321 W Lafayette Blvd Detroit MI 48231

BELTHUIS, LYDA CAROL, educator; b. Parkersburg, Ia., May 29, 1913; d. Alfred William and Aletta (Theerman) Belthuis; B.A., No. Ia. U., 1939; M.A., Colo. State Coll., 1943; Ph.D., U. Mich., 1947. Departmental tchr. Burlington (Ia.) Pub. Schs., 1939-43, grade prin., 1943-45; asst. prof. geography U. Minn., Duluth, 1947-51, asso. prof., 1951-55, prof., 1955—, head dept., 1955-65; geography coordinator Minn., 1952-54. Mem. Am., Canadian, Australian, New Zealand, Minn. geog. socs., Gamma Theta Upsilon, Pi Gamma Mu. Contbr. articles to profl. jours. Home: 100 Elizabeth St Duluth MN 55803

BELTING, ROBERT HENRY, mail order exec.; b. Shelbyville, Ill., Aug. 3, 1919; s. C. Henry and Harriet (Priest) B.; B.S., Kan. State U., 1940; m. Patricia Ann Bush, Apr. 23, 1941. With Joseph Breck & Sons Corp., Boston, 1952-69, treas., 1961-69, pres., 1965-69, also dir.; v.p., gen. mgr. Mason & Sullivan Co. subsidiary of CML Group, Inc., Osterville, 1969—; dir. Sonolite Corp. Served to lt. USNR, 1940-45. Home: PO Box 171 Commaquid MA 02637 Office: 39 Blossom Av Osterville MA 02655

BELTON, WILLIAM, cons., ret. fgn. service officer; b. Portland, Ore., May 22, 1914; s. Francis Hugh and Mary Jane (Sheehy) B.; student U. Ore., 1932-33; A.B., Leland Stanford, 1935; student Nat. War Coll., 1958-59; m. Judy Hyslop, June 12, 1939; children—Barbara (Mrs. Sigfrid Yngvesson), Hugh, Timothy. Clk., Am. legation, Quito, Ecuador, 1936- 37, Bogota, Colombia, 1937-38; apptd. fgn. service officer, 1938; vice consul, Habana, Cuba, 1933-39; 3d sec. legation, and vice consul, Ciudad Trujillo, Dominican Republic, 1940-42; fgn. service officer U.S. D.A., Washington, 1942; vice consul, Fort Willaim, Ont., 1943, Winnipeg, Man., 1943-44; asst. agrl. atache, Ottawa, Ont., 1945-46, consul, Porto Alegre, Brazil, 1946-48; 1st sec., Ciudad Trujillo, 1949-52; officer-in- charge Mexican affairs State Dept., 1952-54, West Coast affairs, 1954-55, dep. dir. Office S. Am. affairs, 1956; counselor Am. embassy, Santiago, Chile, 1956-58, Canberra, Australia, 1960-63; polit. adviser to comdr.-in-chief, with personal rank of minister U.S. So. Command, 1963-65; sr. fgn. service insp., 1965-67, counselor of embassy with personal rank of minister, also consul gen., Rio de Janeiro, 1967-70; retired, 1970; cons. to Dept. State for fisheries and wildlife, 1970—; research collaborator Smithsonian Instn., 1970—. Adviser U.S. delegation 4th Meeting, directing council, Pan American San. Orgn., and 13th Pan Am. San. Conf., Ciudad Trujillo, 1950. Pres. bd. dirs. Carol Morgan Sch., Santo Domingo, 1951. Mem. Am., Royal Australian ornithol. unions, Kappa Sigma. Home: Rocky Hollow

Great Cacapon WV 25422 Office: care Am Consulate Porto Alegre APO New York City NY 09676 also Caixa Postal 119 Gramado RGS Brazil

BELTRAN, ROBERTO SALIDO, Mexican army officer; b. Sonora State, Mexico, Oct. 8, 1912; s. Conrado C. and Altagracia (Beltran) Salido; student Colegio Militar, 1932, Escula Aviacion, 1938, Escula Superior, 1947; m. Alejandrina Reyero, Jan. 27, 1940; children—Alejandrina, Roberto, Jose. Commd. Mexican Army, 1932, advanced through grades to maj. gen.; air staff officer, 1949-53; dep comdr. Air Force, 1953-59; dir. Aviation Sch., 1959-60; dir. Air Coll. Mexico, 1960-65; army and air attache Mexican embassy, Washington, 1965- -. Decorated Merito Militar, Merito Teonico Militar; Legion of Merit (U.S.A.). Roman Catholic. Home: 5881 Nebraska Av Washington DC 20015 Office: 2829 16 St Washington DC 20009

BELTZ, HERBERT ALLISON, constrn. co. exec.; b. Grand Forks, N.D., July 1, 1926; s. Eugene Maurice and Helen (Aune) B.; grad. Minn. Sch. Bus., 1949; m. Opal D. Thomas, Mar. 6, 1948; children—Michael, Mark. Staff accountant Boulay, Anderson, Waldo & Co., Mpls., 1950-58, partner, 1958-65; sec., controller, dir. S.J. Groves & Sons Co., Mpls., 1965—. Served with U.S. Mcht. Marine, 1945-47. C.P.A., Minn. Mem. Am. Inst. C.P.A.'s, Minn. Soc. C.P.A.'s, Financial Execs. Inst. Home: 6015 Manchester Dr Minneapolis MN 55422 Office: 40 Washington Av S Minneapolis MN 55401

BELTZ, LEROY DUANE, univ. dean; b. Pierce, Neb., Apr. 25, 1924; s. Adolph and Caroline (Rohde) B.; B.Sc. in Pharmacy with distinction, U. Neb., 1951; Ph.D. in Pharm. Chemistry, U. Conn., 1956; m. Glenda Marie Reese, Jan. 21, 1944; children—Judith Ann, Glen Duane, David Scott, Keith Stuart. Instr. pharmacy U. Conn., 1952-56; asst. prof. pharmacy U. Fla., 1956-58; asso. prof., then prof. Ferris State Coll., 1958-66; prof. pharmacy, dean Coll. Pharmacy, Ohio No. U., 1966—. Served with USN, 1941-47. Mem. Am., Ohio pharm. assns., Am. Inst. History Pharmacy, Sigma Xi, Rho Chi, Phi Lambda Upsilon, Beta Beta Beta, Phi Eta Sigma, Phi Kappa Phi, Kappa Psi, Alpha Zeta Omega, Gamma Sigma Epsilon. Republican. Mem. Christian Ch. Home: 501 W North St Ada OH 45810 Office: 500-600 S Main St Ada OH 45810

BELURY, NICHOLAS GEORGE, mfg. co. exec.; b. Brockton, Mass., Aug. 4, 1915; s. George N. and Effie (Harris) B.; B.M.E., Purdue U., 1937; m. Elizabeth Beach, Sept. 4, 1948; children—Beverly Beach, Deborah Georgia. With Abex Corp., N.Y.C., 1937—, sales mgr., 1945-46, pres. engineered castings div., 1946-67, group exec., 1967-69, v.p. Abex, 1953-69, 1st. v.p., 1969-70, chief operating officer, 1970-71, pres., chief exec. officer, 1971—; chmn. Abex Industries of Can. Ltd, (Montreal); dir. IC Industries Chgo., Waukesha Foundry Co., Bucyrus-Erie Corp. Served to lt. col. AUS, 1941-45. Episcopalian. Clubs: Woodway Country (Darien, Conn.); Pinnacle, University, Sky (N.Y.C.). Home: 72 St George Lane New Canaan CT 06840 Office: 530 Fifth Av New York City NY 10036

BELYAYEV, PAVEL IVANOVICH, cosmonaut; b. Vologada region, USSR, June 26, 1923; grad. Mil. Air Acad.; m. Tatiana Philipovna; children—Irina, Ludmila. Served as fighter pilot World War II; now col.; comdr. spaceship Voskhod 2 in two man orbital flight, 1965. Mem. Communist Party. Address: Scientific Research Inst Aviation Medicine Petrovsky Park Moscow USSR*

BEMILLER, JAMES NOBLE, biochemist, educator; b. Evansville, Ind., Apr. 7, 1933; s. LaMar N. and Mabel (Gruber) BeM.; B.S., Purdue U., 1954, M.S., 1956, Ph.D., 1959; m. Paraskevi Mavridis, Aug. 6, 1960; children—Byron N., Philip J. Asst. prof. biochemistry Purdue U., 1959-61; asst. prof. biochemistry dept. chemistry So. Ill. U., Carbondale, 1961-65, asso. prof., 1965-68, prof., 1968—, acting chmn. dept. chemistry, 1966-67, prof. biochemistry Sch. Medicine, 1971—, chmn. Faculty Council, 1970-71. Cons. A.E. Staley Mfg. Co., Decatur, Ill., 1962-70. Bd. dirs. Luth. Sch. Theology, Chgo. Mem. Am. Chem. Soc., Am. Assn. Cereal Chemists, A.A.A.S., Am. Phytopath. Soc., Phytochem. Soc. N.Am., Am. Inst. Chemists, Am. Assn. U. Profs., Ill., N.Y. acads sci., Sigma Xi, Alpha Chi Sigma, Alpha Tau Omega. Editor: Industrial Gums, 1959, 71; Methods in Carbohydrate Chemistry, Vols. 1-6, 1962-71; Starch: Chemistry and Technology, Vols. 1 and 2, 1965, 67. Home: Route 1 Murphysboro IL 62966 Office: Dept Chemistry So Ill U Carbondale IL 62901

BEMIS, F. GREGG, Jr., mfg. co. exec.; b. St. Louis, May 25, 1928; s. F. Gregg and Margaret (Houghton) B.; B.A., Stanford, 1950; M.B.A., Harvard, 1954; m. Lisa R. Thacker, Aug. 20, 1952; children—David G., Evalyn S., Ted T., Jennifer L., Stephanie, Tamsen. With Bemis Co., Inc., Boston, 1954-68, dir. allied operations, 1960-62, v.p., 1962-68, dir., 1955-68; pres., dir. Oeconics, Inc., 1969—; v.p., gen. mgr. packaging div. Riegel Paper Co., Co., Charlotte, N.C., 1970—; treas., dir. Boston Waterfront Devel. Corp.; dir. Logetronics, Inc., Lam, Inc. Mem. corp. Emerson Hosp. Finance chmn. Mass. Republican Com., 1968-69. Trustee Wentworth Inst. Served to 1st lt. USMCR, 1950-52. Mem. Marshall Street Hist. Soc. Clubs: Cohasset Yacht, Hochgebirge Ski (Boston); Nashautve Country; Concord Country. Home: 2433 Beretania Circle Charlotte NC 28211 Office: Greenwood Cliff Charlotte NC 28204

BEMIS, JUDSON, packaging co. exec.; b. Cohasset, Mass., July 26, 1913; s. Albert Farwell and Faith (Gregg) B.; grad. Milton Acad., 1932; B.S., Harvard, 1936, postgrad. 1937-38; m. Elizabeth Long, May 13, 1939 (dec. Apr. 3, 1941); 1 dau., Sandra Elizabeth; m. 2d, Barbara White, May 1, 1943; children—Barbara Turney, Ellen Farwell, Gardner, Judson. With Bemis Co., Inc., 1938—, v.p., 1946-56, exec. v.p., 1956-60, pres., chief exec. officer, 1960—, also dir.; chmn. bd. Fed. Res. Bank; dir. Soo Line Ry. Chmn. bd. trustees Fisk U. Home: 3841 Schuneman Rd White Bear Lake MN 55110 Office: 800 Northstar Centre Minneapolis MN 55402

BEMIS, SAMUEL FLAG, educator; b. Worcester, Mass., Oct. 20, 1891; s. Charles Harris and Flora M. (Bemis) B.; A.B., Clark U., 1912, A.M., 1913, hon. D.H.L. 1937; A.M., Harvard, 1915, Ph.D., 1916; grad. study in Eng. and France, 1915- 16; Litt.D., Williams Coll., 1953; L.H.D., Yale, 1963; m. Ruth M. Steele, June 20, 1919 (dec. Oct. 1967); one daughter, Barbara. Instructor in history, Colo. Coll., Colorado Springs, 1917-18, asso. prof., 1918-20; prof. history, Whitman Coll., Walla Walla, Wash., 1920-23; research asso., Carnegie Instn. of Washington, 1923-24; prof. history, George Washington U., 1924-34; director European mission of Library of Congress, 1927-29; lecturer at Harvard, 1934-43; Farnam professor of diplomatic history at Yale, 1935, professor of inter- American relations, 1945, Sterling professor diplomatic history, inter- American relations emeritus, 1960; Carnegie visiting professor to Latin American Universities, 1937-38, Cuba, 1945, 1956. Member American Historical Association (pres. 1961), American Academy Arts and Sciences, Am. Antiquarian Soc., Colonial Soc. of Mass., Mass. Historical Soc., Sociedad Geograficia y Estadistica Mexico). Unitarian. Club: Cosmos. Author historical volumes including: Pinckneys Treaty: A Study of America's Advantage from Europe's Distress 1783-1800, 1926 (Pulitzer prize in letters, 1927); John Quincy Adams and the Foundations of American Fgn. Policy, 1949 (received the Pulitzer award for biography in 1950); John Quincy Adams and the Union, pub. 1956. Editor: The Am. Secretaries of State and their Diplomacy (part author), 10 vols., 1927-29. Contributor to reviews, newspapers, etc. Home: 3030 Park Av Bridgeport CT 06604

BEMIS, WILLIAM HAY, lawyer; b. Cleve., Mar. 3, 1897; s. Alton Adelbert and Elizabeth (Hay) B.; A.B., Dartmouth, 1918; LL.B., Western Res. U., 1922; m. Alice McNeil, Nov. 12, 1927 (dec. Oct. 1956); children—Elizabeth (Mrs. Dean C. Cameron), Rebecca (Mrs. Arthur L. Amiot); m. 2d, Wilma Suits Nye, May 6, 1961. Admitted to O. bar, 1921, since practiced in Cleve.; mem. firm Baker, Hostetler & Patterson, 1924-26, partner, 1927-70, counsel, 1970—. Trustee Shaker Properties; dir. Lincoln Co., Auditorium Hotel Co., Fifty West Broad, Inc., Eumay, Inc. Sec., Lincoln Found. Mem. Am., Ohio, Cleve. bar assns. Clubs: Country, Union, Clevelander (Cleve.). Home: 17306 Aldersvde Dr Shaker Heights OH 44120 Office: Union Commerce Bldg Cleveland OH 44114

BEN, PHILIP, newspaper corr.; b. Lodz, Poland, Mar. 2, 1913; s. Philip and Lina Ben; ed. Sch. Polit. Sci., Paris, Corr. of Maariv, Tel Aviv, Israel, 1948—, of Le Monde, Paris. 1952—. Home: Tel Aviv Israel 305 E 40th St New York City NY 10016

BENACERRAF, BARUJ, educator, physician; b. Caracas, Venezuela, Oct. 29, 1920; s. Abraham and Henriette (Lasry) B.; B. es L., Lycee Janson, 1940; B.S., Columbia, 1942; M.D., Med. Sch. Va., 1945; M.A., Harvard, 1970; m. Annette Dreyfus, Mar. 24, 1943; 1 dau., Beryl. Came to U.S., 1939, naturalized, 1943. Intern, Queens Gen. Hosp., N.Y.C., 1945-46; research fellow dept. microbiology Columbia Med. Sch., 1948-50; charge de recherches Centre National de Recherche Scientique Hopital Broussais, Paris, 1950-56; asst. prof. pathology N.Y. U. Sch. Medicine, 1956-58, asso. prof., 1958-60, prof., 1960-68; chief immunology Nat. Inst. Allergy and Infectious Diseases, NIH, Bethseda, Md., 1968-70; Fabyan prof. comparative pathology, chmn. dept. Harvard Med. Sch., 1970—. Sci. adviser immunology WHO; mem. immunology a study sect. NIH. Trustee, mem. sci. adv. bd. Trudeau Found. Served to capt. M.C., AUS, 1946-48. Fellow Am. Acad. Arts and Scis.; mem. Am. Assn. Immunologists, Am. Assn. Pathologists and Bacteriologists, Am. Soc. Exptl. Pathology, Soc. Exptl. Biology and Medicine, Brit. Assn. Immunology, French Soc. Biol. Chemistry, Harvey Soc., N.Y. Acad. Scis., Alpha Omega Alpha. Editorial bd.: Am. Jour. Pathology, Lab. Investigation Jour. Exptl. Medicine, Jour. Immunology. Home: 111 Perkins St Boston MA 02130

BENADE, ARTHUR HENRY, educator, physicist; b. Chgo., Jan. 2, 1925; s. James Martin and Miriam (McGaw) B.; A.B., Washington U., 1948, Ph.D., 1952; m. Virginia Lee Wassall, June 9, 1948; children—Judith Anne, Martin Daniel. Design engr. McDonnell Aircraft, St. Louis, 1952; instr. physics Case Inst. Tech. (now Case Western Res. U.), 1952-54, asst. prof., 1954-60, asso. prof., 1960-69, prof. physics, 1969—; vis. prof. Indian Inst. Tech., Kanpur, India, 1964-65; cons. instrumentation, archtl. and musical acoustics, nuclear physics. Active Cleve. Music Soc. Served with USAAF, 1943-46. Fellow Accoustical Soc. Am.; mem. Am. Phys. Soc., Calpin Soc., Catgut Acoustical Soc., A.A.A.S., N.Y. Acad. Sci. Home: 3126 Woodbury Rd Shaker Heights OH 44120 Office: Physics Dept Case Western Reserve U Cleveland OH 44106

BENADE, LEO EDWARD, army officer; b. Dubuque, Ia., July 29, 1916; s. Nicholas A. and Jennie (Bruno) B.; student U. Mich. Sch. Law, 1946; J.D., Am. U., 1952; m. Marietta Taylor, Mar. 20, 1943; children—Leonard E., Lawrence M. Enlisted as pvt. U.S. Army, 1941, advanced through grades to maj. gen., 1970; admitted to Va. bar, 1951; adj. gen. U.S. Army Europe, 1966-67; dep. asst. sec. def., Washington, 1968—. Mem. nat. exec. com. U.S.O. Decorated D.S.M. with oak leaf cluster, Legion of Merit with 2 oak leaf clusters, Commendation medal. Mem. Va. State Bar, Am. Judicature Soc., Va. Trial Lawyers Assn., Sigma Nu Phi. Club: Army-Navy Country (chmn. bd. govs. 1970—) (Arlington, Va.). Home: 4031 Justine Dr Annandale VA 22003 Office: Office Asst Sec of Def Manpower and Res Affairs Pentagon Washington DC 20301

BENARIO, HERBERT WILLIAM, educator; b. N.Y.C., July 21, 1929; s. Frederick and Ilse (Kessler) B.; B.A., Coll. City N.Y., 1948; M.A., Columbia, 1949; Ph.D., Johns Hopkins, 1951; m. Janice M. Martin, Dec. 23, 1957; children—Frederick M., John H. Instr. Greek and Latin, Columbia, 1953-58; asst. prof. Greek and Latin, Sweet Briar Coll., 1958-60; mem. faculty Emory U., 1960—; prof. classics, 1967—, chmn. dept., 1968—; dir. Vergilian Soc. Summer Sch. in Italy, 1963, 67, asst. dir., 1957, 59; vis. prof. Intercollegiate Center Classical Studies, Rome, spring 1967, U. Colo., summer 1969; Mem. Latin achievement test com. Coll. Entrance Exam. Bd., 1963-66. Served with AUS, 1951-53. Fulbright grantee, 1956; research grantee Am. Philos Soc. Mem. Am. Philol. Assn., Archaeol. Inst. Am. (pres. Atlanta Soc. 1965- 66, 67-68), Classical Assn. Middle West and South (pres. 1971-72, pres. So. sect. 1968-70), Classical Soc. of Am. Acad. in Rome (pres. 1965), Vergilian Soc. Am. (trustee 1960-65, 69—), Soc. Promotion Roman Studies, Am. Classical League, Phi Beta Kappa (pres. Emory U. chpt. 1968- 69). Author: Tacitus, Agricola, Germany, Dialogue on Orators, 1967. Home: 2278 N Decatur Rd Decatur GA 30033 Office: Emory Univ Atlanta GA 30322

BENARON, JOE, business exec.; b. Winnipeg, Man., Can., 1915; sr. v.p. Warwick Electronics, Inc., Sepulveda, Cal.; pres. chmn. Belvedere Mfg. Co.; chmn. Wilshire Bedding Co., Nat. Foam Rubber Co.; pres. Thomas Organ Co. Office: 8345 Hayvenhurst Av Sepulveda CA 91343*

BENATTAR, CECILIA, holding co. exec.; m. Jack Benattar; 1 son, Simon. Pres. U.S. br. London Merchant Securities, prin. engaged in real estate. Address: 15 Arthur St London EC 4, England.*

BENAVIDES, ALBERTO, mining co. exec.; b. Lima, Peru, Oct. 21, 1920; s. Alberto and Blanca (Quintana) B.; Mining Engr., U. Engring., Lima, Peru, 1941; M.A. in Geology, Harvard, 1944; m. Elsa Ganoza, Sept. 8, 1945; children—Blanca (Mrs. Jose Miguel Morales), Alberto, Mercedes, Roque, Raul. Asst. geologist, geologist, then head exploration dept. Cerro de Pasco Corp., Lima, Peru, 1944-52, then mng. dir., now pres.; mng. dir. Cia de Minas Buenaventura, S.A., 1952-64, asso dir.; dir. Banco de Lima. Mem. Sociedad Geologica del Peru, Instituto de Ingenieros de Minas del Peru. Am. Inst. Mining and Metall. Engrs., Soc. Econ. Geologists. Home: 777 Benavides Miraflores, Lima, Peru. Office: 891 A Wiese Lima Peru

BENBEN, JOHN STEPHEN, educator; b. Chgo., Jan. 25, 1912; s. Stanley P. and Josephine (Siwek) B.; B.S., Northwestern U., 1934, M.A., 1938, Ph.D., 1953; m. Beverlee F. Brown, Jan. 21, 1949; children—Paul Leland, Stephen James Nancy Ruth. Social service casework, Chgo., 1934-37; staff Hull House, Chgo., 1933-36; prin. schs., Midlothian, Ill., 1937-39, dist. supt.,1939-50; prof. No. Ill. U., 1953-56, head dept. edn., 1957-60; prof. ednl. adminstrn. N.Y. U., 1960—. Ednl. adviser Lago Community Schs., Aruba, Netherlands Antilles. Adviser Korean Govt., 1948, V.I. Edn. Dept., 1965, U. P. R., 1966-68; cons. to P.R. sec. edn., 1967-68, 69-71, Presbyn. Hosp., 1968; dir. edn. program Prisoner of War Camp, Koje-Do, Korea, 1951-52; UNESCO adviser Sierra Leone, B.W.I., 1956-57. Mem. Bd. Edn., Ardsley, N.Y., 1963-67. Mem. Ill. Conf. Profs. Ednl. Adminstrn., Ill. Ednl. Assn., Ill. Prins. Assn., Ill. Supts. Assn., Round Table Chgo., Nat. Conf. Profs. Ednl. Adminstrn., Am. Assn. Sch. Adminstrs., Am. Assn. U. Profs., African Resources Conf., Phi Delta Kappa. Author: History of Education, 1965; U.S. Educational Personnel, 1965; For Educational Adminstrators, 1971. Home: 7 Victoria Rd Ardsley NY 10502 Office: NY U Washington Sq New York City NY 10003

BENBOW, CHARLES FRANK, tobacco co. exec.; b. Winston-Salem, N.C., Aug. 22, 1924; s. Charles Frank and Ruth (Harper) B.; B.S. in Commerce, U. N.C., 1945; m. Mary Elizabeth Bexter, Sept. 13, 1947; children—Shirley, Martha, Mary. With R.J. Reynolds Tobacco Co., 1947—, treas., 1968—; treas., dir. Archer Products, Inc.; dir. adv. bd. N.C. Nat. Bank; treas. R.J. Reynolds Foods, Inc., Arjay Equipment Corp. Recipient Victory medal Joslin Diabetic Found., 1968. Rotarian. Home: Route 8 Shattalon Dr Winston-Salem NC 27106 Office: 401 N Main St Winston-Salem NC 27102

BENBOW, JOHN ROBERT, banker; b. Muncie, Ind., June 1, 1931; s. Robert and Thelma Ruth (Parr) B.; B.S., Ind. U., 1954; postgrad. Butler U., 1957-58; m. Marilyn Ann Alhand, Dec. 27, 1958; children—Karen, Susan, Julia. With Ind. Nat. Bank, Indpls; 1954—, mgmt. trainee, 1954-59, asst. cashier, 1959-61, asst. v.p., 1961-63, v.p., 1963-68, exec. v.p., 1968—, dir., 1971—; pres. INB Internat., Inc., Indpls., 1969—, Ind. Nat. Overseas Corp., 1970—; dir. Baker, McHenry & Welch, Inc., MITA, Inc. Pres., gov.'s (Ind.) Economy Program, Inc., 1968—; sec. Indpls. Com. Fgn. Relations, 1966—; v.p. Indpls. Bd. Parks and Recreation, 1970—; bd. dirs. Greater Indpls. Progress Com., 1970—; treas. Ind. Forum, Inc., 1970—; pres. Indpls. Bd. Park Commrs., 1969. Trustee Winona Meml. Hosp., treas., 1968—. Mem. Ind. C. of C. (dir. 1970—), Beta Gamma Sigma. Baptist. Clubs: Kiwanis, Classic Car America, Columbia, Meridian Hills Country. Home: 6868 N Pennsylvania Av Indianapolis IN 46220 Office: 1 Indiana Sq Indianapolis IN 46204

BENBROOK, PAUL, ins. co. exec.; b. Wideman, Ark., July 5, 1912; s. Allen Hervey and Bertie (McSpadden) B.; B.A., M.A., U. Tex., 1937; m. Charlyne Harrison, Dec. 25, 1938; 1 son, Allen Harrison. Tchr. econs. U. Tex., 1937; tchr. econs. and govt. W. Tex. State Tchrs. Coll., 1938; rater casualty div. Tex. Ins. Dept., 1938-39, asst. actuary and casualty actuary, 1941-50; asst. mgr. automobile dept. Cravens Dargan & Co., 1939-41; mgr. Southwestern br. Nat. Bur. Casualty Underwriters, 1950-53; with Am. Gen. Ins. Co., Houston, 1953—, sec., 1956-57, v.p., 1957—; partner gen. ins. firm John L. Wortham and Son, Houston, 1961-65; exec. v.p. Md. Casualty Co., 1966—, also dir.; dir. Agrl. Ins. Co. Served to lt. comdr. USNR, 1944-46. Decorated Bronze Star. Fellow Casualty Actuarial Soc.; mem. Am. Acad. Actuaries, Internat. Congress Actuaries. Home: 4300 N Charles St Baltimore, MD 21218. Office: 701 W 40th St Baltimore MD 21211

BENCH, JOHN, catcher with Cin. Reds Profl. Baseball Team. Address: Central Trust Tower Cincinatti OH 45202*

BENCHER, WALTER SEAMAN, mfg. co. exec.; b. Bklyn., Jan. 21, 1917; s. Alfred and Wilhelmina (Caëmmerling) B.; student Drexel Inst., 1935, Pratt Inst., 1937, St. Johns U., 1941; m. Rita Frugoli, June 16, 1937; children—Anita, Karen, Steven. Accountant, Cities Service Oil Co., 1935-41; engr. Combustion Engring., Inc., 1941-52, asst. controller, 1952, controller, 1953-61, v.p., 1956, v.p. internat. operations, 1961—; pres., dir. Combustion Engring. Overseas, Inc.; vice chmn., dir. Energie-und G.m.b.H.; dir. Lummus Co., CE-rrey, SA (Mexico), Combustion Engring-Superheater Ltd.; Stein et Roubaix, Internat. Combustion (Holdings) Ltd., Combustion Engring. Africa (Pty.) Ltd., Combustion Chems., Inc., Franco Tosi, S.A., Stein Industrie, S.A. Ceramtec, Ltd., Combustion-Stein-Astilleros, S.A., Compagnie des Echanguers de Chaleur, S.A., Uddcomb Sweden, A.B., Ramtite Europ, CESO International, Ltd. Mem. Am. Soc. M.E. Clubs: Union League; Hartford; Wampanoag Country. Home: 2 Copper Hill Terrace East Granby CT 06026 Office: Prospect Hill Rd Windsor CT 06095

BENCHLEY, NATHANIEL GODDARD, writer; b. Newton, Mass., Nov. 13, 1915; s. Robert and Gertrude (Darling) B.; grad. Phillips Exeter Acad., 1934; B.S., Harvard, 1938; m. Marjorie Bradford, May 19, 1939; children—Peter Bradford, Nathaniel Robert. Reporter New York Herald Tribune, 1939-41; asst. editor drama dept. Newsweek, 1946-47. Author: Side Street (novel), 1950; The Frogs of Spring (play), 1953; Robert Benchley (biography), 1955; The Great American Pastime (movie), 1956; One To Grow On (novel), 1958; Sail a Crooked Ship, 1960; The Off Islanders, 1961; Catch A Falling Spy, 1963; A Winter's Tale, 1964; The Visitors, 1965; A Firm Word or Two, 1965; The Monument, 1966; Welcome to Xanadu, 1968; The Wake of the Icarus, 1969; Lassiter's Folly, 1971; also articles and fiction stories pub. various nat. mags. Editor: The Benchley Roundup, 1954. Clubs: Pacific (Nantucket, Mass.); Coffee House; Century Assn. (N.Y.C.). Home: Box 244 Siasconset MA 02564

BENCHOFF, JAMES MARTIN, mfg. co. exec.; b. Hagerstown, Md., May 18, 1927; s. J. Thompson and Marie (Hickey) B.; student U. Pa., 1944-45; m. Mary Louise Kilpatrick, Aug. 12, 1952; children—Helen Marie, James Martin. With Grove Mfg. Co. div. Walter Kidde & Co., Shady Grove, Pa., 1954—, dir., v.p., sales mgr. agrl. div., 1962-65, asst. gen. mgr., 1965-68, exec. v.p., gen. mgr., 1968-69, pres., chief exec. officer, gen. mgr., 1969—; pres. Monta Vista, Inc., Waynesboro, Pa., 1959—, Mar-Penn, Inc., Waynesboro, 1963—. Rotarian. Clubs: Waynesboro Country (dir.); Admirals (N.Y.C.). Home: Route 4 Waynesboro PA 17268 Office: P O Box 21 Shady Grove PA 17256

BENDER, AUSTIN LETHERIDGE, mayor; b. Chattanooga, June 6, 1916; s. George Andrew and Mattie D. (Green) B.; student pub. schs.; m. Rozelle Kelso, June 30, 1938; children— Patricia Ann (Mrs. George Alan Cooper), Frances Kelso, George Andrew. Asst. supt. Tenn. Hwy. Dept., Chattanooga, 1935-41; supt. parks City of Chattanooga, 1946-55; asso. Skiles Realty, Chattanooga, 1955-58; mgr. Hamilton County, Chattanooga, 1958-62; commr. Dept. Pub. Works, Sts. and Airport, Chattanooga, from 1958, now mayor, Chattanooga; former city commr., Chattanooga. Mem. Hamilton County Planning Commn., 1942-46. Served to capt. AUS, 1942-46. Mem. V.F.W., Am. Legion, 40 and 8. Methodist. Elk. Home: 3835 Mission View Av Chattanooga TN 37411 Office: City Hall Chattanooga TN

BENDER, BYRON WILBUR, educator; b. Roaring Spring, Pa., Aug. 14, 1929; s. Ezra Clay and Gertrude (Kauffman) B.; B.A., Goshen Coll., 1949; A.M., Ind. U., 1950, Ph.D., 1963; m. Lois Marie Graber, Aug. 25, 1950; children—Susan Alice, Sarah Marie, Catherine Anne, Judith Lee, John Richard. Lang. adviser Dept. Edn., Trust Ter. Pacific Islands, 1953-59, 62-64; asst. prof. linguistics, anthropology Goshen Coll., 1959-62; asso. prof. linguistics U. Hawaii, Honolulu, 1965-69, prof., 1969—, chmn. dept. linguistics, 1969—, mem. staff Peace Corps tng. programs for Micronesia, 1966-67. Cons. on Maori edn. New Zealand Council for Ednl. Research, 1968-69. Current Anthropology fellow, 1962—. Linguistic mem. Soc. of Am.,

Internat. Linguistic Assn., Polynesian Soc. Mag. editor Oceanic Linguistics, 1965—; co-editor Oceanic Linguistics Special Publs., 1965—. Contbr. articles profl. jours. Home: 7268 Kauhako St Honolulu HI 96821

BENDER, CHESTER ROBEY, coast guard officer; b. Burnsville, W.Va., Mar. 19, 1914; s. John I. and Inez (Harbert) B.; B.S., U.S. Coast Guard Acad., 1936; m. Annamarie R. Ranson, Sept. 1, 1939; 1 son, Mark Alan. Commd. ensign USCG, 1936, advanced through grades to adm., 1970; aviator, 1940; assigned to anti-submarine warfare patrol and air sea rescue, World War II; air sea rescue adviser, liaison officer Hdqrs. Far East Air Force, 1945; aide to comdt., 1946-50; comdr. Air Sta., Traverse City, Mich., 1953-55, Air Detachment, Barbers Point, Hawaii, 1958-59, coast guard cutter Bering Strait, 1959-61; chief adminstrv. mgmt. div. USCG, Washington, 1962-63, chief program analysis div., 1963-64; dist. comdr. 9th Dist., Cleve., 1964-65; supt. U.S. Coast Guard Acad., New London, Conn., 1965-67; comdr. Western area, San Francisco, 1967-70; comdt. USCG, 1970—. Govt. mem. governing bd. U.S. Power Squadrons, 1964—. Decorated Bronze Star, Legion of Merit. Mem. Newcomen Soc. N.Am. Methodist. Clubs: Army-Navy, Aviation (Washington); Army-Navy Country (Arlington, Va.); Bohemian (San Francisco). Home: 6601 Kennedy Dr Chevy Chase MD 20015 Office: 400 7th St SW Washington DC 20591

BENDER, EARL EDWIN, educator; A.B., Marietta Coll., 1931; A.M., U. Ill., 1933. Instr. Physics Marietta Coll. (O.), 1946-47, asst. prof. petroleum sci., 1947-50, asso. prof., 1950-54, dir. Edwy R. Brown Dept. Petroleum Sci., 1950—, Benedum prof. petroleum sci., 1954—. Office: Petroleum Sci Dept Marietta Coll Marietta OH 45740*

BENDER, GEORGE JESSE, investment co. exec., lawyer; b. Brooklyn, Dec. 21, 1906; s. Henry P. and Carolina (Thorn) B.; A.B., N.Y.U., 1929, LL.B., 1932; m. Theresa Roedel, Jan. 7, 1928; children—George J., Philip Lee. Admitted to N.Y., Fed. bars, 1934; asso. N.Y. Trust Co., 1929-36, Sage, Gray, Todd & Sims, 1936-45; v.p. Bklyn. Savs. Bank, 1947-57, trustee, 1953-61, pres., 1957-61; senior v.p. Wallace Investments, Inc., N.Y.C., 1961-64; pres. Wallace Realty Mortgage Co., 1963-64; vice chmn. bd., dir. Fidelity Bank, Beverly Hills, Cal., 1965-66; chmn. Security Investment Co., Los Angeles, 1966—; dir. Security Investment Co., Riverside. Mem. Assn. Bar City N.Y., Am. Bar Assn., Phi Delta Phi, Zeta Psi. Clubs: Bel Air Country; Union League (N.Y.C.); Brooklyn. Home: 10985 Bellagio Rd Los Angeles CA 90024 Office: 1801 Av of Stars Century City Los Angeles CA 90067

BENDER, HOWARD MARVIN, constrn. co. exec.; b. Paterson, N.J., Nov. 10, 1930; s. Jack I. and Dorothy (Blake) B.; student U. Md., 1948-50; m. Sondra Dosik, July 15, 1951; children—Barbara Ann,Ann, Julie Lynn, Eileen Susan, David Stuart. With Blake Constrn. Co., Inc., Washington, 1950—, exec. v.p., 1965—; dir Washington & Lee Savs. and Loan Assn. Bd. dirs. Jewish Community Center of Greater Washington. Mem. Tau Epsilon Phi. Jewish religion. Home: 7400 Radnor Rd Bethesda, MD 20034. Office: 1120 Connecticut Av Washington DC 20036

BENDER, JAMES FREDERICK, psychologist; b. Dayton, O., Apr. 6, 1905; s. Fred Jacob and Bertha (Zimmerman) B.; B.S., Columbia, 1928, Ph.D., 1939; m. Anne Parsons, June 25, 1925; m. 2d, Gertrude Moller, Jan. 21, 1966 (div. 1967); m. 3d, Vera E. Sattler, Jan. 21, 1968. Engaged as psychol. examiner Personnel Bur., Coll. City N.Y., 1928-37; lectr., adj. prof. psychology Bklyn. Poly. Inst., 1928-40; chmn. dept. speech, dir. Speech and Hearing Center, Queens Coll., 1937-44; dir. Nat. Inst. Human Relations, 1944- 54; pres. James F. Bender Assos., 1954—; dir. sales tng. Lehigh Nav. Coal Sales Co., 1953—, also dir.; sr. con-. Kimberly-Clark Corp.; dean Kimberly Clark Marketing Inst., 1958-59; lectr. Columbia, 1950-57, mem. alumni council, 1950-59; prof. bus. adminstrn. Adelphi U., Garden City, 1960- 66, dean Sch. Bus., 1964-66; prof. bus. adminstrn. Pace Coll., 1966-68; prof. C.W. Post Coll. of L.I. U.; dir. Money Mgmt. Inst., 1969—; licensed psychologist, 1958—; cons. Adelphi-Suffolk Coll. Dir. Follett Corp., Tech Products, Profit Motivation Service, Inc., First Multifund. Inc. Sec.-treas. Nat. Schs. Com. Econ. Edn., 1965—; chmn. Career Planning Comm. Nassau County, N.Y., 1966-67. Trustee Queens Speech and Hearing Service Center, 1941—, Friends Acad., 1957-62, Human Resources Found., 1965—. Recipient Distinguished Teaching award Am. Econ. Found.; certificate psychology, N.Y., 1932. Fellow A.A.A.S., Am. Speech and Hearing Assn.; mem. Am. Speech Correction Assn. (past councillor), N.Y. State Assn. Applied Psychology (exec. com. 1942-44), Am. Psychol. Assn., N.Y. Met. Assn. Psychologists, N.Y. Soc. Clin. Psychologists, Nat. Vocational Guidance Assn., Nat. Council Family Relations, Emerson Lit. Soc., Academy Mgmt., Financial Execs. Inst., Sigma Chi. Republican. Mem. Soc. of Friends. Mason. Author: The Technique of Executives Leadership, 1950; Your Way to Popularity and Personal Power, 1950; How to Sleep; Personality Structure of Stuttering; N.B.C. Hndbook of Handbook How to Talk Well; Salesman's Mispronunciations; Make Your Business Letters Make Friends, 1952; Victory Over Fear, 1952; Profits from Business Letters, 1952; How to Sell Well, 1961; 10 Biggest Mistakes Speakers Make, 1963; also articles. Home: 54 Thornwood Lane Roslyn Heights NY 11577 ☆

BENDER, LAURETTA, child psychiatrist; b. Butte, Mont. Aug. 9, 1897; d. John Oscar and Katherine Parr (Irvine) Bender; B.S., U. Chgo., 1922, M.A. in Pathology, 1923; M.D., State U. Ia., 1926; Rockefeller Traveling fellowship, U. Amsterdam, Holland, 1926-27; m. Paul Ferdinard Schilder. 1936 (dec. Dec. 1940); children—Michael, Peter, Jane (Mrs. Henry B. Parkes). Served internship, also resident neurology Billings Hosp., U. Chgo., 1927-28; psychiatric residency Boston Psychopathic Hosp., 1928-29; research asso. Phipps Clinic, Johns Hopkins Hosp., 1929-30; sr. psychiatrist Bellevue Hosp., N.Y.C., 1930-56, charge children's service, 1934-56; with N.Y.U., 1930-58, prof. clin. psychiatry,1951-58, sr. cons. VA tng. program, 1940- 58; psychiat. cons. (children) N.J. State Neuropsychiatric Inst., 1954; prin. research scientist, child psychiatry, N.Y. State Dept. Mental Hygiene, 1956-58, dir. research child psychiatry, 1959—; clin. prof. psychiatry Columbia Coll. Phys. and Surg., 1959-62. Served on various civic orgn. coms. for child welfare. Recipient Adolph Meyer Award, 1953; Med. Woman of Yr. award for N.Y., 1958. Diplomate American Board Psychiatry and Neurology. Mem. Am. Psychiat. Assn. (Agnes Purcell McGavin award 1969), American Neurological Assn., Am. Orthopsychiat. Assn., Am. Psychopath. Assn., Acad. Child Psychiatry, Am. Assn. for Mental Deficiency. Author of Visual Motor Gestalt and Its Clinical Use. 1935. Author, editor; Bellevue Studies in Child Psychiatry. Home: 44 Malone Av Long Beach NY 11561 also 210 E 15th St New York City NY 10003 Office: NY State Psychiat Inst 722 W 168th St New York City NY 10032

BENDER, MAX, educator, chemist; b. Boston, Oct. 23, 1914; s. Samuel and Jennie (Baratz) B.; S.B. in Chem. Engring., Northeastern U., 1936; S.M. in Chem. Engring., Mass. Inst. Tech., 1937; Ph.D. in Chemistry, N.Y.U., 1950; m. May Kaplan, Sept. 7, 1947; children—Sanford Ross, Leslie Marilyn. Research fellow Mass. Inst. Tech., 1937-38; charge lab. Manton-Gaulin Mfg. Co., Everett, Mass., 1938-40; sr. research chemist, group leader Interchem. Corp., N.Y.C., 1941-48, Am. Cyanamid Co., Bound Brook, N.J., 1950-61; prof. chemistry Fairleigh Dickinson U., 1961—; cons. in field, 1961—. Fellow N.Y. Acad. Scis., Am. Inst. Chemists; mem. Am. Chem. Soc., A.A.A.S., Am. Assn. U. Profs., Sigma Xi, Phi Lambda Upsilon. Author research papers. Home: 16 S Woodland Av East Brunswick NJ 08816 Office: Fairleigh Dickinson Univ Teaneck NJ 07666

BENDER, MORRIS B., educator, neurologist; b. Russia, June 8, 1905; s. Boris and Anne (Nemirowsky) B.; came to U.S., 1914, naturalized, 1924; B.S., U. Pa., 1927, M.D., 1931; fellow Yale. 1936-37; m. Sara Spirtes, June 28, 1936; children—Barbara (Mrs. Martin Steiner), Adam, Barnaby, Victor, Leila. Intern Temple U. Hosp., 1931-32; resident neurology Montefiore Hosp., 1932-33, Mt. Sinai Hosp., 1933-35; head lab. exptl. neurology N.Y.U., 1938-43, mem. faculty, 1946-66, prof. clin. neurology, 1951-66; clin. prof. neurology Columbia, Coll. Phys. and Surg., 1953, Goldschmidt prof. neurology, 1968- -; dir. neurology Mt. Sinai Hosp., N.Y.C., 1951—, prof., chmn. dept. neurology Sch. Medicine, 1966—; dir. neurol. service Bellevue Hosp., N.Y.C., 1951-61; cons. visual scis. study sect. USPHS, 1962-64; mem. nat. research council VA, 1948. Mem. council Cerebral Palsy Assn., 1948-51; mem. com. Multiple Sclerosis Soc., 1953. Served to comdr. USNR, 1943-46. Recipient Jacobi medal Mt. Sinai Hosp., 1957; So. Cross for sci. achievement (Brazil). Mem. Am. Neurol. Assn. (vice pres. 1963 pres. elect 1971), Internat. Congress Neurology (treas. 1965—), Am. Physiol. Soc.; hon. mem. French Neurol. Soc., 1970. Author numerous articles in field. Editorial bd. Confinia Neurologica, 1946—, Jour. Mt. Sinai Hosp., 1955—. Spl. research vision perception. oculomotor system, neurophysiology. Home: 400 E Shore Rd Great Neck NY 11024 Office: 1150 Park Av New York City NY 10028

BENDER, MYRON LEE, educator, chemist; b. St. Louis, May 20, 1924; s. Averam Burton and Fannie (Leventhal) B.; B.S. with highest distinction, Purdue U., 1944, Ph.D., 1948; postdoctoral student Harvard, 1948-49; AEC fellow, U. Chgo., 1949-50; m. Muriel Blossom Schulman, June 8, 1952; children—Alec Robert, Bruce Michael, Steven Pat. Chemist, Eastman Kodak Co., 1944-45; instr. U. Conn., 1950-51; from instr. to asso. prof. Ill. Inst. Tech., 1951-60; mem. faculty Northwstern U., 1960—, prof. chemistry, 1962—; cons. to govt. and industry, 1959—. Sloan fellow, 1959-63. Fellow Am. Inst. Chemists; mem. Am. Chem. Soc., Am. Assn. U. Profs., Chem. Soc. (London), Am. Soc. Biol. Chemists, Assn. Harvard Chemists, A.A.A.S., Phi Beta Kappa, Sigma Xi, Phi Lambda Upsilon. Home: 2514 Sheridan Rd Evanston IL 60201

BENDER, PAUL JUNIOR, educator; b. Mansfield, O., Nov. 20, 1917; s. Paul Vermont and Myrtie (Guise) B.; B.S., Sheffield Sch., Yale, 1939; Ph.D. in Phys. Chemistry, Yale, 1942; m. Margaret Jean McLean, May 28, 1943. Faculty U. Wis., Madison, 1942—, prof. chemistry, 1955—. Chmn. chemistry panel, grad. fellowship program NSF, 1961-64; mem. thermochemical panel JANAF, 1959-61, mem. thermochemical working group, 1961-64. Mem. Am. Chem. Soc. (past chmn., councillor Wis. sect.), Sigma Xi, Phi Lambda Upsilon, Gamma Alpha. Co-author: Experimental Physical Chemistry, 7th edit., 1969. Home: 3305 Kingston Dr Madison WI 53713

BENDER, RALPH EDWARD, educator; b. nr. Waldo, O., Dec. 29, 1910; s. George Edward and Nina Amelia (Allmedinger) B.; B.S. in Agr., Ohio State U., 1933, M.A., 1941, Ph.D., 1947; m. Harriett Louise Anspaugh, June 10, 1937; children—John Edward, Susan Jane. Tchr. vocational agr. Anna (O.) High Sch., 1933-37; instr. dept. agrl. edn. Ohio State U. (also tchr. vocational agr. Canal Winchester High Sch.), 1937-47, asst. prof., 1947-48, asso. prof., 1948- 51, chmn. dept. agrl. edn., 1948—, prof., 1951—; vis. prof. Auburn U., 1954, U. Cal., 1957, Colo. State U., 1959, 61, 68, Cornell U., 1962, Pa. State U., 1964; U.S. AID specialist Tchr. Edn. Study in Brazil, 1967; cons.-specialist div. vocational edn. U.S. Office Edn., 1969, 70. Mem. troop com. Boy Scouts; mem. Jr. Fair Bd. Ohio, 1929—. Pres. Bd. of Edn. Mem. adv. com. Sch. Edn., Cornell U., 1962-67. Recipient Distinguished Teaching award A.A.T.E.A., 1969. Mem. Am. Vocational Assn. (pres. tchr. edn., sect. agrl. edn. 1957-58, pres. Central Region agrl. edn. conf. 1963-64, nat. v.p. 1967-70, pres. 1967-70), Ohio Vocational Agricultural Assn. (pres. 1945-46), Ohio Vocational Assn. (pres. 1946-47), Ohio Sch. Bd. Assn., Future Farmers Am. (pres. Ohio 1929-30, nat. v.p. 1930-31), N.E.A., Nat. Vocational Agr. Tchrs. Assn., Ohio Safety Council, Ohio Edn. Assn., Ohio Assn. Adult Edn., Farm Bur., Grange, Alpha Zeta, Gamma Sigma Delta, Phi Delta Kappa, Phi Eta Sigma. Methodist. Mason. Clubs: Lions (pres. 1959), Ohio State University Faculty, Author: The FFA and You-Your Guide to Learning, 1971. Co-author: Teacher Education in Agriculture; Adult Education in Agriculture, 1971. Home: 265 Woodsview Dr Canal Winchester OH 45697 Office: Ohio State U Columbus OH 43210

BENDER, ROBERT FOSTER, corp. exec.; b. Stoyestown, Pa., Sept. 27, 1909; s. Dr. Foster and Edythe (Smith) B.; B.S., U. Pitts., 1931; m. Lenora Norman, Nov. 20, 1938; children—Judith, Robert Foster, Adrienne. Accountant, Asso. Gas & Electric System, Johnstown, Pa., 1931-38; gen. plant accountant Oil Well Supply Co., Oil City, Pa., 1938-40; chief auditor Bendix Aviation Corp., Phila., 1941; controller John B. Stetson Co., Phila., 1941-46, Bigelow- Sanford Carpet Co., Inc., N.Y.C., 1946-51; v.p., treas., dir. Minute Maid Corp., N.Y.C., 1951-57; exec. v.p., dir. Internat. Tel. & Tel. Corp., 1957-60; v.p. Reeves Bros., Inc., 1961-62; v.p., treas. Sperry Rand Corp., 1962-67; pres. Sperry Rand Finance Corp. Mem. Financial Execs. Inst., Sigma Chi. Conglist. Mason. Clubs: India House, Weavers, Patterson, Rockefeller Center Luncheon. Home: 80 N Compo Rd Westport CT 06880 Office: 1290 Av of Americas New York City NY 10019

BENDER, STANLEY SEYMOUR, constrn. co. exec.; b. Paterson, N.J., Jan. 4, 1929; s. Jack I. and Dorothy (Blake) B.; student U. Md., 1948; m. Blanche A. Lewis, July 22, 1955; children—Jerry, Betty. With Blake Contrn. Co., Washington, 1949- -, treas., 1951—; pres. Glade Valley Farms, Inc., Frederick, Md., 1966- -. Mem. Washington Bd. Realtors. Bd. dirs. Bender Found. Served with USNR, 1946-48. Mason (Shriner). Club: Touchdown. Home: 2901 Fessenden St NW Washington, DC 20008. Office: Bender Bldg 1120 Connecticut Av NW Washington DC 20036

BENDER, WELCOME WILLIAM, aerospace engr.; b. Elizabeth, N.J., Nov. 30, 1915; s. Welcome W. and Bertha (Sauer) B.; B.S., Mass. Inst. Tech., 1938, M.S., 1939; m. Mary Virginia Priebe, 1946; children—Deborah, Welcome William, Rebecca, Janet, Heldi, Mary, Gregory. Tech. dir. pilotless aircraft sect. Martin Co., div. Martin-Marietta Corp., 1939-48, mgr. electromech. dept., 1949- 51, chief electronics engr., 1952-55, dir. Research Inst. Advanced Studies, div. Martin Co., 1955-62, dir. research Martin Co., 1962—, dir. research space exploration group, 1964—, project scientist planetary programs, 1966—. Mem. Gov.'s Sci. Resources Adv. Bd., chmn. sci. and engring. edn. com.; edn. counselor Balt. area Mass. Inst. Tech. Fellow I.E.E.E.; asso. fellow Inst. Aero. and Astronautics; mem. Md. Acad. Scis. (sci. council), U.S. C. of C., Balt. Assn. Commerce, Sci. Industry Devel. Council. Patentee in field. Countbr. numerous tech. papers sci. lit. Home: 5005 W King Crest Lane Littleton CO 80123 Office: Martin Marietta Corp PO Box 170 Denver CO 80201

BENDER, WESLEY CHARLES, educator, marketing analyst; b. Bklyn., Aug. 8, 1908; s. George and Mae (Kurtz) B.; student law sch., Cornell U., 1928-30, A.B., 1929; M.A., U. Pitts., 1931; postgrad. Northwestern U., 1934- 35, 36-37, Columbia, 1935; m. Genevieve L. Robolt, Dec. 30, 1933; children—Marilyn, Alane. Instr. marketing Coll. of Commerce, U. Notre Dame, South Bend, Ind., 1931-34, asst. prof. marketing, 1934-37, asso. prof. bus. adminstrn., 1937-43, prof., 1943-46, acting head dept. bus. adminstrn., 1942-46, prof. marketing, 1946—, head dept. marketing, 1946-54. Tchr., Am. Inst. Banking, 1938-41, 46-60; mgr. No. Ind. Adjustment Bur. Mem. Nat. Assn. Credit Men (exec. sec. St. Joseph Valley chpt. 1944-58), Am. Econ. Assn., Am. Marketing Assn. (dir. Michiana chpt. 1967-68), Am. Assn. U. Profs., Michiana World Trade Club (dir. 1957, treas. 1958, pres. 1961-62), Ind. Acad. Social Sci. (v.p. 1940-41, pres. 1941-42, 51), South Bend Civic Music Assn. (dir., 1956-64), Seal and Serpent, Phi Alpha Delta, Beta Gamma Sigma. Editor: Credo (monthly pub. of St. Joseph Valley Chapter Nat. Assn. Credit Men), 1944-58; Notre Dame World Trade Conference Papers, 1953—. Contbr. to retailing jour. Home: 53272 Juniper Rd South Bend IN 46637

BENDER, WILLIAM ERNEST, banker; b. Muskogee, Okla., Mar. 16, 1917; s. William E. and Helen (Jones) B.; B.S., Okla. U., 1939; grad. Sch. Banking. U. Wis., 1954; m. Margaret W. Weaver, Apr. 5, 1941; children—Barbara Ann (Mrs. J. David Lawson), Mary Margaret (Mrs. John R. Hamill V). Office mgr., chief accountant Camp Gruber Exchange (Okla.), 1942-46; owner-mgr. Bender Service Co., Muskogee, 1946-50; asst. cashier Citizens Nat. Bank, Muskogee, 1950-53; with First Nat. Bank & Trust Co., Tulsa, 1953—, sr. v.p., 1968—. Chmn. Tulsa-Rogers County Port Authority; 1st v.p., dir., mem. exec. and membership coms. Ark. Basin Devel. Assn.; trustee, sec.- treas. Tulsa Port of Catoosa Facilites Authority. Recipient Distinguished Service award Muskogee Jr. C. of C., 1952. Mem. Am. Inst. Banking, Okla. Mortgage Bankers Assn., Okla. Bankers Assn., Ind. Petroleum Assn., Tulsa C. of C., Phi Gamma Delta. Methodist (steward). Lion (past pres. Downtown Tulsa club), Mason (32). Clubs: Oaks Country, Propeller, Petroleum (Tulsa). Home: 5234 S Toledo St Tulsa OK 74066 Office: 15 E 5th St Tulsa OK 74066

BENDETSEN, KARL ROBIN, corp. exec.; b. Aberdeen, Wash., Oct. 11, 1907; s. Albert M. and Anna (Bentson) B.; A.B., Stanford, 1929, J.D., 1932; m. Billie McIntosh, Mar. 10, 1938; 1 son, Brookes McIntosh; m. 2d, Maxine Bosworth, 1948; 1 dau., Anna Martha. Admitted to Cal., Ore., Ohio, Wash. bars; practiced law, Aberdeen, Wash., 1934-40; mgmt. counsel, 1946-47; cons. spl. asst. to sec. defense, 1948, asst. and under sec. army, 1950-52; dir. gen. U.S. Railroads, 1950-52; chmn. bd. U.S. Plywood-Champion Papers Inc., 1967, pres. 1969—, also chief exec. officer; dir. Westinghouse Electric Corp. Spl. U.S. rep. to W. Germany, 1956; spl. U.S. ambassador to P.I., 1956; chmn. adv. com. to sec. def., 1962. Served with U.S. Army, 1940-46; col. Gen. Staff Corps; spl. rep. sec. of war to Gen. MacArthur, 1941; directed evacuation of Japanese from West Coast, 1942. Decorated D.S.M. with cluster, Legion of Merit with 2 oak leaf clusters; Croix d'Guerre with Palm, officer Legion of Honor (France); mem. Order Brit. Empire; Medal of Freedom. Mem. Am. Judicature Soc., Theta Delta Chi. Episcopalian (vestryman). Clubs: Links, Metropolitan, Brook (N.Y.C.); Chicago; Wash. Athletic (Seattle); Bohemian, Pacific Union (San Francisco); Houston Country, Petroleum, Tejas, Bayou (Houston). Home: 860 UN Plaza New York City NY 10017 Office: 777 3d Av New York City NY 10017

BENDHEIM, ROBERT AUSTIN, textile exec.; b. N.Y. City, Aug. 5, 1916; s. Julius and Cora (Lowenstein) B.; A.B., Princeton, 1937; student Harvard Bus. Sch., 1941- 42; L.H.D. (honorary), Fordham University, 1966; m. Susan Liebman; children—Lynn, Gail, Kim. Trainee, Spartan Mills, Spartanburg, S.C., 1937-38; in various capacities with M. Lowenstein & Sons, Inc., since 1938, sec. and dir., 1946-47, vice pres., 1947-59, exec. v.p., 1959-64, pres., 1964—, chief exec. officer, 1970—, also dir. Served as lt., U.S.N., 1942-46. Trustee of Mount Sinai Hosp., N.Y.C. Clubs: Princeton, Century, Stanwich. Home: Flagler Dr Greenwich CT 06830 Office: 1430 Broadway New York City NY 10018

BENDICH, AARON, biochemist, educator; b. N.Y.C., June 18, 1917; s. Louis and Ellen (Goldberg) B.; B.S., Coll. City N.Y., 1939; Ph.D., Columbia, 1946; m. Clare Kaufman, Aug. 28, 1940; children—Arnold Jay, Stephen Zachary. Research asst. biochemistry Columbia, 1940-42, mem. sci. staff div. war research, 1943-45, research asst. bacteriology, 1946-47; part-time instr. chemistry Coll. City N.Y., 1946-48, 52, 54, 55, 59; fellow Sloan Kettering Inst., 1947-48, asst., 1948-49, asso., 1949-60, mem., 1960—, chief sect. synthesis lab., 1954-58, chief sect. organic biochemistry, 1958—, chief division of cell biochemistry. 1969—, chmn. postdoctoral studies com., 1960; faculty Sloan-Kettering div. Cornell U. Med. Sch., N.Y.C. 1949—, prof. biochemistry. 1961—. Mem. bd. sci. advisers St. Jude Children's Hosp. and Research Inst., Memphis. Fellow Am.-Swiss Found. Sci. Exchange, 1956; recipient R. Thornton Wilson award genetic and preventive psychiatry, 1960; A.P. Sloan Found. award for cancer research, 1964; Research Career award, NIH, 1964. Fellow N.Y. Acad. Scis.; mem. A.A.A.S., Am. Chem. Soc., Am. Soc. Biol. Chemists, Am. Soc. Human Genetics, Harvey Soc., Lymphold Club, N.Y. State Soc. Med. Research, Nat. Geog. Soc., Sigma Xi. Editor Archives Biochemistry and Biophysics, 1960—. Home: 780 Concourse Village W Bronx NY 10451 Office: 410 E 68th St New York City NY 10021

BENDINER, MARVIN ROBERT, editor, author; b. Pittsburgh, Dec. 15, 1909; s. William and Lillian (Schwartz) B.; student Coll. of City of N.Y., 1928-33; m. Kathryn Rosenberg; children—David, William, Margaret. Mng. editor The Nation, 1937-44, asso. editor, 1946-50. Lectr. Salzburg Seminar in Am. Studies, Austria, 1956; American correspondent The New Statesman. London, Eng., 1957-61. Guggenheim fellow, 1962. Recipient Benjamin Franklin Mag. Award, 1955. Member of Society of Mag. Writers (pres. 1964). Corr. Yank, the Army Weekly, 1944-45. Club: Nat. Press. Author: The Riddle of the State Department, 1942; White House Fever, 1960; Obstacle Course on Capitol Hill, 1964; Just Around the Corner, 1967; The Politics of Schools, 1969. Co-editor: The Strenuous Decade, 1970. Freelance contbr. principal Am. periodicals. Editorial bd. N.Y. Times, 1969—. Home: 45 Central Parkway Huntington NY 11743

BENDITT, EARL PHILIP, educator, med. scientist; b. Phila., Apr. 15, 1916; s. Milton and Sarah (Schoenfeld) B.; B.A., Swarthmore Coll., 1937; M.D., Harvard, 1941; m. Marcella Wexler, Feb. 18, 1945; children—John Milton, Alan, Joshua, Charles. Intern Phila. Gen. Hosp., 1941-43; resident pathology U. Chgo. Clinics, 1944; mem. faculty U. Chgo. Med. Sch., 1945-57, asso. prof. pathology, 1952-57; asst. dir. research LaRabida Children's Sanitarium, Chgo., 1950- 56; prof. pathology, chmn. dept. U. Wash. Sch. Medicine. 1957—; mem. sci. adv. bd. St. Jude Children's Research Hosp. Cons. USPHS-NIH, 1957- -; mem. subcom. NRC, 1957—; Commonwealth Fund fellow, vis. prof. Sir William Dun Sch. Pathology, U. Oxford (Eng.), 1965; mem. Nat. Environmental Health Scis. Adv. Com., 1971—. Recipient Med. Alumni award univ. Chgo., 1968. Mem. Am. Soc. Exptl. Pathology (council 1971—), Am. Soc. Pathologists and Bacteriologists, Soc. Exptl. Biology and Medicine, Phila. Physiol. Soc., Am. Soc. Cell Biology, Internat. Soc. Cell Biology, Am. Assn.

U. Profs. Pathology, Histochem. Soc. (pres. 1963- 64), Phi Beta Kappa, Sigma Xi. Mem. editorial bds. scis. publs. Home: 4528 W Laurel Dr NE Seattle WA 98105

BENDIX, REINHARD, educator, sociologist; b. Berlin, Germany, Feb. 25, 1916; s. Ludwig and Else (Henschel) B.; came to U.S., 1938, naturalized, 1943; B.A., U. Chgo., 1941, M.A., 1943, Ph.D., 1947; m. Jane L. Walstrum, July 5, 1940; children—Karen Moya, Erik Michael, John Steven. Instr. social sci. div. U. Chgo., 1943-46; asst. prof. dept. sociology U. Colo., 1946-47; asst. prof. dept. sociology and social instns., U. Cal. at Berkeley, 1947-51, chmn. dept., 1958-61, asso. prof., 1951-56; prof., 1956—, research sociologist Inst. Indsl. Relations, 1950—. dir. Study Center, Göttingen (Germany) U., 1968—; asst. prof. sociology Columbia, summer 1949; dir. edn. abroad program U. Cal., Göttingen, 1968-70. Fulbright research grant, 1953-54; Carnegie Corp. fellow, 1961-62; Theodor Heuss prof., Free U., Berlin, 1964-65; fellow St. Catherine's Coll. Oxford, 1965. Mem. Am. Sociol. Assn. (council 1959-64, v.p. 1963-64; MacIver award 1958; pres. 1969-70), Pacific Sociol. Assn., International Sociological Assn. (v.p. 1966-70), Am. Acad. Arts and Scis., Phi Beta Kappa (hon.). Author: Higher Civil Servants in American Society, 1949; Work and Authority in Industry, 1956: (with S. M. Lipset) Social Mobility in Industrial Society, 1959; Max Weber: an Intellectual Portrait, 1960; Nation-Building and Citzenship, 1964. Editor: (with S. M. Lipset) Class, Status and Power, 1953, rev. edit., 1966. Contbr. numerous articles profl. publs. Home: 3 Orchard Lane Berkeley CA 94704

BENDIXEN, HAROLD A., food co. exec.; b. Clinton, Ia., Oct. 4, 1910; s. Frederick A. and Katherine (Dierksen) B.; grad. Advanced Mgmt. Program, Harvard, 1953; m. Mildred M. Weaver, Apr. 5, 1941; children—John H., Barbara Jean (Mrs. Russell S. Neilsen), William C. With Clinton Corn Processing Co. div. Standard Brands Inc., Clinton, 1926—, sr. v.p., 1960, pres., 1961—, corp. v.p. parent co., 1962—; dir. Hawkeye Bancorp., First Nat. Bank, Clinton, Ia. Mem. Corn Refiners Assn. (chmn. bd. dirs.). Presbyn. Mason (32). Rotarian. Club: Clinton Country. Home: 3800 Lakewood Dr Clinton IA 52732 Office: Clinton Corn Processing Co Clinton IA 52732

BENECCHI, ROY J., aircraft mfg. co. exec.; b. Brockton, Mass., 1916; grad. Harvard, 1937. Vice pres. Lear Inc., 1943-62; pres., chief exec. officer Clavier Corp., Richmond Hill, N.Y., 1963-65; pres. Aeronca Corp., Torrance, Cal., 1945—. Office: 24751 S Crenshaw Blvd Torrance CA 90505*

BENEDEK, MARTIN HENRY, industralist; b. Budapest, Hungary, Feb. 15, 1904; s. Adolph and Julie (Roth) B.; brought to U.S., 1908, naturalized, 1916; student pub. schs., N.Y.C.; m. Leonore Friedman, Jan. 19, 1935; children—Warren Donald, A. Richard, Barry Paul. Pioneer in devel. components electronic industry; chmn., Gen. Instrument Corp., 1955-69, chmn. exec. com., 1969—, dir., 1955—. Founder Albert Einstein Coll. Medicine; pres., Beledek Found., Inc. Home: 900 Fifth Av New York City NY 10021 Office: 1775 Broadway New York City NY 10019

BENEDETTO, FRANCIS ARISTIDE, educator, physicist; b. Macon, Ga., Mar. 30, 1914; s. Aristide A. and Gertrude (Kennington) B.; A.B., St. Louis U., 1936; M.S., Fordham U., 1940, Ph.D., 1946. Joined Soc. of Jesus, 1931, ordained priest Roman Cath. Ch., 1944; mem. faculty Loyola U., New Orleans, 1947—, prof. physics, 1957—, chmn. dept. physics and math., 1955-57, chmn. dept. physics, 1957-67, chmn. research grants com., 1958-63, chmn. sci. facilities com., 1961-65, exec. asst. to pres., 1966—. Chief radiol. sect. New Orleans Civil Def., 1951-57, dep. chief, 1957—; regional counselor in physics for La., Am. Inst. Physics-Am. Assn. Physics Tchrs., 1961-63, 65-70. Recipient spl. citation and award outstanding record tng. young scientists, Research Corp., 1957. Mem. Am. Phys. Soc., Am. Assn. Physics Tchrs., Am. Geophys. Union, La. Acad. Sci., New Orleans Acad. Sci., Sigma Xi, Sigma Pi Sigma, Blue Key. Spl. research cosmic rays. Author articles. Address: Loyola Univ New Orleans LA 70118

BENEDICT, ANDREW BELL, Jr., banker; b. Nashville, July 6, 1914; s. Andrew B. and Anne Hillman (Scales) B.; student Wallace U. Sch., Nashville; B.A., Vanderbilt U., 1935; student Rutgers U. Grad. Sch. Banking, 1944; m. Sarah Richardson Bryan, Apr. 17, 1937; children—Henriette Richardson (Mrs. Russell F. Morris, Jr.), Andrew Bell III. With Am. Nat. Bank (became First Am. Nat. Bank), Nashville, 1935—, exec. v.p., 1951-60, pres., 1960-69, chmn., 1969—, also dir. Mem. regional adv. com. on banking policies and practices 8th Nat. Bank Region of U.S. Treasury. Mem., past chmn. Commn. Nashville Municipal Auditorium. Past dir. Vanderbilt U. Development Found.; bd. dirs. United Givers Fund, Nashville YMCA; trustee Meharry Med. Coll., Vanderbilt U. Mem. Am. Inst. Banking, Assn. Res. City Bankers (past pres., dir.) Phi Delta Theta, Omicron Delta Kappa. Methodist (mem. bd. publ.). Mason (Shriner, 33), Rotarian. Home: Curtiswood Lane Nashville TN 37204 Office: First American Nat Bank Nashville TN 37202

BENEDICT, BILL CLIFFORD, optical mfg. co. exec.; b. Dallas, Dec. 30, 1925; s. Willie C. and Gladys (Webb) B.; ed. pub. schs.; m. Mary Louise Alford, Mar. 15, 1946; children—Charlotte Ann, Dennis Wayne. With optical industry, 1946- 51; comml. flight instr., 1951-56; pres. Internat. Optical Co., Dallas, 1956—. Served with USNR, World War II. Home: 1220 Toltec St Dallas TX 75232 Office: 11362 Reeder Rd Dallas TX 75222

BENEDICT, CLARENCE CORWIN, mfg. co. exec.; b. Salt Lake City, Aug. 19, 1918; s. Elmer Homer and Sarah (Robinson) B.; certificate Bentley Sch. Accounting and Finance, 1938; student U. Pitts., 1948-50; m. Roberta June Wood, Feb. 21, 1969; children by previous marriage—Jay Lorin, Bruce Corwin, Richard Scott, Stephen Phillip, David Randall. With Goodyear Tire Co., 1938-41, Goodyear Aircraft Co., 1941-43, Standard Brands, Inc., 1946-47, H.J. Heinz Co., 1947-51, 52-53; asst. div. dir. OPS, 1951-52, Nordberg Mfg. Co., 1953-55, Okonite Co., 1955-57; with Chrysler Corp., 1957-68, asst. comptroller, 1965-68; v.p., controller Am. Standard, Inc., N.Y.C., 1968-71; v.p. finance Handleman Co., Detroit, 1971—. Mem. adv. com. wholesale and retail pricing Bur. Labor Statistics, 1967—. Served with USAAF, 1943-46. Mem. Am. Mgmt. Assn. (awards 1958, 62), Planning Execs. Inst. (pres. 1965-66, Ron Hutchinson award 1966, Neil Denen award 1969), Financial Execs. Inst., Nat. Assn. Accountants. Author articles in field. Home: 4793 Valleyview S Orchard Lake MI 48033 Office: 670 E Woodbridge Detroit MI 48226

BENEDICT, DONALD BANKS, chem. engr.; b. Katonah, N.Y., Feb. 10, 1910; s. DeWitt and Grace (Smith) B.; M.S. in Chem. Engring., U. Mich., 1933; m. Winifred Thornhill, Aug. 11, 1935 (dec. Jan. 1967); children—David Banks, Robert Thornhill, Jane Ellen, Helen Elizabeth. With Carbide & Carbon Chems. Co. div. Union Carbide Corp., N.Y.C., 1933—, successively tech. asst., asst. supt., plant supt., works mgr., v.p., 1933-55, div. pres., 1956-57, v.p. corp., 1957—. Pres. Thomas Hosp. Assn., South Charleston, W. Va., 1946-48. Mem. Am. Chem. Soc., Am. Inst. Chem. Engrs., Soc. Chem. Industry (chmn. Am. sect. 1963), Phi Lambda Upsilon, Tau Beta Pi. Holder patents. Home: 257 Millwood Rd Chappaqua NY 10514 Office: 270 Park Av New York City NY 10017

BENEDICT, DONALD LAVERNE, clergyman; b. Detroit, Sept. 12, 1917; s. Leon Boyce and Nina (Hagadorn) B.; A.B., Albion Coll., 1939, D.D. (hon.), 1966; B.D., Union Theol. Sem., N.Y.C., 1948; LL.D., Elmhurst Coll., 1966; 1966; m. Ann Kennette Chare, Jan. 25, 1947; children—Kennette, Sandra, Susan, Ruth. Ordained to ministry United Ch. Christ, 1948; founder E. Harlem Protestant Parish, N.Y.C., 1947-54, Inner City Protestant Parish, Cleve., 1954-60; exec. dir. Community Renewal Soc., 1960—; instr. Chgo. Theol. Sem., 1963—. Liberal Party candidate for N.Y.C. Council, 1953. Served with USAAF, 1944-46; PTO. Home: 5321 S Greenwood Av Chicago, IL 60615. Office: 116 S Michigan Av Chicago IL 60603

BENEDICT, DONALD LEE, ednl. administrator; b. Galesburg, Ill., July 5, 1916; s. Harry Lester and Bertha Nell (Howe) B; A.B., Knox Coll., 1938; Ph.D., U. Wis., 1943; m. Helen Hopkins, Jan. 1, 1944; children—Jane, Lee Hopkins, David Andrew. Teaching asst. U. Wis., 1938-41; asst. in sect. S-E, OSRD, 1941- 42; research physicist Sylvania Elec. Products, Inc., N.Y.C., 1943-45; research fellow electronics Harvard, 1945-49; asso. chmn. engring. research div. Stanford Research Inst., 1949-54, asst. dir., 1954, dir. phys. scis. div., 1956-59, dir. European office, Zurich, Switzerland, 1959-60, dir. phys. and biol. scis. div., 1960-61, asso. dir. for research, 1961-63, dir. Poulter Research Labs., 1963- 66, exec. dir. for phys. and indsl. scis., 1965-66; pres. Ore. Grad. Center, Portland, 1966-69; cons. advanced engrng. edn. AID, Seoul, Korea, 1970—. Recipient Alumni Achievement award Knox Coll., 1961. Mem. Am. Phys. Soc., Am. Math. Soc., I.E.E.E., Am. Inst. Aero. Sci. (dir. edn. San Francisco sect. 1960-64), Sci. Research Soc., Research Soc. Am. (past gov.), A.A.A.S., Sigma Xi. Home: 5051 S W Barnes Rd Portland OR 97221

BENEDICT, HARRY E., corp. exec.; b. Neillsville, Wis., May 20, 1890; s. J. Sidney and Celia Ruth (Reed) B.; B.A., U. Wis.; m. Frances Holmburg, Apr. 16, 1921; children—Russell Reed, Stephen Gordon. Officer, Nat. City Bank, N.Y. C., 1918-19; asso. Frank A. Vanderlip, 1919—; pres. Elcamp Corp.; v.p. Barker Bros., Inc.; chmn. and dir. Palos Verdes Corp.; dir. Am. Airlines, Bill Bros. Pub. Co. Sec. Wis. Highway Commn., 1912-16. Exec. sec. War Savings Commn., Treasury Dept., Washington, 1917-18, War Loan Bd., 1918. Mason (32). Clubs: University India House, Downtown Athletic (N.Y.C.); Sleepy Hollow Country. Office: 1 Pepper Tree Dr Portuguese Bend CA 90274

BENEDICT, MANSON, chem. engr., educator; b. Lake Linden, Mich., Oct. 9, 1907; s. C. Harry and Lena I. (Manson) B.; B. Chemistry, Cornell, 1928; M.S., Mass. Inst. Tech., 1932, Ph.D., 1935; m. Marjorie Oliver Allen, July 6, 1935; children—Mary Hannah (Mrs. Myran C. Sauer, Jr.), Marjorie Alice (Mrs. Martin Cohn). Nat. Research Council fellow chemistry, 1935-36; research asso. geophysics Harvard, 1936-37; research chemist M.W. Kellogg Co., 1938-43; in charge process design gaseous diffusion plant for uranium-235 Kellex Corp., 1943-46; dir. process development Hydrocarbon Research, Inc., 1946-51; tech. asst. to gen. mgr. U.S. A.E.C., 1951-52; prof. nuclear engring. Mass. Inst. Tech., 1951-69, Institute 1969—, prof., 1969—, head dept. nuclear engineering, 1958—; sci. adviser Nat. Research Corp., 1951-58, dir., 1962-67; mem. gen. advisory committee U.S. AEC, 1958-68, chmn., 1962-64; mem. Mass. Adv. council on Radiation Protection; dir. Atomic Indsl. Forum. Forum. Recipient William H. Walker award Am. Inst. Chem. Engrs., 1947, recipient Founders award 1965; Indsl. and Engring. Chemistry award Am. Chem. Soc., 1962; Perkin medal Society of Chemical Industry; Robert E. Wilson award in nuclear chem. engring.; Arthur H. Compton award Am. Nuclear Soc. Fellow Am. Nuclear Soc., Am. Acad. Arts and Sci.; mem. Am. Inst. Chem. Engrs., Nat. Acad. scis., Nat. Acad. Sigma Engring., Sigma Xi. Clubs: Cosmos (Washington, D.C.); Weston (Mass.) Golf. Co-editor: Engineering Developments in the Gaseous Diffusion Process, 1949. Co-author: Nuclear Chemical Engineering, 1957. Home: 25 Byron Rd Weston MA 02193 Office: Dept Nuclear Engring Mass Inst Tech 02139 Cambridge MA 02139

BENEDICTY, MARIO GUSTAVO DE, educator, mathematician; b. Trieste, Italy, July 16, 1922; s. Gustavo Carlo de and Emma (Serti) de B.; D. in Math. Sci., U. Rome, 1946, Libero Docente in Geometria, 1951; m. Alfonsina Mucciante, July 16, 1947; children—Gustavo, Franca. Came to U.S., 1958, naturalized, 1968, assistant, then associate professor University of Rome, 1947-58; mem. faculty U. Pitts., 1958—, prof. math. 1960—, chmn. dept., 1963-69; vis. prof. U. Pitts., 1957, U. B.C., 1960-62. Served with Italian Army, 1943-45. Decorated Bronze medal, War cross. Mem. Unione Matematica Italiana, Circolo Matematico di Palermo, N.Y. Acad. Scis., Canadian Math. Congress, Math. Assn. Am., Am. Math. Soc., A.A.A.S., Sigma Xi. Clubs: Touring (Milan, Italy); University (Pitts.). Co-editor: Introduzione alla Geometria Algebrica, 1948; Lezioni sulle Funzioni Analitiche di piu Variabili Complesse, 1958. Contbr., editor math.; Dizionario Enciclopedico dell'Enciclopedia Italiana, 1952-58, Enciclopedia Italiana Appendix III. Contbr. articles to math. jours. Home: 53 Academy Av Pittsburgh PA 15228

BENEDUM, PAUL GREGORY, bus. exec.; b. Cameron, W. Va., Feb. 17, 1902; s. Charles Yantis and Leota (Hicks) B.; A.B. in Metall. Engring. and Geology, Ohio State U., 1927; LL.D., Capital U., Columbus, O., 1949; D.Sc. (hon.), W. Va. Wesleyan Coll., 1951; LL.D., Waynesburg Coll., 1955, Davis and Elkins Coll., 1961, Ohio State U., 1971; D.Hum., Salem Coll., 1963; m. Beatrice Wileen Ludwig, Apr. 17, 1928; 1 son, Paul G. Jr. Geologist, Benedum-Trees Interests, 1927-30; with M. L. Benedum as head, geol. expdn. to Lake Van region, Turkey, 1930; geologist and dist. mgr., Pa., and later the Southwest, Benedum- Trees, 1930-43; pres., dir. Hiawatha Oil & Gas Co. until 1961, dir., 1961—; pres., dir. Penn-Ohio Gas Co. until 1961, dir., 1961—; pres., chief exec. officer, dir. Plymouth Oil Co., 1961-63; pres., dir. Bentex Oil Corp., 1963-69; pres. Bendum-Trees Oil Co., 1963—, also dir.; v.p. Republic Pipe Line Co., dir. subsidiary cos.; dir. Pitts. Nat. Bank. Active Boy Scouts Am. Pres., Claude Worthington Benedum Found., 1959—; trustee Waynesburg Coll., Shady Side Acad., W. Va. Wesleyan Coll.; bd. dirs. Western Pa. Hosp., Children's Home of Pitts., Western Pa. Sch. for Blind Children; bd. dirs., treas. Fellowship Christian Athletics. bd. mgrs. Children's Hosp. Mem. Nat. Petroleum Council, Military Petroleum Adv. Bd., Def. Services Com. of Am. Petroleum Inst. Mem. Sigma Gamma Epsilon, Kappa Kappa Psi, Delta Chi. Methodist. Clubs: Fox Chapel Golf, Duquesne, Pitts. Athletic Assn. (Pitts.); Gibson Island (Md.) Yacht Squadron, Bayou, Ramada (Houston); Pike Run Country (Jones Mills, Pa.); Army Navy (Washington); Laurel Valley Golf, Rolling Rock (Ligonier); Edgartown (Mass.) Yacht; Ocean Reef (Key Largo, Fla.); Hole-In-The Wall Golf, Naples Sailing, Naples Yacht, Port Royal Beach, Royal Poinciana Golf (Naples, Fla.); Xanadu Yacht and Tennis (Freeport, Grand Bahama Island). Home: McDowell Rd RD 2 Ligonier PA 15658 Office: Benedum-Trees Bldg Pittsburgh PA 15222

BENEDUM, THOMAS RICHARD, lawyer, univ. regent; b. Spencerville, O., Nov. 14, 1905; s. Obediah Harvey and Leona (Cahill) B.; LL.B., U. Okla., 1928; m. Lucille Williams, June 2, 1930; 1 son, Benjamin Thomas. Admitted to Okla. bar, 1928; practice in Norman, 1930—; parnter firm Benedum, Haast Benedum. Dir. City Nat. Bank Norman, Norman Bldg. & Loan Assn., Okla. Facturing Services, Acid Engrs., Inc., Service Chemicals, Inc., Naturizer, Inc. Mem. Okla. Personnel Bd., 1946- 52, chmn., 1948-51. Bd. regents U. Okla., 1947-61, pres., 1954-61; trustee U. Okla. Found.; incorporator, trustee Okla. Bar Found. Recipient citation for pub. service 45th N.G. Div., 1960; citation for achievement U. Okla., 1958, for meritorious service as regent, 1962. Mem. Am., Okla., Cleveland County (past pres.) bar assns., Norman C. of C. (past pres.), Pi Kappa Alpha, Pi Alpha Delta. Democrat. Methodist. Rotarian (past pres. Norman). Home: 501 Lahoma St Norman OK 73069 Office: City Nat Bldg Norman OK 73069

BENENATI, ROBERT F., educator; b. Bklyn., Jan. 28, 1921; s. Frank and Catherine (Traina) B.; B.Chem. Engring., Bklyn. Poly. Inst., 1942, M.Chem. Engring., 1949, Ph.D., 1955; m. Jeanne V. Benenati, Dec. 30, 1944; children—Frank J., Irene A., Robert M., Joseph, John P. Head operating dept. Kellex Corp., 1944-45; with Hydrocarbon Research, Inc., 1945-49; mem. faculty Bklyn. Poly. Inst., 1949—, now prof. chem. engring., also dir. computer center, 1966—; cons. in field, 1952—. Mem. W. Hempstead (L.I.) Sch. Bd., 1960-63. Candidate for N.Y. Senate, 1965, N.Y. State Constl. Conv., 1966. Mem. Am. Inst. Chem. Engring., Am. Chem. Soc., Am. Nuclear Soc., Assn. Computing Machinery, Sigma Xi, Tau Beta Pi, Phi Lambda Upsilon. Mem. Conservative Party. Roman Cath. Home: 75 Deepdale Dr Manhasset NY 11030 Office: 333 Jay St Brooklyn NY 11201

BENEPE, JAMES LORIMER, Jr., hosp. dir.; b. St. Paul, Nov. 3, 1927; s. James Lorimer and Gladys (Bond) B.; B.A., Macalester Coll., 1950; M.D., Washington U., St. Louis; m. Sheila K. Hanson, May 26, 1956; children—James Lorimer III, Mark John. Psychiat. resident U. Minn., 1958; intern Madigan Gen. Hosp., Ft. Lewis, Wash., 1954-55; psychiat. resident VA Hosp., Mpls., 1955-58; staff psychiatrist VA Hosp., Sheridan, Wyo., 1958-60, chief staff, 1960-68; dir. VA Hosp., Northampton, Mass., 1968—. Served with USNR, 1945-46, AUS, 1954-55. Mem. Izaak Walton League (bd. dirs.), Am., Western Mass. psychiat. assns., Nat. Wildlife Fedn., Wilderness Soc., Nat. Rifle Assn., Am. Trapshooters Assn., Duck, Unlimited, Esalen Inst. Republiican. Episcopalian. Elk. Home: VA Hosp., Northampton, MA 01060.

BENERITO, RUTH ROGAN, (Mrs. Frank H. Benerito), chemist; b. New Orleans, Jan. 12, 1916; d. John Edward and Bernadette (Elizardi) Rogan; B.S., H. Sophie Newcomb Coll., 1935; postgrad. Bryn Mawr Coll., 1935-36; M.S., Tulane U., 1938; Ph.D., U. Chgo., 1948; m. Frank Henshaw Benerito, Aug. 22, 1950. Instr. chemistry Randolph-Macon Woman's Coll., Lynchburg, Va., 1940-43, Newcomb Coll., New Orleans, 1943- 47; asst. prof. chemistry Tulane U., New Orleans, 1947-53, mem. grad. faculty, 1960—, lectr. dept. biochemistry med. sch., 1960—; phys. chemist fat emulsion program So. Regional Lab., Dept. Agr., New Orleans, 1953-58, supervisory phys. chemist, head phys. chem. investigations cotton chem. reactions lab., 1958—. Recipient Distinguished Service award U.S. Dept. Agr., 1964, 70, Distinguished Service award New Orleans Fed. Exec. Assn., 1967, Fed. Woman's award U.S. Civil Service Commn., 1968. Fellow Am. Inst. Chemists; mem. Am. Chem. Soc. (So. Chemist award 1968, Garvan medal 1970); Am. Oil Chem. Soc., Am. Assn. Textile Chemists and Colorists, Sci. Research Soc. Am., Sigma Xi, Sigma Delta Epsilon. Contbr. articles profl. publs. Home: 4733 Marigny St New Orleans LA 70122 Office: 110 Robert E Lee St New Orleans LA 70124

BENESCH, ALFRED ABRAHAM, lawyer; b. Cleve., Mar. 7, 1879; s. Isidore Julius and Bertha (Federman) B.; A.B. magna cum laude, Harvard, 1900, A.M., 1901, LL.B., 1903; LL.D., Fenn College, 1955, Western Reserve U., Cleveland, 1965, H.L.D. (hon.), Hebrew Union College, 1962; married to Helen Newman, Nov. 29, 1906. Admitted to Ohio bar, 1903, since practiced law in Cleveland, Ohio; now with firm of Benesch, Friedlander, Mendelson & Coplan. Mem. Cleve. City Council, 1912-13, dir. Pub. Safety, 1914-15; dir. commerce State of Ohio, 1935-39; area rent dir. Northeastern Ohio, 1942-45; mem. Bd. Edn., 1926-63, pres., 1933-34. Presdl. elector Democratic Party, 1941. Vice pres. Nat. Jewish Hosp.; trustee Cuyahoga County Hospital; member bd. of trustees Mt. Sinai Hospital; member Bur. Jewish Edn., Jewish Community Fedn.; v.p. Cleve. Jewish Orphan Home. Recipient Distinguished Service awards Cleve. Community Fund, 1951, Citizens League, 1952, Cleve. C. of C., Jewish Welfare Fedn., Jewish Nat. Fund. Bd. Edn. Mem. Phi Beta Kappa. Mem. B'nai B'rith (past pres. Grand Lodge 2). Clubs: Commerce, Oakwood (Cleve.). Author articles. Home: 2515 Kemper Rd Cleveland OH 44120 Office: Citizens Bldg Cleveland OH 44114

BENET, EDUARDO RAMON, banker;b. Cienfuegos, Cuba, June 13, 1905; s. Eduardo Benet and Teresa (Prieto) Castellon; degree in bus. adminstrn., Champanac Coll., Cienfuegos, 1920; m. Maria Cristina Consuegra, Sept. 12, 1931; children—Eduardo Andres, Gabriel Octavio, Alex. Asst. mgr. Royal Bank Can., Havana, Cuba, 1944; v.p. Trust Co. Cuba, Havana, 1945-56; pres. Banco Continental Cubano, Havana, 1956-60; v.p. internat. banking div. First Wis. Nat. Bank, Milw., 1962-66, sr. v.p., 1966—. Mem. Bankers Assn. for Fgn. Trade, Milw. World Trade Club, Internat. Trade Club Chgo., Nat. Fgn. Trade Council Clubs: Forex, Rotary. Home: 2107 N Terrace Av Milwaukee, WI 53217. Office: 743 N Water St Milwaukee WI 53201

BENET, JAMES, journalist; b. Port Washington, N.Y., Jan. 7, 1914; s. William Rose and Teresa (Thompson) B.; A.B., Stanford, 1935; m. Mary Elizabeth Liles, Dec. 13, 1938 (div. 1952); children—Judith (Mrs. Philip Richardson), Mary Kathleen, Peter; m. 2d, Jane Ann Gugel, Sept. 16, 1954. With New Republic mag., 1936-37, 38-39, N.Y.C. bur. Tass, 1939-46; free-lance writer, 1946-48; mem. staff San Francisco Chronicle, 1948-68, edn. editor, 1957-68; with KQED-TV, San Francisco, 1968—; asso. prof. journalism San Francisco State Coll., 1959-69. Served with Internat. Brigade, Spanish Republican Army, 1937-38. Mem. Am. Newspaper Guild. Democrat. Club: Sierra. Author: A Private Killing, 1948; The Knife Behind You, 1950; A Guide to San Francisco and the Bay Area, rev. edit., 1967; SCSD; The Project and the Schools, 1967. Contbr. to Academics on the Line, 1970. Home: 181 Edgehill Way San Francisco, CA 94127. Office: 525 4th St San Francisco CA 94107

BENET, LAURA, author; b. Ft. Hamilton, N.Y. Harbor; d. James Walker and Frances (Nell) Rose Benet; grad. Emma Willard Sch., Troy, N.Y.; A.B., Vassar Coll.; Litt.D. (hon.), Moravian Coll., Bethlehem, Pa. Settlement worker, Spring St. Settlement, N.Y.C., 1915-17; placement worker Children's Aid Soc., N.Y.C., 1917; sanitary insp. U.S. Red Cross, Augusta, Ga., 1917-19; worker St. Bartholomews House, 1924-25; sec., asst. editor book pages N.Y. Evening Post, 1927-28, N.Y. Evening Sun, 1928-29; book review editor's asst. and book review substitute, N.Y. Times, summer 1930; free lance writer, 1930—. Received medal as honor poet, Nat. Poetry Center, 1936; poems recorded at Library of Congress, 1958. Democrat. Episcopalian. Author: Fairy Bread (poems), 1921; Noah's Dove (poems) 1929; Goods and Chattels (fiction), 1930; Basket for a Fair (poems), 1934; The Boy Shelley (biography), 1937; The Hidden Valley (fiction), 1938; Enchanting Jenny Lind (biography), 1939; Roxana Rampant (fiction), 1940; Young Edgar Allan Poe (biography), 1941; Come Slowly, Eden: A Novel about Emily Dickinson, 1942; Caleb's Luck (for children), 1942; Washington Irving, Explorer of American Legend, 1944; Is Morning Sure? (poems), 1947; Thackeray of the Great Heart and the Humorous Pen (biography), 1947;

Barnum's First Circus and Other Stories (for children), 1949; Famous American Poets, 1950; Coleridge, Poet of Wild Enchantment, 1952; Stanley, Invincible Explorer (biography), 1955; Famous American Humorists, 1959; In Love With Time (book of poems), 1959; Horseshoe Nails, 1965; Famous Poets for Young People, 1964; Famous English and American Essayists, 1966; Famous Storytellers, 1968; Introductions to Classics; articles, verse to periodicals. Mem. Poetry Soc. Am., Women Poets, Craftsmen, P.E.N. Club, Pen and Brush Club (hon.). Home: Hotel Van Rensselaer 17 E 11th St New York City NY 10003 Office: care Dodd Meade & Co 79 Madison Av New York City NY 10016

BENEZET, LOUIS TOMLINSON, univ. pres.; b. La Crosse, Wis., June 29, 1915; s. Louis Paul and Genevieve (Tomlinson) B.; A.B., Dartmouth, 1936, LL.D., 1966; A.M., Reed Coll., 1939; Ph.D., Columbia, 1942; LL.D., Mt. Union Coll., 1949, Pitts., 1953, Waynesburg Coll., 1953, U. Denver, 1950, Knox Coll., 1961, Loyola U., 1963, Colo. Coll., 1963, U. Colo., 1963, U. Cal., 1967; L.H.D., Westminister Coll., 1960, Hebrew Union Coll., 1969; summer study Harvard, 1937, 38; m. Mildred Jean Twohy, June 27, 1940; children—Joel (dec.), Laura, Julia, Barbara, Martha. Instr. The Hill Sch., 1936-38; asso. psychology resident adviser Reed Coll., 1938-40; fellow in psychology Coll. City N.Y., 1941-42; asso. prof. psychology, asst. dir. admissions Knox Coll., 1942-43; asst. dir. extension sch. Syracuse U., 1946, asst. dean Univ. Coll., 1946-47, asst. to chancellor, 1947-48; pres. Allegheny Coll., 1948-55, Colo. Coll., 1955-63, Claremont (Cal.) Grad. Sch. and U. Center, 1963-71, State U. N.Y., Albany, 1971—. Pres. Pa. Assn. of Colls. and Univs., 1951-52; chmn. Ind. Coll. Funds of Am., 1961-62. Mem. Com. on Edn. of Women, 1953-56; adv. com. Vets. Rehab., Edn., VA, Washington, 1955-59; spl. cons. Dept. Health, Edn. and Welfare, 1959-60; organizer, 1st pres. Pikes Peak United Fund, 1961-63; mem. Def. Adv. Com. on Edn. in Armed Forces, 1963-65; chmn. univ. relations com. AID, 1966-67; mem. instnl. relations com. NSF, 1967—, chmn. com., 1969-70; nat. adv. council Upward Bound. Served as ednl. services officer USNR, 1943-46, edn. officer, 7th Fleet, S.W. Pacific, 1944-45. Mem. Western Coll. Assn. (pres. 1969-70), Assn. Am. Colls. (chmn. commn. acad. freedom & tenure 1955-58, commn. liberal edn. 1959-63), Assn. Colls. Colo. (pres. 1959-60), Am. Council on Edn. (mem. exec. com. 1955-58, bd. dirs. 1961-64, chmn. 1965-66), Omicron Delta Kappa (hon.), Phi Beta Kappa, Sigma Alpha Epsilon. Club: Hudson River. Author: General Education in the Progressive College, 1943. Contbr. articles to ednl. periodicals and books. Home: Newtonville NY 12128 Office: Office of Pres State Univ NY Albany NY 12203

BENFEY, OTTO THEODOR, educator, editor; b. Berlin, Germany, Oct. 31, 1925; s. Eduard and Lotte (Fleischmann) B.; B.Sc., Univ. Coll., London, Eng., 1945, Ph.D., 1947; m. Rachel Elizabeth Thomas, Aug. 28, 1949; children—Stephen, Philip, Christopher, Karen. Came to U.S., 1946, naturalized, 1952. Postdoctoral research fellow Columbia, 1947-48; from instr. to asso. prof. Haverford Coll., 1948-55; research fellow Harvard, 1955-56; mem. faculty Earlham Coll., Richmond, Ind., 1956—, now prof. chemistry and history of sci., and chmn. dept. chemistry, 1971—; editor Chemistry, 1964—; lectr., cons. in field. U.S. del. Inter-Am. Conf. Chemistry Teaching, Buenos Aires, 1965, U.S.-Japan Chem. Edn. Conf., Berkeley, Cal., 1968, Internat. Symposium Chem. Edn., Sao Paulo, Brazil, 1971. Del. Soc. Friends World Conf., Oxford, Eng., 1952, Guilford, N.C., 1967. Recipient Doan Distinguished Tchr. Travel award Earlham Coll., 1961; E. Harris Harbison award distinguished teaching Danforth Found., 1967; Chemistry Tchr. award Mfg. Chemists Assn., 1967; Fulbright-Hays research-study award Kwansei Gakuin, Japan, 1970-71. Mem. Am. Assn. U. Profs., History Sci. Soc., Soc. Social Responsibility in Sci., Am. Civil Liberties Union, Assn. Harvard Chemists, Assn. Asian Studies, Am. Chem. Soc. (chmn. div. history chemistry 1966), Sigma Xi. Author: From Vital Force to Structural Formulas, 1964; Classics in the Theory of Chemical Combination, 1963; The Names and Structures of Organic Compounds, 1966; Introduction to Organic Reaction Mechanisms, 1971; also articles, introductions and chpts. books. Translator: (Ernst Cassirer) Determinism and Inderterminism in Modern Physics, 1956. Editorial bd. Revista Iberoamericana de Educacion Quimica, 1966—. Home: 809 SW 5th St Richmond IN 47374

BENGELSDORF, IRVING SWEM, sci. writer; b. Chgo., Oct. 23, 1922; s. Jacob and Frieda (Wiener) B.; B.S., U. Ill., 1943; postgrad. Cornell U., 1943-44; M.S., U. Chgo., 1948, Ph.D. (AEC fellow), 1951; m. Beverly Devorah Knapp, June 12, 1949; children—Ruth Ann, Lea Beth, Judith Eve. Research fellow Cal. Inst. Tech., 1951-52; instr. chem. dept. U. Cal. at Los Angeles, 1952-54, sr. lectr. chemistry, 1966-67, 71; research chemist Gen. Electric Research Lab., Schenectady, 1954-59; research group leader Texaco-U.S. Rubber Research Center, Parsippany, N.J., 1959-60; sr. scientist U.S. Borax Research Corp., Anaheim, Cal., 1960-63; sci. editor Los Angeles Times, 1963-70; dir., lectr. sci. communication Cal. Inst. Tech., 1971—; scientist columnist, contbg. editor Enterprise Sci. Service of Newspaper Enterprise Assn., 1971—. Sr. lectr. Sch. Journalism U. So. Cal., 1967-69, chemistry dept., 1971. Served with USNR, 1944-46; PTO. Recipient Journalism award Cons. Engrs. Assn. Cal., 1963, 65, First Place Safety Story award Am. Trucking Assns., 1963, Thomas L. Stokes award hon. mention Nat. Resources Conservation, 1963, 64, Jean M. Kline Meml. award Am. Cancer Soc., 1965, James T. Grady award Am. Chem. Soc., 1967, Humanitarian award Hadassah, 1967; Claude Bernard Science Journalism award Nat. Soc. Med. Research, 1968, A.A.A.S.-Westinghouse Sci. Writing award, 1967, 69. Mem. A.A.A.S., Am. Chem. Soc., Chem. Soc. (London), Nat. Assn. Sci. Writers, Sigma Xi, Sigma Delta Chi. Author: Spaceship Earth: People and Pollution , 1969. Writer news column Atoms and Men, 1961—. Contbr. profl. jours. Patentee in field. Home: 256 S Arden Blvd Los Angeles CA 90004

BENGERT, GEORGE WENDELL, pharm. mfr.; b. Paterson, N.J.; s. Frank X. and Jennette M. (Derks) B.; student Middlebury Coll., 1918; Ph.C., Columbia, 1922; m. Jane C. Hartigan, Nov. 25, 1935; children—William C., Mary J. With Norwich Pharmacal Co. (N.Y.), 1922—, successively research chemist, asst. dir. lab., asst. supt., supt., v.p., exec. v.p., 1922-56, pres., 1956-64, chmn. bd., 1964—, also chmn. exec. com., dir.; dir. Morton-Norwich Products Inc., Eastern Diversified, Inc., Mid-State Vernon Downs Track, Small Bus. Investment Corp., N.Y. Bd. trustees Norwich YMCA; bd. Health Information Found.; regent LeMoyne Coll.; chmn. bd. trustees Marymount Coll. Served with U.S. Army, 1918. Mem. Am. Chem. Soc., Am. Mgmt. Assn., Pharm. Mfrs. Assn. (dir.), World Med. Assn. (dir. U.S. com.). Home: 26 Hayes St Norwich NY 13815 Office: 17 Eaton Av Norwich NY 13815

BENGTSON, JOHN ROBERT, educator; b. Chgo., Nov. 21, 1919; s. Carl O. and Edith (Matson) B.; B.A., Augustana Coll., Ill., 1946; M.A., U. Ia., 1947, Ph.D., 1953; m. Getrude Raab, Dec. 21, 1945. Tchr., Burlington (Ia.) High Sch. and Jr. Coll., 1947-50; faculty U. Minn., 1953-54; asst. curator newspaper library Minn. Hist. Soc., 1954-59; faculty No. State Coll., Aberdeen, S.D., 1959-61; faculty Wis. State U.-Oshkoh, 1961—, prof. history, 1966—, chmn. social sci. div., 1965-68, chmn. history dept., 1964-71. Served with AUS, 1942-46. Author: Nazi War Aims: The Plans for the Thousand Year Reich, 1962. Home: 1210 E Forest Av Neenah WI 54956 Office: Wis State Univ Oshkosh WI 54901

BENGTSON, THORD ANDERS JOHANNES, diplomat, economist; b. Helsingborg, Sweden, Dec. 10, 1916; s. Sture Henning and Hildur (Aberg) B.; m. Geneva Mae Clark, Dec. 11, 1944; children— Anne, Jan. Attaché Swedish legation, Rio de Janeiro, 1941-46; with Ministry Fgn. Affairs, Stockholm, 1946-47; comml. attaché Swedish legation, Rio de Janeiro, 1947-50; with Ministry Fgn. Affairs, Stockholm, 1950-51; comml. attaché Swedish legation, Pretoria, 1951-57; Swedish consul, Kenya, Tanganyika, Uganda, Zanzibar, 1957-63; 1st sec. comml. Swedish embassy, Lima, Peru, 1963-66; Swedish trade commr., Zambia, 1966-67; Swedish comml. attaché, Manila, 1967-69; spl. econ. advisor Swedish embassy, Washington, also Swedish Mission to UN, N.Y.C., 1969—. Home: 5400 Blackstone Rd Washington DC 20016 Office: 2249 R St NW Washington DC 20008

BEN-GURION, DAVID, Israeli diplomat; b. Plonsk, Poland, Oct. 1886; educated privately and at U. Constantinople; D.H.L., Jewish Theol. Sem. Am., 1952; Ph.D., Hebrew U., Jerusalem, 1957; LL.D., Brandeis U., 1960, Rangoon U., 1961; D.Architecture, Israel Inst. Tech., Haifa, 1962; m. 1917; 3 children. Went to Palestine, then under Turkish rule, 1906; became active in Palestine Labor Party and editor of its jour., 1915; exiled by Turkish govt.; came to U.S. and helped organize pioneers for settlement in Palestine; helped organize and extend Jewish Legion (Am., Brit. and Palestinian vols.) for service in World War I; served as pvt. with 40th Bn., Royal Fusiliers, in Gen. Allenby's operations against Turks; became mem. Gen. Council of Zionist Orgn., 1920; gen. sec. Gen. Fedn. Labor, 1921-35; mem. exec. bd. Jewish Agy. for Palestine, 1933, chmn. bd., 1948; proclaimed Independence of Israel, May 14, 1948; head provisional govt. and minister of def., 1948-49; prime minister of Israel and minister of def., 1949-53, 55-63. Leader of Mapai (Labour) Party. Recipient Bublick prize Hebrew U., 1949; Bialik Lit. prize for Judaica, 1952; Henrietta Szold award Hadassah Women's Zionist Orgn. Am., 1958. Author: PalestineA Historical, Economic and Geographical Research Survey, 1917; We and Our Neighbors, 1930; The Working Class and the Nation, 1933; The Struggle (5 vols.), 1949; Israel at War, 1950; Vision and Implementation, 5 vols., 1951-57; Mimaamad Leam, 1955; Rebirth and Destiny of Israel, 1954; The Sinai Campaign, 1959; Eternity of Israel, 1963; Israel-Years of Challenge, 1963; Ben-Gurion Looks Back, 1965; Dvarim Kehavayatam; Talks with Arabs; Michtavim LePaula, 1969; The Restored State of Israel, 2 vols., 1969; Iyunim Batanach, 1969; Memoirs, 1971; and others. Home: Sdeh Boker Negey Jerusalem Israel

BENGZON, CESAR, judge Internat. Ct. Justice. Address: Internat Ct Justice UN New York City NY 10017*

BEN-HAIM, PAUL, composer; b. Munich, Germany, July 5, 1897; s. Heinrich and Anna (Schulmann) Frankenburger; student Acad. Music and U. Munich, 1915-16, 18-20; m. Helena Acham, Aug. 10, 1934; 1 son, Yoram. Asst. to Bruno Walter, later Knappertsbusch, State Opera Munich, 1920-24; condr. Opera House, Augsburg, Germany, 1924-32; left Germany, 1933, settled permanently in Tel-Aviv, Israel, 1933; tchr. Shulamith Conservatoire, 1933-49; dir. Jerusalem Acad. Music, 1949-54, pedagogical adviser, 1960-66; occasionally condr. own works; works performed throughout world. Recipient Tel-Aviv Municipality prize for 1st symphony, 1945, for 2d symphony, 1953; Israel State prize for The Sweet Psalmist of Israel, 1957; decorated 1st class Cross Merit (German Fed. Republic), 1968. Mem. Israeli Composers League (hon. pres.), Author, Composers and Pubs. Assn. Israel (hon. pres.). Compositions include symphonic and chamber music, songs, chorals works, pieces for several instruments. Address: 11 Aharonowitz St 63566 Tel-Aviv Israel

BEN-HARON, MOHAMED, Malaysian diplomat; b. Malaysia, Apr. 11, 1943; student Malay Coll., 1959- 60, U. Wales, 1961-64. Asst. sec. Ministry Fgn. Affairs, Malaysia, 1964-65; 3d sec. High Commn. for Malaysia, India, 1965-67, 1st sec., 1967-68; 1st sec. Embassy of Malaysia, Washington, 1969-70, counselor, 1971—. Del. 24th Session UN Gen. Assembly. Bd. govs. Muslim Centre, Washington. Home: 2807 N Quebec St Arlington VA 22207 Office: 2401 Massachusetts Av NW Washington DC 20008

BENHIMA, AHMED TAIBI, Moroccan diplomat; b. Safi, Morocco, Nov. 13, 1927; s. Taibi and Rquia (Benhida) B.; grad. Faculty of Law, U. Nancy (France), 1951, Polit. Scis. Inst., Paris, France, 1953. Pres. Moroccan Students Assn., Paris, 1951-54; rep. Independence Party in France, Switzerland and Belgium, 1952-54; cabinet dir. of minister charge negotiations for independence, 1956; sec.-gen. Moroccan delegation which conducted negotiations with France and Spain for independence, 1956; joined Moroccan Fgn. Service, 1956; counsellor, Paris, 1956-57; ambassador to Italy, 1957-59; sec. gen. Ministry Fgn. Affairs, 1959-61; head Moroccan delegation to UN, 1959-64, permanent rep. of Morocco to UN, 1961-64; fgn. minister of Morocco, 1964-67; ambassador of Morocco to UN, 1967—. Home: Park Lane Hotel New York City NY 10001 Office: 342 Madison Av New York City NY 10017

BENICHOU, PAUL, educator, author; b. Tlemcen, Algeria, Sept. 19, 1908; s. Chemoul and Rachel (Serfati) B.; Licence-ès-Lettres, Sorbonne, Paris, France, 1928, Agrégation des Lettres, 1930; student Ecole Normale Supérieure, 1926-29; m. Gina Labin, Dec. 26, 1929; 1 dau., Sylvia (Mrs. Jacques Roubaud). Came to U.S., 1958. Prof. French and classic lits. Lycée Janson de Sailly, 1937, Inst. Francais d'Etudes supèrieures, Buenos Aires, 1943-49, Lycée Condorcet, 1949-58; prof. French lit. Harvard, 1959—. Served with French Army, 1929-30, 39-40. Author: Morales du grand siècle, 1948; L'écrivain et ses travaux, 1967; Creación poética en el romancero tradicional, 1968; Romancero judeo-español de Marrucecos, 1968; Nerval et la Chanson folklorique, 1970; also articles and revs. Home: 139 Av Jean Jaurès Paris 19 France Office: Boylston Hall Harvard Univ Cambridge MA 02138

BENIDICKSON, WILLIAM MOORE, Canadian senator; b. Dauphin, Man., Can., Apr. 8, 1911; s. Christian and Gertrude (Moore) B.; B.A., U. Man., 1932, LL.B., 1936; m. Agnes Richardson, Nov. 27, 1947; children—William James, Kristjan, Kathleen. Mem. Canadian House of Commons from Kenora-Rainy River Dist., 1945-65; parliamentary asst. to minister transp., 1951, to minister finance, 1953- 57; mem. Privy Council, minister mines and tech. surveys, 1963-65; mem. Canadian Senate, 1965—. Office: Canadian Senate Ottawa Ontario Canada

BENINCASA, PIUS A., bishop; b. Niagara Falls, N.Y., July 8, 1913; grad. Buffalo Diocesan Sem., 1931, Propagation U., Lateran U., Rome, Italy, D.C.L., 1952. Ordained priest Roman Catholic Ch., 1937; parish work, Buffalo, 1937-43; sec. Buffalo Diocesan Tribunal, 1947-50, vice-officialis, 1952-54; served with Papal sec. of state, 1954-64; titular bishop of Buruni and aux. bishop Buffalo, 1964—. Chaplain, AUS, World War II. Address: 157 Cleveland Dr Buffalo NY 14215

BENINGTON, HERBERT DAVIDSON, govt. ofcl.; b. Montreal, Can., Oct. 28, 1928; s. Herbert Hingston and Marie-Luce (Beaubien) B.; S.B. in Elec. Engring., Mass. Inst. Tech., 1950; B.A., Oxford (Eng.) U., 1952; m. Anne Merithew Hills, Jan. 11, 1958; children—George Beaubien, Joel Hills, Eliza Merithew. Asso. group head Lincoln Labs., Mass. Inst. Tech., 1953-57; group head RAND Corp., Santa Monica, Cal., 1957; asso. div. mgr. System Devel. Corp., Santa Monica, 1957-63; tech. dir., joint command control requirements group Office Joint Chiefs Staff, Dept. Def., 1963-65; dir. command control communications and intelligence Office Asst. Sec. Def., 1965-67, asst. dir. command and control, def. research and engring., 1967-70, dep. dir. electronics and information systems, def. research and engring., 1970—. Rhodes scholar, 1950. Mem. Assn. Computing Machinery, Operations Research Soc. Am. Home: 6004 Delwood Pl Bethesda MD 20034 Office: The Pentagon Washington DC 20301

BENINI, GINELLO, chem. co. exec.; b. Pisa, Italy, Dec. 8, 1927; s. Zenone and Giulia (Menicanti) B.; LL.D., U. Florence, 1950; m. Maria Frescobaldi, Jan. 11, 1951; children—Ginevra, Domitilla, Vivia, Piero, Stefano. Asst. sec. gen. Pignone SpA, Florence, 1951-52, sec. gen., 1953—; exec. v.p. internat. operations Occidental Chem. Co. div. Occidental Petroleum Corp., Los Angeles, 1970—; exec. v.p. Internat. Ore & Fertilizer Corp., N.Y.C., 1967—; chmn. bd., pres. Internat. Ore & Fertilizers S.p.A., Rome, 1959—. Clubs: Circolo della Caccia (Rome); Golf, Unione (Florence); Clubino (Milan); Olgiata Golf, Tennis and Sailing (Rome); Castiglione della Pescaia. Home: 6 Via dei Tre Orologi Rome Italy 00197 Office: 31 Via Lombardia Rome Italy 00187

BENIRSCHKE, KURT, pathologist, educator; b. Glueckstadt, Germany, May 26, 1924; s. Fritz Franz and Marie (Luebcke) B.; student U. Hamburg (Germany), 1942, 45- 48, U. Berlin (Germany), 1943, U. Wuerzburg (Germany), 1943-44; M.D., U. Hamburg, 1948; m. Marion Elizabeth Waldhausen, May 17, 1952; children—Stephen Kurt, Rolf Joachim, Ingrid Marie. Came to U.S., 1949, naturalized, 1955. Resident, Teaneck, N.J., 1950-51, Peter Bent Brigham Hosp., Boston, 1951-52, Boston Lying-in-Hosp., 1952-53, Free Hosp. for Women, Boston, 1953, Children's Hosp., Boston, 1953; pathologist Boston Lying-in-Hosp., 1955-60; teaching fellow, asso. Med. Sch. Harvard, 1954- 60; prof. pathology, chmn. dept. pathology Med. Sch. Dartmouth, Hanover, N.H., 1960-70; prof. reproductive biology and pathology U. Cal. at San Diego, 1970—; cons. NIH, 1957-70. Served with German Army, 1942-45. Mem. A.M.A., Internat. Acad. Pathology, Am. Coll. Pathology, N.Y. Acad. Sci., Teratol. Soc., Animal Care Panel. Home: 8457 Prestwick Dr LaJolla CA 92037 Office: U Cal at San Diego San Diego CA 92110

BENITES-VINUEZA, LEOPOLDO, diplomat of Ecuador; b. Guayaquil, Ecuador, Oct. 17, 1905; s. Leonidas Benites and Angelina Vineuza; ed. Colegio Vincente Rocafuerte, Guayaquil, U. Guayaquil; D. Honoris Causa, U. Montevideo (Uruguay); m. Margot Sierra, July 26, 1926; children—Leopoldo, Roberto. Prof. Vincente Rocafuerte, 1925-40; prof. philosophy and letters U. Guayaquil, 1940; under sec. Ministry Pub. Works, 1932; minister of Ecuador to Bolivia, 1948; ambassador of Ecuador to UN, 1954—. Founding mem. casa de Cultura Ecuador, 1944. Rep. to Lower House Ecuador, 1944-45. Author: Argonautas de la Selva, Ecuador Dram y Paradoja. Home: 150 E 69th St New York City NY 10017 Office: Ecuador Mission to UN 820 2d Av New York City NY 10017

BENITEZ, AGUSTIN, labor union exec.; b. Vieques, P.R., Nov. 11, 1910; s. Eugenio Benitez Calzada and Engracia Ortiz Benitez; ed. pub. schs., Lieques; m. Luisa Bermudez, May 5, 1935; children—Judith (Mrs. Jim Castro), Luis (Mrs. Isidra Gonzales), Robert E., Lucille. Came to U.S., 1929. Various positions with industry, 1930-57; local union Internat. Brotherhood Elec. Workers, 1945-57; spl. rep. AFL-CIO, N.Y.C., 1957-60; regional dir. region XXIII, AFL-CIO, P.R., 1961—; del. and/or mem. numerous union coms. and orgns. Mem. Small Bus. Adv. Council for P.R. and V.I.; mem. Coop. Devel. Adminstrn. P.R.; adv. council vocational tng. in P.R.; founder Central Labor Council San Juan and vicinity, 1964, mem. exec. bd., 1964—. Charge Spanish com. for registration and presdl. campaign, Kennedy-Johnson, 1960. Bd. dirs. P.R. chpt. A.R.C.; mem. adv. council P.R. Indsl. Relations Sch. Recipient numerous certificates of acknowledgement for civic work. Mem. Am. Arbitration Assn. (council P.R.). Home: Cruz de Malta 351 Round Hill Development Trujillo Alto PR 00760 Office: 804 Ponce de Leon Av Santurce PR 00907

BENITEZ, JAIME, educator; b. Vieques, P.R., Oct. 29, 1908; s. Luis and Candida (Rexach) B.; LL.B., Georgetown U., 1930, LL.M., 1931; A.M., U. Chgo., 1939; LL.D., Poly. Inst., San German, 1950; LL.D., N.Y.U., 1960, Fairliegh Dickinson U., 1961; Catholic Univ. P.R., 1965, U. W.I., 1969, U. Miami, 1970; Litt.D., Temple U., 1969; m. Luz A. Martinez, Aug. 15, 1941; children—Clotilde, Jaime, Margarita Ines. Instr. polit. sci. U. P.R., 1931-41, asso. prof., 1941-42, chancellor univ., 1942-66, pres., 1966-71. Head hearings officer Nat. War Labor Bd., Washington. Del. Gen. Conf. UNESCO, Paris, 1951; mem. U.S. Nat. Commn. UNESCO, 1951-55. Pres. com. of Bill of Rights, P.R. Constl. Conv., 1951; mem. housing com. Fed. Housing Agy., 1957. U.S. del. conf. of Univs., Utrecht, Holland, 1948. Recipient Carnegie Traveling Grant, 1954; traveling grant from Fund for Advancement on Edn., 1956. Fellow Am. Acad. Arts and Scis. Mem. Georgetown U. Alumni Assn., Alumni Assn. U. Chgo., Am. Acad. Polit. and Social Scis., Fed. Bar Assn., Nat. Assn. of State Univs. (pres. 1958), Assn. Caribbean Univs. (pres. 1969), Colegio de Abogados de Puerto Rico. Club: Cosmos (Washington). Author: The Concept of the Family in Roman and Common Law Jurisprudence, 1931; Political and Philosophical Theories of Jose Ortega y Gasset, 1939; Reflexion Sobre el Presente, 1950; La Iniciacion Universitaria y las Ciencias Sociales, 1952; The United States, Cuba and Latin America, 1961; Junto a la Torre, 1963; La Universidad del Futuro, 1964; Discurso en Salamanca, 1965; Sobre el Futuro Cultural y Politico de Puerto Rico, 1966; 25 Años de Direccion Universitaria, 1967; Crisis en el Mundo y en La Educación, 1968; With the Odds Against Us, 1969; Where Is Our Courage?, 1970. Home: U of Puerto Rico Rio Piedras PR 00931

BENJAMIN, ALBERT, ret. oil co. exec.; b. Dorchester, Mass., June 14, 1904; s. Albert and Etta Melissa (Wolcott) B.; B.S., U.S. Naval Acad., 1926; m. Alice Moorhead Jackson, May 25, 1929; 1 son, Albert Jackson. Commd. ensign U.S. Navy, 1926, advanced through grades to capt. USNR, 1943; active duty as naval attache, also naval attache for air Am. embassy, Montevideo, Uruguay, 1941- 45; mem. staff Am. mag., 1951-51, advt. dir., 1947-51; dir. pub. relations, exec. asst. to exec. v.p. Publ. Corp., N.Y.C., 1951-52; exec. asst. to exec. v.p. newspaper relations This Week mag., N.Y.C., 1952-54, mgr. gen. marketing div., 1954-56, mgr. sales devel., 1956-59; mgr. Latin Am. div. employee and pub. relations Texaco Inc., N.Y.C., 1959-60, dir. pub. relations, 1960-69. Mem. pub. information adv. com. U.S. Navy. Decorated Legion of Merit; recipient Distinguished service medal N.Y. State. Mem. Pub. Relations Soc. Am., U.S. Naval Inst., Navy League, S.A.R. Episcopalian. Clubs: University, Cloud, Southern Cross, Dutch Treat (N.Y.C.); Ponte Verda (Fla.), Chevy Chase (Md.); Farmington (Va.). Contbr. popular mags. Home: 40 Old Farm Rd Bellair Charlottesville VA 22901

BENJAMIN, BLANCHE STERNBERGER, civic worker; b. Mayesville, S.C., May 15, 1901; d. Emanuel and Bertha (Strauss) Sternberger; student Wellesley Coll., 1920-21; m. Edward B. Benjamin, Oct. 19, 1921; children—Edward B., W. Mente, Jonathan S. Vice pres. Startmount Co., Greensboro, N.C., 1930-68, Friendly Center Inc., Greensboro, 1955-68; dir. Benjamin Minerals, Inc., New

Orleans, 1947—. Vice pres. New Orleans Garden Soc., 1927-30, New Orleans Philharmonic Soc., 1928-51; mem. orgn. com. Newcomb Presch. and Metairie Park Country Day Sch.; v.p. Benjamin Fund, New Orleans Symphony Soc.; trustee Delgado Art Mus.; co-founder (with husband) Sternberger Hosp. (now Guilford Welfare Center), Starmount Forest Country Club; co-founder Emanuel Sternberger Ednl. Found, Greensboro. Mem. Jr. League Clubs: Orleans (corr. sec. 1947-49), Garden Soc., New Orleans Country, Southern Yacht (New Orleans); Greensboro Country, Assembly, Dogwood Garden (Greensboro); Saratoga Golf (Saratoga Springs, N.Y.). Address: 383 Walnut St New Orleans LA 70115

BENJAMIN, BURTON RICHARD, TV producer-writer; b. Cleve., Oct. 9, 1917; s. Sam and Ruth (Bernstein) B.; A.B., U. Mich., 1939; m. Aline L. Wolff, Apr. 5, 1942; children—Ann Norma, Jane Ruth. Newspaperman with U.P. and NEA Service, Cleve. and N.Y.C., 1939-42, NEA Service, N.Y.C., 1945-46; writer, producer documentary films RKO-Pathe, N.Y.C., 1946-55; exec. producer CBS News series Twentieth Century, also World War I, 1957—, CBS News Series, The 21st Century, 1967—; sr. exec. producer CBS News, N.Y.C., 1968—; writer dramatic and documentary scripts for network TV, 1955—. Trustee Scarborough Sch. Served to lt. USCGR, 1942-45. Co-winner 1st prize Fund for Republic for documentary script Pepito, 1955; recipient Peabody, Overseas Press Club, Emmy, Ohio State U. awards for Twentieth Century series; Certificate achievement sec. army, 1962; meritorious pub. service citation sec. navy, 1963; Emmy and Lasker awards for 21st Century, 1968-69; Emmy, Ohio State and Am. Bar Assn. awards for CBS News Spl., Justice Black and the Bill of Aftermath, Martin Luther King Assassination, 1968. Mem. Writers Guild Am., Nat. sec. navy, 1963; meritorious service certificate, sec. air force, 1966. Mem. Writers Guild Am., Nat. Acad. TV Arts and Scis. Home: Holbrook Rd Scarborough NY 10510 Office: CBS News 524 W 57th St New York City NY 10019

BENJAMIN, CURTIS G., publisher; b. Providence, Ky., July 13, 1901; s. John Baird and Effie (Head) B.; student U. Ky., 1919-21, LL.D., 1957; student U. Chgo., 1921-22; A.B., U. Ariz., 1927, Litt. D., 1961; m. Norma Olson, Sept. 9, 1931; children—Linda Baird (Mrs. Philip C. Smith), John Lucien. Dir., Community Theatre, Tucson, 1927; with McGraw-Hill Book Co., 1928—, mgr. coll. dept., 1932-42, v.p., 1942-46, pres. 1946-60, chmn. bd., 1960-66; cons., dir., McGraw-Hill, Inc., 1966—; dir. McGraw Hill Co. Can., Ltd., McGraw Hill Pub. Co., Ltd., London, Eng. Mem. sci. information council NSF, 1959-60, 64-68; mem. com. on sci. and tech. communications Nat. Acad. Sci., 1967-69; chmn. Govt. Adv. Com. on Internat. Book Programs, 1962-64; adv. com. on library services program U.S. Office Edn., 1964-65. Bd. dirs. Save the Children Fedn. and Community Devel. Found.; trustee Norwalk Hosp. Mem. Am. Textbook Pubs. Inst. (v.p. 1953-55), Am. Book Publishers Council (pres. 1958-59), Sigma Chi, Phi Kappa Phi, Sigma Delta Chi. Democrat. Presbyn. Clubs: University (N.Y.); American (London). Author articles on book pub. and copyright. Home: 36 Kellogg Hill Rd Weston CT 06880 Office: 330 West 42d St New York City NY 10036

BENJAMIN, DONALD MERLE, chem. and pharm. co. exec.; b. Mars Hill, Me., Apr. 6, 1909; s. Chester William and Ora Ann (Bell) B.; student Boston U., 1928-32; evening student N.Y.U., 1935-37; m. Marguerite Renee Rassaert, Dec. 28, 1945. With Am. Cyanamid Co., 1934—, asst. gen. mgr. Lederle div., 1955-58, gen. mgr. mfg. services div. parent co., 1958-61, controller, 1961- -; dir. 1st Nat. Bank of Passaic County, N.J. Bd. dirs. Better Business Bur. Met. N.Y., Inc.; vice chmn. Better Bus. Bureau of Bergen, Passaic and Rockland Counties, 1965—. Councilman, Borough of Montvale, N.J., 1951-57, police commr., 1955-57, pres. borough council, 1956. Trustee Pascack Valley (N.J.) Hosp., 1954-55. Mem. N.Y. Acad. Scis. (treas. 1954-55), Nat. Office Mgmt. Assn., Lambda Chi Alpha. Club: Ridgewood (N.J.) Country, Arcola Country. Home: 16 Sunnyside Dr Montvale NJ 07645 Office: Am Cyanamid Co Berdan Av Wayne NJ 07470

BENJAMIN, EDWARD B., minerals co. exec.; b. New Orleans, La., Nov. 18, 1897; s. Emanuel Victor and Rachel (Goldsmith) B.; A.B. magna cum laude, Harvard, 1918; L.H.D., U. Rochester, 1960; m. Blanche Sternberger, Oct. 19, 1921; children—Edward Bernard Jr., William Mente Sternberger, Jonathan Sternberger. Began in employ of family interests, 1919; past pres. E. V. Benjamin Co., Inc., Myles Salt Co., Starmount Co., Bay Chem. Co., New Orleans, Friendly Center, Inc., Greensboro, N.C.); pres. Benjamin Minerals, Inc., 1947—. Dir. Grayson Found.; pres. Benjamin Fund; donor Benjamin Awards for Restful Music. Trustee, founder (with wife) Sternberger Chidren's Hosp., now Guilford Co. Welfare Center, Greensboro; mem. visiting com. dept. of biology, Harvard, 1953-59. Mem. export adv. com. U.S. Dept. Commerce, 1946. Mem. orgn. com. New Orleans Community Chest, New Orleans Welfare Com., 1930-32; dir. New Orleans Opera House Assn.; chmn. organizing com., 1st pres. Cultural Attractions Fund Greater New Orleans, 1960-61; pres. Community Concert Assn. New Orleans, 1960-68. Bd. dirs. Human Betterment League N.C., U.S. Coast Guard Found. Served with Harvard R.O.T.C., 1917, Camp Lee (Va.), 1918. Clubs: Round Table, Southern Yacht, New Orleans Country (New Orleans); Merchants and Manufacturers, Greensboro Country (Greensboro); Turf and field (N.Y.C.). Author: The Larger Liberalism, 1918; The Restful in Music, 1970. Contbr. articles on religion, sociology, econs., music, yachting to mags. Home: 383 Walnut St New Orleans LA 70118 Office: Whitney Bldg New Orleans LA 70130

BENJAMIN, GARY EDWIN, controls co. exec.; b. Akron, O., Nov. 15, 1941; s. Glenn Eldon and Lillian Mae (Johns) B.; B.S., U. Akron, 1963; m. Marlene Joyce Holle, July 25, 1964; children—Doreen, Dawn, Glenn. Accountant Lybrand, Ross Bros. & Montgomery, N.Y.C. and Newark, 1963-68; controller, chief accounting officer Vikoa, Inc., Hoboken, N.J., 1968-70; controller, chief accounting and financial officer Wellington Computer Systems, Inc., 1970; controller Internat. Controls Corp., Fairfield, N.J., 1970—. C.P.A., D.C. Mem. Am. Inst. C.P.A.'s, Nat. Assn. Accountants, Am. Inst. Corporate Controllers. Home: 6 Tracy Lane Madison NJ 07940 Office: 200 Fairfield Rd Fairfield NJ 07006

BENJAMIN, MARY AVEZZANA, (Mrs. Harold G. Henderson), autograph dealer; b. Yonkers, N.Y., Mar. 25, 1905; d. Walter Romeyn and Carina de Saint Seigne Benjamin; A.B., Barnard Coll., 1925; m. Harold G. Henderson, June 20, 1946. Entered father's firm, Walter R. Benjamin Autographs 1925; mgr. firm, editor, The Collector (established 1887), 1937-43, owner, serving as dir., pub., editor, 1943—. Life mem. N.Y. Hist. Soc.; mem. Manuscript Soc., Antiquarian Booksellers Assn. Am., Internat. League Antiquarian Booksellers. Clubs: Colony, Cosmopolitan. Author: Autographs: A Key to Collecting, 1946; the Presidents-1965; A Survey of Autograph Values. Contbr. articles to mags. Home: 179 E 70th St New York City NY 10021 Office: 790 Madison Av New York City NY 10021

BENJAMIN, RICHARD NEWTON, utility exec.; b. Phila., May 5, 1904; s. Frank Tarbell and Ida (Malone) B.; B.S. cum laude, Harvard, 1925, M.B.A., 1927; m. Linda Tabb, June 26, 1936; children—Richard Dyke, John Tabb, Thomas Bruce, Elizabeth Payne. With Stone & Webster, Inc., 1927-37, pres., 1959-71, chmn. exec. com., 1971—, dir., 1959—; sec. Engrs. Pub. Service Co., 1937-47; v.p. Stone & Webster Service Corp., N.Y.C., 1948-53, pres., dir., 1953-58, chmn., 1959-61; dir. Upper Peninsula Generating Co., 1953-58, dir. subsidiaries; chmn. bd., dir. Pub. Utilities Reports, Inc., Comml. Cold Storage, Atlanta, Georgia, Reddy Kilowatt, Inc. Bd. dirs. Inst. Gas Tech., Chgo. Mem. Nat. Indsl. Conf. Bd. (dir.), Am. Gas Assn. (dir. 1967—), N.Y. Soc. Securities Analysts, Soc. Gas Lighting. Clubs: Links, Recess, Harvard; Echo Lake Country. Home: 267 Woodland Av Westfield NJ 07090 Office: 90 Broad St New York City NY 10004

BENJAMIN, ROBERT S., atty., bus. exec.; b. N.Y.C., May 14, 1909; student Coll. City N.Y., 1924-28; J.D. cum laude, Fordham U., 1928-31; L.H.D. (hon.), Brandeis U., 1971; m. Jean Kortright, 1949; children—Margret Lisa Taylor, Jonathan Adam. Office boy N.Y. Film Bd. of Trade, 1924; clk. in law offices of Phillips & Nizer, 1925, became atty., 1931, partner, 1935, gen. partner, 1938; v.p. Pathe Film Corp., 1937-41; pres. J. Arthur Rank Orgn., Inc., 1945-67, also dir.; v.p., gen. counsel Pathe Inds., Inc., and Eagle-Lion Films, Inc.; v.p., gen. counsel for United World Pictures, Inc., 1945; sr. partner Phillips, Nizer, Benjamin, Krim & Ballon; chmn. bd. United Artists Corp.; dir. Transamerica Corp. Hon. trustee Carnegie Hall Corp., Am.-Israel Cultural Found.; chmn. Nat. Citizens Commn. for Internat. Cooperation Yr., 1965; dir. Urban League Greater N.Y., Joint Def. Appeal; mem. exec. com. Nat. Patrons Soc. of Jewish Theol. Sem. Am.; trustee Eleanor Roosevelt Meml. Found., 1963—, exec. vice chmn., 1963-66, chmn. exec. com.,1966—. Mem. exec. com. Citizens' Com. Internat. Devel.; nat. chmn. U.S. Com. for UN, 1961-64; dir. UN Assn. U.S.A., 1961-64, chmn. nat. bd., 1963-64, pres., 1965-69, chmn. bd. govs., 1969—; sr. adviser U.S. delegation 21st Gen. Assembly UN, del., ambassador 22d Gen. Assembly. Elected to Electoral Coll. for Kennedy, 1960; nat. bd. dirs. Nat. Com. of Bus. and Profl. Men and Women for Kennedy and Johnson; finance chmn. Dem. adv. council Nat. Dem. Com. Vice chmn. bd. trustees Brandeis U.; mem. bd. dirs. Corp. for Pub. Broadcasting. Served as a maj., Signal Corps, U.S. Army, 1942-45. Decorated Legion of Merit; recipient Townsend Harris medal, Peace medal for 1971, Sec.-gen. UN. Mem. Assn. Bar City N.Y. Jewish religion (Conservative). Club: North Shore Country (L.I.). Home: Dock Lane Kings Point NY 11024 Office: 477 Madison Av New York City NY 10022 also 729 7th Av New York City NY 10019

BENJAMIN, THOMAS BROOKE, mech. engr., mathematician; b. Wallasey, Eng., Apr. 15, 1929; s. Thomas Joseph and Ethel (Brooke) B.; B.Eng., U. Liverpool, 1950; M.Eng., Yale, 1952; Ph.D., Cambridge U., 1955; m. Helen Gilda Rakower Ginsburg, July 9, 1956; children—Lesley Anne Brooke, Joanna Helen Brooke, Peter Charles Brooke. Sr. asst. in research Cambridge (Eng.) U., 1955-558, asst. dir. research, 1958-66, lab. dir. dept. applied math. and theoretical physics, 1964-70; prof. math., founder Fluid Mechanics Research Inst., U. Essex, 1970—. Vis. scientist U. Mich., 1962; vis. prof. Inst. Geophysics and Planetary Physics, U. Cal. at San Diego, 1966-67, Clarkson Coll. Tech., 1970; cons. English Electric Co., 1956-67. Recipient L.F. Moody award Am. Soc. M.E., 1966, William Hopkins prize Cambridge Philos. Soc., 1969. Fellow Royal Soc., Inst. Math. and Its Applications. Contbr. articles profl. jours. Office: U Essex Colchester Essex England

BENKE, PAUL ARTHUR, mfg. co. exec.; b. Michigan City, Ind., May 27, 1921; s. Paul Roland and Virginia (Peterson) B.; student Ind. U., 1941-42; A.B., Ind. State Coll., Terre Haute, 1948; M.A., U. Chgo., 1951, M.B.A., 1954; m. Lucy Newlin, Sept. 18, 1942; children—Janet, Eric. Gen. mgr. war prodn. div. Cline Electric Mfg. Co., Chgo., 1951-55; gen. mgr. Paasche Airbrush Co., Chgo., 1955-58; asst. to pres. H. K. Porter Co., 1956-57, gen. mgr. div. Coldform, 1957-58, Thermoid div., 1958-63; pres. Colt's Firearms Div., Hartford, Conn., 1963—; v.p. Colt Industries Inc., 1969—. Served to 1st lt. Ordnance Corps, U.S. Army, 1942-45; CBI. Mem. Beta Gamma Sigma, Alpha Phi Gamma, Pi Gamma Mu, Blue Key. Home: 3 Squirrel Hill Lane West Hartford, CT 06107. Office: 150 Huyshope Av Hartford CT 06102

BENKELMAN, WILLIAM DONALD, plastic co. exec.; b. Royal Oak, Mich., Oct. 23, 1928; s. Harold LeRoy and Isabel (Fletcher) B.; B.A., Mich. State U.; postgrad. U. Utah, 1952; m. Barbara Audrey Ell, May 2, 1952; children—Jeffrey R., James E., Cynthia L. Gen. mgr. Centerport Yacht Club, L.I., N.Y., 1955-56; gen. sales mgr. Cadillac Plastic & Co., Detroit, 1956-65, v.p. marketing, 1964-68, exec. v.p., 1968—; pres., chmn. bd. dirs. Cadillac Plastic Can., Ltd.; sec.-treas. Tuscola Broadcasting, Caro, Mich.; dir. Cadillac Plastic GmbH, Germany. Served to capt. AUS, 1952-54. Decorated Bronze Star. Mem. Soc. Plastics Industry, Soc. Plastics Engrs., Phi Kappa Tau. Republican. Home: 830 Rock Spring Rd Bloomfield Hills MI 48013 Office: 15111 2d Av Detroit IL 48203

BENN, ANTHONY WEDGWOOD, British politician; b. London, Eng., Apr. 3, 1925; s. William Wedgwood (Viscount Stansgate) and Margaret Eadie (Holmes) B.; M.A., New Coll. Oxford U., also LL.D. (hon.) and D. Tech. (hon.); m. Caroline Middleton DeCamp, June 17, 1949; children—Stephen Michael, Hilary James, Melissa Anne, Joshua William. Pres. Oxford Union, 1947; producer BBC N. Am. Service, 1949; mem. parliament for Bristol S.E., 1950-61, 63—; postmaster gen. Britain, 1964; minister of tech., 1966—; lectr. on world affairs in U.S., 1961-62. Chmn. Fabian Soc., 1964—. Mem. Nat. Union Journalists. Home: 12 Holland Park Av London England Office: House of Commons London SW 1 England

BENN, RALPH PHILIP, machinery co. exec.; b. Newark, Nov. 21, 1912; s. Arthur and Anna Louise (Ulrich) B.; B.S. in Mech. Engring., Newark Coll. Engring., 1938; m. Frances Louise Osterhout, Oct. 7, 1939; children—Philip Craig (dec. 1968), Barbara Frances (Mrs. James E. Handley). With Singer Co., N.Y.C., 1946-70, v.p. N. Atlantic consumer products group, 1968-70; pres. Leesona Corp., Warwick, R.I., 1970—. Served to lt. col. AUS, 1940-46. Republican. Club: Rhode Island Country (W. Barrington). Home: Nayatt Point West Barrington RI 02890 Office: 333 Strawberry Field Rd Warwick RI 02887

BENNACK, FRANK ANTHONY, Jr., newspaper publisher; b. San Antonio, Feb. 12, 1933; s. Frank Anthony and Lula W. (Connally) B.; student U. Md., 1954-56, St. Mary's U., 1956-58; m. Luella M. Smith, Sept. 1, 1951; children—Shelley, Laura, Diane, Cynthia, Julie. Advt. account exec. San Antonio Light, 1950-53, 56-58, adv. mgr., 1961-65, asst. pub., 1965-67, pub., 1967—; dir. sales, advt. Jorrie Furniture Co., San Antonio, 1958-61; dir. Alamo Nat. Bank, San Antonio. Vice chmn. bd. San Antonio Symphony. Trustee Our Lady of Lake Coll., hon. trustee Witte Meml. Mus. Served with AUS, 1954-56. Mem. Tex. Daily Newspaper Assn. (bd. dirs. 1969—), Am. Newspaper Pubs. Assn., Greater San Antonio C. of C. (v.p. 1969—). Rotarian (bd. dirs. San Antonio). Home: 401 Squires Row San Antonio TX 78213 Office: 420 Broadway St San Antonio TX 78205

BENNANI, AHMED, Marocca banker; b. Fès, Marocco, Dec. 12, 1926; s. Haj Driss and Khaddouj Bennani; diplmé d'Enseignement Comml. Supérieur, Paris, 1951; Licencié en Droit de la Faculté de Paris, 1952; m. Latifa El Kohen, Mar. 10, 1958; children—Chakir, Omar, Myriam. With Secrétaire Gén. au Ministère des Finances, Rabat, 1960-63, Secrétaire d'Etat au Ministère du Commerce et de l'Industrie, Rabat, 1964-65; dir. Gén. de la Caisse de Dépt et de Gestion, Rabat, 1965-66; with Secrétaire d'Etat aux Affaires Economiques auprès du Premier Ministre, Rabat, 1967-68; vice gov. Banque du Maroc, 1968—; adminstr. de la B.N.D.E., Rabat, de la B.M.C.E., de la C.M.M. et de la Comanav, Casablanca, de l'U.B.A.F., Paris. Decorated officer Order du Trne, 1970. Home: 2 rue de Khénifra Rabat Maroc Office: 277 av Mohammed V Rabat Maroc

BENNE, KENNETH DEAN, educator; b. Morrowville, Kan., May 11, 1908; s. Henry and Bertha Alveen (Thrun) B.; B.S., Kan. State Coll., 1930; A.M., U. Mich., 1936; Ph.D., Columbia, 1941 (scholar advanced sch. edn., 1936-38); L.H.D., Lesley Coll., Cambridge, Mass., 1969. Tchr. of phys. and biol. scis. Concordia (Kan.) H.S., 1930-35; tchr. chemistry Manhattan (Kan.) H.S., 1935-36; asso. social and philos. foundations of edn., Columbia Tchrs. Coll., 1938-41, asso. prof. edn. and research asso., Horace Mann-Lincoln Inst., 1946-48; asst. prof. edn. U. Ill., 1941- 46, prof. edn., 1948-53; editor Adult Leadership, 1952-53; Berenson prof. Boston U., 1953—, dir. Human Relations Center, 1953-61. Vice pres. Boston Adult Center, 1957-60; exec. bd. New Eng. Adult Edn. Inst., 1958-69. Served to lt. comdr. USNR; 1942-46. Mem. Mayor's Civic Unity Com., Boston, 1954-59; mem. Commn. Human Relations, Boston, 1957-65. Recipient Kilpatrick award for distinguished contbn. to Am. Philosophy of Edn., 1943; Bode Meml. lectr. Ohio State U., 1961; Centennial prof. social scis. U.Ky., 1965. Fellow Nat. Council Religion in Higher Edn., Internat. Inst. Arts and Letters. A.A.A.S., Am. Edn. Research Assn.; mem. Adult Edn. Assn. (pres. 1955-56, publs. com. 1956-59), Nat. Assn. Intergroup Relations Ofcl., Am. Sociol. Soc., Soc. for Psychol. Study Social Issues, Am. Philos. Assn., Philosophy of Edn. Soc. (pres. 1950- 51), Am. Edn. Fellowship (pres. 1949-52), N.E.A. (adj. staff, fellow Nat. Tng. Lab. 1959—, dir. 1959-62, 66-70), Phi Delta Kappa, Phi Kappa Phi, Kappa Delta Pi. Author: A Conception of Authority, 1943; Education for Tragedy, 1967. Co-author: Discipline of Practical Judgement, 1943; Mobilizing Educational Resources, 1943; Group Dynamics and Social Action, 1950; Improvement of Practical Intelligence, 1950. Theoretical Foundations of Education, 1952, Social Foundations of Education, 1955; The Planning of Change, 1961; The University and the National Future, 1966; Philosophy and Educational Development, 1966. Co- editor: Reading in Foundations of Education (2 vol.), 1941; Essays for John Dewey's Ninetieth Birthday, 1950; Human Relations in Curriculum Change, 1951; Readings in Social Aspects of Education, 1951; T-Group Theory and Laboratory Method, 1963. Mem. editorial bd. Progressive Edn., 1948-53; bd. cons. editors Teachers College Record, 1962-64; editorial bd. Jour. Applied Behavioral Sci., 1963-68. Home: 8 Kilsyth Terrace Brookline MA 02146 also Lovell ME 04051 Office: 270 Bay State Rd Boston MA 02215

BENNER, CLAUDE L., life ins. exec.; b. Adrian, Mich., June 27, 1892; s. John and Catherine (Ahman) B.; A.B., U. Mich. 1920, A.M., 1921, Ph.D. Robert Brookings Grad. Sch. Econs. and Govt., 1925; m. Marion Jacklin, Nov. 8, 1924; children—Roberta (Mrs. William R. Corkhum), Claude L., Richard Gordon Gordon (dec.). Instructor economics, U. Mich., 1920-21; asst. prof. econ. Ia. State Coll., 1921-23; mem. research staff Brookings Inst., Washington, 1923-25; prof., head dept. econ. U. Del., 1925-28; lectr. in finance U. Pa. Wharton Sch., 1938-42; with Continental Am. Life Ins. Co., Wilmington, Del., 1928—, dir., 1930—, pres., 1949-61, chmn. of board, 1961-63; dir. of Bank Del., New Castle Mut. Ins. Co., Life Ins. Assn. of Am. Mem. Nat. Voluntary Credit Restraint Com., Am. Econ. Assn., Am. Statis. Assn. Republican. Episcopalian. Clubs: Wilmington, Wilmington Country (both of Delaware), Union League (Philadelphia), Author: Federal Intermediate Credit System, 1926; Ten years Intermediate Credits (with Frieda Baird), 1932. Home: 705 du Pont Rd Westover Hills Wilmington DE 19807 Office: Rodney Sq Wilmington DE 19809

BENNER, LORRAINE WINEOW, educator; b. Schenectady, July 30, 1906; d. Stanley J. and Emma (Wineow) Benner; diploma, Illman Kindergarten Tng. Sch., 1926; B.S., Boston U., 1942; M.A., Tchrs. Coll., Columbia, 1946. Kindergarten tchr. Longmeadow (Mass.) Pub. Schs., 1928-41; instr. edn. Wheelock Coll., 1943- 46; asst. prof. child study Smith Coll., 1946-51; asso. prof. psychology and edn., dir. Gorse Child Study Center, Mt. Holyoke Coll., 1951—, prof., 1967—; instr. Vassar Summer Inst. Family and Community Living, 1950-57; Fulbright sr. lectr. child devel. Ochanomizu Womens U., Tokyo, Japan, 1958; Exchange prof. child devel. U.S.-India Womens Coll. Exchange Program, Womens Christian Coll., Madras, India, 1964-65. Dir. Orientation for Head Start Tchrs., 1967; Office Econ. Opportunity cons. Head Start programs, 1966-68. Assn. Childhood Edn. Internat. fellow, 1940- 41. Author: Portfolio for Kindergarten Teachers, 1942. Home: 20 Jewett Lane South Hadley, MA 01075.

BENNER, NOLAN PAUL, found. exec.; b. Hoffman, Pa., Mar. 24, 1893; s. Ulysses F. and Mary Ann (Remaly) B.; student Lehigh U.; m. Nettie Ludwig, Mar. 8, 1919; children—Bettie J. (Mrs. Charles Garrettson), Nolan Paul; m. 2d, Caroline W. Thomas, Feb. 11, 1969. With Trexler Found., Allentown, Pa., 1934—, trustee, 1934—, exec. dir., 1947—. Pres. Cia. Minera Lehigh S.A., Cuba, 1956-59. Mem. Pa. N.G., Mexican Border; served to capt. U.S. Army, World War I. Republican. Clubs: Lehigh Country; Livingston (Allentown). Home: 25 S 15th St Allentown PA 18102 Office: 1227 Hamilton St Allentown PA 18102

BENNETT, ABRAM ELTING, physician; b. Alliance, Neb., Jan. 12, 1898; s. Charles E. and Bertha (Kinsey) B.; B.S., U. Neb. 1919, M.D., 1921; children—Foster (dec.), Ann (dec.), Jeanne. Intern U. Neb. Hosp., 1920-21, Phila. Gen. Hosp., 1922-23; resident neurology Phila. Orthopedic Hosp. and Nervous Infirmary, also Phipps Psychiat. Clinic, Johns Hopkins, 1923-24; practice medicine limited to neurology and psychiatry, Omaha, 1924-48, Berkeley, Cal., 1948—; mem. faculty U. Neb. Coll. Medicine, 1928-47, prof., chmn. neurology and psychiatry, organizer, chief dept. psychiat. Herrick Meml. Hosp., Berkeley, 1948-63; asso. clin. prof. psychiatry U. Cal., 1949-65; founder, 1945, dir. A.E. Bennett Neuropsychiat. Research Found. Dr. A. E. Bennett Psychiat. Pavilion at Herrick Memorial Hospital named in his honor; recipient awards for sci. exhibits A.M.A., 1940, 46, 58; three sci. exhibit research awards A.M.A. Diplomate Nat. Board Med. Examiners, Am. Bd. Psychiatry and Neurology. Fellow A.A.A.S., Am. Psychiat. Assn. (life), A.M.A.; mem. Am. Neurol. Assn., Soc. Biol. Psychiat. (pres. 1953, hon.), Central Soc. Clin. Research, Central Neuro- psychiat., Cal., Alameda County med. socs., Brit. Royal Psychol. Assn. (corr.), Northern Cal. Hugenot Soc. (v.p., 1968), Alpha Omega Alpha, Phi Rho Sigma. Clubs: Berkeley City Commons (pres. 1959- -), Rotary. Author: Psychiatric Nursing Technic (with Avis Purdy), 1940; The Practice of Psychiatry in General Hospitals (with E. A. Hargrove and Bernice Engle), 1956; also articles. Asso. editor Diseases of Nervous System, Quar. Rev. Psychiatry and Neurology, Psychiatry in Gen. Practice. Pioneered modern therapy for mentally ill in gen. hosps.; discovered effective use of convulsive shock in affective disorders; developed use of curare, 1939; original research in alcoholic brain disease. Home: 668 Moraga Rd Moraga CA 94556 Office: 2000 Dwight Way Berkeley CA 94704 ☆

BENNETT, ALVIN LEROY, educator; b. Golden, Ill., July 4, 1914; s. Emery E. and Stella E. (Johnson) B.; B.Ed., Western Ill. State Coll., 1939; M.A., U. Ill., 1946, Ph.D., 1950; m. Pauline M. Anderson, Mar.

5, 1943; children—Linda, Marcia, Patricia. Tchr., Ill. pub. schs., 1934-42; asst. prof. polit. sci. Mich. State U., 1948-54; prof. polit. sci., chmn. dept. Drake U., 1954-62; prof. U. Del., 1962—, chmn. dept. polit. sci., 1962- 68; vis. prof. Western Wash. Coll. Edn., Bellingham, summer 1959. Pres. Des Moines chpt. Am. Assn. UN, 1955-56, v.p. Ia. div., 1959-62. Fellow Fund Advancement Edn., 1951-52. Served with USNR, 1942-46. Mem. Am., Midwest (sec.-treas. 1953-59) polit. sci. assns., Am. Assn. U. Profs., Internat. Studies Assn. Home: 102 Hullihen Ct Newark DE 19711

BENNETT, ALVIN S., rec. co. exec.; b. Joiner, Ark., 1926; Pres., dir. Liberty/UA, Inc., Los Angeles; chmn. All Disc Records, Inc., Liberty/UA Distbg. Corp., Liberty/UA Tape Duplicating, Inc., Research Craft Corp.; chmn., pres. Record Sales of La., Inc.; pres. Record Sales Corp.; v.p., dir. United Artists Corp.; v.p., treas., dir. Bennett-Forrester Implement Co.; dir. Liberty/UA BmbH, Mus. Isle of Mo., United Artists Music Co., Inc. Home: 3755 Longridge Av Sherman Oaks CA 91403 Office: 6920 Sunset Blvd Los Angeles CA 90028

BENNETT, ARTHUR DUANE, mfg. co. exec.; b. Bklyn., Aug. 26, 1916; s.Charles F. and Sophie (Bowers) B.; B.S. in Bus. Adminstrn., N.Y. U., 1937; m. Rita Pastorino, Sept. 3, 1939; children—Barbara, Arthur Duane, Edward, Richard, Anthony. With Nat. Cash Register Co., 1946-51; v.p. sales A. Kimball Co., div. Litton Industries, 1951-64; v.p. Walter Kidde Co., also pres. Dura Corp., div. Walter Kidde Co., 1964—. Mem. Sales Exec. Club Detroit. Clubs: Detroit Athletic; Plum Hollow Country (Oak Point, Mich.). Home: 239 Palmer Ct Ridgewood, NJ 07450. Office: 21800 Greenfield Rd Oak Park MI 00642

BENNETT, ARTHUR LAWRENCE, med. physiologist; b. Oconto, Wis., June 25, 1905; s. Andrew Arthur and Mabel Claire (Durand) B.; A.B. summa cum laude, Lawrence Coll., 1927; Ph.D., U. Chgo., 1933; M.D., Rush Medical Sch., 1937; m. Helen May Schlagenhauf, Sept. 5, 1932; children—Robert Bruce, Jane Carol. Instr. chemistry Lawrence Coll., 1927-28; adj. prof. physiology U. Tex. Coll. Medicine, 1930-31; successively instr., asst. prof., asso. prof. physiology U. Neb. Coll. Medicine, 1934- 40, prof. physiology and pharmacology, 1941—, asst. chmn. dept., 1954-67, chmn. dept. physiology, 1967-70, prof. physiology and biophysics, 1970—. Recipient J. P. Freer prize and medal Rush Med. Sch., 1930. Fellow A.A.A.S.; mem. Physiol. Soc., Am. Assn. Electromyography and Electrodiagnosis, Phi Beta Kappa, Sigma Xi, Alpha Omega Alpha. Home: 1713 Crawford Rd Omaha NB 68144

BENNETT, CARL, discount dept. store exec.; b. Greenwich, Conn., Jan. 27, 1920; s. Mayer and Rebecca (Lipsky) B.; student N.Y. U., 1937-38; m. Dorothy Becker, June 24, 1951; children—Marc Mitchell, Robin Cheryl, Bruce Kenneth. Wholesale liquor salesman, Conn., 1940-51; pres., chmn. bd. Caldor, Inc., discount dept. store chain, Norwalk, Conn., 1951—; dir. Restaurant Asso. Industries, Inc., Restaurant & Waldorf Asso., Incorporated. Chairman bd. Bi-Cultural day Sch., Stamford, Conn., 1965- 67, treas. 1967-68. Served with AUS, 1942-45. Recipient Amudin award outstanding work Hebrew day schs., 1965. Mem. World Bus. Council Inc. (charter). Young Pres. Orgn. (treas. 1964-65, chmn. pub. relations com. 1964-65). Jewish religion (dir. temple, cultural chmn. congregation). Home: Green Briar Lane Stamford CT 06903 Office: 20 Glover Av Norwalk CT 06852

BENNETT, CARROL MORTIMER, financial and mgmt. cons.; b. Clarksburg, W.Va., Dec. 8, 1910; s. Clyde M. and Martha (Martin) B.; student U. Tex.; m. Elizabeth A. O'Beirne, May 29, 1937; children—Carrol Mortimer, Randolph, Barbara A., Betty. J. Engr. Magnolia Petroleum Co., 1931-34; v.p., dir. Dallas, Rupe & Son, investment bankers, Dallas, 1935-55; pres., dir. Bennet, Osborn & Hall, financial, mgmt. cons., Dallas, 1955-60; v.p., dir. Middletown, Inc., Dallas, 1945—; dir. Small Business Investment co. of Southwest; pres. Tex. Pacific Oil Co., Inc.; dir. Distillers Corp., Seagrams, Ltd., Gaz Marina, Gaz Ocean, Paris, Hedge Fund Am., Inc., Summit Capital Funds, Inc. Regional adminstr. Emergency Petroleum Gas Adminstrn. Active A.R.C. Mem. Ind. Petroleum Assn. Am. (exec. com., v.p., dir.), Mid Continent (dir.), W. Central (exec. com.) oil and gas assns., Nat. Petroleum Council, Tex. Research League, Dallas C. of C. (petroleum affairs com.), Am. Petroleum Inst. (dir.). Presbyn. (elder). Home: 6007 St Andrews Dr Dallas TX 75205 Office: 1 Main Pl Dallas TX 75250

BENNETT, CHARLES DANA, exec. cons.; b. Syracuse, N.Y., Apr. 20, 1903; s. Charles Frederick and Katherine Frances (Carroll) B.; student Columbia, 1920-23; LL.D., Okla. Christian Coll.; m. Edith Thoman, Sept. 20, 1924. Pub. relations dir. for Gov. George D. Aiken of Vt., 1940; editor Washington Farm Reporter, 1942-45; pub. relations dir. Nat. Grange, 1942-45, Nat. Coöp. Milk Producers' Fedn. Conv., 1942, Nat. Council of Farmer Coöps. Conv., 1944-45, mem. forest products coordinating com., WPB, 1944-45; cons. to NBC America United Program, 1945; special cons. to Found. for Am. Agr., Liberty, Ill., Washington, Farm Film Found.; cons. Periodical Pubs. Nat. Com., Nat. Paint, Varnish and Lacquer Assn., 1944-55; owner Charles Dana Bennett Assos.; v.p., treas. Elk Run Farms, Inc., 1948-58. Trustee Goddard Coll., 1941- 48; mem. Sec. Forrestal's Joint Orientation Conf. on Nat. Def.; incorporator Crusade for Freedom, chmn. agrl. com.; dir. citizen's com. for Hoover Report, Spl. Cons. agrl. com. Mem. adv. council Nat. 4-H Club Found.; mem. Nat. council Boy Scouts Am.; vice chmn., dir. Nat. Farm City Council, 1955, dir., mem. exec. com., 1956-59, 69—, chmn. spl. events com., 1959—. Naval War Coll. Global Conf., 1953-55; Air War Coll. Conf., 1954; mem. adv. com. Univ. Film Producers Found., 1963—; v.p., exec. com. Coucil on Internat. Non-Theatrical Events, Inc., 1967-69, trustee, 1957—; chmn. adv. com. agrl. div. Am. Vocational Assn. Trustee Nat. Safety Council, Keep Vt. Beautiful, Inc.; gov. Agrl. Hall of Fame, 1958-68. Recipient citation Nat. 4- H Club (with Mrs. Bennett), 1956; Hon. Am. Farmer Degree, Future Farmers Am., 1953; Silver Buffalo award Boy Scouts of America, 1955; Commissioned Ky. col., 1966. Mem. Newcomen Soc. of N.A., Am. Marketing Assn. (1945-55), Nat. Grange (7th Degree), Vt. Farm Bur. Fedn., Nat. Com. for Traffic Safety, President's Hwy. Safety Conf. (com. to organize pub. support 1945-53), Intercollegiate Studies Inst. (exec. com., trustee), Am. Assn. Agrl. Coll. Editors (asso.), Am. Agrl. Editors Assn. (asso.), Nat. Assn. Farm Broadcasters (asso.), Alpha Zeta (hon.), Alpha Tau Alpha (hon.), Sigma Chi. Clubs: Chicago, Union League (Chgo.); Nat. Press (Washington). Contbr. mags. Home: Hedgerow House Vergennes RD 3 VT 05491 Office: 1425 H St Washington DC 20005

BENNETT, CHARLES EDWARD, congressman; b. Canton, N.Y., Dec. 2, 1910; s. Walter James and Roberta Augusta (Broadhurst) B.; J.D., U. Fla., 1934; H.H.D. (hon.) U. of Tampa, 1950; m. Jean Bennett; children—Bruce, Charles, James, Lucinda. Admitted Fla. bar, 1934, practiced in Jacksonville; mem. Fla. Ho. of Reps., 1941; mem. 81st-92d Congresses, 3d Fla. Dist., mem. armed services com., chmn. seapower, real estate coms. Served as pvt. to capt. infantry, U.S. Army, 1942-47; overseas in New Guinea and the Philippines, including guerilla fighting in Luzon. Awarded Silver Star, Bronze Star; Philippine Legion of Honor and Gold Cross, 1968; Distinguished Service award Pres.'s Com. on Employment of Handicapped, 1969. Mem. board of directors of Boys' Home, Red Cross, Tuberculosis Association, Council of Social Agencies, Florida Children's Home Society. Member Disabled American Veterans, American Legion, Vets. Fgn. Wars, Fla. and Jacksonville bar assns., Jacksonville Jr. C. of C. (pres. 1939), U. Fla. Alumni Assn. (pres.). Democrat. Mem. Disciples of Christ Ch. Mason. Author: Laudonniere and Fort Caroline, 1964; Settlement of Florida, 1968; Southernmost Battlefields of the Revolution, 1970. Co-author: Congress and Conscience, 1970. Home: 305 W Adams St Jacksonville FL 32205 Office: House Office Bldg Washington DC 20515

BENNETT, CHARLES LEO, newspaper editor; b. Springfield, Mass., Apr. 11, 1920; s. Samuel T. and Bessie (Holmes) B.; student Hartwick Coll., Oneonta, N.Y., 1940-42; m. Julia Catella, Jan. 1, 1941; children—Judith, Barbara. Sports, state, city editor Geneva (N.Y.) Times, 1946-52; city editor Schenectady Union- Star, 1952-54; mng. editor Elyria (O.) Chronicle-Telegram, 1954-57, Cin. Enquirer, 1957-60; mng. editor The Daily Oklahoman, Oklahoma City Times, 1960—. Home: 8622 Waverly Dr Oklahoma City OK 73120 Office: PO Box 25125 Oklahoma City OK 73125

BENNETT, CLARENCE EDWIN, educator; b. Providence, May 23, 1902; s. George Wilfred and Clara Freeman (Wright) B.; Ph.B., Brown U., 1923, M.S., 1924, Ph.D., 1930; m. Ruth Nason, Sept. 8, 1928; children—Muriel N. (Mrs. Arthur R. McAlister), Ronald Stokes. Instr. physics Brown U., 1923-31, Mass. Inst. Tech., 1931-34; asst. prof. physics U. Me., Orono, 1934-38, asso. prof., 1938-40, prof., 1940-70, prof. emeritus, cons., 1970—, head dept. physics, 1939- 67; with Office Naval Research, 1946-56 Mem. Nat. Acad. Sci. adv. panel Nat. Bur. Standards, 1959-62. Fellow A.A.A.S., Am. Phys. Soc. (chmn. N.E. sect.); mem. Am. Inst. Physics (counselor Me.), Am. Assn. Physics Tchrs., Optical Soc. Am., Am. Assn. U. Profs. Am. Soc. Engrng. Edn. (physics editor), Phi Beta Kappa, Sigma Xi, Phi Kappa Phi, Tau Beta Pi, Sigma Pi Sigma (exec. com.). Mason. Author: Physics, 1935; Physics Without Math. 1949; First Year College Physics, 1954; Physics Problems, 1958. Home: 65 Forest Av Orono ME 04473

BENNETT, DONALD VIVIAN, army officer; b. Lakeside, O., May 9, 1915; s. Louis E. and Mary (Jacka) B.; student Mich. State Coll., 1933-35; B.S., U.S. Mil. Acad., 1940; grad. Command and Gen. Staff Coll., 1951, Army War Coll., 1955; m. Betty Deacon, June 24, 1940; children—Peter A., Mary Lynn. Commd. 2d lt. U.S. Army, 1940, advanced through grades to lt. gen., 1968; comdr. 62d Armored F.A. Battalion, Sicily, 1943; participated in Normandy landing, campaigns in Europe, World War II; assigned dept. tactics U.S. Mil. Acad., 1946-50, Far East Command Hdqrs., 1952, Army Forces Far East, 1953-54; chief staff 3d Armored Div., 1956-57; G-3 sect., 7th Army, Germany, 1957-59; mem. gen. staff Dept. Army, 1959-60; mem. U.S. delegation NATO Mil. Com. and Standing Group, 1960-62; comdr. I Corps Arty., Korea, 1962-63; dir. strategic plans and policy Office Dep. Chief Staff Operations, Dept. Army, 1963-65; supt. U.S. Mil. Acad., 1966-68; comdg. gen. VII U.S. Corps, 1968-69; dir. Def. Intelligence Agy., 1969—. Mem. nat. council Boys Scouts Am., 1967-68. Decorated D.S.C., D.S.M. with one oak leaf cluster Legion of Merit with 3 oak leaf clusters, Bronze Star medal, Army Commendation medal with 1 oak leaf cluster, Purple Heart with 1 oak leaf cluster. Mem. Council Fgn. Affairs. Address: Quarter 27 A Fort Myer VA 22211

BENNETT, EARL DEAN, educator; b. Shattuck, Okla., June 1, 1923; s. Frederick J. and Bertha M. (States) B.; B.S., John Brown U., 1945; M.B.A., Harvard, 1947; Ph.D., U. Mich., 1959; m. Agnes Lucille Evans, June 17, 1951; children—Deborah Elaine, David Eugene. Faculty Coll. Bus. Adminstrn., La. Poly. Inst., 1947-55; asst. prof. Harvard Bus. Sch., 1955- 1955- 60; prof. accounting U. Tex. Coll. Bus., 1960-68, chmn. dept., 1962-65, asso. dean, dir. grad. programs Coll. Bus. Adminstrn., Tex. A. and M. U., College Station, 1968—. Cons. to industry, 1956—. Served to lt. (j.g.) USNR, 1944-46. Scholar, Union Equity Coop. Grain Exchange, 1943-44; Gen. Edn. Bd. fellow, 1950. C.P.A., La. Mem. Am. Accounting Assn., Phi Kappa Phi, Beta Alpha Psi, Kappa Sigma, Delta Sigma. Republican. Methodist. Author: Cost Administration: Cases and Notes, 1960; (with Floyd S. Brandt and Charles R. Klasson) Business Policy: Cases in Managerial Decision Making, 1970. Home: 500 W Dexter St College Station TX 77840

BENNETT, EARL WILLARD, chem. co. exec.; b. White Cloud, Mich., Jan. 18, 1880; s. Frank and Eudorah (Ostrander) B.; student pub. schs., Grand Rapids, Mich., 1897; D.Eng. (hon.), Mich. Sch. Mines and Tech., 1953; m. Eva V. Barclay, Aug. 9, 1905; children—Vada L. (Mrs. Alden B. Dow), Helen L. (Mrs. Alden B. Hanson), Willard V., Grace E. (Mrs. Chas. E. Reed), Barbara, Robert B., David, Thomas J. Clk., Marshall Field & Co., 1897-1900; with Dow Chem. Co., 1900—, beginning as clerk, became v.p., 1931, treas., 1930, dir., 1927—, chmn. bd., 1949, now hon. chmn.; dir. Dow Corning Corp., Dow Chem. Co. Can., Cliffs Dow Chem. Co., Chem. State Savs. Bank. Mem. light metal com. NRC, World War II. Republican. Baptist. Clubs: Midland Country; Saginaw Bay (Mich.) Yacht. Home: 714 W Main St Midland MI 48640 Office: Dow Chemical Co Midland MI 48640

BENNETT, EDWARD HERBERT, Jr., architect; b. Chgo., Dec. 22, 1915; s. Edward Herbert and Catherine (Jones) B.; grad. St. Mark's Sch., 1934; A.B., Harvard, 1938, B.Arch., 1950; 1 son, Edward Herbert III; m. 2d, Katharine F. Phillips, November 4, 1960. Mem. firm Schweikher & Elting, architects, 1953-54, Elting & Bennett, 1954-56; pvt. practice of architecture, 1956—. Dir. Chgo. Regional Planning Assn., 1952-58; vice chmn. Lake County regional planning commission, 1958-60, chairman, 1960-70. Director Lyric Opera of Chgo., 1956—; trustee Chgo. Art Inst., 1958—, Chicago Symphony Orchestra, 1969—. Served to lt. comdr., USNR, 1940-45. Mem. Chgo. Orchestral Assn., A.I.A. Clubs: The Arts (dir.), Cliff Dweller (Chgo.). Address: 332 S Michigan Blvd Chicago IL 60604

BENNETT, EDWARD INSLEY HUNT, banker; b. Easton, Pa., June 14, 1906; s. Howard H. and Margaret (Drake) B.; B.S., Lafayette Coll., 1927; m. Mary Louise Hester, Oct. 18, 1930; children—Edward I.H., Elizabeth H. Auditor, Gen. Electric Co., 1927-36; credit exec. Sears, Roebuck & Co., 1936-45; v.p. Pitts. Nat. Bank, 1945- 60; exec. v.p. Western Pa. Nat. Bank, Pitts., 1960—. Mem., past pres. Mt. Lebanon Bd. Twp. Commrs. Mem. Sales Execs. Club Pitts. (past pres.), Bankers Club Pitts. (past pres.). Clubs: Duquesne, Pittsburgh Athletic, St. Clair Country (Pitts.). Home: 1420 Centre Av Pittsburgh PA 15219 Office: 5th Av and Smithfield St Pittsburgh PA 15222

BENNETT, EDWARD OWEN, coll. dean; b. St. Louis, Mar. 16, 1926; s. Edward Owen and Myrtle Louise (Sager) B.; A.A., Lamar Coll., 1947; B.S., U. Houston, 1949; M.S., State U. Ia. Med. Sch., 1951; Ph.D., Baylor U. Coll. Medicine, 1958; m. Dorothy Louise MacDonald, May 30, 1947; children—James David, Robert Paul. Asst. prof. biology U. Houston, 1951-58, asso. prof., 1958-63, prof., 1963—, chmn. biology dept., 1964-67, asso. dean Coll. Arts and Scis., 1967—; cons. in field. Recipient Gulf Oil Corp. summer faculty fellowship, 1961, 62. Mem. Am. Soc. Microbiology, Soc. Indsl. Microbiology, Sec. Gen. Microbiology, Am. Sec. Mfg. Engrs., Am. Soc. Lubrication Engrs., Soc. Metal Prodn. World, Inc., Sigma Xi, Phi Kappa Phi, Beta Beta Beta. Contbr. articles profl. jours. Patentee in field. Home: 5614 Cerritos St Houston TX 77035

BENNETT, EDWARD PENDLETON, Jr., former life ins. co. exec.; b. Beaumont, Tex., May 3, 1913; s. Edward Pendleton and Lillian Vera (Rush) B.; student So. Methodist U., 1931-32; m. Mary Merle Nevill, on April 27th, 1935 (dec. April 1968); children—Edward Nevill, Carol (Mrs. David L. Cruikshank), Richard Lee; m. 2d, Bertha A. O'Donnell, Sept. 19, 1968. Engaged in loan mortgage loan bus., Dallas, 1937—; with Prudential Ins. Co. Am., 1939-42, Travelers Ins. Co., 1942-44; with Mass. Mut. Life Ins. Co., 1946-70, 2d v.p. charge mortgage loan dept., 1960-62, vice pres., 1962-70; trustee, mem. investment com. Mass. Mut. Mortgage & Realty Investors, Inc., Springfield, Mass.; corporator of Five Cent Savings Bank. Corporator of Wesson Memorial Hosps., Springfield, Mass. Mem. Am. Inst. Real Estate Appraisers, Springfield Bd. Realtors, Delta Chi. Methodist. Home: 56 Williamsburg Dr Springfield MA 01108

BENNETT, EDWARD REO, physician; b. Williamson, N.Y., Dec. 13, 1905; s. Edward Augustus and Sarah (Decker) B.; A.B., Union Coll., Schenectady, 1928; M.D., Albany (N.Y.) Med. Sch., 1933; m. Myrta Lois Warner, Sept. 26, 1936; children—Edward Reo, Drucilla W. Intern Bellevue Hosp., N.Y.C., 1934-35, admitting officer USPHS, S.I., N.Y., 1936; practice medicine specializing in psychiatry, VA hosps. St. Cloud, Minn., Mendota, Wis., Danville, Ill., Sheridan, Wyo., Northport, N.Y., S.I. and Montrose, N.Y., 1937-51; chief of staff VA Hosp., Gulfport, Miss., 1951-57; dir. VA Hosp., Pitts., 1957-65, VA Hosp., Marion, Ind., 1965-70. Bd. dirs. Easter Pageant, Marion. Served to lt. col, M.C., AUS, 1944-46. Recipient Medal of Merit, Jewish War Vets., 1963, Citation Distinguished Service, D.A.V., 1964. Diplomate Am. Bd. Psychiatry and Neurology. Fellow Am. Psychiat. Assn.; mem. A.M.A., Assn. Med. Supts. Mental Hosps. Address: 1207 Colony Ct Lebanon PA 17042

BENNETT, ELMER FRANK, govt. ofcl., lawyer; b. Longmont, Colo., Sept. 17, 1917; s. Herbert A. and Jessie C. (Wharton) B.; A.B., Colo. State Coll. Edn., 1938; LL.B., Stanford, 1941; m. Gertrude A. Turner, Sept. 9, 1939; children—John H., Kathryn H. Admitted to D.C. bar, 1947; adminstrv. work War Dept., 1942-48; trial atty. FTC, 1948-51; legal adviser, exec. sec. U.S. Senator Eugene D. Millikin of Colo., 1951-53; legislative counsel Dept. Interior, 1953-56, asst. to sec. interior, 1956-57, gen. counsel Dept. Interior, 1957-58; under sec. Dept. Interior, 1958-61; mem. firm Ely, Duncan & Bennett, 1961-66; gen. counsel U.S. Pub. Land Law Rev. Commn., 1966-70; spl. asst. to dir. Office Emergency Preparadness, Exec. Office of President, Washington, 1970—. Adminstrv. asst. to chmn. resolutions com. Rep. Nat. Conv., 1952. Served with USNR, 1944. Recipient history scholarship award Phi Alpha Theta, 1938, spl. distinction Forensic Key, Pi Kappa Delta, 1937. Mem. Am. (chmn. mineral law sect. 1965-66), Fed. bar assns., Phi Alpha Delta, Phi Alpha Theta, Blue Key. Republican. Conglist. Home: 5000 Randall Lane Washington DC 20016 Office: Exec Office Bldg Annex Washington DC 20504

BENNETT, ELMER JAMES, lawyer; b. Williamstown, N.J., Apr. 9, 1909; s. Joseph A. and Catherine (Rennebaum) B.; A.B., Lafayette Coll., 1930; LL.B., Harvard, 1933; m. Mary Ann Martin, May 18, 1947; children—James M., David A., Barbara C. Admitted to N.J. bar, 1935, since practiced in Jersey City and Newark; partner firm Carpenter, Bennett & Morrissey, 1947—. Mem. Common Council, Summit, N.J., 1960—, pres., 1964-70, mayor, 1970—. Served with AUS, 1945-46. Mem. Am., N.J. (chmn. client's security fund com. 1962-67, conflict of interest com. 1965—), Essex County bar assns. Presbyn. (pres. bd. deacons 1956). Clubs: Harvard (N.Y.C.); Canoe Brook Country, Beacon Hill (Summit, N.J.). Home: 76 Prospect Hill Av Summit NJ 07901 Office: 744 Broad St Newark NJ 07102

BENNETT, EMMETT LESLIE, Jr., educator, mycenologist; b. Mpls., July 12, 1918; s. Emmett Leslie and Mary (Buzzelle) B.; B.A., U. Cin., 1939, M.A., 1940, Ph.D., 1947; m. Marja D. Adams, June 5, 1942; children—Patrick R., Kathleen L., Cynthia A., John L., S. Christopher. Instr., asst. prof. Yale, 1947-58, U. Tex., 1958-59; vis. lectr., asso. prof., now prof. classics Inst. for Research Humanities, U. Wis., Madison, 1959—; Fulbright Research scholar, 1953-54, 65; mem. Inst. for Advanced Study, Guggenheim fellow, vis. lectr. Greek, Bryn Mawr Coll., 1955-56; vis. prof. arts and humanities U. Colo.; 1967. Mem. Am. Philol. Assn., Archaeol. Inst. Am. Classical Assn. Midwest and South, German Archaeol. Inst. (corr.), Linguistic Soc. Am., Com. Internat. pour les Etudes Myceniennes. Editor: The Pylos Tablets, 1951, 55; The Mycenae Tablets, 1953, 58; Nestor, 1957- -; Mycenaean Studies, 1962. Contbr. articles archeol. jours. Home: 1933 West Lawn Av Madison WI 53711

BENNETT, FRANKLIN SEATON, lawyer; b. Youngstown, O., June 21, 1926; s. James Eugene and Marion (Osborne) B.; B.S., U.S. Mcht. Marine Acad., 1947; B.A., Cornell U., 1951, LL.B., 1954; m. Margaret Rebecca Campbell, Aug. 16, 1952; children-Franklin Seaton, David Campbell, Robert Campbell. Admitted to Ohio bar, 1955, since practiced in Youngstown; asso. law firm Manchester, Bennett, Powers & Ullman, 1955-62, partner, 1963—. Trustee Youngstown Area Urban League, 1955-64, v.p., 1967-69; chmn. capital fund drive, Goodwill Industries Youngstown, 1968; chmn. Health and Welfare Council Youngstown Community Chest, 1968-69. Trustee Goodwill Industries Youngstown, Florence Crittenton Home Youngstown, Youngstown Humane Soc.; trustee, mem. exec. com. Ohio Citizens Council for Health and Welfare. Served with U.S. Mcht. Marines, 1944-47; to lt. USNR, 1950-51. Mem. Am., Ohio, Mahoning County bar assns., Am. Judicature Soc. Home: 31 Poland Manor Poland OH 44514 Office: Union Nat Bank Bldg Youngstown OH 44503

BENNETT, FRED GROCH, naval officer; b. Yazoo City, Miss., Sept. 9, 1915; s. John Patterson and Clara Antoinette (Groch) B.; B.S., U.S. Naval Acad., 1936; M.S., Mass. Inst. Tech., 1944; m. Nancy Kittelle, May 10, 1941; children—Nicholas Lockwood, Christopher Patterson. Commd. ensign U.S. Navy, 1936, advanced through grades to vice adm., 1968; served in U.S.S. Maryland, 1936-42, U.S.S. Topeka, 1944-46, U.S.S. Harwood, 1951-52, U.S.S. Grand Canyon, 1959-60, U.S.S. Newport News, 1960-61; dir. budget and reports Office Comptroller, Navy Dept., 1963-65; comdr. Cruiser Destroyer Flotilla 8, 1965-66; asst. chief naval operations for gen. planning and programming, 1966-68, dir. navy program planning, 1968—. Decorated Legion of Merit, also various area and service ribbons. Home: 3709 Cameron Mills Rd Alexandria VA 22305 Office: Navy Dept Washington DC 20350

BENNETT, G. W., oil and gas co. exec. Controller Hudson's Bay Oil & Gas Corp., Ltd. Office: 3207 The Av SW Calgary 2 Alberta Canada*

BENNETT, GEORGE BAIRD, adj. gen. Idaho; b. Oklahoma City, Sept. 3, 1914; s. George Fenton and Mabel (Gager) B.; student U. Ida. So. Br., 1934, Long Beach (Cal.) Jr. Coll., 1936, U. Ida. 1938; grad. Army Command and Staff Coll., 1950, Army Aviation Flight Sch., 1959, Army Aviation Helicopter Sch., 1961; m. Mary K. Killimann, Apr. 12, 1941; 1 dau., Tracy Lyn. Sec.-treas., Jerome County (Ida.) Agrl. Conservation Assn., 1938-40; served from 2d lt. to col., U.S.

Army, 1940-46; mem. Ida. N.G., 1946—; maj. gen., 1965; adj. gen. Ida., 1965—. Mem. exec. com. Ida. Heart Assn. Decorated Bronze Star with oak leaf cluster. Mem. N.G. Assn. U.S. (exec. com.), Ida N.G. Assn. (past pres.), Adj. Gens. Assn., Boise C. of C., Sigma Alpha Epsilon. Elk, Rotarian. Home: 3430 Woodacres Dr Boise, ID 83705. Office: Box 1098 Boise ID 83701

BENNETT, GEORGE FREDERICK, investment mgr.; b. Quincy, Mass.; Aug. 16, 1911; s. Wallace Cherrington and Lois E. (Williams) B.; A.B. cum laude, Harvard, 1933; m. Helen F. Brigham, Oct. 25, 1935; children—Peter C., George Frederick, Robert B. With First Boston Corp., Boston, 1934-37, Newton, Abbe & Co., Boston, 1937-43; with State Street Research & Mgmt. Co., Boston, 1943—, partner, 1946—; pres. State Street Investment Corp., Boston, Fed. Street Fund, Inc., Boston; dir. Middle South Utilities, Inc., N.Y.C., N.E. Electric System, Commonwealth Oil Refining Co., Inc., P.R., Hewlett Packard Co., Palo Alto, Cal., Fla. Power & Light Co., Miami, Ford Motor Co., John Hancock Mut. Life Ins. Co., Boston, U.S. & Fgn. Securities Corp. Treas. Harvard U., Harvard-Yenching Inst.; trustee Wheaton (Ill.) Coll., Rockefeller U., Com. Econ. Devel., Washington; bd. dirs. Mass. Soc. Prevention Cruelty to Animals. Mem. Pi Eta. Clubs: Harvard (Boston and N.Y.C.); Hingham (Mass.) Yacht; Union (Boston); Cohasset Golf; Links (N.Y.C.). Home: 712 Main St Hingham MA 02043 Office: 225 Franklin St Boston MA 02110

BENNETT, GEORGE KETTNER, psychologist; b. New York, N.Y., Feb. 26, 1904; s. Walter Taylor and Henriette Charlotte (Kettner) B.; A.B., Yale, 1928, Ph.D. in psychology, 1935; m. Marjorie Gelink; children—George Kettner, Deborah Swan. Director of test division of The Psychological Corp., 1936- 44, vice pres., mem. bd. dirs., 1944-47, pres., 1947-70. Mem. applied psychol. panel, Office of Scientific Research and Development, 1943-45; mem. com. on service personnel, Nat. Research Council, 1942-45, vice chmn. div. anthropology and psychology, 1947-48. Diploma in Industrial Psychology American Board of Examiners in Professional Psychology, Fellow American Psychology Assn.; mem. N.Y. State Assn. for Applied Psychology (pres., 1947-48), Sigma Xi. Republican. Episcopalian. Clubs: N.Y. Yacht; Larchmont Yacht. Author or co-author: Test of Mechanical Comprehension, Differential Aptitude Tests, Short Employment Tests, Stenographic Aptitude Test, Stenographic Proficiency Test. Home: Stoneleigh Apts Bronxville NY 10708

BENNETT, GORDON LATTA, ret. librarian; b. Lincoln, Neb., May 20, 1908; s. John Gordon and Marie Letitia (Latta) B.; A.B., U. Neb., 1931; B.S. in L.S., U. Denver, 1937; m. Emma Louise Schwalb, Aug. 28, 1940; 1 dau., Mary Louise (Mrs. Richard David Nass). Library asst. Neb. Legislative Reference Bur., Lincoln, 1928-32; asst. Neb. Pub. Library Commn., 1933- 35; library asst. Lincoln City Library, 1936; asst. reference dept. Denver Pub. Library, 1937-39; librarian Pulaski County Library, Little Rock, 1939-42; exec. sec. W.Va. Library Commn., Morgantown, 1942; librarian Colo. State Library, Denver, 1943-46, 47-70, Amarillo (Tex.) Pub. Library, 1946. Exec. dir. Nat. Library Week, Colo., 1959; trustee Rocky Mountain region Bibliog. Center for Research; nat. ednl. adv. com. Voice of Youth; mem. Council Ednl. TV, Gov.'s Manpower Commn.; mem. adminstrv. council Colo. Dept. Edn. Mem. Am. (dir. pub. library div. 1955-58), Colo. (pres. 1945- 46, exec. bd. 1958-62), Mountain-Plains library assns., Colo. Edn. Assn., Nat. Assn. State Libraries, Colo. P.T.A. (mgr.), Internat. Platform Assn. Presbyn. Contbr. articles profl. jours. Home: 5100 E 17th Denver CO 80220

BENNETT, GORDON RICHARD, coll. pres.; b. Stamford, Tex., Sept. 22, 1904; s. George William and Ella (Reilly) B.; student Wayland Coll., 1922-24; B.A., Baylor U., 1926; postgrad. Tex. Technol. Coll., 1928, U. Tex., 1931; M.A., Hardin-Simmons U., 1944; LL.D., Midwestern U., 1953; m. Lola Juanita McElhaney, May 17, 1930; children—Patricia Lee, Richard Michael. Prin. high sch., Whireflat, Tex., 1928-31; supt. schs., Avoca, Tex., 1931-34; prin. high sch., Hamlin, Tex., 1935-39, supt. schs., 1939-45; mgr. Hamlin Hatchery, 1945-48; v.p. McMurry Coll., Abilene Tex., 1948-58, acting pres., 1958, pres., 1958—. Mem. Jurisdictional Bd. Edn., 1960-64. Mem. com. on interdenominational coop., conf. bd. edn. N.W. Tex. Conf. Meth. Ch.; del. N.W. Tex. Ann. Conf., 1950—, Gen. Conf., 1960, Jurisdictional Conf., 1960. Mem. sch. bd., Hamlin, 1945—, councilman, 1946-48. Mem. Tex. Council Church-Related Colls. (pres. 1962-63), Tex. Meth. Coll. Assn. (pres. 1961-63). Club: Lions (pres. 1957-58). Home: 1632 Sayles Blvd Abilene TX

BENNETT, GRANVILLE ALLISON, physician, pathologist; b. Hiawatha, Kan., Sept. 23, 1901; s. Frank and Abby Chatten (Allison) B.; B.S., U. Ia., 1923, M.D., 1925; A.M. (hon.) Harvard, 1942; m. Leonore Weber, May 15, 1926; 1 dau., Mary Allison (Mrs. Carlos Hudson). Intern. surgery U. Ia. Hosp., 1925-26, clin. asst. surgery and pathology, 1926-27; resident pathologist Peter Bent Brigham Hosp., Boston, 1927-29; instr. pathology Harvard Med. Sch., 1927-34, faculty instr., 1934-35, asso., 1935-37, asst. prof. 1937-42, asso. prof., 1942-43; prof. pathology and bacteriology Sch. Medicine, Tulane U., 1943-44; prof. pathology Coll. Medicine U. Ill., 1944-70, prof. pathology emeritus, 1970—, dean, 1954-67; orthopedic pathologist Children's Hosp., Boston, 1942-43; sr. vis. pathologist Charity Hosp., New Orleans, 1943-44; pathologist-in-chief U. Ill. Research and Ednl. Hosp., 1944-54; cons. Armed Forces Inst. Pathology. Fellow Coll. Am. Pathologist, A.M.A.; mem. Am. Assn. Pathologists and Bacteriologists (past pres.), Soc. Exptl. Pathology, Am. Soc. Clin. Investigation, Internat. Assn. Med. Museums (past pres. Am. and Canadian sect.), Chgo. Pathol. Soc. (past pres.), Central Soc. Clin. Research, Assn. Am. Med. Colls., Am. Soc. Clin. Pathology, Ill. Soc. Pathologists, Inst. Medicine (Chicago), Sigma Xi, Pi Rho Sigma, Alpha Omega Alpha, Phi Kappa Phi. Clubs: University, Harvard, Iowa (Chgo.). Author: Changes in the Knee Joint at Various Ages, 1942. Contbr. med. jours. Editorial bd. Archives of Pathology, 1944-60, chief editor, 1950-54. Home: 3000 Sheridan Rd Chicago IL 60657

BENNETT, HAROLD HARPER, corporation exec.; b. Salt Lake City, Utah, Sept. 20, 1900; s. John F. and Rose (Wallace) B.; A.B., U. of Utah; grad student U. of London, Sch. of Polit. Sci. and Economics; m. Emily Higgs, Aug. 21, 1924; children—John H., Mary E., Michael J., Rose C., Ann C., Peter H., Susan E., Stephen H. Accountant Zion's Coöp. Mercantile Instn., 1926, gen. accounting office, 1927, asst. sec. and controller, Jan. 1928, asst. treas., Dec. 1928-33, sec., 1931-46, sec.-treas., 1933-46, asst. gen. mgr., 1936-46, became v.p., gen. mgr., 1946, exec. vice pres., dir., 1952-58, pres., dir., 1958—; v.p. director Bennett's; pres., dir. Bennett Motor Co., Bennett Leasing Co., Nat. Car Rental of Utah; dir. Standard Ins. Co. of Portland, Zion's 1st Nat. Bank of Salt Lake, Heber J. Grant Co. Mchts. council Inst. Retail Mgmt., N.Y.U.; adv. council mgmt. conf. Brigham Young U. Bd. dirs. Utah Found., Utah Safety Council, Salt Lake Oratorio Soc., Pro-Utah; trustee Com. Econ. Devel., Bennett Assn. Mem. Salt Lake C. of C., Utah Retail Mchts. Assn. (dir.), Nat. Retail Mchts. Assn. (pres. 1962-63, dir., chmn. internat. div. com.), Nat. Council Crime and Delinquency, Utah N.G. (hon. col.). Mem. Church of Jesus Christ of Latter Day Saints. Home: 1187 Harvard Av Salt Lake City UT 84105 Office: 15 S Main St Salt Lake City UT 84101

BENNETT, HARRY, chem. cons.; b. N.Y.C., May 28, 1895; s. Louis and Esther (Cohen) B.; B.S. in chem. engring., N.Y. U., 1917; m. Rose Michaels, Feb. 6, 1921; children—Helene M. (Mrs. D. Martin), Marilyn S. (Mrs. I. Ziegler). Pres. Bennett-Rosendahl Co., Inc., cons., Miami Beach, Fla.; dir. B.R. Lab., Miami Beach, Fla.; holder ten U.S. patents, 1 Canadian, 1 Brit. Compiler and pub., The Chem. Formulary, 17 vols., 1932—. Chmn. Chem. Forum, Miami Beach. Mem. Am. Inst. Chemistry, Soc. Chem. Industry, Am. Chem. Soc., Am. Assn. Textile Chemists and Colorists, A.A.A.S., N.Y. Acad. Scis., Soc. Cosmetic Chemists, Inst. Chem. Engrs., Inst. Food Tech., Oil Chem. Soc., Am. Ceramic Soc., Soc. Plastics Engrs., T.A.P.P.I., Am. Soc. Testing Materials, Am. Inst. Chem. Engrs., Tau Beta Pi. Author numerous books on chemistry. Home: 4747 Collins Av Miami Beach FL 33140 Office: 714 W 51st St Miami Beach FL 33140

BENNETT, HARRY LOUIS, educator; b. Ansonia, Conn., Dec. 22, 1923; s. Louis and Florence (Swole) B; B.A., Yale 1944, M.A., 1948, Ph.D., 1954; m. Claire Davis, July 2, 1949; 1 dau., Lisa Brierley. Welfare investigator, Conn., 1950-51; mem. faculty Quinnipiac Coll., Hamden, Conn., 1951—, prof. history, dean coll., 1956-67, vice president for academic affairs, 1967- 69, prof., chmn. history, 1969—. Sec.-treas. Conn. Conf. Community and Jr. Colls., 1955-62, v.p., 1962- 64, pres., 1964-65; chmn. standing com. accreditation Connecticut Council Higher Edn., 1964-65. Trustee Quinnipiac Coll. Served to 1st lt., inf., AUS, 1944-46; MTO. Mem. Am. Hist. Assn. Catholic. Home: 21 Knollwood Rd Hamden CT 06518 Office: Quinnipiac Coll Hamden CT 06518

BENNETT, HARRY WIGGIN, Jr., advt. and marketing exec.; b. N.Y.C., June 2, 1907; s. Harry Wiggin and Agnes Pattie (Smith) B.; B.S., Cornell U., 1932; m. Virginia Joan Stead, June 8, 1935; children—Joan (Mrs. Edward Moore Kennedy), Candace (Mrs. Robert M. McMurrey). Student tng. Nat. Biscuit Co., 1932-34; salesman Beech-Nut Packing Co., 1934-36; account exec. Compton Advt., Inc., 1936- 47; advt. mgr. Good Luck div. Lever Bros. Co., 1948-50; v.p., account supr. Sherman & Marquette, Inc., N.Y.C., 1950-54, exec. v.p., gen. mgr., dir. successor co. Bryan Houston, Inc., 1954-58; sr. v.p., chief adminstrv. officer N.Y. office Joseph Katz Co., N.Y.C., 1958—; pres. of Robert C. Durham Assos., 1959—; pres., dir. New Horizons Telecasting Corp., Jacksonville, Fla., 1963—, Five Beaches Cable-TV, Inc., Cocoa Beach; pres., dir. The Anchorage, Inc.; pres. Universal Cablevision, Inc., Cocoa Beach, 1965—; pres. Bayou Country Products, Inc., Kenner, La.; dir. chmn. bd. Florida CATV Assn., Inc.; mem. bd. dirs. Vest. Broadcasting Co., 311 W. Ashley St., Rochester, N.Y., China Tung Oil Company, Incorporated (Gainsville, Florida), Tampa Bay Area Telecasting Corp. (St. Petersburg, Fla.) Pub. information officer Westchester (N.Y.) Civilian Def., 1952. Served with USCG Maritime Serv., 1944-46. Mem. Assn. for Propagation of Relaxation (sec.). Westchester Center Spot Players (chmn.), Radio and TV Execs. Soc., N.A.M., A.I.M., Rear Guards (pres.), Radio and Television Execs. Soc., Sales Execs. Club N.Y., U.S. Power Squadron, U.S. Coast Guard Aux., The Players, Zeta Psi. Clubs: New York Athletic (N.Y.C.); Cornell (N.Y.C.) and Westchester, Seminole (Jacksonville); Atlantic Beach (Fla.); Canaveral Press (Fla.). Home: PO Box 301 Inglis FL 32649

BENNETT, HENRY STANLEY, anatomist; b. Tottori, Japan, Dec. 22, 1910 (parents U.S. citizens); s. Henry James and Anna Woodruff (Jones) B.; came to U.S., 1924; Diploma, Germantown Friends Sch., 1928; A.B., Oberlin Coll., 1932; M.D., Harvard, 1936; m. Alice Helen Roosa, July 28, 1935; children—Edith Roosa, Anna Woodruff, Henry James, Patience St. John. Fellow of Nat. Research Council and research fellow, anatomy, Harvard Med. Sch., 1937- 39; instr. in anatomy, 1939-42; asst. prof. of cytology, Mass. Inst. Tech., 1945-48; prof. of anatomy and chmn., dept. of anatomy, U. of Wash. School of Medicine, Seattle, 1948-60; dean div. biological sciences, U. Chgo., 1961-65, dir. Labs. for Cell Biology, Robert R. Bensley prof. biol. and med. scis., 1966-69; Sarah Graham Kenan prof., dir. Labs. for Reproductive Biology, chmn. dept. anatomy U. N.C., Chapel Hill, 1969—. Mem. nat. adv. health council USPHS, 1958-62. Entered M.C., U.S. Navy, as lt. (j.g.), 1942; service in S. Pacific, 1943-45; disch. to Res. as comdr., Jan. 1946; captain MC, U.S.N.R. Vol. Research Res. Unit 13-1, 1948-52. Awarded Legion of Merit. Diplomate Nat. Bd. Med. Examiners. Fellow Am. Acad. Arts and Sciences, A.A.A.S.; mem. Soc. for Clin. Investigation, Am. Assn. of Anatomists (pres. 1959- 60), Am. Physiol. Soc., Soc. Cell Biology, Am. Chem. Soc., Electron Microscope Soc. Am., Am. Assn. Physicians Histochem. Soc., Alpha Omega Alpha, Sigma Xi. Home: Jones Ferry Rd Chapel Hill, NC 27514.

BENNETT, HOWARD CLIFTON, coll. pres.; b. Cleburne, Tex., June 13, 1910; s. Howard C. and Lillie (Freeman) B.; student U. Tenn., 1928-29; B.A., Union U., Jackson, Tenn., 1936; Th.M., So. Bapt. Theol. Sem., Louisville, 1939; D.D., E. Tex. Bapt. Coll., Marshall, Tex., 1948; m. Mary Lee Hurt, May 6, 1935; children—Marilyn (Mrs. George W. Hillyer III), Kate (Mrs. John E. Fite), Susan (Mrs. Kenneth B. Livingston). Ordained to ministry Bapt. Ch., 1935; pastor in Carthage, Tenn., 1939-41, Vivian, La., 1941- 43, Kilgore, Tex., 1943-60; pres. E. Tex. Bapt. Coll., 1960—, trustee coll., 1944-53. Mem. exec. bd. Bapt. Gen. Conv. Tex., 1943-52; mem. Tex. Bapt. Edn. Commn., 1953-60, chmn., 1959-60. Chmn. Gregg County chpt. A.R.C., 1945. Trustee So. Bapt. Theol. Sem., 1958-68; chmn. bd. Roy H. Laird Meml. Hosp., Kilgore, 1952-58. Mem. Marshall C. of C., Sigma Alpha Epsilon. Rotarian. Home: 701 East Av Marshall TX 75670

BENNETT, HOWARD FRANKLIN, educator; b. Worcester, Mass., Jan. 3, 1911; s. Edwin Harlan and Abbie Minerva (Flagg) B.; A.B. magna cum laude, Amherst Coll., 1933; A.M. in Teaching (Homes fellow teaching 1937-38), Harvard, 1939, Ph.D. in Am. History (Edward Austin fellow history 1938-39), 1951; m. Elizabeth Maurine Hoover, Feb. 10, 1951. Tchr., Worcester High Sch., 1933-35, W. Hartford (Conn.) High Sch., 1935-37; asst. history Harvard, 1939-42, asst. Dean's Office, 1939-42; mem. Faculty Northwestern U. Sch. Bus., 1946—, prof. bus. history, 1960—, chmn. dept. bus. history and environment, 1955—, faculty Inst. Mgmt., 1961—, pres. Student Pub. Co., Inc., Northwestern U.; dir. Bus. History and Econ. Life Program, Inc.; mem. staff exec. and mgmt. devel. program Bell Telephone System, 1959-60; faculty Gen. Electric Advanced Mgmt. Program, 1964—, Ill. Bell Telephone Mgmt. Program, 1961—; cons. Field Enterprises Ednl. Corp., 1963—. Served with USNR, 1942-46, 51-53; capt. Res. Mem. Am., Miss. Valley hist. assns., Econ. History Assn., Am. Econ. Assn., Soc. History Tech., Naval Res. Assn., Navy League U.S., Am. Assn. U. Profs., Phi Beta Kappa, Theta Delta Chi. Clubs: Harvard of Chicago; Chicago Amherst (past pres.). Author: Precision Power: The First Fifty Years of Bodine Electric Co., 1959; also articles. Home: 2526 Laurel Lane Wilmette IL 60091 Office: Northwestern Univ Evanston IL 60201

BENNETT, IVAN LOVERIDGE, Jr., physician; b. Washington, Mar. 4, 1922; s. Ivan Loveridge and Ruby (Jenrette) B.; A.B., Emory U., 1943, M.D., 1946; m. Martha Rhodes, June 24, 1944; children—Susan, Paul Bruce, Katherine, Jeffrey Ivan. Med. intern Grady Hosp., Atlanta, 1946-47, chief resident physician, 1951-52; asst. pathologist Johns Hopkins Hosp., Balt., 1949-50, physician, cons. bacteriology, 1954-58; asst. resident physician Duke Hosp., 1950-51; asst. prof. internal medicine Yale, 1952-54; asso. prof. medicine Johns Hopkins, 1954-57, prof. medicine, head biol. div., 1957-58, Baxley prof. pathology, also pathologist-in-chief Johns Hopkins Hosp., 1958-66; dep. dir. Office Sci. and Tech., Exec. Offices of the President Washington, 1966-69; v.p. health affairs, dir. Med. Center, N.Y. U., 1969—, prof., dean Sch. Medicine, 1970—; cons. Va Hosp., Balt., Clin. Center, Nat. Insts. Health, Bethesda; spl. cons. Surgeon Gen., U.S. Army. Mem. Pres.'s Sci. Adv. Com., 1966-70, Commn. on Epidemiological Survey, Armed Forces Epidemiology Bd.; research contract dir. Army Chem. Corps; mem. bd. sci. counselors Nat. Inst. for Dental Research; member exec. com. div. med. scis.; mem. bd. sci. advisers Armed Forces Inst. Pathology; mem. panel on Sci. and Tech., Com. on sci. and astronautics U.S. Ho. of Reps., 1969—; Diplomate Am. Bd. Internal Medicine, 1954. Fellow A.C.P., N.Y. Acad. Scis.; mem. Soc. Exptl. Biology and Medicine, Am. Psychosomatic Soc., Am. Fedn. Clin. Research (pres. 1957- 58), Am. Soc. Clin. Investigation, Assn. Am. Physicians, A.M.A., Biomed. Engring. Soc., Am. Assn. Pathologists and Bacteriologists, Am. Soc. Exptl. Pathology, Am. Clin. and Climatol. Assn., Am. Assn. Immunologists, Internat. Acad. of Pathology, So. Soc. for Clin. Investigation (pres. 1963-64), Johns Hopkins Med. Soc. (pres. 1963-64), Phi Beta Kappa, Sigma Xi, Omicron Delta Kappa, Alpha Omega Alpha, Sigma Chi, Phi Chi. Author tech. articles sci. jours. Editor: Principles of Internal Medicine, rev. edit., 1958, 62, 66, 68. Editorial bd. Ann. Rev. Medicine, 1965-66, Jour. Biochem. and Molecular Pathology, 1947-67. Office: NY U Med Center 550 1st Av New York City NY 10016

BENNETT, JAMES AUSTIN, educator; b. Taber, Alta., Can., Jan. 29, 1915; s. William Alvin and Mary (Walker) B.; came to U.S., 1945, naturalized, 1949; B.S., Utah State U., 1940, M.S., 1941; Ph.D., U. Minn., 1957; m. Dolores Buttars, Sept. 18, 1940; children—James Ralph, Carl Robert and Calleen (twins), Marvin Charles and Marilyn (twins). Livestock asst. Dominion Dept. Agr., Swift Current, Sask., Can., 1941-45; asst. prof. Utah State U., 1945-50, prof., head dept. animal sci., 1950—. Mem. A.A.A.S., Am. Soc. Animal Sci. Am. Genetic Assn., Sigma Xi. Contbr. numerous articles on animal breeding and genetics to profl. jours. Home: 714 N 150th W Logan UT 84321

BENNETT, JAMES EDGAR, cosmetic co. exec.; b. Cranbury, N.J., July 15, 1916; s. Samuel Edgar and Gertrude (Snedeker) B.; grad. Peddie Sch., 1934; B.A. in Econs., Yale, 1938; m. Jessie Milne Silvers, Dec. 26, 1938; children—James Edgar, William Russell, Gertrude Snedeker. With Carnation Milk Co., 1938- 45; with P. Lorillard Co., 1945—, gen. mgr., Louisville, 1949-51, asst. dir. mgr., N.Y.C., 1951-60, dir. mfg., also dir. co., mem. exec. com., 1960-69, vice president, 1961-65, assistant to the president, 1963-65, exec. v.p., 1965, pres., 1965-69; group v.p. Chesebrough-Pond's, N.Y.C., 1970—. Member Beta Theta Pi. Republican. Presbyn. Clubs: Yale Economics, Sales Executive (N.Y.C.); Greenwich Country, Indian Harbor Yacht (Greenwich). Home: 263 Overlook Dr Greenwich CT 06830 Office: 485 Lexington Av New York City NY 10017

BENNETT, JAMES EDWARD, educator, surgeon; b. Burlington, Wis., May 19, 1925; s. John Francis and Florence (Mauer) B.; student Notre Dame U., 1943-44, Mass. Inst. Tech., 1944-45; M.D., Northwestern U., 1950; m. Ellen MacPherson, June 18, 1956; children—David, Martha, Thomas, Jonathan. Intern Milwaukee County Hosp., 1949-50; resident surgery U. Mich. Hosp., 1953-58; gen. practice medicine, Burlington, 1950-51; exchange fellow plastic surgery, Wales, 1956-57; resident plastic surgery U. Tex. Sch. Medicine at Calveston, 1958-61; asst. prof. surgery, dir. plastic surgery Ohio State U. Sch. Medicine, 1961-64; prof. surgery, dir. plastic surgery Ind. U. Med. Center, 1964—. Mem. A.C.S., Plastic Surgery Research Council (chmn. 1970), Frederick A. Coller Surg. Soc., Am. Soc. Plastic and Reconstructive Surgeons, Am. Assn. Surgery Trauma, Am. Assn. Plastic Surgeons, Phi Rho Sigma. Research wound healing, cleft lip-palate. Home: 5865 Hunter Glen Rd Indianapolis IN 46226

BENNETT, JAMES EUGENE Jr., lawyer; b. Youngstown, O., Oct. 23, 1918; s. James Eugene and Marion (Osborne) B.; grad. Phillips Exeter Acad., 1937; A.B., Cornell U., 1941, LL.B., 1948; m. Ruth Eleanor Hillman, Oct. 25, 1941; children—James Eugene 3d, Richard O., Stephen B., Carl H., Alan F. Admitted to Ohio bar, 1948, since practiced in Youngstown; partner firm Manchester, Bennett, Powers & Ullman. Dir. Dollar Savs. & Trust Co., Home Savs. & Loan Co., Poling and Bacon Constrn. Co., Inc. Pres. Youngstown Community Corp.; mem. Mahoning County Bd. Edn., Mahoning County Joint Vocational Sch. Bd. Served with USAAF, World War II. Decorated Air medal, D.F.C. Mem. Am., Ohio, Mahoning County bar assns., Youngstown Area C. of C. (past pres.), Phi Beta Kappa, Order of Coif, Chi Phi. Republican. Mem. Disciples of Christ Ch. Club: Youngstown. Home: 56 Poland Manor Poland OH 44514 Office: Union Bank Bldg Youngstown OH 44503

BENNETT, JAMES JEFFERSON, univ. pres.; b. Owensboro, Ky., June 8, 1920; s. James H. and Amelia (Brownfield) B.; B.S., U. Ala., 1941, LL.B., 1948, LL.D., 1966; m. Christine Thaxton, Oct. 21, 1942; 1 son, James Jefferson. Admitted to Ala. bar, 1948; practice in Fairhope, 1948-50; asst. prof. law U. Ala., 1950-52, asso. prof., asst. dean, 1952-54, prof., 1953-68, asst. to pres. for devel., 1954-56, adminstrv. asst. to pres., 1956-60, adminstrv. v.p., 1960-68, provost, 1968; asst. adminstr. for legislation and pub. policy Health Services and Mental Health Adminstrn., Dept. Health, Edn. and Welfare, 1968-69; exec. dir. Health Edn. Authority of La., New Orleans, 1969-71; pres., vice chancellor U. of South, 1971—. Served to maj. USMCR, 1942-46. Recipient Algernon Sydney Sullivan award, 1964. Mem. Ala. Edn. Assn., Ala. Assn. Sch. Adminstrs. (past pres.), Farrah Order Jurisprudence, Internat. House, Sigma Chi, Omicron Delta Kappa, Phi Delta Phi. Episcopalian. Club: Timberlane Country. Office: Univ of South Shawnee TN 37375

BENNETT, JAMES MURRELL, architect; b. Dallas, Aug. 22, 1904; s. Edward C. and Maude (Ramsey) B.; B.A., So. Meth. U., 1923; B.Arch. with honors, Washington U., St. Louis, 1927; m. Juanita Morgan, Jan. 2, 1926; children—Elizabeth (Mrs. David Schultz), Edward. With archtl. firms, St. Louis, 1926-37; partner charge design Gill & Bennett, Dallas, 1938-42; archtl. rep. in Dallas and Houston, J. Gordon Turnbull, Inc., Cleve., 1942-44; partner Bennett & Crittenden, Dallas, 1945-64; partner Bennett & Bennett, Dallas, 1965—; specializing in design of churches; prin. works include Fain Meml. Presbyn. Ch., 1948, Floral Heights Meth. Ch., Wichita Falls, Tex., 1949, Flow Meml. Hosp., Denton, Tex., 1950, Highland Park Meth. Ch., 1951, Kessler Park Meth. Ch., 1952, Restland Mortuary, 1957, Lovers Lane Meth. Ch., 1958, Zion Luth. Ch., Dallas, 1958, Rowsev Meml. Chapel, Muskogee, Okla., 1960, 1st Presbyn. Ch., Irving, 1st Meth. Ch., Alexandria, La., 1968, Trinity Meth. Ch., Ruston, La., 1971. Mem. city plan commn., University Park, Tex., 1956—, chmn., 1962—; mem. city zone commn., University Park, 1956-62. James Harrison Steedman travelling fellow, Europe, 1928. Fellow A.I.A. (pres. N. Tex. chpt. 1946, Dallas chpt. 1947); mem. Tex. Soc. Architects (chmn. com. archtl. practice 1953-58). Methodist. Lion. Home: 3717 University Blvd Dallas TX 75205 Office: 3308 Oak Grove Dallas TX 75204

BENNETT, JAMES WILLIAM, author; b. Mitchell, Ind., Oct, 15, 1891; s. Benjamin Franklin and Ellen (Munson) B.; A.B., Stanford, 1916; m. Dorothy Graham, July 23, 1924 (div.); m 2d, Linda Annan Wagner, Feb. 6, 1943. With legal dept., U.S. Food Adminstrn., Washington, 1918; vice consul, Shanghai, China, 1918-19, Sydney, Australia, 1919. Lectr. in short story writing St. John's U., Shanghai, 1922-23; historian U.S. Q.M. Corps Depot, Mira Loma, Cal., 1943-45. Mem. Kappa Alpha, Sigma Delta Chi. Author: Plum Blossoms and Blue Incense (short stories), 1926 (translated into Danish, 1930); The Manchu Cloud (novel), 1927; The Yellow Corsair (novel), 1927; (with Dorothy Graham) Brush Strokes on the Fan of a Courtesan (verse), 1927; Dragon Shadows (short stories), 1928; Son of the Typhoon (novel), 1928; Chinese Blake (novel), 1930; Spinach Jade (novel), 1939. Contbr. to leading mags. in Am. and Eng. Home: 514 Lime St Redlands CA 92373

BENNETT, JAMES WILLIAM, Jr., educator; b. Asheville, N.C., July 20, 1920; s. James William and Noreen (Alexander) B.; A.B., Maryville (Tenn.) Coll., 1941; M.S., U. Tenn., 1950; Ph.D., U. Fla., 1955; m. Ruth Maxine Russell, June 10, 1942; children—James William III, Keith R. With Aluminum Co. Am., 1941-42, Tenn. Eastman Corp., 1946-49; instr. Auburn U., 1950-51; mem. faculty U. Tenn., 1952—, now prof. transp. econs. Served with AUS, 1942-45. Mem. Am. Soc. Traffic and Transp. (dir. edn., bd. dirs.), So. Econ. Assn. Home: 106 Hummingbird Dr Maryville TN 37801 Office: Alumni Hall Knoxville TN 37916

BENNETT, JIM, univ. ofcl.; b. Las Animas, Colo., Aug. 26, 1921; s. Rex Marion and Margaret (Walker) B.; student Okla. A. and M. Coll., 1942, Murray State Tchrs. Coll., 1945, U. Ga., 1945, U. Denver, 1947; m. Ernestine Y. Rogers, May 2, 1948; children—Steven Roger, Patti Sue, Deanne Lee. Reporter-printer Las Animas Leader, 1939-41; announcer radio sta. KOKO, La Junta, Colo., 1941-42; newsman radio stas. KFEL and KOA, Denver, 1942; circulation mgr. San Fernando (Cal.) Reporter, 1946; news writer NBC, Hollywood, Cal., 1946; news writer, newscaster radio sta. KLZ, Denver, 1947-71, news dir., 1957-71; dir. univ. communications, instr. tech. journalism Colo. State U., Ft. Collins, 1971—; producer (film) The Road to Nowhere (Emmy award, Sigma Delta Chi TV documentary award, Edward R. Murrow documentary award), 1967. Pres. Sunset Hills Recreation Assn., Westminster, Colo., 1965-66. Served with USNR, 1942-45. Named Outstanding Journalist U. Colo., 1968. Mem. Nat. Press Photographers Assn. (treas. 1960-62, pres. 1963-64, Joseph A. Sprague award 1966, merit award 1961-64, fellowship award 1962), Radio TV News Dirs. Assn. (bd. dirs. 1961-64), Colo. Press Assn., Order DeMolay (master councilor 1939), Sigma Delta Chi (pres. Colo. 1959, TV Reporting award 1956). Club: Hyland Hills Mens Golf (Westminster); Denver Press (Best Spl. Events Broadcast award 1950). Home: 804 Garfield St Ft Collins CO 80521

BENNETT, JOAN, actress; b. Palisades, N.J., Feb. 27, 1910; d. Richard and Adrienne (Morrison) Bennett; ed. pvt. schs.-Miss Chandor's and Miss Hopkins' (N.Y.C.), St. Margaret's (Waterbury, Conn.), L'Ermitage (Versailles, France); m. John Marion Fox, 1926 (div. Aug. 1928); 1 dau., Diana; m. 2d, Gene Markey, writer. Mar. 16, 1932 (div. 1937); 1 dau., Melinda; m. 3d, Walter Wanger, 1940 (div. 1965); children—Stephanie, Shelley. Made stage debut in Jarnegan with father 1928; appeared in films Bull Dog Drummond, Three Live Ghosts, Disraeli, Maybe It's Love, Moby Dick, Putting on the Ritz, Many a Slip, Doctors' Wives, She Wanted a Millionaire, Careless Lady, The Trial of Vivienne Ware, Week Ends Only, Wild Girl, Me and My Gal, Arizona to Broadway, Little Women, Pursuit of Happiness, Man Who Reclaimed His Head, Mississippi, Private Worlds, She Couldn't Take It, 13 Hours By Air, Big Brown Eyes, Wedding Present, Vogues of 1938; also starred in stage play Stage Door, 1938; The Texans, Artists and Models, Trade Winds, The Man in the Iron Mask, Housekeeper's Daughter, Green Hell, House Across the Bay, The Man I Married, Son of Monte Christo, I Married a Nazi, She Knew All the Answers, Man Hunt, Wild Geese Calling, Confirm or Deny, Twin Beds, The Wife Takes a Flyer, Girl Trouble, Margin for Error, The Woman in the Window, Nob Hill, Colonel Effingham's Raid, Scarlet Street, Woman on the Beach, The Macomber Affair, The Secret Beyond The Door, Hollow Triumph, Reckless Moment, Father of the Bride, For Heaven's Sake, Father's Little Dividend, Love that Brute, Lead in Nat. Touring Co. of Bell Book and Candle, 1952. We're No Angels, 1955; Janus; Pleasure of His company; motion picture Desire in the Dust; Love Me Little (stage play); Too Young to Go Steady (TV series); Dark Shadows (TV series); Never Too Late (London), 1963-64. Author: (with Lois Ribbee) The Bennett Playbill, 1970. Home: 150 E 72d St New York City NY 10021

BENNETT, JOE CLAUDE, medical educator; b. Birmingham, Ala., Dec. 12, 1933; s. Claude and Clara Lucille (Clark) B.; A.B., Samford U., 1954; M.D., Harvard, 1958; m. Nancy Miller Bennett, June 17, 1958; children—Katherine Diane, Miller, Cark Barton. Intern Univ. Hosp., Birmingham, 1958-59, resident, 1959-60; practice medicine specializing in rheumatology; with NIH, 1962-64; sr. research fellow div. biology Cal. Inst. Tech., Pasadena, Cal., 1964-65; asst. prof. dept. medicine, asso. prof. dept. microbiology, asst. dir. div. clin. immunology and rheumatology U. Ala. Med. Sch., Birmingham, 1966-70, prof. dept. medicine, dir. div. clin. immunology and rheumatology, prof., chmn. dept. microbiology, 1970—. John and Mary R. Markle Found. scholar in acad. medicine, 1965-70; recipient Research Career Devel. award NIH; fellow Arthritis and Rheumatism Found., arthritis unit Mass. Gen. Hosp., 1960-62. Club: Downtown, Mountain Brook Swim and Tennis (Birmingham). Author: Vistas in Connective Tissue Diseases, 1968. Editorial bd. Arthritis and Rheumatism, 1969—. Home: 4236 Antietam Dr Birmingham AL 35213

BENNETT, JOHN CHARLES, army officer; b. Washington, Dec. 6, 1923; s. Ivan Loveridge and Ruby (Jenrette) B.; B.S., U.S. Mil. Acad., 1945; M.A., Columbia U., 1951; M.A., George Washington U., 1964; student Emory U., 1940-41; m. Jean Hazelton MacKenzie, Sept. 8, 1945; children—Jill Anne (Mrs. Nicholas A. Delmore), John Charles Jr., Judith MacKenzie, Robert MacKenzie. Commd. 2d lt. U.S. Army, 1945, advanced through grades to maj. gen., 1970—; asst. prof. English, U.S. Mil. Acad., 1949-52, comdr. 4th Mechanized Div., also Ft. Carson, Colo., 1970—. Decorated Legion of Merit with 2 oak leaf clusters, Bronze Star, Air medal with nine oak leaf clusters. Mem. Order Daedalians, Sigma Chi. Address: Commanding Gen Fort Carson CO 80913

BENNETT, JOHN COLEMAN, educator, clergyman; b. Kingston, Ont., Can., July 22, 1902; s. William Russell and Charlotte (Coleman) B.; (parents U.S. citizens), prep. edn., Phillips Exeter Acad., 1918-20; A.B., Williams Coll., 1924; B.A., Oxford Univ. (Mansfield Coll.), 1926, M.A., 1930; B.D., Union Theol. Sem., New York, 1927, S.T.M., 1929; hon. D.D., Church Divinity School of the Pacific, 1940, Pacific School Religion, 1943, Williams, 1947, Yale, 1965, Harvard, 1965, Wesleyan U., 1968, Huron College, London Ontario, Canada, 1969; Dr. Sacred Theology, Oberlin Coll., 1961, Columbia U.; LL.D., Holy Cross Coll., St. Peters Coll., Boston Coll., Manhattan Coll., Fordham U.; D.D., Franklin and Marshall Coll., 1962, Lafayette Coll., 1966, Princeton, 1966, Colgate U., 1967, Glasgow U., 1967; S.T.D., Kenyon Coll., 1966; LL.D. from the Jewish Theological Seminary, 1967; m. to Anne McGrew, Oct. 30, 1931; children—Elizabeth, John McGrew, William McGrew. Instr. in theology, Union Theological Seminary, 1930, 31; asst. prof. of Christian theology, Auburn Theol. Sem., 1931-35, asso. prof., 1935-38; prof. of Christian theology and philosophy of religion, Pacific Sch. of Religion, Berkeley, Calif., 1938-43, now vis. prof. religion; Reinhold Niebuhr professor of social ethics Union Theol. Sem., 1943—, dean of faculty, 1955-64, pres., 1964-70, ordained to ministry Congl. Ch., 1939; found. lectr. Queens Theol. Coll., 1938, Chicago Theol. Sem., 1939, Yale U., 1941, Grinnell Coll., 1942, Lancaster Theol. Sem., 1944, Bangor Theol. Sem., 1945, U. of Va., 1945; Hartford Theol. Sem., 1946, Eden Theol. Sem., 1947; found. lectr. Colgate- Rochester Div. Sch., 1950, Berea Coll., 1951, Garrett Bibl. Inst., 1952; sec. sect. on ch. and econ. order Oxford Conf. on Life and Work, 1937. Vice chairman Liberal Party, New York State, 1955-65. Mem. Am. Theol. Soc. (pres. 1954), Soc. of Christian Social Ethics (pres. 1960), Phi Beta Kappa. Author of several books, since 1935, titles including: Social Salvation, 1935; Christian Ethics and Social Policy, 1946; Christianity and Communism, 1947; The Christian As A Citizen, 1955; Christians and the State, 1958; Foreign Policy in Christian Perspective, 1966. Co-author: Christian Values & Economic Life, 1954. Co-editor: Christianity and Crisis. Editor: Nuclear Weapons and the Conflict of Conscience, 1962: Christian Social Ethics in a Changing World, 1966. Contbr. to religious jours. Home: 2340 Virginia St 94709 Berkeley CA 94709 Office: 1798 Scenic Av Berkeley CA 94709 ☆

BENNETT, JOHN FISHER, former rubber co. exec., b. N.Y.C., June 15, 1908; s. John William and Cora (Fisher) B.; grad. Phillips Exeter Acad., 1926; B.S., Mass. Inst. Tech., 1930; m. Anne Gellatly, Oct. 17, 1936; children—Pollyann, Joan. With Goodyear Tire & Rubber Co., 1930—, dir., sec. Goodyear Tire & Rubber Co. (Australia), 1939-42, asst. treas. Goodyear Tire & Rubber Co., also Goodyear Aircraft Corp., 1942-60, treas. Goodyear Tire & Rubber Co., 1960-70. Treas. Akron Community Trust. Home: 239 Aurora St Hudson OH 44236

BENNETT, JOHN MIRZA, Jr., banker, cattleman; b. San Antonio, June 26, 1908; s. John M. and Jamie (Armstrong) B.; graduate Phillips Acad., Andover, Mass., 1927; student Princeton U., 1927-29; B.A., U. Tex., 1931; m. Eleanor Catherine Freeborn, Dec. 18, 1946; children—Eleanor Bennett Marlow, Carolyn Bennett Wood, Davis Graves, John Stephen. With Standard Trust Co., San Antonio, since 1932, now pres., dir.; chmn. bd. Nat. Bank Commerce, San Antonio, Yoakum Nat. Bank, Yoakum, Texas; director Texas and Southwestern Cattle Raisers Association, American General Insurance Company, Houston. Served as colonel, USAAF, 1940-45, maj. gen. USAF Res.; ret. ret. Decorated Silver Star, Legion of Merit, D.F.C. with oak leaf cluster, Bronze Star, Air medal with three oak leaf clusters; Croix de Guerre avec palm (France). Episcopalian. Clubs: La Rinconada (Mexico); Princeton (N.Y.); Argyle, Country (San Antonio). Author: Letters from England, 1945. Home: 417 W Dewey Pl San Antonio TX 78212 Office: Nat Bank of Commerce Bldg San Antonio TX 78205

BENNETT, JOHN TOSCAN, economist, govt. ofcl.; b. Madison, Wis., Jan. 21, 1929; s. Martin Toscan and Cornelia (Van Der Laan) B.; B.A., Harvard, 1950; M.S., U. Cal., 1952, Ph.D., 1958; m. Maria Waschuck, Nov. 26, 1953; children—Kim, Holly, Michael Toscan. Chief econ. sect. Am. Embassy, Saigon, Vietnam, 1963-65; with A.I.D., 1965—, dir. Office of Econ. Policy Vietnam bur., 1968-69, dep. dir., Santo Domingo, Dominican Rep., 1969—; lectr. Am. U., 1966-69. Mem. Am. Econ. Assn., Econometric Soc. Home: 3801 Towanda Rd Alexandria VA 22303 Office: American Embassy Santo Domingo Dominican Republic

BENNETT, JOHN WILLIAM, author, educator; b. Milw., July 18, 1915; s. William Homer and Elsa (Biersach) B.; A.B., Beloit (Wis.) Coll., 1937; M.A., U. Chgo., 1941, Ph.D., 1946; m. Kathryn Goldsmith, Dec. 7, 1940; children—John M., James P. Asst. prof., asso. prof. dept. sociology and anthropology Ohio State U., 1946-48, 52-59; chief Pub. Opinion and Sociol. Research Div., Japan Occupation, 1948-52; prof. dept. sociology and anthropology Washington U., St. Louis, 1959-67, prof., chmn. dept. anthropology, 1967—; mem. social scis. rev. com. Nat. Inst. Mental Health; sr. fellow Center for Biology of Natural Systems. Mem. Mo. adv. com. U.S. Civil Rights Commn., 1966—. Fellow Am. Anthrop. Assn.; mem. Am. Ethnological Soc. (pres.), Soc. for Applied Anthropology (pres. 1960-62), Assn. for Asian Studies, Am. Sociol. Assn., Ecol. Soc. Am., Sigma Xi. Author: In Search of Identity: Japanese in the U.S. and Japan, 1958; Paternalism in the Japanese Economy, 1963; Hutterian Brethren, 1967; Northern Plainsmen, 1969. Cons. editor: Ency. Americana; editorial bd. Ann. Rev. Anthropology, 1971—. Home: 648 Vassar Av St Louis MO 63130

BENNETT, JOSEPH A., educator; b. Owensboro, Ky., Feb. 6, 1912; s. Ira Franklin and Ethel (Allen) B.; B.S. in Engring., U. Mich., 1934, M.A., 1938; student Western Ky. State Coll., 1934-35; m. Grace Elizabeth Edfred, June 20, 1937; children—James Allen, Shirley Kathryn (Mrs. Robert Carlan Dean), Instr., Western Ky. State Coll., 1935-38, Grand Rapids (Mich.) Jr. Coll., 1938-42, 45-48; product engr. Am. Seating Co., Grand Rapids, 1942- 45; mem. faculty U. Ala., 1949—, now prof. engring.; cons. in field. Mem. Am. Soc. Engring. Edn. (pres. S.E. sect. 1966-67), Am. Assn. U. Profs. (pres. U. Ala. chpt. 1965-66), Nat. Soc. Profl. Engrs. Methodist. Kiwanian (sec.-treas. 1968—). Author: Descriptive Geometry, 1961; Problems in Descriptive Geometry, vols. I, II, III; (with others) Engineering Drawing, 1962, Home: 1917 7th Av E Tuscaloosa AL 35401 Office: Box 1934 University AL 35486

BENNETT, KENNETH HERBERT, mfg. co. exec.; b. Red Wing, Minn., Jan. 18, 1927; s. Charles H. and Hannah (Lange) B.; B.S. in Elec. Engring., U. Minn., 1951, B.B.A., 1951; m. Dorothy J. Abplanalp, Oct. 24, 1953; children—Alan J., Bruce C., Janice L., Lori A. With Cutler Hammer, Inc., Milw., 1951—, v.p. finance, treas., 1969—; instr. eve. div. Marquette U., 1959-60. Mem. Greenfield (Wis.) Indsl. Devel. Commn., 1966-69. Trustee Citizens Govtl. Research Bur. Wis. Served with USNR, 1944- 46. Mem. Financial Execs. Inst., Planning Execs. Inst., Greenfield C. of C. (bd. dirs. 1964-67), Milw. Better Bus. Bur. (dir.), Alpha Kappa Psi. Home: 5858 S 43d St Greenfield WI 53220 Office: 4201 N 27th St Milwaukee WI 53216

BENNETT, LERONE, Jr., mag. editor, author; b. Clarksdale, Miss., Oct. 17, 1928; s. Lerone and Alma (Reed) B.; B.A., Morehouse Coll. 1949, D.Letters 1966; m. Gloria Sylvester, July 21, 1956; children—Alma Joy, Constance, Courtney, Lerone III. Reporter, Atlanta Daily World, 1949-51, city editor, 1952-53; asso. editor Ebony mag., Chgo., 1953-58, sr. editor, 1958—; vis. prof. history Northwestern U., 1969. Bd. dirs. Race Relations Information Center, Inst. of Black World; trustee Martin Luther King, Jr. Meml. Center. Recipient Patron Saints award Soc. Midland Authors, 1965, Book of Year award Capital Press Club, 1963. Mem. Black Acad. Arts and Letters. Kappa Alpha Psi. Author: Before the Mayflower: A History of the Negro in America, 1619-1964, 1962, rev., 1964; The Negro Mood, 1964; What Manner of Man; A Biography of Martin Luther King, Jr., 1964; Confrontation: Black and White, 1965; Black Power U.S.A., 1968; Pioneers in Protest, 1968, Contbr. New Negro Poets: USA, 1964, American Negro Short Stories, 1966. Home: 1308 E 89th St Chicago IL 60619 Office: 1820 S Michigan Av Chicago IL 60616

BENNETT, LESLIE LATTY, physiologist, educator; b. Portland, Ore., Nov. 15, 1908; s. Leslie Nathaniel and Matilda Ann (Latty) B.; A.B., U. Cal., 1933, Ph.D., 1937, M.D., 1940; m. Dorothy Isabelle Nelson, Aug. 9, 1935; children—Mary Elizabeth, John Leslie. Instr. physiology and medicine U. Cal. Med. Sch., 1942-43, asst. prof., 1943-45; faculty U. Cal., San Francisco, 1945—, successively asst. prof. physiology and exptl. biology, asso. prof., 1945-50, prof., 1950—, chmn. capt. physiology, 1953-66, acting vice chancellor acad. affairs, 1965-66, vice chancellor acad. affairs, 1966-71, acting chancellor, 1969, Morris Herzstein prof. biology, 1955—; on sabbatical leave, 1948-49, as sr. med. fellow Commonwealth Fund, also research fellow medicine Harvard and asst. in medicine Peter Bent Brigham Hosp., Boston. Mem. endocrine study sect., research grants div. USPHS, 1952-55. Mem. Albany (Cal.) Sch. Bd., 1952-60. Mem. Am. Physiol. Soc., Soc. Exptl. Biology and Medicine, Endocrine Soc., Western Soc. Clin. Research, A.A.A.S., Phi Beta Kappa, Sigma Xi, Alpha Omega Alpha. Contbr. articles profl. jours. Mem. editorial bd. Jour. Clin. Endocrinology and Metabolism. Home: 959 Peralta Av Albany CA 94716 Office: Sch Medicine U Cal San Francisco CA 94122

BENNETT, LOUIS LOWELL, lawyer, educator, social worker; b. N.Y.C., Jan. 15, 1909; s. Maurice and Sarah (Brown) B.; LL.B., St. John's U., 1931, B.S., 1939; M.S., N.Y. Sch. Social Work, Columbia, 1941, Fed. bar, 1931; m. Estelle Goldman, June 8, 1929; children—Peter Charles, Richard. Dir. evening session St. John's U., 1927-41; admitted to N.Y. bar, 1931, practiced in N.Y.C., 1932-41; asst. regional dir. U.S. Office Community War Services, N.Y., 1941-45; dir., organizer, exec. Vets. Service Center, N.Y.C., 1944-45; cons. to adminstr., regional housing expediter Nat. Housing Agy., Washington, also N.Y.C., 1945-47; asst. exec. dir. Am. Jewish Com., N.Y.C., 1947-49; exec. dir. N.Y. Assn. for New Americans, 1949-52; asst. exec. vice chmn. Nat. United Jewish Appeal, 1952-56; exec. dir. Jewish Child Care Assn. of N.Y., 1956-60; asst. exec. dir. Comm. Council Greater N.Y., 1960-62; regional representative Office of Aging, Dept. Health, Edn., Welfare, N.Y.C., 1962-65, regional rep. Bur. Family Services, prin. welfare adminstrn. regional representative, 1965-67; dep. regional commr., dep. equal employment opportunities rep. Social and Rehab. Service, 1967-70; prof., dean students, chmn. dept. student personnel services Baruch Coll., City U. N.Y., 1970—. Cons. War Manpower Commn., 1942-44; lectr. N.Y. Sch. Social Work, 1942-45; lectr., condr. insts. at numerous colls. and univs.; adv. bd. N.Y. state health Preparedness Commn., 1943; hon. dep. commr. N.Y. State Dept. Social Welfare, 1950; cons. N.Y. State Civil Def. Commn., 1950; cons. U.S. Office Edn., 1952-53; chmn. family and child welfare com., chmn., sec. functional planning bd. Community Council Greater N.Y., 1956-60, bd. mem., 1959-60; nominating com. N.Y. State Welfare Conf., 1958-60; bd. dirs. Child Welfare League America, 1960-62; mem. bd. Assn. Children's Instns. N.Y. State, 1956- 60; mem. joint bd. com. Council Social Work Edn.-Nat. Assn. Social Workers, 1960-67; mem. com. psychiatric services for children Dept. Hospitals, 1962-65; mem. examining panel N.Y. State Civil Service Commn., 1968—; mem. examining panel N.Y.C. Civil Service Commn., 1956—; program chmn. combined asso. group meetings Nat. Conf. Social Welfare, 1957; functional planning com. Fedn. Jewish Philanthropies of N.Y., 1957-60. Mem. Nat. Assn. Social Workers (mem. bd. N.Y.C. chpt. 1956-59; nat. treas., nat. bd. 1959-61), Am. Bar Assn., Am. Pub. Welfare Assn., Am. Soc. Pub. Adminstrn. (sr.), N.Y. Sch. Social Work Alumni Assn. (pres. 1945-48, nominating com.), Acad. Certified Social Workers, Council Social Work Edn. (3d v.p., mem. bd., exec. com.), Nat. Council Juvenile Ct. Judges (asso.), Am. Arbitration Assn., Nat. Conf. Social Work, Nat. Conf. Lawyers and Social Workers (co.-chmn. 1965-70, hon. mem. 1970—). Contbr. numerous articles to profl. publs. Home: 2001 Avenue P Brooklyn NY 11229 Office: 17 Lexington Av New York City NY 10010

BENNETT, MAILLARD, hotel exec.; b. Berkeley, Cal., Sept. 9, 1904; s. Oscar M. and Bertha (Olsen) B.; B.S., U. Cal. at Berkeley, 1926; m. Gladys Comstock, Dec. 25, 1932 (dec. Jan. 1961); children—Ardys C., Jane; m. 2d, Mary Carrell, Oct. 22, 1963. Truck, bus tire sales mgr. Firestone Tire & Rubber Co., San Francisco, 1926-36; mgr. Brockway Hot Springs, Lake Tahoe, Cal., summers, 1936—, Ariz. Inn, Tucson, winters, 1936—; pres. Brockway Hotel Co., Brockway Land & Water Co., Oakwood Investment Co.; dir. Hotel Red Book Corp. Mem. hotel adv. com. NPA; v.p., trustee Am. Hotel and Motel Assn. Ednl. Inst.; mem. adv. com. Cal. Dept. Parks and Recreation. Named Compagnon de Bordeaux, Le Grand Counceil L'Académie du Vin de Bordeaux. Mem. Am. Hotel and Motel Assn. (past pres.), Ariz. (dir., past pres.), Cal. No. (hon. dir.), Cal. State (hon. dir.) hotel assns., Internat. Platform Assn., Hotel Greeters Internat., Confrerie de la Chaine des Rotisseurs, Delta Phi Epsilon. Clubs: Old Pueblo, Tucson Country, Rotary, Tucson Sunshine Climate (dir.) (Tucson); Tavern (N.Y.C.); Brockway Country (Lake Tahoe, Cal.); Soc. for Pigeons, (N.Y.C.). Home: Brockway Lake Tahoe CA 95719 Office: Arizona Inn Tucson AZ 85719

BENNETT, MARION TINSLEY, U.S. ct. ofcl.; b. Buffalo, Mo., June 6, 1914; s. Philip Allen and Bertha (Tinsley) B.; A.B., Southwest Mo. State Teachers Coll., 1935; J.D., Washington U., 1938; m. June Young, Apr. 27, 1941; children—Ann (Mrs. Paul B. Guptill), William Philip. Admitted to Mo. bar, 1938, D.C. bar, 1956, U.S. Supreme Court, also other fed. cts.; pvt. practice of law, 1938-43; adminstrv. asst. to father, 1941-43; mem. 78th-79th Congresses, 6th Mo. Dist.; commr. U.S. Ct. of Claims, 1949-64, chief commr., 1964—. Mem. Greene County Republican Central Com., 1938-42. Col. USAF Res. Mem. Fed. Bar Assn. (nat. council), Judge Advocates Assn., Res. Officers Assn., Delta Theta Phi. Republican. Methodist (ofcl. bd.). Club: Exchange. Author: American Immigration Policies, A History, 1963. Home: 3715 Cardiff Rd Chevy Chase MD 20015 also 731 S Pickwick Springfield MO 65802 Office: U S Court of Claims Washington DC 20439

BENNETT, MARY WOODS, coll. dean; b. Oakland, Cal., Apr. 5, 1909; d. Louis W. and Mary (Sperry) Bennett; A.B., U. Cal., 1931, Ph.D., 1937. Faculty Mills Coll., 1935—, successively asst. in child development and coordinator of the Family Council, instr., asst. prof., asso. prof., prof. psychology and child development, dean of faculty, 1953—, provost, 1954—. Mem. Am. Assn. U. Women, Soc. Research Child Development, Phi Beta Kappa, Sigma Xi. Address: Mills College Oakland CA 94613

BENNETT, MICHAEL MOFFETT, coll. pres.; b. Westfield, Ill., May 30, 1916; s. Clayton Moffett and Iva Ruth (Phillips) B.; B.B.A., U. Fla., 1940; M.A., Fla. State U., 1949, Ed.D., 1955; m. Beverly Ann Backus, June 21, 1942; children—Charles, William. Registrar, St. Petersburg Jr. Coll., 1940-47, dean admissions, 1947-49, dean of men, 1949, pres., 1950—. Bd. dirs. Fla. West Coast Ednl. TV, Inc.; trustee St. Petersburg Art Mus. Member So. Assn. Jr. Colls. (pres.), Fla. Assn. Pub. Jr. Colls. (past pres.), So. Assn. Colls. and Secondary Schs. (sec. commn. on higher edn.). Democrat. Episcopalian. Rotarian. Home: 300 Lakeshore Dr N St Petersburg FL 33710

BENNETT, MIRIAM FRANCES, educator; b. Milw., May 17, 1928; d. Stanley Edward and Dorothy (Wheeler) Bennett; A.B., Carleton Coll., 1950; A.M., Mt. Holyoke Coll., 1952; Ph.D., Northwestern U., 1954. Mem. faculty Sweet Briar Coll., 1954—, prof.

biology, 1964. Mem. corp. Marine Biol. Lab. NSF fellow, 1961. Fellow A.A.A.S.; mem. Am. Soc. Zoologists, Ecol. Soc. Am., N.Y., Va. acads. scis., Am. Inst. Biol. scis., Am. Microscopical Soc., Assn. So. Biologists, Sigma Xi. Author articles biol. rhythmicity and endocrinology. Address: Sweet Briar Coll Sweet Briar VA 24595

BENNETT, NEWCOMB BENJAMIN, Jr., civil engr.; b. Sheridan, Wyo., Oct. 14, 1910; s. Newcomb Benjamin and Mabel Lillian (Haywood) B.; student Kemper Mil. Sch., 1928-29; B.S., U. Neb., 1933; m. Thelma Lee Sanders, Oct. 20, 1934; children—Newcomb Benjamin III, Becky Lou. Surveyor U.S. Bur. Reclamation, 1933-35, engr., 1942-53, chief div. project development, 1953-59; asst. commr. for power and gen. engring., 1959-70; resident engr. Dan J. McQuaid Engring. Service, 1935-39; asst. state engr. Wyo., 1939-42; engr.-sec. Wyo. Water Conservation Bd., 1939-42; resources cons. engr, 1970—; dir. Papago Tribal Utility Authority, 1970—. Former chmn. U.S. sect. Internat. Souris-Red River Engring. Bd. of Internat. Waterton-Belly engring. Bd., chmn. U.S. Sect. Internat. Pembina River Engring. Bd.; former mem. adv. bd. office critical tables Nat. Acad. Scis., Nat. Research Council; former mem. exec. com. Federal Construction Council; former member Interior Committee on Research and Development. Recipient Superior Performance award U.S. Department of Interior, 1958, Distinguished Service award, 1968. Fellow Am. Soc. C.E.; mem. Sigma Alpha Epsilon. Mason. Home: 10721 Saratoga Circle Sun City AZ 85351

BENNETT, NORMAN E., publisher; b. Saugus, Mass., Aug. 15, 1917; s. Elmer A. and Mildred J. (Smith) B.; student N.Y.U., 1937-40; m. Eleanor Teel, Dec. 3, 1942; children—Roger, Jeffrey, Alison. Dir. bus. relations, v.p. Nat. Better Bus. Bur., 1946-51; with P.F. Collier Inc., N.Y.C., 1951—, sr. v.p., 1960-65, pres., 1965-68, chmn. bd., 1968—; v.p. Crowell-Collier & MacMillan, Inc., N.Y.C., 1961-67, sr. v.p., 1968—; chmn. bd. Merit Students Ency., Inc., 1968—; pres. P.F. Collier Ltd., Toronto, Ont., Can., 1965-68, chmn., 1968—, also dir.; dir. Collier Services. Mem. at large Nassau County council Boy Scouts Am. Trustee Oceanside (N.Y.) Pub. Library. Served to lt. col., ordnance dept., AUS, 1941-45. Clubs: Rockville Links (Rockville Centre, N.Y.); Army and Navy (Washington). Home: 244 Rockaway Av Oceanside NY 11572 Office: 866 3d Av New York City NY 10022

BENNETT, OTES, Jr., coal co. exec.; b. Barbour County, W.Va., July 30, 1921; s. Otes and Bertha (Cozad) B.; B.S. in Mining Engring., W.Va. U., 1955; m. Naomi Ruth Queen, May 5, 1941; children—Barbara (Mrs. Charles R. Hertzler), Rebecca (Mrs. A.J. Beal), Jeffrey. With N. Am. Coal Co., Cleve., 1955—, 1955—, v.p., 1961-65, pres., 1965-70, pres., chief exec. officer, 1970—. Served with USAAF, 1942-45; ETO. Decorated Air medal with 4 oak leaf clusters. Registered profl. engr., W.Va., Ohio, Pa. Mem. Nat. Coal assn. (bd. dirs.), Bituminous Coal Operators Assn. (bd. dirs.). Home: 2056 Taylor Rd Cleveland OH 44112 Office: 12800 Shaker Blvd Cleveland OH 44120

BENNETT, RAINEY, artist; b. Marion, Ind., July 20, 1907; s. William Rainey and Ethel (Clark) B.; Ph.B., U. Chgo., 1930; suudied art at Art Inst., Chgo., Am. Acad. Art (Chgo.), Art Students League and George Grosz-Maurice Stern Sch., N.Y.; m. Ann Port, Oct. 4, 1936; children—Pamela, Renee, Anthony. Free lance work for book publs., 1931-33; mural Peoples Gas Co. at Century of Progress, Chgo., 1933; supr. Fed. Art Project, Chgo., 1935-38; executed mural for Post Office, Dearborn, Mich., 1937, Rushville, Ill., 1938, Naperville, Ill., 1941; 13-panel mural for The Neil House, Columbus, O., 1939; commd. by Nelson Rockefeller to paint water colors in Venezuela for Standard Oil Co., 3 months, 1939, Brazil, Argentina, Bolivia, Peru, Ecuador, 1941. Exhibited Downtown Gallery (New York), Art Inst. Chgo., Cleve. Mus., Toledo Mus., Whitney Mus., Musee du que de Paume (Paris). Rep. in Met. Mus. Mus. of Modern Art (New York), Cranbrook Mus., Chgo. Art Inst. and varius pvt. collections. Author, illustrator: What Do You Think?, 1958; The Secret Hiding Place, 1960. Home: 5761 Dorchester Chicago IL 60637

BENNETT, RALPH DECKER, consultant; b. Williamson, N.Y., June 30, 1900; s. Edward Augustus and Sarah Jane (Decker) B.; B.S., Union Coll., 1921, M.S., 1923, Sc.D. (hon.), 1945; Ph.D., U. Chgo., 1925; m. Anna Gray, Apr. 15, 1967; children—Sarah Louise, Ralph Decker. Instr. math. Union Coll., 1921-23, asst. prof. physics, 1925-26; NRC fellow Princeton, 1926-27, Cal. Inst. Tech., 1927-28; research asso. U. Chgo., 1928-31; asso. prof. elec. measurements Mass. Inst. Tech., 1931-37, prof., 1937-46; chief mine and depth charge div. Naval Ordnance Lab., 1941-44, tech. dir., 1944-54; mgr. tech. dept. Knolls Atomic Power Lab. General Electric Co., Schenectady, N.Y., 1954-56; mgr. Gen. Electric Vallecitos Atomic Lab., Pleasanton, Cal., 1956-61; dir. research, v.p. nuclear div. Martin Co., Balt., 1961-65, v.p. research, 1965-66; cons. U.S. Navy 1966—, U.S. Coast Guard, 1970—. Bd. dirs. Atomic Indsl. Forum, 1963-69; chmn. Council Edn. for Nuclear Industry, 1968—. Life trustee Union Coll. Served from lt. comdr. to capt., USNR, 1940-47. Recipient USN Distinguished Civilian Service medal, Navy Meritorious Civilian Service award; decorated Legion of Merit; officer Order Brit. Empire. Fellow Am. Phys. Soc., I.E.E.E.; mem. Am. Soc. Engring. Edn., Am. Nuclear Soc., Sigma Xi. Clubs: Mohawk, Cosmos. Author papers in field. Address: 204 San Rafael Av Belvedere CA 94920

BENNETT, REYNOLD, lawyer, assn. exec.; b. Detroit, June 26, 1918; s. Harry S. and Muriel R. (Lynn) B.; B.S., Harvard, 1940; LL.B., Georgetown U., 1948; LL.M., Cambridge (Eng.) U., 1949; m. Dorothy Dyer, May 1, 1953; children—Reynold, Dorothy. Admitted to Mich. bar, 1949, N.Y. bar, 1957; practiced in Detroit, 1949-51; with Office Judge Adv. Gen., Army Hdqrs., Washington, 1951-54; legal staff Bell System, N.Y., 1954-57; with N.A.M., N.Y.C., 1958—, dir. creative industry program, 1962—, v.p., 1967—. Mem. Mich. Gov.'s Legal Study Commn., 1949-51; dir. Pacific Indsl. Property Assn., 1970—; del. Patent Cooperation Treaty Diplomatic Conf., Geneva, Washington, 1970. Bd. dirs. Jr. Engring. Tech. Soc., 1967-70. Served to capt. AUS, 1942-46; PTO, Pentagon. Mem. Am., N.Y., Patent Law, Internat. bar assns., Assn. Internationale pour le Protection de Propriete Industriel, A.A.A.S. Unitarian (pres. All Souls N.Y. Laymen's League 1962—). Author, editor: Living Tomorrow—Today!, 1970. Editor Fed. Bar Jour., 1952-54. Contbr. articles and pamphlets to legal and sci. lit. Home: 903 Park Av New York City NY 10021 Office: care Nat Assn Mfrs 277 Park Av New York City NY 10017

BENNETT, RICHARD EARLE, corp. exec.; b. N.Y.C. Oct. 6, 1919; s. David L. and Augusta (Levanthal) B.; B.Mech. Engring., Coll. City N.Y., 1941; grad. student Stevens Inst. Tech., 1947-49; m. Helen Pitsillidis, Nov. 22, 1961; 1 son, Gerald Richard; 1 dau. by previous marriage, Nancy (Mrs. Hervey Friss). Mfg. engr. Western Electric Co., 1945-50; owner, operator Fairmount Tool Co., Newark, 1950-51; gen. mgr. Daystrom, Inc., later Weston Instruments, Inc., 1952-64; with Internat. Tel. & Tel. Corp., 1964—, exec. v.p. office of pres. operations, 1967—, also dir.; dir. various subsidiaries. Served with AUS, 1942-44. Mason. Patentee wire wrap tool used in electronic assembly. Home: 18 Laurie Dr Englewood Cliffs NJ 07632 Office: 320 Park Av New York City NY 10022

BENNETT, RICHARD JOSEPH, corp. exec.; b. Bklyn., Jan. 20, 1917; s. Richard and Gertrude (McGuire) B.; A.B., Fordham Coll., 1938, LL.B., 1942; m. Eileen P. O'Neill, May 4, 1946; children—Susan, Richard. Admitted to N.Y. bar, 1942; mem. firm Whedon & Bennett, N.Y.C., 1945-46; staff atty. Schering Corp., Bloomfield, N.J., 1947-55, asst. sec., asst. gen. counsel, 1955-59, sec., gen. atty., 1959-70, v.p., sec., gen. counsel, 1970—; v.p., sec., gen. counsel Schering-Plough Corp., 1971—. Served with USAAF, 1942-45. Mem. Am., N.Y. State bar assns., N.Y. County Lawyers Assn., Am. Soc. Corporate Secs. Home: 10 Maple Dr North Caldwell NJ 07006 Office: 60 Orange St Bloomfield NJ 07003

BENNETT, RICHARD MARSH, architect; b. Braddock, Pa., Feb. 4, 1907; s. Herbert George and Florence (Hunter) B.; S.B., Harvard, 1928, M.Arch., 1931; Julia Appleton Amory fellowship, 1931-33; A.M. (hon.), Yale, 1946; m. Susan Jacobson 1957; children by previous marriage—Judy, Mark. Instr. Rensselaer Poly. Inst., 1934-36; vis. lectr. Vassar, 1938-43; partner Hornbostel and Bennett, 1938-43; asst. prof. Yale, 1940-43, prof. design, 1945-47; dir. of design Montgomery Ward, 1943-45; partner Loebl, Schlossman, Bennett & Dart, architects and engrs., 1947—. Prin. works: bldgs. at Wheaton Coll., Norton, Mass.; town of Park Forest, Ill.; hosps., schs., shopping center, apts., religious bldgs. in Chgo. area. Mem. archtl. adv. com. Office of Fgn. Bldg., U.S. Dept. of State, 1956-58. Mem. Nat. Archtl. Accrediting Bd. Fellow A.I.A. Author: (with H.L. Kamphaefer and Paul Thiry) Churches and Temples, 1954. Home: 880 Lake Shore Dr Chicago IL 60611 Office: 333 N Michigan Av Chicago IL 60611

BENNETT, ROBERT RUSSELL, composer, conductor; b. Kansas City, Mo., June 15, 1894; s. George Robert and May (Bradford) B.; studied harmony, counterpoint and composition with Carl Busch and Nadia Boulanger; studied in Paris, Berlin, Vienna and London, 5 yrs.; Dr. Humane Letters, Franklin and Marshall Coll., 1965; m. Louise Edgerton Merrill, Dec. 26, 1919; 1 dau., Jean. Played violin, piano and trombone, Kansas City, 1908-16; copyist, orchestrator, composer of music, N.Y.C., 1916-26; composer and conductor, Europe, 1926-29, 1932, Hollywood, Cal., 1935-40; composer, conductor and commentator, radio stations at N.Y.C., 1940—; composer and conductor television films, 1950—. Awarded fellowship John Simon Guggenheim Memorial Foundation, 2 yrs.; 2 Victor prizes ($5000 each) for symphonic works. Mem. A.S.C.A.P., Nat. Assn. Am. Composers and Conductors (pres. 1947), Bohemians (pres. 1965). Clubs: Tennis (Los Angeles); West Side Tennis (N.Y.). Author in Field. Home: 140 E 56th St New York City NY Office: 30 Rockefeller Plaza New York City NY

BENNETT, ROBERT BARCLAY, chem. mfg. co. exec.; b. Midland, Mich., Oct. 23, 1920; s. Earl Willard and Eva Victoria (Barclay) B.; student U. Mich., 1940-42; m. Bonita Lowden, Aug. 2, 1941; children—Stephanie, Constance. With Dow Chem. Co., Midland, Mich., 1942—, successively accounting clk., asst. credit mgr., credit mgr., asst. treas., 1942-59, treas., 1959—, also dir.; chmn. bd. Dow Banking Corp., Zurich, Switzerland; dir. Chem. State Savs. Bank, Midland, Second Nat. Bank & Trust Co., Saginaw, Michigan. Served with USNR, 1944-46. Home: 1015 W Sunet Rd Midland MI 48640 Office: Dow Chemical Co Midland MI 48640

BENNETT, ROBERT EUGENE, physician; b. Kingston, Pa., Jan. 1, 1913; s. Isaiah L. and Martha L. (Stookey) B.; B.S., Ursinus Coll., 1934, D.Sc. (hon.), 1964; M.D., U. Pa., 1938; m. Ida B. Trout, Aug. 28, 1937; children—Robert Eugene, Herbert Branin. Intern Cooper Hosp., Camden, N.J., 1938-39; psychiat. resident Trenton (N.J.) State Hosp., 1939-42, chief female service, 1945- 47, clin. dir., 1948-52, asst. med. dir., 1952-58; med. dir. Cleve. Receiving Hosp., 1947-48; med. dir., chief exec. officer N.J. Neuro- Psychiat. Inst., Princeton, 1958-68; staff psychiatrist Carrier Clinic, Belle Mead, N.J., 1968—; mem. faculty Western Res. Sch. Medicine, 1947- 48. Trustee N.J. Mental Health Research and Devel. Fund, 1964—. Served as flight surgeon USAAF, 1942-45; CBI. Diplomate Am. Bd. Psychiatry and Neurology. Fellow Am. Psychiat. Assn.; mem. A.M.A., Med. Soc. N.J. Contbr. med. jours. Home: 24 Robin Dr Skillman NJ 08558 Office: Box 147 Belle Mead NJ 08502

BENNETT, ROBERT LEO, Jr., physician; b. Wilkinsburg, Pa., Dec. 18, 1911; s. Robert Leo and Nelle (McGuire) B.; B.S., U. Pitts., 1934, M.D., 1936, D.Sc., 1960; M.S., U. Minn., (fellowship Mayo Clinic, 1937-40), 1940; m. Esther McDowell, July 10, 1937; children—Judith, Susan. Intern Mercy Hosp., Pitts., 1936-37; asst. prof. phys. medicine, U. Wis., 1940-41; dir. phys. medicine Ga. Warm Springs Found., 1941-48, asst. med. dir., 1948-53, med. dir., 1953-58, exec. dir., 1958—; prof. phys. medicine Emory U. Med. Sch., 1945—, chmn. dept. phys. medicine Emory U. Hosp., 1946-65; clin. prof. medicine Sch. Medicine, U. Ga., 1970—; clin. prof. phys. medicine Coll. Medicine, U.S.C., 1970—; Horowitz vis. prof. N.Y.U. Inst. Phys. Medicine and Rehab., 1962. Mem. phys. therapy adv. com. Ga. State Coll., 1969—; mem. Meriwether County Hosp. Authority, Ga.; mem. com. prosthetic research and devel. Nat. Acad. Scis.-NRC; med. dir. Ga. Rehab. Center; cons. area 3, phys. medicine rehab. VA, 1945-65; cons. Ga. Crippled Children's Div., 1947—, to surgeon-gen. phys. med., 1948—; mem. adv. coms. Dept. Health, Edn. and Welfare, Nat. Found., American Rehab. Foundation; v.p. Ga. chpt. Arthritis Found., 1969. Recipient Gold Key award Am. Congress Phys. Medicine and Rehab., 1955. Diplomate Am. Bd. Phys. Medicine and Rehab. (sec. treas. 1947- 53, chmn. bd. 1953-63). Mem. Internat. (v.p. 1957, chmn. exec. com. 1960), Am. (pres. 1951-52) congresses phys. medicine, Internat. Soc. Rehab. Disabled (Am. bd. dirs. 1965—), Am. (chmn. sect. phys. medicine 1961), So. med. assns., Am. Rheumatism Assn., Am. Acad. Phys. Medicine and Rehab., Internat. Rehab. Medicine Assn. (U.S. councillor 1st internat. meeting 1970), Am. Acad. Cerebral Palsy, Am. Acad. Neurology, Sigma Xi, Sigma Chi. Nu Sigma Nu, Cath. Club: Rotary. Author numerous papers in field. Home: Warm Springs Found Warm Springs GA 31830 Office: Emory Hospital Atlanta GA 30322

BENNETT, ROBERT WILLIAM, metall. engr.; b. Denver, Feb. 26, 1917; s. William J. and Augusta J. (Robson) B.; Metall. Engr., Colo. Sch. Mines, 1940; m. Geraldine Carrell, July 4, 1941; children—Robert J., Jeri Janene, Kathleen J. Welding metallurgist Caterpillar Tractor Co., 1940-42; welding research engr. Battelle Meml. Inst., Columbus, O., 1942-49, sr. tech. adviser, 1965—; metallurgist, chief quality control engr. Alco Products, Inc., Dunkirk, N.Y., 1949-54, chief metallurgist charge welding, metall. and chem. engring., Schenectady, 1955-62, dir. research and devel. engring., 1962-63; asst. to gen. mgr., project mgr. atomic fuel div. Westinghouse Electric Corp., 1963-65. Mem. citizens adv. com. Niskayuna Pub. Schs. Registered profl. engr., Ohio Mem. Am. Soc. Metals, Am. Soc. Testing Materials (exec. counicl central N.Y. dist.), Canadian Welding Bur., Am. Ordnance Assn., Pipe Fabrication Inst., Am. Welding Soc., Sigma Xi. Methodist. Odd Fellow, Mason. Author tech. papers, lectr. in field. Home: 4154 Squires Lane Columbus OH 43221 Office: 505 King Av Columbus OH 43201

BENNETT, RUSSELL HOADLEY, engr., rancher; b. Mpls., Nov. 30, 1896; s. Russell Meridan and Helen (Harrison) B.; grad. Phillips Acad., Andover, Mass., 1915; A.B., Yale, 1920; student Columbia, 1920-21; m. Miriam Fletcher, May 31, 1924; children—Winslow W., Helen H. (Mrs. W.J. Beus), Miriam (Mrs. D.S. Leslie, Jr.), Fletcher, Meridan, David T., Noel F. Chmn., Electro Manganese Corp., Knoxville, Tenn., 1941-56; dir. Meriden Iron Co., Mpls.; former chmn. Placer Devel., Ltd.; dir. Sargent Land Co.; trustee Farmers and Mechanics Savs. Bank; owner, operator Shoderee Ranch, Pincher Creek, Alta., Can., 1932—. Commr. representing City Mpls. in Met. Drainage Commn., 1927-31. Chmn. bd. trustees Dunwoody Indsl. Inst. Mpls., 1937-61. Registered profl. engr., Minn. Mem. Am. Inst. Mining and Metall. Engrs. Republican. Methodist. Clubs: Minneapolis, Explorers. Century Assn. (N.Y.C.). Author: The Compleat Rancher: A Decade of Electrolytic Manganese; Quest for Ore; also articles in profl. jours. Home: 2217 E Lake of Isles Blvd Minneapolis MN 55405 also Shoderee Ranch Pincher Creek Alberta Canada Office: Baker Bldg Minneapolis MN 55402

BENNETT, RUSSELL ODBERT, lawyer; b. Dexter, Mo., July 11, 1915; s. Corna Lewman and Nelle (Odbert) B.; A.B., U. Okla., 1936; LL.B., Harvard, 1939; m. Patricia Birch, June 26, 1948; children—Birch Odbert, Russell Andrew. Admitted to Ill. bar, 1939; asso. firm Taylor, Miller, Busch & Boyden, Chgo., 1939- 41; asso. firm Leibman, Williams, Bennett, Baird and Minow, and predecessors, Chgo., 1946-52, partner firm, 1952—. Dir. Doric Corp., Federal Petroleum Co., Oklahoma City. Bd. dirs. Northwestern U. Settlement; bd. dirs. Lawrence Hall-Randall House, 1949- -, pres., 1960-63; trustee Kemper Mil. Sch. Served to maj. AUS, 1941-46. Mem. Am., Ill., Chgo. bar assns., Am. Law Inst., Am. Judicature Soc., Chgo. Council Fgn. Relations, Phi Beta Kappa, Phi Gamma Delta. Republican. Episcopalian. Clubs: Law, Legal, Economic, Attic (Chgo.); Exmoor Country. Home: 918 Locust Rd Wilmette IL 60091 Office: One First National Plaza Chicago IL 60604

BENNETT, SILAS FLEMING, librarian; b. Everson, W.Va., Aug. 20, 1910; s. Jonathan Lloyd and Beulah Gertrude (McIntire) B.; A.B., Fairmont State Coll., 1931; B.L.S., Western Res. U., 1941; student Grad. Library Sch., U. Chgo., 1947-50; m. Violet Marie Mackey, Oct. 20, 1943; children—Carole Roxane, Richard Fleming. Librarian Fairmont Jr. High Sch., 1934-40, Findlay (O.) Sr. High Sch., 1941-42; asst. reference librarian W.Va. U. Library, 1942, 1945-46, chief audio-visual aids librarian, 1946-47; head acquisitions dept. Columbia Libraries, 1950-52; univ. librarian U. Ariz., 1952-64; librarian Inst. Food and Agrl. Scis., U. Fla., 1964-69, asst. dir. libraries U. Fla., 1969—. Pres. bd. trustees Tucson Pub. Library, 1961-64. Mem. A.L.A. (council 1954-59), Assn. Coll. and Research Libraries (chmn. agrl. and biol. scis. 1965-66, chmn. Oberly Meml. award com. 1968-71), Ariz. Library Assn. (pres. 1956-58), Am. Assn. U. Profs., Alpha Psi Omega. Asso. editor Ariz. Librarian, 1959-60, editor, 1962-64. Contbr. articles library jours. Home: 318 SW 40th Terrace Gainesville FL 32601

BENNETT, STEPHEN FREDERIC, engring. co. exec.; b. Birmingham, Eng., Nov. 22, 1908; s. Frederick William and Janet (Best) B.; 1st class honours degree in Math. Tripos, Clare Coll., Cambridge U., 1930; m. Valerie Grace Wade, Sept. 3, 1938; children—Jennifer (now Mrs. Gordon), William Seymour. Sec., Neckar Water Softener Co. Ltd., 1930-31, mng. dir., 1931- 52; dir. Brit. Timken Ltd., 1950-59, asst. mng. dir., 1952-59; mng. dir. Brit. Timken div. Timken Co., 1959-68, chmn., 1963- -; dir. Timken Co., Canton, O. Justice of peace County Northampton, 1963—. Bd. govs. St. Andrew's Hosp., Northampton, Wellingborough Sch., Northamptonshire. Mem. Inst. Dirs., Pilgrims, Magistrates' Assn. Club: Carlton (London). Home: The Manor House Everdon nr Daventry Northamptonshire England Office: British Timken Div Timken Co Duston Northampton England

BENNETT, THEODORE LAKE, educator; b. Portage, N.Y., Sept 24, 1899; s. Charles Benjamin and Mary Leslie (Parmelee) B.; A.B., Cornell U., 1921; A.M. U. Ill., 1923, Ph.D., 1926; NRC fellow, Princeton U., 1928-29; m. Betty Scott, June 1, 1943. Instr. math. U. Ill., 1925-28; asst. prof. math. U. Wis., 1929-37; prof. math. Marietta (O.) Coll., 1937-69, prof. emeritus, 1970—, chmn. dept., 1942-67. Mem. Math. Assn. Am., Phi Beta Kappa, Sigma Xi, Phi Kappa Phi, Gamma Alpha, Kappa Mu Epsilon, Delta Sigma Phi, Omicron Delta Kappa. Home: 327 5th St Marietta OH 45750

BENNETT, TONY, entertainer; b. Long Island City, N.Y., Aug. 3, 1926; s. John and Anna (Suraci) Benedetto; ed. pub. schs., N.Y.C., also Am. Theatre Wing; m. Patricia Beech, Feb. 12, 1952; children—D'Andrea, Daegal. Nightclub entertainer; frequent appearances on TV and in summer stock. Recipient gold records for recordings Because of You; winner 17 popularity polls, also Cash Box mag. best male vocalist award, 1951. Recordings for Columbia Records. Served with inf., AUS, World War II. Home and office: 271 Next Day Hill Ct Englewood NJ 07631

BENNETT, VERUS WARD, Jr., hotel exec.; b. Binghamton, N.Y., June 6, 1923; s. Verus Ward and Ruth (Caldwell) B.; B.S., Mich. State U.; m. Dolores Mae Bileske, Sept. 9, 1945; children—Cheryl Ann (Mrs. Dennis Bement), Debbie Kaye. With Sheraton Hotels, 1960—, gen. mgr. Sheraton Lincoln, Houston, 1968—; tchr. bus. U. Houston. Bd. dirs. Houston Conv. and Visitors Bur.; active Tex. Tourist Commn. Served with USAAF, 1942-46. Mem. Mich. State U. Alumni Assn. Presbyn. Home: 777 Polk St Houston TX 77002

BENNETT, W. T., diversified industry exec. Controller, Armour-Dial, Inc., Chgo. Office: 401 N Wabash Av Chicago IL 60611*

BENNETT, WALLACE FOSTER, U.S. senator; b. Salt Lake City, Nov. 13, 1898; s. John Foster and Rosetta (Wallace) B.; A.B., U. Utah, 1919; m. Frances Marion Grant, Sept. 6, 1922; children—Wallace Grant, Rosemary, David Wells, Frances, Robert Foster. Office clk. Bennett Glass & Paint Co. (now Bennett's), Salt Lake City, 1920-28, sec., treas., 1928-32, gen. mgr., 1932-38, pres. 1938-50, chmn. bd., 1950—; pres. Bennett Motor Co., 1939-50, chmn. bd., 1950—; dir. Utah Home Fire Ins. Co.; U.S. senator from Utah, 1951—. Mem. N.A.M. (dir. 1946-47, regional v.p. 1948, pres. 1949, chmn. bd. 1950). Republican. Mem. Ch. of Jesus Christ of Latter-day Saints (treas. Sunday Sch. Gen. Bd. 1938-66). Clubs: Alta, Rotary, Country Timpanogos (Salt Lake City). Author: Faith and Freedom, 1951; Why I Am A Mormon, 1958. Home: 1430 S 13th St Salt Lake City UT 84115 Office: Senate Office Bldg Washington DC 20510

BENNETT, WALTER EDWARD, photojournalist; b. London, Eng., Aug. 16, 1921; s. Walter Albert Edward and Gladys Mae (Bulger) B.; grad. high sch.; m. June Anne Whittaker, September 11, 1942 (div. 1964); children—Vicki June, Craig; m. 2d, Joy Lynn Furry, Feb. 21, 1970. Came to U.S., 1930, naturalized, 1943. Freelance photographer, 1939-42, 46-52; staff photographer Time magazine, 1952—. Served from pvt. to sgt., USAAF, 1942-46. Member White House News Photographers Assn., Nat. Press Photographers Assn., U.S. Senate Photographers Gallery. Club: Nat. Press. Co-discoverer Wreck of Mantanceros, off southern coast Quintana Roo, Mexico, 1957. Photographer for Diving for Treasure and Pleasure, 1960. Home: 4101 Cathedral Av N W Washington, DC 20016. Office: 888 16th St NW Washington DC 20006

BENNETT, WALTER HARTWELL, polit. scientist; born near Danville, Va., Sept. 6, 1907; s. William Hartwell and Martha Elizabeth (Dodson) B.; A.B., Univ. Richmond, 1930; A.M., Duke, 1935; Ph.D., 1940; m. Mae Maxine Purcell, Sept. 3, 1937; children—Walter Hartwell, Martha Leslie. Teacher public schs. of Pittsylvania and Halifax counties, Va., 1930-32; head social sci. dept., George Washington High Sch., Danville, Va., 1932-34; instr., Ga. Teachers Coll., 1936-38, Univ. of Ala., 1938-41, 1942-43; asst. prof. of economics, Univ. of Miss., 1941-42; asst. prof., polit. science., Univ. of Ala., 1943-46, asso. prof., 1946-47, prof., since 1947; vis. prof. La. State Univ. summer 1948, Duke, summer 1950, Wake Forest College, summer 1962. Member American Assn. Univ. Profs., Am. Polit. Sci. Assn. (exec. council 1952-54), So. Polit. Sci. Association (v.p. 1947, pres. 1954), Am. Soc. Polit. and Legal Philosophy. Episcopalian. Member editorial staff, Journal of Politics, 1942-46. Contbr. articles to Journal of Politics and South Atlantic Quarterly; mem. editorial staff Am. Political Science Review, 1950-52. Author: Am. Theories of Federalism, 1964. Home: Eight Beech Hills Tuscaloosa AL 35401

BENNETT, WILLARD HARRISON, educator, physicist; b. Findlay, O., June 13, 1903; s. Harry and Elsie Mae (Ward) B.; student Carnegie Inst. Tech., 1921-22; A.B., Ohio State U., 1924; M.S., U. Wis., 1926; Ph.D., U. Mich., 1928; m. Mona D. Sheets, Sept. 8, 1928; children—Willard Harrison, Barbara, Bruce, Stephan; m. 2d, Helen Mae Sawyer, Oct. 24, 1948; children—Charles, Ward, Rebecca, NRC fellow Cal. Inst. Tech., 1928-30; from instr. to asst. prof. physics Ohio State U., 1930-38; dir. research Electronics Research Corp., 1938- 41; dir. applied research Inst. Textile Tech., 1945; physicist, sect. chief Nat. Bur. Standards, 1945-50; prof. physics U. Ark., 1950-51; br. head, div. cons. U.S. Naval Research Lab., 1951-61; Burlington prof. physics N.C. State U., 1961—. Mem. Gov. N.C. Sci. Adv. Com. Served to lt. col. AUS, 1941-45. Fellow Am. Phys. Soc., Washington Acad. Sci. Contbr. profl. jours. Patentee in field. Discoverer pinch effect. Home: 604 Appleton Dr Raleigh NC 27606

BENNETT, WILLIAM FRANKLIN, communications exec.; b. Berlin, N.H., Dec. 23, 1917; s. William Lauriston and Frances (Corey) B.; A.B., Dartmouth, 1938; m. Patricia Egan, Feb. 1949; children—William L., Catherine P., James G., Elizabeth C., Robert Egan. Comptroller Colgate-Palmolive Co., N.Y.C., until 1962; v.p., controller Gen. Telephone and Electronics International, Incorporated, 1962-64, president, 1964—. Member of the Financial Execs. Inst. Clubs: Essex Hunt, Dartmouth, Morris County Golf. Home: James St Morristown NJ 07960 Office: 909 3d Av New York City NY 10022

BENNETT, WILLIAM HUNTER, ch. ofcl.; b. Taber, Alta., Can., Nov. 5, 1910; s. William Alvin and Mary (Walker) B.; came to U.S., 1933, naturalized, 1942; B.S., Utah State U., 1936, M.S., 1948; Ph.D., U. Wis., 1957; m. Patricia June Christensen, Apr. 12, 1950; children—Camille Kay, William Bradford, Mary Ann, Julee Hazel, Deborah Pat, Jacqueline, Asst. county agr. agt. Salt Lake County, 1937; county agr. agt. Carbon County, Utah, 1937-42; mem. faculty Utah State U., 1937-70, prof. agronomy, 1956-70, asst. dir. extension 1956-58, dir., 1962-70, acting dean Coll. Agr., 1958-60, dean, 1960-62; asst. to the council of twelve Ch. of Jesus Christ of Latter-day Saints, 1970—. Sec.-treas. Utah Edn. TV Found., 1958-59, v.p., 1959—. Served to capt. inf., AUS, 1942-46. Mem. Crop Sci. Soc. Am., Sigma Xi, Phi Kappa Phi, Alpha Zeta, Alpha Gamma Rho, Phi Sigma, Alpha Tau Alpha, Epsilon Sigma Phi. Mem. Ch. of Jesus Christ of Latter Day Saints (counselor state presidency 1952-60, regional rep. council twelve 1967-70). Rotarian. Author, co-author sci. papers. Home: 757 N 4th E Logan UT 84321

BENNETT, WILLIAM RALBERT, educator; b. Evergreen, Ala., July 2, 1918; s. William Ralbert and Pearla (Moore) B.; B.A., Birmingham So. Coll., 1939; M.B.A., La. State U., 1946; Ph.D., U. Ill., 1950; m. Anne Armstrong, Aug. 10, 1942; children— Patricia Anne, Alan Lee. Instr. U. Ill., 1948; asst. prof. to prof. marketing U. Ala., 1950—, dir. Grad. Sch. Bus., 1963—. Served with AUS, 1942-45. Decorated Bronze Star. Mem. Am., So. (pres. 1965-66) marketing assns., Am. Econ. Assn., Beta Gamma Sigma, Omicron Delta Kappa. Home: 14 Beech Hills Tuscaloosa AL 35401 Office: Box 1896 University AL 35436

BENNETT, WILLIAM RALPH, Jr., educator, physicist; b. Jersey City, Jan. 30, 1930; s. William Ralph and Viola (Schreiber) B.; A.B., Princeton, 1951; Ph.D., Columbia, 1957; M.A. (hon.), Yale, 1965; m. Frances Commins, Dec. 11, 1952; children—Jean, William Robert, Nancy. Research asst. physics Columbia Radiation Lab., 1952-54, mem. Pupin Cyclotron Group, 1954-57; mem. faculty Yale, 1957- 59, 62—, prof. physics and applied sci., 1965—, fellow Berkeley Coll., 1963—; mem. tech. staff Bell Telephone Labs., Murray Hill, N.J., 1959- 62; cons. Tech. Research Group, Melville, N.Y., 1962-67, Inst. Def. Analysis, Washington, 1963—; vis. scientist Am. Inst. Physics Vis. Scientist Program, 1963-64; vis. prof. Brandeis Summer Inst. Theoretical Physics, 1969; cons. mem. bd. dirs. Laser Scis. Corp., Bethel Conn., 1968—. Mem. adv. panels atomic physics and astrophysics Nat. Bur. Standards, 1964-69; cons. CBS Labs., Stamford, Conn., 1967-68; mem. lab. adv. bd. for research Naval Research Adv. Com., 1968—; guest of Soviet Union, 1967, 69. Sloan Found. fellow, 1963-65; Guggenheim fellow, 1967. Fellow Am. Phys. Soc., Optical Soc. Am.; mem. I.E.E.E. (sr.; Morris Liebmann award 1965), Sigma Xi. Author: Aspects of the Physics of Gas Lasers, 1970. Editorial adv. bd. Jour. Applied Physics, Applied Physics Letters, also Jour. Quantum Electronics, 1965-69; guest editor Applied Optics, 1965. Research gas lasers and atomic physics. Co-author basic patents on first several gas lasers. Home: 424 St Ronan St New Haven CT 06511

BENNETT, WILLIAM TAPLEY, Jr., lawyer, ambassador; b. Griffin, Ga., Apr. 1, 1917; s. William Tapley and Annie Mem (Little) B.; A.B., University Georgia, 1937; student University of Freiburg, Germany, 1937-38; LL.B., George Washington U., 1948; D.C.L. (honorary), Indiana State Univ., 1966; m. Margaret Rutherfurd White, June 23, 1945; children—William Tapley, 3d, John Campbell White, Anne Barclay, Ellen Pierrepont, Victoria Ridgely. Instr., polit. sci. U. Ga., 1937; with National Inst. Pub. Affairs, 1939- 40, Dept. Agr., 1940; asst. to coordinator Office of Def. Housing, 1940- 41; with State Dept. since 1941; officer charge Central Am. & Panama Affairs, 1949-51, officer charge Caribbean Affairs, 1951, dep. dir. Office South Am. Affairs, 1951-54; assigned to Nat. War Coll., 1954-55; special assistant to dep. undersecretary of state, 1955-57; counselor embassy, Vienna, 1957-61, Rome, Italy, 1961; counselor with rank of minister, Athens, Greece, 1961-64; U.S. ambassador to Dominican Republic, 1964-66, to Portugal, 1966-69; State Dept. adviser Air U., 1969; dep. U.S. rep., ambassador Security Council, UN, 1971—, U.S. rep. Trusteeship Council, 1971—. Asst. U.S. delegation International Conference on Internat. Orgn., San Francisco, Cal., 1945; adviser U.S. Delegation, 5th Gen. Assembly of U.N., N.Y.C., 1950, Sec. Gen., 4th meeting of fgn. ministers of Am. States, Washington, 1951; mem. U.S. Delegation to inauguration of Pres. Ibanez of Chile, 1952, Eisenhower mission to S.A., 1953; mem. U.S. Delegation 10th Inter-American Conference at Caracas, 1954; mem. U.S. delegation Internat. Atomic Energy Agy. Confs., 1957, 58. Served as lt. U.S. Army, E.T.O., 1944-46. Member Georgia Bar Association, English Speaking Union, Am. Society Internat. Law, Sphinx Soc., Phi Beta Kappa, Phi Kappa Phi, Omicron Delta Kappa, Sigma Chi, Phi Delta Phi. Presbyn. Clubs: Chevy Chase, Metropolitan (Washington); Corsica River Yacht (Centreville, Md.); Piedmont Driving (Atlanta). Address: care Dept State Washington DC 20025

BENNETT, WINSLOW WOOD, metall. engr.; b. Mpls., Mar. 18, 1925; s. Russell H. and Miriam (Fletcher) B.; grad. Phillips Acad., Andover, Mass., 1943; B.Mech. Engring., U. Minn., 1949; m. Adele Wulsin, Oct. 20, 1951; children—Winslow Wood, Peter Wulsin, Frank Babbott, Russell Hoadley II. With Armco Steel Corp., Middletown, O., 1949-51, Electro Manganese Corp., N.Y.C., 1951-56, Foote Mineral Co., Phila., 1956-61, Laird & Co., investment bankers, Wilmington, Del., 1961-63; pres., dir. Molybdenum Corp. Am., N.Y.C., 1963-64; with Placer Devel., Ltd., Vancouver, B.C., Can., 1964-68; pres., dir. Equity Mining Capital, Vancouver, 1968—. Served to lt. (j.g.) USNR, 1943-48. Clubs: Vancouver, Royal Vancouver Yacht. Home: 1341 Matthews Av Vancouver British Columbia Canada Office: 1111 W Hastings St Vancouver British Columbia Canada

BENNINGHOFF, WILLIAM SHIFFER, educator, plant ecologist; b. Ft. Wayne, Ind., Mar. 23, 1918; s. William Nelson and Edith Esther (Shiffer) B.; S.B. magna cum laude, Harvard, 1940, A.M., 1942, Ph.D., 1948; m. Gladys Helen Kunst, Apr. 19, 1941 (div. 1968); children—Valerie Anne, Jonathan William; m. 2d, Anne Louise Stevenson, June 14, 1969. Botanist, U.S. Geol. Survey, Washington, 1948-57, chief Alaska terrain and permafrost sect., 1953-57; mem. faculty U. Mich., 1957—, asso. prof. botany, 1957-60, prof., 1960—, prof. U. Mich. Biol. Sta., Douglas Lake, summers 1957, 61, 63, 66, palynologist Great Lakes Research div. Inst. Sci. and Tech., 1960-63, prof., asst. dir. Bot. Gardens, 1965-66, prof., curator, 1966- -. Mem. com. on polar research, panel on biol. and med. scis. Nat. Acad. Scis., 1962—, chmn., 1966-71; chmn. aerobiology panel U.S. Nat. Com. for Internat. Biol. Program, 1967, dir. aerobiology program, 1968—; convenor Internat. Biol. Program aerobiology working group, 1968- -. Served to lt. USNR, 1942-46; ETO, PTO. Recipient Meritorious Service award Dept. Interior, 1954. Fellow A.A.A.S., Am. Geog. Soc., Geol. Soc. Am., Arctic Inst. N.Am. (gov. 1957-63, 66-71, chmn. research com. 1964-66, vice chmn. bd. 1967-68); mem. Am. Polar Soc. (bd. govs. 1968—, Bot. Soc. Am., Am. Soc. Limnology and Oceanography, Ecol. Soc. Am., Soc. for Cryobiology, Internat. Soc. Plant Geography and Plant Ecology (v.p.), Floristisch- Soziologische Arbeitsgemeinschaft (Hanover), Sigma Xi. Clubs: Explorers (N.Y.C.); Cosmos (Washington). Asso. editor Ecological Monographs, 1965-67. Contbr. numerous articles on Pleistocene biogeography, pollen and spores in atmosphere to sci. jours. Office: Dept Botany U Mich Ann Arbor MI 48104

BENNINGHOVEN, EDWARD DANIEL, banker; b. Chgo., Feb. 16, 1911; s. Daniel and Elsie (Oberg) B.; student Northwestern U., 1934; m. Frances Fairweather, Sept. 23, 1939; children—Daniel II, Christina. With Continental Ill. Nat. Bank & Trust Co., Chgo., 1934—, trust officer, 1947-49, 2d v.p., 1949-51, v.p., 1951- -. Trustee Internat. House, Chgo.; mem. citizens bd. U. Chgo.; bd. assos. Northwestern U.; bd. govs. Chgo. Zool. Soc.; bd. dirs., v.p. Lyric Opera, Chgo. Mem. Chgo. Assn. Commerce and Industry, Lambda Alpha. Clubs: Economic, Bankers, Racquet, Mid America (Chgo.); Barrington Hills Country. Home: Spring Creek Rd Barrington IL 60010 Office: 231 S LaSalle St Chicago IL 60604

BENNINGTON, GEORGE ARTHUR, III, life ins. co. exec.; b. Joplin, Mo., Feb. 1, 1919; s. George Arthur and Julia Annetta (Smoyer) B.; B.S., Central Mo. State Coll.; m. Jean Elizabeth Gorham, Aug. 3, 1938; children—George Arthur IV, James Gorham. With Penn Mut. Life Ins. Co., Phila., 1948—, 2d v.p., supt. agys., 1958-60, v.p., 1960-68, agy. v.p., 1968-71, sr. v.p., 1971—. Dir. Ams. for Competitive Enterprise System, Inc. Bd. corporators Med. Coll. Pa., 1970. Served with Mcht. Marine, World War II. Mem. Nat. Assn. Life Underwriters, Life Ins. Agy. Mgmt. Assn. (mem. agy. officers round table; mem. exec. devel. com.), Sales and Marketing Execs. Phila. (dir., pres. 1970-71). Home: 395 Woodcrest Rd Stafford Wayne PA 19087 Office: Penn Mutual Life Ins Co Independence Sq Philadelphia PA 19106

BENNINGTON, NEVILLE LYNNE, biologist, educator; b. Canton, O., Aug. 8, 1906; s. James William and Leora Bell (Slates) B.; A.B., Coll. of Wooster, 1928; grad. study Franz Theodore Stone Inst. Hydrobiology, summers 1928, 29; M.A., Northwestern, 1930, Ph.D., 1934; m. Virginia Rebecca Tudor, Apr. 19, 1930; children— James Lynne, Ann Tudor. Instr. zoology Northwestern, part-time 1934-35, mem. staff summer session, 1948; instr. biology Coll. of Wooster, 1936; asst. prof. botany and zoology Beloit (Wis.) Coll., 1937-38, asso. prof., 1939-40, prof., 1941-42, prof. biology Cornelia Bailey Williams Found. since 1943; research germ cells and reproductive rhythms of fish; research Oceanographic Labs. Friday Harbor, Washington U., summer 1934; mem. stream survey Ohio Div. Conservation, 1936; biologist in charge lake survey So. area Wis., Wis. Conservation Dept., summer 1946; research consultant to Parker Pen Company, 1955—; head insts. sect. Nat. Sci. Found., 1959-60; cons., 1960—; asst. commr. for profl. edn. state edn. dept. U. State of N.Y., 1962-66; div. dir. pre-coll. edn. in sci. NSF, Washington, 1966-68; dir. faculty research and projects Wis. State U., Oshkosh, 1968—. Mem. A.A.A.S., Am. Assn. U. Profs., Am. Soc. Zoologists, Sigma Xi, Omicron Delta Kappa, Sigma Pi. Home: 833 Windward Ct Oshkosh WI 54901 Office: Wisconsin State University-Oshkosh 800 Algoma Blvd Oshkosh WI 54901

BENNINGTON, RONALD KENT, lawyer; b. Hillsboro, Ohio, July 16, 1936; s. Ralph P. and Delorice (Dudley) B.; B.A., Kenyon Coll., 1958; J.D., Ohio State U., 1961; m. Barbara Schumm, June 19, 1959; children—Scott C., Amy E. Admitted to Ohio bar, 1961; mem. firm Black, McCuskey, Souers & Arbough, Canton, 1961—, partner, 1964—. Sec. Hoover Worldwide Corp., 1968—, Hoover America Latina S.A., Hoover Inc., 1968—; dir. Towne Real Estate & Mgmt. Corp., The Towne Real Estate Co., Accelerated Reading Inst. First vice-pres. Canton chpt. A.R.C. Bd. dirs. Canton YMCA, Canton Urban League. Mem. Stark County, Ohio, Am. bar assns., Canton Jr. C. of C. (v.p. 1965), Delta Tau Delta. Presby. (elder 1971—). Home: 3920 Darlington NW Canton OH 44709 Office: Harter Bank Bldg Canton OH 44702

BENNINK, RICHARD ELLIS, banker; b. Cambridge, Mass., Feb. 1, 1917; s. Arthur S. and Ethel (Powers) B.; A.B., Harvard, 1938; m. Mary Clay Keisker, July 29, 1944; children—Nancy C., Richard Ellis, John P. With Boston Safe Deposit & Trust Co., 1938-41, 46—, asst. treas., 1947-53, treas., 1953—, v.p., 1958—; trustee bd. investment North Av. Savs. Bank, Cambridge; corporator Winchester Savs. Bank. Trustee, v.p. Boys' and Girls' Camps, Inc.; bd. dirs. Winchester Hosp.; mem. bd. of dirs. Nature Conservancy of Massachusetts; exec. com. Roxbury Charitable Soc.; trustee Trustees of Reservations; sec.-treas. Fund for the Preservation of Wildlife and Natural Areas. Served to lt. comdr. USNR, 1941-46. Mem. Greater Boston C. of C. Clubs: Wardroom (Boston), Speakers (Cambridge). Home: 16 Yale St Winchester MA 01890 Office: 1 Boston Pl Boston MA 02106

BENNION, CHARLES GEORGE, shoe machinery co. dir.; b. Enfield, Eng., June 13, 1913; s. Claud and Nora Grace (Jarvis) B.; B.A., Pembroke Coll., Cambridge U., 1934; m. Biddy Chichester Smith, Mar. 25, 1941; children—Miranda, Charles Richard. Dir. Brit. United Shoe Machinery Co. Ltd., 1946—, asst. mng. dir., 1950- 54, dep. mng. dir., 1954-56, mng. dir., 1956—, chmn. co., 1964—; dir. USM Corp., also asso. co., Eng., Australia, South Africa. Served to lt. comdr. Royal Naval Vols. Res., 1939-46. Home: Little Skeffington Leicestershire England Office: British United Shoe Machinery Co Ltd Union Works Belgrave Rd Leicester England

BENNION, GRANT MADISON, pub.; b. Madison, Wis., Jan. 2, 1913; s. Milton and Cora (Lindsay) B.; B.S., U. Utah, 1934; m. Marjorie Ralph, Aug. 17, 1935; children—Deanne (Mrs. Errol Scott), Grant Ralph. Tchr., Salt Lake City, 1934-35; regional mgr. Young Am. Films, 1945-47; with Ginn & Co., 1936- 45, 47—, v.p., 1962-64, pres., chief exec. officer, 1964-71, ret., 1971, also dir. Bd. dirs. Am. Textbook Pubs. Inst., 1964-67. Mem. Sigma Chi. Club: Algonquin (Boston). Home: 330 Beacon St Boston MA 02116 Office: Statler Bldg Boston MA 02115

BENNION, HUGH CLARK, coll. dean; b. Logan, Utah, Sept. 14, 1906; s. Edwin T. and Mary (Clark) B.; B.S. (Danforth Found. fellow 1930), Utah State U., 1931; M.S., Ia. State U., 1939; student U. Ore., 1945-46; Ed.D., Ore. State U., 1950; postgrad. U. Cal., Los Angeles and Berkeley, 1965; m. Rachel Parrish, Sept. 5, 1930 (dec. 1954); 1 dau., Jean (Mrs. Merle W. Johnson). m. 2d, Marjorie Owens, June 10, 1955; children—David, Craig. Mem. faculty Ricks Coll., Rexburg, Ida., 1931-42, 45—, head dept. psychology, 1945-65, dean faculty, 1952—; dir. employee counseling Hill AFB, 1942-45; Mem. subcom. asso. degree programs Nat. League Nursing, 1960-66, steering com. dept. asso. degree programs, 1966-69. Chmn. Madison County Community Chest, 1955. Mem. Am. Coll. Personnel Assn., Soc. Advancement Edn., Ida. Psychol. Assn., Nat., Ia. edn. assns., N.W. Jr. Coll. Assn. (chmn. instl., research com.), Phi Delta Kappa, Psi Chi, Gamma Sigma Delta. Republican. Mem. Ch. of Jesus Christ of Latter Day Saints. Rotarian (past pres. Rexburg). Home: 210 E 2d S St Rexburg ID 83440

BENNION, M. LYNN, educator; b. Salt Lake City, Oct. 4, 1902; s. Milton and Cora (Lindsay) B.; B.S., U. Utah, 1926, M.S., 1932; Ed.D., U. Cal., 1936; m. Katherine Snow, Sept. 1, 1927; children—Annette Bennion Clark, Carolyn Bennion Heston, John, Rebecca Bennion Glade. Tchr., Latter Day Saints Sems., 1926-27, 31-32, 33-34, supr., 1934-35, 44-45; supt. schs., Salt Lake City, 1945-69; adj. prof. ednl. adminstrn. U. Utah, 1969—. Recipient Distinguished Service award Am. Assn. Sch. Adminstrs., 1970. Mem. N.E.A., Salt Lake C. of C., Am. Council Edn., Am. Soc. Sch. Adminstrs., Horace Mann League (past pres.), Soc. Utah Sch. Supts. (exec. sec.), Phi Delta Kappa. Clubs: Rotary; Bonneville Knife and Fork. Author: Mormonism and Education, 1936. Compiler: Oil for Their Lamps, 1943. Home: 18 U St Salt Lake City UT 84103

BENNIS, WARREN G., coll. pres.; b. N.Y.C., Mar. 8, 1925; s. Philip and Rachel (Landau) B.; A.B., Antioch Coll., 1951; hon. certificate econs., U. London (Eng.), 1952; Ph.D., Mass. Inst. Tech., 1955; m. Clurie Williams, Mar. 30, 1962; children—Katharine, John Leslie, Will Martin. Asst. prof. psychology Mass. Inst. Tech., 1953-56, prof., 1959-67; asst. prof. psychology and bus. Boston U., 1956-59; provost State U. N.Y. at Buffalo, 1967-68, v.p. acad. devel., 1968-71; pres. U. Cin., 1971—; vis. lectr. Harvard, 1958-59, Indian Mgmt. Inst., Calcutta; vis. prof. U. Lausanne (Switzerland), 1961-62; cons. editor social scis. and adminstrn. Addison-Wesley Book Co.; cons. in field, 1955—. Mem. Pres.' White House Task Force on Sci. Policy, 1969-70; mem. adv. com. N.Y. State Joint Legislative Com. Higher Edn.; mem. Buffalo Citizens Adv. Council. Bd. dirs. Erie County Dept. Mental Health, Albright-Knox Gallery (hon.); trustee Antioch Coll., Pitzer Coll., Park Sch., Buffalo; adv. bd. Fed. Jud. Center, Fed. Exec. Center, bd. advisers Innovation Group. Served to capt. AUS, World War II. Decorated Bronze Star, Purple Heart. Diplomate Am. Bd. Profl. Psychology. Fellow Am. Psychol. Assn.; mem. A.A.A.S., Am. Sociol. Assn., Am. Acad. Arts and Scis. (co-chmn. policy council 1969-71), Ch. Soc. for Coll. Work (dir.). Author: Planning of Change, 1961; Interpersonal Dynamics, 1963; Personal and Organizational Change, 1965; Changing Organizations, 1966; The Temporary Society, 1968; The Planning of Change, 1968; Organization Development, 1969; American Bureaucracy, 1970. Asso. editor Trans-Action: Jour. Applied Behavioral Sci., Jour. Transpersonal Psychology, Bus. and Pub. Adminstrv. Rev., Community Psychology; cons. editor Jour. Creative Behavior. Address: Univ Cincinnati Cincinnati OH

BENNISON, BERTRAND EARL, physician; b. Boston, Mass., Apr. 18, 1915; s. Harold Bertrand and Ina M. (Sterling) B.; S.B., Mass. Inst. Tech., 1937; M.D., Harvard, 1941; M.P.H., U. Pitts., 1954; m. Lella Brice, Aug. 28, 1943; children—Alice M., John B., Louise A., Charles B. Commd. med. officer USPHS, specializing in malaria, cancer and Tb, 1942-54; asst. dir. med. research div. Esso Research and Engring. Co., 1954-60; asst. dir. research Ortho Pharm. Corp., 1960-65; prof. biol. scis., head dept. biology Drexel Inst. Tech., 1966-71; dir. Leon County Heath Dept., Fla., 1971—. Address: Leon County Health Dept Tallahassee FL 32304

BENNISON, CHARLES ELLSWORTH, bishop; b. Janesville, Wis., July 23, 1917; s. Floyd William and Cleo Leona (Wilson) B.; student Lawrence Coll., 1935-38; B.A., U. Minn., 1939; B.D., Seabury-Western Theol. Sem., 1942, D.D., 1960; m. Marjorie Elizabeth Haglun, June 16, 1942; children—Charles Ellsworth, Mary, John, Ordained priest Episcopal Ch., 1942; rector, Hastings, Minn., 1942-45, Joliet, Ill., 1945-52, St. Luke's Ch., Kalamazoo, 1952-60; bishop Diocese Western Mich., 1960—. Trustee Seabury-Western Theol. Sem. Mem. S.A.R., Beta Theta Pi. Clubs: Torch, Rotary. Home: 3305 Lakehill Dr Kalamazoo MI 49001 Office: Cathedral Ch of Christ the King 2600 Vincent Av Kalamazoo MI 49001

BENNSKY, GEORGE MICHAEL, govt. ofcl.; b. Hickory, N.C., Dec. 22, 1923; s. George M. and Gladyes Ethel (Fisher) B.; B.A., George Washington U., 1949; M.A. in Econs., U. Mich., 1950; postgrad., Nat. War Coll., 1967-68; m. Ruth Maness, July 15, 1960; 1 son, Matthew Maness. Econ. research asst. IMF, 1950-51; economist Treasury Dept., 1951-52, 56, asst. rep. in Mid East, 1952-56; with State Dept., 1956—; economist N.E. affairs, 1956-60; chief, econ. sect., consulate gen., Madras, India, 1960-62; chief, polit. sect., consulate gen., 1962-64; officer-in- charge N.E. econ. affairs, 1964-66, sr. polit.-econ. officer UAR affairs, 1966-67; chief, econ.-coml. sect., asst. dir., acting dep. dir. EMB/AID, Lima, Peru, 1968—. Served with USAAF, 1943-46; CBI. Mem. Am. C. of C. Peru, Am. Fgn. Service Assn., Am. Acad. Polit. and Social Sci. Mem. Ch. of Christ. Clubs: de la Banca Golf, Santa Maria Beach (Lima, Peru). Office: Am Embassy Lima Dept State Washington DC 20521

BENNY, JACK (stage name), radio entertainer; b. Waukegan, Ill., Feb. 14, 1894; s. Meyer and Emma (Sachs) Kubelsky; ed. Waukegan (Ill.) High Sch.; m. Mary Livingstone (actress) Jan. 25, 1927; 1 dau., Joan Naomi (adopted). Began as violinist, 1912; featured player on vaudeville stage; star in motion pictures since 1939; radio entertainer since 1932 also on TV as guest artist and in own program; recent pictures: To Be or Not to Be, George Washington Slept Here, The

Horn Blows at Midnight. Served in U.S. Navy, World War I; spent summers 1943, 44, 45, entertaining armed forces overseas during World War II. Recipient award for best continuing performance by a male entertainer Nat. Acad. Television Arts and Sci., 1957, Spl. award. Club: Friars (proctor). Home: 1002 North Roxbury Dr Beverly Hills CA 90210

BENOIST, LOUIS AUGUSTE, business exec.; b. St. Louis, Oct. 1, 1899; s. Lee and Edith (Turner) B.; B.S., U.S. Naval Acad., 1921; m. Katharine Bentley, Feb. 9, 1942. Commd. ensign, U.S.N., 1920, served, 1921-23; asso. with Ill. Power & Light Co., Chgo., 1923-26; design engr. Dillon Read & Co., 1927; exec. v.p. Bankamerica Co., 1928-32; organizer, pres. Bay Cities Ice & Cold Storage Co., Inc., San Francisco, 1932-36; with Lawrence Warehouse Co. since 1936, exec. v.p., 1941-44, pres. since 1944; pres. Lawrence Investment Co., San Francisco, since 1944, Alamaden Santa Clara Vineyards, Los Gatos, Cal., 1941—, The Lawrence Properties Company, 1958—; now retired. Clubs: Brook (N.Y.C.); Bohemian, Burlingame Country, Pacific Union, Cypress Point (Pebble Beach, Cal.) Home: The Chimneys Warm Springs VA 24484

BENOIT, EMILE, educator, economist; b. N.Y.C., July 14, 1909; s. Isadore and Rosina (Freeman) Benoit-Smullyan; B.A., Harvard, 1932, M.A., 1933, Ph.D., 1938; m. Mary Louise Mincher, Mar. 13, 1936; 1 son, Jon; m. 2d, Etta Leist Fleming, Feb. 11, 1959. Mem. faculty Harvard, 1934-36, U. Ill., 1938-39, Wells Coll., 1939-42; prof. internat. bus. Grad. Sch. Bus. and Sch. Internat. Affairs, Columbia, N.Y.C., 1956—; sr. economist Labor Dept., 1943-47; attache Am. embassy, London, 1948-51, Vienna, 1951-53; economist McGraw Hill Pub. Co., 1954-56; cons. Dept. Def., State Dept., Pfizer Internat. Corp. Dir. research program on econs. arms control Ford Found., Carnegie Corp., and U.S. Arms Control and Disarmament Agy.; dir. research project Effects of Nat. Def. on Devel. Econs., 1968-69. Vice chmn. Ams. for Democratic Action, 1964—. Bd. dirs. N.Y. Friends Group, Soc. Family of Man. Mem. Am. Econs. Assn., Am. Finance Assn., A.A.A.S. Author: Europe at Sixes and Sevens, 1961; Disarmament and the Economy, 1963. Editorial bd. Columbia Jour. World Bus., 1964—; The Internat. Exec., 1962—; Disarmament and Arms Control, 1963—; Jour. of Arms Control, 1963-64, Jour. Conflict Resolution, 1966—, Am. Rev. of East West Trade, 1968—. Editor, contbr. Disarmament and World Economic Interdependence, 1966. Contbr. chpts. to books, articles to profl. jours. Home: 39 Claremont Av New York City NY 10027 also Elka Park Greene County NY 12427

BENOIT, LEROY JAMES, educator; b. Newton, Mass.., Aug. 23, 1913; s. Alexander James and Phoebe Anne (White) B.; A.B., Tufts U., 1936; licence, U. Paris, France, 1938; A.M., Harvard, 1939, Ph.D., 1941; Doctor Honoris Causa, U. Coimbra, Portugal, 1952; m. Edith Doris Meyer, May 26, 1939; children—Peter Allan, Diane (Mrs. J. John Ryan). Asst. prof. French, Harvard, 1938-42; asso. prof. French, Amherst Coll., 1945-47; prof. Romance langs. Johns Hopkins, Balt., 1947-51; cultural attache, Lisbon, Portugal, 1951-54, Brazil, 1954-56; with USIA, Washington, 1956-60; dir. cultural exhibit, USSR, 1960, 63; lang. adviser Dept. Def., Washington, 1963-66; prof. linguistics Cornell U., 1966—. Cons. U.S. Office Edn., U.S. Dept. State, Ford Found. Chmn. Heart Fund, Bethesda, Md., 1960-61; v.p. PTA, Bethesda, Md., 1962-63. Served to maj. USAAF, 1942-45; Africa, Italy, USSR. Decorated Purple Heart, D.F.C.; Order Brit. Empire; Legion of Honor (France). Mem. Modern Lang. Assn., Linguistic Soc. Am., Phi Beta Kappa. Author advanced text in French syntax. Contbr. articles profl. jours. Home: 320 Winthrop Dr Ithaca NY 14850

BENSCH, KLAUS GEORGE, med. educator; b. Miedar, Germany, Sept. 1, 1928; M.D., U. Erlangen (Germany), 1953; married; 3 children. Naturalized Am. citizen. Intern U. Hosps. of Erlangen, 1953-54; resident in anat. pathology U. Tex. and M.D. Anderson Hosp., Houston, 1954-56, Yale, 1956-57; instr. pathology Yale Med. Sch., 1958-61, asst. prof., 1961-64, asso. prof., 1964-68; prof. pathology Stanford, Med. Sch., 1968—. Diplomate in anat. pathology Am. Bd. Pathology. Mem. Am. Assn. Pathology and Bacteriology. Office: Dept Pathology Stanford U Med Sch Stanford CA 94305*

BENSCHOTER, JOHN LEWIS, beef processing co. exec.; b. Falls City, Neb., Sept. 20, 1933; s. Leo Melvin and Ruth (Knickerbocker) B.; B.Sc., U. Neb., 1960; m. Martha Sue Edmonds, Dec. 23, 1962; children—John Lewis, Nancy Ruth. Sr. accountant Touche, Ross & Co., C.P.A.'s, Kansas City, Mo., 1960-64; with Ia. Beef Processors, 1964—, v.p., 1969—. Served with USAF, 1952-56. Mem. Am. Soc. C.P.A.'s, Nat. Assn. Accountants. Home: 4115 Lincoln Way Sioux City IA 51106 Office: Ia Beef Processors Dakota City NB 68731

BENSCOTER, CARL ANDREW, air transp. cons.; b. Brookville, Pa., July 10, 1917; s. Carl T. and Janet (Bunyan) B.; student Am. U., 1935-36, Pa. State Coll., 1936-39, Cornell U., 1948, Harvard, 1962; m. Alice Woods, May 28, 1943; children—Anne, Janet, Carol, Katherine, Carl Andrew, Gail. Pilot, Mohawk Airlines, 1946-50, operations mgr., 1950-51, v.p. operations, 1951-63, dir., 1959-68, exec. v.p., 1963-68; pres., chief exec. officer Air Cal., Newport Beach, 1968-70; pres. CABenscoter & Assos., Newport Beach, Cal., 1970—. Served to comdr. USNR, 1939-46. Decorated D.F.C., Air medal, Order Brit. Empire. Home: 901 Aleppo St Newport Beach CA 92660 Office: 901 Alleppo St Newport Beach CA 92660

BENSEL, FRANCIS SCOTT, lawyer; b. N.Y.C., Oct. 2, 1905; s. Charles E. and Julia (Smith) B.; LL.B., Fordham U., 1926; m. Nora Murphy, Aug. 31, 1929, children—Irene (Mrs. Leland Markley), Francis P., Joan. Admitted to N.Y. bar, 1927, since practiced in N.Y.C.; mem. firm Warren, Clark Carr & Ellis and predecessor, 1936—. Trustee Marymount Manhattan Coll. Fellow Am. Bar Found. mem. Am., N.Y. bar assns., Assn. Bar City N.Y., N.Y. County Lawyers Assn. (pres. 1960-62), Am. Judicature Soc., Cath. Lawyers Guild, Soc. Friendly Sons of St. Patrick. Clubs: Lake Placid (N.Y.); St. Andrews Golf (Hastings-on- Hudson, N.Y.). Home: 200 E 66th New York City NY 10021 Office: 350 Park Av New York City NY 10022

BENSINGER, B. E., corp. exec.; b. Chgo., Dec. 6, 1905; s. Benjamin E. and Rose (Frank) B.; Ph.B., Yale; m. Linda Galston, Nov. 28, 1929; children—B. Edward III, Roger G., Peter B. Asst. to sales mgr. Brunswick Corp. (formerly Brunswick-Balke-Collender Co.), Chgo., 1928-32, dir., 1930—, asst. sec., treas. 1932-36, gen. mgr., 1936, exec. v.p., 1937-50, pres., 1950-54, chief exec. officer, 1954—, chmn. bd., 1963—; dir. Am. Nat. Bank & Trust Co., Chgo., Inland Life Ins. Co. Mem. adv. council U. Chgo. Grad. Sch. Bus.; mem. U. Ill. Citizens Com. Bd. dirs. Michael Reese Hosp., Project Hope, Chgo. Lyric Opera, Chgo. council Boy Scouts Am.; trustee U. Chgo. Mem. Art Inst. Chgo. (life), Soc. Contemporary Art, Lincoln Park Zool. Soc. (founder, life), Northwestern U. Assos. Clubs: Standard, Lake Shore Country, Yale (dir.), Commercial, Tavern (Chgo.); Tryall Ltd. (Jamaica) Home: 945 Dean Av Highland Park IL 60035 Office: 69 W Washington St Chicago IL 60602

BENSINGER, PETER BENJAMIN, state ofcl.; b. Chgo., Mar. 24, 1936; s. Benjamin Edward and Linda Elkus (Galston) B.; B.A., Yale, 1958; 1 son, Peter Benjamin. With Brunswick Corp., 1958-60, sales control mgr., 1958-60; with Brunswick Internat. C.A., 1960-63, gen. mdse. mgr., 1961-63; sales mgr. Brunswick Corp. (U.K.) Ltd., London, Eng., 1963-65, gen. sales mgr. of Europe, 1965-66, spl. products mgr. 1966-69; dir. Ill. Dept. Corrections, Chgo., 1970—. Lincoln Park Zool. Soc., Chgo., 1962—; chmn. Ill. Youth Commn., 1969; former asst. to dir. Ill. Dept. Pub. Safety; exec. council Anti- Defamation League; men's council Art Inst. Chgo. Clubs: Arts, Executives, Lake Shore Country, Mid-America, Standard (Chgo.); Yale (N.Y.C.). Address: State of Ill Bldg Chicago IL 60601

BENSINGER, ROGER GALSTON, mfg. co. exec.; b. Chgo., July 5, 1933; s. Benjamin Edward and Linda Elkus (Galston) B.; B.A., Brown U., 1956; m. Ruth Baker Thomas, June 18, 1955; children—Roger Galston, Terri Thomas, Christopher Staunton, Stephanie Leigh. With Brunswick Corp., Chgo., 1956—, Chgo. S. br. mgr., 1961-62, v.p. Great Lakes region, now pres. community resources div. Mem. Phi Gamma Delta. Presbyn. (treas. Mens Council, 1962—). Clubs: Lake Shore Country (Glencoe); Rainbow Springs Country (Mukwonage, Wis.); Standard, Tavern (Chgo.). Home: 300 Birch St Winnetka IL 60093 Office: 69 Washington St Chicago IL 60602

BENSLEY, EDWARD HORTON, physician; b. Toronto, Ont., Can., Dec. 10, 1906; s. Benjamin Arthur and Ruth (Horton) B.; B.A. (Fulton scholar 1924, Balmer scholar 1924; Blake scholar 1925, Wilson scholar 1926, Bronze medal British Assn. Advancement Sci. 1927), U. Toronto, 1927, M.D. (Gold medal 1930), 1930; D.Sc. (hon.), Acadia U., 1964; m. Catharine Speid, Sept. 9, 1944, Jr. intern Montreal Gen. Hosp., 1930-31, resident pathology, 1931- 32, mem. staff, 1932—, dir. dept. metabolism and toxicology, 1947-61, chem. pathologist-in-chief, 1947-61, sec. med. bd., 1951-60, cons. physician, 1962—; hon. cons. Royal Victoria Hosp., 1962-67; mem. faculty McGill U., 1932-35, 41—, asst. dir. Univ. Med. Clinic, 1952-57, vice dean faculty medicine, 1961-67, prof. exptl. medicine, 1965—, hon. lectr. bio-chemistry, 1956-69, lecturer in the history of medicine, 1968- -; cons. metabolism and toxicology Reddy Meml. Hosp., 1950-61, chmn. nutrition panel Def. Research Bd., 1949-52; mem. Canadian Council Nutrition, 1948-59; cons. nutrition Canadian Forces Med. Council, 1957-60. Served to maj., M.C., Royal Canadian Army, World War II. Decorated Order British Empire. Fellow A.C.P., Royal Coll. Physicians Can., Chem. Inst. Can.; licentiate Med. Council Can.; mem. Nutrition Soc. Can. (past pres.), Canadian Med. Assn. (past chmn. com. nutrition), Canadian Soc. Clin. Chemists (past pres.), Osler Soc. (past hon. pres.), Canadian Fedn. Biol. Socs. (past hon. sec.). Author numerous articles in fields metabolic diseases, clin. chemistry, nutrition, toxicology, med. history. Home: 157 Morrison Av Montreal 305 Quebec Canada Office: 1200 Pine Av W Montreal 112 Quebec Canada

BENSON, BRUCE BUZZELL, educator, physicist; b. Choteau, Mont., Feb. 22, 1922; s. Harry Fort and Mary (Buzzell) B.; B.A., Amherst Coll., 1943; M.S., Yale, 1945, Ph.D., 1947; m. Lucy Peters Wilson, Mar, 30, 1950. Simpson fellow Yale, 1943- 44, instr. physics, 1944-46, research asst., 1946-47; mem. faculty Amherst Coll., 1947—, prof. physics, 1960—; asso. physics Woods Hole Oceanographic Instn., 1957-67. Cons. earth scis. sect. NSF, 1964-67, consultant oceanography section, 1967-68. Guggenheim fellow, 1958-59. Mem. Am. Phys. Soc., Am. Geophys. Union, A.A.A.S., Geochem. Soc., Am. Assn. Physics Tchrs., Am. Assn. U. Profs., Phi Beta Kappa, Sigma Xi. Contbr. profl. jours. Home: 46 Sunset Av Amherst MA 01002

BENSON, CARL FREDERICK, educator; b. Camden, Ark., Feb. 19, 1916; s. Louis Victor and Elizabeth (Walther) B.; student So. State Coll. Ark., 1933-35; B.A., U. Tex., 1937, M.A., 1938; Ph.D., U. Ill., 1948; m. Martha Ellen Blanks, May 29, 1941; children—Stephen Louis, Katherine Ellen. Asst. prof. English, Ark. A. and M. Coll., 1939-41; mem. faculty Auburn (Ala.) U., 1947—, prof., 1962—, Hargis prof., 1964—; vis. prof. N.Y.U., summer 1964. Ford Faculty fellow Harvard and Mass. Inst. Tech., 1955-56; Fulbright lectr. Erlangen (Germany) U., 1960-61. Served with AUS, 1943-46; ETO. Mem. Modern Language Assn., S. Atlantic Modern Lang. Assn. Author: The Idea of Tragedy, 1966. Contbr. profl. jours. Home: 362 Choewacla Dr Auburn AL 36830

BENSON, DAVID WILLIAM, coll. dean; b. N. Branch, Minn., Oct. 13, 1931; s. Fredolf Ernest and Ruth (Rystrom) B.; B.S., U. Cal. at Los Angeles, 1954, M.S., 1958; Ph.D., U. So. Cal., 1966; m. Betty Juan Broders, Feb. 29, 1952; 1 dau., Mary. Instr. U. Cal. at Los Angeles, 1958-61; asst. prof. to prof. phys. edn. San Ferando Valley State Coll., 1961-67, dean acad. planning, dean acad. adminstrn., 1967- -. Served as ensign USNR, 1954-56. Named distinguished tchr., San Ferando Valley State Coll., 1966. Home: 23505 Schoenborn St Canoga Park CA 91304 Office: 18111 Nordhoff St Northridge CA 91324

BENSON, DONALD LEE, lawyer; b. Cherokee, Okla., July 7, 1933; s. Raymond R. and Vesta (Niles) B.; B.B.A., U. Okla., 1959, J.D., 1961; m. Donna M. Garrett, Jan. 1, 1954; children—Brenda Rae, Bryce Thomas. Admitted to Okla. bar, 1961, since practiced in Alva; asst. to John B. Doolin, 1961-63; partner Morford & Benson 1963-65, Morford, Benson & Gruber, 1965—. Dir. N.W. Translator TV, Inc., Woods County Abstract Corp., EWB Ranch, Inc. Chmn. Woods County chpt. A.R.C., 1961-67; mem. bd. Edn. Ind. Dist. No. 1, Woods County, 1968—. Served with AUS, 1953-55. Named Outstanding Young Man of Am., 1965. Mem. Am., Okla., Woods County (pres.) bar assns., Am. Legion, Delta Theta Phi. Democrat. Mem. Christian Ch. Elk, Lion. Club: Alva Quarterback. Home: 518 14th St Alva OK 73717 Office: 615 Barnes St Alva OK 73717

BENSON, DONALD WARREN, anesthesiologist; b. Jamestown, N.Y., Aug. 17, 1921; s. George Elver and Elen Johanna (Peterson) B.; student N. Park Coll., Chgo., 1940-42, U. Ill., 1942-43, Notre Dame U., 1943-44; B.S., U. Chgo., 1949, M.D., 1950, Ph.D. in Pharmacology, 1957; m. Marjorie Ann Maulsby, June 8, 1946; children—Brian Wesley, Jane Ellen, Ruth Ann. Instr., then asst. prof. anesthesiology U. Chgo., 1953-56; asso. prof. anesthesiology Johns Hopkins Med. Sch., 1956-59, prof., 1959—; anesthesiologist-in-charge Johns Hopkins Hosp., 1956—. Served to ensign USNR, 1944-46. Diplomate Am. Bd. Anesthesiology. Mem. Am. Soc. Anesthesiologists, Assn. U. Anesthesiologists, Sigma Xi. Home: Dance Mill Rd Phoenix MD 21131 Office: Johns Hopkins Sch Medicine Baltimore MD 21205

BENSON, EDGAR JOHN, Canadian govt. ofcl.; b. Cobourg, Ont., Can., May 28, 1924; s. Franklin M. and Ann (Minifie) B.; B.Commerce, Queen's U., 1949; m. Marie Louise Van Laer, Mar. 29, 1945; children—Robert, Paul, Peter, Nancy. Partner firm England, Leonard and Macpherson, chartered accountants, Kingston, Ont., 1952-64; asst. prof. commerce Queen's U., 1952-62; mem. Parliament from Kingston Constituency, 1962—; Parliamentary sec. to minister finance, 1963-64; minister nat. revenue, 1964-67; vice chmn. Treasury Bd., 1965-68; minister of finance, 1967—. Served with Canadian Army, 1941-46. Chartered accountant, 1952. Fellow Inst. Chartered Accountants. Home: 44 Strathcona Crescent Kingston Ontario Canada Office: House of Commons Ottawa Ontario Canada

BENSON, EDWARD MUNROE, Jr., oil co. exec.; b. Kansas City, Mo., July 27, 1920; s. Edward Munroe and Margretta (Brown) B.; B.S., U. Cal., Berkeley, 1942; m. Shirley Clymer, Sept. 5, 1942; children—Stuart E., John M., Christine. With Richfield Oil Corp., 1947-66, mgr. land and lease div., Los Angeles, 1959-62, gen. mgr. operations, 1963-66; v.p. mgr. Western region N.Am. Producing div. Atlantic Richfield Co., Dallas, 1966-68, v.p., mgr. exploration and producing operations N.Am. Producing div., 1968—. Mem. earth scis. adv. bd. Stanford; vis. com. dept. petroleum engring. U. So. Cal., 1963—. Bd. dirs. R.M. Pyles Boys Camp. Served to maj. AUS, 1942-46; ETO. Mem. Stanford Bus. Sch. Assn., Am. Petroleum Inst. (past chpt. chmn.), Western Oil and Gas Assn., U. Cal. Alumni Assn. (past dir.), Am. Assn. Petroleum Gologists. Home: 4556 Mill Run Rd Dallas TX 75234 Office: P O Box 2819 Dallas TX 75221

BENSON, EZRA TAFT, former sec. agr.; b. Whitney, Ida., Aug. 4, 1899; s. George Taft and Sarah (Dunkley) B.; student Oneida Stake Acad., Preston, Ida.; Utah State Agrl. Coll., Logan, 1918-21; B.S., Brigham Young U., 1926, Dr. Pub. Service (hon.), 1955; M.S. in Agrl. Econs., Ia. State Coll., 1927, D. Agr. (hon.), 1953; postgrad. U. Cal., 1937-38; H.H.D., Coll. Osteo. Physicians and Surgeons, 1951; LL.D., U. Utah, 1953, Bowdoin Coll., 1955, U. Me., 1956; D. Agr. (hon.), Mich. State Coll., 1955; D.Sc. (hon.), Rutgers U., 1955; m. Flora Smith Amussen, Sept. 10, 1926; children—Reed, Mark, Barbara, Beverly, Bonnie, Flora Beth. Mission for Ch. Jesus Christ Latter-day Saints, Brit. Isles and Europe; pres. Newcastle dist., 1921-23; farm operator, 1923-30; co. agrl. agt., U. Ida. Extension Service, Preston, Ida., 1929-30; extension economist and marketing specialist in charge econ. and marketing work for State of Ida., 1930-38; organizer, sec. Ida. Coop. Council, 1933-38; exec. sec. Nat. Council farmer Coops., 1939-44; mem. exec. com., bd. trustees Am. Inst. Co-op., 1942-52, vice chmn. bd. trustees, 1942-49, chmn. 1952; sec. of agr. U.S. Dept. of Agr. 1953-61; dir. Olson Bros., Inc. Bd. dirs. Farm Found., 1946-50. Mem. Nat. Agrl. Adv. Com., World War II; mem. Nat. Farm Credit Com., 1940-43; U.S. del. 1st Internat. Conf. of Farm Orgns., London, Eng., 1946. Mem. nat. exec. bd. Boy Scouts Am., 1948-66, awarded Silver Antelope, 1951, Silver Buffalo award, 1954. Mem. Boise (Ida.) Stake Presidency, Ch. of Jesus Christ of Latter-day Saints, 1933-37, pres. Boise Stake, 1938-39; pres. Wash. Dist. Council, Eastern States Mission, 1939-40, Washington (D.C.) Stake, 1940-44; ordained apostle of Ch., mem. Council of Twelve, 1943, pres. European Mission, 1946, mem. Gen. Ch. Bd. Edn.; bd. trustees Brigham Young U. Recipient testimonial for distinguished service to agr. U. Wis., 1952; recipient scholarship Gamma Sigma Delta, hon. soc. agr. Ia. State Coll.; fellowship, U. Cal. at Berkeley. Mem. Am. Marketing Assn., Farm Econs. Assn., Delta Nu, Alpha Zeta. Contbr. agrl., coop. and ch. publs. Home: 1907 Quincy St NW Washington DC 20011

BENSON, FRANK THOMAS, educator; b. Rexburg, Ida., Nov. 8, 1925; s. Frank Andrus and Josephine Anna (Thomson) B.; student Colo. Coll., 1945-47; B.S. with honors, U. Utah, 1949, M.S., 1952; Ph.D., U. Minn., 1962; m. Patricia Renee Jensen, Aug. 15, 1947; children—Peter, Jon, Elizabeth, Margaret, Philip. Faculty, U. Minn. Gen. Coll., Mpls., 1953—, prof. philosophy, asst. dean Gen. Coll., 1968—. Served with USMCR, 1943-46. Am. Council Edn. fellow in acad. adminstrn., 1967- 68. Mem. Speech Assn. Am., Am. Philos. Assn., Nat. Creative Leadership Council, Am. Assn. U. Profs., Kappa Sigma. Author: Creating a Speech, 1968. Editor: Gen. Edn. Sounding Bd., 1966-67. Home: 2169 Fulham St St Paul MN 55113 Office: Nicholson Hall U Minn Minneapolis MN 55455

BENSON, FRED JACOB, coll. dean, engr.; b. Grainfield, Kan., Sept. 27, 1914; s. Fred Emerson and Inez (Houser) B.; B.S. with high honors in Civil Engring., Kan. State U., 1935; M.S., A. and M. Coll. of Tex., 1936; m. Marjorie Clara Cooper, Sept. 3, 1937; children—Fred Charles, Joyce Lyn, Clark Alan. Draftsman, Kan. Hwy. Commn., Topeka, 1935, Internat. Boundary Commn., El Paso, Tex., 1937; Instr. Purdue U., 1936-37; from instr. to prof. A. and M. Coll. Tex., 1937-55, dean engring., 1957—; asst. city engr., Wichita Falls, Tex., 1938; city engr., College Station, Tex., 1947-66; exec. officer Tex. Transp. Inst., 1955-62; vice dir. Tex. Engring. Expt. Sta., 1956-57; dir., 1962—. Dir. Tex. A&M Research Found., Bryan Bldg. and Loan Assn., H.B. Zachery Co., Univ. Nat. Bank, Gen. Security Life Ins. Co. Served from ensign to lt. (s.g.), USNR, 1943-46. Mem. Hwy. Research Bd., Am. Road Builders Assn., Am. Pub. Works Assn., Am. Soc. C.E., Sigma Xi, Tau Beta Pi, Phi Kappa Phi, Sigma Tau. Methodist. Club: Cosmos. Contbr. articles tech. jours. Home: 817 N Rosemary Bryan TX 77801 Office: Office Dean of Engring College Station TX 77840

BENSON, GEORGE CHARLES SUMNER, govt. ofcl.; b. N.Y.C., Jan. 16, 1908; s. Eugene Huntington and Helen (Sumner) B.; B.A., Pomona Coll.; A.M., U. Ill., 1929; A.M., Harvard University, 1930, Ph.D., 1931; m. Mabel Gibberd, May 10, 1935; children—Sumner, Brien Gibberd. Instr. Harvard U., 1930- 34, head tutor Lowell House, 1932-34; lectr. U. Chgo., 1934-36; asso. prof. U. Mich., 1936-41; prof. Northwestern U., 1941-44; personnel dir. and dir. Administrative Div., Office of Price Adminstrn., 1940-41; pres. Claremont Men's Coll., 1947-69, also trustee; dep. asst. sec. Def. (Edn.), 1969—. Research dir. U.S. Commn. on Intergovtl. Relations; pres. Western Assn. Schs. and Colls., 1961-63; former mem. Mich. State Planning Commn., Washtenaw County Bd. Supervisors. Served captain, col., U.S. Army, 1942-46. Clubs: Cosmos (Washington, D.C.); Sunset California. Episcopalian. Author: (books) Financial Control and Integration, 1933: Civil Service in Massachusetts, 1934; The State Administrative Board in Michigan, 1938; The New Centralization, 1941; the Politics of Urbanism, 1972. Home: 1600 S Joyce Arlington VA 22202

BENSON, GEORGE STUART, educator; b. Okla. Ter., Okla., Sept. 26, 1898; s. Stuart Felix and Emma (Rogers) B.; B.S., Oklahoma A. and M. Coll., Stillwater, 1924; A.B., Harding Coll., 1925, LL.D., 1932; LL.D., Knox Coll., 1948; M.A., U. Chgo., 1931; m. Sallie Ellis (Hockaday), July 2, 1925; children—Mary Ruth, Fannie Lois. Tchr. rural schs., Okla., 1918- 21; high sch. prin. Harding Coll., 1924-25; missionary and tchr., S. China, 1925-30; prof. english Nat. Sun Yat Sen U., Canton, 1929-30; founder, trustee and pres. Canton (China) Bible Sch., 1930-36; pres. Harding Coll., 1936-65; chancellor Okla. Christian Coll., 1956-67; now producer radio program Behind the News. Pres. Ark. Public Expenditure Council, 1942-44, 52-56; dir. Nat. Thrift Com., Inc. Mem. Nat. Com. for Religion and Welfare Recovery, 1939; mem. adv. com. U.S. Flag Found. Trustee Nat. Council Community Improvement; mem. adv. bd. U.S. Mcht. Marine Acad., Kings Point, L.I., 1953-56; pres. nat. edn. program, Searcy, Ark., 1954—. Recipient several awards Freedoms Found. Mem. Am. Arbitrators Assn. (nat. panel), Nat. Assn. Sch. Adminstrs., C. of C., A.I.M., Pi Kappa Delta. Mem. Ch. of Christ. Kiwanian. Editor: Oriental Christian (pub. Canton, China), 1929-36. Writer syndicated weekly newspaper column Looking Ahead; producer radio program Land of the Free, 1942-55. Tchr., authority on Oriental religions and philosophy. Contbr. religious publs. and secular mags. Home: 15 Cloverdale Searcy AR 72143

BENSON, SIR HENRY ALEXANDER, accountant; b. Johannesburg, South Africa, Aug. 2, 1908; s. Alexander Stanley and Florence Mary (Cooper) B.; ed. in Johannesburg; m. Anne Virginia Macleod, Sept. 2, 1939; children—Peter Macleod, Michael D'Arcy, Phyllida Anne (Mrs. Dare). With Cooper Bros. & Co., London, Eng., 1926—, partner, 1934—. Dir., dep. gov. Hudson's Bay Co., 1953-62; dir. Finance Corp. for Industry Ltd., 1953—. Adviser royal ordnance factories, Ministry Supply, 1943, dir. ordnance factories, 1943-44, mem. adv. com., 1946-50; controller bldg. materials Ministry Works, 1945; ind. mem. Linoleum working party Bd. Trade, 1946- 50; mem. Crawley Devel. Corp., 1947-50; mem. Shipbldg. Costs Com., 1947-49; mem. New Towns Working Party, 1948-49; mem. com. enquire financial orgn. Ministry Food, 1948-50; mem. Royal Ordnance Factories Bd., 1952- 56; mem. com. report cost bldg. power stas. Ministry Fuel and Power, 1952-53; dep. chmn. Fleck com. Nat. Coal Bd., 1953-55; mem. Adv. Com. Legal Aid, 1956-60; mem. tribunal Prevention of Fraud Act, 1939, 1957—, Wilson Com. on Coal, 1959-60; chmn. adv. com. to review mgmt., orgn. and responsibilities of Nat. Trust, 1967; chmn. Racing Industry Com. of Inquiry, 1967; ind. mem. Dockyard Policy Bd., 1970; v.p. Union Europeene des Experts Comptables Economiques et Financiers, 1969-70; mem. com. to inquire into adminstrn. and orgn. Ministry of Def., 1969; also mem. numerous other coms. on behalf Brit. Govt. Served with Grenadier Guards, Brit. Army, 1940- 45. Created comdr. Order Brit. Empire, 1946, knight bachelor, 1964, Knight grand cross, 1971. Fellow Inst. Chartered Accountants Eng. and Wales (council 1956—, pres. 1966-67); internat. asso. mem. Am. Inst. C.P.A.'s. Clubs: Royal Yacht Squadron (Cowes, Isle of Wight); Brooks's (London). Home: The Red House Merstham Surrey England Office: Abacus House Cutter Lane Cheapside London E C 2 England

BENSON, HOMER LESTER, govt. ofcl.; b. Elmore County, Ala., Nov. 14, 1918; s. Lester C. and Bessie (Henderson) B.; B.S., Tuskegee Inst., 1941; student Temple U., 1945-46; M.S.W., Atlanta U., 1948; m. Laurajean Troupe, May 22, 1939; children—Homer Tigner, Beverly Ann. Counselor, Sch. Colored Children, Pomeroy, Pa., 1948; visitor Pa. Dept. Pub. Welfare, 1948-49; parole officer U.S. Penitentiary, Terre Haute, Ind., 1949-62; case analyst U.S. Bur. Prisons, Washington, 1962; mem. U.S. Bd. Parole, 1962-69; classification and guidance coordinator City and County Jails, Denver, 1970—. Served with USAAF, 1941-44. Mem. Assn. Paroling Authorities, Nat. Council Crime and Delinquency, Omega Psi Phi. Democrat. Methodist. Mason. Home: 3872 S Sebring Ct Denver CO 80237 Office: Denver County Jail Denver CO 80202

BENSON, JOHN ALEXANDER, Jr., educator, physician; b. Manchester, Conn., July 23, 1921; s. John A. and Rachel (Patterson) B.; B.S., Wesleyan U., 1943; M.D., Harvard, 1946; m. Irene Zucker, Sept. 29, 1947; children—Peter M., John Alexander III, Susan Leigh, Jeremy P. Intern Univ. Hosps., Cleve., 1946-47; resident Peter Bent Brigham Hosp., Boston 1949-51; instr. medicine Harvard, 1956-59; prof. medicine, head div. gastroenterology U. Ore., 1959—; cons. VA Hosps., Madigan Gen. Army Hosp. Mem. Am. Bd. Internal Medicine. Mem. Ore. Drug Adv. Council, 1965—. Dir. Ore. Med. Ednl. Found., 1967-72, pres., 1969-72. Served with USNR, 1947-49. Diplomate Am. Bd. Internal Medicine and subspecialty bd. gastroenterology. Mem. Am. Gastroenterol. Assn. (sec. 1970-73), Am. Clin. and Climatol. Assn., Phi Beta Kappa, Alpha Omega Alpha. Mem. editorial bd. Am. Jour. Digestive Diseases. Contbr. articles profl. jours. Home: 3935 SW 52d Pl Portland OR 97221

BENSON, JOHN CABOT, lawyer; b. Heron Lake, Minn., Feb. 27, 1890; s. John Wesley and Mary Harriet (Cabot) B.; student Hamline U., U. Wis., also U. Minn.; m. Edna Frances Server, June 10, 1914; children—Margaret Eleanor (Mrs. Clark R. Fletcher, Jr.), Mary Lois (Mrs. Fenton M. Davison); m. 2d, Sara Wingate Jordan, Dec. 29, 1951. Admitted to Minn. bar, 1912; since practiced in that state; mem. Faegre & Benson, Mpls. Pres. Asso. Finance Co.; dir., mem. exec. committee Mpls. Gas Co.; dir. Fed. Cartridge Corp. Counsel, dir., exec. com. Mpls. War Chest, 1941-45; organizer, 1st atty. Mpls. Legal Aid. Mem. Am., Minn., Hennepin County (pres. 1938-39) bar assns., S.A.R., Mayflower Society, Phi Delta Phi, Sigma Alpha Epsilon. Episcopalian. 1964 Kenwood Pkwy Minneapolis MN 55405 Office: Northwestern Bank Bldg Minneapolis MN 55402

BENSON, JOHN KINGSLEY, banker; b. Bridgewater, Mass., Jan. 22, 1910; s. Arthur Davis and Mary and Mary (Churchill) B.; B.A., Dartmouth, 1931, M.C.S., Amos Tuck Sch., 1932; m. Gladys Wilkie, May 23, 1934; children—John Kingsley, Carolyn Wilkie. With Nat. Shawmut Bank Boston, 1932—, v.p., comptroller, 1954-60, senior vice president, 1960-66, exec. v.p., 1966-68, vice chmn., 1968—; pres., dir. Shawmut Assn., Inc, Boston; trustee Union Savs. Bank Boston. Mem. Res. City Bankers, Phi Beta Kappa. Clubs: Down Town, Commercial, Algonquin (Boston). Home: 190 Edgewater Dr Needham MA 02192 Office: 40 Water St Boston MA 02102

BENSON, KEITH STONE, steamship co. exec.; b. Chgo., Sept. 15, 1918; s. August and Ethel (Stone) B.; B.A. summa cum laude, Dartmouth, 1940; LL.B., Western Res. U., 1947; m. Jean Marilyn Sprague, Sept. 25, 1942; children—Karen S., Paula S. Admitted to Ohio bar, 1947; atty. Pickands Mather & Co., Cleve., 1947-55, sec., gen. counsel, 1955-61, then v.p., asst. to pres., dir., pres., chief exec. officer, 1967—; dir. Interlake Steel Co., Parker-Hannifin Corp., Sherwin- Williams Co., Soc. Corp., Soc. Nat. Bank of Cleve. Bd. dirs. Cleve. Growth Bd.; chmn. bd. overseers Case Western Res. U. Served to maj. AUS, 1941-46. Mem. Iron and Steel Inst. (dir.). Home: 22401 McCauley Rd Shaker Heights OH 44122 Office: 2000 Union Commerce Bldg Cleveland OH 44115

BENSON, KENNETH VICTOR, mfg. co. exec., lawyer; b. New Lisbon, Wis., Aug. 2, 1929; s. Carl W. and Ottilia (Olson) B.; B.B.A., U. Wis., 1951, J.D., 1957; m. Alice May Drewry, June 23, 1951; children—Jennifer, Elizabeth, Kenneth, Jonathan, Nathan. Admitted to Wis. bar, 1957; sales trainee, sales corr. Marathon Corp., Menasha, Wis., 1953-54; pvt. practice with Benson & Day, Marshfield, Wis., 1957-58; sec., gen. counsel, dir., exec. com. Kohler Co. (Wis.), 1959—; sec., dir., exec. com. Kohler Can., Ltd. Bd. dirs. Sheboygan (Wis.) United Fund, 1969—, Sheboygan YMCA, 1971—; pres. Sheboygan Community Players and Civic Orch., 1967-69, bd. dirs., 1963-71. Served with AUS, 1951-53. Mem. Sheboygan County Bar Assn. (v.p. 1971). Methodist (chmn. adminstrv. bd.). Club: Sheboygan Kiwanis (dir. 1962-65). Home: 507 Washington Ct Sheboygan WI 53081 Office: Kohler Co Kohler WI 53044

BENSON, LARRY DEAN, educator; b. Sioux Falls S.D., June 20, 1929; s. Joseph Robert and Elsie (Ellis) B.; A.B., U. Cal. at Berkeley, 1955, A.M., 1957, Ph.D., 1959; m. Margaret Owens, Jan. 5, 1951; children—Cassandra, Gavin, Amanda, Geoffrey. Lectr. English, U. Cal. at Berkeley, 1958-59; instr. Harvard, 1959-62, asst. prof., 1962-65, asso. prof., 1966-69, prof., 1969—, Allston Burr sr. tutor Quincy House, 1963-65. Served with USMCR, 1946-48, 50-51. Guggenheim fellow, 1965. Mem. Medieval Acad. Am. (asst. exec. sec. 1965-71). Author: Art and Tradition in Sir Gawain and the Green Knight, 1965; (with T.M. Andersson) The Literary Context of Chaucer's Fabliaux, 1971. Asst. editor, Speculum, 1965—. Home: 24 Woodland Rd Lexington MA 02173 Office: 271 Widener Library Harvard Cambridge MA 02138

BENSON, LAWRENCE KERN, lawyer; b. Lake Charles, La., Jan. 19, 1906; s. George William and Lotta Emma (Tannehill) B.; LL.B., Tulane U., 1927; m. Adele Foster, Aug. 24, 1933; children—Lawrence Kern, Robert George. Admitted to La. bar, 1927, Tex. bar, 1929, U.S. Supreme Court bar, 1964; pvt. practice law, Hammond, La., 1927-29; asso. firm Baker, Botts, Parker & Garwood, Houston, 1929; asso. firm Milling, Saal, Benson, Woodward & Hillyer, and predecessors, New Orleans, 1929-35, partner, 1936—; prof. law Tulane U., 1963-65. Pres. Atchafalaya Land Corp.; dir. La. Land and Exploration Co. Mem. civil law sect., adv. com. mineral law project La. Law Inst. Mem. Council for Better La. Mem. Am., La., New Orleans bar assns., Assn. Bar City N.Y., Mid-Continent Oil and Gas Assn., Land and Royalty Assn. La., Ind. Petroleum Assn. Am., Order of Coif, Sigma Phi Epsilon, Phi Delta Phi. Democrat. Presbyn. (trustee, elder). Clubs: Boston, Internat. House, Petroleum, Plimsoll (New Orleans); City (Baton Rouge). Home: 5544 Jacquelyn Ct New Orleans, LA 70124. Office: Whitney Bldg New Orleans LA 70130

BENSON, LUCY PETERS WILSON, pres. League Women Voters U.S.; b. N.Y.C., Aug. 25, 1927; d. Willard Oliver and Helen (Peters) Wilson; B.A., Smith Coll., 1949, M.A., 1955; L.H.D. (hon.), Wheaton Coll., Norton, Mass., 1965; LL.D. (hon.), U. Mass., 1969; m. Bruce Buzzell Benson, Mar. 30, 1950. With jr. exec. tng. program, Bloomingdale's, N.Y.C., 1949-50; engaged in pub. relations Smith Coll., 1950-53, Mt. Holyoke Coll., 1955; research asst. dept. Am. studies Amherst Coll., 1956-57; pres. League Women Voters, Amherst, Mass., 1957-58, 59-61, dir. Mass., 1957-61, pres. Mass., 1961-63, 63-65, nat. bd. dirs., 1965-66, 2d v.p., 1966-68, nat. pres., 1968—. Trustee Northeast Utilities. Mem. council Nat. Municipal League, 1968—; mem. steering com. Urban Coalition, 1968, exec. com., 1970—; mem. policy council Urban Coalition Action Council, 1970—; exec. com. Common Cause, 1970—; mem. Gov. Mass. Spl. Com. Rev. Sunday Closing Laws, 1961; mem. spl. commn. Mass. Legislature to Study Budgetary Powers of Trustees U. Mass., 1961-62; mem. Gov. Mass. Com. Rev. Salaries State Employees, 1963, Mass. Adv. Bd. Higher Ednl. Policy, 1962-65, Mass. Bd. Edn. Adv. Com. Racial Imbalance and Edn., 1964-65, Mass. adv. com. U.S. Commn. Civil Rights, 1964—; vice chmn. Mass. Adv. Council Edn., 1965-68; mem. Mass. Com. Children and Youth Com. to Study Report by U.S. Children's Bur., Mass. Youth Service Div., 1967; mem. pub. adv. com. U.S. Trade Policy, 1968. Mem. town meeting, Amherst, 1957—, finance com., 1960-66. Trustee Edn. Devel. Center, Newton, Mass., 1967—; mem. nat. adv. council Hampshire Coll., 1968—. Recipient Achievement award Bur. Govt. Research, U. Mass., 1963; Distinguished Service award Boston Coll., 1965; Smith Coll. medal, 1969; Distinguished Civic Leadership award Tufts U., 1965; Radcliffe fellow Radcliffe Inst., 1965-66, 66-67. Mem. Am. Civil Liberties Union, UN Assn., Urban League, N.A.A.C.P., Amherst Human Relations Council, Assn. Am. Indian Affairs, E. African Wildlife Soc., Boston Human Rights Council, Jersey Wildlife Preservation Trust Channel Islands. Home: 46 Sunset Av Amherst MA 01002 Office: 1730 M St N W Washington DC 20036

BENSON, LYMAN DAVID, educator; b. Kelseyville, Cal., May 4, 1909; s. Charles A. and Cora (West) B.; A.B., Stanford, 1930, M.A., 1931, Ph.D., 1939; m. Evelyn Linderholm, Aug. 16, 1931; children—Lyman David, Robert Leland. Instr. Bakersfield Jr. Coll., 1931-38; instr. U. Ariz., 1938-40, asst. prof. botany, 1940-44, asst. botanist Agrl. Expt. Sta., 1938-44; asso. prof., head dept. botany Pomona Coll., 1944-49, prof. botany, head dept., 1949—; asso. prof. botany Claremont Grad. Sch., 1944-49, prof., 1949—; specialist in classification, plant geography and evolution, distbn. and floristics of Ranunculaceae, especially in N.A., Cactaceae of U.S., Gramineae, especially Pleuropogon, Prosopis in U.S., trees and shrubs of S.W. deserts of U.S., vascular flora of Western N.A., especially Cal., Ariz. and Pacific N.W. Recipient Wig Distinguished Prof. award Pomona Coll.; Greater Linnaeus medal Swedish Royal Acad. Scis. Fellow A.A.A.S., Cactus and Succulent Soc. Am. (pres. 1956-57), Cal. Acad. Sci., So. Cal. Acad. Sci.; mem. Am. Soc. Plant Taxonomists (pres. 1960), Soc. Study Evolution, Am. Inst. Biol. Sci., Cal. Bot. Soc., Torrey Bot. Club, Am., Western (pres. 1955) socs. naturalists, Am. Fern Soc., So. Cal. Botanists, (pres. 1949-50), Soc. Mexicana de Cactologia, Assn. Tropical Biology, Internat. Orgn. Succulent Plant Study, Bot. Soc. Am., Internat. Assn. Plants Taxonomists, Phi Beta Kappa, Sigma Xi. Author: The Cacti of Arizona, 1940, 50, 69; The Trees and Shrubs of the South- western Deserts (with Robert A. Darrow), 1945, 54; A Treatise on the North American Ranunculi, 1948; Plant Classification, 1957; Plant Taxonomy, Methods and Principles, 1962; The Native Cacti of California, 1969; also tech. articles. Home: 1430 Via Zurita Claremont CA 91711

BENSON, MARY SUMNER, educator; b. N.Y.C., Apr. 6, 1903; d. Eugene Huntington and Helen (Sumner) Benson; B.A., Pomona Coll., 1923; A.M., Columbia, 1930, Ph.D., 1935. Tchr. high sch., Elk Creek, Cal., 1924-25, jr. high sch., Pomona, Cal., 1925-29; instr. Lindenwood Coll., 1935-40; successively instr., asst. prof., prof., Milw.-Downer Coll., 1940-52; asso. prof. Mt. Holyoke Coll., 1952-66, chmn. history dept., 1958-64, prof., 1966—, asso. acad. dean, 1968-70. Mem. Orgn. Am. Historians, Am. Studies Assn., Am. Assn. U. Profs., Am. Assn. U. Women, Phi Beta Kappa. Episcopalian. Author: Women in Eighteenth Century America, 1935; also articles and book reviews in profl. jours. Home: 30 Ashfield Lane South Hadley MA 01075

BENSON, MERRITT ELIHU, publisher, journalist, educator; b. Sabetha, Kan., July 17, 1902; s. Burritt Ellis and Anna (Markey) B.; student Grinnell Coll., 1920-21; U. Neb., 1922-26; J.D., U. Minn., 1930; A.B., U. Wash., 1942; m. Isabelle Dowle, Mar. 27, 1929; 1 son, Merritt Dowle. Reporter, news exec. Neb. State Jour., Columbus (Neb.) Telegram, Mpls. Tribune, 1921-29; mem. faculty dept. journalism U. Minn., 1929-30; admitted to Minn. bar, 1930; editorial dir. Travel Guild, Inc., 1930-31; mem. faculty Sch. Journalism, U. Wash., 1931—, prof., acting dir. Sch. Communications, 1951-68, emeritus, 1968—; vis. prof. Stanford, 1935, summer 1937, spring 1957, U. Minn., 1945; pub. The Ranger, Ft. Lewis, Wash., 1951—; pres. Ranger Pub. Co., Inc., Tacoma, 1964—. Spl. mediation rep. War Labor Bd., 1942; adv. Office Med. Services, Sec. Def., 1949; asst. to gov. Wash., 1950- 51. Served to lt. comdr. USNR 1943-45; flag sec., adminstrv. officer Fleet Air Wing One and comdr. Okinawa, Mem. Am. Assn. U. Profs., Aircraft Owners and Pilots Assn., Phi Delta Phi, Sigma Delta Chi, Phi Sigma Kappa, Kappa Tau Alpha. Clubs: Seattle Yacht; Shadow Mountain (Palm Desert, Cal.). Home: 5700 Ann Arbor Av Seattle WA 98105

BENSON, MILES, editorial editor Long Island Press. Address: 92-20 168th St Jamaica NY 11433*

BENSON, MORTON, educator; b. Newark, Dec. 13, 1924; s. Jacob and Mollie (Ravin) B.; B.A., N.Y.U., 1947; Certificat, Grenoble U. (France), 1948; student Frankfurt (Germany) U., 1948-50; Ph.D., U. Pa., 1954; m. Evelyn Rose, July 3, 1955; children—Rebecca J., Miriam. Asst. prof. Ohio U., 1954-60; mem. faculty U. Pa., 1960—, prof., chmn. dept. Slavic langs., dir. Slavic Lang. and Area Center, 1966—. Served with AUS, 1943-46, 48-52. Fulbright-Hays research fellow, 1965-66. Mem. Am. Assn. Tchrs. Slavic and E. European Langs. (pres. 1964), Assn. Internat. des Langues and Litteratures Slaves (sec. 1963-66). Jewish religion. Author: Dictionary of Russian Personal Names, 2d edit., 1967; Serbocroatian-English Dictionary, 1971. Asso. editor Slavic and East European Jour., 1960—; mem. editorial bd. Names, 1968—. Home: 219 Myrtle Av Havertown PA 19083 Office: Dept Slavic Langs Univ Pa Philadelphia PA 19104

BENSON, OLIVER EARL, educator; b. Guthrie, Okla., Aug. 20, 1911; s. Earl A. and Ivy (Hurley) B.; A.B., U. Okla., 1932; A.M., 1933; Docteur ès sciences politiques, U. Geneva, 1936; m. June Tompkins, June 1, 1940; children—John, Megan (Mrs. Graydon Hale Doolittle). Instr. govt. U. Okla., Norman, 1936, asst. prof., 1938-41, asso. prof., 1941-47, prof., 1947-67, George Lynn Cross research prof. polit. sci., 1967—, chmn. dept. govt., 1946- 51, 59-62, dir. grad. internat. studies, dir. Bur. Govt. research, 1962-69. Vis. prof. history Peabody Coll., 1940; vis. prof. polit. sci. Northwestern U., 1954-55, 68; vis. prof. govt. U. Tex., 1956-57; vis. prof. polit. sci. U. Minn., 1964; dir. Okla. Inst. Internat. Relations, 1947-51. Mem. Brookings Instn. Seminar U.S. Fgn. Pol., 1952, Naval War Coll. Global Strat. Discussions, 1955. Served with USNR, 1942-46. Fellow Social Science Found., 1964-65. Mem. Hansard Soc., Am., So. polit. sci. assns., A.A.A.S., Am. Soc. Pub. Adminstrn., Am. Acad. Polit. and Social Scis., Inst. Strategic Studies, Am. Assn. U. Profs., Southwestern Social Sci. Assn. (pres. 1970-71), Phi Beta Kappa, Phi Eta Sigma. Democrat. Presbyn. Author: Through the Diplomatic Looking Glass, 1939; How Vulnerable is Communism, 1952; Policy Making in Communist China, 1959; A Simple Diplomatic Game; The Emergent Nations: Problem for the Sixties, 1963; Oklahoma Votes: 1907-62, 1964; Oklahoma Votes for Congress, 1965; Political Science Laboratory, 1969; also articles. Editor of Southwestern Social Sci. Quar., 1947-53. Home: 640 E Boyd St Norman OK 73069 also Kingscourt Allenspark CO 80510

BENSON, OTIS OTTO, Jr., ret. air force physician; b. Sandstone, Minn., Sept. 14, 1902; s. Otis O. and Minnie (Sprague) B.; grad. Antioch Coll. Acad., 1920; A.B., U. Mont., 1924, Sc.D. (hon.), 1955; M.S., U. Ia., 1925; M.D., U. Chgo., 1930; postgrad. Mayo Found. and Harvard, 1939-40, Nat. War Coll., 1948-49; m. Georgia Madelaine Guimont, Dec. 8, 1924; 1 son, Otis Otto III; m. 2d, Dawn McMillan. Intern Presbyn. Hosp., Chgo., 1928-30; fellow medicine Fitzsimons Gen. Hosp., Denver, 1930-32; Commd. 1st lt. M.C., U.S. Army, 1930, advanced through grades to maj. gen., 1956; chief medicine March Field, Cal., 1933-37; sect. chief medicine Schofield Barracks, Hawaii, 1937-39; chief, aeromed. research lab. Wright Field, O., 1940-43; air surgeon 15th Air Force, Africa and Italy 1943-44, AAF, M.T.O.U.S.A., 1944-45; chief surgeon AAF, Center, Fla., 1945; chief, research div. Office Air Surgeon, 1945-48; comdt. USAF Sch. Aviation Medicine, Tex., 1949-53; became dir. med. staffing and edn., hdqrs. USAF, Washington, 1953; comdt. Sch. Aviation Medicine, USAF, 1956-59, comdr. USAF Aerospace Med. Center, Brooks AFB, Tex., 1959-65; staff dir. biosci. and bioengring. Southwest Research Inst., San Antonio, 1965-70. Cons. bioastronautics Aerospace Corp., Los Angeles, Northrop Aircraft Corp., Los Angeles, N. Am. Aviation, Inc., Los Angeles. Decorated Legion of Merit (Oak-Leaf Cluster), Bronze Star Medal, D.S.M., Air Medal; Croix de Guerre with palm, Medal of Honor of Med. Service, Air (France); Honoris Causa Diploma and Observer's Wings (Royal Yugoslav Air Force); recipient John Jeffries award, Inst. of Aero. Sciences, 1951. Diplomate Am. Bd. Preventive Medicine (preventive and aviation medicine) (vice chmn. bd.); mem. Nat. Bd. Med. Examiners. Fellow A.C.P., Aerospace Med. Assn. (pres. 1953- 54; Louis Bauer Founders award 1969); mem. A.M.A., Am. Physiol. Soc., A.A.A.S., Alpha Omega Alpha, Nu Sigma Nu, Delta Tau Delta. Editorial bd. MD Mag. Home: 11821 Persuasion Dr San Antonio TX 78216

BENSON, RALPH CRISWELL, physician, educator; b. St. Louis, Apr. 19, 1911; s. Ernest Beal and Margaret (Rinner) B.; B.A., Lehigh U., 1932; M.D., Johns Hopkins, 1936; m. Jean Bell, June 16, 1937; children—Ralph Criswell, Lynn, Frederick. Intern Johns Hopkins Hosp., 1936-37; resident N.Y. Lying-In Hosp., 1937- 40; prof., head dept. obstetrics and gynecology U. Ore. Med. Sch., Portland, 1956—. Diplomate Am. Bd. Obstetrics and Gynecology. Fellow Am. Coll. Obstetricians and Gynecologists; mem. Pacific Coast Obstetrics-Gynecology Soc., Continental, Am. gynecol. socs., Am. Assn. Obstetricians and Gynecologists. Author: Handbook of Obstetrics and Gynecology, 1966; (with others) Primer on Prematurity and High-Risk Pregnancy, 1966. Home: 1960 SW Vista Av Portland OR 97201

BENSON, REUBEN ALEXANDER, physician and surgeon; b. Alexandria, Minn., June 23, 1904; s. Bennett A. and Thea Gurine (Goli) B.; student S.D. State Coll., 1921-22; B.A., St. Olaf Coll., 1926; student U. Minn., 1926-27; M.D., U. Chgo., 1932; m. Margaret L. Stotts, June 13, 1931; children—Beverly Jane (Mrs. John L. Cahill), David Alan. Commd. lt. (j.g.), M.C., U.S. Navy, 1931, advanced through grades to capt., 1946; pvt. practice medicine and surgery, 1936-41, diagnosis and gen. surgery, 946—; cons. surgeon U.S. Naval Hosp., Bremerton, Wash., 1946—; clin. instr. U. Wash. Med. Sch., 1950—. Chmn., Wash. State med. adv. com. SSS. Recipient Distinguished Alumnus award St. Olaf Coll., 1971. Fellow A.C.S.; mem. A.M.A. (chmn. council nat. security), Assn. Mil. Surgeons, County Med. Soc., Wash. State Med. Assn. (past pres.), Puget Sound Surg. Soc., Bremerton C. of C. (past pres.). Elk. Home: Route 1 Box 40 Allyn WA 98524 Office: 1245 4th St Bremerton WA 98310

BENSON, ROBERT DALE, govt. ofcl.; b. Little River, Kan., June 4, 1912; s. Leslie Robert and Vernena (Sherer) B.; grad. Hutchinson (Kan.) Jr. Coll., 1932; student Northwestern U., 1939-40; grad. Army Indsl. Coll., 1944; m. Nelle Malick Payne, Dec. 23, 1933; children—Robert Payne, Robin Sherwood. Chief accountant Asso. Dairies, Wichita, Kan., 1933-34; chief accountant, comptroller Steffen Ice and Ice Cream Corp., Wichita, 1936; with Spurrier & Wood, C.P.A.'s, Wichita, 1935; partner Spurrier, Wood & Benson, accountants and auditors, Hutchinson, 1941-43; with firm P. H. Willems, accountants and auditors, McPherson, Kan., 1937; partner Willems & Benson, accountants and auditors, McPherson, 1937-43; chief fixed price audits br., also chief termination audits br. Hdqrs. USAAF, 1943-46; chief spl. audits br. Hdqrs. Army Audit Agy., 1946-48; dep. auditor gen. USAF, 1948-53; dep. for accounting and financial mgmt. to asst. sec. air force, 1953- 58; dep. asst. sec. air force, 1958—; guest lectr. George Washington U., 1953-56. Pres. Kan. Jr. C. of C., 1942-43; bd. dirs. Kan. C. of C., 1942-43; v.p. U.S. Jr. C. of C., 1943-44; treas., 1944-45; mem. Bd. U.S. Civil Service Examiners, 1955—. Recipient Exceptional Civilian Service decoration Dept. Air Force, 1953, 55, 69. Mem. Am. Accounting Assn., Am. Soc. Mil. Comptrollers, Fed. Govt. Accountants Assn., Kan. Soc. Licensed Municipal Pub. Accountants, Armed Forces Mgmt. Assn., Air Force Assn., Ordre Des Compagnons Du Bontemps-Medoc (hon. comdr.), Internat. Wine and Food Soc., Les Amis du Vin, Internat. Platform Assn., Kan. State Soc. Rotarian. Clubs: Kenwood Country, Nat. Aviation (Washington). Asso. editor Future mag., Chgo., 1944. Home: 3506 Manor Rd Chevy Chase MD 20015 Office: Dept of Air Force The Pentagon Washington DC 20330

BENSON, ROBERT GREEN, retired publisher; b. Nashville, Mar. 19, 1889; s. John T. and Eva (Green) B.; student Wallace U. Sch., 1902-05; grad. Vanderbilt U., 1909; m. Maggie Mai Phillips, Mar. 29, 1916. Partner Benson Printing Co., Nashville, 1909-68, John T. Benson Pub. Co., 1937-68; dir. Garden Publs. Inc., 1941-60. Mem. U.S., Nashville chambers commerce. Mason. Clubs: Rotary, Bell Meade Country, Cumberland (Nashville). Home: 72 Belle Meade Towers Nashville TN 37205 Office: 136 Fourth Av N Nashville TN 37219

BENSON, ROBERT LOUIS, educator; b. Portland, Ore., Aug. 21, 1925; s. Robert Louis and Hazel (Altman) B.; B.A., U. Cal. at Berkeley, 1950; M.A., Princeton, 1953, Ph.D., 1958; m. Ruth Ann Crego, Jan. 30, 1966; children—Emily, Robert Louis. Instr. history Barnard Coll., 1956-59; asst. prof. history Wesleyan U., Middletown, Conn., 1959-63, asso. prof. history Wesleyan U., 1963-68, prof., 1968—; vis. asso. prof. history Cornell U., 1961-62. Served with USAAF, 1943-45. Am. Council Learned Socs. fellow, 1964-65; Fulbright fellow, 1953-55. Author: The Bishop-Elect, 1968. Home: 417 Main St Portland CT 06480 Office: Dept History Wesleyan U Middletown CT 06457

BENSON, ROY STANLEY, ret. naval officer; b. Concord, N.H., Dec. 7, 1906; s. Charles B. and Ida E. (Johanson) B.; B.S., U.S. Naval Acad., 1929; grad. Nat. War Coll., 1953; m. Vida Wimbrow, Apr. 10, 1948; 1 stepson, Rickart A. Connole. Commd. ensign U.S. Navy, 1929, advanced through grades to rear adm., 1956; comdr. submarines Trigger and Razorback, World War II; dir. pub. information Navy Dept., 1950-52; comdg. officer amphibious ship Bayfield, 1953-54; comdr. Amphibious Sqdn. 6, 1954-55; dir. navy recruiting, 1955-56; asst. chief personnel Navy Dept., 1956-57; comdr. Cruiser Div. One, 1957-58; dep. comdr. Mil. Sea Transp., Washington, 1958-60; comdr. Submarine Force, Pacific Fleet, Pearl Harbor, Hawaii; 1960-62; asst. vice chief naval operations, until 1966; spl. asst. to sec. navy for reorgn. of Navy Dept., 1966-67; comdt. 1st Naval Dist., Boston, 1967-68; retired, 1968; mgmt. cons. New Eng. Telephone Co., 1969—. Decorated Navy Cross (2), Silver Star (2), Legion of Merit (2), Presdl. Unit Citation (2). Royal Order Sword (Sweden). Home: 134 Forest St Needham MA 02192 Office: 495 Sumner St Boston MA 02210

BENSON, STANTON FLOYD, envelope mfg. co. exec.; b. Moreland, Ida., Nov. 3, 1918; s. Hans Andrew and Ida (England) B.; student Shrivenham (Eng.) Am. U., 1945; B.S., Brigham Young U., 1947, m. Marion Gardner, Aug. 12, 1949; children—Mari, Jan, Brooke, Patricia. With Reeves-Wood-Garrett, C.P.A.'s, Salt Lake City, 1947-49; asst. nat. bank examiner, 1949-50; with U.S. Envelope Co., 1952—, treas., 1963—. Mem. Mass. Tax Found. Bd. dis. U.S. Envelope Found. Served to maj. USAAF, 1942-46, USAF, 1950-52. C.P.A., Cal., Utah. Mem. Financial Execs. Inst. (pres. Springfield 1967-68), Am. Inst. C.P.A.'s. Rotarian. Home: 32 Wildwood Glen Longmeadow MA 01106 Office: US Envelope Co Springfield MA 01101

BENSON, WILBUR EARLE, univ. dean; b. Wakefield, Va., Aug. 3, 1921; s. Richard Henry and Ada (King) B.; A.B., George Washington U., 1951, M.B.A., 1952, Ph.D., 1960; student Inst. Chartered Financial Analysts, 1967-69; m. Margaret Elizabeth Benson, Feb. 9, 1946; children—Alan Earle, Janet Marie, Robert Gordon. Asst. prof. George Washington U., 1952-60; asso. prof. U. Ga., 1960-65; prof., asso. dean Fla. Atlantic U., 1965-68; prof., dean U. Akron, 1968-60; prof., dean Clarkson Coll. Tech., 1970—; investment and tax cons.; writer, pub. Dir. Cleve. Trust Co. Mem. Potsdam Welfare Bd., 1970—; mem. Presdl. Manpower Study Commn., 1969. Adviser Potsdam Meml. Hosp. Served with USNR, 1942-46. Decorated Purple Heart. Mem. Am. Finance Assn., Assn. Decision Scis., Financial Analysts Fedn. Home: 2 Ridgewood Lane Potsdam NY 13676

BENSON, WILLIAM ARCHIBALD, printing co. exec.; b. Nashville, Dec. 7, 1886; s. John Thomas and Eva (Green) B.; student Vanderbilt U., 1907; m. Florence Riddle, Apr. 15, 1916; children—William Archibald, Mary (Mrs. Albert Duling, Jr.). Asst. supt. Tenn. Packing Co., 1906-07; salesman Commins-Bennett, 1907-08; partner Benson Printing Co., Nashville, now chmn. bd.; now retired; v.p., dir. Army & Navy Pub. Co., Baton Rouge, 1941-47. Mem. Nashville Printer's Club (pres. 1914), Nashville C. of C., Sigma Chi. Clubs: Hermitage, Uptown Social, Belle Meade Country (Nashville). Home: 426 Page Rd Nashville TN 37205 Office: 136 4th Av N Nashville TN 37219

BENSON, WINSTON MILLARD, coll. dean; b. Clarissa, Minn., July 11, 1922; s. William Henry and Hilma (Nelson) B.; B.S., Bemidji (Minn.) State Coll., 1947; student Ind. U., 1944, U. Minn., 1947; M.A., State U. Ia., 1949, Ph.D., 1951; m. Jean Jacobson, Dec. 21, 1947; children—Winston Craig, Kristin Ann, Julie Karin. Tchr., Tracy (Minn.) High Sch., 1947-48; critic tchr. Univ. High Sch., State U. Ia., 1948-51; prof. polit. sci. Mankato (Minn.) State Coll., 1951-66, chmn. dept., 1964-66, acting asst. acad. dean, 1965-66, grad. dean, 1966; dean Sch. Arts and Scis., Western Ill. U., Macomb, 1966-67; dean Sch. Grad. Studies, Mankato State Coll., 1967—. Pres. interfaculty orgn. Minn. State Colls., 1963—; supr. N.E.A. Washington UN Seminars, summer 1956, 60, 64. Ford Found. fellow, 1955. Mem. Midwest Polit. Sci. Assn. Address: Mankato State Coll Mankato MN 56001

BENSTEAD, HORACE MELVILLE, printing co. exec.; b. Arlington, N.J., Mar. 13, 1891; s. Charles Robert and Henrietta (Butcher) B.; student N.Y.U.; m. Jessie I. Jordan, June 30, 1926; children—Horace M., Dorothy J. Asst. treas. Thomas A. Edison Industries, West Orange, N.J., 1910-17; asst. to pres. Franklin Automobile Co., Syracuse, N.Y., 1919-23; partner E. Naumburg & Co., N.Y.C., 1923-32; dir. Western Publ. Co., Racine, Wis., 1933—. Mem. exec. com., 1952—, chmn., 1952-67; chmn. bd. Horlicks Corp., Racine; dir. First Wis. Bankshares Corp., First Nat. Bank & Trust Co., Racine. Trustee Cove Schs., Racine; pres. St. Lukes Hosp., Racine, Kemper Hall (Kenosha), Athens (Greece) Coll., Ripon Coll.; hon. trustee Anatolla (Greece) Coll.; Served as 1st lt., Signal Corps, AUS 1917-19. Recipient Founders award Ripon Coll., 1967. Mem. Am. Legion, Wis. Hist. Soc. (curator). Episcopalian. Clubs: Milw. Country, Milw.; Racine Country, Somerset, (Racine); Bucks, American (London); Racquet and Tennis (N.Y.C.). Home: 3025 Spring St Racine WI 53405 Office: 1220 Mound Av Racine WI 53404

BENT, DONN NEWBERRY, lawyer; b. Los Angeles, Sept. 20, 1908; s. Charles E. and Gladys N. (Newberry) B.; B.A., Pomona Coll., 1930; LL.B., U. So. Cal., 1933; m. Gail Jones, Aug. 28, 1932; children—Kirke, Devin. Admitted to Cal. bar, 1933; practiced law, Los Angeles, 1933-35; various positions with U.S. Govt., 1935—; exec. sec. NLRB, 1943-47; sec. U.S. Tariff Commn., Washington, 1950-69; atty., Barnes, Richardson & Colburn, 1969—. Served as lt. comdr. USNR, 1944-45. Mem. Cal., Fed., D.C. bar assns., Phi Alpha Delta. Home: 2128 N Pollard St Arlington VA 22207 Office: 1819 H St NW Washington DC 20006

BENT, HENRY EDWARD, educator; b. Oglesby, Ill., Oct. 6, 1900; s. Henry Albert and Josephine (Roberts) B.; A.B., Oberlin (O.) Coll., 1922; M.S., Northwestern U., 1923; Ph.D., U. Cal., 1926; m. Florence E. Demo, Aug. 4, 1924; children—Henry Albert, Robert Demo. Instr. in chemistry, Harvard, 1926-32, asst. prof., 1932-36; asso. prof. of chemistry, U. Mo., 1936-38, prof. 1938—, dean of grad. faculty, 1938-66. Chief of the fellowship section Financial Aid Branch, Office of Education, Washington, 1959-60. Chmn. Council Grad. Schs. of U.S., 1961-62; chmn. council grad. work Assn. Land Grant Colls. and Univs., 1954-55; pres. Assn. Grad. Schs. in the Assn. Am. Univs., 1952-53; chmn. commn. of scholars Ill. Bd. Edn., 1968—. Pres. United Fund, Columbia, Mo., 1958. Mem. S.A.T.C., 1918. Member Nat. Def. Research Com., World War II. Mem. Am. Chem. Soc., A.A.A.S., Am. Assn. U. Profs., Phi Lambda Upsilon, Phi Delta Kappa, Alpha Chi Sigma, Sigma Xi, Phi Beta Kappa. Club: Kiwanis. Contbr. articles to Jour. of Am. Chem. Soc. Home: 210 Westwood Av Columbia MO 65201

BENT, JAMES EDWARD, savs. and loan exec.; b. Lee, Mass., Aug. 15, 1905; s. James Frank and Elizabeth (Collins) B.; student Trinity Coll., Hartford, Conn., 1928; m. Frances Patricia Williams, Sept. 26, 1936. Asst. foreman U.S. Rubber Co., Naugatuck, Conn., 1930-31; sales mgr. Hartford office Page, Steel & Wire Co., 1931-32; organizer Bent & Bent Ins., Inc., Hartford, 1932, pres., 1932-63; activate Hartford Fed. Savs. & Loan Assn., 1935, pres., 1942-65, chmn. bd., 1963—, also chief exec. officer; organizer Bent & Bent Real Estate, Inc., Hartford, 1936, pres., 1936-63; formed Bent Constrn. Co. (now JEB Corp.), Hartford, 1946, chmn. bd., 1947-, also president; dir. Security Ins. Co. Hartford, Indemnity Co., Fire & Casualty Ins. Co. Conn., Security-Conn. Life Ins. Co. Chaben Corp., Ryerson & Haynes Mfg. Co. Mem. of Conn. Adv. Council Banking; savings and loan adv. com. to treas. U.S.; past mem. adv. council FHA; adv. com. coops. AID; past dir. nat. com. emergency preparedness Fed. Home Loan Bank; former savs. and loan tech. adviser AID and Inter-Am. Devel. Bank to Govt. Guatemala and Banco de Guatemala. Mem. Hosp. Council Greater Hartford; adviser Greater Hartford Community Ambassador Project: mem. Com. for Hartford. Republican town chmn., W. Hartford, 1961-62; mem. Conn. Const. Conv., 1965; founder, 1st pres. Conn. Republican Key Man Com. Bd. dirs. Neighborhood Planning Assos., trustee Conn. Inst. Blind; bd. regents U. Hartford. Served to maj. USAAF, World War II. Decorated Commendation medal; recipient Leadership medal Trinity Coll., 1963. Mem. Soc. Residential Appraisers, Greater Hartford C. of C. (pres. 1963-65), New Eng. Conf. Savs. and Loan Assn. and Coop. Banks (past pres.), Fed. Savs. League New Eng. (dir., past pres.), Nat. League Insured Savs. Assn. (past pres.), Newcomen Soc., Defense Orientation Conf. Assn., Psi Upsilon. Methodist. Mason (32, Shriner), Rotarian. Clubs: Hartford, Hartford Golf, University (Hartford); Tunxis (Tolland, Mass.), Lauderdale Yacht, Lago Mar Golf, Landings Yacht (Ft. Lauderdale, Fla.). Home: 343 N Steele Rd West Hartford CT 08117 Office: 50 State St Hartford CT 06101

BENT, LEO GERALD, coll. dean; b. Abrams, Wis., Sept. 16, 1911; s. Walter Herbert and Loretta (Whitcomb) B.; B.E., Whitewater (Wis.) State Tchrs. Coll., 1934; Ph.M., U. Wis., 1939, Ph.D., 1948; m. Irene Haan, Nov. 23, 1944 (dec. Jan. 1961). Tchr. Wis. Pub. Schs., 1934-35, supervising prin., 1935-40; asst. prin., dir. guidance U. Wis. High Sch., 1943-44; dir. personnel research Oscar Mayer & Co., Madison, Wis., 1944; asso. prof. edn., dir. guidance Western Ill. State Coll., Macomb, 1945-48; asso. prof. edn. Bradley U., 1948-52, dir. spl. services, 1948-63, coll. dean, 1952—. Member State Teachers Certification Board; chmn. Ill. Pupil Personnel Services Adv. Bd. Mem. Ill. Schoolmasters Assn., Nat., Ill. (Mickelmann award) guidance and personnel assns., Ill. Edn. Assn., Phi Delta Kappa. Home: 2623 Northmoor Rd Peoria IL 61614

BENT, ROBERT DEMO, educator, physicist; b. Cambridge, Mass., Dec. 28, 1928; s. Henry Edward and Florence (Demo) B.; student U. Mo., 1945-46; B.A., Oberlin Coll., 1950; M.A., Rice U., 1952, Ph.D., 1954; m. Mary Alice Keating, June 9, 1956; children—Lisa Clare, Jason Robert, Alan Demo. Research asso. Rice U., Houston, 1954-55, Columbia, 1955-58; vis. research asso. Brookhaven Nat. Lab., Upton, N.Y., summer 1955; asst. prof. physics Ind. U., Bloomington, 1958-62, asso. prof., 1962-66, prof., 1966—. Guggenheim fellow, Oxford, Harwell, 1962-63. Fellow Am. Phys. Soc. Contbr. articles in nuclear physics to profl. jours. Home: 1315 Longwood Dr Bloomington IN 47401

BENT, ROBERT DUNLOP, petroleum co. exec.; b. Phila., Jan. 31, 1914; s. George Leason and Jane (Lowery) B.; B.S., U. Pa., 1935; postgrad. Wharton Sch., U. Pa., also Columbia; m. Edith Breyer Scott, Oct. 28, 1938; children—Robert David, John Scott, Catherine Ruth (Mrs. Sutton), Ruth Joyce. With Atlantic Refining Co., 1935-66, v.p., dir. 1960-65; company merged, 1965; sr. v.p. Atlantic Richfield Co., 1966—, also pres. chem. subsidiary ARCO Chem. Co. Bd. dirs. Pa. Economy League, University City Sci. Center, Meth. Episcopal Hosp.; trustee J. W. Van Dyke Found., Phila. Mem. Am. Petroleum Inst. (past v.p.), Soap and Detergent Assn., Mfg. Chemists Assn., Am. Mgmt. Assn., Phila. C. of C. (dir.), Alpha Chi Sigma, Sigma Tau. Republican. Methodist. Clubs: Union League (Phila.); Springfield Country; Barnegat Light Yacht (past commodore) (Harvey Cedars, N.J.). Home: 125 N Rolling Rd Springfield PA 19064 Office: 260 S Broad St Philadelphia PA 19101

BENT, WILLARD OSBORN, retail co. exec.; b. Chgo., Dec. 22, 1912; s. Charles H. and Imo (Baker) B.; student Purdue U., 1931-32; m. Ruth Ward, July 15, 1939; children—Christopher, Dennis. Buyer, Montgomery Ward & Co., N.Y.C. 1933- 42; mdse. mgr. Lord & Taylor, N.Y.C., 1946-48, Stewart's, Louisville, 1948-56, Famous-Barr, St. Louis, 1956-60; v.p. J. W. Robinson Co., Los Angeles, 1960-65; pres., chmn. bd., Garfinkel, Brooks Bros., Miller & Rhodes Inc., Washington, 1965—. Bd. dirs. Fed. City Council, Washington, 1966—, Downtown Progress Com., Washington, 1966—; chmn. corp. gifts div. United Givers Fund. Served to lt. (s.g.) USNR, 1943-45. Clubs: Union League (N.Y.C.); University, Burning Tree Country (Washington); Talbot Country (Easton, Pa.); Bull and Bear (Richmond, Va.); George Town. Home: 1671 32d St NW Washington DC 20007 also Baileys Neck Rd Easton MD Office: 1401 F St NW Washington DC 20004

BENTEL, DWIGHT, educator, writer; b. Walla Walla, Wash., Apr. 15, 1909; s. Joseph Eugene and Kate (Essler) B.; A.B., Stanford, 1934, A.M., 1935; Ed.D., (Henry W. Sackett scholarship 1943), Columbia, 1950; m. Edna Fuller, Mar. 28, 1934 (div. Apr. 1956); 1 son, David; m. 2d, Genieva Record, Sept. 8, 1959. Newspaperman, San Jose and San Francisco, 1928-34; head dept. journalism San Jose State Coll., 1934-41, prof., head dept. Journalism and advt., 1945—, asst. to pres., 1960—; mem. staff, div. of edn. Am. Mus. Natural History, N.Y.C., 1942-43; lectr. Coll. Notre Dame, Columbia, 1943; mem. editorial staff Editor & Publisher mag., 1944-45, edn. editor, 1946-62; co-founder, dir. San Jose Savs. & Loan Assn. Mem. Am. Council Edn. for Journalism, 1954-58, Am. Council Radio and TV Journalism, 1958-62. Mem. Am. Acad. Advt., Am. Soc. Journalism Sch. Adminstrs. (pres. 1949-50), Assn. Edn. in Journalism, Cal. Newspaper Pubs. Assn. (sec. central coast div. 1947—, sec., pres. 1960), Sigma Delta Chi. Contbr. publs. on newspaper industry and journalism, edn. Home: 1729 Santa Barbara Dr San Jose CA 95112

BENTEL, MARIA-LUISE RAMONA AZZARONE, (Mrs. Frederick R. Bentel), architect; b. N.Y.C., June 15, 1928; d. Louis and Maria-Teresa (Massaro) Azzarone; B.Arch., Mass. Inst. Tech., 1951; Fulbright scholar Scuola d'Architettura, Venice, Italy, 1952-53; m. Frederick R. Bentel, Aug. 16, 1952; children—Paul Louis, Peter Andreas, Maria Elisabeth. Partner, Bentel & Bentel, Architects, Locust Valley, N.Y., 1955—; pres. Tesstoria Realty Corp., N.Y.C., 1961—; treas. Correlated Designs, Inc., Locust Valley, 1967—. Founding mem. Locust Valley Bus. Dist. Planning Commn., 1968—; mem. Mass. Inst. Tech. Ednl. Council. Registered profl. architect, N.Y., N.J., Va., Vt., N.C. Mem. A.I.A., N.Y. State Assn. Architects, Nat. Council Archtl. Registration Bds., Mass. Inst. Tech. Alumnae Assn., Mass. Inst. Tech. Alumni L.I. (dir.). Archtl. works include Campus Union, Dome Auditorium, C.W. Post Coll. L.I. U., Hempstead Bank, Nassau Centre Office Bldg., North Shore Unitarian Sch., Plandome, N.Y. (N.Y. State Assn. Architects award 1970), Shelter Rock Library, Searingtown, N.Y. (L.I. Assn. Architects award 1970), St. Anthony's Ch., Nanuet, N.Y., Kinloch Farm, Va., Steinberg Learning Center-Woodmere (N.Y.) Acad., St. Francis de Sales Ch., Bennington, Vt. Home: 23 Frost Creek Dr Lattingtown NY 11560 Office: 22 Buckran Rd Locust Valley NY 11560

BENTIA, JOHN, mfg. co. exec.; b. Alliance, O., May 15, 1917; s. John and Rose (Streza) B.; B.S., Mount Union Coll., 1938. Prodn. worker Alliance Drop Forge, 1938-39; auditor Stark County Auditor, 1939-41; with Alliance Mfg. Co. (O.), 1941-, successively asst. purchasing agt., asst. sales mgr., sales mgr., v.p., exec. v.p., 1941-55, pres., dir., 1955-; v.p. Consol. Electronics Industries Corp., N.Y.C., 1955-; sales cons. Alliance Tool & Motor Co., Ltd., Toronto Ont., Can., 1943-46; dir. Midland-Buckeye Fed. Savs. & Loan, First Nat. Bank. Trustee Community Fund, Mt. Union Coll., Rodman Pub. Library, Nat. Profl. Football Hall of Fame; bd. dirs. YMCA, 1957-62. Recipient Horatio Alger award Am. Schs. and Colls. Assn.; named hon. col. Mo., 1964; Man of year award YMCA; named to Alliance High Sch. Hall Distinguished Alumni, 1967. Mem. Mfrs. Assn. Alliance (chmn.), Am. Mgmt. Assn., Nat. Oceanography Assn. (policy com.), Electronics Industry Assn. dir. 1966-69, exec. com., gov. 1969—, Nat. Indsl. Conf. Bd., C. of C. (dir.) Hon. Order Ky. Cols. Elk. Presbyn. (elder). Clubs: Congress Lake Country; Union (Cleve.), Alliance Country (dir.). Home: 2043 S Union Av Alliance OH 44601 Office: Alliance Mfg Co Alliance OH 44601

BENTINCK-SMITH, WILLIAM, univ. adminstr.; b. Boston, Jan. 22, 1914; s. William Frederick and Marion (Jordan) Bentinck-S.; A.B., Harvard, 1937; M.S., Columbia, 1938; m. Phebe Keyes, June 26, 1937; children—Michael, Judy, Nancy, Peter. Reporter, Boston Globe, 1938-40; mng. editor Harvard Alumni Bull., 1940-46, editor, 1946-54; asst. to pres. Harvard, 1954-71, publn. asso., 1971—; hon. curator type specimens and letter design Harvard Coll. Library. Dir. Cambridge Trust Co. Clk., exec. com. WGBH Ednl. Found.; coordinator Lowell Inst. Coop. Broadcasting Council. Sec., Harvard Class of 1937. Served to lt. USNR, 1942-45. Decorated Bronze Star. Mem. Colonial Soc. Mass., Phi Beta Kappa (hon.). Clubs: Odd Volumes, Tavern, Harvard (Boston); Harvard (N.Y.C.). Editor: The Harvard Book, 1953. Home: Peabody St Groton MA 01450 Office: Wadsworth House Harvard U Cambridge MA 02138

BENTLEY, CHARLES HARRY, banker; b. Trenton, N.J., Sept. 26, 1913; s. Frederick and Charlotte (Jones) B.; A.B., Princeton, 1935; M.B.A., U. Chgo., 1951; m. Phyllis Mary Opper, Jan. 14, 1938; children—Charles A., Thomas F., John P. Civil service examiner N.J., 1935-39, Los Angeles, 1939-41; personnel oficer U.S. Govt., 1941-54; with Am. Nat. Bank & Trust Co., Chgo., 1954—, adminstrv. v.p., 1968—. Pres. Des Plaines (Ill.) Civil Service Commn., 1954—. Served with lt. USNR, 1944-46. Conglist. Clubs: Tower, Bankers, Princeton (Chgo.). Home: 1237 Prairie Av Des Plaines IL 60016 Office: 33 N LaSalle St Chicago IL 60690

BENTLEY, CHARLES RAYMOND, educator; b. Rochester, N.Y., Dec. 23, 1929; s. Raymond and Janet Cornelia (Everest) B.; grad. Phillips Exeter Acad., 1946; B.S., Yale, 1950; Ph.D., Columbia, 1959; m. Marybelle Goode, July 3, 1964; children—Molly Clare, Raymond Alexander. Research geophysicist Columbia, 1952-56; Antarctic traverse leader and seismologist Arctic Inst. N.A., 1956-59; project asso. U. Wis., 1959-61, asst. prof., 1961-63, asso. prof., 1963-68, prof. geophysics, 1968—. Mem. council Internat. Antarctic Glaciological Project, mem. com. on polar research Nat. Acad. Sci. Nat. Sci. Found. sr. postdoctoral fellow, 1968-69. Mem. Am. Geophys. Union, Soc. Exploration Geophysicists, A.A.A.S., Glaciological Soc., Seismolog. Soc. Am., Geol. Soc. Am., Am. Geol. Inst., Am. Polar Soc., Am. Assn. U. Profs., Phi Beta Kappa, Sigma Xi. Research on Antarctic glaciology and geophysics, seismic refraction measurements at sea, magnetotelluric exploration of earth structure. Home: 5618 Lake Mendota Dr Madison WI 53705

BENTLEY, ERIC, writer; b. Eng., Sept. 14, 1916; s. Fred and Laura (Evelyn) B.; B.A., Oxford U., 1938, Litt.B., 1939; Ph.D., Yale, 1941. Brander Matthews prof. dramatic lit. Columbia, 1953-69; dramatic critic The New Republic, 1952-56; Norton prof. poetry Harvard, 1960-61; co-producer of DMZ, a political Cabaret, 1968. Guggenheim fellow, 1948-49, 67- 68; recipient George Jean Nathan award, 1966. Mem. Am. Acad. Arts and Scis. Author: A Century of Hero-Worship, 1944; The Playwright as Thinker, 1946; Bernard Shaw, 1947; In Search of Theatre, 1953; The Dramatic Event, 1954; What is Theatre?, 1956; The Life of the Drama, 1964; The Theatre of Commitment, 1967; What is theatre and other reviews, 1968; A Time to Die, 1970; The Red White and Black, 1970. Editor: The Importance of Scrutiny, 1948; From the Modern Repertoire, 1949-56; The Modern Theatre, 1955-60; The Classic Theatre, 1958-61; The Theory of the Modern Stage, 1968; The Great Playwrights, 1970; Thirty Years of Treason, 1971. Adapter, translator plays A Man's a Man, 1962, Mother Courage, 1963, others. Address: 711 West End Av New York City NY 10025

BENTLEY, GERALD EADES, educator; b. Brazil, Ind., Sept. 15, 1901; s. Layton Coval and Josephine Cynthia (Eades) B.; A.B. (Rector scholar), DePauw U., 1923, Litt.D., 1949; A.M., U. Ill., 1926; Ph.D., U. London, 1929; Litt.D., U. Birmingham (Eng.), 1959; L.H.D., U. Ind., 1970; m. Esther Greenwood Felt, Sept. 12, 1927 (dec. 1961); 1 son, Gerald Eades; m. 2d, Ellen Voigt Stern, Aug. 25th 1965. Instr. English, U. Ill., 1923-26, N.M. Mil. Inst., 1926-27; from instr. to prof. English, U. Chgo., 1929-45; prof. English, Princeton, 1945-70, Murray prof., 1952-70. Research fellow Huntington Library, 1938-39, Guggenheim Found., 1944-45; Fulbright sr. research fellow Cambridge U., 1952-53, lectr. Lent term, 1953; lectr. Post Grad. Sch. Elizabethan Studies, U. Birmingham, summers 1947, 53, 57, 62, Harvard, summer 1955. Mem. Jesus Coll. (Cambridge) Soc., Modern Humanities Research Assn., Am. Assn. U. Profs., Malone Soc. (U.S. sec.), Bibliograph. Soc., Am. Philos. Soc., Am. Soc. Theatre Research (mem. bd.), Phi Kappa Psi. Clubs: Century, Princeton, Grolier (N.Y.C.). Author: The Art of the Drama (with Millett), 1935; The Jacobean and Caroline Stage, 7 vols., 1941-68; Shakespeare and Jonson, 2 vols., 1945; The Swan of Avon and the Bricklayer of Westminster, 1948; The Development of English Drama, 1950; Shakespeare, A Biographical Handbook, 1961; Shakespeare and His Theater, 1964; The Profession of the Dramatist in Shakespeare's Time, 1971; also articles. Editor: The Play's the Thing (with Fred B. Millett), 1936; The Alchemist (Jonson), 1947; The Arte of Angling, 1956; Shakespeare's Othello, 1957; The Seventeenth Century Theater, 1968. Home: 24 Brookstone Dr Princeton NJ 08540

BENTLEY, HELEN DELICH, (Mrs. William Roy Bentley), govt. ofcl.; b. Ruth, Nev.; d. Michael and Mary (Kovich) Delich; student U. Nev., 1941-42, George Washington U., 1943; B. J., U. Mo., 1944; LL.D. (hon.), U. Md., 1970; m. William Roy Bentley. Reporter, Ely (Nev.) Record, 1940-42; polit. campaign mgr. for the late Senator James G. Scrugham in White Pine County, 1942; bur. mgr. United Press. Ft. Wayne, Ind., 1944-45; reporter Balt. Sun. 1945-53, maritime editor, 1953-69; chmn. Fed. Maritime Commn., 1969—; TV and film producer, world trade and maritime shows, 1951-69. Recipient 1st prize maritime writings Propeller Club, 1950, 51; spl. world trade award, Men's Advt. Club, 1956; spl. advt. award Am. Mcht. Marine Inst., 1957, 58; award as port personality of 1958, Gov's Com. for World Trade; 1st prize for TV series Grocery Mfs. Assn. Am., 1960; Achievement award Traffic Club of Balt., 1965; Distinguished Service award North Atlantic Ports Assn., 1965; Maritime Service award Maritime Port Council; Distinguished Service award Iron Shipbuilders Council 1966; Am. Mcht. Marine Writers award Propeller Club of U.S., 1967, 68; George Washington Honor medal award Freedom's Found., 1971; decorated Order Maritime Merit, San Francisco Port Commn., 1970. Mem. Md. Hist. Soc., Star Spangled Banner Assn., Md. Am. Women in Radio and TV. Women's Advt. Club (named Advt. Woman of the Year, 1956, 69, chmn. Constellation restoration com. 1964); hon. mem. Maritime Law Assn. U.S.; mem Am. Newspaper Woman's Club, Balt. Pub. Relations Soc., Theta Sigma Phi. Republican. Greek Orthodox. Club: Zonta. Editor: Seaport Histories of Ports of the Americas, History and Development, 1961. Only woman to trek N.W. Passage aboard SS Manhattan, 1969. Home: 408 Chapel Wood Lane Lutherville, MD 21093. Office: 1405 I St Washington DC 20005

BENTLEY, HERSCHEL PAUL, Jr., pediatrician; b. Amory, Miss., Oct. 27, 1928; s. Herschel Paul and Frankie (Boozer) B.; B.S., Jacksonville State Tchrs. Coll., 1950; M.D., Med. Coll. Ala., 1954; m. Nancy Lee Harper, Aug. 25, 1950; children—Paul Crawford, John Franklin. Intern, then resident pediatrics Univ. Hosp., Birmingham, Ala., 1954-56; president pediatrics Univ. Minn. Hosps., 1959- 60; fellow hematology U. Minn., 1959-60; mem. faculty Med. Coll. Ala., 1960—, prof. pediatrics, chmn. dept., 1963—; pediatrician-in-chief Univ. Ala. Hosps. and Clinics, 1963—; prof. dentistry U. Ala. Sch. Dentistry, 1965—; dir. Cystic Fibrosis Care, Research and Teaching Center, Birmingham, 1964—, Nat. Found. Birth Defects Spl. Treatment Center, Birmingham, 1966—. Mem. bd. Girls Clubs Am.; chmn. med. com., mem. bd. Vis. Nursing Assn. Served with USAF, 1957-58. Diplomate Am. Bd. Pediatrics. Mem. Am. Acad. Pediatrics, Am. Soc. Hematology, So. Soc. Pediatric Research, Soc. Pediatric Research, Fedn. Clin. Research, Jefferson County Med. Soc. (trustee 1965—), Jefferson County Pediatric Soc. (pres. 1964), Assn. Am. Med. Colls., Ala. Acad. Sci., Birmingham Acad. Medicine, Am. Assn. U. Profs., Assn. Med. Sch. Pediatric Dept. Chmn., A.A.A.S., Alumni Assn. Med. Coll. Ala., Phi Beta Pi, Alpha Omega Alapha. Methodist (trustee). Author numerous articles in field. Home: 4008 Lenox Rd Birmingham, AL 35213. Office: 1919 7th Av Birmingham AL 35233

BENTLEY, ORVILLE GEORGE, coll. dean; b. Midland, S.D., Mar. 6, 1918; s. Thomas O. and Ida Marie (Sandal) B.; B.S., S.D. State Coll., 1942; M.S. in Biochemistry, U. Wis., 1947, Ph.D., 1950; m. Enolia J. Anderson, Sept. 19, 1942; children—Peter T., Craig E. Asst. prof. animal sci. Ohio Agrl. Expt. Sta., also mem. dept. animal sci. and dept. agrl. biochemistry Ohio State U., 1950-58; dean Coll. of Agr. and Biol. Scis., S.D. State U., 1958-65; dean Coll. Agr., U. Ill. at Urbana, 1965—. Mem. com. animal nutrition NRC-Nat. Acad. Scis., 1958-67; mem. Council U.S. Univs. for Rural Devel. in India, 1967—; mem. Nat. Agrl. Research Adv. Com., 1970—; mem. ad hoc adv. com. Ill. Inst. for Environmental Quality, 1971—. Bd. dirs. Midwest Univs. Consortium for Internat. Activities, Found. for Agr.; vice chmn. bd. dirs. Farm Found. Dir. Busey 1st Nat. Bank, Urbana, Ill. Served to maj., chem. warfare service, AUS, 1942-45. Named Young Man of Year, Wooster Jr. C. of C., 1953. Mem. Am. Soc. Animal Sci. (v.p. midwestern sect. 1963; Am. feed mfrs. award 1958), Am. Chem. Soc., Am. Inst. Nutrition, Am. Soc. Animal Sci., Am. Dairy Sci. Assn., Internat. Union of Nutritional Scis., Farm House (hon.), A.A.A.S. (committeeman-at-large 1971—), Phi Kappa Phi, Sigma Xi. Rotarian. Mem. editorial bd. jour. Animal Sci., 1956-59. Author articles profl. jours. Home: 1106 Eliot Dr Urbana IL 61801

BENTLEY, PHYLLIS ELEANOR, novelist, lit. critic, lectr.; b. Halifax, Eng., Nov. 19, 1894; d. Joseph Edwin and Eleanor (Kettlewell) Bentley. B.A. London U.; D. Litt., Leeds U. Lecture tours in U.S., 1934, 36, 39, 41, Holland, 1934, 51 Belgium, 1950. Decorated Order Brit. Empire. Fellow Royal Soc. Lit.; mem. English-Speaking Union, P.E.N. Club, Author Soc., Fedn. U. Women (London). Author numerous books, including: Inheritance, 1932; Freedom, Farewell!, 1936; The Rise of Henry Morcar, 1946, The Brontes, 1947; Panorama 1952; The House of Moreys, 1953; Noble in Reason, 1955; Love and Money, 1957; Crescendo 1958; Kith and Kin, 1960; The Young Brontes, 1960; O Dreams, O Destinations (autobiography), 1962, Committees, 1962; Public Speaking, 1964; Enjoy Books, 1964; The Adventures of Tom Leigh, 1964; Tales of The West Kiding, 1965; A Man of His Time, 1966; Oath of Silence, 1967; Forgery, 1968; Ring in the New, 1969. Contbr. to Yorkshire Post, others. Home: The Grange Warley Halifax Yorkshire England

BENTLEY, WILLIAM HARRIS, mfg. co. exec.; b. Cin., July 23, 1931; s. Edward B. and Dorothy (Harris) B.; B.Engring. Physics, Cornell U., 1954; M.B.A., Harvard, 1958; m. Dorothy Klausing, Sept. 11, 1954; children—Victoria Anne, Nicholas Klausing. With Xomox Corp., 1970—, v.p., gen. mgr. Tufline div., 1970—. Served as officer USAF, 1954-56. Mem. Cincinnatus, Engring. Soc. Cin., Cincinnatus Assn., Kappa Alpha. Clubs: Harvard Business School, Cornell, University, Tennis (Cin.). Author articles in field. Home: 1241 Edward Rd Cincinnati OH 45208 Office: 4444 Cooper Rd Cincinnati OH 45242

BENTON, BYRL. E., educator; b. Armstrong, Ia., Sept. 4, 1912; s. Howard and Hanna (Hanson) B.; B.S., S.D. State Coll., Brookings, 1935, M.S., 1939; Ph.D., U. Ill., 1946; m. Marjorie Glass, Dec. 31, 1939; children—Carol Benton, Robert John. Asst. in pharmacy S.D. State Coll., 1939-40; instr. pharmacy U. Ill., 1940-46, asst. prof. mfg. pharmacy, 1946-47, asso. prof., 1947-49; prof. of pharmacy, dean Coll. Pharmacy, Drake U., 1949—. Trustee Community Blood Bank Central Ia. Recipient citation for outstanding contbn. in pharm. edn. Ia. Pharm. Assn., 1956; Rexall award for outstanding achievement in pharmacy, 1957. Fellow A.A.A.S.; member Am., Ia. pharm. assns., Ia. Acad. Sci., Drake Chem. Soc., Rho Chi, Phi Delta Chi, Kappa Psi, Omicron Delta Kappa. Presbyn. (bd. elders). Club: Torch. Prescription editor Nat. Assn. Retail Druggists Jour., 1945-47; tech. editor LaFarmacia, 1947, 49, 50. Contbr. profl. jours. Home: 7510 College Dr Des Moines IA 50322

BENTON, CHARLES, ednl. film co. exec.; b. N.Y.C., Feb. 13, 1931; s. William and Helen (Hemmingway) B.; grad. Deerfield Acad., 1949; A.B., Yale, 1953; grad. student Northwestern U., Nat. Coll. Edn.; m. Majorie Craig, June 13, 1953; children—Adrianne, Craig, Scott. With Ency. Britannica Films, Wilmette, Ill., 1953—, v.p. charge distbn., pres., 1964—, also treas., dir.; bd. Ency. Britannica, F. E. Compton & Co. Mem. bd. Progress Devel. Corp., Deerfield, Ill.; chmn. Am. Freedom in Residence Fund; mem. Gov. Ill. Task Force on Edn., v.p. Great Artists, Inc.; asso. Nat. Coll. Edn.; mem. Nat. Com. for Support of Pub. Schs.; mem. Center Human Understanding. Trustee U. Chgo., Hampton Inst.; bd. dirs. Community Music Center N. Shore, Council World Tensions; gov. life mem. Art Inst. Chgo. Club: Arts (bd.) (Chgo.). Home: 2717 Lincoln St Evanston IL 60201 Office: Encyclopaedia Britannica Films 1150 Wilmette Av Wilmette IL 60091

BENTON, CHARLES, Jr., electronic machines mfg. co. exec.; b. Verona, N.J., July 9, 1913; s. Charles and Amy (Vreeland) B.; A.B., Dartmouth, 1935; student Cades C.P.A. Sch.; exec. seminar Mass. Inst. tech.; m. Frances Laura Sparks, Nov. 21, 1945; children—Charles III, Martha Ellen, Barbara. With Merrill Lynch, Pierce, Fenner & Beane, 1936-37; balance sheet auditor Am. Gas & Electric Corp., 1937-39; with IBM Corp., 1939-68, beginning as br. mgr., successively dist. mgr., Eastern regional mgr., asst. to v.p. charge sales, mgr. marketing programs, gen. mgr. mil. products div., 1939-59, pres. fed. systems div., 1959-68, dir. marketing and service fed. systems div., 1962-64, dist. mgr., data processing div., 1964-68; pres., chief exec. officer, exec. com. Computer Usage Corp., 1968-69; chmn. bd., pres. Gen. Information Systems Corp., 1970—; pres. Md. Cablevision, Inc., 1970—. Bd. dirs. Washington Heart Assn., Suburban Hosp. Mem. Assn. Computing Machinery. Clubs: Congressional Country; Rehoboth Beach Country. Home: 12221 Stoney Creek Rd Potomac MD 20854 Office: PO Box 1768 Rockville MD

BENTON, EDWARD LAMAR, lawyer; b. Macon, Ga., July 27, 1906; s. Daniel Morrison and Emma Jane (Crumo) B.; LL.B., Mercer U., 1929; m. Mary Wynelle Willums, Dec. 19, 1928; children—Edward Bruce, Mary Lamar (Mrs. James W. Grimsley). Admitted to Ga. bar, 1929, since practiced in Macon; partner firm Jones, Cork, Miller & Benton, 1968—. Mem. Am., Macon bar assns., State Bar Ga., Am. Judicature Soc., Phi Alpha Delta. Methodist. Mason (32, Shriner), Elk, Moose. Club: Idle Hour Golf and Country (Macon). Home: 3580 Ridge Av Macon GA 31204 Office: First Nat Bank Bldg Macon GA 31201

BENTON, GEORGE STOCK, univ. dean; b. Oak Park, Ill., Sept. 24, 1917; George GEorge and Julia (Davieson) Blumenstock; S.B., U. Chgo., 1942, Ph.D. in Meteorology, 1947; m. Charlotte Ann Russ, June 21, 1945; children—Sandra Jean, Barbara Lea, Jeffrey George, Lauren Ann. With U.S. Weather Bur., Akron, O., also Soil Conservation Service, Washington, 1939-42; instr. meteorology U. Chgo., 1942-45, asst. prof., 1948; operations analyst USAAF, 1945; mem. faculty Johns Hopkins, 1948-66, prof. meteorology, 1957-66, acting chmn. dept. civil engring., 1958-60, chmn. dept. mechanics, 1960- 66; dir. research labs. Environmental Sci. Services Adminstrn., Dept. Commerce, Boulder, Colo., 1966-69; prof. chmn. dept. earth and planetary scis. Johns Hopkins, 1969-70, dean faculty arts and scis., 1970—; astrogeophysics U. Colo., 1967-69. Fellow Am. Meteorol. Soc. (pres. 1969-70), Am. Geophys. Union; mem. Am. Soc. C.E., Am. Assn. U. Profs., Phi Beta Kappa, Sigma Xi, Tau Beta Pi (hon.). Home: 1981 Greenberry Rd Baltimore MD 21210

BENTON, JOSEPH GEORGE, physician, educator; b. N.Y.C., Jan. 20, 1915; A.B., Bklyn. Coll., 1937; M.Sc., N.Y. U., 1938, Ph.D., 1940, M.D., 1945; children—Nancy J., Elizabeth A. Intern Bellevue Hosp., 1945-46; fellow clin. pharmacology Cornell U. Med. Sch., 1946-48; fellow rehab. med. N.Y. U. Coll. Medicine, asso. prof., also Inst. Rehab. Medicine, 1948-58; prof., chmn. dept. rehab. medicine State U. N.Y. Coll. Medicine Downstate Med. Center, 1958—; Distinguished Alumni lectr., 1966, N.Y. U. Coll. Medicine dean Coll. Health Related Professions, 1966—; physiatrist-in-chief Kings County Hosp. Center, State U. Hosp.; cons. L.I. Jewish Hosp., Bklyn. State Hosp., VA Hosp., Maimonedes Hosp., Bklyn. Cumberland Med. Center. Recipient Distinguished Service award Am. Congress Rehab. Medicine, 1968. Mem. Am. Bd. Phys. Medicine and Rehab. Address: 450 Clarkson Av Brooklyn NY 11203

BENTON, MORRIS CAREY BENTON, Jr., trucking co. exec.; b. Kenansville, N.C., Oct. 25, 1917; s. Morris Carey Benton and Mattie (Grady) B.; B.S.C., U. N.C., 1938; m. Elizabeth Holmes, Dec. 25, 1939; children—William Grady, Katherine Stuart, Carey Elizabeth, Alice Holmes. Jr. accountant W.M. Russ and Co., Raleigh, N.C., 1939; with McLean Trucking Co., Winston-Salem, N.C., 1939-43, 45--, v.p., treas., chmn. exec. com., 1956-61, exec. v.p., treas., 1962-70, vice chmn., chmn. exec. com., 1970—, also dir.; exec. v.p., treas. subsidiaries Malja Corp., Modern Automotive Services, Inc.; dir. N.C. Nat. Bank, Winston Salem Hotel Corp., Hercules Steel Co., Winston-Salem and Forsyth County Indsl. Corp. Chmn. Winston-Salem Sch. Bd., 1962-63; mayor of Winston-Salem, 1963—. Pres. bd. regents Presbyn. Orphans' Home, Barium Springs, N.C., 1960-64. Served to 1st lt. USAAF, 1943-45. Mem. Am. Trucking Assn. (past pres., bd. dirs. nat. accounting and finance council), N.C. Motor Carriers Assn. (bd. dirs., past pres. accounting council), U.S. Conf. Mayors, N.C. League Municipalities (pres., dir.). Democrat. Presbyn. (elder). Lion (past pres. Winston-Salem), Elk, Moose. Clubs: Forsyth Country, Pine Brook Country, Twin City (Winston-Salem). Home: 2901 Country Club Rd Winston-Salem NC 27104 Office: PO Box 213 Winston-Salem NC 27102

BENTON, ROBERT AUSTIN, Jr., investment banker, broker; b. Manes, Mo., Mar. 21, 1921; s. Robert A. and Laura (Pridgen) B.; B.S., U. Mo., 1943; postgrad. U. Detroit, 1946-47, Wayne State U., 1947-48; m. Marian Oppenheim, Oct. 2, 1943; 1 son, Robert Austin III. Account exec. Cray, McFawn & Co., Detroit, 1946-47, S. R. Livingstone & Co., Detroit, 1947-50; account exec. Manley, Bennett & Co., Detroit, 1950-52; gen. partner Manley, Bennett, McDonald & Co., Detroit, 1952—, chmn. mgmt. com. mng. partner, 1971—. Allied mem. N.Y. Stock Exchange, 1952—; gov. Detroit Stock Exchange, 1971—. Chmn. Beverly Hills Retirement System. Served with USMCR, 1943-46. Mem. Investment Bankers Assn. Am. (mem. nat. com., past chmn., Service awards 1961, 62), Sales Marketing Execs. (v.p. Detroit), Pi Sigma Epsilon (life), Alpha Gamma Rho. Presbyn. Kiwanian. Clubs: Bond, Savoyard (Detroit). Home: 15810 Reedmere St Birmingham MI 48009 Office: Buhl Bldg Detroit MI 48226

BENTON, ROBERT DOUGLAS, author; b. Dallas, Sept. 29, 1932; s. Ellery Douglas and Dorothy (Spaulding) B.; B.F.A., U. Tex., 1953; student Columbia, 1953-54; m. Sally Rendigs, Oct. 20, 1964; 1 son. John Douglas. Asst. art dir. Esquire mag., 1957-58, art dir., 1958-64. Served with AUS, 1954-56. Recipient N.Y. Film Critics award for best screenplay, 1967. Writers Guild award best origional screenplay and best drama, 1967. Nat. Soc. Film Critics award, 1967. Author: (with Harvey Schmidt) The In and Out Book. 1960. The Worry Book, 1961; (juvenile) Little Brother No More. 1961; (with David Newman) (Broadway mus.) Superman, 1966, (film) Bonnie and Clyde, 1967. (film) There Was a Crooked Man. 1969; (childrens book) What Do You Do With A Seven Foot Bear, 1972. Home: 1065 Lexington Av New York City NY 10021 Office: 200 W 57th St New York City NY 10019

BENTON, THADDEUS GREENE, lawyer; b. Washington, Mar. 23, 1900; s. William Horace and Florence May (Yeatman) B.; LL.B., Georgetown U., 1921; m. Ruth E. Hadley, July 21, 1923 (dec. 1954); childrenElizabeth Seymour, Thaddeus Greene; m. 2d, Ann S. Dixon 1956. Admitted to D.C. bar, 1921, N.Y. bar, 1928; law clk. for solicitor gen. of U.S., 1919-22; spl. asst. to atty. gen. of U.S., 1924-27; practicing atty., Washington, D.C., 1921—, also N.Y., 1927—; formerly v.p., dir. and sec. Middle States Petroleum Corp., also officer subsidiary corps. Gen. counsel, fgn. operations com. of the petroleum industry, apptd. by Petroleum Adminstrn. for War, also gen. com. Dist. No. 1, P.A.W., 1944-45; liaison officer Dept. Def., adminstr. Small Bus. Adminstrn., 1960-61; hearing examiner ICC, 1961—. Mem. Delta Chi. Episcopalian. Home: Crystal Plaza Arlington, VA 22202.

BENTON, THOMAS HART, artist; b. Neosho, Mo., Apr. 15, 1889; s. Maecenus E. and Elizabeth (Wise) R.; ed. Western Mil. Acad., Alton, Ill., 1906; student Art Inst. Chgo., 1906-07, Academie Julien, Paris, France, 1908-11; A.F.D. (hon.), U. Mo.; m. Rita Piacenza, Feb. 19, 1922; children—Thomas Piacenza and Jessie Piacenza. Began as cartoonist Joplin American, 1906, and as profl. painter, 1912; dir. dept. painting Kansas City (Mo.) Art Inst., 1935-41; rep. by murals in New Britain Mus., New Sch. Social Research, N.Y.C.; murals for states Ind. and Mo., Power Authority State N.Y. (2 murals). River Club, Kandas City, Truman Library, Independence, Mo. Served as pvt. U.S. Army, World War I. Recipient gold medal Archtl. League, 1933. Hon. mem. Academia de Bellas Artes (Argentine Republic), Academia Sienesa deglia Intronati (Siena, Italy), Academia Fiorentina della Arti del Disegno (Florence, Italy); mem. Am. Acad. Arts and Scis., N.A.D., Phi Beta Kappa. Democrat. Author: An Artist in America, 1937. Home: 3616 Belleview Av Kansas City MO 64111

BENTON, THOMAS HENRY, stock broker; b. Elizabeth, N.J., Dec. 31, 1895; s. Thomas and Ellen (Clarke) B.; student eve. courses accounting, Columbia; m. Mary E. Zimmerman, Oct. 20, 1923; children—Elnora M. (Mrs. Oliphant), Thomas C., William A. Accountant, Am. Express Co., 1921-24, Crum & Forster Co., 1924-26, Am. Founders Corp., 1926-30; founder, 1931, since sr. partner Benton & Co., N.Y.C. Gov. N.Y. Stock Exchange. Trustee Village of S. Orange, N.J., 1948—. Trustee Blair Acad., 1948—. Mem. Holstein Friesian Assn. Am. (dir.), N.J. Holstein Assn. (chmn. show com), Pure Bred Cattle Assn. (pres.). Clubs: Baltusrol Golf; Downtown Athletic (N.Y.C.). Home: Box 393 Blairstown NJ Office: 71 Broadway New York City NY 10006

BENTON, WILLIAM, publisher; b. Mpls., Apr. 1, 1900; s. Charles William and Elma Caroline (Hixson) B.; grad. Shattuck Sch., Faribault, Minn., 1917; student Carleton Coll., 1917-18, LL.D., 1961; A.B., Yale 1921; LL.D., U. Louisville, 1948, Bard Coll. 1951, Mont. State Coll. 1957, Knox Coll. 1960, Brandeis U., Dartmouth, U. Notre Dame, 1968; m. Helen Hemingway, June 12, 1928; children—Charles, Helen (Mrs. John Nicholas Boley), Louise Hemingway, John Hemingway. With advt. agy. Lord & Thomas, until 1929; co-founder Benton & Bowles, N.Y., advt. agy., pres., 1929-35, chmn. bd., until 1936, then ret. from bus.; v.p. U. Chgo., 1937-45, asst. to chancellor, 1945, trustee 1946; asst. sec. of state, Washington, 1945-47; U.S. senator from Conn., 1949-53; chmn. bd. Ency. Brit. and Ency. Brit. Films, 1943-67, Ency. Brit. Ednl. Corp., 1967—; U.S. mem. exec. bd. with rank of ambassador UNESCO, Paris, France, 1963-68. Adv. com. Co- ordinator Inter-Am. Affairs, 1939-45; vice chmn. bd. trustees Com. Econ. Devel., 1942-45, exec. com. bd. trustees, 1958-63, now bd. mem., vice chmn. U.S. Commn. of Inter-Am. Devel. 1943-45; chmn. U.S. delegations to numerous internat. confs. Mem. platform com. and drafting subcom. Democratic Nat. Conv., 1952, 56, 64, 68. Trustee U. Conn., U. Bridgeport, U. Chgo. (life), Brandeis U., Hampton Inst. (hon.) Carleton Coll. (hon.), Shattuck Sch. (emeritus); bd. dirs. Fair Campaign Practices Com., Eleanor Roosevelt Meml. Found., Kennedy Library Corp., William Benton Found. (chmn.), Am. Assembly (Columbia) Am. Shakespeare Festival Theatre and Acad., Cradle Soc., Aspen Inst., Inst. Internat. Edn. Recipient Ann. award of honor HIAS, 1952; Distinguished Service medal Sch. Journalism, Syracuse U., 1960. Distinguished Honor award Dept. State, 1967; 1st William Benton medal U. Chgo., 1968; Human Relations award Am. Jewish Com., 1968; Kajima Peace award, 1969; Nat. Human Relations award Nat. Conf. Christians and Jews, 1969; Key to Freedom award Hadassah, 1966. Hon. fellow Weizmann Inst. Sci., Israel, 1970; decorated grand cross Nat. Order So. Cross (Brazil); Order of Star of Soliadrity 1st Class (Italy). Mem. Am. Legion. Cleve. Conf., Council Fgn. Relations. Yale Polit. Union (hon.), Am. Fgn. Service Assn. (hon.). Clubs: Chicago; Fairfield (Conn.) Country; Yale, University, River (N.Y.C.); Pequot Yacht (Southport, Conn.); Metropolitan (Washington); Paradise Valley Country (Phoenix); Union Interalliee (Paris). Author: This Is the Challenge, 1958; The Voice of Latin America, 1961; The Teachers and the Taught in the U.S.S.R., 1966. Contbr. to mags. Home: Southport CT 06490 Office: 342 Madison Av New York City NY 10017

BENTONELLI, JOSEPH, (Joseph Horace Benton), lyric tenor; b. Kansas City, Mo., Sept. 10, 1898; s. Oliver Horace and LaMiza (Seawell) Benton; A.B., from University of Oklahoma, 1920, Mus.B., 1921, M.A. in Modern Languages, 1941; studied with Jean de Reszké. Debut in Don Giovanni, at Nice, France, Dec. 1924; created world-premieres of two different operas, Il Vassallo of Smareglia at Trieste, Nov. 1930, and Cecilia of Refice with soprano, Claudia Muzio, at Royal Opera House, Rome, Feb. 1934; with Chicago Civic Opera Co., 1934. Debut with Met. Opera Co. (New York), Jan. 10, 1936, taking place (on 33 hrs. notice) of Richard Crooks because of latter's sudden illness, and subsequently in many roles, including first Am. presentation of Puccini's Gianni Schicchi in English; tenor Met. Opera Quartet since 1936. Voted by Italian Fascist Soc. of Musicians one of Italy's four most popular tenors during 1934 season. Elected to Oklahoma Hall of Fame, 1951. Chmn., adviser dept. of voice U. Okla., Norman, 1944—. Fellow Am. Inst. Vocal Pedagogy of Nat. Assn. Tchrs. of Singing (Geneva); mem. Internat. Inst. Arts and Letters (asso.), Am. Hist. Soc., Am. Biol. Assn., Am. Nat. Opera Assn. (dir.), Pi Kappa Alpha, Phi Beta Kappa, Phi Beta Kappa Assos., Phi Mu Alpha, Phi Delta Kappa, Kappa Delta Pi, Kappa Tau Pi (one of founders). Presbyn. (elder). Mason (32), Lion. Star on 3 major radio hours of Nat. Broadcasting Company, 1934 and guest on 7 other radio hours, NBC and CBS; gives yearly coast-to-coast concert tours and lecture-recitals. Made first English translation of Clovis Nogueira de Sa's new Brazilian novel No Delirio da Vida (In the Delirium of Living). summer 1942; on commn. from novel's author, first translation into Italian as Nel Delirio della Vita, 1943. Hon. Col. on staff of gov. of Okla. Home: 711 College Av Norman OK 73069

BENTRUP, MAUD MERRITT COOK, librarian; b. Baton Rouge, Mar. 25, 1908; d. John Brown and Fannie Elam (Merrit) Cook; A.B., La. State U., 1929, summer student, 1961; B.S. in L.S., U. Ill., 1931; summer student Columbia, 1937, U. S.C., 1950; m. Walter Carl Bentrup, Apr. 15, 1944. Cataloger, La. State U., 1929-43, instr. Library Sch., summer 1939; head cataloger, asso. prof. Stephens Meml. Library, U. Southwestern La., 1943-49, acting head librarian, 1948- 49; librarian McMaster and Hamrick schs., Columbia, S.C., 1950-54; asso. prof. Sandel Library, Northeast La. State Coll., 1954-66, librarian, prof., 1966—. Mem. Am. La. (pres. 1961-62, chmn. coll. and reference sect. 1959-60), Southwestern library assns., La. Coll. Conf. (chmn. coll. sect. 1957-70), Am. Assn. U. Women, Delta Kappa Gamma, Sigma Tau Delta, Kappa Delta. Home: 305 K St Monroe LA 71201

BENTSEN, LLOYD MILLARD, Jr., U.S. senator; b. Mission, Tex., Feb. 11, 1921; s. Lloyd M. and Edna Ruth (Colbath) B.; LL.B., U. Tex., 1942; m. Beryl Ann Longino, Nov. 27, 1943; children—Lloyd M., Lan, Tina. Admitted to Tex. bar, 1942; practice law, McAllen, Tex., 1945-48; judge Hidalgo County, Tex., hdqrs. Edinburg, 1946-48; mem. 80th to 83d congresses from 15th Tex. Dist.; U.S. Senator from

Tex., 1971—. Served to lt. col. AUS, 1942-45. Decorated for bravery. Home: 711 Polk St Houston TX 77002 Office: Senate Office Bldg Washington DC 20510

BENTZ, FREDERICK JACOB, architect; b. McGregor, Ia., Nov. 26, 1922; s. Fred August and Ethel Alice (Kramer) B.; student Eastman Sch. Music, U. Rochester, 1939-41; B.Arch. with distinction, U. Minn., 1948; m. Gladys Ann Ronning, May 31, 1957; children—Mariann Louise, John Ronning. With Long & Thorshov, Inc., Mpls., 1948—; v.p. Thorshov & Cerny, Inc., Mpls., 1959-66; sr. v.p. Cerny Assos., Inc., 1966-71; pres. Frederick Bentz/Mile Thompson & Assos., Inc., Mpls., 1971—. Mem. Citizens' Sch. Facilities Com., 1970-71; chmn. Bus. Involvement Task Force Com., 1970-71. Bd. govs. Minn. Sch. Facilities Council. Served with AUS, 1943-46. Fellow A.I.A.; mem. Mpls. C. of C. (chmn. edn. com.), Am. Assn. Sch. Adminstrs. Mpls. Inst. Arts, Guild Religious Architecture, Luth. Soc. Worship, Music and Arts, U. Minn. Alumni Assn. Lutheran (sec. commn. on architecture Mo. Synod). Clubs: Minneapolis Athletic; University of Minnesota Alumni. Prin. archtl. works include Nekoosa (Wis.) High Sch. (Am. Assn. Sch. Adminstrs. citation 1969), pedestrian bridges, Mpls. (A.I.A. Honor award 1970, Am. Inst. Steel Constrn. award of Merit 1970), Brunswick Meth. Ch., Crystal, Minn. (Liturgical Conf. Hon. Mention 1969). Home: 2778 Thomas Av S Minneapolis MN 55416 Office: 1234 Dain Tower Minneapolis MN 55402

BENTZEL, CHARLES H., steel products co. exec.; b. Balt., 1926; grad. U. Balt., 1951. Vice pres., treas. Roblin Industries, Inc., Buffalo; v.p. finance, dir. United Steel & Wire, Androck Inc., Lake Erie Rolling Mill, Inc.; v.p. finance Duo-Temp Corp., Flange Klamp Industries, Erie Forge & Steel Corp., Bison Mortgage Corp., Motor Tire, Inc., Fleet Tire, Inc., Arrow-Smith Fence Corp., Northland Wire & Supply Co., Noremac Instrument Co. Mason. Home: 21 Tee Ct Williamsville NY 14221 Office: 290 Main St Buffalo NY 14202*

BENWARD, BRUCE CHARLES, educator, musician; b. Churubusco, Ind., June 29, 1921; s. Charles Arthur and Maude (Jones) B.; Mus.B., Ind. U., 1942, Mus.M., 1943; Ph.D.,U. Rochester, 1951; m. Mary Gene Aishe, July 4, 1942; children—Cynthia, Tamara, Nadia. Grad. asst. Ind. U., 1942-43; instr. U. Ida., 1945-46; asst. prof. music U. Ark., 1946-49, prof., chmn. dept., 1951-65; grad. asst. Eastman Sch. Music, 1949-50; prof. music U. Wisc., Madison, 1965—, also chmn. Sch. Music, 1969—; mem. Sopkane Symphony Orch., 1945-46. Recipient Ind. State scholarship, 1939- 43; Grad. award research U. Rochester, 1950; named Ark Traveler, 1965. Mem. Nat. Assn. Schs. Music, Am. Musicol. Soc., Mus. Tchrs. Nat. Assn. (regional officer), Phi Eta Sigma, Kappa Kappa Psi, Phi Mu Alpha. Unitarian. Author: Workbook in Ear Training, 1962; Teachers Manual in Ear Training, 1962; Practical Beginning Theory, 1964; Sightsinging Complete; Workbook in Advanced Ear Training and Sight-Singing, 1969. Home: 5602 Hammersley Rd Madison WI 53711

BENZ, GEORGE W., banker. Chmn. bd., exec. officer bank Am. Nat. Bank & Trust Co., St. Paul. Office: 419 Robert St St Paul MN 55101*

BENZ, JOHN STEPHEN, economist; b. Milw., Aug. 27, 1910; s. Edward and Catherine Benz; B.Ed., Wis. State Coll.; student U. Wis. With Wis. Income Study, 1936-37, div. tax research Treasury Dept., 1938-41, SSS, 1941. Census Bur., 1947-48; assigned ECA mission to U.K., London, 1949-55, ICA mission to Pakistan, Karachi, 1955-59, to Laos, Vientiane, 1959-61; assigned Internat. Coop. Office, State Dept., 1962-64, dep. dir. Office S. Asian Affairs, 1964-66, Kathmandu, 1966-69, Hdqrs. AID, Washington, 1969—. Served to capt. AUS, 1942-46. Co-author: Sterling Area, An American Analysis. Address: Agy Internat Devel Washington DC

BENZEL, CHARLES FREDERICK, Sr., pvt. and spl. investments mgr.; b. Bedford, Ind., June 19, 1905; s. Frederick W. and Maude E. (Campbell) B.; B.S. cum laude, Ind. U., 1927; m. Janet Bass, Nov. 22, 1927; children—Charles Frederick, John E. Asst. v.p. and gen. mgr. Gimbel Bros., Milw., 1928-33; officer, dir. Mayflower Assos., Inc., 1933-40, Pilgrim Exploration Co., 1936-47; v.p., dir. Rockland Corp., 1940—, La Floresta Perdida, Inc., 1940—, Florell Corp., 1940—, Clifton Park Manor, 1948-52, Hetherington, Inc., 1941-58, All Am. Aviation, 1943- 44, Continental Research Corp., 1950-59, United Funds, Inc., 1956-59; pres., dir. Del. Chem. Engring. Co., 1954-68; pres., exec. v.p., dir. Del. Chem. Engring. Corp. (Delfi Am., Inc.), 1964-68, exec. v.p. Blue Ridge Mut. Fund, 1964-68; dir. Piasecki Helicopter, 1947-49, Waddell & Reed Inc., 1952-57, Welex Corp., 1949-55, Coral Drilling Co., 1954-67. Officer, trustee Robert Earll McConnell Found., 1937-42; pres., trustee Averell-Ross Found., 1958- 68. Mem. Nat. Security Indsl. Assn. (trustee, life mem.), Beta Gamma Sigma, Delta Sigma Pi, Phi Gamma Delta (Western Conf. medal 1927). Clubs: Wall Street (N.Y.C.); University, Wilmington Country (Wilmington). Mem. P.E. Ch. (treas. 1950-56). Address: 4004 Kennett Pike Wilmington DE 19807

BENZEL, HOWARD ALFRED, breathing equipment mfg. exec.; b. Buffalo, Sept. 14, 1913; s. William G. and Caroline (Hyback) B.; student U. Buffalo, 1947; m. Lois White Butler, Aug. 28, 1939; children—Penny (Mrs. Richard Powell), Gary H. Mgr. service dept., instr. ground sch. Buffalo Aero. Corp., 1933-41; with Scott Aviation Corp., Lancaster, N.Y., 1941—, sr. v.p., 1961-63, pres., 1963-66; pres. aviation div. Scott Industries Inc., 1966—. Police commr. Lancaster Twp., 1963—. Mem. Indsl. Safety Equipment Assn., Vets. for Safety, Inst. Aero. and Astronautics. Mason (Shriner), Elk. Club: Aero (Buffalo). Home: 28 Lombardy St Lancaster NY 14086 Office: 225 Erie St Lancaster NY 14086

BENZER, SEYMOUR, educator, scientist; b. N.Y.C., Oct. 15, 1921; s. Mayer and Eva (Naidorf) B.; B.A., Bklyn. Coll., 1942; M.S., Purdue U., 1943, Ph.D., 1947, D.Sc. (hon.), 1968; m. Dorothy Vlosky, Jan. 10, 1942; children—Barbara Ann, Martha Jane. Mem. faculty Purdue U., 1945-67, prof. biophysics, 1958-61, Stuart distinguished prof. biology, 1961-67; prof. biology Cal. Inst. Tech., 1967—; biophysicist Oak Ridge Nat. Lab., 1948-49; vis. asso. Cal. Inst. Tech., Pasadena, 1965-67. Research fellow Cal. Inst. Tech., 1949-51; Fulbright Research fellow Pasteur Inst., Paris, France, 1951- 52; sr. NSF postdoctoral fellow, Cambridge, Eng., 1957-58; recipient Award of Honor, Bklyn. Coll., 1956; Sigma Xi research award Purdue U., 1957; Ricketts award U. Chgo., 1961; Gold medal N.Y. City Coll. Chemistry Alumni Assn., 1962, Gairdner award of merit, 1964; McCoy award Purdue U., 1965; Lasker award, 1971. Mem. Nat. Acad. Scis., Am. Acad. Arts and Scis., Am. Philos. Soc., Harvey Soc., A.A.A.S., Animal Behavior Soc. Contbr. papers in field. Home: 195 S Wilson St Pasadena CA 91106

BEN-ZION, artist; b. Ukraine, Russia, July 8, 1897; ed. at Art Academy, Vienna, Austria, for two years. Prepared for rabbinical career until 1917; engaged in Hebrew letters, 1917-31; painting since 1931; art instr. Cooper Union since 1947; exhibited at Am. Artists Gallery, 1936, East River Gallery, 1937; one of founders of "The Ten," with whom exhibited in Paris, 1937; exhibitor at Bonestell Gallery, spring 1939; represented in traveling exhbn. circulated by American Fedn. Art, 1953-54, and with various groups; represented at Mus. Modern Art, N.Y.C., State Dept. Art Abroad, Chicago Art Institute, Duncan Phillips Gallery, Washington, D.C., Tel Aviv Museum, in Israel, New Art Circle, J. B. Newman and Goodyear collections, Marian Willard Gallery, Bertha Schaefer and Buchholz galleries; 2 exhbns. Duveen-Graham Gallery, 1955-56. Mem. United Am. Artists, Artists Congress. Author of poetry, drama and fairy tales in Hebrew; Portfolio of Biblical Etchings, 1950; Portfolio of Prophets, 1953; Portfolio of Ruth, Job, Song of Songs, 1954; DrawingsThe Wisdom of the Fathers, 1960; Judges and Kings, portfolio of etchings, 1964; The Life of A Prophet, portfolio of etchings, 1965; The Epic of Gilgamesh and Enkidu, 1967; In Search of Oneself, 1968. Home and studio: 329 W 20th St New York City NY 10011

BEPLAT, TRISTAN E., banker; b. N.Y.C., June 14, 1912; s. Emanuel T. and Victoria (Govey) B.; student City Coll. N.Y., 1929-33; grad. Am. Inst. Banking, 1937, Advanced Mgmt. Program, Harvard, 1960; m. Margaret Mosher, Sept. 7, 1940. Econ. cons. on Japan, State Dept., 1948; v.p., Far Eastern rep. Mfrs. Hanover Trust Co., N.Y.C., 1952—, sr. v.p. internat. div., 1963—. Bd. dirs. Japan Soc., treas., 1963—; bd. dirs. Am.-Indonesian C. of C., 1962-69; bd. govs. Philippines-Am. Soc.; mem. Adv. Council Ceylon Tourism; mem. Am. businessmen adv. com. State Dept.; adv. council Tea Ceremony Soc. of Urasenke. Served to 1st lt. AUS, 1943-46; PTO. Mem. Asia Soc., Philippine Am. C. of C. (dir., Pres.), Council Fgn. Relations, Korea-Am. Commerce and Industry Assn. (bd. dirs., pres.), Far East- Am. Council Commerce and Industry Assn. (dir. 1964—). Clubs: Philippine. Home: 256 Edgerstoune Rd Princeton NJ 08540 Office: 350 Park Av New York City NY 10022

BERANEK, LEO LEROY, adminstr., scientist; b. Solon, Ia., Sept. 15, 1914; s. Edward Fred and Beatrice (Stahle) B.; A.B., Cornell Coll., 1936, D.Sc., 1946; M.S., Harvard, 1937, D.Sc., 1940; m. Phyllis Knight, Sept. 6, 1941; children—James Knight, and Thomas Haynes. Instr. physics Harvard, 1940-41, asst. prof., 1941-43, dir. research on sound, 1943-45; dir. Electro-Acoustics and Systems Research, Labs., 1945-46; asso. prof. communications engring. Mass. Inst. Tech., 1947-58; lectr., 1958—; tech. dir. Acoustics Lab., 1947-53; pres., dir. Bolt, Beranek & Newman, research, cons., devel., Cambridge, 1953-69, chief scientist, dir., 1969—; Broadcasters, Inc., 1963—; chmn. bd. Mueller-BBN GmbH, Munich, Germany, 1963—. chmn. panel on acoustics Research and Devel. Bd. Nat. Def., 1949-52; mem. com. on hearing and bioacoustics Armed Forces NRC, 1955-58; mem. Mass. Commn. Ocean Mgmt., 1968-70. Charter mem. bd. overseers Boston Symphony Orch., 1968—; mem. vis. com. Center Behavioral Scis. Harvard, 1964-70, adv. com. mgmt. devel. Harvard Bus. Sch., 1965-70; trustee Cornell Coll., 1955-71; dir. Boston Opera Co. (pres. 1961-63). Recipient John Simon Guggenheim fellowship, 1946-47. Presidential certificate of merit, 1948, Cornell Coll. Alumni Citation, 1953; 1st Silver medal le Groupement des Acousticiens de Langue Francaise, Paris, France, 1966. Fellow Acoustical Soc. Am. (Biennial award 1944; mem. exec. council; v.p. 1949-50, pres.-elect, 1953-54, pres., 1954-55; asso. editor, 1946-60, Wallace Clement Sabine Archtl. Acoustics award 1961), Nat. Acad. Engring. Am. Acad. Arts and Scis., Am. Phys. Soc., A.A.A.S., Audio Engring. Soc. (pres. 1967-68), I.E.E.E. (chmn. profl. group audio 1950-51); mem. Am. Standards Assn. (chmn. acoustical standards bd. 1956-68; dir. 1963-68), Cambridge Soc. Early Music (pres. 1963-71 and mem. bd. dirs.), Phi Beta Kappa, Sigma Xi, Eta Kappa Nu. Clubs: Mass. Inst. Tech. Faculty, Winchester Country. Author: Principles of Sound Control in Airplanes (with others), 1944; Acoustic Measurements, 1949; Acoustics, 1954; Music, Acoustics, and Architecture, 1962. Editor, contbr. Noise Reduction, 1960; Noise and Vibration Control, 1971. Editor Magazine Noise Control, 1954-55; asso. editor Sound mag., 1961-63. Contbr. articles on acoustics, audio and speech communications system to tech. publs. Home: 7 Ledgewood Rd Winchester MA 01890 Office: 50 Moulton St Cambridge MA 02138

BERARD, ARMAND, French diplomat; b. Paris, France, May 2, 1904; s. Victor and Alice (Colin) B.; ed. Ecole Normal Supérieure, Paris, 1924-28, Heidelberg (Germany) U., 1925; grad. Paris U., 1928; mem. French Inst. of Madrid, 1929-30; m. Isabelle de Savignac, Jan. 15, 1945; children—Marie-Alice (Mrs. Ponsolle), Monique. Sec. of French embassy, Berlin, 1931-36; sec. French fgn. minister, Paris, 1936-38; sec. French embassy Washington, 1938, Rome, 1939-40; minister counselor French embassy, Washington, 1945-49; minister plenipotentiary, dep. high commr. in Germany, 1949-55; diplomatic adviser to French prime minister, 1955; French ambassador to Japan, 1956-59, to Italy, 1962-67; permanent rep. from France to UN, 1959-62, 67-70. Decorated Grand-officer Legion of Honour. Roman Catholic. Home: 25 rue du Bois de Boulogne Neuilly 92 France Office: 4 E 79th St New York City NY 10021

BERBERIAN, ARA, basso; b. Detroit, May 14, 1930; s. Haroutune and Siroun (Vartabedian) B.; A.B. in Econs., U. Mich., 1952, LL.B., 1955; m. Virginia Harriet Kalfaian, May 16, 1964. Profl. debut Turnau Opera, Woodstock, N.Y., 1958; N.Y.C. Opera debut, 1963; leading resident bass San Francisco Opera, 1966—; performer Marlboro Music, Casals, Aspen Music, Lincoln Center Midsummer Music festivals, others; performer leading roles numerous operas N.Y., TV and throughout U.S., 1958—. Served to sgt. Army Band, AUS, 1956-58. Conglist. Address: 44 Morton St New York City NY 10014 also 28415 Streamwood Lane Southfield MI 48075

BERBERIAN, CATHY, singer; b. Attleboro, Mass.; d. Ervant and Louise (Sudbeaz) Berberian; student Columbia, Conservatorio G. Verdi, Milan, Italy; Fulbright scholar with Giorgina Del Vigo, Milan, Italy, 1950-51; m. Luciano Berio, Oct. 1, 1950; 1 dau., Christina Luisa. Formerly engaged in theatre, also ethnic dancing; appeared European radio, also in concerts Europe, U.S., Can., Iran, Japan, 1958—; performer vocal works avant-garde composers, music written for her by Bussotti, Cage, Milhaud, Pousseus, Stravinsky, Berio, including Circles, Epifanie with Chgo. Symphony Orch., 1967; recordings for Time, Boston, Wergo, Columbia, Philips, Angelicum, RCA, Telefunken records; tchr. U. Vancouver, 1964, Rheiniscle Musikschule, 1965-66. Composer: Stripsody, 1966; Morsicathy, 1969; Anathema con Varie Azioni, 1970; Awake and Read Joyce, 1970-71. Address: 7 Via Moscati Milan Italy

BERCHDORF, MAURICE DONALD, banker; b. Terra Alta, W.Va., July 9, 1929; s. Donald Frederick and Ann (Myers) B.; certificate Bank Mgmt. Sch., U. Cal. at Berkeley, 1961; exec. award grad. Sch. Credit and Financial Mgmt. Sch., Stanford, 1968; m. Audrey Darlene Alderson, May 8, 1954; children—Carol Ann, Steven Donald, Elaine Marie. With Am. Trust Co., San Francisco, 1947-60, v.p., 1967-69; v.p. Wells Fargo Bank (merger Am. Trust Co. and Wells Fargo Bank), San Diego, 1962—. Mem. exec. bd. San Diego council Boy Scouts Am., 1970—. Bd. dirs. Am. Cancer Soc., Camp Fire Girls. Served with AUS, 1951-53. Mem. Am. Banking Inst. Home: 11917 Fuerte Dr El Cajon CA 92020 Office: 500 Broadway San Diego CA 92101

BERCHER, HARRY OLDHAM, mfg. co. exec.; b.. Urbana, Ill., 1906; s. Theodore C. and Daisy C. B.; grad. U. Ill., 1928; m. Audrey Vrooman, 1930; children—Frederick, Nancy. With Internat. Harvester Co. Chgo., 1928—, v.p., 1953-56, exec. v.p., 1956- 62, pres., 1962-68, chmn. bd. dirs., 1968—; dir. Harris Trust & Savs. Bank, Amsted Industries, Inc., Marshall Field & Co., Westinghouse Electric Co., U.S. Gypsum Corp., Gen. Am. Transp. Corp. Trustee Mus. Natural History, Chgo., Mus. Sci. and Industry, Joint Appeal Chgo.; mem. governing bd. Glenwood Sch. for Boys. Republican. Clubs: Chicago, Commercial (Chgo.); Flossmoor Country; Brook. Home: 2321 S Golfview Lane Flossmoor IL 60422 Office: 401 N Michigan Av Chicago IL 60611

BERCHTOLD, WILLIAM EDWARD, business counsellor, writer; b. Chgo., Apr. 9, 1905; s. John Andrew and Mary Ann (Lee) B.; A.B. cum laude, U. Ill., 1927; m. Paula Kathryn Cosby, July 28, 1939. Editor, writer A.P., Champaign, Ill., Cleve., Columbus, O., Washington, 1927-29; dir. advt. and pub. relations Aero. C. of C. Am., 1929-34; v.p., dir. J. Stirling Getchell, Inc., N.Y.C. 1934-42, J. Walter Thompson, 1942-45; exec. v.p., dir. Foote, Cone & Belding, 1945-51; with McCann-Erickson, Inc., 1951-61, v.p., gen. mgr. midwest region, 1953-56; chmn. bd. Marschalk & Pratt, Communications Counselors, Inc., Market Planning Corp., Sales Communications, Inc., 1956-58; sr. v.p., chmn. plans rev. bd. McCann-Erickson Advt. (U.S.A.), 1959-61; dir. Simmonds Precision Products, Inc., 1937—, chmn. bd., 1939—; pres. Pinnacle Products Corp., 1960—; chmn. ICAI, 1968—; pres. Growth Services for Bus., Inc., 1962-68, chmn. bd., 1968—; chmn. bd. Central Westchester Pub. Co., 1961-66. Mem. Delta Chi, Sigma Delta Chi, Kappa Tau Alpha, Pi Alpha Mu. Clubs: University, Circumnavigators (N.Y.C.); Tavern (Chgo.); Grosse Pointe Yacht, Old (Detroit). Contbr. mag. articles. Editor: The Aircraft Year Book, 1929-34. Home: 2 Sutton Pl S New York City NY 10022

BERCKEMEYER, FERNANDO, Peruvian diplomat; b. Lima, Peru, July 24, 1904; s. Gustavo and Maria (Pazos- Varela) B.; student Inst. Lima, 1919, U. Notre Dame, 1917-1922; B.E., Rider Coll., Trenton, N.J., 1923; m. Claribel Rapp, Sept. 29, 1939. Vice consul for Peru, New Orleans, 1921-29, San Francisco, 1929- 31, N.Y.C., 1931; counsul, Seattle, 1932-34; counsul gen., San Francisco, 1934-39, N.Y.C., 1939; chargé d'affaires Peruvian embassy, London, Eng., 1943-44; E.E. and M.P., London, 1944-45, Stockholm, 1945-46; ambassador, London, 1946-49, Washington, 1949—. Del. to UN Assembly, London, Paris, N.Y.C. Bd. dirs. G. Berckemeyer & Co., Lima. Clubs: St. James's, Travelers (London). Roman Catholic. Home: Malecn de los Ingleses Barranco Lima Peru Office: 3001 Garrison St Washington DC 20008

BERDAHL, CLARENCE ARTHUR, univ. prof.; b. Baltic, S.D., June 14, 1890; s. Anders J. and Karen (Otterness) B.; A.B., St. Olaf Coll. 1914, LL.D., 1958; A.M., U.S.D., 1917, LL.D., 1961; Ph.D. (fellow), U. Ill., 1920; m. Evelyn Tripp, June 9, 1926. Cik., Achives Div., War Dept., Washington 1914-15; asst. in periodicals div. Library of Congress, 1916; instr. polit. sci. U. Ill., 1920-22, asso., 1922-25, asst. prof., 1925-29, asso. prof., 1929-30, prof. 1930-61, prof. emeritus, 1961—, chmn. div. social scis., 1935-39, chmn. dept. polit. sci., 1942-48; summer teaching at univs. Tex., 1920, Tulane, 1921, Ohio State, 1923. Colo., 1928, Syracuse, 1929, Columbia, 1934. Stanford, 1950; lectr. L'Institut Universitaire de Hautes Etudes Internationales, Geneva, Switzerland, 1932; vis. prof. govt. So. Ill. U., 1958-67; vis. prof. polit. sci. U. Del., 1965. Chmn. bd. editors Ill. Studies in Social Scis., 1941-52. Cons. U.S. Dept. State 1942-45; on London staff Office Strategic Services, 1944; mem. Internat. Secretariat, UN Conf., San Francisco, 1945; adv. com. on fgn. relations State Dept., 1957-64, chmn. 1963-64, cons. hist. office, summer 1961; mem. exec. com. Commn. To Study Orgn. of Peace, 1933—. Mem. European Conf. Tchrs. Internat. Law and Relations, Carnegie Endowment for Internat. Peace, summer, 1926. Served as pvt. inf., U.S. Army, 1918. Grant-in-aid from Social Science Research Council for study abroad, 1931-32. Mem. Am. Polit. Science Assn. (exec. council 1932-33, 3d v.p. 1939, 2d v.p. 1944), Am., Norwegian-Am. hist. assns., Am. Soc. for Pub. Adminstrn. (council, 1944-47). Ill. Hist. Soc. Midwest Polit. Sci. Conf. (pres. 1957-58), Am. Soc. Internat. Law (exec. council, 1939-42, 43-46, 52-54), Fgn. Policy Assn., Soc. Advancement of Scandinavian Study, Geneva Research Center (adv. com., 1932-36), Conf. Tchrs. Internat. Law and Related Subjects (exec. com., 1933-42, 47-50), Internat. Studies Assn. (adv. com. 1965-69), Phi Beta Kappa (book award com. Ralph Waldo Emerson award 1966-68). Clubs: University, Cosmos (Washington). Author or co-author books including: War Powers of the Executive in the United States, 1921; The Policy of the United States with respect to the League of Nations, 1932; Aspects of American Government, 1950; Toward a More Responsible Two-Party System, 1950; Presidential Nominating Politics, 1952; also articles. Home: 1103 S Douglas Av Urbana IL 61801

BERDICK, MARLAND L., restaurant chain exec.; b. Batavia, N.Y., 1932; grad. Trinity Coll., 1953; U. Mich. Grad. Sch. Bus. Adminstrn., 1958. Treas., controller, dir. Chicken Delight, Inc., Des Plaines, Ill. Elk. Home: 2718 Helen Dr Glenview IL 60018 Office: 1515 S Mt Prospect Rd Des Palines IL 60018*

BERDIE, RALPH FREIMUTH, psychologist, educator; b. Chgo., June 21, 1916; s. Sidney S. and Enid (Freimuth) B.; B.A., U. Minn., 1938, M.A., 1939, Ph.D., 1942; m. Frances Warren Strong, Aug. 6, 1942; children—Phyllis (Mrs. Imre Somlai), Douglas, Carl. Teaching asst. U. Minn., Mpls., 1938-41, counselor 1941- 46, prof. psychology, dir. Student Counselling Bur., 1947-65, prof. psychology, dir. student life studies, 1965—; asso. prof. George Peabody Coll., Nashville, 1946-47; Ford Found. cons. U. Calcutta, 1962; summer teaching appointments Harvard, Stanford, U. Cal. at Berkley, U. Mont., U. Utah, U. So. Cal., U. Pitts. Precinct chmn. Minn. Democratic Party, 1960-68. Pres. E.K. Strong Meml. Found. Served to lt. USNR, 1943-46. Recipient award of profl. achievement Am. Bd. Psychology, 1968. Fulbright research scholar in Australia, 1956-57. Mem. Am. (past pres. div. counseling psychology), Minn. (past exec. sec.) psychol. assns., Am. Student Personnel Assn. (past pres.), Am. Personnel and Guidance Assn. (pres.). Author: After High School-What?, 1954; (with Albert Hood) Decisions for Tomorrow, 1965, The Minnesota Counseling Inventory, 1956, The Revised Strong Vocational Interest Blank, 1968. Editor: Jour. of Counseling Psychology, 1970—. Contbr. articles profl. jours. Home: 2208 Folwell St St Paul MN 55108 Office: 301 Walter Library U Minn Minneapolis MN 55455

BERDING, ANDREW H., orgn. exec.; b. Feb. 3, 1902; s. Andrew and Catherine M. (Weber) B., B.A., Xavier U., 1926; B.A., Oxford (Eng.) U., 1928, M.A., 1931; m. Alice Godley Jones, Dec. 30, 1930; children—Anne Catherine (Mrs. Carl A. Broaddus, Jr.), Andrew R. Newspaper reporter, editor, Cin., 1921-26; fgn. corr. A.P., 1928-37, bur. chief, Rome, Italy, 1933-37, Washington corr., 1937-40; editorial writer, radio commentator Buffalo Eve. News, 1940-42; chief information div. Econ. Coop. Mission to Italy, Rome, 1948-50; dep. dir. information ECA, Washington, 1950-51; dir. information ODM, 1951-52, Mut. Security Agy., 1952, Dept. Def., 1952-53; dep. dir. USIA, 1953-57; asst. sec. state pub. affairs, 1957-61; exec. dir. Washington Internat. Center, Washington, 1964-68; dir. Meridian House Found.; trustee, sec. Consortium Washington Univs., 1968—. Served with the USAAF, 1942-46; lt. col. Res. Decorated Legion of Merit, Bronze Star (U.S.); Croix de Guerre (France). Clubs: Nat. Press, Overseas Writers, Internat., Cosmos (Washington); Kenwood Country. Author: (with Cordell Hull) The Memoirs of Cordell Hull, 2 vols., 1948; Foreign Affairs and You, 1962; Dulles on Diplomacy, 1963; The Making of Foreign Policy, 1966. Home: 2801 New Mexico Av Washington DC 20007 Office: 1717 Massachusetts Av NW Washington DC 20036

BERE, JAMES FREDERICK, mfg. exec.; b. Chgo., July 25, 1922; s. Lambert Sr. and Madeline (Van Tatenhove) B.; student Calvin Coll., 1940-42; B.S., Northwestern U., 1946, M.B.A., 1950; m. Barbara Van Dellen, June 27, 1947; children—Robert Paul, James Frederick, David Lambert, Lynn Barbara, Becky Ann. With Clearing Machine Corp. div. U.S. Industries, Inc., 1946-53, gen. mgr. Clearing Machine Corp., 1953-56, gen. mgr. Axelson Mfg. Co. div., 1956, pres., 1957-61; pres., gen. mgr. Borg & Beck div. Borg-Warner Corp., Chgo., 1961-64, group v.p. Pres. of corp., 1964-66, exec. v.p. automotive, 1966—, pres. corp., 1968—; dir. Abbott Labs., North Chicago, Continental Ill. Nat. Bank & Trust Co. of Chgo. Served as lt. AUS, 1943-45. Mem. Am. Mgmt. Assn., Young Pres.'s Orgn., Alpha Tau Omega. Home: 641 Elm St Hinsdale IL 60521 Office: 200 S Michigan Av Chicago IL 60604

BEREGOVOI, GEORGY, Russian cosmonaut. Cosmonaut, Soyuz 3, which conducted a rendevous with Soyus 2, 1968. Address: Scientific Research Inst Petrovsky Park Moscow USSR*

BERELSON, BERNARD R., orgn. exec.; b. Spokane, Wash., June 2, 1912; s. Max and Bessie (Shapiro) B.; A.B., Whitman Coll., 1934, U. Wash., 1936, M.A., 1937; Ph.D., U. Chgo., 1941; fellow Rockefeller Found., 1941; m. Elizabeth Durand, Apr. 1, 1941; (div. Dec. 1943); 1 son, David Durand; m. 2d, Rosalind Kean, Sept. 20, 1948 (div.); m. 3d, Ruth Palter, Aug. 1953, children—Alice, Lois Ann, William Max, Jennie Bess. Spl. analyst Fgn. Broadcast Intelligence Service, FCC, 1941-44; research dir., bur. applied social research Columbia, 1944-46; from asst. prof., to prof. library sci., social scis. U. Chgo., 1946, dean Grad. Library Sch., 1947, prof. dir. study grad. edn., 1957-60; dir. behavioral scis. div. Ford Found., 1951-57; dir. Bur. Applied Social Research, Columbia, 1960-61; dir. communication research program Population Council, 1962-63, v.p., 1963-68, pres. 1968—. Mem. Am. Sociol. Soc., Population Assn. Am., Am. Assn. Arts and Scis. Author: What Reading Does to People (with D. Waples and F. Bradshaw), 1940; The People's Choice (with Paul Lazarsfeld and H. Gaudet), 1944; The Library's Public, 1949; Content Analysis, 1952; Voting (with Paul Lazarsfeld and William McPhee), 1954; Graduate Education in the United States, 1960; (with Gary Steiner) Human Behavior: An Inventory of Scientific Findings, 1964. Editor: Educator for Librarianship, 1949; Reader in Communication and Public Opinion (with Morris Janowitz), 1930, rev. edit., 1966; Family Planning and Population Programs, 1966. Home: 7 Ardsley Terrace Irvington-on-Hudson NY 10533

BERENDA, CARLTON WARREN, educator; b. Atlantic City, N.J., Apr. 17, 1911; s. Charles Berenda and Sarah (Cash) Weinberg; B.S., Villanova U., 1932; M.A., Columbia, 1935, Ph.D., 1937; m. Ethel Lois Warren, July 21, 1967; 1 son, Steven. Instr. physics Coll. City N.Y., 1941-43, U. Rochester (N.Y.), 1943-44; prof. physics U. Mass., 1944-46; prof. philosophy U. Okla., 1946—, chmn. dept., 1950-60. Chmn. United World Federalists, Norman, Okla., 1948-51. Mem. Am. Phys. Soc., Am. Philos. Assn., Okla. Acad. Sci., Okla. State Psychol. Assn., Okla. Ednl. Assn., Sigma Xi, Sigma Pi Sigma, Psi Chi, Pi Mu Epsilon, Phi Delta Kappa. Unitarian. Author: World Visions and the Image of Man, 1965. Chief staff editor Grolier Soc., N.Y.C., 1940-41. Contbr. articles profl. jours. Home: 805 Jona Kay Terrace Norman OK 73069

BERENGARTEN, SIDNEY, univ. dean; b. Bklyn., May 28, 1911; s. Adolph and Therese (Finkelstein) B.; B.A., N.Y.U., 1932; M.A., Clark U., 1933; M.S. in Social Work, Columbia, 1943; m. Miriam Lindenbaum, June 26, 1932. Successively field worker, unit supr., asst. case supr. N.Y.C. Dept. Welfare, 1934-41; caseworker, supr. N.Y. Community Service Soc., 1942- 43; mem. faculty Columbia Sch. Social Work, 1946—, prof., 1955—, acting dean, 1967-71, asso. dean, 1971—, lectr. nursing edn. Tchrs. Coll., 1947-55; cons. surgeon gen. Army, 1948—; adviser State Dept. and Fulbright Commn., 1965—. Mem. com. tng. and personnel adv. to U.S. Children's Bur. and Bur. Pub. Assistance, Dept. Health, Edn. and Welfare, 1953-57; cons. Mayor N.Y.C. Task Force Tb, 1967-68. Adv. bd. Found. Thanatology. Served to 1st lt. AUS, 1943-46. Mem. Am. Assn. U. Profs., Nat. Assn. Social Workers, Acad. Certified Social Workers, Council Social Work Edn. (chmn. com. admissions policies 1956-65). Author: Admissions Prediction and Student Performance in Social Work Education, 1964; Interviewing and Personality Assessment: Selection of Social Work Students, 1968; also articles. Office: 622 W 113th St New York City NY 10027

BERES, DAVID, psychoanalyst; b. Odessa, Russia, Apr. 1, 1903; s. Nathan and Mary (Best) B.; brought to U.S., 1905, naturalized, 1921; B.S., Coll. City N.Y., 1923; M.D., State U. N.Y. Downstate Med. Center Coll. Medicine, 1928; m. Dinah Schleifer, Mar. 1, 1926; children—Paul, Robert A. Intern Mt. Sinai Hosp., N.Y.C., 1928-30; psychiat. resident Hillside Hosp., Bellerose, L.I., 1940-42; mem. neurology dept. Montefiore Hosp., N.Y.C., 1940-48; staff psychiatrist Jewish Child Care Assn., N.Y.C., 1942-61; pvt. practice, N.Y.C., 1942—; mem. faculty N.Y. Psychoanalytic Inst., 1958—; vis. prof. Coll. City N.Y., 1951-54. Mem. Internat. (v.p. 1963-65), Am. (sec. 1959-60, pres. 1963-64, editorial bd. jour.) psychoanalytic assns., A.M.A., Am. Psychiat. Assn., Am. Orthopsychiat. Assn., A.A.A.S., N.Y. Psychoanalytic Inst. (pres. 1964-66), N.Y. Psychoanalytic Soc. (pres. 1969-71). Editorial bd. Psychoanalytic Quar. Address: 151 Central Park West New York City NY 10023

BERESFORD, HOBART, agrl. engr.; b. Vinton, Ia., Dec. 6, 1896; s. Howard L. and Leah M. (Williams) B.; B.S., Ia. State Coll., 1924, A.E., 1941; m. Lorene M. Kling, Aug. 20, 1925. Instr. U. Ida., 1924-26, mem. faculty, 1928-46; agrl. engr. Ida. Power Co., Boise, 1927-28; mem. faculty Ia. State U., 1946—, prof. agrl. engring., now prof. emeritus. Registered profl. engr., Ia., Ida. Fellow Am. Soc. Agrl. Engrs. (life); mem. Sigma Xi, Gamma Sigma Delta. Contbr. numerous articles on agrl. enging. subjects in profl. jours. Home: Skunk Hollow Box 310 Ames IA 50010

BERESFORD, JAMES ALFRED newspaper and business exec.; b. Wellsville, O., June 16, 1901; s. William Edwin and Martha (McFarland), B.; A.B., U. Mich., 1924; m. Florence Louise Booth, Feb. 7, 1925; children—Mary Louise, John Booth, Virginia Ann, Daniel Booth. With Booth Newspapers, Inc., 1924—, chmn. bd., 1959-63, also dir.; dir. George G. Booth Corp. 1940-60, v.p., 1947- 60; pres., dir., treas. Beresford Co. Mem. local draft board, 1940-47. Commr. City of Bloomfield Hills, Mich., mayor, 1954-55, 61. Chmn. bd. trustees Cranbrook Inst. Sci.; mem. adv. bd. Salvation Army; pres., dir. Beresford Fund; trustee Rotary Found. Mem. Engring. Soc. Detroit, Financial Execs. Inst., Detroit Zool. Soc. (dir.), Delta Upsilon. Episcopalian. Clubs: M (Univ. Mich.); Detroit, Detroit Athletic; Bloomfield Hills (Mich.) Country; University (N.Y.C.); Farm, Metamora Open Hunt (Metamora). Home: Lone Pine Rd Bloomfield Hills MI 48013 Office: 770 S Adams St Birmingham MI 48011

BERG, EUGENE PAULSEN, mfg. co. exec.; b. Chgo., May 25, 1913; s. Christian Paulsen and Mae Olive (Mathews) B.; B.S. in Mech. Engring., Purdue U., 1937; M.B.A., U. Chgo., 1945; m. Margaret Louise Hughes, Jan. 21, 1939; children—Charles, Paula. With Link-Belt Co., Chgo., 1937-60, gen. mgr., 1950-60; exec. v.p. Bucyrus-Erie Co., South Milwaukee, Wis., 1960-62, pres., 1962—, chmn. bd., 1963—, also mem. exec. com.; pres., chmn. bd. Bucyrus-Erie Co. Can., Ltd., Guelph, Ont., 1963—; chmn. bd. Ruston Bucyrus, Ltd., Lincoln, Eng., 1962—; dir. Komatsu-Bucyrus, K.K., Japan, Equipos Mecanicos Bucyrus-Erie S.A., Mexico, Interlake Inc., Chgo. Mem.-at- large Milw. chpt. Boy Scouts Am. Bd. dirs., pres., trustee Bucyrus-Erie Found., Inc. Mem. Am. Soc. M.E. (chmn. Chgo. 1956), Am. Mining Congress (bd. govs. mfrs. div.), Delta Upsilon, Pi Tau Sigma. Clubs: Economic, Yacht (Chicago); Westmoreland Country (Wilmette, Ill.); Bath and Tennis (Lake Forest). Home: 24 Shawnee Lane Lake Forest IL 60045 Office: Bucyrus-Erie Co South Milwaukee WI 53172

BERG, GLEN VIRGIL, educator; b. Mead, Neb., Dec. 17, 1918; s. Emil Gottfred and Rosella (Gibson) B.; B.Sc., U. Neb., 1941, M.Sc., 1955; Ph.D., U. Mich., 1958; m. Margaret Mary Eaton, Aug. 8, 1941; children—Sylvia, Stephanie, Wendy. Jr. engr. Panama Canal, 1941-43, engr., 1946-48; engr. C. Iber & Sons, Peoria, Ill., 1948-50; partner firm Berg-Hartsfield Co., Lincoln, Neb., 1950-53; engr. Capital Steel Co., Lincoln Neb., 1953-55; research asso. U. Mich., 1955-58, prof., 1958—, chmn. dept. civil engring. 1969—; dir. Earthquake Engring. Research Inst. Served to lt. AUS, 1943-46. Mem. Seismol. Soc. Am., Indian Soc. Earthquake Tech., Am. Soc. Civil Engrs., Am. Soc. Engring. Edn., Earthquake Engring. Research Inst., Universities Council Earthquake Engring. Research. Home: 1033 Baldwin St Ann Arbor MI 48104

BERG, HARVEY ALLEN, architect, civil engr.; b. Bklyn., July 20, 1933; s. Louis and Lillian (Dworsh) B.; B.Arch., Rensselaer Poly. Inst., 1955; m. Marja-Tettu Heinonen, June 20, 1956. Partner, Werfel, Weissman & Berg, Architects, Flushing, N.Y., 1962-65, Werfel & Berg, 1965—; mem. faculty Newark Coll. Engring., Sch. for Archtl. Tng., 1968—. Served to lt. (j.g.) USNR, 1956-58. Recipient Alpha Rho Chi award, 1955; Certificate of Merit for Outstanding design N.Y. Assn. Architects, 1962; Nat. Design award Prog. Architecture, 1963; 1st prize in design Queens C. of C.; award in bldg. constrn. N.Y. Soc. Architects, 1963. Fulbright scholar, Finland, 1955-56. Registered profl. architect, N.Y., N.J., Va., Ala.; registered profl. engr., N.J. Mem. A.I.A., N.J. Soc. Architects, Sigma Xi, Tau Beta Pi, Pi Delta Epsilon, Scarab. Home: Shore Dr Blooming Grove NY 10914 Office: 75-19 Vleigh Pl Flushing NY 11367

BERG, IRWIN AUGUST, educator; b. Chgo., Oct. 9, 1913; s. Bertil Sigfried and Clara (Anderson) B.; A.B. cum laude, Knox Coll., 1936; A.M., U. Mich., 1940, Ph.D., 1942; m. Sylvia Maria Taipale, Mar. 4, 1939; 1 dau. Karen Astrid (Mrs. A. C. Kirby). Asst. prof. psychology U. Ill., 1942047; asso. prof. Pomona Coll., 1947-48, Northwestern U., 1948-55; chmn. dept., prof. psychology La. State U., 1955-66, dean coll. arts and scis., prof. psychology, 1966-. Spl. cons. U.S. Dept. Labor, U.S. Va., La. State Dept. Hosps. Mem. La. State Commn. on Law Enforcement and Adminstrn. Criminal Justice, 1968—; mem. La. Bd. Licensing for Sanitarians. Mem. Am. (pres. div. counseling psychology 1964), Southeastern (pres. 1963), Southwestern (pres. 1963-64) psychol. assns., A.A.A.S., Am. Assn. U. Profs., Phi Beta Kappa, Sigma Xi, Phi Kappa Phi, Phi Beta. Author: Workbook in Psychology, 1961; Response Set and Personality Assessment, 1967. Co-editor; Conformity and Deviation,1961; An Introduction to Clinical Psychology, 3d edit., 1966. Home: 853 DuBois Dr Baton Rouge, LA 70808.

BERG, JOHN EDWARD, railroad ofcl.; b. Ansonia, Conn., Oct. 12, 1912; s. John Albin and Amelia (Ekengren) B.; m. Dazma Charlotte Hercher, June 15, 1936; children—Gordon Hercher, Paul Edward. With Ansonia Electric Co., 1929- 30, Standard Oil Co. N.Y., 1930, Sidney Blumenthal & Co., 1931; with N.Y., N.H. & H. R.R. Co., 1931—, various positions in accounting, finance, treasury depts., New Haven, 1931-54, asst. treas., cashier, 1954-58, asst. v.p., 1958-60, asst. v.p. finance, treas., 1960-62, dir. finance, treas., 1962-69, sec., treas., 1969—; dir. Davenport Residence, Inc. Treas., Town of Hamden, Conn., 1959-61. Bd. dirs. No. br. YMCA, Quinnipiac Valley Devel. Corp. Mem. Assn. Am. R.R.s. Republican. Conglist. Kiwanian. Clubs: New Haven Country; High Lane (Hamden). Home: 117 Harmon St Hamden CT 06510 Office: 54 Meadow St New Haven CT 06506

BERG, JOHN ROBERT, geologist, coll. adminstr.; b. Chgo., Feb. 18, 1915; s. Gustav Adolph and Clara (Swanson) B.; B.A., Augustana Coll., Rock Island, Ill., 1938; M.S., U. Ia., 1940, Ph.D., 1942; m. Hazel C. Anderson, Sept. 11, 1940; 1 son, Richard. Machine operator Continental Can Co., Chgo., 1932-36; med. attendant Internat. Harvester Co., 1936-38; research asst., instr. U. Ia. 1939-42; chem. engr. E.I. duPont de Nemours Co., 1942-44; geologist Shell Oil Co., 1944-46; prof., head dept. geology Wichita State U., 1946—, dean Univ. Coll., 1962-69; cons. Govt. Brazil, 1949-50. Bd. Dirs., sec.-treas. Petroleum Resources Fund, Inc. Fellow Geol. Soc. Am., A.A.A.S.; mem. Soc. Econ. Geologists, Am. Chem. Soc., Am. Assn. Petroleum Geologists, Nat. Assn. Geol. Tchrs. (v.p., acting pres. 1956, pres. 1957-58), Am. Inst. Mining and Metall. Engrs., Am. Geophys. Union, Am. Commn. Stratigraphic Nomenclature, Sigma Xi. Home: 1744 N Hillside Wichita KS 67214

BERG, JOSEPH WILBUR, Jr., geophysicist; b. Essington, Pa., Oct. 6, 1920; s. Joseph Wilbur and Anne (Fullerton) B.; B.S., U. Ga., 1948; M.S., Pa. State U., 1952, Ph.D., 1954; m. Lillian Miriam Douglas, June 26, 1950; children—Anne Lillian, Joseph Wilbur III, Frederick Douglas. Instr., Armstrong Coll., Savannah, Ga., 1948-49; research asst. Pa. State U., 1949-55; asst. prof. physics and geophysics U. Tulsa, 1954-55; asso. prof. geophysics U. Utah, 1955-60; geophysicist Inst. for Def. Analyses, Washington, 1960-61; prof. oceanography Ore. State U., Corvallis, 1961-66; exec. sec. div. earth scis. Nat. Acad. Sci., 1966- -; vis. prof. Cornell U., 1969-70, Ga. Inst. Tech., 1970- 71. Mem. Geophys. Soc. Am., Soc. Exploration Geologists, Geol. Soc. Am., Seismol. Soc. Am. Research, publs. in generation and propagation of seismic waves, determination of earth structure from transit times of seismic waves, interpretation of earth gravity in terms geol. structure, conduction of electricity by rocks. Home: 8904 Gallant Green Dr McLean VA 22101 Office: 2101 Constitution Av Washington DC 20418

BERG, LOUIS, psychiatrist, author; b. London, Eng., June 19, 1901; s. Samuel and Ida B., brought to U.S. 1904, naturalized, 1919; A.B., Columbia 1920; M.D., Jefferson Med. Coll., Phila., 1923; grad. study U. Vienna, 1926; m. Lisa Conlin; adopted children—Leslie Lanham Berg, Wendy Lee Berg, Michael David Berg. Intern. Beth David Hosp., N.Y.C., 1923-24; resident Montefiore Hosp., 1924-25; asst. physician Manhattan State Hosp. for Insane, 1924-25; Dist. med. Supr. Dept. of Health, N.Y.C., 1929—; physician to N.Y. Dept. of Correction, Welfare Island, 1928-35; part-time instr. of edn., New York U., 1929-34; med. dir. Henry Meinhard Meml. Health Center 1931—. Medico-legal expert, lectr., 1934—; asso. in neuro-psychiatry Beth David Hosp..; neuro- psychiatrist to the army induction station, Grand Central Palace, N.Y.C., 1943-; mem. impartial specialist panel in neurology Workmens Compensation Bd. Bd. visitors Highland State Tng. Sch. Boys. Served in inf., U.S. Army, 1918. Diplomate Am. Bd. Psychiatry and Neurology. Mem. A.M.A., N.Y. State, N.Y. County med. socs., Am. Psychiat. Assn. Mason. Author: (Novels) Prison Doctor; 1931; Prison Nurse, 1934; Devils Circus, 1934; Twilight Comes Early, 1939; other and later books include: The Human Personality; Sex, Methods and Manners (with Robert Treat), 1953; Psychiatry for the Layman, 1963; The Velvet Underground (with Michael Leigh) 1964. Contbr. articles in field to mags. Address: 17 E 70th St New York City, NY 10021.

BERG, MARSHALL, fgn. service officer; b. Cedar Falls, Iowa, July 21, 1927; s. Anton F. and Clare E. (Marshall) B.; B.A., State U. Iowa, 1950; student Princeton, 1951-52, 67-68; m. Nancy Tate Howay, Sept. 22, 1959; children—Eric Alexander, Kristine Helen. Joined U.S. Fgn. Service, 1957; spl. asst. to dep. dir. USIA, 1957-59; pub. affairs officer, consul, Alexandria, Egypt, 1959-62; cultural attache Am. embassy, Algiers, 1962-65; pub. affairs officer, Quagadougou, Upper Volta, 1965-67; dep. dir. African cultural affairs State Dept., 1968-70; public affairs officer, Istanbul, Turkey, 1970—. Served with USN, 1945-46. Princeton fellow public affairs, 1967-68. Mem. Phi Beta Kappa, Kappa Tau Alpha, Delta Tau Delta. Presbyn. Home: 1911 Martha's Rd Alexandria VA 22307 Office: Am Consulate General Tepebasi Istanbul Turkey

BERG, NORMAN ALF, govt. ofcl.; b. Burlington, Ia., Mar. 14, 1918; s. Alf Fredrick and Mary E. (Rohleder) N.; B.S., U. Minn., 1941; M.P.A., Harvard, 1956; m. Ruth A. Askegaard, Nov. 20, 1941; children—Susan (Mrs. Edward L. Morgan, Jr.), Jane (Mrs. Glenn R. Paulsen), Pamela Ann, Rebecca Ruth. With Soil Conservation Service, Dept. Agr., 1943—, asso. adminstr., 1969—. Mem. Internat. Migratory Bird Com. U.S.-Can., 1962—. Served with USMCR, 1943-46. Ford Fellow, 1956. Fellow Soil Conservation Soc. Am.; mem. Pocatello Jaycees (pres. 1949-50), Farm House Frat. Methodist (ofcl. bd.). Co-author: Modern Supervisory Practice, rev. edit., 1966. Home: 133 St Andrews Rd Severna Park MD 21146 Office: Dept Agr Washington DC 20515

BERG, NORMAN WALTER, clergyman; b. Saginaw, Mich., Mar. 29, 1920; s. Ehrenfried J. and Lydia (Lehman) B.; student Mich. Lutheran Sem., 1937; B.A., Northwestern Coll., Watertown, Wis., 1941; B.D., Wis. Luth. Sem., Mequon, 1944; m. Eleanor M. Martin, Oct. 6, 1946; childrenPeter M., Mary E., John W., Margaret A., Miriam E. Ordained to ministry Luth. Ch., 1946; instr. Northwestern Luth. Acad., Mobridge, S.D., 1944-46; pastor in Globe, Ariz., 1946-50, Tucson, 1950-54, Benton Harbor, Mich., 1954-60, Plymouth, Mich., 1960-68; exec. sec. bd. home missions Wis. Evang. Luth. Synod, Milw., 1968—, v.p. Ariz.-Cal. dist., 1954, chmn. bd. information and stewardship, 1955-61, sec., 1961-62, v.p., 1965-68, pres. Mich. dist., 1962-68, moderator Luth. Free Conf., 1964-68; chmn. Evang. Luth. Confessional Forum, 1967-. Home: 2774 N Grand Blvd Milwaukee, WI 53210. Office: 3512 N North Av Milwaukee WI 53208

BERG, PAUL, educator, biochemist; b. N.Y.C., June 30, 1926; s. Harry and Sarah (Brodsky) B.; B.S., Pa., State U., 1948; Ph.D., Western Res. U., 1952; m. Mildred Levy, Sept. 13, 1947; 1 son, John. Postdoctoral fellow Copenhagen (Denmark) U., 1952-53; postdoctoral fellow Washington U., St. Louis, 1953-54, scholar cancer research, 1954-57, from asst. to asso. prof. microbiology, 1955-59; prof. biochemistry Stanford Sch. Medicine, 1959—, Jack, Lula and Sam Willson prof. biochemistry, 1970. Served to lt. (j.g.) USNR, 1943-46. Recipient Eli Lilly prize biochemistry, 1959; named Cal. Scientist of Year, Cal. Museum Sci. and Industry, 1963. Mem. Nat. Acad. Sci., Am. Acad. Arts and Scis., Am. Soc. Biol. Chemists, Am. Soc. Microbiology. Contbr. profl. jours. Editor Jour. Molecular Biology, 1966-69. Home: 838 Santa Fe Av Stanford CA 94305 Office: Stanford Sch Medicine Palo Alto CA 94304

BERG, ROBERT LEWIS, physician, educator; b. Spokane, Wash., Sept. 10, 1918; s. Evan and Rachel Myfanwy (Lewis) B.; B.S., Harvard, 1940, M.D., 1943; m. Florence Mitcham Foster, June 18, 1943; children—Erik Christian, Astri Maren. Successively intern, resident, chief med. resident Mass. Gen. Hosp., Boston, 1944-46, 50, asst. to dir. research and edn., 1951-54, asst., then asso. physician, 1951-58; Moseley travelling fellow Royal Caroline Inst., Stockholm, 1948-49; from instr. to asst. prof. medicine Harvard Med. Sch., 1951-58, Albert D. Kaiser prof., also chmn. dept. preventive medicine and community health, 1958—; asso. prof. medicine Univ. Rochester, 1958-69, prof. medicine, 1969—, sr. asso. physician Strong Meml. Hosp., 1958-69, physician, 1969—, acting adminstr., 1960-61. Mem. NIH Epidemiology and Biometry Tng. Com., 1962-66, 67-71, chmn., 1969-70; mem. U.S. Com. Vital and Health Statistics, 1965-69, chmn., 1967-69. Mem. Am. Pub. Health Assn., Assn. Tchrs. Preventive Medicine (treas. 1963-69, v.p. 1969-70, pres. 1970—), Internat. Assn. Asthmology, N.Y. Acad. Sci., Mass., N.Y. State med. socs., Assn. Am. Med. Colls., Indsl. Med. Assn., Internat. Epidemiological Assn. Home: 227 Pelham Rd Rochester NY 14610 Office: 260 Crittenden Blvd Rochester NY 14642

BERG, ROBERT RAYMOND, educator, geologist; b. St. Paul, May 28, 1924; s. Raymond F. and Jennie (Swanson) B.; B.A., U. Minn., 1941, Ph.D., 1951; m. Josephine Finck, Dec. 22, 1946; children—James R., Charles R., William R. Geologist, Calif. Co., Denver, 1951-56; cons. Berg and Wasson, Denver, 1957-66; prof. geology, head dept. Tex. A. and M U., 1967—; cons. petroleum geology, 1959—. Served with AUS, 1943-46. Fellow Geol. Soc. Am.; mem. Am. Assn. Petroleum Geologists, Am. Inst. Profl. Geologists (pres. 1971). Author papers in field. Home: 414 Brookside Bryan TX 77801 Office: Geology Dept Tex A and M Univ College Station TX 77843

BERG, ROLAND HOBSBAWN, writer, editor; b. N.Y.C., Feb. 20, 1908; s. Davis and Millie (Hobsbawn) B.; B.S., Fordham U., 1929; Safety Engr., N.Y.U., 1930. Freelance writer, 1934—; writer, producer series of radio and TV dramatizations popularizing sci. advances; dir. sci. information Nat. Found. Infantile Paralysis, 1945-53; sci. editor Farrell Publs., 1948-52; sci., medicine editor Look mag., 1935—, also now sr. editor. Cons. Am. Cancer Soc., USPHS. Recipient Benjamin Franklin mag. award, 1955, Albert Lasker med. journalism award, 1956; Am. Med. Assn. Journalism award, 1967. Mem. Nat. Assn. Sci. Writers Inc. (past pres.), Authors Guild, Radio Writers Guild, Council Advancement of Sci. Writing. Author: Polio and Its Problems, 1946; Challenge of Polio, 1950. Home: 240 Central Park New York City NY 10019 Office: 488 Madison Av New York City NY 10022

BERG, RUDOLF GOTTFRID, refrigeration co. exec.; b. Chgo., Apr. 10, 1908; s. August George and Amanda (Olson) B.; m. Helen Maggison, May 26, 1934; children—Barbara Louise, Donald George. With Am. Radiator Co., Chgo., 1928-29, Zerozone Refrigeration Corp., Chgo., 1929-34; with Copeland Refrigeration Corp., Sidney, O., 1934—, exec. v.p. sales, vice chmn., 1970—, also dir. Pres. Air Conditioning and Refrigeration Inst., Washington, 1959-60. Mem. Am. Soc. Heating, Refrigeration and Air Conditioning Engrs. Mason (32, Shriner), Elk, Club: Piqua Country. Home: 1570 Cedar Ct Sidney OH 45365 Office: Cope Refrigeration Corp Sidney OH 45365

BERG, RUSSELL ALLEN, retired air force officer; b. Chgo., Jan. 6, 1917; s. Werner and Blenda (Ohlson) B.; B.A., Grinnell Coll., 1940; grad. Army Air Corps Advanced Flying Sch., 1941, USAF Command and Staff Sch., 1949, Nat. War Coll., 1957; m. Joan Ada Mortrude, June 24, 1946; children—Marilee Joan (Mrs. John A. Henneberger), Thomas Lee. Commd. 2d lt. USAAF, 1941, advanced through grades to brig. gen. USAF, 1965; tactical reconnaissance group comdr., 1944-46; comdr. Korea reconnaissance wing, 1952-53; chief of staff, asst. vice comdr. Space Systems Div., 1960-65; dep. program dir. Manned Orbiting Lab., 1965-67; dir. Office Space Systems, Sec. of Air Force, 1967-69; chief requirements and devel. div. Orgn. Joint Chiefs of Staff, 1969-70; retired, 1970; cons. Computer Scis. Corp., Los Angeles. Decorated D.S.M., Legion of Merit with 2 oak leaf clusters, D.F.C., Bronze Star, Air medal with 8 oak leaf clusters (U.S.); Distinguished Flying Cross with bar (U.K.); Croix de Guerre (France and Belgium). Episcopalian. Home: 3280 Loma Riviera Dr San Diego CA 92110 Office: 9841 Airport Blvd Los Angeles CA 90045

BERG, RUSSELL K., labor union ofcl.; b. Michigan City, Ind., Jan. 23, 1905; s. Henry and Edith (Kull) B.; ed. pub. schs.; m. Wilma Zimmer, Oct. 16, 1923; children—Mary Ann (Mrs. George Papp), Robert. Bus. mgr. local 647 Internal. Brotherhood Boilermakers, Iron Shipbuilders, Blacksmiths, Forgers and Helpers, 1940-48, internat. v.p., 1948-61, internat. pres., 1962—, also editor union paper and jour. Dir. Brotherhood State Bank, Kansas City, Kan.; v.p., dir. Elexite Corp., Wheatland, Wyo. Bd. dirs. Kaw Valley Heart Assn.; bd. govs. Am. Royal Assn. Mason (Shriner). Club: Optimists. Home: Lake Forest Bonner Springs KS 66012 Office: New Brotherhood Bldgs Kansas City KS 66101

BERG, SHERWOOD OLMAN, univ. dean; b. Hendrum, Minn., May 17, 1919; s. Joseph O. and Ida E. (Tommerdahl) B.; B.S., S.D. State Univ., 1947; M.S., Cornell U., 1948; Ph.D., U. Minn., 1951; m. Elizabeth A. Hall, Aug. 12, 1944; children—Mary E., Bradley J. Head, Berg Hatchery, Hendrum, 1936- 40; undergrad. research asst. agrl. econs. S.D. State Univ., 1940-43; instr. Sch. Agr., Brookings, S.D., 1946-47; research asst. agrl. econs. Cornell U., 1947-48, U. Minn., 1948-51; U.S. agrl. attache, Yugoslavia, 1951-54, Denmark and Norway, 1954-57; prof., head dept. agrl. econs. U. Minn., 1957-63, dean Inst. Agr., 1963—. Cons. econ. research service, mem. econs. research adv. com. U.S. Dept. Agr., 1963-68; personnel cons. ICA. Treas., dir. Experience, Inc., 1963—; dir. North Star Research and Devel. Inst., State Capitol Credit Union. Chmn. Nat. Adv. Commn. Food and Fiber; dir., vice chmn. Minn. Council Econ. Edn.; dir. Westminster Found. Minn.; mem. Pres.'s Commn. Income Maintenance Programs, 1968-70; Served with AUS, 1943-46; ETO; lt. col. Res. Decorated Bronze Star, Combat Inf. badge, Army Commendation ribbon; recipient Superior Service award Dept. Agr., 1956; Danforth Found. fellow, 1942; Caleb Dorr research fellow U. Minn., 1948, Greater Univ. grad. fellow, 1949; Kellogg Found. Travel fellow, 1958. Mem. Agrl. History Soc., Am. Assn. U. Profs., Am. Econ. Assn., Am. Farm Econ. Assn., Am.-Scandinavian Found., Assn. U.S. Army, Internat. Assn. Agrl. Economists (U.S. council), Agrl. History Soc., Atlantic Community Council U.S. (sponsor), St. Paul- Mpls. Com. on Fgn. Relations, Res. Officers Assn., U. Minn. Science Club, Alpha Gamma Rho, Alpha Zeta, Gamma Sigma Delta, Pi Gamma Mu, Phi Kappa Phi. Presbyn. Rotarian. Club: Cosmos. Contbr. articles, bulls., profl. jours. Home: 3261 N Snelling Av St Paul MN 55112

BERG, THOMAS LEROY, educator; b. Glenville, Minn., June 3, 1930; s. Alvin O. and Ruth (Karhoja) B.; B.B.A., U. Minn., 1952; M.S., Columbia, 1956, Ph.D., 1960; m. Toshiko Betsumiya, Mar. 20, 1965. From asst. to asst. prof. marketing Columbia, 1956-64; mem. faculty N.Y.U., 1964—, prof. marketing, 1967—, joint chmn. dept., 1968—; speaker, lectr., cons. in field. Served with USNR, 1952-55. Samuel Bronfman fellow Democratic Bus. Enterprise, 1956- 57; Ford fellow, 1957-58. Mem. Am. Marketing Assn., Beta Gamma Sigma. Author: (with Ralph S. Alexander* Dynamic Management in Marketing, 1965; Mismarketing, 1970; also articles. Editor: (with Abe Shuchman) Product Strategy and Management, 1963. Home: 687 Closter Dock Rd Closter NJ 07624 Office: 100 Trinity Pl New York NY 10006

BERG, WARREN STANLEY, banker; b. Lynn, Mass., Jan. 17, 1922; s. Carl W. and Gladys (Colburn) B.; B.S., Harvard, 1943; grad. exec. devel. program, Cornell U., 1944; m. Marjorie E. Coleman, Mar. 25, 1944; children—Peter C., Carolyn (Mrs. John Spengler), Dana S. Dir. pub. relations and sales promotion Arthur D. Little, Inc., Cambridge, Mass., 1951-65; with Nat. Shawmut Bank, Boston, 1965—, sr. v.p., 1969—; dir. H. Harwood & Sons; corporator Arlington Five Cents Savs. Bank (Mass.). Mem. exec. com. Mass. Bay United Fund. Trustee Museum Sci., Winchester Hosp.; bd. overseers Boys Clubs Boston. Served to 1st lt. USMCR, 1943-46. Mem. Bank Marketing Assn. Pub. Relations Soc. Am. (presdl. citiation for meritorious service 1962). Clubs: Harvard, Harvard Varsity (Boston); Winchester Country; Essex County (Manchester, Mass.). Author: History of Harvard Baseball, 1964; History of Massachusetts Institute of Technology Athletics, 1950. Home: 75 Arlington St Winchester MA 01890 Office: 40 Water St Boston MA 02109

BERG, WILLIAM WILSON, air force officer; b. Logansport, Ind., Mar. 14, 1918; s. Walter W. and Rayna (Wilson) B.; B.S., U. Md., 1956; M.A., George Washington U., 1960; postgrad. U. Pitts., 1951-52; grad. Indsl. Coll. Armed Forces, 1962; m. Vera Moscatelli, Apr. 5, 1948; children—George, Walter, Lucy, Caroline. Commd. 2d lt., U.S. Army, 1943, advanced through grades to maj. gen. USAF, 1968; chief selection bd., chief promotion bd., chief personnel procurement Hdqrs. USAF, Washington, 1956-61; asst. for plans Office Asst. Sec. for Def. for Manpower, Washington, 1962-63; dep. asst. Sec. of Def. for Mil. Personnel Policy, Washington, 1963-68; dir. manpower and orgn., dep. chief of staff for programs and resources Hdqrs. USAF, Washington, 1968—. Decorated D.S.M., Legion of Merit, Army Commendation medal with oak leaf cluster; Cross for War Merit (Italy). Home: 1003 Dalebrook Dr Alexandria VA 22308 Office: Hdqrs USAF/PRM Washington DC 20330

BERGAN, FRANCIS judge; b. Albany, N.Y., Apr. 20, 1902; s. Michael F. and Mary (Henchey) B.; LL.B., Union U., 1923, LL.D., 1964; A.B., Siena Coll., 1946, LL.D., 1949; student N.Y. State Coll. for Tchrs., 1920; m. Marion Wheldon, Apr. 23, 1935; childrenMichael Francis, William Wheldon. Newspaper reporter, 1910-23; admitted to N.Y. State Bar, 1924; asst. to minority leader in N.Y. Assembly, 1927-29; elected justice, Albany City Ct., 1929; spl. asst. atty. gen., N.Y. State, 1931-32; police justice, 1933-37; elected justice, N.Y. Supreme Ct. 1935-63, asso. justice, Appellate Div., 3d Judicial Dept., 1949-60, also temporary assignment 1st Jud. Dept., 1952, presiding justice Appellate Div., 1960-63; asso. judge N.Y. State Ct. Appeals, 1963- -. Vice chmn. N.Y. Com. Revision and Simplification of Constn., 1959—; mem. N.Y. Constl. Conv., 1938; N.Y. State Constl. Conv. Commn., 1956-58; chmn. State Commr. of Edn's Com. on Pub. Library Service, 1956-57. Del. N.Y. Constl. Conv., 1967, chmn. com. edn. Pres., bd. of trustees, Albany Pub. Library, 1946-; trustee Dudley Obs. (div. of astronomy Union U.); trustee, bd. govs., Albany Hosp., v.p., 1952; Trustee Albany Med. Coll., 1951, pres. bd. trustees, 1964; vice chmn. Library Trustees Found. of N.Y. State, 1952, mem. subcom. on laws affecting children over 16, N.Y. State Citizens Com. of 100 for Children and Youth; mem. mng. bd. Albany Jr. Coll.; bd. dirs. Jacob's Pillow Dance Festival, 1962—. Recipient citation of merit as library trustee, A.L.A., 1959. Mem. Am., N.Y. State, Albany County bar assns., N.Y. State Magistrates' Assn., Am. Law Inst., Bar Assn. City of N.Y. Democrat. Roman Catholic. Elk. Clubs: University, Fort Orange (Albany, New York). Contbr. articles on law and criminology to profl. publs. Author of non-criminal traffic infraction plan passed by N.Y. State legislature, 1934; author of County Home Rule and comptroller's pre-audit provisions, N.Y. State Constn., 1938. Contbr. to Ency. of Criminology, 1949. Home: 5 Circle Lane Albany NY 12203 Office: Court of Appeals Hall Albany NY 12207

BERGAN, GERALD T., former bishop; b. Peoria, Ill., 1892; ed. St. Victor's Coll., Bourbonnais, Ill. Was vicar gen. Peoria diocese and pastor St. Mary's R.C. Cathedral; apptd. bishop of Des Moines, Ia., 1934, to succeed the late Bishop Thomas W. Drumm; promoted to archepiscopal see of Omaha, Feb. 1948; archbishop of Omaha; now ret. Address: 6300 Dodge St Omaha NB 68132*

BERGANTZ, JOSEPH ARTHUR, educator; b. Knoxville, Tenn., June 8, 1914; s. George Stanley and Maud Montressor (Manley) B.; B.S. in Chem. Engring., U. Tenn., 1934; M.S., U. Ill., 1937; Sc.D. (Arthur D. Little fellow), Mass. Inst. Tech., 1941; m. Joan Osborn, Apr. 24, 1943; children—Barbara (Mrs. John P.R. Moslow), William, George, James. Engring. aide TVA, Wilson Dam, Ala., 1934-36; instr. to asst. prof. Mass. Inst. Tech., 1939-42; project engr., research mgr. FMC Corp., Buffalo, 1946-60; ind. cons., Buffalo, 1960-61; prof., chmn. dept. chem. engring. State U. N.Y., Buffalo, 1961-68, asso. provost, 1969—, acting provost engring. and applied scis., 1970-71. Trustee Creative Edn. Found. Served with AUS, 1942-46. Hon. research asso. Univ. Coll., London, Eng., 1968. Mem. Am. Inst. Chem. Engrs. (Profl. Progress award Western N.Y. sect. 1962, sect. chmn. 1954), Am. Soc. Engring. Edn. (chmn. chem. engring. div. 1965), Am. Chem. Soc., Sigma Xi, Tau Beta Pi, Phi Kappa Phi, Alpha Chi Sigma, Sigma Chi. Clubs: Buffalo, Canoe, Pundit (all Buffalo). Home: 56 Arlington Pl Buffalo NY 14201

BERGANZA, TERESA, mezzo-soprano; b. Madrid, Spain, 1936; d. Guillermo and Maria (Ascension) Berganza; m. Felix Lavilla, 1957; 1 son, 1 dau. Debut, Madrid, 1955, Glyndebourne, Eng., 1959; appearances include Royal Opera House, Covent Garden, 1959, 60, 63, 64, Royal Festival Hall, 1960, 61, 62, also in Vienna, Milan. Aix-en Provence, Holland, Edinburgh, Israel, Met. Opera Co., Address: Joaquin Maria Lopez 29 Madrid 15 Spain

BERGAUST, ERIK, publisher; b. Baerum, Oslo, Norway, Mar. 23, 1925; B.S. in Chemistry, Frogner Gymnasium, 1943; student Oslo Handelsgymnasium, 1944; m. Jean Cameron Sommers, Jan. 13, 1951; children—Christine C., Erik R., Paul R., Jane. Came to U.S., 1949, naturalized, 1956. Aviation editor Aftenposten, daily newspaper, Oslo, 1946-48; pub. relations dir. Norwegian Aero Club, 1946-48; mgr. Thoftefly Taxiplane Co., 1948-49; free lance aviation writer, 1949-52; mgr. Norwegian Helicopter Service, 1952; project engr., tech. editor Design Service Co., 1952-54; project officer, editor Douglas Engring. Co., 1954-55; rocket engring. editor Aero Digest, 1955-56; missile sci. editor Am. Aviation, 1956; editor Missiles and Rockets mag., 1956-59; pub., editor Space Daily, 1939, Ground Support Equipment mag. and Underwater Engring. mag., 1959-60; Washington dir. Missiles and Space mag.; editor NATO Jour., 1960-62; pres. North Springs, Inc., 1962-64; pub. Bermington & Ross, Inc., Washington; editorial cons. Spartan Books, Inc., 1965—; sr. cons. to Spartan Books, Inc, 1965—, Paul Verdow & Assos., 1962—; mem. information adv. group President's Com. on Scientists and Engrs., 1957. Chmn. Republican Adv. Com. on Space and Aeros., 1962—. Mem. Norweigan Resistance Movement, 1943, Norwegian Exile Army, 1944-45. Mem. Am. Rocket Soc. (past pres. nat. capital sect.), Aviation and Space Writers Assn., Convertible Aircraft Pioneers, Authors Guild, Am. Mil. Engrs., Am. Helicopter Soc., Norsk Astronautisk Forening. Clubs: Nat. Space (founder, pres. 1957-58), Nat. Press (Washington). Author: The Next Fifty Years of Flight, 1954; (with William Beller) Satellite!, 1956; Rockets and Missiles, 1957; Rockets Around the World, 1958; (with Seabrook Hull) Rocket to the Moon, 1958; Satellites and Space Probes, 1959; Rockets of the Navy, 1959; Rockets of the Air Force, 1960; Rockets of the Army, 1960; First Men in Space, 1960; Reaching for the Stars (biography of Dr. Wernher von Braun), 1960; Rocket Aircraft, USA, 1961; Rockets to the Moon, 1961; Rockets to the Planets, 1961; Birth of a Rocket, 1961; Rocket Power, 1961; Space Stations, 1962; Saturn Story, 1962; Our New Navy, 1962; (with William O. Foss) Helicopters in Action, 1962, Coast Guard in Action, 1962; Rocket City, USA, 1963; The Next Fifty Years in Space, 1963; Marine Corps in Action, 1965; Skin Divers in Action, 1965; Illustrated Space Ency., 1965; The Peenemünde Story, 1965. Home: 6360 Waterway Dr Falls Church VA 22044 Office: Munsey Bldg Washington DC 20004

BERGDOLT, VOLLMAR E., educator; B.S. in Mech. Engring., Purdue U., 1939, M.S. in Mech. Engring., 1946, Ph.D., 1956. Now prof. mech. engring., exec. asst. to head head Sch. Engring., Purdue U. Address: Sch Mech Engring Purdue U Lafayette IN 47907

BERGEN, CANDICE, actress; b. Beverly Hills. Cal., May 9, 1946; ed. U. Pa. Model during Coll.; films include: The Group; The Sand Pebbles, The Day the Fish Came Out; Live for Life; The Magus; Soldier Blue; Getting Straight; The Hunting Party; Carnal Knowledge; T. R. Baskin; photo-journalist credits include articles for Vogue, Esquire, Cosmopolitan, Playboy; dramatist (play) The Freezer included in Best Short Plays of 1968. Address: care CMA 8899 Beverly Blvd Hollywood CA 90048

BERGEN, GARRET LAWRENCE, ret. business educator; b. Bklyn., Apr. 28, 1904; s. Samuel White and Anne (Boynton) B.; A.B., Columbia, 1926, M.A., 1928; m. Elsbeth Hendrickson, Apr. 12, 1930 (dec. Jan. 23, 1968); m. 2d, Lucie Jacobs Gorham, Apr. 26, 1969. With Marshall Field & Co., Chgo., 1936-56, div. v.p., 1946-53, v.p., 1953-56; prof. bus. adminstrn. Northwestern U., 1956-70; dir. The Psycho. Corp. Am. certified psychologist. Diplomate indsl. psychology Am. Bd. Examiners Profl. Psychology. Mem. Ill. C. of C. (dir. 1946-52), Nat. Labor-Mgmt. Manpower Policy Com., Chgo. Heart Assn. (gov.), Great Books Found. (past dir.), Indsl. Relations Assn. Chgo. (pres. 1946), Am. Psychol. Assn., Am. Mgmt. Assn. (v.p. personnel div. 1950-52, Distinguished Service award 1957), Nat. Indsl. Conf. Bd., Chgo. Crime Commn., Theta Delta Chi., Beta Gamma Sigma. Conglist. Clubs: Curling, University (Chgo.); Indian Hill (Winnetka). Author: (with William V. Haney) Organizational Relations and Management Action, 1966. Home: 88 Indian Hill Rd Winnetka IL 60093

BERGEN, JOHN VANDERVEER, editor; b. N.Y.C., Nov. 3, 1934; s. Reginald Vanderveer and Janice Agnes (Brotzmann) B.; B.S., Phila. Coll. Pharmacy and Sci., 1956; Ph.D., U. Wis., 1961; m. Ann Taylor Ratcliff, June 14, 1958; children—Lisa Ann, Rebecca Janice. Instr. U. Wis., summer 1959; mem. faculty Ida. State U., Pocatello, 1960-68, dean Coll. Pharmacy, 1963-68, dir. div. med. arts, 1964-68, prof. pharm. chemistry, 1966-68; lectr. U. Kan., 1968-69; asso. dir. Nat. Formulary, Am. Pharm. Assn., 1969, dir., 1970—. Mem. Gov. Ida. Advt. Council Comprehensive State Health Planning, 1967-69; mem. pharmacy rev. com. USPHS, 1968—; mem. U.S. Adopted Names Council, 1970—. Mem. Am. Pharm. Assn., Am. Chem. Soc., Am. Assn. Colls. Pharmacy, Acad. Pharm. Scis., Ida. Pharm. Assn. (Ida. Pharmacist of Year 1967), Sigma Xi, Rho Chi, Phi Lambda Upsilon, Kappa Psi, Phi Delta Chi (hon.). Home: 6405 Lyric Lane Falls Church VA 22044 Office: 2215 Constitution Av NW Washington DC 20037

BERGEN, JULIUS, found. exec.; b. Chgo., Nov. 7, 1896; s. Sophus Theodor and Marie (Tecklenburg) B.; student Ill. Bus. Coll., also extension courses; D.Bus. Adminstrn. (hon.), U. Nev., 1956; m. Mary Elizabeth Wood, Feb. 14, 1927; childrenBarbara Marie (Mrs. Donald L. Phipps), Ann (Mrs. Malcolm Willard Brawn). With Fleischmann Co., Chgo., 1912- 21, sec. mfg. dept., 1920-21; with Fleischmann Co. and Standard Brands, Inc., N.Y.C., 1921-41, asst. to chmn. bd., 1925-41; bus. mgr., agt. for Max C. Fleischmann enterprises, 1941-51; agt. for estate, also chmn., trustee Max C. Fleischmann Found. Reno, Nev., 1951—; dir. Security Nat. Bank Reno, Haida Corp., J. V. Oil Corp. Mem. Reno chpt. Nat. Conf. Christians and Jews, Inc. Bd. dirs. Council Founds., Inc.; adv. investment com. U. Nev.; trustee Santa Barbara Mus. Natural History, Western Speleological Inst.; hon. mem. Nev. State Mus. Served with USCGR, World War II. Mem. Reno C. of C., Reno Execs. Club. Republican. Episcopalian (vestry). Rotarian, Elk. Clubs: Channel City (Santa Barbara, Cal.); Hidden Valley Country (Reno). Home: 1140 Fairfield Av Reno NV 89502 Office: 195 S Sierra St Reno NV 89501

BERGEN, POLLY, actress; b. Knoxville, Tenn; d. William and Lucy (Lawhorn) Bergen; m. Freddie Fields, Feb. 13, 1956; children—Kathy, Pamela, Peter. Motion Pictures include The Stooge, At War with the Army, That's My Boy, Cape Fear, Caretakers, Move Over Darling, Kisses For My President, Guide for Married Man; recording artist for Mercury, Columbia records; star Polly Bergen Show, NBC-TV; other TV appearances include Perry Como Show, Ed Sullivan Show, Playhouse 90, Andy Williams Show, Dean Martin Show, Red Skelton Show. Pres. Kam. Enterprises, Ltd., 1956—, Apache Corp., 1955—, Fashions of the Four Seasons; v.p. Oil Fields, Unlimited, 1957—; dir. F 8 Prodns., Inc.; dir. Peter Bruce Fields Found., Inc.; partner cosmetic firm Oil of The Turtle, Ltd., 1966—; chmn. bd. Polly Bergen Co., Beverly Hills. Mem. Share, Inc.; mem. women's guild Cedar-Sinai Medical Center. Recipient Emmy award as best actress Nat. Acad. TV Arts and Scis., 1957-58; Troupers award Sterling Publs., 1957; Fame award, Top Ten in TV, 1957-58; Editors and Critics award Radio and TV Daily, 1958; named Best Dressed American Woman Entertainer, Costume Designers Guild, 1966; Outstanding Working Woman award Downtown St. Louis, Inc.; Golden Plate award Am. Acad. Achievement 1969; Polly Bergen Cardio-Pulmonary Research Lab., Children's Research Inst. and Hosp., Denver, dedicated, 1970. Mem. Screen Actors Guild, Actors Equity, Am. Guild Variety Artists, A.F.T.R.A. Author: Fashion and Charm. Office: 190 N Canon Dr Beverly Hills CA 90210

BERGEN, WILLIAM BENJAMIN, engr.; b. Floral Park, N.Y., Mar. 29, 1915; s. Oldfield and Hazel (Zernico) B.; B.S., Mass. Inst. Tech., 1937; D. Engring., Drexel Inst. Tech., 1937; D. Engring., Drexel Inst. Tech., 1963; m. Eleanor M. Bergen, Dec. 14, 1968; children (by previous marriage)— William Benjamin, Lynn Louise. With The Martin Company (Aerospace div. Martin Marietta Corp.), Balt., 1937-68, successively vibrations engr., chief flight test engr., chief pilotless aircraft sect., dir. spl. weapons dept., chief engr., v.p., v.p. operations, 1937-55, exec. v.p., 1955-59, president, 1959-67; exec. v.p. Marietta Corp., 1967; group v.p. space and and propulsion N. Am. Aviation, Inc. (co. name changed to N. Am. Rockwell Corp), 1967, pres. space div., 1967-70, corp. v.p., group v.p. aerospace, 1970-71, group pres. aerospace, 1971—; dir. Black & Decker Mfg. Co. Alumni term mem. exec. com. Mass. Inst. Tech.; trustee St. Paul's School, Brooklandville, Md. Served as 1st lt. U.S. CAC Res., 1937-38; cadet Md. N.G., 1938-40. Recipient Sperry award Inst. Aerospace Scis., 1944; Pub. Service Service awards (2), NASA, 1969. Fellow Am. Inst. Aeronautics and Astronautics; mem. Am. Astronautical Soc. Soc. (dir.), Air Force Assn., Aerospace Industries Assn. (hon. chmn. internat. commn.); Nat. Space Club, Soc. Automotive Angrs., Armed Forces Communication Assn., Holland Soc. N.Y., Conquistadores del Cielo. Author tech. articles. Address: 1700 E Imperial Hwy El Segundo CA

BERGENDOFF, CONRAD JOHN IMMANUEL, clergyman, educator; b. Shickley, Neb., Dec. 3, 1895; s. Carl August and Emma Mathilda (Fahlberg) B.; B.A., Augustana Coll., Rock Island, Ill., 1915, B.D., 1921; M.A., U. Pa., 1916; postgrad. Columbia, 1918-19, Lutheran Theol. Sem., Phila., 1918-19; Ph.D., U. Chgo., 1928; postgrad. univs. of Upsala (Sweden) and Berlin, 1926-27; Th.D., (hon.), U. Upsala, 1938; LL.D., Upsala College, 1943; Litt.D. (hon.), Rockford (Ill.) Coll., 1958; D.D. (hon.), Concordia Theol. Sem., 1967; L.H.D. (hon.), Nat. Coll. Edn., 1968, Marycrest Coll., 1968; m. Gertrude Carlson, June 28, 1922; children—Conrad Luther, Beatrice Gertrude, Elizabeth Ann. Asst. prof. English, prof. edn. Augustana Coll., 1916-17; asst. pastor Gustavus Adolphus Luth. Ch., N.Y.C., 1917-19; ordained Augustana Synod Lutheran Ch., 1921; pastor Evang. Luth. Salem Ch., Chgo., 1921-31; prof. systematic theology, also dean Augustana Theol. Sem., 1931; pres. Augustana Coll. and Theol. Sem., 1935-48; pres. Augustana Coll., 1948-62; exec. sec. bd. theol. edn. Luth. Ch. in Am., 1962-64. Cons. Am. Mil. Occupation, Germany, 1948. Has served on several coms. and bd. of ch. on ednl. matters; has been mem. commns. on liturgy of Augustana Synod, Luth. World Fedn.; mem. delegation Nat. Council of Chs. to Russian Orthodox Ch., 1962. Mem. Ill. Bd. Higher Edn., 1962-69, Ill. Arts Council, 1965-68; mem. spl. coms. of Am. Council Edn., N. Central Assn. Colls. and Secondary Schs. Chpt. chmn. A.R.C., Rock Island and Moline, 1964-66. Bd. dirs. Assn. Am. Colls., 1940-41; pres. Augustana Inst. Swedish Culture, 1940-67; trustee Am. Scandinavian Found., 1943-70. Decorated comdr. North Star, Sweden, 1944; hon. mem. Pro Fide et Christianismo (Stockholm), 1941. Mem. Phi Beta Kappa. Republican. Clubs: Rotary, Black Hawk Hiking (Rock 1 Island); Contemporary (Davenport, Ia.); University (Chgo.). Author books in field including: One Holy Catholic Apostolic Church, 1954; The Doctrine of the Church in American Lutheranism, 1956; The Church of the Lutheran Reformation, 1967; History of Augustana College 1860-1935, 1969. Editor: Luther League Manual; Daily Devotions for Luth. Youth; The Luth. Quar., 1949-53; co-editor Augustana Quar. Contbr. hist., ednl. and ch. publs. Translator vol. 40 Luther's Works, 1958. Home: 10 Hawthorne Rd Rock Island IL 61201

BERGENDOFF, RUBEN NATHANIEL, engring. exec; b. Newman Grove, Neb., Jan. 5, 1899; s. Carl August and Emma Mathilda (Fahlberg) B.; B.S. in Civil Engring., U. Pa., 1921; m. Dorothy Lindgren, June 1, 1925; children—Raymond Carl, Robert Perry, Marjorie Ann. With N.C. Hwy. Dept., 1921-22; cons. engr. Harrington, Howard & Ash, 1922-28, Ash, Howard, Needles & Tammen, 1928-39, Howard, Needles, Tammen & Bergendoff, 1940—; designer bridges, expressways, turnpikes in numerous states, also govt. units, pvt. corp. bldgs.; dir. Grand Av. Bank, Kansas City, Mo. Pres. Kansas City Commn. Internat. Relations and Trade, 1958; v.p. Downtown Com., Inc. Bd. dirs. Trinity Luth Hosp.; trustee U. Kansas City. Recipient numerous awards for beautiful bridges Am. Inst. Steel Constrn.; award for distinguished service in engring. U. Mo., 1957. Mem. Am. Soc. C.E., Am. Inst. Cons. Engrs. (v.p. 1967), Mo. Society Profl. Engrs., Am. Ry. Engring. Assn., Am. Pub. Works Assn., Am. Soc. Testing Materials, Theta Xi. Clubs: Kansas City, University, Mission Hills Country, Rotary (pres. 1956) (Kansas City). Home: 1005 W 65th St Kansas City MO 64113 Office: 1805 Grand Av Kansas City MO 64108

BERGENFIELD, BERT KEVIN, holding co. exec.; b. N.Y.C., Jan. 27, 1925; s. David and Celia (Rosdeitscher) B.; student Ohio State U., 1942-43; B.B.A., Coll. City N.Y., 1947; m. Norma Friedwald, June 20, 1948; children—Caren, Glenn. With S.D. Leidesdorf & Co., C.P.A.'s, 1948-51, Maweco Industries, 1951- 61; with Glen Alden Corp., 1963-67, treas., v.p., 1964-67; v.p. finance, dir. Mc- Gregor-Doniger, Inc., 1967—; instr. financial mgmt. and accounting Pace Coll., 1955—. Mem. Am. Mgmt. Assn., Financial Execs. Inst., Am. Assn. U. Profs., Am. Arbitration Assn. Home: 25 Howland St West Caldwell NJ 07007 Office: 666 Fifth Av New York City NY 10019

BERGENHEIM, ROBERT CARLTON, publisher; b. Boston, Jan. 19, 1924; s. Carl O. and Thyra (Branting) B.; student Boston U., 1941-43, 46-53; Nieman fellow, Harvard, 1953-54; m. Elizabeth Darling McKee, Aug. 30, 1947; children—Richard, Carol, Roger, Robert, Christine, Ronald. Copyboy, Christian Sci. Monitor, Boston, 1941-43, Boston City Hall reporter, 1948-57, New Eng. news and city editor, 1957-60, asst. mgr. Christian Sci. Pub. Soc., 1960-69, mgr., 1969—. Active Big Brother Assn. Mem. Gov. Mass. Com. Study Free Press and Fair Trial, 1969-70. Served with USNR, 1943-46; PTO. Mem. Boston U. Alumni Assn., Boston Bar-Press Com. Home: Canoe Tree Way Marshfield Hills MA 02051 Office: 1 Norway St Boston MA 02115

BERGER, ANDREW JOHN, educator, zoologist; b. Warren, O., Aug. 30, 1915; s. Anton A. and Mary (Rodenberger) B.; A.B., Oberlin Coll., 1939; M.A., U. Mich., 1947, Ph.D., 1950; m. Edith Grace Denniston, Aug. 13, 1942 (div. 1969); children—John D., Diana M. From instr. to asso. prof. anatomy U. Mich. Med. Sch., 1950-64; sr. Fulbright lectr. Maharaja Sayajirao U., Baroda, India, 1964-65; prof., chmn. dept. zoology U. Hawaii, 1965—; hon. asso. ornithology Bernice P. Bishop Museum, Honolulu, 1965-71, Lab. Ornithology, Cornell U., 1966—. U. Hawaii rep. adv. council Orgn. Tropical Studies; mem. Gov. Hawaii Com. Preservation Sci. Areas, Gov. Hawaii Animal Species Adv. Com.; co-dir. island ecosystem stability and evolution project Internat. Biol. Program. Guggenheim fellow, 1963. Fellow A.A.A.S., Am. Ornithologists Union; mem. Am. Soc. Zoologists, Am. Assn. Anatomists, Wilson, Cooper ornithol. socs., Assn. Tropical Biology, Hawaiian Audubon Soc., Conservation Council Hawaii, Hawaiian Acad. Sci., Sigma Xi, Phi Sigma, Phi Kappa Phi, Psi Omega (hon.). Club: Explorers (N.Y.C.). Author: Bird Study, 1961; Elementary Human Anatomy, 1964; Hawaiian Birdlife, 1971; (with Josselyn Van Tyne) Fundamentals of Ornithology, 1959; (with J.C. George) Avian Myology, 1966; also articles. Editorial bd. U. Mich. Med. Bull., 1961-64, East-West Center Press, 1968-70. Address: Univ Hawaii Honolulu HI 96822

BERGER, ARTHUR VICTOR, educator, composer, critic; b. N.Y.C., May 15, 1912; s. Louis Charles and Ethel (Gertenzang) B.; B.S. in Music, N.Y.U., 1934; M.A., Harvard, 1936; student Longy Sch. Music, Cambridges, Mass. 1934-36; m. Esther Turitz, May 25, 1937 (dec. 1960); m. 3d, Ellen Phillipsborn Tessman, Dec. 8, 1967; Editor, Musical Mercury, 1934-37; mus. reviewer Boston Transcript, 1934-37; instr. Mills Coll., 1939-41, N. Tex. State Coll., 1941, Bklyn. Coll., 1942-43; music reviewer N.Y. Sun, 1943-46; asso. music Critic N.Y. Herald Tribune, 1946-53; mem. faculty Brandeis U., 1953—, Naumburg prof. music, 1962—, Irving G. Fine prof. music, 1969; composer in residence Berkshire Music Center, 1964. Recipient commns. from CBS, 1944, Dimitri Mitropoulos, 1952, Louisville Orch., 1955, Fromm Music Found., 1959, League Composers, 1951; grantee Am. Council Learned Socs., 1936, award Nat. Inst. Arts and Letters, 1960; Fulbright research grantee, 1960, 61; Naumburg Recording award, 1964; citation for string quartet N.Y. Music Critics Circle, 1962, St. Botolph Club Arts award, 1968. Fellow Am. Acad. Arts and Scis.; mem. Am. Composers Alliance (bd. govs. 1957-59, 63—). Composer: Serenade Concertante for orch., 1944-51, 3 pieces for strings, 1945, Ideas of Order for orch., 1952, Polyphony for orch., 1956, chamber concerto, 1960, woodwind quartet, 1941, string quartet, 1958, chamber music for 13 players, 1956, duos for violin and piano No. 1, 1948, No. 2, 1950, for piano and clarinet, 1957, for cello and piano, 1951, for oboe and clarinet, 1952, for 2 pianos, 1961; also numerous solo piano works. Author: Aaron Copland, 1953; also articles, reviews. Co-founder, editor Perspectives of New Music, 1962-63, editorial bd., 1962—. Office: Brandeis Univ Waltham MA 02154

BERGER, BENNETT MAURICE, educator, b. N.Y.C., May 1, 1926; s. Julius and Ethel (King) B.; A.B., Hunter Coll., 1950; Ph.D., U. Cal. at Berkeley, 1958; m. Jean Kirkham, Dec. 9, 1956 (div. 1971); children—Jane, Nora. Asst. prof., then asso. prof. sociology U. Ill., 1959-63; mem. faculty U. Cal. at Davis, 1963—, prof. sociology, 1965—, chmn. dept., 1956-69. Served with USMCR, 1944-46. Fellow Am. Sociol. Assn.; mem. Am. Assn. U. Profs. Author: Working-Class Suburb, 1960; Looking For America, 1971. Asso. editor Sociometry, 1966-69, Social Problems, 1969—; adv. editor Transaction, 1965—. Home: 6607 Heartwood Dr Oakland CA 94611 Office: 1Voorhies Hall Univ California Davis CA 95616

BERGER, CURTIS JAY, legal educator; b. Rochester, N.Y., Apr. 16, 1926; s. Samuel and Ruth (Taksen) B.; A.B. with high honors, U. Rochester, 1948; LL.B., Yale, 1951; m. Constance Lindau, June 29, 1953; children—Ellen, John, Cathy, Wendy. Admitted to N.Y. bar, 1951; practice in Rochester, 1951-58; instr. law Yale Law Sch., 1958-60, vis. lectr., 1966; asso. prof. U. So. Cal. Law Sch., 1960-62; mem. faculty Columbia Law Sch., 1962—, prof. law, 1964—, chmn. div. urban planning Sch. Architecture, 1969-70; spl. cons. Nassau (N.Y.) County, 1964-66; lectr. U. Miss., 1967, Leiden U. (Netherlands), 1968, N.Y.U., 1969, Amsterdam U., The Netherlands, 1971. Exec. dir. N.J. Commn. to Study Meadowland Devel., 1964-67; chmn. Englewood Redevel. Agy., 1968-69. Democratic candidate for N.Y. State Senate, 1956. Bd. dirs. legal services unit Moblzn. for Youth. Served with USNR, 1944-46. Mem. Am., N.Y. State bar assns., Bar Assn. City N.Y., Am. Assn. U. Profs., Am. Jewish Com., Phi Beta Kappa, Order of Coif, Phi Alpha Delta, Zeta Beta Tau. Club: Columbia Men's Faculty, Author: Land Ownership and Use, 1968; Law and Poverty, 1969; (with Axelrod and Johnstone) Land Transfer and Finance, 1971. Contbr. profl. jours. Home: 129 Meadowbrook Rd Englewood NJ 07631 Office: Columbia Law Sch New York City NY 10027

BERGER, DAVID, lawyer; b. Archibald, Pa., Sept. 6, 1912; s. Jonas and Anna (Raker) B.; A.B. cum laude, U. Pa., 1932, LL.B. cum laude, 1936; m. Harriet Fleisher, Sept. 7, 1939; children—Jonathon, Daniel. Admitted to Pa. bar, 1938; asst. U. Pa. Law Sch., 1936-38; asst. counsel RFC, Phila. Loan Agy., 1938-39; law clk. Justice H. Edgar Barnes, Pa. Supreme Ct., 1939- 40; spl. asst. to dir. enemy alien identification program U.S. Dept. Justice, 1941-42; law clk. to Judge John O'Connell, U.S. Ct. Appeals, 1946; pvt. practice David Berger Law Offices, Washington and Phila.; city solicitor, Phila., 1956-63; counsel Sch. Dist. Phila.; lectr. U. Pa. Med. Sch. Mem. council Pa. Supreme Ct., mem. Jud. Council; mem. adv. com. fed. rules evidence U.S. Supreme Ct. Chmn. Phila. Met. Regional Anti-Defamation League, B'nai B'rith; chmn. Passenger Service Improvement Corp., Phila. Transp. Task Force; chmn. NORPAX; adv. bd. anti-trust and trade regulation report Bur. Nat. Affairs, Inc. Served from lt. (j.g.) to comdr., USNR, 1942-45. Decorated Silver Star, Presdl. unit citation. Fellow Am. Coll. Trial Lawyers, Internat. Acad. Trial Lawyers, Internat. Soc. Barristers; mem. Am. (ho. dels. 1963), Phila. (pres., bd. govs., chancellor) bar assns., Phila. Bar Found. (past pres.), Order Coif. Author numerous articles on legal subjects. Home: 4101 Timber Lane Philadelphia PA 19144 Office: 1622 Locust St Philadelphia PA 19103

BERGER, ERIC, mag. editor; b. N.Y.C., Dec. 18, 1906; s. David and Mary (Friedenberg) B.; student N.Y.U., 1924-25; LL.B., St. John's Coll., Bklyn., 1928; m. Isabelle Gronich, Jan. 5, 1935; 1 son, Neil. Reporter, Bklyn. Daily Eagle, 1929-31, Bklyn. Times, 1931-33; editor Nat. Sci. Publs., Inc., N.Y.C., 1934-39; free-lance writer and editor, 1940-41; with Scholastic Mags., Inc., N.Y.C., 1941-, editor Sr. Scholastic, 1941- 59. World Week, 1942-43, Lit. Cavalcade, 1948-55, editorial dir. Science World, 1960—. Science Tchrs. World, 1959—; dir. Sci. dept. Scholastic Mags., Inc., 1963—, editor in chief high school divison, 1968—. Served with AUS, 1943-45. Recipient Freedoms Found. award for articles on democracy, 1953. Mem. Nat. Assn. Sci. Writers, A.A.A.S. Home: 127 W 96th St New York City NY 10025 Office: Scholastic Magazines Inc 50 W 44th St New York City NY 10036

BERGER, EVELYN MILLER, psychologist; b. Hanford, Cal., Nov. 7, 1896; d. George A. and Margaret (Ross) Miller; grad. State Normal Sch., San Jose, Cal., 1919; spl. student Coll. Pacific, 1915-16, 20, U. So. Cal., 1916-17, U. Mexico, summer 1926, Entro de Estudios Historicos, Madrid, Spain, 1928; A.B., Stanford, 1921, A.M., 1930; Ph.D. (Romlett Stevens scholar), Columbia 1932; Pd.D. (hon.), U. Pacific, 1961; m. Jesse Arthur Berger, June 16, 1939. Sch. tchr. and prin., Panama City, Panama, 1918-19; exec. sec. girls' work, M.E. Ch., Chile and Argentina, 1921-23; tchr. Spanish, San Jose High Sch., 1923- 30, Coll. Pacific, Stockton, Cal., 1929, 30; dean women, asso. prof. Spanish, Allegheny Coll., 1932-36; dean women U. Ida., 1936-38, State Coll., San Diego, 1938-49; lectr. adult study groups family relations, child guidance, Alameda, Berkeley, Albany schs., 1942-44; pres. Cal. Conf. W.S.C.S. (Meth.), 1940-42; adminstr. dir. East Bay Psychol. Center, Oakland, Cal., 1944—; tchr. counseling, cons. clin. psychology Berkeley Baptist Div. Sch., 1962-69; civilian cons. psychol. problems USAF, 1968-69. Trustee Scarritt Coll., 1967-71. Diplomate Am. Bd. Examiners in Psychology. Fellow Am. Psychol. Assn., Am. Assn. Marriage Counselors; mem. Internat. Council Psychologists, Am. Inst. Family Relations, Cal., Western psychol. assns., Nat. Council Family Relations, P.E.O., Phi Beta Kappa, Kappa Delta Pi, Pi Lambda Theta, Phi Sigma Iota, Gamma Phi Beta. Methodist (mem. TV, radio, film commn.). Club: Cal. Writers. Author: Triangle, 1971. Writer on Spanish and ednl. subjects; contbr. articles and short stories to ch. mags. Home: 34 La Salle Av Piedmont CA 94611 Office: 315 14th St Oakland CA 94612

BERGER, FRANK MILAN, scientist, pharm. co. exec.; b. Pilsen, Czechoslovakia, June 25, 1913 ; s. Otto and Martha (Weigner) B.; M.D., U. Prague (Czechoslovakia), 1937, State U. N.Y., 1948; D.Sc. (hon.), Phila. Coll. Sci. and Pharmacy, 1966; m. Bozena Jahodova, Mar. 15, 1939; children—Franklin Milan, Thomas Jan. Came to U.S., 1947, naturalized, 1953. Research fellow pysiology U. Prague, 1934-36, research asst. bacteriology, 1936-38; bacteriologist Czechoslovak State Inst. Health, 1938-39; sr. resident Monsall Hosp. Infectious Diseases, Manchester, Eng., 1941-43; chief pharmacologist Brit. Drug House, London, 1945-47; asst. prof. pediatrics U. Rochester, 1947-49; dir. research Carter Products, Inc., 1949-55, v.p., 1955-58; pres. Wallace Labs., Cranbury, N.J., 1958—; mem. adv. council dept. biology Princeton, 1961—, lectr., prof., 1969—. Discover tranquilizer meprobamate, muscle-relaxant mephenesin, pain-reliever carisoprodol, also method purification penicillin. Fellow N.Y. Acad. Scis., Royal Soc. Medicine, A.A.A.S.; mem. Am., Brit. pharm. socs., Am. Bacteriol. Soc., Soc. Gen. Microbiology, Soc. Exptl. Biology and Medicine, A.M.A., Am. Assn. U. Profs., Am. Chem. Soc., Biometric Soc., Eastern Psychiat. Assn., Sigma Xi. Clubs: Cosmos (Washington); Nassau (Princeton). Home: 145 Constitution Dr Princeton NJ 08540 Office: Wallace Labs Cranbury NJ 08512

BERGER, FRED, painter; b. Chgo., Sept. 24, 1923; s. Carl and Rose (Kaplowitz) B.; student Sch. Art Inst. Chgo., 1942-43; B.S. in Visual Design, Ill. Inst. Tech., 1952; m. Mary Imogene Craig, Oct. 25, 1946; 1 son, Dylan. Tchr. visual fundamentals eve. div. Inst. Design, Ill. Inst. Tech., 1954-56; exhibited in group shows at Art Inst. Chgo., 1947, 51, 53, 56, 57, 58, 60, 62, 63, 60th Ann. Am. Exhbn., Art Inst. Chgo., 1951, Chgo. Artists Exhbn. circulated in France by USIA, 1957-58, Richard Feigen Gallery, Chgo., 1959, Premiere-Bienale de Paris, Musee d'Art Moderne, Paris, France, 1959, 1st and 2d Biennial of Prints, Drawings and Watercolors, Art Inst. Chgo., 1961, 64, U. Ill., Chgo., 1965, Mus. Modern Art, N.Y.C., 1962, Kendall Coll., Evanston, Ill., 1966, DePaul U., Chgo., 1966; one-man exhbns. include Bordelon Gallery, Chgo., 1949, John L. Hunt Gallery, Chgo., 1964, Kendall Coll., 1967, U. Chgo., 1956, Richard Feigen Gallery, Chgo., 1961, Alverno Coll., Milw., 1970; rep. permanent collection Art Inst. Chgo.; work reproduced in numerous magazines. Recipient Pauline Palmer award for drawing, 1960; Frank G. Logan Chgo. Art Inst. medal and award for drawing, 1961; Vielhr award painting, 1962. Mem. Mus. Contemporary Art, Chgo. Mem. fine arts bd. Kendall Coll., 1969-. Address: 3428 N Janssen Av Chicago IL 60657

BERGER, HAROLD, physicist; b. Syracuse, N.Y., Oct. 7, 1926; s. Joseph H. and Fannie A. (Stein) B.; B.S., Syracuse U., 1949, M.S., 1951; m. Dawn Marie Beranek, Dec. 27, 1952; children—Susan, Margaret, Thomas, Joseph, Daniel. Physicist Gen. Elec. Co. x-ray dept., Milw., 1951-59; sr. physicist Battelle Meml. Inst., Columbus, 1959-60; asso. physicist Argonne (Ill.) Nat. Lab., 1960-70, group leader nondestructive testing, 1965—, sr. physicist, 1970—; vis. scientist Centre d'Etudes Nucleaires, Grenoble, France, 1968-69; vis. lectr. U. Grenoble, 1968-69; pres.'s honor lectr. Non-Destructive Testing Soc. G.B., 1971. Mem. Nat. Materials Adv. Bd. ad hoc com. Nondestructive Inspection, 1967-68. Served with USNR, 1944-45. Recipient achievement award Am. Soc. Nondestructive Testing, 1967. Mem. Am. Nuclear Soc., Am. Phys. Soc., Am. Soc. Nondestructive Testing (nat. dir. 1965-68), Sci. Research Soc. Am. Author: Neutron Radiography, 1965; Understanding the Atom, 1965. Tech. editor of Materials Evaluation Jour. of Am. Soc. Nondestructive Testing, 1969—. Contbr. articles profl. jours. Home: 537 Cypress Dr Naperville IL 60540 Office: Argonne Nat Laboratory Argonne IL 60439

BERGER, JOHN TORREY, lawyer; b. Great Bend, Kan., Nov. 25, 1900; s. John Calvin and Haddie (Torrey) B.; student Emporia (Kan.) Coll.; LL.B. (Law Library scholar), Washington U., St. Louis, 1923; m. Maud A. Beattie, Aug. 29, 1928; children—Betty Jo (Mrs. Meyer), Marilyn (Mrs. Engman), John Torrey. Admitted to Mo. bar, 1923, since practiced in St. Louis; partner firm Lewis, Rice, Tucker, Allen and Chubb, and predecessors; formerly city atty., Kirkwood, Mo. Past pres. Kirkwood Park Bd.; mem. Kirkwood Charter Commn.; sec. St. Louis County League Municipalities; pres. Mo. League Municipalities; v.p. Nat. Inst. Municipal Law Officers; mem. Met. St. Louis Freeholders Com. on Transp.; spl. hearing officer Dept. Justice. Co-founder Kirkwood YMCA, then mem. bd. dirs., also mem. met. bd.; pres. Kirkwood Jr.-Sr. High Sch. P.T.A., Kirkwood Choral Club; chmn. Pioneer council Boy Scouts Am., then mem. bd. Eagle rev., and recipient Silver Beaver award. Named Citizen of Year, Kirkwood C. of C., 1965. Mem. Am., Mo., St. Louis bar assns., S.R. (past pres. St. Louis), Kirkwood Hist. Soc. (past pres.), Sigma Phi Epsilon, Phi Delta Phi. Presbyn. (past elder, trustee, del. gen. assembly). Mason (32, Shriner). Rotarian (past sec., pres. Kirkwood, dist. gov.). Republican. Club: Greenbriar Hills Country. Address: Ry Exchange Bldg St Louis MO 63101

BERGER, JOSEPH, educator; b. Bklyn., Apr. 3, 1924; A.B., Bklyn. Coll., 1949; M.A., Harvard, 1952, Ph.D. in Sociology, 1958; married; 2 children. Instr. sociology Dartmouth, 1954-56, asst. prof., 1956-59; asst. prof. Stanford, 1959-62, asso. prof., 1962-68, prof. sociology, 1968—. Served to 1st lt. AUS, 1943-46. Mem. Am. Sociol. Assn. Office: Sociology Dept Stanford U Stanford CA 94305*

BERGER, KARL HEINZ, vibist; b. Germany. Played with groups of Roswell Rudd, Ran Blake, Robin Kenyatta and Steve Lacy; recording artist for ESP Disk Records. Address: 41 Albestrasse 2 Berlin Federal Republic of Germany*

BERGER, LAWRENCE SHERWIN, broadcasting exec.; b. Fargo, N.D., July 17, 1925; s. Benjamin N. and Beatrice (Gillis) B.; student U. Minn., 1947; m. Jacqueline McInnis, Sept. 27, 1955; children—Robert S., William B. Film booker Berger Amusement Co., Mpls., 1947-50; exec. v.p. Standard TV, Beverly Hills, Cal., 1951-55; exec. v.p., gen. mgr. sta. KTWO-AM-TV, Casper, Wyo., 1956-64, sta. KFBB-AM-TV, Great Falls, Mont., 1961-64; pres., gen. mgr. sta. KHVH-AM-TV, Honolulu and sta. KHVO-TV, Hilo, Hawaii, 1964—, instr. U. Hawaii, 1969—. Chmn. Hawaii State Ednl. TV Council, 1967-70; adviser Am. Samoa Dept. Edn., 1970—; chmn. Hawaii State Industry Adv. Com., 1969—; pres. Hawaiian Assn. Broadcasters, 1967-68, 69—. Home: 2457 Makiki Heights Dr Honolulu HI 96822 Office: 1290 Ala Moana Honolulu HI 96814

BERGER, MORRIS ISAIAH, educator; b. N.Y.C., Aug. 5, 1928; s. Victor and Minnie (Waltzer) B.; B.A. Magna cum laude, N.Y. State Tchrs. Coll., 1950, M.A., 1952; Ph.D., Columbia, 1956; m. Sheila Barbara Strongin, Aug. 11, 1957; 1 son, Jamie Thomas. Tchr. history Queensbury High Sch., Glens Falls, N.Y., 1950-52; lectr. Coll. City N.Y., 1954-55; asso. prof. State U. N.Y. Albany, 1956- 63, prof., 1963—, chmn. dept. Foundations of Edn., 1970—; vis. prof. Pa. State U., 1956, 57; Univ. fellow State U. N.Y., 1956; Faculty fellow Columbia, 1957; research fellow State U. N.Y. 1962, 65, 69. Chmn. capital dist. chpt. Am. Civil Liberties Union, 1966; bd. dirs. N.Y. Civil Liberties Union, 1967-68. Mem. Am. Assn. U. Profs. (pres. State U. N.Y. chpt., 1960), Am. Philos. Assn., Philosophy of Edn. Soc. Contbr. books, periodicals, mags., profl. jours. Home: 471 State St Albany NY 12203

BERGER, MORROE, educator, author; b. N.Y.C., June 25 1917; s. Morris and Frieda (Trotiner) B.; B.S.S., Coll. City N.Y., 1940; M.A., Columbia, 1947, Ph.D., 1950; m. Paula Wainer, Mar. 7, 1943; children—Edward Morris, Keneth Harry, Laurence Philip. Mem. faculty Princeton, 1952—, prof. sociology, 1962—, dir. program Near Eastern Studies, 1962-68, chmn. Council on Internat. and Regional Studies, 1968—. Chmn. joint com. Near and Middle East, Social Sci. Research Council and Am. Council Learned Societies, 1963-68; cons. 20th Century Fund, 1957, Congress Cultural Freedom, 1958-61, Ford Found., 1960-63, 67-68; adv. panel on Middle East, Dept. State. Mem. Middle East Studies Assn. (pres. 1967). Served with AUS, 1940-45. Author: Equality by Statute, rev. edit., 1967; Bureaucracy and Society in Modern Egypt, 1957; The Arab World Today, 1962; Islam in Egypt Today, 1970; also articles. Editor, translator: Madame de Stael on Politics, Literature and National Character, 1964. Home: 72 Clover Lane Princeton NJ 08540

BERGER, OSCAR, artist; b. Presov, Eperjes, Czechoslovakia, May 12, 1901; s. Henry and Regina (Berger) B.; art study in Europe; m. Ann Arany I. Varga, Feb. 9, 1937. Came to U.S., 1945, naturalized, 1955. Cartoonist well known personalities drawn from life, including Winston Churchill, Eleanor Roosevelt, Queen Elizabeth II, Prince Philip of Eng., Bernard Shaw, Robert Frost, King Paul I of Greece, Gen. de Gaulle, King Baudouin, King Feisal, Emperor Haille Selassie, Premier Khrushchev, Pope Pius XII, Pope Paul VI, Anna Pavlova, Toscanini, Prof. Einstein, Jacqueline Kennedy Onassis, Pres. Pompidou, Alexei Kosygin, last 8 U.S. presidents; sketched meetings League of Nations, 1925, House of Commons, London, 1935-45, UN confs., 1945-70, UN gen. assemblies, 1946-70; work represented permanent collections Library of Congress, Nat. Portrait Gallery, Met. Mus., also pvt. collections and museums. Club: Nat. Press (Wash.). Author: Tip & Top, 1933, A La Carte, 1948; Aesop's Foibles, 1949; Famous Faces, 1950; My Victims, 1952; I Love You, 1960; The Presidents, 1968. Contbr. am., European publs. Address: Berkeley House 120 Central Park S New York City NY 10019

BERGER, STANLEY, educator; b. N.Y.C., May 9, 1923; B.A., Bklyn. Coll., 1950; M.A., U. Kan., 1955, Ph.D., 1957; married, 1950; three children. Research asso. Bur. Child Research, U. Kan., 1956-57; asst. prof. psychology U. W.Va., 1957-59, U. N.H., 1959-63; prof., chmn. psychology dept. U. R.I., Kingston, 1963—; dir. Behavioral Sci. Center, 1966—. Served with USNR, 1943-46. Mem. A.A.A.S., Psychol. Assn., Soc. Research Child Devel. Contbr. articles to profl. jours. Office: Dept Psychology U RI Kingston RI 02881*

BERGER, THOMAS EDWARD, automotive and aerospace supplier; b. Detroit, Mar. 6, 1936; s. Sidney Bloom and Esther Ruth (Walker) B.; B.B.A., U. Mich., 1958, M.B.A., 1959; m. Sharon L. Vincent, June 17, 1958; children—Thomas Edward, James Vincent, Nancy Elizabeth. Sr. accountant Touche Ross & Co., 1959-63; successively staff accountant, corporate dir. budgets, asst. controller, corporate controller Kelsey-Hayes Co., Romulus, Mich., 1964—. Mem. Urban Affairs Forum of City of Detroit; Detroit area rep. Common Cause; dir. Livonia (Mich.) YMCA. Mem. N.A.M., Am. Inst. C.P.A.'s, Mich. Assn. C.P.A.'s. Prebyn. (elder). Home: 16530 Whitby Dr Livonia MI 48154 Office: 38481 Huron River Dr Romulus MI 48174

BERGER, THOMAS LOUIS, author; b. Cin., July 20, 1924; s. Thomas Charles and Mildred (Bubbe) B.; B.A. with honors, U. Cin., 1948; postgrad. Columbia, 1950-51; m. Jeanne Redpath, June 12, 1950. Librarian, Rand Sch. Social Sci., N.Y.C., 1948-51; staff mem. N.Y. Times Index, 1951-52; asso. editor Popular Sci. Monthly, 1952-53. Served with AUS, 1943-46; ETO. Recipient Rosenthal award Nat. Inst. Arts and Letters, 1965, Western Heritage award, 1965; Dial fellow, 1962. Mem. P.E.N., Authors Guild. Author: Crazy in Berlin, 1958; Reinhart in Love, 1962; Little Big Man, 1964; Killing Time, 1967; Vital Parts, 1970; (play) Other People, 1970; contbr. nat. periodicals. Office: Matson Co 22 E 40th St New York City NY 10016

BERGERON, VICTOR, restauranteur; b. Cal., 1903; s. Victor and Marie (Camount) B.; ed. pub. schs., Cal. Opened restaurant Hinky Dink's, Oakland, Cal., 1934; name of restaurant changed to Trader Vic's, 1938; founder, pres., mgr. of other Trader Vic's in Oakland, N.Y.C., Chgo., Beverly Hills, Portland, Ore., Seattle, Denver, Washington, Scottsdale, Ariz., San Juan, P.R., Vancouver, B.C., Can. and London, Eng. Address: 20 Cosmo Pl San Francisco CA 94109

BERGERON, WILBUR LEE, educator, psychologist; b. Jefferson Parish, La., Aug. 29, 1925; s. V. S. and Sadie (Purifoy) B.; B.A., La. Coll., 1946; M.A., George Peabody Coll., 1947; Ed.D., U. Ark., 1953; m. Ann Hearn, May 14, 1949; 1 dau., Nancy Ann. Asst. prof. psychology La. Coll., 1947-51; psychologist La. State Colony and Tng. Sch., 1949, student counseling service U. Ark., 1951-53; psychology adviser La. Tech. U., Ruston, 1953-63, dir. psychol. services South, Monroe La., 1963-65, prof., head dept. psychology, 1964-70, dir. div. endl. research, 1966—. Vocational cons. Bur. Hearings and Appeals, Social Security Adminstrn., 1962-65; chmn. bd. dirs. Ruston Area Guidance Center; mem. regional mental health com. La. Council Handicapped Children, N. Central La. chpt. Council Exceptional Children; exec. dir. S. Central Region Research Lab., Little Rock, 1966. Mem. Am. Psychol. Assn., Am. Personnel and Guidance Assn., Nat. Vocational Guidance Assn., Nat. Employment Counselors Assn., La. Guidance Assn. (pres. 1965), Ruston C. of C. Research in psychology of adolescence. Home: 1607 Ridge Dr Ruston LA 71270

BERGERON, WILLIAM EMILIEN, ret. govt. ofcl.; b. Marlboro, Mass., Aug. 14, 1902; s. Emilien and Mary Ann (Archambault) B.; B.S., Yale, 1924; m. Josephine Ann Enright, Aug. 22, 1929; children—Josephine Yvonne, Dorothy Helen (dec.), Eileen Anne, William Emilien, Albert Edmund. Survey, constrn. engring., 1924-28; resident engr. constrn., Radburn, N.J., 1928-34; civil engr. Pub. Works Adminstrn., 1934-38; planner housing projects U.S. Housing Authority, 1938-42; asst. dir. Fed. Pub. Housing Authority, Chgo., 1942-48; dir. Pub. Housing Adminstrn., Chgo., 1948-66; asst. adminstr. Chgo. Regional Office of Housing Adminstrn., 1966-69; ret., 1969. Licensed profl. engr., N.J. Mem. Nat. Assn. Housing Ofcls., Yale Engring. Assn., Sigma Xi, Tau Beta Pi. Club: Yale (Chgo.). Home: 433 Prairie Av Elmhurst IL 60126

BERGES, MARSHALL WILLIAM, journalist; b. Chgo.; s. Charles and Beatrice (Marin) B.; Ph.B., Marquette U.; postgrad. U. Chgo.; m. Mildred Adrian; children—Renee Jean, Edward Steven. Mem. staff Time, Inc., 1947—, chief Detroit bur., 1958-60, Los Angeles bur., 1961—. Pres. bd. dirs. Center Theater Group, Music Centers, Los Angeles; bd. dirs. Music Center Operating Co., bd govs. Performing Arts Council, Music Center. Served with USNR, 1942-45. USNR, 1942-45. Mem. Sigma Delta Chi. essays, 1948; Adventures in Journalism and other essays, 1950. Office: 450 N Roxbury Dr Beverly Hills CA 90210

BERGETHON, KAARE ROALD, coll. pres.; b. Tromso, Norway, June 8, 1918; s. Maximilian and Petra Rudd (Olsen) B.; brought to U.S., 1926, naturalized, 1930; A.B., DePauw U., 1938; M.A., Cornell U., 1940, Ph.D., 1945; Litt.D., Brown U., 1959, Franklin and Marshall Coll., 1959; LL.D., Rutgers U., 1959, Muhlenberg Coll., 1959, Lehigh U., 1959, DePauw U., 1961; Waynesburg Coll., 1960; m. Katherine Helen Lind, Apr. 4, 1942; children—Bruce L., Peter R. With Walter Kidde Constrns. Inc., N.Y., 1938-39, 41-44; instr. German, Syracuse U., 1945-46; instr. Brown U., 1946-47, asst. prof. German, asst. to chmn. div. modern langs., 1947- 52, asso. dean, 1952-55, asso. prof. German, 1953-58, dean, 1955-58, prof. German, 1958; pres. Lafayette Coll., Easton, Pa., 1958—. Chmn. nat. exec. com., program of ednl. inquiry Carnegie Found., 1952-53; pres. Presbyn. Coll. Union, 1962-63; mem. adv. bd. of coll. presidents Nat. Scholarship Service, Fund for Negro Students. Bd. dirs. United Fund Easton Area, Community Council Easton, Delaware Valley Area Council Boy Scouts, Sta. WLVT-TV, ednl. TV, Bethlehem, Pa. Mem. Presbyn. Hist. Soc., Modern Lang. Assn. Am., Am. Assn. U. Profs., Am. Assn. Tchrs. German, Found. Ind. Colls. Pa., Pa. Assn. Colls. and Univs. (0p.p.), Middle States Assn. Colls. and Secondary Schs. (accreding commn. on instns. of higher edn.), Ind. Coll. Funds Am., Commn. Ind. Colls. and Univs., Am. Council on Edn., Phi Beta Kappa, Phi Eta Sigma, Phi Kappa Phi, Beta Theta Pi, Sigma Delta Chi, Alpha Phi Omega. Presbyn. Clubs: Kiwanis (dir.), Pomfret (Easton, Pa.); Northampton County Country, University (N.Y.C.). Author: Grammar for Reading German, 1950, alternate edit., 1963; also articles profl. publs. Home: 515 College Av Easton PA 18042

BERGFELD, ALBERT JOSEPH, mgmt. cons.; b. St. Paul, July 15, 1910; s. Charles Daniel and May Adele (Carey) B.; grad. Antioch Coll., Yellow Springs, O., 1934; m. Elizabeth Smith Palmer, June 13, 1941; children—Charles Daniel II, Kristin Palmer, Elisabeth Pennock. With Stevenson, Jordan & Harrison, Inc., N.Y.C., 1934-62, mem. firm, 1942-62, pres., 1958-64; pres. Case and Co., Inc., 1962—; dir. Am. Chain & Cable Co., Inc. Served to lt. USN, World War II. Clubs: Union League, N.Y. Yacht (N.Y.C.); Racquet (Chgo.). Author: (with Dr. James S. Earley, W.R. Knobloch) Pricing for Profit and Growth, 1957. Home: Long Ridge Rd Stamford CT 06905 Office: Case and Co Inc 600 Fifth Av New York City NY 10020

BERGFORS, EMERY E., financial analyst cons.; b. Chgo., Aug. 24, 1910; m. Anne Hulko. With Am.-Marietta Co., Chgo., 1933-61, asst. treas., 1945-61, controller, 1948-61; asst. treas. Martin-Marietta Corp., 1961-65; financial analyst cons. Chgo., 1965—. Republican. Club: Swedish (Chgo.). Home: 10117 Old Orchard Ct Skokie IL 60076 Office: 277 Park Av New York City NY 10017

BERGGREN, RONALD BERNARD, surgeon; b. S.I., N.Y., June 13, 1931; s. Bernard and Florence (Schmidt) B.; B.A., Johns Hopkins, 1953; M.D., U. Pa., 1957; m. Mary Beth Griffith, Nov. 25, 1954; children—Karen Ann, Eric Griffith. Asst. instr. surgery U. Pa., 1958-62, instr., 1962-65; gen. surg. resident Hosp. U. Pa., 1958-62, resident plastic surgery, 1963-64, chief resident plastic surgery, 1964-65; sr. research surgery Phila. Gen. Hosp., 1962-63; asst. prof. surgery Ohio State U. Sch. Medicine, 1965-68, dir. div. plastic surgery, 1965—, asso. prof. surgery, 1968—; attending staff Ohio U. Hosps.; attending staff, dir. div. plastic surgery Children's Hospital, Columbus, O. Diplomate American Bd. Surgery, Nat. Bd. Med. Examiners, Am. Bd. Plastic Surgery. Fellow A.C.S.; mem. Central, Columbus surg. socs., Am. Soc. Plastic and Reconstructive Surgeons, Ohio Valley Plastic Surg. Soc., Am. Cleft Palate Assn., A.M.A., Am. Assn. Plastic Surgeons, Franklin County (O.) Med. Soc., Soc. Cryosurgery, Plastic Surg. Research Council, Soc. Cryobiology, N.Y. Acad. Scis., Am. Assn. Surgery of Trauma, Assn. Academic Surgery, Sigma Xi, Phi Kappa Psi, Alpha Kappa Kappa. Home: 1960 Hampshire Rd Columbus OH 43221 Office: 410 W 10th Av Columbus OH 43210

BERGGREN, WILLARD PAUL, coll. dean; b. Pittsburg, Cal., Aug. 20, 1912; s. Carl Gustaf and Vera Belle (Collins) B.; B.S. in Elec. Engring., U. Cal. at Berkeley, 1931, M.S. in Mech. Engring., 1932, Ph.D. in Mech. Engring., 1934; m. Ruth Mary Noell, June 25, 1938; children—Noel David, Mary Ellen, Gail. Teaching asst. mech. engring. U. Cal. at Berkeley, 1932-35, instr. physics at Davis, 1935-41, supr. war tng. at San Diego, 1941-42, asst. prof. physics at Davis, 1942-45; research engr. Aerojet Corp., Azusa, Cal., 1945-49; asso. prof. aero. engring. Ohio State U., 1949-50; research engr. Oak Ridge Nat. Lab., 1950-53; dir. div. engring. U. Bridgeport (Conn.), 1953-56, dean Coll. Engring., 1956—; cons. to corps. Registered profl. engr., Cal., Conn. Named Engr. of Year, Conn. Soc. Profl. Engrs., 1959. Mem. Am. Soc. M.E., Am. Soc. Engring. Edn., Conn. Acad. Arts and Scis., Am. Inst. for Aeros. and Astronautics, Nat. Soc. Profl. Engrs., Sigma Xi, Tau Beta Pi, Eta Kappa Nu. Home: 212 Rock Major Rd Fairfield, CT 06430. Office: U Bridgeport Bridgeport CT 06602

BERGHOF, HERBERT, actor, dir., educator; b. Vienna, Sept. 13, 1909; s. Paul and Regina Berghof; student U. Vienna, Vienna State Acad. Dramatic Art; pupil of Alexander Moissi, Max Reinhardt, Lee Strasberg; charter mem. Actors Studio, N.Y.C.; m. Alice Hermes (marriage dissolved); m. 2d, Uta Hagen. Theatrical appearances include Don Carlos, 1927; resident mem. St. Gallen Repertory Co., Zurich, 1927-29; mem. Deutsches Volks Theatre, theatre in cler Josefstadt, Vienna, 1929-30; performed Berlin and Salzburg festivals, 1930-33, 33-38; appeared in Romeo and Juliet, Journey's End, The Doctor's Dilemma, Hamlet, All God's Chillun Got Wings, Crime for Crime, Six Characters in Search of an Author, An American Tragedy, Everyman, Ghosts, As You Like It, Candida; dir. The Melody That Got Lost, Vienna; N.Y.C. debut as King Lear, 1941; appearance in Criminals; dir. From Vienna; actor, dir. Reunion in New York, rev. version From Vienna, 1940; actor in France, 1941, Nathan the Wise, 1943, Twelfth Night, 1942, Winter Soldiers, 1942, The Russian People, 1942, The Innocent Voyage, 1943, Oklahoma!, 1943, Jacobowsky and the Colonel, 1944, The Man Who Had All the Luck, 1944, Little Women, 1944, The Beggars are Coming to Town, 1945, St. Lazare's Pharmacy (tour), 1945, The Mayor of Zalemea, 1946, Temper the Wind, 1946, The Whole World Over, 1947, Ghosts, 1948, Hedda Gabler, 1948, Miss Liberty, 1949, Torquato Tasso, 1949, The Lady From the Sea, 1950, Guardsman, 1951, Tovarich, 1952, The Deep Blue Sea, 1952; numerous stock appearances; dir. The Key, 1947, Rip Van Winkle, 1947, Waiting for Godot, N.Y.C., 1956-57, Protective Custody, 1956, The Infernal Machine, 1958, Twelfth Night, 1959; The Queen and the Rebels, 1959; dir., actor The Affairs of Anatol; appeared in The Andersonville Trial, 1959, Krapp's Last Tape, 1960; dir. Do Know The Milky Way?, 1961, This Side of Paradise, 1962; dir. for Lincoln Seize the Day, Tomorrow, Kaspar, Oppenheimer, 1969; film appearances include Assignment Paris, 1952, Diplomatic Courier, 1952, Five Fingers, 1952, Red Planet Mars, 1952, Fräulein, 1958, An Affair of the Skin, 1963, Cleopatra, 1963; numerous radio and TV appearances; tchr. acting Columbia, New Sch. Social Research, Neighborhood Playhouse, Am. Theatre Wing: founder, dir. HB Studio, 1945, HB Playwrights Found., 1964. Mem. Artists Equity Assn., A.F.T.R.A., Screen Actors Guild. Home: 27 Washington Sq N New York City NY 10011 Office: 120 Bank St New York City NY 10014

BERGHOLZ, RICHARD CADY, newspaperman; b. Corvallis, Ore., Apr. 13, 1917; s. William Orville and Mabel (Cady) B.; B.A., U. Wash., 1938; m. Elizabeth True Jamison, Feb. 22, 1941; children—Barbara (Mrs. William T. Stacy), Richard J., Betty Jean. Reporter, Ventura (Cal.) Star-Free Press, 1938-41, A.P., 1941-44; war corr., New Guinea, Philippines, China, Manchuria, 1944-46; reporter Glendale (Cal.) News-Press, 1946-47; polit. editor San Diego Evening Tribune, 1947-54, Los Angeles Mirror, 1954-62; polit. writer Los Angeles Times, 1962—. Mem. Sigma Delta Chi, Pi Kappa Alpha. Home: 929 Crestview Dr Pasadena CA 91107 Office: Times Mirror Sq Los Angeles CA 90053

BERGIN, DANIEL TIMOTHY, lawyer; b. New Rochelle, N.Y., Mar. 21, 1930; s. Daniel Timothy and Elsie (Dillon) B.; student Northwestern U., 1948-49; B.S., U. Ariz., 1952, J.D., 1957; m. Ann Averill Edmunds, July 26, 1958; children-Daniel Hunt, Catherine Ann, Jeffrey Thomas, Brian McCormack. Admitted to Ariz. bar, 1957; practice in San Francisco, 1957-58, Phoenix, 1958—; clk. to Richard H. Chambers chief judge U.S. Ct. of Appeals, 9th Judicial Circuit, San Francisco, 1957-58; asso. Fennemore, Craig, von Ammon & Udall, 1958-63, partner, 1964—. Mem. Am., Ariz., Maricopa County bar assns., Am. Judicature Soc., Lawyers Club Phoenix (bd. dirs. 1970—), Phoenix C. of C., Phi Delta Phi, Phi Gamma Delta. Republican. Roman Catholic. Club: Arizona Country (Phoenix). Home: 3111 N 53d St Phoenix AZ 85018 Office: 411 N Central Av Phoenix AZ 85004

BERGIN, THOMAS FRANCIS, legal educator; b. New Haven, Nov. 17, 1924; s. Frank S. and Cecelia (Phillips) B.; B.A., Princeton, 1948; LL.B., Yale, 1951; m. Marguerite Suzanne Freda, May 18, 1951; 1 dau., Anne. Admitted to N.Y. bar, 1952; asso. firm Kelley, Drye, Newhall & Maginnes, N.Y.C., 1951-57; partner Tompkins, Boal & McQuade, N.Y.C., 1957-60; asst. to pres. Sarah Lawrence Coll., Bronxville, N.Y., 1960-62; asst. to dir. capital funds program Yale Law Sch., 1962-63; asso. prof. law U. Va. Sch. Law, Charlottesville, 1963-65, prof. 1965-70, Lile prof. law, 1970—; mem. Queen's Coll., Cambridge (Eng.) U., 1970—. Mem. Council on Urban Devel., Inst. Human Scis. Served with AUS, 1943-44; with USAAF, 1944-46; CBI. Mem. Am. Civil Liberties Union, Charlottesville Council Human Relations, Order of Coif. Author: (with Paul G. Haskell) Preface to Estates in Land and Future Interests, 1966. Home: Route 5 Box 361 Garth Rd Charlottesville VA 22901

BERGIN, THOMAS GODDARD, educator; b. New Haven, Conn., Nov. 17, 1904; s. Thomas Joseph and Irvinea (Goddard) B.; B.A., Yale, 1925, Ph.D., 1929; Litt.D. (hon.). Hofstra Coll., 1958; L.H.D. (hon.), Fairfield U., 1965; m. Florence T. Bullen, Dec. 30, 1929; children—Winifred Mandeville, Jennifer Mandeville. Instr. Italian, Yale Coll., 1925-30; asso. prof. Italian and Spanish, Western Res. U., Cleve., 1930-35; prof. Romance langs. N.Y. State Coll. Tchrs. Albany, 1935-41; prof. Romance langs., curator Dante and Petrarch collections Cornell U., 1941-48, chmn. div. lit., acting chmn. dept. of English, 1946-48; prof. Italian, Yale 1948—, chmn. dept. Spanish and Italian, 1949-58, Barge prof. Romance langs., 1950-57, Sterling prof. Romance langs., 1957—, master Timothy Dwight Coll., 1953-68; Fulbright scholar, Italy, 1955- 56. Served as maj. in Spl. Res., 1943, promoted lt. col. 1945; with allied commn., Italy, 1943-46. Decorated Bronze Star (U.S.); Order Crown of Italy, Order Sts. Maurice and Lazarus, Order of Civil Merit (Italy), Order Brit. Empire. Mem. Modern Lang. Assn. Am., Am. Assn. Tchrs. Italian (pres. 1947), Medieval Acad. Am., Dante Soc., Am. Assn. U. Profs., Renaissance Soc., Phi Beta Kappa. Clubs: P.E.N., Yale Century (N.Y.C.); Mory's, Elizabethan (pres. 1965-68) (New Haven); Savile (London, Eng.). Author: The New Science of G. B. Vico (with M. Fisch), 1948, Dante's Inferno, 1948; Dante's Purgatory, 1953; Paradise, 1954; Translations from Petrarch, 1955; Master Pieces, 1964; Dante, 1965; perspective on the Divine Comedy, 1964; A Diversity of Dante, 1969; Petrarch, 1970. Editor: Rambaldo de Vaqueiras, Liriche, 1956; Modern Italian Short Stories, 1959; Bertran de Born, Liriche, 1964; Sonnets and Odes of Petrarch 1966; (with E.H. Wilkins) Concordance to the Divine Comedy, 1965. Contbr. to mags. Home: 48 Wyndybrook Lane Madison CT 06443 Office: Dept Romance Langs Yale New Haven CT 06520 ☆

BERGLAND, BOB SELMER, congressman; b. Roseau, Minn., July 22, 1928; s. Selmer Bennett and Mabel (Evans) B.; Sears Roebuck scholar U. Minn., 1946-48; m. Helen Elaine Grohn, June 24, 1950; children—Dianne, Linda, Stevan, Jon, Allan, Billy, Franklyn. Field rep. Minn. Farmers Union, 1948-50; farmer, 1950—; mem. 92d Congress from 7th Dist. Minn. Sec. Roseau County Democratic Farmer- Labor Party, Minn., 1951-52, chmn., 1953-54; chmn. Minn. Agr. Stblzn. and Conservation Service Com., Dept. Agr., 1961-62; dir. Midwest Area Agr. Stblzn. and Conservation Service, 1963-68; candidate U.S. Ho. of Reps., 1968. Recipient Gold Letter award U. Minn. Mem. Minn. Farmers Union, Nat. Farmers Orgn. Lutheran. Mason, Lion, Eagle. Address: Route 3 Roseau MN 56751*

BERGLEITNER, GEORGE CHARLES, Jr., investment banker; b. Bklyn., July 16, 1935; s. George Charles and Marie (Preitz) B.; B.B.A., St. Francis Coll., Bklyn., 1959; M.B.A., Coll. City N.Y., 1961; m. Betty Van Buren, Oct. 29, 1966; children-George Charles III, Michael John, Stephen William. Dir. instl. sales A.T. Brod & Co., N.Y.C., 1965-66; dir. instl. sales Weis, Voisin & Cannon, Inc., N.Y.C. 1966-67; dir. instl. sales C.B. Richard, Ellis & Co., N.Y.C., 1967-68; pres. M.J. Manchester & Co., . Fashion & Time, Inc., Jerome Mackeys Judo Sch., Inc., B.J.B. Graphics, Inc., First Coinvestors, Inc., Smart Fit Foundations, Inc., Macron Corp., Jay Co., Computer Holdings Corp., Anka Research Ltd.., Microlab/FXR, Devon Internat., Ltd., Computer Engrng. Corp. Mem. Nat. Stock Exchange, N.Y. Merc. Exchange, Phila.-Balt.- Washington Stock Exchange. Chmn. Franciscan Fathers Devel. Program, 1967- 71; mem. President's Council, Franciscan Spirit award, 1959—. Regent St Francis Coll.; bd. dirs. Printing Trade Sch. Served with U.S. Army, 1952- 55. Resipient St. Francis Coll. Alumni Fund award, 1965. Mem. Security Traders Assn. N.Y., Nat. Security Traders Assn., A.I.M., Cath. War Vets., Assn. Investment Bankers, St. Francis Coll. (dir.), Coll. City N.Y. alumni assns. Republican. K.C., Moose. Home: 370 E 76th St New York NY 10021 also Hobart NYOffice: 221 W 57th St New York NY 10019

BERGLUND, MILTON EDWARD, mfg. co. exec.; b. Worcester, Mass., Dec. 26, 1903; s. Edward G. and Anna (Anderson) B.; B.S., Worcester Poly. Inst., 1926; m. Mary M. Gibbons, Jan. 19, 1928; children—Anna M., Milton Edward. Test engr. Gen. Electric Co., Lynn, Mass., 1926-27; project engr. Torrington Co., 1927-33, asst. plant supt., 1933-45, asst. gen. works mgr., 1945, gen. works mgr., 1945-47, v.p. charge mfg., dir., 1947-55, exec. v.p., 1955-58, pres., 1958—, chmn. bd., 1967—; dir. Hartford Nat. Bank, Hartford Electric Light Co., Torrington Water Co., Am. Mut. Liability Ins. Co., Wakefield, Mass., MFB Mut. Ins. Providence, R.I. Bd. dirs. Charlotte Hungerford Hosp.; trustee YMCA. Address: 21 Studley Rd Hyannis MA 02601

BERGMAN, ALAN, author of songs; b. Bklyn., Sept. 11, 1925; s. Sammuel and Ruth (Margulies) B.; grad. Ethical Culture Sch.; B.A., U. N.C.; student U. Cal. at Los Angeles; m. Marilyn Keith, Feb. 9, 1958; 1 dau., Julie Rachel. TV dir. CBS, Phila., 1945-53; wrote TV Prodn. numerous for Shower of Stars, spls. for Jo Stafford, songs for Fred Astaire, Marge and Gower Champion; author songs for revues, night clubs, films; stage scores include That's Life, Ice Capades of 1957, Something More. Recipient Acad. award for best song, 1968; Acad. award nomination for What Are You Doing the Rest of Your Life?, 1969 Lyricist (songs) Yellow Bird, Nice 'n' Easy, I've Never Left Your Arms, Marriage-go-Round, (film) Never Be Afraid, Sentimental Baby, Sleep Warm, Sogni D'Oro, That Face, Ol' MacDonald, That's Him Over There; (film) The Windmills of Your Mind; title song for film In the Heat of the Night; other songs for films Make Me Rainbows, I Believed It All, Ask Yourself Why, Maybe Tomorrow, Sweet Gingerbread Man, Summer Me, Winter Me, Pieces of Dreams. Albums include Never Be Afraid; Aesop's Fables. Served with AUS, 1943-45. Mem. A.S.C.A.P. Address: care Freedman & Freedman 911 Gateway West Century City Los Angeles CA 90067

BERGMAN, BERNARD AARON, editor; b. Chillicothe, O., July 8, 1894; s. Eleazer and Carrie (Weiler) B.; B.A., Ohio State U., 1916; spl. student, Universite de Poitiers, 1919; m. Frances Dellar, Mar. 17, 1933 (dec. Oct. 1965). Pub. relations work, N.Y.C., 1919-31; mng. editor New Yorker mag., 1931-33; editor March of Events Page, Hearst Newspapers, 1933-35; successively Sunday editor, feature editor, exec. editor Phil. Record, 1935-42, also feature editor N.Y. Post, 1938; feature editor Pageant mag., 1946; dir. pub. relations Publicker Industries, Inc., 1947-55; editor, dir. Phila. Daily News, 1955-58; editor Jewish Exponent, Phila., 1958-61; editor Sunday mag. Phila. Bull., 1961-66, editor book div., 1966-69, book editor, 1970—; spl. instr. journalism U. Pa., 1951-52, lectr., 1960. Served as sgt. maj. U.S. Army, World War I; lt. col. USAAF, World War II. Recipient journalism award Temple U., 1956. Mem. Phi Beta Kappa, Zeta Beta Tau, Sigma Delta Chi. Democrat. Jewish religion. Clubs: Art Alliance, Peale, Franklin Inn (Phila.). Author: The Smiling Corpse (with Philip Wylie), 1935. Home: 1810 Rittenhouse Sq Philadelphia PA 19103 Office: The Bulletin 30th and Market Sts Philadelphia PA 19101

BERGMAN, EDWIN ALFRED, aluminum co. exec.; b. Chgo., July 18, 1917; s. Sigmund and Eda Eisenstaut) B.; B.A. in Bus. Adminstrn., U. Chgo., 1939; m. Betty Jane Lindenberger, July 10, 1940; children—Carol Ann (Mrs. Douglas Cohen), Robert Henry, Betty Lynn. Vice pres. S.A. Bergman, Inc., Chgo., 1939—; pres. U.S. Reduction Co., East Chicago, Ind., 1940—; dir. 1st Nat. Bank, East Chicago, 1968—. Pres., Young Men's Jewish Council, Chgo., 1950; v.p. Mus. Contemporary Art, Chgo., 1966—; mem. vis. com. humanities U. Chgo., 1965—. Bd. dirs. Assn. Contemporary Art, 1967—, Aluminum Assn., 1960—; trustee Michael Reese Hosp., Chgo., 1952—, St. Catherine's Hosp., East Chicago, 1965—, Hebrew Union Coll., Cin., 1968—. Clubs: Standard (dir. 1960—) (Chgo.); Ravisloe Country (Homewood, Ill.). Home: 6759 S Bennett Av Chicago IL 60649 Office: 4610 Kennedy Blvd East Chicago IN 46312

BERGMAN, EMMETT NORLIN, educator; b. Slayton, Minn., May 6, 1929; s. August and Meda (Norlin) B.; B.S., U. Minn., 1950, D.V.M., M.S., 1953, Ph.D., 1959; m. Mary Margaret Welfare, July 12, 1953; children—Margaret L., Patricia A., Susan M., Emmett Norlin. Instr. physiology U. Minn., 1950-53, 55-59, asst. prof., 1959-61; vet. lab. officer Walter Reed Army Inst. Research, 1953-55; asso. prof. N.Y. Vet. Coll., Cornell U., 1961-66; sr. postdoctoral fellow, Gt. Britain, 1963-64; prof. physiology Cornell U., 1966—; vis. prof. physiology U. Cal. at San Francisco Med. Center, 1969-70; cons. in field. Served to 1st lt. AUS, 1953-55. Mem. Am. Physiol. Soc., N.Y. Acad. Sci., A.A.A.S., Am. Vet. Med. Assn., Conf. Research Work Animal Disease, Sigma Xi, Phi Zeta, Gamma Sigma Delta, Alpha Zeta. Conglist. (deacon 1966-69). Rotarian. Mason. Author articles in field; contbr. book. Home: 212 Enfield Falls Rd Ithaca NY 14850

BERGMAN, G. MERLE, lawyer, motion picture co. exec.; b. Mpls., Apr. 11, 1920; s. George H. and Anna Vera (Bergman) B.; B.A., U. Chgo., 1940, M.A., 1941; J.D., Northwestern U., 1948; LL.D., Kyushu U. (Japan), 1951. Admitted to Ill. bar, 1948, Cal. bar, 1957; asst. prof. law U. Kansas City, 1948-49; research dir., adminstrv. asst. to Adlai E. Stevenson, 1948; legal research analyst state Ill., 1949-50; practice law, Chgo. and Los Angeles, 1948—; gen. counsel v.p., dir. World-Wide Artists' Mgr., Inc., Hollywood, Cal., 1969—; v.p., dir. J.D. Ludwig Corp., Los Angeles, 1968—. Pres. World Council Jurisprudence, 1967-68. Bd. dirs. Soc. of Fellowship, Prep. Tours Acad. Served with USAAF, 1941-45, USAF, 1950-52. Recipient Humanitarian award World Fellowship, 1960; chevalier Internat. Legion Advocates. Diplomate Collegium Internat. Lawyers. Office: 6777 Hollywood Blvd Hollywood CA 90028

BERGMAN, HARRY, physician; b. N.Y.C., Oct. 25, 1912; s. Sam and Pauline (Freedman) B.; M.D., U. Buffalo, 1934; m. Tillie Simon, Feb. 16, 1936 (dec. Feb. 1957); m. 2d, Mollie Holtzman, Apr. 2, 1958.

Intern Lebanon Hosp., N.Y.C., 1934- 36, resident Morrisania City Hosp., N.Y.C., attending urologist, 1958—; practice medicine specializing in urology, N.Y.C., 1936—; attending urologist Bronx Lebanon Hosp. Center, 1953—, Jewish Meml. Hosp., N.Y.C., 1960—; asso. clin. prof. N.Y. Med. Coll., 1966—. Diplomate Am. Bd. Urology. Fellow A.C.S. (exec. com. 1962—, pres. Bronx chpt. 1965—), Am. Urol. Soc., N.Y. Acad. Medicine; mem. A.M.A., Bronx County Med. Soc., New York State Soc. Surgeons dir., Am. Geriatric Soc., Met. Med. Alumni U. Buffalo (pres. gen. alumni 1958—), Magicians Guild Am., Physicians Square Club Am., Alpha Omega Alpha. Mason. Research and publs. on cancer of ureter; new radiol. sign for cancer ureter called Bergman's Sign; designer cancer biopsy instrument, 1947, and new prostate catheter, 1958. Editor-in-chief: The Ureter, 1967, co-editor column Urologic-Radiologic Revs. in N.Y. State Jour. Medicine. Home: 24 Monterey Dr Mt Vernon NY 10552 Office: 1749 Grand Concourse New York City NY 10453

BERGMAN, INGMAR, (Ernest), film writer, dir.; b. Uppsala, Sweden, July 14, 1918; ed. Stockholm U.; m. Käbi Lareti; 1 son. Writer of screenplay Torment, 1943; dir. film Crisis, 1945, (comedy) Lesson in Love, Smiles of a Summer Night (Cannes Film Festival award), 1956, Seventh Seal (Cannes Film Festival award), 1957, Brink of Life (Cannes Film Festival award), 1958, Wild Strawberries (Berlin Film Festival award), 1958, The Virgin Spring (Acad. award), 1960, The Devil's Eye, 1961, Through a Glass Darkly, 1961, Winter Light, 1962, The Silence, 1963, Now About All These Women, 1964, Persona, 1967, Hour of the Wolf, 1968, Shame, 1968, A Passion, 1970; head Royal Dramatic Theatre, Stockholm, 1963-66. Recipient Netherlands' Erasmus award for contbn. to arts, 1965. Address: Svensk Filmindustri Kungsgatan 36 Stockholm Sweden*

BERGMAN, INGRID, actress; b. Stockholm, Sweden; d. Justus and Friedel (Alder) Bergman; ed. Lyceum for Flickor and Sch. Royal Dramatic Theatre, Stockholm; m. Peter Lindstrom, July 10, 1937 (div.); 1 dau., Pia; m. 2d, Roberto Rossellini; children—Roberto, Isabella and Ingrid (twins); m. 3d, Lars Schmidt, Dec. 21, 1958. Began acting in motion pictures and stage plays in Sweden, came to U.S., 1939; has played in motion pictures in U.S.: Intermezzo, 1939; Adam Had Four Sons, 1940; Rage in Heaven, 1940; Dr. Jekyll and Mr. Hyde, 1941; Casablanca, 1942; For Whom the Bell Tolls, 1943; Gaslight, 1944; Saratoga Trunk, 1945; Bells of St. Mary's, 1945; Notorious, 1946; Joan of Arc; Under Capricorn, Stromboli, The Greatest Love; Trip to Italy; Strangers, Fear; Anastasia, 1956; Paris Does Strange Things, 1957; Indiscreet, 1958; Inn of the 6th Happiness, 1958; Goodby Again, 1961; The Visit, 1963; The Yellow Rolls-Royce, 1964; Cactus Flower, 1969; Walk in the Spring Rain, 1969; stage plays U.S.: Lilliom, 1940; Anna Christie, 1941; Joan of Lorraine, 1946, Tea and Sympathy (Paris), 1956-57; Hedda Gabler, 1963; Month in The Country, 1966; More Stately Mansions 1968; Captain Brassbounds Conversion, 1970. Recipient Acad. award Acad. Motion Picture Arts and Scis., 1944, 56, N.Y. Film Critics Award, 1956; TV Acad. award for The Turn of the Screw, 1960. Address: care London Artists Ltd 25 Gilbert St London W 1 England

BERGMAN, MARILYN KEITH, author, lyricist; b. Bklyn., Nov. 10; d. Albert A. and Edith (Arkin) Katz; B.A., N.Y. U.; m. Alan Bergman, Feb. 9, 1958; 1 dau., Julie Rachel. Numerous revues, songs for night clubs and films; stage scores include That's Life, Ice Capades of 1957, Something More!. Recipient Acad. award for best song 1968. Mem. A.S.C.A.P. Author: (songs) Yellow Bird, Nice 'n' Easy, I've Never Left Your Arms, Afraid, Outta My Mind, (film) The Right Approach, Sentimental Baby, That Face, (film) The Windmills of your Mind; (film) In The Heat Of The Night, What Are You Doing The Rest Of Your Life? (Acad. award nominee 1969), Make Me Rainbows, Summer Me, Winter Me, Ask Yourself Why, Pretty World, Sweet Gingerbread Man, Pieces of Dreams. Address: care of Freedman & Freedman 911 Gateway West Century City Los Angeles CA 90067

BERGMAN, MELVIN ROBERT, lawyer; b. Bellevue, O., Aug. 21, 1901; s. Carl Hjälmar and Christina (Carlson) B.; B.A., Ohio State U., 1923, LL.B., 1925; student U. Mich., summer 1925; m. Frances Curson, Apr. 30, 1938 (dec. Feb. 1960); 1 dau., Barbara (Mrs. Eugene Schneider); m. 2d, Doris M. Kransberger, Jan. 29, 1971. Admitted to Ohio bar, 1925; partner firm Eastman, Stichter, Smith & Bergman, Toledo, 1931—. Mem. Am., Ohio, Toledo bar assns., U.S. (sec. 1964-66), Western (pres. 1945-46), Northwestern (sec. 1937-41) lawn tennis assns., Internat. Platform Assn., Am. Judicature Soc., Downtown Coaches Assn., Phi Beta Kappa, Lambda Chi Alpha, Gamma Eta Gamma. Republican. Conglist. Clubs: University, Tennis, Racquet, Inverness (Toledo); Catawba Island. Home: 4243 W Bancroft St Ottawa Hills Toledo OH 43615 Office: 240 Huron St Toledo OH 43604

BERGMAN, WALTER JAMES, business exec.; b. N.Y.C., Jan. 14, 1904; s. Simon and Anna (Bloch) B.; student Wharton Sch. Commerce and Finance, U. Pa., 1922-25; LL.D. Drury Coll. 1954; m. Leona Lefferts, June 19, 1927; 1 dau., Virginia B. Edelman. With Lily-Tulip Cup Corp., N.Y.C., 1929-68, 1st v.p., 1929-43, exec. v.p., 1943-46, pres., 1946-62, chmn. chief exec. officer, 1962-68; pres. Lily Cups, Ltd., Toronto, Can., 1946-62, dir., 1946-68; v.p., dir. Thanks to Scandinavia, Inc.; dir. Owens-Ill., Inc.; founder College Point Nat. Bank (N.Y.), 1927, dir., 1927-29; adv. com. 45th St. br. Chase Manhattan Bank of N.Y.; pres., dir. Red River Paper Mill. Inc.; dir. First Multifund of Am., Inc. Vice pres. Am. Jewish Com.; pres., dir. Sydenham Hosp., 1939-41. Trustee Drury Coll., 1954-68, hon. life trustee; trustee Population Reference Bur.; nat. trustee Nat. Conf. Christians and Jews; chmn. bd. trustees Henry Nias Found.; bd. dirs. Speech Rehab. Inst. Mem. Nat. Dairy Council (dir. at large 1958-60). Clubs: Beach Point Yacht, Harmonie, Pinnacle. Contbr. chpt. Top Mgmt.'s Use of Outside Services. Home: 1185 Park Av New york City NY 10028 (summer) 92 Greenhaven Rd Rye NY 10580

BERGMANN, FREDRICK LOUIS, educator; b. Tecumseh, Kan., Sept. 27, 1916; s. Curt and Minna (Herrmann) B.; A.B., Washburn Coll., 1937; M.A., State Coll. Wash., 1939; postgrad. Columbia, 1941; Ph.D., George Washington U., 1953; m. Jean Marshall, July 6, 1941; children—Juliann (Mrs. Peter Jan Witteveld), John Fredrick. Asst. Washburn Coll., 1939-40; instr. English, DePauw U., 1940-43, asst. prof., 1943-46, asso. prof., 1946-54, prof., 1954—, head dept. English, dir. Conf. Am. Studies, 1956—, James Whitcomb Riley prof. English lit., 1969. Founder Greencastle Summer Theater, 1962; pres. English dept. chmn. Gt. Lakes Colls. Assn., 1968-69. Fellow Folger Shakespeare Library, 1951, Grad. Council George Washington U. Mem. Ind. Coll. English Assn. (pres. 1956, 63), Modern Lang. Assn., Am. Soc. 18th Century Studies, Societe francaise d'Etude du XVIIe Siecle, Am. English-Speaking Union, Sigma Delta Chi (leather medal award for greatest service to DePauw U. 1962), Delta Chi, Episcopalian. Author: (with R.W. Pence) Writing Craftsmanship, 1956; Paragraph Rhetoric, 1967; Sentence Rhetoric, 1969; Essays: Method, Content, Conscience, 1970; also articles profl. jours. Home: 205 Arlington Av Greencastle IN 46135

BERGMANN, GUSTAV, educator; b. Vienna, Austria, May 4, 1906; s. Fritz and Therese (Pollack) B.; Ph.D., Vienna, 1928, J.D., 1935; Doctor honoris causa, U. Goteborg, 1962; m. Leola M. Nelson, Sept. 4, 1943; 1 dau., Hanna Elisabeth (Mrs. Burns H. Weston). Came to U.S., 1938, naturalized, 1943. With State U., Ia., 1939—, successively research asso., lectr., asst. prof., asso. prof., 1939-50, prof. dept. philosophy, 1950—; guest prof. Lund, Goteborg, Stockholm, Uppsala univs. (all Sweden), 1961-62. Mem. Am. Philos. Assn. (pres. 1968-69). Author: The Metaphysics of Logic Positivism, 1954; Philosophy of Science, 1957; Meaning and Existence, 1960; Logic and Reality, 1964; Realism, 1967. Editor: Philosophy of Sci. (Quar.), 1948- -. Home: 124 Grand Av Ct Iowa City IA 52240

BERGMANN, OTTO, educator, physicist; b. Vienna, Austria, Feb. 7, 1925; s. Anton and Emilie (Firszt) B.; Ph.D., U. Vienna, 1949; m. Joyce M. Dunn, Feb. 12, 1957; children—Anton, Elizabeth. Came to U.S., 1958. Scholar, Dublin Inst. for Advanced Studies, 1951-52; sr. research fellow U. Adelaide, S. Australia, 1952-55; sr. research fellow U. New Eng., N.S.W., Australia, 1955-58; research physicst Research Inst. Advanced Sci., Balt., 1958-61; asso. prof. U. Ala., 1961-62; faculty George Washington U., Washington, 1962—, prof., 1967—, mem. Univ. Senate, 1970—. Mem. Am. Phys. Soc., Am. Assn. U. Profs., Osterreichischer Ingenieur and Architekten Verein, German Sch. Soc., German Lang. Soc., Goethe Gesellschaft, Sigma Xi. Contbr. articles profl. jours. Office: George Washington U Washington DC 20006

BERGMANN, PETER GABRIEL, educator, research physicist; b. Berlin, Germany, Mar. 24, 1915; s. Max and Emmy Miriam (Grunwald) B.; student Dresden, Germany, 1931, Freiburg, Germany, 1932, Prague, Czechoslovakia, 1933; Dr.rer.-nat., 1936; m. Margot Eisenhardt, May 23, 1936; children—Ernest, John. Came to U.S., 1936, naturalized, 1942. Research asst. to Prof. A. Einstein, Inst. Advanced Study, 1936-41; asst. prof. physics Black Mountain Coll., 1941, Lehigh U., 1942-44; war work Columbia, also Woods Hole Oceanog. Inst., 1944-47; asso. prof. physics Syracuse U., 1947-50, prof. physics, 1950—; adj. prof. Poly. Inst. Bklyn., 1947-57; vis. prof. physics Yeshiva U., 1959-63, 70—, prof. physics, chmn. dept. physics Belfer Grad. Sch. Sci., 1963-64; vis. faculty King's Coll., London, also Stockholm, 1958; summer Inst. Italian Math., 1958. Mem. Internat. Commn. on Relativity and Gravitation, 1959—. Trustee New Lincoln Sch., 1963—. Fellow Am. Phys. Soc., A.A.A.S.; mem. Am. Inst. Physics (com. physics faculties in colls.), Am. Math. Soc., German Physics Soc., Fedn. Am. Scientists (chmn. 1964), European Phys. Soc., Sigma Xi. Author grad. texts on relativity, introduction to theoretical physics, also The Riddle of Gravitation. Contbr. research articles to various jours.; articles on spl. and gen. relativity in Ency. of Physics. Asso. editor profl. jours. Office: Dept Physics Syracuse U Syracuse NY 13210

BERGMANN, THEODORE GERARD, advt. exec.; b. Bklyn., Sept. 12, 1920; s. Augustus H. and Johanna (Roman) B.; grad. Gov. Dummer Acad., 1937; student Amherst Coll., 1937- 39; m. Patricia Bull, April 27, 1946; children—Theodore, Donald, David, Jonathan, Lisa, Laura. Began with NBC, N.Y.C., 1941-42, 46-47; successively salesman, dir. sales, gen. mgr. DuMont TV Network, N.Y.C., 1947-54, mng. dir., 1954-56; v.p. McCann-Erickson, Inc., 1956-57; pres. Parkson Advt. Agy., Inc., 1957-60, v.p. advt. Revlon, Inc., 1960-62; pres. Charter Producers Corp., 1962-66; v.p. programs Ted Bates & Co., N.Y.C., 1966—. Served as capt. AUS, 1942-46. Decorated Bronze Star. Mem. Nat. Assn. Radio and TV Broadcasters (dir. 1954-56), Acad. TV Arts and Scis. (nat. trustee), Internat. Radio and TV Soc. (gov. 1957-64). Clubs: Friars (N.Y.C.); Plandome Country. Home: 530 Manhasset Woods Rd Manhasset NY 11030 Office: 666 Fifth St New York City NY 10019

BERGNER, ALLEN ALFRED, naval officer; b. Kankakee, Ill., May 29, 1916; s. Alfred and Harriet (Hess) B.; student Northwestern U., 1935-36; B.S., U.S. Naval Acad., 1940, postgrad. study naval engring., 1946-48; m. Jayne Clark, Oct. 30, 1940; childrenJon C., Barbara A. Commd. ensign USN, 1940, advanced through grades to rear adm., 1967; service assignments include command of 3 submarines, submarine div., submarine tender and submarine squadron; operating staff anti-submarine warfare; staff dir. anti- submarine warfare programs Office Chief Naval Operations; comdr. Naval Tng. Center, San Diego, 1967-70; asst. chief Bur. Naval Personnel For Edn. and Tng., 1970. Served on Naval Ct. of Inquiry USS Pueblo, 1969. Active local Boy Scouts Am., Little League; officer San Diego County Combined Fed. Campaign, United Community Fund. Bds. dirs. Armed Services YMCA, San Diego, San Diego A.R.C. Decorated Legion of Merit, Navy-Marine Corps medal, Bronze Star, Navy Commendation medal. Mem. Phi Kappa Psi. Kiwanian. Research, publs. human factor approach to mil. mgmt. Home: 7002 Tyndale St McLean VA 22101 Office: Bureau Naval Personnel Pers C Navy Dept Washington DC 20370

BERGONZI, CARLO, tenor; b. Polesine, Italy, July 13, 1924; student Parma Conservatory, then trained as baritone. Debut as Figaro in Barber of Seville, Lecce; debut in title role of Andrea Chenier, Bari, 1951; appearances at La Scala, San Carlo Opera, Rome, other leading opera houses in Italy, France, Spain; Am. debut at Chgo. Lyric Theatre, 1955; debut with Met. Opera as Radames in Aida, 1956, now mem. opera co.; debut San Francisco Opera, 1969. Address: care Signor A Ziliani Via Paolo de Cannobio 2 Milan Italy*

BERGQUIST, PETER ALDEN, banker; b. Shickley, Neb., Aug. 5, 1905; s. Peter and Erma H. (Stephenson) B.; student Hastings (Neb.) Coll., 1925-26, U. Neb., 1926- 29; m. Janet Schmitz, Oct. 5, 1932; children—Mary Janet (Mrs. Karl W. Wellensiek), Peggy (Mrs. Charles C. Palmer). With First Nat. Bank Chgo., 1929—, sr. v.p., 1929—. Home: 866 Oak Knoll Dr Lake Forest IL 60045

BERGREN, GUSTAV WALTER, educator; b. S.I., N.Y., Sept. 10, 1917; s. Axel L. and Gudrun (Strom) B.; B.S. in Mech. Engring., Colo. State U., 1940; M.S., Purdue U., 1948; m. Virginia Wilkinson Trice, Sept. 15, 1942; children—Walter W., Paul L. Grad. asst. Purdue U., 1940-41, mem. faculty 1945—, prof. mech. engring., adminstrv. dean acad. affairs regional campus adminstrn., 1966—. Served with USNR, 1941-45. Decorated Letter of Commendation. Registerd profl. engr., Ind. Mem. Am. Soc. Engring. Edn., Am. Soc. M.E., A.A.A.S. Rotarian. Home: 1300 Catula Av Lafayette IN 47905

BERGSMA, DANIEL, med. found. exec.; b. Wallington, N.J., Apr. 4, 1909; s. Chris and Henrietta (Hengeveld) B.; A.B., Oberlin Coll., 1932; M.D., Yale, 1936; M.P.H., U. Mich., 1946; m. Nellie Dorothy Arnold, June 1937; children—Donald Roy, Claire. Chief bur. venereal disease control N.J. Dept. Health, 1940-42, dep. dir., 1946-48, state commnr. health, 1948- 59; asso. dir. med. care Nat. Found., 1959-64, dir. med. dept., 1964- 69, v.p. for med. services, 1968-69; dir. profl. edn. dept., v.p. for propl. edn., 1969—. Mem. Interstate San Commn., N.Y., Conn., N.J., 1951-59, Fed. Water Pollution Control Adv. Bd., 1954-57, conf. dir. 2d Internat. Conf. Congenital Malformations, 1963; mem. adv. bd. state ofcls. AEC; chmn. adv. com. div. occupational health USPHS, 1958, past mem. nat. research pub. health study sect. Bd. dirs. Christian Sanitorium, Wyckoff, N.J. Served from capt. to col., M.C., AUS, 1942-46. Decorated Legion of Merit. Diplomate Am. Bd. Preventive Medicine and Pub. Health. Fellow Am. Pub. Health Assn. (chmn. radiol. health program area com. 1957-58; chmn. nonimating com. 1963), N.Y. Acad. Scis., N.J. Acad. Medicine, A.A.A.S.; mem. Am. Soc. Pub. Adminstrn. (exec. bd. N.J. chapt 1950-52, pres. 1951), Am. Social Hygiene Assn. (hon. life), A.M.A. Editor: Birth Defects: Original Article Series, 1965—), Birth Defects Atlas and Compendium, 1972—. Home: 98 Suncrest Av North Haledon NJ 07508 Office: 800 2d Av New York City NY 10017

BERGSMA, STUART, hosp. supt., psychiatrist; b. Grand Rapids, Mich., Nov. 15, 1900; s. Gerrit and Helen (Meyer) B.; B.A., Calvin Coll., 1922; M.D., U. Chgo., 1927; Dr. Tropical Medicine and Hygiene, London (Eng.) Sch. Tropical Medicine and Hygiene, 1928; m. Mildred Bosma, Sept. 9, 1926; children—Stuart Kenneth, Harold Milton, Joan Ellen (Mrs. Stuart J. Kingma). Intern Los Angeles Gen. Hosp., 1926-27; resident Eastern State Hosp., Williamsburg, Va. 1955-57, Neuro-Psychiat. Inst., U. Mich. 1957-58; med. missionary, surgeon and hosp. supt. U.P. Ch. N.Am., Ethiopia, Africa, 1928-34; practice medicine, specializing in surgery, Passaic, N.J., 1935-38, Grand Rapids, 1943-49; med. missionary U.P. Ch., India, 1939-43; med. missionary, surgeon, hosp. supt., asso. prof. surgery Ludhiana Christian Med. Coll., Punjab, India under Christian Reform Ch., Grand Rapids, Mich., 1949-53; generalist-psychiatrist Pine Rest Christian Hosp., Grand Rapids, 1953- 55, psychiatrist, clin. dir., 1959-64, supt., 1964—; resident psychiatry Eastern State Hosp., Williamsburg, Va., 1955-57, Neuro- Psychiat. Inst., U. Mich. Hosp., Ann Arbor, 1957-58; practice medicine, specializing in psychiatry, Grand Rapids, 1958—. Mem. Bd. Fgn. Missions Christian Reformed Ch., 1954-55; mem. Kent County Community Mental Health Services Bd., 1967—. Diplomate Am. Bd. Psychiatry and Neurology. Fellow A.C.S., Royal Soc. Tropical Medicine and Hygiene (London); mem. A.M.A., Mich., Kent County med. socs., Am. Psychiat. Assn., Christian Med. Soc. Author: Rainbow Empire, 1932; Sons of Sheba, 1933; Just One Small Choir, Gabriel, 1964; Speaking With Tongues, 1965; See That Holy Child, Gabriel, 1968; also articles. Home: 3791 Shaffer Av SE Grand Rapids MI 49508 Office: 6850 S Division Av Grand Rapids MI 49508

BERGSMA, WILLIAM LAURENCE, composer; b. Oakland, Cal. Apr. 1, 1921; s. William Joseph and Helen Margaret (Doepfner) B.; student Stanford, 1938-40; teaching fellow Eastman Sch. Music, 1942-44; A.B., U. Rochester, 1942, M.Mus., 1943; m. Nancy Nickerson, 1946. Chmn. composition dept., also chmn. dept. lit. and materials of music, asso. dean Juilliard Sch., 1961-63; dir. School of Music, U. Wash., Seattle, 1963-71. Recipient Town Hall, commn. for Symphony for Chamber Orch., 1942; Bearns prize for String Quartet No. 1, 1943; Koussevitzky Found. Commn., 1943-44; grant Am. Acad. Arts and Letters and Nat. Inst. Arts and Letters, 1945; award Soc. for Publ. Am. Music, 1945; Guggenheim fellow, 1946, 51; Collegiate Chorale Commn., 1946; commn. from Carl Fischer, Inc., for 25th anniversary of League of Composers, 1947; Juilliard Found. Commn., 1953-62; Louisville Commn., 1953; Elizabeth Sprague Coolidge Commn., 1956; Collegiate Choral of Ill. Wesleyan U. Commn., 1956; 1st ann. Edwin Franco Goldman Meml. Commn., 1957; Harvard Mus. Soc. Commn., 1961; Portland Jr. Symphony Commn., 1960; Mid-Am. Chorale Commn., 1963; Mus. Arts Soc. La Jolla Commn., 1965; Phi Beta Commn., 1966; Am. Choral Dirs. Assn. Commn., 1967; Kansas City Youth Symphony Commn., 1967; U. Ala. for Gadek Quarter, 1970; Poncho and Brechemin Family Found. Commn., 1971. Mem. Nat. Inst. Arts and Letters, Phi Beta Kappa, Phi Mu Alpha. Composer: Gold and the Señor Commandante (ballet), 1942; First Quartet, 1942; Symphony for Chamber Orchestra, 1942; Music on a Quiet Theme (orchestra), 1943; Second Quartet, 1944; Six Songs, 1945; Suite from Children's Film, 1945; Symphony, 1949; The Fortunate Islands (string orchestra), 1947, rev. 1956; Tangents (piano solo), 1951; Third Quartet, 1953; A Carol on Twelfth Night (orchestra), 1953; The Wife of Martin Guerre (3 act opera), 1955, rev. 1958; Riddle Me This (3 choruses), 1956; March with Trumpets (band), 1957; Concerto for Woodwind Quintet, 1958; Chameleon Variations (orchestra), 1960; Fantastic Variations (viola and piano), 1961; In Celebration; Toccata for the Sixth Day (orch.), 1962; Confrontation from the Book of Job (chorus, orch.), 1963; Documentary One (orch.), 1963; Serenade to Await the Moon (orch.), 1965; Concerto for Violin and Orchestra, 1966; The Sun, The Soaring Eagle, The Turquoise Prince, The God (chorus, brass, percussion), 1967; Documentary Two (Orch.), 1967; Illegible Canons (clarinet, percussion), 1969; Fourth Quartet, 1970; Changes (solo woodwind quintet, harp, percussion, strings), 1971; Changes for Seven (solo woodwind quintet, percussion, piano), 1971. Office: care School of Music U Wash Seattle WA 98105

BERGSON, ABRAM, economist; b. Balt., Apr. 21, 1914; s. Issac Burk and Sophia (Rabinovich) B.; A.B., Johns Hopkins, 1933; Ph.D., Harvard, 1940; m. Rita S. Macht, Nov. 4, 1939; children—Judith, Emily, Lucy. Instr. econs. Harvard, 1937-38, 1939-40; asst. prof. econs. U. Tex., 1940-42; economist various agys. Fed. Govt., 1942-46; mem. U.S. delgation Moscow Reparations Conf., summer, 1945; asso. prof. econs. Columbia, 1946-50, prof., 1950-56; prof. econs. Harvard, 1956-71, George F. Baker prof. econs., 1971—, dir. the Russian Research Center, 1964-68; cons. Rand Corp., 1948—. Mem. social sci. adv. bd. U.S. Arms Control and Disarmament Agy., 1966—. Fellow Econometric Soc., Am. Acad. Arts and Scis.; mem. Am. Philos. Soc., Am. Econ. Assn., Social Sci. Research Council (dir.-at-large 1963-69). Jewish religion. Author: Structure of Soviet Wages, 1944; Economics of Soviet Planning, 1964; Essays in Normative Economics, 1966; Planning and Productivity under Soviet Socialism, 1968; also other books, and various articles in profl. econ. jours. Co-editor: Economic Trends in the Soviet Union, 1963. Home: 113 Walker St Cambridge MA 02138

BERGSON, HERBERT AUGUSTUS, lawyer; b. Boston, Jan. 14, 1909; s. Harry and Augusta (Cook) B.; student Boston Latin Sch., 1920-26; A.B., Harvard, 1930, LL.B., 1933; m. Bernice A. Weber, Sept. 22, 1933; children—Richard W., Barbara C. (dec.), Paul C., Mary K. Admitted to Mass. bar, 1933, practiced in Boston, 1933-34, Washington, 1950—; trial atty. claims div., Dept. Justice, 1934-36, asst. chief legislation, 1936-43, chief legislation, 1945-48, cons. to atty. gen., 1946-47, acting asst. atty. gen. claims div., 1947-48, exec. asst. to atty. gen., 1948, asst. atty. gen. charge of anti-trust div., June 1948-Sept. 1950; gen. counsel O.D.M. 1951; mem. firm Bergson, Borkland, Margolis and Adler, Washington. Served to lt. USCGR, 1944-45. Mem. Am. (chmn. sect. antitrust law 1957-58), Fed. bar assns., Bar Assn. D.C. Clubs: Harvard, Army and Navy, Nat. Capital Democratic (Washington). Editor: Federal Bar Jour, 1947-48. Home: 2015 Plymouth St Washington DC 20012 Office: 888 17th St NW Washington DC 20006

BERGSON, MARIA, designer; b. Vienna, Austria; d. Egon F. and Therese (Schey) Bergson; came to U.S., 1940, naturalized, 1944; m. Thomas L. Brunner, Jan. 1, 1942. Entered field of indsl. and interior design, specializing in planning and design of offices, banks, hotels, hosps., stores, other comml. interiors; also product design, fabrics, displays and graphic arts; mem. firm Maria Bergson Assos. Exhibited Phila. Art Alliance, 1948, Archtl. League, 1954, various travelling exhibits U.S. and abroad. Recipient Ann. Merit award Chicago Bldg. Congress, 1964; Food Service Honor award Institutions mag., 1964. Fellow Internat. Inst. Arts and Letters; mem. Archtl. League N.Y., Mus. Modern Art, N.Y.C. Postal Council, Indsl. Designers Inst. Episcopalian. Home: 140 E 72d St New York City, NY 10021. Office: 595 Madison Av New York City NY 10022 also 8749 Holloway Dr Los Angeles, CA 90069.

BERGSTEIN, LEONARD, educator, scientist; b. Bilgoraj, Poland, Sept. 1, 1928; s. Shalom and Zlata (Silverminz) B.; ed. U. Vienna (Austria), 1946-47, Tech. U. Stuttgart (Germany), 1947-51; postgrad. Columbia, 1952-57; postgrad. Bklyn. Polytech. Inst., 1958-59, Ph.D. in Physics, 1959; m. Sarah Elallouf, Sept. 8, 1960; children—Solomon Shalom, David Rafael, Ethel. Came to U.S., 1951, naturalized, 1957. Optical engr. Zoomar Corp., Glen Cove, N.Y., 1952-56; mem. faculty City U. N.Y., 1959-60, distinguished vis. prof., 1965-66; mem. faculty Bklyn. Polytech. Inst., 1960—, prof. electro-optical scis., 1965—; vis. prof. Technion-Israel Inst., Haifa, 1967-68; chmn. acad. supervisory council Holon (Israel) U., 1969—; cons. to industry, 1956—. Fellow Optical Soc. Am.; mem. Am. Inst. Physics, I.E.E.E., Phi Beta Kappa, Sigma Xi, Eta Kappa Nu. Research, publs. fields of optics and electro-optics. Patentee in field. Home: 191 Willoughby St Brooklyn, NY 11201.

BERGSTRAND, WILTON EVERET, clergyman; b. Bloomington, Ill., July 16, 1909; s. Rev. John Ivard and Esther (Jernberg) B.; B.A., Gustavus Adolphus Coll., 1930, D.D., 1949; B.D., Augustana Theol. Sem., 1935; m. Dolores Youngren, Oct. 17, 1953; children—John Wilton, Paul William, Lori Esther. Ordained to ministry Lutheran Ch., 1935; prof. English, speech Gustavus Adolphus Coll., 1930-32; pastor Gloria Dei Luth. Ch. Duluth, 1935-38; youth dir. Augustana Luth. Ch., Mpls., 1938-63, chaplain hdqrs., 1942-63, lectr., tchr. Bible, camp program dir., 1963-64; pastor Luth. Ch. of Holy Trinity, Jamestown, N.Y.; dir. internat. youth confs., leadership schs., Bible camps; producer filmstrip series. Chmn. commn. young peoples work Am. Luth Conf., 1943-48; del. World Conf. Christian Youth, Oslo, Norway, 1947; Augustana rep. orgn. meeting Luth., World Fedn., Lund, Sweden, 1947. Mem. Bd. College Edn., Luth. Church in Am. Mem. Greater Gustavus Assn. (pres.). Am. Scandinavian Found., World Council Christian Edn., World Council Chs., (youth dept.). Author: Stitch in Time, 1940; Luther League Scrapbook, 1942; All Smiles, 1943; Centennial Programs, 1945; The Bugles are Calling, 1946; God's Outstretched Hand, 1947; Good Counsel for Counselors, 1956; Leadership, 1956; Youth Round the World, pub. 1958; Youth's Favorite Chuckles, 1958; Christ Unites Us. Co-author: Public Speaking Question-ette, 1942; To Light A Candle, 1946; Open Doors, 1949; Who Will Go?, 1947; Luther League Handbook, 1950; A Leaders Guide, 1950; Dynamic District Leagues, 1950; Living High in High School, 1953; Banquet Lore, 1954; Adventuring with Christ in Church Staff Vocations, 1955; Bible Camp Check List, 1956; Bible Study Notes, 1956. Co-editor: Youth's Favorite Poems, vols. 1-7; Youth's Favorite Songs; Uniting Word: All Yours; The Bible and the Devotional Life, 1970; also numerous mag. articles. Home 95 E Virginia Blvd Jamestown NY 14701 Office: 825 Forest Av Jamestown NY 14701

BERGSTROM, DEDRIC WALDEMAR, paper co. exec.; b. Neenah, Wis., Aug. 21, 1919; s. D. Waldemar and Agnes (Forsythe) B.; grad. Northwestern Mil. and Naval Acad., Lake Geneva, Wis., 1936; student Lawrence Coll., Appleton, Wis., 1936-37; U. Minn., 1938; m. Jane Katherine Gibson, June 14, 1941; children—Dedric Waldemar IV, John F., Richard A., Jennifer M., William A. With Bergstrom Paper Co., Neenah, 1936—, successively gen. mill, office work, purchasing agt., treas., 1950-56, dir., 1950—, dir. purchases, 1950-71, dir. prodn. planning and scheduling, 1957- 71, v.p., sec., 1956-62, exec. v.p., 1962—; dir. Twin City Savs. and Loan Assn., First Nat. Bank of Neenah. Vice pres. Bergstrom Found., 1962—; bd. regents Campion High Sch., 1968—. Served to maj. AUS, 1942-45. Mem. Wis. Paper & Pulp Mfrs. Traffic Assn. (dir.). Roman Catholic. Club: Bergstrom Paper Co. Management. Home: 835 River Lane Neenah WI 54956 Office: Bergstrom Rd Neenah WI 54956

BERGSTROM, NATHAN HOUGH, paper co. exec.; b. Neenah, Wis., Apr. 25, 1895; s. Dedrick W. and Sarah (Hough) B.; student Lawrence Coll., 1912-16; m. Agnes E. Birdsall, June 12, 1919; children—Alice P. (Mrs. Haigh R. Moore), Marjorie S. (Mrs. Franklin Moore, Jr.), Natalie J. (Mrs. H. T. Rindal); m. 2d, Ernestine P. Waite, October 13, 1967. With Bergstrom Paper Co., Neenah, 1915- -, dir., 1919-, treas., 1921-28, sec., 1928-35, v.p., sec., 1935-44, v.p., 1944-48, pres., 1948-62, chmn. bd., 1962-70, hon. chmn. bd., 1970—; dir. First Nat. Bank of Neenah. Mem. city water commn., Neenah, 1947-49; mem. adv. council on library devel., 1965—; mem. nat. Nat. Book Commn., 1965—. Treas., dir. Boys' Brigade Assn., 1929-58; Mfrs. trustee Theda Clark Meml. Hosp., 1949—, chmn. 1958-65. Served with U.S. Army, 1917-19. Mem. Am. Paper and Pulp Assn., Printing Paper Mfrs. Assn., Newcomen Soc. Home: 561 E Wisconsin Av Neenah WI 54956 Office: Bergstrom Paper Co Hwy 41 Neenah WI 54956

BERGSTROM, ROBERT WILLIAM, lawyer; b. Chgo., Nov. 8, 1918; s. C. William and Ellen (Anderson) B.; M.B.A., U. Chgo., 1947; LL.B., Chgo. Kent Coll. Law, 1940, J.D., 1970; m. Ruth Doyle, May 29, 1946; children—Mark Robert, Philip Alan. Admitted to Ill. bar, 1940, also U.S. Supreme Ct.; practice in Chgo., 1940—; partner firm Bergstrom, Rohde, Dahlgren and Olson, and predecessors, 1951—. Legislative asst. Better Govt. Assn. Chgo., 1940-41; participant in drafting, presentation to legislature Ill. Anti-trust Act of 1956; bd. dirs. Ill. Com. Constl. Conv., 1969—, Ill. Constl. Research Group, 1961—; spl. counsel Ill. Joint Legislative Com. to Investigate Met. San. Dist. of Cook County, Ill., 1967, Ill. Senate Municipal Corp. Com., 1970; chmn. Glenbrook (Ill.) Village Caucus, 1961, Elementary Sch. Caucus, Glenview, 1959. Served to lt. USNR, 1942-46. Named Chicagoan of Year in Law and Jurisprudence, 1969. Mem. Ill. (exec. council antitrust sect. 1967), Chgo. (sec. 1969-71); Am. bar assns., Chgo. Assn. Commerce and Industry. Clubs: Executives, Union League (1st v.p. 1970—). Co-author: The Law of Competition in Illinois, 1962. Author articles in field. Home: 820 Windsor Rd Glenview IL 60025 Office: 39 S LaSalle St Chicago IL 60603

BERGSTROM, SWAN EBERHARDT, ret. engring. exec.; b. Rosholt, S.D., Feb. 11, 1902; s. Swan and Anna (Smith) B.; student Purdue, 1921-23, M. Industry (hon.), 1948; m. Dorothy Baldwin, Sept. 24, 1925 (dec. June 1959); one dau., Judith Lynne; m. second, Ruth Burkhard, December 17, 1960. Tool engr., 1923-25; sales engr. Nat. Automatic Tool Co., 1925-27; sales engr., sales mgr. Cin. Milling and Grinding Machines, Inc., 1927-50; v.p. and dir., Cin. Milling Machine Co. 1951-56, exec. v.p., 1956-58, pres., 1958-63, chmn. bd., 1963-70, ret. Dir. metal working equipment div. NPA, 1951-52. Mem. Am. Soc. Tool Engrs., Soc. Automotive Engrs., Cin. Engring. Soc. Mason. Clubs: Queen City, Makatewal Country, Commercial. Home: 3863 Crayton Rd Naples FL 33940

BERGUS, DONALD CLAYTON, fgn. service officer; b. South Bend, Ind., Feb. 26, 1920; s. George Nicholas and Grace Velma (Sprankle) B.; A.B., U. Chgo., 1942; student U. Pa., 1949-50, Nat. War Coll., 1959; m. Elizabeth Ravdin, May 18, 1950; children— Elizabeth Grace, George Ravdin, Priscilla Mary. Joined U.S. Fgn. Service, 1942; officer Am. embassy, Baghdad, 1942-45, Athens, Greece, 1945-46, Patras, 1946-47, Beirut, 1947-48, Jidda, 1948-59, Paris, 1959-62, Cairo, 1962-65, State Dept., 1965-67; prin. officer U.S. interests sect. Embassy of Spain, Cairo, Egypt, 1967—. Mem. U.S. delgation to funeral Gamal Abdul Nasser, 1970. Recipient Arthur Flemming award Outstanding Man in Govt., 1955. Home: Am embassy Box 10 FPO New York City NY 09527 Office: US Interests Section Embassy of Spain Cairo Egypt

BERGWALL, EVAN HAROLD, clergyman; b. Jamestown, N.Y., Sept. 16, 1915; s. A. Elof and Alice H. (Lund) B.; A.B., Taylor U., 1939; B.D., Yale (Tew prize 1942, Julia Archibald High scholar, Day fellow 1943), 1943; postgrad. Yale, N.Y.U., Emory U., Oxford (Eng.) U., D.D., Asbury Theol. Sem., 1955; m. Jean Mitchell Francis, Aug. 30, 1941; children—Evan Harold, David Francis. Ordained to ministry Methodist Ch., 1941; minister Bethelship Ch., Bklyn., 1941-43, Grace Ch., Waterbury, Conn., 1943-45, Lexington Av. Ch., N.Y.C., 1945-48, High St. Ch., Muncie, Ind., 1948-49, First Ch., Kendallville, Ind., 1949-51; pres. Taylor U., Upland, Ind., 1951-59; minister Simpson Methodist Ch., Ft. Wayne, Ind., 1959-67; supt. Elkhart dist. N. Ind. Conf., 1967—. Goodwill ambassador to Meth. Ch. in Germany, 1950; visitor mission stas. Meth. Ch. in Congo and Rhodesia, summer 1963, 70, Middle East, 1953, 63, 70; mem. staff Ft. Wayne Counseling Center of Meth. Ch.; del. Gen. and Jurisdictional confs. Meth. Ch., 1968. Chmn. bd. dirs. Basher Home of United Meth. Ch., Goshen; pres., bd. dirs. Bethel Meth. Home for Aged, Ossining, N.Y., 1947-48; bd. dirs. Child Care Found. Recipient Widsom Award of Honor, 1970. Mem. Am. Assn. Sch. Adminstrs., N.E.A., N. Ind. Conf. Meth. Ch., Chi Alpha Omega. Contbr. religious publs. Address: 1721 Meadowood Dr Elkhart IN 46514

BERHENKE, MARGARET ELIZABETH (Mrs. Luther Frederick Berhenke), church ofcl.; b. Iowa City, June 15, 1910; d. Elijah Asa and Bessie (Elerick) Thomas; B.A., U. Ia., 1931, M.S., 1933, Ph.D., 1935; m. Luther F. Berhenke, June 4, 1935; childrenMartha (Mrs. James Ronald Sherrard), Frederick Thomas. Mem. women's orgn. United Presbyn. Ch., 1935-, mem. Commn. Ecumenical Mission and Relations, 1961-64, nat. pres. United Presbyn. Women, 1964-67; pres. Provisional League Women Voters Midland City and County, 1967—; mem.-at-large gen. council Synod Mich., United Presbyn. Ch. U.S.A., 1968—. Mem. Gen. Fedn. Women's Clubs, Phi Beta Kappa, Sigma Xi (asso.), Phi Mu, Iota Sigma Pi. Address: 4214 Chelsea Ct Midland, MI 48640.

BERICK, MORRIS, lawyer; b. Kobrin, Russia, Mar. 22, 1894; s. Albraham Z. and Bessie (Silberston) B.; came to U.S., 1904, naturalized, 1913; A.B., Columbia, 1916, LL.B., 1918; m. Rebecca Gerdy, Aug. 16, 1923; children—Joseph G., James H. Admitted to Ohio bar, 1918, since practiced in Cleve.; partner firm Burke, Haber & Berick, 1922—. Chmn. adv. bd. Juvenile Ct. and Detention Home. Recipient Profl. Service award Nat. Legal Aid and Defender Assn., 1964. Mem. Cleve. Bar Assn. (pres. 1965-66; fellow found. 1966), Phi Beta Kappa. Home: 13720 Shaker Blvd Cleveland OH 44120 Office: Union Commerce Bldg Cleveland OH 44115

BERINGER, E. ROBERT, educator, physicist; b. Pitts., Oct. 14, 1917; s. Edward W. and Lenore (Pennell) B.; B.S., Washington and Jefferson Coll., 1939; Ph.D., Yale, 1942; m. Ruth Kaolin McVeigh, Oct. 17, 1942; children—Michael, John, Robert. With radiation lab. Mass. Inst. Tech., 1942-46; mem. faculty Yale, 1946—, now prof., physics, dir. heavy ion accelerator lab., fellow Calhoun Coll.; research microwave spectroscopy, nuclear acceleration devel. Mem. Am. Phys. Soc. Home: 3997 Whitney Av Mount Carmel CT 06518 Office: Dept Physics Yale U New Haven CT 06520

BERINGER, FREDERICK MARSHALL, chemist, educator; b. N.Y.C., May 8, 1920; s. Albert F. and Elizabeth (Marshall) B.; B.S., Harvard, 1941; M.S., Columbia, 1944, Ph.D., 1947; m. Priscilla J. Schumacher, Nov. 20, 1944; 1 son, Bruce Clay. Organic chemist Allied Chem. Corp., 1941-43; with Rockefeller Inst., 1947; mem. faculty Poly. Inst. Bklyn., 1948—, prof. organic chemistry, 1959—, head chemistry dept., 1964-68, acting dean of sci., 1967-68, dean of science, 1968—. Mem. Am. Chem. Soc., A.A.A.S., Chem. Soc. (London). Editor: Am. Chem. Soc. Monographs, 1964—. Contbr. articles profl. jours. Home: 800 Fenimore Rd Larchmont, NY 10538. Office: 333 Jay St Brooklyn NY 11201

BERIO, LUCIANO, composer, conductor, educator; b. Imperia Oneglia, Italy, Oct. 24, 1925; s. Ernesto Filippo and Ada (Dal Fiume) B.; student Liceo Classico, 1936- 43; grad. composition and orch. conducting, Conservatorio G. Verdi, Milan, 1951; m. Cathy Berberian, Oct. 1, 1950 (div.); 1 dau., Christina Luisa; m. 2d, Susan Oyama, 1964; children—Marina and Stefano. Founder, 1954, Studio de Fonologia Musicale for electronic music at Italian Radio; founder, 1954, musical rev. Incontri Musicali; tchr. composition Berkshire Festival, 1960, Dartington Summer Sch., 1961, 62, Mills Coll., 1962, 63, Darmstadt Ferienkurse, 1963; tchr. at Juilliard Sch. Music, 1965, also seminars at Harvard, 1966. Composer: Tre Iriche popolari, 1948; Magnificat, 1948; Due Pezzi, 1950; 5 Variazioni, 1951; Chamber Music, 1953; Variazioni, 1953; El Mar la Mar, 1953; Mimusique 1, 1953; Mimusique 2, 1953; Nones, 1954; Quartetto, 1955; Perspectives, 1956; Allelujah II, 1956-57, Serenata, 1957; Thema, 1958; Sequenza, 1958; Allez-Hop, 1953-59; Differences, 1959; Tempi Concertati, 1958-59; Circles, 1960; Momenti, 1960; Epifanie, 1959-61; Visage, 1961; Passaggio 1962; Sequenza II, 1963; Passaggio, 1963; Rounds, 1964; Traces, 1964; Sincronie, 1965; Chemins, 1965; Sequenza III, IV, V, 1966; Folk Songs, 1964; Laborintus, 1965; Gesti, 1966; Chemins II, 1967; Chemins III, 1968; Sinfonia, 1968; Questo Vuol Dire Che, 1969; Opera, 1970; Memory, 1971; Bewegung, 1971; Prayer, 1971. Numerous recordings. Address: 53 Potter Pl Weehawken NJ 07087

BERK, ALAN, corp. exec.; b. N.Y.C., May 11, 1934; s. Phil W. and Mae (Buchberg) B.; B.S. in Econs., Wharton Sch., U. Pa., 1955; M.S., Columbia, 1956; m. Barbara Diane Binder, Dec. 18, 1960; children—Charles Martin, Peter Marshall, Nancy Muriel. With Arthur Young & Co., C.P.A.'s 1956-67, mgr., 1962-66, prin., 1966-67; controller Avco Corp., 1967—, v.p., 1969—; treas., dir. Avco Devel. Corp.; controller Paul Revere Investors, Inc.; v.p., controller Paul Revere Realty; supervisory dir. Avco Overseas Capital Corp. N.V.; dir. Avco Broadcasting Corp., Avco Radio Corp., Cartridge TV, Inc., Carte Blanche Corp. Lectr., Am. Mgmt. Assn., 1962—. Pres. Windsor Park Civic Assn., 1967-68. Served with AUS, 1957-61. C.P.A., N.Y. Mem. Am. Inst. C.P.A.'s, N.Y. State Soc. C.P.A.'s, Financial Execs. Inst. (Westchester chpt.), A.I.M. (fellow pres. council). Club: Board Room (N.Y.C.). Home: Cornelia Dr Greenwich CT 06830 Office: 1275 King St Greenwich CT 06830

BERK, ALFRED GOODMAN, former aluminum co. exec.; b. Chelsea, Mass., Aug. 8, 1905; s. Morris and Sarah (Goodman) B.; grad Bentley Coll. Accounting and Finance, 1935; m. Reva Hart, Oct. 7, 1934; 1 dau., Carolyn (Mrs. Alan Stamler). With Harvey Aluminum, Inc., 1946-71, asst. treas., 1962-71, ret. Served with AUS, World War II. Mem. Am. Ordnance Assn., Nat. Assn. Accountants. Home: 13222A Admiral Av Marina Del Rey CA 90291

BERK, JACK EDWARD, physician, educator; b. Phila., Nov. 24, 1911; s. Samuel and Esther (Pill) B.; A.B., U. Pa., 1932, M.S., 1939, D.Sc., 1943; M.D., Jefferson Med. Coll., 1936; m. Adeline Elizabeth Alberts, June 26, 1937; children—Philip Howard, Richard Hanna. Intern Walter Reed Gen. Hosp., Washington, 1936-37; resident No. div. Albert Einstein Med. Center, Phila., 1938-39; fellow gastroenterology Grad. Hosp., U. Pa., 1939-40; Ross V. Patterson fellow physiology Jefferson Med. Coll., Phila., 1940-41, instr. gastroenterology Grad. Sch. Medicine, 1941-46; asst. prof. medicine Sch. Medicine, Temple U., 1946-54, asst. dir. Fels Research Inst., 1946-54; asso. prof. clin. medicine Coll. Medicine, Wayne State U., 1954-62, prof. clin. medicine, 1962-63; prof., chmn. dept. medicine Coll. Medicine, U. Cal. at Irvine, 1963—; vis. lectr. Grad. Sch. Medicine, U. Pa., 1961—; cons. VA Hosp., Long Beach, Cal., 1963—, Cedars of Lebanon Hosp., 1963—, Mt. Sinai Hosp., 1963—, White Meml. Hosp., 1963—, Meml. Hosp., Long Beach, 1964- -, Sinai Hosp., Detroit, 1963—. U.S. Dept. State rep. to S.Am. countries Cultural Exchange Program, 1961. Served to maj., M.C., AUS, 1941-46. Recipient Distinguished Service award Mich. Med. Soc., 1959; Rudolf Schindler award Am. Soc. Gastro-intestinal Endoscopy, 1966; Rorer award Am. Coll. Gastroenterology, 1970; Faculty Community Service award U. Cal. at Irvine Alumni Assn., 1971. Diplomate Am. Bd. Internal Medicine (subspecialty bd. gastroenterology). Fellow A.C.P.; mem. Am. Gastroent. Assn., Am. Soc. Gastrointestinal Endoscopy (Rudolf Schindler award 1966, past pres.), Am. Fedn. Clin. Research (past chmn. Eastern sect.), Bockus Internat. Soc. Gastroenterology (pres. 1967-71), Am. Coll. Gastroenterology, A.M.A. (chmn. sect. gastroenterology, 1965-66), Detroit Gastroent. Soc. (past pres.), Soc. Exptl. Biology and Medicine, So. Cal. Soc. Gastroenterology (past pres.), A.A.A.S., N.Y. Acad. Scis., Internat. Soc. Internal Medicine, Los Angeles Acad. Medicine; hon. mem. Acad. Med. Ecuador; corr. mem. Soc. Gastroenterology Columbia, Ecuador, Venezuela and Brazilian Soc. of Gastroenterology and Nutrition, Sigma Xi, Alpha Omega Alpha, Pi Gamma Mu. Editorial bd. Current Therapeutic Research, 1959—; Cal. Medicine, 1963—, Am. Jour. Gastroenterology, 1971—. Contbr. chpts. to books, articles to med. jours. Home: 894-C Ronda Sevilla Laguna Hills CA 92653 Office: 101 Manchester Orange CA 92668

BERK, VIOLA GREENHUT, broadcasting co. exec.; b. Cleve., Sept. 21, 1900; d. Max and Gizella M. (Edelstein) Greenhut; student Case Western Reserve U., 1917-19; B.A., Stetson U., 1920; m. S. Bernard Berk, Aug. 28, 1919; children—Roger G., James L. With Summit Radio, Akron, O., 1940—, writer, 1940—, producer, 1940-65, pres., 1966—; dir. WAKR Radio and WAKR-TV, Akron, 1940—, WONE Radio, Dayton, O., 1967—. Bd. dirs. Akron Gen. Hosp. Rotarian. Clubs: Akron City; Rosemont Country. Home: 2365 Covington Rd Akron OH 44313 Office: 853 Copley Rd Akron OH 44320

BERKAW, GEORGE ROBINSON, Jr., banker; b. Colechester, Ont., Can., July 29, 1908; s. George R. and Isabelle R. (Darge) B.; brought to U.S., 1908; A.B., Wayne State U., 1930; M.B.A., Harvard, 1932; m. Helen Joan Baldwin, May 25, 1935; childrenElizabeth Joan (Mrs. Swanson), Margaret Ruth (Mrs. Gerber), David Baldwin, John Darge. Security analyst Union Guardian Trust Co., 1932-33; security analyst, account mgr. Investment Counsel, Inc., 1933-35; with The Detroit Bank, 1935-, successively security analyst, asst. cashier, asst. v.p., 1935-54, v.p., mgr. bond investment dept., 1954-58, v.p., mgr. trust investment dept., 1958-67, sr. v.p., 1967—, (bank now Detroit Bank & Trust Co.). Spl. lectr. U. Mich. Sch. Bus. Adminstrn. Bd. dirs. Met. Detroit YMCA, 1953-, 2d v.p., 1957-60, treas., 1955-57, 60-63; trustee YMCA Found. Met. Detroit, 1958—, treas., 1958-62, pres., 1962-69; trustee, treas. Wayne U. Found., 1952-61; trustee Wayne Alumni Fund, 1958-, pres., 1961-62; trustee, sec. Jack Kittler Found., 1953—; trustee Olivet Coll., 1966—, treas., 1969—. Mem. Nat. Fedn. Financial Analysts Socs. (past dir.), Financial Analysts Soc. Detroit (past pres.), Econ. Club Detroit, Wayne State U. Alumni Assn. (past dir., sec.), Inst. Chartered Financial Analysts (charter). Conglist. Clubs: Detroit, Harvard Bus. Sch. (past pres.) (Detroit). Home: 14231 Penrod St Detroit, MI 48223. Office: 211 W Fort St Detroit MI 48231

BERKE, NATHAN R., lawyer; b. Detroit, July 23, 1912; s. Joseph and Sarah (Garrison) B.; A.B., U. Mich., 1931, LL.B., 1933, J.D., 1968; postgrad. Harvard, 1940; m. Miriam R. Levin, Dec. 28, 1932; 1 dau., Tricia Margot. Admitted to Mich. bar, 1933, Cal. bar, 1951; practice in Detroit, 1933-42, San Francisco, 1954—; atty. fed. govt. agys., 1942-47; atty., hearing officer NLRB, 1947-54; asso. Severson, Davis & McCallum, 1954-55; sr. partner Severson, Werson, Berke & Melchior, San Francisco, 1955—. Dir. Diversified Services, Inc., Budget Rent-A-Car of Miami, Inc. Mem. Cal. Republican Central Com., 1969—. Recipient medallion in appreciation for vol. service Nat. Jewish Hosp., Denver, 1969, plaque from Pres. Nixon for service in 1968 campaign. Mem. Am., Cal., San Francisco, Mich. bar assns., Am. Judicature Soc. Jewish religion. Clubs: World Trade, Merchants Exchange (San Francisco). Author: Design for Foreign Policy, 1969. Contbr. articles profl. jours. Home: 726 El Camino Del Mar San Francisco CA 94121 Office: 433 California St San Francisco CA 94104

BERKELEY, AUSTIN WEST, educator; b. Freeport, Me., Sept. 2, 1914; s. James Percival and Grace Isabelle (Lane) B.; A.B., Bowdoin Coll., 1936; Ph.D., Clark U., 1950; m. Jane Chalfant McConnell, Sept. 21, 1940; children—Charles Melvin, Pennell Jane, Heather Anne. Psychologist, Worcester (Mass.) State Hosp., 1940-52; mem. faculty Boston U., 1952—, prof. psychology, 1958—, chmn. dept. Coll. Liberal Arts and Grad. Sch., 1959-67. Served to capt. AUS, World War II. Mem. Am., Mass. (pres. 1958-60) psychol. assns., Am. Statis. Assn., A.A.A.S. Author: (with L. Alexander, Alene M. Alexander) Multiple Sclerosis: Prognosis and Treatment, 1961. Home: 133 Burgess Av Westwood MA 02090 Office: 64 Cummington St Boston MA 02215

BERKELEY, BUSBY (William Berkeley Enos), dance dir.; b. Los Angeles, Nov. 29, 1895. Started career on N.Y. stage, later joined Warner Bros.; joined MGM, 1939. Pictures include: 42nd Street, Footlight Parade, Hollywood Hotel, Men Are Such Fools, Broadway Serenade, Strike Up the Band, Fast and Furious, Ziegfeld Girl, For Me and My Gal, Gang's All Here, Cinderella Jones, Take Me Out to the Ball Game, Two Weeks with Love, Call Me Mister, Two Tickets to Broadway, Million Dollar Mermaid, Small Town Girl, Easy to Love, Rose Marie. Address: Palm Desert CA 92260*

BERKELEY, LENNOX RANDAL, composer; b. Boars Hill, Oxford, Eng., May 12, 1903; s. Hastings G.F. and Aline (Harris) B.; B.A., Merton Coll., Oxford (Eng.) U., pupil of Nadia Boulanger, 1928-32; m. Elizabeth Freda Bernstein, Dec. 14, 1946; children—Michael, Julian, Nicholas. Mem. music staff BBC, 1942-45; prof. composition Royal Acad. Music, London, Eng., 1946—. Decorated comdr. Order British Empire; Ordre de Merite Cultural (Monaco). Compositions include: (3 act opera) Nelson, 1953; (1 act opera) A Dinner Engagement, 1954; (1 act opera) Ruth, 1956; (1 act opera) Castaway, 1967; also chamber, orchestral choral music, and piano pieces. Address: 8 Warwick Av London W.2, England.

BERKELEY, NORBORNE, Jr., banker; b. Bethlehem, Pa., June 5, 1922; s. Norborne and Dorothea (Randolph) B.; B.A., Yale, 1945; LL.B., U. Va., 1949; m. Diane Gould, June 1951; children-Sally, Anne, Norborne III. Admitted to N.Y. bar, 1950; asso. firm Root, Ballantine, Harlan, Bushby & Palmer, N.Y.C., 1949- 50; with Chem. Bank, N.Y.C., 1950—, exec. v.p., 1968—; dir. Microdot Inc., Greenwich, Conn., Chem. Internat. Finance Ltd., N.Y.C., Chem. Internat. Banking Corp., N.Y.C. Treas. Nat. Fund for Med. Edn., Inc., 1969—. Bd. advisers Pace Coll., N.Y.C.; trustee New Canaan (Conn.) Country Sch.; trustee Nat. Recreation and Park Assn., Washington, treas., 1965—. Served with AUS, 1943-45; ETO. Republican. Episcopalian. Clubs: Links, Yale (N.Y.C.); Nat. Golf Links Am.

(Southampton, N.Y.); New Canaan Country, Winter (New Canaan). Home: 393 Oenoke Av New Canaan CT 06840 Office: 20 Pine St New York NY 10015

BERKELMAN, KARL, nuclear physicist, educator; b. Lewiston, Me., June 7, 1933; s. Robert and Yvonne (Langlois) B.; B.S., U. Rochester, 1955; Ph.D., Cornell U., 1959; m. Mary Bowen Hobbie, Oct. 10, 1959; children—Thomas, James, Peter. Asst. prof. physics dept. Cornell U., Ithaca, N.Y., 1961-63, asso. prof., 1963-67, prof., 1967—; research in exptl. high energy particle physics Cornell Electron Synchrotron. NSF postdoctoral fellow Frascati (Italy) Nat. Synchrotron Lab., 1960-61, NSF sr. postdoctoral fellow European Center for Nuclear Research, Geneva, Switzerland, 1967- 68. Mem. Am. Phys. Soc. Home: 971 E State St Ithaca NY 14850

BERKLEY, CARL, med. engr. Formerly mem. faculty Rockefeller Inst. Med. Research, also mgr. spl. products Allen B. DuMont Labs.; now sci. dir. Found. Med. Tech., also head Lab. Tech. in Environmental Medicine, Mt. Sinai Med. Center, N.Y.C., editor and pub. Med. Research Engring. Mem. N.Y. Acad. Scis. (chmn. dept. instrumentation), Assn. Advancement Med. Instrumentation (bd. dirs. 1956—). Contbr. tech. papers. Patentee electronic and optical instrumentation for oscillography, automatic scanning and image analysis. Address: Mt Sinai Med Center New York City NY 10029

BERKMAN, IRVING JAY, steel co. exec.; b. Chgo., Feb. 8, 1915; s. Louis and Jessie (Bell) B.; LL.B., Chgo.-Kent Coll. Law, 1937; m. Jeanette Fisher, Aug. 11, 1935. Admitted to Ill. bar, 1938; practice in Chgo., 1938-42; exec. v.p. Follansbee Steel Corp. (W.Va.), 1954—; exec. v.p., dir. Screw & Bolt Corp. Am., Pitts., 1961—. Mem. Ill. Bar Assn., N.A.M. Mason (Shriner). Clubs: Steubenville Country; Covenant, Standard (Chgo.); Franklin Hills Country, Standard City (Detroit); Hillcrest Country (Beverly Hills, Cal.). Home: 802 Granard Pkwy Steubenville OH 43952 Office: PO Box 1708 Pittsburgh PA 15230

BERKMAN, JACK NEVILLE, lawyer, corp. exec.; b. London, Eng., Feb. 12, 1905; s. Hyman L. and Sarah (Hellman) B.; brought to U.S., 1908, naturalized, 1922; A.B., U. Mich., 1926; J.D., Harvard, 1929; m. Sybiel B. Altman, Aug. 27, 1933 (dec. May 1964); children—Myles P., Monroe E., Stephen L.; m. 2d Lillian Dubon Rojtman, Jan. 26, 1970. Admitted to Ohio bar, 1930, since practiced in Steubenville. Vice chmn. bd., chmn. exec. com., dir. Rust Craft Greeting Cards, Inc., N.Y.C., Boston; vice chmn. bd., dir. Rust Craft Broadcasting Co., operating WSTV-TV-AM-FM, Steubenville, WJKS-TV, Jacksonville, Fla., WRDW-TV, Augusta, Ga., WSOL-AM, Tampa, Fla.; pres., dir. Rust Craft Broadcasting N.Y., Inc. operating WROC- TV-Am-FM, Rochester, Rust Craft Broadcasting Pa., Inc., operating WRCP-AM-FM, Phila., WPIT-AM-FM, Pitts., Rust Craft Broadcasting Tenn., Inc. operating WRCB-TV, Chattanooga, Radio Buffalo, Inc. operating WWCL-AM-FM; vice chmn., dir. Rust Craft Calde Communications, Mc., Steubenville, operating the CATV's; dir. Cardigan Press, Leeds, Eng., Barker Greeting Cards Cin. Union Savings Bank and Trust Co., Steubenville, Rust Craft, Ltd., Friendship House, Ltd., Volland, Ltd. (all Toronto, Can.), Asso. American Artists, N.Y.C.; sec., dir. Sinclair Bldg. Co. Trustee Sybiel B. Berkman Found. Steubenville; mem. devel. bd. Retina Found.; mem. Am. Jewish Com., N.Y. mem. Internat., Am., FCC, Ohio, Jefferson County bar assns., Am. Soc. for Technion (bd. dirs.), Am. Judicature Soc., Fgn. Policy Assn. (asso.), Ohio Soc. N.Y., Radio and TV Execs. Soc. Elk. Clubs: Steubenville Country; Culver Parents; Broadcasters (Washington); Harvard-Yale-Princeton, Variety (Pitts.); Friars, Harvard Harmonie, Raffles (N.Y.C.). Author: (play) Playing God, 1931; short stories, articles. Home: 120 Lovers Lane Steubenville OH 43952 also 22 E 6th St New York City NY 10021 Office: 320 Market St Steubenville OH 43952 also 680 Fifth Av New York City NY 10019

BERKMAN, LOUIS, business exec.; b. Canton, O., Jan. 15, 1909; s. Hyman L. and Sarah (Galman) B.; m. Sandra Weiss, Apr. 14, 1935; children—Marshall, Donna (Mrs. Robert A. Paul). Pres. Louis Berkman Co., Steubenville, O., 1931—, Parkersburg Steel Corp. (W.Va.), 1946—, Steel Trading Corp., Pitts., 1952—, Follansbee Steel Corp. (W.Va.), 1954—; chmn., pres. Screw & Bolt Corp. Am., Pitts., 1961—. Rust Craft Greeting Cards, Inc., 1958—, Rust Craft, Ltd., Scarborough, Ont., Can., 1958—, Steubenville Motor Hotel Co., 1962—; sr. v.p., treas., dir. Rust Craft Broadcasting Co., 1962—, Radio Buffalo, Inc., 1962—, Rust Craft Broadcasting N.Y., Inc., 1964—, Rust Craft Broadcasting Tenn., Inc., 1962; treas., dir. Neptune Broadcasting Corp., 1965—, Rust Craft Broadcasting of Pa., 1968—, dir. Ampco Metal Co Metal, Inc. Milw., Scott Lumber Co., Bridgeport, O., Union Savs. Bank & Trust Co., Steubenville, Rust Craft Greeting Cards (U.K.) Ltd. Dewbury, Eng. Pres., trustee H.L. Berkman Found., Steubenville, 1952—. Mem. Ohio Valley Devel. Council. Adv. bd. St. John Hosp., Gill Meml. Hosp. Mem. Steubenville C. of C., Pitts. Symphony Soc. Elk; mem. B'nai B'rith. Clubs: Rotary, Steubenville Country, Civic Music (Steubenville); Oglebay Institute (Wheeling, W. Va.); Friars (N.Y.C.); Standard, Concordia (Pitts.). Home: Fort Steuben Motor Hotel Steubenville OH 43952 Office: 330 N 7th St Steubenville OH 43952

BERKOVITS, ELIEZER, clergyman, author; b. Oradea, Rumania, Sept. 8, 1998; s. Bernard and Bella (Kosch) B.; Rabbi, Hildesheimer Rabinical Sem., 1934; M.A., Ph.D., Berlin U., 1933; m. Sali Bickel, Jan. 6, 1933; children—Avraham, Shimshan, Bernard. Came to U.S., 1950, naturalized, 1956. Rabbi, Jewish community, Berlin, Germany, 1936-39, United Hebrew Congregation, Leeds, Eng., 1940-45, Central Synagogue, Sydney, Australia, 1946-50, Adath Jeshurun, Boston, 1950-58; chmn. dept. Jewish philosophy Hebrew Theol. Coll., Skokie, Ill., 1958—. Author: Towards Historic Judaism, 1943; Between Yesterday and Tomorrow, 1945; Judaism: Fossil or Ferment, 1956; God, Man and History, 1959; A Jewish Critique of the Philosophy of Martin Buber, 1962; Prayer, 1963; T'nai Binsuin u' Beget (Hebrew), 1967; Man and God, Studies in Biblical Theology, 1970; others. Home: 8829 N Monticello St Skokie IL 60077

BERKOVITZ, LEONARD DAVID, educator; b. Chgo., Jan. 24, 1924; s. Judea and Esther (Trop) B.; B.S., U. Chgo., 1946, M.S., 1948, Ph.D., 1951; m. Anna Whitehouse, June 18, 1953; children—Dan Michael, Kenneth Eugene. AEC fellow Stanford U., 1951-52; research fellow Cal. Inst. Tech., 1952-54; mathematician RAND Corp., 1954-62; prof. math. Purdue U., 1962—; editor SIAM Jour. Control; asso. editor Jour. Optimization Theory and Applications. Served to lt. USAAF, 1943-46. Mem. Am. Math. Soc., Math. Assn. Am., Soc. Indsl. and Applied Math., Phi Beta Kappa. Jewish religion. Office: Dept Math Purdue U Lafayette IN 47906

BERKOWITZ, ABE, lawyer; b. Meridian, Miss., Nov. 26, 1907; s. Max and Sara (Smokler) B.; LL.B., U. Ala., 1928; m. Estelle Reiss, May 4, 1931. Admitted to Ala. bar, 1928, since practiced in Birmingham; sr. partner Berkowitz, Lefkovits & Patrick, 1950—. Chmn. Birmingham Bar Assn. Aid Trust; Mem. Com. for Civil Rights Under Law. Trustee A.G. Gaston Boys Club, Jewish Community Center. Recipient Freedom medal State of Israel, 1965. Mem. Am., Ala., Birmingham bar assns., Am. Judicature Soc., Zionist Orgn. Am. (past Southeastern pres.). Jewish religion. Clubs: Pine Tree Country, Relay House, The Club (Birmingham). Home: 2112 Cahaba Rd S Birmingham AL 35223 Office: City Nat Bank Bldg Birmingham AL 35210

BERKOWITZ, ABRAM, lawyer; b. Bklyn., Apr. 15, 1892; s. Morris and Bessie (Douglas) B.; student Northeastern U., 1915; LL.B., Boston U., 1916, LL.D., 1962; m. Minna Kroll, Dec. 7, 1917 (dec. Nov. 1947); children—Leonard K., Dorothy (Mrs. Harvey White); m. 2d, Jean Sholkin, Jan. 31, 1963. Admitted to Mass. bar, 1915, since practiced in Boston; with Ropes & Gray, 1907—, legal asso., 1916-30, mem. firm, 1930—; dir. Emile Bernat & Sons Co., Fabreeka Products Co., Zayre Corp. Trustee, past pres. Beth Israel Hosp., trustee Combined Jewish Philanthropies Greater Boston; co-trustee Jacob Ziskind Trust for Charitable Purposes. Served with Q.M.C., U.S. Army, 1917-18. Fellow Brandeis U. Mem. Am., Mass., Boston bar assns., Am. Soc. Technion (dir. Boston chpt.). Jewish religion (trustee temple). Clubs: Palm Beach (Fla.) Country; Belmont (Mass.) Country; Down Town. Home: 80 Park St Brookline MA 02146 Office: 225 Franklin St Boston MA 02110

BERKOWITZ, DAVID SANDLER, educator; b. Pitts., Aug. 20 1913; s. Abraham Jacob and Nellie (Sandler) B.; A.B., Harvard, 1938, A.M., 1940, Ph.D., 1946; m. Jessie Cohen, Sept. 8, 1940; children—Carl Sandler, Naomi Judith. Teaching fellow Harvard, 1939-41, Rogers travelling fellow, 1941-42; asso. prof. history, chmn. dept. social sci. Emerson Coll., Boston, 1946-47; exec. officer Assn. Colls. and Univs. State N.Y., also cons. and liaison officer Commn. Need for State Univ. N.Y., 1946-48; mem. faculty Brandeis U., 1948—, prof. history, 1949—, asst. to pres., dir. univ. planning, 1948-52; vis. lectr. history Harvard, 1957-58. Dir. New Eng. Transp. Co., 1956-62; dir., treas. Berkshire Assos., Inc., 1959—; incorporator Waltham Savs. Bank, 1952—. Bd. dirs. Waltham Family Service Assn., 1949—, pres., 1959-61; incorporator Waltham Hosp., 1952—; bd. dirs. Region West Family Counseling Service, 1963—, mem. exec. com., 1963—, chmn. personnel com., 1963-66, chmn. community relations com., 1966—; bd. dirs. Waltham Community Found., 1971—, pres., 1971—. Recipient Washburn prize history Harvard, 1938; Folger Shakespeare Library fellow, 1965-66, sr. fellow, 1971-72. Mem. Am. Assn. U. Profs., Am. Hist. Assn., Renaissance Soc. Am., Conf. Brit. Studies, New Eng. Renaissance Conf. (permanent chmn. 1965—), Soc. History of Discoveries, Oxford Bibilog. Soc., Phi Beta Kappa. Author: Inequality of Opportunity in Higher Education, 1948; Bibliotheca Bibliographica Britannica, 1963; Catalogue of the Incunabula of Brandeis University Library, 1963; Aldine Dynasty of Humanistic Printers, 1963; Ancient Civilizations and the Founding of Libraries, 1964; From Ptolemy to the Moon; Progress in the Art of Exploration and Navigation, 1965; In Remembrance of Creation 1968. Home: 93 Beaumont Av Newtonville MA 02160 Office: History Dept Brandeis Univ Waltham MA 02154

BERKOWITZ, HOWARD, educator; b. N.Y.C., July 31, 1927; s. Louis Israel and Celia (Goluboff) B.; B.A., N.Y.U., 1949; postgrad. Bklyn. Coll., 1949-51; M.A., MacMurray Coll., 1954; Ph.D., U. Tex., 1957; m. Phyllis Muriel Koenigsberg, June 30, 1951; children—Ruth Ann, Robert Stanley. Asst. prof. Miami U., Oxford, O., 1957-63; prof. psychology State U. Coll. at Oneonta, N.Y., 1963—, head dept. psychology, 1966-70, chmn. dept. ednl. psychology, 1970—, also pvt. practice clin. psychology, 1960—; cons. N.Y. State Dept. Edn. Mem. Oneonta Housing Commn., 1965—; commr. Oneonta City Operations, 1964-65; pres. Otsego County Mental Health Assn., 1964-65. Mem. Am. Psychol. Assn., Am. Ednl. Research Assn., Eastern Psychol. Assn., N.E. Ednl. Research Assn. (v.p.), Phi Delta Kappa. Kiwanian. Home: 33 East St Oneonta NY 13820

BERKOWITZ, LEONARD, educator, social psychologist; b. N.Y.C., Aug. 11, 1926; s. Morris and Goldie (Berkowitz) B.; B.A., N.Y. U., 1948; Ph.D., 1951; m. Nettie Shankler, Jan. 30, 1949; children—Marti Anne, Phyllis Joan. Research psychologist Human Resources Research Center, Randolph AFB, Tex., 1951-55; mem. faculty U. Wis., 1955—, prof., 1962—, chmn. dept. psychology, 1968-70, Vilas research prof., 1969—; vis. asso. prof. Stanford, 1960-61; research Oxford U., 1964-65; vis. prof. Cornell U., 1966-67; fellow Center for Advanced Study Study in Behavioral Sci., 1970-71. Mem. behavioral scis. fellowships panel NIH, 1965-68. Cons. Presdl. Commn. Causes and Prevention Violence, 1968. Served USAAF, 1945-46. Mem. Am. Psychol. Assn., Soc. Study Social Issues. Jewish religion. Author: Aggression: A Social-Psychological Analysis, 1962; Development of Motives and Values in Children, 1964; Roots of Agression, 1969. Editor: (with J. Macaulay) Altruism and Helping Behavior, 1970. Editor Advances in Exptl. Social Psychology, 1963—; asso. editor Jour. Personality and Social Psychology, 1967-68; cons. editor Jour. Exptl. Social Psychology, 1965-67. Home: 5818 Anchorage Av Madison WI 53705

BERKOWITZ, MONROE, educator; b. Exeter, Pa., Mar. 9, 1919; s. Edward and Molly (Kaufman) B.; A.B., Ohio U., 1942; A.M., Columbia, 1946, Ph.D., 1951; m. Shalvo Schwartz, Mar. 6, 1942; 1 son, Edward. Asso. economist NWLB, 1942-44; mem. faculty Rutgers U., 1946—, prof. econs., 1960—, dir. Bur. Econ. Research, 1960-. Mem. arbitration panels Am. Arbitration Assn., Fed. Mediation and Conciliation Service, N.Y.C. Office Collective Bargaining; cons. Nat. Insts. Rehab. and Health Services, Bur. Labor Standards. Mem. Am. Assn. U. Profs. (pres. Rutgers U. chpt. 1958), Nat. Acad. Arbitrators, Am., Indian econs. assns., Indsl. Relations Research Assn., Nat. Rehab. Assn., Indian Soc. Labor Econs., Phi Beta Kappa. Author: (with others) Economics, Experience and Analysis, 1950; Processing Workmen's Compensation cases, 1969. Home: 1791 Middlebrook Rd Bound Brook NJ 08805 Office: Rutgers Univ New Brunswick NJ 08093

BERKOWITZ, MORTIMER, Jr., publisher; b. Brookline, Mass., Nov. 12, 1915; s. Mortimer and Alice Ruth (Seligman) B.; grad. Taft Sch., Watertown, Conn., 1933; B.A., Dartmouth, 1937; m. Marjory Schwalbe, June 13, 1951; children—Hugh James Freund, John Paul, Betsy Lee Freund, Mortimer III. With Westchester County newspapers, 1937; reporter Boston Herald, 1938, Cleve. News, 1939; ad rep. N.Y. Post, 1940; publishers rep. George A. McDevitt Co., 1941, 46-47, Am. Weekly, 1948-51; Eastern advt. mgr. Woman's Day, 1951- 53; nat. mgr. N.Y. Post, 1953-56; advt. dir. Woman's Home Companion, 1956; v.p., account supr. Batten, Barton, Durstine & Osborn, 1957-61; advt. dir. Fawcett Publs., 1961-66; pres. Flower Grower Pub., Inc., also pub. Home Garden mag., 1966—. Trustee Bklyn. Savs. Bank. Mem. Supreme Ct. Appellate div. N.Y. State Joint Com. Jury System. Bd. dirs. Bklyn. Botanic Garden, N.Y. Hort. Soc. Served to lt. comdr. USNR, 1941-45. Mem. Mag. Pubs. Assn. (past bd. govs.). Club: Dartmouth (past bd. govs.) (N.Y.C.). Home: 32 E 64th St New York City NY 10021 Office: 235 E 45th St New York City NY 10017

BERKY, ANDREW SCHULTZ, sch. pres.; b. Pottstown, Pa., Sept. 6, 1922; s. Darius Weller and Mabel (Schultz) B.; student Williams Coll., 1941-42; A.B., Franklin and Marshall Coll., 1950; postgrad. U. Pa., 1951; m. Lucile S. Reiff, June 27, 1946; children—Christopher, Rebecca, Melissa. Dir., Schwenkfelder Library, Pennsburg, Pa., 1950—; headmaster Perkiomen Sch., Pennsburg, 1966-68, pres., 1968—. Dir. Boyertown Burial Casket Co. (Pa.). Pres. Upper Perkiomen Community Chest, 1957-59; dir. Upper Perkiomen Recreation Council, 1957-63, So. Lehigh Sch. Dist., 1960-64. Served as lt. (j.g.) USNR, 1942-46. Mem. German Soc. (dir.). Republican. Mem. Palm Schwenkfelder Ch. Author: Practitioner in Physick, 1954; The Schoolhouse Near the Old Spring, 1955; An Account of Some Hosensack Valley Mills, 1958; co-author The Historians' History of the United States, 1966. Editor: The Journals and Papers of David Schultze, 2 vols., 1952-53; The Challenge to American Life, 1956. Mng. editor of Corpus Schwenckfeldianorum, 1957-61, The Schwenkfeldian, 1955-64. Office: Perkiomen Sch Seminary Av Pennsburg PA 18073

BERL, WARREN HARRY, investment banker; b. San Francisco, Aug. 24, 1920; s. Edwin D. and Selma (Green) B.; A.B., Stanford, 1942; m. Aline Meyer, Jan. 2, 1948; children—Douglas, Cathryn, Susan. Partner, Edwin D. Beri & Sons, investment securities, San Francisco, 1946-57; gen. partner Sutro & Co., investment securities, San Francisco, 1957-69, pres. Sutro & Co. Inc., 1970—. Chmn. bd. Pacific Coast Stock Exchange, 1961; bd. govs. Am. Stock Exchange, 1968-71. Mem. athletic bd. Stanford U., 1968—. Mem. Hall of Fame, Stanford U. Served with USNR, 1942-45. Mem. Investment Bankers Am. (bd. govs. 1970—, chmn. dist. 10, 1971). Clubs: Street, Bond (San Francisco). Home: 3939 Washington St San Francisco CA 94118 Office: 460 Montgomery St San Francisco CA 94104

BERLA, JULIAN EMERSON, architect; b. Newark, Apr. 7, 1902; S.B., Mass. Inst. Tech., 1923. Draftsman, Bertram Goodhue & Assos., 1922, designer, 1925-29; draftsman Edward S. Hewitt, 1924-25; with U.S. Resettlement Adminstrn., 1936-37; with Berla & Abel, Washington, 1941—; cons. architect Dept. Commerce, 1937-39, U.S. Housing Authority, 1938-40, U.S. Golden Gate Commn., 1939, Bldg. Ministry, Kingdom of Denmark, 1951-52, 53-54; cons. Denmark embassy Washington, 1954—; lectr. N.Y.U., 1930-32, N.Y. Met. Mus. Art, 1931; archtl. critic Mass. Inst. Tech., 1958-63; archtl. lectr. and critic U. Va., 1963—. Mem. design adv. panel Dept. Housing and Community Devel., Balt. Fellow A.I.A. (pres. Washington chpt. to 1948). Address: 1330 Massachusetts Av NW Washington DC 20005*

BERLAND, ABEL EDWARD, lawyer, realtor; b. Cin., Aug. 27, 1915; s. Samuel and Ann (Brod) B.; LL.B., DePaul U., 1938; m. Meredith E. Tausig, Aug. 31, 1940; children—Michael Gardner, Richard Bruce, Jay Robert. Admitted to Ill. bar, 1938; pres., dir. Arthur Rubloff & Co., Chgo.; dir. Lake Mich. Mortgage Co.; real estate cons. to chain store orgns., corps., attys. and ednl. instns. Trustee, DePaul U. Fellow Brandeis U., 1958—. Mem. Am., Chgo. bar assns., Nat. Assn. Real Estate Bds. (dir.), Nat. Assn. Real Estate Investment Funds, Nat. Inst. Real Estate Brokers (bd. govs., chmn. comml. property com.), Real Estate Service Investment Funds (sec. 1966), Am. Soc. Real Estate Counselors (pres.), Newberry Library Assos., Pvt. Libraries Assn., Manuscript Soc. Nat., Ill., Chgo. assns. real estate bds. Am. Arbitration Assn. (nat.panel arbitrators), Internat. Real Estate Fedn.), Bibliog. Soc. Am., Bibliog. Soc. of U. Va., Shakespeare Soc. Am., Lex Legio, Wabash Avenue, Assn. (dir.), Pi Gamma Mu, Pi Kappa Delta, Lambda Alpha, Omega Tau Rau. Clubs: Book of California; Caxton, Mid-Day, Brandeis University (founder 1949, pres. 1954), Standard, Executives' Boswell (Chgo.); Grolier (N.Y.C.), Philobiblon (Phila.). Contbr. articles on real estate to profl. scholarly and trade jours. Home. 251 Sylvan Rd Glencoe IL 60022 Office: 69 W Washington St Chicago IL 60602

BERLAND, KENNETH K., shoe co. exec.; b. 1922; grad. Coll. City N.Y.; m. Gloria Berland; children—Alan Lance, Elizabeth Anne. With Melville Shoe Corp., 1957—, v.p., treas., dir., 1966—. Chmn. tax com. Volume FootWear Retailers Assn. Address: 25 W 43d St New York City NY 10036

BERLE, ADOLF AUGUSTUS, lawyer; b. Boston, Jan. 29, 1895; s. Adolf Augustus and Augusta (Wright) B.; A.B., Harvard, 1913, A.M., 1914, LL.B., 1916; LL.D., Oberlin, Wesleyan, Columbia, Detroit, Yankton; Hon. D., U. Brazil, U. Andes, U. Aix-Marseilles; m. Beatrice Bend Bishop, Dec. 17, 1927; children—Alice Bishop (Mrs. Clan Crawford), Beatrice (Mrs. Dean Winston Meyerson), Peter Adolf. Practiced law, Boston, 1916-17, N.Y.C., 1919—; partner Berle & Berle; prof. corp. law Columbia Law Sch., 1927-64, prof. law emeritus 1964—; lectr. Air War Coll., 1951—; dir. SuCrest, N.Y.C., Twentieth Century Fund, N.Y.C., Ecole de L'Europe Libre, France; spl. counsel RFC, 1933- 38; chamberlain of N.Y.C., 1934-38; asst. sec. of state, 1938-44; U.S. ambassador to Brazil, 1945-46; chmn. task force on Latin Am., 1961; cons. to secretary of state, 1961-62. Del. U.S. Govt. to Inter-Am. Conf. for Maintenance of Peace, Buenos Aires, 1936-37, 8th Pan Am. Conf., Lima, Peru, 1938, Pan Am. Conf., Habana, 1940; pres. Internat. Conf. Civil Aviation, Chgo., 1944, and chmn. U.S. delegation. Served from pvt. to 1st lt. inf. O.R.C., 1917-19; expert on staff Am. Commn. to Negotiate Peace with Germany, 1918-19. Decorated Order Cross (Brazil); Order of Merit (Italy) Mem. Phi Beta Kappa. Clubs: Army and Navy (Washington); Pilgrims, Harvard, Century, Players, Anglers. Author: Studies in the Law of Corporation Finance, 1928; Cases and Materials in the Law of Corporation Finance, 1930; (with Dr. G. C. Means) The Modern Corporation and Private Property, 1932; (with Victoria J. Pederson) Liquid Claims and National Wealth, 1934; New Directions in the New World, 1940; (with Prof. Wm. C. Warren) Business Organization; Corporation, 1948; Natural Selection of Political Forces, 1950; The 20th Century Capitalist Revolution, 1954; Tides of Crisis, 1957; Power Without Property, 1959; The American Economic Republic, 1963; The Three Faces of Power, 1967; Power, 1969. Home: 142 E 19th St New York City NY 10003 Office: 70 Pine St New York City NY 10005

BERLE, MILTON, (real name Milton Berlinger), actor; b. N.Y.C., July 12, 1908; m. Joyce Mathews; 2 children; m. 2d, Ruth Cosgrove, Dec. 9, 1953; children—Vicki, Billy. Began profl. work as child actor in silent motion pictures for Biograph; later on stage in vaudeville; appearances on N.Y. legitimate stage include roles in Earl Carroll Vanities, Saluta, Life Begins at 8:40, Ziegfeld Follies; later motion pictures include: New Faces of 1937; Tall, Dark and Handsome, 1941; Sun Valley Serenade, 1941; Over My Dead Body, 1943; Always Leave Them Laughing, 1949; Let's Make Love, 1960; It's a Mad, Mad, Mad, Mad World, 1962; The Oscar; The Loved One; Who's Minding the Mint. Recently conducted radio program; now TV actor; TV series Kraft Music Hall; Jackpot Bowling, 1960-61. Mem. A.S.C.A.P., Am. Guild Authors and Composers, Grand Street Boys, Friar's (re-elected hon. abbot emeritus 1968) (N.Y.C.). Author: Out Of My Trunk, 1945; Earthquake, 1959. Address: Sagebrush Enterprises Inc 151 El Camino Beverly Hills CA 90212

BERLEW, FRANK KINGSTON, co. exec.; b. Bangor, Me., Apr. 9, 1930; s. Herman D. and Lillian (Kingston) B.; A.B., Wesleyan U., Middletown, Conn., 1951; LL.B. magna cum laude, Harvard, 1954; m. Jeanne Cadigan, Aug. 16, 1952; children—Derek Kingston, Sarah. Admitted to Mass. bar, 1954; clk. U.S. dist. ct. judge, Boston, 1956-57; with firm Ropes & Gray, Boston, 1957- 61; regional legal counsel for Near East and S. Asia, AID, 1961-62; dir. for Pakistan, Peace Corps, 1962-64, dep. asso. dir. corps, 1964, asso. dir., 1964-66; legal dir. ITT, London, Eng., 1966-67, exec. v.p ITT Africa and Middle East, 1967—. Served with AUS, 1954-56. Editor Harvard Law Rev., 1952-54. Home: 10 St Stephens Close Avenue Rd London, N.W.8, England. Office: 190 Strand London WC 2 England

BERLIN, IRVING (surname adopted), composer; b. Russia, May 11, 1888; s. Moses and Leah (Lipkin) Baline; brought to U.S., 1893; ed. pub. schs., N.Y.C.; hon. degrees. Bucknell, Fordham and Temple univs.; m. Dorothy Goetz, Feb. 1913 (dec. July 1913); m. 2d, Ellin Mackay, Jan. 4, 1926; children—Mary Ellin (Mrs. Marvin Barrett), Linda (Mrs. Edouard Emmet), Elizabeth (Mrs. Alton Peters). Writer, composer popular songs; pres. The Irving Berlin Music Corp. Served as sgt. Infantry, at Camp Upton, L.I. Mason (Shriner), Elk. Clubs: Lambs, Friars, City Athletic. Composer: Alexander's Ragtime Band; Oh, How I Hate to Get Up in the Morning; When I Lost You; When I Leave the World Behind; What'll I Do?; All Alone; Remember; Reaching For the Moon; Always; Because I Love You; At Peace With the World; Russian Lullaby; Music Box Revues; Cocoanuts; Ziegfeld Follies; Me; Any Bonds Today; White Christmas; This Is the Army (musical comedy revue); Easter Parade (film musical); Annie Get Your Gun, Miss Liberty, Call Me Madam, Mr. President, 1962 (stage musicals); also various others; total songs composed about 800. Recipient Medal of Merit for This Is The Army; Congl. gold medal for God Bless America; decorated Legion of Honor (France). Office: 1290 6th Av New York City NY 10009

BERLIN, ISAIAH, educator; b. Riga, Latvia, June 6, 1909; s. Mendel and Marie (Wolshonock) B.; ed. St. Paul's Sch., London, Eng., 1922-28; scholar Corpus Christi Coll., Oxford (Eng.) U., 1928-32; LL.D., (hon.), Hull (Eng.) U.; D.Litt., Cambridge U., Glasgow U., East Anglia U., Jerusalem U., Brandeis U.; hon. Dr. Columbia; m. Aline De Gunzbourg, 1956. Fellow, All Souls Coll., Oxford U., 1932-38, 50-67, fellow New Coll., 1938-50, lectr. philosophy New Coll., 1932-50, Chichele prof. social and polit. theory at univ., 1957-67, pres. Wolfson Coll., 1966—; vis. prof. Harvard, 1949, 52, 53, 61, Bryn Mawr Coll., 1952, Princeton, 1965; Alexander White prof. U. Chgo., 1955; prof. humanities City U. N.Y., 1966—. First sec. Brit. embassy, Washington, 1942-46, Moscow, USSR, 1945. Mem. com. awards Commonwealth (Harkness) Fellowships, 1961-65, Kennedy Scholarships, 1965—. Bd. dirs. Royal Opera House, London, 1955- 66; bd. govs. U. Jerusalem, 1955—. Decorated comdr. Order British Empire, 1946; created knight, 1957. Fellow British Acad. (v.p. 1958-60); hon. fellow Corpus Christi Coll.; hon. mem. Am. Acad. Arts and Scis., Am. Acad. Arts and Letters. Author books and essays on lit., philosophy, other subjects. Address: Wolfson Coll Oxford Univ Oxford England

BERLIN, J. L., lawyer; b. Salt Lake City, July 4, 1926; s. M. A. and Helen (Converse) R.; student U. Wis.; B.A., Ida. State U., 1950; LL.B. cum laude, Washburn U., 1953; m. Joyce Burnham, June 1, 1950; children—Robert L., Sally Jo., Nancy Anne. Admitted to Ida. bar, 1953; practice in Twin Falls, 1953; partner firm Richards, Haga & Eberle, Boise, 1966-67; partner law firm of Eberle and Berlin, 1967—; with Albertsons, Inc., Boise, 1953-66, exec. v.p., 1962-64, pres., 1964-66; pres., dir. Gold Strike Stamp Co., dir. A. & T. Ins. Co., Boise Bldg. Supply Co., Continental Co. Served with USNR, 1943-46. Mem. U.S., Ida., Boise chambers commerce. Home: 1824 Norcrest St Boise, ID 83701; summer Donnelly, ID Office: Title Ins Bldg Boise ID 83701

BERLIN, NATHANIEL ISAAC, physician; b. N.Y.C., July 4, 1920; s. Louis and Gertrude (Sugarman) B.; B.S., Western Res. U., 1942; M.D., L.I. Coll. Medicine, 1945; Ph.D., U. Cal. at Berkeley, 1949; m. Barbara Ruben, June 14, 1953; children—Deborah Joy, Marc David. Intern Kings County Hosp., Bklyn., 1945-46, resident pathologist, 1946-47; Nat. Cancer Inst. postdoctorate research fellow U. Cal., 1948-50, research fellow, 1949-50, research asso., 1950-51, instr., 1951, lectr. and research asso., 1952-53, lectr., asso. research med. physicist, 1952-53; Nat. Heart Inst. spl. research fellow Nat. Inst. Med. Research, London, Eng., 1953-54; head metabolism service, gen. medicine br. Nat. Cancer Inst., 1956—, chief gen. medicine br., 1959-61, clin. dir., 1961-71, sci. dir. general lab. and clinics, 1969—. Cons. U.S. Naval Hosp., Bethesda, Md., 1955-65, Armed Forces Spl. Weapons Project, Dept. Def., 1957-59; alumni lectr. Downstate Med. Center. Pres. Alta Vista P.T.A., 1962-63; trustee Alta Vista Elementary Sch. Served with AUS., 1943-45; lt. comdr. M.C., USNR, 1954-56; comdr. Res. Recipient Superior Service award Dept. Health, Edn. and Welfare; Alumni medal for distinguished service to medicine State U. N.Y. Fellow A.A.A.S., N.Y. Acad. Sci., Internat. Soc. Hematology; mem. Am. Fedn. Clin. Research, Soc. Exptl. Biology and Medicine, Am. Physiol. Soc., Biochem. Soc. (Eng.), Radiation Research Soc., Am. Soc. Hematology (exec. com.), Assn. Am. physicians, Am. Soc. Clin. Investigation, Western Soc. Clin Research, Mid-Eastern Soc. Nuclear Medicine (sec.-treas. 1957-60), Am. Assn. Cancer Research, Sigma Xi, Alpha Omega Alpha, Zeta Beta Tau, Phi Delta Epsilon. Editorial adv. bd. Cancer Research; editorial bd. Handbook Radioactive Isotopes, Research Communications in Chem. Pathology and Pharmacology. Contbr. articles to med. jours. Home: 6600 Braeburn Pkwy Bethesda MD 20034 Office: Nat Cancer Inst Nat Insts Health Bethesda MD 20014

BERLIN, RICHARD E., publisher; b. Omaha; s. Richard and Sarah (Noonan) B.; student pub. schs., Omaha; m. Muriel (Honey) Johnson, Dec. 21, 1938. Pres., chief exec. officer The Hearst Corp., which owns Hearst Newspapers, Magazines, Radio, etc., also dir. Executor and trustee estate of W. R. Hearst. Bd. dirs. Boys Clubs Am.; trustee Roosevelt Hosp., N.Y.C., Am. Heritage Found., Freedoms Found., Valley Forge. Commr. Saratoga Springs Commn. Served in U.S. Navy, World War I. Recipient Henry Johnson award, 1966. Roman Catholic. Knight of Malta. Clubs: Book; Apawamis (Rye, N.Y.); Deepdale Golf (Great Neck, N.Y.). Home: 835 Fifth Av New York City NY 10021 Office: 959 8th Av New York City NY 10019

BERLIN, SEYMOUR SANFORD, govt. ofcl.; b. Cleve., Aug. 2, 1917; s. David and Marie (Rutsky) B.; B.A., Western Res. U., 1940; m. Edith E. Glinsberg, Oct. 12, 1940; children—Jeffrey S., Marcia B. Personnel interviewer USAAF, Dayton, O., 1941-42; with U.S. Civil Service Commn., 1942-43, 46—, dep. dir. bur. inspections, 1958-61, dir. bur., 1961-67, dir. Bur. Exec. Manpower, 1967—. Pres. Montgomery County Civic Fedn., 1961-62. Mem. adv. com. Montgomery County Sch. Bd., 1958. Served with AUS, 1943-46. Decorated Legion of Merit; recipient Arthur S. Flemming award, 1952. Mem. Am. Soc. for Public Administration (pres. Nat. Capital chpt. 1965- 66), Pub. Personnel Assn., Soc. Personnel Adminstrn., Phi Beta Kappa. Home: 6410 Bannockburn Dr Bethesda MD 20034 Office: Civil Service Commn Washington DC 20415

BERLIN, STANTON HENRY, lawyer; b. Chgo., May 24, 1934; s. Jerome S. and Gertrude (Levy) Weiss; B.B.A., U. Mich., 1955, M.B.A., 1956, J.D., 1959; m. Elinor R. Berlin, Sept. 2, 1958; children—Robert D., Michael J. Admitted to Ill. bar, 1959, since practiced in Chgo.; asso. Bell, Boyd, Lloyd, Haddad & Burns, 1959-67, partner, 1968—. Served with U.S. Army, 1957. Mem. Am., Ill., Chgo. bar assns., Legal Club Chgo., Chgo. Mortgage Attys. Assn., U. Mich. Alumni Assn., Order of Coif, Phi Kappa Phi, Beta Alpha Psi, Beta Gamma Sigma, Tau Epsilon Rho, Sigma Alpha Mu. Home: 1512 W Touhy St Chicago IL 60626 Office: 135 S LaSalle St Chicago IL 60603

BERLIND, BRUCE PETER, educator; b. Bklyn., July 17, 1926; s. Peter Sydney and Mae (Miller) B.; student Mercersburg Acad., 1941-43; A.B., Princeton, 1948; M.A., Johns Hopkins, 1950, Ph.D., 1958; m. Mary Elizabeth Dirlam, Sept. 11, 1954; children—Lise, Anne, John, Paul, Alexandra. Instr. English, Colgate U., Hamilton, N.Y., 1954-58, asst. prof., 1958-63, asso. prof., 1963-66, prof., 1966—, chmn. dept. English, 1967—; poet in residence U. Rochester, 1966. USIS lectr., Germany, 1963. Served to 1st lt. U.S. Army, 1945-46, 50-52. Mem. Modern Lang. Assn., Am. Assn. U. Profs. (mem. council, past pres. N.Y. State Conf.). Author: (poems) Ways of Happening, 1959; Companion Pieces, 1971. Asso. editor: The Hopkins Rev., 1949-53. Contbr. poems, essays, revs. to mags. Home: 62 Broad St Hamilton NY 13346

BERLIND, ROGER STUART, investment banker; b. N.Y.C., June 27, 1930; s. Peter Sydney and Mae (Miller) B.; A.B., Princeton, 1952; m. Helen Polk Clark, July 7, 1962; children—Helen Carroll, Peter Stuart, Richard Clark. Account exec. Eastman Dillon, Union Securities & Co., N.Y.C., 1956-60; gen. partner Carter, Berlind & Weill, N.Y.C., 1960-65; chmn. exec. com. Cogan, Berlind, Weill & Levitt, Inc., N.Y.C., 1965-69; chief exec. officer CBWL-Hayden, Stone, Inc., N.Y.C., 1969—; dir. Downe Communications, Inc., Bartell Media Corp., Unibraze Corp., Topper Corp. Bd. dirs. Unity Hosp., Bklyn. Served with CIC, U.S. Army, 1952-54. Mem. Investment Bankers Assn. Clubs: Princeton (N.Y.C.); Tower (trustee) (Princeton, N.J.). Home: 120 East End Av New York City NY 10028 Office: 767 Fifth Av New York City NY 10022

BERLINER, DONALD MYRON, financial planning exec.; b. N.Y.C., June 21, 1928; s. Fred M. and Henrietta (Garver) B.; student N.Y.U., 1948-51; B.B.A., U. Miami, 1951; m. Janice H. Berzon, June 2, 1957; children—Erik H., Stefan D. Vocalist various Eastern and European orchs. night clubs, 1945-51; v.p. Asso. Bus. Campaigns, Inc., N.Y.C., 1951-56; mgr. Las Vegas (Nev.) C. of C., 1956-58; pres. Service Publs., Inc., Las Vegas, 1958-60; div. mgr. Equity Funding Corp., San Diego, 1960-62; pres. Unity Capital Corp. of Am., Beverly Hills, Cal., 1962-69, chmn. bd., 1969—; pres., dir. Unity Adminstrv. Services, Inc.; pres., sec., dir. Unity Securities Corp.; v.p., sec., dir. Unity Real Estate Corp.; mem. adv. bd. Anchor Nat. Life Ins. Co. Served with USAAF, World War II; ETO. Mem. Alpha Epsilon Pi Alumni Club, Alpha Delta Sigma. Home: 17042 Baruna Lane Huntington Beach CA 92649 Office: 9100 Wilshire Blvd Beverly Hills CA

BERLINER, ERNST, educator, chemist; b. Kattowitz, Germany, Feb. 18, 1915; s. Joseph and Lucy (Selinger-Ehrenhaus) B.; came to U.S., 1940, naturalized, 1949; student univs. Breslau and Freiburg (Germany), 1935-38; M.A., Harvard, 1941, Ph.D., 1943; m. Frances Jean Bondhus, Sept. 11, 1947; 1 dau., Susan Lucy. Mem. faculty Bryn Mawr Coll., 1944—, chmn. dept. chemistry, 1951—, prof., 1953—. Guggenheim fellow, 1962; recipient Coll. Chemistry Tchr. award Mfg. Chemists Assn., 1963. Fellow A.A.A.S.; mem. Am. Chem. Soc. (Phila. Sect. award 1971), Chem. Soc. (London, Eng.), Sigma Xi. Contbr. articles profl. jours. Bd. editors Jour. Organic Chemistry, 1963-68. Home: 219 N Roberts Rd Bryn Mawr PA 19010

BERLINER, JOSEPH SCHOLOM, educator, economist; b. N.Y.C., Sept. 4, 1921; s. Michael and Yetta (Eisenberg) B.; student USCG Acad., 1941-43; B.A., Harvard, 1947, Ph.D., 1954; m. Ann Korenbaum, Nov. 7, 1943; childrenPaul, Carl, Nancy. Asst. dir. Russian Research Center, Harvard, 1953-54; economist Corp. Econ. and Industry Research, Washington, 1954-56; prof. econs. Syracuse U., 1956-63, Brandeis U., 1963-. Mem. Assn. Study Soviet-Type Econs. (exec. sec. 1957-61), Am. Assn. Advancement Slavic Studies (pres. 1964), Am. Econ. Assn. Author: Factory and Manager in the USSR, 1957; Soviet Economic Aid, 1958. Home: 3 Compton Circle Lexington, MA 02173. Office: Dept Econs Brandeis Univ Waltham MA 02154

BERLINER, MILTON RICHARD, journalist; b. Boston, Aug. 18, 1907; s. Louis and Sara (Richard) B.; A.B., Harvard, 1928; B.S., Columbia, 1933; m. Anna Ayer Smyth, May 18, 1940; children—Mary Smyth (Mrs. David Hugh Thompson), Richard Ayer, Peter Louis, Kathleen. Reporter, Boston Traveler, 1933-34, Springfield (Mass.) Republican, 1933-44; feature editor OWI, 1944-45; Capitol Hill corres. Washington Daily News, 1947-67, movie critic, performing arts editor, 1967—. Recipient Interpretive Writing award Washington Newspaper Guild, 1951. Home: 602 Forest Glen Rd Silver Spring MD 20901 Office: 1013 13th St NW Washington DC 20005

BERLINER, ROBERT WILLIAM, physician; b. N.Y.C., Mar. 10, 1915; s. William M. and Anna (Weiner) B.; B.S., Yale, 1936; M.D., Columbia, 1939; m. Leah Silver, Dec. 21, 1941; children—Robert William, Alice (Mrs. Hadler), Henry J., Nancy. Intern Presbyn. Hosp., N.Y.C., 1939-41; resident physician Coldwater Meml. Hosp., N.Y.C., 1942- 43, research fellow 3d div. research service, 1943-44, research asst., 1944-47; asst. medicine N.Y.U. Coll. Medicine, N.Y.C., 1943-44, instr., 1944-47; asst. prof. medicine Columbia, research asso. dept. hosps., N.Y.C. 1947-50; chief lab. kidney and electrolyte metabolism Nat. Heart Inst., NIH, Bethesda, Md., 1950-62, dir. intramural research, 1954-68; dir. lab. and clinics NIH, 1968-69, dep. dir. sci. 1969—; lectr. George Washington U. Sch. Medicine, 1951—; professorial lectr. Schs. Medicine and Dentistry, Georgetown U., 1964—. Mem. Am. Physiol. Soc. (pres. 1967-68), Soc. Gen. Physiol., Am. Soc. Clin. Investigation (pres. 1959-60), Soc. for Exptl. Biology and Medicine, Am. Acad. Arts and Scis., Washington Acad. Medicine, Philos. Soc. Washington, Asso. Am. Physicians, Nat., Washington acads. scis., Am. Soc. Nephrology (pres. 1968-69), Harvey Soc., Sigma Xi, Alpha Omega Alpha. Editorial bd. Jour. Clin. Investigation, Am. Jour. Physiology, Circulation Research. Home: 14 North Dr Bethesda MD 20014 Office: Office of Dir Nat Insts Health Bethesda MD 20014

BERLIS, DOUGLAS A., lawyer; b. Toronto, Ont., Can., Dec. 25, 1920; B.A., Trinity Coll., Toronto, 1942; LL.B., Osgood Hall, 1949. Admitted to Ont. bar, 1949; partner firm Edison, Aird & Berlis, Toronto. Head course on corp. law, bar admission course Osgoode Hall, 1965-69. Mem. Canadian Bar Assn. Office: 111 Richmond St W Toronto 110 Ontario Canada*

BERLITZ, CHARLES FRAMBACH, educator, linguist; b. N.Y.C., Nov. 22, 1913; s. Charles L. and Melicent (Berlitz) Frambach; grad. Riverdale County Sch., 1932; B.A. magna cum laude, Yale, 1936; m. Valerie Anne Seary, Jan. 28, 1950; children—Lin Maria, Marc Daniel. Dir. Berlitz Schs. Langs., N.Y.C., Balt., Boston, Chgo., and S.A. 1937-41, v.p., 1944-; v.p. Berlitz Publs., 1947-66, pres., 1966-; v.p. Berlitz Schs. E. Asia. Served as maj., intelligence officer, AUS, 1941- 46. Mem. Res. Officers Assn., Mil. Order of World Wars. Clubs: Overseas Press; Yale. Author: Berlitz MethodSpanish, 1947, English, 1947, French, 1954, and in 23 other langs. including Chinese, Malay, Hindustani, 1947-; Berlitz Self TeacherFrench, 1949, Spanish, 1949, Italian, 1949; German, 1949, 50, Russian, 1951, English, 1951, Portuguese, 1953, Hebrew, 1953; Phrase Books and Pocket Dictionaries—French, German, Spanish, Italian, 1954; Berlitz Self-Teaching Record Course: French, 1956, Spanish, 1957, German 1957, Italian, 1958; Language Series for Children, 1960; Language Teaching Films, 1962; World Language Phrase Book, 1962; Navajo, 1965. Office: 630 5th Av New York City NY 10020

BERLO, DAVID KENNETH, univ. pres.; b. St. Louis, Mar. 28, 1929; s. Raymond Leo and Audrey (Brucher) B.; A.B., U. Ill., 1953, Ph.D., 1956; m. Patricia Alice Dennis, July 28, 1953; children—Sandra Jean, David Todd, Maryellen, Andrea. Asst. prof. Eastern Ill. State U., Charleston, 1955-56; prof., chmn. dept. communication Mich. State U., East Lansing, 1956-71; pres., prof. psychology Ill. State U., Normal, 1971—; asso. dir. Nat. Project in Agrl. Communication, 1960-61. Adviser Inter-Am. Inst. Agrl. Scis., San Jose, Costa Rica, 1962-70. Chmn. Human Relations Commn., East Lansing, 1964-68; chmn. Ingham County March of Dimes, 1967. Vice chmn. Mich. Republican Council on Arts, Scis. and Professions, 1968; Ingham County Rep. chmn., 1968-71. Bd. dirs. Mich. Dept. Pub. Health. Served with USAF, 1951-54. Mem. Assn. Pub. Opinion Research, Am. Psychol. Assn., Am. Sociol. Assn., Internat. Communication Assn., A.A.A.S., Alpha Epsilon Rho, Delta Sigma Rho, Phi Kappa Phi. Author: Process of Communication, 1960. Home: 903 Randall St Normal IL 61761

BERMAN, ABRAHAM S., educator; b. N.Y.C., May 20, 1921; s. David and Bella (Fein) B.; B.Chem. Engring., Coll. City N.Y., 1942; Ph.D. (duPont fellow 1947-49), Ohio State U., 1949; m. Edith Paster, Feb. 13, 1943; childrenLewis Howard, Mark Allen, Deborah Ruth, Engr., Pa. ordnance works U.S. Rubber Co., Williamsport, Pa., 1942-43; research engr. SAM Labs., Columbia, 1943-46; head flow research dept. Union Carbide Corp., Oak Ridge, 1950-66; prof. fluid mechanics U. Minn., 1966-; cons. to industry, 1966-. Mem. Am. Chem. Soc., Am. Phys. Soc., Research Soc. Am., A.A.A.S. Contbr. profl. jours. Home: 686 Mt Curve Blvd St Paul, MN 55116. Office: Inst Tech Dept Aero Univ Minn Minneapolis MN 55455

BERMAN, ARTHUR IRWIN, educator, physicist; b. N.Y.C., Jan. 1, 1925; s. Elliott and Julia (Meyers) B.; A.B., Bklyn. Coll., 1945; M.S., Stanford, 1949, Ph.D., 1954; m. Clara Marianne Bang, July 15, 1957; children—Jeanne, Xenia, Anya, Ian, Pia, David. Mem. staff Los Alamos Sci. Lab., 1949-52; research asso. Stanford, 1952-54; project physicist United Aircraft Corp., 1954-55; mem. faculty Rensselaer Poly. Inst., 1955-69, prof. physics, 1961-69; cons. in field, 1959—; now sr. research fellow Inst. Studies Higher Edn., U. Copenhagen; Fulbright prof. Tech. U. Denmark, 1952, 67. Asso. fellow Am. Inst. Aeros. and Astronautics, Am. Astronautical Soc.; mem. Am. Phys. Soc., Internat. Astron. Fedn., A.A.A.S. Author: The Physical Principles of Astronautics, 1961. Address: Gammel Strandvej 300 3050 Sletten Denmark Office: Inst Studies Higher Edn U Copenhagen Fiolstraede 24 1171 Copenhagen Denmark

BERMAN, DAVID THEODORE, educator; b. Bklyn., June 14, 1920; s. Morris and Rebecca (Shapiro) B.; B.A., Bklyn. Coll., 1941; D.V.M., Cornell U., 1944; M.S., U. Wis., 1946, Ph.D., 1949; m. Rhoda Hiesiger, Sept. 24, 1944; children—Sara Pauline, Morris D. Mem. faculty U. Wis.-Madison, 1946—, asso. prof., 1954-57, prof., 1957—, chmn. dept. vet. sci., 1964-68, asso. dean Grad. Sch., 1968—. Cons., WHO, 1962, mem. expert com. on Brucellosis, 1963, 70. Trustee Madison Jewish Welfare Council, 1971. Served with AUS, 1943-44. Haight Travelling fellow Wis. Grad. Sch., 1963; Research grantee NIH, 1954—; recipient certificate of appreciation Agrl. Research Ser., 1965. Mem. Am. Vet. Med. Assn., Am. Soc. Microbiology, Assn. Immunologists, A.A.A.S., Sigma Xi. Jewish religion (trustee 1967—, sec. temple bd. 1970—). Contbr. numerous research articles to vet. and Microbiology jours. on infectious diseases. Home: 4738 Lafayette Dr Madison WI 53705

BERMAN, EMILE ZOLA, lawyer; b. N.Y.C., Nov. 3, 1902; s. Eli and Elizabeth Berman; B.S., N.Y. U., 1923, LL.B., 1924; m. Alice R. Gaines, Oct. 20, 1944 (dec.); children—Eliza, Eli; m. 2d, Virginia Anne Berman. Admitted to N.Y. bar, 1925; practice of law, N.Y.C., 1926-; mem. firm Emile Z. Berman & A. Harold Frost, 1956-. Lectr. trial tactics Practicing Law Inst., 1935-41, 46-; lectr. law grad. div. N.Y.U., 1950-55, Columbia U. Law Sch., 1950-51, 55, Law Sci. Inst., U. Tex., 1954-55. Mem. nat. adv. Council Law-Medicine Research Inst., Boston U. Fellow Am. Coll. Trial Lawyers; mem. Assn. Bar City N.Y., Am., N.Y. (past exec. com.) bar assns., Met. Trial Lawyers Assn. (past pres., dir.), Internat. Acad. Trial Lawyers (past pres., trustee), Bklyn.-Manhattan Trial Counsel Assn. (past pres.), Fedn. Ins. Counsel (past gov.), Internat. Assn. Ins. Counsel. Author: Foundations for Evidence (Trial Practice Series), 1956; also articles. Office: 77 Water St New York City NY 10005

BERMAN, EUGENE, painter, designer; b. Russia, Nov. 4, 1899; s. Gustave and Lydia (Manassevitch) B.; student schools in Petrograd, Berlin, Munich, 1911- 14; art edn. in Russia, 1914-18, also Paris and Italy; m. Ona Munson, 1950. Came to U.S., 1937, naturalized, 1944. Leader Neo Romantic Movement since exhbn., Paris, 1925; Guggenheim fellow, 1947, 49. Exhibited since 1930, most of maj. museums and galleries in U.S. and Paris; designed settings and costumes for operas and ballets, U.S. and Europe; works permanently exhibited at Metropolitan and Mus. of Modern Art, N.Y.C., Fogg Art Museum, Cambridge, Mass., Vassar, Smith colls., museums in Boston, Balt., Hartford; also many pvt. collections; executed murals pvt. homes. Mem. Nat. Inst. Arts and Letters. Home: 100 W 55th St New York City NY 10019 Address: care M Knoedler & Co 14 E 57th St New York City, NY 10022.

BERMAN, HAROLD JOSEPH, educator; b. Hartford, Conn., Feb. 13, 1918; s. Saul and Emma Rose (Kaplan) B.; B.A., Dartmouth, 1938; student London Sch. Econs. and Polit. Sci., 1938-39; M.A., Yale, 1942, LL.B., 1947; m. Ruth Carol Harlow, June 10, 1941; childrenStephen Harlow, Jean Carol, Susanna, John Kingsley. Asst. prof. law Stanford, 1947-48; vis. prof. law Harvard, 1958-59, research asso. Russian Research Center, 1948-, mem. exec. com., 1952-, asst. prof. law, 1949-52, prof., 1952-; lectr. law Salzburg Seminar Am. Studies, summer 1955, 67; lectr. Soviet Law Inst. des Hautes Etudes Internationale, Geneva, Switzerland, 1956-57; guest scholar Inst. State and Law, U.S.S.R. Acad. Sci., 1961-62; lectr. Am. law Moscow State U., spring 1962. Served as sgt. AUS, 1942-45. Decorated Bronze Star. Rockefeller Found. grantee to study in Europe, 1956-57; Ford Found. and Am. Council Learned Socs. grantee to study in USSR, 1961-62. Chmn. com. on teaching law outside of law schs. Assn. Am. Law Schs., 1955, 56, 63; gen. reporter Internat. Assn. Legal Sci. study of legal aspects East-West trade, 1956-58; del. Econ. Commn. Europe, Geneva, 1956-57. Mem. Am. Assn. Advancement Slavic Studies, Am. Soc. of Internat. Law, Internat. Law Soc., Am. Soc. Legal History, Am. Fgn. Law Assn., Phi Beta Kappa, Order of the Coif. Author: Justice in U.S.S.R.; An Interpretation of Soviet Law, 1950, rev. edit. enlarged, 1963; Soviet Law in Action; The Recollected Cases of a Soviet Lawyer (with Boris A. Konstantinovsky), 1953; The Russians in Focus, 1953; Soviet Military Law and Administration (with Miroslav Kerner), 1955; On the Teaching of Law in the Liberal Arts Curriculum, 1956; The Nature and Functions of Law, 1958, (with William R. Greiner) 2d edit., 1966; Introduction, The Trial of the U-2, 1960; Soviet Criminal Law and Procedure, 1966; (with Peter B. Maggs) Disarmanent Inspection under Soviet Law, 1967. Editor, translator; Documents on Soviet Military Law and Administration (with Miroslav Kerner), 1955; Basic Laws on the Structure of the Soviet State (with John B. Quigley), 1969; Soviet Statutes and Decisions, vols. 1-5, 1964-69. Editor, co-author Talks on American Law, 1961. Contbr. articles legal, other jours. and mags. Home: 7 Chauncy Lane Cambridge MA 02138

BERMAN, HARRY LOUIS, physician; b. Peoria, Ill., May 7, 1908; s. Max and Golda Rose (Fogelman) B.; B.S., Bradley U., 1927; M.D., Northwestern U., 1933; m. Ellen Jean Stein, June 24, 1934; 1 son, Howard H. Intern Cook County Hosp., Chgo, 1933-34; resident radiology Walter Reed Gen. Hosp., Washington, 1947-48, Presbyn. Hosp., N.Y.C., 1948-50; practice medicine specializing in dermatology, Peoria, 1935-39, specializing in radiology, Balt., 1960—; commd. 1st lt., M.C., U.S. Army, 1939, advanced through grades to col., 1960; with Sta. Hosp., Ft. Dix, N.J., 1939-42; div. surgeon 10th Mountain Div., Camp Carson, Colo., Camp Hale, Colo., Camp Swift, Tex., and Italy, 1942-45; med. instr. Mountain and Winter Warfare Sch., Camp Carson, 1946-47; prof. mil. sci. and tactics Columbia Coll. Phys. and Surgs., 1948-50; successively radiologist U.S. Army Hosp., Ft. Monmouth, N.J., 343d Gen. Hosp., Japan, Atom Bomb Casualty Commn., Hiroshima, Nagasaki, Japan, 1950-52; cons. radiology U.S. 8th Army, Korea, 1952; chief radiation therapy Walter Reed Gen. Hosp., 1953-60; ret., 1960; head div. radiation therapy, and isotopes Sinai Hosp., Balt., 1960—; asst. prof. radiology Sch. Medicine Johns Hopkins; clin. asst. prof. radiology Sch. Medicine George Washington U.; cons. radiation therapy Walter Reed Gen. Hosp., Ft. Howard VA Hosp., Armed Forces Radiobiol. Research Inst. Bd. dirs. Md. div. Am. Cancer Soc., pres. Balt. unit, 1969-71. Decorated Legion of Merit, Bronze Star with cluster. Diplomate in radiology and nuclear medicine Am. Bd. Radiology. Fellow Am. Coll. Radiology, Am. Geriatrics Soc.; mem. A.M.A., Pan Am. Med. Assn., Balt. Med. Soc., Med. and Chirurg. Faculty Md., Radiol. Soc. N. Am., Am. Roentgen Ray Soc., Am. Radium Soc., Soc. Nuclear Medicine, Md. Radiol. Soc., Am. Med. Writers Assn., Am. Soc. Therapeutic Radiologists, A.A.A.S., Assn. Am. Med. Colls., Assn. Mil. Surgeons U.S., Assn. Advancement Med. Instrumentation, Inter-Am. Coll. Radiology, Ret. Officers Assn. Mason. Contbr. articles profl. jours. Editorial bd. Military Medicine. Home: 2754 Deerfield Dr Ellicott City MD 21043 Office: Sinai Hosp Belvedere and Greenspring Av Baltimore MD 21215

BERMAN, HERBERT, lawyer; b. N.Y.C., Nov. 13, 1923; s. Israel and Ida (Leder) B.; B.A., N.Y.U., 1944; J.D. Harvard, 1947; m. Daisy B. Koenig, June 5, 1949; children-Sara, Debra, Nathaniel A. Admitted to N.Y. bar, 1947, since practied in N.Y.C.; asso. atty. Tenzer, Greenblatt, Fallon & Kaplan, 1947-53, partner, 1953—; lectr. Practing Law Inst., 1960—. Del. White House Conf. on Fgn. Trade, 1958, White House Conf. on Children and Youth, 1960, White House Conf. of Aging, 1961; participant White House Conf. of Religious Leaders on Racial Problems, 1963; mem. Real Estate Bd. N.Y., Inc. Mem. Bd. Higher Edn. City of N.Y., 1967—; chmn. Bklyn. Coll. Com., 1969—, vice chmn. com. on grad. div., 1968—, vice chmn. law com., 1969—, chmn. com. on profl. obligations of faculty, 1969—. Bd. dirs. Bklyn. Coll. Student Services Corp., City U. Research Found., Jewish Edn. Com., Union Orthodox Jewish Congregations Am., Am. Assn. Jewish Edn., Am. Com. for Shaare Zedek Hosp. in Jerusalem; mem. exec. com. Am. sect. World Jewish Congress, Nat. Conf. on Religion and Race; bd. overseers Bar-Ilan U. Recipient Robert Bruce Dow medal for distinguished service to Washington Sq. Coll., N.Y.U. Mem. N.Y. County Lawyers Assn. (com. chmn.), Am., N.Y. State, Queens County bar assns., Assn. Bar City N.Y., Internat. Real Estate Fedn., Am. Judicature Soc., Phi Beta Kappa, Tau Kappa Alpha. Club: HArvard (N.Y.C.). Mng. editor: Harvard Law Sch. Record, 1947. Home: 108-19 68th Av Forest Hills NY 11375 Office: 235 E 42d St New York NY 10017

BERMAN, JEROME RICHARD, physician, educator; b. N.Y.C., Aug. 7, 1920; s. Samuel and Sadie Leah (Fox) B.; B.A., U. Cin., 1941, M.D., 1944; m. Estelle L. Brown, June 15, 1946; 1 son, Arthur E. Intern, Cin. Gen. Hosp., 1945, resident medicine, 1946; infectious disease, 1947, gastroenterology, 1948-50; practice medicine specializing in gastroenterology, Cin., 1950—; mem. med. staff U. Cin., 1947—, clin. prof. medicine, 1967—; cons. VA Hosp., Cin., 1955—; mem. exec. bd. Jewish Hosp., Cin., 1971—. Mem. North Avondale Neighborhood Assn., Cin., Charter Com. Cin.; mem. corporate bd. Cin. Coll. Conservatory Music, asso. of coll., 1964—. Served to capt. M.C., AUS, 1946-47, USAF, 1953. Fellow A.C.P., Am. Coll. Gastroenterology; mem. Am. Gastroent. Assn., Am. Soc. Gastrointestinal Endoscopy, Am. Assn. Study Liver Disease, A.A.A.S., Sigma Xi. Jewish religion. Home: 3904 Wess Park Dr Cincinnati OH 45217 Office: U Cin Coll Medicine 2825 Burnet Av Cincinnati OH 45219

BERMAN, JOSHUA MORDECAI, lawyer, mfg. co. exec.; b. Rochester, N.Y., Aug. 4, 1938; s. Jeremiah Joseph and Rose (Rappaport) B.; B.B.A. summa cum laude, Coll. City N.Y., 1958; J.D. cum laude, Harvard, 1961; m. Claire S. Shapiro, Apr. 16, 1961; children—Marc Ethan, Eve. Admitted to Mass. bar, 1961; with firm Goodwin, Procter & Hear, Boston, 1961—, partner, 1969—. Chmn. bd., chief exec. officer Tyce Labs., Inc., Waltham, Mass., 1970—; dir. Prelude Corp., Westport, Mass. Trustee Boston Children's Sch., Inc. Home: 34 1/2 Beacon St Boston MA 02108 Office: 28 State St Boston MA 02109

BERMAN, LAWRENCE, ins. co. exec.; b. Spring Valley, N.Y., Feb. 28, 1929; s. Rubin and Anne (Baron) B.; B.A., in Econs., Mich. State U., 1950; LL.B., Cornell U., 1953; m. Louise Wortman, Nov. 29, 1953; children—Daniel Bruce, Robin Carol, Ralph Andrew. Admitted to N.Y. bar, 1953; with Lehigh Valley R.R., 1955-62, asst. gen. counsel, 1959-62; atty. Western Union Telegraph Co., 1962-63; spl. asst. to pres. Ry. Express Agy., Inc., 1963- 64, sec., 1964-69; sec. R E A Leasing Corp., Fast Service Shipping Terminals, Inc., R E A Express-Seven Arts Transvision, Inc., REXCO, Inc., REXCO Supply Corp., REA, Inc. of Cal., Ry. Express Motor Transp., Inc., REA, Inc., Va., gen. counsel Ins. Rating Bd., 1969-71. Ins. Services Office, 1971—. Served with AUS, 1953-55. Mem. N.Y. County Lawyers Assn., Am. Bar Assn. Jewish religion. Club: Bankers (N.Y.C.). Home: 22 Charlotte Dr Spring Valley NY 10977 Office: 125 Maiden Lane New York City NY 10038

BERMAN, MORTON, educator; b. Syracuse, N.Y., Mar. 21, 1924; s. Irving Joseph and Rose (Lieberman) B.; A.B., U. Ill., 1948; A.M., Harvard, 1950, Ph.D., 1957. Teaching fellow gen. edn. Harvard, 1951-54; instr. English, Boston U., 1954-58, asst. prof., 1958-61, asso. prof., 1961-64, prof. English, 1964—, chmn. dept. English, 1962—; cons. on lit. textbooks Little, Brown & Co., Boston. Served with AUS, 1944-46. Recipient Ruskin prize, 1954. Dexter Travelling fellow, 1954. Mem. Am. Assn. U. Profs., Modern Lang. Assn. Am. Author: (with S. Barnet and W. Burto) The Study of Literature, 1960, Aspects of the Drama, 1962, A Dictionary of Literary, Dramatic, and Cinematic Terms, 1971, Introduction to Literature, 4th edit., 1971; Afterword to George Eliot's The Mill on the Floss, 1965; Collaborator: Eight Great Tragedies, 1957; Eight Great Comedies, 1958; The Genius of the Irish Theater, 1960; The Genius of the English Theater, 1962; Tragedy and Comedy, 1967. Home: 29 Ash St Cambridge MA 02138 Office: Dept English Boston U 236 Bay State Rd Boston MA 02215

BERMAN, MORTON MAYER, rabbi; b. Balt., Aug. 23, 1899; s. Morris and Rose (Frommer) B.; B.A., Yale, 1921; M.H.L., Jewish Inst. Religion, 1926, D.D., 1946; ordained Rabbi, Jewish Inst. Religion, 1926; postgrad. Columbia, 1922-30; U. Grenoble, France, 1926; Hebrew U., Palestine (Israel), 1926-27; Hochshule für die Wissenschaft des Judentums, Berlin, 1927; m. Grayce Sunshine Hofheimer, Oct. 21, 1925 (dec. 1949); 1 son, John Simon; m. 2d, Elaine Ruth Siegel Levy, June 27, 1950; children—Susanna, Stephen, David. Student rabbi, Danbury, Conn., 1923-26; rabbi Temple Emanuel, Davenport, Ia., 1927-29; asso. rabbi and dir. edn. Free Synagogue, N.Y.C., 1929-37; dir. field activities Jewish Inst. Religion, 1929-37; rabbi Temple Isaiah Israel, Chgo., 1937-57, rabbi emeritus; hon. dir. dept. English speaking countries Keren Hayesod United Israel Appeal, Jerusalem, Israel. Past nat. v.p., former chmn. adminstrv. com. Am. Jewish Congress; former chmn. Zionist Council of Chicago; hon. pres. Chgo. Council Jewish Nat. Fund; past pres. Chgo. div. Am. Jewish Congress; past mem. exec. com. World Jewish Congress. past pres. Chgo. Rabbinical Assn.; mem. Central Conf. Am. Rabbis. Trustee AMLI Central Music Library Israel. Chaplain USNR, 1943-46; with 6th Marine Div., Okinawa. Decorated Bronze Star medal. Mem. Phi Beta Kappa, Phi Alpha. Mason (32); mem. B'nai B'rith. Author: A Jew's View of the Crucifixion, 1929; Index to Mielziner's Introduction to the Talmud, 3d, edit., 1925; Role of the Rabbi, 1941; Our First Century, 1952; edited Negro Community to the West, 1940; The Bridge to Life, 1971. Editor Am. Jewish Congress Bull., 1933-34; editor Opinion; contbr. Jewish Forum, Unity. and Congress Weekly. Editorial adv. bd. P.F. Collier & Sons; asst. editor Ency. Judaica. Home: 6 Rehov Berachyahu 6 Bet Hakerem Jerusalem Israel Office: Keren Hayesod United Israel Appeal Jerusalem Israel

BERMAN, MYRON PHILIP, paper co. exec.; b. N.Y.C., Nov. 24, 1916; s. Morris Bernard and Rose (Hecht) B.; student N.Y.U., 1934-38; m. Roslyn Rettich, Dec. 17, 1939; children—Janice Lee (Mrs. David Lawrence), Harvey Alan. Vice-pres. Harlem Card & Paper Co., N.Y.C., 1938-52; pres. Berman Paper Co., N.Y.C., 1952-60; pres., chmn. bd. dirs. Saxon Industries, Inc., N.Y.C., 1960-. Mem. Nat. Paper Trade Assn. (bd. dirs. 1966-70). Jewish religion (pres. temple 1960-62). Clubs: Edgewood Country (Riverdale, N.J.); Putnam Country (Mahopac, N.Y.). Home: 200 Central Park S New York City NY 10019 Office: 450 7th Av New York City NY 10001

BERMAN, SEYMOUR, banker. Sr. v.p. Exchange Nat. Bank Chgo. Office: La Salle and Adams Sts Chicago IL 60690*

BERMAN, SHELLEY, comedian; b. Chgo., Feb. 3, 1926; s. Nathan and Irene (Marks) B.; student Goodman Theatre, Chgo., 1943-47; m. Sarah Herman, Apr. 19, 1947; 1 son, Joshua. Summer and winter stock, Midwest and East, 1947-49; joined Compass Players, Chgo., 1955; debut as comedian Chgo. night club, 1957; numerous TV appearances, night club performances, 1957—; theatrical appearances include The Girls Against The Boys, Broadway, 1959, Damn Yankees, 1960, Mirror Under the Eagle, 1960, Where's Charlie, 1961 (all summer stock), Guys and Dolls, Los Angeles, 1961, A Family Affair, Broadway, 1962; appeared in movie The Best Man, 1963; recordings include Inside Shelley Berman, 1959, Outside Shelley Berman, 1959, Edge of Shelly Berman, 1960, Shelley Berman-A Personal Appearance, 1961, New Sides, 1963, others; now writer of situation comedies for Screen Gems, CBS, Warner Bros.; dir. film Keep Off My Grass, 1971. Recipient award Most Promising New Comedian, Show Bus. Rev., 1958, Grammy award for best comedy records, 1959, Comedian of year award Chgo. Jewish Appeal, 1961. Mem. Am. Guild Variety Artists, Actors Equity Assn., Am. Fedn. Radio and TV Artists, Screen Actors Guild, Writers Guild Am. Screen Dirs. Guild. Author: Cleans and Dirtys, 1965. Office: 9876 Beverly Grove Dr Beverly Hills CA 90210

BERMINGHAM, JOHN REEVE, data processing exec.; b. N.Y.C., Jan. 22, 1926; s. Luke V. and Leslie (Reeve) B.; B.A. in Geology, Princeton, 1946-49; m. Janet Maul, Apr. 15, 1950; children—Leslie J., John Reeve, Geoffrey B. With Standard Oil Co. of N.J., 1949-60, Am. Machine & Foundry Co., 1960-62, Internat. Tel. & Tel. Corp., N.Y.C., 1962-64; v.p., dir. electronic systems center N.Y. Stock Exchange, N.Y.C., 1965-68; v.p., dir. Central Computer Accounting Corp., N.Y.C., 1965-68; dir. systems and planning Hirsch & Co., N.Y.C., 1968-69; exec. v.p., dir. Wall St. Information Services, Inc., N.Y.C., 1968-71; v.p. Irving Trust Co., N.Y.C., 1971—. Served with USNR, 1943-46. Home: 21 Mallard Dr Greenwich CT 06830 Office: 1 Wall St New York City NY 10015

BERN, HOWARD ALAN, educator; b. Montreal, Can., Jan. 3, 1920; s. Simeon and Ethel (Hyman) B.; B.A., U. Cal., Los Angeles, 1941, M.A., 1942, Ph.D., 1948; m. Estelle Claire Bruck, Mar. 30, 1946; children—Alan, Lauren. Instr., asst. prof., asso. prof. zoology U. Cal. at Berkeley, 1948-60, prof., 1960—, research prof. Miller Inst. Basic Research in Sci., 1961; research endocrinologist Cancer Research Genetics Lab., 1960—; vis. prof. pharmacology U. Bristol, 1965-66; vis. prof. zoology U. Kerala, 1967, U. Tokyo, 1971. Served to capt. AUS, 1942-46. Guggenheim fellow, 1951- 52; NSF fellow, 1958-59, 65-66; fellow Center Advanced Study Behavioral Scis., 1960. Mem. Zool. Soc. Calcutta (hon.), Am. Soc. Zoologists (past pres., past div. chmn. comparative endocrinology), Internat. Brain Research Orgn. (neuroendocrinology panel), Endocrine Soc., Am.Assn. Cancer Research, Soc. Exptl. Biology and Medicine, Am. Assn. Anatomists, Société Zoologique de France. Author: (with A. Gorbman) A Textbook of Comparative Endocrinology, 1962. Mem. editorial bd. Endocrinology, Gen. and Comparative Endocrinology, Internat. Rev. Cytology. Home: 1010 Shattuck Av Berkeley CA 94707

BERNABO, RAYMOND ANDREW, lawyer; b. N.Y.C., Jan. 1, 1930; s. Ernest L. and Ethel (Volpi) B.; A.B., Harvard, 1951; Fulbright scholar, U. Rome, 1951-52; LL.B. (Stone scholar), Columbia, 1955. Admitted to N.Y. bar, 1955; asso. Winthrop, Stimson, Putnam & Roberts, N.Y.C., 1955-58; corporate counsel, sec. M & T Chems., Inc., Greenwich, Conn., 1958—. Mem. Assn. Bar City N.Y., Am., N.Y. State bar assns., Am. Soc. Corporate Secs., Phi Delta Phi. Club: Harvard (N.Y.C.). Home: 60 Sutton Pl S New York City NY 10022 Office: American Lane Greenwich CT 06830

BERNAL Y GARCIA PIMENTEL, IGNACIO, archaeologist; b. Paris, Feb. 13, 1910; s. Rafael and Rafaela (Garcia Pimental) B.; M.A. in Anthropology, Escuela Nacional de Antropologia, 1946; Ph.D. in Archaeology, U. Nacional Autonoma de Mexico, 1949; H.H.D. (hon.), U. Am., 1967; L.H.D., U. Cal. at Berkeley, 1969; LL.D., St. Mary's U., 1970; m. Sofia Verea Corcuera, Oct. 14, 1944; children—Ignacio, Rafaela, Carlos, Concepcion. Prof. U. Nacional Autonoma de Mexico, 1948—; dir. anthropology Mexico City Coll., 1948-59; cultural attache Mexican embassy, Paris, 1955-56, also permanent del. Mexico to UNESCO; mem. Internat. Commn. Monuments, UNESCO, 1956—; dir. Teotibuacan Project, 1962-64, Nat. Museum Anthropology, 1962-68, 71—; Pres. Comision Premio Nacional de Arte, 1967, Soc. Am. Archaeology, 1969-70; dir. gen. Inst. Nacional de Antropologia e Historia, 1968-70. Decorated officer Royal Order Orange-Nassau (Netherlands); officer Legion of Honor (France); comdr. Order of Merit (Italy); officer Order of Crown (Belgium); comdr. Order of Merit (Germany); officer Royal Order Dannebrog (Denmark). Fellow Am. Anthrop. Assn., Am. Acad. Arts and Scis.; regular mem. Mexican Acad. History; mem. Soc. Am. Archaeology, Acad. Nacional de Ciencias, Soc. des Americanistes de Paris, Soc. Mexicana de Antropologia, Acad. Nacional de la Investigacion Cientifica. Author: (with Alfonso Caso) Urnas de Oaxaca, 1952; Bibliografia de Arqueologia y Etnografia, Mesoamérica y Norte de Mexico, 1514-1960, 1962; La Ceramica de Monte Alban, 1967; El Museo Nacional de Antropologia, 1967; El Mundo Olmeca, 1968; Ancient Mexico in Colour, 1968; The Olmec World, 1969. Home: 65 Tres Picos Mexico City 5 Mexico Office: Muses Nacional de Antropologia Mexico City 5 Mexico

BERNARD, HUGH YANCEY, Jr., librarian, educator; b. Athens, Ga., July 17, 1919; s. Hugh Yancey and Marguerite (Vonderau) B.; student Piedmont Coll., 1937-38; A.B., U. Ga., 1941; B.S., Columbia, 1947; J.D., George Washington U., 1961. Tchr. high schs., Moultrie, Ga., 1941; acting supr. VA, Atlanta, 1946; cataloger, copyright office Library of Congress, Washington, 1947-52, reviser, 1952-59, sr. cataloger manuscripts sect. Descriptive Cataloging Div., 1959-60; librarian Law Library, Washington U., 1960—; lectr. George Washington U., 1962-67, asso. prof. law, 1968-70, prof. law, 1970—; admitted to D.C. bar, 1961. Dir. 3810 Southern Av., S.C., Inc., Washington, 1952-55, pres., 1955; chmn. bd. Robinson Farm, Inc., Alexandria, Va., 1970—. Founding dir., incorporator Women's Home, Alexandria, Va., 1963. Served with USAAF, 1942-46. Mem. Spl. Libraries Assn., Am. Bar Assn., Am. Judicature Soc., Law Librarians Soc. Washington (v.p. 1964-66 pres. 1966), Am. Assn. Law Libraries, Order of Coif, Phi Beta Kappa, Kappa Delta Pi, Phi Alpha Delta. Democrat. Baptist (deacon). Mason (Shriner). Club: National Lawyers (Washington). Author: The Law of Death and the Disposal of the Dead, 1966; Public Officials, Elected and Appointed, 1969. Co-author: Your Complete Guide to Estate Planning, 1971. Home: 1911 Paul Spring Pkwy Alexandria VA 22308 Office: 716 20th St NW Washington DC 20006

BERNARD, J. PIERRE, banker, b. New Orleans, Jan. 17, 1901; s. George Richard and Jeanne (Wogan) B.; B.S., U.S. Naval Acad., 1923; student N.Y.U. Grad. Sch. Bus. Adminstrn., 1930-31; m. Sibyl Mary Darlington, Aug. 7, 1941; Children—Sibyl Julia (Mrs. Shaun F. O'Malley), Mary Olivia. Vice pres. Annapolis Banking & Trust Co., 1946-50, dir., 1949—, exec. v.p., 1950, pres., 1951-66, chmn. bd., 1966—; vice chmn. bd. Mercantile Bankshares Corp.; dir. Balt. Gas & Electric Co., Annapolis Broadcasting Corp. Dir., past pres. Anne Arundel County Trade Council; bd. dirs. Credit Devel. Corp. Md.; trustee U.S. Naval Acad. Found. Served to comdr. USNR, World War II. Mem. Mil. Order World Wars, Md. Bankers Assn. (past pres.). Clubs: University (N.Y.C.); Army-Navy (Washington); Maryland (Balt.). Home: 207 Hanover St Annapolis MO 21401 Office: Main St and Church Circle Annapolis MD 21401

BERNARD, KENNETH A., educator; m. Dorothy F. Graham; 1 dau., Mrs. Robert N. Larson. Prof. history Boston U.; vis. prof. Wash. State U., summers 1953, 57, 61, U. Ida., summers 1959, 68. Hon. mem. Lincoln Sesquicentennial Commn., 1959-60; pres. Lincoln Group of Boston, 1960-69. Recipient Civil War Round Table Benjamin Barondess award for Lincoln and the Music of the Civil War, 1967. Mem. Phi Beta Kappa. Author: Abraham Lincoln—The Song in His Heart, 1970. Contbr. articles on Lincoln to profl. jours. Office: Boston Univ Boston MA 02215

BERNARD, LAWRENCE GEORGE, naval officer; b. Arpan, S.D., Feb. 9, 1914; s. George Charles and Stephanie (Manseau) B.; B.S., U.S. Navel Acad., 1937; m. Caroline Lenhart, June 10, 1939; children—Lawrence George, Alan C., Jon M. Commd. ensign U.S. Navy, 1937, advanced through grades to rear adm., 1966; comdr. Submarine Flotilla, 1967-68; dir. shore installations div. Office Chief Naval Operations, 1968—. Decorated Silver Star, Legion of Merit, Bronze Star. The Pentagon, Washington, DC 20350.

BERNARD, LOLA DIANE, educator; b. Rockaway Beach, N.Y., Nov. 9, 1928; d. Clark C. and Antoinette (Berger) Bernard; B.A., Roosevelt U., 1949; M.A., U. Houston, 1952; M.S.W., Tulane U., 1954; Ph.D., Bryn Mawr Coll., 1967. Psychometrician counseling and testing dept. Roosevelt U., 1948-49; Rorshach interpreter Dr. Ralph J. Wentworth-Rohr, N.Y.C., 1949-50; psychometrician Dr. J. Sanford Davis Vocational Bur., N.Y.C., 1949-50; psychometrician counseling and testing dept. U. Houston, 1950; psychologist Woman's Fed. Penitentiary, Huntsville, Tex., 1951; social worker M.D. Anderson Hosp. Cancer Research, Houston, 1952; med. social worker Bur. Tb Control, New Orleans, 1954-56; dir. social service dept. Touro Infirmary, New Orleans, 1956-60; instr. Bryn Mawr Coll., 1964-65; field instr. Tulane U., 1958-62, asst. prof., 1965-66, asso. prof., 1966-69; prof., chmn. dept. social work Fla. State U., 1969—; dir. accrediation procedure for profl. membership Council Social Work Edn., 1969-70, mem. nat. accreditation commn., 1970-73. Mem. manpower study Fla. Bd. Regents, 1971-72; Disaster worker A.R.C., 1965-69; mem. Leon County (Fla.) Assn. Community Services, 1970—, Leon County Humane Soc., 1970—, Tallahassee Urban League, 1970—. Bd. dirs. Home for Incurables, New Orleans, 1966-69, Le Moyne Art Found., Tallahassee, 1970—. Nat. Found. Infantile Paralysis grantee, 1952-54, Nat. Inst. Mental Health grantee, 1962-64. Mem. Nat. Assn. social Workers (mem. nat. commn. casework 1967-69), Council Social Work Edn., Nat. Conf. Social Welfare, Am. Assn. U. Profs., So. Regional Ednl. Bd., Psi Chi. Contbr. articles profl. jours. Home: 606 W Call St Tallahassee FL 32304

BERNARD, MICHAEL MARK, city planning cons., lawyer; b. N.Y.C., Sept. 5, 1926; s. H. L. and Henryetta (Siegel) B.; A.B., U. Chgo., 1949; J.D., Northwestern U., 1953; M. City Planning, Harvard, 1959; student Urban Design Consortium, 1971; m. Laura Jane Pincus, Aug. 28, 1958. Admitted to Ill. bar, 1952, N.Y. bar, 1955; gen. practice law, Chgo. and N.Y.C., 1953-55; research Harvard Law Sch., 1955-56; city planning cons., atty.-adviser Puerto Rico, 1956-58; city planner, legal adviser Chgo. Dept. City Planning, 1960-64; cons. planning and zoning, 1964—; lectr. in field, 1959—. Mem. exec. faculty Boston Archtl. Center 1967—; vis. prof. urban and regional planning U. Ia., 1969—. Adviser to gov. on modernization Commonwealth Mass., 1968—. Mem. com. urban devel. and housing World Peace Through Law Center, 1965—; mem. com. transp. law Hwy. Research Bd., 1966—; cons. White House Policy Adv. Com. to D.C., 1966; del. World Congress Housing and Planning, Paris, France, 1962, Tokyo, Japan, 1966. Patron Hull House Assn., Chgo., 1965—. Served with USNR, 1944-46. NRC-Nat. Acad. Scis. grantee, 1964-66. Mem. Am. Bar Assn. (various coms. 1961—), Internat. Fedn. Housing and Planning, Am. Inst. Planners (chmn. legislative com. Met. Chgo. sect. 1963- 65), Am. Soc. Planning Ofcls., Boston Visual Artists Union (sec.-gen. 1971—), Phi Delta Phi. Unitarian. Author. Contbr. profl. jours. Editorial adviser Urban Law Ann. of Washington U. Sch. Law. Address: 25 Stanton Av Newton MA 02166

BERNARD, PAUL PETER, educator; b. Antwerp, Belgium, July 5, 1929; s. Oscar Arthur and Margaret (Fuchs) B.; came to U.S., 1939, naturalized, 1945; student N.Y.U., 1945-46; A.B., U. Denver, 1948, postgrad., 1948-50; postgrad. Columbia, 1950-51; M.A., U. Colo., 1952, Ph.D., 1955; m. Edna Mary Jones, Mar. 24, 1949; children—Steven Leon, James Peter, Alison Rose. Instr. French, U. Colo., 1955; instr. to prof. history Colo. Coll., 1955-68; prof. history U. Ill., 1968—; asso. Center for Advanced Study, 1971. Fulbright fellow, 1953-54; Ford Found. fellow, 1960-61. Mem. Am. Hist. Assn., Conf. Group for Central European History. Author: The Origins of Josephinism, 1964; Joseph II and Bavaria, 1965; Zion Through a Spy Glass, Darkly, 1968; Joseph II, 1968; Jesuits and Jacobins, 1971. Home: 407 Eliot Dr Urbana IL 61801

BERNARD, ROBERT JOHN, transp. co. exec., lawyer; b. Boston, Jan. 27, 1922; s. J. Howard and Emma Jean (Perry) B.; A.B., Boston Coll., 1946, J.D., 1949; m. Katherine G. Cronin, Oct. 21, 1945; children—Elizabeth, Mark, Theresa, Robert. Admitted to Mass. bar, 1949, Ill. bar, 1955; atty., examiner ICC, Washington, 1949-54; atty. Assn. Western Rys., 1954-61; commerce counsel Greyhound Lines, Inc., 1961-65, v.p. commerce, 1966—; v.p., law Greyhound Corp., Phoenix, 1969—; dir. Jefferson Lines, Inc., Tex., N.M. and Okla. Coach Lines, subsidiaries and affiliated cos. of Greyhound Corp. Mem. Skokie (Ill.) Human Relations Commn., 1958-62. Served with USAF, 1943-45. Mem. Nat. Assn. Motor Bus Owners (bd. dirs.), Am. Bar Assn. K.C. Clubs: Ariz.; Camelback Golf. Contbr. articles profl. jours. Home: 6536 N 40th Pl Paradise Valley AZ 85253 Office: Greyhound Tower Phoenix AZ

BERNARD, VIOLA WERTHEIM, psychiatrist; b. N.Y.C., Feb. 22, 1907; d. Jacob and Emma (Stern) Wertheim; B.S., N.Y.U., 1933; M.D., Cornell U., 1936; m. T. C. Bernard, Aug. 1, 1934 (div. June 1938). Intern Jersey City Med. Center, 1937-38; resident in psychiatry Grasslands Hosp., Valhalla, N.Y., 1938-39, N.Y. State Psychiat. Inst. and Hosp., 1939-40; postgrad. tng. N.Y. Psychoanalytic Inst., 1939-42; staff Bur. Child Guidance N.Y.C. Bd. Edn., 1940-43; practice medicine, specializing in psychiatry and psychoanalysis, N.Y.C., 1940—; asso. in psychiatry Columbia, 1948-55, asst. clin. prof., 1955-57, asso. clin. prof., 1957-61, clin. prof., 1961—, dir. div. community psychiatry, dept. psychiatry and School of Pub. Health and Social Adminstrv. Medicine, 1956-69; tng. analyst Columbia Psychoanalytic Clinic, 1946—; faculty N.Y. School Social Work, 1944-57; psychiat. cons. Ethical Culture Schs., 1947- 56, Bank Street Coll. Edn., 1950—; chief psychiat. cons. Louise Wise Services, 1942—. Co-chmn. com. psychiat. services for children City of N.Y. Dept. Hosps., 1961-63; mem. N.Y.C. Mayor's Com. on Cts., 1956-57; spl. cons. to tng. com. Nat. Inst. Pub. Health, USPHS, 1950-54; mem. State of N.Y. Com. for Children, 1971. Bd. dirs., chmn. com. on treatment program Wiltwyck Sch. for Boys, 1942-69; Diplomate Am. Bd. Psychiatry and Neurology. Fellow Am. Pub. Health Assn., Am. Psychiat. Assn. (v.p. 1971-72), Am. Orthopsychiat. Assn.; mem. A.M.A., Am. Acad. Child Psychiatry, Am. Psychoanalytic Assn., A.A.A.S., Group for Advancement Psychiatry (mem. com. social issues), N.Y. Council of Child Psychiatry, N.Y. Acad. Scis., World Fedn. Mental Health. Co-editor: Urban Challenges to Psychiatry, 1969; Crises of Family Disorganization, 1971. Contbr. articles profl. jours. Home and Office: 930 Fifth Av New York City NY 10021

BERNARDI, HERSCHEL, actor. Appears in TV series Arnie. Address: Imperial Theatre 249 W 45th St New York City NY 10036*

BERNARDI, THEODORE C., architect; b. Jugoslavia, Oct. 3, 1903; s. John A. and Vincenza (DePolo) B.; A.B., U. Cal., Berkeley, 1924, postgrad. student, 1925; m. Beatrice Boot, Aug. 1947; children—Gene, Joan V. (Mrs. Howell Breece). Came to U.S., 1912, naturalized, 1921. Draftsman, designer, architect, San Francisco, 1923-43; partner Wurster, Bernardi & Emmons, architects, San Francisco, 1944-64; exec. v.p. Wurster, Bernardi & Emmons, Inc., Architects, San Francisco, 1964—. Lectr. in architecture U. Cal., Berkeley. Chmn. archtl. design com. San Francisco Housing Authority; chmn. Reynolds Award Jury, 1968. Recipient 1st annual award and award of merit, Nat. A.I.A., 1956, also Archtl. Firm award, 1965, and Collaborative Project award, award of merit, 1966; two awards of merit No. Cal. chpt. A.I.A., 1957. Fellow A.I.A.; member San Francisco Planning Urban Renewal Assn. Club: Commonwealth. Home: 99 Miller Lane Sausalito CA 94965 Office: 1620 Montgomery St San Francisco CA 94111

BERNARDIN, DAVID MARIOTTE, banker; b. Kansas City, Mo., Aug. 25, 1929; s. Eugene Phillip and Virginia (Rectonwald) B.; student Grad. Sch. Banking, So. Methodist U., 1960; m. Faye Mynon Mantooth, Sept. 2, 1950; 1 son, David Mariotte. With Mercantile Nat. Bank, Dallas, 1948—, sr. v.p., 1969—; dir. Winn's Stores, Inc., San Antonio. Served with USAF, 1950-52. Club: Salesmanship Club Dallas. Mason (32). Home: 1233 Comanche St Richardson TX 75080 Office: P O Box 5415 Dallas TX 75222

BERNARDIN, JOSEPH LOUIS, bishop; b. Columbia, S.C., Apr. 2, 1928; s. Joseph and Maria M. (Simion) B.; A.B. in Philosophy, St. Mary's Sem., 1948; M.A. in Edn., Cath. U. Am., 1952. Ordained priest Roman Cath. Ch., 1952; asst. pastor Diocese Charleston, S.C., 1952-54, vice chancellor, 1954-56, chancellor, 1956-66, vicar gen., 1962-66, diocesan consultor, 1962-66, adminstr., 1964-65; titular bishop of Lugura, aux. bishop Atlanta, 1966-68; gen. sec. Nat. Conf. Cath. Bishops-U.S. Cath. Conf., 1968—, also mem. exec. com. Mem. Inter-religious Com.; mem. joint working group World Council Chs. and Roman Cath. Ch. Address: 1312 Massachusetts Av NW Washington DC 20005

BERNARDO, JOHN D., business exec. Treas., Darin & Armstrong, Inc., Detroit. Office: 2041 Fenkell Av Detroit MI 48238*

BERNAT, EDWARD, business exec.; b. 1935; grad. Harvard, 1957; married. With Garland Corp., 1957—, pres., chief exec. officer, 1962—, also dir. Office: Garland Plaza Brockton MA 02401*

BERNAT, PAUL, business exec.; b. Hungary, 1902; married. With Garland Corp., Brockton, Mass., 1937—, now chmn. bd., dir. Home: 145 Clyde St Chestnut Hill MA 02167 Office: Garland Plaza Brockton MA 02401*

BERNAT, WILLIAM ALBERT, yarn processing exec.; b. Milton, Mass., June 30, 1928; s. Eugene and Elva (Packer) B.; A.B., Harvard, 1952; m. Eleanor C. Oliva, July 8, 1956; children—Eugene Nicholas, Lisa Michel, Jacqueline. Purchasing and prodn. control Emile Bernat & Sons Co., Boston, 1954-56, exec. v.p., treas., Uxbridge, Mass., 1960-66, pres., treas., 1966—; asst. to pres. design and product devel. coordination Garland Knitting Mills, Boston, 1956-60. Served to 2d lt. arty. AUS, 1952-54. Mem. Am. Mgmt. Assn. Mason. Home: 156 Brigham Hill Rd North Grafton MA 01536 Office: Depot and Mendon Sts Uxbridge MA 01569

BERNAYS, EDWARD L., pub. relations counsel; b. Vienna, Austria, Nov. 22, 1891; s. Ely and Anna (Freud) B.; B.S., Cornell U., 1912; Dr. of Humanities (hon.), Boston U.; m. Doris E. Fleischman, Sept. 16, 1922; children—Doris Fleischman (Mrs. Richard M. Held), Anne Fleischman (Mrs. Justin D. Kaplan). Counsel on pub. relations in partnership with Doris Fleischman Bernays to govt., and industries, corps., trade orgns., 1919—; adjunct prof. pub. relations N.Y. U., 1949-50, Sch. Pub. Communications Boston U., 1968-69; fgn. affairs officer, cons. U.S. State Dept. Bur. Ednl. and Cultural Affairs. Mem. adv. council Sch. Gen. Studies, Columbia, mem. Am. adv. council Ditchley Found. Bd. dirs. New Eng. Conservatory Music; gov. Nat. Guild Community Music Schs. Hon. mem. bd. dirs. Nat. Multiple Sclerosis. Pres. Edward L. Bernays Found., mem. Columbia U. Pub. Communications seminar; mem. adv. bd. Suffolk U. Sch. Bus. Adminstrn.; adv. com. Edward R. Murrow Center Pub. Diplomacy Fletcher Sch. Law and Diplomacy, Tufts U., bd. dirs. Longy Sch. Music; mem. Mass. Com. on Crime and Delinquency. Awarded Officer of Pub. Instrn. (France), King Christian Medal (Danish), 1946; bronze medallion of honor City of N.Y., 1961; Honor Award, Ohio U., 1970. Mem. English Speaking Union, Soc. for Psychol. Study of Social Issues, Columbia Assos. Clubs: Columbia Men's Faculty, Overseas Press, Cornell (New York), Harvard Faculty. Author: numerous books latest being Public Relation, 1952; Your Future in Public Relations, 1961; Biography of an Idea; Memoirs of Public Relations Counsel Edward L. Bernays, 1965. Editor: An Outline of Careers; The Engineering of Consent. Co-editor: The Case For Reappraisal U.S. Overseas Information Policies and Programs, 1970. Contbr. numerous publs. Address: 7 Lowell St Cambridge MA 02138

BERNBACH, WILLIAM, advt. exec.; b. N.Y.C., Aug. 13, 1911; s. Jacob and Rebecca (Reiter) B.; B.C.S., N.Y. U., 1933; m. Evelyn Carbone, June 5, 1938; children—John Lincoln, Paul. Dir. research N.Y. World's Fair, 1939-40; dir. postwar planning Coty, Inc., 1943-44; v.p. Grey Advt. Agy., 1945-49; pres. Doyle Dane Bernbach, Inc., 1949-67, chmn., chief exec. officer, 1968- -. Adj. prof. N.Y.U. Mem. nat. bd. Nat. Library Com., mem. Lincoln Center Film Com. Bd. dirs. Salk Inst. Biol. Studies, Internat. Eye Found. Named Man of Year, Pulse, Inc. 1966; mem. Copywriters Hall of Fame; recipient Madden Meml. award, 1968; named Top Advt. Agy. Exec., 1969; named One Person Who Did Most for the Progress of the Advertising Industry, 1963, 65, 66. Club: N.Y. University Alumni; City Athletic. Home: 870 UN Plaza New York City NY 10017 Office: 20 W 43d St New York City NY 10036

BERNBAUM, MAURICE MARSHALL, ret. fgn. service officer; b. Chgo., Feb. 15, 1910; s. Louis and Anne (Warsaw) B.; S.B., Harvard, 1931; postgrad. econs., U. Chgo., 1931-32; m. Elizabeth R. Hahn, Feb. 5, 1942; children—Edwin Marshall, Louise Marcia. Social worker State Ill., Chgo., 1932- 35; economist, U.S. Tariff Commn., Washington, 1935-36; vice consul, Vancouver, B.C., 1936-38; Singapore, 1938-41; vice consul, 2d sec., Caracas, Venezuela, 1942-45; 2d sec., Managua, Nicaragua, 1945-48; 1st sec. and consul Quito, Ecuador, 1948-50; staff Nat. War Coll., Washington, 1950-51; with Bur. Inter Am. Affairs, Dept. State, 1951-53; counselor of Embassy, Caracas, Venezuela, 1953-55; dir. Office of S. Am. Affairs, Dept. of State, 1955-59; minister-counselor Am. embassy Buenos Aires, Argentina, 1959-60; ambassador to Ecuador, 1960-65; ambassador to Venezuela, 1965-69. Clubs: Harvard, International, Kenwood (Washington). Home: 5108 Westpath Way Washington DC 20016

BERND, JOSEPH LAURENCE, polit. scientist, educator; b. Macon, Ga., Dec. 8, 1923; s. Laurence Joseph and Eva (Bloom) B.; B.A., Mercer U., 1945; M.A., Boston U., 1953; Ph.D., Duke, 1957; m. Ruth Audrey Brady, July 2, 1960; 1 dau., Alison Ruth. Instr. polit. sci. Boston U., 1952-53; asst. prof., asso. prof. High Point (N.C.) Coll., 1957-59; asst. prof., asso. prof. So. Meth. U., 1959-65; prof. Va. Poly. Inst., Blacksburg, 1965—, dept. chmn., 1965-70; 1965-70; cons. former gov. Ga., 1949-50, 54, U.S. Commn. Civil Rights, 1958, NSF, 1965, Duke U. Press., 1966, Harper and Row, pubs., 1970, Nat. Broadcasting, 1969-70, plaintiffs brief in Sanders v. Gray U.S. Supreme Ct., 1963, Myer & Rubin in case on election law; lectr., New Orleans, Vienna, Austria, Atlanta, Lynchburg and Lexington, Va. Founder Young Peoples League for Better Govt., 1947; wage analyst WSB, 1951. Fellow Social Sci. Research Council, 1956-57, Grad. Council Humanities So. Meth. U., 1962-63, Mem. Am., So. (mem. exec. com. 1966-69) polit. sci. assns., Am. Assn. U. Profs. Jewish religion. Author: Grass Roots Politics in Georgia, 1960. Editor: Mathematical Applications in Political Science, Vols. I- IV, 1965-69, co-editor vol. V, 1970. Contbr. articles to profl. jours. Home: 502 Stonegate Dr NW Blacksburg VA 24060

BERND-COHEN, MAX, artist, lectr., critic; b. Macon, Ga., May 7, 1899; s. Max and Ernestine (Golinsky) B.; B.A., Columbia 1920, LL.B., 1922; studied in leading art schs. of Paris and Madrid; under Fernand Leger, Charles Baudouin, Academie Suisse; m. 2d, Mary Churchill Morgan, June 9, 1941; childrenWindreth, Nortina. Instr., Ringling Art Sch., 1932-33; head art dept. Fla. So. Coll. and Stanley E. Jones Found., Lakeland, Fla., 1939- 44; dir. Royal Gorge Art Sch., Canon City, Colo., 1947; portrait, landscape and mural painter; guest prof. lectr. Central Sch. Arts and Crafts. London, 1952-53; vis. artist Dartmouth, 1964; vis. artist, sr. lectr. Carlisle (Eng.) Coll. Art, 1964-65, U. Cal. at San Diego, 1965- 66, 12 one-man exhbns.; selected in open competition to paint mural for Florida Bldg., Chgo. Century of Progress Expn., 1933; chosen to represent Fla. in All States Exhbn. (Heron Art Inst.), 1933. Painted mural, The Sermon on the Mount, now at the First Community Church, Columbus, O. Recipient first prize Chester County Art Assn., 1934. Founder Fla. So. Art League and Museum, also Colo. Friends of Art Mem. Phila. Art Alliance, Zeta Beta Tau, Delta Sigma Rho. Served in S.A.T.C., Columbia University, World War I; With Am. Red Cross in the Pacific, 1945. Mason, Lectr. on art; contbr. to mags. Address: 210 Cowles St W Englewood FL 33533

BERNDT, REXER, univ. adminstr.; b. Bellefontaine, O., Mar. 9, 1920; s. Robert and Delia (Rexer) B.; B.S., U. Denver, 1949, M.B.A., 1950; Ph.D., U. Colo., 1957; m. Geraldine Cowman, Dec. 27, 1941; children—Elizabeth, Katherine, Rexer. Dean Instrn., Ariz. State Coll., Flagstaff, 1965-66; acad. v.p. No. Ariz. U., Flagstaff, 1966-67, exec. v. p., 1967-69; pres. Ft. Lewis Coll., Durango, Colo., 1969—. Served to 1st lt. USAAF, 1942-45. Home: Ft Lewis Coll Durango CO 81301

BERNDTSON, ARTHUR, educator, philosopher; b. Chgo., Jan. 31, 1913; s. Ambrosius and Katherine (Gronlund) B.; A.B., U. Chgo., 1935, Ph.D., 1940; m. Esther Schumm, Dec. 25, 1940; children—Mark Vincent, Keith Alan. Instr. philosophy Earlham Coll., 1941-44; mem. faculty U. Mo., 1945—, prof. philosophy, 1959—, chmn. dept., 1962-67. Ford fellow, 1951-52. Mem. Am., Mo. (pres. 1955-56) philos. assns., Am. Soc. Aesthetics, Soc. for Phenomenology and Existential Philosophy, Am. Assn. U. Profs. (chpt. pres. 1960-61), Inter-Am. Congress Philosophy, Phi Beta Kappa (pres. U. Mo. chpt. 1963). Author: Art, Expression, and Beauty, 1969. Contbr. to jours. and books. Home: 1107 W Rollins Rd Columbia MO 65201

BERNE, CLARENCE JOHN, surgeon; b. Hartley, Ia., Mar. 6, 1904; s. Thomas and Barbara (Wachtel) B.; M.D., U. Ia., 1927; m. Esther Van Cleave, Jan. 3, 1928; children—John Rowna, Thomas Van Cleave. Intern Univ. Hosp., Iowa City, Ia., 1927-28, resident, 1928-32; with U. So. Cal., 1930—, prof., head dept. surgery, 1938—; attending sr. staff Los Angeles Co. Hosp. Served as lt. col. M.C., AUS, 1942-45. Diplomate Am. Bd. Surgery. Fellow A.C.S.; mem. Am., Western, Pacific Coast surg. assns., Societi Internat. De Chirugie. Home: 2023 Redcliff Los Angeles CA 90039

BERNE, ROBERT MATTHEW, physiologist, educator; b. Yonkers, N.Y., Apr. 22, 1918; s. Nelson and Julia (Stahl) B.; A.B., U. N.C., 1939; M.D., Harvard, 1943; m. Beth Goldberg, Aug. 18, 1944; children—Julie, Amy, Gordon, Michael. Intern Mt. Sinai Hosp., N.Y.C., 1943-44, resident, 1946-48; research fellow Western Res. U. Sch. Medicine, Cleve., 1948-49, instr. physiology, 1949- 50, sr. instr., 1950-52, asst. prof., 1952-55, asso. prof., 1955-61, prof., 1961-66; prof., chmn. dept. physiology U. Va. Sch. Medicine, Charlottesville, 1966—. Mem. evaluation com. on post doctoral fellowships in life scis. Nat. Acad. Scis., 1963-65; mem. physiology tng. com. NIH, 1964-65; mem. tng. com. Nat. Heart Inst., 1966-70; mem. cardio-pulmonary tng. program VA, 1968-71; mem. physiology test Com. Nat. Bd. Med. Examiners, 1969-70. Trustee Cleve. Area Heart Soc., 1962-65, pres. sci. council, 1964-65; steering com. Circulation Group Physiol. Soc., 1969-71. Served with M.C., AUS, 1944-46. Mem. Am. Physiol. Soc. (mem. council 1970—; mem. finance com. 1966-70, pres. 1972-73), Am. Soc. for Clin. Investigation, Am. Heart Assn. (com. on med. edn. 1963-66, vice chmn. com. on council basic sci.), A.A.A.S., Cardiac Muscle Club, Assn. Chmn. Depts. Physiology (pres. 1970), Microcirculatory Soc., Phi Beta Kappa, Sigma Xi. Author: (with Matthew N. Levy) Cardiovascular Physiology, 1967. Editor: Circulation Research, 1970. Sect. editor Am. Jour. Physiology, Jour. Applied Physiology, 1964-65; mem. editorial bd. Circulation Research, 1961-67, 68 —, Jour. Molecular and Cellular Cardiology, 1969—, Proc. Soc. Exptl. Biology and Medicine, 1962-64. Home: 1851 Wayside Pl Charlottesville VA 22903

BERNEGGER, E. LLOYD, pharm. mfg. exec.; b. N.Y.C., June 20, 1910; s. John Rudolph and Kathryn (Curley) B.; student Columbia, N.Y. U., Merchants and Bankers and Credit Inst., Advt. Inst., m. Isabel Francis Noell, Oct. 1, 1938; children—Lloyd, James Brian, Kathryn Noell, John Kenneth. Engaged successively as salesman, credit mgr. office mgr. asst. sales mgr. of Veldown div. Internat. Paper Co., 1928-41; asst. gen. sales mgr., dir. sales, v.p., Whitehall Labs. div. Am. Home Products, 1941-49; v.p. sales and advt., dir. U.S. Time Corp., 1949-51; v.p., dir., exec. v. p. Bristol-Myers Products div. Bristol-Myers Co., 1951-59; pres. Warner-Lambert Products div. Warner-Lambert Pharm. Co., Inc., Morris Plains, N.J., 1959- -, corporate v.p. trade relations, 1963—. Bd. dirs., sec. N.J. Arthritis Arthritis Found.; bd. dirs. Morris County (N.J.) council Girl Scouts U.S.A. Home: 14 Lawrence Rd Madison, NJ 07940. Office: 201 Tabor Rd Morris Plains NJ 07950

BERNER, LEWIS, biologist, educator; b. Savannah, Ga., Sept. 30, 1915; s. Joseph Benjamin and Frances (Lax) B.; B.S., U. Fla., 1937, M.S., 1939, Ph.D., 1941; m. Amelia Pauline Brenn, Oct. 7, 1945; children—Roberta Jacqualyn, Cheryl Brenna. Asst. prof. biol. sci. U. Fla., 1946-51, asso. prof., 1951-54, prof., 1954—, chmn. biol. sci. dept., 1959—, acting dir. div. biol. scis., 1970—; prof. entomolgy U. Minn., Lake Itasca, summers 1958-60, 62, 68; entomologist Volta River Project, Govt. of Gold Coast, Brit. W. Africa, 1950, Shire River Project, Govt. Nyasaland, Brit. Central Africa, 1952. Vice pres., bd. dirs. Highlands Biol. Sta. Served to lt. col., Med. Service Corps, AUS, 1941-46; col. Res. ret. 1969. Decorated Legion of Merit; recipient Phi Sigma medal, 1941, Distinguished Service award Fla. Entomol. Soc., 1963, Distinguished Faculty award Blue Key Honor Soc., 1967. Mem. Entomol. Soc. Am. (past sect. chmn.), Assn. Southeastern Biologists, Fla. Entomol. soc. (past pres., editor), Entomol. Soc. Washington, Midwest Benthological Soc., Phi Beta Kappa, Sigma Xi, Phi Kappa Phi, Phi Sigma Alpha Epsilon Delta. Author: The Mayflies of Florida, 1950. Contbr. articles profl. jours. Home: 7080 NW 23d Av Gainesville FL 32601

BERNER, ROBERT FRANK, coll. dean; b. Cleve., Nov. 30, 1917; s. Frank Otto and Marie (Gideon) B.; B.S., U. Buffalo, 1939, M.B.A., 1948; Ph.D., U. Chgo., 1961; m. Ruth Harriet Levis, Nov. 6, 1943; children—Robert Frank, Mary Elizabeth, John David, Jean Harriet. Tchr. Palmyra (N.Y.) High Sch., 1939-41; instr. statistics U. Buffalo, 1946-48, acting chmn. dept., 1948-49, asst. dean Evening Coll., 1949-52, asst. prof. statistics, 1952-63; asso. prof. dept. mgmt. sci. State U. N.Y. at Buffalo, 1963-65, prof. mgmt. sci., and operations analysis, 1965—, acting dean div. continuing edn., 1952-55, dean, 1955—; Fulbright prof. Robert Coll., Istanbul, Turkey, 1968-69. Chmn. adult edn. com. Community Welfare Council Buffalo and Erie County, 1962-64. Dir. Creative Edn. Found., 1969—. Served to capt., F.A., AUS, 1941-45. Decorated Bronze Star, Silver Star. Mem. Assn. Univ. Evening Colls. (past pres.), Nat. Univ. Extension Assn., Am. Council Edn., Am. Assn. Univ. Profs., Am. Assn. Univ. Adminstrs., Am. Soc. Tng. Dirs. (chpt. sec. 1952-56), Theta Chi, Alpha Kappa Psi, Beta Gamma Sigma, Alpha Sigma Lambda (nat. pres.). Home: 69 E Royal Pkwy Williamsville NY 14221 Office: Hayes Hall 3435 Main St Buffalo NY 14214

BERNER, T. ROLAND, lawyer, trustee, corp. exec.; b. N.Y.C., Sept. 23, 1910; s. Irwin Rolston and Cecile (Olin) B.; B.S., Harvard, 1931; LL.B., Columbia, 1935; m. Rosalie Leventritt, Mar. 24, 1938; children—Edgar Rolston, Rosalie, Winifred, Thomas Roland, Richard Olin. Admitted to N.Y. bar, 1936; asso. Gravath, DeGersdorff, Swaine & Wood, 1935-42; pvt. practice of law, and trustee, N.Y.C., 1946—; chmn. bd., pres. Curtiss-Wright Corp.; chmn. bd. Dorr-Oliver, Inc.; dir., exec. com. Amerace ESNA Corp., GAF Corp., Lynch Corp. Bd. dirs. Young Audiences, Inc.; v.p., dir. Edgar M. Leventritt Found.; trustee Marlboro Music Sch. Served as lt. comdr. USNR, 1942-45. Recipient Navy Meritorious Pub. Service citation. Mem. Bar Assn. City of N.Y., Am. Ordnance Assn., Air Force assn., Aerospace Industries Assn. (gov.) Aircraft Builders Council (pres.), Assn. U.S. Army, Nat. Security Indsl. Assn., Soc. Automotive Engrs. Episcopalian. Clubs: Harvard Lunch, Highland Country; Economic (N.Y.C.); Nat. Aviation (Washington). Office: Curtiss-Wright Corp One Passaic St Wood-Ridge NJ 07075

BERNERS, EDGAR HUBERT, architect; b. Port Washington, Wis., Jan. 6, 1898; s. Hubert J. Berners and Catherine (Peters) B.; B.Arch., U. Ill., 1921; m. Zita Davis, Aug. 18, 1923; children—Edgar Davis, Mary Catherine (Mrs. Thomas Kishler). Mem. Berners, Schober & Kilp, architects, and predecessor firm, Green Bay, 1927—; projects designed include: Sacred Heart Hosp., Eau Claire, Wis., St. Joseph Hosp., Joliet, Ill., St. Vincent Hosp., Green Bay, Wis., St. Marys Hosp., Decatur, Ill., St. Joseph Hosp., Elgin, Ill., St. John's Hosp., Springfield, Ill., Mercy Hosp., Urbana, Ill., others: cons. St. Mary's Hosp. Himeji, Japan, St. Francis Hosp., Nagasaki, Japan, also on libraries and ednl. instns. Chmn. architects div. Wis. Registration Bd. Architects and Profl. Engrs.; pres. nat. council Archtl. Registration Bd., 1956-57. Fellow A.I.A. (pres. Wis. chpt. 1949-50, No. Central States rep. nat. bd. dirs. 1952-55); mem. Wis. Soc. Profl. Engrs., Am. Legion. K.C. Rotarian. Office: 310 Pine St Green Bay WI

BERNET, LEWIS HOWARD, business exec.; b. Leesport, Pa., Aug. 3, 1902; s. John L. and Minnie E. (Shappell) B.; student bus. coll.; m. Hazel L. Gehman, Sept. 11, 1930; children—Doris M. (Mrs. Norman C. Brendel), Larry. Former v.p., treas., dir. Am. Casualty Co., Valley Forge Ins. Co., Valley Forge Life Ins. Co.; pres., dir. First Nat. Bank of Leesport. Home: 136 E Wall St Leesport PA 19533

BERNET, WILLIAM G., business exec.; b. Buffalo, N.Y., 1894. Chmn. and dir. U.S. Truck Lines, Inc., of Del., Cleve. Home: 18975 Van Aken Blvd Shaker Heights OH Heights OH South Park Blvd. Office: 1602 Union Commerce Bldg Cleveland OH 44115

BERNHARD, ARNOLD, investment counsel and exec.; b. N.Y.C., Dec. 2, 1901; s. Bernhard and Regina (Steigelfest) B.; B.A., Williams Coll., 1925; m. Janet Marie Kinghorn, Dec. 21, 1929; children—Jean Haxton (Mrs. Edgar M. Buttner), Arnold Van Hoven. Newspaper reporter, 1926-28; security analyst, 1928-31; investment counsel, 1931—; founder, editor, research dir. The Value Line Investment Survey, N.Y., 1936—, The Value Line Over-the-Counter Spl. Situations Service, 1951—, The Value Line Convertible Bond,

Convertible Preferred, Warrant and Merger Service, 1967—; pres., dir. The Value Line Fund, 1950—, The Value Line Income Fund, 1952—, The Value Line Spl. Situations Fund, 1956—, Arnold Bernhard & Co., Inc., 1946—; chmn. The Value Line Devel. Capital Corp., 1968—. Trustee U. Bridgeport, Earlham Coll., Skidmore Coll. Mem. Phi Beta Kappa, Delta Sigma Rho, Delta Upsilon. Clubs: Saugatuck Harbor Yacht; Williams. Author: The Evaluation of Common Stocks, 1959; Fortnightly Commentaries Value Line Investment Survey. Home: Rondelet 21 N Sylvan Rd Westport CT 06880 Office: 5 E 44th St New York City NY 10017

BERNHARD, BERL, lawyer; b. N.Y.C., Sept. 7, 1929; s. Morris and Celia B.; B.A. in Govt. magna cum laude (Rufus Choate scholar), Dartmouth, 1951; LL.B., Yale, 1954; LL.D., Central O. State Coll., 1963; m. Janice Hartman, Aug. 29, 1952; children—Peter Berl, Robin Churchill, Andrew Morris. Grad. instr. polit. sci. Yale, 1952-53; admitted to D.C. bar, 1954, U.S. Supreme Ct. bar, 1957; with firm Davis, Polk, Wardwell, Sunderland & Kiendl, N.Y.C., summer 1953; law clk. to U.S. dist. judge, 1954-56; pvt. practice, Washington, 1956-58; partner Verner, Lipfert, Bernhard & McPherson and predecessor firms, 1958, 63—. Mem. U.S. Commn. on Civil Rights, 1958-63, dep. staff dir., 1959-61, staff dir., 1961-63; cons. undersec. polit. affairs, Sec. State, 1963-67; adj. prof. law Georgetown U. Law Center, 1963-65; counsel Lawyers Com. for Civil Rights Under Law. Gen. counsel Democratic Senatorial Campaign Com., 1967—; spl. counsel Dem. Nat. Com., 1969—. Mem. D.C. Bd. Higher Edn., chmn. finance com. Recipient Arthur S. Flemming award D.C. Jr. C. of C., 1960, Ten Outstanding Young Men award U.S. Jr. C. of C., 1962. Mem. Am. Bar Assn., Bar Assn. D.C., Assn. Interstate Practitioners, Nat. Panel Arbitrators, Am. Arbitration assn., Casque and Gauntlet, Phi Beta Kappa, Sigma Nu, Phi Delta Phi, Casque and Gauntlet, Club: Cosmos (Washington). Contbr. articles to profl.jours. Home: 5405 Blackistone Rd Bethesda MD 20016

BERNHARD, JOHN TORBEN, univ. pres.; b. N.Y.C., June 24, 1920; s. Torben Martin and Mary (Nielsen) B.; B.S., Utah State U., 1941; M.A., U. Cal. at Los Angeles, 1949, Ph.D., 1951; m. Ramona Bailey, June 2, 1941; children—John Gary, Scott Martin, Randall Lee, Julie Ann. Prof. Polit. sci. Brigham Young U., 1959-68, dean humanities and social scis., 1962-68; pres., prof. polit. sci. Western Ill. U., Macomb, 1968—. Served to lt. (j.g.) USCGR. Mem. Am. Assn. Higher Edn., Am. Polit. Sci. Assn., Pi Sigma Alpha, Pi Gamma Mu, Xi Sigma Pi, Sigma Nu, Phi Delta Kappa, Phi Kappa Phi, Pi Delta Epsilon. Mem. Ch. of Jesus Christ of Latter Day Saints. Author: Journey Into Light, 1961; also articles. Home: 555 Meadow Dr Macomb IL 61455

BERNHARD, LEOPOLD FREDERIK, Everhard Julius Coert Karel Godfried Pieter, The Prince of the Netherlands, Prince of Lippe-Biesterfeld; b. Jena, Germany, June 29, 1911; s. Prince Bernhard of Lippe-Biesterfeld; hon. doctorates in law, State U. Utrecht, U. Montreal, U. B.C., U. Mich., in econs., Protestant U. Amsterdam, in tech. scis. Inst. Advanced Tech., Delft; m. Juliana Louise Emma Marie Wilhelmina, Queen of the Netherlands, Jan. 7, 1937; children—Beatrix Wilhelmina Armgard, Irene Emma Elizabeth, Margriet Francisca, Maria Christina. Mem. bd. K.L.M., Royal Netherlands Aircraft Factories Fokker, Royal Netherlands Blast Furnances and Steelworks, Netherlands Trade and Industry Fair; hon. air marshall RAF, 1964—; insp. gen. Netherlands Armed Forces; regent Prince Bernhard Fund, Praemium Erasmianum; chmn. European Cultural Found., Bilderberg Confs.; pres. World Wildlife Fund; hon. mem. Royal Spanish Acad.; referendar juris U. Berlin. Hon. functions and honors number over 100 items. Address: Soestdijk Palaca The Netherlands

BERNHARD, RICHARD, constrn. co. exec.; b. Bklyn., Mar. 10, 1930; s. I. Charles and Florence (Kresky) B.; student U. Colo., 1947-48; B.A., Bard Coll. 1951; m. Joan Murdoch, June 9, 1956; children—Daniel, William, Catherine. Constrn. supt.. Wantagh Rangers, Inc., L.I., N.Y., 1952-53; real estate salesman Islip Assos. (L.I.), 1954; FHA-VA rep. Bildner-Feder Mortgage Brokers, Jamaica, N.Y., 1954-55; partner Laurel Gardens, Inc., 1955-56, Bayamon Housing Corp., San Juan, P.R., 1957-61; exec. v.p. Levitt & Sons P.R., Inc., 1961-68, exec. v.p. operations, Lake Success, N.Y., 1968—. Trustee Presbyn. Hosp., Santurce, P.R. Served with USCGR, 1953-54. Mem. P.R. Golf Assn., P.R. Home Builders Assn. Home: 10 Cedar Lane Sands Point NY 11050 Office: Levitt & Sons Lakeville Rd and Marcus Av Lake Success NY 11040

BERNHARD, ROBERT ARTHUR, investment banker; b. N.Y.C., May 14, 1928; s. Richard J. and Dorothy (Lehman) B.; B.S., Williams Coll., 1951; M.B.A., Harvard, 1953; m. Frances Wells, Dec. 21, 1949; children—Adele, Michael, Susan, Steven ; m. 2d, Joan M. Sommerfield, Aug. 1, 1970. With Lehman Bros., N.Y.C., 1952-71, partner, 1963-71; mng. dir. Lehman Bros., Inc., N.Y.C., 1970—; pres. William Asso., Inc.; v.p., dir. One William Street Fund; dir. H.C.A. Industries, Lehman Corp. Mem. N.Y. Gov.'s Steering Com. on Social Problems; mem. Citizens Commn. on City N.Y. Trustee, v.p. Fedn. Jewish Philanthropies; trustee Worcester Found. Exptl. Biology, Montefiore Hosp., Rye Country Day Sch., Jewish Child Care Assn., pres., bd. dirs. N.Y. Urban League; bd. overseers Albert Einstein Coll. Medicine. Mem. Phi Gamma Delta. Clubs: Madison Square Garden, Williams (N.Y.C.); Century Country (White Plains, N.Y.); City Midday; Harvard Business, Governor's, President's. Home: 46 E 71st St New York City NY 10021 Office: 1 William St New York City NY 10004

BERNHARD, RUSSELL SHERMAN, lawyer; b. Milw., Dec. 24, 1914; s. Raymond S. and Adeline (Lipman) B.; B.S. magna cum laude, Northwestern U., 1936, M.A., 1938; J.D. cum laude, Harvard, 1941; m. Winifred Hermann, Jan. 1, 1944; children-Barbara Anne (Mrs. Robert B. Anderson III), Nancy Ruth. Admitted to D.C. bar; sr. atty. CAB, 1943-46; atty. Air Transport Assn. Am., 1947-56; asst. gen. counsel Air Cargo, Inc., Washington, 1947-56, gen. counsel, 1957—; partner firm Macleay, Lynch, Bernhard & Gregg, Washington, 1957—; gen. counsel Nat. Aviation Club, Washington, 1962—; professorial lectr. trans. Am. U., 1949-62. Mem. Am. Bar Assn., Bar Assn. D.C., Air Force Assn. (legal counsel), ICC Practitioners Assn., Phi Beta Kappa. Home: 4972 N Rock Spring Rd Arlington VA 22207 Office: 1625 K St N W Washington DC 20006

BERNHARD, WILLIAM FRANCIS, thoracic and cardiovascular surgeon; b. Bklyn., Dec. 11, 1924; s. William and Helen (Conroy) B.; B.A., Williams Coll., 1946; M.D., Syracuse U., 1950: m. June Horne, Sept. 17, 1948; children—Susan, William Francis, Christine, Margaret, Catherine, John, Ann, James, Robert, Peter. Intern Syracuse U. Hosp., 1950-51; asst. resident Children's Hosp. Med. Center, Boston, 1951-52, dir. surg. research lab. Children's Hosp., Boston, 1960—, asso. surgeon, 1962-66; sr. asso. in cardiovascular surgery Children's Hosp. Med. Center; asst. resident Peter Bent Brigham Hosp., Boston, 1952-57; resident Bellevue Hosp., Columbia div., N.Y.C., 1957-58, Columbia-Presbyn. Hosp., N.Y.C., 1959; attending surgeon thoracic and cardiovascular surgery VA Hosp., West Roxbury, Mass., 1960- -; clin. asso. surgery Harvard Med. Sch., 1962-66, asst. clin. prof. surgery, 1966-68, asso. clin. prof. surgery, 1968-71, prof. surgery, 1971—. Mem. New Eng. Surg. Soc. (Sr.), Am. Heart Assn., Mass. Med. Soc., Am. Assn. Thoracic Surgery, Soc. Univ. Surgeons, Am. Acad. Pediatrics, New Eng. Cardiovascular Soc., Soc. Vascular Surgery, Am. Soc. Artificial Internal Organs, Am. Surg. Assn. Home: 60 Singletary Lane Framingham MA 01701 Office: 300 Longwood Av Boston MA 02115

BERNHARDT, JACK DOUGLAS, advt. exec.; b. Cin., June 8, 1926; s. Stanley C. and Flo (Young) B.; B.B.A. cum laude in Marketing and Merchandising, Miami U., Oxford, O., 1950; m. Nancy Cox Todd, June 14, 1952; children—Douglas, Amy, Todd, Lisa. Vice pres. Benton & Bowles, 1951-64; sr. v.p. J. Walter Thompson, 1964—. Active local Boy Scouts Am. Rep. town meeting, Darien, Conn., 1957-68. Served with AUS, 1944-46; PTO. Mem. Phi Beta Kappa, Sigma Alpha Epsilon, Phi Eta Sigma, Omicron Delta Kappa. Episcopalian (vestry). Home: 356 Brookside Rd Darien CT 06820 Office: 420 Lexington Av New York City NY 10017

BERNHARDT, JOHN BOWMAN, banker; b. Norton, Va., Aug. 7, 1929; s. Claude Bowman and Mabel (Dixon) B.; B.A., U. Va., 1954, LL.B., 1957; postgrad. Rutgers U., 1967; m. Ada Nuckels, Aug. 29, 1952; children—Jared B., J. Carter. With Peoples Nat. Bank, Charlottesville, 1957-63; asst. v.p. Va. Nat. Bank, Norfolk, 1963- 64, v.p., 1964-68, sr. v.p., 1968-69, exec. v.p., 1969—. Mem. regional adv. council Small Bus. Adminstrn., 1970-72. Bd. dirs. Urban Coalition Norfolk; trustee Leigh Meml. Hosp., Va. Wesleyan Coll. Mem. Am., Va. bankers assns., Nat. Alliance Businessmen (met. chmn.), Hampton Rds. Maritime Assn., Navy League U.S., Newcomen Soc. N.Am., Va., Norfolk chambers commerce. Presbyn. Clubs: Norfolk Yacht and Country, Harbor (Norfolk); Cedar Point (Crittenden, Va.). Home: 925 Hanover Av Norfolk VA 23508 Office: 1 Commercial Pl Norfolk VA 23510

BERNHEIM, DANIEL MARC, advt. agy. exec.; b. Newark, Dec. 25, 1924; s. David and Adeline (Braunschweiger) B.; student U. Ala., 1941-42, U. Newark, 1943-46; m. Frances Ellen Reinfeld, May 29, 1949; children—Adelyn R., Lewis Andrew, Anthony Paul. Account exec. Lewis Advt. Agy., Newark, 1943-46, v.p., 1949-53; pres. Daran Corp., 1946-49; exec. v.p., treas., dir. Reach, McClinton & Co., 1957-65, chmn. bd., 1965—, chmn. exec. com., 1963—; chmn. bd. Bozell & Jacobs, Inc., 1970—; pres. Continental Metal Industries, P.R., 1955—; dir. Old Discovery Distillers, Inc. (Pa.), Renfield Importers, Ltd. Trustee, mem. fund-raising and finance com. Robert Treat council Boy Scouts Am. Mem. Essex County Park Commn., 1968—. Bd. dirs. Pleasant Valley Home for Aged and Sick; trustee Vocational Guidance Bur., Family Problems Bur., Jewish News of Essex County, Daus. of Israel Home for Aged. Served with AUS, 1942-43. Mem. Advt. Club N.J. (dir.). Home: 69 Crest Dr South Orange NJ 07079 Office: 69 Washington St Newark NJ 07102 also 505 Park Av New York City NY 10022

BERNHEIM, ELINOR KRIDEL, (Mrs. Leonard H. Bernheim), social welfare vol.; b. N.Y.C., June 26, 1907; d. Alexander Hayes and Irma (Hernsheim) Kridel; B.A., Vassar Coll., 1928: postgrad. N.Y. Sch. Social Work, 1947-48; m. Leonard H. Bernheim. Mem. bd. and council Assn. for Aid for Crippled Children, 1941—; trustee Fedn. Jewish Philanthropies, N.Y.C., 1942—, v.p., 1955-58, chmn. women's div. fund raising drive, 1943, 44, 49, chmn. women's bd., 1955-58, hon. chmn., 1958—, v.p., 1971—; mem. bd. Jewish Assn. Neighborhood Centers; dir. Nat. Jewish Welfare Bd., 1944—, chmn. women's div., 1954-61, hon. chmn. women's bd., 1961—; mem. bd., exec. com. Nat. Social Welfare Assembly, 1947-51, v.p., 1949-51, chmn. edn. and recreation div., 1959—; adv. com. vol. services, VA 1947-61; bd. dirs. United Neighborhood Houses of N.Y.C., 1949-53; mem. bd. Nat. Council on Social Work Edn., 1952-54, mem. nat. citizens com. on careers, 1961-65; chmn. bd. Social Work Recruiting Com. of Greater N.Y., 1955—; pres. bd. Mosholu Montefiore Community Center, 1958-70; bd. dir. Assn. YM and YWHA's of Greater N.Y., 1958-60, asso. chmn. 1960-69, co-chmn., 1970—; bd. dirs. Community Council Greater N.Y., 1960—, chmn. group work and recreation div., 1961 —, v.p., 1970—; adv. bd. N.Y. Sch. Social Work, Columbia, 1960—; bd. dirs. Community Service Soc., 1961—; mem. N.Y. State Welfare Conf., 1961-63; v.p. Nat. Conf. Social Welfare, 1963; mem. Gov. N.Y. State Com. Children and Youth, 1963; co-chmn. Dimitri Mitropolous Internat. Music Competition, 1961-63; bd. dirs. Young Concert Artists, 1968—; mem. Mayor's Screening Panel to Bd. Higher Edn., N.Y.C., 1964; v.p. Nat. Jewish Welfare Bd., 1967-71; v.p. Columbia Univ. Sch. Social Work, 1968—. Recipient Gen. award N.Y. State Welfare Conf., 1958; Bi-Centennial medal Columbia, 1956; Frank L. Weil award Nat. Jewish Welfare Bd., 1960; Research Inst. citation Nat. Conf. Jewish Center Workers, 1961; Blanche Ittleson award, 1963, Naomi Lehman Meml. Found. award, 1966. Clubs: Women's City, Cosmopolitan (N.Y.C.). author articles in field. Address: 930 Park Av New York City NY 10028

BERNHEIM, FREDERICK, educator, pharmacologist; b. Long Branch, N.J., Aug. 18, 1905; s. George B. and Alice (Rheinstein) B.; B.S., Harvard, 1925; Ph.D., Cambridge (Eng.) U., 1928; m. Mary Christian Hare, Dec. 17, 1928; 1 dau., Cecily Ann (Mrs. Werner K. Honig). NRC fellow Johns Hopkins Med. Sch., 1929-30; mem. faculty Duke Med. Center, 1930—, prof. pharmacology, 1946—, James B. Duke prof. pharmacology, 1963—. Cons. B. Duke prof. pharmacology, 1963—. Cons. Smith Kline and French Labs., 1948-67. Fellow N.Y. Acad. Sci., A.A.A.S.; mem. Am. Soc. Oil Chemists, Am. Soc. Biol. Chemists, Am. Soc. Pharmacology and Exptl. Therapeutics, Am. Soc. Cell Biology, Am. Assn. U. Profs. (pres. Duke chpt. 1951-52), Sigma Xi (pres. Duke chpt. 1939- 40). Author: Interaction of Drugs and Cell Catalysts, 2d edit., 1946; also revs., articles, chpts. in books. Home: 115 Woodridge Dr Durham, NC 27705.

BERNHEIM, LEONARD HENRY, investment banker; b. N.Y.C., Sept. 4, 1902; s. Charles H. and Lillian (Schiff) B.; B.A., Princeton, 1923; m. Elinor Kridel, Dec. 6, 1928; children—Charles Alexander, Leonard Henry. Partner, William E. Lauer & Co., N.Y.C., 1930-38, Stern, Lauer & Co., N.Y.C., 1938—. Pres. Loeb Center Nursing and Rehab., N.Y.C., 1948—. Trustee Fedn. Jewish Philanthropies, Montefiore Hosp., N.Y.C., Jewish Family Service, N.Y.C. Home: 930 Park Av New York City NY 10028 Office: 120 Broadway New York City NY 10005

BERNHEIMER, MARTIN, music critic; b. Munich, Germany, Sept. 28, 1936; s. Paul Ernst and Louise (Nassauer) B.; came to U.S., 1940, naturalized, 1946; B.A. with honors in Music, Brown U., 1958; student Munich Conservatory, 1958-59; M.A. in Musicology, N.Y. U., 1962; m. Lucinda Pearson, Sept. 30, 1961; children—Mark Richard, Nora Nicoll, Marina and Erika (twins). Free-lance music critic, 1958—; mem. music faculty N.Y. U., 1960-62; N.Y. corr. N.Y. corr. for Brit. publ., Opera, 1962-65, Los Angeles corr., 1965—; contbg. critic N.Y. Herald-Tribune, 1959-62; asst. music editor Saturday Rev., 1962-65; mng. editor Philharmonic Hall Program, N.Y.C., 1962-65; 1962-65; music editor, chief critic Los Angeles Times, 1965—; faculty Rockefeller program for tng. music critics at U. So. Cal., 1966—; mem. music faculty U. Cal. at Los Angeles, 1969—. Contbr. articles newspapers, mags. in field, also liner articles newspapers, mags. in field, also liner notes for recordings; radio and TV appearances. Office: Los Angeles Times Times-Mirror Square Los Angeles CA 90053

BERNIAN, BROTHER DANIEL, coll. pres., clergyman; b. Balt., Sept. 10, 1916; s. James J. and Margaret T. (O'Neill) K.; B.A., Cath. U., Washington, 1938; M.A., U. Pa., 1943; Ph.D., Laval U., 1952; LL.D., Villanova U., 1959, St. Joseph's Coll., Phila., 1961, Temple U., 1963. Tchr. French, West Cath. High Sch., Phila., 1938-40, tchr. Spanish, 1941-47; tchr. English, Coll. St. Patrice, Que., 1940-41; tchr. French and Spanish, LaSalle Coll. High Sch., Phila., 1947-49; prof. French, LaSalle Coll., 1951-52, 53-69, dean of men, 1953-54, dean students, 1954-58, v.p., 1954-58, pres., 1958-69, spiritual dir., 1960-69; prof. relig. Cath. U., Washington, 1949-50; prof. English, Colegio Buonanova, Barcelona, Spain, 1953. Chmn. Phila. Commn. Higher Edn.; mem. Phila. Ednl. Nominating Panel. Hon. dir. Phila. Grand Opera Co.; Chmn. bd. National Hemophilia Found.; dir. Columbia Sch.; trustee Phila. Community Coll.; trustee Immaculata Coll.; pres. trustees LaSalle Coll. Recipient edn. award 21 Jewel Square Club. Mem. Am. Cath. Hist. Soc., Adv. Council Naval Affairs, L'Academie Francaise des Etats-unis, Phila. C. of C. (commerce and industry council), Res. Officers Assn., Phi Delta Phi, Alpha Phi Omega.

BERNICK, RICHARD JESSE, lawyer, univ. regent; b. Denver, Jan. 12, 1929; s. Philip and Ethel (Milstein) B.; B.A. cum laude, U. Colo., 1950, LL.B., 1952; m. Margaret Elaine Stark, Mar. 14, 1952 (div.); children—Philip Avery, Amy Elaine, Margaret, Andrew. Admitted to the Colorado State bar, 1952, Fed. bar, 1952; pvt. practice, Denver, 1952—; mem. firm Gould, Moch and Bernick. U.S. Jury Cmmr. for Colo. Mem. Com. on legislation and intergovtl. relations Assn. Governing Bds. State Univs. and Allied Instns.; bd. regents U. Colo., 1958—. Mem. Colo. Democratic State Central Com., mem. exec. com. Denver Dem. Central Com. Judge Adv. Gen. area rep. USAF Res. Mem. Nat. Com. Support Pub. Schs., Pi Gamma Mu, Phi Alpha Delta. Home: 790 Washington St Denver CO 80203 Office: Security Bldg Denver CO 80202

BERNIER, JOSEPH LEROY, oral pathologist; b. Chgo., Apr. 5, 1909; s. Joseph Francis and Mary (Raddle) B.; student Crane Jr. Coll., Chgo., 1927-28; D.D.S., U. Ill. Coll. Dentistry, Chgo., 1932, M.S., Grad. Sch., 1934; m. Bernice Mary O'Rourke, Dec. 26, 1936; children—Beverly R., Joseph W. Instr. dental and oral pathology U. Ill., 1932-34; entered Regular Army Dental Corps 1935, advanced to rank of maj. gen.; served Armed Forces Inst. Pathology, 1937-38, 40-42, 1945—; chief dept. lab., Panama Canal Dept., 1939-41; chief dental and oral path. div. Armed Forces Inst. Pathology, Washington; prof., chmn. dept. oral pathology Georgetown U. Sch. Dentistry, Washington, 1945—; pathologist to Registry of Dental and Oral Pathology, Am. Dental Assn. Mem. nat. dental health council USPHS; chmn. dental research adv. com. Dept. of Army; asst. surg. gen. and chief Dental Corps Dept. of Army, 1960—. Recipient Louis Livingston Seaman award for Research in cancer of the lip, Thomas P. Hinnman award, 1955, Callahan award, 1955; named one of twelve outstanding dentists of all time, USIA, Alfred C. Fones award, 1957, Tufts U. award, 1955, Georgetown U. award of merit, 1957; recipient Pierre Fouchard medal, 1961; Ann. award Sigma Epsilon Delta, 1963; Dentist of Year award R.I. Dental Soc., 1965; S.C. Miller award Am. Acad. Oral Medicine, 1967; Internat. research award Mass. Dental Soc., 1968; William J. Gies award, 1969. Diplomate Am. Bd. Periodontology, Am. Bd. Oral Medicine, Am. Bd. Oral Pathology (sec.). Fellow Am. Coll. Dentists, Internat. Coll. Dentists (master), Royal Coll. Surgeons, Odontological Soc. Dominican Republic (hon.), Royal Acad. Medicine (Eng.); mem. Internat. Dental Fedn., Am. Assn. Endodontists, Am. Acad. Oral Pathology (sec. 1958, pres. 1959), Internat. Assn. Dental Research, Am. Acad. Periodontology (pres. 1959), Am. Assn. Pathologists and Bacteriologists, Assn. Med. Museums, A.A.A.S., Acad. Medicine Washington, Internat. Assn. Research Paradentopathies, Internat. Acad. Pathology, Assn. Oral Surgeons Cuba (hon.); Korean, Taiwan dental assns., 38th Parallel Dental Soc. (hon.), Am. Soc. Oral Surgeons (hon.), Am. Acad. Dental Sci., Omicron Kappa Upsilon, Delta Sigma Delta. Roman Catholic. Club: Cosmos (Washington). Author: Differential Diagnosis Oral Lessons, 1941; Atlas Dental and Oral Pathology, 1948; chpt. Fasicle, in Atlas of Tumor Pathology, 1948, 59; Management of Oral Disease; Improving Dental Practice Through Preventive Measures; sci. publs. Asso. editor Jour. Oral Surgery; cons. editor Jour. Oral Surgery, Oral Pathology and Oral Medicine: editorial bd. Current Dental Comment, 1968. Home: 6905 Hillmead Rd Bethesda MD 20034 Office: Dept of Oral Pathology Georgetown U School Dentistry 3900 Reservoir Rd Washington DC 20007

BERNIKER, HERMAN, lawyer, title ins. exec.; b. N.Y.C., Mar. 10, 1906; s. Louis and Fannie (Feder) B.; LL.B., St. Lawrence U., 1927; m. Viola Rapaport, Sept. 18, 1945; children—Elaine (Mrs. Michael Plaut, Jr.), Michael, Marie. Admitted to N.Y. bar, 1928; spl. dep. supt. ins. State of N.Y. 1933- 38; v.p. Lawyers Title Corp., N.Y.C., 1938-47, 1st v.p., 1947 (merged with Title Guarantee Co., 1948); v.p. Title Guarantee Co., N.Y.C., 1948- 50, exec. v.p., 1950-64, dir., 1964—, also chief exec. officer and trustee; dir. Blacksone Cigar Co. Mem. Am., N.Y. State bar assns., Am. Land Title Assn., Ass. Bar City N.Y., N.Y. State Title Assn., N.Y. C. of C. 34 Park Rd Scarsdale NY 10585 Office: 176 Broadway New York City NY 10038

BERNINGHAUSEN, DAVID KNIPE, librarian; b. Beaman, Ia., Feb. 5, 1916; s. Frederick William and Lillian Jane (Knipe) B.; A.B., Ia. State Tchrs. Coll., 1936; M.A., Drake U., 1943; B.L.S., Columbia, 1941; postgrad. study U. N.C., 1944: Harvard Edn. fellow, 1950-51; m. Elizabeth Sara Smith, Feb. 16, 1940; children—John David, Eric Knipe (dec.). Instr. Edgewood (Ia.) high Sch., 1936-37, Valley Jr. High Sch., West Des Moines, 1937-40; circulation librarian Ia. State Tchrs. Coll., 1941-44; instr. U. N.C., 1944; dir. libraries Birmingham-Southern Coll. 1944-47; librarian, prof. bibliography Cooper Union, 1947-53; dir. library sch. U. Minn., 1953—. Vis. prof., library cons. Nat. Taiwan U., 1962-63. Chmn. Com. for Eastern Coll. Librarians' Conf., 1951-53; mem. Phi Delta Kappa Commn. for Free Pub. Edn., 1952-54; pres. Assn. Am. Library Schs., 1959-60. Mem. A.L.A. (chmn. intellectual freedom com. 1948-50), Am. Assn. U. Profs., Minn. Library Assn. (pres. 1957-58), Blue Key, Theta Alpha Phi. Contbr. to jours., periodicals. Address: 1912 Dupont Av S Minneapolis MN 55403

BERNITT, ELMER W., ret. mfg. exec.; b. Detroit, May 6, 1910; s. William J. and Anna (Carll) B.; B.S., U. Detroit, 1932; postgrad. U. Mich., Lawrence Inst. Tech.; m. Betty L. Thomas, July 2, 1938; children—Lois M., Kathryn H. Engr., Detroit Edison, 1932-35, Plymouth Motors Corp., 1935-38; plant engr. Nash Motors, 1938-47, works mgr., 1947-54; v.p. in charge mfg., procurement Am. Motors Corp., 1954-56, v.p. operations automotive div., 1956-66, v.p. safety and quality assurance, 1966-71; dir. 1st Nat. Bank Kenosha. Bd. dirs. Kenosha Hosp. Mem. Am. Mgmt. Assn. (dir.), Nat. Soc. Profl. Engrs., Nat. Soc. Automotive Engrs. Mason. Home: 4385 Clarke Dr St Clair MI 48079 Office: 14250 Plymouth Rd Detroit MI 48232

BERNIUS, ODELL LEWIS, banker; b. Cin., Apr. 26, 1918; s. George Lewis and Alice (Aufdenberg) B.; student U. Cin., 1946-49; m. June M. Huebner, June 4, 1942; children—Lynn Mary (Mrs. John J. Schiff, Jr.), Craig O. With Fifth Third Bank, Cin., 1936—, sr. v.p., 1965—. Bd. dirs. Cin. Better Bus. Bur. Treas. Hamilton County div. Ohio Republican Finance Com. Served to maj. AUS, 1941-46. Mem. Robert Morris Assos. Episcopalian. Clubs: Bankers (pres.),

Cincinnati, Western Hills Country (Cin.). Home: 810 Matson Pl Cincinnati OH 45204 Office: 1 Fifth Third Center Cincinnati OH 45201

BERNLOHR, ROBERT WILLIAM, biochemist, educator; b. Columbus, O., Apr. 20, 1933; s. William Fredrick and Ruth Elizabeth (Russel) B.; B.S., Capital U., 1955; Ph.D., Ohio State U., 1958; m. Carol Jean Smiley, June 11, 1955; children—David A., Timothy J., Mark W., James R. Research asso. Oak Ridge Nat. Lab., 1958-59; asst. prof. Ohio State U., 1960-62; asst. prof. to prof. microbiology, biochemistry U. Minn., Mpls., 1962—. Cons. NSF, indsl. firms. Vice pres. local sch. P.T.A., 1968-69, pres., 1969-70. Recipient USPHS Career Devel. award, 1962-72. Mem. Am. Soc. Microbiology (sec. to pres. physiology div.), others. Lutheran (pres. council 1969). Mem. editorial bd. Jour. Bacteriology, 1965—. Contbr. articles to profl. jours. Home: 1746 W Skillman Av St Paul MN 55113 Office: 1060 Mayo U Minn Minneapolis MN 55455

BERNS, SEYMOUR, producer-director; b. Chgo., May 29, 1924; s. Isidore and Ella (Spiegel) B.: B.A., U. Cal. at Los Angeles, 1943; m. Ann Sampter, Feb. 12, 1950; 1 dau., Tracy. Dir. CBS Radio, Los Angeles, 1945-48; TV dir. Paramount sta. KTLA, Los Angeles, 1948-49; dir. Red Skelton TV Show, 1953-59, Shower of Stars, 1958; producer-dir. Jack Benny TV Show, 1959-62; producer Red Skelton TV Hour, 1964-68; v.p. Nat. Gen. Television Corp., 1968-70; now pres. Valjon Prodn. Co., Hollywood, Cal. TV adviser to gov. Cal., 1962-64; mem. Cal. Arts Commn., 1964-68. Recipient Emmy award for Jack Benny TV Show, 1960, Christopher award for Edsel Show, 1958, Look mag. award dir. best comedy TV series, 1959, 60, 61. Mem. Nat. Acad. Television Arts and Scis. (sr. v.p. 1964-65, nat. pres. 1968- 70), Radio and TV Dirs. Guild (pres. 1959), Dirs. Guild Am. (bd. govs. 1962—). Home: 705 N Palm Dr Beverly Hills CA 90210 Office: Samuel Goldwyn Studios Hollywood CA 90028

BERNS, WALTER FRED, educator; b. Chgo., May 3, 1919; s. Walter Fred and Agnes (Westergard) B.; B.Sc., U. Ia., 1941; postgrad. Reed Coll., 1948-49, London (Eng.) Sch. Econs. and Polit. Sci., 1949-50; Ph.D., U. Chgo., 1953; m. Irene Sibley Lyons, June 16, 1951; children—Elizabeth, Emily, Christopher. Asst. prof. govt. La. State U., 1953-56; asst. prof. polit. sci. Yale, 1956- 59; mem. faculty Cornell U., 1959-69, prof. govt., chmn. dept., 1963-68; prof. polit. sci. U. Toronto, 1970—. mem. Salzburg (Germany) Seminar Am. Studies, 1959. Served with USNR, 1941-45. Mem. Am. Polit. Sci. Assn. Episcopalian. Author: Freedom, Virtue and the First Amendment, 1957; Constitutional Cases in American Government, 1963. Joint author Essays in the Scientific Study of Politics (H.J. Storing editor), 1963. Home: 118 Roxborough Dr Toronto 5 Ontario Canada

BERNSTEIN, ALBERT BERNARD, lawyer; b. Savannah, Ga., Dec. 24, 1898; s. Jacob and Sarah (Leaf) B.; A.B., U. Ga., 1919; LL.B., Columbia, 1922; m. Muriel Lesser, Mar. 14, 1934; 1 son, John Albert. Admitted to Ga. bar, 1921; practice law, Savannah, 1922-25, Miami, Fla., 1925—; sec., dir., gen. counsel Wometco Enterprises, Inc., Miami, 1943—; sr. mem. firm Bernstein, Hodsdon & Tannen Attys., Miami, 1966—. Lectr. taxation U. Miami Sch. Law, 1945-47. U. Miami Tax Conf. program and/or adv. com., 1959-70. Bd. dirs. Greater Miami Crime Commn., 1952-55, v.p., 1954-55. Mem. Am., Dade County (vice chmn. legal aid com. 1970) bar assns. Jewish religion. Home: DuPont Plaza Apts 300 Biscayne Blvd Way Miami FL 33131 Office: 950 Sybold Bldg Miami FL 33132

BERNSTEIN, ALVIN P., trading stamp co. exec.; b. 1930; B.S., U. Ill., 1956; married. Dept. mgr. Sears, Roebuck & Co., 1947-50; indsl. engr. Gen. Aniline & Film Corp., 1956-57; systems analyst Sperry & Hutchinson Co., N.Y.C., 1957-59, mgr. dept. store sales, 1959-60, mgr. notes receivable, 1960-64, asst. treas., 1964-68, treas., 1968, now v.p. finance, treas. Served with USNR, 1951-54. Office: 330 Madison Av New York City NY 10017

BERNSTEIN, BARRY, educator; b. N.Y.C., Nov. 20, 1930; s. Charles Michael and Louise Ruth (Fried) B.; B.S. magna cum laude, Coll. City N.Y., 1951; M.A., Ind. U., 1954, Ph.D., 1956; m. Ilse Lewenberg, Aug. 23, 1943; children—Lynn, Jill. Mathematician Naval Research Lab., Washington, 1951-53, 56-61, Nat. Bur. Standards, Washington, 1961-65; vis. asso. prof. Purdue U., 1965-66; prof. mathematics Ill. Inst. Tech., 1966—; acting dir. Center Applied Mathematics of Ill. Inst. Tech.; cons. to industry, Nat. Bur. Standards. Recipient award for outstanding achievement Nat. Bur. Standards, 1966. Mem. Rheology Soc., Soc. Indsl. and Applied Mathematics, Am. Math. Soc., Phi Beta Kappa, Sigma Xi. Jewish religion (dir. temple). Research and publs. on large deformations of continuous media, viscoelasticity, math. analysis, biol. applications of mathematics. Home: 1039 N Oak Park Av Oak Park IL 60302 Office: Illinois Inst Tech Chicago IL 60616

BERNSTEIN, BERNARD, lawyer; b. N.Y.C., Nov. 30, 1908; s. Henry and Annie (Goldstein) B.; A.B., Columbia, 1928, J.D., 1930; m. Bernice Lotwin, Aug. 4, 1938; children—Elinor (Mrs. Sigmund Balka), Kate, Anne. Admitted to N.Y. bar, 1931, U.S. Supreme Ct. bar, 1936, D.C. bar, 1947; asso. Mitchell, Taylor, Capron & Marsh, N.Y.C., 1930-33; atty. U.S. Treasury Dept., 1933-42, asst. gen. counsel, 1938—; participated in all litigation relating to govt.'s monetary policies, internat. financial arrangements of Treasury, 1934-42; mem. com. experts that drafted plans for Inter-Am. Bank, 1939-40; active in adminstrn. fgn. funds control by Treasury Dept., 1940-42; U.S. adviser Inter-Am. conf. on systems of econ. and financial control, 1942. Legal adviser Am. Jewish Conf., 1946-48; chmn. Working Com. Jewish Orgns., for treaties with enemy countries, 1946-47; cons. on behalf of coordinating bd. Jewish orgns. to ECOSOC, 1949-53; testified before Senate Com. on Mil. Affairs respecting investigation by Mil Govt. of I.G. Farben, 1945. Commd. lt. col., U.S. Army, 1942, promoted col., 1944; financial adviser to Gen. Eisenhower for Civil Affairs and Mil. Govt., ETO, MTO, U.S.A., 1942-45. Decorated Legion of Merit, European-African theatre ribbon with 6 campaign stars (U.S.), Legion of Honor, Croix de Guerre (France). Mem. N.Y. County Lawyers Assn. (chmn. com. fgn. law and internat. law 1964-69), Am. Soc. Internat. Law, Mil. Govt. Assn., Am., N.Y. State bar assns., Am. Legion, Bar Assn. City N.Y., Am. Fgn. Law Assn. (dir.), Am. Soc. French Legion of Honor, Tau Delta Phi. Mem. B'nai B'rith. Editor: Columbia Law Rev., 1928-30. Home: 34 Elm Ridge Rd Kings Point NY 11024 Address: 745 Fifth Av New York City NY 10022 ☆

BERNSTEIN, CHARLES C., judge; b. St. Louis, June 2, 1904; s. David Charles and Bessie (Gorcester) B.; LL.B., Southwestern U., 1929; m. Blanche Friedman, Dec. 31, 1927. Admitted to Ariz. bar, 1929, began practice in Phoenix; asst. atty. gen. Ariz., 1937- 39; spl. asst. Ariz. Ins. Dept., 1939-43; judge Ariz. Superior Ct., 1949-59, justice Ariz. Supreme Ct., 1959-69; chief justice 1962, 63, 67; now mem. firm Brown, Vlassis & Bain, Phoenix. Mem. Am., Maricopa County bar assns., State Bar Ariz. (mem. com. judicial adminstrn. 1950-69), Sigma Tau. Democrat. Jewish religion. Mason, Elk, Club: Arizona. Address: Supreme Ct Bldg Phoenix AZ 85003*

BERNSTEIN, DAVID, trailer and container mfg. co. exec.; b. Omaha, June 10, 1917; s. Jacob and Ida (Gerelick) B.; B.A., U. Neb., 1938; m. Muriel Thelma Krasne, June 11, 1939; children—Phyllis Ann (Mrs. Richard Glazer), Howard Bruce. With Ind. Metal Products, Omaha, 1938-68, v.p., gen. mgr., 1948-68; exec. v.p. Fruehauf Corp., Detroit, 1968—, dir., 1970—; dir. Crane Fruehauf Trailers Ltd. Fruehauf Fischbach Automation, Jacksonville Shipyards, Inc., Maryland Shipbuilding & Drydock Co.; pres. Daro, Ltd. Mem. Am. Ordnance Assn. (adv. com. 1970—), Truck Trailer Mfrs. Assn. (pres. 1971-72), Economic Club Detroit, Sigma Alpha Mu. Mason. Clubs: Franklin Hills Country; Highland Country (pres. 1966-68); Great Lakes; Standard City. Home: 16500 N Park Dr Southfield MI 48075 Office: 10900 Harper Av Detroit MI 48232

BERNSTEIN, DAVID W., rubber co. exec.; b. Chelsea, Mass., 1908; ed. Mass. Inst. Tech. Chmn., chief exec. officer, dir. Am.-Biltrite Rubber Co., Chelsea, Mass.; chmn., mem. exec. com. Am. Synthetic Rubber Co., Louisville; dir. Am. Rubber & Chem. Co., Louisville. Home: 94 Hammondswood Rd Chestnut Hill MA 02167 Office: 575 Tech Sq Cambridge MA 02139

BERNSTEIN, DOROTHY LEWIS, educator, mathematician; b. Chgo., Apr 11, 1914; d. Jacob L. and Tillie (Lewis) Bernstein; B.A., M.A., U. Wis. 1934; Ph.D., Brown U., 1939. Instr. math. Mt. Holyoke Coll., 1937-40, U. Wis., 1941-42; research asso. U. Cal. at Berkeley, 1942-43; faculty U. Rochester, 1943-59, prof. math., 1957-59; prof. math. Goucher Coll., 1959—, chmn. dept., 1960-70; mem. Inst. Advanced Study, Princeton, 1950-51. Vis. prof. U. Cal. at Los Angeles, 1957-58, Brown U., 1966-67. Mem. Am. Math. Soc., Math. Assn. Am., Soc. Indsl. and Applied Math., Am. Assn. U. Profs., Phi Beta Kappa, Sigma Xi. Author: Existence Theorems in Partial Differential Equations, 1950: also articles. Office: Goucher Coll Baltimore MD 21204

BERNSTEIN, ELMER, composer, conductor; b. N.Y.C., Apr. 4, 1922; s. Edward and Selma (Feinstein) B.; student N.Y. U.; m. Pearl Glusman, Dec. 21, 1946; children—Peter Matthew, Gregory Eames. Concert pianist, N.Y.C., Phila., Chgo., 1946-50; composer music for UN radio shows, 1949: composer mus. scores 1950—, including Man with the Golden Arm, The Ten Commandments, The Magnificent Seven, Summer and Smoke, Walk on the Wild Side, To Kill a Mockingbird (Golden Globe award Hollywood Fgn. Press 1962), The Great Escape, The Birdman of Alcatraz, Hud, Sudden Fear, God's Little Acre, Sweet Smell of Success, Desire Under the Elm, Some Came Running, From the Terrace, Love With the Proper Stranger, Baby the Rain Must Fall, The Caretakers, The Sons of Katie Elder, Cast a Giant Shadow, Hawaii. Pres. Young Musicians Found., 1961—. Recipient Motion Picture Exhibitor Laurel awards 1956, 57, 6 written for TV, Making of a President, 1964, Acad. award for best original music score for Thoroughly Modern Millie, 1968. Mem. Acad. Motion Picture Arts and Scis. (1st v.p. 1963—), The Thalians (v.p. 1959-62), Screen Composers Assn. (bd. dirs.), Nat. Acad. Rec. Arts and Scis. (bd. dirs.). 12127 Iredell St Studio City CA

BERNSTEIN, EUGENE FELIX, medical educator; b. N.Y.C., Oct. 9, 1930; s. Mayer H. and Sarah (Marmerstein) B.; student Coll. Arts and Pure Scis., N.Y.U., 1947-50; M.D., Downstate Med. Center, State U. N.Y., 1954; M.S., U. Minn., 1961, Ph.D., 1964; m. Joan Jordan, Oct. 10, 1954; children—Diane, Steven, Susan. Intern King's County Hosp., Bklyn., 1954-55; resident U. Minn., 1957-64; instr. dept. surgery U. Minn. Med. Sch., 1963-64, asst. prof., 1964-67, asso. prof., 1967-69; prof. surgery U. Cal. at San Diego Sch. Medicine, 1969—; cons. Naval Hosp., San Diego, Gulf Gen. Atomic, Inc., San Diego, Medtronics, Inc., Mpls. Served to capt., M.C., AUS, 1955-57. Postdoctoral research fellow Nat. Heart Inst., 1959-62; Advanced research fellow Am. Heart Assn., 1962-64; John and Mary R. Markle scholar acad. medicine, 1963-68. Diplomate Am. Bd. Thoracic Surgery. Mem. A.C.S., Am. Heart Assn., Am. Soc. Artificial Internal Organs (pres.), Assn. Acad. Surgery, Central Surg. Assn., Internat. Cardiovascular Soc., Soc. Univ. Surgeons, Soc. Vascular Surgery, James E. Moore Surg. Soc., Beta Lambda Sigma, Alpha Omega Alpha. Research cardiovascular physiology, rheoloy of blood, assisted circulation. Home: 2520 Via Viesta La Jolla CA 92037

BERNSTEIN, EUGENE MERLE, educator, physicist; b. Balt., Feb. 13, 1931; s. Isidore and Ethel (Karsh) B.; B.S., Duke, 1953, M.A., 1954, Ph.D., 1956; m. Jean M. Stuesser, Aug. 3, 1960; children—Robert Glen, Lisa Joan. Instr., Duke, 1956-57; instr. U. Wis., 1957-59, lectr., 1960-61; NSF postdoctoral fellow Niels Bohr Inst., Copenhagen, 1959-60; asst. prof. U. Tex., 1961-63, asso. prof., 1963-65, prof., 1967-68; vis. staff mem. Los Alamos Sci. Lab., 1965-67; prof. Western Mich. U., Kalamazoo, 1968—. Mem. Am. Phys. Soc., N.Y. Acad. Scis., Phi Beta Kappa, Sigma Xi. Home: 2417 Acorn Lane Kalamazoo MI 49001

BERNSTEIN, JEREMY, educator; b. Rochester, N.Y., Dec. 31, 1929; s. Philip Sidney and Sophy (Rubin) B.; B.A., Harvard, 1951, M.A., 1953, Ph.D., 1955. Research asso. Harvard, 1955-57, Inst. for Advanced Study, 1957-60, NSF and Brookhaven Nat. Lab., 1960-62; asso. prof. physics N.Y. U., N.Y.C., 1962-67; faculty, dept. physics Stevens Inst. Tech., Hoboken, N.J., 1967—. Cons., RAND Corp., Gen. Atomic Co.; mem. staff New Yorker, N.Y.C., 1962—. Recipient Westinghouse prize for sci. writing, 1964. Mem. Am. Phys. Soc. Club: French Alpine. Author: Analytical Engine: Computers, Past, Present, and Future, 1964; Ascent, 1965. Office: Dept Physics Stevens Inst Tech Hoboken NJ

BERNSTEIN, JOSEPH, lawyer; b. Balt., Jan. 23, 1897; s. David M. and Elizabeth (Zetlin) B.: LL.B., U. Md., 1918; m. Bertha Miller, Oct. 19, 1930; children—Jane (Mrs. Edward H. Friend), David H. Admitted to Md. bar, 1918; practiced in Balt., 1919—; mem. firm Frank, Bernstein, Gutherlet & Conway 1954-66; Frank, Bernstein, Conaway and Goldman, 1966—. Chmn. Legal Aid Bur. Balt., 1943-46. Bd. dirs. Sinai Hosp. of Balt., Inc.; past trustee Commn. on Govtl. Efficiency and Economy. Fellow (life), Md. bar founds.; mem. Am. (ho dels. 1960), Md. (pres. 1960), Balt. (pres. 1950) bar assns. Home: 3900 N Charles St Baltimore MD 21202

BERNSTEIN, LAWSON FREDERICK, lawyer; b. N.Y.C., Feb. 29, 1920; s. Benjamin and Ruth (Kleeblatt) B.; A.B., Columbia, 1940; postgrad. Yale, 1940-41; LL.B., N.Y.U., 1947; m. Charlotte Jane Baer, Dec. 20, 1955 (div. June 1969); children—Lawson Frederick, Richard Douglas; m. 2d, Mio Miriam Fedland, Nov. 22, 1969; 1 dau., Katherine Miriam Celia. Admitted to N.Y. State bar, 1947. U.S. Supreme Court bar, 1953; mem. firm Bernstein & Bernstein, N.Y.C., 1950-63; practice in N.Y.C., 1963-66, 69—; partner firm Pincus, Bernstein & Bernstein & Seeman, N.Y.C., 1966-69, Acting chmn. Nat. Enforcement Commn., 1952-53. Served from pvt. to capt., U.S. Army, 1942-46. Mem. Am., N.Y. State bar assns., N.Y. County Lawyers Assn., Yale Law Sch. Assn., Am. Jewish Soc. for Service (dir.), Assn., Bar City of N.Y. Mem. B'nai B'rith (pres. Midtown lodge 1959-61, dist. dep. 1961-63). Office: 110 E 59th St New York City NY 10022

BERNSTEIN, LEONARD, conductor, pianist, composer; b. Lawrence, Mass., Aug. 25, 1918; s. Samuel Joseph and Jennie (Resnick) B.; A.B., Harvard, 1939; grad. Curtis Inst. Music, 1941; studied conducting with Fritz Reiner and Serge Koussevitsky; studied piano with Helen Coates, Heinrich Gebhard and Isabella Vengerova; numerous hon. degrees from various colls. and univs.; m. Felicia Montealegre Cohn, Sept. 9, 1951; children—Jamie, Alexander, Nina. Asst. to Serge Koussevitzky at Berkshire Music Center, 1942; asst. condr. N.Y. Philharmonic Symphony, 1943-44; condr. N.Y.C. Symphony, 1945-48; mus. adviser Israel Philharmonic Orch., 1948-49; faculty Berkshire Music Center, 1948- 55, head conducting dept., 1951-55; prof. music Brandeis U., 1951-56; co- condr. with Dimitri Mitropoulas of N.Y. Philharmonic, 1957-58, music dir., 1958-69, appointed laureate condr. Philharmonic for life; condr. major orchs. of U.S., Europe in tours, 1946—; frequent condr. Israel Philharmonic Orch., 1947—; condr. opera at La Scala, Milan, also Met. Opera, N.Y.C. and Vienna State Opera; shared transcontinental tour in U.S. with Serge Koussevitzky and Israel Philharmonic, 1951; toured Europe with Vienna Philharmonic Orch., 1970. Works include: Clarinet Sonata, 1942; Seven Anniversaries for Piano, 1942; Song Cycle, I Hate Music, 1943; Piano Pieces, Four Anniversaries for Piano, 1948; Song Cycle, La Bonne Cusine, 1949; Symphony No.2-The Age of Anxiety, 1949; Trouble in Tahiti (1 act opera; also wrote libretto), 1952; Symphony No. 3, Kaddish, 1963; Chichester Psalms for mixed chorus, boys' choir, orch., 1965. Score for musical show On The Town; ballets Fancy Free, 1944, Facsmile, 1946; incidental score for prodn. Peter Pan, 1950, The Lark, 1957; musical score for Broadway prodn. Wonderful Town, 1953, Broadway mus. Candide, 1956, West Side Story, 1957, film On the Waterfront, 1954; songs are Afterthought, Silhouette, 1951, Two Love Songs, 1949; Serenade for violin and string orchestra with percussion, 1954; Five Anniversaries for Piano, 1964; Mass (for opening of John F. Kennedy Center for Performing Arts), 1971. Recipient TV Acad. award for Young People's Concerts, 1960. Author: The Joy of Music, 1959 (Christopher award); Leonard Bernstein's Young People's Concerts for Reading and Listening, 1962, rev. edit., 1970; The Infinite Variety of Music, 1966. Mem. Nat. Inst. Arts and Letters. Office: 205 W 57th St New York City NY 10019

BERNSTEIN, LESTER, mag. editor; b. N.Y.C., July 18, 1920; s. Isidore and Rebecca (Axelrod) B.; A.B., Columbia, 1940; m. Jacqueline Lipscomb, Feb. 6, 1946; children—Lynn, Nina, Paul, Daniel. Reporter N.Y. Times, 1940-48; writer, fgn. corr., editor Time mag., 1948-58; dir. information NBC, 1958-60, v.p. corp. affairs, 1960-62; nat. affairs editor Newsweek, 1963- 65, exec. editor, 1965-69, mng. editor, 1969—. Served with AUS, World War II. Home: 10 Pineapple St Brooklyn NY 11201 Office: 444 Madison Av New York City NY 10022

BERNSTEIN, MARSHALL MENLINE, lawyer; b. N.Y.C., Apr. 21, 1901; s. Saul and Sarah (Menline) B.; A.B., Columbia, 1921, J.D., 1923; m. Beatrice Weilburg, Dec. 28, 1926; children—Carole Brooks, Gerald Marshall. Admitted to N.Y. bar, 1924; since practiced in N.Y.C., mem. firm Saul & Marshall M. Bernstein, 1926-57, Sirota, Bernstein & Steyer, attys., 1957—; gen. counsel, sec., mem. exec. and finance coms. Nat. Container Corp. of Del., dir., 1940-56. Mem. Anti-Defamation League N.Y., N.Y. County Lawyers Assn., Am. Bar Assn. Home: 91 Central Park W New York City NY 10023 Office: 60 E 42d St New York City NY 10017

BERNSTEIN, MARTIN, educator, musicologist; b. N.Y.C., Dec. 14, 1904; s. Joseph and Ida (Colodny) B.; Sc.B., N.Y. U., 1925, Mus.B., 1927; m. Juliet Danziger, Nov. 7, 1930 (dec. June 1948); children—Ellen, James; m. 2d, Virginia Lubkin, Aug. 28, 1949; children—Roger, John. Asst. physics N.Y. U., 1924-25, asst. to asso. prof. music, 1926-47, prof., 1948—, head dept. music, 1955-70. Played with N.Y. Symphony Orch., 1925, N.Y. Philharmonic, 1926-28; condr. Am. Bach Soc., 1949-50; radio commentator CBS, 1956-57. Served to 1st lt. Intelligence Corps., AUS, 1943-46. Decorated Bronze Star medal; recipient Great Tchr. award N.Y. U., 1968. Mem. Am. Assn. U. Profs., Coll. Music Assn., Am. Internat. musicol. socs., Music Library Assn., Phi Beta Kappa. Democrat. Jewish religion. Author: Score Reading, rev. edit., 1949; An Introduction to Music, rev. edit., 1951, (with Martin Picker) 3d edit., 1966. Home: 1 Blackstone Pl New York City NY 10471

BERNSTEIN, MARVER HILLEL, educator; b. Mankato, Minn., Feb. 7, 1919; s. Meyer M. and Esther (Alpert) B.; B.A., M.A., U. Wis., 1940; Ph.D. in Politics, Princeton, 1948; m. Sheva Rosenthal, Sept. 19, 1943. Budget examiner U.S. Bur. Budget, 1942-46; faculty Princeton, 1947—, prof. polit. and pub. affairs, 1958—, Ford research prof. govtl. affairs, 1960-61, chmn. dept. politics, 1961- 64; asso. dir. Woodrow Wilson Sch., 1961-64, dean Woodrow Wilson Sch. Pub. and Internat. Affairs, 1964-69. Cons. orgn., adminstrn. state and fed. agys.; State Comptroller of Israel, 1953-57, A.I.A., 1968-70; asso. staff dir. spl. com. fed. conflict of interest laws Assn. Bar City N.Y., 1958-60; mem. Adminstrv. Conf. U.S., 1961-62; vis. com. John F. Kennedy Sch. Govt., 1966—; mem. Rockefeller Pub. Service Awards Selection Com., 1964-69, mem. Nat. B'nai B'rith Hillel Commn., 1966—, chmn., 1969—; chmn. Pub. and Sch. Employees' Grievance Procedure Study Commn. N.J., 1967. Trustee Nat. Civil Service League, 1967—. Fellow Am. Acad. Arts and Scis.; mem. Nat. Acad. Pub. Adminstrn., Am. Polit. Sci. Assn. (program chmn. 1958, chmn. com. profl. standards and responsibilities), Am. Soc. Pub. Adminstrn., Nat. Acad. Pub. Adminstrn., Am. Acad. Arts and Scis. Clubs: Princeton of N.Y.; Cosmos (Washington). Author: Regulating Business by Independent Commission, 1955; The Politics of Israel, 1957; The Job of the Federal Executive, 1958; (with Robert K. Carr) American Democracy 1951—. Home: 37 McCosh Circle Princeton NJ 08540

BERNSTEIN, PAUL, coll. dean; b. Phila., Jan. 19, 1927; s. Abraham and Jennie (Geek) B.; B.S., Temple U., 1949, M.Ed., 1950; Ph.D., U. Pa., 1955; m. Irma Shuster, Apr. 10, 1949; children—Jay Ira, Lisa Beth. Tchr. social scis. Phila. pub. schs., 1949-55; prof. European history, chmn. social scis. dept. Lock Haven (Pa.) State Coll., 1955-64, Plattsburg (N.Y.) State U. Coll., 1964-66; dean Coll. Gen. Studies, Rochester Inst. Tech., 1966—. Co-chmn. Citizens for Humphrey, Monroe County, N.Y., 1968. Served with AUS, 1944-47. Grantee Am. Philos. Soc., 1959. Mem. Am. Hist. Assn., French History Soc. (exec. bd.), Assn. Gen. and Liberal Studies. Democrat. Jewish religion. Elk. Author: (with R. Green) History of Civilization, 2d edit., 1962; also articles. Mng. editor Lock Haven Bull., 1959-64. Home: 5 Candlewood Circle Pittsford NY 14534 Office: Rochester Inst Tech Rochester NY 14623

BERNSTEIN, PETER L., economist; B.S., Harvard. Economist, Fed. Res. Bank N.Y., comml. banks, N.Y.C.; faculty Williams Coll.; now pres., dir. Bernstein-Macaulay, Inc.; faculty New Sch. for Social Research, N.Y.C. Author: The Price of Prosp. 1963; Primer on Money, Banking and Gold. 1965; (with Robert L. Heilbroner) Primer on Government Spending. Contbr. articles to bus. and econs. jours. Address: care New Sch for Social Research 66 W 12th St New York City NY 10011*

BERNSTEIN, PHILIP SIDNEY, rabbi; b. Rochester, N.Y., June 29, 1901; s. Abraham M. and Sarah (Steinberg) B.; A.B., Syracuse U., 1917-21; Rabbi, M.H.L., Jewish Inst. Religion, 1926, D.D., 1946; postgrad. Columbia, 1922-25, Cambridge U. (Eng.) and Hebrew U., 1925-26; LL.D., Miami U., 1953; D.S.T., Syracuse U., 1954; D.D., U. Rochester, 1959; m. Sophy Rubin, June 11, 1925; children—Jeremy,

Stephen, Alice. Rabbi, Temple B'rith Kodesh, Rochester, N.Y., 1926—; on leave of absence to act as exec. dir. com. on Army and Navy religious activities Jewish Welfare Bd., 1942-46, as adviser on Jewish affairs to theater comdrs., U.S. Forces, ETO, and U.S. Forces, Germany, Austria, 1946-47. Pres. Central Conf. Am. Rabbis, 1950-52; v.p. World Jewish Congress, Am. Jewish Congress, World Alliance Internat. Friendship Through the Churches; trustee Ch. Peace Union; chmn. Citizens' City Planning and Housing Council Rochester, Rochester Jewish Community Council, Am. Israel Pub. Affairs Com.; mem. Gov.'s Commn. on the Aging. Pres. Rochester City Club, 1932-33. Ofcl. mission for War and Navy depts. to pacific theaters of war, 1944-45. Served with S.A.T.C., 1918. Recipient Man of the Year award Rochester Rotary Club, 1958; Rochester (N.Y.) civic medalist, 1962. Author: What the Jews Believe. Contbr. articles to nationally known mags. and religious jours. Home: 140 Windemere Rd Rochester NY Office: 2131 Elmwood Av Rochester NY 14618

BERNSTEIN, RICHARD BARRY, educator, research chemist; b. N.Y.C., Oct. 31, 1923; s. Simon and Stella (Grossman) B.; A.B., Columbia, 1943, M.A., 1944, Ph.D., 1948; m. Norma B. Oliver, Dec. 17, 1948; children—Neil David, Minda Dianne, Beth Anne, Julie Lynn. Mem. research staff SAM Lab., Columbia, 1942-46; asst. prof. chemistry Ill. Inst. Tech., 1948-53; from asst. prof. to prof. chemistry U. Mich., 1953-63; prof. chemistry U. Wis., 1963-66, W.W. Daniells prof., 1966—. Reilly Centennial lectr. and award for honor, U. Notre Dame, 1965; Mack lectr. Ohio State U., 1966; FMC lectr. Princeton, 1966; N.Y. State distinguished lectr. Yeshiva U., 1969; Folk-Plaut lectr. Columbia, 1971; del. Pontifical Acad. Conf., 1966; mem. adv. bds. chemistry Nat. Acad. Sci., 1965-69; adv. bd. Army Research Office, Durham, N.C., 1967-69; Sloan Found. fellow 1956-60; sr. postdoctoral fellow NSF, 1960-61. Fellow Am. Phys. Soc. (chmn. div. chem. physics 1967-68); Am. Acad. Arts and Scis.; mem. Am. Chem. Soc. (chmn. div. phys. chemistry 1965-66), A.A.A.S., Nat. Acad. Scis., Author papers, chpts. in books. Home: 3410 Lake Mendota Dr Madison WI 53705

BERNSTEIN, RICHARD JACOB, educator, philosopher; b. N.Y.C., May 14, 1932; s. Henry S. and Anna (Halperin) B.; A.B., U. Chgo., 1951; B.S., Columbia, 1953; M.A., Yale, 1955, Ph.D., 1958; m. Carol M. Lippit, Sept. 11, 1955; children—Robin, Andrea, Jeffrey, Daniel. Mem. faculty Yale, 1954-66, asso. prof. philosophy, 1964-66; prof. philosophy, chmn. dept. Haverford Coll., 1966—. Fulbright lectr. Hebrew U., 1957-58, vis. prof., 1966-67. Recipient E. Harris Harbison award for distinguished teaching, 1970. Fellow Stiles Coll., Yale. Mem. Am. Philos. Assn. (exec. com. 1967-70), Metaphys. Soc. Am., Charles Sanders Peirce Soc. (pres. 1969), Fullerton Club (pres. 1967). Author: John Dewey on Experience, Nature and Freedom, 1959; Perspectives on Peirce, 1965; John Dewey, 1966; Praxis and Action, 1971. Editor: Perspectives on Peirce, 1967. Editor Rev. Metaphysics, 1964—. Home: 1614 Monk Rd Gladwyne PA 19035

BERNSTEIN, ROBERT LOUIS, book publisher; b. N.Y.C., Jan. 5, 1923; s. Alfred and Sylvia (Bloch) B.; grad. Lincoln Sch., N.Y.C., 1940; B.S., Harvard, 1944; m. Helen Walter, Nov. 23, 1950; children—Peter Walter, Tom Alfred, William Sammuel. Gen. sales mgr. Simon & Schuster, Inc., N.Y.C., 194657; with Randson House, Inc., 1957—, pres., 1966—. Sch. bd. Union Free Sch. Dist. 6, Town Mt. Pleasant. Vice chmn. Assn. Am. Pubs., 1970—. Bd. dirs. Am. Book Pubs. Council, 1967-70. Bd. dirs. Camp Rainbow, Dr. Seuss Found.; trustee Blythedale Childrens Hosp., State U. N.Y. at Purchase Found.; bd. friends Scarsdale Library. Served with USAAF, 1943-46. Clubs: Harvard (N.Y.C.); Century Country (White Plains, N.Y.); Town (Scarsdale). Home: 20 Murray Hill Rd Scarsdale, NY 10585. Office: 201 E 50th St New York City NY 10022

BERNSTEIN, SEYMOUR, educator, physicist; b. Chgo., Feb. 20, 1909; s. Isadore Samuel and Etta (Sher) B.; B.S. in Engring., U. Ill., 1930; Ph.D. in Physics, U. Chgo. (Charles A. Coffin fellow), 1939; m. Adelaide Rubin, Sept. 18, 1938; children—Ruth Alice (Mrs. S. Hillel Hyman), Irene Susan. Research asso., metall. lab. U. Chgo., 1942-44; from asso. physicist to chief physicist Oak Ridge Nat. Lab., 1944-64; lectr. physics U. Tenn., 1949-60; prof. physics Israel Inst. Tech., Haifa, 1955-56, U. Ill. at Chgo. Circle, 1964—; vis. prof. physics U. Miami (Fla.), 1961-62. Vis. scientist Argonne Nat. Lab., summers 1965,67,68. U.S. sci. del. 1st Conf. Peaceful Uses Atomic Energy, Geneva, Switzerland, 1955. Mem. Am. Phys. Soc., A.A.A.S., Sigma Xi, Tau Beta Pi. Contbr. profl. jours. Home: 5405 Howard St Western Springs IL 60558 Office: PO Box 4348 Chicago IL 60680

BERNSTEIN, SID, jazz promoter; student Columbia. Formerly mgr. of Esy Morales, then with Latin music agy.; asst. for Latin Quarter, N.Y.C., 1955; producer play The Year Around, 1955. agt. for Shaw Artists, 1955-59; jazz promoter, 1960—; promotions include Miles Davis, Brook Benton, Fats Domino, 1960 Atlantic City Jazz Festival, 1961 Newport Jazz Festival; with Gen. Artists Corp., 1962-64; promoter The Beatles, now mgr. The Rascals. other artists. Address: 510 Madison Av New York City NY 10022*

BERNSTEIN, SIDNEY RALPH, editor; b. Chgo., Jan. 29, 1907; s. Charles and Jennie R. (Greenblatt) B.; student U. Ill., 1924-25; M.B.A., U. Chgo., 1956; m. Adele Bass, Oct. 5, 1930; children—Janet (Mrs. C.P. Wingis), Henry. Asso. editor and mng. editor Hosp. Mgmt., Chgo., 1925-31; mng. editor Advertising Age, Chgo., 1932-38, editor, 1939-57, editorial dir., 1958-64, pub., 1964-70; dir. research and promotion Crain Communications Inc. (formerly Advt. Pubs., Inc.), Chgo., 1938- 39, v.p., 1938-60, exec. v.p., gen. mgr., 1961-64, pres., 1964- -. Lectr. U. Coll., U. Chgo., Mich. State U., 1950-58; dir. Am. Marketing Assn., 1946-47, v.p. for marketing mgmt., 1963-64. Mem. nat. marketing adv. com. U.S. Dept. Commerce, 1967—. Bd. dirs. Am. Bus. Press, 1970—. Named Advt. Man of Year, Chgo. Post 170 Am. Legion, 1957, Chgo. Federated Advt. Club, 1961, Communications Man of Year, Chgo. Jr. Assn. Commerce and Industry, 1962; elected to Distbn. Hall of Fame, Boston Conf. on Distbn., 1962; named Man of Year, Nat. Advt. Agy. Network, 1964. Mem. Mag. Pubs. Assn. (dir. 1970—), also numerous advt. and sales orgns., Phi Epsilon Pi, Alpha Delta Sigma, Sigma Delta Chi, Beta Gamma Sigma. Clubs: Chicago Press, Arts, Mid-Am., Cliff Dwellers, Tavern (Chgo.); Nat. Press (Washington). Home: 534 Stratford Pl Chicago IL 60657 Office: 740 Rush St Chicago IL 60611

BERNSTEIN, THEODORE MENLINE, editor; b. N.Y.C., Nov. 17, 1904; s. Saul and Sarah (Menline) B.; A.B., Columbia, 1924, B.Litt., 1925; m. Beatrice Alexander, Sept. 2, 1930 (dec. Jan. 1971); 1 son, Eric Menline. Mem. staff N.Y. Times, 1925—, news editor, 1951-52, asst. mng. editor, 1952-69, founding editor internat. edit., Paris, France, 1960, editorial dir. book div., 1969—, exec. editor N.Y. Times Encyclopedic Almanac, 1969—; from asst. to asso. prof. Columbia Sch. Journalism, 1925- 50. Cons. U.S. Panel Ednl. Research and Devel., 1964. Mem. Sigma Delta Chi. Author: (with R.E. Garst) Headlines and Deadlines, 2d edit., 1961; Watch Your Language, 1958; More Language That Needs Watching, 1962; The Careful Writer, 1965; Miss Thistlebottom's Hobgoblins, 1971. Cons. on usage Random House Dictionary, Am. Heritage Dictionary. Home: 2 Fifth Av New York City NY 10011 Office: 229 W 43d St New York City NY 10036

BERNSTEIN, THERESA F., artist; b. Phila.; d. Isidore and Anne (Ferber) Bernstein; student Pa. Acad. Phila. Sch. Design, Art Students League; m. William Meyerowitz, 1919. Dir. Salons of Am., 1924-30, Ind. Artists; life mem. Grand Central Art Galleries, N.Y.; represented in permanent collections U.S. Nat. Mus., Washington Library of Congress, Phillips Meml. Art Gallery, Chgo. Art Inst., Met. Mus. Art, N.Y. Pub. Library, Bklyn. Mus., others; also pvt. collections; represented Art U.S.A. by painting Jazz Players; exhbns. including Carnegie Inst., N.A.D., Cooper Union Mus. Butler Inst. Am. Art, Boston Pub. Library, Phila. Mus. Art; one-man show Nat. Mus., Smithsonian Instn., Fitchburg Art Mus., Doll & Richards, Inc., Boston Publick House, Sturbridge, Mass., U. Me., Orono, 1963, Columbus Mus., Gainesville Mus.; dir. summer art course, Gloucester, Mass. Chmn., Meml. Exhibit Cape Ann Festival, 1958—. Recipient Phillips prize for Progressive Painting, 1946; Green traveling fellow, John Sartain scholar, Phila. Bd. Edn. scholar; Robert Dain prize, 1964; hon. mention Soc. Am. Graphic Artists, 1954, Knickerbocker Artists, 1956, Ogunquit Art Center; Carl Matson portrait award Rockport Art Assn., 1967; New Eng. Artists award N. Shore Arts Assn., 1967; Cantorella prize Nat. Assn. Women Artists, Nat. Acad., N.Y., 1968. Mem. Nat. Assn. Women Artists jury of awards 1948-50, jury oil painting 1959, Margaret Cooper prize for oil portrait Sarah 1951, Jane Peterson prize, 1955, (nominating com. 1963-64), Boston Printmakers Assn., Cape Ann. Soc. Artists, Nat. Assn. Women Painters and Sculptors, (Jury of award 1920-29), N.Y. Soc. Woman Artists (chmn. 1935-36, dir. 1959—, hon. dir. 1969—), North Shore Arts Assn., Cape Ann Soc. Artists, Conn. Acad. Artists of Am. (mem. oil jury 1957-58), Allied Artists Am. Contbr. articles to mags., newspapers. Studio: 54 W 74th St New York City NY 10023 also 44 Mount Pleasant Av East Gloucester MA 01930

BERNSTEIN, VICTOR HEINE, writer, editor; b. N.Y.C., Oct. 7, 1904; s. Chanon A. and Eva (Finn) B.; B.A., Columbia, 1924; B.Lit., Pulitzer Sch. Journalism, 1925; m. Selma Krumgold, Oct. 25, 1935. Reporter, Providence News and Woodland (Cal.) Democrat, 1926-30; contbr. Sunday dept. N.Y. Times, 1931-33; fgn. corr. Jewish Telegraph Agy., Berlin and Vienna, 1937-39; reporter, fgn. corr. in France, Germany, Israel, also fgn. editor PM, newspaper, and N.Y. Star, 1940-49; mng. editor The Nation, N.Y.C., 1952-63; free-lance writer and editor, New Milford, Conn., 1964—. Covered prewar persecution of Jews in Germany and Austria, Austrian anschluss, collapse of Germany, liberation of concentration camps, Nuremberg trials. Mem. Sigma Delta Chi. Author: Final Judgement, the Story of Nuremberg, 1947; (with Justin Gray) The Inside Story of the Legion, 1948. Contbr. periodicals. Home: 120 Chestnut Land Rd New Milford, CT 06776.

BEROL, ALFRED C., pencil mfr.; b. N.Y.C., Oct. 5, 1892; s. Emil and Gella (Goldsmith) B.; student Phillips Exeter Acad., 1909; A.B., Harvard, 1913; m. Madeleine Rossin, May 4, 1922; 1 son, Kenneth. Chmn., dir. Berol Corp., Eagle Pencil Co., N.Y.C., London, Eng., Mexico City, Montreal, Que., Can., Bogata, Colombia, Caracas, Venezuela, Danbury, Conn., Blaisdell All-Rite, Fair-Lawn, N.J.; chmn., dir. Elkins Sawmill, Inc., Anderson, Cal., Hudson Lumber Co., San Leandro, Cal. Mem. Pencil Makers Assn. (pres.). Home: 6 E 61st St New York City NY 10021 also Faraway Farm Cross River NY 10518 also A M K Ranch Moran WY 83013 Office: 375 Park Av New York City NY 10022

BERONIO, JOHN B., motion picture co. exec.; b. 1921; grad. Pace Inst., 1947; married. With Metro-Goldwyn-Mayer, Inc., 1946—. treas., 1967—. Served with AUS, 1942- 45. Address: 1350 Av of Americas New York City NY 10019*

BERQUIST, MILLARD JOHN, pres. theol. sem.; b. Kansas City, Kan., Jan. 29, 1902; s. John Henry and Matilda (Lundquist) B.; A.B., William Jewell Coll., 1932, LL.D., 1960; D.D., Stetson U., 1946; Th.M., So. Bapt. Theol. Sem., 1935, Ph.D., 1942; m. Gladys Elizabeth Stack, June 22, 1927; 1 dau., Barbara Elizabeth. Ordained to ministry Baptist Ch., pastor in Ky. and Ohio, 1934-42, Jacksonville, Fla., 1942-47, Tampa, Fla., 1947-57; pres. Midwestern Bapt. Theol. Sem., Kansas City, Mo., 1957—; preaching missions in Panama, Jamica, P.R. Mem. radio and TV commn. So. Bapt. Conv., 1945-47; pres. Fla. Bapt. Conv., 1949; treas. United Christian Action of Fla., 1956-57; lesson writer Bapt. Sunday Sch. Bd. Trustee So. Bapt. Theol. Sem., 1949-57. Pres. United Fla. Drys, 1953-55. Author: Studies in First Corinthians, 1961. Home: 700 N E Vivion Rd Kansas City MO 64118

BERRA, YOGI, (Lawrence Peter), profl. baseball coach; b. St. Louis, May 12, 1925; s. Peter and Pauline (Longsoni) B.; ed. pub. schs., St. Louis; m. Carmen Short, Jan. 26, 1949; children—Lawrence A., Timothy Thomas, Dale Anthony. Profl. baseball player with N.Y. Yankees, 1946-63, mgr., 1964 (winner Am. League Pennant); coach N.Y. Mets, 1965—. Vice pres. Yoo-Hoo Beverage Co. Served with USNR, 1943-46. Lion, Elk, Moose. Home: 61 Sutherland Rd Montclair NJ 07042 Office: Shea Stadium Flushing NY 11368

BERRETT, WILLIAM EDWIN, educator, lawyer; b. Union, Utah, June 2, 1902; s. Heber Hookway and Ellen Ellener (Walker) B.; A.B., U. Utah, 1924, LL.B., 1933, J.D., 1967; summer student Brigham Young U., 1927-31, LL.D., 1965; m. Eleanor Louise Callister, June 2, 1926; children—Verne Russell, Sharon Louise, Richard Heber, William Brian. Sem. prin. dept. edn. Ch. of Jesus Christ of Latter-day Saints Sem., 1925-31, dir. Inst. Religion, 1931-33, editor dept. edn., 1933-42; admitted to Utah bar, 1933; spl. prosecutor OPA, 1943-46; asst. U.S. atty. 4th Jud. Dist. Alaska, 1946-47; prof. religion Brigham Young U., 1948—, v.p., 1953-63; adminstr. sems., also insts. religion Ch. of Jesus Christ of Latter-day Saints, 1963—. Mem. Utah Com. Children and Youth, 1960-65, chmn., 1961-64; dir. Nat. Council State Coms. Children and Youth, 1963-65; mem. White House Conf. Children and Youth, 1960. Mem. gen. bd. Deseret Sunday Sch. Union, 1936-45, 47- 54; councilor E. Millcreek stake Ch. of Jesus Christ of Latter-day Saints, 1945-46, councilor Fairbanks (Alaska) br., 1946-47. Mem. Tau Kappa Alpha (Spl. Service award 1960), Delta Theta Phi, Phi Kappa Phi. Author: The Restored Church, 1936; Doctrines of the Restored Church, 1940; The Gospel Message, 1938; Teachings of the Doctrine and Covenants, 1954; Teachings of the Book of Mormon, 1952. Co-author: Readings in Latter-day Saints Church History, 3 vols., 1952, 54, 58; Mormonism and the Negro, 1960. Editor: Saga of Sugar, 1940. Home: 404 E 4380 North Provo UT 84601

BERRIAN, ALBERT HARRY, educator; b. Miami, Fla., July 8, 1925; s. Neal and Florence (Peake) B.; B.A. in English, N.Y. U., 1948, M.A. in French, 1949, Ph.D., 1954; m. Mary Miles, Apr. 7, 1945; children—Brenda, Antoinette, Albert Harry II, Derek. Chmn. fgn. lang. dept. Clark Coll., Atlanta, 1942-52, Tex. So. U., 1954-60, Central State Coll., 1956-58, N.C. Coll. at Durham, 1958- 60; prof. French, Plattsburg State Coll., 1962-63; prof. French, dean faculty Hampton (Va.) Inst., 1964—; now asso. commr. higher edn. N.Y. State Edn.; dir. English lang. tng. English lang. Services, AID, Leopoldville, Congo, 1960-62. Asso. commr. for higher edn. N.Y. State Edn. Dept., Albany. Bd. dirs. Hampton Community Action Agy., So. Fellowships Fund. Served with USCGR, 1943-45. Recipient Centennial medallion Hampton Inst., 1968. Author: Notebook for Teachers of African Culture, 1965; Negritude: Essays and Studies, 1968; Education for Life in a Multi-Cultural Society, 1968. Mem. editorial bd. Jour. Human Relations, 1956—. Home: 57 Astor Pl Jersey City NJ 07304 Office: State Edn Dept Albany NY 12335

BERRIGAN, DANIEL J., cleryman, author; b. May 9, 1921; s. Thomas and Frieda (Fromhart) B. Joined Soc. of Jesus, 1939; ordained priest Roman Catholic Ch., 1952; tchr. French and philosophy Bklyn. Preparatory Sch., 1954-57; prof. N.T. studies Le Moyne Coll., 1957-63; dir. United Religious Work Cornell U., 1967—. Author: World for Wedding Ring, 1962; No One Walks Waters (poetry), 1966; Consequences: Trust & . . ., 1967; Go From Here, a Prison Journal; Love, Love at the End (poetry), 1968; They Call Us Dead Men, 1968; Night Flight to Hanoi, 1968; The Trial of the Catonsville Nine, 1970; False Gods, Real Men, 1969. Office: United Religious Work Cornell U Ithaca NY 14850

BERRIGAN, PHILIP FRANCIS, clergyman; b. Two Harbors, Minn., Oct. 5, 1923; s. Thomas William and Freda (Fromhart) B.; A.B. in English, Holy Cross Coll., 1950; B.S. in Secondary Edn., Loyola U. of South, 1959; M.A., Xavier U., New Orleans, 1961. Ordained priest Roman Catholic Ch., 1950; prof. English and religion, also student counselor St. Augustine High Sch., New Orleans; asst. pastor St. Peter Claver Ch., Balt.; worked and demonstrated with So. Christian Leadership Conf., N.A.A.C.P., CORE, SNCC; mem. Fellowship of Reconciliation; co-founder, co-chmn. Cath. Peace Fellowship, Balt. Interfaith Peace Mission; lectr. on race, peace, poverty; theologian within Fellowship of Reconciliation's nat. program on Triple Revolution in Washington, Portland, Ore., Seattle, Louisville, Cin., Chgo. Served with inf. AUS, World War II; ETO. Author: No More Strangers, 1965; The Trial of the Catonsville Nine (play), 1970; Prison Journals of a Priest Revolutionary, 1970. 1546 N Fremont Av Baltimore MD 21217

BERRY, BETTY BLAISDELL, designer, assn. exec.; b. Providence, Oct. 6, 1922; d. Sidney Briggs and Eleanor May (Platt) Blaisdell; B.A., Smith Coll., 1944; student N.Y. Sch. Interior Design, 1951, 52, 54, Craft Students League, 1960-61; M. A., N.Y. U., 1968; m. Robert Gifford Berry, June 14, 1947 (div. Sept. 1970). Adminstrv. asst. Nat. Metal Trades Assn., 1945-46; research asst. Office John D. Rockefeller, Jr., 1950-52; adminstrv. asst. Am. Museum Immigration, 1955-57; bus. mgr., bd. dirs. Goetz Indsl. Design, Inc., N.Y.C., 1958-60; exec. sec. Indsl. Designers Inst., N.Y.C., 1960-62; textile designer, 1962-68; exec. dir. Indsl. Designers Soc. Am., 1971—. Br. sec. N.Y.C. League Women Voters, 1954; mem. Citizens for Eisenhower, 1956. Mem. Mus. Modern Art, Craft Students League (mgmt. com.), Phi Beta Kappa. Co.-author article. Home: 60 W 55th St New York City NY 10019

BERRY, BREWTON, ret. educator; b. Orangeburg, S.C., Aug. 9, 1901; s. Joseph Andrew and Frances Deborah (Pike) B.; A.B., Wofford Coll., 1922; B.D. (Fogg scholarship, Day fellowship), Yale, 1925; Ph.D., U. Edinburgh, 1930; m. Margaret Foley Woods, Sept. 11, 1926; children—Margaret (Mrs. Forrest J. Curtin, Jr.), Deborah (Mrs. Douglas R. Houser). Asst. prof. sociology and anthropology U. Mo., 1931-37, asso. prof., 1937-45, vis. prof., summer 1950, dir. anthrop. collection, 1932-45; dir. Archeol. Survey Mo., 1932-45; prof., head sociology dept. U. R.I., 1945-46; prof. sociology and anthropology Ohio State U., Columbus, 1946-64. Julius Rosenwald fellow, 1943-44; recipient Anisfield-Wolf book award, 1952. Fellow Am. Anthropological Assn., Am. Sociol. Assn.; mem. Mo. Archeol. Soc. (hon. life), Ohio Valley Sociol. Soc. (pres. 1954-55), Sons of Am. Revolution, Phi Beta Kappa (chpt. pres. 1965-66), Sigma Xi. Democrat Episcopalian. Clubs: Scioto Country; Crichton; Torch (chpt. pres. 1967-68), Faculty (Columbus, Ohio); Book and Bond (Yale). Author: You and Your Superstitions, 1940; (with Seba Eldridge) Fundamentals of Sociology, 1950; Race Relations, 1951; Race and Ethnic Relations, 1958, rev. edit., 1965; Almost White, 1963; The Education of American Indians, 1968; also articles, essays, short stories. Editor: Mo. Archaeologist, 1934-45, Ohio Valley Sociologist, 1947-52; asso. editor Am. Sociol. Rev., 1953-56; editorial bd. Ohio State U. Press, 1964—. Home: 2221 Brixton Rd Columbus OH 43221 Office: 1775 S College Rd Columbus OH 43210

BERRY, BRIAN JOE LOBLEY, educator; b. Sedgley, Stafford, Eng., Feb. 16, 1934; s. Joe and Gwendoline (Lobley) B.; B.Sc. with honors, U. Coll., London, Eng., 1955; M.A., U. Wash., 1956, Ph.D., 1958; m. Janet Elizabeth Shapley, Sept. 6, 1958; children—Duncan Jeffrey, Carol Anne, Diane Leigh. Came to U.S., 1955, naturalized, 1965. Instr. geography, civil engring. U. Wash., Seattle, 1957-58; asst. prof. geography U. Chgo., 1958-62, asso. prof., 1962-65, prof., 1965—, faculty Center for Urban Studies, dir. tng. programs in urban studies, 1963—, faculty Com. So. Asian Studies, 1969—. Propr., Spatial Analysis-Systems Planning Consultants, Park Forest, Ill. Mem. Plan Commn., Park Forest, 1966-68. Mem. Am. Geog. Soc., Assn. Am. Geographers, Am. Statis. Assn., Econometric Soc., Regional Sci. Assn., Royal Statis. Soc., Inst. Brit. Geographers, Sigma Xi, Lambda Alpha. Author: Studies of Highway Development and Geographic Change, 1959; Central Place Studies, 1961; Commercial Structure and Commercial Blight, 1963; Commodity Flows and the Spatial Structure of the Indian Economy, 1966; Geography of Market Centers and Retail Distribution, 1966; Spatial Analysis, 1967; Impact of Urban Renewal on Small Business, 1968; Spatial Analysis, 1968; Goals for Urban America, 1968; Geographic Perspectives on Urban Systems, 1970. Home: 304 Gettysburg St PO Box 190 Park Forest IL 60466 Office: Center for Urban Studies Univ of Chgo 5852 University Av Chicago IL 60637

BERRY, C. S., newspaper publisher. Pres., pub. Ark. Democrat, Little Rock; treas., dir. Ark. TV Co. Home: 480 Ridgeway St Little Rock AR 72205 Office: Capitol Av and Scott St Little Rock AR 72203

BERRY, CHARLES ALDEN, flight surgeon; b. Rogers, Ark., Sept. 17, 1923; s. George Valentine and Vera Helen (Whitmore) B.; A.B., U. Cal. at Berkeley, 1945; M.D., U. Cal. at San Francisco, 1947; M.P.H., Harvard, 1956; m. Addella Nance, June 30, 1944; children—Michael A., Charlene A. (Mrs. David Forester), Janice A. (Mrs. Jay Dudley). Rotating intern. U. Cal. Service, San Francisco City and County Hosp., 1947-48; resident aero. space medicine Sch. Aero. Space Medicine, USAF, 1951-52; gen. practice medicine, Coachella, Cal., 1948-51; commd. 1st lt., M.C., USAF, 1951, advanced through grades to lt. col., 1960; dep. command surgeon Carribean Air Command, Albrook AFB, C.Z., 1952-55; chief faculty flight medicine Sch. Aerospace Medicine, 1956-59; tech. adv. for TV, Hollywood, Cal., 1959; chief flight medicine Surgeon Gen. Office, Washington, 1959- 62; resigned, 1963; chief med. programs Manned Spacecraft Center, NASA, Houston, 1962-66, dir. med. research and operations, 1966—; clin. asst. prof. preventive medicine Ohio State U., 1964—. Adv. dir. Nassau Nat. Bank. Mem. med. adv. council Fed. Air Surgeon Bd. Bd. dirs. Gulf Coast Sci. Found., Houston. Pres.-elect Harvard Sch. Pub. Health. Served with USNR, 1942-46. Decorated Commendation ribbon; USAF Certificate Achievement; Wings of Nicaraguan, Recipient Hoyt S. Vandenberg trophy Arnold Air Soc., 1966; Melbourne W. Boynton award Am. Astronautical Soc., 1966; Gold medal Am. Coll. Chest Physicians, 1966; Hubertus Strughold award, 1967; meml. medal Acad. Natural Scis., 1968; Physician Mission award Carlo Erba Found., Milan, Italy, 1969; Silver medal distinguished service Ministry of Health and Welfare of Portugal,

1969; Daniel and Florence Guggenheim Internat. Astronautics award, 1969; Exceptional Sci. Achievement award NASA, 1969; Am. Coll. Surgeons ann. award, 1970. Fellow Am Coll. Preventive Medicine, Aerospace Med. Assn. (editorial bd. jour.; exec. com., council; internat. com.; past pres. space medicine bd.; Arnold D. Tuttle award, 1961; Louis H. Bauer Founders Award, 1966) Internat. Acad. Aviation and Space Medicine, Internat. Acad. Astronautics, Pan Am. Med. Assn., A.C.P.; mem. Am. (spl. aerospace medicine honor citation 1962, 69), Tex., Harris County med. assns., Am. Acad. Gen. Practice, Soc. USAF Flight Surgeons (bd. gov.) Am. Inst. Aero. and Astronautics, Delta Omega, Nu Sigma Nu; hon. mem. Argentina, Australian med. assns. Methodist (bd. mem.). Rotarian. Club: El Lago Keys (pres.) (Seabrook, Tex.). Contbr. articles med. jours. chpts. to books. Home: 422 Terrace Dr El Lago Seabrook TX 77586 Office: Center Med Programs Manned Spacecraft Center NASA Houston TX 77058

BERRY, CHARLES OSCAR, lawyer; b. Washington, Apr. 7, 1907; s. Charles Adams and E. Louise (Payne) B.; A.B., George Washington U., 1933, LL.B., 1932; m. Margaret Anna Fox, Oct. 20, 1934; children—Charles Henry, Louise Margaret. Admitted to D.C. bar, 1932, since practiced in Washington; mem. bar Supreme Ct. U.S., U.S. Circuit Ct. Appeals; gen. counsel, sr. v.p. Washington Gas Light Co.; pres. Gas Distbrs. Information Service. Adv. bd., past pres. D.C. Salvation Army. Past pres. Columbia Hosp. for Women. Mem. Am. (chmn. sect. pub. utility law 1954-55; mem. ho. of dels. 1957), D.C. bar assns., D.C. Bd. Trade, Am. Judicature Soc., Newcomen Soc., George Washington Law Assn., Phi Delta Phi, Sigma Phi Epsilon. Methodist. Mason (Jester). Clubs: Rotary, Metropolitan, Lawyers, Columbia Country (Washington). Home: 4324 43d St Washington DC 20016 Office: 1100 H St Washington DC 20005

BERRY, CHUCK, singer; b. St. Louis, Oct. 18, 1926. Popular artist in rock and roll music; plays guitar, saxophone, piano; rec. artist Chess Records; film Go, Johnny Go. Address: care Chess Records 320 E 21st St Chicago IL 60601

BERRY, DONALD STILWELL, civil engr., educator; b. Vale, S.D., Jan. 1, 1911; s. Stephen C. and May (Stilwell) B.; B.C.E., S.D. Sch. Mines, 1931; M.S., Ia. State Coll., 1933; Ph.D., U. Mich., 1936; m. Helen B. Mitchell, Oct. 30, 1937; children—Judith H., Jeane E. Tng. engr. Nat. Safety Council, Chgo., 1936-43, dir. traffic and transp. div., 1943-48; asst. dir., inst. transp. and traffic engring. U. Cal., Berkeley, 1948-51, prof. transp. engring., 1951-56, chmn. div. transp. engring., 1954-56; prof. transp. engring. Purdue U., 1956-57; prof. civil engring. Northwestern U., Evanston, Ill., 1957-66, Walter P. Murphy prof., 1966—, chmn. dept. civil engring., 1962-68. Mem. Nat. Acad. Engring., Am. Soc. C.E., Inst. Traffic Engrs., Hwy. Research Bd. (chmn. 1965-66), Sigma Xi, Sigma Tau, Chi Epsilon, Phi Kappa Phi, Tau Beta Pi. Home: 2146 Forestview Rd Evanston, IL 60201.

BERRY, EDWIN CARLOS, assn. exec.; ed. Oberlin Coll., Duquesne U.; postgrad U. Pitts., 1943, Western Res. U., 1945; m. Betsy G. Frazier, Sept. 1957; 1 son, Joseph M. With Urban League, Pitts., 1937-45, Portland, Ore., 1945-56; exec. dir. Chgo. Urban League, 1956—. Tchr., guest lectr. numerous univs., including U. Chgo., No. Ill. U., Northwestern U., Roosevelt U., Nat. Coll., Loyola U., 1947—; human relations cons. various indsl. religious, ednl. community groups. Contbr. articles to profl. publs. Home: 1344 E 48th St Chicago IL 60615 Office: Chicago Urban League 4500 S Michigan Av Chicago IL 60615

BERRY, ELLIS YARNAL, former congressman; b. Larchwood, Ia., Oct. 6, 1902; s. William S. and Kitty (Teghtmeyer) B.; student Morningside Coll., 1920-22; LL.B., U. S.D., 1927; m. Rose Hartinger, Mar. 4, 1928; children—Robert Ellis, Nila Lee. Admitted to S.D. bar, 1927, practiced in McLaughlin, 1929—; pub. McLaughlin Messenger, 1938—. Mem. S.D. Senate, 1939,41; mem. 82d-91st U.S. Congresses, 2d S.D. Dist. Mem. Mo. River States com., 1941- 44; State Bd. Regents, 1946-50. Mem. S.D. Press Assn. (pres. 1944-45), Delta Theta Phi, Sigma Delta Chi, Mason (Shriner). Home: McLaughlin SD 57642

BERRY, ERIC, actor, dir.; b. London, Eng., Jan. 9, 1913; s. Frederick William and Anna Lovisa (Danielson) B.; student Royal Acad. Dramatic Art, 1930-32. Came to U.S., 1954, naturalized, 1964. Appeared in numerous plays in London including Judgement Day, 1937-39, Eden End, 1949, The Cherry Orchard, 1948, Hedda Gabler, 1950, Macbeth, 1950, At The Lyric, 1953; U.S. appearances include The Boy Friend, 1954-57, Family Reunion, 1958, The Power and the Glory, 1959, The Beaux Strategem, 1959, Henry IV, 1960, Gideon, 1961, Falstaff, 1962, The White House, 1964, Tiny Alice, 1964- 65; TV appearances include The Invincible Mr. Disreali, 1962, Man from U.N.C.L.E., 1963, Bob Hope Chrysler Hour The Fifth Passenger, 1963; motion pictures include Red Shoes, 1947, The Gilbert and Sullivan Story, 1952; dir. Dial M for Murder, Fallen Angels, 1966; appeared with Helen Hayes in the Circle; with Meadow Brook Theatre, Oakland U., Rochester, Mich. 1966-69; dir. The Spiders Web, 1967, Don Juan in Hell, 1968; dir. Canterbury Tales, nat. tour, also Charley's Aunt, in N.Y.C., 1970, Twelfth Night in Chgo., 1970-71. Served to capt. British Army, 1940- 46. Mem. Ch. Religious Science. Club: Green Room (London). Address: care L K Strauss 400 E 56th St New York City NY 10022

BERRY, FRANKLIN HAYWOOD, lawyer, banker; b. Manahawkin, N.J., May 15, 1904; s. J. Willits and Jessie (Haywood) B.; A.B., U. Pa., 1925, LL.B., 1928; m. Eleanor Lamon, Oct. 10, 1928; 1 son, Franklin Haywood; m. Leonora Patterson, Aug. 14, 1948; children—Margaret L. (Mrs. Margaret Johnson), John Sherwin, Elizabeth R. (Mrs. W. M. Collinsworth). Admitted to N.J. bar, 1928, since practiced in Toms River; partner firm Berry Summerill, Rinck & Berry and predecessor, 1933—; pres. Beach Haven Nat. Bank & Trust Co., 1939-70, chmn. bd., 1970—; v.p., counsel Adm. Farragut Acad., 1946—; dep. atty. gen. N.J., 1946-48; pres. Long Beach Water Co.; em; dir. emeritus First Nat. Bank Toms River. Del. N.J. Constl. Conv., 1947; mem. com. on character and fitness N.J. Supreme Ct. Trustee, Richard Stockton State College. Served from capt. to col., AUS, 1941-46; col. Res. (ret.). Decorated Legion of Merit, Bronze Star medal. Fellow Am. Bar Found.; mem. C. of C., Ocean County Bankers Assn. (past pres.), Am. (mem. ho. of dels., mem. com. on lawyers in armed forces), N.J. (past pres.), Ocean County bar assns., Judge Adv. Assn. (dir., past pres.), N.J. Soc. S.R., Holland Soc. N.Y. Presbyn. (elder). Clubs: Ocean County Lawyers (past pres.); Union League (Phila.); Little Egg Harbor and Toms River Yacht. Home: The Berry Patch Pine Beach NJ 08741 Office: 34 Washington St Toms River NJ 08753

BERRY, GEORGE PACKER, physician, med. research; b. Troy, N.Y., Dec. 29, 1898; s. George Titus and Carrie Electa (Packer) B.; grad. Hill Sch., Pottstown, 1917; 1917; A.B. with highest honors, Princeton, 1921; M.D., Johns Hopkins, 1925; LL.D., Hobart and William Smith Coll., 1949; A.M., Harvard, 1949; Sc.D., Union Coll., 1950, Princeton, 1951, Harvard, 1954, N.Y.U., 1955, U. Rochester, 1955; Litt. D., Tufts U., 1952; L.H.D., Jefferson Med. Coll., 1955, Brandeis U., 1964; Sc. D., Boston U., 1963, U. Pa., 1965, Dartmouth, 1965; LL.D., U. Cal., 1966, Loyola U., 1966; m. Elizabeth L'Estrange Duncan, July 10, 1923 (died Mar. 9, 1926) 1 dau., Caroline Elizabeth (Mrs. Cloyd Laporte). Resident house officer Conn. State Hosp. for the Insane, Middletown, summer, 1923, Bellevue Hosp., 1st Div. (Columbia), summer, 1924, Johns Hopkins Hosp., 1925-27; asst. resident physician in med. Johns Hopkins U. 1927- 28, instr. in medicine, 1928-29; asst. Rockefeller Inst. for Med. Research, 1929-31, asso., 1931-32; prof. bacteriology, head of dept. and asso. prof. of medicine U. Rochester Sch. of Medicine and Dentistry, 1932-49, asst. dean, 1941-47, asso. dean, 1947-49; dean of faculty and dean Harvard Med. Sch., 1949-65, prof. bacteriology Harvard, 1949-65, prof. emeritus bacteriology, 1965—; pres. Harvard Med. Center, 1956-65; spl. cons. to pres. Princeton, 1966—. Chmn. adv. council, dept. biol., mem. Grad. Council Princeton, 1941-56; ednl. cons. Council Rochester Regional Hosps., 1946-49. Bd. dirs. Josiah Macy Found., 1943-65, Nat. Health Council, 1956-57; trustee Am. U. of Beirut, 1952—; charter trustee Princeton, 1956—; mem. med. sch. grants adv. com. Ford Found., 1956-57; mem. Pres. Com. on Med. Edn. Beyond High Sch., 1956-57; v. p. Sex Information and Education Council of U.S., 1964—; trustee Worcester Found. Exptl. Biology, 1965-68; mem. adv. com. edn. VA, 1952—; mem. med. adv. com. Boston Mus. Sci., 1952—; hon. pres. Louis T. Wright Meml. Fund, Inc., 1952—; mem. sci. adv. com. Howard Hughes Med. Inst. 1956-68; mem. adv. med. bd. Am. Hosp. of Paris, 1961-68; cons. med. research and edn. Dept. Health, Edn. and Welfare, 1957-68; mem. adv. com. Mass. Dept. Public Health. 1957-68: cons. Medicine Peter Bent Brigham Hosp., Boston, 1963. Chmn. Panel on Virus, Con. on Growth, NRC, 1945-47. In S.A.T.C., 1918; U.S. Naval Reserve, 1941-53; Operation Crossroads, Bikini, 1946. Diplomate Am. Bd. Internal Medicine. Fellow A.A.A.S., Am. Pub. Health Assn., Rochester Museum of Arts and Scis.; mem. Johns Hopkins Med. Assn., Am. Soc. for Clin. Investigation, Assn. Am. Med. Colls. (chmn. com. on research and edn. 1947-61, mem. exec. council, 1947-52, pres. 1951-52), Harvey Soc. N.Y., Soc. Exptl. Biology and Medicine, Soc. Am. Bacteriologists (chmn. Central N. Y. br. 1934-35, mem. council 1935-40), Boylston Med. Soc. (trustee 1961-62), Am. Assn. Immunologists (council 1938-45, pres. 1939-40), Am. Assn. Pathologists and Bacteriologists, Am. Assn. History Medicine, S.A. R., Phi Beta Kappa, Omicron Kappa Upsilon, Alpha Omega Alpha, Sigma Xi, Kappa Pi Eta. Republican. Presbyn. Clubs: Century Association of New York, Princeton (New York); Newcomen Society (Eng.); Fortnightly, Genesee Valley (Rochester). Harvard of Boston, Martha's Vineyard, New York, Aesculapian, Roxbury Clinical Record, St. Botolph (Boston): Cosmos (Washington). Former mem. editorial bd. Jour. of Bacteriology, asso. Jour. of Immunol. and Bact. Reviews. Contbr. numerous papers to med. and ednl. jours. Home: 84 N Stanworth Dr Princeton NJ Office: Princeton U Princeton NJ 08540

BERRY, GEORGE RONALD, ret. ins. co. exec.; b. Scarborough, Yorkshire, Eng., July 2, 1907; s. George Edwin and Sarah (Streeting) B.; student Lisgar Collegiate Inst., Ottawa, Ont., Can., 1919-24; m. Dorothy Anne Hewit, Nov. 15, 1930; children—Dorothy R., Sally Ann, George Louis, Susan Winifred. With Met. Life Ins. Co., 1924-71, 3d v.p., 1954-60, 2d v.p., 1960, 2d v.p., asst. gen. mgr., 1960-61, v.p., gen. mgr., 1962-71; dir. Montreal Trust Co. Past pres. Ottawa Bd. Trade. Mem. Anglican Ch. Mason. Home: 85 Range Rd Ottawa 2 Ontario Canada

BERRY, HAROLD A., business exec.; b. Clio, Mich. June 12, 1908; s. Vinton W. and Clara (LaDue) B; Ph.B., U. Detroit, 1933, M.A., 1935; m. Eleanor Staley, Nov. 19, 1943; 1 dau., Ellyn. Mgr. purchasing Hotpoint Co., 1948-51; mgr. procurement Ingersoll div. Borg-Warner Corp., 1951-56; mgr. purchases and stores C., R.I. & P. R.R., Chgo., 1956-64, v.p., 1964-65; pres. Afro- Am. Purchasing Center, Inc., N.Y.C., 1965-69, Internat. Fedn. Purchasing, 1970—. Chmn. com. UN Indsl. 1970—. Chmn. com. UN Indsl. Devel. Orgn., 1967. Mem. Nat. Assn. Purchasing Mgmt. (del. to, chmn. profl. devels. for Internat. Fedn. Purchasing), Nat. Assn. Purchasing Agts. (past pres., chmn. edn. com.), Purchasing Agts. Assn. Chgo. (dir., past pres.). Clubs: Union League, Executives (Chgo.). Author: Purchasing Management, 1964; contbg. author Purchasing Handbook. Home: 400 Fisher Park Circle Greensboro NC 27401 Office: 232 N Edgeworth St Greensboro NC 27401

BERRY, HAROLD JAMES, investment banker; b. Westwood, N.J., Apr. 12, 1913; s. Charles William and Ella (Hopper), B.; B.S. in Econs., U. Pa., 1935; m. Anne Sherman; children—Thomas, Elizabeth, Lindsay, Harold James. With Harriman Ripley & Co., Inc., N.Y.C., 1935-66, successively jr. buyer, mgr., 1935- 49, v. p., 1949-59, exec. v.p., 1959-63, pres., chief exec. officer, 1963-66; chmn. Drexel Harriman Ripley, Inc., 1966—; dir. Westvaco Corp., Am. Enka Corp., United Aircraft Corp., R.R. Donnelly & Sons, Inc. Trustee Bklyn. Hosp., Packer Collegiate Inst. Clubs: Recess, University, Links (N.Y.C.). Office: 60 Broad St New York City NY 10004

BERRY, HELEN JANICE, nursing educator; b. Marion, O., Jan. 5, 1925; d. Chester Milton and Mary Mildred (Garver) Berry; B.A., Miami U., Oxford, O., 1950; diploma Miami Valley Hosp. Sch. Nursing, 1948; R.N., Ohio, 1948; M.S. in Nursing Edn., Ind. U., 1960, Ed.D., 1963. Staff nurse Miami Valley Hosp., 1948, asst. head nurse communicable disease and pediatrics, 1950-51; part-time staff nurse Student Health Center, Miami U., 1948-50; asst. to dir. student affiliate programs Dayton State Hosp., 1951-52; obstet. supr. Greene Meml. Hosp., 1952-54, Univ. Hosps., Ann Arbor, Mich., 1954-55; surg. head nurse and supr. Greene Meml. Hosp., 1955-56; surg. clin. instr. and coordinator Good Samaritan Hosp. Sch. Nursing, Dayton, 1956-59, cons. nursing edn., 1961—; vis. asst. prof. div. nursing edn., asst. campus coordinator Korea project Ind. U., 1960-62; prof. nursing, head dept. Ball State U., Muncie, Ind., 1963—; guest lectr. in field, 1963—; mem. adv. bd. Ednl. Films, Inc. Mem. bd. mgmt. Fairborn (O.) YMCA, 1951-54, sec. bd., 1953-54; chmn. Tb survey, Bath Township, O., 1956; mem. edn. com. Delaware County Tb Assn., 1964-66; co-chmn. 2d cancer nursing inst. Delaware County Cancer Soc., 1964-65; mem. subcom. Ind. Regional Planning Com. Mental Health, 1965-66; mem. Delaware div. health Community Services Council, 1967—; mem.-at-large Ohio Ednl. Adminstrs., cons. tchrs. sect. Ohio Nurses Assn., 1959, chmn. a sect. in dist. 10, 1958-60; co-chmn. Stress Inst. Nurses Western Ohio, 1958. Named Ind. Nurse of Yr., 1965. Mem. Muncie Symphony Orch., 1963-65. Mem. Nat., Ind. (chmn. council nursing edn. 1964-66, vice chmn. council nursing edn. 1966-68, bd. dirs. 1964-66) leagues nursing, Am., Ind. nurses assns., Delta Omicron, Pi Lambda Theta (v.p. chpt. 1962-63). Mem. Order Eastern Star. Club: Altrusa. Home: 1704 Belmont Dr Muncie IN 47304

BERRY, JACK, educator; b. Leeds, Eng., Dec. 13, 1918; s. Harry and Nellie (Butterfield) P.; B.A., Leeds U., 1939; Ph.D., London U., 1952; m. Winifred Mary Ingle, Feb. 14, 1942; 1 son, Mark Adrian. Came to U.S., 1963. Lectr., London U., 1946-55, reader, 1955-60, prof., 1960-63; prof. Mich. State U., 1963-64; prof. linguistics Northwestern U., 1964—. Home: 2119 Lincoln St Evanston IL 60201

BERRY, JAMES D., banker; b. Sapulpa, Okla., June 23, 1921; s. James D. and Gertrue (Morrow) B.; B.S., U. Okla., 1943; grad. Rutgers U. Grad. Sch. Banking, 1959; grad. Advanced Mgmt. Program, Harvard, 1963; m. Mary Evelyn Irby, Oct. 16, 1946; children—Beverly, James D., Robert Neil. With Am. Nat. Bank, Sapulpa, 1932-50, asst. v.p., 1948-50; with Republic Nat. Bank, Dallas, 1950—, sr. v.p., 1961-63, exec. v.p., now chmn. bd.; partner I-B Cattle Co. Bd. dirs. Dallas County chpt. A.R.C., Dallas Crime Commn., Dallas Better Bus. Bur., Dallas Heart Assn., Dallas Summer Musicals, Dallas Theatre Center, Goodwill Industries Dallas. Served to capt. AUS, 1943-46. Mem. Inter-frat. Council, Scabbard and Blade, Beta Theta Pi. Mason (32, Shriner). Clubs: Dallas (bd. dirs.), Chaparral (Dallas); Coterie; Northwood. Home: 3901 Lovers Lane Dallas TX 75225 Office: P O Box 5961 Dallas TX 75222

BERRY, JAMES DUFER, Jr., oil producer, cattle breeder; b. Oil City, Pa., Mar. 25, 1914; s. James D. and Helen Caroline (Robinson) B.; student The Hill Sch., Pottstown, Pa., 1929-34; m. Helen Jean Holst, Jan. 2, 1937; children—James Dufer III, Michael Truby, Linda Gay. Oil producer, Penna Field, 1934—; breeder Registered Guernsey cattle, Titusville, Pa., 1939—; chmn. bd. Quaker State Oil Refining Corp., 1960-64, chmn. exec. com., 1964—; dir. Northwest Pa. Bank and Trust Co., Oil City. Mem. Pa. Grade Crude Oil Assn. (dir. 1959), Pa. Guernsey Breeders Assn. Mason (K.T. Shriner). Home and office: Box 245 Titusville PA 16354

BERRY, JAMES FREDERICK, educator; b. Balt., Nov. 11, 1927; s. James Harvey and Atha Mabel (Harer) B.; B.A., Johns Hopkins, 1949; Ph.D., U. Rochester, 1953; m. Catherine Ann Smith, Dec. 27, 1952; children—Barbara, Bonnie, Sarah, Catherine. Research fellow biochemistry U. Western Ont., 1953-55, lectr., 1955-56; fellow Multiple Sclerosis Soc. Inst. Animal Physiology, Babraham, Cambridge, Eng., 1956-57; fellow physiol. chemistry Johns Hopkins Sch. Medicine, 1958-59, lectr., 1959-61; asso. dir. Biochemistry Research div. Dept. Medicine Sinai Hosp., Balt., 1957-61; asso. prof. neurology U. Minn. Med. Sch., 1961-66, prof., chief neurochemistry sect., 1966—. Active Boys Scouts Am., Girl Scouts Am.; mem. Ind. Dist. 623 Sch. Bd., Roseville, Minn. Recipient Silver Beaver award distinguished service to Boys Scouting, 1962. Fellow A.A.A.S., Minn. Acad. Sci., Internat. Soc. Neurochemistry, Am. Inst. Chemists, Assn. Ofcl. Analytic Chemistry, Sigma Xi. Home: 1059 Woodhill Dr Roseville MN 55113 Office: Mayo Bldg Box 289 Minneapolis MN 55455

BERRY, KEEHN W., banker; b. Glen Allen, Mo., Dec. 12, 1894; s. Pinkney Jasper and Ida (Keehn) B.; A.B., U. Mo., 1913, LL.B., 1915; m. Mary Lois Brown, June 5, 1920; children—Keehn W., Mary Ellen. With Whitney Nat. Bank of New Orleans, 1937—, chmn. bd., dir., 1969—. Presbyn. Clubs: Boston, New Orleans Boston, New Orleans Country (New Orleans). Home: 149 Audubon Blvd New Orleans LA 70118 Office: Whitney Natl Bank 228 St Charles Av New Orleans LA 70130

BERRY, LEONARD GASCOIGNE, educator; b. Toronto, Ont., Can., Aug. 17, 1914; s. Francis Richard and Amelia (Gascoigne) B.; B.A., U. Toronto, 1937, M.A., 1938, Ph.D., 1941; m. May Catherine Milthorpe, Apr. 11, 1941; children—Paul Richard, Susan Elizabeth. Geologist Ont. Dept. Mines, summers 1936-40; engr. optical div. Research Enterprises Ltd., Toronto, 1940-44; mem. faculty mineralogy and crystallography Queen's U., Kingston, Ont., 1944—, prof., 1956—, Miller research prof., 1967—. Chmn. Canadian Nat. Com. Crystallography, 1967-70. Recipient Coleman gold and medal geology U. Toronto, 1937, Willet G. Miller gold medal Royal Soc. Can., 1963; Guggenheim fellow, 1953. Fellow Royal Soc. Can., Mineral. Soc. Am. (pres. 1964), Geol. Soc. Am.; mem. Mineral. Soc. Gt. Britain (hon.), Mineral. Assn. Can. (hon.), Am. Crystallographic Assn., Internat. Mineral. Assn. (treas. 1960—). Author: (with Brian Mason) Mineralogy, 1959, Elements of Mineralogy, 1968. Editor: The Canadian Mineralogist, 1956—, X-ray Powder Date File, 1969—. Home: 1693 Hillview Kingston Ontario Canada

BERRY, LEVETTE JOE, microbiologist, educator; b. Birmingham, Ala., June 17, 1910; s. Levette J. and Elizabeth (Fitzgerald) B.; B.S., S.W. Tex. State Coll., 1930; Ph.D., U. Tex., 1939; m. Virginia Lee Goolsby, May 28, 1934; 1 son, James Goolsby. Instr., U. Tex., 1939-40; faculty Bryn Mawr Coll., 1940- 70, asso. prof., 1946-52, prof., 1952-70, chmn. dept. of biology, 1965-70, sec. faculty, 1964-69, acting provost, 1969-70; prof., chmn. dept. microbiology U. Tex., Austin, 1970—. Research asso. nutrition clinic Hillman Hosp., Birmingham, 1943-45; cons. infectious diseases com. VA, 1960-71, chmn., 1968-71; cons. bacteriology and mycology study sect. NIH, 1963—, chmn., 1966-67, cons. internat. fellowship rev. com., 1970—; cons. bacteriology and mycology Lunar Receiving Lab., NASA Space Center, Houston, Tex., 1969-71, chmn., 1971—; adv. com. Army Chem. Corps, 1960-63; cons. life scis. research evaluation com. Office Naval Research, 1970—. Fellow Am. Acad. Microbiology (mem. bd. govs. 1969—, chmn. 1970-71), A.A.A.S.; mem. Am. Soc. Microbiology (councilor-at-large, council policy com., chmn. bd. edn. and tng.), Am. Physiol. Soc., Reticuloendothelial Soc. (pres. 1966-68). Editor Jour. Bacteriology, 1964-68. Home: 4618 Crestway Dr Austin TX 78731

BERRY, LLOYD EASON, univ. chancellor; b. Houston, Aug. 1, 1935; s. Joel Halbert and Fay (Eason) B.; B.A., U. N.C., 1959, M.A. (Carnegie Found. fellow), 1958; Ph.D. (Marshall scholar), Magdalene Coll., Cambridge (Eng.) U., 1960. Asst. prof. English, U. Ill. at Urbana, 1960-63, faculty fellow, 1962, asso. prof., then prof. history, 1963-69, asst. chancellor, 1969—, asso. mem. Center Advanced Study, 1967-68. Commnr. Midwest region Marshall Scholarship Com.; pres. Central Renaissance Conf., 1969-70. Bd. dirs. Camp Howard, 1965-67, Ill. Found. Dance, 1967—, Univ. YMCA, 1969—, Carle Hosp. Found., 1971—, United Community Council, 1969—, Champaign C. of C., 1971—. Am. Philos. Soc. grantee, 1963, 65; Henry H. Huntington Library fellow, 1965; Folger Shakespeare Library fellow, 1965; Guggenheim fellow, 1966-67; recipient Alumnus award Kinkaid Prep. Sch. Mem. Modern Lang. Assn., Modern Humanities Research Assn., Milton Soc. (exec. com.), Renaissance Soc. Am. (adv. com.), Renaissance English Text Soc. (returning officer, mem. exec. com.), Malone Soc., Bibliog. Soc., Cambridge Bibliog. Soc. (sec. U.S. and Can.), Marshall Scholars Assn. (permanent sec.). Baptist. Clubs: Champaign Country; Indian Acres Swim. Author: A Bibliography of Studies in Metaphysical Poetry, 1939-60, 64; The English Works of Giles Fletcher, the Elder, 1964; John Stubb's Gaping Gulf with Letters and Other Relevant Documents, 1968; Rude and Barbarous Kingdom: Russia in the Accounts of Sixteenth-Century English Voyagers, 1968; The Geneva Bible: A Facsimile of the 1560 Edition, 1969; The Dramatic Works of George Chapman, 1970; also articles. Home: 1709 Ridge Rd Champaign IL 61820 Office: Office of Chancellor Univ Ill Urbana IL 61801

BERRY, LOREN MURPHY, business exec.; b. Wabash, Ind., July 24, 1888; s. Charles D. and Elizabeth (Murphy) B.; student Northwestern U., 1909-10; LL.D., Rio Grande (Ohio) Coll.; m. Lucile Kneipple, June 9, 1909 (dec.); children—Loren Murphy, Martha Sue Fraim, John William, Elizabeth Anne Fox; m. 2d, Helen Anderson Henry, Aug. 28, 1938; 1 son, Leland. Newspaper reporter, Wabash, Ind., Joliet, Ill., Chgo.; sold telephone directory advt., Marion, Ind., 1910, St. Louis, Louisville, Indpls., which developed into nat. sales orgn. of L.M. Berry & Co., main office, Dayton, O., now chmn. bd. chief exec. officer; dir. United Utilities, Inc., Kansas City, Mo., Edison Nat. Bank, Ft. Myers, Fla., Super Food Services, Inc., Dayton, O., Fla. Telephone Corp., Ocala, Third Nat. Bank & Trust Co., Laughter Corp., Hulman Realty Co., Mutual Broadcasting Corp., N.Y.C. Mem.

Republican Nat. Finance Com. Trustee Junior Achievement, Dayton, Rio Grande Coll. Mem. U.S. Ind. Telephone Pioneers (pres. 1938-39), Bell Telephone Pioneers Assn. (v.p. N.C. Kingsbury chpt. 1939-40). Episcopalian. Mason (32 Shriner). Clubs: Capitol Hill (Washington); Dayton City, Engineers, Kiwanis, Dayton Country, Dayton Bicycle, Moraine Country (Dayton); Surf (gov.), Committee of 100, Indian Creek (Miami Beach, Fla.); Bohemian (San Francisco). Home: 1155 Ridgeway Rd Dayton OH 45419 also Surf Club Apts 9133 Collins Av Miami Beach FL 33154 Office: 3170 Kettering Blvd Dayton OH 45401 also 3818 Bay Vista Av Tampa FL 33609

BERRY, MARGARET ETHEL, social worker; b. Hermansville, Mich., Mar. 6, 1915; d. Samuel Herbert and Ethel (Collins) Berry; B.A., Albion Coll., 1935; M.S., Western Res. U., 1937. Indsl. sec. Cleve. YWCA, 1935-41; program dir. Soho Community House, Pitts., 1941-47, exec. dir., 1947-51; cons. Youth Leadership Tng. Schs., Germany, 1951-52; staff mem. Nat. Fedn. Settlements & Neighborhood Centers, N.Y.C., 1952-59, exec. dir., 1959-71; exec. dir. Nat. Conf. on Social Welfare, N.Y.C., 1972—. Pres. Nat. Conf. Social Welfare, 1970-71, Internat. Fedn. Settlements. Mem. Nat. Assn. Social Workers, Delta Sigma Rho. Democrat. Methodist. Club: Cosmopolitan (N.Y.C.). Home: 57 Montague St Brooklyn NY 11201 Office: 2 Park Av New York City NY

BERRY, NIXON T., lawyer; b. Caledonia, Ont., Can., Oct. 15, 1905; grad. U. Toronto, Osgoode Hall. Admitted to Ont. bar, 1931; partner firm McMillan, Binch, Toronto. Mem. Canadian Bar Assn. Office: 20 King St W Toronto 1 Ontario Canada*

BERRY, OTHMAR BERARDE, ret. petroleum exec.; b. San Jose, Cal., June 20, 1901; s. Frederick Charles and Pearl (Albaugh) B.; A.B., Stanford U., 1924; m. Velda Hancock, Mar. 18, 1924; children—Wanlyn (Mrs. Benton Bejach), Winifred (Mrs. Keith Lowell), Carol Jean (Mrs. Myles Berg), William Frederick. Pres., dir. Berry Oil Co., Kern County, Cal., 1930-71; with Big Ten Oil Co. 1931—, pres., 1940—; with Berry Holding Co., 1930-71; with Ethel D. Co., 1931-71, v.p., 1951-71; pres., dir. Berry and Ewing Oil Co., 1930-71; dir. Crocker Nat. Bank, Crocker Nat. Corp. Mem. Independent Petroleum Assn. Am., Phi Kappa Sigma. Home: 450 Westridge Dr Menlo Park CA 94025

BERRY, PAUL LUCIEN, librarian; b. San Jose, Cal., Sept. 4, 1921; s. Elmer G. and Nellie (Bush) B.; B.A., Am. U., 1943, postgrad., 1957-63; postgrad. Yale, 1943- 44, Catholic U. Am., 1946-50; m. Doris M. Patterson, Apr. 14, 1945; children—Marsha Joan, Donald Lucien. With Library of Congress, Washington, 1945—, dir. adminstrv. dept., 1967-68. asso. dir. reference dept., 1968-69, dir. reference dept., 1969—. Mem. Am., D.C. library assns., Nat. Microfilm Assn., Am. U. Alumni Assn. (past pres.), Omicron Delta Kappa, Alpha Tau Omega. Contbr. articles profl. jours. Home: 2104 Cascade Rd Silver Spring MD 20902 Office: Library of Congress Washington DC 20540

BERRY, RICHARD EMERSON, educator; b. Washington, N.J., Nov. 11, 1933; s. Vernon Emerson and Estelle Patricia (Peterson) B.; B.S., Lafayette Coll., 1954; M.A., Princeton, 1956, Ph.D., 1958; m. Ruth Helen Enger, Sept. 4, 1954; children—Dirk, Arthur, Richard, Marilyn, Robert. Asst. prof. physics Lafayette Coll., 1958-67; asso. prof. physics Tex. Tech. Coll., 1962-65; prof., chmn. dept. physics Ind. U., Indiana, Pa., 1965—. Mem. Am. Phys. Soc., Am. Assn. Physics Tchrs., Phi Beta Kappa, Sigma Xi, Sigma Pi Sigma. Home: 462 S 7th St Indiana PA 15701

BERRY, RICHARD STEPHEN, chemist, educator; b. Denver, Apr. 9, 1931; s. Morris and Ethel (Alpert) B.; A.B., Harvard, 1952, A.M., 1954, Ph.D., 1956; m. Carla Lamport Friedman, Sept. 3, 1955; children-Andrea, Denise, Eric. Instr., Harvard, 1956-57, U. Mich., 1957-60; asst. prof. Yale, 1960-64; asso. prof. chemistry U. Chgo., 1964-67, prof. chemistry, 1967—; Arthur D. Little prof. Mass. Inst. Tech., 1968; cons. Avco-Everett Research Labs., 1964- -, Am. Oil Co., 1965—; vis. prof. U. Copenhagen (Denmark), 1967. Alfred P. Sloan fellow, 1962-66. Mem. Am. Phys. Soc., Am. Chem. Soc., Sigma Xi. Contbr. articles profl. jours. Home: 5317 S University Av Chicago IL 60615

BERRY, SIDNEY BRYAN, army officer; b. Hattiesburg, Miss., Feb. 10, 1926; s. Sidney Bryan and Lois Elizabeth (Hathorn) B.; student U. Miss., 1943-44; B.S., U.S. Mil. Acad., 1948; M.A., Columbia, 1953; postgrad. Am. U. of Beirut, 1954; m. Anne Florine Hayes, June 18, 1949; children—Bryan Hathorn, Lynn Elizabeth, Nan Nissiat. Commd. 2d lt. U.S. Army, 1948, advanced through grades to maj. gen., 1971; mil. asst. to Sec. of Def., 1961-64; sr. advisor ARVN Inf. Div., Vietnam, 1965-66; inf. brigade comdr., Vietnam, 1966-67; asst. comdt. U.S. Army Inf. Sch., 1968-70; asst. div. comdr. 101st Airborne Div., Vietnam, 1970-71; dep. chief personnel operations Dept. Army, Washington, 1971—. Mem. nat. com. Boy Scouts Am., 1969—. Decorated Silver Star with 3 oak leaf clusters, D.S.M., D.F.C. with oak leaf cluster, Legion of Merit with 3 oak leaf clusters, Bronze Star, Purple Heart with oak leaf cluster. Mem. Council Fgn. Relations (Army fellow 1967-68). Lutheran. Home: 617 Walnut St Hattiesburg MS 39401 Office: Office Personnel Operations Dept Army Washington DC 20310

BERRY, THORNTON GRANVILLE, Jr., judge; b. Sutton, W.Va., Dec. 13, 1904; s. Thornton Granville and Mamie Newlon (Kawalska) B.; A.B., Va. Mil. Inst., 1928; LL.B., Washington and Lee U., 1934; m. Rita Crockett Brewster, June 5, 1934. Admitted to W.Va. bar, 1934; asso. firm Strother & Curd, 1934; mem. firm Strother, Curd & Berry, 1935-37, Stother, Herndon & Berry, 1937-40; asst. U.S. atty. So. Dist. W.Va., 1939-40; pros. atty. McDowell County, W.Va., 1940-42; pvt. practice, Welch, W.Va., 1946-52; judge 8th Jud. Circuit, W.Va., 1952- 58; judge Supreme Ct. Appeals, W.Va., 1959—. Served to lt. comdr. USNR, 1942-46. Mem. Am., W.Va. (past v.p.), McDowell County (past pres.) bar assns., Am. Judicature Soc. (v.p., dir.), W.Va. Jud. Assn., Am. Law Inst., Am. Legion, 40 and 8, S.R., Phi Kappa Psi, Phi Delta Phi. Mason (32, Shriner). Democrat. Presbyn. Home: 1612 Virginia St E Charleston WV 25311 Office: Supreme Ct of Appeals Capitol Bldg Charleston WV 25305

BERRY, TRAVER LAW, utilities exec.; b. Chatham, N.J., Oct. 24, 1911; s. Henry Titus and Jessie (Muchmore) B.; grad. Lawrenceville Sch., 1930; B.S., Syracuse U., 1934; M.B.A., N.Y.U., 1941; m. Frances Isable Mayes, Sept. 17, 1938; children—James Henry, Nancy Traver. Staff accountant Patterson, Teele & Dennis, pub. accountants, N.Y.C., 1934-39, 45-47; tax accountant E.I. duPont de Nemours Co., Wilmington, Del., 1939-42; controller Fred Waring Enterprises, Inc., N.Y.C., Shawnee, Pa., 1948-50; asst. gen. auditor Port N.Y. Authority, N.Y.C., 1950-52; financial analyst export operation Ford Motor Co., Jersey City, 1952-54; asst. controller Conn. Light & Power Co., Berlin, 1954-59, controller, 1959-67; mgr. internal auditing dept. N.E. Utilities Service Co., Berlin, 1967. Vice chmn. High Sch. Bldg. Com., Berling, Mem. Town Council, Boro Florham Park, N.J., 1953-54, also chmn. finance com. Mem. Hartford Symphony Chorale. C.P.A., N.Y., N.J. Mem. Financial Execs. Inst. (past chpt. pres.), Am. Inst. C.P.A.'s, Conn., N.Y. Soc. C.P.A.'s, Am. Gas Assn. (past com. chmn.), Edison Electric Inst. (past com. chmn.), U.S. Power Squadron, Electric Council New Eng. (past com. chmn.), Psi Upsilon, Sigma Beta Chi. Kiwanian (past pres. Berlin, Conn.). Club: Glastonbury Hills Country. Home: 48 Oldewood Rd Glastonbury CT 06033

BERRY, WALTER, baritone; b. Vienna, Austria, Apr. 8, 1929; s. Franz and Hilde (Jelinek) B.; ed. Akademie für Musik und darstellende Kunst, Vienna; m. Christa Ludwig, Sept. 29, 1957, (div. June 1970); 1 son, Wolfgang. Mem. Vienna State Opera, 1950—, guest artist London, Chgo., Buenos aires, Munich, Berlin, Tokyo, Salzburg Festival, Festival Lucerne, Hunter Coll., Carnegie Hall, Metropolitan Opera, Holland Festival, Zurich Festival, Festival de Montreux, others; Mus., Saratoga Festival, Expo Montreal. others; recording artist Electrola, Columbia, Philips, RCA Victor, His Master's Voice, Decca, London, Eurodisc, Deutsche Grammonopphon, C.B.S. Named Kammersänger by Austrian Govt., 1963. Recipient medal King of Sweden, 1965; decorated Ordenen für Kunst und Wissenchaft (Austria). Mem. Schlaraffia Vindobona. Home: Seefeldstrasse 11 Lucerne Switzerland Office: Music and Arts SA Tobelhofstrasse 2 CH-8044 Zurich Switzerland

BERRY, WILLIAM AYLOR, state justice; b. Ripley, Okla., Dec. 28, 1915; s. Thomas Nelson and Harriet Virginia (Patton) B.; B.A. Okla. State U., 1939; J.D., Okla. U., 1940; m. Carolyn Burwell, Jan. 2, 1947; children—Elizabeth Patton, Nichols Burwell. Admitted to Okla. bar, 1940; county atty. Payne County, 1940-41; asst. U.S. dist. atty., 1947-50; County, 1940-41; asst. U.S. dist. atty., 1947-50; pvt. practice, Oklahoma City, 1950-53; county judge Okla. County, 1953-59; asso. justice Supreme Ct. Okla., 1959-66; justice of Supreme Court of Oklahoma, 1966—, vice chief justice, 1969-70, chief justice, 1971—. Served to lt. comdr. USNR, 1942-46; Japanese prisoner of war. County juvenile detention home named Berry House in recognition of work with juvenile delinquents 1960. Mem. Am., Okla., Oklahoma County bar assns., Okla. C. of C. (dir.), Sigma Nu, Phi Delta Phi. Home: 1706 Wilshire Blvd Oklahoma City OK 73116 Office: Supreme Ct State Capitol Oklahoma City OK 73105

BERRY, WILLIAM H., ins. co. exec.; b. Aurora, Ill., 1908; ed. Ill. Inst. Tech., 1929. Exec. v.p. Continential Ins. Cos.; v.p. Fidelity & Casualty Co., Seaboard Fire & Marine Ins. Co., Fireman's Ins. Co., Newark, Nat.-Ben Franklin Ins. Co., Pitts., Comml. Ins. Co., Newark. Home: 73 New England Av Summit NJ 07901 Office: 80 Maiden Lane New York City NY 10038

BERRY, WILLIAM MARTIN, mfg. co. exec.; b. Chgo., June 21, 1920; s. William John and Mary Frances (Martin) B.; B.S. summa cum laude, St. Mary's Coll., Winona, Minn., 1941; M.A., De Paul U., 1949; m. Rose Livovich, June 5, 1943; children—William E., Mary Patricia, Peter D. Div. controller Hughes Aircraft Co., 1951-55, Thomson-Ramo-Wooldridge Co., 1955-58; mgr. mgmt. services Peat Marwick Mitchell & Co., C.P.A.'s, Los Angeles, 1958-61; v.p., controller bus. equipment group Litton Industries, Inc., 1961, now pres. Royal Typewriter group. Served to 1st lt., C.E., AUS, 1941-45; ETO, PTO. Mem. Financial Execs. Inst., Nat. Assn. Accountants. Clubs: Union League (N.Y.C.); Woodland Hills Country. Home: 20349 Clark St Woodland Hills CA 91364 Office: Royal Typewriter Co 850 3d Av New York City NY 10022

BERRY, WILLIAM THOMAS, Jr., assn. exec.; b. Vernon, Tex., Apr. 4, 1921; s. William Thomas and Mattie (Carney) B.; B.S. in Agr., Tex. A. and M. U., 1942, M.S. in Animal Sci., 1955, Ph.D. in Animal Nutrition (Shepardson fellow), 1960; m. Mabel Barbour, Sept. 12, 1942; children—William Thomas III, Judy (Mrs. Michael Spafford), Martha Blanche. Co-owner, mgr. farming, cattle enterprise, Vernon, 1946-53; prof. animal sci. dept. Tex. A. and M. U., 1953-60; operator in-charge cattle, farming Winrock Farms, Morrilton, Ark., 1961-67; exec. sec. Am. Hereford Assn., Kansas City, Mo., 1967—; dir. Armendaris Land Devel. Corp. Mem. cattle adv. com. Internal Revenue Service, Washington, 1970—; mem. Nat. Livestock Tax Com., 1967—. Bd. dirs. Am. Royal Livestock and Horse Show. Served with USAAF, 1942-46; PTO. Recipient Distinguished Achievement award faculty Tex. A. and M. U., named Outstanding Prof., Sch. Agr., 1960. Mem. Am. Nat. Cattlemen's Assn., Am. Soc. Animal Sci., Am. Soc. Assn. Execs., Airplane Pilots and Owners Assn., Sigma Xi, Alpha Zeta. Author: (with others) Basic Animal Science, 1957. Home: 9700 Horton St Overland Park KS 66207 Office: Am Hereford Assn 715 Hereford Dr Kansas City MO 64105

BERRY, WILLIAM WELLS, lawyer; b. Nashville, Sept. 10, 1917; s. Allen Douglas and Agnes (Vance) B.; B.A., Vanderbilt U., 1938, LL.B., 1940; m. Mary John Atwell, May 31, 1941; children—William Wells, Edith Allen. Admitted to Tenn. bar, 1940; practiced in Nashville, 1940-42, 46—; partner Bass, Berry & Slims, 1965—. Mem. adv. com. Dental div. Tenn. Dept. Pub. Health, 1953-57. Pres. Bill Wilkerson Hearing and Speech Center, 1959-67; past bd. dirs. Noel Meml. Found. Served to capt. F.A., AUS, 1942-46. Decorated Air medal with oak leaf cluster. Mem. Am., Tenn., Nashville (dir.) bar assns., Nashville C. of C., Beta Theta Pi, Phi Delta Phi, Tau Kappa Alpha. Democrat. Presbyn. (deacon, elder). Clubs: Belle Meade Country, Cumberland, Hillwood Country (past pres.). Home: 1018 Stonewall Dr Nashville TN 37220 Office: Am Trust Bldg Nashville TN 37201

BERRYMAN, JAMES THOMAS, cartoonist, illustrator; b. Washington, June 8, 1902; s. Clifford Kennedy and Kate Gaddis (Durfee) B.; student George Washington U., 1920- 23, Corcoran Art Sch., 1921-22; m. Louise Marble Rhees, Oct. 23, 1926; 1 son, Rhys Morgan. Reporter N.M. State Tribune, 1923-24; staff artist Washington Star, 1924-30, editorial illustrator, 1930-33; sports cartoonist Evening Star and Sporting News, 1934-41; mag. illustrator, 1936-66; polit. cartoonist, 1941—; editorial illustrator, 1930-33; mag. illustrator, 1936-66; polit. cartoonist King Features Syndicate, 1944-66; now writer, illustrator mag. and news articles; tchr. graphic arts Southeastern U., 1937-38; cartoonist for Assn. Am. R.R.'s, 1948—; pub. dir. art Nat. Rifle Assn., 1941-48. Recipient awards from N.Y. World's Fair, Infantile Paralysis Found., War Bond Com. (U.S. Treasury). A.R.C., Wash. Central H.S. Alumni Assn., Freedoms Found., 1949, 50, 51, 62; Distinguished Service medal Am. Legion, 1950, medal for Merit, 1951; Nat. Cartoonist Soc. award, 1950; Pulitzer prize for cartoon, 1950; Nat. Headliners award, 1953. Hon. life mem. Nat. Rifle Assn.; life mem. Culver Mil. Acad. Fathers; mem. Coast Guard Aux., Delta Tau Delta, Sigma Delta Chi. Presbyn. Clubs: Gridiron, University, Alfalfa; Venice (Fla.) Yacht. Contbg. editor Am. Motorist. Address: 372 Renoir Dr Osprey FL 33559

BERRYMAN, JOHN, author; b. McAlester, Okla., Oct. 25, 1914; s. John Allyn Smith and Martha (Little) B.; student South Kent Sch.; A.B., Columbia U., 1936; B.A., Clare Coll., Cambridge, 1938, M.A., 1968; m. Eileen Patricia Mulligan, Oct. 24, 1942; m. 2d, Ann Levine; m. 3d, Kathleen Donahue; children—Paul, Martha, Sarah. Faculty Wayne State U., 1939-40, Harvard, 1940-43; instr. English, lectr., fellow creative writing Princeton, intermittently, 1943-49; lectr. U. Wash., 1950; Elliston lectr. poetry U. Cin., 1952; now Regents prof. humanities U. Minn., Mpls. Rockefeller fellow humanities, 1944-46; Hodder fellow Princeton, 1950-51; Guggenheim fellow, 1952-54, 66-67; recipient first prize for Imaginary Jew, Kenyon- Doubleday, 1945; Guarantors, Levinson prizes Poetry Mag., 1948; Shelley Meml. award, 1949; Am. Acad. award, 1950; The Harriet Monroe Poetry prize, U. Chgo., 1957; Brandeis award, 1960; Pulitzer prize for poetry, 1965; Acad. Am. Poets fellowship, 1966; Bollingen award Yale, 1967; Nat. Book award, 1968. Mem. Nat. Inst. Arts and Letters, Acad. Am. Poets (chancellor), Am. Acad. Arts and Scis., Phi Beta Kappa. Author: Poems, 1942; The Dispossessed (poems), 1948; Stephen Crane, 1950, Homage to Mistress Bradstreet, 1956; 77 Dream Songs, 1964; Short Poems, 1967; Berryman's Sonnets, 1967; His Toy, His Dream, His Rest, 1968; The Dream Songs, 1969; Love and Fame (poems), 1970. Editor: Unfortunate Traveller (T. Nashe). Contbr. Five Young Am. Poets, 1940; Best American Short Stories, 1946; A Little Treasury of American Prose; verse, anthologies. Contbr. lit. criticism, profl. publs. Home: 33 Arthur Av SE Minneapolis MN 55414

BERRYMAN, MACON MOORE, welfare agy. ofcl.; b. Lexington, Ky., Feb. 17, 1908; s. James Henry and Elizabeth (Bridges) B.; B.A., Lincoln U., 1930, postgrad., 1931, D.C.L., 1967; grad. Atlanta U. Sch. Social Work, 1933; m. Dortha Alice Hackett, June 19, 1943; 1 son, James Henry. Investigator, Emergency Relief Adminstrn., Burlington County, N.J., 1933-34, dist. adminstr., case supr., 1934-36; social worker, parole officer N.Y. State Tng. Sch. Boys, N.Y.C., 1936-45; exec. dir. Sunnycrest Farm for Boys, Cheyney, Pa., 1945-50; dir. insular div. child welfare Dept. Social Welfare, St. Thomas, V.I., 1950-58, acting commr. social welfare, 1958-59, commr., 1959—. Cons. V.I. Commn. on Aging, 1959-67, V.I. Insular Commn. on Children and Youth, 1950-67. Chmn. Gov.'s Com. on Employment of Handicapped, 1959-67; vice chmn. Gov.'s Commn. Human Resources, 1964-69; mem. local bd. SSS, 1964—; mem. V.I. dist. com. Boy Scouts Am., 1964-66, pres. V.I. council, 1966-69, nat. council rep., 1964-67, 69—, mem. Region II com., 1968— (all St. Thomas). Bd. dirs. St. Thomas chpt. Hands Across the Sea Scholarship Com. (treas. 1955-60), St. Thomas Community Chest (treas. 1960—), St. Thomas U.S.O. Recipient Alumni award Lincoln U., 1954. Mem. Am. Pub. Welfare Assn. (welfare policy com. 1959—, nat. membership com., chmn. V.I. membership com. 1959-68), Nat. Assn. Social Workers (mem. cabinet div. social policy and action 1967—), Acad. Certified Social Workers, Lincoln U. Alumni Assn. (pres. V.I. chpt., 1964-67), Alpha Phi Alpha. Anglican. Mason, Rotarian (pres. St. Thomas 1966-67). Home: 26 AC Lindberg Bay St Thomas VI 00801 Office: Dept Social Welfare St Thomas VI 00801

BERRYMAN, ROBERT BENTON, nat. resources co. exec.; b. Brookeland, Tex., Mar. 9, 1924; s. Andrew Andrew Alvin and Effie (McDaniel) B.; B.S. in Mech. Engring., Tex. A. and M. Coll. Coll. 1948; m. Mary Anne Tabb, Aug. 14, 1948. With United Gas Corp., 1948-68, asst. sec., 1958-64, sec., 1965-68; sec. Pennzoil United, Inc. (merger United Gas Corp. and Pennzoil Co.), 1968—. Served to 1st lt., pilot USAAF, 1943-45. Mem. Am. Gas Assn., Ind. Petroleum Assn. Am., Am. Petroleum Inst., Am. Soc. Corporate Secs. Home: 1119 C Post Oak Park Dr Houston TX 77027

BERRYMAN, ROBERT GLEN, educator; b. Freeport, Ill., Nov. 22, 1928; s. Loyd Vernon and Gladys Leone (Hicks) B.; B.S., Northwestern U., 1950, M.B.A., 1952; Ph.D., U. Ill., 1958; m. Ruth Madelyn Bjorngjeld, Aug. 25, 1955; children—Peter, David, Kathryn. Staff accountant Touche Ross & Co., Chgo., 1951-54; instr. U. Ill., 1954-58; prof. accounting U. Minn., Mpls., 1958-69, 70—, chmn. dept., 1963-65, 70—; mgr. Touche Ross & Co., Mpls., 1969-70. Lectr., Northwestern U., 1953-54; dir. Nat. Biocentric, Inc. Ford Found. fellow, 1959-60; recipient Horace Morse Outstanding Tchr. award, U. Minn., 1966. Mem. Am. Accounting Assn., Am. Inst. C.P.A.'s, Nat. Assn. Accountants, Minn. Soc. C.P.A.'s (dir.), Beta Alpha Psi, Beta Gamma Sigma. Lutheran (vice chmn. bd. adminstrn.). Home: 1462 Brenner St St Paul MN 55113 Office: U Minn Minneapolis MN 55455

BERS, LIPMAN, educator, mathematician; b. Riga, Latvia, May 22, 1914; s. Isaac and Bertha (Weinberg) B.; Dr. Rerum Naturalium, U. Prague, 1938; m. Mary Kagan, May 15, 1939; children—Ruth, Victor. Came to U.S., 1940, naturalized, 1949. Research instr. Brown U., 1942-45; asst. prof., asso. prof. Syracuse U., 1945-49; mem. Inst. Advanced Study, 1948-50; prof. N.Y. U., 1950-64, chmn. dept. math., 1959-64; prof. Columbia U., 1964—. Vis. prof. Stanford, summer 1955; vis. Miller Research prof. U. Cal. at Berkeley, 1968; chmn. Com. Support on Research on Math. Scis., Nat. Acad. Scis.-N.R.C., 1966-68; chmn. div. math. scis. N.R.C., 1969-71. Fellow Am. Acad. Arts and Scis., A.A.A.S.; mem. Am. Math. Soc. (v.p. 1963-65), Nat. Acad. Scis. (chmn. math. sect. 1967-70), Math. Assn. Am. Author math. books. Contbr. articles to math. jours. Home: 111 Hunter Av New Rochelle NY 10801 Office: Dept Math Columbia U New York City NY 10027

BERSCH, GEORGE MORTON, cons.; b. Bklyn., May 19, 1906; s. Samuel and Kate (Lemberg) B.; student pub. schs.; m. Anne Kaplan, June 1, 1930; children—Neil Robert, Richard Lawrence, Nona Yavner. Buyer R.H. Macy Co., N.Y.C., 1927-30; mdse. mgr. Bamberger's, Newark, 1930-37, sr. v.p. fashion apparel, 1937-59, sr. v.p., dir. stores, 1950-71, now dir., 1950—; corporate cons. R.H. Macy, Inc., 1971—. pres. Essex County Jewish News, 1960-65. Trustee Newark Beth Israel Hosp., 1946, Newark Hosp. Devel., 1967. Recipient citation N.J. Dept. Def. Home: 200 Central Park S New York City NY 10019 Office: 131 Market St Newark NY 07102

BERSON, JEROME ABRAHAM, chemist, educator: educator; Sanford, Fla., May 10, 1924; s. Joseph and Rebecca (Bernicker) B.; B.S., Coll. City N.Y., 1944; M.A., Columbia, 1947, Ph.D., 1949; m. Bella Zevitovsky, June 30, 1946; children—Ruth, David, Jonathan. Asst. chemist Hoffmann-LaRoche, Inc., Nutley, N.J., 1944; asst. prof. U. So. Cal., 1950-53, asso. prof., 1953-58, prof., 1958-63; prof. U. Wis., 1963-69; prof. Yale, 1969—. Vis. prof. U. Cal., U. Cologne, U. Western Ont.; cons. Riker Labs., Goodyear Tire & Rubber Co. Mem. adv. panel for chemistry NSF; mem. medicinal chemistry study sect. NIH, 1969—. Served with AUS, 1944-46; CBI. Mem. Nat. Acad. Scis., Am. Chem. Soc. (Cal. sect. award 1963, chmn. elect. div. organic chemistry 1970), Chem. Soc. London, Phi Beta Kappa, Sigma Xi, Phi Lambda Upsilon. Mem. editorial adv. bd. Jour. Organic Chemistry, 1961-65. Contbr. profl. jours. Home: 19 Hemlock Hollow Woodbridge, CT 06525. Office: Sterling Chem Lab New Haven CT 06520

BERSTACK, JOSEPH GERHART chemist, educator; b. Chicago, 1928; B.S. in Physics, Yale, 1950; Ph.D. in Chemistry, Harvard, 1956; m. Sally Ann Jones, July 5, 1957; children--Kenneth J., Nancy A. Chemist, Acme Chem. Co., Blue Island, Ill., 1950-51; director of Research Lab., Indsl. Chemicals Corp., Cambridge, Mass., 1956-60; project coordinator environmental sect. Steinmetz Assos., Chgo., 1960-61; v.p. for research Bauer Bros. Chem. Co., Inc., Memphis, 1961-64; asst. prof. chemistry Washington U., St. Louis, 1964-66, asso. prof., 1966-70, prof., 1970--, head of chemistry dept., 1970-71. Vis. prof. So. Ill. U., summer 1967, U. of Ore., 1969. Scoutmaster, Boy Scouts America, University City, Mo., 1968-70. Bd. dirs. Rest Haven Home for Elderly, 1960-61; trustee of the Lutheran Hosp., 1965-71. Served from lt. to capt., AUS, 1951-53. Mem. Am. Chem. Soc., Sci. Research Soc. Am. (chpt. treas. 1967), American Institute Chemists, Ecological Soc. Am. (chpt. sec.), Sigma Xi. Author: (with others) Basic Inorganic Chemistry, 1971. Contbr. articles to profl. jours., encys., also chpts. to books. Home: Fairfax Apts 7291 Windermere Dr University City MO 63105 Office: Dept Chemistry Washington University St Louis MO 63130

BERSTED, ALFRED, mfg. exec.; b. Chgo., June 7, 1898; s. Martin and Julia B.; student pub. pub. schs.; m. Grace Hamberg, Aug. 1923; 1 dau., Ruth. Pres. Bersted Mfg. Co., Fostoria, O., 1919-49; v.p. McGraw Edison Co., Chgo., 1949-57, exec. v.p., 1957-60, pres., 1960-67, chmn. bd., chief exec. officer, 1967-69, chmn. exec. com., 1969—. Address: 333 W River Rd Elgin, IL 60120.

BERSTEIN, IRA BORAH, educator, theoretical physicist; b. N.Y.C., Nov. 8, 1924; s. Aaron M. M. and Rae (Hochberg) B.; B.Chem. Engring., Coll. City N.Y., 1944; Ph.D., N.Y. U., 1950; m. Gioconda Oresti, Apr. 1, 1955; children—Rachel, Adam. Research physicist Westinghouse Research Labs., 1950-54; sr. research physicist Princeton, 1954-64; prof. applied sci. Yale, 1964—. Cons. in field, 1960—. Served with USNR, 1944-46. Fellow Am. Phys. Soc. Home: 70 Killdeer Rd Hamden, CT 06517. Office: Yale Univ New Haven CT 06520

BERSTEIN, ISRAEL, educator, mathematician; b. Briceni, Bessarabia, USSR, June 23, 1926; s. Ephraim and Hana (Brandes) B.; diploma U. Bucharest (Roumania), 1954; Ph.D., Inst. Math. Roumanian Acad., 1958; m. Else-Maj Suolinna, May 28, 1970. Came to U.S., 1962. Research asso. Inst. Math., Roumanian Acad., Bucharest, 1954-61; lectr. Israeli Inst. Tech., Haifa, 1961-62; asst. prof., then asso. prof. Cornell U., 1962-66, prof. math., 1967—; vis. asso. prof. Princeton, 1966-67; vis. prof. State U.N.Y., Buffalo, 1970-71. Served with USSR Army, 1944-45. Author research papers in field. Home: 600 Warren Rd Ithaca NY 14850

BERTALAN, FRANK JOSEPH, univ. adminstr.; b. Edwardsville, Ill., Sept. 18, 1914; s. Frank Joseph and Ida (Barthi) B.; B.Ed., Ill. State U., 1938; B.S. in L.S., U. Ill., 1939, M.S., 1945; Ph.D., Cath. U. Am., 1962; m. Helen G. Scheck, Apr. 6, 1942; children—Edward, Mary, Patricia, Frank, Elaine, John, Joan. Head reference and bibliog. services U.S. Office Edn. Library, Washington, 1946-50; chief library services div. Legislative Reference Service Library of Congress, Washington, 1950-55; head engring. information br. Navy Bur. Aeros., Washington, 1955-58; exec. asst. for sci. information Office Naval Research, Washington, 1958-62; chief emergency measures div. Office Emergency Planning, Exec. Office of Pres., Washington, 1963-65; dir. U. Okla. Sch. Library Sci., Norman, 1965—. Cons. Goddard Space Flight Center Library, NASA Hdqrs. Library, comdt. USCG, U.S. Senate Finance Com.; spl. rep. U.S. Book Exchange, 1962-65. Served to comdr. USNR, 1942-46; ETO. Mem. A.L.A. (nat. chmn. library orgn. and mgmt. sect. 1968—), Assn. Am. Library Schs. (chmn. recruiting and personnel com. 1967—), Spl. Libraries Assn., Okla. Library Assn., Kappa Delta Pi, Kappa Mu Epsilon, Kappa Phi Kappa. Author: Books for Junior Colleges, 1954; Provision of Federal Benefits for Veterans, 1955; Proposed Scope and Coverage of the Goddard Space Flight Center Library, 1963; The Junior College Library Collection, 1968, rev. 1970. Home: 1608 Chestnut Lane Norman OK 73069 Office: 401 W Brooks St Norman OK 73069

BERTELSON, ARTHUR ROBARDS, newspaperman; b. Louisville, July 4, 1907; s. Herman E. and Josephine (Robards) B.; student U. Louisville, 1929-33; m. Jane Elizabeth Horrell, Nov. 28, 1942; children—Elizabeth Stewart (Mrs. Robert Wells Streett), Christine Adkin. Sports writer Louisville Herald-Post, 1933-36; copy editor Chattanooga Times, 1936-37; dir. Star-Times, 1937-40; with St. Louis Post-Dispatch, 1940—, make-up editor, 1948-53, news editor, 1953-58, asst. mng. editor, 1958-62, mng. editor, 1962-68, exec. editor, 1968—; dir. Pulitzer Pub. Co., Ariz. Star, Tucson, Sta. KVOA-TV, Tucson, Sta. KOAC-TV, Albuquerque. Bd. dirs. St. Louis Post-Dispatch Found.; bd. dirs., mem. exec. com. United Fund St. Louis. Served with AUS, 1942. Mem. Sigma Delta Chi. Democrat. Episcopalian. Clubs: Normandie Golf, Media (St. Louis). Home: 911 Glenridge Av Clayton MO 63105 Office: 1133 Franklin Av St Louis MO 63101

BERTERO, VITELMO VICTORIO, educator; b. Esperanza, Argentina, May 9, 1923; s. Victorio and Luci (Risso) B.; Ingeniero Civil, Facultad de Ciencias Mathematicas, 1947; M.Sc., Mass. Inst. Tech., 1955, D.Sc., 1957; m. Nydia Barcelo Vilas, Feb. 25, 1949; children—Maria Treasa, Eduardo Telmo, Robert Charles, Mary Rita, Adolph Victor, Richard Albert. Came to U.S., 1953. Dir. tech. dept. Talleres Metalugicos Angeloni Rosario, 194953; cons. engr. Weder Bertero Firm, Rosario, 1950-53; asst. prof. Facultad de Ciencias Matematicas, Rosario, 1949-53; research engr. Mass. Inst. Tech., 1953- 57; prof. civil engring. U. Cal. at Berkeley, 1958—; cons. engr., 1958-. Recipient award Inst. Universitario de Architecturd di Venezia (Italy). Mem. Am. Concrete Inst., Am. Soc. C.E., Internat. Assn. Shell Structors, Internat. Assn. Bridge and Structural Engring. Soc. Exptl. Stress Analysis, Earthquake Engring. Research Inst. Author papers in field. Home: 1106 Colusa St Berkeley, CA 94707.

BERTHEAU, CESAR JORDAN, ret. banker; b. San Francisco, June 5, 1897; s. Cêsar and Anita (Jordan) B.; A.B., U. Cal., 1919; m. Bernard M. Cameron, Nov. 28, 1941. Mgr. Los Angeles office Am. Nat. Co. of San Francisco, 1925-28; v.p., N.Y.C. rep. Am. Nat. Co. and Am. Trust Co. of San Francisco, 1928-30; v.p., dir. Pacific Trust Co. and Am. Pacific Corp., N.Y.C., 1928-30; v.p. Marine Midland Trust Co., 1930-47; pres., dir. Fidelity Safe Deposit Co., N.Y.C., 1939-47; pres., chmn. exec. com., dir. Anchorage Homes, Inc., Westfield, Mass., 1947; exec. v.p., dir. Peoples Trust Co. of Bergen County, Hackensack, N.J., 1948-51, pres., chief exec. officer, 1951-60, chmn. bd., 1960-70. Vice pres., dir., mem. exec. com. Regional Plan Assn., Inc., N.Y., chmn. N.J. Com. Regional Plan Assn., Inc., 1960-63; mem. Bennington County (Vt.) Regional Planning Assn., 1968- -. Bd. fellows Fairleigh-Dickinson U., 1960-63. Served as 2d lt., arty. U.S. Army, 1918-19; AEF, mem. Res., 1921-26. Mem. Soc. Cal. Pioneers, Psi Upsilon (gov. alumni Assn., N.Y., 1952-60, v.p. exec. council). Republican. Unitarian. Club: Pacific Union (San Francisco). Home: Rock Botton Winhall Hollow Rd Peru VT 05152

BERTHEL, JOHN HALLOCK, librarian; b. Washington, Pa., Mar. 27, 1914; s. Frank H. and Nina B. (Hallock) B.; A.B., Columbia, 1938, M.A., 1939, B.S., 1942; m. Elizabeth Bagby Edwards, Apr. 5, 1941; 1 dau., Deborah Gresham. Librarian Columbia Coll., 1945-47, also faculty mem.; librarian Columbia Coll. and Butler Departmental Libraries, Columbia U., 1947-48, Nicholas Murray Butler Libraries, 1948-54, Johns Hopkins U., Balt., 1954—. Cons., Catholic U., Lima, Peru, 1968, Sch. Advanced Internat. Studies, Bologna, Italy, 1970, Lehigh U., 1968—, George Washington U., 1968—. Mem. Am. Assn. U. Lima, Peru, 1968, Sch. Advanced Internat. Studies, Bologna, Italy, 1970, Lehigh U., 1968—, George Washington U., 1968—. Mem. Am. Assn. U. Profs., Balt. Bibliophiles. Club: 14 West Hamilton St. Baltimore Md. Home: 3701 Patterson Av Baltimore MD 21207

BERTHOFF, ROWLAND TAPPAN, educator, historian; b. Toledo, Sept. 20, 1921; s. Nathaniel and Helen (Tappan) B.; A.B., Oberlin Coll., 1942; A.M., Harvard, 1947, Ph.D., 1952; m. Tirzah Margaret Park, Aug. 5, 1954; children—Thomas Arthur, Margaret Olivia, Andrew Warner, Clarissa Helen. Instr., Princeton, 1953-57, asst. prof., 1957-62; asso. prof. Washington U., St. Louis, 1962-65, prof., 1965—, chmn. history dept., 1968—; Fulbright lectr. U. Edinburgh, 1965-66. Served to 1st lt., inf., AUS, 1942-46. Mem. Am. Hist. Assn., Orgn. Am. Historians. Author: British Immigrants in Industrial America, 1790-1950, 1953; An Unsettled People: Social Order and Disorder in American History, 1971. Home: 7195 Washington Av St Louis MO 63130

BERTHOFF, WARNER BEMENT, educator; b. Oberlin, O., Jan. 22, 1925; s. Nathaniel and Helen (Tappan) B.; B.A., Harvard, 1947, M.A., 1949, Ph.D., 1954; m. Ann Rhys Evans, June 29, 1949; children—Rachel, Frederic. Teaching fellow Harvard, 1949-51; from asst. to prof. English, Bryn Mawr Coll., 1951-67; prof. English, Harvard, 1967—. Vis. prof. U. Catania (Italy), 1957-58, U. Minn., 1961, U. Cal. at Berkeley, 1962-63, U. Warsaw (Poland), 1963, Columbia, 1964, U. Pa., 1967. Served with USNR, 1943-46. Guggenheim fellow, 1968-69. Author: American Literature: Traditions and Talents, 1960; The Example of Melville, 1962; The Ferment of Realism; American Literature, 1884- 1919, 1965; Edmund Wilson, 1968; Fictions and Events, 1971. Home: 35 Belknap St Concord MA 01742 Office: Dept English Harvard Univ Cambridge MA 02138

BERTHOLD, FRED, Jr., educator, clergyman; b. St. Louis, Dec. 9, 1922; s. Fred and Myrtle Bernice (Williams) B.; A.B., Dartmouth, 1944; B.D., U. Chgo., 1947, Ph.D., 1954; D.D., Middlebury Coll., 1959, Concord Coll., 1960, U. Vt., 1961; m. Laura Bell McKusick, Dec. 27, 1945; children—Marjorie Chase, Daniel S., Timothy M., Sarah M. Instr. philosophy Utica Coll. of Syracuse U., 1948-49; ordained to ministry Congl.-Christian Ch., 1949; instr. philosophy Dartmouth, 1949-50, instr. religion, 1950-51, asst. prof. religion, 1951-56, prof., 1956—, chmn. dept., 1951-58, 1962—, dean William Jewett Tucker Found., 1957-62. Mem. Nat. Council Religion Higher Edn., Soc. for Sci. Study Religion, Am. Acad. Religion, Am. Assn. U. Profs., Am. Theol. Soc., Phi Beta Kappa. Author: The Fear of God, 1959. Editor: Basic Sources of the Judaeo-Christian Tradition, 1962. Contbr. to The Future of Empirical Theology, 1969, The Dialogue between Psychology and Theology, 1969. Home: RFD 227 Norwich VT 05055

BERTHOLF, LLOYD M., ret. ednl. adminstr., biologist; b. Kechi, Kan., Dec. 15, 1899; s. Albert Linton and Mable Sarah (Haden) B.; A.B., Southwestern Coll., 1921; A.M. Johns Hopkins, 1925, Ph.D., 1928; post doctoral work U. Munich, 1930-31; LL.D., Southwestern Coll., Winfield, Kan.; L.H.D., Ewha Womans U., Seoul, Korea, 1970; m. Martha Washburn, June 15, 1921; children—Mabelyn Washburn, Max Erwin. Instr. biology Woman's Coll., U. N.C., Greensboro, 1922-24; investigator honeybees U.S. Dept. Agr., summers 1922-37; prof. biology Western Md. Coll., Westminster, 1924-48, dean faculty, 1939-48; dean coll. and prof. zoology U. of Pacific, 1948-58; pres. Ill. Wesleyan U., 1958-68; pres. Central States Coll. Assn., 1968-69; sci. cons. Ewha Womans U., Seoul, Korea, 1969-70; co-ordinator Mid-Ill. Areawide Health Planning Corp., 1971—. Trustee Lincoln Acad. Ill., 1965-68. Served O.T.S., U.S. Coast Arty., 1918. Awarded Nat. Research fellowship to Munich, Germany, 1930-31. Del. Gen. Conf. Meth. Ch., 1949, 52, 56, 60, 64, 66, 68; mem. gen. bd. lay activities Meth. Ch., 1950-58, 60-68, sec. Quadrennial emphasis com., 1968—. Fellow A.A.A.S.; mem. Woods Hole Biol. Lab., N.E.A. (life), Entomol. Soc. Am., Am. Soc. Zoologists, Phi Beta Kappa, Sigma Xi, Beta Beta Beta (pres. 1946-54), Alpha Kappa Psi, Gamma Alpha, Phi Kappa Phi. Democrat. Rotarian. Contbr. articles in field. Home: 1228 Gettysburg Dr Bloomington IL 61701

BERTHOLO, RENE, artist; b. Alhandra, Portugal, Aug. 18, 1935; s. Augusto and Isabel (Costa) B.; ed. Nat. Art Sch., Lisbon; m. Lourdes Castro, Oct. 30, 1956. Exhbns. include Gallerrie Portico, Lisbon, 1954, Gallerie Dragon, Paris, 1963, Gallerie Mathias Fels, Paris, 1965, 66, Gallerie Birch, Copenhagen, 1968; Gallery 20, Amsterdam, 1969, Gallery Kuckels,, Bochum, 1969, Salon de Mai, Paris, Expn., Prix Marzotto 1966, Start Lefabre Gallery, N.Y.C., 1965, Gallery L. Durand, Paris, 1970; a pubiisher KWY mag., 1958—. Author: Livre, 1964; Il Faut Ce Quil Faut, 1963. Address: 71 rue Sts Péres 75 Paris France

BERTHRONG, DONALD JOHN, educator; b. LaCrosse, Wis., Oct. 2, 1922; s. LeRoy M. and Viola (Ritter) B.; student Wis. State U., 1941-42; B.S., U. Wis., 1947, M.S., 1948, Ph.D., 1952; m. Edna E. Marr, Dec. 21, 1942; children—John Hugh, Sherri Lee. With U. Kansas City (Mo.), 1951-52; mem. faculty U. Okla., 1952-70, prof. history, 1964-70, chmn. dept., 1966-70; faculty Purdue U., Lafayette, Ind., 1970—, head dept., 1970—. Fulbright lectr. Lafayette, Ind., 1970—, head dept., 1970—. Fulbright lectr. Hong Kong, 1965-66; cons. for Indian Claims, Dept. Justice, 1957-63. Served with AUS and USAAF, 1942-46. Fellow Social Sci. Research Council, 1949-50, Am. Philos. Soc., summer 1957. Mem. Am. Hist. Assn., Orgn. Am. Historians, Western, Agrl. history assns., Am. Assn. U. Profs. Editor: Joseph Reddeford Walter and the Arizona Adventure, 1956; The Southern Cheyennes, 1963; A Confederate in the Colorado Goldfields, 1970. Contbr. profl. jours. Home: profl. jours. Home: 601 Waldron St West Lafayette IN 47906

BERTHRONG, MORGAN, physician, educator; b. Aurora Hills, Va., July 17, 1918; s. Fred Morgan and Elsie (Edwards) B.; student U. Pa., 1936-39; M.D., Harvard, 1943; m. Patricia Eleanora Kinane, Jan. 4, 1944; children—Patricia, James McDowell, Sonja Buckley, Deirdre Lucy, Mary Olga, Elizabeth Regan. Resident pathologist Johns Hopkins Hosp., 1948-49, surg. pathologist, 1952-53; from instr. to asso. prof. pathology Johns Hopkins Sch. Medicine 1947-54; prof. pathology U. Colo. Sch. Medicine, 1959—, chmn. dept., 1959-60; dir. labs. Penrose Hosp., Colorado Springs, 1954—; vis. prof., acting head dept. pathology Stanford Med. Sch., 1966. Served capt., inf., AUS, World War II. Decorated Bronze Star. Diplomate Am. Bd. Pathology. Mem. A.M.A., Am. Assn. Pathologists and Bacteriologists, Am. Soc. Clin. Pathologists, Am. Coll. Pathologists, Phi Beta Kappa, Alpha Omega Alpha. Home: 9 Cragmor Village Colorado Springs CO 80907 Office: Penrose Hosp Colorado Springs CO 80907

BERTINE, HERBERT WHEATON, lawyer; b. N.Y.C., May 21, 1914; s. Herbert Cable and Esther Alice (Quackenbush) B.; A.B., Princeton, 1935; LL.B.; Columbia, 1938; m. Kathe Janet Vanderhoof, Sept. 17, 1938; children—Herbert Vanderhoof, Kathe Karlyn. Admitted to N.Y. bar, 1939; with firm Menken, Ferguson & Idler, N.Y.C., 1938-42; counsel N.Y. region RFC, 1942-46; asst. counsel, asso. dep. dir. N.Y. region, War Assets Adminstrn., 1946-48; asst. counsel gen. chem. div. Allied Chem. & Dye Corp., 1948-56; sec., gen. counsel Olivetti Corp. Am., N.Y.C., 1956-59, now v.p. sec., dir.; dir. Olivetti Can. Ltd., Geschäftsführer of Mercedes Büromaschinen Werke G.m.b.H., Germany. Dir. chem. and rubber div. Bus. and Def. Services Adminstrn., Dept. Commerce, Washington, 1955. Mem. N.Y. Bar Assn. Home: 30 Leeuwarden Rd Darien CT 06820 Office: 500 Park Av New York City NY 10022

BERTINO, JOSEPH ROCCO, physician, educator; b. Port Chester, N.Y., Aug. 16, 1930; s. Joseph and Madaleine (Posillipo) B.; student Cornell U., 1947-50; M.D., Downstate Med. Center N.Y., 1954; m. Mary Patricia Hagemeyer, Sept. 29, 1956; children—Frederick, Amy Marie, Thomas Allen, Paul Phillip. USPHS Research fellow U. Wash. Sch. Medicine, Seattle, 1958-61; Mem. faculty Yale Sch. Medicine, 1961—, asso. prof. pharmacology and medicine, 1964- 67, prof., 1967—; cons. USPHS, 1966—. N.Y.. State scholar for medicine, 1950-54. Mem. Am. Soc. for Clin. Investigation, Am. Soc. Hematology, Biol. Chemists, Pharmacology and Therapeutics. Contbr. articles profl. jours. Home: 384 Hill St Hamden CT 06514 Office: 333 Cedar St New Haven CT 06510

BERTLAND, CHARLES PERCIVAL, textile mfg. exec.; b. Bklyn., Sept. 10, 1908; s. Joseph and Kathryn (Hollwedel) B.; student N.Y. U.; m. Anna P. Backman, Sept. 18, 1934; 1 son, Stuart Edward. Began as sales exec. various textile firms; salesman, gen. sales mgr. textile fibers div. Tenn. Eastman Corp., 1933-55; exec. v.p. Fibers div. Beaunit Mills, Inc., 1955-59; asst. gen. mgr. Fibers div. Am. Cyanamid Co., N.Y.C., 1959-61; dir. sales fiber devel. dept. Hercules Powder Co., 1961-62; v.p. sales and merchandising Celanese Fibers Co., 1962-66; exec. v.p. Celanese Fibers Marketing Co., subsidiary Celanese Corp., 1966—. Served as lt. col. USAAF, 1942-46. Decorated Bronze Star medal (U.S.); Liberation Cross (Norway). Clubs: Wings (N.Y.C.); City (Charlotte, N.C.). Home: 1300 Queens Rd Charlotte NC 28207 Office: Celanese Fibers Marketing Co Box 1414 Charlotte NC 28201

BERTO, GIUSEPPE, author; b. Mogliano Veneto, Italy, Dec. 27, 1914; s. Ernesto and Norina (Peschiutta) B.; Doctor of Letters, U. Padua (Italy), 1940; m. Manuela Perroni, Apr. 8, 1954; 1 dau., Antonia. Author: Il cielo e'rosso (The Sky is Red), 1947; Il brigante (The Brigand), 1951, Il male oscuro (Incubus), 1964; La cosa buffa (Antonio in Love), 1965. Home: 9 Contrada Capo Vaticano Ricadi (Catanzaro) Italy Office: Via Valerio Anziate 16 Roma Italy

BERTOCCI, PETER ANTHONY, educator; b. Elena, Italy, May 13, 1910; s. Gaetano and Nancy (Guglietta) B.; A.B., Boston U., 1931, Ph.D., 1935; M.A., Harvard, 1932; postgrad. U. Cambridge (Eng.), 1934-35; m. Lucy Soldani, Sept. 2, 1935; children—Peter John, Stephen Paul, Richard Anthony. Prof. psychology and philosophy Bates Coll., 1935-44; prof. Boston U., 1946—, Borden P. Bowne prof. philosophy, 1953—. Fulbright scholar, Italy, 1951, India, 1960-61; Guggenheim fellow, 1967-68. Fellow Am. Psychol. Assn.; mem. Soc. Sci. Study Religion, Am. Cath. Philos. Assn., Soc. Religion and Mental Health, Philosophy of Edn. Assn., Am. Philos. Assn., Am. Theol. Soc. (pres. 1963-64), Metaphys. Soc. Am. (pres. 1963-64), Assn. Bibl. Instrs., Nat. Council Religion in Higher Edn., Am. Assn. U. Profs., Phi Beta Kappa. Author: The Empirical Argument for God in Late British Thought, 1938; The Human Venture in Sex, Love and Marriage, 1949; Introduction to Philosophy of Religion, 1951; Free Will, Responsibility, and Grace, 1957; Religion as Creative Insecurity, 1958; Why Believe in God?, 1963; Sex, Love, and the Person, 1967; (with Richard M. Millard) Personality and the Good, 1963; The Person God Is, 1970. Editor: Person and Reality (E.S. Brightman), 1958. Home: 243 Park Av Arlington MA 02174 Office: 725 Commonwealth Av Boston MA 02115

BERTOIA, HARRY, artist; born San Lorenzo, Italy, Mar. 10, 1915; s. Giuseppe and Maria (Mussio) B.; student pub. schs., Italy and Mich., Arts and Crafts Sch., Detroit, Cranbrook Acad. Art, Bloomfield Hills, Mich., 1937-42; m. Brigitta Valentiner, May 10, 1943; children—Mara Lesta, Val Odey, Celia Marei. Came to the United States, 1930, naturalized, 1947. Student teachers Cranbrook Acad., 1938-43; development war material Evans Products Co., 1943-46; independent artist, jewelry craftsman, 1946-47; with U.S. Electronics Lab., San Diego, Cal., 1948-50; chair designer Knoll Internat., 1950-54; executed sculptural screens for Gen. Motors, New Tech. Center. Mfrs. Trust Bank N.Y., Mass. Inst. Tech. chapel; bronze sculpture View of Earth from Space, Dulles Airport, Washington, 1962; copper and bronze fountain piece Civic Center, Phila. Recipient gold medal Archtl., League N.Y., 1955; gold medal, A.I.A., 1956; Graham Found. scholarship, 1957. Home: Barto PA 19504

BERTOLET, JOHN HERBINE, lawyer; b. Reading, Pa., May 8, 1906; s. William S. and Mary E. (Herbine) B.; A.B., Franklin and Marshall Coll., 1927; LL.B., U. Pa., 1931; m. Margaret Mary Cook, Mar. 4, 1933; children—William C., Frederick C., John C., Mary Margaret (Mrs. Nicholas Triffin). Admitted to Pa. bar, 1931, since practiced in Reading; gen. partner firm Stevens & Lee, 1954—. Dir. Wm. G. Leininger Knitting Co., Kutztown Foundry & Machine Corp. (Pa.), Reading Eagle Co. (pubs. Reading Times and Reading Eagle). Bd. dirs. Vis. Nurse Assn. Reading and Berks County, 1955—. Mem. Am., Pa., Berks County bar assns., Order of Coif, Phi Beta Kappa, Delta Sigma Phi, Phi Delta Phi. Republican. Mem. United Ch. of Christ. Clubs: Endlich Law, Wyomissing (Reading). Home: 500 Friedensburg Rd Reading PA 19606 Office: 607 Washington St Reading PA 19603

BERTOLLI, ROBERT L., pres. Mass. Coll. Art. Office: Mass Coll of Art Boston MA 02139

BERTRAM, HARRY EDWARD, lawyer; b. Milw., Aug. 29, 1903; s. Edmund E. and Emma (Gruendler) B.; J.D., Marquette U., 1934; m. Edna Lenz, Nov. 12, 1932 (dec. 1965); children—Daniel E., Robert E.; m. 2d, Loretta Fechner, Mar. 4, 1967. Mgr. classified advt. Milw. Leader, 1924-34; admitted to Wis. bar, 1934, since practiced in Milw.; sr. mem. firm Bertram & Bertram, 1959—. Dir. Aid Assn. for Lutherans, 1954—, chmn. bd., 1966-68; sec., dir. Entre Nous, Inc. (formerly Harris Corp.), 1951—; dir. Hibbard Machine Co., 1964—, Melvin A. Luedtke, Inc., 1964—, Bultman Trucking Co., E & L Leasing Co. Lectr. advanced estate planning Aid Assn. for Luths., 1963-66. Mem. Luth. Laymens League, Luth. Men in Am.; past pres. Luther Meml. Chapel, Wis. Fedn. Aid Assn. for Luth. Mem. Wis., Milw., Bar assns., Nat. Luth. Lawyers Assn., Am. Judicature Soc., Beta Phi Theta (past pres.), Delta Theta Pi. Clubs: Milwaukee Athletic, North Shore Country (past pres.) (Milw.). Home: 1205 E Hermitage Rd Milwaukee WI 53210

BERTRAMSON, B. RODNEY, agronomist; b. Potter, Neb., Jan. 25, 1914; s. James W. and Gladys D. (Nelson) B.; B.S., U. Neb., 1937, M.S., 1938; Ph.D., Ore. State Coll., 1941; m. Eleanor Anne Maloney, Aug. 28, 1938; children—James Leitch, Christina MacPherson, Susan M. Chemist technician, lab. asst. U. Neb., 1936-37; soil surveyor, U.S. Dept. Agr., 1941; instr. in soils Colo. State Coll., 1941; asst. prof. soils U. Wis., 1946; asso. soil chemist Purdue U., 1946-49; chmn. dept. agronomy Wash. State U., Pullman, 1949-67, dir. resident instrn. Coll. Agr., 1967—, prof. soil chemistry and coordinator agronomic research, 1949—. Entered U.S. Army, 1941; chief of food and agr. for Rheinland, later for Gross Hessen, Mil. Govt., 1945; disch. to Research and Devel., U.S. Army Res. as maj., 1946. Fellow A.A.A.S., Am. Soc. Agronomy (v.p. 1959, pres. 1960); mem. Crop Sci. Soc. Am., Soil Sci. Soc. Am., Soil Conservation Soc. Am., Sigma Xi, Phi Kappa Phi, Alpha Zeta, Gamma Sigma Delta. Prepared course outlines for soil anlaysis and soil chemistry. Contbr. articles in profl. jours. Home: 314 S Spring St Pullman WA 99163

BERTRAND, ANSON RABB, coll. dean; b. Gatesville, Tex., Aug. 19, 1923; s. Rabb Albert and Retta Mildred (Cook) B.; B.S., Texas A. and M., 1947; M.S., U. Ill., 1949; Ph.D., Purdue U., 1955; m. Gloria Jolly, July 27, 1946; children—Cynthia Lynn, Styles Leslie. Instr.

agronomy Purdue U., Lafayette, Ind., 1949-55, asst. prof., 1955-58, asso. prof., 1958-61; dir. So. Piedmont Soil & Water Mgmt. Research Center, Watkinsville, Ga., Agrl. Research Service, U.S. Dept. Agriculture, 1961-64; chief so. br. soil and water research Agrl. Research Service, U.S. Dept. Agriculture, 1964-67; prof., chmn. agronomy div. U. Ga. at Athens, 1967-71; dean Coll. Agrl. Scis., Texas Tech. U., Bubbock, 1971—. Served with AUS, 1942-46. Fellow Am. Soc. Agronomy, Soil Conservation Soc. Am.; mem. Agronomy Soc., Internat. Soil Sci. Soc., A.A.A.S., Nat. (com. agriculture and environment), Ind., Ga. acads. sci., Sigma Xi, Gamma Sigma Delta. Elk, Kiwanian. Co-author: Soil Conservation Textbook, 1959. Asso. editor Jour. Soil and Water Conservation, 1964—; Soil Sci. Soc. Am. Proceedings, 1965-71; Agronomy Jour., 1965-71. Home: 4407 8th Lubbock TX 79416

BERTRAND, CHARLES EDWARD, railroad ofcl.; b. Pine Bluff, Ark., May 30, 1915; s. Charles L. and Kibble (Moore) B.; ed. pub. schs.; m. Ludene A. Asklund, Dec. 23, 1933; children—Cynthia Ludene, Charles Edward. With B. &O. R.R. Co., 1937- gen. mgr. Eastern region, 1960, asst. v.p. operations and maintenance, 1960-61, v.p. operations and maintenance, 1961—; pres., dir. Balt. and Ohio Stores, Inc., B.R.& P. Warehouse, Inc., Camden Warehouses, Inc., Md. Constrn. Co. of Balt., New Gauley Coal Corp., Terminal Storage Co. Washington, Toledo. Lorain & Fairport Co.; v.p., dir. numerous subsidiaries and affiliates B.& O. R.R. Co.; pres. Reading Co.; dir. Central R.R. Co. Republican. Presbyn. Mason (Shriner). Home: 1900 Lismore Lane Baltimore MD Office: B & O R R Co Baltimore and Charles Sts Baltimore MD

BERTRAND, JOHN J., business exec.; b. Chgo., Feb. 8, 1906; s. Edward John and Ann Elizabeth (Smith) B.; student Campion, 1923-25, Loyola Acad., 1925-27, Loyola U., 1927-28; m. Marion Barrett, Sept. 25, 1935; children—Charles, Barbara, Marion. Liquor sales mgr. Kansas City div. McKesson & Robbins, Inc., 1936-44, dist. liquor sales mgr. midwest dist., 1944-46, v.p., gen. liquor sales mgr., 1946—, dir., exec. v.p., 1953—, exec. com., 1963—; pres. McKesson Liquor Co.; exec. v.p., dir. Foremost- McKesson, Inc., 1967—; dir. Licensed Beverage Industries (N. Y.); mem. advisory com. Chase Manhattan Bank. Knight of Malta, Knight of Equestrian Order of Holy Sepulchre Jerusalem. Clubs: Athletic Asso. (Chicago); Larchmont (New York) Yacht; Winged Foot Golf (N.Y.C.); Westchester Country, Madison Square Garden Home: 39 Chestnut Av Larchmont NY 10538 Office: 155 E 44th St New York City NY 10017

BERTRAND, JOHN RANEY, coll. pres.; b. Gray County, Tex., Aug. 3, 1914; s. Bell Otis and Eugenia Theresa (Studer) B.; student West Tex. State Coll., 1933-34; B.S., Tex. Technol. U., 1940, M.S., 1941; student U. Mo., 1941-42; Ph.D., Cornell U., 1950; m. Annabel Lee Hodges, Oct. 23, 1942; children—John Thomas, Diana Carroll, Karen Elizabeth, Janet May. Farmer, White Deer, Tex., 1932-37; vocational agr. tchr., Claude, Tex., 1940; prof., acting dean men Sam Houston State U., 1945-46; asst. prof. rural sociology Tex. A. and M. U., 1946-47, asso. prof., asst. dean agr., 1947-50, dean basic div., 1950-54; dean. Max C. Fleischmann Coll. Agr., U. Nev., 1954-56, dir. Nev. Agrl. Expt. Sta., Nev. Agrl. Extension Service, 1954-56; staff study needs and resources for higher edn. ICA, Libya, 1955; pres. Berry Coll., Mt. Berry, Ga., 1956—, Berry Acad., 1956- -, sec. bd. trustees Berry Schs., 1957—. Trustee, former pres. Ga. Found. for Ind. Colls.; mem. bd. visitors U.S. Naval Acad.; former pres., now mem. exec. com. Assn. Pvt. Colls. and Univs. in Ga. Pres., N.W. Ga. council Boy Scouts Am. Served as officer USNR, 1942-45; comdr. Res. ret. Decorated Silver Star (2), Naval Unit citation, Presdl. Unit citation. Mem. Am. Coll. Personnel Assn., Am. Edn. Research Assn., Am. Sociol. Soc., Assn. Higher Edn., N.E.A., Nat. Soc. for Study Edn., Phi Delta Kappa, Pi Gamma Mu, Phi Eta Sigma, Alpha Chi. Methodist. Rotarian. Club: Army and Navy. Address: Berry Coll Mount Berry GA 30149

BERTSCH, FRANK HENRY, furniture mfg. co. exec.; b. Mpls., Oct. 2, 1925; s. Herbert Thomas and Eleanor Emma (Tuscany) B.; B.S. in Mech. Engring., Northwestern U., 1947; m. Barbara Tiffany Mills, Sept. 12, 1953; children—Jeffrey T., Staven H., Carolyn T. With Flexsteel Industries, Inc., Dubuque, Ia., 1947—, plant engr., 1947-49, plant mgr., 1949-53, v.p., dir. design and devel., 1953-55, pres., 1955—; pres., dir. Retirement Investment Corp., Dubuque, 1967—; developer Heritage Manor Nursing Home, Dubuque, 1969; dir. Am. Trust and Savs. Bank, Dubuque; partner Ryan House, hist. home restoration partnership, Dubuque, 1969—. Bd. dirs. Jr. Achievement of Tri-States, Inc., United Fund Dubuque. Served with USNR, 1944-46. Recipient Distinguished Service award Dubuque C. of C., 1964, Man Behind the Boy award Dubuque Boys Club, 1969. Mem. Am. Legion, Dubuque Shooting Soc. Presbyn. (elder, trustee). Elk. Club: Dubuque Golf and Country. Home: 700 Sunset Ridge Dubuque IA 52001 Office: care Flexsteel Industries Inc PO Box 877 Dubuque IA 52001

BERWALD, HELEN DOROTHY, educator; b. Lac Qui Parle County, Minn., Mar. 15, 1925; B.A., U. Minn., 1948, B.S., M.A., 1951, Ph.D., 1962. Tchr., Robbinsdale (Minn.) High Sch., 1951-52; mem. faculty Carleton Coll., Northfield, Minn., 1952—, now prof. edn. Mem. Nat. Council Accreditation Tchr. Edn., also video tape project. Mem. Phi Beta Kappa, Pi Lambda Theta, Delta Kappa Gamma. Home: 208 Elm St Northfield MN 55057

BERZAK, WILLIAM PETER, govt. ofcl.; b. Czechoslovakia, Mar. 23, 1914; s. Michael F. and Anna (Matlon) B.; came to U.S., 1920, naturalized, 1938; B.S.L., U. Minn., 1938, J.D., 1940; M.P.A., St. Louis U., 1960; m. Maurine McCaskill, Jan. 4, 1947; children—Susan, William, Frank. Admitted to Minn. bar, 1940, also U.S. Supreme Ct. bar; with U.S. Civil Services Commn., 1946—, dep. chmn. bd. appeals and rev. and internat. orgns. Employees Loyalty Bd., 1966, chmn., 1966—. Served to capt. AUS, 1941-46. Mem. Minn., Fed. bar assns., Bar Assn. D.C., Am. Soc. Pub. Adminstrn., Pub. Personnel Assn., Soc. Personnel Adminstrn., Am. Legion, Delta Theta Phi. Contbr. articles to legal jour. Home: 1416 Carrington Lane Vienna VA 22180 Office: 1900 E St NW Washington DC 20415

BES, JEAN, food products co. exec.; b. Miliana, Algeria, Sept. 29, 1921; s. Lucien and Alice (Bourgoin) B.; M.A. in Scis., U. Algiers, 1938-42; postgrad. Ecole Sciences Economiques, Paris, 1950-52; m. Jacqueline Balleyguier, Aug. 1, 1950; children—Philippe, Jean-Marie, Cecile, Monique, Sabine, Pierre. Came to Switzerland, 1956. Civil engr. Port of Tunis (Tunisia), 1946-48; gen. mgr. for W. Africa, Grands Travaux Est, Paris, 1950-56; with Suchard Holding S.A. (name changed to Interfood S.A. 1970), Lausanne, Switzerland, 1956—, dir., 1961—, mng. dir., 1963—; vice chmn. Grey Poupon and Maille, Dijon, France, 1970—; chmn. Chocolat Tobler, Bordeaux, France, 1970—. Served to capt. French Army, World War II. Decorated Croix de Guerre (France). Home: 14 Cure Lausanne 1012 Switzerland Office: Interfood SA 14b St Francois Lausanne 1000 Switzerland

BESANT, ALVIN WILLIAM KENWAY, retail trade exec.; b. Winnipeg, Man., Can., June 20, 1933; s. William Joseph and Lillian Ruth (Kenway) B.; B.A., United Coll., Winnipeg, 1954; postgrad. McGill U., 1965; m. Jean Mary Nicol, Oct. 1, 1956; children—Christopher, Paul, Laura. Trainee Hudson's Bay Co., 1955-56, asst. dept. mgr., 1956-57, dept. mgr., Victoria, B.C., 1957-60, Vancouver, 1960, mdse. mgr., Vancouver, 1960-61; mdse. mgr. Henry Morgan & Co., Ltd., Montreal, 1961-66, store mgr., 1966-67; v.p. marketing Singer Co. of Can., 1967-68; v.p. mdsg. Oshawa Wholesale Dept. Store div. Towers Dept. Stores, Toronto, 1968-69; exec. v.p., chief operating officer Gambles Can., Ltd., Winnipeg, 1969—. Dir. Man. Sports Fedn., 1970. Mem. Am., Canadian mgmt. assns., Montreal, Toronto bds. trade, Winnipeg C. of C., Retail Council of Can., Mdse. Research Inst. N.Y. Home: 3198 Assiniboine Av Winnipeg 22 Manitoba Canada Office: 1530 Gamble Pl Winnipeg 19 Manitoba Canada

BESCH, EVERETT DICKMAN, univ. dean; b. Hammond, Ind., May 4, 1924; s. Ernst Henry and Carolyn (Dieckmann) B.; D.V.M., Tex. A. and M. Coll., 1954; M.P.H., U. Minn., 1956; Ph.D., Okla. State U., 1963; m. Mellie Darnell Brockman, Apr. 3, 1946; children—Carolyn Darnell, Ceryl Lynn, Cynthia Lee, Charlotte Ann, Everett Dickman. Instr. U. Minn., 1954-56; asst. prof. Okla. State U., 1956-64, prof., head dept. vet. parasitology and pub. health, 1964-68; dean Sch. Vet. Medicine, La. State U., 1968—. Served with USN, 1942-48. Mem. Assn. Tchrs. Vet. Pub. Health and Preventive Medicine (pres. 1968-69), Am., La. vet. med. assns., Am. Soc. Parasitologists, Conf. Pub. Health Veterinarians, Helminthological Soc. Washington, Conf. Research Workers Animal Diseases. Author articles, chpt. in book. Reviewer Am. Jour. Vet. Research. Home: 1453 Ashland Av Baton Rouge, LA 70806.

BESHANY, PHILIP ARTHUR, rear adm. U.S. Navy. Address: care Bur Naval Personnel Navy Dept Washington DC 20025*

BESHEARS, JAMES KEITH, r.r. ofcl.; b. Springfield, Mo., Mar. 9, 1914; s. James Robert and Maude (Granthom) B.; student pub. schs.; student exec. devel. program U. Ga., 1953, exec. program bus. adminstrn., Columbia, 1956, advanced mgmt. program U. Hawaii, 1960; m. Mildred Fern Thomas, June 1, 1936; children—Jeri, Judy. With St. L.-S.F. R.R., 1936—. successively brakeman, condr., saftety supr., terminal trainmaster, asst. supt., supt. terminals, div. supt., 1953-55, dir. labor relations, 1955-57, v.p. personnel, 1957—; dir. FTC. Mem. exec. com., bd. trustees Frisco Employees Hosp. Assn. Mem. nat. council YMCA's. Mem. Nat. Def. Transp. Assn. (life; continental membership com. transp. dept.), Am. Mgmt. Assn., Springfield C. of C., Exec. Assn. Grad. Sch. Bus. of Columbia. Presbyn. Mason (Shriner). Club: Hickory Hills Country. Home: Route 12 Box 342-A Arlington Dr Springfield MO 65804 Office: 3253 E Trafficway Springfield MO 65802

BESHEARS, ROBERT GENE, lawyer; b. Charleston, Ark., Aug. 24, 1931; s. Allen and Goldie (Stovall) B.; B.S., U. Ariz., 1958, LL.B., 1959; m. Doris Marie Muchmore, Dec. 31, 1952; children-John Robert, Michael Arthur, Charles Phillip. Admitted to Ariz. bar, 1959, since practiced in Phoenix; partner firm O'Connor, Cavanagh, Anderson, Westover, Killingsworth & Beshears, 1963—. Active numerous fund-raising drives for civic and philanthropic orgns. Served with USAF, 1951-55. Recipient Pima County Bar Aux. scholarship award, 1958. Mem. Internat. Assn. Ins. Counsel, Am. Judicature Soc., State Bar Ariz. (co-chmn. standard interrogatories com. 1965), Am., Maricopa County bar assns., Ariz. Law Alumnae Assn. (charter), Beta Gamma Sigma, Phi Kappa Phi, Phi Delta Phi. Republican. Episcopalian. Club: Paradise Valley Country (Phoenix). Contbr. legal jours. Editor Ariz. Law Rev., 1958-59. Home: 4211 E Highlands Dr Paradise Valley AZ 85253 Office: 3003 N Central Av Phoenix AZ 85002

BESLEY, LOWELL, forester; b. Balt., Aug. 20, 1909; s. Fred Wilson and Bertha Adelaide (Simonds) B.; B.S., Cornell, 1931; M.F. cum laude, Yale, 1932; m. Elizabeth Stewart Wise, Sept. 21, 1932. Field asst. Md. Dept. Forestry, 1925-31; field asst., technicin N.E. and Appalachian Forest expt. sta., U.S. Forest Service, 1931-32, 33-34; research asst. Duke Forest, N.C. 1932-33; supt. CCC Camp, Md., 1933; exec. sec. W.Va. State Planning Bd., 1942; forestry edn. cons. Am. Forestry Assn., 1947, exec. dir. and forester, 1953-56; chmn. woodlands research dept. Pulp and Paper Research Inst. Can., 1956-69, dir. woodlands research div., 1969—; forestry cons. for C.D. Schultz and Assos., B.C., 1951-52; instr. Pa. State Coll., 1934-36, asst. prof. forestry, 1936-37, W.Va. U., 1937, asso. prof., 1938, prof. forestry mgt., 1946-48; prof., head forestry dept. U. B.C., 1948-50, dean faculty forestry, 1950-53; v.p. Besley & Rodgers, Inc., 1955-60, pres., 1960—. Asso. del. 6th Brit. Commonwealth Forestry Conf., Can., 1952; chmn. Natural Resources Council of Am., 1955. Asso. commr. Forest Fire Protection, NRC (Can.), 1960-68. Served as lt. comdr., bur. aero. and Pacific, USNR, 1942-46. Mem. T.A.P.P.I. (U.S.; sect. Can.) Soc. Am. Foresters, Canadian Inst. Forestry (dir. 1951, 59-65, v.p. 1959- 61, pres. 1961-63), Canadian Pulp and Paper Assn. (asso. woodlands sect.), Forest Products Research Soc., Assn. B.C. Foresters (v.p., 1952), Canadian Forestry Assn. (dir. 1952), Sigma Xi, Alpha Chi Rho. Home: 58 Elmwood Av Senneville 830 Quebec Canada Office: 570 Saint John's Rd Pointe Claire 720 Quebec Canada

BESS, HENRY ALVER, educator; b. Newville, Ala., Jan. 21, 1907; s. Henry Cleatus and Mary Jane (Kirkland) B.; B.S., Auburn U., 1927; M.S., U. Fla., 1931; Ph.D., Ohio State U., 1934; NRC scholar, U. Cal. at Riverside, 1935-36; m. Ina Ozeal Green, Aug. 25, 1935; children—Henry David, Stephen Green. Entomologist div. insect. investigations U.S. Dept. Agr., 1936-48; sr. prof. entomologist, sr. entomologist U. Hawaii, 1948—; Fulbright scholar, Ceylon, 1954-55, Kenya, 1960-61; research Japan, S.E. Asia and Africa, summers 1963-66, Ceylon and S.E. Asia, fall 1968. Del. Pacific Sci. Congress, Manila, 1953, Honolulu, 1961, Toyko, 1966, Internat. Congress Entomology, Montreal, Can., 1956, Vienna, Austria, 1960, London, Eng., 1964. Mem. Entomol. Soc. Am., Ecol. Soc. Am., Hawaiian Entomol. Soc., A.A.A.S. Home: 3364 Emekona Pl Honolulu HI 96822

BESS, WILLIAM THOMAS, Jr., paper co. exec.; b. Huntington, W.Va., Mar. 2, 1924; s. William Thomas and Mary (Simpson) B.; student Marshall Coll., Huntington, 1941-42; B.S., U.S. Mil, Acad., 1945; m. Patricia Waldron, Nov. 24, 1945; children—Patricia Ann, William Thomas III, Barbara Jeanne. Commd. 2d lt. USAAF, 1945, advanced through grades to 1st lt., 1949; resigned, 1949; with Union Bag-Camp Paper Corp. (now named Union Camp Corp.), 1950—, gen. mgr. bag div., 1962—, v.p., 1964—, group v.p. bag and container divs., 1966-69, exec. v.p., 1969—, dir., 1966—. Home: 74 Arcadia Rd Allendale NJ 07401 Office: 233 Broadway New York City NY 10007*

BESSE, HARRY WILLIAM, stockbroker; b. Wareham, Mass., June 9, 1898; s. Frank Alden and Mary (Gammons) B.; A.B., Tufts Coll., 1920; m. Olive Brett, Jan. 11, 1927. With Boston Stock Exchange, 1927—, pres., 1946-62; with Stock Clearing Corp., Boston, 1946-62, pres., 1946-62; chmn. bd. Hutchins, Mixter and Parkinson, Inc., Boston, 1949—; dir. Allegheny Airlines, Boston Garden Arena Corp.; pres., dir., chmn. bd. Ventura Internat. Moderator, Town of Gilmanton (N.H.). Served as col. USAAF, 1942-46. Mem. U.S. C. of C. (finance com.). Home: Gilmanton NH 03237 Office: 2 Center Plaza Boston MA 02108

BESSE, RALPH MOORE, lawyer; b. Shadyside, O., Nov. 23, 1905; s. Jesse A. and Hope (Fish) B.; A.B., Heidelberg Coll., 1926, L.H.D. (hon.); J.D., U. Mich., 1929; LL.D., Baldwin-Wallace Coll., Oberlin Coll., Case Inst. Tech., Cleve. Marshall Law Sch., Wilberforce Coll., Western Res. U.; m. Augusta Woodward Mitchell, Apr. 28, 1934; children—Jean Elizabeth (Mrs. Ralph Minehart), William Truman, Robert Allen. Admitted to Ohio bar, 1930; atty. Squire, Sanders & Dempsey, Cleve., 1929-48, partner 1940-48, 70—; v.p. Cleve. Electric Illuminating Co., 1948-53; exec. v.p., 1953-60, pres., 1960-67, chmn. bd., chief exec. officer, 1967-70; dir. Acme- Cleve. Corp., Nat. Machinery Co., Tremco Mfg. Co., Cleve. Electric Illuminating Co., Am. Airlines, Inc., Cleve. Trust Co. Trustee Heidelberg Coll., Tiffin, O., Ursuline Coll., Cleve., Case-Western Res. U., U. Circle Devel. Found., John Huntington Fund of Edn., John Huntington Art and Poly. Trust; chmn. Cleve. Inner City Action Com. 1967-68; mem. Carnegie Commn. on Future of Higher Edn.; chmn. Nat. Adv. Com. Jr. Colls., 1965-66; chmn. Cleve. Commn. on Higher Edn., 1956—; v.p. Friends Cleve. Pub. Library; mem. Nat. Adv. Com. Vocational Edn., 1964-66; v.p., sec. Ednl. Research Council, 1958—; campaign chmn. Cleve. Community Chest, 1956; pres. United Appeal, 1960; dist. chief Cleve. Ordnance Dist., 1951-62; chmn. Ohio Community Coll. Bd., 1962-63; mem. Ohio Interim Commn. on Higher Edn. Beyond High Sch., 1961-62. Mem. Am. Mgmt. Assn. (dir.), Am. Bar Assn. (chmn. pub. utility sect. 1956), Ohio, Cleve. chambers commerce, Ohio Electric Utility Inst. (pres. 1956-58). Republican. Conglist. Clubs: Union, Canterbury Golf, Fifty (pres. 1962-63). Home: 2701 Ashley Rd Shaker Heights OH 44122 Office: 1800 Union Commerce Bldg Cleveland OH 44115

BESSER, ALBERT GORDON, lawyer; b. Newark, Nov. 19, 1924; s. Hyman and Fannie (Bear) B.; B.A., Yale, 1945, LL.B., 1949; m. Gretchen Rous, Dec. 28, 1953; children—James, Neal, Brian. Admitted to N.Y. bar, 1949, N.J. bar, 1953, U.S. Dist. Cts. Eastern and So. Dists. N.Y., Ct. Appeals, 2d and 3d Circuits, U.S. Supreme Ct.; asso. Carter, Ledyard & Milburn, N.Y.C., 1949-53; asst. U.S. atty. Dist. N.J., 1953-56; pvt. practice, Newark, 1956-60; mem. firm Hannoch, Weisman, Stern & Besser, Newark, 1960—; instr. econs. Yale, 1946-47; vis. lectr. law Rutgers Law Sch., 1953-55, 60-62. Chmn. United Community Fund, South Orange, N.J., 1965-66. Served with OSS, AUS, 1943-46; CBI. Mem. Assn. Bar City N.Y., N.J., Essex County bar assns., Order of Coif, Phi Beta Kappa. Editor: Yale Law Jour., 1948-49, N.J. Law Jour., 1970—. Home: 227 Tillou Rd South Orange NJ 07079 Office: 744 Broad St Newark NJ 07102

BESSEY, ROBERT JOHN, educator; b. East Lansing, Mich., Apr. 8, 1916; s. Ernst Athearn and Edith C. (Higgins) B.; B.S., Mich. State U., 1937; M.S., U. Mich., 1938, Ph.D., 1943; m. Winifred Christianson, Oct. 19, 1945; children—John, Richard. Instr., Albion Coll., 1942; instr. U. Ida., 1942-44, asst. prof., 1944-47; asst. prof. U. Okla., 1947-53; asst. prof. U. Wyo., 1953-56, asso. prof., 1956-58, prof. physics, 1958—, dir. various NSF Insts. for Sci. Tchrs. Summer visitor High Altitude Obs., Boulder, Colo., 1961, 62, 63; vis. scientist Sonnenborgh Obs., Utrecht, Nethlands, 1968-69. Mem. Am. Phys. Soc., Am. Astron. Soc., Am. Assn. Physics Tchrs., Colo.-Wyo. Acad. Sci., Sigma Xi, Phi Kappa Phi. Kiwanian. Home: 601 S 15th Laramie WY 82070

BESSEY, WILLIAM HIGGINS, physicist, educator; b. East Lansing, Mich., Mar. 18, 1913; s. Ernst Athearn and Edith Carleton (Higgins) B.; S.B., U. Chgo., 1934; M.S., Carnegie Inst. Tech., 1935, D.Sc., 1940; m. Thelma Moyer Shelly, Sept. 8, 1945; children—Barbara Lynn, Karen Elizabeth. Teaching asst. Carnegie Inst. Tech., 1934-39., instr., asst. prof., 1942-52; instr. S.D. Sch. Mines, 1939-40, N.C. State Coll., 1940-42; asso. prof., then prof. U. Mo. Sch. Mines and Metallurgy, 1952-56; prof., head dept. physics Butler U., 1956—; summer instr. New Paltz (N.Y.) State Tchrs. Coll., 1953, Mich. State U., 1954; summer staff IBM Research Lab., Poughkeepsie, 1956. Fellow A.A.A.S.; mem. Am. Phys. Soc., Am. Assn. Physics Tchrs. (pres. Ind. sect.), Ind. Acad. Sci., Sci. Research Soc. Am., Phi Beta Kappa, Sigma Xi, Phi Kappa Phi, Tau Kappa Epsilon. Home: 7454 N Chester Av Indianapolis, IN 46240.

BESSIE, SIMON MICHAEL, publisher; b. N.Y.C., Jan. 23, 1916; s. Abraham and Ella (Brainin) B.; B.A. magna cum laude, Harvard, 1936; m. Constance Ernst, Sept. 12, 1945; children—Nicholas, Katherine; m. 2d, Cornelia Schaeffer, Dec. 21, 1968. Reporter, Newark Star Eagle, 1936; research dept. RKO-Radio Pictures, 1936-38; editor Market Research Monthly, 1938: free lance writer, Europe, Africa, 1938-39; asso. editor, war editor, war corr. Look mag., 1940-42; editor Harper & Bros., 1946- 52, gen. editor, 1952-59; co-founder Atheneum Publishers, 1959, pres., 1963—. Lectr. English, Columbia, 1953-59; dir. Novel Workshop, New School, 1959-63; dir. Franklin Book programs, 1963—; bd. overseers vis. com. history dept. Harvard, 1964—; dir. Am. Book Publishers' Council, 1964-69; chmn. trade book div. Assn. Am. Publishers, 1970—. Service, Algiers, Sicily, Italy, 1943-44; chief news br. psychol. warfare br. Armed Forces hdqrs. Algiers and Naples, 1943-44; chief psychol. warfare combat team So. France, 1944; dep. dir. USIS, France, 1944-46. Recipient Medal of Freedom, 1946. Mem. Council Fgn. Relations, P.E.N., Phi Beta Kappa. Clubs: Century Assn., Harvard (N.Y.C.); Federal City (Washington). Author: Jazz Journalism, 1938. Contbr. numerous articles mags. Home: Joshuatown Rd Lyme CT 06371 Office: 122 E 42d St New York City NY 10017

BESSIN, HYMAN, corp. exec. Pres. Ackland Ltd., McLennan, McFeeley & Prior Ltd., Shane Distbrs. Lts., B & V Mgmt. Services Ltd., Rachel Investments Ltd., Bob Lalande Motors Ltd., Winston Hall Ltd.; sec. treas. Community Video Ltd.; dir. Mizrachi Bank Israel. Nat. pres. Canadian Zionist Fedn.; trustee Yeshiva U., N.Y.C. Home: 438 Daly Av Ottawa 2 Ontario Canada Office: 1300 Michael St Ottawa Ontario Canada*

BESSMAN, MAURICE JULES, educator; b. Newark, July 31, 1928; s. Edward Seymour and Sara (Greenberg) B.; A.B., Harvard, 1949; M.S., Tufts U., 1952, Ph.D., 1955; m. Zita Goss, Feb. 23, 1952; children—Sheri, Cindee, Edward, Debra. Postdoctoral fellow NIH, Washington U., St. Louis, 1958: mem. faculty Johns Hopkins, 1958—, prof. biology, 1966—. Mem. Am. Soc. Biol. Chemists, Am. Chem. Soc., Am. Assn. U. Profs., A.A.A.S., Md. Acad. Sci., Sigma Psi. Home: 4715 Parmelee Rd Baltimore, MD 21208.

BESSMAN, SAMUEL PAUL, physician, educator; b. Newark, Feb. 3, 1921; s. Edward S. and Sara R. (Greenberg) B.; student Coll. William and Mary, 1938-41; M.D., Washington U., 1944; m. Alice Neuman, July 3, 1945; children—Joel David, Ellen. Intern, asst. resident St. Louis Children's Hosp., 1944-45; asst. prof. pediatrics George Washington U., 1947-54; dir. research Children's Hosp., Washington, 1947-54; asso. prof. pediatrics U. Md., 1954-59, prof. pediatric research, 1959-68, prof. biochemistry, 1962-68; prof., chmn. dept. pharmacology U. So. Cal., 1968—, prof. pediatrics, 1969—; dir. research Rosewood State Hosp., Md., 1962-68, Jewish Home for Retarded Children, Washington, 1962-68. Pres. 1st Dist. Community Council, Balt., 1965. Trustee Robert Lindner Found. Served with USPHS, 1945-47. Recipient Crawford Long award U. Ga., 1963. Fellow Am. Acad. Pediatrics, A.A.A.S.; mem. Am. Soc. Biol. Chemists, Soc. Pediatric Research, Am. Inst. Nutrition, Am. Soc. Pharmacology and Exptl. Therapeutics, Sigma Xi, Alpha Omega

Alpha. Editor Biochem. Medicine; editorial bd. Analytical Biochemistry, Current Med. Digest. Research on treatment of lead poisoning, theoretical basis of coma, mechanism of insulin action chemistry mental retardation. Home: 3111 Chandelle Rd Los Angeles CA 90046

BESSON, FRANK SCHAEFFER, Jr., ret. army officer; b. Detroit, Mich., May 30, 1910; s. Frank Schaeffer and Virginia (Koehler) B.; B.S., U.S. Mil. Acad., 1932; M.S. in Civil Engring. Mass. Inst. Tech., 1935; grad. Engr. Sch., company officers' course, 1937; m. Nancy Sessions Morris, Dec. 3, 1934; children—Woodson Taliaferro, Frank Schaeffer III, Peter Richard. Commd. 2d lt., U.S.A., 1932, advanced through grades to general; asst. to dist. engr., Vicksburg Engr. Dist., 1932-34. Portland (Ore.) Engr. Dist., 1937-40; in devel. of mil. engr. equipment Engr. Bd., Fort Belvoir, Va., 1940-41; chief Devel. Branch, Office of chief engr., Washington, D.C., 1942-43; asst. dir., gen. mgr. 3d Mil. Railway Service, Teheran, Iran, Dec. 1943-May 1944; dir., gen. mgr. May 1944-May 1945; dep. chief. Transp. officer, Army Forces, Western Pacific, June 1945-Aug. 1945; dir., gen. mgr. 3d Mil. Ry. Service, Japan, Sept. 1945-Mar. 1946; transp. officer, 8th Army, Japan, Apr.-July 1946; transp. officer, F.E.C. and S.C.A.P., Japan, Aug. 1946-Nov. 1948; asst. chief transp., Dept. Army, 1948-52, dep. chief of transp., spl. asst. for Army Aviation, 1952-53, comdg. Transp. Tng. Command, Ft. Eustis, Va., 1953-54; asst. chief of staff for logistics SHAPE, 1955- 56, asst. chief of staff for programs, 1956-57; chief of transp. Dept. of Army, Washington, 1958-62; commanding officer Army Materiel Command, 1962-69; chmn. joint logistics rev. bd. Office Sec. Def., 1969-70; retired, 1970; mem. bd. incorporators, dir. Nat. Ry. Passenger Corp., 1970—. Decorated D.S.M. with 2 bronze oak leaf clusters, Legion of Merit (U.S.); comdr. Order of Brit. Empire; Iranian Order of Hoymayoun. Mem. Am. Helicopter Soc., Inc., Am. Soc. C.E. Club: Army and Navy Country (Washington). Address: 1200 Huntley Pl Alexandria VA 20038

BEST, ALBERT MARLIN, agrl. engr.; b. Knox, Pa., Sept. 20, 1919; s. George Washington and Ada A. (Master) B.; B.S., Pa. State U., 1942; m. Florence Jane Evans, June 15, 1946; children—David, Barbara (Mrs. Paul Ruskin), Nancy, Susan. Product design engr. New Holland (Pa.) div. Sperry Rand Corp., 1942-51, research engr., 1951-53, research and devel. mgr., 1953-69, dir. engring. research, 1969—. Treas. New Holland Borough Sch. Dist., 1956-64; sec. New Holland Borough Authority, 1971—. Mem. Am. Soc. Agrl. Engrs. (dir. 1967-69, adminstrv. v.p. 1969-72), Am. Forage and Grassland Council, Am. Soc. Engring. Edn., Nat. Soc. Profl. Engrs., Agrl. Research Inst. div. Nat. Acad. Sci. (dir.). Kiwanian. Patentee farm equipment. Home: 5 Kutz Av New Holland PA 17557 Office: Sperry Rand Corp New Holland PA 17557

BEST, ARTHUR C., wholesale food co. exec.; s. John C. and Kathleen (Cox) B.; B.S., Ia. State U., 1939; M.B.A., Harvard, 1941; m. Ruby Cullins, Jan. 21, 1944; children—Julia Best (Mrs. Erwin), Karen K., Arthur C. Sec., treas. Malone & Hyde Inc., Memphis. 1945—. Served to lt. comdr. USNR. World War II. Home: 60 Eastland Dr Memphis, TN 38111. Office: 1451 Union Av Memphis TN 38104

BEST, CHARLES HERBERT, physiologist, educator; b. West Pembroke, Me., Feb. 27, 1889; s. Herbert Huestis and Luella (Fisher) B.; B.A., U. Toronto, 1921, M.A., 1922, M.D., 1925; D.Sc., U. London (Eng.), 1928, U. Chgo., 1941, Paris, 1945, Cambridge U., 1946, Oxford U., 1947, Paris, 1945, Cambridge U., 1946, Oxford U., 1947, U. Laval, 1952, U. Me., 1955, Northwestern U., 1959, Laurentian U., 1971; hon. degrees univs. of Chile, Uruguay, San Marcos, Peru; Dr. Medicine h.c., univs. of Amsterdam, Louvain and Liege, 1947; LL.D., Dalhousie U., 1949, Queens U., 1950, U. Melbourne, 1952, U. Edinburgh, 1959, U. Toronto, 1970; Hon. Dr., Central U. Venezuela, 1958; Dr. Medicine h.c., Thessaloniki, 1963, (hon.), Freie U. Berlin, 1966; m. Margaret Hooper Mahon, Sept. 3, 1924; children—Charles Alexander, Henry Bruce Macleod. With U. Toronto, 1920—, fellow dept. physiology, 1920-21, research mem. Counaught Labs., 1922-32, research asso. Banting-Best Dept. Medicine Research, 1923-41, dir., 1941- 67, emeritus, 1967—; asst. prof. physiol. hygiene, 1926-29, acting head dept. physiol. hygiene, 1929-41, prof. physiology, 1929—, head dept., 1929-65, dir. emeritus, 1967—, grad. lectr., 1965—; asso. dir. Counaught Labs., 1932-41. Mem. adv. com. on med. research WHO, 1963—; mem. bd. sci. dirs. Jackson Lab. Trustee Nutrition Found. Served as sgt. 70th Battery, 2d Canadian Tanks Corps, with B.E.F., World War I. Dir. med. research div. Royal Canadian Navy, surgeon with rank of capt. Discoverer of insulin with F. G. Banting, 1921. Instrumental in initiation of Canadian serum project for provision of dried human serum of mil. use. Decorated knight comdr. Mil. and Hospitaller Order St. Lazarus of Jerusalem; F.N.G. Starr gold medal Canadian Med. Assn., 1936, Charles Mickle fellowship Council of Faculty Medicine, U. Toronto, 1939; Baly medal Royal Coll. Physicians, 1939; Flavelle medal Royal Soc. Can., 1950; Order Brit. Empire (civil), 1944, Legion of Merit (U.S.), 1947; King Haakon VI Cross of Liberation (Norway) 1947; comdr. Order of Crown, Belgium, 1948; John Phillips Meml. medal A.C.P., 1953; J. Howard Reber medal Phila. Metabolic Assn., 1955; Banting medal Am. Diabetes Assn.; Croonian lectureship The Royal Soc., 1955; Civic award of merit Toronto, 1958; Dale medal Soc. for Endocrinology, 1959; commemorative medal Czechoslovak Soc. Phys. Medicine, 1962; grand silver medal City of Paris, 1962; 1st Joslin medal New Eng. Diabetes Assn., 1965; Centennial medal, 1967; companion Order of Can., 1967, comdr. Order Brit. Empire; Companion of Honor. Fellow Royal Soc. London, Royal Soc. Can., Royal Coll. Phys. and Surg. Can., Physiol. Soc., Biochem. Soc. (Eng.), Royal Coll. Physicians (Edinburgh), Toronto Acad. Medicine (hon.); mem. Am. Soc. Clin. Nutrition (hon.), Am. Diabetes Assn. (hon., pres. 1948, council), Am. Acad. Arts and Sci., Royal Acad. Scis., Amsterdam, Canadian Assn. Gastroenterology (hon.), Acad. Royal de Med. Belgique, Soc. de Farmacol., Buenos Aires; mem. Royal Soc. of Med. (hon.), Am. (council), Canadian physiol. socs., Am. Soc. Biol. Chem., Am. Soc. Clin. Investigation, Nat. Acad. Scis. (fgn. asso.), Am. Philos. Soc., Assn. Am. Physicians, Internat. Union Physiol. Scis. (1st pres. 1953), Physiol. Soc. Gt. Britain (hon.), European Assn. for Study Diabetes (hon.), Pontificial Acad. Scis., Nu Sigma Nu, Alpha Omega Alpha, The Athenaeum. Author: (with F.G. Banting) The Internal Secretion of the Pancreas (original publ. on insulin), 1922; (with N.B. Taylor) The Physiological Basis of Medical Practice, 8th edit., 1966; The Human Body, 4th edit., 1963; The Living Body, 4th edit.; Selected Papers of Charles H. Best, 1963; also numerous publs. on insulin, histaminase, muscular exercise, choline, carbohydrate and fat metabolism, heparin, shock. Home: 105 Woodlawn Av W Toronto 190 Ontario Canada

BEST, ELMER RICHARD, life ins. co. exec.; b. Cin., Jan. 24, 1914; s. Harry and Hattie (Ruediger) B.; A.B., Harvard, 1936, LL.B., 1939; m. Marti Janet Cohan, Aug. 3, 1940; children—Robert Charles, Philip Cohan, Sally Carol. Admitted to Ohio bar, 1939; with Union Central Life Ins. Co., Cin., 1940- -, treas., 1958—, v.p., 1962—. Bd. govs. Cin. Salvation Army. Served to lt. (j.g.) USNR, World War II. Mem. Cin. Financial Analysts Soc., Phi Beta Kappa. Presbyn. (elder). Mason (Shriner). Clubs: Bankers (past bd. govs.), Queen City, Western Hills Country (Cin.). Home: 1976 Beech Grove Dr Cincinnati, OH 45238. Office: PO Box 179 Cincinnati OH 45201

BEST, JAMES MACLEOD, lawyer; b. Watertown, S.D., Nov. 1, 1903; s. Robert and Jessie Isabella (MacLeod) B.; A.B., Carleton Coll., 1925; J.D., U. Chgo., 1927; m. Katherine Denning; 1 son, James Reynolds. Admitted to Ill. bar, 1928; practied in Chgo. as mem. firm Balhatchet & Best, 1928-31; asso. firm Kirkland, Fleming, Green, Martin & Ellis, 1931-32; atty. for RFC charge litigation in Chgo., 1932-35; atty. Quaker Oats Co., 1935-46, gen. counsel, 1946-55; engaged in investments and cons., 1956—. Pres. bd. trustees Unified Sch. Dist., 1960-61. Mem. Am. (sec. div. food, drug and cosmetic law 1948-55), Ill., N.Y. State, Chgo. (bd. mgrs. 1946-48) bar assns., U.S. Trade-Mark Assn. (dir. 1948-55, pres. 1952-53), Clan MacLeod Soc., Isle of Skye (Scotland) Law Club, Legal Club, Phi Alpha Delta. Presbyn. Clubs: University (Chgo.); Executives (dir. 1950-52); Economic. Author papers on food law. Address: 263 Valley View Dr Paradise CA 95969

BEST, JOHN STEVENS, lawyer; b. Arlington Heights, Ill., May 18, 1906; s. Bruce Taylor and Genevieve (Stevens) B.; A.B., U. Wis., 1928, LL.B., 1930; m. Pamelia Laurence, July 9, 1934 (dec.): children—Pamelia, Bruce, Mary (Mrs. Joseph P. Newhauser, Jr.); m. 2d, Helen Meredith. Admitted Wis. bar, 1930, practiced law, Milw., 1938—, asso. Lecher, Michael, Whyte & Spohn, 1938-43; mem. firm Michael, Best & Friedrich, and predecessors, Milw., 1943—. Income tax counsel, gen. counsel Wis. Tax Comm., 1930-38. C.P.A., Wis. Mem. Am., Wis., Milw. bar assns., Sigma Nu, Alpha Kappa Psi, Phi Alpha Delta, Beta Gamma Sigma, Order of Coif. Clubs: Milwaukee, University (Milw.); Madison. Home: Town Line Rd Menomonee Falls WI 53051 Office: 626 E Wisconsin Av Milwaukee WI 53202

BEST, MARSHALL AYRES, publisher; b. N.Y.C., Nov. 26, 1901; s. Albert Starr and Marjorie (Ayres) B.; A.B. summa cum laude, Harvard, 1923; postgrad. U. Grenoble Grenoble (France), 1923-24; m. Elizabeth Hoyt Worthington, 1939 (div.); children—Mary (Mrs. Burt Alcantara), John Ayres. With Viking Press, N.Y.C., 1925—, dir., sec., 1927, gen. mgr., 1935, v.p., 1956-68, sr. editorial cons., 1969—. Dir., mem. exec. com. Am. Book Pubs. Council, 1962-65. Mem. Phi Beta Kappa. Clubs: Century Assn., Harvard (N.Y.C.), P.E.N. (v.p. 1967-70). Author poems, articles, translations. Home: Sharon CT 06069 Office: 625 Madison Av New York City NY 10022

BEST, NORMAN FRANK, advt. exec.; b. Chgo., Jan. 17, 1912; s. Victor Charles and Winnifred Edith (Thomson) B.; student Am. Inst. Banking, N.Y.C., 1931-32, electronic engring. Dayton U., 1943-44; m. Muriel Noreen Atkinson, Dec. 16, 1944; children—Shirley Anne (Mrs. Joseph Lambert) and Roger N., Michael R. With Chase Nat. Bank, N.Y.C., 1929-35; with Lennen & Mitchell, advt., 1936-38; program dir. CBS, Hollywood, Cal., 1939-40; with Erwin Wasey & Co., advt., 1946-58, v.p. account mgmt., 1950-58; dir. Erwin Wasey & Co. Can., 1954-58; v.p., gen. mgr. Campbell- Mithun, Inc., Mpls., 1958-61, exec. v.p., 1961-68, Los Angeles, also dir., mem. finance com.; v.p., account supr. Grey Advt., Inc., Los Angeles, Cal., 1968—. Served as squadron leader RAF, 1940-46. Mem. Los Angeles Advt. Club. Home: 666 Walther Way Los Angeles CA 90049 Office: 3435 Wilshire Blvd Los Angeles CA 90002

BEST, QUESTIN WILLIAM, rock products co. exec.; b. Mpls., July 9, 1901; s. Everett R. and Caroline J. (LaFontaine) B.; student U. Minn.; m. Helene Von Korff, July 23, 1923. Vice pres., dir. Consol Rock Products Co., Los Angeles, 1945- 56, exec. v.p., dir., 1956-61, pres., dir. 1961-71, chmn. bd., chief exec. officer, 1971—. Trustee Am. Library of Information, Cal. Museum Found.; dir. Cal. Assn. for Nat. Cowboy Hall of Fame. Mem. Los Angeles C. of C. (dir. 1954-55; chmn. constrn. industries com. 1954-55), Pacific Coast Hunter, Jumper and Stock Horse Assn. Inc. (pres. 1958, 60, dir.), Am. Horse Shows Assn. Inc. (judge, dir.), Nat. Ready Mixed Concrete Assn. (past pres., dir.), So. Cal. Rock Products Assn. (past pres., dir.), Cal. Mfrs. Assn. (dir.), Mchts. and Mfrs. Assn. (dir.), Am. Charros Assn. Clubs: California, Jonathan (1st v.p. 1957-58, dir. 1955-56, 57-58) (Los Angeles); Rancheros, Visitadores (dir.) (Santa Barbara, Cal.). Home: 1655 Rancho Av Glendale CA 91201 Office: 2730 S Alameda St Los Angeles CA 90054

BESTOR, ARTHUR EUGENE, Jr., historian; b. Chautauqua, N.Y., Sept. 20, 1908; s. Arthur Eugene and Jeanette Louise (Lemon) B.; Ph.B., Yale, 1930, Ph.D., 1938; M.A., Oxford U., 1956; LL.D., Lincoln U., 1959; m. Anne Carr, Mar. 5, 1939 (dec. Feb. 1948); children—William Porter, Thomas Wheaton; m. 2d, Dorothy Alden Koch, Nov. 23, 1949; 1 son, Theodore Charles. Instr., Yale, 1930- 31, 34-36; asso. history Tchrs. Coll., Columbia, 1936-37, asst. prof., 1937-42; asst. prof. humanities Stanford, 1942-45, asso. prof. history, 1945-46; Newberry fellow Newberry Library, Chgo., 1946; lectr. U. Wis., 1947; asso. prof. history U. Ill., 1947-51, prof., 1951-62; prof. history U. Wash., Seattle, 1962—; Harmsworth prof. Am. history, Oxford U., 1956-57; Fulbright vis. prof. U. Tokyo, 1967. Bd. dirs. Univ. Centers for Rational Alternatives, 1970—. Guggenheim fellow, 1953-54,61-62. Mem. Am. Hist. Assn. (Beveridge Meml. award 1946), Orgn. Am. Historians (bd. editors Miss. Valley Hist. Rev. 1951-54, exec. com. 1964-67), Ill. (pres. 1954-55), Wash. hist. socs., Council for Basic Edn. (pres. 1956-57, bd. dirs. 1956—), Am. Assn. U. Profs., Am. Studies Assn. (v.p. 1962), N.A.A.C.P., Phi Beta Kappa. Democrat. Club: Elizabethan (New Haven). Author: David Jacks of Monterey, 1945; Education and Reform at New Harmony, 1948; Backwood Utopias, 1950, 2d enlarged edit., 1970; Educational Wastelands, 1953; The Restoration of Learning, 1955; (with Richard N. Leopold and others) Problems of American History, 1952, 3d edit., 1966; (with David C. Mearns and Jonathan Daniels) Three Presidents and Their Books, 1955; (with John H. Murray and others) The Heritage of the Middle West, 1958; (with William H. Cartwright and others) Interpreting and Teaching American History, 1961; also articles in hist. jours., Proc. Am. Philos. Soc., Daedalus, New Republic, others; several articles reprinted in anthologies. Home: 4553 55th Av NE Seattle WA 98105

BESTOR, CHARLES LEMON, composer, educator; b. N.Y.C., Dec. 21, 1924; s. Arthur Eugene and Jeanette Louise (Lemon) B.; student Yale, 1943-44; B.A., Swarthmore Coll., 1948; M.Mus., U. Ill., 1951; B.S., Juilliard Sch. Music, 1951; m. Ann Newbold Elder, Nov. 1, 1952; children—Charles Elder, Geoffrey Grant, Phillip Russell, Leslie Ann, Wendy Lynn, Jennifer Lee. Mem. faculty Juilliard Sch. Music, 1951-53, 56-59, asst. to dean, 1951-53, concert mgr., 1952-59, bus. mgr., 1955-59; mgr. Juilliard Orch. European tour sponsored by U.S. State Dept., ANTA, 1958; asst. prof. music U. Colo., 1939-64; prof., dean Coll. Music, Willamette U., 1964-71; prof., head dept. music U. Ala., 1971—. Mem. exec. council N.W. Regional Inst. for Music in Contemporary Edn., 1966-68; asso. dir. Peter Britt Music Festival, Jacksonville, Ore., 1966—; mem. Gov.'s Adv. Com. Arts and Humanities, 1963—. Past mem. exec. com. Morningside Heights, Inc. (N.Y.C.). Served to lt. USNR, 1943-46. Mem. Am. Assn. U. Profs., Phi Beta Kappa, Pi Kappa Lambda, Phi Mu Alpha Sinfonia, Phi Kappa Psi (past mem. nat. exec. com.), Theta Alpha Phi, Omicron Delta Kappa. Rotarian. Composer: Undine, 1951; Three Choruses, 1955; J.B., 1962; Piano Sonata, 1963; Measure for Measure, 1963; A Wind in the Willows, 1964; My Love and I, 1966; Suite for Strings, 1968; Concerto Grosso for Percussion and Orchestra, 1968; Improvisation I for Tape Recorder Alone, 1971; Improvisation II for Tape Recorder and Instruments, 1971; In Memoriam to texts by Malcolm X, 1969; Suite for Recorders, 1970. Home: 260 Hansen Av Salem OR 97302

BETANCES, LUIS RAUL, diplomat of Dominican Republic; b. San Francisco de Macoris, Dominican Republic, Sept. 6, 1912; s. Luis Adolfo Betances Coen and Carmen Ricart Cavan; D.Social Scis. and Pub. Law, Licentiate Pub. Adminstrn., U. Havana (Cuba), 1946; m. Ana America Fernandez Delgado, Mar. 19, 1935; 1 dau., Elizabeth Antionette. With Pan Am. Union, 1954—, chief auditor, 1958, dir. dept. adminstrn., 1962, ambassador at large Dominican Republic, 1964; A.E. & P. of Dominican Republic to UN, 1968—. Decorated Order Christopher Columbus, Order Merit Durate, Sanchez and Mella (Dominican Republic); Order Basco Nunez de Balboa (Panama); Order Civil Merit (Spain); Nat. Order Honor and Merit (Haiti); recipient Gold button Nat. Council Tb Cuba. Mem. Inst. Internat. Auditors, Am. Accounting Assn., Hispano-Luso-Am. Press Assn., Boliverian Soc. Ecuador. Home: 6801 Tulip Hill Terrace Washington DC 20016 Office: 144 E 44th St New York City NY 10017

BETCHER, ALBERT MAXWELL, physician; b. Jersey City, June 22, 1911; s. Jacob and Esther (Popkin) B.; B.S., N.Y. U., 1931; M.D., St. Louis U., 1935; m. Gertrude Weinberger, Sept. 22, 1940; children—Diane Elaine (Mrs. Trister), Peter Andrew, Robert William. Rotating intern Jersey City Med. Centre, 1935-36, resident anesthesiology, 1937-38, staff anesthetist, 1938-41; staff anesthetist Hosp. Joint Diseases, N.Y.C., 1946—, dir. dept., 1947—, also sec. med. adv. bd. and asso. editor hosp. jour., 1960-69, pres., 1970—; asst. clin. prof. anesthesiology Albert Einstein Coll. Medicine, 1955-61, asso. clin. prof., 1961-67; prof. anesthesiology Mt. Sinai Sch. Medicine, City U. N.Y., 1967—. Pres., chmn. bd. trustees Wood Library-Mus. Anesthesiology, 1956-69; trustee Anesthesia Found. Served to lt. col. M.C., AUS, 1941- 46. Decorated Purple Heart, Bronze Star. Diplomate Am. Bd. Anesthesiology (dir. 1967—). Fellow Am. Coll. Anesthesiologists, A.C.P.; mem. Am. Soc. Anesthesiologists (treas. 1958-61, pres. 1962-63), N.Y. Acad. Medicine (sec. 1961-63, chmn. sect. anesthesiology and resuscitation 1963-64), N.Y. Soc. Anesthesiologists (pres. 1955, speaker ho. dels. 1956-59), N.Y. State Med. Soc. (chmn. anesthesiology 1959-60), A.M.A. (residency rev. com. for anesthesiology 1969—), N.Y. Acad. Scis., A.A.A.S., Acad. Anesthesiology, World Fedn. Socs. Anesthesiologists (del., mem. finance com.). Author articles in field. Home: 1435 Lexington Av New York City NY 10028 Office: 1919 Madison Av New York City NY 10035

BETH, RICHARD ALEXANDER, physicist; b. N.Y.C., Jan. 14, 1906; s. Otto Carl Heinrich and Frieda (Unger) B.; B.S., Worcester Poly. Inst., 1927, M.S., 1929, D.Sc., 1963; Dr. Phil.-Nat. in Math., U. Frankfurt am Main (Germany), 1932; m. Hettie Sprague, June 26, 1943; children—Richard Sprague, Hettie Virginia. Instr. physics Worcester Poly. Inst., 1927-29, asst. prof., 1932-39; Am. Exchange fellow, Germany, 1929-32, research asso. Palmer Phys. Lab., Princeton, 1934-35; asso. prof. applied math. Mich. State Coll., 1939-40; physicist, Com. on Passive Protection against Bombing, NRC, Washington, 1940-42; cons. com. on fortification design, 1943-45; mem. Div. 2, NDRC, Princeton U. Sta., 1942-44, dept. head 1942-46; Perkins prof., chmn. physics dept. Western Res. U., 1946-55; physicist accelerator dept. Brookhaven Nat. Lab., 1955—. Expert cons. War Dept., G-2, Alsos Mission in Europe, 1945; cons. Joint Army and Navy Exptl. and Testing Bd., 1943-44; mem. council of reps. Argonne Nat. Lab., Chgo., 1947-54; Fulbright guest prof. U. Innsbruck (Austria), 1954-55, U. Bonn (W. Germany), 1963-64. Recipient U.S. Certificate of Merit for work in World War II, 1948. Fellow Am. Phys. Soc.; mem. Cleve. Physics Soc. (pres. 1950-51), Sigma Xi, Tau Beta Pi, Pi Mu Epsilon, Theta Chi. Conglist. Club: Old Inlet. Writer reports for coms. OSRD, NDRC. Asso. editor: Am. Jour. Physics, 1953-56. Contbr. to Handbook of Physics, Encyclopaedic Dictionary Physics, other sci. publs. Exptl. demonstration of angular momentum of light, 1934-35; of scale effect for projectile penetration of targets, 1941-42. Home: 8 Leisurely Lane Bellport NY 11713 Office: Brookhaven Nat Lab Upton NY 11973

BETHE, HANS ALBRECHT, physicist, educator; b. Strassburg, Alsace-Lorraine, July 2, 1906; s. Albrecht Theodore and Anna (Kuhn) B.; ed. Goethe Gymnasium, Frankfurt on Main, U. Frankfort; Ph.D., U. Munich, 1928; D.Sc., Bklyn. Poly. Inst., 1950, U. Denver, 1952, U. Chgo., 1953, U. Birmingham, 1956, Harvard U., 1958; m. Rose Ewald, 1939; children—Henry, Monica. Came to U.S., 1935. Instr. in theoretical physics, univs. of Frankfort, Stuttgart, Munich and Tubingen, 1928-33; lectr. univs. of Manchester and Bristol, Eng., 1933-35; asst. prof. Cornell U., 1935, prof., 1937—; dir. theoretical physics div. Los Alamos Sci. Lab., 1943-46. Head of Presdl. Study Disarmament, 1958; mem. President's Sci. Adv. Com., 1956-60. Recipient A. Cressy Morrison prize N.Y. Acad. Scis., 1938-40; Presdl. Medal of Merit, 1946; Max Planck medal, 1953; Enrico Fermi award AEC, 1961; Nobel Prize in physics, 1967. Fgn. mem. Royal Soc. London; mem. Am. Philos. Soc., Nat. Acad. Scis. (Henry Draper medal 1968), Am. Phys. Soc. (pres. 1954), Am. Astron. Soc. Author: Mesons and Fields, 1953; Elementary Nuclear Theory, 1957; Quantum Mechanics of One-and Two-Electron Atoms, 1957; Intermediate Quantum Mechanics. 1964. Contbr. to (books) Handbuch der Physik, 1933; Reviews of Modern Physics, 1936-37; Phys. Rev. Office: Lab Nuclear Studies Cornell U Ithaca NY 14850

BETHE, ROBERT SUMNER, mfg. co. exec.; b. Malden, Mass., May 23, 1919; s. Herman W. and Edna (Jackson) B.; B.S., Tufts U., 1941; M.B.A., Harvard, 1947. Exec. trainee Am. Can Co., Seattle, 1947-50, chief internal auditor, N.Y.C., 1950-55; with controller Dover Corp., 1955—, v.p., treas., 1971—; 1964—, dir. subsidiaries. Served with USNR, 1941-45. Club: Winged Foot Golf (Mamaroneck, N.Y.). Home: 190 E 72d St New York City NY 10021 Office: 277 Park Av New York City NY 10017

BETHEL, CARLYSLE ALLEN, banker; b. Nottoway County, Va., Sept. 1, 1904; s. Liston Linwood and Lois (Ransone) B.; LL.B., U. Va., 1928; m. Frances Luckett, Apr. 9, 1935; children—Gracey, Lois. Admitted to N.Y. bar, 1928; with Carter, Ledyard & Milburn, attys., N.Y.C., 1928-37; trust officer Wachovia Bank & Trust Co., Winston-Salem, N.C., 1937-51, sr. v.p., sr. trust officer, 1951-56, vice chmn. bd., 1956—; pres. New South Ins. Co., Winston- Salem; dir. Piedmont Pub. Co., Hanes Dye & Finishing Co., Hanes Hosiery Mills Co. Mem. Bankers Assn. (pres. trust div. 1958-59). Clubs: Old Town, Twin City (Winston-Salem). Home: 2665 Grosvenor Pl Winston-Salem NC 27104 Office: Wachovia Bank & Trust Winston-Salem NC 27101

BETHEL, JAMES SAMUEL, educator, forester; b. New Westminster, B.C., Can., Aug. 13, 1915; s. Joseph and Ruth (Wilkinson) B.; B.S. in Forestry, U. Wash., 1937; M.F. (grad. fellow 1937-39), Duke, 1939, D.Forestry, 1947; m. Marinelle Rives, June 8, 1941; children—Ruth Anne, James Samuel, John Patterson. Instr. forestry Pa. State U., 1939-41; asst. prof. biology Va. Poly. Inst., 1941-42; factory mgr. Tidewater Plywood Co., 1946-49; prof. wood tech., dir. wood products lab. N.C. State Coll., 1949-59, acting dean Grad. Sch., 1958- 59; head spl. projects in sci. edn. sect. NSF, 1959-62; prof. forestry U. Wash., 1962-64, dean Coll. Forestry, 1964—. Pres. Forest Products Sales Co., 1947-49; cons. FAO, adviser Govt. Yugoslavia, 1952; cons. Econ. Devel. Adminstrn., P.R., 1956, Gov. N.C. Research Triangle Com., 1958; mem. agrl. sci. com. U.S. Dept. Agr., 1963, mem. agrl. research planning adv. com., 1969; mem.

Wash. Bd. Natural Resources, 1964—. Bd. dirs. U. Wash. Arboretum Found., 1965—; trustee Keep Washington Green, 1964—. Served to capt. with USAAF, 1942-46. Fellow Inst. Wood Sci., A.A.A.S.; mem. Soc. Am. Foresters, Forest Products Research Soc. (chmn. Carolinas-Chesapeake sect. 1957, mem. nat. exec. bd. 1962-63), Am. Inst. Wood Engrs. (chmn. organizing com. 1957, pres. 1958-59), Soc. Wood Sci. and Tech. (pres. 1960-61, chmn. nat. vis. scientists program 1963), Orgn. Tropical Studies (pres.), Assn. State Coll. and Univ. Research Orgns. (pres. 1969-70), IX Internat. Bot. Congress (chmn. local com., mem. nat. com.; treas. 1968—), Inst. Biol. Sciences, Assn. Tropical Foresters, Assn. Tropical Biologists, Sigma Xi, Phi Sigma, Xi Sigma Pi, Gamma Sigma Delta. Club: Rainier. Author: (with N.C. Brown) Lumber, 1938; (with Panshin Harrar and Baker) Forest Products, 1962; also numerous articles. Home: 3816 E Mercer Way Mercer Island WA 98040 Office: Univ Wash Seattle WA 98105

BETJEMAN, JOHN, poet, author; b. London, Eng., Aug. 28, 1906; s. Ernest Edward and Mabel Bessie (Dawson) B.; student Marlborough Coll., 1925-27, Magdalen Coll., Oxford, 1925-28; m. Penelope Chetwode, June 23, 1932; children—Paul, Candida. Book critic Daily Telegraph, 1952—; weekly column The Spectator, 1954—. Recipient Queen's Gold Medal for poetry, 1960; decorated comdr. Order of British Empire. Mem. Athenaeum. Mem. Ch. of Eng. Clubs: Beefsteak (london); Kildare Street (Dublin). Author: (poems) Mount Zion, 1931, Continual Dew, 1937, Old Lights for New Chancels, 1940, New Bats in Old Belfries, 1945, Selected Poems, 1950, A Few Late Chrysanthemums, 1954, Collected Poems, 1958 (Duff Cooper award; Foyle poetry prize); (prose) Ghastly Good Taste, 1933; First and Last Loves, 1944; (with John Piper) Murray's Guides to Books and Bucks and Berks; (with John Piper) Shell Guide to Norfolk, Shell Guide to Wiltshire, Guide to Shropshire, Buckinghamshire and Berkshire; (with Basil Clarke) High and Low, Victorian and Edwardian London, 1969; (with Basil Clarke) English Churches; (anthologies) (with Geoffrey Taylor) English Landscape Poetry, English Love Poetry; A Ring of Bells, 1963; Summoned by Bells, 1960; High and Low, 1967. Home: The Mead Wantage Berkshire England Office: 43 Cloth Fair London England*

BETLER, RUSSELL P., banker; b. Smethport, Pa., July 26, 1907; s. Charles F. A. and Blanche (Vaux) B.; student U. Pitts., 1926-38, U. Wis. Sch. Banking, 1951; m. Carolyn Margaret Camp, Aug. 1, 1927; children—Reta Pauline (Mrs. Phillip Brown), Audrey Mae (Mrs. Patrick Waterloo), Donna Aryl (Mrs. Robert Faith), Russell P. With Peoples State Bank, also Logan Nat. Bank & Trust Co., New Kensington, Pa., 1924-39; nat. bank examiner Treasury Dept., 1939-52; exec. v.p. Peoples Union Bank & Trust Co. (merged Union Nat. Bank Pitts., 1969), McKeesport, Pa., 1952—, also dir. Past chmn. Elizabeth Twp. Planning Commn. Pres., dir. McKeesport YMCA; bd. dirs. McKeesport Boys Club. Mem. McKeesport C. of C. (bd. dirs.). Mason (Shriner), Kiwanian (past pres. McKeesport). Home: 24 Colonial Dr Mount Vernon McKeesport PA 15135 Office: 301 5th Av McKeesport PA 15132

BETO, GEORGE JOHN, state ofcl., clergyman; b. Hysham, Mont., Jan. 19, 1916; s. Louis H. and Margaret (Witsma) B.; student Concordia Coll., Milw., 1930-35, Concordia Sem., St. Louis, 1935-37, 38-39; B.A., Valparaiso U., 1938; M.A., U. Tex., 1944; Ph.D., 1955; m. Marilynn Knippa, Mar. 5, 1943; children—Dan, Lynn, Mark, Beth. Instr. Concordia Coll., Austin, Tex., 1939-49, pres., 1949-59; vis. instr. U. Tex., 1944; pres. Concordia Theol. Sem., Springfield, Ill., 1959-62; dir. Tex. Dept. Corrections, Huntsville, 1962—. Dir. Huntsville Nat. Bank, 1st Nat. Bank, Palestine, Tex. Sec. Tex. Bd. Corrections, 1953-59, mem. Ill. Parole and Pardon Bd., 1961-62; Am. del. UN Conf. on Prevention Crime and Treatment Offender, Kyoto, Japan, 1970; mem. Nat. C. of C. Panel on Crime Prevention and Control; mem. Commn. on Correctional Facilities and Services. Recipient Tex. Heritage Found. medal for devel. ednl. system Tex. Prison System. Mem. Am. Bar Assn., Am. Soc. Ch. History, Am. Correctional Assn. (past pres.), So. States Prison Assn., Am. Angus Assn., Am. Quarter Horse Assn., Phi Delta Kappa, Alpha Delta Kappa. Lutheran. Clubs: Old Capitol (Houston); Citadel, 40-Acres (Austin). Home: 1206 Av I Huntsville TX 77340 Office: Tex Dept of Corrections Box 99 Huntsville TX 77340

BETSCH, BERTRAM M., corp. ofcl.; b. Union City, N.J., Jan. 15, 1906; s. William and Louisa A. (Eberhardt) B.; B.C.S., N.Y.U., 1927; m. Helen D.J. McDonald, Apr. 14, 1932; children—James E., William E. Staff, Haskins & Sells, C.P.A.'s, 1930-43; supervising accountant Western Electric Co., 1943-44; asst. sec., asst. treas. Electric Bond & Share Co., N.Y.C., 1944-48, sec., treas., 1948—. C.P.A., N.Y., N.J. Mem. Am. Soc. Corporate Secs. (pres. 1958-59), N.Y. State Soc. C.P.A.'s, Am. Inst. Accountants, N.Y. Soc. Security Analysts, Mason. Club: Rock Spring. Home: 198 Sagamore Rd Milburn NJ 07041 Office: Electric Bond & Share Co 2 Rector St New York City NY 10006

BETSCH, W.D., utilities exec. Sr. v.p. Columbia Gas of Ohio, Inc., Columbus. Office: 99 N Front St Columbus OH 43215*

BETTELHEIM, BRUNO, educator; b. Vienna, Austria, Aug. 28, 1903; Ph.D., U. Vienna, 1938; m. Trude Weinfeld, May 14, 1941; children—Ruth, Naomi, Eric. Came to U.S., 1939, naturalized, 1944. Research asso. Progressive Edn. Assn., U. Chgo., 1939-41; asso. prof. psychology Rockford (Ill.) Coll., 1942-44; asst. prof. ednl. psychology U. Chgo., 1944-47, asso. prof., 1947-52, prof., 1952—, Stella M. Rowley Distinguished Service prof. edn., prof. psychology and psychiatry, 1963—; Fellow Am. Psychol. Assn., Am. Orthopsychiat. Assn.; mem. Am. Philos. Assn., Am. Assn. U. Profs., Am. Sociol. Assn., Chgo. Psychoanalytic Soc., Am. Acad. Edn. Author: Dynamics of Prejudice (with Morris Janowitz), 1950; Love is Not Enough—The Treatment of Emotionally Disturbed Children, 1950; Symbolic Wounds, 1954; Truants From Life, 1955; The Informed Heart, 1960; Dialogues with Mothers, 1962; The Empty Fortress, 1967; The Children of the Dream, 1969. Home: 5725 Kenwood Av Chicago IL 60637

BETTENCOURT, PIERRE, artist; b. Normandy, France, 1917. Numerous shows in Paris galleries, Rene Drouin, Daniel Cordier, Arditti. Address: care Galerie Arditti Ste, 15 Rue Miromesnil Paris 8e, France.*

BETTERSWORTH, JOHN KNOX, educator, univ. ofcl.; b. Jackson, Miss., Oct. 1909; s. Horace Greely and Annie McConnell (Murphey) B.; B.A. magna cum laude, Millsaps Coll., 1929; Ph.D., Duke, 1937; m. Ann L. Stephens, Oct. 28, 1943; 1 dau., Nancy Elizabeth. Instr. Jackson (Miss.) Central High Sch., 1930-35; grad. fellow Duke, 1935-37, vis. prof., summer 1940; vis. instr. Asheville (N.C.) Normal, summer 1937; instr. history Miss. State U., State College, 1937, asst. prof., 1938-42, asso. prof., 1945-48, prof., 1948—), head dept. history and govt., 1948-61, dir. Social Sci. Research Center, 1950-60, asso. dean for liberal arts,sch. arts and sci., 1956-61, acad. v.p., 1961-66, acad. v.p., dean faculty, 1966—; text editor Miss. Hist. Commn., 1948—; chmn. Miss. Research Clearing House, 1953-55, Pres., So. Conf. Deans Faculty and Acad. v.ps., 1967-68. Trustee Mississippi Dept. Archives and History. Served as lt. (j.g.) USNR, 1942-45. instr. Naval Indoctrination Sch., Tucson. Fellow Internat. Inst. Arts and Letters; mem. Miss. Hist. Soc. (dir. 1953—, v.p. 1955-56, pres. 1961-62), Am., So. hist. assns., Phi Beta Kappa, Omicron Delta Kappa, Phi Kappa Phi, Phi Alpha Theta, Alpha Tau Omega. Democrat. Episcopalian. Club: Starkville Rotary (pres. 1951-52). Author: Confederate Mississippi, The People and Policies of a Cotton State in Wartime, 1943; People's College: A History of Mississippi State, 1953; Mississippi: A History, 1959; Mississippi in the Confederacy: As They Saw It, 1961; Your Old World Past, 1960; Mississippi: Yesterday and Today, 1965; Inventory for Greatness: The Story of Mississippi Power and Light, 1968; (with others) This Country of Ours, 1965; South of Appomattox, 1959; also contbr. articles to profl. publs. Founder, pub. The Miss. Quarterly. Home: 401 Broad St Starkville MD 39759 Office: Drawer B State College MS 39762

BETTES, MRS. TORREY JAMES, banker; b. Brownwood, Tex., Aug. 10, 1896; d. Robert Baker and Elva (Tannehill) Rogers; grad. U. Tex.; 1918; m. Torrey James Bettes (dec.); 1 dau., Elizabeth Ann (Mrs. Roger Dally). Former chmn. bd. dirs. T.J. Bettes Co., Houston, T. J. Bettes Co. Cal. Episcopalian. Clubs: Houston, Houston Country, River Oaks Garden. Home: 1059 Kirby Dr Houston TX 77019 Office: Bettes Bldg 201 Main St Houston TX 77002

BETTES, WILLIAM A., banker; b. St. Johns County, Fla., 1905. First v.p. Atlantic Nat. Bank Jacksonville (Fla.); chmn. Palatka Atlantic Nat. Bank, Normandy Atlantic Bank. Home: 4249 Robin Hood Rd Jacksonville FL 32210 Office: 121 W Forsythe St Jacksonville FL 32203*

BETTI, UGO, Italian playwright; works include Crime on Goat Island, Landslide, Struggle till Dawn, The Fugitive, Corruption in the Palace of Justice, Summertime Queen, The Rebels, Burnt Flower Bed, Inquiry, The Gambler.*

BETTINA, ALBERT ANTHONY, educator; b. DeKalb, Ill., Sept. 12, 1921; s. John and Antonia (Zanco) B.; B.E., No. Ill. U., 1943; M.A., U. No. Colo., 1948; Ed.D., Bradley U., 1953; postgrad. U. Md., 1964, U. Mo., 1957, U. Ill., 1966; m. Frances Hintz, Aug. 28, 1948; children—John Ernest, Elizabeth Ann, Catherine Lynn. Instr., Eastern N.M. U., 1948-51, asst. prof., 1951-57, asso. prof., 1957-61, prof. indsl. edn. and dean Sch. Tech., 1961—; cons. in field. Served with USAAF, 1943-46. Mem. Am. Vocational Assn., Am. Indsl. Arts Assn., N.E.A., N.M. Manpower Adv. Com., N.M. Indsl. Arts Adv. Council, N.M. Trade and Indsl. Adv. Council, Epsilon Pi Tau (recipient laureate award 1969). Kiwanian (pres. 1959). Home: 1511 W 17th Lane Portales NM 88130

BETTIS, VALERIE, dancer, choreographer; b. Houston, Tex.; d. Royal Holt and Valerie Elizabeth (McCarthy) B.; student U. Tex.; m. Bernardo Segall, Sept. 20, 1943 (div. 1955); m. 2d, Arthur A. Schmidt, Sept. 26, 1959. First profl. appearance, 1937, first solo performance, 1941; choreographer, 1942—; made piano-dance recital tour with husband (pianist-composer), Central and South America, 1946; appeared in connection with work at YMHA Dance Center, N.Y.C., 1947; dancer five solo modern dances Jacob's Pillow Festival, Lee, Mass., 1947; dancer legitimate stage prodns. on Broadway: Inside U.S.A., Tiger Lily, Haunted Heart, 1948; As I Lay Dying (YMHA Dance Center), 1949, (N.Y. State Theatre, Lincoln Center, N.Y.C.), 1965; choreographer Paul Whiteman's TV show, 1949; dancer and choreographer TV shows: Colgate Comedy Hour, Philco Playhouse, Your Show of Shows, Chevrolet Hour, Studio One, Omnibus, Kraft TV Theatre, Producers Showcase; dir. If Five Years Pass, N.Y.C., 1962; dancer, actress, singer Great to be Alive, 1949; Bless You All, 1950; ballet Street Car Named Desire, 1954; choreographer Peer Gynt, 1951, Slavenska-Franklin Ballet Co., N.Y.C., 1952, Our Town (NBC Spectacular), 1955; choreographer for films: Affair in Trinidad; Salome, 1952; Athena, 1954; actress The Women (NBC); guest artist Three Penny Opera; actress in Back to Methuselah, 1957-58; stage dir. London prodn. Ulysses in Nighttown, 1958; (revival) Virginia Sampler for 1960 Dallas Civic Ballet Co.; choreographer and performer Golden Round and Early Voyagers. Recipient Donaldson award, Mademoiselle award, 1948. ‡

BETTMANN, OTTO LUDWIG, picture archivist, graphic historian; b. Leipzig, Germany, Oct. 15, 1903; s. Hans and Charlotte (Frank) B.; Ph.D., U. Leipzig, 1927, M.S. in L.S., 1932; m. Anne Clemens Gray, Mar. 4, 1938. Came to U.S., 1935, naturalized, 1939. Asso. editor C.F. Peters Co., music pubs., Leipzig, 1927-28; editor Axel Juncker Pub., Berlin, 1928-30; curator rare books State Art Library, Berlin, 1930-33; founder, 1941, since propr. and pres. Bettmann Archive, Inc. (picture library on history civilization), N.Y.C.; founder Picture House Press, Inc.; pictorial research pubs., advt. agys., TV producers; picture editor, cons. graphic history; organizer picture filing systems. Mem. Am. Inst. Graphic Art, French Inst., Spl. Library Assn. Author: (with Bellamy Partridge) As We Were, Family Life in America, 1946; (with John Durant) A Pictorial History of American Sports, 1952; A Pictorial History of Medicine, 1956; (with Van Wyck Brooks) Our Literary Heritage, 1956; (with Paul H. Lang) A Pictorial History of Music, 1960; The Bettmann Portable Archive, 1966. Picture editor: The New Pictorial Encyclopedia of the World, 1954. Home: 25 Sutton Place S New York City NY 10022 also Siscowit Rd Pound Ridge NY 10576 Office: 136 E 57th St New York City NY 10022

BETTS, ATTIE LESTER, engring. educator; b. Fairy, Tex., July 30, 1916; s. Thomas Lester and Beulah (Richardson) B.; B.S., Tex. A. and M. Coll., 1938, M.S., 1939; Ph.D., U. Tex., 1952; m. Erma Fife, Oct. 5, 1940; children—Judith Lynn, Sheryl Ilene. Teaching asst. elec. engring. dept. Tex. A. and M. Coll., 1938-39; engr. Gulf States Utilities Co., Beaumont, Tex., 1939-41; instr. radio Armored Force Sch., Ft. Knox, Ky., summer 1941; instr. elec. engring. Okla. State U., 1941-42, asst. prof., 1946-48. asso. prof., 1948-53, prof., 1953-55; prof., chmn. dept. elec. engring. Wash. State U., 1955-70, prof., 1970—. Served from 2d lt. to maj. AUS, 1942-46. Registered profl. engr., Okla. Mem. I.E.E.E., Am. Soc. Engring. Edn., Sigma Xi, Eta Kappa Nu, Tau Beta Pi, Sigma Tau. Mem. Ch. of Christ. Rotarian. Home: Route 4 Box 275 Moscow ID

BETTS, AUSTIN WORTHAM, research co. exec.; b. Westwood, N.J., Nov. 22, 1912; s. Irving Wilcox and Bessie Harris (Boardman) B.; B.S., U.S. Mil. Acad., 1934; M.S., Mass. Inst. Tech., 1938; m. Edna Jane Paterson, Dec. 8, 1934; children—Jerry W., Lee W., Lynn P. Commd. 2d lt. U.S. Army, 1934, advanced through grades to lt. gen., 1966; dist. engr. Bermuda Dist., U.S. Engr. Dept., 1942-43; engr. 14th Air Force, 1944-45; asso. dir. Los Alamos Sci. Lab., 1946-48; chief atomic energy br., G-4, Dept. Army, 1949-52; exec. to chief research and devel. Dept. Army, 1952-54; mil. exec. to spl. asst. or dir. guided missiles Office Sec. Def., 1957-59; dir. Advanced Research Projects Agy., Office Sec. Def., 1959-61; dir. mil. application AEC, 1961-64; dep. chief research and devel. Dept. Army, 1964-66, chief research and devel., 1966-70; retired, 1970; v.p. Southwest Research Inst., San Antonio, 1970—. Mem. Assn. U.S. Army, Innovation Group, Soc. Am. Mil. Engrs., Am. Inst. Aeros. and Astronautics, Am. Ordnance Assn. Presbyn. Mason. Home: 6414 View Point San Antonio TX 78229 Office: 8500 Culebra Rd San Antonio TX 78228

BETTS, BERT A., financial cons.; b. San Diego, Aug. 16, 1923; s. Bert A. and Alma (Jorgenson) B.; B.B.A., Cal. Western U., 1950; m. Barbara Lang; children—Terry Lou, Linda Sue, Sara Ellen, Bert Alan, Randy Wayne, LeAnn, John Cauncey, Frederick P., Roby F., Bruce H. Accountant, John R. Gillette, 1946-48; partner Gillette & Betts, 1949-50; pvt. accounting practice, 1951-54; partner Betts & Munden, Lemon Grove, Cal., 1954-57; sr. partner Bert A. Betts & Co., 1958-59; treas. State of Cal., 1958-67; prin. Bert A. Betts & Assos., 1967—; chief exec. officer Internat. Prodn. Assos., 1968—; trustee Fidelity mortgage Investors; gen. partner Sacramento Met. Airport Properties 4, Ltd. 1970—. Mem. Lemon Grove Sch. Bd. 1954-57; Cal. chmn. Max Baer Heart Fund; state employees chmn. Am. Cancer Soc., 1962-64, bd. dirs. county br., 1963-69, Sacramento County campaign chmn., mem. exec. com., 1965, pres. Sacramento chpt. 1967-68. Served as 1st lt. USAAF, 1942-45. Decorated D.F.C., Air Medal with 3 clusters. Recipient Louisville award Municipal Finance Officers Assn. U.S. and Can., 1963; honored by Cal. Municipal Treasures Assn., 1964. C.P.A., Cal. Mem. Am. Inst. Accountants, Nat. Assn. Accountants Nat. Assn. State Auditors, Comptrollers and Treasurers, Municipal Forum of N.Y., Cal. Soc. C.P.A.'s, San Diego Squadron Air Force Assn. (past vice comdr.), Am. Legion, V.F.W., Native Sons Golden West, Foresters, Beta Alpha Psi (hon.), Alpha Kappa Psi (hon.). Presbyn. Mason, Eagle. Clubs: Men's (pres.). Lions (treas.) (Lemon Grove); Commonwealth. Home: 441 Sandburg Dr Sacramento CA 95819 also Betts Ranch Levee Rd Elverta CA 95626 Office: 629 J St Sacramento CA 95814

BETTS, CHARLES JULIUS, state govt. ofcl.; b. Danbury, Wis., July 6, 1914; s. Thomas Britton and Ruby (Slack) B.; student Antioch Coll., 1934-35, Internat. Corr. Schs., 1937-40, U. Colo., 1939-41, Alexander Hamilton Inst., 1961; LL.B., Blackstone Sch. Law, 1960; m. Virginia Dare, Oct. 6, 1935; children—Earl Palmer, Mary Anna (Mrs. Jack A. Wilkerson), Burr Joseph. Architect Roland L. Linder, Architect, 1937-47; cons. architect bd. church extension Disciples of Christ, Indpls., 1947-69; state bldg. commr. State of Ind., Indpls., 1969—. Fellow A.I.A.; mem. Ind. Soc. Architects (pres. 1958-59). Republican. Mem. Disciples of Christ. Contbr. articles profl. jours. Home: 6700 Spring Brook Indianapolis IN 46219 Office: State Office Bldg Indianapolis IN 46204

BETTS, DORIS JUNE WAUGH, author; b. Statesville, N.C., June 4, 1932; d. William Elmore and Mary Ellen (Freeze) Waugh; student Woman's Coll., U. N.C., 1950-53, U. N.C., 1954; m. Lowry Matthews Betts, July 5, 1952; children—Doris LewEllyn, David Lowry, Erskine Moore II. Newspaperwoman, Statesville Daily Record, 1950-51, Chapel Hill (N.C.) Weekly and News-Leader, 1953-54, Sanford Daily Herald, 1956-57; Guggenheim fellow, 1958-59; editorial staff N.C. Democrat. newspaper, 1961-62; editor Sanford (N.C.) News Leader, 1962; lectr. creative writing, English dept. U. N.C., Chapel Hill, 1966—; vis. lectr. creative writing Duke U., 1971. Mem. N.C. Tercentenary Commn., 1961-62. Mem. Sanford City Sch. Bd. Recipient short story prize Mademoiselle mag., booklength fiction prize G. P. Putnam-U. N.C., 1954. Mem. N.C. Writers Assn., Am. Philatelic Soc. Author: (story collection) The Gentle Insurrection, 1954; (novel) Tall Houses in Winter (Sir Walter Raleigh award for best fiction by Carolinian 1957), 1957; Scarlet Thread (Sir Walter Raleigh award 1965); The Astronomer & Other Stories, 1966. Contbr. stories collections, anthologies. Editor: Young Writer at Chapel Hill, 1968. Office: Dept English U NC Chapel Hill NC 27514

BETTS, EDWARD, artist; b. Yonkers, N.Y., Aug. 4, 1920; s. Harrison and Mildred (Waterbury) B.; A.B., Yale, 1942; M.F.A., U. Ill., 1952; m. Jane Burke, June 2, 1949; children—Peter, John, Wendy. Watercolor painter, 1937—; instr. art U. Ill., 1949—, now prof. art, also asso. Center for Advanced Study, 1968-69; one-man show Contemporary Arts Gallery, N.Y.C., 1953,55, John Heller Gallery 1956,59, Charles Feingarten Gallery, Chgo., 1954, 56, 57, Midtown Galleries, N.Y.C., 1961,65,68, Krannert Art Mus., U. Ill., 1970; exhibited Corcoran biennial exbns. Contemporary Am. Painting, 1947,51,55,57, 59, Met. Mus. Am. Painting Today, 1950, Bklyn. Internat. Watercolor Exhbn., 1953,55,61, N.A.D., 1953—, Audubon Artists, Am. Water Color Soc., Cal. Water Color Soc., Bklyn. Mus., 1961, Pa. Acad., 1953-54, 59,61, Nat. Inst. Arts and Letters, 1962, Water color USA, Springfield (Mo.) Art Mus., 1963, 64, 20th Am. Drawing Ann., Norfolk Mus. Arts and Scis., 1963, Hassam Purchase Fund Exhibit, 1961,63, Me. 100 Artists of the 20th Century, Colby Coll., 1964, others; represented in permanent collections Fogg Art Mus., Upjohn Pharm. Co., La Jolla Art Center, Indpls. Mus. Art, Stephens Coll. (Mo.), Sandoz Pharm. Co., Atlanta U., St. Lawrence U., Irving Trust Co., N.Y.C., USIA Art in Embassies Program, New Britain Mus. Am. Art, Kan. State U., Rochester (N.Y.) Meml. Art Gallery, Springfield (Mo.) Art Mus., Davenport (Ia.) Municipal Gallery, Ball State Tchrs., Coll., Va. Mus. Fine Arts, Butler Inst. Am. Art, Cal. Watercolor Soc., also pvt. collections. Recipient 1st prize oil painting Brick Store Mus. exhbn., Kennebunk, Me., 1949, Arts and Artists Along Miss. exhbn., Davenport, Ia., 1950, Grumbacher award for case in Allied Artists, 1950, Audubon Artists, 1951, gold medal of honor Audubon Artists, 1952, silver medal of honor Am. Watercolor Soc., 1953, 59, Pennell medal Phila. Water Color Club, 1953, 2d Altman prize N.A.D., 1954, bronze medal of honor Allied Artists Exhbn., 1956; $100 award Portland Mus. Summer Art Festival, 1957. Benjamin Altman prize $1500), 1957; $2000 Altman prize, N.A.D., 1959,66; Remmey award Am. Watercolor Soc., 1966; Hassam Fund Exhbn. Purchase award, 1966. Mem. N.A.D., Am. Water Color Soc., Art Students League, Ogunquit (Me.) Art Assn. (past pres.), Phila. Water Color Club. Home: 804 Dodds Dr Champaign IL 61820 Office: Art Dept U Ill Champaign IL 61820

BETTS, EMMETT ALBERT, psychologist, educator, author; b. Elkhart, Ia., 1903; s. Albert Henry and Grace L. (Greenwood) B.; B.S., Des Moines U., 1925; M.S., U. Ia., 1928, Ph.D., 1931; m. Thelma Marshall, May 31, 1924; children—Beverly Jean (Mrs. Morris Pitts), Shirley Lee, Margaret Jane (Mrs. Robert Meckley); m. 2d Carolyn Welch, July 15, 1950. Vocational dir. indsl. arts and agr., Orient, Ia., 1922-24; staff physics dept. Des Moines U., 1924-25; supt. schs., Northboro, Ia., 1925-29; research asst. U. Ia., 1929-31; sch. psychologist, elementary prin., Shaker Heights, O., 1931-34; dir. tchr. edn., dir. summer sessions State Tchrs. Coll., Oswego, N.Y., 1934-37; research prof., dir. reading clinic sch. edn. Pa. State Coll., 1937-45; prof. psychology, dir. reading clinic, dept. psychology Temple U., 1945- 54; director Betts Reading Clinic, Haverford, Pa., 1954-61; research prof. Sch. of Edn. Miami U., Coral Gables, Fla., 1961—. Vis. prof. numerous colls. and univs. U.S., 1930—; editorial advisor My Weekly Reader; editor in chief Education; asso. editor Jour. Ednl. Research; cons. state and nat. orgns.; author vision tests. Vice pres. Nat. Aerospace Education Council. Trustee, Lake Placid (N.Y.) Edn. Found. Recipient Apollo award, 1962, Fellow Am. Psychol Assn. (diplomate sch. psychology), Distinguished Service Found. Optometry, Grad. Soc. Optometry; mem. Soc. Advancement Edn., Nat. Council Research in English (chmn. editorial com.), Nat. Conf. on Research Elementary Sch. English, Nat. Soc. Study Edn., Internat. Reading Assn., Nat. Council Tchrs. English, Eastern Psychol. Assn., Internat. Council Exceptional Children (adv. com.), N.E.A., Am. Assn. U. Profs., Am. Assn. Sch. Adminstrs., Am. Assn. Applied Psychology, Am. Edn. Research Assn., Nat. Aeronautics Assn., Aircraft Owners and Pilots Assn., A.A.A.S., Silver Wings (hon. life), Phi Delta Kappa, Beta Sigma Kappa, Psi Chi. Mason (Shriner). Author: Foundation of Reading Instruction, rev. edit., 1957; Betts Basic Readers, 1970; others. Contbr. profl. jours. Home: Royal Caribbean Club 1150 Av Madruga Coral Gables FL 33416

BETTS, ERNEST CLAIRE, Jr., govt. ofcl.; b. Hillsboro, Wis., Aug. 27, 1914; s. Ernest Claire and Cora (Steffen) B.; student Platteville State Coll., 1932-33; tchrs. license Vernon County Normal, Viroqua, Wis., 1934; student U.S. Dept. Agr. Grad. Sch.; m. Gwendolyn Elizabeth Washburn, Mar. 27, 1937; children—Ernest Claire III, Keith Weston, Willis Lee. Tchr., prin. grade schs., Wis., 1934-39; adminstrv. officer, exec. officer U.S. Dept. Agr., 1939-50, asst. to sec., 1953-56, dir. personnel, 1956-61; dep. dir. personnel State Dept., 1961-62, dir. budget, 1962-63; budget officer, attache for adminstrn. U.S. embassy, Beirut, Lebanon, 1950-53; asst. controller Tech. Coop. Adminstrn., 1953; budget officer, dir. Office Budget and Finance, Dept. Treasury, 1964, dep. asst. sec. for adminstrn., 1964-70, asst. sec. for adminstrn. Treasury, 1970—. Mem. bd. lay activities Va. Conf. Meth. Ch. Mem. Am. Soc. Pub. Adminstrn., Soc. Personnel Adminstrn., Pub. Personnel Assn., Internat. Platform Assn. Home: 815 S 26th St Arlington VA 22202 Office: U S Dept Treasury Washington DC 20225

BETTS, GEORGE CORNELIUS, educator; b. Warren, Pa., June 7, 1914; s. George H. and Alice (Titus) B.; B.A., La. State U., 1939; M.A., Kent (O.) State U., 1940; Ph.D., Syracuse U., 1953; m. Eleanor Shoemaker, Jan. 6, 1947 (div.); 1 son, Terence Hanley. Univ. editor Kent State U., 1941-42, dir. univ. relations, 1955-66, exec. dean pub. service and publs., 1966-69, prof. polit. sci., 1969—; editor Martins Ferry (O.) Times-Leader, 1942-43; staff editor OWI overseas br., N.Y.C., 1943-45; pub. affairs officer USIS, Manila, P.I., 1945-46; asst. prof. journalism Syracuse (N.Y.) U., exec. sec. N.Y. State Soc. Newspaper Editors, 1947-50; press officer U.S. Mission to UN, 1950-55. Mem. Am. Soc. Pub. Adminstrn. (pres. N.E. Ohio regional chpt. 1967-68), Am. Polit. Sci. Assn., Pi Sigma Alpha, Omicron Delta Kappa. Home: 314 Rellim Dr Kent OH 44240

BETTS, HOWARD M., ins. co. exec.; b. Howard County, Ind., Nov. 6, 1913; s. Frank and Arda (Ritchey) B.; grad. Kokomo (Ind.) Jr. Coll., 1935; m. Mary Ellen Long, Oct. 10, 1942; children—Marlynn Kay, Dee Ann. With Grain Dealers Mut. Ins. Co., Indpls., 1936—, v.p., 1959-65, pres., 1965—, also dir.; pres., dir. Companion Ins. Co., Indpls., 1962—; dir. Am. Mut. Ins. Alliance, Assn. Mill and Elevator Mut. Ins. Cos. Mem. gov. com. improved risk mutuals Mut. Loss Research Bur.; charter mem., past pres. Indpls. Fire and Marine Underwriters. Mem. Indpls. C. of C., Newcomen Soc. N.Am. Mem. Christian Ch. Rotarian. Club: Columbia (Indpls.). Home: 1601 N Whitcomb Av Indianapolis IN 46224 Office: 1752 N Meridian St Indianapolis IN 46202

BETTS, JACKSON EDWARD, congressman; b. Findlay, O., May 26, 1904; s. John Edward and Elizabeth (Fisher) B.; A.B. cum laude, Kenyon Coll., 1926; LL.B., Yale, 1929; M.A. (hon.), Kenyon Coll., 1952; LL.D., Ohio No. U., 1959, Heidelberg Coll., 1962, Findlay Coll., 1965; m. Martha Neeley, June 12, 1934; 1 dau., Nancy Lou (Mrs. David C. Bowman). Admitted to Ohio bar, 1930; pros. atty., Hancock County, O., 1933-37. Mem. Ohio Gen. Assembly, 1937-47, speaker Ho. of Reps., 1945-46; mem. 82d-92d Congresses, 8th Ohio Dist. Mem. Jud. Council Ohio, 1941-45. Mem. Am., Ohio, Findlay bar assns., Delta Tau Delta, Phi Delta Phi, Corbey Court (Yale). Republican. Episcopalian. Mason, Elk, K.P., Odd Fellow, Rotarian. Home: 3309 Briarcliff Dr Findlay OH 45840 Office: Niles Bldg Findlay OH 45840 also 3 N Main St Mansfield OH 44901 also Rayburn Bldg Washington DC 20525

BETTS, JOHN FREDERICK, Jr., pipe co. exec.; b. St. Louis, Sept. 27, 1909; s. John Frederick and Mary Belle (Howell) B.; student Yale, 1931; m. Roxana Van Sant, Aug. 9, 1962; children—John Frederick III, Christopher Morse. With firms on Wall St., 1932-44, Fiduciary Trust Co., 1944-47; v.p., dir. Lock Joint Pipe Co., East Orange, N.J., 1947-62; exec. v.p., dir. Interpace Corp. (formerly Internat. Pipe and Ceramics Co. formed by merger Lock Joint Pipe Co. and Gladding McBean & Co., 1962-65, pres., 1965-67, chmn. bd., 1967—; dir. Anken Industries Inc., Chesebrough-Ponds, Inc., Eagle Stores Co., Charlotte, N.C., Prudential Ins. Co. Eng., Scandia Ins. Co. Sweden, Instron Corp., Canton, Mass. Mem. council financial execs. Nat. Indsl. Conf. Bd., 1952—, mem. chief execs. council, 1966—, also dir. Bd. trustees Overlook Hosp., Summit, N.J., 1952-56; pres. Short Hills Country Day Sch., 1945-48. Mem. N.A.M. (dir.). Clubs: Stock Exchange Lunch (N.Y.C.); Baltusrol Golf (Springfield, N.J.); California (Los Angeles); Somerset Hills Country (Bernardsville, N.J.); Mid-Ocean (Bermuda); Country of N.C. Home: Post House Rd Morristown NJ 07960 Office: Interpace Corp PO Box 1111 Parsippany NJ 07054

BETTS, REX, banker; b. Chenowith, Wash., June 20, 1928; s. Harold R. and Sylvia (Thornton) B.; student U. Utah, 1945-46; B.B.A., U. Ore., 1956; standard certificate, Am. Inst. Banking, 1961; grad. Bank Adminstrn. Inst., U. Wis., 1970; m. Beulah M. Korn, Feb. 18, 1956; children-Gary, Michael, Craig, Daniel. Asst. cashier 1st Nat. Bank Ore., Portland, 1948-52, examiner, 1956-64; auditor Ida. 1st Nat. Bank, Boise, 1964—. Served with C.E., AUS, 1945-47, 52-54. Mem. U. Ore. Alumni Assn., Am. Legion, Bank Adminstrn. Inst., Kappa Sigma. Methodist. Elk. Home: 10509 Stardust St Boise ID 83705 Office: 10th and Idaho Sts PO Box 7009 Boise ID 83707

BETUMA, SYLVESTER ANDREW chemist, educator; b. Chicago, 1928; B.S. in Physics, Yale, 1950; Ph.D. in Chemistry, Harvard, 1956; m. Sally Ann Jones, July 5, 1957; children--Kenneth J., Nancy A. Chemist, Acme Chem. Co., Blue Island, Ill., 1950-51; director of Research Lab., Indsl. Chemicals Corp., Cambrige, Mass., 1956-60; project coordinator environmental sect. Steinmetz Assos., Chgo., 1960-61; v.p. for research Bauer Bros. Chem. Co., Inc., Memphis, 1961-64; asst. prof. chemistry Washington U., St. Louis, 1964-66, asso. prof., 1966-70, prof., 1970--, head of chemistry dept., 1970-71. Vis. prof. So. Ill. U., summer 1967, U. of Ore., 1969. Bd. dirs. Rest Haven Home for Elderly, 1960-61; trustee of the Lutheran Hosp., 1965-71. Served from lt. to capt., AUS, 1951-53. Mem. Am. Chem. Soc., Sci. Research Soc. Am. (chpt. treas. 1967), Sigma Xi. Author: (with others) Basic Inorganic Chemistry, 1971. Home: Fairfax Apts 7291 Windermere Dr University City MO 63105 Office: Dept Chemistry Washington University St Louis MO 63130

BETZ, BARBARA JEAN, educator, physician; b. Boscobel, Wis., Jan. 25, 1909; s. Jonathan Clymont and Margaret (McKee) Betz; A.B., Mt. Holyoke Coll., 1931; S.M., Johns Hopkins, 1933, M.D., 1938; children—Noel R. Langworthy, Deborah J. Langworthy. Successively intern, resident, instr., asst. prof., asso. prof. psychiatry Johns Hopkins Med. Sch., 1938-55; asso. prof., then prof. psychiatry Cornell U. Med. Coll., 1965-69; clin. prof. psychiatry Dartmouth Med. Sch., 1969—; cons. psychiatry VA, 1948—; dir. edn. Spring Grove State Hosp., 1962-65, Westchester div. N.Y. Hosp., 1965-69, Brattleboro (Vt.) Retreat, 1969-70. Trustee Brattleboro Music Center, 1969—. Diplomate Am. Bd. Psychiatry. Fellow Am. Psychiat. Assn.; mem. Assn. Advancement Psychotherapy, Sigma Xi. Contbr. profl. jours. Home: Box 68 Marlboro VT 05344 Office: 8 Chapin St Brattleboro VT 05301

BETZ, CARL, actor; b. Pitts., Mar. 9; student Duquesne U., Carnegie Inst. Tech. Profl. debut in Pitts. summer stock company; Broadway debut in The Long Watch; films include Powder River, Dangerous Crossing; TV appearances in Love of Life; The Donna Reed Show; Judd For the Defense. Served with AUS, 1942. Recipient Emmy award 1968, Address: care William Morris Agy., 151 El Camino Dr Los Angeles, CA 90212.*

BETZ, CHARLES W., mfg. co. exec.; b. Chgo., Jan. 13, 1922; s. John L. and Florence (Jayne) B.; B.S. in Mech. Engring., U. Mich., 1951; postgrad. Wayne State U., 1955-56; m. Shirley M. Barrett, Apr. 18, 1942; children—Charles W., John S., James E., Frederick L. Project engr. Riley Stoker Corp., 1946- 47, Tucker Corp., 1947-49, Kaiser-Frazer Corp., 1950-51; dir. research project Am. Metal Products Co., 1954-57; v.p. sales, dir. Alliance Ware, Inc., 1957-61; exec. v.p., dir. Briggs Mfg. Co., 1961-64; pres. Borroughs Mfg. Co., 1964-66; pres. Lindsay Co. div. Union Tank Car, St. Paul, 1966—; dir. Crown San. Pottery Co., Briggs-Ohio Co., Hycroft China Co., Am. Nat. Bank St. Paul, Gen. Marking Co. Served with AUS, 1942-46; ETO; served to capt. USAAF, 1952-54. Mem. Triangle, Stoic Honor Soc. (v.p.), Greater St. Paul C. of C. (dir.). Clubs: Chicago Athletic Assn.; Recess; Park; Edina Country; North Oaks Golf. Home: 21 Skillman Lane North Oaks St Paul, MN 55110. Office: 455 Woodlane Dr St Paul MN 55119

BETZ, EUGEN CHRISTOPH, German diplomat; b. Peking, China, Nov. 22, 1907; s. Heinrich Franz and Elisabeth (von Petzel) B.; student law, univs. Muenster, Munich, Berlin and Giessen (Germany), 1926-31; m. Elfriede Bechler, Dec. 13, 1948; 1 son, Rolf-Michael. With various German cts. and pub. agys., 1932- 35; joined German Fgn. Service, 1936; attaché German legation, Prague, Czechoslavakia, 1937, assigned Fgn. Ministry, 1938-39; vice consul, Shanghai, China 1940-45; sec. gen. Adminstrn. Steel and Iron Duesseldorf, 1948-52; 1st sec. Fgn. Ministry, Bonn, 1952; assigned embassy, Athens, Greece, 1954-56, Fgn. Ministry, Bonn, 1956-63; consul gen., Chicago, 1963—. Served with German Army, 1939-40. Decorated knight comdr. Royal Greek Order Phoenix; comdr. Order of Merit of Germany. Mem. Chgo. Federated Advt. Club. Rotarian. Clubs: Executives, Germania, Mid-America, Economic of Chicago, Adventurers, Arts (Chgo.); Oakbrook Polo; Exmoore Country. Office: 104 S Michigan Av Chicago IL 60603

BETZ, EUGENE WILLIAM, architect; b. Dayton, O., Jan. 12, 1921; s. Jesse Earl and Elizabeth Freda (Meyer) B.; B.S., U. Cin., 1944; m. Marjorie Lois Frank, Oct. 30, 1948; children—Douglas William, Gregory Vincent. Draftsman archtl. firm Lorenz & Williams, Dayton, O., 1942; co-op student draftsman archtl. firm Potter Tyler & Martin, Cin., 1943; adminstrv. asst. archtl. firm Schench & Williams, Dayton, O., 1944-55; prin. Eugene W. Betz, architects, Dayton, O., 1956—. Chmn. Bd. Building Standards and Appeals, 1960-63, Kettering Planning Commn., 1957-61. Served with AUS, 1944. Recipient Honor award Architects Soc. Ohio, 1967, 71; Award of Merit, 1968; Nation's Sch. Month award Nat. Council Schoolhouse Constrn. , 1967; Nat. Citation Am. Assn. Sch. Adminstrs. 1967, 71. Mem. Dayton Area C. of C. Mason. Home: 5561 Lotusdale Dr Dayton OH 45429 Office: 2223 S Dixie Av Dayton OH 45409

BETZ, FREDERICK, Jr., geologist; b. Rochester, N.Y., Mar. 11, 1915; s. Frederick and Elisabeth (Filkins) B.; A.B., Columbia, 1934; Ph.D., Princeton, 1938; m. Elisabeth Alma Walter, July 18, 1942; children—Frederick III, Elisabeth Walter, Paul Richard. From asst. to research asso. in geology Princeton, 1936-40; geologist Nfld. Geol. Survey, St. John's, 1936-40, 46-47; mineral economist U.S Bur. Mines, 1941-43; asst. prof. geology Lehigh U., 1946-47; geologist U.S. Geol. Survey, 1943-60, asst. chief mil. geology br., 1948-54, chief team to Europe, 1954-60; sec. Geol. Soc. Am., 1960-62; editor in charge earth scis. program John Wiley & Sons, pubs., N.Y.C., 1962-63; cons. geologist, 1963-64; chief acquisition sect. Clearinghouse Fed. Sci. and Tech. Information, Nat. Bur. Standards, 1964-65; sr. scientist, geoscis. operations, mgr. sci. and tech. information center Sci. Services div. Texas Instruments, Inc., 1965-68; dir. Coastal Plains Regional Commn. Center for Marine Devel. Services, Chevy Chase, Md., 1969—. Fellow Geol. Soc. Am., A.A.A.S.; mem. Geologische Vereinigung, Sigma Xi. Address: 3535 Chevy Chase Lake Dr Chevy Chase MD 20015

BETZ, FRED MCLEAN, Jr., newspaper pub.; b. Lamar, Colo., Nov. 13, 1926; s. Fred McLean and Lennie Maude (Coffman) B.; student Lamar Jr. Coll., 1946-47, Wayne U., 1948; B.A., U. Colo., 1950; m. Barbara Lee Applebach, Aug. 21, 1948; children—Norman Thomas, Rebecca Sue (Mrs. Gerald Larrew), Gregory John, Lynn Marle. Apprentice, Betz Pub. Co., Inc., Lamar, Colo., 1940-44, partner, v.p., 1946—. sec.-treas. Media Cable TV Systems, Lamar, Inc., 1965. Mem. exec. com. Squadron Civil Air Patrol. Nat. del. Sr. Party Conv. Democrats, Chgo.; nat. committeeman Colo. Young Democrats, 1954; Colo. leader for Sen. Estes Kefauver, 1956. Bd. regents U. Colo., 1956-62. Served with USNR, 1941-46, 50. Mem. Rocky Mountain Advt. Men's Assn. (pres. 1954-55). Colo. Press Assn. (pres. 1956-57), Am. Legion, V.F.W., Nat. Planning Assn. (mem. nat. council), Sigma Delta Chi. Methodist. Eagle, Elk. Club: Denver Press. Home: 400 S 2d St Lamar CO 81052 Office: 310 S 5th St Lamar CO 81052

BETZIG EDWARD economist; b. N.Y.C., Dec. 7, 1914; s. dward and Amelia (Frank) B.; B.A., Colgate U., 1936; M.A., Columbia, 1938; m. Varzenik Bedikian, May 7, 1957; children—Dikran, Arda. Tchr. in Latin Am., also free-lance writer, 1946-50; program officer, also operations officer, Saudi Arabia and Iran, 1952-57; program officer/economist AID mission to Costa Rica, 1957-62; regional econ. adviser Central Am. Common Market, AID, Guatemala City, Guatemala, later asst. dir. ROCAP; dir. CIAP/OAS div. AID, Washington 1966-70; audit. mgr. AID/LA, 1970—. Served with AUS, 1941- 45. Mem. Royal Asian Soc., Am. Econ. Assn., A.A.A.S., Wilderness Soc. Home: 9703 Cedar Lane Bethesda, MD 20014. Office: AID New State Bldg Washington DC 20523

BEUKEMA, CHRISTIAN F., civil engr.; b. Grand Haven, Mich., July 20, 1917, s. Fred and Cora (Van Koevering) B.; B.S., Mich. State Coll., 1940; LL.D., Mich. State U., 1967; m. M. Elizabeth Robertson, Sept. 10, 1941; children—John, Robert. Civil engr. Mich. Limestone & Chem. Co., Rogers City, Mich., 1940-41, 46-49, staff. asst. raw materials div. U.S. Steel Corp., 1949-51; dir. raw material planning, 1951-53, gen. mgr. operations Mich. Limestone div. U.S. Steel Corp., 1953-54, v.p., 1954, pres., 1955-59, pres. Oliver Iron Mining div., 1960-63; v.p. ore and limestone operations, U.S. Steel Corp., Pitts., 1964-68, v.p. ore, limestone, and lake shipping, 1968—. Mem. exec. bd. Mich. State U. Alumini Assn. and Devel. Fund; bd. dirs. Minn. Council on Econ. Edn., Northeastern Minn. Devel. Assn.; mem. bus. adv. board Minn. Private College Fund; mem. corporate bd. North Hills Passavant Hosp. Served as major, gen. staff officer of plans and operations, AUS, 1941-46. Mem. Am. Inst. Mining, Metall. and Petroleum Engrs., Am. Iron and Steel Inst., Eastern States Blast Furnace and Coke Oven Assn., Am. Bur. Shipping, Am. Iron Ore Assn. (dir., v.p.), Am. Mining Congress (dir.), Lake Carriers Assn. (dir.), Newcomen Soc. N.Am., Tau Beta Pi, Phi Kappa Phi. Presbyn. Clubs: Wildwood Golf, Duquesne (Pitts.); Kichi Gammi (Duluth). Home: 1568 Hazlett Rd Pittsburgh PA 15237 Office: 600 Grant St Pittsburgh PA 15230

BEUSCHLEIN, MURIEL, educator; b. Chgo., June 14, 1905; d. William Alexander and Agnes (Kennedy) Henderson; B.E., Chgo. Tchrs. Coll., 1949; M.S. Northwestern U., 1951, Ph.D., 1962; m. Louis Beuschlein, Nov. 29, 1933 (div.); children—Vinita (Mrs. Robert Super), Muriel (Mrs. George Babcock), Louis Albert. Sci tchr. Parker Elementary Sch., 1940-51; mng. editor Am. Biology Tchr., 1951-65; asso. prof. biology Ill. Tchrs. Coll., Chgo. State Coll., 1951-62, prof., 1962—, chmn dept. natural scis., 1964-65, chmn. dept. biol. scis., 1965—. Cons. sci. films and filmstrips; coordinator TV sci. series WGN-TV, Chicago, 1960. Recipient Conservation Edn. award from Wildlife Soc., 1964. Fellow A.A.A.S.; mem. Chgo. Acad. Scis., Nat. Assn. Research in Sci. Teaching, Nat. Assn. Biology Tchrs. (pres. 1962), Nat. Sci. Tchrs. Assn., Central Assn. Sci. and Math. Tchrs. Author: Free and Inexpensive Materials for Science Education; co-author: Things to do in Science and Conversation, 1960. Home: 6431 S Richmond Chicago IL 60629

BEUTEL, ALBERT PHILLIP, ret. business exec.; b. Cleve., Nov. 13, 1892, s. William C. and Sophie (Harjes) B.B.S., Case Sch. Applied Sci. Cleve., 1914, Ph.D., 1942; m. Belle Armstrong, Apr. 16, 1916; children—Phillip R., Betty Ann (Mrs. E. B. Hanley), Richard A. Engring. draftsman Dow Chem. Co., Midland, Mich., 1914-21, pipe shop supt., 1921-31, spl. asst. to pres. later asst. gen. mgr., 1931-40, v.p., dir. govt. dept., mem. exec. com. Dow Chemical Co., until 1971; v.p. dir. Dowell division Dow Chemical Co. Midland: dir. First City Nat. Bank (Houston). Bd. dirs. Tex. A. and M. Coll. Fellow Am. Soc. M.E.; mem. Am. Chem. Soc., Am. Petroleum Inst., Am. Inst. Chem. Engrs., Soc. Chem. Industry (Am. sect.). Mason. Home: Box 8 Lake Jackson TX 77566

BEUTEL, FREDERICK KEATING lawyer, educator; b. Montgomery, Ala., Oct. 23, 1897, s. Conrad Frederick and Annie Margaret (Keating) B.; student U. Wash., 1917-19; A.B. Cornell U., 1921; LL.B., Harvard, 1925, S.J.D., 1928; m. Nellie Irene McKinney, June 22, 1924; children—Fiora Ann, Ann, Beatrice Thorndyke. Began as clk. Puget Sound Bank, Tacoma, Wash., 1916; mgr. and propr. Beutel Bus. Coll., Tacoma, 1921-22; critic on editorial staff Ginn & Co., Boston, 1922-25; practiced law Pitts., 1925-27; atty. to county controller, 1927; vis. prof. law U. Pa., 1931-32; dean La. State U. Law Sch., 1935-37; vis. prof. law Northwestern U., 1938- 39; prof. law, Coll. William and Mary, 1939-42; head cons. Coordinator Inter-Am. Affairs, 1941-42; mediator War Labor Bd., 1942; atty. to Alien Property Custodian, 1942-43; asst. solicitor Dept. Interior, 1944-45; dean U. Neb. Coll. Law, 1945-48, prof., 1949- 63; prof. U. Puerto Rico, 1963-65; vis. prof. law U. Ill., 1965-68, State U. N.Y., Buffalo, 1968-69, Ariz. State U., Tempe, 1969, Washington U., St. Louis, 1970—. Mem. Am. Assn. U. Profs., Fed. Bar Assn., Am. Law Inst. (life), Scabbard and Blade. Author: Beutel's Brannon on Negotiable Instruments, 1948; Uniform Commercial Laws, 1950: Experimental Jurisprudence, 1957: Bank Officers Handbook, Banking Law, 1939, 1965, 70; Democracy or the Scientific Method, 1965. Organizer, editor Tulane Law Rev., 1929-31; editor Fed. Bar Jour., 1944. Contbr. law revs. Home: 665 S Skinker St Louis MO 63105

BEVAN, DAVID CRUMLEY, ret. railroad exec.; b. Wayne, Pa., Aug. 5, 1906; s. Howard Sloan and Matilda (Crumley) B.; A.B., Haverford Coll., 1929; M.B.A., Havard, 1931; m. Mary Gilbert Heist, June 10, 1936; children—David Crumley, John Strong. Employee Provident Trust Co. of Phila., 1931, asst. trust officer, 1940, asst. v.p., 1946, dir., 1951-60; with WPB, 1942; mem. Lend Lease Mission to Australia, 1943-44, acting head, 1944; dept. head U.S. Mission Econ. Affairs, London, Eng., 1945; asst. treas. N.Y. Life Ins. Co., 1946, asst. v.p., 1947, treas., 1949-51; v.p. in charge finance Pa. R.R., 1951-63, chmn. finance com., 1963-68; chmn. finance com. Penn Central Co., 1968-70; dir., mem. exec. com. Tropical Gas Co.; dir. Phila. Suburban Water Co., Allegheny Ludlum Steel Corp., Phila. Suburban Corp. Bd. mgrs. Haverford Coll. Mem. Colonial Soc. Pa. Episcopalian. Clubs: Peale (Phila.); Links, (N.Y.C.); Merion Golf (Ardmore, Pa.); Gulfstream Golf (Delray Beach, Fla.). Home: Idlewild Rd Gladwyne PA 19035

BEVAN, FRANK POOLE educator, theatrical designer, b. Scranton, Pa., Nov. 9, 1903; s. Walter Scott and Daisy May (Poole) B.; B.A., Lafayette Coll., 1925; M.F.A. Yale, 1929; m. Margaret strauss, Dec. 22, 1944. Faculty Yale Drama Sch., 1929-70, prof. theatrical design. Home: 120 Dwight St New haven CT 06511

BEVAN, JOHN MORGAN, coll. adminstr.; b. Plains, Pa., Dec. 5, 1924; s. William and Elizabeth (Merrill Jones) B.; B.A., Franklin and Marshall Coll., University M.A., Duke 1948, B.D., 1946, Ph.D., 1952; Sc.D., Fla. Presbyn. Coll., 1967; m. Louise Dabbs, May 25, 1946; children—Brenda, Elizabeth, John Morgan, Megan Anne. Instr. psychology Davidson (N.C.) Coll., 1948; asst. prof. Heidelberg Coll., 1949-51; asso. prof. Davidson Coll., 1952-59; dean faculty Fla. Presbyn. Coll., 1959-67; v.p. acad. affairs U. Pacific, 1967-70, Davidson Coll., 1970—; ct. psychologist Seneca County, Ohio, 1950-51; cons. Ore. Edn. Council, 1968-70, CBS TV, 1954-59, Nat. Life Vt., 1955-59, Mut. Life N.J., 1954-59, George Frye & Assos., N.Y.C., Chgo. and Los Angeles, 1954-59; chmn., 1st All Asia Conf. Higher Edn., Hong Kong, 1969. Sec. St. Petersburg (Fla.) Civic Opera Assn., 1965-68. Trustee Ottawa U., Kans.; bd. dirs. Pacific Med. Center, San Francisco, Inst. Med. Scis., San Francisco. Recipient Vis. Scholar award Duke, 1955, Social Sci. Research Council award, 1956; Cullum scholar U. Ga., 1970. Mem. Council Protestant Colls. and Univs. (bd. dirs.), Am. Council Edn. (policy and planning com. 1969-70), Phi Beta Kappa, Sigma Xi, Pi Gamma Mu, Omicron Delta Kappa, Phi Kappa Phi, Am. Psychol. Assn., Am. Assn. U. Profs. Democrat. Presbyn. (elder). Home: 404 Concord Rd Davidson NC 28036

BEVAN, TIMOTHY HUGH, banker; b. London, Eng., May 24, 1927; s. Francis Hugh and Pleasance Mary Vidal (Scrutton) B.; ed. Eton Coll., 1939-45; m. Pamela Murray Smith, July 12, 1952; children—Nicola Jane, Fiona Sarah, David Mark, Hugh Charles. Called to bar, Eng., 1950; with Barclays Bank Ltd., London, 1950—, local dir., 1957—, dir., 1966—, vice-chmn. bd., 1968—; dir. Barclays Bank Cal., Société Financière, Europeénne, London Bd. Bank New South Wales. Mem. Inst. Internat. d'Etudes Bancaires, Internat. Banking Conf., Ct. Council Fgn. Bondholders. Clubs: Guards, Royal Ocean (London); Royal Yacht Squadron (Cowes, Isle of Wight, Eng.). Home: Tyes Pl Staplefield Near Haywards Heath Sussex England Office: 54 Lombard St London EC3 England

BEVAN, WILLIAM, sci. assn. admistr.; b. Plains, Pa., May, 16, 1922; s. William and Elizabeth Merrill (Jones) B.; A.B. (honors), Franklin and Marshall Coll., 1942; M.A., Duke, 1943, Ph.D., 1948; m. Dorothy Louise Chorpening, Feb. 17, 1945; children—William III, Mark Filbert, Philipp Ross. Instr. psychology Duke, 1947; instr., then asst. prof. psychology Heidelberg (O.) Coll., 1946-48; mem. faculty Emmory U., 1948-59, prof. psychology, 1958-59; prof. psychology, chmn. dept. Kan. State U., 1959-62, dean arts and scis., 1962-63, v.p. acad. affairs, 1963-65; fellow Center for Advanced Study Behavioral Scis., Stanford, Cal., 1965-66; sr. postdoctoral fellow NSF, 1965-66; v.p., provost Johns Hopkins U., Balt., 1966-70, prof. psychology, 1966—; exec. officer A.A.A.S., 1970—, pub. science, 1970—; cons. insts. founds. Mem. adv. council Human Resources Research office George Washington U., 1967-69; trustee Human Resources Research Orgn., 1968—. Fulbright scholar U. Oslo (Norway), 1952-53. Served with USNR, 1944-46. Fellow Am. Psychol. Assn., A.A.A.S.: mem. Aerospace-Med. Soc., Brit. Assn., Study Animal Behavior,

Psychononic Soc., So. Soc., Phil- osophy and Psychology, Am. Ecol. Soc. (asso.), Phi Beta Kappa, Sigma Xi. Contbr. articles profl. journals. Clubs: Cosmos; Johns Hopkins. Home: 901 Hatherleigh Rd Baltimore MD 21212

BEVEL, JAMES LUTHER, clergyman, orgn. exec.; b. Ittabena, Miss., Oct. 19, 1936, s. Dennis and Illie (Murphy) B.; B.A. cum laude, Am. Baptist Theol. Sem., 1961; m. Diane Judith Nash, Nov. 13, 1962; children—Sherrillyn Jill, Douglas John. Ordained to ministry Bapt. Ch., 1959; pastor in Dixon, Tenn., 1959- 61; chmn. Nashville Student Movement, 1960-61; an organizer Student Non-Violent Coordinating Com., 1961, field sec. in Miss., 1961-61; organizer Miss. Free Press, 1961, action program of Albany (Ga.) Movement, 1962; chief organizer, dir. Birmingham movement of So. Christian Leadership Conf., 1963; sponsor Council Fed. Orgns. in Miss., 1962-64; dir. Ala. movement in Selma march, 1965; program dir. Westside Christian parish, Chgo., also project dir. So. Christian Leadership Conf., 1965. Served with USNR, 1954-55. Recipient Peace award War Resistors League, 1963; Rosa Parks award So. Christian Leadership Conf., 1965. Composer freedom songs; Dod-Dog, 1954; I Know We'll Meet Again, 1960; Why Was A Darky Born, 1961.

BEVELANDER, GERRIT, educator; b. West Sayville, N.Y., Apr. 6, 1905; s. John and Alice (Liewen) B.; A.B., Hope (Mich.) Coll., 1926; M.A., U. Mich., 1928; Ph.D., Johns Hopkins, 1932; m. Alice McLaren, Feb. 3, 1949; children—Jill, Karen. With U.S. Bur. Fisheries, 1928-29; instr. Union Coll., N.Y. 1931033; research asso. N.Y. U., 1933-34, instr., 1935-37, asst. prof. anatomy, 1938-40, asso. prof., 1940-47, prof. histology, 1947-62; prof. histology U. Tex. Dental Br., 1962—. Cons. USPHS. Mem. Marine Biol. Lab. (Woods Hole, Mass.), Bermuda Biol. Lab. for Research, Mt. Desert Island Biol. Sta. Fellow A.A.A.S., N.Y. Acad. Sci.; mem. Am. Assn. Anatomists, Am. Soc. Zoologists, Harvey Soc., Soc. Exptl. Biology and Medicine, Internat. Assn. Dental Research, Histochem. Soc., Am. Soc. Oceanography. Home: 689 N Post Oak Lane Houston, TX 77024.

BEVER, ELLIS DORWIN, lawyer; b. Sedan, Kan., Jan. 2, 1903; s. Daniel J. and Tessa (Elliott) B.; student U. Kan., 1922-24; LL.B., George Washington U., 1927, A.B., 1930; m. Dorothy Ann Pennington, Apr. 29, 1933; 1 dau., Vicki. Admitted to Kan. bar, 1927; asst. atty. U.S. Bd. Tax Appeals, Washington, 1927- 33; dir. Kan. Income Tax Dept., Topeka, 1933-37; sr. partner Bever, Dye, Mustard & Belin, specializing in fed. and state tax matters, Wichita, 1937—; partner Carl Todd Drilling Co.; dir. Kansas City Stock Yards Co., (Mo.), Peoples State Bank, Ellinwood, Kan. Bd. dirs., Kan. Crippled Children's Soc. Mem. Am. Bar Assn., Phi Delta Phi, Pi Kappa Alpha. Clubs: Rotary (pres. 1951-52) (Wichita). Home: 560 Broadmoor Wichita KS 67207 Office: First Nat Bank Bldg Wichita KS 67202

BEVER, MICHAEL BERLINER, metallurgist, educator; b. Schmargendorf, Germany, Aug. 7, 1911, s. Rudolf and Maria (Bever) Berliner; came to U.S., 1934, naturalized, 1938; Dr. jur., Heidelbert U., 1934; M.B.A., Harvard, 1937; S.M., Mass. Inst. Tech., 1942, Sc.D., 1944; m. Marion Gordon, Aug. 26, 1936; children—James G., Thomas G., Mary-Ivers. Staff mem. dept. metallurgy 1945-48, asso. prof., 1948-56, prof., 1956-. Member corp. Boston Museam Sci. Registered profl. engr., Mass. Fellow Am. Acad. Arts and Scis.; mem. Am. Inst. Mining, Metall. and Petroleum Engrs., Inst. Metals (Gt. Britain), Am. Soc. Metals, Harvard Musical Assn., Sigma Xi, Unitarian. Contbr. articles profl. jours., books. Co-editor: Basic Open Hearth Steelmaking, 2d. edit., 1951. Cons. editor McGraw-Hill Metallurgy and Metall. Engring. Series, 1956—, Materials Sci. and Engring. Series, 1962—. Home: 23 Highland St Cambridge, MA 02138.

BEVER, WAYNE MELVILLE, educator; b. Lewiston, Ida., Mar. 5, 1904; s. Elmer Edward and Sadie Jane (DeBaun) B.; B.S. in Agr., U. Ida., 1927, M.S., 1928; Ph.D. in Plant Pathology, U. Wis., 1940; m. Velma Myers, July 18, 1931; children—Merilyn Ann, Bernie Wayne. With Agrl. Research Service, Field Crops Research Br., U.S. Dept.Agr., 1928—, pathologist, 1946—; prof. crop pathology U. Ill., 1949—, head dept. plant pathology. Fellow A.A.A.S.; mem. Am. Inst. Biol. Scis., Am. Phytopath. Soc., Sigma Xi, Alpha Zeta, Gamma Sigma Delta. Presbyn. Contbr. Peoples Ency. Home: 609 S Russell St Champaign IL 61820 Office: 218 Mumford Hall Dept of Plant Pathology U Ill Urbana IL 61801

BEVERIDGE, ANDREW BENNIE, lawyer; b. Jellico, Ky., Sept. 28, 1915; s. Andrew and Annie (Bennie) B.; B.S. in Elec. Engring. U. Md., 1936; J.D., George Washington U., 1941; m. Elizabeth Griffith, Aug. 19, 1939; children—Susan W. (Mrs. Pericles G. Perikles), Lynn A. Admitted to D.C. bar, 1941 also U.S. Supreme Ct.; patent atty. Gen. Elec. Co., 1947-51; partner firm Browne, Beveridge & DeGrandi, and predecessors, Washington, 1951—. Served to lt. col. USAAF, 1941-46. Mem. Am. (chmn. sect. patent, trademark and copyright law 1970-71), D.C. (chmn. sect. patent, trademark and copyright law 1963-64), Fed. bar assns., Am. Patent Law Assn., Tau Beta Pi, Omicron Delta Kappa. Democrat. Presbyn. Rotarian. Home: 3910 Calverton Dr Hyattsville MD 20782 Office: 1819 H St Washington DC 20006

BEVERIDGE, JAMES MACDONALD RICHARDSON, univ. pres.; b. Dunfermline, Scotland, Aug. 17, 1912, s. James and Margaret (Spence) B.; B.Sc., Acadia U., Wolfville, N.S., Can., 1937, D.Sc., 1962; Ph.D., U. Toronto, 1940; M.D., U. Western Ont., 1950; LL.D., Mt. Allison U., 1966; m. Jean Frances Eaton, Dec. 26, 1940; children—Catherine, James, Alexander, Robert, Duncan, William, Elizabeth. Research asst. U. Toronto, 1940-44; sci. asst., later asso. biochemist Pacific Fisheries Expt. Sta., Vancouver, B.C., 1944-46; lectr. U. Western Ont., 1946-50; Craine prof. biochemistry, head dept. Queen's U., 1950-64, chmn. bd. grad. studies, 1960-63, dean grad. studies, 1963-64; pres. Acadia U., 1964—. Dir. Canadian Broadcasting Corp., 1966-68; mem. Fisheries Research Bd. Can., 1958-68; mem. Sci. Council Can., 1968—. Fellow Royal Soc. Can., Chem. Inst. Can.; mem. Am. Inst. Nutrition, Internat. Union Biochemistry (chmn. Canadian nat. com. 1959-62), Canadian Biochemistry Soc., Canadian Physiol. Soc. (sec. 1953- 56), Nutrition Soc. Can. (pres. 1965), Alpha Omega Alpha. Mem. United Ch. Can. Contbr. profl. jours. Home: Main St Wolfville Nova Scotia Canada

BEVERIDGE, THOMAS ROBINSON, geologist; b. Sandwich, Ill., June 30, 1918; s. Merritt Hoy and Isabelle Beveridge (Robinson) B.; B.S., Monmouth Coll., 1939; B.S. in Mining Engring., Mo. Sch. Mines, 1942; M.S., U. Ia., 1947, Ph.D., 1949; m. Nancy Mary Lytle, June 12, 1926; children—Nancy L., Mary I. Geologist Ia. Geol. Survey, 1945-47; instr. U. Ia., 1947-49; geologist Mo. Geol. Survey, 1949-55, state geologist and dir., 1955-64; prof. geology and geophysics U. Mo. at Rolla, 1964—, chmn. dept. geology and geophysics, 1965—. Served with Ill. N.G., 1936-40; 1st lt. USAAF, 1943- 45. Fellow Geol. Soc. Am.; mem. Sigma Xi. Presbyn. Home: Route 2 Rolla MO 65401

BEVERLEY, WILLIAM WELBY, ret. army officer; b. Alexandria, Va., Aug. 28, 1917, s. R. H. and Elizabeth (Jones) B.;B.S., U.S. Mil. Acad., 1938; grad. Command and Gen. Staff Coll., 1944, U.S. Armor Sch., 1951, Armed Forces Staff Coll., 1951, Army War Coll., 1955; m. Margaret Rust, Sept. 8, 1938; 1 son, William Welby. Commd. 2d lt. U.S. Army, 1938, advanced through grades to maj. gen., 1960; asst. dir. Army Research Office Chief Research and Devel., Dept. Army, 1960-61; arty. comdr. 2d Armored div., 1961-62; mil. adviser, dir. def. research and devel. Office Sec. Def., 1962-64; dir. enlisted personnel Office Personnel Operations, Dept. Army, Washington 1964-67; chief personnel operations Dept. Army, Washington, 1967-68; comdg. gen. USATC and Ft. Lewis, Washington, 1968-69; chief staff Hdqrs. 8th Army, Korea, 1969-70; ret., 1970. Decorated DSM with oak leaf cluster, Silver Star medal with Oak leaf cluster, Legion of Merit, Bronze Star medal, Croix de Guerre (French), Croix deGuerre (Belgian). Home: 310 Mansion Dr Alexandria, VA 22302.‡

BEVILL, TOM, lawyer, congressman; b. Townley, Ala., Mar. 27, 1921; s. Herman and Fannie Lou (Fike) B.; B.S. U. Ala., 1943; LL.B., 1948; m. Lou Betts, June 24, 1943; children—Susan B., Donald H., Patricia Lou. Admitted to Ala. bar, 1949; pvt. practice law, Jasper, 1948—; mem. Ala. Ho. Reps., 1958-66; mem. 90th-92d Congresses, 7th Dist. Ala. Mem. Am., Ala., Walker County (past pres.) bar assns., Am. Judicature Soc. Home: 1600 Alabama Av Jasper, AL 35501. Office: House Office Bldg Washington DC 20515

BEVILLE, HUGH MALCOLM, Jr., educator; b. Washington, Apr. 18, 1908, s. Hugh Malcolm and Bessie (Hodges) B.; B.S., Syracuse U., 1930; M.B.A., N.Y. U., 1966; m. Eleanor Hudson, Sept. 1, 1939. Statistician NBC, 1930-35, chief statistician, 1935-40, mgr. research, 1940-41, dir. research, 1945-55, v.p., 1956-68, cons., 1968-70. Asso. prof. Southampton Coll., L.I. U., 1966-68, prof., 1968—. Exec. dir. Broadcast Rating Council. Served from 1st lt. to lt. col. AUS, 1941-45. Mem. Am. Marketing Assn., Market Research Council (past pres.), Radio-TV Research Council (past pres.), Am. Assn. U. Profs. Home: 29 Centre Dr Douglaston NY 11363 Office: 420 Lexington Av New York City NY 10017

BEVIN, NEWTON PHILO, architect; b. East Hampton, Conn., Oct. 4, 1895; s. Samuel Mills and Julia (Williams) B.; Litt.B., Princeton, 1917, postgrad., 1919; B. Arch., U. Pa., 1922; m. Elizabeth Hopkins, June 25, 1936. Architect, Milliken & Bevin, N.Y.C., 1927-44; head firm Newton P. Bevin, Architect, N.Y.C., 1944—. Served to 1st lt. U.S. Army, 1917-18; AEF in France. Recipient Ward Melville certificate for Washington (Conn.) community improvement, 1960. Mem. A.I.A., Nat. Inst. Archtl. Edn., N.A.D. Republican. Presbyn. Club: Century (N.Y.C.). Prin. works include residences of Anderson, Mt. Kisco, N.Y., 1930, de Waal, Lexington, Ky., 1938, Shelden, Grosse Pointe, Mich., 1954, Pratt, Frijole, Tex., 1942, Whittemore, Middlebury, Conn., 1961; offices of Telanswer Phone, 1946, N.Y. Airbrake Co., 1953, Rheem Mfg. Co., 1954 (all N.Y.C.); restoration Washington Depot, Conn., 1955; Home: 169 E 78th St New York City, NY 10021. Office: 154 E 61st St New York City NY 10021

BEVIS, DONALD JESSE, accountant; b. Helena, Mont., Oct. 26, 1909; s. Jesse R. and Mabel A. (Bredbeck) B.; M.B.A., U. Mich., 1934; m. Gertrude E. Farley, Sept. 28, 1933 (dec.); children—Frederick, Gregory; m. 2d, Barbara E. Soff, 1962; children—Caroline, Randall, Christopher, Sharon. Staff accountant Ernst & Ernst, 1934-43, asst. mgr., 1943-47; partner George Bailey & Co., 1947 (all Detroit); partner Touche, Ross, Bailey & Smart, Detroit, 1947-61, N.Y.C., 1961—. C.P.A.,Mich., Wis., N.Y., Mo. Treas. Mich. Employer's Unemployment Compensation Bur., 1952—; mem. adv. bd. Wm. A. Paton Fund for Accounting Scholarships and Fellowships at U. Mich. Dir. Detroit Conv. and Tourist Bur., 1958—. Mem. Mich. Mfrs. Assn. (treas., dir.), Am. Accounting Assn., Am. Inst. C.P.A.'s (accounting principles bd., exec. com. council; del. 3d Inter-Am. Accounting Conf. Brazil 1954, v.p. 1957-58), Nat. Assn. Accountants, Mich. Assn. C.P.A.'s (pres. 1953-54, dir. 1948- 54), Detroit Bd. Commerce, Financial Analysts Soc. Detroit, Harrowgate Property Owners Assn. (dir.), Newcomen Soc. Eng. (Am. br.), N.Y. State Soc. C.P.A.'s, Beta Gamma Sigma, Alpha Chi Rho, Beta Alpha Psi, Delta Sigma Pi. Clubs: Union League (N.Y.C.); Larchmont Shore (Larchmont, N.Y.); Sleepy Hollow Country (Scarborough, N.Y.). Home: 22 Carstensen Rd Scarsdale NY 10583 Office: 80 Pine St New York City NY 10005

BEVIS, JOSEPH C., pub. opinion research exec.; b. Harrison, O., Jan. 16, 1910; s. Joseph C. and Helen S. (Norton) B.; A.B., Miami U., Oxford, O., 1931; M.A., Northwestern U., 1932; student Ohio State U., 1931; m. Betsy Ross, Dec. 9, 1934; children—Joseph Ross, James Norton, Cheryl Ann, Beverly Jean. Made pioneer telephone survey of radio audience, 1932; employe, and in full charge, hardware and farm implement store, Harrison, 1932-34; with research div., as dir. surveys of relief population, Fed. Emergency Relief Adminstrn., and successor orgn., WPA, 1934-40; with Opinion Research Corp., Princeton, N.J., 1940-70, v.p., 1945-57, pres., 1957-60, 65-67, chmn. and chief exec. officer, 1960-70; dir. Roper Pub. Opinion Research Center at Williams Coll., 1970—; dir. Roper Orgn., Inc., N.Y.C., 1970—. Mem. Am. Marketing Assn., World, Am. assns. for pub. opinion research, Am. Statis. Assn., Market Research Council N.Y., European Soc. for Opinion and Marketing Research, Market Research Soc. (London), Sigma Alpha Epsilon. Home: 2535 Main St Lawrenceville NJ 08648

BEWKES, EUGENE GARRETT, Jr., holding co. exec.; b. Norwood, Mass., Sept. 28, 1926; s. Eugene Garrett and Helen (Van Vlaanderen) B.; B.A., Colgate U., 1948; LL.B., Yale, 1951; m. Marjorie Louise Klenk, Aug. 20, 1949; children—Eugene Garrett III, Jeffrey Lawrence, Robert David. Admitted to N.Y. bar, 1952; with firm Chapman, Bryson, Walsh & O'Connell, N. Y. C., 1951-55; atty.-adviser also asst. Office Sec. USAF, 1955-57; with Am. Mgmt. Assn., 1957-61, gen. mgmt. div., mgr., 1959-61; gen. counsel, sec., asst. v.p. Reuben H. Donnelley Corp, 1961-67; v.p. law and adminstrn., sec. Canada Dry Corp., 1967-68; v.p., dir. Norton Simon, Inc., N. Y. C., 1968—. Served to ensign USNR, 1945-46. Mem. Am., N.Y. bar assns., Phi Beta Kappa, Delta Kappa Epsilon, Phi Delta Phi. Club: Yale (N.Y.C.). Home: 2 Ox Ridge Lane Darien CT 06820 Office: 277 Park Av New York City NY 10017

BEYCHOK, SHERMAN, educator, biochemist; b. N.Y.C., Sept. 10, 1931; s. Abe and Miriam (Schiffman) B.; B.S., City Coll. N.Y., 1951; Ph.D., N.Y.U., 1957; m. Martha Marcus, Mar. 25, 1950; 1 dau., Cori Bess. Guest chemistry Mass. Inst. Tech., 1956-60; research asso. Children's Cancer Research Found. and Harvard Med. Sch., 1960-61; mem. faculty Columbia, 1962—, prof. biol. scis. and chemistry, 1968—; cons. in field. Mem. Am. Soc. Biol. Chemists, Harvey Soc., Am. Chem. Soc. Author papers in field. Home: 61 Lylewood Dr Tenafly NJ 07670 Office: Dept Biol Scis Columbia Univ New York City NY 10027

BEYEA, HERBERT WRITER, newspaper exec.; b. Howells, N.Y., Mar. 3, 1895; s. George and Emma (Newkirk) B.; student pub. schs.; m. Helen Elizabeth Collins, Feb. 8, 1921; 1 dau., Mary Jane (Mrs. Bartholomew J. Delia). Sec. newspaper reps. co. Cone, Lorenzen & Woodman, 1914-19; with Hearst Newspapers, 1919—; gen. mgr. Hearst Advt. Service, N.Y.C. 1943-56, pres. Bd. dirs. N.Y.C., 1956—; chmn. bd. Hearst Corp. Hearst Found., William Randolph Hearst. Served as chief petty officer USN, 1917-19. Clubs: Metropolitan; Westchester Country: New York Athletic (N.Y.C.). Home: 530 E 72d St New York City, NY 10021. Office: 959 8th Av New York City, NY 10019.

BEYER, EDWARD GEORGE, pharm co. exec.; b. Chgo., July 26, 1910; s. Edward R. and Emma (Knach) B.; grad. Northwestern U., 1934, exec. program bus. adminstrn. Columbia. With Abbott Labs., North Chicago, Ill., 1940—. controller, 1960-64, v.p. finance, 1964-68, v.p. corporate planning, 1968-71, v.p. financial services, 1971—. Mem. Pharm. Mfrs. Assn., Financial Execs. Inst. (dir. Chgo. chpt.), Inst. Mgmt. Scis., Ill. Mfrs. Cost Assn. (mem. exec. com., past pres.), Nat. Assn. Accountants. Home: 4243 Monitor Av Chicago IL 60634 Office: Abbott Labs 14th St and Sheridan Rd North Chicago IL 60064

BEYER, EUGENE EDWARD, Jr., mfg. co. exec.; b. New Brunswick, N.J., Aug. 31, 1920; s. Eugene Edward and Sara (McGowan) (Moore) B.; B.A. magna cum laude, Williams Coll., 1941; LL.B., Yale, 1943; m. Katherine Bozorth, July 15, 1944; children—William Huntley, Alison, Kristi. Admitted to D.C. bar, 1944, Cal. bar, 1946, N.Y. bar, 1950; law clk. to Justice Douglas, 1943-44; spl asst. to atty. gen. tax div. Dept. Justice, 1944-46; asso. Brobeck, Phleger & Harrison, San Francisco, 1946-47; with RCA, 1947-, staff v.p., gen. atty., 1962—. Mem. Assn. Bar City N.Y., Order of Coif, Phi Beta Kappa, Phi Delta Phi, Delta Upsilon. Club: Rockefeller Center Luncheon (N.Y.C.). Editor-in-chief Yale Law Jour., 1942-43. Home: 199 Sagamore Rd Millburn NJ 07041 Office: 30 Rockefeller Plaza New York City NY 10020

BEYER, GERHARD HAROLD, educator; b. Fowler, Mich., July 28, 1923; s. Edwin and Agnes (Rau) B.; B.S., U. Wis., 1944, M.S., 1947, Ph.D., 1949; m. Ruth Anne Zimmerman, May 14, 1947; children—Gerhard Andrew, Jenni Anne, Richard Arnold, Elisabeth Anne. Asso. prof. chem. engring. Ia. State Coll., 1949-55, also asso. engr. Ames Lab.; prof. chem. engring., chmn. dept. U. Mo., 1956-64; prof., chmn. dept. chem. engring. Va. Poly. Inst., 1964-67, prof. chem. engring., 1967—; cons. to industry. Served to lt. (j.g.) USNR, 1944-46. Mem. Am. Inst. Chem. Engrs., Am. Chem. Soc., Am. Soc. Engring. Edn., Sigma Xi, Tau Beta Pi. Home: 1415 Highland Av Blacksburg, VA 24060.

BEYER, KARL HENRY, Jr., pharmacologist; b. Henderson, Ky., June 19, 1914; s. Karl Henry and Lennie Mary (Beadles) B.; B.S., Western Ky. State Coll., 1935; Ph.M., U. Wis., 1937, Ph.D., 1940, M.D., 1943; m. Annette Weiss, Aug. 9, 1940; children—Annette Matilda (Mrs. Richard A. Ellison), Katherine Louise. (Mrs. Kenneth G. Cranson). Asst. dir. pharmacological research Sharp & Dohme, 1943-44, dir. pharmacological research, 1944-50, asst. dir. research, 1950-56; dir. Merck Inst. Therapeutic Research, West Point, Pa., 1956-58, pres., 1961-66; v.p. life scis. Merck Sharp & Dohme, Research Labs., West Point, 1958-66, sr. v.p. research West Point, Merck Sharp & Dohme Research Labs., 1966—; lectr. pharmacology Temple U. Med. Sch., U. Pa. Grad. Med. Sch., Woman's Med. Coll.; lectr. physiology Jefferson Med. Coll.; guest lectr. Swedish U. Med. Schs., 1962. Recipient Gairdner Found. award, 1964; Modern Pioneers in Creative Industry award, Nat. Assn. Mfrs. 1965; Modern Medicine Distinguished Achievement award, 1967; Am. Pharmaceutical Assn. Found. Achievement award, 1967; Distinguished Service award Wis. Alumni Assn., 1968. Fellow Am. Coll. Physicians, A.A.A.S., N.Y. Acad. Scis., Royal Acad. of Medicine; mem. Am. Chem. Soc., Am., Phila. physiol. socs., Soc. for Exptl. Biology and Medicine, Phila. Med. Soc., Am. Soc. for Pharmacology and Exptl. Therapeutics (pres. 1964-65), Fedn. Am. Soc. Exptl. Biology (pres. 1965-66), Am. Therapeutic Soc., Soc. Toxicology, Am. Soc. Nephrology, Am. Heart Assn. (council circulation and renal sect.), Heart Assn. Southeastern Pa. (gov. 1965—), Biol. Abstracts (trustee; treas.), Nat. Acad. Scis. (drug research bd. 1964-70), Canadian Pharm. Soc., Assn. Am. Med. Colls. Author; Pharmacological Basis of Penicillin Therapy, 1950. Contbr. articles profl. jours. Home: Box 276 Gwynedd Valley PA 19437 Office: West Point Merck Sharp & Dohme Research Labs West Point PA 19437

BEYER, LAWRENCE LEONARD, hotel exec.; b. Mpls., Dec. 19, 1908; s. Carl Frederick and Emma (Kesberg) B.; grad. Mpls. Central High Sch., 1927; m. Adelaide R. McNaughton, Oct. 6, 1933; children—Robert, Judith (Mrs. Benjamin Jenkins), Linda (Mrs. Paul Markowitz), Jean Mary. With Curtis Hotel, Mpls., 1928—, mgr., 1945—; sec. Curtis Hotel Co. Home: 5052 Belmont Av S Minneapolis MN 55419 Office: 327 S 10th St Minneapolis MN 55404

BEYER, ROBERT, accountant; b. Milw., Feb. 10, 1913; s. John and Ella (Streidt) B.; B.A., U. Wis., 1935, M.A., 1935; m. Monica Clark, June 24, 1936; children—Tom, Joan (Mrs. Richard Morris), Robert William. Auditor, Ernst & Ernst, C.P.A.'s, Chgo., 1936-47; v.p. Cleaver-Brooks Co., Milw., 1947; partner charge Milw. office Touche, Ross & Co., 1948-62, mng. partner, N.Y.C., 1962—. Guest lectr. U. Wis., 1955, Harvard, 1962—. Mem. bus. adv. council U. Wis., 1965—, sponsor Robert Beyer Professorship in Accounting, 1970—; mem. Pres.'s Commn. on Minority Bus. Enterprise, 1969—; mem. Nat. Indsl. Conf. Bd., 1970—; mem. Com. for Econ. Devel., 1971—; mem. Bus. Adv. Council for the Arts, 1970—. C.P.A., N.Y., Wis., Ill., Mich. Mem. Am. Inst. C.P.A.'s, Nat. Assn. Accountants (exec. com., v.p., nat. bd. chmn. com. research planning, 1966-69), Phi Beta Kappa. Club: University (N.Y.C.). Home: 1205 Wynkoop Rd Colorado Springs CO Office: 1345 Av of Americas New York City NY 10019

BEYER, ROBERT CARLYLE, educator; b. St. Paul, Dec. 7, 1915; s. Thomas Percival and Winifred (Lynn) B.; B.A., Hamline U., 1937; B.A. (Rhodes scholar), Oxford (Eng.) U., 1939, M.A., 1943; Ph.D., U. Minn., 1947; m. Margaret Marie Betterton, Sept. 4, 1950; children—Garrick Warren, Deelan Kay. With Dept. Commerce, 1942; travel and research on coffee industry in Colombia, 1946-47; asst. prof. history U. Miami, 1948-52, aeso. prof., 1952-60, prof., 1960-65, dir. honors, 1960-65; prof. history, dir. honors Coll. William and Mary, 1965—; mem. Klein and Saks Econ. and Financial Mission to Chile, 1955-56. Served from ensign to lt. comdr. USNR, 1942-46, 50-52. Mem. Am. Hist. Assn., Conf. Latin Am. History, Am. Assn. U. Profs., Phi Kappa Phi. Unitarian. Contbr. articles to periodicals. Home: 117 Indian Springs Rd Williamsburg VA 23185

BEYER, ROBERT THOMAS, educator; b. Harrisburg, Pa., Jan. 27, 1920; s. James M. and Mary (Gibney) B.; A.B., Hofstra U., 1942; Ph.D., Cornell U., 1945; M.A. (hon.), Brown U., 1957; m. Ellen Fletcher, Feb. 14, 1944; children—Catherine E., Margaret A., Richard J., Mary L. Teaching asst. Cornell U., 1942-45; instr. physics Brown U., 1945-47, asst. prof., 1947- 51, asso. prof., 1951-58, prof., 1958—, exec. officer dept. physics, 1966-68, chmn. dept., 1968—; vis. prof. Technische Hochschule, Stuttgart, Germany, 1961-62, U. Birmingham (Eng.), 1971. Editor Soviet Physics JETP transl. jour., 1955-57; cons., chmn. Am. Inst. Physics Trans. adv. bd., 1957—; cons. on underwater sound Raytheon, 1962—. Fellow Fund for Advancement Edn., 1953-54. Fellow Am. Phys. Soc., Accoustical Soc. Am. (pres. 1968-69), I.E.E.E. Translated (from German), Practical Analysis by F. A. Willers, 1948; Mathematical Foundations of Quantum Mechanics by Johann von Neumann, 1955; translated (from Russian), Molecular Scattering of Light by I.L. Fabelinskii, 1968. Author: (with A.O. Williams, Jr.) College Physics, 1957; (with Stephen V. Letcher) Physical Ultrasonics, 1969. Editor transl. from

Chinese: Acta Physica Sinica, 1966-68. Home: 132 Cushman Av East Providence RI 02914 Office: Physics Dept Brown U Providence RI 02912

BEYER, WERNER WILLIAM, educator; b. Laporte, Ind., Mar. 22, 1911; s. Franz E.W. and Martha L. (Beyer) B.; A.B. with spl. honors, Columbia, 1934, M.A., 1936, Ph.D., 1945; m. Ruth Katherine Bibos, Nov. 19, 1954; children—Tanya E., Mary Deirdre. Sr. English master Englewood (N.J.) Sch. Boys, 1936-41; instr. English, Drew U., 1943-45; asst. prof. Rutgers U., 1945-48; vis. asst. prof. English, Columbia, 1948; faculty Butler U., 1948—, prof. English, 1951—, Rebecca Clifton Reade prof., head dept., 1967—; vis. prof. Ind. U., 1964-65; Jr. League lectr., 1963—. Cons. Scott Foresman & Co., 1966-67. Mem. English adv. com. Ind. Dept. Edn., 1968—. Lydig fellow, 1941-42; William Bayard Cutting fellow, 1942-43; Ford Found. fellow, 1951-52. Mem. Modern Lang. Assn. (sec., then chmn. comparative lit. VI, 1960-62), Coll. English Assn., Phi Kappa Phi. Presbyn. (deacon 1960-65, elder 1966-68). Author: The Prestige of C.M. Wieland, 1936; Keats and the Daemon King, 1947; The Enchanted Forest, 1963; The World in Literature (bibliography), 1967; also articles, revs. Editor: Oberon W. Sotheby, 1971. Home: 6455 E 96th St Indianapolis IN 46250

BEYLER, ROGER ELDON, univ. dean; b. Nappanee, Ind., May 20, 1922; s. Oscar L. and Ethel (Johns) B.; B.A., North Central Coll., 1944; M.A., U. Ill., 1947, Ph.D., 1949; m. Herberta E. Hasewinkel, Aug. 29, 1944; children—Keith, Eric, Jane. Research chemist pharmaceuticals Merck & Co., Inc., Rahway, N.J., 1949-59; prof. So. Ill. U., Carbondale, 1959—, acting chmn. dept. chemistry, 1965-66, dean Coll. Liberal Arts and Scis., 1966—; vis. lectr. U. Minn., 1963. Served with USNR, 1944-46. OECD Sci. fellow U. Strasbourg (France), 1964. Mem. Am. Chem. Soc., The Chem. Soc. (Eng.), Sigma Xi, Phi Kappa Phi, Alpha Chi Sigma, Phi Lambda Upsilon. Presbyn. Research and publ. in steroid chemistry. Patentee in field. Home: 117 Pinewood Dr Carbondale IL 62901

BEZANSON, GORDON HOFFMAN, banker; b. New Haven, Sept. 21, 1908; s. Harry Brown and Grace (Hoffman) B.; ed. pub. schs.; diploma Am. Inst. Banking, 1955; m. Evelyn A. Myers, Oct. 5, 1932; children—Gordon Hoffman, Dianne (Mrs. Robert J. Keleher). With Hartford Nat. Bank & Trust Co. (Conn.), 1927—, sr. v.p., 1968—; tchr. Am. Inst. Banking, 1955-58. Mem. Probate Ct. Practice Book Com. on Accounting; mem. Estate and Bus. Planning council of Hartford. Mem. Avon Zoning and Planning Commn., 1962-63. Bd. dirs. Avon (Conn.) Pub. Library, 1971—, Avon (Conn.) United Fund, 1966—. Episcopalian. Clubs: City (Hartford); Golf (Avon). Home: 756 W Avon Rd Avon CT 06001 Office: 777 Main St Hartford CT 06115

BEZANSON, PETER FLOYD, banking and finance co. exec.; b. Mpls., Apr. 2, 1915; s. Harry B. and Lilliam M. (Zwicker) B.; B.A., U. Wis., 1937; Postgrad. Columbia, 1960; m. Lorrayne B. Bing, June 17, 1939; children—Judith Rae, Randal Peter. Pres. MorAmerica Financial Corp., also Morris Plan of Ia., Cedar Rapids 1953—, Jackson State Bank & Trust Co., Maquoketa, Ia., 1956—, Bezanson Ins., Inc., Cedar Rapids, 1949—, Ia. Growth Investment Co., Cedar Rapids, 1958—, Lease Am., Inc., DW Co., Cedar Rapids, 1955—, Sunnycrest Nursing Facilities, Inc., Cedar Rapids, 1964—. Chmn. bd. Am. Indsl. Bankers Assn., 1966-68; bd. govs. Nat. Assn. Small Bus. Investment Assn., 1961-68. Chmn. finance com. Hawkeye area council dist. Boy Scouts Am., 1965-69; nat. vice chmn. fund drive A.R.C., 1959-60. Trustee U. Colo. Installment Banking Sch., 1962—. Served with USAAF, 1944-45. Mem. Chi Phi. Presbyn. (trustee). Mason (Shriner), Elk, Rotarian. Club: Cedar Rapids Country. Home: 2111 Cottage Grove Lane S E Cedar Rapids, IA 52401. Office: American Bldg Cedar Rapids IA 52401

BEZANSON, PHILIP THOMAS, educator, composer; b. Athol, Mass., Jan. 6, 1916; s. Claude Edward and Blanche (Redden) B.; Mus.B., Yale, 1940; M.A., U. Ia., 1948, Ph.D., 1951; m. Lillian Elizabeth Carlson, Nov. 28, 1940; children—Carol Ann (Mrs. William Arthur Garrabrant), Thomas Edward. Instr., U. Ia., 1948- 51, asst. prof., 1951-54, asso. prof., 1954-61, prof. composition, 1961- 64; prof., head music dept. U. Mass., Amherst, 1964—. Chmn. music screening com. Internat. Exchange of Persons, Washington, 1968-70. Mem. Mass. Council on Arts and Humanities, 1966-69. Served with USNR, 1945-46. Guggenheim fellow, 1967-68. Mem. Am. Composers Alliance. Publns. include: Prelude and Dance for Brass Sextet, 1961; String Quartet No. 1, 1965; Diversion for Brass Trio, 1968. Composer: Piano Concerto, N.Y. Philharmonic Symphony Orch., 1953; Opera, Golden Child, NBC-TV, Hallmark Hall of Fame, 1961; also solo, chamber, vocal, orchestral works. Home: 15 Highland Circle Hadley MA 01035 Office: U Mass Amherst MA 01002

BEZOU, HENRY CHARLES, clergyman, educator; b. New Orleans, April 28, 1913; s. André Ralph and Lydia Marie (Bouligny) B.; ed. Saint Aloysius Coll., 1929; student St. Joseph Sem., St. Benedict, La., 1932, Notre Dame Sem., New Orleans, 1934, 38; A.M., Cath. U. Am., 1947; Litt.D. (honoris causa), Loyola U. of So., 1952. Ordained priest Roman Cath. Ch., 1938; with Sacred Heart Ch., Montegut, La., 1938-42, St. Charles Ch., Lafourche, La., 1942-43; head Normal Sch., Houma, La., 1940-42; Archdiocesan supt. schs., New Orleans, 1943-68; named Papal Chamberlain with title Very Reverend Monsignor, 1949; domestic prelate with title Rt. Rev. Monsignor, 1954; dir. Cath. com. S. Summer Sch., Loyola U.; pastor St. Patricks Ch., New Orleans, 1951-65, Our Lady Star of the Sea Ch., 1965- 67, St. Francis Xavier, Metairie, La., 1967—; spiritual dir. Ozanam Inn, 1955-65. Mem. Archdiocesan Central Council, Soc. St. Vincent de Paul, 1956-66, archdiocesan cons., 1962—; sec. elementary div. Nat. Cath. Ednl. Assn.; mem. Gov.'s Safety Com.; also other state coms.; mem. Archdiocesan Bldg. Commn.; mem. Mayor's Adv. Coms.: bd. dirs. New Orleans Symphony Soc., New Orleans TB League, La. Soc. for Crippled Children, Community Chest, United Fund, mem schs. com.; mem. adv. com. Juvenile Ct.; cons. supt's div., dept. edn. Nat. Cath. Welfare Conf.; mem. coms. State Dept. Edn.; trustee Greater New Orleans Ednl. TV Found.; mem. White House Conf. on Edn., 1955; regional adv. bd. A.R.C.; adv. bd. Cath. Ency. Sch. and Home. Dir. Information Council of Ams. Chevalier Legion of Honor; recipient Palmes Academiques and title Officer d'Academie, 1949. Mem. Am. Cath. Hist. Assn., Fgn. Policy Assn., Nat. Cath. Edn. Assn. (pres. supts. dept.), Am. Soc. Legion of Honor. Author articles, pamphlets, brochures including: A Course of Study for Catholic Schools in Louisiana; A Handbook of Policies for the Catholic Schools of the Archdiocese of New Orleans; A Brief History of St. Patrick's Church, New Orleans The Second Century. Address: 448 Metairie Rd Metairie LA

BHAGWATI, JAGDISH NATWARLAL, educator; b. Bombay, India, July 26, 1934; s. Natwarlal H. and Saraswati (Amin) B.; B.Commerce, Bombay U., 1954; B.A., Cambridge (Eng.) U., 1956, M.A., 1961; Ph.D., Mass. Inst. Tech., 1964; B.A., Oxford (Eng.) U., 1959; m. Padma Kalidas Desai, Oct. 24, 1970. Came to U.S., 1968. Research asso. internat. econs. U. Chgo., 1959; research fellow Nuffield Coll., Oxford U., 1959-61; prof. econs. Indian Statis. Inst., 1962-63; prof. internat. trade Delhi U., 1963-68; vis. prof. econs. Columbia, 1967-68; prof. econs. Mass. Inst. Tech., 1968—; cons. UN agencies, govts. Turkey and India. Mem. Econometric Soc., Am. Econ. Assn. Author: Economics of Underdeveloped Countries, 1966; The Theory and Practice of Commercial Policy, 1968; Trade, Tariffs and Growth, 1969; Planning for Industrialization: A Study of India's Trade and Industrial Policies, 1970. Editor Jour. Internat. Econs., 1971—, Am. Econ. Rev., 1970—. Contbr. profl. jours. Home: 11 White Pine Lane Lexington MA 02173 Office: Mass Inst Tech Cambridge MA 02139

BHARGAVA, TRILOKI NATH, educator; b. Lucknow, India, Aug. 21, 1933; s. Sri Ram and Kailash (Devi) B.; B.Sc., Lucknow U., 1952, B.Sc. hons., 1953, M.Sc., 1954; Ph.D., Mich. State U., 1962. Came to U.S., 1965. Lectr. Khalsa Coll., Bombay, India, 1954-55, Gujarat U., 1955-57, Agra U., 1957-58; asso. prof. State Tchrs. Coll., Elizabeth City, N.C., 1961-62; asst. prof. to prof. mathematics Kent State U., 1962—; research asso. Center Urban Regionalism. Recipient grant, Nat. Sci. Found., 1963, NASA, 1964-68. Fellow Royal Statis. Soc.; mem. Am. Math. Soc., A.A.A.S., Am. Statis. Assn., Inst. Math. Statistics, Kent Council World Affairs (exec. com.). Home: 2255 Winter Pkwy Cuyahoga Falls OH 44221 Office: Kent State Univ Kent OH 44242

BHERER, WILBROD, mfg. co. exec.; b. Murray Bay, Can., Aug. 11, 1905; s. Wilbrod and Laure (Lapointe) B.; B.A., St. Mary's Coll., 1927; LL.B., Laval U., 1930; m. Francoise Pruneau, 1931; 1 dau., Helene. Called to Bar of Que., 1930; apptd. Queen's Counsel, 1945; chmn. bd. Canadian Vickers, Ltd.; dir. Banque Canadienne Nationale, Montreal, La Prevoyance Compagnie d'Assurance, Trust Gen. du Can., Trans-Can. Corp. Fund, Syndicat de Que. Ltez., Jacques-Cartier Investment Co., Ritz Carlton Hotel Co. Montreal Ltd., Power Corp. Can. Ltd., Gaz du Que. Inc., Longmans Can. Ltd., Ciments Lafarge Que. Ltee. Pres. Commn. Cath. Schs. Que. Gov. bd. trustees Laval U., also pres. Hospitality Center. Home: 835 Av des Braves Quebec Quebec Canada Office: 500 E Grande Allee Quebec Quebec Canada*

BHUMIBOL, ADULYADEJ, See Phumiphon Aduldet, king of Thailand. Address: Thailand

BHUTTO, ZULFIKAR ALL, lawyer; b. Larkana, Sind, Pakistan, Jan. 5, 1928; s. Sir Shah Nawaz Khan and Lady Khurshid Bhutto; B.A. with honors in Polit. Sci., U. Cal. at Berkeley, 1950; M.A. with honors in Jurisprudence, Christ Ch. Coll., Oxford (Eng.) U., 1952; m. Nusrat Ispahani, Sept. 8, 1951; children—BeNazir, Mir Ghulam Murtaza, Sanam-Sema, Shah Nawaz. Called to bar Lincoln's Inn, 1953; practiced law in Karachi, W. Pakistan, 1953-58; lectr. constl. law Sind Muslin Law Coll., Karachi, 1956-58; Pakistanian minister commerce, 1958-60, minister nat. reconstrn. and information, 1959-60, minister Kashmir affairs and minority affairs, 1959-60, minister fuel, power and natural resources, 1960-62, minister industries and natural resources, 1962-63, minister external affairs, 1963-66; lead revolt against Govt. of Ayub Khan, 1969. Pres., Pakistan Islamic Council for Internat. Affairs. Founder, chmn. Pakistan People's Party, 1967, now leader majority party from West Pakistan. Del. from Pakistan, XII session UN Gen. Assembly, 1957; former dep. leader Muslim League, Nat. Assembly; leader Pakistan delegation UN Conf. Law of Sea, Geneva, Switzerland, 1958, XIV and XV sessions UN Gen. Assembly, 1959-60, to USSR for negotiation oil exploration agreement, 1960; Pakistanian chief negotiator Indo-Pakistan talks on Kashmir, 1962; leader Pakistan delegation on demarcation boundary between Pakistan and China, 1963; leader Pakistan delegation to SEATO Ministerial Council Meeting, London, 1965, 14th CENTO Ministerial Council, Ankara, 1966; participant numerous other internat. confs. and meetings. Chmn. bd. govs. Pakistan Adminstrv. Staff Coll., Lahore. Decorated Nishan-i-Hamayun 1st class (Iran); Order of Republic of Indonesia; Gran Cruz de la Order del Libertador Gen. San Martin (Argentina). Mem. Abadgars Assn. Dist. Larkana (pres.), Social Welfare Council W. Pakistan. Author: Myth of Independence, 1968. Home: Bhutto Colony Larkana West Pakistan Office: 70 Clifton St Karachi West Pakistan

BIAGGI, MARIE, congressman; b. N.Y. C., Oct. 26, 1917 s. Salvatore and Mary (Campari) B.; LL.B., N.Y. Law Sch., 1963; m. Marie Wassil, Apr.20, 1941; children—Jacqueline, Barbara, Richard, Mario II. Detective lt. N.Y.C. Police Dept., 1942-65; community relations specialist, N.Y.C., 1961-63; admitted to N.Y. bar, 1963; asst. sec. state N.Y. 1966—; mem. 91st Congress 24th Dist. N.Y. Past 1st v.p. acting pres. Patrolmen's Benevolent Assn.; past bd. dirs. Police Widows Relief Fund. Police Recreation Center, Police Pension Fund. Municipal Credit Union. Recipient medal of honor N.Y.C. Police pres. 1967), Am., Bronx County bar assns., Trial Lawyers Assn., Navy League, Columbia Assns. in Civil Service (pres grand council Office: Longworth House Office Bldg Washington DC 20515

BIAGGINI, BENJAMIN FRANKLIN, R.R. exec.; b. New Orleans, Apr. 15, 1916; s. B.F. and Maggie (Switzer) B.: B.S. St. Mary's of Tex., 1936: advanced mgmt. program Harvard, 1955; m. Anne Payton, Sept. 9, 1937; children— successively rod-man, engring dept., asst. to chief engr., dir. St. Louis Southwestern Ry. Co. Gen Chmn. United Bay Area (dir.), Cal. Chamber of Commerce (director), American Railway Engring. Assn., Harvard Bus. Sch. Assn. Clubs; Burlingame (Cal.) Country; Houston; California (Los Angeles); San Francisco Golf, Stock Exchange, Pacific Union, Bohemian (San Francisco); Links (N.Y.C.); Chicago; Metro- (Washington). Home: 1170 Sacramento St. San Francisco CA 94108 Office: 65 Market St San Francisco CA 94105

BIALKOSKI, HENRY STANLEY, banker; b. N.Y.C., Apr. 7, 1922; s. Walter and Helen (Karaszewski) B.; certificate, Bergen Jr. Coll 1949; B.B.A., Iona Coll., 1951; postgrad. Rutgers U., 1969-70; m. Dorothy Elizabeth Lorenzen, Sept. 27, 1947; children—John, Raymond, Matthew. Jr. accountant T.M. Byxbee & Co., N.Y.C., 1951-53; sr. accountant Lybrand, Ross Bros. & Montgomery, N.Y.C., 1953-56; sr. auditor Standard Brands, Inc., N.Y.C., 1956-61; asst. to financial v.p. Sperry Gyroscope Co. div. Sperry Rand Corp., 1961-69; auditing officer European Am. Banking Corp.-European Am. Bank & Trust Co., N.Y.C., 1969—. Served with USAAF, World War II. C.P.A., N.J. Mem. Am. Inst. C.P.A.'s, N.J. Soc. C.P.A.'s, Inst. Internal Auditors, Bank Adminstrn. Inst. Republican. Club: Toastmasters Internat. (sec.-treas.) (Paramus, N.J.). Home: 581 Stewart St Ridgefield NJ 07657 Office: 52 Wall St New York City NY 10005

BIANCO, JOSEPH, banker; b. Visalia, Cal., Oct. 7, 1913; s. Stephen and Mary L. (Lippolis) B.; B.S., U.San Francisco, 1936; postgrad. U. Cal. at San Francisco, 1939, Columbia, 1958; m. Marcile Miller, Feb. 7, 1967. Br. mgr. Bank of Am., 1936-52; asst. v.p. First Nat. Bank Nev., Reno, 1952-55; v.p. 1st Western Bank & Trust Co., Bakersfield, Cal., 1955- 57; pres. Conrad Nat. Bank, Kalispell, Mont., 1957-60; chmn. bd., pres. Bank of Ida., Boise, 1960—, also dir.; dir. Western Nat. Corp. Past pres. Boise Clearing House Assn., Boise Art Assn. Served with USAAF, World War II. Mem. Am. (exec. council), Ida (past pres.) bankers assns., Greater Boise C. of C. (past pres.), Bank Marketing and Pub. Relations Assn. (past dir.), Am. Legion. Clubs: Hillcrest Country, Arid, Crane Creek (Boise); Hayden Lake (Ida.) Country. Home: 2817 Selkirk St Boise, ID 83702. Office: 700 W Idaho St Boise ID 83701

BIANCOE, GEORGE ANDERS educator, biologist; b. Ames, Ia. Instr., Ia. State U., 1946-47; asst. prof. biology Johns Hopkins, 1947-50, asso. prof., 1950-62, prof., 1962--, chmn. dept., 1963-69; vis. lectr. Stanford, 1970-71. Active Boy Scouts Am., 4-H Club. Served with AUS, 1940-46. Mem. Am. Soc. Biologists, Md. Biologists, A.A.A.S., Am. Acad. Arts and Scis., Phi Beta Kappa.

BIANCOLLI, LOUIS, writer; b. N.Y.C., Apr. 17, 1907; s. Carmine and Achilla (Montesano) B.; A.B., N.Y. U., 1935. A.M., 1936; postgrad. Columbia, 1936-38, Am. Council Learned Socs. grant for studies Russian, Intensive Lang. Programs, 1943; m. Edith Rattner, 1933 (dec. 1957); 1 dau., Margaret (Mrs. Murray Weissbach); m. 2d, Jeanne Mitchell, 1958; children—Lucy, Amy. Music critic N.Y. World-Telegram and Sun. 1928-66; annotator N.Y. Philharmonic Soc., 1941-49. Mem. Music Critics Circle, Phi Beta Kappa. Author: (with Robert Bagar) The Concert Companion, 1947; The Book of Great Conversations, 1948; The Analytical Concert Guide, 1951; (with Mary Garden) Mary Garden's Story, 1951; The Flagstad Story, 1952; The Opera Reader, 1953; The Mozart Handbook, 1954; (with Herbert F. Peyser) Masters of the Orchestra, 1954; (with Ruth Slenczynska) Forbidden Childhood, 1957; (with Roberta Peters) A Debut at the Met, 1967. Translator: Boris Godounoff libretto from Russian, 1952, 64; (in blank verse) Dante's Divine Comedy, 1966; (with Thomas Scherman) The Beethoven Companion, 1972. Contbr. articles to mags. Address: New Preston CT 06777

BIANCULLI, JOSEPH A., educator; b. Pitts., Oct., 24, 1911; s. Vitale and Josephine (Martorano) B., B.S., U. Pitts., 1932, Ph.D. in Organic Chemistry, 1941; B.S. in Pharmacy, Pitts. Coll. Pharmacy, 1935; m. Nancy Viccarelli, Aug. children—Thomas, Paul, Arthur. Grad. asst. Pitts. Coll. Pharmacy, 1936-41; research chemist Am. Cyanamid Co., 1942-45; asst. dir. chem. research Reed and Carnrick, 1945-48; with U. Pitts. Sch. Pharmacy, 1945—, prof. pharm. chemistry, 1954—, chmn. dept., 1955—, now dean. Recipient Alumnus award, 1967. Mem. Galen Pharm. Soc. (hon. life), Am. Chem. Soc., Am. Pharm. Assn., Sigma Xi, Alpha Zeta Omega, Rho Chi, Phi Lambda Upsilon, Kappa Psi, Omicron Delta Kappa (dean 1961). Home: 443 S Braddock Av Pittsburgh PA 15221

BIBB, PEYTON DANDRIDGE, lawyer; b. Elmore, Ala., Oct. 3, 1904; s. Walter Haynie and Florence (Spiers) B.; A.B., U. Ala., 1925, LL.B., 1929; m. Hulda McNeel, Nov. 19, 1932; children-Adele (Mrs. Charles H. Colvin III), Peyton Dandridge. Admitted to Ala. bar, 1929, since practiced in Birmingham; spl. asst. atty. gen. Ala., 1935-39; mem. firm Wingo, Bibb, Foster, Conwell & Strickland and predecessor firms, 1929—; instr. English, U. Ala., 1927- 29; dist. counsel Seaboard Coast Line R.R. and predecessors, 1932—. Dir. Nat. Filtronics, Inc. Vice pres., bd. dirs. Ala. Motorists Assn.; pres. bd. trustees Brooke Hill Sch.; mem. adv. bd. Ala. Boys Indsl. Sch. Served to maj. USAAF, 1942-45. Mem. Am., Ala., Birmingham bar assns., Am. Judicature Soc., Newcomen Soc., Phi Beta Kappa, Phi Delta Phi, Omicron Delta Kappa, Sigma Upsilon, Phi Kappa Sigma, Masons. Democrat. Episcopalian. Clubs: Civitan, Redstone, Relay House (Birmingham). Home: 2835 Argyle Rd Birmingham AL 35213 Office: First Nat Bldg Birmingham AL 35203

BIBBY, BASIL GLOVER, dentist; b. Waipawa, New Zealand, Oct. 6, 1904; s. James Woodhouse and Mary Glover (Tod) B.; came to U.S., 1939; naturalized 1940; B.D.S., U. Otago, New Zealand, 1927, D.Sc. (hon.), 1969; Ph.D., U. Rochester, 1935; D.M.D., Tufts Coll., 1939; Doctor Odontology (honorary), Norway, 1959; m. Beatrice Boardman, July 8, 1933; children—Ruth Mary, Anne Beatrice, Evelyn S., Douglas B. Dental asst. Christchurch (New Zealand) Hosp., 1928-29; instr. operative dentistry U. Otago, 1929- 30; in private practice, Wellington, New Zealand, 1930; Rockefeller dental fellow U. Rochester, 1930-33, Rockefeller sr. fellow, 1933- 35, asst. prof. dentistry, 1936-40; dean Tufts Coll. Dental Sch., Boston, 1940; prof. bacteriology Tufts Med. and Dental Sch., 1940-47; dir. Eastman Dental Center, Rochester, prof. of dentistry, U. Rochester, 1947-70, clin. prof. emeritus, 1971—. Lectr. Internat. Dental Congress of Chile, 1951; Fulbright lectr., New Zealand, 1953; cons. Armed Forces Med. Library, 1950-54, NIH, 1970-71. Alumni trustee Tufts College, 1940-59; regent Nat. Med. Library. Recipient Alfred C. Fones award Conn. Dental Soc., 1961; research award Mass. Dental Soc., 1969. Mem. Soc. American Bacteriologists, Internat. Assn. Dental Research (president 1950-51), Pan Am. Odontalogy Assn. (pres. 1946), Am. Dental Assn., All India Dental Soc., also dental socs. Denmark, Peru, Chile. Presbyn. Clubs: Rotary, Genesee Valley. Contbr. profl. jours. Home: 94 Shoreham Dr Brighton NY 14610 Office: 800 Main St E Rochester NY 14605

BIBBY, DAUSE LEVERIDGE, appliance co. exec.; b. Cisco, Tex., June 7, 1911; s. Ocie Douglas and Carrie Ethel (Leveridge) B.; student Tex. A. and M. Coll., 1928-29; B.B.A. U. Tex., 1933; m. Virginia Martin, Apr. 4, 1937; children—Carolyn, Martha, Douglas. Student salesman IBM Corp., Endicott, N.Y., 1934, sr. salesman, 1935-37, mgr. sales office, 1937-41, asst. to v.p., 1941-43, resident mgr. Poughkeepsie (N.Y.) plant, 1943-46, exec. asst. Endicott plant, 1946, gen. mgr., Poughkeepsie, 1946-49, v.p. corp., 1949-56; exec. v.p., dir. Daystrom, Inc., 1956-59; exec. v.p. Remington Rand div., 1959-60, pres., 1960-64, dir. Sperry Rand Corp., 1959-64, v.p. 1963- 64; pres. Stromberg-Carlson div. Gen. Dynamics Corp., N.Y.C., 1964—. Mem. adv. com. Met. br. Chase Nat. Bank, N.Y.C.; mem. bd. advisers XIII Internat. Mgtm. Congress; 1963. Bd. dirs., v.p. Sheltered Workshop for Disabled, Birmingham, N.Y.: bd. dirs. Youth Consultation Service, N.Y.C., 1961—; hon. chmn. Mid-Hudson Workshop for Disabled; dir.- at-large N.Y. Cerebral Palsy Assn.; v.p. exec. bd. Susequenango council Boy Scouts Am., 1950-53; bd. dirs. Broome County chpt. A.R.C., 1952-53, N.Y. State div. Am. Cancer Soc., also Broome County chpt.; bd. dirs. Bus. Equipment Mfrs. Assn., Council for Internat. Progress in Mgmt. Served as lt. USNR, World War II. Mem. Navy League U.S., Nat. Football Found., Soc. for Advancement Mgmt. (past chmn., past pres.), N.Y. So. Soc., Newcomen Soc., Nat. Fund Med. Edn. (com. Am. industry). Clubs: University, Economic, Manhattan (N.Y.C.); Ardsley (N.Y.C.); Ardsley (N.Y.) Country. Office: 100 Carlson Rd Rochester NY 14603

BIBBY, DOUGLAS EARL, physician; b. Cisco, Tex., Aug. 15, 1922, s. Earl Riss and Eunice (Key) B.; student John Tarleton Agrl. Coll., 1940-42; MD., U. Tex., 1946; m. Elinor Elaine Duncan, May 9, 1945; children—Gayle Elaine, Bonnie Colleen, Lynda Diane. Intern Harris Meml. Hosp., Ft. Worth, 1946-47; resident radiology VA Hosp., McKinney, Tex., 1949-51; practice radiology, Temple, Tex., 1951-52, Ft. Worth, 1952—; asst. prof. radiology U. Tex. Southwestern Med. Sch., 1961—. Trustee Am. Registry Radiol. Technicians, 1962-66. Served with M.C., AUS, 1947-49. Diplomate Am. Bd. Radiology. Fellow Am. Coll. Radiology; mem. A.M.A., Tex. Med. Assn., Tarrant County Med. Soc., Radiol. Soc. N.Am. Home: 3708 Sierra Ct Ft Worth, TX 76109. Office: 1550 W Rosedale St Ft Worth TX 76104

BIBELOW, EUGENE THAYER, banker; b. Boston, Mar. 19, 1913; s. Henry Forbes and Susan (Thayer) B.; A.B., Harvard, 1935; m. Marjorie Benson, Jan. 6, 1953; children—Eugene Thayer, Susan (Mrs. Anthony K. Fisher), Natalie (Mrs. Christopher Cutler), Alice Ann. Mdse. mgr. Burrows & Sanborn, Lynn, Mass., 1935-42; v.p. First Nat. Bank & Trust Co., Santa Barbara, Cal., 1942-52; credit and investment analyst First Nat. Bank of Nev., Reno, 1953, cashier, 1954, v.p.,

1955-61, adminstrv. v.p., 1961-69, sr. v.p., exec. officer trust activities, 1969—. State pres. U.S.O., 1968—; pres. United Fund, Las Vegas, 1967-68; head spl. gifts United Fund, Reno, 1970. Mem. Prospectors. Rotarian. Club: Hidden Valley Country (Reno). Home: 701 Brown St Reno NV 89502 Office: 1 E 1st St Reno NV 89504

BIBERMAN, HERBERT J., writer, dir.; b. Phila., Mar. 4, 1900; ed. U. Pa.; M.A., Prof. Baker's Prof. Baker's 47 Workshop, Yale; m. Gale Sondergaard. Dir. N.Y. plays for Theatre Guild including Roar China, Red Rust, Miracle At Verdun, Green Grow The Lilacs, Valley Forge; dir. films One Way Ticket, Meet Nero Wolfe, Road to Yesterday, The Master Race, Salt of the Earth; author original and screenplay King of Chinatown, Slaves; producer Abilene Town; collaborator original story New Orleans. Address: 263 West End Av New York City NY 10023

BIBERSTEIN, ERNST LUDWIG, vet. med. educator; b. Breslau, Germany, Nov. 11, 1922; s. Hans Harry and Erna (Stein) B.; B.S., U. Ill., 1947; D.V.M., Cornell U., 1951, M.S., 1954, Ph.D., 1955; m. Hannah Hahn, June 26, 1949; children—Michael P., Helen R., Anne D., Julie B. Practice vet. medicine, Akron, O., 1951-52; acting asso. prof. clin. pathology N.Y. State Vet. Coll., 1955-56; faculty U. Cal. at Davis Sch. Vet. Medicine, 1956—, prof. microbiology, 1966—, chmn. dept., 1969—, chief microbiology service Vet. Med. Teaching Hosp., 1967—. Mem. com. animal health, subcom. standards methods for vet. microbiology Nat. Acad. Scis. Served with AUS, 1943-45. Decorated Silver Star. NIH spl. fellow Moredun Inst., Edinburgh, Scotland, 1963-64, 68-69. Diplomate Am. Coll. Vet. Microbiology. Mem. Am. Acad. Microbiology, Am. Vet. Med. Assn., Am. Soc. Microbiology, Path. Soc. Gt. Britain and Ireland, Conf. Research Workers Animal Diseases, Sigma Xi, Gamma Sigma Delta, Phi Zeta, Phi Kappa Phi, Alpha Epsilon Pi. Jewish religion. Co-translator, editor (with R.E. Habel): The Fundamentals of the Histology of Domestic Animals, rev. edit., 1957. Home: 508 12th St Davis CA 95616

BIBLE, ALAN, U.S. senator; b. Lovelock, Nev., Nov. 20, 1909; s. H.H. and Isabel (Welsh) B.; A.B., U. Nev., 1930; LL.B., Georgetown Law Sch., Washington, 1934, LL.D.; LL.D., Rider Coll., U. Nev., 1970; m. Loucile Jacks, Nov. 17, 1939; children—Debra (Mrs. Robert Watkins), Paul Alfred, William Alan, David Milton. Admitted to Nev. bar, 1935; dist. atty. Storey County, Nev., 1935-38, dep. atty. gen., 1938-43, atty.-gen. Nev., 1943-51; U.S. senator from Nev., 1954—. Mem. Am. (state del. of com. on improvement jud. adminstrn.), Nev. bar assns., Western Regional Group of Attys. Gen. (chmn.), Nat. Safety Council (mem.-at-large traffic sect.), U. Nev. Alumni Assn. Democrat. Methodist. Mason, Eagle. Office: 145 Senate Office Bldg Washington DC 20013

BIBLE, HENRY HAROLD, chem. exec.; b. Lawton, Okla., Feb. 13, 1916; s. Minnes and Margaret May (Mosley) B.; B.S. in Chem. Engring., U. Okla., 1938; m. Alice Malene Baber, Jan. 2, 1937; children—Alice Kay, Suzanne Malene, Henry Harold. Engr. Humble Oil & Refining Co., 1938-42; mfg. supr. Lion Oil Co., 1942, later tech. asst. to pres., asst. mgr. mfg., became dir. mfg. when Lion merged into Monsanto Co., St. Louis, 1955, later asst. gen. mgr.; gen. mgr. Lion Oil div., v.p. parent co., 1958, gen. mgr. hydrocarbons div., 1961, hydrocarbons and polymers div., 1965, v.p. adminstrn. Monsanto Co., 1968—, dir. 1969—. Mem. Ind. Petroleum Assn., Am. Chem. Soc., Am. Inst. Chem. Engrs., C. of C. of Metropolitan St. Louis (bd. dirs.) Home: 21 Clermont Lane St Louis MO 63124 Office: Monsanto Co 800 N Lindbergh Blvd St Louis MO 63166

BIBLER, LESTER DAVID, physician; b. Findlay, O., Jan. 13, 1902; s. Anson A. and Rosa A. (Friend) B.; B.S., Ind. U., 1923, M.D., 1925; m. Vera K. Moomaw, June 26, 1922; 1 son, David Anson. Intern Meth. Hosp., Indpls., 1925-26, now mem. active staff; practicing physician, 1926—; active staff Winona Hosp., Methodist Hosp. Vice pres. Muncie Oil & Coal Co., Capitol Med. Bldg., Indpls. Bd. dirs. Ind. div. Am. Cancer Soc. Served to capt. M.C., USNR, 1940-46; condg. officer Vol. Med. Unit 9-3, USNR. Diplomate Am. Bd. Family Practice, also bd. dirs. Mem. Am. Acad. Gen. Practice (past v.p.), A.M.A. (chmn. com. med. practice, past chmn. sect. gen. practice; past trustee; past del. sect. gen. practice), Ind. Med. Assn. (past dist. councilor, past chmn. sect. gen. practice), Ind. Acad. Gen. Practice (past pres.), Indpls. Med. Soc., Indpls. C. of C., Am. Legion (past post comdr.), 40 and 8, Ind. U. Sch. Medicine Alumni Assn. (treas. 1969—), Phi Beta Pi (past pres. Ind.). Mem. Christian Ch. Mason (Shriner, Jester). Clubs: Torch (past pres. Indpls.); Mercator (past nat. pres.). Author articles. Home: 4360 N Pennsylvania St Indianapolis IN 46205 Office: 1815 N Capitol Av Indianapolis IN 46202

BIBO, FRANZ, musical dir., condr.; b. Berlin, Germany, Aug. 2, 1922; s. Guenther and Kate (Naphtali) B.; came to U.S., 1946, naturalized, 1952; B.A. in Music, N.Y. U., 1950; diploma performance and teaching Mannes Coll. Music, 1951; M.S. in Conducting, Juilliard Sch. Music, 1955; m. Jacqueline M. Barbera, Aug. 6, 1961; children—Geoffrey, Jonathan. Mus. dir. City Symphony of N.Y., 1951-61; mus. dir. orch. and opera Oberlin Coll. Conservatory of Music, 1961-66; mus. dir., condr. Youngstown (O.) Symphony Soc., 1967—; instr. music Bklyn. Coll., 1955-56; guest conductor in Germany, Italy, Sweden, Roumania; research specialist Am. Symphony Orch. League, Vienna, Va., 1966-67. Rockefeller Found. grantee, 1956-59, spl. recording grantee, 1960; Ford Found. grantee, 1962. Mem. Nat. Assn. Am. Composers and Conductors. Rotarian. Research specialist Youth Concert Study Am. Symphony Orch. League and Am. U., 1967. Office: 260 W Federal St Youngstown OH 44503

BIBOROSCH, RUDOLPH A., banker; b. 1911. With Mid City Bank, 1928-46; mgr. personal loan dept. Germantown Trust Co., 1946-47; with First Pa. Banking & Trust Co., 1947— , exec. v.p. installment, mortgage and constrn. loan, 1968—. Address: First Pa Banking and Trust Co 15th and Chestnut Sts Philadelphia PA 19101*

BIBRING, GRETE LEHNER, psychiatrist, psychoanalyst; b. Vienna, Austria, Jan. 11, 1899; d. Moritz and Victoria (Stengel) Lehner; M.D., U. Vienna, 1924; LL.D., Brandeis U., 1968; m. Edward Bibring, Dec. 22, 1921 (dec. 1959); children—George L., Thomas. Came to U.S., 1941, naturalized, 1946. Resident, Neurol. Univ. Clinic, Vienna, also Psychiat.-Neurol. Univ. Hosp., U. Vienna, 1924-27; asst. dir. Vienna Psychoanalytic Out-Patient Clinics, 1926-30; tng. analyst, instr. Vienna Psychoanalytic Soc., 1933-38; tng. analyst Brit. Psychoanalytical Soc. and Inst., 1939-41, Boston Psychoanalytic Soc. and Inst., 1941—; spl. lectr. psychoanalytic psychology Simmons Coll. Sch. Social Work, Boston, 1942-64; head dept. psychiatry Beth Israel Hosp., Boston, 1946-55; asso. psychiatry Harvard Med. Sch., 1946-50, asst. prof. 1950-55, asso. clin. prof., 1955-61, clin. prof. psychiatry, faculty of medicine, 1961-65, emerita, 1965—; research cons. in psychoanalytic psychology Radcliffe Coll., Cambridge, Mass., 1965—; tng. analyst Boston Psychoanalytic Inst.; psychiat. cons. Children's Bur., Washington, 1949-54; chmn. ednl. com. Boston Psychoanalytic Soc. and Inst., 1952-54, pres., 1955-58; adv. com. psychol. counseling center Brandeis U., 1954—; vis. prof. psychiatry Sch. Medicine U. N.C., 1955-56; psychiatrist-in-chief Beth Isreal Hosp., 1955-65, psychiatrist-in-chief emerita, 1965—; cons. psychiat. service Faulkner Hosp., Boston, 1966—; adv. bd. psychiat. unit Mt. Auburn Hosp., Cambridge, 1956-58. Recipient Abram L. Sachar silver medallion Brandeis U., 1971. Fellow Am. Acad. Art and Scis., Am. Psychiat. Assn.; mem. A.A.A.S., Am. (councilor 1950-58, pres. 1961-63), Internat. (hon. sec. 1950-52, v.p. 1959-63), psychoanalytic assns., Group Advancement Psychiatry (com. research 1960—), Mass. Med. Soc., N.Y. Acad. Sci., Alpha Omega Alpha (hon.). Author: Lectures in Medical Psychology, 1969. Contbr. to profl. lit. Editorial bd. Psychological Problems in Medicine, 1960—. Editor: The Teaching of Dynamic Psychiatry, 1968. Home: 47 Garden St Cambridge MA 02138

BICAK, L.J., coll. dean; B.S., Wayne State Coll.; M.Ed., U. Neb.; Ph.D., U. Minn. Dean Grad. Sch., Kearney State Coll. (Neb.). Office: Grad Sch Kearney State Coll Kearney NB 68847*

BICE, LORIN TRESSLAR, citrus grower; b. Winnemucca, Nev., Oct. 25, 1903; s. Samuel Otis and Clara (Schwartz) B.; student U. Fla., 1923-24; m. Ruth Cramer, Sept. 18, 1924; children—Doris Jean (Mrs. R.T. Stalnaker), William Thomas, Judy Catherine (Mrs. E.W. Winchester). Engaged in Fla. citrus industry, 1918—; plant supt. Florence Citrus Growers Assn., 1924-35; gen. mgr. Haines City Citrus Growers Assn., 1935-43; exec. v.p., gen. mgr. Lake Hamilton Coop. Inc., 1943-51; pres. W. Coast Growers Coop., 1947-51, 59-60, dir., 1946-70; chmn. Farm Credit Bd., Columbia S.C., 1960, dir., 1956-63; mem. Fed. Farm Credit Bd., Wash., 1963-69, chmn., 1968-69. Mem. Fla. Citrus Commn., 1949-50, Citrus Marketing Agreement Coms., 1941-44, 52- 54; v.p. Fed. Land Bank Assn. of Lakeland, 1952-63; Fla. Citrus Prodn. Credit Assn., 1945-63; mem. gov. com. re-writing and enacting Fla. Citrus Code, 1948-49. Dir. State Bank Haines City. Chmn. bd. trustees Polk Jr. Coll., 1968-69. Mem. Haines City C. of C. Methodist. Rotarian. Home: 1107 Peninsular Dr Haines City FL 33844

BICHY, CHARLES EDWARD, Jr., banker; b. Balt., Aug. 15, 1912; s. Charles Edward and Lula (Dudrow) B.; student U. N.C., 1931-32; B.S., Wharton Sch., U. Pa., 1935; LL.B., U. Md., 1940; m. Lucille Virginia Kirkley, Oct. 28, 1944; children—Charles Edward III, Jane Kirkley. Admitted to Md. bar, 1940; with firm Miles & O'Brien, Balt., 1941-45; v.p., dir. Diamond Ice & Coal Co., 1945-57; v.p., treas. Wilmington Trust Co. (Del.), 1957-68, sr. v.p., treas. , dir., 1968—; v.p., dir. Dover Builders, Inc. (Del.) 1956—. Bd. dirs. Non-Partisan Com. for Good Govt., 1958-60, Recreation, Promotion and Service, 1962. Mem. Am. Inst. Banking, Del. C. of C. (treas., bd. dirs. 1962-64), Navy League, Del. Bar Assn. (asso.). Rotarian (bd. dirs. Wilmington 1965-67), Mason (Shriner). Club: Wilmington. Office: Wilmington Trust Co 10th and Market Sts Wilmington DE 19899

BICKEL, ALEXANDER MORDECAI, educator, lawyer; b. Bucharest, Rumania, Dec. 17, 1924; s. Solomon and Yetta (Schafer) B.; brought to U.S., 1939, naturalized, 1943; B.S., Coll. City N.Y., 1947; LL.B., Harvard, 1949; M.A. (hon.), Yale, 1960; m. Josephine Ann Napolino, Oct. 17, 1959; children—Francesca Ann, Claudia Rose. Admitted to Mass. bar, 1950, U.S. Supreme Ct. bar, 1959; law clk. to chief judge U.S. Ct. Appeals, Boston, 1949-50; law officer State Dept., 1950-52; law clk. to U.S. Supreme Ct. Justice Frankfurter, 1952-53; spl. asst. to dir. policy planning staff State Dept., 1953-54; research asso. Harvard, 1954-56; faculty Yale Law Sch., 1956— prof., 1960- 66, also mem. history faculty and Chancellor Kent prof. law and legal history, 1966—, William Clyde DeVaney prof., 1971-74. Cons. sub-com. on separation powers Senate Com. on Judicary, 90th-91st Congresses; Holmes lectr. Harvard Law Sch., 1969. Served with AUS, 1943-45. Guggenheim fellow, fellow Center for Advanced Study in Behavioral Scis., 1970-71, Decorated Combat Inf. badge. Mem. Am. Acad. Arts and Scis. Author: The Unpublished Opinions of Mr. Justice Brandeis, 1957; The Least Dangerous Branch, 1962; Politics and the Warren Court, 1965; The Supreme Court and the Idea of Progress, 1970; Reform and Continuity, 1971. Contbg. editor New Republic, 1957- -. Home: 261 St Ronan St New Haven CT 06511 Office: Yale Law Sch New Haven CT 06520

BICKEL, CLARENCE ALOIS, investment banker; b. Ft. Wayne, Ind., Sept. 11, 1904; s. Charles and Pauline (Muench) B.; student Walton Sch. Commerce; C.P.A., Northwestern U., 1929; m. Helen I. Crum, June 21, 1928; 1 son, Robert G. With Robert W. Baird & Co., Inc., and predecessor firms, 1933—, pres., 1957—, chmn. bd., 1969—; dir. Aldrich Chem. Co., Smith Investment Co., Heil Co., Kearney & Trecker, Johnson Service Co., W.H. Brady Co., W.A. Krueger Co., E.R. Wagner Mfg. Co., Wayenberg Shoe Mfg. Co. Bd. dirs. St. Mary's Hosp., Milw. Sanitarium. Home: 2004 Bay Point Lane R 3 Hartland WI 53029 Office: 731 N Water St Milwaukee WI 53202

BICKEL, HERBERT JACOB, Jr., gas co. exec.; b. Evanston, Ill., Feb. 20, 1930; s. Herbert Jacob and Jean (Meadows) B.; B.S. in Bus. Adminstrn., U. Fla., 1952; M.S. in Indsl. Mgmt., Ga. Inst. Tech., 1955; postgrad. Mass. Inst. Tech., 1955- 56; m. Joan Hough, July 17, 1954; children—David Alan, Daniel Wayne, John Douglas, Prin. economist Tex. Eastern Transmission Corp., Houston, 1957-66, treas., 1966—; dir. Nassau Bay Nat. Bank. Instr. Ga. Inst. Tech., 1955, Centenary Coll., Shreveport, 1958; vis. lectr. 1957-66, Pa. State U., 1964. Served to 1st lt. AUS, 1952-54. Mem. Am. Econ. Assn., Am. Finance Assn., Soc. Petroleum Engrs., Am. Gas Assn., Nat. Assn. Bus. Economists. Club: Houston. Author: (with others) National Fuels and Energy Study; (with others) Competition and Growth in American Energy Markets, 1947-1985, 1968. Home: 138 Hickory Ridge Houston, TX 77024. Office: Box 2521 Houston TX 77001

BICKEL, WILLIAM HAROLD, educator, surgeon; b. Shamokin, Pa., July 4, 1909; s. Edwin Forrest and Florence (Simon) B.; B.A., Lawrence Coll., 1931; M.S., Northwestern U., 1935, M.D., 1936; M.S., Mayo Found., U. Minn., 1941; m. Annette Ray, Jan. 1, 1937; children—Barbara Carnell, Ruth Ann, Patricia, Priscilla. Intern, St. Luke's Hosp., Chgo., 1935-37; resident Hosp. Milw. Sanatorium, 1936-38; pvt. practice, asst. surgeon Internat. Harvester Co., Milw., 1936-38; fellow orthopedic surgery Mayo Found., U. Minn., Rochester, 1938-42, instr. to asso. prof., 1942-59, prof. orthopedic surgery, 1959—, 1st asst. orthopedic surgery Mayo Clinic, 1940-42, mem. staff, 1942—. Civilian cons. orthopedic surgery Surg. Gen., ETO, 1958; mem. spl. med. adv. group, orthopedic cons. VA; adv. bd. Med. Specialties. Diplomate Am. Bd. Orthopedic Surgery, pres., 1959. Fellow A.C.S.; mem. Am.-Brit.-Canadian Travelling Fellowship Club, Am. Acad. Orthopedic Surgeons (pres. 1964), Minn. Med. Assn., Am., Tex. orthopedic assns., Interurban Orthopedic Soc., A.M.A., Am. Assn. Surgery Trauma, Clin. Orthopedic Soc., Internat. Soc. Surgery and Trauma, Sigma Xi. Home: Mail Route 72 Rochester MN 55901 Office: 200 First St SW Rochester MN 55901

BICKERMAN, ELIAS JOSEPH, historian, educator; b. Russia, July 1, 1897; s. Joseph and Sarah (Marguelies) B.; A.B., U. Petrograd, 1915, Ph.D., 1918; Ph.D., U. Berlin, 1926; él ève deplm , École Pratique des Hautes Études, Paris, France, 1938. Came to U.S., 1942, naturalized, 1948. Privat- dozent U. Berlin, 1929-33; chargé de cours École Pratique des Hautes Études, Paris, 1933-40; chargé de recherches Centre National de la Recherche, 1937-42; prof. New Sch. for Social Research and cole Libre, N.Y.C., 1942-46; research fellow Jewish Theol. Sem., N.Y.C., 1946-50; vis. prof. Columbia, 1948-49, prof. ancient history, 1952-67; with Inst. Advanced Study, Princeton, 1967-68; vis. prof. U. Judaism, Los Angeles, 1950-52, U. Cal. at Los Angeles, 1957, Jewish Theol. Sem., 1968—. Served with Russian Army, 1916-18. Recipient R. Kreglinger Triennal award, U. Bruxelles, 1935, Asso. études grecques, 1938; Guggenheim fellow, 1949, 59. Fellow Am. Acad. Jewish Research; mem. Am. Assn. Internat. de Papyrologues, Società Italiana di storia del diritto. Jewish religion. Author: Der Gott der Makabaer, 1937; Institutions des Seleucides, 1938; From Ezra to the Last of the Maccabees, 1962; Chronology of the Ancient World, 1967; Four Strange Books of the Bible, 1967. Co-editor Revue Internationale des droits de l'Antiquité. Office: 3080 Broadway New York City NY 10027

BICKERSTAFF, THOMAS ALTON, educator; b. Tishomingo, Miss., Sept. 5, 1904; s. John Ramsey and Mary (Blunt) B.; student U. Miss., 1924-29, A.B., 1928; A.M., 1929; Ph.D., U. Mich., 1948; m. Lillian Josephine Russell, Aug. 26, 1933; children—Thomas Alton, David Russell, Carolyn Josephine. Instr. math. U. Miss., 1928-30, asst. prof., 1930-36, asst. prof. and registrar, 1936-47, prof., chmn. dept. math., 1947—, faculty chmn. athletics, 1937—, sec. Southeastern Conf., 1957, spl. coordinator STAR unit Army Specialized Tng. Program, 1942-44; spl. instr. Navy V-12 program U. Mich., 1944-45. Mem. Math. Assn. Am. (past pres. La.-Miss. sect.), Am. Math. Soc., Inst. Math. Statistics, Miss. Acad. Sci., Miss. Ednl. Assn., Sigma Xi, Omicron Delta Kappa, Pi Kappa Alpha, Pi Mu Epsilon. Democrat. Baptist. Mason, Rotarian (past pres.). Home: Box 262 University MS 38677

BICKFORD, EDWARD DAVIDSON, steel co. exec.; b. Toronto, Ont., Can., Jan. 18, 1909; s. Harold Childe and Mary (Davidson) B.; student Yale; m. Ann Watson, June 10, 1937; children—Mary Ann (Mrs. Richard B. Patton), Patricia (Mrs. Allen L. Greenough), Susan (Mrs. Neil Thomas, III), Edward W., Peter W. With Bethlehem Steel Corp., 1929—, asst. v.p., 1963, v.p. sales, 1963-70, sr. v.p. comml., 1970—, also dir. Asst. dir. charge prodn. and distbn., chmn. prodn. directive com. Iron and Steel div. Nat. Prodn. Authority, 1951-52. Mem. Am. Iron and Steel Inst. (chmn. com. to promote use steel 1966-68). Episcopalian. Clubs: Country of N.C.; Brook, Yale, Sky, Links (N.Y.C.); Saucon Valley Country, Bethlehem (Bethlehem); International (Chgo.); The Steel Division. Home: Saucon Valley Rd R D 4 Bethlehem PA 18015 Office: Bethlehem Steel Corp Bethlehem PA 18016

BICKFORD, GEORGE PERCIVAL, lawyer; b. Berlin, N.H., Nov. 28, 1901; s. Gershon Percival and Lula Adine (Buck) B.; A.B. cum laude, Harvard, 1922, LL.B., 1926; m. Clara L. Gehring, Apr. 6, 1933; 1 dau., Louise G. Admitted to Ohio bar, 1926, since practiced in Cleve.; asso. firm Arter & Hadden, partner, 1940—. Instr. Hauchung U., Wuchang, China, 1922-23; instr. taxation Western Res. Law Sch., 1940-47; lectr. Indian history and culture, Cleve. Coll., 1948-50; gen. counsel FHA, Washington, 1958-59. Dir. Cyril Bath Co., Indsl. Electronic Rubber Co., Anderson Spring Co. Hon. Consul of India, 1964—. Mem. moral claims commn. City Cleve. 1935-37. Mem. Cuyahoga County Rep. Exec. Com., 1948-58, 60—. Trustee Am. U. in Cairo; vis. com. fine arts dept. Harvard, 1962-68; trustee, v.p. Cleve. Mus. Art; trustee, v.p. Cleve. Inst. Art. Served with Ohio N.G., 1926-29; from capt. to lt. col., judge adv. gen. dept., AUS, 1942-46. Decorated Legion of Merit. Mem. Fed., Am., Ohio, Cleve. bar assns., Cleve. Council World Affairs (trustee), Cleve. C. of C. Episcopalian (standing com. Diocese Ohio 1951- 63, chancellor 1962—). Clubs: Union Midday, Mayfield Country, Rowfant, Skating (Cleve.); Army and Navy, Capitol Hill (Washington); Harvard (N.Y.C.). Home: 2247 Chestnut Hills Dr Cleveland OH 44106 Office: Union Commerce Bldg Cleveland OH 44115

BICKFORD, REGINALD GEORGE, educator; b. Brewood, Eng., Jan. 20, 1913; s. George and Jessie (Jones) B.; B.A.(Cambridge scholar 1932), St. Catherine's Coll. Cambridge U., 1933, M.D., 1936; student Univ. Coll. Hosp., U. London, 1933-36; m. Joyce Audrey Davis, June 8,1945; children—Michael, Christopher. Resident medicine Univ. Coll. Hosp., London, Eng., 1937; fellow Med. Research Council, 1938-41; research on anoxia Royal Air Force, 1944; research asso. Mayo Found., Rochester, Minn., 1946; asso. prof. physiology U. Minn., 1955-59, prof., 1959; now prof. dept neurosci. U. Cal. at San Diego. Cons. neurophysiology, electroencephalography; mem. computer research study sect. USPHS; mem. NIH Study Group on Computer Research. Served as squadron ldr., M.C., R.A.F., 1942-46. Mem. Royal Coll. Physicians, Am. Electroencephalographic Soc. (pres. 1956), Am. Neurol. Assn., A.A.A.S. Universalist. Author: (with A. Faulconer) Electroencephalography in Anesthesiology. Contbr. numerous research papers. Home: 7378 Via Capri LaJolla CA 92037 Office: Dept Neurosci U Cal San Diego, CA 92037.

BICKHAM, JACK MILES, author; b. Columbus, O., Sept. 2, 1930; s. John Robert and Helen (Miles) B.; B.A., Ohio State U., 1952; M.A., U. Okla., 1960; m. Janie Ruth Wallace, Nov. 24, 1952; children—Robert, Daniel, Stephen, Lise. Prof. journalism U. Okla., Norman, 1969—. Served with USAF, 1952- 54. Recipient 1st Pl. Writing award Am. Coll. Pub. Relations Assn., 1966; Teepee award Okla. Writers Assn., 1968; named Okla. Editor of Yr., 1969, Okla. Writer of Yr., 1970. Mem. Western Writers Am. Democrat. Roman Catholic. Author: Feud Fury, 1959; Padre Must Die, 1967; The Shadowed Faith, 1968; Decker's Campaign, 1970; others: (pseudonym Jeff Clinton) Range Killer, 1962; Wildcat O'Shea series, others. Home: 2603 Beau Rue Norman OK 73069

BICKING, CHARLES ALBERT, research exec.; b. Wilmington, Del., Nov. 22, 1908; s. William Laurence and Clara (Albert) B.; B.S. in Mech. Engring., U. Del., 1930; M.S. in Bus. and Engring. Adminstrn., Mass. Inst. Tech., 1931; m. Blanche Malcom, Feb. 21, 1935; children—Martha (Mrs. Paul J. Nagy), Marjorie, William Laurence II, Charles Malcom. Power sales and rate study engr. Del. Power & Light Co., 1931-41; quality control engr. Hercules Power Co., 1941-51; chief design expt. unit, research and devel. U.S. Army Ordnance, 1951-56; mgr. math. br., research and devel. div. Carborundum Co., 1956-71; lectr. State U. N.Y. at Buffalo, 1971. Cons. exptl. design and quality assurance White Sands Missile Range, 1956-69; mem. rev. bd. quality standards NASA, 1962; U.S. rep. com. statictics in industry Internat. Statis. Inst., 1958-61, ofcl. U.S. del., Rome, 1953, NSF, Japan Soc. Promotion Sci. Seminar, Tokyo, 1965, Honolulu, 1970. Travel grantee NSF, Rio de Janeiro, 1955. Registered quality engr., N.Y. Fellow A.A.A.S., Am. Statis. Assn., Am. Soc. Quality Control (exec. sec. 1965-66, Shewhart medalist 1967), N.Y. Acad. Scis., Internat. Acad. for Quality (dir. information services 1969—), Am. Soc. for Testing and Materials (award of merit 1962, chmn. com. statis. methods 1962-68); mem. Biometric Soc., Operations Research Soc. Am., Am. Inst. Indsl. Engrs., Internat. Assn. for Statistics in Phys. Scis., Soc. de Statistique Paris, Tau Beta Pi, Phi Kappa Phi. Editorial bd. Internat. Jour. Abstracts on Statistics, 1953-59; editorial bd. Indsl. Quality Control, 1954-59, book rev. editor, 1967. Home: 773 The Circle Lewiston NY 14092

BICKING, LLOYD W., steel co. exec.; student Walsh Inst. Accounting, Detroit. Treas. Detroit Steel Corp. Served with AUS. 1944-45. Address: 1025 S Oakwood Av Detroit, MI 48209.*

BICKLEY, WILLIAM ELBERT, entomologist, educator; b. Knoxville, Tenn., Jan. 20, 1914; s. William Elbert and Lucretia (Jordan) B.; B.S., U. Tenn., 1934, M.S., 1936; Ph.D., U. Md., 1940; m. Elizabeth Macgill, Apr. 5, 1941; children—Lucretia Jordan (Mrs.

Lucretia Bickley Pope), James Macgill, David Clarke, Edith Clarke. Tchr. high sch. sci., Tenn., 1935-37; teaching fellow entomology U. Md., 1937-40, instr., 1940-42, asso. prof. etomology, 1949-57, head dept., 1956-71, prof., 1957—; asst. entomologist to sr. asst. sanitarian Malaria Control in War Areas, USPHS, 1942-46; asst. prof. biology U. Richmond, 1946-49; entomologist Va. State Health Dept., 1947-49. Mem. Entomol. Soc. Am., Am. Mosquito Control Assn. (pres. 1961-62), Entomol. Soc. Washington (pres. 1963), Washington Acad. Scis., Am. Inst. Biol. Ser., Am. Soc. Tropical Medicine and Hygiene, Sigma Xi. Home: 6516 40th Av University Park Hyattsville MD 20782 Office: U Md College Park MD 20740

BICKMORE, J. GRANT, banker; b. Brigham City, Utah, Nov. 24, 1916; s. William M. and Ida Luella (Olson) B.; student pub. schs.; m. Marjorie Marshall, June 4, 1940; children—Roger G., William Bradford. Asst. cashier, cashier Downey State Bank (Ida.), 1934-44; bank examiner State of Ida., 1944-48, Fed. Res. Bank, San Francisco, 1948-50; cashier Ida. Bank & Trust Co., Pocatello, 1950, v.p., dir., exec. v.p., 1953-63, pres., 1963—; dir., mgr. Downey State Bank; v.p., dir. Guaranty Fed. Savs. & Loan Assn., Pocatello; dir. Ida. Power Co., Garrett Freightlines, Inc., Comml. Security Bank, Ogden, Utah, KID-TV Corp., Idaho Falls. Mem. Gov.'s State Health Planning Council, 1967—; mem. Ida. Bd. Health, 1966-69; regional dir., pres. Tendoy council Boy Scouts Am., 1966-70; mem. Ida. adv. council Small Bus. Adminstrn. Trustee Found. for Full Service Banks; chmn. adv. bd. Coll. Bus., Ida. State U., Pocatello. Mem. Am. (v.p. Ida.), Ida. (past pres.) bankers assns., U.S. (fiscal policy com.), Ida. (v.p., dir.) chambers commerce. Elk, Rotarian. Home: Juniper Hill Rd Route 3 Pocatello ID Office: PO Box 1788 Pocatello ID 83201

BICKMORE, LEE SMITH, sales exec.; b. Paradise, Utah, June 5, 1908; s. Danford M. and Sarah Jane (Smith) B.; B.S., Utah State Coll., 1932; diploma Dale Carnegie Sch. Effective Speaking, 1947; certificate advanced mgmt. program, Harvard, Bus. Sch., 1949; m. Ellen McMinn, June 30, 1939; children—Beverlee Ann, (Mrs. George Zwerdling), Elizabeth Kay, (Mrs. William Blake Sonne). With J.C. Penney Co., 1927-32; office, warehouse staff Nat. Biscuit Co., 1933-35, salesman, 1935-40, spl. salesman, 1940-43, br. mgr., Pocatello, Ida., 1943-45, asst. mdse. mgr., 1946-47, dist. sales mgr., N.J., 1947-49, adminstrv. asst. to v.p., 1949-50, v.p. in charge sales, advt., 1950, sr. v.p., 1957-59, exec. v.p., dir., mem. exec. com., 1959-60, pres., 1960-61, pres., chief exec. officer, dir., 1961—, chmn. bd. dirs., 1968—, officer, and/or dir. Nabisco subsidiaries; dir. Bankers Trust Co., Western Electric Co. Carrier Corp., Mut. N.Y., Internat. Ednl. Broadcasting Corp. Sherman Oaks, Cal., Hart Schaffner & Marx, Chgo. Bd.; govs.; Arthritis and Rheumatism Found.; trustee Pace Coll., Nutrition Found. Mem. Grocery Mfrs. Am.Inc. (exec., finance coms., dir.), Biscuit and Cracker Mfrs. of Am. Biscuit Bakers Inst. (dir.), Am. Mgmt. Assn. (dir.), Internat. C. of C. (trustee U.S. council), UN Assn. of U.S.A. (dir.), Alpha Kappa Psi. Clubs: Canoe, Brook Country (Summit, N.J.); Fifth Avenue, Economic, Union League, University, Links, Board Room (N.Y.C.); Balustrol Golf (Springfield, N.J.). Home: 15 Randall Dr Short Hills NJ 07080 Office: 425 Park Av New York City NY 10022

BICKNELL, WARREN, Jr., ret. constrn. exec.; b. Wheaton, Ill., Sept. 5, 1902; s. Warren and Anne Sabra (Guthrie) B.; A.B., Williams Coll., Williamstown, Mass., 1925; m. Kate Benedict Hanna, Nov. 4, 1931; children—Constance Hanna (Mrs. Reynolds), Kate Hanna (Mrs. Kirkham), Wendy Hanna, Warren III. Pres., The Cleve. Constrn. Co., 1940-71; dir. Soc. Nat. Bank of Cleve., Hanna Mining Co. Trustee, pres. Cherokee Found.; trustee John D. Archibald Hosp., Western Res. Acad., Hudson, O., Greater Cleve. council Boy Scouts Am. Mem. Delta Kappa Epsilon. Clubs: Fifty (Cleve.); Glen Arvin Country (Thomasville, Ga.); Chagrin Valley Hunt, Union, Tavern, Kirtland Country. Home: 10255 Mitchell's Mills Rd Route 3 Chardon OH 44024 Office: 100 Erieview Plaza Cleveland OH 44114

BIDDINGTON, WILLIAM ROBERT, univ. dean, dentist; b. Piedmont, W.Va., Mar. 30, 1925; s. William M. and Sadie (Vogtman) B.; student Potomac State Coll., 1942-43, Hampden-Sydney Coll., 1943-44; D.D.S. cum laude, U. Md., 1948; m. Dolores E. Berrett, June 14, 1947; 1 son, William Berrett. Gen. practice dentistry, Balt., 1949-59; instr. Balt. Coll. Dental Surgey, Dental Sch. U. Md., 1949-52, asst. prof., 1952-56, asso. prof., 1956-59; prof., chmn. dept. endodontics Sch. Dentistry, W.Va. U., Morgantown, 1959-68, asst. dean, 1966-68, dean, 1968—. Sec. St. Francis Grade Sch. P.T.A., 1961-62; v.p. Cheat Lake Jr. High P.T.A., 1965-66; pres. Cheat Lake Band Boosters, 1965-66, Cheat Lake P.T.A., 1966-67; committeeman Cheat Lake Boy Scout Troop, 1960-67, chmn. advancement com., 1964-67. Served with USNR, 1942-46, 48-49. Diplomate Am. Bd. Endodontics. Fellow Am. Coll. Dentists; mem. Am., W.Va. dental assns., Monongahela Valley, Monongalis County (pres. 1966) dental socs., Internat. Assn. Dental Research, Am. Assn. Dental Schs., Am. Assn. Endodontists, Gorgas Odontological Soc., Psi Omega, Omicron Kappa Upsilon. Home: Route 7 Box 720 Morgantown WV 26505

BIDDLE, ALEXANDER, corp. ofcl.; b. Phila., Apr. 4, 1893; s. Alexander Williams and Anne (McKennan) B.; grad. Groton (Mass.) Sch., 1912; A.B., Harvard, 1916; student U. Pa. Law Sch., 1917; m. Margaret Scull, Sept. 12, 1917; children—Alexander Williams, David Scull. With Charles D. Barney & Co., investment bankers, 1919-31, partner, 1930-31; pres. Pa. Economy League, 1935-42; exec. v.p. Phila.-Balt. Stock Exchange, 1946-64; pres. Phila.-Balt.-Washington Stock Exchange and Stock Clearing Corp., Phila., 1964-65, cons., 1965—. Bd. dirs. Invest in Am. Nat. Council. Served as 2d lt., F.A., U.S. Army, 1917-19; lt. col. AUS, 1943-46; ETO. Clubs: Philadelphia, The Rabbit, Gulph Mills Golf, Midday (Phila.). Home: Bryn Mawr PA 19010 Office: Phila Balt Washington Stock Exchange 17th St and Stock Exchange Pl Philadelphia PA 19103

BIDDLE, CHARLES J., ret. lawyer; b. Andalusia, Pa., Mar. 13, 1890; s. Charles and Letitia (Glenn) B.; A.B., Princeton, 1911; LL.B., Harvard, 1914; m. Katharine J. Legendre, Feb. 10, 1923; children—Charles, James. Admitted to Pa. bar, 1914, practiced law, Phia., from 1914, partner firm Drinker, Biddle & Reath, from 1924; trustee Phila. Sav. Fund Soc.; gen. counsel Phila. Contributionship for Ins. of Houses from Loss by Fire, Drexel Inst. Tech., other instns. Trustee Drexel Inst. Tech., John and Mary R. Markle Found.; chmn. bd. Overbrook Sch. for Blind. Served with U.S.A.A.F., also French Army Air Force in pursuit aviation, 1917-18. Decorated D.S.C, Letters of Commendation from Comdr. in Chief A.E.F., Purple Heart, French Legion of Honor and Croix de Guerre with 4 Palms, Belgian Order of Leopold. Mem. Am. Pa., Phila., Bucks County bar assns., Am. Soc. French Legion of Honor, others. Episcopalian. Author: Way of the Eagle, 1919. Home: Andalusia PA 19020

BIDDLE, ERIC HARBESON; b. Phila., Apr. 27, 1898; s. Frederick Davis and Estelle (Harbeson) B.; student Central High Sch., Phila., 1912-16, Oxford U., (Eng.), 1918- 19, U. Pa., 1919-20; m. Katharine Rogers, Apr. 26, 1927; children—Eric Harbeson, John, Maurice; m. 2d, Janet Mayo Jepsen, 1957. Served with inf., later field arty. Pa. N.G., 1916; lt., pilot RAF (Eng.), 1917-19. Asst. to mfrs., agt., 1920-21; investment banking, 1922-25; mgr. electric ry. and motor bus. cos., 1925-32; varied positions in pub. service, 1932-41; head spl. mission to Gt. Britain, bur. of budget Exec. Office of Pres., 1942-47; mission to Middle East and N. Africa, 1943; missions to Gt. Britain, Germany, France, Italy, etc., 1944-45; adv. to U.S. dels. to internat. confs. 3d council meeting UNRRA, London, UNESCO, London, Nov. 1945; UN at London, Aug. 1945-Feb. 1946; chmn. adv. group of experts on adminstrn., personnel, budget UN, Nov. 1945-Dec. 1946; spl. asst. to sec. gen. UN, 1946; Dept. of State, 1947; spl. asst. to dir. Office Internat. Information and Cultural Affairs; cons. to asst. sec. of state for pub. affairs, Jan. 1947-April 1948; missions to various European countries; spl. asst. for overseas adminstrn. ECA, Apr. 1948; acting chief ECA mission to Korea, Oct. 1948; cons. to chief ECA mission to Italy, Apr. 1949; spl. asst. to dir. of German Affairs div. Dept. of State, Sept. 1949; cons. to chmn. Nat. Security Resources Bd., Dec. 1949; cons., mut. security program ECA, 1951, dir. Middle East planning staff, 1951; cons. to asst. dir. for Europe, to chief of mission to China and Far East programme div. Mut. Security Agy., 1952; spl. cons. to exec. Chmn. tech. assistance bd. UN, 1952-53; various cons. services, 1953-57; v.p. U.S. Leasing Corp., 1958- 61; pres., dir. Biddle Assos., Inc., 1961—; v.p. Childs Securities Corp., 1963-65; chmn. bd. Pan Am. Minerals & Mining, Inc., 1967—; chmn. bd. Nat. Minerals, Exploration, Inc., 1969—. Home: 1200 N Nash St Arlington, VA 22209. Office: 815 Connecticut Av N W Washington DC 20006 ☆

BIDDLE, GEORGE, painter, sculptor; b. Phila., Jan. 24, 1885; s. Algernon Sydney and Frances (Robinson) B.; grad. Groton Sch., 1904; A.B., Harvard, 1908, LL.B., 1911; m. Anne Coleman, 1917 (div.); m. 2d, Jane Belo, 1925 (div.); m. 3d, HélÈe Sardeau, Apr. 1931; 1 son, Michael John. Over 100 one man shows Paris, Vienna, Rome, Mexico City, Tokyo, New Delhi. Bombay, Calcutta, most Am. cities; commd. with Hélène Sardeau to execute fresco and sculpture Supreme Ct. Bldg., Mexico City; commd. to execute fresco Nat. Library, Rio de Janeiro; assisted inauguration fed. art projects, 1933; executed murals Justice Bldg., Washington; chmn. art adv. com. War Dept., sent to N. Africa to assist with pictorial war record, 1943; painter-mem. art adv. com. State Dept.; mem. Fine Arts Commn., 1950; retrospective exhbn. of prints circulated by U.S. Information Agy., Japan, Italy, India, other European countries; works in permanent collections, museums U.S., Berlin, Mexico City, Modern Mus., Tokyo, Butler Inst. Am. Art, Fugg Art Mus., Corcoran Gallery Fine Arts, Walter E. Chrysler collection. Mem. Nat. Coms. for an Effective Congress. Served from 1st lt. to capt. U.S. Army, World War I. Recipient art award, fellowship Huntington Hartford Found., 1954; art award Edward MacDowell Colony, 1956; purchase prize Brandeis U. Mem. Soc. Painters, Gravers and Sculptors (v.p. 1934), Nat. Soc. Mural Painters (pres. 1935), Mural Artists Guild (pres. 1937-38), Nat. Soc. Arts and Letters (v.p. 1962). Club: Century. Author: (text and illustrations) George Biddle's War Drawings, 1944; The Yes and No of Contemporary Art, 1957; (text and drawings) Indian Impressions, 1960; Tahiti Jour. Contbr. to mags. Address: Mount Airy Rd Croton on Hudson NY 10520 (summer) Hog's Back Hollow Truro MA 02666

BIDDLE, GEORGE HENRY, agrl. co. exec.; b. Nashua, Mont., Feb. 10, 1919; s. Royce Edgar and Hulda (Gaukstad) B.; B.S., Mont. State Coll., 1942, M.S., 1943; postgrad. U. Cal. at Davis, 1949, Cal. Poly. Inst., 1950; m. Evelyn Helen Kaiser, Dec. 17, 1950; children—Royce James, Michael William, Mary Suzanne. With Simon Newman Co., Newman, Cal., 1946-47, Berry Seed & Feed Co., Ceres, Cal., 1947; self-employed as Golden Valley Hatchery, Oakdale, Cal., 1948- 49; tchr. Modesto (Cal.) High Sch., 1950-51; instr. Modesto Jr. Coll., 1952-62; propr. Biddle Farms, Modesto 1962—, Lay-D Farms, Inc., Modesto, 1962—, Chico Seed & Feed Co. (Cal.), 1966—, Foothill Layers, Inc., Modesto, 1967—; pres. Valley Pullet Farms, Modesto, 1966—; treas., dir. Sun-Up Farms, Modesto, 1965—; sec., dir. Western Egg Co., 1968—, Cal. Chix, 1970—. Bd. dirs., pres. Pacific Growers, 1963-64, chmn. bd., 1964—; dir. Nulaid Farmers, 1963; dir., mem. exec. com. Poultry and Egg Nat. Bd., 1966—. Mem. Cal. Grain and Feed Assn., Served to 1st Lt. AUS, 1943-46, 51-52. Kiwanian (pres. Modesto 1957-58). Club: Commonwealth of Cal. Author: (with E.M. Jorgensen) Approved Practices in Poultry Production, 1963. Home: 1331 Crawford Rd Modesto CA 95350. Office: 2530 Morrill Rd Modesto CA 95350

BIDDLE, JAMES, mus. curator; b. Phila., July 8, 1929; s. Charles John and Katherine (Legendre) B.; grad. St. Paul's Sch., Concord, N.H., 1942-47; B.A. in Art and Archeology, Princeton, 1951; m. Louisa Copeland, Apr. 25, 1959; children—Letitia C., Pamela, James C. With U.S. Govt., 1951-53; with Met. Mus. Art, 1955—, curator Am. wing, 1963-67; pres. Nat. Trust for Historic Preservation, Washington, 1967—. Mem. Am. Revolution Bicentennial Commn.; chmn. Drawing Soc., Inc. Trustee Am. Fedn. Arts, U.S. Capitol Hist. Soc.; bd. govs. Corcoran Mus.; bd. dirs. White House Hist. Assn. Office: 740-748 Jackson Pl N W Washington DC 20006

BIDDLE, LIVINGSTON LUDLOW, Jr., educator, author; b. Bryn Mawr, Pa., May 26, 1918; s. Livingston Ludlow and Eugenia (Law) B.; A.B., Princeton, 1940; m. Cordelia Frances Fenton, Mar. 15, 1945; children—Cordelia Frances (Mrs. Henry Richard Dietrich, Jr.), Livingston Ludlow IV. Reporter, Phila. Eve. Bull., 1940-42; with Am. Field Service, Middle East, N. Africa, Italy, France, Germany, 1942-45; spl. asst. to U.S. Senator Claiborne Pell, 1963-65; dep. chmn. Nat. Endowment for Arts, Washington, 1965-67; chmn. div. arts Liberal Arts Coll., Fordham U., Lincoln Center, N.Y.C., 1967-70. Pres., Childrens Service, Inc., Phila., 1960-62; chmn. bd. Pa. Ballet, 1971—. Recipient Phila. Athenaeum Best Novel award, 1956. Mem. Internat. Council Fine Arts Deans. Democrat. Episcopalian. Clubs: Philadelphia, Merion Cricket (Phila.); Coffee House, Century Assn. (N.Y.C.); Gulph Mills (Pa.) Golf. Author: Main Line, 1950; Debut, 1952: The Village Beyond, 1956, Sam Bentley's Island, 1960. Home: Apple Tree Farm Box 128 Bryn Mawr PA

BIDDLE, THEODORE WILLIAM, univ. pres.; b. Donora, Pa., March. 2, 1906; s. Rev. Richard Long and Mary Jane (Pitcock) B.; B.S., U. Pitts., 1929, Ed M., 1936; Ed. D., Waynesburg Coll., 1952; m. Ruby Anne Meyer, July 7, 1934; children—Susanna, Theodore Long. Asst. to dean men U. Pitts., 1929-41, acting dean men, 1941-42, dean men, 1942-58; pres. U. Pitts. at Johnstown, 1958—. Mem. exec. com. Greater Johnstown Com. Bd. dirs. Johnstown United Community Chest, Met. YMCA, Pitts. Mem. Greater Johnstown C. of C. (dir.), Am. Arbitration Assn., Nat., Eastern assns. deans and advisers of men, Pitts. Personnel Assn. Nat. Assn. Student Personnel Adminstrs., N.E.A., Pa. Soc., Assn. Higher Edn., Eastern Assn. Coll. Deans (pres. 1950-52), Alpha Phi Omega, Pi Kappa Alpha (ednl. adviser), Omicron Delta Kappa, Phi Eta Sigma, Scabbard and Blade, Druids. Presbyterian. Clubs: University Faculty, University (Pitts.); Bachelor's (Johnstown); Sunnehanna Country. Contbr. articles to ednl. jours. Home: 131 Fayette St Johnstown PA 15905

BIDELMAN, WILLIAM PENDRY, educator, astronomer; b. Los Angeles, Sept. 25, 1918; s. William Pendry and Dolores (De Remer) B.; student U. N.D., 1936-37; S.B., Harvard, 1940; Ph.D., U. Chgo., 1943; m. Verna Pearl Shirk, June 19, 1940; children—Lana Louise (Mrs. Thomas H. Stone), Linda Elizabeth, Billie Jean, Barbara Jo. Physicist, Aberdeen Proving Ground (Md.), 1943-45; instr. astronomy, then asst. prof. Yerkes Obs., U. Chgo., 1945-53; asst. astronomer, then asso. Lick Obs., U. Cal., 1953-62; prof. astronomy U. Mich., 1962-69; prof. astronomy U. Tex. at Austin, 1969-70; prof., chmn. dept. astronomy Case Western Res. U., Cleve., 1970—, also dir. Warner and Swasey Obs. Mem. adv. panel astronomy NSF, 1959-62; mem. NRC adv. com. astronomy Office Naval Research, 1964-67. Mem. Am. Astron. Soc. (councilor 1959-62, participant vis. prof. program 1961-65), Astron. Soc. Pacific (editor publs. 1956-61), Internat. Astron. Union (pres. commn. 45, 1964-67), Phi Beta Kappa. Presbyn. Contbr. profl. jours. Spl. research spectral classification, galactic structure, observational astrophysics. Home: 3171 Chelsea Dr Cleveland Heights OH 44118

BIDLACK, RUSSELL EUGENE, univ. dean; b. Manilla, Ia., May 25, 1920; s. Harold Stanley and Mable (Thompson) B.; B.A. with honors, Simpson Coll., 1947; A.B. in L.S. with honors, U. Mich., 1948, A.M. in L.S., 1949, A.M. in History, 1950, Ph.D. (L.S.), 1954; m. Melva Helen Sparks, June 13, 1942; children-Stanley Alden, Martha Sue, Christopher Joel, Harold Wilford. Instr. library sci. U. Mich., 1951-56, asst. prof., 1956-60, asso. prof., 1960-65, prof., 1965—, dean Sch. Library Sci., 1969—. Served to master sgt. AUS, 1941- 46, Mem. Am., Mich. library assns., Assn. Am. Library Schs., Mich. Hist. Soc. Author: The City Library of Detroit, 1817-1837, 1955; Letters Home, the Story of Ann Arbor's Forty-Niners, 1960; John Allen and the Founding of Ann Arbor, 1962; The Yankee Meets the Frenchman, 1965. Home: 1709 Cherokee Rd Ann Arbor MI 48104 2MC

BIDWELL, ROGER GRAFTON SHELFORD, biologist, educator; b. Halifax, N.S., Can., June 8, 1927; s. Roger Edward Shelford and Mary (Bothamly) B.; B.Sc., Dalhousie U., 1947; B.A., Queen's U., 1950, M.A., 1951, Ph.D., 1954; m. Shirley Mae Rachael Mason, July 1, 1950; children—Barbara, Alison, Roger, Gillian. Came to U.S., 1965. Tech. officer Canadian Def. Research Bd., Kingston, Ont., 1951- 56; asst. research officer Nat. Research Council, Halifax, 1956-59; asso. prof. biology U. Toronto (Ont.), 1959-65; prof. biology Case Western Res. U., Cleve., 1965-69, chmn. dept., 1966-68; prof. biology Queen's U., Kingston, Ont., Can., 1969—. Vis. prof. Cornell U., summers 1961-63; vis. scientist Atlantic Regional Lab., Nat. Research Council, Halifax, summer 1966; cons. Faculty Edn., Simon Fraser U., 1966. Mem. Canadian (founder, past sec.-treas.), Japanese socs. plant physiologists, A.A.A.S., Am. Soc. Plant Physiology, Am. Inst. Biol. Scis., Canadian Bot. Assn., Bot. Soc. Am., N.S. Inst. Sci. Contbr. articles on biochem. mechanisms in plants, protein metabolism and tumors, CO2 metabolism in leaves, photosynthesis and metabolism in marine algae. Office: Queen's Univ Kingston Ontario Canada

BIDWELL, SETH ROLAND, lawyer, business exec.; b. Girard, Mich., May 6, 1900; s. Myron Elezer and Elizabeth Young (Ackerman) B.; J.D., U. Mich., 1924; m. Dorothy E. DeKleine, June 16, 1924; 1 son, Seth Macey. Admitted to Mich. bar. 1924; partner firm Bidwell, Schmidt & Martin, Grand Rapids, Mich., 1924-51; pres., dir. Hasselbring Co.; dir. Niles Chem. Paint Co.; Bijou Theatrical Enterprise Co., Butterfield Mich. Theatres Co., Blodgett Uncrated Furniture Co., Bradfield & Bidwell, Inc.; dir. Lansing bd. Mich. Nat. Bank. Trustee W.S. Butterfield Estate, Grand Rapids Youth Commonwealth; pres. Ingham County unit Am. Cancer Soc.; chmn. Ingham County Chpt. A.R.C., 1952-53. Mem. Nat. Stationers Assn., S.A.R. (past pres. Kent County), Phi Alpha Delta. Mason (K.T., 32°, Shriner). Clubs: Rotary (dir., v.p.), Peninsular (pres.). Kent Country (Grand Rapids); Paradise Valley Country (Scottsdale, Ariz.); Lansing Country (past pres.), Automobile (Lansing); Circumnavigators (N.Y.C.); Scottsdale (Ariz.) Country: Home: Box 553 Baldwin MI 49304 (winter) 5634 N Scottsdale Rd Scottsdale AZ 85253 Office: 310 N Grand Av Lansing, MI

BIDWILL, CHARLES W., Jr., profl. football exec.; b. Chgo., June 9, 1928; s. Charles W. and Violet Margaret (Fulls) B.; B.S., Georgetown U., 1950, LL.B., 1952; m. Patricia Shea, Sept. 3, 1949; children—Mary Christine, Patricia Margaret, Charles W. III, Shauna, Brian. Pres., Chgo. Cardinals Football Club, 1951; now pres. St. Louis Cardinals Football Team; pres. Nat. Jockey Club, Inc. Clubs: Chicago Yacht, Chicago Athletic Assn., North Shore Country. Office: 200 Stadium Plaza St Louis MO 63102

BIDWILL, WILLIAM VOGEL, sports exec.; b. Chgo., July 31, 1931; s. Charles W. and Viola (Fulls) B.; B.S., Georgetown U., 1953; m. Nancy Lavezzorio, Sept. 1, 196O; children—William Vogel, Michael J., Nicole L., Patrick C. Vice pres. St. Louis Football Cardinals, 1951—; treas. Nat. Jockey Club, Chgo., 1965—. Dir. Cosmopolitan Nat. Bank Chgo. Bd. Govs. Cardinal Glennon Meml. Hosp. for Children. Served with USNR, 1954-55. Roman Catholic. Home: 4 Southmoor Dr Clayton, MO 63105. Office: 200 Stadium Plaza St Louis, MO 63102.

BIEBEL, LAWRENCE BURTON, patent lawyer; b. La Grange, Ill., Feb. 24, 19O6; s. Herman M. and Alice (Morris) B.; B.S. in Elec. Engring. with highest honors, U. Pitts., 1927; LL.B., George Washington U., 1931; m. Josephine E. Hopkins, June 27, 1931; children—Jane H., Nancy E. Examiner U.S. Patent Officer, 1928- 30; admitted to D.C. bar, 1931, Ohio bar, 1937; engaged in pvt. practice patent law, Dayton, O., 1930—; sr. partner Maréchal, Biebel, French & Bugg Asso., 1930—. Bd. dirs. Water Refining Co., Inc., Duriron Co., Inc. Mem. Sec. of Commerce adv. com., 1955-56; mem. Nat. Inventors Council, 1956—. Pres. Dayton Opera Assn., 1969-70. Trustee, adv. bd. Sinclair Coll. Mem. Inst. Patent Attorneys Australia, Am. (past pres.), Dayton (pres. 1947) patent law assns., Am., Ohio, Dayton bar assns., Newcomen Soc., Theta Chi, Phi Delta Phi. Club: Dayton Engineers (pres. 1945-46). Home: 631 Garden Rd Dayton, OH 45419. Office: Winters Bank Bldg Dayton OH 45402

BIEBER, DAVID J., univ. pres.; b. Tolstoy, S.D., Nov. 14, 1910; s. John and Kathryn (Trefz) B.; A.B., Union Coll., Lincoln, Neb., 1936; M.A., U. Minn., 1945; m. Eva LaFave, Sept. 5, 1933; 1 son, Donald. Tchr. Oak Park Acad., Nevada, Ia., 1936-39; tchr., prin. Maplewood Acad., Hutchinson, Minn., 1939-45; prin. Hawaiian Mission Acad., Honolulu, 1945-49, Monterey Bay Acad., Watsonville, Cal., 1949-57; pres. Union Coll., Lincoln, Neb., 1957-64, LaSierra Coll., Riverside, Cal., 1965-67, Loma Linda U., 1967- . Rotarian. Home: 5325 Peacock Lane Riverside CA 92505

BIEBER, SAMUEL, coll. provost; b. N.Y.C., Feb. 5, 1926; s. Hyman and Pauline (Sussman) B.; B.A., N.Y. U., 1944, M.S., 1948, Ph.D., 1952; m. Rosalyn Lilah Hewitt, Dec. 18, 1949; children—Susan Ellen, Scott Hewitt. Adj. asst., adj. asso. prof. biology L.I. U., 1957-62, prof. biology 1962-69, asso. dean grad. faculties, 1962-66, dean Richard L. Conolly Coll., 1966-69; campus dean Fairleigh Dickinson U., Teaneck, N.J., 1969-71, provost Teaneck campus, 1971—; teaching fellow N.Y. U., 1948-51; Wellcome Research fellow Wellcome Found., 1951-52; sr. research biologist Wellcome Research Labs., Burroughs Wellcome & Co., 1952-62; vis. scientist Reed Coll., summer 1967; cons. in field, 1952—. Mem. adv. councils Westchester County and Rockland County sci. fairs.; asst. chief radiol. service, New Rochelle, N.Y., 1955-57. Served with USNR, 1944-46. Fellow N.Y. Acad. Scis.; mem. Am. Assn. Cancer Research, Soc. Exptl. Biology and Medicine, Soc. Devel. Biology, Am. Chem. Soc., Am. Soc. Zoologists, A.A.A.S., Sigma Xi, Phi Sigma. Mason, Odd Fellow, Rotarian. Contbr. profl. jours. Home: 1303 River Rd Teaneck NJ 07666

BIEBUYCK, DANIEL PROSPER, educator; b. Deinze, Belgium, Oct. 1, 1925; s. Marcel G. and Bertha (Van Laere) B.; Lic. Classics, Ghent U., 1948, Doctorate Philosophy and Letters, 1954; postgrad. anthropology, London U., 1948-49; m. Laure-Marie de Rycke, Nov. 21, 1950; children—Brunhilde, Anne-Marie, Edwin, Hans, Jean-Christopher, Jean-Marie, Beatrice. Came to U.S., 1961. Research fellow Inst. pour la Recherche Sci. en Afrique Centrale, 1949 57; prof. anthropology Lovanium U., Kinshasa, Congo, 1958-61; govt. anthropologist, Kingshasa, 1958-60; prof. anthropology U. Del., 1961-64, U. Cal. at Los Angeles, 1964-66; H. Rodney Sharp prof. U. Del., 1966—, chmn. dept. anthropology, 1970—; curator African ethnology U. Cal. at Los Angeles, 1964-66; vis. lectr. Liège U., 1957, Yale, 1968-69; vis. prof. London U., 1960-61, Yale, 1969- 70. Fellow Am. Anthrolology Assn., African Studies Assn., Internat. African Inst., Belgian Acad. Royale des Scis. d'Outre-Mer, Inst. des Civilisations Differentes, N.Y. Acad. Scis. Author: De Hond hii de Nvanga, 1958; Congo Tribes and Parties, 1961; African Agrarian Systems, 2d edit., 1965; The Mwindo Epic from the Banyanga, 1969; Tradition and Creativity in Tribal Art, 1969: Anthologie de la littérature nyanga, 1969. Home: 271 W Main St Newark DE 19711

BIEDENHARN, LAWRENCE CHRISTIAN, Jr., educator; b. Vicksburg, Miss., Nov. 18, 1922; s. Lawrence Christian and Willetta (Lyens) B.; B.S., Mass. Inst. Tech., 1944, Ph.D., 1949; m. Sarah Jeffress Willingham, Mar. 25, 1950; children—John David, Sarah Willetta. Research asso. Mass. Inst. Tech., 1949-50; physiciat Oak Ridge Nat. Lab., 1950-52; asst. prof. Yale, 1952-54; asso. prof. Rice U., 1954-61; prof. physics Duke, 1961—. Cons. Los Alamos Sci. Lab., Nat. Bur. Standards, Oak Ridge Nat. Lab. Served with Signal Corps, AUS, 1943-46. Sr. Fulbright fellow, 1958; Guggenheim fellow, 1959; NSF Sr. postdoctoral fellow, 1964-65. Fellow Am. Phys. Soc., Inst. Physics, Phys. Soc. Gt. Britain; mem. Swiss Phys. Soc., A.A.A.S., Am. Assn. U. Profs., European Phys. Soc., Sigma Xi, Kappa Sigma. Author: (with Pieter Brussaard) Coulomb Excitation, 1964; (with H. Van Dam) Quantum Theory of Angular Momentum, 1965. Asso. editor Jour. Math. Physics, 1964-68. Contbr. articles to profl. jours. Home: 2716 Sevier St Durham NC 27705

BIEDERMAN, BARRON ZACHARY, advt. exec.; b. N.Y.C., Sept. 1, 1930; s. William and Sophye (Groll) B.; B.A. with distinction, Cornell U., 1952; postgrad., Columbia Sch. Journalism, 1953, U. London, 1954; m. Susan Howard, May 13, 1967; children—Rachel, David. Copy group head Mogul, Williams & Saylor, N.Y.C., 1955-59; sr. writer Lennen & Newell, N.Y.C., 1960-62; v.p., asso. creative dir. Cunningham & Walsh, N.Y.C., 1962-64; sr. v.p., exec. creative dir. Needham, Harper & Steers, N.Y.C., 1964—. Recipient various advt. awards, including Am. TV Comml. Festival, 1958, 59, 70, 71, Hollywood TV Comml. Festival, 1970, Advt. Club N.Y., 1969-71, Am. Advt. Fedn., 1969-71, Cork (Ireland) Festival, 1970, 71, Cannes (France) Internat. Comml. Festival, 1971; Ford Found. fellow, Eng., India, 1953-55. Mem. Copy Club N.Y. (past dir.). Home: 85 East End Av New York City NY 10028 Office: 909 3d Av New York City NY 10022

BIEGEL, HERMAN CHARLES, lawyer; b. N.Y.C., Aug. 5, 1909; s. David and Tillie (Nusim) B.; B.S.S. cum laude, Coll. City N.Y., 1930; LL.B. (editor Law Jour.), Yale, 1933; m. Shirley Gubert, June 24,1934; children—Richard, Judy. Admitted to N.Y. bar, 1933, D.C. bar, 1938; with office chief counsel Bur. Internal Revenue, 1934-37; pvt. law practice, Washington, 1937—; partner firm Alvord & Alvord, 1942-50, Lee, Toomey & Kent, 1950—. Lectr. tax and law insts.; mem. adv. com. Council Profit-Sharing Industries, 1950—; pension research council Wharton Sch. Finance, U. Pa., 1958—. Served as lt. comdr. USNR, 1944-46. Mem. Am. Bar Assn., Phi Beta Kappa. Contbr. articles law jours., periodicals. Home: 2838 Chesterfield Pl NW Washington DC 20008 Office: 1200 18th St NW Washington DC 20036

BIEGERT, MAURINE, mem. Democratic nat. com.; b. Shickley, Neb., June 6, 1929; d. Willard Hiner and Marie (Kolar) Steyer; student Coll. Arg., U. Neb., 1946-47, 48- 49; m. John Richard Biegert, Oct. 2, 1949; children—Jeffrey Lynn, Deborah Ann, Beth Marie. Rural sch. tchr., 1947-48; 4-H camp counselor Neb., 1948; demonstrator frozen foods Internat. Harvester Co., 1949-50. Organizer Fillmore County Dem Womens Group, 1958; Fillmore County co- chmn. Citizens for Kennedy, 1960; mem. Dem. Nat. Com. for Neb., 1960—. Pres. Fillmore County Extension Bd., 1952-54, Fillmore County Tchrs. Assn., 1947-48, Neb. Homemakers Assn., 1957-58. Bd. dirs. Crippled Childrens Assn. 4-H pub. speaking winner, Neb., 1945, nat. 4-H girls record winner, 1946. Mem. Federated Womens Club (pres. Shickley chpt. 1954-56, Fillmore County 1956-57). Address: Shickley NB 68436

BIEGLER, JOHN CHARLES, accountant; b. Chgo., Aug. 22, 1921; s. John Charles and Josephine (Watson) B.; B.S. with honors, U. Ill., 1943; m. Jeannette Mae Hawkins, Oct. 4, 1947; 1 son, James Cameron. With Price Waterhouse & Co., C.P.A.'s, 1946—, partner, N.Y.C., 1958-69, sr. partner, 1969—. Bd. dirs. Tokeneke Tax Dist., Darien, Conn., 1965—. Served to capt. C.E., AUS, 1943-46; ETO. C.P.A., Ill., N.Y. Mem. Am. Inst. C.P.A.'s, N.Y. State Soc. C.P.A.'s, Beta Gamma Sigma. Episcopalian. Clubs: University, Board Room, Recess (N.Y.C.); Stanwich (Greenwich, Conn.); Metropolitan (Washington); Wee Burn, Tokeneke (Darien, Conn.). Home: 19 Winding Lane Darien CT 06820 Office: 60 Broad St New York City NY 10004

BIEHL, WILLIAM J., mgmt. cons.; b. Brazil, Ind., June 30, 1916; s. William H. and Odessa (Nicosin) B.; B.S., Ind. U., 1937; m. Marie L. Schlueter, Oct. 21, 1938; children—Peter J., David L. Chief indsl. engr. Libby, McNeill & Libby, Honolulu, 1940-42, supr. methods, Chgo., 1942-43; partner Fry Lawson & Co., 1945-46; v.p. George Fry & Assos., Inc., 1946-49, 53-55, pres., 1955-58, chmn., 1958-70; chmn. Fry Consultants Inc., 1958-70, vice chmn., 197—, also dir.; v.p. Comstock Corp., Newark, N.Y., 1949- 51; pres. Internat. Milk Processors, Inc., 1951-53; chmn. bd. Natomas Co., James Dole Engting. Co., Am. Pres. Lines, Ltd. Mem. Soc. Advancement Mgmt. (dir., exec. v.p.), Indsl. Mgmt. Engrs. (pres. 1963), Indsl. Mgmt. Soc. (exec. v.p.). Republican. Presbyn. Clubs: University, Attic, Chicago, Commonwealth (Chgo.); Tucson Nat. Golf (Tucson). Home: 7501 E Ellison Dr Tucson AZ 85704 Office: 4400 E Broadway Tucson AZ 85711

BIELENSTEIN, HANS HENRIK AUGUST, educator; b. Stockholm, Sweden, Apr. 8, 1920; s. Maximilian August Rudolf Gottfried and Elsbeth Margot Erika (von Gruenewaldt) B.; Ph.D., Royal U., Stockholm, 1954; m. Gabrielle Carter Maupin, Jan. 12, 1954; children—Danielle Erika Mary, Andrea Johanna Gabrielle. Came to U.S., 1961. Prof. Oriental langs., head Sch. Oriental Studies, Australian Nat. U., Canberra, 1952-62; prof. Chinese history Columbia, 1961—, chmn. dept. E. Asian langs. and cultures, 1969—. Served with Swedish Vol. Corps to Finland, 1939-40. Decorated Finnish War medal with swords and clasp; Guggenheim fellow, 1967-68. Author books and articles on Chinese history, historiography and demography. Home: 50 Riverside Dr New York City NY 10024

BIEMANN, KLAUS, educator; b. Innsbruck, Austria, Nov. 2, 1926; s. Willibald and Margarethe (Dinkhauser) B.; Ph.D., Innsbruck, 1951; m. Vera Themistocles, July 29, 1956; children—Hans-Peter, Elisabeth. Came to U.S., 1955, naturalized 1965. Postdoctoral fellow Mass. Inst. Tech., Cambridge, 1955-57, instr. chemistry, 1957-59, asst. prof., 1959-62, asso. prof., 1962-63, prof., 1963—. Recipient Tricentennial medal U. Innsbruck, 1970. Fellow Am. Acad. Arts and Scis.; mem. Am., Austrian, Belgium (hon.; recipient gold medal 1962) chem. socs. Author: Mass Spectrometry, 1962. Mem. editorial bd. Organic Mass Spectrometry, 1967—, Analytical Chemistry, 1968-71. Research publs. mass spectrometry. Home: Alton Bay NH 03810 Office: Mass Inst Tech Cambridge MA 02139

BIEMILLER, ANDREW JOHN, labor union ofcl., ex-congressman; b. Sandusky, O., July 23, 1906; s. Andrew Frederick and Pearl (Weber) B.; A.B., Cornell U., 1926; postgrad. U. Pa., 1928-31; m. Hannah Perot Morris, Dec. 20, 1929; children—Andrew John, Nancy Barbara. Tchr. history Syracuse U., U. Pa., 1926-32; newspaper and labor relations positions, 1932-42; mem. Wis. legislature, 1936-42; with WPB, 1942-44; mem. 79th, 81st U.S. congresses, 5th Wis. Dist.; pub. relations counsellor, lectr., writer ; spl. asst. to sec. interior, 1951-52; dir. dept. legislation AFL-CIO, 1956—, chmn. staff com. on atomic energy. Mem. labor-mgmt. adv. com. AEC; mem. mgmt.-labor textile adv. com. Dept. Commerce, 1961—; mem. Presdl. Task Force on Career Advancement, 1966-67; mem. consumer com. on automobile ins. and compensation Dept. Trans.; labor adviser Am. delegation GATT Conf., 1957, 61. Mem. Am. Fedn. Tchrs., Delta Kappa Epsilon. Democrat. Mem. Soc. Friends. Clubs: Kenwood Golf and Country, Nat. Press. Home: 6805 Glenbrook Rd Bethesda MD 20014 Office: 815 16th St NW Washington DC 20006

BIEN, PETER ADOLPH, educator. Prof. English Dartmouth. Office: Dept English Dartmouth Hanover NH 03755*

BIENEMAN, WALTER N., lawyer; b. Chgo., June 8, 1914; A.B., U. Mich., 1935, J.D., 1937. Admitted to Mich. bar, 1937; now mem. firm Matheson, Bieneman, Veale & Parr, Detroit. Mem. Am., Detroit bar assns., State Bar Mich., Motor Carrier Lawyers Assn. Office: 1 Woodward Av Detroit MI 48226*

BIENFANG, RALPH DAVID, educator; b. Jefferson, Wis., Jan. 15, 1905; s. John Matthew and Nellie (Arnold) B.; student U. Colo., 1922-23; B.S., U. Wis., 1926, M.S., 1927, Ph.D., 1929; m. Bess Irene Marriott, June 27, 1934; 1 dau., Jane Marriott B. (Mrs. James G. Barlow, Jr.). Prof., Conn. Coll. Pharmacy, 1929-30; asst. prof. pharmacognosy U. Okla., Norman, 1930-37, asso. prof., 1937-41, prof., 1941-42, prof. pharmacy, 1942-65, David Ross Boyd prof., 1965—. Mem. Am. Pharm. Assn., Wis. Hist. Soc., Sociedade de Farmacia e Quimica de Sao Paulo (hon.), Sociedade de Farmacia de Rio de Janeiro (hon.), Sigma Xi, Rho Chi, Phi Sigma, Kappa Psi, Alpha Sigma Phi. Lutheran. Lion Writer of Poetry. Home: 1114 E Louisiana St Norman, OK 73069.

BIENSTOCK, ABRAHAM LAWRENCE, lawyer; b. N.Y.C., Dec. 30, 1904; s. Alexander Myer and Matilda (Touster) B.; student Coll. City N.Y., 1922-24; LL.B., N.Y. U., 1927; m. Marjorie Cahne, July 12, 1939; children—Patricia Grace Murdock (Mrs. Patricia M. Williams), John James Murdock. Admitted to N.Y. bar, 1928, since practiced N.Y.C., 1928—; sr. mem. firm Abraham L. Bienstock, N.Y.C., 1941—; ltd. partner Hurt Oil Co., Ltd., Houston; chmn. bd. Intsel Corp.; dir., mem. exec. com. R.H. Macy & Co., Inc.; dir. Community Newspapers, Inc. Bd. dirs. Univ. Settlement Soc.; trustee Bethsabee de Rothschild Found. for Arts and Scis., Sciences, Inc. Mem. Council Fgn. Relations, Assn. Bar City N.Y., Am., N.Y. bar assns., N.Y. County Lawyers Assn. Clubs: Wall Street (N.Y.C.); Piping Rock, Locust Valley, Long Island. Home: Berry Hill Rd Syosset NY 11791 also 29 E 63d St New York City NY 10021 Office: 30 Broad St New York City NY 10004

BIENVENU, BERNARD JEFFERSON, educator; b. St. Martinville, La., Apr. 8, 1925; s. Louis Jefferson and Beatrice (Durand) B.; B.S., U. Southwestern La., 1947; M.B.A., Harvard, 1947, D.B.A., 1956; student U. Paris, also U. Lyon (France), 1959. Engaged in stock brokerage bus., 1947-48; asso. gen. agt. Pan Am. Life Ins. Co., 1948-50; prof. bus. adminstrn., dir. alumni relations U. Southwestern La., 1952-53, prof. bus. adminstrn., 1955—, head dept. marketing, 1955-56, head dept. mgmt., 1956—; Ford fellow bus. adminstrn., faculty Harvard Grad Sch. Bus., 1954-55; mgmt. cons. to bus., govt., ch. orgns., 1958—; lectr. nat. orgns.; vis. prof. Institut Superieur Des Affaires, Centre d'Enseignment des Affaires de Jouy- en-Josas, France, 1970-71. Dir., vice chmn. bd. Evangeline Pepper & Foods, Inc., 1963-65. Area chmn. Radio Free Europe drive, 1963; mem. La. Bd. Commerce and Industry, 1960-64; tng. dir. Lafayette United Givers Fund, 1958-59; mem. La. Labor Mediation Bd., 1966—. Pres. faculty senate U. Southwest La., 1966-67. Served with USNR, 1943-46, 50-52; capt. Res. Mem. So. (dir. 1964, v.p. 1966-67, pres. 1968-69), Southwest (pres. 1962-63) mgmt. assns., Am. Assn. U. Profs., Am. Acad. Mgmt. (bd. govs. 1968-69), John Henry Cardinal Newman Honor Soc., Phi Kappa Theta (nat. sec. 1956-57), Phi Kappa Phi. Author: New Priorities in Training-A Guide for Industry, 1969. Contbr. profl. jours. Home: 211 N Main St St Martinville LA 70582 Office: PO Box 598 Univ Southwestern Louisiana Lafayette LA 70505

BIENVENU, PAUL, food products exec.; b. Montreal, Que., Can., May 5, 1897; s. Tancrede and Clara (Martin) B.; ed. Laval U., Que., 1917; m. Raymonde Mercier, May 16, 1922; children—Renée, Madeleine, Claudine, Nicole. Pres., mng. dir. Catelli Food Products, Ltd., 1928—; v.p. Bovril (Can.), Ltd.; chmn. bd. Place Victoria-St. Jacques Co., Inc.; dir. Catelli-Habitant, Ltd., Credit Foncier Franco-Canadien, Bank of Montreal, Ford Motor Co. Can., Molson's Brewery, Ltd., Asbestos Corp., Ltd., Consol. Bakeries, Ltd., Canadian Petrofina, Ltd., Ogilvie Flour Mills, Ltd., Holt, Renfrew & Co., Ltd., No. Electric Co., Ltd., Canadian Tabacofina, Ltd., Royal Exchange-Atlas Group. Bd. dirs. Notre Dame Hosp. Mem. Internat. C. of C. (past pres. Can. council). Clubs: St. Denis Mt. Royal (Montreal); Forest and Stream (Dorval); Laval sur le lac (Que., Can.) Golf. Home: 3010 The Boulevard Montreal Quebec Canada Office: 1980 Sherbrooke W Montreal Quebec Canada

BIER, JUSTUS, museum dir.; b. Nuremberg, Germany, May 31, 1899; s. Jacob and Minna (Honig) B.; student univs. Munich, Erlangen, Jena, Bonn, Munich, 1918-24; Ph.D. magna cum laude, U. Zurich, 1924; D.F.A., Duke U., 1970; m. Senta Dietzel, Mar. 17, 1931; 1 son, Max Robert. Came to U.S. 1937, naturalized 1944. Docent, Inst. Art History, Municipal U., Nuremberg, Germany 1925-30; traveling fellow Notgemeinschaft der Deutschen Wissenschaft, 1928; dir., curator Kestner-Gesellschaft Art Inst., Hannover, Germany, 1930-36; founder, dir. Mus. für das vorbildliche Serienprodukt, 1930-36; asst. prof. art history, acting head dept. fine arts U. Louisville, 1937-41, asso. prof., 1941-46, head dept., 1941-60, prof., 1946-60; Fulbright lectr. and vis. prof. U. Wurzburg Germany, 1960-61; dir. N.C. Mus. Art, Raleigh, 1961-70, dir. emeritus and curator research, 1970—. Bd. dirs. Allen R. Hite Art Inst., U. Louisville, 1946-60; mem. Inst. for Advanced Study, Princeton, 1953-54; art editor, critic The Courier-Jour., Louisville, 1944-56; vis. prof. Free Univ. Berlin, 1956, U. So. Cal., 1958. Bd. dirs. Deutscher Werkbund, Berlin, 1931-34; adv. bd. art edn. U. Ky., 1947; adv. com. Ky. State Fair and Expn. Center, 1949, Jr. Art Gallery, Louisville, 1949-60; mem. Louisville Council Historic Sites and Bldg., 1950-53; profl. adviser Jr. League Louisville 1945-60; lectr. Europe, U.S. Recipient research grant Notgemeinschaft der deutschen Wissenschaft, 1928; Dürer medal, Nuremberg, 1928; August Kestner medal Kestner-Gesellschaft, Hannover, 1938. Guggenheim fellow, 1953-54, 56-57. Mem. Coll. Art Assn. Am., Southeastern (chmn. nominations com.), Midwestern (pres. 1951-52), coll. arts confs., Am. Soc. Aesthetics, So. Art Mus. Dirs. Assn., Internat. Art Critics Assn. (asso. Am. sect.), Assn. German Art Historians (hon.), Friends of Art and History in Mainfranken at Wurzburg (hon.), Delta Phi Alpha, Kappa Pi Epsilon, Phi Kappa Phi. Club: Filson (Louisville). Author: Tilman Riemenschneider Ein Gedenkbuch, 6th edit. 1948, and other books and articles. Mem. editorial council Jour. Aesthetics and Art Criticism, 1951-53. Home: 201 Peartree Lane Raleigh NC 27610 Office: NC Museum of Art 107 E Morgan St Raleigh NC 27601

BIER, STEPHEN JAY, financial exec.; b. N.Y.C., Sept. 4, 1936; s. Mac Daniel and Lillian (Schoengold) B.; B.S., Yale, 1958; M.B.A., Wharton Sch., U. Pa., 1960; m. Karen Mary Conway, Dec. 10, 1961 (div. 1969). Financial analyst Merrill Lynch, Pierce, Fenner & Smith, Inc., N.Y.C., 1960-61; mgr. portfolio analysis dept. Eastman Dillon, Union Securities & Co., N.Y.C., 1961-64; dir. investments Moore-McCormack Lines, Inc., N.Y.C., 1964-65; treas. Moore and McCormack Co., Inc., N.Y.C., 1965-68; treas., dir. Tidewater Terminals, Inc., 1965-68, Comml. Steamship Co., Inc., 1965-68, Trident Leasing Co., Inc., 1965-68; asst. treas. ELTRA Corp. (formerly Electric Autolite Co. and Mergenthaler Linotype Co.), N.Y.C., 1968—, Equilease Corp., N.Y.C., 1970—. Served with USMCR, 1958. Mem. N.Y. Soc. Security Analysts, Financial Analysts Fedn. Clubs: Wall Street, City Midday, Yale (N.Y.C.). Home: 136 E 76th St New York City NY 10021 also Broadview Rd Woodstock NY 12498 Office: 2 Pennsylvania Plaza New York City NY 10001

BIER, WILLIAM CHRISTIAN, clergyman, psychologist; b. Bklyn., May 1, 1911; s. Christian J. and Adelaide M. (Kraus) B.; A.B., Woodstock Coll., 1934, Ph.L., 1935, S.T.L., 1941; M.A., Fordham U., 1939; Ph.D., Catholic U. Am., 1948. Entered Soc. of Jesus, 1928; ordained priest Roman Cath. Ch., 1940; instr. dept. psychology Fordham U. Grad. Sch., 1948-51, asst. prof., 1951-55, asso. prof., 1955-66, prof., 1966—, also chmn. dept., 1958-68. Cetified psychologist, N.Y. State. Fellow Am. Psychol. Assn.; mem. Acad. Religion and Mental Health (profl. bd.), Am. Cath., Eastern, N.Y. State psychol. assns., Sigma Xi. Editor Am. Cath. Psychol. Assn. Newspetter, 1950—; Pastoral Psychology Series, 1962—. Address: Fordham U Bronx, NY 10458.

BIERBAUER, CARL EDMUND, banker; b. Chgo., Feb. 10, 1916; s. John and Theresa (Solderdich) B.; student Am. Inst. Banking, 1946-49, Northwestern U., eves. 1942, 44, 49; grad. Sch. Banking, U. Wis., 1950; m. Edith Mae Dean, Jan. 14, 1939; children—Jean Carol (Mrs. Kenneth Aquino), Paul Dean. With Fed. Res. Bank Chgo., 1933—, sr. v.p., control officer, 1969—. Served with AUS, 1945-46. Office: 230 S LaSalle St Chicago IL 60690

BIERER, JOSHUA, psychiatrist; b. Radautz, Austria, July 1, 1901; Dr. Econ. and Social Sci., U. Vienna (Austria), 1930, Dipl. Individual Psychology, 1926, M.D., 1938. Lectr., Inst. Individual Psychology, Berlin, Germany, 1928-29, Runwell Hosp., London, Eng., 1938-42, 43-44, 46—; med. dir. Inst. Social Psychiatry, London, 1946—, Social Psychotherapy Centre and Marlborough Day Hosp., London, 1948-67; now prof. social and community psychiatry Southeastern U. Fla. Pioneer of Day, Night, Weekend and Turno Hosp., self-governed hostel and therapeutic social club.; founder first psychiat. therapeutic community, 1938; spl. research psychotherapy of schizophrenics. Chmn. Friends of Kibbutz, 1964-67; chmn. Internat. Congress Social Psychiatry, 1964, 69, Israel Med. Assn. British Fellowship, 1965-67. Served as maj. Royal Army Med. Corps,1944- 46. Mem. Brit. Assn. Social Psychiatry, Internat. Assn. Soc. Psychiatry (chmn.). Author: The Day Hospital, 1951; (with R. Evans) Innovations in Social Psychiatry. Editor-in-chief Internat. Jour. Social Psychiatry, 1955—, British Jour. Social Psychiatry, 1967—. Home: 7 Hollycroft Av London NW 3 England Office: 140 Harley St London W 1 England

BIERER, WILLIAM E., banker; b. Uniontown, Pa., Dec. 19, 1929; s. William Edmund and Gertrude (Morley) B.; student U. Pitts., 1954, Stonier Grad. Sch. Banking, Rutgers U., 1965; m. Ruth Sibel, Aug. 22, 1959; children—William E., Nannette. With Westinghouse Electric Corp., Pitts., 1954-61; v.p. Mellon Nat. Bank & Trust Co., Pitts., 1961-68; exec. v.p. Western Pa. Nat. Bank, Pitts., 1968—; dir. Eastern States Bankcard Assn., Consumer Credit Counseling Service. Bd. dirs. North Hills Passavant Hosp., RIDC Indsl. Devel. Fund. Served with AUS, 1948-49, 51-53. Home: Grubbs Rd Wexford PA 15090 Office: 5th and Smithfield Pittsburgh PA 15232

BIERI, BERNHARD HENRY, Jr., naval officer; b. Camden, N.J., Oct. 12, 1915; s. Bernhard Henry and Elsie (Genther) B.; B.S., U.S. Naval Acad., 1937; grad. Naval War Coll., 1953, Nat. War Coll., 1960; m. Margaret Walter, Dec. 23, 1939; children—Margaret (Mrs. David L. Butterfield), Bernhard Henry III. Commd. ensign U.S. Navy, 1937, advanced through grades to rear adm., 1963; supply officer U.S.S. San Francisco, 1942-43; exec. officer Gen. Stores Supply Office, Phila., 1948-51, Naval Supply Depot, Bayonne, N.J., 1951-52; mem. staff Joint Chiefs Staff, 1953-55; spl. asst. to asst. sec. navy, 1955-56; supply officer Long beach Naval Shipyard, 1956- 59; comdg. officer Naval Supply Depot, Seattle, 1962-63; dep. chief naval material, 1963-65; fleet supply officer Pacific Fleet, 1965—. Decorated Legion of Merit, Navy Commendation ribbon. Mem. Nat. Def. Transp. Assn., Def. Supply Assn. Clubs: N.Y. Yacht; Army-Navy, Washington Golf and Country (Washington). Home: Office: care FPO Navy 128 San francisco CA 96614

BIERINGER, LEROY J., pub. relations counsel; b. Chgo., June 14, 1922; s. Benjamin S. and Sylvia (Sternheim) B.; student George Williams Coll., Chgo., 1943-45; m. Annette S. Orenstein, Aug. 12, 1945; children—Steven A., Garry J., Shelly J. Publicity dir. Chgo. council Boy Scouts Am., 1943-45; account exec. Pub. Relations Services, Chgo., 1945-48; owner Leroy J. Bieringer Assos., Chgo., 1948-59; exec. v.p. Harsha-Rotman & Druck, Inc., N.Y.C., 1950—; pres., dir. Bloom/Harshe-Rotman & Druck, Inc., (Dallas); lectr. Am. Mgmt. Assn. Mem. nat. council Boy Scouts Am., 1967—; fund chmn. Hartsdale (N.Y.) A.R.C., 1962. Mem. Hartsdale Bd. Edn., 1963-66, 69—, pres., 1963-66. Served with USAAF, 1942-43. Mem. Pub. Relations Soc. Am. Home: 100 E Hartsdale Av Hartsdale NY 10530 Office: 300 E 44th St New York City NY 10017

BIERINGER, WALTER H., plastic and rubber mfg. co. exec.; b. Boston, Mass., Nov. 17, 1899; s. Leo and Sara (Wolfenstein) B.; A.B., Harvard U., 1921; m. Gertrude Marie Kessel, Aug. 5, 1922; 1 dau., Doris Marie (Mrs. Howard H. Hiatt). Exec. v.p. dir. Plymouth Rubber Co., Canton, Mass., 1921—. Chmn. Gov.'s Commn. on Refugees, 1946—. Trustee Howard U.; bd. overseers Brandeis U. Sch. Social Work; bd. dirs. Joint Distbn. Com., Am. ORT Fedn., United HIAS

Service, Inc. Served with AUS, World War I. Mem. World Trade Center Boston. Home: 26 Wolcott Rd Extension Brookline MA 02167 Office: 1000 Revere Rubber St Canton MA 02021

BIERKOE, ELEANOR, see Tupper, Eleanor, (Mrs. George O. Bierkoe).

BIERKOE, GEORGE OLAF, clergyman, educator; b. Brooklyn, New York, July 2, 1895; s. Johan Arnt and Alvilde (Boe) Bjerkoe; A.B., Muhlenberg Coll., 1922, Litt.D., 1946; B.D., Lutheran Theol. Sem., Mt. Airy, Pa., 1925; A.M., N.Y. U., 1935; postgrad. Boston U., 1935-36, Harvard, summer, 1936, Columbia, 1938-39; Litt.D., U. Cin., 1971; m. Eleanor Tupper June 21, 1933; children—Priscilla, Barbara. With Endicott-Johnson Co., N.Y., 1914- 17; social worker, Lutheran Ch., N.Y., 1923; ordained to ministry Luth. Ch., 1925; pastor Ch. of Good Shepherd, Bellaire, L.I., N.Y., 1925-35; instr. Boston YMCA, 1936-38, Stoneleigh Coll., Rye, N.H., 1937; a founder, pres., chaplain Endicott Jr. Coll., Beverly, Mass., 1939—, also trustee. Entered O.T.C., 1918; served in U.S. Army, Year, during World War; R.O.T.C., Muhlenberg Coll., 2 years. Mem. Mass. Civil League, Boston. Mem. Greater Boston Coop. Soc., Beverly (Mass.) C. of C., Beverly YMCA, Phi Kappa Tau. Republican. Club: Rotary. Founded, organized, built 2 ch. bldgs. and parsonage at Ch. of Good Shepherd, Bellaire. Home: 375 Hale St Beverly MA 01915

BIERMAN, ARTHUR, educator; b. Vienna, Austria, Oct. 14, 1925; s. Jacob and Regina (Wenig) B.; came to U.S., 1939, naturalized, 1944; student Bklyn. Coll., 1942-44; M.A., U. Chgo., 1948, Ph.D., 1954; M.A., Columbia U., 1957; m. Enid Sharp, Aug. 29, 1953; children—Jessica, Cynthia. Asst. prof. Coll. City N.Y., 1958-62; sr. research scientist Lockheed Cal. Co., 1962-64; prof. physics Coll. City N.Y., 1969—, acting asso. provost, 1971. Served with AUS, 1944-46. Fellow Infantile Paralysis Found., 1954-55; research grantee AEC, 1965-71. Mem. Am. Phys. Soc. Contbr. articles physics jours. Home: 137 W 78th St New York City NY 10024

BIERMAN, CLIFFORD DELEF HARM, business exec.; b. Hastings, Neb., Feb. 10, 1910; s. Harry H. and Jessie Emma (Moenck) B.; student Hastings Coll., 1926-29, Ga. Inst. Tech., 1931-32, George Washington U., 1940-41; m. Lucy Marie Fierro, Oct. 20, 1945; 1 dau., Marcia Steele. Sales engr. Rosslyn Steel & Cement Co., Washington, 1936-42; chief engr. Maxon Constrn. Co., Marine Div., Tell City, Ind., 1943-45, yard supt., 1945-47; constrn. supt. Blaw-Knox Chem. Plants, Inc., Pitts., 1947-50, project mgr., 1950-56, mgr. estimating, 1956—. Served with USCG, 1932-36. Mem. Am. Assn. Cost Engrs. (pres. Pitts. sect. 1963-64, nat. dir. 1965-67, 69-70, nat. v.p. 1967-68, nat. pres. 1968-69), Engrs. Soc. Western Pa. Republican. Episcopalian (vestryman, treas. 1960-63). Mason. Club: Pittsburgh Playhouse. Contbr. articles tech. jours. Home: 4828 Old Boston Rd Pittsburgh PA 15227 Office: 1 Oliver Plaza Pittsburgh PA 15222

BIERMAN, HAROLD Jr., educator; b. N.Y.C., June 17, 1924; s. Harold Stahl and Frieda (Zelezney) B.; B.S., U.S. Naval Acad., 1945; M.B.A., U. Mich., 1949, Ph.D., 1955; m. Florence Merwin Kelso, Feb. 2, 1952; children—James Landon, Harold Scott, Donald Bruce, Jonathan David. With Arthur Young & Co., 1949-50; with Shell Oil Co., 1950; faculty La. State U., 1950-51, U. Chgo., 1955-56; mem. faculty Cornell U., Ithaca, N.Y., 1956—, Nicholas H. Noyes prof. bus. adminstrn., 1969—; cons. Ford Found.; adviser to mgmt. program U. W.Indies. Served with USN, 1942-47, 51-53. Mem. Am. Accounting Assn., Am. Finance Assn., Am. Econ. Assn. Author: The Capital Budgeting Decision, 1960, rev., 1966; (with Seymour Smidt) Financial Accounting Theory, 1965; Financial Policy Decisions, 1970. Home: 109 Kay St Ithaca NY 14850

BIERMAN, HOWARD RICHARD, physician; b. Newark, Jan. 27, 1915; s. Philip and Cecile (Cohen) B.; B.Sc., Washington U., 1935, M.D., 1939; m. Doris Rita Simmons, May 18, 1946; children—Barry, Tracy, Dana. Fellow in hematology Sch. Medicine, Washington U., 1939; house officer, dept. internal medicine Barnes Hosp., St. Louis, 1939-41; chief resident St. Louis Isolation Hosp. for Contagious Diseases, 1940; clin. physiologist Nat. Cancer Inst., 1946, chief clin. sect., lab. exptl. oncology, Sch. Medicine, U. Cal., 1947-53, also asso. clin. prof. oncology; med. and sci. dir. Hosp. for Tumors and Allied Diseases, City of Hope Med. Center, Duarte Cal., 1953-56, med. and sci. dir. City of Hope Med. Center, 1956-59, chmn. dept. medicine, 1954-59; clin. prof. medicine Loma Linda U., 1959—; dir. Inst. for Cancer and Blood Research, 1959—; sr. attending physician emeritus Los Angeles County Gen. Hosp.; cons. Nat. Cancer Inst., 1953—; mem. biomechanics com. Protein Found., Harvard U. Served as comdr. USN, 1941-46. Diplomate Am. Bd. Internal Medicine, Pan Am. Med. Assn. Fellow A.C.P., A.A.A.S., Internat., Am. socs. hematology, N.Y. Acad. Scis., Am. Coll. Angiology, Los Angeles County Med. Soc., Am., Cal. socs. for internal medicine, Am. Soc. Clin. Investigation, Western Soc. Clin. Research, Am. Soc. Clin. Oncology, Am. Acad. Cancer Research, Beverly Hills Acad. Medicine (pres. 1969), Am. Fedn. Clin. Research, Soc. Exptl. Biology and Medicine, Am. Soc. for Pharmacology and Exptl. Therapeutics, Western Pharmacology Soc. (charter pres. 1960-61), Sigma Xi, Phi Delta Epsilon, Alpha Omega Alpha. Author: Cancer Learning in Medical Schools, 1952; Cancer Learning in Dental Schools, 1954; Selective Arterial Catheterization, 1969. Editor: American Lectures in Tumors, 1970—. Contbr. over 200 articles to profl. jours. Patentee. Home: 300 Hilgard Av Los Angeles CA 90024 Office: 152 N Robertson Blvd Beverly Hills CA 90211

BIERMANN, LUDWIG FRANZ BENEDLKT, astrophysicist; b. Hamm, Westfalen, Germany, Mar. 13, 1907; s. Dr. Franz and Thea (Schulte) B.; student U. München, 1925-27, U. Freiburg, 1927- 28; Ph.D., U. Goettingen, 1932; D.Sc. (hon.), U. Colo., 1969; m. Ilse Wandel, Jan. 3, 1942; children—Peter B., Christiane, Sabine. Exchange scholar U. Edinburgh, 1933-34, U. Jena, 1934-37, Univs. Sternwarte Berlin and Babelsberg, 1937- 45; dozent U. Berlin, 1938-45, U. Hamburg, 1945-47; spl. prof. U. Hamburg, 1947, U. Goettingen, 1948; head astrophysics sect. Max Planck Inst. Physics, U. Goettingen, 1947-58; dir. Inst.for Astrophysics of Max-Planck-Inst. for Physics and Astrophysics, Munich, 1958—; Geschäftsführender Direktor, Max-Planck-Inst. for Physics and Astrophysics, 1971—; prof. U. Munich, 1959; vis. prof. Cal. Inst. Tech., Haverford Coll. and Princeton, 1955, 61, U. Cal. at Berkeley, 1959-60, Sydney and Canberra (both Australia), 1960; vis. fellow U. Colo., Boulder, 1967, spl. vis. prof., 1968-71. Recipient Catherine Wolfe-Bruce gold medal Astron. Soc. of Pacific, 1967. Mem. Astron. Soc. of the Pacific, Max-Planck-Gesellschaft, Astronomische Gesellschaft, Physikalische Gesellschaft, Internat. Astron. Union, Gesellschaft fur Angewandte Mathematik und Mechanik, Gesellschaft Deutscher Naturforscher und Arzte, Internat. Acad. Astronautics, Bayerische Akademie der Wissenschaften, Royal Astron. Soc., London, Société Royale des Scis. de Liége (Belgium) (corr.). Home: 12 Rohmederstr Munich 23 Germany 8000 Office: Munich 23 Fohringer Ring 6 Germany

BIERMANN, WOLF, poet, balladier; b. Hamburg, Germany, 1936. Author: (vol. poetry) The Wire Harp (transl. by Eric Bentley). Address: East Berlin German Democratic Republic*

BIERSTEDT, ROBERT, sociologist, author; b. Burlington, Ia., Mar. 20, 1913; s. Henry F. and Bertha (Strauss) B.; A.B., U. Ia., 1934; A.M., Columbia, 1935, Ph.D., 1950; fellow Harvard, 1936-37; m. Betty MacIver, Dec. 26, 1939; children—Peter, Karen (Mrs. Paul Migliore), Robin. Lectr. philosophy Columbia, 1937-39, head men's residence halls, 1938-39; instr. social studies div. Bennington Coll., 1939-40; instr. philosophy Bard Coll., 1940-43; asst. prof. sociology U. Wash., summer 1946; asst. prof. Wellesley Coll., 1946-47; asst. prof. U. Ill., 1947-51, asso. prof., 1951-53; prof., chmn. dept. sociology and anthropology Coll. City N.Y., 1953-59; vis. prof. Stanford, summer 1959; Fulbright lectr. U. Edinburgh (Scotland), 1959-60; Barnett lectr. Oxford, 1960; head dept. N.Y. U., 1960-66, prof. sociology, 1960—; Fulbright lectr. London Sch. Econs., 1966-67. Adv. editor Dodd, Mead & Co., 1957—. Served from lt. (j.g.) to lt. USNR, 1943-46. Fellow Am. Sociol. Assn. (past v.p.); mem. Eastern Sociol. Soc. (past pres.), Brit. Sociol. Assn., Sociol. Research Assn., Am. Assn. U. Profs. (pres. City Coll. chpt. 1958-59, council 1963-66), Am. Civil Liberties Union (bd. dirs.), Phi Beta Kappa. Club: Harvard (N.Y.C.). Author: The Social Order, 1957, 3d edit., 1970; (with others) Modern Social Science, 1964; Emile Durkheim, 1966. Editor: The Making of Society, 1959; Florian Znaniecki, 1969. Contbr. articles profl. lit. jours. Home: 110 Bleecker St New York City NY 10012 summer Chilmark MA 02535 Office: NY U Washington Sq New York City NY 10003

BIERWIRTH, JOHN COCKS, diversified mfg. co. exec.; b. Lawrence, L.I., Jan. 21, 1924; s. John E. and Alice (Marguerite) B.; student Lawrence Sch.; grad. Hotchkiss Sch., 1942; B.A., Yale, 1947; LL.B., Columbia, 1950; m. Marion Moise, June 14, 1946. Admitted to N.Y. bar, 1951; asso. firm White & Case, N.Y.C., 1950- 53; asst. v.p. N.Y. Trust Co., 1953-57; asst. treas. Nat. Distillers & Chem. Corp., N.Y.C., 1957-58, v.p., 1958-69, head Internat. div., 1963- 69, exec. v.p., 1969—; dir. Grumman Corp., Bethpage, N.Y., Nat. Distillers and Chem. Corp., Beacon Mfg. Co., Elkhorn Ins., Bridgeport Brass Ltd., N. Ireland, Bridgeport Brass S.p.A., Italy, Bridgeport Argentina S. A. C.I.F., NDC North Pacific Ltd., Japan, Leco Industries Ltd., Can., USI Europe, N.V., Belgium, USI Far East Corp., Taiwan, Holland House Brands, Inc., Indice Argentina SACIFIA. Clubs: Pinnacle, Yale (N.Y.C.); Laurentian (Can.). Office: Nat Distillers & Chem Corp 99 Park Av New York City NY 10016

BIERWIRTH, JOHN E., business executive; b. Bklyn., Apr. 21, 1895; s. Julius Carl and Nettie Gheradine (Cocks) B.; student Hotchkiss Sch., Lakeville, Conn., 1911-13; A.B., Yale, 1917; m. Alice M. Von Bernuth, May 24, 1922; children—John Cocks, Nancy Elizabeth. Vice-pres., dir. Thompson- Starrett Co., Inc., contractors, 1919-29; v.p. N.Y. Trust Co., 1929-41, pres., trustee, 1941-49; pres. Nat. Distillers & Chem. Corp., 1949-58, chmn. bd., dir., chief exec. officer, 1958-70, chmn. bd., 1970—. Dir. Bridgeport Brass Co., Owens Corning Fiberglas Corp., Discount Corp., Reactive Metals, Inc., Merc. Stores Co., Deering Miliken, Inc., Panhandle Eastern Pipe Line Co. Trustee Presbyn. Hospital, N.Y.C. Served as 1st lt. with A.E.F., U.S. Army, 1917-19. Clubs: Yale, Madison Square Garden, Pinnacle, Union League, Sky, Links (N.Y.C.); Rockaway Hunting, Lawrence Beach (L.I.). Home: Briarwood Crossing Lawrence NY 11559 Office: care Nat Distillers & Chem Corp 99 Park Av New York City NY 10016

BIESELE, JOHN JULIUS, biologist, educator; b. Waco, Tex., Mar. 24, 1918; s. Rudolph Leopold and Anna Emma (Jahn) B.; B.A. with highest honors, U. Tex., 1939, Ph.D., 1942; m. Marguerite Calfee McAfee, July 29, 1943; children—Marguerite Anne, Diana Terry, Elizabeth Jane. Fellow Internat. Cancer Research Found., U. Tex., 1942-43, Barnard Skin and Cancer Hosp., St. Louis, also U. Pa., 1943-44; instr. zoology U. Pa., 1943-44; temporary research asso. dept. genetics Carnegie Instn. of Washington, Cold Spring Harbor, 1944-46; research asso. biology dept. Mass. Inst. Tech., 1946-47; asst. Sloan-Kettering Inst. Cancer Research, 1946-47, research fellow, 1947, asso., 1947-55, head cell gorwth sect., div. exptl. chemotherapy, 1947-58, mem., 1955-58, asso. scientist div., 1959—; asst. prof. anatomy Cornell U. Med. Sch., 1950-52; asso. prof. biology Sloan-Kettering div. Cornell U. Grad. Sch. Med. Scis., 1952-55, prof. biology, 1955-58; prof. zoology, mem. grad. faculty U. Texas, Austin, 1958—, also mem. faculty Coll. Pharmacy, 1969—; cons. cell biology M. D. Anderson Hosp. and Tumor Inst., U. Texas at Houston, 1958—, dir. Genetics Found., 1959—. Mem. cell biology study sect. NIH, 1958-63; Sigma Xi lectr. N.Y. U. Grad. Sch. Arts and Scis., 1957; Mendel lectr. St. Peter's Coll., Jersey City, 1958; mem. adv. com. research etiology of cancer Am. Cancer Soc., 1961-64, pres. Travis County unit, 1966, mem. adv. com. on personnel for research, 1969—; counsellor Cancer Internat. Research Coop., Inc., 1962—; mem. cancer research tng. com. Nat. Cancer Inst., 1969—. Gen. chmn. Conf. Advancement Sci. and Math. Teaching, 1966. Research Career award NIH, 1962, 67. Fellow N.Y., Tex. acads. scis., A.A.A.S.; mem. Am. Assn. Cancer Research (dir. 1960-63), Tissue Culture Assn., Histochem. Soc., Am. Soc. Naturalists, Am. Soc. Zoologists, Am. Soc. Cell Biology, Am. Soc. Human Genetics, Internat. Soc. Cell Biology, Am. Inst. Biol. Scis., Phi Beta Kappa, Sigma Xi (pres. Tex. chpt. 1963-64), Phi Eta Sigma. Author: Mitotic Poisons and the Cancer Problem, 1958. Editorial bd. Year Book Cancer, 1959—; editorial adv. bd. Cancer Research, 1960-64, asso. editor, 1969—; cons. editor Am. Jour. Mental Deficiency, 1966-68. Contbr. articles sci. jours., books. Home: 2500 Great Oaks Pkwy Austin TX 78756

BIESER, IRVIN GRUEN, lawyer; b. Dayton, O., June 15, 1902; s. Charles William and Flora Sophia (Gruen) B.; B.S. cum laude, Harvard, 1924, LL.B., 1927; m. Catharine Mary French, Apr. 14, 1936; children—Catharine B., Marvin, Irvin Gruen. Admitted to Ohio bar, 1927, since practiced in Dayton; sr. partner firm Bieser, Greer & Landis, and predecessors, 1932—. Dir. Dayton Power & Light Co., Third Nat. Bldg., Co., Midwest Securities Investment, Inc., City Transit Co.; v.p., dir. Everybody's Office Outfitters, Inc., 1931-69. Trustee Miami Valley Hosp., 1935—, pres., 1948-54; pres. trustee Dayton Law Library Assn.; mem. standing com. on gen. principles of law recognized by community of nations and spl. com. on rev. UN charter World Peace Through Law Center; Care Corp. Southwestern Ohio, 1939—, pres., 1956-58, chmn. 1958-60, trustee, Dayton Art Inst., 1954—, sec., 1956, pres., 1967; trustee Dayton Philharmonic Orch. Assn., 1963-70; v.p., trustee Frank M. Tait Found. Mem. Internat., Am. Ohio (past mem. coms. on taxation, jud. reform). Dayton (pres. 1957-58) bar assns., Am. Judicature Soc., Dayton Lawyers Club (trustee), Alpha Sigma Phi. Republican. Lutheran. Clubs: Rotary, Dayton Country, Moraine Country, Harvard (past pres.), Rod and Reel (Dayton). Mason. Author: Origin and Rise of the Republican Party, 1924. Home: 447 Kramer Rd Dayton, OH 45419. Office: 8 N Main St Dayton OH 45402

BIESTER, EDWARD GEORGE, Jr., congressman; b. Phila., Jan. 5, 1931; s. Edward G. and Muriel (Worthington) B.; B.A., Wesleyan U., 1952; LL.B., Temple U., 1955; m. Elizabeth Ruth Lauffer, Apr. 10, 1954; children— Ann Meredith, Edward George III, James Paul, David Robertson. Admitted to Pa. bar, 1956; practice in Phila., 1956, Biester & Ludwig, 1967-69; asst. dist. atty. Bucks County, Pa., 1958-64; mem. 90th-92d congresses from 8th Dist. Pa. Dist. fund chmn. A.R.C., 1965-66. Bd. dirs. Bucks County Big Bros., 1964-67. Mem. Am., Pa., Phila., Bucks County (bd. dirs. 1956-66) bar assns. Republican. Kiwanian (pres. Doylestown 1963). Home: Lower Mountain Rd Furlong PA 18925 Office: Cannon House Office Bldg Washington DC 20515

BIETER, RAYMOND NICHOLAS, pharmacologist; b. Heron Lake, Minn., Oct. 9, 1900; s. William Adam and Catherine Baptista (Offerman) B.; student Coll. St. Thomas, St. Paul, 1917-19, U. Minn., 1919-29 (B.S., M.S., M.B., M.D., Ph.D.); m. Lorraine Josephine Endres, June 15, 1925; children—William Raymond (dec.), Mary Anne, Ursula Frances, Thomas Godfrey. Instr. pharmacology U. Minn., 1925-29, asst. prof., 1929- 30, asso. prof. pharmacology, 1931-40, prof. pharmacology, 1940—, head dept., 1943-62, dir. spl. ednl. services office dean, 1962- -; asso. physiology Johns Hopkins Sch. Medicine, 1930-31; vis. prof. pharmacology U. Chgo., summer 1941; collaborator, agt. Bur. Plant Industry USDA, 1938-46; sec.-treas. Minn. Bd. Examiners Basic Scis. Mem. Am. Soc. for Pharmacology and Exptl. Therapeutics (sec. 1941-45), A.A.A.S., Minn. Med. Assn., A.M.A., Hennepin County Med. Soc., NRC (com. problems drug dependence Div. Med. Sci.), Am. Assn. U. Profs., Phi Chi, Sigma Xi. K.C. Club: Cos Cnidos (Mpls., St. Paul). Home: 2015 Dayton Av St Paul MN 55104 Office: U Minn Med Sch Millard Hall MN 55455

BIEU, TRAN VAN, govt. ofcl. South Vietnam; b. Saigon, S. Vietnam, Oct. 14, 1928; s. Tran Van and Ma Thi (Chon) Thao; LL.B., Saigon Law Sch., 1965, M.Pub. Law, 1968; m. Chau-thi-Dien, Apr. 29, 1949; children—Quang, Phuong, Chi, Khanh, Thi Thi. Came to U.S., 1968. Protocol officer Ministry Fgn. Affairs, Saigon 1967, chief, Bur. Am. Affairs, 1968—; chief, Bur. Vietnamese Affairs, Vietnam embassy, Washington, 1969—, chief Bur. Consular Affairs, 1970—, 1st sec., 1970—. Mem. Am. Polit. Sci. Assn. Home: 2770 N Washington Blvd Arlington VA 22201 Office: 2251 R St Washington DC 20008

BIGARD, ALBANY BARNEY LEON, clarinetist; b. New Orleans, Mar. 3, 1906; s. Alexander and Emanuella (Marquette) B.; student Straight Coll., New Orleans, 1919-23. With King Oliver, Chgo., 1925-27, Duke Ellington, 1927-42, Freddie Slack Band, 1942-44; leader 6-piece group Barney Bigard Sextette, 1944-47; joined Louis Armstrong All-Stars Concert Group, 1947, 3 European tours, Japan and Australia; African Good Will Tour for State Dept., 1960; also recs., TV and motion pictures; joined jazz group Los Angeles, 1956; free-lance concerts, recs., club work, 1961—; coll. lectr. jazz history, 1969—. Composer songs, including Mood Indigo, Clouds in My Heart, Rocking in Rhythm, Minuet in Blues, Steps Steps Up and Steps Steps Down, Stompy Jones. Recipient silver jazz award Esquire, 1945, 46, 48; gold award West Coast Lamplighter, 1943, 44, 45; award, Hot Club of France, 1947, 64. Mem. A.S.C.A.P. Home: 3837 Gibraltar Av Los Angeles CA 90008

BIGART, HOMER, journalist; b. Hawley, Pa., Oct. 25, 1907; s. Homer S. and Anna (Schardt) B.; student Carnegie Inst. Tech., N.Y. U.; m. Alice Weel, July 6, 1963. War corr. N.Y. Herald Tribune, 1942-45, roving corr., 1945-55; fgn. corr. N.Y. Times, 1955—. Recipient Pulitzer prize for Pacific war reporting, 1945, Korean war articles, 1951. Home: 329 E 58th St New York City NY 10022 Office: 229 W 43d St New York City NY 10036

BIGBIE, JOHN TAYLOR, banker; b. Lynchburg, Va., Sept. 12, 1923; s. William Bright and Maria Woodson (Taylor) B.; B.A., Princeton, 1944; LL.B., U. Va., 1948; m. Nadine de Coninck, Oct. 6, 1956; children-Astrid, John Eric. Admitted to N.Y. bar, 1950; asso. firm Breed, Abbot & Morgan, N.Y.C., 1948-54; counselor Nat. Assn. Life Underwriters, Washington, 1954-61; v.p., sec., trust officer European-Am. Bank & Trust Co., N.Y.C., 1961—; dir. Watkins Salt Co., Compagnie Generale des Salines de Tunisie, G.A. Coleman & Co., Butlers Bank Ltd. Bd. dirs. Manhattanville Community Centers, N.Y.C. Served to lt. (j.g.) USNR, 1944-46. Mem. S.R., Soc. Colonial Wars. Episcopalian. Mason. Clubs: Down Town Assn. (N.Y.C.); Seawanhaka Corinthian Yacht (Oyster Bay, L.I.). Home: 21 E 87th St New York NY 10028 Office: 52 Wall St New York NY 10005

BIGELEISEN, JACOB, educator, chemist; b. Paterson, N.J., May 2, 1919; s. Harry and Ida (Slomowitz) B.; A.B., N.Y.U., 1939; M.S., Wash. State U., 1941; Ph.D., U. Cal. at Berkeley, 1943; m. Grace Alice Simon, Oct. 21, 1945; children—David M., Ira S., Paul E. Research scientist Manhattan Dist., Columbia, 1943-45; research asso. Ohio State U., Columbus, 1945-46; fellow Enrico Fermi Inst., U. Chgo., 1946-48; sr. chemist Brookhaven Nat. Lab., Upton, N.Y., 1948-68; prof. chemistry U. Rochester, N.Y., 1968—, chmn. dept., 1970—; vis. prof. Cornell U., 1953; NSF sr. fellow, vis. prof. Eidgen Techn. Hochschule, Switzerland, 1962-63. Trustee Sayville Jewish Center, 1954-58. Recipient Nuclear award Am. Chem. Soc., 1958, Gilbert N. Lewis lectr., 1963, E. O. Lawrence award, 1964. Fellow Am. Phys. Soc., Am. Chem. Soc., A.A.A.S., Am. Acad. Arts and Sci.; mem. Nat. Acad. Scis., Phi Beta Kappa, Sigma Xi, Phi Lambda Upsilon. Mem. editorial bd. Jour. Chem. Physics, Ann. Rev. Phys. Chemistry, Jour. Phys. Chemistry. Research in photochemistry in rigid media, semiquinones, cryogenics, chemistry of isotopes, quantum statistics of gases, liquids and solids. Home: 835 Allens Creek Rd Rochester NY 14618

BIGELOW, DONALD NEVIUS, govt. ofcl.; b. Danbury, Conn., Aug. 19, 1918; s. Harry R. and Bessie M. (Nevius) B.; B.A. cum laude, Amherst Coll., 1939, M.A., 1945; Ph.D., Columbia, 1950; m. Louise M. Fournel, Sept. 21, 1957; 1 son, Pierre Nevius. Spl. agt. Inland Marine Ins., North Brit. and Merc. Ins. Co., N.Y.C. and Detroit, 1939-43; instr. history Amherst Coll., 1943-45; instr. Columbia, 1947-50, asst. prof., 1951-55; vis. prof. Am. civilization U.S. Ednl. Found. (India), U. Baroda, U. Lucknow; vis. Fulbright prof. U. India, 1954-55; asso. prof. Brandeis U., 1955-60; prof. humanities N.Y. Sch. Music, 1949-56; Fulbright vis. prof. U. So. Fla., 1969—; chief lang. and area centers, 1961—; head task force Nat. Def. Edn. Act Title XI Inst. Program, 1964—; dir. div. ednl. personnel tng. Office Edn., Dept. Health, Edn. and Welfare, Washington, 1965—, dir. div. program adminstrn., 1967—, dir. div. coll. programs Bur. Ednl. Personnel Devel., 1968—; cons. Carnegie Corp., Ford Found. Founder, moderator ABC TV series Seminar, 1954-55. Mem. Am. Hist. Assn. Episcopalian. Club: University (Washington). Author: (with Hiram Haydn) William Conant Church and the Army and Navy Journal, 1952: Makers of the American Tradition Series, 1953-55. Editor: (with introduction, Jacob A. Riis) How the Other Half Lives, 1957; (with Joseph Axelrod) Resources for Language and Area Studies, 1960; (with Lyman H. Legters) Language and Area Centers, 1964; The Non-Western World in Higher Education, 1964. Lectr., contbr. articles to profl. jours. Home: 3314 P St NW Washington DC 20007 Office: US Office Edn Washington DC 20202

BIGELOW, EDWARD LIVINGSTON, banker; b. Boston, Apr. 19, 1899; s. Henry Forbes and Eliza (Davis) B.; A.B., Harvard, 1921; m. Caroline Fessenden, Apr. 30, 1927; children—Edward Livingsotn, Caroline Lee. Mem. firm Tucker Anthony & Co., 1921-34; joined State Street Trust Co., Boston, 1934, v.p., chmn. trust com., 1934-50, pres., 1950, chmn. merged orgn. State St. Bank & Trust, 1955-66, dir., mem. exec. com., 1966-70; dir. Haverhill Gas Co., Employers' Life Ins. Co., Am. Employers' Ins. Co., Employers' Fire Ins. Co.; chmn. trustees Boston Personal Property Trust; trustee Employers' Group Assn., Haverhill Gas Co.; mem. U.S. investment adv. com.

Employers-Comml. Union Ins. Group. Trustee old Sturbridge Village, Mass. Gen. Hosp.; mem. corp. Northeastern U.; treas. Soc. Preservation New Eng. Antiquities, Inc.; trustee, mem. trust investment com. Trustees of Donations to Protestant Episcopal Ch. Clubs: Brookline (Mass.) Country. Home: Coolidge Point Manchester, MA 01944. Office: State Street Bank and Trust Co Boston MA 02101

BIGELOW, GERALD O., bank exec.; Sr. auditor, v.p. Genesee Bank. Office: One E 1st St Flint MI 48502*

BIGELOW, KARL WORTH, educator; b. Bangor, Me., May 10, 1898; s. Bert Elmer and (Annie) Florence (Worth) B.; A.B., Clark U., 1920, L.H.D., 1938; student Cornell U., 1920-21; Ph.D., Harvard, 1929; LL.D., Parsons Coll., 1941, Moravian Coll., 1963; D.Litt., U. E. Africa, 1970; m. Margaret Johnson, Sept. 15, 1921 (dec. 1960); children—Mark Hamilton (dec.), David Hall, Stephen Colton, Paul Jay. Instr. econs. Cornell U., 1920-21; tutor, instr. econs. and sociology Harvard, Radcliffe, 1921-30; asst. prof. econs. U. Buffalo, 1930-31, prof., 1931-37; headmaster Park Sch. of Buffalo, 1933-35; vis. prof. edn. Tchrs. Coll., Columbia, 1936-37, prof., 1937-63, prof. emeritus, 1963—; dir. Afro-Anglo-Am. Program in Tchr. Edn., 1960-69; dir. Inst. for Edn. in Africa, 1962-66; vis. lectr. U. London Inst. of Edn., 1958; Ingalis lectr. Harvard Grad. Sch. Edn., 1964. Mem. overseas liaison com. Am. Council of Edn., 1963—, vice chmn., 1965-71; chmn. com. sent by Dept. State to study relations of Am. vol. agys. with Germany and Austria, 1950; lectr., cons. UNESCO seminar on edn. for internat. understanding, France, 1947, dir. seminar edn. and tng. of tchrs., Eng., 1948; mem. U.S. nat. commn. UNESCO, 1948-54, U.S. mem. governing bd. Inst. for Edn., Germany, 1957-61; student higher edn. and tchr. tng. in Brit. Africa, under auspices Brit. Colonial Office, U. London Inst. Edn. and Inter-univ. Council for Higher Edn., in Colonies, 1952; del. Am. Assn. Colls. Tchr. Edn. to Am. Council Edn., 1951-56, mem. com. on studies, 1954-60; mem. council U. Zambia, 1964—. Served with USN, 1917-19. Fellow African Studies Assn.; mem. Am. Assn. U. Profs., N.E.A., Assn. Higher Edn., Phi Beta Kappa, Kappa Delta Pi, Phi Delta Kappa. Co-author several books including, The Improvement of Teacher Education, 1946; General Education, 1952; Education and Foreign Affairs, 1965. Mem. editorial bd. Internat. Rev. of Edn., 1955-61, Tchr. Edn., 1962—. Contbr. articles on gen., tchr., and African edn. to profl. publs. Home: 430 W 116th St New York City NY 10027 also Temple NH 03084 Office: Teachers Coll Columbia Univ New York City NY 10027 ☆

BIGELOW, LEONARD, librarian; b. Lockport, N.Y., June 27, 1920; s. Harold Louis and Luella (Leonard) B.; B.S. in Edn., State U. N.Y., 1953; postgrad., U. Buffalo, 1953, U. Ill., 1955; m. Rose Marie Rongo, Sept. 5, 1942; 1 son, Richard Alan. Information specialist Gen. Elec., Ithaca, N.Y., 1956-60; library mgr. Honeywell Aerospace Div., Mpls., 1960—. Served with USAAF, 1941-50. Mem. Spl. Libraries Assn., Am. Soc. Information Scis., Soc. for Preservation and Encouragement Barber Shop Quartet Singing Am. Home: 1213 Rhode Island Av N Minneapolis MN 55427 Office: 2600 Ridgeway Pkwy Minneapolis MN 55413

BIGELOW, ROBERT MANSFIELD, shoe machinery mfr.; b. Natick, Mass., Oct. 12, 1906; s. William Reed and Mary Louise (Bigelow) B.; B.S., Mass. Inst. Tech., 1927; m. Helen Miller, Mar. 23, 1929; children—Martha Ann, Jane Gibbs. With Hobart Mfg. Co., Troy, O., 1927-29, United Shoe Machinery Corp. (now USM Corp.), Boston, 1929-68, asst. dir. research, 1947-55, dir. research, 1955-61, v.p., dir. 1959-68. Mem. Alpha Tau Omega. Unitarian. Home: 9 Standish Rd Wellesley Hills MA 02181

BIGELOW, WILLIAM R., utility exec.; b. 1928; B.S., U. Cal., 1950. With Pacific Lighting Corp., San Francisco 1956—, treas., asst. sec., 1966—. Served as 1st lt. USAF, 1951-53. Mem. Cal. Inst. C.P.A.'s, Financial Execs. Inst. Address: 810 S Flower St Los Angeles CA 90017

BIGGER, CHARLES PURCELL, III, educator; b. Richmond, Va., May 18, 1923; s. Charles Purcell and Helen (Smith) B.; B.A., U. Va., 1947, M. A., 1949, Ph.D., 1951; m. Cynthia Hopwood, Nov. 23, 1963; children—Charles, Elizabeth, Ann, Rachel Meredith. Lectr., Hollins Coll., 1949-50; instr. Ohio State U., 1951-52; asso. prof. U. Miss., 1952-57; prof. Southwestern at Memphis, 1957-63; faculty Memphis State U., 1963-64; prof. philosophy, chmn. dept. La. State U., 1964—, dir. honors div. Coll. Arts and Scis. Served with AUS, 1943-46; PTO. Ford Found. fellow, 1955-56; hon. fellow U. Edinburgh (Scotland), 1971-72. Mem. Am. Assn. U. Profs., Am. Philos. Assn., So. Assn. Philosophy and Psychology, Phi Beta Kappa. Mem. editorial adv. bd. So. Jour. Philosophy, 1963—, co-editor, 1963-64. Sol. research Plato, Whitehead. Author: Participation: A Platonic Inquiry, 1968. Home: 1299 Kimbro Dr Baton Rouge LA 70808

BIGGER, RICHARD ANDREW, corporation exec.; b. York, S.C., July 28, 1893; s. James M. and Elizabeth (Mason) B.; student Westminster Sch., Rutherfordton, N.C., Kings Bus. Coll., Charlotte, N.C., 1912-13; m. Hazel Simpson, Apr. 7, 1926; 1 son, Richard Andrew. Vice pres. in charge N.Y. office, dir. B.S. Dickson & Co., Charlotte, N.C., 1920-45, pres., 1945-54; vice chmn., dir. Ruddick Corp., Charlotte; dir. Henry V. Dick Co., Charlotte, Gulf Life Ins. Co., Jacksonville, Fla. Mem. N.Y. So. Soc. Presbyn. Mason (Shriner). Clubs: Commodore Yacht, Charlotte Country, Charlotte City, Myers Park Country (Charlotte). Home: 2131 Roswell Av Charlotte NC 28207 Office: Wachovia Bank Bldg Charlotte NC 28202*

BIGGERS, JAMES RINARD, food co. exec.; b. Buchanan, Ga., Mar. 24, 1924; s. James R. and Nola Alma (Smith) B.; student U. Pa., 1944-45, U. Ga., 1946; m. Johnnie Joyce Brunson, June 2, 1946; children—Brenda Joyce (Mrs. Terrance Byron Quinn), Janice Anita, Bitsy Melinda. Accountant Calloway Mills, LaGrange, Ga., 1941-43, 46-52; dist. sales mgr. Ralston Purina Co., St. Louis, 1952-60; gen. mgr. B & B Poultry, Cypress Gardens Eggs, Inc., also Central Feed & Service Co., 1960-65; pres., chmn. bd. Modern Foods, Inc., Winter Haven, Fla., 1965—; dir. Nat. Egg Co., United Egg Producers, Atlanta, Exchange Nat. Bank, Winter Haven. Served with USAAF, 1943-45. Named Mem. of the Year, Nat. Egg Co., 1970. Mem. Fla. Egg Dealers Assn. (dir.), Nat. Broiler Marketing Assn. (dir.), Nat. Broiler Council (dir.). Baptist. Home: 411 S Lake Florence Dr Winter Haven FL 33880 Office: PO Drawer 2356 Winter Haven FL 33880

BIGGERS, JOHN DENNIS, educator, physiologist; b. Reading, Eng., Aug. 18, 1923; s. Wilfred Norman and Winifrid (Gardner) B.; B.Sc. in Physiology, B.Sc. in Vet. Sci., U. London, 1946, Ph.D. in Physiology, 1952, D.Sc., 1965; m. Barbara Joan Nevill Cobbold, July 24, 1947; children—David John, Philippa Jeanne, Jennifer Ann. Came to U.S., 1959. Demonstrator physiology Royal Vet. Coll., London, 1944-47, sr. lectr. physiology, 1955-59; asst. lectr. physiology U. Sheffield, 1947-48; lectr. vet physiology U. Sydney (Australia), 1948-53, sr. lectr., 1953-55; Commonwealth fellow St. John's Coll., Cambridge (Eng.) U., 1954-55, vis. scientist Strangeways Research Lab., 1954-55; asso. mem. Wistar Inst., Phila., 1959-61; asso. prof. physiology U. Pa. Sch. Vet. Medicine, 1959- 61, King Ranch research prof. reproductive physiology, 1961-66; prof. reproductive physiology Johns Hopkins Sch. Hygiene and Pub. Health, 1966-71; prof. physiology Harvard Med. Sch., Boston, 1971—; mem. corp. Marine Biol. Lab., Woods Hole, Mass., 1965—; mem. study sect. reproductive biology NIH, 1967-71; cons. to the govt., 1963—, also to UNESCO, WHO, NRC. Fellow Royal Statis. Soc., Royal Coll. Vet. Surgeons; mem. Anat. Soc. Gt. Britain, Soc. Endocrinology (U.K.), Physiol. Soc. (U.K.), Internat. Biometrics Soc., Internat. Soc. Cell Biology, Soc. Fertility (U.K.), Soc. Study Reproduction (pres. 1968-69), Am. Statis. Assn. A.A.A.S., Am. Soc. Cell Biology, Sigma Xi, Phi Zeta. Editor: Biology of Reproduction. Home: 313 Tuscany Rd Baltimore MD 21210

BIGGERS, RAY NATHAN, trailer mfr.; b. Arlington, Tex., Apr. 20, 1918; s. James N. and Arrevia (Patterson) B.; student Arlington State Coll., 1936-38; m. Joyce P. Herbert, Aug. 27, 1938; children—Judy (Mrs. Mickey Wilson), Donna (Mrs. Don Moore), Jimmy. Sec. to gen. sales mgr. Hobbs Mfg. Co., Ft. Worth, 1939-40, asst. gen. sales mgr., 1940-46, br. mgr., Lubbock, Tex., 1946- 53, v.p. sales, 1953-55; gen. sales mgr. Hobbs Trailers div. Fruehauf Trailer Co., Detroit, 1955-58, v.p. Hobbs div. 1958—, also gen. mgr.; v.p. Fruehauf Corp., Fruehauf Trailer Co.; dir. Union Bank, Ft. Worth. Mem. Truck Trailer Mfrs. Assn. (dir.). Home: 4102 Shady Valley Dr Arlington TX 76010 Office: 609 N Main St Fort Worth TX 76106

BIGGERSTAFF, JAMES ADAIR, mfg. co. exec.; b. Springfield, Mass., 1923; ed. U. Conn., 1948. With Anchor Hocking Corp., Lancaster, O., sec., 1965-67, v.p., dir. corporate With planning, 1967-70, v.p., Southeast regional mgr., container div., Jacksonville, Fla., 1970—. Home: Anchor Hocking Corp. Lancaster, O., sec., 1965-67, v.p. dir. corporate planning, 1967-70, v.p., Southeast regional mgr., container div., Jacksonville, Fla., 1970—. Home: 7653 Hunter's Grove Rd Jacksonville FL 32216 Office: 4151 Woodcock Dr Jacksonville FL 32207

BIGGERSTAFF, WARREN RICHARD, educator; b. Folsom, N.M., May 2, 1918; s. Walter S. and Matilda (Kempf) B.; B.A., Willamette U., 1940; M.S., Ore. State Coll., 1942; Ph.D., U. Wis., 1948; m. Evelyn Mae Zahradnik, Dec. 30, 1942; children—Mary Louise, Steven Scott, Jennifer Beth. Instr. chemistry U. Wis., 1947-48; faculty Fresno State Coll., 1948—, successively instr., asst. prof., asso. prof., 1948-58, prof. chemistry, 1958—, chmn. dept., 1961-66, asso. v.p. acad. planning, 1969-70. Vis. asso. Sloan Kettering Inst., 1956-57; vis. prof. Lund U. (Sweden), 1967. Recipient Leadership award Fresno State Coll., 1968. Served with AUS, 1944-46. Mem. Am. Chem. Soc., Cal. Assn. Chemistry Tchrs., Sigma Xi, Phi Lambda Upsilon, Phi Kappa Phi. Research in heterocyclics and steroid derivatives. Home: 1187 W Barstow Av Fresno CA 93705

BIGGIO, ALVIN A., cons.; b. New Orleans, Feb. 14, 1904; s. Charles Albert and Louise (Darring) B.; B.S., Auburn U., 1926, LL.B., 1965; m. Mila Justice, Sept. 24, 1926. With Liberty Nat. Life Ins. Co., Birmingham, Ala., 1927-69, gen. mgr. indsl. div., 1938-45, v.p., 1945-58, sr. v.p., 1958-69; dir. Service Ins. Co., Brown-Service Mfg. Co. Bd. dirs. Ala. Goodwill Industries, Auburn U. Ednl. Found. Served to lt. USNR, World War II. Mem. Nat. Assn. Life Underwriters, Life Ins. Agy. Mgmt. Assn., Sigma Chi. Methodist. Kiwanian. Club: Birmingham Country. Home: 41 Fairway Dr Birmingham AL 35213

BIGGS, CLINTON ARTHUR, distbg. co. exec.; b. Canon City, Colo., Aug. 22, 1911; s. Arthur H. and Ethel (McLain) B.; student U. Colo., 1929-32, Stanford, 1933-34; m. Lina May Smith, May 12, 1935; children—Clinton Arthur III, Silmon L., Clyde M. With Biggs Kurtz Co., Grand Junction, Colo., 1932—, exec. v.p., gen. mgr., 1952-63, pres., 1963-70, also dir.; pres. C.A. Biggs Assos., Inc.; dir. Mountain States Tel. & Tel. Co. Active Boy Scouts Am.; mem. adv. bd. nursing Mesa Coll.; pres. adv. bd. St. Mary's Hosp. Trustee Hist. Mus. and Inst. Western Colo. Served to lt. USNR, 1943-46. Mem. Rocky Mountain Distbrs. Assn. (dir. 1946, pres.), Colo. (dir. 1955), Grand Junction (past dir.) chambers commerce, Mesa County Art Assn. Republican. Episcopalian. Mason (32, Shriner). Home: 230 Sunset Hills St Grand Junction CO 81501

BIGGS, DONALD CLAIR, ednl. adminstr.; b. Greenwood, Neb., July 29, 1927; s. James Franklin and Edith (Hartsock) B.; A.B., Stanford, 1950; M.A., San Francisco State Coll., 1952; Ph.D., Univ. Minn., 1968; m. Bernice Louise Prince, June 7, 1952; children—Carrie Jirina, Franklin Warner, Katherina Anne, Donald Allen. Instr. English, San Francisco State Coll., 1952-56, asst. prof. English, 1956-58; dir. Cal. Hist. Soc., San Francisco, 1958-66; lectr. U. Madrid, U. Navarra (Spain), 1966-68; prof. history San Francisco State Coll., 1968-69; dir. admissions Cal. Inst. of Arts, Los Angeles, 1969—. Communications cons. various fed., state, pvt. agys. Trustee Cal. Heritage Council, Pacific Ballet, Inc. Served with USNR, 1945-46. Mem. Am. Assn. State and Local History (nat. council), Am. Hist. Assn., Orgn. Am. Historians, Cal. Geneal. Soc. Clubs: Roxburghe; Book of California. Author: The Pony Express, Creation of the Legend, 1956; Stevenson's Regiment in California: A Study in Social Action, 1971. Contbr. Ency. Brit. Home: 708 2d Av San Francisco CA 94118

BIGGS, EDWARD GEORGE POWER, concert organist; b. Westcliff, Eng., Mar. 29, 1906; s. Clarence Power and Alice Maud (Tredgett) B.; student Hurstpierpoint Coll., 1917-24; grad. Royal Acad. Music (Thomas Threfall Organ scholar), 1929; Mus. D. (hon.) Acadia U., Can., 1963, New Eng. Conservatory Music; D.F.A. (hon.) Coe Coll.; m. Margaret Allen. Came to U.S., 1930, naturalized, 1937. Toured Eng., appearing in numerous historic cathedrals, Queen's Hall, London , 1929; N.Y. debut Wanamaker Auditorium, 1932; organ recitals CBS radio 1942-58; concert tours throughout U.S., Can., Europe, Australia. Decorated knight comdr. Order of Isabella the Catholic; recipient Hubert Kiver Organ prize, 1929; citation for services particularly to Am. music, Nat. Assn. Am. Composers and Condrs., 1952. Fellow Royal Acad. Music (hon.), Am. Acad. Arts and Scis., Royal Coll. Organists (hon.). Author articles mus. publs. Recs. for Columbia Records. Home: 53 Highland St Cambridge MA 02138

BIGGS, HUGH LAWRY, lawyer; b. Burns, Ore., Aug. 28, 1904; s. Dalton and Phebe (Lawry) B.; A.B., U. Ore., 1927, J.D., 1931; postgrad. U. Wash., 1929-30; m. Elra Ware, Mar. 25, 1931; children—Suzanne, Barry Hugh. Asst. dean men U. Ore., 1928-30, acting dean men, 1930-31; admitted to Ore. bar, 1931; dist. atty., Malheur County, Ore., 1933-34; asst. U.S. atty., Ore., 1934-35; practiced in Portland, 1935-43; mem. firm Davies, Biggs, Strayer, Stoel & Boley, and predecessor, Portland, 1943—; gen. counsel S.P. & S. Ry. System, 1960-70. Bd. dirs., sec. Ore. div. Am. Cancer Soc.; bd. dirs., v.p. U. Ore. Develop Fund; bd. govs. Nat. Legal Aid Assn., 1958-62; bd. visitors U. Ore. Law Sch. Fellow Am. Coll. Trial Lawyers; mem. Ore. R.R. Assn. (dir.), Am. (ho. dels.), Ore. (past gov.), Multnomah (past pres.) bar assns., Phi Beta Kappa, Phi Delta Phi, Delta Sigma Rho, Alpha Tau Omega. Democrat. Clubs: Rotary, University (Portland); Arlington, Waverely Country. Home: 6834 SE Reed Coll Pl Portland OR 97202 Office: 1410 Yeon Bldg Portland OR 97204

BIGGS, J. O., gen. industry co. exec.; b. Kansas City, Mo., Feb. 17, 1925; s. John Olin and Parilee Catherine (Story) B.; A.B., U. Kan., 1947, LL.B., 1949; m. Marilyn Frances Sweeney, Dec. 27, 1947; children—Melissa Anne, John Kevin, Brian Sweeney. Admitted to Kan. bar, 1949, Mo. bar, 1950, Ia. bar, 1953; with legal dept. Kansas City Life Ins. Co., 1950-51; exec. asst. to industry members Regional Wage Stblzn. Bd., 1951-52; dir. labor relations Meredith Pub. Co., 1952-58; with Gustin-Bacon Mfg. Co. (merger into Certain-teed Products Corp. 1966), 1958—, v.p., asst. to pres., 1962-63; pres., chief exec. officer, 1963-66, exec. v.p., Ardmore, Pa., 1966-69; pres. Thermo-Kinetic Corp., 1969—; mem. exec. com. Pioneer Hotel Co., Tucson; cons. in field. Active Big Bros. of Tucson. Mem. Am., Mo. bar assns., Lawyers Assn. Kansas City, Am. Mgmt. Assn., Sigma Alpha Epsilon, Phi Alpha Phi. Republican. Presbyn. Clubs: Skyline Country Tucson); Mission Hills Country (Kansas City). Home: 6740 N Casas Abodes Dr Tucson AZ 85704 Office: Pioneer Internat Hotel Tucson AZ 85701

BIGGS, JOHN, Jr., judge, author;b. Wilmington, Del., Oct. 6, 1895 s. John and Rachel Valentine (Massey) B.; prep. edn. Hill Sch., Pottstown, Pa., Litt.B., Princeton 1918, LL.D., 1956; LL.B., Harvard, 1922, LL.D., 1969; LL.D., Lafayette Coll., 1948; LL.D., Temple U., 1958, U. Del., 1960, Dickinson Sch. Law, 1962, Washington and Jefferson Coll., 1963; m. Anna Swift Rupert, April 16, 1925; children—John III, Charles Rupert, Anna Swift Rupert. Admitted to Del. bar, 1922, and since practiced in Wilmington; U.S. referee in bankruptcy, Dist. of Del.; apptd. judge U.S. Circuit Ct. Appeals for 3d Circuit, 1937; chief judge 3d Jud. Circuit of U.S. 1939-65, circuit judge, 1965—. Enlisted in U.S. Army and served in Ordnance and Tank Corps, World War; civilian aide to sec. of war for Del., 1923-37. Recipient Isaac Ray award Am. Psychiat. Assn., 1955. Fellow Am. Psychiat. Assn.; mem. Wistar Assn.; Am., Del. Fed. bar assns., Assn. of Bar City N.Y., Am. Philos. Soc., Soc. Colonial Wars (past gov. Del.), S.A.R., Am. Legion, Century Assn., Am. Orthopsychiat. Assn. (hon.), Order of Coif, Phi Alpha Delta. Mem. Soc. of Friends. Clubs: Metropolitan (Washington); Campus, Nassau (Princeton); Greenville Country; Rittenhouse (Phila.); Wilmington, Wilmington Country; Harvard (N.Y.C.); Grolier. Author: Demigods, 1926; Seven Days' Shipping, 1928; Delaware Laws Affecting Business Corporations (with Stewart Lynch), 1935; The Guilty Mind, Psychiatry and the Law of Homicide, 1955. Contbr. mags., legal periodicals. Home: Wooddale Wilmington DE 19809 Office: Federal Bldg P O Box 2048 Wilmington DE 19899

BIGGS, JOHN H., ins. co. exec.; b. St. Louis, Mo., July 19, 1936; s. Peter Willis and Lillian (Herron) B.; A.B. magna cum laude Harvard, 1958; m. Penelope Frances Parkman, June 13, 1959; children—Andrea, Henry. Group underwriting v.p. Gen. Am. Ins. Co., 1965-67, dir. corp. planning, 1967-70, v.p., controller, 1970—. First v.p. New City Sch., Inc., 1969—. Bd. dirs. St. Louis Com. for Environmental Information, Pastoral Counseling Inst. Fellow Soc. Actuaries; mem. Am. Acad. Actuaries (dir. 1970—), St. Louis Actuaries Club (pres. 1964). Clubs: St. Louis Harvard (pres. 1969-70), Mo. Athletic. Home: 4904 Pershing Pl St Louis MO 63108 Office: 1501 Locust St St Louis MO 63166

BIGGS, JOHN MELVIN, educator; b. Ft. Forth, Jan. 29, 1920; s. John Quincy and Zona (Davidson) B.; S.B., Mass. Inst. Tech., 1941, S.M., 1947; m. Margaret Crozier Thomson, Dec. 14, 1925; children—John Duncan, Andrew Thomson, Judith Ann. Stress analyst Curtiss-Wright Corp., Buffalo, 1941-42; instr. Robert Coll., Istanbul, Turkey, 1942-45; structural engr. Fay, Spofford & Thorndike, Boston, 1945-47; mem. faculty Mass. Inst. Tech., 1947—, Cambridge, Mass., prof. civil engring., 1962—; partner Hansen, Holley & Biggs, cons. engrs., Cambridge, 1954—. Mem. Am. Soc. C.E. (Moissieff award 1955, Wellington prize 1960), Am. Concrete Inst., Boston Soc. C.E. (pres. 1966-67), Am. Soc. Engring. Edn. Author: Introduction to Structural Dynamics, 1964. Research on structural dynamics and computer- aided structural design. Office: Dept Civil Engring Mass Inst Tech Boston MA

BIGGS, KENNETH AUSTIN, chem. co. exec.; b. Edmonton, Alta., Can., Apr. 9, 1929; s. Walter A. and Elizabeth (Rudd) B.; Chartered Accountant, Alta., 1957; m. Leone Ruth Hoffman, Sept. 10, 1958. With Canadian Chem. Co., Ltd., Montreal, Que., Can., 1951-65; asst. controller Chemcell Ltd., Montreal, 1965-68, treas., 1968—, v.p., 1971—. Mem. Canadian Tax Found., 1965—. Mem. Chartered Accountants Alta., Soc. Indsl. Accountants Can. (v.p., dir. 1970—), Engrs. Club Montreal. Home: 249 Percival Av Montreal West 263 Quebec Canada Office: 800 Dorchester Blvd Montreal Quebec Canada

BIGGS, ROBERT MITCHELL, educator, economist; b. Mio, Mich., Aug. 29, 1915; s. Morgan S. and Myrtle A. (Mitchell) B.; B.A., Wayne State U., 1939; M.A., U. Mich., 1940, Ph.D., 1950; m. Jane E. Williams, June 6, 1953; 1 son, Richard Oliver. Teaching fellow U. Mich., 1941-45; instr. Wayne State U., 1946- 49; from instr. to prof. U. Detroit, 1949-61; prof. econs., chmn. dept., also chmn. div. social sci. Jamestown (N.D.) Coll., 1961-63; prof. econs. U. Toledo, 1963—. Chmn. econs. sect. Mich. Acad. Sci., Arts and Letters, 1959. Mem. Am. Econ. Assn., Am. Finance Assn., Phi Beta Kappa, Phi Kappa Phi. Author: National Income Analysis and Forecasting, 1956; also articles. Home: 3145 Scarsborough St Toledo OH 43615

BIGGS, ROBERT WILDER, mfg. co. exec.; b. Elyria, O., Aug. 16, 1907; s. Hardy D. and Bessie (Wilder) B.; B.S. in Mech. Engring., Ohio No. U., 1930; m. Eleanor Hughes, Jan. 30, 1932; 1 son, Robert Wilder. With Nat. Tube Co., 1930- 38, Jones & Laughlin Steel Co., 1938-45; gen. mgr. operations Nat. Electric Products Co., Ambridge, Pa., 1945-51; v.p. mfg. Ball Bros. Co., Muncie, Ind., 1951-54; pres., dir. S. K. Wellman Co., Bedford, O., 1954-65; pres., dir. Brush Berylium Co., Cleve., 1965-69, chmn. bd., 1969—; dir. Ill. Central Ind. Abex Corp. Trustee Ohio No. U. Mem. Soc. Automotive Engrs. Clubs: Country of Cleve., Union. Home: Hillbrook Apts County Line Rd Chagrin Falls OH 44022 Office: 17678 St Claire Av Cleveland OH 44110

BIGGS, STANLEY C., lawyer; b. Toronto, Ont., Can., Dec. 6, 1913; B.A., U. Toronto, 1936, LL.B., 1939; postgrad. Osgoode Hall Law Sch., 1939, Khaki U. (Eng.), 1945. Admitted to Ont. bar, 1939; now partner Payton, Biggs & Graham, Toronto. Mem. Forest Hill Bd. Edn., 1953-59. Queen's Counsel, 1955. Mem. Canadian Bar Assn. (council 1950-51), York County Law Assn., Lawyers Club Toronto (trustee 1958-64, pres. 1963-64). Office: 250 University Av Toronto 110 Ontario Canada*

BIGGS, THOMAS WEST, ret. food co. exec.; b. Ambler, Pa., Mar. 3, 1905; s. Lawrence West and Mable Darling (Vining) B.; B.S., Columbia, 1928; m. Florence Elizabeth Brown, Nov. 22, 1929; children—Barbara Dennison (Mrs. Joseph A. Parini), Thomas William. With Borden Co., 1928-70, asst. v.p., corp. research coordinator, 1960-63, v.p., asst. to pres., 1963-70. Mem. industry adv. com. Nutrition Found., 1958-68; mem. research com. N.A.M., 1962. Chmn. bd. Pelham (N.Y.) chpt. A.R.C., 1955-56. Mem. Theta Xi, Alpha Kappa Phi. Episcopalian (past vestryman, warden). Clubs: Pelham Country (bd. govs., v.p. 1956-58); Woodway Country (Darien, Conn.); Cuttyhunk (Mass.) Anglers. Home: 375 Beach Rd Jupiter Island Tequesta FL 33458

BIGGS, WELLINGTON ALLEN, journalist; b. Platteville, Colo., Mar. 9, 1923; s. Wellington H. and Adeline (Brown) B.; B.A. in Journalism, U. Colo., 1949; m. Laura Jean Mowrey, Dec. 7, 1951; children—Catherine, Joseph, Lorraine, Louise, Jeffrey. Asst. editor Brighton (Colo.) Blade, 1949-50; editor Haywood Pub. Co., Chgo., 1950-52; asst. editor Alamosa (Colo.) Daily Courier, 1952, Wyo. State Jour., Lander, 1952; dir. publs. U. Colo., 1952-56; editor Rocky Mountain Teamster, Denver, 1956-61; pub. relations cons. Colo. Freedom to Bargain Com., 1958; dir. pub. relations, editor Internat. Teamster mag., Washington, 1961—. Precinct committeeman, dist. capt., publicity chmn., pub. relations cons. Boulder County (Colo.) Democratic Party, 1952-61. Served with USNR, 1942-46; PTO. Mem. Sigma Delta Chi, Pi Kappa Alpha. Methodist. Home: 500 Valleybrook Dr Silver Spring MD 20904 Office: 25 Louisiana Av NW Washington DC 20001

BIGGS, WILLIAM RICHARDSON, banker, economist; b. Islip, L.I., N.Y., Sept. 9, 1901; s. Hermann Michael and Frances (Richardson) B.; A.B., Yale, 1922; postgrad. Trinity Coll., Cambridge U., 1922-23; m. Georgene Williams, Nov. 1, 1929; children—Barton M., Jeremy H., Christopher N. Employee Seaboard Nat. Bank (merged with Equitable Trust Co.), N.Y.C. 1923-31; joined Bank of N.Y., 1931, v.p., 1935-64, trustee, exec. v.p., 1964-66, hon. trustee, econ. cons., 1966—; dir. Am. Security Trust, Washington, N.A.M. Reassurance Co., N. Am. Reins. Corp. N.Y., Dome Mines, Ltd., Peoples Life Ins. Co., Washington Rand McNally and Co., Julius Garfinckel Co.; trustee Atlantic Mut. and Centennial Ins. Cos., N.Y.C. Chmn. exec. com., trustee Brookings Inst. Trustee, chmn. finance com. retirement system Nat. A.R.C.; mem. investment com. Nat. Bd. Missions Presbyn. Ch. Vice chmn. War Dept. Price Adjustment Bd., 1944-45; pub. rep. U.S. del. to UN Econ. and Social Council, Geneva, 1954, Presbyn. Clubs: Cosmos, Chevy Chase, Metropolitan (Washington); University (Washington, N.Y.C.). Home: 550 N St SW Washington, DC 20024 Office: 48 Wall St New York City NY 10015

BIGHAM, MILTON ROBERT, ins. co. exec.; b. Santa Rosa, Cal., July 1, 1916; s. William B. and Myrtle L. (Rich) B.; m. Bettie Kennedy, Feb. 10, 1940; children—Sharon L., Deborah D., Cynthia S. With Nat. Fire Ins. Co., San Francisco, 1936- 39; ins. broker, 1939-42; with Von Hamm-Young Co., Ltd., Honolulu, 1950- 57; com. mem., dir., pres. Bd. Underwriters Hawaii, Hawaii Casualty and Surety Rating Bur., mem. governing com. Hawaii Fire Rating Bur., 1951- 57; asst. mgr. Pacific dept. Hartford Ins. Group, San Francisco, 1957- 59; v.p. Hartford Accident & Indemnity Co., 1959- 63, pres. bd., 1963-65, vice chmn. bd., 1965—, also dir.; sr. v.p. corporate devel. U.S. and Europe, Hartford Fire Ins. Co., 1970—; dir. Pacific Ins. Co., Ltd., Sentinel Ins. Co., Ltd., Citizens Ins. Co. N.J., Hartford Life Ins. Co., Twin City Fire Ins. Co., N.Y. Underwriters; trustee Underwriters Labs., Inc., Chgo. Bd. dirs. Hartford YMCA; corporator Hartford Hosp., Inst. Living, Mt. Sinai Hosp. Home: 88 Spring Lane West Hartford CT 06107 Office: 690 Asylum Av Hartford CT 96115

BIGIARETTI, LIBEROM, writer, journalist; b. Matelica, Italy, May 16, 1906; s. Lucano and Rosa (D'Andrea) B.; ed. art Sr. High Sch.; m. Matilde Crespi. Head press office Olvetti Co. Nat. sec. Italian Writers Syndicate. Mem. Press Assn., Pen Club. Author: Esterina, 1943; Il Villino, 1946; Carlone, 1950; 1 Figli (Marzotto prize), 1955; Disamore, 1957; Le Congresso, 1963; Le Indulgenze, 1966; La Controfigura, 1968; Le Dissenso, 1970. Address: 661 Via Francesco Denza Rome Italy

BIGLAND, ERNEST FRANK, ins. co. exec.; b. Cheshire, Eng., Dec. 7, 1913; s. Robert Taylor and Helen Inglis Scott (Hannay) B.; student St. Edwards Sch., Oxford, 1927-30; m. Mary Dalzell, July 15, 1936; children—Robert David Inglis and John Anthony Dalzell (twins), Josephine Helen. With Guardian Assurance Co., Ltd., 1930-69, gen. mgr., 1960-65, dir., group chief gen. mgr., 1965, mng. dir., 1966-69; mng. dir. Guardian Royal Exchange Assurance, Ltd., London, 1969—; dir. numerous firms. Trustee Montagu Motor Mus., Beaulieu, Eng. Served to lt. col. Royal Arty., 1939-45; ETO. Decorated mem. Brit. Empire. Fellow Chartered Ins. Inst. Clubs: Leander, Bath. Home: 9 Moncorvo Close London S W 7 England Office: Royal Exchange London E C 3 P 3 DN England

BIGLER, ELWOOD LLOYD, banker; b. Carlisle, Pa., Sept. 4, 1906; s. Stewart H. and Elizabeth (Smith) B.; student Beckley Coll., Harrisburg, Pa., 1924-26, Wharton Sch., U. Pa., nights 1932-38; C.P.A., 1936; m. Lucille M. Winering, June 21, 1930; children—Jane (Mrs. Paul Spencer), Carolyn (Mrs. John Hartley). Statistician, Bd. Commrs. Navigation, Phila., 1927-29; engaged in pub. accounting, 1929-42; with Bank of N.J., Camden, 1942—, comptroller, 1964—. Tax cons., borough assessor, Audubon, N.J., 1948—. Republican county committeeman, 1948-52. Mem. Bank Adminstrn. Inst. Mason (Shriner). Home: 233 Washington Terrace Audubon NJ 08106 Office: Bank of New Jersey Broadway at Market St Camden NJ 08102

BIGLEY, JAMES PHILIP, telephone co. exec.; b. Viroqua, Wis., July 28, 1912; s. Lawrence A. and Ellen (McCall) B.; m. Dorothy Bent, Aug. 28, 1948. Officer, dir. State Bank of LaCrosse (Wis.), 1930-47, State Bank of Viroqua (Wis.), 1947-55, 70—; dir. Viroqua Telephone Co., 1948—, sec., treas., mgr., 1954-62, pres., mgr., 1962—; pres. Viroqua Bldg. Corp., 1966—; dir. Capital Indemnity Corp., 1959- -, Capital Transam Corp., 1966—. Mem. region 5 USPHS- Comprehensive Health Planning Commn. Exec. sec. Republican party Wis., 1955-57. Served from pvt. to 1st lt., 32d Div., AUS, 1942-46. Mem. U.S. Independent Telephone Assn. (dir. 1966—), LaCrosse Jr. C. of C. (pres. 1939), 32d Div. Vets. Assn. (nat. pres. 1957-58), Am. Legion, V.F.W., Wis. Telephone Assn. (pres. 1962-64). Elk, Eagle (Wis. pres. 1952- 53, internat. pres. 1959-60, financial adviser 1962-69, internat. chmn. program and activities, 1969—). Home: 3 S Washington Heights Viroqua WI 54665 Office: 114 E Court St Viroqua WI 54665

BIGLEY, THOMAS CREVISTON, lawyer; b. Culver, Ind., Mar. 25, 1912; s. Chester G. and Pearl Ann (Creviston) B.; B.S., Ind. U., 1934, LL.B., 1938; m. Rebecca Sharpnack, July 21, 1936 (dec. 1956); children—Thomas Creviston, Stephen S.; m. 2d, Eleanor Clay, July 13, 1958. Admitted to Ind. bar, 1938; with First Bancredit Corp., Indpls.; atty. mfg. div. RCA Indpls., 1940-43; partner firm Sharpnack, Bigley & David, and predecessor firms, Columbus, Ind., 1943—. Mem. Ind. Bd. Financial Instns., 1949-53. Fellow Am. Coll. Probate Counsel; mem. Am. Judicature Soc., Am. (ho. of dels.), Bartholomew County (past pres.), Ind. (pres. 1959-60) bar assns., Columbus C. of C. (pres. 1949), Sigma Alpha Epsilon. Methodist. Clubs: Columbia (Indpls.); Kiwanis (pres. 1946), Harrison Lake Country (Columbus). Home: 3402 Grove Pl Columbus IN 47201 Office: 422 5th St Columbus IN 47201

BIJOU, SIDNEY WILLIAM, educator; b. Balt., Nov. 12, 1908; s. Leon and Leah (Barbert) B.; student Lehigh U., 1929-31; B.A., U. Fla., 1933; M.A., Columbia, 1936; Ph.D., U.Ia., 1941; m. Janet R. Tobias, Aug. 31, 1934; children—Robert Kenneth, Judith Ann. Psychologist, Del. State Hosp. and Mental Hygiene Clinic, 1937-39; research child psychologist Wayne County Tng. Sch., 1941-42, 46-47; asst. prof. Ind. U., 1946-48; asso. prof., prof., dir. Inst. Child Devel. U. Wash., 1948-65; dir. Research Program in Human Devel. U. Ill., Champaign, 1965—; cons. Nat. Inst. Mental Health, 1959- 63, Nat. Inst. Child Health and Human Devel., 1964-67, U.S. Office Edn., NSF. Mem. research adv. bd. Nat. Assn. for Retarded Children, 1965—. Served to capt. USAAF, 1942-46. Nat. Inst. Mental Health Sr. fellow Harvard, 1961-62. Fellow Am. Psychol. Assn. (past div. pres.); mem. Psychonomic Soc., Soc. For Research in Child Devel., Am. Assn. U. Profs., Sigma Xi. Author: (with D.M. Baer) Child Development; A Systematic and Empirical Theory, 1961; Child Development: The Universal State of Infancy, 1965; Child Development: Experimental Analysis of Behaviour, 1967. Editor Jour. Exptl. Child Psychology, 1964-71. Asso. editor Internat. Rev. of Research in Mental Retardation, 1965—, Jour. Behavior Therapy and Exptl. Psychiatry, 1969—. Home: 612 LaSell Dr Champaign IL 61820 Office: 403 E Healey St Champaign IL 61820

BIJUR, HERBERT ISAAC, retail exec.; b. N.Y.C., Feb. 6, 1911; s. Nathan I. and Eugenie (Blum) B.; B.S., Haverford Coll., 1932; m. Marion Halpert, Feb. 1, 1939; children—Peter, Priscilla, Polly. With McCall Corp., 1949-70, v.p., 1957 -70; pres. McCall Pattern Co.; with Erica Wilson, Inc., N.Y.C., 1970—. Mem. citizens adv. com. Parks and Recreation Commn. Home: 502 Orienta Av Mararoneck NY 10543 Office: 40 East End Av New York City NY 10028

BIKEL, THEODORE, actor, singer; b. Vienna, Austria, May 2, 1924; s. Josef and Miriam (Riegler) B.; student U. London (Eng.); grad. Royal Acad. Dramatic Art, London, 1948; m. Rita Weinberg, 1967. Came to U.S., 1954, naturalized, 1961. Apprentice with Habimah Theatre, Tel Aviv, 1942- 44; a founder Tel Aviv Chamber Theatre, 1944-46; theatrical prodns. include A Streetcar Named Desire (London), 1950, the Love of Four Colonels (London), 1950-52, Tonight in Samarkand (N.Y.C.), 1954, Rope Dancers (N.Y.C.), 1957-58, The Lark (N.Y.C.), 1955-56, Sound of Music (N.Y.C.), 1959-61, Fiddler on the Roof (Las Vegas), 1968, (Honolulu), 1969; motion pictures include Blue Angel, 1951, The Little Kidnappers, 1951, I Want to Live, 1958, The Defiant Ones (Academy award nomination 1959), My Fair Lady, 1964, Sands of the Kalahari, 1965, The Russians are Coming, 1966, Sweet November 1967, My Side of the Mountain, 1969, Darker Than Amber, 1970, The Little Ark, 1971; also numerous TV appearances, 1954—; author, star TV prodns. The Eternal Light, 1958, Look Up and Live, 1958-60; host-editor TV prodn. Directions 61, 1961; weekly radio program, At Home with Theodore Bikel, 1958-63; concert folk singer, 1955—; recording artist for Elektra and Reprise. Founder arts chpt. Am. Jewish Congress, 1961-63, nat. v.p. 1963-70, co-chmn. governing council 1970—. Del. Democratic Nat. Conv., 1968. Mem. Acad. TV Arts and Scis. (gov. 1961-65), Actors Equity Assn. (Councillor 1961—, 1st v.p. 1964—), Acad. Motion Picture Arts and Scis., A.F.T.R.A., Screen Actors Guild, Am. Fedn. Musicans. Author: Folksongs and Footnotes, 1960. Address: care William Morris Agy 1350 Av of Americas New York City NY 10019

BIKLE, PAUL FIERY, aero. engr.; b. Wilkinsburg, Pa., June 5, 1916; s. Paul and Elizabeth (Wooden) B.; B. Aero. Engring., U. Detroit, 1939; m.. Anne E. Daily, June 22, 1940; children—Hugh, John, Patricia, Alan. Design engr. Taylorcraft Aircraft Co., Alliance, O., 1939-41; flight engr. Wright Field, Dayton, O., 1940-51; tech. dir. Air Force Flight Test Center, Edwards AFB, Cal., 1951-59; dir. NASA Flight Research Center, Edwards AFB, 1959—. Holder world's altitude record sailplains Fedn. Aero. Internat., 1961—, recipient Lilienthal medal, 1962, medal outstanding leadership NASA, 1962. Mem. Soaring Soc. Am. (pres. 1961-62, dir. 1952-64). Home: 44926 N Raysack St Lancaster, CA 93534 Office: NASA Flight Research Center Edwards 7 CA 93523

BIKLEN, PAUL, advt. exec.; b. Burlington, Ia., Apr. 2, 1915; s. Fred Ludwig and Lydia (Ruckenbrod) B.; m. Anne Chenoweth, Dec. 30, 1939; children—Stephen C., Douglas P. Writer, Gen. Electric Co., 1936-41; pub. relations dir. Kaiser Cargo, Inc., Bristol, Pa., 1941-43; advt. exec. Fuller & Smith & Ross, Inc., N.Y.C., 1947-52; v.p. N.W. Ayer & Son, N.Y.C., 1952-60; sr. v.p. Ogilvy & Mather, Inc., N.Y.C., 1960—, also dir. Bd. dirs. Westport (Conn.) YMCA, 1953-56. Served to lt. USNR, 1943-46. Clubs: Fairfield (Conn.) Country (bd. govs. 1966—); Dublin (N.H.) Lake. Author: (with Robert Breth) The Successful Employee Publication, 1946. Home: 12 North Av Westport CT 06880 Office: 2 E 48th St New York City NY 10017

BILANIUK, OLEXA MYRON, educator, physicist; b. Ukraine, Dec. 15, 1926; s. Petro Yakovytch and Marie (Kunkevytch) B.; student U. Louvain, 1947-51; M.S., U. Mich., 1953, M.A., 1954, Ph.D., 1957; m. Larissa T. Zubal, Nov. 14, 1964; children—Larissa, Laada. Came to U.S., 1951, naturalized, 1957. Postdoctoral fellow U. Mich., 1957-58; research asso., asst. prof. U. Rochester, 1958-64; asso. prof. physics Swarthmore Coll., 1964-70, prof., 1970—, chmn. natural scis. div., 1970—; vis. scholar Argentine Atomic Energy Commn., Buenos Aires, 1961-62; vis. prof., cons. Delhi U., summer 1966, Shivaji U., Kolhapur, India, summer 1969. NSF fellow, Germany, 1967-68, France, 1971-72. Mem. Am. Phys. Soc., Am. Assn. Physics Tchrs., Ukrainian Acad. Arts and Scis. in U.S., Sigma Xi. Research on nuclear structure; with Deshpande and Sudarshan challenged the view that Einstein's relativity precludes possibility of existence of particles that travel faster than light, 1962. Home: 100 Plush Mill Rd Wallingford PA 19086 Office: Swarthmore Coll Swarthmore PA 19081

BILBY, KENNETH W., electronic co. exec.; b. Salt Lake City, Oct. 7, 1918; s. Ralph W. and Marguerite (Mansfield) B.; B.A., U. Ariz., 1941; m. Helen Owen Meeker, Mar. 6, 1948; children—Barbara Windsor, Kenneth Mansfield, Marquerite Mansfield, Robert Bryan. Fgn. corr. Europe and Middle East, N.Y. Herald Tribune, 1947-50; pub. relations rep. RCA Victor, Camden, N.J., 1950-54; v.p. pub. relations, exec. v.p. NBC, 1954-60; v.p. pub. affairs RCA, 1960-62, exec. v.p. pub. affairs, 1962—, also mem. RCA Pres.'s Policy Council. Exec. com., trustee Am. Heritage Found.; bd. dirs. World Press Inst. Served to lt. col. AUS, World War II. Decorated Silver Star medal, Legion of Merit, Bronze Star medal, Combat Infantry Badge; Croix de Guerre; recipient Alumni Achievement award U. Ariz., 1960. Mem. Radio and TV Execs. Soc. (bd. govs.), Phi Delta Theta. Clubs: Apawamis (Rye, N.Y.); Winged Foot Golf (Mamaroneck, N.Y.); Lake Placid (N.Y.); Burning Tree (Bethesda, Md); Bay Hill (Orlando, Fla.); Rockefeller Center Luncheon (N.Y.C.). Author: New Star in the Near East, 1950. Home: 58 Close Rd Greenwich CT 06830 Office: 30 Rockefeller Plaza New York City NY 10020

BILBY, RICHARD MANSFIELD, lawyer; b. Tucson, May 29, 1931; s. Ralph Willard and Marguerite (Mansfield) B.; B.S., U. Ariz., 1955; J.D., U. Mich., 1958; m. Ann Louise Borchert, July 6, 1957; children—Claire Louise, Ellen Markley. Admitted to Ariz. bar, 1959, since practiced in Tucson; law clk. to Chief Justice Chambers, 9th Circuit Ct. Appeals, San Francisco, 1958-59; mem. firm Bilby, Thompson, Shoenhair & Warnock, 1959—, partner, 1967—; conscientious objector hearing officer Dept. Justice, 1959-62; chmn. Pima County Med.-Legal panel, 1968-70. Mem. Tucson Charter Revision Com., 1965-70; chmn. United Fund Profl. Div., 1968, Spl. Gift Div., 1970; chmn. St. Joseph Hosp. Devel. Fund Drive, 1970. Republican state chmn. Vols. for Eisenhower, 1956. Pres. Tucson Conquistadores; v.p. exec. com. St. Josephs Hosp. Served with AUS, 1952-54. Mem. Am. Bd. Trial Advocates, U. Ariz. Alumni Assn. (dir.), Ariz. Acad., Town Hall. Home: 5902 E Miramar Dr W Tucson AZ 85715 Office: Valley Nat Bldg Tucson AZ 85701

BILDERBACK, CLAYTON W., union ofcl. Sec.-treas. Metal Trades Dept. AFL-CIO. Office: 815 16th St NW Washington DC 20006*

BILDERSEE, BARNETT, pub. relations exec.; b. N.Y.C., Apr. 6, 1911; s. Isaac and Selena (Ullman) B.; B.Litt., Columbia, 1932; m. Ada Kogan, June 30, 1934; 1 dau., Adele (Mrs. Jerome Feldman). Reporter N.Y. Evening World, 1928-31; corr. N.Y. Post-Phila. Pub. Ledger Syndicate, London, 1932-33; reporter Providence Jour., 1933-34; cable editor AP, N.Y.C., 1934-40; fgn. news editor, day city editor PM and N.Y. Star newspapers, 1940-49; with Allied Indsl. Research Consultants, Inc., 1949-56, v.p., 1953-54, exec. v.p., 1954-56; also dir.; v.p., chmn. plans bd. Tex McCrary, Inc., N.Y.C., 1957-58, exec. v.p., 1958-61, pres., 1961; pres. Martial & Co., Inc., 1961-63, Bildersee Pub. Relations, N.Y.C., 1963—; dir. N.Y. Dental Service Corp.; lectr. N.Y. U. Sr. field rep. OWI, 1943. Bd. dirs. Brotherhood-in-Action, Inc. Mem. Pub. Relations Soc. Am., Soc. Silurians (gov.), U.S. Power Squadrons, Sigma Delta Chi. Club: Overseas Press. Home: 205 West End Av New York City NY 10023 Office: 103 Park Av New York City NY 10017

BILES, JOHN ALEXANDER, educator; b. Del Norte, Colo., May 4, 1923; s. John Alexander and Lillie (Willis) B.; B.S., U. Colo., 1944, Ph.D. (AEC fellow), 1949; m. Margaret Pauline Off, June 19, 1943; children-Paula M. (Mrs. Patrick Murphy), M. Suzanne. Prof. pharm. chemistry Midwestern U., 1949-50; asst. prof. pharmacy Ohio State U., 1950-52; asst. prof. pharm. chemistry U. So. Cal., Los Angeles, 1952-53, asso. prof., 1953-57, prof., 1957-68, dean, prof. biomedicinal chemistry, 1968—; cons. Allergan Pharms., 1953-68. Mem. Nat. Adv. Council, Edn. for Health Professions, 1970—. Trustee, Portals House, Recipient Lehn and Fink Scholarship award, 1944, S.C. Assos. award for excellence in teaching, 1962. Mem. Am., Cal. pharm. assns., Am. Cancer Soc. (mem. sci. adv. com. Los Angeles County), Acad. Pharm. Scis., Am. Assn. Colls. Pharmacy. Home: 400 Surfview Dr Pacific Palisades CA 90272 Office: U So Cal Sch Pharmacy University Park Los Angeles CA 90007

BILHEIMER, ROBERT SPERRY, clergyman; b. Denver, Sept. 28, 1917; s. Gus Steven and Katherine Elizabeth (Sperry) B.; grad. Phillips Exeter Acad.; B.A., Yale, 1939, B.D., 1945; D.D. (hon.), Chgo. Theol. Sem., 1954, Butler U., 1954; m. Dorothy Stevenson Dodge, June 13, 1942; children—Robert Edwin, Richard Sperry, Roger Stevenson. Ordained to ministry Presbyn. Ch.; exec. sec. The Inter-sem. Movement, 1945-48; pastor Westminster Presbyn. Ch. of Cedar Manor, N.Y.C., 1947-54; adminstrv. sec. First Assembly World Council Chs., 1948, exec. sec. 2d assembly, 1954, program sec. in N.Am., 1948-54, asso. gen. sec., dir. div. of studies, Geneva, Switzerland, 1954-63; sr. minister Central Presbyn. Ch., Rochester, N.Y., 1963-66; dir. internat. affairs program Nat. Council Chs. of Christ U.S.A., 1966—. Author: What Must the Church Do?, 1947; The Quest for Christian Unity, 1952. Gen. editor: The Interseminary Series (4 vols.), 1947. Home: 60 Pinewood Gardens Hartsdale NY 10530 Office: 475 Riverside Dr New York City NY 10027

BILL, MAX, architect, artist, educator; b. Winterthur, Switzerland, Dec. 22, 1908; s. Erwin and Marie (Geiger) B.; ed. Sch. Arts and Crafts, Zurich, Switzerland, also Bauhaus, Dessau, Germany; m. Binia Spoerri, Jan. 22, 1931; 1 son, James. Propr. archtl. office, Zurich, 1932—; co-founder, dir., head archtl. dept., also head product design dept., Inst. Design, Ulm, Germany, 1951-56; prof. environmental design State Coll. Arts, Hamburg, 1967—; chief architect cultural sect. Swiss Nat. Exhbn., Lausanne, 1962- 64; works represented in permanent collections Albright-Knox Art Gallery, Buffalo, Bush-Reisinger Mus., Cambridge, Mass. Detroit Inst. Arts, N.Y.U. Art Gallery, Art Inst. of Chgo., Art Gallery of Toronto, Art Gallery Montreal, Musé d'art contemporian Montreal, Storm King Art Center Mountainville, N.Y., Hirshhorn Collection. Mem. Swiss Nat. Parliament, 1967—. Recipient grand prix Swiss Pavillion, Milan Triennal Exhbn., 1936, 51, Kandinsky prize, 1946, 1st Internat. Sculpture prize Biennal de Sao Paulo, 1951; Art prize City of Zurich, 1968. Honorary fellow A.I.A.; member of the Union Swiss Architects, Swiss Assn. Art and Industry (hon.). Author: Robert Maillart, 3d edit., 1966; Le Corbusier and Pierre Jeanneret, 1938; Mies Van Der Rohe, 1955; Fifteen Variations on a Single Theme, 1938; Form, a Balance Sheet of Mid-Twentieth Century Trends in Design, 1952; Kandinsky, 2d edit., 1951; also monographs. Home: Rebhusstr 50 Zumikon Zurich Switzerland Office: Albulastrasse 39 CH8048 Zurich Switzerland

BILLANE, J. MICHAEL, rubber mfr. Chmn. bd. Dunlop Tire & Rubber Corp., Buffalo. Office: Dunlop Tire & Rubber Corp River Road and Sheridan Dr Buffalo NY 14207*

BILLERA, I. JOHN, corp. exec.; b. N.Y.C., July 20, 1912; s. Frank and Mary (Quartaro) B.; B.B.A., Coll. City N.Y., 1933; m. Frieda Tumbarello, Oct. 27, 1940; 1 dau., Mary Ann. Corp. officer Edward Ermold Co., 1946-51, Noma Electric Corp., 1951-53; sr. v.p. U.S. Industries, Inc., 1953-60, exec. v.p., 1960-65, pres., chmn. bd., 1965-66, chmn. bd., chief exec. officer, 1966—, also dir.; dir. USI P.R., Inc., USI de Venezuela SA., USI Philippines, Inc., USI Gt. Britain Ltd., USI Engring., Ltd., USI Worldwide Corp. Clubs: Union League (N.Y.C.); Country Club of Darien (Conn.). Home: West Cross Rd New Canaan CT 06820 Office: 250 Park Av New York City NY 10017

BILLETDOUX, FRANCOIS-PAUL, actor, producer; b. Paris, France, Sept. 7, 1927; student Charles Dullin Sch. Dramatic Art, 1944, Inst. Higher Cinematic Studies, 1945; m. Evelyne Colin, Aug. 2, 1947; children—Virginie, Rafaele. Actor, prod. Radiodiffusion Francaise, 1946; dir. programs Radiodiffusion-Francaise, Fort-de-France, Martinique, 1949, dir. overseas program Soc. Radiodiffusion de la France, 1957; actor or producer Thirteen Plays to Praise, Theater of Latin Quarter, 1951, At Night, It's Night, one-act comedy, L'Animal from La Table Ronde, 1955, also Hi-Fi, variety show Theater des Trois-Baudets, A Rose for Charles Cros (Grand Prix du Disque), Royal Garden Blues from editon of Robert Laffont, 1957, Tchin- Tchin, comedy, Theatre de Poche-Montparnasse, Prix U., Prix Lugne-Poë, 1959, The Bredburry's Behavior, comedy Theatre des Mathurins, 1960, Chez Torpe, comedy Studio of Champs Elysees, A Man and His Master, also Theatre from la Table Ronde, and Monologues pour rire, cabaret numbers on records, 1961, For Dellany, 1962, How Goes the World Sir? (Prix du Cercle Internat. de la Jeune Critique, Pass Through the Clouds, Theatre II from la Table Ronde, 1964, Je n' etais pas Chez Moi, 1968, Quelqu'un devrait Faire Quelque Chosa, 1969, Musique pour une Ville, 1969, Famine Chez les Rats, 1970, Femmes Paralleles, 1970, Cantique des Creatures, 1970, Ai-je Dit que Je suis Bossu?, 1971, Rintru Pa Trou Tar Hin!, , 1971. Recipient Prix de l'Unanimité for literary prodn., C.N.E., 1965; Silence! L'arbre remue encore. . . créé au Festival d'Avignon, 1967; Pitchi Poi ou la parole donnée, Eurovision, 1967. Home: 31 Montsouris Sq Paris 14 France

BILLETT, ROY OREN, prof. edn.; b. Martel, O., June 17, 1891; s. Edward Elmore and Ida Lenora (Earley) B.; ed. Bliss Business Coll., 1917; Bowling Green State Normal Sch., 1918; B.Sc., Ohio State U.,

1923, M.A., 1927, Ph.D., 1929; Ed.D. (Hon.), R.I. Coll. Edn., 1958; m. Edna Mae Cunningham, Sept. 14, 1912; 1 dau., Evelyn Margaret. Tchr., supt., village schs., Morrow County, O., 1912-18; supt. New Bloomington Centralized Schs., Marion County, O., 1918-22; prin. Thomas W. Harvey Meml. High Sch., Painesville, O., 1923-28; instr. Ohio State U., 1929; specialist in sch. adminstrn. U.S. Office Edn., 1930-32; prof. lectr. on edn. Grad. Sch., Am. U., 1930-32, George Washington U., 1931-32; mem. staff Survey of Higher Instns. of Learning, Ark., 1930; mem. staff Nat. Survey of Secondary Edn., 1930-32; asso. prof. secondary edn., supervisor practice teaching, Ill. State Normal U., 1932-33; lectr. edn. Grad. Sch. Edn., Harvard, 1933-34; asso. prof. edn. Boston U., 1934-35, prof., 1935-57, prof. edn. emeritus, 1957—, chmn. dept. edn., Grad. Sch., 1944; vis. prof. edn. Fla. Atlantic U., 1966—. Mem. staff Survey of Pub. Schs., Cin., 1935; dir. Survey Pub. Edn., Harford County, Md., 1945-46; lectr. edn., U. B.C., 1946, 1951; vis. prof. U. So. Cal., 1948, Duke U., 1955, U. Fla., 1959, Fla. State U., 1960. Dir. Two Year Revision Program, Coop. Study Secondary School Standards, 1948. Mem. Nat. Assn. Secondary Sch. Prins., Am. Assn. U. Profs., Am. Ednl. Research Assn., Nat. Soc. for Study of Edn. (mem. yearbook com., 1936), Internat. Reading Assn., Nat. Council on Measurements in Edn., Phi Data Kappa. Club: Boston Authors'. Author: Administration and Supervision of Homogeneous Grouping; Aims and Activities of Supervisors; Provisions for Individual Differences, Marking and Promotion; Fundamentals of Secondary-School Teaching; Growing Up and Related Manuals; Youth Problems Inventories; Teaching in Junior and Senior High Schools; Improving the Secondary School Curriculum; also articles in field. Home: 5921 NE 15th Av Fort Lauderdale FL 33308

BILLICK, STANLEY RICHARD, lawyer; b. Oskaloosa, Ia., Sept. 8, 1923; s. Gilbert Wayne and Zora (Gray) B.; student Ill. Wesleyan U., 1940-43; B.S., U. Ill. 1947, J.D., 1948; m. Shirley Anne Armour, July 3, 1946; children—Stanley Richard II, Nancy Anne. Admitted to Ill. bar, 1948; mem. firm Chapman and Cutler, Chgo., 1948-59; partner firm Holland & Billick, Chgo., 1960-67, Norman & Billick, Chgo., 1968—. Dir. First Nat. Bank of Mt. Prospect, Ill. Business Capital Corp. Served to capt. USAAF, 1943-45. Decorated D.F.C., Air medal. Mem. Ill. Bar Assn., Order of Coif, Pi Kappa Delta, Tau Kappa Epsilon, Phi Delta Phi. Methodist. Club: Inverness Golf. Home: 702 S Salem Av Arlington Heights IL 60005 Office: 69 W Washington St Chicago IL 60602

BILLINGHAM, RUPERT EVERETT, educator; b. Warminster, Eng., Oct. 15, 1921; s. Albert E. and Helen (Green) B.; B.A., Oriel Coll., Oxford, Eng., 1943, M.A., 1944, D.Phil., 1950, D.Sc., 1957; m. Jean Mary Morpeth, Mar. 29, 1951; children—John David, Peter Jeremy, Elizabeth Anne. Lectr. zoology U. Birmingham (Eng.), 1947-51; research fellow Brit. Empire Cancer Campaign, hon. research asso. dept. zoology Univ. Coll., London, Eng., 1951-57; mem. Wistar Inst., Wistar Prof. zoology U. Pa., Phila., 1957-65, prof., chmn. dept. med. genetics, dir. Henry Phipps Inst., U. Pa. Med. Sch., 1965-71; prof., chmn. dept. cell biology U. Tex. Southwestern Med. Sch., Dallas, 1971—. Adv. editor Jour. Exptl. Medicine, 1963—; asso. editor Jour. Immunology, 1964—; mem. allergy and immunology study sect. NIH, 1959-62; mem. transplantation immunology com. Nat. Inst. Allergy and Infectious Diseases, NIH, 1968-70; mem. sci. adv. bd. St. Jude Children's Research Hosp., Memphis, 1965-70. Served to lt. Royal Navy, 1942-46. Recipient Alvarenga Prize, Coll. Physicians, Phila., 1963; hon. award Soc. Plastic Surgeons, 1964. Fellow Royal Soc. (London), N.Y. Acad. Scis., Am. Acad. Arts and Scis.; mem. Am. Assn. Immunologists, Transplantation Soc. Contbr. articles to profl. jours. Home: 5211 Meaders Lane Dallas TX Office: Dept Cell Biology U Tex Southwestern Med Sch Dallas TX 75235

BILLINGS, BRUCE HADLEY, physicist; b. Chgo., July 6, 1915; s. Thomas H. and Grace (Hadley) B.; grad. Phillips Exeter Acad., 1932; A.B., Harvard, 1936, A.M., 1937; Ph.D., Johns Hopkins, 1943; m. Sarah Winslow, June 23, 1938; children—Sally Frances, Bruce Randolph, Jane Winslow, Peter Fayssoux. Tchr. math. sci. Am. Community Sch., Beirut, Lebanon, 1937-40; jr. instr. physics Johns Hopkins, Balt., 1940-41; physicist Polariod Corp., Cambridge, Mass., 1941-47; mem. radiol. safety sect. atomic bomb test, Bikini, 1946; dir. research Baird-Atomic, Inc. Cambridge, 1947-63, exec. v.p., 1955-59, v.p. and tech. dir., 1960-63; v.p., gen. mgr. labs. operation Aerospace Corp., Los Angeles, 1963-68; Am. commr. Joint Commn. on Rural Reconstrn., spl. asst. to Am. ambassador for sci. and tech., Taipei, Taiwan, 1968—; dir. Ealing Corp., Diffraction, Ltd., Inc. Mem. Air Force Sci. Adv. Bd., 1962—; asst. dir. def. research and engring. Dept. Defense, 1959-60; U.S. del. Marseille Conf. on Thin Films, 1949; mem. U.S. nat. com. Intnl. Commn. Optics; research asso. Harvard Coll. Obs. Fellow Am. Acad. Arts and Scis. (sec.); mem. Am. Phys. Soc., Acoustical Soc. Am., Optical Soc. Am. (asso. editor jour. 1956-60, pres. elect 1970), A.A.A.S., Sigma Xi. Club: St. Botolph. Asso. editor Am. Inst. Physics Handbook; subject editor: Applied Optics. Contbr. tech. articles profl. jours. Home: care Box 2 Am Embassy APO San Francisco CA 96263 Office: Am Embassy Taipei Taiwan Republic of China

BILLINGS, EDWARD ROBERT, accountant; b. Blunt, S.D., Nov. 6, 1913; s. Edward C. and Lydia (Abendroth) B.; B.S., U. Ill., 1940, B.A., 1940; m. Paula W. Knickrehm, July 11, 1936; children—Edward A., Bruce P., David W. Jr. accountant Haskins & Sells, C.P.A.'s, Chgo., 1940-52, partner, 1952-63, mng. partner Detroit office, 1963-69, partner, exec. officer, N.Y.C., 1969—. Home: 44 Byfield Lane Greenwich CT 06830 Office: 2 Broadway New York City NY 10004

BILLINGS, FRED CHESTER, banker; b. N.Y.C., Dec. 22, 1902; s. Albert William and Gilberta (Seiders) B.; student Princeton, 1919-21; B.S., U.S. Naval Acad., 1925; m. Kathryn Susan Frazier, June 17, 1953; children—Blanche (Mrs. James C. Smith), Fred Chester. Sec., Peoples State Bank S.C., Charleston, 1929-33; asst. v.p. J. P. Morgan & Co., N.Y.C., 1933-51; v.p. Exchange Nat. Bank Tampa (Fla.), 1951-52, exec. v.p., 1952-69, dir., 1954-69; vice chmn. Southeast Bank of Tampa, 1969—; v.p., dir. Draper Groves, Inc.; dir. Brandon State Bank. Pres., Merchants Assn. Tampa, 1957-58, hon. dir., 1958—. Pres. Boys Clubs Tampa, 1965; treas. Fla. Financial Forum, 1964—. Counselor, U. Tampa, 1965—; trustee Naval Acad. Found., 1966—. Served with USN, 1925-28, as comdr., USNR, 1941-46. Named to Lacrosse Hall of Fame, 1962. Mem. A.I.M. (pres.'s council), Ye Mystic Krewe of Gasparailla, Naval Acad. Alumni Assn. Episcopalian. Clubs: University (pres. 1956), Palma Geia Golf and Country, Tampa Yacht and Country, Lions (Tampa). Home: 2401 Bayshore Blvd Tampa FL 33609 Office: PO Box 3283 Madison and Morgan Sts Tampa FL 33611

BILLINGS, FREDERIC TREMAINE, Jr., physician, educator; b. Pitts., Feb. 22, 1912; s. Frederic Tremaine and Romaine (LeMoyne) B.; A.B., Princeton, 1933; B.Sc., (Rhodes scholar), Balliol Coll., Oxford, Eng., 1936; M.D., Johns Hopkins, 1938; m. Ann Howe, Feb. 21, 1942; children—Frederic Tremaine III, Ann Howe, John Howe. Postgrad. tng. medicine Johns Hopkins, Vanderbilt U. hosps., 1938-42; instr. medicine Vanderbilt U. Sch. Medicine, 1946-49, asst. prof., 1949-53, asso. prof., 1953-63, clin. prof. medicine, 1963—, dean students, 1960-67, asso. dean for med. center devel. programs, 1967—, interim dir. Vanderbilt Center for Health Services, 1971—; prof. medicine Meharry Med. Coll., 1950-60, chmn. dept., 1950-57, also trustee. Sec. State Selection Com. Rhodes Scholars, Tenn. Mem. U.S. delegation to Soviet Union on Health Services Research, 1970. Past dir. Nat. Med. Fellowships, Inc.; trustee Princeton, 1956-60, Choate Sch. Served from capt. to lt. col. AUS, 1942-46; asst. med. cons. S.W. Pacific area, 1944; chief gen. medicine br. med. consultants div. Office Surgeon Gen., 1945- 46. Diplomate Am. Bd. Internal Medicine, 1946. Fellow A.C.P., A.M.A.; mem. Assn. Am. Rhodes Scholars (past dir.), Am. Clin. and Climatological Assn. (sec.-treas. 1958-68, pres. 1968-69), Assn. Am. Physicians, Soc. U.S. Med. Cons. Armed Forces, A.A.A.S., Am. Heart Assn., Am. Fedn. Clin. Research, Med. Library Assn., Phi Beta Kappa, Alpha Omega Alpha. Clubs: Ivy; Rolling Rock (Ligonier, Pa.); Belle Meade Country (Nashville). Contbr. articles to profl. publs. Home: 3906 Woodlawn Dr Nashville TN Office: Medical Arts Bldg Nashville TN 37212 also Vanderbilt Medical Center 21st and Garland Nashville TN 37203

BILLINGS, JOHN SHAW, former editor; b. Beech Island, S.C., May 11, 1898; s. John S. and Katharine (Hammond) B.; grad. St. Paul's Sch., Concord, N.H., 1916; student Harvard, 1916-17, 1919-20; m. Frederica Washburn Wade, Apr. 19, 1924 (dec.); 1 dau., Frederica Wade (dec.); m. 2d, Elise Lake Chase, Sept. 10, 1963. Reporter Bklyn. Daily Eagle, 1921, Washington Corr., 1921-29; nat. affairs editor Time, 1929-33, mng. editor, 1933-36; mng. editor Life, 1936-44; editorial dir. all Time Inc. publs., Time, Life, Fortune, 1944-54. Served as ammunition truck driver French Army, 1917; 2d lt. Air Service, U.S. Army, 1918-19. Home: "Redcliffe Beech Island SC 29842

BILLINGS, MARLAND PRATT, geologist, educator; b. Boston, Mar. 11, 1902; s. George Bartlett and Helen Agnes (McDonough) B.; student Roxbury Latin Sch., 1913-19, A.B., Harvard, 1923, A.M., 1925, Ph.D., 1927; D.Sc., Washington U., St. Louis, 1960, U. N.H., 1966; m. Katharine Stevens Fowler, Apr. 23, 1938; children—George, Betty. Asst. in geology Harvard, 1922- 25, instr., 1925-28, asst. prof. geology Harvard, 1930-39, asso. prof., 1939-46, prof., 1946—; chmn. div. geol. scis., 1946-51; asso. Bryn Mawr Coll., 1928-29, asso. prof., 1929-30; asst. geologist, U.S. Geol. Survey, 1929-38, 1940-43, asso. geologist, 1943-44, geologist, 1945; curator Geol. Mus., Harvard U. Civilian tech. observer U.S. Army, 1944. Fellow Geol. Soc. Am. (v.p. 1951, 58, pres. 1959), Mineral Soc. Am.; mem. Am. Acad. Arts and Scis.; Seismol. Soc. Am., Nat. Acad. Scis., A.A.A.S. (v.p. 1947), Am. Assn. Petroleum Geologists. Author: Geol. Map. of N.H.; Bedrock Geology of New Hampshire, 1956; Structural Geol. and contbr. numerous geol. articles. Home: 18 Ocean Blvd Box 327 North Hampton, NH 03862 Office: Dept Geol Scis Harvard U Cambridge MA 02138

BILLINGS, ROGER, former ins. exec.; b. Tewksbury, Mass., Mar. 20, 1901 s. Henry Milton and Alice Maud (Foristall) B.; student Philips Exeter Acad., 1918-19; B.A., Dartmouth, 1923; m. Dorothy Kelley, Aug. 1925; children—Roger, Stanley D.; m. 2d, Ruth Adele MacBeane; 1 dau., Marcia Elizabeth (Mrs. Crombie S. Dallin). With Mass. Indemnity and Life Ins. Co., Boston, 1923-68, dir., 1926-68, asst. sec., 1926-32, sec., 1932-35, gen. mgr., 1934-64, pres., 1935-64, chmn. bd., 1964-68. Mem. Bostonian Soc., Sigma Chi. Mason. Clubs: Braeburn Country, Sarasota Yacht, Eastward Ho Country, Sarasota Dartmouth, Ivy League; Bird Key Yacht (Sarasota). Home: 65 White Oak Rd Wellesley Hills 82, MA (winter) 643 Mourning Dove Dr Bird Key, Sarasota, FL;(summer) Chatham, MA 02633

BILLINGS, STEPHEN ELLSWORTH, editor; b. Ripton, Vt., Oct. 18, 1909; s. S. Jason and Blanche A. (Newton) B.; ed. pub. schs.; m. Antonietta Sannino, June 25, 1945; children—Bianca, Marcia, Patricia. Mem. staff Barre (Vt.) Daily Times, 1928-37, 45—, editor editorial page, 1945—, also book editor; state news editor Rutland (Vt.) Herald, 1937-41. Pres. Ward Five P.T.A., 1960. Sec. Barre (Vt.) Republican Com., 1947—. Served with AUS, 1942-45, ETO. Mem. Barre C. of C. (dir.), Poetry Soc. Vt., Vt. Hist. Soc. Methodist (steward). Home: 7 Humbert St Barre VT 05641 Office: 34 N Main St Barre VT 05641

BILLINGS, WILLIAM DWIGHT, ecologist, educator; b. Washington, Dec. 29, 1910; s. William Pence and Mabel (Burke) B.; B.A., Butler U., 1933; M.A., Duke, 1935, Ph.D., 1936; D.Sc., Butler U., 1955; m. Shirley Ann Miller, July 29, 1958. Instr. botany U. Tenn., 1936-37; instr. biology U. Nev., 1938-40, asst. prof., 1940-43, asso. prof., 1943-49, prof., chmn. biology dept., 1949-52; asso. prof. botany Duke, 1952-58, prof., 1958-67, James B. Duke prof., 1967—. Mem. adv. panels NSF, Washington, 1954-57. Fulbright research scholar, New Zealand, 1959; recipient Certificate of Merit, Bot. Soc. Am., 1960, Mercer award Ecol. Soc. Am., 1962. Mem. Ecol. Soc. Am. (v.p. 1960), Brit. Ecol. Soc., Bot. Soc. Am. Author: Plants and the Ecosystem, 1964; Plants, Man and the Ecosystem, 1970. Editor: Ecology, 1952-57, Ecological Monographs, 1969—. Contbr. articles tech. jours. Home: 1628 Marion Av Durham NC 27705

BILLINGSLEA, CHARLES, army officer; b. Chgo., May 16, 1914; s. Charles and Mabel Billingslea; B.S., U.S. Mil. Acad., 1936; grad. Army War Coll., 1953, Nat. War Coll., 1958; grad. Advanced Mgmt. Program, Harvard, 1957; m. Bettina Hill, Dec. 17, 1939; 1 son, Charles. Commd. 2d lt. U.S. Army, 1936, advanced through grades to maj. gen., 1963; various assignments U.S. and Hawaii, 1936-41; with II Corps and Allied Forces Hdqrs., Eng., 1942; with Hdqrs. USAAF, 1st Brit. Parachute Brigade, 5th Army, Morocco, Algeria and Tunisia, 1942-43; exec. pathfinder Parachute Brigade, Sicily, Italy, 1943; exec. officer 504th Parachute Inf., Eng. and Italy, 1943-44; regtl. comdr. 325th Glider Inf., Eng., Central Europe and Berlin, 1944- 45; chief staff 82d Airborne Div., 1945-46; with plans sect. Army Field Force, Ft. Monroe, Va., 1946-49; mem. staff and faculty Command and Gen. Staff Sch. and War Coll., 1949-51; assigned ORO, Korea and Washington, 1951-52; chief plans SHAPE, Paris, France, 1953-56; dep. chief European region OSD, ISA, Washington, 1958-61; dep. chief staff 8th U.S. Army, Korea, 1961-62; assigned Hdqrs. 2d Div., Ft. Bragg, N.C., 1962; comdg. gen. 2d Inf. Div., Fort Benning, Ga., 1962-64; now dep. comdg. gen. Combat Devel. Command, Fort Belvoir, Va. Decorated D.S.C. with oak leaf cluster, Bronze Star medal with oak leaf cluster, Army Commendation ribbon with oak leaf cluster; Fouragerre (Belgium); Orange Lanyard, knight 4th class Militarie Willems Order (Netherlands); Red Star (Russia); Korean Order Merit 3d class. Mem. Assn. U.S. Army. Rotarian. Home: Quarters 59 Fort Belvoir VA 22060 Office: Dep Comdg Gen USA Combat Devel Comnd Fort Belvoir VA 22060

BILLINGSLEY, HASCAL SANDERS, beverage co. exec.; b. Wylie, Tex., Dec. 26, 1905; s. James Clement and Eva (Sanders) B.; student Advanced Accounting Sch., U. Tex., 1926-27; m. Mary Louise Bruss, Nov. 15, 1935; children—Hascal Bruss, Martha Joan (Mrs. Ralph D. Bowman). Accountant, Peat, Marwick, Mitchell & Co., C.P.A.'s, Dallas, 1927-30; with Dr. Pepper Co., Dallas, 1931, pres., 1966-69, chmn. bd., 1969—. Bd. dirs. Dallas chpt. A.R.C. Mem. Dallas C. of C. (dir.), Salesmanship Club Dallas (bd. dirs. 1953-54, sec. 1953-54), All Sports Assn., Beta Alpha Psi. Clubs: Dallas City, Chapparal, Northwood (Dallas). Home: 4818 Melissa Lane Dallas, TX 75229 Office: 5523 E Mockingbird Lane Dallas TX 75222

BILLINGSLEY, HENRY EDMUND, bus. and govt. cons.; b. Indpls., Nov. 12, 1915; s. Allen Loren and Alma Lee (Mohr) B.; A.B., Yale, 1938; student Western Res. U. Law Sch.,, 1939-41, George Washington U. Law Sch., 1948, Am. U. Grad. Sch., 1950-52, Georgetown U. Grad. Sch., 1952- 54; m. Ann Moneta O'Keefe, June 8, 1946; children—Catherine Ann, Allyn Elizabeth, Lauren Keefe, Henry Edmund II, Charles Arthur. Marketing and pub. relations cons. to instns. and indsl. firms, 1938-41, 48-50; fgn. affairs officer State Dept., 1947-48; asst. Office Sec. Def., 1952-58; dir. internat. programs NASA, 1958-59; cons. Com. Fgn. Affairs, U.S. Ho. of Reps., 1959-61; cons. ICA, 1961; chief U.S. Mission to West Africa, 1962; pres. Analog Corp.; adminstr. The Moly Group; v.p., sec. Space, Ltd.; cons. Geo-surveys Co., and Internat. Community Devel. Corp., Washington; dir., treas. Rand Internat. Corp. (N.Y.C.) dir. Pilot Markets, Inc., (N.Y.C.); dir., v.p. Rippon Corp. (Va.); chmn. bd. dir. Hasco Corp. (Phila.); sr. partner Billingsley & Assos., Washington. Mem. long range studies com., adminstr.'s staff group, NASA, 1958-59; mem. U.S. delegation 3d gen. assembly UNESCO, 1947, UN Conf. Freedom Information, 1948, World Meteor. Orgn. Conf., 1948, NATO Council Ministers, 1952-54, UN Gen. Assembly com. outer space, 1959. Pres. Old Georgetown Rd. Citizens Assn., 1957, N. Bethesda Congress of Citizens Assns., 1958; chmn. citizens adv. bd. Cabin John Valley, Montgomery County, Md., 1957-58. Mem. Yale, govt. and social scis. coms. Yale U. Council, 1958—. Served to lt. comdr. USNR, 1941-46, 50-52; comdr. Res. Mem. Am. Rocket Soc. (space law and sociology com.), Am. Polit. Sci. Assn., Order Founders and Patriots Am., Newcomen Soc. Am. Arbitration Assn., Calvert County (Md.) Hist. Soc., Cleve. Council World Affairs, Cum Laude Soc., Book and Snake Sr. Soc. (permanent class agt.), S.A.R., Beta Theta Pi. Clubs: Kirtland, Chagrin Valley Hunt, Union, City (Cleve.); Yale (past pres., dir.), Grolier, Canadian (N.Y.C.); Duquesne (Pitts.); Metropolitan Kenwood, Fed. City, City Tavern (Washington). Home: 9319 Old Georgetown Rd Bethesda MD 20014 Office: Otis Bldg 810 18th St NW Washington DC 20006

BILLINGSLEY, PATRICK P., educator; b. Sioux Falls, S.D., May 3, 1925; s. Paul Raymond and Frances (Bulot) B.; B.S. in Elec. Engring., U.S. Naval Acad., 1948; M.A. in Math., Princeton, 1952, Ph.D., 1955; m. Ruth Newberry Thomas, Sept. 26, 1953; children—Frances, Patricia, Julia, Martha, Paul. Mem. faculty U. Chgo., 1958—, prof. statistics and math., 1967—. Served with USN, 1948- 57. Fellow Inst. Math. Statistics; mem. Am. Math. Soc. Author papers and books in field. Home: 5630 Kimbark Av Chicago IL 60637 Office: Univ Chicago Chicago IL 60637

BILLINGTON, DAVID PERKINS, educator, civil engr.; b. Bryn Mawr, Pa., June 1, 1927; s. Nelson and Jane (Coolbaugh) B.; B.S. in Engring., Princeton, 1950; postgrad. (Fulbright fellow) U. Louvain, 1950-51, U. Ghent, 1951-52 (both Belgium); m. Phyllis Bergquist, Aug. 26, 1951; children—David Perkins, Elizabeth N., Jane N., Philip N., Stephen N., Sarah L. Structural engr. Roberts & Schaefer Co., N.Y.C., 1952- 60; vis. lectr. Princeton, 1958-60, asso. prof., 1960-64, prof. civil engring., 1964—. Mem. U.S. delegation to observe concrete and prestressed concrete engring., USSR, 1958. NSF Sci. Faculty fellow, Delft, 1966-67. Registered profl. engr., N.Y., N.J. Mem. Am. Soc. C.E., Am. Contrete Inst., Prestressed Concrete Inst., Internat. Assn. Shell Structures, Internat. Assn. Bridge and Structural Engring., Princeton Engring. Assn., Sibma Xi. Republican. Episcopalian. Author: Thin Shell Concrete Structures, 1965; research and design publs. in field. Home: 109 Broadmead Princeton NJ 08540

BILLINGTON, JAMES HADLEY, historian, educator; b. Bryn Mawr, Pa., June 1, 1929; s. Nelson and Jane (Coolbaugh) B.; B.A., Princeton, 1950; D.Phil. (Rhodes scholar), Oxford (Eng.) U., 1953; m. Marjorie Anne Brennan, June 22, 1957; children—Susan Gilbert, Anne Holmes, James Hadley, Thomas Keator. Instr. history Harvard, Cambridge, Mass., 1957-58, asst. prof., research fellow Russian Research Center, 1958-61; Fulbright prof., Helsinki, Finland, 1960-61; Guggenheim fellow, 1960-61; Hodder fellow Council Humanities, Princeton, 1961-62, asso. prof. history, 1962-64, prof., 1964—; guest lectr. U. Leningrad (USSR), 1961, 65, Moscow, 1965; guest research prof. Inst. History, Moscow, 1966-67. Served with AUS, 1953-56. Mem. Council Fgn. Relations, P.E.N., Assn. Am. Rhodes Scholars (dir.), Am. Assn. Advancement Slavic Studies (dir., vice chmn. bd. fgn. scholarships), Phi Beta Kappa. Episcopalian. Author: Mikhailovsky and Russian Populism, 1958; The Icon and the Axe: An Interpretive History of Russian Culture, 1966. Home: 6 McCosh Cirlce Princeton NJ 08540

BILLINGTON, RAY ALLEN, historian; b. Bay City, Mich., Sept. 28, 1903; s. Cecil and Nina (Allen) B.; Ph.B., U. Wis., 1926; M.A., U. Mich., 1927; Ph.D., Harvard, 1933; M.A., Oxford U., 1953; Litt.D., Bowling Green U., 1958, U. Redlands, 1965; LL.D. (hon.), Park Coll., 1961, Occidental Coll., 1969, U. Toledo, 1970; L.H.D., Northwestern U., 1971; m. Mabel R. Crotty, Sept. 6, 1928; children—Anne, Allen. Instr., asst. prof. history Clark U., 1931-37; asst. prof. Smith Coll., 1937-38, asso. prof., 1938-44, prof., 1944; prof. history Northwestern U., 1944-49, William Smith Mason prof. history, 1949-63; sr. research asso. Huntington Library, 1963—; Harmsworth prof. Am. history Oxford U., 1953. Guggenheim Meml. fellow, 1943-44; Schouler lectr. Johns Hopkins, 1944; Taft lectr. U. Cin., 1954; Blazer lectr. U. Ky., 1960. Hist. editor Dryden Press, 1949-56, Rinehart and Co., 1956-60; hist. cons. Ency. Americana, 1962-69. Trustee Newberry Library, Westerners Internat., Occidental Coll.; bd. dirs. Social Sci. Research Council. Mem. Am. Studies Assn. (pres. 1959-61), Am. Hist. Assn., Orgn. Am. Historians (pres. 1962- 63), Hist. Assn. Eng. and Wales (hon.), Hist. Soc. So. Cal., Agrl. History Soc., Econ., So., Western (pres. 1962-63) history assns., Phi Beta Kappa, Phi Beta Kappa Assos., Hermitage Frat., Sigma Delta Chi. Author: The Protestant Crusade, 1938; Westward Expansion, 1949; American History Since 1865, 1950; American History Before 1877, 1951; The Far Western Frontier, 1830-1860, 1956; Historians' Contribution to Anglo-American Misunderstanding, 1966; America's Frontier Heritage, 1966; Genesis of Frontier Thesis, 1971; articles. Co-author: The United States, American Democracy in World Perspective, 1947; The Making of American Democracy, 1950. Editor: The Jours. of Charlotte L. Forten, 1953; The Westward Movement in the United States, 1959; Frontier and Section, 1961; The Frontier Thesis, 1966; The Reinterpretation of Early American History, 1966; America's Frontier Story, 1969; Dear Lady: The Letters of Frederick Jackson Turner and Alice Forbes Perkins Hooper, 1970; Histories of American Frontiers series, 1962—. Bd. editors Am. Heritage, 1959-62, Ariz. and West, 1959—, Am. West, 1962—, America: History and Life, 1964—, Pacific Historian, 1965—, Western Historical Quar., 1970—. Home: 2375 Lombardy Rd San Marino CA 91108 Office: Huntington Library San Marino CA 91108 ☆

BILLMAN, CARL, assn. exec.; b. Winchester, Mass., June 23, 1913; s. Christopher Lewis and Lilian (Livermore) B.; A.B., Harvard, 1935, M.A., 1936. Asst. in history Harvard, 1937-41; instr. St. Marks Sch., 1941-42; tariffs and schedules analyst Am. Airlines, Inc., 1942-46; asst. sec. United Chpts. of Phi Beta Kappa, 1946-47, exec. sec., 1947—. Office: 1811 Q St NW Washington DC 20009

BILLMAN, JOHN HENRY, educator, chemist; b. Bklyn., Feb. 8, 1912; s. Frederick and Marie (Van Schoonhoven) B.; B.S., U. Va., 1934; A.M., Princeton, 1935, Ph.D., 1938; m. Nannie Belle

Humphries, Aug. 16, 1937; children—Betty V., William F. Mem. faculty U. Ill., 1937-39; prof. chemistry Ind. U., Bloomington, 1939—; vis. prof. U. Wis., 1946, Yale, 1946, U. Del., 1958. Cons. numerous indsl. firms; responsible investigator OSRD; mem. pharmacology endocrinology fellowship panel Dept. Health. Sr. fellow USPHS, 1959-60. Fellow Ind. Acad. Sci.; mem. Am. Chem. Soc., Sigma Xi, Alpha Chi Sigma, Phi Lambda Upsilon, Alpha Epsilon Delta. Author: Methods of Synthesis in Organic Chemistry, 1954. Contbr. numerous articles to profl. jours. Research in areas of catalysis, spl. reducing agts., synthesis of amino acids, metal chelating agts., field of medicinal chemistry. Home: 910 S Dunn St Bloomington IN 47401

BILLMEYER, FRED WALLACE, Jr., educator, chemist; b. Chattanooga, Aug. 24, 1919; s. Fred W. and Eleanor (Salmon) B.; B.S., Cal. Inst. Tech., 1941; Ph.D., Cornell U., 1945; m. Annette M. Trzcinski, Aug. 4, 1951; children—Fred S., Eleanor A., Dean W., David M. With plastics dept. E.I. du Pont de Nemours & Co., 1945-64; lectr. high polymers dept. chemistry U. Del., 1951-64; vis. prof. chem. engring. Mass. Inst. Tech., 1960-61; prof. analytical chemistry Rensselaer Poly. Inst., 1964—. Cons. com. colorimetry Internat. Commn. Illumination (CIE), 1964—; mem. U.S. Nat. Com. CIE, 1968—. Trustee Munsell Color Found. Fellow Am. Phys. Soc., Optical Soc. Am.; mem. Am. Chem. Soc., N.Y. Soc. Paint Tech., Soc. Plastics Engrs., Am. Assn. Textile Chem. Colorists, Inter-Soc. Color Council (pres. 1968-70, sec. 1970—), A.A.A.S., Am. Soc. Testing and Materials, Sigma Xi, Phi Kappa Phi. Author: Textbook of Polmer Chemistry, 1957; Textbook of Polymer Science, 1961, 2d edit., 1971; (with Max Saltzman) Principles of Color Technology, 1966; also articles. Asso. editor Jour. Color and Appearance, 1971—; adv. bd. series Macromolecular Revs., 1965—; editorial adviser Optical Spectra, 1967—. Home: 2121 Union St Schenectady NY 12309 Office: Rensselaer Poly Inst Troy NY 12181

BILLOCK, WILLIAM BYRON, oil co. exec.; b. Pitts., July 7, 1911; s. John and Julia (Conick) B.; B.S., U. Pitts., 1933; LL.B., Duquesne U., 1938; m. Florence Berg, Jan. 12, 1946; 1 son, William Byron. With Gulf Oil Corp., 1934—, v.p., 1961—. Admitted to Pa. bar, 1942. Mem. ILO adv. council to U.S. C. of C. Bd. dirs., Foremanship Found., Rehab. Center, Jr. Achievement S.W. Pa. Served with USNR, 1942-46; ETO, PTO. Mem. C. of C. Greater Pitts., Pitts. Conv. and Visitors Bur. (mem. bd.), Am. Petroleum Inst. (chmn. ILO com.), Pitts. Personnel Assn., Pa. Bar Assn., Beta Gamma Sigma, Sigma Alpha Epsilon. Mason. Clubs: Duquesne, Pittsburgh Field, 525 (Pitts.). Home: 3024 Swansea Crescent W Allison Park PA 15101 Office: Gulf Bldg Pittsburgh PA 15230

BILLOTTE, PIERRE, govt. ofcl.; b. Mar. 8, 1906; ed. Ecole Militaire de Saint-Cyr. Mil. rep. Free France in Moscow, 1941-42; chief staff to Gen. de Gaulle, London, 1942-44; comdr. brigade under Gen. Leclerc, 1944; asst. gen. chief staff nat. def., 1945-46; French mil. rep to UN, 1946-50; ret., 1950; mem. Chamber of Deps., 1951-55, 62- -; minister nat. def. and armed forces, 1955; rep. of France on various UN coms., 1955-62; v.p. U.N.R. group in Nat. Assembly, 1962—; minister of state for overseas depts. and territories, 1966; mayor of Creteil, 1965. Decorated comdr. Legion of Honor; Compagon de la Liberation. Home: 39 Blvd du Commandant-Charcot 92 Neuilly-sur-Seine France Office: Nationale Assemblee Paris 7 France*

BILLS, MARK WHITEZEL, ednl. adminstr.; b. Alexandria, Ind., Nov. 22, 1902; s. Fred Aaron and Grace (Whitezel) B.; A.B., DePauw U., 1923; postgrad. U. Ill., summer 1924; Mus.B., U. Mich., 1935, Ph.D., 1945; D.H.L., Bradley U., 1962; m. Jeanetta McWethy, June 6, 1923; children—Robert N., Mary Ann (Mrs. William Trapp); m. 2d, Sara McEwen, Dec. 22, 1939; 1 son, Mark McEwen. Dir. athletics Levinson High Sch., Noblesville, Ind., 1923-24, Central High Sch., Ft. Wayne, Ind., 1924-27, North Side High Sch., 1927- 33; profl. concert, radio, opera singer, Phila., N.Y.C., 1935-38; head voice dept., dir. Men's Glee Club, U. Mo., 1938-41; instr. voice dept. U. Mich., 1941-43, lectr. grad. sch., 1943-45, instr. extension div. grad. sch., 1945; dean Flint (Mich.) Jr. Coll., 1945-46; supt. schs., Flint, Mich., 1946-52, Kansas City, 1952-55, Peoria, Ill., 1955—. Vis. prof. Mich. State Coll., summers 1948, 1950, Purdue U., summer 1951, Central State Tchrs., College, Mich., summer 1952. Mem. Kansas City Safety Council, Council Social Agys., Mental Health Found. Bd. dirs. Kansas City Area council Boy Scouts Am., Peoria Y.M.C.A., Kansas City Inst. Art, Philharmonic Orch.; adv. bd. adult edn. U. Ill.; trustee Eureka Coll. Recipient Service award Amvets, 1959. Member Peoria C. of C., N.E.A., Am. Assn. Sch. Adminstrs., Am. Ednl. Research Assn., Am. Assn. Sch. Bus. Ofcls., Ill. Tchrs. Assn., Ill. Assn. Bus. Ofcls., Lambda Chi Alpha, Phi Delta Kappa, Kappa Delta Pi. Elk, Rotarian, Mason (K.T., Scottish Rite, Shriner). Club: Advertising. Home: 1524 W Barker Av Peoria IL 61606

BILLS, ROBERT EDGAR, educator; b. Nutley, N.J., Dec. 15, 1916; s. Willis Minard and Leah (Condit) B.; B.S., Western Ky. U., 1938; M.A., U. Ky., 1946; Ed.D., Columbia, 1948; m. Annie Tartleton Carley, Dec. 22, 1944; children—Mary Ann, Leah Catherine. Sci. tchr., Breathitt County Bd. Edn., Jackson, Ky., 1938-42; sci. tchr. Anchorage (Ky.) Bd. Edn., 1943-44, prin., 1944-45; critic tchr. sci. U. Ky. Coll. Edn., 1945-46, faculty Coll. Arts and Scis., 1948-56, asso. prof. psychology, 1948-56, chmn. div. biol. scis., 1950-51; grad. asst. Columbia Tchrs. Cll., 1947-48; vis. summer prof. U. Fla., 1952, 53; cons. sch. plant planning Mich. State U., summer 1956; prof. psychology, chmn. dept. Auburn U., 1956-61; vis. summer prof. U. Wash., 1963; prof. ednl. psychology U. Ala., 1961-69, asst. dean for research, 1961-63, interim dean Coll. Edn., 1963-65, dean, 1965-69, research prof. edn., 1969—; cons. in field, 1948. Chmn. Ky. Bd. Examiners Psychologists, 1954-56; pres. Ky. Psychol. Assn., 1952-53; mem. council psychol. resources of South, So. Regional Edn. Bd., 1953-56; bd. dirs. Southeastern Ednl. Corp., 1966- 67; scholar Clemson U. Lecture Series, 1967; sec. Ala. Coalition for Better Edn., 1969-70, pres., 1971-72. Served with AUS, 1942-43. Fellow Am. Psychol. Assn. (chmn. membership com. div. teaching, psychology 1958-61, 61-62, sec.-treas. 1963-66), A.A.A.S.; mem. Am. Edn. Research Assn., Ala., Southeastern psychol. assns., Nat., Ala. edn. assns., Assn. Supervision and Curriculum Devel. (bd. dirs. 1962-64), Phi Delta Kappa, Kappa Delta Pi, Psi Chi. Author numerous articles, revs., bulls. in field. Home: 73 Woodland Hills Tuscaloosa AL 35401

BILLUPS, FREDERICK HARDING, gas co. exec.; b. Norfolk, Va., Apr. 13, 1903; s. Charles Elmo and Elizabeth Allison (Borden) B.; B.S., Va. Poly. Inst., 1925; m. Marian Louise Porter, Mar. 13, 1934; children—Elizabeth Allison (Mrs. Nicholson), Frederick Harding. Asst. auditor Inglesby-Patterson S.S. Co., Norfolk, Va., 1920-21; in coal and shipping bus., 1925-28; service sta. attendant Standard Oil Co. N.J., 1928, Norfolk dist. mgr., 1928- 36, staff mem., later managerial positions Va., 1936-43, marketing operations for U.S. Co., N.Y.C., 1943-46; marketing adviser affiliated cos., Europe, No. Africa, Near East, Latin Am. Standard Oil Co. (N.J.), 1946-50, N.A. and S.A., 1950-51, apptd. to implement merger several affiliates, pres., dir. Esso Standard Oil S.A., Havana, Cuba, 1951-54; chmn. pres., chief exec. officer Tropical Gas Co., Inc., Coral Gables, Fla., also pres., chief exec. officer Tropigas, Inc. Fla., subsidiary Compania Cubana Toda Onda. S.A., affiliated cos.; pres. Industrias Magic-Gas de Cuba. S.A.; pres., chmn. bd. Southeastern Natural Gas Corp., Miami, 1958—; pres. Standard Oil Co. Portugal, 1948-51; dir. Standard Francais de Petroles, Paris, France, 1948-50; Ancon Ins. Co., Balboa Ins. Co., Havana, 1st Nat. Bank Miami, Exec. Jet Aviation, Inc., Columbus, O. Mem. exec. bd. Boy Scouts Am.; bd. govs. Dade Found.; mem. Fla. Council 100, Orlando; treas. Orange Bowl Com., Miami; trustee United Fund Dade County; past chmn., dir. Dade County chpt. A.R.C. Asso. ofcl. capacity Petroleum Adminstr. for War, Va., 1941-45. Mem. Am. Petroleum Inst., Greater Miami (bd. govs.), Fla. (dir.) chambers commerce, Pan-Am. Soc., N.Y. So. Soc. Democrat. Episcopalian. Clubs: Athletic (N.Y.C.); Havana Yacht, Country, American (Havana); Riviera Country (past pres., gov.), Coral Gables Country, Century (past pres., gov.) (Coral Gables); Kiwanis; Bath, Miami, Committee of 100 (v.p., dir.) (Miami Beach, Fla.); Biscayne Bay Miami, Country of Miami, Coral Reef Yacht (Miami, Fla.). Home: 8805 Arvida Dr Coral Gables FL 33156

BILSKY, MANUEL, educator; b. Bklyn., Mar. 25, 1910; s. Harry and Minnie (Haber) B.; M.A., U. Mich., 1947, Ph.D., 1951. Asst. prof. U. Chgo., 1949-58; asso. prof. Roosevelt U., Chgo., 1958-60; prof. philosophy Eastern Mich. U., 1960—, also chmn. dept. Served to 1st lt. AUS, 1942-46. Mem. Am. Philos. Assn. Author: Logic and Effective Argument, 1956; Patterns of Argument, 1963; (with H.G. Duffield) Tolstoy and the Critics, 1965; also articles, book revs. Home: 1820 Alhambra St Ann Arbor, MI 48103 Office: Eastern Mich Univ Ypsilanti MI 48197

BILSON, BRUCE, television dir.; b. Bklyn., May 19, 1928; s. George and Hattie (Dratwa) B.; B.A. in Theatre Arts, U. Cal. at Los Angeles, 1950; m. Mona Weichman, Aug. 31, 1955; children—Daniel, Julie. Film editor Groucho Marx show, 1953-54; asst. dir. various TV shows, 1954-64; asso. producer CBS-TV, 1964-65; dir., 1965—; TV credits include Get Smart, Hogan's Heroes, Doris Day Show, Bewitched, Gidget, Patty Duke Show, Please Don't Eat the Daisies, Love American Style. Founder Sponsors for Ednl. Opportunities, Los Angeles. Served with USAF, 1951-53. Recipient Emmy award for outstanding directorial achievement in comedy, 1968. Mem. Dirs. Guild Am. (dir.), Nat. Acad. TV Arts and Scis. Home: 16968 Encino Hills Dr Encino CA 91316 Office: care Shapiro-Lichtman Artists Mgrs 116 N Robertson Blvd Los Angeles CA 90048

BILTZ, NORMAN HENRY, realtor, cattle raiser; b. Bridgeport, Conn., July 6, 1902; s. Charles F. and Lucie B. (Kingman) B.; student Peekskill Mil. Acad., 1920; m. Esther J. Auchincloss, June 2, 1930; children—Jeanne A. (Mrs. William L. McLaughlin), Sheila (Mrs. Biltz O'Brien), Esther A. (Mrs. Paul Langham). Pres., dir. Greenridge Mgmt. Corp.; partner Red Rock Ranch, Ltd., Heizer-Biltz Exploration; v.p. Nevada Properties Corp., Donner Lake Utility Co.; dir. Donner Lake Devel. Co. Elk. Clubs: Bohemian (San Francisco); Prospectors (Reno). Home: 125 Greenridge Dr Reno NV 89502 Office: 103 Mill St Reno NV 89501

BIMROSE, ARTHUR SYLVANUS, Jr., editorial cartoonist; b. Spokane, Mar. 18, 1912; s. Arthur Sylvanus and Jane E. (Lee) B.; student San Francisco Art Inst. Coll., 1931; U. Ore., 1933; m. Olga Radilovich, Sept. 4, 1937; 1 son, Jack Joseph. Free-lance comml. artist, 1934-37; staff artist The Oregonian, Portland, 1937-49, editorial cartoonist, 1949—; cartoon rep. permanent collections State Hist. Soc. Mo., Wayne State U., Library of Congress. Served with AUS, World War II. Recipient Freedoms Found. award, 1952, 61, 65. Mem. Assn. Am. Editorial Cartoonists, Sigma Alpha Epsilon. Home: 1632 SW Westwood Ct Portland OR 97201 Office: 1320 SW Broadway Portland OR 97201

BIMSON, CARL ALFRED, former banker; b. Berthoud, Colo., Mar. 15, 1900; s. Alfred George and Margaret (Eichman) B.; M.E., Colo. A. & M. Coll., 1923; m. Irene M. Hildreth, Oct. 25, 1927. With Mt. States Tel. & Tel. Co., 1924-30, dist. cashier, Colorado Springs, Colo., dist. sales supr. Pueblo; real estate, investment, property mgmt. Denver, 1931-32; with Valley Nat. Bank, Phoenix, since 1933, mgr. installment loan dept., 1936-39, asst. v.p., 1939-40, v.p., 1940-49, exec. v.p., 1949-53, pres., 1953-62, vice chmn. bd., chmn. exec. com., 1962-70, dir., 1941-70; pres. Concho Investment Co., Concho Ins. Co.; mem. exec com., asst. sec. Valley Nat. Ins. Co. Mgr. Financial relations F.H.A., Ariz., 1934-36. Dir. Sun Angel Found., Maricopa County Better Bus. Bur. (past pres.), Municipal Indsl. Devel. Corp., Mchts. and Mfrs. Credit Bur.; dir. Maricopa County Chpt. A.R.C.; v.p., dir., mem. adv. com. Phoenix YMCA; past pres. Phoenix Credit Bur.; mem. Phoenix Growth Com; chmn. finance com. Maricopa County Planning Com.; mem. adv. council Ariz. Bus.-Industry-Edn. Council; v.p., mem. bd. Jr. Achievement Met. Phoenix; mem. board exec. com. Phoenix Devel. Assn. Recipient degree Hon. State Farmer, Future Farmers of America; Significant Sig award Sigma Chi, 1963. Mem. Future Farmers America (v.p. 1959, pres. 1960, mgmt., adminstrv., govt. borrowing coms.), Ariz. (past pres.), Am. (past pres.) bankers assns., Nat. Assn. Better Bus. Burs. (past mem. bd. of govs.), Financial Pub. Relations Assn. (third v.p.), Phoenix Clearing House Assn. (past pres.), Nat. Retail Credit Men's Assn. (past dir.), Robert Morris Assos., U.S. (finance com.), Phoenix (past pres.) C.'s of C., Phoenix Thunderbirds, Sigma Chi. Clubs: Kiwanis, Country (Phoenix); Paradise Valley Country, Kiva, Arizona. Contbr. articles trade jours. Home: 5221 N Saddle Rock Dr Phoenix AZ 85018 Office: Valley Nat. Bank Phoenix AZ 85036

BIMSON, EARL LEE, banker; b. Evanston, Ill., May 17, 1921; s. Walter R. and Florence (Early) B.; student Mass. Inst. Tech., 1939-41; m. Betty C. Guilfoyle, May 3, 1946; children—Pamela Lee, Earl Lee, Mark Lee. Tool designer Douglas Aircraft, Long Beach, Cal., 1941, Santa Monica, 1941-42; tool designer, tool project engr. Goodyear Aircraft Corp., Litchfield Park, Ariz., 1942-43, supr. modification machine shop, 1943-44, mgr. modification exptl. dept., 1944-45; long range trainee Valley Nat. Bank, Phoenix, 1946-49, asst. auditor, 1950-53, asst. auditor personnel and tng., 1950-53, comptroller, 1954-60, controller, v.p., 1960-63, exec. v.p., 1963-67, pres., 1967—. Mem. staff Nat. Assn. Bank Auditors and Controllers, Madison, Wis., 1958-64; trustee Nat. Assn. Bank Auditors and Controllers Research Inst., 1961-64; mem. planning com. Corpora-Phoenix, 1959-68; mem. ednl. council Mass. Inst. Tech., 1955—. Chmn. fund drive United Fund, Phoenix, 1960, pres. bd. dirs., 1961. Trustee Orme Sch., 1963-68. Served with USNR, 1945-46. Mem. Phoenix C. of C., Phoenix Thunderbirds, Ariz. Zool. Soc. (pres. bd. dirs.), Financial Execs. Inst. (chpt. pres. 1963-64, nat. dir. 1964—), Bank Adminstrn. Inst. (v.p. 1967-68, pres. 1968-69),. Clubs: Phoenix Country, Kiva (Phoenix). Home: 3303 E Manor Dr Phoenix AZ 85014 Office: 141 N Central Av Phoenix AZ 85001

BIMSON, WALTER REED, banker; b. Berthoud, Colo., Apr. 25, 1892; s. A.G. and Margaret (Eichman) B.; student U. Colo., U. Chgo.; LL.D., Ariz. State U., 1957; L.H.D., U. Ariz., 1965; m. 1917; children—Lloyd Alfred (dec. 1967), Earl Lee; m. 2d, Nancy Johnson, Jan. 21, 1938; 1 dau., Vicki (Mrs. Aaron Rosenberg); m. 3d, Isabel Sclater, July 2, 1970. With Berthoud (Colo.) Nat. Bank, 1912-16, Harris Trust & Savs. Bank, Chgo., 1920-33; pres. Valley Nat. Bank, Phoenix, 1933-53, chmn. bd., 1953-70, chmn. emeritus, 1971—; pres. Arizona Bancorp., 1953-63, now dir.; dir. Allison Steel Co., Bagdad Copper Co. Bd. dirs. Am. Inst. Fgn. Trade. Served with USN, 1917-18. Mem. Phoenix Fine Arts Assn. (chmn.), Assn. Applied Solar Energy (dir.). Clubs: Arizona, Phoenix Country, Paradise Valley Country, Kiva. Home: 23 Biltmore Estates Phoenix AZ 85036 Office: Valley Nat Bank Phoenix AZ 85003

BINDA, H. JEFFREY, govt. ofcl.; b. Boston, July 10, 1920; s. Paul-Jean Hubert and Margaret Ellen (Hayes) B.; student Duke U., 1943-44; B.S., M.S. with honors, Georgetown U., 1958; m. Margaret Anne Smith, Mar. 29, 1959; 1 dau., Hilary Janine; children by earlier marriage—Marc Christian Jeffrey, Solange Carinne Dominique. Mem. faculty dept. English and linguistics Georgetown U., 1955-58; lectr. in Russian, Am. U., 1959-60, head dept. Russian, 1960-61; vis. lectr. Boston U. Sch. African Research and Studies, 1961; vis. prof. English and linguistics U. Lovanium, Republic of Congo, 1962-66; cons. internat. edn. to U.S. Govt., North Africa and Asia, 1959; dir. U.S. Govt. internat. edn. programs, Guinea and Republic of Congo, 1960-66; exec. asst. to dir. VISTA, 1966-70; sr. adviser Office Econ. Opportunity, 1970—. Served to capt. USMCR, 1942-55; ETO, PTO, CBI. Mem. Linguistic Soc. Am., Am. Assn. Tchrs. Slavic and East European Langs., Am. Assn. Advancement Slavic Studies, Nat. Assn. Fgn. Student Advisers. Club: Internat. (Washington). Author-editor 66 textbooks in 13 fgn. langs. for use in teaching fgn. langs. in U.S., fgn. countries, 1958-62. Home: 308 N Pitt St Alexandria VA 22314 Office: Office Econ Opportunity 1200 19th St NW Washington DC 20506

BINDER, DAVID, fgn. corr. N.Y. Times, N.Y.C. Office: New York Times 229 W 43d St New York City NY 10036*

BINDER, FREDERICK MOORE, coll. pres., b. Atlantic City, Nov. 18, 1920; s. Paul Reginald and Kathryn (Moore) B.; B.A., Ursinus Coll., 1942, LL.D., 1960; M.A., U. Pa., 1948, Ph.D., 1955; Litt.D., Wagner Coll; 1964; L.H.D., Rider coll., 1967; Pd.D., Susquehanna U., 1969; m. Grace Irene Brandt, May 27, 1943; children—Janet Karen, and Roberta Lynn. Tchr., Somerville (N.J.) High Sch., 1946; asst. registrar Temple U., 1946-47, dept. history, 1947-55; dean, asso. prof. history Thiel Coll., 1955-57, acad. v.p. prof. history, 1957- 59, acting pres., 1959; pres. Hartwick Coll., 1959-69; asso. commr. for higher edn. N.Y. State Edn. Dept. 1969-70, pres. Whittier (Cal.) Coll., 1970—. Mem. N.Y. State Regents Exams. Bd., 1962-68; treas. Ind. Coll. Fund Assn., 1965; chmn. Ind. Coll. Funds. Am., 1966-67. Served at lt. (j.g.) USNR, 1942-45, lt. comdr., 1954-. Recipient Newcomen award for contbn. to cause of material history Newcomen Soc. in N. Am., 1955; Fulbright lectr. in Yugoslavia, 1967-68. Mem. Newcomen Soc., Pa. Acad. Deans (chmn. 1959), Am. Hist. Assn., Orgn. Am. Historians, Am. Assn. U. Profs., Empire State Found. for Ind. Liberal Arts Colls. (chmn. 1962-63), Phi Alpha Theta, Alpha Chi Rho (nat. scholarship officer 1957-59). Lutheran. Kiwanian. Contbr. book revs. and articles profl. publs. Address: Office of President Whittier College Whittier CA 90608

BINDER, HEROLD KULL, freight co. exec.; b. Newark, Sept. 7, 1902; s. Albert and Emma (Kull) B.; ed. pub. schs.; m. Helena Marie Allen, June 20, 1928; children—Barbara (Mrs. Robert Mehlin), Janet (Mrs. Richard Hurd). Clk., then chief accountant Universal Carloading & Distbg. Co., N.Y.C., 1924- 38, dir., 1960—; with U.S. Freight Co., N.Y.C., 1938-71, treas., 1961- 67, v.p., 1967-71; dir. Western Carloading Co., Inc., Stor Dor Forwarding Co., Mcht. Shippers, Internat. Forwarding Co., Internat. Expediters, Inc., Universal Transcontinental Corp., Pioneer Carloading Co., Pacific Forwarding Co., Western Freight Assn., Caribbean Transp., Miami Terminal Transport Co., Universal Terminal Warehouse Co., Colonial Warehouse Co., Westcartage Co., Inc., Wescar Terminal Co., Robertson Drayage Co., Pioneer Car Co., Custom Cartage Co., Lasham Cartage Co., Western Terminal Co., Empire Freight Co., Universal Air Freight Corp. Home: 4 Brantwood Terrace Short Hills NJ 07078 Office: 711 3d Av New York City NY 00017

BINDER, LEONARD, educator; b. Boston, Aug. 20, 1927; s. Morris and Mollie (Winer) B.; B.A., Harvard, 1952, Ph.D., 1956; postgrad. Princeton, 1952-53, Oxford U., 1953-54; m. Yona Shander, June 29, 1947; children—Naava, Guyora. Asst. prof. U. Cal. at Los Angeles, 1956-60; asso. prof. U. Chgo., 1961-64, prof., 1965—, chmn. dept. polit. sci., 1964-67. Dir. Center for Comparative Study Polit. Devel.; mem. Social Sci. Research Council Com. on Comparative Politics. Served with AUS, 1945-46. Ford Found. fellow, 1953-56, Rockefeller fellow, 1960-61, Social Sci. Research Council fellow, 1958-59, fellow Center for Advanced Study in Behavioral Scis., 1967-68. Fellow Middle East Inst.; founding mem. Middle East Studies Assn. Author: Religion and Politics in Pakistan, 1961; Iran, Political Development in a Changing Society, 1962; The Ideological Revolution in the Middle East, 1964. Editor: Politics in Lebanon, 1966. Home: 5512 S Harper St Chicago IL 60637

BINDER, RAYMOND CHARLES, educator; b. Chgo., July 25, 1907; s. Robert Edwin and Theresa (Schindler) B.; B.S., Mass. Inst. Tech., 1939; M.S., Cal. Inst. Tech., 1933, Ph.D., 1936, m. Elizabeth Biggs Timberlake, Aug. 18, 1937; 1 dau., Carol. With Met. Water Dist So. Cal., 1933-36; instr. mech. engring. Purdue U., 1936-37, asst. prof., 1937-40, asso. prof., 1940-44, prof. mech. engring., 1944-59; prof. mech. engring. U. So. Cal., Los Angeles, 1960—; coordinated instrn. and research in fluid mechanics at Purdue U. for other agys., 1944-59; cons. for Navy Missile Center, Point Mugo, Ca. Fellow Am. Soc. M.E. (meters com.), Inst. Aero. Scis., Am. Soc. Engring. Edn., Sigma Xi, Tau Beta Pi, Pi Tau Sigma. Author: An Introduction to Fluid Dynamics and Fluid Machinery, 1951; Mechanics of The Roller Chain Drive, 1956; Advanced Fluid Mechanics, Vol. I & II, 1958. Contbr. Jour. Applied Mechanics, Jour. Engring. Edn., Jour. of Franklin Inst., Machine Design, Power, Product Engring., other sci. publs. Home: 2711 Manning Av Los Angeles CA 90064

BINFORD, CHAPMAN HUNTER, physician; b. Darlington Heights, Va., Oct. 3, 1900; s. Charles F. and W. Ava (Chilton) B.; A.B., Hampden-Sydney Coll., 1923, D.Sc. (hon.), 1962; M.D., Med. Coll. Va., 1929; m. Thelma Lynette Beauchamp, June 8, 1929; children—Charles C., M. Lynette. Commd. officer USPHS, 1930, med. dir., 1948; cancer investigator Harvard Med. Sch., 1931-32; with Leprosy Research Inst., Honolulu, 1933-36; pathology investigations NIH, 1936- 37; pathologist USPHS hosps., 1937-51; rep. USPHS at Armed Forces Inst. Pathology, Washington, 1951-60; ret., 1960, chief geog. pathology Leonard Wood Meml. Leprosy Research Lab., 1960-62, med. dir. Leonard Wood Meml. (Am. Leprosy Found.), also chief spl. mycobacterial diseases br. Armed Forces Inst. Pathology, 1963—. Registrar for leprosy Am. Registry Pathology, 1951—; expert com. leprosy WHO, 1964—; chmn. U.S. coordinating com. Internat. Com. Socs. Pathology, 1966-69. Diplomate Am. Bd. Pathology. Mem. Wash. Soc. Pathologists (pres. 1954-55), Coll. Am. Pathologists, A.M.A., Am. Assn. Pathologists and Bacteriologists, Am. Soc. Clin. Pathologists, Internat. Acad. Patholgoy (pres. 1958-59, rep. to internat. intersoc. com. pathology 1962-70, editor bull. 1960- 65), Internat. Leprosy Assn. (v.p. for Ams. 1968—), Am. Soc. Tropical Medicine and Hygiene, Societe Belge De Medecine Tropicale (asso.), Phi Beta Kappa, Alpha Omega Alpha. Author: (with Emmons and Utz) Medical Mycology, 1970; also numerous articles. Home: 6046 N 23d St Arlington VA 22205 Office: 1200 18th St NW Washington DC 20036

BING, KURT, educator; b. Cologne, Germany, Apr. 30, 1914; s. Adolf and Alice (Isaacson) B.; M.S., Hebrew U., 1946; Ph.D., Harvard, 1953; m. Patricia Ross Smith, June 26, 1952; children—Thomas Abraham, Andrew Daniel. Came to U.S., 1949, naturalized, 1955. Teaching fellow Harvard, 1950-52; asso. math. U. Cal., Berkeley, 1952-53; asst. prof. math. Rensselaer Poly. Inst., Troy, N.Y., 1953-56, asso. prof. math., 1956-62, prof. math., 1962—. Served with Brit. Army, 1941-46. Mem. Am. Math. Soc., Assn. Symbolic Logic, Math. Assn. Am., Fedn. Am. Scientists, Am. Assn. U. Profs., Sigma Xi. Research in math. logic. Home: 22 Kuhl Blvd Troy NY 12180

BING, R.H., educator, mathematician; b. Oakwood, Tex., Oct. 20, 1914; s. Rupert Henry and Lula May (Thompson) B.; B.S., S.W. Tex. State Tchrs. Coll., 1935; M.Ed., U. Tex., 1938, Ph.D., 1945; m. Mary Blanche Hobbs, Aug. 26, 1938; children—Robert H., Susan Elizabeth, Virginia Gay, Mary Patricia. High sch. tchr., Tex., 1935-42; instr., then asst. prof. math. U. Tex., 1942-46; faculty U. Wis., 1947—, prof. math., 1952—, chmn. dept., 1958- 60; acting prof. U. Va., 1949-50; vis. prof. U. Tex., 1971-72; dir. Summer Inst. on Set Theoretic Topology, Madison, Wis., 1955; mem. Inst. Advanced Study, Princeton, 1957-58, 62-63, 67. Mem. Nat. Sci. Bd., 1968—; chmn. div. math. Nat. Acad. Acad. Scis. - NRC, 1967-69. Mem. Conf. Bd. Math. Sci. (chmn. 1965-66), Nat. Acad. Scis., Math. Assn. Am. (pres. 1963-64, vis. lectr. 1954-55, 61-62, chmn. Wis. sect. 1952), Am. Math. Soc. (councilor 1952-54, 58-60, v.p. 1967-68), A.A.A.S. (v.p., chmn. sect. A, 1959), Pi Mu Epsilon (vice dir. gen. 1960-63). Presbyn. (elder). Home: 3509 Blackhawk Dr Madison WI 53705

BING, RUDOLF, opera mgr.; b. Vienna, Austria, Jan. 9, 1902; s. Ernest and Stefanie (Hoenigsvald) B.; student schs. in Vienna; Mus.D. (hon.), Lafayette Coll.; L.H.D., Temple U., Wagner Coll., Dickinson Coll., N.Y. U.; LL.D., Jacksonville U.; m. Nina Schelemskaya, Dec. 7, 1929; naturalized British subject, 1946; came to U.S., 1949. Connected with operatic and concert agencies and opera houses, Germany, 1921-33; gen. mgr. Glyndebourne Festival, Eng., 1934-49; artistic dir. Edinburgh Internat. Festival, 1947-49; gen. mgr. Met. Opera Assn., N.Y.C., 1950-72. Decorated comdr. Order Brit. Empire; chevalier Legion of Honor; comdr.'s cross Order of Merit (Germany); Grand Silver medal Honor (Austria); grand officer Order Merit (Italy). Office: Metropolitan Opera Assn New York City NY 10023

BINGAY, JAMES SCLATER, life ins. co. exec.; b. Seattle, Oct. 10, 1919; s. Pierson Livingston and Janet Gibson (Sclater) B.; B.A., U. Wash., 1942; grad. advanced mgmt. program Harvard, 1960; m. Margaret Anita Blackstock, Mar. 4, 1942; children—James Sclater, Janis Lynn. With Mut. Life Ins. Co. N.Y., N.Y.C., 1945—, v.p. sales, 1962-63, sr. v.p., 1963-67, exec. v.p., 1967—. Mem. Life Ins. Agy. Mgmt. Assn., Agy. Officers Round Table, Life Underwriters Assn. N.Y.C., Sales Execs. Club N.Y.C., Theta Chi. Clubs: Innis Arden Country (Old Greenwich, Conn.); Metropolitan (N.Y.C.); Washington Athletic (Seattle). Home: Colonial Lane Riverside CT 06878 Office: 1740 Broadway New York City NY 10019

BINGAY, WOOLSEY, banker; b. Seattle, Jan. 26, 1916; s. Pierson L. and Janet (Sclater) B.; B.A. in Bus. Adminstrn., U. Wash., 1939; B.A. in Accounting Pacific Coast Banking Sch., 1958, certificate completion, 1962; m. Wilma C. Loeffler, May 30, 1942; children—Richard W., Charles P., Marybeth J. Purser, Puget Sound Navigation Co., Seattle, 1936-38; with People Nat. Bank Wash., Seattle, 1939—, sr. v.p., 1961—. Active various community fund drives. Served to capt. AUS, 1942-45; ETO. Decorated Bronze Star. Mem. Am. Inst. Banking, Theta Chi. Episcopalian (past officer). Club: Washington Athletic (Seattle). Home: 4309 N E 87th St Seattle WA 98115 Office: 1414 4th Av Seattle WA 98111

BINGER, CARL A.L., psychiatrist; b. Long Branch, N.J., Aug. 26, 1889; s. Gustav and Frances (Newgass) B.; A.B., Harvard, 1910, M.D. cum laude, 1914; m. Clarinda Garrison, June 3, 1926; children—David G., Beatrice, Katherine G. Austin teaching fellow, lectr. on history sci. Harvard, 1914; study, tng., research, 1914-33; asst. attending physician N.Y. Hosp., 1933-47, asso. attending psychiatrist, 1947-54; asst. prof. clin. med. in psychiatry Cornell U. Med. Coll. and later asst. prof. clin. psychiatry, 1933-47, asso. prof., 1947-54; cons. psychiatrist Med. Dept. Radcliffe Coll., 1954—; hon. cons. Harvard U. Health Services, 1964—; vis. prof. psychiatry U. Cin. Med. Coll., 1956-68; ednl. cons. Psychiat. Tng. Faculty of Mass., 1956-58; spl. cons. psychiat. unit Peter Bent Brigham Hosp., Boston; lectr. psychiatry Harvard Med. School, Boston, 1954-56; vis. psychiatrist Mass. Gen. Hosp., 1954-58, hon. physician, 1958—; with rehab. clinic Payne Whitney Clinic, 1943-46; cons. Selective Service System, 1943-46; cons. neuropsychiatry VA, 1955-56; rev. editor Psychosomatic Medicine, 1945-47, editor-in-chief, 1947-62, mem. editorial bd., 1962—; dir. Mary Conover Mellon Fund for Advancement of Edn. at Vassar Coll., 1949-51; chmn. com. to study neuropsychiat. problems in Tb, VA. Served as 1st lt. M.C. (A.E.F.), U.S. Base Hosp. No. 6, 1917-19. Awarded citation by Gen. Pershing, Purple Heart; Order of St. Geoge (Greece); Mil. medal of Greece. Diplomate Am. Bd. Internal Medicine, Am. Bd. Neurology and Psychiatry. Fellow A.M.A., Am. Acad. Arts and Scis., N.Y. Acad. Medicine, Am. Psychiat. Assn.; mem. Internat. Congress on Mental Health, Internat. Com. Mental Hygiene to WHO (mem. interim governing bd., exec. com.), Nat. Com. for Mental Hygiene (bd. dirs., del. to Internat. Congress on Mental Health, Eng., Aug. 1948, gave opening address Congress 1948), Mental Health Film Bd. (pres. 1952), Am., Mass. psychoanalytic assns., Mass. Med. Soc. Clin. Investigation, Assn. Psychoanalytic Med. Assn. (pres. 1943-44), Am. Psychosomatic Soc. (pres. 1963-64), Group Advancement Psychiatry (ex-chmn. com. on pub. edn.), Harvey Soc., Am. Legion, Alpha Omega. Clubs: Harvard, Century Assn. (N.Y.C.); Sakonnet Yacht. Author: The Doctor's Job, 1945 (winner Norton award 1945); Personality in Arterial Hypertension (monograph, with others), 1945; More About Psychiatry, 1949; Revolutionary Doctor, Benjamin Rush 1746-1813, 1966; The Two Faces of Medicine, 1966; Thomas Jefferson, a Well-Tempered Mind, 1970; also sci. popular articles Address: 21 Lowell St Cambridge MA 02138

BINGER, JAMES HENRY, mfr., lawyer; b. Mpls., May 16, 1916; s. Henry E. and Vida E. (DeBar) B.; A.B., Yale, 1938; LL.B., U. Minn., 1941; m. Virginia E. McKnight, June 24, 1939; children—James McKnight, Cynthia, Judith. Admitted to Minn. bar, 1941; asso. Fletcher, Dorsey, Barker, Colman & Barber, Mpls., 1941-43; joined Honeywell, Inc. (formerly known as Mpls.-Honeywell Regulator Co.), 1943, asst. sec., 1945-46, asst. v.p., 1946-50, v.p., gen. mgr. valve div., Phila., 1950-55, co. v.p., 1952-61, pres., 1961-65, chmn. bd., 1965—, chief exec. officer, 1964—, dir., 1959—; dir. N.W. Airlines, Inc., Northwestern Bell Telephone Co., Northwest Bancorp. Mem. Order of Coif, Phi Delta Phi. Clubs: Woodhill Country (Wayzata, Minn.); Minneapolis; Gulfstream Bath and Tennis (Delray Beach, Fla.); Everglades (Palm Beach, Fla.). Home: 2511 Crosby Rd Wayzata MN 55391

BINGHAM, ALBERT YOUNG, portfolio mgr.; b. Chgo.; s. Horace W. and Amy M. (Young) B.; A.B., U. Ill.; m. Helen M. Worst, 1932; children—Poppy (Mrs. Quattlebaum), Albert Y. II. Asso. Continental Ill. Nat. Bank & Trust Co., 1927-36; with Walter P. Murphy, 1936-42; financial v.p. Chgo. Title & Trust Co., 1942-67, chmn. finance com., 1968-69, dir., 1954—; chmn. exec. com. Halsey, Stuart & Co., 1968-69, dir., 1967—; dir. Am. Ins. Co., 1960-69, Nat. Survey Corp., 1960-69, Transatlantic Reins. Co., 1960-69. Life-term trustee Highland Park Hosp.; bd. dirs. Sarah Hackett Stevenson Meml. Home. Founder Financial Analysts Fedn. (former dir.), Investment Soc. Chgo. (pres. 1946-47). Republican. Clubs: Zeta Psi, University, Chicago, Attic, Commercial (Chgo.). Home: 331 Sheridan Rd Winnetka IL 60093 Office: 111 W Washington St Chicago IL 60602

BINGHAM, BARRY, editor; b. Louisville, Feb. 10, 1906; s. Robert Worth and Eleanor (Miller) B.; student Middlesex Sch., Concord, Mass., 1921-23; A.B. magna cum laude, Harvard, 1928; LL.D., U. Ky., Kenyon Coll., Center Coll.; Litt.D., U. Louisville, U. Cin.; m. Mary Clifford Caperton, June 9, 1931; children—Worth (dec.), Barry, Sarah (Mrs. Michael Iovenko), Jonathan (dec.), Eleanor. With Courier-Jour. and Louisville Times Co., 1930—, successively reporter, sec., asso. pub., pub., 1930-45, editor, pub., 1945-71; chmn. bd., 1971—; chmn. bd. WHAS, Inc., Standard Gravure Corp. Chmn. bd. Historic Homes Found.; trustee Berea Coll., Pine Mountain Settlement Sch.; overseer U. Louisville; dir. Asia Found.; chmn. Internat. Press Inst., 1964-66; chmn. adv. bd. Am. Press Inst., 1963-68, now mem.; mem. adv. bd. on Pulitzer Prizes, 1956-68. Chief of mission to France, ECA, 1949-50. Nat. chmn. Vols. for Stevenson-Kefauver; 1956. Served to comdr. USNR, 1941-45; ETO, PTO. Decorated comdr. Order Brit. Empire, comdr. Legion of Honor; recipient Sullivan award, U. Ky. Mem. Sigma Delta Chi (hon. nat. chmn.). Democrat. Episcopalian. Clubs: Pendennis, River Valley, Wynn-Stay, Louisville Country (Louisville), Century Assn. Home: Glenview KY 40025 Office: Courier-Journal and Times Louisville KY 40202

BINGHAM, CURTIS HARRY, investment banker; b. Rockford, Ill., Nov. 3, 1898; s. Charles and Lola (Curtis) B.; B.S., Ore State Coll., 1921; m. Mary Decker, Aug. 12, 1922; children—Mary Jane, Charles, Richard. With Bateman Eichler, Hill Richards, Inc. (formerly Bingham, Walter & Hurry, Inc.), Los Angeles, 1933—, pres., 1933—, chmn. exec. com., 1966—, also dir. Bd. dirs. Travelers Aid of Los Angeles, Soc. for Prevention Cruelty to Animals. Mem. Nat. Assn. Securities Dealers (gov.), Investment Bankers Assn. Am. (gov.; chmn. Cal. group; past pres.). Club: Bond (Los Angeles, past pres.). Home: 1811 Spruce St South Pasadena CA 91030 Office: 460 S Spring St Los Angeles CA 90013

BINGHAM, GEORGE BARRY, see Bingham, Barry.

BINGHAM, JAMES LYMAN, ret. assn. exec.; b. Brookfield, Mo., Feb. 25, 1892; s. Lyman and Carrie Elizabeth (Van Brunt) B.; A.B., U. Denver, 1916; m. Helen Hess Wright, Aug. 20, 1919; children—Barbara Ann, Betty Jean. Instr. Loveland (Colo.) High Sch., 1916-17; dir. athletics U. Denver, 1919-30; asst. to pres. Amateur Athletic Union U.S., Chgo., 1930-50. Served as lt. F.A., U.S. Army, 1917-18, Gen. mgr. track and field athletics Olympic Games Los Angeles, 1932; sec. sport com. Chgo. Centry of Progress; mem. adv. com. N.Y. World's Fair; chef de mission and asst. treas. U.S. Winter Olympic Team, St. Moritz, Switzerland, also London, 1948, asst. treas., gen. gen. mgr., Oslo Norway, 1952; gen. mgr. U.S. Olympic Team, Helsinki, Finland, 1952. Exec. dir. U.S. Olympic Assn., 1950-65; dir. fund raising U.S. Olympic Com., 1966-68; gen. mgr. U.S. Team, 1st Pan-Am. Games, Buenos Aires, 1951; gen. mgr. U.S. Team II Pan-Am. Games, Mexico City, 1955, Olympic winter games, Cortina, Italy, 1956, Melbourne, Australia, 1956, U.S. Team III, Pan Am. Games, Chgo., 1959, U.S. Olympic Team, Rome, Italy, 1960, Pan Am. Games, Sao Paulo Brazil, 1963, Winter Olympic Games, Innsbruck, Austria, 1964; chef de mission Games of XVIII Olympiad, Tokyo, Japan, 1964. Mem. Sigma Phi Epsilon. Republican. Baptist. Mason (Shriner). Home: 247 Coachlight Sq Montrose NY 10548 Office: 57 Park Av New York City NY 10016

BINGHAM, JONATHAN BREWSTER, congressman; b. New Haven, Apr. 24, 1914; s. Hiram and Alfreda (Mitchell) B.; student Groton Sch.; B.A., Yale, 1936. LL.B., 1939; m. June Rossbach, Sept. 20, 1939; children—Sherrell (Mrs. James E. Bland), June Mitchell (Mrs. Erik Esselstyn), Timothy Woodbridge, Claudia Rossbach (Mrs. Hall). Admitted to N.Y. State bar, 1940, practiced in N.Y.C., 1939-41, 46-51, 53-54, 59-61; with O.P.A., 1941-42; chief Alien Enemy Control Sect., Dept. State, 1945-46, asst. dir. Office Internat. Security Affairs, 1951, dep. adminstr. Tech. Coop. (Point Four), 1951-53; mem. firm Goldwater & Flynn, 1959-61; sec. to gov. N.Y. State, 1955-58; U.S. rep. in UN Trusteeship Council, 1961-62, pres., 1962, prin. adviser to U.S. rep. (amb.) to UN on colonial and trusteeship questions, 1961-62; U.S. rep. UN Econ. and Social Council, 1962-63, also alternate rep. 15th-18th Gen. Assemblies; mem. U.S. Mission UN, 1961-64; mem. 89th-92d congresses from 23rd N.Y. Dist. Pres. Bronx County Soc. Mental Health, 1960-62. Mem. and past pres. Bronx Boys Club; trustee 20th Century Fund; mem. bd. Scholarship Edn. and Def. Fund for Racial Equality. Served from pvt. to capt., U.S. Army, 1943-45. Fellow Yale Corp., 1949-51. Recipient Staff citation, War Dept., 1945. Mem. Am. N.Y. State, Bronx County bar assns., Assn. Bar City of N.Y., Council Fgn. Relations N.Y.C. Club: Century Assn. (N.Y.C.). Author of: Shirt Sleeve Diplomacy-Point 4 in Action, 1954; (with Alfred M. Bingham) Violence and Democracy, 1970; also articles. Home: 5000 Independence Av Bronx NY 10471 Office: House Office Bldg Washington DC 20515

BINGHAM, MARY CAPERTON, (Mrs. Barry Bingham), newspaper exec.; b. Richmond, Va., Dec. 24, 1904; d. Clifford R. and Helena (Lefroy) Caperton; B.A., Radcliffe Coll., 1928; postgrad. (Charles Eliot Norton fellow) Am. Sch. Classical Studies, Athens, 1929; D.Litt., U. Louisville, 1954; m. Barry Bingham, June 9, 1931; children—Robert W. (dec.), G. Barry, Sarah M. (Mrs. Michael Iovenico), Jonathan W. (dec.), Eleanor M. Vice pres., dir. Courier-Jour., Louisville Times, WHAS, Inc., 1942—; editor World of Books column Louisville Courier Jour., 1943-67; v.p. Louisville Courier-Jour. Times, 1942—. Mem. library services com. Nat. Book Com., 1956-57; pres. Council Basic Edn., Washington. Trustee Radcliffe Coll., 1942-60; mem. bd. Nat. Associated Councils of Arts. Mem. Colonial Dames. Clubs: River Valley, Louisville Country (Louisville); Cosmopolitan (N.Y.C.); Glenview Garden. Home: Glenview KY 40025 Office: 525 W Broadway Louisville KY 4202

BINGHAM, ROBERT, mag. editor; b. Lima, O., Apr. 10, 1925; s. Rankin and Miriam (Kamerer) B.; grad. Phillips Exeter Acad., 1943; A.B. cum laude, Harvard, 1948; m. Janet McPhedran, May 13, 1950; children—Thomas, Anne, Peter. With Time mag., 1948; with The Reporter mag., 1948-64, mng. editor, 1957-64; mem. editorial staff New Yorker mag., 1965—. Served with AUS, 1943-36. Home: 25 Bradley St Dobbs Ferry NY 10522

BINGHAM, WOODBRIDGE, educator; b. Cambridge, Mass., Nov. 24, 1901; s. Hiram and Alfreda (Mitchell) B.; A.B., Yale, 1924; A.M., Harvard, 1929; Ph.D., U. Cal., 1934; m. Ursula W. Griswold, June 28, 1928; children—Anne (Mrs. Richard N. Pierson, Jr.), Clarissa (Mrs. James S. Junge), Evelyn (Mrs. Richard S. Prosser), Marian (Mrs. William B. Hubbell, Jr.). Instr., Yale-in-China, Chang-sha, China, 1924-25; instr. Far Eastern history U. Cal., 1937-40, asst. prof., 1940-46, asso. prof., 1946-52, prof., 1952-69, prof. emeritus, 1969—, dir. Inst. East Asiatic Studies, 1949-57. Vis. prof. Centre of Asian studies, U. Hong Kong, 1970-71. Mem. Nat. Com. U.S.-China Relations. Served as lt. USNR, 1943-45. Mem. Assn. Asian Studies, Am. Hist. Assn., Am. Oriental Soc., Psi Upsilon. Club: University (N.Y.C., San Francisco). Author: The Founding of the T'ang Dynasty: The Fall of Sui and Rise of T'ang, 1941; (with Hilary Conroy, Frank W. Ikle) History of Asia, vol. I: Formation of Civilizations from Antiquity to 1600, 1964, vol. II, Old Empires, Western Penetration and the Rise of New Nations, since 1600, 1965. Home: 27 Tamalpais Rd Berkeley CA 94708

BINION, RUDOLPH, educator, historian; b. N.Y.C., Jan. 18, 1927; s. Stephen Rudolph and May (Bunimowitz) B.; B.A., Columbia, 1945; diplôme Inst. d'Etudes Politiques, Paris, France, 1949; Ph.D., Columbia, 1958; m. Alice Lemée Lemée Aug. 30, 1952. Statis. asst. UNESCO, Paris, France, 1950-53; instr. Rutgers U., 1955-56, Mass. Inst. Tech., 1956-59; asst. prof., then asso. prof. Columbia, 1959-67; prof. history Brandeis U., Waltham, Mass., 1967—. Served with AUS, 1945-46. Recipient Clarke F. Ansley award Columbia, 1958; George Louis Beer prize Am. Hist. Assn., 1960. Author: Defeated Leaders, 1960; Frau Lou, 1968. Home: 62 Pinckery St Boston MA 02114 Office: Brandeis Univ Waltham MA 02154

BINION, WILLIE CLAYTE, Jr., newspaper editor; b. Houston, June 7, 1912; s. Willie Clayte and Mattie (Sayers) B.; student Southwestern U., Georgetown, Tex., 1929-31, Stephen F. Austin Coll., Nacogdoches, Tex., 1931-32, U. Tex., 1932-35; m. Sara Dell Newsom, Mar. 28, 1937; children—Clayte III, Jack Russell, Emma Lee (Mrs. David V. Wilson), Tommy Sayers. With Lufkin (Tex.) Daily News, 1937-42, 45-48, mng. editor, 1942, 47-48; mem. pub. relations dept. Jefferson Amusement Co., Beaumont, Tex., 1942-43; with sports copy desk Beaumont Enterprise, 1948-49; with Houston Chronicle, 1949—, mng. editor, 1965-71, exec. dir., 1971—, also dir. Pulitzer prize Juror Journalism Jury, 1969, 70. Mem. newspapers editors com. U. Tex. Served with USMCR, 1944-46; PTO. Mem. Nat., Tex. (pres. 1971) U.P.I. editors assns., Am. Soc. Newspaper Editors, Nat., Tex. A.P. (pres. 1969—), mng. editors assns., Harris County Hist. Soc., Houston C. of C., S.A.R., Sons of Republic of Tex., Kappa Sigma, Sigma Delta Chi. Methodist. Clubs: Houston, Yacht, Old Capitol. Pres. Farm and Ranch (Houston). Home: 5502 Pebble Springs St Houston TX 77040 Office: Houston Chronicle Travis St Houston TX 77001

BINKERD, GORDON WARE, composer; b. Lynch, Neb., May 22, 1916; s. Archie Abiijah and Verna Blanche (Jones) B.; Mus.B., S.D. Wesleyan U., 1937; Mus.M., U. Rochester, 1941; M.A., Harvard, 1952; m. Frances Patricia Walker, Sept. 11, 1942. Prof. music faculty U. Ill., 1949-71, asso. mem. Center Advanced Studies, 1963. Guggenheim fellow, 1959; recipient award Nat. Inst. Arts and Letters, 1964. Served with USNR, 1942-45. Mem. A.S.C.A.P. Composer: Symphony 1, 1955; Symphony 2 (commn. Fromm Mus. Found. 1957), 1957; Symphony 3, 1959; Symphony 4 (commn. St. Louis Symphony Orch. 1963), 1963; Sonata for Cello and Piano, 1952; String Quartet 1, 1958; String Quartet 2, 1961; Piano Sonata, 1955; Aspects of Jesus for double chorus (commn. Ford Found. 1964), 1964; also choral, organ, vocal solo and chamber music. Home: Rural Route 2 Urbana IL 61801

BINKERT, ALVIN JOHN, hosp. exec.; b. Ft. Atkinson, Wis., Oct. 20, 1910; s. John and Clara (Burrow) B.; B.A., U. Wis., 1931; m. Lucile Latton, June 4, 1939; children—Barbara L., Cynthia R. With Haskins & Sells, C.P.A.'s N.Y.C., 1931-41; comptroller Presbyn. Hosp., N.Y.C., 1941-48, asst. v.p., 1948- 54, v.p., gen. mgr., 1954-57, exec. v.p., 1957-70, pres., 1970—; lectr. pub. health, adminstrv. medicine Columbia, 1954—. Past bd. dirs. Asso. Hosp. Service. C.P.A., Wis., N.Y. Mem. Greater N.Y. Hosp. Assn. (past pres., bd. govs.), Hosp. Assn. N.Y. State (past pres., trustee, del.), Am. Coll. Hosp. Adminstrs. Clubs: Scarsdale (N.Y.) Golf; University (N.Y.C.). Home: 50 Grandview Blvd Yonkers NY 10710 Office: 622 W 168th St New York City NY 10032

BINKLEY, LUTHER JOHN, educator; b. Wernersville, Pa., Oct. 7, 1925; s. Harry Garfield and Jennie Theresa (Yoder) B.; A.B., Franklin and Marshall Coll., 1945; B.D., Lancaster Theol. Sem., 1947; Ph.D., Harvard, 1950; m. Betty Jane Bowman, June 5, 1964. Instr. philosophy Franklin and Marshall Coll., 1949-51; asst. prof., 1951-56, asso. prof., 1956-62, Elijah E. Kresge prof. philosophy and ethics, chmn. dept. philosophy, 1962—; ordained to ministry Evang. and Ref. Ch., 1949; vis. fellow Cambridge U., 1959-60, Princeton, 1967, 69; tchr. grad. courses Lancaster Theol. Sem., 1963-64, 67-68, Temple U., 1965—. Recipient Lindback Found. award for distinguished coll. teaching, 1962. Mem. Am. Assn. Univ. Profs. (pres. chpt. 1962-63), Am. Philos. Assn., Am. Soc. Aesthetics, Metaphys. Soc., Soc. Sci. Study Religion, Phi Beta Kappa (pres. Theta chpt. of Pa. 1970-71), Delta Sigma Phi, Pi Gamma Mu. Clubs: Lancaster Torch (pres. 1956-57); Fullerton (Bryn Mawr, Pa.). Author: The Mercersburg Theology, 1953; Contemporary Ethical Theories, 1961; Conflict of Ideals; Changing Values in Western Society, 1969. Home: 445 N President Av Lancaster PA 17603

BINKLEY, MAX ARTHUR, univ. adminstr.; b. Dayton, O., May 29, 1920; s. Arnold G. and Ruth (Hart) B.; B.S., Miami U., Oxford, O., 1942; M.S., U. Ill., 1947, Ph.D., 1953; m. Lois A. Akerstrom, Feb. 23, 1946; children—David, Janice, Sara. Instr. Miami U., 1945-46, U. Ill., 1946-50; auditor ECA, Western Germany, 1950- 52; staff accountant C F & I Steel Corp., Pueblo, 1953-61, divisional controller, 1962-65, controller, Denver, 1965-67; v.p. finance Colo. State U., Ft. Collins, 1968—. Chmn. budget com. Pueblo Single Fund, 1960-65. Mem. bus.-alumni adv. council U. Colo., 1966-67; chmn. family service budget com. Ft. Collins United Fund, 1971—. Served with USAAF, 1942-45. Republican. Methodist. Home: 1300 Stover St Fort Collins CO 80521

BINKLEY, OLIN TRIVETTE, clergymen, sem. pres.; b. Harmony, N.C., Aug. 4, 1908; s. Joseph and Minnie (Trivette) B.; A.B. magna cum laude, Wake Forest Coll., 1928; Th.B., So. Baptist Theol. Sem., 1930; D.D., Wake Forest (N.C.) Coll., 1951, U.N.C., 1964; B.D., Yale, 1931, Ph.D., 1933; m. Pauline Eichmann, Aug. 24, 1933; children—Pauline Edith, Janet Margaret. Ordained to ministry Bapt. Ch., 1928; asso. pastor Calvary Bapt. Ch., New Haven, 1931-33; pastor Chapel Hill (N.C.) Bapt. Ch., 1933-38; lectr. sociology U. N.C., 1937-38; head dept. religion Wake Forest Coll., 1938-44; asso. prof., acting head dept. ethics and sociology So. Bapt. Theol. Sem., 1944-46, prof., head dept., 1946-52; prof. Christian sociology and ethics Southeastern Bapt. Theol. Sem., 1952—, dean, 1958-63, pres., 1963—; vis. fellow Yale Divinity Sch., New Haven, 1951. Dir. Central Carolina Bank. Pres. N.C. Com. Social Service, 1957-58, recipient Social Service award, 1967. Pres. bd. mgrs. Louisville Children's Agy., 1948-50; trustee Ministry Studies Bd., Children's Homes Soc. N.C., Bapt. Children's Homes N.C., Meredith Coll. Mem. Am, Assn. Marriage Counselors, Am. Assn. Theol. Schs. (pres.; commn. research and counsel), Am. Sociol. Soc., So Bapt. Conv. (Christian life and social service commns.), Phi Beta Kappa. Clubs: Rotary (past pres.), Louisville Torch. Author: Frontiers for Christian Youth, 1942; From Victory Unto Victory, 1945; The Churches and the Social Conscience, 1948; How to Study the Bible, 1969. Home: Durham Rd Wake Forest NC 27587

BINNEY, ARTHUR FREMONT, research analyst; b. Big Rapids, Mich., Nov. 25, 1905; s. Rupert Fremont and Bessie Ruth (Westfall) B.; B.S., U.S. Naval Acad., 1928; postgrad. Harvard, 1936, Naval War Coll., 1951; LL.D., Ferris Inst., Big Rapids, Mich., 1962; m. Jean Elizabeth Shacklette, June 7, 1928; children—Douglas Craig, Elizabeth Jean (Mrs. Carol Sidney Hartley). Commd. 2d lt., USMC, 1928, designated naval aviator, 1930, advanced through grades to maj. gen., 1957; participated 2d Nicaraguan campaign, 1931-33, Central Pacific, World War II; naval attaché, C.A., 1945-48; dir. electronics div. Bur. Aero., Navy Dept., 1949-50; with 1st Marine Aircraft Wing, Korean campaign, 1951-52, comdg. gen., Western Pacific, 1956-57; comdg. gen. 2d Marine Aircraft Wing, Air Sta., Cherry Point, N.C., 1958-59; dir. Marine Corps Aviation, 1959-61, dep. comdr. Fleet Marine Force, Atlantic, 1961-63; ret., 1963; cons. Research Analysis Corp., McLean, Va., 1965-68, analyst, 1968—. Cons., Ins. for Def. Analysis. Clubs: Army and Navy, Army and Navy Country (Washington). Home: 2815 Cathedral Av NW Washington DC 20008 Office: Research Analysis Corp McLean VA 22101

BINNINGTON, ARTHUR A., lawyer; b. Toronto, Ont., Can., Nov. 6, 1931; B.Commerce, U. Toronto, 1953, LL.B., 1956. Admitted to Ont. bar, 1958; partner firm Tory, Tory, DesLauriers & Binnington, Toronto. Mem. Canadian Bar Assn. Office: 11 King St W Toronto Ontario Canada*

BINNION, JOHN EDWARD, educator; b. Paris, Tex., July 14, 1918; s. Roy Cecil and Johnnie Mary (Garner) B.; A.A., Chaffey Coll., Ontario, Cal., 1936; B.B.A., U. Tex., 1945; M.A., N.M. Highlands U., 1951; Ed.D., Okla. State U., 1953; m. Doris Lee Cambell, Mar. 30, 1945; children—Margaret Anne, John Edward II, Mary Virginia, Dianna Lee. Accountant, D & B Emsco Mfg. Co., Dallas, 1945-46; accountant, office mgr. Lumber Dealer's Supply Co., Long Beach, Cal., 1946-47; tchr. Sawyer (Kan.) High Sch., 1947-50; asst. prof. bus. edn. and bus. adminstrn., also supr. USAF clk.-typist program N.M. Highlands U., 1951-52; asso. prof. bus. edn. and accounting Southwestern State Coll., Weatherford, Okla., 1953-55; mem. faculty U. Denver, 1955-65, prof. bus. edn., chmn. dept. 1957-65; prof. bus. edn. charge grad. program bus. edn. Tex. Tech. U., Lubbock, 1965-68; nat. dir. edn.; edn. div. Lear Siegler Inc., 1968—. Textbook cons. U.S. Armed Forces Inst., 1955-68; text coordinator, profl. standards program Nat. Assn. Ednl. Secs., 1965-69; mem. Policies Commn. Bus. and Econ. Edn., 1962-66; commr. Accrediting Commn. Bus. Sch., 1963-69; mem. Colo. Adv. Com. Bus. Edn., 1955-65; mem. U.S. Office Edn. Adv. Council Insured Loans to Vocational Students, 1966-69; cons. Acad. Ednl. Devel., 1965-67, Ednl. Testing Service. Served to capt. AUS, 1940-44. Decorated Purple Heart. C.P.A., Okla., Tex. Mem. Adminstrv. Mgmt. Soc. (Merit award 1965), Mountain Plains Bus. Edn. Assn. (pres. 1964-65), N.E.A., Nat. Assn. Bus. Tchr. Edn. (sec. 1957-59), Am. Legion, Mil. Order of Purple Heart (nat. vice comdr. 1967- 69, nat. insp. 1970—), Am. Inst. C.P.A.'s Tex., Okla. Socs. C.P.A.'s, Inst. for Certifying Secretaries (mgmt. mem), Delta Pi Epsilon (nat. treas., 1958-61, nat. exec. secretary, 1962-66), Pi Omega Pi, Phi Beta Lambda, Alpha Kappa Psi, Beta Alpha Psi, Kappa Kappa Psi, Delta Tau Delta, Phi Delta Kappa. Democrat. Methodist. Author: Equipment Standards for Business Classrooms, 1954; Selected Authorities in Business Education, 1965. Co-author: College Accounting for Secretaries, 1971. Editor: Western Bus. Rev., 1958-62; Colo. Study Guides for Bus. Edn., 1957-65. Contbr. articles to profl. publs. Home: 3891 S Quebec St Denver CO 80237 Office: 1275 Sherman St Denver CO 80203

BINNS, JAMES EDWARD, banker; b. Alameda, Cal., Oct. 5, 1931; s. Guy Vivian and Beatrice (Jury) B.; student U. Nev., 1950-51; grad. Sch. Bank Audit and Control, U. Wis., 1963, Am. Inst. Banking, 1964; m. Marjean Friesen, Feb. 21, 1951; children—Cheryl Jean, Jana Lee, Lori LeAnn. With Sierra Pacific Power Co., Reno, 1948-50; with First Nat. Bank of Nev., Reno, 1951—, asst. cashier, 1957-63, asst. to cashier, 1963-65, auditor, 1965—, also asst. v.p., 1968—; instr. Am. Inst. Banking. Mem. Nat. Assn. Accountants, Am. Inst. Banking (past pres. Sierra Nev. chpt., past nat. asso. councilman), Bank Adminstrn. Inst. (chartered bank auditor), Data Processing Mgmt. Assn. (charter mem. Sierra-Nevada chpt., dir.), Reno (Nev.) Jr. C. of C. (past treas.). Mason. Club: Reno Toastmasters (past pres.). Home: 1720 Allen St Reno NV 89502 Office: PO Box 461 First and Virginia St Reno NV 89504

BINNS, JAMES HAZLETT, indsl. exec.; b. Salida, Colo., Dec. 23, 1912; s. Hazlett C. and May (Lacey) B.; A.B., U. Denver, 1934; m. Ruamie Hill, Dec. 29, 1936; 1 son, James Hazlett. Dir. placement and field work U. Denver, 1934-35; with Armstrong Cork Co., Lancaster, Pa., 1935—, successively sales trainee floor div., salesman floor div., Atlanta, acting dist. mgr., dist. mgr., asst. sales mgr., Lancaster, Pa., asst. gen. mgr. munitions div., asst. gen. sales mgr. floor div., gen. sales mgr., 1935-60, v.p., gen. mgr. floor and indsl. operations, 1961-62, sr. v.p., 1962-68, pres., 1968—, also dir.; dir. Campbell Soup Co. Mem. bldg. materials sub-council Nat. Indsl. Pollution Control Council. Bd. dirs. Lancaster Gen. Hosp., Lancaster Heart Assn. Mem. Pa. Soc. N.Y., Newcomen Soc. N. Am., Lancaster C. of C. (past dir.), Omicron Delta Kappa, Kappa Sigma. Presbyn. Clubs: Pinehurst (N.C.) Country; Lancaster Country, Hamilton (Lancaster); Skytop (Pa.); Economic of N.Y. Home: 111 Eshelman Rd Lancaster PA 17601 Office: Armstrong Cork Co Liberty and Charlotte Sts Lancaster PA 17604

BINSWANGER, HERBERT, psychiatrist; b. Kreuzlingen, Switzerland, Sept. 6, 1900; s. Robert and Marie Luise (Meyer) B.; fed. exam., Zurich, Switzerland, 1926; student surgery and internal medicine, Germany; m. Ruth Elisabeth Frick, 1932. Head Dr. Sanatorium Schloss Knonau, 1938-48; head Dr. Sanatorium Schlössli, Octwil, 1948-51; pvt. practice psychiatry, 1951—; mem. dept. psychiatry U. Zurich. Fellow Am. Acad. Psychoanalysis; mem. Swiss Psychol. Assn., Psychol. and Neurol. Assn. Zurich, Assn. Dr. Canton Zurich; corr. mem. German Psychoanalytical Assn. Author: Zur forensischen Psychiatrie nichtgeisteskranker Personen, 1941; Leitfaden der Forensischen Psychiatrie, 1948; Kurzes Lehrbuch der Psychiatrie, 1949; Der Objektverlust, 1957. Address: Im Düggel 5 8700 Küsnacht-Zurich Switzerland

BINSWANGER, MILLARD IRVING, glass co. exec.; b. Richmond, Va., July 2, 1908; s. Moses I. and Ada Ada (Binswanger) B.; B.S., U. Va., 1927; M.B.A., Harvard, 1929; m. Frances Weil, Nov. 14, 1933; children—Ann (Mrs. Richard S. Levinson), Millard Irving. With Binswanger Glass Co., Richmond, 1929—, chmn. bd., chief exec. exec. exec. officer, 1959—; chmn. bd. Hamilton of Ind., Inc., Vincennes, 1963—; dir. Central Nat. Bank, Richmond; adv. dir. Liberty Mut. Ins. Co., Richmond. Mem. bd. Robert E. Lee council Boy Scouts Am. Served to capt. USAAF, 1942-45. Recipient Thompson award of merit Flat Glass Jobbers Assn., 1952. Club: Jefferson-Lakeside (pres.), Richmond. Home: 7751 Riverside Dr Richmond, VA 23225. Office: 3300 W Leigh St Richmond VA 23230

BINTZER, HARRY RUSELL, mgmt. executive; b. Perkasie, Pa., Oct. 3, 1913; s. Harry O. and Viola M. (Weeks) B.; B.S., Drexel Inst. Tech., 1936, M.S., 1952; m. Helen Lichtfuss, July 3, 1938; 1 dau., Beverly. Coordinator, Fenn Coll., 1936- 38, Drexel Inst. Tech., 1938-42, asst. to pres., 1945-54; fund dir. Washington U., 1954-57; v.p. devel. Carnegie Inst. Tech., 1957- 66, Cal. Inst. Tech., Pasadena, 1966-68; pres. John Price Jones Co., N.Y.C., 1968—. Served with USNR, 1942-45. Recipient Alumni citation Drexel Inst. Tech., 1962. Mem. Am. Coll. Pub. Relations Assn. (trustee 1960—, pres. 1962-63), Am. Soc. Engring. Edn. (chmn. coop. edn. div. 1953-54, chmn. relations with industry div. 1957-58), Soc. Pa, Lambda Chi Alpha, Omicron Delta Kappa. Mason. Home: Scarborough Manor Scarborough NY 10510 Office: 30 E 42d St New York City NY 10017

BINZ, LEO, archbishop; b. Stockton, Ill., Oct. 31, 1900; s. Michael and Thecla (Reible) B.; student Loras Coll., Dubuque, Ia., 1914-18, LL.D., 1944; A.B., St. Mary's Sem., Baltimore, 1919, A.M., 1920; student Sulpician Sem., Washington, 1920-21, North Am. Coll., Rome, 1921-24; S.T.D., U. "de Propaganda Fide," Rome; Ph.D., Gregorian U., 1926; LL.D., St. Mary's College, Winona, Minn., 1948, St. Ambrose Coll., 1956, Creighton U., 1962; S.T.D., Pontificium Athenaeum Angelicum, Rome, 1956. Ordained priest, Roman Cath. Ch., Rome, Mar. 15, 1924; instr. N.A. Coll., Rome, 1924-26; asst. pastor St. Mary's Ch., Sterling, Ill., 1927- 28; sec. to Bishop of Rockford, Ill., 1928-29; chancellor, Diocese of Rockford, 1929-32; pastor St. Rita's Ch., Cherry Valley, Ill., 1929-32, St. Peter's Church, Rockford, 1932-33, St. James' Church, Belvidere, Ill., 1933-36; diocesan consultor, 1932-36; sec. to Apostolic Delegation, 1936-42; chaplain, St. Rose Sch., Washington, D.C., 1938-42; titular bishop of Pinara, coadjutor bishop of Winona, Minn., and apostolic adminstr. of Winona, 1942-49; titular archbishop of Silyum, Coadjutor to the archbishop of Dubuque, 1949-54, archbishop of Dubuque, 1954-61, St. Paul, 1961; asst. at the Pontifical Throne, 1954; pallium conferred, 1958, 62; consultor Commn. on Bishops and Govt. of Dioceses, 2d Vatican Council, 1962-65, mem. Post-Counciliar Commn. Bishops and Govt. of Dioceses, 1966; adminstrv. bd. Nat. Cath. Welfare Conf., 1963—. Episcopal chmn. dept. lay orgns., 1963-66. Address: 226 Summit Av St Paul MN 55102

BIOSSE DUPLAN, JACQUES, textile co. exec.; b. Paris, France, Aug. 14, 1914; s. Auguste and Elizabeth (Cartier-Bresson) B.-D.; diploma Ecole des Hautes Etudes Commerciales, Paris, 1934, diploma law U. Paris, 1934; m. Anne-Marie de Seze, Jan. 15, 1938; children—Guillaune, Jeanne-Marie (Comtesse d'Angosse-Mieulle), Pierre, Jean-Félix. Mem. bd. Thiriez & Cartier-Bresson, Paris, 1940-50, dep. chmn., 1950—; pres. Dollfus-Mieg & Cie, Paris, 1962—, chmn., 1968—; mem. bd. L'Union des Industries Textiles, France, 1970—. Served with French Army, 1934-35, 39-45. Decorated chevalier de l'Ordre National de la Legion d'Honneur. Home: 16 rue du Général-Foy Paris 8e 75 France Office: 86 Blvd Sébastopol Paris 3e 75 France

BIOW, MILTON H., bus. exec.; b. N.Y.C., July 24, 1892; s. Harry L. and Lena (Deckinger) B.; H.H.D., Wilberforce U., 1958; m. Sophie Taub, July 5, 1917; children—Richard M., Patricia; m. 2d, Melise Banning, Jan. 9, 1944. Advt. bus., 1917—; pres. The Biow Co., Inc., N.Y.C., 1918-53, chmn. bd., 1953—. Mem. Eisenhower's Com. Govt. Employment Policy. Recipient Cuban Cross, Carlos Finley Inst., 1942. Home: Mimosa Ridgefield CT 06877 Office: 375 Park Av New York City NY 10022

BIRBECK, HERBERT EVANS, educator; b. King City, Mo., Feb. 25, 1929; s. Verna Ray and Mary Ella (Evans) B.; A.B., Tarkio Coll., 1950; M.A., U. Mo., 1954; Ph.D., U. Ia., 1960; m. Marilyn Mildred Beerier, Aug. 25, 1957; children—Victoria Jean, Thomas Herbert, James Lester. Tchr., Oregon (Mo.) High Sch., 1950-51; dir. speech correction Ferguson-Florisant schs., St. Louis County, Mo., 1954-58; tchr. severely handicapped children Hosp. Sch., U. Ia., 1958-60; asst. prof. edn. Ida. State U., 1960-61; prof., chmn. dept. spl. edn. Mankato (Minn.) State Coll., 1961—. Bd. dirs. Christian Concern, Mankato Rehab. Center, Open Arms Day Activity Center, Minn. Council Exceptional Children. Served with AUS, 1951-53. Mem. Am. Psychol. Assn., Am. Assn. Mental Deficiency, Council Exceptional Children, N.E.A., Minn., Nat. assns. retarded children, Phi Delta Kappa. Rotarian. Author: Parental Attitudes in Familiers Where Cerebral Palsy is Present, 1960; Study of Day Activity Centers in Minnesota, 1964. Home: 1515 N Broad St Mankato MN 56001

BIRCH, ALBERT FRANCIS, educator; b. Washington, Aug. 22, 1903; s. George Albert and Mary Clayton (Hemmick) B.; B.S. in Elec. Engring., Harvard, 1924, M.A., 1929, Ph.D. (John Tyndall scholar 1928-31), 1931; student Univ. of Strasbourg, France (Am. Field Service fellow), 1926-28; m. Barbara Channing, July 15, 1933; children—Anne Campaspe, Francis Sylvanus, Mary Narcissa. Engr., N.Y. Telephone Co., 1924-26; instr., tutor physics Harvard, 1931-34, research asso. geophysics, 1932-37, asst. prof., 1937-43, asso. prof. 1943-46, prof., 1946—; on leave Mass. Inst. Tech. 1941-42. Sturgis-Hooper prof. geology, 1948. Served as lt. comdr. to comdr. USNR, 1924-45. Recipient Legion of Merit; Arthur L. Day medal Geol. Soc.; William Bowie medal Am. Geophys. Union, 1960; Nat. medal of sci. Fellow Royal Astron. Soc., Am. Phys. Soc., Am. Acad. Arts and Scis., Geol. Soc. Am. (pres. 1964); mem. Am. Geophys. Union, Seismol. Soc. Am., Nat. Acad. Sci., Am. Philos. Soc., Sigma Xi. Editor: Handbook of Physical Constants. Office: Dept Geology Harvard Univ Cambridge MA 02138

BIRCH, ARTHUR JOHN, educator; b. Sydney, Australia, Aug. 3, 1915; s. Arthur Spencer and Lily (Bailey) B.; M.Sc., Sydney U., 1938; D.Phil. (1851 Exhbn. scholar 1938- 41, research fellow 1941-48), Oxford U., 1948; Smithson fellow Royal Soc., Cambridge U., 1948-52; m. Jessie Williams, Oct. 21, 1948; children—Susan, Michael, Francis, Rosemary, Christopher. Prof. organic chemistry U. Sydney, 1952-55, U. Manchester, 1955-67; prof. organic chemistry Sch. Chemistry, Australian Nat. U., Canberra, Australia, 1967—, dean research, 1967-70. Recipient Fritzsche award Am. Chem. Soc., 1963. Fellow Australian Acad. Sci. (treas.), Royal Soc., Royal Inst. Chemistry. Author: How Chemistry Works, 1948. Author numerous research articles and papers. Office: Sch Chemistry Australian Nat U Canberra Australia

BIRCH, FRANK VICTOR, advt. and pub. relations exec., mfr.; b. Stevens Point, Wis., Dec. 14, 1894; s. Albert V. and Helen (Church) B.; A.B., U. Wis., 1918; m. Marion Yost, July 5, 1919 (div.); children—Frank Victor, John Richard, Thomas Merrill; m. 2d, Roa Kraft, Nov. 24, 1943. Newspaper editorial writer, 1913-18; editor The Badger, U. Wis., 1918; export advt. J. Roland Kay, 1919; copy dir. Klau-Van Pietersom-Dunlap, Inc., 1919-23, account exec., 1923-39, exec. v.p., 1935-51, pres., 1951-54, chmn. bd., 1954-57, chmn. spl. projects, 1957-60; pres., treas. Birch Kraft, Inc., Milw.; dir. Hilldale Shopping Center, Madison; v.p., sec. ROA's films, Milw., 1960—; dir. Green Bay Packers. Pres. U. Wis. Found., 1956-62, chmn. bd., 1962-66, hon. v.p., 1966—, mem. President's Club, 1966—; mem. Nat. Boys and Girls Week Com.; vice chmn. Milw Community Chest, 1956; bd. dirs. Milw. Civic Progress Commn. Served as 2d lt. USAAF, 1918. Decorated Carlos Manuel de Cespides (Cuba), 1938. Mem. Wis. Alumni Assn. (dir. 1938-39), Am. Legion, Acadia, Order of Good Time of N.S., Sigma Delta Chi, Beta Gamma Sigma. Presbyn. Mason (32). Clubs: University, National W. (pres. 1955-56), Advertising (pres. 1956-57), Milwaukee Press, Lions (pres. Milw. 1927-28, Wis. dist. gov. 1929-30, internat. dir. 1931-33, v.p. 1934-37, internat. pres. 1937-38; life dir. Milw.; chmn. pub. relations and publicity com. internat. 1958-68); Rosarians (Portland, Ore); Islamorada (Fla.) Fishing. Home: 1696 N Astor St Milwaukee WI 53202 Office: Birchkraft Bldg Milwaukee WI 53202

BIRCH, JACK WILLARD, psychologist; b. Glassport, Pa., Nov. 27, 1915; s. Samuel Rush and Anna (Zimmerman) B.; B.S., Cal. State Coll., 1937; M.Ed., Pa. State U., 1941; Ph.D., U. Pitts., 1951; m. Barbara Jane Roof, June 22, 1940; children—Dee Ann, Barbara Joan. Tchr. pub. schs., Berks and Miflin counties, Pa., 1937-41; psychologist county schs. and courts, supr. spl. edn., Somerset, Pa., 1941-48; dir. spl. edn., ednl. clinic Bd. Edn., Pitts., 1948-58; lectr. dept. psychology School Edn., U. Pitts., 1948—, now prof. psychology and spl. edn. and rehab., asso. dean Sch. Edn. Served from pvt. to 1st lt. AUS, 1943-46. Diplomate Am. Bd. Psychology. Fellow Am. Psychol. Assn. (ednl. and sch. Psychol. sects., mem. Thayer com.); mem. Pa. (chmn. clin. div.), Pitts. (pres. 1949) psychol. assns., Am. Assn. Mental Deficiency (regional chmn. coms. on psychology, edn., nomenclature and standards), N.E.A., N.Y. Acad. Sci., Council Exceptional Children (mem. governing bd., asso. editor Exceptional Children; pres.), Sigma Xi, Phi Delta Kappa. Presbyn. Clubs: University (Pitts.); Cosmos (Washington). Home: University Square 1 Pittsburgh PA 15213

BIRCH, JOSEPH DAVID, educator, psychologist; b. Cedar Rapids, Ia., Oct. 20, 1925; s. Joseph and Clara (Sundberg) B.; B.S., Ia. State Coll., 1948; M.A., State U. Ia., 1951, Ph.D., 1952; m. Dorothy Thomas, Nov. 22, 1950; children—Rebecca Jo, Thomas David. Mem. faculty U. Mich., 1952—, prof. psychology, 1963—, co-dir. lang. devel. program Center Human Growth and Devel., 1965-69. Mem. Psychonomic Soc., N.Y. Acad. Sci., Am. Psychol. Assn., Sigma Xi, Phi Kappa Phi. Author: Nebraska Symposium on Motivation, 1961; Motivation; A Study of Action, 1966; The Dynamics of Action, 1970. Home: 1701 Morton Av Ann Arbor MI 48104

BIRCHARD, GLEN ROBBINS, air force officer; b. Grand Rapids, Mich., Feb. 5, 1914; s. Glen R. and Lula Mae (Garrison) B.; A.B., Bay City (Mich.) Jr. Coll., 1934, U.S. Army A.C. Flying Sch., 1939, Air War Coll., 1953; m. Virginia Leigh Brooks, Jan. 11, 1941; children—Geoffrey Robbins, Christopher. Commd. 2d lt. USAAF, 1939, advanced through grades to lt. gen. USAF, 1966; comdr. 307th Bombardment Group, Solomon Islands, 1942-44; operations officer Berlin Airlift, 1948-49; dep. comdr. Airlift Force, Korea, 1950-51; comdr. 1707th Transp. Tng. Wing, 1951-52; staff officer Hdqrs. USAF, 1953-56; dep. chief staff operations Mil. Air Transp. Service, 1958-61; comdr. Western Transp. Air Force, 1961-63; vice comdr. Mil. Air Transport Service, 1963-66; comdr. in chief Hdqrs. Alaskan Command, Elmendorf AFB, Alaska, 1966-67. Decorated Legion of Merit with two oak leaf clusters, D.F.C., Air medal with 9 oak leaf cluster; Order Brit. Empire. Home: 1314 McKinley Av Bay City MI 48706

BIRCKHEAD, OLIVER WILLIAM, Jr., banker; b. Bklyn., June 20, 1922; s. Oliver William and Ethel G. (Hardy) B.; grad. Nichols Coll., Dudley, Mass., 1942, Stonier Grad Sch. Banking, 1955; m. Elizabeth Edwards Winzeler, June 28, 1947; children—Oliver William III, Randall E. With Peoples Nat. Bank, White Plains, N.Y., 1946; asst. nat. bank examiner, 1946-48; with Chem. Bank N.Y. Trust Co., 1948-51; with Central Trust Co., Cin., 1951—, exec. v.p., 1967-69, pres., 1969—, also dir.; v.p., dir. Central Bancorp.; dir. Union Central Life Ins. Co. Cin. Adv. bd. Cin. Salvation Army, Children's Dental Care Assn., Cin.; active United Fund Drives; treas. United Negro Coll. Fund. Served with USAAF, 1942-46. Mem. Assn. Res. City Bankers, Newcomen Soc., Greater Cin. C. of C. (treas., exec. com., dir.). Clubs: University, Tennis, Recess, Cin. Country, Commonnwealth, Ohio Valley Tennis Assn., Queen City (Cin.) Home: 3109 N Farmcrest Dr Cincinnati OH 45213 Office: Central Trust Co 4th and Vine Sts Cincinnati OH 45202

BIRD, DONALD ARTHUR, educator; b. Beloit, Wis., July 12, 1919; s. Arthur Roland and Grace Marie (Reimer) B.; student Beloit Coll., 1936-37; B.A., U. Wis., 1940, M.A., 1941, Ph.D., 1950; m. Rita Ann Marricco, Mar. 17, 1948 (dec. 1950). Instr. English, Ohio State U., 1946-49; mem. faculty U. Cal. at Los Angeles, 1949-56, asst. prof., 1950-56; mem. faculty Cal. State Coll. at Los Angeles, 1956—, prof. English, 1963—, dean grad. studies, 1964-67. Member Curriculum Commn., State of Cal. Recipient Outstanding Prof. award Cal. State Coll. at Los Angeles, 1964. Mem. Linguistic Soc. Am., Am. Dialect Soc., Mediaeval Acad. Am., Modern Lang. Assn., Nat. Council Tchrs. English, Am. Name Soc., Coll. English Assn. Democrat. Co- author: Patterns of Thinking and Writing, 1959; Your Language, book 5, 1960, book 6, 1962. Adv. bd. Am. Speech, 1965-66. Home: 1637 N Dillon St Los Angeles, CA 90026.

BIRD, FRANCIS MARION, lawyer; b. Comer, Ga., Sept, 4, 1902; s. Henry Madison and Minnie Lee (McConnell) B.; A.B., U. Ga., 1922, LL.B., 1924; LL.M., George Washington U., 1925; m. Mary Adair Howell, Jan. 10, 1935; children—Francis Marion, Mary Adair, Elizabeth Howell, George Arthur. Admitted to Ga. bar, 1924. D.C. bar, 1925, since practiced in Atlanta; with U.S. Senator Hoke Smith, 1925; pvt. practice, 1930-45; mem. firm Bird & Howell, 1945-49, Jones Bird & Howell, 1949—; served as part-time U.S. referee in bankruptcy, 1945-54; spl. asst. to atty. gen. as hearings officer Nat. Selective Service Act. Mem. commn. for preparation plan of govt. City of Atlanta and county area; mem. permanent rules com. Ga. Supreme Ct.; mem. Met. Atlanta Commn. Crime and Juvenile Delinquency, chmn., 1969-70; co-chmn. Tech.-Ga. Devel. Fund. Trustee Young Harris Coll., U. Ga. Fund., Atlanta Lawyers Found., Interdenominational Theol. Center; trustee, mem. exec. com. Emory U., Atlanta. Chmn. Ga. Bd. Bar Examiners, 1954-61. Recipient Distinguished Service citation U. Ga. Law Sch. Fellow Am. Bar Found; mem. Am. Judicature Soc. (bd. dirs.), Am. Law Inst. (council), Am., Ga. (past pres.), Atlanta (past pres.) bar assns., Assn. Bar City N.Y., Atlanta C. of C. (pres. 1957, dir. Atlanta Civic Service award 1957), U. Ga. Alumni Assn. (past pres., certificate of merit, 1952), George Washington U. Alumni (achievement award 1965), Phi Kappa Phi, Sigma Chi, Phi Delta Phi. Methodist. Kiwanian (dir. Atlanta). Clubs: Peachtree Golf, Atlanta Athletic (past pres.), Piedmont Driving (Atlanta); Capital City; Lawyers (past pres.); Augusta (Ga.) Nat. Golf. Mem. permanent editorial bd. Uniform Comml. Code. Home: 89 Brighton Rd NE Atlanta GA 30309 Office: Haas—Howell Bldg Atlanta GA 30303

BIRD, GEORGE LLOYD, ret. educator; b. Francisco, Ind., Aug. 29, 1900; s. George William and Ella (Caraway) B.; B.S., Allegheny Coll., 1922; A.B., U. Wis., 1923, M.A., 1925, Ph.D., 1937; postgrad. U. Fla., summers 1930, 34; m. Jeanne Pinard, Sept. 11, 1937 (dec. 1953); 1 son, Jon Pinard. Copyreader, reporter Tribune Republican, Meadville, Pa., summer 1923; head Warren bur. Youngstown (O.) Telegram, 1924, copyreader, 1925; copyreader New Bedford (Mass.) Eve. Standard, 1925; publicity dir. Lawrence Developing Co. and Bd. Trade, Keystone Heights, Fla., 1925-28; asst. to editor News-Herald of Franklin (Pa.), 1926-28; publicity dir. Fla. Chautauqua, 1926-28; prin. high sch., Keystone Heights, 1927-28; instr. journalism and English, dir. pub. relations, editor Alumni News, Bradley U., Peoria, Ill., 1928-29; dir. courses journalism, instr. asst. prof. DePauw U., Greencastle, Ind., 1929-33, dir. tri-weekly newspaper, exec. sec. press bd., 1929-32; lectr. journalism U. Wis., 1933-36; acting head dept. sociology U. Fla., summer 1935; research sociologist N.R.P.

Community Study, Brazil, Ind., 1936-37; asst. prof. Syracuse (N.Y.) U., 1937-41, asso. prof., 1941-45, prof. journalism, 1945-68, dir. div. grad. studies, 1940-63, prof. emeritus, 1968—; missionary journalist, 1969. Active in A.R.C. drive and Community Chest, 1941-53; mem. Natural Resources Council Onondago County, Fayetteville Planning Com.; mem., elder Christian and Missionary Alliance, 1965—. Bd. dirs. Limestone Creek Improvement Assn.; trustee Fayetteville Free Library. Mem. Am. Assn. Tchrs. Journalism, Am. Assn. U. Profs. (pres. Syracuse chpt. 1956- 57), Phi Beta Kappa, Sigma Delta Chi, Pi Delta Epsilon, Pi Kappa Delta, Alpha Kappa Delta, Phi Gamma Delta. Club: Faculty (Syracuse, N.Y.). Author: How Life Begins, 1935; Employment and Unemployment in a Depressed Labor Market; Brazil, Ind., 1937; Article Writing and Marketing, 1948, rev. edit., 1956; How to Go to College, 1951; Modern Article Writing, 1967; also articles and monographs. Co-author: The Newspaper and Society, 1942; The Press and Society, 1951. Contbr. to Christian Life, Ch. Herald, Christianity Today, Eternity. Home: 305 Elm St Fayetteville NY 13066

BIRD, GEORGE RICHMOND, educator; b. Bismarck, N.D., Jan. 25, 1925; s. George Francis and Mary Helen (Hoppin) B.; A.B., Harvard, 1949, A.M., 1952, Ph.D., 1953; m. Doris Elinor Forgue, June 12, 1948; children—George Peter, Elizabeth Newell, Margaret Allison. Asst. prof. chemistry Rice U., 1954-58; scientist, mgr. phys. chem. lab. Polaroid Corp., Cambridge, Mass., 1958-69; prof. chemistry Rutgers U., New Brunswick, N.J., 1969—, dir. Sch. Chemistry, 1971—. Served from pvt. to 1st lt., AUS, 1943-46. Fellow Soc. Photog. Scientists and Engrs., Optical Soc. Am.; mem. Am. Phys. Soc., Am. Chem. Soc. Inventor (with Maxfield Parrish, Jr.) wire grid optical polarizer; discoverer of collision-narrowing in optical spectrum of H. Home: 85 Red Hill Rd Princeton NJ 08540

BIRD, HORACE VIRGIL, naval officer; b. Ryan, Okla., June 16, 1912; s. Homer V. and Ellen (Jackson) B.; B.S., U.S. Naval Acad., 1933; grad. Naval War Coll.; m. Elsa Ruth Melhorn Feb. 15, 1936; 1 son, Richard Kent. Commd. ensign U. S. Navy, 1933, advanced through grades to rear adm., 1963; various assignments Atlantic Fleet to 1942; asst. dir. naval officer procurement, 1942-44; gunnery officer U.S.S. Missouri, 1944-45; charge arrangements for surrender ceremonies, Tokyo Bay, Sept. 2, 1945; spl. asst. to chief naval personnel for Congl. liaison, 1945-48; exec. officer U.S.S. Springfield, 1948-49; comdg. officer U.S.S. Rogers, 1949- 51; aide to Sec. Navy, 1951-53; chief staff Destroyer Flotilla Two, 1954- 55; comdr. Destroyer Squadron 22, 1955-57; chief staff Naval Force Philippines, 1957-59; dep. and chief staff to comdr. First Fleet, 1959- 61; naval aide to Vice Pres. U.S., 1961-62, chief legislative affairs Navy Dept., 1962-63; comdr. Cruiser Destroyer Flotilla 11, 1963-64; comdr. naval forces Marianas, comdr.-in-chief Pacific Rep. Mariana-Bonin Islands, 1964-67; comdr. mineforces Pacific, also comdr. U.S. Naval Base, Los Angeles, 1967—. Decorated Navy Commendation medal with 4 oak leaf clusters; Legion of Honor (P.I.), Legion of Merit. Clubs: Nat. Press, Nat. Aviation, Army-Navy Country (Washington); Army-Navy (Manila); Lakeside Country (Los Angeles); Virginia Country (Long Beach, Cal.). Author: Don't Tread on Me, 1954; also short stories and articles for mags. Home: 3824 Del Mar Av San Diego CA Office: Internat Food Research Box 514 Santec CA 92071

BIRD, JACK DEE, banker; b. Wichita, Kan., Oct. 18, 1917; s. Isaac Henry and Lola (Stanley) B.; grad. Pacific Coast Banking Sch., Seattle, 1956; m. Dorothy Jean Merrill, June 14, 1947; children—John, Phyllis, Rodney. With U.S. Nat. Bank, Portland, Ore., 1936—, sr. v.p., exec. trust officer, 1968—; dir. Almanor R.R. Co. Big Creek & Telocast Co., Collins Pine Co., Fremont Lumber Co., Lakeview Logging Co., Lynnridge Investment Co., Ostrander Constrn. Co. Mem. exec. bd. Albertina Keer Homes, 1957- 66; exec. bd. Ore. United Appeal, 1958-68, pres., 1966-67, chmn. bd., 1967-68; mem. exec. bd. Columbia Pacific council Boy Scouts Am., 1968—. Served with USNR, 1942-46. Mem. Am. Bankers Assn., Am. Soc. Corp. Secretaries. Methodist (trustee 1963—). Home: 7801 SW 49th Av Portland OR 97219 Office: PO Box 3168 Portland OR 97208

BIRD, JOHN ALEXANDER, editor; b. Hays, Kan., Feb. 14, 1910; s. John Sterling and Martha (Henderson) B.; student Ft. Hays State Coll., 1926-27; B.S. in Journalism, Kan. State Coll., 1932; m. Katherine Edna Taylor, Oct. 3, 1930; 1 dau., Judith Ann. Asst. to pres. Wheat Farming Co., 1930-31; sr. sec. to congl. rep. 6th Dist. of Kan., 1933-34; asst. chief press sect. A.A.A., Washington, 1934-36; asso. prof. journalism Kan. State Coll., 1936-38; dir. information Fed. Crop Ins. Corp., Washington, 1938-40; prin. writer Office Land Use Coordination, Dept. Agr., 1940-42; asso. editor Country Gentleman mag., 1942-55; asso. editor Sat. Eve. Post, Phila., 1955-60, sr. editor, 1960-64, editor-at-large, 1964-69; freelance writer, editorial cons., 1969—. Mem. Citizens Com. for Outdoor Recreation Resources and Rev. Commn. Mem. Presdl. Trade mission, Central and So. Europe, 1954. Speech writer Republican Presdl. Campaign, 1952. Served as lt. (j.g.) USNR, 1944-45. Eisenhower exchange fellow, 1956. Mem. Soc. Internat. Devel., Beta Theta Pi, Sigma Delta Chi. Clubs: National Press (Washington); Springhaven (Wallingford); Quill. Contbr. articles popular mags. Home: 506 Oak Crest Lane Wallingford PA 19086

BIRD, JOHN BRIAN, educator; b. Birmingham, Eng., Aug. 28, 1923; s. George Harold and Edna (Attwood) B.; B.A. (hons.), Cambridge U., 1947, M.A., 1949; m. Marjorie Beryl Briggs, Dec. 31, 1947; children—Joanne M., D. Neil, Colin R. Lectr. U. Toronto, 1947-50; mem. faculty McGill U., 1950—, prof., 1962—, chmn. dept. geography, 1967—. Chmn. Canadian nat. com. Internat. Geog. Union, 1960-64; adv. bd. Inst. Arctic and Alpine Research of U. Colo., 1969—; chmn. organizing com. 22d Internat. Geog. Congress, 1969; leader sci. expdn. to Arctic, 1948, 50, 52, 54, 55, 58, 66. Councillor, Town of Preville, Que., 1966-69. Served to capt. Royal Marines, 1942-45. Fellow Arctic Inst. N.A.; mem. Canadian Assn. Geographers (pres. 1958-59), Assn. Am. Geographers, Inst. Brit. Geographers, Hakluyt Soc. (hon. sec.), Sigma Xi. Author: Physiography of Arctic Canada, 1967. Home: 27 Rue de Lombardie Preville Quebec Canada Office: McGill Univ PO Box 6070 Montreal 101 Quebec Canada

BIRD, JOHN I., lawyer; b. Wimbledon, Eng., 1917; B. Comm., U. B.C. (Can.), 1938; LL.B., Dalhousie Law Sch. (Can.). Admitted to B.C. bar, 1946; partner firm Owen, Bird & McDonald, Vancouver, B.C. Mem. Canadian Maritime Law Assn., Alpha Delta Phi. Office: Bentall Centre 505 Burrard St Vancouver 1 British Columbia Canada*

BIRD, ROBERT BYRON, educator, chem. engr.; b. Bryan, Tex., Feb. 5, 1924; s. Byron and Ethel (Antrim) B.; student U. Md., 1941-43; B.S. in Chem. Engring., U. Ill., 1947; Ph.D. in Chemistry, U. Wis., 1950; student U. Amsterdam, 1950-51. Asst. prof. chemistry Cornell U., 1952-53; mem. faculty U. Wis., 1951- 52, 53—, prof. chem. engring., 1957—, C.F. Burgess distinguished prof. chem. engring., 1968—, chmn. dept., 1964-68; lectr. Lectures in Sci., Humble Oil co., 1959, 61, 64, 66; lecture tour Am. Chem. Soc., 1958, Canadian Inst. Chemistry, 1961, 65; cons. to industry, 1965—. Mem. adv. panel engring. sci. div. NSF, 1961-64. Served to 1st lt. AUS, 1943-46. Decorated Bronze Star; Fulbright Fellow, Holland, 1950, Fulbright lectr., 1958; Guggenheim fellow, 1958; Fulbright lectr., Japan, 1962. Fellow Am. Phys. Soc.; mem. Am. Chem. Soc. (chmn. Wis. sect. 1966; unrestricted research grant Petroleum Research Fund 1963), Am. Inst. Chem. Engrs. (William H. Walker award 1962, Profl. Progress award 1965), Am. Assn. Engring. Edn. (Curtis McGraw award 1959, Westinghouse award 1960), Soc. Rheology, Brit. Soc. Rheology, Dutch Phys. Soc., Royal Inst. Engrs. (Holland), Japanese Soc. Chem. Engrs., Nat. Acad. Engring., Sigma Xi, Tau Beta Pi, Alpha Chi Sigma, Phi Kappa Phi, Omicron Delta Kappa, Sigma Tau. Author: (with others) Molecular Theory of Gases and Liquids, 2d edit., 1964, Russian edit., 1961, Transport Phenomena, 10th printing, 1971, Spanish edit., 1965, Czech edit., 1966, Italian edit., 1970; Een Goed Begin: A Contemporary Dutch Reader, 1963, 2d edit., 1971; also numerous research publs. Am. editor: Applied Sci. Research, 1969—. Office: Chem Engring Dept Univ Wis Madison WI 53706

BIRD, ROBERT MONTGOMERY, medical educator; b. Charlottesville, Va., Feb. 1, 1915; s. Robert Montgomery and Caroline (Reid) B.; B.S. in Medicine, U. Va., 1937, M.D., 1939. Intern N.Y. Hosp., 1939-40, asst. resident medicine, 1940-42; fellow physiology Am. Cancer Soc., Cornell U. Med. Coll., 1946-48, from research asso. to asst. prof. physiology, 1946-50, instr. medicine, 1947-52; from asst. physician to physican outpatients N.Y. Hosp., 1946-52; pvt. practice internal medicine, N.Y.C., 1950-52; asso. prof. medicine U. Okla. Sch. Medicine, Oklahoma City, 1952-61, prof. medicine, 1961—, prof. physiology, 1962—, vice chmn. dept. medicine, 1961-65, asso. dean planning and devel. 1965-70, dean Sch. Medicine, 1970—; from attending to cons. medicine Oklahoma City VA Hosp., 1953—. Mem. constrn. sch. med. rev. com. Dept. Health, Edn. and Welfare, 1967-70, cons. div. physician manpower, 1967—; chmn. com. B institutional research program evaluation VA, 1970-71. Mem. Okla. Sci. and Arts Found., Oklahoma City Symphony Soc. Served with M.C. AUS, 1942-46. Recipient U. Okla. Regents award for superior teaching, 1969. Mem. A.C.P. (gov. Okla. 1970—), Am. Physiology Soc., Am. Soc. Hematology, A.A.A.S., Am. Clin. and Climatol. Assn., A.M.A., Am. Fedn. Clin. Research, Central Soc. Clin. Research, Harvey Soc., So. Soc. Clin. Investigation, N.Y. Acad. Scis., Okla. City Acad. Medicine, Sigma Xi. Alpha Omega Alpha, Omicron Delta Kappa. Episcopalian. Contbr. articles profl. jours. Home: 205 NE 28th Oklahoma City OK 73105

BIRD, ROBERT STEWART, writer; b. Amesbury, Mass., July 16, 1904; s. Patrick S. and Marcella (Burke) B.; student Columbia; 1 son by previous marriage, Robert Stewart; m. 2d, Hester Faison, Sept. 27, 1947. Reporter N.Y. Times, 1925-43, N.Y. Herald Tribune, 1943-63, nat. corr., 1963- 66; sr. editor for nat. affairs Sat. Eve. Post. N.Y.C., 1966-69; mem. staff Parade mag. N.Y.C., 1969—. TV cons. Recipient Lasker award for best newspaper med. reporting, 1957; Page-One awards (4), Newspaper Guild. Mem. Nat., Overseas press clubs. Contbr. articles to popular mags. Home: 120 E 34th St New York City NY 10016 Office: 733 3d Av New York City NY 10017

BIRD, ROBERT WILSON, farm equipment co. exec.; b. Brady, Mont., Sept. 2, 1918; s. Frank W. and Cora (Lincoln) B.; LL.B., U. Wis., 1943; m. Hedda M. Cimoli, Dec. 29, 1946; children—Frank A., Robert M., Michael J. Admitted to Wis. bar, 1943, Ill. bar, 1952; with firm Schmitt & Bird, Merrill, Wis., 1947-50; with Oliver Corp., Chgo., 1950—, asst. to pres., 1960-68, sec., 1963- -, v.p., 1968—. Mem. labor relations adv. com. U. Wis. Mgmt. Inst., 1964—. Served to capt., inf. AUS, 1943- 47; MTO. Decorated Bronze Star; Crown of Italy, Order St. George (Italy). Mem. Wis., Chgo. bar assns., U.S., Ill. chambers commerce, N.A.M., Farm and Indsl. Equipment Inst., Indsl. Equipment Mfrs. Council, Phi Beta Kappa, Order of Coif. Club: Univ. Wisconsin Alumni (bd. dirs.) (Chgo.). Office: 2 N Riverside Plaza Chicago IL 60606

BIRD, VIOLA AVIS FOSTER, librarian; b. Fall River, Wis., June 7, 1905; d. John and Mary Louis (Babcock) Foster; B.A., Lawrence Coll., 1927; J.D., U. Washington, 1950, M.L.L., 1953; m. Winfred Wylam Bird, Dec. 26, 1928; children—Marilyn Jane (Mrs. Harold B. Valendine), Elizabeth Louise (Mrs. Gerald D. Turman). Asst. law librarian U. Wash., 1953—. Mem. Am. Assn. Law Libraries (mem. exec. bd. 1968-70, v.p., pres. 1971-72). Home: 5233 Pullman Av NE Seattle WA 98105

BIRD, WALLACE SAMUEL, Canadian provincial govt. ofcl.; b. Marysville, N.B., Can., Dec. 7, 1917; s. Charles Edwin and Catherine (Yeomans) B.; student pub. schs.; LL.D., St. Thomas U., 1968; D.Com.Sc., U. Moncton, 1968; LL.D., U. N.B., 1968; D.C.L., Mt. Allison U., 1969; m. Phyllis M. Bailey, June 4, 1941; (dec. Dec. 1970); children—Richard, Nancy, David, Michael. With Mussens, Ltd., Fredricton, N.B., 1946—, dir., 1951—, exec. v.p., 1959—; pres. Mack Maritime Distbrs., Ltd., Atlantic (Mussens), Ltd. Pres., chmn. bd. dirs. N.B. Devel. Corp., 1966—. Lt. gov. Province of N.B., 1968—. Chmn. bd. govs. Beaverbrook Art Gallery, 1968—. Mem. Fredericton Bd. Trade (past pres.). Decorated Knight of Grace of Order of St. John of Jerusalem, 1968. Mason (Shriner, Jester). Clubs: Fredericton Golf, Fredericton Curling. Home: 837 Charlotte St Fredericton New Brunswick Canada Office: Legislative Bldg Fredericton New Brunswick Canada

BIRDSALL, CHARLES KENNEDY, educator, elec. engr.; b. N.Y.C., Nov. 19, 1925; s. Charles Griffen and Irene (Fitzgerald) B.; B.S., U. Mich., 1946, M.S., 1948; Ph.D., Stanford U., 1951; m. Betty Jean Hansen, June 18, 1949; children—Elizabeth (dec.), (dec.), Anne, Barbara, Thomas, John. Research physicist Hughes Aircraft Co., Culver City, Cal., 1951-55; group leader electron physics group Gen. Electric Co., Palo Alto, Cal., 1955-59; prof. elec. engring. U. Cal., 1959—; cons. to industry, Lawrence Radiation Lab. of U. Cal.; prof. Miller Inst. Basic Research in Sci., 1963-64; grantee U.S.-Japan Coop. Sci. Program, 1966-67. Served with USNR, 1944-46. Fellow I.E.E.E.; mem. Am. Phys. Soc., A.A.A.S., Sigma Xi, Tau Beta Pi, Eta Kappa Nu. Roman Catholic. Author: (with W.B. Bridges) Electron Dynamics of Diode Regions, 1966. Contbr. articles profl. jours. Patentee in field. Home: 3745 Meadow Lane Lafayette CA 94549 Office: University of California Berkeley CA 94720

BIRDSALL, GUY HENRY, former govt. ofcl, lawyer; b. Algoma, Wis., Apr. 18, 1893; s. Asa and Alice (Perry) B.; pre-legal, State Coll., Stevens Pt., Wis., 1916; J.D., Georgetown U., 1922; m. Lillian May Koken, Jan. 29, 1927; 1 dau., Marjorie (Mrs. Edwin F. Irish). Teacher, grade sch., Kewaunee Co., 1912-13; asst. prin., Blair, Wis., 1916-17; admitted to D.C. bar, 1922; supervision, rating and adjudication of claims VA, 1922-29, legislative counsel, asst. solicitor, 1930-46; asst. adminstr. for legislation and congressional liaison, 1946-56, general counsel, 1956-60, ret.; mem. President's Com. Employment Handicapped; legislative and legal cons hist. and probate matters. Active Friendship Citizens' Assn., Washington and Federation of Citizen's Associations, 1941-45. Served with U.S. Army, 1917-19. Mem. Am. Legion, Vets. of Fgn. Wars, Disabled Am. Vets. Episcopalian. Mason (33, Shriner). Compiler handbooks and resumes of vets. laws. Home: 6130 Massachusetts Av Washington DC 20016 Office: President's Committee on Employment of Handicapped Washington DC 20425

BIRDSALL, J. FRANK Jr., hotel exec.; b. Lexington, Mich., June 26, 1913; s. J. Frank and Brittie May (Alton) B.; B.S. in Hotel Adminstrn, Cornell U., 1935; m. Jane Power, June 1, 1942; 1 dau., Jill. Cook, Dearborn (Mich.) Inn., 1935-40; mgr. Brass Rail Restaurant, N.Y. World's Fair, 1940; with Treadway Inns, 1954—, v.p., 1958-63, pres., 1963-71; dir. First Nat. Bank, Rochester, N.Y. Served with AUS, 1942-48. Mem. N.Y. State Hotel and Motel Assn. (past pres.), Am. Hotel and Motel Assn. (v.p.), Cornell Soc. Hotelmen (past pres.). Home: 360 Alexander St Rochester NY 14607 Office: 384 East Av Rochester NY 14607

BIRDSALL, RICHARD DAVENPORT, educator; b. Tuxedo, N.Y., June 28, 1924; s. Merwin Davenport and Sophia (Smith) B.; B.A., Yale, 1945, M.A., 1947; Ph.D., Columbia, 1954; m. Virginia Ann Ogden, Sept. 8, 1950; children—Caroline, Hugh, Meredith. Instr. history Rensselaer Poly. Inst., 1952-55; instr. history Conn. Coll., 1955-58, asst. prof., 1958-64, asso. prof., 1964-67, prof., 1967—; vis. prof. Helsinki U., 1962-63, Brown U., 1968-69. Served with USNR, 1943-46. Guggenheim fellow, 1959-60. Mem. Am. Hist. Assn., New Eng. Am. Studies Assn. (pres. 1969-70). Author: Berkshire County: a Cultural History, 1959. Home: 73 Oswegatchie Rd Waterford CT 06385 Office: Connecticut Coll New London CT 06320

BIRDSONG, CINDY, vocalist, mem. The Supremes; recordings include; A'Go-Go, At the Copa, Bit of Liverpool, Country Western and Pop, I Hear a Symphony, Sam Cooke, Where Did Our Love Go. Address: care Motown Records 2457 Woodward Detroit MI 48208*

BIRDSONG, WILLIAM HERBERT, Jr., army officer; b. Mayersville, Miss., Mar. 16, 1918; s. William H. and Julia Morgan (Pearl) B.; B.S., Miss. State Coll., 1939; grad. Army Inf. Sch., 1940, Command and Gen. Staff Coll., 1950, Armed Forces Staff Coll., 1954, Nat. War Coll., 1958; m. Onylene Joyce Lepper, Apr. 5, 1941; children—William H. III, Joyce O. (Mrs. Carl R. Murphy), Mary H. Commd. 2d lt. U.S. Army, 1939, advanced through grades to brig. gen., 1963; command and staff positions, 5th and 1st Inf. Divs., Europe and U.S., 1939-54; assigned army staff, Pentagon, 1954-57, UN, Korea, 1958-59, Inf. Sch., 1960-62; asst. div. comdr. 3d Inf. Div., Germany, 1963-65; chief of staff Landsoutheast NATO Hdqrs., Turkey, 1965-67; joint staff Pentagon, 1967-70; comdg. gen., Ft. Campbell, Ky., 1970—. Decorated Silver Star, Legion of Merit with oak leaf cluster, B.S.M. with 3 oak leaf clusters, Army Commendation Medal with oak leaf cluster, Purple Heart (U.S.), Croix de Guerre (France). Home: 1541 Cole Park St Fort Campbell KY 42223 Office: Commanding General Fort Campbell KY 42223

BIRENBAUM, WILLIAM M., coll. pres.; b. Macomb, Ill., July 18, 1923; s. Joseph and Rose (Whiteman) B.; student Ia. State Tchrs. Coll., 1943; J.D., U. Chgo., 1949; L.H.D., Columbia Coll., Chgo., 1970; m. Helen Bloch, Mar. 8, 1951; children—Susan, Lauren Amy, Charles. Dir. student affairs U. Chgo., 1949-54; mem. faculty social scis. coll of univ., 1950-54, dean students Univ. Coll., 1955-57; dir. research, conf. bd. Asso. Research Councils, Ford Found. project study post-doctoral internat. ednl. exchanges, 1954-55; asst. v.p. Wayne State U., 1957-61; dean New Sch. Social Research, N.Y.C., 1961-64; v.p., provost Bklyn. Center, L.I. U., 1964-67; pres. Edn. Affiliate, Bedford-Stuyvesant Devel. & Services Corp., Bklyn, 1967-68; pres. Staten Island Community Coll., 1968—; mem. faculty N.Y. U. Grad. Sch. Edn., 1969-70. Cons., Austrian Ministry Edn., Vienna, 1969. Founder, Nat. Student Assn., 1946-48, chmn. nat. faculty bd., 1950-54; pres. Assn. Community Councils Met. Chgo., 1955-57; chmn. Mich. Cultural Commn., 1960-61; founder, original dir. Detroit Adventure, vol. assn. cultural instns, 1958-61; mem. Bd. Edn., dists. 21-22, N.Y.C., 1962-64; bd. dirs. Bklyn. chpt. Am. Civil Liberties Union, 1967—, chmn. acad. freedom com., 1967—; chmn. edn. com. Met. council Am. Jewish Congress, 1967—, chmn. acad. freedom com., 1967—; St. N.Y.C., 1963—; bd. adv. Bklyn. Acad. Music, 1965—; mem. mass media program com. Religion in Am. Life, 1969—; mem. adv. council Korean Student Assn. N.Y., 1969—; adv. bd. ERIC Clearinghouse for Jr. Coll., Los Angeles, 1970—; mem. commn. on curriculum Am. Assn. Jr. Colls., 1970—; mem. nat. adv. council Eastern Va. Med. Sch., 1971—. Trustee Friends World Coll., Westbury, N.Y. Mem. Chgo. Bar Assn., Delta Sigma. Author: Overlive: Power, Poverty and the University, 1968; Something for Everybody is Not Enough: An Educator's Search for His Education, 1971. Home: 108 Willow St Brooklyn NY 11201 Office: Staten Island Community College Sunnyside NY 10301

BIRES, JOSEPH JOHN, banker; b. Throop, Pa., Feb. 13, 1908; s. John J. and Elizabeth (Hurney) B.; student Pa. State U., U. Wis.; m. Katherine C. Kovacs, Feb. 21, 1935; 1 son, Robert J. Teller, accountant Franklin Savs. Bank, N.Y.C., 1929-50, asst. sec., 1950-60, auditor, 1960—; free lance artist. Home: 9 Lisa Dr Dix Hills NY 11746 Office: 656 8th Av New York City NY 10036

BIRGE, KINGSLEY HARLOW, educator; b. Worcester, Mass., Feb. 6, 1916; A.B., Dartmouth, 1938; Ph.D., Yale, 1945. Instr. sociology Colby Coll., Waterville, Me., 1946-50, from asst. prof. to asso. prof., 1950-64, prof., 1964—, also chmn. dept. sociology. Mem. Am. Sociol. Assn., Am. Anthrop. Assn., Am. Acad. Polit. and Social Sci. Office: Dept Sociology Colby Coll Waterville ME 04901*

BIRGE, RAYMOND THAYER, ret. educator, physicist; b. Bklyn., Mar. 13, 1887; s. John Thaddeus and Caroline S. (Raymond) B.; A.B., U. Wis., 1909, A.M., 1910, Ph.D., 1914; LL.D., U. Cal., 1955; m. Irene Adelaide Walsh, Aug. 12, 1913; children—Carolyn Elizabeth, Robert Walsh. Instr. in physics Syracuse U., 1913-15; asst. prof., 1915-18; instr. in physics U. Cal., 1918; successively asst. and asso. prof., prof., 1926-55, prof. emeritus, 1955—, chmn. dept., 1933-55. Co-operating expert in Internat. Critical Tables; mem. adv. com. Office of Critical Tables. Physics Bldg. at U. Cal at Berkeley named in his honor. Fellow Am. Phys. Soc. (v.p. 1954, pres. 1955), Optical Soc. Am., A.A.A.S.; mem. Nat. Acad. Scis., Am. Philos. Soc., Am. Assn. Physics Tchrs., Am. Inst. Physics (governing bd. 1955-58), Phi Beta Kappa, Sigma Xi. Contbr. to Phys. Rev., others. Home: 1639 La Vereda St Berkeley CA 94709

BIRKE, HELEN MORSE (Mrs. William D. Birke), ret. publisher; children—John M., Julia M. Publisher, Herald Dispatch, 1963-71; pres. Blangid Trading Co., Norway Av. Land Co.; dir. Huntington Publishing Co. (W.Va.). Bd. dirs. United Community Services, 1967—. Mem. Am., So. newspaper pubs. assns., W.Va. Arts and Humanities Council, W.Va. Fedn. Republican Women. Jewish religion (treas. congregation 1966-68). Address: 261 High Dr Huntington WV 25705

BIRKELAND, CHARLES JOHN, horticulturist, educator; b. Warwick, N.D., Apr. 16, 1916; s. John and Harriett Agnes (Watts) B.; B.S., Mich. State Coll, 1939; M.S., Kan. State State Coll., 1941; Ph.D., U. Ill., 1947; m. Wilma Florine Evans, Dec. 25, 1941; children—Charles Evans, Janis Lynn, John Richard. Grad. asst. Kan. State Coll., 1939-41, asst. horticulturist, 1941-46; grad. asst. U. Ill., 1946-47, asst. prof. dept. horticulture, 1947-49, acting head, 1949-50, prof. and head, 1950—. Served as lt. USNR, port dir. operations, San Francisco, Okinawa, 1942-46. Fellow A.A.A.S.; mem. Bot. Soc. Am., Ill. Hort. Soc., Ill. Vegetable Assn., Ill. Florists Assn., Ill. Nursery Men's Assn., Am. Inst. Biol. Scis., Am. Soc. Hort. Sci., Am. Pomol. Soc., Vegetable Growers Assn. Am., Am. Genetics Assn., Ill. Acad., Naval Res. Officers Assn., Sima Xi (research award), Phi Kappa Phi, Phi Alpha Xi, Alpha Zeta, Gamma Sigma Delta, Phi Sigma, Alpha Gamma Rho. Republican. Unitarian. Clubs: Rotary,

Lincoln Debate, University, Urbana Golf and Country, Author bulls. and articles in sci. and hort. jours. Home: 2111 Zuppke Dr Urbana IL 61801

BIRKENSTOCK, JAMES WARREN, bus. machine mfr.; b. Burlington, Ia., May 7, 1912; s. George Louis and Anna (Flynn) B.; student Burlington Jr. Coll., 1933; B.S., U. Ia., 1935; m. Jean Lois Hale, Nov. 30, 1935; children—Robert Hale, Joyce Ann. With IBM Corp., 1935—, successively student salesman, St. Louis, jr. salesman, sr. salesman, asst. mgr., St. Louis, br. mgr., Kansas City, spl. sales exec. World Hdqrs., gen. sales mgr., mgr. future demands, spl. adminstrv. asst. corporate ofcls., exec. asst. to pres., exec. dir. product planning and market analysis div., dir. comml. devel., 1935-58, v.p. comml. devel., 1958-70, v.p. corporate relations, 1971—; dir. The Vendo Co., Kansas City, Mo., IBM World Trade Corp. Trustee Fairfield U. Fairfield, Conn.; bd. dirs. Charles E. Culpeper Found., Inc. Mem. Bus. Equipment Mfrs. Assn., Beta Gamma Sigma, Delta Sigma Pi. Clubs: Westchester Country (Rye, N.Y.); Metropolitan (N.Y.C.). Home: 506 Country Club Rd W New Canaan CT 06840 Office: Armonk NY 10504

BIRKERTS, GUNNAR, architect; b. Riga, Latvia, Jan. 17, 1925; s. Peter and Meria (Shop) B.; Diplomingeneur Architekt, Technische Hochschule, Stuttgart, Germany, 1949; m. Sylvia Zvirbulis, July 29, 1950; children—Sven Peter, Andra Sylvia, Erik Gunnar. Came to U.S., 1949, naturalized, 1954. Designer, Perkins & Will, Chgo., 1950-51, Eero Saarinen & Assos., Bloomfield Hills, Mich., 1951-55; prin. chief designer Minoru Yamasaki & Assos., Birmingham, Mich., 1955-59; pres. Gunnar Birkerts & Assos., Inc., Birmingham, 1959; prin. works include Schwartz House, Northville, Mich. (First Honor award A.I.A. 1961, Merit award Mich. chpt. A.I.A. 1962, Archtl. Record award 1961); Univ. Reformed Ch., Ann Arbor Mich. (award Ch. Archtl. Guild Am. 1962); Peoples Fed. Savs. & Loan Bank, Royal Oak, Mich. (Merit award Mich. chpt. A.I.A. 1962); Fisher Adminstrv. Center, Detroit (award of merit Mich. Soc. Architects 1967; Merit award Mich. chpt. A.I.A. 1967); Detroit Inst. Arts addition; 1300 Lafayette Apts., Detroit; Tougaloo (Miss.) Coll.; Vocational-Tech. Campus, So. Ill. U., Carbondale; Glen Oaks Community Coll. Campus, Centreville, Mich.; Lincoln Sch., Columbus, Ind. (A.I.A. First Honor award 1970); Fed. Res. Bank, Mpls.; exhbns. include Akron Inst. Art, 1954, 40 Under 40, U.S.A.-N.Y. Architects League, 1965, Sao Paulo (Brazil) Bienniale, 1961, Mus. Modern Art, N.Y.C., 1971; asst. prof. architecture U. Mich., 1961, asso. prof., 1963-69, prof., 1969—, Graham fellow, 1970. Named Young Designer of Year, Akron Inst. Art, 1954; recipient 1st prize Internat. Furniture competition, Cantu, Italy, 1955; 3d prize Internat. competition for Cultural Centre, Belgian Congo; Design award Progressive Architecture mag., 1957, 59, 61; Nat. Gold medal Tau Sigma Delta, 1971. Fellow A.I.A.; mem. Mich. Soc. Architects, Ch. Archtl. Guild, Hon. Order Ky. Cols. Home: 1830 E Tahquamenon Ct Bloomfield Hills MI 48013 Office: 909 Haynes St Birmingham MI 48011

BIRKETT, JOHN HOOPER, chem. co. exec.; b. Montreal, Que., Can., Oct. 16, 1925; s. Leonard Harris and Gertrude (Caughill) B.; B.Commerce, McGill U., Montreal, 1949; m. Joan Louise Macklaier, Dec. 27, 1952; children—Peter, Jennifer, Timothy, Elisa. Dist. supr. Canadian Liquid Air Co., 1949-54; sales service mgr. Canadian Chm. & Cellulose Co., Ltd., Montreal, 1955-57, asst. sec., 1959-61; asst. sec. Columbia Cellulose Co. Ltd., 1958-59; asst. sec. Canadian Chem. Co. Ltd., Montreal, 1962-63; asst. sec. Chemcell Ltd., Montreal, 1963-64, sec., 1964-71, v.p., sec., 1971—, also dir. subsidiaries; sec. Millhaven Fibres Ltd. Co-chmn. financial campaign Montreal YMCA, 1969-71, bd. mgmt., 1969—, exec. com., 1970—. Served with Royal Canadian Navy, 1944-45. Mem. Chartered Inst. Secs. Mem. Anglican Ch. Clubs: Royal Montreal Golf, Red Birds Ski, Ski Hawks (Montreal). Home: 1 Poplar Pl Baie d'Urfé Quebec Canada Office: 800 Dorchester Blvd W Montreal 101 Quebec Canada

BIRKHAUG, KONRAD ELIAS, bacteriologist; born Bergen, Norway, October 12, 1892; son Karl Anderssen and Elise Marie (Olsen) B.; student Jamestown (N.D.) Coll. Acad., 1912-14; A.B., Jamestown Coll., 1917; M.D., Johns Hopkins, 1924; M.S., Rochester U., 1927; grad. study Univs. of Berlin and Hamburg, summers, 1922, 24, 32; m. Marie Mustad Berner, Mar. 8, 1938 (div. 1944). Came to U.S., 1911, naturalized, 1917. Hosp. sec. Internat. Y.M.C.A., Russia, 1917-19, prisoner of war relief, Internat. Y.M.C.A., Verdun, France, 1919-20; interne Sydenham Hosp., Baltimore, Md., 1923- 24; asst. in medicine and Charlton fellow in med. research, Johns Hopkins Hosp., 1924-25; asso. in bacteriology, U. of Rochester, 1925-26, asst. prof., 1925-28, asso. prof., 1928-34; resident bacteriologist Strong Memorial Hosp., Rochester, 1925-32; sous-chef, Institut Pasteur Lab. Tuberculosis, Paris, 1932-35; mem. Christian Michelsen Inst., Bergen, Norway, 1935-45; dir. Norwegian Nat. Tuberculosis Vaccine (BCG) Lab., Bergen, 1937-45; bacteriol advisor, Sahlgrenska Hosp., Gothenburg, Sweden, 1945-46; asso. med. bacteriologist dir. Tuberculosis Vaccine (BCG) Lab., State Dept. Health, Albany, 1946-50, principal medical bacteriologist, 1950-53; asso. prof. pathology and bacteriology Albany Med. Coll., 1954; cons. USPHS. Vice pres. 1st Internat. BCG Congress, Paris, 1948. Exhibitor sculptres, aquarelles. Active with A.R.C. Norway, World War II. Recipient Awards Tb, Red Cross Work, Diploma of Honor, Am. Acad. Tb physicians, 1949. Diplomate Am. Bd. Preventive Medicine and Pub. Health. Fellow A.A.A.S., A.C.P., Am. Med. Assn.; mem. N.Y. State Pub. Health Assn., N.Y. State Assn. Pub. Health Labs., N.Y. State Med. Soc., Med. Soc. City Albany, Am. Trudeau Soc., Am. Assn. Immunologists, Internat. Leprosy Assn., Am. Association Pathologists and Bacteriologists. Am. Soc. Bacteriol., Soc. for Expt. Biology and Medicine, Sigma Xi, also fgn. soc. Author books including; Telavaag, 1946; It Happened in Norway, 1967; Physician at the End of the Road, 1968, also articles relating to field. Sculptor. Home: Kalvedalsvei 51 Bergen, Norway.

BIRKHEAD, GUTHRIE SWEENEY, Jr., educator, polit. scientist; b. Holden, Mo., Oct. 28, 1920; s. Guthrie Sweeney and Yula Donna (Glass) B.; A.A., Jefferson City (Mo.) Jr. Coll., 1940; A.B., U. Mo., 1942, A.M., 1947; M.A., Princeton, 1949, Ph.D. in Politics, 1951; m. Louise Gartner, Aug. 16, 1952; children—Guthrie Sweeney III, Richard Gartner, Evan Clark. Mem. faculty Syracuse U., 1950—, prof. polit. sci., 1960—, chmn. dept., 1959-62, 66-67, dir. met. studies program, 1968—, also dir. pub. adminstrn. programs Maxwell Sch., 1959-62; dir. research UN Inst. Pub. Adminstrn. for Turkey and Middle East, 1955-56; cons. Pakistan Adminstrv. Staff Coll., Lahore, 1962-64, Ford Found., Pakistan, 1967-68. Chmn. pub. finance com. Community Renewal Plan, Syracuse, N.Y.; 1970—; exec. dir. com. on local govt. and home rule N.Y. State Constl. Conv., 1967. Served with inf. AUS, 1942-46. Fellow Nat. Municipal League, 1952-53. Mem. Am. Polit. Sci. Assn., Am. Soc. Pub. Adminstrn., Am. Assn. U. Profs., Phi Beta Kappa. Author articles. Co-author: River Basin Administration and the Delaware, 1960; Science and State Government in New York, 1960; Decisions in Syracuse, 1962. Editor: Administrative Problems in Pakistan, 1966. Home: 220 Lockwood Rd Syracuse NY 13214

BIRKHEAD, KENNETH MILTON, govt. ofcl.; b. St. Louis, Nov. 15, 1914; s. Leon Milton and Agnes (Schiereck) B.; A.B., Mo. Valley Coll., Marshall, 1949; M.A., U. Mo., 1950; m. Barbara Belwood, May 17, 1943; children—David, Scott. Research dir., also exec. dir. Friends of Democracy, 1938-48; asso. dir. pub. relations Democratic Nat. Com., 1948; asst. to dir. Dem. Congl. Campaign Com., 1951; asst. to Dem. whip U.S. Senate, 1952-55; nat. dir. Am. Vets. Com., 1956-57; finance dir. Dem. Nat. Com., 1958-59; cons. Albert and Mary Lasker Found., 1960; asst. to sec. Dept. Agr., 1961-66, adminstr. rural community devel. service, also vice asst. to the sec., 1966-68, nat. exec. dir. Citizens for Humphrey, 1968; spl. asst. to U.S. Senator Thomas J. McIntyre, 1969—. Served to 1st. USAAF, World War II. Mem. Am. Vets. Com. (nat. bd.). Clubs: Nat. Capital Dem. (gov.); Internat. Town and Country (Falls Church). Home: 6445 Queen Anne Terrace Falls Church VA 22044 Office: Senate Office Bldg Washington DC 20510

BIRKHOFF, GARRETT, educator, mathematician; b. Princeton, N.J., Jan. 10, 1911; s. George David and Margaret (Grafius) B.; A.B., Harvard, 1932, Soc. of Fellows, 1933-36; postgrad. Cambridge U., 1932-33; hon. degree U. Nacional Mexico, 1951, U. Lille, 1960, Case Inst. Tech., 1964; m. Ruth Collins, June 21, 1938; children—Ruth W., John D., Nancy C. Instr. Harvard, 1936-38, asst. prof., 1938-41, asso. prof., 1941-46, prof., 1946—; cons. to govt. and pvt. industry; Walker-Ames lectr. U. Wash., Taft lectr. U. Cin., 1947. Chmn. organizing com. Internat. Congress Mathematicians, 1950. Guggenheim fellow, 1948. Mem. Am. Math. Sco. (v.p. 1958). Math. Assn. Am. (v.p. 1971-72), Am. Acad. Arts and Scis. (v.p. 1966-68), Nat. Acad. Sci., Conf. Bd. Math. Sci. (chmn. 1969-70), Assn. Computing Machinery, Soc. Indsl. Applied Math. (pres. 1967-68), Am. Nuclear Soc.; hon. mem. Sociedad Math. Mex., Acad. Ciencias Lima. Mem. Soc. of Friends. Author: Survey of Modern Algebra (with S. MacLane), 1941, rev. edit. 1965; Lattice Theory, 1940, rev. 1967; Hydrodynamics, 1950, rev. 1960; Jets, Wakes and Cavities (with E. Zarantonello), 1957; (with G.C. Rota) Ordinary Differential Equations, 1962, rev. edit, 1969; (with S. Maclane) Algebra, 1967. Home: 45 Fayerweather St Cambridge MA 02138

BIRKHOFF, ROBERT D., educator, physicist; b. Chgo., Jan. 29, 1925; s. Robert D. and Ellen (Gleason) B.; B.S., Mass. Inst. Tech., 1945; Ph.D., Northwestern U., 1949; m. Ariel Frances Jewett, Nov. 4, 1945. Asso. prof. U. Tenn., Knoxville, 1949-55, prof. physics and astronomy, 1965—; physicist Oak Ridge Nat. Lab., 1955—, cons., 1950-55; head radiol. def. State of Tenn., 1952-55. Mem. Am. Phys. Soc., Health Physics Soc. Author: Handbuch der Physik, Vol. 34, 1958; Health Physics, 1967; also articles. Measured cross sects. for plasmon excitation, electron flux in irradiated media, optical properties of metals, liquids, scintillators, electron diffusion in metals, plasmon and bremsstrahlung light from irradiated metals. Home: 1433 Whitower Dr Knoxville TN 37919

BIRKMEYER, KARL MARTIN, educator, art historian; b. Hamburg, Germany, Nov. 13, 1918; s. Karl and Ruth (Zimmerman) B.; Ph.D. in Art History, Humboldt U., Berlin, Germany, 1943. Came to U.S., 1948, naturalized, 1955. Chief adviser and adminstr. fine arts and archives sect. Am. Mil. Govt. Bavaria, 1945-48; asst. prof. art history Stanford, 1950-53; mem. faculty U. Cal. at Los Angeles, 1953—, prof. art history, 1962—. Mem. Coll. Art Assn. Am., Renaissance Soc. Am. Contbr. profl. jours., bulls. Home: 11310 Elderwood St Los Angeles, CA 90049.

BIRKS, HENRY GIFFORD, jeweller; b. Montreal, Can., Sept. 6, 1892; s. William Massey and Miriam Childs (Gifford) B.; student McGill U., 1911-12; m. Lilian Cockshutt Drummond, June 12, 1917; children—G. Drummond, Sheila G. (Mrs. Laird W. Bovaird), Willa K. (Mrs. James H. McDougall). Asso. with Henry Birks & Sons, Ltd., Montreal, Que., Can., 1911—, chmn. bd., 1944—; pres. Birmanco, Ltd., 1911—, chmn. bd., 1944—; pres. Central Investment Corp., Ltd., Montreal; dir. RCA Victor Co., Ltd.; hon. dir. Royal Trust Co. Councillor, Montreal, Que., 1940-44. Served with Canadian Army, 1914-17. Fellow Chartered Inst. Secretaries; mem. Montreal Bd. Trade (past pres.) Home: 1227 Sherbrooke St W Montreal 25 Quebec Canada Office: 1240 Phillips Sq Montreal 111 Quebec Canada

BIRLENBACH, SCRIBNER, transp. co. exec.; b. Louisville, Apr. 7, 1904; s. William and Anna (Scribner) B.; B.E., U. Cal. at Los Angeles, 1928; m. Helen Woodfill, June 25, 1960. Editorial staff Pacific Coast Wall St. Jour., Los Angeles, 1930-32; investment banker, Los Angeles, 1932-41; pres. Southwestern Freight Line, Phoenix, 1942-46; with Transcon Lines, Los Angeles, 1946-70, pres., chief exec. officer, 1946-62, chmn. bd., chief exec. officer, 1962-70. Clubs: Stock Exchange, Jonathan, Los Angeles Country (Los Angeles). Home: 314 S Las Palmas Av Los Angeles CA 90005

BIRMINGHAM, FREDERIC ALEXANDER, editor; b. N.Y.C., Nov. 13, 1915; s. John Francis and Louise (Westher) B.; A.B., Dartmouth, 1933; m. Ruth Frances Atherton, Nov. 8, 1941. Eastern editor Apparel Arts mag., 1935-36; mem. editorial staff Time mag., 1936-37; editor Ogden-Watney Pubs., 1938-39; sales promotion mgr. Esquire mag., 1941-45; mng. editor, 1952, editor-in-chief, 1952-56; exec. editor Gentleman's Quar., 1950-52; fashion editor Playboy mag., 1957-58; editorial dir. Gen. Pub. Co., 1959-62; editor Cavalier mag., 1963-66; spl. project editor Reader's Digest Assn., 1966-67; editoral dir. Status-Diplomat mags., 1967-68; sr. editor Status mag., N.Y.C., 1968-71; mng. editor Saturday Eve. Post, 1971—; lectr. Radcliffe Coll., U. Mo., Northwestern U., N.Y. U., Coll. City N.Y., C.W. Post Coll., New Sch. Social Research. Sr. editor OWI 1942-43. Served to lt. comdr. USNR, 1943-46. Mem. Overseas Press Club, Alpha Iota Epsilon, Sigma Phi Epsilon. Clubs: Tabard Inn, U. Mo (Columbia, Mo.); Sanborn House, Dartmouth (Hanover, N.H.). Author: The Writer's Craft, 1957; It Was Fun While It Lasted, 1960; The Cookbook for Men, 1961; The Ivy League Today, 1962; How to Succeed at Touch Football, 1963; The Wedding Book, 1964. Author-editor: Girls From Esquire, 1953; The Esquire Book of Etiquette, 1954; The Esquire Drink Book, 1956; The Esquire Fashion Guide, 1958. Contbr. articles mags. and newspapers. Home: 801 Olive St Scranton, PA 18500. Office: 1100 Waterway Blvd Indianopolis IN 46202

BIRMINGHAM, STEPHEN, author; b. Hartford, Conn., May 28, 1931; s. Thomas J. and Editha (Gardner) B.; grad. Hotchkiss Sch., 1946; B.A., Williams Coll., 1950; m. Janet Tillson, Jan. 5, 1951; children—Mark, Harriet, Carey. Mem. New Eng. Soc. of City N.Y. Democrat. Episcopalian. Club: Coffee House (N.Y.C.). Author: Young Mr. Keefe, 1958; Barbara Greer, 1959; The Towers of Love, 1961; Those Harper Women, 1963; Fast Start, Fast Finish, 1966; Our Crowd; The Great Jewish Families of New York, 1967; The Right People, 1968; Heart Toubles, 1968; The Grandees, 1971; The Late John Marquand, 1972. Address: Hidden Spring Lane Rye NY 10580

BIRMINGHAM, WILLIAM THOMAS, lawyer; b. Chgo., Aug. 17, 1928; s. William Thomas and Ann (Garrity) B.; B.S., U. Ariz., 1948, LL.B., 1951; m. Laura V. Biberstein, Aug. 16, 1958; children—Robert W., Thomas M., Ann E., Julie F. Admitted to Ariz. bar, 1951, also U.S. Supreme Ct.; asst. atty. gen. Ariz., 1953-54; partner firm Jennings, Strouss & Salmon, Phoenix, 1954—. Bd. dirs. Ariz. State Hosp., 1970—. Served to 1st lt. AUS, 1951-53. Mem. Maricopa County, Ariz. bar assns., Am. Bd. Trial Advocates, Assn. Ins. Attys., Internat. Assn. Ins. Attys., Fed. Ins. Counsel, Phoenix Def. Counsel, Def. Research Inst., Phi Delta Phi, Sigma Chi. Office: 111 W Monroe Phoenix AZ 85003

BIRNBAUM, HENRIK, educator; b. Breslau, Germany, Dec. 13, 1925; s. Immanuel and Lucie (Richter) B.; Fil. kand., Stockholm (Sweden) U., 1949, Fil. mag., 1952, Fil. lic., 1954, Fil. dr., 1958; m. Marianna Daisy Laszlo, July 3, 1965; children—Ewa Lucia, Björn Staffan. Came to U.S., 1961. Docent, Stockholm U., 1958-61; vis. lectr. Harvard, 1960; mem. faculty U. Cal. at Los Angeles, 1961—, prof. Slavic langs. and lit., 1964—, dir. Russian Russian and East European Studies Center, 1968—; cons. RAND Corp., 1962-66. Served with Swedish Army, 1948-49. Swedish Govt. fellow, 1961; Guggenheim fellow, 1964-65; Am. Council Learned Socs. grantee, 1969-70. Author books and articles Slavic linguistics and lit., Balkan linguistics and linguistic theory. Home: 17350 Sunset Blvd Pacific Palisades CA 90272

BIRNBAUM, HENRY, librarian; b. Switzerland, Mar. 7, 1917; s. Isaac and Fanny (Hauser) B.; came to U.S., 1929, naturalized, 1941; B.A. in Internat. Relations magna cum laude, U. Colo., 1952; M.S. in L.S., Columbia, 1954. Personal service mgr. Hoover Mfg. & Sales Co., N.Y.C., 1936-41; adminstrv. asst. Library of Congress Mission in Europe, 1945-46; library asst. Library Congress, 1946-47; research analyst Office Chief Counsel War Crimes, Nurnberg, Germany, 1947-48; asst. case editor, 1948-49; asst. acquisition div. Bklyn. Coll. Library, 1952-54, catalog librarian, 1954- 57, chief circulation librarian, 1957-61; chief librarian Pace Coll., N.Y.C., 1961-66, dir. libraries, 1966—, sec. senate, 1969-71. Served with AUS, 1941-45. Mem. A.L.A. (chmn. ad hoc com. circulation librarians 1959-60, chmn. circulation services discussion group, library adminstrn. div. 1961-62, chmn. planning and action com., circulation service sect. 1968-70), Assn. Coll. and Research Libraries, N.Y. Tech. Services Librarians (chmn. social com. 1958-59), N.Y. Library Club (mem. council 1963-64, treas. 1964-66, v.p., pres.-elect 1971-72), Library Assn. City Colls. N.Y. (del. Bklyn. Coll. to exec. council 1956-59), Archons of Colophon (convener 1966-67), N.Y. Hist. Soc., Phi Beta Kappa, Pi Gamma Mu, Delta Phi Alpha. Author of monograph. Contbr. articles profl. jours. Home: 40 E 10th St New York City NY 10003 Office: Pace Coll Pace Coll Plaza New York City NY 10038

BIRNBAUM, HOWARD KENT, educator; b. N.Y.C., Oct. 18, 1932; s. Jack and Ida (Kornblau) B.; B.S., Columbia, 1953, M.S., 1954; Ph.D., U. Ill., 1958; m. Freda Ethel Silber, Dec. 25, 1954; children—Elisa, Scott, Shari. Asst. prof. U. Chgo., 1958-61; asso. prof. U. Ill., 1961-63, prof. metallurgy, 1963—; metall. cons. Oak Ridge Nat. Lab., Dow Chem. Corp. Guggenheim fellow, 1968; recipient Rhodes prize, 1953; Union Carbide fellow, 1954-57; Campbell Meml. fellow, 1953-54; H. Krumb scholar, 1952-53. Mem. Am. Inst. Mining and Metall. Engring., Am. Phys. Soc., A.A.A.S., Sigma Xi, Tau Beta Pi. Contbr. articles profl. jours. Patentee in field. Home: 800 Hamilton Dr Champaign IL 61820 Office: Univ Illinois Urbana IL 61801

BIRNBAUM, NATHAN, chemist; b. N.Y.C., July 14, 1907; s. Jacob and Sarah (Schutzberger) B.; B.A. cum laude, Coll. City N.Y., 1929; M.A., Columbia, 1932, Ph.D., 1937; m. Jeanne D. Pancoast, Jan. 16, 1931. Mem. faculty dept. chemistry Coll. City N.Y., 1929—, beginning as fellow, successively tutor, instr., asst. prof., asso. prof., 1929-56, prof., 1956—, chmn. dept., 1954-69. Mem. Nat. Def. Research Com., Columbia, 1941; mem. radiol. safety sec. Bikini atomic weapons test, 1946; civilian cons. to Chem. Corps, U.S. Army, 1947-49, 52-65; cons. FDA, 1965-67; mem. Nat. Com. Radiation Protection, 1950-51; chief Chem. Corps group Operation Greenhouse, Eniwetok, 1951. Served from capt. to lt. col. AUS, 1942-47, 49-52; col. Res. Decorated Army, Navy, Air Force commendation ribbons. Mem. Am. Chem. Soc., A.A.A.S., Phi Beta Kappa, Sigma Xi, Phi Lambda Upsilon. Home: 119 Knapp Terrace Leonia NJ 07605 Office: City Coll NY New York City NY 10031

BIRNBAUM, NORMAN, educator, author; b. N.Y.C., July 21, 1926; s. Silas Jacob and Jean (Bermen) B.; B.A., Williams Coll., 1947; M.A., Harvard, 1951, Ph.D., 1958; m. Gudrun Apel, Aug. 21, 1955 (div. July 1970); children—Anna, Antonia; m. 2d, Edith Kurzweil, Feb. 20, 1971. Editor, OWI, 1943-45; teaching fellow Harvard, 1948-52, tutor Adams House, 1949- 52; asst. lectr. London Sch. Econs. and Polit. Sci., U. London, 1953-55, lectr., 1955-59; fellow Nuffield Coll., Oxford (Eng.) U., 1959-66; vis. prof. faculty letters and human scis. U. Strasbourg (France), 1964-66; prof. grad. faculty New Sch. Social Research, 1966-68; prof. Amherst Coll., 1968—. Mem. founding editorial bd. New Left Rev., London, 1959; chmn. com. sociology religion Internat. Sociol. Assn., 1959—, chmn., 1970—; mem. interim com. New Univs. Com., 1968. Guggenheim fellow, 1971. Author: Sociological Study of Ideology (1940-60), 1962; Crisis of Industrial Society, 1969; Towards a Critical Sociology, 1971; also articles. Mem. editorial bd. Praxis, 1966—; contbg. editor Change mag. of higher edn., 1970—. Home: 50 Lincoln Av Amherst MA 01002

BIRNBAUM, ZYGMUNT WILLIAM, educator; b. Lwow, Poland, Oct. 18, 1903; s. Ignacy and Lina (Nebenzahl) B.; LL.M., U. Lwow, 1925, Ph.D. in Math., 1929; postdoctoral research U. Goettingen (Germany), 1929-31; m. Hilde Merzbach, Dec. 20, 1940; children—Ann Miriam, Richard Franklin. Came to U.S., 1937, naturalized, 1943. Math. instr. Gymnasium, Lwow, 1926-29; chief actuary Life Ins. Co. Phoenix in Poland, 1931-36; research biometrician N.Y.U., 1937-39; mem. faculty U. Wash., Seattle, 1939—, prof. math., 1950—, dir. lab. statis. research, 1948—; vis. prof. Stanford, 1951-52, U. Paris (France), 1960- 61, U. Rome (Italy), 1964; cons. Boeing Co., 1956—, Dept. Health, Edn. and Welfare, 1963—. Guggenheim fellow, 1960-61. Fellow Inst. Math. Statistics (pres. 1963-64), Am. Statis. Assn.; mem. Am. Math. Soc., Math. Assn. Am., Soc. Indsl. and Applied Math., Am. Assn. U. Profs. Editor Annals of Math. Statistics, 1967-70. Home: 14620 SE 55th St Bellevue WA 98006 Office: Math Dept Univ Wash Seattle WA 98105

BIRNEY, ROBERT CHARLES, ednl. adminstr., psychologist; b. Westmont, N.J., May 2, 1925; s. Charles Alexander and Florence (Moore) B.; B.A., Wesleyan U., Middletown, Conn., 1950; M.A., U. Mich., 1951, Ph.D., 1955; m. Margaret Ann Momerak, June 18, 1949; children—Reed Charles, Ruth Elizabeth, Barbara Ann, Robert Carl. Mem. faculty Amherst Coll., 1954-67, prof. psychology, 1965-67; dean Sch. Social Scis., Hampshire Coll., 1968-70, v.p., 1971—; vis. prof. Ruhr (W. Germany) U., 1966-67; spl. research human motivation. Mem. adv. council, assos. program Danforth Found., 1963-66. Served to lt. USAAF, 1943-46. Decorated Air medal with 3 oak leaf clusters. Mem. Am., New Eng. (steering com.) psychol. assns., Am. Assn. U. Profs., Phi Beta Kappa, Sigma Xi. Editor: (with Richard Teevan) Van Nostrand Insight Series, 1961-70. Home. 85 Alpine Dr Amherst MA 01002

BIRNIE, JOSEPH EARLE, banker; b. Greenville, S.C., Nov. 30, 1903; s. James and Annie Curran (Earle) B.; student Washington and Lee U., 1923-24; grad. cum laude, Am. Inst. Banking Sch., Richmond, Va., 1929; grad. Naval Tng. Sch., Quonset Point, R.I., 1943; m. Octavia Norfleet Riley, June 4, 1941; 1 dau., Ada Lea Norfleet Dew. Clk., Alexander Nat. Bank, St. Petersuburg, Fla., 1925-27; clk., later officer. Bank of Va., Richmond, 1927-33; exec. sec., treas., Morris Plan Bankers' Nat. Assn., 1933-38, pres. 1945-46; pres., dir. Nat. Bank of Ga. (formerly Bank of Ga.), Atlanta, 1938-69), chmn. bd. dirs., 1969—; dir. Ga. Internat. Life Ins. Co., Ga. Internat. Corp., Abbey Internat. Corp. Trustee Met. YMCA, A.R.C.; nat. dir. Jr.

Achievement Inc.; trustee Atlanta Art Mus., hon. life trustee, past pres. Atlanta Tb Assn.; pres. Atlanta Symphony Orch. Comdg. officer of Aeros. Rep. Mid-Western Procuremetnt Dist., U.S. Navy, 1943-44 Apptd. by Fed. Deposit Ins. Corp., Washington, as mem. 3-man bd. to examine applicants for FDIC examiners, 1942. Mem. adv. council Furman U. Trustee Washington and Lee U., Met. Found. Atlanta, bd. visitors Emory U. Recipient commendation for meritorious performance of duty, U.S. Navy, 1946. Mem. Am. (v.p. Ga. savs. div. 1940, exec. council 1965-68), Ga. (exec. council 1969—) bankers assns., Consumer Bankers Assn. (pres., 1945- 47), Newcomen Soc. Am., Soc. of Cincinnati, Soc. Colonial Wars in Va., Nat. Alumni Assn. of Washington and Lee U. (1st v.p. 1931), Alumni Assn. of Richmond (pres. 1935), of Atlanta (pres. 1946), Mil. Order of World Wars, Ga. C. of C. (dir.), Sigma Alpha Epsilon, Omicron Delta Kappa. Nat. treas. Washington and Lee U. bicentennial. Republican. Episcopalian (vestryman). Clubs: Piedmont Driving, Capital City, The Nine O'Clocks (Atlanta); Commonwealth (Richmond); Keowee; Homosassa. Contbr. numerous articles on banking subjects to nat. pubs. Home: 3130 Habersham Rd Atlanta GA 30305 Office: 34 Peachtree St Atlanta GA 30303

BIRNIE, WILLIAM ALFRED HART, editor; b. Springfield, Mass., Aug. 4, 1910; s. Walter and Loraine Field (Hart) B.; A.B., Williams Coll., 1931; student univs. Munich, Bonn (Germany), 1931-33; m. Jean Whittlesey, Sept. 22, 1939; children—Loraine Jean, Whittlesey B. Hart, William Alfred Hart, Christine (dec.). Reporter Berkshire Eve. Eagle, Pittsfield, Mass., 1933- 34; reporter, rewrite, drama editor N.Y. World Telegram, 1934-38; staff writer and asst. editor American mag., 1938-42; mng. editor The Woman's Home Companion, 1942, editor-in-chief, 1943-52, pub., 1952-54; v.p. Crowell- Crowell- Collier Pub. Co. until 1957; fgn. affairs attache USIA, Bonn, Germany, 1957-60; sr. editor The Reader's Digest, 1960—; dir. radio sta. WKNE, Keene, N.H. Mem. Chi Psi, Gargoyle Soc., Silurians, Sigma Delta Chi. Clubs: Pequot Yacht (Southport, Conn.); Dutch Treat. Home: Farm CT Office: Readers Digest Pleasantville NY 10570

BIRNKRANT, NORMAN HOWARD, lawyer; b. N.Y.C., Aug. 22, 1908; s. Maurice H. and Tillie (Schellberg) B.; J.D., Detroit Coll. Law, 1928; postgrad. U. Mich., 1928-32, U. Detroit, 1938; m. Phyllis Zelens, Apr. 30, 1956; children—Terry Joy (Mrs. Gordon R. Miller), Madge Sue (Mrs. Thomas Grossman). Admitted to Mich. bar, 1929, since practiced in Detroit; mem. firm Birnkrant, Birnkrant & Birnkrant, 1928—, sr. mem., 1946—; Mich. consul for Republic of Austria, 1954—, Austrian consul gen., 1965—; sec. Detroit Consular Corps, 1966—; dean Consular Corps Coll. and Internat. Consular Acad., 1971. Mem. World affairs com., internat. adviser world trade Greater Detroit Bd. Commerce, 1954—; sec. Inter-Am. Affairs Center, State Dept., 1942; guest lectr. internat, affairs Wayne State U., 1955—. Recipient Gold medal of honor for services behalf Republic Austria, 1959; Max-Reinhardt medal from mayor of Salzburg Austria, 1961. Mem. State Bar Mich., Am., Internat., Fed. (2d v.p.), Detroit bar assns., Am. Soc. Internat. Law, Am. Trial Lawyers Assn., Am. Arbitration Assn., World Trade Club Detroit, Detroit Jr. C. of C. Alumni Assn. (pres. Detroit and Windsor 1952), Detroit Econ. Club (v.p., chmn. reception com.). Club: Cirumnavigators (N.Y.C. and Detroit). Home: 1525 Balmoral Dr Palmer Woods Detroit, MI 48203. Office: First Nat Bldg Detroit MI 48226

BIRON, ROBERT HENRY, Jr., land developer; b. Mpls., Aug. 12, 1912; s. Robert Henry and Alice (Brugger) B.; student Carleton Coll., 1929; B.A., U. Minn., 1933, LL.B., 1935; m. 2d, Jean Machamer, Apr. 14, 1951; 1 dau., Patricia. Asst. sec. Mpls.-Honeywell Regulator Co., 1936-43; asst. to dir. indsl. relations Consol. Vultee Aircraft Corp. (now Convair div. Gen. Dynamics Corp.), 1943-45; v.p. Northrop Aircraft, Inc., 1945-47; v.p. Transcontinental & Western Air, Inc., 1947-48; v.p. adminstrn. Convair div. Gen. Dynamics Corp., 1948-61, sr. v.p. Gen. Dynamics, 1961-64; vice chancellor for bus. and finance U. Cal. at San Diego, 1964-68; pres. Rancho LaJolla, Inc., land devel., 1968—; v.p. La Jolla Village Corp.; dir. San Diego Electric Co. Trustee Scripps Clinic and Research Found. Mem. Theta Delta Chi, Phi Delta Phi. Republican. Home: Linea del Cielo Rancho Santa Fe CA 92067 Office: 3299 Holiday Ct LaJolla CA 92037

BIRR, HERMAN THEODORE, stock broker; b. Oakland, Cal., June 28, 1907; s. H.T. and Elizabeth (Carstenn) B.; student U. Cal. ext., 1923-26; m. Antoinette Corriea, May 25, 1929; children—Herman Theodore III, Robert Roger. Asst. mgr. Bank of Am. (formerly Bank of Italy), 1924-30; mgr. Reinhard & Co., 1930-32; dist. mgr. Asso. Am. Distbrs., 1932-37; v.p. Bankamerica Co., 1937-45; chmn. pres. First Cal. Co., 1945-57; chmn. Blair, Rollins & Co., Inc., N.Y.C., 1951-54; v.p. Walston & Co., Inc., 1958-59; chmn. bd. Birr, Wilson & Co., Inc. (formerly Birr & Co., Inc.), 1959-71, exec. vice chmn. bd., chief exec. officer, 1971—; chmn. bd. dirs. 1st Nat. Fund, dir. San Francisco-Oakland Helicopter Airlines, Inc. Mem. N.Y. Stock Exchange, Pacific Coast Stock Exchange; asso. mem. Am. Stock Exchange. Bd. dirs., pres. Los Gatos Cemetery Assn., A.P. Giannini Scholarship Found. Mem. Cal. Hist. Soc., Beta Phi Sigma. Clubs: Commercial, Stock Exchange, Merchants Exchange, Bond (San Francisco); Wall St. (N.Y.C.); Claremont Country; Prospectors (Reno). Home: 21 Selborne Dr Piedmont CA 94611 Office: 155 Sansome St San Francisco CA 94104

BIRR, KENDALL ALBERT, educator, historian; b. Wheaton, Ill., Feb. 10, 1924; s. Edward Louis and Gertrude (Nuechterlein) B.; B.A., Cornell Coll., 1947; M.S., U. Wis., 1948; Ph.D., 1952, M. Marcia K. Rukwid, Aug. 4, 1963 (dec.); 1 son, Christopher. Lectr. U. Cal. at Berkeley, 1951-52; fellow Am. studies Amherst Coll., 1956-57; mem. faculty State U. N.Y. at Albany, 1952-, professor history, 1959—, chmn. div. social scis., 1962-66. chmn. dept. history, 1966-68. Served with AUS, 1943-46. Mem. Orgn. Am. Historians, Econ. History Assn., Soc. History Tech. Lutheran. Author: (with Merle Curti) Prelude to Point Four, 1954; Pioneering in Industrial Research, 1957; also articles. Home: 24 Herrick Av Delmar, NY 12054. Office: Dept History State Univ NY Albany NY 12203

BIRRELL, GEORGE ANDREW, oil co. exec.; b. Warren, O., Apr. 25, 1921; s. George Henry and Mary Ann (Rook) B.; B.A., Yale, 1942, LL.B., 1947; m. Lelia Torrey Pannill, Aug. 7, 1948; children—Lelia Carter, Amanda Griswold, Ellen Torrey, Laura Tudor, George William. Admitted to N.Y. bar, 1948; asso. firm Donovan, Leisure, Newton and Irvine, N.Y.C., 1947-55, partner, 1956-58; with Mobil Oil Corp., 1959—, gen. counsel, 1970—. Mem. planning commn., Rye, N.Y., 1957-60, bd. zoning appeals, 1962-67, mem. city council, 1968—, acting mayor, 1970—. Mem. adv. bd. Internat. and Comparative Law Center, also Internat. Oil and Gas Ednl. Center, Southwestern Legal Found. Served to 1st lt. USAAF, 1943-45. Mem. Am. Bar Assn., Assn. Bar City N.Y., Assn. Gen. Counsel, Chi Psi. Republican. Episcopalian. Mason. Clubs: Golf, Manursing Island (Rye); Pinnacle (N.Y.C.). Home: 195 Milton Rd Rye NY 10580 Office: 150 E 42d St New York City NY 10017

BIRRELL, JAMES R., utility exec.; b. 1911; B.B.A., U. Denver; married. With Pub. Service Co. Colo., 1941—, v.p. accounting, sec., 1968—. Served with AUS, 1945-46. Address: 550 15th St Denver CO 80202*

BIRSH, ARTHUR THOMAS, publisher; b. Englewood, N.J., Oct. 6, 1932; s. Abraham S. and Mary (Levinsohn) B.; grad. Lawrenceville N.J. Sch., 1950; B.A., Yale, 1954; m. Judith Roseberg, June 29, 1955; childrenAndrew, Philip, Joanne. Engaged sales Western Pub. Co., Poughkeepsie, N.Y., 1956-58; founder Cross Road Press, Hyde Park, N.Y., 1958, pres., 1958-60; with Playbill mag., N.Y.C., 1960-, publisher, 1965-; exec. v.p. Am. Theatre Press, Inc., 1961—, v.p., 1961-68; group v.p. Metromedia, Inc., 1968-. Served with AUS, 1954-56. Home: 4671 Delafield Av New York City, NY 10471. Office: 277 Park Av New York City, NY 10017.

BIRZGALIS, ALFREDS ARTURS, physician; b. Riga, Latvia, Mar. 3, 1908; s. Peters and Helena (Lapins) B.; M.D., State U. Latvia, 1932; m. Berta Caucis, June 29, 1935; children—Eriks Peters, Ivars Alfreds. Came to U.S., 1950, naturalized, 1955. Surgeon army hosps., Riga and Liepaja, Latvia, 1932-40; asst. urologist City Hosp., Riga, 1941-44; village physician Buttenwiessen, Swabia, Germany, 1945; physician-surgeon UNRRA Hosp., Dilligen, Swabia, 1945-46, camp physician, Klein-Kotz, Swabia, 1946-47; physician charge Tb clinic Internat. Refugee Orgn., Leipheim, Swabia, 1948-50; anesthetist St. Luke's Hosp., Marquette, Mich., 1950; mem. staff Ionia (Mich.) State Hosp., 1950—, med. supt., 1961—; rotating intern Edward W. Sparrow Hosp., Lansing, Mich., 1952-53. Mem. A.M.A., Mich., Ionia-Montcalm County (pres. 1963) med. socs., Am. Psychiat. Assn., Mich. Soc. Psychiatry and Neurology, Ionia C. of C. Rotarian. Address: Ionia State Hosp Ionia MI 48846

BISBEE, FRANK DOAN, bus. exec.; b. Knoxville, Tenn., Nov. 13, 1891; s. William Adolphus and Harriet Anne (Backus) B.; prep. edn., St. Paul's Sch., Concord, N.H., Harstrom Sch., Norwalk, Conn.; student U. Pa., 1911-13; m. Ella Taylor Slemons, Oct. 25, 1921; 1 son, Frank Doan. Bank runner, Fla. Nat. Bank, Jacksonville, 1912; mgr. Bisbee Bldg.; pres. Frank D. Bisbee & Co. (became Brisbee-Baldwin Corp.), office bldg. mgmt., ins., real estate, mortgage loans; chmn. bd. Bisbee-Baldwin Corp.; pres. Bisbee Investment Co.; v.p. Holly Point Devel. Co.; trustee Profit Sharing Plan of Bisbee-Baldwin Corp.; dir. Barnett First Nat. Bank. Vol. with French Ambulance Corps., 1916, 1st lt., later capt. inf., U.S. Army, World War I; ensign. USCG Aux., World War II. Former lt. col. personal staff, Gov. Spessard Holland of Fla. Ex-chmn. Selective Service System, Duval County Local Board No. 5; past facility security officer Fla. under OCD. Mem. City Council, Jacksonville, 1923-25. Vice pres., dir. Children's Home Soc.; past pres. N.E. Fla. Div. Children's Home Soc.; past pres. Travelers' Aid Soc.; dir. com. Jacksonville Community Chest; past v.p. N.E. Fla. Heart Assn. Mem. S.A.R., Am. Legion, U.S., Fla., Jacksonville chambers commerce, Newcomen Soc. Eng., Camellia Soc. N. Fla. (dir.), Internat., Am. (permanent judge) camellia socs., Phi Kappa Sigma. Democrat. Episcopalian. Clubs: River, Men's Garden (dir.) (Jacksonville); Meninak, Seminole (past pres.), Fla. Yacht, Timuquana Country. Home: 1611 S McDuff Av Jacksonville FL 32205 Office: 341 W Forsyth St Jacksonville FL 32202

BISBEE, ROYAL DANIEL, govt. ofcl.; b. Godhra, India, Feb. 21, 1923 (parents U.S. citizens); s. Royal Daniel and Pearl Bertha (Gosnell) B.; B.A., U. Wash., 1947; M.A., George Washington U., 1964; m. Barbara Beeler, Jan. 7, 1946; 1 dau., Renee D. (Mrs. Peter T.E. Miller). Joined U.S. Fgn. Service, 1947; vice consul, Bombay, India, 1947-48; vice consul, adminstrv. officer embassy, New Delhi, India, 1948-50; spl. tng. in S. Asian regional affairs U. Pa., 1950-51; chief Hindu unit Voice of Am., 1951; dir. USIS, Lucknow, India, 1952-56, Salonika, Greece, 1956-58, Lahore, Pakistan, 1959-61; program and policy officer for India, Nepal and Ceylon, USIA, 1961-63; assigned Nat. War Coll., 1963-64; dir. USIS, Freetown, Sierra Leone, 1964-66, Pretoria, S. Africa, 1966-69; dep. dir. USIS, Manila, Philippines, 1970—. Served with AUS, 1943-46. Recipient certificate of commendation State Dept., 1950. Mason, Rotarian. Club: Army and Navy (Manila). Author: Tibet: Communist Road to India, 1950; China's Traditional National Interests in the Borderlands of the Himalayas, 1964. Address: American Embassy (IS) APO San Francisco CA 96528

BISCHOFF, CHARLES MICHAEL, accounting exec.; b. N.Y.C., Nov. 25, 1927; s. Charles John and Grace (Hurley) B.; B.S., Seton Hall U., 1951; m. Marilyn A. Guilmette, Sept. 15, 1951; children—Cheryl Ann, Susan Grace. Staff accountant Haskins & Sells C.P.A.'s, Newark, 1951-57, semi sr., 1952-55, sr., 1955-57; financial accountant Houdaille Constrn. Materials, Morristown, N.J., 1957-59; divisional controller R.H. Wright, Inc., Ft. Lauderdale, Fla., 1959-61; divisional controller Houdaille Duval Wright div., Jacksonville, Fla., 1961-62; tax mgr. Houdaille Industries, Inc., Buffalo, 1963-64, corp. controller, 1964—. Mem. accounting council Canisus U., 1967—. Served with USNR, 1945-48. Mem. Am. Inst. C.P.A.'s Home: 27 North Lane Orchard Park NY 14127 Office: 1 M & T Plaza Buffalo NY 14203

BISCHOFF, ELMER, artist; b. Berkeley, Cal., July 9, 1916; s. John A. and Elna (Nelson) B.; B.A., U. Cal. at Berkeley, 1938, M.A., 1939. Chmn. grad. program San Francisco Art Inst., 1957-63; tchr. art dept. U. Cal. at Berkeley, 1963—; 1963—; represented in permanent collections Art Inst. Chgo., Mus. Modern Art, Oakland (Cal.) Mus. Art, Whitney Mus. Am. Art, Rockefeller Inst., Chase Manhattan Bank, N.Y.C., Hallmark Cards, Inc., Kansas City, Mo., also pvt. collections; permanent exhibit with Staempfli Gallery, N.Y.C. Grantee Ford Found., 1959, Nat. Inst. Arts and Letters, 1963. Served with USAAF, 1942-46; ETO. Home: 109 Strathmoore Dr Berkeley CA 94705 Studio: 2571 Shattuck Av Berkeley CA 94704

BISCHOFF, KENNETH BRUCE, educator, chem. engr.; b. Chgo., Feb. 29, 1936; s. Arthur William and Evelyn Mary (Hansen) B.; B.S., Ill. Inst. Tech., 1957; Ph.D., 1961; m. Joyce Arlene Winterberg, June 6, 1959; children—Kathryn Ann, James Eric. Mem. faculty U. Tex., Austin, 1961-67; asso. prof., then prof. U. Md., 1967-70; Walter R. Read prof. engring., dir. Sch. Chem. Engring., Cornell U., 1970—; cons. Esso Research and Engring., NIH, Environmental Protection Agy. Mem. council thrombosis Am. Heart Assn., 1971—. Shell Found. fellow, 1959; NSF fellow, 1960, Ghent, 1960-61. Fellow Am. Inst. Chemists; mem. Am. Inst. Chem. Engrs. Am. Chem. Soc., Am. Soc. Engring. Edn., A.A.A.S., Am. Soc. Artificial Internal Organs, Catalysis Soc., Am. Assn. U. Profs., N.Y. Acad. Scis., Sigma Xi, Tau Beta Pi, Phi Lambda Upsilon, Omega Chi Epsilon, Alpha Chi Sigma. Author: (with D.M. Himmelblau) Process Analysis and Simulation, 1968. Editor: (with E.L. Dedrick and E.F. Leonard) The Artificial Kidney. Contbr. articles to research publs. Editorial bd. Chem. Reaction Engring. Revs., Jour. Biopharmaceutics and Pharmacokinetics. Home: 4 Beanhill Lane RD 1 Ithaca NY 14850

BISCHOFF, RALPH FREDERIC, educator; b. Boston, May 16, 1906; s. Rudolph P. and Louise P. (Burkhardt) B.; B.S., Wesleyan U., 1927; LL.B., Harvard, 1930, A.M., 1931. Ph.D., 1937; student Berlin U., Hochschule, 1933-34; m. Elizabeth F. Fauver, Sept. 11, 1937; children—Elizabeth Ann, David Fauver, John Frederic. Instr. govt. Wesleyan U., 1934-38, asst. prof., 1938-46, asso. prof., 1946, dir. admissions, 1942-46, exec. sec., 1946; asso. prof. law N.Y.U., 1946-49, prof. since 1949, sec. law Sch., 1948-51, asst. dean, 1951-57, asso. dean, 1957-64, vice dean, 1964-66, Charles L. Denison prof. law, 1965—; specialist U.S. Dept. State, Germany, 1956. Project dir. N.Y. State Commn. on Constl. Conv., 1957-60. Pub. panel mem. W.L.B. 1943-46; cons. N.Y. State Commn. on Fiscal Affairs 1953, 1955-59. Trustee Conn. Wesleyan U., 1960—, Bennett Jr. Coll., 1955-59; mem. board corporators Middlesex (Conn.) Hosp.; mem. bd. edn. Middletown, 1945-46; mem. Westport (Conn.) Bd. Edn., 1959-63, chmn., 1961-63; chairman of Westport-Weston Community Council, 1965-66. Mem. Am. Arbitration Assn., Phi Beta Kappa, Phi Nu Theta. Author: Nazi Conquest through German Culture, 1942. Contbr. articles to law jours. Home: Kings Highway Westport CT 06880 Office: New York University New York City NY 10003

BISCHOFF, WILLIAM NORBERT, educator, historian; b. Yakima, Wash., June 27, 1916; s. Adolph Julius and Mary (Clark) B.; B.A., Gonzaga U., 1940, M.A., 1942; S.T.B., U. Santa Clara, 1948; Ph.D., Loyola U., Chgo., 1950. Joined Soc. of Jesus, 1933, ordained priest Roman Catholic Ch., 1947; mem. faculty Gonzaga U., 1940-42, 50-67, prof. history, 1961-67, chmn. dept., 1960-67; prof. history Sophia U., Tokyo, Japan, 1968-69, Seattle U., 1969—; cons. Coeur d'Alene and Kalispel Indian claim suits. Mem. adv. bd. historic sites and monuments Wash. Parks Commn., 1950-56, chmn., 1955-56. Mem. Am. Hist. Assn., Ida., Mont., Ore., Wash. hist. socs. Author: Jesuits in Old Oregon, 1947; We Were Not Summer Soldiers, 1971. Address: Seattle U Seattle WA 98122

BISGYER, MAURICE, former social work exec.; b. Bklyn., Aug. 28, 1897; s. Joseph and Sara (Flaumenhaft) B.; B.A., N.Y. U., 1918, M.A. with honors, 1919; L.H.D., Hebrew Union Coll. Jewish Inst. Religion; m. Hoda Adele Rosenberg, July 7, 1925; children—Jay Lewis, Doris. Instr. N.Y. U., 1918-19; exec. dir. Jewish Ednl. Alliance, Balt., 1919-22; dir. YMHA, Trenton, N.J., 1922-23; dir. Jewish Community Center, Washington, 1923- 37; sec. B'nai B'rith (Internat), Washington, 1937-56, exec. v.p., 1956- 66, hon. exec. v.p. 1966—; pres. Nat. Assn. Jewish Center Workers; mem. Nat. Adv. Com. on Edn. apptd. by presidents Herbert Hoover and Franklin D. Roosevelt; sec.-gen. Coordinating Bd. Jewish Orgns. to ECOSOC; exec. com. U.S. nat. commn. for UNESCO. Exec. com., later budget com., Community Chest, Washington; mem. presdl. inaugural com., 1929, 1948; mem. atty. Gen.'s com. on Juvenile Delinquency; v.p. Nat. Citizenship Conf. Fellow N.Y. U.; bd. govs. Nat. Jewish Ednl. Assn., Nat. Conf. Jewish Social Welfare, Zionist Orgn. Am. (editorial bd.), Phi Beta Kappa. Jewish religion. Author: Henry Monsky—The Man and His Work (with Daisy Monsky), 1947; also series for N.Y. Daily Mirror, 1948; Challenge and Encounter, 1967. Home: 5500 Friendship Blvd Chevy Chase MD 20015

BISH, GLENN FREDERICK, ret. oil co. exec.; b. nr. Carolina, O., Nov. 22, 1904; s. James Newton and Marie (Bauer) B.; student U. Tex., 1925; grad. Advanced Mgmt. Program, Harvard, 1950; m. Eunice Herring, Feb. 5, 1930; children—James H., Sally Anne, Martha Louise. With Marathon Oil Co. (formerly Ohio Oil Co.), 1926—, beginning as mem. land and geol. dept., Artesia, N.M., successively mem. prodn. dept., Casper, Wyo., supt. prodn., Hobbs, N.M., div. supt. prodn., Houston div., mgr., Grand Rapids, Mich., also Tulsa, 1926-54, asst. mgr. prodn., Findlay, O., 1954-69, v.p. 1959-64, sr. v.p. prodn., 1964-69, also dir. Pres., dir. Tulsa YMCA, 1948-55. Mem. Am. Inst. Mining, Metall. and Petroleum Engrs., Am. Petroleum Inst., Mid-Continent Oil and Gas Assn. Episcopalian. Clubs: Ramada (Houston); Tulsa (pres., past gov.), Southern Hills Country (Tulsa); Findlay Country; Los Angeles Country. Home: 2928 N Main St Findlay OH 45840

BISHER, JAMES FURMAN, journalist, author: b. Denton, N.C., Nov. 4, 1918; s. Chisholm and Mamie (Morris) B.; student Furman U., 1934-36; A.B. in Journalism, U. N.C., 1938; divorced; children—Roger, James Furman, Monte. Editor Lumberton (N.C.) Voice, 1938-39; reporter High Point (N.C.) Enterprise, 1939-40; reporter, state editor Charlotte (N.C.) News, 1940-43, sports editor Atlanta Constitution, 1950-57, Atlanta Jour, 1957—; moderator weekly TV show, Football Rev., 1950—. Chmn. Ga. Christmas Seal campaign, 1961; mem. Atlanta-Fulton County Stadium Authority. Served to lt., Air Corps., USNR, 1943-46. Recipient Best Sports Stories of Year award 14 times, Ga. A.P. sports writing award 9 times. Mem. Football Writers Assn. Am. (pres. 1959-60), Chi Psi. Named Ky. col., 1958; hon. Tar Heel, 1961; recipient 10 Sportswriting awards Ga. A.P. Presbyn. Clubs: Jockey (Miami, Fla.); Canongate Golf Atlanta Country, Capital City (Atlanta); Gridiron (U. Ga.); Druid Hills Golf. Author: With A Southern Exposure, 1962; Miracle in Atlanta, 1966; Strange But True Baseball Stories, 1966; Aaron, RF, 1968; Arnold Palmer—The Golden Year, 1971; also numerous articles and included in anthologies. Home: 3135 Rilman Rd NW Atlanta GA 30327 Office: 10 Forsyth St Atlanta GA 30302

BISHOP, AVERY ALVIN, educator; b. Delta, Utah, Aug. 27, 1913; s. John Avery and Lemira (Walker) B.; B.S. in Civil Engring., Utah State U., 1934, M.S. in Agrl. Engring., 1938; Ph.D. (NSF fellow), Colo. State U., 1961; m. Anna Beth Reeder, Nov. 10, 1938; children—Alvin Bruce, Janet, Carol Anne (Mrs. Hugh Denniston), Dan Roger. Draftsman, topographic engr., irrigation engr., civil engr. various fed. agys., 1934-46; faculty agrl. and irrigation engring. Utah State U., Logan, 1946—, prof., 1954—, head dept., 1965—. Cons. engr. City Logan, 1948—; irrigation cons. fgn. agrl. service Agr. Dept., 1953, 55, FAO, UN, 1956, 58, 61, Aichi Irrigation Pub. Corp., Japan, 1957, AID, 1965, 66, 68, 70; lectr. SEATO Grad. Sch. Engring., Bangkok, Thailand, 1963. Planner, condr. Nr. East-S. Asia Irrigation Practices Seminars, also tech. editor Procs. Seminars, 1966, 68, 70; mem. council U.S. Univs. for Soil and Water Mgmt. in Arid and Sub-Humid Lands, 1968—. Utah State U. Faculty honor lectr., 1971. Fellow Am. Soc. C.E. (exec. sec. irrigation and drainage div., editor div. Jour.); mem. Am. Soc. Agrl. Engrs., Am. Soc. Engring. Edn. Kiwanian. Home: 725 North 14 East Logan UT 84321

BISHOP, BARBARA JANET, ret. marine corps officer; b. Boston, Oct. 2, 1920; d. Sidney Lewis and Jessie Currie (Bruce) Bishop; B.F.A., Yale, 1943; M.A., U. Chgo., 1948. Commd. 2d lt. USMC, 1943, advanced through grades to col., 1964; comdg. officer Woman Recruit Tng. Bn., 1956-59; mil sec. to comdr.-in- chief Allied Forces So. Europe, Naples, Italy, 1962-63; dir. Women Marines, 1964-69, congl. liaison officer to senate, 1969; sr. personnel analyst City of Hartford (Conn.), 1970—. Home: Bushnell Plaza Hartford CT 06103 Office: Municipal Bldg 550 Main St Hartford CT 06103

BISHOP, BARRY LEE, journalist; b. Floresville, Tex., Oct. 7 1906; s. Charles Milton and Zella (Riggs) B.; student U. Tex., 1923-28; m. Josephine Foester, Dec. 1, 1929; 1 son, Barry Louis (dec.). Asst. state house corr. Dallas Morning News, 1926-29, reporter, staff writer, corr. specializing city planning and racial integration progress, 1929-45, Latin Am. corr., 1945- 50, staff corr. Washington bur., 1951; press-information officer Am. embassy, Mexico City, 1951-54; chief Latin Am. press service USIA, Washington, 1955-58; information officer Am. embassy, Buenos Aires, Argentina, 1958-59; apptd. attache Am. embassy, La Paz, Bolivia, 1960; became pub. affairs officer-attache Am. embassy, Madrid, Spain, 1962; Latin Am. corr. Chgo. Tribune Press Service, Mexico City, 1967—. Mem. Sigma Delta Chi. Mason (Shriner). Clubs: Overseas Press (N.Y.C.); Nat. Press (Washington); American (Buenos Aires). Office: care Chgo Tribune Press Service 435 N Michigan Av Chicago IL 60611 also Paseo de la Reforma 46 Mexico City Mexico

BISHOP, CAROLYN BENKERT, magazine editor; b. Monroe, Wis., Aug. 28, 1939; d. Arthur Churchill and Delphine (Heston) Benkert; student Purdue U., 1957-58; B.S., U. Wis., 1961; grad. Tobe-Coburn Sch., 1962; m. Lloyd Francis Bishop, June 15, 1963. Writer, asst. editor Co-ed Mag., N.Y.C., 1962-63; copywriter Woodward & Lothrop, Washington, 1963-65; home furnishings editor Co-ed Mag., 1965-68; editor Budget Decorating Mag., N.Y.C., 1968-69; home furnishings editor Family Circle Mag., N.Y.C., 1969—; free lancer writer. Recipient T award Tobe Coburn, 1967, award Burlington House, 1969. Mem. Nat. Home Fashions League (v.p. edn. N.Y. chpt. 1968-69), Am. Inst. Interior Designers (press asso.), Am. Home Econs. Assn., Home Economists in Bus., Tobe-Coburn Alumnae Assn., U. Wis. Alumnae Assn. Author: 25 Decorating Ideas Under $100 1968; Make Room for Guests, 1969; How to Decorate on a Budget, 1969. Home: 245 E 25th St New York City NY 10010 Office: 488 Madison Av New York City NY 10022

BISHOP, CHARLES EDWIN, educator, economist; b. Campobello, S.C., June 8, 1921; s. Fred and Hattie Bess (Wall) B.; B.S., Berea Coll., 1946; M.S., U. Ky., 1948; (Farm Found. fellow 1948-49), U. Chgo., 1952; m. Dorothy Anderkin, Feb. 13, 1943; children—Susan Ann, Mary Catherine, Charles Edwin. Research asst. agrl. econs. U. Ky., 1947-48; research asso. econs. U. Chgo., 1949- 50; mem. faculty N.C. State Univ., 1950-67, prof. agrl. econs., 1956- 67, head dept. agrl. econs., 1957-65, head dept. econs., 1965-67 William N. Reynolds distinguished prof., 1957-67; v.p. U. N.C., Chapel Hill, 1967-70, exec. dir. Agrl. Policy Inst., 1960-66, chancellor U. Md., College Park, 1970—; vis. prof. U. Va., 1961-63; vis. lectr. Va. Poly. Inst. extension, Lima, Peru, 1961; mem. Nat. Com. Agrl. Policy, 1958—, Nat. Planning Assn., 1961—; agrl. bd. Nat. Acad. Scis., 1963—; sci. adv. com. to sec. agr., 1962—; mem. Nat. Manpower Adv. Com., 1962-68; Mem. Am. Agr. Econ. Assn. (pres. 1967- 68), Am. Econ. Assn., Internat. Assn. Agrl. Econs., Alpha Zeta, Phi Kappa Phi, Gamma Sigma Delta. Co-author: Introduction to Agricultural Economic Analysis, 1958. Home: 7012 Hunter Lane Hyattsville MD 20782

BISHOP, CHARLES SEAMAN, ret. banker; b. Elizabeth, N.J., Sept. 3, 1904; s. Charles Edward and Helen Mae (Oakley) B.; B.S., Dartmouth, 1926; m. Edith L. Good, May 19, 1928; children—Barbara Ann, Charles S., Richard G. Sales staff, sales mgr. Guaranty Co. of N.Y., 1926-34; sales rep. E.B. Smith & Co., Smith Barney & Co., 1934-41, Lazard Freres & Co., 1941-48; asst. v.p. Central Hanover Bank & Trust Co., 1948-50; v.p. Hanover Bank, 1950-61; v.p. Mfrs. Hanover Trust Co., N.Y.C., 1961-62, sr. v.p., 1962-69; dir. N.Y. Hanseatic Corp. Mem. Phi Kappa Psi. Presbyn. Clubs: Duquesne (Pitts.); Recess, Bond, Anglers (N.Y.C.); Bond, Dartmouth (N.J.); Detroit; Baltusrol Golf. Home: 13A Sussex Way Rossmoor Jamesburg NJ 08831 Office: 60 Broad St New York City NY 10015

BISHOP, DAVID WAKEFIELD, educator, physiologist; b. Phila., May 23, 1912; s. Jacob Van Sciver and Maud (Lipman) B.; B.A., Swarthmore Coll., 1934; Ph.D., U. Pa., 1942; m. Donna Thorpe, Dec. 9, 1953; children—Timothy, Jane. Instr. zoology U. Pa., 1935-41; research asso. physiology Swarthmore Coll., 1941-42; asst. prof. zoology U. Colo., 1946-47, U. Ill., 1947-48; prof. physiology U. Mass., 1948-51; vis. prof. zoology Cal. Inst. Tech., 1951-52; vis. fellow Max Planck Inst. Med. Research, Heidelberg, Germany, 1956-57; staff mem. dept. embryology Carnegie Instn. Washington, 1952-67; vis. prof. Cornell U., Ithaca, N.Y., 1967-68; prof. physiology Med. Coll. Ohio At Toledo, 1968—. Cons. NSF, 1963—, Lalor Found., 1962—; fellow cons. Planned Parenthood Fedn. Am., 1951-52; v.p. 24th Internat. Physiol. Congress, Washington, 1968. Served with USAAF, 1942-46. Fellow A.A.A.S. (chmn. sect. F. 1968-70, v.p. 1968-70); mem. Am. Physiol. Soc., Am. Soc. Cell Biology, Am. Soc. Zoologists (chmn. sect. on developmental biology 1967), Marine Biol. Lab., Soc. Exptl. Biology and Medicine (pres. Md. sect. 1961-63), Soc. Gen. Physiologists (sec. 1961-63, pres. 1965-66), Soc. Study Growth and Devel., Soc. for Study Reprodn. (dir. 1970—), Soc. for Study Fertility. Democrat. Presbyn. Author: Comparative Animal Physiology, 1950; Spermatozoan Motility, 1962; also research publs. reproductive physiology, enzymology, autoallergy. Editorial bd. Biol. Bull., 1960-63, Am. Zoology, 1961-62, Jour. Exptl. Zoology, 1964-66. Home: 5720 Summit St Sylvania OH 43560

BISHOP, DONALD FRANCIS, investment counselor; b. Phila., Oct. 8, 1897; s. Clarence Meecham and Harriet Baxter (Peirce) B.; student U. Pa., 1922-23; m. Janet Redman, Feb. 10, 1923; children—Nancy Janet, Jane. Investment banker, Eastman, Dillon & Co., Phila., 1920-36; investment counselor Bishop & Co., Phila., 1936-41; v.p. Provident Trust Co., Phila., 1941-46; pres. Bishop & Hedberg, Inc., Phila., 1946-64; pres. Bishop & Assos., Inc., 1963-66, chmn. bd., 1966—. Trustee Rittenhouse Fund. Mem. Musical Fund Soc. Phila., Financial Anaiysts. Club: Union League (Phila.). (Phila.). Home: 249 St Joseph's Way Philadelphia PA 19106 (summer) Loon Ledge Lincolnville Me 04849 Office: 2 Penn Center Plaza Philadelphia PA 19102

BISHOP, DONALD GERST, educator; b. Altoona, Pa., May 16, 1907; s. Walter M. and Maona V. (Mason) B.; A.B. with honors, U. Akron, 1928; M.A., Princeton, 1929; Ph.D., Ohio State U., 1939; m. Iona Fay Maxwell, July 3, 1937. Instr. polit. sci. U. Akron, 1931-32; tchr. Akron pub. schs., 1932-35; grad. asst. polit. sci. Ohio State U., 1935-38; mem. faculty Maxwell Sch., Syracuse U., 1938-72, chmn. citizenship program, 1941-48, prof. polit. sci., 1952-72, chmn. dept. polit. sci., 1965-66, chmn. internat. relations program, 1950-65; prof. polit. sci. Slippery Rock (Pa.) State Coll., 1972—; lectr., news analyst Chautauqua Instn., 1956-68; adj. prof. U. State N.Y., Albany, 1959-63; vis. prof. Tunghai U., Taiwan, 1966-67. Cons. U.S. Govt., 1955—. Mem. Am., N.Y. State (pres. 1960-61) polit. sci. assns., Am. Assn. U. Profs., UN Assn. Central N.Y. Presbyn. Author: (with M.J. Fisher) Municipal and Other Local Governments, 1950; Soviet Foreign Relations, 1952; The Administration of British Foreign Relations, 1961; The Roosevelt-Litvinov Agreements: the American View, 1965; The Administration of United States Foreign Policy Through the United Nations, 1967. Contbr. jours., yearbooks. Office: Dept Polit Sci Slippery Rock State Coll Slippery Rock PA 16057

BISHOP, ELIZABETH, poet; b. Worcester, Mass., Feb. 8, 1911; d. William Thomas and Gertrude (Bulmer) B.; A.B., Vassar Coll., 1934; LL.D., Smith Coll., 1968. Houghton Mifflin poetry fellow., 1945; Guggenheim fellow, 1947; Lucy Martin Donnelly fellow, Bryn Mawr, 1951, Amy Lowell fellow, 1957; lectr. English, Harvard, 1970-71. Cons. poetry Library of Congress, 1949-50. Recipient Am. Acad. Arts and Letters award, 1951; Shelley Meml. award, 1952; Partisan Review fellowship, 1956; Pulitzer prize for poetry, North & South, 1956; award Acad. Am. Poets, 1964, Poetry Soc. Am., 1964; Merrill Found. award, 1969; Nat. Book award, 1969; Order Rio Branco (Brazil), 1971. Nat. Inst. Arts and Letters, Acad. Am. Poets (chancellor 1966—). Author: North & South (poems), 1946; Poems, 1955; Brazil, 1962; Questions of Travel, 1965; Selected Poems, Chatto and Windus, 1967; Complete Poems, 1969. Contbr. poems, stories to mags. and anthologies. Address: Union Sq care Farrar Straus & Giroux New York City NY 10003

BISHOP, GEORGE WESLE educator; b. N.Y.C., Jan. 13, 1910; s. George Wesley and Anna (Farrington) B.; A.B., Coll. William and Mary, 1935; M.B.A., N.Y. U., 1955, Ph.D., 1959; m. Helen Young, Dec. 22, 1942; children—Georgelen Elizabeth Kuhn, George Wesley III. With Union Carbide Corp., N.Y.C., 1935-36, U.S. Gypsum Co., N.Y.C., 1936-42; account exec., portfolio analyst Merrill Lynch, Pierce, Fenner & Smith, N.Y.C., 1947-50, 54-56, 57-59; adminstrv. asst. to dean Grad. Sch. Bus. Adminstrn., N.Y. U., 1956-57; with U. Tenn, 1959-65, asst. prof. finance, 1959-60, asso. prof., 1960-64, prof., 1964-65; prof., head dept. finance No. Ill. U., DeKalb, 1965—; research fellow dept. history Yale, 1970-71; cons., expert witness Fed. Ct. Served with USNR, 1942-46, 50-54. Mem. Omicron Delta Kappa, Delta Sigma Pi, Pi Kappa Alpha, Beta Gamma Sigma. Episcopalian. Author: Charles H. Dow and the Dow Theory, 1960. Editor: Charles H. Dow, Economist, 1967. Contbr. articles profl. jours. Home: 120 Ridge Dr DeKalb IL 60115

BISHOP, HAROLD FRANCIS, educator, physician; b. Barnes City, Ia., May 7, 1908; s. Howard F. and Nelle R. (Dawson) B.; student Ia. Wesleyan Coll., 1926-27; B.A., U. Wis., 1930, M.D., 1933. Intern Phila. Gen. Hosp., 1933-35, resident anesthesiology, 1935-36, med. anesthetist, 1936-37; resident anesthesiology Hartoford Hosp., 1937-38; prof., chmn. dept. anesthesiology N.Y. Med. Coll., 1968—; chmn. anesthesiology Grasslands Hosp.; dir. anesthesiology Grasslands Hosp.; cons. anesthesiology VA Area I, United, Phelps Meml., St. Francis, Vassar Bros., Mt. Vernon, St. John's Riverside, St. Agnes, Greenwich, Yonkers Gen. hosps.; attending anesthesiologist VA Hosp. (Bronx). Active Met. Opera Guild, Westchester Heart Assn. Served as col. M.C., AUS, World War II; chief operating sect. Walter Reed Gen. Hosp., 1941-44, Halloran Gen. Hosp., 1944-46. Fellow N.Y. Acad. Medicine, Westchester Acad. Medicine, Am. Coll. Anesthesiology; mem. A.M.A., Am. Surg. Assn., Alpha Omega Alpha. Contbr. articles profl. jours. Home: Ardsley-on-Hudson NY 19503 Office: 1249 Fifth Av New York City NY 10029

BISHOP, HEWLETT RYDER, assn. exec.; b. Patchogue, N.Y., Feb. 12, 1909; s. Henry J. and Ethelinda (Ryder) B,; ed. Merchant Marine Tng. Center, Bklyn.; m. Ruth H. Truex, July 17, 1938; children—Hewlett Ryder, Marcia Louise. With Roosevelt Steam Ship Co., also U.S. Lines, 1927-41; designated master, 1938; port capt. U.S. Maritime Commn., 1941-42; mgr. cargo operations Atlantic Coast dist. War Shipping Administrn., 1942-45; Atlantic Coast dir. Maritime Adminstrn., Dept. Commerce, 1945-64; exec. v.p. Nat. Cargo Bur., N.Y.C., 1964—. U.S. rep. to Intergovt. Maritime Consultative Orgn., London, 1964—, chmn. internat. sub-com. on bulk cargoes, 1964-68, chmn. internat. sub-com. on containers and cargoes, 1969—; adviser municipal state and fed. groups; devel. macanno deck on tankers enabling additional cargo, World War II. Vice Chmn. Fed. Exec. Bd., 1962-63; mem. marine sect. Nat. Safety Council. Exec. com. Am. Merchant Marine Library Assn. Recipient Meritorious Service medal Dept. Commerce, 1956, Career Service award Nat. Civil Service League, 1963, Distinguished Service medal for Americanism, Am. Legion, 1952. Mem. Am. Nat. Standards Inst., Maritime Assn. Port N.Y., Fed. Bus. Assn. (pres.), Propeller Club U.S. (gov.), Nat. Cargo Bur., Nat. Fire Protection Assn., Water Island Assn. Methodist. Mason. Clubs: India House, Whitehall. Author articles. Home: 188 N Long Beach Av Freeport NY 11520 Office: 99 John St New York City NY 10038

BISHOP, ISABEL (Mrs. Harold G. Wolff), artist; b. Cin., Mar. 3, 1902; d. John Remsen and Anna Bartram (Newbold) Bishop; ed. Wicker Art Sch., Detroit, 1917-18, N.Y. Sch. Applied Design for Women, 1918-20, Art Students League N.Y., 1920-22, 1927-30; A.F.D. (hon.), Moore Inst., Phila.; m. Harold George Wolff, Aug. 9, 1934. Instr. life painting and composition Art Students League, N.Y.C., 1936-37; instr. Snowhegan Sch. Painting and Sculpture, 1957, lectr., 1957, 60, 62, 64, 66, Rep. Mus. Bibliotheque Nationale, Paris, Victoria and Albert Mus., London, Des Moines Art Center, and art galleries, collections Paul Sachs, Johnson Collection, others. Exhibited expns.; 6 one-man shows in N.Y.C., one-man show at Berkshire Museum, Pittsfield, Mass., 1957. Awards include W.A. Clark Prize ($1,000), Bronze Medal, Corcoran Gallery, Washington, 1945; Mrs. H. S. Noyes and Am. Artists Group prizes, 1947; Benjamin Franklin fellow Royal Soc. Art, 1965; first Altman prize N.A.D., 1967; Asso. mem. N.A.D., 1940; elected Nat. Academician, 1941. Fellow Royal Soc. Arts London; mem. Nat. Inst. Arts and Letters, Am. Soc. Painters, Sculptors and Gravers, Soc. Am. Etchers, Nat. Arts Club, Phila. Water Color Club, Am. Group Cosmopolitan Club. Home: 355 W 246th St Fieldston New York City NY 10463 Studio: 857 Broadway New York City NY 10003

BISHOP, JACK GARLAND, educator, physiologist; b.. Ft. Worth, Tex., Sept. 12, 1919; s. James Garland and Sallie (Blackwell) B.; B.S., N. Tex. State U., 1946, M.S., 1949; Ph.D, Ind. U., 1955; m. Mary Frances Stubblefield, Aug. 2, 1946; 1 dau., Julia Anne. From undergrad. asst. to instr. biology N. Tex. Sta U., 1945-51; grad. asst. physiology, then research asst. Ind. U., 1951- 54; mem. faculty Baylor U. Coll. Dentustry, 1954—, prof. physiology, chmn. dept., 1959-69, asst. dean grad. study and research, 1969, asso. dean Grad. Sch., 1970—. Cons. program-project com. NIH, 1968—. Bd. dirs. Med. Research Found. Tex., 1961. Served with USAAF, 1941-44. Fellow A.A.A.S.; mem. Soc. Exptl. Biology and Medicine, Tex. Acad. Sci., Am. Physiol. Soc., Internat. Assn. Dental Research, Sigma Xi. Author articles in field. Home: 5011 Horseshoe Trail Dallas TX 75209

BISHOP, JIM, author: b. Jersey City, Nov. 21, 1907; s. John Michael and Jenny Josephine (Tier) B.; student Drakes Secretarial Coll., 1923; Litt.D., St. Bonaventure U., 1958; Litt.D., Belmont Abbey Coll., 1968; m. Elinor Margaret Dunning, June 14, 1930 (dec. Oct. 1957); children—Virginia Lee, Gayle Peggy; m. 2d, Elizabeth Kelly Stone, May, 1961; children—Karen, Kathleen. Copy boy N.Y. News, 1929-30; reporter N.Y. Daily Mirror, 1930-32, asst. to Mark Bellinger, columnist, 1932-34, rewriteman, feature writer Daily Mirror, 1934-43; asso. editor Colliers mag., 1943-44, war editor, 1944-45; exec. editor Liberty mag., 1945-47; dir. lit. dept. Music Corp. Am., 1947-49; founding editor Gold Medal Books, 1949-51; exec. editor Catholic Digest, founding editor Catholic Digest Book Club, 154-55; v.p. Royalty Prodns., Inc. (TV), Jacksonville. Club: Dutch Treat (N.Y.C.). Author: The Glass Crutch, 1945; The Mark Hellinger Story, 1952; Parish Priest, 1953; The Girl in Poison Cottage, 1953; The Making of a Priest, 1954; The Day Lincoln Was Shot, 1955; The Golden Ham, 1956; The Day Christ Died, 1957; Go With God, 1958; Some of My Very Best; 1960; The Day Christ Was Born, 1960; The Murder Trial of Judge Peal, 1962; Honeymoon Diary, 1963; A Day in the Life of President Kennedy, 1964; Jim Bishop; Reporter, 1965; A Day in the Life of President Johnson, 1967; The Day Kennedy was Shot, 1968. Columnist, King Features Syndicate. Contbr. nat. mags. Home: Golden Isles 442 Tamarind Dr Hallandale FL 33009

BISHOP, JOEY, (Joseph Abraham Gottlieb), comedian; b. Bronx, N.Y., Feb. 3, 1918; ed. pub. schs. Phila.; m. Sylvia Ruzga; 1 son, Larry. Comedian, Eastern burlesque circuit, 1938-42, Vine Gardens, N.J., 1948-49, Chez Paree, Chgo.; motion pictures include The Deep Six, Onionhead, The Naked and The Dead, Ocean's 11, Sargents 3; TV appearances include Keep Talking, Jack Paar Show; summer stock appearance in Who Was That Lady I Saw You With?, 1960; star Joey Bishop Show, 1961-69; guest appearances TV and nightclubs. Home: 1025 Chevy Chase Dr Beverly Hills CA 90210

BISHOP, JOHN H., lawyer; b. Monterey, Va., Jan. 14, 1896; s. Vergil B. and Mary Jane (Miller) B.; LL.B., U. Va., 1918; m. Mildred Charleen, 1928. Admitted to Ill. bar, 1920, since practiced in Chgo.; partner firm Fink, Lowes & Bishop, 1920-28, Woods & Bishop, 1928-30, Bishop & Burdett, 1930- 35, Bishop, Mitchell, Burdett, 1935-45, Bishop & Burdett, 1945-46, Bishop, Ericson, & Flynn and predecessor firm, 1946—; dir. 1st Nat. Bank in Harvey (Ill.), Chgo. Rawhide Mfg. Co., S.J. Reynolds Co., Kenwood Constrn. Co., Phillips Drill Co., Williams Press, Inc., John W. Clarke & Co. Mem. Am., Ill., Chgo. bar assns. Clubs: Chicago Athletic, Attic, Olympia Fields Country. Home: 1310 Ritchie Ct Chicago IL 60610 Office: 141 W Jackson Blvd Chicago IL 60604

BISHOP, JOSEPH WARREN, Jr., lawyer, educator; b. N.Y.C., Apr. 15, 1915; s. Joseph Warren and Edna Priscilla (Dashiell) B.; grad Deerfield Acad., 1932; A.B., Dartmouth, 1936; LL.B., Harvard, 1940; m. Susan Carroll Oulahan, May 6, 1950; 1 son, Joseph Warren III. Admitted to D.C. bar, 1941, N.Y. bar, 1954, Conn. bar, 1963; spl. asst. to undersec. war, 1940-42; with Office Solicitor Gen., Dept. Justice, 1947-50; asst. to gen. counsel U.S. High Commn. Occupied Germany, 1950-52; dep. gen. counsel, acting gen. counsel Dept. Army, 1952-53; pvt. practice law, N.Y.C., 1953-57; prof. law Yale Law Sch., 1957—, Richard Ely prof. law, 1968—; vis. prof. law U. Muenster (West Germany), 1965; faculty Salzburg Seminar Am. Studies, 1967; asst. counsel trustees New Haven R.R. 1961—. Expert cons. SEC, 1958. Served with AUS, 1943-46. Recipient exceptional civilian service citation Dept. Army, 1953. Mem. Am., New Haven County bar assns. Democrat. Club: New Haven (Conn.) Lawn. Author: (with G.T. Washington) Indemnifying the Corporate Executive, 1963; Obiter Dicta, 1971; also articles book revs. Home: 83 E Rock Rd New Haven CT 06511

BISHOP, LEO KENNETH, clergyman, educator; b. Britton, Okla., Oct. 11, 1911; s. Luther and Edith (Scovill) B.; A.B., Phillips U., 1932; L.H.D., 1958; M.A. Columbia U., 1944; M.B.A., U. Chgo., 1957; Litt.D., Kansas City Coll. Osteopathy and Surgery, 1964; m. Pauline T. Shamburg, Sept. 15, 1935; 1 dau., Linda Paulette. Ordained to ministry Christian Ch., 1932; asso. minister Univ. Place Ch., Okla. City, 1932-35; minister First Ch., Paducah, Ky., 1935-41, Central Ch., Des Moines, 1941-45; dir. St. Louis office Nat. Conf. Christians and Jews, 1945-48, v.p., dir. central div., Chgo., 1949-63; dir. pub. affairs People-to-People, Kansas City, Mo., 1963-66; v.p. Chgo. Coll. Osteopathy, 1966—, also lectr. Cons. Community Social Planning Council, Mayor's Race Relations Com., YMCA, St. Louis; Am. del. Conf. World Brotherhood, Paris, 1950; bd. dirs. Am. Heritage Found. Recipient Jr. C. of C. Most Useful Citizen award, Puducah, 1937, Distinguished Service award Dore Miller Found., 1958, Freedom Found. of Valley Forge award, 1961; named Chicagoan of Year, 1960. Clubs: Rotary, Union League. Contbr. religious and ednl. jours. Developed radio series Storm Warning, TV series, The Other Guy, 1954. Home: 4940 East End Av Chicago IL 60615 Office: 5200 S Ellis Av Chicago IL 60615

BISHOP, LEONARD A., ins. co. exec.; b. Elizabeth, N.J., Sept. 8, 1908; ed. in N.J. With Great Am. Ins. Co., 1930-70, sec., 1959-70, v.p., 1963; also v.p., sec. Am. Nat. Fire Ins. Co. Mem. accounting adv. com. Coll. of Ins. Mem. Ins. Accountants Soc., Ins. Accounting and Statis. Assn. Mason: Home: 380 Irvington Av Elizabeth NJ*

BISHOP, LUTHER DOYLE, educator; b. Graham, Tex., Oct. 31, 1921; s. Luther Whitfield and Clara Bell (Rowe) B.; student Baylor U., 1939-40; B.B.A., U. Tex., 1948, M.B.A., 1950; Ph.D., Ohio State U., 1959; m. Nan Alice Schneider, Mar. 15, 1942. With Clifton Mfg. Co., Waco, Tex., 1940-42, Brown and Boot Constrn. Co., Texarkana, Tex., 1942; mgr. vets dormitories U. Tex., 1948- 49, instr. mgmt. dept., 1949-51; faculty U. Okla., Norman, 1951—, prof. bus. mgmt., 1959—, chmn. dept., 1959-68, 70—. Grad. asst. in bus. orgn. Ohio State U., 1953-54. Served with USNR, 1942-45. Mem. Acad. Mgmt., Am. Assn. U. Profs., Indsl. Mgmt. Soc., Soc. Advancement Mgmt., Southwestern Social Sci. Assn., Beta Gamma Sigma. Home: 1201 Avondale Dr Norman OK 73069

BISHOP, MARGARET STEARNS, (Mrs. Barton Phelps Bishop), educator, author; b. Lewiston, Mich., June 21, 1906; d. Harry Lindley and Lizzie (Christman) S.; A.B., U. Mich., 1929, M.S., 1931, Ph.D., 1933; m. Barton Phelps Bishop, Aug. 14, 1937; children—Harry Barton, Richard Stearns. Jr. geologist Pure Oil Co., 1929-30, 33-35, asst. to chief geologist, 1935-38, cons., 1938-53; asst. prof. U. Houston, 1953- 57, asso. prof., 1957-65, prof., 1965—, dir. Earth Sci. Insts., 1965—. Mem. Am. Assn. Petroleum Geologists, Nat. Assn. Geology Tchrs., Geol. Soc. Am., Tex. Acad. Sci., Houston Geol. Soc., Phi Beta Kappa, Sigma Xi, Phi Kappa Phi. Author: Subsurface Mapping, 1960. Focus on Earth Science, 1969. Home: 1921 Brunson St Houston TX 77025 Office: U Houston 3800 Cullen Blvd Houston TX 77004

BISHOP, MORRIS GILBERT, educator, author; b. Willard, N.Y., Apr. 15, 1893; s. Edwin Rubergall and Bessie (Gilbert) B.; A.B., Cornell U., 1913, A.M. 1914, Ph.D., 1926; Dr. honoris causa, U. Rennes, 1948; D.Litt., Union Coll., 1953, U. Laval, 1954, Hofstra Coll., 1956, Colgate U., 1959; Litt.D. (hon.) Trent U., 1969; m. Alison Mason Kingsbury, June 14, 1927; 1 dau., Alison. Instr. Romance langs. Cornell U., 1921-26, asst. prof., 1926-36, prof., 1936-60, faculty trustee, 1957-60, curator Cornell Dante and Petrarch Coll., 1970—; vis. prof. Am. civilization U. Athens, 1951-52; faculty trustee Cornell U., 1957-60. Mem. Am. Relief Adminstrn. Mission to Finland, 1919. Served as lt. in inf. U.S. Army, World War I; with O.W.I., N.Y. and London, 1942-44, Psychol. Warfare Div., AUS 1944-45. Decorated Order White Rose (Finland); Officier d'Académie, Chevalier Legion d'Honneur (France). Fellow A.A.A.S.; mem. Modern Lang. Assn. Am. (pres. 1964), Am. Assn. Tchrs. French, Phi Beta Kappa (senator 1958-64). Unitarian. Clubs: P.E.N., Century (N.Y.C.). Author: Champlain, The Life of Fortitude, 1948; The Life and Adventures of La Rochefoucauld, 1951; A Bowl of Bishop, 1954; College Survey of French Literature, 1955; White Men Came to The St. Lawrence, 1961; A History of Cornell, 1962; Petrarch and His World, 1963; Blaise Pascal, Life and Works, 1966; Letters from Petrarch, 1966; The Horizon Book of the Middle Ages, 1968; The Exotics, 1969. Editor: A Medieval Storybook, 1970; A Classical Storybook, 1970; A Renaissance Storybook, 1971; A Romantic Storybook, 1971. Translator: Eight Plays of Moliere, 1957. Home: 903 Wyckoff Rd Ithaca NY 14850

BISHOP, RICHARD EVETT, artist; b. Syracuse, N.Y., May 30, 1887; s. Richard Whitney and Minnie (Blackall) B.; M.E., Cornell U., 1909; m. Mary Helen Harrington, 1915. Elec. engr. Cutler Hammer Mfg. Co., Milw., 1909-17; sec. and sales mgr. Harrington Co., Phila., 1919-33; retired from bus., 1933, began etching as profession; specializes etchings and paintings wild fowl and game birds; decorator of glassware, service plates, medals, tiles, jewelry and linen with game birds. Exhibited Acad. Fine Arts, Phila., Chgo. Art Inst., Cleve. Mus. Art, Bklyn. Mus., Nat. Acad., N.Y.C., Nat. Mus., Washington, others. Served as capt. Chem. Warfare Service, U.S. Army, 1917-19. Mem.

WPB, 1942-44, chief dep. regional dir., region 6, 1944. Mem. Am., Chgo. socs. etchers, Print Makers Cal., Zoöl. Soc. Phila. (dir.), Acad. Natural Scis., Franklin Inst., Ducks Unlimited (hon. trustee), Delta Upsilon. Clubs: Rittenhouse, Philadelphia Cricket, Wilderness, Boon and Crockett, Lacota. Author: Bishop's Birds, 1936; Bishop's Wildfowl, 1948; co-author Ways of Wild Fowl, 1971. Address: 6706 Springbank St Philadelphia PA 19119 summer studio: Enoch's Acres Gaysville VT 05032

BISHOP, ROBERT LYLE, economist, educator; b. St. Louis, June 4, 1916; s. Lyle Austin and Helen (Craden) B.; A.B., Harvard, 1937, M.A., 1942, Ph.D., 1949; postgrad. Princeton, 1938-39; m. Joan Frances Fiss, Sept. 12, 1942. Instr. econs. Harvard, 1939-42; faculty Mass. Inst. Tech., 1942—, successively instr., asst. prof., asso. prof., 1942-57, prof. econs., head dept. econs. and social sci., 1958-65, dean Sch. Humanities and Social Scis., 1964—; vis. lectr. Harvard; vis. prof. Brandeis U. Mem. Am. Econ. Assn., Econometric Soc., Am. Acad. Arts and Scis., Phi Beta Kappa. Home: 27 Amherst Rd Wellesley MA 02181 Office: Mass Inst Tech Cambridge MA 02139

BISHOP, ROBERT MILTON, stock exchange ofcl.; b. Elmira, N.Y., June 5, 1921; s. Milton W. and Florence E. (Crofutt) B.; A.B., Union Coll., Schenectady, 1943; A.M., Trinity Coll., Hartford, Conn., 1955; m. Anne Selene Rowan, Oct. 30, 1943; children—Donald M., Anne Selene (Mrs. Donald R. Bennett), Elizabeth M., Robert Milton, Regina J.M., Rowan J.S. Asst. dir. pub. relations Union Coll., Schenectady, 1945-47; dir. pub. relations Trinity Coll., 1947- 55; mem. staff N.Y. Stock Exchange, 1955—, dir. dept. mem. firms liaison, asst. dir. dept. mem. firms, 1961-63, v.p., asso. dir. dept. mem. firms, 1963-65, v.p., dir. dept. mem. firms, 1965-71, v.p. spl. projects, 1971—. Served as pilot USAAF, 1943-45. Episcopalian. Author booklets, securities tng. manuals. Home: 4 Kimball Circle Westfield NJ 07090 Office: NY Stock Exchange 4 New York Plaza New York City NY 10004

BISHOP, ROBERT W., ednl. adminstr.; b. Waynesville, N.C., May 24, 1902; s. Jesse Norman and Adelphia Elizabeth (Marshburn) B.; ed. Maryville Coll., U. Mich., YMCA Grad. Sch., U. N.C., U. Cin.; m. Helen Rebecca Chapman, June 18, 1930; 1 son, Barry Chapman. Exec. dir. U. Cin. YMCA, 1929-45; dean men U. Cin., 1946-60, dean summer sch., 1960. Mem. nat. bd. Student YMCA, 1937-41. Bd. dirs. Cin. Social Health Soc., 1962-64. Mem. Assn. Coll. Honor Socs. (pres. 1949-51), Nat. Conf. Coll. Frats. and Socs. (pres. 1951-54), Nat. Assn. Student Personnel Adminstrs., Nat. Assn. Coll. and Univ. Summer Schs., Phi Eta Sigma, Theta Chi, Pi Delta Epsilon, Theta Alpha Phi, Omicron Delta Kappa (mem. gen. council 1935—, nat. sec. and editor The Circle, 1937-64, nat. pres. 1964-68, cons. and adviser gen. council 1970—), Scabbard and Blade, Pershing Rifles. Club: Cincinnati Faculty. Office: U Cin Cincinnati OH 45221

BISHOP, SAMUEL WORTH, aerospace co. exec.; b. Lometa, Tex., Aug. 16, 1916; s. Archie Lee and Ora Christian (Bradford) B.; B.B.A., U. Tex., 1947; grad. Advanced Mgmt. Program, Harvard; m. Rebecca Page Stone, June 17, 1944; children—Rebecca Stone, Samuel Worth, Conrad, David. Commd. 2d lt. U.S. Army Air Corps, 1940, advanced through grades to col. USAF, 1952; ret. dep. chief staff material, Hdqrs., Air Research and Devel. Command, 1961; pres., dir. Electronic Communications, Inc., St. Petersburg, Fla., 1961—; now v.p. Nat. Cash Register Co.; dir. 1st Nat. Bank, St. Petersburg, Milton Roy Co. Mem. Fla. Council of 100. Decorated Silver Star, Legion of Merit, Purple Heart. Mem. Air Force Assn., Army Ordnance Assn., Armed Forces Communications and Electronics Assn. (dir.), Navy League, St. Petersburg C. of C. (bd. govs. 1962-65), Pinellas County Com. 100 (exec. com. 1965-66), Newcomen Soc. Episcopalian. Clubs: Suncoasters, Golden Triangle Assn., St. Petersburg Yacht, Sunset Country (St. Petersburg). Home: 1833 Brightwaters Blvd St Petersburg FL 33704 Office: 1501 72d St N St Petersburg FL 33733

BISHOP, SIDNEY WILLARD, lawyer; b. Denver, Oct. 28, 1926; s. Sidney W. and Helen (Marihugh) B.; B.S., Regis Coll., Denver, 1949; J.D., U. Denver, 1950; m. Betty Lou Dolan, May 10, 1947; children—Linda, Thomas, Nancy, Joan, Ann, Mary, Elizabeth, Sidney Willard III, Jane. Admitted to Colo. bar, 1950, Cal. bar, 1958; with January & Yegge, Denver, 1949-50; dep. dist. atty. Cheyenne County, Colo., 1951-56; pvt. practice, Cheyenne Wells, Colo., 1950-56; with Prudential Ins. Co. Am., Los Angeles, 1956-61, 64-68; asst. counsel law dept., 1958-61, asst. gen. solicitor, 1964-66, dir. govt. relations, 1966-68; gen. counsel Am. Ins. Assn., N.Y.C., 1968-70; mem. firm Svenson & Garvin, Van Nuys, Cal., 1970—; confidential asst. to postmaster gen. U.S., 1961; asst. postmaster gen. bur. facilites, 1962-63, dep. postmaster gen., 1963-64. So. Cal. vice chmn. Statewide Water Devel. Com., 1959-60. Served with USNR, 1944-46. Home: 6519 Langdon Av Van Nuys CA 91406 Office: 6842 Van Nuys Blvd Van Nuys CA 91405

BISHOP, THOMAS EDWARD, govt. ofcl.; b. Cin., Aug. 18, 1917; s. William H. and Mary (Brennan) B.; A.B., U. Cin., 1939; LL.B., Chase Coll. Law, Cin., 1950; m. Carleen E. Stephens, Mar. 1, 1946; children—Patricia Ann, Kevin R. Spl. agt. FBI, Washington, 1941-54, asst. spl. agt in charge, 1954-60, spl. agt. in charge, 1960-65, inspector, 1965-67, inspector in charge, 1967-68, asst. dir., 1968—. Mem Phi Alpha Delta. Home: 8820 Stark Rd Annandale VA 22003 Office: Justice Bldg Washington DC 20535

BISHOP, WARNER BADER, indsl. exec.; b. Lakewood, O., Dec. 13, 1918; s. Warner Brown and Gladys (Bader) B.; A.B., Dartmouth, 1941, M.B.A., Amos Tuck Grad. Sch., 1942; grad. Advanced Mgmt. Program, Harvard, 1955; m. Katherine Sue White, Dec. 15, 1944; children—Susan, Judith, Katharine, Jennifer; m. 2d, Barrie Osborn, Feb. 4, 1967; children—Wilder, Brooks. With Archer-Daniels-Midland Co., Cleve., 1946-59, successively sales rep., export mgr., sales mgr., divisional gen. mgr., asst. v.p., 1946-56, v.p., 1956-59; pres. Fed. Foundry Supply Co., 1957-59, Wyodak Clay & Chem. Co., 1957-59, Basic, Inc., until 1963; chmn. bd., pres. Union Financial Corp., Union Savs. Assn., Cleve., 1963—; chmn. Cowles Tool Co., Copifyer Lithograph Corp.; dir. Port Clinton Nat. Bank, Bell Intercontinental, Pacific Industries, Aurora Corp., Nat. Cleve. Corp.; trustee Nat. Mortgage Fund. Sec. Foundry Ednl. Found., 1956-60; gen. campaign mgr. Cleve. Area Heart Soc., bd. chmn., 1960-61; mem. corp. Fenn Coll. Bd. dirs. Ohio Heart Soc.; chmn. Highland Redevel. Corp., 1963-68; pres. Council High Blood Pressure. Served to lt. USNR, 1942-45; comdg. officer escort vessels. Foundrymen's Soc., Am. Inst. Mining and Metallurgy, Refractories Inst., Dolomitic Refractories Assn. (v.p.), Cleve. C. of C., Internat. Inst. Gen. Semantics, Cleve. Art Assn., Cleve., Citizens League, Phi Gamma Clubs: Kirtland Country (Willoughby, O.); Dartmouth, Union, Tavern (Cleve.). Contbr. articles to trade jours. Home: 2965 Fairmount Blvd Cleveland Heights OH 44118 Office: 232 Superior Av Cleveland OH 44114

BISHOP, WILLIAM WARNER, Jr., educator, lawyer; b. Princeton, N.J., June 10, 1906; s. William Warner and Finie Murfree (Burton) B.; A.B., U. Mich., 1928, J.D., 1931; postgrad. Harvard, 1928-29, Columbia, 1938-39; m. Mary Fairfax Shreve, July 19, 1947; 1 dau., Elizabeth Shreve. Admitted to Mich. bar, 1931, U.S. Supreme Ct., 1941; asst. reporter Harvard Research Internat. Law, 1932- 35, mem. exec. com., 1949—; asso. Root, Clark, Buckner & Ballantine, N.Y.C., 1935-36; lectr. politics Princeton, 1936-38; asst. legal adv. Dept. State, 1939-47; vis. prof. internat. law Law Sch., U. Pa., 1947-48, Columbia, 1948; research, teaching asst. Law Sch., U. Mich., 1931-35, prof. law, 1948—. Legal adviser to U.S. delegation Council Fgn. Ministers and Paris Peace Conf., 1946; lectr. Hague Acad. Internat. Law, 1961, 65. Mem. Am. Bar Assn., Mich. State Bar, Institut de Droit Internat. (asso.), Am. Soc. Internat. Law (v.p. 1960-61, 65-66, hon. v.p. 1969—), Internat. Law Assn. Author: International Law Cases and Materials, 1962, 70; articles legal jours. Mem. bd. editors Am. Jour. Internat. Law, 1947—, editor-in-chief, 1953-55, 62-70; contbg. editor Ann. Digest of Pub. Internat. Law Cases, 1931-40. Home: 1612 Morton Av Ann Arbor MI 48104

BISHOPRIC, KARL, advt. exec.; b. Greensboro, N.C., Jan. 5, 1925; s. James Robert Karl and Frances (Farrell) B.; student U. N.C., 1941-44; m. Rose Anne Straub, Mar. 4, 1944; children—Robert Lewis, James Nelson (dec.), Bruce Graham. With Houck & Co., Roanoke, Va. and Miami, Fla., 1946-54; pres. Houck & Co. Fla., 1948-54; pres. Bishopric & Fielden, Inc., Miami and N.Y.C., 1954-68, chmn. bd., 1968—; treas. Woody Kepner Asso., Inc., Miami, 1957—; v.p., dir. Advt. & Marketing Internat. Network, Inc.; dir. Fla. Nat. Bank & Trust Co., Miami. Pres. United Fund Dade County, 1967-68, trustee, 1963—; chmn. Port Action Com., 1969-71; bd. dirs. Community TV Found. S. Fla., 1965-67, v.p., 1969—; dir. citizens bd. U. Miami, 1966—; bd. dir. Econ. Soc. S. Fla., 1969—, Urban Coalition Greater Miami, 1968—; bd. dirs. Urban League Greater Miami, 1956-65, pres., 1956-60; chmn. budget leaders conf. United Funds and Community Councils Am., 1968. Served to lt. (j.g.) USNR, 1944-46. Recipient Printer's Ink Silver medal. Mem. Am. Assn. Advt. Agys., Greater Miami C. of C. (dir.), Young Pres. Orgn., Alpha Delta Sigma, Beta Theta Pi. Home: 60 Casuarina Concourse Coral Gables FL 33143 Office: 3361 SW 3d Av Miami FL 33145

BISHTON, ROBERT ARTHUR, fgn. service officer; b. Ilion, N.Y., Dec. 31, 1922; s. Frederick and Helena Augusta (Bagans) B.; B.A., U. Md., 1944; postgrad. Georgetown U., 1946-47, Cornell U., 1953-54; m. Jane Elizabeth Plitt, Jan. 5, 1945; children—Patricia (Mrs. Kent Swanson), Sandra (Mrs. Robert Oliver Stevens), Robert, Michael, David. Joined U.S. Fgn. Service, 1948; vice consul, Dublin, Ireland, 1948-50; asst. comml. attache, Bangkok, Thailand, 1951-53; consul, Surabaya, Indonesia, 1954-58; 2d sec., consul Am. embassy, Djakarta, Indonesia, 1958-59; consul, Rotterdam, Netherlands, 1959-63; fgn. affairs officer Dept. State, 1963-67; consul gen., Saigon, Vietnam, 1967-69, Buenos Aires, Argentina, 1969—. Served with USNR, 1945-46. Mem. Alpha Tau Omega, Omicron Delta Kappa. Address: Dept State Buenos Aires Washington DC 20521

BISKUP, GEORGE JOSEPH, clergyman; b. Cedar Rapids, Ia., Aug. 23, 1911; s. Frank L. and Julia (Kuda) K.; A.B., Loras Coll., 1933; student Gregorian U., Rome, 1933-37. Ordained priest Roman Cath. Ch., 1937; curate St. Raphael's Cathedral, Dubuque, Ia., 1937-39; faculty Loras Coll., 1939- 48; head art dept. Loras Coll., 1941-48; minutante sacred congregation Oriental Ch., Vatican City, 1948-51; chancellor of Archdiocese of Dubuque, 1951-52, vicar gen., 1952-65; bishop of Des Moines, 1965-67; bishop of Indpls., 1967-70, archbishop, 1970—; pastor St. Joseph's Ch., 1951-52; chaplain Mt. Loretta Convent, Dubuque, 1952-58; archdiocesan dir. Cath. Cemeteries, 1953-58, aux. bishop, 1957- 65; pastor Ch. of Nativity, 1958-65. Vice pres. Archdiocese Dubuque, Inc., 1952-65. Papal chamberlain, 1949, domestic prelate, 1951. Address: 1350 N Pennsylvania St Indianapolis IN 46202

BISPLINGHOFF, RAYMOND LEWIS, educator; b. Hamilton, O., Feb. 7, 1917; s. Roscoe Earl and Isabelle (Lewis) B.; A.E., U. Cin., 1940, M.Sc., 1942; Sc.D., 1963; Sc.D., Swiss Fed. Inst. Tech., 1957; D.Eng. (hon.), Case Inst. Tech., 1965; m. Ruth Doherty, June 20, 1944; children—Ross Lee, Ron Sprague. Engr. Aeronca Aircraft Corp., 1937-40, Wright Field, 1940-41; instr. U. Cin., 1941-43; engr. Bur. Aero., Navy Dept., Washington, 1943-46; asst. prof. Mass. Inst. Tech., 1946-48, asso. prof., 1948-53, prof., 1953-62; dir. Office Advanced Research and Tech., NASA, Washington, 1962-63, asso. adminstr., 1963-65, spl. asst. to adminstr., 1965- 66; prof., head dept. aeros. and astronautics Mass. Inst. Tech., Cambridge, 1966-68, dean Coll. Engring., 1968-70; dep. dir. NSF, 1970—; cons. Dept. Def., adminstr. NASA, FAA; Wright Brothers lectr., Inst. Aero. Scis., 1955; Samuel P. Langley lectr. U. Pitts., 1962; 3d Ann. von Karman lectr. Am. Inst. Aeros. and Astronautics, 1965; dir. Allied Research Assos., Allied Systems Ltd., Gen. Aircraft Corp.; mem. corporate adv. council Eastern Air Lines; mem. sci. adv. bd. USAF; chmn. research and tech. adv. council NASA. Mem. advanced policy studies adv. com. George Washington U.; U.S. mem. Internat. Council Aero. Scis.; mem. vis. com. Princeton, Carnegie-Mellon U. Recipient certificate of Merit, USAF; Sylvanus Reed award Inst. Aero. Scis., 1958; Distinguished Service medal NASA, 1967; Extraordinary Service medal FAA, 1968. Fellow Am. Acad. Arts and Scis., A.A.A.S., Inst. Aero. Scis., Am. Astronautical Soc., Am. Inst. Aeros. and Astronautics (pres. 1966), Royal Aero. Soc.; mem. Nat. Acad. Engring., Nat. Acad. Sci., Def. Sci. Bd., Internat. Acad. Astronautics, Engrs. Council for Profl. Devel. (dir.), Engrs. Joint Council (dir.), Sigma Xi, Tau Beta Pi. Mason. Club: Cosmos (Washington). Author: Aeroelasticity (with others), 1955; Principles of Aeroelasticity (with H. Ashley), 1962; Solid Mechanics (with J.W. Mar and T.H.H. Pian) 1966; also numerous profl. papers. Assos. editor Jour. of Franklin Inst.; cons. editor McGraw Hill Ency. Technology. Home: 15 Fife Rd Wellesley Hills MA 02181 Office: National Science Found Washington DC 20418

BISQUE, RAMON E., geochemist, educator; b. Stambaugh, Mich., Sept. 1, 1931; s. Edward and Camilla (Zyskowski) B.; B.S., St. Norbert Coll., 1953; M.S. in Chemistry, Ia. State U., 1956, M.S. in Geology, 1957, Ph. D., 1959; m. Marie L. Young, July 31, 1954; children—Camille Luise, Stephen Michael, Laura L., Thomas Matthew, Daniel Ramon, Matthew Livingston. Asst. prof. chemistry Colo. Sch. Mines, 1959-62, asso. prof., 1962-68, dir. Earth grad. dean Colo. Sch. Mines, 1967—. Bd. dirs., co-founder Earth Scis., Inc.; cons. Inst. for Def. Analyses. Mem. Geochem. Soc., Am. Chem. Soc., Geol. Soc. Am., Am. Inst. Profl. Geologists, Sigma Xi. Distinguished lectr. Am. Assn. Petroleum Geologists, 1968. Research on global tectonics and earth's core; developed with G.E. Rouse theory that stresses at interface in earth's interior (globally) control distbn. of surface features, such as mountains, deep oceanic trenches, mineral belts, island arcs, etc.; theory asserts that quakes, volcanoes,, rifts fall into ordered pattern and are not chance happenings; provides possibility for prediction of earthquakes; asserted that intergalactic and interplanetary magnetic fields may react sufficiently with earth's magnetic field to cause core to rotate a little differently than earth does on regular turning around axis. Office: Colo Sch Mines Golden CO 80401

BISSELL, ALFRED ELLIOTT, investment banker; b. Wilmington, Del., Feb. 11, 1903; s. George Perkins and Jessie Lane (Elliott) B.; grad. magna cum laude, Hill Sch., 1921; A.B., Yale, 1925; LL.D., U. Del., 1965; m. Julia du Pont Andrews, June 1, 1929; children—Julia du Pont (Mrs. Edward B. Leisenring), Antonia Valerie (Mrs. Walter J. Laird, Jr.), Alfred Elliott, Susan Patten, (Mrs. George M. Parker, Jr.). With firm Laird, Bissell & Meeds, Wilmington, 1926—, partner, 1930—, now dir.; dir. Del. Trust Co., Wilmington, 1948—, mem. exec. com., 1952—, chmn. 1966—; dir. Farmers Bank of Del., Wilmington, 1934—, exec. com., 1946—; trustee, v.p., Del. Park, Inc., Wilmington, 1962—; dir. Del. Steeplechase and Race Assn., Wilmington; chmn. finance com., trustee Group Hosp. Service, Inc., Wilmington, 1961-70. Treas., Layton Home for Aged Persons. Wilmington, 1936; bd. dirs., pres. Old Brandywine Village, Inc., Wilmington, 1962- 70; bd. dirs. Del. chpt. A.R.C., 1930-50, chmn., 1934-36; Catholic Diocese Found., 1962-70, mem. finance com. Wilmington Med. Center, 1967—; pres. past treas. U. Del. Library Assos.; chmn. finance com. Home of Merciful Rest, 1948-70; treas. Friends of H.F. du Pont Winterthur Mus., 1966-70; trustee, exec. and finance coms. Hill Sch., 1951-54; trustee, treas. U. Del. Friends of Library, 1959-61; v.p., trustee Copeland-Andelot Found., 1956—; treas. trustee Winterthur Corp., 1957—, trustee Unidel Found., 1962- -; treas. mem. bd. mgmt. Wilmington Inst. Free Library, 1952—; trustee, v.p. Bredin Found. 1966—; trustee, treas. Tower Hill Sch., 1950-69. Served to capt. USAAF, 1942-45. Mem. Wilmington Savs. Fund Soc., Hist. Soc. Del., Nat. Trust Hist. Preservation, Soc. Colonial Wars, Wilmington Soc. Fine Arts, Conferie des Chevaliers du Tastevin. Clubs: Tennis, Palmetto Golf (Aiken, S.C.); Camp Harmony Angling Assn. (Matapedia, Que., Can.); Cotton Bay (Eleuthera, Bahamas); Tuscarora (Margaretville, N.Y.); Wilmington, Vicmead Hunt (Wilmington). Home: 1106 Hopeton Rd Westover Hills Wilmington DE 19806 Office: Du Pont Bldg Wilmington DE 19899

BISSELL, CHARLES OVERMAN, editorial cartoonist; b. Nashville, June 29, 1908; s. Charles Jay and Adelaide (Overman) B.; ed. pub. schs.; m. Lolita Hannah, June 5, 1943; 1 son, Charles William. Lithographic artist, 1924-45; mem. staff Nashville Tennessean, 1943—, art dir. Sunday mag., 1945-70, editorial cartoonist, 1943—. Recipient Cartoon award Nat. Headliners Club, 1963; Distinguished Service award Sigma Delta Chi, 1964; Pub. Service award Nat. Nat. Safety Council, 1966. Mem. Assn. Am. Editorial Cartoonists, Nat. Cartoonist Soc. Creator cartoon feature Bissell's Brave New World, 1962. Home: 4221 Farrar A Nashville, TN 37215. Office: 1100 Broadway Nashville TN 37202

BISSELL, CLAUDE THOMAS, educator; b. Meaford, Ont., Can., Feb. 10, 1916; s. George Thomas and Maggie Editha (Bowen) B.; B.A., U. Toronto, 1936, M.A., 1937; Ph.D., Cornell U., 1940; D.Litt., U. Man., 1958; LL.D., McGill U., 1958, Queen's U., 1959, U. N.B., 1959, Carleton U., 1960, U. Montreal, 1960, St. Lawrence U., 1962, U. B.C., 1962, U. Mich., 1963, Columbia, 1965, York U., 1967, Prince of Wales Coll., 1967, U. Windsor, 1968; D. es L., Laval U., 1966; m. Christina Flora Gray, Sept. 12, 1945; 1 dau., Deirdre MacFarlane. Instr. English, Cornell U., 1938-41; lectr. dept. English, Univ. Coll., U. Toronto, 1941-47; asst. prof., 1947-51, asso. prof., 1951-56, dean in residence, 1946-56, asst. to pres., 1948-52, v.p., 1952-56, pres., 1958-71, prof. English, 1962—; pres. Carleton U., 1956-58; vis. prof. Canadian studies Harvard, 1967-68, prof., 1971—. Chmn., Can. Council, 1960-62; pres. Nat. Conf. Canadian Univs. and Colls., 1962-63, World Univ. Service Can., 1962-63; chmn. Canadian Univs. Found., 1962-63. Served with Canadian Inf. Corps, 1942-46. Decorated companion Order Can. Fellow Royal Soc. Can. Mem. United Ch. Can. Clubs: Arts and Letters; University, York (Toronto); Rideau (Ottawa, Ont.). Editor: University College: A Portrait, 1853-1953, 1953; Canada's Crisis in Higher Education, 1957; Our Living Tradition, 1957; Great Canadian Writing, 1966. Author: The Strength of the University, 1968; also articles on lit. in U.S. and Canadian jours. Home: 229 Erskine Av Toronto 12 Ontario Canada

BISSELL, CUSHMAN BREWER, lawyer; b. St. Marys, O., July 20, 1900; s. John Winthrop and Rowena (Brewer) B.; A.B., U. Ill., 1923; LL.B., Harvard, 1926; J.D., John Marshall Law Sch., 1927; LL. D. (hon.), Loyola U., Chgo., 1965; m. Marion Bremner, July 3, 1928; children—Deborah, Cushman B. Admitted to Ill. bar, 1926; asso. Lord, Wire & Cobb, 1926-28; pvt. practice, 1928-31; partner Lord, Lloyd & Bissell, 1931-38, Lord Bissell Chgo.); pres. N.W. Nat. Bank Chgo., 1943, chmn. bd., 1944-63, chmn. exec. com., 1963—; gen. counsel dir. General Outdoor Advt. Co., 1942—; dir. Tremont Lumber Co., La. Cypress Lumber Co., Joyce Lumber Co., Old Republic Ins. Co., Nova Chrome, Inc., Currier-Lee Warehouses, Inc., Waylite Co. Mem. exec. com. Nat. Cath. Community Service, 1950—; Chgo. Indsl. Sch. for Girls, 1934—, Ill. Assn. for Crippled, 1946—, U.S.O., 1951-54, United Def. Fund, Inc., 1951-57; mem. Chgo. Crime Commn., 1944—, dir., 1946-64; pres. Cath. Charities Chgo., 1949-53, dir. mem. exec. com., 1953—; pres. dir. Chgo. Charitable Found., 1949—; v.p . Chgo. Community Fund, 1949- 54; trustee U. Ill., 1952-59, U. Retirement System of Ill., 1953-59; trustee Art Inst. Chgo., Loyola U. organizer, dir. Citizens Greater Chgo., Inc.; mem. adv. com. adv. com. to pres. Notre Dame and Loyola Univs.; mem. council Harvard Law Sch., 1956-60. Decorated Knight of St. Gregory by Pope Pious XII. Mem. Nat. Conf. Realtors and Lawyers, 1943. Mem. Am. (chmn. law list com. 1942-45), Ill., Chgo. (pres. 1951-52) bar assns., Harvard Law Sch., Assn. (council), Pi Kappa Alpha, Phi Alpha Delta, Alpha Alpha Alpha. Clubs: Chicago, Attic Commercial, Law (Chgo.); Lincoln Inn Editor Biographical Survey Harvard Law Sch. Class 1926, 51. Home: 1530 N State Pkwy Chicago IL 60610

BISSELL, GEORGE K., brewing co. exec.; b. N.Y.C., 1926; ed. Boston U. Formerly pres., chmn., dir. Drewrys Ltd. U.S.A., Inc.; pres., dir. Pepsi-Cola Mokan Bottlers, Inc.; dir. Piel Bros., Inc. 747 Country Club Lane South Bend IN Office: 1408 Elwood Av South Bend IN*

BISSELL, HERBERT DEMING, marketing exec.; b. Pitts., June 29, 1907; s. Robert DeLos and Margaret Isabel (Haddock) B.; A.B., Dartmouth, 1929; m. Rachel Collins Pfieffer, Sept. 22, 1931; children—Carol, Joan. Account exec. Ford Motor Co. account, N.W. Ayer, advt. agy., 1929-40; gen. advt. mgr. Electric Auto Lite Co., 1941-49; dir. merchandising Honeywell, Inc. (formerly Mpls.-Honeywell Regulator Co.), Mpls., 1950-56, v.p., 1956-62, v.p. marketing, 1962—; dir. Imperial Capital Fund, Imperial Growth Fund, Mpls. Gas Co. Bd. dirs. YMCA, Abbott-Northwestern Hosp., Youth Research Center. Presbyn. Home: 3810 W Calhoun Blvd Minneapolis MN 55410 Office: 2701 4th Av S Minneapolis MN 55408

BISSELL, MARSHALL PHILIP, life ins. co. exec.; b. Bloomfield, N.J., June 20, 1914; s. Robert B. and Mary (Campbell) B.; B.S., U. Va., 1936; m. Claire Marie Flint; children—Beverley Anne (Mrs. Charles F. Wilson), Robert W., Marilyn B. With N.Y. Life Ins. Co., 1936—, beginning as mgr. bank relations successively asst. v.p., sec., 1936-58, became v.p., 1958, formerly v.p. and controller, sr. v.p., 1965-69, exec. v.p., 1969—. Home: 13 Robert Dr Chatham NJ 07928 Office: 51 Madison Av New York City NY 10010

BISSELL, PELHAM ST. GEORGE 3d, judge, orgn. ofcl.; b. N.Y.C., Oct. 20, 1912; s. Pelham St. George and Mary Valentine Yale (Bissell) B.; grad. St. George's Sch., Newport, R.I., 1931; student Columbia, 1931-34; A.B., Rutgers U., 1936; LL.B., N.Y.U., 1939; m. Mary Alascia, Dec. 24, 1934. Admitted to N.Y. bar, 1941; asso. firm Barnes, Richardson & Colburn, N.Y.C., 1939-41, 45-51; law sec. to judge Ct. Gen. Sessions, N.Y. County, 1945-51; judge Civil Ct. City N.Y., 1952—. Mem. S.R., 1933—, gen. pres., 1961-64; asst. gov. gen. Soc. Mayflower Descs., 1960-63; comdr.-in-chief Soc. Am. Wars in U.S.A., 1961-64, Mem. adv. bd. Grand St. Boys Assn. Served to Lt. col., inf., AUS, World War II; col. Res. Decorated Bronze Star medal;

French Croix de Guerre, Belgian Croix de Guerre. Mem. Bar Assn. City N.Y., N.Y. County Lawyers Assn., Am., N.Y. State bar assns., Mil. Order Fgn. Wars (past comdr. N.Y. State), Am. Legion (past post comdr.), Soc. Colonial Wars, St. Nicholas Soc., Vets. Corps Arty. Soc. 1st Div., St. George's Soc., St. David's Soc., New Eng. Soc., Colonial Order Acorn, V.F.W., 40 and 8, Order of Founders and Patriots. Republican. Episcopalian. Mason (33), Elk. Clubs: Union League, Columbia University, N.Y. Athletic, Church (N.Y.C.); Army and Navy (Washington); St. Anthony. Author: Descendents of Captain John Bissell, 1966. Home: 22 E 36th St New York City NY 10016 Office: 111 Centre St New York City NY 10013

BISSELL, PHIL (Charles P. Bissell), cartoonist; b. Worcester, Mass., Feb. 1, 1926; s. Ralph Kenneth and Dorothy Earle (Pennell) B.; student Sch. Practical Arts, Boston, 1945- 47; hon. degree Art Instrn., Inc. Mpls.; m. Beverly Barrows, Sept. 17, 1948; children—Steven Barrows, Christopher W. Theatrical and editorial sports cartoonist Christian Sci. Monitor, 1949-53; editorial sports cartoonist Boston Globe, 1953-65; free lance comml. art, 1965-67; editorial cartoonist, sports cartoonist Worcester (Mass.) Telegram and Evening Gazette, 1967; represented in permanent collections Basketball Hall Fame, Springfield, Mass., Football Hall Fame, Canton, O. Home: 162 W Main St Box 155 Westborough MA 01581 Office: 20 Franklin St Worcester MA 01608

BISSELL, RICHARD, writer; b. Dubuque, Ia., June 27, 1913; s. Frederick Ezekiel and Edith Mary (Pike) B.; grad. Phillips Exeter Acad., 1932; B.S., Harvard, 1936; m. Marian Van Patten Grilk, Feb. 5, 1938; children—Thomas St. George, Nathaniel Gaylord, Anastasia, Samuel Pike, With Polarizing Instrument Co., N.Y., 1937; factory supt. H.B. Glover Co., Dubuque, Ia., 1938- 40, supt., stylist, 1944-52, v.p., 1944-60; mate and pilot towboats Central Barge Co., 1940-44; pres. Bissell Towing & Transport Co., Dubuque, 1958—. Recipient Antoinette Perry award for best musical play, 1954, Donaldson award for outstanding achievement in theatre, 1954-55. Holder pilot license all tonnage, Upper Mississippi and Monogahela rivers. Mem. Sons and Daus. of Pioneer Rivermen, Dramatists Guild, Screen Writers Guild, New Zealand Antartic Society (hon.). Clubs: Harvard, Lambs (N.Y.C.); Peosta Boat (Dubuque). Author: A Stretch on the River, 1950; The Monongahela, 1952; 71/2 Cents, 1953; High Water, 1954; Say Darling, 1957; Good Bye Ava (novel), 1960; You Can Always Tell a Harvard Man, 1962; Pursuit of the Happy Cabbage, 1964; Still Circling Moose Jaw Game, (With Abe Burrows, Marian Bissell) Say Darling; How Many Miles to Galena, 1968; Julia Harrington, 1913, 1969. Contbr. short stories to nat. mags., coll. textbooks, anthologies. Home: 6 Rocky Point Rd Bell Island Rowayton CT 06853 Office: American Trust Bldg Dubuque IA

BISSELL, RICHARD MERVIN, Jr., economist; b. Hartford, Conn., Sept. 18, 1909; s. Richard Mervin and Marie (Truesdale) B.; student Kingswood Sch., 1916-22, Groton Sch., 1922- 28, London Sch. Econs., 1932-33; A.B., Yale, 1932, Ph.D., 1939, M.A. (hon.), 1949; m. Ann Cornelia Bushnell, July 6, 1940; children—Richard Mervin, Ann Harriet, Winthrop Bushnell, William George, Thomas Erickson. Research asst. Yale, 1934, instr. econs., 1935-39, asst. prof., 1939-42; staff mem. Bur. Fgn. and Domestic Commerce, Dept. Commerce, 1941-42; economist Combined Shipping Adjustment Bd., asst. to dep. adminstr. War Shipping Adminstrn., 1942-43; dir. ship requirements, U.S. exec. officer Combined Shipping Adjustment Bd., 1943-45; econ. adviser to dir. War Mblzn. and Reconversion, 1945-46, dep. dir., 1946; asso. prof. econs. Mass. Inst. Tech., 1942-48, prof., 1948-52; exec. sec. President's Com. Fgn. Aid (Harriman Com.), 1947-48; asst. adminstr. program E.C.A., 1948-51, acting adminstr., Sept.-Dec. 1951; staff mem. Ford Found., 1952-54; spl. asst. to dir. CIA, 1954-59, dep. dir. plans, 1959-62; pres. Inst. for Def. Analyses, 1962-64; dir. marketing and econ. planning United Aircraft Corp., East Hartford, Conn., 1964—; dir. Mut. Ins. Co. of Hartford. Cons. to dir. Mut. Security, 1952; cons. various intervals Conn. Pub. Utilities Commn., Fortune Mag., Social Sci. Research Council, Cosmopolitan Shipping Co., U.S. Steel Corp., Scudder, Stevens & Clark, Brightwater Paper Co., Asiatic Petroleum Co. Bd. regents, chmn. ednl. policies com. U. Hartford. Recipient Nat. Security medal, 1962. Mem. Am. Econ. Assn., Am. Geog. Soc., Econometric Assn., Council on Fgn. Relations, Fgn. Policy Assn., Washington Inst. Fgn. Affairs, Conn. Acad. Arts and Scis. Clubs: Hartford; Graduate Club Assn. (New Haven); Yale (N.Y.C.). Author articles econ. jours. Prin. editor, contbr.: (report of President's Com. Fgn. Aid) European Recovery and American Aid. Home: 22 Mountain Rd Farmington CT 06032 Office: United Aircraft Corp 400 Main St East Hartford CT 06108

BISSELL, THOMAS ASHLEY, assn. exec.; b. Buffalo, Apr. 24, 1899; s. Frederick Olds and Nellie Caught (Smith) B.; M.E., Cornell U., 1923; m. Katherine Romer Albertson, Dec. 23, 1938. Maintenance engr. Carborundum Co., Niagara Falls, N.Y., 1923-24; sales engr. Lamson Co., Syracuse, N.Y., 1925-26; design engr. Dunlop Tire & Rubber Co., Buffalo, 1927-29; plant engr. Gould Coupler Co., Depew, N.Y., 1929-30; asst. editor Maintenance Engring., McGraw-Hill Pub. Co., N.Y.C., 1931-32; sales engr. Chgo. Belting Co., 1934-35; tech. editor SAE Jour., N.Y.C., 1936-42; mgr. meetings div. Soc. Automotive Engrs., N.Y.C., 1943-57; exec. sec. Soc. Plastics Engrs., Inc., Stamford, Conn., 1957-62; pres. Assn. Adminstrn. & Services, Inc., N.Y.C., 1962-64; cons. Engring., Index Inc., N.Y.C., 1964—. Civilian staff prodn. div. Bur. Aeronautics, Navy Dept., 1942. Trustee, Mid Fairfield County Youth Museum, 1958—, chmn. bd., 1968-70. Served as pvt. Recipient S.A.T.C., 1918. award merit for editorial achievement Indsl. Marketing, 1941. Mem. Soc. Automotive Engrs., Phi Kappa Psi. Clubs: Cornell (N.Y.C.); Shorehaven Golf (East Norwalk, Conn.). Author: (with Norman G. Shidle) Motor Vehicles and Their Engines, 1941; (with Norman G. Shidle, Joseph Heitner) Automotive Mechanics, 1942. Contbr. motor vehicle sect. Ency. Brit., 1940. Home: 21 Old Hill Farms Rd Westport CT 06880 Office: 345 E 47th St New York City NY 10017

BISSELLE, MORGAN FITCH, lawyer, ins. co. exec.; b. N.Y.C., Mar. 25, 1908; s. Luther Cleaveland and Lillian (Jones) B.; A.B., Colgate U., 1929; J.D., Yale, 1932; m. Lucille Florence Marks, Oct. 21, 1933; children—Philip Morgan, Walter Cleaveland. Admitted to N.Y. bar, 1933, U.S. Supreme Ct. bar, 1950; practiced in N.Y.C., 1933-35, Utica, 1939-53, New Hartford, 1953—; confidential clk. Asso. Justice Rowland L. Davis Appellate Div., Supreme Ct., 2d Judicial Dept., Bklyn., 1935-38; mem. firm Hart, Senior & Nichols, 1939-43; mem. firm Tucker & Bisselle, 1943-65; pvt. practice, 1965—; gen. counsel Utica Mut. Ins. Co., 1943—, sec., 1968—. Trustee Savs. Bank of Utica. Pres. Bd. Edn., New Hartford Central Sch., 1952; mem. New Hartford Planning Bd., 1962- 68. Mem. Am., N.Y. State, Oneida County (past pres.) bar assns., Internat. Assn. Ins. Counsel, Def. Research Inst., Am. Judicature Soc., Sigma Nu, Phi Alpha Delta. Republican. Presbyn. Mason. Club: Fort Schuyler (Utica). Home: 133 Paris Rd New Hartford NY 13413 Office: 180 Genesee St New Hartford NY 13413

BISSETT, JAMES ROBERT, civil engr.; b. Junction, Tex., May 9, 1910; s. Joe B. and Mary (Lanan) B.; student Tex. A. and M. Coll., 1927-29; B.S., U. Tex., 1941; M.S., U. Ill., 1950; m. Ila Louise Knight, July 13, 1935; 1 son, Joe Knight. Instrumentman, field engr. Tex. Hwy. Dept., 1932-39, bridge design engr., Austin, Tex., 1944-47; constrn. engr. Corps Engrs., Ft. Sam Houston, 1941-44; asst. prof. civil engring. U. Ark., 1947-49, asso. prof., 1950-51, prof. civil engring., 1951—, also asso. dir. Engring. Expt. Sta., 1951-61; instr. U. Ill., 1949-50. Alderman City of Fayetteville. Mem. Am. Soc. C.E., Nat., Ark. socs. profl. engrs., Hwy. Research Bd., Assn. Asphalt Paving Tech., Am. Soc. Engring. Edn., Sigma Xi, Tau Beta Pi, Chi Epsilon. Home: 1230 Eastwood Dr Fayetteville AR 72701

BISSHOPP, KENNETH EDWARD, educator; b. Beloit, Wis., July 14, 1909; s. John and Maud Alice (Lufkin) B.; A.B. in Math., U. Ill., 1930; M.S. in Math., Ill. Inst. Tech., 1946, Ph.D. in Mech. Engring., 1954; m. Beatrice Lenora Ortmann, June 16, 1932; 1 son, Frederic Edward. Design calculator Fairbanks Morse and Co., 1930-32, research engr., 1934-44, cons., 1950-55; mech. engr. Sun Shipbldg. & Dry Dock Co., Chester, Pa., 1932-34; research engr. Armour Research Found., Chgo., 1944-48, st. engr., 1948-55; prof. mechanics Hartford Grad. Center, Rensselaer Polytech. Inst., East Windsor Hill, Conn., 1955-57, prof. mech. engring., Troy, N.Y., 1957—, chmn. dept. mech. engring., 1957-67. Mem. Am. Soc. M.E. (lectr. 1959-60), Am. Math. Soc., Am. Soc. Engring. Edn., Sigma Xi, Tau Beta Pi. Contbr. articles to profl. jours. Home: 3 Clinton Pl Troy NY 12183

BISSINGER, BARNARD HINKLE, educator; b. Lancaster, Pa., Jan. 27, 1918; s. John Barnard and Marion (Killian) B.; A.B., Franklin and Marshall Coll., 1938; M.A., Syracuse U., 1940; Ph.D., Cornell U., 1943; m. Ruby Etta Green, Mar. 1, 1951; children—Gail Susan, Karen Lynn. Instr. math. Syracuse U., then Cornell U., 193843; research asst. NRC, Columbia, 1944; operations analyst USAAF, 1944-45; exec. v.p. George Gillis Athletic Shoe Mfg. Corp., 1945-53; mem. faculty Lebanon Valley Coll., 1953-70, successively prof. math., Lehman prof., chmn. dept., also chmn. sci. div.; NSF summer vis. lectr. insts. at Vt., Rutgers U., Pa. State U.; math. cons. U.S. Navy Supply System, 1958—; dir. vis. scientists lectr. program secondary schs. in Pa., 1962-67; acting chmn. math. Grad. Center, Pa. State U., Middletown, 1965-70, coordinator math. scis. Capitol Campus Grad. Center, 1970—; lectr. 5 Nat Def. Edn. Act programs in math. to secondary and elementary tchrs. Lebanon County, Pa., 1962-67. NSF fellow Princeton, 1958-59. Mem. Math. Assn. Am., Am. Math. Soc., Am. Statis. Assn., Inst. Math. Statistics, London Math. Soc., Econometric Soc., Operations Research Soc. Am., Inst. Mgmt. Scis., Soc. Indsl. and Applied Math., Brit. Operational Research Soc., Indian Math. Soc., Nat. Council Tchrs. Math., Soc. Math. France, Biometric Soc., Japanese, Belgian, Finnish, Australian math. socs., Australian Statis. Soc. New S. Wales, Sigma Xi, Pi Mu Epsilon, Sigma Pi Sigma, Phi Kappa Psi. Author numerous articles in field. Home: 281 W Main St Middletown PA 17057

BISSINGER, FREDERICK LEWIS, corp. exec.; b. N.Y.C., Jan. 11, 1911; s. Jacob Frederick and Rosel (Ensslin) B.; M.E., Stevens Inst. Tech., 1933, M.S., 1936; J.D., Fordham U., 1938; m. Julia E. Stork, Aug. 4, 1935; children—Frederick Lewis, Elizabeth Julia. Instr. chemistry Stevens Inst. Tech., 1933-36; admitted to N.Y. bar, 1939, asso. Pennie, Davis, Marvin & Edmonds, N.Y.C., 1936-42; with Indsl. Rayon Corp., Cleve., 1942-61, v.p. charge research, 1948-57, group v.p. marketing and research, 1957-59, v.p., gen. mgr., 1959-60, pres., chief exec. officer, 1960-61, following merger, group v.p. Midland-Ross Corp., 1961-62; v.p., dir., mem. exec. com. Stauffer Chem. Co., 1962-65; v.p. Allied Chem. Corp., N.Y.C., 1965-66, exec. v.p., 1966-69, pres., chief operating officer, 1969—, dir., 1966—; dir. Rheingold Corp. Trustee Stevens Inst. Tech., Fordham U.; bd. dirs. Nutrition Found. Mem. Am. Chem. Soc., Soc. Chem. Industry, Synthetic Organic Chem. Mfrs. Assn. (pres.), N.A.M. (dir.), A.A.A.S. Clubs: Union League, Economic of N.Y., Chemists' (N.Y.C.); Siwanoy Country, Sakonnet Golf (Little Compton, R.I.); Pinnacle. Home: 11 Westway Bronxville NY 10708 Office: 1411 Broadway New York City NY 10018

BISSON, EDMOND EMILE, mech. engr.; b. East Barre, Vt., July 16, 1916; s. Eugene and Annabella (Desilets) B.; student U. Vt., 1934-35; B.S. with honors, U. Fla., 1938, M.E., 1954; m. Fernande M. Trottier, May 24, 1947; children—Roland Andre, Colette Marie, Michelle Denise. Research engr. NACA, Langley Field, Va., 1939-43; successively sect. head, br. chief, asso. chief fluid system components div. Lewis Research Center of NASA, 1943—; tchr. short courses U. Cal. at Los Angeles, Case Western Res. U. Recipient medal for exceptional sci. achievement, NASA, 1968, nat. award Am. Soc. Lubrication Engrs., 1967, Jacques de Vaucanson medal French Soc. Groupement pour l'Avancement de La Mecanique Industrielle, 1966, Alfred E. Hunt meml. medal Am. Soc. Lubrication Engrs., 1954. Registered profl. engr., Ohio. Fellow Am. Soc. M.E., Am. Soc. Lubrication Engrs.; mem. N.Y. Acad. Scis., Phi Kappa Phi, Tau Beta Pi, Sigma Tau. Roman Catholic. Author: (with W.J. Anderson) Advanced Bearing Technology, 1964. Contbr. articles profl. jours. Home: 20786 Eastwood Av Fairview Park OH 44126 Office: 21000 Brook Park Rd Cleveland OH 44135

BISSON, WHEELOCK ALEXANDER, physician; b. Key West, Fla., 1898; s. George Henry and Sarah Jane (Kemp) B.; B.S., Fla. A. and M. U., 1922; M.D., Meharry Med. Coll., 1929; m. Maude Lee Voorhies, June 2, 1930. Intern, Royal Circle Hosp., Memphis, 1931-33; gen. practice, Memphis, 1931—; clinician Memphis and Shelby County Health Dept., 1932—. Named Tenn. Doctor of Year by Vol. State Med. Assn., 1962, 63; recipient citation, Key to City, Memphis and Shelby County Health Dept., 1965; Practitioner of Year award Nat. Med. Assn., 1967. Mem. Am. Thoracic Soc., Tenn. Acad. Sci., Am., Tenn., Nat. (2d v.p. 1966—), Vol. State (1st v.p. 1965) med. assns., Bluff City, Memphis, Shelby County med. socs. Address: 2312 Park Av Memphis TN 38114

BISSONNETTE, GEORGES LOUIS, clergyman; b. Central Falls, R.I., July 22, 1921; s. George Joseph and Alida (Provost) B.; B.A., Assumption Coll., 1943; S.T.B., Laval U., 1947, S.T.L., 1949; M.A., Fordham U., 1953; M.H., Columbia, 1957, Ph.D., 1962; fellow at the Russian Inst., Columbia, 1957. Instr., Assumption Coll., 1943-45, 49-51; ordained priest Roman Cath. Ch., 1949; chaplain of Americans in USSR and apostolic adminstr. of USSR, 1953-55; dir. sch. fgn. affairs Assumption Coll., also dean of faculty, prof. polit. sci., 1962-68, pres., 1968—; lectr.-cons. U.S. Army Command and Gen. Staff Coll., Leavenworth. Recipient 175th Anniversary medal of honor Georgetown U., 1964. Author: Moscow Was My Parish, 1956. Home: 88 Darling St Central Falls RI 01609 Office: Assumption Coll Worcester MA 01609

BISTA, KIRTI NIDHL, fgn. minister of Nepal; b. Kathmandu, Nepal, Dec. 5, 1927; s. Chandra Nidhi and Ghana (Kumari) B.; M.A. in Polit. Sci., Lucknow U., 1951; m. Bodh Kumari, July 1940; childrenNanu, Binod, Sarda, Kamala, Rajani. Journalist for jours. in Kathmandu, 1957-58; active revolutionary movement against Rana Regine, 1951; mem. Rastriya Panchyat (nat. legislature), 1963-; mem. standing com. State Council, 1967-; asst. minister, then cabinet minister edn., 1962-64; vice chmn. Council Ministers, also minister fgn. affairs 1964-67; dep. prime minister, fgn. affairs and edn., 1967; dep. prime minister, minister fgn. affairs and econ. planning, 1967-69; premier of Nepal, since 1969-; a delegate and/or leader of numerous Napalese delegations to UN and other internat. meetings. Decorated Gorkha Dakshina Babu, Trisakti Patta (Nepal); grand cross order Orange Nassau grand officer Legion of Honor (France). Home: Chhetrapati Kathmandu, Nepal. Office: Ministry Foreign Affairs Kathmandu, Nepal

BISTLINE, JAMES ADAMS, r.r. exec., lawyer; b. Newport, Pa., June 18, 1915; s. George P. and Laura (Adams) B.; A.B. summa cum laude, Duke, 1937; J.D., Columbia, 1940; m. Lillian Hunter, Mar. 12, 1949; children—James, Scott, Mark. Admitted to N.Y. bar, 1941, D.C. bar, 1954; lawyer Sage, Gray, Todd & Sims, N.Y.C., 1940-42; with So. Ry. Co., 1948—, gen. solicitor, 1965-67, gen. counsel, 1967—, asst. v.p., Washington, 1969—. Served to maj. AUS, 1942-47; col. Res. Mem. Assn. ICC Practitioners (pres. 1969-70), Judge Adv. Gen. Assn. (dir. 1967—), Am., Internat. bar assns., Phi Beta Kappa. Presbyn. (elder 1962—). Republican. Mason. Home: 7711 Ridgecrest Dr Alexandria VA 22308 Office: PO Box 1808 Washington DC 20013

BITKER, BRUNO VOLTAIRE, lawyer; b. Milw., Feb. 5, 1898; s. Jacob Louis and Sarah Ann (Rubin) B.; LL.B., Cornell U., 1921; m. Marjorie M. Mayer, 1957. Admitted to Wis. bars, 1921; gen. practice law, Milw., 1921—. Mem. Sewerage Commn. Milw., 1931-53; fed. ct. trustee Milw. Rapid Transit Line, 1950-52; spl. counsel to Gov. Wis., 1937, State Banking Commn., 1938; chmn. Citizens' Adv. Com. on Greendale, 1938; cons. OPM, Washington, 1941; Wis. state counsel, dist. dir. OPA, 1942-44; spl. pros. atty. Milw., 1948; chmn. State Pub. Utility Arbitration Bd., 1947; mem., officer Gov.'s Commn. on Human Rights, 1947-56; chmn. Milw. Com. on Living Cost and Food Conservation, 1947; chmn. Commn. on Econ. Study Milw., 1948; mem. Mayor's Commn. on Econ. Study Milw., 1948; mem. Mayor's Commn. on Human Relations, 1948-52; U.S. del. Internat. Conf. Local Govts., Geneva, 1949; U.S. observer 1st World Conf. Lawyers, Athens, 1963; chmn. Municipal Commn. on Mass Transp., 1954; lectr. div. continuing edn. Marquette U., 1961; mem. Gov.'s Com. UN, 1959—, Wis. adv. com. U.S. Commn. Civil Rights, 1960—. Nat. Citizens' Commn. Internat. Coop., 1965, U.S. Nat. Commn. for UNESCO, 1965-70, Pres.'s Commn. for Observance Human Rights Year, 1968-69; U.S. rep. Internat. Conf. on Human Rights, Teheran, 1968; cons. Dept. State, 1968—. Trustee, adv. council Milw. Art Inst., 1957—. Recipient City of Milw. citation for distinguished pub. service, 1944; Amity award, 1950; Jr. Achievement award, 1959. Served as lt. inf. U.S. Army, World War I. Mem. Am., Wis., Milw. bar assns., Fed. Bar Assn. Wis. (pres. 1945), World Peace through Law Center (charter, Geneva). Clubs: University, Cornell Alumni of Wis. (Milw.). Contbr. articles to legal jours; treatises on U.N. affairs. Home: 2330 E Back Bay Milwaukee, WI 53202 Office: 208 Wisconsin Av Milwaukee WI 53202

BITNER, HARRY, law librarian; b. Kansas City, Mo., July 22, 1916; s. Barney and Helen (Samberg) B.; B.A., U. Mo. at Kansas City, 1941, J.D., 1939; B.S. in L.S., L.S., U. Ill., 1942; m. Anne Goldstein, Sept. 15, 1940; 1 dau., Lorraine Ellen. Instr. law U. Kansas City, 1942-43, law librarian, 1939-42; reference law librarian Biddle Law Library, U. Pa., 1946; asso. law librarian Columbia Law Sch., 1946-54; librarian Dept. Justice, 1954-57; law librarian Yale Law Sch., 1957-65; law librarian, prof. law Cornell U. Law Sch., Ithaca, N.Y., 1965—. Sec. bd. dirs. New Haven Jewish Community Council, 1962-64, v.p., dir., 1963- 65; sec. bd. dirs. New Haven Bur. Jewish Edn., 1960-63, treas., dir., 1963-65, 2d v.p., 1965; bd. dirs. New Haven Jewish Family Service, 1961-65, 2d v.p., 1965. Served with AUS, 1943-46. Mem. Internat., Internat., Am. (exec. bd. 1951-54, pres. 1963-64) assns. law libraries, Am., Conn. library assns., Spl. Libraries Assn., Council Nat. Library Assns. (vice chmn.), Am. Soc. Legal History, Beta Phi Mu. Jewish religion (pres. temple 1965). Author: (with Price) Effective Legal Research, 3d edit., 1969. Contbr. profl. jours. Home: 406 Winthrop Dr Ithaca NY 14850

BITTENBENDER, WILLIAM ALBERT, chemist, mfg. co. exec.; b. Ames, Ia., Sept. 7, 1914; s. Harrie Artley and Bess (Chase) B.; A.B., Wittenberg Coll., 1936; M.S., Purdue U., 1938, Ph.D. (duPont fellow), 1941; postgrad. Harvard, 1950, U. Pa., 1958; m. Mary McClelland, June 9, 1941; children—David, Charles. With Merck & Co., Inc., Rahway, N.J., 1941-55, dir. product devel., 1952-54, asso. dir. chem. control, 1954-55; tech. asst. to pres. Merck, Sharp & Dohme div. Merck & Co., Inc., West Point, Pa., 1955-56, dir. prodn., psychology U.S. Fla., Tampa, 1970—. Fell engring., 1956-60; corp. dir. research, dir. Glidden Co., Cleve., 1961- 65; tech. asst, to pres. Sherwin-Williams Co., Cleve., 1965-66, gen. mgr. auxs., chem., 1966—. Mem. Am. Chem. Soc., A.A.A.S., Soc. Chem. Industry, Sigma Xi, Phi Kappa Psi, Theta Chi Delta, Phi Lambda Upsilon. Home: 11 Pepper Ridge Rd Cleveland, OH 44124 Office: 101 Prospect Av NW Cleveland OH 44101

BITTER, JOHN, ins. exec.; b. N.Y., Apr. 8, 1909; s. Karl and Marie Agnes (Schevill) B.; grad. Curtis Inst. Music, Phila., 1931; m. Dorothy Michelson, 1934; 1 dau., Ursula; m. 2d, Barbara Pinion, Feb. 22, 1947; children—Robin Simonetta, Noel Lesley, Marietta. Condr., Jacksonville (Fla.) Symphony Orch., 1934-36, Fla. State Symphony, 1936-39; asso. condr. Leopold Stokowski's All Am. Youth Orch., 1940-41; condr. symphony orch. U. Miami, 1940-59, dean sch. music, 1951-63, asst. to pres., lectr. humanities, 1963-64; v.p. Parker, Kolodny Assos., Inc., Miami, Fla., 1964—; condr. summer symphony, 1951—, guest condr. Berlin Philharmonic Orch., Berlin Staatsoper, Hamburg Philharmonic, Radio Italiana, others, 1946-67. Consul for Germany in Miami. Served as maj., AUS, 1942-46. Awarded Allied Artists prize for composition, 1939; Nat. Sales Achievement awards, 1968-71. Mem. Nat. Assn. Schs. Music (v.p. 1959), Phi Mu Alpha Sinfonia (hon.), Phi Kappa Phi. Rotarian. Home: 5671 SW 98th Terrace Miami FL 33156

BITTERMAN, MORTON EDWARD, educator, psychologist; b. N.Y.C., Jan. 19, 1921; s. Harry Michael and Stella (Weiss) B.; B.A., N.Y.U., 1941; M.A., Columbia, 1942; Ph.D., Cornell U., 1945; m. Shirley Subke, Oct. 1, 1952 (div. Apr. 1964); children—Joan, Ann; m. 2d, Mary Gayle Foley, June 26, 1967; 1 dau., Sarah Fleming. Instr., then asst. prof. Cornell U., 1945-50; asso. prof. U. Tex., 1950-55; mem. Inst. Advanced Study, 1955-57; asso. prof. Bryn Mawr Coll., 1957-60, prof. psychology, 1960-70, chmn. dept., 1957-67; prof. psychology U. S.Fla., Tampa, 1970—. Fellow Am. Psychol. Assn.; mem. Psychonomic Soc. Editor Am. Jour. Psychology, 1955—. Cons. editor Jour. Behavioral Research Methods and Instruments, 1968—, Psychonomic Sci., 1971—. Spl. research evolution of intelligence. Home: 10037 N 53d St Temple Terrace FL 33617 Office: Dept of Psychology Univ of South Fla Tampa FL 33620

BITTINGER, DESMOND WRIGHT, coll. ofcl.; b. Eglon, W.Va., Dec. 16, 1905; s. Jonas H. and Mary Etta (Fike) B.; A.B., Elizabethtown Coll., 1927; A.M., U. Pa., 1934, Ph.D., 1940; advanced study U. Chgo., 1948; m. Irene Frantz, June 15, 1927; children—Stanley, Patricia (Mrs. Irven Stern), Richard, Marianne (Mrs. Lyle Dobson). Prin., Tchr. Tng. Inst., Nigeria, W. Africa, 1931-38; prof. sociology and edn. McPherson (Kan.) Coll., 1940-44, pres., 1950-66; dean The Floating Campus, U. of Seven Seas, 1966, 68, 71; chancellor Chapman Coll., Orange, 1966-68, head dept. sociology and anthropology, 1968—; editor Messenger, Ch. of Brethren, 1944-50; Fulbright lectr. in Taiwan, 1962-63. Mem. gen. brotherhood bd. Ch. of Brethren, 1950-61, nat. moderator, 1950-51, 58-59, alternate nat. moderator, 1955-56; chmn. Brethren Service

Com., 1954-61; bd. dirs. Ch. World Service, 1960-69; dir. Brethren Pub. House, 1940-44. Pres. Kansas Found. Pvt. Colls. and Univs., 1953-54, 58-60. Mem. Quivera dist. Boy Scouts Dirs., 1941-44; pres. Kan. Debating League, 1941-44. Mem. Phi Delta Kappa, Pi Kappa Delta. Author: An Educational Experiment in Its Cultural Setting in West Africa, 1941; Black and White in the Sudan, 1941; Sudan's Second Sunup, 1938; Land of the Monkey Bread Tree, 1939; Snow Ball, a story, 1945; The Church of the Brethren, 1954. Co-author: The Adventurous Future, 1959; In the Unity of the Faith, 1960; Brethren Trail Blazers, 1960; Wu Feng: Companion of Head Hunters, 1963; The Church of the Brethren from its European Origins, 1969; Man, Culture and Religion, 1970; Die Kirchen der Welt, 1971. Contbr. Am. Church, Annals Am. Acad. Polit. Sci. Quar. Home: 904 E Everett Pl Orange CA 92667 Office: Chapman Coll Orange CA 92666

BITTINGER, DONALD S., pub. utility exec.; b. Washington, Feb. 19, 1909; s. Henry E. and Mary C. (Leishear) B.; A.B., Am. U., 1929; B.Engring., Johns Hopkins, 1932; m. Jean R. Hunt, Oct. 23, 1943; children—Andrew H., Edmund S., Paul D. With Washington Gas Light Co., 1933—, v.p. operations, 1953-58, pres., 1958—, chief exec. officer, 1960—, chmn. bd., 1969—; dir. Security Storage Co., Woodward & Lothrop, Union Trust Co.; trustee Equitable Life Ins. Co. Mem. Pres.'s Commn. on Crime in D.C.; past chmn. Citizens Zoning Adv. Com. D.C. Zoning Commn. Trustee Johns Hopkins U., 1962-68, Am. U., Landon Sch., Greater Washington Ednl. TV Assn., Children's Hosp.; past pres. United Givers Fund D.C., Goodwill Industries Washington; v.p. Fed. City Council; bd. dirs. Met. Washington Urban Coalition, Jr. Achievement Met. Washington, Washington Bd. Trade, Downtown Progress, Inc. A.R.C. of D.C. Recipient Distinguished Alumni award Am. U., 1963, Johns Hopkins, 1969; Distinguished Service award Am. Gas Assn., 1965, Cosmos Club, 1966; named Man of Year, Met. Washington Bd. Trade, 1970. Registered profl. engr., D.C. Mem. engineer, District Columbia. Member of Washington Board Trade Am. Gas Assn. (2d v.p., dir.), D.C. Soc. Profl. Engrs. Presbyn. (elder). Mason, Rotarian. Clubs: University, Columbia Country, Metropolitan. Home: 3910 Livington St NW Washington DC 20015 Office: 1100 H St NW Washington DC 20005

BITTKER, BORIS IRVING, educator; b. Rochester, N.Y., Nov. 28, 1916; s. Albert and Minnie (Rubens) B.; B.A., Cornell U., 1938; LL.B., Yale, 1941; m. Anne Elizabeth Stern, 1949; children—Susan Emilie, Daniel Albert. Admitted to N.Y. bar, 1942, Conn. bar, 1951; law clk. to Judge Jerome N. Frank, U.S. Ct. Appeals, 2d Circuit, N.Y.C., 1941-42; staff Lend Lease Adminstrn., 1942-43, Alien Property Custodian's Office, 1945-46; faculty Yale Law Sch., 1946—, successively asst. prof., asso. prof., 1946-51, prof., 1951-66, Southmayd prof. law, 1958-70, Sterling prof. law, 1970—; Fulbright lectr. Univs. Pavia, Siena (Italy), 1955-56; vis. prof. Stanford Law Sch.; Ford Distinguished Vis. prof. N.Y. U. Sch. Commerce, 1965; Charles Inglis Thomson prof. law U. Colo., 1966. Served with AUS, 1943-45. Mem. Am., Conn. bar assns., Am. Law Inst. Author: Federal Income, Estate and Gift Taxation, 1958; Professional Responsibility and Federal Tax Practice, 1965. Contbr. articles to profl. jours. Home: 445 St Ronan St New Haven CT 06511

BITTLE, BILLY MCMILLAN, Jr., mfg. co. exec.; b. Tupelo, Miss., Aug. 16, 1921; s. Billy McMillan and Thelma M. (Milstead) B.; student Miss. State Coll., 1940; m. Mary Barbara Martin, Oct. 9, 1943; children—James M., Susan C. (Mrs. Bart Frary), Judith A., Charles W. With Woodward Governor Co., Rockford, Ill., 1945-66, gen. mgr., 1958-60, pres., gen. mgr., 1960-66, dir.; pres., owner P.F. Jackson Co., Inc., designers and mfrs. kitchens and cabinetry, Rockford, Ill., 1966—; dir. Park State Bank, Loves Park, Ill. Bd. counselors Rockford (Ill.) Coll. Served to capt., navigator USAAF, World War II. Mem. Am. Soc. M.E., Inst. Aero. Scis., Chgo. Presidents Orgn., Young Presidents' Orgn. Mason (Shriner, Jester), Elk, Rotarian. Clubs: Chicago Athletic Assn.; Forest Hills Country (Rockford). Home: 7118 N 2d St Rockford IL 61111 Office: 1011 E River Lane Rockford IL 61111

BITTMAN, WILLIAM OMAR, lawyer; b. Milw., Aug. 6, 1931; s. Omar A. and Lyda (Schneider) B.; B.S., Marquette U., 1956, student Law Sch., 1956-57; J.D., DePaul U., 1959; m. Carole Jean Chiletti, Aug. 25, 1956; children—Michael John, Barbara Jean, Mary Elizabeth, William Omar, Robert James, Julie Anne, Carrie Lynn. Admitted to Ill. bar, 1960, D.C. bar, 1967; with Dept. Justice, 1960-67, spl. atty., Washington, 1965-67; partner firm Hogan & Hartson, Washington, 1967—; lectr. trial techniques, 1962—. Served with USNR, 1951-53. Named one of Chicago's 10 outstanding young men, 1964; recipient Sustained Outstanding Performance award Dept. Justice, 1964, Spl. Act. Meritorious Achievement award, 1967. Chief prosecutor in govt. trial of James R. Hoffa, 1964, of Robert G. Baker, 1967. Mem. Am., Fed., D.C., Ill. bar assns. Roman Catholic. Home: 9116 Bradley Blvd Potomac MD 20854 Office: 815 Connecticut Av Washington DC 20006

BIUNNO, VINCENT P., lawyer; b. Newark, Feb. 2, 1916; s. James and Margaret (George) B.; student Columbia, 1932-33; LL.B. magna cum laude, N.J. Law Sch., 1937; m. Mary Ann Zocchi, June 8, 1941. Admitted to N.J. bar, 1937, counselor 1940; mem. firm Lum, Biunno & Tompkins, and predecessors, Newark, 1937- 46, partner, 1946-58, 60—. Counsel to Gov. N.J., 1958-60; mem. N.J. Gov.'s Study Com. Legalized Games of Chance, 1953-54; counsel Legislative Com. to Revise Law of Evidence, 1955-57, to pres. N.J. Senate, to rules com. N.J. Supreme Ct. Dir. Prudential Ins. Co. Am. Mem. Glen Ridge Devel. Bd. Pres., trustee N.J. Law Inst., 1955—; adv. bd. Western Res. U. Sch. Library Sci.; mem. com. indexing statutory law Am. Bar Found. Mem. N.J. Gov.'s Milk Study Com., 1962-64; mem. N.J. Commn. on Def. of Indigent; N.J. pub. rate counsel, utilities, 1970—. Served with Signal Corps, AUS, 1942-43. Fellow Am. Bar Found.; mem. Am. (mem. com. electronic data retrieval 1958—, mem. ho. of dels. 1968—), N.J. (gen. council 1962—, chmn. jud. selection com. 1968—), Essex County (pres. 1963—, trustee) bar assns., Nat. Conf. Bar Presidents, Alpha Sigma Phi. Club: Glen Ridge Country. Editorial bd. N.J. Law Jour. Author articles on legal research. Home: 321 Forest Av Glen Ridge NJ 07028 Office: 550 Broad St Newark NJ 07102

BIVENS, GORDON ELLSWORTH, educator; b. Nevada, Ia., Feb. 5, 1927; s. Clarence E. and Hazel (Markland) B.; B.S., Ia. State U., 1950, M.S., 1953, Ph.D., 1957; m. Muriel Katherine Collier, Feb. 14, 1953; children—Dale Mark, Carol Sue, Bruce Alan, Paul Wayne. Instr., asst. prof., asso. prof. Ia. State U., 1954-62; asso. prof., prof. econs., founding dir. Center for Consumer Affairs, U. Wis., Milw., 1962-68; consumption economist Consumer and Food Econs. Research div. Agrl. Research Service, Dept. Agr., 1967-68; prof. family econs. and agrl. econs. U. Mo. at Columbia, 1968—. Mem. Consumer Task Force, White House Conf. on Food, Nutrition and Health, 1969; cons. President's Com. on Consumer Interests, Office Econ. Opportunity, Glick & Lorwin, John Wiley & Sons. Trustee Am. Home Econs. Assn. Found. Served with USMCR, 1945-46. Mem. Am. Econ. Assn., Am. Home Econs. Assn., Am. Agrl. Econ. Assn., Am. Assn. for Consumer Research (mem. adv. bd.), Am. Council on Consumer Interests (past pres., mem. exec. bd.), Tau Kappa Epsilon, Phi Kappa Phi, Alpha Zeta, Gamma Sigma Delta. Editor Jour. Consumer Affairs. Mem. Soc. Friends. Home: Route 3 Columbia MO 65201

BIVENS, WILLIAM JAMES, ret. lawyer; b. Tampa, Fla., Nov. 28, 1899; s. Thomas A. and Annie (Varn) B.; LL.B., U. Fla., 1922; m. Louise Bragdon, Dec. 5, 1943; step- children—Wilmer Thomas Coram, Carol Louise Meader, James Michael Coram. Admitted to Fla. bar, 1922, Ill. bar, 1955; mem. firm Worth, Bivens & Lively, Tampa, 1937-40; mem. Fla. Ho. of Reps., 1928-30; law specialist USN, 1940-54; legal officer Naval Operating Base, Argentina, Nfld., 1941-43; atty. gen. Am. Samoa, 1945-47; tchr. naval and internat. law Gen. Line Sch., Newport, R.I., 1947-50; condr. corr. courses internat. and advanced internat. law Naval War Coll., 1950-52; legal officer U.S. Naval Sta., Tongue Point, Astoria, Ore., 1952-54; atty. U.S. Army Signal Corps, 1954-62; research and devel. counsel in legal div. Office of Chief Signal Officer, 1958-61, asst. gen. counsel for procurement, 1961-62; atty. Office Gen. Counsel, Army Materiel Command, 1962-69, Sec. Tampa Election Bd. Served with U.S. Army, 1917. Mem. Fla. Bar, Am., Fed. bar assns., Judge Advs. Assn., Phi Delta Phi, Theta Chi, Blue Key. Episcopalian. Home: 7710 Bristow Dr Annandale VA 22003

BIVINS, HOWARD JACKSON, textile co. exec.; b. Haddock, Ore., Dec. 23, 1902; s. Jackson C. and Mattie (Skinner) B.; student Ga. Mil. Acad., 1917-20; B.Sc., Mercer U., 1925; m. Katherine Armstrong, Oct. 19, 1932; children—Jack, Guy, Ben, Charlotte (Mrs. Roland K.Knight). With Bibb Mfg. Co., Macon, Ga., 1925- -, treas., 1948—. Trustee Oliver S. Porter Fund, Bibb Benevolent Fund, Inc. Mem. Ga. Soc. C.P.A.'s. Baptist. Clubs: Civitan (pres. 1960-61), Idle Hour Golf and Counrty (Macon). Home: 110 DeSoto Pl Macon GA 31204 Office: 237 Main St Macon GA 31208

BIXBY, HAROLD GLENN, business exec.; b. Lamotte, Mich., July 14, 1903; s. Charles Samuel Samuel and Laura (Schenk) B.; A.B., U. Mich., 1927; m. Pauline Elizabeth Summy, July 3, 1928; children—Mary Louise and Richard Glenn (twins). Began in accounting dept. Ex-Cell-O Corp., Detroit, 1928, asst. sec., 1929, controller, 1933, sec., treas. and dir., 1937, became v.p., treas., treas., dir., 1947, pres., gen. mgr., 1951-70, chmn. bd., chief exec. officer, 1970—; dir. Detrex Chem. Industries, Inc., Mich. Bell Telephone Co., Mich. Chrome & Chem. Co. Detroit, Mfrs. Nat. Bank, Detroit, Detroit Edison Co. Bd. dirs. Project. Hope, United Found., Com. for Nat. Trade Policy; trustee New Detroit, Inc., Kalamazoo Coll., Grace Hosp. Detroit; bd. bd. dirs., chmn. U. Mich. Devel. Council. Mem. Greater Detroit Bd. Commerce, Tau Kappa Epsilon. Clubs: Economic, Detroit Athletic, Detroit Golf, Detroit. Home: 18510 Bretton Dr Detroit, MI 48223 Office: 14310 Hamilton Av Highland Park MI 48232

BIXBY, J. E., corp. exec.; b. Houston, 1922; B.B.A., U. Houston, 1949. Sr. auditor Hughes Tool Co., 1941-51; controller, asst. sec. asst. treas. W.S. Bellows Constrn. Corp., 1951-55; treas. Tex. Eastern Transmission Corp., 1956-63, v.p., treas., 1963-66, comptroller, 1966-68, v.p. finance, 1968—; v.p., treas. La Gloria Oil & Gas Co.; v.p., dir. Transwestern Pipeline Co. Home: 1311 Briarmead Dr Houston TX 77027 Office: PO Box 2521 Houston TX 77001*

BIXBY, JOSEPH R., ins. co. exec.; b. Apr. 7, 1925; s. Walter Edwin and Angeline I. (Reynolds) B.; ed. U. Mo.; m. Marilyn Swartzel, Aug. 28, 1947; children—Kathryn Ann, Nancy Lea. Various positions Kansas City Life Ins. Co. (Mo.), until 1950, asst. sec., 1950-55, asst. regional supr., 1952- 55, v.p., asst. sec., 1955-62, adminstrv. v.p., 1962-64, pres., 1964—. also dir.; dir. Commerce Trust Co., Kansas City, Mo., Glasgow, Mo., Memphis Bank. Bd. dirs. Kansas City Heart Assn.; trustee U. Kansas City. Served with USAAF, 1944-46. Mem. Navy League U.S., USCG Aux. Clubs: Kansas City, River, Kansas City Country. Home: 1035 W 65th St Kansas City MO 64113 Office: 3520 Broadway Kansas City MO 64141

BIXBY, PAUL WARREN, educator; b. Richville, Minn., Dec. 22, 1913; s. John L. and Cora (Davis) B.; B.Ed., St. Cloud State Coll., 1937; M.A., U. Minn., 1943; Ed.D. (grad. fellow 1943-44), Columbia, 1944; m. Ruth Jane Lowry, June 1, 1935; children—Jean (Mrs. Robert Wiegand), Mark, Mary (Mrs. Bert Kisner). Rural tchr., Ottertail County, Minn., 1932-35; tchr. secondary sch., St. Cloud, 1937-42; prin. Cos Cob Sch., Greenwich, Conn., 1944-46, Milburn (N.J.) Sch., 1946-48; mem. faculty Pa. State U., 1948—, prof. edn., 1951—, head elementary edn. dept., 1948-58, asso. dean Coll. Edn., 1962-70, univ. coordinator internat. programs, 1966-69; vis. prof. U. Philippines, Quezon City, 1955-56; dir. tng. for Philippine program Peace Corps, 1961-62. Mem. N.E.A., Am. Assn. U. Profs., Phi Delta Kappa. Home: 224 Ridge Av State College PA 16801 Office: Coll Education Pennsylvania State Univ University Park PA 16802

BIXBY, R. BURDELL, lawyer, state ofcl.; b. Schenectady, Oct. 11, 1914; s. Raymond O. and Mabel A. (Rumsey) B.;A.B., Colgate U., 1936; LL.B., Albany Law Sch., 1940, J.D., 1968; m. Anne M. Hardwick, Oct. 25, 1941; 1 son, Robert Hardwick. Admitted to N.Y. bar; 1940; partner firm Dewey, Ballentine, Bushby, Palmer & Wood, N.Y.C., 1955—; asst. sec. gov. State N.Y., 1948-50, exec. asst., 1950-52, sec., 1952-54; sec.-treas. N.Y. State Thruway Authority, 1950-60, chmn., sec., treas., 1960-61, chmn., sec., 1961—. Trustee, Hudson City Savs. Instn. (N.Y.). Treas. N.Y. State Republican Com., 1959-61. Trustee Albany Law Sch., Darrow Sch., New Lebanon, N.Y. Served with USAAF, 1942-46. Mem. Am., N.Y. State, Columbia County bar assns., Assn. Bar City N.Y., N.Y. County Lawyers Assn., Am. Legion, Mason. Club: City Midday (N.Y.C.). Home: 7 Joslen Pl Hudson NY 12534 Office: 140 Broadway New York City NY 10005 also Delaware Plaza Elsmere NY 12054 12054

BIXBY, WALTER EDWIN, business exec.; b. Champaign, Ill., Aug. 20, 1896; s. Walter Albert and Lizzie (Holmes) B.; student Culver (Ind.) Mil. Acad., 1914-15, Drury Coll., U. Mo.; LL.D., Drury Coll., 1967; m. Angeline I. Reynolds, Apr. 11, 1923 (dec.); children—Joseph Reynolds, Walter Edwin; m. 2d, Louise T. Bogart, Apr. 8, 1964. Field timekeeper Liquified Petroleum Gas Co. of Okla., Tulsa, 1921-23; clk. Kansas City Life Ins. Co. (Mo.), 1923-24, asst. sec., 1924-37, exec. v.p., 1937-39, pres., 1939-64, chmn. bd., 1964—; past Life Ins. Med. Research Fund; past pres. Am. Life Conv.; gov. Am. Royal. Past mem. bd. dirs. Salvation Army, Boy Scouts Am., Jackson County Chpt. A.R.C.: past mem. Kansas City Crime Commn.; trustee Midwest Research Inst., past trustee U. Mo. at Kansas City. Mem. Inst. Life Ins. (past dir.), Sigma Alpha Epsilon. Democrat. Episcopalian. Clubs: Kansas City, University, Country, River, Casper (Wyo.) Country; Tavern (Chgo.). Home: The Walnuts 5049 Wornall Rd Kansas City MO 64112 also Bar BX Ranch Glenrock WY 82637 Office: 3520 Broadway PO Box 139 Kansas City MO 64141

BIXBY, WILLIAM COURTNEY, author; b. San Diego, June 15, 1920; s. Vernon Chamberlain and Courtney (Rudd) B.; B.S., Va. Poly. Inst., 1942; m. Elizabeth Knight, Jan. 22, 1944; children—William Courtney, Barbara Ruth. Staff writer Cowles Mags., Inc., N.Y.C., 1945-47, 49-50; free lance writer, N.Y.C., 1948; asso. editor Time, Inc., Archtl. Forum, N.Y.C., 1950-52; free lance writer, 1953—. Tchr. secondary sch. and coll.; museum dir., 1968—. Served to 1st lt. AUS, 1942-45. Author: The Impossible Journey of Sir Ernest Shackleton, 1960; Havoc, The Story of Natural Disasters, 1961; The Race to the South Pole, 1961; Skywatchers—The U.S. Weather Bureau in Action, 1962; McMurdo Antarctica, 1962; Waves-Pathways of Energy, 1963; Great Experimenters, 1964; The Universe of Galileo and Newton, 1964; Track of the Bear, 1965; The Forgotten Voyage of Charles Wilkes, 1966; Seawatchers-Oceanographers at Work, 1967; Of Animals and Men, 1968; Rebel Genius, 1970; Robert Scott, 1970; A World You Can Live In, 1971. Home: 248 Stone House Lane Guilford CT 06437

BIXER, EDMOND P., curtain mfr.; b. N.Y.C., Mar. 15, 1899; s. Herman and Hannah (Petzal) B.; grad. high sch. Pres., dir. Bartmann & Bixer, Inc., curtain mfrs., N.Y.C.; dir. United Mchts. & Mfrs., Inc. Served with USNR, World War II. Clubs: Turf and Field; Lambs, Athletic (N.Y.C.). Home: 45 Sutton Pl S New York City NY 10022 Office: 339 Fifth Av New York City NY 10016

BIXLER, JOHN EDMUND, business exec.; b. Lafayette, Ind., Aug. 25, 1902; s. John E. and Ruth (Miller) B.; B.S., Purdue U., 1924; m. Jim Lindley, Apr. 15, 1933; 1 dau., dau., Joyce. Gen. sales mgr. Duncan Electric Co., Lafayette, 1929-49, v.p., 1949-50, pres., 1950-67, chmn. bd., 1967—; dir. Lafayette Nat. Bank, Lafayette Life Ins. Co. Bd. dirs. Purdue Research Found. Mem. Ind. Mfrs. Assn. (pres. 1956), Purdue Alumni Assn. (pres. 1948-51), Am. Inst. E.E., Ind. Soc. of Chgo., Greater Lafayette C. of C., Tau Beta Pi, Phi Gamma Delta, Sigma Delta Chi, Pi Tau Sigma, Scabbard and Blade. Presbyn. (elder). Clubs: Columbia (Indpls.); Lafayette (Ind.) Country. Home: 610 Ridgewood Dr West Lafayette IN 47906 Office: care Duncan Electric Co Inc Lafayette IN 47902

BIXLER, JULIUS SEELYE, ret. coll. pres.; b. New London, Conn., Apr. 4, 1894; s. James Wilson and Elizabeth James (Seelye) B.; A.B., Amherst Coll., 1916, A.M., 1920, D.D., 1939; Ph.D., Yale, 1924; student Union Theol. Sem., 1917-18, Harvard, 1923-24, U. Freiburg (Germany), 1928-29; hon. M.A., Harvard, 1942, L.H.D., Union Coll., 1947, Wesleyan U., 1954, Bates Coll., 1958, Harvard, 1960, Carleton Coll., 1964; LL.D., U. Me., 1948, Brown U., 1948, Bowdoin, 1952, Colby Coll., 1960; D.C.L., Acadia U., N.S., 1949; Litt. D., Am. Internat. Coll., Springfield, Mass., 1961; Sc.D., Worcester Poly. Inst., 1962; m. Mary Harrison Thayer, Sept. 21, 1918; children—Mary Harriet (Mrs. John N. Sinnock), Elizabeth Seelye (Mrs. Fred C. Bonner), Martha Harrison, Nancy Emerson (Mrs. Sanford M. Isaacs). Instr. Latin and English, Am. Coll., Madura, India, 1916-17; dir. religious activities Amherst Coll., 1919-20; lectr. philosophy Am. U., Beirut, Syria, 1920-22; asst. prof. religion and Bibl. lit. Smith Coll., 1924-25, asso. prof., 1925-29, prof., 1929-33; lectr. theology Harvard, 1932-33, Bussey prof. theology, 1933-42, acting dean Div. Sch., 1937, 40; pres. Colby Coll., Waterville, Me., 1942-60, pres. emeritus, 1960—, Ingraham lectr., 1967; ednl. cons. Thammasat U., Bangkok, 1962-63; lectr. U. Hawaii; fellow Center Advanced Studies, Wesleyan U., Middletown, Conn., 1961-62; Donald J. Cowling vis. prof. philosophy Carleton Coll., 1964; vis. prof. philosophy Bowdoin Coll., 1965; Distinguished vis. prof. U. Me., 1969; Phi Beta Kappa vis. scholar, 1961-62; lectr. Salzburg Seminar in Am. Studies, 1951, 59, 61; lectr. Am. U. Beirut, 1966. Former trustee Smith Coll., Amherst Coll., Colby Coll., Radcliffe Coll.; pres. bd. dirs. Nat. Council on Religion in Higher Edn., 1934-39. Mem. Am. Theol. Soc. (sec. 1930-35; pres. 1935-36), Am. Philos. Assn., Am. Acad. Arts and Scis., Phi Beta Kappa, Alpha Delta Phi, Delta Sigma Rho. Conglist. Author: Religion in the Philosophy of William James, 1926; Immortality and the Present Mood (Ingersoll lecture), 1931; Religion for Free Minds (Lowell Lectures), 1939; Resources of Religion and Aims of Higher Education (Hazen Lectures), 1942; Conversations with an Unrepentant Liberal (Terry Lectures), 1946; A Faith that Fulfills (Ayer Lectures), 1951; Education for Adversity (Inglis Lecture), 1952. Editor: (with R.L. Calhoun and H.R. Niebuhr) and contbr. to The Nature of Religious Experience, 1937; contbr. to other symposia and theol. jours. Home: RFD 1 Box 244 Jaffrey NH 03452

BIXLER, RAY HERBERT, psychologist, educator; b. Emerson, Neb., May 15, 1917; s. Ray Andrew and Josephine Olivia (Gress) B.; B.Ed., Ill. State Normal U., 1939; M.A., Ohio State U., 1942, Ph.D., 1951; m. Marjorie Marie Martin, Jan. 28, 1956; children—Deveney, Danae, Dike, Minda, Andrea. Psychologist, Akron (O.) Child Guidance Center, 1943-44; counselor U. Minn. Counseling Center, 1944-46; psychologist Minn. Psychiat. Inst. 1946-48; mem. faculty U. Louisville, 1948—, prof. psychology, 1959—, chmn. dept. 1957-67, coordinator Freshman Symposium, 1971—, cons. children's and youth project Sch. Medicine; coordinator psychol. service Central State Hosp., 1968—. Cons., Ky. Dept. Mental Health. Mem. Louisville Human Relations Commn. Docent, U. Hamburg (Germany), 1952-53; Fulbright lectr. Bogotá, Colombia, 1964-65. Mem. A.A.A.S., Am. Psychol. Assn., Soc. Research Child Devel., Sociedad Interamericana de Psicologia, Phi Kappa Phi, Delta Phi Alpha, Phi Delta Kappa, Psi Chi. Author articles in counseling, psychotherapy and ethics. Home: 3912 Chenoweth Run Rd Jeffersontown KY 40299 Office: U Louisville Louisville KY 40208

BJARNASON, PAUL HAROLD ERLING, drug co. exec.; b. Wynyard, Sask., Can., Apr. 14, 1915; s. Paul and Halldora (Johnson) B.; student Western Coll. Pharmacy, 1937-38; student Banff Sch. Advanced Mgmt., 1958; m. Evelyn Jonasson, Aug. 29, 1939; children—Darel (dec.), Karen (Mrs. Michael Apps), Sigrid, Stefan. Apprentice Wynyard (Sask.) Pharmacy, 1933-37; apprentice pharmacist Cunningham Drug Stores Ltd., Vancouver, B.C., Can., 1937-38, asst. store mgr., 1938-42, store mgr., 1942-44, store supr., 1944-47, personnel mgr., 1947-50, mdse. mgr., 1950-56, v.p., gen. mgr., 1956-63, exec. v.p., 1963-69, pres., 1969—; pres. Western Wholesale Drug Ltd.; dir. Koffler Stores Ltd. Pres. Vancouver Assn. Retarded Children, 1958-60, pres. B.C. Assn. for Mentally Retarded, 1962-65; v.p. Can. Assn. for Mentally Retarded, 1966-69; chmn. adv. council B.C. Mental Retardation Inst., 1967-69; dir. B.C. Rehabilitation Assn., 1968-69. Mem. B.C. Profl. Pharmacists' Soc., Can. Pharmaceut. Assn., Pharmaceut. Assn. B.C. Home: 1927 W 18th Av Vancouver British Columbia Canada Office: 2780 E Broadway Vancouver British Columbia Canada

BJERKNES, JACOB AALL BONNEVIE, educator; b. Stockholm, Sweden, Nov. 2, 1897; s. Vilhelm Friman Koren and Honoria Sophia (Bonnevie) B.; Ph.D., U. Oslo, 1924; LL.D., University of California, 1967; m. to Hedvig Borthen, July 11, 1928; children—Vilheim, Kirsten. Came to U.S., 1939, naturalized, 1946. Meteorologist, Meteorol. Obs., Bergen, Norway, 1918-20; supt. Weather Forecast Center, 1920-31; prof. meteorology Geophys. Inst., 1931-40; prof. of meterology U. Cal., Los Angeles, 1940—; Fulbright & Guggenheim research asso., 1957-58. Lectr. Mass. Inst. Tech., 1933, 34; cons. in weather forecasting, Zurich, Switzerland, 1922-23, London, 1925-26, 1935- 36, Toronto, 1933, 39, Washington, 1939, 40, 46; lectr., exchange program Nat. Acad. Scis.-Soviet Acad. Scis., Moscow, Leningrad, 1963. Served as cons. USAAF, Eng., North Africa, Italy, Hawaii, Guam, 1943-45. Recipient Symons medal Royal Meteorol. Soc., London, 1940, Bowie medal, Am. Geophys. Union, 1942, Vega medal, Swedish Society Anthropology and Geography, WMO medal World Meteorol. Orgn., Losey medal Inst. Aerospace Scis. Decorated Royal Norwegian Order of St. Olav, 1947. Recipient the Nat. Medal Sci., 1966. Hon. mem. Royal Meteorol. Soc. of London; mem. Am.

Acad. Arts and Scis., Royal Norwegian, Nat., N.Y., Indian acads. scis. Danish Acad. Tech. Scis., Royal Swedish Acad. Scis., Internat. Assn. Meteorology (pres. 1948-51), Am. Meteorol. Soc. (v.p., hon.), Am. Acad. Achievement. Author: Polar Front theory and initiator of weather map analysis methods based on same, 1920; Theory on Pressure variations as function of flow pattern, 1944; Theory on the gen. circulation of the atmosphere, 1942; research on atmosphere-ocean interaction. Home: 1201 Ocean Av Santa Monica CA 90401 Office: University of California Los Angeles CA 90024

BJONER, INGRID, lyric-dramatic soprano; b. Kraakstad, Norway, Nov. 8, 1927; d. Johan and Alma (Prestangen) Bjoner; student Miss Boellemose, Conservatory Music, Oslo, Norway, 1946-51, Prof. Paul Lohmann, Music Hochschule, Frankfurt- M, Germany, 1951-57; grad. phamacist U. Oslo, 1951; m. Thomas R. Pierpont, Sept. 28, 1960. Operatic debut as Donna Anna in Don Giovanni, Oslo, 1957; mem. Wuppertal Opera, 1958-60, Deutsche Oper am Rhein, Dusseldorf, 1960-62; 1st lyric-dramatic soprano Bayerische Staats Oper, Munich, Germany, 1961—; summer guest appearances at Vancouver Internat. Festival, 1959, Stockholm Festival, 1959, Wagner Festival, Bayreuth, 1960; U.S. debut at San Francisco and Los Angeles Opera, 1961; debut Met. Opera, 1961; debut at La Scala, 1965; rec. artist for Deutsche Grammophon, Ariola. UNESCO scholar, 1955-56; recipient Norwegian Music Critics Soc. award, 1959-60; decorated Order St. Olav 1st class (Norway); named Kammersängerin, Bavarian Ministry Culture, 1965; decorated Bavarian Order of Merit. Mem. Soc. New Music (Oslo), Norwegian Pharm. Soc. Home: Birnauerstrasse 2 8 Munich 13 Germany

BJORAKER, WALTER THOMAS, educator; b. Steele County, Minn., Jan. 19, 1920; s. Lewis I. and Mary (Barsness) B.; B.S. with distinction, U. Minn., 1942, M.S., 1948, Ph.D., 1952; m. Delores E. Johnson, Feb. 15, 1947; children—Barbara Jeanne, Gary Thomas, Gordon Lee. Instr. vocational agr. Harmony (Minn.) High Sch., 1942-43; asst. supr. agrl. edn. Minn. Dept. Edn., 1946; instr. vocational agr., Rochester, Minn., 1946-48; instr. agrl. edn. U. Minn., 1948-50; prof. agrl. and extension edn. U. Wis., 1950—; chmn. dept. 1953—. Sec. nat. adv. committee to the National Center for Advanced Study and Research in Agriculture, 1965; U. Wis. and U.S. AID Study Team Edn. Feasibility in Nigeria, 1964, 65; cons. on Nigeria, UN, 1966; cons. AID, Rio Grande do Sul, Brazil, 1966; cons. on edn. in agr. Govt. of Brazil, 1969. Served with USAAF, 1943-45. Mem. Am. Vocational Assn. (regional research rep. 1958-61; mem. credential and accreditation com. 1966), Wis. Edn. Assn., Wis. Assn. Vocational Agr. Instrs., Nat. Vocational Agr. Assn., Am. Assn. U. Profs., Wis. Acad. Sci., Rural Edn. Assn., Ygdrasil Literary Society, Farm House Frat., Alpha Zeta, Delta Theta Sigma, Gamma Sigma Delta, Phi Delta Kappa, Phi Kappa Phi. Author: Introduction to Agriculture, 1956. Contbr. articles profl. jours., bulls. Home: 5701 Midmoor Rd Madison WI 53716

BJORK, ALTON JOSEPH, educator; b. Marion, N.D., Jan. 22, 1913; s. Albert Clarence and Minda (Halvorson) B.; B.A., State Tchrs. Coll., Valley City, N.D., 1937; Ed.D., Columbia Tchrs. Coll., 1942; m. Adeline Marie Hoge, Apr. 18, 1943; children—Mary, David, Paul, John, Ruth. Rural elementary tchr., Montpelier, N.D., 1931-34; high sch. bus. edn. tchr., Manistique, Mich., 1937-40; prof. edn. U. N.D., 1946-55, chmn. dept. edn., 1955-66, dir. grad. study, 1966-68; prof. edn. Ill. State U., Normal, 1968—. Served with USAAF, 1942-45. Mem. N.E.A., Nat. Soc. Study Edn., Ill. Edn. Assn., Soc. Profl. Edn., Am. Ednl. Studies Assn., Phi Delta Kappa, Kappa Delta Pi. Home: 905 Broadway Normal, IL 61761.

BJORK, CHRISTOPHER, bank exec. Gen. auditor Fed. Res. Bank Mpls. Office: 73 S 5th St Minneapolis MN 55440*

BJORKLUND, FREDERICK, savs. and loan assn. exec.; b. St. Paul, Feb. 17, 1913; s. Edward and Hanna (Bodin) B.; B.B.A., U. Minn., 1935; m. Doris Dunlap, Aug. 28, 1937. With Minn. Fed. Savs. & Loan Assn., St. Paul, 1940—, pres., 1959—, chmn. bd. dirs., 1965—; vice chmn., dir. FHLB, Des Moines, Ia., 1963- 66; trustee Minn. Mut. Life Ins. Co., Bd. dirs. Port Devel. Assn.; pres. Indianhead council Boy Scouts Am., 1968-69; bd. dirs. Charles T. Miller Hosp., 1966—, St. Paul YMCA, 1960— 68, St. Paul Jr. Achievement, 1962-69. Served to 2d lt. AUS, World War II. Recipient Silver Beaver award Boy Scouts Am., 1954. Mem. U.S. Savs. and Loan League (bd. dirs. 1965-67), Savs. and Loan League Minn. (past bd. dirs.), St. Paul Bd. Realtors (past bd. dirs.), St. Paul Home Builders Assn. (past bd. dirs.), Saint Paul Area C. of C. (pres. 1965-67), Savs. Council Twin Cities (past pres.), Am. Legion. Presbyn. (trustee). Mason (Shriner). Clubs: Kiwanis (past pres.), St. Paul Athletic (past bd. dirs.), Town and Country (pres. 1969—) (St. Paul). Home: 1937 Highland Pky St Paul MN 55116 Office: 355 Minnesota St St Paul MN 55101

BJORLIE, LIV LUNDEBY, mem. Democratic Nat. Com.; b. Tolna, N.D., Dec. 30, 1932; d. Fredrick and Anna (Iverson) Lundeby; student Valley City (N.D.) Tchrs. Coll; m. Elmer Peter Bjorlie, Apr. 14, 1952; children—Peter, Anna, John, Paul, Laura. Chmn. Dem. Women's Orgn. Barnes County, N.D., 1958-60; mem. exec. com. N.D. Dem. Women, 1959-65, pres., 1960-64; mem. Dem. Nat. Com. for N.D., 1964—; treas., mem. exec. com. Dem. Mid West Conf.; mem. Dem. Nat. Rules Commn., 1968-72, dem. Nat. Site Com., 1968-72. Mem. adv. council Peace Corps; mem. Pres.'s Council for Youth, 1967. Mem. Internat. Platform Assn. Club: Zonta. Address: 1380 E Av N Valley City ND 58072

BJORNSON, VAL (Kristjan Valdimar Bjornson), state treas.; b. Minneota, Minn., Aug. 29, 1906; s. Gunnar B. and Ingibjorg Augustine (Hurdal) B.; B.A. summa cum laude, U. Minn., 1930; m. Gudrun Jonsdottir, Feb. 20, 1946; children—Helga, Kristin, Jon, Valdimar, Maria. With Father printer's trade weekly newspaper Minneota Mascot, 1918, editor, 1925-27, 31-35; radio commentator sta. KSTP, St. Paul-Mpls., 1935-42; editorial writer Mpls. Jour., 1935-36, Mpls. Tribune, 1937-41; asso. editor St. Paul Pioneer Press and Dispatch, 1947- 50, 55-56; Minn. state treas., 1951-55, 56—. Former pres., now dir. Minn. chpt., mem. nat. bd. Am.-Scandinavian Found.; hon. consul for Iceland, Minn., 1942, 47-50. Rep. nominee, U.S. senator, 1954. Served with USN, Iceland, 1942-46; disch. as lt. comdr. Decorated comdr. Order of Falcon (Iceland), 1946; Knight Order St. Olav, 1st class (Norway), 1949. Mem. Phi Beta Kappa, Delta Sigma Rho, Sigma Delta Chi. Lutheran. Mason. Home: 2914 46th Av S Minneapolis MN 55406 Office: State Adminstration Bldg St Paul MN 55101

BJORSETH, WALTER DAVID, electronics co. exec.; b. Aurora, Ill., July 15, 1921; s. John J. and Astrid (Aksdal) B.; student U. S.C., 1943, U. N.C., 1945, Harvard U. Grad. Sch. Bus. Adminstrn., 1945; B.S., U. Ill., 1947; m. Betty Kandalec, Dec. 4, 1948; children—Jeffry David, Melinda Marie. Accounting mgr. UARCO, Inc., Chgo., 1947-52; mgmt cons. Booz Allen & Hamilton, Chgo., 1953-54; controller Borg Warner Corp., Decatur, Ill., 1954-58; sec., treas. Pyle Nat. Co., Chgo., 1958-65, v.p. finance, 1965- 67; v.p. Admiral Corp., Chgo., 1967—, treas., 1968—, sec., 1969, also dir.; treas., dir. Admiral Credit Corp. Served with Supply Corps, USNR, 1942-46, 50-52. Republican. Home: 1870 Buckingham Av Westchester IL 60153 Office: Admiral Corp 3800 Cortland St Chicago IL 60647

BJURMAN, GEORGE D., investment executive; b. Huntington, Pa., March 11, 1906; son Andrew and Augusta (Bert) B.; B.S., U. Cal. at Berkeley, 1929; m. Dorothy Mary Kuhlmeyer, Oct. 1, 1936; children—Susan A., George Andrew. Investment analyst Wells Fargo Bank & Union Trust Co., San Francisco, 1929-36; trust investment officer Bank of Am., Los Angeles, 1936-46; v.p. charge investments, Occidental Life Ins. Co. of Cal., Los Angeles, 1946- v.p., 1964-70, chmn. finance com., dir. 1964—; member executive com. Pacific Finance Corporation, Transamerica Insurance Company; director, member of investment com. Mt. Beacon Ins. Co., Olympic Ins. Co., Marathon Ins. Co., Spartan Ins. Co., Pacific Fidelity Life Ins. Co.; dir. Transam. Indemnity Co., Transam. Life Ins. pres., dir., chief exec. Transam. Investment Counselors, Inc., until 1970; pres., chief investment officer George D. Bjurman & Assos., Los Angeles, investment com. Countrywide Life Ins. Co. Chmn. endowment com., dir. Mem. Businessmen's Garden Club of Los Angeles (dir.). Clubs: California, Stock Exchange, Bond, Los Angeles Country (Los Angeles); Lincoln. Home: 786 Tortuoso Way Bel-Air Los Angeles, CA 90024 Office: 1800 Century Park E Los Angeles CA 90069

BLACHER, BORIS, composer, educator; b. China, Jan. 3, 1903; s. Eduard B. and Helene (Wolff) B.; student of Friedrich E. Koch, also univ. courses in music, m. Gerty Herzog, 1945. Tchr., Dresden Conservatory, later dir. High Sch. for Music, Berlin. Composer; (oratorio) Der Grossinquisitor; (operas) Preussisches Marchen, Romeo and Juliet; Concertante Musik; Variations on a Theme by Paganini; Music for Cleveland; Studie im Pianissimo; Thirteen Ways of Looking at a Blackbird; also ballets, concerti, chamber music, piano works, songs.*

BLACK, ARTHUR LEO, educator; b. Redlands, Cal., Dec. 1, 1922; s. Leo M. and Marie A. (Burns) B.; B.S., U. Cal. at Davis, 1948, Ph.D., 1951; m. Trudi E. McCue, Nov. 11, 1945; children—Teresa (Mrs. William Townsend), Janet, Patti. Faculty physiol. chemistry Sch. Vet. Medicine U. Cal., Davis, 1951—, prof., 1962—, chmn. dept. physiol. scis., 1968—. Cons. NIH, 1970—; chmn. Nutritional Scis. Tng. Com., 1971—. Served to 1st lt. USAAF, 1943-46. Recipient Sci. Faculty award NSF, 1958. Research grantee NSF, NIH, 1952—. Mem. Am. Soc. Biol. Chemists, Am. Physiol. Soc., Am. Inst. Nutrition (Borden award 1963), Sigma Xi, Phi Beta Kappa, Phi Zeta. Contbr. papers to profl. lit. Home: 891 Linden Lane Davis CA 95616

BLACK, BARRON FOSTER, lawyer; b. Norfolk, Va., Nov. 27, 1893; s. Foster and Jennie M. (Tilley) B.; B.A., U. Va., 1917, LL.B., 1920; m. Aileen Pettit Taylor, Nov. 24, 1925; children—Anna (Mrs. C. Randolph Hudgins), Aileen (Mrs. Walter B. Martin, Jr.), Jane (Mrs. David Clark). Admitted to Va. bar, 1920, since practiced in Norfolk, mem. Hughes, Vandeventer & Eggleston, 1922-25, Vandeventer, Eggleston & Black, 1925-35, Vandeventer & Black, 1935-51, now Vandeventer, Black, Meredith & Martin, 1951—; Norfolk, Va.; dir. Bank of Va. Rector U. Va., mem. bd. visitors, 1945-56, chmn. Alumni Fund, vice pres. U. Va. Law Assn.; chmn. U.S. Savs. Bond Campaign, 1958; overseer Sweet Briar Coll., 1954-56; chmn. Norfolk Pub. Library; chmn. distbn. com. Norfolk Found. Served as sgt. U.S. Army, Am. Field Service, French Army, World War I. Named first citizen of Norfolk, 1959; Mr. Hampton Roads, Hampton Roads Maritime Assn.; recipient Commerce Builder award Hampton Roads Fgn. Commerce Club, 1961, Brotherhood citation Norfolk chpt. Nat. Conf. Christians and Jews. Fellow Am. Bar Assn.; mem. Hampton Roads Maritime Asso. (past pres.), Norfolk, Portsmouth (past pres.) bar assns., Maritime Law Assn. U.S., Raven Soc., Phi Gamma Delta, Omicron Delta Kappa, Phi Beta Kappa. Clubs: Virginia (pres.), German, Norfolk Yacht and Country (Norfolk), Harbor. Home: 7409 Glencove Pl Norfolk VA 23510 Office: Virginia Nat Bank Bldg 1 Commercial Pl Norfolk VA 23510

BLACK, BENJAMIN MARDEN, surgeon; b. Salt Lake City, July 4, 1910; s. B.W. and Jean (Blackburn) B.; A.B., Stanford, 1931, M.A., 1933, M.D., 1936; M.S., U. Minn., 1940; m. Eleanor Weber, Nov. 14, 1942. Intern Alameda County Hosp., Oakland, Cal.; instr. anatomy Stanford, 1932-33; fellow surgery Mayo Found., 1937-41, instr. surgery, asst. and asso. prof. surgery, 1950-57, prof., 1957—. Diplomate Am. Bd. Surgery. Mem. Am. Surg. Assn., Phi Beta Kappa, Sigma Xi. Contbr. articles profl. jours. Home: 432 SW 10th Av Rochester MN 55901 Office: 200 1st St SW Rochester MN 55901

BLACK, BRADY FORREST, newspaper editor; b. Lawrence Co., Ky., July 31, 1908; s. Fred Nixon and Melissa (Cornwell) B.; student pub. schs.; m. Edra Dailey, Sept. 17, 1930; children—Brenda Gayle, Brady Brent, Lisa Ann. Sports editor Ashland (Ky.) Independent, 1927-38, city editor, 1938-40; with Cin. Enquirer, 1940—, beginning as copyreader, promoted through various positions to Ky. corr., 1946, Ohio corr., 1948, mng. editor, 1956-57, editor editorial page, 1957-59, exec. editor, 1959-64, v.p., editor, 1964—. Mem. Ky. Harness Racing Commn. Mem. Inter Am. Press Assn. (dir.), Newcomen Soc., Ohio C. of C. (v.p., mem. board directors), Sigma Delta Chi (pres. Central Ohio profl. chpt. 1955-56). Home: 1870 Dixie Hwy Lookout Heights KY 41101 Office: 617 Vine St Cincinnati OH 45201

BLACK, CARL BRAHAM, sales exec.; b. Mt. Pleasant, Pa., Jan. 2, 1904; s. John Roland and Ida (Braham) B.; student Ohio State U., 1921-24; m. Pauline Horlocker, June 19, 1926; children—Barbara (Mrs. J. B. Bloomstrom), Marilyn (Mrs. J.B. Auchterlonie), Carol (Mrs. Howard D. Hobbs), Helen (Mrs. Ned W. Bechthold). With Standard Steel Spring Co., 1924-53, v.p. sales, 1940- 53, dir., 1945-53; v.p., dir. Rockwell Spring & Axle Co., 1953-57; exec. vice pres., dir. Rockwell-Standard Corp., 1957-67; exec. v.p. Rockwell- Standard divs. N. Am. Rockwell Corp., 1967-71; dir. Ontario Steel Products Co. Ltd., Toronto, Mem. Soc. Automotive Engrs. Republican Presbyn. Clubs: Detroit, Detroit Athletic, Recess (Detroit); Duquesne (Pitts.); Bloomfield Hills (Mich.) Country; Hole-in- the-Wall Golf (Naples, Fla.). Home: 150 Marblehead Dr Bloomfield Hills MI 48013 Office: Clifford at Bagley Detroit MI 48231

BLACK, CHARLES ALLEN, educator; b. Lone Tree, Ia., Jan. 22, 1916; s. Guy Cameron and Katharine Lavina (Loehr) B.; B.S. in Chemistry and Agronomy, Colo. State U., 1937; M.S. in Soil Fertility, Ia. State U., 1938, Ph.D., 1942; m. Marjorie Anderson, June 11, 1939; children—Carol Anne, Richard Allen, Marilyn Jean. Mem. faculty Ia. State U., 1939—, prof. soils, 1949—, Distinguished prof., 1967—; vis. prof. Cornell U., 1955; senior postdoctoral fellow Nat. Sci. Found., 1964-65; research asso. Kearny Found., U. Cal., 1964, U. Cal., 1965. Served USNR, 1945-46, Fellow Am. Soc. Agronomy (exec. com. 1961-63; Soil Sci. award 1957, nat. pres. 1970-71), Am. Inst. Chemists; mem. Soil Sci. Soc. Am. (chmn. div. 2, 1954, nat. pres. 1962), Internat. Soc. Soil Sci. (sec. commn. 2, 1960). Author: Soil-Plant Relationships, 1957, 2d edit., 1968. Editor-in-chief Methods of Soil Analysis, 1965. Home: 624 Agg Av Ames IA 50010

BLACK, CHARLES LUND, Jr., educator; b. Austin, Tex., Sept. 22, 1915; s. Charles Lunn and Alzada Helena (Bowman) B.; B.A., U. Tex., 1935, M.A., 1938; LL.B., Yale, 1943; m. Barbara Ann Aronstein, Apr. 11, 1954; three children—Gavin Bingley, David Alan, Robin Elizabeth. Admitted to the N.Y. bar, 1946, U.S. Supreme Ct. bar; practiced New York City, 1946-47; asst. professor law Columbia, 1947-49, asso. prof., 1949-52, prof., 1952-56; Henry R. Luce prof. jurisprudence Yale, 1956—; vis. prof. law U. Tex., 1955; mem. faculty Salzburg Seminar in Am. Studies, 1956; Edward Douglas White lectr. La. State U., 1968; Holmes Devise lectr. U. Washington, 1970; Bye fellow Queens' Coll., Cambridge, Eng., 1966-67. Counsel, Supreme Ct. briefs in school segregation, civil rights cases; legal cons. N.A.A.C.P. Legal Def. and Edn. Fund. Mem. adv. com. on admiralty rules Jud. Conf. U.S. Fellow Jonathan Edwards College, Yale. fellow of the Queens College, Cambridge, 1966-67; Mem. Assn. Am. Indian Affairs, Am. Assn. U. Profs., Maritime Law Assn. U.S., Phi Delta Phi, Kappa Sigma, Order of Coif. Club: Elizabethan. Author: The Law of Admiralty (with Grant Gilmore), 1957; The People and the Court, 1960; The Occasions of Justice, 1963; Perspectives in Constitutional Law, 1963; Telescopes and Islands (poetry), 1963; Structure and Relationship in Constitutional Law, 1969; also articles and poems in mags. and jours. in field. Office: Yale U Law Sch New Haven CT 06520

BLACK, CLAIR WILE, univ. ofcl.; b. Emlenton, Pa., Oct. 4, 1905; s. Colonel Warren and Iva (Wile) B.; A.B., U. Pitts., 1929, M.A., 1935; Ed.D., Tchrs Coll., Columbia, 1955; m. Katherine Wells, Feb. 16, 1946; children—Edwin Clair, Clair, Sandra Louise. Chmn. math. dept. pub. schs., South Brownsville, Beaver Falls, Ford City, Pa., 1929-41; tchr. math pub. schs., Irvington, N.J., 1941-43; faculty Fairleigh Dickinson U., Rutherford, N.J., 1943—, chmn. sci. and engrng., 1943-56, dean Coll. Sci. and Engring., 1955-58, dean Rutherford Campus, 1958-66, v.p. for govtl. affairs, 1966-71, dir. instructional services, 1971—. Faculty Pa. State U. Extension, Newark Coll. Engring., Upsala Coll., 1939-43. Conf. lay leader bd. laity, Conf. bd. trustees, v.p. bd. religious edn. No. N.J. Conf. Methodist Ch.; mem. Nat. Com. for Instructional Television Fixed Service, 1968-70. Trustee United Methodist Methodist Homes Homes of N.J. Mem. Am. Assn. U. Profs., Rutherford C. of C. (pres. 1966-67), Am. Am. Assn. for Higher Edn., Nat. Edn. Assn. Methodist. Mason (K.T.), Rotarian. Home: 328 Colonial Blvd Westwood NJ 07675 Office: Fairleigh Dickinson University Montross Av Rutherford NJ 07070

BLACK, CREED CARTER, newspaper editor; b. Harlan, Ky., July 15, 1925; s. Creed Carter and Mary (Gole). B.; B.S., with highest distinction and honors in Polit. Sci., Northwestern U., 1949; M.A. U. Chgo., 1952; m. Mary C. Davis, Dec. 28, 1947; children—Creed Carter, Steven D., Douglas S. Reporter Paducah (Ky.) Sun-Democrat, 1942-43, 46; editor Daily Northwestern, 1947; copy editor Chgo. Sun-Times, 1949, Chgo. Herald-American, 1950; editorial writer Nashville Tennessean, 1950-57, exec. editor, 1957-59; v.p., exec. editor Savannah (Ga.) Morning News, and Savannah Evening Press, 1959-60, Wilmington, (Del.) Morning News and Evening Jour., 1960-64; mng. editor Chgo. Daily News, 1964-68, exec. editor, 1968-69; assistant sec. for edn. commr. Office Edn. U.S. Dept. Health, Edn. and Welfare, 1969-70; editor Phila. Inquirer, 1970—. Served with 100th Inf. Div., AUS, WW II; ETO. Decorated Bronze Star Medal. Mem. Am. Soc. Newspaper Editors, treas., 1967—, bd. dirs. A.P. Mng. Editors Assn., Nat. Conf. Editorial Writers (chmn. 1962), Northwestern Alumni Assn. (v.p.), Chgo. Econ. Club, Sigma Delta Chi, Kappa Tau Alpha, Lambda Chi Alpha. Methodist. Clubs: Mid-America, Kenilworth, Chicago Press.; Indian Hill. Office: Phila Inquirer Philadelphia PA

BLACK, CYRIL EDWIN, educator; b. Bryson City, N.C., Sept. 10, 1915; s. Floyd Henson and Zarafinka (Kirova) B.; student U. Besancon, 1934-35, U. Berlin, summer, 1935; A.B., Duke, 1936; A.M., Harvard, 1937, Ph.D., 1941; m. Corinne Manning, June 30, 1951; children—James Manning, Christina Ellen. Mem. faculty Princeton, 1939—, asst. prof., 1946-49, asso. prof., 1949-54, prof. history, 1954—, dir. Center Internat. Studies, 1968—; fellow Behavioral Studies Center, 1960-61; officer Dept. State, 1943-44, fgn. service auxiliary officer assigned Eastern Europe, 1944-46; mem. U.S. delegation UN Commn. Investigation Concerning Greek Frontier Incidents, 1947; adviser, alternate U.S. mem. subcommn. on prevention discrimination and protection minorities, 1949-52; mem. U.S. delegation to observe Soviet elections, 1958; civilian faculty Nat. War Coll., 1950. Mem. Am. Hist. Assn., Am. Polit. Sci. Assn., Council Fgn. Relations. Author: Establishment of Constitutional Government in Bulgaria, 1943; Twentieth Century Europe: A History (with E.C. Helmreich), 4th edit., 1971; The Dynamics of Modernization, 1966; (with R.A. Falk, K. Knorr, O.R. Young) Neutralization in World Politics, 1968. Editor: Challenge in Eastern Europe, 1954; Rewriting Russian History, 1956; The Transformation of Russian Society, 1960; (with T.P. Thornton) Communism and Revolution, 1963 (with R.A. Falk) The Future of the International Legal Order, 3 vols. 1969-71. Contbr. profl. jours. Home: 182 Western Way Princeton NJ 08540

BLACK, DAVID, theatrical producer; b. N.Y.C., Nov. 20, 1931; s. Algernon and Elinor (Goldmark) B.; grad. Fieldston Sch., Riverdale, N.Y.C., 1949; B.A., Harvard, 1952; m. Linda Cabot, Dec. 21, 1951; children—Sophie, Alexander Goldmark, Jeremiah Wellington. Engaged in investment bus., 1959-62, co- producer Broadway prodn., Look: We've Come Through!, 1961; producer Broadway prodns. The Aspern Papers, 1962, Semi-Detached, 1963, Cambridge Circus, 1964, Ready When You Are, C.B.!, 1964; off Broadway prodn. The Knack, 1964; in London, The Ides of March, 1963; The Impossible Years, 1965; Those That Play the Clowns, 1966; The Natural Look, 1967; To Clothe the Naked, 1967; Broadway prodn. George M!, 1968; Fire, 1969, Paris Is Out, 1969, Salvation, 1969, W.C., 1971. Home: 190 Olmstead Hill Rd Wilton CT 06897 Office: 1564 Broadway New York City NY 10036

BLACK, DAVID STATLER, lawyer; b. Everett, Wash., July 14, 1928; s. Lloyd Llewelyn and Gladys (Statler) B.; B.A., Stanford, 1950; LL.B., U. Wash., 1954; m. Nancy Haskell, July 26, 1952; children—David Lloyd, Andrew Haskell, Kathleen Louise. Admitted to Wash. bar, 1954; D.C. bar, 1969; asso. firm Preston, Thorgrimson & Horwitz, Seattle, 1954-57; asst. atty. gen. Wash. State, also counsel Wash. Pub. Service Commn., 1957-61; gen counsel Bur. Pub. Roads, Dept. Commerce, 1961-63; vice chmn. Fed. Power Commn., 1963-66; adminstr. Bonneville Power Adminstrn., 1966-67; under sec. of interior, 1967-69; v.p. The Dreyfus Corp., 1969-70; mem. firm Ball & Dowd, Washington, 1970—. Bd. regents U. Portland. Mem. Wash. State Bar Assn., Phi Delta Phi, Delta Kappa Epsilon. Office: 1000 Ring Bldg Washington DC 20036

BLACK, EDWIN FAHEY, aerospace co. exec.; b. New Orleans, Aug. 17, 1915; s. Edwin Gregory and Lillian (Fahey) B.; B.S. in Civil Engring., U.S. Mil. Acad., 1940; M.A. in Internat. Relations, George Washington U., 1962; grad. Nat. War Coll., 1962; m. Margaret Cobey, Nov. 26, 1945; children—Star, Christopher, Noel, Nicholas, Brian, Bruce. Commd. 2d lt. U.S. Army, 1940, advanced through grades to brig. gen., 1965; comdg. officer 2d bn. 505th Airborne Inf., 82d Airborne Div., Fort Bragg, N.C., 1950-51, 2d battle group 19 Infantry, 25th Div., Schofield Barracks, Honolulu, 1957-58; mil. asst. to dep. sec. def. Washington, 1959-61; comdg. gen. U.S. Army Support, Thailand, 1967-69; asst. comdr. 25th Inf. Div., Vietnam, 1969; asst. chief of staff U.S. Army Pacific, Honolulu, 1970; ret., 1970; dir. bus. plans S.E. Asia, LTV Aerospace Corps, Bangkok, Thailand, 1971—. Exec. v.p. Freedoms Found., Valley Forge, Pa., 1970—. Decorated Legion Merit with 2 oak leaf clusters, Bronze Star; Order Crown (Thailand), 1969; Cross of Gallantry with palm and star (Rep. S. Vietnam). Mem. Council Fgn. Relations. Clubs: Cercle Sportif

(Saigon, South Vietnam); Outrigger Canoe (Honolulu); Royal Bangkok Sports (Bangkok, Thailand); Army-Navy Country (Washington). Contbr. profl. jours. Home: 4910 Kahala Av Honolulu HI 96815 Office: PO Box 5003 Dallas TX 75222

BLACK, ELI M., corp. ofcl; chmn. bd. United Brands Co.; dir. PEC Israel Econ. Co. Trustee Alfred (N.Y.) U. Office: 245 Park Av New York City NY 10017

BLACK, ERNEST GORDON, gas utility exec.; b. San Antonio, Oct. 4, 1909; s. Ernest Franklin and Florence (McKellar) B.; student Rice U., 1927-29, McGill U., 1929-31; m. Everitt Mattison, Oct. 11, 1940; childrenGordon McKellar, Dale Everitt. Chartered accountant, McDonald Currie & Co., Montreal, 1932-39; audit dir. Brit. Purchasing and Air Commns., N.Y.C., 1939-42; asst. to controller Ingersoll Rand Co., N.Y.C., 1946-50; v.p., treas. Wis. Gas Co., Milw., 1950-, also dir. Served to lt. comdr. USNR, 1943-46. Decorated Commendation ribbon. Mem. Financial Execs. Inst., Zeta Psi. Club: University, (Milw.). Home: 2837 E Park Pl Milwaukee, WI 53211 Office: 626 E Wisconsin Av Milwaukee, WI53202

BLACK, EUGENE, former judge U.S. Tax Court; b. Blossom, Tex., July 2, 1879; s. Alexander Wesley and Talula Ann (Shackelford) B.; LL.B., Cumberland U., 1905, LL.D., 1937; m. Mamie Coleman, Mar. 15, 1903; children—Margaret, Lyda Gene, Adelle, Rachel, Harold, Barbara. Admitted to Texas bar, 1905, and practiced at Clarksville; mem. 64th to 70th Congresses 1915-29, 1st Texas Dist.; mem. U.S. Board of Tax Appeals now Tax Court of U.S. 1929- 66, chmn., 1933-37. Democrat. Methodist. Home: 5206 Colorado Av NW Washington DC 20011

BLACK, EUGENE ROBERT, banker; b. Atlanta, May 1, 1898; s. Eugene Robert and Gussie (Grady) B.; grad. U. Ga., 1917; LL.D. (honorary), U. Chattanooga, 1951, Columbia, 1954, Oglethorpe U., 1955, Syracuse U., 1957, Macalester Coll., U. Ark., Rutgers U., 1959, Yale, Princeton, Harvard, Williams, 1960. Manchester (Eng.), Bishops (Can.), Hartford, 1961, Emory, Oxford (Eng.), 1962; LL.D. (honorary), U. Sussex, 1962; Dr. Econs. and Social Scis., U. Hamburg (Germany), 1962; Dr. Pub. Adminstrn., Northeastern U., 1962; m. Susette Heath, Jan. 25, 1930; children—Elizabeth (Mrs. Campbell), Eugene Robert (by former marriage), William Heath. Employed Harris, Forbes & Co., Atlanta, 1931-33, asst. v.p., 1933; with Chase Nat. Bank, N.Y.C., 1933-47, 2d v.p., 1933-37, v.p., 1937-47; exec. dir. for U.S., Internat. Bank for Reconstrn. and Devel., Wash., 1947-49, pres., chmn. exec. dirs., 1949-62; chmn., pres. Internat. Finance Corp., 1961-62; dir., cons. Chase Manhattan Bank, 1963-70; cons. Am. Express Co., 1970—; dir. Boise Cascade Corp.; mem. adv. bd. Colonial Fund, Inc., Colonial Growth Shares, Inc., Colonial Income Fund, Inc., dir. Hartford Fire Ins. Co., Hartford Accident Indemnity Co.; now spl. financial cons. to sec. gen. UN; mem. permanent adv. com. evaluate U.S. fgn. aid programs; dir. Chase Internat. Investment Corp.; chmn., dir. Howmet Corp., Internat. Tel. & Tel. Co., N.Y. Times Co., Cummins Engine Co., Inc., Trust Co. of Ga.; trustee Bowery Savs. Bank. Mem. World Bank Pension Fund. Financial adviser to Shaikh of Kuwait. Trustee, chmn. bd. Pierpont Morgan Library, Johns Hopkins; trustee Conservation Found., Population Council, Inc.; dir. Atlantic Council, Project Hope, Internat. Exec. Service Corps.; mem. Nat. Com. Internat. Devel., Dag Hammarskjold Found.; mem. bd. trustees, also pres. Am. Shakespeare Festival. Chmn. men's adv. com. Girls Clubs Am.; vice chmn. Planned Parenthood-World Population; mem. bd. overseers vis. com. Harvard U. Center Internat. Affairs. Mem. Phi Beta Kappa. Author: The Diplomacy of Economic Development. Home: 178 Columbia Heights Brooklyn, NY 11201. Office: 65 Broadway New York City NY 10006

BLACK, FISCHER SHEFFEY, utility Co. exec.; b. Bryson City, N.C., Jan. 27, 1911; s. Stanley Warren and Marianna (Fischer) B.; grad. Riverside Mil. Acad., Gainesville, Ga, 1929; B.S., U. N.C., 1933; LL.B., Nat. U. Law Sch., Washington, 1939, M.P.L., 1939; m. Elizabeth Clark Zemp, June 20, 1936; children—Fischer S., Janice Blakeney, Louis Engleman. With Nantabala Power & Light Co., Franklin, N.C., 1933-34; engr. Potomac Elec. Power Co., Washington, 1934-42; asst. system planning engr., 1942-46, asst. to pres., 1946-48; editor Elec. World, McGraw-Hill Pub. Co., N.Y.C., 1948-54, pub., editor, 1954-59; v.p. adminstrn. Tampa Electric Co., 1959-61, exec. v.p., 1961-67, pres., 1967-71, vice chmn. bd., 1971—; chmn. bd. Founders Financial Corp., George Thompson Corp. Registered profl. engr., Va. Mem. I.E.E.E., Beta Theta Pi, Alpha Sigma Phi, Delta Theta Phi. Presbyn. Clubs: Palma Ceia Golf; University; Tampa Yacht and Country; Rotary. Home: 930 Golfview Av Tampa FL 33609 Office: 111 N Dale Mabry Highway Tampa FL 33609

BLACK, GARY, newspaper exec.; b. Balt., Nov. 26, 1914; s. Van Lear and Jessie Augusta (Gary) B.; student Gilman Country Sch., 1934; m. Catharine Bond Jackson, June 10, 1939 (Div.); children—Gary, and Catherine Wilder (Mrs. Frederick B. Peterson); m. Nancy Byers Martin, Dec. 30, 1955; step children— John William Young Martin, Jr., Carolyn Lee Martin (Mrs. James N. Carrigan), Alexander Byers Martin, Peter Young Martin. Vice chmn. bd. A.S. Abell Co., pubs. Balt. Sun, 1950-56, chmn. bd., 1956—; dir. mem. exec. com. Maryland Nat. Bank, Balt., Fidelity & Deposit Co. of Md., Balt. Trustee Johns Hopkins U., Gilman Country Sch. Clubs: Maryland (bd. govs.), Green Spring Valley Hunt (Balt.). Home: Snow Hill Farm Glyndon, MD 21071 Office: Fidelity Bldg Baltimore, MD 21201.

BLACK, GEORGE, JR., lawyer; b. Portland, Ore., Jan. 2, 1899; student U. Ore.; LL.B., Yale, 1923. Admitted to Ore. bar, 1923; now mem. firm Black, Kendall, Tremaine, Boothe & Higgins. Mem. Am., Ore., Multnomah County bar assns., Phi Delta Phi. Office: 520 SW 6th Av Portland OR 97204

BLACK, HAROLD STEPHEN, research engr.; b. Leominster, Mass., Apr. 14, 1898; s. Stephen A. and Julia S. (Bushnell) B.; B.S., Worcester (Mass.) Polytech. Inst., 1921, D.Eng., 1955; m. Meta C. Spreen, July 1, 1934. With engring. dept. Western Electric Co., 1921-25; mem. tech. staff Bell Telephone Labs., Inc., Murray Hill, N.J., 1925-63; prin. research scientist serving on a consulting basis with aerospace group General Precision, Inc., Little Falls, N.J., 1963-66; communications cons., Summit, N.J., 1966—; devel. and research on amplifiers, multichannel carrier telephone and telegraph systems, pulse microwave radio relay systems, laminated conductors, advanced communication and guidance feedback techniques pertaining to aerospace interests, telecommunications, advanced circuit techniques, new types feedback, feedback- feedforward systems. Mem. biomechanics com. Rusk's Inst. for Rehab. Medicine, 1970. Recipient Nat. best Paper prize Am. Inst. E.E., 1934, Lamme gold medal, 1957; Modern Pioneer award N.A.M., 1940; John Price Wetherill medal Franklin Inst., 1941; certificate of appreciation U.S. War Dept., 1946; Research Corp. sci. award, 1952, John H. Potts Meml. Award, 1959; medal Engrs. Club Phila., 1961; Honor award Wisdom Soc., 1969. Fellow I.E.E.E., A.A.A.S., Intercontinental Biog. Assn., N.Y. Acad. Scis.; mem. Audio Engineering Soc. (hon.), Am. Inst. Aeros. and Astronautics, Am. Ordnance Assn., Franklin Inst., Telephone Pioneers Am., N.J. Acad. Sci., Sigma Xi, Tau Beta Pi. Author: Modulation Theory, 1953; also tech. articles. Patentee in field. Address: 120 Winchip Rd Summit NJ 07901

BLACK, HENRY FRANKLIN, lawyer; b. Newport, Vt., Mar. 27, 1906; s. Harry A. and Jane M. (Gates) B.; B.S., Norwich U., 1928; LL.B., George Washington U., 1933; m. Beatrice M. Skinner, Sept. 12, 1930; children—Harry A., Roy S. Admitted to Vt. bar, 1934; state's atty. Windsor County, Vt., 1937-41, superior judge, 1941-49; practice law, White River Junction, Vt., 1949—; sr. partner Black & Plante, White River Junction, 1959—; lectr. med. juris prudence Dartmouth Med. Sch., 1968—. Dir., gen. counsel Vt. Mut. Fire Ins. Co., No. Security Ins. Co. (both Montpelier, Vt.); dir. Twin State Fruit Corp., White River Junction, Dartmouth Nat. Bank of Hanover, N.H. Mem. Vt. Bd. Edn., 1950-53; chmn. Town of Hartford (Vt.) Planning Commn., 1958-61; corporator Mary Hitchcock Meml. Hosp., Hanover; mem. World Conf. Peace Through Law, 1968—. Fellow Am. Coll. Trial Lawyers, Am. Coll. Probate Counsel, Am. Bar Found.; mem. Am. (mem. ho. dels. 1961—), Inter-Am., Vt. (pres. 1956-57, certificate of merit 1963), Windsor County (pres. 1938) bar assns., Am. Fedn. Ins. Counsel, Am. Trial Lawyers Assn., Inter-Am. Bar Assn., Assn. Ins. Attys. Republican. Episcopalian. Mason (Shriner), Rotarian, Elk. Author: Some Observations Relative to Vermont's Judicial System, 1956. Home: Passumpsic Av Wilder VT 05001 Office: White River Junction VT 05001

BLACK, HENRY MONTGOMERY, educator, mech. engr.; b. Reinbeck, Ia., May 13, 1907; s. Alexander Melvin and Sarah (Montgomery) B.; B.S., Ia. State U., 1929; M.S., Harvard, 1934; m. Bernice Bernard, Oct. 6, 1936 (dec. May 1961); children—Bruce Bernard, Bernice (Mrs. Loyal Durand); m. 2d, Alice Redington, Dec. 22, 1969. Instr. mech. engring. Ia. State U., Ames, 1929-32, prof., head dept. mech. engring., 1946—; mech. engr. Berlin & Swern, architects, Chgo., 1934-36; mech. engr. Sargent & Lundy, engrs., Chgo., 1936-41; v.p. Ames Bldg. & Loan Assn.; cons. engr. Chmn. Ia. Bd. Engring. Examiners, 1967-70; bd. dirs. Engrs. Council for Profl. Devel., 1967-70. Pres. Boy Scout Dist., 1961-62, v.p. Talleorn Area council, 1962-64; pres. Community Chest of Ames, 1959. Bd. dirs., trustee Ames YMCA. Served from capt. to col., C.E., AUS, 1941-46; ETO. Decorated Bronze Star with oak leaf cluster, Legion of Merit, Croix de Guerre (France). Registered profl. engr., Ia., Ill. Fellow Am. Soc. M.E. (v.p.); mem. Am. Soc. Engring. Edn., Ia. Engring. Soc. (pres. 1952, John Dunlap award 1954), Delta Sigma Phi, Tau Beta Pi, Phi Kappa Phi. Republican. Conglist. (deacon, trustee). Rotarian. Home: 2819 Ross Rd Ames IA 50010

BLACK, HUGO LAFAYETTE, justice U.S. Supreme Ct.; b. Harlan, Clay County, Ala., Feb. 27, 1886; s. William La Fayette and Martha Ardellah (Toland) B.; ed. pub. schs. Ashland, Ala.; LL.B., U. Alabama 1906; m. Josephine Foster, Feb. 1921 (dec. Dec. 1951); children—Hugo LaFayette, Sterling Foster, Martha Josephine; m. 2d, Elizabeth Seay DeMeritte, Sept. 11, 1957. Began practice Ashland, Alabama, 1906-07, Birmingham, Alabama, from 1907; served as police judge 18 months, 1910-11; solicitor (pros. atty.) Jefferson County, Ala., 1915-17; in gen. practice, Birmingham, 1919-27; U.S. Senator from Ala., 2 terms, 1927-37; asso. justice U.S. Supreme Court, 1937-71. Entered 2d O.T.C., Ft. Oglethorpe, Ga., Aug. 3, 1917; commd. capt. F.A.; served in 81st F.A. and as adj. 19th Ary. Brigade. Died 1971. Home: Alexander VA Office: Supreme Ct Bldg Washington DC 20543 and 619 Lee St Alexandria VA 22314

BLACK, JAMES FARLIN, advt. exec.; b. Elizabeth, N.J., May 20, 1919; s. Thomas and Ethel (Farlin) B.; student Rutgers U., 1941; m. Virginia H. Twyman, May 22, 1942; children—Kendra (Mrs. Jerome L. Power), James Farlin, Robert, Peter and Patricia (twins), David. With sales promotion dept. Gen. Outdoor Advt. Co., 1940-41; zone sales mgr. Ford Motor Co., N.Y. area, 1945-50; field supr. William H. Weintraub Agy., 1950-53; account exec. Benton & Bowles, v.p., 1953-57; with Kudner Agy., Inc., 1957-65, exec. v.p., 1963-65; vice chmn. bd., mem. exec. com., mgmt. dir. Tatham-Laird & & Kudner, Inc., 1965—. Served with AUS, 1941-45. Mem. Am. Trucking Assn., Chi Psi. Republican. Clubs: Union League, (N.Y.C.); Manasquan (N.J.) River Golf. Home: 600 Holly Hill Dr Brielle NJ 08730 Office: 605 3d Av New York City NY 10016

BLACK, JAMES HAY, assn. exec.; b. Pitts., Aug. 14, 1921; s. Alexander and Ruth (Hay) B.; A.B. in Chemistry, Cornell U., 1943; B.S., U. Pitts., 1948, M.S., 1949, Ph.D., 1954; hon. alumnus Carnegie-Mellon U., 1954; m. Mary Lucretia Garland, Feb. 4, 1950; children—Ruth Hay (Mrs. Charles Linden Vess), Alexander Chisholm, Patricia Anne. Research chemist Koppers Co., Inc., Pitts., 1943; instr. U. Pitts., 1950-52; fellow Mellon Inst. Indsl. Research, Pitts., 1952-54; asst. project engr. Standard Oil Co., Ind., 1954-55; sr. technologist, supervising technologist U.S. Steel Corp., Monroeville, Pa., 1955-62; prof., head chem. engring. U. Ala., 1962—; exec. sec. Am. Assn. Cost Engrs., 1964—; cons. in field. Mem. Nat. Air Pollution Techniques Adv. Com., Dept. Health, Edn. and Welfare, Washington, 1969—; cons. Tuscaloosa (Ala.) Environmental Quality Control Com., 1969—; mem. tech. panel U.S. Office Coal Research, Washington. Served to 1st lt. AUS, 1943-46. Registered profl. engr., Pa., Ala. Mem. Am. Inst. Chem. Engrs., Am. Chem. Soc., Am. Inst. Chemists, Soc. History Tech., Sigma Xi, Tau Beta Pi, Sigma Tau, Phi Lambda Upsilon, Omega Chi Epsilon. Episcopalian. Clubs: Tuscaloosa Racquet; University. Contbg. author: Cost and Optimization Engineering, 1970. Contbr. articles profl. jours. Home: 96 Arcadia Dr Tuscaloosa AL 35401 Office: PO Box 6312 University AL 35486

BLACK, JEAN PHYLLIS, ret. librarian; b. Duluth, May 22, 1903; d. David Gilmour and Justine Justine (Shannon) Black; B.A. magna cum laude, Mt. Holyoke Coll., 1924; M.A., U. Mich., 1925, Ph. D. (fellow history 1924-26), 1928; B.S. in L.S., U. Wash., 1932. Librarian Seattle Art Mus., 1933-36; asst. prof. library sci. Rosary Coll., River Forest, Ill., 1941-43; librarian Iowa Historical Society, 1943-46; librarian and prof. at the Portland (Oregon) State U., 1946-69, instr. history and polit. sci. Coll. St. Catherine, St. Paul, 1928-29; research asso. Hoover Library, Stanford, 1937-39; asst. prof. history and polit. sci. Our Lady of the Lake Coll., San Antonio, Tex., 1939-41. Eleanor Duse fellow Italy-Am. Soc., N.Y., 1926-27; postdoctoral fellow Social Sci. Research Council, 1929-30. Member Am. Pacific Northwest, Oregon (pres. 1963-64) library assns., Assn. Coll. and Research Libraries, Phi Beta Kappa. Home: 2210 NW Everett St Portland OR 97210

BLACK, JOHN J., business exec. With Pub. Service Coordinated Transport, 1927—, sec., treas., 1967—. Office: 180 Boyden Av Maplewood NJ 07040*

BLACK, JOHN SAMUEL, Jr., assn. exec.; b. New Orleans, Nov. 12, 1912; s. John S. and Iris (Johnson) B.; A.B., Dartmouth, 1933; LL.B., U. Mich., 1936; m. Jean Elaine Royce, Sept. 11, 1937; children—John Samuel III, Royce Ann, Susan MacLendon. Admitted to Conn. bar, 1937, N.Y. bar, 1939; practiced in N.Y.C., 1936- 43; gen. counsel Stanley Works, New Britain, Conn., 1943-68, sec., 1944- 70, director, 1955-70; exec. dir. Am. Soc. Corporate Secs., N.Y.C., 1970—; sec. dir. Goss & deLeeuw Machine Company. Bd. dirs. New Britain Gen. Hosp., New Britain Inst. Mem. Am. Soc. Corporate Secs. (nat. pres. 1962-63). Conglist. Home: 1 Rock Ridge Rd New Britain CT 06052 Office: 9 Rockefeller Plaza New York City NY 10020

BLACK, JOHN WOODLAND, lawyer b. Spokane, Sept. 22, 1925; s. Hugh James and Margaret (Woodland) B.; student Colo. U., 1944-45; A.B., U. Wash., 1947; M. Internat. Affairs, Columbia, 1949; J.D., George Washington U., 1959; m. Iryne Codon, Sept. 3, 1959; children—John McKenzie, Catherine Louise, Bridget Dianne, James Joseph, Ian Andrew, Timothy Matthugh. Interne State Dept., 1949-50; fgn. service officer, Germany and Haiti, 1950-55; mem. profl. staff, commerce com. U.S. Senate, 1955-61; spl. asst. to sec. commerce, 1961; dept. dir. U.S. Travel Service, 1961-64, named dir., 1965. Admitted to D.C. bar, 1960, Cal. bar, 1971; since practiced in Santa Ana, Cal. Mem. Cal. Democratic State Central Com., 1971—. Served as ensign USNR, 1945-46. Mem. Am. Bar Assn., Pacific Area Travel Assn. (pres. 1966-67, Nat. Salesman of Year 1968), Internat. Union Ofcl. Travel Orgns. (v.p. 1967-68). Home: 1646 Irvine Av Newport Beach CA 92660 Office: 615 Civic Center Dr W Santa Ana CA 92701

BLACK, JOSEPH, transp. co. exec.; b. Plainfield, N.J., Feb. 8, 1924; s. Joseph and Martha T. (Watkins) B.; B.S., Morgan State Coll., 1950; postgrad. Rutgers U., 1959, Seton Hall U., summers 1959-60; m. Mae Nell Rogers, children—Joseph Frank, Martha Jo. Profl. baseball player Balt. Elite Giants, Negro Nat. League, 1944-50; baseball player Latin Am. Baseball, Venezuela, Cuba, Dominican Republic, 1947, 50-51, 51-52, 55, Internat. League-Montreal Royals, 1951, Am. Assn., St. Paul, 1951, Nat. League-Bklyn. Dodgers, 1952-55, Cin. Reds, 1955-56, Am. League- Washington Senators, 1957; tchr. Plainfield Bd. Edn., 1958-63; spl. markets rep. Greyhound Lines, Inc., N.Y.C., 1962-63, dir. spl. markets, Chgo., 1963-67, v.p. spl. markets, 1967-69; v.p. spl. markets Greyhound Corp., Chgo., 1969—; instr. Mgmt. Tng. Sch. 2d Congl. Dist.-Bus. and Profl. Womens Club, Chgo., 1965-67. Trustee George Williams Coll. Served with AUS, 1943-46. Mem. Nat. Alliance Businesses (mem. operations com. Nat. Office), Nat. Assn. Market Developers (nat. pres. 1967-68, chmn. bd. 1968-69), Omega Psi Phi. Office: 10 S Riverside Dr Chicago IL 60611

BLACK, JOSEPH E., found. exec.; b. Blanding, Utah, Sept. 14, 1921; s. Henry G. and Louise (Brown) B.; B.A., Utah State U., 1947; M.A., Northwestern U., 1949, Ph.D., 1950; m. Gertrude Nelson, Sept. 8, 1948; children—Burton Kenneth Jo Lynne, Carol Ann, Sandra Lee. Tchr., Lovell (Wyo.) High Sch., 1946-47; mem. faculty Miami U., Oxford, O., 1950-63, prof. polit. sci., chmn. dept., 1958-63; vis. prof. U.E. Africa, 1963; prof. polit. sci., dean faculty social scis. U. Ibadan (Nigeria), 1963-65; dir. humanities and social scis. div. Rockefeller Found., 1965—. Served with USAAF, 1943- 46. Mem. Council on Foreign Relations, Am. Polit. Sci. Assn. Author: (with Kenneth Thompson) Foreign Policies in a World of Change, 1963. Home: 3 Heathcote Rd Scarsdale, NY 10583 Office: 111 W 50th St New York City NY 10020

BLACK, JOSEPH LAURENCE, telephone co. exec.; b. Sackville, N.B., Can., May 28, 1900; s. Frank Bunting and Eleanor Louisa (Wood) B.; student Upper Can. Coll., Toronto, 1917-18; grad. Royal Mil. Coll. of Can., 1921; m. Gwendolyn McDonald, June 18, 1935; children—Joseph Laurence, Janet (Mrs. Richard Alexander), John Donald. With J.L. Black & Sons, Ltd., Sackville, 1921—, pres., 1945—; pres. Moncton Broadcasting Co., 1933-46; dir. N.B. Telephone Co., 1945—, v.p., 1959, pres., 1959-62, chmn. bd., 1965—; dir. Bell Telephone Co. of Can., Atlantic Industries (N.B.), Ltd., Merc. Bank of Can. Bd. dirs. Mt. Allison U., Army Cadet League Can.; trustee, bd. dirs. Maritime Hosp. Assn. Served with Canadian Army, 1940-44. Fellow Royal Soc. Arts; hon. life mem. Maritime Hosp. Assn., Canadian Cav. Assn. Clubs: Sackville Golf and Country, Sackville Curling; Aesculapins Fishing Assn. (Miramichi River, N.B.); Albert Fishing (McFadden Lake, N.B.). Address: PO Box 68 Sackville New Brunswick Canada

BLACK, KENNETH, Jr., univ. dean; b. Norfolk, Va., Jan. 30, 1925; s. Kenneth and Virginia (Wolf) B.; A.B., U. N.C., 1948, M.S., 1951; Ph.D., U. Pa., 1953; m. Mabel Folger, Sept. 20, 1948; children—Kenneth III, Kathryn Anne. Partner Colonial Ins. Agy., Chapel Hill, N.C., 1948-50; instr. U. Pa., 1952-53; chmn. ins. dept. Ga. State U., 1953-69, regents' prof. ins., 1959—, dean Sch. Bus. Adminstrn., 1969—. Dir. N. Am. Reins. Corp., N. Am. Reassurance Co. (N.Y.C.). Vice pres. President's Commn. R.R. Retirement, 1971—. Trustee Village of St. Joseph, 1969—. Mem. lay adv. bd. Marist Sch., 1968—; exec. dir., trustee Ednl. Found., Inc., 1969—, Harold T. Dillon Found., Inc., 1964—. Served with USNR, 1944-46. Mem. Am. Risk and Ins. Assn. (pres. 1964), Phi Beta Kappa, Beta Gamma Sigma, Omicron Delta Kappa, Alpha Kappa Psi. Roman Catholic. Author: (with Russell) Human Behavior and Life Insurance, 1963; (with Keir and Surrey) Cases in Life Insurance, 1965; (with Huebner and Cline) Property and Liability Insurance, 1968; (with Huebner) Life Insurance, 7th edit., 1969. Editor Jour. Am. Soc. C.L.U.'s, 1959—. Home: 2 Hanover West Ct NW Atlanta GA 30327

BLACK, KENNETH CHAPMAN, architect; b. Cedar Springs, Mich., Dec. 23, 1901; s. Lee and Nellie Manley (Chapman) B.; B.Arch., U. Mich., 1925; George G. Booth traveling fellow architecture, Am. Acad., Rome, Italy, 1925-26; m. Marie C. MacKenzie, Dec. 27, 1929; 1 son, Duncan MacKenzie. Archtl. designer James Gamble Rogers, N.Y.C., 1926-30; partner Lee Black & Kenneth C. Black 1930-59; pres. Kenneth C. Black Assos., Inc., architect & Engrs., 1959—. Mem. Lansing Bd. Park and Cemetery Commrs., 1932-33; sec. Lansing City Plan Commn., 1933-39; mem. Mich. Planning Commn., 1939-46; vice chmn. Lansing City Plan Board, 1966-70, chmn., 1970—; mem. Michigan State Council for the Arts, 1967-71. Fellow A.I.A. (dir. Detroit chpt. 1940-42, Gt. Lakes dist., 1947- 50); mem. Mich. Soc. Architects (pres. 1938-40, recipient gold medal 1962), Lansing C. of C. (pres. Jr. sect. 1933-34, dir. senior section), Mich. Jr. C. of C. (dir. 1934-35), Mich. Engring. Soc., Mich. Acad. Sci., Arts and Letters, Nat. Assn. Housing Ofcls., Nat Assn. Planning Ofcls. Clubs: City (dir. 1949- 52), Country (dir. 1948-54). Automobile (Lansing). Home: 1501 Cambridge Rd Lansing MI 48910 Office: Stoddard Bldg Lansing MI 48933

BLACK, KENNETH EUGENE, ins. exec.; b. Rockaway, N.J., May 15, 1904; s. Milton John and Elizabeth J. (Munson) B.; student pub. schs. Rockaway; m. Ethel Johnson, 1928; children—Janet, Peter. Employed Liberty Mut. Ins. Co., 1924-29, D.F. Broderick Corp., 1929-42; with Home Ins. Co., 1942—, v.p., 1950, dir., 1951—, pres., 1954—; chmn. bd., 1968—; pres., dir. Home Indemnity Co., chmn. bd. Peoples-Home Life Ins., Co., Ind.; dir. Chem. Bank N.Y. Trust Co., Hawaiian Ins. & Guaranty Co., Seaboard Coast R.R. Co., Seaboard Surety Co., Sperry & Hutchison Co., Gen. Cable Corp.; trustee Harlem Savs. Bank. Home: 7 Harwood Dr Madison NJ 07940 Office: 59 Maiden Lane New York City NY 10038

BLACK, LEON HAROLD, dental equipment mfr.; b. Kirksville, Mo., 1918; s. Ernest R. and Letha M. (Scott) B.; grad. Coe Coll., 1941; m. Cheryl J. Hampton, June 12, 1941; children—Karen, Jon, Barbara. With W. A. Sheaffer Pen Co., Ft. Madison, Ia., 1946—, asst. purchasing agent, 1946-53, exec. vice pres., 1957-60, v.p. internat. relations, 1960-69; gen. mgr. Den-Tal-Ez Mfg. Co., 1970—, also dir.; pres. W.A. Sheaffer Pen Co. of Can., Ltd., Goderich, Ont., Can., 1953-57. Mason, Elk. Club: Wakonda Golf and Country. Office: 1201 SE Diehl Des Moines IA 50313

BLACK, MARTIN LEE, Jr., educator; b. Charlotte, N.C., Jan. 7, 1905; s. Martin L. and Edna (Rigler) B.; A.B., Duke, 1926; M.B.A., Northwestern U., 1933; m. Ann Biggerstaff, Apr. 18, 1931; children—John, Jane. Accountant, Peat, Marwick, Mitchell & Co., Chgo., 1926-30; prof. accounting Duke, 1930—; chief accountant OPA, 1941-43; cons. AEC, 1949-53, Office of Price Stabilization, 1951; Fulbright lecturer to Japan, 1961-62, to Australia, 1968; cons. Agy. Internat. Devel. Mission to Kenya, 1965. Commr. Eastern Carolina Housing Authority; pres. N.C. Bd. C.P.A. Examiners; Fulbright lectr., Australia, 1956-57, 1968. C.P.A., Ill., N.C. Mem. Am. Inst. C.P.A.'s (council), Am. Accounting Assn. (past president), Nat. Assn. Accountants, N.C. Assn. C.P.A.'s (p.p.), Nat. Soc. Accountants for Coops. (sec.-treas.), Financial Execs. Inst., Phi Delta Theta, Omicron Delta Kappa, Alpha Kappa Psi, Beta Alpha Psi. Editor: Cooperative Accountant. Author articles. Home: 135 Pinecrest Rd Durham NC 27705

BLACK, MAX, educator; b. Baku, Russia, Feb. 24, 1909; s. Lionel and Sophia (Divinska) B.; B.A., Queens Coll., U. Cambridge, 1930; student U. Göttingen, 1930-31; Ph. D., U. London, 1939, D.Lit., 1955; m. Michal Landsberg, Aug. 21, 1933; children—Susan Naomi, Jonathan. Came to U.S., 1940, naturalized, 1948. Lectr., tutor U. of London Inst. Edn., 1936-40; prof. philosophy U. Ill., 1940-46; became prof. philosophy Cornell, 1946, Susan Linn Sage prof. philosophy and humane letters, 1954—; dir. The Society for the Humanities, 1965-70; vis. prof. U. Washington, 1951-52; vis. mem. Princeton Inst. Advanced Study, 1970-71. Guggenheim fellow, 1950-51. Fellow Am. Acad. Arts and Scis.; mem. Am. Philos. Assn. (pres. 1958), Aristotelian Soc., Assn. Symbolic Logic, Internat. Inst. Philosophy (v.p. 1970). Author: Philosophical Studies (with others), 1948; Science and Civilization (with others), 1949; Language and Philosophy, 1949; The Nature of Mathematics, 1950; Critical Thinking (rev. edit.), 1952; Translations from the Philosophical Writings of Gottlob Frege (with P. T. Geach); Problems of Analysis, 1954; Models and Metaphors, 1962; A Companion to Wittgenstein's Tractatus, 1964; The Labyrinth of Language, 1968; Margins of Precision, 1970. Editor: Philosophical Analysis, 1950; The Social Theories of Talcott Parsons, 1961; The Importance of Language, 1962; Philosophy in America, 1965; The Morality of Scholarship, 1967. Editor Philos. Rev., 1946—. Home: 408 Highland Rd Ithaca NY 14850 ☆

BLACK, MYRON L., business exec.; b. Rochester, N.Y., Sept. 24, 1906; student Phillips Exeter Acad. 1922-23; A.B., Harvard, 1927; married. Exec. sec. Am. C. of C. for the Levant and editor of the Levant Trade Rev., Istanbul, 1927-28; mem. exec. staff 1st Inter Civil Aeronautics Conf., Washington, 1928; asst. trade commr. and comml. agt. U.S. Dept. of Commerce, Washington, Wellington, New Zealand and N.Y.C., 1928-37; spl. fgn. rep. Isbrandtsen S.S. Co., N.Y.C., 1937-44; sec. Danish Shipping Commn., N.Y.C. 1940; mem. War Shipping Adminstrn., State Dept. mission to S.A., 1942; field dir., div. fgn. service War Shipping Adminstrn., 1942-44; mem. Anglo-Am. Shipping and Ports Mission to Africa and the Middle East, 1942; dir., field operations staff Fgn. Econ. Adminstrn., 1944-45, spl. rep. to Denmark and spl. asst. to Am. Minister to Denmark, 1945; adviser on shipping for Mediterranean area Am. embassy, Rome, 1945-48; 1st sec., consul Am. embassy, Rome, 1948-50, Am. embassy, Colombo, Ceylon, 1950; consul gen. Halifax, N.S., 1953-54; counselor Am. embassy, Ottawa, Ont. 1954-58; with Dept. State, Washington, 1958-60; v.p., Washington rep. Isbrandtsen Co., Inc., 1960-66. Mem. U.S. del. 1st session Prov. Maritime Consultative Council, Paris, 1947; spl. adviser Am. Miss. Aid to Greece, Athens, 1947-50; adviser U.S. del. U.N. Maritime Conf., Geneva, 1948, Tri-Partite Maritime Commn., London, 1947; alternate U.S. del. meeting Consultative Com. for Econ. Development South and S.E. Asia, Colombo, 1951; adviser U.S. Delegation to 13th, 14th sessions contracting parties Gen. Agreement on Tariffs and Trade, Geneva, 1958, 59. Home: 3217 Klingle Rd NW Washington DC 20008 Office: 2000 K St Washington DC 20006

BLACK, PETER, sulphur co. exec., artist; b. Boston, Sept. 4, 1918; s. Percy Gamble and Doris (Taylor) B.; B.S., Harvard, 1942; m. Caroline Sears Warren, Feb. 3, 1945; children—Sylvia, Caroline, William Murray. Vice pres. Harold Cabot and Co., Boston, 1945-51; asst. to dir. Office Devel. Moblzn., 1951- 53; v.p. Freeport Sulphur Co., N.Y.C., 1953—; pres., dir. subsidiary Sul-Sulphur Export Corp., 1958-61, Freeport Internat. Inc., 1961-64; pres., dir. Internat. Marketing & Investment Corp., 1964—; also pres., dir. Delta Marketing and Shipping Corp.; dir. Sulpetro of Can., Ltd. One man exhbns. Dayton, (O.) Art Inst., 1955, Witte Meml. Mus., San Antonio, 1957, Empire Studio, New Canaan, Conn., 1959, River Gauche Gallery, Darien, Conn., 1961. Served to lt. comdr. USNR, 1942-45. Mem. Council Fgn. Relations, Silvermine Guild Artists. Mason. Clubs: Metropolitan (Washington); River, Harvard (N.Y.C.). Home: Southerly Royal Oak MD 21662 Office: 711 3d Av New York City NY 10017

BLACK, RICHARD BLACKBURN, ret. research coordinator; b. Grand Forks, N.D., Aug. 10, 1902; s. George Edgar and Mary Emeline (Hogue) B.; B.S. in C. E., U. of North Dakota, 1926, D.S., 1958: grad. study Floating U. U. Travel Add.m 1926-27; m. Ruth Carolyn Schlabert , Aug. 30, 1928 (dec.. Jan. 21, 1934, Douglas Francis Blackburn; m. 2d. Aviza Olga Johnson, Aug. 19, 1937; children—Brenda Baylis (dec.), Debra Jane; adopted daughter—Carrie Elizabeth. Various civil and mining engineering Engineerly positions U.S. and Can., 1927-33; surveyor, asst. to scientists Byrd Antarctic Expdn. II, 1933-35; field rep. div. territories and island possessions Dept. Interior, also comdr. East Base, U.S. Antarctic Service Expdn., 1936-41; spl. rep. econ. rehabilitation Micronesian Islands, U.S. Commercial Co., 1946-48; asst. dir. Hawaii Aero. Commn,, 1948-50; operations analyst Operations Research Office, Johns Hopkins, 1950-52; operations analyst mil. operations and geography brs. Office Naval Research, 1952-54, 57; Antarctic Task Force, 1954-56; staff U.S. Antarctic programs, 1956-57; lectr. in field; U.S. observer with Belgian Antarctic expdn., 1960-61; 5th Antarctic trip on Operation Deep Freeze, 1965; research coordinator Office Naval Research, Washington, until 1967; cons. ManTech Corp., N.J.; dir. The Am. Bank, Woodbridge and N.Va., Devel. Resources Transp. Co. Mem. exec. board Nat. Capital Area council Boy Scouts Am. Served active duty USNR, PTO, 1941-46; capt. USNR, 1954-57, retired as rear adm., 1959. Decorated Silver Congressional medal of Byrd Antarctic Expedition, 1933-35, Gold Congressional medal. U.S. Antarctic Service Expdn., 1939-41, Antarctic medal for operations after World War II; Bronze Star medal, Presdl. unit citation; Gold Eagle of the Cincinnati, Mil. Order Revolutionary Officers. Fellow Royal Am. geog. socs.; mem. Soc. Cincinnati, Washington Acad. Scis., S.A.R., Am. Polar Soc., Va. Hist. Soc., Antarctican Soc. (bd.), Sigma Alpha Epsilon. Clubs: N.Y. Yacht, Explorers, Army and Navy. Home: Rippon Lodge Woodbridge VA 22191

BLACK, RICHARD HERBERT, retail merchandising co. exec.; b. Littleton, Ill., Mar. 28, 1910; s. John Warren and Pearl (Chockley) B.; B.S., U. Neb., 1932; LL.B., Detroit Coll. Law, 1949; m. Phyllis M. Meyers, June 24, 1939; 1 dau., Dorothy Gayle. Tchr. math., commerce Neb. high schs., 1932-36; asst. mgr. S.S. Kresge Co., Detroit, 1936-41, asst. to buyers, 1941-43, asst. treas., 1945-64, treas., 1964—; instr. math. U.S. Naval Tng. Sta., Dearborn, Mich., 1943-44. Pres. Players Guild, Dearborn, 1954-55; mem. finance com. Detroit Symphony Orch. Mem. Greater Detroit Bd. Commerce, Pi Kappa Psi, Sigma Nu Phi. Kiwanian. Home: 22930 Law St Dearborn, MI 48224 Office: 2727 2d Av Detroit MI 48232

BLACK, ROBERT BRUCE, fgn. service officer; b. Mass., May 23, 1920; s. Samuel Bruce and Adele (Bergner) B.; grad. Phillips Exeter, 1938; B.S., Harvard, 1942; M.A., 1948, Ph.D., 1950; m. Martha Mooney, July 12, 1947 (dec. Mar. 1963); children—Brenda, Rebecca; m. 2d. Jeannetta Wilson Rado, June 14, 1964. Fiscal analyst U.S. Bur. Budget, 1949-52; program officer ICA and predecessor agys., 1952-58, dep. dir. U.S. Operations Mission, Tunisia, 1958-61; dir. U.S. AID Mission, Senegal, 1961-62; assigned Nat. War Coll., 1963-64; chief mil. assistance div. AID, Washington, 1964-67, dir. AID mission, Costa Rica, 1967-68; dir. Office of Population, Social and Civic Devel., Dept. of State. Home: 6655 MacArthur Blvd Washington DC 20016 Office: Dept State Washington DC 20525

BLACK, ROBERT COLEMAN, lawyer; b. Greenville, Ala., July 3, 1934; s. James Monroe and Mabel (Coleman) B.; B.S. in Commerce and Bus. Adminstrn., U. Ala., 1960, LL.B., 1961; m. Carolyn Musselwhite, Dec. 20, 1960; children—Elizabeth Anne, Robert C., Carolyn Jane. Admitted to Ala. bar, 1961; law clk. to justice Ala. Supreme Ct., 1961-62; partner firm Hill, Hill, Stovall & Carter, Montgomery, Ala., 1968—, spl. asst. atty. gen. Ala., 1969—; prof. law Jones Law Sch., Montgomery; instr. bus. law U. Ala. at Montgomery, Auburn U. City chmn. March of Dimes, 1966. Mem. campaign staff Albert Brewer for gov. Bd. dirs. March of Dimes Found., 1966—. Served with USMCR, 1954-57. Mem. Am., Ala., Montgomery County (chmn. exec. com. 1969-70, pres. 1971) bar assns., Phi Delta Phi, Beta Gamma Sigma. Author article. Home: 3379 Walton Dr Montgomery AL 36101 Office: Hill Bldg Montgomery AL 36101

BLACK, ROBERT EARL LEE, educator, zoologist; b. Cassville, Mo., Nov. 20, 1928; s. Luther R. and Myrtle (Taylor) B.; student N.E. Okla. A. and M. Coll., 1946-49; B.A., William Jewell Coll., 1951; Ph.D., U. Wash.; m. Shirley Ann Whitesell, June 26, 1953; children—Bradford Eugene, David Evan, Jennifer Lynn. NSF postdoctoral fellow U. Wash., 1955-56; USPHS fellow Cal. Inst. Tech., 1957-59; faculty Coll. William and Mary, 1959—, prof. biology, 1964—. Mem. Am. Soc. Zoologists, A.A.A.S., N.Y. Acad. Sci., Va. Acad. Sci. Author research articles. Home: 98 Gilley Dr Williamsburg VA 23185

BLACK, ROBERT FOSTER, educator; b. Dayton, O., Feb. 1, 1918; s. Stanley C. and Margaret (Martin) B.; B.A., Coll. Wooster, 1940; M.A., Syracuse U., 1942; student Cal. Inst. Tech., 1942-43; Ph.D., Johns Hopkins, 1953; m. Hernelda R. Lone, Feb. 12, 1944; children—John R., Dean S. Geologist, Roosevelt Wildlife Conservation Dept., N.Y. State, 1941-42, U.S. Geol. Survey, 1943-59; mem. faculty U. Wis., 1956—, prof. geology, 1959-70; prof. geology U. Conn., 1970—; cons. in field, 1942—. Fellow Geol. Soc. Am., Arctic Inst. N. Am., Soc. Econ. Geologists; mem. A.A.A.S., Am. Geophys. Union, Am. Soc. Photogrammetry, Wis. Acad. Sci., Am. Inst. Profl. Geologists. Author papers in field. Home: Route 3 Saw Mill Brook Lane Willimantic CT 06226 Office: University Connecticut Dept Geology Storrs CT 06268

BLACK, ROBERT G., lawyer; b. Provost, Alta., Can., 1922; B.A., LL.B., U. Alta. Admitted to Alta. bar, 1945; partner firm Saucier, Jones, Peacock, Black, Gain, Stratton & Laycraft, Calgary, Alta. Mem. Canadian, Calgary bar assns., Law Soc. Alta. Office: 444 7th Av SW Calgary Alberta Canada*

BLACK, ROBERT PERRY, banker; b. Hickman, Ky., Dec. 21, 1927; s. Burwell Perry and Veola (Moore) B.; B.A., U. Va., 1950, M.A., 1951, Ph.D., 1955; m. Mary Rives Ogilvie, Oct. 27, 1951; children—Patty Rives, Robert Perry. Part-time instr. U. Va., 1953-54; research asso. Fed. Res. Bank, Richmond, Va., 1954-55, asso. economist, 1956-57, economist, 1958-60, asst. v.p., 1960-62, v.p., 1962-68, 1st v.p., 1968—; asst. prof. U. Tenn., 1955-56; lectr. U. Va., 1956-57. Served with AUS, 1946-47. Mem. Am., So. econ. assns., Am., So. finance assns., Am. Inst. Banking, Raven Soc., Robert Morris Assos., Phi Beta Kappa, Beta Gamma Sigma, Alpha Kappa Psi, Kappa Alpha. Methodist. Rotarian. Clubs: Focus, Country of Virginia (Richmond). Contbr. articles profl. jours. Home: 10 Dahlgren Rd Richmond VA 23233 Office: Fed Res Bank 9th and Franklin Sts Richmond VA 23213

BLACK, ROBERT SMALLWOOD, former found. exec.; b. Zanesville, O., Jan. 13, 1909; s. Robert Smallwood and Dollie (VanVoorhis) B.; B.A., Dartmouth, 1932; M.A., Columbia, 1935; m. Barbara T. Bell, Mar. 22, 1941. Tchr. English, Stearns Sch., Mount Vernon, N.H., 1932-34, Am. U., Beirut, Lebanon, 1935-37, Friends Sch., Wilmington, Del., 1937-42, Detroit U. Sch., Grosse Pointe Woods, Mich., 1946-48; fgn. service res. officer Am. embassy, Cairo, Egypt, 1948-51; chief secretariat bd. fgn. scholarship IES, Dept. of State, 1952-55; fgn. service officer Am. embassy, Tokyo, Japan, 1955-57; consul Am. consulate, Tampico, Mexico, 1958-61, Am. consulate, Surabaya, Indonesia, 1961-63; appointed consul gen. Am. consulate gen., Halifax, N.S., Can., 1964-67; exec. dir. U.S. Ednl. Found., Thailand, 1967-69, ret., 1969. Served with USNR, 1942-45; lt. comdr. Address: Old County Rd Cape Neddick ME 03902

BLACK, ROE CODDINGTON, editor; b. Milw., Jan. 15, 1926; s. Roe R. and Avis (Coddington) B.; A.B. summa cum laude, Dartmouth, 1949; m. Carolyn Lapp, Jan. 19, 1947; children—Donna, Avis, Thomas, Phillip. Mgr. Black Ranches, Inc., San Antonio, and Aurora, Neb., 1949-53; field editor The Corn Belt Farm Dailies, Chgo. and Aurora, 1953-64; field editor Farm Jour., Inc., Phila. and Aurora, 1964-69; editor Top Operator mag., Farm Jour., Inc., Phila., 1969—. Served with AUS, 1944-46; PTO. Mem. Am. Assn. Agrl. Coll. Editors (asso.), Am. Legion, Dartmouth Alumni Assn., Phi Beta Kappa, Delta Upsilon. Club: Dartmouth (Phila.). Home: PO Box 352 Huntingdon Valley PA 19006 Office: 230 W Washington St Philadelphia PA 19105

BLACK, ROGER ANTRIM, elec. mfg. co. exec.; b. Mansfield, O., July 29, 1905; s. Frank B. and Jessie (Baxter) B.; A.B., Princeton, 1927; m. Elizabeth Thomas, Nov. 6, 1931; children—Frank T., R. Gordon, David B., Edith T. (Mrs. Joseph E. Humphrey). With counsular service Dept. State, 1927-30, serving as vice consul, Brisbane, Australia, 1928-30; with Ohio Brass Co., Mansfield, 1930—, beginning as salesman, successively mgr. fgn. trade, gen. factory mgr., v.p., 1930- 56, pres., 1956-67, chmn. bd., 1967—; dir. Farmers Savs. & Trust Co., Richland Hotel Co. (both Mansfield), Cyclops Corp., Pitts. Mem. I.E.E.E., Nat. Elec. Mfrs. Assn. Clubs: Union (Cleve.); Princeton (N.Y.C.); Westbrook Country, Rotary (Mansfield). Home: 955 Marion Av Mansfield OH 44906

BLACK, SHIRLEY NORMAN, museum ofcl.; b. Gardner, Mass., Sept. 26, 1916; s. Henry Warren and Ella (Thompson) B.; B.S. in Commerce and Bus. Adminstrn., U. Ala., 1938; M.B.A. with distinction, Harvard, 1954; student George Washington U., 1955; grad. Air U., 1959; m. Kathryn Mary Linser, Mar. 19, 1947; 1 son, Peter Norman. Commd. 2d ltd. USAF, 1938, advanced through grades to col. USAF, 1953; exec. dir. finance Hdqrs. USAF, 1951-62; dep. chief staff, comptroller hdqrs. Crew Tng., 1955-57; dir. accounting and finance Hdqrs. Air Tng. Command, 1957-58, Hdqrs. Pacific Air Force, 1950-60; dep. chief staff, comptroller Hdqrs. 5th Air Force, Japan, 1960-62; dir. accounting and finance Hdqrs. Air Def. Command, 1962-63; ret., 1963; comptroller, asst. treas. Art Inst. Chgo., 1963—, also adminstr.; past pres., dir. pres., dir. Restaurant Food Buyers, Inc. Pres., dir. Restaurant Food Buyers Investment Co. Active local Boy Scouts Am., Little League. Decorated Bronze Star medal, Commendation medal with oak leaf cluster. Mem. Air Force Assn., Ret. Officers Assn., Am. Mgmt. Assn., Am. Soc. Mil. Comptrollers (outstanding Achievement certificate 1959), Chgo. Assn. Commerce and Industry, Harvard Bus. Sch. Assn. Chgo., Heroes of '76, Nat. Sojourners. Clubs: Army Navy Country (Arlington, Va.); Toastmasters (pres. Scott AFB chpt. 1954). Home: 451 Beverly Pl Lake Forest IL 60045 Office: Art Institute Michigan Av at Adams St Chicago IL 60603

BLACK, THEODORE MICHAEL, publisher; b. Bklyn., Oct. 3, 1919; s. Walter Joseph and Elsie (Jantzer) B.; A.B. summa cum laude, Princeton, 1941; grad. Inf. Officers' Candidate Sch., Ft. Benning, Ga., 1943; Litt.D. honoris causa, Siena Coll., Loudonville, N.Y., 1971; m. Barbara A. Somerville, Nov. 10, 1956; children—Walter Joseph II, Theodore Michael Black; step-children—Mrs. Beverly A. Paulak, Mrs. Dorothy B. Scharkopf. With Walter J. Black, Inc., 1945—, v.p., 1952-58, pres., treas., 1958—; gen. partner Black's Readers Service Co., 1949—, pres., 1958—; pres. The Classics Club, Detective Book Club. Alumni pres. Class of 1941, Princeton; area chmn. Mercy Hosp. Ball Com., 1966; chmn. county fund drive Nassau Heart Assn., 1967; mem. adv. com. Nassau council Girl Scouts, Inc., 1972; mem. Nassau-Suffolk com. U.S.O., 1972. Staff publicity div. Democratic Nat. Com., 1940; exec. dir. Citizens for Nixon-Lodge, Nassau County, N.Y., 1960; chmn. Citizens for Congressman S.B. Derounian, 1962-64; del. 1967 Constl. Conv.; mem. Port Washington Rep. Club; chmn. Seldin for Congress, 1968; mem. minority research staff N.Y. State Assembly, 1968; dir. Fair Campaign Practices Com., 1971. Exec. com. Alumni Council, Princeton, 1950-63; bd. dirs. Long Island Assn. Mem. N.Y. State Bd. Regents, 1969—. Served from pvt. to capt. CIC, AUS, 1941-45, lt. col. Army Res., retired 1967. Decorated Bronze Star medal with cluster (U.S.); Belgian, French Fourragere; recipient medal S.A.R. Mem. N.A.M., U.S. C. of C., Direct Mail Advt. Assn., M.I. Res. Soc. (chmn. res. affairs 1956-59, pres. 1961-62), Res. Officers Assn. U.S., Assn. U.S. Army, Mil. Order Fgn. Wars, Nat. CIC Assn., 3d Armored Div. Assn., Am. Legion, Mil. Order World Wars, Phi Beta Kappa. Republican. Roman Catholic. Elk, Lion. Clubs: University (N.Y.C. and Albany, N.Y.); North Hempstead Country, Port Washington (N.Y.) Yacht; Capitol Hill (Washington); Nassau (Princeton, N.J.). Author: Know Your Stamps, 1934; Democratic Party Publicity in the 1940 Campaign, 1941; How To Organize and Run a Citizens' Committee for Your Candidate, 1964. Home: 47 Cornwell's Beach Rd Sands Point NY 11050 Office: Northern Blvd Flower Hill Roslyn NY 11576

BLACK, THEREL R., educator; b. Ferron, Utah, June 30, 1917; s. William L. and Clyda (Barton) B.; B.S., Brigham Young U., 1939; M.A., La. State U., 1941; Ph.D., U. Wis., 1951; m. Vera Jerrilyn Clark, June 16, 1944; children—Beth (Mrs. Roy W. Esplin), LaDonna (Mrs. Steven Kemmerle), Bonnie. Asst. prof. Okla. State U., 1946-49; vis. prof. Mich. State U., summer 1953; asst. prof. to prof. Utah State U., Logan, 1950—, head dept. sociology, 1964—; mem. Utah Population Work Com.; former chmn. Western States Social Research Adv. Com. in Sociology for Land Grant Colls. and Univs. Served with AUS, 1942-46. Fellow Am. Sociol. Assn.; mem. Internat. Union for Sci. Study Population, Rural Sociol. Soc., Population Assn. Am. Mem. Ch. of Jesus Christ of Latter-day Saints. Author: (with James D. Tarver) Age and Sex Population Projections of Utah Counties, 1965; (with Vernon L. Israelsen) Economic and Social Effects of a Highway Bypass, American Fork, Utah, 1968. Contbr. articles profl. jours. Home: 441 E 1 N Logan UT 84321

BLACK, THOMAS HOWARD, Jr., advt. exec.; b. Washington, Feb. 23, 1912; s. Thomas Howard and Anna Morton (Roberts) B.; grad. Kiskiminetas Springs Sch., 1930; m. Alice Esch, Apr. 11, 1938; children—Karen (Mrs. Cecil Burgin), Christine (Mrs. Richard Bluestein); m. 2d, Dorothy Chambers Dailey, Aug. 17, 1945; children—Thomas Howard III, William Rea, Margaret Chambers, Dorothy Elizabeth. With T. Howard Black Advt., Atlantic City, 1930-36; with W. Earl Bothwell Advt., 1936-49, exec. v.p., 1946-49; with Ted Bates & Co., Inc., 1949—, sr. v.p., 1961—, also dir. Home: Cedarwood Dr Greenwich CT also Old Mill Point West Harwich MA 02645 Office: 666 Fifth Av New York City NY 10019

BLACK, THOMPSON, Jr., educator; b. Berwick-upon-Tweed, Eng., Sept. 20, 1909; s. Thompson and Naval Acad., 1933; M.A., U. Cal. at Los Angeles, 1949, Ph.D., 1954; m. Katherine Antoinette Becker, June 16, 1935; children—Robert Thompson, Virginia, Ruth Ann, Bruce Richard. Commd. ensign U.S. Navy, 1933, advanced through grades to comdr., 1944; asst. prof. naval sci. U. Notre Dame, 1941-43; injured during Anzio campaign, 1944; asso. prof. naval sci. U. Cal. at Los Angeles, 1944-45, exec. officer Naval Res. Officer Tng. Corps, 1945-46; retired, 1947; teaching fellow U. Cal. at Los Angeles, 1948-49; faculty Cal. State Coll. at Los Angeles, 1949—, prof. govt., 1959-67, prof. polit. sci., 1967—, chmn. dept. of govt., 1955-61, chmn. div. social scis., 1961-64, dir. coll. found., coordinator, 1965—. Chmn. Joint Coll. Federal Service Am. Soc. Legal History (chmn. Pacific Coast br. 1960), So. Cal. Polit Sci. Assn. (chmn. 1959), Los Angeles World Affairs Council, Western Polit. Sci. Assn., Cal. Employees Assn., U.S. Naval Inst., Blue Key, Pi Sigma Alpha, Phi Delta Kappa. Decorated Purple Heart. Home: 1641 Courtney Av Los Angeles CA 90046

BLACK, W. G., transp. co. exec.; b. Winnipeg, Can., 1927; ed. U. Man. Sec., v.p. finance Can. Steamship Lines Ltd.; dir. Canadian Shipbldg. & Engring. Ltd., Provincial Transport Enterprises, Ltd. Home: 242 Bruton St Beaconsfield Quebec Canada Office: 759 Victoria Sq Montreal 126 Quebec Canada

BLACK, WENDELL CONDREY, ret. coll. pres.; b. Puyallup, Wash., Mar. 21, 1909; s. A. Lawrence and Alice (Wallace) B.; A.B., U. Redlands, 1930, L.H.D. (honorary), 1966; M.A., U. So. Cal., 1935; m. Sarah Ifland, Dec. 27, 1930; children—Mary Ann (Mrs. Robert A. Knox), John Wallace, Wendy Jean, William Keith. Instr., Cal. schs., 1931-47; mem. faculty Los Angeles City Coll., 1947-58, dean, 1953-58; pres. Los Angeles Harbor Coll., Wilmington, Cal., 1958-71. Mem. exec. bd. Wilmington chpt. A.R.C. Served to lt. (s.g.) USNR, World War II. Mem. So. Cal. (pres. 1959-60, exec. Delta Kappa, Pi Kappa Delta, Epsilon Pi Tau (Laureate citation 1959). Methodist. Home: 245 Calle Mayor Redondo Beach CA 90277

BLACK, WILLIAM, philanthropist, restaurant exec.; b. Bklyn.; grad. Columbia, 1926, L.H.D. (hon.), 1967; m. Jean Martin, 1951 (div. 1962); 1 dau., Melinda; m. 2d, Page Morton, Mar. 27, 1962. Checker, Washington Market; retail mcht. shelled nuts, N.Y.C.; organizer chain of stores Chock Full O' Nuts, N.Y.C., converted to restaurants, past pres., chmn. bd., chief exec. officer; also owner coffee producing firm.

Founder Parkinson's Disease Found., 1957; bd. dirs. New Rochelle Hosp. Home: Premium Point New Rochelle NY 10802 Office: 425 Lexington Av New York City NY 10017*

BLACK, WILLIAM, Jr., banker; b. Kansas City, Mo., Nov. 19, 1921; s. William Byron and Alice (Monihan) B.; B.S. with honors, U. Neb., 1947; M.B.A. with honors, U. Pa., 1949; postgrad. Rutgers U., 1960; m. Claire Hyland, June 27, 1943; children—Adrienne H., William Byron III, Christopher Durrill. With bus. devel. dept. Nat. Bank of Commerce, Houston, 1949; mgr. civic affairs dept. Houston C. of C., 1949-52, asst. gen. mgr., 1951-54; v.p., mgr. bus. devel. dept. Bank of S.W. Nat. Assn., Houston, 1955-58, v.p., mgr. banking relations dir., sec. mgmt. com., 1958—, pres. dir. Houston Intercontinental Nat. Bank, sr. v.p., 1964—; dir. 1st Nat. Bank, Longview, Tex., Gulf Coast Nat. Bank, Houston. Vice pres. Houston Area council Boy Scouts Am., 1960—; mem. pres. adv. council U. Houston Coll. Bus. Adminstrn. Bd. dirs. Houston Grand Opera, Houston Heart Assn.; pres., exec. com. Mus. Natural Sci. Served to capt. AUS, 1942-45. Mem. Am. Bankers Assn., Assn. Res. City Bankers, N.A.M., Houston C. of C. (hon. life). Episcopalian. Clubs: Lakeside Country, Forest (Houston), Houston Racquet (dir. pres.). Home: 6517 Bayou Glen Houston TX 77027 Office: PO Box 2629 Houston TX 77001

BLACKADAR, ALFRED KIMBALL, educator, meteorologist; b. Newburyport, Mass., July 6, 1920; s. Walter Lloyd and Harriett (White) B.; A.B., Princeton, 1942; Ph.D., N.Y.U., 1950; m. Beatrice J. Fenner, Mar. 23, 1946; children—Bruce Evan, Russell Lloyd, Thomas Alan. From instr. to asso. prof. N.Y.U., 1946-56; lectr. climatology Columbia, 1953-55; mem. faculty Pa. State U., 1956—, prof. meteorology, 1961—, head dept. meteorolgy, 1967—; bd. dirs. Univ. Corp. Atmospheric Research, 1962-68, mem. exec. com., 1965-68. Exec. com. div. earth scis. NRC, 1966-69. Sec. Univ. Christian Assn., 1964-68. Served to maj. USAAF, 1942-46; Iceland. Fellow A.A.A.S., Am. Meteorol. Soc. (sec. 1965-69, pres. 1971—; editor monographs 1962-65), Am. Geophys. Union; fgn. mem. Royal Meteorol. Soc. Baptist. Editor: Meteorological Research Revs., 1957. Home: 805 W Foster Av State College PA 16801 Office: Deike Bldg University Park PA 16802

BLACKALL, ERIC ALBERT, educator; b. London, Eng., Oct. 19, 1914; s. Frederick and Lillie (Stanger) B.; student Latymer Upper Sch., London; B.A., Gonville and Caius Coll., Cambridge, 1936, M.A., 1940; Ph.D., U. Vienna, 1938; Litt. D., Cambridge U., 1960; m. Jean Hargrave Frantz, June 25, 1960; 1 son, Roger Nicholas Blackall. Became naturalized citizen, 1965. Lectr. English lang. and lit. U. Basel, Switzerland, 1938-39; lectr. German, Cambridge U., 1939-58; vis. prof. German lit. Cornell U., 1957-58, chmn. dept. German lit., 1958-65, Avalon Found. prof. in humanities, 1964-67, Schurman prof. of German lit., 1967—; vis. prof. U. Heidelberg (Germany), 1968. Guggenheim fellowship, 1965. Fellow Am. Acad. Arts and Scis.; mem. Modern Lang. Assn., English Goethe Soc., Am. Philos. Soc., Assn. Am. Tchrs. of German, Am. Assn. U. Profs., Phi Beta Kappa. Author: Adalbert Stifter, 1948; The Emergence of German as a Literary Language, 1959; Die Entwicklung des Deutschen zur Literatursprache, 1966. Author articles, reviews on German studies. Recipient J. G. Robertson prize in German Studies, U. London, 1962. Home: 811 Triphammer Rd Ithaca NY 14850

BLACKARD, EMBREE HOSS, clergyman; b. Trenton, Tenn., Nov. 18, 1900; s. James Washington and Louisa (White) B.; A.B., Emory U., 1921, B.D., 1922, D.D., 1934; Th.B., Yale, 1923, M.A., 1924, grad. student, 1925; student Johns Hopkins, 1934; m. Margaret Lounsbury Griffith, June 16, 1925; children—Margaret Lee (Mrs. Harry Inman), Dr. Embree Hoss, Dr. William Griffith. Ordained deacon Meth. Ch., 1921, elder, 1925; pastor, Cheshire, Conn., 1922-24, Epworth Ch., New Haven, 1924-25, Melrose Ch., Kansas City, Mo., 1925-31, Wilson Meml. Ch., Balt., 1931-36, Wesley Meml. Ch., High Point, N.C., 1936-41, Myers Park Meth. Ch., Charlotte, N.C., 1941-45; supt. Charlotte dist., 1945-47, 61-63; pastor Main Street Ch., Gastonia, N.C., 1947-49, Central Ch., Asheville, N.C., 1949-61, supt. Asheville dist., 1963-67; chaplain, cousellor Morris Funeral Home, 1967—; Brit.-Am. exchange preacher, 1966. Mem. of World Conf. on Faith and Order, Edinburgh, 1937, Ecumenical Conf., Springfield, Mass., 1947, conf. World Council of Chs., Amsterdam, 1948, Evanston, 1954; mem. joint radio com. Gen. and Jurisdictional Confs., Meth. Ch., 1944, 48, 52, 56, 60, 64, coordinating council, 1948-60. Pres. Western N.C. Conf., Bd. Edn., 1956-60, pres. bd. of evangelism, 1960-61; mem. World Meth. Council, 1956-60; del. World Meth. Conf., 1961, 66. Trustee Emory U., Brevard Coll., Meth. Home for Aged, Charlotte. Mem. Theta Phi. Rotarian. Office: 274 Lakeshore Dr Asheville NC 28804

BLACKBIRD, WILLIAM H., justice; b. Coalgate, Okla., May 26, 1894; s. Robert and Agnes (Phillips) B.; student Okla. Sch. Mines, 1914, Okmulgee Law School, 1922- 27; m. Anne Courtney, 1915; m. 2d, Daisey Hawley, Dec. 1, 1954. County judge, Okmulgee County, Okla., 1933-43, dist. judge, 1943-53; asso. justice Supreme Ct. Okla., 1953, now chief justice. Mem. Okla. Bar Assn. Mason. Home: Okmulgee OK 74447 Office: PO Box 3122 State Capitol Oklahoma City OK 73105

BLACKBURN, BENJAMIN BENTLEY, III, congressman; b. Atlanta, Feb. 14, 1927; s. Benjamin Bentley Jr. and Sara (Medlock) B.; B.A., U. N.C., 1947; LL.B., Emory U., 1954; m. Mary A. Pandora, 1952; children—Michael, Robert, Kathryn, David. Admitted to Ga. bar, 1954; practice in Atlanta, 1956-66; mem. staff Atty. Gen. Ga., 1955- 56; partner firm of Peek, Whaley, Blackburn and Haldi, 1963-66; member 90th to 92d Congresses, 4th Dist. Ga. Mem. deKalb County Republican Exec. Com., 1964-67; sec. 4th Congl. Dist. Rep. Exec. Com., 1966-67. Served with USNR, 1944-46, 50-52; now lt. comdr. ret. Mem. Am., Ga., Atlanta bar assns., Lawyers Club Atlanta, Phi Delta Phi. Episcopalian. Club: Peachtree Optimist. Home: 9603 Hillridge Dr Kensington MD 20795 Office: Longworth House Office Bldg Washington DC

BLACKBURN, CLARK WARING, social worker; b. Seneca, S.C., Nov. 15, 1908; s. Charles Stanley and Res. U., 1935; m. Virginia Mitchell, June 15, 1935; children—Clark Waring, Mary Jane, Bennett Sykes. Supr., Cuyahoga County Relief Adminstrn., Cleve., 1935-37; field cons. N.C. Bd. Charities and Pub. Welfare, Raleigh, 1937-39; exec. sec. United Family and Children's Soc., Plainfield, N.J., 1939-43, Family Service Soc., Hartford, Conn., 1943-44, Family and Children's Service, Mpls., 1944-52; gen. dir. Family Service Assn. Am., N.Y.C., 1952—. Treas. Social Work Vocational Bur., N.Y., 1954-56; mem. bd. Nat. Social Welfare Assembly, 1954-60, 64-68, Nat. Legal Aid and Defender Assn., 1956-62, Sex Information and Edn. Council U.S., 1968-70, Nat. Found. Consumer Credit, 1968—; mem. bed. Nat. Council Homemaker Service, 1963- -, v.p., 1968-70; corporate mem. Nat. Assembly for Social Policy and Devel., 1968—, mem. bd., 1970—; mem. adv. com. on consumer credit protection act Fed. Res. Bd., 1968-70; chmn. U.S. com. Internat. Union Family Orgns., 1965—, v.p., 1970—; bd. mem. Nat. Council Family Relations, 1971—; 1st v.p. Nat. Conf. Social Welfare, 1961-62; del. White House Conf. on Children, 1960, 70, White House Conf. on Aging, 1961. Mem. Nat. Assn. Social Workers. Presbyn. (elder). Co-author: How to Stay Married, 1969. Home: 28 Montrose Rd Scarsdale NY 10583 Office: 44 E 23d St New York City NY 10010

BLACKBURN, CLEO W., coll. pres., social worker, clergyman; b. Port Gibson, Miss., Sept. 27, 1909; s. J. David and Sarah (Sneed) B.; A.B., Butler U., 1932; postgrad. U. Pa., 1934-35; M.A., Fisk U., 1936; Rosenwald fellow, Ind. U., 1941-42; D.D., N.W. Christian Coll., 1955; D.D. (hon.), Drake U., 1955; D.Humanities, Ind. Central Coll., 1966; D.H.L., Wabash Coll., 1968, Butler U., 1970; m. Fannie Elizabeth Scott, May 9, 1934 (dec. Nov. 1965); children—Harriet Virginia (Mrs. Collins J. Reynolds III), Walter Scott, Sarah Ann (Mrs. Edward I. Kimbrough); m. 2d, Dora Oma Atkins Powell, Aug. 27, 1966. Ordained to ministry of Disciples of Christ; sociology research asst. Fisk U., 1932; research dir. study for Chester (Pa.) Tb Assn., 1933; instr. sociology Knoxville Coll., also research asso. Tuskegee Inst., 1934; exec. dir. Flanner House, Indpls., 1936—; pres. Jarvis Christian Coll., 1953-64; exec. dir. Bd. Fundamental Edn., Indpls., 1954—. Mem. Ind. Bd. Edn., 1943-45; v.p., dir. Nat. Fedn. Settlements, 1947-50; del. nat. health assembly Nat. Commn. Children and Youth, 1948. Active N.A.A.C.P.; mem. adv. council Ind. Employment Security Div., 1949-53; mem. Indpls. Rent Control Bd., 1948-52, Indpls. Pub. Housing Authority, 1951-52. Recipient Distinguished Service award Indpls. Jr. C. of C., 1940. Mem. Fed. Council Chrs. Christ Am., Nat. Soc. Study Edn., Am. Sociol. Soc., Nat. Council Family Relations (dir.), Am. Anthrop. Assn., Am. Acad. Polit. and Social Scis., U.S. C. of C. (dir. 1971—). Home: 2518 Boulevard Pl Indianapolis IN Office: 333 W 16th St Indianapolis IN 46202 also 156 E Market St Indianapolis IN 46204

BLACKBURN, DAVID RICHARD, banker; b. Britton, Tex., Mar 6, 1914; s. Dave E. and Zola Mae Blackburn; ed. pub. schs., Tex.; m. Carmelita Kilp, Dec. 1, 1924. Engaged in constrn. work, 1932-34; bookkeeper Groce Parrish Wholesale Grocery Co., 1934-36; with Victoria Bank & Trust Co. (Tex.), 1936—, now chmn., chief exec. officer, dir.; dir. First State Bank & Trust Co., Pt. Lavaca, Tex., Jackson County State Bank, Edna, Tex., Bank Southwest N.A., Houston. Served with AUS, World War II. Mem. Am. (bd. govs.), Tex. (exec. com., past v.p., pres.) bankers assns., Assn. State Chartered Banks Tex. (bd. govs.). Home: Arlington Apts Victoria TX 77901 Office: Victoria Bank & Trust Co PO Box 1698 Victoria TX 77901

BLACKBURN, FRANCIS MARION, librarian; b. Akron, O., May 31, 1917; s. Chester A. and Angeline (Schumacher) B.; A.B., Kent State U., 1941, M.A., 1946, M.A. in L.S., 1951; m. Geraldine Springer, Mar. 4, 1941 (dec. Dec. 1962); 1 son, Thomas Scott; m. second, Carolyn G. Holmes, Sept. 2, 1968. Proprietor of Blackburn's Book Store, Akron, 1948-51; acquisitions librarian Matthews Library, Ariz. State Coll., 1951-53; base librarian Sheppard AFB, Wichita Falls, Tex., 1953-56; asst. to librarian U. Mo. Library, 1956-58; librarian W. Tex. State U., Canyon, 1958—. Mem. Tex. librarians com. for Nat. Library Week, 1960. Served with USAAF, 1942-46. Mem. Am., Southwestern, Tex. (chmn. dist. 1, 1960-62) library assns., Am. Assn. U. Profs. Tex. Assn. Coll. Tchrs. Home: 413 Taylor Lane Canyon TX 79015

BLACKBURN, FREDERICK GEORGE, corp. exec.; b. Pitts., Mar. 11, 1892; s. William W. and Harriet (Bloom) B.; A.B., Yale, 1914; B.S., Carnegie Inst. Tech., 1928; m. Madelaine F. Walton, June 2, 1923 (dec. Sept. 28, 1945); children—Madelaine W. (Mrs. E. S. Lewis), Harriet Elizabeth (Mrs. Moses Taylor); m. 2d, Maxwell D. Church Blair, Oct. 24, 1947. Metallurgist Carnegie Steel Co., 1915-29; partner Moore, Leonard & Lynch, 1929-32; v.p. City Deposit Bank & Trust Co., 1932-35, pres., 1935; v.p. Union Trust Co. of Pitts., 1935-46, Mellon Nat. Bank and Trust Co., 1946-57; pres. Tremarco Corp., 1956-67; mem. bd. mgrs. Homewood Cemetery; dir. Haugh & Keenan Storage & Transfer Co.; trustee Dollar Savs. Bank. Dir. Western Pa. Sch. for Blind Children; trustee Carnegie Inst., Carnegie-Mellon Univ., Child Guidance Center, Chatham Coll. Mem. Carnegie Hero Fund Commn., adv. bd. Salvation Army. Vice chmn. Pitts. Sinking Fund Commn. Served as 1st lt. U.S. Army F.A., 1917-19. Mem. Phi Beta Kappa, Alpha Delta Phi, Wolf's Head (Yale). Republican. Presbyn. (elder). Clubs: Pittsburgh Golf, Duquesne (Pitts.); Yale (N.Y.C.); Rolling Rock (Ligonier, Pa.). Home: 1055 Devon Rd Pittsburgh PA 15213 Office: 530 6th Av Pittsburgh PA 15219

BLACKBURN, JACK BAILEY, educator; b. Sterling, Okla., Oct. 19, 1922; s. Raymond Wasden and Vonnie Irene (Bailey) B.; B.S., Okla. U., 1947; M.S., Purdue U., 1949, Ph.D., 1955; m. Janice Ann Keller, Sept. 2, 1949; children—Judith Ann (Mrs. Charles Ray Cameron), Jo Ann. Grad. asst., research asst., research engr. Joint Hwy. Research Project, Purdue U., 1947-55; asso. prof. civil engring., asso. dir. Md. Hwy. Research Program, U. Md., 1955-58; transp. planning engr. Harland Bartholomew and Assos., St. Louis, Memphis, 1958-60; prof. civil engring., dir. Ariz. Transp. and Traffic Inst., U. Ariz., Tucson, 1960-63; prof., head, civil engring. dept. Kan. State U., Manhattan, 1963—. Mem. Nat. Acad. Sci./Nat. Acad. Engring. bldg. research adv. bd., 1968-71. Served with AUS, 1943-46. Mem. Am. Soc. Testing and Materials (chmn. subcom. on evaluation of data of C-9 com. on concrete 1956-58), Am. Soc. C.E., Engrs. Council Profl. Devel. (ad hoc visitors list 1964-69; chmn. publns. com., urban planning and devel. div. 1971—), Manhattan C. of C. (dir. 1968-71), Nat. Soc. Profl. Engrs. (exec. bd. engrs. in edn. practice sect. 1968-71, sec. 1971—), Am. Arbitration Assn. Home: 908 Garden Way Manhattan KS 66502

BLACKBURN, JOHN LESLIE, ednl. adminstr; b. Malta Bend, Mo., Dec. 21, 1924; s. Clarence Oliver and Vivian (Mitchener) B.; B.S., Mo. Valley Coll., 1950; M.Ed., U. Colo., 1952; Ph.D., Fla. State U., 1969; m. Gloria Bullington, June 10, 1950; 1 dau. Holly. Accounting clk. fed. account div., Agrl. Adjustment Adminstrn., 1942-43; personnel mgmt. instr. Air Force Career Guidance Tng. Sch., 1951-52; counselor to men Fla. State U., 1952-56; asst. dean men U. Ala., 1956-58, dean men, 1958-68, dean for student devel., 1968-69; vice chancellor for student affairs U. Denver, 1969—. Mem. Mayor's Program Policy Adv. Bd. Denver Model City Program. Served with AUS, 1943-46; CBI. Mem. Nat. Assn. Student Personnel Adminstrs. (v.p. 1964-65, dir. profl. devel. and standards 1967-69), Am. Coll. Personnel Assn., Am. Personnel and Guidance Assn., Am. Assn. U. Adminstrs. (mem. exec. com., dir.), Alpha Sigma Phi (pres. 1968-70), Phi Delta Kappa, Phi Alpha Theta, Phi Eta Sigma, Pi Gamma Mu, Alpha Phi Omega, Omicron Delta Kappa. Office: U Denver Denver CO 80210

BLACKBURN, JOHN OLIVER, univ. adminstr.; b. Miami, Fla., Sept. 13, 1929; s. Elmer E. and Proxie (Hughes) B.; A.B., Duke, 1951; postgrad. U. Miami (Fla.), 1951-52; Ph.D., U. Fla., 1959; m. Jeanne Elise Miles, Nov. 29, 1957; children—Katherine Elise, John Parkinson, David Laurence. Asst. prof. econs. Duke, 1959-61, 62-63, asso. prof., 1963-68, prof. econs., 1968—, provost, 1970—; asst. prof. bus. adminstrn. Am. U., Beirut, Lebanon, 1961-62; dir. United Durham, Inc. Bd. dirs. Carolina Friends Sch. Served with USNR, 1952-55. C.P.A., Fla. Mem. Am., So. econs. assns., Phi Beta Kappa, Chi Phi. Democrat. Presbyn. Home: 208 Pineview Rd Durham NC 27707

BLACKBURN, MORRIS ATKINSON, painter; b. Phila., Oct. 13, 1902; s. James Meyers and Emma (Brightly) B.; student Pa. Acad. Fine Arts; William Emlen Cresson traveling scholar to Europe, 1928, 29; m. Sarah Elizabeth Thompson, May 1, 1937; 1 dau., Patricia Joan. Faculty Bryn Mawr Coll., 1946-48, Temple U., 1948-52, Phila. Mus. Sch. Indsl. Art, 1933-40; faculty Pa. Acad. Fine Arts, 1952- -, Phila. Mus. Art, 1946—; works exhibited U.S., also France, Eng., Italy, Holland, Yugoslavia, India, Pakistan and New Zealand; works represented in collections Phila. Mus. Art, Acad. Fine Arts, Butler Inst. Am., Capehart Collection, Lessing J. Rosenwald Collection, Brooks Meml. Art Gallery, Clearwater Mus., Dept. State, Free Library of Phila., Library of Congress, Woodmere Art Gallery, Pa. State U., U. Mont., Mus. N.M., U.S. embassies abroad. Recipient John Gribbel prize Phila. Print Club, 1942, Lessing J. Rosenwald prize and Mary S. Collins prize, 1950; gold medal award Pa. Acad. Fine Arts, 1946, fellowship prize, 1949, Harrison S. Morris prize, 1951, Thornton Oakley prize, 1955, Pyramid Club award, 1957; Gugenheim fellow painting and graphic art, 1952, Zimmerman prize, 1960, Artist of Year, Ocean City, N.J., 1968, Phila. Water Color Club medal of award, 1969. Mem. Am. Water Color Soc., Phila. Water Color Club, Print Club, Allied Artists, Audubon Soc., Art Alliance, Taos Art Assn. Home: 2104 Spring St Philadelphia PA 19103 (summer) Taos NM 87571

BLACKBURN NORMAN, educator; b. Huddersfield, Eng., May 27, 1930; s. Ernest and J. Elsie (Warwick) B.; B.A., Ph.D. Trinity Coll., Cambridge, 1950-58; m. Joan P. Herbert, Sept. 3, 1960; children—Virginia Ellen, Caroline Mary. Came to U.S., 1965. Faculty U. Manchester (Eng.), 1958-65, lectr., 1961-64, sr. lectr., 1964-65; prof. math. U. Ill. at Chgo. Circle, 1965—. Mem. London, Am. math. socs. Home: 1317 Judson Av Evanston IL 60201 Office: Dept Math U Ill Chicago IL 60201

BLACKBURN, PAUL PRICHARD, Jr., naval officer; b. Seattle, Jan. 13, 1909; s. Paul P. and Nellie (Carey) B.; B.S., U.S. Naval Acad., 1930; grad. Air War Coll., 1949, Nat. War Coll., 1953; m. Marian Alice Moulden, May 16, 1931; children—Paul Prichard III, William Stewart. Commd. ensign U.S. Navy, 1930, advanced through grades to rear adm., 1958; designated naval aviator, 1932; pilot various carrier observations and patrol planes with fleet, 1932-42; aviation officer staff 1st Am. naval task force with Brit. Home Fleet, Mürmansk convoy operations, 1942-43; carrier officer Pacific campaigns, World War II; comdg. officer flagship comdr. Middle East Force, Persian Gulf, 1951-52, carrier U.S.S. Intrepid, 1955-56; chief staff comdr. Naval Air Force, Atlantic Fleet, 1956-57; comdr. U.S. Taiwan Patrol Force, 7th Fleet, 1958-59; dir. strategic analysis div. Office Chief Naval Operations, Navy Dept., 1959-61; comdr. carrier div. 3, 1961-62; chief joint command and control requirements group Office Joint Chiefs Staff, Washington, 1962-64; sr. mem. UN Armistice Commn., Korea, 1964, 65; comdr. U.S. 7th Fleet, 1965-66; chief of staff U.S. Strike Command, 1966—. Active Boy Scouts Am.; pres. Uniformed Services Benefit Assn. Mem. bd. control U.S. Naval Inst., 1955—. Decorated Bronze Star; Medal of Pao-Teng (Nationalist China), Legion of Merit, D.S.M. Episcopalian. Club: Army-Navy (Washington). Author articles. Home: Medomak ME 04551 Office: US Strike Command MacDill AFB Tampa FL 33608

BLACKBURN, ROBERT HAROLD, librarian; b. Vegreville, Alberta, Can., Feb. 3, 1919; s. John Hiram and Palma Gertina (Olson) B.: B.A., U. Alberta, 1940, M.A., 1941; B.L.S., U. Toronto, 1942; M.S., Columbia, 1948; LL.D., Waterloo U., 1965; m. Frances Patricia Gibson, Dec. 31, 1942; children—Robert Gibson, Karen Margaret, John Henry. Gen. asst. Calgary Pub. Library, 1945-46; asst. librarian U. Toronto, 1947-54, chief librarian, 1954—, also lectr. library adminstrn.; editorial adviser Collier's Ency., 1953—. Chmn. bd. Center for Research Libraries, 1967. Chmn. Streetsville (Ont.) Pub. Library, 1957-65. Served as flight lt. Royal Canadian Air Force, 1942-45. Mem. Assn. of Research Libraries, Canadian (pres.. 1958-59), Ont. library assns., A.L.A., Canadian Assn. Coll. and U. Libraries (past pres.). Mem. United Ch. of Can. Editor Newfoundland Supplement, Ency. of Can., 1949; Joint Catalogue of Serials in Libraries, City of Toronto, 1953. Author articles, poems, short stories. Home: Durle Rd Streetsville Ontario Canada Office: University of Toronto Library Toronto Ontario Canada

BLACKBURN, WILLIAM F., newspaper pub. and editor; b. Joliet, Ill., Oct. 15, 1916; s. George J. and Anna (McGowan) B.; ed. parochial schs., Joliet; m. Catherine Jean Plitt, Sept. 5, 1946; children—Catherine, William, Janet, James, Mary, John Dennis, Judith, Carol, Jeffrey. With Joliet Herald- News, 1930—, pub., editor, 1966—; v.p., dir. Copley Press, 1967—; dir. First Nat. Bank Joliet, 1968—, Ill. Daily Newspaper Markets, 1968- -. Pres. United Crusade Will County, 1967-68, campaign chmn., 1966. Adv. bd. St. Joseph Hosp., Coll. St. Francis; bd. dirs. Downtown Devel. Council, Boy Scouts Am. Served with AUS, 1943-46. Mem. Joliet Advt. Club (pres. 1954-55), Joliet Region (v.p., dir. 1967-68), Ill. chambers commerce, Am. Newspaper Pubs. Assn., Internat. Newspaper Advt. Execs. Assn., No. Ill. Editorial Assn. Republican. Roman Catholic. Lion (pres. Joliet 1957-58), Elk. Club: Joliet Country. Home: 601 Western Av Joliet IL 60435 Office: 78 N Scott St Joliet IL 60431

BLACKBURN, WILLIAM H., telephone co. exec.; b. Coffeen, IL., 1922; ed. Washington U., St. Louis, 1950. Vice pres., treas. Continental Telephone Corp. Elk. Home: 355 Medina Dr St. Louis, MO 63122. Office: 130 S Bemiston Av St Louis MO 63105

BLACKERBY, PHILIP EARLE, found. exec.; b. Erlanger, Ky., Aug. 9, 1910; s. Philip Earle and Helen Clara (Young) B.; A.B., U. Louisville, 1930, D.D.S., 1933, H.H.D. (hon.), 1970; grad. student U. Ill., summers 1934-37; M.S. in Pub. Health, U. Mich., 1941; D. Honoris Causa, U. Montreal, 1948; LL.D. (hon.), Dalhousie U., 1958, U. Ky., 1966; m. Clara Mae Hartmetz, June 1, 1935; children—Linda Clare (Mrs. Fred F. Vaughan), Nancy Mary (Mrs. Thomas E. Stone). Instr. U. Louisville Sch. Dentistry, 1934-36, prof., 1942-45, dean, 1944-45; dir. dental health Tenn., Dept. Pub. Health, 1936-42; dir. div. dentistry W.K. Kellogg Found., Battle Creek, Mich., 1945—, asso. gen. dir., 1956-65, v.p. programs, 1966-67, 70—, pres., 1967-70, trustee, 1957—; hon. prof. U. Costa Rica Faculty Dentistry. Dental dir. USPHS Res., 1942—; spl. cons. WHO, 1950, 54, 56—; mem. Pres. Nat. Adv. Com. White House Conf. Children and Youth, 1958-60; mem. adv. bd. health services A.R.C., 1946-50; bd. med. edn. and research U. Pa., 1955-56; panel dentistry Pres.'s Commn. Health Needs of Nation, 1952; steering com. dental sect. Nat. Health Assembly, 1949; cons. USPHS, 1947-52, 55-69. Recipient Distinguished Service certificate U. San Carlos (Guatemala) Faculty Dentistry, 1952; Sesquicentennial award U. Mich., 1967; William J. Gies award Am. Coll. Dentists, 1967. Decorated Order of Southern Cross (Brazil). Mem. Am. Bd. Dental Pub. Health (founder 1950, pres. 1958-59), Am. Assn. Pub. Health Dentists (pres. 1951-52; Especial Service award 1951, Distinguished Service award 1961), Am. Coll. Dentists (bd. regents 1957-62, pres. 1962-63), Am. Dental Assn. (chmn. council dental edn. 1954-55), Am. Pub. Health Assn. (chmn. council profl. edn. 1955-59), Internat. Dental Fedn., Internat. Assn. Dental Research, Am. Soc. Dentistry Children, Am., Latin Am. assns. dental schs., Latin Am. Assn. Pub. Health Dentistry (hon. mem.), Psi Omega, Omicron Kappa Upsilon, Delta Omega; hon. mem. N.C., Ky. (Centennial award 1960) dental assns., Guatemalan Dental Soc., Chilean Soc. Dentistry Children, Fla. Dental Soc., Am. Assn. Dental Examiners. Author articles, contbr. textbooks. Home: 138 Northside Dr E Battle Creek MI 49017 Office: 400 North Av Battle Creek MI 49017

BLACKETT, DONALD WATSON, educator; b. Boston, May 2, 1926; s. Charles Wesley and Josephine Sewall (Parsons) B.; A.B., Harvard, 1947; A.M., Princeton, 1948, Ph.D., 1950; m. Shirley Jane Allart, July 7, 1951. Instr. Princeton, 1950-51, research asso., 1951-53; asst. prof. math. Boston U., 1953-57, asso. prof., 1957-62, prof., 1962—. Mem. Am. Math. Soc., Math. Assn. Am. Conglist. Author: Elementary Topology, 1967. Home: 97 Eliot Av West Newton MA 02165 Office: Boston Univ Boston MA 02215

BLACKETT, PATRICK MAYNARD STUART, physicist, b. London, Eng., Nov. 18, 1897; s. Arthur Stuart and Caroline (Frances) B.; grad. Royal Naval Colls., 1914; student Magdalene Coll., 1919-23; fellow King's Coll., 1923-33; D.Sc. (hon.), New Delhi U., 1947, U. Strasbourg, 1947, U. Reading, 1948, Queen's U., Belfast, 1953, Cambridge, 1954; LL.D. Glasgow, 1955, Dalhousie U. Halifax, N.S., 1960; m. Costanza Bayon, Mar. 17, 1924; children—Giovanna, Nicolas Maynard. Prof. physics Brikbeck Coll., 1933- 37; Langworthy prof. physics U. Manchester, 1937-53, pro-vice chancellor, 1950-52; prof. physics Imperial Coll. Sci. and Tech., U. London, 1953-65, sr. research fellow, 1965—, pro rector Imperial Coll., 1961-64. Mem. Council Dept. Sci. and Indsl. Research, 1955-60; mem. council and exec. com., Overseas Devel. Inst., 1960—; councillor Inst. for Strategic Studies, 1958-61. Served in the Royal Navy, 1914-19, lt. 1919. Recipient Royal medal, Royal Soc., 1940, Copley medal, 1956; Am. medal of Merit, 1947; Nobel Laureate for physics, 1948; hon. fellow Magdalene Coll., 1948, Weizmann Inst. Sci., Israel, 1954. Fellow Royal Soc. (pres. 1965-70); mem. Inst. France, Acad. Scis., Berlin Acad. Sci., Brit. Assn. Advancement Sci. (pres. 1957-58). Club: Athenaeum (London). Author: Military and Political Consequences of Atomic Energy, 1948; Lectures on Rock Magnetism, 1956; Atomic Weapons and East-West Relations, 1956; Studies of War, 1962; also sci. papers in field. Home: 806 Nelson House Dolphin Sq London SW 1 England

BLACKFIELD, WILLIAM, builder, engr., lawyer; b. Stockton, Cal., July 20, 1914; s. David and Mina (Schwartzfeld) B.; B.A., LL.B., U. Cal. at Berkeley, 1938; m. Cecilia Malik, Dec. 25, 1941; childrenLeland Gregory, Pamela Esther, Karen Ann. Founder William Blackfield Orgn., San Francisco, 1944, chmn. bd., 1950-; chmn. bd. Rex Devel. Co., Mortgage Advisors, Inc., (both San Francisco), Leeward Devel. Corp., Waical Devel. Co., Tract Devel. Corp., Realty Sales Corp., Leeward Shopping Center, Ltd., Realty Mortgage Corp. (all Honolulu); pres., dir. Leeward Realty Corp.; dir. United Title Ins. Agy., Honolulu. Mem. citizens adv. com. fire protection and residential safety Cal. Legislature; mem. Gov. Cal. Environmental and Planning Com., 1964-65, Pres.'s Citizens Adv. Com., 1964, Small Bus. Adv. Council, Washington, 1964-65, Mayor Honolulu Financial Adv. Com., 1965. Chmn. trustees Western Mortgage Investors; trustee Hawaii Loa Coll.; bd. dirs. Columbia Park Boys Club, San Francisco; mem. exec. bd. Am. Jewish Com. Recipient citation gov. Hawaii and Hawaii Econ. Planning Commn., 1959; Commendation award achievement home bldg. field Cal. Legislature, 1964. Mem. Asso. Home Builders San Francisco (past pres., dir.), Nat. Assn. Home Builders (dir., mem. exec. com., past pres.), Home Builders Assn. Hawaii (dir.), Mortgage Bankers Assn. Clubs: Federal City, Nat. Capital Democratic (Washington); Concordia, Argonaut, Lake Merced Golf and Country (San Francisco); Waialae Country, Waikiki Yacht. Elks (Honolulu). Home: 5900 Manchester Dr Oakland, CA 94618. Office: 612 Howard St San Francisco, CA 94105.

BLACKFORD, BENJAMIN, banker; b. Bklyn., Jan. 26, 1913; s. Benjamin and Elizabeth (McArthur) B.; B.S., St. Lawrence U., 1935; LL.B., Bklyn. Law Sch., 1938, J.S.D., 1940; grad. Sch. Banking, Rutgers U., 1949; m. Jeanne Fraser, Feb. 9, 1946. Admitted to N.Y. bar, 1939; trust dept. adminstrn. Manufacturers Trust Co., N.Y.C., 1935-41; officer mgr. Empire Finished Steel Corp., Newark, 1941-42; asst. sec.-treas. Greenwich Trust Co., 1945-46, treas., trust officer, 1946-47, v.p., trust officer, 1947-49, exec. v.p., v.p., 1949-57, dir., 1953-58, pres., 1957; pres., dir. State Nat. Bank of Conn., Bridgeport, 1958—; dir. Sperry and Hutchinson Co. Pres., dir. Greenwich Boys Club; bd. dirs. Boys Club Am. Served from ensign to lt. (s.g.), USNR, 1942- 45. Mem. N.Y. State Bar Assn., Beta Theta Pi, Phi Delta Phi. Republican. Conglist. Home: Sky Ridge Rd Greenwich CT 06830 Office: 2834 Fairfield Av Bridgeport CT 06605

BLACKIE, WILLIAM, mfg. exec.; b. Glasgow, Scotland, 1906; s. William and Catherine (Hyne) B.; m. Florence M. Hewens, Aug. 7, 1934; 1 son, Bruce L. Chartered accountant's apprentice, Glasgow, Scotland, 1924-29; staff Price, Waterhouse & Co., C.P.A.'s, Chgo., 1930-39; controller Caterpillar Tractor Co., Peoria, Ill., 1939-43, v.p., 1943-54, charge accounting, mdse, and traffic depts., adminstrv. coordinator all plants and subsidiaries, pres., dir., until 1966, chmn. bd., 1966—; dir. Caterpillar Americas Co., Caterpillar Far East, Ltd., Caterpillar of Can., Ltd., Caterpillar Tractor Co., Ltd. (Gt. Britain), Caterpillar of Australia, Caterpillar Belgium S.A., Towmotor Corp., Shell Oil Co., Caterpillar Argentina S.A., Ampex Corp.; Internat. Exec. Service Corps.; mem. internat. adv. com. Chase Manhattan Bank. Mem. Adv. Council Japan-Am. Econ. Relations. Trustee Conf. Bd. Inc. Decorated officer Order of Crown (Belgium). C.P.A., Ill., Wis.; chartered accountant, Scotland. Mem. Am. Inst. C.P.A.'s, Nat. Assn. Accountants, Soc. Automotive Engrs., British-N.Am. Com. Clubs: Chicago, Union League (Chgo.); Pacific Union (San Francisco). Home: 493 E High Point Dr Peoria IL 61614 Office: Caterpillar Tractor Co 100 NE Admas St Peoria IL 61602

BLACKIE, WILLIAM MCALISTER, business exec.; b. Nashville, May 24, 1904; s. George F. and Medora (McAlister) B.; B.E. summa cum laude, Vanderbilt U., 1925; m. Van Meter Proctor, June 10, 1926; children—Martha Van Meter (Mrs. Henry M. Bailey, Jr.), William McAlister. Office mgr. Gen. Shoe Corp. (now Genesco), Nashville, 1928-31, sec.-treas., 1932-36, v.p., dir., 1936-54, exec. v.p., 1954—, chmn. exec. com., 1958; dir. S. H. Kress & Co., Bonwit Teller, Nashville & Decatur R.R., 3d Nat. Bank. Mem. Vol. Footwear Retailers Association (past pres., mem. bd. dirs.), Beta Theta Pi. Presbyn. (elder, trustee). Clubs: University (N.Y.C.); Belle Meade Country, Cumberland (Nashville); Colemere. Home: 1645 Tune Blvd Nashville TN 37215 Office: Genesco Bldg Nashville TN 37202

BLACKISTON, HENRY CURTIS, lawyer; b. Hampton, Va., Oct. 11, 1909; s. Henry Curtis and Mary (Marrow) B.; grad. Episcopal High Sch., Alexandria, Va. 1928; B.S., Princeton, 1932; LL.B., Harvard, 1935; m. Elizabeth Parker Nugent, June 28, 1932; children—Henry Curtis, III, George Howland. Admitted to N.Y. bar, 1935; asso. Lord, Day & Lord, N.Y.C., 1935-43, 46-49, mem. firm. 1949—. Mem. Internat. Maritime Com., Antwerp, Belgium. Mem. Maritime Law Assn. U.S. (pres. 1960-62), Am. Bar Assn., Assn. Bar City of N.Y., Maritime Assn. Port N.Y. Episcopalian. Clubs: Ivy, (Princeton, N.J.); Down Town Assn., Church, Century Assn., Anglers' (sec.) (N.Y.C.). C.). Home: 1088 Park Av New York City NY 10028 Office: 25 Broadway New York City NY 10004

BLACKLEDGE, WILLIAM WESLEY, lawyer; b. Wichita, Kan., Dec. 15, 1923; s. Haskell Reginald and Mildred (Hockett) B.; LL.B., Oklahoma City U., 1954; m. Wilma Dean Trotter, Oct. 22, 1966; children—Larry Wesley, David Eugene, Stephen Ed, Celia Dianne, Trent Eugene. Asst. traffic mgr. Oklahoma City C. of C., 1948-58; traffic mgr. Okla. Dept. Commerce and Industry, Oklahoma City, 1958-62; admitted to Okla. bar, 1954, Tex. bar, 1966; pvt. practice law, Oklahoma City, 1962-64; counsellor Plains Cotton Coop. Assn., Lubbock, Tex., 1964-66, sec., counsellor, 1966—. Served with USAAF, 1942-46. Mem. Am., Okla. bar assns., State Bar Tex., Asso. Traffic Clubs, Delta Nu Alpha. Home: 3908 54th St Lubbock TX 79413 Office: 3301 NE 50th St Lubbock TX 79404

BLACKLER, ANTONIE WILLIAM CHARLES, biologist; b. Portsmouth, Eng., Oct. 19, 1931; s. Leslie Guy and Florence (Harris) B.; B.S. in Zoology, U. Coll., London, 1953, Ph.D., 1956; m. Rochelle Lois Melkin, Mar. 12, 1970. Came to U.S., 1964. Professeur Extraordinaire U. Geneva, Switzerland, 1961-64; prof. zoology, Cornell U., Ithaca, N.Y., 1964—. Mem. Internat. Soc. Devel. Biology, Am. Soc. Zoologists, Swiss Zoological Soc. Research on origins of sex. Home: The Carriage House Ithaca NY 14850 Office: 246 Emerson Hall Cornell Univ Ithaca NY 14850

BLACKLIDGE, RICHARD HENRY, newspaper pub.; b. Kokomo, Ind., June 7, 1914; s. Kent H. and Bernice (Kautz) B.; B.S. in Chem. Engring., Purdue U., 1936; m. Marian Reinertsen, Jan. 5, 1938. With Kokomo Tribune, 1936—, chief exec. officer, pub., 1938—; exec. com., dir. Union Bank and Trust Co., Kokomo, 1942—; dir., sec. Kokomo Opalescent Galss Co., 1940—; bd. dirs. Pub. Service Ind. Active Howard County Tb Assn., United Fund. Served with USAAF, 1944-45. Mem. Inland Daily (pres. 1960- 61), Hoosier (past pres., dir.) press assns., Am. Newspaper Pubs. Assn. (dir., chmn.; dir., chmn. research inst.), Am. Legion. Elk. Club: Kokomo Country (past pres.). Home: 1771 W Taylor St Kokomo IN 46901 Office: 300 N Union St Kokomo IN 46901

BLACKMAN, ALFRED CHURCHILL, safety engr.; b. N.Y.C., Apr 21, 1908; s. Alfred O. and Janette E. (Kitching) B.; B.S. in Mech. Engring., Cornell U., 1929; m. Jeanne D. Reuling, Aug. 14, 1954; children—Joanne, James Kragh, Judy Kragh, Judy Blackman, David. Supervising safety engr. Liberty Mut. Ins. Co., 1931- 47; chief Cal. Div. Indsl. Safety, 1947-59; mng. dir. Am. Soc. Safety Engrs., 1959—, sec., 1959—. Mem. Am. Indsl. Hygiene Assn., Vets. of Safety, Chgo. Soc. Assn. Execs. (pres. 1970-71), Am. Soc. Assn. Execs. Episcapalian. Home: 920 Sheridan Rd Wilmette, IL 60091. Office: 850 Busse Hwy Park Ridge IL 60068

BLACKMAN, HERBERT NEIL, govt. ofcl.; b. Bklyn., Dec. 20, 1913; s. Morris and Freda (Schachet) B.; B.S.S., Bklyn. Coll., 1934; M.A., Columbia, 1936; student Am. U., George Washington U.; m. Edythe Penzner, July 28, 1937; children—Meredith (Mrs. Stephen Kellner), Leslie (Mrs. James H. Landsman). With Treasury Dept., 1936-38; economist WPB, 1940-45; chief economist textile div. Civilian Prodn. Adminstrn., 1945-46; with Dept. Commerce, 1946-61, internat. economist, 1955-61; economist Census Bur., 1961-63; with Dept. Labor, 1963—. adminstr. Bur. Internat. Labor Affairs, 1967-70, dep. asst sec. labor for trade and adjustment policy, 1970—. Vice pres. Montgomery County Council P.T.A.'s, 1960-63. Recipient Menitorious Service award Dept. Labor, 1963. Mem. Am. Econ. Assn., Am. Statis. Assn. Home: 7004 Wilson Lane Bethesda, MD 20034. Office: Dept of Labor Washington DC 20210

BLACKMAN, HONOR, actress; b. London, U.K., Aug. 22, 1929; d. Frederick and Edith Eliza (Blackman) Thomas; licentiate drama, Guildhall Sch. Music and Drama, 1945; m. Maurice H. Kaufmann, Dec. 18, 1961; children—Carlotta Lucy, Barnaby Frederick. Played in The Gleam, Globe Theatre, London, 1946, The Blind Goddess, Apollow Theatre, 1947-48, Cambridge Theatre, 1954, Fifth Season, Strand Theatre, 1966, Wait Until Dark, Piccadilly Theatre, 1966, Who Killed Santa Claus, 1970; originated Avenger series, 1962-64; films include Shalako, Goldfinger, Virgin and The Gypsy, Something Big. Author: Honor Blackman's Book of Self Defense. Home: 39 Tregunter Rd London 10 SW England Office: CMA 22 Grafton St London W1 England

BLACKMAN, PAUL DAVID, perfume co. exec.; b. N.Y.C., May 8, 1922; s. David M. and Sylvia (Schoenberg) B.; student N.Y. U., 1940, Washington and Lee U., 1941; m. Nancy de Roy Rittmaster, June 19, 1947; children—Diane Lynn, Linda Anne. Gen. mgr. Bellins Wonderstone, 1946-49, Helene Pessl, Inc., 1949-54, gen. beauty products div. Coty, 1954-58; pres. House of Fragrance, 1958- 62; v.p. internat. Rayette-Faberge, Inc., 1965-67; exec. v.p. Faberge, Inc., 1966-71. Chmn. cosmetic and fragrance com. Kennedy for President, 1968. Served to capt. AUS, 1942-46. Mem. Fragrance Found., Toilet Goods Assn. (past bd. dirs.). Home: 47 E 88th St New York City NY 10029 Office: 5 W 54th St New York City NY 10019

BLACKMAN, PERCY C., business exec.; b. Rock Hill, S.C., 1907; student N.C. State U., 1924-25, U. of South, 1925-27; married. With Synalloy Corp., Spartanburg, S.C., 1945—, chmn., pres., 1968-70, chmn., chief exec. officer, 1970—. Pres., dir. Multifab, Inc., Balco Realty Co., Delmar Equipment Co.; dir. Eckerd Drugs, Inc. Home: 1016 Glendalyn Circle Spartanburg SC 29302 Office: PO Box 5627 Spartanburg SC 29301*

BLACKMAN, RAYMOND VICTOR BERNARD, editor; b. Portsmouth, Hampshire, Eng., June 29, 1910; s. Leo Albert Martin and Laura Gertrude (Thomas) B.; student So. Grammar Sch. 1922-28; m. Alma Theresa Joyce Hannah, Sept. 28, 1935; children—Jill, Martin. Naval corr., free lance tech. journalist, 1935—; editor Jane's Fighting Ships, London 1949—; broadcasts B.B.C., 1951—. Served in His Majesty's Ship Vernon and Admiralty Mine Design Dept., 1939-45. Decorated Order Brit. Empire. Fellow Royal Instn. Naval Architects, Inst. Marine Engr. Clubs: Anchorites; Press (London); Royal Naval (Portsmouth). Author: The Modern World Book of Ships, 1950; The World's Warships, 1955, 60, 63, 69. Contbr. to Statesman's Year-Book, Brit. Book of the Year, The Engr., The Navy, The Sea Cadet, Sunday Times, Lloyd's List, and other London newspapers. Address: 72 The Brow Widley Portsmouth England

BLACKMAN, SAMUEL GARRISON, newspaperman; b. Port Jervis, N.Y., Oct. 22, 1904; s. Samuel Garrison and Mathilde Emilie (Jardin) B.; Litt.B., Rutgers U., 1927, M.A., 1930, Doctor of Letters (honorary), 1964; m. Jeannette Finn, August 29, 1931; children—Carolyn (Mrs. Glenn E. Jacoby, Jr.), Ann Towers. Asst. city editor Long Branch (N.J.) Daily Record; city editor New Brunswick (N.J.) Home News, 1930-31; with Asso. Press, 1931, chief N.Y. bur., 1945-58, gen. news editor, 1958-69. Home: 105 Creston Av Tenafly NJ 07670 Office: care Associated Press 50 Rockefeller Plaza New York City NY 10020

BLACKMAR, CHARLES BLAKEY, lawyer; b. Kansas City, Mo., Apr. 19, 1922; s. Charles Maxwell and Eleanor (Blakey) B.; A.B. summa cum laude, Princeton, 1942; J.D., U. Mich., 1948; m. Ellen Day Bonnifield, July 18, 1943; children—Charles A., Thomas J., Lucy E., Elizabeth S., George B. Admitted to Mo. bar, 1948, and practiced in Kansas City; mem. firm Swanson, Midgley, Jones, Blackmar & Eager, and predecessors, 1952-66; professorial lectr. U. Mo. at Kansas City, 1949-58; prof. law St. Louis U.; spl. asst. atty. gen. of Missouri, 1969—; labor arbitrator. Chmn. Fair Pub. Accommodations Commn. Kansas City, Mo., 1964-66; mem. Commn. Human Relations, Kansas City, Mo., 1965-66. Mem. Jackson County Republican Com., 1952-58, Mo. Rep. Com., 1956-58. Served to 1st lt., inf., AUS, 1943-46. Decorated Silver Star, Purple Heart, Combat Inf. badge. Mem. Am. Law Inst., Mo. Bar (spl. lectr. insts.), Phi Beta Kappa, Order of Coif. Mem. Disciples of Christ Ch. Author (with Volz and others) Missouri Practices, 1953, West's Federal practice Manual, 1957, 71; (with Devitt) Federal Jury Practice and Instructions, 1970. Contbr. numerous articles on probate law to profl. publs. Home: 7305 Maryland Av St Louis MO 63130 Office: 3642 Lindell St St Louis MO 63108

BLACKMON, DON E., sch. adminstr.; b. Calion, Ark., July 7, 1913; s. Orland B. and Laura (Hux) B.; A.B., Henderson State Tchrs. Coll., 1937; M.A., U. Ark., 1940; m. Hester Wylie, Aug. 21, 1937; children—Betty Ann (Mrs. R. Wm. Petty), Lynda Janice. Supt., Cotten (Ark.) Pub. Schs., 1937-41; supt. Dyess (Ark.) Pub. Schs., 1941-46, Wynn (Ark.) Pub. Schs., 1946-52; asst. state commr. edn., Little Rock, 1952-55; supt. Dell (Ark.) Pub. Schs., 1955-59; sch. supt. Pulaski County, Little Rock, 1959—; pres. Asso. Edcators. Mem. Ark. Edn. Assn. (past pres.). Mason (Shriner), Lion (pres. Little Rock 1971-72). Home: 8711 Cantrell Rd Little Rock AR 72207 Office: County Court House Little Rock AR 72201

BLACKMON, ROSEMARY BARNSDALL, magazine editor, writer; b. Buffalo; d. Jay Thornton and Grace (Devine) Barnsdall; A.B., Barnard Coll., 1943; m. William Andrew Blackmon, Jr., Aug. 1, 1945; children—Rosemary, William Andrew III. Staff editor Am. Coll. Dictionary, 1946-47, Thorndike-Barnhart dictionaries, 1949; researcher, then feature writer Vogue mag., 1952-61, mng. editor, spl. features writer, 1962—. Mem. Fashion Group, Municipal Art Soc. Democrat. Collaborator: (with Irving Penn) Moments Preserved, 1960. Home: 24 Bank St New York City NY 10014 Office: Vogue Magazine 420 Lexington Av New York City NY 10017

BLACKMUN, HARRY ANDREW, asso. justice U.S. Supreme Ct.; b. Nashville, Ill., Nov. 12, 1908; s. Corwin Manning and Theo H. (Reuter) B.; B.A. summa cum laude, Harvard, 1929, LL.B., 1932; m. Dorothy E. Clark, June 21, 1941; children—Nancy Clark, Sally Ann (Mrs. D.R. Funk), Susan Manning (Mrs. Roger M. Karl). Admitted to Minn. bar, 1932; law clk. for John B. Sanborn, judge 8th circuit, U.S. Ct. of Appeals, St. Paul, 1932-33; asso. Dorsey, Owen, Barker, Scott & Barber, Mpls., 1934-38, jr. partner, 1939-42, gen. partner, 1943-50; instr. St. Paul Coll. Law, 1935-41, U. Minn. Law Sch., 1945-47; resident counsel Mayo Clinic, Mayo Assn., Rochester, 1950-59, mem. sect. adminstrn., 1950-59; judge 8th Circuit, U.S. Ct. of Appeals, 1959-70; asso. justice U.S. Supreme Ct., 1970—. Mem. bd. members Mayo Assn. Rochester, 1953-60; bd. dirs., mem. exec. com. Rochester Meth. Hosp., 1954-70. Trustee Hamline Univ., St. Paul, 1964-70, William Mitchell Coll. Law, St. Paul, 1959—. Mem. Am., Minn., Olmsted County, 3d Jud. Dist. bar assns., Phi Beta Kappa, Contbr. profl. articles legal, med. jours. Office: Supreme Ct US Washington DC 20543

BLACKNER, BOYD ATKINS, architect; b. Salt Lake City, Aug. 29, 1933; s. Lester Armond and Anna (McDonald) B.; B.Arch., U. Utah, 1956, B.F.A., 1956; m. Elizabeth Ann Castleton, June 4, 1955; children—Catherine, David, Elizabeth, Genevieve. Asst. landscape architect Nat. Park Service, Mt. Rainier, Wash., 1956; job capt. Cannon, Smith & Gustavson, Salt Lake City, 1957, Snedaker, Budd & Monroe, Salt Lake City, 1958, Hellmuth, Obata & Kassabaum, St. Louis, 1958-59, Caudill, Rowlett & Scott, Houston, 1959-60; project architect Victor A. Lundy, Sarasota, Fla. and N.Y.C., 1960-63; pvt. practice architecture, Salt Lake City, 1963—; vis. jury mem. U. Utah dept. arch. Vice-chmn. Utah Advanced Gift Heart Fund drive, 1964; co-chmn archtl. div. United Fund drive, 1964. Recipient Danforth Honor award, 1951; also numerous A.I.A. awards. Registered architect, Fla., Utah, Wyo. Mem. A.I.A. (dir. Utah chpt. 1968, 71). Rotarian. Clus: Alta; Salt Lake Swim and Tennis. Home: 1203 4th Av Salt Lake City UT 84111 Office: 22 E 1st S Salt Lake City UT 84031

BLACKSHEAR, PERRY LYNNFIELD, Jr., educator; b. Atlanta, July 19, 1921; s. Perry Lynnfield and Dorothy (Breitenbucher) B.; B.S., Ga. Inst. Tech., 1943, M.S., 1947; Ph.D., Case Inst. Tech., 1956; m. Gertrude Julianna Liebl, June 17, 1948; children—Perry Justin, Edmund David, Joseph Lynnfield, Elizabeth Julianna, David Alexander, Dorothy Magdeline. Aero. research scientist Lewis Research Center, NACA, NASA, Cleve., 1947-56, head combustion dynamics sect., 1956, asso. prof. U. Minn., Mpls., 1956-57, prof., head power and propulsion div. mech. engring. dept., 1957—, also dir. bioengring. lab.; cons. Amercon Corp., Aerospace Corp., Avco, Everette Research Lab., Mayo Clinic engring. sect., NIH, Nat. Heart Inst., Naval Radiol. Def. Lab., Medtronics; cons. artificial kidney program NIH. Mem. fire research com. Nat. Acad. Sci., 1965-67; NSF fellowship com. 1961-66; Fulbright Engring. Fellowship com., 1962-67; mem. Columbia Seminar Biomaterials, 1967—. Mem. Planning Commn., Mahtomedi, Minn., 1963—, mem. Park Commn., 1968—; councilman Village of Mahtomedi, 1971. Vice chmn. bd. dirs. White Bear Lake Art Council. Served to 1st lt. AUS, 1943-45; CBI. Fulbright lectr. Stuttgart, 1962. Mem. Combustion Inst., Am. Inst. Aeros. and Astronautics, Am. Soc. Artificial Internal Organs, Tau Beta Pi, Pi Tau Sigma, Chi Phi. Home: 29 Birchwood Rd Mahtomedi MN 55115 Office: Dept Mech Engring U Minn Minneapolis MN 55455

BLACKSTOCK, LEROY, lawyer; b. El Reno, Okla., Apr. 19, 1914; s. Herbert Austin and Ethel Mae (Gwin) B.; grad. Draughon's Bus. Inst., Tulsa, 1933; LL.B., U. Tulsa, 1938; m. Virginia Lee Lowman, Dec. 29, 1939; children—Craig, Priscilla, Birch, Lore, Trena. With Phillips Petroleum Co., Tulsa, 1933- 41, asst. credit mgr., 1939-41; admitted to Okla. bar, 1938; gen. practice, Tulsa, 1941—; now sr. partner law firm Blackstock Joyce & Pollard; dir., gen. counsel Tulsa Homebuilders Assn., 1959-68; dir. Fourth Nat. Bank Tulsa, Owasso First State Bank (Okla.); pres. Skelly Stadium Corp., 1964—. Mem. nat. adv. com. Practicing Law Inst. Pres. Gt. Western Investment Trust, Jud. Reform Okla., 1966—, Tulsa Sci. Center, 1968—; chmn. Citizens Adv. Com. County Commrs., 1963-66; pres., dir. Tulsa County Bar Found., 1962-66; mem. Gov.'s Acad. for State Govt., 1966-68; pres. Tulsa Camp Fire Council, 1971—, Pres. Tulsa Baptist Laymen's Corp., 1962-66. Bd. dirs. Tulsa County Mental Health Assn., 1963—, Tulsa Psychiat. Found., 1964-67; pres. Tulsa County Legal Aid Soc., 1961-62, bd. dirs., 1958-66. Served with USNR, 1943-46. Recipient Distinguished Citizens award Okla. Psychol. Assn., 1963. Mem. Am. (ho. dels. 1965-67), Okla. (pres. 1966), Tulsa County (pres. 1962, Outstanding Atty. award 1961) bar assns., Tulsa County Hist. Soc. (founding mem.). Republican. Baptist (chmn. deacons 1962, chmn. bldg. com. 1951—). Author: Paper Dolls; Lawyers' Fees. Home: 3740 Terwilleger St Tulsa OK 74105 Office: Petroleum Club Bldg Tulsa OK 74119

BLACKSTOCK, ROBERT WILLIAM, lawyer; b. Drumright, Okla., Feb. 28, 1927; s. Boyd Lee and Pearl Catherine (Parks) B.; student Okla. State U., 1944; B.A., U. Okla., 1949, LL.B., 1951; m. Elaine Eda Cartwright, July 18, 1953; children—Roger Brent, Katherine Ann, Robert Keith Benjamin. Admitted to Okla. bar, 1951, since practiced in Bristow, specializing trial and appellate law state and fed. cts. Pres. Bristow Industries, Inc., 1959; dir. Woolaroc Oil Co. Chmn., mem. council Blue Cross-Blue Shield, 1955- 59. Mem. Okla. Gov.'s Council Water Devel.; dist. chmn., exec. bd. Indian Nations council Boy

Scouts Am., 1965—; chmn. law center commn. U. Okla. Coll. Law, 1971—. Bd. dirs., exec. bd. U. Okla. Assn.; trustee Bristow Meml. Hosp. Found., Okla. Bar Found., Frontiers of Sci. Found. Okla., Inc. Served with USAAF, World War II. Mem. Am. (ho. of dels.), Okla. (pres. 1963, chmn. negligence sect. 1958, chmn. banking, corporate and bus. law sect. 1959), Creek County (pres. 1960, exec. council 1962) bar assns., Bristow C. of C. (pres. 1954), Deep Fork Watershed Assn. (pres. 1964), U. Okla. Alumni Assn. (mem. at large exec. bd. 1967—, pres. 1968-69), Delta Tau Delta, Phi Alpha Delta. Editor Okla. Bar Jour. Home: 506 W 11th St Bristow OK 74010 Office: Blackstock-McMillan Bldg Bristow OK 74010

BLACKSTONE, DONALD LEROY, educator, geologist; b. Chinook, Mont., June 16, 1909; s. Donald Leroy and Sarah H. (McKibbin) B.; B.A., U. Wash., 1931; M.A., Mont. State U., 1934; Ph.D., Princeton, 1936; m. Helen F. Bookman, Nov. 10, 1936; children-Andrew J., Mary E., William J., Sarah J. Geologist, Carter Oil Co. (now Humble Oil & Refinery), 1936-39, 41-45; asst. prof. U. Mo., 1939-41; asso. prof. U. Wyo., 1947-50, prof., 1950—, head dept., 1963- 68. Wyoming state geologist, 1967-69. Distinguished lectr. Am. Assn. Petroleum Geologists, 1957; co-dir. Internat. Field Inst. Alps, 1962; cons. petroleum geology and groundwater, research regional tectonics Rocky Mountain region. Fellow Geol. Soc. Am. (past councillor); mem. Am. Assn. Petroleum Geologists, Am. Geophys. Union, Wyo. Geol. Assn. (life), Rocky Mountain Assn. Geologists, Sigma Xi, Phi Beta Kappa (hon.). Home: 1415 Steele St Laramie WY 82070

BLACKSTONE, HENRY, elec. engring. co. exec.; b. American Falls, Ida., Aug. 2, 1915; s. Henry A. and Lena Marie (Walder) B.; B.S., Mass. Inst. Tech., 1937, M.S. in 1938. Began career as a test engr. Gen. Electric Co., 1936; jr. engr. San Diego Gas & Electric, 1938; mem. Hillyer & Blackstone, consultants, 1939-44; dir. electromechanical engring. Fairchild Camera & Instrument Co., 1944-46; pres. Servo Corp. of Am., Hicksville, L.I., 1946—, chmn., 1946—; dir. L.I. Commercial Review, Plainview, N.Y. Mem. guided missile div. NDRC, 1943-46; adminstrv. vice chmn. Small Bus. Adminstrn., 1953-67. Trustee, Adelphi Coll.; mem. governing bd. Railway Progress Inst. Mem. I.E.E.E., Inst. Navigation (vice pres.), Young Pres.' Orgn. (v.p.), Chief Execs. Forum, The Conf. Bd. (exec. council). Office: 111 New South Rd Hicksville NY 11801

BLACKSTONE, WILLIAM THOMAS, educator; b. Augusta, Ga., Dec. 8, 1931; s. Thomas Watson and Katie (Curtis) B.; B.A., Elon Coll., 1953; M.A., Duke, 1955, Ph.D., 1957; m. Norma Jean Tew, Mar. 27, 1954; children—Lisa Brooks, Jeffrey Thomas. Asso. prof. philosophy Elon Coll., 1957-58; asst. prof. U. Fla., 1958- 61; mem. faculty U. Ga., 1961—, prof. philosophy, head dept. philosophy and religion, 1964—, chmn. div. Social Scis. Author: The Problem of Religious Knowledge, 1963; Frances Hutcheson and Contemporary Ethical Theory, 1964; Education and Ethics, 1968; Concept of Equality, 1969; Meaning and Existence, 1971; also articles. Home: Barnett Shoals Rd Athens GA 30601

BLACKWELL, BETSY TALBOT, ret. editor; b. N.Y.C.; d. Hayden and Benedict (Bristow) Talbot; grad. Acad. St. Elizabeth, N.J., 1923; Litt.D., Dickinson Coll.; m. Bowden Washington, Dec. 11, 1925; m. 2d, James Madison Blackwell, Apr. 10, 1930; 1 son, James Madison IV. Fashion reporter for The Breath of the Avenue, New York 1923; successively asst. to fashion editor, beauty editor and fashion editor of Charm, 1923-31; advt. mgr. Sisholz Bros. dept. stores, 1931; with Tobe, fashion service, 1931-33; asso. Women's Orgn. for Nat. Prohibition Repeal, 1933; with Tobe 1933-35; fashion editor Mademoiselle 1935-37, editor in chief 1937-71; dir. Hanes Corp., Winston-Salem, N.C. Del. Am. Assembly; mem. Columbia U. Sch. of Gen. Studies Council; v.p. Fashion Group, Inc., 1959-60, chmn. bd. govs., 1961-62; mem., past chmn. Coty Am. Fashion Critics' Awards; mem. adv. council Tobé-Coburn Sch. for Fashion Careers. Mem. lay council Internat. Cardiology Found.; mem. council Hofstra U.; chmn. pub. relations com. Girls Club Am. Recipient Pres.'s citation Lake Erie Coll. Mem. Am. Soc. Mag. Editors (charter, exec. com.). Clubs: Women's Nat. Press Club; Women's Nat. Republican Club, Inc. Presbyn. Home: 226 West Lane Ridgefield CT 06877

BLACKWELL, CECIL, assn. exec.; b. Enterprise, Miss., Oct. 29, 1924; s. George Dewey and Neely (Baggett) B.; B.S., Miss. State U., 1951; M.S., U. Md., 1955; postgrad. U. Ark., 1953-54; m. Louise McLendon, May 27, 1944; children—Cecil Carl, Donna Lynn, Gregory Dale. Asst. horticulturist Truck Crops Br. Expt. Sta., Crystal Springs, Miss., 1951; research asst. U. Md., College Park, 1951-52; instr., jr. horticulturist U. Ark., 1952-54; extension horticulturist U. Ga., 1954-56, head extension hort. dept., 1956-59; hort. editor Progressive Farmer, Birmingham, Ala., 1959-65; exec. dir. Am. Soc. Hort. Sci., editor Hort. Sci., St. Joseph, Mich., 1965—. Served with USAAF, 1944-46. Decorated Air medal. Gen. Edn. Bd. fellow Rockefeller Found., 1951-52. Mem. Internat., Am. socs. hort. sci., Am. Inst. Biol. Scis., A.A.A.S., Alpha Zeta. Mem. Ch. of God. Author: (with L.A. Niven) Garden Book for the South, 1961. Home: 2200 Pioneer Rd St Joseph MI 49085 Office: 914 Main St St Joseph MI 49085

BLACKWELL, DAVID, educator, statistician; b. Centralia, Ill., Apr. 24, 1919; s. Grover and Mabel (Johnson) B.; A.B., U. Ill., 1938, A.M., 1939, Ph.D., 1941, D.Sc., 1966; m. Ann Madison, Dec. 27, 1944; children—Ann, Julia, David, Ruth, Grover, Vera, Hugo, Sara. Instr. math. Southern U., 1942-43, Clark Coll., 1943-44; asst. prof., then prof. math. Howard U., 1944-54; prof. statistics U. Cal. at Berkeley, 1954—. Fellow Inst. Math. Statistics (pres. 1955); mem. Am. Math. Soc., Am. Statis. Assn. Co-author: Theory of Games and Statistical Decisions, 1954. Home: 3021 Wheeler St Berkeley CA 94705

BLACKWELL, EARL, publisher; b. Atlanta, May 3, 1913; s. Samuel Earl and Carrie (Lagomarsino) B.; student Culver Mil. Acad., 1928; A.B., Oglethorpe U., 1933; student Columbia. Co-founder Celebrity Service Inc., offices N.Y.C., London, Paris, Rome, Hollywood, pres., 1939—; owner, pub. Celebrity Bull., Theatrical Calendar, Contact Book, pub., co-editor Celebrity Register; contbg. editor Town & Country mag., N.Y.C., 1964—, now also internat. editor Town & Country; pres. Celebrity Register, Ltd., 1957—; pres. Embassy Found., Inc., 1958-67; radio commentator, Celebrity Table, 1955-56; founder, chmn. bd. Raffles Club, N.Y.C.; lectr. on celebrities, 1963-64. Prod. Pres. Kennedy's Birthday Celebration, Madison Sq. Garden, 1962. Founder, pres. Nine O'Clocks of N.Y. dir. Mayor N.Y.C. Com. for Scholastic Achievement, 1957-65; bd. dirs. Soldiers, Sailors, Airmens Club, N.Y.C. Mem. Pi Kappa Phi, The Boar's Head. Republican. Roman Catholic. Clubs: N.Y. Athletic (N.Y.C.); Tamboo (Bahamas). Author: (play) Aries is Rising, prod. 1939. Contbr. articles on celebrities to mags. Home: 171 W 57th St New York City NY 10019 also 450 W Paces Ferry Rd Atlanta GA Office: 171 W 57th St New York City NY 10019

BLACKWELL, GORDON WILLIAMS, univ. pres.; b. Timmonsville, S.C., Apr. 27, 1911; s. Benjamin L. and Amelia (Williams) B.; A.B., Furman U., 1932, LL.D., 1958; M.A., U. N.C., 1933, LL.D., 1967; A.M., Harvard, 1937, Ph.D., 1940, L.H.D., Rollins Coll., 1961; LL.D., U. Miami (Fla.), 1964, The Citadel, 1968, William Jewell Coll., 1968; m. Elizabeth Blair Lyles, Aug. 21, 1937; children—Gordon Lyles, Randolph Williams, Elizabeth Blair, Amelia Mayo. Research asst. U. N.C., 1932-33; research N.C. Emergency Relief Adminstrn., 1933-34, W.P.A., 1935-36; fellow Harvard, 1936-37; prof. and head dept. sociology Furman U., 1937-41; asso. prof. sociology and research asso. Inst. for Research in Social Science, U. N.C., 1941, study of community understanding in teacher edn. Com. on Teacher Edn., 1942, dir. Inst. for Research in Social Sci., and research prof. sociology U. N.C., 1944-57, became Kenan prof. sociology, 1955; chancellor Woman's Coll. of U. N. C., 1957-60; pres. Fla. State U., 1960-65, Furman U., 1965—; field instr. Columbia U., summers, 1939-41, vis. prof., summers 1948, 49. Mem. com. on computing activities NSF, 1967—. Dir. Peoples Nat. Bank. Mem. staff Greenville County Council for Community Devel., 1937-41; chief, tng. sect. and community problems sect. Civilian War Services branch Office Civilian Def., 1942-43. Mem. Am. Council on Edn. (com. on adminstrv. affairs 1962-63), Am. Assn. Colls., Am. Sociol. Soc., So. Sociol. Soc. (chmn. com. on research, 1946; 1st v.p. 1947), Rural Sociol. Soc. (chmn. com. on research 1945, com. on extension 1948, 49; v.p. 1948), Am. Assn. U. Profs., Blue Key, Phi Beta Kappa, Phi Kappa Phi, Omicron Delta Kappa, Alpha Phi Omega, Kappa Sigma, Alpha Kappa Delta, Pi Gamma Mu. Baptist. Clubs: Quaternion, Poinsett, Green Valley. Author: (with L. M. Brooks and S. H. Hobbs, Jr.) Church and Community in the South, 1949; (with R. F. Gould) Future Citizens All, 1952; Addresses of Gordon W. Blackwell, 1960-65, 1965. Dir. Study of College Teaching of Social Science in So., for So. Assn. Colls. and Secondary Schs., 1944-48; dir. and editor Studies of So. Resources, for So. Assn. Sci. and Industry, 1948-50; library adv. bd. Air U., 1951-54; editor Social Forces, 1954-57; asst. editor Am. Sociol. Rev., 1946-50; adv. com. Ency. Internat. Contbr. to profl. publs. Home: 68 Kensington Rd Greenville SC 29609

BLACKWELL, HAROLD RICHARD, educator; b. Harrisburg, Pa., Jan. 16, 1921; s. Jefferson Davis and Lucy Salome (Love) B.; B.S., Haverford Coll., 1941; A.M., Brown U., 1942; Ph.D., U. Mich., 1947; m. Olive Gladys Mortenson, June 12, 1943; children—Laird Richard, Bryan Richard. From instr. to asso. prof. depts. psychology, ophthalmology U. Mich., 1945-58; prof. biophysics, ophthalmology and physiol. optics, dir. Inst. Research Vision, Ohio State U., 1958—. Tech. aide to exec. sec. vision com. Armed Forces Nat. Research Council, 1945-55. Recipient Lomb medal Optical Soc. Am., 1950, Army-Navy Certificate Appreciation for World War II research, 1947. Fellow Optical Soc. Am., Illuminating Engring. Soc., Am. Academy Optometry, Am. Assn. Advancement Sci., Am. Inst. Physics; mem. Assn. Research Vision and Ophthalmology. Contbr. articles in field to tech. jours. Home: 3160 Herrick Rd Columbus OH 43221

BLACKWELL, JOHN DAVENPORT, banker; b. Richmond, Va., Nov. 30, 1918; s. Karl S. and Mary (Ball) B.; B.A., U. Va., 1941; grad. in trusts Stonier Grad. Sch. Banking, Rutgers U., 1953; m. Doris Conway Fleming, Aug. 19, 1950; children—Doris Conway, John Davenport, Carl F., Ellen B. Salesman, Virginia Paper Co., Richmond and Charlotte, N.C., 1941-44; with First & Merchants Nat. Bank, Richmond, 1945—, v.p., trust officer, 1961-66, sr. v.p., trust officer, 1966—. Mem. Estate Planning Council Richmond. Pres., Protestant Episcopal Ch. Home, Grace and Holy Trinity Endowment Fund; trustee St. Andrews Assn.; bd. dirs. A.R.C.; bd. govs. St. Christophers Sch. Mem. Am. Bankers Assn. (com. mem.), Phi Kappa Sigma. Episcopalian. Clubs: German, Hundred, Society. Virginia Creepers, Commonwealth, Country of Virginia, Downtown (Richmond). Home: 6124 St Andrews Lane Richmond VA 23226 Office: PO Box 26903 Richmond VA 23261

BLACKWELL, LLOYD PHALTI, forester; b. Lynchburg, Va., Nov. 4, 1910; s. Allen Owen and Mary Elizabeth (Martin) B.; B.A., Lynchburg (Va.) Coll., 1931; Va. collegiate teaching certificate, Lynchburg Coll., 1932; M.F., Yale, 1937; m. Eva Ray Mackey, June 30, 1938; 1 dau., Mary Ellen. Field and staff asst. U.S. Forest Service, Lynchburg, Va., Elkins, W. Va., Charleston, S.C., Columbia, S.C., 1931-35; forester and woodlands mgr. The Urania (La.) Lumber Co. Ltd., 1937-46; prof. and head Sch. Forestry, Coll. Life Scis., La. Tech. U., 1946—. Served with USNR June 1942-Nov. 1945; transport duty Pacific and Atlantic; Dunkeswell, Eng. Permanent sec. Yale Forestry Class, 1937. Pres. Presbyn. Young Peoples Conf. for State of Va., 1928. Chmn. La. Tree Farms System, 1950-55. Fellow Soc. Am. Foresters (mem. nat. com. of income taxation 1949, chmn. La. chpt. Gulf States sect. 1961-62, Outstanding La. Forester Gulf States sect. 1963); mem. La. Forestry Assn. (bd. dirs., exec. com. 1947—; chmn. N. La. group foresters 1941—), Am. Legion (dir. 1947, vice comdr. 1948), Phi Kappa Phi, Tau Kappa Alpha, Alpha Psi Omega. Presbyn. Mason. Clubs: Masquers of Hollywood (hon. mem. 1942-43), Kiwanis (past pres.). Author: Selective Land Utilization in the Piedmont Region of South Carolina, 1936; Puerto Rico and its Forests, 1937. Compiler, pub. Louisiana Forest Laws. Contbr. to trade jours, on forestry and related subjects. Home: 1212 Dubach St Ruston LA 71270

BLACKWELL, MENEFEE DAVIS, lawyer; b. Lexington, Mo., Feb. 17, 1916; s. Horace F. and Berrien (Menefee) B.; A.B., U. Mo., 1936; J.D., U. Mich., 1939; m. Mary Louise Harris, Apr. 25, 1942; 1 son, Stephen M. Admitted to Mo. bar, 1939, since practiced in Kansas City; partner firm Blackwell, Sanders, Matheny, Weary & Lombardi. Dir. Kansas City Title div. Chgo. Title Ins. Co., Inter-State Cattle Loan & Oil Co., Westport Bank Cook Paint & Varnish Co., Percy Kent Bag. Co. Bd. dirs. Chas. R. Cook and Minnie K. Cook Found., Charles T. and Marion M. Thompson Found., trustee William Rockhill Nelson Trust, Louetta M. Cowden Found., Jacob L. Loose Charity Fund Assn., Midwest Research Inst. Served from 2d lt. to maj., 14th Armored Div., AUS, 1942-46. Decorated Silver Star medal, Bronze Star medal with cluster, Purple Heart. Mem. Am., Mo., Kansas City bar assns., Phi Beta Kappa, Phi Delta Theta, Phi Delta Phi, Order of Coif. Episcopalian. Clubs: Kansas City Country, Mission Hills Country, Kansas City, University (Kansas City). Home: 1215 W 57 Terrace Kansas City MO 64113 Office: Fed Res Bank Bldg Kansas City MO 64106

BLACKWELL, RICHARD JOSEPH, educator; b. Cleve., July 31, 1929; s. Edward and Cecelia (Koch) B.; A.B., John Carroll U., 1950; M.A., St. Louis U., 1952, Ph.D., 1954; m. Rosemary Gallagher, Jan. 16, 1954; children—Richard Joseph, Thomas. Instr., John Carroll U., Cleve., 1954-57, asst. prof. philosophy, 1957- 61; asso. prof. St. Louis U., 1961-66, prof. philosophy, 1966—. Served with U.S. Army, 1954-56. Mem. Philosophy Sci. Assn., Am., Am. Cath. philos. assns. Roman Catholic. Author: Discovery in the Physical Sciences, 1969. Co-translator Commentary on Aristotle's Physics, 1963; translator Preliminary Discourse on Philosophy in General, 1963. Home: 7700 Missy Ct St Louis MO 63123

BLACKWELL, SARA ELIZABETH, educator; b. Dunbar, Pa., Aug. 9, 1916; d. Grant R. and Anabelle (Rankin) Blackwell; B.S., Pa. State U., 1938, M.S., 1944; Ph.D., U. Minn., 1950. Homemaking tchr. Pa. schs., 1938-45; research asst. U. Minn., 1945-47; ednl. cons. Gen. Mills Inc., Mpls., 1947-48; asst. prof., asso. prof. home econs. edn. N.Y. State Coll. Home Econs., Cornell U., 1948-58, prof., head dept. home econs. edn., 1958-69; prof. community service edn. N.Y. State Coll. Human Ecology, Cornell U., 1969—; asso. research div. Ednl. Testing Service, Princeton, N.J., 1955-56. Mem. Am. Home Econs. Assn., Am. Vocational Assn., Am. Ednl. Research Assn., A.A.A.S., Pi Lambda Theta, Omicron Nu, Phi Kappa Phi. Home: 104 Christopher Circle Ithaca NY 14850

BLACKWELL, WILLIAM ALLEN, educator; b. Ft. Worth, May 17, 1920; s. Charles Clarence and Lilly (Hartsfield) B.; B.S. in Elec. Engring., Tex. Tech. Coll., 1949; M.S., U. Ill., 1952; Ph.D., Mich. State U., 1958; m. Sherry LaRue Tibbets, June 1, 1949; children—David Allen, Rebecca Rae. Project engr. Gen. Dynamics Corp., 1959-61; prof. elec. engring. So. Meth. U., 1961, Okla. State U., 1961-66; prof. elec. engring., head dept. Va. Poly. Inst., State U., 1966—. Served with USAAF, 1941-45. Mem. I.E.E.E., Am. Soc. Engring. Edn., A.A.A.S. Author: (with H.E. Koenig) Electromechanical System Theory, 1961; Mathematical Modeling of Physical Networks, 1968; also articles. Home: 801 Dickerson Lane Blacksburg VA 24060

BLACKWELL, WILLIAM RAY, city mgr.; b. Lockhart, Tex., Jan. 13, 1927; s. Joseph Vernon and Mary Katherine (Tate) B.; B.S. in Civil Engring., Tex. A. and M. U., 1955; m. Joyce Rheinlander, Feb. 8, 1948; children—Diane, Cheryl Ann, David Alan. Student engr. Profl. baseball player St. Louis Cardinals, 1948-55; civil engr. Lockwood, Andrews & Newnam, cons. engrs., Victoria, Tex., 1955-59; city mgr. Freeport, Tex., 1959-64, Galveston, 1964-67, Lubbock, Tex., 1967—. Served with USNR, 1945-46. Mem. Tex. City Mgrs. Assn. (pres. 1970-71), Internat. City Mgrs. Assn., Tau Beta Pi. Presbyn. Rotarian. Home: 3811 61st St Lubbock TX 79413 Office: PO Box 2000 Lubbock TX 79457

BLACKWOOD, ALLISTER CLARK, educator; b. Calgary, Alta., Can., Nov. 22, 1915; s. Allister Chester and Bessie (Saunders) B.; B.Sc., U. Alta., 1942, M.Sc., 1944; Ph.D., U. Wis., 1949; m. Mildred Marsh, May 1, 1943; children—Alan, Marsha, Susan. With Canadian Nat. Research Council, 1944-46, 48-57, sr. research officer Saskatoon, Sask., 1956-57; prof. microbiology Macdonald Coll., McGill U., 1957—, chmn. dept., 1957-68. Fellow Royal Soc. Can.; mem. Canadian Soc. Microbiologists (pres. 1964-65), Que. Soc. de Microbiologie, Am. Soc. Microbiology, Soc. Gen. Microbiology, Soc., Applied Bacteriology, Sigma Psi, Kappa Sigma. Research microbial physiology and fermentations. Home: Windcrest Rd Hudson Quebec Canada

BLACKWOOD, EASLEY, composer, concert pianist, educator; b. Indpls., Apr. 21, 1933; s. Easley and Beatrice (Overall) B.; Mus.B., Yale, 1953, Mus.M., 1954; student French Nat. Conservatory Music, 1954-57. Prof. music U. Chgo.; commissions by Fromm Foundation, Koussevitzky Music Found., Walter W. Naumburg Found., G. Schirmer Co., Yale, Cin. Orch., Chgo. Symphony, Indpls. Symphony; grantee Nat. Inst. Arts and Letters. Composer: Sonata for Viola and Piano, Opus 1, 1953; Chamber Symphony for 14 Winds, 1954; Symphony No. 1, 1955; Quartet No. 1, 1957; Concertino for 5 Instruments, 1959; Quartet No. 2, 1959; Sonata for Violin and Piano, 1960; Fantasy for Violoncello and Piano, 1960; Symphony No. 2, 1960; Sonatas for Violin, Viola; Concertos for Flute, Oboe, Violin and Piano; 3 symphonies. Recipient Creative Arts award citation Brandeis U., 1968; Quantrell award U. Chgo., 1970. Mem. A.S.C.A.P. Home: 5300 South Shore Dr Chicago IL 60615 Office: care Melvin Kaplan Inc 85 Riverside Dr New York City NY

BLACKWOOD, GEORGE W., chem. co. exec.; b. Boston, 1914; A.B., Harvard, 1937. With Dewey & Almy Chem. Co., 1937-54; v.p. container and chem. specialties div., pres. Dewey & Almy Chem. div., group exec. indsl. chemistry group W.R. Grace & Co., 1954-67, exec. v.p., dir., 1968—; dir. Am. Synthetic Rubber Corp., Am. Rubber & Chem. Co.; corporator Charlestown Savs. Bank, Boston. Home: 29 Wedgemere Av Winchester MA 01890 Office: 62 Whittemore Av Cambridge MA 02040*

BLADEN, VINCENT WHEELER, educator; b. Stoke-on-Trent, Eng., Aug. 14, 1900; s. Joseph Clement and Easter Gertrude (Cleverley) B.; B.A., Balliol Coll., Oxford (Eng.) U., 1921, M.A., 1926; LL.D., U. Western Ontario, Carleton U., McGill U.; Litt.D., Acadia U.; D.Sc. Soc., Laval U.; m. Margaret Landon Briggs, June 12, 1929; children—Sarah Landon (Mrs. Lloyd Banbury), Katharine Mary, Norah Cleverley (Mrs. W. B. Ferguson). Mem. faculty U. Toronto, 1921—, prof. polit. economy, 1940-70, prof. emeritus, 1970—, chmn. dept. 1953-59, dir. Inst. Indsl. Relations, 1946-50, dir. Inst. Bus. Adminstrn., 1950-53, dean faculty arts and scis., 1959-66, dean emeritus, 1970—. Royal commnr. to inquire into Canadian automotive industry, 1960-61; chmn. Commn. Financing Higher Edn. Can., 1964-65; chmn. Adjustment Assistance Bd., 1965-71. Fellow Royal Soc. Can. (pres. sect. 11, 1958); mem. Can. Polit. Sci. Assn. (pres. 1947-48), Royal Econ. Soc., Am. Econ. Assn., Econ. History Assn. Editor Canadian Jour. Econs. and Polit. Sci., 1936-47. Home: 400 Walmer Rd Toronto 10 Ontario Canada

BLADES, BRIAN BREWER, surgeon; b. Scottsville, Kan., July 4, 1906; s. Samuel Thomas and Martha Minette (Hoffmeister) B.; A.B., U. Kan., 1924-28; M.D., Washington U. Sch. Medicine, 1928-32; fellow in surgery, 1936- 38; m. Virginia Layton, Jan. 1, 1932; childrenBeverly, Judith, Brian. Surg. intern Henry Ford Hosp., Detroit, 1932-33; 2d (Cornell) div., Bellevue Hosp., N.Y., 1934-36; instr. clin. surgery, Washington U. Sch. Medicine, 1938-41; asst. prof. 1941—; asst. surg. Barnes Hosp., Children's Hosp. and Maternity Hosp., St. Louis; vis. surgeon Mo. Pacific R.R. Hosp., St. Louis; Lewis Saltz prof. surgery, George Washington U. Sch. Medicine, Washington, D.C., 1946—. Served as lt. col., M.C., AUS, World War II; chief thoracic surg. sect. Walter Reed Gen. Hosp., Washington, cons. surgeon gen. in thoracic surgery, USAF. Awarded Legion of Merit (U.S.). Mem. Am. Assn. Thoracic Surgery, So. Surg. Assn., Am. Coll. Surgeons, Soc. Clin. Surgery, Am. Surg. Assn., Alpha Omega Alpha, Sigma Xi, Beta Theta Pi. Club: Halsted. Assoc. editor, Jour. Thoracic Surgery. Contbr. to current med. jours. on thoracic surgery. Home: 5317 Albermarle Westmoreland Hills Washington DC 20016 Office: George Washington Univ Hosp 2150 Pennsylvania Av Washington DC 20037

BLADES, HERBERT WILLIAM pharm. co. exec.; b. Dubuque, Ia., Apr. 27, 1908; s. Walter and Nellie (Quilliam) B.; B.S., Northwestern U., 1931; m. Jane Larison Marshall, June 1, 1933; children—John William, William Stoddard. Gen. mgr. John Wyeth and Bro., Can., Ltd., 1935-38; v.p., gen. mgr. Kolynos Co., 1938- 43; asst. to pres. Am. Home Products Corp., 1943-46, exec. v.p., 1960—, also dir.; exec. v.p. Wyeth Labs. div., 1946-56, pres., 1956-71, chmn. bd., 1971—; dir. Carlo Erba, S.p.A., Milan, Italy, Provident Mutual Life Ins. Co. Phila., Phila. Nat. Bank, Phila. Cons. White House Conf. on Aging, 1961; dir. Pa. Plan to Develop Scientists Med. Research. Bd. dirs. Bryn Mawr (Pa.) Hosp., Pharm. Mfrs. Assn. Found., Inc. Recipient Order of Honneur et Merite (Republic Haiti), 1959. Mem. Pharm. Mfrs. Assn. (dir.), Delta Upsilon. Presbyn. (elder, trustee). Clubs: Racquet (Phila.); St. Davids (Wayne). Home: 3 Fenimore Lane St Davids PA 19087 Office: PO Box 8299 Philadelphia PA 19101

BLADES, WILLIAM HAMLET, lawyer; b. Athens, Tex., Aug. 5, 1894; s. Joseph Robert and Ida Irene (Deupree) B.; LL.B., U. Texas, 1920; m. Agnes Mills, Aug. 5, 1924; children—Joseph Hamlet, Betty

Agnes (Mrs. Ted B. Reed), Bonnie Lynnette (Mrs. George N. Allen, Jr.). Licensed to practice, 1920, since practiced in Tex.; sr. partner Blades, Crain & Winters; local atty. Atlantic Richfield Oil Co. 1956—; gen. atty., gen. counsel, dir. Houston Oil Co. Tex. 1921-56. Former v.p. bd. trustees Meth. Hosp., Houston. Served as capt., inf., U.S. Army, World War I. Mem. Am., Houston bar assns., State Bar Tex., Delta Kappa Epsilon. Democrat. Methodist. Mason. Clubs: Good Samaritan (founder, dir.), Houston. Home: 1245 Wood Hollow Houston TX 77027 Office: San Jacinto Bldg Houston TX 77002

BLADY, JOHN VALENTINE, surgeon; b. Milw., Dec. 16, 1905; s. Valentine and Kathryn (Grolewski) B.; B.S., U. Wis., 1929; M.D., Duke 1932; m. Mary Esther Fisher, Aug. 9, 1939 (dec. 1962); children—John Fisher, Kathryn Diane (Mrs. John T. McNeill, III); m. 2d, Rose Dina Cadman, Oct. 20, 1962; 1 stepdau., Mary Frances Dina McElroy. Surg. intern Duke Med. Sch., 1932-33; resident radiology Temple U. Hosp., 1933-35; surg. resident, postgrad. cancer surgery Rockefeller fellow, Meml. Hosp., N.Y.C., 1936-39; practice specializing surgery head and neck, Phila., 1939—; dir. tumor clinic Temple U. Med. Center, 1940—; clin. prof. surgery Temple U. Health Scis. Center, 1950—; cons. oncology Taylor Hosp., Ridley Park, Pa., Delaware Hosp., Wilmington, Shriner's Hosp., Phila., VA Hosp., Phila. Bd. dirs. Phila. div. Am. Cancer Soc., 1945—, pres., 1959-60. Recipient award contbns. cancer control Am. Cancer Soc., 1950. Mem. Phila. County Med. Soc. (bd. dirs. 1956-68, pres. 1967), James Ewing Soc. (pres. 1947-48), Wainwright Tumor Clinic Assn. (pres. 1957-58), Am. Radium Soc. (sec. 1968, pres. 1971-72), A.C.S., Soc. Head and Neck Surgeons, A.M.A., Pa. Med. Soc., Phila. Coll. Physicians, Phila. Acad. Surgery, Med. Club Phila., Doctors Golf Assn. Phila. (pres. 1968). Clubs: Phila. Country, Union League (Phila.); Atlantic Country. Research radium applicator for treatment cancer nasopharynx, study sialography, salivary gland tumors, restoration of facial function with nerve grafts, treatment cancer oral cavity, larynx and hypopharanx. Home: 2009 Stone Ridge Lane Villanova PA 19085 Office: 2201 Benjamin Franklin Pwky Philadelphia PA 19130

BLAEDEL, WALTER JOHN, educator, chemist; b. N.Y.C., May 26, 1916; s. George L. and Marie T. (Grundler) R.; B.A., U. Cal. at Los Angeles, 1938, M.A., 1939; Ph.D., Stanford, 1942; m. Barbara Jeane Bennett, Feb. 1, 1942; children—Mark Edward, Kenneth Lee, Robert Walter. Instr., Northwestern U., 1941-44; research asso. Manhattan Project, U. Chgo., 1944-46, U. Cal. at Berkeley, 1946-47; mem. faculty U. Wis., 1947—, prof. chemistry, 1957—. Mem. com. postdoctoral fellowships Nat. Acad. Sci., 1964-68, adv. panel 31,000, 1968-70. Recipient award OSRD, 1945. Manhattan Project, 1945. Mem. Am. Chem. Soc. (chmn. Wis. sect. 1965-66), Phi Beta Kappa, Sigma Xi, Alpha Chi Sigma, Phi Lambda Upsilon. Author: Elementary Quantitative Analysis, 2d edit., 1963; also articles. Mem. adv. bd. Analytical Chemistry, 1966-68. Home: 6201 S Highlands Av Madison, WI 53705.

BLAES, EMMET ANDREW, lawyer; b. Cherryvale, Kan., Apr. 18, 1907; s. Mathias and Theresa (Koehler) B.; J.D., Creighton U., 1931; m. Anna Sebron Kranda, Oct. 3, 1933; children—Charles Emmet, Robert Eugene, Elizabeth Ann. Admitted to Kan. and Neb. bars, 1931; practice in Wichita, Kan., 1931—; sr. partner firm Jochems, Sargent & Blaes, 1960—. Asst. sec., dir. Kan. Beef Industries, Inc.; sec., dir. Met. Devel. Co., Inc.; dir. Union Nat. Bank, Wichita, Kansas. Pres. Wichita Community Planning Council, 1948-49, Nat. Council Catholic Men, 1948-50. Bd. dirs. Cath. Diocese Wichita; trustee Benedictine Coll., Atchison, Kansas. Decorated knight St. Gregory, Benemerenti medal. Mem. Am., Kan., Wichita bar assns., Wichita C. of C. (past dir.), Wichita Urban League (past pres.), Kan. Catholic Conf. (bd. govs.), Kan. Jud. Council (adv. com.), Delta Theta Phi, Phi Kappa Theta, Alpha Sigma Nu. Democrat. Roman Catholic. K.C. (past dept. Kan.). Clubs: Wichita Country, Wichita. Home: 2011 Porter Wichita KS 67203 Office: Farmers and Bankers Life Bldg Wichita KS 67202

BLAESSER, WILLARD WILLIAM, educator; b. Cedarburg, Wis., Nov. 11, 1912; s. George William and Lydia (Jochem) B.; B.S., U. Wis., 1934, M.A., 1940; Rockefeller Found. fellow mental hygiene, Columbia, summer 1939; Ed.D., George Washington U., 1953; m. Helen Ann Geimer, Oct. 4, 1941; children—Ann Marie, Jean Margaret, Brian William. Tchr. high sch., Sheboygan, Wis., 1934-36; asst. dir. div. social edn., instr. edn. U. Wis., 1936-39, asst. dean men, coordinator student personnel, 1939-45; asst. dean students, dir. counseling center, U. Chgo., 1945-46; dir. student personnel, asso. prof. edn. U. Mont., 1946-47; dean students, asso. prof. edn. Wash. State U., 1947-50, on leave, 1949-50; head student personnel programs div. higher edn. U.S. Office Edn., 1949-53; dean students, prof. ednl. psychology U. Utah, 1953-62; prof. edn., dean students Coll. City N.Y., 1962-69; prof. counseling and psychology Ariz. State U., 1969—. Fellow Nat. Tng. Inst. for Applied Behavioral Sci., 1957—; chmn. policy com. Intermountain Group Devel. Lab., 1958-62; sr. asso. Leadership Resources, Inc. Spl. cons., editor war service opportunities Am. Council Edn., 1943, adv. com. Japanese univs. student personnel insts., 1952-57; cons. Haile Selassie I U., 1960; Asia Found. cons. U. Ceylon, 1966-67; mem. adv. com. Scarsdale Adult Edn. Sch., 1963-68; mem. edn. policy com. Dept. of Def., 1950-53. Pres. Greater N.Y. Council for Fgn. Students, 1963-65. Bd. dirs. Nat. Tng. Inst. for Applied Behavioral Sci. Mem. Nat. Assn. Student Personnel Adminstrs. (chmn. internat. relations com. 1964—, mem. exec. com. 1965—), Am. Coll. Personnel Assn. (v.p. 1947-48, executive council 1943-50, 1953-55, president 1955-57), Am. Personnel and Guidance Assn. (member executive council 1955-57), Am. Psychol. Assn. (chmn. com. counselor tng., div. counseling and guidance 1950-51), Council Guidance and Personnel Assns. (chmn. com. manpower utilization 1950-51), Western Personnel Inst. (chmn. acad. council 1959-61), N.E.A. (adv. com. ednl. policies commn.). Bd. editors Personnel and Guidance Jour., 1956-60, Jr. Coll. Student Personnel, 1971—. Home: 314 E Del Rio Dr Tempe AZ 85281

BLAGGINI, BENJAMIN FRANKLIN, R.R. exec.; b. New Orleans, Apr. 15, 1916; s. B.F. and Maggie (Switzer) B.; B.S. St. Mary's of Tex., 1936; advanced mgmt. program Harvard, 1955; m. Anne Payton, Sept. 9, 1937; children—Connie Sue (Mrs. James S. Malott), Anne (Mrs. David M. Krattebol). With So. Pacific Co. (Tex. and La. lines), 1936-56, successively rod-man, mem. engring dept., asst. to chief engr., exec. asst., asst. to exec. v.p., 1936-56, v.p. S.P. Co., San Francisco, 1956-63, exec. v.p., 1963-64, pres., 1964—, chief exec. officer, 1968—, dir., 1963—, dir. St. Louis Southwestern Ry. Co. Gen Chmn. United Bay Area Crusade, 1962, pres., 1968; trustee Nat. Indsl. Conf. Bd.; adv. council Stanford Grad. Sch. Bus. Mem. Assn. Am. Railroads (dir.), Cal. Chamber of Commerce (director), American Railway Engring. Assn., Harvard Bus. Sch. Assn. Clubs: Burlingame (Cal.) Country; Houston; California (Los Angeles); San Francisco Golf, Stock Exchange, Pacific Union, Bohemian (San Francisco); Links (N.Y.C.); Chicago; (Washington). Home: 1170 Sacramento St San Francisco CA 94108 Office: 65 Market St San Francisco CA 94105

BLAGONRAROV, ANATOLI ARKADYEVICH, Soviet scientist; b. Ankovo, Russia, June 1, 1894; student Mikhailovskaya Sch. Arty., then Higher Sch. Arty.; grad. Military- Tech. Acad., 1929; Dr. Tech. Scis., 1938. Charge dept. small arms Acad. Arty., later founder and dir. Inf. Weapons Research Center, also developed ednl. program for ordnance engrs.; charge Dzerzhinski Mil. Acad., World War II, specializing improvement arty. weapons, instr., research scientist, 1929-46, prof., 1938—; head Soviet Acad. Arty. Sci., 1946-64; head Soviet delegation Internat. Congress on Missiles, Paris, 1956; chmn. Soviet delegation Internat. Rocket and Satellite Conf., U.S., 1957; dir. Inst. Study of Machines, Moscow, 1953—. Served as comdr. units Red Army, Bolshevik Revolution; lt. gen. arty., World War II. Decorated Order of Lenin (3 times), Order of Red Banner of Labor (3 times); named meritorious sci. and tech. worker Soviet Union, 1940; recipient Stalin prize for contbn. to arty., 1941. Mem. Soviet Acad. Scis. (academician-sec. Dept. Scis. 1957-63; chmn. commn. on study and use of space; v.p. com. space research), Czechoslovak Acad. Scis. Author: Foundations of Design of Automatic Armaments, 1931; also numerous sci. monographs on inf., aviation armament, ballistics, kinematics, rockets and automatic weapons. Editor-in-chief Mashinovedenie (Study of Machines). Address: care Academy of Science of USSR 14 Lenin Prospekt Moscow USSR

BLAHERTY, FRANK, (John Francis), journalist; b. Caledon, Ont., Can., Dec. 18, 1903; s. James and Anne (Wallace) F.; B.A., U. Toronto, 1925, M.A., 1928; student Osgoode Hall Law Sch., 1925-28; m. Dorothy Eva Rhodes, Aug. 28, 1934; children—Mary Anne (Mrs. Hubert Dittmann), Helen Theresa (Mrs. John Dempster), Roderick John, Kathleen Dorothy. Reporter, Toronto Daily Star, 1925-26; reporter, wire-editor, Parliamentary corr. Canadian Press, 1927-45; Parliamentary corr. Toronto Globe and Mail, 1946-47; Canadian corr. Chgo. Daily News, 1947-70; pub. nat. bus. news report Buchanan's Bull., 1945-69; pres., mgr. Nat. Editorial Bur., 1965—. Organized pub. relations and information services for Marian Congress Ottawa. Mem. Canadian Inst. Internat. Affairs, Canadian C. of C. (first Bowater award for journalism 1956), Parliamentary Press Gallery, Sigma Delta Chi. Clubs: Nat. Press Can. (past pres.), University (Ottawa). Home: 539 Hilson Av Ottawa Ontario Canada Office: 150 Wellington St Ottawa Ontario Canada

BLAIK, EARL HENRY, mfg. corp. exec.; b. Detroit, Feb. 15, 1897; s. William Douglas and Margaret Jane B.; A.B., Miami U., Oxford, O., 1918, LL.D. (honorary), 1959; B.S., U. S. Mil. Acad., 1920; student Cavalry Sch., Fort Riley, Kan., 1920-21; m. Merle McDowell, Oct. 20, 1924; children—William McDowell, Robert McDowell. Commd. 1st lt. cav. U.S. Army, 1920; served with 8th cav., 1922-23; resigned 1923; Mem. firm M.D. and E.H. Blaik, builders, Dayton, O., 1923-34; head football coach Dartmouth Coll., 1934-40; part time football coach U.S. Mil. Acad., West Point, 1927-34; 1941, dir. athletics, 1949, serving as lt. col. U.S. Army, 1943, col. cav., 1944; v.p., dir. Avco Corp., N.Y.C., 1959-60, dir., chmn. exec. com., 1960—; chmn. exec. com. Blaik Oil Co., Oklahoma City trustee John F. Kennedy Library; mem. adv. bd. MacArthur Meml. Found.; sponsor Hampton Inst. Named Coach of the Yr., 1946; Coach of Yr., Washington Touchdown Club, 1953; named to Nat. Football Hall of Fame, 1959; State of Va. Sportsman Club award, Touchdown Club of N.Y. award, 1958, Gold Medal award Nat. Football Found. and Hall of Fame, 1966. Mem. Assn. Grads. U.S. Mil. Acad. (trustee), Assn. U.S. Army (adv. bd.), Beta Theta Pi, Tau Kappa Alpha. Clubs: Blind Brook, Metropolitan (N.Y.); Burning Tree (Washington); La Quinta (Palm Desert, Cal.). Contbr. to mags. Home: 73-165 Fiddleneck Lane Palm Desert CA 92260 Office: 750 3d Av New York City NY 10017

BLAIN, DANIEL, physician; b. Kashing, China, Dec. 17, 1898; s. John Mercer and Claudia (Grier) B.; student McCallie Sch., 1916; B.A., Washington and Lee U., 1921; pre-med., U. Chgo., 1924; M.D., Vanderbilt U. Sch. Medicine, 1929; m. Sarah Logan Starr, Oct. 15, 1936; 1 son, Daniel. Intern, Peter Bent Brigham Hosp. and Boston City Hosp., 1929-31; fellow Austen Riggs Found., Stockbridge, Mass., 1931-32, resident physician Silver Hill Sanitarium, New Canaan, Conn., 1932-35; pvt. practice, N.Y.C., 1932-42; chief, neuro-psychiatry service, Dept. Medicine and Surgery, VA, 1945-48; capt. USPHS 1942-45; medical dir., War Shipping Adminstrn.; chmn. Dept. Psychiatry, Georgetown U. Sch. Medicine 1947-48, clin. prof. psychiatry 1948-58; prof. clin. psychiatry U. Pa., 1958; project dir. mental health tng. and research Western Interstate Commn. Higher Edn., Boulder, Colo., 1958-59; state dir. mental hygiene, Cal., 1959-63; cons. social psychiatry Pa. Hosp; director of the Philadelphia State Hospital; prof. clin. psychiatry U. Pa. Med. dir. Am. Psychiat. Assn., 1948- 58; cons. Nat. Assn. Mental Health, 1958—. Cons. VA; mem. expert com. mental health WHO. Diplomate Am. Bd. of Psychiatry and Neurology. Fellow Am. Psychiat. Assn. (pres. 1964-65), A.M.A., A.C.P.; mem. Am. Psycho-analytic Assn., Soc. for Research in Nervous and Mental Diseases, Alpha Omega Alpha, Beta Theta Pi. Rotarian. Home: 2100 Clarkson Av Philadelphia PA 19144 Office: Phila State Hosp Philadelphia PA 19114

BLAINE, CHARLES GILLESPIE, lawyer; b. N.Y.C., Mar. 12, 1925; s. James G. and Marion (Dow) B.; grad. St. Paul's Sch., 1943; student Amherst Coll., 1946; LL.B., U. Va., 1948; m. Gloria Beckwith, Dec. 16, 1944; children—Cathryn D. (Mrs. J.D. Muzzy), Susan B. (Mrs. J.B. Nesbitt), Charles Gillespie. Admitted to N.Y. bar, 1949, since practiced in Buffalo; now partner firm Phillips, Lytle, Hitchcock, Blaine & Huber. Dir. Marine Midland Bank-Western, Marine Midland Banks, Inc., Monroe Abstract & Title Corp., Birge Co., Inc., H.R. Hunt Motor Corp. Pres., dir. Legal Aid Bur. Buffalo, 1967-68; mem. Bd. Edn. City of Buffalo, 1970—; bd. dirs. State U. Coll. at Buffalo, N.Y., 1965—, Childrens Aid Soc., 1967—. Mem. Buffalo Fine Arts Acad., 1970—. Served to lt. (j.g.) USNR, 1943-46. Mem. Am., N.Y. State (chmn. banking, corp. and bus. law sect. 1966-67), Erie County bar assns., Assn. Bar City N.Y., Buffalo & Erie County Hist. Soc., Grosvenor Soc. Episcopalian. Clubs: Saturn, Mid-Day, Pundit, Marshall, Lawyers (Buffalo); Cherry Hill (Ridgeway, Ont., Can.); Metropolitan (Washington). Home: 20 Berkeley Pl Buffalo NY 14209 Office: Marine Trust Bldg Buffalo NY 14203

BLAINE, GRAHAM B., investments; b. Taunton, Mass., Mar. 26, 1894; s. Charles H. and Emma J. (Burt) B.; A.B., Harvard, 1917; m. Katharine W. Tweed, Jan. 5, 1918; children—Dr. Graham B., Jr., Katharine W. Swan, Lorna B. Halper, Charlotte W. Vaughn. Vice pres., treas. Kidder Peabody Acceptance Corp., Boston, 1922-27; v.p. Internat. Acceptance Bank and Internat. Manhattan Co., Inc., N.Y.C., 1927-32; v.p. Bank of Manhattan Co., 1932-48, vice chmn. Chase Manhattan Bank, 1955-57; limited vice chmn. Chase Manhattan Bank, 1955-57; gen. partner Tucker Anthony & R. L. Day, N.Y.C., investment bankers, 1957-68; trustee Dollar Savs. Bank, N.Y.C. Episcopalian. Clubs: Harvard, Century Assn., Down Town Association (N.Y.C.); Somerset (Boston). Home: 101 E 85th St New York City NY 10028 Office: 120 Broadway New York City NY 10005

BLAINE, VIVIAN, actress; b. Newark, Nov. 21, 1924; d. Lionel P. and Wilhelmina (Tepley) Stapleton; student pub. schs.; m. Manny G. Frank, Jan. 10, 1945 (div. 1956); m. 2d, Milton R. Rackmil, June 1959 (div. 1961). Motion picture actress 20th Century Fox Studios, Hollywood, Cal., 1942—, starring in Greenwich Village, Something for the Boys, Nob Hill, State Fair, Doll Face, Three Little Girls in Blue, If I'm Lucky, for Metro Goldwyn Mayer in Skirts Ahoy, headline performer Roxy Theatre, N.Y.C., Chgo. Theatre, others in U.S. and Eng., 1946-50; starring stage role in Guys and Dolls, N.Y.C., 1950, London Coliseum, 1953, command performance Coliseum Theatre, Eng., 1954, motion picture version for Samuel Goldwyn, 1955; guest star maj. TV programs; star motion picture Public Pidgeon No. 1 for RKO, also Broadway prodn. Hatful of Rain, 1956. Recipient Donaldson award for best debut performance, stage prodn. Guys and Dolls, 1951, named best dressed woman Fashion Acad., 1952. Mem. Am. Guild Variety Artists, Screen Actors Guild, A.F.T.R.A. Actors Fund, Artists Equity. Home: Sutton Pl S New York City NY 10022 Office: 1601 Lindacrest Dr Beverly Hills CA 90210

BLAIR, BENJAMIN FRANKLIN, ins. co. exec.; b. Lansdowne, Pa., July 13, 1908; s. Joel Allen and Grace (Webster) B.; B.A., Haverford Coll., 1930; M.A., Princeton, 1931; m. Ann Redman Willits, Dec. 9, 1939; children—Judith Ann (Mrs. Louis R. Santiago), Elizabeth (Mrs. A. Thomas Andrews III), Benjamin F. With Provident Mut. Life Ins. Co., Phila., 1931—, actuarial asst., 1942-46, asst. actuary, 1946-49, asso. actuary, 1949-57, actuary, 1957—, v.p., 1959—. Fellow Soc. of Actuaries. Republican. Quaker. Author various articles pub. in profl. jours. Home: 64 Princeton Rd Havertown, PA 19083. Office: 4601 Market St Philadelphia PA 19101

BLAIR, BOWEN, investment banker; b. Bar Harbor, Me., Aug. 4, 1918; s. William McCormick and Helen Haddock (Bowen) B.; grad. Groton Sch., 1936; B.A., Yale, 1940; postgrad. Harvard, 1940-41; m. Joan Halpine Smith, Dec. 9, 1950; children—Joan Bowen. With William Blair & Co., Chgo., 1946- -, partner, 1950—; dir. Continental Casualty Co., Continental Assurance Co., CNA Financial Corp., Nat. Fire Ins. Co. Hartford, Valley Forge Ins. Co., Transcontinental Ins. Co. of N.Y., Nat. Fire Co. of Hartford, Peoples Gas Co., Am. Casualty Co. of Reading, Spaulding & Co., Transp. Ins. Co. N.Y. Trustee Art Inst., Chgo., Chgo. Hist. Soc. Field Museum Natural History, Beloit Coll., Cradle Soc., Graceland Cemetery. Clubs: Chicago; Onwentsia (Lake Forest, Ill.); Racquet and Tennis (N.Y.C.). Home: 3 S Green Bay Rd Lake Forest IL 60045 Office: 135 S LaSalle St Chicago IL 60603

BLAIR, CHARLES EMMETT, dept. store exec.; b. Laramie, Wyo., Mar. 29, 1905; s. Charles E. and Elizabeth (Norholm) B.; student U. Wyo., 1923-24; B.S., Armour Inst. Tech., 1927; m. Elinor Beatrice Morrissey, July 17, 1924; children—Elizabeth (Mrs. Richard Starkey), Charlotte (Mrs. Thomas Sand), Charles Emmett III. With White House Dept. Store, Laramie and Sidney, Neb., 1928-31; successively store mgr., dist. mgr., operating mgr. v.p. Scott Burr Stores, div. Butler Bros., Chgo., 1932-48; v.p., treas. J.M. McDonald Co., Hastings, Neb., 1948-60, pres., dir., 1960—; dir. City Nat. Bank; pres. Hastings Corp., 1952-53. Trustee Neb. Found. Pvt. Colls., 1971—. Mem. Hastings C. of C. (pres. 1961), Neb. Assn. Commerce and Industry (pres. 1969). Elk, K.C. Home: 739 N Pine Av Hastings NB 68901 Office: 2635 W 2d St Hastings NB 68901

BLAIR, CHARLES MELVIN, mfg. co. exec.; b. Vernon, Tex., Oct. 24, 1910; s. Charles Melvin and Sallie (Gilliland) B.; B.A., Rice Inst., 1931, M.A., 1932; Ph.D., Cal. Inst. Tech., 1935; m. Catherine E. Stone, June 12, 1936; children—Charles Melvin, Sally. Research chemist Tretolite div. Petrolite Corp., St. Louis, 1935-43, research dir. for corp., 1943-53, pres., 1953- 64, dir. Southeastern Gas Devel. Co., Olney, Ill., Blair Petroleum Co., Fullerton, Cal., Am. Petroleum Internat., Inc., Los Angeles; vice chancellor, treas. Washington U., St. Louis, 1964-67; chmn. bd. Magna Corp., Santa Fe Springs, Cal., 1967—. Mem. Am. Council Edn., Am. Chem. Soc., A.A.A.S., Am. Petroleum Inst., Phi Beta Kappa, Sigma Xi, Phi Lambda Upsilon. Clubs: Hacienda, Petroleum (Los Angeles). Patents and publs. in surface chemistry and petroleum processing. Home: 3625 Coronado Dr Fullerton CA 92632 Office: 11808 S Bloomfield Av Santa Fe Springs CA 90670

BLAIR, CLAUDE MACLARY, banker; b. Columbia, Tenn., May 5, 1913; s. Anderson McClary and Lucy (Howell) B.; LL.B., Atlanta Law Sch., 1949; m. Rose Bottagaro, June 9, 1945; children—Randy, Barbara, Julie. With Am. Tel. & Tel. Corp., 1930-57, v.p. space communications programs, 1961-64; v.p., gen. mgr. Mountain States Tel. & Tel. Co., 1958-60; v.p., dir. Pacific N.W. Bell Telephone Co., 1960-61; president Ohio Bell Telephone Co., 1964-67; pres. Nat. City Bank, Cleve., 1967—, also dir.; dir. Gould Inc., J.M. Smucker Co., University Circle Inc., Trustee Boy Scouts Am. Served to maj. Signal Corps, AUS, 1942-46, 51-52. Mem. Mus. Arts Assn. (trustee), Armed Forces Communications Assn. (dir. Washington 1955), Ga. Bar Assn. Clubs: Union, Country, Pepper Pike, Clevelander, Tavern. Home: 2711 Sherbrooke Shaker Heights OH 44120 Office: Nat City Bank 623 Euclid Av Cleveland OH 44114

BLAIR, CLAY DREWRY, Jr., writer, editor; b. Lexington, Va., May 1, 1925; s. Clay Drewry and Marie Louise (Barreto) B.; student Tulane U., 1946-48, Columbia, 1948-49; m. Agnes Kemp Devereux, Nov. 25, 1950; children—Marie Louise, Clay Drewry III, Joseph Devereux (dec.), Sibyl Devereux, Kemp Devereux, Robert Augustus Drewry, Christopher Ryan. Correspondent Time mag., 1949-55; mil. corr. Life Mag., 1955-57; asso. editor Saturday Evening Post, 1957-61, asst. mng. editor, 1961-62, mng. editor, 1962, editor, 1963-64; v.p., editorial dir. Curtis Pub. Co., 1962, sr. v.p., editor-in-chief, 1963-64, exec. v.p., dir., 1964; spl. research 16th, 17th, 18th Century naval history and marine archaeology, 1957—. Served with USNR, 1943-46. Decorated Submarine Combat insignia. Member Beta Theta Pi. Roman Catholic. Clubs: Metropolitan (Washington); Chevy Chase (Md.). Author: The Atomic Submarine and Admiral Rickover, 1954; (with James Shepley) The Hydrogen Bomb, 1954; Beyond Courage, 1955; (for Maj. Ward Millar) Valley of the Shadow, 1955; Nautilus 90 North (with Comdr. William R. Anderson), 1959; Diving for Pleasure and Treasure, 1960; Always Another Dawn (with A. Scott Crossfield), 1960.

BLAIR, DAVID, ballet dancer; b. Halifax, Yorkshire, Eng., July 27, 1932; s. John and Zette Carolyne Elizabeth (Whiteley) B.; ed. Trinity Sch., Halifax, also Royal Ballet Sch., London; m. Maryon Lane, June 22, 1957; children—Catherine and Diana (twins). Mem. Sadler's Wells Ballet (now Royal Ballet), 1948—, premier dancer, 1955—; prin. roles include The Catch, 1948, Children's Corner, 1948, Capt. Belaye in Pineapple Poll, 1950-51, 59, Franz in Coppelia, 1951, Blue Bird, 1950, Red Knight in Checkmate, 1953, the miller in Three-Cornered Hat, 1953, prince in Cinderella, 1956, prince in Sleeping Beauty, 1955, prince in Swan Lake, 1955, Albrecht in Giselle, 1955, lead in premiere Prince of the Pagodas, 1957, Petroushka, 1959, Rake, 1950, Satan in Job, 1959, Colas in La Fille Mal Gardee, 1960; partner Alicia Markova in Giselle, 1957, Margot Fonteyn, 1956; U.S. tours with ballet company, 1951-52, 53, 55, 57, 60, 63, 65; choreographer Swan Lake for Am. Ballet Theatre at Met. Opera House, N.Y.C., 1967, Giselle, 1968. Decorated comdr. Order of British Empire. Home: 19 Holland Park Rd Kensington London W 14 England Office: Royal Opera House Covent Garden London W C 2 England

BLAIR, EDWARD MCCORMICK, investment banker; b. Chgo., July 18, 1915; s. William McCormick and Helen Haddock (Bowen) B.; grad. Groton Sch., 1934; B.A., Yale, 1938, M.B.A., Harvard, 1940; m. Elizabeth Graham Iglehart, June 28, 1941; children—Edward McCormick, Francis Iglehart. With William Blair & Co., Chgo., 1946—, partner, 1950—; chmn. bd. Growth Industry Shares, Inc., Chgo.; dir. Gen. Binding Corp. (Northbrook), Indsl. Nucleonics Corp.

(Columbus, Ohio), Field Enterprises, Inc., World Book Encyclopedia (Chgo.), Barber-Greene Co., Inc. (Aurora, Ill.), Marshall Field & Co. (Chgo.), Powers Regulator Co. (Skokie, Ill.), Del Monte Properties Co., Pebble Beach, Cal., Herman Miller, Inc., Zeeland, Mich. Bd. dirs. George M. Pullman Ednl. Found.; trustee James C. King Home Evanston, Ill., U. Chgo., Rush-Presbyterian-St. Luke's Med. Center, Chgo., Ill. Inst. Tech. Served to lt. comdr. USNR, 1941-46. Home: Crab Tree Farm Sheridan Rd Lake Bluff IL 60044 Office: 135 S LaSalle St Chicago IL 60603

BLAIR, EDWARD PAYSON, educator; b. Woodburn, Ore., Dec. 23, 1910; s. Oscar Newton and Bertha (Myers) B.; A.B., Seattle Pacific Coll., 1931; S.T.B., Bib. Sem. N.Y., 1934; Ph.D., Yale, 1939; Two Brothers fellow, Am. Sch. Oriental Research, Jerusalem, Palestine, 1935-36; m. Vivian Elizabeth Krisel, Sept. 13, 1934; children—Phyllis Marie, Sharon Louise. Prof. Bible, Seattle Pacific Coll., 1939-41, dean Sch. Religion, 1940-41; prof. O.T. lang. and lit. Bib. Sem. N.Y., 1941-42; faculty Garrett Theol. Sem., Evanston, Ill., 1942—, prof. N.T. interpretation, 1947-60, Harry R. Kendall prof. N.T. interpretation, 1960—. Cond. archaeol. soundings, Anata, Palestine, 1936; staff mem. excavation N.T. Jericho, Hashemite Kingdom Jordan, 1951, staff mem. excavation Shechem, Jordan, 1966, 68. Rep. Garrett Theol. Sem. on corp. Am. Schs. Oriental Research. Mem. Soc. Bib. Lit. and Exegesis, Am. Acad. Religion, Chgo. Soc. Bib. Research, Am. Assn. U. Profs. Author: The Acts and Apocalyptic Literature, 1946; The Bible and You, 1953; Getting to Know the Bible, 1956; Jesus in the Gospel of Matthew, 1960; Deuteronomy-Joshua, 1964. Editor: Jour. Bibl. Research, 1964-66; contbr. cons. editor The Illustrated Family Ency. of the Living Bible, 1968; The Interpreter's Dictionary of the Bible; Interpreter's One-Volume Commentary on the Bible. Home: 2021 Harrison St Evanston IL 60201

BLAIR, FRANK, TV personality; b. Yemassee, S.C., May 30, 1915; ed. Charleston Coll.; m. Lillian Stoddard, 8 children. Newsman on Today show, 1951-. Served with USNR as flight instr. and transport pilot. Roman Catholic. Address: Ocean Dr Stamford CT 06902

BLAIR, GEORGE KEITH, shoe co. exec.; b. Toronto, Ont., Can., Sept. 29, 1924; s. Andrew and Georgetta (Mossop) B.; B.Commerce, U. Toronto, 1947; m. Ailene Holmes, Aug. 20, 1947; children—Barbara Lynn, David Andrew. With Can. Life Ins. Co., 1947-48; with Massey Ferguson Ltd., Toronto, 1948-69, gen. credit mgr., 1957-61, treas., 1961-66, comptroller, 1966-68, asst. to pres., 1968-69; dir. finance Bata Shoe Orgn., 1969—. Home: 9 Ashwood Crescent Toronto Ontario Canada Office: 59 Wynford Dr Don Mills Ontario Canada

BLAIR, GEORGE SIMMS, educator; b. Homewood, Kan., May 31, 1924; s. William Horace and Mary (Simms) B.; A.B., Kan. State Tchrs. Coll., Emporia, 1948, B.S. in Edn., 1948, M.S., 1949; Ph.D., Northwestern U., 1951; m. Gloria Jean Barnes, Sept. 10, 1949; children—David Lawrence, Rebecca Lynn. Asst. prof. polit. sci. U. Tenn., 1951-53; asst. prof. polit. sci. U. Pa., 1953-56, asso. prof., 1956-60; asso. prof. govt. Claremont (Cal.) Grad. Sch., 1960-64, prof., 1964—. Mem. Claremont City Planning Commn., 1964—. Mem. Scholars for Rockefeller, 1960, 68, Scholars for Nixon, 1960, 68, Scholars for Reagan, 1969-70. Bd. dirs. Greater Los Angeles Consortium. Served with AUS, 1943-46; PTO. Mem. Am. Polit. Sci. Assn., Am. Assn. U. Profs., Am. Soc. Pub. Adminstrn., Pi Sigma Alpha, Pi Gamma Mu. Republican. Methodist. Author: (with S.B. Sweeney) Metropolitan Analysis, 1958 (Fruin-Colnan award 1959); Cummulative Voting in Illinois, 1960; American Local Government, 1964; El Gobierno Local en Los Estados Unidos, 1966; American Legislatures, 1967; (with H.I. Flournoy) Legislative Bodies in California, 1967. Bd. editors: Western Polit. Quarterly, 1964-68. Home: 509 Bowling Green Dr Claremont CA 91711

BLAIR, GLENN MYERS, educator; b. Portland, Ore., Oct. 2, 1908; s. Oscar Newton and Bertha (Myers) B.; A.B., Seattle Pacific Coll., 1930; A.M., U. Wash., 1931; Ph.D., Columbia, 1938; m. Ruth Virginia Van Ness, June 7, 1934; children—Glenn Myers, Sally Virginia (Mrs. Donald Lee Leach). Arthur A. Denny fellow U. Wash., 1931-32; instr. math. Sedro-Woolley High Sch., 1932-33; head math. dept. Bremerton (Wash.) High Sch., 1933-36; dir. guidance and research Everett (Wash.) pub. schs., 1936-37; Tchrs. Coll. fellow Columbia, 1937-38; vis. prof. ednl. psychology U. Wash., summer 1937, U. Kan., 1938, Stanford, 1950; prof. ednl. psychology U. Ill., Urbana, 1938—, chmn. dept., 1948-52; spl. lectr. U. Chgo., Northwestern U., U. Wis., Syracuse U., U. Miami, U. W.Va., U. Mo.; co-dir. Reading Clinic, U. Ill., 1938-48. Fellow Am. Psychol. Assn. (past mem. exec. com.), Am. Ednl. Research Assn.; mem. Nat. Soc. Coll. Tchrs. Edn., Phi Delta Kappa, Kappa Delta Pi, Psi Chi. Author: Prediction of Freshman Success in the University of Washington, 1931; Mentally Superior and Inferior Children, 1938; Diagnostic and Remedial Teaching, 2d edit., 1956; Educational Psychology; Its Development and Present Status, 1948; Educational Psychology, 3d edit., 1968; Psychology of Adolescence for Teachers, 1964. Editor: The Words You Use, 1958. Home: 305 W Delaware Urbana IL 61801

BLAIR, GORDON WILLISTON, mfg. co. exec.; b. Phila., June 24, 1901; s. Gordon Munsey and Mary Elizabeth (Weldon) B.; student pub. schs., Can.; m. Patricia Kelley Brooke, July 3, 1937; children—Mary G. (Mrs. Charles A. White), Nancy V., Marcia B. Prin., Price Waterhouse & Co., C.P.A.'s, N.Y.C., 1924-29, 32-51; v.p. treas., Foreman State Corp., Chgo., 1929-32; mgmt. cons., N.Y.C., 1951-59; v.p., treas., dir. Crown Cork & Seal Co., Inc., Phila., 1959-71, now dir.; financial cons. U.S. Govt., Dept. Defense, USAF, Bur. of Budget, Ho. of Reps. Appropriation Com., Commerce, State Dept. Financial control exec. Citizens for Eisenhower-Nixon Com., 1952. Served to pilot officer RAF, World War I. C.P.A., N.Y., N.J., Pa., Ohio. Home: 245 Welsh Rd Huntingdon Valley PA 19006 Office: 9300 Ashton Rd Philadelphia PA 19114

BLAIR, HERBERT ARTHUR, utility exec.; b. Peoria, Ill., Feb. 29, 1912; s. Arthur C. and Catherine C. (Torris) B.; student pub. utilities exec. course, U. Mich., 1959; m. Marcella L. Coates, Oct. 3, 1934; children—Suzanne, Richard. With Central Ill. Light Co., Peoria, 1928—. Comptroller, 1958-66, sec., 1958-64, v.p. 1963-66, sr. v.p. finance, 1966-67, exec. v.p., 1967- 70, chmn. bd., chief exec. officer, 1970—, also dir. Dir. Jefferson Trust and Savs. Bank of Peoria. Mem. Ill. C. of C., Peoria Assn. Commerce. Clubs: Rotary, Creve Coeur (Peoria); M. Hawley Country. Home: 1728 W Baywood St Peoria IL 61614 Office: 300 Liberty St Peoria IL 61602

BLAIR, JAMES BIRNEY, broadcasting co. exec.; b. Spokane, Wash., Aug. 22, 1921; s. Harvey O. and Edna L. (Thompson) B.; B.A., Whitman Coll., 1945; m. Cleila Marcille Bohn, June 2, 1946; 1 dau., Pamela (Mrs. D. Elden Hopp). With KHQ, Inc., Spokane, Wash., 1946—, news editor, 1946-49, promotion dir., 1949-50, radio sales, 1950-51, radio sales mgr., 1951-55, television sales mgr., 1955-70, pres., gen. mgr., 1970—. Financial bd. dirs. Pacific N.W. Indian Center. Served to lt. col. AUS, 1942-46, 50-51; ETO. Decorated Bronze Star. Mem. Spokane C. of C., Wash. State Assn. Broadxasters (dir.), Athletic Round Table, Spokane Press Club, Sigma Chi. Club: Manito Golf and Country (Spokane). Home: S 5216 Perry Spokane WA 99203 Office: S 4202 Regal Spokane WA 99203

BLAIR, JAMES BURTON, lawyer; b. Elkins, Ark., Oct. 27, 1935; s. William Joe and Mildred (Woolsey) B.; B.A. cum laude, U. Ark., 1955, J.D., 1957; m. Margaret Ann Gibson, Aug. 24, 1957; children-Heather Elaine, Arden Sue, James Rufus. Admitted to Ark. bar, 1957; practiced in Fayetteville, 1957—, Springdale, 1958—; pvt. practice, 1957; asso. Crouch & Jones, 1958; partner Crouch, Blair, Cypert & Waters and predecessor firms, 1959—. Dir. Springdale Savs' & Loan Assn., Chicken Hut Systems, Inc., Razorback Farms, Inc., Sprindale Service & Loan Corp., NW Ark. Investment Corp., Lawyers Investment Corp., N.W. Ark. Corp. Pres. Conf. Local Bar Assns. Ark., 1970—; legal counsel Com. to Defend U.S. Constn., 1970—. Gen. counsel Democratic Party Ark., 1968—, mem. exec. com., 1968—; del. Dem. Nat. Conv., 1968. Bd. dirs. Tyson Found. Mem. Am., Ark. (mem. exec. com.), Washington County bar assns., Motor Carrier Lawyer Assn., Assn. Ins. Attys., Am., Ark. trial lawyers assns., Mensa, Blue Key, Acacia, Phi Eta Sigma, Delta Theta Phi. Baptist. Editor-in-chief Ark. Law Review and Bar Assn. Jour., 1956. Home: Route 2 Dogwood Springes Fayetteville AR 71701 Office: 111 Holcomb St Springdale AR 72764

BLAIR, JANET, (Martha Janet Lafferty), actress; b. Altoona, Pa., Apr. 23, 1921; d. Fred Blair and Florence (Crawford) Lafferty; grad. Altoona High Sch.; student Juilliard Sch. Music, N.Y.C.; m. Louis Ferdinand Busch, July 12, 1943; m. 2d, Nick Mayo; 1 daughter, 1 son. Vocalist Hal Kemp band, 1939-41; motion picture actress Columbia Pictures, 1941—; motion pictures include Three Girls About Town, Broadway, My Sister Eileen, Something to Shout About, Tonight and Every Night, Gallant Journey, I Love Trouble, Fuller Brush Man, Boys' Night Out; on tour in South Pacific, 1950-52; TV appearances on Caesar's Hour, Ed Sullivan Show, others; mem. cast TV show The Smith Family, 1970—; appearances in night clubs. Recipient Look mag. award, 1943. Mem. Motion Picture Acad. Dramatic Arts and Scis., Screen Actors Guild, Radio Guild, Radio and TV Women of Am. (dir.). Home: 2901 Antelo View Dr Los Angeles CA 90024

BLAIR, JOHN LOUIS, mail order co. exec.; b. Warren, Pa., Oct. 29, 1920; s. John Leo and Maude (Hall) B.; A.B.A., Nichols Coll., Dudley Mass., 1942; m. Orpha Thompson, Nov. 26, 1945; children—John Louis, Wendy Ann (Mrs. Kevin Quinn). Started his career with the Lake Erie Engrng. Corp., Buffalo, 1943-45; v.p. New Process Co., Warren, 1945-61, pres., 1962—, also dir.; dir. Warren Nat. Bank. Clubs: Conewango Valley Country, Conewango (Warren); Wanakah Country (Hamburg, N.Y.); Saturn (Buffalo); Yacht, Seagate Beach, Gulf Stream Bath and Tennis, Delray Beach (Delray Beach, Fla.). Home: 108 East St Warren PA 16365 Office: 220 Hickory St Warren PA 16365

BLAIR, JOHN MORRIS, educator; b. Russellville, Ark., May 24, 1919; s. Morris Meyers and Corinne (Brown) B.; B.S. in Elec. Engring., Okla. A. and M. Coll., 1940; Ph.M. in Physics, U. Wis., 1942; Ph.D., U. Minn., 1947; m. Kay A. Winger, Sept. 17, 1947; children—John T., Carl E. Jr. scientist Los Alamos Sci. Lab., 1943-45; research asso. U. Minn., Mpls., 1947-48, faculty, 1950—, prof. physics, 1962—; asso. scientist Argonne (Ill.) Nat. Lab., 1948-50. Fellow Am. Phys. Soc.; mem. Sigma Xi. Home: 1582 Vincent St St Paul MN 55108 Office: Sch Physics U Minn Minneapolis MN 55455

BLAIR, LORRAINE LOUISE, financial cons.; b. Milw.; d. Robert and Mina (Hesse) Schiller; student Mil. Downer Sem. and Coll.; childrenLouise (Mrs. Richard Drury), Betty (Mrs. Carl Vaughn). Mgr. woman's dept. Mut. Life of N.Y., Milw.; gen. agt. Continental Assurance Co.; mgr. woman's dept. Conn. Mut. Life Ins. Co., Chgo.; ins. broker, Chgo.; v.p. The Marshall Co., investments, Milw.; pres., treas. Lorraine L. Blair, Inc., investments and mut. funds, Chgo.; owner Lorraine L. Blair Ins. Agy. Founder, exec. dir. Finance Forum of Am. Mem. Pres.'s Citizens Adv. Council on Status of Women, Community Adv. Council Small Bus. Adminstrn. Mem. Nat. League Am. Pen Women, Midland Authors, Japan Soc. Chgo., Ill. Opera Guild, English-Speaking Union, Ind. Broker Dealers' Trade Assn. (bd. govs.). Episcopalian. Republican. Clubs: Chicago Press (Chgo.); Organized, directed ednl. and pub. relations meetings Chgo. Stock Exchange, 1949; TV show Finance Forum of the Air. Lectr. before clubs and orgns. on finance, related subjects. Author: Answers to Your Everyday Money Questions, 1968. Home: 2400 Lakeview Av Chicago IL 60614 Office: 11 S LaSalle St Chicago IL 60602

BLAIR, LOUIS BLISS, hosp. adminstr.; b. Cin., Dec. 24, 1909; s. Louis Gillette and Charlotte (Bliss) B.; B.A., Maryville (Tenn.) Coll., 1932; postgrad. U. Cin., 1933-34; m. Ernestine Melissa Smith, July 24, 1935; children—Alice Bryant (Mrs. Joseph L. Riley, Jr.), Mary Bliss (Mrs. Charles R. Moser), John Charles, Virginia Louise. With bus. office Cin. Gen. Hosp., 1935-40; bus. mgr., supt. Lawrence County Gen. Hosp., Ironton, O., 1940-42; supt. Ohio State U. Hosps., Columbus, 1942-48, St. Luke's Meth. Hosp., Cedar Rapids, Ia., 1948—;preceptor, lectr. hosp. adminstrn. State U. Ia., U. Mich., Washington U. Mem. United Meth. Health and Welfare Certification Council, 1967—; mem. Linn County Pub. Health Nursing Bd., 1967—, Linn County Mental Health Assn. Bd., 1950—, Linn County Mental Health Clinic Bd., 1970—; mem. governing council AHA Hosp. Schs. Nursing, 1971; pres. Upper Midwest Hosp. Conf., 1953-54. Mem. Am. Coll. Hosp. Adminstrs., Am. Hosp. Assn., Ia. Hosp. Assn. (pres. 1951-52, 54-55), Nat. Assn. Meth. Hosp.. and Homes (pres. 1966-67), Am. Prot. Hosp. Assn. (dir.), Ia. Inter-Profl. Soc. (pres. 1957), Nat. League for Nursing, Cedar Rapids C. of C., Republican. Methodist. Club: Cedar Rapids Rotary (dir.). Home: 662 29th St Cedar Rapids IA 52402 Office: 1026 A Av Cedar Rapids IA 52402

BLAIR, LUCY, phys. therapist, assn. exec.; b. Peterborough, N.H., Nov. 6, 1904; d. Ned Goodhue and Julia Alice (Moore) Blair; ed. Simmons Coll., Children's Hosp. Sch. Nursing; grad. courses phys. therapy, Harvard Med. Sch.; M.A., Columbia, 1948. Phys. therapist Vis. Nurse Assn., Boston; supr. phys. therapy Vis. Nurse Assn. Milw.; cons. phys. therapy Wis. Dept. Pub. Instrn.; cons. Nat. Orgn. Pub. Health Nursing, N.Y.C.; now exec. dir. Am. Phys. Therapy Assn., N.Y.C. Cons. phys. therapy U.S. Army. Served with WAVES, World War II. Recipient citation for work with Gamma Globulin and Salk vaccine, 1955. Mem. Delta Kappa Gamma, Kappa Delta Pi. Home: 319 Av C New York City NY 10009 Office: 1740 Broadway New York City NY 10019

BLAIR, PAXTON, lawyer; b. New Orleans, Sept. 30, 1892; s. Joseph Paxton and Eugenie (Kruttschnitt) B.; grad. Lawrenceville (N.J.) Sch., 1910; A.B., Princeton, 1914; J.D., Harvard, 1917; m. Gertrude Hubbard Grosvenor, Dec. 5, 1925 (div. 1938); children—Joan Grosvenor (Mrs. Henry Paul Sullivan), Edwin Augustus Grosvenor, Joseph P.; m. 2d, Edna D. von Rynkofski, Nov. 16, 1940; 1 son; David P. Admitted to N.Y. bar, 1918, and began practice in N.Y.C.; asst. corp. counsel N.Y.C., 1934-43; justice Supreme Ct. State N.Y., 1945; solicitor gen. State of N.Y., 1957-65. Trustee Child Edn. Found., 1931, pres. 1942-53. Mem. N.Y. State Bd. Social Welfare, 1946-56; dir. Council for Basic Edn., 1956, pres., 1958-59. Dir. N.Y. County Lawyers' Assn., 1958-60. Served as 2d lt., inf., U.S. Army, AEF, World War I. Mem. S.A.R., Am. Jud. Soc., Am., N.Y. State bar assns., Assn. Bar City of N.Y., Pilgrims, Phi Beta Kappa. Republican. Episcopalian. Clubs: Church, University (N.Y.C.); Fort Orange (Albany). Author: Breach of Contract Due to War, 1940. Contbr. to Harvard Law Rev. Columbia Law Rev. N.Y. State Bar Bull. Address: Breezy Hill Rd Hillsdale NY 12529

BLAIR, ROBERT NOEL, artist; b. Buffalo, Aug. 12, 1912; s. Charles Frances and Grace Ethylin (McGonegal) B.; student Albright Art Sch., 1931, Sch. Mus. Fine Arts, 1931-33, Art Inst. Buffalo, 1937; U. Buffalo, 1951; m. Jeannette Kenney, Aug. 8, 1943; children—Jeanne Elizabeth (dec.), David Francis, Bruce Allen. Painted western N.Y., no. Vt. subjects, 1933-43; instr. Art. Inst. Buffalo, 1939-42, dir., 1945-49; instr. Buffalo Mus. Sci., 1939- 42, U. Buffalo, 1952. One-man shows, Buffalo, 1937-41, 45, 53, N.Y.C., 1938-41, 53, 62. Albright Art Gallery, Buffalo, 1942, 54-55, U. Ala., 1944, others; paintings exhibited Internat. Water Color Exhibit. Bklyn., Art Inst., Chgo., exhbns. Nat. Gallery, Washington, Fleming Mus., Vt., State U. Coll., Buffalo, 1966, others; painter murals Fifth area Chapel, Fort McClellan, Ala., 1943, Post Hosp., 1944, Bethlehem Steel Plant, Lackawanna, 1947, Olean (N.Y.) House, Unitarian Ch., East Aurora, N.Y., Lake View Hotel, Lake View, New York; works in permanent collection of the Colgate U., Met. Mus., N.Y.C., Munson Williams Proctor Inst., Utica, Dubuque and Bryn Mawr art assos. Butler Art Inst., Ford Motor Co., Buffalo State U. Coll., U. State N.Y. Served with AUS, 1942-45. Awarded water color prize western N.Y. exhibit, 1940-44, 1947-51; Guggenheim fellowships, 1946-51; Silver and Gold medals, Buffalo Soc. Artists 1947, 50; Ala. Water Color Soc., 1947; water color prize Art Inst. Chgo., 1948; watercolor prize N.Y. State Exhbn., 1950; Waugh prize Buffalo Soc. Artists Ann., 1951, 54, gold medal 1955, 57-68, silver medal, 1956, 62, 69, water color prize 2d Spring Art Exhibit. Buffalo, 1957; 1st watercolor prize Youngstown (O.) Nat., 1953, Western N.Y. Exhbn., 1963, Chautaqua Nat. Exhibit. 1963; watercolor prize, Balt. Water Color Club, 1954; Buffalo Soc. Artists annual painting prize, 1958, 62-65, 70, watercolor prize, 1959; Silvermine Guild watercolor prize, 1958; drawing prize Indsl. Niagara Art Exhbn.; 1st painting prize Cooperstown N.Y. Nat. Exhbn., 1970; 1st Watercolor prize White Mountain Art Festival, Sholow, Ariz., 1970; others. Mem. Am. Water Color Soc., Patteran Soc., Buffalo Soc. Artists, Western N.Y. Watercolor League. Address: RFD 1 Olean Rd Holland NY 10021

BLAIR, THOMAS S. steel co. exec.; b. New Castle, Pa., Apr. 15, 1922; s. George Dike, Jr. and Hazel (Slingluff) B.; grad. Hill Sch., Pottstown, Pa., 1939; A.B., Williams Coll., 1943; m. Phyllis Emmerich, Sept. 17, 1946; children—Joan Dix, George Dike, Hadden Slingluff. With Manhattan Project, 1942-47; asso. editor Iron Age mag., 1947-49; pres., chmn. bd. Blair Strip Steel Co., New Castle, 1949—; dir. Columbia Gas System, Inc., Columbia Gas Pa., Inc., Columbia Gas Md., Inc., First Nat. Bank Lawrence County, Tuscarora Plastics, Inc., Matflo Corp., Southeastern Plastics Corp. Home: 2906 Old Plank Rd New Castle PA 16105 Office: Blair Strip Steel Co New Castle PA 16103

BLAIR, WALTER, univ. prof.; b. Spokane, Wash., Apr. 21, 1900; s. John J. and Emma (Merritt) B.; PH.B., Yale, 1923; M.A., U. of Chicago, 1926, Ph.D., 1931; m. Carol Conrad, Sept. 21, 1925; 1 dau., Paula. Newspaper reporter, Spokane, Wash., 1923-25; instr. English, U. Chgo., 1926-30, asst. prof., 1930-39, asso. prof., 1939-44, prof. English, 1944-68, chmn. dept., 1951-60, prof. emeritus, 1968—; vis. prof. Goethe U., Frankfort, Germany, 1949-50. Mem. Modern Lang. Assn. (chmn. Am. lit. group 1958), Am. Studies Assn. (Christian Gauss award com. 1958-60), Nat. Council Tchrs. English, Phi Delta Theta. Club: Quadrangle (Chgo.). Author: Tall Tale America, 1944; Davy Crockett, Frontier Hero-Truth and Legend, 1955; Hawthorne in Eight American Authors, 1956; Mark Twain and Huck Finn, 1960 (recipient of the Thurmod Monsen award, 1961); Native American Humor, rev. edit. 1960; (with Theodore Hornberger, Randall Stewart and James E. Miller) American Literature: A Brief History, 1964. Editor: Literature of the United States (with Theodore Hornberger and Randall Stewart) 2 Vols., 1946, 47, 53, 54, 65, 69, 70, 3 Vols., 1969. (with F. J. Meine) Half Horse Half Alligator: The Mike Fink Legend, 1956; Selected Shorter Writings of Mark Twain, 1962; (with Hamlin Hill) The Art of Huckleberry Finn, 1962, revised edit., 1969; Mark Twain's Hannibal, Huck and Tom, 1969. Mem. editorial boards of Am. Lit., 1943-51; Publs. Modern Lang. Assn., 1945-51; Mark Twain Papers, 1967—; Collected Works of Mark Twain, 1970—; editorial adviser Coll. English, 1952; departmental editor Ency. Brit., 1951—. Office: English Dept U Chicago 1050 E 59th St Chicago IL 60637

BLAIR, WILBUR TYLER, retired corp. ofcl.; b. Youngstown, O., Dec. 7, 1912; s. Wilbur Tyler and Magda S. (Normann) B.; student U. Mich., 1930-33; LL.B., U. Cin., 1936; grad. student sch. banking, Rutgers U., 1949; m. Margaret Roemer, June 17, 1931; children—Barbara B. Legg, Robert Henry, David Alan. Admitted to Ohio bar, 1936, mem. firm Manchester, Ford, Bennett & Powers, Youngstown, since 1936; prof. contracts Cleve. Marshall Law Sch., 1940-50; asst. sec. Fed. Res. Bank of Cleve., 1945-48, counsel, sec., 1948-51, v.p., counsel, sec., 1951-53, v.p. charge Cin. br. since 1953; v.p., treas., gen. counsel, sec. Sharon Steel Corp. (Pa.), 1953-70, dir., 1957-70; dir. Macomber Inc., Canton, O., 1963-70, Union Steel Corp., Piscataway, N.J., 1963-70; sec.-treas., dir. Carpentertown Coal & Coke Co., Pitts., 1953-70; v.p., sec.-treas., dir. Sharon Bldg. and Land Corp. (Pa.); sec.-treas., dir. Summit Systems, Inc., Piscataway, N.J., 1968-70; v.p., treas. NVF Co. (Del.); sec., treas. Aviation Leasing Corp., Ohio. Asso., Cleve. 1969-70. Ordnance Dist. War Dept., 1942-45. Mem. Am. Bar Assn. Clubs: Youngstown, Youngstown (O.) Country; Sharon Country; Duquesne (Pitts.). Author: Selected Ohio Key Cases, 1937; Appraising Boards of Directors in Security Analysis, 1949. Home: 343 Silver Moss Dr John's Island Vero Beach FL 32960

BLAIR, WILLIAM DRAPER, Jr., govt. ofcl.; b. Charlotte, N.C., May 3, 1927; s. William D. and Mary- Eula (Mason) B.; B.A., Princeton, 1949; m. Jane Fraser Coleman, June 25, 1949; children—Jane Coleman, Elizabeth Mason. Successively reporter, Korean war corr., European corr. Balt. Sunpapers, 1949-52; successively asst. editor, corr., London, Eng., chief Bonn (Germany) bur., then chief Paris (France) bur., Newsweek mag., 1953-59; press officer, then dep. dir. Office Spl. Projects, State Dept., 1959-62, dir. Office Media Services, 1962-70, dep. asst. sec. for pub. affairs, 1970—. Served with USMCR, 1945-46. Recipient Meritorious Honor award State Dept., 1964, Superior Honor award, 1967. Mem. Am. Fgn. Service Assn. (chmn. pub. affairs com., 1964-67), Audubon Naturalist Soc. Central Atlantic States (bd. dirs. 1966—, pres. 1968-70). Clubs: Princeton, (bd. dirs. 1966-69), Metropolitan, Internat. (bd. govs. 1970—) (Washington); Chevy Chase; Univ. Cottage (Princeton, N.J.). Office: Dept of State Washington DC 20520

BLAIR, WILLIAM FRANKLIN, zoologist; b. Dayton, Tex., June 25, 1912; s. Percy Franklin and Mona (Patrick) B.; B.S., U. Tulsa, 1934; M.S., U. Fla., 1935; Ph.D., U. Mich., 1938; m. Fern Antell, Oct. 25, 1933. Research asso. Lab. Vertebrate Biology, U. Mich., 1937-46; mem. faculty U. Tex., 1946—, now prof. zoology. Mem. adv. panel environmental biology NSF, 1958-62, mem. adv. com. div. biology and medicine, 1967-69; chmn. U.S. nat. com., mem. spl. com. for Internat. Biol. Program, 1968—, v.p., 1969—, mem. internat. environmental programs Com. NAS/NRC, 1970—; mem. monitoring commn. spl. com. on problems environment Internat. Council Scientific Unions, 1970—; chmn. adv. panel U.S. Bur. Reclamation,

1971—. Fellow A.A.A.S.; mem. Am. Soc. Ichthyologists and Herpetologists (bd. govs. 1951-55, 56-61, 62—, v.p. 1955), Am. Soc. Mammalogists, Am. Soc. Naturalists (editorial bd. 1957-58), Am. Inst. Biol. Scis. (mem. exec. com. 1969—, v.p. 1971—), Am. Soc. Internat. Law (mem. panel internat. law and global environment 1969—), Ecol. Soc. Am. (editorial bd. 1960-62, pres. 1963, chmn. public affairs com. 1967-68), Am. Soc. Zoologists (chmn. ecology sect. 1965), Genetics Soc. Am., Soc. Study Evolution (mem. council 1959-61, pres. 1962, asso. editor 1961-62), Soc. Systematic Zoology (council 1968—). Author: The Rusty Lizard, 1960. Sr. author: Vertebrates of the United States, 1957, rev. edit., 1968. Editor: Vertebrate Speciation, 1961. Home: 5401 E 19th St Austin TX 78721

BLAIR, WILLIAM GRANGER, newspaper exec.; b. Chgo., Nov. 17, 1925; s. William Mitchell and Martha (Granger) B.; grad. Kent (Conn.) Sch., 1943; A.B. cum laude, Princeton, 1950; m. Sue Cunningham, Apr. 19, 1952, (div.); children—Robert, Bruce, Laura; m. 2d, Ellen Lopin, Sept. 29, 1970. Reporter, Kansas City (Mo.) Star, 1950-53; mem. staff N.Y. Times, 1953—, fgn. corr., Paris, 1956-62, Jerusalem, 1962-65, London, Eng., 1965-67, mgr. employee communications, 1968, mgr. pub. relations, N.Y.C., 1969-70, dir. pub. relations, 1970—. Served with USMCR, 1943-46; PTO. Home: 320 E 52d St New York City NY 10022 Office: NY Times 229 W 43d St New York City NY

BLAIR, WILLIAM MCCORMICK, lawyer; b. Chicago, Ill., May 2, 1884; s. Edward Tyler and Ruby (McCormick) B.; B.A., Yale, 1907; LL.D., Northwestern U., 1964; Litt.D., Lake Forest Coll., 1963; m. Helen Bowen, Feb. 10, 1912. Partner William Blair & Co. Past pres., life trustee Art Inst. Chgo.; life trustee U. Chgo., Chgo. Natural History Mus. Decorated chevalier French Legion of Honor, comdr. Royal Order of Vasa. Presbyterian (trustee, pres. congregation). Clubs: Chicago, Shoreacres, Commercial, Old Elm (Chgo.); Racquet and Tennis (N.Y.C.). Home: 1416 Astor St Chicago IL 60610 also Lake Bluff IL 60044 Office: 135 S La Salle St Chicago IL 60603

BLAIR, WILLIAM MCCORMICK, Jr., orgn. exec.; b. Chgo., Oct. 24, 1916; s. William McCormick and Helen (Bowen) B.; A.B., Stanford, 1940; LL.B., U. Va., 1947; m. Catherine Gerlach, Sept. 9, 1961; 1 son, William McCormick III. Admitted to Ill. bar, 1947; asso. firm Wilson & McIlvaine, Chgo., 1947-50; adminstrv. asst. to Gov. Adlai E. Stevenson of Ill., 1950-52; partner firm Stevenson, Rifkind & Wirtz, Chgo., 1955-61, Paul, Weiss, Rifkind, Wharton & Garrison, N.Y.C., 1957-61; U.S. ambassador to Denmark, 1961-64; U.S. ambassador to Philippines, 1964-67; now gen. dir. John F. Kennedy Center. Bd. dirs. Juvenile Protective Assn. Chgo., Washington Internat. Exhbn. Found., Lasker Found., N.Y.C., Am.-Scandinavian Found., N.Y.C. Served to capt. USAAF, 1942-46. Decorated Bronze Star (U.S.); officer Order of Crown (Belgium); Order of Sikatuna (Philippines). Mem. Phi Delta Phi. Democrat. Clubs: Federal City (Washington); River (N.Y.C.). Office: 726 Jackson Pl NW Washington DC 20566

BLAIR, WILLIAM MELLVILLE, newspaper reporter; b. Cleve., June 14, 1911; s. Mellville Clifton and Margaret (O'Grady) B.; student Ohio State U., 1930-34; m. Helen Stern, Oct. 26, 1936; children—Jonathan Stern, Christopher Jo, Jeffery William. With publicity dept. Ohio State U. radio sta. WEAO, 1933-34; reporter-editor Canton (O.) Repository, 1934-36, Pitts. Sun-Telegraph, 1936-37; with Pitts., Harrisburg and Phila. bureaus A.P. 1937-42; mem. staff N.Y. Times, 1942—, reporter Washington bur., 1953—. Recipient U.S. Navy commendation, 1946; award Nat. Council Farmer Coops., 1950; J.S. Russell Meml. award Newspaper Farm Editors Assn., 1962; Conservation Service award U.S. Dept. Interior, 1969. Mem. bd. mgmt. Central YMCA. Mem. Sigma Delta Chi. Clubs: Washington Athletic (bd. govs. 1958-61, 63-66, 68-70), Nat. Press (sec. 1962-64, pres. 1965) (Washington). Home: 5602 Namakagan Rd Washington DC 20016 Office: 1920 L St NW Washington DC 20036

BLAIR, WILLIAM RICHARDS, Jr., lawyer; b. Loudon County, Va., Aug. 30, 1910; s. William Richards and Florence (Smith) B.; B.A., Harvard, 1933, LL.B., 1938; m. Jean Szepesi, Oct. 13, 1945; children—Theresia F. and Florence R. (twins), Stephanie K. Admitted to N.J. bar, 1939; asso. firm Parsons, Labrecque, Canzona & Combs (now Parsons, Canzona, Blair & Warren), Red Bank, N.J., 1939-47, partner, 1947—. Recorder, Borough of Fair Haven, 1948; atty. Boroughs of Fair Haven, 1948—, Little Silver, 1965—, Monmouth Beach, 1961—, Rumson, 1961—; mem. N.J. Bd. Bar Examiners, 1963-67, chmn., 1966-67; trustee Clients Security Fund Bar N.J., 1969—. Served with AUS, 1942-45. Mem. Am., N.J., Monmouth County bar assns. Mason. Clubs: Harvard (N.Y.C.); Navesink Country; Shrewsbury River Yacht; Lions (pres. 1962-63) (Red Bank, N.J.). Home: 48 Gillespie Av Fair Haven NJ 07701 Office: 18 Wallace St Red Bank NJ 07701

BLAIR, WILLIAM SUTHERLAND, publisher; b. Glasgow, Scotland, Sept. 18, 1917; s. Duncan and Ada (Sutherland) B.; B.A., Lincoln Coll., Oxford (Eng.) U., 1940; student Princeton Grad. Sch., 1940-41; m. Mary Seymour Barnes, Feb. 17, 1945; children—Colin Campbell, Fiona Seymour, Sheila Sutherland, Felicity Duncan. Came to U.S., 1950, naturalized, 1961. Econs. and statistic officer Internat. Air Transp. Assn., Montreal, 1946-49; v.p. Ogilvy & Mather, N.Y.C., 1950-57; pres. Harper-Atlantic Sales Inc., N.Y.C., 1957- 68; Harper's mag., N.Y.C., 1968—. Served with Canadian Army, 1943-46. Home: 24 Gramercy Park S New York City, NY 10003. Office: 2 Park Av New York City NY 10016

BLAIR, WREN ALVIN, profl. hockey team mgr.; b. Lindsay, Ont., Can., Oct. 2, 1925; s. Joseph Alvin and Audrey Viola (Cook) B.; student Oshawa Collegiate and Vocational Inst., 1939-42; m. Elma Juanita Harriet Pearce, June 30, 1945; children—Daniel Wren, Jill Audrey. Salesman, Beaton's Dairy, Oshawa, Ont., 1945-53; appraiser Can. Central Mortgage and Housing Corp., 1953-60; in profl. hockey, 1960—, gen. mgr. Minn. North Stars Nat. Hockey League, 1966—; dir., pres. Haliburton Youth Devel. Ltd., 1965—; pres. B & G Enterprises, Haliburton, Ont., 1966—. Served with Canadian Army, 1942-45. Named Hockey Exec. of Year, 1958. Home: 6309 Loch Moor Dr Edina MN 55435 Office: 7901 Cedar Av S Bloomington MN 55420

BLAIS, LEO, Cath. aux. bishop Montreal. Address: 2000 Sherbrooke St W Montreal 25 Quebec Canada*

BLAISDELL, GEORGE GRANT, business exec.; b. Bradford, Pa., June 5, 1895; s. Philo C. and Sarah (Grant) B.; student Ricker Classical Inst., Horance Mann Sch.; m. Miriam Barcroft, Feb. 21, 1922 (dec.); children—Harriett (Mrs. Robert H. Wick), Sarah (Mrs. Tom Blauser); m. 2d, Barbara Thompson, Apr. 20, 1957. Gen. mgr. Blaisdell Machinery Co., Bradford, 1917- 20; owner Blaisdell Oil Co., Bradford, 1930-50; pres. Zippo Mfg. Co., 1933—, now also treas., dir., pres. Blaisdell Bros., N.Y.C., 1936-37; dir. Bradford Nat. Bank, 1950—. Clubs: Pennhills (dir.), Bradford (Bradford); La Gorce Country, Indian Creek Country (Miami, Fla.); Westchester Country (Rye, N.Y.). Home: 160 Jackson Av Bradford PA 16701 Office: Zippo Mfg Co 33 Barbour St Bradford PA 16701

BLAISDELL, RICHARD KEKUNI, physician; b. Honolulu, Mar. 11, 1925; s. William Kahai and Marguertie Multnomah (Piltz) B.; A.B. cum laude, U. Redlands, 1945; M.D., U. Chgo., 1947; m. Irene Hiroko Saito, Aug. 25, 1962; children—Mitsunori Kamakanikailialoha, Helen Kaleleonalani. Intern Osler Med. Service Johns Hopkins Hosp., 1948-49; asst. resident Tulane Med. Service Charity Hosp., New Orleans, 1949-50; asst. resident, instr. dept. Pathology Duke, 1954-55; asst. resident, resident dept. medicine U. Chgo., 1955-57, instr. 1957-58, asst. prof., 1958, 61-66; prof. dept. medicine U. Hawaii, Honolulu, 1966—, chief div. hematology, 1966—, chmn. dept. medicine, 1966-69; practice medicine, specializing in hematology, Chgo., 1957-66; chief hematology, research asso. Atomic Bomb Casualty Commn., Hiroshima, Nagasaki, Japan, 1959-61. Served to maj., M.C., U.S. Army, 1950-54. Recipient Lederle Med. Faculty award, 1965. Mem. A.A.A.S., Am. Fedn. Clin. Research, Am. Assn. History Medicine, Assn. Am. Med. Colls., Internat., Am., Japan hematology socs., Phi Beta Kappa, Sigma Xi. Home: 3333 Koahinani Dr Honolulu HI 96817

BLAIZE, REGINALD NICHOLAS, oil industry cons.; b. Pass Christian, Miss., Dec. 20, 1911; s. Reginald Nicholas and Julia (Olivari) B.; student Tulane U.; 1929-31; B.S. in Chem. Engring., La. State U., 1934; grad. Advanced Mgmt. Program, Harvard, 1954; m. Vivian Goodwin, Dec. 20, 1936; 1 son, Reginald Nicholas III. Chem. engr. Lion Oil Co., 1934-40; with Eastern States Petroleum & Chem. Corp., Houston, 1940-60, exec. v.p., 1950-58, pres., 1958-59; (Merger with Signal Oil and Gas Co., 1959), v.p. gen. mgr. Houston div., 1959-61, v.p. mfg., Los Angeles, 1961-68, v.p. mfg., petro- chem. sales, research and devel., 1968—, also dir.; partner Blaize-Armstrong Engring. Co., Houston, 1945-48. Registered profl. engr., Tex. Mem. Am. Inst. Chem. Engring., Am. Petroleum Inst., Houston Engring. and Sci. Soc. Roman Catholic K.C. Clubs : Harvard Bus. Sch., Petroleum (Los Angeles). Home: 30025 Avenida Elegante Palos Verdes Peninsula CA 90274 Office: PO Box 17126 Foy Station Los Angeles CA 90017

BLAKE, ALFRED GREENE, mining co. exec.; b. Pitts., June 22, 1902; s. William F. and Blanche (Johnson) B.; C.E., Lehigh U., 1925; spl. student U. Pa., 1933-34; m. Mildred I. Cordeaux, July 27, 1929; children—Johnson C., Phyllis I. Spl. rep. Standard San. Mfg. Co., Pitts., 1925-32; mgr. dealer div. Phila. Gas Works Co., 1932-37; mgr. Eastern operations Ruud Mfg. Co., Pitts., 1937-45; partner Rogers & Slade, mgmt. cons., N.Y.C., 1945-50; v.p. Edgar Bros. Co., Metuchen, N.J., 1950-54, (co. merged with 4 other cos. to form Minerals and Chems. Corp. Am.), exec. v.p., dir., mem. exec. com., 1954-60; exec. v.p., dir., mem. exec. com. Minerals & Chems. Philipp Corp., 1960-64, pres. chief exec. officer minerals and chems. div., 1964-67, (co. merged with Engelhard Industries to form Engelhard Minerals & Chems. Corp., 1967) exec. v.p., dir., mem. exec. com., 1967—, pres. minerals and chems. div., 1967-69, chmn. div., 1969—, v.p., dir. Porocel Corp., 1954-67, pres., dir., 1967-70, chmn., dir., 1970—; v.p., dir. Chemstone Corp., 1955-67, pres., dir., 1967-70; chmn., dir., 1970—, v.p., dir. Cuyahoga Lime Co., 1955-67, pres., dir., 1967-70 chmn., dir., 1970—; pres., dir. Commonwealth Bank of Metuchen Eastern Magnesia Talc Co., 1967-70; chmn., dir., 1970—; dir. Commonwealth Bank of Metuchen (N.J.) Bd. dirs., pres. Syracuse U. Pulp and Paper Found.; dir. operations U.S. Govt. tng. within industry div. War Manpower Commn., 1942-45; trustee Tng. Within Industry Found., Summit, N.J., Lehigh U. Mem. Am. Petroleum Inst., T.A.P.P.I., Lehigh U. Alumni Assn. (dir., mem. exec. com.), Am. Pulp and Paper Assn. Mason. Clubs: Union League (N.Y.C.); Colonia (N.J.) Country: Baltusrol (N.J.) Golf; Saucon Valley Country (Pa.). Home: 970 Glenwood Av Plainfield NJ 07060 Office: Menlo Park Edison NJ 08817

BLAKE, EMMET REID, ornithologist; b. Abbeville, S.C., Nov. 29, 1908; s. John Rennie and Blanche (Ammen) B.; A.B., Presbyterian Coll. S. C., 1928, D.Sc. (honorary), 1966; M.S., U. Pitts., 1933; m. Margaret Newcomb Bird, Oct. 18, 1947; children—Margaret Newcomb, Elizabeth Wier. Grad. instr. zoology U. Pitts., 1929-30; tech. asst. Nat. Geog. Soc. Brazilian- Venezuelan Expdn., 1930-31; mem. Mandel-Field Mus. Venezuelan Expdn., 1931-32, Guatemalan Expdn., 1933-34, Carnegie Mus. Brit. Honduras Expdn., 1935, Stanley Field Brit. Guiana-Brazilian Expdn., 1937-38, Sewell Avery Brit. Guiana Expdn., 1938-39, Southwestern Zool. Expdn., 1941, Mexican Field Studies, 1953, Conover Peru Expdn., 1958; asst. curator birds Chgo. Natural History Mus. (now Field Museum), 1935-47, asso. curator birds, 1947-55, curator birds, 1955—. Capt. M.I., U.S. Army, 1942-46. Recipient of the Alumni award Presbyterian Coll., 1938; scroll of honor Anderson (S.C.) Daily Mail, 1941. Fellow Am. Ornithol. Union, A.A.A.S.; mem. Ill. Audubon Soc. (dir. 1947-50), Wilson Ornithol. Club, Cooper Ornithol. Soc., CIC Assn., Sigma Xi, Chi Beta Phi. Club: Kennicott (Chgo.). Author: Birds of Mexico, 1953. Home: 1139 Judson Av Evanston IL 60202 Office: Field Museum of Natural History Chicago IL 60605

BLAKE, EUGENE CARSON, ch. ofcl.; b. St. Louis, Nov. 7, 1906; s. Orville P. and Lulu (Carson) B.; A.B., Princeton U., 1928, D.D. (hon.), 1952; student New Coll., Edinburgh, Scotland, 1929-30; Th.B., Princeton Theol. Sem., 1932; D.D., Occidental Coll., 1941, Lake Forest Coll., 1954; Lafayette Coll., 1959, U. Pitts., 1961, Grinnell Coll., 1962, Yale, 1962, Morgan State Coll.; HH.D., Coll. Ida., 1951, Ohio Wesleyan U.; LL.D., Mo. Valley Coll. 1951, Macalester Coll. 1961, Alma Coll. 1962, Fordham U. New York City, 1966; LaSalle Coll. Phila., 1969; Litt. D., Beaver Coll., 1952; D.Cn.L., Bloomfield Coll. and Sem., 1952; L.H.D., Parsons, Coll., 1955; S.T.D., Maryville Coll., 1958; m. Valina Gillespie, Sept. 12, 1929. Teacher Forman Christian Coll., Lahore, India, 1928-29; asst. pastor Collegiate Church of St. Nicholas, N.Y. City, 1932-35; pastor First Presbyn. Ch., Albany, 1935-40, Pasadena Presbyn. Ch., 1940-51; stated clk. Gen. Assembly of the Presbyn. Ch. U.S.A., 1951-58; stated clk. Gen. Assembly, U.P. Ch. in U.S.A., 1958-66; gen. sec. World Council Chs. Geneva, Switzerland, 1966—. Vis. lectr. religion Williams Coll., 1938-40. Pres. Nat. Council Chs. Christ U.S.A., 1954-57 Trustee Princeton Sem., Occidental Coll., San Francisco Theol. Sem., Hawaii Loa Coll., John F. Kennedy Library; former trustee Princeton U. Recipient Woodrow Wilson award Princeton U., 1967; named Clergyman of Year, Religious Heritage of Am., 1967. Author: He is Lord of All; Challenge to the Church; The Church in the Next Decade, 1966. Home: Country Club Rd New Canaan CT 06840 Office: World Council of Churches 150 Route de Ferney Geneva Switzerland

BLAKE, FREDERICK JULIUS, banker; b. Pitts., Aug. 21, 1909; s. Julius and Minnie (Bordt) B.; B.B.A., Westminster Coll., 1932; M.B.A., Harvard, 1934; m. Florence Helen Groth, Oct. 19, 1935; children—Carolyn Ann (Mrs. C.N. Reed), Robert Frederick. Sales mgr. Simmons Mfg. Co., 1936-41; asst. cashier Fed. Res. Bank Cleve., 1941-45; asst. v.p., sec. Sterling & Welch Co., 1945-53; v.p. Central Nat. Bank, Cleve., 1953-62, gen. mgr. banking offices, 1963-65, sr. v.p. sales and marketing, 1966-70, sr. v.p. retail and comml. sales, 1970-71, sr. v.p. corporate and urban affairs, 1971—; pres. Linwood Park Co., Vermilion, O.; lectr. Stonier Grad. Sch. Banking Rutgers U., Ohio Sch. Banking Ohio U., Sch. Bank Marketing Northwestern U. Past pres. Citizens League Cleve., 1968-70; councilman Pepper Pike (O.), 1965-69. Trustee Westminster Coll., New Willmington, Pa., 1969—. Recipient Distinguished Service award Jr. C. of C., 1945. Mem. Bank Marketing Assn. (1st v.p. 1968-69, pres. 1969-70), Pub. Relations Soc. Am. (bd. dirs. 1956-59), Cleve. Advt. Club. (treas. 1959-65). Kiwanian (past pres.). Clubs: Vermilion Yacht; Harvard Bus. Sch. (past pres., trustee), Cleveland Athletic (Cleve.); Shaker Heights (O.) Country. Home: 33400 S Woodland Rd Pepper Pike OH 44124 Office: 800 Superior Av Cleveland OH 44114

BLAKE, HARLAN MORSE, educator, lawyer; b. Huron, S.D., Oct. 21, 1923; s. Ambrose Barnum and Martha (Fardig) B.; B.A., U. Chgo. 1946, M.A., 1947, J.D., 1954; student Yale, 1947-48; m. Barbara Barke, July 17, 1957. Asst. dean, lectr. econs. Univ. Coll., U. Chgo., 1948-52, acting dean, 1950-51; admitted to N.Y. bar, 1955; with firm Cravath, Swaine & Moore, N.Y.C., 1954-57; prof. law U. Minn., 1957-59; mem. faculty Columbia Law Sch., 1960—, prof. law, 1963—. Mem. Joint com. econs. and law Am. Econ. Assn.-Assn. Am. Law Schs., 1965—; mem. trade regulation council Assn. Am. Law Schs., 1964—; cons. Inter-Am. Law Center, 1968—. Served to lt. (j.g.) USNR, 1943-46. Mem. Assn. Bar City N.Y. (dir. European common market research project 1964-68), Am., Inter-Am. bar assns., Phi Beta Kappa, Sigma Chi, Order of Coif. Club: Taurino (founder, dir.) (N.Y.C.). Author: Cases and Materials on Antitrust Law, 1967; also articles. Editor: Business Regulation in the Common Market Nations, 3 vols, 1969. Home: 125 Riverside Dr New York City NY 10024

BLAKE, HENRY SEAVEY, physician, surgeon; b. Des Moines, Oct. 5, 1911; s. Henry Seavey and Grace (Riebeth) B.; B.S., Washburn Coll., 1933; M.D., Cornell U., 1937; m. Alice Lee Scott, Aug. 29, 1935; children—Susan Riebeth (Mrs. Onis Lemon), Sally Scott (Mrs. D.M. Bentobji), and Henry Seavey III. Resident surgeon at the Harper Hosp., Detroit, 1937-42; pvt. practice surgery, 1946—. Pres. Kan. Blue Shield, 1952-54; bd. trustees Nat. Blue Shield, 1955-66, vice chmn., 1958-61, chmn., 1961-64. Mem. Topeka Recreation Commn., 1954-55; pres. Council Social Agys., 1949. Pres. Capper Found. Crippled Children, 1956—. Served to lt. comdr. M.C., USNR, 1942-45. Decorated Presdl. unit citation. Diplomate Am. Bd. Surgery. Fellow A.C.S., Acad. Internat. Medicine; mem. Kan., Shawnee County med. socs., Nat. Med. Vets. Soc. (pres. 1953-54), A.M.A. Rotarian. Home: 2024 Birchwood Lane Topeka KS 66604 Office: 918 W 10th St Topeka KS 66604

BLAKE, H. WILLIAM, banker; b. Shawno, Wis., 1905; grad. U. Minn., 1929. Dir. Northwestern Nat. Bank St. Paul, Title Ins. Co. Minn., Telmont Corp., Farwell Ozmun, Kirk & Co.; trustee Minn. Mut. Life Ins. Co. Home: 665 Goodrich Av St Paul MN 55105 Office: 55 E 5th St St Paul MN 55101

BLAKE, JOHN BALLARD, historian; b. New Haven, Oct. 29, 1922; s. Francis Gilman and Dorothy Palmer (Dewey) B.; B.A., Yale, 1942; M.A., Harvard, 1947, Ph.D., 1954; m. Jean Place Adams, Apr. 2, 1949; children—Catherine Curtis, John Gilman, Ann Ballard, James Adams. Fellow history of medicine Johns Hopkins, 1951-52; research fellow history of medicine Yale, 1952-55; asst. historian Rockefeller Inst. Med. Research, N.Y.C., 1955-57; asso. curator div. med. scis. U.S. Nat. Museum, Smithsonian Instn., 1957-59, curator, 1959-61; chief history medicine div. Nat. Library Medicine, Washington, 1961—. Served as 1st lt. USAAF, 1943-46. Recipient hon. M.D. degree Conn. Med. Soc., 1966. Mem. Med. Library Assn., Am. Hist. Assn., History Sci. Soc., Am. Assn. History Medicine (sec.-treas. 1956-67, v.p. 1970—), Phi Beta Kappa. Author: Benjamin Waterhouse and the Introduction of Vaccination: A Reappraisal, 1957; Public Health in the Town of Boston, 1630-1822, 1959. Editor: Medical Reference Works, 1967; Education in the History of Medicine, 1968; Safeguarding the Public, 1970. Contbr. articles profl. jours. Home: 3038 Newark St NW Washington DC 20008 Office: Nat Library Medicine Bethesda MD 20014

BLAKE, JOHN LEWIS, govt. ofcl.; b. Providence, June 11, 1921; s. Jacob Stephen and Hortense (Hayes) B.; student Mich. State U., 1949-52, B.A., 1961; m. Rose Marie Kornegay, Feb. 13, 1952; children-Kim Renee, Edward Marshall. Tchr. bus. West High Sch., Rochester, N.Y., 1961-66; dep. dir. Monroe County Human Relations Com., Rochester, 1966-67; tng. coordinator Sybron Corp., Rochester, 1967-68; gen. mgr. Rochester Bus. Corp., 1968; asst. sec. Marine Midland Bank, Rochester, 1968-69; dep. manpower adminstr. Dept. Labor., 1969—. Trustee Rochester Inst. Tech., 1970—. Served With USMCR, 1943-46. Recipient award Am. Mgmt. Assn., 1969, Nat. C. of C., 1969. Mem. Am. Soc. for Tng. and Devel., N.E.A., Kappa Alpha Psi. Home: 11215 Oak Leaf Dr Silver Spring MD 20901 Office: 14th and Constitution Av Washington DC 20010

BLAKE, MARTIN IRVING, educator; b. Paterson, N.J., Oct. 20, 1923; s. Jacob and Rose (Leen) B.; B.S., L.I. U., 1947; M.S., Rutgers U., 1950; Ph.D., Ohio State U., 1951; m. Sylvia Coonin, Nov. 25, 1948; children—Rhonda Lynne, David Robert, Kenneth Paul, Harriet Ann. Asst. prof. pharmacy Duquesne U., Pitts., 1951-55; prof. pharmacy N.D. State U., 1955-59; research asso. Argonne (Ill.) Nat. Lab., 1959-60, cons., 1961—; prof., head dept. pharmacy U. Ill. Med. Center, Chgo., 1960—; cons. Hines VA, 1967—; mem. Nat. Formulary Bd., 1965—, U.S. Pharmacopeia Revision Com., 1970—. Served with inf., AUS, 1943-46; ETO. Sigma Xi lectr. N.D. State U., 1958, Phi Kappa Phi lectr. U. Ill., 1968. Fellow A.A.A.S.; mem. Am. Pharm. Assn., Am. Chem. Soc., Am. Assn. U. Profs., Sigma Xi. Author: Systematic Organic Chemistry, 1957. Contbr. articles profl. jours. Home: 9023 Kenton St Skokie IL 60076 Office: 833 S Wood St Chicago IL 60612

BLAKE, MARTY, gen. mgr. St. Louis Hawks Profl. Basketball Team. Address: 9011 Manchester Rd St Louis MO 63144*

BLAKE, NORMAN PERKINS, airline exec.; b. Malden, Mass., Apr. 17, 1914; s. Warren L. and Ella F. (Perkins) B.; grad. Bridgton Acad., 1934; B.S., U. Mass., 1938; m. Eleanor L. Adams, Sept. 2, 1940; children—Norman P., Leslie E. Sales staff Socony Vacuum Co., 1938; with Pan Am. Airways, 1939-41, central and western regional traffic and sales mgr., 1950-51, regional dir. Middle East, Asia, 1951-54, exec. asst. to v.p., 1954-56, div. mgr., 1956-57, v.p., 1958-64, v.p., asst. to the pres., 1964-66, v.p. sales, 1966, sr. v.p. traffic and sales, 1967—: sr. v.p. Europe, Seaboard World Airlines; asst. to v.p. sales European traffic and sales mgr. Am. Overseas Airlines, 1945-50 (merged Pan Am. Airways 1950). Served from 2d lt. to lt. col. USAAF, 1941-45. Decorated Order Cedars of Lebanon; Haakon VII Liberation Cross. Mem. Lambda Chi Alpha. Home: Mayo Av Greenwich CT 06830 Office: Pan Am Bldg New York City NY 10017

BLAKE, PETER JOST, architect, editor; b. Berlin, Germany, Sept. 20, 1920; s. Frederic and Kate Maria (Salmon) Blach; student U. London, Eng., 1939, U. Pa., 1940- 41; B.Arch., Pratt Inst., 1948; m. Martha Howard, Dec. 21, 1944; 1 dau., Christina Howard; m. 2d, Loretta Ann Nelson, Oct. 3, 1953; 1 son, Casey Nelson. Came to U.S., 1939, naturalized, 1944. Asso. various archtl. firms, London, Phila., N.Y.C., 1938-42; writer Archtl. Forum, 1942-43, asso. editor, 1950-54, 58-61, mng. editor, 1961-64, editor, 1964—; curator architecture and design Mus. Modern Art, N.Y.C., 1948-50; archtl. editor House and Home, 1955-57; partner Peter Blake & Julian Neski, 1958- 61, James Baker & Peter Blake, architects, N.Y.C., 1964—. Techr. architecture Pratt Inst., Cooper Union, Yale, Cornell. Bd. dirs. Municipal Arts Soc. N.Y. Served as 1st lt. AUS, 1943-47. Mem. Archtl. League N.Y. (v.p.). Author: The Master Builders, 1960; God's

Own Junkyard, 1965. Contbr. articles to popular mags., newspapers. Home: 108 E 81st St New York City NY 10028 Office: Archtl Forum 111 W 57th St New York City NY 10019 also Baker & Blake Carnegie Hall New York City NY 10019

BLAKE, RAN, pianist, composer; b. Springfield, Mass., Apr. 20, 1935; s. Philip Randall and Alison (Powers) B.; B.A., Bard Coll., 1960. Appeared at Monterey Festival, 1962, Antibes (France) Music Festival, 1963; appeared on TV shows, Flemish TV, radio, 1963, 66-67; concerts in ten European countries; tchr. New Eng. Conservatory, Boston, 1967-; music columnist Morningsider, 1960-62. Mem. Am. Com. For Democracy in Greece, 1967. Recipient RCA Album First prize in Germany, 1963. Composer: (with Jeanne Lee) Newest Sound Around, 1962; R.B. Plays Solo Piano, 1966; The Blue Potato and Other Outrages, 1969. Address: New Eng Conservatory 290 Huntington Av Boston, MA 02115.

BLAKE, ROBERT, actor; b. Nutley, N.J., Sept. 18, 1938; student Jeff Corey's drama sch.; m. Sondra Kerry. Appeared in film The Treasure of the Sierra Madre, 1943, Town without Pity, PT-109, The Connection, This Property is Condemned, In Cold Blood, 1968, Tell Them Willie Boy is Here; also TV roles. Served with AUS. Address: care United Artists 15130 Ventura Sherman Oaks CA 91413*

BLAKE, ROBERT O., fgn. service officer; b. Los Angeles, Apr. 7, 1921; s. Frank O. and Marjorie (Edwards) B.; A.B., Stanford, 1943; M.A., Johns Hopkins, 1947; m. Sylvia Whitehouse, July 28, 1956; children—Robert O., Lucy, George. Mem. Fgn. Service, 1947—; 3d sec., Managua, Nicaragua, 1947-49, 2d sec., Moscow, U.S.S.R., 1950-52, Tokyo, Japan, 1952-54; chief Soviet desk Dept. of State, 1955-57; 1st sec., Tunis, Tunisia, 1957-60; U.S. del. to UN, 1961-63; apptd. counselor of embassy Am. embassy, Kinshasa, Congo, 1963; U.S. dep. ambassador to France, until 1970; ambassador to Mali, 1970—. Home: 6722 S Friends Av Whittier CA 90601 Office: Dept State Washington DC 20510

BLAKE, STEWART PRESTLEY, ice cream co. exec.; b. Jersey City, Nov. 26, 1914; s. Herbert P. and Ethel (Stewart) B.; student Trinity Coll., 1934-35; m. 2d, Setsu Matsukata, June 8, 1971; children by previous marriage—Nancy (Mrs. Basil Yanakakis), Benson Prestley. Co-founder, chmn. Friendly Ice Cream Corp., retail shops 7 states, hdqrs. North Wilbraham, Mass., 1935—; dir. Valley Bank & Trust Co., Springfield, Mass. Trustee Wesson Meml. Hosp., Springfield, Bay Path Jr. Coll., Longmeadow, Mass.; student adviser Smith Coll., South Hadley, Mass. Mem. New Eng. Asso. Retail Ice Cream Mfrs. Kiwanian. Clubs: Colony (Springfield); Longmeadow Country. Home: Hall Hill Rd Somers CT 06071 Office: 1855 Boston Rd North Wilbraham MA 01067

BLAKE, THOMAS LOUIS, assn. exec.; b. Tuscaloosa, Ala., July 20, 1922; s. Julius Otto and Esther (McGowin) B.; student U. Ala., 1947, 50, 51; diploma in C. of C. adminstrn. U. N.C., 1957; certificate advanced mgmt., U. Ga., 1968; m. Maude Kelly Greene, Oct. 17, 1942; children—Donna Elizabeth, Robert McGowin, Thomas Louis. Salesman, supr. Montgomery Coca-Cola Bottling Co. (Ala.), 1940-48; sales mgr. Coca-Cola Bottling Co., Tuscaloosa, 1948-53; partner, v.p. T & G Cleaners & Laundry, Montgomery, 1953; tourist and conv. dir. Montgomery C. of C., 1954-56, indsl. and econ. devel. dir., 1956-61, exec. v.p., 1961—. Instr., C. of C. Inst., U. Ga., 1965-66; lectr., cons. U. Ala., Air U., Maxwell AFB, Ala.; hon. faculty mem. Air Force Command staff coll. Bd. dirs., com. chmn. Tukabatchee and Black Warrior council Boy Scouts Am., 1949-66; bd. regents U.S. Chamber Insts. Served with USAAF, 1942-45; MTO. Decorated Air medal with 2 silver and 3 bronze oak leaf clusters. Recipient Paul Revere Leadership medal Greater Boston C. of C., 1962; named certified chamber exec., Am. C. of C. Exec. Assn. Fellow Am. Indsl. Devel. Council; mem. Chamber Execs. Assn. Ala. (pres. 1966-67), So. Indsl. Editors Assn. (pres. 1960), Sales and Marketing Execs. Montgomery (pres. 1970- 71), Am., So. chamber execs., So. Indsl. Devel. Council. Baptist. Rotarian. Club: Montgomery Country. Home: 2169 Meadowlane Dr Montgomery AL 36106 Office: 41 Commerce St Montgomery AL 36101

BLAKE, WILLIAM DEWEY, educator; b. Summit, N.J., June 27, 1918; s. Francis Gilman and Dorothy Palmer (Dewey) B.; A.B., Dartmouth, 1940; M.D., Harvard, 1943; m. Mary Robbins Anderson, June 14, 1942; children—Pamela Ballard (Mrs. Lolax), William Dewey. Successively intern, resident, research, fellow medicine Columbia- Presbyn. Med. Center, N.Y.C., 1944, 47-49; instr., then asst. prof. physiology Yale Sch. Medicine, 1949-52; asso. prof. physiology U. Ore. Sch. Medicine, 1952-60; prof. physiology, head dept. U. Md. Sch. Medicine, 1960—; spl. research neuroendocrine control kidney function. Served to capt., M.C., AUS, 1945-46. Mem. A.A.A.S., Am. Physiol. Soc., Am. Soc. Clin. Investigation, Phi Beta Kappa, Sigma Xi, Alpha Omega Alpha. Asso. editor: (Fulton) Textbook on Physiology, 17th edit., 1956. Mem. editorial bd. Communications in Behavioral Biology. Home: 1211 Bolton St Baltimore MD 21217

BLAKE, WILLIAM HAROLD, lawyer; b. South Orange, N.J., June 20, 1915; s. George Harold and Carolyn Hunt (Rittenhouse) B.; Princeton, 1937; LL.B., Rutgers U., 1939. Admitted to N.J. bar, 1939; atty. Pub. Service Electric & Gas Co., Newark, 1940-46, apptd. gen. solicitor, 1946, v.p. in charge law, dir., 1951—; dir. Pub. Service Coordinated Transport, Newark, since 1951. Mem. Am. N.J. bar assns., Fed. Power Bar Assn., I.C.C. Practitioners Assn. Clubs: Univ. Cottage (Princeton, N.J.); Essex (Newark); Seaview Country (Absecon, N.J.). Home: 17 Oyster Bay Dr Rumson NJ 07760 Office: 80 Park Pl Newark NJ 07101

BLAKEFIELD, WILLIAM HENRY, army officer; b. Sturgeon Bay, Wis., Dec. 28, 1917; s. Harry William and Vivian (Klinkenberg) B.; B.A., Ripon (Wis.) Coll., 1939; postgrad. Command and Gen. Staff Coll., 1950, Armed Forces Staff Coll., 1957, U. Pitts., 1958, Nat. War Coll., 1960; m. Doris Fairweather, Feb. 12, 1941; children—Nancy Elizabeth (Mrs. Thomas F. Dooley), William J.S. Commd. 2d lt. U.S. Army, 1939, advanced through grades to maj. gen., 1965; comdg. officer 1st BG, 7th Cav., 1st Cav. Div., Korea, 1960-61; mem. staff and faculty U.S. Army Command and Gen. Staff Coll., Ft. Leavenworth, Kan., 1961-64; chief Army sect. Joint U.S. Mil. Mission for Aid to Turkey, Ankara, 1964-66; asst. div. comdr. 3d Inf. Div., Wurzburg, Germany, 1966- 67; comdg. gen. U.S. Army Intelligence Command, Ft. Holabird, Md., 1967- 70; chief U.S. Army Adv. Group, Korea, 1970; chief of staff 8th U.S. Army, 1970—. Decorated Silver Star medal, Legion of Merit, Bronze Star medal with V and oak leaf cluster, Joint Service Commmendation medal, Army Commendation medal with three oak leaf clusters, Purple Heart, Combat Inf. badge, Croix de Guerre with star (French). Mason (32). Home: Quarters 7086 Yongsan Seoul Korea Office: Chief of Staff 8th US Army APO San Francisco CA 96301

BLAKELEY, GERALD W., Jr., realty investment co. exec.; b. Newton, Mass., Nov. 8, 1920; s. Gerald W. and Mabel E. (Roy) B.; B.S., Bowdoin Coll., 1943; married; children—Gerald W. III, Robert Whitcomb, Bradford William, Geoffrey Lowe, Amanda C.; stepchildren—Jacqueline Tagle, Terry Tagle. With Cabot, Cabot & Forbes Co., Boston, 1948—, pres., trustee, 1957—; dir. Abethaw Constrn. Co., Boston Co., Pennwalt Corp., INA Corp.; trustee New Eng. Indsl. Center, Suffolk Franklin Savs. Bank, Chase Manhattan Mortgage & Realty Trust. Bd. dirs. Boys Clubs Am., Inc., Avon Old Farms Sch.; chmn. Pine Manor Jr. Coll. Bd. dirs. Boys Club Am., Big Bros. Am.; overseer Bowdoin Coll.; trustee, Mass. Found., N.E. Aquarium; mem. corp. New Eng. Center Hosp.; mem. vis. com. Joint Center for Urban Studies Mass. Inst. Tech., Harvard. Served from ensign to lt., USNR, 1942-46. Mem. Greater Boston C. of C. (dir. 1956-72). Home: 70 Codman Rd Brookline MA 02146 also 12 Lagomar Rd Palm Beach FL Office: 28 State St Boston MA 02109

BLAKELY, JOHN BYRNE, photographic mfg. co. exec.; b. St. Joseph, Mo., Feb. 15, 1910; s. Samuel Abraham and Emma Belle (Montgomery) B.; A.B., Park Coll., 1930; A.M., Columbia, 1934; m. Marion Carolyn Nelson, June 8, 1934; children—Nelson Montgomery, Susan Carolyn, James William. Prodn. supr. E.I. duPont de Nemours & Co., 1935-50; with Anken Chem. & Film Corp., Newton, N.J., 1951-71, v.p., 1952-59, chmn. bd., 1959-71, also dir. Chmn. Sussex County Employer Legislative Com., 1962-66. Mem. Nat. Assn. Photographic Mfrs. (bd. dirs. 1961-64, pres. 1963-64), Employers Assn. N.J. (bd. dirs. 1963-65). Methodist. Elk. Clubs: Newton Country; Culyer Lake (N.J.) Golf. Home: 438 N Post Oak Lane Houston TX 77024

BLAKELY, NEWELL HILLIS, educator; b. Prescott, Ark., July 23, 1919; s. Irvin A. and Clarice (Baker) B.; B.A., Ouachita Coll., 1943; Ph.M., U. Wis., 1944; LL.B., U. Tex., 1947; LL.M. (Cook Research fellow), U. Mich., 1954; m. Mildred P. Skinner, Feb. 20, 1944; children—Mark H., Samuel I. Admitted to Tex. bar, 1947; mem. Blakely & Sloan, Harlingen, Tex., 1947-49; asst. prof. law U. Houston, 1949-52, asso. prof., 1952-55, prof., 1955—, asst. dean, 1951-56, acting dean, 1956-57, dean, 1957-65. Mem. Am., Tex., Houston bar assns., Phi Delta Phi. Home: 438 N Post Oak Lane Houston TX 77005

BLAKELY, ROBERT JOHN, writer; b. nr. Ainsworth, Neb., Feb. 24, 1915; s. Percy Lee and Mary Frances (Watson) B.; B.A. with highest distinction, State U. Ia., 1937; scholar Harvard Grad. Sch., 1937-38; m. 2d, Alta M. Farr, 1964; 3 children. Editorial writer, Chgo. Daily News, 1964-67, editor sch. page, 1967-68; with Register and Tribune, Des Moines, 1938-42, 46-48; asst. to dir. domestic br. O.W.I., 1942-43, charge bur. spl. operations; editorial page editor St. Louis Star Times, 1948-51; mgr. central regional office Fund for Adult Edn., 1951-56, v.p., 1956-61; dean extension State U. Ia., 1961-62; adj. asso. prof. adult edn. Syracuse U., 1969-71; appeared numerous radio, T.V. broadcasts, author scripts for plays. Exec. com. Adult Edn. Council, Des Moines, 1939-41, St. Louis, 1948-51. Served from pvt. to 1st lt., USMCR, 1943-46. Author: Adult Education in a Free Society, 1958; Toward a Homeodynamic Society, 1965; Knowledge Is The Power to Control Power, 1969; The People's Instrument: A Philosophy for Public Television, 1971. Contbr. chpts. profl. publs., articles mags. Home: 5418 S Blackstone Av Chicago IL 60615

BLAKELY, THOMAS, journalist. Motion picture, theatrical editor Pitts. Press. Office: 34 Blvd of Allies Pittsburgh PA 15230*

BLAKEMAN, ROYAL E., lawyer; b. N.Y.C., June 9, 1923; s. Jesse H. and Edythe (Siegel) B.; B.A., Hofstra Coll., 1941; B.A. cum laude, N.Y. U., 1947; m. Edith Hughes, Sept. 1, 1945; 1 dau., Carol. Admitted to N.Y. bar, 1947, since practiced in N.Y.C.; partner firm Marshall, Bratter, Greene, Allison & Tucker, specializing in theatrical law, 1953—; officer, dir. Red Wing Prodns., Inc., Goodson-Todman Asso., Inc., Goodson-Todman Enterprises, Ltd., Telecast Enterprises, Inc., January Enterprises, Inc., Royal Crown Beverage Co., Los Angeles. Served with USMCR and USNR, 1942-46. Recipient George M. Esterbrook Distinguished Service award Hofstra Alumni Assn., 1966. Mem. Nat. Acad. TV Arts and Scis. (pres., bd. govs. N.Y.C. chpt.; past nat. pres., trustee), Nat. Youth Council. Club: Dad's (past pres.) (Long Beach). Home: 454 E Harrison St Long Beach NY 11561 Office: 430 Park Av New York City NY 10022

BLAKEMORE, CLAUDE COULEHAN, banker; b. Los Angeles, Apr. 26, 1909; s. Claude Payne and Agnes C. (Coulehan) B.; student U. Cal. at Los Angeles, 1928-29, U. Ia., 1929; grad. Stonier Sch. Banking, Rutgers U., 1951; m. Violet E. Alt, Aug. 27, 1937; children—Susan (Mrs. Gary Manley), Bruce A. With First Nat. Bank Santa Ana, Cal., 1930-41; comptroller of currency, asst. nat. bank examiner, 1941-42; bank examiner Fed. Res. Bank San Francisco, 1942-45; with First Nat. Bank San Diego, 1945-70, sr. v.p., 1962-64, pres., 1964- 70, chief exec. officer, 1966-70; pres; chief exec. officer So. Cal. First Nat. Corp., 1969—. dir., sec.-treas. San Sacto Co.; dir. Fathoms Plus. Dir. San Diego County Med. Rehab. Center Assn.; pres. dir. San Diego County council Boy Scouts Am.; treas., dir. San Diego Hall of Sci.; dir. San Diego Symphony. Mem. Am. (exec. council), Cal. (pres., dir.) bankers assns., San Diego C. of C. (dir.), Econ. Devel. Corp. Mem. Cal. Bankers Assn. (bd. dirs., chmn. trust Navy League U.S., Sigma Pi. Clubs: DeAnza Desert Country (Borrego Springs, Cal.); Cuyamaca (San Diego). Home: 1822 Altamira St San Diego CA 92103 Office: 530 B St San Diego CA 92101

BLAKEMORE, NEVILLE, banker; b. Louisville, Apr. 10, 1905; s. Marcus Throckmorton and Josie (Morris) B.; A.B., Cornell U., 1927; m. Elleanor Gray, Mar. 2, 1935; children—Neville, Elizabeth B. (Mrs. William M. Kinnaird). Engaged as investment banker and counsel, N.Y.C. and Louisville, 1927-35; with Ky. Trust Co., Louisville, 1935-71, pres., 1965-71, also dir.; treas., dir. Louisville Ladder Co.; trustee First Nat. Bank and affiliates, Louisville; dir. First Nat. Bank, First Ky. Co., Campbell Co., Fabrico, Inc., Vibranetics, Inc., Midland Warehouse Co. (all Louisville). Campaign chmn. Louisville Community Chest, 1946. Trustee Ky. Jud. Retirement Bd.; pres., bd. govs. J.B. Speed Art Mus., treas., dir. Community Chest Jefferson County; past treas., trustee Children's Hosp., Louisville. Served to maj. USAAF, 1942- 45. Mem. Louisville Com. Fgn. Relations (chmn. 1952), Soc. Colonial Wars (treas. Ky. chpt.), English Speaking Union, Newcomen Soc., Kappa Sigma, Quill and ville); Cornell (N.Y.C.). Co-founder, Blakemore & Gathright, pub. legal fiduciary forms, 1955. Home: 81 Warrier Rd Louisville KY 40207 Office: 352 Starks Bldg Louisville KY 40201

BLAKEMORE, WILLIAM BARNETT, Jr., educator, clergyman; b. Perth, Western Australia, July 22, 1912 (parents U.S. citizens); s. William Barnett and Nell (Porter) B.; B.S., Washington U., St. Louis, 1933; A.M., U. Chgo., 1937, D.B., 1938, Ph.D., 1941; m. E. Josephine Gilstrap, June 2, 1942; children—William B., Josephine Jory. Tech. salesman G.S. Robins & Co., St. Louis, 1933-35; mem. counselling and directional staff, Am. Youth Found. St. Louis, 1936-40 faculty, 1948—, trustee, 1957—; ordained to ministry Disciples of Christ Ch., 1941; instr. psychology of religion U. Chgo., 1941-43, asst. prof., 1943-48; asso. prof. practical theology, 1948—, mem. cabinet Federated Theol. Faculty, 1945-61, asst. to dean. Disciples Divinity House, 1941-45, acting dean, 1945-46, dean 1946—, asso. dean Rockefeller Meml. Chapel, 1959-66; minister Normal Park Baptist Ch., Chgo, 1950-51. Mem. dept. pastoral services Fed. Council Chs. of Christ in Am., 1947-57; mem. bd. higher edn. Disciples of Christ, 1945—, mem. council of agys., 1945-68, sec., 1956-58; bd. dirs. Ill. Disciples of Christ, 1950-56; mem. Disciple Panel of Scholars, 1956-62, chmn., 1958-62; mem. central com. Brotherhood Commn. on Restructure, 1961-69; del. Ch. Fedn. Greater Chgo., pres., 1967-68; del. assembly World Council Chs., New Delhi, India, 1961, Uppsala, 1968; mem. Council Christian Unity; chmn. Dept. Ecumenical Studies, 1961-66; mem. Ill. Commn. on Ministry; del.-observer Vatican Council II, 1964, 1965; del. to 4th World Conf. on Faith and Order, Montreal, 1963; fraternal del. Faith and Order Commn., Bristol, 1967; adviser central com. World Council of Chs., Canterbury, 1969, Addis Ababa, 1971. Recipient Susan Colver Rosenberger prize for meritorious research U. Chgo., 1938; travelling fellow. Disciples Divinity House, 1938-39. Mem. Association Disciples Theol. Discussion, Am. Theol. Soc. (midwest br.), Campbell Inst., Disciples of Christ Hist. Soc., Assn. Theol. Profs. in Practical Field. Club: Quadrangle (Chgo.). Author: The Cornerstone and the Builders, 1955; A Needy One Stands Before Thee, 1956; Encountering God, 1965; The Discovery of the Church, 1966; The Bible Enlightens Our Lives, 1968; Quest for Intelligence in the Ministry, 1970. Editor of: Disciples in Illinois, 1959; mem. editorial bd. Pastoral Psychology, 1949-54; editor, contbr. The Renewal of Church, 3 vols., 1963; The Challenge of Christian Unity, 1963. Contbr. to religious periodical. Home: 5629 University Av Chicago IL 60637

BLAKEMORE, WILLIAM STEPHEN, surgeon, educator; b. Stockdale, Pa., June 22, 1920; s. Isaac Thompson and Mary Jane (Crockett) B.; B.S. Washington Jefferson Coll., 1942; M.D., U. Pa., 1945; postgrad. in pharmacology George Washington U., 1947; m. Elaine Hooven, Apr. 2, 1949; children—William Stephen, Holly Hooven, Karin Jane, Stephenie Elaine, Mary Jane, Laurel Claire. Intern U. Pa. Hosp., 1945-46, asst. resident surgery, 1946, 48-51, resident surgery, 1951-52; asst. resident pediatric surgery Children's Hosp., Phila., 1949; mem. faculty U. Pa. Med. Sch., 1948—, J. William White asso. prof. surg. research, 1960-62, asso. dir Harrison dept. surg. research, 1961—, prof. surgery, 1962—, prof., chmn. dept. surgery, Grad. Sch. Med., 1962-64, prof., chmn. grad. dept. surgery, 1964—; asso. surgeon Hosp. U. Pa., 1952—; attending physician thoracic surgery Phila. Gen. Hosp., 1952—; chief surgery Emergency Am. Med. Team to Algeria, 1962; surgeon-in-chief Grad. Hosp. of U. Pa., 1962—; mem. dean's com. VA Hosp., Wilmington, Del., 1962-66; mem. com. blood and transfusion problems NRC, 1962-66; mem. exec. bd. Care-Medico, Phila.; mem. study sect. on surgery NIH, 1965-69. Pres., Merion Home and School Assn., 1962. Trustee Washington and Jefferson Coll.; bd. govs. Middle East Inst., Washington. Served to lt. (j.g.), M.C., USNR, 1946-48. Scholar Am. Cancer Soc., 1952-57; I.S. Ravdin travelling fellow, 1953-54; vis. fellow with Prof. C. Crafoord, Karolinska Hosp., Stockholm, Sweden, 1953-54; recipient Nat. Humanitarian award Order Ahepa, 1962. Diplomate Am. Bd. Surgery, Am. Bd. Thoracic Surgery. mem. A.A.A.S., Am. Assn. Cancer research, Am. Assn. Thoracic Surgery Am. Assn. U. Profs., A.C.S., A.M.A., Am. Physiol. Soc., Am. Surg. Assn., Biochemistry Club Phila., Coll. Physicians Phila., Internat. Cardiovascular Soc., John Morgan Soc. Phila. (pres. 1957), Laennec Soc. Phila. (pres. 1966) N.Y. Acad. Medicine, Pa. Thoracic Soc., Phila. Physiol. Soc., Phila. Acad. Surgeons, Soc. Nuclear Medicine, Soc. Univ. Surgeons, Soc. Vascular Surgery, Internat. Soc. Surgery, Soc. Med. Consultants to Armed Forces, Sigma Xi, Alpha Kappa Kappa (pres. 1944), Alpha Omega Alpha. Editor: (with I.S. Ravdin) Current Perspectives in Cancer Therapy, 1966; (with L. Kraeer Ferguson) Current Perspectives in Gastroenterology, 1967; (with W.T. Fitts) Current Perspectives in Management of Injured Patients, 1969. Consulting editor Jour. of Trauma, 1968—. Asso. editor Surgery, 1965—. Contbr. numerous articles profl. jours. Home: 631 Winsford Rd Bryn Mawr PA 19010 Office: Grad Hosp Univ Pennsylvania 19th and Lombard Sts Philadelphia PA 19146

BLAKESLEE, ALTON LAUREN, sci. writer; b. Dallas, June 27, 1913; s. Howard Walter and Marguerite Alton (Fortune) B.; student Duke, 1931-33; A.B., Columbia, 1935; m. Virginia Boulden, July 3, 1937; children—Dennis, Carolyn Sandra. Reporter Jour. Every Evening, Wilmington, Del., 1935-39; staff Asso. Press, 1939—, Balt., 1939-42, N.Y. fgn. news staff, 1942-46, sci. reporter, 1946, sci. editor, 1969—, Asso. Press corr. U.S. Navy Antarctic Expdn., 1946-47. Recipient George Westinghouse sci. writing award, A.A.A.S., 1952, George Polk award, 1952, Lasker Med. Journalism award, 1954, 62, 64, bronze medallion, 1954, Blakeslee award, 1963, Am. Heart Assn., James T. Grady medal Am. Chem. Soc., 1959; Honor award for distinguished service U. Mo., 1966; Distinguished Service award Sigma Delta Chi, 1965; Sci. Writers' award Am. Dental Assn., 1967. Fellow Rochester Mus. Arts and Scis. Mem. Nat. Assn. Sci. Writers (pres. 1954-55). Author: Polio and the Salk Vaccine, 1956; What You Should Know About Heart Disease, 1957; Your Heart Has Nine Lives (Blakeslee award Am. Heart Assn. 1964; Lasker award 1965), 1963. Home: 13 Vista Way Port Washington NY 11050 Office: AP 50 Rockefeller Plaza New York City NY

BLAKESLEE, WILLIAM SHERMAN, Jr., mfg. co. exec.; b. Grand Rapids, Mich., Oct. 10, 1914; s. William Sherman and Mary Hazel (Shannessy) B.; A.B., Dartmouth Coll., 1935; student Wayne U. Law Sch., 1938-41; m. Ann Louise Miller, May 25, 1942; children—Mary Miller, William Sherman III, Ann Louise. Sales mgr. Gar Wood Industries, Wayne, Mich., 1946-54; dir. govt. relations Chrysler Corp., 1954-58, gen. mgr. def. operations div., 1958-62, v.p. and group exec. def. space, 1962—. Active in the United Found. of Detroit. Served to lt. col. AUS, 1941-46. Mem. Assn. U.S. Army, Army Ordnance Assn. Clubs: Country of Detroit, Detroit Athletic (Detroit). Home: 22 Warner Road Grosse Pointe Farms MI 48236 Office: 341 Massachusetts Av Highland Park MI 48203

BLAKEY, ART, jazz drummer; b. Pitts., Oct. 11, 1919. Joined Fletcher Henderson band, 1939; with pianist Mary Lou Williams, 1940; with own group at Tic-Toc, Boston, 1941; with Billy Eckstine Band, 1944-47, Lucky Millinder, 1949, Buddy De Franco's Quartet, 1951-53; appeared Birdland, 1954; formed Jazz Messengers, 1955; recordings include Three Blind Mice; with Jazz Messengers on tour U.S., Europe and Japan. Recipient New Star award Down Beat Critics, 1953. Address: Shaw Artists Corp 565 Fifth Av New York City NY 10017*

BLAKEY, RICHARD WATSON, lawyer; b. Janesville, Wis., Oct. 17, 1911; s. Richard Watson and Jean (White) B.; B.A., Beloit Coll., 1933; LL.B., U. Wis., 1936; m. Dorothy Jean Jones, May 17, 1941; children—Jean Clare, Richard Watson. Admitted to Wis. bar, 1936, Nev. bar, 1945; practice in Beloit, Wis., 1936-42, Reno, 1946-47, 51—; litigation atty. OPA, Nev., 1944-45; dep. city atty., Reno, 1947-51; mem. firm McCarren, Rice, Wedge & Blakey, 1951-55, Woodburn, Forman, Wedge, Blakey, Folsom & Hug, 1955—. Mem. adv. com. rules of civil procedure Supreme Ct. Nev., 1951—. Mem. Reno Civil Service Commn., 1963—. Trustee Nev. Children's Found., 1947—. Mem. Am., Washoe County (pres. 1954-55) bar assns., State Bar Nev. (chmn. bd. bar examiners 1955-63, bd. govs. 1962—, pres. designate 1971-72), Inst. Judicial Adminstrn., Am. Judicature Soc., Nat. Assn. R.R. Trial Lawyers, Am. Law Inst. Clubs: Hidden Valley Country, Prospectors (Reno). Home: 2225 Lindley Way Reno NV 89502 Office: 1 E 1st St Reno NV 89501

BLAKINGER, RICHARD JEROME, lawyer; b. Aurora, Ill., June 19, 1922; s. Leo A. and Loretta C. (Dirkers) B.; B.A., Cornell Coll., Mt. Vernon, Ia., 1946; J.D., Northwestern U., 1949; m. Barbara B.

Bowman, Aug. 24, 1944; children—Charles, Dan, Betsy, John, Jean. Admitted to Ill. bar, 1949, Pa. bar, 1952; instr. Northwestern U. Sch. Law, 1949; profl. staff mem. Majority Policy Com., U.S. Senate, 1949-50; with Hamilton Watch Co., Lancaster, Pa., 1951-70, v.p., 1960-67, pres., 1967-70, also dir. Bd. dirs. Lancaster County Community Chest, 1957-68, pres., 1959; bd. dirs. Nat. Conf. Christians and Jews, 1968—, Lancaster Gen. Hosp.; bd. dirs. Urban League Lancaster County, 1965—, pres. 1968; trustee Millersville (Pa.) State Coll., 1961-67. Recipient Distinguished Service award Lancaster Jr. C. of C., 1957, Alumni Achievement award Cornell Coll., 1961. Mem. Am., Pa., Lancaster County bar assns., Phi Beta Kappa, Order of Coif. Home: 1461 Hunsicker Rd Lancaster PA 17602 Office: 49 N Duke St Lancaster PA 17602

BLAKLEY, WILLIAM A., lawyer, found. exec.; b. 1898; student U. Okla. Admitted to bar, 1933; part-time lawyer; chmn. bd., dir. Blakley-Braniff Found., Dallas. Trustee Southwestern Med. Found., Inc., Dallas. Mem. Am. Bar Assn. Address: Blakley-Braniff Found PO Box 35212 Exchange Park Dallas TX

BLALOCK, CHARLES DILLARD, textile mills exec.; b. Union, S.C., May 28, 1913; s. Charles Dillard and Cynthia Pearl (Betenbaugh) B.; B.S., Furman U., 1936; m. Dorothy Elizabeth Hart, Aug. 29, 1953. Sr. accountant Elliott, Davis & Co., C.P.A.'s, Greenville, S.C., 1936-42, 44-49; mem. civilian staff U.S. Army Quartermaster, 1943; with Greenwood Mills, Greenwood, S.C., 1949—, v.p., 1965-68, treas., 1962-68, exec. v.p., 1968—, dir., 1958—; dir. Greenwood Mills, Inc., Ninety Six Mfg. Co., Central Trust Co., Greenwood Motor Lines, Textile Investment Co., Bankers Trust of S.C. Active YMCA, Community Chest, Trustee, treas. Self Found., Greenwood, Mathews Found., Greenwood; trustee, v.p. Self Meml. Hosp., Greenwood; trustee Connie Maxwell Childrens Home, Greenwood. Baptist. Rotarian, Moose. Home: 703 Nelson St Greenwood SC 29646 Office: Drawer 1017 Greenwood SC 29646

BLALOCK, JOSEPH ROGERS, psychiatrist; b. Rockingham, N.C., Nov. 18, 1897; s. Joseph Gooch and Minnie (Janie) B.; B.A., M.A., Wake Forest Coll., 1918; M.D., Johns Hopkins, 1922; Sc.D., Columbia, 1935; m. Marie Ella Miller, Oct. 9, 1931 (dec.); 1 son. Joseph Rogers; m. 2d Mildred Hester Brant, Aug. 18, 1962; children—Henry Hester, James Herman. Intern Harper Hospital, Detroit, Mich., 1922-23; resident Detroit Receiving Hosp., 1923-25; practice medicine, Detroit, 1925-26, Pueblo, Colo., 1926-29; mem. staff N.Y. Psychiat. Inst. Hosp., 1929-38; supt. Southwestern State Hosp., Marion, Va., 1938-71, retired, 1971. Mem. Gov. Va. Adv. Bd. Mental Hygiene, 1938—. Diplomate Am. Bd. Psychiatry and Neurology. Fellow A.C.P., Am. Psychiat. Assn.; mem. A.M.A., Va. Neuropsychiat. Soc., Va. Mental Hygiene Soc., So. Psychiat. Assn., So. Electroencephalogram Soc., Va. Mental Health Soc. Baptist. Contbr. articles med. jours. Address: Box 670 Marion VA 24354

BLANC, PETER, (William Peters Blanc), sculptor, painter; b. N.Y.C., June 29, 1912; B.A., Harvard; LL.B., St. Johns U.; postgrad. Corcoran Sch. Art.; M.A., Am. U. Exhibited one man shows including Passedoit Gallery, 1951, 53, Albert Landry Gallery, N.Y., 1960, La Galeria Escondida, Taos, N.M., 1955, Hudson River Mus., 1961, 65, Amel Gallery, N.Y.C., 1964, Ft. Worth Art Center, 1966; exhibited group shows including Whitney Mus. Am. Art, 1952, City Art Mus. St. Louis, 1951, Washington Water Color Club, 1949, 51, 52, Riverside Mus., 1950, 54, 56, 58, 64, New Sch. for Social Research, Springfield Mus. Art, 1952, Nat. Collection Fine Art, Washington, 1953, Balt. Mus. Art, 1953, Bklyn. Mus., 1955, Fogg Mus. Art, 1959, N.Y. U., 1960, St. Paul Gallery, 1961, Internat. Gallery N.Y., 1961, Fort Worth Art Center, 1963; Asso. Art Gallery, Washington, 1962, Hudson River Mus., 1965, Parrish Art Mus., Southampton, N.Y., 1965, Benson Gallery, Bridgehampton, N.Y., 1966, 67, Daniels Gallery, N.Y.C., 1965, East Hampton Guild Hall, N.Y.C., 1966, 67, Southampton Coll., N.Y., 1967, 68, 69, 70, Iona Coll., N.Y., 1968, Mercy Coll., N.Y., 1970; one-man shows include: Thomson Gallery, N.Y.C., 1969; Benson Gallery, Bridgehampton, N.Y., 1969. Instr., Am. U., Washington, 1950-53. Recipient awards Corcoran Gallery Art, 1949, Soc. Washington Artists, 1951, Washington Water Color Club, 1952. Mem. Spiral Group, Artists Equity Assn. (dir. 1963-70), Soc. Washington, Artists Proto-V Group. Address: 161 W 75th St New York City NY 10023

BLANC, WILLIAM ANDRE, pathologist; b. Geneva, Switzerland, Sept. 28, 1922; s. Marcel J. and Blanche (Probst) B.; B.A., Coll. Geneva, 1940; M.D., 1947, U. Geneva, D. Med. Sc., 1951; m. Corinne Pasche, June 6, 1954; 1 dau., Catherine. Came to U.S., 1953, naturalized, 1957. Prof. pathology Columbia Coll. Phys. and Surg., 1966—, head div. devel. pathology, 1963—; formerly career scientist Health Research Council N.Y.; cons. NIH, USPHS, VA; prin. research work in medicine of unborn child. Home: 11 E 86th St New York City NY 10028 Office: 622 W 168th St New York City NY 10032

BLANCHAR, CARROLL HENRY, utility co. exec.; b. Windsor, Wis., Apr. 3, 1912; s. John C. and Amelia (Eggleson) B.; B.A., U. Wis., 1933; C.P.A., U. Ill., 1943; grad. Advanced Mgmt. Program Harvard, 1951; m. Cecile Cunningham, Dec. 24, 1934; children—Beverly, Patricia, Thomas. Accountant, Arthur Andersen & Co., C.P.A.'s, 1933-37; auditor Commonwealth Edison Co., 1937-43; comptroller United Air Lines, Inc., 1943-52; v.p. finance Roddis Plywood Corp., 1952-58, pres., 1958-60; pres. Pub. Service Co. of Indiana, Inc., 1960-68, chmn. bd., chief exec. officer, 1968—, also dir.; dir. Merchants Nat. Bank & Trust Co., Indpls., Am. United Life Ins. Co., Indpls. Mem. bd. govs. Asso. Colls. Ind.; mem. bd. mgrs. Rose-Hulman Inst. Tech.; bd. dirs. Edison Electric Inst. N.Y. Mem. Ind. C. of C. (dir., officer), Alpha Kappa Psi, Beta Alpha Psi. Clubs: Union League (Chgo.); Columbia, Indianapolis Athletic (Indpls.); Meridian Hills Country. Home: Riley Towers Apt 2602 Indianapolis IN 46204 Office: 1000 E Main St Plainfield IN 46168

BLANCHARD, CARL RICHARD architect; b. New Haven, Mar. 17, 1912; s. Carl Russell and Mary (Dann) B.; Cert. Constrn. Pratt Inst., 1933, Cert. Design, 1934; m. Rachel Estelle Begor, Jan. 8, 1937; children—Mary Ludia (Mrs. James Bradford Kallock), Susan Anne (Mrs. Mohamed Ahmed Fadl). Job capt. Fletcher Thompson, Bridgeport, Conn., 1937-40; designer Lorenzo Hamilton, Meriden, Conn., 1935-37; pvt. practice architecture, New Haven, Conn., 1937—. Dir. New Haven Savs. & Loan Assn. Mem. Conn. Archtl. Registration Bd.; mem. Town Plan Commn. N. Haven, Conn. Trustee Center Church Home for Aged; bd. dirs. New Haven chpt. A.R.C., Fellow A.I.A.; mem. New Haven C. of C., Conn. Bldg. Congress, Ch. Archtl. Guild Republican. Mem. United Ch. Christ. Kiwanian. Home: 44 Barton Circle North Haven CT 06473 Office: 74 Forbes Av New Haven CT 06512

BLANCHARD, CONVERSE HERRICK, educator, physicist; b. Boston, Sept. 25, 1923; s. Lindall Converse and Miriam (Herrick) B.; A.B., Harvard, 1944; Ph.D., U. Wis., 1950; m. Margaret Alice Wheatley, June 29, 1946; children—Elizabeth, Margaret, Jean, Brian. With Nat. Bur. Standards, 1950-53; asst., prof., then asso. prof. Pa. State U., 1953-61; mem. faculty U. Wis., 1961—, prof. physics, 1963—, asst. chmn. dept., 1961—. Mem. New Democratic Coalition. Served with USNR, 1943-46. Fellow Am. Phys. Soc.; mem. Am. Assn. U. Profs., Am. Civil Liberties Union, Madison Area Peace Action Council. Home: 2021 Van Hise Av Madison WI 53705

BLANCHARD, GEORGE SAMUEL, army officer; b. Washington, Apr. 3, 1920; s. George S. and Elizabeth (Blanchard) B.; student Am. U., 1938-40; B.S., U.S. Mil. Acad., 1944; M.S., Syracuse U., 1948; grad. Advanced Mgmt. Program, Harvard, 1966; m. Beth Howard, June 9, 1944; children—Kate E., Marylou C. (Mrs. John Hennessey), Deborah E., Blythe H. Commd. 2d lt. AUS, 1944, advanced through grades to maj. gen., 1970; served as co. comdr. and staff officer, Europe, 1944-47; adviser, Taiwan, 1955-57; with 82d Airborne Div., U.S., 1958-60, Korea, 1961-62, Vietnam, 1966-68, comdr., Ft. Bragg, N.C., 1970—; mem. Pentagon staff, 1962-66, 68-70. Decorated D.S.M. with 2 oak leaf clusters, Silver Star with oak leaf cluster, Bronze Star with oak leaf cluster. Mem. Assn. U.S. Army, Army Aviation Assn. Episcopalian. Club: Army-Navy Country (Washington). Contbr. to Ency. Britannica. Home: 24 Capron St Fort Bragg NC 28307 Office: 82d Airborne Division Fort Bragg NC 28307

BLANCHARD, HENRY G., banker; b. Purcell, Okla., Nov. 10, 1904; s. John A. and Blanche N. Blanchard; B.C.S., Drake U., 1927; m. Catherine Remus, Aug. 29, 1929; 1 son, Robert H. Cashier, Nodaway Valley Bank, Maryville, Mo., 1927-47; with Comml. Nat. Bank, Kansas City, Kan., 1947—, now chmn. bd. Pres. Kansas City (Kan.) Clearing House Assn. Treas. Kansas City (Kan.) United Funds, Cancer Soc. Wyandotte County, Kan.; pres. Kaw council Boy Scouts Am., bd. dirs., mem. exec. council region VIII. Bd. dirs. Am. Royal Hosp., Kansas City, Kan., Bethany Hosp., Kansas City, Kan. Recipient Silver Beaver award Boy Scouts Am. Mem. Am. (v.p. Kan.), Kan. (chmn. legislation com.) bankers assns., Kan. (past dir.), Kansas City (Kan.) (past pres.) chambers commerce, Delta Sigma Pi. Mason (Jester, Shriner). Home: 3801 W 52d St Terrace Shawnee Mission KS 66208 Office: 6th and Minnesota Avs Kansas City KS 66117

BLANCHARD, LAWRENCE ELEY, Jr., corp. exec.; b. Lumberton, N.C., Mar. 7, 1921; s. Lawrence Eley and Anna Neal (Fuller) B.; A.B., Duke, 1942; J.D., Columbia, 1948; m. Frances Hallum, May 6, 1944; children—Lawrence Eley III, Neal H., Sally H., Charles A. Admitted to Va. bar, 1948; asso., then partner firm Hunton, Williams, Gay, Powell & Gibson, Richmond, 1948-66; exec. v.p., dir., mem. exec. com. Ethyl Corp., Richmond, 1967-; dir. State Planters Bank of Commerce and Trusts, First Colony Life Ins. Co., Overnite Transp. Co. Trustee Va. Episcopal Sch., 1959-65. Served to lt. USNR, 1942-46. Mem. Am., Va. bar assns., Phi Beta Kappa, Omicron Delta Kappa. Democrat. Presbyn. (elder). Clubs: Commonwealth, Country of Virginia, Downtown (Richmond); Sky (N.Y.C.). Home: 4101 Sulgrave Rd Richmond, VA 23221. Office: 330 S 4th St Richmond VA 23217

BLANCHARD, RICHARD FRANK, financial service co. exec.; b. Hartford, Conn., Jan. 21, 1920; s. Maurice L. and Maude Elizabeth (Hurst) B.; grad. Loomis Sch., 1937; A.B., Dartmouth, 1946, M.C.S., 1947; m. Margaret Rodgers Lyon, May 15, 1944; children—Margaret Hurst, Anne Forbes and Elizabeth Brooks (twins). With Brown Bros. Harriman & Co., 1947-52; with Am. Express Co., 1952—, sr. v.p., 1964-68, exec. v.p., 1968—; vice chmn. bd. Am. Express Internat. Banking Corp., 1971—; exec. v.p. Firemen's Fund Ins. Served to maj. USAAF, 1940-45. Mem. N.Y. Soc. Security Analysts. Club: Broad Street (N.Y.C.); Morris County (N.J.) Golf. Home: Canfield Rd Convent Station NJ 07961 Office: 65 Broadway New York City NY 10006

BLANCHARD, ROGER WILSON, bishop; b. Brockton, Mass., Sept. 11, 1909; s. Charles Francis and Grace (Wilson) B.; A.B., Boston U., 1932; B.D., Episcopal Theol. Sch., Cambridge, Mass., 1936; D.D., Lake Erie Coll., Kenyon Coll., 1958; m. Patricia Goodwillie, June 11, 1936; children—David Dennen, Joan, Peter Sherrill. Ordained deacon Protestant Episcopal Ch., 1936, priest, 1937; curate St. Stephens Ch., Lynn, Mass., 1936-38; rector St. Peters Ch., Beverly, Mass., 1938-42, Calvary Ch., Columbia, Mo., 1943-49; exec. sec. div. coll. work Nat. Council Episcopal Ch., 1950-56; dean St. John's Cathedral, Jacksonville, Fla., 1956-58; bishop co-adjuster Diocese of So. Ohio, 1958-59, bishop, 1959-70; exec. v.p. Protestant Episcopal Ch. U.S.A., N.Y.C., 1970—. Bd. dirs. Local chpt. A.R.C., Travelers Aid, Boy Scouts Am.; bd. dirs. Children's Hosp., Cin, Kenyon Coll. Address: 815 2d Av New York City NY 10017

BLANCHARD, RUSSELL ALLEN, banker; b. Camak, Ga., Oct. 2, 1907; s. Walter and Rachel (Chapman) B.; student Augusta Coll., 1928; grad. Stonier Grad. Sch. Banking, Rutgers U., 1947; m. Catherine Jones, Dec. 22, 1932; children-Russell Allen and Thomas Walter (twins), John Richard. With Ga. R.R. Bank & Trust Co., Augusta, 1928—, pres., 1969—, also dir.; v.p. dir. Ga. R.R. and Banking Co., First R.R. & Banking Co. Ga.; dir. Bankers Trust S.C., First Ga. Devel. Corp. Profl. Bldg., Inc., Riverside Mills, Inc., Hamburg Industries, Inc. Past pres., chmn. loa ed exec. United Fund Augusta; chmn. nominating com., past dir. Augusta Jr. Achievement; bd. dirs. Com. 100, Augusta. Mem. Adv. bd. Furman U.; trustee Tuttle-Newton Home: chmn. trustees Augusta Coll. Found.; trustee, chmn. endowment com. Ga. Baptist Found. Mem. Am. (past v.p. Ga., past pres. state bank div., mem. exec. com. 1964—), Ga. (past pres.) bankers assns., Augusta C. of C. (past dir., treas.). Rotarian. Clubs: Augusta Country, Pinnacle (Augusta). Home: 3027 Bransford Rd Augusta GA 30904 Office: 699 Broad St Augusta GA 30904

BLANCHE, FRED ALEXANDER, lawyer; b. Monroe, La., Jan. 12, 1898; s. John S. and Pauline (Wetzel) B.; B.S., La. State U., 1919, M.S., 1923, LL.B., 1927; m. Amy Moran, Nov. 21, 1919; children—Fred Alexander, Amy (Mrs. Robert M. Slowey). Admitted to La. bar, 1927; mem. firm Watson, Blanche, Wilson, Posner & Thibaut, Baton Rouge. Mem. La. Ho. of Reps., 1928-32, La. Senate, 1934- 36. Mem. Am., La. (pres. 1959-60), Baton Rouge (pres. 1951-52) bar assns., Phi Delta Phi. Mason (Shriner), Kiwanian. Clubs: City, Baton Rouge County (past pres.). Home: 3465 E Lakeshore Dr Baton Rouge LA 70808 Office: 505 North Blvd Baton Rouge LA 70821

BLANCHET, GEORGE ARTHUR, lawyer; b. Manchester, N.H., July 31, 1902; s. George and Mary (Shea) B.; A.B., Holy Cross Coll., 1924; LL.B., Harvard, 1927; m. Lucille A. Kennedy, Apr. 4, 1932; children—Lucille (Mrs. John J. Conklin, Jr.), Beverly (Mrs. Theodore J. Reiss), Margaret Ann, Rosamond Blanchet, Carole (Mrs. Michael Brown). Admitted to Mass. bar, 1927, N.Y. bar, 1931; partner firm Bigham Englar, Jones & Houston, N.Y.C. 1937—. Mem. Internat. Assn. Ins. Counsel (pres. 1958-59), Am. Bar Assn., Maritime Law Assn. U.S. Clubs: India House (N.Y.C.); International (Chgo.). Home: 315 E 72d St New York City NY 10021 Office: 99 John St New York City NY 10038

BLANCHET, WALDO WILLIE EMERSON, coll. pres.; b. New Orleans, Aug. 6, 1910; s. Louis Alexander and Hattie (D'Astugue) B.; A.B., Talladega Coll., 1931; M.S., U. Mich., 1936, Ph.D., 1946; m. Josephine Lavizzo, Oct. 13, 1943; children—Geri Therese, Waldo Willie Emerson. Tchr. sci. Fort Valley (Ga.) Normal and Indsl. Sch., 1932-35, dean, 1936-38; instr. Fort Valley State Coll., 1939, prof. phys. sci., 1939—, admistrv. dean, 1939-66, now pres. coll., 1966—. Cons. sci. edn. Ga. Dept. Edn., NSF Sci. Insts. in Albany and Atlanta, 1960-61. Mem. Nat. Adv. Council on Edn. of Disadvantaged Children. Mem. Assn. Higher Edn., Nat. Assn. Research Sci. Teaching (pres. 1956-57), Nat. Inst. Sci., A.A.A.S., Phi Kappa Phi, Phi Delta Kappa. Contbr. articles to tech. lit. Home: 110 Lamar St Fort Valley GA 31030

BLANCHETTE, ROBERT WILFRED, lawyer; b. New Haven, July 7, 1932; s. Wilfred H. and Dora R. (deJordy) B.; B.A., U. Conn., 1953; Woodrow Wilson fellow, Fulbright scholar, U. Grenoble (France), 1953-54; LL.B. cum laude, Yale, 1957; m. Marna Madelaire Nielsen, May 17, 1969. Admitted to Conn. bar, 1957, since practiced in New Haven; partner Adams, Blanchette & Evans, 1957-62; gen. counsel N.Y., N.H.&H. R.R., 1963-68; gen. atty. New Eng. Penn Central Co., 1969-70; exec. dir. America's Sound Transp. Rev. Orgn., Washington, 1969-70; counsel to trustees Penn Central Transp. Co., Phila., 1970—. Tutor Law Sch. Yale, 1961-68. Served to 1st lt. USAF, 1958-60. Mem. Am., Conn., New Haven bar assns., Order of Coif. Roman Catholic. Club: Yale (N.Y.C.). Contbr. to Moore's Fed. Practice. Home: 2 Livingston St New Haven CT 06511 Office: 6 Penn Center Plaza Philadelphia PA 19104

BLANCHETTE, ROMEO ROY, bishop; b. St. George, Ill., Jan. 6, 1913; s. Oscar and Josephine (Langlois) B.; B.A., St. Mary of Lake Sem., Mundelein, Ill., 1934, M.A., 1936, S.T.B., 1935, S.T.L., 1937; J.C.B., Pontifical Gregorian U., Rome, Italy, 1938, J.C.L., 1939. Ordained priest Roman Cath. Ch. 1937; notary Met. Tribunal Archdiocese Chgo., 1939-49, also asst. pastor Holy Name Cathedral; chancellor Diocese Joliet (Ill.), 1949-65, officialis, 1949-59, vicar gen., 1958-66, aux. bishop, 1965-66, bishop Diocese of Joliet, 1966—. Chaplain Young Christian Students and Young Christian Workers, 1939-49; treas. Joliet Cathedral Bldg. Fund, 1950, Joliet High Sch. Bldg. Fund, 1953; bd. dirs. Joliet Sem. Bldg. Fund, 1960. Bd. dirs. Lewis Coll., Joliet Cath. Charities. Named domestic prelate, 1950, protonotary apostolic, 1959. Mem. Canon Law Soc. Am. (bd. dirs.). Address: 425 Summit Joliet IL 60435

BLANCHFORD, JOHN A., ins. co. exec.; b. Hartford, Conn., Oct. 8, 1906; s. James E. and Anne (Sullivan) B.; student Hartford Coll. Law; m. Margaret J. Halloran, Jan. 26, 1931. With Aetna Life Ins. Co., 1924-, v.p. life dept., 1957-62, sr. v.p., 1962-; dir. Hartford Home Savs. & Loan Assn. Mem. bldg. fund U. Hartford; corporator Hartford Hosp. Served with AUS, 1943-45. Mem. Greater Hartford C. of C. (dir.), C. of C. U.S. (dir.), Internat. Claim Assn. (past pres.). Home: 43 Woodridge Circle West Hartford CT 06007 Office: 151 Farmington Av Hartford, CT 06115.

BLANCK, JACOB NATHANIEL, bibliographer, author; b. Boston, Nov. 10, 1906; s. Selig and Mildred R. (Friedman) B.; student Boston schs.; L.H.D. (hon.), Brown U., 1969; m. Stella Balicer, Aug. 28, 1938; 1 dau., Rosamunde. Rare book editor Publishers Weekly and Antiquarian Bookman, 1936-52; bibliographer Americana, Library of Congress, 1939-41; cons. bibliography Ind. Hist. Soc., 1942; editor Bibliography of Am. Lit., 1943—. Mem. Mass Hist. Soc., Bibliog. Soc. Am., Am. Antiquarian Soc., Antiquarian Bookseller's Assn. of Am., (hon.), Phi Beta Kappa (hon.). Club: Odd Volumes (Boston). Mason. Author: Peter Parley to Penrod, 1938, rev. edit. 1961; Harry Castlamon, Boy's Own Author, 1941; Jonathan and the Rainbow, 1948; The King and the Noble Blacksmith, 1950. Editor: Merle Johnson's American First Editions, 3d and 4th edits. 1936, 41. Contbr. Ency. Brit. Year Books, profl. jours. Home: 19 Reservoir Rd Chestnut Hill MA 02167 Office: care Houghton Library Harvard U Cambridge MA 02138

BLANCO, TEODORA, artist in ceramics; b. Santa Maria. Atzompa, Mexico. Apr. 1, 1929; d. Amado and Carmen (Nunez) Blanco; m. Antonio Garcia, Feb. 5, 1953; children—Luis Garcia, Irma Garcia, Arturo Garcia, Leticia Garcia. Roberta Garcia. Exhbns. include Museo de Artese e Industria Populares. Mexico City. Casa Yera, Mexico City, Anthrop. Mus., Mexico City, also in U.S. and Can. Address: Santa Maria Atzompa Oaxaca Mexico

BLAND, CARL C., corp. exec.; b. Dallas, 1911; ed. U. So. Cal., 1935. Sr. v.p., dir. Balfour, Guthrie & Co., Ltd. Home: 10 N Ridgewood Rd Kentfield, CA 94904 Office: 256 California St San Francisco CA 94111

BLAND, CHESTER, elec. mfr.; b. Hartford, Conn., June 2, 1908; s. Herman and Anna (Levy) B.; A.B., Clark U., 1929, A.M., 1930; student U. Basle, Switzerland, 1933-34; m. Shirley Levenson, June 11, 1933; children—Linda, Deborah. Pres. Bland Burner Co., 1935-68, H.P. Townsend Mfg. Co., 1944-69; pres., dir. Ohio Electric Mfg. Co., 1946-59; chmn. bd. Howell Electric Motors Co. (Mich.), 1959-66, SFM Corp., 1969—; dir. Tubutron Corp., Trans Lux Corp., Rogers Corp. Bd. dirs. Conn. State Prison, 1949-51, mem. bd. parole, 1949-51; trustee Clark U., Worcester, Mass. Home: 1028 Farmington Av West Hartford CT 06107 Office: Brook St Elmwood CT 06110

BLAND, DUANE ALVIN, petroleum co. exec.; b. Rudolph, O., Nov. 9, 1932; s. George DeWayne and Evelyn (Durfey) B.; B.S. in Bus. Adminstrn., Bowling Green State U., 1956; M.B.A., U. Toledo, 1960; m. Delores Rae Hamm, Sept. 4, 1955; children—Cheryl DeAnn, Douglas Duane, David Alan, Shelia Diane. Tax and staff analyst Marathon Oil Co., Findlay, O., 1956-61, staff analyst, accounting supr., Tulsa, 1961-64; staff accountant, accounting supr. Skelly Oil Co., Tulsa, 1964-66, mgr. accounting, 1966-69, controller, 1969—. Served with AUS, 1953-55. C.P.A., Okla. Mem. Financial Exec. Inst., Nat. Accounting Assn. (chpt. dir. 1968-69, treas. 1969-71), Petroleum Accounting Assn. Okla. (dir. 1968-70). Home: 5030 S Irvington Av Tulsa OK 74135 Office: PO Box 1650 Tulsa OK 74102

BLAND, EDWARD FRANKLIN, physician; b. W.Point, Va., Jan 24, 1901; s. James Edward and Mary L. (Bowden) B.; B.S., U. Va., 1923, M.D., 1927; research fellow Univ. Coll. Hosp., London, Eng., 1930-31; m. Frances Poinier, Sept. 7, 1935; children—Frances (Mrs. Herbert M. Berk), James Edward, Robert Poinier. Intern Mass. Gen. Hosp., 1927-29, resident, 1929-30, chief cardiac unit, 1949-64, cons. vis. physician, 1960-; pvt. practice specializing in cardiology, Boston, 1932-; sr. vis. physician House of Good Samaritan, Children's Med. Center, 1962-; mem. cons. staff W. Roxbury, VA, Winchester, Malden, Brockton, Framingham and Gloucester hosps.; asso. clin. prof. medicine Harvard Med. Sch., 1954-64, clin. prof. medicine, 1964-67, clin. prof. medicine emeritus, 1967—. Civilian cons. to surgeon gen. U.S. Army, 1946-50; mem. tng. rev. com. Nat. Heart Inst., 1965-. Served to lt. col., M.C., AUS, 1942-45; MTO. Decorated Bronze Star medal. Mem. Am. Clin. Investigation, Am. Clin. and Climatol. Assn., Assn. Am. Physicians, New Eng. Cardiovascular Soc. (past pres.), Am. (past bd. dirs.), Mass. (past pres.) heart assns. Clubs: Aesculapian (Boston); Country (Brookline, Mass.). Mem. editorial bd. Cardiology Digest, 1965-. Home: 232 Woodland Rd Chestnut Hill, MA 02167. Office: Zero Emerson Pl Charles River Park Boston MA 02114

BLAND, GUY EMERY, savs. and loan exec.; b. Blandburg, Pa., Dec. 31, 1906; s. Frederick Jacob and Christina Maud (Tabor) B.; A.B., Bucknell U., 1928; m. Hazel Marie Troxell, Nov. 21, 1929. Prin., Bigler Twp. High Sch., Madera, Pa., 1928-40, supervising prin.,

1940-42; supr. indsl. edn. Aluminum Co. Am., Bridgeport, Conn., 1942-45; asst. sec. Mt. Lebanon Fed. Savs. and Loan Assn., Pitts., 1948-51, sec., 1951-68, pres., 1968—; tchr. Am. Savs. and Loan Inst., 1950-55. Mem. Nat. Soc. Controllers and Finance Officers of Savs. Instns. (past pres.), Pa. (dir.), Allegheny County (past pres. and dir.) savs. and loan leagues, Mt. Lebanon Fed. Savs. and Loan Assn. (dir.), Mt. Lebanon C. of C. (dir.), Lambda Chi Alpha. Presbyn. (past trustee). Kiwanian (dir.), Mason (Shriner). Clubs: University (Pitts.); Reade Sportsman Glasgow, Pa.). Home: 631 Highview Rd Pittsburgh PA 15234 Office: 733 Washington Rd Pittsburgh PA 15228

BLANDAU, RICHARD JULIUS, educator, physician; b. Erie, Pa., Aug. 5, 1911; s. Richard Albert and Kate (Lubbers) B.; A.B., Linfield Coll., McMinnville, Ore., 1935; Ph.D. in Biology, Brown U., 1939; M.D. with honor, U. Rochester, 1948; m. Olive Lewellen, Oct. 9, 1937; 1 son, Richard Lewellen. Fellow anatomy and psychobiology NRC, Yale, 1937-38; instr. biology Brown U., 1939-42; instr. anatomy Harvard Sch. Medicine, 1942-43; mem. faculty U. Rochester, 1943-49, Buswell fellow urology and surgery, Sch. Medicine and Dentistry, 1948-49; mem. faculty U. Wash., 1949—, prof. Anatomy 1949—, asso. dean Sch. Medicine, 1960-64; Harry Burr Ferris lectr. Yale U., 1965. Cons. in histopathology Manhatten Dist., 1947; Solomon Theron DeLee lectr. U. Chgo., 1954; mem. Wash. Basic Sci. Examining Bd., 1951—; cons. Childrens Orthopedic Hosp. and Med. Center, Seattle, 1965—. Recipient Vienna Film Festival award 1959. Mem. Am. Assn. Anatomists (pres. 1968-69), Soc., Problems in Growth, Soc. Exptl. Biology and Medicine, Am. Soc. Study Sterility Isidor Rubin award in 1952. Ortho Research award in 1956, Ortho medal award in 1969), Am., Soc. Cell. Biologists, Am. Soc. Teratologists, Am. Soc. Med. Illustrators (hon), Los Angeles Surg. Soc. (hon), Los Angeles Obstet. Assembly (hon.), Am. Fertility Soc. (pres. 1967-68), Sigma Xi, Alpha Omega Alpha (Borden Research award medicine 1948). Republican. Presbyn. (elder). Asso. editor Jour. Am. Anatomy, 1961, Am. Jour, Fertility and Sterility, 1963—. Home: 540 Edmonds Way Edmonds WA 98020 Office: Univ Wash Med Sch Seattle WA 98105

BLANDFORD, JOHN RUSSELL, lawyer; b. Buffalo, Feb. 20, 1918; s. Raymond S. and Mary (Perkins) B.; B.A. cum laude, Hobart Coll., 1939; LL.B., Yale, 1946; m. Barbara Jane Waterhouse, July 28, 1944; 1 dau., Marcia Ann (Mrs. Irwin Raymond Hoener II). Admitted to N.Y. bar, 1947, D.C. bar, 1957, also U.S. Supreme Ct.; practice in Buffalo, 1947; counsel com. armed services U.S. Ho. of Reps., Washington, 1947-63, chief counsel, 1963-. Served to maj. USMCR, 1941-46; PTO. Recipient Rockefeller Pub. Service award, 1966. Mem. Phi Beta Kappa, Tau Kappa Alpha. Methodist. Mason. Home: 4520 N 39th St Arlington, VA 22207. Office: Rayburn House Office Bldg Washington DC 20515

BLANDIN, AMOS NOYES, Jr., judge; b. Bath, N.H., Dec. 20, 1896; s. Amos N. and Katherine (Woods) Blandin; grad. Exeter Acad., 1914; A.B., Dartmouth, 1918, LL.D., 1951; LL.B. Harvard, 1921; J.S.D., Suffolk U., 1948; LL.D., U.N.H., 1968; m. Alberta Bell, July 15, 1937; children—Dale M., Joanna Bell, Jane Noyes. With Streeter, Demond, Woodworth & Sulloway, Concord, N.H., 1921; mem. firm Remick & Blandin, 1922-23; asso. of Murchie & Murchie, 1923-29; mem. firm Murchie, Murchie & Blandin, 1929-41; mem. corp. Loan & Trust Savs. Bank, Concord, N.H., 1938-41; justice of Superior Ct., 1941-1945, chief justice 1945-47; asso. justice Supreme Ct. of N.H., 1947-66; judicial referee, 1966—; mem. N.H. Jud. Council, 1945-47; mem. N.H. Board Probation, 1947-63, chmn., 1961-63; lectr. law schs., colls. Chmn. N.H. Gov.'s Commn. on Pub. Disturbances, 1965-69. Trustee N.H. State Library, 1938-43. Coll. Advanced Sci., Canaan, N.H., 1961-63, Mary Hitchcock Meml. Hosp., Hanover, 1960-63; chmn. N.H. Pub. Library Commn., 1943-50. Served as 2d lt. F.A., U.S. Army, World War I. Mem. Am., N.H. (sec., treas. 1924- 29) bar assns., Am. Judicature Soc., Nat. Probation and Parole Assn. (adv. council judges), Am. Law Inst. (adv. group subject of agy.), Kappa Kappa Kappa, Dragon Sr. Soc. Democrat. Roman Catholic. Home: 6 Chase Rd Hanover NH 03755

BLANDINE, SISTER MARY, hosp. adminstr. Adminstr. St. Francis Hosp., Tulsa. Office: 6161 S Yale Av Tulsa OK 74135*

BLANDING, ROBERT J., bank exec. Vice pres. operations, exec. officer bank Mich. Nat. Bank, Lansing, Mich. Office: 124 W Allegan St Lansing MI 48904*

BLANDING, SARAH GIBSON, educator; born Lexington, Ky., Nov. 22, 1898; d. William and Sarah Gibson (Anderson) Blanding; certificate New Haven Normal Sch. of Gymnastics, 1919; A.B., U. of Ky., 1923; M.A., Columbia U., 1926; student London Sch. of Economics, London, 1928-29, Columbia U., summers, 1933, 34; LL.D., Syracuse U., U. Ky., U. Pa., Skidmore Coll., Russell Sage Coll., Rollins Coll., U. Louisville, Mills Coll., Smith Coll., Brown U., N.Y.U., The Woman's College, U.N.C., Mt. Holyoke Coll., Knox Coll., U. Mich., Bennett Coll., Williams Coll., Chatham Coll.; L.H.D., Keuka Coll. Instr. phys. edn. U., Ky., 1919-23 acting dean of women, 1923-24, dean of women and asst. prof. polit. sci., 1926-37, dean of women asso. prof. polit. science, 1937-41; dir. New York State Coll. of Home Economics, Cornell U., 1941- 42, dean, 1942-46; pres. Vassar Coll., 1946-64, pres. emeritus, 1964-. Nat. adv. com. UN Assn. U.S.A.; charter trustee Eisenhower Coll.; nat. adv. council Girl Scout U.S.A.; sponsor women's planning com. Japan Internat. Christian U. Found.; mem. nat. com. and adv. council, acad. freedom com. Am. Civil Liberties Union. Trustee, Scoville Library, Salisbury, Conn. Mem. Kappa Kappa Gamma. Democrat. Episcopalian (vestry). Club: Cosmopolitan (N.Y.C.). Home: Lakeville CT 06039

BLANFORD, FRED R., trucking co. exec.; b. Terre Haute, Ind., 1915; grad. Ind. U., 1939. Treas., dir. Aero Mayflower Transit Co., Indpls. Home: 5206 Radnor Rd Indianapolis IN 46226 Office: 863 Massachusetts Av Indianapolis IN 46204*

BLANK, SAMUEL, bottling co. exec., b. N.Y.C., Apr. 23, 1896; s. Morris and Jennie (Polonsky) B.; m. Beatrice Miller, June 20, 1915; children—Marion (Mrs. Stanley Frehling), Rose (Mrs. Sanford Kramer), Jerome. Chmn. bd. Nat. Brands, Inc. and affiliated cos. (all in Miami, Fla.); chmn. bd. Nat. Beverages, Inc., Pepsi-Cola Bottling Co. of Lakeland Inc., Seven-Up Bottling Co. Inc., Daytona Beach, Fla., Seaboard Warehouse Terminals, Inc., Miami; partner State Beverages, Miami; dir. City Nat. Bank of Miami. Trustee emeritus U. Miami; life trustee, founder Mt. Sinai Hosp.; annual mem. United Fund of Dade County; bd. dirs. Goodwill Industries of Dade County. Mem. regional exec. bd. Nat. Conf. Christians and Jews. Mem. Fla., Miami-Dade County, Miami Beach chambers commerce, Nat. Beer Wholesalers Assn. of Am., Greater Miami Jewish Fedn. Mason (Shriner), Elk; mem. B'nai B'rith. Clubs: Standard of Greater Miami (hon. chmn. govs.), Westview County (Miami), Variety of Greater Miami. Home: 5255 Collins Av Miami Beach FL 33140 Office: 11077 NW 36th Av Miami FL 33168

BLANK, SAMUEL ALLAN, lawyer; b. Phila., June 22, 1910; s. Philip and Olga (Millis) B.; B.S. in Econs., Wharton Sch. of U. Pa., 1929; LL.B., 1932; LL.D., Phila. Coll. Osteo. Medicine, 1963; m. Ruth Saler, May 19, 1938; children—Robert Saler, Jeffrey Charles. Admitted to Pa. bar, 1932, since practiced in Phila.; sr. partner firm Blank, Rome, Klaus & Comisky, and predecessor firm, 1946—. Dir. Continental Bank, Indsl. Cold Storage & Warehouse Co., Title Ins. Corp. Pa., Pa. Refrigerated Terminals, Inc., Kardon Enterprises, Inc., Am. Bag & Paper Corp. Mem. Pa. Ho. of Reps. from Phila. County, 1936-37, Trustee Acad. Natural Scis., Fedn. Jewish Agys. Phila., Moss Rehab. Hosp., Cardiovascular Inst. Heart Research; chmn. bd. trustees Phila. Coll Osteo. Medicine. Mem. Am., Pa., Phila. bar assns. Clubs: Philmont Country, Urban, Locust (gov. Phila.). Office: 4 Penn Center Plaza Philadelphia PA 19103

BLANK, SHELDON HAAS, educator; b. Mt. Carmel, Ill., Sept. 17, 1896; s. Solomon Henry and Byrde (Haas) B.; A.B., U. Cincinnati, 1918; A.M. 1920; Rabbi, Hebrew Union Coll., Cincinnati, 1923; Ph.D., U. Jena (Germany), 1925; m. Amy Kirchberger, July 21, 1926; children—Miriam Elizabeth. Mem. faculty, Hebrew Union Coll., 1926—, prof. Bible 1936—, chmn. of faculty, 1947-55, now Nelson Glueck prof. Bible. Mem. Am. Oriental Soc. (pres. Middle West br., 1937-38), Soc. Bib. Lit. and Exegesis (pres. Midwest sect., 1947, nat. prs. 1952). Author: Prophetic Faith in Isaiah, 1958; Jeremiah; Man and Prophet, 1961; Understanding the prophets, 1969; sci. articles on Hebrew Scriptures. Home: 201 Lafayette Circle Cincinnati OH 45220

BLANKENHEIMER, BERNARD, govt. ofcl.; b. N.Y.C., July 6, 1920; s. Benjamin and Anna (Barach) B.; B.A., Bklyn. Coll., 1941; postgrad., N.Y. U., 1941-42; M.A. in Econs., George Washington U., 1950; m. Rosalind Brescher, Dec. 4, 1943; children—Alan Howard, Susan Leslie. With Commerce Dept., 1942—, jr. economist European div., 1942, asst. economist, 1945-47, internat. economist Africa sect. Brit. Commonwealth div., 1948-50, chief, African sect. Africa-Near East div., 1950-61, dep. dir. Africa Div., 1961, dir., 1962-68, U.S. Fgn. Service sr. comml. officer Am. consulate gen., Johannesburg, Republic South Africa, 1968-70, dep. dir. Office Import Programs, Washington, 1970—. Dir. U.S. Trade Mission to Liberia, Ghana, Sierra Leone, Guinea, 1960, Mission to Kenya, Uganda, Tanganyika, 1963; adviser U.S. del. 22d session GATT, Geneva, 1965; mem. U.S. Observer delegation UN Econ. Commn. for Africa Symposium on Industrialization, Cairo, 1966; mem. 9th Sr. Seminar in Fgn. Policy, State Dept., 1966-67; lectr. African studies Johns Hopkins Sch. Advanced Internat. Studies, 1957-62, Am. U. Sch. Bus. Adminstrn., 1967, Howard U., 1962-68. Served with AUS, 1942-45. Recipient Meritorious Service award for distinguished authorship Commerce Dept., 1960. Fellow African Studies Assn., Royal Geog. Soc. Contbr. articles to govt., profl. jours. Home: 9508 Wadsworth Dr Bethesda MD 20034 Office: U S Dept Commerce Washington DC 20230

BLANKENSHIP, GEORGE TONY, state govt. ofcl.; b. Oklahoma City, Mar. 11, 1928; s. George Tony and Daisy (Dean) B.; B.A., U. Okla., 1951, LL.B., 1954; m. Elizabeth Katherine Warren, June 8, 1951; childrenMatthew Steven, Elizabeth Ann, Julie Kay. Admitted to Okla. bar, 1954; pvt. practice, Oklahoma City 1956-61; mem. firm Lampkin, Wolfe & Blankenship, Oklahoma City, 1961-64; mem. Okla. Ho. of Reps. from Okla. County, 1960-66, minority floor leader, 1964-66; atty. gen. Okla., 1967-. Campaign chmn. Okla. Mental Health Assn., 1962. Served with USAF, 1954-56. Mem. Sigma Nu, Phi Alpha Delta. Republican. Mason (Shriner), Kiwanian. Home: 1600 Elmhurst Av Oklahoma City, OK 73120. Office: State Capitol Bldg Oklahoma City, OK 73105.

BLANKENSHIP, JOSEPH, univ. dean; b. Pulaski, Va., Dec. 8, 1917; s. Richard Conrad and Florence (Mills) B.; B.S., Ohio U., 1939; Mus.M., Cin. Conservatory Music, 1946, certificate in Piano Tech., 1947; Ph.D., U. Tex., 1956; m. Ruth Marian Johnson, Dec. 26, 1963; 1 dau., Victoria. Vocal and instrumental music tchr., Perry County, O., 1939-43; instrumental music tchr., supr., Portsmouth, O., 1943-44; instr. oboe and piano tech. Cin. Conservatory Music, 1945-47; piano technician Baldwin Piano Co.; music prof. U. Tex., Austin, 1947-60; chmn. dept. music U. N.M., 1960-69; dean U. Mo.-Kansas City Conservatory Music, 1969—; adjudicator music contests; conductor and clinician All-State Music Festivals; instl. examiner Nat. Assn. Schs. Music. Maj., N.M. Wing staff Civil Air Patrol, 1960-68; U.S. State Dept. rep. Teenage Tour in Europe, 1957; chmn. overseas com. Nat. Music Council, United Service Orgn., Dept. Def., 1970- -. Bd. dirs. Albuquerque Symphony Orch., Kansas City Philharmonic Assn., Youth Symphony Bd. Served with USAAF, 1944-45. Recipient Boss of Year award Am. Bus. Womens Assn., 1963-64. Mem. Nat. Assn. Schs. Music (chmn. Region 1), Kappa Kappa Psi, Phi Mu Alpha, Pi Kappa Lambda (nat. v.p.). Home: 5713 Metcalf Ct Overland Park KS 66202 Office: 4420 Warwick Blvd Kansas City MO 64111

BLANKERTZ, DONALD FREDERIC, educator; b. Monroe, Mich., Dec. 6, 1912; s. Ferdinand Jacob and Amalia Johannes (Lindeman) B.; A.B., U. Mich., 1934, M.B.A., 1935, Ph.D., 1942; m. Eloise Evelyn Strecker Hettinger, July 1, 1942; 1 son, Donald Edwin. With Keeler Brass Co. and Gen. Motors Corp., 1935-37; instr. marketing Ind. U., 1937-40; lectr. Wharton sch. finance and commerce U. Pa., 1941- 42, asst. prof., 1946-49, asso. prof., 1949-51, prof. marketing, 1951—, dir. Wharton grad. div. bus. and govt. administrn., 1953-69, vice dean, 1958-69; various positions War Production Board, and Office Civilian Requirements, 1942-44; with reports and control office, asst. chief of air staff materiel and supply Hdqrs. USAAF and spl. research asst. to chief supply division, Hdgrs. USAAF, 1944-46; mgmt. and research cons. Mem. Am. Marketing Assn., Eastern Mgmt. Assos. (bd. dirs.). Club: Lenape. Author: Marketing Cooperatives, 1940; Profitable Retail Advertising (with J. Rowen), Cases and Problems in Marketing Research (with R. Ferber and H. Wales), 1954. Contbr. profls. jours. Home: 7119 Lincoln Dr Philadelphia PA 19119

BLANKNER, FREDERIKA, educator, poet; d. Frederick and Irene (Aiken) Blankner; student Detroit Jr. Coll., 1918-20; Ph.B., U. Chgo., 1922, A.M. (grad. honor scholar, fellow, 1923; Alice Freeman Palmer fellowship for research abroad, Wellesley Coll., 1925-26; Litt. D., Royal U. Rome, 1926; student Abel Sch. Music, Detroit, 1919-20, 1921, Am. Conservatory of Music, Chgo., 1921-23. Acting chmn. dept., asst. prof. Italian, Vassar Coll., 1931-33; asst. prof. Romance langs. Western Res. U., 1935-42; prof. modern langs. Marymount Coll., 1942-43; poet in residence, prof., chmn. dept. classical civilization, langs. and lits., Adelphi Univ., Garden City, N.Y., 1943—. Mem., charter sponsor Found. for Integrated Edn., also mem. editorial bd., its publ. Main Currents in Modern Thought 1948—. Recipient numerous awards for lit., poetry, plays, 1923—, latest being 1st Hermes Lit. award, UN (for play From Cave to Cosmos), 1959; Prix de Paris for drama, 1961; 1st prize for drama Nat. League Am. Pen Women, 1962. Fellow MacDowell Colony, Internat. Inst. Arts and Letters (life); mem. Am. Coll. Minute Men (founder), Am. Soc. Baltic Studies (founder N.Y.C. 1958), Poetry Soc. Gt. Britain, Authors League Am., Am. Musicol. Soc. Nat. League Am. Pen Women, Am. Assn. U. Women, Womens' Press Club, Am. Philol. Assn., Am. Classical League, Classical Soc. Am. Acad. Rome, Dante Soc., Virgilian Soc., Modern Lang. Assn., Mediaeval Acad. Am., Nat. Council Tchrs. English, A.A.A.S., Am. Polit. Sci. Assn., Phi Beta Kappa., Phi Beta Kappa Assos., Eta Sigma Phi, Delta Tau Alpha, Mu Phi Epsilon, other learned socs. Co-author, editor, compiler, translator; History of the Scandinavian Literatures (with Richard Beck and Adolph Benson), 1938. Author publs. relating to field, including plays, essays, verse; also contbr. to Am., fgn. publs. Lectr., reader original poetry. Home: 1 W 67th St New York City NY 10023 Office: Adelphi Coll Garden City NY 11530 ☆

BLANSETT, BRUCE EDWARD, investment co. exec.; b. Versailles, Ill., Oct. 7, 1923; s. Paul Laverne and Velma (Myers) B.; B.S., U. Ill., 1946; student Mass. Inst. Tech., N.Y. U.; m. Melva Jean Coulter, Sept. 27, 1952; children—Jean, Peter Coulter. Account mgr. Arthur Andersen & Co., C.P.A.'s, N.Y.C., 1948-62; treas. Equity Corp., N.Y.C., 1962—, Bell Intercontinental Corp., N.Y.C., 1966-71; pres., dir. Garden City Co., N.Y.C., 1966—, 101-103 Park Av., Inc., N.Y.C., 1966—; dir. Cornwall Trading Corp., Bell Aluminum Co. Served to capt. USAF, 1943-46, 51-52. Home: 3945 Wolkow Av Seaford NY 11783 Office: 26 Broadway New York City NY 10004

BLANSHARD, BRAND, educator, philosopher; b. Fredericksburg, O., Aug. 27, 1892; s. Francis G. and Emily (Coulter) B.; A.B., U. Mich., 1914; A.M., Columbia, 1918; B.Sc., Oxford (Eng.) U., 1920; Ph.D., Harvard, 1921; Litt.D., Swarthmore Coll., 1947, Concord Coll., 1962, Albion Coll., 1966; L.H.D., Bucknell U., 1954, Colby Coll., 1956, Trinity Coll., 1957, Roosevelt U., 1959, Simpson Coll., 1961, Kenyon Coll., 1961, U. N.M., 1968; LL.D., Oberlin Coll., 1956, U. St. Andrews (Scotland), 1959; m. Frances Bradshaw, Nov. 3, 1918 (dec. 1966); m. 2d, Roberta Yerkes, June 6, 1969. Asst. prof. philosophy U. Mich., 1921-25; asso. prof. Swarthmore Coll., 1925- 28, prof., 1928-45; prof. philosophy Yale, 1945-61, chmn. dept., 1945- 50, 59-61; Dudleian lectr. Harvard, 1945, Noble lectr., 1948, Whitehead lectr., 1961; Gifford lectr. St. Andrews U., 1952-53; Hertz lectr. British Acad., 1952; Adamson lectr. U. Manchester (Eng.), 1953; Howison lectr. U. Cal. at Berkeley, 1954; Matchette lectr. Wesleyan U., Middletown, Conn., 1957, Bklyn. Coll., 1962; Carus lectr. Am. Philos. Assn., 1959; vis. prof. U. Minn., 1962. Sec. British YMCA, Mesopotamia and India, 1915-17; served with U.S. Army, 1918-19; AEF in France. Rhodes scholar, 1913-15, 1919-20; Guggenheim fellow, 1929-30; fellow Center Advanced Studies, Wesleyan U., 1961-62; recipient sr. award Am. Council Learned Socs., 1959; medal of honor Rice U., 1962; hon. fellow Merton Coll., Oxford U. Corr. fellow British Acad.; mem. Am. Theol. Soc. (pres. 1955-56), Am. Philos. Assn. (pres. Eastern div. 1942-44), Am. Acad. Arts and Scis., Phi Beta Kappa. Mem. Soc. Friends. Author: The Nature of Thought, 2 vols., 1940; Reason and Goodness, 1960; Reason and Analysis, 1962; (with others) Philosophy in American Education, 1945; Preface to Philosophy, 1946. Editor: Education in the Age of Science, 1959. Home: 4 St Ronan Terrace New Haven CT 06511

BLANSHARD, PAUL, author; b. Fredericksburg, O., Aug. 27, 1892; s. Francis George and Emily (Coulter) B.; A.B., U. Mich., 1914; LL.B., Bklyn. Law Sch., 1937; grad. study Harvard, Columbia, Union Theol. Sem.; m. Julia Anderson, Oct. 20, 1915 (dec. 1934); children—Paul, Rufus; m. 2d, Mary W. Hillyer, Hillyer, August 1, 1935 (dec. 1965); m. 3d, Beatrice Mayer. Ordained to ministry Conglist Ch., 1917, pastor First Ch., Tampa, 1917-18; ednl. dir. Amalgamated Clothing Workers Am., Rochester, N.Y., 1920-24; field sec. League Indsl. Democracy, 1925-33; asso. editor The Nation, 1928-29; dir. city affairs com., N.Y.C., 1930-33, commr. investigations and accounts, 1934-38; admitted to N.Y. bar, 1938, practiced 1939-41; econ. analyst, cons. Caribbean Commn. State Dept., 1942-46; writer, 1946—. Mem. of the Phi Beta Kappa, Delta Sigma Rho. Unitarian. Author: An Outline of the British Labor Movement, 1923; (with Norman Thomas) What's the Matter with New York, 1932; Democracy and Empire in the Caribbean, 1947; American Freedom and Catholic Power, 1949; Communism, Democracy and Catholic Power, 1951; The Irish and Catholic Power, 1953; The Right to Read, 1955; God and Man in Washington, 1960; Freedom and Catholic Power in Spain and Portugal, 1962; Religion and the Schools, 1963; Paul Blanshard on Vatican II, 1966; others. Home: Thetford Center VT 05075

BLANTON, HARRY CULLEN, lawyer; b. Paris, Mo., July 5, 1891; s. Charles Lee and Mary Agnes (Cullen) B.; J.D., Georgetown U., 1914; m. Maureen Daily, Feb. 12, 1918; children—Rosemary Louise (Mrs. Harry K. Barr, Jr.), Patricia Daily (Mrs. Dudley T. Kavanagh), Maureen Margaret (Mrs. Jean Klein), John David, Anne Madeleine (Mrs. J. Patrick Tlapek), Henry Joseph Cullen, Charles Lewis Michael, Harry Augustine. Engaged in practice law, Sikeston, Mo.; mem. firm Blanton, Blanton & Rice; city atty., Sikeston, 1915-16; pros. atty. Scott County, Mo., 1917-18; chmn. Dem. Congl. Com., 14th Mo. Dist., 1922; chmn. Scott County Democratic Com., 1922-28; mem. Mo. Supreme Court Commn. to regulate practice and procedure, 1933, 34; U.S. atty. Eastern Dist. Mo., 1934-47. Admitted to practice before U.S. Supreme Court and all state and fed. cts. Eastern Mo. Past pres. Fed. Bus. Assn. of St. Louis, Sikeston (Mo.) Bldg. & Loan Assn. Served as mem. 1st O.T.C., Ft. Riley, Kan., and as mem. Hdqrs. Troop, 10th Div. Camp Funston, Kan., later mem. Central Machine Gun O.T.S., Camp Hancock, Ga. Pres. S.E. Mo. Council Boy Scouts Am., 1950-52 (Silver Beaver award 1955). Fellow Am. Bar Found., Am. Coll. Trial Lawyers; mem. Am., St. Louis, Scott County (former pres.), Fed. (past pres. St. Louis chpt.) bar assns., Mo. Bar, Mo. Bar Integrated (bd. govs. 1956-60, trustee 1960-68), Am. Judicature Soc., Am. Legion (dept. comdr. 1929-30, dept. judge adv. 1930-31), Delta Chi. Roman Catholic (pres. Cape Girardeau Deanery Archdiocesan Council Cath. Men 1955). K.C., Kiwanian. Home: 1023 N Ranney Sikeston MO 63801 Office: PO Box 805 Sikeston MO 63801

BLANTON, JACK SAWTELLE, oil co. exec.; b. Shreveport, La., Dec. 7, 1927; s. William Neal and Louise (Wynn) B.; B.A., U. Tex., 1947, LL.B., 1950; m. Laura Lee Scurlock, Aug. 20, 1949; children—Elizabeth Louise, Jack Sawtelle, Eddy Scurlock. Admitted to Tex. bar, 1950; with Scurlock Oil Co., Houston, 1950—, v.p., 1956-58, pres., 1958—, dir., 1956—; v.p. Eddy Refining Co., Key Oil Co.; dir. Chem. Bank & Trust Co. Vice pres. Sam Houston area council Boy Scouts Am.; founder, 1st pres. Parents League Houston. Mem. bd. mgrs. Harris County Hosp. Dist.; trustee Meth. Hosp.; mem. bd. devel. So. Meth. U., Lon Morris Coll.; v.p. Mus. Natural Sci.; pres. Scurlock Found. Named Houston's outstanding young man of year, 1960. Mem. Houston C. of C. (life), Sons Rep. of Tex. (past pres. San Jacinto chpt.), Sam Houston Meml. Assn., Nat. Tennis Assn., U.S. Lawn Tennis Assn., Am. Petroleum Inst., Tex. Ind. Oil Producers and Refiners, Young Pres.'s Orgn., (past pres. S.E. Tex. chpt.), Delta Kappa Epsilon, Phi Delta Phi, Phi Alpha Delta, Ex-Students Assn. U. Tex. (past pres.). Clubs: Houston (past pres.), River Oaks Country (Houston). Home: 3390 Inwood Dr Houston TX 77019 Office: Houston Club Bldg Houston TX 77002

BLANTON, LEONARD RAY, congressman; b. Hardin County, Tenn., Apr. 10, 1930; s. Leonard Alonza and Ova A. (DeLaney) B.; B.S., U. Tenn., 1951; m. Betty Jane Littlefield, July 23, 1949; children—Deborah, Jane, David Ray, Paul Derik. Tchr., Moresville, Ind., 1951-53; with B-B Constrn. Co., Adamsville Tenn., 1954- 67; mem. Tenn. Ho. of Reps. from McNairy County, 1965-66; mem. 90th-92d congresses 7th Dist. Tenn. Mem. Tenn. Plant-Mix and Asphalt Assn. (past v.p.), U. Tenn. Alumni Assn. Democrat. Methodist (chmn. bd.). Lion, Moose, Mason (Shriner). Home: Old Shilo Rd Adamsville TN 38310 Office: Longworth House Office Bldg Washington DC 20515

BLASBAND, ALFRED, cab co. exec.; b. Phila., Aug. 31, 1905; s. Benjamin and Mollie (Sobel) B.; eve. student Wharton Sch., U. Pa., 1929; m. Gertrude Leventon, Nov. 10, 1928; children—Richard A., David. Exec. v.p. Bankers Securities Corp. until 1951, v.p., 1960-64, now dir.; pres. Shellenburgs, 1952-59; pres. Yellow Cab Co., Phila. 1961—; dir. Loft Candy Corp., Ben Franklin Hotel Co., Bankers Bond & Mortgage Guaranty Co. Am. Chmn. Mayor Phila. Traffic Safety Adv. Com. Bd. dirs. United Fund Phila., Fedn. Jewish Charities, Phila. Mem. C. of C. Greater Phila. (bd. dirs.). Home: 1801 John F Kennedy Blvd Philadelphia PA 19103 Office: 105 S 12th St Philadelphia PA 19130

BLASER, LORENZ PAUL, oil co. exec.; b. Markinch, Sask., Can., Feb. 12, 1916; s. Paul and Barbara (Appenheimer) B.; B.Sc. in Chem. Engring., U. Sask., 1938; m. Marjorie Jean Orr, July 4, 1942; children—Barbara Lynn, Paula Jean, David Lorenz Paul. With Gulf Oil Canada Limited (formerly British American Oil Co. Ltd.), 1939—, chief engr., Toronto, 1954-58, gen. mgr., mfg., 1958-63, v.p. mfg., 1963-66, world wide coordinator refining Gulf Oil Co., Pitts., 1966-67, sr. v.p., 1967—. Bd. dirs. Canadian Opera Assn. Registered profl. engr., Ont. Mem. Ont. Soc. Profl. Engrs., Am. Petroleum Inst., Toronto C. of C., Canadian C. of C. Engrs.' Club Toronto. Clubs: Donalda, Canadian, Granite, National. Home: 37 Daneswood Rd Toronto 317 Ontario Canada Office: 800 Bay St Toronto 5 Ontario Canada

BLASICK, HENRY JOHN, librarian; b. Swoyersville, Pa., Oct. 26, 1919; s. Teofil L. and Josephine (Shultz) B.; A.B., Stetson U., 1952; M.L.S., Fla. State U., 1955; m. Mary Nelle Martin, July 28, 1952; children—James David, Martin Laurence. Br. and bookmobile librarian Orlando (Fla.) Pub. Library, 1955- 56; base librarian McCoy AFB, Orlando, 1956-57; head librarian Hayner Pub. Library, Alton, Ill., 1957-58; dir. libraries Suwanne River Regional Library, Live Oak, Fla., 1958-61; city librarian Sterling Municipal Library, Baytown, Tex., 1961-64; librarian-recruiter Mo. State Library, Jefferson City, 1964-65; dir. Mobile Pub. Library, 1965-71; state library dir. Fla. State Library, Tallahassee, 1971—. Served with AUS, 1942-45; PTO. Mem. Am., Southeastern, Ala. library assns. Rotarian. Contbr. profl. jours. Home: 2302 Mission Rd Tallahassee FL 32304 Office: Supreme Ct Bldg Fla State Library Tallahassee FL 32304

BLASIER, COLE, educator; b. Jackson, Mich., Mar. 16, 1925; s. Stewart Parnell and Helen (Cole) B.; A.B., U. Ill., 1947; postgrad. U. Mexico and U. Chile, 1947-48; A.M., Columbia, 1950, certificate Russian Inst., 1950, Ph.D. in Polit. Sci., 1955; m. Martha Hiett, Sept. 20, 1947; children—Peter Cole, Martha Hamilton. Joined U.S. Fgn. Service, 1951; polit. econ. officer Am. embassy, Belgrade, Yugoslavia, 1951-54, Bonn, Germany, 1954-56, Moscow, USSR, 1958, Washington, 1959-60; resigned, 1960; exec. asst. to pres., sec. bd. trustees Colgate U., 1961-63; vis. prof. Universidad del Valle, Cali, Colombia, 1963-64, asso. prof., 1964-67; prof. polit. sci. U. Pitts., 1967—, dir. Center Latin Am. Studies, 1964—. Trustee Ellis Sch., Pitts. Served with USNR, 1943-46. Rotary Found. fellow, 1947-48; Rockefeller Found. grantee, 1963-64. Mem. Am. Polit. Sci. Assn., Latin Am. Studies Assn. Presbyn. Club: Pittsburgh Golf. Editor: Constructive Change in Latin America, 1968. Contbr. articles profl. jours. Home: 5306 Westminster Pl Pittsburgh PA 15232

BLASIER, ROBERT DALTON, business exec.; b. Jesup, Ia., Jan. 3, 1911; s. William W. and Ula E. (Dalton) B.; A.B., Grinnell Coll., 1932; J.D. cum laude, Harvard, 1935; m. Helen J. Talbott, Aug. 20, 1935; children—Susan Elizabeth (Mrs. John Butler), Diane Talbott, Marcia Jean (Mrs. Dirk Schindel), Robert Dalton, William Eugene. Admitted to N.Y. bar, 1937; with Cravath, Swaine & Moore (formerly Cravath, de Gersdorff, Swaine & Wood), 1935-42; sr. atty., law dept. Westinghouse Electric Corp., 1942-48, asst. to v.p. law dept., 1948-52, now v.p. indsl. relations. Trustee, Indsl. Hygiene Found. Mem. Am. Bar Assn., Harvard Law Sch. Assn., Am. Acad. Polit. Sci., Am. Mgmt. Assn., Phi Beta Kappa. Mason (Shriner). Clubs: Youghiogheny Country (McKeesport, Pa.); Duquesne (Pitts.); Lakeview Country (Morgantown, W. Va.). Home: High Tor 356 Old Clairton Rd Pleasant Hills Pittsburgh PA 15236 Office: Westinghouse Bldg Gateway Center Pittsburgh PA 15222

BLASINGAME, FRANCIS JAMES LEVI, physician, educator; b. Hot Springs, Ark., Jan 17, 1907; s. John Mitchell Coleman and Lillian Adams (White) B.; A.B., U. Tex., 1929, M.D. 1932; m. Dorothy Isbel Rugeley, June 8, 1932; children—Mary Lillian, Betty Nan, John Chester, Rebecca Louise, James Edward. Intern, Henry Ford Hosp., Detroit, 1935-36; instr. anatomy, med. br. U. of Tex., 1932-33, adj. prof., 1933-35, asso. prof., 1936-37, lectr. anatomy 1937- 58; mem. staff Rugeley and Blasingame Clinic-Hosp., Wharton, Tex., 1937- 58; exec. v.p. Am. Med. Assn., Chgo., 1958-68; now cons. in the health field, Chmn. bd. edn. Wharton Co. Jr. Coll.; pres. state bd. dirs. Blue Cross and Blue Shield of Tex. Fellow A.C.S., Am. Coll. Hosp. Adminstrs. (hon.); mem. A.M.A. (trustee), Southwestern Surg. Congress, State Med. Assn. Texas (pres.), Cook County Med. Soc., Phi Chi, Alpha Omega Alpha. Episcopalian. Mason (Shriner), Rotarian. Author articles in profl. jours. Home: 1350 Astor St Chicago IL 60610

BLASINGAME, RALPH UPSHAW, Jr., librarian; b. State College Pa., Oct. 9, 1920; s. Ralph Upshaw and Sue (Combs) B.; B.A., Pa. State Coll., 1942; B.S., Columbia U. Sch. Library Service, 1947, M.S., 1950; Doctor of Letters, St. Francis Coll., 1963; m. Mariann L. Carpino, Aug. 30, 1943; childrenGail, Karen, Jill. Library asst. Coll. City N.Y., 1947-49; research asst. Columbia U. Sch. Library Service, 1949-50, asst. to dean, 1950-52; asst. state librarian, Cal., 1952-57; state librarian Pa., 1957-64; prof. Grad. Sch. Library Service, Rutgers U., 1964—; chmn. Pa. Bd. Regional Library Resources Centers, 1961-64. Bd. dirs. Union Library Catalogue. Served in USAAF, 1942-46; lt. col. Res. Mem. A.L.A. (council; A.L.A.-N.E.A. joint com.; adv. com. library tech. project; pres. library adminstrn. div. 1961-62, commn. on nat. plan for library edn. 1963, chmn. adv. com. recruiting project 1963, treas. 1964- 68), Pa. Library Assn. Author: (with M.F. Tauber, others) Technical Services in Libraries, 1954; Punched Card (vol. 4, part 3 The State of the Library Art); Library Services in West Virginia; Present and Proposed: Survey of Ohio Libraries and State Library Services, 1968. Contbr. articles profl. jours. Home: 24 Pine Ridge Dr East Brunswick NJ 08816 Office: Rutgers The State U New Brunswick NJ 08903

BLASKA, GREGORY DARWIN, coop. exec.; b. Marshall, Wis., May 25, 1926; s. John M. aand Rose F. (Schuster) B.; student U. Wis., 1943-45; m. Laura M. Klein, Sept. 11, 1948; children—John, Jeffrey, Margaret, Barry. Sec.-treas., dir. Dairyland Coop. Assn., Juneau, Wis., 1954-59; sec., dir. Pure Milk Assn., Chgo., 1959-69; dir. Asso. Milk Producers, Inc., San Antonio, 1969—; life ins. underwriter, 1958—. Gen. chmn. 1970 Wis. Farm Progress Days. Treas. Sun Prairie (Wis.) Joint Sch. Bd., 1970-71. Democrat. Roman Catholic. Rotarian, Cath. Order of Foresters. Home: Route 2 Marshall WI 53559 Office: Box 32287 San Antonio TX 78216

BLASKE, FLOYD HUGH, transp. co. exec.; b. St. Louis, June 30, 1913; s. Hugh C. and Elsa (Heldman) B.; A.B., Central Coll., Fayette, Mo., 1935; m. Dorothy Francis Hellrung, June 27, 1940; children—Roger H., Stephen F., Stanley J., Jeffrey C., Mark D., Marilyn F. Partner, Blaske Boat and Barge Co., Alton, Ill., 1937-45; v.p. Blaske Lines, Inc., Alton, 1943-56; v.p. Am. Comml. Barge Line Co. (now Am. Comml. Lines, Inc.), Jeffersonville, Ind., 1956-58, exec. v.p., 1958-60, pres., 1960—, also dir.; now v.p. Inland Waterways Services (subsidiary Tex. Gas Transmission Corp.), Houston; adv. bd. Liberty Mut. Ins. Co.; dir. Citizens Fidelity Bank & Trust, Jeffersonville. Mem. Louisville and Jefferson County Riverport Authority. Bd. dirs. Ohio Valley Improvement Assn. Served from ensign to lt. USNR, 1942-46. Mem. Am. Bur. Shipping. Clubs: Harmony Landing Country (dir. 1964—) (Goshen, Ky.); Nat. Propeller (v.p.). Home: 5814 Aura Rd Louisville KY 40222 Office: 2919 Allen Pkwy Houston TX 77019

BLASS, BILL, clothing designer; b. Ft. Wayne, Ind., June 22, 1922; s. Ralph Aldrich and Ethyl (Keyser) B.; student Parsons Sch. Design, N.Y.C., 1941. Asst. designer for Anna Miller, 1950-59; designer Maurice Rentner, 1959—, partner, 1961—, v.p., 1963—; pres. Bill Blass, Inc.; pres. Bill Blass Ltd., 1970—. Served with AUS, World War II. Recipient Coty award Am. Fashion Critics, 1961, 63, Spl. Coty award, 1968; Neiman Marcus award, 1969, Coty Hall of Fame award, 1970; Am. Fashion Critics Hall of Fame award, 1970. Mem. Council Fashion Designers Am. (v.p.). Home: 444 E 57th St New York City NY 10021 Office: 550 7th Av New York City NY 10018

BLASS, GERHARD ALOIS, educator; b. Chemnitz, Germany, Mar. 12, 1916; s. Gustav Alois and Anna (Mehnert) B.; Abitur, Oberrealschule Chemnitz, 1935; Dr. rer. nat., Universität Leipzig, 1943; m. Barbara Siegert, July 16, 1945; children—Andrew, Marcus, Evamaria, Annamaria, Peter. Came to U.S., 1949, naturalized, 1955. Asst., Instutut fur Theoretische Physik, Leipzig, 1939-43; research cons. Siemens & Halske, Berlin, 1943-46; dozent math. and physics Oberrealschule, Nuremberg, 1946-47; dozent math. and physics Ohm Polytechnikum, Nuremberg, 1947-49; prof. physics Coll. St. Thomas, St. Paul, 1949-51; prof. physics U. Detroit, 1951—, chmn. dept., 1962-71. Fellow A.A.A.S.; mem. Am. Phys. Soc., Math. Assn., Am. Ordnance Assn., Detroit Astron. Soc. (pres.), Sigma Pi Sigma. Roman Catholic. Author: Theoretical Physics, 1962. Home: 16636 Wildemere Av Detroit MI 48221

BLASS, NOLAND, Jr., architect; b. Little Rock, Ark., May 28, 1920; s. Noland and Isabel (Ringelhaupt) B.; B.Arch., Cornell U., 1941; m. Elizabeth Weitzenhoffer, Oct. 21, 1947; children—Elizabeth Victoria, Wilhelmina Louise. Designer-draftsman Erhart, Eichenbaum, Rauch (name changed to Erhart, Eichenbaum, Rauch and Blass), Little Rock, Ark., 1946-56, partner, 1956—; dir., mem. exec. com. Pleasant Valley Inc., 1960—. Pres. elect Ark. Arts Center, 1971; mem. Little Rock Planning Commn., 1960-69; pres. Pulaski Metropolitan Y.M.C.A., 1967-68; mem. Gov.'s Inauguration Com., 1971. Trustee A.I.A. Ednl. Endowment Fund. Served with AUS, 1941-45. Fellow A.I.A. (pres. Ark. 1958-59); mem. Tau Beta Pi, Zeta Beta Tau. Jewish religion. Mason (32). Home: 217 Normandy Rd Little Rock AR 72207 Office: Continental Bldg Little Rock AR 72201

BLATAS, ARBIT, artist; b. Kaunas, Lithuania, Nov. 19, 1908; s. Ilya Arbit and Ida (Neercik) B.; ed. elementary and high schs., Russia and Lithuania; painted and studied in Germany, 1924-25; studied Acad. Julien, Paris, also alone, 1925; m. Sylvia Satenstein, July 13, 1933; 1 dau. Dorothée Renée (Mrs. Christian Gas). Came to U.S. 1939. Exhibited in Lithuania, 1926, Paris, France, 1948-52, Galerie Van Leer, Paris, 1933; Pierre Matisse Gallery, N.Y.C., 1934; Galerie de l'Elysee, Paris, 1937, 54; Galeria Mouradian and Valloton, Paris, 1939, 54; also French Art Galleries, N.Y.C., 1940, 1941 and 1942; Robert C. Vose Gallery, Boston, 1941; annually at Salon des Tuileries and Salon d'Automne, Paris, 1929-39; World's Fair Expn., Paris, 1937; Galerie Bernheim Jeune, for the Prix Paul Guillaume, 1938, Fine Arts Assos., 1956, Hirschl & Adler Galleries, N.Y.C., 1957, Marcel Marceau, N.Y.C., 1958, Carnegie Inst., Rochester, N.Y., 1959; had one-man show Providence (R.I.) Mus., Dayton (O.) Mus., Wichita (Kan.) Mus., San Francisco Mus., Colorado Mus., Asso. Am. Artists, 1943, Gallerie de L'Elysee (Paris), 1945-46, Bignou Gallery (N.Y.C.), 1946. Represented in Musee National de Jeu-de-Paume, Paris; Mus. of Grenoble, France; Nat. Mus. of Lithuania; Mus. of Modern Art, N.Y.C.; Providence Mus.; Wichita Mus.; Richmond Mus.; Mus. of Modern Art, Paris (purchased by French govt.), also various private collections in France, Eng., U.S. Met. Mus. Art, Montclair Mus., Whitney Mus., Carnegie Inst., Rochester. Home: 50 W 56th St New York City NY 10019

BLATCHFORD, JOSEPH HOFFER, govt. ofcl.; b. Milw., June 7, 1934; s. George Nason and Zoe Mae (Hoffer) B.; B.A. in Polit. Sci., U. Cal. at Los Angeles, 1956, LL.D., at Berkeley, 1961; L.H.D., Seton Hall U., 1969; L.H.D., Chapman Coll., 1970; L.H.D., Kenyon Coll., 1970; m. Winifred Anne Marich, Dec. 29, 1967; 1 dau., Andrea Nicole. Legislative asst. U.S. Congress, 1957; founder ACCION en Venezuela, 1960-64; founder, exec. dir. ACCION Internat., 1965-68; founder Acao Comunitaria do Brazil, 1966-67; dir. Peace Corps, Washington, 1969—. Capt. NCAA Championship Tennis Team, U. Cal., Los Angeles, 1956. Republican candidate for U.S. Congress, Cal., 1968. Served to 2d lt. U.S. Army, 1956-57. Recipient Distinguished Service award U. Cal. at Los Angeles, 1970. Mem. Phi Kappa Psi. Home: 3036 P St NW Washington DC 20007 Office: 806 Connecticut Av NW Washington DC 20525

BLATCHFORD, NICHOLAS, journalist; b. Winnetka, Ill., May 6, 1919; s. Nathaniel Hopkins and Margaret (Copeland) B.; B.A., Harvard, 1940; m. Lois Greeley, June 3, 1944; children—Anne Hathaway, Kim Copeland, Nicholas Mark. With Washington Daily News, 1947—, asst. mng. editor, 1958-66, mng. editor, 1966-68, asso. editor, 1968—. Bd. dirs. D.C. Bur. Rehab. Served with AUS, 1941-45. Home: 2945 Cedar Lane Fairfax VA 22030 Office: 1013 13th St NW Washington DC 20005

BLATNIK, JOHN A., congressman, educator; b. Chisholm, Minn., Aug. 17, 1911; s. John and Margaret (Kochevar) B.; B.E. cum laude, Winona, (Minn.) State Tchrs. Coll., 1935; student U. Chgo., summer 1938; grad. work in pub. adminstrn., U. Minn., 1941-42; m. Gisela Hager, Apr. 9, 1955; children—Thomas, Stephanie, Valerie. Bagan as tchr. in a country sch., 1930-31; ednl. adviser Civilian Conservation Corps, Superior Nat. Forest, Minn., 1935-37; chem. instr. Chisholm (Minn.) High Sch., 1937-39; asst. to St. Louis County (Minn.) Supt. Schs., 1939-41; mem. Minn. State Senate, 1941-46; mem. 80th-92nd U.S. Congresses, 8th Minn. Dist. Chmn. Pub. Works Com., 1971—. Co.-founder, past chmn. Dem. Study Com. Former chmn. N.E. Minn. Rehab. Com., 1940- 42. Minn. Democratic nat. committeeman, 1962—; chmn. Minn. delegation Democratic Nat. Conv., 1968. Served in Army Air Corps Intelligence and Office of Strategic Services; spent 8 months behind enemy lines with Yugoslav Partisans in northern Yugoslavia, liaison for Allied Hdqrs. in Italy; disch. as paratrooper capt., Jan. 1946. Awarded Bronze star medal with Oak Leaf cluster, Air medal; recipient Gold Key award as outstanding young man in community, 1941; Bernard M. Baruch prize, 1968; Water Conservation and Mgmt. award Great Lakes Commn., 1969; State Conservation award Minn. Izaak Walton League, 1970. Active in Boy Scout work for ten years, was Eagle Scout; Jr. C. of C. work for 5 yrs. Mem. Minn. Am.-Jugoslav Assn. (state pres. 1939-41), Izaak Walton League, Am. Legion, V.F.W., Am. Vets. Com., Kappa Delta Pi. Mem. Democratic-Farmer-Labor Party of Minn. Roman Catholic. Home: 417 1/2 Fourth St SW Chisolm MN 55719 Office: Rayburn Office Bldg Washington DC 20515

BLATNY, PAVEL, composer; b. Brno, Czechoslovakia, Sept. 14, 1931; s. Josef and Anna (Sekerová) B.; student musicology U. Brno, 1953-58, Music Acad., 1955-59, Berklee Sch. Music, Boston, 1968; m. Libuse Orálkova, Aug. 24, 1956; children—Renata, Marek. Condr. symphony or jazz orch. 1954; piano player, 1950—; private tchr. composition, 1965—; TV speaker, 1963—; composition played at various festivals; recording artist for Supraphon, Panton, Edition Modernist for München Schott's Söhne-Mainz, Saba, R. Mellin records. Recipient 1st award composition Prague Internat. Competition, 1966, 67, Down Beat Jazz poll, 1965, 66, 67, 68. Compositions include: Music for Piano and Orchestra, 1955; Concerto for Orchestra, 1956; Concerto for Chamber Orchestra, 1958; 10, 30 for Symphonic Orchestra, 1965; Concerto for Jazz Orchestra, 1962; Study for 1/4 Tone Trumpet and Jazz Orchestra, 1964; Pour Ellis, 1966. Address: 24 Drobneho Brno Czechoslovakia

BLATT, ALBERT HAROLD, educator; b. Cin., Jan. 9, 1903; s. Joseph and Fannie (Krebs) B.; B.S., Harvard, 1923, M.A., Ph.D., 1926; student Coll. de France, 1923-24; m. Therese Herman, Jan. 30, 1935; 1 son, Joel. Research asso. Harvard, 1926- 28; asst. to gen. mgr. Columbus-McKinnon Chain Co., 1928-30; research asso. U. Buffalo, 1930-32; asso. prof. Howard U., 1932-39; mem. faculty Queens Coll., 1939—, prof. chemistry, 1948—, chmn. chemistry dept., 1961-68. Mem. div. 8 NDRC, also mem. London mission OSRD, 1941-46. Recipient Naval Ordnance Devel. award, 1946, Certificate of Merit, 1948. Mem. Am. Chem. Soc., Am. Assn. U. Profs., Am. Civil Liberties Union. Author: (with James B. Conant) Chemistry of Organic Compounds, 5th edit., 1959. Editor: Organic Syntheses Collective, Vol. I, 1941, vol. II, 1943. Editorial bd. Organic Syntheses, 1938-43, Organic Reactions, 1948-70. Home: 415 E 52d St New York City NY 10022 Office: Queen's Coll City Univ of NY Flushing NY 11367

BLATT, BURTON, educator; b. Bronx, N.Y., May 23, 1927; s. Abraham and Jennie (Starr) B.; B.S., N.Y.U., 1949; M.A., Columbia Tchrs. Coll., 1950; Ed.D., Pa. State U., 1956; m. Ethel Draizen, Dec. 24, 1951; children—Edward Richard, Steven David, Michael Lawrence. Tchr. mentally retarded children, N.Y.C., 1949-55; grad. scholar, grad. asst. Pa. State U., 1955- 1955- 56; asso. prof., coordinator spl. edn. So. Conn. State Coll., 1956-59, prof., chmn. spl. edn. dept. 1959-61; prof. chmn. spl. edn. dept. Sch. Edn., Boston U., 1961—; dir. div. spl. edn. and rehab. Syracuse U., 1969—; former commr. mental retardation Mass. Dept. Mental Health. Former prin. cons. to R.I. Commn. to Study Edn. of Retarded Children; cons. U.S. Office Edn.; mem. adv. bd. Joseph P. Kennedy Jr. Found.; past bd. dirs. Epilepsy League Mass., former chmn. Mass. Task Force on Edn. Mentally Handicapped; past mem. nat. adv. bd. Nat. Soc. Prevention Blindness; Past mem. Mass. Gov's Com. on Services to Children, Conn. Gov.'s Adv. Council Mental Retardation. Recipient Ann. award Mass. Psychol. Assn., 1967, Mass. Assn. for Retarded Children. Fellow Am. Assn. Mental Deficiency (editorial staff of Mental Retardation, v.p.); mem. Council Exceptional Children (past state pres., state dir., div. pres.), Phi Delta Kappa. Jewish religion. Author: (with S. Sarason, K. Davidson) The Preparation of Teachers, 1962; The Intellectually Disfranchised; Impoverished Learners and Their Teachers, 1967; (with F. Kaplan) Christmas in Purgatory, 1967; The Educability of Intelligence, 1969; Exodus from Pandemonium, 1970. Contbg. author: Mental Retardation—Readings and Resources, 1961; also articles, monographs on spl. edn. Home: 106 Cedar Heights Dr Jamesville NY 13078 Office: 805 S Crouse Av Syracuse NY 13210

BLATT, GENEVIEVE, lawyer; b. East Brady, Pa., June 19, 1913; d. George F. and Clara (Laurent) Blatt; A.B., U. Pitts., 1933, M.A., 1934, J.D., 1937; LL.D., St. Francis Coll., 1959, Villanova U., 1960, St. Joseph's College, 1964, Barry Coll., 1966, Seton Hall Coll., 1968. Faculty U. Pitts., 1934-38; admitted to Pa. bar, 1938; sec., chief examiner Civil Service Commn., City of Pitts., 1938-42; asst. city solicitor, Pitts., 1942-45; dep. state treas. Pa., exec. dir. State Treasury Dept., 1945- 49; sec. internal affairs Pa., 1955-67; asst. dir. to the Office Econ. Opportunity, 1967-68; dir. departmental audits Pa. Auditor Gen.'s Office, 1969; counsel to Morgan, Lewis & Bockius, Attys., 1970—; spl. cons. Shared Services Assn. Founder, exec. dir. Pa. Intercollegiate Conf. on Govt., 1934—; sec. Pa. Indsl. Devel. Authority Bd., 1956-67; vice chmn. Interstate Oil Compact Commn., 1959. Mem. weights and measures adv. com. Nat. Bur. Standards, 1960-67; mem. adv. com. women in armed services Def. Dept., 1964-67; mem. President's Consumer Adv. Council, 1964-66, President's Commn. on Law Enforcement and Adminstrn. Justice, 1965-67. Sec. Pa. Dem. State Com., 1948-70; Dem. nominee for auditor gen. Pa. 1952; delegate-at-large and vice chmn. Pa. delegation to Democratic Nat. Conv., 1956; pres. Young Dem. Clubs Pa., 1942-50; exec. bd. Pa. Fedn. Dem. Women, 1940—; dist. del. Dem. Nat. Conv., 1936, 44, 48, del.-at-large, 1960, 64, 68; Dem. nominee for United States Senate, 1964; Dem. nat. committee woman Pa., 1970—. Mem. bd. of dirs. Tri-County and Pa. united funds; bd. mgrs. Holy Spirit Hosp.; pres.'s council Mt. Mercy Coll.; bd. trustees La Roche Coll., Allison Park, Pa., St. Joseph's Coll., Emmetsburg, Md. Recipient Distinguished Dau. of Pa. award, 1956; named Woman of the Year in Govt., Pitts., 1959; also by Who's Who of American Women, 1963; Mother Gerard Phelan gold medal Marymount Coll., 1965; Pro Ecclesia et Pontifice medal Pope Paul VI, 1968; Louise de Marillac medal St. Joseph's Coll.; Dubois medal Mount St. Mary Coll., 1970. Mem. Am., Pa., Allegheny County bar assns., Nat. Assn. Women Lawyers, Am. Assn. U. Women, League Women Voters, Bus. and Profl. Women, Cath. War Vets. Auxiliary, Nat. Council Cath. Women, Mortar Bd., Phi Beta Kappa, Delta Sigma Rho, Pi Tau Phi, Pi Sigma Alpha. Home: Grayco Apts Harrisburg PA 17101 800 N 3d St Harrisburg PA 17101

BLATT, JOSEPH DUV, civil engr.; b. N.Y.C., Apr. 16, 1913; s. Bernard and Gertrurde (Bernfus) B., B.S. in Engring., Coll. City N.Y., 1934, M. Civil Engring., 1935; m. Ethel Dimitman, June 9, 1934. With FAA, and predecessors, 1937-70, asso. adminstr. devel., 1965-70; cons. engr., 1970—; cons., tchr. in field, 1957—. Head U.S. delegation conf. Internat. Civil Aviation Orgn., also Internat. Air Transp. Assn. Recipient honor grad. award Sch. Tech., Coll. City N.Y. 50th anniversary for outstanding govt. service, 1969; FAA decoration for exceptional service and adminstr's. career achievement award, 1970. Registered profl. engr., Mo. Fellow Am. Soc. C.E. (chmn. exec. com. air transp. div. 1956-57); mem. Soc. Airways Pioneers. Clubs: Nat. Aviation, Nat. Press (Washington); Wings (N.Y.C.). Home: 4201 Cathedral Av NW Washington DC 20016

BLATT, SOLOMON, state legislator; b. Blackville, S.C., Feb. 27, 1896; s. Nathan and Mollie (Blatt) B.; LL.B., U. S.C., 1917; m. Ethel Green, Mar. 18, 1920. Mem. firm Blatt & Fales, Barnwell, S.C.; mem. S.C. Ho. of Reps., Columbia, 1933—, Speaker of House, 1935-45, 51—. Trustee Barnwell Sch., U.S.C., 1936-48. Served with U.S. Army, World War I. Address: SC Ho of Reps State Capitol Columbia SC 29201

BLATTER, L. PRESTON, airline exec.; b. Idaho Falls, Ida., 1916; grad. Benjamin Franklin U., 1947. Pres., gen. mgr., dir. Alaska Airlines, Inc., Seattle. Office: Seattle-Tacoma Airport Seattle WA 98158*

BLATTNER, RUSSELL JOHN, pediatrician, educator; b. St. Louis, July 3, 1908; s. Rudolph Frederick and Lydia (Bergmann) B.; A.B., Washington U., St. Louis, 1929, M.D., 1933; m. Marian Koeneke, June 24, 1939; childrenFrederick Russell, William Albert. Intern Barnes Hosp., St. Louis, 1933-34; resident Children's Hosp., St. Louis, 1934-37, Princess Elizabeth of York Hosp. Children, London, Eng., 1937; faculty Washington U. Sch. Medicine, 1937- 47, chmn. dept. pediatrics Baylor U. Coll. Medicine, 1947-, distinguished service prof. pediatrics, 1968—; physician-in- chief Texas Childrens Hosp., Houston, 1954—. Recipient Alumni citation Washington U. Sch. Medicine, 1956. Fellow Am. Acad. Pediatrics; mem. Pan Am. Med. Assn., Am. Pediatric Soc., Soc. Pediatric Research, A.A.A.S., N.Y. Acad. Scis., Am. Soc. Human Genetics; affiliate mem. Royal Soc. Medicine. Club: Horse Shoe (London, Eng.). Author articles virus epidemiology, congenital malformations, human genetics. Editorial bd. Jour. Pediatrics. Home: 2227 Bellefontaine St Houston TX 77025

BLATZ, DURAND BARRETT, silver co. exec.; b. Ventnor, N.J., July 27, 1918; s. John B. and Ethel (Barrett) B.; A.B., Cornell U., 1940; m. Joan Ipsen, Mar. 29, 1941; children—Durand Barrett, Ann Galen, Megan Eller, John Balthazar, Estelle Elizabeth. Treas. George C. Lewis Co., Phila., 1946-50; gen. controller Crosley and Bendix divs. Avco Mfg. Corp., Cin., 1951-57; with Insilco Corp. (formerly Internat. Silver Co.), Meriden, Conn., 1957—, v.p., treas., 1959-65, pres., 1965-66, pres., chief exec. officer, 1966—, also dir.; dir. Hartford Nat. Bank & Trust Co., Aetna Life & Casualty Co., Hartford. Served to lt. col. AUS, 1940-46, Mem. Delta Upsilon. Republican. Episcopalian. Home: 23 Beaumont Av Wallingford CT 06492 Office: 1000 Research Pkwy Meriden CT 06450

BLATZ, GEORGE JOSEPH, former sugar co. exec.; b. Bklyn., Dec. 7, 1908; s. Adolph and Katherine (Knapp) B.; grad. N.Y.U. Sch. Commerce, 1932; m. Elsie Elizabeth Franke, Apr. 28, 1934; 1 dau., Linda (Mrs. Linda West). With Amstar Corp. (formerly Am. Sugar Co.), 1927—, beginning as jr. clk., successively cost clk., cost accountant mgr. cost and statis. dept., asst. comptroller, 1927-54, controller, 1957-69, now ret. Mem. Financial Execs. Inst. Nat. Assn. Accountants. Presbyn. (deacon). Home: Hideaway Estates Mattituck NY 11952

BLAU, ABRAM, psychiatrist, psychoanalyst; b. Montreal, Can., Jan. 19, 1907; s. Nathan and Molly (Lobel) B.; B.Sc., McGill U., 1927, M. Sc., 1929, M.D., Master in Surgery, 1931; m. Anna Phyllis, Aug. 1931 (dec. 1966); children—Donald (dec.), Meryl. Eugene Meyer fellow in pathology Mt. sinai Hisp., N.Y.C., 1931-32, sucessively asst. neuro—pathologist, resident in psychiatry and neurology, Isadore Abrahamson Meml. fellow in psychiatry and neurology, adj. psychiatrist, associate psychiatrist, 1947-53, attending psychiatrist, 1953—; asst. psychiatry N.Y. U., 1934-36, instr. psychiatry, 1936-39, asst. clin. prof., 1939-51; chief psychiatrist, N.Y. Univ. Clinic, 1937-49; asst. alienist, Bellevue Psychiatric Hosp., 1934-37; cons. neuropsychiatrist, N.Y.U. Med. Group, 1947-51; asst. neuro psychiatrist Univ. Hosp. N.Y.U. 1949-51; research fellow Friedsam Fdn. Child Neurol. Research, 1937-39; sch. adj. psychiatrist and neurologist Beth Israel Hosp.,j 1937-39; sch. psychiatrist Bur. Child Guidance, N.Y. City Bd. Edn., 1940-46; psychiatrist in charge child psychiatry Mt. Sinai Hosp., 1947-; lectr. psychiatry, tng. psychoanalyst State U. N.Y. Coll. Medicine, 1955-62, asso. clin. prof. psychiatry, 1962—; clin. prof. psychiatry Mt. Sinai Sch. Medicine, City U.N.Y., 1966—. Served as lt. comdr., M.C., USNR, 1944-46, Diplomate Am. Bd. Psychiatry and Neurology. Fellow Am. Orthopsychiatric Assn., N.Y. Acad. Medicine, American Psychiatric Assn., Am. Acad. Child Psychiatry (treas. 1959-62); mem. A.M.A. Assn. for Research in Nervous and Mental Disease, Am. Psychoanalytic Assn., Am. Group Therapy Assn., Am. Psychosomatic Society, N.Y.Neurol. Society, N.Y. Psychoanalytic Soc., N.Y. Soc. Clin. Psychiatry (council 1957-60), Psychoanalytic Assn. N.Y., Internat. Psychoanalytic Assn., N.Y. State Med. Soc., Med. Soc. County N.Y., N.Y. Psychoanalytic Inst. (trustee) 1949-52, treas. 1950-52), N.Y. Council on Child Psychiatry (pres. 1962-63). Contbr. articles to med. jours. Home: 47 E 88th St New York City NY 10028 ☆

BLAU, CLARENCE ISAAC, former govt. ofcl.; b. Cin., Aug. 24, 1907; s. Joel and Rachel (Woolf) B.; A.B., Columbia, 1926; student London Sch. Econs., 1927-28; LL.B., Harvard, 1931; m. Edith Spivack, June 18, 1929; children—Miriam (Mrs. Neil Grabois), Ruth (Mrs. Peter Robertson). Admitted to N.Y. bar, 1932; law clk., atty. Bank of U.S. in Liquidation, 1931-34; asst. counsel NRA, 1934-35; sect. chief legal div. Resettlement Adminstrn., 1935-36; sect. chief, then div. chief and asso. solicitor, Solicitors Office, Dept. of Agr., 1936-43; asst. gen. counsel Fgn. Econ. Adminstrn., 1943-45; with Dept. of Commerce, 1945-64, dir. internat. resources staff, bur. fgn. commerce, 1957-61, asst. dir. bur. internat. commerce, 1962-64; sr. adviser Econ. and Social Affairs U.S. Mission to UN, 1964-67, counsellor econ. and social affairs, 1967-70. Dir. U.S. Trade Mission Fedn. Rhodesia and Nyasaland, 1960; others. Mem. Phi Beta Kappa. Home: 907 Fifth Av New York City NY 10021

BLAU, EDWARD, lawyer; b. N.Y.C., Aug. 3, 1922; s. Morris and Lillian (Levy) B.; B.B.A., Coll. City N.Y., 1948; LL.B., Harvard, 1951; m. Rita Alpert, Mar. 23, 1958; children—Gary, Rona, Sharon. With Harvard Grad. Sch. Bus. Adminstrn., 1945; group statis. control officer Army Airways Communications System. 1946; engaged in pub. accounting; admitted to N.Y. bar, 1951, Cal. bar, 1955; with legal dept. Music Corp. Am., 1952; partner firm Pacht, Ross, Warne, Bernhard & Sears, Los Angeles, 1960—. Trustee Los Angeles Copyright Assn. Served to 1st lt. USAAF. World War II. Mem. Am., Beverly Hills, Los Angeles bar assns. Home: 3156 Club Dr Los Angeles CA 90064 Office: Gateway East Bldg Century City Los Angeles CA 90067

BLAU, HARVEY RONALD, lawyer, instrument co. exec.; b. N.Y.C., Nov. 14, 1935; s. David and Rose (Kuchinsky) B.; A.B., N.Y.U., 1957; LL.B., Columbia, 1961; LL.M., N.Y.U., 1965; m. Arlene Joan Garrett, Mar. 21, 1964; children—Stephanie Elizabeth, Melissa Karen, Victoria Gayle. Admitted to N.Y. bar, 1961; practiced in N.Y.C., 1961—; asst. U.S. atty. So. Dist. N.Y., 1962-63; v.p., sec., dir., counsel Instrument Systems Corp., Jericho, N.Y., 1966—. Chmn. com. corp. and Securities law Fed. Bar Council. Served to capt., Judge Adv. Gen.'s Corps, AUS, 1958-66. Mem. Am., Fed. bar assns., Assn. Bar City N.Y. Home: 125 Wheatley Rd Old Westbury NY 11568 Office: 410 Jericho Turnpike Jericho NY 11753

BLAU, HENRY HESS, phys. chemist; b. Dayton, O., May 16, 1897; s. Samuel and Lena (Bowman) B.; B.S. in Chem. Engring., Carnegie Inst. Tech., 1919; M.S., Dupont Fellow), Mass. Inst. Tech., 1920; Ph.D., U. Pitts., 1935; m. Edith Elizabeth Piersol, Sept. 9, 1924; children—Elizabeth (Mrs. John T. Stickney), Henry Hess, Carol (Mrs. Thomas-Morris Perot, IV). Research chemist Macbeth-Evans Glass Co., 1920-36; dir. research, 1925-36, asst. gen. mgr., 1927-36; research and exec. positions Corning Glass Works, 1936-41; gen. mgr. Fed. Glass Works, 1941—, v.p., 1943—; prof. glass sci. Ohio State U., 1945—; v.p., dir. Fed. Glass Co.; v.p. Fed. Paper Board Co. Chmn. ceramic data com., com. ceramic chemistry NRC; chmn. adv. com. on ceramics Internat. Critical Tables. Served with Engrs. Res. Corps., W.W. I; sci. cons. Joint Chiefs of Staff, 1945-46. Recipient S.B. Meyer Jr. award, Toledo award in glass and ceramics, both from Am. Ceramic Soc.; Albert Victor Bleininger Meml. award Am. Ceramic Soc., 1965; Alumni Merit award Carnegie Inst. Tech. Fellow A.A.A.S., Am. Ceramic Soc. (chmn. Pitts. sect. 1932; chmn. glass div. 1934, treas. 1963-65), Brit. Soc. Glass Tech. (hon. Am. treas.); mem. Sci. Research Soc. Am., Am. Inst. Chem. Engrs., Am. Inst. Ceramic Engrs., Am. Chem. Soc., Illuminating Engring. Soc., Keramos, German Soc. Glass Tech., Phi Lambda Upsilon, Tau Beta Pi, Sigma Xi, Clubs: University (Columbus); Faculty (Ohio State U.); Chemists (N.Y.C.); Rotary. Author: Technology of German and Austrian Glass Industry, 1946; other publs. in field. Patentee in field. Home: 2841 S Dorchester Rd Columbus OH 43221

BLAU, JOSEPH LEON, educator; b. Bklyn., May 6, 1909; s. Joel and Rachel (Woolf) B.; A.B., Columbia, 1931, M.A., 1933, Ph.D., 1945; m. Eleanor S. Weslock, June 23, 1940; children—Rachel M. (Mrs. Robert St. Cyr du Plessis), Judith L. (Mrs. Richard S. Katz). Tchr., N.Y.C. high schs., 1933-46; mem. faculty Columbia, 1944—, prof. religion, 1962—, chmn. dept., 1966-68; vis. prof. U. Ark., fall 1950-51, Cal. Inst. Tech., 1961-62, Vassar Coll., spring 1969, Hunter Coll., 1970-71. Mem. com. history religious Am. Council Learned Socs., 1963—, chmn., 1966—. Exec. sec. Conf. Jewish Social Studies, 1946-47, bd. dirs., 1963—, v.p., 1965—. Mem. Am. Studies Assn. (exec. com. 1959- 62), Am. Soc. Study Religion (exec. com. 1962-65), Am. Philos. Assn., Am. Assn. U. Profs., Am. Acad. Jewish Research. Author: The Christian Interpretation of the Cabala in the Renaissance, 2d edit., 1966; Men and Movements in American Philosophy, 1952; The Story of Jewish Philosophy, 1962; Modern Varieties of Judaism, 1966. Editor: Social Theories of Jacksonian Democracy, 1947; Cornerstones of Religious Freedom in America, 2d edit., 1964; (with S.W. Baron) Judaism, Post Biblical and Talmudic Periods, 1954; The Jews of The United States, 1790-1840, A Documentary History, 1963. Home: 3636 Greystone Av Bronx NY 10463

BLAU, WILLIAM ROBERT, Jr., chemist, educator; b. Chicago, 1928; B.S. in Physics, Yale, 1950; Ph.D. in Chemistry, Harvard, 1956; m. Sally Ann Jones, July 5, 1957; children--Kenneth J., Nancy A. Chemist, Acme Chem. Co., Blue Island, Ill., 1950-51; director of Reseach Lab., Indsl. Chemicals Corp., Cambridge, Mass., 1956-60; project coordinator environmental sect. Steinmetz Assos., Chgo., 1960-61; v.p. for reseach Bauer Bros. Chem. Co., Inc., Memphis, 1961-64; asst. prof. chemistry Washington U., St. Louis, 1964-66, asso. prof., 1966-70, prof., 1970--, head of chemistry dept., 1970-71. Vis. prof. So. Ill. U., summer 1967, U. of Ore., 1969. Scoutmaster, Boy Scouts America, University City, Mo., 1968-70. Bd. dirs. Rest Haven Home for Elderly, 1960-61; trustee of the Lutheran Hosp., 1965-71. Served from lt. to capt., AUS, 1951-53. Mem. Am. Chem. Soc., Sci. Research Soc. Am. (chpt. treas. 1967), Sigma Xi. Author: (with others) Basic Inorganic Chemistry, 1971. Contbr. articles to profl. jours., encys., also chpts. to books. Home: Fairfax Apts 7291 Windermere Dr University City MO 63105 Office: Dept Chemistry Washington University St Louis MO 63130

BLAUSTEIN, AL, artist; b. N.Y.C., Jan. 23, 1924; s. Sydney and Sophie (Silbersher) B.; grad. Cooper Union Art Sch., 1947, Skowhegan Sch. Painting, 1946; m. Lotte Heilbrunn, on May 5, 1949; one son, Marc D. Blaustein. One man shows include Nordness Gallery, N.Y.C., 1959, 61, 62, Phila. Art Alliance, 1962, Galleries Läubli, Zurich, Switzerland, 1962, Phila. Print Club, 1964, Albany Art Insr., 1965, Randolph-Macon Coll., 1967, Troup Gallery, Dallas, 1968, Terry Dintenfass Gallery, N.Y.C., 1969; rep. permanent collections Whitney Mus., Phila. Mus., Butler Art Inst., Hartford Atheneum, Met. Mus., Boston Mus., Bklyn Mus., Chgo. Art Inst., Library of Congress, Syracuse U., Albany Art Inst., Norfolk Mus., also pvt. collections; now asst. prof. Pratt Inst. Guggenheim fellow, 1957-59, 61-62; fellow Am. Acad. Rome, 1954-57; grantee Am. Inst. Arts and Letters, 1957. Address: 141 E 17th St New York City NY 10003

BLAUSTEIN, ALBERT PAUL, legal educator; b. N.Y.C., Oct. 12, 1921; s. Karl Allen and Rose (Brickman) B.; A.B., U. Mich., 1941; J.D., Columbia, 1948; m. Phyllis Migden, Dec. 21, 1948; children—Mark Allen, Eric Barry, Dana Beth. Admitted to N.Y. bar, 1948, N.J. bar, 1962; reporter, rewrite man City News Bur., Chgo., 1941-42; pvt. practice law Blaustein & Blaustein, N.Y.C., 1948-50, 52-55; asst. prof. law, law librarian N.Y. Law Sch., 1953-55; asso. prof. law, law librarian Rutgers U. Sch. Law, Camden, 1955-59, prof. law, law librarian, 1959-69, prof. law, 1969—. Spl. studies cons. Survey Legal Profession, 1948-55; profl. relations adviser Nat. Assn. Claimants Compensation Attys., 1955-57; cons. U.S. Commn. Civil Rights, 1962-63; cons. desegregation problems Sch. Dist. Phila., 1963-64; law library cons. Haile Selassie I U., Addis Ababa, Ethiopia, 1963-68; law library cons. SAILER Program Inst. Internat. Edn. and Internat. Legal Center for Legal Instns. African Nations, 1963—; cons. legal materials for drafting 1967 S. Vietnamese Constn. for USIS, 1966-67; cons. Commn. on Age of Majority, U.K., 1967; cons. legal research and law book resources Ministry Justice and Nat. Assembly S. Vietnam, for U.S. AID, 1967; cons. legal devel. S. Vietnam Supreme Ct. and law faculties U. Saigon, Hue and Cantho, Asia Found., 1969; lectr. on wills Bar Rev., Rutgers Inst. Continuing Legal Edn., 1963-66; lectr. Council State Govts., 1968—, N.D. State Constl. Conv., 1970—; cons. N.J. Div. on Civil Rights, 1971—; expert witness legal aspects population control U.S. Senate Com., 1966. Nat. bd. dirs. Zero Population Growth, 1968—, Abortion and Birth Control Coalition N.J., 1970—; bd. mgrs. Jewish Community Center, Camden, N.J., 1966—, pres. Bangla Desh-Am. Found., Inc. Served to maj. AUS, 1944-46, 50-52. Ford fellow U. Wis., summer 1962. Mem. Am. Camden County (N.J.) bar assns., Assn. Bar City N.Y., Am. Assn. Law Libraries (chmn. publs. com. 1965-69), Assn. Am. Law Schs. (chmn. legislation round table council 1965-67), Anti-Slavery Soc. (Gt. Britain). Author: (with others) Public Relations for Bar Associations, 1952, 1953; The American Lawyer, 1954; Fiction Goes to Court, 1954; Desegregation and the Law 1957, 1962; Doctors' Choice, 1957; Deals with the Devil, 1958; Invisible Men, 1960; Civil Affairs Legislation, Selected Cases and Materials, 1960; Fundamental Legal Documents of Communist China, 1962; Manual on Foreign Legal Periodicals and their Index, 1962; Civil Rights U.S.A.; Public Schools in Cities in the North and West Philadelphia, 1962; Human and Other Beings, 1963; Law in Communist China, 1963; Civil Rights U.S.A., 1963, Public Schools in Camden and Environs, 1964; Civil Rights and the American Negro, 1968; Civil Rights and the Black American, 1970; Law and the Military Establishment, 1970; Intellectual Property: Cases and Materials (1960-70), 1971. Co-founder, 1st editor-in-chief Columbia Law Sch. News, 1947; 1st editor Am. Bar Assn. Pub. Relations Bull., 1953-54. Contbr. articles profl. jours., chpts. in books, book revs. Home: 415 Barby Lane Cherry Hill NJ 08034 Office: Rutgers Univ School of Law Camden NJ 08102

BLAUVELT, FOWLER, mfg. co. exec.; b. Bronxville, N.Y., Feb. 8, 1925; s. Charles and Kate (Garthwaite) B.; Sc.B. in Engring., Brown U., 1945; grad. Exec. Devel. Program, Cornell, 1959; m. Norma Emerson, Oct. 3, 1953; children—Whitney, Richard Emerson, Margaret Jane. With Owens-Corning Fiberglas Corp., 1946—, br. mgr. Cin., 1956-61, mgr. Central Region, 1962- 63, v.p. central region, 1963-64, v.p. Fiberglas Indsl. Materials div., 1964-68, v.p. marketing 1968-69, group v.p. textile and indsl. group., 1969—. Served with USNR, 1945-46. Mem. Soc. Plastics Engrs., Brown Engring. Assn. Home: 2450 Underhill Rd Toledo OH 43615 Office: Owens-Corning Fiberglas Corp Toledo OH 43604

BLAUVELT, HOWARD W., oil co. exec.; b. N.Y.C., Feb. 11, 1917; s. Harry and Lilian (Woelfert) B.; B.A., Yale, 1939; student Columbia Grad. Sch. Bus. Adminstrn., nights 1939-42; m. Margaret D. Hahn, Sept. 2, 1939 (dec. Feb. 1970); children—Harry, Margaret; m. 2d, Mary E. Cassity, July 25, 1970. Controller Continental Oil Co., Houston, v.p. charge coordinating and planning, now pres. Conoco Chems. div. also mem. bd. dirs. Served with USNR, 1944-46. C.P.A., N.Y. Mem. Financial Execs. Inst., Am. Petroleum Inst., Phi Beta Kappa, Beta Gamma Sigma, Presbyn. Home: 59 Londonderry Dr Greenwich CT 06830 Office: 30 Rockefeller Plaza New York City NY 10020

BLAUVELT, JOHN CLIFFORD, Jr., chem. co. exec.; b. Nyack, N.Y., Feb. 22, 1920; s. John Clifford and Henrietta (Lane) B.; B.S., Houghton Coll., 1940; postgrad. N. Tex. State Coll., 1940, N.Y.U., 1946-48; m. Laura Biddleman, July 29, 1944; children—Laura Lane (Mrs. Elliott Simons), John Clifford III. With Am. Cyanamid Co., Wayne, N.J., 1940—. prodn. mgr. Lederle Labs. div., Pearl River, N.Y., 1960-64, asst. gen. mgr., 1967-68, asst. to Pres., 1969-69, controller Am. Cyanamid Co., 1969—. Served to lt. USNR, 1943-46. Mem. Soc. Chem. Industry. Registered profl. engr., N.Y. Home: 17 Glenwood Dr Salle River NJ 07548 Office: Am Cyanamid Co Wayne NJ 07470

BLAYDES, GLENN WILLIAM, educator; b. Roachdale, Ind., Sept. 30, 1900; s. William T. and Nettie L. (Hinkle) B.; A.B., Ind. U., 1924; A.M., Ohio State U., 1926, Ph.D., 1931; m. Bernice Winstel, Sept. 22, 1928; 1 son, David Fairchild. Instr. botany Ohio Wesleyan U., 1924-26, asst. prof., 1926-28; instr. botany Ohio State U., 1928-32, asst. prof., 1932-37, asso. prof., 1937-45, prof. botany and plant pathology, 1945—. Asso. histologist U.S. Dept. Agr., 1942-44. Mem. Bot. Soc. Am., A.A.A.S. (coop. com. sci., math. teaching 1945—), Am. Genetics Assn., Ohio Acad. Sci. (pres. 1952-53), Am. Soc. Plant Taxonomists, Sigma Xi. Author: Methods and Materials for Teaching Biological Sciences, rev. edit., 1962; Gen. Botany Workbook, rev. edit., 1966; also numerous articles. Editor Ohio Jour. Sci., 1941- 51. Home: 214 Westwood Rd Columbus OH 43214

BLAYNEY, KEITH DALE, univ. dean; b. Anamosa, Ia., Feb. 8, 1937; s. Darrell Price and Evelyn (Thompson) B.; B.S., U. Ia., 1959, M.A., 1961, Ph.D., 1966; m. Joyce Ann Bryan, Sept. 14, 1961; children—Michael Bryan, Steven Price. Instr. grad. program in hosp. adminstrn. U. Ia., 1964-66; acting dir. Regional Tech. Inst. for Health Occupations, Birmingham, Ala., 1966-67; dir. Bur. Research and Community Service, U. Ala., Birmingham, 1967-69, adminstr. U. Ala. Hosps. and Clinics and dir. Sch. Health Services Adminstrn., 1969-71, dean Sch. Community and Allied Health Resources, 1971—; asso. prof. dept. pub. health and epidemiology, 1968-71, asso. prof. Sch. Community and Allied Health Resources, 1971—. Mem. Nat. Adv. Allied Health Professions Council, Dept. Health, Edn. and Welfare, Washington, 1970—; cons. Appalachian Regional Health Planning Com., Washington; mem. Task Force on Allied Health Profls. div. edn. and communication Nat. Program for Dermatology. Served with Med. Service Corps, USAF, 1961-64. Decorated USAF Commendation medal; recipient USPHS traineeship, 1965, Outstanding Pub. Speakers award N.M., 1963. Mem. Am., Ala., Birmingham Regional hosp. assns., Am. Coll. Hosp. Adminstrs., Am. Pub. Health Assn., Ala. Regional Med. Program, Community Service Council Jefferson County, Assn. Am. Med. Colls. Home: 3009 Sterling Rd Birmingham AL 35213

BLAYNEY, LINDSEY, educator; b. Lebanon, Ky., Dec. 3, 1874; s. Rev. John McClusky and Lucy Weisiger (Lindsey) B.; A.B., Centre Coll., Ky., 1894, A.M., 1897; univs. Göttingen, Geneva, Grenoble, and Faculty of Lit., Florence; Ph. D., U. Heidelberg, 1904; LL.D., Southwestern U., Loyola U., New Orleans, U. Notre Dame, 1923, Austin (Texas) Coll., 1926, Centre Coll., Ky., 1947; m. Gertrude South, Sept. 9, 1896 (dec. 1945); children—Lucy L. (dec.), John McC., Lindsey; m. 2d, Dr. Ida Walz Kubits, Mar 24, 1948. Expdn. interior Morocco, 1899; vice consul, Mannheim, Germany, 1901-04; prof. modern langs., and history European art Central U. Ky., 1904-12; prof. German, William M. Rice Inst., Houston, 1912-24; pres. Tex. State Woman's Coll., 1924-26; dean Carleton Coll., 1926-45, chmn. dept. German, 1926-46; chmn. first Houston City Planning Commn.; as pres. Houston Art League, planned, negotiated for present site Houston Mus. Art, and self- perpetuating bd. trustees. Am. Albert Kahn fellow to Orient, 1914-15. Served from maj. to lt. col. AEF, 1917-19. Decorated Croix de Guerre with palm (2), officer Legion of Honor (France); hon. officer Chasseurs Alpins; Order White War Eagle, Serbia; Chevalier Order St. Sauveur (Greece); Comdr. Order Corwn of Italy; 6 citations for D.S.M.; Order Purple Heart (U.S.). Am. Legion del. 17th Congress FIDAC, Warsaw; del. Internat. Ednl. Congress, Heidelberg. Mem., fellow nat. and internat. orgns., Rice U. Alumni Assn. (hon.). Vice pres. Am. Fed. Arts, 1910. Presbyn. Mason, Rotarian (hon.). Author: Thomas Moore, als irisch-galischer Dichter, 1906; Ideals of Orient, 1916; To Our Country (verse series); Am. Ideals and Traditions. Contbr. Am., fgn. and lit. press. Pioneered history of art Am. Colls. and univs. Article on Philippine independence credit with slowing down Congressional action. Home: Shady Terrace Marine-on-St Croix MN 55047 Died Mar. 13, 1971

BLAYTON, JESSE BEE, educator, business exec.; b. Garden, Okla., Dec. 6, 1899; s. Lester Benjamin and Mattie Elizabeth (Carter) B.; student Langston U., 1919-22; diploma Walton Sch. Commerce, Chgo., 1932; student U. Chgo., 1933-35; LL.B., Am. Extension Sch. Law, 1936; m. Willia Mae Daniels, Dec. 27, 1920; children—Doris Ada, Jesse Bee. Prof. accounting Morehouse Coll., 1925-30; faculty Atlanta U., 1931—, Carnegie prof. bus. adminstrn., 1931—. Co-founder Mut. Fed. Savs. & Loan Assn., Atlanta, 1925, pres., 1956—; chmn. bd. Radio Atlanta, Inc. (sta. WERD), 1949—; prin. J.B. Blavton & Co., C.P.A.'s 1928—; dir. Citizens Trust Co., Atlanta. Mem. Bd. License Appeals, Atlanta, 1968—, Goals Commn., Ga. Dept. Edn., 1969—. Mem. cabinet U. Chgo.; bd. dirs. Atlanta Urban League, 1936—, chmn. bd., 1956-69; bd. dirs. Butler St. YMCA; exec. com. adv. bd. Atlanta Urban Renewal; commr. Atlanta Housing Authority. Named Most Outstanding Alumnus, Langston U., 1961. C.P.A., Ga. Mem. Am. Assn. U. Profs., Nat. Assn. Accountants, Assn. Practising and Profl. Accountants (Great Britain), Am. Tax Assn., Am. Accounting Assn., A.I.M., Am. Soc. Social and Polit. Sci., U.S. Savs. and Loan League, Am. Inst. C.P.A.'s, Nat. Council Chs. (finance com.), Omega Psi Phi (treas.), Sigma Pi Phi. Baptist (trustee). Author: Fundamentals of Accounting, 1945; also articles. Home: 1235 Hunter Rd NW Atlanta GA 30314

BLAZER, REXFORD SYDNEY, oil co. exec.; b. Aledo, Ill., Sept. 1, 1907; s. Frederick B. and Elizabeth E. (Niederlander) B., A.B., U. Ill., 1928; D.Sc., Pikeville Coll., 1969; m. Mary Elizabeth Vary, 1935 (dec.); 1 dau., Mary Linda; m. 2d, Frances Montross Green, 1942 (div.); 1 son, Richard; m. 3d, Lucile Thornton Scott, 1954; 1 son, Rexford Sydney; stepchildren—Dan W. III, W. Thornton Scott. Joined Allied Oil Co., Cleve., 1928, dir., 1935-59, v.p., 1938, pres., 1948-59; dir. Ashland Oil & Refining Co. (Ky.) (name now Ashland

Oil, Inc.), 1949—, pres., 1951-57, chmn. bd., 1957—; dir. 3d Nat. Bank of Ashland. Mem. Nat Petroleum Council, 1960-61. Mem. Eastern Ky. Regional Planning Commn., Ky. Indsl. Devel. Bd., 1956-59; mem. adv. com. Ohio Valley Improvement Assn., Nat. Waterways Conf. Dir. Spindletop Research Center; bd. dirs. U. Ill. Found., U. Ill. Pres.'s Club; trustee Ky. Ind. Coll. Found., 1952-64; mem. exec. commn. U. Ky. Devel. Council, also fellow, hon. alumnus U. Ky.; regent, U. of South. Recipient of Alumni Achievement award U. Ill., 1968. Mem. Am. Petroleum Inst. (v.p. transp. 1970, exec. com., dir.), Nat. Petroleum Assn. (past pres.), Asphalt Inst. (dir.), Nat. (dir., mem. exec. com., finance com.), Western (v.p. 1957-61) petroleum refiners assns., Ky. (pres. 1955-56), Ohio (dir.) chambers commerce, Ky. Oil and Gas Assn. (dir.), Cleve. Petroleum Club (pres. 1947), 25-year Club Petroleum Industry (gov.), Hwy. Users Fedn. for Safety and Mobility (trustee, chmn.), Psi Upsilon (chmn. bd. govs. Omicron chpt., exec. council). Episcopalian. (sr. warden 1959; mem. exec. council Lexington diocese 1958-62). Rotarian. Clubs: Bellefonte Country (Ashland); Pendennis, Filson (Louisville); Idle Hour Country (Lexington); Westwood Country (Cleve.). Home: 2711 Seminole Av Ashland KY 41101 Office: 1401 Winchester Av Ashland KY 41101

BLEAKNEY, WALKER, educator; b. Elderton, Pa. Feb. 8, 1901; s. Robert Wilson and Wilda (Hall) B.; B.S., Whitman Coll., 1924, D.Sc. (hon.), 1955; student Harvard, 1924-25; Ph.D., U. Minn., 1930; grad. study Princeton, 1930-32; m. Dorothy Clyde Thomas, July 16, 1931. Mem. faculty Princeton, 1932—, prof. physics, 1945-70, Class of 1909 prof. emeritus, 1970—, chmn. dept., 1960-67. Fellow Am. Phys. Soc., Am. Acad. Arts and Scis.; mem. Nat. Acad. Scis., Phi Beta Kappa, Sigma Xi, Phi Delta Theta. Home: 4681 La Espada Dr Santa Barbara CA 93105

BLECHMAN, HARRY, oral microbiologist; b. Bklyn., Aug. 22, 1918; s. Bernard and Mollie (Shalov) B.; B.S., Coll. City of N.Y., 1938; student Bklyn. Coll., 1939- 41, John Hopkins Sch. Pub. Health and Hygiene, 1943-44; D.D.S., N.Y.U., 1951; M.A., Hunter Coll., N.Y.C., 1959; m. Zara Ehrich, Nov. 6, 1943; children—Enid Ellen, Betsy. Sr. bacteriologist Harlem Hosp., 1946-47; asst. prof., chmn. dept. microbiology N.Y.U. Coll. Dentistry, 1951-53, prof., chmn. dept., 1960-64, asst. dean, 1964-67, dean Coll. Dentistry, 1967—, prof., 1964-71, prof. endodontics, 1971—, chmn. dept. microbiology, 1964-68, asso. prof. preventive med. and hygiene, dir. clin. pathology lab., 1952-60. Exec. sec. Murry and Leonie Guggenheim Found. Inst. Dental Research, 1953-67. Served as capt. Med. Service Corps, AUS, 1943-46; maj. USAR, 1946—. Diplomate Am. Bd. Endodontics. Fellow Am. Acad. Endodontists, Am. Coll. Dentists, N.Y. Acad. Scis., Am. Acad. Dental Medicine, Am. Acad. Gen. Dentistry; mem. Am. Bd. Endodontics, Am. Dental Assn. (chmn. council nat. bd. dental examiners), Am. Assn. Endodontists, A.A.A.S., Internat. Assn. Dental Research, Soc. Am. Bacteriologists, Harvey Soc., Research Soc. Am., Sigma Xi, Omicron Kappa Upsilon. Author: Laboratory Manual in Microbiology, rev. edit. 1960; Contbr. author: Textbook on Oral Microbiology, 1968. Home: 110 Bleecker St New York City NY 10012

BLECKER, HARRY HERMAN, chemist, educator; b. Phila., Apr. 10, 1927; s. Herman and Eva (Hahn) B.; B.S., Bucknell U., 1951; M.S., Rutgers U., 1953, Ph.D., 1955; m. Charlotte Wetklo, June 16, 1951; children—Harry S., Barbara R., Marian L., Karen E. Asst. prof. Bucknell U., 1956-57; asst. prof. U. Mich., Flint, 1957-61, asso. prof., 1961-65, prof., chmn. dept. chemistry, 1965- -. Mem. Am. Chem. Soc., Sigma Xi, Phi Lambda Upsilon, Alpha Chi Sigma. Author: Properties and Products of Algae, 1970; The Fatty Acids in Blue-Green Algae, 1968. Home: 6382 Springdale Blvd Grand Blanc MI 48439 Office: U Mich 1321 E Court St Flint MI 48903

BLECKWELL, EDGAR HALE, chem. mfg. co. exec.; b. Phila., Sept. 7, 1911; s. Edward Augustus and Eva Anna (Hale) B.; M.E., Cornell U., 1933; student bus. mgmt., U. Pa., 1934; m. Mary E. Curtis, Aug. 14, 1935; 1 dau., Joan (Mrs. Earl S. McHugh). With engring. dept., then textile fibres dept. E. I. duPont de Nemours & Co., Inc., 1934-62; v.p. research and devel. Remington Arms Co., Inc., Bridgeport, Conn., 1962-63, v.p., asst. gen. mgr., 1963-66; exec. v.p. DuPont Co. of Can., Ltd., 1966-69, pres., chief exec. officer, 1969—, dir., 1966—; dir. Royal Bank Can. Mem. univ. council, alumni fund com. Cornell U. Mem. Tau Beta Pi. Clubs: Forest and Stream; Toronto; St. James's, Mt. Royal (Montreal). Home: 2 Westmont Sq Montreal 216 Canada Office: 555 Dorchester Blvd W Montreal 128 Canada

BLEDSOE, LEIGHTON MCLELLON, lawyer; b. Bisbee, Ariz., Mar. 27, 1903; s. Frank C. and Irene (McLellon) B.; A.B., Stanford, 1926, J.D., 1928; m. Katheryn Turner, June 36, 1930; children—Margaret Irene (Mrs. Wilfred Schofield), Turner. Admitted to Cal. bar, 1929, since practiced in and around San Francisco; mem. Bledsoe, Smith, Cathcart, Johnson & Rogers, 1955—; trial atty. defending ins. firms, drs., hosps.; mem. hearing tribunal, discipline of state bar. Mem. town council Los Altos Hills, Cal., 1956- 58, dep. mayor, 1958. Mem. Am., San Francisco bar assns., State Bar Cal., Sigma Alpha Epsilon, Phi Alpha Delta. Mason (K.T., Shriner). Clubs: Commonwealth of California; Commercial (San Francisco). Home: 25525 Moody Rd Los Altos Hills CA Office: 650 California St San Francisco CA 94108

BLEE, MYRON ROY, educator b. Paw Paw, Ill., Feb. 25, 1917; s. Roy T. and Martha (Fox) B.; B.Ed., No. Ill. State Tchrs. Coll., 1938; M.A. in Polit. Sci., U. Ill., 1939, D.Ed., 1958; m. Charlotte Marie Leverenz, Jan. 1, 1941; 1 dau., Kathleen Marie. Tchr., also teaching prin. elementary schs., Lake County, Ill., 1939-42; asso. dean men, instr. Am. Govt. No. Ill. State Tchrs. Coll., 1946-48; asst. supt. instrn. Community Unit Sch. Dist. 271, Ashton, Ill., 1948-52; asso. dir. Fla Legislative Reference Bur., Tallahassee, 1952-54, Council Study Higher Edn. in Fla., 1954-56; ednl. and research officer Fla. Bd. Control Higher Edn., 1956-62; dir. Fla. Inst. Continuing Univ. Studies, Tallahassee, 1962-65; asso. dean acad. affairs Fla. Atlantic U., 1965- 66; dep. dir. Office Emergency Planning, exec. Office of Pres., 1966-67; pres. Jr. Coll. Broward County, Ft. Lauderdale, Fla., 1967-68; pres. Asso. Consultants in Edn., Inc., 1968—; vis. prof. higher edn. Fla. State U., 1970—. Mem. Fla. Ednl. TV Commn., 1960-66; bd. edn. Fla. Annual Conf. Methodist Ch., 1960-68. Trustee Bethune Cookman Coll., Daytona Beach, 1961-. Served to lt. comdr. USNR, 1942-46; PTO. Mem. Am. Assn. Adminstrs., N.E.A., Fla., Adult edn. assns., Kappa Delta Pi, Phi Delta Kappa. Democrat. Club: Internat. Torch. Home: 1447 Marion Av Tallahassee FL 32303 Office: 114 W Pensacola St Tallahassee FL 32505

BLEE, THOMAS JOSEPH, advt. exec.; b. Ft. Wayne, Ind., Jan. 29, 1930; s. Robert T. and Agnes M. (Becker) B.; A.B. cum laude, Ind. U., 1951; m. Phyllis A. Grothouse, June 9, 1951; children—Kathleen, Timothy, Michael, Mary Beth, Thomas M. With advt. and sales promotion dept. Gen. Electric Co., 1951-56; sr. account exec., mem. plans bd. Fuller & Smith & Ross, Pitts., 1956-59; with Bonsib, Inc., Ft. Wayne, 1959—, v.p., dir., 1961—; pres. Bonsib, Inc., 1966—. Dir. pub. relations Citizens for Decent Lit.; past pres. Neighbors, Inc.; v.p. Ft. Wayne United Fund, Ft. Wayne United Community Services. Served with USMCR, 1951-53. Mem. President's Assn., Ft. Wayne Advt. Club (pres. 1968-69), Ft. Wayne C. of C. (v.p.), Phi Beta Kappa. Catholic. Clubs: Ft. Wayne Country, Pine Valley Country (Ft. Wayne); Quest. Home: 11117 Carriage Pl Fort Wayne IN 46805 Office: 927 Harrison St Fort Wayne IN 46805

BLEGEN, CARL WILLIAM, archeologist; b. Mpls., Jan. 27, 1887; s. John H. and Anna B. (Olsen) B.; B.A., Augsburg Sem., Mpls., 1904, U. Minn., 1907; B.A., Yale, 1908, Ph.D., 1920, (hon.) M.A., 1927; student Am. Sch. Classical Studies, Athens, Greece, 1910-13 hon. doctorate, U. Oslo (Norway), 1951, Thessaloniki (Greece), 1951, U. Athens, 1963; D. Litt., Oxford, 1957; LL.D., U. Cin., 1958; L.H.D., Hebrew Union Coll., Jewish Inst. Religion, 1963; Litt. D., Cambridge U., 1963; m. Elizabeth Denny Pierce, July 11, 1924 (dec. 1966). Sec. Am. Sch. Classical Studies, 1913-20, asst. dir., 1920-26, actg. dir., 1926- 27; prof. classical archeology Grad. Sch. Arts and Scis., U. Cin., 1927-57, prof. emeritus, 1957—. Distinguished Service prof. emeritus, 1969—, became fellow, 1927; head dept. classics, 1950-57; field dir. U. Cin. Archaeol. Expdn., Turkey and Greece; on leave of absence, with OSS, Washington, 1942-45; cultural relations attaché, Am. Embassy, Athens, Greece, 1945-46; dir. Am. Sch. Classical Studies, Athens, 1948-49. With A.R.C. in Greece, 1918-19. Recipient gold medal Archaeol. Inst. Am., 1965, gold medal Soc. Antiquaries of London, 1966, Gold medal U. Cin., 1969. Corresponding fellow Brit. Acad. Fellow Am. Acad. Arts and Scis.; mem. Am. Philos. Soc., Am. Philol. Assn., Archeol. Inst. Am., Am. Assn. Univ. Profs., German Archeol. Inst., Archaeol. Soc. Athens (hon. v.p.), Soc. Promotion of Hellenic Studies, London, Eng. (hon.) Royal Soc. Letters of Lund (Sweden), Swedish Royal Acad. Letters, History and Antiquities, Norwegian Acad. Sci. and Letters, Phi Beta Kappa (hon.), Sigma Xi. Lutheran. Clubs: Literary, University (Cinn.); Yale (New York); Cosmos (Washington); Royal Yacht (Greece). Author: Korakou, A Prehistoric Settlement near Corinth, 1921; Zygouries, A Prehistoric Settlement in the Valley of Cleonae, 1928; Acrocorinth (with R. Stillwell, O. Broneer and A. Bellinger), 1930; Prosymna, the Helladic Settlement Preceding the Argive Heraeum (with Elizabeth Blegen), 1937; Troy, Vol. I (with J.L. Caskey, M. Rawson, J. Sperling), 1950, Troy, Vol. II (with J.L. Caskey and M. Rawson), 1951, Vol. III, 1953, Vol. IV (with C. Boulter, J.L. Caskey, M. Rawson), 1958; Troy and the Trojans, 1963; (with M. Rawson) The Palace of Nestor at Pylos, Vol. I, 1966. Contbr. to archaeol. publs. Home: 9 Plutarch St Athens 139 Greece Office: U Cin Cincinnati OH 45221

BLEIBERG, GERMAN, author, educator; b. Madrid, Mar. 14, 1915; s. Jose and Anselma (Gottlieb) B.; Licenciado en Filosofia y Letras, U. Madrid, 1947, Ph.D., 1958; m. Maria Antonia Muniz, Sept. 8, 1936; children—Alicia (Mrs. Fernando de Teran), Fabiola. Came to U.S., 1961. Editor, cons. pub. house Revista de Occidente, Madrid, 1947—; co-founder 1963, since dir. Tamesis Books Ltd., London; vis. prof. U. Notre Dame, 1961-62; prof. Vanderbilt U., 1962-66; prof. U. Mass., 1966-67; prof. Hispanic studies Vassar Coll., 1967—, Andrew Mellon prof., 1971—. Recipient Nat. Lit. Book award Spain, 1938; grantee Am. Philos. Soc., 1965, Am. Council Learned Socs., 1968. Mem. Hispanic Soc. Am., Modern Lang. Assn. Roman Cath. Author: Sonetos Amorosos, 1936; Más allaá des las ruinas, 1947; La Mutua primavera, 1948; also numerous articles. Editor: (with Julian Marias) Diccionario de literatura Espaola, 4th edit., 1971; Diccionario de Historia de Espaua, 3 vols., 2d edit., 1969; Antologia de Elogios de la Lengua Espanola, 1951; (with E.I. Fox) Spanish Thought and Letters in the Twentieth Century, 1966; Antología de la Literatura Espaola, 4 vols., 1970-71. Address: Vassar Coll Poughkeepsie, NY 12601.

BLEIBERG, ROBERT MARVIN, financial mag. editor; b. Bklyn., June 21, 1924; s. Edward and Frances (DuBroff) B.; B.A., Columbia, 1943; M.B.A., N.Y. U., 1950; m. Harriet Evans, May 1948 (div. Mar. 1953); 1 dau., Ellen; m. 2d. Sally Diane Beverly, Oct. 25, 1956; 1 son, Richard Beverly. Asso. editor Prudden's Digest of Investment and Banking Opinions, N.Y.C., 1946; asso. editor Barron's Nat. Bus. and Financial Weekly, N.Y.C., 1946-54, editor, 1955- . Served with inf. AUS, 1943-45; PTO. Decorated Purple Heart. Mem. N.Y. Soc. Security Analysts. N.Y. Financial Writers Assn., Phi Beta Kappa. Home: 25 Central Park W New York City, NY 10023. Office: 30 Broad St New York City, NY 10004.

BLEIBTREU, JACOB, stockbroker; b. Frankfort am Main, Germany, Sept. 30, 1886; s. Nathan and Auguste (Homburger) B.; grad. Comml. High Sch., Frankfurt am Main, 1902; m. Helen Reinthaler, Oct. 27, 1924; children—John N., Ann-Louise (Mrs. Hugh Thornton). Came to the U.S., 1909, naturalized, 1916. With Lazard-Speyer-Ellissen, Frankfurt am Main, 1902-09, Speyer & Co., bankers, N.Y.C. 1909-19; sr. partner Abraham & Co., N.Y.C., 1919-71, limited partner, 1971—. Mem. N.Y. Stock Exchange, 1921—, gov., 1954-60. Chmn. war record bur. Greater N.Y. Jewish Welfare Bd., 1944-47; mem. com. Wall St. Fedn. Jewish Charities; chmn. Wall St. com. Am. Jewish Com. Dir., v.p. Arthritis and Rheumatism Found. of N.Y. Trustee Hillside Hosp., Long Island. Served with U.S. Army, 1918-19; gen. staff 2d Army, AEF; instr. Air Force Intelligence Sch., Harrisburg, Pa., 1942-45. Mem. Am. Legion. Clubs: New York Stock Exchange Luncheon; Buttonwood (dir. sec. of club and found.); Sunningdale Country (Scarsdale, N.Y.). Home: 262 Central Park W New York City NY 10023 also 26 Lincoln Av Port Chester NY 10573 Office: 120 Broadway New York City NY 10005

BLEICH, CLEMENTS HARRY, food co. exec.; b. Jackson, Tenn., Dec. 1, 1911; s. Clements Harry and Serena (McCutchen) B.; B.S., Washington U., St. Louis, 1934; m. Betty Jane Jess, Oct. 18, 1941; children—John North, Susan McCutchen. With Cal. & Hawaiian Sugar Refining Corp., 1935-60, v.p., 1955-60; v.p., dir. Dole Corp., 1961-66; v.p. marketing Sunshine Biscuits, Inc., Long Island City, N.Y., 1966-69; pres. Cal. Agrl. Specialties div. Heggblade-Marguleas-Tenneco Inc., Indio, Cal., 1969-70, Cal-Date Co. subsidiary Heggblade-Marguleas-Tenneco Inc., 1970—. Dir. Rod McLellan Co. Served to lt. comdr. USNR, 1942-46. Mem. Sigma Chi. Republican. Episcopalian. Clubs: Bohemian (San Francisco); Union League (N.Y.C.); Marrakesh Country (Palm Desert, Cal.); Home: 47-483 Tangier Dr Palm Desert CA 92260 Office: 82-625 Interstate 10 Indio CA 92201

BLEICH, HANS HEINRICH, civil engr., educator; b. Vienna, Austria, Mar. 24, 1909; s. Friedrich and Antonie (Stern) B.; C.E., Tech. U., Vienna, 1933, D.Sc., 1934. Came to U.S. 1945, naturalized, 1950. Designing engr. of bridges and indsl. plants, Austria, 1934-39; sr. engr. Braithwaite & Co., Ltd., London, Eng., 1940-44; research engr. Chance Vaught Aircraft div. United Aircraft, 1945; asso. engr. Hardesty & Hanover, N.Y.C., 1945-50; lectr. civil engring. Columbia, 1946-50, asso. prof., 1950-52, prof., 1953—, dir. Inst. Air Flight Structures, 1954—. Mem. Am. Soc. Civil Engrs., Am. Soc. Mech. Engrs., Am. Inst. Aeros. and Astronautics, Internat. Assn. Bridge and Structural Engring., Sigma Xi. Author: Design of Suspension Bridges, 1935. Editor: Buckling Strength of Metal Structures, 1952. Address: School of Engring Columbia U New York City NY 10027

BLEICKEN, GERHARD DAVID, ins. exec.; b. Newton, Mass., Aug. 29, 1913; s. Gerhard and Beatrice (Douglas) B.; student Gettysburg Coll., 1931-32; J.D. cum laude, Boston U., 1938; sch. indsl. mgmt. Mass. Inst. Tech., 1958; m. Ellene T. Mailhot, Mar. 6, 1936 (div.); children—Kurt Douglas, Eric, Carl Weeman; m. 2d, Ann M. Meacham, Sept. 9, 1967; children—David H., Neil G. Admitted to Mass. bar, 1938; with John Hancock Mut. Life Ins. Co., Boston, 1939—, successively att., asst. counsel, asso. counsel, 2d v.p., counsel and 2d v.p., 1939-55, sec., 1955-66, v.p., 1958-61, sr. v.p., 1961-66, exec. v.p., 1966-67, sr. exec. v.p., 1967-70, vice chmn. bd., 1969-70, chmn. bd., chief exec. officer, 1970—, also dir.; dir. First Nat. Bank of Boston, Am. Research and Devel. Corp. Mem. program adv. com. Office Emergency Preparedness, 1958—. Mem. Am. Battle Monument Commn. Mem. Republican Nat. Finance Com. Trustee Boston U., Boston Urban Found.; chmn. trustee council Boston U. Med. Center; vis. com., U. Cal. at Los Angeles; dir. Mass. Higher Edn. Assistance Corp. (pres. 1962-64), World Affairs Council; trustee Blood Research Inst., Boston. Served as lt. USNR, 1943- 46. Mem. Am. Law Institute, Conf. Bd: Episcopalian. Clubs: Algonquin, University, St. Botolph, Commercial (Boston); Wianno (Mass.); Internat. (adv. council) (Washington). Home: 18 Wood Rd Sherborn MA 01770 Office: 200 Berkeley St Boston MA 02117

BLEIER, RICHARD M., water co. exec.; b. N.Y.C., Dec. 29, 1913; s. William David and Irma (Stiefel) B.; B.S., Cornell U., 1935; m. Jeanette Guinzburg, Sept. 5, 1938; children—Richard Jay, Steven Randolph, Ralph Kleinert. Mgr. stitching machine service engring. dept. Am. Machine & Foundry Co., 1935- 41; plant engr. I.B. Kleinert Rubber Co., N.Y.C., 1945-49, asst. to pres., 1950-54, v.p. sales, 1954-1962, pres., 1962-67, chmn. of bd., 1967-69, also mem. bd. dirs.; supt., pres., also dir. New Castle Water Co., 1945—. Mem. bd. govs. Am. Jewish Com.; vice pres. Fedn. Employment and Guidance Service. Served to maj. C.A.C., AUS, 1941-45. Mem. Pi Lambda Phi. Jewish religion (pres. temple). Clubs: New Castle (N.Y.) Town (pres.), Sheldrake Yacht. Home: 715 King St Chappaqua NY 10514 Office: 735 King St Chappaqua NY 10514

BLEITZ, DONALD LOUIS, engr., author, ornithologist, naturalist; b. Los Angeles, Oct. 1, 1915; s. Louis Rollin and Violet Mae (Trout) B. Owner, operator photog. mfg. firm, pharm. mfg. plant, various tech. labs. and optical mfg. concerns; founder, pres. Bleitz Wildlife Found., 1952—; color photographs, descriptive manuscripts over 650 species birds of N.Am., 1940—, produces and shows slides, lectures sci. ornithol. groups. Recipient award Am. Acad. Achievement, 1964. Mem. Los Angeles County Mus. Bd. dirs., v.p. San Pedro Heart Found. Mem. Nat. Audubon Soc. (life), Cooper Ornithol. Soc., Wilson Ornithol. Club (life), Am. Ornithologists Union (life), Cal., So. Cal. acads. sci., Internat. Soc. Bird Protection, Western (life), Eastern, Inland bird banding assns. Clubs: Thunderbird Country; Los Angeles (founder, v.p., director). Author: Birds of the Americas (22 folio vols. in compilation). Contbr. feature articles (in color), Sat. Eve. Post, Readers Digest, Ariz. Hwys., also various sci. jours., news media periodicals. Patentee in field of optics, emulsions, photog. equipment. Office: 5334 Hollywood Blvd Hollywood CA 90027

BLEND, CHARLES DANIELS, educator, author; b. Marion, Ind., July 18, 1918; s. Gordon B. and Huldah (Daniels) B.; B.A., Ohio State U., 1949, M.A. 1951, Ph.D. 1955; postgrad. Universite D'Aix Marseille, 1949-50, Mex. City Coll., 1946; m. Rhoda Cook, Jan. 2, 1953; children—Jonathan, Patricia. Asst. prof. French, then asso. prof. Ohio State U., 1955-62; prof., chmn. Romance langs. U. N.C., Greensboro, N.C., 1962-66; prof., chmn. Romance langs. Mich. State U., 1966—. Served with AUS, World War II; ETO. Decorated Combat Inf. badge; Fulbright fellow; Am. Philos. Soc. grantee; Am. Council of Learned Socs. grantee. Mem. Am. Assn. U. Profs., Modern Lang. Assn., Am. Assn. Tchrs. French. Author: Andre Malraux, Tragic Humanist, 1963. Contbr. articles profl. jours. Home: 1651 Birchwood Okemos MI 48864 Office: Dept Romance Languages Wells Hall Michigan State University East Lansing MI 48823

BLENDER, DOROTHEA KLOTZ, lawyer, publisher; b. Carthage, Ill., Nov. 25, 1908; d. William and Meda (Klotz) Blender; student Bradley U., 1926-29; Ph.B., U. Chicago, 1930, J.D., 1932. Admitted to Ill. bar, 1932; editor Commerce Clearing House, Inc., pubs. law reporst, N.Y.C., Chgo., Washington, 1932-36, pub. relations mgr., 1940, asst. pres., 1939-56, v.p. 1957—. Mem. Am. Assn. Law Libraries, Spl. Libraries Assn., Am. (ho. of dels. 1954- 56), Chgo. bar assns., Women's Bar Assn., Ill. (president 1947-48), National Assn. Women Lawyers (pres. 1952-54, exec. bd. 1948-56, 2d v.p. 1950-51, 1st v.p. 1951-52), Kappa Beta Pi. Editor of Women Lawyers Jour., 1948-50. Home: 908 Pleasant Lane Glenview IL 60025 Office: 4025 W Peterson Av Chicago IL 60646

BLENKO, WALTER JOHN, lawyer; b. London, Eng., Mar. 4, 1899; s. William J. and Sarah (Balman) B.; came to U.S. in infancy; B.S., Carnegie-Mellon U., 1921, M.E., 1941; J.D., Duquesne U., 1924, LL.D., 1963; m. Ardis L. Jones, Sept. 15, 1921; children—Walter J., Don Balman. Admitted to Pa. bar, 1924, since practiced in Pitts. Bd. dirs. Duquesne U.; trustee Carnegie Inst., Carnegie-Mellon U., trustee Duquesne U. Found. Mem. Newcomen Soc. N.Am., Am. Acad. Polit. and Soc. Sci., N.Y. Acad. Scis., Sigma Alpha Epsilon, Phi Kappa Phi, Tau Beta Pi, Pi Tau Sigma, Omicron Delta Kappa. Clubs: University, Duquesne, Fellows. Home: 4073 Middle Rd Allison Park PA 15101 Office: North American Rockwell Bldg Pittsburgh PA 15222

BLESH, RUDI (Rudol author, artist; b. Guthrie, Okla., Jan. 21, 1899; s. Abraham Lincoln (M.D.) and Theodora Bell (Pickett) B.; student Dartmouth, 1917-20; B.S., with honors, U. Cal., 1924; m. Editha Tuttle, Feb. 22, 1925; 1 dau., Editha Hilary; m. 2d, Barbara Lamont, July 1939. Furniture, archtl., indsl. designer, 1924-43; founder, v.p. Circle Sound Inc., N.Y.C., phonograph documentation pure Afro-American music; one-man show abstract paintings Art of This Century, N.Y.C., 1946. Prof. music Queens College, also prof. Am. arts N.Y.U. Mem. Phi Gamma Delta, Pi Delta Upsilon. Author: This is Jazz, 1943; Shining Trumpets: A History of Jazz, 1946; (with Harriet Janis) They All Played Ragtime, 1950; Modern Art USA, 1956; (with Harriet Janis) Stuart Davis, 1960; De Kooning, 1960; (with Harriet Janis) Collage, 1962; Keaton, 1966; Combo USA, 1971. Writer, narrator radio programs This is Jazz, Our Singing Land, Jazz Saga, Dimensions of Jazz. Editor: O Susanna, 1960. Home: 38 E 4th St New York City NY 10003 (summer) Hillforge Gilmanton NH 03237

BLESSER, WILLIAM BENJAMIN, educator; b. Warren, Pa., Feb. 19, 1924; s. Benjamin and Rebecca (Reiderman) B.; B. Mech. Engring., Rensselaer Poly. Inst., 1950; M. Elec. Engring., Bklyn. Poly. Inst., 1958; m. Leatrice Crown, Nov. 18, 1951; children—Danna, Bonnie. Plant engr. Beaunit Mills Inc., 1950-52; chief mech. engr. Anton Electronic Labs., N.Y.C., 1952-53; engr. Bulova Research and Devel. Co., N.Y.C., 1953-54; mem. faculty Bklyn. Poly. Inst., 1954—, prof. elec. and mech. engring., 1965—. Engring cons. AROD; bioengring. cons. Downstate Med. Center, also Mt. Sinai Sch. Medicine. Served with USAAF, 1942-45. Mem. Sigma Xi, Pi Tau Sigma, Eta Kappa Nu. Author: Systems Approach to Biomedicine, 1969; also articles. Home: 11 Sexton Rd Syosset NY 11791 Office: 333 Jay St Brooklyn NY 11201

BLESSEY, WALTER EMANUEL, civil and structural engr.; b. New Orleans, Oct. 2, 1919; s. Sidney H. and Carrie (Grabert) B.; B.S., Tulane U., 1940, M.S., 1943; m. Ruth Adele Peterson, Nov. 11, 1941; 1 son, Walter Emanuel. Rodman, instrumentman on hydrog. surveys, Atchafalaya Basin, C.E., U.S. Engring. Dept., 1938, on land surveys

Red River Basin, 1939; asst. S.W. La. dist. engr., United Gas Pipe Line Co., 1940-41; asst. city engr., New Orleans, 1941-42; estimator George P. Rice, cons. engr., New Orleans, 1942; asst. prof. exptl. engring. Tulane U., 1942-45, asso. prof. bridge, structural and found. engring. dept. civil engring., 1946-56, prof., 1956—, head dept. civil engring., 1959—; structural detailer, designer Jones & Laughlin Steel Co., New Orleans, 1946; cons. engr. structures, foundations and bridges, 1949—; engr. with W. Horace Williams Co., engrs. and contractors, 1948-49; structural and found. cons. Fromherz Engrs., New Orleans, 1949-51; cons. Gulf Refining Co. on design of wharf at Gretna, La., 1953. Mem. Bd. of Levee Commrs., Orleans Levee Dist.; mem. dean's adv. com. La. Stadium and Exposition Dist. Served as an ensign, C.E., USNR, 1945-46. Nominated one of 10 outstanding young men in U.S., New Orleans Jr. C. of C., 1951. Registered civil engr., La. Mem. Am. Soc., C.E. (pres. La. sect., chmn. mech. properties engring. materials com. engring. mechanics div. 1965-66), La. Engring. Soc., Am. Concrete Inst., Am. Soc. Engring. Edn., Sigma Xi, Tau Beta Pi, Phi Kappa Sigma, Omicron Delta Kappa. Methodist. (steward, trustee, chmn. ofcl. bd.). Clubs: Roundtable, New Orleans Country, Pickwick (New Orleans). Contbr. profl., edn. jours. Home: 5546 Dayna Ct New Orleans LA 70124 Office: Tulane U New Orleans LA 70118

BLETTNER, EDWARD FREDERICK, banker; b. Chgo., Dec. 9, 1907; s. Edward F. and Mary (Klaner) B.; A.B., Harvard, 1928; M.B.A., 1930; LL.B., John Marshall Law Sch., 1935; m. Margaret Maw, Mar. 19, 1943; children—Margaret Jean (Mrs. Christopher Angell), Elizabeth Mary. With First Nat. Bank of Chgo., 1930—, successively trust dept. investment div., asst. trust officer, asst. v.p., 1930-49, v.p., term loan div., 1950-60, sr. v.p., 1961, exec. v. p., 1962-67, pres. 1968-69, vice chmn. of the bd., 1969—, also dir.; vice chmn. bd., dir. First Chgo. Corp., dir. First Chgo. Internat. Banking Corp., First Chgo. Internat. Finance Corp., First Nat. Bank Chgo. (Lebanon) S.A.L., First Capital Corp. Chgo., Internat. Minerals & Chem. Corp., Pabst Brewing Co., Zenith Radio Corporation. Mem. bd. trustee vice chmn. of bd. Rush Presbyn.-St. Luke's Med. Center, Chgo.; pres., dir. Lyric Opera Chgo.; governing mem. Orch. Assn. Chgo.; governing life mem. Art Inst. Chgo.; mem. bd. of trustees Ill. Inst. Tech., McGraw Edison Profit Sharing Trust. Served from capt. to lt. col., AUS, 1942-45. Conglist. Clubs: Chicago, University, Commercial (Chgo.); Indian Hill (Winnetka, Ill); Old Elm (Lake Forest, Ill.). Home: 596 Maple St Winnetka IL 60093 Office: 1 First National Plaza Chicago IL 60670

BLEVINS, HERBERT HARNER, controller, pharm. co. exec.; b. Keats, Kan., Aug. 11, 1916; s. Walter T. and Hazel V. (Harner) B.; B.S., Kan. State Coll., 1938; m. Neva J. Payne, Oct. 26, 1939; children—Robert Leigh, Patti Lynn. Auditor, Lybrand, Ross Bros. & Montgomery, 1938-41; mgr. internal auditing Merck & Co., Inc., 1946-53, controller chem. div., 1953-56, exec. dir. adminstrn. Merck Sharp & Dohme Research Labs., 1956-58, asst. controller Merck & Co., Inc., 1958, controller, 1958-68, v.p. mgmt. information systems, 1968—. Trustee Union Coll., Cranford, N.J. Served from 1st lt. to lt. col., USAAF, 1941-46. Mem. Financial Execs. Inst. of Am. (pres. Newark 1958- 59; nat. dir. 1960-62, v.p. Eastern area 1967- 68, internat. pres. 1969-70, chmn. bd. dirs. 1970-71). Presbyn. (elder). Mason. Club: Lions (Fanwood N.J.; past pres.). Home: 2231 Woodland Terr Scotch Plains NJ 07076 Office: Merck & Co Inc Rahway NJ 07065

BLEVINS, ROBERT WINSTON, ins. co. exec.; b. Dallas, Sept. 5, 1927; s. John L. and Ruby (Henslee) B.; student U. Tex., 1944-47; m. Jeanie C. McGilvray, Sept. 6, 1947; children—Janet Lynn, Donald Lee, Jon Scott. With Southland Life Ins. Co., 1952—, v.p. underwriting, 1967—. Chmn. for Tex., Health Ins. Council. Co-chmn. advanced gifts div. Dallas United Fund, 1968. Served with AUS, 1952-53. Fellow Life Office Mgmt. Assn.; mem. Home Office Life Underwriters Assn. (past pres. Tex.), Health Ins. Assn. Mason (Shriner). Home: 9440 Dartridge Dr Dallas TX 75238 Office: PO Box 2220 Dallas TX 75221

BLEWETT, EDWARD Y., former coll. pres.; b. Yonkers, N.Y., Mar. 22, 1905; s. Howard B. and Ada Maude (York) B.; A.B., Univ. of N.H., 1926, A.M., O. State U., 1940; LL.D., Colby Coll., 1961, New Eng. Coll., 1961; Litt. D., U. N.H., 1967; Ped. D., U. Me., 1967; LL.D., St. Francis Coll., 1970; m. Marion Elizabeth Arthur, Aug. 11, 1928; children—Elizabeth (Mrs. Richard F. Stevens), Edward, John. With Ginn & Co., ednl. pubs., 1926-27; alumni sec., U. N.H., 1927, exec. sec., 1929- 37, asst. to pres., 1937-39, chmn. summer session, 1938-39, dean Coll. of Liberal Arts, 1939-58; pres. Westbrook Jr. Coll. 1958-70, pres. emeritus, 1970—. Cons. to Surgeon Gen. U.S. Army, 1966-69. Mem. nat. adv. dental research council USPHS, 1954-58. Staff mem., State of Washington Ednl. Survey, Jan.- April, 1946. Regional v. chmn. Boy Scouts Am., 1954-56; chmn. Me. Commn. on Arts and Humanities, 1966-67; pres. New Eng. Jr. Coll. Council, 1964-65. Commd. 2d lt. Infantry O.R.C., 1926, active duty as maj., 1941, advanced through ranks to col., 1943; served as chief, Enlisted Branch, Personnel Div., Air Staff and mem. Enlisted Branch, Personnel Div., War Dept. Gen. Staff, 1942-43. Chmn. arts and sci. div. Assn. Land Grant Colls. and Univs., 1948-49. Mem. New Eng. Assn. Colls. and Secondary Schs. (coll. com. chmn., mem. exec. com., editor 1950-62), Lambda Chi Alpha, Phi Delta Kappa, Pi Gamma Mu, Phi Kappa Phi. Episcopalian. Rotarian (past gov.), Mason. Contbr. profl. jours. Home: Trundy Rd Cape Elizabeth ME 04107

BLEWITT, THOMAS HUGH, physicist; b. Cleve., Feb. 8, 1921; s. Reginald T. and Ethyl (Arstall) B.; B.S. in Physics, Case Inst. Tech., 1942; B.S. in Meteorology, N.Y. U., 1943; D.Sc. in Physics, Carnegie Inst. Tech., 1950; m. Agnes Winifred Herr, Sept. 4, 1943; children—Kenneth Thomas, Carol Alice. AEC fellow Carnegie Inst. Tech., 1948-50; physicist Oak Ridge Nat. Lab., 1950-61; exchange scientiest Atomic Energy Establishment, Harwell, Eng., 1957-58; prof. Enrico Fermi Summer Sch., Ispra, Italy, 1960; sr. physicist Argonne Nat. Lab., Lemont, Ill., 1961—; prof. materials engring. U. Ill. Chgo. Circle Campus, 1965—; cons. Internat. Atomic Energy Agy.; vis. scientist Argentine Atomic Energy Com., 1969-70. Served to capt. USAAF, 1942-46. Mem. Am. Phys. Soc., Am. Soc. Metals. Contbr. children—Phyllis jours. Home: 1610 Center Av Wheaton, IL 60187. Office: Materials Sci Div Argonne Nat Lab Argonne IL 60439

BLEY, ELMER O., bank exec. Sr. v.p., controller Mercantile Safe Deposit & Trust Co., Balt. Office: Calvert and Redwood Sts Baltimore MD 21203*

BLEY, PAUL, jazz pianist; b. Montreal, Que., Can., Nov. 10, 1932; s. Joseph and Betty Bley; studied violin and piano, jr. diploma McGill Conservatory at age 11; studied composition, conducting at Juilliard Sch. Music, 1950-52; m. Carla Bley (divorced 1968). Started musical career as leader of high sch. bank; organized quartet Chalet Hotel, Montreal, 1945-48; with Ozzie Roberts, Clarence Joines, played at Alberta Lounge, 1949-50; weekly TV show Jazz Workshop, Montreal, 1952; with Stan Kenton in movie short dealing with jazz history; played N.Y.C. clubs, midwestern colls., 1955, nightclubs, Los Angeles, 1956-58, also group shows with Ornette Coleman and Don Cherry, 1958; coll. concert Cal., 1957-59; with Charlie Mingus, 1960; with Jimmy Guiffre, 1960-61, toured Germany, 1961; coll. concerts including Town Hall and Lincoln Center, 1962-63; member Sonny Rollins' quartet, 1963; tours in U.S., Europe, also appeared Newport Jazz Festival, WNDT-TV network show, concert tour of Japan,, and RCA Victor Recordings, 1964; formed own trio for Bard Coll. concert, 1964, trio recorded for E.S.P. Records, 1965, tour Europe, 1965, 66, 67, tour Eastern U.S. colls., 1967, recorded for Mercury-Limelight Records, Milestone Records, also for Douglas International Records; commissioned to write and to play for Norddeutcher Rundfunk, Hamburg, W. Germany, 1969. Home: 639/ Hudson St New York City NY 10014

BLEYHL, NORRIS ARTHUR, librarian; b. Snyder, Neb., May 7, 1915; s. Otto and Mabel (Becker) B.; A.B., U. Neb., 1936, B.L.S., U. Denver, 1938; M.A., U. Minn., 1947, Ph.D., 1955; m. Zella E. Smith, June 17, 1950; 1 son, David F. Circulation asst. Lincoln (Neb.) Pub. Library, 1936-37; student U. Denver Library Sch., 1937-38; cataloger U. Omaha Library, 1938-39; asst. periodical dept., bus. library Temple U., 1939-43; librarian Mesa Coll., Grand Junction, Colo., 1947-49, Chico State Coll., 1951—. Mem. A.L.A., Cal. Library Assn., Phi Alpha Theta. Conglist. Home: 237 W Lincoln Av Chico CA 95926

BLEYMAIER, JOSEPH SYLVESTER, constrn. co. exec., ret. air force officer; b. Austin, Tex., Dec. 31, 1915; s. Jacob and Mary Ann (Frish) B.; B.B.A. U. Tex. 1950; grad. Air Command and Staff Sch., 1950, Air War Coll., 1954; m. Rosemary Josephine Mathias June 25, 1942; children—Joseph Sylvester, Marianne, Theodore, John, Eugene. Commd. 2d lt. USAAF, 1942, advanced through grades to maj. gen., 1967; chief equipment div. Hdqrs. Air Research and Devel. Command, 1954-56, dep. dir. astronautics, 1956- 58, also dir. subsystems devel.; asst. dep. comdr. ballistics missiles Air Force Ballistic Missile Div., 1958-60; dep. for launch vehicles, systems program dir., also dep. comdr. manned systems Hdqrs. Space Systems Div., 1961-65; comdr. Air Force Western Test Range, Vandenberg AFB, Cal., 1965-67; dep. dir. MOL program USAF, also dep. comdr. SSD MOL, Los Angeles, 1967-69; retired, 1969; v.p. bus. devel. Morrison-Knudsen Co., Boise, Ida., 1969—. Decorated Air medal with 10 oak leaf clusters, D.S.M., Army Commendation medal, Legion of Merit; recipient John F. Kennedy Meml. award Arnold Air Soc., 1965. Mem. Am. Inst. Aero. and Astronautics (astronautics award 1965), Soc. Mil. Engrs., Air Force Assn., Am. Ordnance Assn., Am. Mgmt. Assn. Roman Cath. K.C. Address: 627 Lawrence Av Boise ID 83705 Office: Morrison-Knudsen Co Inc Box 7808 400 Broadway Boise ID

BLEZNICK, DONALD WILLIAM, educator; b. N.Y.C., Dec. 24, 1924; s. Louis and Gertrude (Kleinman) B.; B.A., Coll. City N.Y., 1946; M.A., Universidad Nacional de Mexico, 1948; Ph.D., Columbia, 1954; m. Rozlyn Burakoff, June 15, 1952; children—Jordan, Susan. Instr. romance langs. Ohio State U., 1949-55; prof. romance langs. Pa. State U., 1955-67; head, romance langs., prof. U. Cin., 1967—. Served with CIC, 1946-47. Am. Philos. Soc. research grantee, 1964. Downer fellow Coll. City N.Y., 1947-48. Mem. Am. Assn. Tchrs. Spanish and Portuguese, Modern Lang. Assn. Am., Am. Assn. U. Profs., Midwest Modern Lang. Assn., Phi Beta Kappa (pres. Delta chpt. of Ohio 1971-72), Sigma Delta Pi (state dir. Ohio 1968-70, Order of Don Quijote 1970), Phi Sigma Iota, Kappa Delta Pi. Bibliographer, Modern Lang. Assn. Internat. Bibliography, 1966—; rev. editor: Hispania, 1965—, El Ensayo Espanol del Siglo Veinte, 1964, El Ensayo Espanol, 1964; editor: Duelo en el Paraiso (Goytisolo), 1967, Madrugada (Buero Vallejo), 1969, Quevedo, 1971; editor (with Walter T. Pattison) Representative Spanish Authors, 1971; contbr. articles to profl. jours., Ency. Americana. Home: 7870 Elbrook Av Cincinnati OH 45237

BLICK, CHARLES AUGUSTUS, naval officer; b. Jersey City, June 2, 1911; s. John James and Letitia (Parker) B.; B.S., U.S. Naval Acad., 1933; M.B.A., Harvard, 1947; m. Carmelitta DaCosta, Aug. 10, 1936; children—VanWitt Charles, Timothy Augustus. Commd. ensign U.S. Navy, 1933, advanced through grades to rear adm., 1961; asst. comdr. Adm. Farragut Acad., Toms River, N.J., 1933; mem. staff Comdr. Amphibious Group 3, World War II, supply officer U.S.S. Procyon, carrying med. needs after surprise attack Pearl Harbor; exec. dir. procurement and prodn. Def. Supply Agy., 1962-65; comdg. officer Navy Ship's Store Office, Bklyn., 1966-68; ret. 1968; mgr. fed. govt. services microfilm products div. 3 M Co., Washington, 1968—; established intra-govt. procurement adv. council for drugs Def. Supply Agy., for improvement procurement practices and quality control standards for drugs, 1963, chmn., 1963-65. Decorated Bronze Star with combat V, various ribbons, Legion of Merit with gold star. Mem. Harvard Bus. Sch. Alumni Assn. Clubs: Army-Navy (Washington); N.Y. Yacht; Hurlingham (London, Eng.). Home: 4121 48th St NW Washington DC 20016 Office: 3 M Co 1750 Pennsylvania Av NW Washington DC 20006

BLIGHT, JOHN, 1953-63. Pres. Urban League N.J., 1955. Served with USNR, 1943-46. Mem. Mabel (Crago) B.; m. Margaret M. Collicutt Oct. 3, 1946; 1 dau., Judith M. With various pipeline companies, 1939-42, 46-50; accountant Interprovincial Pipe Line Co., Edmonton, Alta., Can., 1950-54; chief accountant Lakehead Pipe Line Co., Superior, Wis., 1955-59, treas., 1960- 64, sec.-treas., 1964—; chief accountant Interprovincial Pipe Line Co., 1960, treas., 1960-64, sec.-treas., 1964—. Served to 1st lt. Canadian Army, 1942-45. Mem. Financial Execs. Inst. Clubs: National (Toronto); Thornhill (Can.) Country. Home: 199 Burbank Dr Willowdale 432 Ontario Canada Office: 7 King So E Toronto 210 Ontario Canada

BLINDER, ABE LIONEL, rep. of Denmark to UN, 1967—. Home: (Goldstein) B.; Ph.B., U. Chgo., 1931; m. Henriette Levin, Oct. 19, 1947; children—Henry David, Jonathan. Circulation mgr. Apparel Arts, Chgo., 1932-33; circulation mgr. Esquire, Inc., Chgo., 1933-36, circulation dir. 1936-45, dir., 1945—, v.p., 1945-51, exec. v.p., 1952-61, pres., 1961—. dir. Ideal Toy Co. Mem. Phi Beta Kappa. Clubs: Harmonie (N.Y.C.); Metropolis Country. Home: 5 Horseguard Lane Scarsdale NY 10583 Office: 488 Madison Av New York City NY 10022

BLINKEN, MAURICE HENRY, investment co. exec.; b. Kiev, Ukraine, Apr. 26, 1900 (father U.S. citizen); s. Mayer and Anna (Turefskoy) B.; B.C.S., N.Y. U., 1921, LL.B., 1924, LL.M., 1925; C.P.A., U. State N.Y., 1921; m. Ethel Horowitz, Oct. 9, 1924; children—Donald M., Robert J., Alan J. Partner accounting firm Blinken, Eisner & Philip, N.Y.C., 1921-25; admitted to N.Y. bar, 1925, also U.S. Supreme Ct. bar; practiced law, 1925-45; chmn. bd., treas. MITE Corp., New Haven, 1962—; treas., dir. Fifth Av. and 59th Corp., N.Y.C., 1952—; dir. PEC Israel Econ. Corp.; former partner law firm Cabell, Ignatius, Lown & Blinken, N.Y.C. Mem. bd. edn., Yonkers, N.Y., 1934-35, pres., 1935. Trustee Horace Mann Sch. Boys, N.Y.C., 1936- 52, Yonkers Pub. Library, 1936. Served with U.S. Army, 1918. Mem. Assn. Bar City N.Y., Delta Mu Delta (past pres.), Tau Delta Phi (past pres.). Mason; mem. B'nai B'rith. Home: 300 Seminole Av Palm Beach FL 33480 Office: 446 Blake St New Haven CT 06515

BLINKEN, ROBERT JAMES, mfg. co. exec.; b. N.Y.C., Apr. 18, 1929; s. Maurice Henry and Ethel (Horowitz) B.; grad. Horace Mann Sch., N.Y.C., 1946; B.S. cum laude, Harvard, 1950; m. Jeanne Pagnucco, Mar. 5, 1955 (div. Jan. 1967); children—Robert James, Rachel; m. 2d, Allison Matsner, Dec. 14, 1967. Vice pres. Exchange Trading Corp., N.Y.C., 1953- 57; pres. Teleprinter Corp., Paramus, N.J., 1954-61; v.p. Mite Corp., New Haven, 1961-63, pres., 1963—, also dir. Served to 1st lt. USAF, 1950-53. Home: 400 Blake St New Haven CT 06515 Office: 446 Blake St New Haven CT 06515

BLINKS LAWRENCE ROGERS, biologist; b. Michigan City, Ind., Apr. 22, 1900; s. Walter Moulton and Ella Little (Rogers) B.; student Kalamazoo Coll., 1918-19; Stanford Univ., 1920-21; S.B., Harvard, 1923; A.M., 1925, Ph.D., 1926; m. Anne Catherine Hof, July 27, 1928; children—John Rogers, David (dec.), Samuel (dec.). Investigator Bermuda Biol. Sta. and Rockefeller Inst. Lab., Bermuda, various years between 1923-37, 70, Carnegie Instn., Dry Tortugas, Fla., summers 1926-29, Woods Hole, 1923, 33, 40, Cold Spring Harbor, 1940; asst. Rockefeller Inst. for Med. Research 1926-29, asso., 1929-33; asso. prof., plant physiology Stanford U., 1933-36, prof. biology, 1936-65, emeritus, 1965—; prof. U. Cal., Santa Cruz, 1965—, chmn. dept. biology, 1965-67; fellow Crown Coll., 1967—; chief scientist Te Vega Expdn., winter 1965; mem. Alpha Helix Expdn. Great Barrier Reef, 1966; dir. Hopkins Marine Sta. Stanford U., Pacific Grove, Cal., 1943-65. John Simon Guggenheim Meml. fellow, 1939-40, 49, 57; Am.-Scandinavian fellow (hon.), 1949; Fulbright Scholar, Cambridge, 1957. In war research in aviation medicine under OSRD, 1942-44, Bikini Scientific Resurvey, 1947; cons. Nat. Sci. Found., asst. dir., 1954-55; mem. adv. bd. Guggenheim Found., 1956-60, Marine Resources Inst. (U. Cal.), 1957-61. Fellow Am. Acad. Arts and Sci., A.A.A.S. (v.p. 1955), Cal. Acad.; mem. Botanical-Zool. Soc. of Vienna, Nat. Acad. Scis. (com. sci. and pub. policy 1963-66), Soc. Gen. Physiologists (pres. 1951-52), Western Soc. Naturalists (pres. 1950), Bot. Soc. Am., Am. Soc. Plant Physiologists (Stephen Hales award 1952), Bermuda Biol. Sta., Inc., Am. Assn. U. Profs., Sigma Xi. Club: Faculty (Stanford). Contbr. sci. papers on electrobiology, permeability of cells, photosynthesis, algal physiology to profl. jours. Mem. editorial bd. jour. Gen. Physiology, 1951-62, hon. editor, 1967—; mem. editorial bd. Botanica Marina. Home: Ranche Aguajito Route 3 Box 522 Carmel CA 93921 Office: Hopkins Marine Stat Pacific Grove CA 93950

BLINN, KEITH WAYNE, oil co. exec.; b. Hutchinson, Kan., July 28, 1917; s. Alonzo Cary and Clifton (Wright) B.; A.B., Washington and Lee U., 1940; LL.B. (Sterling fellow), Yale, 1951; m. Ellen Young, Aug. 31, 1940; children—John Randolph, Stephen David. Admitted to Wis. bar, Conn.); Pine Orchard Yacht. Home: Valley Rd New Canaan CT 06840 Office: 30 Rockefeller Plaza New York City NY 10020 1941, Tex. bar, 1953, N.Y. bar, 1966; atty. TVA, 1942, NLRB, 1942-46; prof. law U. N.D., 1946-52; vis. prof. law U. Ida., 1952; v.p. gen. counsel Continental Oil Co., N.Y.C., 1962—; lectr., seminar participant, 1964—; arbitrator Am. Arbitrator Assn., 1961—. Atty. adviser OPA, 1951; chmn. regional enforcement commn. WSB, Mpls., 1952. Mem. bd. zoning appels, Bellaire, Tex., 1957, mem. city council, 1959. Mem. Am. Bar Assn., Assn. Bar City N.Y., Order of Coif, Phi Delta Phi. Episcopalian (vestryman). Clubs: Stamford (Conn.) Yacht; Wee Burn Country (Darien,

BLISS, A. HARRY, sanitarian; b. Saginaw, Mich., June 10, 1909; s. Fred L. and Janet (Smith) B.; B.S., U. Cal., Berkeley, 1931, M.S., 1934, M.P.H., Los Angeles, 1950; Dr. Pub. Adminstrn., U. So. Cal., 1958; m. Ella Whiton, June 21, 1933; 1 dau., Barbara Janet (dec.). With USPHS, Fresno, Cal., 1935-36, Alameda County (Cal.) Health Dept., 1936-40; camp ins. div. housing State of Cal., 1940-42; lectr. Pub. health U. Cal., Berkeley, 1946-47, cons. Sanitarian, 1950-59, asso. prof. sch. pub. health, 1959-70, prof. pub. health emeritus, mgmt., 1971—; chmn. dept. pub. health U. Cal., Los Angeles, 1947-55, asst. prof., 1950-53, asso. prof., 1953-59, asso. prof. preventive medicine Sch. Medicine, 1955-59; statewide coordinator environmental health and safety Office of the President, 1959-62. Cons., mem. food sanitation adv. com. USPHS, 1956-66, cons. Bur. Health Services, 1968, cons., conducting survey and evaluation environmental health program Div., Indian Health, 1967-68; developed Sch. Pub. Health, U. West Indies, cons., WHO-Pan Am. Health Assn., 1967-68; mem. Sanitarians Joint Council, 1958-66, Nat. Health Forum, 1965-68, Nat. Council on Environmental Health for Health Care Facilities; pres. Nat. Council for Sanitarians Residencies; cons. to the Los Angeles Met. Sanitation Dirs. Group. Served as maj. San. Corps, USAAF, 1942-46. Recipient Walter S. Mangold award Nat. Assn. Sanitarians, 1960. Registered sanitarian, Cal. Diplomate Am. Intersoc. Bd. Certification sanitarians (bd. mem.), Fellow Am. Pub. Health Assn. (pres. Western br. 1956-57; sanitarian's joint council 1958-66), A.A.A.S.; mem. Nat. (hon.; past pres.; chmn. bd. examiners), Cal. assns. sanitarians, Conf. Municipal Pub. Health Engrs. Am. Coll. Health Assn., Assn. Food Industry Sanitarians, Inst. Sanitation Mgmt. (v.p. 1959), Nat. Safety Council, Western Govtl. Research Assn., No. Cal., So. Cal. (pres. 1957) Pub. Health assns., Am. Soc. Pub. Adminstrn., Nat. Environmental Health Assn. (hon. life, bd. dirs. 1965—), Tau Kappa Epsilon, Phi Delta Kappa, Delta Omega. Presbyn. (elder). Editor, pub. The Sanitarian, 1948-56, asso. editor, 1956-64; editor Jour. Environmental Health, 1964—; mem. editorial bd. Internat. Jour. Environmental Studies, 1969—. Honored by establishment A. Harry Bliss award Cal. Assn. Sanitarians, 1964. Office: Univ of Cal Sch of Public Health Berkeley CA 94720

BLISS, ANTHONY ADDISON, lawyer; b. N.Y. C., Apr. 19, 1913; s. Cornelius Newton and Zaidee (Cobb) B.; B.A., Harvard, 1936; LL.B., U. of Va., 1940; m. Barbara Field, Dec. 22, 1937 (div. Dec. 1941); 1 dau., Barbara (Mrs. Luis Mestre); m. 2d, Jo Ann Sayers, June 9, 1942 (div. July 12, 1967); children—Eileen (Mrs. Eileen Bliss Andahazy), Anthony Addison, John Wheeler; m. 3d, Sally Brayley, July 24, 1967; children— Mark Brayley, Timothy Newton. Admitted to the New York State bar, 1943; member firm Milbank, Tweed, Hadley & McCloy, New York City. Trustee U.S. Trust Co. N.Y. Member bd. dirs., member executive committee Metropolitan Opera Association, pres., 1956-67; chmn. bd. Found. for Am. Dance, Inc.-City Center Joffrey Ballet; mem. adv. panel on dance Nat. Endowment for Arts; vice chmn. bd. Nat. Opera Inst. Served in USNR, 1942-45. Decorated Air Medal. Mem. Am., Internat., N.Y. State, Nassau County bar assns., Assn. Bar City New York. Clubs: Rockefeller Center Luncheon, Wall Street, River, Creek. Home: Centre Island Oyster Bay NY 11771 Office: One Chase Manhattan Plaza New York City NY 10005

BLISS, CHARLES ANDRESSEN, educator; b. Napa, Cal., June 20, 1904; s. Charles Humphrey and Helen Margaret (Andressen) B.; A.B., U. Cal., 1926, A.M., 1929; Ph.D., Columbia, 1939; A.M., Harvard, 1946; m. Gertrude Reaske, June 16, 1932; 1 son, Charles Michael. Exec. sec., Nat. Bur. Econ. Research, N.Y.C., 1932-37; instr. statistics, Columbia, 1930-37; asso. in research, Harvard 1937-38, asst. prof. bus. statistics, 1938-41, asso. prof., 1941-46, prof. bus. adminstrn., 1946-66, Royal Little prof. bus. adminstrn., 1966-70, prof. emeritus, 1970—. Mem. Phi Beta Kappa. Author: Structure of Manufacturing Production, Nat. Bur. Econ. Research, 1939. Home: 1425 Howell Mt Rd Anqvin CA 94508

BLISS, CHARLES MELBOURNE, banker; b. Evanston, Ill., Oct. 9, 1921; s. Charles H. and Hazel (Whitmore) B.; A.B., Harvard, 1943, student Bus. Sch., 1942-43; M.B.A., Northwestern U., 1947; m. Margaret Soule, Jan. 1, 1943; children—Charles Melbourne, Marian Elizabeth, Emily Margaret. With Harris Trust & Savs. Bank, Chgo., 1944—, sr. v.p., 1969-71, exec. v.p., 1971—; lectr. finance Am. Inst.

Banking, Northwestern U., 1945-52. Bd. dirs. Scholarship and Guidance Assn., Family Service Assn., Winnetka and Northfield, Ill., Citizen Traffic Safety Bd. Met. Chgo. Served with AUS, 1943. Mem. Phi Beta Kappa, Beta Gamma Sigma. Episcopalian (bd. dirs.). Home: 585 Somerset Lane Northfield IL 60093 Office: 111 W Monroe St Chicago IL 60690

BLISS, CHARLES MITCHELL, bank exec.; b. Washington, Jan. 20, 1904; s. Charles Lincoln and Edith (Little) B.; student N.E. Conservatory Music, 1921-23, Babson Inst., 1923-24; m. Ella Flanders, Aug. 22, 1926; children—Richard M., Marjorie. With Shenango Penn Mold Co., 1924-28, Equitable Trust Co., and Chase Nat. Bank (upon merger), 1929-31; became v.p. Bank of N.Y., N.Y.C., 1942, then exec. v.p., was chmn. bd., 1963-69, now dir. Dir. The Home Life Ins. Co., N.Y.C.; chmn., pres. Elizabeth Arden Sales Corp.; trustee The Seamens Bank for Savs., N.Y.C.; dir. Prudential Ins. Co. Gt. Britain, Phoenix Assurance Co. N.Y. Dir., mem. Fgn. Bondholders Protective Council, Inc. Trustee Bd. Home Missions, Congl. Ch., N.Y.C., Annuity Fund for Congl. Ministers, N.Y.C. Pres. bd. mgrs. St. Barnabas Hosp. Chronic Diseases. Home: 535 Park Av New York City NY 10021 Office: 48 Wall St New York City NY 10005

BLISS, DANIEL, clergyman; b. Upper Montclair, N.J., Mar. 15, 1898; s. Howard Sweetser and Amy (Blatchford) B.; student Am. Community Sch., Beirut, Lebanon, 1905-14; grad. Hill Sch., Pottstown, Pa., 1916; B.A., Amherst Coll., 1920, D.D., 1950; grad. student Am. U. Beirut, 1925; B.D. magna cum laude, Union Theol. Sem., 1926; student div. sch. Harvard, 1930-34; m. Winifred Rouse, June 22, 1926; children—Mary Hallock, Howard Blatchford, John Williams. Faculty Am. U., Beirut, 1920-23; student asst. Brick Presbyn. Ch., N.Y.C., 1924-26; ordained to ministry Conglist. Ch., 1926, home mission pastor, Lander, Wyo., 1925; minister Monson, Mass., 1926-29; asso. minister Old South Ch., Boston, 1929-35; instr. Emerson Coll., Boston, 1932-35; minister 2d Ch., Greenwich, 1936-57; sec. bd. Am. Bd. of Commrs. for Fgn. Missions, Boston, 1957-60; acting sr. minister 2d Ch. (Congl.), Newton, Mass., 1962; pres., chmn. exec. com. Am. Middle East Rehab. Inc., N.Y.C., 1968-70; vice chmn. Am. Near Internat. Coll., Beirut, Lebanon, 1961—. Em. prudential com. A.B.C.F.M., 1949-57; dean Congl. Youth Confs. of Conn., Storrs, 1940-42. Pres. Crispus Attucks Assn. (social center), Greenwich, 1946-55; dir. Union Theol. Sem.; trustee Am. U., Beirut, Domascus (Syria) Prep. So., Near East Coll. Assn., N.Y.C. Recipient Gold medal of Merit, Republic of Lebanon, 1959. Served with Inf. in S.A.T.C., 1918; capt. Chaplains Corps, USAAF, 1943-46. Mem. Nat. Chaplains Fellowship Congl. Chs. (pres.), Missions Council Nat. Congl. Chs. (chmn. 1951-53), Gen. Assn. Congl. Ministers Conn. (moderator), Am. Legion, Res. Officers Assn., Amateur Astronomers Assn., Alpha Delta Phi. Clubs: Century (N.Y.C.); Rotary. Author: How to Increase Church Attendance, 1936; The Spiritual Diary, 1941; Strength for Service to God and Country, 1942; Strength for the Day, 1943. Contbr. articles religious publs. Address: Route 3 Box 438 Orlando FL 32811

BLISS, FRANCIS ROYSTER, educator. Prof. classics and Greek U. Vt., Burlington. Office: Dept Classics U Vt Burlington VT 05401*

BLISS, FRANCIS WALTER, lawyer; b. Gilboa, N.Y., Apr. 27, 1892; s. Franklin W. and Alberta (Becker) B.; A.B., Cornell U., 1913; LL.B., Albany Law Sch., 1915; LL.D., LL.D., Central Coll., Pella, Ia., 1939; m. Margaret E. Shaeffer, June 22, 1918 (dec. June 24, 1956); children—Janet Schaeffer (Mrs. Snyder), Margaret Ellen (Mrs. Berdan), Martha Ann (Mrs. Grogan); m. 2d, Margaret A. Nethaway, Oct. 31, 1957. Admitted to N.Y. bar, 1915; practiced in Middleburgh, 1916-30; county atty. Schoharie County N.Y., 1922-26; Sci., Am. justice Supreme Ct., N.Y., 1930-44, Appellate Div., 1933-44; mem. firm Bliss & Bouck, Schoharie, Albany, N.Y., 1945-62; pvt. practice, practice, Schoharie, 1963—. Pres., Howe Caverns, Inc. (N.Y.). Mem. Am., N.Y. State Schoharie County bar assns. Mem. Reformed Ch. (bd. edn.). Mason. Club: Fort Orange (Albany). Home: Middleburgh NY 12122 Office: 316 Main St Schoharie NY 12157

BLISS, GEORGE WILLIAM, newspaperman; b. Denver, July 21, 1918; s. William Lane and Marie (Bresnan) B.; student Northwestern U., 1938; m. Helen Jeanne Groble, June 29, 1940 (dec. June 1959); children—William R., George L., Dennis M., Marianne, Carol, Helen Jeanne; m. 2d, Therese O'Keefe, Aug. 11, 1960; 1 son, Terrence. With Chgo. Evening Am., 1937-42; with Chgo. Tribune, 1942-68, 71—, labor editor, 1953-68, dir. investigative task force, 1971—; chief investigator Better Govt. Assn., 1968-71, also acting exec. dir. Served with USNR, World War II. Recipient Edward Scott Beck award Chgo. Tribune, 1954, 58; Spot News Reporting award Chgo. Newspaper Guild, 1957, A.P., 1958, 59; Pulitzer prize for local reporting, 1962. Mem. Chgo. Newspaper Reporters Assn. Clubs: Press, Ill. Athletic Assn. (Chgo.). Home: 9605 S Lawndale Av Evergreen Park IL 60642 Office: 435 N Michigan Av Chicago IL 60611

BLISS, GEORGE LAURENCE, S., William S. Staff mem. radiation lab. Mass. Inst. Tech., 1942-43, instr. math. 1944-46, asst. prof. mech. engring., 1947-51, asso. B.S. in Econs., U. Pa., 1919 (1918); m. Corinne Constance Sawyer, June 1, 1921; children—George Donald, Arthur Sawyer (dec.), Janet. With Fisk Rubber Co., Chicopee Falls, Mass., N.Y.C., 1919-22; asst. to pres. Franklin Soc. for Home-Bldg. & Savs., 9 alumni Indsl. and Applied Math., Am. Math. Soc., Loan Bank System, Washington, 1936-37), dir., 1954-57, vice chmn., 1955-57; pres. Century Fed. Savs. & Loan Assn., Electromechanical Systems, 1968. Editor: Random Vibration Savs. Instns., 1966—. Pres., Met. League Savs. Assn., 1928-29, N.Y. State League Savs. and Loan Assns., 1931-32; chmn accounting div. U.S. Savs. and Loan League, 1934-40, chmn. legislative com., 1950-54, director, 1956-58, mem. exec. com., 1958-61; vice chmn. Nat. Thrift Com., 1949-63; mem. council of Internation Union Bldg. Soc., 1956-58. Mem. Pres. Eisenhower's Adv. Com. on Housing, Contbr. papers on numerical analysis, applied mechanics, vibrations, acoustics. Home: Tabor Hill Rd Lincoln MA 01773 Office: Massachusetts Inst Technology Cambridge MA 02139 Fellow Royal Soc. Arts (London, Eng.); mem. Am. Savs. and Loan Inst. (pres. 1930-31), Am. Finance Assn., Nat. Assn. Bus. Economists, Am. Legion, 316th Inf. Assn. (pres. 1941-42), Internat. Benjamin Franklin Soc. (pres. 1948—). Republican. Conglist. Rotarian. Clubs: Army-Navy (Washington); University of Pennsylvania (N.Y.C.). Home: 49 Esplanade Mount Vernon NY 10553 also 42 Butler Pl Northampton MA 01060 Office: 50 E 42d St New York City NY 10017

BLISS, HARDING, educator; b. St. Louis, July 14, 1911; s. Carl Crider and Elizabeth (Harding) B.; B.S., U. of Ill., 1932; Ph.D., Yale, 1935; m. Gretchen Elizabeth Evans, Feb. 12, 1941. Dir. semi works, Rohm & Haas Co., Phila., 1935-37; asst. prof. chem. engring., U. of Pa., 1937-39; asst. prof., Yale, 1939-42, asso. prof., 1942-47, prof. chem. engring., 1947- -. Cons. State Water Commn., Nat. Def. Research Commn., World War II. Mem. Am. Inst. Chem. Engrs. (former editor jour.), Am. Chem. Soc., Sigma Xi, Tau Beta Pi. Contbr. sects. and chpts. in books; articles chem. publs. Home: Todd St Mt Carmel CT 06518 Office: 9 Hillhouse Av New Haven CT 06511

BLISS, HARVEY JOHN, lawyer; b. Toronto, Ont., Can., Oct. 6, 1933; s. Henry and Ida (Hoffman) B.; B.Commerce, U. Toronto, 1955; LL.B., 1958; m. Eileen May Sullivan, Feb. 4, 1966; children—Kimberley Anne, Deborah Leigh. Called to bar with honors barrister, 1960; practice in Toronto; partner Levinter, Dryden, Bliss, Maxwell & Hart, Toronto, 1965—. Instr. trial practice Bar Admission Course, 1962—; lectr. trial practice Osgoode Hall Law Sch., York U., 1970—. Chmn. constn. com. Toronto and Dist. Liberal Assn., 1966—, also Liberal Party in Ont., 1971—. Mem. Canadian Bar Assn. (chmn. Ont. civil justice sect. 1966-67, mem. dominion council 1968—), Internat. Bar Assn., Internat. Commn. Jurists, Advs. Soc. Lawyers Club, Toronto Medico-Legal Soc., County of York Law Assn., Sigma Alpha Mu. Home: 19 Chelford Rd Don Mills Ontario Canada Office: 100 Adelaide St W 1300 Toronto 1 Ontario Canada

BLISS, LOUIS G., minerals exec.; b. Rahway, N.J., June 17, 1907; s. Frank H. and Lulu (Ganong) B.; B.S., Rutgers U., 1929, M.S., 1931; m. Margaret Nola, Feb. 22, 1935; 1 son, Stephen M. Grad. asst. Rutgers U., 1931-33; sales research engr. Foote Mineral Co., Phila., 1933-36, sales mgr., 1938-52, v.p. charge sales, 1952-56, pres., 1956-60, pres., chmn. bd., pres., 1961-67, pres., chief exec. officer, 1968, pres., chmn. bd., chief exec. officer, 1968-70, chmn. bd., chief exec. officer, 1970—, also dir.; sales dept. Meckling Bros., also Gen. Chemical Co., Camden, N.J., 1936-38. Mem. bd. dirs., also exec. com. Phila. Mfrs. Mutual Ins. Co., Mfg. Chemists Assn. Mem. Am. Chem. Soc. Home: 335 Dreshertown Rd Fort Washington PA 19034 Office: Rte 100 Exton PA 19341

BLISS, RALPH KENNETH, ret. agrl. educator; b. Diagonal, Ia., Oct. 30, 1880; s. Horace and Mary and Mary Ellen (Day) B.; B.S. in Agr., Ia. State U., 1905, D.Sc., 1958; m. Ethel Eveleth McKinley, Sept. 14, 1912 (dec. 1945); children—Robert Sessions (pres. elect McKinley, William Ralph, Richard Kenneth; m. 2d, Ella Luick, Kappa, Alpha 1957. Farm mgr., 1906; in charge animal husbandry extension, 1906-11, actg. supt. agrl. extension, 1912, Ia. State Coll., prof. animal husbandry U. Neb., 1912-14; dir. agrl. extension Ia. State Coll., 1914-46, dir. emeritus, 1946—. Chmn. extension section Am. Assn. Agrl. Coll. and Expt. Stas., 1917; Sec. War Emergency (Atha) Food Com. of Ia., 1917; state dir. of Boy's Working Reserve, 1917-18; chmn. State Seed Stocks Com., 1917; chmn. com. on extension orgn. and policy of Land Grant Coll. Assn., 1933 and 1936; mem. Ia. State Corn-Hog Adjustment Com., 1933-35; chmn. State Adv. Com., Soil v.p., 1958-64, Conservation Service, 1937-46; chmn. State Land Use and Program Devel. Com., 1939-42; mem. State Farm Security Advisory Com., 1939- 46, State Agrl. Adjustment Com., State Soil Conservation Dist. Law Com., 1939-46, State U.S. Dept. Agrl. War Bd., 1941-46; rep. War Food Adminstrn. on State Manpower Priorities Commn. Recipient Nat. Award for distinguished service to Am. agr. Am. Farm Bur. Fedn., 1943; Alumni Merit Award from Chgo. alumni of Ia. State Coll., 1946; nat. citation for leadership in 4-H Club work, 1950; plague for outstanding leadership in soil conservation by Ia. State Soil Conservation Soc., 1950; hon. award Soil Conservation work, Soil Conservation Soc., 1951; faculty citation Ia. State Coll., 1952; Am. Country Life Assn. award, 1953; Ruby award, 1958. Mem. Epsilon Sigma Phi, Delta Sigma Rho, Phi Kappa Phi. Republican. Conglist. Author: History of Extension Work in Iowa, 1960; also various bulls. and articles on agrl. subjects. Compiler, editor; spirit and Philosophy of Extension, 1952. Radio commentator. Home: 2316 Burnett St Ames IA 50010

BLISS, RAY CHARLES, mem. Rep. Nat. Com.; b. Akron, O., Dec. 16, 1907; s. Emil and Emilie (Wieland) B.; A.B., U. Akron, 1935, L.H.D., 1968; m. Ellen F. Palmer. Sec., treas. Wells & Bliss, Inc., 1933-37; pres. Tower Agys., Inc., gen. ins., Akron, 1947—. Mem. Summit County Bd. Elections, 1936—, chmn. bd., 1949- 50. Chmn., Summit County Republican Central Com., 1942-64, Ohio Rep. State Central and Exec. Com., 1949-65, mem., 1944—, mem. finance com., 1949—; mem. Rep. Nat. Com., 1952—, mem. exec. com. 1952—, vice chmn., 1960- 65, chmn., 1965-69; del.-at-large Rep. Nat. Conv., 1952, 56, 60, 64, 68, chmn. delegation, 1956, vice chmn. subcom. to select 1960 conv. site, chmn. 1968 site com., vice chmn. Ohio delegation, 1960; chmn. Midwest and Rocky Mountain Rep. State Chmns. Assn., 1953-65; chmn. Rep. com. on big city politics, 1961; chm. Rep. State Chairmen's Adv. Com., 1963-65; adviser exec. com. on Pres. United Rep. Nat. Conv. arrangements Com., 1964, chmn. conv. arrangements com. 1968. Trustee Akron U. appt. chmn. subcom. on devel., mem. subcom. on finance. Recipient U. Akron Alumni Honor award, 1965. Mem. Phi Kappa Tau, Episcopalian. Mason (32, Shriner), Kiwanian. Clubs: City, Portage Country, Fairlawn Country (Akron); Columbus (O.); Cleveland, Union (Cleve.); 1925 F Street (Washington). Home: Editors, Sigma Delta Chi, 2535 Addyston Rd Akron, OH 44313. Office: First Nat Tower Akron OH 44308

BLISS, RICHARD MITCHELL, banker; b. Washington, Dec. 19, 1929; s. Charles Mitchell and Ella (Flanders) B.; grad. Phillips Exeter Acad., 1947; B.A., Yale, 1951; M.B.A., N.Y. U., 1957; m. 2d, Alicia G. Guerrero Vallejo, July 18, 1970; children by previous marriage—Jacqueline, Richard Mitchell, Stephen, Laura. With Bankers Trust Co., N.Y.C., 1954-71, sr. v.p., head internat. dept., 1967-71; pres. R.M. Bliss, Inc., internat. financial services, 1971—; pres. Bankers Internat. Corp.; vice chmn. S.G. Warburg, Inc.; dir. LEASCO Data Processing Equipment Corp. Served with AUS, 1951-54. Home: 501 E 87th St New York City NY 10028 Office: 280 Park Av New York City NY 10017

BLISS, ROBERT LANDERS, pub. relations cons.; b. Binghamton, N.Y., Nov. 19, 1907; s. George Calvin Sherwood and Katherine Barbara (Scheider) B.; A.B., Mary Cornell U., 1930; m. Friede Smidt, May 16, 1942; children—John Smidt, Friede Sherwood (now Mrs. Thomas Mark Brayton). With Gen. (dec.), Tire & Rubber Co., N.Y.C., 1933-36, Arthur B. Treman & Co., mem. N.Y. Stock Exchange, N.Y.C., 1936-38; asst. chief press Bur. J. Walter Thompson, N.Y.C., 1938-40; asst. to pub. and promotion mgr. PM Newspaper, 1940, Compton Advt., Inc., 1941-46; dir. pub. relations, Nat. Assn. Ins. Agts., N.Y.C., 1946-49; exec. v.p. Pub. Relations Soc. Am., N.Y.C., 1949-56; mng. editor pub. Pub. Relations Jour., 1950-56; editor Pub. Relations Register, 1949-56; pres. Robert L. Bliss Inc., pub. relations cos., 1956—. Owner Vegaline Kennets, purebred show beagles. Chmn. Ardn-House on Bus. prize, 1967; Henry Russel Lectureship, and Politics, 1959, Am. Bus. Conf. on Practical Local Politics, N.Y., Service award U. Mich., 1957. 1960. Mem. Cornell U. Rep. town chmn., New Canaan, 1951-62; mem. Rep. State Central Com., 1954-56; treas., chmn. Fairfield County Rep. Com., 1960-64; mem. Conn. Senate, 1962-67; counsel Weicker for U.S. U.S. Senate Com., 1970. Pres., trustee Playfair Found., 1967—. Served from 2d lt. to maj., USAAF, 1942-46. Mem. Pub. Relations Soc. Am. (charter, pres. N.Y. chapter 1962), Internat. Pub. Relations Assn. (founding council mem. 1955; chmn. research com.; mem. council, v.p., pres. 1965-67; gen. rapporteur 2d World Congress on Pub. Relations, Venice 1961; exec. com., program chmn. 3d World Congress, Montreal, Que. 1964), Nat. Soc. State Legislators (1st v.p.), S.A.R., Psi Upsilon. Baptist. Clubs: New Canaan Country; Wings, University, Down Town Assn. (N.Y.C.). Contbr., feature writer mags., ins. and pub. relations, jours.; contbr. Brit. Book of the Year. Wesleyan Home: 162 Park St New Canaan CT 06840 Office: 103 Park Av New York City NY 10017

BLISS, ROBERT LEWIS, architect, educator; b. Seattle, May 21, 1921; student Black Mountain Coll., 1939-42; B.Arch. (Emerson Fund scholar), Mass. Inst. Tech., 1949. Prin. firm Bliss & Campbell, Salt Lake City, 1956—; prof., chmn. dept. architecture, U. Utah, 1963—. Pres., Utah Heritage Found. Bd. dirs. Shorewood (Minn.) Planning Commn., 1956-63. Served with U.S. Mcht. Marine, 1944-46. Recipient award for design Carrier Corp., merit award Minn. Soc. Architecture, 1960, others. Mem. A.I.A. (dir. Mpls. chpt.), Am. Assn. Coll. Schs. Architecture (pres. 1967-69). Works include Stillwater Club, Minn., 1958, Jones Summer Pavilion, Wayzata, Minn., 1959. Office: 27 University St Salt Lake City UT 84102*

BLISS, WALTER ERNEST, lawyer; b. Greeley, Colo., May 3, 1918; s. Walter Ernest and Artie (Sterling) B.; B.A., LL.B., U. Colo., 1942; m. Audrey Pratt, Nov. 10, 1945; children—Walter Ernest, Wendy Marie. Admitted to Colo. bar, 1943, Hawaii bar, 1946; spl. agt. FBI, 1942-44; practiced in Honolulu, 1946—; partner firm Jenks, Kidwell, Goodsill & Anderson, and predecessors, 1957- -. Past pres. Legal Aid Soc. Hawaii. Mem. Bar Assn. Hawaii (exec. com. 1966, chmn. ethics com. 1968, v.p. 1969, pres. 1970), Am. Bar Assn., Beta Theta Pi, Phi Delta Phi. Home: 44-023 Kaimalu Pl Kaneohe HI 96744 Office: Castle & Cooke Bldg Honolulu HI 96801

BLISS, WILLIAM J. corp. exec., lawyer; b. Bklyn., 1915; ed. Sch. Commerce, N.Y.U., 1949; LL.B., Bklyn. Law Sch., 1958. Vice Pres., sec., gen. counsel Amcorp Nat. Services, Inc.; sec., gen. counsel, dir. Am. Match Co., Boatel, Inc., Crotty Bros., Inc.; asst. sec., dir. Canadian Book Wholesale Co., Ltd. Mem. N.Y. Bar. Home: 174 Wellington Rd Garden City NY 11530 Office: 131 Varick St New York City NY 10013*

BLISSITT, CHARLES WILLIAM, coll. dean; b. College Park, Ga., Aug. 1, 1932; s. Hayden C. and Rosilee (Moore) B.; B.S. in Pharmacy, Mercer U., 1954; Ph.D. (U. Fla. fellowship), U. Fla., 1958; m. Gail Parker Allison, Dec. 29, 1959; children—Allison Lee, Karin Hendrix, Robert Hayden. Asst. prof. pharmacy W.Va. Med. Center, 1958-64; dean Coll. of Pharmacy, St. Louis, 1964-70; dean Coll. of Pharmacy, Norman, Okla., 1970—, also prof. Mem. city council, Morgantwn, W.Va., 1960-62, mayor, 1962-64. Am. Found. for Pharm. Edn. fellow, 1958. Mem. Am. Ill., Mo., Okla. pharm. assns., Am. Soc. of Hosp. Pharmacists, Yellow Dog Soc., Sigma Xi, Kappa Psi, Rho Chi, Gamma Sigma Epsilon, Phi Sigma. Rotarian. Contbr. articles profl. jours. Home: 324 Merkle Dr Norman OK 73069

BLISTEIN, ELMER MILTON, educator; b. Pawtucket, R.I., Sept. 17, 1920; s. Philip and Lena (Melnick) B.; A.B., Brown U., 1942, A.M., 1947, Ph.D., 1953; m. Sophia P. Schaffer, Nov. 27, 1946; children—Adam Dara, David Schaffer. Asst. dept. English, Brown U., 1942, instr., 1946-53, asst. prof., 1953-59, asso. prof., 1959-65, prof., 1965—. Mem. Pawtucket (R.I.) Sch. Com., 1954-58; mem. Gov.'s Commn. on Fair Housing Legislation, 1960. Served with AUS, 1942-45. Mem. Malone Soc., Renaissance Soc. Am., Modern Language Assn. Am., Am. Assn. U. Profs., Am. Arbitration Assn., Phi Beta Kappa. Author: Comedy in Action, 1964; (with others) The Order of Poetry, 1961, The Variety of Poetry, 1964; editor George Peele's David and Bethsabe, 1970; editor The Drama of the Renaissance; Essays for Leicester Bradner, 1970. Home: 99 Alumni Av Providence RI 02906

BLITCH, JAMES BUCHANAN, architect; b. Charleston, S.C., Sept. 2, 1923; s. Norman Henry and Louise (Buchanan) B.; B.Arch., Tulane U., 1950; m. Hilda Goodspeed Mouledoux, Nov. 24, 1945; children—James Buchanan, John Crandell, Ronald Buchanan, Judith Ann (dec.), Courtney Ann, David Alan, Leslie Ann, Lisi Maria. Owner J. Buchanan Blitch & Asso., 1958-66; pres. J. Buchanan Blitch & Asso., Inc., 1966—. Trustee Asso. Cath. Charities, St. Elizabeth's Home for Girls; chmn. E. Jefferson Hosp. Found. Served with USNR, 1943-45. Named papal knight of Holy Sepulchre. Fellow A.I.A.; mem. La. Architects Assn. (pres.), New Orleans C. of C. Democrat. Roman Catholic. Home: 1703 Haring Rd Metairie LA 70001 Office: 1070 St Charles Av New Orleans LA 70130

BLITCH, LORIMER HENRY, retired grocery co. exec.; b. Clearwater, Fla., Sept. 27, 1905; s. Hallie and Eva Davis (Hughey) B.; student University of Fla., 1924-25; m. Mary Landis Kinsey, Nov. 23, 1927 (dec. Apr. 1966); 1 son, Lorimer Henry; m. Doris Knight Dismore, Dec. 15, 1966. With Blitch Grocery Co., Jacksonville, Fla., 1925-28; with Winn Dixie Stores, Inc., and predecessors, Jacksonville, 1928-33, 37-71, v.p., 1958—; with So. Food Stores, Inc., Tampa, Fla., 1933-36, Bonacker Bros., food brokers, Tampa, 1936-37; v.p. Monterey Canning Co., 1957-71; dir. Westside Atlantic Bank, Jacksonville. Mem. Jacksonville C. of C. (dir. 1959-61). Episcopalian (past sr. warden). Clubs: Rotary (pres. 1956-57), Timuquana Country (pres. 1962-63), University (Jacksonville, Fla.), Florida Yacht (Jacksonville). Home: 1560 Lancaster Terrace Jacksonville FL 32204

BLITMAN, CHARLES H., cons. engr.; b. Central Nassau, N.Y., Oct. 10, 1893; s. Charles and Anna (Penn) B.; C.E., Rensselaer Poly. Inst.; m. Anna Palestine, Oct. 10, 1921; children—Howard N., Doris Lucy (Mrs. Rudolph Stafall). Pres. Blitman Constrn. Corp., N.Y.C., 1926—, Taylor Woodrow Blitman Inc., N.Y.C., 1964—; sr. partner Blitman & Tischler, sons. engrs., N.Y.C., 1944—; tchr. Coll. Engring., U. Minn., 1916-17. Dir. Mimonedes Med. Center, Bklyn. Served as 1st lt., Air Force, U.S. Army, World War I. Mason. Home: East Stars Plane Rd Danbury CT 06810 Office: 101 Park Av New York City NY 10017

BLITMAN, HOWARD NORMAN, constrn. co. exec.; b. N.Y.C., Dec. 9, 1926; s. Charles H. and Anna (Palestine) B.; C.E., Rensselaer Poly. Inst., 1950; postgrad. Grad. Faculty New Sch. Social Research, 1962-67; m. Barbara Joffe, Sept. 8, 1957. Field engr. Drier Structural Steel Co., N.Y., 1950-51; design engr. Blitman & Tischler, N.Y.C., 1952-60; project engr. Blitman Constrn. Corp., N.Y.C., 1960-61, coordinator, 1961-62, exec. v.p., 1962-69, pres., 1969—. Mem. housing com. State Constnl. Conv., 1968. Mem. bd. Jewish Child Care Assn., Beth Israel Med. Center. Served to 2d lt. Chem. Corps, AUS, 1944-47, to 1st lt., 1951-53. Recipient Norman Tishman Human Relations award, 1967. Registered profl. engr., N.Y., N.J., Conn. Mem. N.Y. Soc. Profl. Engrs., Am. Soc. C.E., Am. Soc. M.E. Mason. Club: Harmonie (N.Y.C.). Home: 45 Sutton Pl S New York City NY 10022 Office: 101 Park Av New York City NY 10017

BLIVEN, BRUCE, editor; b. Emmetsburg, Ia., July 27, 1889; s. Charles F. and Lilla C. (Ormsby) B.; A.B., Stanford, 1911; m. Rose Emery, May 17, 1913; 1 son, Bruce. Editorial staff, San Francisco Bulletin, 1909-12; mag. contbr. and advertisement writer, 1912-14; dir. dept. of journalism, U. of Southern Calif., 1914-16; editorial staff. Printers' Ink, 1917-18; mem. editorial bd. N.Y. Globe, 1919-23; mem. editorial bd. New Republic, 1923- 55; N.Y. corr. Manchester Guardian, 1925-47; lectr. communication and journalism Stanford U., 1956—. Director of the Twentieth Century Fund, 1923-57. Author: The Men Who Make the Future, 1942; Preview for Tomorrow, The Unfinished Business of Science, 1953; The World Changers, 1965; Five Million Words Later (autobiography), 1970. Editor: What the Informed Citizen Needs to Know, 1945; Twentieth Century

Unlimited, 1950. Contbr. to Sat. Eve. Post, Ladies' Home Jour., Readers Digest, Harper's, Redbook, etc. Address: Kingscote Gardens Lagunita Dr Stanford CA 94305

BLIVEN, BRUCE, Jr., writer; b. Los Angeles, Jan. 31, 1916; s. Bruce and Rose (Emery) B.; A.B., Harvard, 1937; m. Naomi Horowitz, May 26, 1950; 1 son, Frederic Bruce. Reporter Manchester (Eng.) Guardian, 1936; editorial asst. New Republic mag., 1937-38; editorial writer N.Y. Post, 1939-42; contbr. nat. mags., 1946—. Tchr. Ind. U. Writers Conf., 1955, 66. Served from pvt. to capt. F.A., AUS, 1942-45. Decorated Bronze Star with oak leaf cluster. Mem. Soc. Mag. Writers, Authors Guild, Authors Guild Council, Soc. Am. Historians. Author: The Wonderful Writing Machine, 1954; Battle for Manhattan, 1956; (juveniles) The Story of D-Day, 1956; The American Revolution, 1958; From Pearl Harbor to Okinawa, 1960; From Casablanca To Berlin, 1965; (with Naomi Bliven) New York: the Story of the World's Most Exciting City, 1969. Office: care Theron Raines Lit Agt 244 Madison Av New York City NY 10016

BLIVEN, CHARLES WATSON, educator, pharmacist; b. Dakota City, Neb., Nov. 22, 1911; s. Leslie Sides and Mazie (Wingett) B.; B.S., U. Neb., 1934, M.S., 1936; grad. work U. Mich., George Washington U.; D.Sc., Phila. Coll. Pharmacy and Science, 1960; m. Marjorie Bennett Brew, June 5, 1938; children—Virginia Louise, John Leslie. Mem. faculty, coll. pharmacy U. Neb., 1935-38; pharm. analyst Geo. A. Breon Co., 1938-40; mem. faculty George Washington U., 1940-61, prof. pharmacy, 1947-61, acting dean, 1946-47, dean, 1947-61; exec. sec.-treas. Am. Assn. Colls. Pharmacy, 1961—. Pres., Nat. Drug Trade Conf., 1967-68; vice chmn. Fedn. Assn. Schs. of Health Professions, 1971. With U.S. Maritime Service, assigned to Hosp. Corps Sch., 1942-43; with U.S.N.R., 1943-46. disch. as lt. Mem. Am. Pharm. Assn., Sigma Xi, Omicron Delta Kappa, Phi Lambda Upsilon, Kappa Psi, Alpha Sigma Phi. Home: 812 Heron Dr Silver Spring MD 20910 Office: 850 Sligo Av Silver Spring MD 20910

BLIVEN, NAOMI, book reviewer; b. N.Y.C., Dec. 28, 1925; d. Frederic and Minnie (Goodfriend) Horowitz; A.B., Hunter Coll., 1945; m. Bruce Bliven, Jr., May 26, 1950; 1 son, Frederic Bruce. Mem. editorial staff New Republic, 1945-47, Random House, 1949-54; book reviewer New Yorker mag., 1958-. Mem. Phi Beta Kappa. Author: (with Bruce Bliven, Jr.) New York: The care The New Yorker 25 W 43d St New York City NY 10036

BLIZZARD, ROBERT M., educator; b. E. St. Louis, Ill., June 20, 1924; s. Robert Watson and Gertrude (Oechsner) B.; B.S., Northwestern U., 1949, M.D., 1952; postgrad. tng. Johns Hopkins Sch. Medicine, 1955-57; m. Gladys Schmelter, June 24, 1952; children—Janice Lyn, Robert Steven. Intern Ia. Meml. Hosp., Des Moines, 1952-53; resident pediatrics Blank Meml. Hosp. Children, Des Moines, 1953-55; asst. prof. Pediatrics and medicine Ohio State U. Sch. Medicine, 1957-60; mem. faculty Johns Hopkins Sch. Medicine, 1960—, dir. nat. pituitary agy., 1963-67, prof. pediatrics, 1967—. Mem. Am. Thyroid Assn., Soc. Pediatric Research, Am. Pediatric Soc., Am. Fedn. Clin. Research, Endocrine Soc., Sigma Xi. Author med. textbooks, articles. Home: PO Box 22 Gibson Island MD 21056 Office: Johns Hopkins Hosp Baltimore MD 21205

BLOCH, CHARLES JULIAN, lawyer; b. Baton Rouge, Oct. 10, 1893; s. Michel and Lena (Blum) B.; student La. State U., 1909-10; A.B., U. Ga., 1913; student Mercer U. Law Sch., 1913-14; J.D. Suffolk U., 1959; m. Marie L. Klein, Nov. 8, 1917; children—Eleanor (Mrs. Jerome K. Small), Marian (Mrs. Richard A. Hecht). Admitted to Ga. bar 1914, mem. Hall, Grice & Bloch, 1919-33, Hall & Bloch, 1933-54, Bloch, Hall, Groover & Hawkins, Macon, Ga., 1954-68, Bloch, Hall, Hawkins, & Owen, 1968—; div. counsel (for Ga.), So. Ry. System. Chmn. rules com. Supreme Ct. of Ga., 1946—; bd. regents U. System of Ga., 1950-57. Del. Dem. Nat. Conv., 1932, 44, 48, 52, 60. Fellow Am. Coll. Trial Lawyers, Am. Bar Found.; mem. Am., Ga. (pres. 1944-45), Macon bar assns., Jud. Council Ga. (chmn. 1945-57), Phi Delta Phi, Phi Kappa Phi. Jewish religion. Clubs: Commerce (Atlanta, Ga.); Idle Hour Country (Macon, Ga.). Author: States' Rights—The Law of the Land, 1958. Editor Ga. Bar Jour., 1958-66. Home: 2703 Hill Crest Av Macon GA 31204 Office: Ga Power Bldg Macon GA 31201

BLOCH, E. MAURICE, educator, art historian; b. N.Y.C.; s. Leonard and Rose (von Auspitz) B.; B.F.A., N.Y.U., 1939; student Harvard, 1941-42; A.M., N.Y.U., 1942, Ph.D., 1957. With Met. Mus. Art, 1943; instr. art history U. Mo., 1943-44; lectr. art history N.Y.U., 1945-46, U. Minn., 1946-47; Keeper drawings and prints, prof. chalcography Cooper Union, 1949-53; prof. art history curator graphic arts, dir. Grunwald Graphic Arts Found., U. Cal. at Los Angeles, 1956—. Bd. dirs. Tamarind Lithograph Workshop, Los Angeles, Print Council Am. Tamarind Inst., U.N.M., Albuquerque, Louis Corinth Meml. Found., N.Y., U. Cal. at Los Angeles Art Council. Recipient Founders Day award of achievement N.Y.U., 1957, Western Heritage Center award, 1968; Belgian Am. Ednl. Found. traveling fellow, Belgium, 1951; Am. Council Learned Socs. grant-in-aid, 1962. Mem. Coll. Art Assn. Am., Art Historians So. Cal., Art Students League, Manuscript Soc., Hist. Soc. Mo. Author: George Caleb Bingham; Evolution of an Artist, 1967; Catalogue Raisonne, 1967; also articles, revs., mus. and art gallery publns. Regional editor Jour. of West. Home: 2253 Veteran Av Los Angeles CA 90064

BLOCH, FELIX, prof. of physics; b. Zurich, Switzerland, Oct. 23, 1905; s. Gustav and Agnes (Mayer) B.; student Fed. Inst. Tech., Zurich, Switzerland, 1924- 27; Ph.D., Leipzig, Germany, 1928; m. Lore C. Misch, Mar. 14, 1940; children—George J., Daniel A., Frank S., Ruth. Lectr. theoret. physics., Leipzig, 1932; asso. prof. physics, Stanford U., Calif., 1934-36, prof. since 1936, war research Stanford University, Los Alamos, Harvard, 1942-45. Recipient Nobel Prize in Physics, 1952. Lorentz Found. fellow, Holland, 1930, Oersted Found. fellow, 1931, Rockefeller Found. fellow, 1933. Fellow Am. Phys. Soc. (pres. 1965-66), Am. Acad. Arts and Scis., Royal Soc. Edinburgh; mem. Nat. Acad. Scis., Royal Dutch Acad. Scis. Contbr. about 50 articles on atomic physics to sci. publs., since 1927. Home: 1551 Emerson St Palo Alto CA 94301 Office: Dept Physics Stanford Univ CA 94305

BLOCH, HENRY SIMON, economist; b. County Kehl (Baden), Germany, April 6, 1915; s. Edward and Claire (Bloch) B.; Dr. Laws (Econs.), U. Nancy, 1937; Dr.h.c. in Econs., Polit. and Social Scis., Free U. of Brussels, 1969; fellow Acad. Internat. Law, The Hague, summer 1937; 1 dau., Miriam. Came to U.S., 1937, naturalized, 1943. Research asst. U. Chicago, 1938; lectr. Inst. for Mil. Studies, U. Chgo., 1941-42, instr. economics, 1943, instr., research supervisor Civil Affairs Tng. Sch. for Army and Navy Officers, 1943-45; cons. Fgn. Econ. Adminstrn., 1945; economist Treasury Dept., 1945-46 (mem. Treasury del. participating in tax treaty negotiations with govts. France, Belgium, Holland, Luxembourg, 1946); chief sect. Dept. Security Council Affairs, U.N., 1947-49; dep. prin. sec. U.N. Commn. to India and Pakistan, 1948), acting dir. fiscal div., Dept. Econ. Affairs, U.N., 1949-51, dir., 1951; dir. fiscal and financial br. UN, 1955- 62, acting dir. Bur. Econ. Affairs, 1958-59, dir. Bur. Tech. Assistance Operations, 1959-62, dep. commr. for tech. assistance, 1961-62; pres. Zinder Internat. Ltd., 1962-66; v.p., dir. E.M. Warburg & Co., Inc., N.Y.C., 1967—; sr. v.p., dir. E.M. Warburg, Pincus & Co., Inc., 1970—; dir. Am. Bank & Trust Co., N.Y.C.; tech. assistance expert, Haiti, 1950, Israel, 1951, Cuba, 1952, Bolivia, 1954, Ghana, Liberia, 1957; tech. assistance mission Somalia, 1960, Bunche mission to Congo, 1960; vis. prof. econs. Yale 1955; lectr. law Columbia, 1955-63, adj. prof. law and internat. relations, 1963—; guest prof. U. Chile, summer 1958. Bd. patrons dept. applied econs. Free U. of Brussels. Adv. council Internat. Bur. Fiscal Documentation, Amsterdam, Holland; adviser UN Consultative Com. for Asian Devel. Bank, Bangkok, Thailand. Mem. Am. Econ. Assn., Institut Internat. de Finances Publiques (Paris), Soc. Royale d'Economie Politique de Belgique (hon.). Jewish. Clubs: Cosmos (Washington), Faculty (Columbia). Author: The Challenge of the World Trade Conference, 1965; Financial Strategy for Developing Nations—Afterthoughts to the Amsterdam Panel, 1969; co-author: Yale Law Journal Symposium on World Organization, 1946; Technical Aid and the Progress of Underdeveloped Countries, 1952; Legal-Economic Problems of International Trade, 1961; The Global Partnership, International Agencies and Economic Development, 1968; Financial Integration in Western Europe, 1969. Contbr. Ency. Brit., econ., legal jours. Office: 60 Broad St New York City NY 10004

BLOCH, HENRY R., lawyer; b. Toledo, Aug. 9, 1903; student Phillips Exeter Acad.; B.A., Yale, 1925; LL.B., 1927. Admitted to Ohio bar, 1927; now firm Marshall, Melhorn, Bloch & Belt, Toledo. Mem. Am., Ohio, Toledo bar assns. Office: 1434 National Bank Bldg Toledo OH 43604*

BLOCH, HERBERT, educator; b. Berlin, Germany, Aug. 18, 1911; s. Ludwig and Alice (Gutmann) B.; Dott. Lett., U. Rome, Italy, 1935, diploma in ancient history, 1937; A.M. (hon.), Harvard, 1947; m. Clarissa Holland, Nov. 23, 1943 (dec. Aug. 1958); children—Mary Alice, Anne Coolidge; m. 2d, Ellen Cohen, 1960. Came to the U.S., 1939, naturalized, 1946. Excavated at Ostia, Italy, 1938-39; jr. fellow Harvard, Dumbarton Oaks, 1941-42; instr. Greek and Latin, Harvard, 1941-42, faculty instr., 1942- 46, asst. prof., 1946-47, asso. prof., 1947-53, prof., 1953—; prof.-in- charge sch. classical studies Am. Acad. in Rome, 1957-59; sr. fellow Soc. of Fellows Harvard, 1964—. Member Inst. for Advanced Study, 1953-54; Guggenheim fellow, 1950-51. Fulbright fellow in Italy, 1950-51. Trustee Loeb Classical Library, 1964—. Fellow Am. Acad. Arts and Scis.; mem. Am. Philol. Assn. (pres. 1969), Archaeol. Inst. Am., German Archaeol. Inst., Mediaeval Acad. Am., Am. Assn. U. Profs., Istituto di Studi Romani, Pontificia Acc. Romana di Archeologia, American Philos. Soc., Phi Beta Kappa. Author: I bolli laterizi e la storia edilizia romana, 1947; Supplement to Vol. XV, 1 of the Corp. Inscr. Latinarum, 1948; Abhandlugen zur griechischen Geschichtschreibung von Felix Jacoby, 1956. Co-author: Scavi de Ostia I, 1953, III, 1958. Contbr. profl. jours. Home: 524 Pleasant St Belmont MA 02178

BLOCH, HERBERT R., Jr., dept. store exec.; b. Cin., Oct. 29, 1916; s. Herbert R. and Jean (Kaufman) B.; grad. Taft Sch., 1935; B.A., Yale, 1939; m. Jean Freiberg, Jan. 1, 1969; 1 son, Peter Millard. Research dir. John Shillito Co., Cin., 1940-46, personnel dir., 1946-50, controller, 1950-56, v.p., treas., 1956-67, exec. v.p., 1967—; dir. Wolf Machine Co. Vice-chmn. bd. dirs. Hebrew Union Coll., Jewish Inst. Religion; bd. dirs. Cin. Symphony, Jewish Fedn. Cin., Bellefaire, Better Bus. Bur. Cin.; pres. Shillito Store Found. Served with USAAF, World War II. Mem. Financial Execs. Inst., Bankers Club Cin. Jewish religion. Clubs: Losantiville Country; Queen City. Home: 1617 E McMillan St Cincinnati OH 45206 Office: Shillito Co 7th and Race Sts Cincinnati OH 45202

BLOCH, INGRAM, educator; b. Louisville, Aug. 27, 1920; s. Oscar Edgeworth and Katharine (Armstrong) B.; B.A. in Physics, Harvard, 1940, M.S., U. Chgo., 1941, Ph.D., 1946; m. Muriel Holzhauer, Aug. 4, 1945 (dec. Jan. 1959); m. 2d, Mary Lee Henry, Dec. 27, 1960; step-children—Daniel Lee Henry, Paul Harold Henry. Asst. in math. biophysics U. Chgo., 1941-42, asst. instr. electronics, 1942-43; jr. scientist Manhattan Project, U. Chgo., also Los Alamos, 1943-46; research asso. in nuclear theory U. Wis., also Yale, 1946-48; asst. prof. physics Vanderbilt U., 1948-51, asso. prof., 1951-57, prof., 1957—. Fellow Am. Phys. Soc. (vice chmn. Southeastern sect. 1960-61, chmn. 1961-62); mem. Am. Assn. Physics Tchrs., Am. Assn. U. Profs., Am. Civil Liberties Union (state bd. dirs.), Sigma Xi. Home: 926 Cantrell Av Nashville TN 37215

BLOCH, JULIUS MARCUS, educator; b. Montclair, N.J., Apr. 2, 1911; s. Marcus and Lena (Marcus) B.; A.B., Cornell U., 1932, M.A., 1934; Ph.D., Harvard, 1941; m. Lynn Epstein, Sept. 1936; children—Peter, Lawrence. Grad. teaching asst. history Harvard and Radcliffe Coll., 1936-39; lectr., instr. Queens Coll., N.Y.C., 1942-43, instr. history and comtemporary civics, 1946-50, from asst. prof. to prof. history, 1950—, chmn. dept., 1964—; cons. in field. Asso. com. econ. research Social Sci. Research Council, 1940-41. Dir. Inst. Early N.Y.C. History. Served with AUS, 1943-45; PTO. Mem. Am., Miss. Valley hist. assns., Soc. Am. Archivists, N.Y. Gen. and Biog. Soc., Am. Assn. U. Profs. (pres. Queens Coll. chpt. 1962-63), Phi Beta Kappa. Author: Miscegenation, 1958: co-author and co-editor: An Account of Her Majesty's Revenue in the Province of New York, 1701-1709, 1966. Home: 84-23 Charlecote Ridge Jamaica Estates New York City NY 11432 Office: Queens Coll Flushing NY 11367

BLOCH, KONRAD, biochemist; b. Neisse, Germany, Jan. 12, 1912; s. Frederick D. and Hedwig (Steimer) B.; Chem.Eng., Technische Hochschule, Munich, Germany, 1934; Ph.D., Columbia, 1938; m. Lore Teutsch, Feb. 15, 1941; childrenPeter, Susan. Came to U.S., 1936, naturalized, 1944. Asst. prof. biochemistry U. Chgo., 1946-50, prof., 1950-54; Higgins prof. biochemistry Harvard, 1954—. Recipient Nobel Prize in physiology and medicine, 1964. Fellow Am. Acad. Scis.; mem. Nat. Acad. Scis., Am. Philos. Soc. Home: 16 Moon Hill Rd Lexington MA 02173 Office: 38 Oxford St Cambridge MA 02138

BLOCH, RAY E., business exec.; b. Marshallville, O., Sept. 10, 1894; s. Charles E. and Margaret (Stotler) B.; m. Rhea Garman, Dec. 16, 1915; 1 dau., Mary Ellen. With Mohawk Rubber Co. 1913—, pres., gen. mgr., dir., Akron, 1935, now chmn. bd., also with Mohawk Rubber Co. of N.Y., Inc., 1935—; dir. Citizens Av. & Loan Co. Adv. com. rubber industry O.P.M., W.P.B. Dir. Akron Art I st., Akron chpt. A.R.C.; trustee Peoples Hosp. Akron, Mt. Union Coll. Mem. Akron C. of C. (dir.), Newcomen Soc. Methodist (trustee). Mason (Shriner, Jester). Clubs: City (dir.), Portage Country (dir.), Kiwanis, Liedertafel (Akron); Rockwell Springs Trout. Home: 701 Delaware Av Akron OH 44303

BLOCH, THOMAS MOFFAT, mfg. exec.; b. Wheeling, W.Va., Feb. 13, 1907; s. Jesse A. and Jessie Thornton (Moffat) B.; grad. Phillips Exeter Acad.; B.S., Princeton, 1929; LL.D., Davis and Elkins Coll., 1962; Dr. Bus. Adminstrn., Bethany Coll., 1965; m. Nancy Fulton, June 11, 1932; children—Stuart Fulton, Quarrier (Mrs. Robert McK. Jones III), Martha McE. (Mrs. Duer McLanahan, Jr.). Asso. with Bloch Brothers Tobacco Co., Wheeling, 1929—, dir., 1931—, pres., 1947-70, chmn. of bd., 1970, dir. mem. exec. com. Helme Products Inc. Mem. exec. com., region IV, exec. bd. Nat. Trail council Boy Scouts Am. Dir., v.p. Ohio Valley Gen. Hosp., Wheeling; dir. Children's Home City Wheeling, House of Friendship. Mem. alumni council Phillips Exeter Acad. Mem. W.Va. Mfrs. Assn. (v.p., dir.). Presbyn. (elder). Clubs: Williams Country (Weirton, W.Va.); Ft. Henry (Wheeling); ton (N.Y.C); Nassau Priceton Charter (Princeton); Country (Moundsville, W.Va.); Mid-Ocean (Bermuda); Lakeview Country (Morgantown, W.Va.); Royal and Ancient (St. Andrews, Scotland). Home: Elm Hill 366 Oglebay Dr Wheeling WV 26003 Office: 4000 Water St Wheeling WV 26003

BLOCH, WILLIAM ALBERT, chem. co. exec.; b. Newton, Mass., Feb. 26, 1912; s. Ferdinand and Augusta (Mattis) B.; grad. Bentley Coll., 1931; B.B.A., Northeastern U., 1936; grad. Advanced Mgmt. Program, Harvard, 1956; m. Emma F. Hartwig, Nov. 10, 1935; children—Linda (Mrs. Robert L. Sturtevant), William Albert, Kenneth Amon. With Cabot Corp., Boston, Mass., 1936-68, comptroller, 1952-66, treas., 1966-68; treas., dir. Lookout Farm, Inc. Trustee Bentley Coll. Accounting and Finance. Mem. Financial Execs. Inst., Nat. Assn. Accountants, Pi Tau Kappa. Lutheran. Home: 153 Lowell Rd Wellesley Hills MA 02181

BLOCH-LAINE, FRANCOIS, French govt. ofcl.; b. Paris, France, Mar. 25, 1912; s. Jean Frederic and Suzanne (Laine) B.-L.; student Ecole Gerson, Lycee Janson-de-Sailly, Law Sch. of Paris; m. Anne-Marie d'Abbadie D'Arrast, June 8, 1935; children—Jean-Michel, Jean-Francois, Jean-Louis, Olivier. Insp. finances, 1936, insp. gen., 1963—; asst. dir. Treasury, 1944, dir., 1947; financial counsellor in China and chief French Financial Mission in Far-East; dir. gen. Caisse des Depots, 1953; pres. Credit Lyonnais, 1967; adminstr. Societe Nationale des Petroles D'Aquitaine, Banque de Bruxelles, Credit Nat., Credit Foncier Franco-Canadien; mem. supervisory com. Compagnie Bancaire; bd. dirs. Commerce Exterieur, Institut Pasteur. Pres. Found. for French Med. Research. Decorated comdr. Legion D'Honneur, Comdr. Palmes Academiques, Croix de Guerre, Medaille de la Resistance. Author: L'Emploi des Loisirs Ouvriers et L'Education Populaire; La Zone Franc; Le Tresor Publique; La Reforme de L'Entreprise. Home: 11 rue de l' Hotel Colbert Paris 5e France Office: 19 Boulevard des Italiens Paris 2e France

BLOCK, ADOLPH, sculptor; b. N.Y.C., Jan. 29, 1906; s. Henry and Dora (Wolpin) B.; student Beaux Arts Inst. Design, Fontainebleau Sch. Fine Arts; m. Tilda M. Frishman, June 29, 1930. Sculptor, works exhibited N.A.D., Archtl. League N.Y., Pa. Acad. Fine Arts, Whitney Mus., Jewish Mus., French and Argent Galleries, Salamagundi Club, Lever House; works installed at Bayonne (N.J.) Pub. Library, William Cullen Bryant High Sch., Morris High Sch., Queens Vocational High Sch., Beth-El Hosp. (all N.Y.C.), Garfield Restaurant, Bklyn., Saxony Restaurant, Newark, Concord Restaurant, Jamaica, L.I.; designer Spencer, Grady medals Am. Chem. Soc., Karl Taylor Compton medal Am. Inst. of Physics, Long Lines Medal of Am. Tel. & Tel. Co., Allen medal Am. Soc. Human Genetics, 63d medal Soc. Medallists, bronze portrait medallions Tobacco Industry Hall Fame, bronze portrait plaque Dr. Franz J. Kallman, Columbia Presbyn. Med. Center, N.Y.C., 1967, Washington Irving medal N.Y. U. Hall Fame Series, 1968, others; designed eight 9-foot figure panels Nat. Shrine Immaculate Conception, Washington; has done bronze busts of Spinoza, Simon Barer and others; designed Nathan Hale Coin medal for Nat. Commemorative Soc., 1969, Simon Newcomb medal for N.Y.U. Hall of Fame series, 1970. Del. Fine Arts Fedn. N.Y., 1954-64, dir., chmn. sculpture, 1955-56; mem. faculty Nat. Acad. Sch. Fine-Arts, 1959—. Tiffany Found. fellow, 1926; Fontainebleau fellow, 1927; Beaux-Arts Architects Silver medal, 1926, Beaux Arts Inst. Paris prize, 1927, 1st award for sculpture at ann. exhbns. Fontainebleau Alumni Assn., 1932, 34, 38, hon. mention for sculpture Nat. Gold Medal Exhbns., Archtl. League N.Y., 1955-56, Lindsay Morris prize, bas reliefs, Allied Artists Am., 1956, Gold Medal of Honor, 1958, 1st Lindsay Morris prize for bas relief sculpture, 1969; Lindsay Morris prize for medals, Nat. Sculpture Soc., 1958, Herbert Adams Meml. medal and citation, 1961; 1st Mrs. John Newington prize Hudson Valley Art Assn., 1960, gold medal of honor for sculpture, 1961; Henry Hering Meml. medal and citation, 1961; Harriet Mayor Meml. award for sculpture Am. Artists Profl. League, 1961; Gold Plate award Acad. Achievement, 1961; Silver medal Nat. Sculpture Soc. Ann. Exhbn., 1967, cash award for most notable service, 1970; cash award for portrait bust Nat. Arts Club, 1969. First v.p. Altruists chpt. City of Hope, 1954-56. Fellow Nat. Sculpture Soc. (rec. sec. 1953-56, sec. 1956-59, chmn. membership com., 1956-63, 1st v.p. 1959-62, pres. 1963-65); academician Nat. Acad. Design; mem. Allied Artists Am. (v.p. 1958-61, chmn. jury of selection 1958, dir. bd. govs., v.p., pres. 1964-65, Lindsay Morris Meml. prize for bas-relief 1963, Therese Richard Meml. prize for religious sculpture 1964), Internat. Assn. Plastic Arts (2d v.p. U.S. com. 1960-62), Fine Arts Fedn. N.Y. (dir. 1954-63, 70—, chmn. sculpture), Archtl. League N.Y., Fontainebleau Alumni Assn. Editor Nat. Sculpture Rev., 1958—. Home: 319 W 18th St New York City NY 10011 Studio: 400 W 23d St New York City NY 10011

BLOCK, EDWARD K., trust co. exec. Vice pres., comptroller U.S. Trust Co. N.Y., N.Y.C. Office: 45 Wall St New York City NY 10005*

BLOCK, FRANK EMMANUEL, banker; b. Ashville, N.C., May 15, 1925; s. Hamilton and Evelyn Gayle (Johnson) B.; B.S. with honors in Mech. Engring., Yale, 1948, B.S. in Indsl. Adminstrn., 1949; m. Anne Nimmons Burckhardt, Aug. 31, 1948; children—Frank Emmanuel, Jeannette B. Vice pres. Citizens & So. Nat. Bank, Atlanta, 1949-70; sr. v.p. Girard Trust Bank, Phila., 1970—; dir. Studley Schupert Phila., Inc., 1971—. Served with AUS, 1943-45. Mem. Inst. Chartered Financial Analysts (v.p. 1971—). Financial Analysts Fedn. (pres. 1969-70; Graham and Dood award 1964). Episcopalian. Clubs: Piedmont Driving (Atlanta); Yale (N.Y.C.). Editor: Personel Trust Investment Management, 1969; asso. editor Financial Analysts Jour., 1965—. Contbr. articles profl. jours. Home: 535 Maison Pl Bryn Mawr PA 19010 Office: Girard Trust Bank 1 Girard Plaza Philadelphia PA 19101

BLOCK, HASKELL MAYER, educator; b. Chgo., June 13, 1923; s. Abraham M. and Edith (Hymen) B.; A.B., U. Chgo., 1944; A.M., Harvard, 1947; Doct. d'Univ., U. Paris, 1949; m. Elaine Carlin, June 27, 1948; children-Randall, Laurie, Linda. Instr. English, Queens Coll., N.Y.C., 1949-52; asst. and asso. prof. comparative lit. U. Wis., 1952-61; prof. comparative lit. Bklyn. Coll., 1961—; prof. comparative lit., exec. officer Doctoral Program in Comparative Lit., City U. N.Y., 1968—; vis. prof. U. Hawaii, summer 1963, U. Ill., 1966-67, U. Colo., summer 1967, Harvard, summer 1968; cons. editor Random House, Inc., N.Y.C., 1961—; mem. screening com. for Western Europe, Fgn. Area Fellowship Program, 1965-68. Served with USAAF, 1944-45. Fulbright research scholar U. Cologne, 1956-57, U. Paris, 1968-69. Mem. Internat. (past sec.), Am. (mem. adv. bd.) comparative lit. assns., Modern Lang. Assn., Modern Humanities Reerach Assn., Dante Soc. Am., Phi Beta Kappa. Clubs: Harvard Faculty (Cambridge, Mass.); Chicago (N.Y.C.); Whitehall (Chicago). Author: (with Herman Salinger) The Creative Vision, 1960; (with Robert G. Shedd) Masters of Modern Drama, 1962; Mallarmé and the Symbolist Drama, 1963; Naturalistic Triptych, 1970; Nouvelles Tendances ed Littérature Comparée, 1970. Home: 209 Argyle Rd Brooklyn NY 11218 Office: 33 W 42d St New York NY 10036

BLOCK, HENRY DAVID, mathematician, engr., educator; b. N.Y.C., Feb. 22, 1920; s. Isaac and Celia (Gottschall) B.; B.S. cum laude, Coll. City N.Y., 1940, B.C.E., 1943; M.S., Ia. State U., 1947, Ph.D., 1949; m. Phoebe T. Goggin, May 12, 1946; 1 son, David Lee. Exptl. flight test engr., stress analyst Goodyear Aircraft Corp., Akron, O., 1943-45; aerodynamicist Fairchild Engine & Aircraft Corp., Jamaica, L.I., N.Y., 1946; teaching fellow Ia. State U., 1946-47, faculty, 1947-53; asst. prof. U. Minn., 1953-55; mem. faculty Cornell U., 1955—, prof. theoretical and applied mechanics, 1961—; vis. prof. applied electrophysics U. Cal. at San Diego, LaJolla, 1966-67. Chmn. Gordon Research Conf. on Biomath., Andover, N.H., 1969-70. Guggenheim Meml. Found. fellow for research in biomath., 1970-71. Mem. Am. Math. Soc., Math. Assn. Am., Assn. Computing Machinery, I.E.E.E., Phi Beta Kappa, Sigma Xi, Tau Beta Pi, Pi Mu Epsilon, Phi Kappa Phi. Author: An Introduction to Tensor Analysis, 1962. Contbr. articles profl. jours. Home: Lansing Apts West N Triphammer Rd Ithaca NY 14850

BLOCK, HERBERT LAWRENCE, (Herblock), editorial cartoonist; b. Chgo., Oct. 13, 1909; s. David Julian and Tessie (Lupe) B.; student Lake Forest (Ill.) Coll., 1927-29, LL.D., 1957; LL.D., Rutgers U., 1963; student Art Inst. Chgo. (part time classes); unmarried. Editorial cartoonist, Chgo. Daily News, 1929-33; NEA Service, 1933-43, U.S. Army 1943-45; Editorial cartoonist The Washington Post, 1946—. Received Pulitzer prize, 1942, 54; Am. Newspaper Guild award, 1948; Heywood Broun award, 1950; Sigma Delta Chi Nat. Editorial Awards, 1949, 50, 52, 57, Sidney Hillman award (for book), 1953, Reuben Award, Nat. Cartoonists Soc., 1957, Lauterbach Award for civil liberties, 1960; U. Mo. distinguished service journalism award, 1961; Golden Key award, 1963; Capital Press Club award, 1963, Bill of Rights award, 1966. Fellow Am. Acad. Arts and Scis.; mem. Phi Beta Kappa (hon.). Clubs: Fed. City, Cosmos (Washington). Author: The Herblock Book, 1952; Herblock's Here and Now, 1955; Herblock's Special for Today, 1958; Straight Herblock, 1964. Designed U.S. postage stamp commemorating 175th anniversary Bill of Rights, 1966. Address: The Washington Post Washington DC 20005

BLOCK, HERMAN BERNHARDT, mfg. co. exec.; b. Crawfordsville, Ind., Aug. 8, 1904; s. Morris and Frances (Goldberg) B.; student Harvard Mil. Acad., Los Angeles, 1919-20, U. Wis., 1922-25; m. Lillian Shirley Callin, Apr. 12, 1927 (dec. 1958); children—Francine Joan Krupp, Richard Morse; m. 2d, Florence Joyce Boden, May 11, 1960; 1 son, Ronald Jay. Dept. store mgmt., 1927-35; owner indsl. salvage firm, 1935-45; sales indsl. supplies, 1946-52; subcontract mgr. Merritt-Chapman & Scott Corp., 1952-54, v.p. procurement, 1956-57, exec. v.p. procurement, 1958-66; pres. Practical Mfg. Co., 1966—; dir. purchasing Devoe & Raynolds Co., Inc., 1954-56; dir. Merritt- Chapman & Scott Corp. Served as lt. comdr. USNR, 1943-46. Mem. Phi Sigma Delta. Elk; mem. B'nai B'rith. Clubs: Chemists (N.Y.C.); Rock Ridge Country (Newtown, Conn.); Haresfoot (U. Wis.). Home: New Fairfield CT 06810 Office: 250 W 57th St New York City NY 10019

BLOCK, JOSEPH DOUGLAS, utility exec. lawyer; b. Three Lakes, Wis., Apr. 18, 1919; s. Max and Rose (Chaimson) B.; B.A., U. Wis., 1939, J.D., 1941; LL.M., Harvard, 1946; m. Doris R. Schoenewald, Sept. 26, 1958. Admitted to Ill. bar, 1946, practiced Chgo. 1946-70; partner Aaron, Aaron, Schimberg & Hess, 1957-70; spl. asst. atty. gen. Ill., 1951-53; v.p., gen. counsel Consol. Edison Co. N.Y., 1970—. Served with CIC, AUS, 1942-45. Mem. Am., Ill., Chgo., Wis. bar assns., Order of Coif, Phi Kappa Phi. Home: 920 Park Av New York NY 10028 Office: 9 Irving Pl New York NY 10003

BLOCK, JOSEPH DOUGLAS, elec. co. exec.; b. Three Lakes, Wis., Apr. 18, 1919; s. Max and Rose (Chaimson) B.; B.A., U. Wis., 1939, J.D., 1941; LL.M., Harvard, 1946; m. Doris Ruth Schoenewald, Sept. 26, 1958. Admitted to Wis. bar, 1941, Ill. bar, 1947, N.Y. bar, 1971; atty. OPA, Washington, 1942, 45-46; asso. Swiren and Heineman, Chgo., 1946-56; partner Aaron, Aaron, Schimberg & Hess, Chgo., 1957-70; v.p., gen. counsel Consol. Edison Co. N.Y., Inc., N.Y.C., 1970—. Spl. asst. atty. gen. Ill., 1951-53. Served with CIC, AUS, 1942-45. Mem. Am., N.Y. State, Wis. bar assns., Bar Assn. N.Y.C., Edison Elec. Inst. (legal com.), N.Y.C. C. of C. Home: 920 Park Av New York City NY 10028 Office: 4 Irving Pl New York City NY 10003

BLOCK, JOSEPH L., steel co. exec.; b. Chgo., Oct. 6, 1902; s. Leopold E. and Cora (Bloom) B.; student Cornell U., 1920-22; LL.D., St. Joseph's Coll., 1957, Bradley U., 1959, Roosevelt U., 1965, Ill. Inst. Tech., 1968, Northwestern U., 1968; D.Eng., Rose Poly. Inst., 1961; m. Lucille Eichengreen, Jan. 19, 1924; children—Joseph Jr. (dec.), Mrs. Susan B. Rubnitz. With sales dept. Inland Steel Co., 1923-27, asst. v.p., 1927-30, v.p., dir., 1930-36, v.p. charge sales, 1936, vice chmn., 1949, exec. v.p., chmn. finance com., 1952, pres., 1953-59, chmn., chief exec. officer, 1959-67, now dir., chmn. exec. com.; dir. Chgo. Bd. Trade, Commonwealth Edison Co., Chgo., 1st Nat. Bank, Chgo. With Steel Div. WBP, Washington, 1941-44. Mem. President's Adv. Com. on Labor- Mgmt. Policy, 1961-66, President's Commn. for Observance 25th Anniversary of UN, 1970-71; mem. Adv. Commn. on Labor Mgmt. Policy for Pub. Employees (Ill.), 1966-67; dir. Nat. Merit Scholarship Corp. Pres., Crusade of Mercy, 1965-66; mem. Ill. Bd. Higher Edn., 1967—; chmn. adv. com. Cook County Dept. Pub. Aid, 1968—. Bd. dirs. Community Fund., Chicago, pres. 1961-63; trustee Ill. Inst. Tech., Com. for Econ. Devel., Jewish Fedn. Chgo. (dir. 1931-52, pres. 1947-50), Mus. Sci. and Industry. Recipient many awards, including Silver plaque Nat. Conf. Christians and Jews, 1968. Mem. Chgo. Assn. Commerce and Industry (pres. 1957-58, sr. council), Am. Iron and Steel Inst. (dir. 1953-67, hon. v.p.). Clubs: Lake Shore Country (Glencoe, Ill.); Standard, Commercial, Executives, Mid-America, Tavern, Chicago (Chgo.). Home: 1325 Astor St Chicago IL 60610 Office: 30 W Monroe St Chicago IL 60603

BLOCK, KENNETH LEROY, mgmt. cons.; b. Newark, May 14, 1920; s. Herman J. and Flora E. (Wiehle) B.; B.B.A., U. Minn., 1942; B.S., Mass. Inst. Tech., 1947; M.B.A., U. Mich., 1948; m. Margaret Sally Sheratt, Aug. 22, 1947; children—Kenneth Lee, Timothy Douglas, Elizabeth Ann. With Mpls.-Honeywell Regulator Co., 1940, Ford Co., 1941, Chevrolet Aviation Engine Co., 1942; instr. Sch. Bus. Adminstrn., U. Mich., 1947-48; Pres., also dir. A.T. Kearney & Co., Inc., Chgo., 1948—; dir. Chgo. Rawhide Mfg. Co., 1962—; dir. Bank of Elmhurst, Ill., 1968—, Littlefuse, Inc., Des Plaines, Ill., 1960—; mem. pres.'s adv. council Elmhurst Coll., pres., 1966-69; bd. dirs. Mid-Am. chpt. A.R.C., 1965—; life mem. Mus. Natural History; sustaining mem. Chgo. Art Inst.; mem. Joint Civic Com. on Elections, Chgo.; pres., dir. Chgo. Crime Commn.; fire and police commr. Village of Glen Ellyn, 1962-65; bd. dirs. Chgo. Met. YMCA; v.p. exec. bd. dirs. Chgo. council Boy Scouts Am., 1965—; chmn. mgmt. standards and cons. com., 1966-69; vice chmn. budget com. Community Fund of Chgo., 1967-69, bd. dirs., 1969—. Bd. dirs., chmn. membership and operations com. Central Du Page Hosp., 1963-69, pres., 1966-69. Served with USAAF, 1942-45 45. C.P.A., Ill.; registered profl. engr., N.H. Mem. Assn. Cons. Mgmt. Engrs. (v.p. 1970—), Nat. Assn. Citizens Crime Commns. (pres. 1970—), Inst. Mgmt. Cons. (pres. 1971—), Beta Gamma Sigma, Delta Sigma Phi, Iron Wedge. Clubs: Sunday Evening (dir. 1970), Union League (dir., v.p. 1969—) (Chgo.); Glen Oak Country; Chicago. Author numerous articles in field. Contbg. editor Prodn. Handbook, 1959. Home: 11 Woodley Rd Winnetka IL 60093 Office: 100 S Wacker Dr Chicago IL 60606

BLOCK, LEROY BENATAR, advt. exec.; b. Stamford, Conn., Jan. 14, 1918; s. William and Abigail (Benatar) B.; B.A., Dartmouth Coll., 1938; m. Jean Fraser McCarraher, July 31, 1945. With Grey Advt. Inc., N.Y.C., 1947—, sr. v.p., mgmt. supr., 1969—, marketing adviser, 1970—; adj. asst. prof. communications arts dept. N.Y. Inst. Tech., Old Westbury, N.Y., 1970—. Served to capt. Intelligence, AUS, 1941-46. Home: The Blockhouse 123 Old Winkle Point Dr Eaton's Neck Northport NY 11768 Office: 170 E 78th St New York City NY 10021

BLOCK, MARVIN AVRAM, physician; b. Buffalo, Jan. 11, 1903; s. Robert and Sarah (Sernoffsky) B.; B.S., M.D., State U. N.Y. at Buffalo, 1925; student U. Vienna (Austria), 1931; m. Lillian Kevitt, Nov. 29, 1933. Intern Buffalo Gen. Hosp., 1924-25, Buffalo City Hosp., 1925-26; mem. faculty State U., N.Y. at Buffalo Med. Sch., 1927—, asst. prof. clin. medicine, 1945—; pvt. practice specializing internal medicine, 1945—, alcoholism and addictive diseases, 1950—; mem. staff Buffalo Gen. Hosp., 1951—; bd. mgrs. Meyer Meml. Hosp., Buffalo, 1943-44, U. Buffalo Rehab. Center, 1949-51; vis. lectr. U. Nev., U. Tex.; U. Utah Sch. Alcohol Studies, McMaster U., Inst. Alcohol, U. Colo. Sch. Alcohol Studies, Columbia Sch. Social Studies, U. Miss. Sch. Alcohol Studies, U. Witwatersrand (South Africa), U. U. Capetown (South Africa), U. Stellenbosch (South Africa), U. Melbourne (Australia). Cons. South Africa Nat. Council Alcholism, 1960, Australian Council Alcoholism, 1960, New Zealand Council Alcoholism, 1960, Dept. Hosps. and Med. Facilities of A.M.A., 1964, also Malvern (Pa.) Inst., B.C. project of Am. Psychiat. Assn., Nat. Inst. Mental Health, Buffalo Police Dept., Dept. Health, N.Y. State Motor Vehicle Bur.; founder, 1950, 1950, N.Y. State Council Coms. Alcoholism, pres., 1954-60; pres. Western N.Y. Com. Edn. Alcoholism, 1954-59, bd. dirs., 1949—; bd. dirs. Nat. Council Alcoholism, v.p., 1963; adv. bd. Erie dean acad. affairs State U. N.Y. Coll., 1964—; dean County Mental Health Assn., Internat. Inst. Alcoholism; adv. com. narcotics N.Y. State Dept. Health, N.Y. State Dept. Mental Hygiene; NSF del. Am.-Japanese Conf. on Addictions, 1964. Pres. Liberty Loan Co., Inc., Buffalo. Mem. exec. com. Erie County Community Welfare Council, 1963; bd. dirs. Buffalo and Erie County Community Chest, 1956-60. Pres. Marvin A. and Lillian K. Block Found.; bd. dirs. Rosa Coplon Home and Infirmary, Jewish Fedn. Social Service, Nag. Council Joint Distbn. Recipient M. & R. award A.A.G.P., 1953, Buffalo Evening News award, 1955, citation of merit Malvern Inst., 1962, Wisdom Award of Honor, Wisdom Soc., 1966. Fellow Am., N.Y. State pub. health assns., Assn. Am. Med. Colls.; mem. A.M.A. (chmn. com. alcoholism council mental health), N.Y. State (chmn. subcom. alcoholism and narcotics pub. health com.), Erie County (chmn. spl. com. problems alcoholism) med. socs., Buffalo Acad. Medicine, A.A.A.S., Am. Acad. Polit. and Social Scis., N.Y. Acad. Scis., N.Y. State Soc. Med. Research, Am., Western N.Y. geriatrics socs., Profl. Assn. Alcoholism, World Med. Assn., British Soc. Study Alcholism, N.Y. State Assn. Professions, Acad. Psychosomatic Medicine, Buffalo Fine Arts Acad., Buffalo Philharmonic Orch. Soc., Buffalo Chamber Music Soc., Erie County Soc. Prevention Cruelty Animals, Am. Jewish Physicians Com., Cleve. Health Mus., Salvation Army Assn., Am. Jewish Com., Alumni Assn. State U. N.Y. at Buffalo, Am. Red Mogen David for Israel, Zionist Orgn. Am., Am. Edn. Found., Maimonides Med. Soc., Am. Med. Society on Alcoholism (v.p.). Mem. B'nai B'rith. Clubs: Montefiore, Automobile (Buffalo); Westwood Country (Williamsville, N.Y.) Author: Alcohol—Its Facets and Phases; also numerous works in field. Address: 371 Linwood Av Buffalo NY 14209

BLOCK, MARY LASKER (Mrs. Leigh Block), civic leader; b. Chgo., Sept. 16, 1904; d. Albert Davis and Flora (Warner) Lasker; grad. Vassar Coll., 1926; m. Leigh B. Block, Oct. 21, 1942. Vice pres. Foote, Cone & Belding Advt. (formerly Lord & Thomas), 1937-41. Mem. women's bd., trustee Art Inst. Chgo.; mem. nat. bd. Recording for the Blind, 1955-63, Skowhegan Sch. of Painting and Sculpture, 1953-63; charter mem., mem. exec. com., bd. dirs. Mayor's Com. for Econ. and Cultural Devel. Chgo.; mem. Ill. Arts Council; mem. women's bd. U. Chgo.; trustee Lincoln Acad.; mem. bd., corr. sec. women's bd. Lyric Opera Chgo.; charter mem. women's bd. Field Mus. Natural History; chmn. awards com. Chgo. Beautiful Com.; mem. citizens council Chgo. Ednl. TV Assn. Vice chmn. Chgo. chpt. A.R.C., 1939- 44; bd. dirs. U.S.O. Recipient Camelia award Loyola U., 1966. Mem. English-Speaking Union (exec. com.), Chgo. Hist. Soc., Oriental Inst. (U. Chgo.), Antiquarian Soc., Alliance Francaise. Clubs: Arts of Chicago. Home: 1260 Astor St Chicago IL 60610 Office: 30 W Monroe St Chicago IL 60603

BLOCK, MURRAY HAROLD, univ. adminstr.; b. N.Y.C., Feb. 14, 1924; s. Joseph and Rebecca (Wollendler) B.; B.B.A., City Coll. N.Y., 1945; M.A., Columbia, 1947, Ed.D., 1953; m. Estelle M. Kleckner, May 27, 1948; children—Richard Neil, Paul Alan, Jo- Carol. Mem. faculty N.Y.C. Community Coll., 1947-50, dir. eve. div., 1950-60, dean, 1960-62, acting pres., 1962-65; pres. Borough Manhattan Community Coll., 1965-70; dep. to the chancellor State U. N.Y., 1970—. Bd. dirs. Council Higher Ednl. Instns. N.Y.C., 1965-70; vice chmn. Nassau County Adv. Com. Legislation, 1967—; pres. Council Community Coll. Pres. N.Y. State, 1967-69; mem Regents Adv. Council Two-Year Edn., 1966—; commn. mem., also chmn. Am. Assn. Jr. Colls., 1965-70. Served with USAAF, 1943-46. Mem. Assn. Higher Edn., Phi Delta Kappa, Delta Pi Epsilon. Home: 9 Heather Lane Delmar NY 12054 Office: State U NY 8 Thurlow Terrace Albany NY 12201

BLOCK, PAUL JR., newspaper pub., chemist; b. N.Y.C., May 11, 1911; s. Paul and Dina (Wallach) B.; grad. Hotchkiss Sch., Lakeville, Conn., 1929; A.B. Yale, 1933; student Columbia, 1933-34, Harvard, 1934-35; Ph.D., Columbia, 1943; m. Eleana Barnes Conley, 1940 (div. 1947) 1 s., Cyrus P.; m. 2d, Marjorie McNab Main, May 26th, 1948 (dec. Sept. 30, 1960); children—Allan James, John Robinson; m. 3d, Mary Gall Petok, 1965; 3 children by previous marriage. Reporter Toledo Blade, 1935, became polit. writer, 1938, asst. editor, 1941, co-pub., 1942; co- pub. Pitts. Post Gazette, 1944—; fellow Mellon Inst. Indsl. Research, Pitts., 1943-44, hon. fellow, dept. pharmacology, Yale U., 1948-49. Mem. Nat. Adv. Health Manpower Council, 1967—. Chmn. bd. trustees Med. Coll. Ohio, Toledo. Mem. Am. Chem. Soc. N.Y. Acad. Scis., Am. Soc. Newspaper Editors, Internat. Press Inst. (chmn. Am. com. 1958-61), Sigma Xi. Home: 4059 River Rd Toledo OH 43614 Office: Toledo Blade Toledo OH 43604

BLOCK, PHILLIP D., Jr., business exec.; b. Chgo., June 25, 1906; s. Philip D. and Celia (Leopold) B.; student Phillips Acad., Andover, Mass., 1922-24; B.S., Sheffield Sci. Sch. Yale, 1928; m. Margaret L. Selz, Nov. 28, 1934; children—Philip D., III, Andrew K. With Inland Steel Co., Chgo., 1928—, asst. v.p., 1934-48, dir. 1942—, became v.p. in charge raw materials, 1948, later, sr. v.p., vice chmn. 1959-67, chmn. bd., 1967-71, chmn. exec. com., 1971—; mem. exec. com. Chgo. community Trust, 1962—; dir. Continental-Ill. Nat. Bank & Trust Co. of Chgo. Bd. dirs. Jewish Children's Bur., Chgo., 1930- 50, United Charities of Chgo. 1939-58, pres., 1951-52; bd. dirs. Jewish Fedn. of Chgo., 1954-59; trustee U. Chgo., 1957—. Home: 1540 Lake Shore Dr Chicago IL 60610 Office: 30 W Monroe St Chicago IL 60603

BLOCK, RALPH, writer; b. Cherokee, Ia., June 21, 1889; s. Sigfried and Doris (Count) Block.; A.B., U. Mich., 1911; m. Mary Greenacre; children—Beulah (dec.), Bridget. Reporter, Louisville Courier Jour., Detroit News, dramatic editor Kansas City Star until 1917; with N.Y. Evening Sun, dramatic editor N.Y. Tribune, 1917-18; Washington staff New Republic, 1918; Washington corr. N.Y. Tribune, 1918-19; asso. editor Goldwyn Picture Corp., 1919-22; with Paramount-Famous Players-Lasky Corp., 1922-27, editor in chief, 1926-27; became asso. producer Pathe Studios 1927; with Fox Film Corp., 1929; later free-lance writer of screen plays; in Europe observing motion picture prodn., 1936-37; asst. regional dir. 9th Civilian Def. Region, U.S. Office Civilian Def., 1942; spl. asst. to personal rep. U.S. Pres. in India, 1943; gen rep. in India overseas operations U.S. OWI and spl. asst. to U.S. commr. India, 1944-45; chief pub. affairs officer Am. Mission, New Delhi, India, 1945-46; spl. asst. to dir. Office Internat. Information, U.S. Dept. State, 1947, information policy adviser to asst. sec. state for pub. affairs, 1949-50, acting dir. fgn. information policy staff, 1951-52, dir. gen. staff, policy and plans. div. Internat. Information Administrn., 1952-53; spl. asst. to chief policy and program staff USIA, 1954, spl. adviser information center service, chief bibliog. div., 1954-60. Hon. trustee Motion Picture Relief Fund, Hon. fellow Harry S. Truman Library Inst. Recipient Medal of Freedom, War Dept., 1946; Merit citation Nat. Civil Service League, 1958; Superior Service award USIA, 1959. Mem. Screen Writers' Guild of Authors League Am. (past pres.), Am. Fgn. Service Assn., Phi Beta Kappa, Michigamua. Clubs: Players, Coffee House (N.Y.C), Fossils (Chevy Chase, Md.). Home: 6314 32d St Washington DC 20015.

BLOCK, ROBERT CHARLES, physicist; b. Newark, Feb. 11, 1929; s. George and Sue (Ehrenkranz) B.; B.S. in Elec. Engring., Newark Coll. Engring., 1950; M.A. in Physics, Columbia, 1953; Ph.D. in Nuclear Physics, Duke, 1956; m. Rita Adler, June 28, 1952; children—Keith, Robin. Elec. engr. Nat. Union Radio Corp., W. Orange, N.J., 1950-51, Bendix Aviation Co., Teterboro, N.J., 1951; physicist Oak Ridge Nat. Lab., 1955-66; vis. scientist Atomic Energy Research Establishment, Harwell, Eng., 1962-63; prof. nuclear engring. and sci. Rensselaer Poly. Inst., 1966—; vis. scientist Am. Inst. Physics, 1961—; cons. AEC, 1969—, Gen. Electric Co., 1968—. Mem. nuclear cross sect. adv. com. AEC, 1969—. Mem. A.A.A.S., Am. Phys. Soc., N.Y. Acad. Scis., Am. Nuclear Soc., Sigma Xi, Sigma Pi Sigma, Phi Beta Tau, Tau Beta Pi. Research on neutron physics. Co-Author chpt. in book. Home: 1163 Fernwood Dr Schenectady NY 12309 Office: Rensselaer Poly Inst Troy NY 12181

BLOCK, S. LESTER, dept. store exec.; b. Trenton, N.J., Jan. 10, 1917; s. Maurice R. and Jeanne (Finkle) B.; A.B., Princeton, 1938; LL.B., U. Pa., 1941; m. Ruth Harris, Mar. 21, 1942; children—John D., Richard H. Admitted to N.Y. bar, 1945, N.J. bar, 1947; asso. Proskauer, Rose, Goetz & Mendelsohn, N.Y.C., 1945-54; labor atty. R.H. Macy & Co., Inc., N.Y.C., 1954-67, v.p., labor atty., 1967-70, sr. v.p. govt. relations, labor counsel, 1970—; lectr. N.Y. State Sch. Indsl. and Labor Relations. Chmn. labor-mgmt. law com. Am. Arbitration Assn., 1967, mem. arbitration com., 1959; mem. N.Y. State Bus. Adv. Com. Mgmt. Improvement, 1970—; mem. planning com. N.Y.U. 24th Annual Conf. Labor, 1970; mem. regional adv. conf. adminstrn. NLRB, 1960-63; mem. Fed. Adv. Council Employment Security, 1960-62. Mem. Bergen County Jewish Welfare Council, 1958-66, Teaneck (N.J.) Jewish Community Council, 1954-60. Served from pvt. to capt., Signal Corps, AUS, 1941-45. Mem. Assn. Bar City N.Y., Am. Retail Fedn. (exec. com., dir.), Am. Mgmt. Assn., N.Y. C. of C., Commerce and Industry Assn. N.Y., Indsl. Relations Soc., Inc., Nat. Retail Mchts. Assn., Nat. Acad. Arbitrators, Phi Beta Kappa, Order of Coif. Home: 1181 W Laurelton Pkwy Teaneck NJ 07666 Office: 151 W 34th St New York City NY 10001

BLOCK, STANLEY MARLIN, educator; b. Mpls., Feb. 4, 1922; s. Herman J. and Flora (Weihle) B.; B. Mech. Engring. with high distinction, U. Minn., 1943, M.B.A., 1950, Ph.D. in Mech. Engring., 1956; m. Isabelle Jeanette Kirk, Aug. 15, 1947; children—Patricia Sue, Carol Jean, Beverly Ann, Priscilla Jo. Indsl. engr. Minn. Mining and Mfg. Co., 1947-49; from instr. to asst. prof. U. Minn. 1949-59; prodn. planner Mpls.-Honeywell Co., 1951; time standards engr. Whirlpool Corp., 1952; human engring. cons. USAF, 1953; asso. prof. prodn. mgmt. Grad. Sch. Bus., U. Chgo., 1959-62; prof. indsl. engring., chmn. dept. Ill. Inst. Tech., 1962—; prin. S.M. Block and Assos., Olympia Fields, Ill., 1955—; pres. Vienna Woods Devel. Corp., Olympia Fields, 1961-69; acad. adviser Student Project for Amity among Nations group to S. Africa, 1957; lectr. Japan Mgmt. Assn., 1964, Nat. Mgmt. and Devel. Found., Johannesburg, S. Africa, 1965. Pres. Vienna Woods Landowners Assn., 1962-66; mem. finance com., Village of Olympia Fields, 1961; U.S. rep. Internat. Fellowship Evangelical Students, Lausanne, Switzerland, 1966—. Bd. dirs. Inter-Varsity Christian Fellowship, 1958-65, 66—; pres. Abundant Life Found., 1968—. Served with AUS, 1943-46. Registered profl. engr., Minn. Mem. Am. Inst. Indsl. Engrs., Operations Research Soc. Am., Am. Arbitration Assn. (labor panel 1962—), Am. Sci. Affiliation, Hosp. Mgmt. Systems Soc., Sigma Xi. Pi Tau Sigma, Tau Beta Pi, Alpha Pi Mu. Mem. Christian Brethren Ch. Clubs: University, Armour Faculty (pres. 1969) (Chgo.). Inventor sequential electronic motion timer and recorder. Contbr. profl. jours. Home: 2002 Quilchena Crescent Vancouver 13 British Columbia Canada Office: Ill Inst Tech Chicago IL 60616

BLOCK, WILLIAM, mfg. co exec.; b. Kankakee, Ill., Dec. 26, 1930; s. William F. and Agnes (Bottary) B.; B.S., Northwestern U., 1952; m. Frances A. Drew, Oct. 7, 1954; children-Deoborah, John, Mark, Steven, Gary. Controller, Dura Corp., Detroit, 1964-67; v.p., controller A.T.O. Inc., Cleve., 1967—. Served with AUS, 1952-54. Mem. Financial Execs. Inst. Home: 15189 S Deepwood Lane Chagrin Falls OH 44022 Office: 55 Public Sq Cleveland OH 4411

BLOCK, WILLIAM, newspaper publisher; b. N.Y.C., Sept. 20, 1915; s. Paul and Diana (Wallach) B.; A.B., Yale, 1936; m. Maxine Horton, Mar. 23, 1944; children—William, Karen, Barbara, Donald. With circulation, other depts. Toledo (Ohio), Blade, 1937-39, asst. to gen. mgr., 1939-41; co-pub. Pitts. Post- Gazette and Toledo Blade, 1941—; pres. Post-Gazette; v.p. Toledo Blade. Bd. dirs. Pitts. Regional Planning Assn., Pitts. Communications Found.; sponsor Allegheny Conf. on Community Development. Served as pvt., inf., A.U.S., 1941-42; officer C.A.C. (Anti-Aircraft), 1942-46; disch. capt.; served in mil. govt. in Korea, Sept. 1945- June 1946. Mem. Am. Soc. Newspapers Editors, Pitts. Symphony Soc. (bd. dirs.). Home: 5050 Warwick Terrace Pittsburgh PA 15213 Office: 50 Blvd of Allies Pittsburgh PA 15222

BLOCK, WILLIAM JOSEPH, educator; b. Mattoon, Ill., Mar. 10, 1918; s. Archie Carl and May (McQuown) B.; B.S., Eastern Ill. State Coll., 1948; M.A., U. Ill., 1948, PH.D., 1956; m. Miriam Josephine Preston, July 12, 1941; children—Christina Jo, Carla Jean, Cheryl Jane. Asst. prof. polit. sci. The Citadel, 1951-57; asst. prof. polit. sci. N.C. State U., Raleigh, 1957-60, asso. prof., 1960-63, prof., 1963—, head dept. politics, 1967—. Served to 1st lt. AUS, 1942-46. Mem.

Am., So. polit. sci. assns., Am. Soc. for Pub. Adminstrn., Am. Assn. U. Profs., Phi Kappa Phi. Democrat. Methodist. Author: The Separation of the Farm Bureau and the Extension Service, 1960; Rural Zoning: People, Property and Public Policy, 1967. Home: 5227 Melbourne Rd Raleigh NC 27606

BLOCKER, DAN, actor; b. Bowie County, Tex., 1929; s. Shack and Mary Blocker; ed. Tex. Mil. Inst., Hardin-Simmons U.; M.A., Sul Ross State Coll.; postgrad. U. Cal. at Los Angeles; m. Dolphia Parker, 1952; children—Danna and Debra (twins), David, Dennis. Formerly sch. tchr., Sonora, Tex., Carlsbad, N.M.; later substitute tchr. Glendale (Cal.) High Sch.; actor NBC-TV weekly series, Bonanza, 1959—. Served with 45th Div. AUS, 1950-52; Korea. Democrat. Address: Herman Gold Agy 9034 Sunset Blvd Hollywood CA 90069

BLOCKER, TRUMAN GRAVES, Jr., surgeon; b. Westpoint, Miss., 1909; M.D., U. Tex., 1933. Intern Pa. Gen. Hosp., 1933-35; resident surgery, then attending surgery and plastic surgery John Sealy Hosp., Galveston, Tex., 1935-36; med. adminstr., then dean clin. faculty Univ. Branch Hosps., 1950-55; instr. Columbia Coll. Phys. and Surg., 1936-37; mem. faculty U. Tex. Med. Sch., 1937—, prof. surgery, 1946—, chmn. dept., 1960-64, exec. dir., dean, 1964-67, pres. 1967—. Served to col., M.C., 1942-46; brig. gen. Res. Diplomate Am. Bd. Surgery. Fellow A.C.S. (v.p.), Am. Assn. Plastic Surgery; mem. A.M.A., Am. Surg. Assn. (v.p.), So. Surg. Assn., Am. Assn. Plastic and Reconstructive Surgery. Address: Office of Pres Univ Tex Med Sch Galveston TX 77550

BLODGETT, HUGH CARLTON, psychologist, educator; b. Zamora, Cal., Nov. 21, 1896; s. Carlton Salmon and Esther Cornelia (Heard) B.; A.B., U. Cal. at Berkley, 1921, Ph.D., 1925; m. Georgia Colombat, Sept. 20, 1926 (dec. July 1932); childrenJoan, Carlton Colombat; m. 2d, Yvonne Bledsoe, Sept. 9, 1932; 1 dau., Carol Yvonne. Teaching fellow U. Cal. at Berkeley, 1922-23, research asst., 1923-25; research asst. Stanford, 1925; teaching asst. Harvard, 1926-27; instr. Lehigh U., 1927-28; faculty U. Tex., Austin, 1928—, prof. psychology, 1944-69, prof. emeritus, 1969—, chmn. dept., 1948-50, 60-62, research scientist def. research lab., 1951-64, radiobiol. research lab., 1957- 64; vis. scientist Bekhterev Inst. of Brain, Leningrad, USSR, 1932; vis. prof. U. Cal. at Los Angeles, 1950; participant Mercury space project S.A.M., NASA, 1959-60. Served to ensign U.S. Navy, 1917-19. Fellow Am. Psychol. Assn. (council reps. 1949-51); mem. Tex. (pres. 1954), S.W. psychol. assns., Psychonomic Soc., A.A.A.S., Sigma Xi. Contbr. to profl. jours. Home: 1314 Westover Rd Austin TX 78703

BLODGETT, RALPH HAMILTON, economist, educator; b. North Adams, Mass., Dec. 25, 1905; s. Charles Raymond and Lillian (Morits) B.; B.S. in Econs., U. Vt., 1927; A.M., Syracuse U., 1928; Ph.D., U. Pa., 1933; m. Loretta Neunfeldt, June 14, 1930 (dec. Dec. 1957); children—Moyra Loretta (Mrs. James F. Schaeffner), Sanda Elizabeth (Mrs. Stuart A. McIntosh); m. 2d, Margaret Adkins, July 18, 1958. Grad. asst. econs. Syracuse U., 1927-28; instr. econs. Valparaiso U., 1928-29; instr., asst. prof. economics U. Pa., 1929-37; asst. prof. econs. U. Ill., 1937-41, asso. prof., 1941-45, prof., 1945-50; prof. econs. U. Fla., 1950—, acting head econs. dept., 1964-65, bd. editors U. Fla. Social Sci. Monograph Series. Vis. prof. econs., U. So. Cal., summer, 1949; econ. cons., expert witness various law firms; econ. cons. TVA, 1959-61, NASA, 1964-65; Dept. Housing and Urban Devel., 1965-67. Mem. Am., So., Midwest (v.p. 1946-47) econ. assns., Am. Assn. U. profs., Am. Contract Bridge League (life master), A.A.A.S., Phi Beta Kappa, Omicron Delta Epsilon, Sigma Alpha Epsilon, Alpha Kappa Psi, Beta Gamma Sigma. Democrat. Episcopalian. Clubs: University of Fla. Bridge; Gainesville Golf and Country. Author: Cyclical Fluctuations in Commodity Stocks, 1935; Principles of Econs., 1941, rev. edit. 1946, 1951; Comparative Econ. Systems, 1944, 49; Our Expanding Economy: An Introduction, 1955; co-author: An Econ. Question Book, 1931; Contemporary Econ. Problems, 1932; Getting and Earning, 1937; Econ.; Principles and Problems, 1937, rev. edits., 1942, 48; Current Economic Problems, 1939, 1947; Comparative Economic Development, 1956. Author numerous articles and monographs in econs. Home: 6401 S W 35th Way Route 4, Gainesville, FL. 32601.

BLODI, FREDERICK CHRISTOPHER, ophthalmologist, educator; b. Vienna, Austria, Jan. 11, 1917; s. Adolph and Bertha (Grueger) B.; M.D., U. Vienna, 1940; m. Ottilie Schmakal, Apr. 22, 1946; children—Christopher F., Barbara Ann. Came to U.S., 1947, naturalized, 1950. Intern City Hosp., Vienna, 1940-42; resident eye clinic U. Vienna, 1942-45; instr. U. Vienna, 1946-47; research fellow Columbia, 1947-52; asst. prof., prof. ophthalmology U. Ia., Iowa City, 1952-67, head dept. ophthalmology, 1967—; cons. to surgeon gen., 1960- -. Served with German Army, World War II. Diplomate Am. Bd. Ophthalmology. Mem. Assn. U. Profs. Ophthalmology (sec.-treas.), Am. Ophthal. Soc., Verhoeff Soc. Unitarian. Mem. editorial bd. Am. Jour. Ophthalmology, 1965—. Home: 1105 Dill St Iowa City IA 52240 Office: U Hosp Iowa City IA 52240

BLOEDE, VICTOR GUSTAV, advt. exec.; b. Balt., Jan. 31, 1920; s. Victor Gustav, Jr. and Helen (Yoe) B.; student St. John's Coll., Annapolis, Md., 1939. U. Md., 1941; m. Merle Huie, Mar. 11, 1945; children—Victor Gustav, Susan Lohn. Vice pres., copy chief French & Preston, N.Y.C., 1947-50; with Benton & Bowles, Inc., N.Y.C., 1950—, v.p., creative dir., 1957-61, sr. v.p., 1961-62, sr. v.p. charge creative services, 1962-63, exec. v. p., 1963-68, chmn. plans bd., 1963-67, pres., chief exec. officer, 1968-71, chmn. bd., chief exec. officer, 1971—, dir. at large Am. Assn. Advt. Agys.; dir. Am. Advt. Fedn., Nat. Outdoor Advt. Bur., travelers Aid Soc. N.Y. Trustee Am. Fund for Dental Health. Served to capt. USAAF, 1942-45. Decorated Air medal with 6 oak leaf clusters. Mem. Phi Sigma Kappa. Clubs: Sands Point, Sands Point Golf (L.I.) Bath and Tennis (v.p., bd. govs. 1962); Coral Beach (Bermuda); Manhasset Bay Yacht, Windermere Island, Economic (New York). Contbg. author: The Copy Writer's Guide, 1958. Home: 160 Bayview Rd Plandome Manor Long Island NY 11030 Office: 909 3d Av New York City NY 10022

BLOEDORN, FERNANDO GERMANE, educator, physician; b. Varginha, Brazil, Oct. 12, 1913; s. Reynaldo and Maria (Pasquale) B.; M.D., U. del Litoral, Rosario, Argentina, 1936; m. Nelida Ansaldi, Feb. 10, 1938. Came to U.S., 1951, naturalized, 1957. Instr. anatomy U. del Litoral, 1933-36; intern Hosp. Centenario, Rosario, 1934-36; dir. surgery pvt. clinic, San Pedro, Argentina, 1936-49; asst. surgeon Hosp. San Pedro, 1943-48; scholar British Council in Eng., 1948-51; sr. resident radiotherapy Frances Delafield Hosp., N.Y.C., 1951; asso. radiotherapist M. D. Anderson Hosp. and Tumor Inst., Houston, 1951-55; head div. radiotherapy U. Md. Hosp., 1955—, asso. prof. radiology Sch. Medicine, 1955-60, prof., 1960—; asst. prof. radiology Johns Hopkins Sch. Medicine, 1958—; now chmn., prof. dept. therapeutic radiology at Tufts-New Eng. Med. Center; cons. numerous hosps. in area, 1956—. Mem. radiation study sect. NIH, 1963-67, 70—. Diplomate Am. Bd. Radiology. Mem. Inter-Am. Coll. Radiology (sec. 1968-70), Balt. Med. Soc., Med. and Chirurgical Faculty Md., A.M.A., Am. Soc. Therapeutic Radiologists (pres. elect), Am. Coll. Radiology, Am. Radium Soc. (pres. 1969-70) Md. Radiol. Soc., Radiol. Soc. N.Am., Pan Am. Med. Assn.; hon. mem. numerous fgn. med. assns. Contbr. profl. jours. Home: Prudential Center Boyleston Bldg Boston MA 02199 Office: Dept Therapeutic Radiology New Eng Med Center Hosps 171 Harrison Av Boston MA 02111

BLOEMBERGEN, NICOLAAS, Physicist, educator; b. Dordrecht, Netherlands, Mar. 11, 1920; s. Auke and Sophia M. (Quint) B.; B.A., Utrecht U., 1941, M.A., 1943; Ph.D., Leiden U., 1948; M.A. (hon.), Harvard, 1951; m. Huberta D. Brink, June 26, 1950; childrenAntonia, Brink, Juliana. Came to U.S., 1952, naturalized, 1958. Teaching asst. Utrecht U., 1942-45; research fellow Leiden U., 1948; mem. Soc. Fellows, Harvard, 1949-51. asso. prof., 1951- 57, Gordon McKay prof. applied physics, 1957—. Recipient Buckley prize for solid state physics Am. Phys. Soc., 1958; Morris Liebmann award Inst. Radio Engrs., 1959; Stuart Ballantine medal Franklin Institute, 1961. Fellow Am. Phys. Soc., Am. Acad. Arts and Scis., I.E.E.E.; mem. Nat., Royal Dutch acads. Scis., Dutch Physicists Soc. Author: Nuclear Magnetic Relaxation, 1948; Nonlinear Optics, 1965; also articles profl. jours. Home: 3 Stonewall Rd Lexington MA 02173 Office: Pierce Hall Harvard Univ Cambridge MA 02138

BLOETJES, MARY KIEFER, hosp. adminstrn. cons.; b. Ramsey, N.J., Dec. 28, 1904; d. Raymond A. and Elizabeth B. (Wanamaker) Kiefer; B.S., Columbia, 1939, M.A., 1942; postgrad. U. Copenhagen, Denmark, 1952; Ph.D., Cornell U., 1953; m. Louis E. Bloetjes, July 23, 1930 (dec.). Dir. nutrition Hosp. for Joint Diseases, N.Y.C., 1929-49; nutrition exec. Montefiore Hosp., 1949; prof., head dept. instn. adminstrn. Sch. Home Econs., Fla. State U., 1953-55; prof., head dept. instn. mgmt. Coll. Home Econs., Cornell U., 1955-70, prof. emeritus, 1970—; cons. hosp. adminstrn., 1970—. Recipient John G. Bergquist internat. fellowship Am.-Scandinavian Found., 1947-48, Mary Swartz Ross fellowship Am. Dietetic Assn. and Nutrition Found., 1952. Mem. Danish, Am. dietetic assns., Am. Home Econs. Assn., Assn. Allied Health Professions, Am. Pub. Health Assn., Royal Soc. Health (London), Am. Assn. U. Profs., Am. Assn. U. Women, A.A.A.S., Am. Econ. Assn., Am. Hosp. Assn., Royal Soc. Medicine United Kingdom (affiliated), Phi Kappa Phi. Contbr. profl. jours. Travelled Europe, Scandinavian Countries, Hawaii. Home: 400 Triphammer Rd Ithaca NY 14850

BLOM, DANIEL CHARLES, lawyer, ins. co. exec.; b. Portland, Ore., Dec. 13, 1919; s. Charles D. and Anna (Reiner) B.; B.A. magna cum laude, U. Wash., 1941, postgrad., 1941-42; J.D., Harvard, 1948; postgrad. U. Paris, 1954-55; m. Ellen Lavon Stewart, June 28, 1952; children-Daniel Stewart, Nicole Jan. Teaching fellow speech U. Wash., 1941-42; law clk. to Judge Supreme Ct. Wash., 1948-49; admitted to Wash. bar, 1949, since practiced in Seattle; asso. Graves, Kizer & Graves, 1949-51; gen. counsel Northwestern Life Ins. Co., 1952-54; partner Case & Blom, 1952-54; asso., partner Ryan, Carlson, Bush, Swanson & Hendel, 1956—; sr. v.p., gen. counsel, dir. Family Life Ins. Co., 1964—; v.p., dir. Family Life Bldg. Co. Vice chmn. Wash. Bd. Bar Examiners, 1970—. Mem. industry adv. com. Nat. Assn. Ins. Commrs., 1966-68. Bd. dirs. Crisis Clinic. Served to 2d lt. AUS, 1942-45; PTO. Decorated Bronze Star medal. Mem. Am., Wash., Seattle bar assns., Am. Judicature Soc., Harvard Law Sch. Assn., Am. Arbitration Assn., Wash. Ins. Council, Phi Beta Kappa, Tau Kappa Alpha. Editor: Wash. State Bar Jour., 1951-52. Home: 2424 Magnolia Blvd W Seattle WA 98199 Office: PO Box 12620 Republic Bldg Seattle WA 98111

BLOMGREN, PAUL BROWN, coll. dean; b. Winterset, Ia., Dec. 8, 1920; s. Lawrence L. and Aletha (Brown) B.; B.A., State U. Ia., 1942, M.A., 1947; D.B.A., Ind. U., 1952; m. Aleen Helen Trask, Aug. 21, 1942; children—Paul Brown, Richard H., Barbara A., Robert C. Instr. econs. DePauw U., 1947-50; from teaching fellow to asso. prof. transp. Ind. U. Sch. Bus., 1950-56; asso. prof. marketing and transp. Mich. State U., 1956-59; prof. bus. adminstrn., dean Sch. Bus., Mont. State U., 1959-63; dean sch. Bus. Adminstrn. and Econs. San Fernando Valley State Coll., Northridge, California, 1963—. Mem. Gov's Com. Econ. Studies, Mont. Small Bus. Adminstrn. Adv. Council, adv. com. Pacific N.W. Econ. Base Study, exec. com. Mo. Basin Research and Devel. Council; pres. Western Mont. Council Boy Scouts Am. Served with USNR, 1942-46. Mem. Am. Econ. Assn., Am. Soc. Traffic and Transp., Order Artus, Beta Gamma Sigma, Theta Xi. Rotarian. Office: San Fernando Valley State Coll Northridge CA 91324

BLOMQUIST, AGNES, real estate co. exec.; b. Platte, S.D., Jan 2, 1911; d. Patrick Richard and Eva (Anderson) Blomquist; student Woodbury Coll., Los Angeles, 1927-28. With P.A. Palmer Inc., Pasadena, Newport Beach, Cal., 1928—, sec.-treas., dir., 1945—, also dir.; exec. v.p. Newport Balboa Savs. & Loan Assn., 1936-52, pres., mng. officer, 1962-69, also dir.; pres. Lido Ins. Agy., Newport Beach, 1953-69, also dir.; pres. Lido Isle Properties, Inc. Newport Beach, 1949—, also dir.; dir. Imperial Savs. of Newport-Pasadena. Pres. Newport Beach United Fund, 1964; asso. mem. Assistance League Newport Beach, 1964—; pres. Town and Gown Club, U. Cal. at Irvine, 1965-66; charter mem., founding bd. mem. Com. Profl. Women for Los Angeles Philharmonic Orch. Named Woman of Year, Los Angeles Times, 1962; Outstanding So. Cal. Businesswoman, Los Angeles chpt. Nat. Assn. Accountants, 1963; recipient Outstanding Community Service award Zonta Club, 1963; Outstanding Citizen award Orange Coast Coll., 1970. Mem. Nat. Fedn. Bus. and Profl. Womens Clubs (pres. Newport Harbor club 1938-39, 48-49; Women of Achievement award Cal. Fedn. 1966). Clubs: Newport Harbor Yacht, Irvine Coast County, Soroptimist (hon.), Altrusa (hon.) (Newport Harbor); Balboa Bay Club. Home: 130 Via Xanthe Newport Beach CA 92660 Office: 3333 West Coast Hwy Newport Beach CA 92660

BLOMQUIST, ALFRED THEODORE, educator; b. Chgo., Nov. 16, 1906; s. Alfred and Charlotte Amelia (Lindgren) B.; A.B. summa cum laude, U. Ill., 1928, M.S., 1929, Ph.D., 1932; m. Sara Amelia Moffat, Aug. 21, 1931; children—Alfred Theodore, Charlotte (Mrs. William C. Jensen), James Moffat. NRC fellow Cornell U., 1932-33; sec. H. M. Stevenson Co., Chgo., 1943-41; faculty Cornell U., 1941—, prof. chemistry, 1950—, prin. investigator univ. group on high explosives, 1942-45; mem. RDX com. Nat. Def. Research Council, 1942-45; cons. organic chemistry B.F. Goodrich Co., 1946-47; Sloan vis. prof. chemistry Harvard U., 1962. Cons. editor Acad. Press, Inc., 1961—. Recipient Naval Ordnance Devel. award, 1946, Certificate of Appreciation, War and Navy Depts., 1947. Mem. Nat., N.Y. acads. scis., Am. Chem. Soc., A.A.A.S. Sigma Xi, Phi Beta Kappa, Theta Delta Chi. Home: 208 Iroquois Rd Ithaca NY 14850

BLOMSTER, RALPH NORMAN, educator; b. Lynn, Mass., May 18, 1931; s. George Alfred and Ranghild (Johnson) B.; B.S., Mass. Coll. Pharmacy, 1953; M.S., U. Pitts., 1958; Ph.D., U. Conn., 1963; m. Merilyn Gay Christenson, May 19, 1962; children—Kirsten Joy, Erik Bjrn. Instr., U. Pitts., 1958-59, prof., 1963- 66, asso. prof., 1966-68; prof., chmn. dept. pharmacognosy U. Md., Balt., 1968—; cons. Amazon Natural Drug Co. Served with AUS, 1953-55. Fellow A.A.A.S., N.Y. Acad. Scis.; mem. Am. Soc. Pharmacognosy, Am. Assn. Coll. Pharmacy, (sec. sect. tchrs. biology and sci. 1966—), Am. Pharm. Assn., Acad. Pharm. Sci., A.A.A.S., Soc. Econ. Botany, Am. Inst. Biological Sci., Am. Forstry Assn., Sigma Xi, Kappa Psi, Rho Chi. Editor, Am. Soc. Pharmacognosy Newsletter, 1968—; asso. editor Lynn Index. Home: 108 Hillside Rd Catonsville MD 21228 Office: 636 W Lombard St Baltimore MD 21201

BLOOD, ARCHER KENT, govt. ofcl.; b. Chgo., Mar. 20, 1923; s. Francis Earle and Hazel Mary (Brown) B.; B.A., U. Va., 1943; postgrad., U. Va., 1946-47, Army War Coll., 1962-63; M.A., George Washington U., 1963; m. Margaret Lloyd Millward, May 14, 1948; children—Shirley Millward, Barbara Kent, Peter Ross, Archer Lloyd. With State Dept., 1947—; vice consul, Salonica, Greece, 1947-49, Munich, Germany, 1949-50; 2d sec., Athens, Greece, 1950-52; vice consul, Algiers, Algeria, 1953; civil mil. relations officer, Bonn, Germany, 1953-55; internat. affairs officer, Washington, 1956-60; consul, Dacca, Pakistan, 1960-62, consul gen., 1970-71; personnel officer, Washington, 1963-65, counselor of embassy, dep. chief of mission, Kabul, Afghanistan, 1965-68; counselor for polit. affairs, Athens, Greece, 1968-70; asst. dir. for personnel, Washington, 1971—. Served to lt. (j.g.) USNR, 1944-46. Recipient State Dept. Meritorious Honor award, 1971; Christian A. Herter award, 1971. Mem. Phi Beta Kappa, Omicron Delta Kappa, Sigma Phi Epsilon. Home: 7501 Glendale Rd Chevy Chase MD 20015 Office: Dept of State Washington DC 20520

BLOOD, GORDON FISK, air force officer; b. Washington, Sept. 30, 1919; s. Fred Ethelburt and Emma (Fisk) B.; student Command and Gen. Staff Sch., Ft. Leavenworth, Kan., 1943, Air Command and Staff Sch., Maxwell AFB, Ala., 1949. Combat Crew Tng. Sch., Nellis AFB, Nev., 1951, Air War Coll., Maxwell AFB, 1959; B.S., U. Md., 1962; postgrad. George Washington U., 1962-63; m. Alice Catherine Tydings, Mar. 18, 1942; children—Jane Elizabeth (Mrs. William Michael Abbott), Nancy Lee. Commd. 2d lt. USAF, 1941, advanced through grades to maj. gen., 1967; comdg. officer, dir. operations and tng. 316th Troop Carrier Group, Sewart AFB, Tenn., 1950-51; dep. comdr., comdr. 49th Fighter Bomber Group, Korea, 1952; chief Combat Operations Div. 5th Air Force, Korea, 1952-53; dir. operations and tng. 9th Air Force, Shaw AFB, S.C., 1953-56; comdr. 413th Fighter-Day Wing, George AFB, Cal., 1956-58; chief planning and programming Force Structure br., dep. dir. for war plans Hdqrs. USAF, Washington, 1959-60, asst. chief, chief Force Plans Div., dept. dir. plans for war plans, 1960-63; comdr. 36th TFW, Bitburg Air Base, Germany, 1963-64; dep. chief of staff operations 4th ATAF, Ramstein Air Base, Germany, 1964-66; chief Objectives Plans and Programs Div. J-5, JCS, Washington, 1966-67; dept. chief of staff operations Hdqrs. 7th Air Force, Pacific Air Forces, 1967-69; dep. chief of staff operations Hdqrs. USAF in Europe, 1969-70; dep. chief of staff operations and intelligence Hdqrs. AFCENT, Brunssum, The Netherlands, 1970—. Decorated D.S.M., Silver Star medal, Legion of Merit with four oak leaf clusters, D.F.C. with two oak leaf clusters, Air medal with two oak leaf clusters, Vietnam 1st Class AF Distinguished Service Order. Mem. Air Force Assn. Daedalions Soc. Rotarian. Home: #7 Dennenberg Bunde The Netherlands Office: Hdqrs AFCENT SHAPE APO New York City NY 09011

BLOODGOOD, DON EVANS, engr., educator; b. Whitewater, Wis., Feb. 1, 1903; s. Erwin Asa and Anna Velna (Evans) B.; B.S., U. of Wis., 1926, C.E., 1935; student Ind. Univ. extension, 1937; m. Margaret Verne Austin, Nov. 12, 1927; children—Don Austin, Thomas Wylie, Natalie Ann. Lab. asst. Milw. Sewerage Commn., 1926-27, asst. research chemist, 1927-29; san. engr. Indpls. Sanitary Dist., 1929-36, mgr. disposal plants, 1936-43; asso. prof. Sanitary engrng. Purdue U., 1943-47, prof., 1947-71, prof. emeritus, 1971—, dir. sanitary engrng. research projects 1943—, sanitary engrng. extension activities, 1943—; cons. on waste problems to industry. Mem. Ind. State Bd. Health, 1949—. Mem. Am. Soc. C.E., Am., Ind. pub. health assns., Water Pollution Control Fedn., Sigma Pi, Sigma Xi, Chi Epsilon. Presbyn. Clubs: Torch (Wabash Valley), University, Kiwanis. Cons. editor Water and Wastes Engineering. Contbr. articles to various publs. Home: 334 Leslie Av West Lafayette IN 47906

BLOODWORTH, J. M. BARTOW, Jr., educator, physician; b. Atlanta, Feb. 21, 1925; s. J. M. Bartow and Elizabeth (Dimmock) B.; student Emory, 1942-43, M.D., 1948; student Stanford, 1944; m. Jean Stone, Nov. 26, 1947; children—Lowell Ann, Joyce Lynn, Elizabeth Carol. Intern, then asst. resident pathology Columbia- Presbyn. Med. Center, N.Y.C., 1948-50; instr. pathology Columbia. 1949- 50; asst. resident medicine U. Ia. Hosp., 1950-51; mem. faculty Ohio State U. Coll. Medicine, 1951-62, prof. pathology, 1960-62; prof. pathology U. Wis., 1962—; chief div. pathologic anatomy Ohio State U. Hosp., 1954-61; pathologist Columbus State Hosp., 1954-57; chief lab. service Madison VA Hosp., 1962—. Served with AUS, 1941-45. Recipient Fight for Sight Citation Am. Assn. Research in Opthalmology, 1964. Mem. Am., Wis. med. assns., Dane County Med. Soc., Wis. Soc. Pathologists, Am. Assn. Pathologists and Bacteriologists, Am. Soc. Exptl. Pathology, Histochem. Soc., Am. Diabetes Assn. (Lilly award 1963), Am., Wis. heart assns., Soc. Exptl. Biology and Medicine, Internat. Acad. Pathology, Am. Soc. Clin. Pathology, Am. Assn. Neuropathologists, Nat. Soc. Med. Research. Am. Soc. Cell Biology, Am. Legion, Endocrine Soc., Sigma Nu, Phi Chi. Club: Gyro Internat. (pres. Columbus 1962). Author numerous articles in field. Editor: Endocrine Pathology, 1968. Home: 4833 Sheboygan Av Madison WI 53705

BLOODWORTH, JAMES NELSON, state justice; b. Decatur, Ala., Jan. 21, 1921; s. Benjamin M. and Marguerite (Nelson) B.; student Athens Coll., 1938-39; B.S., U. Ala., 1942, LL.B., 1947; m. Mary Jean Gregg, Sept. 27, 1963; children—Catherine, Sandra, Jean Marguerite. Admitted to Ala. bar, 1947; mem. firm Calvin and Bloodworth, Decatur, 1947-58; judge Recorder's Ct., Decatur, 1948-51; solicitor Morgan County, Decatur, 1951; judge 8th jud. Circuit Ct. Ala., 1959-68; asso. justice Ala. Supreme Ct. 1968—, lectr. in law, 1963—. Co-chmn. Circuit Judges Seminars Ala., 1960-66; chmn. Ala. Pattern Jury Instrn. Com., 1966-68; pres. Morgan County Jury Com., 1966-68. Pres. Decatur Boys Club, 1951; moderator N. Ala. Presbytery, 1965; mem. Ala. Bd. Pardons and Paroles, 1951-52. Chmn. Ala. Democratic Campaign Steering Com., 1961-63. Bd. dirs. Morgan County chpt. A.R.C., 1959-60. Served to capt. AUS, World War II. Decorated Bronze Star medal, Combat Inf. badge. Mem. Ala. Res. Officers Assn. (chpt. pres. 1959), Ala., Morgan County (pres. 1955) bar assns, Phi Delta Phi, Kappa Alpha, Omicron Delta Kappa. Presbyn. (elder). Mason (K.T., Shriner), Rotarian (pres. Decatur 1953-54). Co-author: Index to Alabama Constitutional Convention of 1901, 1948. Home: 1834 Shoreham Dr Montgomery AL 36101 Office: Judicial Bldg Capitol Montgomery AL 36106

BLOOM, BENJAMIN S., educator; Ph.D., U. Chgo. Now Charles H. Swift distinguished service prof. edn. U. Chgo. Author: Stability and Change in Human Characteristics, 1964; (with A. Davis and R. Hess) Compensatory Education for Cultural Deprivation, 1965. Address: Grad Sch Edn Univ Chgo 5801 Ellis Av Chicago IL 60637*

BLOOM, CLAIRE, actress; b. London, Eng., Feb. 15, 1931; d. Edward Max and Elizabeth (Grew) Blume; student Badminton Sch., Bristol, Eng., Fern Hill Manor, New Milton, Eng.; pub. schs., Fla., N.Y.; m. Rod Steiger, Sept. 19, 1959; 1 dau., Anna. Appeared as Ophelia, Stratford-Upon-Avon, 1948; plays include Lady's Not for Burning, also Ring Around the Moon, London, 1949- 51; in Romeo and Juliet, others, for Old Vic, also as Juliet in Old Vic tour of U.S.; film roles in Limelight, Man Between, Richard III, Alexander the Great, Brothers Karamazov, Buccaneer, Look Back in Anger; Three Steps to Freedom, 1960; The Brothers Grimm, The Chapman Report, 1962; The Haunting, 1963; 80,000 Suspects, 1963; Alta Infidelita,

1963; Il Maestro di Vigeuono, 1963; The Outrage, 1964; Spy Who Came In from the Cold, 1965; appeared Broadway in Rashomon, 1959, at Royal Court Theatre, London, in Altona, 1960; Charley; The Illustrated Man; 3 into 2 Won't Go; also various roles Brit. and U.S. Television.

BLOOM, EDWARD ALAN, Educator, author; b. Michigan City, Ind., May 24, 1914; s. Robert and Tillie (Leibovitz) B.; B.S. in Journalism, U. Ill., 1936, M.A., 1939, Ph.D. in English, 1947; A.M. (hon.), Brown U., 1957; m. Lillian Doris Blumberg, June 17, 1947. Newspaper reporter, corr., editor Midwestern Papers & Press Service, 1936-38, also free lance mag. writer; asst., instr. English U. Ill., 1939-42, 46-47; faculty dept. English. Brown U., 1947—, prof. English, 1959—, chmn. dept., 1960-67, Nicholas Brown prof. oratory and belles lettres, 1960-67. Served from pvt. to capt., AUS, 1942-46. Huntington Library fellow for 1963-64, 67-68. Decorated Bronze Star; Guggenheim fellow, 1969-70. Mem. Am. Assn. U. Profs., Modern Lang. Assn. Am., Sigma Delta Chi. Author: Samuel Johnson in Grub Street, 1957; (with C.H. Philbrick, E. M. Blistein) The Order of Poetry, 1961; (with L. D. Bloom) Willa Cather's Gift of Sympathy, 1962; The Order of Fiction, 1964; (with L.D. Bloom) Joseph Addison's Sociable Animal, 1971; also articles on 18th Century and contemporary English, and Am. lit. problems. Editor: Shakespeare 1564-1964, 1964; Frances Burney's Evelina, 1968; (with L.D. Bloom) The Variety of Fiction. 1969; editor English and Am. lit. Blaisdell Pub. Co., 1964-70; (with L.D. Bloom) Camilla, 1972. Co-editor: The Variety of Poetry, 1964. Sr. editor; Novel: A Forum on Fiction, 1967—; The Variety of Fiction, published 1969. Contbr. book reviews short stories to newspapers, nat. and internat. jours. Home: 21 Creston Way Providence RI 02906

BLOOM, FREDERICK STUART, engring. exec., univ. trustee; b. Mansfield, O., Aug. 30, 1898; s. William H. and Alice (Daugherty) B.; B.S., Carnegie Inst. Tech., 1921; m. Christine E. Moyer, June 30, 1927; children—Eleanor A. (Mrs. John M. Simpson, Jr.), Nancy M. (Mrs. James E. Johns). Engr., Jones & Langhlin Steel Corp. at S.S. Works, 1921-25; mech. engr. Pa. Salt Mfg. Co., Natrona, Pa., 1925-27; indsl. gas sales mgr. Columbia Gas & Electric Corp., Pitts., 1927-31; pres. Bloom Engring. Co., Inc., 1931-68, chmn. bd., 1968—. Sec. Am. Flame Research Com., 1956-66. Life trustee Carnegie Mellon U. Mem. Iron and Steel Engrs., Pa. Soc. Profl. Engrs., Engring. Soc. Western Pa., Pitts. C. of C., Alumni Assn. Carnegie Mellon U. (pres. 1953-54), Pa. Soc., Newcomen Soc., Tau Beta Pi. Presbyn. Clubs: Pitts. Athletic Assn., Duquesne, University, Longue Vue; Seaview Country (Absecon, N.J.); Marco Polo (N.Y.C.). Patentee in field. Contbr. articles tech. lit. Home: 758 Valley View Rd Pittsburgh PA 15243 Office: Bloom Engring Co Inc Horning and Curry Rds Pittsburgh PA 15236

BLOOM, HAROLD, educator; b. N.Y.C., July 11, 1930; s. William and Paula (Lev) B.; B.A., Cornell U., 1951; Ph.D., Yale, 1955; m. Jeanne Gould, May 8, 1958; children—Daniel Jacob, David Moses. Mem. faculty Yale, 1955—, prof. English, 1965—; vis. prof. Breadloaf Summer Sch., 1965-66, Hebrew U., Jerusalem, 1959. Society for Humanities, Cornell U., 1968-69. Recipient John Addison Porter prize Yale, 1955; Newton Arvin award, 1967; Melville Cane award Poetry Soc. Am., 1970; Guggenheim fellow, 1962; Fulbright fellow, 1955. Author: Shelley's Mythmaking, 1959; The Visionary Company, 1961; Blake's Apocalypse, 1963; Yeats, 1970; The Ringers in the Tower, 1971. Home: 179 Linden St New Haven CT 06511

BLOOM, HYMAN, artist; b. Latvia, Apr. 11, 1913; came to U.S. 1920, naturalized, 1934; student public schs.; m. Celestine Eustis Bohlen, Sept. 1954. Instr. Wellesley Coll., 1949-51, Harvard, 1951-53. Exhbns. Mus. Modern Art, 1942, Stuart Gallery, Boston, 1945, Mirski Gallery, Boston, 1949, Venice Biennal, 1950, Durlacher Bros., N.Y., 1946, 48, 54, Grover Cronin Galleries, Waltham, Mass., 1954, Lowe Gallery, U. Miami, Fla., 1955, Whitney Mus., N.Y.C., 1955, 68, Jewett Arts Center (Wellesley, Mass.), 1959, Mus. Fine Arts (Boston), 1959, San Francisco Mus., 1968, U. Conn., 1968, others. Trustee Pan Orient Arts Found. Guggenheim Fellow, 1949. Recipient Nat. Inst. Arts and Letters award, 1953, Ford Found. grant, 1959. Mem. Am. Acad. Arts and Scis. Address: 1 Winchester St Brookline MA 02146

BLOOM, LEE HURLEY, lawyer; b. N.Y.C., June 21, 1919; s. Harry and Harriet (Bresel) B.; B.S., Mass. Inst. Tech., 1940; LL.B., Harvard, 1943; m. Mary Louise Tolan, Dec. 15, 1945; children—Daniel, Louise, Douglas. Admitted to Mass. bar, 1947, N.Y. bar, 1951; atty. legal div. Lever Bros. Co., N.Y.C., 1947-67, v.p., sec., gen. counsel, 1968-70, adminstrv. v.p., gen. counsel, dir., 1970—. Chmn. bd. Larchmont (N.Y.) Red Cross, 1961-63. Mem. Town of Mamaroneck (N.Y.) Rep. com., 1957- 69; mem. Mamaroneck Planning Bd., 1959-69, Town Bd., 1969—. Served to lt. comdr. USNR, 1941-46. Mem. Soap and Detergent Assn. (chmn. legal com. 1964—), Grocery Mfrs. Am. (mem. exec. com., legal com. 1969—). Home: 22 Myrtle Blvd Larchmont NY 10538 Office: Lever Bros Co 390 Park Av New York City NY 10022

BLOOM, MARTIN HARVEY, educator; b. N.Y.C., May 19, 1921 s. Morris and Esther (Cohen) B.; B.S., L.I. U., 1941; B. Mech. Engring., Bklyn. Poly. Inst., 1946, M.S., 1949; Ph.D. in Applied Mechanics, 1951; m. Phyllis Levine, June 25, 1947; children—Matthew, Robert, Alene. With engring. research dept. Celanese Corp. Am., 1942-46; mem. research staff Poly. Inst. Bklyn., 1947-51, mem. faculty, 1951—, prof. aerospace engring., 1959—, head dept. aerospace engring., 1964-66, dean engring., also dir. gas dynamics research, 1966—; cons. to industry, govt. Served with AUS, 1946-47. Asso. fellow Am. Inst. Aero. and Astronautics; mem. Am. Soc. for Engring. Edn., Am. Soc. M.E. Author, patentee in field. Home: 576 Church Av Woodmere NY 11598 Office: 333 Jay St Brooklyn NY 11201 also Route 110 Farmingdale NY 11735

BLOOM, MURRAY TEIGH, author; b. N.Y.C., May 19, 1916; s. Louis I. and Anna (Teighblum) B.; B.A., Columbia, 1937, M.S., 1938; m. Sydelle J. Cohen, Apr. 30, 1944; children—Ellen Susan (Mrs. Michael B. Lubell), Amy Beth. Reporter, N.Y. Post, 1939; free-lance mag. writer, 1940—. Founder, past trustee United Community Fund Great Neck, N.Y.; founder, past pres. Soc. Mag. Writers. Served with AUS, 1942-46; corr. Stars & Stripes, Paris-Berlin, 1944-45; dept. head Sch. Journalism Biarritz-Am. U., 1945. Recipient 50th Anniversary award Columbia Grad. Sch. Journalism. Mem. Soc. Mag. Writers, Dramatists Guild of Authors League Am. Author: Money of Their Own, 1957; The Man Who Stole Portugal, 1966; (play) Leonora, 1966; The Trouble with Lawyers, 1969. Address: 40 Hemlock Dr Great Neck NY 11024

BLOOM, PAULINE, author, educator; d. Max and Meta (Landau) Bloom; student Bklyn. Coll., Hunter Coll., N.Y.C. Instr. fiction writing Bklyn. Coll., 1951—; dir. Pauline Bloom Workshop Writers, corr. course, 1950—; lectr., critic, cons., 1950—. Mem. Authors Guild (past mem. council), Mystery Writers Am. (sec., mem. bd. 1964—), Nat. League Am. Pen Women (pres. N.Y. State 1965-67, pres. Manhattan br. 1970—). Author: Toby, Law Stenographer, 1959. Contbr. nat. publs. Address: 20 Plaza St Brooklyn NY 11238

BLOOM, ROBERT LOUIS, educator; b. Hot Springs, Ark., Aug. 12, 1911; s. Louis Ellsworth and Esther (Killingsworth) B.; B.S., Shippensburg (Pa.) State Coll., 1936; M.A., Duke, 1941; Ph.D., Columbia, 1952; m. Dorothy Chandler Stuart, Feb. 26, 1945; children—Stuart Ellsworth, Alan Robert, Jonathan Richard, Instr., social studies Tyrone (Pa.) High Sch., 1936-42, Monmouth (N.J.) Jr. Coll., 1946-49; mem. faculty Gettysburg Coll., 1949—, prof. history, chmn. dept., 1959-69. Sec. bd. Gettysburg Battlefield Preservation Assn., 1958—. Served with USAAF, 1942-45. Mem. Am., Pa. (pres. 1969—) hist. assns., Hist. Soc. Pa., Orgn. Am. Historians, Am. Assn. U. Profs., Phi Alpha Theta, Phi Sigma Phi, Alpha Tau Omega. Democrat. Lutheran. Home: 108 Artillery Dr Gettysburg PA 17325

BLOOM, WALTER LYON, educator, physician; b. Ont., Can., Dec. 14, 1917; s. Jacob Isaac and Pauline (Breslav) B.; student Emory U., 1933-36; M.D., Yale, 1940; m. Suzanne Ferst, Aug. 2, 1942; children—Walter Lyon, Clement Alan. Asst. medicine, New Haven, 1940-41; resident in research Goldwater Meml. Hosp., N.Y.C., 1942-43; physiol. investigator dept. medicine Columbia Coll. Phys. and Surg., 1943-44; James Hudson Brown research fellow dept. medicine and physiol. chemistry New Haven Hosp., Yale Sch. Medicine, 1946-47; asso. in biochemistry Emory U. Sch. Medicine, Atlanta, 1947-48, faculty medicine, 1947-55, lectr. biochemistry, 1952-57, asso. prof. medicine, 1955-57, dir. med. edn. and research Piedmont Hosp., 1957-67; asso. v.p. acad. affairs, prof. biology Ga. Inst. Tech., Atlanta, 1967—. Contbr. articles profl. jours. Home: Route 12 Bloomland Farm Marietta GA 30060 Office: Ga Inst Tech Atlanta GA 30332

BLOOM, WILLIAM, anatomist; b. Baltimore, Md., Sept. 15, 1899; s. Mayer and Bertha (Singer) B.; A.B., Johns Hopkins, 1919, M.D., 1923; Doctor honoris causa (biology) Cracow, 1964, m. Margaret Abt, June 6, 1928. Began as asst. pathologist Michael Reese Hosp., Smith fellow in anatomy, U. Chgo, 1926-28, asst. prof. anatomy, 1929-33, asso. prof., 1933, prof. 1941, mem. Inst. Radiobiology and Biophysics, 1946-54, com. on biophysics, 1954-64, dept. biophysics, 1964—, also Charles H. Swift Distinguished Service prof., 1957-65. Distinguished Service prof. emeritus, 1965—. Recipient Gold Key award Univ. of Chicago, 1968. Mem. Nat. Acad. Scis., A.A.A.S., Am. Assn. Anatomists, Am. Soc. Exptl. Pathology. Author: Textbook of Histology (with Don W. Fawcett), 9th edit., 1968. Office: 5640 Ellis Av U Chgo Chicago IL 60637

BLOOM, WILLIAM JOSEPH, apparel co. exec.; b. Fall River, Mass., Feb. 12, 1925; s. William and Marie (Belshaw) B.; B.B.A., Western Reserve U., 1949; m. Betty Jean Westemier, June 12, 1948; children—Kathleen, William Thomas, Thomas Mitchell. Cost supr. Reliance Electric and Engring. Co., Cleve., 1948- 52; with Joseph & Feiss Co., Cleve., 1953-69, sec.-treas., 1965-69; corp. treas. Phillips-Van Heusen Corp., N.Y.C., 1969—. Chmn. Richmond Heights, O., Civil Service Commn., 1964-69; mem. Ohio Bd. Nat. Kidney Found., 1969. Trustee Cleve. Lutheran Children's Aid Soc., 1965-68. Served to 1st lt. USAAF, 1943-45. Mem. Financial Execs. Inst. (sec. Cleve. 1959), Delta Upsilon. Lutheran. Club: Downtown Toastmasters (pres. 1959-62) (Cleve.). Home: 358 Holly Dr Wycoff NJ 07481 Office: Phillips Van Heusen Corp 417 Fifth Av New York City NY 10016

BLOOM, WINFRED COLBY, corp. exec.; b. Bklyn., July 18, 1918; s. Winfred Colby and Ida (Tonyes) B.; B.S., Rutgers U., 1940; m. Lily Murphy, Oct. 3, 1941; childrenJanet Stewart, Kathryn Hanton, Winfred Colby III. Treas. Raymond Internat., Inc., N.Y.C., 1958—, dir., 1963—, v.p., 1964, now sr. v. p. for finance; also officer subsidiaries. Served with USCGR, 1943-46. Presbyn. Home: 8 Whitehall Blvd Garden City NY 11530 Office: 2 Pennsylvania Plaza New York City NY 10001

BLOOMBERG, WARNER, Jr., educator; b. Massillon, O., Mar. 2, 1926; s. Warner Sol and Sara (Brockman) B.; Ph.B., U. Chgo., 1947, M.A. in Social Sci., 1950, Ph.D. in Sociology, 1961; m. Carol Jean Shulan, Mar. 19, 1950; children—Warner S. III, Joel David, Victor Daniel, Jason Michael. With Gary Works, United Steel Corp., 1950-52; with Union Edn. Service, U. Chgo., 1952-53, instr. in coll., 1953-57; asst. prof. Syracuse U., 1957-63; asso. prof. U. Wis.-Milw., 1963-66, prof., 1966—, chmn. dept. urban affairs, 1967-70. Bd. govs. Dominican Coll., Racine, Wis., Council U. Insts. Urban Affairs. Served with USNR, 1944-46. Mem. Am., Midwest sociol. assns., Am. Assn. U. Profs., Planned Parenthood, Phi Beta Kappa. Jewish religion. Author: Suburban Power Structures and Public Education, 1963; Power, Poverty, and Urban Policy, 1968; The Quality of Urban Life, 1969. Home: 2908 N Stowell Av Milwaukee WI 53211

BLOOMER, HENRY HARLAN, educator; b. Roseville, Ill., Aug. 1, 1908; s. Henry M. and Mertie (Harlan) B.; A.B., U. Ill., 1930; M.A., U. Mich., 1933, Ph.D., 1935; m. Hope Frances Hartwig, Aug. 26, 1941; children—Harlan Hartwig, Thomas Yocom. Instr. English, Lincoln Jr. Coll., 1931-32; instr. speech U. Mich., 1935-38, asst. prof., 1939-42, asso. prof., 1942- 47, prof. speech, 1947—, prof. of otorhinolaryngology Med. Sch. 1962-68, prof. speech pathology, dept. phys. medicine and rehab., 1969—, dir. Speech Clinic, head speech and hearing sci. sect., phys. medicine and rehab., 1969—; speech therapist Nat. Speech Improvement Camp, Northport, Mich., summers 1935- 38. Pres. Ann Arbor Bd. Edn., 1958-59. Served as lt. USNR, 1943-46; lt. comdr. USNR 1950. Mem. Mich. Assn. Tchrs. Speech, Mich. Speech and Hearing Assn., Mich. Assn. for Better Hearing, Am. Speech and Hearing Assn. (pres. 1955, mem. grad. edn. and tng. bd.), N.Y. Acad. Scis., Am. Cleft Palate Assn. (exec. council 1958- 61), Speech assn. Am. (exec. council 1947-50), Am. Congress Rehab. Medicine, Internat. Assn. Logopedics and Phoniatrics, Omicron Kappa Upsilon, Phi Sigma, Phi Eta Sigma, Phi Kappa Phi, Alpha Kappa Lambda. Club: Rotary (pres. Ann Arbor 1962-63). Author articles speech profl. jours. Asso. editor Speech Monographs, 1950; editorial cons. Jour. Speech and Hearing Disorders, Cleft Palate Jour. Home: 726 Soule Blvd Ann Arbor MI 48103

BLOOMER, JOHN WELLMAN, newspaper editor; b. Wabash, Ind., Apr. 23, 1912; s. John W. and Floy (Hubbard) B.; student Ind. U., 1932-34; m. Margaret Schornick, Nov. 10, 1935. Editor, Elizabethton (Tenn.) Daily Star, 1935-39; exec. editor Kingsport (Tenn.) Times & News, 1939-42, 46; mng. editor Sarasota (Fla.) Herald-Tribune, 1947-52, Columbus (Ga.) Ledger and Sunday Ledger- Enquirer (Pulitzer prize meritorious pub. service 1955), 1952-56; pub.- editor Portsmouth (Va.) Daily Times, 1956-57; state editor Birmingham (Ala.) News, 1957-59, asso. editor, 1959-61, mng. editor, 1961—. Founder Sarasota Community Chest, 1949. Bd. dirs. Jefferson County Mental Health Assn., Tri-Counties A.R.C., Ala. Tb Assn.; chmn. bd. Rural Cleanup in Ala.; co-founder Fla. W. Coast Symphony Orchestra, 1949; mem. program adv. com. So. Newspaper Pubs. Assn. Found.; chmn. adv. bd. Ala. Beautification. Mem. Ala. Press Assn., Am. Soc. Newspaper Editors, Newcomen Soc., Sigma Delta Chi (pres. Ala. profl. chpt. 1963). Episcopalian. Elk, Kiwanian. Author articles on newspaper problems. Home: 2717 Highland Av North Birmingham AL 35205 Office: 2200 4th Av North Birmingham AL 35205

BLOOMER, MILLARD J., Jr., lawyer; b. N.Y.C., June 10, 1899; s. Millard J. and Nellie Adams (Crist) B.; A.B., Columbia, 1920, LL.B., 1923; m. Patricia Foss, Sept. 12, 1962; 1 son, George L. Admitted to N.Y. bar, 1924, since practiced in N.Y.C.; asso. Cravath, Swaine & Moore, 1923-40; mem. firm Rand, French & Carpenter, 1940, Bloomer & Jacobi, 1941, Wickes, Riddell, Bloomer, Jacobi & McGuire, 1941—. Dir. Res. Bank of Peru, Caja de Depositos y Consignaciones Peru. Chmn. Columbia Class of 1920 Reunion Com., 1945-70, chmn. Columbia Law Sch. Fund Class of 1923, 1957-65, mem. Columbia Coll. Council, 1959-63, chmn., 1962-63, exec. com., 1960-62, chmn. com. on budget, 1960-62, chmn. nominating com., 1960-61; 1st v.p., bd. dirs., mem. exec. com. Met. Opera Guild; v.p., mem. exec. com. Masterpieces of Art Exhibit, N.Y. Worlds Fair, 1939-40; bd. dirs. Met. Opera Assn., YMCA Greater N.Y.; bd. mgrs. YMCA McBurney Br. Recipient Columbia Alumni Fedn. Alumni medal, 1961. Mem. Am., N.Y. State bar assns., Assn. Bar City N.Y., N.Y. County Lawyers Assn., Am. Judicature Soc., Acad. Polit. Sci. (life), Municipal Art Soc. N.Y., France-Am. Soc., John Jay Assos., Sr. Soc. Sachems, Kent Moot Ct., Soc. Older Grads., Columbia U. Club Found., Columbia Assos., Down Town Assn., Sigma Sci. Clubs: Wall Street (N.Y.C.); Garden City (L.I.) Golf; The Creek (Locust Valley, L.I.); Club de Golf (Sotogrande, Spain). Extensive travel in Europe and S.Am.; mem. Am. Olympic Fencing Team, 1920. Home: 825 Fifth Av New York City NY 10021 and Tejas Verdes Alvarado 10 Sotogrande Cadiz Spain Office: 59 Maiden Lane New York City NY 10038

BLOOMER, ROBERT OLIVER, educator, geologist; b. N.Y.C., May 3, 1912; s. Alfred Thomas and Marie Argel (Heffermann) B.; B.S., U. Va., 1937, M.S., 1938; Ph.D., U. N.C., 1941; m. Vera Lillian Daniel, Sept. 6, 1938; children—Alfred Travers, Lilliam Marie, Daniel R. Instr. geology U. N.C., 1939-41, U. Va., 1941-44; geologist Va. Geol. Survey, 1939-51; asst. prof. geology St. Lawrence U., Canton, N.Y., 1944-45, head dept., prof. geology, 1947—, James Henry Chapin prof. geology and mineralogy, 1953—; asst. prof. geology Syracuse U., 1945-47; research fellow Harvard, 1947-48. Fellow Geol. Soc. Am., NRC; mem. Am. Geophys. Union, A.A.A.S., Geochem. Soc., Va., N.Y. Acads. sci., Soc. Econ. Geologists, Sigma Xi, Sigma Gamma Epsilon. Episcopalian. Mason, Rotarian. Author: Laboratory Manual for Elementary Physical Geology (pamphlet), 1954; also several articles various periodicals. Home: Canton NY 13617

BLOOMFIELD, ARTHUR IRVING, educator; b. Montreal, Can., Oct. 2, 1914; s. Samuel and Hanna (Brown) B.; B.A., McGill U., 1935, M.A., 1936; Ph.D., U. Chgo., 1942. Came to U.S., 1936, naturalized, 1945. Economist, Fed. Res. Bank of N.Y., 1942- 58, sr. economist, 1953-58; prof. econs. U. Pa., 1958—; cons. govt. agys. and commns., adviser to fgn. govts., 1945-71; cons. Agy. Internat. Devel., 1966-68, U.S. State Dept., 1970-71; vis. prof. econs. Johns Hopkins, 1961, Princeton, 1963, City U. N.Y., 1965. Fellow Social Sci. Research Council, 1939-40, Rockefeller Found., 1957- 58; Ford Foundation Faculty Research fellow, 1962-63. Mem. Am. Econ. Assn., Royal Econ. Soc. Author: Capital Imports and the American Balance of Payments, 1934-39, 1950; Banking Reform in South Korea, 1951; Speculative and Flight Movements of Capital in Postwar International Finance, 1954; Monetary Policy under the International Gold Standard, 1880-1914, 1959; Short-Term Capital Movements under the Pre-1914 Gold Standard, 1963. Also articles, contbns. to symposia. Home: Rittenhouse Claridge Philadelphia PA 19103

BLOOMFIELD, COLEMAN, ins. co. exec.; b. Winnipeg, Man., Can., July 2, 1926; s. Samuel and Bessie (Staniloff) B.; B.Commerce, U. Man., 1948; m. Shirley Rosenbaum, Nov. 4, 1948; children—Catherine, Laura, Leon, Diane, Richard. Came to U.S., 1952, naturalized, 1958. With Commonwealth Life Ins. Co., Louisville 1948-51; actuary, sr. v.p. Minn. Mut. Life Ins. Co., St. Paul, 1952-70, exec. v.p., 1970-71, pres., chief exec. officer, 1971—. Mem. St. Paul Arts and Scis. Com., 1963—. Bd. dirs. St. Paul Health and Welfare Planning Council. Fellow Soc. Actuaries; mem. St. Paul C. of C. (dir.), Am. Mgmt. Assn., Am. Life Conv., Life Ins. Assn., Group Ins. Com. Home: 1748 Hampshire Ct St Paul MN 55116 Office: Victory Sq St Paul MN 55101

BLOOMFIELD, LINCOLN P., educator; b. Boston, July 7, 1920; S.B., Harvard, 1941, M. Pub. Adminstrn., 1952, Ph.D., 1956; m. Irirangi Pamela Coates, 1947; children—Pamela, Lincoln, Diana. Various positions Dept. State, Washington, 1946-57, spl. asst. to Asst. Sec. State, 1952-57; dir. UN Project, Center for Internat. Studies, Mass. Inst. Tech., Cambridge, 1957-60, dir. Arms Control Project, numerous other research projects, 1960—. Mem. Presdl. Commn. on 25th Anniversary of UN, 1970-71; co-chmn. Joint Harvard-Mass. Inst. Tech. Faculty Arms Control Seminar; lectr. fgn. affairs and related topics, Eng., USSR, Rumania, Yugoslavia, Austria, Australia, New Zealand; vis. prof. Inst. Grad. Internat. Studies, Geneva, Switzerland; lectr. Nat. War Coll., Army War Coll., Navy War Coll., Canadian Def. Coll.; cons. Dept. State, U.S. Arms Control and Disarmement Agy., Ford. Found., fgn. govts. and pvt. industry. Bd. dirs. World Affairs Council of Boston. Served to lt. USNR, 1942-46. Recipient Chase prize Harvard, 1956; Littauer fellow, 1952, Rockefeller fellow, 1954. Mem. Am. Polit. Sci. Assn., Council on Fgn. Relations, Hudson Inst., Inst. Strategic Studies (London), UN Assn. (bd. dirs.). Author: Evolution or Revolution? The U.N. and The Problem of Peaceful Territorial Change, 1957; The United Nations and U.S. Foreign Policy: A New Look at the National Interest, rev. edit. 1967; Krushchev and the Arms Race, 1966; Outer Space: Prospects for Man and Society, rev. edit. 1968; Controlling Small Wars: A Strategy for the 1970's, 1969; co-author, editor: International Military Forces, 1964. Bd. editors Internat. Orgn. Contbr. numerous articles and monographs for profl. jours. Research in devel. of conflict data computer system. Home: 37 Beach St Cohasset MA 02025 Office: 30 Wadsworth St Cambridge MA 02139

BLOOMFIELD, MIKE B., musician; b. Chgo., July 28, 1943; s. Harold and Dorothy (Eller) B.; m. Susan Jay Smith, Sept. 4, 1962. Formerly lead guitarist with Paul Butterfield Blues Band; now leader own group The Electric Flag; performed 1st annual Monteray Pop Music Festival. Address: 404 Wellsley St Mill Valley CA 94941

BLOOMFIELD, MORTON WILFRED, educator; b. Montreal, Can., May 19, 1913; s. Samuel and Hanna Mai (Brown) B.; B.A., McGill U., 1934, M.A., 1935; grad. study. U. London, Eng., 1935-36; Ph.D., U. Wis., 1938; A.M., Harvard, 1961; m. Caroline Lichtenberg, Mar. 16, 1952; children—Micah Warren, Hanna, Samuel. Came to U.S., 1936, naturalized, 1943. Faculty McGill U., 1934-35, U. Wis., 1938-39, U. Akron, 1939-46; asst. prof. English, Ohio State U., 1946-51, asso. prof., 1951-54, prof., English, Harvard, 1961—, chmn. dept. English, 1968—; Henry W. and Albert A. Berg prof. English and Am. Lit., Washington Sq. Coll., N.Y.U., 1955-56. Spl. civilian cons. Sec. War, 1945-46. Trustee Center for Applied Linguistics, 1966-68. Served with AUS, 1942-45. Decorated Bronze Star medal. Moyse fellow, 1935-36, Guggenheim fellow, 1949-50, 64-65; Elizabeth Clay Howald fellow, 1953- 54; hon. research asso. U. Coll., U. London, 1953-54; Am. Council Learned Socs. grantee, 1958-59, fellow, 1964-65; fellow Center for Advanced Study in Behavorial Scis., Stanford. 1967-68. Fellow Mediaeval Acad. Am. (Haskins medal 1964); mem. Modern Lang. Assn. Am. (exec. com. 1966-69),

Renaissance Soc. Am., Am. Dialect Soc., Canadian Linguistic Assn., Nat. Council Tchrs. English, Dante Soc. Am. (mem. council 1971—), Internat. Assn. U. Profs. English (cons. com.), Modern Humanities Research Assn., Soc. Internationale pour l'etude de la Philosophie Medieval, Am. Acad. Arts and Scis. (councilor 1969—), Linguistic Soc. Am., Phi Beta Kappa (hon.). Author: the Seven Deadly Sins, An Introduction to the History of a Religious Concept, 1952; "Piers Plowman" as a Fourteenth-Century Apocalypse, 1962; (with Leonard Newmark) A Linguistic Introduction to the History of English, 1963; Essays and Explorations, Studies in Language and Literature, 1970; also articles. Editor: (with R.C. Elliott) Ten plays, 1951, rev. as Great Plays: Sophocles to Brecht, 1965; (with E. Robbins) Form and Idea, 1953, rev. edit. 1961; Editorial adv. bd. Funk & Wagnalls New Coll. Standard Dictionary; editorial bd. Annuale Medieval. Duquesne U., Manuscripta, Chaucer Rev., New Literary History; editorial adv. bd. Language and Style. Home: 13 Kirkland Pl Cambridge MA ☆

BLOOMFIELD, RICHARD JOSEPH, fgn. service officer; b. Conn., 1927; s. John J. and Alice (Boland) B.; B.S., Georgetown U., 1950; M.P.A., Harvard, 1960; m. Jean MacDonald Duvall (dec.); 5 children; m. Patricia A. Koepfle Schiller, July 29, 1967. Joined U.S. Fgn. Service, 1952; assigned La Paz, Bolivia, Salzburg, Austria, Monterrey, Mexico, Montevideo, Uruguay, assigned State Dept., 1962-68, econ. counselor, asso. AID dir., Rio de Janeiro, Brazil, 1968—. Served with USCGR, 1945-46, USAF, 1950-51. Office: Am Embassy Rio de Janeiro, Brazil.

BLOOMGARDEN, KERMIT, theatrical producer; b. Bklyn., Dec. 15, 1904; s. Zemad and Annie (Groden) B.; B.C.S., N.Y. U., 1926; m. Kinda Lee, 1939 (dec. Aug. 1942); m. 2d, Virginia Kaye. Sept. 29, 1943 (div. Jan. 1965); children—David, John. Practice as certified pub. accountant, 1922-33; gen. mgr. Arthur Beckhardt, theatrical producer, 1933-34, Herman Shumlin, 1935-45; theatrical producer, 1945-; plays prod. include Deep Are the Roots, Woman Bites Dog, Command Decision, Death of a Salesman (Pulitzer prize, Tony award, N.Y. Critics Circle award), The Crucible, (Tony award), Legend of Sarah, View from the Bridge, Diary of Anne Frank (Pulitzer prize, N.Y. Critics Circle award, Tony award), The Lark, Most Happy Fella (N.Y. Critics award), Autumn Garden, Another Part of the Forest, Look Homeward, Angel (Pulitzer prize, N.Y. Critics Circle award 1958), The Music Man (Tony award, N.Y. Critics Circle award 1958), The Gang's All Here, The Fighting Cock, Toys in the Attic (New York Critics Circle Award 1960), Anyone Can Whistle, The Playroom, Ilya Darling. Mgr., Stage Door Canteen. Mem. League N.Y. Theatres (dir.), Council Living Theatre (dir.), Am. Theatre Wing (dir.). Office: 1545 Broadway New York City, NY 10036.

BLOOMINGDALE, ALFRED S., corporation exec.; b. N.Y.C., Apr. 15, 1916; s. Hiram C. and Rosalind (Schiffer) B.; grad. Brown U. 1938; m. Betty Lee Newling, Sept. 14, 1946; children—Lee Geoffrey, Elisabeth Lee, Robert Russell. Asst. mdse. mgr. Bloomingdale Brothers, N.Y.C., 1938; Broadway and Hollywood producer, 1939-49; v.p. Diners' Club, 1950-55, pres., 1955—, chmn. bd., dir. 1964-70; chmn. bd., dir. Internat. Flotels, Inc., 1968—, Aerooceanic Corp., 1970—, (all Los Angeles); dir. Lyman G. Realty Co., B. Bros., Realty Co., Mil. Purchase Systems (all N.Y.C.), Diners Club Asia, Diners Club France, Paris, Henry Engring., Santa Ana, Cal. (N.Y.C.), Sheraton Mediterranean, Ltd. Trustee emeritus Brown U.; mem. bd. regents Marymount Coll., St. John's Hosp. Decorated knight comdr. of St. Gregory. Mem. Acad. Motion Picture Arts and Scis., Westminster Alumni Assn. (exec. com.), Delta Kappa Epsilon. Clubs: Lambs (N.Y.C.); Brown University (Los Angeles). Home: 131 Delfern Dr Los Angeles CA 90024 Office: Gateway West Century City Los Angeles CA 90067

BLOOMQUIST, FRANCIS EDWARD, paint co. exec.; b. Moline, Ill., June 16, 1909; s. Edward Robert and Frances (Timberlake) B.; student Augustana Coll., 1927; B.S., U. Ill., 1931; m. Charlotte Ann Jones, Nov. 30, 1932; 1 adopted son, James Joseph. Staff accountant Ernst & Ernst, C.P.A.'s, Indpls., 1932; staff accountant Horwath & Horwath, C.P.A.'s, Chgo., 1933-36; chief of staff McGladrey, Hansen, Dunn & Co., C.P.A.'s, Cedar Rapids, Ia., 1936-41; field auditor War Dept., Ill. and Ia. Ordnance Plant, Carbondale, Ill., 1941-43; with Sherwin-Williams Co., Cleve., 1946—, comptroller, 1964-70, exec. comptroller, 1970—; vice chmn. bd., dir. Homewood Savs. & Loan Assn. (Ill.). Served with AUS, 1943-46. C.P.A., Ia. Mem. Am. Inst. C.P.A.'s, Ohio Soc. C.P.A.'s. Office: 101 Prospect Av NW Cleveland OH 44101

BLOOMQUIST, HOWARD RICHARD, mgmt. cons.; b. Mpls., Sept. 16, 1918; s. Richard P. and Ruth M. (Holmgren) B.; student U. Minn., 1937-40; grad. Advanced Mgmt. Program, Harvard, 1958; m. Ingrid M. Brostrom, Feb. 14, 1941; children—Dennis, Diane, Laurel. Asst. advt. mgr. Pillsbury Mills, Inc., 1941-46; advt. mgr. Toni div. Gillette Co., 1946-49; gen. mgr. Lever Bros. Co., 1949- 53; with Gen. Foods Corp., 1953-68, gen mgr., 1962-63, v.p., 1963-67, group v.p., 1967-68; dir., sr. partner McKinsey & Co., 1969—. Trustee Greenwich Acad. Mem. Am. Mgmt. Assn., Assn. Nat. Advertisers. Mem. Community Ch. (vice chmn. bd. trustees). Clubs: Stanwich (Greenwich, Conn.); Pinnacle, Harvard Business School (N.Y.C.). Home: Round Hill Rd Greenwich CT 06830 Office: 250 North St White Plains NY 10605

BLOSL, THOMAS LOUIS, advt. exec.; b. Seattle, May 22, 1934; s. Otto L. and Clara J. (Pederson) B.; B.A., U. Wash., 1956; m. Phyllis M. Zilmer, Mar. 16, 1956; children—Douglas R., Jamine M. Asst. account exec. Botsford-Constantine & Gardner, Seattle, 1956-58; sales promotion mgr. KIRO AM/FM/TV, Seattle, 1958-59; dir. radio-tv, media dir. Botsford Constantine & McCarty, Seattle, 1960-64, account exec., 1965-67; account supr. Botsford, Ketchum, San Francisco, 1968-70, exec. v.p., mgmt. supr., 1970—, also dir.; dir. Botsford-Ketchum Internat.; instr. U. Wash., 1959-60. Mem. Acad. TV Arts and Scis. (charter gov. Seattle chpt.), Am. Marketing Assn., U. Wash. Alumni Assn. Alpha Delta Sigma. Club: Bankers (San Francisco). Home: 1056 Sanders Dr Morage CA 94556 Office: 114 Sansome St San Francisco CA 94104

BLOSS, MEREDITH, librarian; b. Cressey, Mich., Dec. 17, 1908; s. George Henry and Gracia (Butler) B.; A.B., Oberlin Coll., 1932; B.S. in L.S., Columbia, 1940; m. Elizabeth Maureen Williams, June 17, 1955; 1 son, William Meredith. Asst. librarian Hartford (Conn.) Pub. Library, 1940-43; librarian Adriance Meml. Library, Poughkeepsie, N.Y., 1946-48; asst. librarian Pub. Library Youngstown and Mahoning County (O.), 1948-52; asst. city librarian Milw. Pub. Library, 1952-59; city librarian New Haven (Conn.) Free Pub. Library, 1959—. Bd. dirs. James Blackstone Meml. Library, Branford, Conn. Served with USAAF, 1943-45; as 1st lt. AUS, 1945-46. Mem. Am., Conn. (pres. 1966-67) library assns. Kiwanian (pres. New Haven 1964). Clubs: Graduate of New Haven (Connecticut); Adirondack Mountain. Editor Conn. Libraries. Home: 65 Beckett Av Short Beach CT 06405 Office: 133 Elm St New Haven CT 06510

BLOSS, MERRILENE ESTHER, educator; b. Blossvale, N.Y., Feb. 17, 1903; d. Charles Herbert and Mary (Forward) Bloss; A.B., Cornell U., 1923; M.A., Columbia. 1932; Ph.D., 1938. Chmn. Social studies Baldwin (L.I.) High Sch., 1927-45; asso. prof. sociology Tex. Women's U., Denton, 1945-46; asst. prof. Hofstra Coll., Hempstead, L.I., 1946-47, Adelphi Coll., Garden City, L.I., 1947- 53; prof. sociology, chmn. dept. sociology and anthropology Gettysburg (Pa.) Coll., 1953-68. Mem. Am., Eastern sociol. assns., Am. Assn. U. Profs. Author: Labor Legislation in Czechoslovakia, 1938. Home: 339 E Lincoln Av Gettysburg, PA 17325.

BLOSSER, ROBERT DANIELS, newspaper co. exec.; b. Versailles, Mo., Nov. 21, 1914; s. John and Anna (Daniels) B.; grad. Jefferson City (Mo.) Sr. High Sch., 1933; m. Marjorie Ferguson, May 22, 1948; children—John, Jim, Martha Jo. With News Tribune Co., Jefferson City, 1932—, pres., 1966—; v.p., gen. mgr. Jefferson TV Co., 1955-66. Served with AUS, 1942-45. Decorated Bronze Star. Mem. Mo. Asso. Dailies (pres.), Mo. Press Assn. (v.p.). Mem. Christian Ch. Home: 1329 Moreland St Jefferson City MO 65101 Office: 210 Monroe St Jefferson City MO 65101

BLOSSMAN, ALFRED RHODY, bank exec.; b. Madisonville, La., Oct. 21, 1931; s. Alfred Rhody and Mabel (Perrin) B.; A.B. in Gen. Bus., La. State U., 1955; m. Royanne Elaine Hurd, Dec. 28, 1957; children—Alfred Rhody III, Roy Edward, Gary Bennett, Christopher Hurd, David Quintin, John Eric. Pres., Comml. Capital Systems, Inc.; dir. Blossman Investment Corp., WARB, Inc., Comml. Mortgage Corp., Comml. Capital, Inc., Comml. Bank and Trust Co., WRKN, Inc.; chmn. bd. Parish Nat. Bank, Bogalusa, La. Pres. bd. dirs. River Forest Acad. Mem. Phi Delta Theta. Democrat. Roman Catholic. Clubs: Southern Yacht; Pontchartrain Yacht (past commodore); Covington Country (dir., gov.) Home: 406 Country Club Dr Covington LA 70433 Office: Suite 2 Bogue Falaya Plaza Covington LA 70433

BLOSSOM, SUMNER NEWTON, former editor and publisher; b. Kansas City, Mo.; s. Reubin Sumner and Elizabeth Orr (Hay) B.; ed. public schs. and U. of Mo.; m. Edna A. Stroh, Feb. 4, 1920; children—Sumner N. (dec.), Robert S., Elizabeth O. (Mrs. Robert R. Metz). With Kansas City Star, 1912-14; Asso. Press, Topeka, Kansas City, Chgo., and other Western and Midwestern Cities, 1914-17; Corp. Pershing Expedition in Mexico, 1916; with N.Y. Daily News, 1919-22; editor Popular Sci. Monthly. 1922-29; editor The Am. mag., 1929-56; dir. Crowell-Collier & Macmillan, Inc., 1944-69, v.p. 1956, exec. v.p., 1957, pres., 1957-61, vice chmn., 1961-69. Mem. internat. supreme council of the Order of DeMolay; exec. com. SAME. Served at lt. USNRF, 1917-19. Adviser various times, a number of govt. agys. Mem. Delta Upsilon. Mason. Club: Dutch Treat. Home: Babylon Sands Point NY 12123

BLOT, ROBERT MARIE CAMILLE, banker; b. Limoges, France, Oct. 11, 1914; s. Joseph and Marie-Therese (Brissaud) B.; ed. Faculty of law and letters U. Paris; m. Genevieve de Bonnefoy des Aulnais, Aug. 3, 1945; children—Marie-Odile, Marie-Chantal, Dominique, Armelle, Nicolas, Emmanuel, Nathalie. Dep. gov. Credit Foncier de France, Paris. Decorated officer Legion of Honor. Office: 19 Rue des Capucines Paris France*

BLOTNER, NORMAN DAVID, retail clothing chain exec.; b. Boston, Dec. 6, 1918; s. Leon and Sarah (Weinstein) B.; A.B., Harvard, 1940, J.D., 1947; m. Helen Whitman, Aug. 13, 1954; 1 son, James B. McClain III. Admitted to N.Y. bar, 1948; atty. Spiro, Felstiner, Prager & Treeger, N.Y.C., 1947-52; asst. to pres. Lane Bryant, Inc., N.Y.C., 1952-66, v.p. real estate, 1965—, asst. corporate sec., 1960-68, corp. sec., dir., 1968—. Served from ensign to lt. comdr., USNR, 1942-46. Home: 140 Overlook Rd New Rochelle NY 10804 Office: 1501 Broadway New York City NY 10036

BLOUGH, CARMAN GEORGE, accountant; b. Johnstown, Pa., Nov. 11, 1895; s. Silas S. and Mary Alice (Wertz) B.; A.B., Manchester Coll., 1917, LL.D., 1944; M.A., U. Wis., 1922; student Harvard, 1932-33; m. Lillie Katherine Flory, Aug. 17, 1922; 1 dau., Elizabeth Jean (Mrs. John W. Martin, Jr.). Tchr., 1917-22; with Wis. Tax Commn., 1922-27; dir. budget State of Wis., 1927-29; prof. U. N.D., 1929-33, Armour Inst. Tech., 1933-34; chief acct. SEC, 1934-38; partner Arthur Andersen & Co. Chicago, 1938-42; dir. procurement policy div. WPB; mem. price adjustment bds., 1942-44; mem. U.S. War Contracts Price Adjustment Bd., cons. on renegotiation and termination WPB, 1944-45; dir. research Am. Inst. C.P.A.'s, 1944-61, research cons., 1961-63; adj. prof. accounting Columbia 1947-61; accounting cons., 1961—; vis. prof. accounting U. Fla., winters 1961-65; Distinguished vis. prof. Pa. State U., 1963; vis. lectr. U. Va., 1964; vis. prof. accounting U. Ill., Champaign, 1965-66; ednl. dir. Internat. Accountants Soc., 1964-71; vis. scholar Piedmont U. Center N.C., 1966; Regents lectr. U. Cal. at Berkeley, 1967. Recipient award Alpha Kappa Psi; mem. Accounting Hall of Fame, Ohio State U.; honored Carmen G. Blough chair of accounting U. Va., 1969. C.P.A. Wis., N.D., N.Y., Va. Mem. Am. Inst. C.P.A.'s (Distinguished Service award 1953). Am. Accounting Assn. (past pres.), Delta Sigma Pi, Beta Gamma Sigma, Beta Alpha Psi. Republican. Mem. Ch. of Brethren. Clubs: Harvard (N.Y.C.); University (Washington); Spotswood Country, Rotary (Harrisonburg, Va.). Author: Practical Applications of Accounting Standards, 1957. Contbr. articles of tech. accounting and bus. jours. Home: Penn Laird VA 22846 Office: Nat Bank Bldg Harrisonburg VA

BLOUGH, DONALD S., educator; b. Madison, Wis., Sept. 13, 1929; s. Roy and Marie (Goshorn) B.; B.A., Swarthmore Coll., 1951; M.A., Harvard U., 1954, Ph.D., 1955; m. Patricia Irene McBride, June 19, 1954; children—Douglas Earle, Stephen Richard, Kathryn Marie. Psychologist, Nat. Inst. Mental Health, Bethesda, Md., 1954-58; asst. prof. Brown U., 1958-61, asso. prof., 1961-66, prof., 1966—. Mem. psychobiology rev. panel NSF, 1963-67; mem. small grants com. Nat. Inst. Mental Health, 1968—. Served with USPHS, 1954-58. Mem. Am., Eastern, R.I. psychol. assns., Psychonomic Soc., Soc. Exptl. Psychologists, Am. Acad. Arts and Sci., A.A.A.S. Author (with Patricia M. Blough) Experiments in Psychology, 1964. Home: 169 Brown St Providence RI 20906

BLOUGH, GLENN ORLANDO, author, educator; b. Edmore, Mich., Sept. 5, 1907; s. Levi and Catherine (Thomas) B.; student Central Mich. Coll. Edn., 1922-24, LL.D., 1950; B.A., U. Mich., 1929, M.A., 1932; postgrad. Columbia, summers 1935-37, U. Chgo., 1938. Tchr. secondary schs., Mich., 1925-27, 29-31; instr. State Tchrs. Coll., Ypsilanti, Mich., 1932-36; asst. prof. sci. edn. State Tchrs. Coll., Greeley, Colo., 1937-38; instr. U. Chgo., 1939-42; specialist sci. U.S. Office Edn., Dept. Health, Edn. and Welfare, Washington, 1947-55; prof. edn. U. Md., 1956—. Recipient Distinguished Service to Sci. Edn. citation Nat. Sci. Tchrs. Assn., 1971; Spl. Recognition for contbn. to sci. edn. Council Elementary Sci. Internat., 1971. Served as lt. comdr. USNR, World War II. Mem. N.E.A., Assn. Supervision Curriculum Devel., Assn. Childhood Edn., Am. Assn. U. Profs., Nat. Council Elementary Sci. (pres. 1947), Nat. Sci. Tchrs. Assn. (pres. 1957-58, adviser ednl. policies commn.), Elementary Prins.' Assn., Phi Delta Kappa, Phi Sigma. Author: Monkey With A Nation, 1948; Beno The Riverburg Mayor, 1949; The Tree on the Road to Turntown, 1953; Jr. Lit. Guild selections: Not Only for Ducks, The Story of Rain, 1954; Lookout for the Forest, 1955; After the Sun Goes Down, 1956; Who Lives in This House, 1957; When You Go to the Zoo, 1957; Young Peoples Book of Science, 1958; Soon After September, 1959; Discovering Dinosaurs, 1959; Who Lives in This Meadow?, 1960; Christmas Trees and How They Grow, 1961; Who Lives at the Seashore, 1962; Bird Watchers and Bird Feeders, 1963; Discovering Plants, 1966; Discovering Insects, 1967; also textbooks. Contbr. numerous articles sci., popular publs. Home: 2820 Ellicott St NW Washington DC 20008 Office: U Md College Park MD 20740

BLOUGH, ROGER M., lawyer, steel co. exec.; b. Riverside, Pa., Jan. 19, 1904; s. Christian E. and Viola (Hoffman) B.; A.B., Susquehanna U., 1925, LL.D., 1953; LL.B., Yale, 1931; LL.D. Baylor U., 1955, Washington and Jefferson Coll., 1956, Rollins Coll., 1958, Trinity Coll., 1958, Syracuse U., 1959, Roanoke Coll., Gettysburg Coll., Allegheny Coll., 1960, Wartburg Coll., 1963, Washington U., 1966, Dickinson Coll. Law, 1967; Akron U., 1970; D.C.S., U. Pitts., 1957; D.C.L., U. of South, 1958, Bucknell U., 1961; H.H.D., Pace Coll., 1964, Wagner Coll., 1965; m. Helen Martha Decker, June 13, 1928; children—Jane (Mrs. French), Judith Ann (Mrs. Wentz). Admitted to bar, N.Y., Pa. cts., U.S. Supreme Ct. bar; practiced law with White & Case, N.Y.C., 1931-42, partner, 1969—; gen. solicitor U.S. Steel Corp. of Del., 1942-51; exec. v.p. law, sec. U.S. Steel Corp., 1951, vice chmn., dir., mem. finance com., 1952, gen. counsel, 1953-55, chmn. bd. dirs., chief exec. officer, 1955-69, now dir., mem. exec. com., finance com.; dir. Commonwealth Fund. Fellow Pierpont Morgan Library; asso. fellow Timothy Dwight Coll. of Yale; trustee U.S. Steel Found., 1955, Grand Central Art Galleries; trustee, chmn. finance com. Hawley Library Assn.; trustee, mem. exec. com. Internat. C. of C.; trustee, lifetime councilor Conf. Bd.; chmn. bd. dirs. Council for Financial Aid to Edn.; bd. dirs., founding mem. Bus. Com. for Arts; chmn. emeritus nat. adv. bd. Nat. Football Found. and Hall of Fame. Fellow Inst. Jud. Adminstrn. (pres.); mem. Met. Mus. Art (life), Council Fgn. Relations, Pa. Soc. (past pres., mem. council), Bus. Council (past chmn.), Am. (Found. fellow), N.Y. State, Allegheny County (Pa.) bar assns., Am. Iron and Steel Inst. (hon. v.p.), Yale Law Sch. Assn. (hon. mem. exec. com.), Pilgrims U.S., Acad. Polit. Sci. (life), Met. Opera Assn., Nat. Legal Aid and Defender Assn., Bar Assn. City N.Y., New York County Lawyers Assn., Am. Forestry Assn. (life), Legal Aid Soc., Constrn. Users Anti-Inflation Roundtable (chmn.), Center for Inter-Am. Relations, Com. for Econ. Devel. (hon. trustee), Japan Iron and Steel Fedn. (hon.). Presbyn. (trustee). Clubs: Duquesne (Pitts.); Pine Valley Golf (Clementon, N.J.); Rolling Rock (Ligonier, Pa.); Economic, Grolier, Links, The Board Room, Recess (N.Y.C.); Blind Brook (Portchester, N.Y.); Riverview Quail (Camilla, Ga.); Links Golf (Roslyn, L.I.); Cotton Bay (Eleuthera, Bahamas); Lords Valley Country, Blooming Grove Hunting and Fishing (Hawley); Augusta (Ga.) Nat. Golf; Skytop (Pa.). Home: Blooming Grove Hawley PA 18428 also 580 Park Av New York City NY 10021 Office: 4 Wall St New York City NY 10005

BLOUGH, ROY, economist; b. Pitts., Aug. 21, 1901; s. Silas S. and Mary (Wertz) B.; A.B., Manchester Coll., 1921, LL.D., 1944; A.M., U. Wis., 1922, Ph.D., 1929; L.H.D., Columbia, 1954; m. Marie Goshorn, May 19, 1923; children—Richard, William, Donald. Asst. prof. history and econs. Manchester (Ind.) Coll., 1922-24, asso. prof., 1924-25; dir. tax research U.S. Treasury Dept., 1938- 46, asst. to sec., 1944-46; prof. econs. and polit. sci. U. Chgo., 1946-52 (on leave, 1950-52); mem. Council Econ. Advisers to Pres., 1950-52; mem. Tax Adv. Mission to Turkish Govt., 1949; prin. dir. Dept. Econ. Affairs, UN, 1952-55; prof. internat. bus. Columbia, N.Y.C., 1955-66, S. Sloan Colt prof. banking and internat. finance, 1966-70, S. Sloan Colt prof. emeritus, 1970—. Mem. UN Tax Adv. Mission to Govt. of Peru 1957, 59, UN Adv. Mission to Govt. of Chile, 1959; cons. Com. for Econ. Devel., 1965—. Mem. Am. Econ. Assn. (v.p. 1954), Nat. Tax Assn., Am. Finance Assn., Council on Fgn. Relations, Am. Polit. Sci. Assn., Mem. Ch. of Brethren. Club: Cosmos (Washington). Author: (with others) Facing the Tax Problem, 1937; Federal Taxing Process, 1952; International Business Environment and Adaptation, 1966. Editor: Nat. Tax Journal, 1947-50. Contbr. articles to jours. Home: 450 Riverside Dr New York City NY 10027

BLOUIN, FRANCIS JOSEPH, govt. ofcl.; b. Northbridge, Mass., July 23, 1910; s. Lucien and Agnes (Cournoyer) B.; B.S., U.S. Naval Acad., 1933; grad. Naval War Coll., 1948; m. Rosalie Van Auken, June 12, 1935; children—Gloria (Mrs. K.R. Bailey), Peter. Commd. ensign U.S. Navy, 1933, advanced through grades to vice adm., 1966; served in U.S.S. Cole, 1940, U.S.S. Tuscaloosa, 1941; comdr. destroyers U.S.S. Sterett, 1944, U.S.S. Ingersoll, 1945; exec. officer U.S.S. Manchester, 1946; comdr. Destroyer Div. 12, 1951; mem. staff comdr. in chief Pacific Fleet, 1952; comdr. U.S.S. McKinley, 1958-59, Amphibious Force, 6th Fleet, 1959, Amphibious Force 7th Fleet, Far East, 1962-63; aide to Fleet Adm. Leahy, then chief staff to comdr. in chief Armed Forces U.S., 1947-48; mem. working group for Geneva Conf. Summit Meeting and Fgn. Ministers Meeting, 1955; mem. Joint Staff, also staff chmn. Joint Chiefs Staff, 1954-57; sec. to Joint Chiefs Staff, 1960-62; dir. Far East region Office Asst. Sec. Def. Internat. Security Affairs, 1963-66; comdr. Amphibious Force, U.S. Pacific Fleet, 1966-68; dep. chief naval operations, 1968-71, ret., 1971; mem. Bd. Nat. Estimates, CIA, 1971—. Decorated D.S.M.; Silver Star, Legion of Merit, Bronze Star. Club: Chevy Chase. Home: 3900A Watson Pl Washington DC 20016 Office: CIA McLean VA

BLOUKE, PIERRE, architect; b. Chgo., May 27, 1894 s. Milton Baker and Ola Louise (Matthews) B.; B.S., Mass. Inst. Tech., 1917; affiliated fellow Am. Acad. in Rome; m. Jessie M. Scott, Nov. 11, 1939; children—Morley Matthews, Peter Scott, Susan, Miton Baker II, Martha. Practiced in Chicago, 1920—; cons. architect Greeley & Hansen, engrs. Architect adviser HOLC, Washington, D.C., 1934-51. Trustee Francis W. Parker School. Served as 2d lt. Air Service, United States Army, World War. Mem. Nat. Panel of Arbitrators, Am. Arbitration Assn.; mem. Mil. Order World Wars, Am. Legion. Former pres. Chicago Architectural Exhibition League. Fellow A.I.A. (past director Chgo. Chpt.); mem. Chgo. Engrs. Club, Chgo. Archtl. Club (pres. 1925), Art Inst. Chgo. (life), Am. Aberdeen Angus Assn. (life), Old Town Triangle Assn. (past pres.), Lincoln Park Conservation Assn. (v.p.), Ala. Cattleman's Assn., Delta Tau Delta. Clubs: Boswell (pres.), Arts (Chicago); Cosmos (Washington); Kiwanis (pres. Chatoem). Home: Box 411 Chatom, AL 36518.

BLOUNT, ROBERT ESTES, ret. army officer, univ. dean; b. Bassfield, Miss., July 21, 1908; s. Estes Nathan and Mary Leola (Hathorn) B.; B.S., Millsaps Coll., 1928; M.D., Tulane U., 1932; postgrad. Med. Field Service Sch., 1934-35, Tropical Med. Sch. Walter Reed Army Hosp., 1945; m. Alice Boyd Ridgway, Oct. 17, 1930; children—Robert Estes, Richard B., Jane Elizabeth (Mrs. Warren E. Traub, Jr.). Intern New Orleans Marine Hosp., 1932-33; commd. 1st lt., M.C., U.S. Army, 1932, advanced through grades to maj. gen., 1966; preceptor internal medicine, Ft. Slocum, N.Y., 1935-38; asst. Vanderbilt Clinic, 1935-38; chief medicine, Ft. Stotsenberg, P.I., 1938- 41; comdr. 129th Gen. Hosp., ETO, World War II; chief dept. medicine Oliver Gen. Hosp., 1946-47, Brooke Gen. Hosp., 1951-55, 59-60; chief profl. services office Surgeon Gen., 1960-62; comdg. gen. Army Med. Research and Devel. Command, 1963-65, William Beaumont Gen. Hosp., 1965- 66, Fitzsimons Gen. Hosp., 1966-68; chief cons. in medicine Far East Command, Tokyo, 1947-50, U.S. Army, Heidelberg, Germany, 1955-58; ret., 1968; prof. medicine Grad. Sch., Baylor U. Sch. Medicine, 1952-55, clin. prof. medicine, 1959-60; clin. prof. medicine Med. Field Service Sch., 1951-55; clin. prof. medicine U. Colo. Med. Sch., 1966-68; prof. medicine, asso. prof. preventive medicine, asst. dean U. Miss. Med. Sch., Jackson, 1968-70, dean Med. Sch., dir. Med. Center, 1970—.

Mem. com. medicine NRC, 1961-65; mem. Nat. Bd. Med. Examiners, 1960-62. Coach army baseball N.Y. Harbor League, also Manila Bay League; chmn. Boy Scouts Am. activities Tokyyo-Yokohama, 1959-50; internist Project Mercury, 1960-64. Decorated Legion of Merit, D.S.M. Diplomate Am. Bd. Internal Medicine. Fellow A.C.P.; mem. Am., Central, Miss. med. assns., Am. Clin. and Climatol. Assn., Assn. Am. Med. Colls., Am. Heart Assn., Am. Rheumatism Assn., Am. Soc. Tropical Medicine and Hygiene, Assn. Mil. Surgeons, Alpha Omega Alpha, Pi Kappa Alpha, Nu Sigma Nu, Omicron Delta Kappa. Home: 241 Ridge Dr Jackson MS 39216

BLOUNT, ROY A., banker; b. Hosford, Fla., Oct. 9, 1913; s. N.C. and Lou Allie (Wylie) B.; student Ind. U., 1960-61; m. Louise Floyd, June 10, 1938; children—Roy A., Susan Louise. Office mgr. Libby, McNeill & Libby, 1934-46; regional mgr. Packard Motor Car Corp., 1946-56; dist. mgr. Ford Motor Co., 1956-58; with Decatur Fed. Savs. & Loan Assn. (Ga.), 1958—, pres., 1960—, also dir. Bd. dirs., Met. Atlanta Rapid Transit Authority, 1965—, chmn., 1971. Trustee Wesley Woods Home, Decatur, 1964—. Mem. U.S. (exec. com.), Ga. (past pres.) savs. and loan leagues, Dekalb County C. of C. (pres. 1963). Methodist (chmn. trustee). Rotarian. Home: 3199 Wynn Dr Avondale Estates GA 30002 Office: 250 E Ponce DeLeon Av Decatur GA 30030

BLOUNT, WILLIAM HOUSTON, marketing exec.; b. Union Springs, Ala., Jan. 3, 1922; s. Winton Malcolm and Clara Belle (Chalker) B.; student U. Ala., 1939-42; grad. Advanced Mgmt. Program, Harvard, 1959; m. Mary Frances Dean, Aug. 5, 1945; children—Barbara Dean, William Houston, Beverly, David, Frances. Partner, Blount Bros. Corp., Montgomery, Ala., 1946-48, dir., 1946—; pres., dir., Southeastern Sand & Gravel Co., Tallahassee, Ala., 1948-54; v.p. So. Cen-Vi-Ro Pipe Corp., Birmingham, 1954-57; pres. concrete pipe div. Vulcan Materials Co., Birmingham, 1957-59, corp. v.p., dir., 1959- -, also pres. Southeast div., exec. v.p. constrn. and materials group; v.p., dir. Birmingham & Southeastern R. R. Co.; dir., mem. exec. com. Allied Life Ins. Co. Active devel. fund drive Birmingham-So. Coll., 1962; chmn. Birmingham Girl Scout drive, 1963, Birmingham Arthritis drive, 1964. Served as pilot USNR, World War II. Methodist (steward). Clubs: Mountain Brook, Birmingham Country, Downtown, Relay House (Birmingham). Home: 4117 Old Leeds Lane Birmingham AL 35213 Office: 1 Office Park Birmingham AL 35223

BLOUNT, WINTON MALCOLM, postmaster gen.; b. Union Springs, Ala., Feb. 1, 1921; s. Winton Malcolm and Clara B. (Chalker) B.; student U. Ala., 1939-41; L.H.D., Judson Coll., 1967; Dr. Humanities, Huntingdon Coll., 1969; LL.D., Birmingham-So. Coll., 1969; D.C.L., Southwestern U., 1969; D.Sc., U. Ala., 1971; D.Pub. Service, Seattle-Pacific Coll., 1971; m. Mary Katherine Archibald, Sept. 12, 1942; children—Winton Malcolm III, Thomas A., S. Roberts, Katherine, Joseph W. Pres., chmn. bd. Blount Bros. Corp., Montgomery, Ala., 1946-68; chmn. bd. Benjamin F. Shaw Co., Wilmington, Del., 1967-68; postmaster gen., Washington, 1969—. Mem. Pres.'s Domestic Affairs Council Fed. City Council, Cabinet Com. on Constrn., Pres.'s Com. on Vietnam Vet., Pres.'s Com. Employment of Handicapped, Nat. Council Organized Crime, Pres.'s Council Youth Opportunity, Cabinet Com. on Edn., Cabinet sub-com. White House Conf. on Children and Youth, nat. adv. com. Jobs for Vets. Program. Hon. mem. Nat. Council Boy Scouts Am. Chmn. Ala. Citizens for Eisenhower, 1952; Southeastern dir. Nixon-Lodge, 1959-60. Bd. dirs. United Appeal Montgomery; bd. dirs. Montgomery YMCA, also life mem.; trustee So. Research Inst., U. Ala.; bd. visitors Maxwell AFB; mem. adv. council U.S. Army Aviation Mus., Ft. Rucker, Ala. Served with USAAF, 1942-45. Named one of four Outstanding Young Men Ala., 1956; Man of Year, Montgomery, 1961; recipient Ct. Honor award Montgomery Exchange Club, 1969; Nat. Brotherhood award Nat. Conf. Christians and Jews, 1970; Silver Quill award Am. Bus. Press, 1971. Mem. N.A.M. (Golden Knight Mgmt. award Ala. Council 1962), Ala. State Soc. U.S. (nat. pres. 1968), Ala. (pres. 1962-65) chambers commerce, Newcomen Soc. N. Am. Presbyn. (deacon). Rotarian. Home: Route 4 Box 43 Vaughn Rd Montgomery AL 36111 Office: PO Dept Office Postmaster Gen 1200 Pennsylvania Av Washington DC 20260

BLOUSTEIN, EDWARD J., coll. pres.; b. N.Y.C., Jan. 20, 1925; s. Samuel and Celia (Einwohner) B.; B.A., N.Y. U., 1948; B. Phil. (Fulbright Scholar), Wadham Coll., Oxford (Eng.) U., 1950; Ph.D., Cornell U., 1954, J.D., 1959; m. Ruth Ellen Steinman, Oct. 6, 1951; children—Elise, Lori. Polit. analyst State Dept., 1951-52; instr. logic and philosophy Cornell U., 1954-55; admitted to N.Y. bar, 1959; prof. law N.Y. U. Law Sch., 1961-65; pres. Bennington (Vt.) Coll., 1965-71, Rutgers U., 1971—. Address: 1245 River Rd Piscataway NJ 08854

BLOUT, ELKAN ROGERS, biol. chemist; b. N.Y.C., July 2, 1919; s. Eugene and Lillian B.; grad. Phillips Exeter Acad., 1935; B.A., Princeton, 1939; Ph.D., Columbia, 1942; A.M. (hon.), Harvard, 1962; m. Joan E. Dreyfus, Aug. 27, 1939; children—James E., Susan L., William L. With Polaroid Corp., Cambridge, Mass., 1943-62, successively research chemist, asso. dir. research, 1943-58, v.p., gen. mgr. research, 1958-62; asso. Harvard, 1950-52, 57—, prof. biol. chemistry, 1962-64, Edward S. Harkness prof. biol. chemistry, 1964—, head dept. biol. chemistry, 1965-69; research asso. Childrens Med. Center, Boston, 1950-52, cons. chemistry, 1957—. Mem. sci. adv. com. Blood Research Inst., Inc., also Mass. Gen. Hosp. Mem. vis. com. dept. chemistry Carnegie-Mellon U.; bd. visitors Faculty Health Scis., State U. N.Y. Buffalo Fellow NRC, Harvard, 1942-43. Fellow A.A.A.S., Am., N.Y. acads. arts and scis., Optical Soc. Am. (past pres. New Eng. sect.); mem. Nat. Acad. Scis., Am. Chem. Soc. (nat. councillor 1958-61), The Chem. Soc., Biophys. Soc. Mem. adv. bd. Jour. Polymer Sci.; editorial bd. Biopolymers; contbr. articles profl. jours. Patantee Sci.; editorial bd. Biopolymers, Am. Chem. Soc. Monograph Series; editorial adv. bd. Macromolecules. Contbr. articles profl. jours. Patentee in field. Home: 111 Fletcher Rd Belmont MA 02178 Office: 25 Shattuck St Boston MA 02115

BLOXOM, ELLIOTT, naval officer; b. Hampton Va., Jan. 17, 1916; s. Ritzhugh Perry and Louisa (Elliott) B.; B.S., Coll. William and Mary, 1937; grad. U.S. Naval Supply Corps Sch., 1947, U.S. Naval War Coll., 1961; m. Margie Allen Hoskins, July 5, 1941; children—Margaret Jemison (Mrs. Charles F. Shultz), Louisa Elliott, Elliott Lawrence. Commd. ensign U.S. Navy, 1941, advanced through grades to rear adm.; line officer Atlantic and Pacific theatres, World War II; assigned U.S.S. Salem, then hdqrs. Navy Dept.; dep. comdr. operations Mil. Traffic Mgmt. and Terminal Service. Decorated numerous area and theatre ribbons. Mem. Nat. Def. Transp. Assn., Pi Kappa Alpa. Home: 4012 N Tazewell St Arlington, VA 22207. Office: Hdqrs MTMTS Hassif Bldg Washington DC 20315

BLOY, FRANCIS ERIC, bishop; b. Birchington, Eng., Dec. 17, 1904; s. Francis Joseph Field and Alice Mary (Pointer) B.; brought to U.S., 1911; A.B., U. Mo., 1925; postgrad. Georgetown U. Sch. of Fgn. Service, 1925-26; B.D., Va. Theol. Sem., 1929; D.D., Occidental Coll. Los Angeles, 1953, Va. Theol. Sem., 1953; D.D., Ch. Div. Sch. Pacific, 1942, S.T.D., 1948; S.T.D., U. So. Cal., 1955; m. Frances Forbes Cox, July 30, 1929. Ordained deacon Episcopal Ch., 1928, priest, 1929; rector All Saints' Ch., Reisterstown, Md., 1929-33; asso. rector St. James'-by-the-Sea, La Jolla, Cal., 1933-35, rector, 1935-37; dean St. Pauls' Cathedral, Los Angeles, 1937-48; conscerated bishop Los Angeles, 1948. Pres. Ch. Fedn. Los Angeles 1946; pres. Univ. Religious Conf., 1956; chmn. bd. trustees Good Samaritan Hosp.; trustee Occidental Coll., Ch. Div. Sch. of the Pacific, Gen. Theol. Sem. Mem. Town Hall. Office: 1220 W 4th St Los Angeles CA 90017

BLUE, GEORGE R., lawyer, state legislator; b. Dec. 10, 1916; B.A., Tulane U. 1937, D.J.S., 1939; m. Elizabeth Lida Beard (div.); children—K.F. II, Leslie R., George R.; m. 2d, Catherine Colquitt Bruce. Admitted to La. bar, 1939; practiced in New Orleans; mem. firm Beard & Blue; notary pub. Parish of Orleans, 1938—; spl. agt. F.B.I., 1940-45; U.S. atty. Eastern Dist. La., 1953-56; mem. firm Beard, Blue, Schmitt & Treen, and predecessor firm, New Orleans, 1956—; pres. Found. Plan, Inc. Republican candidate, 2d Dist. La. for Congress of U.S.; mem. La. Ho. of Rep., 1964—, chmn. standing com. of ins., chmn. Gov.'s spl. com. on automobile ins., vice chmn. exec. com. Mem. adv. com. on rules of criminal procedure U.S. Supreme Ct.; mem. Nixon's Task Force Crime and Adminstrn. Justice Bd. dirs. La. Assn. for Mental Health, 1969—; bd. advisers Salvation Army, 1962—. Served 2d lt. USMCR, 1937-41. lt. (j.g.), USNR, O.N.I., 1949-51. Mem. Am. Judicature Soc., Am., La., New Orleans bar assns., Internat. Assn. Ins. Counsel, Soc. Former Spl. Agts. F.B.I., Inc. (former nat. v.p.), Phi Delta Phi. Clubs: Metairie Country; Southern Yacht. Home: 500 Sena Dr Metairie LA 70005 Office: 833 Howard Av New Orleans LA 70113

BLUEFARB, SAMUEL MITCHELL, physician; b. St. Louis, Oct. 15, 1912; s. Sol and Pauline (Brown) B.; B.S., U. Ill., 1936; M.D., 1937; m. Grace Parsons, Jan. 1, 1944; 1 son, Richard Alan; m. 2d, Leah Rose Vendig Pollock, Jan. 24, 1968; children—Fred, Nancy Pollock. Intern Cook County Hosp., Chgo., 1937-38; resident Bellevue Hosp., N.Y.C., 1939-41; practice medicine specializing in dermatology, 1941—; sr. attending dermatologist, chmn. dept. Cook County Hosp., 1952-58; attending dermatologist VA Research Hosp., 1954—; sr. attending staff Chgo. Wesley Meml. Hosp., Passavant Hosp.; prof., chmn. dept. dermatology Northwestern U. Med. Sch. Diplomate Am. Bd. Dermatology and Syphilology. Fellow Am. Acad. Dermatology and Syphilology (dir. 1969), A.C.P.; mem. A.M.A., Ill. (past pres. dermatol. sect.), Chgo. med. socs., Soc. Investigative Dermatology, Chgo. Dermatol. Soc. (past pres.), Am. Dermatol. Assn. Club: Ravisloe Country. Author books and articles. Home: 910 Lake Shore Dr Chicago IL 60611 Office: 30 N Michigan Av Chicago IL 60602

BLUHDORN, CHARLES G., corp. exec.; b. Vienna, Austria, Sept. 20, 1926; came to U.S., 1942; student Coll. City N.Y., Columbia. Treas., KSB Co., Inc. exporters, N.Y.C., 1946-49; pres. Intamex Devel. Corp., importers, N.Y.C., 1949-56, chmn. bd., dir., mem. exec. com. Gulf & Western Industries, Inc., N.Y.C., 1958—; dir. Paramount Pictures Corp., H.C. Bohack Co., Inc., Ward Foods, Inc. (all N.Y.C.). Trustee Trinity Sch., N.Y.C. Trustee Freedoms Found. at Valley Forge. Served with USAAF, 1945. Office: Gulf & Western Bldg 1 Gulf & Western Plaza New York City NY 10023

BLUHM, HEINZ, educator; b. Halle, Germany, Nov. 23, 1907; s. Fritz and Luise (Henke) B.; B.A., Northwestern Coll., 1928; M.A., U. Wis., 1929, Ph.D., 1932; postgrad. Yale, 1930-31, M.A. (hon.), 1950; m. Helen McClure Berry, Aug. 15, 1938; children—Peter, Louise, Margaret, Christopher. Came to U.S., 1925, naturalized, 1931. Instr. German, U. Wis., 1931-37; instr. German, Yale, 1937-39, asst. prof., 1939-44, asso. prof. 1944-50. prof., 1950-67, chmn. dept. Germanic lang., 1954-63, Leavenworth prof. German lang. and lit., 1957-67; prof. Germanic studies Boston Coll., 1967—, dir. Germanic studies, 1967-68, chmn. dept., 1968—. Vis. prof. German, Dartmouth, 1964, U. Cal. at Berkeley 1968. Decorated Grand Cross of Order of Merit. (Fed. Republic W. Germany). Fellow Pierson Coll., Yale; Guggenheim fellow, 1957, Newberry fellow, 1958-60, sr. Newberry fellow, 1967. Mem. Modern Lang. Assn. Am., Renaissance Soc. Am. Club: Elizabethan. Author: Martin Luther, Creative Translator. 1965; contbr. to Luther for an Ecumenical Age, 1967. Editor: Letters and Diaries of the Goethe Family, 7 vols., 1961—; Newberry Library, Essays in Language and Literature, 1965; Luther's Essays on Christian Culture and Education, 1968. Contbr. articles on German lit. to profl. periodicals. Address: Boston Coll Chestnut Hill MA 02167

BLUM, ALEXANDER HENRY, savs. and loan assn. exec.; b. N.Y.C., June 12, 1904; s. Leo N. and Emma (Tannenbaum) B.; B.A., U. Pa., 1926; J.D., N.Y. U., 1929; m. Esther Feldman, July 10, 1929. Admitted to N.Y. bar, 1931; now sr. partner firm Blum & Ross, Lawrence, N.Y. Dir., chmn. bd. Lawrence-Cedarhurst Fed. Savs. & Loan Assn. Village atty. Inc. Village Hewlett Neck, N.Y.; fire dist. atty. Woodmere (N.Y.), Fire Dist. Served with USCGR, 1943-45. Mem. Am., Nassau County, Criminal Ct. (past pres.) bar assns. Club: Exchange. Home: 1063 E Broadway Woodmere NY 11598 Office: 389 Central Av Lawrence NY 11559

BLUM, ANNA OTTILLIA, lawyer; b. Monroe, Wis., Apr. 6, 1908; d. Samuel and Ottillia (Marty) Blum; B.A., U. Wis., 1929, LL.B., 1943. Admitted to Wis. bar, 1943, since practiced in Monroe; mem. firm Blum & Blum. Mem. Wis. Devel. Authority. Pres. Green County Womens Republican Club, 1951-54. Mem. Am., Wis. (rep. to gov. body 1947-54), Green County (pres. 1955-71) bar assns., Nat. Assn. Women Lawyers (pres. 1961-62, Wis. del. 1969-70), Green County Hist. Soc. (pres. 1951-54, treas, 1958-69), Am. Legion Aux., Womens Relief Corps, Bus. and Profl. Women's Club, Order of Coif, Phi Beta Kappa, Kappa Beta Pi. Mem. Order Eastern Star. Home: 1742 14th St Monroe WI 53566 Office: 1508 11th St Monroe WI 53566

BLUM, DAVID, conductor; b. Los Angeles, Sept. 7, 1935; s. Edwin Harvey and Beatrice (Gindick) B.; student Aspen Inst. Music, 1954, Juilliard Sch. Music, 1955; m. Sara Teitelbaum, July 23, 1956; 1 dau., Pamina. Condr., Young Artists Chamber Orch., Los Angeles, 1952-53, Debut Orch., Los Angeles, 1953-55, David Blum Chamber Orch., Los Angeles, 1958-59; guest condr. orchs. Berlin, Munich, Frankfurt, Mannheim and London, 1959- 60, Israel, 1961; condr., mus. dir. Esterhazy Orch. Found., specializing 18th Century and Haydn's neglected symphonies, N.Y.C., 1962- -; orch. tours nationally, records for Vanguard Records; benefit concert given for Dr. Schweitzer's hosp., 1965. Mem. Am. Symphony Orch. League. Composer: (string orch.) A Memory, 1961; (tone poem) Cyrano de Bergerac, 1959. Home: 7 Cornell Dr Great Neck NY 11024 Office: PO Box 47 Manhassett NY 11030

BLUM, EDWARD KENNETH, educator; b. Dec. 1, 1923; s. Jacob and Esther (Lipschultz) B.; B. Mech. Engring., Cooper Union, 1943; A.M., Columbia, 1947, Ph.D., 1952; m. Dolores Shaw, Dec. 27, 1953; children—Deborah, Beth Ann, Laura Amy. Lectr., Columbia, 1947-52; postdoctoral fellow U. Md., 1952-53; mathematician Naval Ordnance Lab., 1953-56; dir. computer center Ramo- Wooldridge Corp., 1956-62; prof. math. Wesleyan U., Middletown, Conn., 1962-66, U. So. Cal., Los Angeles, 1966—. Mng. editor Jour. Computer Scis. Served with USNR, 1944-46. Mem. Am. Math. Soc., Assn. Computing Machinery, Sigma Xi. Home: 880 Leonard Rd Los Angeles CA 90049

BLUM, GERALD SAUL, educator, psychologist; b. Newark, Mar, 8, 1922; s. Benjamin Paul and Augusta (Cohen) B.; B.S., Rutgers U., 1941; M.A., Clark U., 1942; Ph.D., Stanford, 1948; m. Myrtle Wolf, Mar. 3, 1946; children—Jeffrey, Nancy. Clin. psychology intern Palo Alto (Cal.) VA Hosp., 1946-48; mem. faculty U. Mich., 1948-68, prof. psychology, 1959-68; prof., chmn. dept. U. Cal. at Santa Barbara, 1968—; cons. clin. psychology VA, 1949-59. Served with USAAF, 1942-46. Fulbright research scholar, 1954-55; fellow Center Advanced Study Behavioral Scis., 1959-60; fellow Social Sci. Research Council, 1962-63. Fellow Am. Psychol. Assn.; mem. Phi Beta Kappa, Sigma Xi. Author: Psychoanalytic Theories of Personality, 1953; A Model of the Mind, 1961; Psychodynamics: The Science of Unconscious Mental Forces, 1966. Cons. editor Bobbs-Merrill reprint series in psychology. Inventor of Blacky Pictures, 1950. Home: 1227 Viscaino Rd Santa Barbara CA 93103

BLUM, HAROLD F., scientist; b. Escondido, Cal., Feb. 12, 1899; s. Robert Frederick and Dora (Batschy) B.; A.B., U. Cal., 1922, grad. student Med. Sch., 1922-23, Ph.D., 1927; student Harvard Med. Sch., 1923-24; m. Mabel Muriel Gilham, Sept. 19, 1930; 1 dau., Jannet Susan. Asst. prof. U. Ore., 1927-28; instr. Harvard Med. Sch., 1928-30; asst. prof. U. Cal., 1930-36. asso. prof., 1936-38; with Nat. Cancer Inst., USPHS, 1939-43, 47-67; prin. biophysicist Naval Med. Research Inst., 1943-45; vis. prof. dept. biology Princeton, 1947-67; prof. dept. biol. sci. State U. N.Y., Albany, 1967—. Served Signal Corps AEF, U.S. Army, 1918-19. Recipient medal U. Liege, Belgium, 1933; John Simon Guggenheim Meml. fellow, 1936, 46, 53; fellow Belgian Am. Ednl. Found., 1953; U.S. Pub. Health Spl. Research fellow, 1957-58. Fellow A.A.A.S., Cal. Acad. Scis.; mem. Société Philomathique de Paris, Assn. Physiologists Lang. France, Soc. Gen. Physiologists (pres. 1950). Author: Photodynamic Action and Disease Caused by Light, 1941, rev. edit. 1964; Time's Arrow and Evolution, revised edit. 1968; Carcinogenesis by Ultraviolet Light, 1959. Asso. editor Jour. Cellular and Comparative Physiology, 1956-67. Contbr. chpts., articles sci. publs. Home: 8 Providence St Albany NY 12203

BLUM, HENRIK LEO, educator; b. San Francisco, Nov. 11, 1915; s. Haiman and Pauline (Leplin) B.; B.S. in Chemistry, U. Cal. at Berkeley, 1937, M.D. at San Francisco, 1942; M.P.H., Harvard, 1949; m. Marian Hass Ehrich, Dec. 24, 1938. Intern U.S. Marine Hosp., San Francisco, 1942-43; asst. physics Johns Hopkins, 1944-45; fellow medicine Stanford, 1946-47; chief preventive med. services San Diego Country Health Dept., 1948-50; health officer Contra Costa County, Cal., 1950-66; asst. prof. clin. medicine Stanford Med. Sch., 1957-, clin. prof. pub. health U. Cal. at Berkeley, 1963-68, prof. community health planning, 1968-. Mem. health adv. com. region IX, USPHS, 1968-; mem. com. social and phys. environmental variables as determinants mental health Nat. Inst. Mental Health, 1956- 65, mem. spl. grants rev. com., 1962-64, mem. spl. tng. grants and rev. com., 1967-; mem. Cal. Adv. Hosp. Council, 1961-65, Gov. Cal. Com. Children and Youth, 1964-67; cons. ad hoc com. Community Health Services and Facilities. Office Surgeon Gen., 1962-63. Recipient Western States Tb award, 1961. Mem. Am. Pub. Health Assn. (gov. council 1967-), Am. Coll. Preventive Medicine, Alemeda-Contra Costa, Am., Cal. med. assns. Author: (with others) Vision Screening for Elementary Schools; The Orinda Study, 1959; (with A. L. Leonard) Public AdminstrationA Public Health Viewpoint, 1963; (with G.M. Keranen) Control of Chronic Disease in Man, 1966; (with others) Notes on Comprehensive Planning for Health, 1968; also articles. Home: 1148 Grizzly Peak Blvd Berkeley CA 94708

BLUM, JEROME, educator; b. Balt., Apr. 27, 1913; s. Moses and Fannie (Herzfeld) B.; A.B., Johns Hopkins, 1933, Ph.D., 1947. Faculty Princeton, 1947—, prof. history, chmn. dept., 1961-67, James Madison preceptor, 1952-55, master Grad. Coll., 1957—, Henry Charles Lea prof. history, 1966—; Lawrence lectr. Conn. Coll., 1968. Pres. bd. mgrs. N.J. State Home for Girls, 1965-69; chmn. Ad Hoc. Com. on Children's Services N.J., 1966-68, bd. dirs. Morrow Assn. on Correction, 1968—; trustee Princeton U. Press, 1966-70. Served to capt. F.A., AUS, 1942-46. Guggenheim fellow, 1951-52, 71-72; Shreve fellow Princeton, 1952. Mem. Am. Hist. Assn. (Herbert Baxter Adams prize 1962), Conf. on Slavic and East European History (exec. council), Econ. History Assn., Agrl. History Soc., Council Research in Econ. History, Center for Research Libraries (council 1969—). Clubs: Cosmos (Washington); Nassau (Princeton). Author: Noble Landowners and Agriculture in Austria, 1815- 1848, 1948; Lord and Peasant in Russia from the Ninth to the Nineteenth Century, 1961; co-author: The European World. 1966. Bd. editors Jour. Modern History, 1956-58; editorial bd. Jour. Econ. History, 1963-68; also articles. Home: Grad Coll Princeton U Princeton NJ 08540

BLUM, JEROME W., ret. mdse. exec.; b. N.Y.C., Mar. 8 1904; s. Jacob and Lillian (Langenzen) R.; student Columbia, 1927; m. Edith Victorson, Nov. 28, 1929; 1 dau., Jerri Ann; m. 2d, Dorothy B. Steckler; childrenEdward, Roger. With Langdon Textile Co., N.Y.C., 1924-28, A.H. Vandam Co., 1928- 35; formerly mdse. mgr. men's wear div. Cohn-Hall-Marx Co., N.Y.C., past v.p. United Mchts. & Mfrs., Inc., N.Y.C.; collector-dealer in antiques and art bus. Mem. taxation and pub. works coms. Scarsdale (N.Y.) Village. Mem. Textile Fabrics Assn. (pres.), Textile Distbrs. Assn. Inc. (chmn. bd. dirs.), Am. Printed Fabrics Council Inc. (pres., dir.), Am. Arbitration Assn. (dir.). Clubs: Wood (N.Y.C.)., Town (Scarsdale). Contbr. articles to Am. Antiques, also occasional articles in daily press. Home: Ross Hill Rd Lisbon CT 06351

BLUM, JOHN CURTIS, govt. ofcl.; b. Terryville, Conn., July 5, 1915; s. John A. and Marion D. (Curtis) B.; B.S., U. Conn., 1937, M.S., 1939; postgrad. U. Wis., 1941, Dept. Agr. Grad. Sch., 1946; student Indsl. Coll. Armed Forces, 1965-66; m. Mable L. Brooks, Oct. 21, 1939; children—Joanne M. (Mrs. Kogut), John Curtis, Nancy J. With Dept. Agr., 1939—, asst. dir. dairy div. Agrl. Marketing Service, 1960-61, dir. div., 1961-63, economist Office of Adminstr., 1963-64, asst. dept. adminstr. Consumer and Marketing Service, 1964-67, dep. adminstr., 1967—. Violinist, Fairfax County (Va.) Symphony Orch., 1957—, bd. dirs., 1957-70, pres., 1959-61, treas., 1965-67; dist. dir. North Va. dist. P.T.A., 1961-63; treas. Va. Congress Parents and Tchrs., 1963-65, regional v.p., 1965-67, chmn. extension com., 1967-69, budget chmn., 1969—, bd. mgrs., 1961—. Served to lt. (j.g.) USNR, 1944-46; PTO. Mem. Am. Acad. of Polit. and Social Sci., Am. Agr. Econ. Assn., Grange. Home: 7501 Walton Lane Annandale VA 22003 Office: Dept of Agriculture Washington DC 20250

BLUM, JOHN LEO, educator; b. Madison, Wis., May 2, 1917; s. John E. and Kathryn (Cullen) B.; B.S., U. Wis., 1937, M.S., 1939; Ph.D., U. Mich., 1953; m. Anna M. Raick, Jan. 25, 1947; children—Colette (Mrs. Ronald Meister), Suzanne (Mrs. Charles Brooks), Annette. From instr. to prof. biology Canisius Coll., Buffalo, 1941-63; mem. faculty U. Wis.-Milw., 1963—, prof. botany, 1966—, asso. dean Coll. Letters and Sci., 1967-69. Pres. Niagara Frontier chpt. Izaak Walton League, 1959-62. Served with AUS, 1943-45. Cole fellow U. Mich., 1952-53. Fellow A.A.A.S.; mem. Ecol. Soc. Am., Bot. Soc. Am., Phycological Soc. Am., Internat., phycological socs., Am. Inst. Biol. Scientists, Internat. Soc. Limnology, Internat. Assn. Great Lakes Research, Wis. Acad. Sci., Arts and Letters, Sigma Xi. Author: The Vaucheriaceae, 1972. Home: 2961 N Marietta Av Milwaukee WI 53211

BLUM, JOHN MORTON, educator, historian; b. N.Y.C., Apr. 29, 1921; s. Morton Gustave and Edna (LeVino) B.; grad. Phillips Acad., 1939; A.B., Harvard, 1943, M.A., 1947, Ph.D., 1950; M.A., Cambridge (Eng.) U., 1963; D.H.L., Trinity Coll., 1970; m. Pamela Louise Zink, June 28, 1944; children—Pamela, Ann, Thomas Tyler. Research asso., then asst. prof. history, asso. prof. Mass. Inst. Tech., 1948-57; prof. history Yale, 1957—. Pitt prof. Cambridge U., 1963-64. Trustee Buckingham Sch., 1954-56, Hotchkiss Sch., 1964-70; mem. Andover Alumni Council, 1957-60. Served from ensign to lt., USNR, 1943-46. Fellow Harvard, 1970—. Mem. Am., Conn. acads. arts and scis., Am., Mass. hist. assns., Phi Beta Kappa. Author: Joe Tumulty and the Wilson Era, 1951; The Republican Roosevelt, 1954; Woodrow Wilson and the Politics of Morality, 1956; From the Morgenthau Diaries, Vol. I, 1959, Vol. II, 1965, Vol. III, 1967; Yesterday's Children, 1959; The Promise of America, 1966; Roosevelt and Morgenthau, 1970. Asso. editor: (with Elting E. Morison) Letters of Theodore Roosevelt (8 vols.), 1951-54.; editor The National Experience, 1963. Home: 34 Edgehill Rd New Haven CT 06511

BLUM, JOHN ROBERT HALSEY, lawyer; b. Bklyn., July 21, 1929; s. Robert Edward and Ethel Mildred (Halsey) B.; grad. Hotchkiss Sch., 1947; B.A., Yale, 1951; LL.B., Harvard, 1956; m. Susanne Holcomb Delatour, June 9, 1950, (dec. Mar. 1970); children—Anne Beeckman, John Robert Halsey, Sara Delatour, Jane Wilder, Robin Elizabeth, Alice Packard, Suzette Florence Blum; m. 2d, Jeanne Colton Thompson, 1971. Admitted to N.Y. State bar, 1956; asso. firm Milbank, Tweed, Hope & Hadley, 1956-62; dep. dir. N.Y. State Div. for Youth, 1961-62; asso. David Rockefeller, 1962-69; pres. Kings Lafayette Corp., Bklyn., 1969-71; chmn. bd. Kings Lafayette Bank, Bklyn., 1969-71; dir. Cinema 5, Inc., Wood Cemetery Corp. Commr. N.Y. State Park Commn. for N.Y.C. Trustee Met. Mus. Art, Hotchkiss Sch., Bedford-Stuyvesant D & S Corp., Yale Art Gallery, Bklyn. Inst. Arts and Scis., Jackson Lab.; sec. Mus. Primitive Art. Mem. Am. Bar Assn. Clubs: Century Assn.; Wall Street; Rockefeller Center Lunch, Yale (N.Y.C.) Rembrandt (Bklyn.); Seal Harbor (Me.) Yacht; Harbor (Me.); Northeast Fleet; Lyford Cay. Home: Dawn Harbor Riverside CT 06878 Office: 1 E 53d St New York City NY 10022

BLUM, JULIUS RUBIN, educator; b. Nuremberg, Germany, Feb. 1, 1922; s. Max A. and Antonia (Blum) B.; came to U.S., 1937, naturalized, 1943; A.B. highest honors, U. Cal. at Berkeley, 1949, Ph.D., 1953; m. Rhoda Rosenbloom, Feb. 12, 1944; children—Mark A., Howard A. Instr. to asso. prof. math. dept. Ind. U., 1953-59; mem. tech. staff Sendia Corp., Albuquerque, 1959-62, cons., 1963—; prof. math. U. N.M., Albuquerque, 1962—, chmn. dept., 1963-69. Served with AUS, 1943-46. Fellow Inst. Math. Statistics, A.A.A.S.; mem. Am. Math. Soc. Author: (with Bell, Lewis, Rosenblatt) Modern Calculus, 1964; Probability and Statistics, 1969. Contbr. numberous profl. papers in math. Home: 6116 Mossman Pl NE Albuquerque NM 87110

BLUM, LAWRENCE PHILIP, educator; b. Webster, Wis., Feb. 14, 1917; s. Gustav Henry and Mary (Demuth) B.; B.S., U. Wis., 1939, M.S., 1943, Ph.D., 1947; m. Lucille A. Bloy, June 6, 1940; children—Karen Lynn, Kristine Ellen. High sch. tchr., Phillips, Wis., 1939-41; social worker, Chicago Heights, Ill., 1941-42; asst. prof. edn. Mich. State U., 1946-49; mem. faculty U. Wis.-Milw., 1949—, prof. ednl. psychology, 1960—; vocational cons. Social Security Adminstrn. Served with USAAF, 1943-46. Named Mental Health Man of Year, Wis. Assn. Mental Health 1966. Mem. Phi Kappa Phi, Phi Delta Kappa. Author: (with others) Communication, 1964; (with others) Cases and Projects in Communication, 1964; also articles, chpts. in books. Home: 400 E Lexington Blvd Whitefish Bay WI 53217 Office: Univ Wis Milwaukee WI 53201

BLUM, LESTER, educator; b. N.Y.C., June 25, 1919; s. Morris and Rae (Altman) B.; B.S. cum laude, Mich. State U., 1942; M.S., Ia. State U., 1944, Ph.D., 1949; m. Harriet Schlesinger, Apr. 11, 1943; childrenDilys Ellen, Sydney Laura, Galen Elizabeth. Economist OPA, 1942-43; instr., research and extension asso. Ia. State U., 1943-47; faculty Colgate U., Hamilton, prof. econs., 1959—, chmn. dept., 1962-70. Cons. OPS, 1951-52; pub. N.Y. State Minimum Wage Bd. for Cleaning and Dyeing Industry, 1956-57. Fellow Fund for Advancement Edn., Stanford, 1950-51; Asian Study Israel 1967-68. Mem. Am. Econ. Assn., Am. Assn. U. Profs. (pres. Colgate chpt. 1952-53). Author articles in field. Home: East Lake Rd Hamilton NY 13346

BLUM, ROBERT EDWARD, bus. exec.; b. Bklyn., May 8, 1899; s. Edward C. and Florence (Abraham) B.; A.B., Yale, 1921; Litt. D., L.I. U., 1959; m. Ethel Mildred Halsey, Aug. 15, 1928; children—John Robert Halsey, Alice Elizabeth Packard (Mrs. Robert H. Yoakum). Joined Abraham and Straus, Inc., Bklyn., 1922, v.p., 1930-37, 42-64, sec., 1936-60; dir. Equitable Life Assurance Soc. U.S., Bklyn. Union Gas Co., Church & Dwight Co., Inc., Lyford Cay Investments, Ltd., New Providence Devel. Co., Ltd.; trustee Dime Savings Bank Bklyn. Mem. council, hon. v.p. Bahamas Nat. Trust also former pres.; mem. N.Y. State Bd. Social Welfare, 1954-64; mem. of Temporary N.Y. State Commn. on Edn. Finance. Hon trustee Am. Mus. Nat. History; trustee N.Y. Zool. Soc.; former trustee, v.p. Bklyn. Pub. Library; dir. N.Y. World Fair Corp., 1964-65; bd. dirs., pres. Am. Friends of Bahamas Found., Inc., gen. chmn. Prospect Park Centennial, 1966; mem. Mayor's Com. for Cultural Affairs, N.Y.C., 1967; v.p., dir. Bklyn. War Meml., Inc.; dir. emeritus, past treas. Lincoln Center Performing Arts; vice chmn., mem. Bklyn. Sports Center Authority; mem., past pres. Art Commn. City of N.Y. mem. distbn. com. N.Y. Community Trust. Served as 2d lt., F.A., AUS, World War I; maj., Ordnance Dept., AUS, World War II. Mem. Bklyn. Inst. Arts and Scis. (pres. 1951-60, trustee 1936—, hon. chmn. governing com. Bklyn. Mus.), C. of C. (past v.p., dir.), Better Bus. Bur. N.Y.C., Downtown Bklyn. Assn. (former pres., dir.). Clubs: Yale (N.Y.C.); Rembrandt, Century Assn., Brooklyn; Bar Harbor, Northeast Fleet, Kebo Valley (Bar Harbor, Me.), Woods Hole (Mass.) Yacht; Mt. Desert (Me.) Yacht; Creek; Deepdale Golf; Lyford Cay (Nassau); Seal Harbor Yacht. Home: Ore Mine Rd Lakeville CT 06039 also Indian Point Mt Desert ME 04660

BLUM, ROBERT JOSEPH, paper mfr.; b. Cin., June 1, 1906; s. Henry P. and Marie (McHugh) B.; student U. Cin., 1924; m. Elizabeth Hickey, June 20, 1933; children—Elizabeth Ann Buse, Robert Joseph, Mary Gay (Mrs. Connolly), Julianne (Mrs. Thesing). Clk. LaBoiteux Co., 1924, successively salesman, N.Y. office mgr., sales mgr., v.p. and treas., 1924-45; pres. Excello Paper Products div. Mead Corp., 1943-59; exec. v.p. Mead Board Sales, Inc., 1946-57, pres., 1957-70; pres. Piedmont Paper Products, 1950—; v.p. Mead Corp., Dayton, O. Home: 6500 Wyman Lane Cincinnati OH 45243 Office: Central Trust Tower N 7162 Reading Rd Cincinnati OH 45243

BLUM, SIGMUND FRANCIS, architect; b. New Rochelle, N.Y., Jan. 16, 1926; s. Nicholas and Sarah (Feldman) B.; B.A., U. Ill., 1951; m. Carlotte Evangelista, Aug. 1, 1955; children—Diana, Alex. With various archtl. firms, N.Y.C., 1951-53; designer Kelly & Gruzen, N.Y.C., 1953-56; designer, project dir. Ketchum & Sharp, N.Y.C., 1956-59; chief designer, v.p. Smith, Hinchman & Grylls, Detroit, 1959-71; prin. Office Sigmund Blum, Detroit, 1971—; vis. critic U. Detroit, Ill., Mich., Lawrence insts. tech. Mem. nat. com. design A.I.A., 1971; chmn. Detroit Civic Design Com., 1961; prin. works include First Fed. Savs., Detroit, 1960; United Terminal Bldg. Wayne County Airport, 1961; Med. Teaching Center, U. Louisville, 1965; State Capitol, Mich., 1967; S.S. Kresge Co. Hdqrs., Troy, Mich., 1971; Mich. Bell Service Center, Detroit, 1970; work displayed Expo-70 Osaka, Japan, Trade Fair, Roznan, Poland, 1957. Bd. dirs. Friends of Modern Art, Detroit Inst. Art. Served with Air Corp AUS, 1943-45. Decorated Air medal; recipient Nat. Design award A.I.A., 1967, Mich. chpt. design award, 1965, 66, 68, 70, 71, Detroit chpt. design award, 1965, 66, 67, 70, 71, Prestressed Concrete award, 1968. Mem. A.I.A. (nat. honor award jury 1968), Founders Soc., Art Museum Nat. Panel Arbitrators, Tau Delta Phi. Clubs: Franklin Hills Country; Recess, Economic (Detroit). Home: 27070 14 Mile Rd Franklin MI 48025 Office: Fisher Bldg Detroit MI 48202

BLUM, VICTOR JOSEPH, educator; b. Defiance, Ia., Mar. 30, 1907; s. John Peter and Elizabeth (Rushenberg) B.; student St. Louis U., 1927-30, M.A., 1933, M.S., 1936, Ph.D., 1944; A.B., Xavier U., 1931. Instr. geophysics St. Louis U., 1944- 48, asst. prof., 1948-51, asso. prof., 1951-58, prof., 1958—, asso. dean Inst. Tech., 1950-56, dean, 1956-68. Trustee U. Corp. for Atmospheric Research, 1961-67, St. Louis U., 1955-67. Registered profl. engr., Mo. Mem. Nat. Soc. Profl. Engrs., A.A.A.S., Seismol. Soc. Am. (sec. 1951-54; chmn. Eastern sect. 1954-55), Am. Soc. Engring. Edn. (chmn. Mo.-Ark. sect. 1953-54), Am. Geophys. Union, Soc. Exploration Geophysicists, Am. Meteorol. Soc., Am. Soc. Testing Materials (dist. chmn. 1966-68), Sigma Xi. Contbr. articles to profl. jours. Home: 221 N Grand Av St Louis MO 63122

BLUM, VIRGIL CLARENCE, educator; b. Defiance, Ia., Mar. 27, 1913; s. John Peter and Elizabeth (Rushenberg) B.; student Creighton U., 1932-34; A.B., St. Louis U., 1938, M.A., 1945, Ph.D., 1954; student U. Chgo., 1950-51. Joined Soc. of Jesus, 1934, ordained priest Roman Cath. Ch., 1947; tchr. Campion High Sch., Prairie du Chien, Wis., 1941-44; asst. prof. Creighton U., 1953- 56; mem. faculty Marquette U., 1956—, prof. polit. sci., 1961—, chmn. dept., 1961-65, 70—. Chmn. Children's Equal Opportunities Com., 1965—; mem. exec. com. Citizens for Ednl. Freedom, 1964—; mem. steering com. Citizens Nat. Com. Higher Edn., 1963-. Mem. Am. Assn. Polit. Sci., Midwest Conf. Polit. Sci. Author: Freedom of Choice in Education, 1958; Freedom in Education, 1965; Education: Freedom and Competition, 1967; Catholic Education: Survival or Demise, 1969; also articles. Home: 1131 W Wisconsin Av Milwaukee, WI 53233.

BLUM, WALTER J., lawyer, educator; b. Chgo., Aug. 17, 1918; A.B., U. Chgo., 1939, J.D., 1941; m. Natalie Richter; children—Wendy (Mrs. David R. Coggins, Jr.), Catherine (Mrs. Daniel T. Hogan). Admitted to Ill., D.C. bars; atty. OPA, 1941-43; faculty U. Chgo. Law Sch., 1946—, prof., 1953—, mem. planning com. tax conf., 1947—; legal counsel Bull. Atomic Scientists. Trustee Coll. Retirement Equity Fund. Mem. Am., Chgo., (past bd. mgrs.) bar assns., Am. Law Inst. Chgo. Fed. Tax Forum, Order of Coif, Phi Beta Kappa. Author: (with Harry Kalven, Jr.) The Uneasy Case for Progressive Taxation, 1953, Public Law Perspectives on a Private Law Problem; Auto Compensation Plans, 1964; (with Stanley A. Kaplan) Materials on Reorganization, Recapitalization and Insolvency, 1968; also articles. Home: 5724 S Kimbark Av Chicago IL 60637

BLUMBERG, HERBERT KURT, corp. exec.; b. N.Y.C., May 25, 1925; s. Morris and Lucille (Newton) B.; B.A., Princeton, 1946; m. Doris R. Gaines, June 25, 1950; children—Kurt, Charles Newton, Ann Catherine. Sr. asst. dept. mgr. R.H. Macy & Co., 1948-51; v.p. sales Television Program of Am., 1951-58; bus. exec. Metromedia, Inc., 1958-66; chmn. bd. dirs., chief exec. Irvin Industries, Inc., Greenwich, Conn., 1966—; dir. K.F. Products, Inc., Payne Assos., Inc., Irvin Fallskarms A.B., Irvin Manifatture Industriali S.P.A., Irvin G.B., Ltd., Parachute Industries of S. Africa (Pty.), Ltd. Bd. advisers Sch. Bus. Adminstrn. of St. John's U., 1968—. Served to comdr. USNR, World War II; PTO; mem. Res. Mem. Hon. Order Ky. Cols. Mem. Navy League, Res. Officers Assn. Office: 51 Weaver St Greenwich CT 06830

BLUMBERG, JOE MORRIS, ret. army officer, physician; b. Balt., June 27, 1909; s. A.W. and Hortense (Morris) B.; B.S., Emory U., 1930, M.D., 1933; postgrad. Balliol Coll., Oxford U., (Eng.), 1945; M.D. with honors, Cath. U., Seoul, Korea, 1966; m. M. Catherine Weller, Aug. 29, 1935. Intern. Md. Gen. Hosp., Balt., 1933-34; resident Balt. City Hosp., 1934-36; gen. practice medicine, Balt., 1936- 41; commd. 1st lt. U.S. Army, 1935, advanced through grades to maj. gen., 1966; chief lab. service, Ft. Eustis, Va., 1941-44; chief lab. service 115th Gen. Hosp., ETO, 1944-45; pathologist Army Inst. Pathology, Washington, 1945-46; chief Histopathol. Center, Oliver Gen. Hosp., Augusta, Ga., 1946-47, chief lab. service, 1947-50; pathologist Walter Reed Gen. Hosp., 1950-53, chief lab. services, 1953; pathologist Army Med. Service Grad. Sch., Washington, 1953-54; comdg. officer 406th Med. Gen. Lab., Tokyo, cons. pathology and lab. service to chief surgeon U.S. Army Forces Far East and 8th Army, 1954-57; dep. dir. Armed Forces Inst. Pathology, 1957; dep. dir., chief lab. services cons. div. Directorate Profl. Service, Office Surgeon Gen., 1957-63, dir., 1963-67; comdg. gen. Med. Research and Devel. Command, Washington, 1967- 69; spl. asst. to surgeon gen. research and devel., 1967-69; clin. prof. pathology Sch. Medicine Georgetown U., 1963—, Sch. Medicine George Washington U., 1963—. Spl. adviser Republic Korea Army, 1956, spl. adviser, cons. Minister Health P.I., 1956; ICA, 1956; med. adviser U.S. Embassy, Manila, 1956; sci. dir. Am. Registry Pathology, 1959-63. Chmn. Emory U. Merit Program for Greater Washington Area, 1967-69. Bd. dirs. Gorgas Meml. Inst. Tropical Medicine and Preventive Medicine, 1964-70; mem. Smithsonian Assos.; sponsor Corcoran Art Gallery. Decorated Legion of Merit, D.S.M.; recipient Hektoen Bronz medal A.M.A., 1961, Stitt award Assn. Mil Surgeons, 1961, Seale Harris award So. Med. Assn., 1963, Founders medal Assn. Mil. Surgeons, 1964, award of honor Med. Alumni Assn. Emory U., 1966, Clin. Scientist of Year, 1968, Ward Burdick award, 1969. Diplomate Am. Bd. Pathology. Fellow Coll. Am. Pathologists (gov.), Am. Soc. Clin. Pathologists (past v.p., com. chmn.), A.C.P., A.M.A., Am. Soc. Cytology, Kansas City Acad. Medicine, Inter Soc. Cytology Council, So. Soc. Cancer Cytology; mem. Am. Pub. Health Assn., Am. Soc. Exptl. Pathology, Am. Assn. Pathologists and Bacteriologists, A.A.A.S., Acad. Medicine Washington, (hon.) Assn. Mexican Pathologists, (hon.) Am. Med. Soc. Vienna, Am. Assn. Study Neoplastic Diseases. Assn. Clin. Scientists (past v.p.), Aerospace Med. Assn., (life) Assn. Mil. Surgeons U.S., Electron Microscope Soc., Japanese Washington (past. pres.) socs. pathologists, N.Y. Acad. Scis., Internat. Acad. Pathology. (life) So. Med. Assn., Friends of Nat. Zoo. Mem. editorial adv. bd. Cancer, Jour. Am. Cancer Soc., 1966-68. Contbr. articles to profl. jours. Home: 5007 Jamestown Rd Washington DC 20016 Office: Oscar B Hunter Meml Lab 915 19th St NW Washington DC 20006

BLUMBERG, NATHAN BERNARD, educator, journalist; b. Denver, Apr. 8, 1922; s. Abraham Moses and Jeannette B.; B.A., U. Colo., 1947, M.A., 1948; Ph.D. (Rhodes scholar). Oxford U., Eng., 1950; m. Lynne Stout, June 29, 1946 (div. Feb. 1970); children—Janet Leslie, Jenifer Lyn, Josephine Laura. Reporter Denver Post. 1947-48; asso. editor Lincoln (Neb.) Star, 1950-53; asst. to editor Ashland (Neb.) Gazette, 1954-55; asst. city editor Washington Post and Times Herald, 1956; from asst. prof. to asso. prof. journalism U. Neb., 1950-55; asso. prof. journalism Mich. State U., 1955-56; dean, prof. sch. Journalism U. Mont., 1956-68, prof. journalism, 1968—; vis. prof. Pa. State U., 1964, Northwestern U., 1966-67, U. Cal. at Berkeley, 1970. Mem. Assn. Am. Rhodes Scholars, Nat. Conf. Editorial Writers, Kappa Tau Alpha. Author: One-Party Press?, 1954. Contbr. articles mags. and jours. Office: Sch Journalism U Mont Missoula MT 59801

BLUMBERG, PHILLIP IRVIN, lawyer, educator; b. Balt., Sept. 6, 1919; s. Hyman and Bessie (Simons) B.; A.B. magna cum laude, Harvard, 1939, LL.B. magna cum laude, 1942; m. Janet Helen Mitchell, Nov. 17, 1945; children—William A.M., Peter M., Elizabeth B., Bruce M. Admitted to N.Y. bar, 1942, Mass. bar, 1970; practiced in N.Y.C., 1942—; with firm Willkie, Owen, Otis, Farr & Gallagher, 1942-43, Szold & Brandwen, 1946-49; partner firm Szold, Brandwen, Meyers & Blumberg, 1949-66; pres., chief exec. officer United Ventures, Inc. (formerly Kirkeby-Natus Corp.), 1962-67, now dir.; pres., chief exec. officer Federated Devel. Co. (formerly Federated Mortgage Investors), 1966-68, chmn. finance com., 1968—, also trustee; prof. law Boston U. Sch. Law, 1968—; dir. Verde Exploration, Ltd., Mitchell Rand Mfg. Corp. Pres. Adult Sch. Montclair, N.J., 1955-57, trustee, 1958-64. Mem. Essex County (N.J.) Democratic Com., 1956-57. Trustee Edward A. Filene Goodwill Fund. Served with USAAF, 1943-46; ETO. Decorated Bronze Star. Mem. Am. Bar Assn., Nat. Planning Assn. (nat council), Nat. Assn. Real Estate Investment Funds (gov. 1966-68), Assn. Bar City N.Y., Boston Bar Assn., Phi Beta Kappa, Delta Upsilon. Clubs: Wall Street, Harvard (N.Y.C.); Harvard (Boston). Bd. editors Harvard Law Rev., 1940-42., treas. 1941-42. Contbr. articles to legal jours. Home: 35 Foxcroft Rd Winchester, MA. 01890; also Fernfield Wallingford VT 05773 Office: 40 Wall St New York City NY 10005 also Boston School of Law 765 Commonwealth Av Boston MA 02215

BLUMBERG, RICHARD WINSTON, physician, educator; b. Winston-Salem, N.C., Nov. 10, 1914; s. Alexander Webster and Hortense (Morris) B.; B.S., Emory U., 1935, M.D., 1938; m. Rotating intern Grady Meml. Hosp., Atlanta, 1938-39; intern pediatrics Vanderbilt U. Hosp., 1939-40, resident, 1940-41, chief resident, 1941-42; chief outpatient clinic Children's Hosp., Cin., 1945-47, research asso., 1945-47; mem. faculty Emory U. Sch. Medicine, 1948—, Francis Winship Walters prof. pediatrics, chmn. dept., 1959—; chief pediatric service grady Meml. Hosp., 1959—. Served to maj., M.C., AUS, 1942-45. Diplomate Am. Bd. Pediatrics. Mem. Am. Acad. Pediatrics, Am. Pediatric Soc., Soc. Med. Cons. to Armed Forces, Alpha Omega Alpha, Omicron Delta Kappa. Contbr. to Cyclopedia Medicine. Author articles in field. Home: 69 Butler St SE Atlanta GA 30303

BLUME, ALBERT MAX KARL, educator; b. Hof, Bavaria, Germany, Mar. 6, 1902; s. F.P. Bruno Sophie Luise (Beck) B.; came to U.S., 1904, naturalized, 1921; A.B., Yale, 1928, B.Mus., 1929, M.A., 1936, Ph.D., 1940; m. Gertrude Clara Rast, Aug. 21, 1948; 1 dau., Ruth Gertrude. Tchr. St. John's Evang. Lutheran Sch., Meriden, Conn., 1921-24; dir. music Hebron Acad., 1929- 31; master music, German, Choate Sch., 1931-33; instr. German, Yale, 1933-34; instr. German, U. Vt., 1938-42, instr. math., 1943-44; tchr. math., music Westover Sch., 1944-46; asst. prof. German, Syracuse U., 1946-47; asso. prof. German, Bucknell U., Lewisburg, Pa., 1947-57, prof., 1957-, chmn. dept. German and Russian, 1962-68. Served with AUS, 1942-43. Mem. Modern Lang. Assn., Am. Assn. Tchrs. German, Pa. Modern Lang. Assn., Phi Beta Kappa. Home: 19 Verna Rd R D 1 Lewisburg PA 17837

BLUME, BERNHARD, ret. educator; b. Stuttgart, Germany, Apr. 7, 1901; s. Paul and Hedwig (Grabowski) B.; student U. Munich, 1920-21, U. Berlin, 1921-22, Tubingen, 1919-20, 1922-23, Staatsexamen, 1923; Ph.D., Stuttgart, 1935; M.A. (hon.), Harvard, 1956; LL.D., Mills Coll., 1965; m. Carola Rosenberg, June 21, 1927; children—Michael Wolfgang, Frank Reinhart. Came to U.S., 1936, naturalized, 1942. Author and playwright, Germany, 1924-36; vis. prof. German, Mills Coll., 1936-37, asso. prof., 1937-41, prof. German, 1941-45, convenor Sch. Lang. and Lit., 1939-42; prof. German and chmn. dept. Ohio State U., 1945-56; Kuno Francke prof. German Art and Culture, Harvard, 1956-66, emeritus, 1966-, chmn. div. modern langs., 1961-63; prof. German lit. U. Cal. San Diego, 1966-71, emeritus, 1971—. Recipient Gold medal Goethe Inst., 1964. Guggenheim Meml. Found. fellow, 1954-55, 63-64. Mem. Am. Acad. Arts and Scis., Modern Lang. Assn. Am., Deutsche Akademie für Sprache und Dichtung (corr.), Am. Assn. U. Profs., Am. Assn. Tchrs. German, Phi Beta Kappa. Author: Fahrt nach der Sudsee, 1924; Bonaparte, 1926; Treibjagd, 1927; Feurio, 1928, and other plays; Das Withshaus zum roten Husaren, 1936; Das Weltbild Arthur Schnitzlers, 1936; Thomas Mann and Goethe, 1949. Home: 7390 Via Capri La Jolla CA 92037

BLUME, LOUIS JOHN, univ. pres.; b. Chgo., Dec. 21, 1913 s. John A. and Helen (Berger) B.; B.S., Dayton U., 1933; M.A., Catholic U. Am., 1941; Th.D., St. Meinrad, Ind., 1945. Joined Soc. of Mary, 1931, ordained priest Roman Catholic Ch., 1945; faculty South Side Cath. High Sch., St. Louis, 1934-37; dean men Charminade Coll., Clayton, Mo., 1937-40; prof. English, St. Anselme, Que., Can., 1941-42; chaplain St. Mary's U., San Antonio, 1945-46, pres., 1947-53, 63—; v.p. Maryhurst Normal, Kirkwood, Mo., 1946-47; pres. Ch. Related Colls. in Tex., 1952-53; pres. Chaminade Coll. Prep., 1955-61; sabbatical leave, Rome, 1961-62; founder Villa St. Jean Internat. Sch., Fribourg, Switzerland, 1962-63. Chmn. bd. dirs. Tex. Found. Voluntarily Supported Colls. and Univs.; mem. exec. com. Ch.-Related Colls. in South; bd. dirs. KLRN Ednl. TV; mem. conf. com. Tex. Commn. Higher Edn. Mem. Fiesta San Antonio Commn. Trustee S.W. Research Inst., San Antonio Library. Mem. Nat. Cath. Edn. Assn. (regional del. exec. com.), Tex. Council Chs. (commn. on scholarships). C. of C., Nat. Conf. Christians and Jews, Def. Orientation Conf. Assn., Newcomen Soc., Assn. U.S. Army, K.C. (state comdg. officer, state com. Cath. higher edn.). Clubs: Antonians, Torch. Address: St Mary's U San Antonio TX 78228

BLUME, PETER, artist; b. Russia, Oct. 27, 1906; s. Harry and Rose (Gopin) B.; brought to U.S., 1911, naturalized, 1921; student pub. schs., N N.Y.C., Art Student Ednl. Alliance, 1919-24, Art Students League, N.Y.C., Beaux Arts; m. Grace Douglas Gibbs Craton. Mar. 9, 1931. Exhibited at Daniel Gallery, N.Y.C., 1926-31, Cleve., Columbus, Phila., Detroit, Balt., San Francisco, Buffalo, and Whitney museums, Mus. Modern Art, N.Y.C. Century of Progress Expn., Chgo., Internat. Venice, Italy, Julien Levy Gallery, Currier Gallery, Wadsworth Atheneum, Kennedy Gallery, N.Y.C., 1968, Danenberg Gallery, 1970. Recipient first prize Carnegie Art 1934, 2d purchase award Artists for Victory Exhbn. Met. Mus. of Art, 1942, for his "South of Scranton Exhbn.", Durlacher Bros., 1947. Guggenheim Found. Fellow, 1932, 36. Mem. Am. Acad. Nat. Inst. arts and letters. A.N.A. Home: Route 1 Box 140 Sherman CT 06784

BLUMENAUER, THOMAS WILLIAM, Jr., savs. and loan assn. exec.; b. Washington, Oct. 16, 1917; s. Thomas William and Edna (Schaeffer) B.; B.S.C., Benjamin Franklin U., 1938, M.S.C., 1939; grad. Savs. and Loan Grad. Sch., Ind. U., 1949; m. Julia Elizabeth Bistline, May 17, 1941; children—Kathleen Louise, Margery Ellen, William George. With Northwestern Nat. Ins. Co., Washington,

1935- 38; with Columbia Fed. Savs. & Loan Assn., Washington, 1938—, sr. v.p., 1958-68, pres., 1968—, also dir. Bd. dirs. Downtown Progress, Inc.; mem. personnel and finance com. health and welfare council United Givers Fund Washington. Mem. Montgomery County Republican Finance Com., 1968- 69. Mem. Am. Savs. and Loan Inst. (instr., past pres. Washington chpt.), Savs. and Loan Controllers Assn. (past pres. Washington), D.C. Savs. and Loan League (past pres.), Newcomen Soc. Mem. Reformed Ch. (pres. 1966- -). Mason (Shriner, Jester). Club: Washington Sertoma (past treas., dir.). Home: 7617 Carter Ct Bethesda MD 20034 Office: 730 11th St NW Washington DC 20001

BLUMENFELD, HAROLD, newspictures editor; b. N.Y.C., July 12, 1905; s. Jacob and Jennie (Schagrin) B.; student N.Y. U.; m. Gerry Krasner, Feb. 21, 1932; 1 dau., Judith P. Dolgins. Reporter NEA Service, Inc., 1923-26; editor Acme Newspictures, 1926-51; exec. newspictures editor U.P.I., N.Y.C., 1952- 68, dir. spl. projects, 1968—. Named Editor of Year, Nat. Press Photographers Assn., 1959, Joseph A. Sprague award, 1969. Mem. Soc. Silurians, Sigma Delta Chi. Co-editor: Four Days; Churchill (The Life Triumphant); The Pilgrim Pope; Gemini; Flying Saucers; Youthquake; Swift Sword; Israel; Morals; Assasination—Robert F. Kennedy, 1925-68. Home: 320 Central Park W New York City NY 10025 Office: 220 E 42d St New York City NY 10017

BLUMENFIELD, SAMUEL M., educator, rabbi; b. Letichev, Russia, Sept. 13, 1901; s. Max and Fanny (Waxman) B.; B.S., Coll. City N.Y., 1925; M.A., Columbia, 1926; M.H.L. and Rabbi, Jewish Inst. of Religion, 1930, D.H.L., 1944, D.D. (hon.), 1957; m. Rose Mazel, Jan. 8, 1930; children—Tamar Ephrimina, Rena Sarah, Naomi Judith. Ednl. dir. Jewish Communal Center, Bklyn., 1925-29; instr., extension dept., Tchrs. Inst., Jewish Theol. Sem. Am., 1926-30; dir. Dept. Youth and Ednl. Bd. of Jewish Edn., Chgo., 1930-34; dean, dir. Coll. Jewish Studies, Chgo., 1934-47, pres., 1947-54, also prof. edn.; former dir. edn. and culture dept. The Jewish Agy.; prof. Hebrew culture Hofstra Univ., 1968—; lectr. U. Chgo., 1935—, Roosevelt U., 1947, New Sch. for Soc. Research, N.Y.C.; cons. commn. on tchr. edn. and religion of Am. Assn. Colls. for Tchr. Edn., 1953—; ednl. cons. World Conf. of Jewish Orgns.; cons. World Jewish Edn. Conf. Mem. War Labor Bd., 1941-43. Pres. Nat. Council for Jewish Edn., Chgo. Rabbinical Assn. Hon. pres. Soc. for Advancement Hebrew Culture; chmn. Jewish Book Month Council, Army, Navy com. U.S.O. Author: Master of Troyesa study of Rashi, The Educator, 1946; Maimonides, the Educator; Education in the American Jewish Community. Contbr. Ency. Brit., Brit. Book of the Year, 1954—, Am. Educators Ency., Great Jewish Personalities, Ency. Judaica, Great Jewish Ideas, also to various ednl. and religious publs. Home: 1330 E 17th St Brooklyn NY 11230

BLUMENKRANZ, JOSEPH, cons. health facilities; b. Jaroslau, Austria, Aug. 19, 1902; s. Samuel and Sally (Arzt) B.; B.S., Imperial-Royal Higher Tech. Sch., Austria, 1920; postgrad. Beaux-Arts Inst. Design, 1923-25, Columbia, 1930-36; m. Rose Fund, Oct. 20, 1925. Came to U.S., 1920, naturalized, 1925. Mem. N.Y.C. Hosp. Planning Bd., 1938-41; hosp. cons. Govt. of P.R., 1944; cons. planning of health facilities as Jos. Blumenkranz & Assos., N.Y.C., 1944—, prof. hosp. planning Columbia Sch. Pub. Health and Adminstrv. Medicine, 1969—. Chief hosp. cons. U.S. War Dept., 1947; lectr. health care facilities govt. agys., univs., U.S., S.Am., Europe, 1950—. Fellow N.Y. Acad. Scis., A.I.A. Contbr. numerous aritcles profl. jours. Home: 26 Lockwood Rd Scarsdale NY 10583 Office: Blumenkranz & Bernhard 227 E 45th St New York City NY 10017

BLUMENSCHEIN, CARL MARTIN, business exec.; b. Chgo., 1907; s. J. George and Clara M. (Mader) B.; student Northwestern U.; m. Rose Vogt Pfau, Aug. 18, 1934; children—Carol E., George R. With Container Corp. of Am., 1928—, controller, 1945-61, v.p., 1954-61, sr. v.p., controller, 1961-67, sr. v.p. finance, 1967—, dir.; v.p., controller Marcor, 1968-70. Mem. Financial Execs. Inst. United Ch. of Christ. Clubs: Mid-Day, Executives (Chgo.); Economic; Commercial. Home: 265 Winthrop Av Elmhurst IL 60126 Office: 38 S Dearborn St Chicago IL 60603

BLUMENSTOCK, DAVID ALBERT, surgeon; b. Newark, Feb. 14, 1927; s. Albert G. and Marion (Dickson) B.; B.S., Union Coll., 1949; M.D., Cornell U., 1953; m. Audrey J. Webster, Aug. 2, 1952; childrenMary Beth, David Albert II, Kristen Lee. Intern Mary Imogene Bassett Hosp., Cooperstown, N.Y., 1953-54, resident surgery, 1954-55, 56-58, research surgeon, 1960-63, surgeon in chief, 1963-; resident surgery Columbia-Presbyn Med. Center, N.Y.C., 1955-56; clin. instr. thoracic surgery U. Mich. Sch. Medicine, 1958-60; clin. prof. surgery Columbia Coll. Phys. and Surg., 1963-; spl. research biology tissue and organ transplantation, living organs and tissues. Served with AUS, 1946-47; ETO. Recipient Research Career Devel. award USPHS, 1962-63. Diplomate Am. Bd. Surgery, Am. Bd. Thoracic Surgery. Fellow A.C.S.; mem. Am. Assn. Thoracic Surgery, Soc. U. Transplantation Soc., Sigma Xi, Alpha Omega Alpha. Home: Shelterwood RD 2, Cooperstown, NY 13326. Office: Mary Imogene Basset Hosp Cooperstown NY 13326

BLUMENTHAL, ANDRE, bus. exec.; b. N.Y.C., Jan. 23, 1904; s. Sidney and Lucy (Picard) B.; grad. Ethical Culture Sch., 1921; B.A., Yale, 1925; m. Mildred Wimpfheimer, Nov. 23, 1927; children—William, Thomas, Elizabeth. With Sidney Blumenthal & Co., Inc., 1926-57, dir., 1930-57, pres., 1953, vice chmn. bd., treas., 1954; now pres. Norwalk Powdered Metals, Inc. Chmn. Conn. Bd. Mental Health, 1957-59; v.p. Conn. Hosp. Planning Commn. Hon. trustee Norwalk Hosp., pres., 1960-62; mem. adv. bd., past chmn. Conn. Mental Health Center. Comdr. USNR, ret. Pres. Conn. Hosp. Assn. 1956, Textile Research Inst., 1952- 53. Home: Chestnut Hill Rd Norwalk CT 06851 Office: Muller Park Norwalk CT 06851

BLUMENTHAL, HERMAN BERTRAM, public accountant; b. Phila., Sept. 30, 1916; s. Bertram and Florence (Wax) B.; student Oxford U., Birmingham U., Eng., Edinburgh U., Scotland; B.S., Wharton Sch., U. Pa., 1938; m. Elaine J. Belsinger, May 25, 1941; children—Bonni Ann, Herman Bertram III. Sr. partner Shestack, Blumenthal & Stein, C.P.A.'s, Phila., 1964—; pres. Harlan Products. Inc., Phila., 1958—; dir. Colebrook-Terry, Inc. (Pa.), Willem Wirtz Garden Assos., Palm Beach, Fla.; former lectr. Cambridge U., Eng. Mem. nat. panel arbitrators Am. Arbitration Assn. Sec., Greater Phila. Council of Temple Brotherhoods. Chmn. bd. trustees Montgomery County Community Coll., 1969—. Served to capt. USAAF, 1940-46. Mem. Mensa (internat. treas. 1970—), Intertel. Jewish religion. Mason; mem. B'nai B'rith (trustee). Home: 1021 Melrose Av Philadelphia PA 19126 Office: Wyncote House Township Line Rd and Washington Lane Wyncote PA 19095

BLUMENTHAL, LEONARD MASCOT, mathematician, educator; b. Athens, Ga., Feb. 27, 1902; s. George Henriette (Hirschfeld) B.; B.S. in Civil Engring., Ga. Inst. Tech., 1923; M.S., U. Chgo., 1924; Ph.D., Johns Hopkins, 1927; postgrad. (Nat. Research fellow in mathmetics) Inst. for Advanced Study, Princeton, 1933-34, U. Vienna (Austria), 1934-35; m. Eleanor Berger, June 23, 1926. Research asst. Inst. for Advanced Study, 1935-36; asst. prof. U. Mo., Columbia, 1936-39, asso. prof., 1939-42, prof., 1942—, Defoe Distinguished prof. 1968—; Math. cons. Inst. Numerical Analysis, Nat. Bur. Standards, Los Angeles, 1951-52; Fulbright prof. U. Leiden (Netherlands), 1954-55, U. Madrid (Spain), 1962- 63, U. Buenos Aires (Argentina), 1967; mem. fellowship bd. div. mathematics NRC; Symposium lectr. Am. Math. Soc. 1942. Recipient Gold T, Ga. Inst. Tech., Breitenbach Medal, 1922; Distinguished Faculty award (00) U. Mo., 1964. Mem. Royal Acad. Scis. of Spain (corr. fgn. mem.); Math. Assn. Am. (gov.; vis. mathematician 1961-67), Am. Math. Soc., Am. Assn. U. Profs., Sigma Xi, Pi Mu Epsilon, Tau Epsilon Phi (chancellor 1921-22). Jewish religion. Author: Distance Geometries, 1938; Theory and Applications of Distance Geometry, 1953; A Modern View of Geometry, 1961; (with Karl Menger) Studies in Geometry, 1970; also monographs in Am., German and Spanish jours. Collaborator, Math. Reviews, 1940—; asso. editor Am. Math. Monthly, 1942-51. Home: 205 E Ridgeley Rd Columbia MO 65201

BLUMENTHAL, PHILIP, cosmetic co. exec.; b. Newark, 1905; B.A., N.Y. U., 1927, LL.B., 1929. Sec., counsel Revlon, Inc. Home: 315 E 72d St New York City NY 10021 Office: 767 Fifth Av New York City NY 10022*

BLUMENTHAL, ROBERT LOUIS, lawyer; b. Houston, Oct. 15, 1930; s. Charles and Lillian (Wolf) B.; B.B.A., U. Tex., 1951, LL.B., 1953; LL.M., Harvard, 1954; m. Beverly Renee Brand, Aug. 30, 1953; children—Pamela Joan, Karen Frances, Brad Brand. Admitted to Tex. bar, 1953; practice in Houston, 1953, N.Y.C., 1954, Dallas, 1957—; partner firm Carrington, Coleman, Sloman, Johnson & Blumenthal, 1970—. Dir., sec. Am. Title Co. of Dallas; dir. Fox & Jacobs Constrn. Co., Inc.; dir., sec. Interblock, Inc. Bd. dirs. Spl. Care Sch., West Dallas Community Centers, Dallas Home and Hosp. for Jewish Aged. Served with USAF, 1954-57. Mem. Am., Dallas bar assns., U. Tex. Ex-Students Assn. (past pres. Dallas chpt.), Am. Judicature Soc. Mailing Address: Office: 3000 One Main Pl Dallas TX 75250

BLUMENTHAL, SIDNEY, educator, physician; b. N.Y.C., June 24, 1909; s. Jacob and Lena (Uhran) B.; B.S., U. Ia., 1930, M.D., 1933; m. Elaine Levy, Apr. 4, 1953; children—Patricia (Mrs. Gilbert Schedler), Peggy. Intern Milw. Children's Hosp., 1933-34; resident Mt. Sinai Hosp., N.Y.C., 1934-36; pvt. practice pediatrics, N.Y.C., 1936-50; dir. pediatric cardiology Mt. Sinai Hosp., N.Y.C., 1950-58, Babies Hosp., N.Y.C., 1955-70; prof. clin. pediatrics Columbia Coll. Phys. and Surg., 1959-70; prof. pediatrics, dean postgrad. edn. U. Miami (Fla.), 1970—; cons. L.I. Jewish Hosp., Vassar Bros. Hosp., Poughkeepsie, N.Y.; sr. cons. N.Y.C. Health Dept.; vis. prof. pediatric cardiology Nat. Taiwan U., Taipei, 1964. Bd. dirs. N.Y. Heart Assn., 1959—; bd. dirs. Am. Heart Assn., 1965—, chmn. council on rheumatic fever and congenital heart disease. Served to lt. col., M.C., Aus., 1942-45. Decorated Bronze Star. Diplomate Am. Bd. Pediatrics (chmn. sub-bd. pediatric cardiology). Mem. Alpha Omega Alpha. Office: Univ Miami Miami FL 33146

BLUMENTHAL, WERNER MICHAEL, bus. exec.; b. Germany, Jan. 3, 1926; s. Ewald and Rose Valerie (Markt) B.; B.Sc., U. Cal. at Berkeley, 1951; M.A., M.P.A., Princeton, 1953, Ph.D., 1956; m. Margaret Eileen Polley, Sept. 8, 1951; children—Ann Margaret, Gillian, Jane Eileen. Came to U.S., 1947, naturalized, 1952. Research asso. Princeton, 1954-57; labor arbitrator State of N.J., 1955- 57; v.p. dir. Crown Cork Internat. Corp., 1957-61, also dir. overseas affiliated cos.; became dep. asst. sec. state for econ. affairs Dept. State, 1961; apptd. President's deputy spl. rep. for trade negotiations with rank of ambassador, 1963; pres. Bendix Internat., 1967- 70; dir. Bendix Corp., 1967—, vice chmn. 1970-71, pres., chief operating officer, 1971—. U.S. rep. commn. internat. commodity trade UN Econ. and Social Council, 1961, 1962; U.S. adviser spl. meeting Inter- Am. Econ. and Social Council, 1961; chmn. U.S. del. UN Coffee Conf., 1962. Charter trustee Princeton. Mem. U.S. C. of C. (dir.), Salzburg Seminar Am. Studies (dir.), Nat. Com. U.S.-China Relations (dir.), Center for Inter-Am. Relations; Emergency Com. Am. Trade Am. Econ. Assn., Council Fgn. Relations, Atlantic Council U.S. (dir., gov.), Phi Beta Kappa. Clubs: Princeton (N.Y.C.); Barton Hills Country. Home: 505 Barton North Dr Ann Arbor MI 48105 Office: Bendix Corp Exec Offices Bendix Center Southfield MI 48076

BLUMER, HERBERT, educator; b. St. Louis, Mo., Mar. 7, 1900; s. Richard George and Margaret (Marshall) B.; A.B., U. Mo., 1921, A.M., 1922; Ph.D., U. Chgo., 1927; m. Marguerite Barnett, Aug. 16, 1922; 1 dau. Katharine; m. 2d, Marcia Jackson, Aug. 22, 1942; children—Linda, Leslie. Instr. sociology U. Mo., 1922-25; instr. sociology U. Chgo., 1925-30, asso. prof., 1931-47, prof., 1947-52; prof. sociology, U. Mich., 1936-37; prof. sociology U. Hawaii, 1939; prof. sociology and chmn. dept. U. Cal. at Berkeley 1952—, chmn. social sci. council, 1956-58, dir. Inst. Social Scis., 1958-66. Chmn. bd. dirs. Trans- action. Mem. research staff Motion Picture Research Council, 1929-31; prin. liason officer between OWI and Bd. Econ. Warfare, Washington, 1943; pub. panel chmn. WLB, 1943-44; permanent arbitrator, Armour & Co., 1944-45; chmn. bd. arbitration U.S. Steel Corp., 1945-47. Mem. Inst. Internat. de Sociologie, Soc. Study Social Problems (pres. 1955), Sociol. Research Assn., Internat. Soc. Sci. Study Race Relations, Am. (pres. 1956), Internat. (v.p. 1962-66), Pacific (pres. 1971-72) sociol. assns., Phi Beta Kappa, Delta Sigma Rho. Author sci. books and articles. Editor Publs. of Am. Sociol. Soc., 1931-36, Am. Jour. Sociology, 1940-52; editor Sociology Series, pub. by Prentice-Hall, Inc., 1934—. Chmn. bd. editors Integrated Edn., 1965—. Home: 350 Pine Creek Rd Walnut Creek CA 94598 Office: U Cal Berkeley CA 94720 ☆

BLUMGART, HERRMAN LUDWIG, physician; b. Newark, July 19, 1895; s. David and Sophie (Hiller) B.; S.B., Harvard, 1917. M.D. 1921, ScD., 1962, Moseley Traveling Fellow, London and Europe, 1923; m. Margaret Stein, July 18, 1931; 1 dau., Ann. Med. interne Peter Bent Brigham Hosp., 1921-22; asst. Thorndike Meml. Lab., Boston City Hosp., 1924-28, asso. prof. medicine Harvard, 1928-46, prof. medicine, 1946-62, now prof. emeritus, spl. cons. to dean of faculty Harvard Medical Sch., 1962-66; vis. physician Beth Israel Hosp., 1928-46, physician in chief and dir. med. research, 1946-62, now physician in chief emeritus; cons. in medicine and tropical medicine Br. Area 1, VA; cons. Peter Bent Brigham Hosp., Harvard Health Service. Served from lt. col. to col., M.C., AUS, 1943-46. Decorated Legion of Merit with oak leaf cluster; recipient Gold Heart award, Am. Heart Assn. Diplomate Am. Bd. Internal Medicine. Fellow A.C.P. (hon. master), Am. Coll. Cardiology (hon., first James Bryan Herrick award), Indian (hon.), Spanish (hon.) cardiologic socs.; mem. Am. Soc. Clin. Investigation, Assn. Am. Physicians, Am. Physiol Soc., Am. Acad. Arts and Scis., Soc. Cons. of World War II, A.M.A. (chmn. sect. internal medicine), Am., Mass. (past pres.) heart assns., Mass. Med. Soc., New Eng. Cardiovascular Soc. (past pres.); Harvard Med. Sch. Alumni Assn. (past pres.), Am. Nuclear Soc. (hon., recipient Pioneer award). Former editor-in-chief Circulation, Journal Am. Heart Assn.; past mem. editorial bd. New Eng. Jour. Medicine. Home: 987 Memorial Dr Cambridge MA 02138 Office: Harvard Med Area Health Service 275 Longwood Av Boston MA 02115

BLUNCK, HERBERT CHRISTOPHER, hotel exec.; b. Seattle, Oct. 3, 1904; s. John Frederick and Emma Wilhemina (Buttner) B.; student U. Cal.; m. Janet Elizabeth Edwards, Oct. 23, 1932; 1 son, Brooks Edwards. Staff Fairmont Hotel, San Francisco, also Huntington Hotel, Pasadena, Cal., 1925-31; mgr. El Cortez, Bellevue hotels, San Francisco, 1934-39, Hotels Statler Co., Inc., N.Y.C., St. Louis, 1939-41, William Penn Hotel, Pitts., 1941-42; gen. mgr. Detroit Statler, 1942-44, Statler Hilton, Washington, 1944-66; sr. v.p. Hilton Hotels Corp.; dir. No. Va. Bldg. & Loan Assn.; adv. bd. Nat. Bank of Washington. Co-chmn. people to people com. Hotel Industry. Mem. Fed. City Council. Pres. Community Chest Fedn., 1954-55; incorporator United Givers Fund. Bd. dirs. Washington chpt. A.R.C.; adv. com. Mem. Inaugural Com., 1953-57; trustee Washington Hosp. Center. Mem. Am. Hotel and Motel Assn. (pres. 1970, chmn. 1970—), Hotel Assn. Washington (past pres.), Detroit Hotel Assn. (past pres.). Episcopalian. Mason (Shriner, K.T.). Clubs: Burning Tree Golf, Columbia Country, Loudoun Country (Washington). Home: 2500 Calvert St NW Washington DC 20008 Office: Statler Hilton Hotel Washington DC 20036

BLUNDELL, HARRY, electric utility exec.; b. Salt Lake City, May 11, 1925; s. Henry James and Ellen (Terry) B.; B.S., U. Utah, 1949; m. Beverly Mae Martin, Aug. 26, 1944; children—Martin, James, John, Peter, Amy, Ann, Todd. With Utah Power & Light Co., 1949—, now treas., v.p. adminstrn., also dir. Served with USNR, 1943-45. Home: 3191 Crestview Circle Bountiful UT 84010 Office: 1407 West North Temple Salt Lake City UT 84116

BLUNDELL, WILLIAM RICHARD CHARLES, elec. equipment mfg. co. exec.; b. Montreal, Que., Can., Apr. 13, 1927; s. Richard Charles and Aileen (Payne) B.; B.A.Sc. in Engring. Physics, U. Toronto, 1949; m. Monique Audet, Mar. 20, 1959. Children—Richard Paul, Emily Claire, Michelle Ann, Louise Chantale. With Canadian Gen. Electric Co. Ltd., 1949—, treas., 1966-68, v.p. finance, dir., 1968-71, v.p. consumer products div., 1971—. Mem. Anglican Ch. Clubs: Granite (Toronto). Home: 35 Daneswood Rd Toronto 12 Ontario Canada Office: 221 Dufferin Toronto Ontario Canada

BLUNDEN, GORDON ARTHUR, savs. and loan assn. exec.; b. Detroit, Nov. 20, 1920; s. Henry and Margaret (Thiel) B.; B.A., U.Cal. at Los Angeles, 1942; children—Craig, Gale, Carol. With Coast Fed. Savs. and Loan Assn., Los Angeles, 1946-50; v.p. Lynwood Savs. and Loan Assn., Lynnwood, Cal., 1950-55; pres., mng. officer Provident Fed. Savs. & Loan Assn., Riverside, Cal., 1956—; dir. Frontier Fidelity Savs. & Loan Assn., Las Vegas. Served to 1st lt. USAAF, 1942-46. Mem. Riverside C. of C. Kiwanian. Home: Riverside CA Office: 3756 Central Av Riverside CA 92506

BLUNT, CARLETON, lawyer; b. Evanston, Ill., Aug. 27, 1905; s. John Ellsworth and Carlene (Curtis) B.; A.B., Dartmouth, 1926; J.D., Northwestern U., 1929; m. Rebecca Loomis Prentiss, Oct. 31, 1931; children—Frances Laird, Patricia Prentiss, Carlene Curtis. Practiced in Chgo., 1929—; asso. firm Cutting, Moore & Sidley, until 1934; Fisher, Boyden, Bell, Boyd & Marshall, 1934-35; mem. firm Bell, Boyd & Marshall, 1935—, now Bell, Boyd, Lloyd, Haddad & Burns. Dir. Laird, Norton Trust Co., Seattle, Rand McNally & Co., Weyerhaeuser Co., Acme Cleve. Corp., Am. Horse Shows Assn., U.S. Equestrian Team, Inc.; dir., pres. Par Club Fla., Inc.; gen. counsel Western Golf Assn., 1935-45, pres., 1957. Mayor, Village of Golf (Fla.), 1957—. Life trustee Northwestern U.; chmn. bd. trustees Evans Scholars Found.; campaign chmn. Community Fund Chgo., 1949. Mem. Gen. Assn. Alumni of Dartmouth Coll. (pres. 1950-51, chairman 1952), Law Club, Legal Club, Chicago Commonwealth Club (v.p. 1954), Phi Beta Kappa Assos., Phi Beta Kappa, Psi Upsilon, Phi Delta Phi, Order of Coif. Republican. Clubs: Commercial, Chicago, Attic, Glen View, Old Elm; Gulf Stream, Seminole, Lake Placid, Country of Fla. (pres. 1956—). Ocean of Fla. (pres. 1961-71) (Delray Beach). Home: Glen View Club Golf IL (winter) Box 550 Delray Beach FL 33444 Office: 135 S LaSalle St Chicago IL 60603

BLY, CHAUNCEY GOODRICK, coll. pres.; b. Kikungshan, Honan, China, June 14, 1920 (parents Am. citizens); s. John Marius and Minnie (Saboe) B.; B.A. summa cum laude, St. Olaf Coll., 1941; M.S., U. Rochester, 1946, M.D., 1946, Ph. D., 1953; m. Ruth Madeline Henion, June 1, 1946; children—Susan Jean, John Charles, Judith Anne, David Alan, Chauncey Goodrich. Grad. research asst. U. Rochester, 1941-42, intern, then resident pathology Med. Sch., 1946-47; instr. pathology U. Ill. Med. Sch., 1948-49; AEC postdoctoral research fellow U. Rochester, 1949-51; scholar cancer research Am. Cancer Soc., also asst. prof. pathology and oncology U. Kan., 1951-54, asso. prof., 1954-57; clin. asst. prof. pathology U. Rochester, also dir. pathol. labs. Highland Hosp., 1957-59; asso. prof. pathology Duke, 1959-60; prof. pathology Bowman Gray Sch. Medicine, 1960-61; pres. Thiel Coll., 1961—, also trustee. Pres. Kan. Soc. Pathologists, 1957-58; cons. radioisotopes and pathology VA in Kan. and N.C., 1954-61; spl. cons. Nat. Cancer Inst., 1960-61. Mem. exec. com. Central States Synod, Lutheran Ch., 1954-57, Luth. Laymens Movement, 1954-61, United Luth. Ch. Men, 1960-62; bd. fgn. missions United Luth. Ch. Am., 1956-62, ofcl. del. biennial convs., 1954-66; mem. div. coll. and univ. work Nath. Luth. Council, 1957-60; chmn. med. com. bd. world missions Luth. Ch. Am., 1962—; chmn. com. edn. and world affairs Council Protestant Colls. and Univs., 1962—. Mem. leg. adv. com. to Congressman Weaver, 1962—. Bd. dirs. Johnson County chpt. Am. Cancer Soc., 1951-57, Durham County chpt., 1959-60, Monroe County chpt., 1957-59; bd. dirs. Pa. Mental Health Assn., 1961-65; mem. exec. bd. dirs. Mercer County council Boy Scouts Am., 1961—; trustee Lenoir Rhyne Coll., 1959-61. Served to capt., M.C., AUS, 1947-49. Recipient Centennial award in sci. Augustana Coll., 1961. Diplomate Am. Bd. Pathology. Fellow A.A.A.S.; mem. Kan., N,C, Pa., Christian med. socs., A.M.A., Am. Soc. Exptl. Pathology, Am. Assn. Path. Bacteriologists, Internat. Acad. Pathology, N.Y., Pa. acads. sci., Newcomen Soc., Radiation Research Soc., Assn. Am. Med. Colls., Greenville Businessmens Assn., Phi Beta Kappa, Sigma Xi, Blue Key, Alpha Omega Alpha. Clubs: Duquesne (Pitts.); Iroquois, Greenville Country. Rotarian. Republican. Author numerous profl. articles. Home: 40 Eagle St Greenville PA 16125

BLY, ROBERT ELWOOD, poet; b. Madison, Minn., Dec. 23, 1926; s. Jacob Thomas and Alice (Aws) B.; student St. Olaf Coll., 1946-47; A.B., Harvard, 1950; M.A., U. Ia., 1956; m. Carolyn McLean, June 24, 1955; children—Mary, Bridget, Noah Matthew Jacob, Micah John Padma. Editor, pub. Sixties Press, Madison, 1958—. Co- chmn. Am. Writers vs. Vietnam War, 1966—. Served with USNR, 1944-45. Recipient award Nat. Inst. Arts and Letters, Nat. Book award in poetry, 1968. Fulbright grantee, 1956-57; Amy Lowell fellow, 1964-65; Guggenheim fellow, 1965-66; Rockefeller Found. fellow, 1967. Author: (poems) Silence in the Snowy Fields, 1962, The Light Around the Body, 1967; (prose poems) The Morning Glory. Editor: Forty Poems Touching on Recent American History, 1967; A Poetry Reading Against the Vietnam War, 1966; The Sea and the Honeycomb (poems), 1966. Translator: (from Swedish) (Selma Lagerlöf) The Story of Gösta Berling, 1962, (Gunnar Ekelöf) I Do Best Alone at Night, 1968; (from Norwegian) Hunger, 1967; (from German) Twenty Poems of Georg Trakl, 1961; (from Spanish) Twenty Poems of Cesar Vallejo, 1963, Forty Poems of Juan Ramón Jiménez, 1967, Twenty Poems of Pablo Neruda, 1967. Address: Odin House Madison MN 56256

BLYDEN, LARRY, (Ivan Lawrence Blieden), actor, dir., producer; b. Houston, June 23, 1925; s. Adolph and Marian (Davidson) Blieden; student Southwestern La. Inst., 1943-44; B.S., U. Houston, 1948; studied performing arts with Stella Adler, Ethel Meyers, Frank Wagner, Matt Mattox; m. Carol Haney, Apr. 17, 1954 (div. 1961); children—Joshua, Ellen. Made N.Y.C. debut in Mr. Roberts, 1948; since appeared in N.Y. plays The Miser, 1950, Wish You Were Here, 1952, Oh, Men! Oh, Women! 1953, Italian Straw Hat, 1957, Who Was That Lady I Saw You With? 1958, Flower Drum Song, 1958, Foxy, 1964, Luv, 1965, The Apple Tree, 1968, You Know I Can't Hear You When the Water's Running, 1969; appeared in The Time of Your Life, Brussels World's Fair, 1958, Foxy, Dawson City, Yukon, Can., 1962; dir. Harold, N.Y.C., 1962; appeared in films Bachelor Party, 1957, Kiss Them for Me, 1957, On a Clear Day You Can See Forever, 1969, TV programs What Makes Sammy Run? 1960, Joe and Mabel, 1954, Harry's Girls, 1963, others; master ceremonies TV program Personality, 1967-69, The Movie Game, 1969-71. Served to lt. USMCR, 1943-46. Mem. Actors Equity Assn., Am. Fedn. TV and Radio Actors, Screen Actors Guild. Home: 205 W 57th St New York City NY 10019 Office: care International Business Management 641 Lexington Av New York City NY 10022

BLYTH, ANN MARIE, actress; b. N.Y.C., Aug. 16, 1928; d. Harry and Anne (Lynch) Blyth; grad. Cathedral Sch., N.Y.C., 1941; L.H.D., St. Joseph's Coll., Emmittsburg, Md., 1959, U. Portland (Ore.), 1968; m. Dr. James V. McNulty, June 27, 1953; children—Timothy, Maureen, Kathleen, Terence, Eileen. Theater prodns. Watch on the Rhine, 1941; Our Town, 1954; motion picture appearances include Mildred Pierce, 1945; Rose Marie, 1953; Student Prince, 1955; Kismet, 1956; The Buster Keaton Story, 1957; Jazz Age; Slander: The Helen Morgan Story. Address: 6 Toluca Estates North Hollywood CA 91602

BLYTH, COLIN ROSS, math. statistician, educator; b. Guelph, Ont., Can., Oct. 24, 1922; s. Colin McDonald and Gladys (Martin) B.; B.A., Queen's U., 1944; M.A., U. Toronto, 1946; postgrad. U. N.C., 1946-48; Ph.D., U. Cal., 1950; m. Valerie Thompson, Aug. 27, 1955; children-Mary Alice, Georgina, Colin M., Heather, Alexander, Donald. Asst. prof. U. Ill. at Urbana, 1950-54, asso. prof., 1954-59, prof. math., 1959—. Mem. A.A.A.A. Am. Statis. Assn. Am. Math. Soc., Inst. Math. Statistics. Home: 701 W Michigan Av Urbana IL 61801

BLYTH, E.G., glass mfg. co. exec. Vice pres. finance and adminstrn., treas. Dominion Glass Co., Ltd., Montreal, Que., Can. Office: Dominion Glass Co Ltd 1080 Beaver Hall Hill Montreal Quebec Canada*

BLYTH, JOHN WILLIAM, mgmt. cons.; b. Burlington, Wis., Oct. 27, 1909; s. Robert Bayne and Jane (Broadfoot) B.; A.B., Haverford Coll., 1931; M.A., U. Ia., 1932; postgrad. U. Berlin (Germany), 1934-35; Ph.D., Brown U., 1936; m. Renée Fourgous, Aug. 29, 1936. Faculty Hamilton Coll., 1936-62, asst. to pres., dir. summer session, 1946, dean faculty, 1946-48, prof. philosophy, 1947-62, John Stewart Kennedy prof., 1952-62, coordinator teaching machine project, 1959-61; dir. ednl. systems dept. Diebold Group, Inc., 1962-65; v.p. Argyle Pub. Corp., 1965-68; sr. v.p. Metromedia div. AnaLearn Assos., Inc., 1968-70; pres. Blyth Assos., Inc., New Canaan Conn., 1970—. Vice pres., dir. Hamilton Research Assos., Inc., 1959-62. Ford faculty fellow, 1951-52. Mem. Am. Philos. Assn., Am. Assn. U. Profs., Phi Beta Kappa. Author: Whitehead's Theory of Knowledge, Vol. VIII, 1941; A Modern Introduction to Logic, 1957. Co-author: Programmed Text in Logic, 6 vols., 1963. Contbr. articles to profl. Jours. Co-inventor teaching machine. Address: 258 Dan's Hwy New Canaan CT 06840

BLYTH, ROBERT BROADFOOT, banker; b. Burlington, Wis., Mar. 4, 1905; s. Robert Bayne and Jane (Broadfoot) B.; A.B., Oberlin Coll., 1927; M.B.A., Harvard, 1929; m. Henrietta Monroe, May 5, 1936; 1 dau., Cynthia Neale. With Union Trust Co., Cleve., 1929-33; with Nat. City Bank of Cleve., 1933—, v.p., 1943- 55, 56-59, sr. v.p., dir., 1959-60, 1st v.p., 1960-67, vice chmn. bd., 1967- -; dir. Endowment Adv. Services; asst. to sec. Dept. Treasury, Washington, 1955; dir. Nat. City Bldg. Corp., New Eng. Bldg., Inc., Celina Financial Corp. Trustee Oberlin Coll., 1958—; bd. govs. Western Res. U., 1959—. Mem. Am. Bankers Assn., Investment Bankers Am., Assn. Res. City Bankers, C. of C. Conglist. Clubs: Union, Harvard Mid-Day (Cleve.). Author articles on finance. Home: 17445 Shelburne Rd Cleveland Heights OH 44118 Office: 623 Euclid Av Cleveland OH 44101

BLYTHE, DAVID KNOX, educator; b. Georgetown, Ky., May 18, 1917; s. Ivie and Mellie (Featherston) B.; B.S. in Civil Engring., U. Ky., 1940, C.E., 1948; M.C.E., Cornell U., 1950; student hwys. and traffic, U. Cal. at Berkeley, 1955; m. Jeanie Jamieson, Nov. 7, 1942; children—Susan, Peggy, Sheila. Jr. civil engr. U.S. Forest Service, 1940-41; materials engr. U.S. Corps Engrs., 1946-47; prof. civil engring., chmn. dept. U. Ky., Lexington, 1947-69, asso. dean Coll. Engring., 1968—; planning cons. Ky. Dept. Hwys., 1954-57; civil engring. cons. Spindletop Research, Inc. Sr. vis. fellow OEEC, U. Durham (Eng.), 1961; Fulbright lectr., Ecuador, summer 1969. Served from 2d lt. to maj. USAAF, 1941-46; group comdr. Ky. Div. Civil Def., 1956-61. Registered profl. engr., Ky. Fellow Am. Soc. C.E.; mem. Am. Soc. Engring. Edn., Nat. Soc. Profl. Engrs., Am. Cong. Survey and Map, Tau Beta Pi, Omicron Delta Kappa. Home: 975 Edgewater Dr Lexington KY 40502

BLYTHE, STUART OAKES, editor, writer; b. Rochester, N.Y., Mar. 5, 1890; s. Samuel George and Carolyn Hamilton (Oakes) B.; student Dartmouth, 1911, Ia. State Coll., 1912-13; A.B., U. of Wis., 1912; m. Gertrude Tunstall Edwards, Oct. 9, 1920; children—Kathleen Hamilton and Isabel Wilson (twins), Samuel George, 2d. Reporter, Oregon Jour., Portland, 1913-17; news staff U.S. Com. on Pub. Information, 1917-18; with Emergency Fleet Corp., 1918-19; asso. editor Country Gentleman, 1919-28, Washington rep., 1924-28; asso. editor Ladies' Home Jour., 1928-35; with Farm Jour., Inc. 1935-36; asso. editor Cal. Mag. of Pacific, 1936-39; asst. dir Am.-Cavalcade of a Nation, Golden Gate Internat. Expn., 1940; with Office Censorship, San Francisco, 1942-45, Cal. Dept. Employment, 1945-52. Mem. Theta Delta Chi, Sigma Delta Chi. Episcopalian. Club: Family (San Francisco). Home: Carmel CA 93921

BLYTHE, WILLIAM BREVARD, educator, physician; b. Huntersville, N.C., Sept. 23, 1928; s. William LeGette and Esther (Farmer) B.; A.B., U. N.C., 1948, student Sch. Medicine, 1949-51; M.D., Wash. U. Sch. Medicine, 1953; m. Gloria Eleanor Nassif, Feb. 4, 1956; children—William LeGette II, Anne Dewar, David Samuel Brevard, John Alexander. Intern, then resident N.C. Meml. Hosp., Chapel Hill; instr. medicine U. N.C. Sch. Medicine, 1960-62, asst. prof., 1962-65, asso. prof., 1965-70, prof., 1970—, dir. Clin. Research Unit, 1966—. Served to capt. AUS, 1955-57. Mem. A.M.A., Am. Physiol. Soc., Am. Soc. Nephrology, Am. Soc. Artificial Internal Organs, Am. Fedn. Clin. Research, So. Soc. Clin. Investigation, Alpha Omega Alpha. Research renal physiology and renal disease. Home: Hillcrest Circle Chapel Hill NC 27514

BLYTHE, WILLIAM LEGETTE, author; b. Huntersville, N.C., Apr. 24, 1900; s. William Brevard and Hattye (Jackson) B.; A.B., U. N.C., 1921, LL.D., 1969; Litt.D., Davidson Coll., 1950; m. Esther Emily Farmer, May 31, 1926; children—William Brevard, Samuel LeGette, Esther Lovelace (Mrs. Joseph C. Pugh). Tchr., Greensboro (N.C.) pub. schs., 1921-22; successively reporter, columnist, editorial writer Charlotte (N.C.) News, 1922-24; with N.Y. Eve. Post, 1924; pub. N. Mecklenburg News, Huntersville, 1925-26; editor Mecklenburg Times, Charlotte, 1926-27; successively reporter, columnist, editorial writer, lit. editor Charlotte Observer, 1927-50; full time writer, 1950—; writer in residence U. N.C. at Charlotte, 1967—. Chmn. N.C. Writers Conf., 1965; mem. Gov. N.C. Commn. Library Resources, 1964. Commnr. gen. assembly Presbyn. Ch. U.S., 1952; moderator Mecklenburg Presbytery, 1955-56; mem. permanent com. hist. matters Presbyn. Synod N.C., 1967—, mem. sesquicentennial observance com., 1963; chmn. Pres. Andrew Johnson Sesquicentennial Commn., 1958; mem. Mecklenburg County Econ. Devel. Commn., 1966—, Huntersville Planning and Zoning Commn., 1967—, Mecklenburg Presbytery Centennial Com., 1968, Mayflower Award Jury, 1938, 47, 52. Charlotte Bicentennial Com., 1968. Recipient Mayflower award, 1953, 61; Cannon cup for hist. research, 1961; named Huntersville's Man of Year, 1955. Mem. N.C. Writers Conf., N.C. Lit. and Hist. Assn., Mecklenburg Hist. Assn., N.C. Folklore Soc., Phi Beta Kappa, Omega Delta, Sigma Upsilon, Delta Tau Delta. Democrat. Lion. Club: Charlotte Philosophy. Author: The Chatham Rabbit, 1921; Marshal Ney: A Dual Life, 1937; Alexandriana, 1940; Shout Freedom!, 1948; Bold Galilean, 1948; William Henry Belk: Merchant of the South, 1958; A Tear for Judas, 1951; Miracle in the Hills, 1953; Voice in the Wilderness, 1955; James W. Davis: North Carolina Surgeon, 1956; The Crown Tree, 1957; Yes, Ma'am, Miss Gee, 1957; Gift from the Hills, 1958; Call Down the Storm, 1958; Thomas Wolfe and His Family, 1961; Hear Me, Pilate!, 1961; Hornets' Nest: The Story of Charlotte and Mecklenburg County (with Charles R. Brockman), 1961; Echo in My Soul, 1962; Mountain Doctor, 1964; Man on Fire, 1964; Robert Lee Stowe: Pioneer in Textiles, 1965; 38th Evac, 1966; The Hornets' Nest, 1968; Brothers of Vengeance, 1969; Meet Julius Abernethy: Trader and Philanthropist, 1969; also articles, revs., short stories. Address: College St Huntersville NC 28078

BOAK, RUTH ALICE, physician, educator; b. Auburn, N.Y., May 25, 1906; d. Spencer J. and Jane (Clark) Boak; B.S., Cornell U., 1927, M.S., 1927, Ph.D., 1929; M.D., U. Rochester, 1940; m. Donald L. Ferris, May 30, 1942; childrenBoak J., Don R. Research asst. Cornell U., 1927-28; instr. Albany Med. Sch., 1928-30; asso. U. Rochester, 1930-47; house officer Johns Hopkins Hosp., 1940-41; pvt. practice medicine, Greenwich, Conn., 1944; asso. prof. infectious diseases and pediatrics U. Cal. Sch. Medicine, Los Angeles, 1947-57, prof., 1957-, prof. med. microbiology, immunology, pediatrics and pub. health, 1966—. Vis. prof. Airlongga U. Sch. Medicine, Surabaja, Indonesia. 1963-66. Named Woman of the Year in Medicine, Los Angeles Times, 1955. Fulbright award, 1954-55, 59-60. Fellow Am. Pub. Health Assn.; Soc., Mexican Border Pub. Health Assn., Med. Research Soc. Los Angeles. Home: 10639 Mason Av Chatsworth CA 91311 Office: Univ of Cal Med Center Los Angeles CA 90024

BOAL, ARTHUR MCCLURE, lawyer; b. Cherry Tree, Pa., Feb. 14, 1889; s. William McClure and Hannah Waller (Camp) B.; grad. Phillips-Exeter Acad., 1910; A.B., Harvard, 1914, LL.B., 1916; m. Sara Elizabeth Metzner, Apr. 2, 1921; children—Elizabeth (Mrs. William R. Hogan), Arthur McClure. Admitted to Mass. bar, 1917, N.Y. bar, 1930; asso. with William J.E. Sander, Boston, 1917, Whipple, Sears & Ogden, Boston, 1917-19; admiralty atty. U.S. Shipping Bd., Washington, 1919-23, asst. admiralty counsel, 1923-25, admiralty counsel, 1925-29; mem. Chapman, Snider, Duke & Boal, 1930-32; partner Boal, McQuade & Fitzpatrick and predecessor firms, 1932—. Mayor Village of Pelham, N.Y., 1949-53. Chmn. adjudication, arbitration internat. courts Southwestern Legal Found. Dir. Pelham Community Chest, campaign mgr., 1940-41, pres., 1942-43; chmn. Pelham Red Cross War Fund campaign, 1945-46; v. chmn. Westchester County chpt. A.R.C., 1946-49; mem. Pelham Bd. Edn., 1960-67, pres., 1965-67. Mem. Coast Arty. Sch., 1918. Mem. Maritime Law Assn. U.S. (pres. 1958-60, chmn. com. on Comite Maritime Internat. 1960—), N.Y. Bar Assn., Internat. Law Assn., Assn. Bar City N.Y. (mem. com. on judiciary 1962-64). Clubs: Downtown, Harvard (N.Y.C.); Author's (London, Eng.); Men's (pres. 1943-44), Pelham (N.Y.) Country. Contbr. Am. part article on admiralty jurisdiction Ency. Brit., 14th edit. Home: 246 Corona Av Pelham NY 10803 Office: 116 John St New York City NY 10038

BOARD, JOSEPH BRECKINRIDGE, Jr., educator, polit. scientist; b. Princeton, Ind., Mar. 5, 1931; s. Joseph Breckinridge and Rachel Eleanor (Unthank) B.; A.B. with highest honors, Ind. U., 1953, J.D., 1958, Ph.D., 1962; B.A. (Rhodes scholar 1953-55), Oxford (Eng.) U., 1955, M.A., 9161; m. Kjersti E. Danielson, Dec. 31, 1955; children—Ian Robert, Annika Caroline. Teaching fellow govt. Ind. U., 1955-58, lectr. govt., 1958; asst. prof. polit. sci. Elmira Coll., 1959- 61; asso. prof. polit. sci., chmn. dept. Cornell Coll., 1961-64; prof. polit. sci., chmn. dept. Union Coll., Schenectady, 1964—. Mem. Rhodes Scholarship Selection Com. Neb., 1961-62, Ia., 1963-64; mem. regional selection com. for Woodrow Wilson Fellowships, 1966—; mem. exec. council Ia. Conf. Polit. Scientists, 1963-65; spl. adv. coll. and univ. affairs Young Citizens for Johnson, 1964; cons. Nat. Endowment Humanities, 1968, N.Y. State Dept. Edn., 1968; Fulbright lectr. Sweden, 1968-69; Central Am. fellow Asso. Colls. Midwest, 1962; Nat. Def. Edn. Act. postdoctoral fellow in Portuguese, 1963. Mem. Am. Assn. Rhodes Scholars, Am. Polit. Sci. Assn., Am. Assn. U. Profs., Ind. Bar, Am-Scandinavian Found., Acacia, Phi Beta Kappa. Democrat. Episcopalian. Author: The Government and Politics of Sweden, 1970. Home: 15 Sunnyside Rd Scotia NY 12302 Office: Union Coll Schenectady NY 12308

BOARDMAN, ARTHUR GODDARD, Jr., banker; b. New Bedford, Mass., Aug. 20, 1910; s. Arthur G. and Sarah Clifton (Price) B.; B.A., Dartmouth, 1931, M.C.S. 1932; m. Jean Richardson, Nov. 22, 1941; children—James R., Nancy G. With Irving Trust Co., N.Y.C., 1932—, asst. sec., 1941-47, asst. v.p. 1947-49, v.p., 1949-57, sr. v.p., 1957-61, exec. v.p., 1961-69, sr. exec. v.p., 1969-70, pres., 1970—, also dir.; dir. Irving Internat. Banking Corp., Irving Internat. Financing Corp., Gen. Cable Corp., Internat. Comml. Bank, Australian Internat. Finance Corp. Ltd. Mem. adv. council Pres. Assos. of Pace Coll. Served as lt., USNR, 1943-46. Mem. St. George's Soc., The Pilgrims. Club: Rock Spring. Home: 61 Adams Av Short Hills NJ 07078 Office: 1 Wall St New York City NY 10005

BOARDMAN, DONALD CHAPIN, educator, geologist; b. Adna, Wash., Nov. 18, 1913; s. George Parshall and Grace (Rice) B.; student U. Cal. at Santa Barbara, 1933-34; B.S., Wheaton (Ill.) Coll., 1938; student Northwestern U., 1938-39; M.S., U. Ia., 1942; Ph.D., U. Wis., 1952; m. Elizabeth Banford Baillie, Aug. 31, 1938; children—Elizabeth Ann (Mrs. Robert Hein), Barbara Lowell (Mrs. Richard Herd), Donald Chapin. Faculty Wheaton Coll., 1940, prof. geology, 1957—, chmn. dept., 1958—, dir. sci. sta., Rapid City, S.D., summers 1951-65, 69—. SEATO prof. geology U. Peshawar, West Pakistan, 1959-60; cons. in field, 1950—. Mem. bd. edn., Wheaton, 1961-67, pres., 1962-67. Served to lt. comdr. USNR, 1942-46. Named Alumnus of Year, Wheaton Coll., 1967. Fellow Geol. Soc. Am., Am. Sci. Affiliation (nat. pres. 1970-71); mem. Am. Assn. Petroleum Geologists, Am. Inst. Profl. Geologists, Soc. Vertebrate Paleontology, Soc. Econ. Paleontologists and Mineralogists, Ill. Acad. Sci., Am. Assn. U. Profs., Nat. Assn. Geology Tchrs. (pres. central sect. 1961-62), Sigma Xi. Contbr. articles to profl. jours. Home: 311 E Franklin St Wheaton IL 60187

BOARDMAN, EUGENE POWERS, educator; b. Aurora, Ill., Oct. 5, 1910; s. Charles Watkins and Irmgard (Heth) B.; B.A., Beloit (Wis.) Coll., 1932; M.A., U. Wis., 1937; M.A. Harvard, 1939, Ph.D., 1947; m. Elizabeth Reynolds Jelinek, June 21, 1940 (div. June 1969); children—Susan, Sarah, Christopher, Erika, Andrew, Benjamin. Tchr. English prep. dept. Am. U., Beirut, Lebanon, 1932-35; tchr. social studies, French, Delavan (Wis.) High Sch., 1935-36; prof. charge courses, grad. work East Asian history U. Wis., Madison, 1946—. Lobbyist with U.S. Congress for a New China Policy under auspices Friends Com. Nat. Legislation, 1965-66. Served as maj. USMCR, 1941-46. Decorated Legion of Merit. Mem. Am. Hist. Assn., Assn. for Asian Studies (past program chmn.), Phi Beta Kappa, Delta Sigma Rho. Mem. Soc. of Friends. Author: Christian Influence on the Ideology of the Taiping Rebellion, 1851-54; Madison, 1952. Home: Apt 203C 6110 Century Av Middleton WI 53562 Office: U Wis Madison WI 53706

BOARDMAN, FRANCIS, govt. ofcl.; b. N.Y.C., Oct. 2, 1915; s. Francis and Anne Macdonald (Calef) B.; grad. Deerfield (Mass.) Acad., 1934; B.A., Williams Coll., 1938; m. Anne Dwight Hooker, Sept. 10, 1953; 1 dau., Pamela Dwight. Instr. English and Journalism Am., U. Beirut, Lebanon, 1938-41; analyst Fgn. Econ. Adminstrn., 1942-44; area specialist comml. policy div. Middle East br. U.S. Dept. of State, 1944- 48, attache Am. Embassy, Ankara, Turkey, 1948-50, in Office Near Eastern Affairs, 1951-56; 1st sec., consul Am. Embassy, Beirut, Lebanon, 1956- 59; prin. econ. officer Turkish sect., 1959-60; with Near East and S. Asia div. Export-Import Bank, 1962—. Asst. to econ. adviser U.S. delegation to Paris Peace Conf., 1946. Mem. Middle East Inst. (bd. govs., sec.-treas.), Fgn. Service Assn., Alpha Delta Phi. Episcopalian. Club: Metropolitan (Washington; also Williams (N.Y.C.). Author: Institutions of Higher Learning in the Middle East, 1961. Contbr. articles to periodicals. Home: 5035 Lowell St NW Washington DC 20016 Office: 811 Vermont Av NW Washington DC 20511

BOARDMAN, JOHN J., bishop; b. Bklyn., Nov. 7, 1894; LL.D., St. John's U., 1952. Ordained priest, Roman Cath. Ch., 1921; titular bishop of Gunela and auxiliary, 1952—. Mem. Soc. Propagation of Faith (nat. treas.). K.C. Home: 245 Prospect Park W Brooklyn NY 11209 Office: 7320 4th Av Brooklyn NY 11209

BOARDMAN, KATHRYN, journalist. Book editor St. Paul Pioneer Press and Dispatch. Office: Northwest Publs Inc 55 E 44th St St Paul MN 55101*

BOARDMAN, NEWELL STEPHEN, lawyer; b. New Richmond, Wis., May 1, 1894; s. Stephen Charles and Adelia (Clapp) B.; A.B., U. Wis., 1918, LL.B., 1922; m. Maryan Hosford, May 30, 1936; 1 dau., Jane Abbott (Mrs. Robert Homburg). Admitted to Wis. bar, 1922, U.S. Supreme Ct. bar, 1942. Ill. bar, 1943; mem. firm Boardman, Jones & Hamilton, and predecessors, Mineral Point, Dodgeville, Wis., 1922-50, Lord, Bissell & Brook, and predecessors, Chgo., 1942—, dist. atty. pro tem., then dist. atty. Iowa County, Wis., 1923-26; regional atty., then asst. gen. counsel, regional dir. Resettlement Adminstrn., 1937-38; chief asst. atty. gen. of Wis., 1938-42; Served as 2d lt. U.S. Signal Corps., 1918. Mem. Am., Ill., Wis., Chgo. bar assns., Phi Kappa Psi, Phi Delta Phi. Republican. Conglist. Mason. Club: University (Chgo). Home: 23 W Walnut St Hinsdale IL 60521 Office: 135 S LaSalle St Chicago IL 60603

BOARDMAN, PAUL LAWRENCE, banker; b. Indpls., Oct. 22, 1906; s. Fred Lawrence and Nettie Rae (Beaver) B.; extension student Ind. U.; student Am. Inst. Banking, Grad. Sch. Banking, Rutgers U.; m. Mary C. Mackey, Apr. 12, 1928. With Am. Fletcher Nat. Bank & Trust Co., Indpls., 1923-71, v.p., 1957-64, sr. v.p., 1964-71, ret., 1971. Mem. Am. Inst. Banking (chmn. pub. relations com. 1954), Ind. Bankers Assn., Indpls. C. of C., Ind. Soc. Pioneers. Mason (Shriner). Club: Hillcrest Country (Indpls.). Home: 1101 N Mitchner Av Indianapolis IN 46219 Office: 101 Monument Circle Indianapolis IN 46204

BOARDMAN, RICHARD STANTON, paleontologist; b. Oak Park, Ill., July 16, 1923; s. Stanton Knight and Irma (Crouch) B.; student Denison U., 1943; B.S., U. Ill., 1948, M.S.,1952, Ph.D., 1955; m. Phyllis Orwig, Apr. 6, 1946; childrenWilliam Richard, James Mark. Geologist U.S. Geol. Survey, 1952-57; asso. curator Smithsonian Instn., Washington, 1957-60, now curator. Served 1943-46. Mem. Paleontol. Soc., Paleontol. Assn., Soc. Systemic Zoology, Soc. Econ. Paleontologists and Mineralogists, Am. Assn. Petroleum Geologists, Sigma Xi. Author papers taxonomy, morphology, evolution fo Paleozoic Bryozoa. Home: 7004 Richard Dr Bethesda MD 20034 Office: Smithsonian Instn Washington DC 20560

BOARDMAN, THOMAS LESLIE, newspaper editor; b. Arcadia, Mo., Aug. 31, 1919; s. Albert Jefferson and Jessie Dent (Davis) B.; A.B., Oberlin Coll., 1939; Litt. D., Baldwin-Wallace Coll., 1970; m. Cynthia Sergeant, May 12, 1945; children—Thomas Leslie, Caroline Clare. Reporter Cleve. Press, 1939-41, labor editor, 1945-48, asst. city editor, 1948-52, editorial writer, 1952-57, chief editorial writer, 1957-62, editor, 1966—; editor Indpls. Times, 1962-66. Chmn. Recreation Bd., Shaker Heights, O., 1960-62; pres. Golden Age Centers Cleve., 1956-61. Trustee Cuyahoga County Library, 1957-62, Oberlin Coll. Served to lt. comdr. USNR, 1941-45; capt. Res. Mem. Advt. Club Cleve. (pres. 1970), Am. Soc. Newspaper Editors, Sigma Delta Chi. Episcopalian. Clubs: Columbia (Indpls.); Mid-Day, City (pres. 1957), Union (Cleve.). Home: 2739 Green Rd Shaker Heights OH 44122 Office: 901 Lakeside Av Cleveland OH 44114

BOARDMAN, WILLIAM WADE, lawyer; b. New Richmond, Wis., Jan. 25, 1905; s. Stephen Charles and Adelia (Clapp) B.; student N.D. State U., 1923-26; LL.B., U. Wis., 1930; m. Elizabeth Tucker, Sept. 11, 1929; 1 dau., Elizabeth (Mrs. John W. Prussing). Admitted to Wis. Bar, 1930, since practiced in Madison;; mem. firm Boardman, Suhr, Curry & Field; lectr. law U. Wis. Law Sch., 1934- 46. Mem. bd. State Bar Commrs., 1946—, pres., 1953—; mem. Wis. State Jud. Council, 1950-53. Mem. Am., 7th Fed. Circuit, Dane County (past pres.) bar assns., State Bar Wis., Am. Bar Found., Am. Coll. Probate Counsel (regent), Order of Coif, Phi Kappa Phi, Phi Kappa Phi, Phi Delta Phi. Club: Madison. Home: 2921 Colgate Rd Madison WI 53705 Office: 110 E Main St PO Box 2 97 Madison WI 53701

BOAS, HERBERT ALLAN, JR., mfg. co. exec.; b. Pelham, N.Y., Mar. 2, 1917; s. Herbert Allan (Chase) B.; student Princeton, 1940; m. Mildred C. Lowry, Sept. 20, 1941; children—Bonnie Chase (Mrs. B.G.Balmer), Deborah Mead (Mrs. R.B. 1937-39; expediter Pratt & Whitney Aircraft div. United Aircraft Corp., 1942-47; asst. to pres., dir. advt. and pub. relations Bristol Brass Co. (Conn.), 1947-51; asst. dir. advt. and pub. relations Sinclair Oil Corp., N.Y.C., 1951-53; mgr. tire, battery and accessories sales Sinclair Refining Co., N.Y.C., 1955-58; dir. marketing Budd Co., Phila., 1958-59, v.p. marketing,

1959-64; v.p., asst. to pres. Gen. Steel Industries, Inc., Granite City, Ill., 1965-66; exec. v.p. Faillace Prodns., Inc., N.Y.C., 1966-67; v.p. marketing Diners Club, N.Y.C., 68; pres. H.C. Cook Co., Ansonia, Conn., 1968—, Chmn. bd., 1970—; Co., 1968—, chmn. bd., 1970—; pres. Lighter Corp. Am., 1 1968—, chmn. Conn.). Clubs: Country of New Canaan (Conn.); Rolling Rock (Ligonier, Pa.); Princeton (N.Y.C.); Egypt Mills (Bushkill, Pa.); Racebrook Country (Orange, Conn.). Home: 226 Silvermine Rd New Canaan CT 06840 Office: 28 Beaver St Ansonia CT 06401

BOAS, RALPH PHILIP, Jr., educator; b. Walla Walla, Wash., Aug. 8, 1912; s. Ralph Philip and Louise (Schutz) B.; A.B., Harvard, 1933, Ph.D., 1937; m. Mary Elizabeth Layne, June 12, 1941; children—Ralph Layne, Anne Louise, Harold Philip. Nat. Research fellow Princeton and Cambridge U. (Eng.), 1937-39; instr. Duke, 1939-41, U.S. Navy Pre-Flight Sch., Chapel Hill, N.C., 1942-43; vis. lectr. Harvard, 1943-45; exec. editor Math. Revs., Brown U., 1945-50; lectr. Mass. Inst. Tech., 1948-49; prof. math. Northwestern U., Evanston, Ill., 1950—, chmn. dept., 1957—, pres. fellow, 1961-62; Henry S. Noyes prof., 1962—. John Simon Guggenheim Meml. fellow, 1951-52. Fellow A.A.A.S.; mem. Am. Math. Soc. (v.p. 1959-60, trustee 1966-71), Math. Assn. Am. (chmn. undergrad. program in math. 1968-71), London, Indian math. socs., Phi Beta Kappa, Sigma Xi. Author: Entire Functions, 1954; A Primer of Real Functions, 1960; (with R.C. Buck) Polynomial Expansions of Analytic Functions, 1958; Integrability Theorems for Trigonometric Transforms, 1967. Home: 2440 Simpson St Evanston IL 60201

BOAST, WARREN BENEFIELD, educator; b. Topeka, Dec. 13, 1909; s. Charles W. and Lulu (Robinson) B.; B.S. in Elec. Engring., U. Kan., 1933, M.S., 1934; Ph.D., Ia. State Coll., 1936; m. Ruth J. Hansen, Nov. 28, 1936; children—Richard, Charles, Thomas. Asst. elec. engring. Ia. State U., 1934, prof., head dept., 1954—. Fellow I.E.E.E., Illuminating Engring. Soc., Am. Soc. Engring. Edn., Sigma Xi, Eta Kappa Nu, Tau Beta Pi. Author: Illumination Engineering, 1942, 53; Principles of Electric and Magnetic Fields, 1948, 56; Principles of Electirc and Magnetice Circuits, 1950, 57; Vector Fields, 1964. Home: 225 Parkridge Circle Ames IA 50010

BOATNER, CHARLES KNOX, govt. ofcl.; b. Lawrence, Mass., Oct. 29, 1913; s. James William and Mary (Barfield) B.; student Tex. Christian U., 1934; m. Alice Beatrice McCulloch, July 24, 1937; children—James Knox, Charles Knox, Arvel Davis. With Carter Publs., Inc., Ft. Worth, 1935-61, war corr., Pacific Theater, 1945, city editor, 1947-61; spl. asst. to Vice Pres. Johnson, 1961-63; asst. to sec., dir. information dept. Interior, 1964-70; asst. dir. S.W. region Nat. Park Service, Santa Fe, 1970—. Methodist. Home: 1072 Calle Largo Santa Fe NM 87501 Office: National Park Service Santa Fe Trail PO Box 728 Santa Fe NM 87501

BOATNER, EDMUND BURKE, educator; b. Potts Camp, Miss., Mar. 20, 1903; s. Franklin Pierce and Mary Edwards (Wills) B.; student Millsaps Coll., 1919-21, U. Ill., 1921-22; C.E., U. Miss., 1925; A.M., Gallaudet Coll., 1933, Litt.D., 1952; postgrad. Pa. State Coll., Columbia, 1934-45; m. Maxine Tull, July 19, 1928; 1 dau., Barbara. Civil engr. flood control work for U.S. Govt. on Miss. River, New Orleans, 1925-26; civil engr. I.C. R.R., Chgo., 1926- 27, B.W. Constrn. Co., 1927-28; civil engr., asst. dir. purchases H.K. Ferguson Co., engrs., Cleve., 1928-32; vocational prin. N.Y. Sch. for Deaf, N.Y.C., 1933-35; exec. dir., headmaster Am. Sch. for Deaf, Hartford, Conn., 1935-70, dir. devel., 1970—. Sec. Conf. Execs. Am. Schs. Deaf, 1939-51, v.p., 1951-54, pres. 1954-57, chmn. accreditation com.; founder, pres. Captioned Films for the Deaf, Inc., 1954-60. Pres. Conn. Assn. Child-Caring Instns., 1944-45; trustee, mem. exec. com. Soc. for Savs. Corporator Mt. Sinai Hosp., Hartford Hosp., St. Francis Hosp.; dir. West Hartford Sch. Music; pres. Boys Club of Greater Hartford, 1949-52. Chmn. West Hartford (Conn.) War Finance Com., 1944-46. Recipient Outstanding Service award Conf. Execs. of Am. Schs. for Deaf, 1964; Silver Keystone award, 1969. Mem. Nat. Assn. Deaf (hon.), Am. Inst. Archaeology, Twentieth Century (pres. 1951-52), Antiquarian and Landmarks Soc. Conn. (trustee, membership chmn.), Council on Edn. of Deaf, S.A.R. (Conn. chpt.), Pi Kappa Alpha. Congregationalist. Mason, Rotarian (pres. 1956-57) Clubs: Hartford Golf, 20th Century (Hartford); Cosmos (Washington). Contbr. articles. Home: 115 Cliffmore Rd West Hartford CT 06107

BOATWRIGHT, HELEN (Mrs. Howard L. Boatwright), singer; b. Sheboygan, Wis.; d. Gustav A. and Amalia B. (Karth) Strassburger; student Lakeland Coll., Plymouth, Wis., 1933-35; Mus.B., Oberlin Coll., 1939, Mus.M., 1943; student Syracuse U., 1939, Tanglewood, Opera Dept., 1942; m. Howard Leake Boatwright, June 26, 1943; childrenHoward Leake III, Alice Karth, David Alexander. Performances as soprano include San Antonio Civic Opera Co., 1944-45, Bach Festival, Bethlehem, Pa., 1946, Town Hall appearance, 1946, 52, 53, 54, 55, 56, Carnegie Hall, N.Y.C., 1955, 58. Nat. Symphony Constitution Hall, 1955, Boston Symphony Hall, 1956, Cambridge Sanders Theater, 1949, 53, 57, also others including Can.; Mass. Inst. Tech. Choral Soc. on tour in Germany, summer 1956; soloist with New Haven Symphony in Beethoven's Ninth Symphony, 1952, 55, joint concert with husband, violinist, in Mexico, 1944, N.Y.C., 1946, Bermuda, 1954; before Queen Mother of Eng., Williamsburg, Va., 1954; tour to India, 1959, Europe, 1960, 61, 62; soloist with N.Y., Boston, Cleve., Detroit, Los Angeles orchs.; recs. for Overtone, Urania, Columbia, Kantate. Home: 7153 W Genesee St Fayetteville NY 13066 Office: Judson O'Neill Beall and Steinway 119 W 57th St New York City NY 10019.

BOATWRIGHT, HERBERT LEE, III, banker; b. Washington, Feb. 13, 1933; s. H(erbert) Lee, Jr. and Suzanne (Pollard) B.; grad. Woodberry Forest Sch., 1950, Phillips Exeter Acad., 1951; B.A., U. Va., 1955, M.B.A., 1960; m. Joyce Harley Jordan, Aug. 23, 1958; children—Joyce Jordan, Lee Pollard, Mary Virginia. With Wachovia Bank & Trust Co., Winston-Salem, N.C., 1960-63, asst. v.p., Wilmington, N.C., 1963-66; v.p. Merc.-Safe Deposit & Trust Co., Balt., 1966-69; with Balt. br. Fed. Res. Bank of Richmond, 1969—, sr. v.p. charge br., 1970- -. Mgr., goals and allocations com. United Fund Central Md. First v.p., bd. dirs. Balt. Goodwill Industries; bd. dirs. Balt. U.S.O.; trustee, pres. alumni council Woodberry Forest Sch. Served to lt. USNR, 1955-58. Mem. Robert Morris Assos. (dir. Chesapeake chpt.), Bank Adminstrn. Inst. (dir. Balt. chpt.), Alumni Assn. U. Va. Grad. Sch. Bus. Adminstrn. (dir.). Episcopalian. Clubs: Maryland (Balt.); L'Hirondelle (Ruxton, Md.); Jamestowne Society (Richmond, Va.). Home: 4207 Underwood Rd Baltimore MD 21218 Office: Fed Reserve Bank Lexington and Calvert Sts Baltimore MD 21202

BOATWRIGHT, HOWARD LEAKE, JR., educator, musician; b. Newport News, Va., Mar. 16, 1918; s. Howard Leake and Inex (Alexander) B.; Mus.B., Yale, 1947, Mus.M., 1948; pupil of Paul Hindemith; m. Helen Johanna Strassburger, June 25, 1943; children—Howard Leake III, Alice Karth, David Alexander. Debut as violinist Town Hall, N.Y.C., 1942; tours of U.S. and Mexico, 1943-44; asso. prof. violin U. Tex., 1943-45; asst. prof., then asso. prof. music theory Yale, 1948- 64; dean Sch. Music, Syracuse U., 1964—; condr. Yale Orch., 1952-60; dir. music St. Thomas' Ch., New Haven, 1949-64; concertmaster New Haven Symphony, 1950-62; concertizing and conducting throughout U.S. and Europe, 1961-62, 67. Bd. dirs. Syracuse Symphony, 1964-; mem. music commn. and liturgical commn. Episcopal Diocese Central N.Y., 1964—. Recipient Grand Prix du Disque for recording Passion According to St. John, 1958; Publn. award Soc. for Pub. Am. Music for Quartet for Clarinet and Strings, 1962; Fulbright lectr., India, 1959-60; Rockefeller Found. grantee study S. Indian violin playing, 1960. Mem. Soc. Asian Music (charter, bd. dirs. 1960-), Coll. Music Soc. (council 1960-62), A.S.C.A.P. Episcopalian. Author: Introduction to the Theory of Music, 1956; A Handbook on Staff Notation for Indian Music, 1960. Editor: Essays Before a Sonata and Other Writings by Charles Ives, 1962. Composer: Quartet for Clarinet and Strings, 1958; The Passion According to St. Matthew, 1962; Canticle of the Sun, 1963; Music for Temple Service, 1964; The Ship of Death, 1966. Home: 7153 W Genesee St Fayetteville, NY 13066. Office: Crouse Coll Syracuse Univ Syracuse, NY 13210.

BOATWRIGHT, LINTON SINCLAIR, army officer; b. Washington, Apr. 29, 1920; s. Arthur Sinclair and Estelle (Alexander) B.; B.S., U.S. Mil. Acad., 1941; grad. Command and Gen. Staff Coll., 1943, Armed Forces Staff Coll., 1954, Army War Coll., 1960; m. Lucille Paton, Dec. 15, 1945; children—Edward Paton, Clair. Commd. 2d lt. U.S. Army, 1941, advanced through grades to maj. gen., 1969; assigned 3d Army, World War II; battalion comdr., Korea, 1951; tested Army's only atomic cannon, 1952-53; asst. chief staff operations, chief staff I Field Force, Vietnam, 1965-67; comdg. gen. 24th Inf. Div., 1968-69; dir. individual tng. Army Staff, 1970—. Decorated D.S.M., Silver Star, Legion of Merit, Bronze Star with 4 oak leaf clusters. Home: 2657 Fort Scott Dr Arlington VA 22202 Office: Dir Individual Tng Dept Army Washington DC 20310

BOATWRIGHT, MCHENRY RUTHERFORD, baritone, concert artist; b. Tennille, Ga., Feb. 29, 1928; s. Levi and Lillie (Rutherford) B.; Mus.B. in Piano, New Eng. Conservatory Music, 1950, Mus.B. with honors in Voice, 1954. Debut as singer Jordan Hall, Boston, 1956; appeared with Boston Symphony Orch., Boston Pops Orch., Toast of the Town, and other radio shows; guest soloist Chgo. Philharmonic, N.Y. Philharmonic, Los Angeles Philharmonic, Hollywood Bowl, Phila. Orch.; recording artist RCA Victor Co., Boson Records; opera debut New Eng. Opera Theater (Boris Goldavsky); concert tours U.S., Can., Japan, Alaska, P.I., Hong Kong, others. Recipient award nat. competition for soloist Boston Pops Orch., 1949, Boston Post Music Festival, Chicagoland Music Festival, 1953; Marian Anderson award, 1953, 54; award Nat. Fedn. Music Clubs, 1957. Mem. Pi Kappa Lambda, Kappa Gamma Psi. Mason. Home: 13 Albermarle St Boston MA 02115 Office: care Nat Artists Corp 711 Fifth Av New York City 22 NY

BOAZ, MARTHA TEAROSSE, educator; b. Stuart, Va.; d. James Robert and Kate (Gilley) Boaz; B.S., Madison Coll., 1934; B.S. in L.S., George Peabody Coll., 1937; Ph.D., U. Mich., 1955. Sch. librarian, critic tchr. pub. schs., Va., Ky., 1935-40; asst. librarian Madison Coll., Harrisonburg, Va., 1940-49; asso. prof. library sci. U. Tenn., 1951-52; instr. library sci. U. Mich., 1952-53; asso. prof. library sci. U. So. Cal., Los Angeles, dean Sch. Library Sci., 1955—. State Dept. rep. to Pakistan, 1962, Vietnam, 1967. Mem. Am. (chmn. intellectual freedom com. 1964-66, pres. library edn. dir. 1968-69), Cal. (pres. 1962) library assns., Am. Documentation Inst. (pres. So. Cal. chpt. 1962), Am. Assn. Library Schs. (past pres.), Kappa Delta Pi, Delta Kappa Gamma, Beta Phi Mu (pres. 1962). Author: (with Nancy Raisbeck) A Guide to General Book Publishers in the United States, 1950; A Qualitative Analysis of the Criticism of Best Sellers, 1955; (with LeRoy Charles Merrill and Kenneth S. Tisdel) Reviews in Library Book Selection, 1958; Fervent and Full of Gifts, 1961. Editor: A Living Library, 1958; Modern Trends in Documentation, 1959. Compiler: The Quest for Truth, 1961. Contbr. articles to profl. jours. Home: 1849 Campus Rd Los Angeles CA 90041

BOBALEK, EDWARD GEORGE, educator; b. Chgo., Oct. 13, 1915; s. Stephen J. and Emelia (Peterka) B.; B.S., St. Mary's (Minn.) Coll., 1938; M.S., Creighton U., 1940; postgrad. U. Chgo., 1940; Ph.D., Ind. U., 1942; m. Gretchen Marie Roemer, Aug. 22, 1942; children—Stephen, Margaret, Elizabeth, John, Thomas, Charles, Philip. Research chemist Dow Chem. Co., 1942-45; dir. resin research Arco Co., 1945-49; from asst. prof. to prof. chem. engring. Case Inst. Tech., 1949-63; Gottesman research prof. U. Me., Orono, 1963—, chmn. dept. chem. engring. Dir. Structural Fibers, Inc., Charbon, O. Guest lectr. Newman Clubs, also profl., charitable and ch. related socs., 1950-63. Mem. Am. Chem. Soc. (chmn. div. organic coatings and plastics chemistry 1960, publs. bd. jours. 1962-65), Soc. Plastics Engrs. (publs. com.), Fedn. Socs. Paint Tech. (publs. com.), Am. Inst. Chem. Engrs., Cleve. Soc. Paint Tech. (hon.), Am. Assn. U. Profs., Am. Soc. Engring. Edn., Sigma Xi, Alpha Chi Sigma, Phi Delta Upsilon, Delta Epsilon Sigma, Tau Beta Pi. Roman Catholic. Editor: (with W. von Fischer) Organic Protective Coatings, 1953. Contbr. articles to profl. jours., encys. Home: 193 Main St Orono ME 04473

BOBBITT, ARCHIE NEWTON, lawyer; b. Eckerty, Ind., Sept. 3, 1895; s. Irvin and Ida Mae (Newton) B.; student Central Normal Coll., Danville, Ind., 1913, 15, 19; LL.B., Benjamin Harrison Law Sch., 1927, Ind. U.; m. Frances Bringle Adams, Aug. 21, 1921. Grade sch. tchr., 1915; prin. high sch., Alton and Marengo, Ind., 1916-17, Marengo, 1920; auditor Crawford Co., (Ind.), 1921-25; gasoline tax collector State Ind., 1925-29, state auditor, 1929-31; admitted to Ind. bar, 1927, since practiced in Indpls.; sr. mem., firm Bobbitt, Martz and Beattey, 1942-51; city atty. City of Indpls., 1943-44, Corp. counsel, 1944-48; judge Supreme Ct. of Ind., 1951-63; sr. mem. firm Ruckelshaus, Bobbitt & O'Connor, 1964—. Republican nominee for judge Appellate Ct. Ind., 1934; del. Rep. Nat. Conv., 1948, chmn. Ind. del. and state chmn.; co. chmn. Crawford Co., 1922-25; mem. state com. rep. 3d Congl. dist. 1924-26, state chmn. 1937-41. Served with U.S. Navy, World War I. Mem. Am., Ind. (chmn. ho. of dels. 1966-68), Indpls. bar assns., N.Am. Gasoline Tax Conf. (pres., exec. sec. 1933-39), Am. Legion, 40 and 8, Sigma Delta Kappa. Republican. Methodist. Mason (32, Shriner). Clubs: Columbia, Service (Indpls.); Indiana Society (Chgo.). Author: Indiana Appellate Practice and Procedure; Babbitts' Revision—Works Indiana Practice and Procedure (9 vols.). 3635 Totem Lane Indianapolis IN 46208 Office:; 129 E Market St Indianapolis IN 46204

BOBBITT, JOSEPH MATTHEW, psychologist; b. St. Joseph, Mo., Oct. 26, 1908; s. Joseph Matthew and Della Pearl (Carlin) B.; A.B., U. So. Cal., 1931, A.M., 1932; Ph.D., Northwestern U., 1937; m. Katherine C. Long, June 16, 1949; 1 son, Bruce Long. Instr. psychology Mich. State Coll., 1937-41, asst. prof., 1941-42; mem. profl. services br. Nat. Inst. Mental Health, USPHS, 1946-50, acting chief profl. services br., 1950-51, chief, 1951-57, asst. dir. Nat. Inst. Mental Health, 1957-60, asso. dir., 1960-64; asst. dir. manpower devel., acting asso. dir. program planning, acting asso. dir. communications Nat. Inst. Child Health and Human Devel., NIH, USPHS, 1964-66, asst. dir. for behavioral scis. Office Planning and Evaluation, Nat. Inst. Child Health and Human Devel., 1969—; exec. dir. Joint Commn. on Mental Health of Children, 1966-69. Mem. research com. Adv. Council to Pres.'s Com. on Traffic Safety. Served from lt. (j.g.) to lt. comdr., USCGR, 1942-46. Recipient Harold M. Hildreth Meml. award Div. Psychologists in Pub. Service Am. Psychol. Assn., 1967. Fellow Am. Psychol. Assn.; mem. Eastern, D.C. psychol. assns., Am. Psychopath. Assn., Soc. Research Child Devel., Phi Beta Kappa, Sigma Xi, Psi Chi, Phi Delta Kappa. Club: Cosmos (Washington). Home: 9411 Corsica Dr Bethesda MD 20014

BOBBITT, OLIVER BEIRNE, Jr., physician, educator; b. Charleston, W.Va., Jan. 10, 1917; s. Oliver Belrne and Belle (Graves) B.; student Hampden-Sydney Coll., 1934-36; B.S., U. Ga., 1939; M.D., U. Va., 1943; m. Betty Kearse, Nov. 13, 1943; children—Oliver Beirne III, Wesley R., Timothy G. Postgrad. med. tng. U. Va. Hosp., Duke U. Hosp., 1943-44, 46-47; tng. clin. pathology U. Va. Hosp. and Med. Sch., asst. prof. clin. pathology U. Va., Charlottesville, 1949-52, asso. prof., 1952-57, chmn. dept., 1952-71, prof., 1957—. Served as lt., M.C., USNR, World War II. Diplomate Am. Bd. Pathology. Fellow Coll. Am. Pathologists, Am. Soc. Clin. Pathologists. Home: 1857 Westview Rd Charlottesville VA 25311

BOBBITT, ROBERT LEE, lawyer; b. Hillsboro, Tex., Jan. 24, 1888; s. Joseph A. and Laura (Duff) B.; student Carlisle Mil. Acad., 1907; N. Tex. Normal Coll., 1908-11; LL.B., U. Tex., 1915; m. Mary B. Westbrook, Apr. 20, 1918; 1 son, Robert Lee Jr. Admitted to Tex. bar, 1915; jr. partner firm Hicks, Hicks, Dickson & Bobbitt, Laredo and San Antonio, 1916-28; dist. atty. 49th Judicial Dist. Tex., 1928; atty. gen. Tex., 1929-30; asso. justice San Antonio Ct. Civil Appeals, 1935-37; chmn. Tex. Hwy. Commn., 1937-43; sr. partner Bobbitt, Brite, Bobbitt & Allen, 1944—. Pres. Central Securities Co., San Antonio, chmn. bd. S. Tex. Nat. Bank, San Antonio. Active local Boy Scouts Am., Salvation Army, YMCA. Mem. Tex. Ho. Reps., 1923-28, speaker, 1927-28; chmn., keynote speaker Tex. Democratic Conv., 1934. Mem. Tex. Dem. Exec. Com., 1923—. Presdl. Elector from Texas, 1944. Chmn. bd. trustees Tex. A. and I. College, 1932-35; regent N. Tex. State Coll., Denton. Served to capt., 90th Div., U.S. Army, 1917-19. Mem. Am., Tex., San Antonio bar assns., Am. Judicature Soc., Philos. Soc. Tex., Tex. Hist. Assn., Newcomen Soc., S. Tex. C. of C., Am. Legion, Chancellors (U. Tex.), Phi Delta Phi. Presbyn. (elder). Rotarian (pres., dist. gov.), Elk (Laredo). Home: St Anthony Hotel San Antonio TX 78205 Office: Alamo National Bldg San Antonio TX 78205

BOBBITT, VERNON LEROY, educator; b. Pella, Ia., July 27, 1911; s. Lee Roy and Alta (Goodell) B.; student Denison U., 1929-31; B.F.A. Louis Comfort Tiffany fellow, State U. Ia., 1941, M.A., 1946; m. Mary Reed, Feb. 11, 1942; children—Susan, Cara. Instr. art Central Coll., Pella, 1937-42; prof., chmn. art dept. Albion (Mich.) Coll., 1946—; one-man exhbns. Weyhe Gallery, N.Y.C., 1956, Grand Rapids Art Gallery, 1957, Ankrum Gallery, Los Angeles, 1970; mem. staff Bay View (Mich.) Summer Coll. Liberal Arts, 1957-68. Served with USAAF, 1942- 45. Mem. Coll. Art Assn., Mich., Midwestern coll. art assn., Albion Hist. Soc., Am. Assn. U. Profs., Coll. Art Assn., Mich. Art Museums Group. Home: 606 Linden Lane Albion MI 49224

BOBBITT, WILLIAM HAYWOOD, state supreme ct. justice; b. Raleigh, N.C., Oct. 18, 1900; s. James Henry and Eliza May (Burkhead) B.; A.B., U. N.C., 1921, LL.D., 1957; LL.D., Davidson Coll., 1953; m. Sarah Buford Dunlap, Feb. 28, 1924 (dec. Oct. 1965); children—Sarah (Mrs. John W. Carter), William Haywood (dec.), Buford (Mrs. Ekkehart Sachtler), Harriet (Mrs. Dan S. Moss). Admitted to N.C. bar, 1922; gen. practice law, Charlotte, 1922-38; judge Superior Ct., 14th Jud. Dist., 1939-54; asso. justice Supreme Ct. N.C., 1954-69, chief justice, 1969—. Mem. N.C. Jud. Council, 1949-54, chmn., 1966-69. Trustee Brevard (N.C.) Coll. 1933-52. Mem. Am., N.C. bar assns., Am. Judicature Soc., Gen. Alumni Assn. U. N.C. (pres. 1954-55). Methodist. Club: Civitan (past pres, Charlotte). Home: Boylan Apts Raleigh NC 27603 Office: Justice Bldg Raleigh NC 27601

BOBER, JOHN D., corp. exec.; b. Jersey City, Apr. 27, 1922; s. Dmitro and Eva (Fickanich) B.; B.S. in Accounting, L.I. U., 1949; m. Eva Lazorik, May 23, 1948; children—Michaele, John. With Purolator, Inc., Rahway, N.J., 1950—, treas., treas., controller, 1959—; dir. Purolator Argentina, Purolator India, Ltd., Purolator de Venezuela C.A.; dir. Indsl. Workmen's Savs. & Loan Assn., Rahway, N.J., 1967—. Bd. dirs. Rahway YMCA, 1965—. Served with USAAF, 194245. Mem. Nat. Assn. Accountants. Home: 830 Milton Blvd Rahway NJ 07065 Office: 970 Brunswick Av Rahway NJ 07065

BOBER, SAM HENRY, former govt. ofcl.; b. Borzova, Ukraine, Nov. 14, 1891; s. Benjamin Benjamin and Hannah (Sonenschein) B.; came to U.S. 1906, naturalized, 1911; grad. Baron de Hirsch Agrl. Sch., Woodbine, N.J., 1912; student agr. Mich. State U., 1913, S.D. State Coll., 1916, Harvard, 1937; D.Sc., S.D. State U., 1966; m. Rose Stolar, Apr. 13, 1916 (dec. Dec. 1968); children—Louis, Mira Lee (Mrs. Henry Goldstein), Jack; m. 2d, Rachel Silverman, Oct. 1968. Sci. asst. animal husbandry U.S. Dept. Agr., 1916-23; grower, distbr. field seeds; mem. Fed. Farm Credit Bd., 1955-62. Chmn. adv. com. U.S. Expt. Farm, 1948-67, Nat. Farm Loan Assn., 1950-54; chmn. dirs. adv. com. Fed. Land Bank of Omaha, 1950-54. Chmn. war drives Butte County chpt. A.R.C., 1940-45. Candidate for Congress, S.D., 1952. Bd. govs. Agrl. Hall of Fame. Recipient 1st prize for alfalfa Internat. Grain Shows, 1927, 52, other prizes State Crop Improvement Shows, S.D. Fairs. Mem. Am. Farm Bur. Fedn., Newcomen Soc. N.A., Nat. Planning Assn. (nat. council, nat. agrl. com.), Aberdeen Angus Breeders Assn., S.D. Crop Improvement Assn. Contbg. editor: Dakota Farmers, 1919-22. Home: 3473 E Seneca St Tucson AZ 85716

BOBINSKI, GEORGE SYLVAN, librarian; b. Cleve., Oct. 24, 1929; s. Sylvan and Eugenia (Sarbiewski) B.; B.A., Western Reserve University, 1951, M.S. in Library Science, 1952; M.A. Univ. of Michigan, 1961, Ph.D., 1966; m. to Mary Lillian Form, Feb. 20, 1953; children-George Sylvan, Mary Anne. Research asst. Bus Information Bur., Cleve. Pub. Library, 1954-55; asst. dir. Royal Oak (Mich.) Pub. Library, 1955-59; head librarian State U. Coll. at Cortland, N.Y., 1960-67, also dir. libraries State Univ. Coll. at Cortland; asst. dean, prof. Sch. Library Sci., U. Ky., 1967-70; dean, prof. Sch. Information and Library Studies, State U. N.Y. at Buffalo, 1970—; cons. Mich. State Library, 1958, 1959-60, Clawson (Mich.) Pub. Library, 1956-57. Chmn. Conf. State U. N.Y. Head Librarians, 1963-64; treas. Eastern Coll. Librarians, 1963-64. Served with AUS, 1952-54. Mem. Am., N.Y. (dir. coll. and univ. sect. 1964-66) library assns., Polish Am. Hist. Assn., Polonus Philatelic Soc., Assn. Am. Library Schs. Author: A Brief History of the Libraries of Western Reserve University, 1826-1952, 1955; Carnegie Libraries, Their History and Impact on American Public Library Development, 1969; also articles. Chmn. editorial bd. Choice (A.L.A.). Home: 40 William Sq Williamsville NY 14221 Office: Sch Information and Library Studies State Univ at Buffalo Buffalo NY 14214

BOBLETER, LOWELL STANLEY, artist, educator; b. New Ulm, Minn., Dec. 24, 1902; s. John Edward and Alma (Dunkel) B.; student Bishop Brissman Inst., 1920-23, St. Paul Sch. Art, 1923-25; D.F.A., Sch. Asso. Arts, 1965; m. Mabel M. Wendt, Sept. 15, 1924. Dir., St. Paul Gallery and Sch. Art, 1940-42; supt. fine arts Minn. State Fair, 1942-48; prof. art. chmn. Sch. Fine Arts Hamline U., 1942-48; pres. Sch. Asso. Arts, St. Paul, 1948—; exhibited group and one-man shows at Met. Mus. Art, 1944-47, Mus. Modern Art, 1945, Carnegie Inst., 1940-42, U.S. Library of Congress, 1938-45, Nat. Gallery, 1943- 45,

Corcoran Gallery, 1938-47, Art Inst. Chgo., 1940-45, museums in Rome, 1938-39, Italy, 1939-40, Oslo, Norway, 1940-42, Paris, 1938-40, N.Y.C., 1938-65, Phila., 1938-60, Boston, 1938-60, Chgo., 1938-65, Denver, 1940-45, San Francisco, 1938-55, Los Angeles, 1940-47, Buffalo, 1943, New Orleans, 1945, Kansas City, 1940-50, Washington, 1938-45, Mpls., 1930-65, Balt., 1940-47, Seattle, 1940-50; rep. permanent collections Library Congress, Met. Mus. Art, Nat. Gallery Art, Pa. Acad. Fine Arts, Cal. State Library, Flint Inst. Art, Soc. Am. Etchers, Parkersburg Arts Center, Chgo. Art Inst., Smithsonian Inst., N.Y. Pub. Library, Mpls. Inst. Art, Walker Art Center, Harbor Beach Pub. Library, Chgo. Soc. Etchers. Mem. Nat. Com. for Preservation Cultural Resources, 1940-45; mem. Minn. Art. Commn., 1942-48. Recipient numerous first awards, medals in exhbns. throughout U.S. Mem. Am. Assn. U. Profs., Nat. Assn. Mus. Dirs., Coll. Art Assn., Artists Equity, Minn. Artists Assn. (pres.), Nat. Soc. Interior Designers, Am. Fedn. Art. Home: 2040 Berkeley Av St Paul MN 55105 Office: 344 Summit Av St Paul MN 55102

BOBO, GAUDENZLO, Italian industrialist; b. May 17, 1901; Dr. Eng., Politecnico, Turin, Italy. Mng. dir., gen. mgr. Fiat, Turin until 1969, vice chmn. mng. dir. 1969—; dir. several Italian companies. Chmn. Galileo Ferraris Nat. Elec. Engring. Inst. Decorated cavaliere del Lavoro; knight grand cross Italian Republic. Address: 10 Corso Marconi Turin, Italy.

BOBO, JAMES ROBERT, educator; b. Marion County, Ala., Aug. 16, 1923; s. Robert Lee and Lenora (Vickery) B.; B.S., Florence State U., 1950; M.A., George Peabody Coll., 1952; Ph.D., La. State U., 1961; m. Cala Sue Reid, Mar. 27, 1969; 1 dau., Harriet Seretha. Tchr. East Central Jr. Coll., 1952-58; asst. prof. La. State U. at New Orleans, 1961-63; dean Sch. Bus. of N.E. La. State U., 1963-64; prof. econs., dir. div. research La. State U. at New Orleans, 1964-69, prof. econs., dean Grad. Sch., 1969—, on leave as exec. dir. Met. Goals Found. Council, 1970-71; cons. Served with AUS, 1943-46. Mem. Am., So. econ. assns., Regional Sci. Assn., South Western Social Sci. Assn. Club: Rotary (New Orleans). Compiler: Statistical Abstract of Louisiana, 1965. Home: 5734 Chatham Dr New Orleans LA 70122

BOBONIS, AUGUSTO, educator; b. Humacao, P.R., June 20, 1907; s. Augusto and Leonor (Diaz) B.; A.B., U. P.R., 1927, S.M., 1934; Ph.D., U. Chgo., 1939; m. Etta Lang, June 20, 1936; children—Etta, Augusto, Jorge, Elisa. Prof. math. U. P.R. at Rio Piedras, 1927-48, 70—, dir. dept. math., 1944-48, dir. secondary edn. edn., 1948-57, dean Sch. of Edn., 1958-70; cons. NSF, 1962, Dept. Health, Edn. and Welfare, 1964. Mem. Acad. Arts and Scis. P.R., Am. Math. Soc., Sigma Xi. Contbr. articles profl. jours. Home: 575 de Diego Rio Piedras PR 00931

BOBRITZKY, GEORGE VICTOR, artist; b. Znamenka, Russia, Apr. 23, 1917; s. Victor and Maria (Timoshenko) B.; came to U.S., 1949; student Art Students League. N.Y.C., 1951-52, Gewerbschule, Salzburg, Austria, 1948; m. Ulse Straubingerm, Jan. 31, 1948; 1 dau., Helene. Scenic artist, Charkow, Russia; comml. artist, 1949-58; scenic artist, N.Y.C., 1958—; one-man exhbns. drawings include Salzburg, 1965, Frankfurt, 1966; group exhbns. include ann. drawing biennale, Norfolk, Va., 1963, 69, Drawing USA, St. Paul, 1964, Butler Inst., Youngstown, O., 1967, Painters and Sculptors of N.J., Jersey City, 1967, Audubon Artists, N.Y.C., 1968, Nat. Acad. Design, 1968, Nat. Arts Club, N.Y.C., 1963, 64, 68, ann. drawing biennale Smithsonian Instn. travelling exhbn. 1969. Recipient medal of honor Painters and Sculptors N.J., 1967; Saltus gold medal of merit Nat. Acad. Design, 1968; sterling silver award Nat. Arts Club, N.Y.C., 1968. Mem. Yonkers Art Assn. Address: 201 N Broadway Yonkers NY 10701

BOBROW, DAVIS BERNARD, educator; b. Boston, Sept. 2, 1936; s. Robert and Elizabeth (Gelfand) B.; B.A. in Gen. Edn. (Ford Found. scholar), U. Chgo., 1955, B.A. in Communication (Ford Found. fellow), 1956; B.A. in Philosophy-Politics-Econs. (Rhodes scholar), Queen's Coll., Oxford U., 1958; Ph.D. (Social Sci. Research Council fellow), Mass. Inst. Tech., 1962; m. Sue Ellen Berryman, June 25, 1960. Lectr. dept. politics Princeton, 1961-62, asst. prof., 1962-64; sr. social scientist dir.'s div. Oak Ridge Nat. Lab., 1964-68; acting dir. Behavioral Scis. Office, Advanced Research Projects Agy., 1969-70; spl. asst. behavioral and social scis. Office of Dir. Def. Research and Engring., 1968-70; prof. dept. polit. sci. Sch. Pub. Affairs, U. Minn., Mpls., 1970—, dir. Quigley Center Internat. Studies, 1970—; professorial lectr. Sch. Advanced Internat. Studies, Johns Hopkins, 1970; cons. Office Sec. Def., RAND Corp., Fgn. Policy Assn. Mem. USAF Sci. Adv. Bd.; mem. exec. com. Consortium on Peace Research Edn. and Devel. Editor, co-author: Components of Defense Policy, 1965; Weapons System Decisions: Political and Psychological Perspectives on Continental Defense, 1969. Co-editor, co-author: Computers and the Policy-Making Community: Applications to International Relations, 1968. Asso. editor: Policy Sciences, 1969—. Editorial asso. Public Opinion Quarterly, 1963-64. Home: 1725 Emerson Av S Minneapolis MN 55403

BOBRYTZKE, FRANK, banker. Chmn. exec. com., dir. Mfrs. Nat. Bank Chgo. Office: 1200 N Ashalnd Av Chicago IL 60622*

BOCHER, MAIN ROUSSEAU, (Mainbocher), designer; b. Chgo., Oct. 24, 1890; s. George R. and Luella (Main) B.; student piano with Claire Osborn Reed, 1907, with Frank La Forge, 1914; student art, Chgo., 1908-09, N.Y.C., 1909-11, Munich, Germany, 1911-12; student singing with Henri Albers and Giulia Valda, 1919. With Paris studio E. A. Taylor, 1913-14; began fashion drawing, 1922; illustrator Harper's Bazaar, Paris, 1922-23; editor French Vogue, 1923-29; founder, pres. Mainbocher, Paris, 1930-39, Mainbocher, Inc., N.Y.C., 1940—; designer WAVES uniforms, 1942, Women Marine Corps uniforms, 1951, Girl Scout uniforms, 1946, Red Cross Uniforms, 1948, Passavant Hosp. (Chgo.) nursing sch. uniforms, 1949. Served with hosp. unit, France, 1917; with U.S. Army, 1918. Illustrator: Aucassin and Nicolette, 1914; play, Tiny Alice. Office: 609 Fifth Av New York City NY 10017

BOCHIN, FRANK, Jr., greeting card co. exec.; b. Cleve., Mar. 11, 1932; s. Frank and Edith (Eyman) B.; B.B.A. magna cum laude, Fenn Coll., 1959; m. Jeraldine I. Bishop, Mar. 27, 1954; children—Stephanie Anne, Elizabeth Joyce. Sr. accountant Ernst & Ernst, C.P.A.'s Cleve., 1955-62; mgr. systems and procedures Harris-Seybold Co., Cleve., 1962-65; staff asst. to controller Premier Indsl. Corp., Cleve., 1965-66; controller Am. Greetings Corp., Cleve., 1966—. Bd. mgrs. West Side YMCA. C.P.A., Ohio. Mem. Am. Inst. C.P.A.'s Ohio Soc. C.P.A.'s, Cleve. Treasurers Club. Home: 14551 Concord Trail Middleburg Heights OH 44130 Office: 10500 American Rd Cleveland OH 44144

BOCHNER, SALOMON, educator; b. Cracow, Poland, Aug. 20, 1899; s. Joseph and Rude (Haber) B.; Ph.D., U. Berlin, 1921; m. Naomi Weinberg, Nov. 1, 1937; 1 dau., Deborah. Came to U.S., 1933, naturalized, 1938. Internat. Edn. Bd. fellow, 1925-27; lectr. Munich U., 1927-32; faculty Princeton (N.J.), 1933—, prof. math., 1946—, Henry Burchard Fine prof. math., 1959-68; Edgar Odell Lovett prof. math. Rice U., Houston, 1968—. Vis. prof. U. Cal. at Berkeley, 1953; cons. Los Alamos project, Princeton, 1951, NSF, 1952. Mem. Nat. Acad. Scis., Am. Math So. Author: Fouriersche Integrale, 1932; Several Complex Variables, 1948; Fourier Transforms, 1949; Curvature and Betti Numbers, 1953; Harmonic Analysis and The Theory of Probability, 1955; Fourier Integrels, 1959; The Role of Mathematics in the Rise of Science, 1966; Eclosion and Synthesis: Perspectives on the History of Knowledge, 1969. Editorial bd. Scribner's Dict. History of Ideas. Contbr. math. publs. Home: 184 Springdale Rd Princeton NJ 08540 Office: Dept Math Rice U Houston TX 77001

BOCK, DONALD DAVID, ednl. cons.; b. Gasconade, Mo., Aug. 27, 1924; s. Hugo Theodore and Mabel (Schuth) B.; student Ga. Mil. Coll., 1942; B.S. in Pub. Adminstr., U. Fla., 1954; m. Richie Sue Parham, June 15, 1956; children—Donald David, John, Peter. Exec. asst. Central and So., Fla. Flood Control Dist., 1955-56; dir. planning and research div. Fla. Flood Control Dist., 1956- 58; dep. exec. dir. mgmt. A.L.A., 1958-64; pres., gen. mgr. Auto Transcript Inst., Inc., Gainesville, Fla., 1964-66; ednl. coordinator So. region Assoc. Ednl. Services Corp., N.Y.C., 1964-66; div. dir. Advance Distbrs., Inc., 1966-70; ednl. asso. Ednl. Reading Service, Inc., 1966-70; dep. dir. Council for Family Financial Edn., Silver Spring, Md., 1970—. Mem. Gov. Fla. Com. Resource Use Edn., 1956-58; regional dir. Nat. Rivers and Harbors Congress, 1957-58; cons. Pres.'s Com. on Consumer Interests. Adviser Evanston Boys Club. Mem. Assn. Execs. Forum Chgo., Fla. Blue Key, Delta Sigma Pi. Editor: Teaching Consumer Edn. and Financial Planning. Home: 18024 Lafayette Dr Williamsburg Village Olney MD 20832 Office: Twin Towers Bldg 1110 Fidler Lane Silver Spring MD 20910

BOCK, EDWARD JOHN, chem. mfg. co. exec.; b. Ft. Dodge, Ia, Sept. 1, 1916; s. Edward J. and Maude (Juday) B.; M.S. in Mech. Engring., Ia. State U., 1940; m. Ruth Kunerth, Aug. 9, 1941; children—Barbara (Mrs. Lundstrom), Edward, Nancy, Roger. With Monsanto Co., St. Louis, 1941—, asst. gen. mgr. Inorganic Chems. div., 1958-60, v.p., gen. mgr. Inorganic Chems. div., 1960-65, v.p. adminstrn., mem. exec. com., dir., 1965-68, pres., chief exec. officer, chmn. corporate mgmt. and exec. coms., dir., 1968—; dir. Monsanto Research Corp., First Nat. Bank in St. Louis. Trustee Nat. Safety Council, Deaconess Hosp., Ladue Chapel, Narcotics Service Council; bd. govs. Ia. State U. Found.; Recipient Silver Anniversary All-Am. Football award Sports Illustrated, 1963; elected to Nat. Football Found. Hall of Fame, 1970. Mem. Am. Soc. M.E., St. Louis Ambassadors, Inc., Mfg. Chemists Assn. (dir.), Nat. Indsl. Conf. Bd., Civic Progress, Inc., Sigma Chi, Tau Beta Pi. Clubs: St. Louis, Old Warson Country, Bogey. Home: 7 Huntleigh Woods St Louis MO 63131 Office: 800 N Lindbergh Blvd St Louis MO 63166

BOCK, FRITZ, banker; b. Vienna, Austria, Feb. 26, 1911; s. Fritz and Lina (Boeck) B.; LL.B., U. Vienna, 1935; D.Polit. Sci. (hon.), Boston U., 1966; m. Anny Doerrich, Sept. 2, 1939; children—Fritz, Maria-Theresia (Mrs. Klaus Bauer). Active Catholic youth and students' movement; in concentration camp, Dachau, 1938-39; engaged in pvt. business, 1940-45; joined Austrian People's Party, 1945, mem. social policy sect., 1947-54; mem. Parliament, 1949-62; sec. state Fed. Ministry Trade and Reconstrn., 1952, Fed. Ministry Finance, 1955; fed. minister trade and reconstrn., 1956; vice chancellor, fed. minister commerce, trade and industry, 1966-68; chmn. bd. dirs. Credit/anstalt-Bankverein, Vienna, 1969—. Vice pres. Oesterreichischer Wirtschaftsbund, 1961—; pres. Donaueropaeisches Inst., 1957—. Bundeskonferenz der Kammern der freien Berufe Oesterreichs, 1969—. Named hon. sentaor Univ. and Comml. U. Vienna, 1965, hon. citizen Tech. U. Vienna, 1962; recipient Bene Merito medal Austrian Acad. Sci., 1965; decorated Grand Golden Order Merit with ribbon; Grand Golden Order Merit with star; Bavarian Order Merit; grand cross star and ribbon Maltese Knights Order Merit; knight Order Holy Scpulchre; grand cross Belgian Crown-Order, Dutch Order Orange Nassau, Finnish Lion Order, German Order Merit, Greek Order Phoenix, Liberian Order Star Africa, Luxembourg Order Merit, Norweigian Order St. Olav, Papal Order St. Gregory, Portuguese Order Christ, Spanish Order Merit, Swedish North Star Order, Thai Order White Elephant. Author: German Property, 1956; Not Included in the Protocol, 1969; also articles. Home: 47 Braungasse Vienna 1170 Austria Office: 6 Schottengasse Vienna 1010 Austria

BOCK, HAROLD PATTENDON, ret. hotel exec.; b. London, Eng., Aug. 27, 1901; s. Henry Joseph and Elizabeth Harriet (Pattendon) B.; student pvt. schs., Belgium, Austria; m. Dorothy Celeste Hazard, June 3, 1933; 1 son, Philip Hazard. Came to U.S., 1926, naturalized, 1932. Employee hotels, Austria, 1916- 26; with Berkeley-Carteret, Asbury Park, N.J., 1926-27, Drake Dorset hotels, N.Y.C., 1927-30, Carlyle, N.Y.C., 1930-44; gen. mgr. Homestead, Hot Springs, Va., 1945-49, Bismarck Hotel, Chgo., 1949-56, Sheraton Hotel, Chgo., 1956-58, Sheraton-East Hotel, N.Y.C., 1958-66; v.p., gen. mgr. Sheraton-Ambassador Corp., 1967-71, Carlyle Hotel N.Y.C., 1967-71. Mem. Am., Internat., N.Y.C. (food rationing chmn. during World War II) hotel assns. Clubs: Hotel Execs. (past pres.), Ye Host's Square, Fort Dearborn-Chicago Camera (past pres.), Tavern. Home: Hickory Lane Ridgefield CT 06877 Office: The Carlyle New York City NY 10021

BOCK, JERRY, (Jerrold Lewis), composer; b. New Haven, Nov. 23, 1928; s. George Joseph and Rebecca (Alpert) B.; student U. Wis., 1945-49; m. Patricia Faggen, May 28, 1950; children—George Albert, Portia Fane. Writer score for high sch. mus. comedy My Dream, 1945, score for original coll. musical Big as Life, 1948; with Larry Holofcener, wrote songs for TV show Admiral Broadway Revue, also Show of Shows, 1949-51; composer Camp Tamiment, summers 1950, 51, 53; writer continuity sketches Mel Torme show, CBS, 1951, 52; writing staff Kate Smith Hour, 1953-54; writer original songs for night club performers, including night club revue Confetti; wrote songs for Wonders of Manhattan (hon. mention Cannes Film Festival, 1956); composer music for Broadway show Catch a Star, 1955, Mr. Wonderful, 1956; collaborated with Sheldon Harnick on The Body Beautiful, 1958, Fiorello, 1959 (Pulitzer prize, Drama Critics award, Antoinette Perry award), Tenderloin, 1960, She Loves Me, 1963, The Apple Tree, 1966; London prodn. of She Loves Me, 1964; Fiddler on the Roof, 1964; wrote series of children's songs now pub. under title Sing Something Special, also recorded album, N.Y. Bd. Edn. radio broadcasts, 1961—. Mem. Wilderness Soc., Hort. Soc. N.Y., Broadcast Music Inc., Am. Civil Liberties Union. Home: 145 Wellington Av New Rochelle NY

BOCK, ROBERT HOWARD, univ. adminstr.; b. Chgo., Feb. 1, 1932; s. Ralph Edward and Gertrude (Lux) B.; B.S., Purdue U., 1954, M.S., 1955, Ph.D., 1960; m. Sharon Lee Ambler, Sept. 4, 1954; children—Mark Winston, Frank Andrew, Natalie Louise. Teaching asst. Purdue U., 1954-55, research asso. agrl. econs., instr. indsl. adminstrn., 1957-60; asst. prof., asso. prof. Grad. Sch. Bus., Northwestern U., 1960-65; v.p., dean U. Puget Sound, Tacoma, 1965-69; dean Sch. Bus. Adminstrn., U. Miami (Fla.), 1969—. Trustee Annie Wright Sem. Served with USAF, 1955-57. Mem. Tacoma C. of C. (trustee). Conglist. (trustee). Mason, Rotarian. Author: Production Planning and Control, 1963. Home: 7200 SW 129th St Miami FL 33156

BOCK, ROBERT M., univ. dean; b. Preston, Minn., July 26, 1923; s. Glen E. and Hilda (Snyder) B.; B.S., U. Wis., 1949, Ph.D. in Chemistry, 1952; postgrad. Cal. Inst. Tech. 1955, Cambridge (Eng.) U., 1961; m. Ruth Golbien, Sept. 21, 1947; children—Karen, Susan. Mem. faculty U. Wis., Madison, 1952—, prof. molecular biology, 1965—, dean Grad. Sch., 1967—. Sci. adviser Gov. of Wis., 1969—. Mem. Am. Chem. Soc., Am. Soc. Cell. Biologists, Soc. Exptl. Biologists. Contbr. profl. jours. Home: 4816 Hillview Terrace Madison WI 53706

BOCK, RUSSELL SAMUEL, author; b. Spokane, Wash., Nov. 24, 1905; s. Alva and Elizabeth (Mellinger) B.; B.B.A., U. Wash., 1929; children—Beverly A. (Mrs. Robert Wunderlich), James Russell. Part-time instr. U. So. Cal., U. Cal. at Los Angeles, 1942-50; with Ernst & Ernst, C.P.A.'s Los Angeles, 1938, partner, 1951-69, cons., 1969—. Dir., treas. Community TV So. Cal.; dir. v.p., treas. So. Cal. Symphony-Hollywood Bowl Assn.; trustee Internat. Center for Ednl. Devel., Claremont Men's Coll., 1964-70. Mem. Am. Inst. C.P.A.'s (council 1953-57, trial bd. 1955-58, v.p. 1959-60), Cal. Soc. C.P.A.'s (past pres.), Los Angeles C. of C. (dir. 1957-65, v.p. 1963), Sigma Phi Epsilon, Beta Alpha Psi, Beta Gamma Sigma. Clubs: Los Angeles Country (Los Angeles); California Yacht; Waikiki Yacht; Oahu Country (Honolulu). Author: Guidebook to California Taxes, annually, 1950—; Taxes of Hawaii, annually, 1964—; also numerous articles. Office: 615 S Flower St Los Angeles CA 90017

BOCKELKEN, HAROLD EVERETT, petroleum co. exec.; b. N.Y.C., Jan. 12, 1927; s. John A. and Margaret (Kopf) B.; B.A., Adelphi Coll., 1951; m. Dorothy K. Fritch, Mar. 13, 1954. Staff Cities Service Co., N.Y.C., 1951-59, asst. sec., mgr. corporate records dept., 1959—, dir., 1962—, also v.p., sec., asst. sec., asst. treas. subsidiaries. Served with AUS, 1945-46. Home: 62 Daley St New Hyde Park NY 11040 Office: 60 Wall Tower New York City NY 10005

BOCKELMAN, CHARLES KINCAID, physicist, educator; b. San Francisco, Nov. 29, 1922; s. Bernhardt Jacob and Ruth (Kincaid) B.; Ph.B., U. Wis., 1947, Ph.D., 1951; m. Elizabeth Ann Button, June 18, 1950; 1 dau., Faith. Research asso. Mass. Inst. Tech., 1951-55; faculty Yale, 1955—, prof. physics, 1965—, dep. provost for scis., 1969—; spl. research nuclear structure. Served with USAAF, 1942-45. Fellow Am. Phys. Soc.; mem. Sigma Xi. Home: 96 Killdeer Rd Hamden CT 06517 Office: 252 Gibbs Lab Yale Univ New Haven CT 06520

BOCKHOFF, FRANK JAMES, educator; b. Tiffin, O., Mar. 26, 1928; s. Cornelius F. and Helen O. (Bormuth) B.; B.S., Case Inst. Tech., 1950; M.S., Western Res. U., 1952, Ph.D., 1959; m. Esther I. Camperchioli, Jan. 27, 1951; children—Frank Matthew, Susan Virginia, Celia Marie, James Paul. Grad. asst. Western Res. U., 1950-51; instr. Fenn Coll., Cleve., 1951-54, asst. prof., 1954-60, asso. prof., 1960-62, chmn. chemistry, 1962-65; prof., chmn. chemistry Cleve. State U., 1965—. Tech. cons. Am. Agile Corp., Bedford, O., 1953-56, asso. dir. research, devel., 1956-61; cons., dir. Signal Chem. Mfg. Co., Bedford, 1960-62, Reox Corp., Cleve., 1962-69; cons. Apex Reinforced Plastics, Cleve., 1961-63. Trustee Northeastern Ohio Sci. Fair, 1961-64. Named Outstanding Engring. Tchr. Ohio sect. Am. Soc. E.E. 1960; recipient Jr. Tech. Achievement award Cleve. Tech. Soc. Council, 1961; Distinguished Faculty award Cleve. State U., 1965. Registered profl. engr., Ohio. Fellow Am. Inst. Chemists; mem. A.A.A.S., Am. Chem. Soc., Sigma Xi, Tau Beta Pi, Alpha Chi Sigma. Author: Welding of Plastics, 1959; Elements of Quantum Theory, 1969. Contbr. articles and revs. profl. jours. Home: 3015 Scarborough Rd Cleveland Heights OH 44118

BOCKHOFF, HARRY W., tool mfg. exec.; b. Indpls., Apr. 5, 1895; s. William Frederick and Julia (Kloecker) B.; student U. Ill., 1919, Cornell U., 1920; m. Harriet E. Luscomb, Aug. 17, 1918; children—Phyllis (Mrs. John E. Crane), William Frederick II, Camilla Ann (Mrs. John E. Ellis). With Nat. Automatic Tool Co., Inc., Richmond, Ind., 1916—, v.p., mgr., 1918- 28, past pres., chmn., 1958—; vis. prof. U. Ghana, Accra, W. Africa, 1969—; dir. Second Nat. Bank, Radio Sta. WKBV (both Richmond). Mem. Richmond's Com. of 100, Nat. Machine Tool Builders Assn., Am. Soc. of Agrl. Engrs. (sr.). Elk. Clubs: Rotary, Columbia (Indpls.). Home: RR 3 Henley Rd S Richmond IN 47374 Office: National Rd W Richmond IN 47374

BOCKHOP, CLARENCE WILLIAM, agrl. engr., educator; b. Paullina, Ia., Mar. 28, 1921; s. Fred Henry and Sophie Dorothea (Laue) B.; B.S. in Agrl. Engring., Ia. State U., 1943, M.S. in Agrl. Engring., 1955, Ph.D. in Agr. Engring. and Theoretical and Applied Mechanics, 1957; m. Virginia Buhman, July 9, 1949; children—Barbara Lucille, Nancy Jeanne, Bryan William, Karl David. Service and edn. mgr. Stewart Co., Dallas, 1948-53; mem. faculty Ia. State U., Ames, 1953-57, 60—, prof. agrl. engring., 1960—, head dept., 1962- ; prof., head dept. agrl. engineering U. Tenn., 1957-60. Served to capt. AUS, 1943-48. Mem. Am. Soc. A.E. (chmn. Tenn. sect. 1958- 59, chmn. mid-central sect. 1960-61, chmn. Ia. sect. 1963-64, chmn. edn. and research div. 1966-67), Am. Soc. Engring. Edn. (chmn. agrl. engring. div. 1966-67), Sigma Xi, Gamma Sigma Delta, Phi Kappa Phi, Phi Mu Alpha, Tau Beta Pi. Lutheran. Gen. reporter VIth Internat. Congress Agrl. Engring., Lausanne, Switzerland, 1964. Author articles in field. Home: 1419 McKinley St Ames IA 50010

BOCKIUS, GEORGE HAMLIN, corp. exec.; b. Canton, O., Jan. 24, 1895; s. Edward Graham and Florence (Hamlin) B.; M.E., Cornell, 1917; m. Irene Catherine Blake, Apr. 4, 1942. Plant engr. Gordon Tire & Rubber Co., Canton, 1919-21; draftsman Diebold, Inc., Canton, 1921-35, dir., 1930—, dir. purchases, 1935-43, v.p., asst. gen. mgr., 1943-44, v.p., gen. mgr., 1944-45, pres., gen. mgr., 1945-52, chmn. exec. com. 1952—; dir. Canton Nat. Bank. Trustee Aultman Hosp. Mem. C. of C., Ohio Soc. Profl. Engrs. Clubs: Canton, Brookside Country. Home: 2745 Dunkeith Dr N W Canton OH 44708 Office: 818 Mulberry Rd Canton OH 44702

BOCKRATH, GEORGE EUGENE, aero. engr.; b. Chgo., Feb. 15, 1911; s. George A. and Linda (Scheidt) B.; B.S. in Engring., U. Mich., 1933; m. Mary Margaret Kelly, July 17, 1940; children—George P., James E., Joseph F., Thomas A., John M. Instr., Catholic U. Am., 1936-40; engr. Crane Co., Chgo., 1935-36, Douglas Aircraft Co., Inc., 1940-68, McDonnell Douglas Astronautics Co., 1968—; with engring. dept. City of Joliet (Ill.), 1934-35; tchr. night classes U. So. Cal., 1943, U. Cal. at Los Angeles, 1942-43. Recipient Wright Brothers award Soc. Automotive Engrs., 1963. Asso. fellow Am. Inst. Aero. and Astronautics. Patentee aircraft control, aircraft gust alleviating control means, gust alleviating control means for airplanes, also flexible engine pylon. Home: 1021 Claiborne Dr Long Beach CA 90807 Office: 5301 Bolsa Av Huntington Beach CA 92647

BOCKRIS, JOHN O'MARA, phys. chemist, educator, author; b. Johannesburg, South Africa, Jan. 5, 1923; s. Alfred and Emmeline Mary (McNally) B.; student Withdean Hall, Brighton, Eng., 1931-34, Xaverian Coll., Brighton, 1934-38; B.Sc., Brighton Tech. Coll., 1943; Ph.D., Imperial Coll., London U., 1945, D.Sc., 1952; m. Dorothy May Sainty, Aug. 12, 1946 (div. 1964); children—Anna Mary, Victor Francis; m. 2d, Halina S. Wrobel, 1964 (div. 1971). Came to U.S., 1953, naturalized, 1962. Asst. lectr. chemistry U. London (Eng.), 1945, lectr. chemistry, 1948; vis. prof. chemistry U. Pa., Phila., 1953, prof., 1954-62, prof. electrochemistry, 1962-72, adj. prof. chemistry, 1972; prof. physical chemistry Flinders U. Adelaide, Australia,

1971—; lectr. Recipient Medaille d'Honnour, U. Louvain, Belgium, 1953. Fellow Royal Inst. Chemists; mem. Electrochem. Soc. (Richards Meml. lectr. 1951), Bunsen Gesellschaft, Internat. Com. Electrochem. Thermodynamics and Kinetics (dir.), Phi Lambda Upsilon. Author: (330 original papers) Textbook of Electro-chemistry (with G. Kortum), 1951; Technique of High Temperature Measurements, 1959; (with G. Razumney) Fundamental Aspects of Electrocrystallization, 1966; (with A.K.N. Reddy) Modern Electrochemistry an Interdisciplinary Approach, 1969; (with S. Srinivasan) Fuel Cells, Their Electrochemistry, 1970. Editor, author: Modern Aspects of Electrochemistry (with others), Vol. I, 1954, Vol. II, 1959, Vol. III, 1964, Vol. IV, 1966, Vol. V, 1969; Vol. VI, 1970; Electrochem. Acta. Home: 2107 Grad Towers 3600 Chestnut St Philadelphia PA 19104

BOCKUS, HENRY L., physician; b. Newark, Del., Apr. 18, 1894; s. William Jones and Luella (Whiteman) B.; M.D., Jefferson Med. Coll., 1917, D.Sc. 1958; D.Sc., Dickinson Coll., 1946, U. Pa., 1961; Dr. Honoris Causa, U. Central Venezuela, 1965, U. Cordoba (Argentina), 1967; m. Rosalynd Foss, Jan. 13, 1935; 1 dau., Barbara Ann. Resident physician Lenox Hill Hosp., N.Y.C., 1920-21; began practice as physician, Phila., 1921; now internist specializing in gastro-intestinal disorders and as gastroenterologist; organizer stomach clinic Grad. Hosp., U. Pa., 1921, asso. clinic, 1921—; prof. gastroenterology Grad. Sch. Medicine, U. Pa., 1931—, prof., chmn. dept. medicine, 1949-60. prof. medicine emeritus, 1960—; cons. physician Grad. Hosp.; chmn. bd. dirs. MEDICO, 1960-69; v.p. bd. dirs. CARE; cons. gastroenterologist Bryn Mawr Hosp., Abington Meml. Hosp., Phila. Naval Hosp.; hon prof. medicine U. Antioquia (Colombia), 1964. Chmn. World Congress in Gastroenterology, Washington, 1958; hon. prof. U. Nacional de Cordoba, 1967. Trustee Jefferson Med. Coll., 1965-68. Served as lt., M.C., USN, 1917-19. Decorated Comdr. Order Hipolito Unanue (Peru); Order al Merito de Chile; El Sol de Peru (Peru); comdr. Order Rio Branco (Brazil); Order de Andres Bello (Venezuela); Order of Merit Duarte (Dominican Republic); recipient Caldwell Medal, Am. Roentgen Ray Soc., 1950; Strittmater award Phila. County Med. Soc., 1951; Modern Med. award for achievement, 1962. Fellow A.C.P. (master), Royal Soc. Medicine (London) (hon.), Royal Soc. Arts (London), Nat. Acad. Medicine Mex. (hon.); hon. mem. Gastroenterol. Assns. of Central Am., Chile, Cuba, Venezuela, Peru, Brazil, Argentina, Uruguay, Canada, Ecuador, Dominican Republic, Spain, India, Belgium, Germany, Colombia, Bockus Research Inst. of U. Pa., Bockus Internat. Soc. Gastroenterology, Orgn. Mundiale Gastroenterologia (pres. 1958-62, hon. pres. 1962—), Am. Gastroenterol. Assn. (past pres., recipient Friedenwald medal 1962), A.M.A. (former chmn. sect. gastroenterology and proctology), Am. Bd. Internal Medicine (founder mem. subsplty. bd. gastroenterology), Phila. Coll. Physicians, Phila. Pathologic Soc.; hon. asso. Am. Proctologic Assn., Phila. Art Alliance, Alpha Omega Alpha. Presbyn. Clubs: Philadelphia Country, (Phila.); Peale. Author: Gastroenterology, 3 vols., 1943-46, rev., 1963-65 (translated into Portuguese, Spanish, Italian); Postgraduate Gastroenterology, 1950. Contbr. sci. articles to med. jours. Home: 1810 Rittenhouse Sq Philadelphia PA 19103 Office: 250 S 18th St Philadelphia PA 19103

BOCQUET, PHILIP EDMUND, chem. engr., educator; b. Beeville, Tex., Oct. 6, 1918; s. Oscar Jacob and Anne (Henderson) B.; B.S. in Chem. Engring., Tex. A. and M. U., 1940; M.S. in Engring., U. Mich., 1947, Ph.D., 1953; m. Helen Bratton Boudreaux, June 10, 1958; stepchildren—Ray Michael Boudreaux, Ann Gay Boudreaux, Phillip Bratton Boudreaux; 1 dau., Lisa Margaret. Engr. Humble Oil & Refining Co., Ingleside, Tex., 1940-42; research asst. dept. physiology U. Mich. Med. Sch., 1948-51; research group supr. prodn. research Continental Oil Co., Ponca City, Okla., 1953-57; asso. prof. engring. U. N.M., 1957-61; prof. chem. engring., head dept. chem. engring. U. Ark., Fayetteville, 1961-69, asso. dean engring., 1969—. Fulbright lectr. U. Madrid, 1968-69. Served to capt. USAAF, 1942-46. Registered profl. engr., Okla., N.M. Mem. A.A.A.S., Am. Chem. Soc., Am. Inst. Chem. Engrs., Am. Soc. Engring. Edn., Electrochem. Soc., Nat. Soc. Profl. Engrs., Sigma Xi, Tau Beta Pi, Phi Lambda Upsilon, Phi Kappa Phi, Tau Sigma. Home: 555 E North St Fayetteville, AR 72701.

BODA, JAMES MARVIN, educator; b. Mt. Victory, O., July 3, 1924; s. Arthur Wayne and Clarinel Ione (Harvey) B.; B.S., U. Cal. at Davis, 1948, Ph.D., 1953; m. Margaret Elaine Evans, June 6, 1953; 1 dau., Wanda Lynn. Research asst. U. Cal. at Davis, 1948-52, instr., 1952-54, asst. prof., 1954-58, asso. prof., 1959-65, prof., 1965—, chmn. dept. animal physiology, 1968—. Served to lt. (j.g.) USNR, 1943-46. Fulbright research scholar, 1960-61. Mem. Am. Physiol. Soc., Am. Soc. Zoologists, Endocring Soc., Sigma Xi. Contbr. sci. articles to profl. jours. Home: 875 Linden Lane Davis CA 95616

BODANSKY, OSCAR, biochemist, physician; b. Elisabethgrad, Russia, Aug. 21, 1901; s. Phineas and Eva (Geiro) B.; brought to U.S., 1907, naturalized, 1923; B.A., Columbia, 1921, M.A. in Chemistry, 1922, Ph.D. in Chemistry, 1924; M.D., U. Chgo., 1938; m. Barbara Biber, May 31, 1929; 1 dau., Margery (Mrs. Raymond S. Franklin). Asst. and research asst. chemistry Columbia, 1921-25; research asso. biochemistry U. Cal., 1926-27; instr., Med. Sch. U. Tex., 1927-28, adj. prof., 1928-29, asso. prof., 1929-30; instr. pediatrics, Coll. Medicine N.Y.U., 1930-37, lectr. pediatrics, postgrad. div., 1946-55; biochemist children's med. div. Bellevue Hosp., 1930-37; clin. asst. pediatrics Beth Israel Hosp., N.Y.C., 1939-40, asst. adj., 1940-42, asso., 1946-48; research asso., Med. Coll. Cornell U., 1946-48, asso. prof. clin. pharmacology, 1948-51, prof. biochemistry Sloan-Kettering inst., 1951-71, mem., chief biochemistry div., 1956-71, v.p., 1966-71, mem. emeritus, 1971—; attending clin. biochemist, chmn. dept. biochemistry Meml. Hosp. for Cancer and Allied Diseases, N.Y.C., 1948-67, emeritus, 1967—, dir. research tng., 1967-71; vis. clin. biochemist James Ewing Hosp., N.Y.C., 1951-67; cons. biochemistry Hosp. Spl. Surgery, 1958—; Chmn. adv. com. on research on pathogenesis of cancer Am. Cancer Soc. 1964-69; mem. panel gen. biochemistry, com. of growth, NRC, 1955-56. Served from capt. to lt. col. M.C., AUS, 1942-46; chief biochem. sect., med. div. C.W.S., 1943-45, dir. med. research, 1945-46. Decorated Legion of Merit; recipient Distinguished Service award Med. Alumni U. Chgo. Med. Sch., 1952; Alfred P. Sloan award in cancer research, 1962; Van Slyke award in clinical chemistry, 1965. Diplomate Am. Bd. Pathology. Mem. A.M.A., Am. Soc. Biol. Chemists, N.Y. Acad. Medicine, N.Y. State, N.Y. County med. socs., Am. Soc. Pharmacology and Exptl. Therapeutics, Soc. Exptl. Biology and Medicine, Harvey Soc., Am. Assn. Cancer Research, Coll. Am. Pathologists, Ret. Officers Assn., Phi Beta Kappa, Sigma Xi. Author: (with M. Bodanky) Biochemistry of Disease, 2d edit. 1952. Member editorial bd. Anesthesiology, 1946-54, Cancer, 1950—, Cancer Research, 1965-68, Biochem. Medicine, 1967—; asso. editor Jour. Pharmacology, 1946-56. Contbr. articles profl. jours. Home: 535 E 86th St New York City NY 10028 Office: 410 E 68th St New York City NY 10021

BODDE, DERK, educator; b. Brant Rock, Mass., Mar. 9, 1909; s. Theodore and Margaret (Peddle) B.; B.A., Harvard, 1930, postgrad. 1930-31; fellow Harvard-Yenching Inst., Peiping, China, 1931-35; Ph.D. in Chinese, U. Leiden, 1938; m. Galia Speshneff, July 9, 1935; 1 son, Theodore Alexis. Faculty, U. Pa., Phila., 1938—, prof. Chinese, 1950—. Mem. bd. overseers East Asian civilization vis. com. Harvard, 1957-62. Served with OSS and OWI, World War II. Fulbright research fellow, Peking, China, 1948-49; Guggenheim fellow, 1970-71. Mem. Am. Acad. Arts and Scis., Am. Assn. U. Profs., Am. Civil Liberties Union, Am. Oriental Soc. (pres. 1968-69), Am. Philos. Soc., Assn. for Asian Studies (dir. 1968-71). Author: Shakspere and the Ireland Forgeries, 1930; China's First Unifier. 1938; Statesman, Patriot and General in Ancient China, 1940; China's Gifts to the West, 1942; Chinese Ideas in the West, 1948; Tolstoy and China, 1950; Peking Diary, 1950; China's Cultural Tradition: What and Whither, 1957; (with Clarence Morris) Law in Imperial China; also numerous articles. Translator from Chinese: Annual Customs and Festivals in Peking, 1936; A History of Chinese Philosophy, 2 vols., 1952-53. Home: 29 W Phil Ellena St Philadelphia PA 19119

BODDY, FRANCIS MURRAY SOMERVILLE, educator; b. Owen Sound, Ont., Can., Sept. 21, 1906; s. James Newton and Eva (Pearce) B.; B.B.A., U. Minn., 1930, M.A., 1936, Ph.D., 1939; m. Evelyne P. Josephson, Dec. 26, 1936; children—Susan Jane, Stephanie Ruth, Sara Ann, Sherril Elizabeth, William Francis. Faculty, U. Minn., 1930—, successively asst., instr., lectr., asst. prof., asso. prof., 1930-46, prof. econs., 1946—, asso. dean Grad. Sch., 1961—. Cons. Nat. Resources Planning Bd., Washington, 1939-42, OPA, 1942-43, U.S. Treasury Dept., 1950-53; mem. Gov.'s Tax Study Com., 1955-57; pres. Citizens League, Mpls., 1968-69; chmn. Minn. Gov.'s Council Econ. Advisers, 1971—. Served from lt. (j.g.) to lt., USNR, 1943-46. Fellow A.A.A.S.; mem. Am., Royal, Scottish econ. assns., Am. Statis. Assn., Am. Accounting Assn., Econometric Soc., Regional Sci. Assn., Res. Officers Assn., Mont Pelerin Soc., Am. Vets. Com., Am. Assn. U. Profs. Author: (with F. Benham) Principles of Economics, 1947; (with others) Applied Economic Analysis, 1948, Soviet Union, Paradox and Change, 1962; Profits in the Modern Economy, 1967. Editor: (with others) Savings in the Modern Economy, 1953. Home: 4102 Linden Hills Blvd Minneapolis MN 55410

BODE, ALBERT WILLIAM, architect; b. Cin., Oct. 11, 1932; s. Albert Hagenbeck and Dorothy (Mercer) B.; student Carnegie Inst. Tech., 1952-53; B.S., U. Cin., 1957; m. Anna Jeanette Ainsworth, Apr. 16, 1955; children—Pamela, Mark, Grace, Elaine, Albert. Architect, partner Seminoff-Bowman-Bode, Oklahoma City, 1960—. Mem. region 7 adv. panel on architecture Gen. Services Adminstrn.; 1971—. Mem. Oklahoma County Republican Exec. Com., 1967-69. Mem. bd. Village Library, 1967-69; v.p., bd. govs. Licensed Architects of Okla.; life mem. Oklahoma City Arts Center. Recipient Ohio Soc. of A.I.A. award of merit, 1957. Mem. A.I.A., Oklahoma City C. of C., Beta Theat Pi. Mem. Christian Ch. Important works include Dermatology Clinic Okla. U. Med. Center (Okla. A.I.A. award of excellence), 1970, Seminoff Home (Okla. A.I.A. Archtl. Merit award), 1970, Fagin Home (Okla. A.I.A. Archtl. Merit award), 1971; supervisory architect Mummers Theatre, Oklahoma City, 1970. ‡

BODE, CARL, educator, writer; b. Milw., Mar. 14, 1911; s. Paul Christian and Celeste Helene (Schmidt) B.; Ph.B., U. Chgo., 1933; M.A., Northwestern U., 1938, fellow, 1940-41, Ph.D., 1941; m. Margaret Emilie Lutze, Aug. 3, 1938; children—Barbara, Janet, Carolyn. Tchr. Milw. Vocational Sch., 1933-37; asst. prof. English, U. Cal. at Los Angeles, 1946-47; prof. English, U. Md., College Park, 1947—, exec. sec. Am. Civilization program, 1950-57; cultural attache Am. embassy, London, 1957-59, (on leave from U. Md.); chmn. U.S. Ednl. Commn. in U.K., 1957-59; vis. prof. Cal. Inst. Tech., Claremont Colls., Northwestern U., U. Wis., Stanford. Ford Found. fellow, 1952-53, Newberry Library fellow, 1954, Guggenheim Found. fellow, 1954-55. Served with AUS, 1944-45. Fellow Royal Soc. Lit. U.K. (hon.); mem. Am. Assn. U. Profs. (council 1965-68). Am. Hist. Assn., Am. Civilization Conf. (sec. 1950-51), Am. Studies Assn. (founder, 1st pres. 1952), Coll. English Assn. (pres. Middle Atlantic sect. 1951-52, dir., 1957-59), Modern Lang. Assn., Thoreau Soc. Am. (dir. 1955-57, pres. 1960-61), English Speaking Union, Emerson Soc., Phi Beta Kappa (hon.), Alpha Tau Omega. Democrat. Episcopalian. Club: Cosmos (Washington). Author: The Sacred Seasons (poems), 1953; The American Lyceum, 1956; The Man Behind You (poems), 1959; The Anatomy of American Popular Culture, 1840-1861, 1959 (repub. as Antebellum Culture, 1970); The Half-World of American Culture, 1965; Mecken, 1969. Editor: Collected Poems of Henry Thoreau, 1943, enlarged edit., 1964; The Portable Thoreau, 1947, rev. edit., 1964; American Life in the 1840s, 1967; The Selected Journals of Henry David Thoreau, 1967, 2d edit., 1971; Ralph Waldo Emerson, A Profile, 1969. Co-editor: American Heritage, 2 vols., 1955; The Correspondence of Henry David Thoreau, 1958; American Literature, 3 vols., 1966. Editor and contbr.: The Young Rebel in American Literature, 1959, The Great Experiment in American Literature, 1961. Contbr. articles to encys., poetry and revs. to Brit. and Am. jours. Home: 4321 Woodberry St Univ Park Hyattsville MD 20782 Office: Dept English U Md College Park MD 20740

BODE, HENDRIK WADE, research engr., educator; b. Madison, Wis., Dec. 24, 1905; s. Boyd Henry and Bernice (Ballard) B.; B.A., Ohio State U., 1924, M.A., 1926, D.Sc., 1970; Ph.D. Columbia, 1935; m. Barbara Poore, Nov. 18, 1933; children—Katharine Anne, Beatrice Anne Hathaway. With Bell Telephone Labs., 1926-67, beginning with research elec. network theory and application to long distance communications facilities, successively devel. electronic fire control devices, in charge math. research group, dir. math. research, 1944-55, dir. research phys. scis., 1955-58, v.p. mil. devel. and systems engring., 1958-67; Gordon McKay prof. systems engring. Harvard, 1967—. Trustee Research Analysis Corp. Mem. various govt. mil. adv. groups. Recipient Presdl. certificate of merit, 1948. Fellow I.E.E.E. (Edison medal 1969), Am. Acad. Arts and Scis., Am. Phys. Soc.; mem. Nat. Acad. Engring., Nat. Acad. Sci., Am. Math. Soc., Phi Beta Kappa. Author: Network Theory and Feedback Amplifier Design; Synergy: Technical Integration and Technological Innovation in the Bell System. Also tech. papers. Holder patents in fields electric circuit theory, mil. devices. Home: 26 Garden St Cambridge MA 02138

BODE, RICHARD ALBERT, transp. co. exec.; b. Oak Park, Ill., July 26, 1931; s. Charles John and Esther (Burgert) B.; student Loras Coll., 1949-51; B.S., DePaul U., 1953; M.B.A., U. Detroit, 1960; m. Majorie Ann Lane, July 28, 1962; children—Anne, Julie, John. With Baumann, Finney & Co., pub. accountants, Chgo., 1953-56; staff accountant Nat. Tea Co., Chgo., 1956- 58, divisional controller, Detroit, 1958-62; asst. controller Eagle Food Centers, Rock Island, Ill., 1962-63; comptroller Brinks, Inc., Chgo., 1963-68, treas., 1968-69, v.p., treas., 1970. Mem. Plans Commn., Village of Hinsdale, 1969- -; mem. adv. com. for devel. parish accounting systems Archdiocese of Chgo., 1970. Served with M.C., AUS, 1953-55. C.P.A., Ill. Mem. Ill. Soc. C.P.A.'s (mem. career opportunities com.). Home: 20 Springlake St Hinsdale IL 60521 Office: 234 E 24th St Chicago IL 60616

BODE, ROBERT W., free-lance art dir., designer, artist; b. N.Y.C., Nov. 20, 1912; s. William L. and Wilhelmina (Talmon) B.; grad. Sch. Fine and Applied Arts, Pratt Inst., 1933; m. Dorothy Lounsbery, Nov. 20, 1937; children—Susan, Glenn. Art dir. N.Y.C. advt. agencies, 1944-69; now free-lance art designer. Nat. exhibitor water color shows; designer Davy Crockett and Johnny Appleseed stamps for Post Office Dept. lectr. on art and design. Recipient prizes from nat. and local art shows. Mem. Am. Water Color Soc. (recipient prizes), Soc. Illustrators, Art Dirs. Club N.Y.C. Club: Whippoorwill Golf. Home: 8 McClelland Pl Chappaqua NY 10514

BODEM, DENNIS RICHARD, state archivist; b. Milw., July 27, 1937; s. Frederick William and Helen Margaret (Bandow) B.; B.A., Wabash Coll., 1959; postgrad., U. Wis., 1959-61; m. Beverly Ann Jacobson, Sept. 21, 1963; children—Heather, Dawn, Brent. Asst. archivist Wis. Hist. Soc., Madison, 1961-64; chief, resources div. Buffalo and Erie County Hist. Soc., Buffalo, 1964-66; state archivist Mich. Hist. Commn., Lansing, 1966—. Mem. Soc. Am. Archivists, Am. Records Mgmt. Assn. (founding pres. Mid-Mich. chpt.), Nat. Archives (exec. council, chmn. com. Region 5 Adv. Council), Mich. Archival Assn. (exec. council 1970—), also nat. and state orgns. Contbr. articles, revs. to profl. publs. Home: 1315 Poxson Av Lansing MI 48910 Office: 3405 N Logan St Lansing MI 48918

BODENSTEIN, DIETRICH H. F. A., biologist, educator; b. Corwingen, East Prussia, Germany, Feb. 1, 1908; s. Hans and Charlotte (Lilienthal) B.; student U. Königsberg, (Germany), 1926-28, 1926-28, U. Berlin, 1928-33; Ph.D., U. Freiburg (Germany), 1953; m. Jean Coon, July 22, 1947; 1 dau. by previous marriage, Evelina (Mrs. William C. Suhler). Came to U.S., 1934, naturalized, 1940. Research asst. Kaiser Wilhelm Inst. Biology, Berlin, 1928-33; research asso. German-Italian Inst. Marine Biology, Rovigno d'Istria, Italy, 1933-34, Stanford Sch. Biology, 1934-41; John Simon Guggenheim Meml. Found. fellow dept. zoology Columbia, 1941-43; asst. entomologist Conn. Agrl. Expt. Sta., New Haven, 1944; insect physiologist, med. div. Army Chem. Center, Md., 1945-57; embryologist gerontology br. Nat. Heart Inst., Balt. City Hosps., 1958-60; Lewis and Clark prof. biology, chmn. dept. U. Va., Charlottesville, 1960—. Mem. Am. Acad. Arts and Scis., Am. Soc. Zoologists, Genetics Soc. Am., Am. Soc. Naturalists, Am. Assn. Anatomists, Soc. for Study Devel. and Growth, Nat. Acad. Sci., Soc. Biology Brazil (hon.), Sigma Xi, Contbr. articles to profl. and sci. publs. Home: 536 Valley Rd Charlottesville VA 22903

BODIAN, DAVID, educator; b. St. Louis, May 15, 1910; s. Harry and Tillie (Franzel) B.; B.S., U. Chgo., 1931, Ph.D., 1934, M.D., 1937; m. Elinor Widmont, June 26, 1944; children—Helen, Marion, Brenda, Alexander, Marc. Asst. in anatomy U. Chgo. 1935-38; NRC fellow medicine U. Mich., 1938, anatomy, Johns Hopkins, 1939- 40; asst. prof. anatomy Western Res. U., 1940-41; research on problems poliomyelitis, faculty dept. epidemiology Johns Hopkins, 1942-57, asso. porf. epidemiology Sch. Hygiene and Pub. Health, 1946-57, prof. anatomy, dir. dept., 1957—; tech. com. poliomyelitis vaccine, USPHS, 1957- 64; vaccine adv. com. Nat. Found., 1956—; cons. NIH; mem. bd. sci. counselors, div. biol. standards NIH, 1957-59, mem. bd. sci. advisers Nat. Inst. of Neurol. Diseases, 1968—. Served as lt. USNR, World War II. Recipient E. Mead Johnson award in pediatrics Am. Acad. Pediatrics, 1941. Mem. Am. Assn. Anatomists (pres. 1971-72), Am. Acad. Arts and Scis., Nat. Acad. Scis., A.A.A.S., Am. Physiol. Soc., Neurosci. Soc., Assn. Research Nervous and Mental Diseases, Phi Beta Kappa, Sigma Xi. Author: Neural Mechanisms in Poliomyelitis, 1942. Mng. editor Am. Jour. Hygiene, 1948-57; mem. editorial bds. Anatomical Record, Exptl. Neurology, Jour. Comparative Neurology. Contbr. science articles profl. jours. Researcher on structure and diseases of nervous tissue. Home: 906 Rolandvue Av Baltimore MD 21204 Office: 725 N Wolfe St Baltimore MD 21205

BODIE, BELIN VOORHEES, r.r. exec.; b. Pitts., Jan. 13, 1910; s. Charles William and Edna W. (Cree) B.; B.S. in Engring., Johns Hopkins, 1933; m. Thelma Louise Barbee, Sept. 15, 1940; children—Charles William, Belin Frederick. Clk. car service dept. B.&O. R.R., Balt., 1928; rodman U.S. Geodetic Survey, Belair, Md., 1933-34; signalman helper Pa. R.R., Balt., 1934-35; with G., M.&O. R.R. (formerly Alton R.R.), 1935—, successively rodman, instrumentman div. engrs. Eastern div., Bloomington, instrumentman, Chgo., asst. train master, Bloomington, train master, supt., Bloomington, chief engr., Mobile, Ala., asst. v.p. chief engr., gen. mgr., 1935-58, v.p., gen. mgr., 1958, now exec. v.p., gen. mgr.; v.p. New Orleans Gt. No. R.R. Co.; dir. Joliet Union Depot Co., Gulf Transport Co., Trailer Train Co., Kansas City Terminal Ry. Co., Miss. Export R.R. Co., G.M. & O. R.R. Co. Bd. dirs., Southwestern at Memphis. Mem. Ala., Ill., Mobile chambers commerce, Am. Ry. Bridge and Bldg. Assn., Am. R.R. Supts. Assn., Am. Ry. Engring. Assn., Roadmasters and Maintenance of Way Assn., Kappa Alpha. Clubs: Rotary (Mobile); Mississippi Valley Maintenance of Way (St. Louis). Home: 4210 Bellevue Lane Mobile, AL 36608 Office: 104 St Francis St Mobile AL 36602

BODIE, BENJAMIN TILLMAN, real estate exec.; b. Batesburg, S.C.; s. William Obediah and Julia Ann (Cromer) B.; A.B., Newberry Coll., 1917; m. Frances Price, May 11, 1920; children—Armand Francis, Paul Benjamin. Sales mgr., buyer, treas., then v.p. P.C. Price & Co., Columbia, S.C., 1920-47; pres. Eau Claire Ins. & Real Estate Agy., Columbia, 1948-66; exec. sec. Eau Claire Co. of C., 1948-55. Mayor, Eau Claire, 1955 (now merged with Columbia). Exec. com. Luth. Laymen's Movement, 1946-56; sec. bd. trustees Newbury Coll., 1946- 51. Mem. Brotherhood S.C. Luth. Synod (pres. 1947-49), Brotherhood United Luth. Ch. (pres. 1956-57), United Luth. Ch. Men (pres. 1957-59), Luth. Ch. Men Am. (council 1956—, exec. com. council 1959-60), United Ch. Men (bd. mgrs. 1955-60), S.C. Council Chs. (exec. com. 1959-62), Luth. Men S.C. Synod (mem. exec. com., 1959-68). Mason (Shriner, past master); mem. Order Eastern Star (past patron), Internat. Order King's Daus. and Sons (pres. S.C. 1969—, mem. central council). Club: Eau Claire Exchange, (pres. 1955). Address: 613 Townes Rd Columbia SC 29210

BODINE, JAMES FORNEY, banker; b. Villanova, Pa., June 16, 1921; s. William Warden and Angela (Forney) B.; grad. St. Paul's Sch., Concord, N.H., 1940; B.A., Yale, 1944; M.B.A., Harvard, 1948; m. Jean G. Guthrie, June 25, 1949; children—Jane G., Margaret F., Murray G., Tracy W. With First Pa. Banking & Trust Co., Phila., 1948—, v.p., 1958-63, sr. v.p., 1963-65, exec. v.p., 1965-68, sr. exec. v.p., dir., 1968—; dir. Commonwealth Tel. Co., Pennwalt Corp., Penn Mut. Life Ins. Co., Phila. Trustee, Phila. Orch. Assn.; bd. mgrs. Children's Hosp. Phila. Home: 1200 Old Gulph Rd Rosemont PA 19010 Office: First Pa Banking & Trust Co 15th and Chestnut St Philadelphia PA 19101

BODINE, JOHN WEEKS, ret. mus. adminstr.; b. Phila., Jan. 3, 1912; s. George Imlay and Katharine (Weeks) B.; grad. Germantown Friends Sch., 1929; A.B., Wesleyan University, 1933; B.A. (Rhodes scholar), Oxford (Eng.) University, 1935, B.C.L., 1936, M.A., 1953; m. Elizabeth J. Reimann; children—Susanna, Amelia, Lucy, Cornelia. Admitted to Pa. bar, 1937, practiced in Phila.; asso. Drinker, Biddle & Reath, 1937-48, partner, 1948- 59; pres. Pa.-N.J.-Del. Met. Project, Inc., 1959—, exec. dir. 1959-64; pres., chief exec. officer Acad. Natural Scis., Phila., 1963-70, trustee, 1963—. Sec. Assn. Am. Rhodes Scholars, 1949-67, bus. mgr. The American Oxonian, 1949-67, sec. Pa. com. Selection Rhodes Scholars, 1946-56, mem. Mid-Atlantic com., 1950-56. Mem. planning commn., Springfield Twp., Montgomery County, Pa., 1950-68, chmn., 1960-68; mem. Phila. Commn. on Higher Edn., 1962—; pres. Citizens Council on City Planning, 1953-56; mem. Phila. Urban Traffic and Transp. Bd., 1954-56, 58-60; mem. President's Task Force on Air Pollution, 1970. Trustee Samuel S. Fels Fund, 1960—, Balliol Coll. Alumni Fund, 1949—; trustee Wesleyan U., 1956—, sr. vice chmn., 1969—; trustee Community Coll. of Phila., 1964-69, Wistar Inst., 1964—; sec. Inst.

for Cancer Research, 1946-59, trustee 1959—; chmn. Community Leadership Seminar, 1964-69. Served to lt. USNR, 1944-46. Recipient Distinguished Alumnus award Wesleyan U., 1963. Mem. Phila. Bar Assn., A.A.A.S., (air conservation commn.), Am. Assn. Museums. Unitarian. Clubs: Philadelphia, Franklin Inn; Sunday Breakfast. Home: 525 Jarden Rd Wyndmoor PA 19118

BODINE, WILLIAM WARDEN, Jr., orgn. exec.; b. Villanova, Pa., May 29, 1918; s. William Warden and Angela Richardson (Forney) B.; grad. St. Paul's Sch., Concord, N.H., 1938; student Harvard, 1942; m. Louise Richardson Dilworth, May 26, 1946; children—William Warden III, Lawrence D., Anne D., Barbara W. With Penn Mut. Life Ins. Co., Phila., 1951—, asst. sec., 1952, financial sec., 1954-59; pres. Jefferson Med. Coll. and Med. Center, 1959-66, life trustee; pres. Arthur C. Kaufmann & Assos., Inc., mgmt. cons., Phila., 1967-69; pres. World Affairs Council Phila., 1969—. Bd. dirs., mem. exec. com. United Fund of Phila.; v.p., mem. exec. com. YMCA, Phila.; bd. dirs., chmn. fund campaign Mental Health Assn. Southwestern Pa.; trustee Temple U., Episcopal Acad.; chmn. bd. Thomas Jefferson U., 1970—; bd. dirs. Woods Schs., Crime Commn. of Phila.; 1st v.p. Free Library of Phila.; chmn. citizens adv. com. Center for Blind. Mem. Pa. Republican Finance Com. Served as lt. col. AUS, World War II. Decorated Legion of Merit, Purple Heart; Croix de Guerre with palm (France); selected Young Man of Year, Phila., 1950. Mem. Mil. Order World Wars, Nat. Conf. Christians and Jews (dir. Phila. region), Harvard Alumni Assn. (nat. dir.). Home: County Line Rd Villanova PA 19085 Office: John Wanamaker Store 13th and Market Sts Philadelphia PA 19107

BODLEY, JAMES RUSSELL, educator; b. Palo Alto, Cal., May 13, 1902; s. Homer S. and Lydia E. (Wood) B.; Mus.B., Coll. Pacific, 1923, A.B., 1924; Mus.M., Eastman Sch. Music, 1932; Mus.D., U. Puget Sound, 1962; m. Beatrice J. Walton, Aug. 22, 1926; children—H. Walton, Derrill G. Faculty, U. Pacific, Stockton, Cal., 1923—, dir. A Cappela Choir, 1934—, prof. music theory, 1932—, dean conservatory music, 1955-66. Guest dir. Stockton Symphony Orch., 1942, 46,48,54,56, festival choruses Cal. and region. Mem. Music Educators Nat. Conf., Am. Choral Dirs. Assn., Cal. Choral Condrs. Guild, Pi Kappa Lambda, Phi Mu Alpha, Theta Alpha Phi, Phi Kappa Phi. Composer: De Glory Road, 1939, A Chant out of Doors, 1941 (both for a capella choir). Home: 170 W Stadium Dr Stockton CA 95204

BODLEY, RONALD VICTOR COURTENAY, author; b. Paris, France, Mar. 3, 1892; s. J.E.C. and Evelyn (Bell) B.; student Eton Coll., Windsor, Eng., Royal Mil. Coll., Sandhurst, Eng.; m. Harriet Moseley, Nov., 1949. Mil. attaché Brit. embassy, Paris, France, taking part in Peace Conf. 1919; while there became friend of Lawrence of Arabia and as a result left army and went to live among nomad Arabs in desert, remaining 7 years; then set out on long series of voyages to Dutch Indies, China, Japan, Manchuria, Korea, Mongolia and South Sea Islands; came to U.S. and wrote screen plays for several years for Metro-Goldwyn-Mayer, Charlie Chaplin; returned to Europe in 1939 and remained until German invasion; escaped to Spain, then Portugal, eventually reaching U.S. Served to rank col. with King's Royal Rifle Corps, Brit. Army, 15 years, ret. Decorated Mil. Cross, Legion of Honor, Crown of Rumania, Mons Star, etc. Mem. Ch. of Eng. Clubs: Garrick, Marylebone Cricket, Naval and Military (London, Eng.). War corr. London Sphere during Sino-Japanese War, 1932-34. Contbr. numerous articles on travels to Am. and Brit. newspapers. Author: The Messenger, 1946; The Quest, 1947. The Warrior Saint, 1953; In Search of Serenity, 1955; The Soundless Sahara, 1968. Home: Chailey Newburyport MA 01950 Office: care A M Heath 35 Dover St London W 1 England ☆

BODMAN, HENRY TAYLOR, banker; b. Detroit, Jan. 26, 1906; s. Henry Edward and Florence (Taylor) B.; student Detroit U. Sch., student Hotchkiss Sch., Lakeville, Conn., 1922-24; B.S. cum laude, Princeton, 1928; m. Marie- Louise McMillan, May 8, 1930; children—Henry E. II, Thayer B. Cluett, Richard S. With Guardian Detroit Bank and affiliated instns., 1928-33; asst. cashier Nat. Bank of Detroit, asst. v.p., asst. trust officer, v.p., 1945-46, v.p., asst. to pres. 1949, gen. v.p. 1950-58, pres. 1958—, chmn., 1964, dir., 1953—; dir. Mich. Bell Telephone Co., Nat. Steel Corp., S.S. Kresge Co. Vice chmn., trustee Am. Enterprise Inst. Pub. Policy Research; bd. dirs. Henry Ford Hosp., Met. Detroit Bldg. Fund, United Found., Detroit Grand Opera Assn.; trustee Citizens Research Council Mich. Served from maj. to col., ordnance, AUS, 1942-46. With OPM Washington, 1941-42; Republican mem. bd. dirs. RFC Washington, 1946-48. Decorated Legion of Merit. Mem. Am., Mich. bankers assns., Assn. Res. City Bankers, Detroit Bd. Commerce. Episcopalian. Clubs: Economic, Bloomfield Hills Country, Grosse Pointe, Detroit, Country, Yondotega (Detroit); Chevy Chase (Md.); Metropolitan (Washington). Author several articles on econ. subjects. Home: 46 Lake Shore Rd Grosse Pointe Farms MI 48236

BODMAN, RALPH, architect; b. Memphis, Apr. 9, 1903; s. Ralph E. and Rose (mason) B.; student Tulane U., 1923-26; m. Barbara Darlington Mitchell, Oct. 14, 1931; children—Joan Darlington, Earl Kingsley. Partner Bodman & Murrell, Baton Rouge, 1933-50, Bodman & Murrell & Smith, 1950-61, Bodman Murrell, Laundry and Webb, 1961-64, Bodman & Webb, Inc., 1969, projects include library La. State U., master plan Lake Charles AFB, Temple B'Nai Israel of Baton Rouge, St. Joseph's Gymnasium, Cin., indsl. bldgs. Ethyl Corp., Esso Standard Oil Co., Dow Chem. Corp. Mem. La. Bd. Archtl. Examiners, 1942-56, sec. bd., 1950-56. pres. United Givers, 1967. Recipient citation Gulf States Regional Conf., New Orleans. Fellow A.I.A.; mem. La. Architects Assn. (pres. 1949), C. of C. (dir., mem. exec. com.), Pub. Affairs Research Council La. Clubs: Rotary (dir.), City, Country (Baton Rouge). Home: 9555 Jefferson Hwy Baton Rouge LA 70809 Office: 1175 Nicholson Dr Baton Rouge LA 70802

BODMER, ARNOLD RUDOLPH, educator, physicist; b. Frankfurt am/Main, Germany, May 23, 1929; s. Ernest Julius and Sylvia (Bodmer) B.; B.Sc., Manchester (Eng.) U., 1949, Ph.D., 1953; m. Doris E. Zerbe, Aug. 14, 1956; children—Edward C.F., Sylvia E., Richard E., Anne D. Came to U.S., 1963. Sci. officer Royal Armament Research and Devel. Establishment, Eng., 1953-56; postdoctoral research fellow Manchester U., 1956-57, lectr., 1958-63; with European Orgn. Nuclear Research, Geneva, Switzerland, 1957-58; physicist Argonne (Ill.) Nat. Lab., 1963—; prof.physics U. Ill., Chgo. Circle Campus, 1965—. Vis. prof. nuclear physics dept. Oxford (Eng.) U., 1970-71. Mem. Am. Brit. phys. socs., Inst. Physics. Research theoretical nuclear physics, nuclear structure and nuclear many-body problems, physics of hypernuclei, hypernuclear interactions. Home: 239 55th Pl Downers Grove IL 60515 Office: Dept Physics SES Univ Ill Chicago Circle Campus Chicago IL 60680

BODMER, WALTER FRED, educator; b. Frankfurt-am-Main, Germany, Jan. 10, 1946; s. Ernest J. and Sylvia (Bodmer) B.; B.A., Cambridge U. (Eng.), 1956, Ph.D., 1959; m. Julia Gwynaeth Pilkington, Aug. 11, 1956; children—Mark, Helen, Charles. Research fellow Clare Coll. Cambridge U., 1958-61, ofcl. fellow, 1961, demonstrator in genetics, 1960-61; fellow Stanford Sch. Medicine, 1961- 62, asst. prof. genetics, 1962-66, asso. prof. 1966-68, prof., 1968-70; prof. genetics Oxford U., 1970—; mem. NSF Genetics Panel, 1964-67, Nat. Inst. Allergy and Infectious Diseases com. transplantation and immunology, 1964-67, Genetics Study sect. NIH, 1969-70. Mem. Am. Soc. Human Genetics, Genetics Soc. Am., Biometrics Soc. Author: (with L. L. Cavelli-Sforza) The Genetics of Human Populations, 1971. Contbr. articles profl. jours. Home: Manor House 15 Mill Lane Old Marston Oxford England

BODSWORTH, CHARLES FREDERICK, naturalist, author b. Port Burwell, Ont., Can., Oct.11, 1918; s. Arthur John and Viola (Williams) B.; student pub. schs., Port Burwell; m. Margaret Neville Banner, July 8, 1944; children—Barbara, Nancy, Neville. Reporter, St. Thomas (Ont.) Times-Jour., 1940-43; reporter, editor Toronto (Ont.) Daily Star, 1943-46; staff writer, editor Maclean's Mag., Toronto, 1947-56; novelist, 1956—. Mem. Fedn. Ont. Naturalists (pres. 1964-66). Clubs: Men's Press, Ornithological, Field Naturalists (past pres.), Brodie (Toronto). Author: Last of the Curlews, 1954; The Strange One, 1960; The Mating Call, 1961; The Atonement of Ashley Morden, 1964 (also pub. in Eng., fgn. translations); The Sparrow's Fall, 1967; The Pacific Coast, Illustrated Natural History of Canada series, 1970. Address: 294 Beech Av Toronto 13 Ontario Canada

BOE, ARCHIE R., ins. co. exec.; b. Estherville, Ia., Feb. 27, 1921; s. Berge B. and Regina B. (Nelson) B.; B.C.S., Drake U., 1941; M.B.A., U. Chgo., 1951; m. Dorothy E. Schmidt, Apr. 19, 1943 (dec. Dec. 1965); 1 son, Michael A.; m. 2d, Christina S. Wolf, June 9, 1967. With Allstate Ins. Co., 1941—, v.p., sec., 1960-66, pres., 1966—, vice chmn., 1968—, dir.; v.p., sec. Allstate Enterprises, Inc., 1960-66, pres., 1966-, vice chmn., 1968-, also dir. Served with USNR, 1942-45. Mem. U. Chgo. Exec. Program Club, Newcomen Soc. N. Am. Clubs: University, Executives, Economic, Mid- America (Chgo.); Woodstock (Ill.) Country. Home: 1012 Cherry Valley Rd McHenry, IL 60050. Office: Allstate Plaza Northbrook IL 60062

BOE, NILS ANDREAS, govt. ofcl.; b. Baltic, S.D., Sept. 10, 1913; s. Nils and Sissel C. (Finseth) B.; A.B., U. Wis., 1935, LL.B., 1937. Admitted to Wis. bar, 1937, S.D. bar, 1938, D.C. bar, 1970; practice in Sioux Falls, S.D., 1938—; lt. gov. S.D., 1963-64, gov., 1965-69; dir. Office of Intergovtl. Relations exec. office of Pres., Washington, 1969—. Mem. S.D. Ho. of Reps., 1951-57, speaker, 1955, 57. Served with USNR, 1942-46. Mem. Am. Legion, V.F.W., Phi Alpha Delta. Republican. Lutheran. Elk, Odd Fellow. Home: 504 S Duluth Av Sioux Falls SD 57104 Office: Exec Office Bldg Washington DC 20506

BOECK, WILLIAM CHARLES, physician; b. Olivia, Minn., Feb. 18, 1894; s. Gotlieb and Kathryn (Dennstedt) B.; B.S., Carleton Coll., 1915; M.A., U. Cal. 1916, Ph.D., 1918; M.D., Harvard, 1926; M.S., U., Minn. m. Lura Dell Dinsmore, May 8, 1919; children-Mary Kathryn, (dec. 1935), Joan Dinsmore (Mrs. Peter B. Sullivan), William Charles. Teaching fellow U. Cal. at Berkeley, 1915- 17, research fellow, 1917-18; Rockefeller research fellow Johns Hopkins, 1919-20; Spl. investigator USPHS, 1920-21; asst. comparative pathology Harvard, 1922-26; fellow medicine Mayo Clinic, 1925-29, mem. med. staff, 1929-31; practice internal medicine and gastroenterology, Los Angeles, 1931-69; asso. prof. medicine Coll. Med. Evangelicals, 1931-36; asso. clin. prof. medicine U. So. Cal. Med. Sch., 1937-43; clin. prof. medicine U. Cal. at Los Angeles Med. Sch., 1952-69; attending physician St. Vincent's. Good Samaritan, Hollywood Presbyn., St. John's Hosps. Served with U.S. Army World War I; AEF in France. Diplomate Am. Bd. Internal Medicine. Fellow A.C.P., A.M.A.; mem. Am. Gastroent. Assn., Cal. Heart Assn., Cal. Soc. Internal Medicine, Cal. Med. Assn., Los Angeles Acad. Medicine, Los Angeles County Med. Assn., So. Cal. Soc. Gastroenterology (founder, past pres.), Beverly Hills Acad. Medicine, Am. Coll. Gastroenterology (hon.), Phi Beta Kappa, Sigma Xi, Phi Kappa Phi, Alpha Omega Alpha, Sigma Nu. Republican. Club: Los Angeles Country. Author numerous articles in field. Home: 1512 Club View Dr Los Angeles CA 90024

BOECKLIN, ROLAND, educator; b. Fiesole, Italy, Sept. 29, 1900; s. Carlo and Nadia (von Gringmuth) B.; diploma Colonial Inst., Florence, Italy, 1922; Ph.D., Yale, 1935; m. Peg Pitman, June 16, 1941; 1 son, Arnold P. Came to U.S., 1923, naturalized, 1929. Instr. German and Latin, Eastern prep. schs., 1936-46; asso. prof. U. Mass., Ft. Devens, 1946-48; asso. prof. Ohio Wesleyan U., Delaware, 1948-54, prof., 1954-71, prof. emeritus, 1971—, Found. prof. lang. and lit., 1954-71, chmn. dept. classics, 1948-71. Cons. Ohio State U. Research Found., 1963. Mem. Modern Lang. Assn., Classical Assn. Middle West and South, Am. Philol. Assn., Am. Assn. U. Profs. Home: 52 Westgate Dr Delaware OH 43015

BOEGEHOLD, ALAN LINDLEY, educator; b. Detroit, Mar. 21, 1927; s. Alfred Lindley and Katherine (Yeager) B.; A.B., U. Mich., 1950; A.M., Harvard, 1954, Ph.D., 1958; postgrad. Am. Sch. Classical Studies, Athens, Greece, 1955-57; m. Julie Ellizabeth Marshall, Apr. 3, 1954; children—Lindley, David Marshall, Alison, Alan Marshall. Instr. classics U. Ill., Champaign-Urbana, 1957-59, asst. prof., 1959-60; faculty Brown U., Providence, R.I., 1960—, asso. prof., 1964-67, prof. classics, 1967—, chmn. dept. classics, 1966-70; dir. summer session Am. Sch. Classical Studies, Athens, 1963-64, vis. prof., 1968- 69, sec., exec. and mng. com., 1964—; vis. lectr. history Harvard, 1967. Served with AUS, 1945-46. Mem. Archeol. Inst. Am. (exec. com. 1963-69), Am. Philol. Assn. Studies in ancient Greek history, lit., archeology, 1959—. Home: 38 Barnes St Providence, RI 02906.

BOEHL, HERBERT F., lawyer; b. Louisville, Nov. 16, 1894; LL.B., U. Louisville, 1918. Admitted to Ky. bar, 1918; now mem. firm Boehl, Stopher, Graves & Deindoerfer, Louisville. Dir. Louisville Trust Co., other corps. Life mem. Speed Mus. Trustee U. Louisville Alumni Law Found.; mem. bd. overseers U. Louisville. Recipient Distinguished Alumni certificate U. Louisville Sch. Law and Alumni Assn., 1963. Mem. Am., Ky., Louisville bar assns., Internat. Assn. Ins. Counsel, Fedn. Ins. Counsel, Def. Research Inst. U. Louisville Alumni Assn. (organizer, past pres.), Round Table Louisville (past chmn.), Am. Legion, English Speaking Union, Louisville C. of C. (charter mem.). Clubs: Exchange of Louisville (past pres.), Affiliated Exchange Clubs of Ky. (past pres.), National Exchange (past v.p., dir.; hon. life mem.), Filson (life), Arts of Louisville; National Golf Links America; Pendennis. Office: Kentucky Home Life Bldg Louisville KY 40202

BOEHLE, WILLIAM RANDALL, Jr., educator; b. Waxahachie, Tex., July 1, 1919; s. Wilhelm Reinhold and Ruby (Connally) B.; Mus.B., Hardin-Simmons U., 1941: Mus.M., La. State U., 1948; Ph.D., U. Ia., 1954; m. Emma Jean Belk, Dec. 10, 1943; children—Dulcy Jean, Alison Lee. Asst. prof. music Chadron (Neb.) State Coll., 1949-52, chmn. div. fine arts, 1952-60; chmn. dept. music U. N.D., Grand Forks, 1960—. Mem. N.D. Council Arts and Humanities, 1966—. Served with AUS, 1942-46. Mem. Music Tchrs. Nat. Assn. (past nat. chmn. student activities), Nat. Assn. Am. Composers and Conductors, Neb. Music Tchrs. Assn. (past pres.) Home: 406 22d Av S Grand Forks, ND 58201.

BOEHM, CHARLES HAROLD, coll. adminstr.; b. Kintnersville, Pa., Mar. 18, 1903; s. Edward R. and Lizzie (Adams) B.; A.B., Franklin and Marshall Coll., 1923; A.M., Columbia, 1926; Ed.D., Rutgers U., 1949; spl. work Internat. U., Geneva, Switzerland, Lehigh U.; LL.D., Phila. Coll. Osteopathy, 1958; D.Sc., Phila. Coll. Pharmacy and Sci., 1958; D.Sc., Incca U. Bogota (Colombia, S.Am.); m. Caroline E. Stauffer, June 17, 1929; children—Dorine, Charles, Edward. Tchr., athletic and debating coach Woodbridge (N.J.) High Sch., 1923-36; supervising prin. Richboro, Pa., 1926-29; prin. Morrisville (Pa.) High Sch., 1929-31; asst. supt., Bucks County, Pa., 1931-41, supt., 1941-56; supt. pub. instrn. Pa. Dept. Pub. Instrn., 1956-64; chmn. U.S. AID team attached to Nat. Planning Mission, Ministry of Edn. Colombia, 1963-65; ednl. planning specialist, adminstrv. asst. to pres. Phila. Coll. Osteopathy, 1965—; also exec. dir. Pa. Pvt. Acad. Assn. Accrediting Commn.; vis. prof. Pa. State U., 1951, U. Wis., 1954, Lehigh U., 1956, Temple U., 1966, 1968. Mem. nat. adv. com. on Econ. Edn., Higher Edn. Commn. on Accreditation, Service Experiences, nat. adv. commn. for Exchange of Tchrs.; co-chmn. Nat Commn. on Intermediate Unit; chmn. Pa. Coop. Project for County Supts. Trustee Aerospace Found., Pa. State U., Temple U. Mem. nat. adv. com. Boy Scouts Am. Recipient Vandenberg trophy, Am. Educator's medal, Freedom's Found.; Am. Legion medal and nat. awards. Mem. N.E.A., Pa. Edn. Assn., Am. Assn. Sch. Adminstrs. (yearbook commn. 1958). Author articles in field, Contbr. to popular mags. Guest of Swedish Govt., also Govt. of North Rhine-Westphalia. Address: 1203 Yardley Rd Morrisville PA 19067

BOEHM, FELIX HANS, educator, physicist; b. Basel, Switzerland, June 9, 1924; s. Hans G. and Marquerite (Philippi) B.; M.S., Inst. Tech., Zurich, 1948, Ph.D., 1951; m. Ruth Sommerhalder, Nov. 26, 1956; children—Marcus F., Claude N. Came to U.S., 1952, naturalized, 1964. Research asso. Inst. Tech., Zurich, Switzerland, 1949-52; Boese fellow Columbia, 1952-53; faculty Cal. Inst. Tech., Pasadena, 1953—, prof. physics, 1961—. Fellow Am. Phys. Soc. Research on nuclear physics, nuclear beta decay. Home: 2510 N Altadena Dr Altadena CA 91001 Office: Cal Inst Tech Pasadena CA 91109

BOEHM, KARL, opera conductor; b. Graz, Austria, Aug. 28, 1894; s. Leopold and Franz Boehm; student Gymnasium Graz, Vienna, Austria; m. Thea Linhard, May 2, 1927; 1 son, Karlheinz. Dir. Staatsoper, Hamburg, Dresden, Wien, Buenos Aires; condr. opera numerous countries. Home: Himmelstr 41 Vienna XIX Austria Office: Vienna Staatsoper Vienna, Austria.

BOEHM, WERNER WILLIAM, univ. dean; b. Oberlangenstadt, Germany, June 19, 1913; s. Karl and Bertha (Oppenheimer) B.; LL.B., U. Dijon (France), 1936, D.L., 1937; M. Social Work, Tulane U., 1941; m. Bernice Roseburg Brower, June 5, 1948; 1 son Andrew. Came to U.S., 1937, naturalized, 1944. Asso. prof. social work U. Minn., 1952-58, dir., coordinator U.S. and Canadian social work curriculum study, prof. social work, 1958-63; prof., dean Grad. Sch. Social Work, Rutgers U., 1963—. Vice pres. Minn. Welfare Conf., 1954-55; mem. U.S. Com. on Internat. Social Work, 1955-61; vice chmn. commn. 10th Internat. Conf. Social Work, Italy, 1961, rep. 11th Conf., Brazil, 1962; mem. continuing edn. tng. rev. com. Nat. Inst. Mental Health, 1969—; chmn. Commn. I, XVth Internat. Conf., Manila, 1970; mem. Sr. Fulbright travel grant Italo-U.S. Conf. on Ednl. Exchange in Social Welfare, Rome, 1969; sr. Fulbright appointment, Italy, 1971; mem. gov.'s council on aging, 1960; mem. N.J. Crime Commn., 1966-68. Recipient Cassidy Meml. research award U. Toronto, 1959. Mem. Am. Assn. U. Profs., A.A.A.S., Nat. Assn. Social Workers (chmn. commn. edn. 1965-68, dir., mem. exec. com. 1966-67), Nat. Commn. for Social Work Careers (mem. bd. of dirs.), Society Psychol. Study Issues, Council Social Work Edn. (mem. exec. com. 1967-69, chmn. commn. on ednl. services 1969—), Nat. Conf. on Social Welfare (1st v.p. 1969-70), N.J. Welfare Council (exec. com.). Author: Objectives of the Social Work Curriculum of the Future, 1959; The Social Casework Method in Social Work Education, 1959. Contbr. articles profl. jours. Home: 35 N 8th Av Highland Park NJ 08904 Office: Rutgers U Grad School Social Work New Brunswick NJ 08903

BOEHMLER, ERWIN WILLIAM, business and financial cons.; b. Chgo., Jan. 13, 1899; s. G. William and Ida Selma (Hillger) B.; B.S., Northwestern U., 1923, J.D., 1927, M.B.A., 1931; m. Lucile Margaret Roth, July 6, 1935; children—Erwin William, Jean Elizabeth. Admitted to Ill. bar, 1928; accountant Am. Bottle Co., Chgo., 1920-22; instr. manual arts, Evanston, 1922-27; feature editor and mgr. statis. dept. Chgo. Jour. Commerce, 1927-34; mem. staff Sheridan, Farwell & Morrison, Inc., 1934-39; lectr. Sch. Commerce, Central Y.M.C.A. Coll., 1933-38, prof., chmn. dept. bus. adminstrn., 1938-39, dean, 1939-45; dir. training and pub. relations, George Fry & Assos., cons. mgmt. engrs., 1945-48; ednl. dir. Investment Bankers Assn. Am. in Chgo., 1948-54, Washington, D.C., 1954-66, ednl. dir. emeritus and cons., 1966—. Professorial lectr. finance Northwestern U. Sch. Commerce, 1946-54, George Washington U., 1955-63; co- dir. Inst. Investment Banking, Wharton Sch., U. Pa., 1951- 66, now emeritus. Coordinator Rensselaer Inst. Tech., Indsl. Council Conf., The Am. Securities Bus., 1956; nat. adv. com. on econ. edn. Invest-in-Am.; joint com. on edn. Am. Securities Bus.; mem. adv. council OTC Bur., Nat. Security Traders Assn., 1962—. Instnl. edn. dir. engring. sci. and mgmt., War Training Program, U.S. Office Edn.; instl. rep., vocational rehab. tng. VA; mem. organizing com. Chgo. Speakers Bur., Ill. War Savings Staff, 1941-42. Served with USN, 1918. Mem. Am. Assn. Univ. Profs., Am. Econ. Assn., Pub. Relations Soc. Am., Financial Pub. Relations Assn., Am. Finance Assn., Chgo. Investment Analysts Club (pres., 1933-34), Washington Soc. Assn. Execs., Accacia; Delta Theta Phi, Beta Alpha Psi, Beta Gamma Sigma. Methodist. Mason; Kiwanian. Clubs: Kenwood Golf and Country (Bethesda, Md.), National Press. Editor I.B.A. publs., 1948-66. Editor and co-author: (with R. I. Robinson, F. H. Gane and L. C. Farwell) Financial Institutions, rev. edit., 1955. Author: Investment Trusts, 1930; General Management Funds, 1931. Contbr. bus. and financial publs. Home: 3218 Gleneagles Dr Silver Spring MD 20906

BOEHNING, JOSEPH FREDERICK, architect; b. Albuquerque, Mar. 27, 1931; s. Albert William and Henrietta (Marohn) B.; B.S. in Archtl. Engring., U.N.M., 1953, B. Arch., 1961; m. Bonnie Jean Snider, Aug. 6, 1952; children—Joanne, Paula, David Frederick. Archtl. designer A.W. Boehning, Albuquerque, 1955-61, prin. firm, Albuquerque, 1961—. Vice pres. Albuquerque Boys Clubs, 1968. Served to 1st lt. USAF, 1953-55. Registered architect. N.M., Ariz., Colo., Okla., Mo.; registered profl. engr., N.M. Mem. A.I.A., N.M. Soc. Architecture (pres. 1970). Am. Arbitration Assn. (mem. N.M. adv. council 1970—), U. N.M. Alumni Assn. (pres. 1969). Club: Tennis (Albuquerque). Home: 1800 Aliso Dr NE Albuquerque NM 87110 Office: 2005 Carlisle Blvd NE Albuquerque NM 87110

BOEKELHEIDE, VIRGIL, educator; b. Chelsea, S.D., July 28, 1919; s. Charles F. and Eleonor (Toennies) B.; A.B., U. Minn., 1939, Ph.D., 1943; m. Caroline A. Barrett, Sept. 1, 1945; children—Karl, Anne, Erich. Instr. U. Ill., 1943- 46; from asst. to prof. organic chemistry U. Rochester, 1946-60; prof. organic chemistry U. Ore., Eugene, 1960—. Cons., 1962—; mem. adv. panel NIH, 1962-66; chmn. chemistry div. NRC-Nat. Acad. Scis., 1970—. Guggenheim fellow, 1953-54; Swiss-Am. Found. lectr., 1960. Mem. Nat. Acad. Scis. Bd. editors Organic Synthesis, 1956—, Organic Reactions, 1956—, Jour. Am. Chem. Soc., 1962—. Home: 2017 Elk Dr Eugene OR 97403

BOELL, EDGAR JOHN, educator; b. Rudd, Ia., Oct. 30, 1906; s. Albert Emil and Gertrude (Van der Las) B.; A.B., U. Dubuque, 1929, D.Sc., 1963; Ph.D., State U. Ia., 1935; postgrad. Cambridge U. (fellow Rockefeller Found.), 1937-38; A.M. (hon.), Yale, 1946; m. Mildred Cottingham, June 3, 1932; children—Carl David, Dorothy Eleanor. Research asso. State U. Ia., 1934-37; faculty, Yale, 1938—, prof. zoology, 1946-47, Ross Granville Harrison prof. exptl. zoology, 1947—, chmn. dept. zoology, dir. zool. labs., 1956-62, acting dean Yale Coll., 1968-69. Asso. prof. zoology, U. Cal., summer 1941. Fulbright award Carlsberg Lab., 1953-54; Guggenheim Meml. fellow, 1963-64. Fellow Am. Acad. Arts and Scis.; mem. Am. Soc. for Cell Biology, Soc. for Developmental Biology (pres. 1952-53), Internat. Soc. Developmental Biology, Am. Physiol. Soc., Am. Soc. Zoologists (exec. com. 1959-63, mem. organizing com. 16th internat. congress zoology), Corp. Marine Biol. Lab., Conn. Acad. Arts and Scis., Sigma Xi (pres. Yale chpt. 1945-46). Cons. editor Zoology (McGraw-Hill Book Co.), 1949-62; co-mng. editor Jour. Exptl. Zoology; asso. editor Am. Scientist. Contbr. articles on chem. embryology to profl. jours. Home: 577 Skiff St North Haven CT 06473 Office: Kline Biol Tower Yale U New Haven CT 06520

BOENNING, HENRY DORR, Jr., investment banker; b. Phila., Oct. 16, 1914; s. Henry Dorr and Clara Virginia (Smith) B.; B.S., U. Pa., 1935; postgrad. Harvard Bus. Sch., 1935-37; m. Clare Huston Miller, Feb. 18, 1946; m. 2d, Sara Ann Perkins, Aug. 19, 1964. Partner Boenning & Co., Phila., 1946-70; v.p. Boenning & Scattergood, Inc., 1970—. Served from 2d lt. to maj., AUS, 1939-46. Mem. Phi Gamma Delta. Home: 936 Rock Creek Rd Bryn Mawr PA 19010 Office: 1809 Walnut St Philadelphia PA 19103

BOER, BENJAMIN C, lawyer; b. Alton, Ia., Apr. 25, 1889; s. John and Grace (Kuiper) B.; B. Engring., State U. Ia., 1913; LL.B., Western Res. U., 1917; m. Louise Burton, July 30, 1919; 1 dau., Barbara Louise (Mrs. L. M. Irwin). Faculty dept. engring. State U. Ia., 1913-14, Case Inst. Tech., 1914-17; admitted to Ohio bar, 1917, since practiced in Cleve.; mem. firm Boer, Mierke, McClelland & Caldwell, and predecessors, 1943—. Mem. exec. council Nat. Conf. Bar Presidents, 1953-55. Fellow Am. Bar Found., mem. Am. (spl. com. on disciplinary procedures, 1952-56; Ho. Dels., 1955-56), Ohio (exec. com., 1945-50; v.p. 1950-51, pres. 1951-52), Cleve. (exec. com., 1939-41) bar assns., Soc. Benchers of Western Res. Law Sch., Order of Coif, Sigma Xi, Tau Beta Pi. Home: 11820 Edgewater Dr Lakewood OH 44107 Office: Williamson Bldg Cleveland OH

BOERMA, ADDEKE HERDRIK, UN ofcl.; b. Anlo, Holland, Apr. 3, 1912; s. Harm and Janke (Wilkens) B.; diploma agrl. engring. Agrl. U., Wageningen, Holland, 1934; m. Maretta Postuma, Aug. 1, 1935; children—Janke, Johanna, Maretta; m. 2d, Dinah Johnston, Apr. 13, 1953; children—Maureen, Pauline. Dir. Crop Marketing Bd., also dir. Dutch Purchasing Office for Agrl. Produce, 1942- 44; govt. commr. for food and agr. in liberated Holland, 1944-45, acting dir. gen. food, 1945-46; govt. commr. for fgn. agrl. relations, 1946-48; with FAO, 1948—, dir.-gen., 1968—. Decorated knight Order Lion (Netherlands); comdr. Order Leopold II (Belgium): officer de l'ordre duMerit agricole (France). Home: Via Erodoto 11 Casal Palocco Via Cristoforo Colombo km 22 Rome Italy Office: FAO Via delle Terme di Caracalla Rome Italy

BOES, WARREN NORMAN, librarian; b. Grand Rapids, Mich., Sept. 3, 1929; s. John and Marguerite Isabel (Smith) B.; A.B. (Regents-Alumni scholar 1947-51), U. Mich., 1951, M.A., 1953, M.A. in L.S. (Library Service scholar 1953-54), 1954; m. Margaret Owen Camp, July 23, 1960; children—Rachel Marguerite, Richard Camp. Jr. circulation librarian U. Mich., 1954, sr. circulation librarian, 1955, asso. divisional librarian charge Chemistry-Pharmacy Library, 1956-57; dir. libraries Poly Inst. Bklyn., 1958-64; asso. dir. Syracuse (N.Y.) U. Libraries, 1964-66, dir. libraries, 1966—. Library cons. Council of Higher Ednl. Instns. in N.Y.C., 1962-65. Chmn. bd. trustees Five Asso. U. Libraries, 1970—, pres. Central N.Y. reference and research region, 1970—. Mem. A.L.A., Am. Soc. Engring. Edn. (chmn. engring. sch. libraries com. 1963-64), Am. Assn. U. Profs., Spl. Libraries Assn., N.Y. Library Assn., N.Y. Library Club (treas. 1961), Met. Coll. Inter-Library Assn. (pres. 1961). Conglist. Club: Appalachian Mountain (N.Y.C.). Home: 124 Circle Rd Syracuse, NY 13210.

BOESCHE, FRANK E., banker; b. Gaylord, Kan., Mar. 19, 1922; s. John P. and Eunice (Kiefner) B.; student Sch. Banking, Madison, Wis., 1958-60; m. Mary Ann Dutton, Oct. 22, 1949; children—Karen, Kathy, Kevin, Kurt. With Commerce Bank, Kansas City, Mo., 1940—, sr. v.p., 1968—. Mem. Corp. bd. Blue Cross-Blue Shield. Served to maj. AUS, 1942-46. Decorated Army Commendation medal. Clubs: Kansas City; Brook Ridge Country. Home: 3819 W 52d St Shawnee Mission KS 66205 Office: P O Box 248 Kansas City MO 64141

BOESCHENSTEIN, HAROLD, mfr.; b. Edwardsville, Ill., July 21, 1896; s. Charles and Bertha (Whitbread) B.; A.B., U. Ill., 1920; hon. degrees Bowling Green (O.) State U., Defiance Coll., Juniata Coll., Clemson Coll., Oberlin Coll., U. Toledo; m. Mary Elizabeth Wade, Mar. 30, 1922; children—William Wade, Nancy Ann (Mrs. Hart Fessenden), Harold. With Edwardsville (Ill.) Nat. Bank, 1920, Ill. Terminal R.R., Alton, Ill., 1921; various adminstrv. positions Ill. Glass Co., also subsidiaries and affiliates, 1921-26 v.p., 1926-29, (merger Ill. Glass Co. and Owens Bottle Co. 1929), v.p., gen. sales mgr. Owens-Ill. Glass Co., Toledo, 1929-33, v.p., gen. mgr., dir., 1934-38, pres. dir. Owens-Corning Fiberglas Corp., Toledo, 1938-63, chmn. bd., 1963-67, chmn. exec. com., dir., 1967—; chmn. bd. Fiberglas Can. Ltd., Owens-Corning Fiberglas Columbia, S. Am., Owens-Corning Fiberglas Europe, S. Am.; dir. Dow Jones & Co., Inc., Nat. Distillers & Chem. Corp., Edwardsville (Ill.) Nat. Bank & Trust Co., Asahi Fiber Glass Co. Ltd., Tokyo, Vitro Fibras, S. Am., Mexico City. Mem. WPB, 1942-45, vice chmn. operations, 1943-45; bus. council U.S. Govt., 1951—, chmn., 1954-56; chmn. Pres. adv. com. on Soviet Econ. Competition, 1957; mem. adv. com. on Army orgn., 1953. Pres. Toledo Mus. Art; co-chmn. A.R.C. Fund Raising Campaign, 1969-70. Trustee Am. Mus. Natural History (N.Y.), Stanford Research Inst., Rutherford B. Hayes Found., other civic and philanthropic orgns.; bd. dirs. U. Ill. Found. Served to lt. U.S. Army, 1917-19. Decorated Pres.'s Medal for Merit, 1946; recipient Distinguished Citizens citation Denison U. 1956; Distinguished Illini, U. Ill., 1961; Certificate of Appreciation, U.S. Army, 1953; Distinguished Service award Treasury Dept., 1968. Mem. Sigma Chi, Sigma Delta Chi. Episcopalian. Clubs: Links, University, (N.Y.C.); Metropolitan, 1925 F Street (Washington); University (Chgo); Pacific-Union, Bohemian (San Francisco); Toledo, Toledo Country; Belmont, Carranor Hunt and Polo (Perrysburg, O.); Cypress Point (Pebble Beach, Cal.). Home: 28449 E River Rd Perrysburg OH 43551 Office: Fiberglas Tower PO Box 901 Toledo OH 43601 also 717 Fifth Av New York City NY 10022

BOESCHENSTEIN, WILLIAM WADE, glass products mfg. exec.; b. Chgo., Sept. 7, 1925; s. Harold and Elizabeth (Wade) B.; student Phillips Acad., 1944; B.S., Yale, 1950; m. Josephine H. Moll, Nov. 28, 1953; children—William Wade, Michael M., Peter H., Stephens. With Owens-Corning Fiberglas Corp., 1950—, br. mgr., Detroit, 1955-59, v.p. central region, 1959-61, v.p. sales br. operations, Toledo, 1961-63, v.p. marketing, 1963-67, exec. v.p., 1967-71, pres., 1971—, dir. 1967—; dir. Am. Electric Power Co., N.Y.C., Kroger Co., Cin. Trustee Toledo Hosp. Mem. The Conf. Bd., Elec. Mfrs. Club, Delta Kappa Epsilon. Clubs: Grosse Pointe (Grosse Pointe Farms, Mich.); Links, Economic, Fifth Avenue (N.Y.C.); Economic, Country (Detroit); Toledo, Inverness (Toledo); Belmont Country (Perrysburg, O.). Home: 3 Locust St Perrysburg OH 43551 Office: Owens-Corning Fiberglas Corp Fiberglas Tower Toledo OH 43601

BOESE, ELSIE JEAN MCGIVNENY, (Mrs. Herman Lamar Boese), mem. Republican Nat. Com.; b. New Orleans, Jan. 19, 1925; d. John Roderick and Elsie (Buist) McGiveny; B.A., Sophie Newcomb Coll., 1945; m. Herman Lamar Boese, May 20, 1946; 1 son, Robert Lamar. Caseworker A.R.C., 1945-46; script writer Tulane U. Ednl. TV, 1954-55; tchr. Sunny Ct. Sch. For Retarded Children, 1954-55; vice chmn. La. Rep. Central Com., 1964-68, mem., 1964—; vice chmn. Rep. Polit. Action Council La., 1965-68; del. Rep. Nat. Conv., 1964, 68; mem. Rep. Nat. Com. from La., 1968—. Legislative chmn. St. Frances Cabrini Hosp. Aux., 1963-68; mem. La. Consumer Adv. Council, La. Meat Inspection Adv. Bd. Recipient Freedom award La. State Farm Bur. Fedn., 1965-69, Distinguished Service award 12th Dist. V.F.W., 1967. Mem. Central La. Community Theatre, Poets' Circle, Woman's Aux. Rapides Parish Med. Soc. (pres.), Alpha Delta Pi. Roman Catholic. Home: 831 City Park Blvd Alexandria LA 71301

BOESEL, MILTON CHARLES, Jr., lawyer; b. Toledo, July 12, 1928; s. Milton Charles and Florence (Fitzgerald) B.; B.A., Yale, 1950; LL.B., Harvard, 1953; m. Lucy Laughlin Mather, Mar. 25, 1961; children—Elizabeth Parks, Charles Mather, Andrew Fitzgerald. Admtted to Ohio bar, 1953, Mich. bar, 1953; partner firm Ritter, Boesel & Robinson, Toledo, 1956—. Chmn. bd. Hall-Toledo Corp., 1966—. Served to lt. USNR, 1953-56. Episcopalian. Mason. Clubs: Toledo, Toledo Country; Yale (N.Y.C.). Home: 3427 Kirkwall Rd Toledo OH 43606 Office: 240 Huron St Toledo OH 43604

BOETTCHER, ARTHUR HENRY lawyer; b. Chgo., Nov. 10, 1886; s. Charles and Barbara (Reinel) B.; student Lewis Inst., 1904-05; LL.B., Chicago Kent Coll. Law, 1908; spl. student U. Wis., 1908-09; m. Rose Cecil Krieger, May 29, 1912; childrenBarbara Mary (Mrs. C. Lyman Emrich, Jr.), Stephen Arthur. Admitted to Ill. bar, 1908; practicing lawyer, specializing in patent law, Chgo., 1909—; with Brown & Williams, 1909-12; mem. Brown, Williams, Bell, Hanson & Boettcher, 1912-14, Brown, Hanson & Boettcher, 1914-17, Brown, Boettcher & Dienner, 1919-27, Brown, Jackson, Boettcher & Dienner, 1927—. Served with the flying corps, USNR 1917-18, lt. comdr. (ret.). Decorated Navy Cross (with citation for invention of pilot directing feature of bomb-sights). Mem. Am., Chgo. bar assns., Am., Chgo. (pres. 1941) patent law assns., Alpha Sigma Phi. Republican. Presbyn. Clubs: University (Chicago); Glen View (Golf, Ill.). Home: The James C King Home Evanston, IL 60201.

BOETTCHER, BYRON KURTH, mfg. co. exec.; b. Prairie Farm, Wis., Nov. 24, 1917; s. Arthur Otto and Edna Augusta (Kurth) B.; B.A. in Math., North Central Coll., 1941; m. Dorothy Edith Finck, July 6, 1942; children—Barbara Ann, Robert Byron. Mgr., Dayton office, then dir. central region Avco Corp., 1953-63, Washington rep., 1964, v.p. def. and indsl. products group, 1964-67, v.p., gen. mgr. Avco Precision Products div., Richmond, Ind., 1967—. Chmn. civic affairs-spl. events com. Dayton Area C. of C., 1960-62, Chmn. def. adv. council, 1962-64. Served to lt. col. USAAF and USAF, 1941-53. Charter mem. Air Force Mus. Found; mem. Nat. Aviation Hall of Fame. Mem. Armed Forces Mgmt. Assn., Res. Officers Assn., Am. Ordnance Assn. (dir. 1969—), Am. Inst. Aeros. and Astronautics, Nat. Def. Transp. Assn., Army Aviation Assn., I.E.E.E., Nat. Security Indsl. Assn. (pres. Dayton 1966-67), Assn. U.S. Army, Richmond Area C. of C. (dir. 1968-70). Clubs: Dayton Country; Forest Hills Country (Richmond). Home: 1941 Northmont Lane Richmond IN 47374 Office: Avco Precision Products Division Sheridan St Richmond IN 47374

BOETTCHER, HAROLD PAUL, educator; b. Eagle, Wis., July 24, 1923; s. Emil Ernst and Henrietta (Seefeld) B.; B.S., U. Wis., 1947, M.S., 1950, Ph.D., 1954; m. Dorothy Strandberg, Feb. 1, 1948; children—David Paul, John Harold, Mark Alan. Instr. mechanics U. Wis., Madison, 1946-54; research dir. electric motor lab. A.O. Smith Corp., Milw., 1954-61; asso. prof. U. Wis., Milw., 1961- 65, prof., 1965—, chmn. dept., 1965-69, Served with USN, 1944-46. Registered profl. engr., Wis. Mem. I.E.E.E., Am. Soc. Engring. Edn. Home: 19285 Lothmoor Dr Lower Brookfield WI 53005 Office: U Wis Milwaukee WI 53201

BOETTGER, FRANK AUGUST, airframe mfg. co. exec.; b. Cin., Sept. 21, 1905; s. Arthur and Mathilda (Marischen) B.; Comml. Engr., U. Cin., 1926; m. Mabel E. Cook, Nov. 4, 1930; children—Martha Lee (Mrs. Dean Glasco), William A., Jane S. (Mrs. Robert Fry). Asst. comptroller Inland div. Gen. Motors Corp., Dayton, O., 1926-42; with Cessna Aircraft Co., Wichita, Kan., 1942-71, sr. v.p., 1961-71; chmn. bd. Parklane Savs. & Loan Assn., Wichita, 1957-; dir. Kathol Petroleum Co., Wichita, Union Nat. Bank, Wichita. Dir. Wichita State U. Athletic Corp., Wichita Community Planning Council; chairman bd. trustees St. Joseph's Hosp.; trustee Cessna Found. Mem. Mfrs. Aircraft Assn. (dir.), Nat. Assn. Accountants. Conglist. Clubs: Rotary, Wichita Country, Wichita (dir.); Moon Valley Country (Phoenix). Home: 564 N Broadmoor Wichita KS 67206

BOETTICHER, BUDD, producer, dir.; b. Chgo., July 29, 1916; ed. Ohio State U. Dir. for Eagle Lion Pictures, 1946, then Universal Pictures; ind. producer, 1954—; dir. Behind Locked Doors, Assigned to Danger, Black Midnight, Killer Shark, Wolf Hunters, Bullfighter and the Lady, Cimarron Kid, Bronco Busters, Red Ball Express, Horizons West, City Beneath the Sea, Seminole, Man from the Alamo, Wings of the Hawk, East of Sumatra, Killer is Loose, Seven Men from Now; author, dir. Magnificent Matador. Address: care Columbia Pictures 1438 N Gower St Hollywood CA 90028*

BOETTNER, JOSEPH EMERY, life ins. co. exec.; b. Phila., Jan. 12, 1903; s. William E. and Hattie M. (Umholtz) B.; student evening sch., U. Pa., 1927; C.L.U., Am. Coll. Life Underwriters, 1934; m. Ruth E. Robinson, June 30, 1927. With Phila. Life Ins. Co., 1951—, exec. v.p., 1956-57, pres., 1957—, also dir. Clubs: Union League, Midday (Phila.); Overbrook Golf (Bryn Mawr). Home: 73 Brennan Dr Bryn Mawr PA 19010 Office: 111 N Broad St Philadelphia PA 19107

BOGAN, RALPH A.L., Jr., food chain exec.; b. Hibbing, Minn., Oct. 31, 1922; s. Ralph A. L. and Ann (Gerzin) B.; B.A., Dartmouth, 1944; m. Peggy Wickman, Apr. 3, 1951; children—Pamela, Sandra, Karen, Diane. Exec. trainee Greyhound Corp., 1946-48; v.p. Chgo. Door Corp., 1948-58; agt. Sylvania Electric Products Co., 1958-59; asso. Blunt, Ellis & Simmons, Chgo., 1959-62; Chgo. mgr. Dominick & Dominick, 1962-64, v.p. Dominick & Dominick, Inc., Chgo., 1964—; dir. Atlas Press Co., Ordnance Engring. Assos., Tech. Pub. Co., Old Orchard Bank & Trust Co. Trustee Lake Forest Acad. Served lt. (j.g.) USNR, 1943-46. Mem. Alpha Delta Phi. Presbyn. Clubs: Attic, Chicago, Tavern, Bond, Executives, Economic (Chgo.); Bob 'O Link (Highland Park, Ill.); Shoreacres (Lake Bluff, Ill.); Pine Valley (Clementon, N.J.). Home: 815 Timberline Dr Glenview IL 60025 Office: 39 S LaSalle St Chicago IL 60603

BOGAN, S.T., Jr., business exec.; b. 1918; B.S., Okla. State U., 1958; married. Asst. treas. Mercury Oil Refining Co., 1948-56; with Am. Petrofina Inc., N.Y.C., 1956—, adminstrv. asst. to v.p. and treas., 1964-65, asst. sec., asst. treas., 1965-70, controller, 1970—. Served with AUS, 1941-45. Office: 50 Rockefeller Plaza New York City NY 10020*

BOGARD, BENJAMIN TAYLOR, univ. dean; b. Ruston, La., Dec. 19, 1914; s. Frank and Lelia May (Tait) B.; B.S. in Mech. Engring., La. Poly. Inst., 1935; M.S., La. State U., 1936; m. Erma Louise Oxley, Apr. 25, 1945; children—Mary B., Frank E., Jean L., Sarah E., Jane E. Fellow mech. engring. La. State U., 1935-36; instr. mech. engring. La. Poly. Inst., 1937-38, successively asst. and asso. prof. mech. engring., asst. dept. head, dept. head, now dean engring.; cons. operations research office Johns Hopkins, 1949-53; pres. Delta Research and Devel. Corp., 1952-71. Mem. La. Bd. Registration Engrs. and Surveyors, 1950-71, chmn., 1962-65; mem. Nat. Council Engring. Examiners, 1950-71, chmn. engrs. council profl. devel. com., 1963-66; chmn. La. Industry-Engring. Coll. Council, 1960. Trustee Lincoln Gen. Hosp., Inc., 1958-71, pres. 1963, 70. Served as capt. Ordnance Corps, AUS, 1942-46. Mem. Nat. Soc. Profl. Engrs., Am. Soc. M.E., Am. Soc. Engring. Edn. (chmn. Gulf-S.W. sect. 1970), La. Engring. Soc. (pres. 1961), La. Coll. Conf. (pres. 1960-61), Engrs. Council Profl. Devel. (mem. council 1960-66, exec. com. 1962-66), C. of C. (pres. 1955), Jr. C. of C. (pres. 1948-49), Lambda Chi Alpha, Pi Tau Sigma, Omicron Delta Kappa, Tau Beta Pi, Phi Kappa Phi. Democrat. Presbyn. Kiwanian (pres. 1958), Lion (v.p. 1947-48). Patentee on rockets. Home: 36 University Dr Ruston LA 71270

BOGARD, MORRIS RAYMOND, educator; b. St. Louis, Oct. 26, 1926 s; Alred Raymond and Mary Elizabeth (Moore) B.; Ph.B., Ill. Wesleyan U., 1950, M.A., 1952; Ph.D., U. Ill., 1961; student Cornell U., Ithaca, N.Y., 1954; m. Norma Jean Shingleton, June 20, 1948; children—Lawrence Joseph, Robert Scott, Peter Shelby, Kenneth Douglas. Asst. instr., rural drama adviser for extension service U. Ill., 1950-53; mem. faculty State U. N.Y. at Cortland, 1953—, prof. speech and theatre arts, 1954—, chmn. dept., adminstr. Fine Arts Center 1963—, asso. v.p. acad. affairs, 1971—. Actor, technician summer theatre, 1951-57; cons., Choice mag., 1964—; dir. Coll. Centennial Year, 1967-68. Claremont Inst. Higher Edn. fellow 1970. Mem. N.Y. Theatre Festival Assn. (pres. 1966), N.Y. Speech Assn. (mem.-at-large exec. com.), ANTA, Blue Key, Phi Gamma Delta, Theta Alpha Phi, Delta Psi Omega. Democrat. Presbyn. (deacon). Author: American Theatre 1900-1930, 1966; Play Production in the Secondary Schools; 1970; also articles. Theatre editor Reports, 1964—. Home: 15 Cowance St Cortland NY 13045

BOGARD, TRAVIS MILLER, educator; b. San Francisco, Jan. 25, 1918; s. Verner Edward and Gertrude (Travis) B.; A.B., U. Cal. at Berkeley, 1939, M.A., 1940; Ph.D., Princeton, 1947; m. Jane Malmgren, June 21, 1947; children—John George, Sara Snow. Faculty U. Cal. at Berkeley, 1947—, prof. English and dramatic art, 1960—. Served with AUS, 1942-46. Guggenheim fellow, 1958. Author: The Tragic Satire of John Webster, 1955. Editor: (with W.I. Oliver) Modern Drama, Essays in Criticism, 1965. Home: 7 W Parnassus Ct Berkeley CA 94708

BOGARDE, DIRK VAN DEN BOGAERDE, actor; b. London, Eng., Mar. 28, 1921; s. Ulric Jules and Margaret (Niven) vdB; student Univ. Coll., Hampstead, London, 1932. Theatrical appearances, 1938—, latest being Jezabel, 1959; motion pictures include Stranger in Between, 1949, Doctor in the House, 1950, Song without End, 1959, The Servant, 1964, King and Country, 1964, Darling..., 1964, Modesty Blaise, Accident, Our Mothers House, Quartet, Doctor at Sea, Cast of Dark Shadow U.S. Tv appearances include Blythe Spirit, Hallmark, 1966. Served to maj. Brit. Army, 1940-47: CBI. Recipient Best Performance award in Servant, Brit. Acad., 1964, award for Darling . . ., 1966. Home: Adams Farm Sweethaws Sussex England Office: Grade Organisation London W 1 England

BOGARDUS, EMORY STEPHEN, sociologist, editor, educator; b. nr. Belvidere, Ill., Feb. 21, 1882; s. Henry Brown and Eliza Maria (Stevenson) B.; A.B., Northwestern U., 1908, A.M., 1909; Ph.D., U. Chgo., 1911; Litt. D., U. So. Cal., 1945, U. Ariz., 1960; L.H.D., U. Redlands, Cal., 1946; LL.D., Boston U., 1950; m. Edith Mildred Pritchard, Aug. 9, 1911; 1 dau., Ruth Mildred. Fellow Northwestern U. Settlement, Chgo., 1908-09; fellow in sociology U. Chgo., 1909-11; asst. prof. sociology and econs. U. So. Cal., 1911-13, asso. prof., 1913-15, prof. sociology, 1915—, also organizer and first chmn. same dept., dir. Social Work div. 1920-37, dean, 1937-39, acting dean Grad. Sch. 1926-27, ann. research lectr., 1937, dean, 1945-49. Vis. prof. sociology Northwestern U., summer 1926, U. Wash., summer 1928. Regional research dir. (So. Cal.) Pacific Coast Race Relations Survey, 1923-25; social research dir. Boys Work Survey of Los Angeles, 1924-25. Pres. Los Angeles Social Service Commn., 1916-18; mem. bd. Goodwill Industries of So. Cal., 1919-49; trustee All Nations Found., 1940-55. Recipient Merit award Northwestern U., 1933. Registered social worker, Cal. Mem. Am. Assn. Social Workers (pres. Los Angeles chpt. 1923-25), Am. (pres 1931), Pacific (pres. 1929) Sociol. socs., Phi Beta Kappa, Delta Sigma Rho, Phi Kappa Phi, Alpha Pi Zeta, Alpha Kappa Delta (nat. pres., 1924-28, and 1947), Phi Delta Kappa. Editor: Jour. Sociology and Social Research, 1916-61, ann. proceedings, Pacific Sociol. Society, 1930-39; univ. editor U. So. Cal., 1942-45; adv. editor Dictionary of Sociology, 1944; editor Research News, U. So. Cal., 1945-49. Author numerous books, 1912—, latest being: Fundamentals of Social Psychology, 4th edit., 1950; The Making of Public Opinion, 1951; Principles of Cooperation, 1952, 3rd edit., 1964 Spanish edit., 1964; Sociology Applied to Nursing (with Brethorst) 3rd edit., 1952; Sociology, 4th edition, 1954; The Development of Social Though, 4th edit., 1960, also Spanish, Indian, Portuguese edits., 1964-65; History of Cooperation, 2d edit., 1965; The Traveler, 1956; Social Distance, 1959; Problems of Cooperation, 1960; The Explorer, 1961; Much Have I Learned, 1962; Toward a World Community, 1964; Thrice-Seven Wonders of the World, 1965; The Observer, 1966; A Forty-Year Racial Distance Study, 1967; The Wonderful Work of Sonnets, 1968; New Concepts for Sociology, 1969; Personal Tributes to Friends, 1970. Contbr. articles. Address: U Southern Cal University Park Los Angeles CA 90007

BOGARDUS, JOHN ROBERT, hotel exec.; b. Hoosick Falls, N.Y., Feb. 16, 1923; s. Phillip M. and Eileen H. (Cunningham) B.; B.S., Cornell U., Ithaca, N.Y., 1949; m. Nancy Ann Bard, Feb. 20, 1948; children—John Robert, Pamela. With Drake Hotel, Chgo., 1946, 48-63, successively asst. mgr., front office mgr., exec. asst. mgr., dir. food and beverage, 1958-61, gen. mgr., 1961-63; v.p., gen. mgr. Hotels Ambassador, Chgo., 1963-65; innkeeper Holiday Inn Lake Shore Drive, Chgo., 1965-68; regional dir. charge European and Middle Eastern operations Holiday Inns of Am., Memphis, 1968-70; v.p. Western Cities Hotels, Inc., Dallas, Tex., 1970—; mem. front office staff Broadmoor Hotel, Colorado Springs, Colo., 1947; on leave to become island hotel mgr. Gen. Electric Confs., Association Island, Henderson Harbor, N.Y., 1954; v.p. Gt. Western United, Denver, 1969-70; pres. Transcontinental Motor Inns, Inc., Dallas, 1970—. Bd.

dirs. Chgo. Conv. Bur. Served to lt. USAAF, 1942-45. Mem. Greater Chgo. Hotel/Motel Assn. (dir., 1st v.p.), Cornell Soc. Hotelmen (dir.), Escoffier Soc., Sigma Alpha Epsilon. Home: 4718 Mill Creek Rd Dallas TX 75235 Office: One Elm Pl Dallas TX 75202

BOGART, FRANK ARTHUR, govt. ofcl., ret. air force officer; b. Warren, Pa., Jan. 12, 1909; Frank C. and Minnie Josephine (Weeks) B.; B.S., U.S. Mil. Acad., 1931; student Coast Arty. Sch., Ft. Monroe, Va., 1938, Nat. War Coll., 1950; m. Mary Maher, Mar. 31, 1932. Commd. 2d lt., C.A.C., U.S. Army, 1931, advanced through grades to lt. gen., USAF; attached USAF, 1947-64; asst. chief staff logistics Alaskan Dept., J-4 Alaskan Joint Command. 1947; logistic planner SHAPE, Paris, 1951; dir. budget Hdgrs. Air Force, 1954-58; dir. Plans and Programs, Hdgrs. Air Materiel Command, 1958-59, dir. supply, 1959-61, comptroller Air Force, Washington, 1961-64; ret., 1964; dir. mgmt. operations, manned space flight NASA, 1964-65, dept. asso. adminstr. for manned space flight (mgmt.), 1965-69, asso. dir. manned Spacecraft Center, Houston, 1969—. Decorated D.S.M. with cluster, Legion of Merit with cluster; recipient Distinguished Service medal NASA. Home: 18623 Martinique Dr Houston TX 77058 Office: NASA Manned Spacecraft Center Houston TX 77058

BOGART, PAUL, director; b. N.Y.C., Nov. 21, 1919; s. Benjamin and Molly (Glass) B.; ed. pub. schs., N.Y.C.; m. Alma Jane Gitnick, Mar. 22, 1941; children—Peter Gareth, Tracy Katherine, Jennifer Jane. Puppeteer-actor with Berkeley Marionettes, 1946-48; TV stage mgr., asso. dir. NBC, 1950- 52; free-lance dir., 1952—; prodns. include Goodyear Playhouse, Armstrong Circle Theatre, U.S. Steel Hour, 1953-60, The Defenders, 1963, Ages of Man, 1965, Final War of Ollie Winter, 1966, Marlowe (Metro-Goldwyn-Mayer), 1968, Halls of Anger (United Artists), 1969, Skin Game (Warner Bros.), 1971. Lectr. New Sch. Social Research, 1960, ANTA, 1960. Served with USAAF, 1944-46. Recipient Christopher award 1955; Emmy award for 700 Year-Old-Gang (Defenders), 1964-65; Emmy award for Dear Friends (CBS Playhouse), 1967-68; Emmy award for Shadow Game (CBS Playhouse), 1970; Human Arts award Community Relations Conf. So. Cal., 1964. Mem. Dirs. Guild Am. (council 1962—), Soc. Stage Dirs. and Choreographers. Home: 15060 Corona del Mar Pacific Palisades CA 90272 Office: Tiber Productions Inc 760 N LaCienega Blvd Los Angeles CA 90069

BOGDAN, CORNELIU, Rumanian diplomat; b. Bucharest, Rumania, Nov. 5, 1921; s. Horia and Silvia (Lupascu) B.; grad. Inst. Econ. Scis., Bucharest, 1948; m. Emilia Milco. Sept. 14, 1949; children—Svetlana, Ileana, Olga. Counselor, Rumanian legation, Washington, 1951-53; dep. dir., then dir. Ministry Fgn. Affairs, 1953-67; ambassador of Rumania to U.S., 1967—; mem. Rumanian delegation to UN Gen. Assembly, 1956-61; dep. rep. UN Security Council, 1962. Recipient awards of Socialist Republic Rumania. Home: 2236 Massachusetts Av N W Washington, DC 20008. Office: 1607 23d St N W Washington DC 20007

BOGDANOFF, JOHN LEE, educator; b. East Orange, N.J., May 25, 1916; s. Paul George and Louise (Oswald) B.; B.M.E., Syracuse U., 1938; S.M., Harvard, 1939; Ph.D., Columbia, 1950; m. Ruth Franklin Brown, Sept. 9, 1945; children—Sue Carroll, Paul Lawson. Asst. project dir. Wright Aero. Corp., Paterson, N.J., 1939-46; instr. civil engring. Columbia, 1946-50; faculty Purdue U., Lafayette, Ind., 1950—, prof. scis., 1953—, head Sch. Aero., Astronautics and Engring. Schs., 1967—, dir. Center Applied Stochastics, 1962—. Cons. to industry, 1950; past v.p., dir. Midwest Applied Sci. Corp., Lafayette. Mem. Am. Soc. M.E., Am. Phys. Soc., Sigma Xi. Research in dynamics, vibration, application of stochastic processes to engring. problems. Author articles in field. Home: 327 Laurel Dr West Lafayette IN 47906 Office: Sch Aero Astronautics and Engring Scis Purdue Univ Lafayette IN 47907

BOGDANOVICH, JOSEPH JAMES, food co. exec.; b. San Pedro, Cal., May 9, 1912; s. Martin Joseph and Antoinette (Simich) B.; student Sch. Commerce, U. So. Cal., 1934; m. Nancynell Swaffield, Apr. 3, 1937; children—Martin, Robert, Joseph James, With Star-Kist Foods, Inc., Terminal Island, Cal., 1926—, adminstrv. asst., 1937-44, pres., 1944—; dir. H.J. Heinz Co. Mem. Cal Marine Research Com., 1960-66; ofcl. adviser joint U.S.-Japanese Tuna Conf., 1959,62. Bd. dirs. Marymount Coll., South Palos Verdes Estates, Cal. Club: Virginia Country (Long Beach, Cal.). Home: 31 Saddleback Rd Rolling Hills CA 90274 Office: Star-Kist Foods Inc Terminal Island CA 90731

BOGDANOWICZ, WITOLD MICHAEL, educator, scientist; b. Kiev, Ukraine, Jan. 4, 1933; s. Michael Andrew and Anastasia (Chikrygin) B.; B.S., U. Warsaw, 1953, M.S., 1955; Ph.D., Polish Acad. Scis., 1960; m. Ulla Eva-Maria Seeger, Nov. 12, 1968; children—Nina Ania, Michael Andrew. Came to U.S., 1961. Asst. mathematics U. Warsaw, 1952-55, instr., 1955-60, asst. prof., 1960-61; research asso. U. Md., 1961-62; asst. prof. Georgetown U., 1962-63, asso. prof., 1963-64; asso. prof. Cath. U. Am., 1964-66, prof. mathematics, 1966—. Recipient 1st prize, Math. Olimpiad, Poland, 1950, Nat. Sci. Found. research grant, 1963-64. Mem. Am., Polish, London math. socs. Editorial bd. Commentationes Mathematicae, 1959-62. Research linear methods summability, theory distbns., almost periodic differential equations, vectorial integration theory, spectral theory operators. Home: 13012 Pacific Av Rockville MD 20853 Office: Catholic Univ Washington DC 20017

BOGDONOFF, MORTON DAVID, physician, educator; b. N.Y.C., Dec. 8, 1925; s. M. Myron and Minnie (Alpher) B.; M.D., Cornell U., 1948; m. Jano Segal, July 1, 1951 (d. 1971); children—Reid, Ladd, Jesse, Drue. Intern, jr. asst. resident, sr. asst. resident dept. medicine N.Y. Hosp., N.Y.C., 1948-50; sr. asst. surgeon USPHS, Nat. Heart Inst., Balt., 1950-52; sr. asst. resident dept. medicine Duke Hosp., 1952-53, Eli Lilly Research fellow div. endocrinology and metabolism, 1953-54, resident dept. medicine, 1954-55; attending physician, chief metabolic div. Durham VA Hosp., 1955-56, cons., 1959-62; asso. prof. clin. medicine Med. Sch. U. Miami, 1956-57; asso. dept. medicine Med. Sch. Duke, 1955-56, asst. prof. medicine, 1957-59, asso. prof., 1959-62, prof. Med. Center, 1962- 69, asst. dean grad. med. edn., 1967-69; prof., chmn. dept. internal medicine U. Ill., Chgo., 1970—; cons. Ft. Bragg Hosp., 1959-62; cons. VA Hosps., Fayetteville, Durham, West-Side, Chgo.; mem. study sect. health services research NIH, 1966-70. Diplomate Nat. Bd. Med. Examiners, Am. Bd. Internal Medicine. Fellow A.C.P.; mem. Am. Fedn. Clin. Research (past pres.), Am., So. socs. clin. investigation, Assn. Am. Physicians, A.A.A.S., Endocrine Soc., Psychosomatic Soc. (past nat. councillor), Soc. Exptl. Biology and Medicine, A.M.A., Alpha Omega Alpha. Editor: Clinical Research, 1959-64. Chief editor: Archives of Internal Medicine, 1967—. Contbr. med. jours. Home: 21 E Scott St Chicago IL 60610

BOGDONOFF, SEYMOUR MOSES, educator; b. N.Y.C., Jan. 10, 1921; s. Glenn and Kate (Cohen) B.; B.S., Renssaeler Poly. Inst., 1942; M.S., Princeton, 1948; m. Harriet Eisenberg, Oct. 1, 1944; children—Sondra Sue, Zelda Lynn, Alan Charles. Asst. sect. head fluid and gas dynamics sect. Langley Meml. Aero. Lab., NASA, 1942-46; research asso. aero. engring. dept. Princeton, 1946-53, asso. prof., 1953-57, prof., 1957-63, Henry Porter Patterson prof. aero. engring., 1963—, head gas dynamics lab. James Forrestal Research Campus. Cons. aero. engr.; mem. adv. council NASA; mem. sci. adv. bd. Dept. of Air Force. Recipient Exceptional Civilian Service award Dept. Air Force, 1968. Fellow Am. Inst. Aeros. and Astronautics (dir.); mem. Internat. Acad. Astronautics of Internat. Astronaut. Fedn. (corr.), Sigma Xi. Home: 39 Random Rd Princeton NJ 08540

BOGER, LAWRENCE LEROY, educator, economist; b. DeKalb County, Ind., Sept. 26, 1923; s. Lester Elmer and Lazeal (Witt) B.; B.S., Purdue U., 1947; student Harvard, U. Chgo.; M.A., Mich. State U., 1948, Ph.D., 1950; m. Frances June Wilbur, Sept. 2, 1945; children—Richard Lee, Judith Ann. Faculty dept. agrl. econs. Mich. State U., 1948—, beginning as instr., successively asst. prof., asso. prof. 1948-54, prof., head dept., 1954—, dean coll. Agr. and Natural Resources, 1969—; cons. U.S. Crop Reporting Service, Dept. Agr., 1953-56, cons. Bur. Census and Statis. Reporting Service, 1965—; cons. village devel. program for Pakistan govt., Ford Found., 1957; cons. programs econ. assistance Nat. U. of Colombia, S.Am., Kellogg Found., 1959; mem. Nat. Com. on Use of Electronic Data Processing in Farm Mgmt.; dir.-at-large Central Bank for Coops., FCA, 1967—; mem. joint univ. adv. com. U. Nigeria. Mem. Am. Econ. Assn., Am. Farm Econs. Assn. (v.p. 1960-61), Internat. Conf. Agrl. Econs. (Am. council). Home: 988 Lantern Hill Dr East Lansing MI 48823

BOGERT, HENRY LAWRENCE, banker; b. N.Y.C., Oct. 7, 1911; s. Henry Lawrence and Elizabeth Blodget (Sanford) B.; grad. St. Paul's Sch., Concord, N.H., 1930; B.A., Yale, 1934; m. Margaret Milbank, Apr. 25, 1936; children—Henry Lawrence III, Jeremiah M. With Bankers Trust Co., N.Y.C., 1934-42; with Eastman, Dillon & Co., 1946—, gen. partner, 1948-56; gen. partner Eastman Dillon, Union Securities & Co., Inc., 1956-71, sr. v.p., dir., 1971—. Trustee, Provident Loan Soc. N.Y. Trustee Buckley Sch. of N.Y., Boys Club N.Y. Mem. Investment Bankers Assn. Am. (pres. 1966-67, gov.), Soc. of Cincinnati. Clubs: Bond, Links, River, Down Town Assn. (N.Y.C.); Fishers Island (N.Y.) Country (gov.); Island (Hobe Sound, Fla.) (v.p., gov.). Office: 1 Chase Manhattan Plaza New York City NY 10005

BOGGESS, WILLIAM RANDOLPH, forester, educator; b. Oakvale, W.Va., Apr. 9, 1913; s. Bernard F. and Maude (Boyd) B.; A.B., Concord Coll., 1933; M.F., Duke, 1940; m. Effie Cowan, Apr. 9, 1938; children—Randolph, Sam, Mary (Mrs. Carol Ray Daniel), Elizabeth (Mrs. R.W. Sullivan). Biology tchr. Mercer County Schs., 1933-35; staff Ala. Poly. Inst., Auburn, 1939-43, asso. forester, 1946-47; mem. faculty Dixon Spring Agr. Center, U. Ill. at Urbana, 1948- 58, prof. forestry, 1958—, head dept. forestry, 1968—. Mem. Am. Water Resources Assn. (dir. 1965—, editor Water Resources Bull., 1965-68, pres. 1970), Soc. Am. Foresters, Ecol. Soc. Am., Soil Sci. Soc. Am., A.A.A.S., Soil Conservation Soc. Am., Ill. Acad. Sci. Contbr. articles profl. jours. Home: 509 W Washington St Urbana IL 61801

BOGGESS, WILLIAM VERNON, lawyer; b. Noble County, Ind., June 30, 1921; s. John H. and Viola G. (Snyder) B.; student Huntington (Ind.) Coll., 1939-40, Ball State Tchrs. Coll., Muncie, Ind., 1940-41; LL.B., Ind. U., 1948; m. Gloria J. Wilson, Jan. 7, 1950; 1 dau., Barbara Suzanne. Admitted to Ind. bar, 1948, Alaska bar, 1951, U.S. Ct. Appeals, 1954, U.S. Supreme Ct., 1957; practice in Lafayette, Ind., 1948-49, Fairbanks, Alaska, 1951—. Mem. Alaska Bd. Edn., 1960—; mem. Fairbanks Home Rule Charter Commn., 1960. Served to 1st lt. USAAF, 1942-45. Decorated D.F.C., Air medal with 3 clusters. Mem. Am. (chmn. for Alaska), Alaska (bd. govs. 1959-63, pres. 1962-63) bar assns., Phi Delta Phi, Pi Gamma Mu. Home: 1114 Sunset Dr Fairbanks AK 99701 Office: Barnette St Fairbanks AK 99701

BOGGS, DANE RUFFNER, educator, physician; b. Orton, W.Va., Apr. 21, 1931; s. Earl R. and Leni (Rohrabaugh) B.; B.A., U. Va., 1952, M.D., 1956; m. Sallie Slaughter, Aug. 14, 1969; children—Dane Ruffner, Keith W., Richard E., J. Eric, Toni L. Intern U. Va. Hosp., 1956-57; med. resident U. Utah Hosp., 1959- 60; instr., then asst. prof. U. Utah Sch. Medicine, 1961-67; asso. prof. Rutgers U. Sch. Medicine, 1967-69; prof. medicine U. Pitts. Sch. Medicine, 1969—, chief div. hematology, 1967—. Clin. asso. Nat. Cancer Inst., 1957-59; Faculty research asso. Am. Cancer Soc., 1965-70; recipient John Horseley Meml. Research award U. Va., 1970. Diplomate Am. Bd. Internal Medicine. Mem. Am. Soc. Clin. Research, Am. Fedn. Clin. Research, Western Soc. Clin. Research, Am. Soc. Hematology, Internat. Soc. Hematology, A.A.A.S., Soc. Exptl. Biology and Medicine, Reticuloendothelial Soc., Phi Beta Kappa, Alpha Omega Alpha, Beta Theta Phi, Sigma Phi Epsilon. Democrat. Author: White Cell Manual, 1968; also chpts. in books, articles. Home: 441 Maple Av Edgewood Pittsburgh PA 15218

BOGGS, ELIZABETH MONROE, (Mrs. Fitzhugh W. Boggs), civic worker, assn. ofcl.; b. Cleve., Apr. 5, 1913; d. Adair and Elizabeth (McNairy) Monroe; B.A. summa cum laude, Bryn Mawr Coll., 1935; Ph.D., Cambridge (Eng.) U., 1941; postgrad. Newark State Coll., Rutgers U.; m. Fitzhugh W. Boggs, Sept. 20, 1941; 1 son, J. David. Research asst. dept. chemistry Cornell U., 1940-42; lectr. physics U. Pitts., 1942-43; research asso. Explosives Research Lab. OSRD, Bruceton, Pa., 1943-45. Del. White House Conf. on Children and Youth, 1950, White House Conf. on Edn., 1955; mem. Pres.'s nat. com. 1960 White House Conf. Children and Youth; bd. dirs. Nat. Health Council, 1958-61; mem. Pres.'s Panel on Mental Retardation, 1961-62. Bd. dirs. Nat. Assn. Retarded Children, 1950-63, 2d v.p., 1957, 1st v.p., 1957-58, pres., 1958-60; mem. bd. N.J. Welfare Council, 1952-59, 61-66, 71—, pres., 1956-58; 1st v.p. N.J. Assn. Mental Health, 1964-66; pres. N.J. Assn. Retarded Children, 1966-67; mem. Joint Commn. on Mental Health of Children, 1967-71; mem. Nat. Adv. Child Health and Human Devel. Council; adv. council Grad. Sch. Social Work, Rutgers U., 1964-68, 71—; mem. Pa. Adv. Council Mental Health and Mental Retardation, 1968-71, N.J. Mental Retardation Planning Bd., 1970-71, N.J. Gov.'s Task Force on Welfare Mgmt., 1969-71; mem. N.J. State Developmental Disabilities Council, 1971—; staff cons. Fairleigh Dickinson U., 1971—. Bryn Mawr European fellow, 1935-36; Margaret E. Maltby fellow Am. Assn. U. Women, 1938-39. Fellow Am. Assn. on Mental Deficiency. Home: RD 1 Hampton NJ 08827

BOGGS, J. CALEB, U.S. senator; b. Cheswold, Del., May 15, 1909; s. Edgar J. and Lettie Lettie (Vaughan) B.; A.B. U. Del., 1931; LL.B., Georgetown U., 1937; Army Command and Gen. Staff Coll., Ft. Leavenworth, Kan., 1942; m. Elizabeth Muir, Dec. 26, 1931; children—J. Caleb, Marilu. Admitted to bar of Supreme Court of Del., 1938, Supreme Court of U.S., 1946; judge Family Court, New Castle County, Del., 1946; U.S. Rep. in Congress, 1947-53; gov. of Del., 1953-60; U.S. senator from Del., 1961—. Apptd. mem. joint com. on Economic report, 82d Congress. Served to rank of col. AUS, 1941-46. Decorated French Croix de Guerre with Palm, Legion of Merit, Bronze Star with Oak Leaf Cluster, European Theater Operations ribbon with 5 campaign stars. Mem. Am., Del. bar assns., Am. Legion, V.F.W. Republican. Protestant. Club: Kiwanis. Home: 1203 Grinnell Rd Wilmington DE 19803 Office: Senate Office Bldg Washington DC 20510

BOGGS, JAMES HARLOW, ednl. adminstr.; b. Beaumont, Tex., Dec. 10, 1921; s. James H. and Lillie (Collier) B.; B.S. in Mech. Engring., Okla. State U., 1943, M.S., 1948; Ph.D., Purdue U., 1953; m. Jimmie Lea Evans, Jan. 7, 1943; children—Carolyn Jan, James Harlow III, Steven Evans. With Curtiss Wright Airplane Co., St. Louis, 1943; with Okla. State U., Stillwater, 1943—, asst. prof., 1948-53, asso. prof., 1953-57, prof., acting head dept. mech. engring., 1957, head dept., 1958-64, dean Grad. Sch., 1964-66, v.p. for acad. affairs, 1966—, research coordinator, 1968—. Cons. engr. on fluid flow, heat transfer, thermodynamics; mem. Nat. Adv. Research Resources Council, NIH, 1970—. Bd. dirs. Stillwater YMCA; dir. fund drive United Fund. Served from ensign to lt. (j.g.). USNR, 1944-46. Mem. Am. Soc. M.E. (chmn. nat. com. mech. engring. dept. heads 1963-64), Am. Soc. Engring. Edn., Stillwater C. of C. (dir. 1967), Sigma Xi, Sigma Tau, Pi Tau Sigma, Phi Kappa Phi, Sigma Nu. Rotarian. Author book. Editor: Mech. Engring. News, 1963-64. Contbr. papers to publs. Home: 1326 N Washington St Stillwater OK 74074

BOGGS, JEAN SUTHERLAND, art historian, educator; b. Negritos, Peru, June 11, 1922; d. Oliver Desmond and Marguerite (Sutherland) Boggs; B.A., U. Toronto, 1942; A.M., Radcliffe Coll., 1947, Ph.D., 1953. Asso. prof. U. Cal. at Riverside, 1954-62; curator Art Gallery Toronto, Can., 1962-64; Steinberg prof. history of art Washington U., St. Louis, 1964-67; dir. Nat. Gallery Can., 1966—. Fellow Royal Soc. Can.; mem. Coll. Art Assn. Am., Assn. Art Mus. Dirs. Author: Portraits by Degas, 1962. Address: Nat Gallery of Canada Ottawa Ontario Canada

BOGGS, JOHN CAMPBELL, educator; b. Norfolk, Va., Apr. 4, 1896; s. William George and Lula Massenberg (Parham) B.; A.B., Duke U., 1917; LL.D., Randolph-Macon Coll., 1964; m. Mattie Walton Epes, June 14, 1924; children—John Campbell, Charles Epes. Tchr. Ashland (Va.) High Sch., 1919, Blackstone (Va.) Mil. Acad., 1919-27, comdt., 1920-27, Randolph-Macon Acad., Bedford, Va., 1927-33; pres., treas. Randolph- Macon Acad., Front Royal, Va., 1933-65, pres. emeritus, 1965—. Mem. Meth. Commn. on Chaplains, Gen. Commn. on Army and Navy Chaplains. Served to 1st lt. 1st Div., A.E.F.; capt. O.R.C. Decorated D.S.C., Purple Heart. Mem. Nat. Assn. Mil. Schs. (dir.), Meth. Com. Christian Higher Edn., Sigma Chi. Democrat. Methodist. Mason, Rotarian. Home: 9403 Avalon Dr Richmond VA 22630

BOGGS, RALPH STUART, lawyer; b. Toledo, June 6, 1917; s. Nolan and Sarah (MacPhie) B.; A.B., Denison U., 1939; LL.B., U. Mich., 1942; m. Mary Frances Sharp Wiggins, Sept. 7, 1940; children—Sally Ann (Mrs. Thomas H. Brymer), William S., Robert A. Spl. agt. FBI, 1942-45; admitted to Ohio bar, 1942; practiced in Toledo, 1946—; partner Boggs, Boggs & Boggs, 1946—. Pres., dir. J-Sal, Inc.; sec., dir. Master Chem. Corp., Sec., dir. Mar-Mil Corp.; dir. Conforming Matrix Corp. Mem. Maumee Bd. Edn., 1953-69; mem. Maumee Recreation Com., 1954-69. Pres. Maumee Men's Republican Club, 1947-48. Chmn. bd. trustees Presbytery of Maumee, Inc. Mem. X-FBI Agts. Soc., Am., Ohio, Toledo bar assns. Presbyn. (elder), Mason (33, Shriner). Home: 720 E Carisbrook Dr Maumee OH 43537 Office: 413 Michigan St Toledo OH 43624

BOGGS, STEPHEN TAYLOR, educator, anthropologist; b. Chgo., July 13, 1924; s. Judge and Jeanette (Neligh) B.; A.B. summa cum laude, Harvard, 1947; Ph.D., Washington U., St. Louis, 1954; m. Joan Whitehorn, July 10, 1948; children—Christofer H., Ellen E., Andrew K. Shaw fellow Harvard, 1947-48; Social Sci. Research Council fellow among Am. and Canadian Ojibwa Indians, 1951-52; asst. prof. sociology Stanford, 1953-56; social anthropologist Nat. Inst. Mental Health, 1957-60; instr. anthropology Cath. U., 1959, 62; exec. sec. Am. Anthrop. Assn., 1961-66; asso. prof. anthropology U. Hawaii, Honolulu, 1966—. Panel mem. Nat. Acad. Scis. NRC. Mem. Am. Anthrop. Assn. (chmn. adv. com. anthropology curriculm study project), Soc. Anthropology. Roman Catholic. Contbr. articles to profl. jours. Home: 3020 Manoa Rd Honolulu HI 96822

BOGGS, THOMAS HALE, congressman; b. Long Beach, Miss., Feb. 15, 1914; s. William Robertson and Claire Josephine (Hale) B.; B.A., Tulane U., 1935, LL.B., 1937; m. Corinne Claiborne, Jan 22, 1938; children—Barbara Rowena (Mrs. Paul Eugene Sigmund), Thomas Hale, Corinne (Mrs. Steven Roberts). Admitted to La. bar, 1937, general practice civil law, 1943, 46; mem. 77th Congress, 80th to 92d Congresses from 2d La. Dist.; majority leader U.S. Ho. of Reps. Vice chmn. Democratic Nat. Com., 1956—; parliamentarian Dem. Nat. Conv., 1964, chmn. platform com., 1968. Mem. Pres.'s Commn. on Causes and Prevention of Violence; mem. Pres.'s Commn. on Assassination of President Kennedy, 1964. Served with USNR, World War II. Recipient Cunningham award International House, 1958. General manager Tulane U. Alumni Assn., 1937-40; mem. Family Service Soc. of New Orleans. Mem. Am., La., New Orleans bar assns., New Orleans C. of C., Am. Judicature Soc., S.A.R., Am. Legion, Am. Vets. World War II, Internat. Assn. Ports and Harbors (hon.), Phi Beta Kappa, Beta Theta Pi, Omicron Delta Kappa. Democrat. Roman Catholic. K.C. Club: Congressional (Washington). Home: 2801 St Charles Av New Orleans LA 70130 Office: Rayburn House Office Bldg Washington DC 20515

BOGGS, THOMAS HALE, Jr., lawyer; b. New Orleans, Sept. 18, 1940; s. Thomas Hale and Corinne (Claibourne) B.; A.B., Georgetown U., 1961, LL.B., 1965; m. Mary Barbara Denechaud, Dec. 27, 1960; children—Hale, Elizabeth, Douglas. Economist, Joint Econ. Com., U.S. Congress, 1961-65; spl. asst. to dir. Office Emergency Planning, 1965-66; admitted to D.C. bar, 1965; practice in Washington, 1966—; mem. firm Patton, Blow, Verrill, Brand & Boggs, 1966- -. Vice chmn. Md. dist. Am. Cancer Soc., 1966. Asst. scheduling mgr. Johnson Campaign, 1964; Democratic candidate for U.S. Ho. of Reps. 8th Dist. Md., 1970; coordinator Rocky Mountain states and Va. Humphrey Campaign, 1968. Trustee Goodwill Industries; bd. govs. Georgetown Prep. Sch. Mem. Am. Judicature Soc., Am. Bar Assn. (com. chmn.), Delta Theta Phi. Author: Private Trade Barriers in the Atlantic Community, 1964. Home: 6 E Kirke St Chevy Chase MD 20015 Office: 1200 17th St NW Washington DC 20036

BOGIN, BENJAMIN, publishing co. exec.; b. Bklyn., Dec. 25, 1900; s. Joseph and Ida (Lipsin) B.; student Columbia, intermittently 1934-43; m. Yetta Silberman, Dec. 29, 1923; children—Jacqueline Levine, Bruce. With Conde Nast Publs., Inc., N.Y.C., 1923—, comptroller, 1934-45, dir., exec. mgr., 1945-47, v.p., dir., mem. exec. com., 1947—, vice chmn. bd. dirs., 1957—; dir. Stamford Savs. Bank, 1951—. Mem. nat. panel arbitrators Am. Arbitration Assn.; bd. dirs. Stamford-Greenwich Mfrs. Council, 1947—, chmn. bd., 1950-51; exec. mem. Labor-Mgmt.-Citizens Com., Stamford Area council Girl Scouts U.S.A., Y.W.C.A., mens adv. bd.; pres. bd. Community Chest, 1951-52; vice chmn. Interfaith Council (award 1954); past dir. Rehab. Center for Physically Handicapped, 1958; chmn. Stamford chpt. A.R.C., 1953-54; trustee Ferguson Library, pres., 1960-61; treas., bd. dirs. Stamford Forum for World Affairs; bd. dirs. U. Conn. Br. Bldg. Fund, 1960; gen. chmn. Stamford United Jewish Appeal, 1960-61. Lt., Conn. N.G., World War II. Recipient Central Labor Union award, 1958; Joint Def. award, 1959; McAuliffe Medal award, 1962. Mem. Internat. Printing Pressmen and Assts. Union of N.Am. (hon.). Jewish religion. Club: Rockrimmon Country (past pres.). Home: 1540 Hope St Springdale CT 06907 Office: 420 Lexington Av New York City NY

BOGLE, HENRY CHARLES, lawyer; b. Ann Arbor, Mich., 1892; s. Thomas A. and Alice (Burgard) B.; LL.B., U. Mich., 1915; m. Mathilde Masson, Oct. 15, 1927; children—Suzanne, David, Peter. Admitted to Mich. bar, 1915, since practiced in Detroit: mem. firm Bodman, Longley, Bogle, Armstrong & Dahling, 1933—. Served as lt., U.S. Army, 1917-19. Mem. Am., Detroit bar assns., State Bar Mich., Phi Delta Phi, Psi Upsilon. Clubs: Detroit, Country of Detroit. Home: 356 Lakeland Av Grosse Pointe MI 48230 Office: Buhl Bldg Detroit MI 48226

BOGLE, HUGH ANDREW, engring. cons.; b. Lenoir City, Tenn., June 14, 1909; s. Hugh Andrew and Cornelia (Monger) B.; B.S. in Chem. Engring., U. Tenn., 1929; m. Mary Johnson Davis, Nov. 25, 1935 (dec. 1959); 1 son, Edwin Davis; m. 2d, Ethel L. Mitchell, July 28, 1961 (div.). With E.I. du Pont de Nemours & Co., Inc., Wilmington, Del., 1929-66, mgr. indsl. engring. cons. sect., 1954-58, cons. engring. and econ. evaluations, 1958-66; chmn. bd. West Chester Chem. Co. (Pa.), 1966—; v.p., chief engr. Rubco Products Corp., West Chester, 1966—; v.p. sales, dir. Sealants Internat., Inc., West Chester, 1966—; pres. Bolmar Corp. Am. Soc. M.E. rep. to Fedn. Mgmt. Oriented Orgns., 1959-66, v.p., 1961-62, pres., 1962; mem. council indsl. engring. Nat. Indsl. Conf. Bd., 1951-67, chmn. 1959; mem. Grantt Medal Award Bd., Am. Soc. M.E.-Am. Mgmt. Assn., 1960-63, Wallace Clark Award Bd., Am. Soc. M.E.-Soc. Advancement Mgmt.-Am. Mgmt. Assn.-Am. Soc. I.E., 1962-66. Fellow Soc. Advancement Mgmt.; mem. Am. Inst. Indsl. Engrs. (sr.), Am. Soc. M.E. (chmn. mgmt. div. 1960), Council Internat. Progress Mgmt. (dir. 1962-67, exec. com. 1963-65, sec. 1964-66), Kappa Alpha, Alpha Chi Sigma. Episcopalian. Clubs: Aronimink (Pa.) Golf; Plays and Players (Phila.); Drexelbrook (Pa.). Home: Dutton Mill Rd RD 3 West Chester PA 19380 Office: 439 S Bolmar St West Chester PA 19380

BOGLE, JOHN CLIFTON, investment co. exec.; b. Montclair, N.J., May 8, 1929; s. William Yates, Jr. and Josephine (Hipkins) B.; grad. Blair Acad., Blairstown, N.J., 1947; A.B., Princeton, 1951; m. Eve Sherrerd, Sept. 22, 1956; children—Barbara, Jean, John Clifton, Nancy, Sandra. With Wellington Mgmt. Co., Phila., 1951—, sec., 1959-62, adminstrv. v.p., 1962-66 exec. v.p., 1966-67, pres., chief exec. officer, 1967—, also dir.; was chmn. bd. Mass. Investors Trust; exec. v.p., dir. Wellington Fund, Windsor Fund. Mem. Investment Co. Inst. (chmn. bd. govs. 1969—). Clubs: Merion Cricket, Merion Golf (Haverford). Author chpt. in book. Home: 418 N Rose Lane Haverford PA 19041 Office: 1630 Locust St Philadelphia PA 19103

BOGNER, CHARLES NEALE, univ. dean; b. Lakewood O., Mar. 26, 1915; s. Charles and Lydia (Mueller) B.; A.B., Baldwin-Wallace Coll., 1936; M.A., Western Res. U., 1942, Ed.D., 1959; m. Jean Parkinson, Oct. 3, 1936; children—Nancy Jean (Mrs. Robert Enos), Jon Charles, Margaret Ann. With intangible sales staff Prudential Ins. Co., 1936-42; tchr. secondary schs., Cleve., 1942-43; faculty Baldwin-Wallace Coll., 1946-53; asst. supt. schs., Berea, O., 1953-55; asst. to pres. Miami U. (O.). 1955-59, dean Sch. Edn., 1959—. Past dir. Butler County Mental Health Fedn. Mem. Newcomen Soc., Am. Assn. Sch. Adminstrs., N.E.A., Ohio Edn. Assn., Ohio Assn. Sch. Adminstrs., Kappa Phi Kappa, Phi Kappa Tau, Kappa Delta Pi, Phi Delta Kappa. Episcopalian. Mason (Shriner, 32). Club: Cincinnati. Contbr. articles to profl. jours. Home: 11 Olde Farm Rd Oxford OH 45056

BOGNER, WALTER FRANCIS, architect; b. Providence, Oct. 7, 1899; s. Henry and Rosa (Rohn) B.; student State Tech. Sch., Austria, 1914-19, Grad. Sch. Architecture, Harvard, 1922-23, M.A. (hon.), 1948; student Am. Acad. Rome, 1925-26; Rotch traveling fellow, 1925-27; m. Edith L. Penman, Aug. 27, 1932; 1 son, Walter P. Draftsman, designer, Milw., Boston, 1919-25; partner Bogner & Billings, 1928-30; faculty Harvard, 1929—, instr., 1929-31, asst. prof., 1935-45, prof. architecture, 1946-66, prof. architecture emeritus, 1966—; pvt. practice architecture, Cambridge, Mass., 1930-47, 52—; partner Bogner & Richmond, 1947-52. Sch. bldg. cons. Ednl. Service Assos., 1948-52; chmn. ECA Housing Selection Com. Germany, 1951; cons. Housing Ministry, Fed. Rep. Germany, 1951-52; vice chmn. nat. com. Urban Devel. and Housing, 1953; asso. Boston Center Architects for Back Bay Center Devel., 1953. Mem. Lincoln (Mass.) Planning Bd., 1956-61. Recipient 1st prize Greater Boston Contest, 1944. Fellow A.I.A. (nat. chmn. com. house criteria 1948, nat. chmn. com. community planning 1956-69, edn. 1960—); mem. Boston Soc. Architects, Assn. Collegiate Schs. Architecture, Boston Archtl. Center. Club: Harvard (N.Y.C.). Author: Report on School Plant Needs, 1945-50; Planning a Schoolhouse for Tomorrow's Citizens, 1952; From School Program to School Plant. Contbr. Ency. Brit., 1947, 54, Brit. Book of Year, 1939-46. Home: Woods End Rd South Lincoln MA 01773 Office: RFD Lincoln MA 01773

BOGOLYUBOV, NIKOLAI NIKOLAEVICH, math. physicist; Dr. Honoris Causa, U. Chgo., 1967. Now dir. Joint Inst. for Nuclear Research, Dubna, USSR. Recipient Dannie Heineman prize for math. physics, for 1st rigorous proof of dispersion relations for nonforward scattering of elementary particles Am. Inst. Physics - Am. Phys. Soc., 1966. Mem. Am. Acad. Arts and Scis. (hon. fgn. mem.), U.S. Nat. Acad. Scis. (fgn. asso.). Address: Joint Institute for Nuclear Research Head Post Office P O Box 79 Moscow USSR

BOGORAD, LAWRENCE, plant physiologist; b. Tashkent, U.S.S.R., Aug. 29, 1921; s. Boris and Florence (Bernard) B.; brought to U.S., 1922; B.S., U. Chgo., 1942, Ph.D., 1949; m. Rosalyn G. Sagen, June 29, 1943; children—Leonard Paul, Kiki M. Lee. Instr. botany U. Chgo., 1948-51, asst. prof. dept. botany, 1953-57, asso. prof., 1957-61, prof., 1961-67; prof. biology Harvard, Cambridge, Mass., 1967—; vis. investigator Rockefeller Inst., N.Y.C., 1951-53. Served with AUS, 1943-46. Merck fellow, 1951-53, Fulbright fellow, 1960; recipient Career Research award NIH, 1963. Fellow Am. Acad. Arts and Scis.; mem. Am. Soc. Biol. Chemistry, Am. Soc. Cell Biology, Am. Bot. Soc., Am. Inst. Biol. Sci., Nat. Acad. Scis., Am. Soc. Plant Physiologists (pres. 1968-69), Botanical Soc. Am., A.A.A.S., Sigma Xi. Editor: (asso.) Botanical Gazette, 1958; Plant Physiology, 1965-66; editoral com. Annual Rev. Plant Physiology, 1963-67; editorial bd. Biochimica Biophysica Acta, 1967-69, Jour. Cell Biology, 1967-70. Office: Dept of Biology Harvard 16 Divinity Av Cambridge MA 02138

BOGORAD, SAMUEL NATHANIEL, educator; b. New Bedford, Mass., Apr. 7, 1917; s. Sidney and Rebecca (Eisenstadt) B.; A.B. summa cum laude, Brown U., 1939, A.M., 1941; Ph.D., Northwestern U., 1946; m. Ruth Pollack, Sept. 10, 1944. Instr. English, Northwestern U., Evanston, Ill., 1942-45; instr. U. Vt., Burlington, 1946-47, asst. prof., 1947-52, asso. prof., 1952-57, prof., 1957—, Frederick Corse prof. English lang. and lit., 1968—, chmn. English dept., 1961-1969. Vis. asst. prof. Brown U., 1948-49; vis. prof. William and Mary Coll., summer 1951, U. Colo., summer 1958. Chmn. planning commn., South Burlington, Vt., 1952-55, town moderator, 1955-61. Mem. commn. on insts. of higher edn. New Eng. Assn. Colls. and Secondary Schs. Mem. Modern Lang. Assn. Am., Nat. Council Tchrs. English, Coll. English Assn. (pres. New Eng. 1966-67, nat. dir. 1968-71, v.p. 1971—), Am. Assn. U. Profs. (pres. U. Vt. chpt. 1954-55), Phi Beta Kappa (pres. New Eng. dist. United chpts. 1961—, com. on Qualifications United chpts., mem. Senate). Author: (with J. Trevithick) The College Miscellany, 1952; (with C. Graham) Atlantic Essays, 1958. Home: 1425 Hinesburg Rd South Burlington VT 05401 Office: University of Vermont Burlington VT 05401

BOGUE, DONALD JOSEPH, sociologist, educator; b. Ogden, Utah, Feb. 2, 1918; s. Lloyd L. and Anna (Stringer) B.; A.B., U. Ia., 1939; M.A., Wash State U., 1940; Ph.D., U. Mich., 1949; m. Elizabeth J. Mullen, Dec. 23, 1944: children—Erna Lynne, Gretchen Elaine. Asst. dir. Scripps Found. For Research in Population Problems, Miami U., 1947-54; faculty dept. sociology U. Chgo., 1954—, prof. sociology, 1961—, dir. Community and Family Study Center, 1961—; tech. assitance expert UN, India, 1959-60, Chile, 1963-64; cons. U.S. Bur. Census, 1949-50, U.S. Bur. Budget, 1958-65. Bd. dirs. Planned Parenthood Assn. Am. Served to lt. (s.g.) USNR, 1942-46. Mem. Am. Statis. Assn., Am. Sociol. Assn., Internat. Union For Sci. Study Population, Population Assn. Am. (pres.). Author: Structure of the Metropolitan Community, 1949; Population of the United States, 1959; Skid Row in American Cities, 1962; Principles of Demography, 1969. Editor Jour. Demography, 1964-69. Home: 5801 Dorchester St Chicago IL 60637 Office: 1126 E 59th St Chicago IL 60637

BOGUE, PHILIP ROBERTS, accountant; b. Seattle, Dec. 22, 1924; s. Freeman Snowden and Nina (Reck) B.; B.A., U. Wash., 1947; M.B.A., Harvard, 1949; m. A. Suzanne Weatherly, June 9, 1951; children—Scott Weatherly, Nancy Sue. With Arthur Andersen & Co., C.P.A.'s, 1949—, partner, 1956—, resident mng. partner, Portland, Ore., 1961—. Bd. dirs. Columbia Pacific council Boy Scouts Am., Ore. Council Econ. Edn., Tri-County Community Council, Multnomah County Sch. Dist. 51; trustee Ore. Episcopal Schs. Served to lt. (j.g.) USNR, 1943-46. C.P.A., Ore., Wash., Cal. Mem. Ore. Soc. C.P.A.'s Am. Inst. C.P.A.'s, Portland C. of C. (dir.), Phi Beta Kappa, Beta Gamma Sigma, Beta Alpha Psi. Republican. Episcopalian. Home: 11519 S W Breyman Av Portland OR 97219 Office: Morgan Bldg Portland OR 97205

BOGUSCH, EDWIN ROBERT, educator; b. Mason, Tex., June 6, 1905; s. Robert Carl and Wilhelmina (Clark) B.; A.B., U. Tex., 1928, A.M., 1928, Ph.D., 1943; postgrad. U. Ill., 1928-30; m. Ethel Elnora Molby, June 15, 1929; children—George Edwin, Robert Lowell. Instr., State Coll. Wash., 1930-34; botanist USDA, 1935-36; sci. supr. Cuero (Tex.) Schs., 1936-41; prof. biol. scis. Tex. Arts and Industries U., Kingsville, 1941-69, prof. grad. studies, lectr. prof., 1969—, head dept. biology, 1949-68, dir. biol. research, 1963—. Cons. sci. teaching Corpus Christi (Tex.) Schs., 1950-57; cons. pub. sch. sci. curriculum studies; lectr. on wildlife sci.; Nat. Audubon Film lectr., 1969—. Pres. Bogusch Biology Meml. Scholarship Fund, Inc. Fellow A.A.A.S.; mem. Southwestern Assn. Naturalists, Nat. Audubon Soc., Phi Beta Kappa, Sigma Xi. Methodist. Author: Keys to 2500 Plants of Texas, 1945; Laboratory Manual for General Biology, 1949; Hoofbeats Along The Liano, 1955; also articles in sci. jours. Lectr. in field. Spl. work in time-lapse photography of plant growth. Home: 629 W Nettle St Kingsville TX 78363

BOGUSLAVSKY, GEORGE WILLIAM, educator, psychologist; b. Razdolnoye, Russia, Oct. 17, 1911; s. Vasilii P. and Anna (Lysenko) B.; came to U.S., 1930, naturalized, 1939; B.A., U. Wash., 1939, M.S., 1941; postgrad. U. Chgo., 1941-42, Yale, 1947-49; Ph.D., Cornell U., 1953; m. Geneva K. Bowers, Jan. 8, 1943. Instr., U. Conn., 1947-51; asst. prof. Cornell U., Ithaca, N.Y., 1953-57; prof. psychology Rensselaer Poly. Inst., Troy, N.Y., 1957—, exec. officer dept., 1966-68, chmn. dept., 1968—. Cons. Am. Inst. Research, 1952—, Pergamon Inst., 1959-62, N.Y. State Dept. Edn., 1957-59; adviser Rensselaer County Judge Family Ct., 1958-60. Served to capt. AUS, 1942-46; PTO. Mem. Am., Eastern psychol. assns., A.A.A.S., Pavlovian Soc. Am., Sigma Xi. Home: 320 Liberty Rd RD 6 Troy NY 12180

BOHAN, MARC, fashion designer; b. Paris, France, Aug. 22, 1926; s. Alfred and Genevieve (Baudoux) Bohan; received baccalaureat; m. Dominque Gaborit, Feb. 23, 1950 (dec. 1962); 1 dau., Marie Anne. Asst. designer at Piquet, Paris, 1945-49, at Molyneux, 1949-51; designer at Patou, 1951-58, Christina Dior-London, 1958-60; chief designer, artistic dir. Christian Dior S.A., Paris, 1960—. Home: 18 Rue Fean-Goujon Paris 8e, France. Office: Christian Dior 30 av Montaigne Paris France

BOHAN, MERWIN LEE, Latin Am. cons., b. Chgo., Jan. 21, 1899; s. Daniel Joseph and Delia (Lee) B.; ed. Am. Grammar Sch., Mexico City, Mexico, 1909-13; grad. Dallas High Sch., 1916; m. Harriet Davis, Feb. 5, 1921; children—Elizabeth Rowe, Harriet Davis, Clk. Pierce Fordyce Oil Assn., Dallas, 1916, Cia. Mex. de Petroleo " El Aguila," Mexico City, 1917, Am. consulate, 1919, Am. embassy, Mexico, 1920; asst. mgr. U.S. Rubber Export Co., 1920-22; with Dallas C. of C. (fgn trade sec. and publicity mgr.), 1922-26; trade commr. U.S. Dept. Commerce, Havana, 1927, asst. comml. attaché, 1927; comml. attaché, Guatemala, San Salvador and Honduras, 1928-31, Peru and Ecuador, 1931- 33, Chile, 1933-40, Colombia, 1940-41; chief U.S. Econ. Mission to Bolivia, 1941-42; counselor of embassy for econ. affairs Am. embassy, Buenos Aires, 1942; assigned to Dept. of State, 1944-45; counsellor of embassy for econ. affairs, Mexico City, 1945- 49, ret. 1949; prof. internat. relations Am. Inst. Fgn. Trade, Phoenix, 1949-50; mem. U.S. delegation GATT Conf., Torquay, Eng., 1950-51; U.S. ambassador Inter-Am. Econ. and Social Council, 1951-55; U.S. commr. Joint Brazil U.S. Econ. Devel. Commn., 1952-53; ret. 1955; cons. to U.S. and internat. agys., Dept. State, AID, UN, OAS, others, 1955—. Decorated grand cross Order of So. Cross (Brazil, 1956), grand officer Order of Quetzal (Guatemala) 1962. Mason. Author publ. Investment in Cuba. 1956; Investment in Chile, 1960. Home: 6902 Westlake Dr Dallas, TX 75214.

BOHANNAN, PAUL JAMES, anthropologist, educator; b. Lincoln, Neb., Mar. 5, 1920; s. Hillory and Linnie Hazel (Truex) B.; B.A., U. Ariz., 1947; B.Sc. (Rhodes scholar 1947-49), Oxford (Eng.) U., 1949, D.Phil. (Rhodes scholar 1950-51), 1951; m. Laura Marie Smith, May 15, 1943; 1 son, Denis Michael. Field research among Tiv of Nigeria, 1949-53, among Wanga of Kenya, 1955, among middle-class Am. divorcees, 1964—; lectr. social anthropology Oxford U., 1951-56; asst. prof. anthropology Princeton, 1956-59; prof. anthropology Northwestern U., Evanston, Ill., 1959-67, Stanley G. Harris prof. social sci., 1967—, chmn. Center for Social Sci. Research, 1959-64. Exec. dir. human environments in middle Africa project Nat. Acad. Scis., 1958-60. Decorated Legion of Merit. Mem. African Studies Assn. (pres. 1963-64, dir.), Am. Anthrop. Assn., Am. Ethnol. Soc. (dir. 1967-70), Royal Anthrop. Inst., Assn. Social Anthropologists, A.A.A.S., Internat. African Inst. Author: Justice and Judgment Among the Tiv, 1957; Homicide and Suicide in Africa, 1960; Social Anthropology, 1963; Africa and Africans, 1964, 2d edit. (with Philip Curtin), 1971; (with Laura Bohannan) Tiv Economy, 1968; Divorce and After, 1970. Gen. editor Am. Mus. Natural History Sourcebooks in Anthropology. Home: 405 Deerfield Rd Deerfield IL 60015 Office: Dept Anthropology Northwestern U Evanston IL 60201

BOHANNON, GEORGE WILDER, r.r. exec.; b. Duluth, Dec. 2, 1902; s. Eugene William and Mary (Carney) B.; student Cornell U., 1920-23; B.S., U. Minn., 1926; m. Elizabeth Schmitt, Oct. 7, 1930; children—Sarah B. Van Hagen, Jean B. Havano, Mary Elizabeth. Mech. draftsman D.M. & I. Ry., Proctor, Minn., 1926-27, mech. engr., 1927-44; asst. to chief mech. officer charge mech. engring. C. & N. W. Ry., Chgo., 1944-45, asst. chief, 1945-48, chief mech. officer, 1948-51; mgr. purchases and stores Pullman Co., Chgo., 1951-52, gen. mgr., 1952-53, operating v.p., 1954-58; dir., pres., chief exec. officer, 1958-71, dir., 1971—. Fellow Am. Soc. M.E.; mem. Sigma Chi. Mason. Clubs: Chicago; Oak Park (Ill.) Country. Home: 716 N East Av Oak Park IL 60302

BOHANNON, RICHARD LELAND, research dir.; b. Dallas, Oct. 11, 1907; s. Llewellyn Macey and Gussie Anna (Hodges) B.; student So. Meth. U.; M.D., Baylor U., 1932; m. Josephine Adelia Read, June 11, 1932; children—Richard Leland, Carol Josephine, Virginia Macey. Intern, Parkland Hosp., Dallas, 1932-33; commd. 1st lt. U.S. Army Res., 1932, advanced through grades to lt. gen. USAF, 1965; assigned various posts U.S., 1933-45; command surgeon XII Tactical Air Command, Germany, 1945-47; base surgeon Castle AFB, Cal., 1948-49; command surgeon 2d Air Force, Barksdale AFB, La., 1949-53, 15th Air Force, March AFB, Cal., 1953-58, 5th Air Force, Tokyo, Japan, 1958- 59, PACAF, Hawaii, 1959-61; dep. surgeon gen. Hdgrs. USAF, Washington, 1961-63, surgeon gen., 1963-67; ret.; dir. profl. services Doctors Hosp., Washington, 1968-71; exec. dir. Inst. Aerobics Research, Dallas, 1971—. Decorated various service and area medals; recipient Distinguished Alumnus award Baylor Med. Coll., 1964, So. Meth. U., 1968. Diplomate Am. Bd. Preventive Medicine. Mem. Indsl. Med. Assn., Am., Cal. colls. preventive medicine, A.M.A., Aerospace Med. Assn., Nat. Jogging Assn. (pres. 1958—.), Assn. Mil. Surgeons, Civil Aeromed. Assn. Methodist. Office: Institute for Aerobics Research Dallas TX 75221

BOHANON, LUTHER L., U.S. judge; b. Ft. Smith, Ark., Aug. 9, 1902; s. William Joseph and Artelia (Campbell) B.; LL.B., U. Okla., 1927; m. Marie Swatek, July 17, 1933; 1 son, Richard L. Admitted to Okla. bar, 1927, U.S. Supreme Ct. bar; gen. practice law, Seminde, Okla. and Oklahoma City, 1927-61; U.S. dist. judge No., Eastern, Western and So. dists. Okla., 1961—. Mem. platform com. Democratic Nat. Conv., 1940. Served to maj. USAAF, 1942- 45. Mem. Oklahoma City C. of C., Sigma Nu, Phi Alpha Delta. Methodist. Mason (Shriner, 32, K.T., Jester), Kiwanian. Home: 1617 Bedford Dr Oklahoma City OK 73116 Office: US Courthouse 4th and Robinson Sts Oklahoma City OK 73102

BOHEMAN, ERIK, airline exec., former Swedish diplomate; b. Stockholm, 1895; s. Carl and Ellen (Abramson) B.; LL.B., U. Stockholm, 1918; m. Margaret Mattsson, Mar. 16, 1932; children—Louise, Carl Henrik, Monica, Carl Anders. Entered diplomatic service, 1918; with Paris and London legations, 1918-19; fgn. office, Stockholm, 1919, head polit. dept., 1928; minister to Turkey and Greece, 1931-34, to Roumania, 1934, to Poland, 1934-37; undersec. State, Fgn. Affairs, 1938-45; minister to France, 1945-47; ambassador to Gt. Brit., 1947-48, to U.S., 1948- 58; mem. Swedish senate, 1958-70, speaker of First Chamber, 1965- 70; del. UN Gen. Assembly, 1950, 51, 60, 61, 62; vice chmn. bd. Saab-Scania Co., L.M. Ericsson Telephone Co., Swedish Match Co. Attended League of Nations confs., 1920-32, disarmament confs., 1931-32; headed various missions during World War II to Gt. Brit., U.S.A., U.S.S.R. Served as lt. 4th Hussars, 1915. Home: Anneberg Graenna Sweden Office: Stockholms Enskilda Bank Stockholm Sweden

BOHEN FREDERICK OWEN, mag. publisher; b. Waseca, Minn., May 25, 1895; s. Thomas Thaddeus and Amelia Francis (McLaughlin) B.; student N.Y. U., 1923; LL.D., Drake U., 1956; m. Mildred Meredith, Nov. 26, 1919; 1 dau., Barbara Meredith (Mrs. Friedl Pfeifer). Asso. Mpls. Jour., Mpls. Tribune, St. Paul Daily News, Portland Ore. Jour., Des Moines Capital, 1909-21; with Meredith Corp. (formerly Meredith Pub. Co.), Des Moines, 1921—, gen. mgr., 1927-28, pub., gen. mgr., 1928—, pres., chief exec. officer, 1929-65-66, now chmn. bd.; dir. Central Life Assurance Co., Des Moines, Allis-Chalmers Mfg. Co., Milw., C., R.I.&P. Ry. Co. Mem. Bus. Council Washington, 1954—. Bd. dirs. Nat. 4-H Service Com. Chgo., Greater Des Moines Com.; trustee Midwest Research Inst., Kansas City, Mo., Hawley Welfare Found., Des Moines, Thunderbird Grad. Sch. Internat. Mgmt., Phoenix; trustee, mem. exec. com. Drake U., Des Moines, 1929- -; pres., bd. dirs. Meredith Found., 1956—, Bohen Found., 1958—; bd. govs. Ia. State U. Found., Ames, 1959—, bd. dirs., 1967—; bd. dirs. Advt. Council (industries adv. com.), N.Y.C., Washington. Rotarian. Clubs: Wakonda, Des Moines, Embassy (Des Moines); Chicago, International, Tavern (Chgo.); Minneapolis; Marco Polo (N.Y.C.); Paradise Valley Country (Phoenix). Home: 2801 Fleur Dr Des Moines, IA 50321. Office: 1716 Locust St Des Moines IA 50303

BOHL, ROBERT WALTER, educator; b. Peoria, Ill., Sept. 29, 1925; s. Francis John and Ella (Ziegenbein) B.; B.S., U. Ill., 1946, M.S., 1949, Ph.D., 1956; m. Florence Marie Reace, May 30, 1947; children—Nancy (Mrs. Theodore Williams), Betty, Barbara, Robert F. Faculty, U. Ill., Urbana, 1946—, now prof. metall. and nuclear engring.; cons. Caterpillar Tractor Co., U.S. Steel Co., Argonne Nat. Lab., Battelle Meml. Inst. Bd. dirs. Univ. YMCA. Mem. Am. Soc. Metals, Am. Soc. Engring. Edn., Am. Inst. Mining, Metall. and Petroleum Engrs., Sigma Xi, Tau Beta Pi, Phi Kappa Phi, Alpha Sigma Mu, Sigma Tau. Contbr. articles profl. jours. Home: 2014 G Huff Dr Urbana IL 61801

BOHLE, BRUCE WILLIAM editor; b. St. Louis, July 21, 1918; s. Edward F. and Emma W. (Fricke) B.; B.A., Washington U., St. Louis, 1939. Film critic St. Louis Star-Times, 1946-51, drama and music critic, 1950-51; asst. mgr. St. Louis Symphony Orch., 1951-53; asso. editor Grolier Soc., N.Y.C., 1960- 64; editor Theatre Arts mag., N.Y.C., 1953-63; usage editor Am. Heritage Dictionary, Am. Heritage Pub. Co., N.Y.C. 1964—. Served with USAAF, 1942-46; PTO. Recipient Harvard Book prize, 1935. Mem. Phi Beta Kappa. Editor: The Home Book of American Quotations, 1967. Home: 260 Audubon Av New York City, NY 10033 Office: 551 Fifth Av New York City NY 10017

BOHLEN, CHARLES EUSTIS, investment co. exec., b. Clayton, N.Y., Aug. 30, 1904; grad. St. Paul's Sch.; A.B., Harvard, 1927; LL.D., (hon.), Columbia, 1968; m. Avis Howard Thayer; children—Avis T., Charles E., Celestine E. Fgn. service officer, 1929-69; vice consul, Prague, 1929-31, Moscow, 1934; sec. in diplomatic service, 1934; 3d sec., Moscow, 1934; with Dept. State, 1936, 42; sec. U.S. delegation Internat. Sugar Conf., London, 1937; 2d sec., Moscow, 1937; sec. U.S. delegation Conf. of Brussels, 1937; consul, Moscow, 1938; 2d sec., Tokyo, 1940- 41; asst. chief Div. European Affairs, 1943; accompanied Sec. of State to Moscow Conf., 1943; attended Tehran Conf., 1943; 1st sec., Moscow, 1942-44; chief Div. Eastern European Affairs, 1944; area adviser U.S. Group, Dumbarton Oaks Conversations on Internat. Orgn., Washington, 1944; asst. to sec. of State for White House Liaison, 1944; accompanied Pres. Roosevelt to Crimea Conf., 1945; polit. and liaison ofcr., U.S. del. U.N. Conf. on Internat. Orgns., San Francisco, 1945; polit. adviser U.S. delegation Berlin Conf., 1945; asst. to U.S. mem. Meeting of Council Fgn. Ministers, London, 1945; detailed to Meeting of Fgn. Secs., Moscow, 1945; polit. adviser U.S. del. 2d session Conf. Fgn. Ministers, Paris, 1946; polit. adviser, U.S. del. Paris Conf., 1946; spl. polit. adviser U.S. del., Paris Conf., N.Y.C., 1946; apptd. spl. asst. to sec. of State, 1946;

polit. adviser, U.S. del., 4th session Council Fgn. Ministers, 1947; apptd. counselor Dept. State, 1947, 51; adviser, U.S. del. Gen. Assembly, UN, N.Y., 1947; adviser U.S. del. to Council Fgn. Ministers, London, 1947; adviser, U.S. del., Gen. Assembly U.N., Paris, 1948; minister at Paris, 1949; U.S. ambassador to Russia, 1953-57, Philippines, 1957-59. France, 1962-68; spl. asst. to sec. of state for Soviet affairs, 1959-61; dep. under sec. state for polit. affairs, Washington, 1968-69; ret. 1969; pres. Italamerica, S.A., 1969—. Home: 2811 Dumbarton Av Washington DC 20007

BOHLIN, ERIC QUARFORDT, pencil mfg. exec.; b. Bklyn., Sept. 23, 1909; s. John and Anna (Quarfordt) B.; B.C.S., N.Y. U., 1930; certificate in design Pratt Inst., 1935; m. Ann Wehmeyer, May 19, 1935; children—Peter, Nancy (Mrs. Alfred Merritt), Susan. With Eberhard Faber, Inc., Wilkes-Barre, Pa., 1929—, successively merchandising asst., merchandising mgr., asst. supt., gen. supt. plant, v.p. charge mfg., exec. v.p., 1929-63, pres., 1963—, also chmn. bd.; chmn. bd. Hanover Nat. Bank of Wilkes-Barre (Pa.). Mem. Lead Pencil Mfrs. Assn. (past pres.), Nat. C. of C., Delta Sigma Pi, Delta Mu Delta. Lutheran. Club: Westmoreland (Wilkes-Barre). Home: White Haven Rd Bear Creek PA 18602 Office: Eberhard Faber Inc Wilkes-Barre PA 18703

BOHLING, AL, journalist. Editorial writer Kansas City Star. Office: 1729 Grand Av Kansas City MO 64108*

BOHLINGER, ALFRED J., lawyer; b. N.Y.C., Oct. 19, 1902; LL.B., N.Y. Law Sch. Admitted to N.Y. bar, 1926; dep. supt. ins., State of N.Y., 1944-50, supt. ins., 1950-55. Trustee N.Y. Law Sch. Mem. Am., N.Y. State bar assns., Assn. Bar City N.Y., N.Y. New York County Lawyers Assn. Office: 122 E 42d St New York City NY 10017*

BOHLMANN, ARTHUR ERWIN, clergyman; b. Crescent City, Ill., Dec. 15, 1903; s. John and Dora (Meyer) B.; student St. John's Coll., 1924, Concordia Sem., St. Louis, 1928; m. Anne F. Weeke, Aug. 22, 1928; children—Gloria (Mrs. Harley S. Stigge), Ralph A., Victor A., John P., Mark P. Ordained to ministry Lutheran Ch.-Mo. Synod, 1928; pastor in N D., Mont., Neb., Ore., 1928-49, Grace Luth Ch., Western Springs, Ill., 1949—. Sec. and/or chmn. pastoral conf. S. Neb. dist. Luth. Ch.-Mo. Synod, 1935-42, N.Ill. dist., 1950-62, mem. dist. policy bd., 1960-61, circuit counselor, 1956-62; pastoral counselor Luth. Women's Missionary League, Neb. dist., 1942-43; mem. bd. finance and stewardship No. Ill. dist., 1962—; mem. systematic theology com., commn. ch. lit. Luth. Ch.- Mo. Synod, 1959—; sec. Luth. Synodical Conf. N. Am., 1962-70. Mem. city planning commn., West Point, Neb., 1946-49. Civilian chaplain, mgr. Luth. Service Center, Chgo., 1944-46. Mem. Internat. Walther League (chmn. Christian service dept. Neb. dist. 1937-42). Home: 4041 Johnson Av Western Springs IL 60558 Office: Grace Luth Ch 41st St and Wolf Rd Western Springs IL 60558

BOHM, HENRY VICTOR, univ. adminstr.; b. Vienna, Austria, July 16, 1929; s. Victor Charles and Gertrude (Rie) B.; A.B., Harvard, 1950; M.S., U. Ill., 1951; Ph.D., Brown U., 1958; m. Lucy Margaret Coons, Sept. 2, 1950; children— Victoria Rie, Jeffrey Ernst Thompson. Came to U.S., 1941, naturalized, 1946. Jr. physicist Gen. Electric Co., 1951, 53-54: teaching, research asst. Brown U., 1954-58, research asso., summer 1958; staff mem. Arthur D. Little, Inc., Cambridge, Mass., 1958-59; asso. prof. physics dept. Wayne State U., Detroit, 1959-64, acting chmn. physics dept., 1962-63, prof., 1964—, v.p. for grad. studies and research, 1968—. Bd. dirs. Center for Research Libraries, Chgo, 1970—. Served to lt. (j.g.) USNR, 1951-53. Fellow Am. Phys. Soc. Home: 13348 Talbot Huntington Woods MI 48070 Office: Wayne State Univ Detroit MI 48202

BOHM, MAGNUS RICHARD, food co. exec.; b. Tell City, Ind., Aug. 1, 1916: s. Frank and Nellie (Anson) B.; student Evansville (Ind.) Coll., 1946-47; m. Frances Canida, May 18, 1941; children—Virginia (Mrs. Wallace S. Campbell), Nancy. With Gen. Foods Corp., 1938—, v.p., 1963—, pres., gen. mgr. Gen. Foods Ltd., Toronto, Can., 1963-64, gen. mgr. Birds Eye div., 1964-65, pres. Gen. Foods Internat., 1965-67, sr. v.p. corp., 1967-68, exec. v.p., 1968- -, dir., 1968—. Served with AUS, 1943-46; PTO. Mem. Am. Legion. Home: 778 Silvermine Rd New Canaan CT 06840 Office: 250 North St White Plains NY 10625

BOHMAN, GEORGE VROOM, educator; b. Princeton, Ill., Sept. 24, 1908; s. Oscar William and Rachel Maude (Vroom) B.; A.B., Monmouth Coll., 1929; M.A., U. Wis., 1934, Ph.D., 1947; m. Gladys Presley, June 22, 1940; children—Robert Presley, Eric James. Instr. speech Dakota Wesleyan U., 1930-33, asst. prof., head dept., 1933-37; instr. pub. speaking Dartmouth, 1937- 39, asst. prof., 1939-47, chmn. dept. pub. speaking, 1941-45, dir. speech in Naval English V-12 course, 1943-45; prof. speech, grad. chmn., chmn. Wayne State U., Detroit, 1947—. Mem. Hanover (N.H.) Democratic Town Com., 1944-47, chmn., 1946-47. Trustee Congl. Found. for Theol. Studies, 1963-70, 71—, chmn., 1966-70. Mem. Am. Assn. U. Profs., Speech Communications Assn. (chmn. com. on microfilm and microcard materials 1949-50, com. on history Am. pub. address 1952-55, com. on problems in speech edn. in colls. and univs. 1942-45), Eastern Pub. Speaking Conf. (sec.- treas. 1942-45), Central States Speech Assn., Ill., Bureau County (Ill.) hist. socs., Pi Kappa Delta (nat. council 1934-37), Tau Kappa Alpha, Phi Kappa Phi, Sigma Omicron Mu, Delta Sigma Rho. Conglist. (del. Gen. Council 1954-56; moderator Mich. State Assn. 1961-62, exec. com. Mich. conf. 1962—). Co-author: History of the First Presbyterian Church of Princeton, Ill., 1937; editor, author: History of the First Congregational Church, Royal Oak, Mich., 1967. Contbr. articles to speech and hist. jours. Home: 1014 Edgewood Royal Oak MI 48067 Office: Wayne State Univ Detroit MI 48202

BOHMAN, VERLE RUDOLPH, educator, nutritionist; b. Peterson, Utah, Dec. 29, 1924; s. Victor R. and Nancy (Fernelius) B.; student Cornell U., 1950-52; B.S., Utah State U., 1950, M.S., 1951, Ph.D., 1952; m. Renee Jorgensen, June 22, 1945; children—Margaret Louise, Verle Duane, Jolene Renee, Van Reid, Gregory Nathan. Faculty, U. Nev., Reno, 1952—, prof. nutrition, 1962—, chmn. animal sci. div., 1960—. Mem. Am. Inst. Nutrition, A.A.A.S., Am. Dairy Sci. Assn., Am. Soc. Animal Sci., Sigma Xi, Phi Kappa Phi, Alpha Zeta. Editor-in-Chief: Jour. Animal Sci., 1970-72. Research and numerous publs. on devel. techniques in range livestock nutrition, molybdenum toxicity, utilization of lipids by ruminant, measurement of fallout products using domestic animals. Home: 916 Sbragia Way Sparks NV 89531 Office: Animal Sci Div U Nev Reno NV 89507

BOHME, KURT, singer; b. Dresden, Germany, May 5, 1908; s. Oswald B. and Sidonie (Börner) B.; ed. Dresden Conservatory Music; m. Inge Heinicke, 1949. Mem. Dresden State Opera, 1930—, Munich State Opera, 1950—, Vienna State Opera, 1955—; guest appearances include London, Paris, N.Y.C., Bayreuth, Salzburg, Lisbon, Barcelona, Brussels, Antwerp, Monte Carlo, Florence, Rome, Buenos Aires. Address: 7 Geibelstrasse Munich Germany also care of Tillett & Holt Ltd 122/124 Wigmore St London W 1 England*

BOHMONT, DALE WENDELL, univ. dean; b. Wheatland, Wyo., June 7, 1922; s. J.E. and Mary (Armann) B.; B.S., U. Wyo., 1948, M.S., 1950; Ph.D., U. Neb., 1952; M.P.A., Harvard, 1959; children—Dennis E., Craig W. Pub. sch. tchr., Rock River, Wyo., 1941-42; from research asst. to head plant scis. U. Wyo., 1946-60; asso. dir. expt. sta. Colo. State U., 1961-63; dean, dir. agr. U. Nev., Reno, 1963-68, dean agr., 1969—. Cons., Devel. & Resources Corp., N.Y.C., 1968-69. Served with USAAF, 1942-45. Fellow A.A.A.S., Agronomy Soc.; mem. Western Crop Sci. Soc. (pres. 1962-63), Nat. Expt. Sta. Dirs. Assn. (chmn. 1967-68), Am. Range Mgmt. Soc., Farm House (dir. 1962—), Sigma Xi, Gamma Sigma Delta (pres. 1964-66), Alpha Zeta. Alpha Tau Alpha, Phi Kappa Phi. Contbr. articles to profl. jours. Editorial bd. Crops and Soils, 1962—. Home: 280 Island Av Reno NV 89501

BOHMRICH JOHN JACOB, motor vehicle parts mfr.; b. Milw., Feb. 4, 1909; s. Louis G. and Stella (Kenzy) B.; B.A., U. Wis., 1931; m. Genevieve Cofta, July 1, 1932; children—John L., Jay J. Eastern dist. sales mgr. College Inn Food Products Co., Chgo., 1937-41; div. mgr. A. O. Smith Corp., Milw., 1942-50, group exec., 1950- 54; asst. to pres. Fruehauf Trailer Co., Detroit, 1954-57, v.p., 1957; group v.p. Electric Auto-Lite Co., Toledo, 1957—; pres., dir. Prestolite Internat. Corp., Toledo, 1962-64, dir., 1964—; pres., dir. Indsl. Devel. Internat., Ltd., Toledo, Jay Internat. Corp., Chgo., Jay Internat. Corp. Can. Ltd., J.J. Bohmrich & Assos., Inc., Milw., Automark Industries, Inc., Palatine, Ill., 1970—. Indsl. cons. ICA. Mem. A.I.M., Am. Mgmt. Assn., Soc. Automotive Engrs., Internat. Platform Assn. Clubs: Milwaukee Athletic, University (Milw.); Marco Polo (N.Y.C.). Home: Route 5 West Bend WI 53095 Office: 641 Vermont Rd Palatine IL 60067

BOHMRICH, LOUIS, ret. fgn. service officer, lectr., writer; b. Milw., Apr. 19, 1904; s. Louis and Stella (Knauber) B; B.S. cum laude, Harvard, 1926; student George Washington Grad. Law Sch., 1935-37; m. Elizabeth Spalding, Dec. 23, 1934; children—Harriet (Mrs. William Cullen), Betsy (Mrs. Thoms Janke), Lois (Mrs. James Moc), Roger; m. 2d, Marion Letcher, Feb. 28, 1955. Investment counsel Scudder, Stevens & Clark, Boston, 1928-32; rep. SEC. corporate reorgn. cases under Fed. Bankruptcy Act, Washington, 1934-41; chief adminstrv. div. overseas missions Office Lend Lease Adminstrn. and successor agy. FEA, Washington, 1942-45; chief adminstrv. officer U.S. Mission to UN, N.Y.C., 1945-55, chief adminstrv. officer U.S. delegation UN Gen. Assembly, Paris, 1948, 51-52; 1st sec. Am. embassy, Djakarta, Indonesia, 1955-57; chief adminstrv. officer office U.S. commr. to Brussels (Belgium) Worlds Fair, 1957-59; 1st sec. Am. embassy, Ankara, Turkey, 1959-61; profl. lectr. and writer on world affairs and UN, 1962—; cons. on internat. trade and indsl. devel. Mem. internat. relations com. Council for Christian Social Action, United Ch. of Christ. Mem. Internat. Platform Assn. (gov.), Am. Fgn. Service Assn., UN Assn. N.Y. (dir., chmn. speakers com.), Soc. for Prevention of World War III (dir.). Club: Pi Eta (Cambridge, Mass.). Address: 1505 Kendall Dr Boulder CO 80302

BOHN, ERNEST JOHN, lawyer, univ. lectr.; b. Austria-Hungary, May 12, 1901; s. Frank J. and Juliana (Kiry) B.; came to U.S., 1911, naturalized, 1920; A.B. cum laude, Adelbert Coll., Western Res. U., 1924, J.D., 1926, LL.D., 1951. Admitted to Ohio bar, 1926, practiced in Cleve., 1926-38; mem. Ohio Gen. Assembly, 1929-30; mem. Cleve. City Council, 1930-40; mem. Internat. Housing Commn., 1934-40; archtl. adv. com. Fed. Pub. Housing Authority, 1939; cons. U.S. Housing Authority, Resettlement Adminstrn., Def. Housing div. Fed. Works Agy. Pub. Housing Adminstrn.; former dir. Cleve. Met. Housing Authority; now lectr. urban and environmental studies Case Western Res. U.; dir., organizer Regional Assn. Cleve.; bd. dirs. Nat. Housing Conf.; dir. 2d Fed. Savs. and Loan Assn. Cleve.; former chmn. City Planning Commn. Cleve.; adv. bd. Urban Renewal Agy. Cleve.; mem. Ohio Urban Devel. Commn., Midwest Regional Planning Commn.; mem. policy com., planning com. and health goals and central planning bd. coms. Cleve. Welfare Fedn.; mem. Regional Planning Commn. Cuyahoga Country (O.); formerly mem. exec. com. Internat. Fedn. Housing and Town Planning, The Hague; exec. com. Pres. Eisenhower's adv. com. housing policies; past exec. com. Am. Council to Improve our Neighborhoods; mem. Nat. Action Council of Urban Am., Nat. Urban Coalition, Nat. Council on Aging, com. on housing for elderly, adv. com. housing and community devel. and housing for sr. citizens HHFA, Washington; adv. com. on retired workers UAW, Detroit; U.S. del. housing com. UN Econ. Commn. for Europe, Geneva, Switzerland, 1959; nat. com. White House Conf. Children and Youth, 1960, panel on phys. environment Pres.'s Commn. Nat. Goals, 1960; nat. adv. com. White House Conf. on Aging, 1961; cons. subcom. problems aged and aging U.S. Senate; mem. Ohio Gov.'s Commn. on Aging, also adv. bd. Ohio Div. Aging; mem. adv. com. Ohio Civil Rights Commn.; panel cons. on aging Dept. Health. Edn., Welfare; trustee Better Homes and Neighborhoods Cleve.; mem. Cleve. Met. Services Commn; adv. bd., past chmn. Cath. Charities Bur.; trustee, mem. exec. com. Cath. Charities Corp.; citizens adv. com. Cuyahoga County Hosp. Bd., DePaul Infant Home, others; mem. council of Civil Def. adv. bd. St. Vincent's Charity Hosp., Garden Center, Cleve.: adv. com. Notre Dame Coll., Cleve.; chmn. Devel. Council Greater Cleve.; mem. Cuyahoga County Govtl. Consol. Com. Past pres. League Rep. Clubs of Cuyahoga county. Mem. Cuyahoga County Republican Exec. Com. Past mem. vis. com. Harvard Grad. Sch. Design; mem. vis. com. Western Res. U. Sch. Applied Soc. Scis.; trustee Goodrich Social Settlement House; dir. Golden Age Center, Roadside Council; bd. dirs., past pres. Ohio Planning Conf. Cleve. Forum for Community Devel., Citizens' Action Com. on Nursing Homes. Trustee, Vis. Nurses Assn. Recipient many awards for pub. service; Archbishop Edward F. Hoban medal for distinguished service, 1964: silver medal Am. Soc. Planning Ofcls., 1966. Mem. Nat. Assn. Housing and Redevel. Ofcls. (a founder, 1st pres.), Am. Soc. Planning Ofcls. (pres. 1951), Adult Edn. Assn., Consumers League, Nat. Conf. Social Welfare, Cleve. Bar Assn., Western Reserve U. Law Sch. Alumni Assn. (pres. 1952). Roman Catholic. K.C. (past pres. Cleve. dist.). Club: Mid-Day. Author: (with others) A Housing Program for the U.S., 1934. Wrote and obtained passage of Ohio Housing Authority Law (1st in nation), 1933. Home: The Chesterfield 1801 E 12th St Cleveland OH 44104 Office: Case Western Reserve Univ Crawford Hall Cleveland OH 44106 ☆

BOHN, HAROLD C., educator; b. N.Y.C., Dec. 25, 1903; s. Alfred and Emily (Sohn) B.; A.B., Hamilton Coll., Clinton, N.Y., 1922-26; M.A., Harvard, 1929; Ed.D., Columbia, 1954; m. Mary Ellen Warriner, July 24, 1937; children—Emily Ellen Warriner (Mrs. B. Andrew Mudryk), Norman Warriner. Tchr., Irving Sch., Tarrytown, N.Y., 1926-28; mem. faculty Montclair (N.J.) State Coll., 1929—, prof. emeritus, 1970—; tchr. Columbia Tchrs. Coll., 1946-51. Life mem. N.E.A.; mem. N.J. Edn. Assn., Nat. Council Tchrs. English, Modern Long Assn. Conglist. (dir. religious edn. 1953-60, deacon 1962-65, trustee 1968-70, pres. 1968-69). Dormitory named Harold C. Bohn Hall. Home: 82 Gates Av Montclair NJ 07042

BOHN, RALPH CARL, educator; b. Detroit, Feb. 19, 1930; s. Carl and Bertha (Abrams) B.; B.S., Wayne State U., 1951, Ed. M., 1954, Ed. D., 1957; m. Adella Stanul, Sept. 2, 1950; children—Cheryl Ann, Jeffrey Ralph. Part-time instr. Wayne State U., 1954-55, summer, 1956; faculty San Jose (Cal.) State Coll., 1955—, prof. indsl. arts, 1961—, chmn. dept. indsl. studies, 1960-69, asso. dean ednl. service, 1968-70, dean ednl. services, 1970—. Guest summer faculty Colo. State Coll., 1963, Ariz. State U., 1966, U.P.R., 1967, So. Ill. U., 1970, Ore. State U., 1971; cons. U.S. Office Edn., 1965-70, Cal. Pub. Schs., 1960, Nat. Assessment Ednl. Progress, 1968—, Ednl. div. Philco-Ford Corp., 1970—, Am. Inst. Research, 1969—, Far West Labs for Ednl. Research Devel., 1971—; dir. project Vocational Edn. Act, 1965-67, Nat. Def. Edn. Act, 1967, 68; co- dir. Project Edn. Profession Devel. Act, 1969, 70. Served to lt. (j.g.) USCGR, 1951- 53. Recipient Am. Legion award, 1945; scholar Wayne State U., 1953. Mem. Am. Indsl. Arts Assn. (pres. 1967-68, recipient Ship's citation, 1971), Am. Council Indsl. Art Tchrs. Edn. (pres. 1964-66, recipient Man of Year award 1967), Nat. Assn. Indsl. Tchr. Educators (past v.p.), Cal. Indsl. Edn. Assn. (recipient State Ship's citation 1971), Am. Drive Edn. Assn., Nat. Fluid Power Soc., Am. Vocational Assn. (recipient Service awards 1966, 67), N.E.A., Nat. Assn. for Summer Sessions, Lutheran Acad. Scholarship, Cal. Employees Assn. (pres. San Jose State Coll. chpt. 1966-67), Western Assn. Summer Session Adminstrs. (Newsletter editor 1970—). Author: (with G.H. Silvius) Organizing Course Materials for Industrial Education, 1961; (with others) Fundamentals of Safety Education, 1964; (with A. MacDonald) Power- Mechanics of Energy Control, 1970, The McKnight Power Experimenter (4 lab. manuals), 1970. Indsl. arts editor Am. Vocational Jour., 1963-66; editor Jour. Indsl. Tchr. Edn., 1962-64; (with Ralph Norman) Graduate Study in Industrial Arts, 1961. Home: 1874 Harris Av San Jose CA 95124

BOHN, SHERMAN ELWOOD, educator, mathematician; b. New England, N.D., Mar. 11, 1927; s. Paul T. and Josephine (Connadson) B.; B.A., Concordia Coll., 1949; M.A., U. Neb., 1951, Ph.D., 1961; student U. Minn., 1952-53; m. Dorothy V. Solberg, June 15, 1952; children—Jeffrey Andrew, Corinn Jo, Jon Paul. Aero. research scientist NACA, 1951-52; instr., then asst. prof. Concordia Coll., 1953-56; instr. U. Neb., 1957-59; asso. prof. Wartburg Coll., 1959-61; asst., then asso. prof. Bowling Green State U., 1961-64; mem. faculty Miami U., Oxord, O., 1964—, prof. math., 1966—, chmn. dept., 1965—. Author articles in field. Home: 416 Sandra Dr Oxford, OH 45956,

BOHNE, CARL JOHN, Jr., accountant; b. Cuero, Tex., Oct. 24, 1916: s. Carl John and Byrd (White) B.; B.B.A. with highest honors, U. Tex., 1947, M.B.A., 1948; m. Lelon Maurine Brautigam, June 25, 1948; children—Carl John III, Lelon Maurine. With Arthur Andersen & Co., C.P.A.'s, 1949—, dir. tng., Chgo., 1956—, also partner; instr., then asst. prof. accounting U. Tex., 1947-48; cons. U.S. Army Audit Agy., 1954-58. Asst. treas. Evanston (Ill.) Hosp. Assn., 1956—; chmn. profl. accounts solicitation Chgo. Heart Assn., 1957. Served to maj. AUS, 1941-45. Decorated Purple Heart, Bronze Star medal; recipient Elijah Watts Sells Gold medal for C.P.A. exam, 1948. C.P.A., Tex., Ill. Mem. Am. Inst. C.P.A.'s, Ill. (chmn. com. profl. devel. 1957), Tex. socs. C.P.A.'s. Beta Gamma Sigma. Episcopalian (vestryman 1958-60, warden 1969-70). Clubs: Union League (dir.), Lake Shore (Chgo.). Home: 1221 Chestnut Av Wilmette IL 60691 Office: 69 W Washington St Chicago IL 60602

BOHNEN, ELI AARON, rabbi; b. Toronto, Ont., Can., Sept. 16, 1909; s. Max Jacob and Nellie (Brill) B.B.A., U. Toronto, 1931; rabbi, Jewish Theol. Sem., 1935, D.H.L., 1955, D.D., 1967; L.H.D., U. R.I., 1967; D.D., Brown U., 1970; m. Eleanor Rosenthal, July 2, 1939; children—Judith (Mrs. Mayer Levitt), Michael Joseph. Asst. rabbi, Phila., 1935-39; rabbi Buffalo, 1939-48; rabbi Temple Emanuel, Providence, 1948—. Pres. Rabbinical Assembly Am., 1966-68. Bd. overseers, bd. govs. Jewish Theol. Sem. Served as chaplain AUS, 1943-46. Decorated Bronze Star. Mason, Rotarian. Home: 500 Elmgrove Av Providence RI 02906 Office: 99 Taft Av Providence RI 02906

BOHNENBLUST, HENRY FREDERIC, educator; b. Neuchatel, Switzerland, Mar. 22, 1906; s. Jules Otto and Bertha (Hostettler) B.; Ph.D., Princeton, 1931; m. Eleanor Young, July 26, 1937. Came to U.S., 1928 naturalized, 1938. Inst., Princeton, 1931-33, asst. prof., 1933-39, asso. prof. 1939-46; prof. Ind. U., 1945-46; prof. Cal. Inst. Tech., Pasadena, 1946—, dean grad. studies, 1956-71. Mem. Am. Math. Soc., Math. Assn. Am., A.A.A.S. Co-editor Annals of Mathematics, 1931-45. Home: 1798 Pepper Dr Altadena CA 91001

BOHNERT, HERBERT GAYLORD, educator, philosopher; b. Cleve., Mar. 24, 1918; s. Herbert F. and Margaret (Sharp) B.; A.B., U. Chgo., 1940; Ph.D., U. Pa., 1961. Instr., Queen's Coll., 1947-50; asst. mathematician RAND Corp., 1950-51; asst. prof. Swarthmore Coll., 1953-54; computing engr. N.Am. Aviation, 1955-57; sr. scientist Litton Industries, 1958; asso. Planning Research Corp., 1969; mem. research staff IBM Research Center, 1961-68; prof. philosophy Mich. State U., 1968—; Fulbright lectr. Am. philosophy U. Cuyo, Mendoza, Argentina, 1966. Mem. Am. Philos. Assn., Assn. Symbolic Logic, Assn. Computing Machinery, Philosophy Sci. Assn. Author articles in field. Home: 819 Huntington Rd East Lansing MI 48823

BOHNING, RICHARD HOWARD, coll. dean; b. Hope Valley, R.I., Sept. 16, 1919; s. Clarence Minot and Annie Delhia (Lewis) B.; B.S., R.I. State Coll., 1940; M.S., Ohio State U., 1941, Ph.D., 1948; m. Evelyn Maxon Bitgood, Oct. 7, 1938; 1 son, Richard Howard. Mem. faculty Ohio State U., 1946—, prof. botany, 1961- -, dean Coll. Biol. Scis., 1969—. Served with USNR, 1943-46. NSF Sci. Faculty fellow, 1957. Fellow Ohio Acad. Sci.; mem. Bot. Soc. Am., Am. Inst. Biol. Scis., A.A.A.S., Am. Soc. Plant Physiologists, Sigma Xi, Phi Kappa, Phi Epsilon Phi, Alpha Zeta, Gamma Sigma Delta, Gamma Alpha. Co-author: Introduction to Plant Physiology, 1960. Home: 1179 Regency Dr Columbus OH 43220 Office: 484 W 12th Av Columbus OH 43210

BOHR, AAGE NIELS, Danish physicist; b. June 19, 1922; Ph.D., U. Copenhagen (Denmark); postgrad. research work, London, Eng., 1943-45. Research asst. Inst. Theoretical Physics, (now Niels Bohr Inst.), U. Copenhagen, 1946—, prof. physics, 1956—; dir. Niels Bohr Inst. Recipient Dannie Heineman prize, 1960, Pope Pius XI medal, 1963, Atoms for Peace award, 1969. Mem. Danish, Norwegian acads. scis., Royal Physiograph. Soc. (Lund, Sweden), Am. Acad. Arts and Scis., Am. Philos. Soc. Author: Rotational States of Atomic Nuclei, 1954; (with Ben R. Mohlelson) Nuclear Sturcture, Vol. I. Research quantum physics; specialist nuclear physics. Home: Granhojen 10 Hellerup Copenhagen Denmark Office: Niels Bohr Inst Biegdamsvej 15-17 Copenhagen 0 Denmark

BOHRMAN, IRVING G., corp. exec.; b. Waukesha, Wis., 1904. Pres. Perfex Corp., PerfexIowa Inc.; pres., dir. Perfex Radiator Co.; dir. Onmi Lab. Inc., Hillsboro Mile Ocean Apts. Bd. dirs. Wis. Mfrs. Assn. Bd. dirs. St. Luke's Hosp. Assn., Blue Shield, Blue Cross, Jr. Achievement Southeaster Wis.; mem. Carroll Coll. Council Met. Milw.; mem. adv. com. Wis. Found. Ind. Colls. Home: 3062 E Newport Ct Milwaukee WI 53217 Office: 500 W Oklahoma Av Milwaukee WI 53207

BOHROD, AARON, artist; b. Chgo., Nov. 21, 1907; s. George and Fannie (Feingold) B.; student Crane Coll., Chgo., 1925-26, Art Inst. Chgo., 1927-29, Art Students League, N.Y.C., 1930-32; D.F.A., Ripon Coll., 1960; m. Ruth Bush, Dec. 27, 1929; children—Mark, Georgi (Mrs. Stephen Rothe), Neil. Paintings reproduced in Time, Life, Fortune, Holiday, Coronet and Esquire mags.; Illustrator The Illinois by James Gray, The Golden Watch by Albert Halper, A

Pottery Sketch Book (book drawings) by U. Wis., 1959. Artist in residence So. Ill. U., 1942-43; U. Wis., Madison, 1948—. With War Art Unit, South Pacific War Area, on Govt. assignment, served as artist war corr. Life mag., Normandy, Cherbourg, Eng., Luxembourg, Germany, 1943-45. Painted series pictures of Kansas City for Mo. Documentary Art Project, 1946, series on Pitts. for Pa. Documentary Art Project, 1947; on Mich. for Mich. Documentary Art Project, 1947; series of symbolic still life paintings for Look mag., Great Religious of America, 1957-60. Rep. in Met. Mus. Art, Whitney Mus. Am. Art, N.Y.C., Art Inst. Chgo., Bklyn. Mus., Boston Mus. Art, Pa. Acad. Art, Corcoran Mus., Washington, Swope Gallery Art, Terre Haute, Butler Art Inst., Youngstown, U. Ariz., Walker Art Center, Mpls., Norton Art Inst., Telfair Art Acad. (Fla.), Davenport (Ia.) Art Inst., Library of Congress, Witte Meml. Mus., San Antonio, Springfield (Mass.) Mus. Fine Arts, New Britain (Conn.) Art Mus., Detroit Inst. Arts, Wichita State U., Mich. State U., Hartford Gallery Modern Art, Finch Coll., N.Y., Milw. Art Center, Oshkosh Pub. Mus., Madison Art Center, U. Ill., Miami U., Bergstrom Art Center, Neenah, Wis., Clinton (Ill.)Art Center, U. Mo., Ohio U.; represented ceramics (with F. Carlton Ball) in permanent collections Cleve. Mus. Art, Detroit Art Inst., U. Ill., Syracuse U., U. Wis., Beloit Coll. Nat. academician. Awarded Carr landscape prize, 1935, Tuthill watercolor prize, 1935; Logan prizes and Art Inst. medals, 1937-45; awarded Brower prize Art Inst. Chgo., 1947; hon. mention San Francisco Golden Gate Expn., 1939, Carnegie Internat. Exhbn., 1939; first award of merit Cal. Water Color Soc., 1940; first prize Phila. Water Color Soc. (Pa. Acad. Fine Arts), 1942; 5th Purchase prize Artists for Victory Expn., Met. Mus. Art, 1942; Corcoran 2d prize, W.A. Clark prize and silver medal, 1943, A.N.A., 1951, N.A., 1953; 1st prize Profl. Art Exhbn., Ill. State Fair, 1955; hon. mention Miami Nat. Ceramic Exhbn., 1956; Saltus Gold medal N.A.D., 1961; Hassam Purchase award, 1962; Kirk Meml. award, 1965; Fine Arts award Gov. Wis., 1969. Guggenheim fellow in creative art, 1936-37, 37- 38. Author: A Decade of Still Life, 1966. Home: 4811 Tonyawatha Trail Madison WI 53716 Office: 438 Farm Pl Madison WI 53706

BOIES, LAWRENCE RANDALL, otolaryngologist; b. Renville, Minn., Nov. 7, 1898; s. Walter Randall and Gertrude (Olufsen) B.; A.B., U. Wis., 1922, A.M., 1923; M.D., Columbia, 1926; postgrad. Harvard, 1929; m. Louise Marty, Sept. 11, 1928; children—Lawrence Randall, David Blandford, William (dec.). Resident physician in otolaryngology Mass. Eye and Ear Infirmary, 1929- 31; practice medicine specializing in otolarynology, Mpls., 1931—; instr. otolaryn. U. Minn. Med. Sch., 1931-36, clin. asst. prof., 1936-39, clin. asso. prof., 1939-41, dir. div. otolaryngology, 1941-67, clin. prof., 1942-55, prof., head dept., 1955-67, emeritus, 1967—; dir. med. affairs Deafness Research Found., 1967-70. Served with U.S. Army, 1917-18. Dir., Am. Bd. Otolaryngology, pres., 1963-68. Mem. Am. Acad. Ophthalmology and Otolaryngology (bd. secs. 1947-56, pres. 1962), Minn., Mpls. acads. medicine, Minn. Acad. Ophthalmology and Otolaryngology, A.M.A. (chmn. sect. laryngology, otology, rhinology 1961), Am. Laryngol., Rhinol. and Otol. Soc. (pres. 1957-58), Am. Otol. Soc. (pres. 1962), Am. Laryngol. Assn. (pres. 1967), Am. Broncho-Esophological Soc., Hennepin County Med. Soc. (pres. 1946-47), Alpha Kappa Lambda, Alpha Kappa Kappa. Author sect. diseases the ear in Specialties in Medical Practice, 1943; Fundamentals of Otolaryngology, 1949. Contbr. numerous articles to profl. jours. Home: 410 Cottage Downs Hopkins MN 55343 Office: Box 396 University Hospital MN 55414

BOISEN, HAROLD LOUIS, former librarian; b. Omaha, June 22, 1901; s. Louis Nanstedt and Margaret (Olsen) B.; Denver, 1938; A.M., U. Chgo. Library Sch., 1939; m. Lilian Carpenter Gates, Sept. 12, 1933. Librarian, Duncan Y.M.C.A., Chgo., 1939; asst. librarian Northwestern U., Chgo. br., 1940; librarian Washington Coll., Chestertown, Md., 1940-41, 42-46; head librarian Butler U., Indpls., 1946-68, librarian emeritus, 1968—, prof., head dept. library sci., 1946-48. Mem. Am. Assn. U. Profs., A.L.A., Assn. Coll. and Reference Librarians, Ind. Acad. Sci., Ind. Hist. Soc., Ind. Library Assn., Art Assn. Indpls. Mason. Contbr. to library periodicals. Home: 5744 Brockton Dr Indianapolis IN 46220

BOISFONTAINE, CURTIS RICH, lawyer; b. New Orleans, June 30, 1929; s. Albert Sidney and Margaret (Toomer) B.; B.A., Tulane U., 1951; LL.B., 1952; m. Joan Mercer Capdevielle, June 9, 1951; children—Suzanne Baker, Curtis Rich, Eugenie Wright. Admitted to La. state bar, 1952; practice in New Orleans, 1952- 53; asso. Porteous & Johnson, New Orleans, 1955-61; partner Sessions, Fishman, Rosenson, Snellings & Boisfontaine, New Orleans, 1961—. Served with Judge Adv. Gen.'s Corps, USAF, 1953-55. Mem. Am., La. (sec.-treas. 1969-71), New Orleans bar assns., Am. Judicature Soc., Internat. Assn. Ins. Counsel, Fed. Ins. Counsel, La. bd. dirs. 1966-68, sec.- treas. 1968-69, v.p. 1969-70, 1st v.p. 1970-71, pres.-elect 1971-72), New Orleans assns. defense counsel. Home: 4917 St Charles Av New Orleans LA 70115 Office: Bank New Orleans Bldg New Orleans LA 70112

BOISSONNEAULT, GLEN ALVIN, journalist; b. Saginaw, Mich., Dec. 4, 1917; s. Edward Joseph and Florence (Stoddard) B.; student U. Mich., 1937-39; m. Dorothy Jean Lang, Aug. 21, 1954; 1 dau., Kathleen. Clk., Consumer Power Co., Saginaw, 1935- 37; from reporter to editor Saginaw News, 1946-66; editor Flint (Mich.) Jour., 1966—; discussion leader Am. Press Inst., Columbia. Juror, Pulitzer awards, 1969, 70. Active local Red Feather, Boy Scouts Am., YMCA. Served from pvt. to capt. AUS and USAAF, 1942 and 46. Decorated Purple Heart, Air medal two oak leaf clusters. Mem. Am. Soc. Newspaper Editors, Inter-Am. Press Assn., Mich. Press Assn., Sigma Delta Chi. Clubs: Univ. Press of Mich. (pres.) (Ann Arbor, Mich.), Detroit Press; Flint Golf, University (Flint), Saginaw. Home: 2020 Stoneybrook Ct Flint MI 48502 Office: 200 E First St Flint MI 48502

BOITEUX, MARCEL PAUL, economist; b. Niort, Deux Séures, France, May 9, 1922; s. René and Suzanne (Vèzes) B.; student Ecole Normale Supérieure, 1943-46, Agrégation de Mathematiques, 1946; Diplme de l'Institut d'Etudes Politiques, sect. economic, 1947; m. Juliette Barraud, July 5,1946; children—Jean- Paul, Catherine, Martine. With Centre National de la Recherche Scientifique, 1947-49; with Electricité de France 1949—, pres., 1967—; chmn. Comité consultatif Recherche Scientifique et Technique, 1965-66. Mem. Econometric Soc. (pres. 1959), Assn. Francaise d' Informatique et de Recherche Operationelle, Internat. Fedn. Operational Research Socs. (sec. 1965-66), Inst. Mgmt. Scis. (chmn. European sect. 1962), Académie des Sciences Commerciales, Assn. French Econ. Sci. Home: 26 av George V Paris 8 France Office: Electricité de France 2 rue Louis Murate Paris 8 France

BOJANOWSKI, JERZY, former symphony condr.; b. Poland, June 18, 1895; s. Kamil Adam Wincenty and Wladyslawa Teresa (Bujalska) B.; student Mus. Coll., Warsaw, 1907-12, Mus. Acad., Vienna, 1913-14, Vienna U., 1913-14, Kharkoff U. (law), 1915-16; m. Frances Krenz Welzant, 1937. Condr., Warsaw Grand Opera, 1918-19, Opera of Pozman, 1919-25; mus. dir. Torun Opera, 1925- 27, Lwow Opera, 1927-28; condr. Warsaw Grand Opera and Warsaw Philharmonic, also tour of European cities, 1928-32; condr. Chgo. Symphony Orch., World's Fair, Chgo., Tulsa, Milw., Mpls., 1936-37, other cities in Middle West, 1932-38; condr. Polish Ballet on European tour N.Y. World's Fair, 1939, Chgo. Opera, 1941-42, Woman's Symphony Orch. Chgo., 1944-45, Milw. "Stars" Symphony Orch., 1941-51; mus. dir. Polonaise Found., Chgo. Recipient Honor awards Am. Council Polish Cultural Clubs, 1966; Milw. Soc. PNA, 1968; condr. WTMJ-TV Peabody award concert, 1966; award Merit, minister of culture and art Poland, 1971. Fellow Internat. Inst. Arts and Letters. Address: Hotel Astor Milwaukee WI 53202

BOK, BART JAN, educator; b. Hoorn, Holland, Apr. 28, 1906; s. Jan and Gesina Annetta (Van Der Lee) B; student U. Leiden (Holland), 1924-27, U. Groningen, 1927-29; Ph.D., 1932; m. Priscilla Fairfield, Sept. 9, 1929; children—John Fairfield, Joyce Annetta. Came to U.S., 1929, naturalized, 1938. Asst. in astronomy U. Groningen, 1927-29; R.W. Willson fellow in astronomy Harvard, 1929-33, asst. prof., 1933-39, asso. prof., 1939-46, Robert Wheeler Wilson prof. astronomy, 1947- 57; prof., head dept. astronomy Australian Nat. U., 1957-66, dir. Mt. Stromlo Obs., nr. Canberra, 1957-66; prof. astronomy U. Ariz., Tucson, 1966—, head dept. and dir. Steward Obs., 1966-70. Past pres. commn. 33, Internat. Astron. Union. Decorated Orange-Nassau medal (Netherlands); recipient Adion medal French Astronomers, 1971. Fellow Australian Inst. Physics, Australian Coll. Edn., Royal Astron. Soc. (London, asso.); mem. Internat. Astron. Union (v.p. 1970—), Am. Astron. Soc. (pres. elect 1971-72), A.A.A.S., Nat. Acad. Scis., Am. Acad. Arts and Scis., Royal Soc. Scis., Uppsala, Sigma Xi; hon. mem. Royal Astron. Soc. Can., Royal Astron. Soc. New Zealand, Astron. Soc. Australia; corr. mem. Royal Netherlands Acad. Arts and Scis. Author: The Distribution of Stars in Space, 1937; (with Priscilla F. Bok) The Milky Way, 1941, 3d edit., rev., 1957; (with F.W. Wright) Basic Marine Navigation, 1944; The Astronomer's Universe, 1958. Home: 200 Sierra Vista Dr Tucson AZ 85719

BOK, DEREK CURTIS, univ. pres.; b. Ardmore, Pa., Mar. 22, 1930; s. Curtis and Margaret (Plummer) B.; B.A., Stanford, 1951; LL.B., Harvard, 1954; M.A., George Washington U., 1958; m. Sissela Ann Myrdal, May 7, 1955; children—Hilary Margaret, Victoria, Thomas Jeremy. Fulbright scholar, Paris, France, 1954-55; faculty Harvard Law Sch., Cambridge, Mass., 1958-71, prof. 1961-71, dean Law Sch., 1968-71; pres. Harvard U., Cambridge, 1971—. Served to 1st lt. AUS, 1956-58. Mem. Am. Bar Found., Am. Law Inst., Phi Beta Kappa, Phi Kappa Sigma. Author: (with Archibald Cox) Labor Law, 1962; (with John T. Dunlop) Labor and the American Community, 1970. Home: 33 Elmwood Av Cambridge MA 02138 Office: University Hall Cambridge MA 02138

BOKASSA, JEAN BEDEL, pres., prime minister Central African Republic; b. Feb. 22, 1921; ed. Ecole Sainte Jeanne-d'Arc, M'Baiki, Ecole Missionnaire, Bangui, Ecole Missionnaire, Brazzaville. Joined French Army, 1939, advanced through grades to capt., 1961; organized Army of Central African Republic; comdr.-in-chief Central African Republic Army, 1963—; pres., prime minister, 1966—, minister Def., 1966—, minister Justice, 1966-70, minister Information, 1970—, minister Agr. and Stockbreeding, 1970—. Pres. M.E.S.A.N., 1970. Decorated Legion d'Honneur, Croix de Guerre. Address: Office of President Bangui Central African Republic*

BOKAT, GEORGE, govt. ofcl.; b. N.Y.C., Nov. 15, 1904: s. Max and Ida (Levy) B.; student Coll. City N.Y.; LL.B., N.Y.U., 1927; m. Golda Shurack, Nov. 24, 1929; children—Robert Bruce, Stephen Arthur. Admitted to N.Y. bar, 1928; pvt. practice, N.Y.C., 1928-37; mem. firm Bokat & Bokat, N.Y.C., 1935-37; with NLRB, 1937—, chief trial examiner, 1961—. Mem. Am. Bar Assn., Fed. Bar Assn., Fed. Trial Examiners Conf. Home: 7607 Holiday Terrace Bethesda MD 20034 Office: 1717 Pennsylvania Av NW Washington DC 20570

BOKUM, RICHARD D., II, mining co. exec.; b. Chgo., 1918; ed. Princeton, 1940. Pres., chmn. bd. Bokum Corp. Address: 1135 Kane Concourse PO Box 6277 Surfside Station FL 33154

BOLAN, JAMES THOMAS, utility co. exec.; b. Toledo, July 26, 1909; s. Michael H. and Lena (Mattimore) B.; A.B., St. John's Coll., 1931; m. Kathryn Gruhler, Nov. 28, 1936; children—Seanne, James Thomas, Mary Ann, Virginia, Micaela. With Natco Corp., 1964-66, chmn. bd., 1965-66, also dir.; pres., treas., dir. Great Lakes Industries, Inc., 1960-66; v.p. Kewanee Oil Co., Bryn Mawr, Pa., 1963-66, exec. v.p., 1966—, dir., 1963—; dir. N.M.S. Industries, Inc. Home: 104 Oxley Ct Greene Countrie Village Newtown Square PA 19073 Office: Kewanee Oil Co P O Box 591 Bryn Mawr PA 19010

BOLAND, EDWARD P., congressman; b. Springfield, Mass., Oct. 1, 1911; student Boston Coll. Law Sch. Mem. Mass. Legislature, 1935-40; register of deeds, Hampden County, Mass., 1941-52; mem. 83d-92d congresses from 2d Mass. Dist. Served to capt. AUS, World War II; PTO. Democrat. Home: Springfield MA 01101 Office: House Office Bldg Washington DC 20515

BOLAND, EDWARD WARD, physician; b. Redlands, Cal., Dec. 18, 1907; student Santa Clara U., 1926-28; B.S., St. Louis U., 1931, M.D., 1933; M.S. in Medicine, U. Minn., 1938; m. Jane Pauline Rooney; children—Paul, Peter, Philip, Patrick, Ann. Intern, San Bernardino County (Cal.) Gen. Hosp., 1933-34; resident medicine St. Vincent's Hosp., Los Angeles, 1934-35, chmn. dept. medicine, 1956-61, dir. medicine, 1958-61, pres. staff, 1962-63; mem. attending staff Hosp. of Good Samaritan, Los Angeles County Hosp., 1960—; clin. prof. medicine U. So. Cal. Mem. adv. bd. Am. Hosp. of Paris, Alumni Assn. Mayo Found. Med. Edn. and Research, v.p., 1966-67, pres., 1968-69. Mem. president's council Loyola U., Los Angeles; bd. regents U. Santa Clara, bd. founders, 1968—. Fellow in medicine Mayo Clinic, 1935-38. Served to maj. M.C., AUS, 1942-46. Recipient Outstanding Achievement award U. Minn., 1964. Diplomate Am. Bd. Internal Medicine. Fellow A.C.P. (gov. for So. Cal. 1970—); mem. A.M.A. (cons. drugs council), Cal., Am., Internat. socs. internal medicine, Pan-Am. League Against Rheumatism, Ligue Internationale Contre le Rhumatisme, Arthritis and Rheumatism Found. (v.p. 1947-64, chmn. med. and sci. com. 1959-60, gov. 1952—), Brazilian Rheumatism Soc. (hon.), Argentine Rheumatism Assn. (hon.), Am. Heart Assn., Am. Therapeutic Soc., Am. Rheumatism Assn. (pres. 1954-55), Los Angeles Soc. Internal Medicine (pres. 1952), Los Angeles Acad. Medicine (v.p. 1966-67, pres. 1967-68), Mexican Rheumatism Soc. (hon.), Internat. Coll. Physicians, N.Y. Acad. Scis., Cal. Med. Assn., Los Angeles Heart Assn., So. Cal. Rheumatism Assn., Sigma Xi, Alpha Omega Alpha, Alpha Sigma Nu. Club: Jonathan (Los Angeles). Author numerous publs. in field, also chpts. med. textbooks. Asso. editor Annals of the Rheumatic Diseases, London; Arthritis and Allied Conditions. Co-editor: Rheumatism Reviews. Editorial bd. California Medicine. Office: 321 N Larchmont Blvd Los Angeles CA 90004

BOLAND, FRANCIS HALSEY, mfg. exec.; b. N.Y.C., Aug. 3, 1905; s. Francis H. and Agnes Thompson (Murray) B.; A.B., U. Cal., 1926; postgrad. Grad. Sch. Bus. Adminstrn., Harvard, 1931; m. Edna Isabell Beck, 1950. With Trainer & Assos., N.Y.C., 1931-34, Irving Trust Co., 1934-36, Fahnestock & Co., 1936-40; v.p. Am. Internat. Corp., 1945-58; v.p. Adams Express Co., N.Y.C., 1946-58, bd. mgrs., 1947-58; dir., exec. com. Joy Mfg. Co.; exec. v.p., dir. George Fry & Assos., mgmt. cons., 1958-61; dir. v.p. ACF Industries, Inc., gen. mgr. Am. Car and Foundry div., 1961-64, v.p. mfg. and engring., 1964-69; dir. AMP, Inc., Madison Fund, Inc., Warner-Lambert Pharmacal Co. Pres., trustee Internat. Found.; trustee Gen. Douglas MacArthur Meml. Found., Norfolk, Va., Am. U. Served from 2d lt. to capt., U.S. Inf. Res., 1926-36, to col. AUS, 1941-46, maj. gen. Res., 1961. Decorated D.S.M., Legion of Merit. Mem. Phi Beta Kappa, Pi Kappa Phi. Clubs: Olympic (San Francisco); N.Y. Athletic, Union League (N.Y.C.). Editorial bd. Harvard Bus. Rev., 1929-31 Home: 68 Old Nyack Turnpike Monsey NY 10952 Office: 180 Central Park S New York City NY 10019

BOLAND, FRANCOIS, composer, pianist; b. Namur, Belgium, Nov. 6, 1929. Played with Bob Shots at Paris Jazz Festival, 1949; in Germany with Al Goyens, 1950; arrangements for jazz sessions, 1951-54; pianist-arranger Aime Berelli Band, 1954-55; tour Germany, France and Italy with Chet Baker, 1955-56, U.S., 195758; recording artist for Blue Note, Atlantic, Columbia records. Address: Neue Kantstrasse Berlin 19 Federal Republic of Germany

BOLAND, GEORGE BERNARD, lawyer, ins. co. exec.; b. Omaha, Aug. 15, 1897; s. Peter G.H. and Alice V. (Cocur) B.; A.B., Creighton U., 1920, LL.B., 1923; m. Helen Forster, July 7, 1920. Admitted to Neb. bar, 1923, since practiced in Omaha with firm Boland, Mullin, Walsh & Cooney; dir. Nat. Am. Fire Ins. Co., 1958-60, United Benefit Fire Ins. Co., 1958-61, United Benefit Life Ins. Co., 1963—. Chmn. adv. bd. Vols. Am.; vice chmn., asso. bd. trustees St. John Vianney Sem.; bd. regents Creighton U. Served to 2d lt., F.A., U.S. Army, 1918. Fellow Am. Coll. Trial Lawyers; mem. Neb. (v.p. 1947), Omaha (pres. 1943-44) bar assns., 40 and 8 (nat. comdr. 1952, nat. atty. 1951, 54-64), Alpha Sigma Nu. Home: Elkhorn NB 68022 Office: Farm Credit Bldg Omaha NB 57102

BOLAND, JOHN FRANCIS, Jr., lawyer; b. Yonkers, N.Y., July 23, 1915; s. John Frances and Celeste (Kinalley) B.; B.A., Fordham U., 1935, J.D., 1946; m. Jean Clayton Smith, Sept. 15, 1942; children-John Francis III, Richard P., Christopher J., Katherine B., Patricia, Anne, Pegeen. Admitted to N.Y. bar, 1946, Ariz. bar, 1949; practiced in White Plains, N.Y., 1946-48, Tucson, 1949-50, Phoenix, 1951—; asso. McCarthy & Gaynor, 1946-48; partner Boland & D'Antonio, 1949-50; partner Evans, Kitchel & Jenckes, 1951—, mng. partner, 1966—; Mem. Ariz. Selective Service Bd. of Appeals, 1964—. Served to capt., Signal Corps, AUS, 1941-46. Mem. Am., Ariz., Maricopa County bar assns., Am. Inst. Mining, Metall. and Petroleum Engrs., Am. Mining Congress (cons. labor-mgmt. subcommittees). Clubs: Phoenix Country, University (Phoenix). Home: 902 W Augusta Av Phoenix AZ 85021 Office: 363 N 1st Av Phoenix AZ 85003

BOLAND, LAWRENCE, metals co. exec.; b. Robesonia, Pa., Jan. 3, 1917; s. Thomas N. and Gertrude (Flanagan) B.; student Wharton Sch., U. Pa., 1937-38, Cath. U. Am., 1938-41; m. Anna Louise Lebengood, Apr. 11, 1948; children—Lawrence F., Joseph P., Michael C., Stephen E., Elizabeth Anne. Prodn. mgr. Beryllium Corp., Reading, Pa., 1947-52, gen. sales mgr., 1952-56, v.p., 1956-60, exec. v.p., 1960, also dir.; dir. Nonotuck Mfg. Co., Holyoke, Mass., Chem. Pollution Scis., Inc., Consol. Beryllium, Ltd., LLondon, Eng. Trustee St. Joseph's Hosp., Reading, Pa. Mem. Am. Soc. Metals, Am. Ordnance Assn., Copper Devel. Assn., Am. Inst. Aeros. and Astronautics, Reading C. of C. K.C. Clubs: Wyomissing, Berkshire Country, Young Republican (Reading). Home: Golf Rd Greenfields Reading PA 19601 Office: PO Box 1462 Reading PA 19603

BOLAND, THOMAS ALOYSLUS, archbishop; b. Orange, N.J., Feb. 17, 1896; s. John Peter and Ellen (O'Rourke) B.; A.B., A.M., Seton Hall Coll., 1919, LL.D., 1940; D.D., North Am. Coll., 1923. Tchr. moral theology and canon law Immaculate Conception Sem., Darlington, N.J., 1923-38; chancellor Archdiocese of Newark, 1938-40; titular bishop of Hirina, aux. to archbishop of Newark and rector Immaculate Conception Sem., 1940-47; bishop Paterson (N.J.), 1947-53; archbishop Newark, 1953- -. Address: 74 Mountain Av Llewellyn Park West Orange NJ 07052

BOLANDER, HENRY HUSTON, farm coop. exec.; b. nr. Indpls., Ind., Sept. 2, 1912; s. Henry O. and Clara (Albea) B.; ed. pub. schs., Central Bus. Coll., LaSalle Extension U.; m. Hester L. Campbell, July 25, 1936; 1 dau., Barbara J. (Mrs. David H. Kingsbury). With Ind. Farm Bur. Coop. Assn., Inc., Indpls., 1934-42, 45—, internal auditor, 1945-49, controller, 1949—, asst. sec., 1951—, asst. treas., 1952—; supr. tabulating, timekeeping and payroll Farmsworth Television & Radio Corp., 1942-45. Mem. Nat. Soc. Accountants for Coops. (past nat. dir., past chpt. pres.), Nat. Assn. Accountants (past chpt. dir.). Mason. Home: 1650 N Spencer Av Indianapolis IN 46218 Office: 47 S Pennsylvania St Indianapolis IN 46204

BOLCOM, WILLIAM ELDEN, composer; b. Seattle, May 26, 1938; s. Robert Samuel and Virginia (Lauermann) B.; B.A., U. Wash., 1958; M.A., Mills Coll., 1961; postgrad. Paris Conservatoire de Musique, 1959-61, 64-65; D. Mus. Art, Stanford 1964; student piano with Berthe Poncy Jacobson; student composition with George F. McKay, John Verrall, Darius Milhaud, others. Acting asst. prof. music dept. U. Wash., Seattle, 1965-66; lectr., asst. prof. music Queens Coll., Flushing, N.Y., 1966-68; vis. critic music theater Drama Sch., Yale, 1968-69; composer in residence Theater Arts Program, N.Y.U., N.Y.C., 1969—. Recipient Kurt Weill award for composition 1962, William and Noma Copley award, 1960, Marc Blitzstein award for excellence in mus. theatre Am. Acad. Arts and Letters, 1965. Guggenheim Found. fellow, 1964, 68; Rockefeller Found. grant, 1969-70. Composer: symphonies, 1957, 64; string quartets, 1950-65; Décalage for violin cello and piano, 1961-62; Fantasy-Sonata for piano, 1960-62; Concertante for Flute, Oboe, Violin, and Orch., 1960; (opera) Dynamite Tonite, 1960-61, rev., 1966; Octet, 1962; Session for Chamber Ensemble, 1965; 12 Etudes for Piano, 1959-66; Fives, Double Concerto for Violin, Piano and Strings, 1966; Morning and Evening Poems, Cantata, 1966; Session II, violin and viola, 1966; Session III, clarinet, violin, cello, piano, percussion, 1967; Session IV, chamber ensemble, 1967; Black Host for organ, percussion and taped sounds, 1967; Piano Rags, 1967-70; (opera) Greatshot, 1967-69; Circuit, Supermart, electronic-music ballets, 1969-70; Praeludium for vibro-phone and organ, 1969; Dark Music for tympani and cello, 1969; Duets for Quintet, 1970; Unpopular Songs, 1970; Whisper Moon, chamber ensemble, 1971. Home: 118 Christopher St New York City NY 10014

BOLD, HAROLD CHARLES, educator; b. N.Y.C., June 16, 1909; s. Edward and Louise (Krüsi) B.; B.A., Columbia, 1929, Ph.D., 1933; M.S., U. Vt., 1931; m. Mary Eloise Douthit, June 8, 1943. Instr. botany U. Vt., 1929-31; faculty Vanderbilt U., 1932-39, 46-57, prof. biology, 1949-57; prof. botany U. Tex., Austin, 1957—, chmn. div. biol. scis., 1969—. Served with USNR, 1942-45. Mem. Bot. Soc. Am. (sec. 1955-58, v.p. 1965, pres. 1966, editor-in-chief jour. 1958-65), Phi Beta Kappa, Sigma Xi, Omicron Delta Kappa, Phi Kappa Phi, Delta Chi. Roman Catholic. Author: Morphology of Plants, 1957, 67; The Plant Kingdom, 1964, 70; (with C.J. Alexopoulos) Algae and Fungi, 1967. Address: 3221 Duval St Austin TX 78712 ‡

BOLDREY, EDWIN BARKLEY, neurol. surgeon, educator; b. Morgantown, Ind., July 17, 1906; s. Edwin H. and Florence B. (Barkley) B.; A.B., De Pauw U., 1927; M.A., Ind. U., 1930, M.D., 1932; M.Sc., McGill U., 1936; m. Helen B. Eastland, June 16, 1932;

children—Nancy J., Edwin E., Susan E. Intern Montreal Gen. Hosp., 1932-34, admitting officer, spl. grad. student pathology, 1934-35; research fellow Montreal Neurol. Inst., 1935-36, 40, house officer neurology and neurol. surgery, 1936-37, fellow neuropathology, 1938, resident neurology and neurol. surgery, 1939; mem. faculty U. Cal. Sch. Medicine, 1940—, instr. surgery, 1940-44, asst. clin. prof. surgery, 1944-47, asst. clin. prof. neurol. surgery, 1947-48, asso. prof. neurol. surgery, 1948-60, prof., 1960—, chmn. dept., 1951-56, neurol. surgeon- in-chief of hosps, 1956—; attending neurol. surgeon Langley Porter Clinic, 1945—; cons. neurol. surgeon San Francisco Shriner's Hosp. for Crippled Children, 1948—, US Naval Hosp., Camp Pendleton, Cal., VA, Washington, San Francisco Hosp., 1951—, Parks AFB Hosp., 1955-58, May T. Morrison Rehab. Center, 1956-62, Ft. Miley VA Hosp., 1957—, Travis AFB Hosp., 1958—, Barrow Neurol. Inst., Phoenix, Letterman Gen. Hosp., USN Hosp., San Diego; lectr. neurol. surgery Oakland Naval Hosp., 1966—; cons. Nat. Inst. Neurol. Disease and Blindness, 1960-64, 66—. Mem. nat. clin. adv. United Cerebral Palsy, 1953-63, bd. dirs., San Francisco, 1958—, mem. med. adv. bd., 1961—; adv. council neurol. surgery A.C.S., 1956-61; cons. USPHS, 1966—, mem. med. adv. bd. Epilepsy Found., 1966—. Diplomate Am. Bd. Neurol. Surgery (dir. 1958-64). Fellow A.C.S.; mem. A.M.A., Assn. for Research and Nervous and Mental Disease, Pan Pacific Surg. Assn., Am. Neurol. Assn., Am. Acad. Neurol. Surgery (pres. 1958-59), Soc. Neurol. Surgeons (pres. 1965- 66), Am. Assn. Neurol. Pathology, A.A.A.S., Harvey Cushing Soc. (v.p. 1964-65), N.Y., Cal. Acads. sci., Cal Acad. Medicine, Canadian, San Francisco (a founder, pres. 1948-49) neurol. socs., Canadian, Western (a founder, pres. 1964-65) neurosurg. socs., Phi Delta Theta, Phi Chi, Alpha Omega Alpha. Clubs: Commonwealth, University (San Francisco). Author articles, contrbr. med. books, encys. Home: 924 Hayne Rd Hillsborough CA 94010 Office: U Cal Med School San Francisco CA 94122

BOLDT, GEORGE HUGO, judge; b. Chgo., Dec. 28, 1903; s. George F. and Christine (Carstensen) B.; A.B., U. Mont., 1925, LL.B., 1926; LL.D., Coll. Puget Sound, 1954; grad. Command and Gen. Staff School, Ft. Leavenworth, 1943; LL.D., U. Mont., 1961; m. Eloise Baird, Nov. 17, 1928; children—Joan (Mrs. Hugh C. Sobottka), Virginia (Mrs. T. R. Riedinger), George B. Admitted to Mont. bar, 1926, Wash. bar, 1928; asso. W.D. Rankin, Helena, Mont., 1926-27; partner firm Ballinger, Hutson & Boldt, Seattle, 1928-45, Metzger, Blair, Gardner & Boldt, Tacoma, 1945-53; U.S. dist. judge, West dist. Wash., 1953-71, chief judge, 1971—; asst. atty. gen. State of Wash., 1940, 50. U.S. del. 1st UN Congress on prevention of crime and treatment of offenders, Geneva, 1955; mem. com. on jud. facilities Am. Bar Assn.- A.I.A.; mem. com. on operations and appraisals Fed. Jud. Center; Jud. Conf. rep. Sec. State Adv. Com. Internat. Law. Trustee, U. Mont. Found. Served as lt. col. AUS, World War II. Mem. Am., Fed., Washington State, Pierce County bar assns., Am. Judicature Soc., Inst. Jud. Adminstrn., Am. Law Inst., Internat. Inst. Juridical Studies (gen. sci. com.), U.S. Jud. Studies (gen. sci. com.), U.S. Jud. Conf. (various coms.), Am. Legion, Phi Delta Phi, Sigma Chi. Republican. Presbyn. Mason (32, Shriner). Co-author, editor: Manual for Complex and Multi-district Litigation. Home: 9144 Edgewater Dr SW Tacoma WA 98499 Office: Federal Bldg Tacoma WA 98402

BOLEN, AMOS ALONZO, lawyer; b. Knott County, Ky., Oct. 1, 1909; s. J. Monroe and Charlotte (Hicks) B.; A.B., Washington and Lee U., 1934, LL.B., 1937; m. Helen Johnston, Oct. 30, 1938; children—Robert Amos, Richard Johnston. Admitted to Va. and W.Va. bars, 1937, since practiced in Huntington, W.Va.; partner firm Huddleston, Bolen, Beatty, Porter and Copen, and predecessors, 1952—. Vice pres. W.Va. Bd. Regents, 1970-71. Served to lt. USNR, 1943-46. Fellow Am. Coll. Trial Lawyers; mem. Am., W.Va. (pres. 1965-66) bar assns., Am. Law Inst., Am. Judicature Soc., Internat. Assn. Ins. Counsel, W.Va. C. of C. (dir.), Order of Coif, Phi Beta Kappa, Phi Delta Phi, Omicron Delta Kappa, Alpha Tau Omega. Democrat. Episcopalian. Home: 2122 Holswade Dr Huntington WV 25701 Office: First Huntington Nat Bank Bldg Huntington WV 25722

BOLEN, CHARLES WARREN, univ. dean; b. W. Frankfort, Ill., Sept. 27, 1923; s. William and Iva (Phillips) B.; B. Mus. Edn., Northwestern U., 1948; M.Mus., Eastman Sch. Music, 1950; Ph.D., Ind. U., 1954; m. Maxine Sheffler, Aug. 1, 1948; children—Ann, Jane. Instr. music Eastern Ill. U., 1950-51; chmn. music dept. Ripon (Wis.) Coll., 1954-62; instr. flute Nat. Music Camp, summers 1954-62; dean Sch. Fine Arts, U. Mont., Missoula, 1962-70; dean Coll. Fine Arts, Ill. State U., Normal, 1970—. Chmn. Mont. Arts Council, 1965-70; mem. Pres.' Adv. Council to Arts, Pres.'s Adv. Council to J.F. Kennedy Center for Performing Arts, 1970; cons. Chancellor's Panel on Univ. Purposes, State U. N.Y., 1970. Mem. Music Tchrs. Nat. Assn. (pres. East central div. 1961-62, nat. v.p. states and divs. 1962-65), Music Educators Nat. Conf., Am. Musicol. Soc., Internat. Council Fine Arts Deans (chmn. 1969- 70), Fedn. Rocky Mountain States (arts and humanities com. 1966-70), Assn. Western Univs. Contbr. articles to profl. jours. Home: 1007 Barton Dr Normal IL

BOLENDER, CARROLL HERDUS, air force officer; b. Cin., Nov. 2, 1919; s. Oscar H. and Kathryn L. (Baughman) B.; B.S., Wilmington Coll., 1941; M.B.A., Ohio State U., 1949; m. Virginia I. McWilliams, Nov. 7, 1942; children—Carol S. (Mrs. James B. Walden), Robert A. Commd. 2d lt. USAAF, 1941, advanced through grades to brig. gen. USAF, 1965; dep. chief of staff plans and operations Eglin Air Force Base, Fla., 1963-64; study coordinator Office of Vice Chief of Staff, Hq. USAF, Washington, 1964-65; Apollo Mission dir. NASA, Washington, 1965-67; program mgr. for lunar module NASA, Houston, 1967-69; dep. dir. devel. and acquisition Dep. Chief of Staff Research and Devel., Hdqrs. USAF, Washington, 1969—. Decorated Air Force Distinguished Service medal, Legion of Merit, D.F.C. with oak leaf cluster, Air Medal with 8 oak leaf clusters, Air Force Commendation Medal; Croix de Guerre with palm and gold star (France); recipient Apollo Achievement award, exceptional service medal, distinguished service medal, all NASA. Home: 3846 N 26th St Arlington VA 22207 Office: Hdgrs HQ USAF/RDP Washington DC 20330

BOLENIUS, WILLIAM C., business exec.; b. Auburn, N.Y., Dec. 18, 1898; s. Frederic A. and Alice (Bain) B.; A.B., Hamilton Coll., 1921; m. Lucy J. Hallock, Oct. 3, 1925. With N.Y. Telephone Co., N.Y.C., 1921, various positions, Buffalo, Rochester, Syracuse, Elmira, v.p., gen. mgr. for Upstate N.Y., 1943—; pres. Wis. Telephone Co., 1946-48; v.p. Am. Tel. and Tel. Co., 1948-58, exec. v.p., 1958-61, vice chmn., 1961-63; dir. Jaeco, Internat. Nickel Co. Can., Ltd., Am. Fletcher Mortgage Investors; dir., adv. council Morgan Guaranty Co. Trustee, chmn. finance com. St. Vincent's Hosp. Presbyn. Clubs: Links, Inc., North Fork Country; University. Home: Cox Lane Cutchogue NY 12729 Office: 195 Broadway New York City NY 10007

BOLES, C. E., lawyer; b. Barren County, Ky., July 3, 1887; s. Charles E. and Eliza Jewell B.; A.B., Bethel Coll., 1906; LL.B., Columbia, 1915; m. Charlotte Bohannan, June 28, 1916 (dec. Oct. 1961); m. 2d, Margaret Pedigo Richey, July 30, 1969. Tchr., Marlin Tex., 1907-09, 1910-12, Terrell, 1909-10; legal practice, Glasgow, Ky., 1915-17, legal work, espionage, trading with enemy acts Solicitors Office, Post Office Dept., 1917-19; atty., examiner Internal Revenue, 1919-21, I.C.C., 1921-52; asst. dir. bur. finances, I.C.C., 1936-48, dir. bur. finance 1948-54; legal practice, Washington, 1954-59, Glasow, Ky., 1962—; admitted to practice Supreme Ct. Dist. Dir. Ky. Hist. Highway Marker Program. Candidate for Democratic nomination U.S. Senate, 1968. Mem. Ky. Bar Assn., Glasgow C. of C., Phi Gamma Delta, Democrat. Baptist. Mason. Clubs: The Filson (Louisville), Nat. Press; Rotary; Glasgow Golf and Country. Home: 307 W Brown St Glasgow KY 42141 Office: Michell-Terry Bldg Glasgow KY 42141

BOLES, EWING THOMAS, financial cons.; b. Williamstown, Ky., May 4, 1895; s. John R. and Sarah Sheriff (McGowan) B.; student U. Ill., 1915; A.B., Centre Coll., 1916; student Coll. Law, U. Ky., 1916-17; m. Katherine Dwyer, June 19, 1920; children—Ewing Thomas Jr., Helen Anne (Mrs. W.B. Hardy, Jr.). Asso., Halsey, Stuart & Co., Chgo., 1926-29; sales mgr. BancOhio Securities Co., Columbus, O. 1929-35, pres., 1935; pres., dir. of its successor The Ohio Co., 1942-64, chmn., 1964-65; financial cons., 1966—; dir. Atlas Realty, Inc., ATO, Inc., Ohio Valley Pub. Co., Ohio Rvier Collieries, Brodhead-Garrett Co., Huber Corp., Federated Pubs., Inc., life mem. bd. trustees Centre Coll. Mem. Investment Bankers Assn. Am. (past pres.), Phi Kappa Tau (past nat. pres.). Clubs: Columbus Athletic, Columbus. Home: 2750 Crafton Park Columbus OH 43221 Office: 8 E Long St Columbus OH 43215

BOLES, HAROLD WILSON, educator; b. Trafalgar, Ind., July 25, 1915; s. Forest Joseph and Audra (Foster) B.; B.S., Ind. State U., 1937; M.A., Ohio State U., 1950, Ph.D., 1957; postgrad. U. Colo., 1951, U. Chgo., 1968; m. Esther Lucile Bowers, Nov. 2, 1944; children—Sharon Kaye (Mrs. William Douglas Ames), Deborah Dee, David Brian, Dennis Ray. Tchr., dept. head Morton Meml. High Sch., Knightstown, Ind., 1937-41; sect. mgr. L.S. Ayres & Co., Indpls., 1946-47; prin. Mad River High Sch., Westville, O., 1947-48; supt. Mad River Schs., Urbana, O., 1948-50; supt. Madison Local Schs., London, O., 1950-51; instr. Ohio State U., 1951-52; supt. Marion Local Schs., Columbis, O., 1952-55; ednl. facilities cons. Joseph Baker & Assos., architects, Newark, O., 1955-61; asso. prof., prof., dept. head Western Mich. U., Kalamazoo, 1961—; vis. lectr. Ariz. State U., 1963, Wash. State U., 1965; cons. sch. bldg. projects, 1955—. Served with USNR, 1941-46. Mem. Am., Mich. assns. sch. adminstrs., Nat. Council Profs. Ednl. Adminstrn., Mich. Assn. Profs. Ednl. Adminstrn., Phi Delta Kappa. Author textbooks. Contbr. articles profl. jours. Home: 1225 Brent Av Kalamazoo MI 49002

BOLES, JOHN KEITH, Jr., army officer; b. Manila, P.I., July 19, 1916; s. John Keith and Irene (Lowe) B.; B.S., U.S. Mil. Acad., 1939; grad. Advanced Mgmt. Program, Harvard, 1960; M.A. in Internat. Affairs, George Washington U.,, 1963; m. Mary Brooke Lucas, June 15, 1946; children—John Keith III, Judith Brooke. Commd. 2d lt. U.S. Army, 1939, advanced through grades to maj. gen., 1963; tank battalion comdr. 3d Armored Div., World War II; instr. Command and Gen. Staff Sch., 1950-54; comdr. 6th Armored Cav. Regt., Germany, 1955-57; assigned Army Research and Devel. Command, 1959-63, Joint Research and Test Activity, Vietnam, 1964-66; comdr. 1st Armored Div., 1968-70; chief staff NATO Hdqrs., Izmir, Turkey, 1970—. Explorer chmn. for Greece, Turkey and Ethiopia, Boy Scouts Am. Decorated Silver Star, Legion of Merit with 1 oak leaf cluster, D.F.C., Soldier's medal with 1 oak leaf cluster, Bronze Star with 2 oak leaf clusters, Air medal with 5 oak leaf clusters, Purple Heart with 1 oak leaf cluster. Life mem. Nat. Rifle Assn.; mem. 3d Armored Div. (v.p.). Home: care OC Pearce 104 N 13th St Fort Smith AK 72901 Office: Chief Staff NATO Izmir APO New York City NY 09224

BOLES, RUSSELL SAGE, physician; b. Phila., Sept. 27, 1889; s. George H. and Rhoda (Borden) B.; M.D., U. Pa., 1912; postgrad. U. Halle, Germany, Berlin, Vienna, Austria, Hungary, 1914; m. Mary McNeely, Nov. 29, 1916; children— Mary Laird (Mrs. T. Baird McIlvain), Russell Sage. Intern, Phila. Gen. Hosp., 1912-13, chmn. med. div., 1940-43, pres. med. bd., 1943-47, vis. physician, 1929-55, sr. med. chief dept. medicine, 1952-55, hon. cons. dept. medicine, 1955; asso. prof. medicine Grad. Sch., U. Pa., 1947- 52, prof. clin. medicine U. Pa., 1952-55; emeritus prof. clin. medicine, 1955—; chief gastroenterology Bryn Mawr (Pa.) Hosp., 1937-41; spl. cons. Nat. Cancer Inst. USPHS; formerly mem. sci. com. Research council on Problems of Alcohol; former adv. com. Nat. Com. for Edn. on Alcoholism; del. 1st Internat. Congress Gastroenterology, Brussels, 1935. Mem. adv. bd. Woods Sch., Langhorne, Pa.; former mem. bd. dirs. Phila. Civic Opera Co. Served as lt. M.C., USN, World War 1; cons. Pa. Adv. Bd. I, World War II. Recipient Julius Friedenwald medal Am. Gastroent. Assn., 1959. Diplomate in gastroenterology Am. Bd. Internal Medicine. Fellow A.C.P. (life), Phila. Coll. Physicians; mem. Am. Gastroent. Assn. (sec. 1933-39, v.p. 1940-41, pres. 1942), World (founder mem. U.S. com.), Pan-Am. (pres. sect. gastroenterology 1953), Am. (chmn. sect. gastroenterology and proctology 1950), Pa., Montgomery Co., Philadelphia County med. assns., A.A.A.S., Musical Fund Soc. (mem. bd.). Republican. Episcopalian (vestryman). Clubs: Rittenhouse, Philadelphia Country, The Orpheus, Univ. of Pa. Faculty. Author articles in sci. books, jours., lay mags. Mem. gen. com. revision U.S. Parmacopeia, 1950-60; book rev. editor Gastroenterology. Russell S. Boles Med. Research Fund established U. Pa., 1959. Home: 135 S 19th St Philadelphia PA 19103 Office: Rittenhouse Plaza 1901 Walnut St Philadelphia PA 19103

BOLEY, BRUNO ADRIAN, educator; b. Gorizia, Italy, May 13, 1924; s. Orville F. and Rita (Luzzatto) B.; came to U.S., 1939, naturalized, 1945; B.C.E., Coll. City N.Y., 1943; M. Aero. Engring., Poly. Inst. Bklyn., 1945, D. Aero. Engring., 1946; m. Sara R. Boley, May 12, 1949; children—Jacqueline, Daniel L. Asst. dir. structural research, aero. engring. dept. Poly. Inst. Bklyn., 1943-48; engring. specialist Goodyear Aircraft Corp., 1948- 50; asso. prof. aero. engring. Ohio State U., 1950-52; asso. prof. civil engring. Columbia, 1952-58, prof., 1958-68; Joseph P. Ripley prof. engring., chmn. theoretical and applied mechanics Cornell U., Ithaca, N.Y., 1968—, also asso. chmn. dept. mechanics. Asso. fellow Am. Inst. Aero. and Astronautics; mem. Soc. Engring. Scis. (v.p.), Am. Soc. M.E. (exec. com.; pres. applied mechanics div.), Assn. Chmn. Depts. Mechanics (pres.), Internat. Union Theoretical and Applied Mechanics (mem. Cougress com.), Am. Acad. Mechanics, N.Y. Acad. Scis. (named Outstanding Educator of Am. 1971). Author: Theory of Thermal Stresses, 1960; Structures and Material, 1964; Thermoinelasticity, 1970, also articles, numerous tech. papers. Bd. editors Internat. Jour. Solids and Structures, Internat. Bull. Mech. Engring. Edn., Jour. Mech. Sci. Home: 101 Edgecliff Pl Ithaca NY 14850

BOLEY, FORREST IRVING, educator, physicist; b. Ft. Madison, Ia., Nov. 27, 1925; s. Ira Everett and Olive (Conlee) B.; B.S., Iowa State U., 1946, Ph.D., 1951; M.A. (hon.), Wesleyan U., Middletown, Conn., 1959, Dartmouth, 1967; m. Marjorie Lovell, Dec. 26, 1946 (div. 1969); children—Kathleen, Sandra, Philip, John; m. 2d, Barbara Bishop Fellows, Dec. 31, 1969. Faculty, Wesleyan U., 1951-61; prof. physics and astronomy, 1959-61; physicist U. Cal. at Berkeley, 1961-64; prof. physics and astronomy Dartmouth, Hanover, N.H., 1964—. Served with USNR, 1943-46. Mem. Am. Phys. Soc., Am. Astron. Soc., Am. Assn. Physics Tchrs. Author: Plasmas-Laboratory and Cosmic, 1966. Editor: Am. Jour. Physics, 1966—. Home: 20 Occom Ridge Hanover NH 03755

BOLEY, LOYD EDWIN, veterinarian; b. Topeka Kan., Oct. 21, 1909; s. Frank John and Mayme (Richards) B.; D.V.M., Kan. State U., 1932; M.S., U. Ill., 1942; postgrad. U. Mich.; m. Esther Clara Stuewe, July 27, 1935; childrenPatricia Kay, Diane Jane, Practitioner, Burlingame, Kan., 1932- 34: meat inspection div. Bur. Animal Industry, 1934-36: staff asst., div. vet. pathology and hygiene U. Ill., 1936-42, asst. prof. dept. vet. pathology and hygiene, 1942-47, asso. prof. dept. vet. clin. medicine, 1947-49, prof., head dept. Coll. Vet. Medicine, 1949—. asst. dean Coll. Vet. Medicine, 1962-66, asso. dean Coll. Vet. Medicine, 1966-. Served from 1st lt. to lt. col. Vet. Corps, AUS, 1942- 46. Mem. Am., Ill. vet. med. assns., U.S. Livestock San Assn., Research Workers N.A., Sigma Xi, Phi Kappa Phi, Phi Zeta, Gamma Sigma Delta. Lutheran. Club: Exchange (Urbana). Home: 311 W William St Champaign IL 61820

BOLEY, PAUL LEROY, lawyer; b. Chillicothe, Mo., Mar. 5, 1910; s. George Washington and Edyth Elizabeth (Williams) B.; A.B., Lawrence Coll., 1935; LL.B., Harvard, 1940; m. Margaret Synnesvedt, Apr. 29, 1939; children—Barbara Ann, Robert Edward, Patricia Jean, Nancy Tess, Michael Terry. Admitted N.Y. bar, 1942, Ore. bar, 1943; practice in Portland, 1943—; mem. firm Davies, Biggs, Strayer, Stoel & Boley, and predecessors, 1944—; dir. Fred Meyer, Inc., Tektronix, Inc., Pacific N.W. Aviation, Inc. Portland, Ore. Founder, chmn. bd., past pres. Tucker-Maxon Oral Sch. Trustee, Lewis and Clark Coll.; trustee Herbert A. Templeton Found., Max and Rose Tucker Found., Millicent Found., St. Vincent Med. Found. Mem. Am., Ore., Multnomah County bar assns., Phi Beta Kappa, Phi Delta Theta (past nat. scholarship commn.). Episcopalian. Republican. Clubs: Waverley Country; Arlington (Portland, Ore.). Home: 17403 S Viewpoint Lane Lake Oswego OR 97304 Office: 900 SW Fifth Av Portland OR 97204

BOLGER, RAY, actor; b. Boston, Mass., Jan. 10, 1904; s. James Edward and Anne (Wallace) B.; ed. pub. schs., Boston; m. Gwendolyn Rickard, July 9, 1929. Began acting career with Bob Ott Repertory Co., 1923-25; with Ralph Sanford as A Pair of Nifties, vaudeville 1925; with Gus Edwards in Ritz Carton Nights, 1926-28; appeared on Broadway in Shubert revue The Merry Whirl, 1925; revues: George White's Scandals of 1931; Heads Up, 1929; (with Bert Lahr) Life Begins at 8:40, 1934; starred in On Your Toes, 1936; under MGM picture contract made Rosalie, Sweethearts, Wizard of Oz, 1938- 40; starred on Broadway in Keep Off the Grass, 1940, By Jupiter, 1942; with MGM 1941-42, 45—, appearing in The Harvey Girls, 1945, starring in Three to Make Ready, 1946, and in Warner Bros. film Silver Lining; starred on Broadway in Where's Charley?, produced by wife, Gwen Rickard, 1948-51, filmed Where's Charley?, 1951; co-starred in April in Paris, 1952; star motion picture Babes in Toyland, 1961; NBC TV debut Comedy Hour, 1952; filming weekly Ray Bolger Show, ABC-TV, 1953- 55; Washington Square, NBC-TV series, 1956—; starred in Broadway mus. All American, 1962, Come Summer, 1968-69; summer theatres The Happy Time, 1969; appearing in one-man show a Musical Comical Concert, various concert halls and nightclubs; lectr. on various subjects throughout U.S. With U.S.O. Camp Shows entertained soldiers in Caribbean, Brit. Guinea area, 1941; with Little Jack Little entertained in Pacific combat zone, 1943; made 1st war bond tour for Treas. Dept. Recipient Silver medal for Treasury activities during World War II; 2 Donaldson award for best performances; drama critics poll best musical comedy performance, 1946; N.Y. Newspapers Guild Page One award, 1943, 50; Antoinette Perry award, 1948-49; Decency in Entertainment award Notre Dame Club Chgo., 1967. Clubs: Players; Bel-Air Country (Cal.); Valley (Montecito); Bohemian (San Francisco); Burlingame Country (Cal.); Swallows (Pebble Beach, Cal.). Home: 618 N Beverly Dr Beverly Hills CA 90210 Office: care Wm Morris Agency 151 El Camino Beverly Hills CA 90210

BOLGER, T.E., telephone co. exec.; b. Norfolk, Neb., 1927; ed. S.D. Sch. Mines. Pres., chief exec. officer, dir. Pacific Northwest Bell Telephone Co., Seattle; pres., dir. Chesapeake & Potomac Tel. Co. of Md., 1970—; also subsidiary cos. of Va., D.C., W.Va., 1970—. Home: 4120 94th S E Mercer Island Washington DC 98040 Office: 821 2d Av Seattle WA 98104*

BOLIN, ROGER HARRISON, ret. marketing cons.; b. Brazil, Ind., May 29, 1905; s. Charles H. and Julia (Daugherty) B.; B.S. in Elec. Engring., Rose Poly. Inst., 1925; m. Gertrude Lewis, Aug. 11, 1931; children—Charles Philip, Julia Ellen, Kathleen. With Westinghouse Electric Corp., Pitts., 1925-70, mgr. appliance advt. and promotion, 1937-49, asst. to v.p. consumer product group, 1949-54, mgr. gen. advt., 1954-57, dir. advt., 1957-64, dir. marketing communications, 1964-70. Dir. Better Bus. Bur. Greater Pitts., 1966-70, Advt. Council, 1965, Advt. Research Found., 1966. Recipient Hall of Fame award Am. Bus. Press. 1965. Mem. Assn. Nat. Advertisers (chmn. 1961; Paul B. West award, 1963), Pitts. Advt. Club (pres. 1958-59), Pitts. C. of C. Roman Catholic. Home: 241 Shadowlawn Av Pittsburgh PA 15216

BOLIN, WILLIAM HARVEY, banker; b. Dallas, Dec. 8, 1922; s. William Harvey and Bertha (Dickey) B.; B.A. in Internat. Relations, U. Cal. at Berkeley, 1947; student Nat. U. Mexico, 1947; m. Jane Davis, July 9, 1949; children-Teresa, Patricia. Joined Bank of Am., N.T. & S.A., San Francisco, 1947, asst. v.p. Latin Am. div., 1956, mgr. Guatamala br., 1957-60, asst. v.p. Middle East and Africa div., 1960, v.p. Middle East and Africa div., 1961, v.p., head Latin Am. div., 1965-69, sr. v.p., 1969—; sr. v.p. Bank Am. Internat. Fla., 1970—; v.p. Bank Am., N.Y., 1961—; dir. Corporacion Nicaraguense de Inversiones, Managua, Nicaragua, Banque Marocaine du Commerce Exterieur, Casablanca, Morocco, 1961-65, Latin Am. Agribus. Corp., 1970- -, Financiera de Am., S.A. Mem. consultative council Financial Corp. Overseas Countries and United Overseas Bank, Geneva, Switzerland, 1962- 65; mem. Andean com. Nat. Fgn. Trade Council, 1967; mem. Central Am. com. Council Latin Am., 1967. Bd. dirs. Near East Found., N.Y.C.; trustee Pan Am. Devel. Found., Washington. Served from 2d lt. to capt., inf., AUS, 1942-46. Mem. Pan Am. Soc. San Francisco (pres. 1968), World Trade Assn. San Francisco, Am. Inst. Banking, World Affairs Council No. Cal., Bankers Assn. for Fgn. Trade, World Trade Club San Francisco, Delta Phi Epsilon. Mem. United Ch. Christ. Home: 30 St Stephens Dr Orinda CA 94563 Office: 555 California St San Francisco CA 94104

BOLING, EDWARD JOSEPH, univ. pres.; b. Sevier County, Tenn., Feb. 19, 1922; s. Sam R. and Nerissa (Clark) B.; B.S. in Accounting, U. Tenn., 1948, M. S. in Statistics, 1950; Ed.D. in Ednl. Adminstrn., George Peabody Coll. Tchrs., 1961; m. Carolyn Pierce, Aug. 8, 1950; children—Mark Edward, Brian Marshall, Steven Clark. With Wilby-Kinsy Theatre Corp., Knoxville, Tenn., 1940-41, Aluminum Co. Am., 1941-42; instr. statistics U. Tenn., 1948-50; research statistician Carbide & Carbon Chem. Corp., Oak Ridge, 1950, supr. source and fissionable materials accounting K-25 plant, 1951- 54; budget dir. Tenn., 1955-59, commr. finance and adminstrn., 1959-61; v.p. U. Tenn., 1961-70, pres., 1970—. Dir. Nashville br. Fed. Res. Bank Atlanta, Magnavox Corp., Benco Plastics, Inc., Swan's. Mem. So. Regional Edn. Bd., 1957-61, 70—; mem. Edn. Commn. of States, 1970—; mem. Nat. Govs. Conf. Good Will Tour to Brazil and Argentina, 1960. Dir. Bill Wilkerson Speech and Hearing Center, Nashville. Served with AUS, 1943-46; ETO. Mem. Am. Statis. Assn., Assn. Higher Edn., Nat. Assn. Land-Grant Colls., Am. Coll. Pub.

Relations Assn. (trustee, chmn. com. taxation and philanthropy), Am. Alumni Council, Knoxville C. of C. (v.p.), Am. Legion, L.Q.C. Lamar Soc., Phi Kappa Phi (Scholarship award 1947), Beta Gamma Sigma (charter pres. Alpha chpt. 1948), Phi Delta Kappa, Omicron Delta Kappa. Democrat. Author: (with D. A. Gardiner) Forecasting University Enrollment, 1952; Methods of Objectifying The Allocation of Tax Funds to Tennessee State Colleges, 1961. Home: 940 Cherokee Blvd Knoxville TN 37919

BOLING, LLOYD RAYNOR, engring. co. exec.; b. Fresno, Cal., Mar. 13, 1910; s. John W. and Lorena (Kendall) B.; B.S., U. Cal. at Berkeley, 1933; m. Esther M. Williams, June 22, 1934. Controller, Cal. Spray-Chem. Corp., Richmond, 1934-41, Oliver United Filters, Inc., Oakland, Cal., 1941-56; v.p. Dorr- Oliver, Inc., Stamford, Conn., 1956-59, pres., 1959-66, chmn. bd., 1966, dir., 1966—; dir. Nat. Filter Media, New Haven, Dorr-Oliver-Long, Orillia, Ont., Can., Dorr-Oliver N.V., Amsterdam, Holland, Regents Controls Co., Stamford. Mem. Financial Execs. Inst. (pres. San Francisco 1949). Presbyn. Home: Route 2 West Redding CT 06896 Office: Dorr-Oliver Inc Havemeyer Lane Stamford CT 06904

BOLINGER, DWIGHT LEMERTON, educator; b. Topeka, Aug. 18, 1907; s. Arthur Joel and Gertrude (Ott) B.; B.A., Washburn Coll., 1930, Litt.D., 1963; M.A., U. Kan., 1932; Ph.D., U. Wis., 1936; A.M. (hon.), Harvard, 1963; m. Louise Ida Schrynemakers, July 1, 1934; children—Bruce Clyde, Ann Celeste (Mrs. McClure). Instr., U. Wis., 1936, Kansas City (Mo.) Jr. Coll., 1937; asso. prof. Washburn Coll., 1937-44; asst. prof., then prof. U. So. Cal., 1944-60, head dept. Spanish, Italian and Portuguese, 1947-59; prof. Spanish, U. Colo., 1960- 63, Harvard, Cambridge, Mass., 1963—. Sterling fellow linguistics Yale, 1943-44; research fellow speech Haskins Labs., N.Y.C., 1956-57; fellow Center for Advanced Study in Behavioral Scis., 1969-70. Mem. Linguistic Soc. Am. (pres. 1972), Am. Assn. Tchrs. Spanish and Portuguese (pres. 1960), Am. Dialect Soc., Phonetic Soc. Japan, Modern Lang. Assn., Societas Linguistica Europaea, Am. Civil Liberties Union. Author: Interrogative Structures of American English, 1957; (with others) Modern Spanish, 1960; Forms of English, 1965; Aspects of Language, 1968; the Phrasal Verb in English, 1971. Home: 52 Scott Rd Belmont MA 02178 Office: Boylston Hall Harvard Univ Cambridge MA 02138

BOLL, CHARLES RAYMOND, engine co. exec.; b. Columbus, Ind., Mar. 29, 1920; s. Charles Raymond and Hestella (Snyder) B.; B.S. in Elec. Engring., Purdue U., 1941; m. Mary Genevieve Lortz, Nov. 6, 1943; children—Charles Raymond III, Cynthia Ann. With Cummins Engine Co., Inc., Columbus, 1941—, sales engr., 1941-42, asst. regional mgr., Cleve., 1947, mgr. engine sales, 1948-52, gen. sales mgr., 1953- 55, v.p. sales, 1955-60, exec. v.p. marketing, 1960-64, pres. Internat. div., 1965-66, exec. v.p., 1966—, also dir.; Mem. Columbus Bd. Aviation Commrs. Served to 1st lt., Signal Corps AUS, 1943-46. Mem. Soc. Automotive Engrs. Home: 2940 Washington St Columbus IN Office: 1000 5th St Columbus IN 47201

BOLLARD, RICHARD JOHN HOLDEN, educator, cons. engr.; b. Hamilton, New Zealand, July 13, 1927; s. Robert John and Marne (Holden) B.; B.S., Canterbury Coll., U. New Zealand, 1948, M.S., 1949; Ph.D., Purdue U., 1954; m. Evamae Habig, Jan. 27, 1955; children—Sandra Jill, Robert John, Timothy, Barbara. Came to U.S., 1952. Cons. structural engr., Aukland, N.Z., 1949-52, cons. aero. engr., 1954-56; lectr. engring. U. New Zealand, 1954-56; prof. aero. and engring. scis. Purdue U., 1956-61; prof., head dept. aeronautics and astronautics U. Wash., 1961—; engring. cons. aerospace structures, 1956—; asso. dir. aerospace scis. lab. Purdue U., 1956-61. Dir. Math. Scis. Corp. Asso. fellow Inst. Aero. and Astronautics (dir. Pacific N.W. sect.), Royal Aero. Soc., Sigma Xi, Tau Beta Pi. Rotarian. Author papers in field. Home: 6810 51st NE Seattle WA 98115

BOLLAY, WILLIAM, cons. engr.; b. Stuttgart, Germany, Jan. 14, 1911; s. Frederick J. and Dorothea Frieda (Kramer) B.; came to U.S., 1924, naturalized, 1929; B.S., Northwestern U., 1933, Sc.D. (hon.), 1959; Ph.D., Cal. Inst. Tech., 1936; m. Jeanne Marie Brinsley, Aug. 30, 1934; 1 dau., Melody Jeanne (Mrs. George A. Kladnik). Instr. Cal. Inst. Tech., 1936-37, Harvard, 1937-41; with aerophys. lab. N. Am. Aviation, 1945-51; tech. dir. Aerophys. Devel. Corp., 1951-58; cons. engr. 1958-62; vis. prof. Stanford U., 1963-68, Mass. Inst. Tech., 1962-63, U. Cal. at Los Angeles, 1948-54; cons. engr., Santa Barbara, Cal., 1968—. Mem. sci. adv. bd. USAF, 1949-54, U.S. Army Aviation, 1961—; mem. NACA and NASA subcoms., 1941—; dir. Commn. Engring. Edn., 1962-65. Served with USNR, 1941-45. Decorated Legion of Merit; recipient Wright Bros. lecture award, 1951. Fellow Am. Inst. Aeros. and Astronautics (dir. 1968-70). With Werner von Braun developed concept of first U.S. satellite. Address: 4592 Via Vistosa Santa Barbara CA 93110

BOLLE, ARNOLD WILLIAM, univ. dean; b. Watertown, Wis., Oct. 5, 1912; s. Charles Frederich and Anna (Riedelbach) B.; B.A., Northwestern Coll., Watertown, Wis., 1934; B.S., U. Mont., 1937; M.P.A., Harvard, 1955, Dr. Pub. Adminstrn., 1960; m. Helen Swan, July 24, 1937; children—Stanton Gene, Susan Swan, Charles Kenneth. Forester, U.S. Forest Service, Mont., 1937; conservationist U.S. Soil Conservation Service, Wyo., 1938-46; dude rancher, Wyo., 1946-48; conservationist Soil Conservation Service, Wash., Ore., Washington, 1949-55; asso. prof. forestry, conservation U. Mont., Missoula, 1955-60, prof., 1960-62, dean Sch. Forestry, dir. Forest and Conservation Expt. Sta., 1962—, chmn. Sch. Adminstry. Leadership, 1962—. Cons. resources program staff Office Sec. Dept. Interior; past pres. Mont. Conservation Council; pres. Mont. Woodland Council, Mont. Natural Resources Council; mem. panel natural resources Nat. Acad. Sci., mem. com. on support of dissertation research in recreation and leisure; chmn. com. to study Nat. Forest harvesting practices in Mont. by Congl. delegation; mem. Nat. Adv. Board Pub. Lands, Adv. Bd. Congl. Ad Hoc Committee on Environment. Dir., Environment and Resources Analysis Center. Mem. Assn. State Coll. and Univ. Forest Research Orgns. (nat. exec. bd.), Forestry Sch. Execs. (chmn., past pres.), Phi Kappa Phi. Contbr. articles to profl. jours. Home: 1630 Jackson Dr Missoula MT 59801

BOLLE, DONALD MARTIN, educator; b. Amsterdam, The Netherlands, Mar. 30, 1933; s. Maarten C. and Petronella (Kramer) B.; B.Sc., Durham U. (Eng.), 1954; Ph.D., Purdue U., 1961; M.A., Brown U., 1966; m. Barbara June Girton, Nov. 29, 1957; children—Alan Martin, Thomas Raymond, John Kenneth, Cornelis Adrianus. Came to U.S., 1955, naturalized, 1961. Asst. prof. elec. engring. Purdue U., 1961-62; NSF postdoctoral fellow Dept. Applied Math. and Theoret. Physics Cambridge U. (Eng.), 1962-63; asst. prof. engring. Brown U., 1963-66, asso. prof., 1966-70, prof., 1970—; Richard Merton vis. prof. Technische Hochschule, Braunschweig, Germany, 1967; cons. in field. Mem. Am. Soc. Engring. Edn., I.E.E.E., A.A.A.S., Am. Assn. U. Profs., Am. Civil Liberties Union, Wilderness Soc., Sigma Xi, Tau Beta Pi, Eta Kappa Nu. Home: 105 Arlington Av Providence RI 02906

BOLLENGIER, ALBERT EMILE, Jr., mfg. co. exec.; b. Pawtucket. R.I., June 7, 1913; s. Albert E. and Alice (Bollengier) B.; B.S. in Bus. Adminstrn., U. So. Cal., 1935; m. Edith Lodema Kennerd, Nov. 25, 1936; children—Berta (Mrs. Shaw), William E. With Price Waterhouse & Co., C.P.A.'s, 1936-42; treas., controller Hal Rouach Studios, Inc. and Eagle Lion Studios, also Eagle Lion Film Inc., also asst. studio controller Universal Pictures Co., Inc., 1945-51; treas., controller United Artists Corp., 1951-56; financial v.p., treas. United Artists Theatre Circuit, 1956-66; v.p., controller W. R. Grace & Co., 1967—. C.P.A. Mem. Cal. Soc. C.P.A.'s, Beta Alpha Psi. Home: 1 Beresford Lane Larchmont NY 10538 Office: 3 Hanover Sq New York City NY 10005

BOLLENS, JOHN CONSTANTINUS, educator; b. Pitts., Dec. 27, 1920; s. Constantinus John and Annie (Free) B.; A.B., Coll. of Wooster, 1942; A.M., Duke, 1948; Ph.D., U. Wis., 1948; m. Virgene Ruth Anderson, Sept. 21, 1945; children—Ross John, Scott Alan. Research dir. Municipal League Seattle, 1945-47; adminstrv. analyst U. Cal. at Berkeley, 1947-50, lectr. polit. sci., 1949-50; asst. prof. polit. sci. U. Cal. at Los Angeles, 1950-55, acting dir. Bur. Govtl. Research, 1954-55, asso. prof., 1955-60, dir. urban studies, 1958-62, prof., 1960—. Cons. govt., pvt. orgns.; exec. sec. Western Govtl. Research Assn., 1947-50; spl. asst. to dir. Internat. City Mgrs. Assn., 1950; dir. met. areas study Council State Govts., 1955-56; exec. officer, research dir. Met. St. Louis Survey, 1956-57; exec. dir. Met. Community Studies, Dayton, O., 1957-59; dir. study city charter, govtl. orgn. Los Angeles, 1962-63; mem. Los Angeles County Citizens Economy and Efficiency Com., 1964—, Los Angeles Citizens Com. Zoning Practices and Procs., 1967-69; cons. to Adv. Commn. on Intergovtl. Relations, 1967—. Mem. Am. Polit. Sci. Assn., Am. Soc. Pub. Adminstrn. (pres. Los Angeles area chpt. 1962-63), Phi Beta Kappa. Author: The Problem of Government in the San Francisco Bay Region, 1948; Appointed Executive Local Government, 1952; California Government and Politics, 4th edit., 1967; The States and the Metropolitan Problem, 1956; Special District Governments in the United States, 1957; Exploring the Metropolitan Community, 1961; A Study of the Los Angeles City Charter, 1963; The Metropolis: Its People, Politics and Economic Life, 1965; Communities and Government in a Changing World, 1966; A Program to Improve Planning and Zoning in Los Angeles, 1968; Governing a Metropolitan Region: The San Francisco Bay Area, 1968; American County Government, 1969; The City Manager Profession: Myths and Realities, 1969; A Study of the Los Angeles County Charter, 1970. Home: 14801 Pampas Ricas Blvd Pacific Palisades CA 90272

BOLLES, EDMUND BLAIR, corp. exec.; b. St. Louis, Feb. 25, 1911; grad. Philips Exeter Acad., Exeter, N.H., 1929; student, Yale, 1929-30, 31-32; m. Mona Byrnina Dugas, Apr. 19, 1941; children—Edmund B., Charles DeV., Zoe L. (Mrs. Jalabert), Harry P. Wrote for newspapers and mags., 1925-32; tchr. grammar, Latin and algebra Gunston Sch., Centreville, Md., 1930-31; in advt. office Palais Royal Dept. Store, Washington, 1932; reporter, Washington Sun, also Washington Herald, 1933; congl. corr. Universal Service, 1934, 34-35; rewrite man. N.Y. Am., 1934; with Washington Star, 1935-44, successively as writer on N.R.A. and A.A.A. diplomatic corp.; dir. Washington bur. Fgn. Policy Assn., 1944-51, Washington corr., 1951-53; U.S. editor France Actuelle, 1952-53: European corr. Toledo Blade, 1953-57, asso. editor, 1957-59; v.p. marketing, dir. water div. Fairbanks, Morse and Co., 1959-64; v.p. govt. relations Colt Industries, Inc., 1964-67, 68—, v.p. internat., 1966-68; regular contbr. Washingtonian Sunday edit. N.Y. Times, 1938; contbr. on fgn. affairs N. Am. Newspaper Alliance; reg. contbr. on polit. affairs, Toronto Star Weekly; polit. writer for mags. 1936—. Spl. adviser F.A.O. Conf., UN, Copenhagen, 1946. Decorated Royal medal of St. Olav (Norway). Fellow Am. Geog. Assn.; mem. A.I.M., Nat. Security Indsl. Assn. (v.p.), Anglo-Am. Press Assn. Paris, White House Corrs. Assn. Roman Catholic. Clubs: Cosmos, Nat. Press (Washington); Yale (N.Y.). Author: America's Change of Peace, 1939; Arctic Diplomacy, 1948; Military Establishment of the United States, 1949; U.S. Military Policy, 1950; Tyrant from Illinois, 1951; How To Get Rich in Washington, 1952; Armed Road to Peace, 1952; The Big Chance in Europe, 1958: Men of Good Intentions. 1960; Corruption in Washington, 1961. Contbr. to nat. mags. Home: 4831 Linnean Av Washington DC 20008 Office: 1801 K St NW Washington DC 20006

BOLLES, JAMES CHADBOURN, textile co. exec.; b. Southport, N.C., Sept. 2, 1905; s. Charles Pattison (M.D.) and Abbie Ellis (Chadbourn) B.; grad. Culver Mil. Acad., 1925; B.S., U. Pa., 1929; m. Rosemary White, Jan. 27, 1940; children—James Chadbourn, Rosemary Louise duBrutz, William W., Linwood W., Jane M. Asst. trust officer N.C. Bank & Trust Co., Greensboro, 1930- 31; asso. trust officer Am. Trust Co., Charlotte, N.C., 1932-38; pres., chmn. bd. Rufus D. Wilson, Inc. (now Chadbourn Gotham, Inc.), Burlington, N.C., 1938—, treas.; former pres., chmn. bd. Full Knit Hosiery Mills, Inc., Burlington; pres., treas., dir. Shannon Hosiery Mills, Inc.; pres., dir. Owen Osborne Hosiery Mills, Inc., Gainsville, Ga., Charlotte Packaging Corp.; dir. Shenandoah (Va.) Knitting Mills, Inc., Gaybourn Mills, Inc., Gainesville, Lassiter Press, Inc., Consol. Credit Corp. Trustee Charlotte Country Day Sch. Mem. Sigma Alpha Epsilon. Democrat. Episcopalian. Clubs: Charlotte Country, City (Charlotte, N.C.); The Surf (Wrightsville Beach, N.C.); New York Athletic (N.Y.C.). Home: 424 Eastover Rd Charlotte NC 28207 Office: 2417 N Davidson St Charlotte NC 28205

BOLLES, JOHN SAVAGE, architect; b. Berkeley, Cal, June 25, 1905; B.S. in Civil Engring., U. Okla., 1926; M.Arch. (Austin Tuition scholar), Harvard, 1932. Mem. Carnegie Inst. Washington expdn. to Yucatan 1931-35, Med. Acad. of Am. to Cluny, France, Oriental Inst., U. Chgo. to Turkey, Egypt, Iran; draftsman Cal. Commn. for G.G.I.E., 1938; architect for numerous archaeol. expdns.; propr. John S. Bolles, architect, and John Bolles Gallery, San Francisco, 1954—; prin. works include S&H, Sperry & Hutchinson Co. distbg. bldg., South San Francisco, 1958, IMB Corp. bldgs., San Jose, Cal., 1959-70, Paul Masson Champagne plant, Saratoga, Cal., 1959, Giants Stadium (Candelstick Park), San Francisco, 1960, Macy's Stores, Stanford, San Francisco, Concord, Sacramento, Stockton, Monterrey, 1958—, Ping Yuen Housing North, San Francisco Chinatown, 1961, McGraw Hill Pub. Co., 1964, No. Waterfront, San Francisco, 1968, Embarcadero Plaza, San Francisco, 1969, Downtown Plaza, Sacramento, 1969, numerous banks in Cal., Sheraton-Harbor Island Hotel, San Diego, 1970, numerous others. Mem. San Anselmo (Cal.) Planning Commn., 1938-40. Area project dir. engr. U.S. Housing Authority, No. Cal., 1941-42; tech. dir. San Francisco Housing Authority, 1943-44; chmn., San Francisco Bldg. Industry Code Commn., 1954-55. Chmn. bd. dirs. San Francisco Art Inst., 1960-64. Recipient Outstanding Contbn. to Art and Architecture award Artists Equity, 1952. Fellow A.I.A. (sec. N. Cal. chpt.); mem. Cal. Council Architects (1st pres. 1946), Cal. Assn. Architects (pres. 1945), San Francisco Downtown Assn. (dir. 1960—). Office: 14 Gold St San Francisco CA

BOLLES, ROBERT STEPHEN, educator; b. McCook, Neb., Oct. 30, 1908; s. Stephen DeWitt and Sarah Elizabeth (Oyster) B.; certificate Inst. Musical Art, N.Y.C., 1934; B.S., Columbia Tchrs. Coll., 1936, M.A., 1938, Ed.D., 1948; m. Georgia Coy, Aug. 17, 1935; children—Robert Coy, John Louis. Head sch. music dept. Peabody Conservatory of Music, Balt., 1939-42; prof., asst. dir. div. music U. Fla., Gainesville, 1948-56, head dept. music, 1956-60, asst. dean Coll. Architecture and Fine Arts, 1960-65, acting dean, 1965-66, dean, 1966—. Served from lt. (j g.) to comdr. USNR, 1942-45. Mem. Music Educators Nat. Conf., Fla. Music Educators Assn., Music Tchrs. Nat. Assn., Fla. Tchrs. Assn., Phi Mu Alpha. Mason, Kiwanian. Author: A Compendium of Solo Flute Literature for Teachers and Students of the Flute, 1948. Home: 2213 NW 11th Av Gainesville, FL.

BOLLES, THOMAS DARLEY, athletic dir.; b. Willow River, Minn., Sept. 25, 1902; s. Henry Albert and Edith (Lewis) B.; A.B., U. Wash., 1926, M.A., 1936; student Harvard Grad. Sch. Arts and Scis., 1937-40; m. Catharine Hope, Sept. 3, 1936 (dec. 1968); children—Lemuel Harry, Hope Catharine; m. 2d, Doris F. Lewis, Aug. 15, 1970. Coach U. Wash. Freshmen, 1928-36; head rowing coach, Harvard, 1937-51 (from 1937-50 the Harvard Varsity crew lost only one race to Yale; 1939 and 1950 Varsity crews won the Grand Challenge Cup at Henley Regatta, Eng.; the 1947 Varsity won the Lake Washington Regatta 2000 meter sprint race, setting a world's record of 5:49), dir. Athletics, Harvard, 1951-63, dir. emeritus, 1963—, mgr. U.S. Olympic Rowing Team, 1952, 56; chmn. U.S. Olympic Rowing Com., 1964. Served as lt. comdr. USNR, World War II. Elected to Helms Hall of Fame, 1956. Mem. Rowing Coaches Orgn. Am. (pres., 1943-46), Am. Legion, Fellowship of U.S.-Brit. Comrades, London, Eng., Mil. Order of World Wars. Republican. Conglist. Clubs: Harvard Faculty; Carolina Country (Raleigh). Author of rowing articles included in Robert F. Herrick's Red Top, 1948. Home: 2504 St Mary's St Raleigh NC 27609 Office: Harvard Dept Athletic 60 Boylston St Cambridge MA 02138

BOLLING, LANDRUM RYMER, educator, journalist; b. Parksville, Tenn., Nov. 13, 1913; s. Landrum Austin and Carrie Mae (Rymer) B.; B.A., U. Tenn., 1933; M.A., U. Chgo., 1938; LL.D., Valparaiso U., Wabash Coll., Oberlin Coll., Alderson- Broadus Coll., Beloit Coll., Rose Polytech. Inst.; L.H.D., Anderson Coll., Ind. Tech. Coll.; m. Frances Morgan, July 6, 1936; children—Roger Landrum (dec.), Brian Austin, David Morgan, Rebecca Lucy, Daniel Wade, Sarah Middleton. Adminstrv. asst. personnel div. TVA, also housing mgr. Town of Norris, editor Norris News, 1933-36; freelance writer, 1936-37; instr. polit. sci. Brown U., 1938-40; assisted in orgn. Community Service, Inc., Yellow Springs, O., also editor and pub. Yellow Springs News, 1940- 41; instr. to asso. prof. polit. sci. Beloit Coll., 1942-46; war corr. Mediterranean Theater, 1944-45; fgn. corr., Berlin and Central Europe, 1946-48; prof. polit. sci. Earlham Coll., 1948—, gen. sec., 1955-58, pres., 1958—; journalistic, editorial assignments, N.Y., Europe, 1949, 52-53. Mem. Gov. of Ind. Commn. on Post High Sch. Edn., 1968; mem. Pres.'s Commn. on 25th Anniversary UN, 1970; chmn. Internat. Quaker Working Party on Middle East Peace, 1968—. Mem. Assn. Am. Colls. (bd. dirs.), Gt. Lakes Colls. Assn. (chmn. bd. dirs. 1962-64), Ind. Conf. Higher Edn. (pres. 1961-62). Mem. Soc. of Friends. Rotarian. Author: City Manager Government in Dayton, 1940. Co-author: (Settel et al) This is Germany, 1950; Search for Peace in the Middle East, 1970. Home: 312 College Av Richmond IN 47374

BOLLING, RICHARD WALKER, congressman; b. N.Y.C., May 17, 1916; s. Richard Walker and Florence (Easton) B.; A.B., U. of South, 1937, A.M., 1939; postgrad. Vanderbilt U., 1939-40; LL.D., Rockhurst Coll., 1971; m. Jim Grant, Jan. 13, 1964; 1 dau. (by previous marriage), Andrea Walker. Dir. student activities and vets. affairs U. Kansas City, 1946-47; nat. vice-chmn. Am. Vets. Com., 1947-48; mem. 81st-92d congresses from 5th Mo. Dist., mem. Ho. Rules Com., Joint Econ. Com., Ho. Com. on Rec. Studios; chmn. Urban Affairs Subcom.; Chubb fellow Yale, 1965; fellow Center for Advanced Studies, Wesleyan U., 1962-64. Served with AUS, 1941-46. Decorated Legion of Merit, Bronze Star; recipient Congl. Distinguished award Am. Polit. Sci. Assn., 1961; named to Sports Illus. 25th Anniversary All-Am. Football Team. Mem. Phi Beta Kappa, Phi Delta Theta. Democrat. Episcopalian. Author: House Out of Order, 1965; Power in the House, 1968. Home: 722 Walnut St Kansas City MO 64106 Office: US Federal Court Bldg Kansas City MO 64106 also Rayburn House Office Bldg Washington DC 20515

BOLLINGER, EVANGELINE GRACE, coll. dean; b. Detroit, Nov. 30, 1922; A.B., Madison Coll., 1944; M.A., U. Mich., 1945, Ph.D. in English (fellow), 1951. Instr. English, Stephens Coll., 1945-46, U. Mich., 1950-51, St. Joseph Coll., Conn., 1951-54; instr. U. Dayton (O.), 1954-55, asst. prof., 1955-57; asst. prof. English, St. Xavier Coll., Chgo., 1957-58, prof., head dept., 1958—, chmn. div. liberal arts and humanities, 1961-66, dean, 1967—, v.p. for acad. affairs, 1969—. Mem. Modern Lang. Assn., Coll. English Assn., Nat. Council Tchrs. English. Research on Dante. Address: St Xavier Coll 103d St and Central Park Chicago IL 60655

BOLLINGER, LOWELL MOYER, physicist; b. Greene County, Va., Apr. 28, 1923; s. Amsey Floyd and Florence (Moyer) B.; A.B., Oberlin Coll., 1943; Ph.D., Cornell U., Ithaca, N.Y., 1951; m. Margaret Jeffries, Nov. 5, 1944; children—Lesley, Jeffrey, Priscilla. Physicist aircraft engine research lab. NACA, Cleve., 1943-46; neutron physicist Argonne Nat. Lab. (Ill.), 1951—, dir. physics div., 1963—. Guest physicist Atomic Energy Research Establishment, Harwell, Eng., 1961-62. Fellow Am. Phys. Soc. Conglist. Home: 1741 Prairie Av Downers Grove, IL. Office: Argonne Nat Lab Argonne IL

BOLLMAN, JESSE L., physician; b. Springfield, Ill., Feb. 19, 1896; s. George and Emma (Frischot) B.; student U.S. Naval Acad., 1914-15; A.B., U. Ill., 1917, B.S., 1921, M.D., 1923; M.S., U. Mich., 1918; m. Mildred Lee Montgomery, Nov. 29, 1922; children—Elizabeth Lee, Jean, Jesse Louis. Instr. bacteriology U. Mich. Med. Sch., 1917-18; asst. physiol. chemistry U. Ill. Med. Sch., 1919-23; instr. pathology U. Minn., Grad. Sch., Mayo Found., Rochester, 1924-26, asst. prof., 1926-30, asso. prof., 1930-40, prof., 1940-61, prof. emeritus, 1961—. Mem. Minn. Gov's Commn. Mental Health, 1954-58. Recipient Julius Friedenwald medal, 1961; John Phillips Meml. award A.C.P., 1964. Mem. A.M.A., A.A.A.S., Am. Soc. Exptl. Pathology (council, v.p., pres., 1938-41), Am. Gastroenterol. Assn., Am. Chem. Soc., Am. Animal Hosp. Assn. (hon.), Soc. for Exptl. Biology and Medicine, Central Soc. for Med. Research, Minn. Acad. Sci., Alumni Assn. Mayo Found., Am. Assn. Study of Liver Disease (council, v.p., pres., 1952-55), N.I.H. (gen. medicine study sect. 1960-64), Sigma Xi, Nu Sigma Nu. Author chpts. on physiology. Contbr. articles to med. and sci. jours. Home: 410 6th Av SW Rochester MN Office: Rochester State Hosp Rochester MN

BOLLMAN, MARK B., Jr., credit card co. exec.; b. 1925; A.B., Princeton, 1947; M.B.A., Harvard, 1951; married. From trainee to pres. Interpub. Group of Cos., 1951-68; sr. v.p., dir. Benton & Bowles Inc., 1968-70; exec. v.p., dir. marketing Diners' Club Inc., N.Y.C. Served to sgt. AUS, 1944-46. Office: 10 Columbus Circle New York City NY 10019*

BOLLMAN, VERNON LEROY, educator; b. Omaha, Apr. 26, 1908; s. George and Mary (Hendricksen) B.; B.S. in Elec. Engring., U. Neb., 1931, M.S. in Physics, 1933; Ph.D., Cal. Inst. Tech., 1936; m. Frances Louise Lamberton, Aug. 1927; 1 dau., Martha. Instr., Occidental Coll., 1936- also v.p. acad. 38, dean of men, 1938-43, prof., 1943—, dean of faculty, 1958-67, also v.p. acad. affairs. Mem. Am. Phys. Soc., Am. Assn. Physics Tchrs., Phi Beta Kappa, Sigma Xi, Sigma Sigma Pi Sigma, Sigma Tau, Pi Mu Epsilon. Home: 1142 N Campbell St Glendale, CA 91207.

BOLOMEY, ROGER HENRY, sculptor; b. Torrington, Conn., Oct. 19, 1918; s. Henry Albert and Ida (Vurlod) B.; student Acad. Fine Arts, Florence, Italy, 1947, U. Lausanne (Switzerland), 1947-48, Cal. Coll. Arts and Crafts, Oakland, 1948-50; m. Alice Susanne Ryser, June 11, 1948; children—Florence Susanne, Yvonne Marguerite. Prof., Herbert H. Lehman Coll., City U. N.Y. Painter, 1948- 60; sculptor, 1960—; exhibited one-man shows including Bolles Gallery, San Francisco, 1960, Royal Marks Gallery, N.Y.C., 1964, 65; numerous group exhbns., 1960—, including Chgo. Art Inst., 1962, Salon de Mai, Paris (France) Mus. Art, 1963, 64, Whitney Mus., 1964, Larry Aldrich Mus., Ridgefield, Conn., 1964, Carnegie Inst. Internat. Exhbn., 1964, Whitney Mus., 1964, 66, Highlights 1964-65, Larry Aldrich Mus., 1965, Quatrieme Expn. Suisse de Sculpture, Bienne, Switzerland, 1966, Amerikanische Kunst aus Schweizer Besitz, St. Gallen, Switzerland, 1966, Contemporary Am. Painting and Sculpture, U. Ill. at Urbana, 1967; represented permanent collections Mus. Modern Art, Whitney Mus., Larry Aldrich Mus., Bundy Art Gallery, Waitsfield, Vt., San Francisco Art Inst., Oakland Mus., Los Angeles County Mus., U. Cal. Mus. Art, Berkeley, Chase Manhattan Bank, N.Y.C., also numerous pvt. collections. Recipient 1st prize, commn. large mural San Jose (Cal.) State Coll. competition, 1962; 1st prize, purchase award Bundry Art Gallery competition, 1963; Sculpture prize San Francisco Art Inst. 84th Ann., 1965; chosen to execute 2 large sculptures for state office bldg., Albany, N.Y., 1967, sculpture for new Nassau County Supreme Ct. Bldg., 1968. Mem. San Francisco Art Inst., Am. Fedn. Arts. First to use polyurethane from its fluid form as a medium of art. Address: Wingdale NY 12594

BOLOTOWSKY, ILYA, educator, artist; b. St. Petersburg, Russia, July 1, 1907; s. Jules J. and Anastasia (Shapiro) B.; student Gymnasia, Baku, Caucasus, 1915-19, Coll. St. Joseph, Constantinople, Turkey, 1920-23, French Coll., 1920-23, N.A.D., N.Y. Sch. Art, 1924-30; postgrad. research art U. Wyo., 1949- 51; m. Meta Cohen, Sept. 17, 1947; 1 son, Andrew. Came to U.S., 1923, naturalized, 1929. Head dept. art Black Mountain Coll., 1946-48; asso. prof. art U. Wyo., 1948-57; prof. art Coll. Edn., New Paltz, N.Y., 1957-65; adj. prof. Hunter Coll., 1963-64; chmn. dept. fine arts Southampton Coll. (L.I.), 1965—; vis. prof. Bklyn. Coll., 1954-56. One-man shows G.R.D. Studios, N.Y.C., New Art Circle, 1946-52, Pinacotheca, 1947, 50, Borgenicht Gallery, 1954, 56, 58, 59, 61, 63, 65, 68, 70, retrospective one-man show, 1969-70, London (Eng.) Arts Gallery, 1971, London Arts Gallery, Detroit, 1971; exhibited in shows U.S. Western Europe, Japan, Argentina, traveling show U. Colo., U. Art Mus., Albuquerque, Ia. Mus. Art, Newport Harbor Art Mus., Balboa, Cal.; rep. permanent collections Whitney Mus., Phillips Gallery, Washington, Yale U. collection, Phila. Mus., Munson-Williams-Proctor Inst., Utica, N.Y., Guggenheim Mus., Brandeis U., Frederick Oslen Found., Guilford, Conn., Mus. Modern Art, N.Y.C., Lyman Allyn Museum, New London, Conn., Rhode Island Sch. Design, Chase Manhattan Bank, Walter Chrysler Mus., Provincetown, Mass., Mus. Fine Art, Birla Inst., Calcutta, India, The Moll, Albany, N.Y.; represented Musee d'Art Moderne, Ceret, France, Götheborg, Sweden, Walker Art Center, Mpls., Larry Aldrich Mus., Ridgefield, Conn.; represented pvt. collections; executed mural Cinema I, N.Y.C.; developed painting style on 3 dimensional constrns., 1961; creative writer, playwright. Served with AUS 1942-43, USAAF, 1943-45. Recipient 1st prize for painting N.A.D., 1929, 30; for editorial work and translation Mil. Dictionary, 1942; grant for exptl. film work, State U. N.Y. Research Found., 1959-60; 1st prize Midwest Film Festival for film Metanola, 1963; prize Nat. Inst. Arts and Letters, 1971. Fellow Internat. Inst. Arts and Letters (life); mem. Am. Abstract Artists (pres. 1957-58), Nat. Soc. Mural Painters, Fedn. Modern Painters and Sculptors. Home: 69 Tiemann Pl New York City NY 10027 Office: Grace Borgenicht Gallery 1018 Madison Av New York City NY

BOLSTAD, MILO MYRUM, educator; b. Dawson, Minn., July 17, 1915; s. Alfred Christian and Mertie (Myrum) B.; B.S. in Mech. Engring., U. Minn., 1936, Ph.D., 1949; S.M. in Mech. Engring., Mass. Inst. Tech., 1938; m. Margaret Susan Thomes, Aug. 15, 1938; children—Susan Mertie, William Milo, Sally Elizabeth. Faculty U. Mo., 1938-44, 45—, prof. mech. engring., 1955—, chmn. dept., 1958-67; mem. sci. staff Manhattan Project, Los Alamos, 1944-45. Chmn. water and light adv. bd., City of Columbia, 1962—. Co-recipient Wolverine award best tech. article Am. Soc. Refrigerating Engrs., 1950. Registered profl. engr., Mo. Fellow Am. Soc. Heating, Refrigerating and Air Conditionng Engrs.; mem. Am. Soc. M.E., Am. Soc. Engring. Edn., Mo. Soc. Profl. Engrs., Sigma Xi, Tau Beta Pi, Pi Tau Sigma. Episcopalian. Editor-in-chief Refrigerating Data Book, Design, vol. 9, 1955. Home: 835 Greenwood Ct Columbia MO 65201

BOLSTAD, REUBEN WILMER, former theatre co. exec.; b. Fertile, Minn., Mar. 16, 1901; s. Willie K. and Josephine (Johnson) B.; ed. pub. schs., Fertile; m. Ethel E. Hall, Sept. 3, 1923; 1 dau., Shirley Irene (Mrs. David W. Ashworth). With Famous Players Canadian Corp., Toronto, Ont., 1930-68, pres., mng. dir., 1963-68; also former dir., officer asso. companies in theatre, TV and community antenna operations. Mem. Canadian Picture Pioneers. Clubs: Variety, National (Toronto). Home: 130 Old Forest Hill Rd Toronto 10 Ontario Canada

BOLSTER, ARTHUR STANLEY, Jr., educator; b. Bismarck, N.D., Jan. 30, 1922; s. Arthur S. and Gertrude (Pierce) B.; A.B., Dartmouth, 1943; M.A., Harvard, 1947, Ph.D., 1954; m. Elizabeth Barker Winkfield, Oct. 8, 1949; children—Stephen Clark, Gregory Pierce. Tchr. history Grosse Pointe (Mich.) High Sch., 1952-57, Pelham (N.Y.) High Sch., 1957-59; faculty Harvard, Cambridge, Mass., 1959—, prof. edn., 1967—. Served to lt. USNR, 1943-46. Mem. Orgn. Am. Historians, Nat. Council Social Studies, New Eng. History Tchrs. Assn. (pres. 1968- 69, Kidger award 1970), Phi Beta Kappa, Phi Delta Kappa. Mem. United Ch. of Christ. Author: James Freeman Clarke, Disciple to Advancing Truth, 1954. Home: 30 Valley Rd Lexington MA 02173 Office: Longfellow Hall Harvard Grad Sch Edn Cambridge MA 02138

BOLSTER, EDWARD ANDREW, business exec.; b. Berkeley, Cal., Aug. 1, 1912; s. Fred Harvey and Anna Elizabeth (Keyes) B.; student Pasadena (Cal.) Jr. Coll., 1932-33; B.C.S., Strayer Coll., Washington, 1938; B.A., George Washington U., 1945; m. Elizabeth Dawson Killian, Mar. 5, 1937; children—Warren Edward, Janet Elizabeth. Retail grocer, 1933-34; accountant Am. Dairy Supply Co., 1935-36; statistician SEC, 1936-40; economist Bur. of Budget, 1940-45; div. chief CAB, 1945-52; chief Aviation Div., Dept. State, 1952-56; with Nat. War Coll., Washington, 1956-57; 1st sec. Am. embassy, Tokyo, 1957-59; dir. Office Transport and Communications, Dept. State, 1960-63; Am. consul gen., Sydney, Australia, 1963-65; dir. Office Aviation, Dept. State, Washington, 1966-68; v.p. Systems Analysis & Research Corp., Washington, 1968—. Mem. Nat. Aero. Assn., Pi Gamma Mu. Presbyn. Club: International. Home: 4305 40th St N Arlington VA 22207 Office: 1100 Connecticut Av NW Washington DC 20036

BOLT, BRUCE ALAN, educator; b. Largs, Australia, Feb. 15, 1930; s. Donald Frederick and Arlene (Stitt) B.; B.S. with honors, New Eng. U. Coll., 1952; M.S., U. Sydney (Australia), 1954, Ph.D., 1959; m. Beverley Bentley, Feb. 11, 1956; children—Gillian, Robert, Helen, Margaret. Math. master Sydney (Australia) Boys' High Sch., 1953; lectr. U. Sydney, 1954-61, sr. lectr., 1961-62; research seismologist Columbia, 1960; dir. seismographic stas. U. Cal. at Berkeley, 1963—, prof. seismology, 1963—. Mem. com. on seismology Nat. Acad. Scis., 1966—. Recipient H.O. Wood award in seismology, 1967, Fulbright scholar, 1960. Fellow Am. Geophys. Union; mem. Seismol. Soc. Am. (editor bull. 1965—, dir. 1965- 71), Assn. Seismology and Physics Earth's Interior (exec. com. 1964-67), Earthquake Engring. Research Inst., Australian Math. Soc., Royal Astron. Soc., Sigma Xi. Research on dynamics, elastic waves, earthquakes, reduction geophys. observations; discovered more detail on structure in upper mantle and portions earth's core; cons. on seismic hazards. Home: 1508 Le Roy Av Berkeley CA 94708

BOLT, RICHARD HENRY, educator; b. Peking, China, Apr. 22, 1911 (parents Am. citizens); s. Richard Arthur and Beatrice (French) B.; A.B., U. Cal., 1933, A.M., 1937, Ph.D., 1939; m. Katherine Mary Smith, June 24, 1933; children—Beatrice Bolt Scribner, Richard Eugene, Deborah Bolt Haberstron. Asso. in physics U. Ill., 1940; research asso. Mass. Inst. Tech., Cambridge, 1941-43, asso. prof. physics, 1946-54, prof. acoustics, 1954-64, lectr. polit. sci., 1964-70, dir. acoustics lab., 1946-57; asso. dir. NSF, 1960-63; prin. cons. biophysics and biophys. chemistry study sect. N.I.H., Bethesda, Md., 1957-60; chmn. bd. Bolt, Beranek & Newman, Inc., cons., Cambridge, 1953—. Sci. liaison officer OSRD, London, 1943-44; chief tech. aide Nat. Def. Research Com., 1944-45; mem. Armed Forces-Nat. Research Council chmn. com. on hearing and bio-acoustics, 1953-1955. Fellow Center for Advanced Study in Behavioral Sciences, Stanford, 1963-64. Fellow Accoustical Soc. Am. (pres. 1949-50), I.E.E.E., Am. Acad. Arts and Scis., N.Y. Acad. Scis.; mem. Internat. Commn. on Acoustics (pres. 1951-57), A.A.A.S. (dir. 1969—), Am. Inst. Physics (gov. bd. 1957-63). Clubs: Cosmos (Washington). Author: Sonics (with others), 1959; also numerous articles in sound, acoustics, noise control, sci. and public policy. Home: Tabor Hill Rd Lincoln MA 01773 Office: 50 Moulton St Cambridge MA 02138

BOLT, ROBERT, playwright; b. Manchester, Eng., Aug. 15, 1924; s. Ralph and Leah (Binnion) B.; B.A. with honors in History, Manchester U., 1949; m. Celia Anne Roberts, Nov. 1948; children—Sally, Benedict, Joanna. Office-boy ins. office, Manchester, Eng., 1941-42; tchr. village sch., Bishopsteignton, Devonshire, 1950-51, Millfield Sch., Summerset, Eng., 1951-58; playwrighter, screen script writer, 1958—. Served with RAF and Brit. Army, 1943-46. Author: (plays) Flowering Cherry, 1958; The Tiger in the House, 1960; A Man for All Seasons, 1960; Gentle Jack, 1963; (film script) Lawrence of Arabia, 1962; Dr. Zhivago, 1965; A Man for All Seasons, 1966 (Acad. award 1966, N.Y. film critics award 1966. Brit. Film Acad. award). Address: 15 Chelsea Embankment SW 3 London England

BOLTE, BROWN, advt. exec.; b. Winnetka, Ill., Dec. 23, 1908; s. John Willard and Jessie (Brown) B.; student Butler U., 1930; U.S. Army Sch. for Spl. Services, Washington and Lee U., 1943; m. Bernice Nicholson, Jan. 4, 1930; 1 dau., Celia (Mrs. John William Griese, Jr.). Western and So. sales mgr. Rytex Co., Indpls., 1930-35; asst. to pres. in charge marketing Scott & Browne, Inc., Bloomfield, N.J., 1935-41; account exec. Benton & Bowles, Inc., 1941-50, v.p., 1950, exec. v.p., 1955, chmn. plans bd., 1957; pres. Sullivan, Stauffer, Colwell & Bayles, Inc., 1958-60, vice chmn. bd., 1961-65; chmn. bd. Bolté Advt.-Suburban N.Y., Inc. 1965—, Bolté Advt.-Hartford, Inc. 1965—; gen. partner Bolté Advt.-Yonkers, N.Y., 1970—; chmn. Bolté, Lukin & Assos., Inc., Palm Beach, Fla., 1970—. Mem. pres.'s adv. council Butler U., Indpls., 1968—. Trustee Norwalk Hosp. Assn., 1958-65, YMCA New Canaan, 1967—; bd. dirs. New Canaan chpt. A.R.C., 1953-54, Eleanor Roosevelt Found., 1961, Child Welfare League Am., 1962-63, Community Mental Health Center, West Palm Beach, 1970—. Served from 2d lt. to maj. AUS, 1942-45. Mem. Am. Assn. Advt. Agys. (gov. 1956, chmn. eastern region 1957), Inst. Outdoor Advt. (dir., chmn. bd. 1967), Advt. Council (dir. 1966—), Nat. Def. Transp. Assn. (exec. com., chmn. pub. relations. com. 1956-58), A.S.C.A.P., Am. Guild Authors and Composers, Newcomen Soc. N. Am., Sigma Chi. Clubs: Union League (N.Y.C.); Preston Mountain (Kent, Conn.); Lost Tree (Lost Tree Village, Fla.); Beach, Ocean (Palm Beach, Fla.); Club Unlimited. Home: 11804 Lake House Ct Lost Tree Village North Palm Beach FL Office: 41 Midland Av Port Chester NY also 24 Culbro Dr West Hartford Industrial Park West Hartford CT also 242 S County Rd Palm Beach FL 33480

BOLTE, CHARLES GUY, found. exec.; b. N.Y.C., Jan. 19, 1920; s. Guy Willard and Marian (Stewart) B.; A.B., Dartmouth, 1941, L.H.D., 1970; B.Litt. (Rhodes scholar 1947), Oxford (Eng.) U., 1949; m. Mary Brooks Elwell, Aug. 1, 1943; children—Guy Willard II, John Cox, Brooks. Newspaper reporter, 1937-41; spl. writer O.W.I., 1943-44; organizer, chmn. Am. Vets. Com., 1944-47; mil. corr. The Nation, 1944; exec. sec. Am. Book Pubs. Council, 1952; v.p. Viking Press, 1956-61, exec. v.p., 1961-66; v.p. Carnegie Endowment for Internat. Peace, N.Y.C., 1966-71, counsellor, 1971—. Served as lt. Brit. Army, 1941-43. Author: The New Veteran, 1945; The Price of Peace: A Plan for Disarmament, 1956. Home: Riverside CT New York City NY Office: Carnegie Endowment for Internat Peace 345 E 46th St New York City NY 10017

BOLTON, ARTHUR KEY, atty. gen. Ga.; b. Griffin, Ga., May 14, 1922; s. Herbert Alfred and Eunice (Maddox) B.; grad. N. Ga. Coll., 1941; LL.B., U. Ga., 1943; m. Marion Lee Cashen, Sept. 30, 1946; children—Arthur Key, Marian Lee. Practice law, Griffin, 1947—; mem. Ga. Ho. of Reps., 1949-65; floor leader, 1963-65; judge Criminal Ct. Griffin, 1952-65; county adminstr., 1950-65; atty. gen. Ga., 1965—. Served to capt., inf., AUS, World War II; ETO. Decorated Silver Star, Purple Heart, 3 Battle Stars; recipient Statesmanship award Ga. Gen. Assembly, 1961-62; Pub. Service award Ga. Municipal Assn., 1965, Key Citizenship award, 1970; man of Yr. award Griffin, Ga., 1962. Mem. V.F.W., Am. Legion, Phi Delta Phi. Baptist. Elk. Address: Griffin GA 30223

BOLTON, DONNELLY PAUL, army officer; b. Chgo., May 9, 1919; s. Joseph V. and Edith (Berntzen) B.; student U. Ky., 1937-38; B.S., U.S. Mil. Acad., 1942; postgrad. George Washington U., 1963-64; m. Margaret Matthews, July 15, 1944; children—Beth, Ellen. Commd. 2d lt. U.S. Army, 1942, advanced through grades to maj. gen., 1970; inf. company comdr., ETO, 1944-45; instr. Inf. Sch., 1949-52; bn. comdg. officer, Korea, 1952-53; with So. European Task Force, No. Italy, 1957-59; mem. Army Gen. Staff, 1960-62, Joint Chiefs of Staff, 1962-64; brigade comdg. officer 1st Armored Div., 1964-66; asst. div. comdr. RVN, 1966-67; staff officer Hdqrs. MACV, 1967-68; dir. operations Hdqrs. Dept. Army, Washington, 1968—. Decorated D.S.M., Silver Star, D.F.C., Legion of Merit, Bronze Star, Army Commendation medal, Purple Heart. Home: Quarters 21b Fort Myers VA 22211 Office: The Pentagon Washington DC 20310

BOLTON, EARL CLINTON, ednl. cons; b. Los Angeles, Aug. 22, 1919; s. John R. and Hazel A. (Van Order) B.; A.B. magna cum laude, U. So. Cal., 1941, J.D., 1948; LL.D., U. San Diego, 1963; m. Jean Studley, June 27, 1942; children—Barbara (Mrs. Sigmar Hoffmann), Elizabeth Ann, William Earl. Staff, Coordinator Inter-Am. Affairs, N.Y.C., also Washington, 1941; v.p., treas. Nat. Public Discussions, Inc., N.Y.C., 1942; lectr. polit. sci. dept. U. So. Cal., 1946-48, asst. prof. Coll. Liberal Arts and Sch. Commerce, 1948-50, asso. prof. law and v.p. planning, 1952-60; spl. asst. to pres. U. Cal. at Berkeley, 1960-61, v.p. univ. relations, 1962- 64, v.p. adminstrn., 1964-66, v.p. govtl. relations, 1966-68, v.p. adminstrn., 1968-70; v.p. Booz, Allen & Hamilton, Inc., Chgo., 1970—. Admitted to Cal. bar, 1949, also U.S. Supreme Ct.; mem. Cal. Gov.'s Mental Health Adv. Com., Citizens' Legislative Adv. Com.; past chmn., founding mem. Cal. Scholarship Com. Served to capt. USNR, 1942-46, 50- 52. Mem. State Bar of Cal., Order Coif, Phi Beta Kappa, Phi Kappa Phi. Editorial bd. Law Rev., U. So. Cal., 1947-48. Home: 1310 Ritchie Ct Chicago IL 60610 Office: Booz Allen & Hamilton Inc 135 S LaSalle St Chicago IL 60603

BOLTON, EDWIN LYMER, newspaperman; b. Tomah, Wis., Mar. 7, 1918; s. Raymond L. and Leila (Janes) B.; B.A., U. Minn., 1939; m. Arlene Bryant Hansen, Apr. 18, 1970; children by previous marriage—Jean E., Douglas E., Brian G. Reporter, news editor Marshall (Minn.) Daily Messenger, 1939-41; sports editor Winona (Minn.) Republican-Herald, 1942-44, city editor, 1944-46; with Mpls. Star, 1947—, books and arts editor, 1968—; tchr. journalism S.W. State Coll., Marshall, 1968-69; judge annual dist. auditions Met. Opera; art show judge. Past pres. Mpls. Civic Opera Co. Recipient 1st pl. award critical commentary Newspaper Guild Twin Cities, 1969, 70, 71. Home: 3520 W 32d St Minneapolis MN 55416 Office: 425 Portland Av Minneapolis MN 55415

BOLTON, FRANCES PAYNE, former congresswoman; b. Cleve., Mar. 29, 1885; d. Charles William and Mary Perry (Payne) Bingham; ed. Hathaway-Brown School, Cleve., Dieudonne Bornel, Oise, France, 1899-1900; grad. Miss Spence's Sch. for Girls, 1904; student Mannes Music Sch., N.Y. City; LL.D., Colgate U., 1940, Ohio Wesleyan U., 1942, Fenn Coll., 1953, Oberlin Coll., 1953, Heidelberg Coll., 1954, Western Coll. for Women, Oxford, O., 1957, U. Me., 1960; L.H.D., Baldwin-Wallace Coll., 1944, Kenyon Coll., 1947, Coll. Wooster, 1948, Western Reserve U., 1944; Tuskegee Inst., 1957, Johns Hopkins, 1959, others; m. Chester Castle Bolton, Sept. 14, 1907; children—Charles Bingham, Kenyon Castle, Oliver Payne, Elisabeth (dec.). Mem. 76th to 89th Congresses, 22d Ohio Dist.; ranking Rep. mem. fgn. affairs com.; U.S. del. 8th General Assemby UN, 1953; first woman mem. Congress to head mission abroad, 1955; U.S. del. Brit.- Am. Parliamentary Conf., 1961; alt. del. NATO Parliamentary Conf., Paris, 1966; U.S. delegate Ghana Independence ceremonies, 1957; U.S. del to Council of Europe, Strasbourg, France, 1966. Mem. Rep. State Central Com., 1938-40; vice chmn. Nat. Rep. Program Com., 1937-40; del., mem. platform com. Rep. Nat. Conv., 1956, 60, 64, 68; hon. mem. Rep. Executive Com. Cuyahoga County. Vice regent from Ohio, Mount Vernon Ladies' Assn. in charge of George Washington Nat. Shrine at Mount Vernon, Va.; trustee Lakeside Hosp.; hon. trustee Mus. African Art; bd. Sch. Advanced Internat. Studies; bd. women's Africa Com., African-Am. Inst.; adv. council Sch. Nursing of Western Reserve U. (all Cleve.); trustee U.S. Hist. Soc., Nat. Trust Historic Preservation, Lake Erie Coll., Tuskegee Inst., Meharry Med. Coll.; adv. com. Aid to African Students Phelps-Stokes Fund, Rep. Women's Com. Spl. Activities. Recipient William Freeman Snow award, 1949; M. Adelaide Nutting award, 1951; Women for Achievement Inc., nat. award, 1951; Officer French Legion of Honor, 1956; award for achievement in govt. Zonta Internat. 1956; service plaque State Dept., 1961; community service plaque V.F.W. Cleve., 1961, award, 1963; Distinguished Achievement award Nat. Assn. Colored Women's Clubs, 1963; award Operation Crossroads Africa, 1965; named hon. flight nurse U.S. Air Force, 1968, others. Hon. fellow Cleve. Medical Library Assn. Mem. D.A.R., Am. Social Hygiene Assn. (v.p., hon. mem.), Nat. League for Nursing (hon.), Soc. Women Geographers, Alumni Assn. Army Sch. Nursing, Edward Angle Soc. Orthodontia (hon.), Capitol Hill Assos. (bd.), League Women Voters, U.S. Capitol Hist. Soc.; hon. mem. Alpha Iota, Beta Sigma Phi, Delta Kappa Gamma, Phi Delta Gamma, Theta Sigma Phi. Presbyn. Clubs: Women's City (Cleve.); Women's Nat. Republican, Pen and Brush (N.Y.C.); League of Republican Women, Internat. (Washington); Women's Advt. of Cleve. (hon.). Home: 1800 Richmond Rd Lyndhurst OH Office: 888 16th St NW Washington DC 20006 also 2490 Lee Blvd Cleveland Heights OH 44118

BOLTON, FREDERICK ROLSHOVEN, lawyer; b. Detroit, Sept. 27, 1896; s. Edwin Cyrus and Therese (Rolshoven) B.; Engr., U. Mich., 1918; LL.B., Detroit Coll. Law, 1921, J.D., 1968; B.E., Wayne State U., 1927; M.A., U. Detroit, 1931; m. Mabel Carey, Dec. 28, 1925 (dec.); 1 dau., Ann Therese (Mrs. Norman Dodge); m. 2d, Elwyn Walker Milroy, Oct. 19, 1968. Admitted to Mich. bar, 1921, since practiced in Detroit; mem. firm Shock, Bolton & Graham, 1937-60; partner Lacy, Lawson, Kirkby & Bolton, and predecessor firm, 1960-70, Bolton & Coon, 1970—; treas., dir. Harper Safety Center, Inc.; dir. Sq. Deal Heating and Cooling, Inc., Woolf Aircraft Products, Inc. Bd. dirs., sec., treas. Detroit and Mich. Artists Meml. Served as ensign USNRF, World War I; comdr. USNR, World War II. Mem. Am., Mich., Detroit bar assns., Am. Soc. Assn. Execs., Assn. Execs. of Mich. (v.p. 1957), Mich. Execs. Forum (chmn. 1957), Judge Advs. Assn. (1st v.p. 1961-62, pres. 1962-63, dir.), Mich., Detroit hist. socs., Newcomen Soc. N.Am., Soc. Automotive Engrs., Nat. Assn. Execs., Am. Legion (past comdr.), Mil. Older World Wars (regional comdr.), Delta Theta Phi (nat. chancellor 1957-59). Republican. Episcopalian. Mason (K.T., sec.-treas. 1969—). Clubs: Detroit Athletic, Detroit Golf, Harmonie, Savoyard (Detroit); Outrigger Canoe (Honolulu); Army and Navy, (Washington). Home: 8120 Jefferson Av Detroit MI 48214 Office: Buhl Bldg Detroit MI 48226

BOLTON, ISABEL, (see Miller, Mary Britton), writer.

BOLTON, JAMES R., automobile mfg. exec. Comptroller, Buick Motor div. Gen. Motors Corp. Office: Buick Motor Div Gen Motors Corp 902 E Hamilton Av Flint MI 48550*

BOLTON, JAMES ROBERT, educator, chemist; b. Swift Current, Sask., Can., June 24, 1937; s. James Linden and Margaret (McFadden) B.; B.A., U. Sask., 1958, M.A., 1960; Ph.D., Cambridge U., Eng., 1962; m. Wilma Burdette Hall, Dec. 26, 1959; children—Judith Louise, James Thomas. Research asso. Columbia, 1962-64; asst. prof. U. Minn., Mpls., 1964-66, asso. prof., 1966-69, prof., asso. chmn. phys. chemistry, 1969-70; prof. U. Western Ont., London, 1970—. Sloan fellow, 1966-68. Mem. Am. Chem. Soc., Chem. Soc. London, Chem. Inst. Can., Canadian Assn. U. Profs. Co-author: Electron Spin Resonance, 1971. Research, publs. on devel. electron spin resonance spectroscopy as tool to provide detailed information about electronic structure of molecules with unpaired electrons. Home: 485 Coombs Av London Ontario Canada

BOLTON, PRESTON MORGAN, architect; b. College Station, Tex., Aug. 12, 1920; s. Frank Cleveland and Lura (Morgan) B.; B.Arch., Tex. A. and M. U., 1942; m. Pauline Wells, June 30, 1960; children—Dean, Teresa, Elizabeth, Mary. Partner, Bolton & Barnstone, Houston; owner P.M. Bolton Assos., Architects, Houston, 1961—; vis. critic Rice U., 1966-67. Pres. Contemporary Arts Mus., 1952-68, 70-71, Arts Council, 1957-58, Alley Theatre, 1959-60; mem. adv. com. Coll. Architecture Tex. A. and M.U., 1969-71. Bd. dirs. Young Audiences Inc., Houston, 1968-70, Miller Theatre Adv. Council, Houston, 1968-70; pres. Houston Found. for Ballet, 1962-63. Served with AUS, 1942-45; ETO. Decorated Bronze Star. Fellow A.I.A. (pres. Houston chpt. 1965, chmn. nat. com. auditor and theatre architecture 1966-68, nat. sec. 1968-72); mem. Tex. Soc. Architects (dir. 1968- 70; Llewelyn W. Pitts award 1971), English Speaking Union (dir. Houston br. 1968-70), Mus. Fine Arts, Mus. Natural Sci., Houston Symphony Soc., Contemporary Arts Mus., Friends' Bayou Bend, Friends' Houston Pub. Library-Mus. Fine Arts. Rotarian (chmn. civic affairs com. 1967-68). Clubs: Racquet, University (Houston). Home: 266 Pine Hollow Houston TX 77027 Office: 1101 S Post Oak Rd Houston TX 77027

BOLTZ, GERALD EDMUND, govt. ofcl.; b. Dennison, O., June 1, 1931; s. Harold E. and Margaret E. (Hecky) B.; A.B., Ohio No. U., 1953, J.D., 1955; m. Janet Ruth Scott, Sept. 19, 1959; children—Gretchen Elizabeth, Eric Scott, Jill Marie. Admitted to Ohio bar, 1955; pvt. practice, Uhrichsville, O., 1957-58; asst. atty. gen. Ohio, 1958-59; trial atty. sec., 1959-60, legal asst. to commnr., 1961, trial atty. Denver regional office, 1961-64, spl. counsel Denver regional office, regional adminstr. Ft. Worth regional office, 1967—. Served with AUS, 1955-57. Mem. Am., Fed. (chpt. treas., v.p.), Ohio bar assns., Sigma Phi Epsilon, Delta Theta Phi. Republican. Presbyn. Clubs: Rotary, Civitan (Denver). Home: 4709 Comita St Fort Worth TX 76132 Office: US Courthouse Fort Worth TX 76102

BOLWELL, HARRY JAMES, mfg. co. exec.; b. Bloomfield, N.J., May 17, 1925; s. Harry George and Ann Lillian (Seymour) B.; B.S., U. Vt., 1949; M.S., Stevens Inst. Tech., 1952; m. Suzanne Ruth Polachik, Sept. 24, 1949; children—Brian, Suzanne. Gen. mgr. Combustion Engring., Inc., Chattanooga, 1959-61; v.p., gen. mgr. Surface Combustion div. Midland-Ross Corp., Toledo, 1961-65, group v.p. corp., 1965-69, pres., chief operating officer, Cleve., 1969—. Campaign chmn. Jr. Achievement Cleve., 1969-70. Mem. bd. advisers Boys Club Cleve.; bd. dirs. Cuyahoga unit Am. Cancer Soc.; trustee U. Vt., Laurel Sch. for Girls, Golden Age Center of Cleve., Cleve. Soc. Christians and Jews. Served to 1st lt. USAAF, 1942-45. Decorated D.F.C., Air medal. Mem. Ohio, Cleve. chambers commerce, Am. Ordnance Assn., Newcomen Soc. Am., Sigma Alpha Epsilon. Clubs: The Clevelander, The Country, Cleve. Racquet, Pepper Pike, Union. Home: Roundwood Rd Chagrin Falls OH 44022 55 Public Sq Cleveland OH 44113

BOLZ, HAROLD AUGUST, coll. dean; b. Cleve., May 27, 1911; s. William and Amelia A. (Waechter) B.; B.S. in Mech. Engring., Case Inst. Tech., 1933, M.S., 1935; Dr. Engring., Purdue U., 1964; m. Harriett Seymour Hallock, Aug. 7, 1937; children—William Scott, Everett Arthur, Eric Harold. Devel. engr. Weatherhead Co., Cleve., 1935-38; instr. machine design Purdue U., Lafayette, Ind., 1938-40, asst. prof. mech. engring., 1940-42, asso. prof., 1942-46, head dept. gen. engring., prof. indsl. engring., 1946-54; asso. dean Ohio State U. Coll. Engring., Columbus, 1954-58, dean, 1958—, also prof. mech. engring., dir. Engring. Expt. Sta. Trustee Edward F. Orton Jr. Ceramic Found. Registered profl. engr., Ind., Ohio. Fellow A.A.A.S., Am. Soc. M.E., mem. Am. Soc. Engring. Edn. (v.p. 1964-66, pres.-elect 1970-71, pres. 1971—), Nat., Ohio socs. profl. engrs., Sigma Xi, Sigma Pi, Tau Beta Pi, Pi Tau Sigma, Theta Tau. Editor Materials Handling Handbook. Contbr. articles on machine design, engring. and personnel relations to profl. jours. Home: 3097 Herrick Rd Upper Arlington Columbus OH 43221

BOLZ, LOTHAR, govt. ofcl.; b. Gleiwitz, Germany, Sept. 3, 1903; student univs. Munich, Kiel; J.D., U. Breslau. Practice law, 1930-33; publicist, sch. tchr., journalist while in exile, Poland and USSR, 1933-47; justiciary, 1947-48; minister reconstrn. Govt. of German Democratic Republic, Berlin, 1949-53; dep. prime minister, 1950-67, minister fgn. affairs, 1953-65. Dep. chmn. Nat. Democratic Party of Germany, 1948—. Recipient Vaterländischer Verdienstorde in Gold, Orden Banner der Arbeit. Address: Friedrichstrasse 65 Berlin W8 Germany

BOLZ, NORMAN ALEXANDER, accountant; b. Detroit, June 12, 1920; s. Alexander F. and Elsie Ellen (Kneale) B.; B.S., Wayne State U., 1942; postgrad. Walsh Inst. Accountancy, 1946, Detroit Coll. Law, 1949-53; m. Betty Jane Sitlington, Feb. 23, 1946; children—Karen Jeanne, Norman Alexander, James Carleton. Partner, mem. exec. com. Lybrand, Ross Bros. & Montgomery, Detroit, 1942—. Mem. Greater Detroit Bd. Commerce, Central Bus. Dist. Assn., Better Bus. Bur. Met. Detroit. Bd. dirs., chmn. finance com. Detroit Symphony Orch.; mem. deferred gifts com. Wayne State U.; mem. exec. com., bd. dirs. Econ. Devel. Corp. of Detroit; trustee Walsh Inst. Accountancy. Served with AUS, 1942-46. Mem. Am. Inst. C.P.A.'s, Mich. Assn. C.P.A.'s, Nat. Assn. Accountants, Inst. Internal. Auditors, Mich. Assn. Professions, Founders Soc. of Detroit Inst. Arts, Inst. Econ. Edn., Mich. C. of C., Wayne State U. Alumni Assn., Newcomen Soc. N.Am., Alpha Kappa Psi. Clubs: Detroit, Country of Detroit, Detroit Athletic; Grosse Pointe Yacht. Home: 26 Winthrop Pl Grosse Pointe Farms MI 48236 Office: 211 W Fort St Detroit MI 48226

BOLZ, RAY EMIL, educator; b. Cleve., Oct. 24, 1918; s. William and Amelia Anne (Waechter) B.; B.S. in Engring., Case Inst. Tech., 1940; M.S., Yale, 1942, D.Engring., 1949; m. Jean Kathryn Hoeft, Oct. 4, 1944; children—Elaine Kathryn, Nancy Jane, Patricia Lynn, Janet Gail. Research scientist NACA, 1942-46, head jet engine combustion sect., 1944-46; asst. prof. aero. engring. Rensselaer Poly. Inst., 1947-50; faculty Case Western Res. U., 1950—, prof. aero. engring., coordinator research, 1952-55, head dept. mech. engring., 1956-60, head engring. div., 1960- 67, dean Sch. Engring., 1967—. Cons. to industry, 1950—; mem. adv. panel to engring. div. NSF, 1958-61, adv. panel to course content and improvement sect., 1961-66, applied mechanics reviewer, cons. on dept. sci. grants, 1968—. Recipient award for advancement basic and applied sci. Yale U., 1957; Outstanding Alumni award Case Western Res. U., 1968. Mem. Am. Soc. Engring. Edn., Am. Soc. M.E.'s (v.p., chmn. policy bd. edn. 1968-70), Am. Inst. Aero. and Astronautics, Cleve. Engring. Soc., Engring. Council Profl. Devel. (chmn. region II 1963-68), Sigma Xi. Unitarian (trustee 1964-68, pres. bd. trustees 1967-68). Home: 16104 Aldersyde Dr Shaker Heights OH 44120 Office: School of Engineering Case Western Reserve U Cleveland OH 44106

BOMAN, JOHN HARRIS, Jr., lawyer; b. Anniston, Ala., Mar. 8, 1910; s. John Harris and Myrtle (Creen) B.; A.B., Marquette U., 1930; J.D., U. Mich., 1933; m. Marie Askew, Aug. 17, 1935; children—John Harris III, Scott A., Proctor C. Admitted to Ga. bar, 1933, since practiced in Atlanta; asso. firm Grenshaw & Hansell, 1933; sr. mem. Hansell, Post, Brandon & Dorsey, 1939—. Sec., dir. Jackson Packing Co. (Miss.), 1946—. Gen. counsel Atlanta Area council Boy Scouts Am.; pres. bd. Atlanta Legal Aid Soc., 1956; sec. Met. Found. of Atlanta; trustee Atlanta Lawyers Found. Served to lt. comdr. USNR, World War II. Mem. Am., Ga., Atlanta bar assns., Lawyers Club Atlanta (pres. 1950), State Bar Ga., Am. Law Inst. Methodist (steward). Clubs: Capital City, Commerce (Atlanta). Home: 3497 Paces Valley Rd NW Atlanta GA 30327 Office: 1st Nat Bank Bldg Atlanta GA 30303

BOMAR, STEVE HERREN, banker; b. Atlanta, Aug. 13, 1907; s. James Spencer and Iva (Camp) B.; LL.B., Atlanta Law Sch., 1937; grad. Stonier Grad. Sch. Banking, Rutgers U., 1941; m. Reba Murphy, July 3, 1930; children—Steve Herren, William Joseph, Reba Nancy, Lynda Anne. Admitted to Ga. bar, 1938; with Trust Co. Ga., 1925—, sr. v.p., treas., 1957-59, sr. v.p., sec.-treas., 1959-64, exec. v.p., sec.-treas., 1964—; v.p., sec.-treas. Trust Co. Ga. Assos., 1948—, also dir. Mem. banking com. emergency operations of adv. com. comml. bank preparedness Am. Bankers Assn., 1955; adv. com. to Pres. for improving presentation fed. budget U.S. C. of C., 1962. Mem. Nat. Assn. Accountants (dir. 1951-52), Adminstrv. Mgmt. Assn. (Leffingwell award 1968), Bank Adminstrn. Inst. (pres., dir. 1956-58, recipient Key award 1961), Financial Execs. Inst. (pres. 1962-63, chmn. bd. 1963-64, dir. 1963-66, dir. research found. 1962-64), Better Business Bur. Atlanta (sec.- treas., dir. 1961-63, 68-70), Ga., Atlanta bar assns., Atlanta C. of C., Sigma Delta Kappa. Presbyn. (deacon, past chmn. finance com., bd. deacons). Mason. Clubs: Capital City, University Yacht (Atlanta); Civitan. Home: 3516 Paces Pl NW Atlanta GA 30327 Office: PO Box 4418 Atlanta GA 30302

BOMAR, WILLIAM PURINTON, corporate exec.; b. Lookout Mountain, Tenn., Aug. 9, 1886; s. David Terry and Anna E. (Purinton) B.; B.S., Yale, 1908; m. Jewel Nail, Nov. 2, 1915 (dec. Oct. 1965); 1 son, William Purinton; m. 2d, Portia Goulder Hamilton, July 1, 1966. With Bewley Mills, Fort Worth, 1909-57, pres., gen. mgr., 1943-57; past pres. Inland Investment Co.; chmn. bd. Chicasha Cotton Oil Co., 1961—; past chmn. bd. Houston Gen. Ins. Group; dir. Tex. Utilities Co., Tex. Electric Service Co., State Res. Life Ins. Co., Southwestern Expn. and Fat Stock Show, Flour Mills Am., Inc., Mo.-Kan.-Tex. R.R. Co. Pres. Ft. Worth Grain and Cotton Exchange, 1925. Chmn. bd. W. I. Cook Childrens Hosp., Ft. Worth, 1928—; bd. dirs. Tex. Research Found., Retina Found., Boston. Mem. Millers Nat. Fedn. (past pres.), Am. Mixed Feed Mfrs. Assn. (past pres.), Ft. Worth C. of C. Presbyn. (chmn. bd. trustees). Mason. Clubs: Ft. Worth (past pres.), Rivercrest Country (Ft. Worth). Address: 1503 Hillcrest St Fort Worth TX 76107

BOMBERGER, SAMUEL WILLIAM, banker; b. Lancaster, Pa., Mar. 1, 1927; s. Paul Samuel and Emma Elizabeth (Stoneroad) B.; B.S. in Bus. Adminstrn., Rider Coll., 1950; postgrad. Bank Adminstrn. Sch. U. Wis., 1965; m. Elizabeth Mae Hofmann, June 20, 1953; children—Letitia Elizabeth, Paula Mae. Expediter, Paul S. Bomberger Bldg. Contractor, Lancaster, 1950-57; mgmt. trainee Lancaster County Nat. Bank, 1957-59, asst. auditor, 1960-63; sr. auditor Lancaster County Farmers Nat. Bank, 1963-70; sr. auditor Nat. Central Bank, Lancaster, 1970—. Treas. Arthritis and Rheumatism Assn., 1963-67. Bd. dirs. Rider Council Alumni Assn., Rider Coll. Devel. Council. Served with USNR, 1945-46, 50-52; ETO. Recipient distinguished service award Arthritis and Rheumatism Found., 1964. Mem. Am. Inst. Banking, Assn. Internal Auditors (treas. chpt.), Delta Sigma Pi. Presbyn. (trustee, elder). Elk, Mason. Clubs: Beach Haven (N.J.) Surf; Conestoga Country (treas.) (Lancaster). Home: 723 N President Av Lancaster PA 17603 Office: 23 E King St Lancaster PA 17604

BOMELI, EDWIN CLARENCE, educator; b. Peoria, O., Sept. 16, 1920; s. Edward Jacob and Alma Dean (Hoffman) B.; B.Sc. in Bus. Adminstrn., Ohio State U., 1942; M.A., Butler U., 1949; Ph.D., Mich. State U., 1963; m. Doreen Elizabeth Swaim, May 6, 1945; children—David Edwin, Daniel Richard, Paul William, Deborah, Timothy. Staff accountant Keller, Kirschner, Martin & Clinger, Columbus, O., 1942-45; asso. prof. accounting Butler U., 1946-51, 54-56; treas. Motor Express, Inc., Indpls., 1951-52; asso. prof. econs. and bus. adminstrn. Muskingum Coll., New Concord, O., 1952-54; prof. accounting Bowling Green (O.) State U., 1956—, chmn. dept., mem. grad. faculty, 1960—. Ordained to ministry Disciples of Christ Ch., 1949. C.P.A., Ohio, Ind. Mem. Am. Inst. C.P.A's, Ohio Soc. C.P.A.'s Financial Execs. Inst., Am. Accounting Assn. Author: (with Gilbert Cooke) Business Financial Management, 1967. Contbr. articles to profl. jours. Home: 258 S Church St Bowling Green OH 43402

BOMSTAD, GERALD, Jr., corp. exec.; b. 1927; student Mlps. Bus. Coll., also U. Cal.; married. Accountant, office mgr. Tribune Printing Co., 1949-52; with Automation Industries Inc., and predecessors, 1952—, treas., controller, 1968—. Address: Automation Industries Inc 1901 Building Century City Los Angeles CA 90067*

BONACCOLTO, GIROLAMO, ophthalmologist; b. Italy, 1899; s. Giuseppe and Anna (Viola) B.; B.S., Coll. City N.Y., 1919; M.D., Royal U., Rome, Italy, 1926; m. Patricia Ethel McKenzie, June 1943. Clin. prof. ophthalmology N.Y. U.; asso. clin. prof. ophthalmology Columbia, 1946-48; cons. ophthalmologist Manhattan Eye, Ear and Throat Hosp.; dir. ophthalmology St. Clare's Hosp., now dir. emeritus; attending ophthalmologist Univ. and Bellevue hosps.; cons. ophthalmologist Kings Park (N.Y.) State Hosp., N.Y. Police Dept., 1932, Correction Hosps., N.Y.C., Columbus Hosp., Mother Cabrini Hosp. Mem. bd. SSS, 1941-47. Decorated comdr. Order Merit (Italy), 1966; recipient citation scoll Am. Legion, 1968. Diplomate Am. Bd. Ophthalmology. Fellow A.C.S., Am. Acad. Ophthalmology and Otolaryngology, Internal. Coll. Surgeons, N.Y. Acad. Medicine, Am. Acad. Compensation Medicine, Pan Am. Assn. Ophthalmology, Soc. Francaise d'Optalmologie, Soc. Mexico de Oftal. (hon.), Central Ill. Soc. Ophthalmology and Otolaryngology (hon.), Central N.Y. Eye, Ear, Nose and Throat Soc. (hon.), A.M.A., Assn. Research Ophthalmology, N.Y. Ophthalmological socs. Clubs: Metropolitan, New York University (N.Y.C.). Contbg. author Principles and Practice of Ophthalmic Surgery (Spaeth). Contbr. articles to profl. jours. Translator: Fundus Oculi (di Marzio). Office: 123 E 61st St New York City NY 10021

BONADIO, FRANK, labor union ofcl.; b. Pitts., Mar. 19, 1904; s. Felice and Amelia (Torchia) B.; ed. pub. schs.; m. Carmela Doccolo, June 1, 1930; children—Felice A., Francis Charles, Joseph James. Bus. agt. for local of Sheet Metal Workers Union, 1936-48, internat. rep., 1948-54, v.p., 1956-60; v.p., treas. Balt. Bldg. and Trades Council, 1941-42; sec.- treas. bldg. and constrn. trades dept. AFL-CIO, 1954—. Mem. Nat. Joint Bd. Settlement Jurisdictional Disputes, 1949-54. Democrat. Roman Catholic. Home: 3203 Beverly Rd Baltimore MD 21214 Office: 815 16th St NW Washington DC 20006

BONAFEDE, VINCENT IGNATIUS, physician; b. Buffalo, Mar. 5, 1906; s. Joseph and Providence (Anselmo) B.; M.D., U. Buffalo, 1930; m. Carolyn Constantine, Sept. 18, 1943; children—Virginia Isabel, Mary Lee. Intern, Allied Sisters Hosps., Buffalo, 1930-31; resident Meyer Meml. Hosp., Buffalo, 1931; asst. physician St. Lawrence State Hosp., Ogdensburg, N.Y., 1931-32; asst. physician, sr. psychiatrist, supervising psychiatrist Craig State School, Sonyea, N.Y., 1933-52, asst. dir., 1952-60, dir., 1960—; cons. psychiatrist Mt. Morris TB Hosp., 1935-71; psychiatrist Elmira Reformatory, 1959-63. Med. examiner S.S.S., 1943-71. Chmn., Sonyea Community Chest, 1941-50; exec. bd. Genesee council Boy Scouts Am., 1967-71. Diplomate Am. Bd. Psychiatry and Neurology (psychiatry). Fellow Am. Psychiat. Assn. (certified mental hosp. adminstr.), Am. Assn. on Mental Deficiency; mem. A.M.A., N.Y. State (pres. 7th dist. br. 1965-67), Livingston County (past pres.) med. socs., Am. Epilepsy Soc., Central N.Y. Psychiat. Soc., Neuron Club (sec. 1959-71), Assn. Med. Rehab. Dirs. and Coordinators (med. rehab. dir.). Republican. Roman Catholic. K.C., Elk, Rotarian (past pres. Mt. Morris, gov.'s aide Dist. 712, 1961-62). Address: Craig State School Sonyea NY 14556

BONAN, SEON PIERRE, constrn. co. exec., realtor; b. N.Y.C., Feb. 6, 1917; s. Salvator and Matilda (Fox) B.; B.S., Columbia, 1938; LL.B., Bklyn. Law Sch., 1946; m. Janet Ross, Apr. 22, 1948; children—Elizabeth Janet, Charles Sauveur, Virginia Allegra. Admitted to N.Y. bar, 1946; dir., mem. exec. com. Williams-McWilliams Industries, New Orleans, 1955-56; pres. Charles River Park, Inc., Boston, 1956—, Univ. Towers Inc., New Haven, 1957-61, Thomas Jefferson Sq. Corp., Phila., 1958-61, Cadman Plaza North, Inc., Brooklyn Heights, 1961—, Whitman Close Corp., Brooklyn Heights, 1961—, Phoenix Urban Corp. Mass., 1960—, Bonan Equity Corp., N.Y.C., 1961—; partner urban renewal project Joint Venturer S.E. Quadrant, Stamford, Conn., 1960—, Kern Site, Detroit, 1970; a pioneer organizing, financing and constrn. housing devel., urban redevel. projects. Trustee, Greenwich (Conn.) Acad.; adviser N.Y. Council Civic Affairs. Served to lt. USNR, 1941-46. Recipient Congl. Record tribute, 1966. Mem. Young Pres. Orgn. Clubs: Bass River (Mass.) Yacht; Burning Tree Country (Greenwich). Home: Dublin Hill Greenwich CT 06830 Office: 122 E 42d St New York City NY 10017

BONANSEA, BERNARDINO MARIA, author, educator; b. Pinerolo, Turin, Italy, Sept. 27, 1908; s. Joseph and Josephine (Savino) B.; grad. Studio Liceale, Casale Monf. (Italy), 1927; postgrad. Studio Teologico, Turin, 1927-28; grad. Collegio Internazionale (S.Antonio, Rome, Italy), 1928-31; M.A., Cath. U. Am., 1952, Ph.D., 1954. Came to U.S., 1950. Prof. English, religion, music Cath. Middle Sch., Changsha, Hunan, China, 1933-48; prof. Italian, Hunan Province Music Sch., Changsha, China, 1946-47; supt. Cath. Schs., Archdiocese of Changsha, 1940-48; asst. prof. philosophy Siena Coll., Loudonville, N.Y., 1955-57; instr. Cath. U. Am., Washington, 1957, asst. prof., 1958, asso. prof., 1960, prof. philosophy, 1964—; supt. Cath. Hosp., Changsha, 1945-48; prof. English, Cath. Nursing Sch., Changsha, 1946-48; vis. prof. St. John's U., Jamaica, N.Y., 1968. Sec. Hunan Province Cath. Relief Com., China, 1945-48; sec. ad interim Apostolic Delegation, Washington, 1954, 60. Named Lector Generalis by Minister Gen. of Order of Friars Minor, 1960. Mem. Am. Cath. Philos. Assn., Renaissance Soc. Am. Author: The Theory of Knowledge of Tommaso Campanella, 1954. Editor: Duns Scotus: The Basic Principles of His Philosophy, 1961; Tommaso Campanella: Renaissance Pioneer of Modern Thought, 1969. Co-editor: John Duns Scotus, 1265-1965, 1965; translator, editor: My Conversations with Teilhard de Chardin on the Primacy of Christ, 1971. Contbr. articles to philos. mags. and encyclopedias. Home: 1400 Quincy St NE Washington DC 20017

BONAWITZ, IRVING MAURICE, educator; b. Nanticoke, Pa., Oct. 17, 1923; s. Maurice I. and Margaret (Carbonovage) B.; B.S., Bowling Green (O.) State U., 1949; M.B.A., Northwestern U., 1951; D.B.A., Mich. State U., 1964; m. Barbara H. Anderson, May 19, 1959 (div.); children—Steven C., Douglas I. Asst. controller Rauland-Borg Corp., Chgo., 1953-55; partner John Seybold & Co., C.P.A.'s, Chgo., 1955; dir. Grad. Sch. Pub. Accounting, Northeastern U., Boston, 1963-64; chmn. accounting dept. Bus. Sch., Fla. Atlantic U., Boca Raton, 1964-66; prof., chmn. accounting dept. Bus. Sch., State U. N.Y., Albany, 1968—. Served with USAAF, 1943-45; CBI. C.P.A., D.C., Ill., Ohio. Mem. Am. Accounting Assn., Am. Inst. Decision Scis., Am. Inst. C.P.A.'s, Financial Execs. Inst., Nat. Assn. Accountants, Inst. Mgmt. Scis., Beta Alpha Psi, Beta Gamma Sigma, Kappa Sigma. Home: 105 Ten Eyck Pl Guilderland NY 12084 Office: Accounting Dept Bus Sch State U NY Albany NY 12084

BONAZZA, BLAZE ODELL, educator; b. Hancock, N.Y., Aug. 20, 1921; s. Joseph and Phoebe (Odell) B.; A.B., Cornell U., 1943; M.A., Los Angeles State Coll., 1954; Ph.D., U. So. Cal., 1961; m. Marion Sweeney, Feb. 3, 1945; children—Marita, Lisa (Mrs. Keith Esher Davis). Mem. faculty Cerritos Coll., Norwalk, Cal., 1959-64, Fullerton (Cal.) Jr. Coll., 1957-59, Cal. State Coll. at Fullerton, 1964-66; prof. English, chmn. dept. Cal. State Coll. at Long Beach, 1966—. Mem. Modern Lang. Assn., Phi Beta Kappa, Phi Kappa Phi, Alpha Phi Delta. Author: Shakespeare's Early Comedies, 1965; Studies in Fiction, 1971; Studies in Drama, 1968; Read and Write, 1965. Home: 21661 Dirigo Circle Huntington Beach CA 92646

BONBRIGHT, CARL W., banker; b. Muncie, Ind., 1896; ed. Princeton, 1918; LL.D., Alma Coll., 1961. Chmn. bd., dir. Genesee Mchts. Bank & Trust Co., Flint, Mich.; dir. Gen. Foundry Mfg. Co., Grand Trunk Western Ry. Trustee emeritus Alma Coll. Home: 2700 Parkside Dr Flint MI 48502 Office: Genesee Towers E 1st St Flint MI 48502

BONBRIGHT, DANIEL CHARLES, mgmt. cons.; b. Cin., Sept. 1, 1909; s. Stephen Stone and Ellen (Kennelly) B.; B.S. in Bus. Adminstrn., Ohio State U., 1933; J.D. magna cum laude, U. Detroit, 1942; m. Janet Stewart Smith, Nov. 6, 1942; children—Daniel Charles, Bruce. Sec. Investment Counsel Inc., Detroit, 1933-37; chief examiner Mich. Corp. and Securities Commn., 1937-42; admitted to Mich. bar, 1942, Cal. bar, 1946; chief renegotiation sect. Detroit ordnance dist. War Dept., 1942-45; vice chmn. bd., dir., gen. counsel, chief financial officer Capitol Records Inc., Hollywood, Cal., 1945-66; mgmt. cons., Honolulu, Hollywood, 1966—. Instr. econs., bus. adminstrn. and law U. Detroit, Wayne State U., Detroit Sch. Tech., 1934-39, 45; prof. bus. law U. Hawaii, 1967—. Vice pres., bd. dirs. Hollywood Bowl Assn., 1949-63; pres. Hawaii Opera Theatre, 1970; bd. dirs. Honolulu Symphony Assn. Mem. Am. Bar Assn., Honolulu Power Squadron (comdr. 1971), Theta Chi, Gamma Eta Gamma, Beta Gamma Sigma. Kiwanian (pres. Hollywood 1952), Rotarian (pres. Waianae 1971). Clubs: Waikiki Yacht, Hawaii Yacht; Hollywood Yacht. Address: Box 925 Waianae HI 96792

BONBRIGHT, JAMES CUMMINGS, educator; b. Evanston, Ill., Dec. 5, 1891; s. Daniel and Alice D. (Cummings) B.; B.S., Northwestern U., 1913, LL.D., 1956; Ph.D., Columbia, 1921; m. Martha Jane Earnest, Apr. 4, 1933; children—Alice Vivian (Mrs. John F. Merrifield), James C., Daniel Irving. With Bonbright & Co., investment bankers, N.Y.C., 1913-14; instr. econs. Columbia, 1920-21, asst. prof. finance, 1921-23, asso. prof., 1923- 27, prof. finance in grad. sch. bus., prof. emeritus, 1960—, on grad. faculty polit. sci., 1927—, also Ford Found. faculty fellow. Cons. econ. asst. President's Inquiry Commn., 1917-18; mem. N.Y. Commn. Revision Pub. Service Commns. Law, 1929-30; econ. cons. Com. on Interstate and Fgn. Commerce, Ho. of Rep. investigation of ry. holding cos., 1930; trustee Power Authority State N.Y., 1931-46, vice chmn., 1934-39, chmn., 1943-46; mem. Gov.'s com. on N.Y. State's Power Resources, 1959. U.S. del. World Power Conf., Stockholm, 1933. Trustee Tchrs. Ins. and Annuity Assn., 1943-46. Mem. Am. Econ. Assn., Am. Assn. U. Profs., Am. Acad. Arts and Scis., Am. Philos. Soc., Wranglers, Phi Beta Kappa. Author numerous books. Contbr. Columbia Law Rev. and econ. jours. Home: 29 Claremont Av New York City NY 10027

BONCHER, HECTOR PETER, former mfg. exec.; b. Luxemburg, Wis., Apr. 13, 1904; s. Hector and Catherine (Arendt) B.; Comml. Engr., U. Cin., 1928; m. Elizabeth Day, Jan. 27, 1939; children—William H., John D. Sales mgr. Dresser Mfg. div., Bradford, Pa., 1938-42, gen. mgr., 1942-55; operating v.p. Dresser Industries, Inc., Dallas, 1955-59, v.p. marketing, 1959-66, v.p. pub. relations, 1966-69. Home: 9507 Meadowbrook Dr Dallas TX 75220

BOND, ARTHUR CHALMER, educator; b. Salem, W.Va., Feb. 14, 1917; s. Arthur Chalmer and Agnes Lydia (Ashdon) B.; B.S., Mich. State U., 1939; M.S., U. Mich., 1940, Ph.D., 1951; m. Lulu Eleanor Bradley, Mar. 10, 1945; 1 son, Charles Bradley. Research asst. NDRC. OSRD research projects, U. Chgo., 1941-46; asst. prof. chemistry U. Rochester (N.Y.), 1951-57; faculty Rutgers U., New Brunswick, N.J., 1957—, prof. chemistry. 1967—. Mem. Am. Chem. Soc. (asst. editor Jour. 1951-57), A.A.A.S., Sigma Xi. Asst. editor Jour. Phys. Chemistry, 1951-57. Home: 27 Meadowbrook Lane Piscataway NJ 08854 Office: Dept Chemistry Rutgers State U NJ New Brunswick NJ 08903

BOND, ARTHUR STANLEY, Jr., real estate co. exec.; b. Oconto, Wis., June 29, 1927; s. Arthur Stanley and Ida M. (Van Valkenbrugh) B.; A.B. cum laude, Lake Forest (Ill.) Coll., 1949; J.D., U. Mich., 1952; m. Patricia R. Bowen, Aug. 4, 1951; children—Arthur Stanley III, Cathy Ann, Diana Louise. Admitted to Mich. bar, 1952; mem. corp. sec.'s and orgn. staff Chrysler Corp., 1952-54, asst. sec., 1964-65, sec., 1965-69; v.p. Chrysler Realty Corp., Detroit, 1969—. Alumni bd. govs. Lake Forest Coll., 1966—. Served with USNR, 1945-46. Mem. Mich. Bar Assn. Clubs: Detroit Athletic, Detroit Boat; Oakland Hills Country (Birmingham, Mich.). Home: 30897 Lincolnshire E Birmingham MI 48010 Office: 341 Massachusetts St Detroit MI 48231

BOND, CHARLES RANKIN, Jr., air force officer; b. Dallas, Apr. 22, 1915; s. Charles Rankin and Nola (Turner) B.; grad. USAAF Pilot Tng. Sch., 1939; B.S. in Mgmt. Engring., Tex. A. and M. Coll., 1949; grad. Air War Coll., 1951; m. Doris Inez Walker, Sept. 14, 1942; children—Rebecca Ruth (Mrs. Reid Henderson), Cynthia Sue (Mrs. Charles Rogers Gilmer), Mary Jean, Charles Rankin III. Commd. 2d lt. U.S. Army Air Force, 1939, advanced through grades to maj. gen., 1958; mem. Am. volunteer group in China, Flying Tigers, 1941-42; chief current operations div. Hdqrs. Air Def. Command, 1949; chief air def. plans br., dir. plans, orgn. and requirements Hdqrs. Continental Air Command, 1949-50; mem. U.S. Mil. Mission to USSR, 1943-44; dir. air def. Newfoundland, 1951-54, dir. operations U.S. N.E. Command, 1952, comdr. 64th Air Div., 1954-54; asst. dep. operations Hdqrs. Continental Air Def. Command, 1954-55; acting dep. operations CONAD, 1955; comdr. 25th Air Div., McCord AFB, Wash., 1957-59, 28th Air Div., Hamilton AFB, Cal., 1959-60; dep. comdr. 5th Allied Tactical Air Force, 1960-63; vice comdr. 9th Air Force, 1963-66; dep. comdr. 7th AF/13th AF Hdqrs., Udorn RTAFB, Thailand, 1966-68, comdr., 1968—. Decorated Legion of Merit with oak leaf cluster, Distinguished Flying Cross (Eng.); 5th Order Cloud Banner, 7 Star Wing medal (China); Order Southern Cross (Brazil); named Outstanding Dallasite, Dallas Jr. C. of C., 1942. Mgm. Daedalian Soc., Tau Beta Pi. Office: Hdqrs USAF The Pentagon Washington DC 20000

BOND, DONALD FREDERIC, former educator; b. Frankfort, Ind., Nov. 27, 1898; s. Jesse Fred and Almeda (Norris) B.; Ph.B., U. Chgo., 1922, A.M., 1923, fellow, 1929, Ph.D., 1934; m. Judith Strohm, Sept. 1, 1927; children—James, Deborah. Instr. English, Washington U., St. Louis, 1923, asst. prof., 1924-28; mem. faculty U. Chgo., 1930-67, asst. prof., 1940-47, asso. prof., 1947-52, William H. Colvin research prof., 1961-62, now prof. emeritus; vis. prof. No. Ill. U., 1969-71. Mem. Palos Park (Ill.) Library Bd., 1943-58; chmn. com. on curriculum Citizens Com. Edn., 1949; mem. bd. edn. Cook County High Sch. Dist. 230, 1948-58. Guggenheim fellow, 1958-59, 66-67. Mem. Modern Humanities Research Assn., Bibliog. Soc., Internat. Assn. U. Profs. English, Modern Lang. Assn. Am., Phi Beta Kappa, Lambda Chi Alpha. Republican. Episcopalian. Author: books including: A Reference Guide to English Studies, 1962; The Spectator, a critical edit., 5 vols., 1965; The Age of Dryden, 1970; Critical Essays from the Spectator, 1970. Editor: A Critical Bibliography of French Literature (Vol. 4; with G.R. Havens), 1951. Editorial bd. Modern Philology, 1952-59, editor, 1959-67. Author articles and revs., profl. jours. Home: 501 Balra Dr El Cerrito CA 94530

BOND, DOUGLAS DANFORD, physician; b. Waltham, Mass., July 2, 1911; s. Earl Danford and Grace (Newson) B.; A.B., Harvard, 1934; M.D., U. Pa., 1938; fellow Inst. of Pa. Hosp., 1940-41; research fellow in physiology Harvard Med. Sch.; 1941-42; D.Sc., U. Heidelberg, 1953; m. Helen Cannon, July 3, 1937; children—Peter Danford, Thomas Cannon, Sharon, Barbara. Resident psychiatry Butler Hosp., Providence, 1939-40; candidate Boston Psychoanalytic Inst., 1941-42; chief lab. psychiatry, Sch. Aviation Medicine, Randolph Field, Tex., 1942-43; chief div. psychiatry 1st Central Med. Establishment, 8th Air Force, 1943-45; Central Med. chief cons. in psychiatry Army Air Forces, Washington, 1945; prof. psychiatry Case Western Res. U. Med. Sch., 1945—, Cleve., head dept., 1945-69, dean Med. Sch., 1959-66, dir. psychiatry Univ. Hosps. 1945-69. Expert cons. to sec. of army on personnel mgmt., 1946; cons. in psychiatry to med. dir. of VA, 1946-48. Mem. adv. bd. A.R.C., 1948—; mem. com. neuropsychiatry Nat. Research Council 1940-51; mem. adv. com. psychiatry USPHS, 1954-59; adv. com. to dir. NIH, 1965-69; mem. bd. sci. counsellors Nat. Inst. Mental Health, 1966—. Pres., Grant Found., 1966—. Mem. Am. Psychoanalytic Assn. (sec. 1955-57), Ohio Psychiat. Assn. (pres. 1952-53), A.M.A., Am. Psychiat. Assn., Ohio Med. Assn., Cleve. Acad. Medicine, Med. Consultants of World War II, Am. Acad. Arts and Scis. Clubs: Union; 50 (Cleve.); Century Assn. (N.Y.C.); Harvard. Author: Love and Fear of Flying, 1952. Contbr. chpt. in Teaching Psychotherapeutic Medicine, 1948; also articles on physiology and psychiatry to pubs. Home: 3017 Fairmount Blvd Cleveland Heights OH 44118 Office: University Hospitals Cleveland OH 44106

BOND, EDWARD LUPTON, Jr., advt. exec.; b. Clarksboro, N.J., July 18, 1913; s. Edward Lupton and Hannah (Peaslee) B.; grad. George Sch., 1931; student Washington and Lee U., 1931-35, N.Y. U., 1935-36; m. Ruth Lee Lambie, Feb. 19, 1943; children—Linda, Candace. Account exec. Young & Rubicam, Inc., N.Y.C., 1946-53, v.p., account supr., 1953-58, v.p., dir. contact dept. (now account mgmt. dept.), 1958-59, sr. v.p., dir. contact dept., mem. exec. com., 1959-61, exec. v.p., gen. mgr., 1961- 63, pres., 1963-68, chief exec. officer, 1965-70, chmn. bd., 1968—, also dir.; mem. E. Midtown adv. bd. Mgrs. Hanover Trust Co. Mem. commerce information adv. com. U.S. Dept. Commerce, adv. council Religion in Am. Life, information com. Com. Econ. Devel., nat. adv. com. Hampshire Coll.; chmn. com. N.Y. Met. Area, U.S. Savs. Bond Drive, 1971. Trustee, mem. exec. com. Nat. Council Crime and Delinquency; bd. dirs. N.Y. chpt. A.R.C., Nat. Multiple Sclerosis Soc., Internat. Exec. Services Corp., Nat. Alliance Businessman, Thunderbird Grad. Sch. Internat. Mgmt.; adv. bd. Young Ams. for Responsible Action, Council Financial Aid to Edn.; sec. bd. dirs. Council Better Bus. Burs. Served to maj. 45th Inf. Div., AUS, World War II. Mem. Am. Assn. Advt. Agys. (chmn. 1968-69). Bus. Council for Internat. Understanding (dir.), Internat. C. of C. (trustee U.S. council), Econ. Club N.Y., Exec. Assn. Grad. Sch. Bus. of Columbia, Commerce and Industry Assn. N.Y. (dir.), Internat. Radio and TV Soc. Mem. Soc. Friends. Clubs: Union League, Pinnacle (N.Y.C.); Blind Brook, New York Yacht. Home: Belden Hill Rd Wilton CT 06897 Office: 285 Madison Av New York City NY 10017

BOND EUGENE F., appliance mfg. co. exec.; b. Chgo., Feb. 21, 1913; s. William L. and Florence (Young) B.; B.A., U. Ill., 1934; m. Barbara Johnson; children—Sharon (Mrs. Gaylord D. Clark), Linda G. (Mrs. Robert Matson), Terrell J. Accountant, Frigidaire div. Gen. Motors Corp., Chgo., 1937-39, Utility Sales & Engring. Co., Oak Park, Ill., 1939-42; accountant Sunbeam Applicance Service Co., Chgo., 1948-51, v.p., 1951-60, also dir.; v.p. internat. operations Sunbeam Corp, Chgo., 1963—; dir. Sunbeam Corp. (Can.), Ltd., 1960-63, now dir., Republican. Presbyn. Home: 23762 Av Barbizon W Oak Brook IL 60521 Office: Sunbeam Corp 5400 W Roosevelt Rd Chicago IL 60650

BOND, FLOYD ALDEN, economist, educator; b. Farmington, Mich., Aug. 20, 1913; s. Isaac and Ada C. (Wolfe) B.; A.B. cum laude, honors in econs. (Mandlebaum fellow), U. Mich., 1938, A.M., 1940, Ph.D., 1942; m. Jean E. Marrow, June 29, 1939; children—Richard Alden, Robert Lowell. Faculty dept. econs. Ann Arbor, U. Mich., 1938-46, faculty Horace H. Rackham Grad. Sch., 1942-46, dean, prof. bus. econs. Grad. Sch. Bus. Adminstrn., 1960—; asso. prof. econs. Carleton Coll., 1946-48, acting chmn. dept. econs., spring 1948; prof. econs. on Stedman-Sumner Found., chmn. dept. econs. Pomona Coll. 1948-60, Distinguished prof., 1955-60, dir. Social Sci. Research Center, 1951-55, chmn. Social Sci. div., 1951-52; prof. econs. Claremont Grad. Sch., 1948-60. Dir., Clark Equipment Co. (exec. com.), Nat. Bank of Jackson (Mich.), Asso. Corp. N.Am., Hayes-Albion Corp., Mass. Mut. Mgmt. Realty Investment Trust. Bd. dirs. U. Hawaii Conf. on Econ. Edn., 1953, Cal. Conf. on Econ. Edn., 1951, 54, 56, Nat. Pilot Program of Residential confs. on Liberal Arts for Bus. Execs., 1956-60; vis. prof. U. Wis., 1955, U.B.C., 1958; dir. bus.-edn. div. Com. for Econ. Devel., 1959-60; cons. So. Cal. Research Council, 1952-60; trustee Joint Council on Econ. Edn., 1960-70, Cal. Council Econ. Edn. (vice chmn. 1953-60); exec. sec. Nat. Task Force Econ. Edn. 1961. Fed. Res. Banking fellow, 1950; Ford Found. faculty fellow, 1954-55. Mem. Western (sec.-treas. 1951-52, v.p. 1953-54, pres. 1956-57), So. Cal. (trustee 1956-60), Midwest (v.p. 1947-48), Am. econ. assns., Am. Assn. U. Profs. (pres. Asso. Colls. chpt. 1953-54), Am. Assn. Collegiate Schs. Bus. (sec.-treas. 1966-67, v.p. 1967-68, pres. 1968-69), Sphinx (hon.), Katholepistemiad, Phi Beta Kappa (pres. Gamma chpt. of Cal. 1950-51), Phi Eta Sigma, Phi Kappa Phi. Author: Public Regulation in Action, 1948; (with others), Our Needy Aged, 1954, Preparation for Business Leadership—Views of Top Executives, 1964; also articles in profl. jours. Home: 2533 Londonderry Rd Ann Arbor MI

BOND, GEORGE HOPKINS, Jr., lawyer; b. Syracuse, N.Y. Oct. 28, 1909; s. George Hopkins and Florence (Woodford) B.; A.B., Williams Coll., 1933; LL.B., Syracuse U., 1936; m. Margaret Wade, Oct. 22, 1931 (div. 1939); children—Suzanne, Margot; m. 2d, Sally Van Santvoord Pyle, May 24, 1940 (dec. Sept. 1947); children—Anita, George, Sari; m. 3d, Ulla Ouchterlony, Aug. 9, 1949; 1 dau., Margrethe. Admitted to N.Y. bar, 1936, since practiced in Syracuse; partner firm Bond, Schoeneck & King, 1941—. Sec., dir. Syracuse China Corp. Trustee Everson Mus. Served to lt. comdr. USNR, 1942-45. Mem. Am., N.Y. State (head young lawyers sect. 1941), Onondaga County bar assns., S.A.R., Delta Kappa Epsilon, Phi Delta Phi. Mason. Clubs: Century (Syracuse); DKE, Racquet and Tennis (N.Y.C.); Church Street Social (Millbrook, N.Y.) Home: Shore Acres Cazenovia NY 13035 Office: State Tower Bldg Syracuse NY 13202

BOND, HAROLD LEWIS, educator; b. Newton, Mass., July 19, 1920; s. Harold Charles and Alice (Dixon) B.; A.B., Dartmouth, 1942; Ph.D., Harvard, 1955; m. Nancy Ewart, Nov. 16, 1946; children—Katherine, Carolyn, Annie, Elizabeth. Instr. English, Mass. Inst. Tech., 1947-48, Wellesley Coll. 1951-52; mem. faculty Dartmouth, 1952—, prof. English, 1960—, chmn. dept., 1963-67. Served to capt., inf., AUS, 1942-45. Decorated Silver Star, Bronze Star with oak leaf cluster. Mem. Modern Lang. Assn. Author: The Literary Art of Edward Gibbon, 1960; Return to Cassino, 1964; also articles. Home: Box 594 Hanover NH 03755.

BOND, HORACE MANN, ednl. adminstr.; b. Nashville, Nov. 8, 1904; s. Dr. James and Jane (Browne) B.; A.B., Lincoln U., Pa., 1923, LL.D., 1941; A.M., U. Chgo., 1926, Ph.D., 1936; LL.D., Temple U., 1952; m. Julia Agnes Washington, Oct. 11, 1930; children—Jane Marguerite, Horace Horace Julian, James George. Head dept. of edn., Langston U., Okla., 1924-27; dir. of extension, Ala. State Coll., 1927-28; instr. Fisk U., Nashville, 1928-29, asst. prof., 1932-34, head and prof., dept. of edn. 1937-39; research asst. Julius Rosenwald Fund, 1934-37; pres. Fort Valley State Coll., Ga., 1939-45; pres. Lincoln U., 1945-57, pres. hon., 1957—; dean Sch. Edn., Atlanta U., 1957-66, dir. bureau of ednl. and social research, 1966—; summer lectr. Tuskegee Inst., Ala., 1929, Garrett Biblical Inst., Evanston, Ill., 1943. Mem. Joint Army and Navy Com.; staff mem. UNESCO seminar, Ashbridge, Eng., summer 1948; ednl. survey West Africa, 1949, 60-61. Chmn. bd. Am. Soc. African Culture; mem. bd. dirs. Southeastern Ednl. Corp. Recipient Ednl. Research Assn. Am. award for book, Education in Alabama; A Study in Cotton and Steel, 1940; Susan Colver Rosenberger prize for outstanding thesis in social science, U. of Chicago, 1936. Author: The Education of the Negro in the American Social Order, 1934; Education in Alabama, A Study in Cotton and Steel, 1936; The Search for Talent. Contbr. profl. jours. Home: 361 Westview Dr SW Atlanta, GA 30310. Office: 223 Chestnut St SW Atlanta GA 30314

BOND, HORATIO LOCKERBY, cons. safety engr.; b. Barnstable, Mass., Nov. 30, 1900; s. Horatio Simmons and Ella Jessup (Lockerby) B.; S.B., Mass. Inst. Tech., 1923; m. Dorothy Anderson Gere, Sept. 21, 1925. Asst. econs. Mass. Inst. Tech., 1923-24; engr. Nat. Fire Protection Assn., 1924-39, chief engr., 1939-69; cons. engr. to various cities and govt. coms., 1969—. Mem. corp. Mass. Inst. Tech., 1954-59. Mem. Internat. Assn. Chiefs Police, Internat. Assn. Fire Chiefs (hon.) Nat. Acad. Scis. (com. on fire research of NRC 1956-65), Am. Water Works Assn., Am. Soc. Pub. Adminstrn., Nat. Fire Protection Assn. (hon.), Fire Protection Assn. Britain, Soc. Fire Protection Engrs., Inst. Fire Engrs. Britain (hon.), Alumni Assn. Mass. Inst. Tech. (pres. 1953-54). Mason, Club: Hyannisport (Mass.). Editor and author technical books and articles. Address: PO Box 393 Hyannis Port MA 02647

BOND, JOSEPH DIXON, r.r. ofcl.; b. Ft. Worth, Feb. 13, 1908; s. Dixon John and Amy (Kitzmiller) B.; student U. Minn., 1924-28; m. Harriet E. Lovett, Aug. 25, 1934; children—Dixon J., Marsha P., Joseph Dwight. With M., St.P. & S.S.M. Ry., 1928—, beginning as clk. accounting dept., successively asst. to comptroller, asst. to v.p. and gen. mgr., asst. to pres. and co. sec., gen. mgr., 1956-58, dir., 1957—, v.p., 1958-60, exec. v.p., 1961—; dir. Belt Ry. Chgo., Minn. Transfer Ry. Co., St. Paul Union Depot Co., Tri State Land Co., Midland Nat. Bank of Mpls., Packers Car Line Co., Mackinac Transp. Co., Midland Continental R.R.; pres. Soo System Radio Corp. Mem. adv. bd. Salvation Army. Bd. dirs. Abbott-Northwestern Hosp. Mem. Nat. Def. Transp. Assn. (dir.), Citizens League Mpls., Theta Xi. Republican. Presbyn. Clubs: Minneapolis; Western Railway (Chgo.). 4506 Sunnyside Rd Minneapolis, MN 55424. Office: Soc Line Bldg Minneapolis MN 55440

BOND, JOSEPH FRANCIS publishing co. exec.; b. Troy, N.Y., Feb. 17, 1927, s. John A. and Catherine (Waters) B.; B.B.A. cum laude, Siena Coll., Loudonville, N.Y., 1950; m. Jane A. Powers, Oct. 4, 1952; children—Joseph Francis, Mary Marcia, John Matthew, Mary Louise. With Behr-Manning, Inc., Troy, 1950- 57; with Gen. Electric Co., 1957-60, Gen. Aniline & Film Corp., Renssalaer N.Y., 1960-62; controller Crowell Collier and Macmillian, Inc., 1963-67, v.p., 1966-67, sr. v.p. finance, 1967-68, exec. v.p., dir., 1968—, also dir. subsidiaries. Bd. dirs. Rennssalaer County chpt. A.R.C., 1955-57, Troy Area Community Chest, 1957-60. Served with USNR, 1945-46. Mem. Financial Execs. Inst. (dir. N.Y.C. chpt.), Am. Mgmt. Assn., Nat. Assn. Accountants (dir. 1961-62, mgmt. accounting practices com. 1970—). Clubs: Economic (N.Y.C.); Plainfield Country. Home: 756 Norgate Westfield, NJ. Office: 866 3d Av New York City NY 10022

BOND, JULIAN, legislator, civil rights leader; b. Nashville, Jan. 14, 1940; s. Horace Mann and Julia Agnes (Washington) B.; B.A., Morehouse Coll., 1971; LL.D., Dalhousie U., 1969, U. Bridgeport, 1969, Wesleyan U., Conn., 1969, U. Ore., 1969, Syracuse U., 1970, Eastern Mich. U., 1971, Tuskegee Inst., 1971, Howard U., 1971, Morgan State U., 1971, Wilberforce U., 1971; D.C.L., Lincoln U., 1970; m. Alice Louise Clopton, July 28, 1961; children—Phyllis Jane, Horace Mann, Michael, Jeffrey, Julia. A founder Com. Appeal for Human Rights, 1960, exec. sec., 1961; a founder Student Nonviolent Coordinating Com., 1960, communications dir., 1961-66; reporter, feature writer Atlanta Inquirer, 1960-61, mng. editor, 1963; mem. Ga. Ho. of Reps. from Fulton County, 1965—; barred from house because of Vietnam statements, 1966; U.S. Supreme Ct. ruled his Constl. rights were violated, 1966. Bd. dirs. So. Conf. Edn. Fund, Robert F. Kennedy Meml. Fund, So. Regional Council, Highlander Research and Edn. Center, Nat. Sharecroppers Fund, So. Elections Fund, Delta Ministry project Nat. Council Chs., Voter Edn. Project, New Democratic Coalition. Mem. N.A.A.C.P., So. Corr. Reporting Racial Equality Wars. Office: 361 Westview Dr SW Atlanta GA 30310

BOND, KENNETH EDWARD, food co. exec.; b. Waynesboro, Miss., June 15, 1939; s. Robert Cecil and Willie Sarah (Jones) B.; B.S., Centenary Coll., 1961; m. Gail Elizabeth Stimpert, June 3, 1960; children—Beth Margaret, William Shea. Sr. Accountant Peat-Marwick, Mitchell & Co., Houston, 1964-67; successively internal auditor, mgr. financial services, asst. sec., mgr. evaluations and planning, corporate sec. Riviana Foods Inc., Houston, 1967—; dir. Riviana Internat. Inc., Cisco Foods, Inc.; partner Difersified Bus. Services, Internat. Marketing Assos., Documents Handling Ltd. Served to capt. AUS, 1962-64. Mem. Am. Inst. C.P.A.'s, Kappa Alpha. Methodist (res. bd.). Home: 1901 Bolsover St Houston TX 77005 Office: PO Box 2636 Houston TX 77001

BOND, LEWIS HONYMAN, banker; b. Ashport Tenn.; July 31, 1921, s. Lewis H. and Ruth (Bowman) B.; B.S. in Petroleum Engring., U. Okla., 1947; m. Le Kathrin Ozbirn, June 7, 1947; children—Kathrin, Susan Lee, Jane Ann. Petroleum engr. Stanolind Oil & Gas Co., 1947-52; petroleum engr. Ft. Worth Nat. Bank, 1952-53, asst. v.p., petroleum engr., 1953-54, v.p., petroleum engr., 1954-59, pres., dir., 1959—; pres., dir. Fort Worth Nat. Corp.; dir., mem. exec. com. State Res. Life Ins. Co., Ft. Worth; dir. Tex & Pacific Ry. Co., Millers Ins. Group. Trustee Austin Coll.; bd. dirs. Tarrant County United Fund, pres., 1962-63; bd. dirs. Fort Worth's Progress, Inc., Downtown Fort Worth Assn., Tex. Christian U. Research Found., Carter Blood Center, Southwestern Expn. and Fat Stock Show; trustee Saint Joseph Hosp., Ft. Worth Country Day Sch. Mem. Ft. Worth C. of C. (past pres., bd. dirs.), Res. City Bankers Assn. (mem. pub. relations com.), Am. Bankers Assn. (state v.p. Tex.), Tex. Bankers Assn. (mem. legislative com.), Texas Research League (dir., mem. adv. com.), Pi Kappa Alpha, Tau Beta Pi, Sigma Tau. Presbyn. (elder). Club: Ft. Worth. Home: 429 Rivercrest Dr Fort Worth TX 76107 Office: PO Box 2050 Fort Worth TX 76101

BOND, NILES WOODBRIDGE art museum adminstr.; b. Newton, Mass., Feb. 25, 1916, s. George Wood and Clara Mehitabel (Bonney) B.; A.B., U. N.C., 1937; A.M., Fletcher Sch. Law and Diplomacy, Medford, Mass., 1938; m. Julia Rice Folsom, June 25, 1940; children—Ellen Dudley, Nancy Kenneth. U.S. fgn. service officer, 1939-68; vice consul, Havana, Cuba, 1939-40, Yokohama, Japan, 1940-41, interned in Japan upon outbreak of war, repatriated on S.S. Gripsholm, Aug. 1942; 3d sec., vice consul, Madrid, Spain, 1942- 45, 2d sec., 1945-46; adviser to U.S. delegation to 4th session Econ. and Social Council, 1947; 2d sec., vice consul, Bern, Switzerland, 1947, 1st sec. and consul, 1947; asst. chief div. N.E. Asian affairs, Dept. State, 1947-49, officer in charge Korean affairs, 1949-50; adviser to U.S. delegation to 4th session UN Gen. Assembly, 1949; 1st sec. Office of U.S. Polit. Adviser to Supreme Comdr. Allied Powers, Tokyo, Japan, 1950; acting chmn. Allied Council for Japan, 1952; counselor embassy, Tokyo, 1952, Seoul, Korea, 1953-54, Rome, Italy, 1956-58; dir. Office UN Polit. and Security Affairs, Dept. State, 1954-56; counselor of embassy, vis. lectr. Bologna Center, Johns Hopkins, 1957-58; research fellow Center for Internat. Affairs, Harvard, 1958-59; minister-counselor embassy, Rio de Janeiro, Brazil, 1959-63; coordinator interdeptl. seminar Dept. State, 1963; minister, consul gen., São Paulo, Brazil, 1964-68; asst. sec. bd. trustees, sec. bd. govs. Corcoran Gallery Art, Washington, 1970—. Adviser, São Paulo Bienal, 1969. Clubs: Marco Polo (N.Y.C.); University (Washington). Author: Arcanum (poetry), 1965; Elegos (poetry), 1967. Home: 2440 Virginia Av NW Washington DC 20037 Office: Corcoran Art Washington DC 20006

BOND, RICHARD GUY educator, civil engr.; b. Beecher Falls, Vt., Dec. 9, 1916, s. Richard Henry and Annie (Bassett) B.; B.S. in Civil Engring., U. N.H., 1938; M.S. in San. Engring., U. Ia., 1940; M.P.H., U. Minn., 1948; m. Betty Telford Wells, Sept. 29, 1953, Pub. health engr. Ia. Dept. Health, 1940-47; vis. lectr. U. Minn. Sch. Pub. Health, 1943-45, 47-48; asst. prof. civil engring. Cornell U., 1947-49; faculty U. Minn., Mpls., 1949—, prof. Sch. Pub. Health, 1958—. dir. environmental health and safety, 1949-62, dir. environmental health div., 1962—. Cons. in field, 1958—; chmn. planetary quarantine adv. com. Am. Inst. Biol. Scis., 1966—; lectr. seminar community health workers from overseas Central Council Health Edn., Britain, 1964; mem. 3d Nat. Conf. Pub. Health Tng., 1967; health planning adv. council Minn. Planning Agy., 1967—; campus safety assn. Nat. Safety Council, 1955-62. WHO travel fellow S.E. Asia, 1960. Registered profl. engr., Minn., Ia. Diplomate Am. Acad. Environmental Engrs. Fellow Am. Pub. Health Assn. (gov. council 1962-65, 69—, chmn. hosp. facilities com. 1955-65), Am. Soc. C.E., Royal Soc. Health Britain (hon.); mem. Pub. Health Insps. Assn. Britain (hon.), Am. Coll. Health Assn. (gov. council, exec. bd. 1958-64; Ruth E. Boynton award 1968), Health Physics Soc., Nat., Minn. socs. profl. engrs., Water Pollution Control Fedn., Alpha Tau Omega. Episcopalian. Club: Campus (Univ. Minn.). Home: 3307 48th Av S Minneapolis MN 55406

BOND, RICHARD RANDOLPH, coll. pres.; b. Lost Creek, W. Va., Dec. 1, 1927; s. Harley Donovan and Marcella (Randolph) B.; B.S., Salem Coll., 1948; M.S., W. Va. U., 1949; Ph.D. (NSF fellow 1952-53), U. Wis., 1955; m. Reva Stearns, Apr. 20, 1946; children—H. David, Philip S., Josette, Michael R. Asst. prof. biology Milton (Wis.) Coll., 1949-51; asso. prof. biology Salem Coll., 1955-58, dean men, 1957-58; vis. investigator R.B. Jackson Lab., summer 1958; Mich. fellow Coll. Adminstrn., U. Mich., 1958-59; dean faculty Elmira (N.Y.) Coll., 1959-63, asso. prof. biology, 1959-65; prof. acad. adminstrn. Cornell U., Ithaca, N.Y., 1963-66, coll. curriculum specialist Cornell Team to U. Liberia, acting dean Coll. Liberal Arts, 1963-64, chief of party Cornell Project Team, 1964-66; v.p. acad. affairs, dean faculty, prof. zoology Ill. State U., 1966-71; pres. U. No. Colo. at Greeley, 1971—. Chmn. acad. council Conf. Midwestern Univs. Trustee, Salem Coll. Served with AUS, 1946-47. Recipient Outstanding Young Men of Am. award, 1965. Fellow A.A.A.S.; mem. Ecol. Soc. Am., Am. Ornith. Union, Assn. Higher Edn., Soc. Animal Behavior and Sociobiology, Sigma Xi, Alpha Phi Omega. Contbr. articles to profl. jours. Home: 1862 10th Av Greeley CO 80631

BOND, ROLAND S., corp. exec.; b. Van Alstyne, Tex., 1898. Dir., Pan Am. Sulphur Co., Consumers Gas Co., Pioneer Am. Ins. Co.; chmn. bd. Bond Oil Corp. Home: 4600 Brookview Dr Dallas TX 75220 Office: 2600 Republic Nat Bank Bldg Dallas TX 75201

BOND, THOMAS JACKSON, educator, chemist; b. Ennis, Tex., Aug. 16, 1912; s. John Henry and Frances (Puckett) B.; B.S., North Tex. State U., 1938, M.S., 1939; Ph.D., U. Tex., 1950; m. Edith Lyle Gorman, June 3, 1939; children—Anedith (Mrs. Jeffrey E. Nash), Thomas Jackson, Robert Gorman. Instr. chemistry Tex. Coll. Arts and Industries, Kingsville, 1941-43; faculty Baylor U., Waco, Tex., 1943—, prof. chemistry, chmn. dept., 1965—. Mem. Am. Chem. Soc., Am. Soc. Biol. Chemists, Sigma Xi. Mason. Spl. research growth factors, intermediate metabolism, comparative studies effects chem. carcinogens and non-carcinogens on essential cell constituents. Home: 209 Harrington Waco TX 76706

BOND, VAN HUGO, army officer; b. Gardner, Tenn., Apr. 30, 1908; s. John Benjamin and Heyttye (Kesselus) B.; student Vanderbilt U., 1926-27; B.S., U.S. Mil. Acad., 1931; m. Judith Octavia Carter, Aug. 17, 1947; 1 son, John Charles. Commd. 2d lt. U.S. Army, 1931, advanced through grades to maj. gen., 1961; comdr. 39th Inf. Regt., World War II; dir. manpower mgmt. Dept. Army, 1958-60; dir. Joint Mil. Assistance Adv. Group, Korea, 1960-62; comdg. en. XXI U.S. Army Corps, 1963—. Decorated Silver Star (4), Legion of Merit (2), Bronze Star medal with two oak leaf clusters, Purple Heart. Mem. Assn. U.S. Army, Res. Officers Assn., Delta Tau Delta. Club: Army-Navy Country (Arlington, Va.) Office: Hdqrs XXI US Army Corps IGMB Anneville PA 17003

BOND, WILLIAM HENRY, librarian, educator; b. York, Pa., Aug. 14, 1915; s. Walter Loucks and Ethel (Bossert) B.; A.B., Haverford Coll., 1937; M.A., Harvard, 1938, Ph.D., 1941; m. Helen Elizabeth Lynch, Dec. 6, 1943; children—Nancy Barbara, Sally Lynch. Research fellow Folger Shakespeare Library, 1941-42; asst. to librarian Houghton Library, Harvard, Cambridge, Mass., 1946-48, curator manuscripts, 1948-61, librarian, 1965—; lectr. bibliography Harvard, 1964-67, prof., 1967—; asst. keeper manuscripts Brit. Mus., 1952-53. Trustee, Emerson Meml. Assn., 1964—, Heritage Found., Deerfield, Mass., 1965—, Concord (Mass.) Free Pub. Library, 1966-71. Served to lt. USNR, 1943-46. Fellow Am. Acad. Arts and Scis.; mem. Bibliog. Socs. London (hon. sec. for Am.), Am., Assn. Internat. de Bibiophilie, Grolier Club, Club of Odd Volumes, Am. Antiquarian Soc., Mass. Hist. Soc., Colonial Soc. Mass., The Johnsonians, Phi Beta Kappa. Club: Century Assn. Editor: (Christopher Smart) Jubilate Agno, 1954; Supplement to Census of Medieval and Renaissance Manuscripts in the United States, 1962; The Houghton Library, 1942-67, 1967; Records of a Bibliographer, 1967; 18th Century Studies in Honor of Donald F. Hyde, 1970. Home: 109 The Valley Rd Concord MA 01742 Office: Houghton Library Cambridge MA 02138

BOND, WILLIAM LEWIS, aerospace exec.; b. Detroit, Jan. 3, 1934; s. Joseph B. and Vesta (Rogers) B.; B.S., U. Ill., 1958; m. Delores Dee Smith, Mar. 16, 1956; children—Cynthia, Mark, David, Joseph. Sr. staff accountant Price Waterhouse & Co., Chgo., 1958-63; staff asst. Amphenol Electronics Corp., Chgo., 1963-65; controller Information Supplies Corp., Chgo., 1965-66; v.p. finance Hayes Internat. Corp., Birmingham, Ala., 1966—. Served with AUS, 1953-55. Mem. Financial Execs. Inst. (sec. Birmingham chpt.), Phi Kappa Sigma. Home: 3744 Rockhill Rd Mountain Brook AL 35223 Office: PO Box 2287 Birmingham AL 35201

BOND, WILLIAM ROBERT, iron and steel co. exec.; b. Pitts., Feb. 28, 1912; s. Robert Coster and Harriet (Bowman) B.; B.S. in Metall. Engring., U. Pitts., 1935; m. Grace Carrico (dec.); children—Robert W., Anne Penelope, William Gregory; m. 2d, Lucile Turner, Feb. 26, 1953. With Crucible Steel Co. Am. 1935-46; gen. supt. Lone Star Steel Co., 1947-49, gen. mgr., 1949- 50, v.p. operations, 1950-54; v.p. operations, dir. Woodward Iron Co. (Ala.), 1958-68; pres. Woodward Div., exec. v.p. Mead Corp. (merger Mead Corp. and Woodward Corp.), 1968—; dir. So. Ry. System, 1st Nat. Bank Birmingham, Am. Smelting and Refining Co. Recipient Johnson award for contbns. to blast furnace tech., beneficiation E. Tex. iron ores, 1952. Mem. Am. Inst. Mining Engrs., Iron and Steel Inst., Am. Foundryman Soc., Eastern States, Chgo. Dist. blast furnace assns., So. Research Assn. (trustee). Home: 3508 Redmont Rd Birmingham AL 35213 Office: Woodward Iron Co Woodward AL 35189 also 118 W 1st St Dayton OH 45402

BONDA, ALVA TED, car rental and service industry exec.; b. Cleve., June 1, 1917; s. Jacob Nathan and Nettie (Wasserman) B.; student pub. schs.; m. Marie C. Ermisch, Oct. 27, 1940; children—Penny (Mrs. Merrill Solomon), Joel, Thomas. Owner, operator car rental bus., 1945-49; pres. Airport Parking Co., 1949-68; chmn. bd. dirs. Avis Rent a Car, also ITT Consumer Services Corp., Cleve., 1968—. Active Nat. Conf. Christians and Jews, Jewish Community Fedn., Jewish Welfare Fund, Glenville YMCA, Cleve. Police Athletic League. Chmn. bd. Bellefaire Home, 1966-71; fellow Brandeis U., 1970—. Served as sgt. AUS, 1941-45. Mem. Am. Soc. Travel Agts. Clubs: City, Oakwood Country (Cleve.). Home: 2 Bratenahl Pl Cleveland OH 44108 Office: 1700 Investment Plaza Cleveland OH 44114

BONDE, RUTH LILLIAN, home economist, educator; b. Bloomington, Minn., Feb. 25, 1905; d. Gottfrid and Caroline (Holt) Bonde; student State Teachers Coll., St. Cloud, Minn., 1922-24; B.S., U. Minn., 1936, postgrad., 1947; M.S., Ia. State Coll., 1940; postgrad. U. Chgo., summers, 1938, 44, 45. Teacher, Clarissa (Minn.) pub. schs., 1924-25, Janesville (Minn.) 1925-28, Mpls., 1928-37; instr. Iowa State Coll., Ames, 1937-40; asst. prof. Pa. State Coll., State College, 1940-43; asso. prof., dir. family life edn. Macalester Coll., 1943-44; Ida C. Cook prof. home econs. Northwestern U., Evanston, Ill., 1944—. Ofcl. rep. 10th Internat. Congress on Home Econs., Paris, 1963, 11th, Bristol, Eng., 1968. Bd. dirs. Assn. for Family Living, 1962-70. Mem. Am. Sociol. Soc., Am. Assn. U. Profs., Am. (sec. 1949-51), Ill. (pres. 1952-54) home econs. assns., Nat. Council Family Relations, Am. Econ. Assn., A.A.A.S., Internat. Enseignement Menager, Nat. Council Adminstrs. Home Econs. (pres. founding orgn. 1960-63), Omicron Nu, Phi Upsilon Omicron. Author: Management in Daily Living, 1944. Editor and contbr.: The Individual, Marriage and the Family, 1962, 67. Home: 1511 Hinman Av Evanston IL 60201

BONDS, ALFRED BRYAN, Jr., coll. pres.; b. Monroe County, Ark., Nov. 3, 1913, s. Alfred Bryan Sr. and Nellie Belle (Hasley) B.; A.B. Henderson State Tchrs. Coll., Arkadelphia, Ark., 1935; M.A., La. State U., 1936, postgrad., 1936-38, Julius Rosenwald fellow, U. N.C., 1940-41; LL.D., Ohio Wesleyan U., Cleve.-Marshall Law Sch., 1956; m. Georgianna Arnett, Feb. 23, 1939; children—Anna Belle, Alfred Bryan, III, Alexandra Burke, Stephen Arnett. Asst. to dean Grad. Sch., La. State U, 1936-41; coordinating officer So. Grad. Sch. Survey and Work Conf., Tulane U., 1941-42; chief ednl. surveys br. Nat. Roster Sci. and Specialized Personnel, War Manpower Commn., Washington, 1942-43; chief edn. div. retraining and re-employment adminstrn., U.S. Dept. Labor, 1946; asst. exec. sec., Pres.'s Commn. on Higher Edn., 1946-48; dir. tng. AEC, Washington, 1948-49; Ark. commr. edn., Little Rock, 1949-53; chief U.S. Ednl. Commn., Egypt, co-dir. Egyptian-Am. Joint Commn. for Edn., 1953-55; pres. Baldwin-Wallace Coll., 1956—. Cons. FSA; council advisers U.S. Commn. Edn.; gov.'s adviser Council on Land Utilization; mem. exec. com. Bd. Control for So. Regional Edn.; dir. Ark. Tchrs. Retirement System; mem. Cleve. Com. Higher Edn.; bd. dirs. Cuyahoga Co. Library, Lake Erie Jr. Mus., St. Luke's Hosp., Cleve., YMCA, Cleve. Mem. World Council on Methodism; v.p. Ohio Council Chs.; mem. coordinating council Gen. Conf. Meth. Ch.; mem. program council Gen. Conf. Meth. Ch.; delegate to World Meth. Council, London, England, 1966, World Family Life Conf., London, 1966, del. to Consultation on Evangelism, World Meth. Council, Frankfurt, 1970. Trustee Lake Erie Opera Assn. Served from ensign to lt. (s.g.) USNR, 1943-46. Decorated officer's cross Order of Merit (West Germany); recipient medal of honor Nat. Assn., League of New England Women. Mem. Ohio Coll. Assn. (pres. 1970), Am. Soc. Internat. Law, Am. Polit. Sci. Assn., N.E.A., Am. Assn. Sch. Adminstrs., Ark. Edn. Assn., Phi Gamma Mu, Omicron Delta Kappa. Methodist. Rotarian, Mason (33). Clubs: Union, University, Midday. Prepared basic plan and survey for UNESCO publs., Study Abroad, 1948. Editor: Essays on Southern Life and Culture, 1941. Contbr. articles to profl. jours. Home: 329 Beech St Berea OH 44017

BONDS, MARGARET, pianist, composer works including: Spiritual Suite for Piano, The Ballad of the Brown King, Migration, 3 Dream Portraits, The Negro Speaks of Rivers, Peter and the Bells, Mass in D. Troubled Water. Home: 4373 S Van Ness Av Los Angeles CA 90062

BONDURANT, ARTHUR POLK, ret. distillery exec.; b. Bristol, Tenn., Feb. 6, 1907; s. George Edward Caldwell and Mary Mildred (Caines) B.; B.S., Washington and Lee U., 1928; postgrad. Yale, 1948; grad. Advanced Mgmt. Program, Harvard Sch. Bus. Adminstrn., 1952; m. Frances Lee Day, June 30, 1934 (dec. June 1962); 1 dau., Mary Chiles; m 2d, Elizabeth Hillerich, Aug. 2, 1963; 1 stepdau., Mary Ward. Sales promotion Reynolds Metals Co., N.Y.C., 1929-33; advt. mgr. Glenmore Distilleries Co., Louisville, 1934-42, v.p., 1946-67, 1st v.p., 1967-70, marketing cons., 1970—; dir., 1958—; dir., marketing cons. Hillerich & Bradsley, sporting goods mfrs., Louisville. Past dir. Summer Opera, Better Bus. Bur. Served as lt. col. USAAF, World War II. Decorated Legion of Merit. Mem. Air Tech. Service Command Supply Div. Alumni Assn. U.S. Air Force (pres. 1950-54), C. of C. (past dir.), Bourbon Beef Cattle Assn. (dir.). Episcopalian (past sr. warden). Clubs: Louisville Country, Pendennis, Advertising, Harvard (Louisville); Moraine Country (Dayton, O.); Army-Navy (Washington); Little Harbor (Harbor Springs, Mich.); Wequetonsing Golf (Mich.); University (N.Y.C.). Home: 504 Ridgewood Rd Louisville KY 40207

BONDURANT, BYRON LEE, educator; b. Lima, O., Nov. 11, 1925; s. Earl Smith and Joy Koneta (Gesler) B.; student Case Inst. Tech., 1943-44, Rensselaer Poly. Inst., 1944; B.S. in Agrl. Engring., Ohio State U., 1949; M.S. in Civil Engring., U. Conn., 1953; m. Lovetta May Alexander, Feb. 28, 1944; children—Connie Jane (Mrs. John Jaycox), Richard Thayne, Cindy Lynn. Dist. agrl. engr. western N.Y., N.Y. State Coll. Agr., Cornell U., 1949-50; instr. agrl. engring., extension agrl. engr., dept. agrl. engring. U. Conn., 1950-53; asso. prof. agronomy and agrl. engring., extension agrl. engr. dept. agronomy and agrl. engring. U. Del., 1953-54; prof. agrl. engring., head dept. U. Me., 1954-64; prof. agrl. engring. Ohio State U., 1964—, also adviser to dean, later dean Coll. Agrl. Engring., Ludhiana, India, 1964-67, 69-71. Registered profl. engr., Me. Fellow A.A.A.S.; mem. Indian Soc. Agrl. Engrs. (life), Am. Soc. Agrl. Engrs. (vice chmn. N. Atlantic sect. 1956-57, chmn. Acadia sect. 1961-62), Am. Assn. U. Profs., Am. Soc. Engring. Edn. (chmn. agrl. engring. div.) Nat., Me. (pres. 1963) socs. profl. engrs., Sigma Xi, Sigma Pi Sigma, Tau Beta Pi, Gamma Sigma Delta. Home: 2073 Neil Av Columbus OH 43210

BONDY, PHILIP KRAMER, physician, educator; b. N.Y.C., Dec. 15, 1917; s. Eugene Lyons and Irene (Kramer) B.; A.B., Columbia, 1938; M.D., Harvard, 1942; M.A. (hon.), Yale, 1961; m. Sarah B. Ernst, Mar. 18, 1949; children—Jonathan L., Jessica, Steven M. Intern Peter Bent Brigham Hosp., Boston, 1942-43; mem. staff Grady Meml. Hosp., Atlanta, 1943-48, chief resident medicine, 1947-48; faculty Emory U., 1947, 49-52, asst. prof. medicine, 1951-52; Alexander Browne Coxe fellow physiol. chemistry Yale, New Haven, 1948-59, faculty, 1948-49, 1952—, prof. medicine, 1961-65, C.N.H. Long prof. medicine, 1965—, chmn. dept. internal medicine, 1965-72, chmn. com. outpatient services, 1960-62. Mem. med. vis. com. Brookhaven Nat. Labs., 1969-72; mem. program project com. NIH-Nat. Inst. Arthritis and Mental Disease, 1964-68, chmn., 1966-68. Sec. library bd. Woodbridge, Conn., 1960-67. Served to capt., M.C., AUS, 1943-46. Recipient Edward Sutliffe Brainard prize Columbia, 1938; Research Career award NIH, 1962, 66. Fellow N.Y. Acad. Scis.; mem. Endocrine Soc. (councillor 1964-67, publs. com. 1965—, chmn. 1968—), Assn. Am. Physicians, Am. Soc. for Clin. Investigation, Am. Fedn. Clin. Research, Soc. Exptl. Biology and Medicine, Interurban Clin. Club, Laurentian Hormone Conf., Boylston Soc., Phi Beta Kappa, Sigma Xi, Alpha Omega Alpha. Editor-in-chief Jour. Clin. Investigation, 1957-62; editor Yearbook of Endocrinology and Metabolism, 1963-64; editorial bd. Conn. Medicine, 1959-61, Yearbook of Medicine, 1954—, Medicine, 1963—, Merck Manual, 1969—. Home: 9 Chestnut Lane Woodbridge CT 06525 Office: 333 Cedar St New Haven CT 06510

BONDY, PHILIP LEDERER, cigar co. exec.; b. N.Y.C., Mar. 12, 1910; s. Richard C. and Bessie (Gross) B.; student Choate Sch., 1924-28; m. Rae Emily Parish, Sept. 30, 1938; children—Sally Rae (Mrs. William T. Herndon), Susan Ann (Mrs. David Gordon Willoughby), Richard C., Sandra Lee. Salesman, Gen. Cigar Co., Inc., N.Y.C., 1929-49, v.p., 1949-61, dir., 1949—, sr. v.p., 1961-70, exec. v.p., 1970—. Mem. Brit. Admiralty Delegation, 1942-46. Recipient King's medal for service in cause of freedom, 1946. Mem. Masters of Foxhounds Assn., Goldens Bridge Hounds, Cigar Inst. Am. (dir.). Clubs: Sales Executives (N.Y.C.), Waccabuc Country (N.Y.), Desert Forest Golf (Carefree, Ariz.). Home: North Salem NY 10560 Office: 605 3d Av New York City NY 10016

BONDY, ROBERT EARL, social welfare cons.; b. Dover, Minn., Aug. 13, 1895; s. Robert William and Hannah Ida (Glidden) B.; grad. U. Chgo., 1917; m. Ruth Dunn, Sept. 10, 1917 (div. Aug. 1948); children—Ruth Eleanor, Robert Earl; m. 2d, Marjorie Knapp Workman, Sept. 18, 1948 (dec. Dec. 1967); stepchildren—Ann Workman Sheldon, Jenny Workman, Julia Workman Sterrett; m. 3d, Jeanne Hale, Aug. 5, 1968 (dec. June 1969). Mgr. soc. service bur. C. of C., Columbus, O., 1917-18; with A.R.C., Washington, 1919-39, dir. field service, dept. civilian relief, lake div., Cleve., 1919-20, asst. mgr. southwestern div., St. Louis, 1920-22, nat. dir. war service, Washington, 1922-27, mgr. eastern area, Washington, 1927-31, nat. dir. disaster relief, 1931-39, dir. reconstrn. Miss. Valley Flood Relief, 1927, dir. drouth relief Eastern States, 1930-31, exec. dir. cotton distbn. program, 1932-33, dir. relief operations, spring floods, 1936, asso. gen. dir. Ohio-Miss. Valley Flood Operations, 1937, Am. del. to League of Red Cross Socs., Internat. Conf. on Disaster Relief and Nursing, Paris, France, 1937, dir. relief operations New Eng. hurricane, 1938; dir. pub. welfare, D.C., Washington, 1939-41; adminstr. Services to Armed Forces, A.R.C., Washington, 1941-46; adminstrv. trips to ETO, PTO, 1943, 44, 45; dir. Nat. Social Welfare Assembly, N.Y., 1946-65; social welfare cons., 1966—; chmn. adv. council on participation of nat. orgns., mid-century White House Conf. on Children and Youth; vice chmn. 1960 White House Conf. on Children and Youth; chmn. sect. religion White House Conf. on Aging. Pres. Montgomery County Civic Fedn., 1933-35; chmn. Nat. Social Work Council, N.Y.C., 1940-45; chmn. welfare and consumer interest com. D.C. Council of Def., 1940-41; chmn. Nat. Com. on Service to Vets. 1944-46; cons. F.C.D.A., Dept. State, 1951-53; mem. bd. Am. Immigration Conf.; mem. adv. com. U.S. Displaced Persons Commn., 1948-53; chmn. Health and Welfare Adv. Council, AFL-CIO Community Services Com., 1959-66; mem. bd. Nat. Health and Welfare Retirement Assn., 1957-66; various coms. Nat. Council Chs. of Christ, chmn. commn. on social welfare, 1965-68; mem. consultation on role of churches in social service World Council of Chs., 1962. Trustee, Citizens Conf. on State Legislatures, 1964—. Served with U.S. Army, 1918. Mem. Nat. Assn. Social Workers, Nat. Conf. Social Welfare (various offices, coms. 1917—), Phi Gamma Delta, Sigma Delta Chi. Mem. bd. of deacons Riverside Ch., N.Y.C. Contbr. articles to A.R.C. and social work publs. Address: 31 W 10th St New York City NY 10011

BONE, ALFRED RUFUS, Jr., airline exec.; b. Chgo., Jan. 25, 1907; s. Alfred R. and Estelle Kennedy (Aldrich) B.; A.B., Bethany (W.Va.) Coll., 1928; m. Lois Mitchell, Jan. 20, 1933. With Am. Airlines and predecessor cos., 1928—, asst. to v.p. sales, 1937-39, western sales mgr., 1940-44, regional v.p., Los Angeles, 1944—; dir. McDanel Refractory Porcelain Co., San Joaquin Estates. Mem. Beta Theta Pi. Clubs: California, Annandale Golf, Bohemian (San Francisco). Home: 399 Mooresque Dr Pasadena CA 91105 Office: 7000 World Way W Los Angeles CA 90009

BONE, ARTHUR E., business exec.; b. 1914; student Mich. State Coll.; married. Regional mgr. Phillips Petroleum Co., 1936-47; asst. to pres. Suburban Propane Gas Corp., 1947-51; pres. Eastern Propane Gas. Co., 1951-59, Ugite Gas Inc., 1959—; exec. v.p. UGI Corp., 1968-71, pres., chief exec. officer, 1971—, also dir. Office: 1401 Arch St Philadelphia PA 19105*

BONE, HUGH ALVIN, Jr., polit. scientist, educator; b. Sycamore, Ill., Jan. 14, 1909; s. Hugh Alvin and Florence Lydia (Crowder) B.; B.A., North Central Coll., Naperville, Ill., 1931; M.A., U. Wis., 1935; Ph.D., Northwestern U., 1937; m. Elizabeth Browning Purdy, June 11, 1938; children—Christopher Hugh, William James. Teaching asst. Northwestern U., 1935-37; instr., asst. prof. U. Md., 1937-42, Queens Coll., N.Y.C., 1942-48; faculty U. Wash., Seattle, 1948—, prof. polit. sci., 1948—, chmn. dept., 1959-68. Summer vis. prof. Hunter Coll., 1944, Conn. Coll., 1946-48, Columbia, 1952, U. Hawaii, 1962; vis. prof. Stanford, 1949; research asso. N.Y. State Joint Com. Indsl. and Labor Conditions, 1945-48; dir. Wash. State-No. Ida. Center Edn. in Politics, 1952-71. Ford fellow, 1954-55. Mem. Am. (exec. council 1950-52), Western (pres. 1961-62), Pacific N.W. (pres. 1959-60) polit. sci. assns., Pi Gamma Mu, Pi Sigma Alpha, Author: "Smear" Politics: Analysis of 1940 Campaign Literature, 1941; Grass Roots Party Leadership, 1952; American Politics and the Party System, 1971; Party Committees and National Politics, 1958; co-author; Washington Politics, 1960; Politics and Voters, 1971. Home: 6001 51st St NE Seattle WA 98115

BONE, JACK NORMAN, coll. dean; b. Montrose, Colo., Feb. 10, 1919; s. James J. and Sarah (Rives) B.; B.S. in Pharmacy, U. Colo., 1941, M.S., 1948; Ph.D., U. Wash., 1953; m. Evelyn M. Pilon, Dec. 7, 1940; children—Jay, Timothy, Pharm. research blood fractionation Cutter Lab., Berkeley, Cal., 1941- 45; instr. pharmacy U. Colo., 1945-48; mem. faculty U. Wyo., 1948—, dean Coll. Pharmacy, 1966—, dean Coll. Health Scis., 1968—. Mem. Am., Wyo. pharm. assns., Sigma Xi, Rho Chi, Phi Delta, Chi. Contbg. author Husa's Pharmaceutical Dispensing, 5th and 6th edits., 1959, 66. Home: 2602 Park Laramie WY 82070

BONE, MAURICE EDGAR, lawyer; b. East St. Louis, Ill., Mar. 1, 1924; s. Edgar William and Margaret (Jett) B.; student Washington U., St. Louis, 1941-42; B.S., St. Louis U., 1947, J.D., 1951; m. Phyllis Jean Frick, June 5, 1955; children—Stephen, Gregory, Larry, David. Admitted to Mo. bar, 1951, Ill. bar, 1951; practice in St. Louis, 1951-53, East St. Louis, 1953-56, Bellville, 1956—; partner Kassly, Weihl & Bone and predecessor firms, 1956—. Partner, treas. 6400 W. Main Land Trust. Pres. St. Clair County Young Republicans, 1954. Served with USAAF, 1943-45, USAF, 1951-53. Decorated Air medal with four oak leaf clusters. Mem. Am., Ill., St. Clair County (pres. 1966-67) bar assns., Am. Trial Lawyers Assn. Clubs: East St. Louis Optimist (pres. 1956), East St. Louis Toastmasters (pres. 1957). Home: 9 Powder Mill Rd Bellville IL 62223 Office: 7705 W M St Bellville IL 62223

BONE, ROBERT GEHLMANN, ret. univ. pres.; b. Springfield, Ill., June 2, 1906; s. Eugene E. and Alice (Gehlmann) B.; A.B., Coll. of Wooster, 1928; A.M., U. Ill., 1932, Ph.D., 1937; certificate U. Freiburg-in-Breisgau, Germany, 1938; LL.D., Lincoln Coll., 1966, Ill. State U., 1968; m. Karin Levanius, Sept. 26, 1944; children—John Levanius, Robert Gehlmann. Tchr., Am. Coll., Alexandria, Egypt, 1928-31, acting dir., 1930-31; prof. history, dir. forensics Lincoln (Ill.) Coll., 1932-34; instr. history U. Ill., 1934-42; prof. history, head dept. Shrivenham Am. U., Eng., 1945-46; prof. history U. Ill., 1951-56; dir. div. spl. services for war vets, 1947-52, dir. div. gen. studies, 1946-52, acting dean Coll. Edn., 1952-53. asst. provost, 1954-56; pres. Ill. State U., Normal, 1956-67, now emeritus; vis. prof. Coll. of Wooster, 1969-71. Cons. Ford Found. Campaign chmn. Tb Seal, 1966-67. Pres. bd. dirs. Adlai E. Stevenson Lectures on Internat. Affairs, 1965-67, David Davis Meml. Home, 1960-65. Bd. mem. Inst. Oriental Students (Brent House) Chgo., 1938-48, U. YMCA, 1946-56; mem. Civil War Centennial Commn.; exec. com. Ill. Lincoln Sesquicentennial Commn. Mem. nat. com. on standards Nat. Council for Accrediting Tchr. Edn., mem. commn. on colls. and univs. North Central Assn.; bd. dirs. Ill. Certification Bd., 1958-62; chmn. Ill. Commn. Coll. Testing, 1959-67; trustee Winston Churchill Coll., Pontiac, Ill., 1965—; bd. dirs. Multiple Sclerosis Assn., 1965—; trustee Eureka (Ill.) Coll., 1968—; bd. regents Lincoln Acad. Ill., chancellor, 1968-71. Served as maj. A.C., AUS, 1942-46; ETO. Recipient Centennial Year Alumni award Coll. of Wooster, 1966; Educator of Year award Ill. Edn. Assn., 1966; Spl. Edn. award Ill. Congress Parents and Tchrs., 1966; Spl. Citizen award McLean County Jaycees, 1967, Outstanding Citizen award for Normal, 1968. Mem. Assn. State Colls. and Univs. (dir. 1963-67), Am. Assn. Colls. Tchr. Edn., Archeol. Inst. Am.,

N.E.A., Am. Assn. Higher Edn. (dir., nat. pres. 1956-57), Am., Ill. (dir.) hist. socs., Am. Assn. Coll. Tchrs. of Edn. (nat. com. on tchr. edn.), S.A.R., Phi Kappa Delta, Phi Kappa Phi, Zeta Psi, Phi Alpha Theta, Chi Gamma Iota, Kappa Theta Gamma, Phi Kappa Epsilon, Phi Alpha Phi, Phi Delta Theta, Alpha Tau Alpha, Alpha Phi Omega, Omicron Delta Kappa, Phi Eta Sigma. Presbyn. Author: Ancient History, 1939, rev. edit., 1955; Shrivenham American University, 1946. Home: 2 Clinton Pl Normal IL 61761

BONEBRAKE, ROY CONRAD, lawyer; b. Waynesboro, Pa., Dec. 2, 1906; s. Jacob M. and Lillie (Mickley) B.; A.B., Gettysburg Coll., 1928; LL.B., Stanford, 1932; m. Jean Aument, Dec. 24, 1939. Admitted to Cal. bar, 1932, N.Y., 1941; asso. firm Call & Murphey, Los Angeles, 1932-39; counsel, v.p. Newmont Mining Corp., N.Y.C., 1939—, also dir.; dir. O'ckiep Copper Co., Ltd.; chmn. bd. dirs., gen. counsel Magma Copper Co., N.Y.C., 1950—; v.p., dir., gen. counsel Newmont Oil Co.; dir. Foote Mineral Co., Palabora Mining Co. Ltd., Tsumeb Corp. Ltd., So. Peru Copper Corp., Carlin Gold Mining Co.; trustee Empire Savs. Bank Mem. Cal., N.Y. bar assns., Phi Beta Kappa. Home: 30 Sutton Pl New York City NY 10022 Office: 300 Park Av New York City NY 10022

BONER, CHARLES PAUL, constrn. co. exec.; b. Nocoma, Tex., Feb. 8, 1900; s. Charles Wilbur and Sally Elizabeth (Lee) B.; A.B., U. Tex., 1920, M.A., 1922, Ph.D., 1929; postgrad. (Whiting fellow) Harvard, 1927-28; m. Marian Oldfather, Sept. 9, 1930; children—Donald Stephen, Charles Randall, Richard Elwood. Tutor dept. physics U. Tex., Austin, 1920-22, instr., 1922-24, 25-27, adj. prof., 1928-35, asso. prof., 1935-36, prof., 1936-42, 45-70, dir. Def. Research Lab., 1945-65, cons. to dir. of lab., 1965-70, dean Coll. Arts and Scis., 1949-54, dean Univ., 1953-54, v.p. acad. affairs, 1954-57, exec. dir. Office Govt. Sponsored Research, 1949-54, 57-65; radio engr. A.E. Hancock Co., Austin, 1924-25; asso. dir. Underwater Sound Lab., Harvard, 1942-45; accoustical cons. in design broadcast studios, auditoriums and pub. bldgs., 1937—; partner C.P. Boner & Assos., Austin, 1968—. Expert cons., research and devel. bd. Dept. Def., 1948-53. Recipient Naval Ordnance Devel. award, 1945; certificate of appreciation OSRD, 1945; Joint Army-Navy certificate of appreciation, 1948. Fellow Acoustical Soc. Am. (exec. council 1947-50, pres. 1963), A.A.A.S., Tex. Acad. Sci., Audio Engring. Soc.; mem. Phi Beta Kappa, Sigma Xi, Sigma Pi Sigma (hon). Democrat. Baptist. Club: Town and Gown. Editorial bd. Rev. of Sci. Instruments, 1947-49. Contbr. tech. papers to jours. Home: 1508 Hardouin Av Austin TX

BONER, J. RUSSELL, editor; b. Boulder, Colo., July 25, 1930; s. J. Russell and Lillian (Morris) B.; B.A., Yale, 1952; m. Darryl Anne Alkire, Dec. 22, 1954; children—Allyn, Polly, Andrew Case. Reporter, Internat. News Service, Atlanta, 1956-57, bur. mgr., Hartford, Conn., 1957-58; staff reporter U.P.I., Hartford and Buffalo, 1958-59, Wall St. Jour., Chgo., Pitts. and London, Eng., 1959-70; editor-in-chief Internat. Mgmt. mag., London, 1970—. Served to 1st lt. USAF, 1952-56. Home: 61 Cadogan Pl London SW 1 England Office: McGraw-Hill House Maidenhead Berkshire England

BONESTEEL, CHARLES HARTWELL III, ret. army officer; b. Plattsburg, N.Y., Sept. 26, 1909; s. Charles H. and Caroline Mead (Hudson) B.; B.S., U.S. Mil. Acad., 1931; B.A. (Rhodes scholar), Oxford U., 1934; m. Alice M. Pratt, June 16, 1934; 1 son, Charles H. IV. Commd. 2d lt., U.S. Army, 1931, advanced through grades to gen., 1966; asst. resident engr. Bonneville Dam, 1936-37; war service, Europe, 1940-44; War Dept. rep. Council Fgn. Ministers, Paris, N.Y.C., Moscow, 1946-47; spl. asst. to under sec. of state, 1947-48; spl. asst. to ambassador at large Marshall Plan, 1948-50; def. mem. planning bd. NSC, 1953-56; sec. Gen. Staff, U.S. Army, 1958-60; asst. to chmn. Joint Chiefs of Staff, 1960-61; comdg. gen. 24th Inf. div. 1961-62, 7th Corps, 1962-63; dir. spl. studies Office Chief of Staff of Army, Washington, 1963-66; U.S. Army mem. UN Mil. Staff Com., 1966; sr. comdr. in chief UN Command, Korea, also comdg. gen. 8th U.S. Army, 1966-69; ret., 1969; cons. Stanford Research Inst. Trustee, Inst. Def. Analysis. Decorated D.S.M., Legion of Merit (U.S.); Order Brit. Empire; Croix de Guerre (France), Ulchi medal; Order of Nat. Service merit 1st class (Korea), Order of Cloud and Banner (Rep. of China); knight comdr. Most Exalted Order of White Elephant (Thailand). Mem. Assn. Am. Rhodes Scholars, Assn. U.S. Army (v.p. 1971—). Home: 1701 N Kent St Arlington VA 22209

BONET, FRANK JOSEPH, restaurant exec.; b. N.Y.C., Apr. 6, 1937; s. Frank and Alexandra (Roots) B.; B.A. magna cum laude, St. John's U., 1958, LL.B. (asso. editor law rev.), 1961; m. Mary Ellen Mathews, July 14, 1962; children—Catherine Ann, Frank Joseph, Elizabeth Mary, Jean Marie. With Horn & Hardart Co., N.Y.C., 1961—, corporate sec., head corporate legal dept., 1969—; sec. Neilsen Restaurants, Inc., The Neilsen Corp.; treas. Vendedge Corp. Capt. Merrick Democratic Club, 1965-68. Mem. Assn. Bar City of N.Y. Contbr. articles profl. jours. Home: 23 Chestnut St Merrick NY 11566 Office: 600 W 50th St New York City NY 10019

BONEY, LESLIE NORWOOD, Jr., architect; b. Wallace, N.C., Jan. 25, 1920; s. Leslie Norwood and Mary Lily (Hussey) B.; B.S. in Archtl. Engring., N.C. State U., 1940; m. Lillian Maxwell Bellamy, May 8, 1954; children—Emmett Hargrove Bellamy, Mary Grist Bellamy, Leslie Norwood III. Partner Leslie N. Boney, Architect, Wilmington, N.C., 1940-41, 45—. Mem. N.C. Exec. Mansion Fine Arts Com., 1966—; Exec. Com. N.C. Governor's Adv. Com. Beautification, 1966—; pub. relations com. N.C. State U., 1965—; mem. City-County Planning and Devel. Commn., 1960—; N.C. adv. com. U.N.C.-Charlotte New Coll. Arch., 1965—. Trustee Union Theol. Sem., 1948-68, St. Andrews Presbyn. Coll., 1954-70; pres. N.C. State U. Archtl. Found., 1953. Served to maj., C.E., AUS, 1941-45; PTO. Decorated Bronze Star. Fellow A.I.A. (pres. N.C. 1965, pres. Eastern N.C., 1956, jud. bd. 1971—, chmn. task force state govtl. affairs 1971—); mem. N.C. Planning Assn. (pres., 1965-66), N.C. State U. Gen. Alumni Assn. (pres., 1957-58), Lower Cape Fear Hist. Soc. (pres. 1960-61), Phi Kappa Phi. Presbyn. (ruling elder, moderator 1968). Mason. Principal works include N.C. Nat. Bank, 1969, New Hanover Meml. Hosp., 1966, Solomon Towers Apts. for Elderly, 1970, Creekwood South Housing Project, 1971, Dormitory, U. N.C., Wilmington, 1971, Coop. Savs. & Loan Assn., 1955 (all Wilmington); Rockingham Community Coll., Wentworth, N.C., 1966; Reid Ross High Sch., Fayetteville, N.C., 1968; Lenoir Community Coll., Kinston, N.C., 1968; Waccamaw Bank & Trust Co. Hdqrs. Bldg., Whiteville, N.C., 1969; Duplin Gen. Hosp., Kenansville, N.C., 1971; Residence Hall, Marietta (O.) Coll., 1965; Dormitories, N.C. State U. at Raleigh, 1967; Adminstrn. bldgs. E.I. Du Pont de Nemours Co., Inc., Brunswick County, Fayetteville, and Healing Springs, N.C., 1971. Home: 2305 Gillette Dr Wilmington NC 28401 Office: 120 S 5th St Wilmington NC 28401

BONGARTZ, ROY, writer; b. Providence, Dec. 8, 1924; s. Royal and Emma (Asplund) B.; B.A., Miami U., Oxford, O., 1950, M.A., 1951; m. Cecilia Leigh, June 15, 1955; 1 son, Joe Michael. Served with AUS, 1943-46. Author: (play) The Applicant, 1961; (stories) Twelve Chases on West Ninety-Ninth Street, 1965. Contbr. stories, articles to Sat. Eve. Post, New Yorker, Nation, New Statesman, others. Home: Foster RI 02825

BONGIE, LAURENCE LOUIS, educator; b. Turtleford, Sask., Can., Dec. 15, 1929; s. Louis Basil and Madalena (Pellizzari) B.; B.A., U.B.C., 1950; Ph.D., U. Paris (France), 1952; m. Elizabeth A.E. Bryson, July 14, 1958; 1 son, Christopher. Lectr. U.B.C., 1953-54, instr. II, 1954-56, asst. prof. French, 1956-61, asso. prof., 1961-66, prof., head dept., 1966—. Humanities Research Council fellow, 1955-56; Can. Council sr. fellow, 1963-64; recipient French medal, 1950. Mem. French, Internat., Am., Canadian socs. 18th Century studies. Club: University (Vancouver, B.C.). Author: David Hume, Prophet of the Counter-Revolution, 1965; also articles. Home: 3746 W 13th Av Vancouver 8 British Columbia Canada

BONGIOVANNI, ALFRED MARIUS, physician, educator; b. Phila., Sept. 22, 1921; s. Joseph Nathaniel and Elisa (DiSilvestro) B.; B.S., Villanova U., 1940; M.D., U. Pa., 1943. Investigator, Marine Lab., Woods Hole, Mass., 1939-41; instr. pharmacology Phila. Coll. Pharmacy and Sci., 1947-49; asst. physician Rockefeller Inst., 1949-51; asst. prof. Johns Hopkins Sch. Medicine, Balt., 1950-52; faculty U. Pa. Sch. Medicine, Phila., 1952—, prof. pediatrics, chmn. dept., 1963—; physician-in-chief Children's Hosp., Phila., 1963—; mem. staff Hosp. U. Pa., Phila. Gen. Hosp., Pa. Hosp., Children's Seashore House, Atlantic City, N.J.; pediatric dir. Elwyn Inst. Mem. sci. adv. bd. St. Jude's Hosp., Memphis; mem. com. research Am. Cancer Soc.; cons. Dept. Health, Welfare and Edn.; chmn. child devel. and mental retardation tng. rev. com. NIH; sci. adv. bd. Child Devel. Group Miss. Trustee South Jersey Med. Research Found. Recipient award League of Children's Hosp., Phila., 1962; Shaffrey medal St. Joseph's Coll., Phila., 1965; Mendel medal Villanova U., 1968. Fellow N.Y. Acad. Scis., A.C.P.: mem. Endocrine Soc. (Ciba award 1956), Am. Soc. Clin. Investigation, Am. Pediatric Soc., Am. Acad. Pediatrics (Mead Johnson award 1957, drug dosage com.), Pediatric Research Soc., Assn. Am. Physicians, Royal Soc. Medicine (affiliate), U.S. Pharmacopoeia, Alpha Omega Alpha (hon.). Presbyn. Club: Union League (Phila.). Editorial staff Pediatrics, Am. Jour. Med. Scis., Jour. Clin. Endocrinology and Metabolism. Contbr. articles to profl. jours. Home: 238 S 3d St Philadelphia PA 19106 Office: Children's Hosp of Phila 1740 Bainbridge St Philadelphia PA 19146

BONGO, ALBERT BERNARD, pres. Gabon Republic; b. Lewai, Gabon, Dec. 30, 1935; s. Basile Undimba and Jeanne Eboli; grad. comml. sect. College Technique de Brazzaville (Congo), 1958; m. Josephine Kama, Oct. 31, 1959; children—Alain, Albertine. Attache minister fgn. affairs, Libreville, Gabon, 1960-62; dir.-adj., then dir. charge information and tourism, Cabinet of Pres. of the Republic, 1962-64, dir. charge nat. def., 1964-65; minister charge nat. def. and coordination, 1965-66, charge information and tourism, 1966; v.p. govt., 1966-67; v.p. Republic, 1967, pres. Republic, 1967—. Founder, 1968, since sec.-gen. Parti Democratique Gabonais. Served with l'Armee de l'Air, 1958-60. Decorated grand croix, grand maitre Ordre de l'Etoile Equatoriale; grand croix Ordre National du Niger, grand croix Ordre National Tchadien; grand croix Ordre National de la Valeur du Cameroun; grand croix Ordre National Centrafricain du Merite; grand croix Ordre National Mauritanien de Merite; grand croix de l'Ordre Nat. de Cote d'Ivoire; grand croix de l'Ordre Nat. du Dahomey; grand croix Ordre National (Togolais) de Mono; grand cordon Ordre des Nuages Propices (Chine Nationaliste); grand cordon Ordre National du Leopard (Republique Democratique du Congo); grand cross St. George and St. Michael (Gt. Britain); grand croix Ordre National de la Legion d'Honneur, grand croix Ordre National du Merite (France). Club: Rotary. Address: Presidence de la Republique BP 546 Libreville Gabon

BONHAM, HOWARD BRYAN, editor, publisher; b. Vian, Okla., Dec. 11, 1900; s. Thomas Eldon and Addie (Coleman) B.; student Okla. U., 1921, E. Central Coll., 1922-23; m. Aubrey Estelle Combs, Apr. 21, 1925; children—Howard B., Jane Eldon. City editor Times Record, Fort Smith, Ark., 1924-27; corr. AP, 1926-27; news editor Muskogee Times Democrat, 1927; mng. editor Sapulpa (Okla.) Democrat News, 1928-30; staff A.R.C., 1931, dir. pub. relations, 1942, v.p. in charge pub. relations, 1945-51; editor and pub. East Okla. Tribune, Sallisaw; founder, pub. The County News, Warner, Okla., 1969—. Cons., Nat. Assn. Mental Health, N.Y.; founded and became exec. dir. U.S. Rating Bur., Washington. Chpt. chmn. A.R.C. Hon. adm. Ark. River Navigation dedication com., 1971. Mem. Nat. Inst. Social Scis. (N.Y.C.), Nat. Publicity Council for Health and Welfare Service (bd. dirs., mem. pub. relations com.), Nat. Social Welfare Assembly, Am. Pub. Relations Assn., Okla. Press Assn. Democrat. Mem. First Christian Ch. Rotarian (pres. 1968-69). Clubs: Hardscrabble Country (Fort Smith, Ark.); National Press (Washington); Town. Co-author: Your Public Relations. Home: 614 E Mary Av Sallisaw OK 74955 Office: East Oklahoma Tribune Sallisaw OK 74955

BONHAM, LEWIS F., pharm. co. exec.; b. Des Moines, Mar. 8, 1913; s. John Rhule and Rilla (Jolly) B.; A.B., Drake U., 1934; Ph. Sc., Hartwick Coll., 1964; m. Jean O'Neil, Sept. 15, 1935; children—Linda (Mrs. Wesley M. Buckner), John Rhule III. With Continental Oil Co., 1934-35, Joseph Dixon Crucible Co., 1935-37; merchandising mgr. Personal Products div. Johnson & Johnson, 1937-44; dir. sales and advt. Mennen Co., 1944-50; pres. Alfred D. McKelvy Co. div. Richardson-Merrill, Inc., 1950-54; pres., dir. Bourjois, Inc., 1954-58; pres. Barbara Gould, Inc. and Monico, Inc., 1954-58; v.p. dir. Miles Labs., Inc., Elkhart, Ind., 1958-62; pres. Miles Products div. Miles Labs., Inc., 1958-62; exec. v.p., dir. Norwich Pharm. Co., 1962-64, pres., 1964-69, vice chmn. bd., 1969—; pres., chief exec. officer, dir. Morton- Norwich Products, Inc., 1969—; dir. Morton Internat., Inc., 1970—; Morton Industries of Can., Ltd., 1970—, Canadian Salt Co., 1970—; chmn., pres. Norwich Inter-Am., Inc., Eaton Inter-Am., Inc., Austin Labs., Inc., Norwich Pharm. Co., Ltd.; chmn. Norwich Pharmacal Co. de Panama, Norwich Pharmacal Co. de Panama Surcusal de Colombia, Norwich Pharmacal Co. de Mexico, Eaton Ingram, S.A. de C.V., Texize Chems. Inc.; dir. Nat. Bank and Trust Co. Norwich, Orphahell, N.V. Mem. Assn. Nat. Advertisers, Advt. Fdn. Am., Audit Bur. Circulations, Advt. Council, Proprietary Assn. (pub. relations and finance coms., exec. com.), Pharm. Mfrs. Assn. (dir. 1968). Roman Catholic. Elk. Clubs: Ponte Vedra (Fla.); Hartford (Mich.) Hunt; Lost Pond; Union League; Chicago. Home: 610 Red Barn Lane Fox Point Barrington IL 60010 Office: 110 N Wacker Dr Chicago IL 60606

BONHARD, FLORENCE MADELEINE, educator; b. Cleve., May 18, 1900; d. Alfred and Rea (Weberman) Bonhard; A.B., Stanford, 1921; M.A., Columbia, 1927; Ph.D., U. So. Cal., 1946; postgrad. U. Mexico, summer 1923, Centro de Estudios Historicos, Madrid, Spain, 1930, U. Paris (France), 1931. Tchr., Inglewood (Cal.) High Sch., 1923-26, Poly. High Sch., Long Beach, Cal., 1927-30; asst. prof. Romance langs. Western State Tchrs. Coll., Kalamazoo, 1934-35; instr. French and Spanish, Glendale (Cal.) City Coll., 1935-36, Long Beach City Coll., 1940-42, 46-48; lectr. U. So. Cal., 1942-45; instr. Los Angeles City Coll., 1948-49; prof. Spanish, Los Angeles State Coll., 1949-65, prof. emeritus, 1965—, head dept. fgn. langs., 1959-64. Decorated Palmes Academiques (France). Mem. Modern Lang. Assn., Am. Assns. Tchrs. French and Spanish, Renaissance Soc. Am., Modern Lang. Assn. So. Cal., Fgn. Lang. Assn. No. Cal., Am. Assn. U. Profs., Alliance Francaise, Pi Lambda Theta (hon.), Sigma Delta Pi (nat. v.p. 1956-65), Pi Delta Phi. Mem. Nat. Womans Party. Contbr. articles in field. Spl. research on growth and devel. of French and Spanish in Middle Ages, contemporary novel Spain and Hispanic Am., French contemporary theatre. Home: 83 Fremont Pl Los Angeles CA 90005

BONI, ALBERT, publisher; b. N.Y.C., Oct. 21, 1892; s. Charles and Bertha (Seltzer) B.; ed. Cornell U., 1909-10; Harvard, 1910-12; m. Nell van Leeuwen, Sept. 14, 1917; 1 son, William F. Founded Washington Square Players, 1915, later the Theatre Guild; established the Little Leather Library, 1915-17, Boni and Liveright, 1917; Albert and Charles Boni, Inc., 1923, pres., 1923—. Invented Microprint and Readex reading projector; pres. Readex Microprint Corp., 1940—; chmn. bd. Readex Microprint Corp. (U.K.), Ltd. Founder Modern Library. Recipient citation Rochester Mus. Arts and Scis., 1944; Pioneer medal Nat. Microfilm Assn., 1961. Fellow Nat. Microfilm Assn., F.R.M.; mem. Am. Documentation Inst., A.L.A., Optical Soc. Am., Royal Soc. Photography, Soc. Motion Picture and Television Engrs., Soc. Photographic Scientists and Engineers. Editor: Modern Book of French Verse, 1920; A Guide to the Literature of Photography and Related Subjects, 1943; Photographic Literature-A Subject Catalogue and Index to two million books and articles, 1962. Co-inventor silver haloid film eliminating gelatin and capable of 200x reduction. Home: 59 W 12th St New York City NY 10011 Office: 5 Union Square New York City NY 10003

BONICA, JOHN JOSEPH, physician; b. Filicudi Messina, Italy, Feb. 16, 1917: s. Antonino and Angela (Zagame) B.; came to U.S., 1927, naturalized, 1928; student L.I. U., 1934-37; B.S., N.Y. U., 1938; M.D., Marquette U., 1942; m. Emma Louise Baldetti, June 7, 1942: children—Angela, Charlotte, Linda, John. Intern, St. Vincent's Hosp., N.Y.C., 1942-43, resident, 1943-44; practice medicine specializing in anesthesiology; attending anesthesiologist St. Joseph's Hosp., Med. Arts Hosp., Tacoma, 1947-60; dir. anesthesiology U. Wash. Med. Center, Seattle, 1960—, Harborview Med. Center, 1960—; dir. dept. anesthesiology Tacoma Gen. Hosp., 1947-63, Pierce County Hosp., 1947-63; clin. asso. dept. anatomy U. Wash., Seattle, 1948-60, prof., chmn. dept. anesthesiology, 1960—, dir. Pain Clinic, Med. Center and affiliated hosps., 1961—, dir. Anesthesia Research Center, 1967—. Vis. prof. lectr. various Am., European, Latin Am. univs.; sr. cons. anesthesiology Madigan Army Hosp., Ft. Lewis, Wash., VA Hosp., Seattle, No. Pacific Beneficial Assn. Hosp., Tacoma, McNeil Island Penitentiary; mem. anesthesia tng. com. NIH, 1965-69, chmn. gen. med. research program-project com., 1970—; cons. ministry of Health, Argentina, 1959-63, Brazil, 1955-69, Italy, 1954-59, Sweden, 1969—. Ministry Edn., Japan, 1969, Ministry Edn. and Health, Venezuela. Served from lt. to maj., M.C., AUS, 1944-46. Decorated commendatore Order of Merit (Italy); recipient Silver medal Swedish Med. Soc. Diplomate Am. Bd. Anesthesiology. Fellow Am. Coll. Anesthesiologists, Internat. Coll. Anesthetists, Am. Acad. Anesthesiology; mem. A.M.A., King County, Wash. State med. socs., Assn. Univ. Anesthetists (pres. 1969), A.A.A.S., World Med. Assn., Am. (pres. elect 1964-65, pres. 1965-66), Wash. State (pres. 1952) socs. anesthesiologists, Internat. Anesthesia Research Soc., Assn. des Anesthesiologistes Europeens (hon.), Soc. Academic Anesthesia Chairmen, Am. Assn. U. Profs., Assn. Am. Med. Colls., Am. Soc. Pharm. and Experimental Therapy; Royal Coll. Medicine, World Fedn. Socs. Anesthesiologists (chmn. sci. adv. com. 1968—), Alpha Omega Alpha, hon. mem. Cuban, Mexican, Italian (hon. pres. 1954), Argentinian (hon. pres. 1955), Venezuelan, Columbian, Brazilian, Chilean, Swedish anesthesioloy Socs. Author: Management of Pain, 1953; Il Dolore, 1959; Tratamiento del Dolor, 1959, Clinical Applications of Diagnostic and Therapeutic Blocks, 1959, Manual of Anesthesiology for Medical Students, Interns and Residents, 1947; Obstetrical Complications, 1965; Principles and Practice of Obstetric Analgesia and Anesthesia, 1967; Regional Anesthesia, 1969; also articles profl. jours. Asso. editor Survey of Anesthesiology, 1957—, cons. editor Far East Jour. Anesthesiology, 1956-66; fgn. editor Minerva Anestesiologica, 1955—, Revista Mexicana de Anestesiologia, 1958-66. Home: 4732 E Mercer Way Mercer Island WA 98040 Office: Dept Anesthesiology Univ Washington Seattle WA 98195

BONILLA, CHARLES FRANCIS, educator; b. Albany, N.Y., July 11, 1909; s. Rodrigo and Lucy E. (Smith) B.; A.B., Cuenca Inst., Spain, 1925; A.B., Columbia, 1928, B.S., 1930, Chem. E., 1932, Ph.D., 1933; m. Sigrid Isabel Johnson, Oct. 28, 1938; children—Laurence Huguet, Elisabeth Blair. Tutor chem. engring. Coll. City N.Y., 1932-37; asst. prof., later asso. prof. and prof. chem. engring. John Hopkins, 1937-49, chmn. dept. chem. engring., 1943-49; prof. chem. engring. Columbia, N.Y.C., 1948—, prof. nuclear engring., 1960—. Cons. Bd. Econ. Warfare, Fgn. Econ. Adminstrn., Washington, 1942-46; mem. U.S. Indsl. Mission to Brazil, 1942, U.S. Tech. Mission to Cuba, 1943, Atoms for Peace Mission to S.A. 1956; nuclear exchange specialist to Spain, 1956, Nat. Acad. Sci. mission to Chile, 1960; cons. Phillips Petroleum Co., Bartlesville, Okla., 1942-46, U.S. Naval Engring. Expt. Sta., 1946-51, Brookhaven Nat. Lab., 1948-56. Knolls Atomic Power Lab., Schenectady, 1952-55, E.I. du Pont de Nemours & Co., 1955-62, Bettis Atomic Power Div., 1956-62, Atomic Power Devel. Assos., 1960-68, Gen. Elec. Co., 1960—, Nat. Lead Co., 1961—; v.p. research Chlormetals, Inc., 1964-67; dir. Belfort Instrument Co., Balt., 1956—, chmn. bd., 1962—; dir. P.R. Nuclear Center, AEC, 1957-59. Dir. research projects Rubber Res., Air Force, NASA, A.E.C. Registered profl. engr., N.Y., Md. Mem. Am. Inst. Chem. Engrs., Am. Chem. Soc., Am. Soc. M.E. (chmn. com. K-7, 1968-71), Am. Nuclear Soc., I.E.E.E., Phi Beta Kappa, Sigma Xi, Tau Beta Pi, Phi Lambda Upsilon, Phi Sigma Kappa. Club: Mens Faculty (Columbia); Knickerbocker Country. Editor Nuclear Engineering (book); Nuclear Engring. and Design (jour.). Contbr. articles on indsl. chemistry, chem. engring. theory, heat transfer and liquid metals to tech. publs. Home: 7 Coppell Dr Tenafly NJ 07670

BONIN, GARLAND L., state govt. ofcl.; b. St. Martinville, La., Apr. 2, 1912; s. Luke and Blanche (Durand) B.; grad. U. Southwest La., 1933; m. Aline Lallande, June 13, 1936; 1 dau., Yvette (Mrs. Hargett). Mem. sch. bd. Lafayette (La.) Parish, 1950-62; mem. La. senate, 1962-65; commr. welfare La., 1965—. Mem. Tau Sigma Delta. Roman Catholic. Home: 143 Parduton St Lafayette LA 70501 Office: Div Pub Welfare State Welfare Bldg Baton Rouge LA 70801

BONINI, WILLIAM EMORY, educator; b. Washington, Aug. 23, 1926; s. John Emory and Thelma (Scrivener) B.; B.S. in Engring., Princeton, 1948, M.S., 1949; Ph.D., U. Wis., 1957; m. Rose Rozich, Dec. 4, 1954; children—John Allen, Nancy Mara, James Prior, Jennifer Adra. Mem. faculty Princeton, 1953—, prof. civil and geol. engring., 1966-70, George J. Magee prof. geophysics and geol. engring., 1970—. Pres. Yellowstone- Bighorn Research Assn., Red Lodge, Mont., 1959-60, 71—, v.p., 1966-71. Served with USNR, 1945-46. Fellow Geol. Soc. Am., Royal Astron. Soc.; mem. Am. Assn. Petroleum Geologists, Soc. Exploration Geophysicists, European Assn. Exploration Geophysicists, Assn. Engring. Geologists (chmn. N.Y.-Phila. section 1971—). NSF sr. postdoctoral fellow U. Newcastle upon Tyne (Eng.); 1963-64. Research on gravity anomalies and crustal structure, seismic crustal studies, geophys. exploration engring. and groundwater studies, environmental geology. Author articles in field. Home: 74 Robert Rd Princeton NJ 08540

BONISTEEL, ROSCOE OSMOND, lawyer; b. Sidney Crossing, Ont., Can., Dec. 23, 1888; s. Milton Fremont and Frances Anna (Whyte) B.; brought to U.S., 1891; student Dickinson Coll., 1908, LL.D., 1952; LL.B., U. Mich., 1912, LL.D., 1964; D.Sc., Cleary Coll., 1953; m. Lillian Coleman Rudolph, Sept. 12, 1914; children—Jean Ellen (Mrs. William C. Knecht), Betty Dame (Mrs. Wm. Judson Johnson), Frances Coleman (Mrs. Willis Allan Fisher), Roscoe Osmond, Nancy Ann (Mrs. Harry Calcutt). Admitted to Mich. bar., 1912, since practiced law; dir. Mich. Life Ins. Co., R & B Machine Tool Co., State Bank of Frankfort, Ann Arbor Bank, Northwestern Savs. & Loan Assn. (Traverse City). County, city atty. Ann Arbor, 1921-28; del. Republican State Convs.; del. Rep. Nat. Conv., Kansas City, 1928, Chgo., 1944, presdl. elector, 2d Mich. Congl. Dist., 1932; mem. Mich. Constl. Conv., 1961-62. Served as capt. U.S. Air Service, 1918-19; mem. Mich. War Preparedness Commn., Washtenaw County, 1918. Chmn. bd. appeals Mich. Selective Service. Dir. U. Mus. Soc. U. Mich.; dir. Mich. Soc. for Crippled Children, 1934, 35: regent U. Mich., 1946-60; bd. govs. Wayne State U., 1956-59, William L. Clements Library, U. Mich.; trustee Rackham Fund, U. Mich.; trustee Dickinson Coll., Cleary Coll.; chmn. bd. trustees Nat. Music Camp, Interlochen, Interlochen Arts Acad. Mem. State Bd. Law Examiners Mich., 1945-52. Mem. Am. Bar Assn. (mem. resolutions com. 1937-39; ho. of dels. 1936-41, mem. (Mich.) on com. uniformity of legislation in U.S. 1943-61), State Bar Mich. (pres. 1936-37), Hist. Soc. Mich. (pres. 1961- 62), Am. Law Inst., Am. Legion (judge adv. Mich. 1934-35), Huguenot Soc. Can., Huguenot Soc. Mich., Phi Kappa Sigma. Republican. Presbyn. Mason (33), Rotarian (dist. gov. 1934-35), Kiwanian (hon.). Clubs: University, Dickinson College Alumni of Mich. (pres.), Ann Arbor, Ann Arbor Golf and Outing, Detroit, Detroit Athletic, Home: 1138 Fair Oaks Pkwy Ann Arbor MI 48104 Office: Wolverine Bldg Ann Arbor MI 48108

BONN, PAUL VERNE, lawyer; b. N.Y.C., Mar. 11, 1939; s. Milton J. and Dorothy (Bresky) B.; B.A., Cornell U., 1960; LL.B., Yale, 1963; m. Barbara J. Switzer, Feb. 20, 1959; children—Lori Sue, Gregg Evan; m. 2d, N. JoAnne Ashinhurst, Sept. 29, 1969; 1 dau., Rachel Lynne. Admitted to Ariz. bar, 1963, since practiced in Phoenix; law clk. Judge James A. Walsh, U.S. Dist. Ct. Ariz., 1963-64; asso. Brown, Vlassis & Bain, 1964-67, partner, 1967—. Mem. Am., Ariz., Maricopa County bar assns. Home: 2232 N 7th Av Phoenix AZ 85007 Office: 222 N Central Av Phoenix AZ 85004

BONNELL, ALLEN THOMAS, coll. pres.; b. Colon, Panama, Apr. 7, 1912; s. Leander P. and Florence Matilda (Wellington) B.; A.B., Oberlin Coll., 1933, M.A., 1934; Exchange fellow U. Bonn, 1935-36; Ph.D., U. Ill., 1937; Litt.D. (hon.), Drexel Inst. Tech., 1969; m. Dorothy Peyton Haworth, June 14, 1937; children—Annette Peyton, Thomas Haworth, David Wellington, Daniel Churchill. Instr. econs. St. Louis U., 1937-38; asst. prof. econs. U. N.C., 1938-42; relief adminstr. in unoccupied France, Am. Friends Service Com., 1940-41, past chmn. fgn. service exec. com., mem. exec. bd., Phila.; with Office Fgn. Relief and Rehab., Dept. State, 1942-43, Bur. Agrl. Econs., Dept. Agr., 1943-44; div. dir. Bur. Supply, UNRRA, 1944-48; v.p. Drexel Inst. Tech., Phila., 1948-65, provost, 1963-65; pres. Community Coll. Phila., 1965—. Pres. bd. Small Bus. Opportunities Corp.; v.p. Met. Phila. Ednl. Radio and TV Corp., W. Phila. Corp. Past chmn. family div. adv. com., mem. bd. dirs. Phila. Health and Welfare Council. Fellow A.A.A.S. (sec. sect. indsl. sci.); mem. Am. Pub. Relations Assn. (mem. bd. Phila. Forge), Am., So. econs. assns. Mem. Soc. of Friends. Author: German Control Over International Economic Relations, 1930-40; Industrial Science-Present and Future (arranged by Bonnell, edited by Ruth C. Christman), 1952. Home: 11 Single Lane Wallingford PA 19086 Office: 34 S 11th St Philadelphia PA 19107

BONNELL, HETTIE HAZLETT, former Republican Nat. Com.; b. Wheeling, W.Va., Feb. 4, 1898; d. Edward Edward and Jessie (List) Hazlett; student Smith Coll., 1916-17; B.S. in Social Sci., Carnegie Inst. Tech., 1920; m. Robert Owen Bonnell, June 23, 1923; children—Edwina Hazlett (Mrs. Rex Havens), Robert Owen. Recreational dir. Nat. YWCA, 1919; survey staff, spl. field rep. Nat. Child Labor Com., 1920-21; exec. sec. Children's Code Commn., W.Va., 1921-23; 1st woman chmn. U.S. Assay Commn., 1953. Pioneer Ten O'Clock Club for Rep. presdl. campaigns, 1948, 52; v.p. Md. Fedn. Rep. Women, 1954-56; organized taught polit. workshops, 1954; vice chmn. Rep. State Cent. Com.; Com.; mem. Rep. Nat. Com. for Md., 1958-65. Co-chmn. Orthopedic Workshop for Handicapped, Barnes Hosp., St. Louis; nat. bd. dirs. Women's Med. Coll. Pa.; Pa.; bd. dirs. Balt. Family and Children's Soc., Children's Hosp. Sch., James Lawrence Kernan Children's Hosp., Jr. League of St. Louis, Balt.; pioneer, past chmn. Service Men's Club, Episcopal Diocese of Md. Methodist (mem. bd., exec. com.). Author: Political Primer, 1954. Home: 114 St Dunstans Rd Baltimore, MD 21212.

BONNELL, JOHN SUTHERLAND clergyman; b. P.E.I., Can., Jan. 10, 1893; s. Abraham and Catherine (Cameron) B.; came to U.S., 1935; B.A., Dalhousie U., Halifax, N.S., 1919; B.D., Pine Hill Div. Hall, Halifax, 1927, D.D., 1934; LL.D. (hon.), Washington and Jefferson Coll., 1943, U. N.B., 1958, St. Dunstan's Roman Cath. U., P.E.I., Can., 1963; Litt.D. (hon.), Dickinson Coll., 1960; D.D., Lafayette Coll., 1950; m. Bessie Louise Carruthers, June 1923; children—George Carruthers, Catherine Cameron, Elizabeth Louise, Jessie Margaret. Ordained Presbyn. minister, 1922; pastor St. Andrew's Ch., New Brunswick, Can., 1923-29, Westminster Ch., Winnipeg, Can., 1929-35; Fifth Av. Presbyn. Ch., N.Y.C., 1935-62, now minister emeritus; pres. N.Y. Theol. Sem., N.Y.C., 1966-69. Lectr. Theol. Sem., Princeton, N.J., 1938-60; on goodwill preaching mission to Britain, spl. del. to Gen. Assembly of Ch. of Scotland (Edinburgh) from Presbyn. Ch. in the U.S.A., 1941; Sprunt lectr. Union Theol. Sem., Richmond, Va., 1943; chancellor's lectr., Queens U., Kingston, Ont., Can., 1944; Norton lectr., So. Bapt. Theol. Sem., Louisville, 1944; Ashlin lectr. 1st Presbyn. Ch., Morresville, N.C., 1949; Perkins lectr. 1st Meth. Ch., Wichita Falls, Tex., 1950; Charles Claudius Beam lectr. 1st Presbyn. Ch. Charlotte, (N.C.), 1953; Weber Meml. lectr. Moravian Theol. Sem., Bethlehem, Pa., 1956; Edward lectr. Shadyside Ch., Pitts., 1958. Chmn. Royal Commn. on Higher Edn. in P.E.I., 1964. Bd. govs. Silver Hill Found. Served as sgt. 5th Canadian Siege Battery, Canadian Army, 1916-18. Made study of religious situation in 10 European countries, 1948. Broadcast each Sunday over WABC for 20 years. Awarded The King's Medal for service in cause of freedom King George VI, 1949. Mem. Protestant Council N.Y. (pres. 1961), Canadian Soc. N.Y. (pres. 1959-60), Nat. Conf. Christians and Jews (co-chmn. religious commn.). Clubs: Canadian (hon. mem.), University (N.Y.C.). Author books including: What are You Living For, 1950; The Practice and Power of Prayer, 1954; Heaven and Hell; No Escape from Life, 1958; I Believe in Immortality, 1959; Certainties for Uncertain Times, 1962; You Want to be Healed?, 1971. Contbr. articles to mags. Office: 468 Riverside Dr New York City NY 10027 ☆

BONNER, EMMETT PEYTON, naval officer; b. Macon, Ga., Feb. 27, 1918; s. Emmett Peyton and Bessie (Napier) B.; B.S. in E.E., U.S. Naval Acad., 1939; m. Elizabeth Healy, Sept. 2, 1942; children—Emmett Peyton III, Mark Healy, Vance, Gregory Beauregard. Commd. ensign U.S. Navy, 1939, advanced through grades to rear adm., 1966; served in cruisers and amphibious group staff, World War II; active guided missile devel. program; dir. Terrier Missile Program, 1961- 63; comdr. Naval Support Activity, Danang, Vietnam, 1963-70; sr. Navy mem. weapons systems evaluation group Office Sec. Def., Washington, 1970—. Decorated Legion of Merit, Joint Services Commendation medal, numerous unit and area ribbons. Home: 2533 N Quincy St Arlington VA 22207 Office: Office Sec Def Washington DC

BONNER, FRANCIS TRUESDALE, chemist; b. Salt Lake City, Dec. 18, 1921; s. Walter Daniel and Grace (Gaylord) B.; B.A., U. Utah, 1942; M.S., Yale, 1944, Ph.D., 1945; m. Evelyn Hershkowitz, Jan. 17, 1946; children—Michael David, Joan Alisa, Rachel Pearl. Chemist, Manhattan Project S.A.M. Labs. Columbia, 1944-46; chemist Clinton Labs., Oak Ridge, 1946-47; scientist Brookhaven Nat. Lab., Upton, N.Y., 1947-48, research collaborator, 1958—; asst. prof. chemistry Bklyn. Coll., 1948-54; Carnegie vis. fellow Harvard, 1954-55; research phys. chemist Arthur D. Little, Inc., Cambridge, Mass., 1955- 58; prof. dept. chemistry State U. N.Y., Stony Brook, 1958—, chmn. dept., 1958-70; cons. editor Addison-Wesley Pub. Co., Reading, Mass., 1956—; Rockefeller Found. adviser on curriculum, instl. devel. Universidad Del Valle, Cali, Colombia, 1961-62, 64, Ford Found. adviser, 1968; Ford Found. adviser to Universidad de Antioquia, Medellin, Colombia, 1962- 64; dir. N.Y. Met. Area Center Chem. Edn. Materials Study, 1961- 62; mem. Coll. Entrance Examination Bd. Com. for Chemistry, 1962-63; mem. coll. proficiency examination com. chemistry N.Y. State Edn. Dept., 1963-64, 66—; NSF sr. postdoctoral fellow Service des Isotopes Stables. Centre d'Etudes Nucleaires de Saclay, Gif-Sur-Yvette, France, 1964-65. Mem. bd. edn. Central Sch. Dist. 6, Huntington, N.Y., 1968—. Fellow A.A.A.S.; mem. N.Y. Acad. Scis., Am. Chem. Soc., Geochemical Soc., Am. Geophys. Union, Am. Assn. U. Profs., Sigma Xi. Author: (with Melba Phillips) Principles of Physical Science, 1957, 2d edit., 1971. Contbr. articles profl. jours. Home: 27 Stratford Av Greenlawn, NY 11740. Office: Dept Chemistry State U NY Stony Brook NY 11790 NY 11790

BONNER, FRANCIS WESLEY, coll. dean; b. Lanett, Ala., Jan. 28, 1917; s. Oscar Arnold and Cora Eunice (Strother) B.; student Snead Jr. Coll., 1935-37; A.B., U. Ala., 1939, M.A., 1940; Ph.D., U. N.C., 1949; postgrad. Harvard, 1952-53; m. Nilaouise Carnes, Aug. 3, 1941; children—Arnold Frank, Elizabeth Ann. Instr. English, U. Ala., 1939-40; head English dept. Marietta (Ga.) High Sch., 1940-42; asso. prof. English, Furman U., Greenville, S.C., 1949-54, prof. English, 1954—, dean men's coll., 1953-61, chmn. dept. English, 1956-61, dean univ., 1961—, v.p., 1964—. Served as capt. USAAF, 1942-45. Mem. Am. Assn. U. Profs., Modern Lang. Assn. Am., Medieval Acad. Am., So. Conf. Deans Faculties and Acad. Vice Presidents (pres. 1971), South Atlantic Modern Lang. Assn., Phi Beta Kappa, Phi Delta Kappa, Kappa Delta Pi. Baptist. Rotarian. Editor Furman Studies, 1951-53. Contbr. articles to profl. publs. Home: Route 3 Stratford Forest Greenville SC

BONNER, JAMES, educator; b. Ansley, Nbe., Sept. 1, 1910; s. Walter Daniel and Grace (Gaylord) B.; A.B., U. Utah, 1931; Ph.D., Cal. Inst. Tech., 1934; m. Ingelore Silberbach, Nov. 10, 1967; children by previous marriage—Joey, James, Jose. NRC fellow Univs. Utrecht, Leiden, Zürich, 1934-35; faculty Cal. Inst. Tech., Pasadena, 1935—, prof. biology, 1946—. Mem. Nat. Acad. Scis. Author: Plant Biochemistry, 1950; Principles of Plant Physiology, 1952; The Next 100 Years, 1957; The Nucleohistones, 1964; The Molecular Biology of Development, 1965; The Next 90 Years, 1967. Home: 3119 Mesalca Lane Pasadena CA 91107

BONNER, JAMES BROWN, drug store exec.; b. Herrin, Ill., Nov. 16, 1910; s. James and Ollie Frances (Knisell) B.; M.B.A., U. Mich., 1933; m. Jennie Lyon, June 22, 1935; children—James Lyon, John George. Accountant, Standard Oil Co. Ind., Grand Rapids, Mich., 1933-37; accountant Ernst & Ernst, Detroit, 1937-45; controller Cunningham Drug Stores, Inc., Detroit, 1945-52, sec., 1952-63, sec., treas. 1963—. Trustee Cunningham Drug Co. Found. Mem. Detroit Retail Mchts. Assn. (dir.), Am. Soc. Corporate Secs. (past pres. Detroit region), Mich. Chain Store Council (treas.), Am. Inst. C.P.A.'s, Nat. Assn. Accountants, Am. Accounting Assn. Presbyn. (treas.). Rotarian. Club: Detroit Athletic. Home: 4019 Parkway Royal Oak MI 48072 Office: 1927 12th St Detroit MI 48216

BONNER, JOHN TYLER, biologist; b. N.Y.C., May 12, 1920; s. Paul Hyde and Lilly Marguerite Marguerite (Stehli) B.; grad. Phillips Exeter Acad., 1937; B.Sc., Harvard, 1941, M.A., 1942, Ph.D., 1947; D.Sc. (hon.), Middlebury Coll., 1970; m. Ruth Anna Graham, July 11, 1942; children—Rebecca, Jonathan Graham, Jeremy Tyndall, Andrew Duncan. Asst. to asso. prof. Princeton, 1947-58, prof., 1958—, chmn. dept. biology, 1965—; lectr. embryology Marine Biol. Lab. Woods Hole, Mass., 1951-52; spl. lectr. U. London, 1957; Bklyn. Coll., 1966; trustee Biol. Abstracts, 1958-63. Mem. bd. editors Princeton U. Press, 1965-68, 71—. Served from pvt. to 1st lt. USAC, 1942-46; staff aero. med. lab. Wright Field, Dayton, O. Sheldon traveling fellow, Panama, 1941, Rockefeller traveling fellow, France, 1953, Guggenheim fellow, Scotland, 1958, 71-72; recipient Selman A. Waksman award for contbns. to microbiology Theobold Smith Soc.; NSF sr. postdoctoral fellow, 1963. Fellow Am. Acad. Arts and Scis.; mem. Am. Soc. Naturalists, Soc. Gen. Physiologists, Soc. Growth and Devel. Mycological Soc. Am., Phi Beta Kappa, Sigma Xi. Author: Morphogensis, 1952; Cells and Societies, 1955; The Evolution of Development, 1958; The Cellular Slime Molds, 1959, rev. edit. 1966; The Ideas of Biology, 1962; Size and Cycle, 1965; The Scale of Nature, 1969; also scientific papers. Editor: Growth and Form, 1961. Asso. editor Am. Scientist, 1961-69; editorial bd. Am. Naturalist, 1958-60, 66-68, Jour. Gen. Physiology, 1962-69, Growth, 1955—. Home: 148 Mercer St Princeton NJ 08540

BONNER, OSCAR DAVIS, educator; b. Jackson, Miss., May 9, 1917; s. Oscar Davis and Bertha Elizabeth (Basser) B.; B.S., Millsaps Coll., 1939; M.S., U. Miss., 1948; Ph.D., U. Kan., 1951; m. Vaudie Vee Ball, Aug. 3, 1940; children—Davis Roy, Richard Edward, Timothy George. Chemist, Miss. Testing Labs., 1940-42, Filtrol Corp., 1946-47; mem. faculty U. S.C., Columbia, 1951—, prof. chemistry, head dept., 1960-70, R.L. Sumwalt prof. chemistry, 1970—. Fulbright advanced research scholar, Germany, 1957-58. Served to lt. comdr. USNR, 1942-46. Mem. Am. Chem. Soc., S.C. Acad. Scis., Sigma Xi, Phi Lambda Upsilon. Home: 5012 Furman Av Columbia SC 29206

BONNER, ROBERT WILLIAM, forest co. exec.; b. Vancouver, B.C., Can., Sept. 10, 1920; s. Benjamin York and Emma Louise (Weir) B.; B.A. in Econs. and Polit. Sci., U. B.C., 1942, LL.B., 1948; m. Barbara Newman, June 16, 1942; children—Barbara Carolyn, Robert York, Elizabeth Louise. Called to B.C. bar, 1948, created Queen's counsel, 1952; with firm Clark Wilson White Clark & Maguire, Vancouver, 1948-52; atty. gen. Province B.C., 1952-68; sr. v.p. adminstrn. MacMillan Bloedel Ltd., 1968-70, exec. v.p. adminstrn., 1970-71, vice chmn., 1971—, also dir.; dir. Canadian Cablesystems Ltd. Mem. B.C. Legislature for Cariboo Constituency, 1966-69. Bd. dirs. Canadian Council Christians and Jews. Served to maj. Royal Canadian Army, 1942-45; lt. col. Res. Mem. Canadian Export Assn. (bd. dirs.), Canadian Bar Assn., Law Soc. B.C., Delta Upsilon. Mem. Social Credit Party. Mason. Club: Union (Victoria). Home: 5679 Newton Wynd Vancouver 8 British Columbia Canada Office: 1075 W Georgia St Vancouver 105 British Columbia Canada

BONNER, THOMAS NEVILLE, univ. pres.; b. Rochester, N.Y., May 28, 1923; s. John Neville and Mary (McGowan) B.; A.B., U. Rochester, 1947, M.A., 1948; Ph.D., Northwestern U., 1952; m. Joan Nadine Compton, Oct. 12, 1947; children—Phillip Lynn, Diana Joan. Acad. dean William Woods Coll., 1951-54; prof. history, chmn. dept. social sci. U. Omaha, 1955-62; Fulbright lectr. U. Mainz, Germany, 1954-55; prof., head history dept. U. of Cin., 1963-68, v.p. acad. affairs, provost, 1967-71; pres. U. N.H., Durham, 1971—. Democratic candidate for Congress, 1962; legislative aide to Senator McGovern, 1962-63. Served with Radio Intelligence Corps, AUS, 1942-46; ETO. Guggenheim fellow, 1958-59, 64-65. Mem. Am. Hist. Assn., Orgn. Am. Historians, Phi Beta Kappa, Pi Gamma Mu, Phi Alpha Theta. Author: Medicine in Chicago, 1957; The Kansas Doctor, 1959; (with others) The Contemporary World, 1960; Our Recent Past, 1963; American Doctors and German Universities, 1963. Editor, translator: Journey Through the Rocky Mountains (Jacob Schiel), 1959. Home: 74 Main St Durham NH 03824

BONNER, WILLARD HALLAM, educator, writer; b. Lynn, Mass., May 13, 1899; s. Arthur and Josephine (Whitaker) B.; student U. Ala., 1916; A.B., Coll. of Pacific, 192O; A.M., Stanford 1921; Ph.D., Yale, 1931; m. Kathryn Cummings, Mar. 27, 1926 (dec. 1950); children—Willard Hallam, Anne Cummings; m. 2d, Elda O. O. Baumann, Jan. 19, 1951. Asst. in English, Stanford, 1921; instr. English, Mich. State U., 1921-22; successively instr., asst. prof., asso. prof., prof. English, U. Buffalo, 1922-65, James H. McNulty prof. English, 1960-68, emeritus, 1968—, dir. grad. studies in English, 1958-63, editor univ. publs., 1923-39, 40-48. Mem. Am. Assn. U. Profs., Modern Lang. Assn. Am., Phi Beta Kappa. Club: Internat. Torch. Author: Pirate Laureate, the Life and Legends of Captain Kidd, 1947; The Journals and Letters of Sarah and William Hazlitt, 1922-1831, 1959. Contbr. articles to nat. mags. and learned jours. Home: 11Meadowbrook Rd Brunswick ME 04011

BONNER, Z. DAVID, chem. co. exec.; b. San Antonio, Feb. 23, 1919; s. Zora David and Willia Clyde (Calhoun) B.; B.S., U. Tex., 1941; m. Dorothy Shaw, Feb. 28, 1942; children—David Calhoun, Julie Ann. With Gulf Oil Corp., Pitts., 1941-66; v.p. Goodrich-Gulf Chems., Inc., Cleve., 1966, now pres. Gulf Oil Chems. Co., Pitts. Served Gulf Oil Chems. Co., Pitts. Served to lt. comdr. USNR, World War II. Recipient Distinguished Grad. award U. Tex., 1968. Mem. Tau Beta Pi, Phi Lambda Upsilon. Clubs: Pittsburgh, Longue Vue (Pitts.). Patentee in field. Home: 30 Wedgewood Lane Pittsburgh PA 15215 Office: Gulf Bldg Pittsburgh PA 15219 †

BONNET, PHILIP DIRLAM, educator; b. Worcester, Mass., May 28, 1911; s. Frederic and Anne Howard (Binns) B.; A.B., Wesleyan U., 1932; M.D., Harvard, 1936; m. Esther Caroline Bechtold, Sept. 7, 1940; children—Caroline, Philip Austin, Priscilla, Christopher, Deborah. Intern Grad. Hosp. U. Pa., 1936- 38; chief resident physician Lankenau Hosp., Phila., 1938-40, med. dir., 1940-48; adminstr. Mass. Meml. Hosps., Boston, 1948-65; cons. adminstr. Univ. Hosp., Boston, 1965-67; v.p., trustee Mass. Hosp. Service (Blue Cross); asso. prof. hosp. adminstrn. Boston U. Sch. Medicine, 1960-63, clin. prof. hosp. adminstrn., 1963-66; prof. med. care and hosps. Johns Hopkins Sch. Hygiene, Balt., 1967—. Vis. fellow Nuffield Provincial Hosps. Trustee, King Edward's Hosp. Fund, Eng., 1966; mem. health services research study sect. NIH, 1960-64; mem. rev. com. on med. and dental edn. facilities USPHS, 1964-66; pres. bd. New Eng. Hosp. Assembly, 1959-60. Fellow Am. Coll. Hosp. Adminstrs. (regent 1960-63); mem. Am. (pres. 1965-66), Mass. hosp. assns., Soc. Med. Adminstrs., A.M.A., Am. Pub. Health Assn., Phi Beta Kappa. Republican. Lutheran. Home: 500 W University Pkwy Baltimore MD 21210

BONNEY, GEORGE WILLIAM, lawyer; b. Midwest, Wyo., Aug. 22, 1923; s. George William and Bertha Anne (Ormsby) B.; A.B., U. Wis., 195O, LL.B., 1952; m. Kerminette Schweers, Aug. 27, 1949; children—Susan Mary, George William III, Michael Kermit. Admitted to Cal. bar, 1952, since practiced in San Jose; partner firm Rankin, Oneal, Luckhardt, Center, Ingram, Bonney, Marlais & Lund, 1967—. Dist. chmn. Santa Clara County chpt. Boy Scouts Am., 1967—, mem. exec. bd., 1967—; commr. Parks and Recreation Commn., City of Saratoga, 1970—. Served as pilot USAAF, 1942-46. Mem. Am., Cal. (conf. dels.), Wis., Santa Clara County (trustee) bar assns., Wis. Alumni Assn., Sigma Phi Epsilon. Home: 12740 Carniel Av Saratoga CA 95070 Office: First Nat Bank Bldg San Jose CA 95113

BONNEY, SHERWOOD MUNHALL, lawyer; b. Pen Argyl, Pa., May 27, 1909; s. John Kent and Ada Pearl (Rinker) B.; A.B., Dickinson Coll., 1931; LL.B., Harvard, 1937; m. Harriet Jane Brady, July 1, 1938; children—Kent Louis, Jean. French tchr. The Hill Sch., Pottstown, Pa., 1931-34; with tax dept. Arthur Andersen & Co., C.P.A.'s N.Y.C., 1937-42, becoming mgr.; jr. partner Dunnington, Bartholow & Miller, lawyers, 1942-43; with Sun Chem. Corp., 1946-55, sec.-treas., dir. corp. and its 9 subsidiaries until 1955; treas. Johnson & Higgins, 1955-58, v.p., treas., 1958—, dir., 1960—; trustee Am. Savs. Bank. Trustee Dickinson Coll. Served as lt. USNR, 1943-45. Mem. Camp Fire Club of Am. (Chappaqua, N.Y.), Beta Theta Pi (past pres.), Omicron Delta Kappa. Republican. Presbyn. Clubs: Scarsdale Golf (Hartsdale, N.Y.); Wall Street (N.Y.C.). Home: 44 Walworth Av Scarsdale NY 10583 Office: 95 Wall St New York City NY 10005

BONNEY, WESTON LEONARD, banker; b. Lewiston, Me., Sept. 9, 1925; s. Leonard W. and Olive (Jones) B.; A.B. in Econs., Bates Coll., Lewiston, Me., 195O; m. Elaine Gilbert, June 29, 1946; children—Melody Elaine, Merrilee, Michael, Melissa Jane. With Union Mut. Life Ins. Co., 1950-52, Fed. Res. Bank Boston, 1952-63; corp. services officer First Nat. Bank Boston, 1963-65; with Depositors Corp., Augusta, Me., 1966—, pres., 1970—, also dir., with Depositors Trust Co., Augusta, 1965—, pres., sr. adminstrv. officer, 1967-71, pres., chief exec. officer, 1971—, also dir.; dir. Me. Fidelity Life Ins. Co. Trustee Bates Coll., Kents Hill Sch.; commr. Me. Commn. Arts and Humanities. Served with USNR, 1943-46. Home: 49 Ganneston Dr Augusta ME 04330 Office: 286 Water St Augusta ME 04330

BONNICK, ALBERT THOMAS, telephone co. exec.; b. Dayton, Ky., Nov. 4, 1917; s. Albert James and May (Honerkamp) B.; certificate in Accounting, U. Cin., 1948, B.S. in Commerce, 1955; m. Joyce Estelle Poate, Apr. 25, 1942; children—Albert T., Marilyn K., Susan L. With Cin. Bell (formerly Cin. & Suburban Bell Telephone Co.), 1936—, chief accountant, 1957-63, comptroller, 1963-67, v.p., dir., 1967-70, v.p., comptroller, dir., 1970—. Chmn. United Appeal Audit Div., 1965-66; exec. com. allocations div. Community Chest, 1967—. Served form pvt. to maj. AUS, 1941-46. Mem. Financial Execs. Inst. (dir. Cin. chpt.), C. of C., Delta Mu Delta. Clubs: Cincinnati, Queen City (Cin.). Home: 34 St Nicholas Pl Fort Thomas KY 41075 Office: 225 E 4th St Cincinnati OH 45202

BONNIWELL, DONALD RAYMOND, investment banker; b. Kankakee, Ill., Nov. 15, 1909; s. Charles A. and Zita M. (Welch) B.; ed. parochial schs.; m. Ana Power y Morera, June 3, 1944; children—Donald Raymond, Ana Patricia, Charles Anthony, Michelle Ann. Asst. v.p. Bond & Mortgage Co., Chgo., 1928-30;

account exec. Foreman Nat. Bank, Chgo., 1930-31, v.p. Kneeland & Co., Chgo., 1931-35, 38- 43; pres. Bonniwell, Neil & Camden, Chgo., 1935-38; financial and econ. adviser, finance dir. Govt. Devel. Bank for P.R., San Juan, 1943-54; gen. partner Cruttenden, Podesta & Miller, Chgo., 1954-63 (consol. with Walston & Co., Inc. 1963), v.p., money market adviser, head fiscal agy. operations Walston & Co., Inc., Chgo., 1963—, now sr. v.p.; dir. Host Internat., Inc. Mem. finance com. Boys' Town P.R., 1949-51; chmn. Gov. Ill. Legislative Com. Indsl. Devel., 1961-62; chmn. Ill. State Toll Hwy. Commn., 1963—; mem. adv. com. Mayor City Chgo. - Chgo. Calumet Skyway and Toll Bridge Com., 1965—; chmn. Indsl. Devel. Authority Ill., 1961-63; mem. com. for site acquisition and devel. Weston (Ill.) Atomic Accelerator, 1967—; mem. Fathers' Assn. Lake Forest (Ill.) Acad., 1964-66; pres. finance bd. Convent Sacred Heart, Chgo., 1965—. Regent, trustee bursar, rector faculty of finance Lincoln Acad. Ill., 1964—. Mem. Soc. Union Vets. Civil War, S.A.R., Soc. War 1812. Clubs: Oak Brook (Ill.) Polo; Municipal Bond of Chgo., City, Attic Saddle and Cycle (Chgo.); Bankers (N.Y.C., San Juan, P.R.). Author: Liquidation of Joint Stock Land Banks Under Federal Farm Loan Emergency Act, 1933; Analysis of Liquidation of Utility Holding Corps., series of 3, 1937; To the Bulls and Bears on the West Virginia Turnpike, 1955; Crystal-Balling the Future for New Toll Highways, 1966; Chicago Calument Skyway Revenue Bonds - A Speculative Buy or Pie in the Sky, 1968. Address: 505 N Lake Shore Dr Chicago IL 60611

BONNY, JOHN BRUCE, former constrn. exec.; b. San Francisco, Feb. 8, 1903; s. Bruce and Mabel Abbey (Lewis) B.; B.S., U. Cal., 1925; m. Mary Louise McDaniels, 1923 (div. 1927); 1 dau., Jean Bruce (Mrs. McCauley); m. 2d, Dorothy Ernestine Black, May 23, 1929 (div. 1953); 1 dau., Dorothy Ann; m. 3d, Marie Womack, 1954 (dec. 1969); m. 4th, Marion Peel Crawford, 1969. Contractor Derbon Constrn. Co., Seattle, 1926-29; project mgr., supt. Morrison Knudsen Co., Inc., Boise, Ida., 1930-34, dist. mgr., Los Angeles, 1934-47, v.p., div. mgr., 1942-47, v.p., gen. mgr. Boise, 1947—, pres., 1960-69, chmn. bd., 1969, now ret.; dir. Kaiser Cement & Gypsum, Albertson's, Inc., Boise. Mem. Moles, Beavers (pres., dir. 1970-71). Clubs: Pacific Union (San Francisco), California (Los Angeles). Author: Fifty Years of Construction Progress, 1962; author, editor: Handbook of Construction Management and Organization, 1971. Home: Pioneerville Route Idaho City ID 83631

BONNYCASTLE, LAWRENCE CHRISTOPHER, holding co. exec.; b. Russell, Man., Can., Nov. 19, 1907; s. Angus L. and Ellen M. (Boulton) B.; B.A., U. Man., 1929; B.A. in Jurisprudence, Oxford U., 1932; m. Mary F. Andrews, Jan. 20, 1934; children—John Christopher, Michael Kurt, Stephen Rodney. Treas. No. Life Assurance Co. of Can., 1938-39; treas. John Labatt, Ltd., 1940-45, v.p., asst. gen. mgr., 1948-49; gen. mgr. Nat. Life Assurance Co. of Can., 1949-52, v.p., dir., 1951—; v.p. mng. dir. Canadian Corporate Mgmt. Co., Ltd., 1952-63, pres. 1963—. Fellow Actuarial Soc. Clubs: Toronto; University (Toronto and Montreal). Home: 9 Wychwood Park Toronto Ontario Canada Office: 50 King St W West Toronto Ontario Canada

BONNYMAN, GEORGE GORDON, mining co. exec.; b. Knoxville, Tenn., Oct. 22, 1919; s. Alexander and Frances (Berry) B.; B.S., Princeton, 1941; m. Isabel Fouche Ashe, May 20, 1942; children—Isabel Ashe (Mrs. Brooke Herford Stanley), George Gordon, Anne Berry, Alexander Ashe, Brian Andrew. With the Blue Diamond Coal Co., Knoxville, Tenn., 1945—, asst. gen. mgr., gen. mgr., pres., 1953-70, chmn. bd., 1970—. Served as capt. F.A., AUS, World War II. Decorated Silver Star medal, Bronze Star medal with oak-leaf cluster, Purple Heart. Mem. Princeton Engring. Soc., Soc. Mining Engrs., Am. Inst. Mining, Metall. and Petroleum Engrs. Home: 6633 Sherwood Rd Knoxville TN 37919 Office: Blue Diamond Coal Co PO Box 10080 Knoxville TN 37919

BONO, CHER, singer; b. El Centro, Cal., May 20, 1946; d. Georgia and Gilbert LaPiere; student drama coach Jeff Corey; m. Sonny Bono, Oct. 27, 1964; 1 dau., Chastity. Singer with husband as team Sonny and Cher, 1964—; numerous recordings, TV, concert and benefit appearances with husband; appearance with husband in motion picture Good Times, 1966, Chastity, 1969. Address: care Reprise Records 4000 Warner Blvd Burbank CA 91505 ☆

BONO, GAUDENZIO, mfg. co. exec.; b. May 17, 1901; Dr. Eng., Politecnico, Turin, Italy. Mng. dir., gen. mgr. Fiat Co., Turin until 1969, vice chmn. mng. dir., 1969—. Chmn. Galileo Ferraris Nat. Elec. Engring. Inst. Decorated Cavaliere del Lavoro; Knight Grand cross Italian Republic. Address: 10 Corso Marconi Turin Italy*

BONO, PHILIP, aircraft mfr.; b. Bklyn., Jan. 13, 1921; s. Julius and Marianna (Culcasi) B.; B.E., U. So. Cal., 1947; postgrad. U. So. Cal., 1948-49; m. Gertrude Camille King, Dec. 15, 1950; children—Richard Philip, Patricia Marianna, Kathryn Camille. Research and systems analyst N. Am. Aviation, Inglewood, Cal., 1947; engring. design specialist Douglas Aircraft Co., Long Beach, Cal., 1948-49; preliminary design engr. Boeing Airplane Co., Seattle, 1950-59; dep. program mgr. Douglas Aircraft Co., Santa Monica, Cal., 1960-62, tech. asst. to dir. advanced launch vehicles and space stas., Huntington Beach, Cal., 1963-65; br. mgr. advanced studies, sr. staff engr. advanced tech. McDonnell Douglas Astronautics Co., Huntington Beach, 1966—; lectr. seminars, univs. and insts. including Soviet Acad. Scis., 1965. Served with USNR, 1943-46. Recipient Golden Eagle award Council Internat. Nontheatrical Events, 1964, A. T. Colwell merit award Soc. Automotive Engrs., 1968, M.N. Golovine award Brit. Interplanetary Soc., 1969; named engr. of distinction Engrs. Joint Council, 1971. Fellow A.A.A.S., Royal Aero. Soc., Brit. Interplanetary Soc. (editorial adv. bd.), Am. Inst. Aeros. and Astronautics (asso.); sr. mem. Am. Astronautical Soc.; mem. N.Y. Acad. Scis., Internat. Acad. Astronautics, Am. Soc. M.E. Author: (with K. Gatland) Frontiers of Space, 1969. Contbr. articles profl. jours., chpts. in books. Inventor recoverable single-stage spacecraft booster. Home: 1951 Sanderling Circle Costa Mesa CA 92626 Office: 5301 Bolsa Av Huntington Beach CA 92647

BONO, SONNY SALVATORE, singer, composer; b. Detroit, Feb. 16, 1940; children—Santo, Jean Bono; m. 2d, Cher LaPiere, Oct. 27, 1964; 1 dau., Chastity. Song writer, later artist and repertoire man for Speciality Records; singer with wife as team Sonny and Cher, 1964—; numerous recordings, TV, concert and benefit appearances with wife; appearance with wife in motion picture, also composer, lyricist Good Times, 1966; producer film Chastity, 1969. Composer: Koko Joe, You Bug Me Baby, Needles and Pins, Baby Don't Go, Dream Baby. Address: care Reprise Records 4000 Warner Blvd Burbank CA 91505 ☆

BONSAL, DUDLEY BALDWIN, judge; b. Bedford, N.Y., Oct. 6, 1906; s. Stephen and Henrietta Fairfax (Morris) B.; A.B., Dartmouth, 1927; LL.B., Harvard, 1930; m. Lois Abbott Worrall, May 16, 1931; children—Lois (Mrs. Frederic B. Osler, Jr.), Stephen. Admitted to N.Y. bar, 1932; asso. firm Curtis, Mallet-Prevost, Colt & Mosle, N.Y.C., 1930-38, mem. firm, 1938-42, 45-61; U.S. dist. judge, So. dist. N.Y. 1961—; chief counsel Office Inter-Am. Affairs, Washington, 1942-45; mem. U.S. delegation Inter-Am. Conf. on Problems of War and Peace, Mexico City, 1945; legal adviser Fgn. Bondholders Protective Council, Conf. on German Debts, London, 1951, 52; mem. Internat. Commn. of Jurists, Geneva, Switzerland; chmn. spl. com. on fed. loyalty-security program Assn. Bar City N.Y., 1955-57, mem. com. on criminal justice act Jud. Conf. of U.S., 1964—. Trustee Inst. Internat. Edn., 1948-64, Sterling and Francine Clark Art Inst., Williamstown, Mass., William Nelson Cromwell Found., Practising Law Inst.; dir., v.p. Am. Bar Found. Mem. Am., N.Y. bar assns., Assn. Bar City N.Y. (pres.1958-60), N.Y.C. Council on Fgn. Relations. Club: Century Assn. (N.Y.C.). Home: St Mary's Church Rd Bedford NY 10506 Office: US Ct House Foley Sq New York City NY 10007

BONSAL, PHILIP WILSON, former ambassador; b. N.Y.C., May 22, 1903; s. Stephen and Henrietta (Morris) B.; ed. Institute Sillig, Vevey, Switzerland, 1914- 16, St. Paul's Sch., Concord, N.H., 1916-20; A.B., Yale, 1924; m. Margaret Lockett, April 10, 1929. Exec. with telephone cos. in Cuba, Spain, Chile, 1926-35; telephone expert for Fed. Communications Commn., 1935-37; apptd. vice consul at Havana, April, 1938, 3d sec. embassy, Aug., 1938; with Dept. of State, 1939, acting chief Am. Republics div., 1940, chief, 1942-44, 1st sec. embassy in Madrid 1944- 46, charge d'affaires a.i., Madrid, 1946-1947; counselor Am. embassy, The Hague, 1947-48; polit. adviser to W. Averell Harriman, U.S. spl. rep. in Europe, Econ. Cooperation Adminstrn. Paris; minister-counselor Am. Embassy, Paris, 1950; dir. Office of Philippine and S.E. Asian Affairs Dept. State; ambassador to Colombia 1955-57, Bolivia, 1957- 59, Cuba, 1959-61, Morocco, 1961-62; assigned to Dept. State, 1962-65. Served as 2d lt. Field Arty., Officers Res. Corps. 1924-29. Mem. Columbian Acad. Bogota (corr.). Clubs: Metropolitan (Washington); Century (N.Y.C.). Author: Cuba, Castro, and the United States, 1971. Contbr. articles and book revs. on fgn. affairs to mags. Home: 3142 P St NW Washington DC 20007

BONTE, FREDERICK JAMES, educator, physician; b. Bethlehem, Pa., Jan. 18, 1922; s. Frederick R. and Harriett (Stoudt) B.; B.S., Western Res. U., 1942, M.D., 1945; m. Cecile Poetzel; children—Frederick William, Stephen J., John A., Therese A., Suzanne M., Anne E. Intern, Huntington Meml. Hosp., Pasadena, Cal., 1944-46; resident Univ. Hosp., Cleve., 1948-52; practice medicine, specializing in radiology, Dallas, 1956—; mem. faculty Western Res. U. Sch. Medicine, 1952-56, asst. prof., 1952-56, chief radiotherapy and nuclear medicine, 1954-56; prof. U. Tex. Southwestern Med. Sch., Dallas, 1956—, chmn. dept. radiology, 1956—; dir. dept. radiology Parkland Meml. Hosp., Childrens Med. Center, VA Hosp., Presbyn. Hosp. (all Dallas). Mem. bd. Nat. Council Radiation Protection and Measurements, 1966—; radioloty tng. com. Nat. Insts. Gen. Med. Scis., USPHS, 1966-70; residency rev. com. radiology A.M.A., 1966-69. Pres. Dallas County unit Am. Cancer Soc., 1965-67, bd. dirs. Tex. div., 1965—. Served to capt. USAAF, 1946-48. Diplomate Am. Bd. Radiology (trustee 1969—). Fellow Am. Coll. Radiology; mem. Am. Roentgen Ray Soc. (mem. exec. com), Radiol. Soc. N.Am. (counselor), Nuclear Med. Soc. (dir.), Sigma Xi. Contbr. articles profl. jours. Research exptl. nuclear medicine. Home: 11138 Wonderland Trail Dallas TX 75229 Office: 5323 Harry Hines St Dallas TX 75235

BONTECOU, LEE, artist; b. Providence, Jan. 15, 1931; s. Russell and Margaret (Jones) B.; student Art Student's League, 1952-55. One man shows Gallery, N.Y.C., 1958, Leo Castelli, Inc., 1960, 62; exhibited group shows including Festival of Two Worlds, Spoleto, 1958, Martha Jackson Gallery, 1960, 61, Whitney Mus. Am. Art Annuals, 1961, 63, 64, Carnegie, 1961, Mus. Modern Art, 1961, 63, VI Sao Paulo Biennial, 1965, Chgo. Art Inst., 1962, 63, Albright Mus., Buffalo, 1963; represented in permanent collections including Albright Mus., Chase Manhattan Bank, Chgo. Art Inst., Corcoran Gallery, Cornell U., Dallas Mus. Fine Arts, Houston Mus. Fine Arts, Mus. Modern Art, Pa. Acad. Fine Arts, Whitney Mus. Am. Art. Fulbright scholar, 1956-58; recipient Louis Comfort Tiffany grant, 1959- 60; George D. Widerman medal Pa. Acad. Fine Arts, 1959. Address: 147 Wooster St New York City NY 10012*

BONTEMPS, ARNA WENDELL, author; b. Alexandria, La., Oct. 13, 1902; s. Paul Bismarck and Marie Carolina (Pembroke) B.; prep. edn., San Fernando (Cal.) Acad., 1917- 20; A.B., Pacific Union Coll., 1923; A.M., U. Chgo., 1943; L.H.D., Morgan State Coll., 1969; m. Alberta Johnson, Aug. 26, 1926; children—Joan Marie, Paul Bismark, Poppy Alberta, Camille Ruby, Constance Rebecca, Arna Alex. Tchr. pvt. schs., 1923-38; librarian Fisk U., Nashville, Tenn., 1943-65; prof. U. Ill., Chgo. Circle, 1966-69; lectr., curator Yale, 1969—. Julius Rosenwald fellow, 1938-39, 42-43. Awarded Crisis poetry prize, 1926; Alexander Pushkin poetry prize, 1926,27; Opportunity (jour. of Negro Life) short story prize, 1932; Jane Addams Children's Book Award, 1956. Mem. P.E.N., Authors League, Dramatists Guild, Sigma Pi Phi, Omega Psi Phi, Phi Mu Alpha. Editor: Golden Slippers, An Anthology, 1941; Father of the Blues (by W. C. Handy), 1941. Author numerous books latest publs.: Black Thunder, 1936, reissued 1968; Story of the Negro, 1948; The Poetry of the Negro (anthology, co- editor with L. Hughes), 1949; Chariot in The Sky, 1951; Story of George Washington Carver, 1954; Lonesome Boy, 1955; The Book of Negro Folklore (anthology, co-editor with L. Hughes), 1958; Frederick Douglass: Slave- Fighter-Freeman, 1959; One Hundred Years of Negro Freedom, 1961; American Negro Poetry, 1963; Personals, 1964; Famous Negro Athletes, 1964; (with J. Conroy) Anyplace But Here, 1966 (Dow award Soc. Midland Authors 1967); Hold Fast to Dreams, 1969; Great Slave Narratives, 1969; Free at Last: the Life of Frederick Douglass, 1971. Co-author with Countee Cullen: (play) St. Louis Woman, 1946. Editor: American Negro Poetry, 1963. Home: 3506 Geneva Circle Nashville TN 37209 ☆

BONTHRON, ROBERT JOHN, univ. dean; b. Chgo., Nov. 12, 1922; s. John R. and Beatrice (Milroy) B.; B.S., Ill. Inst. Tech., 1944, M.S., 1952, Ph.D., 1962. Dean of student Ill. Inst. Tech., 1968—. Home: 489 E South St Elmhurst, IL 60126.

BONYNGE, RICHARD, condr.; b. Sydney, Australia, Sept. 1930; m. Joan Sutherland, 1954. Debut as condr. Santa Cecelia Orch., Rome, 1962; condr. in Am. for Met. Opera, San Francisco Opera, Phila. Lyric Opera, Boston Opera, Seattle Opera, New Orleans Opera, Am. Opera Soc.; condr. in Can. for Vancouver Opera, Stratford Festival; condr. in Europe for Royal Opera House, London, Hamburg (Germany) State Opera, Edinburg, Florence, Vienna festivals; condr. in S.Am. at Colon, Buenos Aires; concert tours with Joan Sutherland, U.S., Can., Europe. Artistic dir., prin. condr. Sutherland Williamson Opera Co., tour Australia, 1965. Recordings for London Records include: Alcina, Don Giovanni, Beatrice di Tenda, Norma, Puritani, SomnambuLa, Semiramide, Les Huguenots, Faust, Lakmé, Griselda, Montezuma, Rosina (operas); Giselle, La Diable à Quatre, La Péri, Coppelia; also recordings 18th, 19th century vocal and instrumental music; (with Joan Sutherland) recital discs. Scholar 18th and early 19th century vocal and instrumental music; influential revival bel canto period. Office: care Ingpen and Williams 14 Kensington Ct London W8 England

BONZON, PAUL-JACQUES, educator, author; b. Sainte Marie du Mont, Manche, France, Aug. 31, 1908; s. Alphonse and Marie (Flaux) B.; Superior Diploma, Tng. Tchrs. Coll. Saint-Lo, Manche, 1927; m. Aimee Philippon, Oct. 26, 1949; children—Jacques, Isabelle. Tchr., Chabeuil Sch., Drome, France 1929-49; dir. Saint-Laurent Sch., Drome, 1949-59. Vice pres. Acad. Letters, Scis. and Arts, 1960—. Recipient 1st prize Comite national de l'Enfance for Childhood of the World, 1955; grand prize du Salon de l'Enfance de Paris for L'eventail de Seville, 1958; 1st prize Jeunesse, for Youth, 1952. Author: (juveniles) Loutsichien, 1946; Du gui pour Christmas, 1952; Mamadi, 1953; J-an-Lo, 1955; Les orphelins des Simitra, 1955; Le petit passeur du lac, 1956; La Ballerine de Majorque, 1956; Mon Vercors en feu, 1956; Tout-Fon, 1956; Le voyageur saus visage, 1958; La princesse saus nom, 1956; La Crois d'or de Santa-anna, 1960; Les six compagnons, (several vols.), 1961, 64. Works have been translated into numerous langs. Address: 6 Rue Louis Barthou Valence Drome France

BOO, BEN, mayor; b. Mpls., Jan. 21, 1925; s. Benjamin Charles and Henrietta (Mergens) B.; student U. Minn., 1943, U. Mo., 1944; m. Mary Daley, Oct. 12, 1948; children—Chris, Peter, Michael, Mary, Richard, Matthew. Adminstrv. asst. Minn., 195O-58; purchasing agt. St. Louis County, Minn., 1958-66; mayor of Duluth, Minn., 1966—. Home: 102 E Arrowhead Rd Duluth MN 55803 Office: City Hall Duluth MN 55802

BOOCHEVER, LOUIS CHARLES, fgn. service officer; b. Madison, Ga., May 33, 1920; s. Louis Charles and Miriam (Cohen) B.; A.B., Cornell U., Ithaca, N.Y., 1941; M. Pub. Adminstrn., Harvard, 1947, M.A., 1948; m. Virginia K. Outwin, Dec. 28, 1945; children—David Robert, Emily Louise, Mary Virginia, John Outwin. Adminstrn. fellow Littauer Center, Harvard, 1941-42, teaching and research fellow, 1947-48; with Dept. State, 1945-46, economist fiscal and trade policy div. ECA, 1948-50, Office European Regional Affairs, Dept. State, 1950-56, fgn. service officer, 1956—, dep. U.S. rep. European Coal and Steel Community 1956; dep. to U.S. rep. to OECD, Paris, 1960-61; dep. dir. internat. devel. orgn. staff AID, 1962-64; econ. counsellor Am. embassy, Belgrade, Yugoslavia, 1965-70; dep. chief mission, Brussels, 1971—. Counselor, U.S. Mission to European Communities, 1959. Served in OSS, AUS, 1942-45. Recipient Demobilization award Social Sci. Research Council, 1946-47. Mem. Am. Econ. Assn., Phi Beta Kappa, Phi Kappa Phi. Clubs: International, Cornell (Washington); Avala Tennis (Belgrade). Home: 5000 River Hill Rd Washington DC 20016 Office: care Dept of State Washington DC 20525

BOOCHEVER, ROBERT, lawyer; b. N.Y.C., Oct. 2, 1917; s. Louis C. and Miriam (Cohen) B.; A.B., Cornell U., 1939, LL.B., 1941; m. Lois Colleen Maddox, Apr. 22, 1943; children—Barbara K., Linda Lou, Ann Paula, Miriam Deon. Admitted to N.Y. bar, 1944, Alaska bar, 1947; asst. U.S. atty., Juneau, 1946-47; partner firm Faulkner, Banfield, Boochever & Doogan, Juneau, 1947—. Dir. First Nat. Bank Juneau, 1955-61; mem. adv. bd. Nat. Bank of Alaska. Chmn., Juneau chpt. A.R.C., 1949-51, Juneau Planning Commn., 1956-61; mem. Alaska Devel. Bd., 1949-52; adv. bd. Juneau-Douglas Community Coll. Served to capt. inf., AUS, 1941-45. Fellow Am. Coll. Trial Attys.; mem. Am., Alaska (pres. 1961-62), Juneau (pres. 1971-72), bar assns., Am. Judicature Soc. (dir.), Juneau C. of C. (pres. 1952, 55), Alaskans United (chmn.). Rotarian (pres. Juneau 1966-67). Club: Explorers (chmn. Juneau br.). Home: 1700 Angus Way Juneau AK 99801 Office: 311 Franklin St Juneau AK 99801

BOODBERG, PETER ALEXIS, educator; b. Vladivostok, Russia, Apr. 8, 1903; s. Baron Alexis Paul and Valentine (Nazoroff) B.; A.B., U. Cal. at Berkeley, 1924, Ph.D., 1930; m. Helen S. Petroff, 1928; 1 dau., Xenia (Mrs. Richard Henry Lee III). With U. Cal. at Berkeley, 1932—, successively instr., asst. prof., asso. prof., Agassiz prof. Oriental langs. and lit., 1960—. Fellow Am. Acad. Arts and Scis.; J.S. Guggenheim fellow, 1939, 56. Mem. Am. Oriental Soc., Linguistic Soc. Am., Am. Assn. U. Profs., Mediaeval Acad. Am. Author articles in field. Home: 555 Santa Barbara Rd Berkeley CA 94707

BOODELL, THOMAS J., lawyer; b. Harvard, Ill., June 15, 1906; s. John H. and Annette Cullen) B.; LL.B., U. Ill., 1929; m. Mary Elizabeth Houze, Oct. 4, 1933; children—Thomas J., Mary H. (Mrs. R. Donald Prescott, Jr.), William C., Leslie Jane (Mrs. Charles D. Floro). Admitted to Ill. bar, 1929 and since in pvt. practice law; sr. partner firm Boodell, Sears, Sugrue & Crowley, and predecessor firms, 1949—; sec., dir. various corps. Bd. dirs. Am. Bar Endowment, 1969—. Fellow Am. Bar Found. (chmn. 1964-65); mem. Am. (chmn. standing com. on regional meetings 1959, 61, 62, chmn. com. to cooperate with A.M.A. 1964, 65, assembly del. 1960-69, standing com. profl. ethics 1968—, chmn. scope and correlation of work com. 1969—), Ill., Chgo. (bd. mgrs. 1951-53, 63-67, pres. 1965-66) bar assns., Nat. Conf. Lawyers and Bankers (chmn. conf. 1958—), Am. Judicature Soc., Law Club Chgo., Chi Psi (trustee ednl. trust), Phi Delta Phi. Clubs: University, Mid-Day, Saddle and Cycle (Chgo.); Skokie Country (Glencoe, Ill.); Seven Lakes Country (Palm Springs, Cal.). Home: 1500 N Lake Shore Dr Chicago IL 60610 Office: 33 N LaSalle St Chicago IL 60602

BOOHER, EDWARD E., publisher; b. Dayton, O., July 29, 1911; s. Wilfred Elsworth and Cora Maybelle (Middlestader) B.; A.B., Antioch Coll., 1936; m. Selena Read Knight, Aug. 5, 1939 (div. 1961); children—David Knight, Carol Read, Bruce Edward; m. 2d, Agnes Martin Whitaker, 1961. Interviewer, sec. N.Y. State Employment Service, N.Y.C., 1935; joined McGraw-Hill Book Co., Inc., 1936, became v.p., 1944, dir., 1951—, exec. v.p., 1954-60, pres., 1960-68, chmn. bd., chief exec. officer, 1968-70; group v.p. books and edn. services, dir. McGraw-Hill, Inc.; dir. Fidelity Union Trust Co. Chmn. N.J. Bd. Higher Edn.; mem. Community Colls. Task Force for Edn. Commn. of States; mem. chancellor's panel univ. purposes for State N.Y. Bd. dirs. Franklin Book Programs, Inc. Trustee Antioch Coll., The Asia Soc. Mem. N.Y. Acad. Pub. Edn., Century Assn., Am. Soc. Engring. Edn. Club: Nassau. Office: 330 W 42d St New York City NY 10036

BOOK, HOWARD A., coll dean; B.A., Asbury Coll., 1936; M.A., U. Cal., 1938; Ph.D., U. Kan., 1947; postgrad. Ohio State U., 1962-63. Dean of the coll., Manchester Coll., North Manchester, Ind. Office: Manchester Coll North Manchester IN 46962*

BOOKER, HENRY GEORGE, scientist; b. Barking, Essex, Eng., Dec. 14, 1910; s. Charles Henry Henry and Gertrude Mary (Ratcliffe) B.; student Palmer's Sch., Grays, Essex 1921- 30; B.A., Christ's Coll., Cambridge, 1933, Ph.D., 1936; Guggenheim fellow Cambridge U., 1954-55; m. Adelaide Mary McNish, July 9, 1938; children—John Ratcliffe, Robert William, Mary Adelaide, Alice. Came to U.S. 1948, naturalized 1952. Fellow Christ's Coll., 1935-48; sci. officer, Ministry Aircraft Prodn., London, 1940-45; lectr. Cambridge U., 1945-48; prof. elec. engring. Cornell U., 1948-65, dir. sch. elec. engring., 1959-63, asso. dir. Center Radio Physics and Space Research, IBM prof. engring. and applied math., 1962-65; prof. applied electrophysics U. Cal. at San Diego, 1965—. 1965—. Jr. intermediate and sr. county scholarships, Essex, Eng., 1920-30; Entrance scholarship, Christ's Coll., 1930, Allen scholarship, 1934-35, Smith's prize, 1935; Duddell, Kelvin and instn. premiums Instn. Elec. Engrs., London, 1948-50. Fellow Royal Meteorol. Soc., Inst. Radio Engrs.; mem. Inst. Elec. Engrs. (asso.), Am. Astron. Soc. Nat. Acad. Scis., Am. Meteorol. Soc., Sigma Xi. Author: An Approach to Electrical Science, 1959; A Vector Approach to Oscillators, pub. 1965; also sci. papers on radio wave propagation. Home: 8696 Dunaway Dr La Jolla CA 92037 Office: Dept Applied Physics and Information Sci U Cal at San Diego La Jolla Jolla CA 92037.

BOOKHAMMER, EUGENE DONALD, state govt. ofcl.; b. Lewes, Del., June 18, 1918; s. William and Winifred (Jenkins) B.; student Am. Tech. Soc., 1938; m. Catherine Williams, Jan. 31, 1942; children—Joy, Jean. Owner-pres. Bookhammer Lumber Mill, Lewes, 1939-71, Joy Beach Devel. Co., Lewes, 1955-71; pres. Rehoboth Bay Dredging Co., Lewes, 1963-71; mem. Del. Senate, 1962-68; lt. gov. Del., 1969—. Dir. Farmers Bank of Del. Delegate Republican Nat. Conv., 1952, 56, 60; chmn. Sussex County Rep. Party, 1964-66. Bd. dirs. Beebe Hosp. Served with AUS, 1944-46; ETO. Decorated Purple Heart. Life mem. Boy Scouts Am. Mem. Am. Legion, Del. C. of C., V.F.W., Am. Inst. Banking, Tall Cedars of Lebanon. Mason (32, Shriner), Lion. Home: RD 2 Lewes DE 19958 Office: Legislative Hall Dover DE 19901

BOOKHOLT, WILLIAM JOHN, govt. ofcl.; b. Patterson, N.J., Aug. 30, 1916; s. James and Bella (Van Haste) B.; diploma accounting and bus. adminstrn. Pace Coll., 1939; student Rutgers U., 1938-40, Newark U., 1945; LL.B., Woodrow Wilson Coll. Law, Atlanta, 1950; postgrad. U. Ga., 1951-52; m. Marian E. Bell, June 30, 1943; children—Robert G., Barbara G. Field auditor Equitable Life Assurance Soc. N.Y., 1935-41; with Internal Revenue Service, 1946—, dist. dir., Atlanta, 1958-59, regional commr., Atlanta, 1959—; admitted to Ga. bar, 1950. Bd. dirs. United Appeal Atlanta. Served to capt. AUS, 1941-45. C.P.A., Ga. Mem. Ga. Soc. C.P.A.'s (Key award 1951, Outstanding Pub. Service award 1956), Ga. Bar Assn. Home: 2435 Tanglewood Rd Decatur GA 30033 Office: Peachtree St NE Atlanta GA 30303

BOOKMAN, GEORGE BARUCH, pub. relations ofcl; b. N.Y.C., Dec. 22, 1914; s. Arthur and Judith (Wertheim) B.; B.A., Haverford Coll, 1936; student Ecole des Sciences Politiques, Paris, France, 1934-35; postgrad. internat. studies, Geneva, Switzerland, 1936; m. Janet Schrank, Sept. 22, 1944; children— Ellen Jean (Mrs. Alan J. Fincke). Charles Arthur. Asso. editor U.S. News and World Report, Washington, 1938-40, 45-48; White House reporter Washington Post, 1940- 41; with OWI in Africa, Lebanon, Syria, Egypt, Italy, Austria, 1941-45; Washington corr. Time mag., 1948-58, nat. econ. corr., N.Y.C., 1958-60; bd. editors Fortune mag., 1961-62; dir. pub. information and press relations N.Y. Stock Exchange, 1962—. Mem. N.Y. Financial Writers Assn., Phi Beta Kappa, Sigma Delta Chi. Clubs: Nat. Press (Washington); Overseas Press (N.Y.C.). Home: 1085 Park Av New York City NY 10028 also Millbrook NY 12545 Office: 11 Wall St New York City NY 10005

BOOKOUT, JOHN FRANK, Jr., oil co. exec.; b. Shreveport, La., Dec. 31, 1922; s. John Frank and Lena (Hagen) B.; student Ia. Wesleyan Coll., 1943; Centenary Coll., 1946-47; B.Sc., U. Tex., 1949, M.A., 1950; m. Mary Carolyn Cook, Dec. 21, 1946; children—Beverly Carolyn, Mary Adair and John Frank III (Twins). Geologist Shell Oil Co., Tulsa, 1950-59, div. exploration mgr., 1959-61, area exploration mgr., Denver, 1961-63, The Hague, The Netherlands, 1963-64, exploration mgr., New Orleans, 1964, mgr. exploration and prodn. economics dept., N.Y.C., 1965, v.p. Denver exploration and prodn. area, 1966, v.p. Southeastern exploration and prodn. region, New Orleans, 1967-70, pres., chief exec. officer, dir. Shell Canada Ltd., Toronto, Ont., Can., 1970—; pres. Shell Investments Ltd.; dir. Inter-provincial Pipe Line Co. Mem. adv. council Geology Found. U. Tex.; bd. visitors Tulane U. Served with USAAF, 1942-46. Decorated Air medal with 3 oak leaf clusters. Home: 272 Forest Hill Rd Toronto 7 Ontario Canada Office: Shell Canada Ltd 505 University Av Toronto 2 Ontario Canada

BOOKSTAVER, ALEXANDER, corp. exec.; b. Sag Harbor, N.Y., Apr. 11, 1911; s. Samuel and Jennie (Lekus) B.; student Coll. City N.Y., 1929-32; student bus. adminstrn., N.Y.U., 1933-34; grad. Am. Inst. Banking, 1936; m. Dorothy Ravitt, Sept. 3, 1936; 1 son, Richard. With trust dept. Hanover Bank, N.Y.C., 1930-41; with comptroller's dept. Schroder Trust Co., N.Y.C., 1941-46; v.p., comptroller Amalgamated Bank N.Y., 1946-56; controller, dir. investment dept. Internat. Ladies Garment Workers Union, N.Y.C., 1956-61; dir. investment dept. AFL-CIO, Washington, 1961-68; v.p. instl. relations Anchor Corp., Elizabeth, N.J., 1968-69; pres. PMH Mgmt. Corp., Seaford, N.Y. 1969—; investment adviser to Churchill Fund, Inc.; dir. Peoples Nat. Bank of Md., Suitland. Mem. adv. com. housing and urban devel. AID, 1963-68; mem. adv. bd. Nat. Found. Health, Welfare and Pension Plans, 1963-68. Bd. dirs. Hebrew Inst. of L.I. Editorial adv. bd. Pension and Welfare News. Home: 8200 Kennedy Blvd E North Bergen NJ 07047 Office: PMH Mgmt Corp 3774 Merrick Rd Seaford NY 11783

BOOKSTAVER, DAVID RICHARD, lawyer, educator; b. Sag Harbor, N.Y., June 23, 1905; s. Charles and Annie (Jarvis) B.; A.B., Cornell, 1926; J.D. cum laude, Yale 1928, Sterling fellow, 1928-29; m. Rachael S. Booth, Aug. 16, 1941; children—Jane Merritt, Ellen, John. Research asst. law sch. Yale 1928-29; asso. Taylor, Blanc, Capron & Marsh, N.Y.C., 1929-34; practice law, East Hampton, N.Y. 1934-42; mem. firm Stephens & Bookstaver, East Hampton, 1938-42; chief counsel services br. O.P.A., 1942-43; spl. atty. chief fgn. agts. registration sect. Dept. Justice, 1943-47; prof. law Washington Coll. Law, Am. U., 1947-57; dean Washington Coll. Law 1951- 56; prof. law U. Pitts., 1957—. Vis. prof. law U. So. Cal., 1962, U. N.C., 1964; lectr. Practicing Law Inst., N.Y.; vis. prof. U. Cal., Hastings Sch. Law, 1967. Research cons. N.Y. State Law Revision Commn. Mem. Am. Bar Assn., Am. Law Inst., Order of Coif, Alpha Kappa Delta, Sigma Nu Phi. Author: New York Wills - Testamentary Trusts (with Elmer Lee Fingar), 1949; New York Will and Trusts (with Elmer Lee Fingar and John G. McQuaid), 1961; (with Elmer Lee Fingar) New York Will Manual, 1954; Pennsylvania Will Manual, 1965. Gen. editor Will Manual Service. Home: 83 Markham Dr Pittsburgh PA 15228

BOOM, AARON M., educator; b. Balden, Neb., Sept. 15, 1918; s. John Albert and Nettie Nettie (Morey) B.; A.B., U. Neb., 1940, A.M., 1941; Ph.D., U. Chgo., 1948; m. Kathleen Williams, Aug. 14, 1948; childrenBrian M., Alan D. Interim lectr. history Albion Coll., 1948-49; mem. faculty Memphis State U., 1949—, prof. history, 1958—, chmn. dept. 1964—. Served to lt. USNR, 1942-46. Decorated Purple Heart; grantee Am. Philos. Soc., 1958-59. Mem. Am., Miss. Valley, So. hist. assns., Am. Assn. U. Profs., Phi Beta Kappa. Contbr. profl. jours. Home: 1235 Elkwood St Memphis, TN. 38111.

BOOMA, HAROLD ELLSWORTH, shoe machinery mfg. exec.; b. Lynn, Mass., July 4, 1908; s. Scott Clayton and Annie May (Stevens) B.; B.S., Dartmouth, 1930; m. Dorothy Mae Cromwell, Dec. 26, 1931, children—Scott Cromwell, Richard Allan. With Dawn Cigarettes, Inc., N.Y.C., 1930-31, USM Corp. (formerly United Shoe Machinery Corp.), Boston, 1931—, various positions comml. and research divs., 1931-62, v.p. corp., mgr. shoe industry group, 1962-67, exec v.p., dir. 1967—; mem. mgmt. Converter Corp., Mears Heel Co., United Awl & Needle Corp., United Shank & Findings Co.; dir. Hoague Sprague Corp., United Shoe Machinery Can. Corp. Mem. Phi Gamma Delta, Paleopitus, Sphinx, Green Key. Home: 136 Galloupes Point Rd Swampscott MA 01907 Office: 140 Federal St Boston MA 02107

BOOMSLITER, PAUL COLGAN, educator; b. Urbana, Ill., Oct. 24, 1915; s. George Paul and Alice (Colgan) B.; A.B., W.Va. U., 1935; postgrad. La. State U., 1937; M.A., U. Ia., 1938; Ph.D., U. Wis., 1942; postgrad. Northwestern U., 1948; m. Patricia A. Flynn Himes, July 19, 1968; children—Paula Elise, Ann Dekker, Sara Ransone, Paul Lon, Mary Elizabeth Himes, Peter Edmund Himes. Asst. prof. Goucher Coll., Balt., 1940-46; asst. prof. Cornell U., 1946-48; prof. State U. N.Y., Albany, 1948—, chmn. speech pathology and audiology, 1969—; research asso. prof. Albany Med. Coll., 1968—; profl. dir. Northeastern N.Y. Speech Center, 1958-63, cons., 1963—; cons. speech pathology and audiology Albany VA Hosp., 1956—, Albany Study Center for Learning Disabilities, 1963—, Albany Child Guidance Center, 1963—, N.Y. State Dept. Mental Hygiene, 1969—. Served with USAAF, 1942-46. Recipient certificate of clin. competence in speech Am. Speech and Hearing Assn., 1950. Mem. Acoustical Soc. Am., A.A.A.S., Am., N.Y. State, Capital Area speech and hearing assns., N.Y. Acad. Scis., Modern Lang. Assn. Episcopalian. Author: The Referential Search Organ, 1960; The Boomsliter-Creel Test of Tonal Processing, 1965; Language Capacity and Language Learning, 1970. Contbr. articles profl. jours. Home: 8 Lawnridge Av Albany NY 12208 Office: 1400 Washington Av Albany NY 12203

BOONE, BYRON VEST, newspaper pub.; b. Gainesville, Mo., Feb, 27, 1908; s. George W. and Lu (Comer) B.; student U. Tulsa, 1926, LL.B., 1929; m. Audray Sipes, Feb. 17, 1934; 1 dau., Brenda Jo. Pub., Tulsa Daily World, 1959—; v.p., dir. Standard Life & Accident Ins. Co.; dir. Farmers & Mchts. Bank & Trust Co., Sloan Oil & Gas Co. Trustee U. Tulsa, Hillcrest Med. Center. Mem. Am., Okla. bar assns. Clubs: Tulsa, Southern Hills Country (Tulsa). Home: 2150 Forest Blvd Tulsa OK 74114 Office: World Bldg Tulsa OK 74103

BOONE, DANIEL, architect; b. Waco. Tex., Dec. 4, 1913; s. Harry Holmes and Clara (Whiteman) B.; student U. Tex., 1938; m. Margaret Conant, Mar. 14, 1941; children—Daniel, Mark Conant. Asso. Edward L. Wilson, Architect, Ft. Worth, 1939-40; designer Robert & Co., Jacksonville, Fla., 1940-42; asso. David S. Castle Co., Abilene, Tex., 1948-56; parnter Boone & Pope Architects and Engrs., Abilene, 1956—; works include Abilene Civic Center, Abilene City Hall, Taylor County Coliseum, Fine Arts Center of McMurry Coll., Sid Richardson Sci. Bldg. of Hardin-Simmons U. Pres. Nat. Council Archtl. Registration Bds., 1971-72. Chmn. St. John's Sch., Abilene, 1953-60. Served to capt., C.E., AUS, World War II; ETO. Fellow A.I.A. (dir. 1969-72); mem. Tex. Soc. Architects (pres. 1967), Alpha Tau Omega. Episcopalian. Home: 3434 S 9th St Abilene TX 79605 Office: 244 Leggett Dr Abilene TX 79605

BOONE, DANIEL C., Jr., steel co. exec.; b. Mt. Sterling, Ky., Feb. 23, 1920; s. Daniel C. and Grace (Salyer) B.; certificate in accounting, Marquette U., 1947; m. Jayne Deardoff, July 28, 1970; 1 son, Terry. With Superior Lawrence Bag Co., 1937-41, Haskins & Sells, C.P.A.'s, Cin., 1947; with Armco Steel Corp., 1941-42, 47—, controller steel div., 1958- 65, corp. controller, 1965-68, v.p. finance, 1967-69, sr. v.p. finance, 1969—; dir. Armco Steel Corp., Boothe Computor Corp., Winters Nat. Bank, Crystal Tissue Corp. Trustee Ohio Pub. Expenditure Council. Served with USAAF, 1942-45. Mem. Financial Execs. Inst., Ohio C. of C. (dir.). Republican. Home: 2105 Tullis Dr Middletown OH 45042 Office: Armco Steel Corp Middletown OH 45042

BOONE, EDGAR JOHN, educator; b. Varnado, La., June 27, 1930; s. John W. and Daisy M. (Holmes) B.; B.S., La. State U., 1951; M.S., U. Wis., 1955, Ph.D. (Kellogg fellow), 1959; m. Ethel Bower, July 19, 1959; children—John Bower, David Warner. County agt., La., 1951-56; asst. prof. La. State U., 1956-59; prof. extension adminstrn. U. Ariz., 1959-60, U. Wis., 1960-63; prof., head, dept. adult and community coll. edn. N.C. State U., also asst. dir. N.C. Agrl. Extension Service, 1963—. Cons., AID, Jamaica, 1962, U.S. Office Edn., 1968, Tuskegee Inst., 1969—, So. Assn. Colls. and Schs., 1971; mem. Nat. Com. on Adult Edn. Research, 1963—, Nat. Extension Curriculum Com., 1965—, N.C. Coastal Plains Planning and Devel. Commn., 1968—, accreditation commn. N.C. Dept. Community Colls., 1969—, Commn. Profs. Adult Edn. U.S., 1965—. Mem. Bd. Edn., United Meth. Ch. N.C., 1968—. Bd. dirs. Tuskegee Inst. Nat. Resource Devel. Center. Recipient Gov.'s Citizenship award, 1968; named Tar Heel of Week News and Observer, Raleigh, N.C., 1971; named to Acad. Outstanding Tchrs. N.C. State U., 1971—. Mem. Adult Edn. Assn. U.S. (chmn. nat. resources planning commn., 1967—, sec. 1968-69, v.p. 1970-71, pres. elect 1971-72), Rural Sociol. Soc., Epsilon Sigma Phi, Phi Delta Kappa. Democrat. Methodist. Author: Public Affairs Education in Yuma County, Arizona, 1961; A Programming Guide for University Extension, 1964; Curriculum Development in Adult Basic Education, 1967; A Conceptual Schema of Programming in the Cooperative Extension Service, 1971; also articles; editor books and jours. Home: 4918 Rembert Dr Raleigh NC 27609

BOONE, ENOCH MILTON, educator; b. Millersburg, Ky., Feb. 17, 1903; s. Robert Edmondson and Mary Alice (Clarke) B.; B.A. cum laude, U. Colo., 1926, M.S., 1932; M.S. in Elec. Engring., U. Mich., 1937; m. Nevada Atkinson, June 15, 1927; 1 dau., Mildred Louise. Instr. engring. math. U. Colo., 1926-28, instr. physics, 1928-30; research physicist Pittsfield Works lab. Gen. Electric Co., 1930-32; head engring. dept. Amarillo Coll., 1932-37; asst. prof. dept. elec. engring. Ohio State U., Columbus, 1937-44, asso. prof., 1944-47, prof. elec. engring., 1947—, dir. electron device lab., 1947-65, dir. Research Found., 1963-65; tech. staff Bell Tel. Labs., 1944-45. Recipient univ. distinguished teaching award, 1970. Fellow I.E.E.E. (dir. region 4 1955-56, mem. nat. coms. 1946-69); mem. Phi Beta Kappa, Sigma Xi, Tau Beta Pi, Eta Kappa Nu. Author: Circuit Theory of Electron Devices, 1953. Home: 2579 Berwyn Rd Columbus OH 43221

BOONE, JAMES BUFORD, newspaper pub.; b. Newnan, Ga., Jan. 8, 1909; s. James Edwin and Maude (McKoy) B.; A.B., Mercer U., 1929; m. Frances Herin, Sept. 15, 1929; children—Janette (Mrs. Younkin), James B. Reporter, Macon (Ga.) Telegraph and News, 1929-38, city editor, 1938-40, mng. editor, 1940-42; spl. agt. FBI, 1942-46; editor Macon Telegraph, 1946-47; pub. Tuscaloosa News, 1947-68; pres. Tuscaloosa Newspapers, Inc., 1954-68, chmn. bd., 1968—; pres. Tuscaloosa Hotel Co., 1963-65. Pres. Black Warrior council Boy Scouts Am., 1949; chmn. YMCA bldg. fund campaign, 1954; mem. Pulitzer awards jury, 1958. Recipient Pulitzer prize for editorial writing, 1957; George Washington medal for editorial writing Freedoms Found., 1957; Lovejoy award Colby Coll., 1957; Algernon Sydney Sullivan award U. Ala., 1968. Mem. Tuscaloosa C. of C. (v.p. 1954), Ala. Press Assn. (v.p. 1962). Baptist. Clubs: Rotary (pres. 1950-51), Country. Home: 2306 Glendale Gardens Tuscaloosa AL 35401 Office: 2001 6th St Tuscaloosa AL 35401

BOONE, JERRY NEAL, psychologist; b. Corinth, Miss., Feb. 15, 1927; s. Frank B. and Zettie (Nelms) B.; B.A., U. Miss., 1949; M.A., U. Fla., 1951; Ph.D., Vanderbilt U., 1961; m. Frankie Elizabeth Smith, Aug. 26, 1949; children—Jerrilyn Sue, Mary Elizabeth, Robert Arthur, Rebecca Ann. Spl. edn. cons. Tenn. Dept. Edn., 1949-50; sr. speech therapist Wilkerson Speech Center, Nashville, 1951-52; dir. speech clinic E. Tenn. State U., Johnson City, 1952-56; asso. prof., then prof. psychology Memphis State U., 1962-69, dean Univ. Coll., 1968-69; asst. prof. pediatrics U. Tenn. Coll. Medicine, 1964-66, asso. prof., 1966-69; pvt. practice, cons. clin. psychology, 1961-69; asso. dir. acad. affairs Tenn. Higher Edn. Commn., Nashville, 1969-70. Mem. Tenn. Bd. Examiners Psychology, 1965-69, chmn. 1968—. Mem. Am. Psychol. Assn. Home: 500 5th Av N Nashville TN 37219 Office: Jackson Office Bldg Nashville TN 37219

BOONE, PAT, (Charles Eugene Boone), singer, actor; b. Jacksonville, Fla., June 1, 1934; s. Archie and Margaret (Prichard) B.; student North Tex. State Tchrs. Coll., David Lipscomb Coll.; grad. magna cum laude, Columbia, 1958; m. Shirley Foley, Nov. 7, 1953; children—Cheryl Lynn, Linda Lee, Deborah Ann, Laura. Winner on Ted Mack TV Show, 1953, Arthur Godfrey Show, 1954; recs. Dot Records, 1955; singer Arthur Godfrey TV Show CBS, 1955; motion picture contract 20th Century Fox, 1957; star Pat Boone TV Show, ABC, 1957; appeared in the Greatest Story Ever Told, 1965. Dir. Northeastern Inst. Christian Edn., 1958—; mem. pres.'s bd. Pepperdine Coll., 1959. Selected 3d Top Ten Box Office Attractions, 1957; named Top Ten Record Artists, 1955; Top 15 Namepower Stars, 1959. Mem. Church of Christ. Author: Twixt Twelve and Twenty, 1958; Between You, Me and the Gatepost, 1960; The Real Christmas, 1961; Care & Feeding of Parents, 1967. Home: Beverly Hills Los Angeles CA 90213 Office: 9033 Wilshire Blvd Beverly Hills CA 90211

BOONE, RICHARD ALLEN, actor., dir.; b. Los Angeles, June 18, 1917; s. Kirk and Cecile (Beckerman) B.; student San Diego Army and Navy Acad., 1929-32, Stanford, 1934-37, Neighborhood Playhouse, N.Y.C., 1945-47; m. Clair McAloon, Apr. 27, 1951; 1 son, Peter. Actor, appeared in plays including Medea, 1947, MacBeth, 1949, The Man, 1950, also live TV, N.Y.C., 1947-50; motion picture actor 20th Century Fox, 195O-53, films include Halls of Montezuma, The Robe, Way of a Gaucho, Vickie; independent films The Raid, Lizzie; other films include War Lord, 1965, HOmbre, 1967; TV series, Medic (as Dr. Konrad Styner), as Mr. Paladin in Have Gun Will Travel; The Richard Boone Show. Served with USNR, World War II. Four times nominated for Emmy award, 1954. Mem. Acad. TV Arts and Scis., Acad. Motion Picture Arts and Scis. Tau Theta Xi.‡

BOONE, WALTER FREDRICK, consultant; b. Berkeley, Cal., Feb. 14, 1898; s. Thomas Lee and Lily Herman (Reid) B.; student Stanford; B.S., U.S. Naval Acad., 1920, postgrad., 1929; m. Pauline Haller Currey, June 7, 1922. Commd. ensign, U.S. Navy, 1920, advanced through grades to adm.; duties in scouting, fighter and patrol plane types, including comd. of carrier based fighting squadron and patrol seaplane squadron; aviation test and development work, Naval Proving Ground, Dahigren, Va., 1933-35; in charge armament sect. Bur. of Aeronautics, Navy Dept., Washington, D.C., 1939-42; exec. officer in U.S.S. Enterprise, 1942-43; chief of staff, Carrier Task Force, 1943-44; comdr. naval air bases, 12th Naval Dist., 1944; comdg. officer in U.S.S. Yorktown, 1945; chief of staff, Comdr. Naval Naval Forces Western Pacific, 1945-47; mem. gen bd. Navy Dept., 1947; asst. chief Naval Operations for Strategic Plans, 1947-49; comdr. Carrier div. Five, acting comdr. 7th Fleet, 1949-50; dep. comdr.-in- chief Naval Forces Eastern Atlantic and Mediterranean, 195O-51; comdr. Naval Forces Eastern Atlantic, 1951-52; with joint chiefs of staff, 1952- 54, supt. U.S. Naval Acad., 1954-56; comdr.-in-chief, U.S. Naval Forces, Eastern Atlantic and Mediterranean, 1956-58; U.S. mem. NATO standing group and mil. com., 1958-60; ret. as adm. USN, 1960. Cons. McDonnell Aircraft Corp., St. Louis, 1960-62; dep. asso. adminstr. def. affairs NASA, Washington, 1962-66, asst. adminstr. def. affairs, 1966-68; now cons. Decorated Silver Star, Legion of Merit (U.S.); Order of British Empire, D.S.M.; recipient Exceptional Service award NASA. Member U.S. Naval Acad. Alumni Assn. (pres. 1963-64), Chi Psi. Methodist. Home: 4000 Massachusetts Av NW Washington DC 20016

BOONE, WILLIAM BRUCE, investment banker; b. Redlands, Cal., Sept. 18, 1913; s. Charles Jay and Maude (Van Leuvan) B.; student U. Cal. at Berkeley, 1931-35; m. Madeleine Fretz, Sept. 30, 1936; children—Bruce, Ellen Storey, Dennis Jackson, Maria Thresa. With Dean Witter & Co., 1935-42, 49—, account adviser, Portland, Ore., 1936-42, mgr. Portland Office, 1949—, partner, 1954-69; v.p., N.W. corporate finance rep., 1969—; with Blyth & Co., Portland, 1945-49. Pres. Portland Rose Festival Assn., 1958, bd. dirs., 1950—; chmn. Multnomah County March Dimes, 1956, Multnomah County drive Am. Cancer Soc., 1952; recruitment chmn. blood bank program Multnomah County chpt. A.R.C., 1949. Bd. regents U. Portland (Ore.). Served to lt. (j.g.) USNR, 1942-45; MTO. Named First Citizen of Portland, Portland Realty Bd., 1958. Mem. Nat. Assn Security Dealers (chmn. dist. 1, 1953-54), Portland Security Dealers Assn. (pres. 1961-62), Investment Bankers Assn. (chmn. Pacific N.W. group 1960, nat. bd. govs. 1961—), Delta Upsilon. Republican. Roman Catholic. Home: 2432 SW Broadway Dr Portland OR 97201 Office: 1100 SW 6th Av Portland OR 97204

BOONISAR, RICHARD, hotel exec.; b. Boston, June 27, 1907; ed. Harvard, 1929; m. Barbara Manson, June 16, 1937; childrenRichard M., Philip L. With Sheraton Corp., 1953-. Bd. dirs. Family Counseling and Guidance Centers Boston, Mem. nat. adv. Council Small Bus. Adminstrn., 1967. Served to maj. USAAF, World War II. Home: 150 Bristol Rd Wellesley, MA 02181. Office: 47O Atlantice Av., Boston 02210.

BOONSTRA, CLARENCE A., foreign service officer b. Grand Rapids, Mich., Jan. 5, 1914; s. James and Jennie (Brouwer) B.; A.B., Mich. State Coll., 1936; A.M., La. State U., 1937, Ph.D., 1942; spl. studies at U. Wis., 1939, U. Chgo., 1940; m. Mildred Sharp Fereira, Oct. 27, 1944 (dec.); children—Sandra Ann, Carl Albert; m. 2d, Margaret Ellen Beshore, August 13, 1966; children— Tara Elena, Alex Kathleen. Engaged in private business, 1937-38; economist U.S. Dept. Agr., Baton Rouge, 1939; instr. La. State U., 1940—41; information and adminstrv. officer U.S. Dept. Agr., 1942, asst. agrl. attache Am. embassy, Havana, Cuba, 1942-45, agrl. attache, Manila, P.I., 1945-47, 2d sec. and agrl. attache, Lima, Peru, 1947-49, 1st sec. and agrl. attache, Buenos Aires, Argentina, 1949-53; 1st sec. Rio de Janeiro, 1953-55; conselor for econ. affairs, Havana, 1955-57; Nat. War Coll., Washington, 1957-58; dep. dir. Office S. Am. Affairs, Dept. of State, 1958; dep. dir. Office of East Coast Affairs, 1958-59, dir., 1959-61; minister, polit. adviser Caribbean Command, Canal Zone, 1961-63; minister-counselor of Am. embassy, Mexico City, 1963-67; U.S. ambassador to Costa Rica, 1967-69; vis. prof. U. Colo., 1969-70; minister Am. embassy, Rio de Janeiro, Brazil, 1970—. Author tech. econs. bulls. and articles pub. by U.S. Govt. and La. State U. Address: American Embassy Rio de Janeiro Brazil also Dept of State Washington DC 20525

BOORKMAN, CHARLES JOHN, librarian; b. Aurora, Ill., Mar. 31, 1909; s. Charles John and Clara (Frey) B.; A.B., U. Ill., 1933, B. Library Sci., 1938; M.A., U. So. Cal., 1954; m. Ruth Ellen Reuss, Sept. 19, 1939; children—Jo Anne, Mary Elizabeth. Librarian regional project Nat. Youth Adminstrn., Quoddy Village, Me., 1938-42, Fifth Service Command, War Dept., Columbus, O., 1942-43; sci. librarian San Jose State Coll., 1945-48; librarian Los Angeles State Coll., 1948-49, Cal. State Coll., Long Beach, 1949—. Served with USNR, 1943-45. Mem. Am., Cal. library assns., Am. Assn. U. Profs., Kappa

Delta Rho, Phi Kappa Phi. Rotarian. Author bibliographies for Nat. Youth Adminstrn. Home: 6441 DeLeon St Long Beach CA 90815 Office: 6101 E 7th St Long Beach CA 90801

BOORMAN, BRUCE E., ins. co. exec.; b. Buffalo, Jan. 8, 1919; B.A., Duke. With Liberty Mut. Ins. Cos., 1941—; now sec. Liberty Mut. Ins. Co., Liberty Mut. Fire Ins. Co., Liberty Life Assurance Co.; dir. Traffic Safety of Mich., Maugus Corp. Bd. dirs. Jr. Achievement Eastern Mass., Back Bay Planning and Devel. Corp. Mem. Am. Soc. Corp. Secs., Phi Delta Theta. Home: 46 Lincoln Rd Wellesley Hills MA 02181 Office: 175 Berkeley St Boston MA 02144*

BOORMAN, JOHN, dir. motion picture Point Blank. Address: care Metro-Goldwyn-Mayer Films 10202 West Blvd Culver City CA 90230*

BOORSCH, JEAN, educator; b. Anzin, France, Jan. 25, 1906; s. Auguste René and Laure (Renotte) B.; Agrégation-és Lettres, Sorbonne, Paris, 1929; M.A. (hon.), Yale, 1953; L.H.D. honoris causa, Middlebury Coll., 1971; m. Louise Heathwood Totten, Dec. 16, 1933; children—James, Suzanne, Marie-Louise, John Peter. Asst. prof. Middlebury (Vt.) Coll., 1929-34; successively asst. prof. to asso. prof. Yale, 1934-53, Street prof. modern langs., 1953—. Decorated Chevalier Legion of Honor (France). Mem. Modern Modern Lang. Assn., Assn. Tchrs. French, Société des Professeurs Français en Amérique. Author: Etat Présent des Etudes sur Descartes, 1937; Recherches sur la technique dramatique de Corneille, 1943; Méthode orale de Français, 1948; Structure d'esprit de Montaigne, 1955. Home: 61 Millbrook Rd Hamden CT 06518 Office: Pierson Coll Yale New Haven CT 06504

BOORSE, HENRY A., physicist, coll. adminstr.; b. Norristown, Pa., Sept. 18, 1904; s. Henry A. and Martha (Godshall) B.; B.S. with distinction, U.S. Naval Acad., 1926; A.M., Columbia, 1933, Ph.D., 1934; post-doctoral research Cambridge U., 1934-35; m. Margaret V. Hazelton, Mar. 12, 1931; children— Ronald H., Michael (dec.), Suzanne (Mrs. Gilbert Hawkins). Asst. in physics Columbia, 1928-31, instr., 1931-33, Barnard fellow, 1933-34, Lydig fellow, 1934-35; instr. Coll. City of N.Y., 1935-37; asst. prof. Barnard Coll., 1937-43, asso. prof., 1943- 48, prof., 1948-70, prof. emeritus, 1970, chmn. dept., 1937-68, acting dean of faculty, 1957, dean of faculty, 1959-70, dean emeritus, 1970, spl. lectr. physics, 1970—, asst. to pres., 1970—, acting pres., 1962, 67; Ernest Kempton Adams fellow, Columbia 1938-40; on leave of absence for war research, Manhattan Dist. (Atomic Bomb) Project, 1942-45; S.A.M. Labs., Manhattan Project, 1942-46, div. dir., 1945-46. Contract for spl. services with AEC, 1946-58; cons. Brookhaven Nat. Lab., 1946-58. Served as ensign U.S. Navy, 1926-28. Fellow Am. Phys. Soc.; mem. Sigma Xi, Phi Beta Kappa (hon.). Republican. Presbyn. Clubs: Century; Faculty (Columbia U.) Del. Fedn. of American Scientists to Internat. Conf. of Atomic Scientists at Oxford, Eng., July, 1946, and observer for Carnegie Endowment for Internat. Peace. Chmn. Calorimetry Conf., 1956-57, London award com., 1964- 66; mem. commn. I, Internat. Inst. of Refrigeration; mem. U.S. Nat. Com. for I.R.R. and vice chmn. com. on basic sci. Contbr. to science jours. on research in very low temperature physics. Author: (with Lloyd Motz) World of the Atom, 2 vols., 1966. Home: 338 Summit Av Leonia NJ 07605

BOORSTIN, DANIEL J., mus. dir., author; b. Atlanta, Oct. 1, 1914; s. Samuel and Dora (Olsan) B.; A.B. summa cum laude, Harvard, 1934; B.A. first class honors (Rhodes scholar), Balliol Coll., Oxford U., 1936, B.C.L. first class honors, 1937; postgrad. Inner Temple, London, 1934-37; J.S.D. (Sterling fellow), Yale, 1940; Litt.D., Cambridge U., 1967; m. Ruth Carolyn Frankel, Apr. 9, 1941; children—Paul Terry, Jonathan, David West. Admitted as barrister-at-law Inner Temple, 1937; instr., tutor history and lit. Harvard and Radcliffe Coll., 1938-42, lectr. legal history Harvard Law Sch., 1939-42; asst. prof. history Swarthmore Coll., 1942- 44; asst. prof. U. Chgo., 1944-49, asso. prof., 1949-56, prof. Am. History, 1956-69, Walgreen lectr. Am. instns., 1952; dir. Nat. Mus. History and Tech., Smithsonian Instn., Washington, 1969—. Fulbright vis. lectr. Am. history, U. Rome, Italy, 1950-51, Kyoto U., Japan, 1957; cons. Social Sci. Research Center, U. P.R., 1955; lectr. for U.S. Dept. State in Turkey, Iran, Nepal, India, Ceylon, 1959-60, Indonesia, Australia, New Zealand, Fiji, 1968; 1st incumbent of chair Am. history U. Paris, 1961-62; Pitt prof. Am. history and instns. U. Cambridge, 1964-65; sr. fellow Huntington Library, 1969. Admitted to Mass. bar, 1942; sr. attorney Office Lend Lease Adminstr., Office Asst. Solicitor Gen., Washington. Fellow Trinity Coll., 1964-65. Trustee, Colonial Williamsburg; bd. visitors U.S. Air Force Acad. Recipient Bowdoin prize Harvard, 1934, Jenkins prize, Younger prize Balliol Coll., 1935, 36. Mem. Colonial Soc. Mass., Am., So. hist. assns., Orgn. Am. Historians, Internat. House Japan, Phi Beta Kappa. Jewish religion. Mem. Am. Revolution Bicentennial Commn. Clubs: Cosmos; Elizabethan (Yale); Reform (London, Eng.). Author: The Mysterious Science of the Law, 1941; Delaware Cases, 1792-1830 (3 vols.), 1943; The Lost World of Thomas Jefferson, 1948; The Genius of American Politics, 1953; The Americans: The Colonial Experience, 1958 (winner Bancroft award 1959); America and the Image of Europe, 1960; The Image or What Happened to the American Dream, 1962; The Americans: The National Experience, 1965 (Francis Parkman prize 1966); The Landmark History of the American People, 2 vols., 1968, 70; The Decline of Radicalism, 1969; The Sociology of the Absurd, 1970. Editor: Chicago History of American Civilization (23 vols.); An American Primer, 1966. Editor Am. history, Ency. Brit., 1951-55. Author articles, book reviews. Home: 3541 Ordway St NW Washington DC 20016 Office: National Museum of History and Technology Washington DC 20560

BOOS, FERNINAND R., educator; B.A., De La Salle Coll., 1932; M.S., Cath. U. Am., 1939, Ph.D., 1943. Now prof. chemistry, chmn. dept. Detroit Inst. Tech., also acting dean Coll. Arts and Scis. Address: Dept Chemistry Detroit Inst Tech Detroit MI 48201*

BOOT, HENRY ALBERT HOWARD, physicist; b. Birmingham, Eng., July 29, 1917; s. Henry James and Ruby May (Beeson) B.; grad. King Edward's High Sch. for Boys, Birmingham, 1935; B.Sc. with honors in Physics, U. Birmingham, 1938, Ph.D., 1941; m. Penelope May Herrington, May 1, 1948; children—Nicholas John Henry, Christopher James. Jr. Nuffield research fellow U. Birmingham, 1941-45, sr. fellow, 1945-48; prin. sci. officer Services Electronic Research Lab., Baldock, Herts; Eng., 1948-54, sr. prin. sci. officer, 1954—; research high-power microwave generation, prodn. high-temperature plasma and thermonuclear research. Mem. Brit. delegation 2d Conf. Peaceful Uses of Atomic Energy, Geneva, 1958. Recipient award Royal Commn. on Awards to Inventors (with others), 1949, John Price Wetherell medal Franklin Inst. (with others), 1958, John Scott award City of Phila. (with others), 1959. Mem. Inst. Physics, Instn. of Elec. Engrs. Club: Athenaeum (London, Eng.). Home: Old Mill Cottage Rushden Buntingford England Office: Services Electronic Research Laboratory Baldock Herfordshire England

BOOTH, ARCH NEWELL, orgn. exec.; b. Wichita, Kan., July 9, 1906; s. Winfield Milton and Laura Belle (Parker) B.; A.B., Wichita State U., 1927; Nat. Inst. Comml. and Trade Orgn. Exec., Northwestern U., 1932-43; LL.D., Hillsdale Coll., 1953; m. Wilma Grace Harrison, Feb. 2, 1929; children—Joan, Robert Harrison, Donald A. Spl. rep. Wheeler- Kelley Hagney Trust Co., Wichita, 1927-29; asst. mgr. C. of C., Wichita, 1929-38, gen. mgr., 1938-43; asst. gen. mgr. C. of C., U.S., 1943-47, mgr., 1947-50, exec. v.p. 1950—; pub. Nations Bus. Mag. 1950—; dir., mem. exec. Com. Union Trust Co., Washington. Recipient gold medal Freedoms Found., 1952, Spl. Freedom Leadership award, 1963; named vol. leader of year Am. Assn. Orgn. Execs., 1960. Mem. Pi Kappa Delta. Methodist. Mason (Shriner). Club: Metropolitan (Washington). Home: 3520 Overlook Lane NW Washington DC 20016 Office: 1615 H St Washington DC 20006

BOOTH, CHARLES LOOMIS, corp. exec.; b. East Orange, N.J., Oct. 24, 1901; s. Thomas Gearing and Lulu May (Loomis) B.; student Townsend Harris Hall, N.Y.C., 1916-19; B.S., U.S. Mil. Acad., 1924; grad. Air Tactical Sch., 1939; m. Nancy Washington Miller, Dec. 24, 1929; children—Charles Loomis, Elizabeth Tyler. Commd. 2d lt. U.S. Army, 1924, and advanced through grades to brig. gen., Nov. 1943; assigned to Field Arty., 1924-41; with Air Force, 1941; asst. chief of staff, A-4, 8th Air Force, 1942, Northwest African Air Forces, 1942-1943, Mediterranean Air Forces, 1944; dep. comdr. material and maintenance, 1944-1945; asst. chief Staff A-4, U.S. Strategic Air Forces (Pacific), 1945, ret. 1947; v.p., gen. mgr. Société des Eaux d'Athenes et Piree, 1948-67, ret., 1967; cons. Equity Corp. N.Y., 1968—. Decorated Legion of Merit with oak leaf cluster, Bronze Star medal; Croix de Guerre with Palm, Legion of Honor (France); comdr. Order of British Empire; Croix de Guerre (Belgium). Clubs: Propeller (Port of Piraeus, Greece); Tennis, Royal Yachting (Athens, Greece). Home: 2500 Q St Washington DC 20007 also Sotogrande La Linea (Cadiz) Spain

BOOTH, CHARLES THOMAS, former naval officer; b. Penacook, N.H., Jan. 12, 1910; s. Charles Herbert and Fannie May (Chamberlin) B.; B.S., U.S. Naval Acad., 1931; grad. U.S. Navy Postgrad. Sch., 1939; S.M., Mass. Inst. Tech., 194O; grad. Nat. War Coll., 1954; m. Peggy Maltman, Apr. 10, 1933; children—Peter B., Peggy Scott (Mrs. William E. Ramsey), Thomas B. Commd. ensign U.S. Navy, 1931, advanced through grades to vice adm., 1965; designated naval aviator, 1933; served aboard U.S.S. Oklahoma, U.S.S. Saratoga and two U.S.S. Rangers; asst. flight test officer Naval Air Test Center, Patuxent River, Md., 1943-46; mem. staffs Carrier Div. 12 and 7, 1944-46; exec. officer U.S.S. Princeton, 1946-47; assigned Bur. Aero. and Office Chief Naval Operations, Washington, 1947-5O; comdg. officer Composite Squadron 4, 195O-51; dir. electronics test Naval Air Test Center, 1951-53; comdg. officer U.S.S. Badoeng Strait, 1954-55; mem. staff comdr. in chief Pacific Fleet, 1955-57; comdg. officer carrier U.S.S. Ranger, 1957-58; chief staff, aide to comdr. Naval Air Force, Atlantic Fleet, 1958-59; asst. chief program mgmt. Bur. Naval Weapons, Navy Dept., 1959-61; comdr. Carrier Div. 5, Pacific Fleet, 1961-62; dir. devel., programs Naval Operations, 1962-63, dep. chief Naval Operations (devel.), 1963-65; comdr. Naval Air Force, Atlantic Fleet, 1965-69; ret. 1969. Decorated Navy Cross, Legion of Merit, D.S.M. Home: Conn House Naval Base Norfolk CT 06852

BOOTH, DONALD PRENTICE, ret. army officer, assn. exec.; b. Albany, N.Y., Dec. 21, 1902; s. Alfred James and Anna May (Roe) B.; B.S., U.S. Mil. Acad., 1926; C.E., Cornell U., 1928; grad. U.S. Army Engr. Sch., Ft. Belvoir, Va., 1930, Comd. and Gen. Staff Sch., 1940; m. Dee Morrison, Dec. 27, 1928 (div. Mar. 1947); m. 2d, Rose Carolyn Krusich, Apr. 21, 1948. Commd. 2d lt., C.E., U.S. Army, 1926, advanced through grades to lt. gen., 1957; served with 1st U.S. Engrs., Ft. Dupont, Del., 1926-27, with 29th Engrs., Ft. Humphreys, Va., Ft. Bragg, N.C., Ft. Dix, N.J., 1928- 29, with 3d Engrs., Hawaiian Div., Schofield Barracks, T.H., 1930-33; asst. to dist. engr., Rock Island, Ill., 1934-35; instr. math. U.S. Mil. Acad., West Point, 1935-39, with 2d Engrs., Ft. Sam Houston, Tex., 1940; asst. to dist. engr., Seattle, Wash., 1940-42; with Persian Gulf Command, 1942-45, successively dir. ports, asst. chief of staff for operations, chief of staff, 1942-44, comdg. gen., 1944-45; office Under Sec. of War, 1945; exec. to under-sec., 1946-47; dep. dir. for logistics, joint chiefs staff, 1947-50; asst. for planning coordination, office chief of staff U.S. Army, 1950-51; asst. div. comdr. 4th Inf. Div., Germany, 1952-53; comdg. gen. 28th inf. div., 1953-54; comdg. gen. 9th inf. div., Germany, 1954; dep. asst. chief of staff G/l, U.S. Army, The Pentagon, 1954-55, asst. chief of staff G-l, 1955-56; dep. chief staff for personnel, 1956-58; U.S. high commr. Ryukyu Islands, 1958-61; comdg. gen. 4th U.S. Army, 1961-62, ret. 1962; now treas., dir. Citizens Planning Assn., Inc., Santa Barbara County, Cal. Decorated D.S.M., two Oakleaf Clusters to D.S.M. (U.S.); Imperial Order of Humayan, ll Class (Iran); Honorary Comdr. Mil. Order Brit. Empire, 1947; Russian Order of Kutezov; Japanese Order of Rising Sun; Korean Order of Mil. Merit, Taeguk with Silver Star. Mem. Am. Soc. C.E., Am. Soc. Mil. Engrs. Home: 1377 School House Rd Santa Barbara CA 93108 Office: Citizens Planning Assn Studio G El Presidio Santa Barbara CA 93101

BOOTH, FRANK EWEN, mfg. co. exec.; b. Long Beach, Cal., Oct. 4, 1910; s. Harry Wills and Bertha (Bickel) B.; B.A. in Econs., Stanford, 1932, M.B.A., 1934; m. Arleen Kay King, Dec. 29, 1934; children—Karen Kay (Mrs. John C. Carlson). Bonnie G. (Mrs. Richard F. Holt, Jr.). Accountant with Standard Oil Co. Cal., 1934-41; mem. finance dept. mail order div. Montgomery Ward & Co., 1941-43; controller Grayson Heart Control Co., 1943-45; asst. gen. mgr. Gen. Tire & Rubber Co. Cal., 1945-47; chmn. bd. Interstate Engring Corp., Anaheim, Cal., 1947—. Mem. Dept. Commerce Trade Mission to Austria, 1957. Mem. adv. council Stanford Bus. Sch. Mem. Mchts. and Mfrs. Assn. (sec., dir.). Stanford Bus. Sch. Alumni Assn. (pres.), U.S. Olympiads. Clubs: California (Los Angeles); Balboa Bay, Lincoln Orange County (Newport Beach, Cal.); Yuma (Ariz.) Golf and Country; El Dorado Country (Palm Desert). Home: 102 Irvine Cove Dr Laguna Beach CA 92651 Office: 522 E Vermont Av Anaheim CA 92805

BOOTH, GEORGE, physician; b. Pitts., Jan. 16, 1901; s. Harry John and Ella (Youngson) B.; B.S., Allegheny Coll., 1922, D.Sc. (hon.), 1964; M.D., Harvard, 1926; m. Adelaide Earley Rieck, Oct. 4, 1936; children—Albert G., Letitia R. (Mrs. Isherwood), Edward E., John E. Intern West Penn Hosp., Pitts., 1926-27; resident Peter Bent Brigham Hosp., Boston, 1927-28; practice internal medicine, Pitts., 1929-67; pres. med. bd. West Penn Hosp., Pitts., 1956-64, med. dir., 1963-66; instr. medicine U. Pitts. Med. Sch., 1937-40, asst. prof. medicine, 1940-50. Contbr. med. jours. Home: 1340 Bennington Av Pittsburgh PA 15217

BOOTH, HENRY SCRIPPS, found. exec.; b. Detroit, Aug. 11, 1897; s. George Gough and Ellen (Scripps) B.; B.Arch., U. Mich., 1924; m. Carolyn E. Farr, Sept. 27, 1924; children—Stephen Farr, David Gagnier, Cynthia B., Melinda B. (Mrs. Thomas Dale Hubbard), Martha B. (Mrs. Scherer). Chmn. bd. trustees Cranbrook Found., Bloomfield Hills, Mich., 1946—; dir. Booth Newspapers, Inc., Detroit News. Hon. pres. Oakland Citizens League, Cranbrook Music Guild; bd. dirs. sec. Cranbrook Writers Guild; bd. dirs. Cranbrook Gardens Aux., Met. Detroit Council Churches; mem. archtl. commn. Diocese of Mich. Bd. dirs. Birmingham-Bloomfield Council Human Relations; trustee Inst. for Advanced Pastoral Studies, Mariners' Ch., Detroit. Mem. Oakland Citizens League (dir.), Am. Fedn. Arts, Archives Am. Art, Soc. Arts and Crafts, Mich. Hist. Soc., Nat. Trust for Historic Preservation, Nat. Cathedral Assn. Home: 700 Cranbrook Rd Bloomfield Hills MI 48013 Office: The Branbrook Foundation 500 Lone Pine Rd Bloomfield Hills MI 48013

BOOTH, J. HAROLD, corp. exec.; b. Detroit, 1907; grad. John Marshall Law Sch., 1944. Pres., dir. Polaroid Corp., Cambridge, Mass. Home: 212 Bal Bay Dr Bal Harbor FL 33154 Office: Polaroid Corp 730 Main St Cambridge MA 02139

BOOTH, JOHN EDWARD, lawyer; b. N.Y.C., Nov. 7, 1897; s. John T. and Mary (Larkin) B.; A.B., Amherst Coll., 1923; LL.B., Fordham U., 1927; m. Katherine Keeler, June 10, 1928; children—John T., Grace-Mary G. Admitted to N.Y. bar. 1927, since practiced in N.Y.C.; dir. Iroquois Industries, J. W. Wilson Glass Co. Chmn. North Suffolk County chpt. A.R.C. Bd. dirs. Huntington (N.Y.) Hosp., 1940-47, pres. bd., 1943-47. Trustee North Country Sch., Lake Placid; trustee, treas. Nightingale- Bamford Sch., N.Y.C. Served as lt. (j.g.) USNR, 1917-21. Mem. St. George Soc. N.Y.C., Delta Kappa Epsilon. Club: National Arts (bd. govs., pres.). Home: 1 Lexington Av New York City NY 10010 Office: 50 Broadway New York City NY 10004

BOOTH, JOHN LORD, Mary (Batterman) B.; student Yale, 1926-28; m. Louise Preston Camper, Aug. 26, 1944; children—John L. II, Ralph H. II, Doreen (Mrs. George Hamilton III), Winifred, and Jacklyn (Mrs. Robert C. Coleman). Pvt. sec. to Am. Ambassador to Denmark June 1930; v.p., treas. Ralph H. Booth Corp., 1931-38; founder, pres., owner Booth American Co., 1939—; founder, pres., owner Booth Broadcasting Co. (WJLB and WMZK, Detroit; WABQ and WXEN, Cleve.; WTOD and WKLR, Toledo; WIBM and and WBBC, Jackson, Mich.; WSGW and WSBM, Saginaw, Mich.; WIOU and WKMO, Kokomo; Ind.; WJVA and WRBR, South Bend, Ind.; founder, pres., owner Booth Communications Co. (Muskegon TV Cable System, Summit Leoni (Jackson) TV Cable System, Cadillac TV Cable System, Manistee TV Cable System, Holland Zeeland TV Cable System, Mt. Pleasant TV Cable Co. (all Mich.), Salem TV Cable System, Pulaski TV Cable System, Blacksburg Christiansburg TV Cable System (all Va.), Rocky Mount (N.C.) TV Cable System; dir. Booth Newspapers, Inc., owning and operating Grand Rapids Press, Flint Journal, Saginaw News, Bay City Times, Muskegon Chronicle, Kalamazoo Gazette, Jackson City Patriot, Ann Arbor News. Mem. Mayor's Good Citizenship Commn. Trustee Detroit Inst. Arts; patron Grand Rapids Art Gallery, Flint Inst. Arts, Saginaw Mus. Arts. Served as lt. (s.g.), USNR World War II. Decorated Stella della Solidarieta Italiana. Knight Order of Solidarity (Italy). Mem. N.A. Yacht Racing Union, Detroit Hist. Soc., Greater Detroit Bd. Commerce, Yale Alumni Assn. Mich., Andover Alumni Assn. Republican. Episcopalian (vestryman). Mason. Clubs: Detroit, Detroit Athletic, Country, Economic, University, Bayview Yacht (Detroit); Grosse Pointe, Tennis House (Grosse Pointe, Mich.); Radio Executives (N.Y.C.); Otsego (Mich.) Ski; Farmington Country (Charlottesville, Va.); Roanoke (Va.) Country; Saginaw (Mich.); The Old (St. Clair Flats); Seagate Beach (Delray Beach, Fla.); Edgartown (Mass.) Yacht and Tennis. Editor: The Collaborator, Museum of Arts and Science, U. Mich., 1959—. Home: 309 Lake Shore Rd Grosse Pointe Farms MI (winter) 625 Seagate Dr Delray Beach FL 33444 Office: Buhl Bldg Detroit MI 48226

BOOTH, JOHN NICHOLLS, clergyman; b. Meadville, Pa., Aug. 7, 1912; s. Sydney Scott and Margaret (Nicholls) B.; B.A., McMaster U., 1934; B.D., Meadville Theol. Sch., 1942; Litt.D., Portia Law Sch. and Calvin Coolidge Coll., 1950; m. Edith Kriger, Oct. 1, 1941; 1 dau., Barbara Anne (Mrs. Peter Christie). Profl. magician, 1934-40: ordained to ministry Unitarian Ch., 1942; minister Unitarian Ch., Evanston, Ill., 1942-48, First Ch., Belmont, Mass., 1949- 57, Second Ch., Boston, 1958-64, Unitarian Ch., Long Beach, Cal., 1964-71; photographer full length feature travel documentary films for TV, lecture platforms made in India, Africa, S.Am., Indonesia, South Seas, Himalayas; own regularly scheduled TV broadcasts WBKB, Chgo., 1940s; presented first illustrated color travelogue on TV in U.S. over NBC, 1949; panel mem. radio program Churchmen Weigh The News, Boston, 1951-52; co-founder Japan Free Religious Assn., Tokyo, 1948; spl. corr. in Asia for Chgo. Sun-Times, 1948-49; by-line writer Boston Globe, 1952-62; producer motion picture Heart of Africa, 1954; ministerial adviser to liberal students Mass. Inst. Tech., 1958-59; mem. books selection com. Gen. Theol. Library Boston, 1960-63; co-founder Mass. Meml. Soc., 1962, dir., 1962-64; photographer films Golden Kingdoms of the Orient, 1957, Treasures of the Amazon, Ecuador and Peru, 1960, Adventurous Britain, 1962, South Seas Saga in Tahiti, Australia and New Guinea, summer 1966, The Amazing America of Will Rogers, 1970. Pres. Long Beach Mental Health Assn., 1964-66; adv. council Fair Housing Found. Decorated by King of Morocco Officer Ouissam Alaouite Cherifien, 1954; selected for Wall of Fame Town Hall, N.Y.C., 1967; Star of Magic award N.Y.C., 1971. Mem. Unitarian-Universalist Ministers Assn. (past dir.), Am. Unitarian Assn. (past com. chmn.), Internat. Brotherhood Magicians (past pres. Ring 96), Unitarian Ministers Pacific S.W. (v.p.), Clergy Counseling Service So. Cal., UN Assn. (member speakers bureau Long Beach chapter). Author: Super Magical Miracles, 1930; Magical Mentalism, 1931; Forging Ahead in Magic, 1939; Marvels of Mystery, 1941; The Quest for Preaching Power, 1943; Fabulous Destinations, 1950; Story of the Second Church in Boston, 1959. Contbr. articles mags., newspapers. Home: 12032 Montecito Rd Rossmoor CA 90720

BOOTH, JOHN THOMAS, investment banker; b. Bklyn., Oct. 21, 1929; s. John E. and Katherine (Keeler) B.; grad. Deerfield Acad., 1947; B.A., Amherst Coll., 1951; LL.B., Harvard, 1957; m. Anne C. Mott, Feb. 26, 1960; children—Alison McAdam, Anne Katherine, Roxanna Norton. Admitted to N.Y. bar, 1957; practice in N.Y.C., 1957-61; mem. buying dept. Eastman Dillon, Union Securities & Co., N.Y.C., 1961—, partner, 1963—, mng. partner, 1970—, vice chmn. policy and planning com. bd. directing partners, 1968—; exec. v.p., dir. Eastman Dillon, Union Securities & Co., Inc., 1971—; dir. SCM Corp., J.W. Wilson Glass Co., Filmways, Inc., chmn. bd. Eastdil Realty, Inc. Asst. to dir. Harvard Def. Studies Program, 1956-57; counsel N.Y. State Assembly Com. on N.Y.C., 1960, Com. on Judiciary, 1961. Adv. bd. Winant and Clayton Vols., Inc.; trustee Carnegie Hill Neighborhood Conservation Project, Inc.; bd. dirs. Natural Resources Def. Council, Eastman Dillon Union Securities Found. Served from ensign to lt. (j.g.), USNR, 1951-54. Mem. Am. Bar Assn., N.Y. Bar, Down Town Assn., Bond Club, Newcomen Soc., Pilgrim Soc., Delta Kappa Epsilon, Delta Sigma Rho. Republican. Episcopalian. Clubs: Links University, (N.Y.C.); Nat. Arts. Home: 123 E 92d St New York City NY 10028 Office: 1 Chase Manhattan Plaza New York City NY 10005

BOOTH, KENNETH LORING, furniture mfg. co. exec.; b. Quincy, Mass., July 12, 1916; s. Gilbert Alexander and Grace (Dunn) B.; B.S., Harvard, 1939; postgrad. Columbia, 1946; m. Miriam Ward, Dec. 19, 1943; children—Kenneth Loring, Jackson R., James A. With Ward Furniture Mfg. Co., Ft. Smith, Ark., 1947—, exec. v.p., 1968-69, pres., 1969—. Served to col. AUS, 1939-46, 50-52: Korea. Decorated Bronze Star, Silver Star, Legion Merit; named Polymer Man of Year, Soc. Plastics Industry, 1970. Mem. Southwest Furniture Marketing Assn. (pres. 1965-66, bd. dirs. 1963-70), Dallas Market Center (chmn. bd. govs. 1970-71), So. Furniture Mfrs. Assn. (bd. dirs. 1968—), Nat.

Assn. Furniture Mfrs. (bd. dirs. 1970—). Contbr. trade jours. Home: 3822 Country Club St Fort Smith AR 72901 Office: 1201 N 1st St Fort Smith AR 72901

BOOTH, LAVAUGHN VENCHAEL, clergyman; b. Covington County, Miss., Jan. 7, 1919; s. Frederick Douglas and Mamie (Powell) B.; A.B., Alcorn A. and M. Coll., Lorman, Miss., 1940; postgrad. Gammon Theol. Sem., Atlanta, 1940-41; B.D., Howard U., 1943; M.A., U. Chgo., 1945; L.H.D., Wilberforce U., 1964, Central State U., Wilberforce, O., 1969; D.D., Morehouse Coll., 1967; m. Georgia Anna Morris, June 3, 1942; children—Lavaughn V., William D., Anna Marie, Paul Michael, Georgia Annita. Ordained to ministry Baptist Ch., 1941; pastor in Warrenton, Va., 1942-43. Gary, Ind., 1944-52, Zion Bapt. Ch., Cin., 1952—. An organizer Progressive Nat. Bapt. Conv., 1961, exec. sec., 1963; chmn. Opportunities Industrialization Center, Cin., 1966—. Leader Berry for Council, 1963. Pres. Negro Sightless Soc. Cin., 1961-63; trustee Nannie H. Burroughs Sch., Washington, 1967—, U. Cin. Recipient Community Dad award Cin. Jr. C of C., 1959; named Cin. Man of Year. 1961. Mem. Am. Bible Soc. (spl. sec. dept. ch. relations). Author radio sermons, articles. Editor, founder Nation's Prayer Call, 1954—, Progressive Record, 1965—. Home: 3860 Spring House Lane Cincinnati OH 45217 Office: 630 Glenwood Av Cincinnati OH 45229

BOOTH, NICHOLAS HENRY, Jr., coll. dean; b. Hannibal, Mo., Oct. 22, 1923; s. Nicholas Henry and Ruby (Swan) B.; D.V.M., Mich. State U., 1947; postgrad. U. Mich., summer 1949; M.S., Colo. State U., 1951; Ph.D., U. Colo., 1959; m. Jean Rawson Atyeo, Sept. 29, 1944; children—Richard R., Debra Jean, Diane Marie. Pvt. practice vet. medicine, Hannibal, 1947-48; faculty dept. physiology and biophysics Colo. State U., Ft. Collins, 1948-66, head of dept., 1956-66, dean Coll. Vet. Medicine and Biomedical Scis., 1966—; cons. div. physician manpower Bur. Health Manpower, Dept. Health, Edn. and Welfare, 1967-68; chmn. vet. drug panel NRC, Nat. Acad. Scis., 1966-68; mem. vet. medicine review com. Bur. Health Professions Edn. and Manpower Tng., NIH, Dept. Health, Edn. and Welfare, 1969; prin. research investigator projects sponsored by Colo. Heart Assn., Nat. Heart Inst., NIH, USPHS. Served with AUS, 1943-44; with USNR, 1944-46, Mem. Am. Vet. Med. Assn. (past chmn.), Am. Physiol. Soc., N.Y. Acad. Scis., A.A.A.S., Am., Colo. heart assns., Soc. Exptl. Biology and Medicine, Am. Inst. Biol. Scis., Sigma Xi, Phi Kappa Phi, Phi Zeta (past nat. pres.), Gamma Sigma Delta. Author: (with L. Meyer Jones) Veterinary Pharmacology and Therapeutics, 1965. Contbr. articles profl. jours. Home: 829 Pitkin St Fort Collins CO 80521

BOOTH, PHILIP, poet, educator; b. Hanover, N.H., Oct. 8, 1925; s. Edmund Hendershot and Jeanette (Hooke) B.; A.B., Dartmouth, 1948; M.A., Columbia, 1949; Litt.D. (hon.), Colby Coll. 1968; m. Margaret Tillman, Aug. 3, 1946; children—Margot, Carol (Mrs. Patrick Walker), Robin. Instr., Bowdoin Coll., 1949-50; asst. to dir. admissions Dartmouth, 1950-51, instr., 1954; instr. to asst. prof. Wellesley Coll., 1954-61; asso. prof. Syracuse (N.Y.) U., 1961-65, prof. 1966—. Served with USAAF, 1944-45. Recipient Hokin prize, Poetry mag., 1955, Lamont prize Acad. Am. Poets, 1956, Saturday Rev. Poetry award, 1957, Phi Beta Kappa Poet Columbia, 1962, Emily Clark Balch prize Va. Quar. Rev. 1964, award for poetry Nat. Inst. Arts. and Letters, 1967, Guggenheim Meml. fellow, 1958-59, 65; Rockefeller fellow, 1968; Theodore Roethke Poetry prize Northwest mag., 1970. Mem. Dennett's Wharf Hist. Soc., Slocum Soc., Amphibicon Assn., Sphinx, Alpha Delta Phi. Club: Castine Yacht (past commodore) (Castine, Me.). Author: Letter from a Distant Land, 1957; The Islanders, 1961; Weathers and Edges, 1966; Beyond Our Fears, 1968; Margins, 1970. Editor: The Dark Island, 1960; Syracuse Poems, 1965, 70. Contributor poems and essays to jours. Home: N Eagle Village Rd Manlius NY 13104 Office Dept English Syracuse U Syracuse NY 13210

BOOTH, RICHARD EARL, fund raising exec.; b. Toledo, June 10, 1919; s. Earl Arthur and Adelen (Bianchi) B.; Ph.B., U. Toledo, 1941; postgrad. Ohio State U., 1941-42; m. Ruth Eleanor Fisher, June 17, 1944. Asst. to gen. mgr. Rochester (N.Y.) Community and War Chest, 1942-44; dir. indsl. dept. Community Chest Met. Detroit, 1944-49; asst. gen. mgr., campaign dir. United Found., Detroit, 1949-54; exec. dir. St. Louis Community Chest, 1954-55; exec. v.p. United Fund Greater St. Louis, 1955-57; exec. dir. Greater N.Y. Fund, N.Y.C., 1957—, United Fund Greater N.Y., 1968—; mem. conf., fund raising adv. coms. United Way of Am., Inc. Bd. dirs. Boys Club New Rochelle (N.Y.), Am. Hearing Soc., Washington. Recipient Distinguished Service award community services com. N.Y.C. Central Labor Council AFL-CIO. 1966. Mem. Ohio Soc. N.Y. (trustee), Sigma Phi Epsilon. Republican. Methodist. Clubs: Wykagyl Country (New Rochelle, N.Y.); University (Detroit). Home: 51 Flint Av Larchmont NY 10538 Office: 100 E 42d St New York City NY 10017

BOOTH, RICHARD WILLIAM, physician, educator; b. Cin., Mar. 17, 1924; s. Rudolph William and Kathryn (Hehemann) B.; B.S., Xavier U., Cin., 1948; M.D., U. Cin., 1952; m. Catherine J. Ballmann, Dec. 22, 1945; children—Patrick M., Marcia L., Michelle M. Rotating intern U. Wis. Gen. Hosp., 1952-53; jr. asst. resident medicine Ohio State U., 1954-55; resident cardiology, trainee Nat. Heart Inst., U. Cin., 1955-56; clin. instr. medicine Donald L. Mahanna research fellow Central Ohio Heart Assn., Ohio State U. Hosp. 1956-59; asst. prof. medicine, instr. aviation and preventive medicine Ohio State U., 1959-61, attending physician medicine, 1959-61; cons. Dayton (O) VA Hosp., 1956-61; mem. faculty Creighton U. Sch. Medicine, 1961—, prof. medicine, 1964—; dir. cardiac lab. Creighton Meml.-St. Joseph Hosp., 1961—. Area Cons. cardiology Dept. Health, Edn. and Welfare, 1963—; bd. dirs. Neb. Heart Assn., 1961- 69, Douglas County Heart Assn., 1965-69; adv. com. Neb.-S.D. Regional Med. Program, 1967-68, planning com., 1967-69, mem. heart task force, 1967—, chmn., 1967-68; mem. Gov. Neb. Rehab. Com., 1967-68, exec. com., 1967-68. Bd. dirs. Omaha Civic Opera Soc., 1964—. Served with AUS, 1943- 46. Fellow Am. Coll. Cardiology (gov. for Neb. 1966-69), A.C.P., Am. Heart Assn. (rep council clin. cardiology 1968—, chmn. Great Plains regional research adv. com. 1966-67, chmn. Great Plains regional profl. edn. com. 1967—); mem. Neb. Heart Assn. (pres. 1967-68), Alpha Omega Alpha, Phi Chi (pres. Creighton U. chpt. 1963—). Author articles in field. Home: 8555 Woolworth St Omaha NB 68124

BOOTH, ROBERT EDMOND, educator; b. Bridgeport, Conn., May 21, 1917; s. George Robert and Sophie (Anderson) B.; A.B., Wayne State U., 1941; B.S. in L.S., Columbia, 1942; A.M. in L.S., U. Mich., 1943; Ph.D., Western Res. U., 1960; m. Ada Margaret Pfohl, Aug. 19, 1944; children—Ellen Caroline, Margaret Anne. Student library asst. Wayne State U., 1936-41; grad. asst. Columbia Library, 1942, U. Mich. Library, 1943; jr. asst. Detroit Pub. Library, 1943-44; editor, bibliographer Univ. Microfilms Corp., 1944-46; reference librarian Peabody Inst. Library, Balt., 1946-47; asso. librarian Mass. Inst. Tech., 1947-56; research asso., instr. Western Res. U., 1956-60; mem. faculty Wayne State U., 1960—, prof. library sci., chmn. dept., 1964—, head information services Center Application Scis. and Tech., 1965-68. Mem. Founders Soc. Detroit Inst. Art; mem. Friends Detroit Pub. Library; mem. Friends Grosse Pointe (Mich.) Pub. Library; program chmn. Detroit Children's Book Fair, 1963. Scholar Nat. Council Christians and Jews, 1958. Library fellow Queen's Coll., 1941-42. Mem. Am., Mich. (pres. 1969-70) library assns., Spl. Libraries Assn., Am. Soc. Information Sci., Am. Assn. U. Profs., Beta Phi Mu, Phi Delta Kappa. Republican. Episcopalian. Author: Culturally Disadvantaged—A Bibliography and Index, 1967; co-author: Index to Poverty, Human Resources and Manpower Information, 1966; Index to Minority Group Employment Information, 1967. Home: 872 Balfour Rd Grosse Pointe MI 48230 Office: Library Sci Dept Wayne State U Detroit MI 48202

BOOTH, ROBERT MERMOD, Jr., lawyer; b. Rosiclare, Ill., Oct. 16, 1911; s. Robert Mermod and Rose Finch (Sherwood) B.; B.S. in Elec. Engring., Purdue U., 1933; LL.B., Salmon P. Chase Coll. Law, 1941; m. Edna Hannold Booth; children—Pamela Pamela Sherwood, Peter Ruchlmann. Radio broadcast sta. engr. sta. WLW, Cin., 1933-40; admitted to Ohio bar, 1942, D.C. bar, 1945, U.S. Supreme Ct. bar, 1959; practice in D.C., 1945—; founder, 1948, since v.p., dir. Logansport Broadcasting Corp. (Ind.) (sta. WSAL); sr. partner Booth & Lovett; gen. counsel, asst. sec., dir. Knorr Broadcasting Corp. (WKNR), Detroit, 1947—; gen counsel, asst. sec. (Mich. Sta WKMH), Jackson Broadcasting Corp., 1951—; dir., gen. counsel., asst. sec. So. Mich. Broadcasting Corp., Battle Creek, Mich., 1958—; counsel Am. Radio Relay League, Hartford, Conn., 1961—. Mem. nat. industry adv. com. FCC, 1959—. Served to comdr. USNR, 1941-45. Registered profl. engr., D.C., Ohio. Mem. Fed. Communications Bar Assn. (exec. com. 1954-56, pres. 1961-62), Am. Bar Assn., Bar Assn. D.C., I.E.E.E. Club: Exchange (v.p. 1969-70) (Washington). Home: 9509 E Bexhill Dr Rock Creek Hills Kensington MD 20795 Office: 1150 Connecticut Av NW Washington DC 20036

BOOTH, SHIRLEY, actress; b. N.Y.C., Aug. 30, 1909; d. Albert James and Virginia (Wright) Ford; ed. pub. schs., N.Y.C.; m. Edward F. Gardner, 1929 (div. 1941); m. 2d, William H. Baker, 1943 (dec. 1951). Played stock in several large cos. throughout U.S.; first major prodn. was Three Men on a Horse; appeared in Philadelphia Story, My Sister Eileen, Goodby My Fancy, A Tree Grows in Brooklyn; had leading roles Broadway prodns. Come Back Little Sheba, 1949-50, Time of The Cuckoo, 1952-53, By the Beautiful Sea, 1954, Desk Set, 1956, Miss Isobel, 1957, Juno, 1959, Nina, 1959, A Second String, 196O; movies include Come Back, Little Sheba, 1952, Main Street to Broadway, About Mrs. Leslie, 1954, Hot Spell, Matchmaker, 1958; TV series Hazel (as Hazel), 1961—. Recipient Academy award for Come Back, Little Sheba, 1952; Perry award for role in Time of the Cuckoo, 1953; named World's Best Actress, 6th Internat. Film Festival, Cannes, France, 1953; Sarah Siddons award as Actress of Yr., 1957; 1963 Emmy award for best actress Hazel series.

BOOTH, THEODORE HARRINGTON, bronze co. exec.; b. Buffalo, Mar. 24, 1904; s. Charles Arthur and Mabel Louise (Morse) B.; grad. Phillips Acad., 1921; M.E., Cornell, 1925; m. Carol Spitzmiller, June 25, 1927; children—Carol (Mrs. Bayard K. Fox), Charles H., T. William, Timothy M. With Gen. Electric Co., 1927, Buffalo Forge Co., 1927-37; works mgr. Walworth Co., then asst. v.p. mfg., 1952; v.p. Carborundum Co., Niagara Falls, N.Y., 1953-57; pres. Frontier Bronze Corp., Niagara Falls, 1957—; dir. Barclay-Westmoreland Trust Co., Greensburg, Pa., 1946-52, Atlas Steel Casting Corp., Buffalo. Pres. local Community Chest, 1949-51. Mem. Alpha Delta Phi. Clubs: Niagara, Buffalo, Royal Canadian Yacht; Youngstown (N.Y.) Yacht (commodore); Lake Yacht Racing Assn. (pres.). Home: Youngstown NY 14174 Office: Frontier Bronze Corp Niagara Falls NY 14304

BOOTH, THORNTON YOUNG, educator; b. Provo, Utah, Mar. 14, 1918; s. Alfred Lewis and Edith (Young) B.; A.B.. Brigham Young U., 1941; Ph.D., Stanford, 1951; m. Nan Chipman, Dec. 26, 1945; children—Geoffrey Lewis, James Raymond. Instr., Stanford, 1946-50; instr., then asst. prof. Brigham Young U., 1946, 50- 51; mem. faculty Utah State U., 1953—, prof. English, 1961—, acting dean, 1962, head dept., 1966-70. Committeeman Cache Valley council Boy Scouts Am., 1958—. Served as capt. AUS, 1941-45, 52-53; PTO, Korea. Decorated Commendation ribbon. Mem. Am. Assn. U. Profs., Modern Lang. Assn., Nat. Council Tchrs. English, Utah Acad. Scis., Arts and Letters. Author: Mastering the Event: Commitment to Fact in George Meredith's Fiction, 1967. Home: 1371 Juniper St Logan UT 84321

BOOTH, WALTER BURDICK, advt. exec.; b. Marshall, Ill., Dec. 14, 1909; s. Newton R. and Nettie S. (Shaw) B.; B.S., U. Ill., 1932; m. Virjean Dix, Jan. 25, 1936; children—Peter, Patricia. With Erwin, Wasey & Co., Ltd., Chgo., 1933-42; with Campbell-Ewald Co., Detroit, 1945—, now exec. v.p. Served as lt. USNR, World War II. Club: Adcraft (Detroit). Home: 1775 Huntingwood Lane Bloomfield Hills MI Office: Campbell-Ewald Co Gen Motors Bldg Detroit MI 48202

BOOTH, WARREN S., newspaper pub.; b. Detroit, Mich., Apr. 18, 1894; s. George Gough and Ellen Warren (Scripps) B.; student Lawrenceville (N.J.) Sch.; Ph.B., Yale (Sheffield Sch.) 1916; m. Alice Sedgwick Newcomb, May 14, 1921; children—Barbara (Mrs. Gordon Craig), Marjorie (Mrs. Victor C. Koch) dec., Sally (Mrs. William R. Fitzgerald), Dorothy (Mrs. Herbert W. Lester). Peter. Clk. advt. department Detroit News, 1916-17, asst. bus. mgr., 1919-25, dir. Evening News Assn. (pub. Detroit News, owners, licenses Sta. WWJ-AM-FM-TV), 1925-70, treas., 1927-52, pres., pub., 1952-63, chmn., 1963-70, counselor to bd. dirs., 1970—; dir. Booth Newspapers, Inc. 1932- 69, v.p., 1935-46, pres., 1946-52. Commd. 1st lt. F.A., 329th F.A., 85th Div. Camp Custer, Mich., Aug. 15, 1917. Capt., battalion adj., Mar. 19, 1918; saw action Meuse-Argonne, Metz, World War I. Trustee Cranbrook Found. Republican. Episcopalian. Clubs: Detroit, Bloomfield Hills Country, Grosse Pointe (Mich.); Orchard Lake Country, Old (Saint Clair Flats), Bayview Yacht (Detroit); Key Largo Anglers, Ocean Reef (Key Largo); Crown Colony (Chib Cay, Bahamas). Home: 1010 W Maple St Birmingham, MI. 48009. Office: The Detroit News Detroit MI 48231

BOOTH, WAYNE CLAYSON, educator; b. American Fork, Utah, Feb. 22, 1921; s. Wayne Chipman and Lillian (Clayson) B.: A.B., Brigham Young U., 1944; M.A., U. Chgo., 1947, Ph.D., 1950; D. Litt. (hon.), Rockford Coll., 1965, St. Ambrose Coll., 1971; m. Phyllis Barnes, June 16, 1946; children—Katherine, John Richard (dec.), Alison. Instr., U. Chgo., 1947-50; asst. prof. Haverford Coll., 1950-53; prof. English, chmn. dept. Earlham Coll., 1953-62; George M. Pullman prof. English, U. Chgo., 1962—, dean coll. U. Chgo., 1964-69; vis. cons. (with wife) S. African schs. and univs., 1963. Examiner, N. Central Assn. Colls. and Univs., 1959—. Trustee Earlham Coll. Served with inf. AUS, 1944-46. Ford Faculty fellow, 1952-53; Guggenheim fellow, 1956-57, 69-70; fellow Ind. U. Sch. Letters, summer 1962; recipient Christian Gauss prize Phi Beta Kappa, 1962. Mem. Modern Lang. Assn., Am. Assn. U. Profs., Nat. Council Tchrs. English (Russell prize 1966, Coll. Conf. Composition and Communication, Nat. Council on Religion in Higher Edn. Democrat. Mem. Ch. of Jesus Christ of Latter-Day Saints. Author: The Rhetoric of Fiction, 1961; Now Don't Try To Reason With Me: Essays and Ironies for a Credulous Age, 1970. Editor: The Knowledge Most Worth Having, 1967; editorial bd. Novel. Home: 5411 Greenwood Av Chicago IL 60615

BOOTH, WILLIAM WALLACE, lawyer; b. Allegheny, Pa., Nov. 2, 1896; s. Harry J. and Ella (Youngson) B.; B.S. in Econs., U. Pitts., 1920, LL.B., 1922; m. Adelaide Skelton Lanz, June 27, 1925; children—William Wallace, James Youngson, Cynthia Skelton (Mrs. Herbert P. Van Ingen). Admitted to Pa. bar, 1922, practice in Pitts., 1922—; mem. firm Reed, Smith Shaw & McClay, 1935—. Dir. William M. Bailey Co., also Am. Shim Steel Co., A.E. Anderson Constrn. Corp. Chmn. alumni com. on trustees' elections U. Pitts., 1940, mem. alumni council, 1941-47, trustees univ., 1941-69, mem. exec. com., 1955-68; trustee Presbyn. U. Hosp.: founder Bellefield Ednl. Trust, 1946. Served as 2d lt., A.C., U.S. Army, 1917-19. Mem. Am., Pa., Allegheny County bar assns., Am. Judicature Soc., Scottish Am. Soc., Omicron Delta Kappa, Sigma Alpha Epsilon, Beta Gamma Sigma, Phi Delta Phi. Order of Daedalians. Presbyn. Mason (Jester). Clubs: University (pres. 1957-58), Duquesne (Pitts.); Rolling Rock (Ligonier, Pa.); Ox 5 Club America. Home: 3955 Bigelow Blvd Pittsburgh PA 15213 also Marble Top Rd 4 Ligonier PA 15658 Office: Union Trust Bldg Pittsburgh PA 15219

BOOTH, WINDSOR PEYTON, newspaper exec.; b. Little Rock, Apr. 19, 1912; s. John Samuel and Alpha Louisa (Windsor) B.; student Little Rock Jr. College, 1929-31; B.J., U. Mo., 1933; m. Harriet Ellis Evans, Oct. 5, 1938; children—Windsor Peyton, Philip Saffery Evans, Mary Louisa, Robert. Reporter, Little Rock (Ark.) Democrat, 1928-31; librarian Phila. Public Ledger, 1933; feature writer N.Y. Eveniing Post, 1933-34; editor Washington Post News Service, 1934-37, mgr., 1937- 42; Washington Corr. Boston Post and Springfield (Mass.) Republican, 1935-51; chief Phila. Record Washington Bur., 1942-44; Washington corr. Time mag., 1944-51; chief Nat. Geog. Soc. News Service, 1951—. Mem. Soc. Am. Travel Writers (pres. 1964-65), Washington Inst. Fgn. Affairs, Sigma Delta Chi. Clubs: Alfalfa, National Press (pres. 1966), White House Correspondents (Washington); Explorers (N.Y.C.). Home: 15 W Kirke St Chevy Chase MD 20015 Office: Nat Geog Soc Washington DC 20418

BOOTHBY, BRYCE CORYDON, banker; b. Benton Harbor, Mich., May 24, 1924; s. Bryce and Dorothea (Ryno) B.; B.A., U. Mich., 1950, M.Pub. Adminstrn., 1951; m. Bette Jane Johnston, June 18, 1949; children—Bryce Corydon, Russel, Diane, James, Wayne, Laurie. With Harris Trust & Savs. Bank, Chgo., 1951-55; with I.C. R.R., Chgo., 1955-69, exec. asst. to pres., 1967-69; v.p., sec. Ill. Central Industries, Inc., Chgo., 1969-70; v.p., dir. Matteson-Richton Bank (Ill.), 1970—; v.p., sec., dir. Palladium Pub. Co., Benton Harbor, Mich., 1967—; dir. Herald Press Co., St. Joseph. Mayor, Village of Flossmoor, Ill., 1969—. Bd. dirs. Suburban Cook County Tb Sanitarium Dist. Served with AUS, 1943-46. Mem. Assn. Am. R.R.s (hon. mem. treasury div.), Chi Phi. Republican. Club: Flossmoor Country. Home: 2540 Brookwood Dr Flossmoor IL 60422 Office: 21155 Governor's Hwy Matteson IL 60411

BOOTHBY, NORMAN B., artist, dean; b. Colorado Springs, Colo., Aug. 31, 1919; B.S. in Edn., B.F.A., Temple U., 1942, M.F.A., 1947; student Middlebury Coll., 1937- 38. Scene designer, tech. dir. Weston (Vt.) Playhouse, 1942; art tchr. Metairie Park Country Day Sch., New Orleans, 1942-45; instr. Conn. Dept. Edn., Middletown, 1945-46; instr. art Wesleyan U., Middletown, 1946-5O, tech. dir. 1892 Theatre, 1950-51; dir. Putney Sch. Summer work Camp, 1950-52; instr. Hartford Art Sch., 1950-52; asst. prof. Bard Coll., Annandale-on-Hudson, N.Y., 1952-53; dean Parsons Sch. Design, N.Y.C., 1953-59, Sch. Art Inst. Chgo., 1959-66; dean sch. Dayton (O.) Art Inst., 1965-67—; prof., chmn. dept. art Newcomb Coll., Tulane,1967—. One man show Design Assos., Hartford, Conn.; rep. numerous exhbns.; designer furniture, ceramics, jewelry; commns. include sculpture, sculptural murals; dir. self-study grant to Parsons Sch. Design, Ford Found. Fund Advancement Edn., 1953-54; staff research project Inst. Internat. Edn., 1959. Pres. bd. dirs. Summer sch. Painting, Saugatuck, Mich.; 1st vice chmn. Found. Integrated Edn. in Liberal Arts and Professions. Faculty fellow Ford Found. Fund for Advancement Edn., 1951-52; recipient lst prize in sculpture New Orleans Art Assn., 1943, prize in sculpture Springfield Art League, 1952. Home: 1000 Adams St New Orleans, LA.70118.

BOOTHBY, WILLARD SANDS, Jr. investment banking co. exec.; b. Phila., Nov. 11, 1921; s. Willard Sands and Mable (Edgar) B.; grad. Deerfield Acad., 1940; student Cornell U., 1940-42; B.S. in Mech. Engring., Lehigh U., 1946; student Wharton Sch., U. Pa., 1946-48; m. Florence E. Clifford, Jan. 22, 1946; children—Willard Sands III, Richard C., Ann C. Trainee, salesman, corporate finance Drexel & Co., Phila., 1946-50; mgr. municipal bond dept. Eastman Dillon Union Securities & Co., N.Y.C., 1950-54, gen. partner, 1954-57, partner in charge Pa. div., 1957-63, partner in charge br. offices, 1963-66, chief operating partner, 1966-70, chief exec. partner, 1970-71; pres. Eastman Dillon Union Securities & Co., Inc., 1971—; dir. Commonwealth Tel. Co., Getty Oil Co. Mem. Com. of Seventy, Phila., 1954-56. Committeeman Republican Party, Phila., 1952-54. Trustee Episcopal Hosp., Springside Sch. (both Phila.). Mem. Secutity Analysts Assn., Investment Bankers Assn. Am. (chmn. municipal securities div. Pa. 1955). Clubs: Municipal Bond (gov. 1953, 56, 57), Bond (pres. 1961), Philadelphia Cricket, Sunnybrook Golf, Racquet, Cornell (dir. 1954-58), Lehigh (dir. 1950-58) (Phila.); Links (N.Y.C.). Home: 460 W Chestnut Hill Av Philadelphia PA 19118 Office: Eastman Dillon Union Securities & Co Inc 1 Chase Manhattan Plaza New York City NY 10005

BOOTHBY, WILLIAM MUNGER, educator; b. Detroit, Apr. 1, 1918; s. Thomas Franklin and Florence (Munger) B.; A.B., U. Mich., 1941, M.A., 1942, Ph.D., 1949; m. Ruth Robin, June 8, 1947; children—Daniel, Thomas, Mark. Instr., Northwestern U., 1948-51, asst. prof., 1951-59; fellow Am.-Swiss Found. for Sci. Exchange, Swiss Fed. Inst. Tech., Zurich, 1950-51; asso. prof. Washington U., St. Louis, 1959-62, prof., 1962—; NSF sr. postdoctoral fellow Inst. for Advanced Study, Princeton, N.J., 1961-62, U. Geneva, Switzerland, 1965-66; professeur associe U. Strasbourg, France, 1971—. Served with USAAF, 1942-46. Mem. Am. Math. Soc., Math. Assn. Am., Soc. Math. de France, Sigma Xi. Contbr. articles profl. jours. Home: 6954 Cornell Av University City MO 63130 Office: Dept Math Washington U St Louis MO 63130

BOOTHE, A., newspaper editor. Mng. editor Winnipeg Free Press. Office: 300 Carlton St Winnipeg 2 Manitoba Canada*

BOOTHE, ARMISTEAD LLOYD, sem. ofcl.; b. Alexandria, Va., Sept. 23, 1907; s. Gardner Lloyd and Eleanor (Carr) B.; A.B., U. Va., 1928; B.A., Oxford (Eng.) U., 1931, M.A., 1940; m. Elizabeth Ravenel Peells, June 30, 1934; children—Julie (Mrs. Charles S. Perry), Eleanor (Mrs. John M. Smith), Elizabeth (Mrs. Lee F. Davis Jr.). Admitted to Va. bar, 1929; pvt. practice, Alexandria, 1931-70, sr. partner firm Boothe, Dudley, Koontz, Blankingship and Stump, Alexandria, Va., 1950-70; dir. United Virginia Bank, First & Citizens Nat. Bank; dir. devel. Va. Theol. Sem., 1970—, counsel, 1945—, trustee, 1951—. Spl. asst. atty. gen. U.S., 1934-36; atty. City Alexandria, Va., 1938-43. Mem. Va. Ho. Dels., 1948-56, Va. Senate, 1956-64. Trustee Colonial Williamsburg Found. Served with USNR, 1943-45. Mem. Lit. Soc. Washington, Raven Soc., S.A.R., Phi Beta Kappa, Beta Theta Pi. Clubs: Cosmos Club, Commonwealth Club. Home: 913 Vicar Lane Alexandria VA 21302

BOOTHE, CLARE, (Clare Boothe Luce), playwright, former congresswoman, former ambassador; b. N.Y.C.; d. William F. and Ann (Snyder) Boothe; ed. St. Mary's Garden City, L.I., N.Y., 1915-17, The Castle, Tarrytown, N.Y., 1917-19; Litt.D., Colby Coll., Fordham U., Mundelein Coll.; LL.D., Temple U., Creighton U., Georgetown U., Seton Hall Coll.; A.F.D., St. John's U.; m. George Tuttle Brokaw, Aug. 10, 1923 (div. 1929); m. 2d, Henry R. Luce, Nov. 23, 1935 (dec.). Asso. editor Vogue, 1930, Vanity Fair, 1931-32, mng. editor, 1933-34; newspaper columnist, 1934; playwright 1935—; mem. 78th and 79th Congresses, 4th Conn. Dist., 1943-47; U.S. ambassador to Italy, 1953-57. First vice chmn. Nat. Rev. Bd., East-West Center. Mem. Acad. Polit. Sci., Am. Inst. Fgn. Trade. Republican. Roman Catholic. Club: Overseas Press. Author: Stuffed Shirts, 1933; Europe in the Spring, 1940; (plays) Abide with Me; The Women, 1937; Kiss the Boys Goodbye, 1938; Margin for Error, 1939; Child of The Morning, 1951. Contbr. articles and fiction to mags. Collected and edited Saints for Now, 1952. Home: New York City NY 10027 also Honolulu HI 96813

BOOTHE, DYAS POWER, Jr., indsl. leasing co. exec.; b. Berkeley, Cal., Dec. 23, 1910; s. Dyas Power and Margaret (Stewart) B.; A.B., Stanford, 1931; m. Margaret Kempenich, June 28, 1933 (div. 1966); children—Margaret Joanne (Mrs. William F. Hook), Barry Power; m. 2d, Catherine Causey, 1967; 1 dau., Catherine Elizabeth. Pres. Boothe Fruit Co., Modesto, Cal., 1946-59, Boothe Leasing Corp., San Francisco, 1954- 67; chmn., chief exec. officer Boothe Computer Corp., Armco-Boothe Corp., GATX-Boothe Corp., also domestic and fgn. subsidiaries; dir. Armco Steel Corp., Gen. Am. Transp. Corp., Vacu-Dry Co. Served to comdr. USNR, 1942-46; PTO. Mem. Delta Tau Delta. Clubs: University, Commercial, Bankers (San Francisco); Meadow (Fairfax, Cal.); Metropolitan (N.Y.C.). Home 33 San Carlos Av Sausalito CA 94965 Office: 355 California St San Francisco CA 94104

BOOTHE, FERRIS F., lawyer; b. Modesto, Cal., Feb. 18, 1923; A.B., Stanford, 1947, LL.B., 1950. Admitted to Cal. bar, 1950, Ore. bar, 1950; mem. firm Black, Kendall, Termaine, Boothe, and Higgins, Portland, Ore.; instr. Northwestern Sch. Law Lewis and Clark Coll., 1951—. Mem. Am., Multnomah County bar assns., Ore. State Bar, State Bar Cal., Phi Delta Phi, Phi Beta Kappa. Office: Cascade Bldg Portland OR 97204*

BOOTLE, WILLIAM AUGUSTUS, judge; b. Colleton County, S.C., Aug. 19, 1902; s. Philip Loraine and Laura Lilla (Benton) B.; A.B., Mercer U. 1924, LL.B., 1925; m. Virginia Childs, Nov. 24, 1928; children—William Augustus, Ann, James C. Admitted to Ga. bar, 1925, since practiced in Macon; mem. Carlisle & Bottle, 1933-54; U.S. dist. atty. Middle Ga. Dist., 1929- 33; acting dean Mercer U. Law Sch., 1933-37, part-time prof. law, 1926-37; judge, U.S. Dist. Ct., Middle Dist. Ga., 1954—. Trustee Mercer U., 1936-38, 40-41, 42-46, 52, 54-58, 60-64, 66—, chmn. exec. com., 1941-46, 48-53; trustee Walter F. George Sch. Law Found., 1961—, v.p., 1963-65, pres., 1965-66. Recipient Distinguished Alumnus award Mercer U., 1971. Mem. Phi Alpha Delta, Phi Delta Theta. Republican. Baptist. Mason (33, Shriner). Club: Civitan (pres. 1936). Home: Old Club Rd Macon GA 31204 Office: Post Office Macon GA 31208

BOOTY, JOHN EVERITT, educator; b. Detroit, May 2, 1925; s. George Thomas and Alma (Gamauf) B.; A.B., Wayne State U., 1952; B.D., Va. Theol. Sem., 1953; M.A., Princeton, 1957, Ph.D., 1960; m. Catherine Louise Smith, June 10, 1950; children—Carol Holland, Geoffrey Rollen, Peter Thomas, Catherine Jane. Ordained to ministry Episcopal Ch., 1953; curate Christ Episcopal Ch., Dearborn, Mich., 1953-55; asst. prof. ch. history Va. Theol. Sem., 1958-64, asso. prof., 1964-67; prof. ch. history Episcopal Theol. Sch., Cambridge, Mass., 1967—. Fulbright scholar U. London (Eng.), 1957-58; fellow Folger Shakespeare Library, 1964. Chmn. Nat. Youth Commn., P.E. Ch., 1948-50. Recipient Am. Philos. Soc. award, 1964. Mem. Am. Hist. Assn., Am. Soc. Ch. History, Renaissance Soc. Am. Author: John Jewel as Apologist of the Church of England, 1963. Contbr. articles to profl. jours. Home: 27 St Johns Rd Cambridge MA 02138 Office: 99 Brattle St Cambridge MA 02138

BOOYSEN, OWEN F. DE VILLIERS, diplomat; b. Graaff-Reinet, Republic of S. Africa, 1921: student Kingswood Coll., Grahamstown, Republic of S. Africa; bachelor's degree Rhodes U.; m. Bunty Halsted; 2 daus. Joined Dept. Fgn. Affairs, Republic of S. Africa, 1947, 3d sec. S. African Embassy, Washington, 1951-54; 2d sec. S. African Embassy, Rome, 1954-60; head legal and treaties sect. Dept. Fgn. Affairs, Pretoria, 1961-64; counsellor S. African Embassy, Hague, Netherlands, 1964-67, counsul-gen., N.Y.C., 1967—. Mem. S. African Delegation to Gen. Assembly UN, 1967. Served in armed forces, forces, 1940-43. Address: S African Consulate-Gen 655 Madison Av New York City NY 10021

BOOZ, DONALD ROBERT, mgmt. cons.; b. Evanston, Ill., Oct. 19, 1920; s. Edwin G. and Helen (Hootman) B.; A.B., Williams Coll., 1942; Indsl. Adminstr., Harvard, 1943, M.B.A., 1947. Faculty Harvard Bus. Sch., 1946-50; with Jewel Tea Co., Inc., 1951-58; engaged in mgmt. cons., 1958—; pres. Donald R. Booz and Assos., Inc., Chgo., 1961—. Served as officer USAAF, World War II. Mem. Harvard Bus. Sch. Assn. (exec. council). Clubs: Chicago Economic, Harvard Business School (past pres.) (Chgo.). Author: (with Learned and Ulrich) Executive Action, 1951; (with Ulrich and Lawrence) Management Behavior and Foreman Attitude, 1949. Home: 1130 N Lake Shore Dr Chicago IL 60611 Office: 20 N Wacker Dr Chicago IL 60606

BOOZER, ROBERT CHARLES, lawyer; b. Birmingham, Ala., June 18, 1930; s. Herman Wyse and Teressa (Maybin) B.; A.B., Emory U., 1952; J.D., Harvard, 1955; postgrad. Netherlands Inst. Econs., Rotterdam, 1955-56; m. Sidney Cooper Wesley, Oct. 6, 1961; children-Katherine Wyse, Wesley Robert, Margaret Maybin. Admitted to Ga. bar, 1954; practice in Atlanta, 1956—; partner firm Sanders, Hester, Holley, Ashmore & Boozer, 1968—; lectr. law Woodrow Wilson Coll., Atlanta, 1959-61. Pres. Choral Guild Atlanta, 1959-60. Served with USAF, 1951-52. Mem. Am. Arbitration Assn., Phi Beta Kappa, Kappa Alpha, Alpha Kappa Psi, Omicron Delta Kappa. Lutheran. Club: Lawyers (Atlanta). Home: 899 W Wesley Rd NW Atlanta GA 30327 Office: Candler Commerce Bldg Atlanta GA 30303

BOPP, KARL RICHARD, ret. banker; b. Kirkwood, Mo., Feb. 2, 1906; s. Andrew Theodore and Christina (Raaf) B.; A.B., B.S., U. Mo., 1928, M.A., 1929, Ph.D., 1931, LL.D., 1961; LL.D., Temple U., 1960, Cedar Crest Coll., 1964; m. Ruth Callies, June 12, 1931; children—Karl Richard, Joanna Ruth (Mrs. Albert V. Bear). Asst. to asso. prof. U. Mo., 1931-41; dir. research Fed. Res. Bank of Phila., 1941-47, v.p. charge research, 1947-58, pres., 1958-70, ret., 1970. Dir. Atlantic City Electric Co. Lectr. finance U. Pa., 1946-58, Princeton, 1947; faculty Stonier Grad. Sch. Banking Rutgers U., 1950-58, Central States Sch., U. Wis., 1954-58, exec. program bus. adminstrn. Columbia, 1955-58, Tech. sec. Bretton Woods Monetary Conf., 1944; spl. temporary asst. to chmn. bd. govs. Fed. Res. System, 1948. Fellow Social Sci Research Council, 1932-33, Guggenheim Found., 1939-40. Mem. Am. Econ. Assn., Am. Philos. Soc. (councillor 1961-64, sec. 1965-67), Am. Acad. Polit. and Social Sci. (dir.), Am. Statistics Assn., Phi Beta Kappa. Clubs: Cosmos (Washington); Sunday Breakfast (Phila.). Author: Agencies of Federal Reserve Policy, 1935; Hjalmar Schacht: Central Banker, 1939; also articles. Home: 665 Church Rd Wayne PA 19087

BOPP, WALTER STENECK, mfrs. rep.; b. N.Y.C., Nov. 29, 1913; s. Walter Frederick and Josephine (Steneck) B.; A.B., Brown U., 1935; m. Mary Zilla Clarke, Aug. 14, 1943; children—Karen, Linda, Walter Steneck, Peter. Div. controller Lord & Taylor, N.Y.C., 1936-40; sales mgr. internat. div. RCA, 1950-54; with internat. div. Philco Ford Corp., 1958-70, gen. mgr., 1962-64, v.p., 1964-70, ret.; v.p., dir. Eurpac Service, Inc., Greenwich, Conn., 1970—. Served with USNR, 1942-46. Decorated Commendatore dell' Ordine al Merito della Republica Italiana, 1967. Mem. Electropic Industry Assn. (exec. com.), Internat. Execs. Assn. Club: Larchmont Yacht. Home: 9 Bonnie Briar Lane Larchmont NY 10538 Office: Eurpac Service Inc 170 Mason St Greenwich CT 06830

BORCH, FRED J., elec. mfg. co. exec.; b. Bklyn., Apr. 28, 1910; s. Frederik and Antonette (Mikkelsen) B.; A.B., Western Res. U., 1931; D.Engring. (hon.), Clarkson Coll., 1964; m. Martha A. Kananen, July 7, 1934 (dec.); children—Kay B. Otterstrom, Richard; m. 2d, Lucia M. Lowles, Aug. 15, 1970. With Gen. Electric 1931—, sales mgmt. positions lamp div., Cleve., cons., mgmt. consultation services, 1935-53, v.p. marketing, N.Y.C., 1954-59, v.p., group exec. consumer products group, 1959-62, exec. v.p. operations, dir., 1962-63, pres., chief exec. officer, 1963-68, chmn., chief exec. officer, 1968—; dir. Utah Constrn. and Mining Co. Mem. Nat. Indsl. Pollution Control Council, Bus. Council; mem. N.Y.C. Econ. Devel. Council. Trustee Com. Econ. Devel., Case-Western Res. U. Clubs: University, Links (N.Y.C.); Metropolitan (Washington); Royal Poinciana, Hole-in-the-Wall Golf, Naples Yacht (Naples, Fla.); Wee Burn Country (Darien, Conn.); Blind Brook (Port Chester, N.Y.); Augusta (Ga.) Nat. Golf. Office: 570 Lexington Av New York City NY 10022

BORCH, OTTO ROSE, diplomat; b. Aarhus, Denmark, Sept. 1, 1921; s. Adolf and Ninna (Lassen) B.; LL.M., U. Copenhagen, 1948; Rotary fellow, Columbia, 1948-49; m. Astrid Lundbye, Apr. 19, 1951; children—Elizabeth Lundbye, Birgitte Lundbye. Joined Danish Fgn. Service, 1948; with Danish Embassy, Bonn, 1954-59; with Fgn. Ministry, 1959-64; minister counsellor, dep. permanent rep. of Denmark to NATO, Paris, 1964-67; ambassador, permanent rep. of Denmark to UN, 1967-. Home: 34 Sunnybrook Rd Bronxville, NY.10708. Office: 235 E 42d St New York City NY 10017

BORCHARDT, LESTER FERDINAND, cons.; b. Mpls., May 30, 1907; s. Ferdinand A. and Marie (Bemmels) B.; B. Elec. Engring., U. Minn., 1929, postgrad. physics, teaching fellow, 1929-33; grad. Advanced Mgmt. Program, Harvard, 1960; m. Elsie Helen Rohath, June 25, 1929; children—Lester Ferdinand, Gail Elsie. With Central Research Labs., Gen. Mills, Inc., 1933-68, dir. phys. research, activity, also mng. dir., 1960-63, dir. research, 1963- 68, v.p. parent co., 1963-69; chmn. bd. Provesta Corp., 1968-69, ret.; asso. Webber, Barton, Morrison, Connell & Assos., Mpls., 1970—. Member A.A.A.S., Am. Phys. Soc., Sigma Xi, Eta Kappa Nu, Tau Beta Pi. Home: 5508 15th Av S Minneapolis MN 55417

BORCHERT, JOHN ROBERT, educator; b. Chgo., Oct. 24, 1918; s. Ernest J. and Maude Anna (Gorndt) B.; A.B., DePauw U., 1941; M.A., U. Wis., 1946, Ph.D., 1949; m. Jane Anne Willson, June 10, 1942; children—Dianne, William, Robert, David. Instr. U. Wis., 1947-49; asst. prof. U. Minn., 1949-51, asso. prof. 1951-56, prof., 1956—, chmn. dept. geography, 1956-61, now dir. Center for Urban and Regional Affairs. Chmn. earth scis. div. NRC, 1967-69. Served as maj. USAAF, World War II. Mem. Assn. Am. Geographers (councillor 1963-66, v.p. 1967-68, pres. 1969- 70), Am. Inst. Planners, Sigma Xi. Author geography text series. Home: Cedarcliff on St Croix Scandia MN 55073

BORCIANI, PAOLO, violinist; b. Reggio Emilia, Italy, Dec. 21, 1922; s. Mario and Nayr (Gorisi) B.; violin master degree Conservatoir A Boito, Parma, Italy, 1940; classical sch. degree Llceo Classico L, Spallanzani, Reggio Emilia, 1940; m. Elisa Pegreffi, Jan. 24, 1953; 1 son, Mario. Founder, 1945, since lst violinist Quartetto Italiano; numerous tours Europe, 1946—, U.S., 1951—, S. Am., 1968, South Africa, 1970; tchr. Conservatoir G. Verdi, Milan, 1960—. Decorated cavaliere dell'ordine Al Merito Della Repubblica Italiana; recipient Deutschen Schailplattenkritik prize, 1966; prize Critica Discografica Italiana, 1968. Rec. artist Decca, Philips, Columbia. Address: Piazza Giolitti 6 Milano Italy

BORDALLO, MADELEINE MARY (Mrs. Ricardo Jerome Bordallo), mem. Democratic Nat. Com. ; b. Graceville, Minn., May 31, 1933, d. d. Christian Peter and Mary Evelyn (Roth) Zeien; student St Mary's Coll., South Bend, Ind., 1952; A. A. St. Kaatherines Cooll., St. Paul. 1953; hon. hon. degree for community service U. Guam, 1968; m. Ricardo Jerome Bordallo, June 20, 1953; 1 dau., Deborah Josephine. Presented in voice recital Guam Acad. Music, Agana. 1951, 62; mem. Civic Opera Co., St. Paul, 1952- 53; mem. staff KUAM Radio-TV sta., Agana, 1954-63; free lance writer local newspaper, fashion show commentator, coordinator, civic leader, 1963; nat. Dem. committee woman for Guam, 1964—; del. Nat. Dem.. Conv., 1964, 68; pres. Womens Dem. Party Guam, 1967-69; rep. Presdl. Inauguration, Washington, 1965; del. Dem. Western States Conf., Reno, 1965, Los Angeles, 1967, Phoenix, 1968, conf. sec., 1967-69; delegate Democratic Women's Campaign Conf., Wash., 1965. Pres. Guam Womens Club, 1958-59; del Gen. Fedn. Women's Clubs Convs., Miami Beach, Fla., 1961, New Orleans, 1965, Boston, 1968; v.p. Fedn. Asian Women's Association, 1964-67, pres., 1967-69; pres. Guam Symphony Soc., 1967-71; delegate conventions, Manila, P. I., 1959, Taipei, Formosa, 1960, Hong Kong, 1963, Agana, 1964; chmn. Guam Christmas Seal Drive, 1961: bd. dirs. Guam chpt. A.R.C. 1963—, sec., 1963-67; pres. Marianas Assn. For Retarded Children, 1968-69: bd. dirs. Guam Theatre Guild; mem. Guam. Meml. Hosp. Vols. Assn., 1966—, v.p., 1966-67, pres., 1970-71; chmn. Hosp. Hosp. Charity Ball, 1966. Mem. Internat. Platform Assn., Guam Rehab. Assn. (asso.). Club: Spanish of Guam. Address: PO Box 1458 Agana, Guam 96910.

BORDEN, CHARLES FRED, steel exec.; b. Shoshone, Ida., July 1, 1910; s. Charles Frederick and Lenora Alice (Parker) B.; B.A., U. Wash., 1933; M.B.A., Stanford U., 1936; m. Madelyn Hughes, Nov. 28, 1940; children—Joan Alice, Holly Elizabeth, Frederick Hughes. Sales dept. Columbia Steel Co., 1936-42, asst. to v.p., 1942-44; with Kaiser Steel Corp., Oakland, Cal., 1945—, asst. gen. sales mgr., 1946-47, gen. sales mgr., 1947-50, v.p. charge sales, 1950-59, exec. v.p., 1959—, also dir.; sr. v.p. Kaiser Industries, 1968—, Mem. steel industry adv. com. N.P.A., 1950—. Mem. Am. Iron and Steel Inst., Am. Steel Warehouse Assn., Am. Ordnance Assn., San Francisco, Los Angeles, Oakland chambers commerce. Methodist. Clubs: Orinda (Cal.) Country; San Francisco Golf, Family (San Francisco). Home: 544 Miner Rd Orinda CA 94563 Office: Kaiser Center 300 Lakeside Dr Oakland CA 94604

BORDEN, CRAIG WARREN, physician, educator; b. Springboro, O., Aug. 31, 1915; s. Carl C. and Ethel (Pence) B.; A.B., Oberlin Coll., 1937; M.D., Harvard, 1941. Intern Boston City Hosp., 1941-42; fellow medicine U. Cin., 1942-43; resident medicine U. Minn., 1946-47, mem. faculty, 1947-53, asst. prof. medicine, 1950-53; mem. faculty Northwestern U. Sch. Medicine, 1953—, prof. medicine, 1960—; chief med. service VA Research Hosp., Chgo., 1954—; sr. staff physician Passavant Meml. Hosp., Chgo., 1963. Served with USAAF, 1943-46. Recipient Chief Med. Dirs. commendation VA, 1963. Diplomate Am. Bd. Internal Medicine (sec.-treas. 1967, vice chmn. 1968, 69) Fellow A.C.P.; mem. Am. Heart Assn., Central Soc. Clin. Research, A.M.A. (residency rev. com. internal medicine 1966-71). Contbr. med. jours. Home: 244 E Pearson St Chicago IL 60611

BORDEN, HENRY, barrister, solicitor; b. Halifax, N.S., Sept. 25, 1901; s. Henry Clifford and Mabel (Ashmere) Barnstead B.; B.A., McGill U., 1921; postgrad. Dalhousie Law Sch., 1922-24, LL.D., 1968; B.A. (Rhodes scholar), Exeter Coll., Oxford, 1926; LL.D., St. Francis Xavier U., 1960; D.C.L., Acadia U., 1960; m. Jean Creelman MacRae, June 1, 1929; children—Robert, Ann, Perry, Mary Jean, Henry. With Royal Bank Can., 1921-22; admitted to bar, Lincoln's Inn, London, 1927, Nova Scotia bar, 1927, Ontario bar, 1927; King's Counsel, 1938; gen. counsel Dept. Munitions and Supply, Ottawa, 1939-42; chmn. Wartime Industries Control Bd., Ottawa, co-ordinator of controls Dept. Munitions and Supply, 1942-43; past lectr. corp. law Osgoode Hall Law Sch.; sr. mem. Borden, Elliot, Kelley & Palmer, 1936-46; chmn. Royal Commn. on Energy, 1957-59; mem. adv. bd. Indsl. Estates Ltd.; pres. Brascan, Ltd., 1946-63, chmn., 1963-65, now dir.; chmn. Canadian board Norwich Union Life Ins. Soc., Norwich Union Fire Ins. Soc., Can. Security Assurance Co.; dir. IBM Can., Ltd., Bell Can., Canadian Investment Fund, Ltd., Massey Ferguson, Ltd., Canadian Fund, Inc., Tinto Holdings Can. Ltd., British Newfoundland Corp. Ltd., Churchill Falls (Labrador) Corp. Ltd., Rio Algom Mines Ltd., Huron & Erie Mortgage Corp. Hon. pres., dir., mem. exec. com. Royal Agrl. Winter Fair. Chmn. bd. govs. U. Toronto, 1964-68, hon. chmn. bd. govs., 1968-71. Created comdr. Order St. Michael and St. George, 1943; grand officer Nat. Order So. Cross (Brazil), 1962. Recipient medal of service Order Can., 1969. Mem. Phi Kappa Phi. Mem. Anglican Ch. Clubs: York, Toronto, Canadian of Toronto (past pres.) (Toronto). Co-author: Hand Book of Canadian Companies, 1931. Editor: Robert Laird Borden, His Memoirs, 1938. Home: Tannery Hill Farm Rural Route 2 King Ontario Canada Office: 25 King St W Toronto 105 Ontario Canada

BORDEN, JOHN C., tool mfg. co. exec.; b. Mayville, N.D., Oct. 25, 1903; s. Michael J. and Bertha (Dymack) B.; B.E.E., U. Minn., 1929; m. Dorothy Gehrke, Jan. 28, 1933; children—John A., J. Michael, Judith Ann. With Cutler-Hammer, Inc., Milw., 1929—, sales dept., 1930-35, mgr. parts sales, 1935-42, spl. assignments, 1943-47, comptroller, 1947-66, v.p., 1956- 66, exec. v.p., 1966—, dir. Chief elec. equipment sect. tools div. WPB, 1942-43. Mem. Engrs. Soc. Milw., Comptrollers Inst. Clubs: University, Milwaukee, Rotary (Milw.), Home: Elm Grove WI 53122 Office: 780 N Waler St Milwaukee WI 53216

BORDEN, MARY FRANCES, librarian; b. Tacoma, Nov. 23, 1919; d. Lindon A. and Mary Cecelia (Donnelly) Borden; B.A. in History, U. Wash., 1943, B.A. in Librarianship, 1944. Asst. br. librarian in charge work with children Mottet br. Tacoma Pub. Library, 1944-45, br. librarian, 1945-49, br. librarian Moore br., 1950-55, asst. dir. Tacoma Pub. Library, 1955-70, dir., 1970—. Chmn. Wash. Community Library Council, 1970-72. Mem. A.L.A. (chmn. membership com. Wash. 1957-60, chmn. library adminstrn. div. nominating com. 1971), Pacific N.W., Wash. (exec. bd. 1957-59, state exec. dir. Nat. Library Week 1965, treas., exec. bd. 1969-71, 71-73) library assns., Am. Assn. U. Women (2d v.p., membership chmn. Tacoma 1958-59), Ladies Aux. to Brotherhood R.R. Trainmen (past pres. Tacoma), Internat. Platform Assn., Tacoma Symphony Guild, Allied Arts of Tacoma. Roman Catholic. Club: Quota (sec. 1957-58, 1st v.p. 1960-61, pres. 1961-62) (Tacoma). Home: 3827 101st St S W Tacoma WA 98499 Office: 1102 Tacoma Av S Tacoma WA 98402

BORDEN, OLE, fashion designer; b. Elsinore, Denmark, Nov. 4, 1922; s. Ole Christian and Marie (Bech) Olesen; grad. textile design, Royal Acad. Art, Copenhagen, 1940; grad. fashion art, Kunstgewerbe Schule, Vienna, Austria, 1942; grad. textiles fashion, Ecole des Beaux Arts, Lausanne, Switzerland, 1945; m. Vibeke Valentin-Hansen, Feb. 1, 1946; children—Mark, Michele, Christine, Lars. Came to U.S., 1952, naturalized, 1957. Fashion designer, Stockholm, Sweden, 1946-48, Paris, France, Rome, Italy and London, Eng., 1948-52, N.Y.C., 1952—; designer Rembrandt, 1964—; cons. designer European firms, also in field archtl. and indsl. design; specializing in young contemporary clothes; designer exclusive young collection for Lord & Taylor, N.Y.C., 1959-64. Recipient Lord & Taylor award for creative Am. Fashion designs, pioneering first total Am. jr. look. Home: 4 Park Av New York City NY 10016 Office: 498 7th Av New York City NY 10018

BORDEN, R.W., finance co. exec.; b. Hastings, Me., 1913; ed. U. Neb., 1934. Vice pres. finance, treas. Pacific Finance Corp.; v.p., treas. Olympic Ins. Co., Pacific Finance Corp. Can., Ltd., Transam. Internat., Spartan Ins. Co., Mt. Beacon Ins. Co., Marathon Ins. Co., Transam. Financial Co., Bankers Comml. Corp.; v.p., treas., dir. Transam. Leasing Co., First Credit Corp., Pacific Finance Loans (Cal.). Home: 535 Curson Av Los Angeles CA 90036 Office: 1150 S Olive St Los Angeles CA 90015*

BORDEN, SAM WHEATLEY, savs. and loan assn. exec.; b. Bethesda, Md., Apr. 22, 1899; s. Thomas Thomas Sheppard and Frances Caroline (Wheatley) B.; student George Washington U., 1923-24; m. Ruth Walters, Apr. 1, 1938. With Perpetual Bldg. Assn., Washington, 1921-24; asst. chief clk. Supreme Ct. for D.C., 1924-26; exec. v.p. Loyola Fed. Savs. and Loan Assn., Balt., 1929-48, pres., dir., 1948-67, chmn. bd., chief exec. officer, 1967—; chmn. bd., dir. State Title Co., Balt., 1956—, Ins. Mgmt. Corp., Balt., 1956—; pres., dir. Gibson Island Corp. (Md.), 1944-46; dir. lst Mortgage Ins. Co., Greensboro, N.C., Home Protection Life Ins. Co., Sentinel Ins. Agy. Corp., Hato Rey, P.R., Fed. Home Loan Bank, Greensboro; mem. exec. com., dir. Blue Ridge Ins. Co., Hagerstown, Md., 1956-61. Mem. Commn. To Modernize Govt. of Md., 1965—, chmn. natural resources sub-com. 1965—; mem. adv. com. Balt. Planning Commn.; mem. Charles Center Planning Commn., 1964-66. Bd. dirs. Mt. Vernon Improvement Assn., 1955-67, Charles Street Assn., 1948-50. Served with USAAC, 1918-21; to lt. USNR, 1942-44. Mem. Nat. League Insured Savs. Assn. Assn. (exec. gom., dir. state govs.), Md. League Bldg. Savs. and Loan Assn. (dir., past pres.), Internat. Union Bldg. and Savs. Soc., Newcomen Soc. N. Am. Episcopalian (past trustee treas.). Clubs: Chevy Chase (Md.); Maryland, Center, Governors, Advertising, Advertising, Merchants (Balt.); Army-Navy (Washington); Gibson Island, Gibson Island Yacht. Home: Gibson Island MD 21056 Office: 1300 N Charles St Baltimore MD 21201

BORDEN, WILLIAM SILVERS, ins. exec.; b. Groveville, N.J., Feb. 1, 1893; s. Edward and Susan M. M. (Lewis) B.; A.B., Princeton, 1915; m. Lida M. Scheidnagel, Dec. 28, 1920; children—William Silvers, Barbara Louise (Mrs. William F. Floyd), Walter Johnson. Social worker Essex County Children's Aid Soc., 1915-17; examiner N.J. Civil Service Commn., 1919; pres. W.S. Borden Co., ins. and real estate, Trenton, 1920-68, chmn., 1968—; dir. finance Mer- County,

1922-31. Sec. Trenton and Mercer County Meml. Bldg. Commn., 1931-62; chmn. Trenton Central Planning Bd., 1960-68. Pres. Del. Valley United Fund, 1954; adv. bd. Mercer St. Friends Center. Chmn. Mercer County County Rep. Com., 1939-49; mem. N.J. Rep. Com., 1949-53. Trustee, Rutgers U., 1954-58. Served as capt. F.A., U.S. Army, 1917-19. Mem. Trenton Council Human Relations (exec. bd.). Mason. Clubs: Terrace (Princeton, N.J.); Trenton, Trenton Country. Home: 932 Riverside Dr Trenton NJ 08618 Office: 124 W State St Trenton NJ 08608

BORDERS, WILLIAM ALEXIS, air line co. exec.; b. Mayhew, Miss., Aug. 23, 1904; s. Isaac D. and Sara (Gillespie) B.; A.B., U. Mo., 1926; m. Kate Edmonstone Thompson, June 15, 1929; children—Guy Thompson, Carolyn Grey (Mrs. Donald Danforth, Jr.), Kate Edmonstone (Mrs. Morton S. Glazer), William Alexander, John Gillespie. With Halsey, Stuart & Co., investments, St. Louis, 1926-33; fed. bank examiner, 1934-40; v.p. Mercantile Trust Co., St. Louis, 1947- 51; pres. St Louis County Nat. Bank, 1951-57, Security Trust Co., St. Louis, 1957-65; vice chmn. bd. Merc. Trust Co. St. Louis, 1965-70, dir., 1965—; chmn. bd. Ozark Air Lines, 1971—; dir. Central States Paper & Bag Co., Lee-Rowan Co., Mercantile Trust Co. St. Louis, Inc. Served to col. AUS, 1941-46. Decorated Croix de Guerre with palm. Mem. Mo. Bankers Assn. (pres. 1954-55), Phi Beta Kappa. Clubs: Racquet, St. Louis Country, Noonday (St. Louis). Home: 4 N Kingshighway St Louis MO 63108 Office: Ozark Air Lines St Louis MO 63145

BORDERS, WILLIAM DONALD, bishop; b. Washington, Ind., Oct. 9, 1913; s. Thomas M. and Zelpha Ann (Queen) B.; M.S. in Edn., U. Notre Dame, 1947; D.D., LL.D., Notre Dame Sem., 1969. Ordained priest Roman Cath. Ch., 1940; instr. U. Notre Dame, 1946-47; chaplain Cath. Student Center La. State U., 1947-62; rector St. Joseph's Cathedral, Baton Rouge, 1962-68, St. Joseph's Prep. Sch., 1962- 68; bishop Diocese of Orlando, Fla., 1968-69. Dir. Diocesan Council Catholic Men and Women, Baton Rouge, 1959-68. Mem. planning council United Givings Fund, Baton Rouge, 1959-68; mem. Inter-racial Council Orlando, 1968—. Chmn. bd. Notre Dame Sem., 1965-68; bd. dirs. Communities Service, Baton Rouge 1957-59. Served as chaplain AUS, World War II. Decorated Bronze Star. Address: PO Box 3069 Orlando, FL 32802.

BORDIN, EDWARD S., educator, psychologist; b. Phila., Nov. 7, 1913; s. Morris and Jennie (Zarovsky) B.; B.S.C., Temple U., 1935, M.A., 1937; Ph.D., Ohio State U., 1942; m. Ruth Birgitta Anderson, June 2O, 1941; children—Martha Christine (Mrs. Steven A. Hillyard), Charlotte Anna (Mrs. Sung P. Lin). Asst. to co-ordinator, also counselor univ. testing bur. U. Minn., 1939- 42, acting dir. bur., 1945-46; personnel technician War Dept., 1942-45; asso. prof. psychology Wash. State U., 1946-48, U. Mich., Ann Arbor, 1948-55, prof., 1955—. Mem. Am. Psychol. Assn. (pres. div. counseling psychology 1955), A.A.A.S. Author: Psychological Counseling, 1955, 2d edit. 1968. Editor Jour. Cons. Psychology, 1959-64. Spl. research theory psychotherapy. Home: 1000 Aberdeen Dr Ann Arbor MI 48104

BORDINAT, EUGENE, Jr., automobile mfg. co. exec.; b. Toledo, Feb. 10, 1920; s. Eugene and Maude Agnes (Hogan) B.; student U. Mich., 1937-39, Cranbrook Acad., Bloomfield Hills, Mich., 1940-41; m. Edelgard Lietz, Jan. 15, 1954; children— Kevin, Kimberly, Kent. Automotive stylist Gen. Motors Corp., Detroit, 1930-42, supr. Fisher tank program, 1942-44; sr. automotive stylist, 1945-47; with Ford Motor Co., Dearborn, Mich., 1947—, successively supr. advanced styling, supr. exterior styling, mgr. Lincoln-Mercury styling, chief stylist Mercury, chief stylist Lincoln-Mercury styling studio, 1947-61, v.p. design, 1961—. Mem. adv. com. Art Center, Coll. Design, Los Angeles. Trustee St John's Mil. Acad., Delafield, Wis., Cranbrook Acad. Art; trustee, mem. exec. bldg. fund com. Bloomfield Country Day Sch. Served as aviation cadet USAAF, 1944-45. Recipient ann. design award for Lincoln Premiere design Indsl. Designers Inst., 1956, for Lincoln Continental design, 1961, ann. design award for Mustang, 1964. Fellow Am. Inst. Indsl. Design (dir., mem. adv. council, fellowship com.). Presbyn. (trustee). Home: 6233 Dakota Circle Birmingham MI 48010 Office: 21175 Oakwood Blvd Dearborn MI 48124

BORDLEY, JOHN EARLE, physician; b. Balt., Nov. 8, 1902; s. James and Margaretta Carroll (Hollyday) B., Ph.B., Yale, 1925; M.D., Johns Hopkins, 1929; m. Ellen Bruce Fisher, July 3, 1930; children—Ellen Bruce, Anne. Intern surgery Union Meml. Hosp., Balt., 1929-30; intern, asst. resident, resident otolaryngology Johns Hopkins Hosp., 1930-33, otolaryngologist in charge, 1952-69, emeritus, 1969—; instr. laryngology and otology Johns Hopkins U. Sch. Medicine, 1933-36, asso. laryngology, otology, 1936-42, asso. prof., 1942-52, prof., dir. dept., 1952-69, Andelot prof. of otolaryngology 1962-69, now emeritus, asso. prof. physiol. hygiene, div. audiology and speech Sch. Hygiene and Pub. Health, 1949-50, asso. prof. environmental medicine, 1950-52, adj. prof. environmental medicine, div. laryngology and otology, 1952-59, prof. environmental medicine div. audiology and speech, 1959-69, now emeritus; vis. otolaryngologist Prince Alfred Hosp., Sydney, Australia 1943—; chief cons. Balt. City Hosps. 1946—; regional cons. audiology VA 1946—; mem. nat. adv. neurol. diseases and blindness council, 1960-64; cons. neurol. and sensory disease service program U.S. Bur. State Services, 1962-63; cons. Surgeon- Gen. USPHS, 1957, mem. nat. adv. neurol. and diseases council; cons. otolaryngology USAF, Lackland AFB; chmn. communicative disorders program project rev. com. Nat. Inst. Neurol. Diseases and Strokes, 1969-71; mem. adv. council on Preventative and Chronic Diseases of Md., 1969—. Served as lt. col. M.C., AUS, 1942-46; chief ear, nose and throat div. 118th Gen. Hosp., 1942-46, chief surg. div. 1944-45. Diplomate Am. Bd. Otolarynology, bd. dirs., 1964—. Mem. A.C.S. (gov.), Am. Otol. Soc. (pres. 1970-71), Am. Council Otolaryngolgy Council (exec. dir. 1969—), Internat. Fedn. Otolaryngology-Rhino-Laryngol. Socs. (chmn. com. edn. 1968—), Am. Laryngol. Soc., Am. Laryngol. Rhinol, Otological Soc. (pres. 1964), Collegium Oto-Rhino-Laryngologicum, Am. Acad. Ophthalmology and Otolaryngology (com. otolaryngic pathology), Am. Broncho-Esophagological Assn., Soc. Med. Cons. to Armed Forces, Nat. Bd. Rehab., Soc. U. Otolaryngologists (pres. 1963- 65, council 1967), Am. Soc. Head and Neck Surgeons (council 1966), Am. Assn. U. Profs., Assn. Mil. Surgeons U.S., Sigma Xi, Delta Kappa Epsilon, Alpha Omega Alpha. Protestant. Clubs: Elihu (Yale); Elkridge, Balt. Editorial bd. The Laryngoscope, Mil. Medicine, 1964-65. Home: 5510 Woodlawn Rd Baltimore MD 21210 Office: Johns Hopkins Hospital Baltimore MD 21205

BORDT, FREDERICK JOHN, Jr., educator, mech. engr.; b. Bellevue, Pa., Aug. 2, 1916; s. Frederick John and Luella (Schwerin) B.; B.S., Carnegie Inst. Tech., 1938; postgrad. Rensselaer Poly. Inst., 1938, U. Mich., 1941; m. Katherine Elizabeth Thomas, June 30, 1938; 1 dau., Marian Jean (Mrs. James A. Patterson). Draftsman, George J. Hagan Co., Pitts., 1934-38, design engr., summers 1939-40; mem. faculty Rensselaer Poly. Inst., 1938—, prof., 1952—, project head thermo-electric space heater, 1948—, project head high speed traversing system, 1950—; cons. in field, 1956—. Mem. Am. Soc. M.E. (sect. rep. gas turbine div.), Am. Soc. Engring. Edn., A.A.A.S., Soc. Engrs. Eastern N.Y., Sigma Xi (pres. Rensselaer chpt. 1956). Club: Crystal Lake Yacht (commodore 1965-66, bd. dirs. 1967-69) (Frankfort, Mich.). Patentee in field. Home: 2 Thais Rd RD 1 Averill Park NY 12018 Office: Ricketts Bldg Rensselaer Poly Inst Troy NY 12181

BOREI, HANS GEORG, educator; b. Stockholm, Sweden, Feb. 7, 1914; s. Emil Johan Boreus and Elise (Edlund) Påhlson; M.A., U. Stockholm, 1937; Ph.D., 1940, F.D., 1945; m. Ellen Österlin, 1938; children—Karin, Sven, Ragnar. Came to U.S., 1951. Asst. prof. exptl. zoology and cell research U. Stockholm, 1945, asso. prof., 1947, head dept. developmental physiology and genetics Wenner-Gren Inst., 1947-50, head dept. biophysics, 1950-52, acting head Inst., 1948, 50; research Carlsberg Lab., Copenhagen, Denmark, 1946, Molteno Inst., Cambridge (Eng.) U., 1948-49, Mt. Desert Island Biol. Lab., 1955-64, Kristineberg Zool. Sta., Sweden, 1961; vis. prof. U. Pa., also Cal. Inst. Tech., 1951; prof. zoology U. Pa., Phila., 1953—, prof. gen. physiology, 1955-60, dir. research group marine biology, author coll. manuals gen. physiology, invertebrates and biochemistry. Pres., Swan's Island Marine Sta., 1966—. Fellow A.A.A.S.; mem. Biochem. Soc. Eng., Am. Chem. Soc., Soc. Exptl. Biology, Internat. Soc. Cell Biology, Soc. Gen. Physiologists, Sigma Xi. Contbr. profl. jours. Home: 3725 Hamilton St Philadelphia PA 19104

BOREL, ARMAND, educator; b. Chaux-de-Fonds, Switzerland, May 2l, 1923: Master Mathematics, Federal Sch. Tech., Zurich, Switzerland. 1947; Dr. Degree, U. Paris, France, 1952; m. Gabrielle Pittet, May 8, 1952; children— Dominique, Anne-Christine. Asst. Federal Sch. Tech., Zurich, 1947-49, prof., 1955-57; attaché de Recherches, French Nat. Center Sci. Research, Paris, 1949-50; supplying prof. algebra U. Geneva, Switzerland, 1950-52; mem. Inst. Advanced Study, Princeton, 1952-54, prof., 1957-; vis. prof. U. Chgo., 1954-55. Mem. Am., Swiss, French math. socs. Home: 106 Battle Rd Circle Princeton NJ 08540

BOREL, PAUL ARNOLD, govt. ofcl.; b. Zurich, Switzerland, Mar. 15, 1912; s. Jules Arnold and Juliette (Pascal-Rudhardt) Borel-Jacquet; came to U.S., 1917, naturalized, 1923; B.S. in Civil Engring., U. Kan., 1934; M.B.A., Harvard, 1938; M.A., Columbia, 1944; J.D., George Washington U., 1951; grad. Nat. War Coll., 1950; m. Miriam Eleanor Chesham, Oct. 28, 1939; children—Nancy (Mrs. John N. Ellis), Elaine (Mrs. Thomas D. Foster), Julia, Jane Franklin, Douglas, Mark. With Sun Oil Co., 1934-35, Black & Veatch, cons. engrs., Kansas City, Mo., 1935-36, Phillips Petroleum Co., 1939- 40; with CIA, 1947—, dir. central reference service, 1957-63, asst. dep. dir. intelligence, 1964-66, dir. intelligence support, 1966- 67, spl. adviser, 1967-68, dir. Fgn. Broadcast Information Service, 1969—; admitted to D.C. bar, 1952, U.S. Supreme Ct. bar. Served to capt. USNR, 1940-46; ETO. Mem. Tau Beta Pi, Sigma Tau, Alpha Kappa Lambda, Theta Tau. Club: Riverbend Golf and Country. Home: 3175 Holmes Run Rd Falls Church, VA 22042. Office: CIA Washington DC 20505

BORELLA, VICTOR, mgmt. cons.; b. Plymouth, N.H., Oct. 13, 1906; s. Gaspar and Giuditta (Moruzzi) B.; student Norwich U., Northfield, Vt., 1926-27; A.B., Dartmouth, 1930; m. Cecelia O'Connell, July 2, 1934 (dec. 1956); m. 2d, Eleanor Dwinell, May 11, 1957. Dir. personnel Terminal Transp. System, 1930-34; with Gen. Motors Corp., 1934-39; asst. coordinator U.S. Office Inter-Am. Affairs, 1942-45; with Rockefeller Center, Inc., 1939-42, 45- 65, exec. v.p., 1958-65, now dir. Vice chmn. N.Y.C. Mgmt.-Labor Council, 1968-70; labor adviser to Gov. Rockefeller, 1959—; bd. dirs. Am Arbitration Assn., 1962-70, chmn. exec. com., 1965; chmn. Gov. N.Y. Workmen's Compensation Rev. Com., 1962; mem. Presdl. Mission to Latin Am., 1969. Home: 200 E 66th St New York City NY 10021 Office: One Rockefeller Plaza New York City NY 10020

BOREMAN, HERBERT STEPHENSON, judge; b. Middlebourne, W.Va., Sept. 21, 1897; s. Kenner S. and Eva (Wells) B.; LL.B., W.Va. U., 1920; m. Cornelia K. Campbell, July 23, 1924; children—Evelyn (Mrs. C. A. Parks), Cornelia (Mrs. McVey Graham), Herbert Stephenson. Admitted to W.Va. bar, 1920; practice of law, Parkersburg, W.Va., 1920-54; asst. U.S. Dist. Atty., 1923-27; pros. atty. Wood County, W.Va., 1929-33; mem. W.Va. Senate, 1942-50; judge No. Dist. of W.Va., U.S. Dist. Ct., Parkersburg, 1954-59, U.S. Court of Appeals, 4th Circuit, 1959—. Mem. W.Va. Commn. Uniform State Laws, 1950-54; nominee for gov. W.Va., 1948. Bd. govs. W.Va. U., 1932-36, vis. com. coll. law, 1950-54. Mem. Am., W.Va. (v.p.), Wood County (pres. 1934) bar assns., W.Va. U. Alumni Assn. (pres.). Republican. Presbyn. Home: 901 Juliana St Parkersburg WV 26101 Office: Federal Bldg Parkersburg WV 26101

BOREMAN, LEONARD, lawyer; b. Pitts., Sept. 13, 1912; s. Harry and Rae (Rosecrans) B.; A.B., U. Pitts., 1933, LL.B., 1936; m. Dolores Jean Farkas, Nov. 29, 1956; children—Rachel Ellen, Hugh David. Admitted to Pa. bar, 1937, since practiced in Pitts., 1937—; mem. firm Baskin, Boreman, Wilner, Sachs, Gondelman & Craig, 1965—; spl. counsel Allegheny County (Pa.), 1949- 53. Served to lt. USNR, 1942-45. Mem. Am., Pa., Allegheny County bar assns. Home: 6415 Monitor St Pittsburgh PA 15217 Office: Frick Bldg Pittsburgh PA 15219

BOREN, ARTHUR RODNEY, sales mgmt. exec.; b. Dayton, O., June 14, 1916; s. Herbert S. and Katharine Maria (Miller) B.; A.B., Kenyon Coll., 1938; m. Charlotte Poock, Mar. 14, 1942; children—Katharine Elizabeth, A. Rodney. With Mead Corp., 1949-61, asst. to v.p., 1951-53, asst. v.p., 1953-57, v.p. 1957- 61; with Ga. Kraft Co., 1952-61; asst. to pres., 1956-61; with Fourdrinier, Kraft Bd. Inst., 1961—, pres., treas. Past bd. dirs. YMCA, local chpt. A.R.C.; trustee Kenyon Coll. Served to lt. comdr. USNR, 1940-47; maj. to col., Ohio Air N.G., 1947-52. Mem. Nat. Paperboard Assn. (past dir.), Eastern Conservation Commn. (past dir.), Delta Tau Delta. Clubs: Canadian Union League (N.Y.C.); Moraine Country, Miami Valley Hunt and Polo (Dayton). Home: 1401 Runnymede Rd Dayton OH 45419 Office: 280 Park Av New York City NY 10017

BOREN, BENJAMIN N., lawyer; b. Dallas, 1909; s. Samuel H. and Ella (Chilton) B.; student Terrill Sch., Dallas; LL.B., U. Tex., 1933; m. Martha Ruth Moore, Sept. 1, 1931; children—Martha Ann, Benjamin Chilton. Admitted to Tex. bar. 1933, since practiced in Dallas; mem. firm Locke, Purnell, Boren, Laney & Neely, 1947-. Mem. Am., Dallas bar assns., State Bar Tex., Phi Delta Phi. Home: 4135 Windsor Pkwy Dallas TX 75205 Office: Republic Nat Bank Tower Dallas TX 75201

BOREN, CARTER EXCELL, educator; b. Troy. Tex., Apr. 21, 1912; s. Carney Excell and Osee B. (Carter) B.; B.A., Tex. Christian U., 1936; M.A., U. Chgo., 1937, D.B., 1939, Ph.D., 1952; m. Jovan Vanderslice, Dec. 25, 1938 (div. 1957): children—Linda Carol, Alice Jeanne (Mrs. Barry K. Woodward). Ordained to ministry Christian Ch., 1931; minister Bethany Christian Ch., Houston, 1939-42; ad-interim Rosemont Ch., Dallas, 1944-45; asst. prof. philosophy and religion U. Houston, 1946-48, asso. prof., dean religious activities, 1948-50, chmn. philosophy and religion, 1948-55, prof., 1950-55; dean Christian Coll. of Ga., U. Ga., 1955-56; exec. sec. Tex. Pvt. Jr. Coll. Found., Houston, 1956-59; asst. prof. philosophy Arlington State Coll., 1959-62, asso. prof., 1962-69; prof. philosophy U. Tex., Arlington, 1969—. Pres. Select Products, Inc., Houston, 1954-55. Served to 1st lt. AUS, 1943-44. Mem. Am., S.W. philos. assns., S.W. Social Sci. Assn., Am. Ch. History Assn., S.W. Renaissance Soc., So. Hist. Assn., Tex. Hist. Soc., Tex. Assn. Coll. Tchrs., Midwestern Philos. Assn., Am. Assn. U. Profs., Campbell Inst., Phi Delta Kappa, Phi Kappa Phi, Alpha Chi. Lion, Rotarian. Author: Religion on the Texas Frontier, 1968; also articles. Home: 800 W Border St Arlington TX 76010

BOREN, JAMES HARLAN, pub. relations exec. b. Wheatland, Okla., Dec. 10, 1925; s. James Basil and Una Lee (Hamilton) B.; A.B. in Econs., U. Tex., 1948, Ph.D., 1969; A.B. in Edn., Long Beach (Cal.) State Coll., 1950; A.M. in Econs., U. So. Cal., 1950; L.H.D., Nathaniel Hawthorne Coll., 1967; m. Irene Cheek, Aug. 16, 1946; children— Richard Vincent, James Stanley. High sch. tchr., night dir. recreation dept., Oxnard, Cal., 1950-52; chief accounting div. Tex. Dept. Agr., 1952-54; prof. edn., head dept. Arlington (Tex.) State Coll., 1954-56; pres. Boren Oil & Gas Corp., 1956-57; adminstrv. asst. to U.S. Senator Yarborough, 1957-61; dep. dir. USOM to Peru, 1961, AID mission to Peru, 1961-63; spl. asst. to U.S. coordinator Alliance for Progress, 1963-69; dir. Partners of Alliance Programs, AID, 1963-69; engaged in pub. relations, Washington, 1969—. Campaign mgr. Ralph Yarborough for gov. Tex., 1956, for U.S. senator, 1957. Served with USNR, 1943-46. Recipient Outstanding Alumnus award Long Beach State Coll., 1961, Meritorious Honor award AID; 1964, Spl. citation, 1970. Mem. Ednl. Communications Assn. (dir.), Soc. for Internat. Devel., Nat. Assn. Profl. Bureaucrats (founder-pres.), U.S. Senate Adminstrv. Assts. Assn., Order Artus, Phi Delta Kappa. Methodist. Club: Nat. Press (Washington). Home: 1803 Paul Spring Pkwy Alexandria VA 22308 Office: Nat Press Bldg Washington DC 20004

BORER, HAROLD PETER, shipping exec.; b. Bklyn., Oct. 4, 1892; s. Emil V. and Jennie (Newman) B.; student pub. schs.; m. Elizabeth Meyer, Jan. 25, 1916; childrenHarold, Kenneth, Donald. With Cunard Steam-Ship Co., Ltd., N.Y.C., 1910—, gen. passenger mgr., 1934-45, gen. mgr. U.S., 1945—; v.p., dir. Beach Blvd. Marina Inc.; pres., dir. Twenty-Five Broadway Corp. Decorated comdr. Order Brit. Empire; knight Order of White White White Rose (Finland), Knight of Malta. Mem. N.Y. Shipping Assn. (dir.), Brit. Mcht. Navy Club (dir.), Maritime Assn. N.Y. (dir.), St. George's Soc., Pilgrims of Am. Clubs: Ponte Vedra; India House. Home: Ponte Vedra FL 32082 Office: 25 Broadway New York City NY 10004

BORES, FRANCISCO, artist; b. Madrid, 1898. Mem. Ultraist group, Madrid, 1922; influenced by Surrealist movement, Paris, 1925; style in form of personal fantasy, 1929; oneman shows include Galerie Carrie, 1956, Galerie Viland- Galanis, 1966-67. Address: 16 Villa St Jacques Paris 14e France*

BORESI, ARTHUR PETER, educator, author; b. Toluca, Ill., Aug. 27, 1924; s. John Peter and Eva (Grotti) B.; student Kenyon Coll., 1943-44; B.S. in Elec. Engring., U. Ill., 1948, M.S., 1949, Ph.D., 1953; m. Clara Jean Gordon, Dec. 28, 1946; children—Jennifer Ann (Mrs. William Francis Hill), Annette, Nancy Jean. Research engr. N. Am. Aviation, 1950; materials engr. Nat. Bur. Standards, 1951; mem. faculty U. Ill. at Urbana, 1953—, prof. theoretical and applied mechanics and nuclear engring., 1959—; distinguished vis. prof. Clarkson Coll. Tech., Potsdam, N.Y., 1968-69; cons. in field. Served with USAAF, 1943-44, AUS, 1944-46. Founding mem. Am. Acad. Mechanics; mem. Am. Soc. M.E., Am. Soc. C.E., Soc. Exptl. Stress Analysis, Am. Soc. Engring. Edn., Sigma Xi. Author: Engineering Mechanics, 1959; Elasticity in Engineering Mechanics, 1965; also articles. Home: 1715 Lynwood Dr Champaign IL 61820 Office: Talbot Lab Univ Ill Urbana IL 61801

BORETZ, BENJAMIN AARON, composer and music critic; b. N.Y.C., Oct. 3, 1934; s. Abraham and Leah (Yollis) B.; A.B., Bklyn. Coll., 1954; M.F.A., Brandeis U., 1957; M.F.A., Princeton, 1960, Ph.D., 1970; m. Naomi Messinger, Sept. 1, 1954; 1 son, Avron Albert. Mem. faculty Brandeis U., 1955-57, 62-63, U. Cal. at Los Angeles, 1957-59, N.Y. U., 1964-69, also dir. group computer synthesis; mem. faculty Columbia, 1969—, vis. prof. Princeton U., 1967-68, 70-71; Fulbright-Hays lectr. U. Southampton, Eng., 1971-72; music critic The Nation, 1962-69; editor Perspectives of New Music, 1962—; editorial bd. Contemporary Music Newsletter; composer-participant Princeton Seminar Advanced Music Studies, 1959; panel participant congress Internat. Musicol. Soc., Salzburg, Austria, 1964. Recipient composition award Fromm Music Found., Aspen, 1956; Ingram-Merrill Found. grantee in music, 1966. Mem. Am. Composers Alliance, Am. Soc. U. Composers (sec., mem. exec. com.), Am. Musicol. Soc., N.Y. Music Critics Cricle, Internat. Soc. Contemporary Music. (exec. bd.). Composer: Violin Concerto, 1956-57; String Quartet, 1958-59; Donne Songs, 1959-60; Ensemble Variations, 1962-64; Group Variations I, 1967, II, 1969; Composition for flute and piano, 1969-71. Author: Meta-Variations, 1970. Editor: Perspectives on Schoenberg and Stravinsky, 1968; Perspectives on American Composers, 1971; Perspectives on Contemporary Music Theory, 1971. Address: 225 W 86th St New York City NY 10024

BORG, ALFRED FRANCIS, educator; b. Pateros, Wash., Jan. 13, 1918; s. Charles Theodore and Emma Ethel (Shinbur) B.; student Wash. State U., 1934-35; B.S., U. Wash., 1940, M.S., 1943, Ph.D., 1948; m. Betty Eleanor Watson, Dec. 27, 1941; children—Carol Christine, David Gregory, Jennifer Anne. Bacteriologist, Biochem. Research Found., Newark, Del., 1948-49; asst. prof. bacteriology U. Ill., 1949-53; asso. prof. N.C. State Coll., 1953- 57; prof. bacteriology, chmn. dept. Kan. State U., Manhattan, 1957-67, acting dean Grad. Sch., 1961-62, spl. research microbial ecology, cellular slime molds. Research intern No. utilization research and devel. div. Dept. Agr., Peoria, Ill., 1952; chmn. Inter-Soc. Com. on Lab. Services Related to Health, 1952-55; spl. cons., spl. programs in sci. edn. sect. NSF, 1958-66, program dir. sci. curriculum improvement, 1967-70, dep. dir., div. undergrad. edn. in sci., 1970—. Served with AUS, 1942-46. NSF sci. faculty fellow, 1963-64. Fellow Am. Acad. Microbiology; mem. Am. Soc. Profl. Biologists (exec. sec. 1956-57), Am. Soc. Microbiology (pres. Mo. Valley br. 1960-61), A.A.A.S., Soc. Gen. Microbiology, Am. Assn. U. Profs., Sigma Xi. Home: 5514 Cedar Pkwy Chevy Chase MD 20015 Office: NSF Washington DC 20550

BORG, ALVIN ANDREW, former drug chain store exec.; b. Ludington, Mich., Apr. 8, 1904; s. Andrew and Ida (Gustafson) B.; A.B., U. Mich., 1927; m. Marjorie Mailler, Mar. 25, 1931; children—Betty (Mrs. Stanley D. Whitford, Jr.), Judith (Mrs. Rody Biggert), Alvin Andrew, Christine. With Walgreen Drug Co. Chgo., 1928—, beginning as mfg. supr., successively mgr. constrn., dir. engring. and equipment, 1928-54, dir. 1952—, dir. engring., 1955-60, v.p., treas. 1961-63, pres., 1963-69; dir. Sanborn Hnos., Mexico City. Mem. Tau Kappa Epsilon. Episcopalian. Clubs: Chicago Athletic, North Shore Country, Executives (Chgo.) Home: 1154 Seneca Rd Wilmette IL 60091 Office: 4300 Peterson Av Chicago IL 60646

BORG, ANDY LEROY, lawyer; b. Superior, Wis., May 17, 1911; s. Andy and Katherine (Shufelt) B.; B.E., Wis. State U., 1933; LL.B., U. Minn., 1936; m. Syla Olson, June 14, 1941; children—Andy, Willie, Kamie. Admitted to Wis. bar, 1936, since practiced in Superior; asso. mem. Crawford & Crawford, 1936-44; dist. atty., Douglas County, 1946-50; mem. firm Borg, McGill & Moodie, 1951—. Comdr-in-chief

V.F.W. U.S., 1965; mem. Pres.'s Vets. Adv. Commn., 1967-69. Vice chmn. Wis. Geat Lakes Port Com., 1958-59; mem. Police and Fire Commn., Superior, 1958-69; chmn. Douglas County Juvenile Guidance Com., 1948-49; mem. State Labor Conciliation Panel, 1949-50; chmn. U.S. sect. Permanent Joint Bd. Def., Can. -U.S., 1969—. Bd. dirs. Superior Community Chest, Superior No. League Baseball League. Served to lt. USNR, 1944-46. Mem. Am., Wis., Douglas County bar assns., Wis. Dist. Attys. Assn. (past v.p.), Superior Assn. Commerce (past pres.), Am. Legion, United Comml. Travelers. Mason (Shriner, Jester), Moose, Elk, Eagle. Club: Kitchi Gammi (Duluth, Minn.). Home: 820 7th Av E Superior WI 54882 Office: Telegram Bldg Superior WI 54881

BORG, DONALD GOWEN, newspaper editor; b. N. Bergen, N.J., Jan 19, 1906; s. John and Hazel (Gowen) B.; grad. Hill Sch., 1924; B.A., Yale, 1928; m. Flora B. Austin, Aug. 9, 1935; children—Malcolm A., Gregory G. With Bergen County County (N.J.) Record, 1929—, editor, 1932, pub., 1949-70; pres., Bergen Eve. Record Corp., 1949-70, chmn. bd., 1957—; pres., chmn. bd. Call Printing & Pub. Co., Paterson, N.J., 1964-69. Mem. Palisades Insterstate Park Commn., 1953—, sec., 1960-70, v.p., 1970—; pres. Grand Jurors Assn. Assn. Bergen County, 1952—; mem. exec. bd. N.J. Grand Jurors Assn., 1960—, pres., 1970. 1970. Bd. mgrs. Bergen Pines County Hosp., 1941—, pres., 1946—; bd. dirs., 2d v.p. Bergen County United Fund, 1962—; bd. govs. Hackensack Hosp., 1945—; chmn. Bergen County Charter Study Commission, 1967; mem. State Tax Policy Com., 1970. Recipient Good Scout award N. Bergen council Boy Scouts Am., 1964; Howard G. Law medal civic achievement, 1949; brotherhood award Nat. Conf. Christians and Jews, 1964; Citizens award Acad. Medicine N.J., 1969; hon. M.D., Bergen County Med. Soc. Mem. Nat. Parks Assn. (life), Palisades Nature Assn. (life). Home: 655 Summit Av Hackensack, NJ 07601. Office: 150 River St Hackensack NJ 07602

BORG, DOROTHY, educator, author; b. Elberon, N.J., Sept. 4, 1902; d. Sidney C. and Madeleine (Beer) Borg; A.M., Ph.D., Columbia; divorced. Research asso. Am. Inst. of Pacific Relations, 1939-58, E. Asian Research Center, Harvard, 1960-61; research asso. E. Asian Inst., Columbia, also mem. faculty, 1962-; lectr. Peking (China) Nat. U., 1947. Recipient Bancroft prize, 1965. Mem. Am. Hist. Assn., Assn. Asian Studies, Acad. Polit. Scis. Author: American Policy and the Chinese Revolution 1925-28, 1947; The United States and The Far Eastern Crisis 1933-1938, 1964. Home: 172 Sullivan St New York City, NY 10012.

BORG, GRANT KENNETH, civil engr., educator; b. American Fork, Utah, Nov. 11, 1912; s. Kenneth and Leona (Dunn) B.; B.S., U. Utah, 1937, M.S., 1949; m. Margaret Schwenck, Nov. 8, 1945. Engr., gen. mgr. E. Jordan Irrigation Co., 1937-41; pvt. cons., Salt Lake City, 1946-49; asst. prof. civil engring U. Utah, Salt Lake City, 1950-53, asso. prof., 1953— prof., 1953—, head dept., 1956-65, dir. U. Utah Ann. Hwy. Conf.; dir. Municipal Water and Sewage Works for Utah. Mem. Utah Water Pollution Control Bd., chmn., 1955-57; dir. Western zone Nat. Council Engring. Examiners, 1968-70. Served as lt. col. AUS, 1941-46. Mem. Am. Soc. Engring. Edn., Am. Soc. Mil. Engrs., Inter-Am. Assn. San. Engring., Coop. Research Found., Am., Utah (past pres.) pub. health assns., Am. Water Works Assn., Water Pollution Control Assn., Nat., Utah socs. profl. engrs., Am. Soc. C.E., Am. Acad. Environmental Engrs., Theta Tau, Tau Beta Pi, Chi Epsilon, Phi Kappa Phi. Home: 2762 Morningside Dr Salt Lake City UT 84117

BORG, KIM, basso; b. Helsinki, Finland, Aug. 7 1919; s. Kaarlo and Hilkka (Stenius) B.; student Inst. Tech., Helsinki, 1937-45; M.Sc., Sibelius-Acad., Helsinki, 1948-49; m. Ebon Ringblom, Feb. 10, 1950; children—Mette, Matti. Engaged as scientist, 1945-48, as photographer, 1948-49, as singer, 1949—; tours in Europe, Am., Asia, Australia, Africa; operatic appearances at Met. Opera Co., State Opera Hamburg (Germany), Royal Opera, Stockholm, Sweden; guest appearances Bolshoi Theatre, Moscow, USSR, State Opera Vienna (Austria); composer orchestral songs, chamber music. Served to sr. 1st lt. with Finnish Army, 1940-44. Decorated Cross of Liberty 4th class (Finland), knight 1st class of White Rose; hon. cross for sci. and arts (Austria). Home: 158 Osterbrog Copenhagen Denmark Office: Dispeker 59 E 54th St New York City NY 10022

BORG, SIDNEY FRED, educator, engr.; b. N.Y.C., Oct. 3, 1916; s. Herman Leo and Pauline (Leibman) B.; B.S. in Civil Engring., Cooper Union Inst. Tech., 1937; M.C.E., Poly. Inst. Bklyn., 1940; E.D., Johns Hopkins, 1956; M.Eng. (hon.), Stevens Inst. Tech., 1958; m. Audrey Iva Elliott, Apr. 4, 1944; children—Nicholas Elliott, Andrew Douglas, Jill Debora, Kenneth Jeremy. Engr. position city N.Y., U.S. War Dept., Turner Constrn. Co., Gen. Motors Co., 1937-43; with Grumman Aircraft Corp., 1951-52; asst. prof. civil engring. U. Md., 1943-45; asst. and asso. prof. aero. engring. U.S. Postgrad. Sch., 1945-51; head dept. civil engring., asso. prof. civil engring. Stevens Inst. Tech., 1952-56, prof., 1956-68, prof. applied mechanics, 1968—; Fulbright lectr. Royal Danish Tech. U., 1965-66; vis. prof. Technische Hochschule, Stuttgart, Germany, summer 1966; sci. exchange prof. Polish Acad. Scis.-Nat. Acad. Scis., summer 1968; vis. prof. Air Force Inst. Tech., summer 1969; post doctoral fellow in biophysics Marine Biol. Lab., Woods Hole, Mass., summer 1971; vis. prof. Technione Israel Inst. Tech., summer 1970; cons. engr. bd. dirs. Kreisler-Borg Constrn. Co., Scarsdale, N.Y. Recipient Distinguished Alumnus award Poly. Inst. Bklyn., 1957. Licensed profl. engr. Fellow A.A.A.S., N.Y. Acad. Sci., Am. Soc. C.E.; mem. Am. Soc. Engring. Edn., Sigma Xi, Tau Beta Pi. Author: (textbook) An Introduction to Matrix-Tensor Methods in Applied Mechanics, 1956; Advanced Structural Analysis, 1959; Fundamentals of Engineering Elasticity, 1962; Matrix Tensor Methods in Continuum Mechanics, 1963; Modern Structural Analysis, 1969. Editor textbook series. Home: 2 9th St Hoboken NJ 07030

BORGATTA, EDGAR F., educator, social psychologist; b. Milan, Italy, Sept. 1, 1924; s. Edgar A. and Francis (Zinelli) B.; came to U.S., 1929, naturalized, 1934; B.A., N.Y. U., 1947, M.A., 1949, Ph.D., 1952; m. Marie Lentini, Oct. 6, 1946; children—Lynn, Kim, Lee. Instr., N.Y. U., 1949-51, lectr., prof., 1954-59; lectr., research asso. Harvard, 1951-54; social psychologist, asst. sec. Russell Sage Found., 1954-59; prof. sociology Cornell U., Ithaca, N.Y., 1959-61; Brittingham Research prof. U. Wis., 1961—, chmn. dept. sociology, 1962-65, chmn. div. social studies, 1965-68. Cons. to bus. and govt., 1953—, Russell Sage Found., 1970—; cons. editor Rand McNally & Co., 1961—. Certified psychologist, N.Y., Vt. Fellow Am. Psychol. Assn., Am. Sociol. Assn.; mem. Psychometric Soc., Vt. Sociol Assn., Vt. Psychol. Assn., Sociol. Research Assn. Editor Sociol. Methodology, Sociol. Methods and Research; co-editor Handbook of Personality Theory and Research. Contbr. profl. jours. Home: Rupert VT 05768

BORGE, VICTOR, comedian, pianist; b. Copenhagen, Denmark, Jan. 3, 1909; s. Bernhardt and Frederikke (Lichtinger) B.; ed. Borgerdydskolen; m. Sarabel Sanna Scraper, Mar. 17, 1953; children—Sanna J., Victor Bernhardt, Frederikke; children by previous marriage—Ronald, Janet. Naturalized U.S. citizen, 1948. Began study of music age 5; on concert stage, 1922-34; studied at Conservatory of Copenhagen, 1925, music in Vienna and Berlin with Egon Petri and Frederic Lammond, 3 years; appeared in mus. rev., 1934, and combined music ability and humor, creating new vogue of sophisticated mus. satire; wrote and directed own shows; entered motion pictures, 1937; became Denmark's foremost comedian, writing script, composing mus. scores and playing the lead; Scandinavian tour, 1938, while appearing in Sweden, Denmark was invaded and so came to U.S., 1940; spent 1st year in U.S. seeing three or four movies daily to learn English; guest 54 weeks on Kraft Music Hall; headed Victor Borge show, Lower Basin St. and other radio programs; soloist with many famed orchs.; one-man show at Golden Theatre, N.Y.C., 1953; 849 consecutive performances; appeared coast to coast with one man show, numerous one man TV shows U.S., Gt. Britain; ltd. engagement Palace Theatre, London, 1957; tour British Isles, 1958, N.Z., Australia, Thailand, P.I., Hong Kong, 1963. Nat. chmn. pub. service com. CARE, 1959. Awarded many honors for command performances before kings and royal families of Sweden and Denmark; named Funniest Man in Music, 1951; Comedian of Year, 1954; decorated Royal Order Daneborg, Denmark, 1956; Brotherhood award, 1957; TV Father of Year, 1958. ‡

BORGEN, BJORN KROGH, finance co. exec.; b. Aandalsness, Norway, Sept. 22, 1937; s. Truls Krogh and Helene (Lillease) B.; came to U.S., 1948, naturalized, 1957; B.S., U. Wis., 1962; M.B.A., Harvard, 1966; m. Katherine Elizabeth Sharp, Aug. 15, 1964; 1 dau., Kaia Helene. Financial analyst Gen. Electric Co., Lynn, Mass., 1962-64; v.p. portfolio mgmt. Financial Programs, Inc., Denver, 1966-69; exec. v.p. Founders Mut. Depositor Corp., Denver, 1969—, also dir.; v.p., dir. Founders Growth Fund, Founders Spl. Fund; v.p. Founders Securities Corp., Founders Income Fund. Mem. Phila.-Balt.-Washington Stock Exchange. Mem. Denver Soc. Security Analysts, Sigma Alpha Epsilon. Home: 3131 E Alameda Av Denver CO 80209 Office: First Nat Bldg Denver CO 86202

BORGENICHT, GRACE, art dealer; b. N.Y.C., Jan. 25, 1915; d. Samuel L. and Jeanette (Salny) Lubell; M.A., Columbia, 1937; student Andre Lhote, Paris, France, 1934; m. Jack Borgenicht, Jan. 20, 1938 (div. 1954); childrenJan, Berta, Lois; m. 2d, Norman Sachs, Jr., July 17, 1956 (div.); m. 3d, Warren Brandt, Dec. 27, 1960. Dir., owner Grace Borgenicht Gallery, Inc., 1951-; adviser Tupperware Art Found. Scholarship and Bus. Meets the Arts, Young Pres.' Orgn. One man exhbns. include Laurel Gallery, N.Y.C., 1947, 48, 50, Philbrooks Mus., Tulsa, 1948. Everhart Mus., Scranton Pa., 1948; group exhbns. include Nat. Assn. Women Artists, 1948, 49, L'Association Nationale des Femmes Artistes Americaines, 1949, Internat. Watercolor Exhbn., 1949, 53, 1955, 59, Contemporary Am. Painting, 1951, N.Y. Soc. Women Artists, 1953, Whitney Mus. ann. exhbn., 1954, Aquarelles Contemporaines aux Etats-Unis, France, 1954, Martha Jackson Gallery, N.Y.C., 1955; represented in permanent collections of Philbrook Mus., Everhart Mus. Recipient first prize watercolor Nat. Assn. Women Artists, 1949. Mem. N.Y. Soc. Women Artists, Nat. Assn. Women Artists, Art Dealers Assn. Am. Club: Artists (N.Y.C.). Home: 138 E 95th St New York City NY 10028 Office: 1018 Madison Av New York City NY 10021

BORGER, HUGH DONALD, former utility exec.; b. Edgewood, Pa., Sept. 22, 1905; s. William Edward and Alice Annetta (McCune) B.; student Duquesne U., U. Pitts.; m. Gladys Ellerton, 1935; 1 dau., Nancy Jean. With Peoples Natural Gas Co., Pitts., 1922-70, chief accountant, 1934, asst. treas. 1934-42, treas., dir., 1942-51, v.p. 1951-54, exec. v.p. 1954-55, pres. 1955-70, ret.; exec. v.p. operations Consol. Natural Gas Co., 1963-64, pres., 1964-66, chmn. chief exec. officer, 1966-70; dir. Pitts. Nat. Bank. Mem. Allegheny Conf. on Community Devel. Bd. dirs. Suburban Gen. Hosp. Mem. Am. Gas Assn. Presbyn. Address: Blackburn Rd RD 4 Sewickley PA 15143

BORGES, JORGO LUIS, author, educator; b. Aug. 24, 1899; ed. in Switzerland, also Cambridge (Eng.) and Buenos Aires (Argentina) univs. Formerly prof. English and N. Am. lit. Buenos Aires U.; now dir. Nat. Library Buenos Aires Recipient Premio de Honor, 1961, Fondo de les Artes, 1963; co-recipient Prix Formentor, 1961; named hon. knight Brit. Empire. Mem. Acad. Argentina de Letras. Author: Luna de Enfrente; Cuaderno San Martin; Historia de la Eternidad; Antologia Clasica de la Literatura Argentina; (with Margarita Guerrere) El Marin Fierro; La Poesia Gauchesca; El Aleph; El Jardin de Desiderios que se bifurcan; Inquisiciones; Otras Inquisiciones; Historia de la Eternidad; Historia Universal de la Infamia; Fervor de Buenos Aires; Ficciones; Labyrinthe; Libro de Cielo y del Infierno (poems), 1960; El Hacedor, 1960; Antologa personal, 1961. Address: Mexico 564 Buenos Aires Argentina*

BORGIUM, JAMES LINCOLN DE LA MOTHE sculptor, photographer; b. Stamford, Conn., Apr. 9, 1912; s. John Gutzon and Mary (Montgomery) B.; student Lukin Mil. Acad., San Antonio, Tex. 1925-27, Valley (Wyo.) Ranch Sch., 1928-30; studied sculpture under father for 12 years, also in Europe, 1929, 31; m. Louella Jones, Dec. 16, 1937 (dec. Nov. 1963); children—Anna Mary April, James Gutzon; m. 2d, Mrs. Richard Ellsworth, Apr. 9, 1964; children—Richard, Paul, Robert Ellsworth. Apprentice W. Tex. Pub. Utilities Co., Abilene, 1931; with Mt. Rushmore Nat. Meml., Black Hills, S.D., 1932—, charge measurements and enlarging models, 1934-38, apptd. supt. Meml. by Mt. Rushmore Meml. Commn., 1938, apptd. sculptor to complete Meml. following his father's death, 1940, mem. commn,, 1960—; apptd. supt. by Nat. Park Service, U.S. Dept. Interior; tech. adv. in carving worlds largest known sapphires in likeness Washington, Jefferson, Eisenhower; executed statue Our Lady of Loreto, La Bahia Mission, Goliad, Tex., bust Pres. Johnson, near Keystone, S.D. Hon. mem. Lincoln Sesquicentennial Commn. Trustee Mt. Rushmore Nat. Meml. Soc. Black Hills, Rapid City, S.D. Pres. Whooping Crane council Girl Scouts U.S.; mem. Beeville City Council, 1955-61. Mem. So. Tex. Hereford Assn. Club: Rotary. Has exhibited color photography work in salons at Milw., Rochester, N.Y., N.Y.C.; colored photographs used for covers of This Week and Sat. Eve. Post. Author: My Father's Mountain, 1965. Home and Office: Box 2325 Harlingen TX 78550

BORGLUND, WILLIAM HOLT, newspaper exec.; b. Muskogee, Okla., Feb. 6, 1912; s. John and Nettie Gertrude (Holt) B.; grad. Muskogee Jr. Coll., 1934; A.B., B.S. in Journalism, U. Okla., 1936; m. Onlee Katherine West, Jan. 6, 1938; children—Kristin, John. Salesman, Griffin Wholesale Grocery Co., Muskogee, Okla., 1930-32; with Newspaper Enterprise Assn., Inc., 1936—, successively mem. sales staff, Cleve., Southwest bus. mgr., Dallas, Midwest mgr., Chgo., 1936-48, sales mgr., Cleve., 1946-63, gen. sales mgr., 1963—, v.p., 1953—, dir., 1953—. Mem. plan commn., zoning bd. city Shaker Heights (U.), 1954-62. Mem. Nat. Sales and Marketing Execs. Assn., Sales Execs. Club of Cleve. (pres. 1955-56), Pi Sigma Epsilon, Kappa Sigma. Republican. Prebyn. (trustee). Clubs: Cleveland Athletic, Canterbury Golf (Cleve.). Home: 11 Pepperwood Lane Pepper Pike OH 44124 Office: 1200 3d St Cleveland OH 44113

BORGMAN, LUCILLE CO., educator; B.A., U. Mich., 1925, M.A., 1925. Now prof. math., chmn. dept. Detroit Inst. Tech. Address: Dept Math Detroit Inst Tech Detroit MI 48201

BORGMEYER, ERNEST, journalist. Bus., finance editor Omaha World-Herald. Office: 14th and Dodge Sts Omaha NB 68102*

BORGNINE, ERNEST, actor; b. Hamden, Conn., Jan. 24, 1917; s. Charles B. and Anna (Boselli) B.; student pub. schs. New Haven; m. Rhoda Kemins, Sept. 3, 1949 (div.); 1 dau., Nancy; m. 2d, Katy Jurado, Dec. 31, 1960 (div. 1963); m. 3d, Ethel Merman, 1964 (div.); m. 4th, Donna Granoucci Rancourt; 1 dau. Appeard in N. Y. stage plays Harvey, Mrs. McThing; actor Columbia Pictures Corp., Metro-Goldwyn Mayer, 2Oth Century-Fox; motion pictures include The Mob, From Here to Eternity, Bad Day at Black Rock, Demetrius and the Gladiators, Violent Saturday, Marty, Square Jungle, The Catered Affair, The Best Things in Life Are Free, Three Brave Men, Hell Below, Badlanders, Rabbit Trap, Man on String, Barabbas, Flight of the Phoenix, 1966, The Oscar, 1966, The Dirty Dozen, 1968, Willard, 1971; also appears on TV, starred in McHale's Navy. Recipient Oscar for Best Performance of Year, 1956. Served with USNR, World War II. Mason. Office: 9390 Brighton Way Beverly Hills CA 90210

BORG OLIVIER, GEORGE, prime minister Malta; b. Valletta, July 5, 1911; ed. Lyceum and Royal U. Malta; hon. D.Litt. Elected to Council of Govt., 1939, to Legislative Assembly, 1947; minister Works and Reconstruction, 1950-55; leader of Opposition, 1955-58; prime minister and minister Econ. Planning and Finance, 1962—, also minister Commonwealth and Fgn. Affairs, 1965—. Leader Nationalist Party. Decorated knight Grand Cross Order of St. Sylvester and Order Pius IX (Vatican). Address: Auberge d'Aragon Valletta Malta*

BORGSTEDT, DOUGLAS, cartoonist, editor; b. Yonkers, N.Y., Jan. 3, 1911; s. Henning and Jennie (Klotz) B.; student S. Kent Sch., 1927-29, Haverford Coll., 1929- 31, Pa. Mus. Sch. Art, 1932; m. Jean MacLatchie, Mar. 29, 1958. Cartoon editor Sat. Evening Post, 1940-42, photography editor, 1945-63; editorial cartoonist King Features Syndicate, 1964—, Phila. Evening and Sunday Bull., 1968—; cartoons exhibited at Mus. Modern Art, Met. Mus., Berkshire Mus., Pittsfield, Mass.; lectr. at univs., 1964—; represented permanent collection Syracuse U. manuscript collection. Served with AUS, 1943-45. Decorated Bronze Star medal, Legion of Merit. Mem. Assn. Am. Editorial Cartoonists, Nat. Cartoonists Soc. Home: Valley Forge PA 19481 Office: Editorial Offices Phila Evening and Sunday Bull Philadelphia PA 19101

BORGSTROM, GEORG ARME, educator, scientist; b. Gustav Adolf, Sweden, Apr. 5, 1912; s. Algot and Anna (Littorin) B.; B.S., U. Lund (Sweden), 1932, M.S., 1933; D.Sc., 1939; m. Greta Ingrid Stromback; children—Lars, Gerd (Mrs. Arne Linder). Sven. Came to U.S., 1956, naturalized, 1962. Asso. prof. plant physiology U. Lund, 1940-43; head Inst. Plant Research and Food Storage, Nynähamn, Sweden, 1941-48; head Swedish Inst. Food Preservation Research, Göteborg, Sweden, 1948-56, prof. 1953-56; prof. food sci. Mich. State U., 1956—. Prof. geography, 1966—. Recipient Internat. Socrates prize, 1968, Distinguished Faculty award Mich. State U., 1969. Fellow World Acad. Arts and Scis., Royal Inst. Health, Am. Inst. Nutrition, Royal Swedish Academies Engring. and Agrl. Scis.; mem. Inst. Food Technologists, Assn. Am. Geographer, Am. Soc. Plant Physiologists. Author: The Transverse Reactions of Plants, 1939; Japan's World Success in Fishing, 1964; The Hungary Planet, 2d edit., 1967; Principles of Food Science, 2 vols., 1968; Too Many—A Study of Earth's Biological Limitations, 1969. Editor: Fish as Food, 4 vols., 1960-64; Atlantic Ocean Fisheries, 1961. Home: 4550 Commanche Dr Okemos MI 48864 Office: Dept Food Sci Mich State Univ East Lansing MI 48823

BORIS, WALTER RAOUL, utility exec.; b. Amsterdam, N.Y., Sept. 7, 1921; s. Michael and Mary (Hewa) B.; B.S. in Engring., U. Mich., 1948, LL.B., 1950; m. Dorothy Dake, Dec. 28, 1946; children—Charry Dake, Percilla Dake, Emily Dake. Admitted to N.Y. and Mich. bars, 1952; with Consumers Power Co., Jackson, Mich., 1950—, sec., 1956, now v.p. finance; dir. Mich. Gas Storage Co., S.H. Camp Co. Pres. Union Sch. Dist., 1965, Family Service Jackson, 1956; v.p. Land o'Lakes council Boy Scouts Am., 1967, chmn. regional planning, 1967. Bd. dirs. Samuel High Camp Found., Citizens Research Council Mich.; trustee Jackson YWCA, 1956- 67. Served to capt. USAAF, 1941-46. Decorated Air medal, D.F.C. Mem. Alpha Tau Omega, Phi Alpha Delta. Republican. Baptist. Mason, Rotarian (pres. Jackson 1967-68). Home: 2017 Glen Dr Jackson MI 49203 Office: 212 W Michigan Av Jackson MI 49201

BORISON, HERBERT LEON, educator, pharmacologist; b. Bklyn., May 20, 1922; s. Solomon and Beckie (Garber) B.; B.S., City Coll. N.Y., 1941; M.S., N.Y.U., 1942; Ph.D., Columbia, 1948; m. Rosaline Lackowitz, Nov. 5, 1944; children—Ellen Ariel, Adam Bruce. Instr. physiology Columbia, 1947-50; mem. faculty U. Utah, 1950-62, asso. prof. pharmacology, 1955-62; prof. pharmacology Dartmouth Med. Sch., 1962—; cons. in field, 1957—. Guggenheim fellow, 1957. Spl. research brain-stem physiology and pharmacology.

BORK, LESTER SKENE, ret. army officer, cons.; b. Astoria, N.Y., Dec. 26, 1906; s. Paul Daniel and Elizabeth Fredericka (Bayer) B.; student Coll. of City N.Y., also N.Y.U., 1923-25; B.S., A.B., U.S. Mil. Acad., 1929; spl. student U. Va. Law Sch., 1938-39; m. Betty B. Safford, Apr. 23, 1932; childrenSally (Mrs. Earle F. Lasseter), Susan Fernald. Commd. 2d lt. U.S. Army, 1929; instr. law U.S. Mil. Acad., 1939-42, acting prof. law, 1942-43; regtl. comdr., 1943-45; acting judge adv. 8th Army, also chief def. counsel Japanese mil. war criminal trials, 1946; assigned Armed Forces Staff Coll., 1947; Hawaiian sector chief staff, 1947-50; chief plans for fgn. mil. aid, then chief distbn. Office Asst. Chief Staff for Logistics, Washington, 1950-52; assigned Nat. War Coll., 1952-53; asst. chief staff U.S. Army Europe, 1953-55; asst. comdr. 8th Div., Ft. Carson, Colo. 1955-56; chief U.S. Army Mil. Dist., Mich., 1956-58; sr. army adviser Nationalist China, 1958-60; comdr. Armor and Arty. Firing Center, Ft. Stewart, Ga., 1960-62; ret., 1962; pres. Econ. Club of Detroit, 1962-69; sr. cons. NEJ, Inc., Washington, 1969—; dir. Detroit Mortgage & Realty Co. Decorated Bronze Star (3), Purple Heart, Legion of Merit, Combat Infantry badge (U.S.); Croix de Guerre with palm (France); various medals Nationalist China, Sweden. Clubs: Detroit Athletic, Detroit Yacht; Grosse Ile Golf and Country; St. Clair Golf and Country. Home: 1620 Oak Lane McLean VA 21101 Office: NEJ Inc City Bldg 1612 K St NW Washington DC 20006

BORK, ROBERT HERON, lawyer, educator; b. Pitts., Mar. 1, 1927; s. Harry Philip and Elizabeth (Kunkle) B.; B.A., U. Chgo., 1948, J.D., 1953; m. Claire Davidson, June 15, 1952; childrenRobert Heron, Charles E., Ellen E. Admitted to Ill. bar, 1953; asso. and mem. firm Kirkland, Ellis, Houston, Chaffetz & Masters, Chgo., 1955-62; asso. prof. Yale Law Sch., 1962-65, prof. law, 1965—. Served with USMCR, 1945-46, 50-52. Home: 142 Huntington St New Haven CT 06511

BORKE, MITCHELL LOUIS, educator; b. Warsaw, Poland, Mar. 23, 1919; s. Ignacy and Luba (Portugal) B.; student U. Warsaw Med. Coll., 1937-39; B.S., U. Ill., 1951, M.S., 1953, Ph.D., 1957; m. Helene Finke, Dec. 27, 1949; children—Louise Ilene, Susan Elizabeth. Came to U.S., 1947, naturalized, 1950. Asst. chemistry U. Ill., 1951-55, instr., 1955-57; asst. prof. Sch. Pharmacy Duquesne U., 1957-61, asso. prof., 1961-64, prof., 1964—; dir., instr. AEC/NSF Insts. Nuclear Sci. High Sch. Sci. Tchrs., 1964-69; Fulbright vis. lectr. radiochemistry

Nat. Tsing Hua U., Taiwan, 1969-70. Mem. Am. Chem. Soc., Am. Pharm. Assn., Acad. Pharm. Scis., Am. Assn. U. Profs., Sigma Xi, Rho Chi, Sigma Pi Sigma. Home: 5459 Covode St Pittsburgh PA 15217

BORKH, INGE, soprano; b. Mannheim, Germany, 1924; studied acting Reinhardt Sch., voice in Vienna and Italy. Operatic debut, Switzerland; appeared Berlin and Munich festivals, 1951; appeared prin. opera houses, Germany, Italy, Eng. and Portugal; Am. debut as Electra, San Francisco Opera Co., also solo appearances Los Angeles, Chgo.; Buffalo, Montreal, Phila. orchs.; appeared La Scala, Milan, Italy in Fiamma, 1955, in Irish Legend at Salzburg Festival; debut Met. Opera House, 1958. Designated Kammersängerin. Home: 9405 Wienacht Switzerland Office: care Eric Semon 31 W 57th St New York City NY 10019

BORKO, HAROLD, information scientist, psychologist, educator; b. N.Y.C., Feb. 4, 1922; s. George and Hilda (Karpel) B.; student Coll. City N.Y., 1939-41; B.A., U. Cal. at Los Angeles, 1948; M.A., U. So. Cal., 1949, Ph.D. in Psychology, 1952; m. Hannah Levin, June 22, 1947; children—Hilda, Martin. System tng. specialist Rand Corp., 1956-57; with System Devel. Corp., Santa Monica, Cal., 1957-68, asso. staff head lang. processing and retrieval staff, 1965-68; instr. psychology U. So. Cal., 1957-65; instr. Sch. Library Service, U. Cal. at Los Angeles, 1965-68, prof., 1968—. Served with AUS, 1942-46; to capt., Med. Service Corps, AUS, 1950-56. Mem. Am. Documentation Inst. (pres. 1966), Assn. Computing Machinery, Am. Psychol. Assn., Phi Beta Kappa, Sigma Xi, Phi Gamma Mu. Author: Computer Applications in the Behavioral Sciences, 1962; Automated Language Processing, 1967. Asso. U.S. editor Information Storage and Retrieval, 1963—; editor Library and Information Science series, 1970—; book rev. editor Jour. Ednl. Data Processing, 1963—. Home: 11507 National Blvd Los Angeles CA 90064

BORLAND, BRUCE SYLVESTER, former transp. exec.; b. Youngstown, O., Mar. 27, 1902; s. Samuel and and May Jane (Jones) B.; student U. Pitts; m. Mary Elizabeth Henninger, Apr. 4, 1928; childrenBruce H., John H., Richard S. Banker, Butler County Nat. Bank, 1920-25; nat. bank examiner, 1925-27; staff Ernst & Ernst, C.P.A.'s, 1927-31; with Gen. Am. Transp. Corp., Chgo., 1931-70, treas., 1959-70, ret., 1970. Treas., dir. Christopher House, Community Neighborhood House. Presbyn. (deacon elder). Mason. Home: RR 2 Box 290 South Sylvan Dr Mundlein IL 60060

BORLAND, CHAUNCEY BLAIR, real estate exec.; b. Chgo., Nov. 26, 1878; s. John Jay and Harriet (Blair) B.; grad. Lawrenceville (N.J.) Sch., 1897; A.B., Harvard, 1901, postgrad. Law Sch.; m. Belle McCullough, June 23, 1904; children— Harriet, Beatrice, Martha. With John H. Wrenn & Co., 1902-03, No. Trust Co., Chgo., 1903-04; in charge of Borland properties and bldgs., Chgo., 1904—, also mgr., pres. Borland Mfg. Co.; partner Betts Borland & Co. Mem. Chgo. Crime Commn. Trustee Presbyn.-St. Lukes Hosp. Episcopalian. Clubs: Harvard (Chgo., N.Y., Boston); Chicago, Commercial, University, Chicago Athletic (Chgo); New York Yacht. Home: 2450 Lake View Av Chicago IL 60614 Office: 231 S LaSalle St Chicago IL 60604

BORLAND, HAL, (Harold Glen), author; b. Sterling, Neb., May 14, 1900; s. William Arthur and Sarah M. (Clinaburg) B.; student U. Colo., 1918-20, Litt. D., 1944; B.Litt., Columbia, 1923; m. 2d, Barbara Ross Dodge, 1945; children by previous marriage—Harold (dec.), Donal, Neil (dec.), Diana (stepdau.) Mrs. James C. Thomson, Jr.). Reporter Denver Post, 1918; asso. editor Flagler (Colo.) News, 1920-21; reporter Bklyn. Times, 1921, U.P. N.Y.C., 1921-22; with King Feature Service, N.Y.C., 1922; various positions with Salt Lake City, Carson City, Fresno, San Diego and Marshall (Tex.) papers, 1923-24; telegraph editor Asheville, N.C., 1924; publicity (Ivy Lee), 1925; pub. Stratton (Colo.) Press, 1925-26; asst. night editor Phila. Morning Sun, 1927-28; editorial writer Phila. Morning Ledger, 1929-33; lit. editor morning and evening Ledgers, Phila., 1934-37; staff writer N.Y. Times Sunday mag., 1937-43, outdoor editorial essayist N.Y. Times, Sunday editorial page, 1942—; editorial page columnist Pitts. Press, 1966—; columnist Berkshire Eagle, Pittsfield, Mass., 1958-68. Dir. non-fiction sect. Writers Conf. Rocky Mountains, U. Colo., 1955. Bd. Suprs. Bartholomew's Cobble Nature Reservation, Ashley Falls, Mass., 1963—. Served in USNRF, 1918. Recipient Westerners' Buffalo award for best nonfiction, 1957; ann. book award Secondary Edn. Bd., 1957, Journalism Alumni award Columbia, 1962; John Burroughs award and medal, 1968: Edward J. Meeman Conservation Writing award, 1967. Mem. Phi Gamma Delta, Sigma Delta Chi. Mason. Club: Century Assn. (N.Y.). Author: Heaps of Gold (verse), 1922; Rocky Mountain Tipi Tales, 1924; Valor, 1934; Wapiti Pete, 1938; What Is America? (play, with Philip Dunning), 1942; America Is Americans (poems), 1942; An American Year, 1946; High, Wide and Lonesome, 1956; How To Write and Sell Non-Fiction, 1956; This Hill, This Valley, 1957; The Amulet (novel), 1957; The Enduring Pattern, 1959; The Seventh Winter (novel) 1960; The Dog Who Came to Stay, 1961; Beyond your Doorstep, 1962; The Youngest Shepherd, 1962; When the Legends Die (novel), 1963; Sundial of the Seasons, 1964; King of Squaw Mountain (novel) 1964; Countryman: A Summary of Belief, 1965; Hill Country Harvest, 1967; Homeland, A Report from the Country, 1969; Christmas Plants, 1969; Country Editor's Boy, 1970; (under pseudonym Ward West) Trouble Valley, 1934, Halfway to Timberline, 1935. Editor: Our Natural World, 1965. Collaborator (with Barbara Dodge Borland) novelettes and other fiction, popular mags., 1946-56. Contbg. editor Audubon Mag., 1967—. Address: RFD 1 Salisbury CT 06068

BORLAND, WILLIAM F., banker; b. Chgo.; grad. Harvard, 1941. Chmn. bd. Mitchell, Hutchins & Co., Inc. Trustee Presbyn.-St. Lukes Hosp., Chgo. Clubs: University, Onwentsia, Shoreacres, Attic (Chgo); Links (N.Y.C.); Cypress Point. Home: 215 Ahwahnee Rd Lake Forest IL 60045 Office: Two First Nat Plaza Chicago IL 60670

BORLAUG, NORMAN ERNEST, agronomist; b. Cresco, Ia., Mar. 25, 1914; s. Henry O. and Clara (Vaala) B.; B.S. in Forestry, U. Minn., 1937, M.S. in Plant Pathology, 1940, Ph.D., 1941; Sc.D. (honoris causa) Punjab (India) Agrl. U., 1969; Dr. Agr. honoris causa Norge Landbrukshogskole, 1970; D.Sc., Luther Coll., 1970; L.H.D., Gustavus Adolphus Coll., 1971; m. Margaret G. Gibson, Sept. 24, 1937; children—Norma Jean (Mrs. Richard H. Rhoda), William Gibson. With U.S. Forest Service, 1938-39; instr. U. Minn., 1941; research scientist DuPont de Nemours Found., 1942- 44; research scientist in wheat Rockefeller Found., Mexico, 1944, Centro Internacional de Mejoramiento de Maiz y Trigo, Mexico, 1966—. Leonard L. Klinck lectr. Agrl. Inst. Can., 1966. Recipient citation and award from govt. and farmers of Tlaxcala, Mexico, 1955, wheat farmers Yacqui Valley Ciudad Obregon, Sonora, Mexico, 1962; diplomas of honor Wheat Farmers Queretaro, Mexico, 1956, Wheat Farmers and State of Zacatecas, Mexico, 1958; Outstanding Achievement award U. Minn., 1959, E.C. Stakman award, 1962; Distinguished Citizen award Cresco, 1966; Nat. award Agrl. Editors Assn., 1967; Ann. award Nat. Council Comml. Plant Breeders, 1968; Distinguished Service medal, Pakistan, 1968; citation, street named in honor Citizens of Sonora and Rotary Club, 1968; Internat. Agronomy award Am. Soc. Agronomy, 1968; citation and award Farmers of Punjab, Haryana and Himachel Pradesh, 1969; Nobel Peace prize, 1970. Hon. fellow Indian Soc. Genetics and Plant Breeding; mem. Nat. Acad. Sci. Home: Sierra Gorda 69 Lomas de Chapultepec Mexico City Mexico Office: Londres 40 Mexico City 6 Mexico

BORMAN, CLYDE EDWARD, banker; b. Trenton, N.J., Aug. 9, 1917; s. Albert and May (Mittler) B.; A.B., McKendree Coll., Lebanon, Ill., 1952; postgrad. Wis. U., 1952; m. Rosaia Volpentesta. Vice pres., dir. Alton Banking 138 Trust Co. (Ill.), 1946-62; pres. Am. Bank 138 Trust Co., South Bend, Ind., 1962-64; was pres. Citizens Bank 138 Trust Co., Park Ridge, Ill., 1964. Pres. Piasa Bird council Boy Scouts Am., 1960-62. Served with USNR, 1942-46. Recipient Silver Beaver award Boy Scouts Am., 1962. Mem. Am., Ill. (past div. pres.) bankers assns., U.S., Park Ridge chambers commerce. Rotarian, Elk. Contbr. articles profl. jours. Home: 333 Capri Terrace Wheeling IL 60090

BORMAN, FRANK, former astronaut, airlines exec.; b. Gary, Ind., Mar. 14, 1928; s. Edwin Borman; B.S., U.S. Mil. Acad., 1950; M. Aero. Engring., Cal. Inst. Tech., 1957; grad. USAF Aerospace Research Pilots Sch., 1960; m. Susan Bugbee; children—Fredrick, Edwin. Commd. 2d lt. USAF, advanced through grades to col., 1965, ret., 1970; assigned various fighter squadrons, U.S. and Philippines 1951-56; instr. thermodynamics and fluid mechanics U.S. Mil. Acad., 1957- 60; instr. USAF Aerospace Research Pilots Sch., 1960-62; astronaut With Manned Spacecraft Center, NASA, until 1970; command pilot on 14 day orbital Gemini 7 flight, Dec. 1965, including rendezvous with Gemini 6; command pilot Apollo 8, 1st lunar orbital mission, Dec. 1968; sr. v.p. for operations Eastern Air Lines, Inc., Miami, Fla., 1970—. Decorated Distinguished Service award NASA, 1965; Collier Trophy. Nat. Aero. Assn., 1968. Address: Eastern Air Lines Inc Miami International Airport Miami FL 33148

BORMAN, PAUL, corp. exec.; b. Detroit, 1932; ed. Mich. State U., 1954. Formerly v.p., now pres. Borman, Inc. (formerly Borman Food Stores, Inc.), also dir. Home: 1346 Ardmoor Birmingham MI 48010 Office: 12300 Mark Twain Av Detroit MI 48227

BORMANN, FREDERICK HERBERT, educator, ecologist; b. N.Y.C., Mar. 24, 1922; s. Carl B. and A. Gertrude (Andle) B.; B.A., Rutgers U., 1948; M.A., Duke, 1950, Ph.D., 1952; m. M. Christine Williamson, June 20, 1952; children—Rebecca E., Bernard T., Amelia E., Lincoln H. Instr., then asst. prof. Emory U., 1952-56; from asst. prof. to prof. Dartmouth, 1956-66; prof. forest ecology Yale, 1966—. Cons. Ford Found., 1967—; mem. vis. com. AEC, 1965- -; mem. ecology adv. com. Brookhaven Nat. Lab., 1961—. Served with USNR, 1942-45. Recipient George Mercer award Ecol. Soc. Am., 1954. Mem. Ecol. Soc. Am., Am. Inst. Biol. Scis., A.A.A.S., Am. Civil Liberties Union. Spl. research ecology of pine, root grafting, nutrient cycling in ecol. systems. Home; Carriage Hill Dr Brantford CT 06405 Office: 370 Prospect St New Haven CT 06511

BORMANN, SISTER MARY CLARA, librarian; b. Cedar Rapids, Ia., Sept. 17, 1914; d. John Henry and Gertrude (McLaughlin) Bormann; A.B., Clarke Coll., 1940; B.L.S., Coll. St. Catherine, 1944; M.L.S., U. Mich., 1954. Tchr., Gesu Sch., Milw., 1937-38; library asst. Mundelein Coll., Chgo., 1938-44, asst. librarian, 1944-50, librarian, 1950—. Mem. Am., Ill., Catholic (com. chmn.) library assns. Democrat. Editor: Periodical Holdings in Eleven College Libraries in the Chicago Area, 1962. Address: 6363 Sheridan Rd Chicago, IL 60626.

BORN, ERNEST ALEXANDER, architect; b. San Francisco, 1898; A.B., U. Cal., 1922, M.A., 1923; Taussig traveling fellow, 1923; certificate Am. Sch., Fontainbleau, 1928; student Paris Painting Acads., 1928. Designer, John Reid, Jr., 1924-25, John Galen Howard, 1926, George Kelham, 1927, Gehron Ross, 1928-30, Shreve, Lamb & Harmon, 1930-31; pvt. practice architecture, San Francisco, 1937—; prin. works include War Meml., Graniteville, Mass., 1946, housing project, San Francisco, 1951; cons. architect H.E. Fletcher Co., West Chelmsford, Mass., 1930-63; design, editorial cons. Archtl. Record, Archtl. Forum, 1931-36; prof. architecture U. Cal., 1953- 57. Mem. San Francisco Art Commn., 1947-50. Recipient Burch Burdette Long prize Archtl. League N.Y., 1930; C. Valentine Kirby award No. Cal. chpt. A.I.A., 1951, award of high honor, 1954. Guggenheim fellow, 1960-61. Fellow A.I.A.; mem. San Francisco Planning and Housing Assn. (dir. 1945), San Francisco Art Assn. (pres. 1951), Tau Beta Pi, Tau Sigma Delta. Author: The New Architecture in Mexico, 1937; A Plan for Fisherman's Wharf (for San Francisco Port Authority), 1961. Home: 2020 Great Hwy San Francisco CA 94116 Office: 730 Montgomery St San Francisco CA 94111

BORN, HAROLD JOSEPH, educator, physicist; b. Evansville, Ind., Nov. 22, 1922; s. Harold O. and Marie J. (Gronotte) B.; student Evansville U., 1940-42; B.S., Rose Poly. Inst., 1949; M.S., Ia. State U., 1958, Ph.D., 196O; m. Betty Jean Rasche, Apr. 15, 1950; children—Christopher Paul, David William. Design engr. Electronics Research Corp., Evansville, Ind., 1949-52; equipment engr. Phillips Petroleum Co., Bartlesville, Okla., 1952-55; research asst. Ames (Ia.) Lab. AEC, 1955-60; physicist Whirlpool Corp., 1960-61; mem. faculty Ill. State U., Normal, 1961—, prof. physics, head dept., 1966—. Mem. Normal Human Relations Commn., 1964-69, chmn., 1967-68. Mem. Am. Phys. Soc., Am. Assn. Physics Tchrs., Sigma Xi. Roman Catholic. Spl. research low temperature solid state physics. Contbr. articles in field. Home: 806 Highpoint Rd Normal IL 61761

BORNE, MORTIMER, artist; b. Rypin, Poland, Dec. 31, 1902; s. Harry and Lena (Warshaw) B.; student schs. U.S. and abroad; m. Rachel Zipes, Feb. 28, 1929. Came to U.S., 1916, naturalized, 1921. Exhibited major graphic exhbns., 1926—; one-man shows New Gallery, Jerusalem, Israel, 1935 Internat. Coll., Springfield, Mass., 1940, Cedar Rapids (Ia.) Art Assn., 1940, Corcoran Gallery of Art, Washington, 1941, Mus. Fine Arts, Montreal, Can., 1942, Grand Central Art Galleries, N.Y.C., 1943, Smithsonian Instn., Washington, 1944, Currier Gallery, Manchester, 1945, Connoisseur Gallery, N.Y.C., 1959, Tel-Aviv, 1965, Tappan Zee Art Center, Nyack, N.Y., 1962, 69; lectr. Sweet Briar Coll., 1945; lectr. art New Sch. Social Research, N.Y.C., 1945-67; works reproduced various mags., newspapers; represented permanent collections Mus. Modern Art, Library Congress, Nat. Mus., Syracuse, Rochester, N.J. State museums, N.Y. Pub. Library, Rosenwald Collection, Met. Mus. Art (100 etchings and drypoints), U. Judaism, Los Angeles, British Mus., Israel Mus., Jerusalem, Boston Pub. Library, Nat. Gallery Art, Washington; pioneer in technique for color drypoint using 3 plates; originator new method for woodcuts. Recipient J. Frederick Talcott prize Soc. Am. Etchers, 1939, Noyes prize for best print Soc. Am. Etchers 28th Ann. Exhbn., 1943. Developed methods chromatic wood sculpture; "Family of Peoples" (chromatic wood sculpture) in permanent collection Municipal Mus., Ramat-Gan, Israel. Author articles on art. Address: 107 S Broadway Nyack NY 10960

BORNEMANN, ALFRED, educator, metallurgist; b. Montclair, N.J., Apr. 6, 1906; s. Emile L. and Marie (Kidde) B.; M.E., Stevens Inst. Tech., 1927; D.Eng., Sachsische Technische Hochschule, 1930; m. Lieselotte Helene Just, Aug. 2, 1930; children—Peter, Barbara Just (Mrs. Stainton), Toni Marie (Mrs. McKerrow). Asst. prof. chem. engring. Stevens Inst. Tech., Montclair, N.J., 1930-39, asso. prof., 1939-48, prof. metallurgy, head dept., 1948- -; cons. Trustee, pres. Stevens Acad. Mem. Maria Mitchell Assn. of Nantucket (Mass.) (v.p.), Am. Soc. Metals (author, co-editor Metals Tech. 1954), Am. Soc. Testing and Materials, Am. Chem. Soc., Am. Inst. Mining and Metall. Engrs., Inst. Metals (Eng.), Am. Foundrymen's Soc., Beta Theta Pi. Episcopalian. Clubs: Cosmopolitan (Montclair); Nantucket Yacht. Home: 60 Gates Av Montclair NJ 07042

BORNEMEIER, WALTER CARL, surgeon; b. Cass County, Neb., Apr. 22, 1901; s. Charles and Lena (Schlueter) B.; B.A., North Central Coll., 1923, L.H.D., 1970; M.D., Northwestern U., 1929; m. Mabel Kemp, May 29, 1926; children—Lois Mary (Mrs. Louis John Kettle), Beatrice Ann, (Mrs. Ralph Fiedler), Walter Carl II. Practice in Chgo., 1929—; mem. staff Ill. Masonic Hosp., 1934—, sr. attending surgeon, 1938—; hon. cons. surgeon Resurrection Hosp.; instr. surgery Northwestern U. Med. Sch., 1934-52. Pres. Tb Inst. Chgo. and Cook County, 1962-64. Pres. Niles Township High Sch. Bd. Edn., 1952. Hon. trustee North Central Coll. Served to maj., M.C., AUS, World War II; MTO. Recipient Distinguished Alumnus award North Central Coll., 1962; Merit award Northwestern U., 1971. Diplomate Am. Bd. of Surgery. Fellow A.C.S.; mem. A.M.A. (pres. 1970-71), Chgo. (past pres.), Ill. med. socs., Chgo. Surg. Soc. Rome (hon.), World Med. Assn., Phi Chi, Scabbard and Blade. Lutheran. Contbr. med. jours. Address: 4665 W Peterson Av Chicago IL 60646

BORNHOLDT, WALLACE JOHN, heavy vehicle mfg. co. exec.; b. Peoria, Ill., Dec. 28, 1907; s. John and Barbara Katherine (Kohl) B.; student U. Ill., 1925-28; m. Esteleen M. Allen, June 17, 1939. With Caterpillar Tractor Co., 1928—, v.p., 1963—. Mem. Am. Soc. Metals, Am. Ordnance Assn. Mason. Club: Country of Peoria. Home: 7316 McNear Ct Peoria IL 61614 Office: 100 NE Adams St Peoria IL 61602

BORNHUETTER, RONALD LAWRENCE, ins. co. exec.; b. Newark, June 17, 1932; s. Benjamin and Marguerite (Isler) B.; B.A., Coll. Wooster, O., 1953; M.B.A., Columbia, 1959; m. Cynthia Dillman, Sept. 8, 1956; childrenRonald Lawrence, Linda J. With Nat. Bur. Casualty Underwriters, 1953-66, actuary, 1964-66; v.p., actuary Gen. Reinsurance Corp., N.Y.C., 1966-. Served with U. S. Army, 1955-57. Fellow Casualty Actuarial Soc. (sec.-treas. 1969—); mem. Internat. Congress Actuaries, Am. Acad. Actuaries. Home: 87 Tanglewood Dr Summit, NJ 07901. Office: 400 Park Av New York City NY 10022

BORNING, BERNARD CARL, educator; b. Echo, Minn., June 19, 1913; s. Barney J. and Bertha (Preuss) B.; B.A., U. Minn., 1936, Ph.D., 1951; m. Coralie Jean Hamilton, June 10, 1949; childrenAlan, Katherine, Copywriter, layout man Brown & Bigelow, St. Paul, 1937-41; mem. faculty U. Ida., 1949-, prof. polit. sci., 1962-, chmn. dept. 1959-; Fulbright lectr., Korea, 1963-64; research, teaching U. Ife, Nigeria, 1970-71. Pres. Moscow United Fund, 1959. Mem. local sch. bd., Moscow, 1954-56. Served to capt., F.A., AUS, 1942-46; PTO. Decorated Bronze Star. Mem. Am., Western polit. sci. assns., Am. Assn. U. Profs., Am. Civil Liberties Union. Author: The Political and Social Thought of Charles A. Beard, 1962. Home: 494 Ridge Rd Moscow, ID 83843.

BORNKAMM, GUENTHER, educator; b. Görlitz, Germany, Oct. 8, 1905; s. George and Martha (Rooseboom) B., Dr. Theology U. Marburg (Germany), also hon. doctor; hon. doctor, U. Heidelberg (Germany); D.D., U. Glasgow, 1965; m. Elisabeth Zinn, Aug. 13, 1938; children—Anne Elisabeth (Mrs. Dieter Conrad), Katharina, Georg Wilhelm, Aleida (Mrs. Jan Afsmann), Joachim. Asst. prof. U. . Königsburg (Germany), 1934-37; removed by Nazis; prof. U. Goettingen (Germany), 1946-49, U. Heidelberg, 1949—; reverend at Bethel, Germany, 1937-45; dean theology faculty U. Heidelberg, 1950-51, 58-59, selected senator, 1961-62, rector, 1965-66, prorector, 1966-68. Mem. Acad. der Wissenschaffen Heidelberg; hon. mem. Soc. Bib. Studies (Australia). Author: Jesus of Nazareth, 1956; Collected Essays, Vol. 1, 1952, Vol. 2, 1959, Vol. 3, 1968; Tradition and Interpretation in St. Matthew, 1963. Address: 4 Bahofeveg Heidelberg Federal Republic of Germany

BORNSTEIN, ELI, painter, sculptor; b. Milw., Dec. 28, 1922; B.S., U. Wis., 1945, M.S., 1954; student Art Inst. Chgo., U. Chgo., 1943, Academie Montmartre of Fernand Leger, Paris, 1951, Academie Julian, 1952; m. Christine; 2 children. Tchr. drawing, painting and sculpture Milw. Art Inst., 1943- 47; tchr. design U. Wis., 1949; tchr. drawing, painting, sculpture, design and graphics U. Sask. (Can.), 1950—, prof., head art dept., 1963- -; painted in France, 1951-52, Italy, 1957. Exhibited widely, 1943—, retrospective exhbn. (works 1943-64) Mendel Art Gallery, Saskatoon, 1965; one man shows Kazimir Gallery, Chgo., 1965, 67; represented in numerous pvt. collections; executed marble sculpture now in permanent collection Walker Art Center, Mpls., 1947; aluminum constrn. for Sask. Tchrs. Fedn. Bldg., 1956; structurist relief in painted wood and aluminum for Arts and Scis. Bldg., U. Sask., 1958; structurist relief in enamelled steel for Internat. Air Terminal, Winnipeg, Man., Can., 1962; model version of structurist relief in 5 parts, 1962, now in collection Nat. Gallery, Ottawa, Ont. Recipient Allied Arts medal Royal Archtl. Inst. Can., 1968; honorable mention for 3 structurist reliefs 2d Biennial Internat. Art Exhbn., Colombia, S.Am., 1970. Editor (with Baljeu) periodical Structure, 1958; founder, editor ann. publ. The Structurist, 1960—. Contbr. articles, principally on Structurist art to various publs. Address: Box 41 RR 5 Saskatoon Saskatchewan Canada

BORNSTEIN, MORRIS, educator, economist; b. Detroit, Sept. 4, 1927; s. Samuel and Elizabeth (Goldenstein) B.; A.B., U. Mich., 1947, A.M., 1948, Ph.D., 1952; m. Reva Rice, Apr. 7, 1962; children—Susan, Jane. Economist, U.S. Govt., 1951- 52, 55-58; mem. faculty U. Mich., Ann Arbor, 1958—, prof. econs., 1964—, dir. Center Russian and E. European Studies, 1966-69. Asso., Harvard U. Russian Research Center, 1962-63; vis. research fellow Hoover Instn., Stanford, 1969-70; cons. in field, 1959—. Served with AUS, 1953-55. Ford Found. faculty fellow, 1962-63. Mem. Am. Econ. Assn., Am. Assn. Advancement Slavic Studies, Assn. Study Soviet-Type Economies (exec. com. 1965-67). Author: Soviet National Accounts for 1955, 1961; The Soviet Economy, 1962, 3d edit., 1970; Comparative Economic Systems, 1965, 2d edit., 1969; also articles. Home: 1503 Warwick Ct Ann Arbor MI 48103

BORNSTEIN, SAM, newspaper editor; b. Boston, Dec. 3, 1913; s. Harry and Anna (Phillips) B.; B.S. in Journalism, Boston U., 1935; m. Ruth Novogroski, Jan. 4, 1938; children—Marjorie, Harold. Engaged as a reporter with Boston Am., 1936-38; city editor Boston Sunday Advertiser, 1938-42, mng. editor, 1942-71; exec. editor Boston Record Am. and Sunday Advertiser, 1971—. Mem. Sunday Editors Assn., Am. Soc. Newspaper Editors, A.P. Mng. Editors Assn., Boston U. Alumni Assn., Sigma Delta Chi. Home: 780 Boylston St Boston MA 02199 Office: 5 Winthrop Sq Boston MA 02106

BOROW, HENRY, educator, psychologist; b. Phila., May 31, 1917; s. Samuel and Freda (Seresky) B.; B.A., Pa. State U., 1939, M.S. 1942, Ph.D., 1945; m. Marion Edith Sperling, Sept. 26, 1943; children—Carolyn Jean, Nancy Joan. Personnel research technician, engring., sci. and mgmt. war tng. program Pa. State U., 1942-44, instr. psychology, 1944-46; civilian expert Dept. Army, Japan, 1951-52; research asso. Horace Mann-Lincoln Inst., Columbia Tchrs. Coll.,

Personnel and Guidance Assn. (chmn. internat. relations com. 1959-61), Am., Minn. psychol. assns., Psychometric Soc. Sr. author: Vocational Planning for College Students, 1959, Editor: Man in a World at Work, 1964. Dept. editor Jour. Counseling Psychology, 1960—, cons. editor, 1962-64; editorial bd. Personnel and Guidance Jour.; editorial adv. Ency. Edn. Home: 565 Otis Av St Paul MN 55455 Office: General Coll Univ Minnesota Minneapolis MN 55455

BOROWIEC, MATTHEW WILLIAM, lawyer; b. Walkerville, Ont., Can., Apr. 10, 1934; s. Joseph J. and Gladys (Pietrzak) B.; came to U.S., 1951, naturalized, 1956; B.A., Assumption U., Windsor, Ont., 1956; postgrad. Detroit Coll. Law, 1958- 59; J.D., U. Ariz., 1962; m. Margaret L. Hardy, July 6, 1957; children—Joel Patrick, William Matthew, Anne Margaret. With claims dept. Fireman's Fund Ins. Co., Detroit, 1958; adjuster Retail Credit Co., Detroit, 1959; admitted to Ariz. bar, 1962, since practiced in Bisbee; mem. firm Gentry, McNulty & Borowiec and predecessor firms, 1962—. Treas. Cochise County Democratic Central Com., 1968-70; Dem. precinct committeeman Cochise County, 1968-70. Sec. bd. govs. Cochise Coll., Douglas, Ariz. Served to lt. (j.g.) USNR, 1957. Mem. Am., Ariz., Cochise County bar assns., Bisbee C. of C. (dir.). Phi Alpha Delta. Kiwanian. Club: Bisbee Country. Home: 53 Gila Dr Box 622 Bisbee AZ 85603 Office: PO Box 87 Copper Queen Plaza Bisbee AZ 85603

BOROWITZ, DAVID, research found. exec.; b. Louisville, May 30, 1906; s. Abraham and Frieda (Lapoff) B.; LL.B., U. Louisville, 1925, Dr. Humane Letters (hon.), 1969; postgrad. U. Chgo., 1925-26; m. Anne Wolkenstein, 1927 (dec. 1959); children—James, Albert; m. 2d, Lulu Cohen. Various positions men's wear store to 1927; with Crescent Novelty Co., 1927-29; founder Bradley Mfg. Co., Chgo., 1929. Active A.R.C., Community Fund; gen. chmn. Combined Jewish Appeal, 1955-56, pres., 1957-58; mem. Jewish Bd. Edn. Bd. overseers Jewish Tehol. Sem. N.Y.; bd. govs. Haifa Inst. Tech.; trustee Chgo. Med. Sch.; David Borowitz Collection of Am. Lit. at Brandeis U., Lulu and David Borowitz Collection of English Lit. at U. Louisville Research Found.; bd. dirs. Jewish Welfare Fund, Chgo. Recipient Humanitarian of the Year award B'nai B'rith, 1960; Brandeis U. fellow. Mem. Am. Technion Soc. (mem. nat. bd., pres Midwest Chpt.), Am. Jewish Com., Am. Friends of Hebrew U. (nat. v.p.), Brandeis U. Assos. (pres. Chgo. chpt.), Arthur Machen Sco., Baker St. Irregulars, Cabbages and Kings Soc. (internat. pres. 1964—). Mem. B'nai B'rith (founding pres. lodge). Clubs: Standard, Briarwood Country, Quadrangle, City, Ill. Athletic (Chgo.); Grolier, Lotos (N.Y.C.). Author: Geroge Crurkshank, Mirror of an Age, 1970. Home: 20 Cedar St Chicago IL 60611 Office: 412 N Orleans St Chicago IL 60610

BOROWITZ, SIDNEY, educator, physicist; b. Bklyn., June 12, 1918; s. Morris and Rose (Cohen) B.: B.S., Coll. City N.Y., 1937; M.S., N.Y. U., 1941, Ph.D., 1948; m. Ruth Aaron Meyer, June 20, 1943; children—Michael Joseph, Elizabeth Ann. Jr. physicist Navy Dept., 1941-42; engr., Sect. Chief engring. Western Electric Co., 1942- 45; editor Public Domain mag. 1945-46; instr. N.Y.U., 1946-48, Harvard, 1948-50; mem. faculty N.Y.U., 1950—, prof. physics, 1959—, chmn. dept., 1961—, asso. dir. electromagnetics div., Courant Inst. Math. Sci., 1957-59, dean Coll. Arts and Sciences, 1969—. Cons. panel lasers Nat. Acad. Sci., 1963; mem. radiation weapons analysis study group USAF, 1960-68. J. F. Kennedy Meml. Research fellow Weizmann Inst. Israel, 1965-66, Fellow Am. Phys. Soc. (chmn. div. electron and atomic physics 1969); mem. Phi Beta Kappa, Sigma Xi, Author: (with A. Beiser) Essentials of Physics, 1966; Fundamentals of Quantum Mechanics, 1967; (with L. Borstein) A Contemporary View of Elementary Physics, 1968. Home: 1170 Loring Pl Bronx NY 10453

BORREGO, EDWARD CANDELAIRO, oil co. exec.; b. Saguache, Colo., Sept. 3, 1905; s. Conde and Quirina (Garcia) B.; student Colo. Sch. Mines, 1927, Harvard, 1943; m. Mary A. Mohrbacher, Mar. 22, 1946; children—Sarajane, Theodore, Mary Karen, John Edward, Margaret Ann. With Mexico Huasteca & Transcontinental Petroleum Co., 1927-38, Carter Oil Co., 1938-39; dist. supt. Venezuela, Creole Petroleum Corp., 1939-43; petroleum attache Am. embassy, Rome, Italy, 1945-46; pres., gen. mgr. Societa Petrolifera Italiana, 1946-50; asst. gen. mgr. Internat. Petroleum Co., Lima, Peru, 1950-51, gen. mgr. exec. rep., Bogota, Colombia, 1951-55; asst. exec. devel. coordinator, Creole Petroleum Corp., Caracas, 1955; mgr. Libyan Am. Oil Co., 1955-58, v.p., dir.,1956-64; v.p. dir. Tex. Gulf Producing Co., 1958-64; mng. dir., v.p. Companie de Petroleo Ganso Azul, Ltda., Lima, 1958-64; v.p. Kerr McGee Oil Industries (now Kerr-McGee Corp.), Oklahoma City, 1964-71, v.p. internat. devel., 1966—. Served to maj. AUS, 1943-45; ETO. Mem. Newcomen Soc. (life), Am. Inst. Mining, Metall.and Petroleum Engrs., Am. Soc. Petrolem Engrs. (life). Episcopalian (mem. Bishop and Council Okla.) Home: 8217 Lakehurst Dr Oklahoma City, OK 73120. Office: Kerr McGee Bldg Oklahoma City OK 73102

BORRELLI, FRANK JAMES, physician; b. Pitts., Dec. 24, 1905; s. Aniell and Josephine (Pagano) B.; B.S., U. Pitts., 1929; M.D., N.Y. Med. Coll., 1933; m. Wanda Anne Dubiel, July 1, 1936; children—Frank, Niel, Sandra. Intern Flower Hosp., N.Y.C., 1933-34, resident in radiolgy, 1934-35; chief radiologist Flower-Fifth Avenue Hosp., 1935-71, dir., 1941—; chmn. chmn. hosp. com. N.Y. Med. Coll.-Flower-Fifth Av. Hosp., radiologist Met. Hosp., 1938-50, chmn., prof., 1942-70, dir. radiology, 1950-70, pres. med. bd., 1957; dir. radiology, Otisville Municipal Sanatorium, 1941-55; dir. radiology Bird S. Coler Hosp., N.Y.C., pres. med. bd., 1957; cons. radiology Yonkers Hosp., Madison Hosp., Queen's Gen. Hosp., St. Joseph's Hosp., St. Mary's Hosp., N.J., St. Mary's Hosp., Waterbury, Conn., Booth Meml. Hosp.; dir. radiology Gracie Sq. Hosp., Manhattan; spl. tng. Mayo Clinic summer 1936; med. aspects of atomic explosion, Army Dept. Research and Graduate Sch., Army Med. center Washington, 1948; mem. faculty N.Y. Med. Coll., 1933—, prof. radiology 1942-70, now emeritus, also chmn. dept. radiology, chmn. isotope com.; advanced course in isotopes Oak Ridge Inst. Nuclear Studies, 1953. Chmn. spl. com. on radiology N.Y. County, 1955—. Trustee La Guardia House. Diplomate Am. Bd. Radiologists. Fellow Am. Coll. Radiology (councilor), Am. Coll. Chest Physicans, Am. Coll. Gastronenterology (past pres.), N.Y. Acad. Medicine, Royal Coll. Medicine, Medicine, London, Eng., Internat. Acad. Proctology (hon.); mem. A.M.A., Radiol. Soc. N.A. World Med. Assn. (U.S. com), Indsl. Med. Assn. (A.S.A. liaison com.) N.Y. County, N.Y. State (del.) Med. socs. Alpha Kappa Kappa (grand pres.). Home: 65 Minerva Dr Yonkers NY 10710

BORREN, JAMES G., hosp. adminstr. Supt., Hissom Meml. Center, Sand Springs, Okla. Office: Hissom Meml Center Sand Springs OK 74063*

BORRIE, WILFRID JOHN, investment cons.; b. New Westminster, B.C., Can., Apr. 3, 1895; s. Robert Gibb and Sarah Ann (Masterman) B.; student pub. schs. B.C.; m. Elizabeth Taylor, Mar. 10, 1923 (dec.); children—Harry R., Betty Doreen. Clk. city Vancouver (B.C., Can.), 1911-14; salesman W. H. Malkin Co., 1920-23, Pemberton & Son, 1923; pres. Pemberton Securities Ltd., 1940-61, chmn. bd. 1961-71; chmn. bd. Dillingham Corp. Can. Ltd.; dir. Pacific Western Airlines Ltd., Can. Permt. Trust Co., John Labatt Ltd., White Rock Water Works. Pres. B.C. Internat. Trade Fair., 1961, 64. Bd. dirs.; past pres. Pacific Nat. Exhbn.; bd. dirs. Presbyn. Extension Fund (B.C.) Ltd.; gov. Leon and Thea Koerner Found.; adv. bd. Canadian Scholarship Trust Plan. Served with C.E., Canadian Army, 1914-19, F.A. Res., 1939-44. Decorated Mil. Medal, 1914-15, Can. Medal, Russian Order of St. George. Mem. Canadian C. of C. (past pres., dir.), Investment Dealers Assn. (past pres. and chmn. Pacific div., hon. pres.), Vancouver Bd. of Trade (past pres., now mem. council), also Vancouver Execs. Assn. Mason (32, Shriner, Jester). Clubs: Terminal City, Canadian Legion, Fourndex of Canada, Canadian, Vancouver. Home: 1025 Gilford St Vancouver British Columbia Canada Office: 744 W Hastings St Vancouver British Columbia Canada

BORROFF, MARIE, educator; b. N.Y.C., Sept. 10, 1923; d. Albert Ramon and Marie (Bergersen) Borroff; Ph.B., U. Chgo., 1943, M.A. 1946; Ph.D., Yale, 1956. Teaching asst. U. Chgo., 1946-47; instr. dept. English, Smith Coll., 1948-51, asst. prof., 1956-59, asso. prof., 1959; vis. asst. prof. English, Yale, 1957-58, vis. asso. prof., 1959-6O, asso. prof. English, 1960-65, prof., 1965—. Fellow Ezra Stiles Coll., Yale. Recipient James Billings Fiske poetry prize U. Chgo., 1943; Eunice Tietjens Meml. prize Poetry mag. 1945; Margaret Lee Wiley fellow Am. Assn. U. Women, 1955-56; Guggenheim fellow, 1969-70. Mem. Modern Lang. Assn. Am., Medieval Acad. Am., Phi Beta Kappa. Author: Sir Gawain and the Green Knight; A Stylistic and Metrical Study, 1962 (with J.B. Bessinger, Jr., recorded dialogues read in Middle English 1965); Sir Gawain and the Green Knight: A New Verse Translation, 1967. Editor Wallace Stevens, A Collection of Critical Essays, 1963. Home: 311 St Ronan St New Haven CT 06511

BORROWMAN, MERLE L., educator; b. Idaho Falls, Ida., May 12, 1920; s. Lorus P. and Violet (Norton) B.; B.A., Brigham Young U., 1942; M.A., U. Ida., 1947; Ed. D., Columbia, 1953; m. Ellen Louise Young, June 1, 1962; children—Steven, Betty Jo (Mrs. Sherwood Chang), Phyllis, Erik, Alison. High sch. tchr., prin., Sugar City, Ida., 1945-52; instr. to asst. prof. Columbia, 1950-54; asst. prof., asso. prof., prof. ednl. policy studies, history U. Wis., Madison, 1954-69, chmn. dept. ednl. policy studies, 1963-67; dean Sch. Edn., U. Cal. at Riverside, 1969-71, U. Cal. at Berkeley, 1971—; cons. editor Scott Foresman Co., 1963—; cons. Ednl. Testing Services, 1966-67. Pres. Ida. Interscholastic Activities Assn., 1946-47; v.p. Ida. Sch. Adminstrv. Assn., 1947-49. Served to capt. USMCR, 1943-46. Guggenheim fellow, 1967-68. Mem. History of Edn. Soc. (past pres.), Am. Hist. Assn., Orgn. Am. Historians. Author: The Liberal and Technical in Teacher Education, 1956; Teacher Education in America, 1964; What Doctrines to Embrace, 1968. Contbr. profl. jours. Home: 90 Parnassus Rd Berkeley CA 94708

BORSODY, BENJAMIN FRANK, cons. engr.; b. Budapest, Hungary, Feb. 15 1901; s. Ferenc and Mathilda (Gould) B.; came to U.S., 1907, naturalized, 1923; student Cooper Union, Princeton, Tehran U.; m. Edith Nora Veronica Corcoran, Feb. 17, 1924; children—Edith Ann (Mrs. Victor J. Lindbergh, Jr.), Frank Joseph, Eleanor Caroline (Mrs. William G. Battaile), Robert Peter. Various positions Western Union Co., Western Electric cos., RCA, on freight and passenger steamships, 1924-36; engr., mgr. radio system N.Y.C. Fire Dept., 1936-42; chief engr. constrn. overseas radio stas. for AUS and USAAF, 1942-43; research program for radio mfg. corp., 1946-48; engr., negotiator internat. mil. and civil radio frequency allocations Dept. Def. 1948-52; chief engr. radio air navigational aids constrn. and installation, USAF, 1952-57; profl. engr., organizing adviser communications Iranian Nat. Police and INTERPOL, 1957, Korean Nat. Police, Seoul, 1961; chief adviser to minister communications, Rep. Korea, 1962; chief adviser dir. telecommunications, Rep. Vietnam, Saigon, 1964-65; partner Borsody & Bairey, cons. registered profl. engrs.; pres. B&B Engring. & Sales Co., Washington. Served with U.S. Army, 1918-19; AEF in France; with USNR, 1943-46; PTO. Recipient numerous citations for U.S. govt. work. Mem. Soc. Am. Mil. Engrs., I.E.E.E. (sr.), Vet. Wireless Operators Assn., Am. Radio Relay League, Nat. Soc. Profl. Engrs. Author govt. manual. Patentee in field. Home: 905 25th Av West Palmetto FL 33561 Office: Box 3746 Washington DC 20007

BORST, LYLE BENJAMIN, physicist; b. Chgo., Nov. 24, 1912; s. George William and Jean Carothers (Beveridge) B.; A.B., U. Ill., 1936, A.M., 1937; Ph.D., U. Chgo., 1941; m. Barbara Mayer, Aug. 19, 1939; children—John Benjamin, Stephen Lyle, Frances Elizabeth. Instr., U. Chgo., 1940- 41, research asso. metall. lab., 1941-43, sr. physicist Clinton Labs., Oak Ridge, 1943-46 (both labs. working on atomic bomb project); asst. prof. dept. chemistry Mass. Inst. Tech., Cambridge, 1946; chmn. dept. reactor sci. and engring. Brookhaven Nat. Lab., 1946-51; prof. physics U. Utah, 1951; chmn. dept. physics Coll. Engring N.Y. U., 1954-61; prof. physics State U. N.Y. at Buffalo, 1961—; master Clifford Furnas Coll., 1969—. Fellow Am. Phys. Soc.; mem. A.A.A.S., Am. Civil Liberties Union (nat. bd. 1958-62, chmn. Niagara Frontier chpt. 1967-69), Phi Beta Kappa, Tau Beta Pi, Sigma Pi Sigma. Home: 17 Twin Bridge Lane Williamsville NY 14221

BORSTING, JACK RAYMOND, educator; b. Portland, Ore. Jan. 31, 1929; s. John S. and Ruth (Nelson) B.; B.A., Ore. State U., 1951; M.A., U. Ore., 1952. Ph.D., 1959; m. Peggy Anne Nygard, Mar. 22, 1953; children—Lynn Carol, Eric, Jeffrey. Instr. math. Western Wash. Coll., 1953-54; teaching fellow U. Ore., 1956- 59; mem. faculty Naval Postgrad. Sch., 1959—, prof. operations research, chmn. dept. 1964—; vis. prof. U. Colo., summers 1967, 69, 71; vis. distinguished prof. Ore. State U., summer 1968; IBM lectr., 1966-69; bd. dirs. Mil. Operations Research Soc., 1965—, pres., 1970-71, chmn. edn. com., 1968-69. Chmn. Carmel (Cal.) Citizens Math. Curriculum Rev. Com., 1966; mem. adv. bd. for personnel labs. U.S. Naval Research, 1971—. Served with USAF, 1954-56. Mem. Inst. Mgmt. Sci., Inst. Math. Statistics, Am. Statis. Soc., Operations Research Soc. Am. (chmn. edn. com. 1965-70, dir. vis. lectureship program 1967-70, council mem. 1969-72), Math. Assn. Am., Soc. Indsl. and Applied Math., Sigma Xi, Pi Mu Epsilon, Beta Theta Pi. Episcopalian. Contbr. profl. jours. Home: Route 2 Box 1087 Carmel CA 93921 Office: Dept Operations Analysis NPGS Monterey CA 93940

BORTEN, PER, prime minister of Norway; b. 1913; ed. Norwegian Agrl. U. Entered politics 1945; regional sec. Norwegian Farmers Union, 1945-47; a founder Rural Youth League; chmn. Municipal Council of Fla. 1946, chmn. Provincial Council Sor-Trondelag, 1948; mem. Parliament for Sor- Trondelag for Agarian (later Centre) Party, 1950—, chmn. party, 1955—, Parliamentary leader, 1957-; pres. lower chamber Parliament, 1961-; dep. chmn. state owned housing bank, 1955; mem. council Farmers Bank, 1965—; chmn. council United Life Ins. Companies Norway, 1959—; prime minister of Norway, 1965-. Address: Office: Prime Minister Oslo Dep Norway

BORTHICK, M.D., banker. Adminstrv. v.p. Walker Bank and Trust Co., Salt Lake City. Office: Main St at 2d St S Salt Lake City UT 84110*

BORTHWICK, ANDERSON, former banker; b. Yonkers, N.Y., Dec. 25, 1899; s. George and Marion Marion (Anderson) B.; student U. Cal., 1920, Grad. Sch. Banking, Rutgers U., 1941-42; children-Marion (Mrs. E. L. Flood, Jr.), Donald T.; m. 2d, Georgia Mathias, June 24, 1949. With First Nat. Bank San Diego, 1915-68, asst. cashier, 1929-40, asst. v.p. 1940-47, v.p., 1947. exec. v.p. 1947-50, pres. 1950-64, chmn. bd. 1965-68; dir. Pacific Tel. and Tel. Co., Cal. Cubic Corp. Pres. Rees Stealy Research Found. Mem. San Diego Zool. Soc. (pres.). Clubs: Kiwanis, San Diego Country, Cuyamaca, Rowing, University. Home: 785 Bangor St San Diego CA 92106 Office: 530 B St San Diego CA 92101

BORTHWICK, HARRY ALFRED, plant physiologist; b. Wright County, Minn., Jan. 7, 1898; s. Alfred Ellenwood and Frances Estella (Humphrey) B.; student U. Minn., 1917-19; A.B., Stanford, 1921, M.A., 1924, Ph.D., 1930; m. Mytis Vietta Hall, June 4, 1923; 1 son, Howard Hall. Research asst. div. botany U. Cal., 1922-30, asst. prof., 1930-36; morphologist Dept. Agr., Beltsville, Md., 1936-44, botanist, 1944-48, plant physiologist, 1948-68, ret., 1968, collaborator, 1968—. Recipient Distinguished Service award U.S. Dept. Agr. 1959; Charles Reid Barnes Life Membership award in plant physiology, 1960; Norman Jay Coleman award in horticulture, 1962; recipient (with S.B. Hendricks) Hoblitzelle award, Stephen Hales award in plant physiology, 1962; Nessim Habif World prize U. Geneva, 1963. Fellow Am. Acad. Arts and Scis.; mem. Nat. Acad. Scis., A.A.A.S., Am. Soc. Plant Physiologists (pres. 1956), Botanical Soc. Am., Washington Acad. Sci., Washington Biol. Soc., Washington Bot. Soc. (pres. 1952), Am. Soc. Hort. Sci., Sigma Xi, Phi Beta Kappa, Alpha Gamma Rho. Contbr. articles sci. publs. Home: 13700 Creekside Dr Silver Spring MD 20904 Office: Plant Industry Station US Dept Agriculture Beltsville MD 20705

BORTNER, DOYLE MCCLEAN, coll. dean; b. Gettysburg, Pa., Apr. 4, 1915; s. Homer and Mary A. (McClean) B.; A.B., Gettysburg Coll., 1936; M.A., Pa. State Coll., 1937; Ed.D., Temple U., 1950; m. Alba Pignatiello, Apr. 24, 1943. Tchr. social studies Perkiomen Prep. Sch., Pennsburg, Pa., 1938-41; tchr. social studies and English, Bernardsville (N.J.) High Sch., 1945-46; instr. secondary edn. Temple U., 1946-48; prof. edn., chmn. dept. edn. and psychology Bates Coll., 1948-52; vis. prof. edn. U. Me., summers 1950-52; prof. edn., chmn. div. edn. and grad. studies Hofstra Coll., 1952-61; dean coll. Jersey City State Coll., 1961-64; asso. dean, prof. edn. Sch. Edn., Coll. City N.Y., 1964-66, dean Sch. Edn., 1966—; vis. prof. U. P.R., summer 1959, N.Y.U., summer 1960. Served as capt. AUS, 1941-45. Mem. N.Y. State Collegiate Assn. Devel. Ednl. Adminstrn. (pres. 1960), Nat. Sch. Pub. Relations Assn., N.E.A., Am. Asso. Sch. Adminstrs., Am. Assn. Higher Edn., Am. Assn. U. Profs., Phi Beta Kappa, Phi Delta Kappa, Kappa Phi Kappa, Phi Sigma Iota, Pi Delta Epsilon, Kappa Delta Pi. Unitarian. Author: Public Relations for Teachers, 1959; also articles profl. publs. Home: 66 Clinton Av Montclair NJ 07042 Office: Coll City NY New York City NY 10010

BORTOLAZZO, JULIO LAWRENCE, educator; b. Santa Barbara, Cal., Sept. 17, 1915; s. Santo and Vittoria (Raccanello) B.; B.A., Santa Barbara State Coll, 1936; M.S., U. So. Cal., 1939; Ed.M., Harvard, 1942, Ed.D., 1949; m. Alyce Corbin, Sept. 11, 1940; children—Richard Alan, Gerald William, Paul Lawrence. Tchr. Santa Barbara Junior High Sch., 1936-41; tchr., counselor San Francisco City Coll., 1946; prin. Ainsworth Elementary Sch., Portland, Ore., 1946-48, Jefferson High Sch., Portland, 1948-50; faculty grad. sch. edn. Harvard, 1948; faculty San Diego State Coll., 1949, extension center U. Ore., 1949-52; supt. schs., Lake Oswego, Ore., 1950-52; faculty summer session U. Me., 1946, U. Wash., 1951, 53; pres. Stockton Coll., 1952-56; supt. San Mateo Jr. Coll. Dist., also pres. Coll. San Mateo, 1956-68; supt., also pres. San Joaquin Delta Coll., 1968-69, Santa Barbara (Cal.) City Coll., 1969—; ednl. cons., lectr. Cons. to Italian Govt. in Vocational Edn., 1955. Ford Found. Study of Italian Edn., 1960; ICA ednl. cons. in vocational tech., Liberia, 1959; mem. Commn. Accreditation of Service Experiences, Am. Council Edn. 1961- -; mem. Vocational Edn. Study Adv. Com., Commn. Acad. Affairs, 1965—; mem. jr. coll. adv. panel Cal. Bd. Edn.; cons. higher edn. Colombia U., 1966—. Pres. Boys and Girls Aid Soc., Portland. Served as lt. USNR, 1942-46. Mem. Am. Legion., N.E.A., Cal. Jr. Coll. Assn. (pres. 1966-67), Am. Assn. Jr. Colls., Am. Assn. Sch. Adminstrs., Cal. Tchrs. Assn., Phi Kappa Phi, Phi Delta Kappa, Kappa Delta Pi, Sigma Alpha Kappa. Mason. Clubs: Commonwealth of Cal., Kiwanis. Address: 100 Oceano Av Santa Barbara CA 93105

BORTON, HUGH, educator; b. Moorestown, N.J., May 14, 1903; B.S., Haverford Coll., 1926; M.A., Columbia, 1932; student Imperial U. (Tokyo), 1931-37; Ph.D., Rijksuniversiteit (Leyden, Holland), 1937; research asst., Inst. Pacific Relations, summer 1938; LL.D., Temple U., 1960, U. Pa., 1961, Haverford Coll., 1969; m. Elizabeth Wilbur; children—Anne Carter, Anthony. Mem. faculty Columbia, 1937-57, asso. prof. Japanese and asst. dir. East Asian Inst., 1947-50, prof. Japanese and dir. E. Asian Inst., 1950-57; pres. Haverford Coll., Pa., 1957-67; sr. research asso. E. Asian Inst., Columbia, 1967—; on leave for govt. duty, 1942-48; served as mem. faculty War Dept. Sch. Mil. Govt., Charlottesville, Va., 1942, also in various positions with Dept. of State, including chief Northeast Asian Affairs div. and spl. asst. office of dir. Far Eastern Affairs, 1942-48. Chmn. U.S. delegation, co-chmn. U.S.-Japan Ednl. and Cultural Conf., Japan, 1962-66, Washington, 1963, U.S. delegate, 1970—. Mem. Harvard vis. com. Far Eastern Civilizations; v.p. Japan Soc., Inc.; dir. Am. Friends Service Com.; v.p. Japan Internat. Christian U. Found. Fellow Internat. Inst. Arts and Letters (life); mem. Century Assn., Assn. Asian Affairs (mem. com. coll. and world affairs), Phi Beta Kappa. Author: Japan Since 1931; Its Political and Social Development; Peasant Uprisings in Japan, 1968; Occupation of Japan, Korea and Mandated Islands, 1945-47; Japan's Modern Century, 1970. Co-author: A Selected List of Books and Articles on Japan; Japan between East and West, 1957. Editor: Japan 1951. Contbr. numerous articles on Japanese history and politics. Home: 5 Windsor Dr Princeton Junction NJ 08550

BORTREE, ALFRED LEE, educator; b. Peterborough, N.H., Oct. 13, 1916; s. Alfred Dawson and Edna (Lee) B.; B.S., Pa. State U., 1939; M.S., Mich. State U., 1942, D.V.M., 1944; m. Jean Elisabeth Howland, Mar. 26, 1943; children—Ronald Lee, Scott Howland. Mem. faculty Mich. State U., 1944-48; prof. vet. sci. Pa. State U. at University Park, 1948—, head dept. vet. sci., 1953—, chmn. div. animal sci. and industry, 1964-70. Chmn. Explorer Post com. Boy Scouts Am., State College, Pa., 1968-71. NSF sci. fellow U. Cal. at Davis, 1960-61. Mem. Am. Vet. Med. Assn., Conf. Research Workers Animal Diseases, Am. Dairy Sci. Assn., Alpha Gamma Rho, Gamma Sigma Delta. Rotarian. Home: 920 Taylor St State College PA 16801

BORTS, GEORGE HERBERT, educator, economist; b. N.Y.C., Aug. 29, 1927; s. Elias Alexander and Etta (Silberg) B.; A.B., Columbia, 1947; A.M. in Econs., U. Chgo., 1949, Ph.D., 1953; m. Muriel Levenson, Dec. 26, 1948; children—David, Richard, Robert. Research asso. Nat. Bur. Econ. Research, 1954-55; mem. faculty Brown U., 1950—, prof. economics, 1960—, chmn. dept., 1964-67; mng. editor Am. Econ. Rev., 1969—. Fellow Social Sci. Research Council, 1949-50; Ford Found. fellow 1960- 61. Mem. Am. Econ. Assn., Econometric Soc., Phi Beta Kappa. Author: Regional Business Cycles, 1960; (with J.L. Stein) Economic Growth in a Free Market, 1964. Home: 220 Slater Av Providence RI 02906

BOS, L.J., turbine mfg. co. exec. Treas., De Laval Turbine, Inc., Trenton. Office: 803 Nottingham Way Trenton NJ 08602*

BOSA, LOUIS, artist; b. Codroipo, Udine Province, Italy, Apr. 2, 1905; s. Gabriel and Anna (Galassi) B.; ed. grammar and high sch., (Italy); Art Students League, N.Y.C.,; m. Theresa Krakowska, Nov. 26, 1929; 1 dau., Anna. Artist in drawing, painting and wood sculpture; one-man shows Kleeman Galleries (12), Schneider Gabriel Galleries, 1940 (both N.Y.C.), Springfield (Mass.) Mus., Coy Gallery, Fla., Cleve. Inst. Art, Oehlschlaeger Gallery, Chgo., 1954, 59, 65, Milch Gallery, N.Y.C., 1958, 60, 63, 65; exhibited at Carnegie Inst., N.A.D., Pa. Acad. Fine Arts, Art Inst. Chgo., Corcoran Galleries, Met., Atlanta, Rochester, Bklyn., Whitney, Buffalo, Boston, Springfield, Worcester, Montclair, Wilmington, Wis. museums, Mus. Modern Art, Audubon Artists, Pitts. Internat., Kansas City, Phila., Delgadeo museums, Herron Art Inst., Columbus mus. Arts and Crafts, numerous others; represented in collections of Pa. Acad., Springfield Mus., Ency. Brit., Worchester, Montclair, Clearwater and Isaac Delgado museums, IBM collection, Met. Mus. Art, N.Y.C.; instr. advanced painting Cleve. Inst. Art. Recipient John Wanamaker award for Gravel Quarry, 1938; 3d prize Pepsi-Cola Competition, also hon. mention Nat. Acad. for Sidewalk Market, 1944, 1st prize Rockport Art Assn., 1947, award from Paintings of the Year, 1947, from Acad. Arts and Letters, 1948, 1st prize Los Angeles County Fair, 1948, Purchase prize U. Ill., 1949, gold medal Audubon Artists, 1949, 4th prize Internat. Hallmark, 1949, N.A. Whitney Mus. Purchase Prize, 1954, $500 N.A.D., $750 Hallmark Internat. Competition, 1957, $900, 1958; $1000 Butler Ann. Exhbn., 1960; $400 N.A.D., 1961; $750 purchase prize State of N.J., 1963. Mem. N.A.D., Artists Equity (dir.) Audubon Artists (dir.), Art Students League. Home: Upper Black Eddy Bucks County PA 18972

BOSCH, ALLAN WHITWORTH, coll. dean; b. Lebanon Ky., Mar. 1, 1923; s. Frederick William Archibald and Vivian Stewart (Whitworth) B.; student S.W. Mo. State Coll., 1940- 41, 46, Va. Poly Inst., 1943-44; B.S., Davidson Coll., 1947; M.A., U. Chgo., 1950, Ph. D., 1965; m. Louise Coats, Aug. 12, 1946; children—Allan Whitworth II, Anne Louise, Stephen Joel, Susan Carol, Jennifer Lynne. Tchr., Neosha (Mo.) High Sch., 1947-48; from asst. to prof. history Westmінister Coll., Salt Lake City, 1952-57, registrar, chmn. dept. history 1957-61, acad. v.p., dean coll., 1961-65; asst. dean, dir. instl. studies Marietta (O.) Coll., 1965-67, dean coll., 1967—. Served with AUS, 1943-45. Decorated Purple Heart, Bronze Star. Mem. Am. Conf. Acad. Deans, Phi Beta Kappa, Omicron Delta Kappa, Beta Theta Pi, Alpha Phi Omega, Phi Mu Alph. Presbyn. Rotarian. Home: 109 Wildwood Dr Marietta, OH 45750.

BOSCH, GULNAR KHEIRALLAH, Islamicist, art historian; b. Lake Preston, S.D., Oct. 31, 1909; d. George I. and Anna (Griewisch) Kheirallah; B.F.A., Art Inst. Chgo., 1929; M.A. (Carnegie scholar) in Art History and Archaeology, N.Y.U., 1940; Ph.D. in Oriental Langs. and Lit., U. Chgo., 1952; m. Gerhard Bosch, Dec. 23, 1932 (div. 1964); child, Jarir (dec.). Carnegie fellow Inst. Art and Archaeology, U. Paris, summer 1939; Am. Council Learned Socs. fellow Princeton Grad. Coll. Islamic Seminars, 1938, 41; research asst. Oriental Inst., U. Chgo., 1943-45; asst. prof. art Fla. State Coll. for Women, 1940-43; Catherine Comer prof. art history, chmn. dept. art Wesleyan Coll., 1945-57; prof. art history, chmn. dept. fine arts La. State U., 1957-60; prof. art history, head art dept. Fla. State U., 1960—, dir. Study Center, Florence, Italy, 1967-68. Research grant, La. State U., XXV Internat. Congress Orientalists, Moscow, grant Fla. State U. To XXVI congress, New Delhi; participant Iranian Conf., Hoover Inst., Stanford U., 1971. Mem. Am. Oriental Soc., Nat., Southeastern coll. art assns. La. Coll. Conf. (sec. art sect. 1959), Southeastern Coll. Art Conf. (pres. 1957-58, v.p., 1965-67), Am. Assn. U. Profs. Contbr. articles profl. jours., revs., encys. Home: 1501 Hilltop Dr Tallahassee FL 32303

BOSCH, JORGE JOSE, distilling co. exec.; b. Havana, Cuba, June 8, 1925; s. Jose M. and Enriqueta (Schueg) B.; came to U.S., 1960, naturalized, 1966; grad. Phillips Exeter Acad., 1943; B. Engring., Yale, 1947; m. Yvelise Molina, Sept. 2, 1950; children—Jose Ignacio, Jorge Alejandro. Master brewer, asst. tech. dir. Hatuey Breweries, Santiago de Cuba, 1949-58; v.p. Bacardi Corp., San Juan, P.R., 1958-63, pres., 1963—; dir. P.R. Cement Co. Trustee Presbyn. Hosp., San Juan; bd. dirs. P.R. Jr. Achievement. Decorated knight Order Holy Sepulchre. Mem. Am. Chem. Soc., Tau Beta Pi. Home: 23 R Ferrar Urn San Patricio San Juan PR 00920 Office: GPO Box 3549 San Juan PR 00936

BOSCH, JOSE MARIO, rum distiller; b. Santiago, Cuba, Apr. 30, 1898; s. Jose and Josefa (Lamarque) B.; student Lehigh U., 1916; m. Enriqueta Schueg Bacardi, July 17, 1922; children—Jorge J., Carlos E. Mgr., Esperanza and Marimon Sugar Mills, Guantanamo, Cuba 1917-21; pro mgr. First Nat. City Bank, Havana, Cuba, 1925-31; mgr. Bacardi & Co. of Mexico, 1932-50, pres., 1950-65; founder, pres. Bacardi Corp., San Juan, P.R., 1934-66; founder, pres. other Bacardi subsidiaries, 1932—; dir. Trust Co. of Cuba and many others, Nimar Corp., Bahamas, pres., 1961—, Campana Ltd., Bermuda, pres., 1965—. Sec. Treasury Cuba, 1950-51. Clubs: Lyford Bay (Nassau); Surf, American (Miami, Fla.); Bankers (San Juan); Ocean Roof (Key Largo, Fla.). Address: PO Box 4897 Nassau Bahamas

BOSCH, LEON ARTHUR, educator; b. Holland, Mich., Nov. 5, 1907; s. John S. and Anna (Jonkman) B.; A.B., Hope Coll., 1929; A.M., U. of Ill., 1930; Ph.D., Northwestern U., 1948; m. Virginia French, Aug. 24, 1935; 1 dau., Patricia Lee. Mem. faculty Northwestern U. Grad. Sch. Mgmt., 1931—, prof. and chmn. dept. bus. administrn., 1948-53, asso. dean, dir. Grad. School Bus. Adminstrn., 1953-62, prof. mgmt., chmn. policy and environment dept. Grad. Sch. Mgmt., 1969—; sales training, research dir. Oscar Mayer & Co., Chicago, 1940-42; meat and food rationing exec., ration adminstr. O.P.A., Washington, 1942-46; cons. bus. firms and trade assns. Trustee, Hope Coll., 1971—. Mem. Am. Assn. U. Profs., Beta Gamma Sigma, Delta Sigma Pi. Republican. Presbyn. Clubs: University (Evanston); Economic (Chgo.) Home: 2449 Marcy Av Evanston IL 60201 Office: 1914 Sheridan Rd Evanston IL 60201

BOSCHEN, ARTHUR L., drug mfr.; b. N.Y.C., Aug. 31, 1910; s. Henry and Matilda (Keller) B.; B.A., Cornell U., 1932; m. Shirley E. Bower, Dec. 21, 1935; children—Arthur L., Elaine P., Elizabeth K. Credit reporter Dun & Bradstreet, Inc., 1932-35; successively accountant, comptroller, v.p. finance Richardson-Merrell, Inc., N.Y.C., 1935—. Mem. Financial Execs. Inst. (pres. 1961-62). Clubs: American Yacht (Rye, N.Y.); Union League (N.Y.C.). 11 Lavender Lane Rye NY 10580 Office: 122 E 42d St New York City NY 10017

BOSCHEN, HENRY CHARLES, constrn. and engring. co. exec.; b. N.Y.C., July 4, 1906; s. Henry and Matilda (Keller) B.; M.E., Cornell U., Ithaca, N.Y., 1928; m. Nancy Hotchkiss, Mar. 9, 1935; children—Henry Charles, Thomas Eugene, Georgia Edith (Mrs. Jay Roelof). With Raymond Internat. Inc., and predecessor, 1928—, pres., 1960-68, chmn. bd., 1967—, also dir. Mem. Scarsdale (N.Y.) Planning Commn., 1960-63. Bd. dirs. Robert Coll. Mem. Am. Soc. C.E., Cornell Alumni Assn. Clubs: N.Y. Yacht, Cornell (N.Y.C.); Larchmont (N.Y.) Yacht; Camp Fire (N.Y.C.). Home: 69 Louise Lane New Canaan CT 06840 Office: Two Pennsylvania Plaza New York City NY 10001

BOSE, AMAR GOPAL, educator; b. Phila., Nov, 1929, s. Noni Gopal and Charlotte (Mechlin) B.; S.B., S.M., Mass. Inst. Tech., 1952, Sc.D., 1956 m. Prema Sarathy, Aug. 17,1960; children-Vanu Gopal, Maya. Mem. faculty Mass. Inst. Tech., 1956-, prof. elec. engring., 1966-. Chmn. bd., tech. dir Bose Corp., Natick, Mass., 1964-. Fulbright fellow India, 1956-57; recipient Baker Teaching award Mass. Inst. Tech., 1964, Teaching award Am. Soc. Engring. Edn., 1965. Mem. I.E.E.E., Sigma Xi, Tau Beta Pi, Eta Kappa Nu, Author: (with Kenneth N. Stevens) Introductory Network Theory, 1965. Patentee in acoustics, nonlinear systems, communications. Home: 113 Sherman Rd Chestnut Hill, MA 02167. Office: 77 Massachusetts Ave Cambridge MA 02139

BOSE, LEWIS C., lawyer; b. Indpls., Apr. 21, 1917; s. Donald Lester and Jeanne (Crowder) B.; A.B., Swarthmore Coll., 1939; LL.B., Yale, 1942; m. Charlotte Marie Hofmann, Aug. 10, 1946; children—Thomas N., Carl L., John C., Anne, William H. Admitted to Ind. bar; asso. firm Barnes, Hickam, Pantzer & Boyd, Indpls., 1946-50; partner firm Bose Buchanan McKinney & Evans, Indpls., 1950—; dir. First Fed. Savs. & Loan Assn. of Indpls. Bd. dirs. Vols. of Am.; v.p., bd. dirs. Family Services Assn. Served to lt. USNR, 1942-46. Mem. Am., Ind. State (chmn. law sect. 1968, chmn. state legislative com. 1970-71), Indpls. bar assns., Indpls. Lawyers Commn., Ind. Statute Revision Commn. Home: Route 1 Box 302A Westfield IN Office: First Fed Bldg Indianapolis IN 46204

BOSHART, JAMES STEWART, banker; b. Fonda, N.Y., Aug. 1, 1916; s. James Stewart and Jennie (Burke) B.; grad. Stonier Grad. Sch. Banking, 1959; m. Geraldine L. Lombaer, Dec. 24, 1942; children—Diane, James Stewart III, John, Jeffrey, Joseph. With Franklin Nat. Bank, Hauppauge, N.Y., 1945—, sr. v.p., 1967—. Pres. Suffolk County council Boy Scouts Am.; vice chmn. Suffolk County Indsl. Commn. Bd. visitors Pilgrim State. Served with USAAF, 1942-45. Mem. L.I. Bankers Assn. (bd. dirs.), Newcomen Soc. N.Am. Mason. Home: 8 Ridge Dr Huntington Station NY 11743 Office: 730 Veterans Memorial Hwy Hauppauge NY 11788

BOSHELL, EDWARD O. gas co. exec.; b. Melvin, Ill., June 1, 1902; s. H.N. and Anna (Gash) B.; ed. Culver Mil. Acad., 1919; B.S., U. Ill. Sch. Commerce; LL.B., U. Ill., 1926; m. Margie Iehl, Sept. 10, 1929; children—Edward O., Betsey Potter. Admitted to Ill. bar, 1926; with firm Knapp and Campbell, Chgo., 1926-28; asst. gen. atty. Consol. Electric and Gas Co., 1928-33; atty. Stone & Webster Service Corp., 1933- 38, v.p. finance, 1938-48; chmn. bd., pres. Standard Gas & Electric Co., 1948-53, Phila. Co., 1948-51; pres. Westinghouse Air Brake Co., 1951-56, chmn. bd., 1951-57; chmn. exec. com., mem. gov. bd. Ry. Progress Inst., 1955-57; mem. exec. council Fedn. Ry. Progress, 1955-58; dir. Duquesne Light Co.; dir., chmn. exec. com. South Jersey Gas Co. Mem. Beta Theta Pi, Phi Delta Phi, Alpha Kappa Psi. Presbyn. Mason. Clubs: Knickerbocker Country (Englewood, N.J.); Everglades (Palm Beach, Fla.); Rolling Rock (Ligonier, Pa.); Seaview (Atlantic City). Address: Palm Beach FL 33480 also 2001 Atlantic Av Atlantic City NJ 08401

BOSHES, BENJAMIN, physician, educator; b. Chgo., Feb. 15, 1907; s. Jacob and Ethel (Laffer) B.; grad. Crane Jr. Coll., Chgo., 1926; M.B., Northwestern U., 1929, B.S., 1930, M.D., 1931, M.S., 1934, Ph.D., 1938; m. Virginia Tarlow, June 14, 1931 (dec. Dec. 1969); children—Janet (Mrs. Charles A. Stern), Roger Arnold; m. 2d, Mrs. Adeline C. Caro, Sept. 9, 1970. Intern Cook County Hosp., Chgo., 1930-31; faculty Northwestern U. Med. Sch., 1932—, chmn. dept. neurology, 1952—; psychiatrist Inst. Juvenile Research, 1936-41; practice of medicine, specializing neurology and psychiatry, Chgo., 1931—; sr. cons. neurology VA Hosp., Hines, Ill.; cons. neuropsychiatry VA Hosp., Downey, Ill.; sr. cons. neuropsychiatry VA Research Hosp., Chgo.; cons. Fed. Aviation Agy., 1968—. Served from capt. to lt. col. AUS, 1941-46; chief neuropsychiatry service 12th Gen. Hosp. Mem. Am. Acad. Neurology (v.p.), A.M.A., Am. Neurol. Assn. (v.p. 1969), Am. Psychiat. Assn., Chgo. Neurol. Soc. (pres. 1954-55), Ill. Psychiat. Soc. (pres. 1948), Central Neuropsychiat. Assn. (pres 1955), Assn. Research Nervous and Mental Diseases, Am. Epilepsy Society, Sigma Xi, Alpha Omega Alpha. Author articles on neurology, psychiatry. Home: 175 E Delaware Pl Chicago IL 60611 Office: 251 E Chicago Av Chicago IL 60611

BOSHES, LOUIS D., physician; b. Chgo., Oct. 15, 1908; s. Jacob and Ethel (London) B.; B.S., Northwestern U., 1931, M.D., 1936; m. Rhea Amber, Jan. 4, 1942; children—Arlene Phyllis (Mrs. Dennis C. Hirschfelder), Judi Myrl. Intern Michael Reese Hosp., Chgo., 1935-36, Cook County Hosp., 1936-37; pvt. practice medicine, specializing in neurology and psychiatry; fellow psychiatry Ill. Neuro-psychiat. Inst., Chgo., 1941-42, 46-47; sr. attending neurologist and psychiatrist, chief neurology clinic Michael Reese Hosp. and Med. Center, 1958—; asst. prof. dept. neurology, psychiatry Northwestern U. Sch. Medicine, 1955-63; asso. prof. neurology U. Ill. Coll. Medicine, 1963; asso. prof. neurology U. Ill. Coll. Medicine, 1963—, attending neurologist Ill. Research and Ednl. Hosps., 1963- -, dir. consultation clinic for epilepsy, 1963—; asso. neurologist Cook County Hosp., 1947-53, mem. attending staff, 1962—; sr. cons. neurology Downey VA Hosp., 1952-60; cons. neuropsychiatry Woodlawn, Columbus Meml., Louis A. Weiss hosps., Chgo., Ill. State Psychiat. Inst. Mem. med. adv. com. Cook County chpt. Nat Found., 1947-55, Cook County chpt. March of Dimes, 1956- -; mem. med. adv. com. Epilepsy Assn. Am., 1964—, bd. dirs., 1966—; med. adv. com. Am. Epilepsy Soc., 1964—; ambassador Internat. Bur. Epilepsy, 1969—; mem. profl. adv. com. Nat. Parkinson Found., 1960—, Nat. Myasthenia Gravis Found., 1963—, Epilepsy Found Am., profl. adv. bd. United Cerebral Palsy. Served to lt. comdr. M.C., USNR, 1942-46. Diplomate Am. Bd. Psychiatry and Neurology, neurology and psychiatry Pan Am. Med. Assn. Fellow A.C.P., Am. Acad. Neurology, Am. Psychiat. Assn., Inst. Medicine Chgo.; mem. A.M.A. (cons Jour.), Central Neuropsychiat. Assn., Ill. Psychiat. Soc. (sec- treas. 1949-50), Chgo. Neurol. Soc. (pres. 1964—), Michael Reese Hosp. and Med. Center Alumni Assn. (pres. 1961—), Assn. for Research in Nervous and Mental Diseases, Internat., Am., Ill. (med. adv. com.) leagues against epilepsy, Ill. (chmn. sect. neurology and psychiatry 1961—), Chgo. med. socs., World Fedn. Neurology, A.A.A.S., Central Assn. Electroence-Phalographers, Sigma Xi, Phi Delta Epsilon, Alpha Omega Alpha. Author, contbr. to books, med. jours. Asso. editor Diseases of the Nervous System, 1962; asso. editor Internat. Jour. Neuropsychiatry. 1965—, New Physician; cons. editor Current Med. Digest, 1962—; editor Chgo. Neurol. Soc. Bull., Behavioral Neuropsychiatry. Home: 3470 N Lake Shore Dr Chicago IL 60613 Office: 30 N Michigan Av Chicago IL 60602

BOSHKOV, STEFAN HRISTOV, educator, mining engr.; b. Sofia, Bulgaria, Sept. 29, 1918; s. Hristo and Karla (Lubich) B.; came to U.S., 1938, naturalized, 1944; diploma Am. Coll., Sofia, Bulgaria, 1938; B.S. Columbia, 1941, E.M., 1942; m. Bianca G. Amaducci, Aug 28, 1943; children-Lynn Karla, Stefan Robert. Mem. faculty Columbia, 1946-, prof. Henry Krumb Sch. Mines, 1951-, chmn., 1967—; distinguished prof., sr. scientist (Fulbright program), Yugoslavia , 1969; cons. engr., 1950—. Mem. internat. organizing com. Internat. Mining Congress, 1962—. Chmn. 4th Internat. Conf. Strata Control and Rock Mechanics, N.Y.C., 1964. Pres. Harrison (N.Y.) No. 7 Sch. Bd., 1954-63. Served to lst lt. AUS, 1943-46; CBI. Mem. Am. Inst. Mining, Metall. and Petroleum Engrs., Am. Arbitration Assn., Sigma Xi. Presbyn. (trustee 1965-69). Mason. Mem. editorial bd. Internat. Jour. Rock Mechanics and Mining Scis.,1964-. Home: 119 White Plains Ave White Plains NY 10604 Office: Mudd Bldg Columbia Univ New York City NY 10027

BOSHOLM, GERHARD W., banker. Sr. v.p., exec. officer Farmers & Mechanics Savs. Bank, Mpls. Office: 90 S 6th St Minneapolis MN 55402*

BOSKOVSKY, WILLY, musician; b. Vienna, Austria, 1909; ed. Vienna Acad. Music. Violinist, Vienna Philharmonic Orch., 1933—, leader, 1939—, now also concertmaster; head violin dept. Vienna Acad. Music, 1935; founder Boskovsky Trio, 1937, Boskovsky Quartet, 1948; also mem. Vienna Octet; tours throughout world. Address: 51 Jacquinstrasse Vienna Austria*

BOSLEY, HAROLD AUGUSTUS, clergyman; b. Burchard, Neb., Feb. 19, 1907; s. Augustus and Effie (Sinclair) B.; A.B., Neb. Wesleyan Coll., 1930, D.D., 1943; D.D., Northwestern U., 1950; B.D., U. Chgo., 1932, Ph.D., 1933; D.S.T. (hon.), Ripon Coll., 1953; L.H.D. (hon.), Cornell Coll., 1953; D.D., Manchester Coll., 1964; m. Margaret Marie Dahlstrom, July 21, 1928; children—Paul Shailer, Sidney Stanton (dec.), Norman Keith, Diane Marie, David Merrill. Entered ministry Meth. Ch. as local preacher, 1924; ordained elder by Neb. Conf., 1933; dir. religious activities Ia. State Tchrs. Coll., 1934-38; minister Mt. Vernon Place Meth. Ch., Balt., 1938-47; dean Div. Sch., also preacher to Duke U., Durham, N.C., 1947-50; minister 1st Meth. Ch., Evanston, Ill., 1950-62; sr. minister Christ Ch. Meth., N.Y.C., 1962—. Lectr. at various confs., also religious emphasis weeks at various colls. and univs; lectr. Earl Found., Pacific Sch. Religion, 1942, Ayer Found., Rochester Colgate Div. Sch., 1944, Russell Found., Tufts Coll., 1948, Carnahan sems. and schs. in Latin Am., 1951, Japan, Korea, 1955; Mendenhall lectr. DePauw U., 1957; Wilson lectr. McMurry Coll., Abilene, Tex., 1959. Mem. Am. Philos. Assn. Author: The Quest for Religious Certainty, 1939; The Philosophical Heritage of the Christian Faith, 1945; On Final Ground, 1946; Main Issues Confronting Christendon, 1948; The Church Militant, 1952; Preaching on Controversial Issues, 1953; What Did the World Council Say to You?, 1955; Sermons on the Psalms, 1956; Sermons on Genesis, 1958; Doing What is Christian, 1960; He Spoke to Them in Parables, 1963; The Mind of Christ, 1966; The Character of Christ, 1968; The Deeds of Christ, 1969. Home: 135 Elmsmere Rd Bronxville NY 10708 Office: 520 Park Av New York City NY 10021

BOSLEY, TOM, actor; b. Chgo., Oct. 1, 1927; s. Benjamin and Dora (Heyman) B.; ed. high sch., Chgo.; student De Paul U., 1946, Radio Inst. Chgo., 1947-48; studied with Lee Strasberg, 1952; m. Jean Eliot, Mar. 8, 1962. Actor various roles TV programs Alice in Wonderland, 1953, Arsenic and Old Lace, 1962, Focus, 1961, Of Thee I Sing, The Right Man, The Nurses, Law and Mr. Jones, The Perry Como Show; actor numerous theatrical prodns. in stock companies, also off-Broadway prodns., 1952-56; Broadway debut as Fiorello LaGuardia in Fiorello (Pulitzer Prize play), 1959; Broadway roles include musical Nowhere to Go But Up, 1962, play Natural Affection, 1963, play A Murderer Among Us, 1964; film roles include Love with a Proper Stranger, 1963, The World of Henry Orient, 1964. Served with USNR, World War II. Recipient Antoinette Perry award for 1959-60 season as best actor in featured role of musical; Newspaper Guild of Am. Page One award and ANTA award for distinguished contbn. to theatre, 1960; N.Y. Drama Critics award for performance in Fiorello, 1960; Festival of Leadership award, Chgo. Mem. Actors Equity Assn. (governing council 1961—), A.F.T.R.A., Screen Actors Guild.‡

BOSLOW, HAROLD MEYER, psychiatrist; b. N.Y.C., Apr. 30, 1915; s. Sigmond and Helen (Corman) B.; M.D., U. Va., 1939; m. Helen Leora King, July 23, 1943. Resident and staff psychiatrist VA, Perry Pt., Md., 1946-50; med. officer Supreme Bench Balt., 1954—; vis. staff Phipps Clinic, Johns Hopkins, 1950-54; dir. Patuxent Instn., Jessup, Md., 1952—, also mem. med. faculty, 1952—; asst. prof. Johns Hopkins Sch. Medicine. Cons. Surgeon Gen., 1953, Md. Mental Hosps., 1953-58, Nat. Inst. Mental Health, 1970, UN Social Def. Research Inst., 1969-70; ad hoc cons. to White House on mental retardation and antisocial behavior, 1964. Served to maj. USAAF, 1940-46. WHO fellow, 1966. Diplomate Am. Bd. Psychiatry. Fellow Am. Psychiat. Assn., N.Y. Acad. Sci. Home: Route 175 Jessup MD 20794 Office: Patuxent Instn Jessup MD 20794

BOSS, KENNETH JAY, educator; b. Grand Rapids, Mich., Dec. 5, 1935; s. Orrie and Margaret (Oosting) B.; B.A., Central Mich. U., 1957; M.Sc., Mich. State U., 1959; Ph.D., Harvard, 1963. With Bur. Comml. Fisheries, Interior Dept., Washington, 1963-66; asst. curator in malacology Harvard, 1966-69, curator, 1969-70, prof. biology, 1970—. Mem. Inst. Malacology, Am. Malacological Union, A.A.A.S., Marine Biol. Assn. U.K. Home: 24 Fernald Dr Cambridge MA 02138

BOSS, WALLACE LAMONT, ret. banker; b. St. Paul, Oct. 31, 1905; s. Andrew and Evalena (LaMont) B.; B.S., U. Minn., 1928; m. Charlotte Bullen Wells, July 20, 1929; children—Wallace Andrew, Garrett Wells, Janet Charlotte. Clk., Mchts. Nat. Bank, St. Paul, 1923-24, 28-29; rep. First Nat. Bank, St. Paul, 1929-38, asst. cashier, 1938-46, v.p., 1946-68, sr. v.p., exec. officer, 1968-70; dir. St. Anthony Park State Bank. Past chmn. St. Paul Open Golf Tournament; past regional dir. Minn. War Finance Com.; past state campaign chmn. Minn. div. Am. Cancer Soc. Mem. St. Paul Jr. (past treas.), U.S. Jr. (past treas.), St. Paul Area (past treas., past dir.) chambers commerce, Minn. Bankers Assn. (past pres.), U. Minn. Alumni Assn. (past treas., past dir.), King Boreas XX of St. Paul Winter Carnival, Ramsey County Hist. Soc. (dir.). Presbyn. (elder). Home: 1861 Bayard Av St Paul MN 55116

BOSSERMAN, JOSEPH NORWOOD, educator; b. Harrisonburg, Va., July 12, 1925; s. Joseph Astir and Ethel (Wise) B.; B.S., U. Va., 1948; M.F.A., Princeton, 1952. Designer, C. W. Wenger, Harrisonburg, 1948-50, Kenneth Franzheim, Houston, 1952-54; acting asst. prof. architecture U. Va., 1954, asst. prof. architecture, 1954-60, asso. prof. 1963-64, asst. dean Sch. Architecture, 1965, acting dean, prof., 1966, dean, 1967—; vis. prof. architecture Kingston Sch. Art, Kingston-upon-Thames, Eng., 1960-61; sr. Fulbright prof. Technische Hochschule, Stuttgart, Germany, 1964-65. Bd. dirs. Va. Found. Archtl. Edn., Inc.; bd. govs. Am. Assn. Archtl. Bibliographers. Served with USAAF World War II; PTO. Fellow Royal Soc. Arts. (Eng.); mem. A.I.A., Raven Soc., Alpha Rho Chi, Omicron Delta Kappa. Democrat. Mem. United Ch. of Christ. Mason. Clubs: Colonnade (Charlottesville); Keswick (Va.). Home: 422 1st St N Charlottesville, VA 22901.

BOSSERT, ROY GARNER, educator, chemist; b. Monongahela City, Pa., Feb. 21, 1908; s. James Morange and Jennie J. (McCutcheon) B.; B.S., Coll. of Wooster, 1930; M.S., Ohio State U., 1933, Ph.D., 1936; m. Mildred Mary-Ann Boss, Dec. 23, 1933; children—James Robert, William Wallace. Instr. chemistry U. Ky., 1936-37; instr. chemistry Ohio Wesleyan U., Delaware, 1937-38, asst. prof., 1938-44, asso. prof., 1946-49, prof., 1949—, chmn. dept. chemistry, 1962-70; fellow Mellon Inst., Pitts., 1944-46; research chemist Inst. Paper Chemistry, summer 1941; vis. asso. prof.

chemistry Ohio State U., summers 1947-48; asso. program dir. Summer Insts., NSF Washington, 1960-61; cons. NSF, 1961-68. Recipient Research Corp. N.Y. research grants, 1949, 51, Faculty research grant Ohio Wesleyan, summer 1958. Fellow Am. Inst. Chemists, Ohio Acad. Sci.; mem. Am. Chem. Soc. (chmn., councilor Columbus sect.), Sigma Xi, Phi Lambda Upsilon, Phi Gamma Delta. Republican. Presbyn. (elder). Author: (with C.E. Boord and Wallace R. Brode) Laboratory Outlines and Notebook for Organic Chemistry, 3d edit., 1955; (with Wallace R. Brode) Laboratory Text and Notebook for Organic Chemistry, 1968. Home: 17 Westgate Dr Delaware OH 43015

BOSSON, JEAN MICHEL, French diplomat; b. Ambilly, France, Oct. 30, 1929; s. Francois Alexandre and Mathilde Marie (Thusy) B.; grad. Ecole des Hautes Etudes Commerciales, 1945; license Faculte de Droit de Paris, 1945; m. Edith D. Thompson, Apr. 29, 1950; 1 dau., Francois Michel. Comml. attache, Rio de Janeiro, Brazil, 1946-49, Los Angeles, 1949-52, Washington, 1952-57; export promotion dir. Ministry Finance, Paris, 1957-62; sec. gen. Nat. Center for Fgn. Trade, Paris, 1962-64; comml. counselor, New York City, 1964-71, Washington, 1971—. Decorated chevalier Ordre Merite Commercial, chevalier Ordre Economie Nationale, chevalier Legion of Honor. Home: 4546 Cathedral Av NW Washington DC 20016 Office: 1100 Conneticut Av NW Washington DC 20036

BOST, RAYMOND MORRIS, coll. pres.; b. Maiden, N.C., Aug. 18, 1925; s. Loy Robert and Virginia (Anderson) B.; A.B. Lenoir Rhyne Coll., Hickory N.C., 1949; B.D., Luth. Theol. So. Sem., 1952; M.A., Yale, 1959, Ph.D., 1963; m. Margaret Martha Vedder, Aug. 16, 1947; children—Timothy Lee, Penelope Ruth, Peter Raymond, Jonathan Otto. Ordained to ministry Luth. Ch., 1952; pastor in Spartanburg, S.C., 1952-53, Raleigh, N.C., 1953-57; prof. ch. history, dir. field work Luth. Theol. So. Sem., 1960-66; acad. dean Lenoir Rhyne Coll., Hickory, N.C., 1966-68, pres., 1968—. Contact minister Nat. Luth. Council, N.C. State U., 1953-57, Yale, 1957-59; part-time instr. sociology Columbia Coll., 1962-65; mem. Com. to Implement Rufugee Act, 1953; chmn. com. pub. affairs N.C. Council Chs., 1956; pres. Raleigh Ministerial Assn., 1957; treas. N.C. Found. Ch. Related Colls., 1969-70, sec., 1969—; mem. bd. theol. edn. Luth. Ch. Am., 1969-69, mem. standing com. on approaches to unity, 1971—, del. 1970, 72 conv.; bd. dirs. Luth. Ednl. Conf. N. Am., 1970—. Trustee Luth. Theol. So. Sem., 1969—. sec. bd. dirs. Piedmont U. Center N.C., 1970—. Served with USMCR, 1943-47. Luth. Brotherhood Sem. Grad. scholar, 1957-58, Faculty fellow, 1960; Martin Luther fellow Nat. Luth. Ednl. Conf., 1959; Faculty fellow Am. Assn. Theol. Schs., 1959-60. Mem. Am., So. hist. assns., Am. Soc. Ch. History, Orgn. Am. Historians. Rotarian. Home: 741 4th St NE Hickory NC 28601

BOSTED, NELSON P., corp. exec.; b. Indpls., 1923; ed. Bucknell U., 1953. Pres., mem. exec. com., dir. Internat. Rectifier Corp., also dir. Dallons Instruments div.; dir. Rachelle Labs., Inc., Internat. Rectifier Europe, S.A., Internat. Rectifier Co. (G.B.) Ltd., Internat. Rectifier Corp., Italiana, S.P.A., USHA Rectifier Corp., (India), Ltd., Internat. Rectifier (Netherlands, Switzerland, Denmark, France, Germany, Belgium, Japan), Xaloy, S.A., (Belgium). Mem. Am. Physics Soc. Home: 1105 Tower Rd Beverly Hills CA 90211 Office: 9220 Sunset Blvd Los Angeles CA 90069*

BOSTER, DAVIS EUGENE, fgn. service officer; b. Rio Grande, O., Sept. 14, 1920; s. Ernest Gordon and Nelle Emily (Davis) B.; A.B., Mt. Union Coll., Alliance, O., 1942; m. Mary Elizabeth Shilts, Dec. 26, 1942; children—Davis Eugene, Janis Elizabeth, James Shilts, Thomas Daniel, Barbara Anne. Newspaper reporter Canton (O.) Repository, 1939-42; joined U.S. Fgn. Service, 1947; attache Am. embassy, Moscow, 1947-49; Soviet Union desk officer State Dept., 1949- 54; assigned Japanese Peace Conf., San Francisco, 1951; 2d sec. Am. embassy, Bonn, Germany, 1954-58; staff asst. to sec. of state, Washington, 1958-59; officer charge Soviet Union polit. affairs State Dept., 1959-62; 1st sec. Am. embassy, Mexico City, Mexico, 1963-64; spl. asst. to asst. sec. state Inter-Am. affairs, 1964-65; spl. asst. to under sec. state for econ. affairs, 1965-66; counsellor for polit. affairs Am. embassy, Moscow, 1966-67; dep. chief mission Am. embassy, Kathmandu, Nepal, 1967-70. Served to lt. (s.g.) USNR, 1942-47. Mem. Sigma Nu. Home: 6213 Lakeview Dr Falls Church VA 22041

BOSTIAN, CAREY HOYT, educator; b. China Grove, N.C., Mar. 1907; s. William Russell and Nonie (Cress) B.; student Heidelberg Coll., Tiffin, O., 1924-25; B.S., Catawba Coll., Salisbury, N.C., 1928, D.Sc., 1953; M.S., U. Pitts., 1930, Ph.D. 1933; D.Sc., Wake Forest Coll., 1954; D.H.C., Nat. U. Engring., Lima, Peru, 1957; m. Neita Corriher, June 5, 1929; children—Richard Lee, Lloyd Russell, Karl Eugene. Teaching fellow zoology U. Pitts., 1928-30; asst. prof. zoology N.C. State Coll., 1930-36, asso. prof. zoology and poultry genetics, 1936-44, prof., 1944—, asst. dir. instrn. Sch. Agr., 1944-48, dir. instrn. Sch. Agr. and prof. genetics, 1948-53, chancellor, 1953-59, prof. genetics, 1959—. Fellow A.A.A.S.; mem. Genetics Soc. Am., N.C. Acad. Sci., Am. Soc. Human Genetics, Sigma Xi, Gamma Sigma Delta, Phi Sigma, Phi Kappa Phi, Alpha Zeta, Phi Sigma, Phi Kappa Phi, Alpha Zeta. Presbyn. Rotarian. Contbr. articles to profl. jours. Home: 1002 Lake Boone Trail Raleigh NC 27607

BOSTIAN, RICHARD LEE, educator, musician; b. Raleigh, N.C., Jan. 14, 1932; s. Carey Hoyt and Neita (Corriher) B.; B.A., U. N.C., 1954, M.A., 1958, Ph.D., 1961; m. Barbara Ann Bunai, Sept. 10, 1955; children—Russell James, Holly Ann, Bradley Earl, Mary Ann, Carey Hoyt. Asso. prof. music Radford Coll., Radford, Va., 1961-62, prof., head div. fine arts, 1962-66; prof. music, chmn. dept. Denison U., 1966—, coordinator of the arts, 1969—. Founder Radford Community Arts Assn., 1963; cons. music curriculum and phys. facilities; minister of music 1st Presbyn. Ch. Mem. Am. Musicol. Soc., Music Educators Nat. Conf., Coll. Music Soc., Phi Beta Kappa. Research on music of 18th and 20th centuries. Home: Rt 2 Dorrence Rd Granville OH 43023

BOSTICK, J. BENJAMIN, banker; b. Charleston, S.C., 1911; grad. The Citadel, 1931. Exec. v.p. N.C. Nat. Bank, Charlotte. Pres., dir. Frazier Realty. Home: 2001 Stonebridge Lane Charlotte NC 28211 Office: 200 S Tyron St Charlotte NC 28202

BOSTICK, WINSTON HARPER, educator; b. Freeport, Ill., Mar. 5, 1916; s. William Frederick and Alice (Johnson) B.; B.S., U. Chgo., 1938, Ph.D., 1941; m. Virginia Halton Lord, June 16, 1942; children—Joel Lord, Verity Jo Reed, Kent Anthony. Staff in charge pulse transformer devel., radiation lab. Mass. Inst. Tech., 1941-45; asso. prof. physics Tufts U., 1948-54; staff radiation lab. U. Cal. at Livermore, 1954-56; head physics dept., George Meade Bond prof. Stevens Inst. Tech., 1956—. NSF Sr. postdoctoral fellow Centre d'Etudes Nucléairs and Culham Lab., 1961-62; mem. spl. adv. com. on elec. power systems NASA, 1959-61; UNESCO cons. exptl. plasma physics U Buenos Aires, 1970. Candidate for Congress in N.J. Democratic Primary, 1966; del. Dem. Nat. Conv., 1968. Recipient 1st prize Gravity Research Found. essay contest, 1961. Fellow Am. Phys. Soc.; mem. Phi Beta Kappa, Sigma Xi. Contbr. plasma acceleration sect. in Nuclear Energy Series; spl. work in vortex phenomenon in plasma physics. Home: Parker Rd Chester NJ 07930 Office: Stevens Institute Castle Point Hoboken NJ 07030

BOSTOCK, HAROLD DAVIES, former banker; b. Northwich, Cheshire, Eng., Aug. 2, 1907; s. Thomas W. and Mary (Davies) B.; came to U.S., 1910, naturalized, 1918; grad. Stonier Grad. Sch. Banking, Rutgers U., 1953; m. Mary A. Carlen, Apr. 2, 1932; children—Jean Marilyn (Mrs. Warren J. Ahr), Norman Wayne. With Wells Fargo Bank, San Francisco, 1925-70, v.p., sec., 1961-63, v.p., sec.-treas., 1963-70, ret. Mem. adv. com. San Francisco Clearing House Assn., 1961-70; bd. dirs. Better Bus. Bur. San Francisco, 1963-69. Bd. dirs., treas. San Francisco Bay council Girl Scouts Am., 1966-68; mem. St. Francis Hosp. Assn., San Francisco, 1966—. Mem. Am. Soc. Corp. Secs., Cal., San Francisco chambers commerce. Rotarian (treas., past dist. gov.). Home: 1366 Sunnyhills Rd Oakland CA 94610

BOSTWICK, RICHARD RAYMOND, lawyer; b. Billings, Mont., Mar. 17, 1918; s. Leslie H. and Maude (Worthington) B.; student U. Colo., 1937-38; A.B., U. Wyo., 1943, J.D., 1947; m. Margaret Florence Brooks, Jan. 17, 1944; children—Michael, Patricia, Ed, Dick. Admitted to Wyo. bar, 1947; claim atty. Hawkeye Casualty Co., Casper, Wyo., 1948-49; partner Murane, Bostwick, McDaniel & Scott, Casper, 1949—; dir. Nagsco of Casper, Inc., Banta Petroleum, Inc., Depke, Inc., Knapp Supply & Equipment Co., UCOR, Inc., Wyo. Paint & Glass Co. Past trustee Casper YMCA; dep. dir. Civil Def., 1954-58; chmn. local SSS, 1952- -; mem. curriculum coordinating com. Natrona Co. Sch. Dist. 2, High Sch. Dist. Served to capt. AUS, 1943-46. Decorated Bronze Star medal; recipient Silver Merit awards Am. Legion. Mem. Am., Wyo. (pres. 1964-65), Natrona County (pres. 1956) bar assns., Am. Judicature Soc., Internat. Assn. Ins. Counsel, Nat. Conf. Bar Pres. (exec. council 1970—.), Internat. Soc. of Barristers (dir. 1971—), Am. Legion (dir. 1951-58, post comdr. 1953-54), Wyo. Alumni Assn. (trustee 1955- 57), Casper C. of C. (chmn. legistlative com. 1955-57, dir. 1959-62, v.p.). Presbyn. Mason (Shriner, K.T.). Contbr. articles profl. jours. Home: 1137 Granada Av Casper WY 82601 Office: Wyoming Building Casper WY 82601

BOSWELL, DOROTHYE HARRIS, govt. ofcl.; b. Welch, W.Va., Oct. 12, 1924; d. John and Clara (Smith) Harris; student Western Res. U., 1944-45, U. So. Cal., 1966, Los Angeles City Coll., 1967; m. Manisee Boswell, Jr., Apr. 8, 1950 (div. Mar. 1957). Asst. price clk. OPA, Cleve., 1943-45; sec. Urban League, Cleve., 1945-46; clk. War Assets Adminstrn., Cleve., 1946-47; corr. supt. U.S. Navy Dept., Cleve., 1950-59; clerical asst. U.S. Air Force, Los Angeles, 1959-66; adminstrv. asst. U.S. Equal Employment Commn., Los Angeles, 1966-68, equal employment officer, 1968—. First v.p. Nat. Sickle Cell Disease Research Found., 1970-71; nat. youth pres. Nat. Conv. Gospel Choirs and Choruses, Inc., 1944-54, pub. relations chmn., 1954-59; chmn. community relations adv. com. Am. Cancer Soc.; vol. Arthritis Found. Named Vol. of Yr., Jr. Women's Civic League, Cleve., 1958; recipient Service award Los Angeles Urban League Guild, 1966. Mem. Nat. Assn. Negro Bus. and Profl. Women's Clubs Inc. (nat. editor publ. 1967—, commn. on devel.—equal and enriching 1967—, 1st v.p. Los Angeles club 1964-66, gen. conv. chmn. 1965, pres. 1966-70, financial sec. 1970—, Sojourner Truth award 1964, Superior Service award 1965), Women in Govt. Service (founder), Los Angeles Urban League, Los Angeles N.A.A.C.P. Mem. Order Eastern Star. Home: 4408 Presidio Dr Los Angeles CA 90008

BOSWELL, JAMES GRIFFIN, II, cotton co. exec. b. Greensboro, Ga., Mar. 10, 1923; s. William W. and Kate (Hall) B.; B.A., Stanford, 1947; m. Rosalind Murray, Apr. 17, 1947; children—Jody, James W., Lorraine. With J. G. Boswell Co., 1948—, pres., 1952—, also dir.; dir. Safeway Stores, Inc. 2d lt. AUS, 1943-46. Home: 271 Glen Summer Rd Pasadena CA 91105 Office: 510 South Spring St Los Angeles CA 90013

BOSWELL, LORIN ALBERT, dairy exec.; b. Fort Worth, Nov. 14, 1899; s. William Edward and Margie (Huffmaster) B.; B.A., Tex. Christian U., 1937, LL.D., 1967; m. Annie Josephine Shaw, Dec. 21, 1935; children—Lorin Albert, Loretta Gayle (Mrs. Thomas P. Gordon, Jr.). Pres., Boswell Dairies, Fort Worth, 1958-63, chmn. bd., 1963—; dir. Univ. State Bank. Past pres. Dairy Products Inst. Tex., Better Bus. Bur. Fort Worth. Chmn. bd. trustees Tex. Christian U.; hon. chmn., past pres. Van Cliburn Internat. Quadrennial Piano Competition Found., Fort Worth; pres. bd. dirs. Boswell Found., 1958-69. Recipient Nat. citation Nat. Conf. Christians and Jews, 1955. Mem. S.A.R. (past pres.), Newcomen Soc. N.Am., Internat. Assn. Ice Cream Mfrs. (nat. councillors to U.S. C. of C. 1950-57), Beta Gamma Sigma (hon.), Phi Kappa Sigma, Alpha Chi. Mem. Christian Ch. Clubs: Fort Worth (bd. govs. 1961-69), Knife and Fork (past pres.), Exchange (past pres.) (Fort Worth); Rivercrest Country. Author: The Wayside School, 1966; Gustavus Boswell and Descendants, 1970. Address: 6301 Greenway Rd Fort Worth TX 76116

BOSWELL, VICTOR RICKMAN, horticulturist; b. Joplin, Mo., Aug. 8, 1900; s. Ammie Victor and Mattie Pearl (Rickman) B.; B.S.A., U. Mo., 1922; M.S., U. Md., 1923, Ph.D., 1926; m. Dorothy Green, Aug. 20, 1928; 1 son, Victor Rickman. Teaching, research U. Md., 1922-28; sr. horticulturist in charge vegetable crops research USDA bur. plant industry, 1928-35, prin. horticulturist, 1935-51, head sect. vegetable crops, 1951-57, chief vegetable and ornamental research br., 1957-65, asst. dir. crops research div., 1965-68, asst. dir. current research information system, Washington, 1968-69, ret. Sci. cons. G.H.Q., Supreme Comdr. Allied Powers, Tokyo, Japan, 1946. Mem. Washington Acad. Scis., Am. Soc. Hort. Sci. (pres. 1939), Vegetable Growers Assn. Am., Sigma Xi, Alpha Zeta, Phi Kappa Phi, Alpha Gamma Rho. Club: Cosmos (Washington). Contbr. articles sci. jours., popular and trade publns. Home: 6206 43d St Hyattsville MD 20781

BOSWELL, WILLIAM O., former fgn. service officer; b. Vancouver Barracks, Wash., Oct. 24, 1913; s. Walter Osgood and Anne (Orr) B.; grad. Phillips Andover Acad., 1932; A.B., Stanford U., 1936; m. Janine Werner, Sept. 5, 1944; children—Eric, Steven, Philip, Peter, Christopher. Entered as officer Fgn. Service U.S., 1939, vice consul, LeHavre, 1939-40, Georgetown, Brit. Buiana, 1940-41, Martinique, 1941; 3d sec., Lisbon, 1941-45, Vienna, 1945-47; 2d sec., Paris, 1947-49; div. fgn. service personnel Dept. State, 1950-53; 1st sec., Rome, 1953-55; consul gen., Milan, Italy, 1955-58; assigned Fgn. Service Inst., 1958- 59; dir. Office of Security, 1959-62; minister-counselor, Cairo, Egypt, UAR, 1962-65, office of dir. gen., 1965-68; dir. Office Internat. Confs., 1968-70, ret., 1970. Mem. Beta Theta Pi. Home: 5712 Warwick Place Chevy Chase MD 20015

BOSWELL, WILLIAM PERSHING, fgn. service officer; b. Jersey City, Aug. 20, 1918; s. Alfred Moore and Louise (Baylor) B.; A.B., Wilberforce U., 1941; student Am. U., 1947-48; m. Dorothy Ernestine Austin, Jan. 31, 1945; children—William Austin, Robert Ernest, Richard Alan. Asst. security officer State Dept. 1945, intern, 1947-48; joined U.S. Fgn. Service, 1948; disbursing officer, Monrovia, Liberia, 1948-50; vice consul, Ponta Delgada, Azores, Portugal, 1950-53, LaHavre, France, 1953-56; consul, sec., Tokyo, Japan, 1956-61; dep. dir. reception center, Honolulu, 1961-63; assigned Fgn. Service Selection Bd., 1963; consul, 1st sec., Buenos Aires, Argentina, 1964-66; consul, prin. officer Am. consulate, Cali, Colombia, 1966-69; chief Upper Great Lakes div. Office Econ. Opportunity, Chgo., 1969-71; coordinator consular tng. Fgn. Service Inst., Dept. State, 1971—. Served with AUS, 1941-45. Mem. Am. Fgn. Service Assn., Omega Psi Phi. Home: 8358 Glastonbury Ct Annandale VA Office: care Fgn Service Inst Dept State Washington DC

BOSWORTH, EDWIN CARPENTER, ret. educator; b. Foxboro, Mass., Mar. 13, 1890; s. Arthur H. and Annie Frances (Marsh) B.; Ph.B., Brown U., 1911, M.C.S. (hon.), 1927; m. Lucinda Eliza Jeffrey, May 15, 1912; childrenLucinda Caroline, Anne Frances (Mrs. Robert S. Beall), Ruth Margaret (Mrs. Chester C. Hustead). Prof. mathematics Leland U., New Orleans, 1911-11; prof. commerce Detroit YMCA, 1912-14; dean Pace Inst. of Accountancy, Detroit, 1914-17, Washington, 1917-22; with Benjamin Franklin U., 1925-71, dean, 1926-71. Mem. Mayflower Soc., Am. Accounting Assn., Phi Beta Kappa, Phi Alpha Delta, Sigma Phi Epsilon. Republican. Presbyn. Co-author: Manual of Charting, 1923. Home: 2002 R Street Washington DC 20009

BOSWORTH, FREDERIC MANNING, lawyer; b. Lakewood, O., Sept. 2, 1900; s. Frederick C. and Sarah (Manning) B.; student Case Inst. Tech., 1917-20; E.E., Ohio State U., 1921; LL.B., Western Res. U., 1925; m. Lucy Sawyer, July 1, 1931; 1 dau., Constance (Mrs. Paul Eric Kriikku). Admitted to Ohio bar, 1925, U.S. and Canadian patent offices, 1928, Fed. Ct. bar, 1928, now partner firm Bosworth, Sessions, Herrstrom & Cain, Cleve. Trustee Palmer Fund Phi Delta Theta. Served as pvt. 3d class, U.S. Army, 1918. Registered mech. engr., Ohio. Mem. Cleve. bar assn., Am., Cleve. (pres. 1956-57), patent law assns., Newcomen Soc. N.Am., Soc. Mayflower Descs., Tau Beta Pi, Phi Delta Phi, Eta Kappa Nu, Phi Delta Theta. Clubs: Clifton, University, Rowfant, Avon Oaks. Home: 21130 Aberdeen Rd Rocky River OH 44116 Office: Nat City Bank Bldg Cleveland OH 44114

BOSWORTH, HOWARD WILSON, physician; b. Corry, Pa., Nov. 26, 1894; s. George H. and Bertha (Wilson) B.; B.S., Allegheny Coll., 1920, D.Sc. (hon.), 1952; M.D., U. Buffalo, 1921; m. Rebecca Chamness Marshall, May 28, 1928. In private practice of medicine, Buffalo, 1921- 23; resident physician, Barlow San., Los Angeles, 1925-37, med. dir. and supt., 1937-67; emeritus attending staff Los Angeles County Gen. Hosp., Hosp. of Good Samaritan, Queen of Angels Hosp.; cons. USPHS, 1945-54, VA, Washington, 1949-51, San Francisco Area, 1951-66, San Fernando Hosp., 1951-71, Long Beach (Cal.) VA Hosp., 1959—; instr. U. So. Calif. Med. Sch., 1934-40, asst. clin. prof., 1940-43, asso. clin prof., 1943-45, clin prof. medicine, 1945-60, emeritus, 1960- -. Mem. of the Tb adv. com. Los Angeles County Dept. Instns., 1937-52; chmn. chest. bd. Los Angeles City sch. system. Mem. A.M.A., Cal., Los Angeles County med. assns., Nat. Tb Assn. (bd. dirs., 1945-69, v.p. 1950-51, pres., 1956-57, Trudeau medallist, 1949), Cal. Tb Assn. (pres. emeritus 1968—, dir. 1943-50; Cal. medallist, 1953), Los Angeles Tb Assn. (past pres., dir., 1938-43), Los Angeles County Tb Assn. (past pres., dir. 1943-50), Internat. Union Against Tb (councilor 1955-58), Am. Coll. Preventive Medicine, Am. Thoracic Soc. (past pres.), Calif. Thoracic Soc. (past pres.), Los Angeles Thoracic Soc. (past pres.), Am. Pub. Health Assn. (also Western br.), Am., Cal., Los Angeles heart assns., Am. Clin. and Climatol. Assn., D.A.V., Am. Legion, Welfare Council Met. Los Angeles, Los Angeles Acad. Medicine, Phi Gamma Delta, Nu Sigma Nu. Republican. Methodist. Mason. Club: University. Contbr. articles to profl. mags. Home: 31766 Broad Beach Rd Malibu CA 90265 Office: 1444 Portia St Los Angeles CA 90026

BOSWORTH, RAYMOND FRANCIS, educator; b. New Haven, July 19, 1904; s. Leland W. and Sarah B. (Cook) B.; B.S., Middlebury Coll., 1929, A.M., 1931; Diploma Litt., Univ. of London, 1930; m. Helen R. Walter, June 8, 1934; 1 dau., Sarah Elizabeth. Tchr. pvt. and public schs., 1930-35; instr. English, Simmons Coll., 1935-40; asst. prof. English, 1940-45, prof. English, dir. Sch. of Publication, 1945-71, prof. English emeritus, 1971, lectr. on editorial procedures, 1971—; instr. Breadloaf Sch. of English, 1932-41; lectr. Harvard U. Extension, 1946-58. Capt. USNR, ret. Mem. Am. Assn. U. Profs., Navy League, Nat. Graphic Arts Assn., Assn. Edn. Journalism, Am. Soc. Journalism Sch. Adminstrs., Coll. English Assn., Soc. Tech. Writers, Delta Kappa Epsilon. Author: Happy the Bride, Family Plot, Once a Pupil, Three Cents a Day, and other one-act plays and articles. Home: 549 High Rock St Needham MA 02192 Office: Simmons College Boston MA 02115

BOSWORTH, ROBINSON, Jr., mfg. co. exec.; b. St. Paul, Jan. 21, 1916; s. Robinson and Russel (Sprake) B.; B.A., Dartmouth, 1937, student Amos Tuck Sch. Bus. Adminstrn. and Finance, 1937; m. Marian Denison Thompson, June 17, 1939 (div. Jan. 1970); children—Judy (Mrs. Jose M. Roesset), Robinson III, Leslie Pamela (Mrs. Robert Stelzl), Timothy Thompson; m. 2d, Martha Carter Caddell, June 7, 1970. With Will Ross, Inc., Milw., 1937—, pres., 1962-68, chmn. bd., 1968—, also dir.; dir. First Wis. Bankshares Corp., Wehr Corp., First Wis. Nat. Bank, Nalco Chem. Co., Northwestern Nat. Ins. Co., Cutler-Hammer, N N Corp., Wrought Washer Mfg. Co. Trustee Milw. Auditorium and Arena. Home: 1626 N Prospect Av Milwaukee WI 53202 Office: PO Box 2012 Milwaukee WI 53201

BOTEIN, BERNARD, lawyer; b. N.Y.C., May 6, 1900; s. Herman William and Sarah (Leonson) B.; student Coll. City N.Y., 1917-19; LL.B., Bklyn Law Sch., 1924; LL.D., N.Y. Law Sch., 1959, N.Y.U., 1964, Jewish Theol. Sem., 1965, Yeshiva U., 1965, Bklyn. Law Sch., 1966; m. Marian Berman, Oct. 13, 1940; childrenStephen William, Michael Harris. Admitted to N.Y. bar, 1926; practiced, N.Y.C., 1926-41; asst. dist. atty. N.Y. County, 1929-36; justice N.Y. State Supreme Ct., 1941-53, asso. justice appellate div., 1953-57, presiding justice appellate div., 1957-69, ret.; sr. partner firm Botein, Hays, Sklar & Herzberg, N.Y.C., 1969—. Head N.Y.C. Accident Fraud Investigation, 1936, N.Y. State Ins. Fund Investigation, 1938, N.Y. State Printing Investigation, 1940; Cardozo lectr.; vis. lectr. U. P.R. Law Sch., 1960; chmn. Nat. Conf. on Bail and Criminal Justice; chmn. exec. br. N.Y. State Constl. Conv., 1967. Bd. dirs. Nat. Legal Aid and Defender Assn.; trustee-at-large Fedn. Jewish Philanthropies; trustee William Nelson Cromwell Found., Vera Inst. Justice, N.Y. U. Law Found., N.Y.C. Rand Inst., Practicing Law Inst.; v.p. YMHA, YWHA, 1949-59. Served with U.S. Army, World War I. Recipient medal Assn. Bar City N.Y., 1963; New Sch. medal for distinguished service to N.Y.C., 1965; Chief Justice Stone award, 1965, Citizens Union award, 1970, Gold medal St. Nicholas Soc. of N.Y., 1970. Fellow Am. Coll. Trial Lawyers; mem. Am., N.Y. State (Gold medal 1970) bar assns., Assn. Bar City N.Y. (pres. 1970—), N.Y. County Lawyers Assn., Jud. Conf. N.Y. (mem. adminstrv. bd. 1957-68), Century Assn., Am. Arbitration Assn. (exec. com.), Order of Coif (hon.). Jewish religion (pres. Met. Council Synagogues 1948-50). Author: (with Irving W. Halpern) The Slum and Crime, 1935; Trial Judge, 1952; The Prosecutor, 1956; (with Murray A. Gordon) The Trial of the Future. Home: 1010 Fifth Av New York City NY 10028 Office: 200 Park Av New York City NY 10017

BOTHA, MATTHYS IZAK, South African diplomat; b. Bloemfontein, South Africa, Oct. 31, 1913; s. Johannes Hendrik Jacobus and Anna Martina Johanna (Joubert) B.; B.A., Pretoria U., 1936, LL.B., 1938; m. Hester LeRoux Bosman, June 29, 1940; children—Matthys Johannes, Gerhard. With South African Dept. Finance, 1931-44, Dept. Fgn. Affairs, 1944—; posted South African embassy, Washington, 1944-51, permanent mission to UN, 1951-55;

head polit. div., Pretoria, 1955-58; E.E. and M.P. to Switzerland, 1959-60; minister South African embassy, London, Eng., 1960-62; ambassador, permanent rep. to UN, N.Y.C., 1962-70; ambassador to Can., Ottawa, Ont., 1970—. Del. to confs. UN, specialized agys., other internat. confs. Office: 15 Sussex Dr Ottawa 2 Ontario Canada

BOTHMER, BERNARD V., Egyptologist; b. Charlottenburg, Germany, Oct. 13, 1912; s. Willy and Marie (Freiin von und zu Egloffstein) von B.; student U. Berlin, 1931-32, 32-36, U. Bonn-am-Rhein, 1932; m. Oct. 18, 1951; children—Yvette Marina, Nicolas B. (dec.). Naturalized U.S. citizen, 1944. Asst. dept. Egyptian, State Museums, Berlin, Germany, 1932-38; staff O.W.I., N.Y.C., 1942-43, fgn. lang. sect. War Dept., 1943; asst. dept. Egyptian art Mus. Fine Arts, Boston, 1946-53, asst. curator 1954-56; asst. treas. Am. Research Center in Egypt, Inc., 1950-56, gen. sec., 1953-54, field dir. in Egypt, 1954-56; asst. curator Ancient art Bklyn. Mus., 1956-58, asso. curator, 1958-64, curator ancient art, 1964—, vice dir. mus., 1969-70; adj. prof. fine arts Inst. Fine Arts N.Y. U., 1960—. Fulbright Research fellow, Egypt, 1954-56, 63-64. Served with Intelligence Corps, AUS, 1943-46. Mem. Am. Assn. Museums, Archaeol. Inst. Am. (gen. sec. 1952-54), Egypt Exploration Soc., Compagnie de la Toison d'Or (Dijon, France), Am. Research Center Egypt, Coll. Art Assn. Address: Brooklyn Museum Brooklyn NY 11238

BOTHMER, DIETRICH FELIX VON, archaeologist, mus. curator; b. Eisenach, Thuringia, Oct. 26, 1918; s. Wilhelm Friedrich Franz Karl and Marie Julie A. Karoline (Freiin von und zu Eglofftein) von B.; student Friedrich Wilhelms U., Berlin, 1937-38; diploma classical archaeology (Rhodes scholar), Wadham Coll., Oxford, 1938; Internat. House fellow, U. Cal. at Berkeley, 1940. Alfred B. Jordan fellow, 1940-41, univ. fellow, 1941-42, Ph.D. in Classical Archaeology, 1944; Martin Ryerson fellow U. Chgo., 1942-43; m. Joyce Marquise de la Bégassiere, May 28, 1966; children—Bernard Nicholas, Maria Elizabeth. Came to U.S., 1939, naturalized, 1944. Asst. curator Greek and Roman art Met. Mus. Art, 1946-51, asso. curator, 1951-59, curator, 1959—. Adj. prof. N.Y. U.; book rev. editor Am. Jour. Archeol., 1950-57. Served as pvt. AUS, 1943-45. Decorated Bronze Star medal. John Simon Guggenheim Meml. Found. fellowship, 1966. Mem. Archaeol. Inst. Am. (benefactor), Grand Jury Assn., N.Y., Soc. Promotion Hellenic Studies, Deutsches Archaeol. Inst., Vereinigung der Freunde Antiker Kunst (Basle, Switzerland). Club: Piping Rock. Author: Amazons in Greek Art, 1957; Ancient Art from New York Private Collections, 1961; An Inquiry into the Forgery of the Etruscan Terracotta Warriors, 1961; Corpus Vasorum Antiquorum, USA fasc. 12, 1963. Home: Centre Island Rd Oyster Bay NY 11771 Office: Metropolitan Museum Art New York City NY 10028

BOTHNER-BY, AKSEL ARNOLD, chemist; b. Mpls., Apr. 29, 1921; s. Aksel Conrad and Merle Marie (von Hagen) Bothner-by; student U. Nanking (China), 1939; B.Chemistry, U. Minn., 1943; M.S., N.Y.U., 1947; Ph.D., Harvard, 1949; m. Christine Treuner, Oct. 15, 1949; children—Peter Ole, Anne Sigrun. Scientist, Brookhaven Nat. Lab., 1949-53; fellow Am. Cancer Soc., 1952-53; instr., lectr. Harvard, 1953-58; cons. Retina Found., 1957-58; staff fellow Mellon Inst., 1958—, dir., 1960-61, mem. adv. com., 1962—, chmn.. dept. chemistry Carnegie-Mellon U., 1967-70, dean Mellon Inst. Sci., 1971—. Fulbright lectr. U. Munich (Germany), 1962-63; adjunct prof. U. Pitts., 1964—. Served with AUS, 1943-45. Mem. Am. Chem. Soc., Sigma Xi. Author papers in field of theoretical organic chemistry. Home: 6317 Darlington Rd Pittsburgh PA 15217 Office: Mellon Inst 4400 5th Av Pittsburgh PA 15213

BOTHWELL, DORR, artist; b. San Francisco, May 3, 1902; d. John Stuart and Florence Isabel (Hodgson) Bothwell; student Cal. Sch. Fine Arts, Rudolph Schaeffer Sch. Design, U. Ore. Painter, Tau, Mau'a, Am. Samoa, 1928-29, France, 1930-31, Eng., 1960-61, W. Africa and N. Africa, 1966-67; instr. Cal. Sch. Fine Arts, San Francisco, 1945-58, Rudolph Schaeffer Sch. Design, 1960-61, Mendocino (Cal.) Art Center, 1962—, San Francisco Art Inst., 1961. Prof., Sonoma State Coll., summer 1964, U. Cal., Mendocino Art Center, summers 1965-71; faculty Ansel Adams Yosemite Workshop, 1964-71; exhibitor West Coast exhbns., 1927—, 3d biennial Sao Paulo, Brazil, Pitts. Internat., 1952, 55, Art: U.S.A., 1958; works in permanent collection San Diego Gallery Fine Art, Crocker Gallery, Sacramento, San Francisco Mus. Art, Whitney Mus. Am. Art, Bklyn. Mus., Mus. Modern Art, Fogg Mus., Met. Museum, Victoria and Albert Museum, London, Eng., Bibleotheque Nationale, Paris, France; one-man show De Young Meml. Mus., San Francisco, 1957, 63. Recipient 1st prize, 4th ann. exhbn. San Francisco Soc. Women Artists, 1929; Pres.'s purchase prize, 1941; Leisser-Farnham award 7th ann. exhbn. San Diego Art Guild, 1932; hon. mention 7th ann. exhbn. So. Cal. Artists, 1933, spl. prize 9th ann. exhbn., 1937; Artists Fund prize ann. exhbn. drawings and prints San Francisco Art Assn., 1943; hon. mention 2d spring ann. Cal. Palace Legion of Honor, San Francisco, 1947. Notan: The Principle of Dark-Light Design, 1968. Home and studio: Post Office Box 27 Mendocino CA 95460

BOTHWELL, FRANK EDGAR, mathematician; b. Saginaw, Mich., Feb. 25, 1918; S.B. in Applied Math., Mass. Inst. Tech., 1940, S.B. in Elec. Engring., 1941, Ph.D., 1946; m. 1945; 8 children. Staff mem. radiation lab. Mass. Inst. Tech., 1941-45, instr. math., 1945-47; mathematician U. Chgo., 1947-50; asso. prof. elec. engring. Northwestern U., 1950-51; dir. planning Naval Ordnance Testing Sta., 1951-58; dir. Labs. for Applied Scis., U. Chgo., 1958-62; chief scientist Center Naval Analyses, 1962—. Address: 422 East Jefferson St Falls Church VA 22046

BOTKIN, BENJAMIN ALBERT, writer, b. Boston, Feb. 7, 1901; s. Albert and Annie (Dechinick) B.; A.B., Harvard, 1920; M.A., Columbia, 1921; Ph.D., U. Neb., 1931, Litt.D. (hon.), 1956; m. Gertrude Fritz, Aug. 30, 1925; children—Dorothy Ann (Mrs. Jerome Alan Rosenthal), Daniel Benjamin. From instr. English to asso. prof. U. Okla., 1921-40; asst. instr. U. Neb., 1930-31; tchr. summer sessions U. Mont., 1932, N.M. Normal U., 1933; Julius Rosenwald fellow, 1937; folklore editor Fed. Writers Project, Washington, 1938-39; chief editor writers unit Library of Congress Project, 1939-41; resident fellow folklore Library of Congress, 1940-42, hon., 1943-55, asst. in charge, then chief Archive Am. Folk Song, 1942-45; Guggenheim fellow, 1951. Mem. subcom folk music Office Cultural Presentations, Bur. Ednl. and Cultural Affairs, Dept. State, 1967-70; expert cons. Nat. Com. Folk Arts U.S., 1935-70; mem. nat. adv. council Nat. Folk Festival, 1934-67, bd. dirs., 1967—; spl. folklore cons., 1971—; chmn. Workshop for Cultural Democracy, 1956-58; Louis M. Rabinowitz Foundation grant, 1965; sr. fellow Nat. Endowment for the Humanities, 1967. Fellow Am. Folklore Soc. (pres. 1944-45, del. Am. Council Learned Socs. 1951-53); mem. Manuscript Soc., Internat. Folk Music Council, Internat. Soc. Ethnology and Folklore, Folklore Soc. Greater Washington, N.Y. (hon. v.p.), Northeastern folklore socs., The Westerners, Phi Beta Kappa. Author: The American Play-Party Song, 1937, reprint, 1963; editor: Folk-Say, A Regional Miscellany, 4 vols., 1929-32, reprint, 1970; The Southwest Scene, 1931; Space, Vol. I, Nos. 1-12, 1934-35, reprinted 1970; Lay My Burden Down: A Folk History of Slavery, 1945, German version, 1963; A Treasury of American Folklore, 1944; A Treasury of New England Folklore, 1947, rev., 1965; Sidewalks of America, 1954; N.Y.C. Folklore, 1956; (with Carl Withers) The Illustrated Book of American Folklore, 1958; A Civil War Treasury of Tales, Legends and Folklore, 1960; numerous other folklore treasuries. Asso. editor N.Y. Folklore Quar.; contbr. to Ten Eventful Years, Ency. Brit., 1947; Standard Dictionary of Folklore, Mythology, and Legend, 1949-50; Collier's Ency., 1950; The World Book Ency., 1960; The Book of the American West, 1963; The Reader's Adviser, 1969; editorial cons. the Life Treasury of American Folklore, 1961; The Badmen, Columbia Records Legacy Collection, 1963; cons. on games The Random House Dictionary of the English Language, 1966; editor-in-chief Folklore and Soc. and Rediscovering Am. reprints Johnson Reprint Corp., 1966—; others. Address: 45 Lexington Dr Croton-on-Hudson NY 10520

BOTKIN, HENRY, artist; b. Boston, Apr. 5, 1896; s. Albert and Anna (Dachinick) B.; student Mass. Sch. Art, 1915-19, Art Students League, Paris; m. Rhoada Lehman, Sept. 16, 1930; children—Toinette, Glenn. Illustrator Sat. Evening Post, Harpers Bazaar, Vogue and others, 1919-28; painter, 1929—; represented in permanent collection, numerous museums, including Met. Museum of Art, Library of Congress, Mus. Modern Art, Boston, Mus. Fine Arts, Whitney Mus., and others throughout U.S.; pvt. collections throughout U.S.; 61 one-man exhbns., Paris, Boston, Washington, Kansas City, Denver, Los Angeles, San Francisco, N.Y.C.; Chgo., other cities; group shows including Whitney, Carnegie Internat., Corcoran, Art Inst. Chgo. Recipient numerous awards. Fellow Internat. Inst. Arts and Letters; mem. Am. Abstract Artists (pres. 1954-55), Fedn. Modern Painters and Sculptors (pres. 1958-59, 60-61), Artists Equity (pres. 1952-53). Contbr. to George Gershwin, 1938, Esquire, 1943. Co-editor Abstract Art, 1957. Rep. by 16 paintings Walter P. Chrysler, Jr. collection. Studio: 56 West 11th Street New York City NY 10011 Gallery: Rehn Gallery 655 Madison Av New York City NY 10021

BOTKIN, WILLIAM LOYD, internat. union ofcl.; b. Kansas City, Kan., Oct. 11, 1911; s. Arthur Harold and Grace (Rhoades) B.; student Wash. State U., 1930; m. Madge McSpadden, Feb. 25, 1943; children—William Loyd, Michael Lynn. Mem. Internat. Woodworkers Am., 1937—, sec.-treas., 1955—. Home: 6127 NE 17th St Portland OR 97211 Office: 1622 N Lombard St Portland OR 97217

BOTOND, ISTVAN, architect, planning cons.; b. Gyongyos, Hungary, Apr. 17, 1921; s. Peter and Julia (Fabian) B.; Dipl. Architect, Palatine Joseph Poly. U., Faculty Architecture and Engring., Budapest, Hungary, 1955; M.Arch. in Urban Design, Harvard, 1961; m. Patricia Potter, Mar. 15, 1958; children—Krisztina Lee, Andrew Istvan. Came to U.S., 1956. With various archtl. firms in Hungary prior to 1956; head architecture/planning dept. Regional Planning Inst. for Northeastern Hungary, 1955-56; archtl. cons. to indsl. plants, Hungary; archtl. designer I.M. Pei & Partners, N.Y.C., 1956-63; head design dept. Perkins & Will Partnership, Washington, 1963-65; prin. Istvan Botond, architect/planning cons., Washington, 1965—. Bd. dirs. Am.-Hungarian U. Assn., N.Y.C., 1960-62; trustee Kossuth Found., N.Y.C.; mem. adv. com. Am.-Hungarian Cultural Center, Washington. Recipient Andrea Palladio award Centro Internazionale di studi di Architettura, 1961. Mem. A.I.A. (chmn. internat. visitors com.), Nat. Council Archtl. Registration Bds. Clubs: Harvard (Washington); Bathing Corp. of Southampton. Important works include Bicentennial Park, Smithsonian Instn., Conceptual Plans for large mus./park complex, Devel. Plan for Kraemer Point, Fla. (condominium apts. project), housing project Ivory Coast, W. Africa. Home: 2152 Wyoming Av NW Washington DC 20008 Office: 1875 Connecticut Av NW Washington DC 20009

BOTSFORD, DAVID, Jr., advt. exec.; b. Portland, Ore., Nov. 15, 1916; s. David and Alice (Himes) B.; student Nat. U. Mexico, 1937; B.A., Stanford, 1938; postgrad. Columbia, 1939; m. Margot Seward, Feb. 8, 1941; children—Peter, Christopher, Ardsley (Mrs. Harald Fischer). Reporter, San Francisco Chronicle, 1938-39; copywriter J. Stirling Getchell, Inc., N.Y.C., 1939-41; with Botsford Ketchum, Inc. (formerly Botsford, Constantine & McCarty, Inc.), San Francisco, 1941-43, 46—, copywriter, 1946-49, creative dir., 1949-52, San Francisco mgr., 1952-56, pres., 1956-59, chmn. bd., 1959—; pres. Botsford Ketchum Internat., Tokyo, Japan, 1962—; vice chmn. Ketchum Internat., Inc., N.Y.C. and London, Eng., 1967—; sr. v.p. Ketchum, MacLeod & Grove, Inc., N.Y.C., 1970—. Mem. World Affairs Council No. Cal., San Francisco Symphony Assn., Stanford U. Assos. Served with OWI, AUS, 1943-45; CBI. Mem. Am. Assn. Advt. Agys. (bd. dirs. 1968-69, chmn. Western region 1968-69, trustee ins. trust 1970—), Internat. Advt. Assn. (pres. Western N. Am. 1966-69, 71—), Pacific Area Travel Assn. (bd. dirs. 1967-69), Sierra Club, Alpha Delta Sigma, Sigma Delta Chi. Democrat. Rotarian. Club: Commercial (San Francisco). Home: 111 Floresta Way Menlo Park CA 94025 Office: Botsford Ketchum Inc 114 Sansome St San Francisco CA 94104 also 90 Park Av New York City NY 10016

BOTT, JOHN ROBERT, newspaper editor; b. Grand View, N.Y., June 3, 1914; s. Alfred D. and Katherine (Helm) B.; student Drake Bus. Coll.; m. Mary McLeroy, Nov. 20, 1943; children-Robert, Betsy (Mrs. Mayer), Patricia. With N.Y. Post, 1936—, city editor, 1960—. Home: 78 Cove Rd Oyster Bay NY 11771 Office: 210 South St New York NY 10002

BOTT, LAWRENCE LESTER, chem. co. exec.; b. Chgo., July 22, 1924; s. Lester L. and Vivian (Neisch) B.; B.A., U. Ill., 1947; M.A., Rice U., 1949, Ph.D., 1951; m. Jeanette Ruth Petersen, Aug. 30, 1947; children—Barbara Ann, Susan Frances. Research leader chem. div. Armour & Co., 1951-54; with Nalco Chem. Co., Chgo., 1954—, exec. v.p., 1965-69, pres., 1969—, also dir.; dir. Katalco Corp. Served with AUS, 1943-46. Mem. Am. Petroleum Inst., Ill. C. of C., Ill. Mfrs. Assn. (dir.). Home: 927 Forest Av Oak Park IL 60302 Office: 180 Michigan Av Chicago IL 60601

BOTT, RAOUL, educator; b. Budapest, Hungary, Sept. 24, 1923; s. Rudolph and Margit (Kovacs) B.; B.Engring., McGill U., 1945, M.Engring., 1946; D.Sc., Carnegie Inst. Tech., 1949; A.M. (hon.), Harvard, 1959; m. Phyllis Hazell Aikman, Aug. 30, 1947; children—Anthony, Jocelyn, Renee, Candace. Came to U.S., 1947, naturalized, 1959. Mem. Inst. Advanced Study, Princeton, 1949-51, 55-57; instr. math. U. Mich., 1951-52, asst. prof., 1952-55, prof., 1957-59; prof. math. Harvard, 1959-67, Higgins prof. math., 1967—; spl. research network theory, topology and geometry. Recipient Veblen prize in geometry Am. Math. Soc., 1964. Mem. Nat. Acad. Sci., Am. Math. Soc. (council), Am. Acad. Arts and Sci. Editor: Topology. Asso. editor: Annals of Math, 1958—. Home: 77 Kirkstall Road Newtonville 60, MA Office: 2 Divinity Av Cambridge 38 MA

BOTTELLI, ROMOLO, Jr., architect; b. Newark, Dec. 18, 1902; s. Romolo and Annie (Brown) B.; student Columbia, 1922-27; m. Genevieve A. Donahue, Oct. 3, 1925; children—Joan (Mrs. Marcel Mersch), Patricia (Mrs. Edward Allen), Richard J. Propr. archtl. office, Maplewood, N.J., 1929—; prin. works include high rise apt. houses. Chmn. Maplewood Planning Bd., 1959-62. Fellow A.I.A. (pres. N.J. br. 1955-56); mem. N.J. Soc. Architects (pres. Newark 1948-50, N.J. br. 1955-56), Maplewood C. of C. (dir.). Home: 168 Oakland Rd Maplewood NJ Office: 1878 Springfield Av Maplewood NJ

BOTTHOF, CHARLES LAURY, publisher; b. Highland Park, Mich., Feb. 15, 1916; s. Walter E. and Elsa (Laury) B.; A.B., Princeton, 1939; postgrad. Northwestern U., 1939-40; m. June, 1940; children—Charles Laury, Richard Allan; m. 2d, Joan Lightner Stroud Loveland, May 29, 1948; foster children—Richard S. Loveland, Tena Loveland (Mrs. William Findlay, Jr.); 1 son, Kendrick Lance. With Standard Rate and Data Service, Inc., 1939—, treas., 1940-48, pres., 1946—, also dir.; chmn. bd., dir. Nat. Register Pub. Co.; sr. v.p. Crowell Collier and Macmillan, Inc.; pres.; dir. Abrasive Action, Inc.; dir. Lake Shore Nat. Bank of Chgo., Media Daten, Germany, Tarif Media, France, Dati e Tariffa Pubblicitarie, Italy, Medios Publicitarios Mexicanos, Mexico City. Mem. Nat. Coll. Edn. Assos., Northwestern U. Assos., Chgo. Pres.'s Orgn., Lincoln Acad. Ill. Clubs: Tavern, Mid-America, Executives (Chgo.); Elm (Princeton, N.J.); Indian Hill (Winnetka, Ill.); Westmoreland Country (Wilmette, Ill.); Princeton (N.Y.C.). Home: 54 Hibbard Rd Winnetka IL 60093 Office: 5201 Old Orchard Road Skokie IL 60076

BOTTIGLIA, WILLIAM FILBERT, educator; b. Bernardsville, N.J., Nov. 23, 1912; s. Vincent Richard and Quintilia (Mastrobattista) B.; A.B., Princeton, 1934, A.M., 1935, Ph.D., 1948; m. Mildred MacDonald, Dec. 21, 1943 (dec. Oct. 1966); stepchildren—Martha (Mrs. Milton Morris), Janet. Part-time, then full-time instr. modern langs. Princeton, 1934-42; engaged in industry, 1942-47; gen. mgr. J & S Tool Co., East Orange, N.J., 1946-47; asst. prof. English, St. Lawrence U., 1948; prof. Romance langs. and lits., chmn. dept. Ripon Coll., 1948-56; mem. faculty Mass. Inst. Tech., 1956—, prof. fgn. lit. and humanities, 1960—, head dept. fgn. lit. and linguistics, 1964—. Mem. Modern Lang. Assn., Am. Assn. Tchrs. French, Am. Assn. Tchrs. Italian, New Eng., Modern Lang. Assn., Dante Soc. Am., Phi Beta Kappa. Author: Voltaire's Candide: Analysis of a Classic, 2d edit., 1964; (with others) Voltaire (Twentieth Century Views), 1968. Editor: Reports of N.E. Conf. on the Teaching of Fgn. Langs., 1957, 62, 63. Home: 50 Windsor Road Needham MA 02192 Office: Mass Inst Tech Cambridge MA 02139

BOTTKE, KARL GEORGE, educator; b. Indpls., Sept. 22, 1908; s. Eugene G. and Ida (Eberhardt) B.; B.A., Butler U., 1929; M.A., U. Wis., 1931, Ph.D., 1940; Am. Field Service fellow, U. Paris, 1933-34. Asst. prof. dept. French and Italian, U. Wis., Madison, 1941-48, asso prof., 1949-54, prof., 1955-69, prof. emeritus, 1969—, chmn. dept., 1962-63. Mem. Am. Assn. Tchrs. French (past chpt. pres.), Am. Assn. Tchrs. Italian, Internat. Phonetics Assn., Modern Lang. Assn., Am. Assn. U. Profs., Societe Linguistique Romane, Phi Kappa Phi. Author: Brief Oral French Review, 1947; (with J. Palmeri) Practical Italian, 1947; (with G. Joyaux) Aspects de la France, 1968. Contbr. articles profl. jours. Home: 3825 Monona Dr Madison WI 53714

BOTTKOL, JOSEPH MCGRATH, educator; b. Menominee, Mich., July 14, 1909; s. Joseph Alois and Hannah Louisa (McGrath) B.; A.B., Harvard, 1932, A.M., 1934, Ph.D., 1937; m. Rosalie Orr Horton, Aug. 31, 1937 (dec. Feb. 1967); children—John, Matthew Stephen. Asst. English, Harvard, 1933-37; instr. English, Yale, also fellow Jonathan Edwards Coll., 1937-39; asst. prof. Coll. William and Mary, 1939-43; with OSS, 1943-45; mem. faculty Mt. Holyoke Coll., 1945—, prof. English, 1954—; Fulbright research scholar U. Rome, also Biblioteca Apostolica Vaticana, 1951-53; vis. Fulbright prof. Aristotelian U. of Thessaloniki (Greece), 1959-60; vis. lectr. Harvard, Yale, Amherst Coll. Four-Coll. grantee, Japan, summer 1967; Mt. Holyoke grantee, Japan, summer 1968. Democrat. Club: Oxford and Cambridge (London). Contbr. articles profl. jours. Editor: (Henry James) Aspern Papers, The Europeans, 1950. Home: 7 Ashfield Lane South Hadley MA 01075

BOTTLER, EDGAR O. can co. exec.; b. Bartlesville, Okla., Nov. 6, 1923; s. Joseph S. and Helen (Souther) B.; B.S. Chem. Engring., Rice U., 1944; LL.B., U. Tex., 1949; children—Claire, Carolyn. Spl. asst. to U.S. atty. gen., 1954; asst. U.S. atty. So. Dist. Tex., 1955-58, 1st asst. U.S. atty., 1957-58; atty. Gulf Interstate Gas Co., 1958-59; sec., counsel Columbia Gulf Transmission Co., 1959-63; sr. atty. Columbia Gas System Service Corp., 1963-67; sec., legal counsel Continental Can Co., N.Y.C., 1967—. Mem. council Rice U. Fund. Bd. dirs. Greenwich Philharmonia. Mem. Am., Fed. Power, Tex. bar assns., Rice U. Alumni Assn. (exec. bd.), Theodore Gordon Flyfishers, Inc., Defenders Wildlife. Home: 584 Riversville Rd Greenwich CT 06830 Office: 633 3d Av New York City NY 10017

BOTTOMS, JOHN WATSON, naval officer; b. Graceville, Fla. July 7, 1911; s. James Fletcher and Elizabeth (Boldon) B.; B.S., U.S. Naval Acad., 1935; grad. Advanced Mgmt. Program, Harvard, 1950; m. Ruth Geraldine Hill, June 1, 1939; children—John W., Carolyn M. (Mrs. Dana Alden), Christine Ann. Commd. ensign U.S. Navy, 1935; stationed U.S.S. Arturus, U.S.S. Santa Fe; staff comdr. Naval Air Force, Pacific Fleet, World War II; aide to asst. sec. navy; assigned Bur. Aero. Washington. now Def. Supply Office, Camfron Sta., Alexandria, Va. 22314. Recipient D.S.M., 1968. Mem. Armed Forces Mgmt. Assn. (pres. Washington chpt. 1966-67), Nat. Def. Transp. Assn. Newcomen Soc. N.Am. Episcopalian. Club: Army Navy (Washington). Home: 1600 S Gaos St Arlington VA 22202. Office: Defense Supply Office Camfron Sta Alexandria VA 22314

BOTTORFF, CHARLES RUSSELL, hardware mfr. exec.; b. Goshen, Ky., Mar. 1, 1889; s. Robert and Mattie (Moore) B.; ed. pub. schs.; m. Norma Herzer, Oct. 8, 1913 (dec. 1955); 1 dau., Anne (Mrs. William H. Fields); m. 2d, Mildred G. Miller, Mar. 2, 1957. With Beklnap Hardware & Mfg. Co. (now Belknap Inc.), Louisville, 1907—, specialty sporting goods and cutlery salesman, buyer, dir., asst. treas., dir. sales, pres., 1930-55, chmn. bd., 1955-69, dir., cons., 1969—; dir. First Nat. Bank, Ky. Trust Co., First Ky. Co. Bd. dirs. Louisville Community Chest, Louisville Found. Named Hardware Man of Year, Phila. Assn. Mfrs., 1953. Presbyn. Mason. Clubs: Louisville Country, Pendennis (Louisville). Home: 260 Leland Court Louisville KY 40207

BOTTORFF, ORVILLE ORIS, concert mgr.; b. Cortland, Ind., Jan. 15, 1896; s. Milas Frank and Ellen (Whitted) B.; student Northwestern U., 1915-17; m. Lillian Johnston, July 1924 (dec. 1932); m. 2d, Marguerite Zender, June 30, 1936. Rep. and circuit mgr. Redpath Chautauqua and Lyceum Bur., Chgo., 1917-28; also assisted in pioneering civic music assn., organized audience movement and Community concert assns., 1921—; audience promotional dir. Chgo. Civic Opera Co., 1928-31; with Civic Concert Service, Inc., Chgo., 1935-, successively asst. mgr., v.p., dir. and gen. mgr., pres., 1941- ; founder, co-owner, v.p., dir. Nat. Concert and Artist Corp., N.Y.C., 1941-, pres., 1949-. Pres., sr. exec. officer, mem. bd. The Broadway Theatre Alliance, Inc. Mem. Sigma Nu. Clubs: N.Y. Athletic, Bohemians, Lotus (N.Y.C.); Town (Scarsdale). Author articles trade jours. Home: Edgewater Arms Galt Ocean Drive Fort Lauderdale, FL 33308.

BOTTORFF, ROBERT INGRAM, editor; b. Columbus, Ind., Aug. 30, 1907; s. Dean Miles and Gertrude (Eckelman) B.; A.B., DePauw U., 1929; m. Katherine Stoner, May 2, 1930 (dec. 1944); childrenPeter, Katherine; m. 2d, Mary Edna Davis, Feb. 14, 1947; childrenSusan, Sally. Copy editor Pacific Coast edit. Wall St. Jour., 1930-32, news editor, 1932-42, mng. editor 1942-51, mng. editor Midwest 1955-57, exec. editor, 1957-63; v.p., gen. mgr. Dow Jones & Co., 1966-70, ret., 1970; chmn. bd. Dow Jones-Irwin, Inc., 1965-70;

former vice pres. and sec. The Newspaper Fund, Inc. Mem. Alpha Tau Omega, Sigma Delta Chi. Clubs: Echo Lake Country (Westfield, N.J.); Harbor View (N.Y.C.); Dunes Golf (Myrtle Beach, S.C.); Seaview Country. Home: 925 Wyandotte Trail Westfield, NJ Office: 44 Broad Street New York City NY

BOTTS, GUY WARREN, banker, lawyer; b. Milton, Fla., July 12, 1914; s. Alonzo O'Hara and Margaret (Land) B.; LL.B., U. Fla., 1937; LL.B. (hon.), Jacksonville U., 1967; m. Edith M. Huddleston, Nov. 4, 1939; children—Edith, William. Admitted to Fla. bar, 1937; mem. firm Fleming, Hamilton, Diver & Jones, Jacksonville, 1937-39, 40-42; with law dept. Fla. br. Prudential Ins. Co. Am., Lakeland, Fla., 1939-40; mem. firm Fleming, Scott & Botts, and predecessor, 1942-55, sr. partner, 1955-57; sr. partner Botts, Mohoney, Chambers & Adams, and predecessor, Jacksonville, 1957-63; gen. counsel, dir. Barnett Nat. Bank of Jacksonville, 1955-63, pres., chief exec. officer, dir., 1963-70, vice chmn., 1970—; pres., chief exec. officer The Charter Co., 1960-63; chmn., dir. Charter Mortgage & Investment Co., 1960-63; pres. Barnett Banks Fla., Inc. (formerly Barnett Nat. Securities Corp.), 1963—; dir. Fla. Pub. Co., Council Tool Co., Argyle So. Co. Past mem. Fla. Devel. Commn.; commr. Uniform State Laws Fla., 1955-59. Chmn. bd. trustees Jacksonville U., dir., past pres. Duval County Legal Aid Assn. Recipient Gold Key award U.S. Jr. C. of C., 1946; Ted Arnold award Jacksonville C. of C., 1963. Mem. Newcomen Soc., Am. Coll. Probate Counsel (past regent), Jr. (past pres.), U.S., Jacksonville Area (past pres.) chambers commerce, Am., Jacksonville (past pres.) bar assns., Fla. Bar (gov.), Fla. Bankers Assn., Phi Eta Sigma, Phi Alpha Delta, Alpha Kappa Psi, Delta Tau Delta. Clubs: River, University, Meninak, Florida Yacht, Ponte Vedra, Timuquana Country. Compiled Brit. Statutes in Force in Florida, 1943. Editor Banks and banking statutes sect. Fla. Law Practice. Home: 3013 Doctors Lake Dr Orange Park FL 32073 Office: 100 Laura St Jacksonville FL 32202

BOTTS, ROBERT WILLIAM, lawyer; b. Hope, N.M., Aug. 12, 1909; s. Clarence M. and Lessie (Fletcher) B.; A.B., U. N.M., 1930; LL.B., Harvard, 1933; m. Margaret Shortle, May 13, 1934; children—Mary Alice, Robert William, James Shortle. Admitted to N.M. bar, 1933; practice of law, Albuquerque, 1933- 35, 1937-43, 1945—; law clk. U.S. circuit ct. judge Sam G. Bratton, 1935-37; mem. Botts, Botts and Mauney and predecessor firm, 1945—. Bd. dirs. Albuquerque Civic Council; mem. N.M. bd. bar commrs., 1947-53. State exec. com. Republican Party, 1947-53. Regent of N.M. Sch. Mines, 1953-57. Served with AUS, 1943-45. Mem. Am. Law Inst., Am. Bar Assn., Bar Assn. N.M. (pres. 1953), Pi Kappa Alpha. Home: 2605 Cutler St NE Albuquerque NM 87106 Office: Simms Building Albuquerque NM 87101

BOTVINNIK, MIKHAIL MOISSEYEVICH, internat. chess grand master; b. Leningrad, USSR, Aug. 17, 1911; s. Moisey Lvovich and Serafina (Rabinovich) B.; student Poly. Inst. Leningrad, 1928-32; Candidate degree Tech. Sci., 1937, D. degree Tech. Sci., 1951; m. Gayane Davydovna Ananova, Apr. 28, 1935; 1 dau., Olga (Mrs. Andrey Fioshkin). Sci. asso. Sci. Research Inst. Power Engring., Moscow, 1955—. Chess master, 1927, grand master, 1935; chess champion of USSR, 1931, 33, 39, 41, 44, 45, 52; world chess champion, 1948, 51, 54, 58, 61; former mem. presidium, also editorial collegium Federation Internationale de Echecs, frequent del. to internat. chess congresses. Named USSR Champion, 1931, Absolute USSR Champion, 1941; decorated with 2 badges of Honor, Order of Red Banner of Labor, Order of Lenin. Mem. USSR-Netherlands Soc. (pres.). Author numerous articles and books on chess and sci. including: Champion Chess, 1951; One Hundred Selected Games, 1960 (both translated by Stephen Garry); Static Stability Synchronous Machines, 1950; Asynchronized Synchronous Machines, 1964 (translated by L.A. Thompson); (with Yuri Shararian) Alternating Current Synchronous Machines, 1969; An Algorithm for Chess (translated by Arthur Brown), 1968; Computers, Chess and Long Range Planning, 1970. Former mem. editorial bd. mag. Shakhamaty USSR. Home: 7 3Frunzenskaja Moscow USSR

BOTZUM, WILLIAM ALBERT, univ. dean; b. Akron, O., Aug. 20, 1916; s. Charles and Margaret (Trockle) B.; B.A., U. Notre Dame, 1938; Ph.D., U. Chgo., 1950. Instr. philosophy U. Notre Dame, 1948-50, instr. edn., 1950-51; asst. prof. U. Portland, 1951-53, asso. prof., head dept. psychology, 1953-58, prof. psychology, 1958-66, dean grad. sch., 1956-66; prof. psychology U. Notre Dame, 1966—, asst. dean grad. sch., 1966-67, asso. dean, 1967-71, asst. v.p. grad. instrn., 1971—. Mem. Am. Psychol. Assn., Psychometric Soc. Address: Univ Notre Dame Notre Dame IN 46556

BOUATTOURA, TEWFIK, diplomat of Algeria; b. Algeria, Jan. 30, 1936; student philosophy; m. Officer in the Army of Nat. Liberation, 1957-58; mem. Provisional Govt. Republic Algeria, 1958-62; minister armed forces, 1959-60; polit. sec. for Afro-Asian affairs, 1960; polit. sec. for Arab affairs, then ambassador to Ghana; at this time also Algerian del. numerous internat. confs. and meetings; after independence mem. Algerian delegation to XVII session Gen. Assembly UN; dep. dir. Office Minister Fgn. Affairs, 1963, dir. polit. affairs, 1963-64; permanent rep. Algeria to UN Security Council, 1964—, pres. Econ. and Social Council, 1966. Office: Algerian Delegation to United Nations 750 3d Av New York City NY 10017

BOUCHER, CARL OPDYCKE, dentist, educator; b. Ft. Wayne, Ind., October 14, 1904; s. Charles Foster and Winifred (Opdycke) B.; student Ohio State U., 1922, D.D.S., 1927; m. Florence Leona Griess, May 9, 1931; 1 son, James Bradford. Instr. Ohio State U., 1928, asst. prof., 1939-40, asso. prof., 1940-42, chmn. prosthetic div. Coll. Dentistry, 1940-71, prof., 1940—, chmn. dental lab. tech., 1947-57; gen. practice dentistry, Columbus, O., 1927-35, prosthodontist, 1935—; cons. AUS, 1942—, VA, 1950—, USAF, 1954, Walter Reed Army Hosp. Trustee, Ohio Dental Care Corp., 1961-68; mem. med. adv. bd. Services for Crippled Children, Ohio Dept. Pub. Welfare, 1959—. Mem. Joint Commn. Accreditation Dental Labs., 1964-68. Recipient Callahan Meml. award (gold medal) Ohio Dental Assn., 1970. Mem. Ohio Dental Assn. (pres. 1963-64), Columbus Dental Soc. (pres. 1946-47), Acad. Denture Prosthetics (pres. 1950-51), Am. Dental Assn. (past sec. prosthetic dental service com.), Am. Bd. Prosthodontics (pres. 1952-53), Am. Assn. Cleft Palate Rehab. (past v.p.), Southeastern Acad. Prosthodontics (hon.), Carl O. Boucher Prosthodontic Conf. (hon. pres.), Am. Dental Soc. Europe (hon.), Academia Brasiliera de Odontologia (corr. mem.), Am. Assn. Dental Editors, Am. Equilibration Soc., Pierre Fauchard Acad., Am. Acad. Dental Sci., Internat. Assn. Dental Research, Am. Acad. Maxillofacial Prosthetics (hon.), Am. Prosthodontic Soc. (hon.), Am. Coll. Dentists, Fedn. Dentaire Internat., Pacific Coast Soc. Prosthodontics (hon.), Fedn. Prosthodontic Orgns. (pres. 1965-67), Prosthodontic Soc. South Africa (hon.), Dental Assn. South Africa (hon.), Sigma Xi, Psi Omega (supreme grand master 1952-53), Omicron Kappa Upsilon. Author: Dental Prosthetic Laboratory Manual, 1947; author, editor Glossary of Current Clinical Dental Terminology, 1963; Swenson's Complete Dentures, 5th edit., 1964, 6th edit., 1970. Editor of Journal of Prosthetic Dentistry 1949—, Ohio Dental Jour., 1958-60. Home: 3107 Halesworth Road Columbus OH 43221 Office: Beggs Building Columbus OH 43215

BOUCHER, CHARLES GENE, baritone; b. Tagbilaren, Bohol, Philippines, Dec. 6, 1933 (parents Am. citizens); s. Archie D. and Inez (Vince) B.; B.A., Westminster Coll., Fulton, Mo., 1955; Diplome du chant, Conservatoire de Lille (Nord, France), 1957. Winner, Am. Opera Auditions, 1958; debut Teatro Nuovo, Milan, Italy, 1958; soloist Little Orch. Soc. N.Y., Cin. Symphony Orch., Am. Symphony Orch., Orch. Am., Robert Shaw Chorale, Dessoff Choir, Eastman-Rochester Orch., Am. Opera Soc., Chgo. Symphony Orch., N.Y. Choral Soc., Bethlehem Bach Festival (Pa.), Newport (R.I.) Festival; debut Met. Opera Co., 1965; other opera appearances include Cin. Summer Opera, Phila. Lyric/Grand Opera, Washington Opera Soc., Met. Opera Studio; N.Y. premiere Help! Help!, The N.Y.C. Center, 1969; recorded world premiere Howard Hanson's Four Psalms for Baritone and Strings, 1964. Mem. Am. Guild Mus. Artists (bd. govs. 1964—, 3d v.p. 1970—). Address: 244 West 72d St New York City NY 10023

BOUCOT, ARTHUR JAMES, educator, paleontologist; b. Phila., May 26, 1924; s. Joseph Ronald and Katharine (Rosenbaum) B.; A.B., Harvard, 1948, A.M., 1949, Ph.D., 1953; m. Barbara Pierce, June 12, 1948; children—Hannah Gray, Katharine Marsh, Samuel Gordon, Peter Morris. Geologist, U.S. Geol. Survey, 1951-56; asst. prof., then asso. prof. geology Mass. Inst. Tech., 1957-61; asso. prof. then prof. paleontology Cal. Inst. Tech., 1961-68; prof. paleontology U. Pa., 1968-69; prof. geology Ore. State U., 1969—; research asso. Smithsonian Instn., 1967—; adj. prof. U. Ore., 1970—. Served with USAAF, World War II. Decorated D.F.C., Air medal with 6 oak leaf clusters. Guggenheim fellow, 1956-57. Fellow Geol. Soc. Am., Mineral Soc. Am.; mem. Paleontol. Soc., Palaeont. Assn. (Gt. Brit.), Geol. Soc. Washington, Geol. Soc. Sweden (hon. corr. mem.). Democrat. Contbr. profl. jours. Home: 2850 SW Fairmont Dr Corvallis OR Office: Dept Geology Ore State U Corvallis OR

BOUCOT, KATHARINE ROSENBAUM (Mrs. Samuel Booth Sturgis), physician; b. Phila., Sept. 6, 1903; d. Morris and Hannah (Rottenberg) Rosenblaum; student U. Pa., 1921-22, Pa. State Coll., 1934-35; M.D., Woman's Med. Coll. Pa., 1942, Dr. Med. Sci., 1969; M.P.H., Johns Hopkins Sch. Hygiene and Pub. Health, 1954; D.H.L., Keuka Coll., 1960; D.Sc. (hon.), Beaver Coll., 1967; m. Joseph Ronald Boucct (dec.); children—Arthur James, Nancy George (Mrs. Milton Curtis Cummings, Jr.); m. 2d, Samuel Booth Sturgis, Nov. 18, 1964. Intern, Hosp. Woman's Med. Coll. Pa., 1942-43; resident chest diseases Herman Kiefer Hosp., Detroit, 1944; vis. chief div. chronic chest diseases Phila. Gen. Hosp., 1952-56, cons. div., 1959-66; cons. VA Hosp., Phila., 1953-66, Landis State Hosp., Phila., 1963-66; dir. chest x-rays surveys Phila. Tb. and Health Assn., 1945-52; dir. municipal Phila. chest x-rays surveys, 1947-68; asso. internal medicine Grad. Sch. Medicine U. Pa., 1951-63; prof. and chmn. preventive medicine Woman's Med. Coll. Pa., Phila., 1952-68, emeritus, 1968—, clin. prof. medicine, 1952-68. Bd. dirs. Pa. Tb and Research Devel. Soc., Phila. div. Am. Cancer Soc., William B. Lake Found., Moore Coll. Art. Hon. trustee Beaver Coll. Recipient Blackwell citation Public Health Control Tb, 1956; distinguished service to humanity award Albert Einstein Med. Center Woman's Aux., 1967; named Distinguished Dau. of Pa., 1964; recipient Phila. Gimbel award, 1968; Trudeau medal 1969; Pa. State Woman of Yr., 1967. Fellow Am. Coll. Preventive Medicine (pres. 1969-70), Am. Pub. Health Assn., Coll. Physicians Phila. (v.p. 1969—), A.C.P.; mem. A.M.A., Am. Thoracic Soc. (hon. mem., past pres. Eastern sect., v.p. 1960), Am. Epidemiol. Soc., Am. Acad. Occupational Medicine, Am. Med. Women's Assn. (hon.), Laennec Soc. Phila. (past pres.), Assn. Tchrs. Preventive Medicine, Pa. (ho. of dels.), Phila. County (pres. 1968) med. socs., Pa. Pub. Health Assn. (exec. com. 1963, spl. citation 1963), Woman's Med. Coll. Alumnae Assn. (past pres.; alumnae achievement award 1970), Phila. Art Alliance, Alpha Omega Alpha. Episcopalian. Clubs: Cosmopolitan; Medical Women (Phila.). Chief editor A.M.A. Archives Environmental Health, 1960-71. Contbr. articles profl. jours. Home: 349 Wister Rd Wynnewood PA 19096

BOUDART, MICHEL, educator; b. Belgium, June 18, 1924; s. Francois and Marguerite (Swolfs) B.; B.S., U. Louvain (Belgium), 1944, M.S., 1947; Ph.D., Princeton, 1950; m. Marina D'Haese, Dec. 27, 1948; children—Mark, Baudouin, Iris, Philip. Came to U.S., 1947, naturalized, 1957. Research asso. James Forrestal Research Center, Princeton, 1950-53; mem. faculty Princeton, 1954-61; prof. chem. engring. U. Cal. at Berkeley, 1961-64; prof. chem. engring. and chemistry Stanford, 1964—. Cons. to industry, 1955—; Humble Oil Co. lectr., 1958; Am. Inst. Chem. Engrs. lectr., 1961; Sigma Xi nat. lectr., 1965. Chmn. Gordon Research Conf. Catalysis, 1962. Belgium-Am. Ednl. Found. fellow, 1948; Procter fellow, 1949. Recipient Curtis-McGraw research award Am. Soc. Engring. Edn., 1962. Mem. Am. Chem. Soc., Catalysis Soc. (dir.), Am. Inst. Chem. Engrs., Faraday Soc., Soc. Belge des Ingenieurs et Industriels, A.A.A.S., Am. Assn. U. Profs. Author: Kinetics of Chemical Processes, 1968. Mem. adv. editorial bd. Jour. Catalysis, 1964—, Internat. Chem. Engring., 1964—, Advances in Catalysis, 1968—, Catalysis Review, 1968—, Annual Review of Materials Sci., 1969—. Home: 15 Peak Lane Portola Valley CA 94026 Office: Dept Chem Engring Stanford Univ Stanford CA 94305

BOUDEMAN, ROBERT MEIER, pharm. co. exec.; b. Kalamazoo, June 21, 1917; s. Dallas, Jr. and Freda (Meier) B.; B.A., Kalamazoo Coll., 1939; m. Carol Gilmore, June 14, 1938; children—Sherwood M., Martha (Mrs. Thomas Vander Molen), Carol (Mrs. Donald Coggan), Mary Jane (dec.). With Upjohn Co., Kalamazoo, 1939- -, dir. internat. adminstrn., internat. controller, v.p., exec. v.p., 1966, now pres., dir.; pres., Upjohn Internat. Inc., 1962-68, dir., 1968—; dir. 1st Nat. Bank and Trust Co., Kalamazoo. Trustee Kalamazoo Coll. Served to lt. (j.g.) USNR, 1943-45. Mem. Pharm. Mfg. Assn., Gull Lake Star Fleet. Clubs: Gull Lake Country (pres., dir.) (Richland, Mich.); Park (Kalamazoo). Home: 5382 Sheffield Lane Hickory Corners MI 49060 Office: Upjohn Co 7000 Portage Rd Kalamazoo MI 49001

BOUDREAU, HENRY CLEMENT, fgn. service officer; b. Waterville, Me., Oct. 21, 1918; s. Henry Peter and Frances Alberta (Daniels) B.; B.A. in Econs., U. Me., 1948; student Nat. War Coll., Washington, 1965-66; m. Betty Jane Furey, Nov. 18, 1945; children—Paul Edward, Joan Ellen. With Dept. Army, 1940-42, 46; with Dept. State, 1949—, economist, 1949-50, personnel officer, 1950-52, orgn. and mgmt. budget officer, 1953-56; 1st sec., consul Am. embassy, Norway, 1956-59; 1st sec., consul, Warsaw, Poland, 1959-62; exec. dir. Office Sec. State, 1966-69; counselor embassy, Rome, Italy, 1969—. Served to maj. USAAF, 1942-46. Decorated D.F.C., 4 Air medals. Mem. Am. Fgn. Service Assn., Sigma Alpha Epsilon. Office: Am Embassy Rome Italy

BOUDREAUX, PHILIP HENRY, Jr., rail transp. co. exec.; b. New Orleans, July 21, 1924; s. Philip Henry and Bertha (LaBauve) B.; B.B.A., U. Houston, 1953; postgrad. Tex. A. and M. U., 1965; m. Leah Marie Wedelich, May 3, 1947; children—Ann Marie, Janet Marie, Karen Marie, Philip Henry III. With S.P. Co., 1942-67; supr. field data control So. Pacific Transp. Co., Houston, 1967—. Chmn. So. Pacific United Fund Campaign, 1961-62. Served with USAAF, 1943-45; ETO. Recipient Key award Houston Jr. C. of C., 1955, 56. Ky. Col. Mem. Assn. ICC Practitioners (pres.), Houston C. of C. (chmn. park and recreation sub-com. 1969). Republican. Roman Catholic. K.C. Home: 2119 Persa St Houston TX 77019 Office: 913 Franklin St Houston TX 77001

BOUDREAUX, WARREN LOUIS, bishop; b. Berwick, La., Jan. 25, 1918; s. Alphonse Louis and Loretta Marie (Senac) B.; student St. Joseph's Sem., Benedict, La., 1931-36; student Notre Dame Sem., New Orleans, 1937, 42, LL.D., 1963; student Grand Sem. de St. Sulpice, Paris, France, 1938-39; J.C.D., Catholic U. Am. 1946; D.D. (hon.), Pope John XXIII, 1962. Ordained priest Roman Cath. Ch., 1962, apptd. aux. bishop Diocese Lafayette (La.), 1962; asst. pastor, Crowley, La., 1942-43; vice chancellor Diocese Lafayette (La.), 1946-54, officialis, 1949-54; pastor St. Peter's Ch., New Iberia, La., 1954—; vicar gen. Diocese Lafayette, 1957-71, also diocesan consultor; bishop of Beaumont, 1971—; dean New Iberia Deanery, 1954—. Vice pres. Southwest La. Registry Newspaper, 1957—. Mem. New Iberia Community Relations Council, 1963—, U.S. Bishops Liturgical Commn., 1966-70, U.S. Bishop's Louvain Coll. Commn., 1970—, U.S. Cath. Conf. adv. council, 1969—. Bd. dirs. Southwest Ednl. Devel. Lab., Iberia Paris Youth Home, Consolata Home for Aged, New Iberia. Pres. Archdiocesan Conf. Chancery Ofcls. Archdiocese New Orleans, 1950-51, bd. dirs., 1952-55. Address: 108 Saint Peter St New Iberia LA 70561

BOUGHTON, WALTER LEROY, educator; B.A., Brown U., 1941, M.A., M.F.A., Yale, 1951; M.A., (hon.), Amherst Coll., 1964; m. Georgia Aune; childrenJames White, Ross Byron, Andrew Wood. Now Stanley King prof. dramatic arts, also dir. Kirby Meml. Theatre, Amherst Coll. Mem. Nat. Theater Conf., Am. Edn. Theatre Assn., Am. Nat. Theater Assn., Am. Assn. U. Profs. Address: Dept Dramatic Arts Amherst College Amherst MA 01002

BOUHEBENT, ANDRE, advt. agy. exec.; b. Bordeaux, France, Feb. 3, 1913; s. F. Paul and Jeanne (Letertre) B.; A.M.P., Harvard, 1961; m. Maire-Jeanne Biguerie, Jan. 18, 1936. 1 dau., Annie (Mr. Philippe Marquezy). Pres., gen. mgr. Provente-Monfort, Norman, Craig & Kummel, Clichy, France. Office: 98 Blvd Victor Hugo 92 Clichy France*

BOUKER, ALBERT RALPH, Jr. mfg. exec.; b. Lima, O., Apr. 1, 1932; B.S., U. San Francisco, 1954; M.S., Stanford University, 1956; m. Rosemarie Lois Brown, May 15, 1955; 1 son, Anthony Robinson. Sales rep. Ames-Brockton Fabricated Products, Akron, O., 1956-58, sales mgr. Coshocton, Ohio, 1959-61, gen. manager plant, 1961-68, v.p. sales, 1968--. Instr. bus. Coshocton Jr. College, 1968-69. Named Man of Year, Coshocton Junior Chamber of Commerce, 1968. Mem. Coshocton C. of C. (vice president 1967-68, pres. 1969-70), English Speaking Union, Coshocton Sertoma Club, Nat. Assn. Mfrs., Sales Executives Institute, Phi Beta Kappa, Sigma Chi, Phi Mu. Democrat. Mem. Christian Ch. (lay leader). Mason (32, Shriner). Clubs: Coshocton Country, Coshocton City, Running Deer Country. Home: 2d Av Coshocton OH Office: 3d Av Coshocton OH

BOUKER, JOHN GRISWOLD, former marine officer; b. Greenfield, Mass., July 27, 1914; s. Gilbert Wiley and Anna (Griswold) B.; grad. Deerfield Acad., 1932; A.B., Dartmouth, 1936; postgrad. Nat. War Coll., 1959; m. Jane Gehring, May 27, 1938; children—Ann Chamberlain (Mrs. Frederick L. Webber), Peter Gehring. Underwriter, Liberty Mut. Ins. Co., 1936-39; commd. 2d lt. USMC, 1941, advanced through grades to maj. gen., 1966; prof. naval sci. Cornell U., Ithaca, N.Y., 1953-56; sta. Okinawa, Japan, 1956-57; mem. joint staff Joint Chiefs Staff, 1959-61; comdg. gen. 4th Marine Expeditionary Brigade, Santa Domingo, 1965; dep. comdg. gen. Fleet Marine Force Pacific, Okinawa, 1967-68, ret., 1968. Decorated Legion of Merit with oak leaf cluster, Bronze Star medal. Mem. Marine Corps Assn., Naval Inst. Episcopalian. Home: River Rd Bernardston MA 01337

BOULANGER, NADIA JULIETTE, tchr. composition, condr., lectr.; b. Paris, Sept. 16, 1887; d. Ernest and Raissa (Princess Mychetsky) Boulanger; studied Paris Nat. Conservatory; hon. Mus.D., Russell Sage Coll., Brown U., Washington Coll. Music, Harvard, Brown U., U. So. Ill. and Smith Coll. Formerly head of theory dept. Ecole Normale de Musique, Paris; came to U.S. in 1924, 35, 40, 58; was faculty mem. Longy Sch. Music, Cambridge, Mass.; instr. composition Peabody Conservatory; now dir., hon. prof. Nat. Conservatory Music, Paris; prof., dir. Am. Conservatory in Fontainebleau; formerly lectr. Radcliffe Coll., Wellesley Coll. Guest condr. Boston Symphony Orch., Royal Philharmonic, London, N.Y. Philharmonic, Phila. Orch., Washington Symphony. Decorated Officier Legion of Honor (France); Officer Arts et Letters (France); Comdr. Polonia restituta (Poland); Officer St. Charles (Monaco); Henry Hadley medal, 1949. Mem. Soc. of Authors, Composers and Editors of Music (France). Roman Catholic. Composer of songs, cello pieces, an opera in collaboration with Raoul Pugno (La Ville Morte). Contbr. to musical mags. Recordings for La va'x de son Maitu, Decca. Address: 36 rue Ballu Paris IX France also 122 Bay State Rd Boston MA 02215

BOULBY, MARK, educator; b. Leeds, Eng., Mar. 7, 1929; s. Mark and Jane (Morgan) B.; B.A. Jesus Coll., Cambridge, 1949, M.A. 1953; Ph.D. U. Leeds, 1952; m. Jean Margaret Saxby, Mar. 31, 1956; children—Marion Jane, Sarah Margaret. Lectr. German, U. Leeds (Eng.), 1955-61, U. Hull (Eng.) 1961- 63; vis. lectr. Coll. City N.Y., 1963-64; asso. prof. Case Western Res. U., 1964-70, prof. 1967-70, also dept. chmn.; prof. U. B.C., 1970—. Served with RAF, 1951-54. Mem. Modern Lang. Assn. Am. Author: Hermann Hesse: His Mind and Art, 1967. Editor texts, contbr. articles on lit. to profl. jours. Home: 4355 W 15th Av Vancouver 8 British Columbia Canada

BOULDIN, WALTER, lawyer, former utility exec.; b. Scottsboro, Ala., July 30, 1905; s. Virgil and Irene (Jacoway) B.; A.B., U. Ala., 1925, LL.D., 1966; LL.B., Harvard, 1928; LL.D., Samford U., 1967; m. Elizabeth Donovan, Aug. 27, 1932 (dec. Nov. 1967); 1 son, Walter Virgil. Admitted to Ala. bar, 1928, practiced in Birmingham; mem. Martin, Turner, Blakey & Bouldin and predecessor firm, 1935-52; financial v.p. Ala. Power Co., Birmingham, 1952-54, exec. v.p., 1955-57, pres., 1957-69, chmn. bd., 1969-70, ret., 1970; pres. Southeastern Electric Exchange, 1968-69; former v.p., dir. So. Electric Generating Co. Mem. U.S. Indsl. Payroll Savs. Com. Treasury Dept., 1963-64. Chmn. bd. trustees, mem. exec. com. So. Research Inst.; vice chmn. adv. bd. Salvation Army; mem. U.S. com. Internat. Edison Birthday Celebration; trustee Gorgas Scholarship Found., 1965-66, Tuskegee Inst., 1966-68, Central Ala. Regional Sci. Fair, Thomas Alva Edison Found., Ala. man of bd. Birmingham Centennial Corp.; bd. dirs. Festival Arts, 1965-67; dir., past pres. Anti-Tb Assn. Jefferson Co.; Ala. chmn. Crusade for Freedom, 1960. Mem. Edison Electric Inst. (pres. 1963-64, dir. 1961-67), Am. Ordnance Assn. (dir.), Am., Ala., Birmingham bar assns., Ala. (dir., pres. 1967—), Birmingham (past pres., dir.) Acad. Sci., Freedom Ednl. Found., Newcomen Soc. N. Am., Ala. Hist. Soc., Nat. Assn Electric Cos. (dir., mem. exec. com.), Phi Beta Kappa, Kappa Alpha, Beta Gamma Sigma. Democrat. Presbyn. Clubs: Rotary (dir. 1965-67) (Birmingham); Mountain Brook (Ala.); The Club, Downtown Relay House; Metropolitan (Washington). Home: 2611 Watkins Road Birmingham AL 35223

BOULDING, KENNETH EWART, coll. prof., economist; b. Liverpool, Eng., Jan. 18, 1910; s. William Couchman and Elizabeth Ann (Rowe) B.; scholar New Coll., Oxford, 1928-32, B.A. first class honors, Oxford, 1931, M.A., 1939; Commonwealth fellow U. Chgo., 1932-34; m. Elise Biorn-Hansen, Aug. 31, 1941; children—Russell, Mark, Christine, Philip, William. Came U.S., 1937; naturalized, 1948. Asst. U. Edinburgh (Scotland), 1934-37; instr. Colgate U., 1937-41; economist League of Nations Econ. and Financial Sect., 1941-42; prof. Fisk U., 1942-43; asso. prof. Ia. State Coll., 1943-46; Angus prof. polit. economy McGill U., 1946-47; prof. Ia. State Coll., 1947-49; prof. econs. U. Mich., 1949-68, research dir. Center for Research in Conflict Resolution, 1964-66; vis. prof. U. Colo., Boulder, 1967-68, prof., 1968—, dir. program on gen. social and econ. dynamics Inst. Behavioral Sci., 1967—. Vis. prof. Univ. Coll. W. I., Kingston, Jamaica, 1959-60; Danforth vis. prof. Internat. Christian U., Tokyo, 1963-64. Recipient John B. Clark medal Am. Econ. Assn., 1949, prize for distinguished scholarship in humanities Am. Council Learned Socs., 1962. Fellow Center Advanced Study Behavior Scis., Palo Alto, Cal., 1954-55. Fellow Am. Acad. Arts and Sciences, International Institute of Arts and Letters, American Philosophical Society, World Acad. Art and Sci.; mem. American Economic Association (pres. 1968), Soc. Gen. Systems Research (pres. 1955-58), Internat. Studies Assn. (v.p. 1969-70), Peace Research Soc. Internat. (pres. 1969-70), Assn. Study Grants Economy (pres. 1969—. Mem. Society Friends. Author: (books) Economic Analysis, 1941, 4th rev. edit., 1965; Economics of Peace, 1945; There Is a Spirit (The Naylor Sonnets), 1945; A Reconstruction of Economics, 1950; The Organizational Revolution, 1953; The Image, 1956; Principles of Economic Policy, 1958; The Skills of the Economist, 1958; Conflict and Defense, 1962; (with W.A. Spivey) Linear Programming and the Theory of the Firm, 1960; (with Emile Benoit) Disarmament and the Economy, 1963; The Meaning of the Twentieth Century, 1964; The Impact of the Social Sciences, 1966; Beyond Economics, 1968; Economics as a Science, 1970; A Primer on Social Dynamics, 1970; The Prospering of Truth. (Swarthmore Lecture), 1970; Peace and the War Industry, 1970; Collected Papers, Vols. 1-5, 1971. Editor: (with Tapan Mulcerjee) Economic Imperialism, 1971. Home: 890 Willowbrook Road Boulder CO 80302

BOULENGER, ALBERT LEON, hosp. exec.; b. Maumee, O., May 12, 1924; s. Albert and Helen (Shiperd) B.; B.S., Bowling Green State U., 1949; M.S., Washington U., St. Louis, 1953; m. Joyce E. Terrill, July 10, 1948; children—Suzanne, Joy Annette, Albert Leon. Adminstrv. resident Univ. Hosp., Birmingham, Ala., 1952-53, asst. adminstr., 1953-54; adminstr. Good Samaritan Hosp., Vincennes, Ind., 1954-62; asso. dir. Barnes Hosp., St. Louis, 1962-64; dir. hosps. Hosp. and Welfare Bd., Hillsborough County Div. Hosps., Tampa, Fla., 1964; now exec. v.p. Swedish-Am. Hosp., Rockford, Ill. Lectr. Washington U. Program in Hosp. Adminstrn., 1958—; adviser St. Louis and Hillsborough Jr. Coll. Mem. Greater Tampa Citizens Safety Council, Community Coordinating Council, 1965. Served with M.C., AUS, 1942-45: ETO. Mem. Am. Hosp. Assn., Am. Coll. Hosp. Adminstrs., Greater Tampa C. of C. Republican. Methodist. Rotarian. Home: 2081 Jonquil Pl Rockford IL

BOULEZ, PIERRE, composer, condr.; b. Montbrison, nr. Clermont-Ferrand, France, Mar. 26, 1925; s. Leon and Antoinette (Calabre) B.; pupil Olivier Messiaen at Paris Conservatory (recipient 1st prize 1945). Apptd. dir. music Jean-Louis Barrault's Theater Co., 1948; toured Orient, Europe, North and South Am. with Barrault; now tchr., lectr., condr. and pianist; musical adviser, prin. guest condr. Cleve. Symphony Orch., 1970-71; musical dir. N.Y. Philharmonic Orch., 1971—; conducting appearances include Edinburgh Festival, 1965, Bayreuth Festival, 1966. Compositions include: Sonatina for flute and piano, 1946; Symphonic concertante for piano and orchestra, 1950; Le Soleil des eaux for voice and orchestra, 1948; Structures, 1952; Le Marteau sans maitre, 1955; Deux improvisations sur Mallarme, 1957 (performed Hamburg, 1958); Polyphony (performed Aix en Provence Festival 1958); Doubles for orchestra, 1958; Tombeau (on text of Mallarmé), 1959; Pli selon pli, 1960; Structures II, 1962; Eclat, 1964; Domaines, 1968; Multiples, 1970; Cummings 1st der Dichter,, 1970. Author musical criticism and analysis, including Penser la Musique d'Anjourd'hui. Address: 9 Kapuzinerstrasse Baden-Baden Germany

BOULGER, FRANCIS WILLIAM, metall. engr.; b. Mpls., June 19, 1913; s. Francis J. and Mary (Armstrong) B.; Metall. Engr., U. Minn., 1934; M.S. (Battelle fellow), Ohio State U., 1937. With A.P., 1929-34; engr. Minn. Dept. Hwys., 1935-36; metallurgist Republic Steel Corp., Cleve., 1937; research metallurgist Battelle Meml. Inst., Columbus, O., 1938-45, div. chief, 1945-67, sr. tech. adviser, 1967—; cons. USAF, Materials Adv. Bd., OECD. Named Man of Year, Columbus Tech. Council, 1966. Gold medalist Soc. Mfg. Engrs., 1967. Fellow Am. Soc. Metals; mem. Am. Soc. M.E., Am. Inst. Mining, Metall. and Petroleum Engrs. (Hunt medal 1955), Soc. Mfg. Engrs., Internat. Inst. for Prodn. Research, Sigma Xi. Republican. Roman Catholic. Author: (with others) Forging Materials and Practices, 1968; Tri- Lingual Dictionary of Production Engineering, 1969; also articles. Home: 1816 Harwich Rd Columbus OH 43221 Office: 505 King Av Columbus OH 43201

BOULGER, JAMES DENIS, educator; b. N. Adams, Mass., June 9, 1931; s. James Francis and Marguerite (O'Brian) B.; A.B., Coll. Holy Cross, 1953; Ph.D., Yale, 1957; M.A. (hon.), Brown U., 1964; m. Jean Marie Stumpf, July 13, 1957; children—Ellen, James, John, Geoffrey. Instr. English, Yale, 1957-61; fellow St. Catharine's, Cambridge, 1961-62; asst. prof. Yale, 1962-64; asso. prof. English, Brown U., 1964-69, prof., 1969—. Mem. Modern Lang. Assn. Am. Author: Coleridge as Religious Thinker, 1961. Editor: Rime of Ancient Mariner, 1969; various essays on lit., 1961—. Home: 81 Blackstone Blvd Providence RI 02906

BOULLE, PIERRE FRANCOIS, author; b. Avignon, France, Feb. 20, 1912; s. Eugene and Therese (Seguin) B.; Licencié ès Sciences, Ecole Superieure d'Electricité , 1932, Ingenieur, 1933. Elec. engr. Clermont-Ferrand, 1933-35; on rubber plantation, Malaya, 1935-48; writer, 1948—. Recipient Acad. award for best screen play, 1957. Author: William Conrad (Not the Glory), 1950; Le Sacrilége Malais, 1951; The Bridge Over the River Kwai, 1952; Contes de l'Absurde, 1953; La Face (Face of a hero), 1953; Le Bourreau, 1954; L'épreuve des hommes blancs (The Test), 1955; E-MC 2, 1957; Les Voies du Salut (The Other Side of the Coin), 1958; Noble Profession, Sacrilege in Malaya, 1960; Planet of the Apes, 1963; Garden on the Moon, 1964; Time Out of Mind, 1966; My Own River Kwai,, 1967; others. Home: 18 rue Duret Paris 16e France Office: care Vanguard Press Inc 424 Madison Av New York City NY 10017

BOULLIOUN, ERNEST HERMAN, Jr., aerospace co. exec.; b. Little Rock, Nov. 3, 1918; s. Ernest Herman and Georgie (Little) B.; student Subiaco (Ark.) Coll., 1935-36; m. Jane Marie Hoefer, July 4, 1941; children—Jeffrey Ernest, Thomas Arthur, Susan Jane. With Boeing Co., Seattle, 1940—, asst. missile br. mgr. aero-space div., 1962-64, v.p., missile br. mgr. aero-space div., 1964-65, v.p., gen. mgr. comml. airplane div., 1965-67, v.p., gen. mgr., 1967—, group v.p. Comml. Airplane Group, 1969—. Home: 7223 West Mercer Way Mercer Island WA 98040 Office: 7755 E Marginal Way Seattle WA 98124

BOULOS, SAMI IBRAHIM, educator; b. Cairo, UAR, Feb. 27, 1922; s. Ibrahim and Ester (Ibrahim) B.; B.S., U. Cairo, 1941; H.D.Ed., U. Ein-Shams, 1943, M.A., 1957; Ed.D., U. Fla., 1960; m. Jeanne Makari Salib, July 31, 1949; children—Kamal, Fouad, Michael. Came to U.S., 1958, naturalized, 1968. Sci. tchr. campus sch. U. Ein Shams, Cairo, 1943-47; tchr. biology, gen. sci. pub. secondary schs., Cairo, 1947-51; tchr. sci. methods, ednl. psychology, tchr. tng. insts., UAR, 1951-55; sci. and math. cons. State U. of N.Y. Coll. of New Paltz, 1959-62, prof. sci., math., evaluation, 1962-69, prof. sci. edn., chmn. dept. edn., 1969—. Field reader U.S. Office Edn., 1966—; sci. cons. pub. sch. systems; speaker before civic and ednl. groups. Recipient Point 4 award AID, 1955-56. Mem. State U. Fedn. Tchrs. (pres.), Nat. Sci. Tchrs. Assn., Nat. Assn. Research in Sci. Teaching, Am. Fedn. Tchrs., Higher Edn. Assn., Kappa Delta Pi, Phi Delta Kappa. Author: Biology for the Senior High Schools, 1955; also articles. Home: B13 Duzine Rd New Paltz NY 12561

BOULT, SIR ADRIAN CEDRIC, symphony conductor; b. Chester, Eng., Apr. 8, 1889; s. Cedric Randal and Katharine Florence (Barman) B.; Mus.D., Christ Church, Oxford, 1912; M.A. Royal Conservatory, Leipzig, 1913; LL.D., Birmingham U., 1930; hon. Mus.D., U. Edinburgh, 1922, Cambridge U., 1953; m. Ann Mary Grace Bowles, July 1, 1933. Mem. musical staff Royal Opera, Covent Garden, London, 1914; mem. teaching staff, Royal Coll. Music, 1919-30, 62-68; dir. music Brit. Broadcasting Corp., 1930-42; chief conductor BBC Symphony Orch., till 1950, London Philharmonic Orch., 1950-57; condr. City of Birmingham Orch., 1924-30, 59- 60; guest condr. Royal Philharmonic Orch., Liverpool Philharmonic Soc., London Symphony, also symphonies in Vienna, Prague, Barcelona, Zurich, Budapest, Paris, New York, Boston, Sweden; pres. London Philharmonic Orch. Served War Office and Commission Internat. de Ravitaillement, 4 years, World War. Decorated Companion of Honor; recipient gold medal Harvard Glee Club, 1956. Fellow Royal Coll. of Music; hon. mem. Royal Acad. Music; hon. fellow Christ Church, Oxford U. Clubs: Athenaeum, (London). Author: The Technique of Conducting; thoughts on Conducting. Contbr. to musical jours. Office: 38 Wigmore Street London W 1 England

BOULTER, CEDRIC GORDON, archaeologist; b. Tryon, P.E.I., Can., May 9, 1912; s. James Wilfred and Charlotte Wright (Muirhead) B.; student Prince Wales Coll., 1927-30, Johns Hopkins, 1933-34, Am. Sch. Classical Studies, Athens, Greece, 1934-35; B.A., Acadia U., 1933; Ph.D., U. Cin., 1939; m. Elizabeth Neils, May 28, 1953; children—John, Edward. Came to U.S., 1933, naturalized, 1953. Staff mem. U. Cin. excavations at Troy, 1937; instr. classics U. Cin., 1939-45, asst. prof., 1945-52, asso. prof., 1952-54, prof., 1954—, fellow Grad. Sch., 1965—. Ann. prof. Am. Sch. Classical Studies, Athens, 1965-66. Served from sub-lt. to lt. comdr., Royal Canadian Navy, 1942-45. Mem. Archaeol. Inst. Am. (gen. sec. 1955-57, pres. Cin. soc. 1958-70), Am. Philol. Assn., Soc. Promotion Hellenic Studies. Club: University (Cin.). Contbr. articles archaeol. publs. Home: 1 Rawson Woods Circle Cincinnati OH 45220

BOULTING, ROY, film producer-director; b. Nov. 21, 1913; s. Arthur and Rose (Bennett) B.; ed. Reading Sch. Formed ind. film prodn. co. with brother, 1937; now producer-dir. Charter Films Prodns. Ltd.; dir. Brit. Lion Films Ltd.; producer Brighton Rock, 1947; Seven Days to Noon, 1950; Private's Progress, 1955; Lucky Jim (Edinburgh Festival), 1957; I'm All Right, Jack, 1959; Heavens Above, 1962; dir. Pastor Hall, 1939; Thunder Rock, 1942; Fame is the Spur, 1947; The Guinea Pig, 1948; High Treason, 1951; Singlehanded, 1952; Seagulls of Sorrento, 1953; Crest of the Wave, 1953; Josephine and Men, 1955; Run for the Sun, 1955; Brothers-in-Law, 1956; Happy is the Bride, 1958; Carlton-Browne of the F.O., 1958-59; I'm All Right, Jack, 1959; The Risk, 1960; The French Mistress, 1960; Suspect, 1960; The Family Way, 1966; Twisted Nerve, 1968; There's a Girl in My Soup, 1970; films include Desert Victory; Burma Victory. Served with RAC, 1939-45. Home: Broadwick House Broadwick St London W1 England Office: Charter Films Prodns Ltd Broadwick House Broadwick St London W1 England

BOULTON, CHARLES VINCENT, coll. ofcl.; b. Ogdensburg, N.Y., May 25, 1918; s. Harold S. and Pearl G. (Knapp) B.; B.S.C., Northwestern U., 1939; m. Dorothy Falk, May 16, 1942; childrenCatherine, Ann, Christopher, Mary (dec.), John, Stephen. With IBM, 1939-65, successively student sales rep., mgr. Chgo. service bur., asst. to Chgo. br. mgr., mgr. Pueblo (Colo.) office, mgr. methods, N.Y.C., dir. budgets, controller, 1939-55, treas., N.Y.C., 1955-61, asst. treas., 1961-65; asst. to pres., asst. treas. Stevens Inst. Tech., Hoboken, N.J., 1966—. Served from pvt. to lt. col., AUS, 1941-45. Mem. Am. Mgmt. Assn., Financial Execs. Inst., Phi Kappa Sigma. Episcopalian. Clubs: Ridgewood (N.J.) Country; University (N.Y.C.). Home: 6 Stratford Lane Ho-Ho-Kus, NJ 07423. Office: Castle Point Sta Hoboken NJ 07030

BOULTON, LAURA CRAYTOR, musicologist, lectr.; b. Conneaut, O.; d. Herbert Orleans and Emma Lucy (Nottingham) Craytor; student Western Res. U.; A.B., Denison U., L.H.D., 1965; postgrad. U. Chgo., Chgo. Mus. Coll., The Sorbonne, U. London; m. W. Rudyerd Boulton (div. 1941). Ethnologist, musicologist Straus Central African expdn. for Am. Mus. Natural History, 1929, South African expdn. for Carnegie Mus., 1930, Pulitzer Angola expdn., 1931, Straus West African expdn. for Field Mus., 1934, Mandel West Indies expdn., 1938; leader Crane Mexican expdn. for Mus. Modern Art, 1940, Southwest Indian expdn. for Dept. Interior, 1940; dir. coast-to-coast film and rec. project on peoples of Can. for Canadian govt., Nat. Film Bd., 1941-43, including Canadian N.W. expdn., Eastern Arctic expdn., 1942; Alaskan expdn. for Dept. Interior, 1946; Haiti expdn., African expdn. for U. Cal., 1947-48, Asiatic expdn. Am. Mus. Natural History and Buffalo Mus. Sci., 1949-50; European Folk Music Survey including Balkans and UNESCO, 1951; rec. projects as guest of govts. Spain, Portugal, Greece, Turkey, 1952-54, African-Asian expdn., 1956; expdn. to Balkans and Eastern Europe, 1957-58, Near East, 1959, South and Central Am., 1960, Harvard U.-Dumbarton Oaks Byzantine Project, 1960- -; lectr. primitive music U. Chgo., 1931-33, music faculty U. Cal., 1946- 49; dir. Laura Boulton Collection traditional and liturgical music Sch. Internat. Affairs, Columbia U., also dir. research project on world music, 1962—; asst. dir. Center for Studies in Ethnomusicology, 1965—; music dept. Columbia; prod., dir. documentary films nat. groups, primitive tribes; broadcaster radio and TV; del. numerous nat. and internat. confs.; lectr. U.S. and abroad; mem. Com. African Music, UNESCO, Com. for Comparative Music, Berlin, Com. for Liturgical Music, Rome. Winifred Cullis Lectr. Fellowship, English Univs., 1965. Recipient grants for research Am. Council Learned Socs., Am. Philos. Soc., Carnegie Corp., Harvard U.-Dumbarton Oaks. Fellow Am. Geog. Soc., Royal Geog. Soc.; mem. Internat. Inst. Comparative Musical Studies Berlin, Inst. Liturgical Music Rome, Asia Soc., Am. Anthrop. Assn., Am. Musicol. Soc., Inst. Indigenista Interamericano, Internat. Folk Music Council, Internat. Council Women, Soc. Ethnomusicology, Speakers Research Bur. UN, Phi Beta Kappa, Delta Omicron. Recorded and published albums with accompanying booklets: African Music-Rhythm in the Jungle, 1940; Indian Music of the Southwest, 194; Indian Music of Mexico, 1942; Songs and Dances of Yugoslavia, 1952; Songs and Dances of Switzerland, 1953; The Eskimos of Hudson Bay and Alaska, 1954; Songs and Dances of Turkey, 1955; Christmas Songs of Spain, 1955; Christmas Songs of Portugal, 1955; Ukrainian Christmas Songs, 1955; Indian Music of the Northwest, 1956; Ethnic Music of Yugoslavia, 1956; French Folk Songs, 1957. Author: The Laura Boulton Story, 1965. Contbr. to sci. and popular mags. Home: 1 East 66th St New York City NY 10021 Office: Music Dept Columbia U New York City NY 10027

BOULWARE, LEMUEL RICKETTS, ret. indsl. exec.; b. Springfield, Ky., June 3, 1895; s. Judson A. and Martha Price (Ricketts) B.; A.B., U. Wis., 1916; L.H.D., Center Coll., 1953, Carroll Coll., 1954; LL.D., Union Coll., 1957; ScD., Clarkson Coll., 1962; m. Norma Brannock, Dec. 28, 1935. Tchr. bus. adminstrn. U. Wis., 1916-17; tchr. Bklyn. night schs., 1919-20; comptroller E. W. Bliss Co., Hastings (Mich.) div., 1919; purchasing agt., factory mgr. H. B. Sherman Mfg. Co., Battle Creek, Mich., 1920-25; gen. sales mgr. Easy Washing Machine Corp., Syracuse, N.Y., 1925-35; v.p., gen. mgr. Carrier Corp., Syracuse, 1936-39, Celotex Corp., Chgo., 1940-42; asst. to chmn. WPB, 1942, dep. comptroller shipbuilding, 1942-43, operations vice chmn., 1943-44; mem. prodn. exec. com. and standardization of shipbuilding design com. of Combined Chiefs of Staff; with Gen. Electric Co. as marketing cons. and in charge affiliated mfg. cos., 1945; v.p., 1945-47, in charge employee, community and union relations, 1947-56, v.p. public and employee relations, 1956-59, v.p. cons. relations services, 1959-61. Served as capt., inf. U.S. Army 1917-19. Recipient Medal of Merit for War Service; Distinguished Am. Citizen award Harding Coll., 1963. Baptist. Clubs: Century (Syracuse); Triton (Can.); Santee (S.C.); Blind Brook (Purchase, N.Y.); Gulfstream Golf (Fla.); Gulfstream Bath and Tennis. Author: The Truth about Boularism: Trying To Do Right Voluntarily, 1969. Lectr., writer, cons. Home: 1115 Fifth Av New York City NY 10028 also 1045 S Ocean Blvd Delray Beach FL 33444

BOUMAN, HARRY DAAN, physician; b. Amsterdam, Netherlands, June 27, 1907; s. Zweitse Pieter and Riemke (Slaterus) B.; candidate deg. in physics U. Amsterdam, 1928, M.D., 1933; m. Elizabeth S. Loeks, June 15, 1940; 1 dau., Jeanne Marie. Came to U.S., 1931, naturalized, 1943. Research instr. Oberlin (O.) Coll., 1931-32; staff mem. Univ. Eye Clinic Amsterdam, research asso. physiology U. Amsterdam, 1932-35, 36- 39; asst. prof. psychology U. Rochester, 1941-44; asst. prof. phys. medicine Northwestern U., 1944-47; prof. phys. medicine U. Wis., 1947-64; prof., chmn. dept. phys. medicine and rehab. U. Cin. Coll. Medicine, 1965-68; physician VA, 1968-70, dir. phys. medicine rehab. service VA Central Office, Washington, 1971—. Stokvis Found. fellow physiology U. Paris, 1928; Rockefeller fellow Univ. Coll., London, Eng., 1935-36; research fellow physiology and orthopedics U. Rochester, 1940-41, orthopedics, 1941-44; research fellow physiology Washington U., 1940. Recipient Gold medal for original research in physiology U. Amsterdam, 1931. Fellow Am. Psychol. Assn., A.A.A.S.; mem. Am. Physiol. Soc., The Biophys. Soc., Audio Engring. Soc. Author papers med. and sci. jours. Editor Am. Jour. Phys. Medicine. Address: PO Box 219 Benjamin Franklin Station Pennsylvania at 12th St Washington DC 20044

BOUMEDIENNE, HOUARI, pres. of Algeria; b. 1927; ed. Islamic Inst., Constantine and Cairo. Former tchr., Guelma; promoted rebel activities Oran area, Algeria, 1955; comdr. of Wilaya, 1955-57; chief staff F.L.N., 1960-62, minister of def., Algeria, 1962—, 1st dep. premier, 1963-65; chmn. Revolutionary Council, 1965—; prime minister, 1965—, now also pres. Algeria. Address: Cabinet Building Algiers Algeria*

BOURAS, HARRY, artist; b. Rochester, N.Y., Feb. 13, 1931; s. Harry James and Alice (LaPriesse) B.; B.A., U. Rochester, 1951; postgrad. U. Chgo., 1955-56; m. Arlene Marie Aklin, Aug. 18, 1951; 1 dau., Lorraine Ann. Artist-in- residence U. Chgo., 1962-64, faculty, 1959—; artist-in-residence Columbia Coll., Chgo., 1964—, faculty, 1959—; faculty Northwestern U., 1965-67; weekly radio program Critic's Choice, 1965—; exhibited in numerous one-man shows in U.S., fgn. countries, 1956—; represented in permanent collections Mus. Modern Art, N.Y.C., Art Inst. Chgo., Rochester, N.Y., Tokyo; important sculpture works Chgo., Aspen, Detroit, N.Y., New Delhi, Tokyo. Bd. dirs. Creative Student Writers Found. Recipient Pauline Palmer award Chgo. Art Inst., 1962, Logan Gold medal for sculpture, 1964; Hokins Found. grantee, 1969; Guggenheim Found. fellow, 1971-72. Clubs: Cliff Dwellers, Arts of Chgo. Contbr. articles on art to publs. Home: 850 Castlewood Terrace Chicago IL 60640 Office: 540 Lake Shore Dr Chicago IL 60611

BOURCIER, CLAUDE LOUIS, coll. dean; b. Paris, France, July 15, 1910; s. Albert Leon and Jeanne (Roig) B.; ed. Lycées de Bordeaux and Louis-le-Grand, Paris, 1928-32; fellow Ecole Normale Supérieure, Paris, 1932-35, Agrégation des lettres, 1935; m. Almira Darrow Coulter, June 24, 1942; childrenClaudia-Anne Marie, Gerard Pierre-Michel. Came to U.S., 1935. Instr., U. Me., 1935- 36; mem. faculty Middlebury (Vt.) Coll., 1937—, prof. French, 1946—, chmn. dept., 1963-69, dean French Sch., 1947—, dir. Grad. Sch. French, France, 1949-50, 57-58, 62-63, 66-67, 69—; vis. lectr. Inst. Sci. Franco-Canadien, U. Montreal, 1945; acad. cons. Acad. Year Abroad, Paris, 1962-63, mem. adv. council, 1963—; lectr. Alliance Francaise groups, others, Sec., bd. dirs. Vt. Council World Affairs, 1953-57; chmn. Vt. br., v.p. New Eng. council United World Federalists, 1951-57. Mem. bd. Spring Lake Ranch, Cuttingsville, Vt., 1952—. Served to 2d lt. French Army, 1936-37. Decorated chevalier Legion of Honor, Palmes Académi#83ques. Mem. Am. Assn. Tchrs. French, Modern Lang. Assn. Am., Am. Am. Assn. U. Profs. Author: (with M. Raymond) Elementary French Series, 1960- -. Contbr. Columbia Dictionary Modern European Literature. Home: 11 Adirondack View Middlebury VT 05753 Office: Reid Hall 4 Rue de Chevreuse Paris 6 France

BOURDIER, JAMES AARON, photographer; b. Opelousas, La., Feb. 28, 1929; s. James Merrick and Lillian (Jacobs) B.; B.A. in Journalism, La. State U., 1950; m. Charlotte Mozelle Fuller, Dec. 6, 1964; children by previous marriage—Alica Angel, Kayne Lamar. Photographer, Opelousas Daily World, 1955-61; mem. staff A.P., 1961—, now photographer Miami (Fla.) bur. Served as pilot USAF, 1950-55. Recipient 1st place pictures of year Nat. Press Photographers Assn., World Book and U. Mo., 1966; George Polk Meml. award, 1966; citation Overseas Press Club, 1966; Mike Ackerman award Miami Press Photographers Assn., 1966; Top A.P. Photog. award A.P. Mng. Editors Assn., 1966. Mem. Sigma Delta Chi, Delta Kappa Epsilon. Home: 1814 SW 100th Av Miami FL 33165 Office: 2125 Biscayne Blvd Miami FL 33137

BOURDO, ERIC ALBERT, Jr., forester, educator; b. Muskegon, Mich., Jan. 15, 1917; s. Eric Albert and Rose (Beckman) B.; B.S., Mich. Coll. Mining and Tech., 1943; A.M., U. Mich., 1951, Ph.D., 1955; m. Charline Vivian Leady, Mar. 22, 1942; children—Eric Albert III, Laura Lynn, Michael Forest. Rubber compounder Goodyear Tire & Rubber Co., Akron, O., 1943-46; forester Pomeroy & McGowan Co., Wilmar, Ark., 1946; instr. Mich. Coll. Mining & Tech., 1947-51, asst. prof., 1951-55, asso. prof., 1955-58, prof., 1958—; dir. Ford Forestry Center, Mich. Technol. U., Houghton, 1955-68, dean Sch. Forestry and Wood Product, 1968—, prof. forestry, 1958—. Mem. Soc. Am. Foresters, Ecol. Soc. Am., Am. Soc. Agronomy, A.A.A.S., Mich., Wis. acads. sci., Wilson Ornithol. Soc., Sigma Xi, Delta Sigma Phi. Elk, Lion. Contbr. articles profl. jours. Home: Route 2 L'Anse MI 49946 Office: Mich Technol U Houghton MI 49931

BOURDON, HAROLD LEO, motor mfg. exec.; b. South Bend, Ind., Feb. 27, 1906; s. Leo and Eva (Richards) B.; m. Marjorie A. Clark, Sept. 15, 1928; children—Jack Alan, Janet (Mrs. Marion L. Stanforth), Richard, Mary Jane (Mrs. Wayne Parks). With Outboard Marine Corp., 1925—, with Johnson Motors div., successively chief accountant Gale Products div., office mgr., 1925-49, div. mgr. Gale Products, 1949—, v.p. Outboard Marine Corp., 1952—; pres. Galesburg Realty Corp. (financing Galesburg Airport), OMC Distbrs., Inc.; dir. Bank of Galesburg. Home: 375 Fair Acres Dr Galesburg IL 61401 Office: Gale Products Div Outboard Marine Corp Galesburg IL 61401

BOURGAIZE, ROBERT G., banker; sr. v.p., dir. Peoples Nat. Bank Washington; pres. Central Bank, N.A., Tacoma, University Pl. Water Co., Central Capital Corp. Treas. Pierce County Heart Assn., Tacoma. Mem. Tacoma Clearing House Assn. (pres.), English Speaking Union (pres. Tacoma br., dir. on nat. bd.), India Soc. Seattle (pres., dir.). ‡

BOURGAULT, ROY FRANCIS, educator; b. Worcester, Mass., Feb. 25, 1920; s. Louis Joseph and Evelyn (Richardson) B.; B.S., Worcester Poly. Inst., 1942; M.S., Stevens Inst. Tech., 1953; m. Betty Mae Arp, Aug. 9, 1946; children—Robert Louis, Edward Norman, Susan Elizabeth, Richard Douglas. Indsl. engr. U.S. Steel Corp., 1942-43, 46-48, metallurgist, 1948-51; research asso. Stevens Inst. Tech., 1951-53; chief metallurgist Warner Hudnut, Inc., Livingston, N.J., 1953-55; mem. faculty Worcester Poly. Inst., 1955—, prof. mech. engring., 1967—; cons. in field, 1955—. Active local Boy Scouts Am., 1957—; moderator Worcester Assn. Congl. Chs., 1965-66. Served to 1st lt. USAAF, 1943-46. Recipient Silver Beaver award Boy Scouts Am., 1964; Good Citizenship medal S.A.R., 1965. Registered profl. engr., Mass. Mem. Am. Soc. Metals (past chpt. chmn.), Am. Inst. Mining, Metall. and Petroleum Engrs., Am. Soc. Engring. Edn., Sigma Xi, Pi Tau Sigma. Mem. United Ch. Christ. Address: 9 Einhorn Road Worcester MA 01609

BOURGEOIS, A. DONALD, lawyer; b. Chgo., May 12, 1929; s. Prescott A. and Mary Lou (Giles) B.; student Xavier U., New Orleans, 1946-48; LL.B., Loyola U., Chgo. 1951; m. Norma C. Ponquinette, Oct. 7, 1950; children—A. Donald, Yolane Marie, Michael. Dep. dir. St. Louis Human Devel. Corp., 1965-66; dir. St. Louis Model Cities Agy., 1966-68; West coast area dir. Urban Coalition, Washington, 1968-69; exec. dir. Gov.'s Office of Human Resources, Springfield, Ill., 1969-70; prof. edn. Ohio State U., 1970—. Faculty advisor Choking Times. Mem. N.W. Human Relations Council. Mem. bd. Malcolm X Community Coll., Chgo., 1970—. Mgr. Dick Gregory presdl. campaign, 1968. Served with Ill. N.G. Mem. Alpha Phi Alpha. Home: 1888 Willow Way Circle Columbus OH 43220

BOURGEOIS, ANDRE MARIE GEORGES, educator; b. Orleans, France, Dec. 1, 1902; s. Maurice M. and Yvonne (Assire) B.; B.A., U. Paris, 1921, LL.B., 1923; certicats etudes superieures, 1930, doctorat, 1945; M.A., U. Tex., 1934; m. May Hander, July 1, 1940; children—Maxime W., June Katherine Marie. Came to U.S., 1927, naturalized, 1936. Mem. faculty Rice U., 1928—, prof. French, 1954—, acting chmn. dept., 1957-61, Favrot prof. French lit., 1969—, chmn. dept., 1970—. Vis. prof. U. Houston, 1947, 60, U. Tex., 1940, Tulane U., 1939; asst. dir. Le Petit Theatre Francais de Houston, 1933-38; asso. pub. Le Bayou, 1936-61. Served to maj. AUS, 1942-45; ETO. Decorated Bronze Star; Croix de Guerre (France); officer Ouissam Alaouite Cherifien, Palmes Academiques, Corona d'Italia; recipient Medaille d'Honneur, U. Nancy (France). Mem. Modern Lang. Assn., Assn. Tchrs. French, S. Central Modern Lang. Assn., Houston Philos. Soc., Soc. des Gens de Lettres Alliance Francaise. Roman Catholic. Author: Ballades Louisianaises, 1938; Practical French Grammar, 1940; Pastels and Sanguuines, 1947; Rene Boylesve, le peintre de la Touraine 1945; Rene Boylesve, et le probleme de l'amour, 1950; La vie de Rene Boylesve, 1958; Rene Boylesve, le Poete, 1967. Home: 2070 Southgate Blvd Houston TX 77025

BOURGEOIS, LOUISE, sculptor; b. Paris, France, Dec. 25, 1911; d. Louis and Josephine (Fauriaux) Bourgeois; baccalauréat, Lycée Fénelon, 1932; student Sorbonne, 1932-35, Ecole du Louvre, 1936-37, Ecole des Beaux-Arts, Paris, 1936-38, Acad. Ranson, 1936-37, Acad. de la Grande Chaumiere, 1937-38, Acad. F. Leger, 1938; m. Robert Goldwater, Sept. 12, 1938; children—Michel, Jean-Louis, Alain. Came to U.S., 1938, naturalized, 1957. One-man exhbns. include Norlyst Gallery, N.Y.C., 1947, Peridot Gallery, N.Y.C., 1949, 50, 53, Frumkin Gallery, Chgo., 1953, White Art Mus., Cornell U., Ithaca, N.Y., 1953, Stable Gallery, N.Y.C., 1964, Rose Fried Gallery, 1964; represented permanent collections Mus. Modern Art, Whitney Mus., R.I. Sch. Design, N.Y. U., also pvt. collections; docent The Louvre, 1937-38; instr. sculpture Bklyn. Coll., 1963, 68, Pratt Inst., 1965-67, Goddard Coll., 1970. Address: 347 West 20th Street New York City NY 10011

BOURGET, MAURICE, Canadian senator; b. Lauzon, Que., Oct. 20, 1907; s. Philippe T. and Elmire (Gosselin) B.; B.A. Sc. in Engring., cole Polytech., Montreal, 1932; m. Marguerite Cleary, Aug. 31, 1949; children—Suzanne, Louise. Engaged as cons. engr., Que., Can.; dir. Brit. Newfoundland Corp., 1963— , Hall Corp. Can., 1964—; mem. Canadian Ho. of Commons from Quebec Province, 1940-62; Canadian del. to UN, Paris, France, 1951; parliamentary asst. to minister pub. works, 1953-57; del. Gen. Conf. Commonwealth Parliamentary Assn., London, Eng., 1961; joint chmn. Canadian delegation 7th meeting Can.-U.S. Interparliamentary Group, Washington, 1964; mem. Canadian Senate, 1963—, speaker, 1963-66; called to Privy Council for Canada, 1966. Mem. Engring. Inst. Can., Profl. Engrs. Corp. Que. Mem. Liberal Party. Catholic. K.C. Clubs: Reform, Garrison, Cercle Universitaire (Quebec). Home: 3 Place Baribeau Lévis Quebec Canada Office: The Senate Ottawa Ontario Canada

BOURGUIBA, HABIB, Jr., former Tunisian diplomat, investment co. exec.; b. Paris, France, Apr. 9, 1927; s. Pres. Bourguiba of Tunisia; ed. in Arabic in primary grades; law degree U. Paris and Grenoble (France); m., 3 children. Collaborator nat. liberation movement, 1951-54; practice of law, Tunis, 1954-55; assisted establishment Dept. Fgn. Affairs; counselor Tunisian embassy, Washington, 1955-57; Tunisian ambassador to Rome, 1957-58, Paris, 1958-60; spl. mission to Congo, Leopoldville, 1960; mem. Tunisian delegation to UN Assembly, Sept.-Dec. 1960; Tunisian ambassador to U.S., Can. and UN, 1961-62, to U.S. and Mexico, 1962-63; mem. Parliament, 1964; sec. state for fgn. affairs, Tunis, 1964-70, ret., 1970; chmn., gen. mgr. Société Nationale D'Investissements, Tunis, 1971—. Decorated Grand Cordon, Order of Republic (Tunisia); Cordon, Order of Independence.

BOURGUIBA, HABIB BEN ALL, pres. of Tunisia; b. Monastir, 1903; grad. in law and polit. sci. U. Paris. Mem. Destour Party, 1921, formed Neo-Destour Party, 1934; imprisoned by French, 1934- 36, 1938-43; voluntarily exiled 5 years to tour world to promote Tunisian Independence 1945-49; arrested and banished by French, 1952, released, 1954; returned to Tunisia, June 1955; pres. Tunisian Nat. Assembly, prime minister, pres. council, minister fgn. affairs and def., 1956; acting pres. Republic of Tunisia, 1957-59, elected pres., 1959—. Mem. 11th Gen. Assembly UN. Mem. editorial staff La Voix du Tunisien, 1930; established L'Action Tunisienne, also Al-Amal newspapers. Address: Palais Présidentiel de Carthage Tunis Tunisia

BOURGUIGNON, SERGE EDOUARD, film writer, dir.; b. Maignelay, France, Sept. 3, 1929; s. Maurice and Simone (Camus) B.; student Ecole des Arts Appliques a L'Industrie, 1945- 50, Institut des Hautes Etudes Cinematographiques, 1950-51. Mem. French Expdn. to Borneo, 1954-55; chief French Expdn. to No. India, 1955-56; film writer, dir. numerous films including Sikkim or the Language of the Smile, 1958, Jeune Patriarche (Gold medal Florence Film Festival), 1959, Escale, Le Montreur D'Ombres, L'Etoile de Mer, Le Sourire, 1960 (Grand prix Cannes), Sundays and Cybele, 1962, prix spl. Festival Venise 1962, also prix Maschere) Victoire, 1963, The Reward, 1964. Lectr. for Alliance Francaise in India, Mexico; mem. several French cultural delegations; pres. Jury Cork (Ireland) Film Festival, 1962. Decorated knight Order Arts and Letters; recipient Goldwyn award Fgn. Press in Hollywood, 1963; I.F.I.D.A. award in N.Y.C., 1963; Acad. award for best fgn. film in Hollywood, 1963. Home: 18 Rue du General Malleterre Paris-16e France Office: CIMURA 2 Rue Paul-Cezanne Paris-8e France

BOURJAILY, MONTE FERRIS, editor, publisher; b. Republic of Lebanon, Feb. 28, 1894; s. Ferris M. and Terkman E. (Bourjaily) B.; Syracuse U., 1917, Sch. Mil. Aeros., Ohio State U., 1918 m. Barbara Webb (dec.); m. 2d, Norma Sparlin; children— Monte Ferris, Paul Paine, Vance Nye, Valerie Evelyn (Mrs. Donald Hymes), Hale Bradt, Abigail Alice (Mrs. Thomas Campi). Dale Anne. Reporter, Syracuse (N.Y.) Herald, 1914-17, Cleve. Plain Dealer, 1919-20; commr. information and research City of Cleve., 1921; editor-pub. Press, Lakewood, O., 1922; asst. editor-in-chief Scripps-Howard Newspapers (Ohio group), 1922-26; pub. New Haven (Conn.) Union, and Yonkers (N.Y.) Statesman, 1926-27; bus. rep. United Press, 1927-28; editor and gen. mgr. United Feature Syndicate, 1929-36, widely syndicated Charles Dickens' Life of Our Lord, also world statesmen, leading columnists, cartoons, comic strips; editor- pub. Mid-Week Pictorial, Judge Mags., 1936-37; pres., editor Globe Syndicate, 1937—; editor Bangor (Me.) Daily News, 1940-41; editor-pub. Grafton (W.Va.) Sentinel, 1951—, Bangor (Me.) Patriot, 1954-55; lectr. newspaper and syndicate practices. Chief div. Bd. Econ. Warfare, spl. asst. to asst. commerce sec. for internat. trade U.S. Govt., 1941-46; mem. Reparations Commn. U.S. Peace Mission. Served as 2d lt. AC U.S., 1917-18, adj., comdg. officer 499th Aero Squadron, personnel office Chief of AS, Tours, France, asst. adj. Port of Embarkation, Marseilles, France. Roman Catholic. Club: N.Y. Athletic. Author: daily column Everyday Editorials, 1951—. Home: Spring Lake NJ 07762 Office: The Sentinel Grafton WV 26354

BOURJAILY, VANCE, novelist; b. Cleve., Sept. 17, 1922; s. Monte Ferris and Barbara (Webb) B.; A.B., Bowdoin Coll.; m. Bettina Yensen, 1946; children—Anna (dec.), Philip, Robin. Newspaperman, TV dramatist, playwright, lectr.; asso. prof. U. Ia. Writers Workshop; co-founder, editor Discovery, 1951-53; cultural mission to S. Am. auspices State Dept., 1959; distinguished vis. prof. Ore. State U., summer 1968. Mem. campaign staff Hughes for Senate, 1968. Served with Am. Field Service, 1942-44, AUS, 1944-46. Author: The End of My Life, 1947; The Hound of Earth, 1953; The Violated, 1958; Confessions of a Spent Youth, 1960; (non-fiction) The Unnatural Enemy, 1963; The Man Who Knew Kennedy, 1967; Brill Among the Ruins, 1970 (nominated Nat. Book Award for fiction 1971). Home: Redbird Farm Route 1 Iowa City IA Office: care Russell & Volkenning 551 Fifth Av New York City NY

BOURKE, GEGGE, journalist. Motion picture, theatrical editor Miami Herald. Office: Herald Plaza Miami FL 33101*

BOURKE, JAMES A., banker; b. Chgo., July 12, 1908; s. James A. and Jessie (Hill) R.; diploma in commerce, Northwestern U., 1937; m. Irene Lynch, Nov. 20, 1943; children—James P., Thomas K., John B., Mary K., Patricia A., Sheila J. With First Nat. Bank of Chgo., 1924—, v.p., 1955—; dir. Young Radiator Co., Racine, Wis., Morgan Co., Oshkosh, Wis., L.E. Myers Co., Chgo. Mem. faculty U. Wis. Grad. Sch. Banking, Nat. Comml. Lending Sch., U. Okla.; mem. nat. bd. field advisers Small Bus. Adminstrn., 1955—. Treas. Cath. Youth Orgn., K.C. Underprivileged Youth Fund. Trustee Ill. Benedictine Coll., Lisle, Ill., St. Joseph's Coll., Rensselaer, Ind. Mem. Robert Morris Assos. (dir. 1952). K.C. Clubs: Chicago Athletic, Serra (Chgo.); Glen Oak Country (Elmhurst). Home: 140 Elmwood Terrace Elmhurst IL 60126 Office: One First National Plaza Chicago IL 60670

BOURKE, VERNON JOSEPH, educator; b. North Bay, Ont., Can., Feb. 17, 1907; s. Joseph Walter and Therese (Trudeau) B.; B.A., U. Toronto, 1928, M.A., 1929, Ph.D., 1937; m. Aileen Baechler, Aug. 15, 1932 (dec. 1945); children—Jane (Mrs. Ray Luckhaupt), Thomas, Nancy (Mrs. Vernal G. Beckmann); m. 2d, Janet Leahy, June 12, 1947. Came to U.S., 1931, naturalized, 1944. Lectr. ancient philosophy U. Toronto, 1928-31; instr. philosophy St. Louis U., 1931-46, prof., 1946—; adv. editor Christian Wisdom Series, Macmillan Co., 1952- 68. Chmn. Catholic Commn. on Cultural and Intellectual Affairs, 1950. Bd. dirs. Thomistic Inst., St. Louis U. Recipient Gov. Gen. and Cardinal Mercier Gold medals Toronto, 1928, Loyola U. (Chgo.) Gold Key award, 1960, Aquinas medal Am. Cath. Philos. Assn., 1963. Mem. Mediaeval Acad. Am., Am., Am. Cath. (past pres.) philos. assns., World Union Cath. Philos. Socs. (past pres.). Republican. Author: Pocket Aquinas, 1960; Will in Western Thought, 1964; The Essential Augustine, 1966; Ethics in Crisis, 1966; History of Ethics, 1968. Asso. editor: Am. Jour. Jurisprudence, 1956—, Speculum, 1950-66, The Modern Schoolman, 1948—, Augustinian Studies, 1969—. Contbr. Ency. of Philosophy, 1967. Home: 638 Laven-Del Lane Kirkwood MO 63122 Office: St Louis U 221 N Grand St Louis MO 63103

BOURKE-WHITE, MARGARET, photographer; b. N.Y.C., June 14, 1906; d. Joseph and Minnie Elizabeth (Bourke) White; student Columbia, 1922-23, U. Mich., 1923-25, A.F.D. (hon.), 1951; A.B., Cornell, 1927; Litt.D. (hon.), Rutgers U., 1949; m. Everett Chapman, 1925; married 2d, Erskine Caldwell, 1939 (div. 1942). Indsl. photographer since 1927. Has photographed Am. industries including steel, mining farming, railroads, shipping; (Canada) newsprint; (Germany) AEG, I. G. Farben, (South America) coffee; (airplane) Trans Western Airways, Eastern Airlines; Pan Am. Airways, Brazil. Has taken photographs in 34 countries including Arctic region; Asso. editor Fortune Mag., 1929-33, Life Mag. since 1936; U.N. war corr. in Korea for Life Mag., 1952. Accredited war corr.-photographer for Life Mag. to the U.S. Air Forces in Gt. Britain, North Africa and Europe, 1942-45. Photomurals for Aluminum Co. Am., 1933; Lehigh Portland Cement Co., 1938. Awards: 1st prize, Cleve. Mus. Art, 1928, Art Dirs. Club, N.Y., 1930; Am. Woman of Achievement Award, 1951; 2d ann. ASMP-U. Miami Photojournalism Conf., 1958. Rep. in Library of Congress, Bklyn. Mus., Cleve. Museum of Art, Mus. of Modern Art, New York. Author: Eyes on Russia, 1931; U.S.S.R., A Portfolio of Photographs, 1934; You Have Seen Their Faces (with Erskine Caldwell), 1937; North of the Danube (with Erskine Caldwell), 1939; Say: Is This the U.S.A.? (with Erskine Caldwell), 1941; Shooting the Russian War (text & photographs), 1942. They Called It Purple Heart Valley, 1944; Dear Fatherland, Rest Quietly 1946; Halfway to Freedom, A Study of the New India, 1949; A Report on The American Jesuits (with Father John Lafarge), 1956; Portrait of Myself, 1963. Home: Darien CT 06820 Address: Time and Life Building Rockefeller Center New York City NY 10020

BOURLAND, FREDERICK MITCHEL, savs. and loan exec.; b. Peoria, Ill., Aug. 6, 1914; s. Frederick Bailey and Rachel (Mitchel) B.; A.B., Bradley Poly. Inst., 1935; m. Jane Peters, June 8, 1940; children—Rebekah (Mrs. Dennis W. Hansen), Rachel (Mrs. Larry K. Lankton), Andrew M., Peter M. (dec.). With Bourland Realty Co., Peoria, 1935-53; with First Fed. Savs. & Loan Assn., Peoria, 1953—, exec. v.p., 1965-71, pres., 1971—; v.p. Peoria Devel. Corp., 1963—. Mem. Pub. Bldg. Commn., Peoria, 1968—. Mem. Bd. Edn. Peoria, 1953-68. Bd. dirs. Proctor Community Hosp., Hopedale Med. Found.; trustee Bradley U. Served with USNR, 1944-45. Mem. Peoria Assn. Commerce (pres.), Peoria Bd. Realtors (past pres.). Episcopalian. Rotarian. Home: 240 NE Randolph St Peoria IL 61606 Office: 111 NE Jefferson St Peoria IL 61602

BOURNE, EDWARD WALTER, lawyer; b. New Haven, June 17, 1898; s. Edward Gaylord and Annie Thomson (Nettleton) B.; student Taft Sch., Watertown, Conn., 1910-15; A.B., Yale, 1919, postgrad. Law Sch., 1919-20; m. Margaret Watson, July 5, 1930; children—Margaret Gaylord (Mrs. Austin B. Pedersen), Susan Holdrege (Mrs. Nikolaus H. Brinkama), Edward Gaylord, Jane Thomson, James Russell. Admitted to N.Y. State Bar, 1922; asso. firm Alexander & Green, N.Y.C., 1920-29, partner firm, 1929-67, counsel, 1967—. Served as 2d lt., F.A., U.S. Army, 1918; govt. appeal agt., Local Bd. 42, N.Y.C., 1940-43; mem. alien enemy hearing bd., No. 3, N.Y.C., 1943-45. Mem. Am., N.Y. State bar assns., Assn. Bar City N.Y. Soc. of N.Y. Hosp. (hon. gov.), Phi Beta Kappa. Republican. Episcopalian. Clubs: Century Assn., Downtown Assn. Home: West West Cornwall CT 06796 Office: 120 Broadway New York City NY 10005

BOURNE, FRANK CARD, educator; b. Wells, Me., July 17, 1914; s. Moses Avander and Grace (Card) B.; A.B., Princeton, 1936, M.A., 1940, Ph.D., 1941. Mem. faculty Princeton, 1946—, prof. Classics, 1966—, master Grad. Coll., 1954-58. Served with USAAF, 1941-45. Mem. Vergilian Soc. Am. (sec.-treas. 1951-54), Classical Assn. Atlantic States (pres. 1957), Am. Philol. Assn., Assn. Internat. d'Epigraphie Latine, Assn. Internat. de Papyrologues. Author: Public Works of Julio-Claudians and Flavians, 1946; A History of the Romans, 1966; (with Johnson and Norton) Ancient Roman Statutes, 1961. Editor: Decline and Fall (Gibbon); 1963. Home: RD 1 Wells, ME 04090. Office: East Pyne Building Princeton NJ 08540

BOURNE, HENRY CLARK, Jr., educator; b. Tarboro, N.C., Dec. 31, 1921; s. Henry Clark and Marion (Alston) B.; B.S., Mass. Inst. Tech., 1947, M.S., 1948, D.Sc., 1952; m. Margaret Barr Thomas, Aug. 15, 1953; children—Katherine Wimberley, Henry Clark III, Thomas Franklin, Margaret Alston. Asst. prof. Mass. Inst. Tech., 1952-54; asst. prof., then asso. prof. U. Cal. at Berkeley, 1954-63; prof. elec. engring., chmn. dept. Rice U., Houston, Tex., 1963—. Cons. editor Harper & Row, N.Y.C., 1961-67; cons. elec. engring., 1952—. Served to 1st lt. C.E., AUS, 1943-46. Sci. Faculty fellow NSF, 1960-61; hon. research asso. Univ. Coll. London (Eng.), 1961. Registered profl. engr., Cal., Tex. Mem. I.E.E.E., Am. Phys. Soc., Soc. Engring. Sci., Am. Soc. Engring. Edn., Sigma Xi, Tau Beta Pi, Eta Kappa Nu, Delta Tau Delta. Episcopalian. Author tech. papers in field of magnetics. Home: 4439 Lymbar Dr Houston TX 77035

BOURNS, MARLAN E., elec. mfg. co. exec.; b. Brighton, Mich., May 28, 1920; s. Frank E. and Bernice (Muir) B.; B.S., U. Mich., 1944; m. Rosemary R. Miller, July 7, 1947; children—Gordon, Linda, Anita, Denise. Research U. Mich., 1944-45; research asst. Cal. Inst. Tech., 1945; research Gen. Tire & Rubber Co., 1945-46; pres. Bourns, Inc., Riverside, Cal., 1946—. Joint chmn. Reagan TV Com., 1968; mem. Century Club Republican Party. Recipient Silver Beaver award Boy Scouts Am. Mem. World Bus. Council, Young Presidents Orgn., Phi Beta Kappa. Patentee in field. Office: 1200 Columbia Av Riverside CA 92507

BOURS, B. WALKER, Jr., corp. exec.; b. 1908; married. With Price Waterhouse & Co., C.P.A.'s, 1936-38, Standard Oil Co. Cal., 1938-43; gen. auditor Rheem Mfg. Co., 1943-47; auditor J.L. Stuart Mfg. Co., 1947-50; controller paint and wallpaper operations Sears, Roebuck & Co., 1950-56; with DeSoto, Inc., 1956—. treas., 1968—. Address: 1700 Mt Prospect Rd Des Plaines, IL. 60018

BOUSFIELD, HUMPHREY GAMBIER, librarian, educator; b. Newark, Dec. 29, 1903; s. Robert William and Edith Hooper (Eddis) G.; A.B., N.Y.U., 1927, M.A., 1931; M.S. in Library Sci., Columbia, 1935; m. Mary Meldon Gorman, Sept. 1, 1928; 1 dau., Patricia. Gen. asst. N.Y. U. Library, Univ. Heights, N.Y.C., 1923-27, evening asst., 1926-27; supr. evening service Wash. Square Library N.Y. U., 1927-29; instr. English high sch. Columbia Grammar Sch., N.Y.C., 1928-29; chief, readers dept., N.Y.U., 1929-40; asst. librarian, 1940-43; asso. dir. U. Ill. Library, 1943-44; chief librarian, prof., chmn. library dept. Bklyn. Coll., 1944—. Mem. library adv. com. Council Higher Ednl. Instns. in N.Y.C. Mem. A.L.A., Am. Assn. U. Profs., N.Y. Library Club. Author: Circulation Work in College and University Libraries (with Charles H. Brown), 1933. Contbr. articles to library jours. Home: 22 Sagamore Road Bronxville NY 10708 Office: Brooklyn College Library Brooklyn NY 11210

BOUSFIELD, WESTON ASHMORE, phychologist; b. Sao Ching, China, Apr. 22, 1904; s. Cyril Eustace and Lillie (Snowden) B.; came to U.S., 1904, derived citizenship, 1906; B.M.E., Northeastern U., 1927; A.M., Boston U., 1928; A.M., Harvard, 1932, Ph.D., 1933; m. Thelma Knight, July 4, 1935; children—Brenda Lee, Aldridge Knight. Instr., Tufts Coll., 1929-39; mem. faculty U. Conn. since 1939, prof., psychology, 1946-71, emeritus, 1971—, head psychology dept. 1939-60. Fellow Am. Psychol. Assn.; mem. Eastern Psychol. Assn. (treas. 1947-50), Conn. State Psychol. Soc. (pres. 1947), Conn. Valley Assn. Psychologists, Sigma Xi, Phi Kappa Phi. Contbr. articles to psychol. jours. on child devel., motivation, verbal behavior. Home: South Eagleville Rd Storrs CT 06268

BOUTEFLIKA, ABDUL AZIZ, Algerian diplomat ; b. Melilla, Algeria, 1937; ed. Morocco. Former capt. Nat. Liberation Army, minister of sports, fgn. affairs, 1963; mem. F.L.N. Polit. Bur., 1964, Revolutionary Council, 1965; fgn. minister of Algeria, 1966—. Address: Cabinet Building Algiers Algeria*

BOUTELL, CLARENCE BURLEY CLIP, editor and columnist; b. Washington, Feb. 8, 1908; s. Roger Sherman Gates and Avis (Burley) B.; student Stanford U., 1926-27; m. Helen Paulsen, May 25, 1935; children—Patricia Carley, William Burley, Christine Blodgett. Advt. mgr. Alfred A. Knopf, 1930-32; promotion mgr. Saturday Rev. of Lit. 1933-37; advt. and publicity mgr. G. P. Putnam Sons, Coward-McCann and John Day, 1937-43; author syndicated literary column Authors Are Like People, New York Post and other newspapers, 1943-47; editor Fiction Book Club, 1947-48; copy chief Denhard & Stewart, 1953-55, Christian Herald, 1955-65, Famous Writers Sch., Westport, Conn., 1965-67. Original organizer, first chmn. Council on Books in Wartime. Co-editor: Speak of the Devil, 1945. Author: The Fat Baron, 1946. Contbr. mags. Home: 190 Westport Road Wilton CT 06897

BOUTIN, BERNARD LOUIS, coll. pres.; b. Belmont, N.H., July 2, 1923; s. Joseph L. and Annie E. (LaFlam) B.; student Cath. U. Am., 1942-43; Ph.B., St. Michael's Coll., Winooski Park, Vt., 1945, LL.D., 1963; H.H.D., Franklin Pierce Coll., 1969; L.H.D., U. N.H., 1970; m. Alice M. Boucher, Apr. 2, 1945; children—Edmund, Joseph, Bernadette, Michelle, Marie, Louis, Elizabeth, John, Paul, Suzanne, Bernard II. Pres., treas. Boutin Ins. Agy., Inc., Laconia, N.H., 1948-63; propr. Boutin Real Estate Co., 1955-63; incorporator Laconia Savs. Bank; adminstr. Gen. Services Administrn., Washington, 1961-64; exec. v.p. Nat. Assn. Home Builders, 1964-65; dep. dir. Office Econ. Opportunity, 1965-66; adminstr. Samll Bus. Adminstrn., 1966-67; asst. to pres. Sanders Assos., Inc., 1967-69; pres. St. Michael's Coll., Winooski, Vt., 1969—. Dir. Burlington (Vt.) Fed. Savs. & Loan, Hi-G, Inc., Windsor Locks, Conn. Mem. Nat. Council Ind. Colls. and Univs. Com. on Equal Employment Opportunity, President's Com. on Employment Physically Handicapped; chmn. N.H. State Bd. Edn., 1968-69. Mayor, City of Laconia. 1955-59. Dem. nat committeeman for N.H., 1956-60; Dem. nominee for gov. N.H., 1958, 60. Mem. Am. Soc. Pub. Adminstrn., Am. Mgmt. Assn. K.C. (past state dep.), Elk (past exalted ruler N.H.). Address: Saint Michael's College Winooski VT 05404

BOUTWELL, ALBERT BURTON, lawyer; b. Montgomery, Ala., Nov. 13, 1904; s. Clarence C. and Lydia (Sweatt) B.; LL.B., U. Ala., 1928; m. Helen Balfour Drake, Nov. 23, 1934; children—Helen Linder, Albert Burton, Charles Drake. Admitted to Ala. bar, 1928, since practiced in Birmingham. Co-founder, dir. Vulcan Life & Accident Ins. Co., Birmingham; exec. v.p., dir. Merit Oak Flooring Co., Inc., Birmingham, 1956—. Sec., Joint U.S. Congl. Com. on Forestry, 1939- 40. Mem. Ala. Senate, 1946-58; became lt. gov. Ala., 1958; mayor of Birmingham, 1963-67; del.-at-large Dem. Nat. Conf., Chgo., 1944. Mem. U.S. Jr. (nat. v.p. Birmingham, 1963-67; del.-at-large Dem. Nat. Conf., Chgo., 1944. Mem. U.S. Jr. (nat. v.p. 1935-36), Birmingham chambers commerce, Am. Bar Assn., Blue Key, Sigma Delta Delta Kappa, Alpha Kappa Psi (hon.). Methodist (steward). Elk (past exalted ruler), Eagle, Mason (Shriner, Jester), Lion. Clubs: Vesta-via Country, The Club (Birmingham). Home: 4461 Clairmont Av Birmingham AL 35222 Office: First Nat Bldg Birmingham AL 35203

BOUVIER, JOHN ANDRE, Jr., lawyer, corp. exec.; b. nr. Ocala, Fla., May 16, 1903; s. John Andre and Ella (Richardson) B.; student Davidson Coll., 1922-24; A.B., U. Fla., 1926, LL.B., 1929, J.D., 1969; M.B.A., Northwestern U., 1930; m. Helen A. Schaefer, June 6, 1928; children—Helen Elizabeth (Mrs. William Spencer), John Andre III, Thomas Richardson. Admitted to Fla. bar, 1929, pvt. practice, Gainesville, 1929, Miami, 1930—, specialist corp., real estate and probate law, cons. atty.; gen. counsel Patterson & Maloney, Ft. Lauderdale; chmn. exec. com. Permutit Co.; chmn bd. Prosperity Co. div., vice chmn. bd. Ward Indsl. Corp., 1958; chmn. bd., pres. Pantex Mfg. Corp., 1960, Nat. Leasing Inc., Miami; pres. bd. Knaust Bros., Inc., 1962, K-B Products Corp., 1962, Iron Mountain Atomic Storage Vaults, Inc., 1962, pres. West Kingsway, Inc., East Kingsway, Inc., South Kingsway, Inc.; sec. 50th St. Heights, Inc., Knight Manor, Inc., Dade Constrn. Co. (all Miami), Karen Club Apt. Hotel, Ft. Lauderdale; dir. Farquhar Machinery Co., Consol. Bankshares of Fla., Ocean 1st Nat. Bank. Commr., Dade County council Boy Scouts Am.; chmn. Malecon Com. Dade County; dir. Syracuse Govtl. Research Bur.; mem. Planning Council Zoning Bd. Miami; chmn. Coxsackie-Athens Area Redevel. Com.; vice chmn. Nat. Parkinson Found. Trustee Windham Coll. Mem. Internat. Platform Assn., Am. Judicature Soc., Am., Fla., Dade County, Broward County bar assns., C. of C., Sigma Chi. Presbyn. (chmn. bd. trustees). Mason (Shriner), Elk, Rotarian. Clubs: Miami Beach Rod and Reel, Surf, Riviera Country, Skaneateles Country. Author monographs, newspaper articles in field. Home: 2756 NE 17th St Fort Lauderdale FL 33305 also Beinvenue Blowing Rock NC 28605 Office: 6888 NW 7th Av Miami FL 33150 also 3103 N Federal Hwy Fort Lauderdale FL 33306

BOUWMAN, ROLAND JOSEPH, lawyer, utility exec.; b. Heerlen, Holland, Oct. 11, 1922; s. Christian Jacobus and Josephine (Batta) B.; LL.B., U. B.C., 1955; m. Joyce Warwick, Oct. 14, 1949; children—Christian, Mark. Dep. city prosecutor City of Vancouver, B.C., 1956-68; gen. counsel, sec. B.C. Telephone Co., Vancouver, 1968—; sec. Okanagon Telephone Co.; sec., dir. N.W. Telephone Co. Dir. Centennial Mus., H.R. MacMillan Planetarium. Served to flight lt., R.C.A.F., World War II. Mem. Law Soc. B.C., Canadian Bar Assn., Vancouver Bd. Trade, Canadian C. of C. Home: 6864 East Blvd Vancouver 13 British Columbia Canada Office: 768 Seymour St Vancouver 2 British Columbia Canada

BOUWMEESTER, JOHN HENRY, electronics co. exec.; b. Hoogeveen, Netherlands, Sept. 22, 1917; s. John and Jentge (Wams) B.; came to U.S., 1925; ed. pub. schs.; m. Lauretta Radke, Oct. 26, 1940 (div. May 1963); children—Alan John, Lois Jane; m. 2d, Bernadine Vargo, June 8, 1963. Gen. foreman Internat. Harvester Co., Milw., 1936-48; gen. supt. Am. Bosch Corp., Providence, 1948-50; v.p., dir. Ind. Steel Products Corp., Valparaiso, Ind., 1950-55; v.p. Gen. Ceramics Corp., Keasbey, N.J., 1955-56, exec. v.p., 1956-57, pres., 1958-59, also dir.; exec. v.p. Ind. Gen. Corp., Valparaiso, 1959-64, pres., 1964-69, also dir., mem. exec. com.; chmn., pres. Ind. Steel Products Co. of Can., Ltd., Kitchener, Ont., 1964-69; dir. Doughboy Industries, Inc. Exec. bd. Pottawattomie council Boy Scouts Am.; chmn. advanced gifts div. United Fund Porter County. Mem. Am. Mgmt. Assn. Clubs: Naples (Fla.) Sailing; Moorings Country. Home: 211 Bay Point Naples FL 33940 Office: 405 Elm St Valparaiso IN 46383

BOUWSMA, OETS KOLK, educator; b. Muskegon, Mich., Nov. 22, 1898; s. Joachum and Helen (Kolk) B.; A.B., Calvin Coll., 1922; Ph.D., U. Mich., 1928; m. Gertrude Elsie de Vries, Aug. 10, 1922; children—William James, Charles Edmond, Gretchen Ellen (Mrs. R. Bruce Emmous). Instr. English, U. Mich., 1922- 28; prof. philosophy U. Neb., 1928-65; prof. U. Tex., 1965—; vis. prof. Smith Coll., 1949-50; John Locke lectr. Oxford (Eng.) U., 1951. Fulbright Prof.'s Research grantee Oxford U., 1950-51; Woods Study grantee U. Neb., London, Eng., 1956. Mem. Phi Beta Kappa. Author: Philosophical Essays; also essays in philos. jours. Home: 6002 Spancreek Circle Austin TX 78731

BOUWSMA, WILLIAM JAMES, educator; b. Ann Arbor, Mich., Nov. 22, 1923; s. Oets Kolk and Gertrude (DeVries) B.; A.B., Harvard, 1943, M.A., 1947, Ph.D., 1950; m. Beverly Jean Hancock, July 9, 1944; children—John Roger, Philip Hancock, Paul Joseph, Sarah Elizabeth. Instr. to asso. prof. U. Ill., 1950-56; asso. prof. history U. Cal., 1956-61, prof., 1961-68, chmn. dept., 1966-67, vice chancellor for acad. affairs, 1967-69; prof. history Harvard, 1969—. Served with AUS, 1943-46. Fulbright fellow, 1959-60; Guggenheim fellow, 1960; Behavioral Sci. Center fellow, 1963-64. Mem. Am. Hist. Assn., Renaissance Soc. Am. (council), Am. Soc. Reformation Research (pres. 1963). Author: Concordia Mundi: Career and Thought of Guillaume Postel, 1957; Interpretation of Renaissance Humanism, 1959; Venice and the Defense of Renaissance Liberty, 1968. Home: 12 Orchard St Belmont MA 02178

BOVAIRD, DAVIS DOUTHETT, petroleum equipment exec.; b. Bradford, Pa., Sept. 27, 1896; s. William J. and Anna L. (Davis) B.; student Coll. of Emporia, 1914-17, LL.D.; A.B., U. Mich., 1918, B.S. in Mech. Engring., 1920; m. Florence Hettinger, Sept. 21, 1921; children—Ruthanna, William J., Mary Florence. Field salesman Bovaird Supply Co., Tulsa, 1920-22, plant mgr., Independence, Kan., 1922- 27, v.p., treas. 1927-49, pres., 1949-62, chmn. bd., 1962—; dir. Pub. Service Co. of Okla., First Nat. Bank & Trust Co., Tulsa, Pennzoil Co. of Pa. Trustee U. Tulsa. Bd. dirs., chmn. bd. Hillcrest Med. Center Mem. Am. Petroleum Inst., Petroleum Equipment Suppliers Assn. (dir.), Kappa Sigma. Presbyn. Clubs: Tulsa, Southern Hills Country. Home: 2215 E 26th Pl Tulsa OK 74103 Office: 823 S-Detroit St PO Box 2590 Tulsa OK 74103 ‡

BOVARD, JAMES MOORHEAD, president Carnegie Inst.; b. Greenburg, Pa., April 14, 1901; son Harry Foster and Mary (Moorhead) B.; A.B., Yale, 1924; LL.B., U. of Pittsburgh, 1927, LL.D., 1950; m. Carroll E. Donner, Jan. 30, 1942; stepchildrenJoseph William, Carroll Donner. Asso. or partner law firm of Moorhead & Knox, 1927-48; pres. Forbes Nat. Bank of Pitts., 1939-48; pres. bds. of trustees of Carnegie Inst. and Carnegie Library of Pitts., 1948-67, pres. emeritus, 1967-; trustee Carnegie-Mellon U., 1948—, chmn. 1948-66, now hon. chmn.; dir. Equitable Gas Co.; trustee Dollar Savs. Bank Dir. Pitts. Regional Planning Assn., Eye and Ear Hosp. Pitts. Trustee Sarah Mellow Scaife Found. Served as lt. col. USAAF, 1942-45. Home: Park Mansions Apts Pittsburgh, PA 15213.

BOVE, JANUAR D., Jr., lawyer; b. Wilmington, Del., Aug. 17, 1920; s. Januar D. and Teresa A. Bove; grad. with honors, U. Del.; LL.B., Harvard, 1948; m. Lillian Briggs, 1949; children—Jeffrey, Nancy, Kathryn. Admitted to Del. bar, 1949, U.S. Supreme Ct., 1959; practiced in Wilmington, Del., 1949—; partner Connolly, Bove & Lodge, 1953—; asst. city solicitor, 1949-50, city solicitor, 1953-57; dep. atty. gen. Del., 1950-53, atty. gen., 1958-62; dir. T.B. O'Toole, Inc. Bd. dirs. Del. Citizen's Crime Commn. Trustee, Tatnall Sch. Past sec. Republican Com. of Del.; chmn. Crusade for Freedom, Del., 1958. Served from 2d lt. to maj. AUS, World War II. Recipient Good Govt. award Com. of 39, 1962. Mem. Am., Del. bar assns., Nat. Assn. Attys. Gen. (Wyman award 1962), Harvard Law Sch. Assn. (pres. Del. 1962-63), Del. C. of C. (dir. 1967-70), Phi Kappa Phi. Club: Harvard (Wilmington). Home: 714 Princeton Rd Westover Hills Wilmington DE Office: Farmers Bank Bldg Wilmington DE 19801

BOVET, DANIEL, scientist; b. Switzerland; Italian citizen, 1947—. Prof. pharmacology Faculty Medicine, U. Sassari (Italy); dir. inst. psychobiology and psychopharmacology Consiglio Nazionale delle Richerche, Rome, Italy. With French colleague pioneered research on anti-histamine, 1937; later, in research relating to method permitting complete muscular relaxation in extensive surgery, developed synthetic curare drugs. Recipient Nobel prize in medicine and physiology, 1957. Home: 30 Via de Rossi Rome, Italy.

BOVEY, EDMUND CHARLES, gas co. exec.; b. Calgary, Alta., Can., Jan. 29, 1916; s. Charles A. and Dorothy (Smith) B.; student Victoria (B.C., Can.) Coll., 1931, U. B.C., 1935; m. Margaret Snowdon, Jan. 29, 1941; children—Charles Gordon, Myra. Asst. to pres. No. and Central Gas Corp. Ltd. 1958-60, v.p., 1960-65 pres., 1965—, chief exec. officer, chmn. exec. com., 1968—, also dir.; pres., dir. Le Gaz Provincial du Nord de Qué. Lté dir., mem. exec. com. Gaz pret., Zuc.; dir. Champion Pipe Line Corp., Ltd., Greater Winnipeg Gas Co., Westeel-Rosco Ltd., Abitibi Paper Co. Ltd., Dominion Assurance Corp.; chmn. exec. com., dir. Canadian Indsl. Gas & Oil Ltd. Bd. govs. Seneca Coll. Applied Arts and Tech.; bd. dirs. Toronto Symphony; past pres., also trustee Art Gallery Ont., Canadian Exec. Service Overseas. Mem. Canadian Gas Assn. (past pres., bd. dirs.), Royal Ont. Museum (life). Clubs: Rosedale Golf, Royal Canadian Yacht, Granite, Sales Research Empire (life itd. dirs.) (Toronto). Mem. Anglican Ch. (past warden). Home: 33 York Ridge Rd Willowdale Ontario Canada Office: 4600 Toronto-Dominion Centre Toronto Ontario Canada

BOVEY, JOHN ALDEN, Jr., fgn. service officer; b. Mpls., Apr. 17, 1913; s. John Alden and Margaret Eugenia (Jackson) B.; grad. Blake Sch., Mpls., 1931; B.A., Harvard, 1935, M.A., 1938, postgrad., 1938-42; graduate Nat. War Coll., 1960; m. Marcia Peterson Palmer, July 31, 1943; 1 dau., Rosamond Jackson. Pub. relations, advt. Gen. Mills, Inc. 1935-37; instr. Harvard, 1938-42; vice consul, Rotterdam, 1946-49; consul, Casablance, 1949-54; mem. U.S. delegation Internat. Ct. Justice, The Hague, Netherlands, 1952; apptd. Dept. State, Washington, 1954-59; dep. dir. Office North African Affairs, 1958-59; 1st sec. polit. sect. Am. Embassy, Paris, France, 1960-64, counselor for polit. affairs, 1964-65; counselor Am. embassy, Oslo, Norway, 1965-69, Am. embassy The Hague 1969-. Served from ensign to lt. USNR, 1942-45. Mem. YMCA, Fgn. Service Assn., Phi Beta Kappa. Contbr. articles, stories to mags. Address: Am Embassy The Hague Netherlands.

BOVIER, RALPH FREDERICK, utility exec.; b. W. Franklin, Pa., Mar. 4, 1908; s. Frederick H. and Inez (Stevens) B.; Indsl. Mech. Engr., Pratt Inst., 1932; grad. student U. Mich., 1955; m. Alice Paterson, June 30, 1934 (dec. Dec. 1967); childrenRuth Ann (Mrs. Robert F. Witt), Dorothy Jean (Mrs. Harold C. Gueritey); m. 2d, Harriet C. Cummins, 1968. With No. Pa. Power Co., 1932-54; with Pa. Electric Co., 1954-, pres., chief exec. officer, 1967-69, also dir.; v.p. Saxton Nuclear Exptl. Corp., 1960-; pres., chief exec. officer Jersey Central Power & Light Co., 1969-; dir. Trust Co. Nat. Bank, Morristown, N.J., Utilities Mutual Ins. Co., N.Y., N.J. C. of C. Trustee Pratt Inst. Registered profl. engr., Pa. Mem. Pa. Electric Assn. (past pres.), Newcomen Soc. Presbyn. (trustee). Rotarian (bd. dirs. Johnstown). Mason. Clubs: Sunnehanna Country, Bachelors (Johnston); Morris County Golf. Home: 21 Kensington Rd Basking Ridge, NJ 07920 Office: Madison Av at Punchbowl Rd Morristown NJ 07976

BOW, FRANK TOWNSEND, legislator; b. Canton, O., Feb. 20, 1901; s. Charles Clinton and Anna (Withrow) B.; LL.D., Ohio No. U., 1961, Mount Union Coll., 1963; m. Caroline Denzer, May 12, 1923; children—Robert Lee, Joseph Withrow. Admitted to Ohio bar, 1923; practiced at Canton. Mem. Ohio State Rep. Com., 1945-46; counsel to Congl. Com. investigating publicity and propaganda 80th Congress, 1947-48, to Select Com. 80th Congress investigating F.C.C., 1948; mem. 82d-92d Congresses, 16th Dist. Ohio. Mem. bd. regents Smithsonian Instn. Served as war corr. Ohio 37th Div., World War II; PTO. Mem. Ohio Bar Assn. (v.p. 1944-46, exec. com. 1946-50), Sigma Pi. Republican. Presbyn. Elk. Home: 1718 Market Av NW Canton OH 44708 Office: Rayburn Office Bldg Washington DC 20515

BOWATER, SIR NOEL V. BARONET, paper co. exec.; b. Forest Hill, London, Eng., Dec. 25, 1892; s. Sir Frank Henry and Ethel Anita (Fryar) B.; student Rugby Sch., 1906-10; m. Constance Heiton Bett, Feb. 1, 1921; children—Anne Patricia, Jane Gillian (Mrs. Christopher Beeson), Euan David Vansittart. Joined W.V. Bowater & Sons, London, Eng., 1912, joint mng. dir. W.V. Bowater & Sons, Ltd., also Bowaters' Lloyds Sales Co., Ltd., 1927-52; joint vice chmn. The Bowater Paper Corp. Ltd., London, 1952—. Mem. Ct. Common Council, 1937-41; alderman Castle Baynard Ward, 1944-69; sheriff London, 1948-49; Lord Mayor of London 1953- 54. Commd. in Territorial Army, 1913, served as capt. RAF; France, 1915- 19. Decorated Mil. Cross; knight Grand Cross Order Brit. Empire Knight St. John; knight comdr. Royal Order North Star Sweden, Order of Menelik the 2d of Ethiopia. Mem. Worshipful Co. Vintners (liveryman 1919—, master 1954-55). Clubs: St. James, Guildhall, City Livery, United Wards. Home: Conifers St George's Hill Weybridge Surrey & Riscombe Exford Somerset England

BOWDEN, A. BRUCE, banker; b. New Martinsville, W.Va., Aug. 17, 1908; s. George S. and Ora (Zimmerman) B.; B.A., Washington and Jefferson Coll., 1929; grad. Rutgers U. Grad. Sch. Banking, 1952; m. Mildred Bastian, June 26, 1937; 1 son, Alan Bruce. With Mellon Securities, Pitts., 1937-42, Gulf Oil Corp., 1942-44; with buying dept. Mellon Securities Corp., Pitts., 1946-47; asst. v.p. First Boston Corp., 1947-48; with Mellon Nat. Bank & Trust Co., Pitts., 1948—, v.p., 1951-63, sr. v.p., 1963-65, exec. v.p., 1965-66, pres., 1967—; dir. Allegheny Ludlum Steel Corp., Dresser Industries, Inc., Dravo Corp.; chmn. Regional Indsl. Devel. Corp. Southwestern Pa. Vice pres. bd. dirs. Western Pa. Hosp.; trustee Tb League of Pitts. Served as lt. USNR, World War II. Home: 537 Glen Arden Dr Pittsburgh PA 15208 Office: Mellon Nat Bank & Trust Co Mellon Sq Pittsburgh PA 15230

BOWDEN, ALFRED F., former tobacco exec.; b. N.Y.C., Mar. 2, 1906; s. Frank and Emma (Stickles) B.; student parochial schs. N.Y. City; m. Emily C. Wolff, Nov. 11, 1933; children—Barbara, Juliana, Emily, Pamela. Asst. to pres. Am. Tobacco Co., N.Y.C., 1939-57, v.p., 1957-70, dir. pub. relations, 1943-64, dir., 1951-70, pres. cigar div., 1964-70. Roman Catholic. Home: 20 Lefferts Rd Garden City NY 11530

BOWDEN, BURNHAM, business exec.; b. Melrose, Mass., Sept. 22, 1900; s. Frederick Prescott and Mary Eunice Lord (Burnham) B.; A.B., Harvard, 1922, M.B.A., 1923; m. Margaret Loughridge Cornelison, July 24, 1929; children—Mary Alice (Mrs. Robert Lyman), Elizabeth Forsyth (Mrs. Marshall L. Freimer), Burnham, Margaret Loughridge (Mrs. Andrew B. Murray). With Lord & Burnham Co., 1923—, v.p., 1927—, v.p. Burnham Boiler Corp., 1932, pres., 1933—; pres. Burnham Corp. (consolidation Lord & Burnham Co., Burnham Boiler Corp.), 1933-69, chmn. bd., 1969—; treas. J.C. Turner Lumber Co. (now Turner Corp.), 1933-65, v.p., 1933-69, dir., 1921—, chmn. bd., 1970—; mem. Mid-Atlantic adv. bd. Arkwright-Boston Mut. Ins. Co., 1961—; dir. Felters Co., Arbeka Webbing Co. Mem. Soc. Am. Florists, Harvard Engring. Soc. Republican. Unitarian. Clubs: N.Y. Florists, Harvard Business Sch., Appalachian Mountain, Corinthians, Huguenot Yacht. Home: 7 Bertha Place Irvington NY 10533 Office: 2 Main St Irvington NY 10533

BOWDEN, DANIEL JOSEPH, former educator; b. Norfolk, Va., June 14, 1906; s. Daniel Jackson and Josephine (Barrett) B.; B.S. in Mech. Engring., Va. Poly. Inst., 1928; B.D., Yale, 1933, Ph.D., 1937; m. Charlotte McHose, June 10, 1934; children—Douglas McHose, Charles Barrett, Bruce William. Ordained to minister Congl. Christian Ch., 1936; student in indsl. mgmt. Gen. Motors Corp., Pontiac div., 1928-30; mem. faculty Elon (N.C.) Coll., 1935-53, chmn. dept. philosophy and religion, 1935-46, prof. philosophy and religion, 1935-53, dean coll. and dean of men, 1944-53; dir. Indiana Sch. Religion, 1953-70; lectr. Ind. U., Bloomington, 1956-66, asst. dir. scholarship aid, 1965-71, ret., 1971. Mem. com. on student counseling for the Edward W. Hazen Found., 1948-53; chmn. So. Hazen Conf. on Student Counseling, 1947, mem. ., planning com., 1949, 50. Awarded first S.A.R. citizenship medal Maury High Sch., Norfolk, Va., 1924. Mem. Am. Philos. Assn., Am. Acad. Religion, Archeol. Inst. Am., Ind. Council on Religion in Higher Edn. (exec. sec. 1954-62), Ind. Assn. Coll. and Univ. Tchrs. Religion (pres. 1956-57, 63-64, sec.-treas. 1956-63), Metaphys. Soc. Am., So. Ind. Theol. Soc. (sec. 1959-64), Omicron Delta Kappa, Pi Gamma Mu. Mem. Christian Ch. (elder). Clubs: Rotary, Torch. Author monographs. Contbr. chpt. on religion in Society Under Analysis, 1942. Home: 936 S High St Bloomington IN 47401

BOWDEN, EDWIN TURNER, educator; b. Milledgeville, Ga., June 5, 1924; s. Edwin T. and Allie (Myrick) B.; grad. Phillips Exeter Acad., 1942; B.A., Harvard, 1948; Ph.D., Yale, 1952; children—Elisabeth, Susan, Edwin Eric. Instr. English, Yale, 1952-56, asst. dir. Am. studies for fgn. students, 1954-55; mem. faculty U. Tex., 1956—, prof. English, 1966—; vis. prof. U. N.M., 1965. Served with USAAF, 1943-46. Fulbright fellow Cambridge (Eng.) U., 1949-50. Mem. Tex. Inst. Letters, Modern Lang. Assn., English Inst. Author: The Themes of Henry James, 1956; An Introduction to Prose Style, 1956; The Dungeon of the Heart, 1961. Editor The Satiric Poems of John Trumbull, 1962; Washington Irving's History of New York, 1964; James Thurber: A Bibliography, 1968. Address: Dept English Univ Texas Austin TX 78712

BOWDEN, HENRY LUMPKIN, lawyer; b. Atlanta, July 23, 1910; s. John and Mattie (Turner) B.; B.Ph., Emory U., 1932, LL.B., 1933, LL.D., 1959; m. Ellen Marian Fleming, June 30, 1937; children—Ellen Fleming, Mary Lamar, Anne Turner, Henry Lumpkin. Admitted to Ga. bar, 1933, since practiced in Atlanta; asso. firm William E. Arnaud, 1933-39; partner firm Lokey & Bowden, 1939—; city atty. City of Atlanta, 1963—. Dir., 1st Nat. Bank, Atlanta. Mem. U.S. Regional Loyalty Bd., 1950- 52, U.S. Loyalty Rev. Bd., 1952-53. Trustee Emory U. (now chmn. bd.), Wesleyan Coll., Macon, Ga., Clark Coll. Served from 2d lt. to lt. col., AUS, 1941-46. Recipient Alexander Meiklejohn award Am. Assn. U. Profs., 1963. Mem. Am., Fed., Ga. (pres. 1955-56), Atlanta (pres. 1947), Inter-Am. bar assns., Am. Law Inst., Phi Beta Kappa, Phi Delta Theta, Phi Delta Phi, Omicron Delta Kappa. Methodist. Clubs: Capital City, Lawyers, Piedmont Driving (Atlanta); Homossa Fishing (Fla.). Home: 2542 Habersham Rd NW Atlanta GA 30305 Office: First Nat Bank Bldg Atlanta GA 30305

BOWDEN, JESSE EARLE, newspaper editor; b. Altha, Fla., Sept. 12, 1928; s. Jesse Walden and Earline (Rackley) B.; B.S. in Journalism and Polit. Sci., Fla. State U., 1951; m. Mary Louise Clark, Feb. 4, 1951; children-Steven Earle, Randall Clark. Reporter, columnist Panama City (Fla.) News-Herald, 1950; sports editor Pensacola (Fla.) News-Jour., 1953-57, news editor, 1957-65, editorial page editor, 1965-66, editorial cartoonist, 1965—, editor-in- chief, 1966—. Charter mem. Pensacola Hist. Commn. Trustee Pensacola Jr. Coll.; bd. dirs. Fla. Hist. Soc. Served to capt. USAF, 1951-53. Recipient Distinguished Citizen award Pensacola Jr. Coll., 1966; nat. award editorial writing Freedoms Found. at Valley Forge, 1968, awards for editorials and cartoons, 1967, 68, 69. Mem. Am. Soc. Newspaper Editors, Nat. Conf. Editorial Writers, Fla. Soc. Newspaper Editors (pres. 1970). Rotarian. Home: 3725 Bonner Rd Pensacola FL 32503 Office: 101 E Romana St Pensacola FL 32501

BOWDEN, OWEN CHANDLER, corp. official; b. Lexington, Okla., 1900. Chmn., pres. Sterchi Bros. Stores, Inc.; dir. Hamilton Nat. Bank, Cole Drug Co., Inc. Home: 618 Cheowa Circle Knoxville TN 37920 Office: 114 S Gay St Knoxville TN 37920

BOWDEN, ROBERT JOHN, educator; b. Conemaugh, Pa., Feb. 14, 1915; s. George S. and Ora (Zimmerman) B.; A.B. cum laude Waynesburg Coll., 1937; S.T.B., Western Theol. Sem., 1940; M.Ed., U. Pitts., 1942, Ph.D., 1946; m. Sara Catherine Klingensmith, Oct. 7, 1940; children—Robert John II, William B. Ordained minister, Presbyterian Ch., 1940; pastor Smithfield & Bloomfield Presbyn. Chs., Ohio, 1940-46; dean Uniontown Center of Waynesburg Coll., 1946-50; prof. Bible and philosophy Waynesburg Coll., 1950-51, prof. English, chmn. dept., 1951-70, prof. religion, 1970—. Mem. Am. Assn. U. Profs., Nat. Council Tchrs. English, U.S. Power Squadrons. Republican. Presbyn. Author: Were You There, 1963. Home: 500 N West St Waynesburg PA 15370

BOWDEN, WARREN WILLIAM, educator; b. South Penobscot, Me., Nov. 25, 1925; s. Ole Lester and Bernice (Perkins) B.; B.S., U. Me., 1949; M.S. Rose Poly. Inst., 1959; Ph.D., Purdue U., 1965; m. Evelyn Louise Patterson, July 4, 1953; children— Warren R., Rex C., Gilbert H. Research engr. Comml. Solvents Corp., Terre Haute, Ind., 1949-54; instr. chem. engring. Rose-Hulman Inst. Tech., Terre Haute, 1956-59, asst. prof., 1959-65, asso. prof., 1965-69, prof., 1969—; dir. air pollution control dept. Vigo Co., Terre Haute, 1967-68; cons. in field. Served with AUS, 1953-56. Mem. Am. Chem. Soc., Am. Inst. Chem. Engring., A.A.A.S., N.Y. Acad. Scis., Sigma Xi, Tau Beta Pi. Home: 519 S 5th St Terre Haute IN 47807

BOWDISH, LEWIS STANTON, lawyer; b. Bklyn., Aug. 12, 1912; s. Lewis F. and Jessie Edna (Fordham) B.; B.A., Wesleyan U., 1933; student Cornell, 1933-34; J.D., N.Y.U., 1937; m. Margaret E. McClymont, July 25, 1943; children—James L. S., David Lawe. Admitted to N.Y. bar, practicing lawyer, N.Y.C., 1937- 68; mem. Remsen, Millham, Bowdish & Spellman, and predecessors; atty. gen. Am. Samoa, 1951-52; exec. v.p., dir. Bank of Am. Samoa; dir. KMC Semicondr. Corp., Miracle Adhesives Corp., Cayuga Assos., Inc.; pres. bd. edn., commr. pub. safety (all Am. Samoa). Served as intelligence officer, B-29 Group, U.S. Air Corps, Tinian, Mariannas. World War II; maj., A.U.S. Res. Mem. Am., N.Y. State bar assns., Assn. Bar City of N.Y., Phi Beta Kappa, Delta Sigma Rho, Phi Delta Phi, Phi Nu Theta. Methodist. Office: 550 S Flower St Los Angeles CA 90017

BOWDITCH, FREDERICK WISE, auto mfg. co. exec.; b. Jamaica, L.I., N.Y., Nov. 17, 1921; s. Frederick Tryon and Eleanor (Wise) B.; B.S. in Mech. Engring., U. Ill., 1943; M.S., Purdue U., 1948, Ph.D., 1951; m. Dorothy Vucic, June 17, 1944; children—Karalyn A., Dierdra E. Sr. research engr. fuels and lubricants Gen. Motors Research Labs., 1951-66, staff engr. emission control Gen. Motors Engring. Staff, 1966-68, dir. automotive emission control Gen. Motors Environmental Activities Staff, Warren, Mich., 1968—. Served to lt. (j.g.) USNR, 1943-46. Mem. Air Pollution Control Assn. (dir. 1968-71), Automobile Mfrs. Assn. (past chmn. air quality com.), Soc. Automotive Engrs. (vice chmn. automotive and air pollution com. 1969—. Horning Meml. award 1952). Presbyn. (elder 1971—). Club: Hidden Valley Resort (Gaylord, Mich.). Home: 2777 Orchard Trail Troy MI 48084 Office: Gen Motors Environmental Activities Staff Gen Motors Tech Center Warren MI 48090

BOWDITCH, JOHN, 3d, educator; b. Youngstown, O., Oct. 15, 1914; s. John and Martha Angeline (Willits) B.; A.B. magna cum laude with high honors in History, Amherst Coll., 1936; M.A. (Amherst Meml. fellow 1936-38), Harvard, 1937, Ph.D., 1949; m. Helen Ernestine Wharton, Dec. 9, 1945; childrenAnneliese, John Christopher, James Wharton. Instr. Simmons Coll., 1946-47; faculty history U. Minn., 1947-60, prof., 1959-60, chmn. dept., 1958-60; prof. history U. Mich., 1960—, chmn. dept., 1960-65. Rockefeller fellow, 1955-56. Served to capt. AUS, 1942-46; ETO; col. Res. ret. Mem. Am. Hist. Assn., Econ. History Assn., Society for French Hist. Studies (pres. 1966), Am. Assn. U. Profs., Phi Beta Kappa. Author: The Anzio Beachhead, 1947; (with others) From the Volturno to the Winter Line, 1945. Contbr. A History of the Fifth Army, 1946, chpt. in Modern France, 1950, chpt. in Teachers of History, 1954. Co-editor: Economic Man and the Industrial Revolution, 1957. Home: 703 Berkshire Rd Ann Arbor MI 48104

BOWDITCH, NATHANIEL RANTOUL, banker; b. Boston, Feb. 28, 1932; s. Richard Lyon and Mabel Lowel (Rantoul) B.; grad. Deerfield Acad. (Mass.), 1951; B.A., Cornell U., 1955; M.B.A., Stanford, 1959; m. Margaret Cluverius Parsons, Dec. 21, 1959; children—Elizabeth, Nathaniel L., Edward R., William P. Mgr. dept. Strawbridge & Clothier, Phila., 1959-62; asst. treas. First Pa. Bank, Phila., 1962-68, v.p., 1968, sr. v.p., 1968—; dir. Va. Chems., Norfolk, 1969—. Mem. exec. com. Urban Affairs Com., 1968—. Bd. dirs. Me. Coast Heritage Trust, Phila. Council Internat. Vistas, So. Homes for Children. Served with AUS, 1955-57. Home: 5 E Hampton Rd Philadelphia PA 19118 Office: 15th and Chestnut Sts Philadelphia PA 19118

BOWDLER, WILLIAM G., U.S. ambassador; b. Argentina, Mar. 27, 1924; B.A., U. Richmond, 1948; M.A., Fletcher Sch. Law and Diplomacy, 1949; m.; 3 children. Came to U.S., naturalized, 1945. Research asst. Dept. State, 1950-51, internat. adminstrn. officer, 1951-52, internat. relations officer, 1952- 54, fgn. affairs officer, 1954-56; officer charge Antarctica and Internat. Geophys. Yr. affairs, 1956; sec. Inter-Am. Com. for Pres. Reps., OAS, 1956; 2d sec., consul, Havana, Cuba, 1957-61; internat. relations officer Dept. State, 1961, officer charge spl. polit. affairs (Latin Am.), 1961-64, dep. coordinator Cuban affairs, 1964-65; sr. staff mem. for Latin Am., NSC, 1965-68; U.S. ambassador to El Salvador, 1968-71; U.S. ambassador to Guatemala, 1971—. Served with AUS, 1944-46. Address: Dept of State (Guatemala) Washington DC 20521

BOWDOIN, WILLIAM REDDING, banker; b. Atlanta, July 21, 1913; s. William Henry and Pauline (Collins) B.; LL.B., U. Ga., 1933; m. Margaret Stoddard, July 30, 1942; children—William Redding, John Collins. Admitted to Ga. bar, 1934; with Peoples Bank, Winder, Ga., 1936-41; pres. First Nat. Bank, East Point, Ga., 1946-48; with Trust Co. Ga., Atlanta, 1948—, vice chmn. bd., 1964—, also dir.; chmn., pres. Trust Co. Ga. Assos., 1964—; dir. First Nat. Bank & Trust Co., Augusta, Ga., DeKalb Nat. Bank of Brookhaven, Atlanta, Fourth Nat. Bank, Columbus, Ga., First Nat. Bank & Trust Co., Macon, Ga., First Nat. Bank, Rome, Ga., Liberty Nat. Bank & Trust Co., Savannah, Ga. Chmn. Ga. Ports Authority, 1953-55; gov. Ga. Commn. Efficiency and Improvement, 1963-64; supr. purchases Ga., 1959. Co-chmn., Atlanta Meml. Cultural Center campaign, 1964; treas. Ga. Assn. Crippled Children, 1964; adv. com. Ga. Vocational Assn., 1963-64. Trustee Emory U., Ga. Found. Ind. Colls.; vice chmn. bd. Berry Schs.; bd. dirs. Lovett Sch. Served to maj. AUS, 1941-46. Recipient Ga. Citizen of Year award Ga. Assn. County Commnrs., 1963; Nat. Citizenship award Future Farmers Am., 1964; hon. mem. Gridiron Secret Soc. (U. Ga). Episcopalian. Home: 3845 Club Dr NE Atlanta GA 30319 Office: Trust Co of Georgia Pryor St and Edgewood Av PO Box 4418 Atlanta GA 30302

BOWDOIN, WILMOTH BOWEN, univ. dean; b. Coffee Springs, Ala., Dec. 4, 1915; s. James Oscar and Maggie (Covington) B.; B.S., State Tchrs. Coll., Troy, Ala., 1941; M.A., George Peabody Coll., 1947, Ph.D., 1952; m. Ruth Shiver, May 5, 1939. Tchr. elementary sch., Coffee Springs, Ala., 1938-39, prin., 1939-41, tchr. high sch., 1941-38; asst. prof. edn. Middle Tenn. State Coll., Murfreesboro, 1948-51, head dept. edn., 1951-63, dir. Sch. Edn., 1963- 65, dean, 1965—. Mem. Tenn. Curriculum Com., 1955—. Mem. Assn. Supervision and Curriculum Devel. (dir.), Tenn. Assn. Supervision and Curriculum Devel. (past pres.), N.E.A., Tenn. Edn. Assn., Assn. Student Teaching, Kappa Delta Pi, Phi Delta Kappa. Baptist (deacon). Home: 220 Wilson Av Murfreesboro TN 37130

BOWE, SISTER MARY CAMILLE, educator, former coll. pres.; b. Waseca, Minn., May 28, 1903; d. Thomas R. and Mary Ann (Bourchier) Bowe; A.B., Coll. St. Teresa, Winona, Minn., 1935; D. Litt., Sorbonne, U. Paris, 1939. Mem. Sisters of St. Francis, 1922—; tchr. schs. Order St. Francis, 1924-34; head dept. modern langs. Coll. St. Teresa, Winona, Minn., 1939—, v.p., 1946-52, pres., 1952-69, pres. emeritus, 1970—. Past pres. Minn. Pvt. Coll. Council; mem. exec. com. Minn. Pvt. Coll. Fund, 1956-57, 63- 64, 67-68. Adviser women's sect. Mpls. Symphony Orch. Recipient prix de la langue francaise French Acad., 1939; Officer d'Academie, French Govt., 1956. Mem. Assn. Am. Colls. (commn. on internat. understanding), Nat. Council Accreditation Tchrs. of Edn., Modern Lang. Assn., Am. Assn. Tchrs. French, Assn. Minn. Colls. (pres. 1954-55), Cath. Renascence Soc. (dir., past chmn.), Nat., French, Nat. Spanish honor socs., Pi Delta Phi, Sigma Delta Pi. Author: Francois Rio, sa place dans le renouveau Catholique au X1X siecle, in collection Etudes de Litterature Etrangere et Comparee, 1939. Translator critical apparatus and notes for Mary Magdalene (by Raymond Bruckberger, O.P.), 1953; transl. from French: Credo in Unun Deum included in Toward The Summit (R. L. Bruckberger). Editor: The Modern Revolt Against Puritanism, 1954. Author and translator articles and book revs. Editorial adviser of Renascence. Office: College of St Teresa Winona

BOWELL, GORDON STEPHEN JOHNSON, pulp and paper mfr.; b. Vancouver, Can., Dec. 27, 1918; s. Stephen Robert and Charlotte (Johnson) B.; B.A. (Rhodes scholar), Queen's U., 1941; M.B.A., Harvard, 1947; m. Frances Ellen Webb, Jan. 20, 1919; children—Shelley, Christopher. With MacMillan Bloedel, Ltd., Vancouver, Can., 1947—, v.p. pulp and paper, 1957—; exec. v.p., dir. Rayonier Can. (B.S.), Ltd., 1964-66, pres., 1966-71; pres., chief exec. officer Weldwood Can. Ltd., 1971—. Served as maj., arty., Canadian Army, 1941-45. Decorated Order Brit. Empire. Mem. Anglican Ch. Club: Vancouver. Home: 1806 SW Marine Dr Vancouver 14 British Columbia Canada Office: 1055 W Hastings Vancouver 2 British Columbia Canada

BOWEN, ALBERT REEDER, lawyer; b. Logan, Utah, Apr. 13, 1905; s. Albert Ernest and Aletha (Reeder) B.; A.B., U. Utah, 1930; J.D., Leland Stanford Jr. U., 1932; m. Lucile Ross, Nov. 17, 1934 (dec. 1952); children—Barbara (Mrs. Ted O. Brunker), David Ross, Beverly (Mrs. Michael W. Walker), Albert Ross, Robert K. Bowen; m. 2d, Margret Jenson, Mar. 29, 1954; children—Mark J., Julie, Stephen J. Admitted to Utah bar, 1932, since practiced in Salt Lake City; partner firm Ray, Quinney & Nebeker, and predecessors, 1945—. Sec., mem. Utah Sch. Study Com., 1963- 64. Del. Republican Nat. Conv., 1964. Bd. regents U. Utah, 1951-55. Fellow Am. Coll. Trial Lawyers; mem. Am., Utah bar assns. Mem. Ch. of Jesus Christ of Latter Day Saints. Clubs: Timpangogas, Bonneville Knife and Fork (bd. dirs. 1962-65), Fort Douglas (Salt Lake City). Home: 1847 Laird Av Salt Lake City UT 84108 Office: Deseret Bldg Salt Lake City UT 84111

BOWEN, CATHERINE DRINKER, author; b. Haverford, Pa.; d. Henry Sturgis and Aimée Ernesta (Beaux) Drinker; student Peabody Inst., Inst. Mus. Art; Litt.D., U. Pa., Temple U., Boston U., Rochester, Coll., Lafayette Coll., Lehigh Coll.; other hon. degrees; m. Ezra Bowen; children—Catherine Drinker, Ezra; m. 2d, Thomas McKean Downs, July 1, 1939. Author numerous books, latest publs.; Beloved FriendBiography of Tchaikowsky (with Barbara Von Mech), 1937 (Book-of-Month); Yankee from OlympusJustice O. W. Holmes and His Family (Book of the Month), 1944; John Adams and the American Revolution (Book of the Month), 1950; The Lion and the Throne, 1956 (History Book Club); Adventures of A Biographer, 1959; Francis Bacon, 1963 (Book-of-Month); Miracle at Philadelphia, 1966 (Book-of-the-Month); Biography; The Craft and The Calling, 1969; Family Portrait, 1970. Trustee emeritus Free Library System Phila., Nat. Portrait Gallery Commn. Recipient Nat. Book award, Phila. award, Phillips award Am. Philos. Soc., 1957; Nat. Achievement award, 1958. Mem. Nat. Inst. Arts and Letters (mem. council 1965—), Royal Soc. Literature, Phi Beta Kappa. Home: 260 Booth Lane Haverford PA 19041 ☆

BOWEN, CHARLES CLARK, educator, biologist; b. Detroit, Mar. 18, 1917; s. Charles Clark and Geraldine (Jarvis) B.; student U. Mich., 1935-39; B.A., Mich. State U., 1949, M.S., 1951, Ph.D., 1953; m. Vada Robinson, Aug. 28, 1947; children—Clark, Gail (Mrs. Marvin Lindmark), Jean (Mrs. Dean Smith), Lecia (Mrs. William Riva). Postdoctoral fellow NIH at Brookhaven Nat. Lab., 1953-55; faculty Ia. State U., Ames, 1955—, prof., 1962—, chmn. grad. program cell biology, 1966—, asst. dean scis. and humanities, 1967—. Mem. Bot. Soc. Am., Am. Soc. Cell Biology, Radiation Research Soc., Electron Microscope Soc. Am., A.A.A.S., Sigma Xi. Contbr. articles profl. jours. Home: RR3 Ames IA 50010

BOWEN, CHARLES CORBIN, mgmt. cons., accountant; b. Monson, Cal., May 20, 1897; s. William Lee and Serepta Jane (Wicker) B.; B.S., U. Cal., 1921; M.B.A., Harvard, 1923; m. Mildred Virginia Moore, Feb. 5, 1928; 1 dau., Jane. Econ. statistician USDA, spl. assignments Europe and Asia, 1923-24; export mgr. Sun Maid Raisin Growers, Fresno, Cal., 1924-25; head research dept. Tucker, Hunter Dulin & Co., Los Angeles, 1926-28; chief Cal. Bur. Commerce, Sacramento, 1929-30; v.p., dir. Am. Trust Co., affiliates, San Francisco, 1931-33; exec. v.p. Bishop Trust Co., Honolulu, 1935-37; asst. to dir. RFC, Washington, 1934; C.P.A., mgmt. cons. Charles C. Bowen & Co., San Francisco, 1938—; exec. v.p., treas., dir. Klamath Machine & Locomotive Works of Cal., San Francisco; exec. v.p., treas., dir. Pacific Assos. of Cal., Empire Factors, San Francisco; pres., dir. Pacific Assos., Inc., San Francisco, Portland Transit Co.; pres., treas., dir. Landport Co., Inc., Portland, Ore.; pres. treas., dir. Rose City Transit Co., Portland, 1956—; civilian expert cons. U.S. Army Engrs. and Q.M. Corps, 1942-44. Served as ordnance officer AEF, U.S. Army, 1918-19. Mem. Am. Transit Assn. (dir.), S.A.R., Am. Inst. C.P.A.'s, Cal. Soc. C.P.A.'s, Phi Sigma Kappa, Beta Alpha Psi, Alpha Kappa Psi. Republican. Mason. Clubs: Olympic, Merchants Exchange (San Francisco); California (Los Angeles); Arlington, Multnomah (Portland, Wash.); Harvard (N.Y.C.); Capitol Hill (Washington). Contbr. articles profl. jours. Home: 1902 Green St San Francisco CA 94123 Office: Russ Bldg San Francisco CA 94104

BOWEN, CHARLES HUGH, Jr., electronics engr.; b. Belle Ellen, Ala., Jan. 8, 1923; s. Charles Hugh and Lavada (Lawley) B.; student U. Ariz., 1939-40, 46, U. So. Cal., 1946-47; B.S. in Engring. Electronics, Naval Postgrad. Sch., 1953, M.S., 1954; grad. Naval War Coll., 1961; m. Nina Gwen Stevens, July 29, 1945; children—David Hugh, Charles Hugh III. Commd. ensign U.S. Navy, 1943, advanced through grades to capt., 1965; flight tng., 1942-43; pilot and flight officer, PTO, 1944-45; flight instr. Aviation Tng. Unit 5, 1947-49; radar projects supr., VX-1 Key West, Fla., 1949-51; operations officer Attack Squadron 55, 1954-55; aviation electronics engring. officer, staff Comdr. Naval Air Force Pacific Fleet, 1956-58; assigned spl. studies sect. Spl. Projects Office, Bur. Weapons, 1958-60; student replace air tng. group Attack Squadron 122, 1961; comdg. officer Attack Squadron 115, 1962-63; navigator U.S.S. Kitty Hawk, 1963-64, exec. officer, 1964; tchr. elec. sci. U.S. Naval Acad., also head sci. dept., 1965-67; command U.S.S. Vesuvius, 1967-68; advanced devel. engr. Sylvania Electronics Systems, Mountain View, Cal., 1968—. Decorated D.F.C. with gold star, Air medal with silver star. Mem. I.E.E.E., Naval Inst., Internat. Platform Assn. Democrat. Home: 824 La Crosse Ct Sunnyvale, CA 94087. Office: Sylvania Electronics Systems 100 Ferguson Dr Mountain View CA 94040

BOWEN, CHARLES PARNELL, Jr., mgmt. cons.; b. West Collingswood, N.J., Feb. 20, 1914; s. Charles P. and Helen (Sheets) B.; B.S., Mass. Inst. Tech., 1935; m. Hope Ludlow, Dec. 24, 1937; children—Geoffrey, Carla, Deborah, Eve. Time study engr. Gen. Electric Co., 1935-40; indsl. engr. Carnegie Ill. Steel Co., 1940- 41, Ingersoll Steel & Disc div. Borg-Warner, 1941-43, Bell Aircraft, 1943-44; with Booz, Allen & Hamilton, N.Y.C., 1944—, partner, 1948-62, coordinating partner Eastern region, mem. exec. com., 1957-61, pres., dir., 1962-70, chmn., dir., 1970—. Mem. Newcomen Soc. Clubs: Chicago (Chgo.); University, Sky (N.Y.C.); Indian Harbor Yacht; Belle Haven; Economic. Home: 10 Cedarwood Dr Greenwich CT 06830 Office: 245 Park Av New York City NY 10017

BOWEN, DON LESLIE, educator; b. Spanish Fork, Utah, Apr. 16, 1922; s. Leslie and Hortense (Lieshman) B.; B.S., Utah State U., 1944; M.S., U. Denver; 1945; Ph.D., Syracuse U., 1949; m. Janice Applegate, Dec. 25, 1944; children—Stephen Leslie, Kathryn Ann. Instr., asst. prof. dept. govt. U. Okla., 1946-49; dir. research, acting dir. Okla., Legislative Com., 1949- 51; exec. sec. to Congressman John Jarman, Okla., 1951-53; dir. Bur. Govt. Research, asso. prof. govt. U. Md., 1953-56; asst. dir. edn. and research, asso. dir. Am. Soc. Pub. Adminstrn., Chgo., 1956-62, exec. dir., 1962-70; Ford Found. grant Govtl. Affairs Inst., Washington, 1970-71; coll. adviser for pub. service edn. programs Bowie (Md.) State Coll., 1971. Vis. prof. Utah State U., summer 1958; lectr. U. Chgo., Dept. Agr. Grad. Sch.; cons. U.S. Gen Accounting Office, U.S. Office Edn., Md. Dept. Health, Okla. Personnel Bd. Mem. Citizens Com. Constl. Revision Okla., 1948; mem. Prince Georges County Study Commn., 1966-67, chmn. County Merit System Rev. com., 1968-69; mem. governing bds. Pub. Am. Service, Govtl. Affairs Inst. (exec. com.). Mem. Am., Western, So. polit. sci. assns., Western Govt. Research Assn., Am. Soc. Pub. Adminstrn. (past pres. Md. chpt., past v.p. Wash. chpt.), Nat. Acad. Pub. Adminstrn., Phi Kappa Phi, Pi Sigma Alpha (past nat. pres.). Unitarian. Author: Judicial Personnel, 1949; Judicial Organization and Management, 1949; (with R.S. Friedman) Local Government in Maryland, 1955. Co-editor: Administrative Leadership in Government: Selected Papers, 1959, Program Formulation and Development: The Role of the Government Executive, 1960; Methods and Goals in Public Managements, 1961. Contbr. articles to profl. jours., mags. Home: 4401 College Heights Dr University Park MD 20782 Office: Govtl Affairs Inst 1766 Massachusetts Av NW Washington DC 20036

BOWEN, DOUGLAS MALCOMSOM, educator; b. Wellesley, Mass., Sept. 24, 1917; s. Frederick S. and Lillian May (Adriance) B.; A.B., Harvard, 1937, A.M., 1939, Ph.D., 1940; m. Louise Thompson Hayward, Oct. 23, 1943; children—Douglas Malcomson, Alison H. Instr. Harvard, 1941-45; asst. prof. chemistry Dartmouth, 1945- 53, prof., 1953—, registrar, 1968—. Mem. Am. Chem. Soc., New Eng. Assn. Chemistry Tchrs. Home: 8 Chase Rd Hanover NH 03755

BOWEN, EDWARD WOODVILLE, banker; b. Detroit, Oct. 1, 1911; A.B., U. Mich., 1933; m. Barbara Payson, Oct. 14, 1939 (dec. 1962); children—Barbara B., Louise T.; m. 2d, Elizabeth J. Danielson, 1969. Vice pres. Bay Trust Co., 1938-48, Peoples Comml. & Savs. Bank, 1949-50; exec. v.p., cashier Peoples Nat. Bank & Trust Co., Bay City, Mich., 1950-60, dir., 1950—, pres. 1960—. Bd. govs. Clements Library of U. Mich. Mem. Mich. Bankers Assn. (pres. 1971). Presbyn. Clubs: Bay City Country; Saginaw (Mich.). Home: 136 Carroll Rd Bay City MI 48706 Office: 300 Center Av Bay City MI 48706

BOWEN, ELIZABETH DOROTHEA COLE, (Mrs. Alan Charles Cameron), author; b. Dublin, Ireland, June 7, 1889; d. Henry Cole and Florence (Colley) Bowen; ed. Downe House, Downe, Kent, Eng.; D.Litt. (hon.), Trinity Coll., Dublin, 1949; Litt.D., Oxon, 1954; m. Alan Charles Cameron, Aug. 4, 1923. Author short stories, novels, essays. Comdr. Order of Brit. Empire. Mem. Am. Acad. Arts and Letters (hon.). Author: Encounters, 1923; Ann Lee's, 1926; The Hotel, 1927; The Last September, 1929; Joining Charles, 1929; Friends and Relations, 1931; To the North, 1932; The Cat Jumps, 1934; The House in Paris, 1935; The Death of the Heart, 1938; Look at All Those Roses, 1941; Bowen's Court, 1942; Seven Winters, 1943; The Demon Lover, 1945; The Heat of the Day, 1949; Collected Impressions, 1950; Shelbourne Hotel, 1951; A World of Love, 1955; A Time in Rome, 1960; Afterthoughts, 1962 (essays); Little Girls, 1964; Good Tiger, 1965; A Day in the Dark, 1965; Eva Trout, 1968. Home: Carbery Church Hill Hythe Kent England

BOWEN, GEORGE HAMILTON, Jr., educator; b. Tulsa, June 20, 1925; s. George H. and Dorothy (Huntington) B.; B.S. with honor, Cal. Inst. Tech., 1949, Ph.D., 1952; m. Marjorie Evelyn Brown, June 19, 1948; children—Paul Huntington, Margaret Irene, Carol Ann, Dorothy Elizabeth, Kevin Leigh. Asso. biologist Oak Ridge Nat. Lab., 1952-54; asst.prof. physics Ia. State Coll., 1954-57; asso. prof. physics Ia. State U., 1957-65, prof., 1965—. Served with USNR, 1944-46. Recipient Ia. State U. Outstanding Tchr. award, 1970, Faculty citation Ia. State U. Alumni Assn., 1971. Mem. Am. Assn. Physics Tchrs. (chmn. Ia. sect. 1966-67), A.A.A.S., Sigma Xi, Tau Beta Pi. Home: 1919 Burnett Av Ames IA 50010

BOWEN, HAROLD GARDINER, Jr., naval officer; b. Annapolis, Md., Oct. 15, 1912; s. Harold Gardiner and Margaret Edith (Brownlie) B.; B.S., U.S. Naval Acad., 1933; M.S., Carnegie Inst. Tech., 1942; grad. Naval War Coll., 1950; m. Constance Kathryn Baker, May 28, 1938; children—Constance Ruth (Mrs. Camp), Margaret Edith (Mrs. Easley), Kathryn Anne (Mrs. Woodward), Charlotte Elizabeth. Commd. ensign U.S. Navy, 1933, advanced through grades to vice adm., comdr. U.S.S. Conway, 1943-44, U.S.S. Samuel N. Moore, 1945-46, Destroyer Div. 92, 1952-53, U.S.S. Neosho, 1957-58, U.S.S. Northampton, 1959-60, Cruiser Destroyer Flotilla 4, 1962-63, Operational Test and Evaluation Force, 1963-65; dir. atomic energy div. Office Naval Operations, 1958- 59; dep. dir. naval intelligence Navy Dept., 1960-62; dep. chief naval operations (devel.), 1965-67, comdr. Anti-Submarine Warfare Force Pacific, 1967-69; vice adm. U.S. Navy Dep. Asst. Sec. Def. (Intelligence), 1969—. Decorated D.S.M., Legion of Merit (2), Bronze Star (3), Navy Commendation medal (3). Mem. Newcomen Soc. N. Am., U.S. Naval Inst. Office: Dep Asst Sec Def Pentagon Washington DC 20301

BOWEN, HENRY LUMPKIN, utilities exec.; b. Pelham, Ga., Dec. 14, 1906; s. Alma Lumpkin and Alma (Miller) B.; B.S., Ga. Inst. Tech., 1930; m. Florence Allene Brown, Dec. 24, 1931 (dec.); children—Henry Lumpkin, Judith Elaine. With Ga. Power Co., 1926—, mgr. indsl. relations, Augusta, 1950-58, v.p., Atlanta, 1958-66, sr. v.p., dir., 1966—; dir. So. Electric Generating Co. Mem. Atlanta C. of C. Baptist. Kiwanian. Club: Commerce (Atlanta). Home: 88 Pine Lake Dr NW Atlanta GA 30327 Office: 270 Peachtree St NW Atlanta GA 30303

BOWEN, HOWARD ROTHMANN, economist; b. Spokane, Wash., Oct. 27, 1908; s. Henry G. and Josephine (Menig) B.; B.A., Wash. State U., 1929, M.A., 1933; Ph.D., U. Ia., 1935; LL.D., Cornell Coll., 1956, Knox Coll., 1964, Drake U., 1968; L.H.D., Coe Coll., 1965, Loras College, 1963, Marycrest Coll., 1968; D. Litt., Grinnell Coll., 1964; m. Lois B. Schilling, Aug. 24, 1935; children—Peter Geoffrey, Thomas Gerard. Instr. econs. U. Ia., 1935-38, asst. prof., 1938-40, asso. prof., 1940-42; economist U.S. Dept. Commerce, 1942-44; chief economist Joint Congl. Com. on Internal Revenue Taxation, 1944-45, economist Irving Trust Co., 1945-47; dean Coll. Commerce and Bus. Adminstrn., prof. econs. U. Ill., 1947-52; prof. econs. Williams Coll. 1952-55; pres. Grinnell (Ia.) Coll., 1955-64, U. Ia., Iowa City, 1964-69; now pres. emeritus; prof. econs. Claremont Grad. Sch., chancellor Claremont U. Center, 1969—. Dir. Bankers Life Co. mem. Tax Mission to Japan for U.S. Army, 1949; econ. cons. Nat. Council Chs., 1949-53; chmn. Gov.'s Commn. Econ. and Social Trends in Ia., 1958; mem. Nat. Com. Govt. Finance, Brookings Instn., 1960-65; chmn. Ia. Coordinating Council for Post High Sch. Edn., 1967-68; mem. Fed. Adv. Com. Intergovtl. Relations, 1961-64; chmn. Nat. Commn. Tech., Automation and Econ. Progress, 1964-66; chief U.S. Mission to Thailand, 1961; mem. Ford Found. Mission to Yugoslavia, 1962; chmn. Nat. Citizens Com. for Tax Revision and Reform, 1963; bd. commrs. Nat. Commn. on Accrediting, 1965-69; mem. Council for Financial Aid to Edn., 1968-69; mem. Argonne Univs. Assn., 1966-69, chmn., 1967-69. Trustee Common Fund, Sun Valley Forum on Nat. Health, Nat. Planning Assn., Citizens Conf. on State Legislatures; bd. visitors Tulane U. Soc. Sci. Research Council fellow for study in Eng., 1937-38, chmn. com. on bus. enterprise research, 1954-56. Mem. Am. Finance Assn. (pres. 1950), Am. Econ. Assn. (dir. study grad. edn. econs. 1951-53), Royal Econ. Soc. (Eng.), Phi Kappa Phi, Beta Gamma Sigma, Phi Beta Kappa. Author: English Grants in Aid, 1939; Iowa Income, 1934; Unemployment Compensation Applied to Iowa, 1936; Toward Social Economy, 1948; Social Responsibilities of the Businessman, 1953; Graduate Education in Economics, 1953; Christian Values and Economic Life, 1954; (with Garth L. Mangum) Automation and Economic Progress, 1966; The Finance of Higher Edn., 1968; (with Gordon Douglass) Efficiency in Liberal Education, 1971; also numerous pamphlets and articles. Home: 723 Alamosa Dr Claremont CA 91711

BOWEN, IRA SPRAGUE, astronomer; b. Senece Falls, N.Y., Dec. 21, 1898; s. James Henry and Philinda May (Sprague) B.; A.B., Oberlin Coll., 1919, D.Sc., 1948; postgrad. U. Chgo., 1919-21; Ph.D., Cal. Inst. Tech., 1926; Ph.D., U. Lund, 1950; Sc.D., Princeton, 1953; m. Mary Jane Howard, July 12, 1929. Asst. in physics U. Chgo., 1919-21; instr. physics Cal. Inst. Tech., 1921-26, asst. prof., 1926-28, asso. prof., 1928-31, prof. 1931-45; dir. Mount Wilson Obs., 1946-64, Palomar Obs., 1948-64, Distinguished Service staff mem., 1964-69. Morrison research asso. Lick Obs., 1938-39. S.A.T.C., 1918. Recipient Potts medal Franklin Inst., 1946; Ives medal Optical Soc. Am., 1952. Mem. Nat. Acad. Sci. (Draper medal 1942), Am. Philos. Soc., Am. Acad. Arts and Scis. (Rumford Premium 1949), Am. Astron. Soc. Astron. Soc. Pacific (asso., Bruce medal 1957), Royal Astron. Soc. (Gold medal 1966). Contbr. articles to sci. jours. Home: 2388 N Altadena Dr Altadena CA 91001

BOWEN, JOHN CLYDE, judge; b. Newbern, Tenn., May 12, 1888; s. William Allen and Maryette (Featherston) B.; A.B., U. Tenn., 1913; LL.B., Harvard, 1916; m. Ruth Welsh Tuttle, Sept. 1, 1961. Prin. high sch., Timberville, Miss., 1909-10; admitted to Tenn. bar, 1916, Hawaii bar, 1917, Wash. bar, 1919; practiced at Seattle; U.S. dist. judge, Seattle, 1934—. Mem. Wash. Senate, 1931; legal adviser to Gov. 1933; mem. Columbia River Basin Commn. which promoted Grand Coulee Dam project and assisted in letting that project's first constrn. contract, 1933-34; collector Internal Revenue Service dist. Wash. and Alaska, 1933-34. Served with U.S. Army, 1917-18, 2d lt. F.A.R.C. Mem. Am., Wash., Seattle bar assns., Am. Legion, Maritime Law Assn. U.S., Order of Coif (hon.). Democrat. Baptist. Mason. Clubs: Rainier, Harvard (Seattle). Office: US Court House Seattle WA 98104

BOWEN, JOHN SHEETS, advt. exec.; b. Chelsea, Mass., Feb. 4, 1927; s. Charles Parnell and Helen (Sheets) B.; B.A., Yale, 1949; m. Catherine Leigh Stander, June 28, 1952; children—Mark Stander, Charles Parnell III, Holly Leigh. Salesman, Procter & Gamble Co., 1949-51, unit mgr., 1952; account exec. McCann-Erickson, Inc., 1952-58; with Benton & Bowles, Inc., 1959—, mgmt. supr., 1964—, sr. v.p., 1965-68, exec. v.p., 1968-71, pres., 1971—, also dir. Trustees Inst. Advanced Advt. Studies. Served with AUS, 1943- 46; ETO. Mem. Am. Assn. Advt. Agys. (gov. Eastern region). Episcopalian. Home: 44 Grace Church St Rye NY 10580 Office: 909 3d Av New York City NY 10022

BOWEN, KENNETH EDWARD, utility co. exec.; b. Oskaloosa, Ia., July 11, 1915; s. Edward Asher and Ina (Mitchell) B.; student Defiance Coll., 1934; B.S. in Bus. Adminstrn., Ohio State U., 1939; M.S. in Indsl. Mgmt. (Sloan fellow), Mass. Inst. Tech., 1953; m. Betty Jean Raney, Aug. 21, 1943; children—Pamela, Stephen, Donna, Deborah. Jr. engr. Ohio Gas, Light & Coke Co., Bryan, 1939-41; engring. clk. Central Ill. Pub. Service Co., Springfield, 1941-42, div. indsl. engr., Beardstown, 1946-47, div. mech. engr., 1947-52, mgr. gas operations, Springfield, 1953-59, div. mgr., Mattoon, 1959-65, then v.p., dir., Springfield, now pres.; dir. Electric Energy, Inc., Joppa, Ill., Ill. Nat. Bank, Springfield. Served to lt . comdr. USNR, 1942-45. Registered profl. engr., Ill. Mem. Am. Mgmt. Assn., Ill. C. of C., Springfield C. of C., Beta Gamma Sigma. Republican. Episcopalian. Mason (32, Shriner). Home: 101 Linden Lane Springfield IL 62707 Office: 607 E Adams St Springfield IL 62700

BOWEN, LEM WARNER, mfg. co. exec.; b. Detroit, July 31, 1915; s. Julian Perry and Louise Hopkins (Chapman) B.; A.B., Dartmouth, 1937; m. Elizabeth R. Pollock, Oct. 1, 1945; children—Susan E., Louisa H. With Burroughs Corp., Detroit, 1937-42, 46—, treas., 1963—; dir. Mfrs. Appraisal Co. Trustee McGregor Fund, Merrill-Palmer Inst.; bd. dirs. Detroit Symphony Orch. Served with AUS, 1942-46. Home: Grosse Pointe MI Office: Burroughs Pl Detroit MI 48232

BOWEN, MERLIN SHELLEY, educator; b. Eureka, Cal., Aug. 7, 1910; s. Shelley M. and Nellie (Lee) B.; B.A., U. Chgo., 1936, M.A., 1947, Ph.D., 1957; m. Ruth Helen Collette, Feb. 15, 1941; children—John S., Jeffery C. Tchr. English, Francis W. Parker Sch., Chgo., 1941-46; mem. faculty U. Chgo., 1947—, prof. English and humanities, 1967—; Fulbright lect. Am. lit. U. Athens (Greece), 1960-61, U. Bucharest (Romania), 1971-72. Von Marwitz fellow, 1956; recipient Quantrell award excellence undergrad. teaching U. Chgo., 1963. Mem. Phi Beta Kappa. Author: The Long Encounter: Self and Experience in the Writings of Herman Melville, 1960; also articles. Home: 5515 Woodlawn Av Chicago IL 60637

BOWEN, ORLANDO MOORE, hosp. adminstr.; b. Camden, N.J., Aug. 8, 1918; s. Orlando M. and Blanche I. (Moyer) B.; B.S. in Hotel Adminstrn., Cornell U., Ithaca, N.Y., 1940; m. Betty Jane Davis, Oct. 5, 1940; children—Barbara (Mrs. Anthony Kluczník), Robert, Richard, John. Unit mgr. food service Trans World Airlines, 1941-42; asst. mgr. Stouffer's, Cleve., 1942-47; asst. supt. Allentown (Pa.) Hosp., 1947-54, adminstr., 1954-. Bd. dirs. Lehigh Valley Crippled Childrens Soc., 1950-64; trustee Lehigh County Community Coll., 1966-68. Served to lt. (j.g.) USNR, 1944-46. Fellow Am. Coll. Hosp. Adminstrs.; mem. Hosp. Assn. Pa. (past bd. dirs.; pres. 1968-69). Rotarian (pres. Northampton, Pa. 1954-55, pres. Allentown, Pa. 1967-68). Home: 721 S 25th St Allentown, PA 18103. Office: Allentown Hosp 17th and Chew St Allentown PA 18102

BOWEN, RAYMOND L., utility co. exec.; b. 1897; married. Pres., Community Pub. Service Co., Fort Worth, 1935-62, gen. mgr., chmn. bd., chief exec. officer, 1962-68, chmn. bd., 1968—, also dir. Office: 501 W 6th St Fort Worth TX 76102*

BOWEN, RICHARD L., univ. pres.; b. Avoca, Ia., Aug. 31, 1933; s. Howard L. and Donna (Milburn) B.; B.A., Augustana Coll., 1957; M.A., Harvard, 1959, Ph.D., 1967; m. Constance Sikkink, July 7, 1956; children—Catherine, David, Thomas. Fgn. service officer State Dept., 1959-60; research asst. to U.S. Senator Francis Case, 1960-62; legislative asst. to U.S. Senator Karl Mundt, 1962-65; minority cons. sub-com. exec. reorgn. U.S. Senate, 1966-67; asst. to pres., asso. prof. polit. sci. U. S.D., Vermillion, 1967-69, pres., 1969—. Served with USNR, 1951-54. Recipient Outstanding Alumnus award Augustana Coll., 1970. Woodrow Wilson fellow, 1957; Fulbright scholar, 1957; Congl. Staff fellow, 1965. Home: 109 Austin St Vermillion SD 57069

BOWEN, ROBERT ALLEN, food co. exec.; b. Sheridan, Ill., Mar. 9, 1915; s. Ai P. and Myra Belle (Wallace) B.; B.S., U. Ill., 1937, postgrad. 1938-39; m. Helen Aleksiun, July 2, 1939; children—Ken, Pat. With Arthur Andersen & Co., C.P.A.'s, Chgo., 1937-38, 39-45, Quaker Oats Co., Chgo., 1946—, controller, 1963-66, v.p., controller, 1966—. C.P.A., Ill. Mem. Am. Inst. C.P.A.'s, Financial Execs. Inst. Home: 3911 Johnson Av Western Springs IL Office: Quaker Oats Co Merchandise Mart Chicago IL 60654

BOWEN, THEODORE, educator; b. Evanston, Ill., Mar. 19, 1928; s. Harvey Newland and Sylvia (Turner) B.; Ph.B., U. Chgo., 1947, M.S., 1950, Ph.D. (AEC fellow), 1954; m. Lillian Ann Neill, Mar. 4, 1961; 1 stepson Warren M. Alter. Research asst. U. Chgo., 1953-54; research fellow Centro Brasileiro de Pesquisas Fisicas, Rio de Janeiro, Brazil, La Paz, Bolivia, 1954-55; research asst. Princeton, 1956, research asso., 1957-62, research physicist, 1962; asso. prof. U. Ariz. at Tucson, 1962-64, prof. physics, 1964—; NASA/Nat. Acad. Scis. sr. research asso. Goddard Space Flight Center, 1968. Fellow Am. Phys. Soc., A.A.A.S.; mem. Sigma Xi, Phi Beta Kappa. Contbr. articles profl. jours. Home: 2233 E Waverly St Tucson AZ 85719

BOWEN, WILLIAM GORDON, univ. adminstr., economist; b. Cin., Oct. 6, 1933; s. Albert A. and Bernice (Pomert) B.; B.A., Denison U., 1955; Ph.D., Princeton, 1958; m. Mary Ellen Maxwell, Aug. 25, 1956; children—David Alan, Karen Lee. Mem. faculty Princeton, 1958-, prof. econs., 1965-, dir. grad. studies Woodrow Wilson Sch. Pub. and Internat. Affairs, 1964-66, provost, 1967—. Cons. Council Econ. Advisers, Office Edn. Trustee Denison U., 1966—, Center for Advanced Study in the Behavioral Scis. Mem. Am. Econ. Assn., Indsl. Relations Research Assn., Phi Beta Kappa. Author: The Wage-Price Issue; A Theoretical Analysis, 1960; Wage Behavior in the Postwar Period; An Empirical Analysis, 1960; Economic Aspects of Education: Three Essays, 1964; (with W. J. Baumol) Performing Arts: The Economic Dilemma, 1966; (with T.A. Finegan) The Economics of Labor Force Participation, 1969. Home: 10 Maclean Circle Princeton, NJ 08540.

BOWEN, WILLIAM HARVEY, lawyer; b. Altheimer, Ark., May 6, 1923; s. Robert James and Lois Ruth (Falls) B.; student Henderson State Tchrs. Coll., 1941-42; LL.B., U. Ark., 1949; LL.M. in Taxation, N.Y. U., 1950; m. Mary Constance Wanasek, Aug. 31, 1947; children—Cynthia Ruth, William Scott, Mary Patricia. Admitted to Ark. bar, 1949, also U.S. Supreme Ct.; atty. adviser U.S. Tax Ct., Washington, 1950-52; trial atty. tax div. Dept. Justice, Washington, 1952-54; asso. firm Mehaffy, Smith & Williams, Little Rock, 1954-57, participating mem., 1957-62; partner firm Smith, Williams, Friday & Bowen and predecessor, Little Rock, 1962—. Ark. chmn. Radio Free Europe Fund drive, 1963-64; campaign chmn. Pulaski County United Fund, 1964; pres. Urban Progress Assn., 1965-66; pres. U. Ark. Endowment and Trust Fund, 1968-69. Trustee Philander Smith Coll., Little Rock, Ark. Served to ensign USNR, 1943-46. Named Little Rock Man of Year, Ark. Democrat, 1962. Mem. Am., Fed., Pulaski County bar assns., Little Rock C. of C. (past pres.), U. Ark. Alumni Assn. (pres. 1966-67), Delta Theta Psi, Sigma Alpha Epsilon. Mason. Home: 2200 Beechwood St Little Rock AR 72207 Office: Boyle Bldg Little Rock AR 72201

BOWEN, WILLIAM JACKSON, gas co. exec.; b. Sweetwater, Tex., Mar. 31, 1922; s. Berry and Annah (Robey) B.; B.S., U.S. Mil. Acad., 1945; m. Annis K. Hilty, June 6, 1945; children—Shelley Ann, Barbara Kay, Berry Dunbar, William Jackson. Petroleum engr. Delhi Oil Corp., Dallas, 1949-57; v.p. Fla. Gas Co., Houston, 1957-60, pres., Winter Park, Fla., 1960—. Trustee, Barnett Morgage Trust; dir. 1st Nat. Bank at Orlando (Fla.). Bd. dirs. Fla. Council 100, Orange Bowl Com., Loch Haven Art Center, Orange County YMCA; trustee Rollins Coll. Served with AUS, 1945-49. Registered profl. engr., Tex. Mem. Ind. Natural Gas Assn. Am. (dir.), Am. Gas Assn. (dir.), Delta Kappa Epsilon. Presbyn. Home: 1821 Pinetree Rd Winter Park FL 32789 Office: PO Box 44 Winter Park FL 32789

BOWER, BEVERLY, soprano; b. Olean, N.Y.; d. Archie M. and Esther (Salmonson) Bower; m. John C. Kaufmann; 1 son, Mark Douglas. Operatic debut in La Traviata, N.Y.C. Opera, 1956; debut in Tosca, Vienna (Austria) State Opera, 1963; debut in Die Valkyries, Met. Opera Co., 1964; concert appearances with leading orchs. U.S. and Can., also radio, TV appearances. Recipient Key to City, Olean, N.Y. Mem. D.A.R. Address: Metropolitan Opera Assn 147 W 39th St New York City NY 10018

BOWER, J. LEEDS, lawyer; b. Mattoon, Ill., Oct. 21, 1931; s. Albert A. and Mildred (Leeds) B.; B.A., U. Ill., 1953, J.D., 1957; m. Gail Mary Kuehnle, Dec. 21, 1952; children-Bruce Albert, Brian Leeds, Douglas Joseph, Karen Mildred. Admitted to Ill. bar, 1957; Internal Revenue Service; practiced in Charleston, 1957—; mem. firm Brainard & Bower, 1961-70; mem. firm Brainard, Bower & Kramer, 1970—; spl. asst. atty. gen. Ill., 1969—. Dir. Columbian Savs. & Loan Assn. Republican precinct committeeman, 1960- -. Served to 1st lt., inf. U.S. Army. 1954-56. Mem. Ill. (mem. probate and trust council), Coles-Cumberland bar assns., Theta Delta Chi, Phi Alpha Delta. Presbyn. (trustee). Mason (Shriner), Elk, Rotarian, Moose. Home: 408 Cedar Dr Charleston IL 61920 Office: Linder Bldg Charleston IL 61920

BOWER, MARVIN, mgmt. cons.; b. Cin., Aug. 1, 1903; s. William J. and Carlotta (Preston) B.; Ph.B., Brown U., 1925; LL.B., Harvard, 1928, M.B.A., 1930; m. Helen M. McLaughlin, Aug. 17, 1927; children—Peter Huntington, Richard Hamilton, James McKinsey. Admitted to Ohio, Mass. bars, 1928; lawyer Jones, Day, Cockley & Reavis, Cleve., 1930-33; asso. McKinsey & Co., 1933-35, partner, 1935-50, mng. partner, 1950-56; mng. dir. McKinsey & Co., Inc. 1956-67, dir., 1956—. Cons. to USAF, AUS, Bur. Budget, 1941-43. Chmn., Bronxville Planning Commn. Chmn. McKinsey Found. Mgmt. Research, Inc.; trustee bd. edn., Bronxville, 1945-48. Trustee, Brown U., Com. Econ. Devel.; chmn. bd. trustees Case-Western Res. U.; chmn. Joint Council on Econ. Edn. Mem. vis. com. Harvard Bus. Sch. Mem. Harvard Bus. Sch. Assn. (pres. 1941-42), Alpha Tau Omega, Tau Beta Pi. Clubs: Blind Brook (Port Chester, N.Y.); Sky (N.Y.C.); Union (Cleve.). Author: The Will to Manage, 1966. Editor: Development of Executive Leadership, 1949. Contbr. various mags. Home: 44 Greenfield Av Bronxville NY 10708 Office: 245 Park Av New York City NY 10017

BOWER, RICHARD STUART, educator, economist; b. N.Y.C., Aug. 1, 1928; s. Jacob and Elsie (Vander Beugle) B.; A.B., Kenyon Coll., 1949; M.B.A., Columbia, 1955; Ph.D., Cornell U., 1962; m. Dorothy Ann Hagberg, June 23, 1953; children—Gari Ellen, Laura Jane, Nancy Lynne. Instr. econs. Kenyon Coll., 1949-50, Alfred U., 1955-57; asst. prof. econs. and bus. Vanderbilt U., 1959-62; prof. bus. econs. Dartmouth, 1962—; cons. Chase Manhattan Bank, Paine, Webber, Jackson & Curtis, Am. Stock Exchange. Corporator Manchester Savs. Bank; dir. Boston Financial Tech. Group, Inc. Served with USNR, 1951-55. Mem. Am. Econ. Assn., Am. Finance Assn., Phi Beta Kappa, Beta Gamma Sigma, Phi Kappa Phi. Author: Investment and Liquidity: A Case Study of Clay Construction Products, 1965. Contbr. articles profl. jours. Home: South Esker Hanover NH 03755

BOWERMAN, RICHARD H., lawyer; b. Newark, 1917; B.A., Yale, 1939, LL.B., 1942. Admitted to Conn. bar, 1946; pres. So. Conn. Gas Co., Bridgeport; former partner, now counsel firm Tyler, Cooper, Grant, Bowerman and Keefe, New Haven. Mem. Am. (chmn. jr. bar sect. Conn. 1946-49, nat. vice-chmn. 1951-52, nat. chmn. 1952-53, sec., treas. 1957-61), New Haven County bar assns., State Bar Assn Conn. (pres. 1967). Office: 880 Broad St Bridgeport, CT 06609.

BOWERS, CHARLES EDWARD, educator; b. Hanna, Wyo., Sept. 3, 1919; s. Harry M. and Mary (Baldwin) B.; B.S. in Civil Engring., U. Wyo., 1937-42; M.S. in Civil Engring., U. Minn., 1948; m. Audrey S. Hanson, June Minn., 1948; m. Audrey S. Hanson, June 29, 1946; children—Nancy Lynne, John Edward. Hydraulic engr. Bur. Reclamation, 1949-50; with St. Anthony Falls Hydraulic Labs., U. Minn., 1950-58, mem. faculty, 1958—, prof. civil engring. and hydraulics, 1961- -. Served with USNR, 1944-45. Fellow Am. Soc. C.E. (student award 1942, Collingwood award 1949); mem. Am. Soc. Engring. Edn., Internat. Assn. Hydraulic Research, Sigma Tau, Tau Beta Pi, Kappa Sigma. Roman Catholic. K.C. Contbr. profl. jours. Patentee mobile breakwater. Home: 3385 N Oxford St St Paul MN 55112 Office: Dept Civil Engring and Hydraulics Univ Minn Minneapolis MN 55455

BOWERS, CLAUDE THOMAS, state ofcl.; b. Littleton, N.C., July 18, 1899; s. T.R. and Mary (Dowtin) B.; student N.C. State Coll., 1918; m. Hattie Connell, 1925; 1 dau., Mrs. Stanley S. Betts. Former distbr. petroleum products; adj. gen. State of N.C., Raleigh, 1960—. Mem. Warren Bd. Town Commrs., 1947-51; pres. Warren County Devel. Corp., 1953—; chmn. bd. dirs. Bute Devel. Corp., 1955—; chmn. N.C. Vets. Commn., 1958-61. Trustee Meredith Coll. Served with U.S. Army, 1918; from pvt. to col., AUS, 1940-46. Recipient Silver Beaver award Boy Scouts Am., 1951. Mem. Am. Legion (past post comdr.), 40 and 8, N. G. Assn. U.S. (treas. 1963—). Democrat. Baptist (past deacon, chmn. finance com.). Lion (past Pres. Warrenton). Address: Office Adj Gen Raleigh NC 27611*

BOWERS, EDWARD THOMAS, natural gas co. exec.; b. Detroit, Apr. 24, 1912; s. Thomas F. and Anna (Best) B.; student Rider Coll.; m. Verna Kate Sheffield, Nov. 27, 1946; childrenBarbara Kay, Edward Thomas, Laura Ann. Sec.- treas. Southwest Gas Producing Corp., 1941-42; asst. treas. Tex. Gas Transmission Corp., 1946-51, comptroller, 1951-. Bd. dirs. Owensboro YMCA, 1956-63, pres., 1959-60; bd. dirs. Cliff Hagan Boys Club, 1967-71, pres., 1971. Served with USAAF, 1942-45. Mem. Am., So. (chmn. accounting sect. 1964) gas assns. Presbyn. (elder). Club: Owensboro Country (bd. dirs. 1961-62, pres. 1962). Home: 2036 Fernwood Dr Owensboro, KY 42301. Office: PO Box 1160 Owensboro KY 42301

BOWERS, ELLIOTT TOULMIN, univ. pres.; b. Oklahoma City, Aug. 22, 1919; s. Lloyd and Enah (McDonald) B.; B.S., Sam Houston State U., 1941, M.A., 1942; Ed.D., U. Houston, 1959; m. Frances Ann Handley, May 29, 1940; children—Linda Lu (Mrs. Charles Rushing), Cynthia Ann (Mrs. Wayland Vincent). Dir. music Huntsville High Sch., 1937-42; mem. faculty Sam Houston State U., 1946—, v.p. univ. affairs and dean of students, 1964-70, acting pres., 1963-64, pres., 1970—. Active Salvation Army, Am. Cancer Soc.; pres. bd. Wesley Found., 1962-63. Served with USAAF, 1943-46. Mem. Am., Tex. personnel and guidance assns., Assn. Higher Edn., Criminal Justice Council Tex., N.E.A., Huntsville C. of C. (past pres.), Alpha Pi Omega, Kappa Delta Pi. Mason, Kiwanian. Home: 1802 16th St Huntsville TX 77340

BOWERS, FRANCIS ROBERT, educator; b. N.Y.C., May 4, 1920; s. William Leo and Catherine (Callahan) B.; B.A., Cath. U. Am., 1946, Ph.D., 1959; M.A., Fordham U., 1952. Tchr. Ascension Sch., N.Y.C., 1946-48, St. Augustine's High Sch., Bklyn., 1948-51, St. Peter's High Sch., Staten Island, 1951-53; instr. De La Salle Coll., Washington, 1953-59; asso. prof. English and world lit. Manhattan Coll., 1959—, chmn. dept., 1967-70, chmn. grad. English dept., 1961-70, dean arts and scis., 1970—. Trustee De La Salle Coll., 1969—; trustee scholarship Cath. U., 1953-58. Recipient Finn grant, 1962. Mem. Nat. Conf. Tchrs. of English, Modern Lang. Assn., Am. Conf. Acad. Deans, Am. Assn. Higher Edn., Nat. Cath. Edn. Assn., Phi Beta Kappa. Author: Characterization in Narrative Poetry of George Crabbe, 1959. Address: Manhattan Coll Bronx NY 10471

BOWERS, FREDSON THAYER, educator; b. New Haven, Apr. 25, 1905; s. Fredson Eugene and Hattie (Quigley) B.; Ph.B., Brown U., 1925, D.Litt., 1970; Ph.D., Harvard , 1934; Litt.D., Clark U., 1970; m. Hyacinth Sutphen, Nov. 11, 1924; children—Fredson, Joan (Mrs. Donald Stout), Stephen, Peter; m. 2d, Nancy Hale, Mar. 16, 1942. Instr. English, tutor modern langs. Harvard, 1926-36; instr. English, Princeton, 1936-38; asst. prof. English, U. Va., 1938-45, asso. prof., 1945-49, prof. English 1949—; professorial lectr. English, U. Chgo., 1950-65, chmn. dept., 1961-68, Linden Kent prof. English 1968—, dean faculty arts and scis., 1968-69. Fulbright fellow advanced research, U.K., 1952-53; Sandars reader in bibliography Cambridge (Eng.) U., 1958; James Lyell reader in bibliography Oxford U., 1959; Guggenheim fellow, 1958-59, 71-72; regional chmn. Woodrow Wilson Nat. Fellowship Found., 1956-59; Phi Beta Kappa vis. scholar, 1962-63; vis. fellow All Saints Coll., Oxford, 1972. Served as comdr. USNR, Washington, 1942-45. Recipient Bicentennial medal Brown U., 1964; Thomas Jefferson award U. Va., 1971. Corr. fellow Brit.

Acad.; mem. S. Atlantic Modern Lang. Assn. (pres. 1969), Modern Lang. Assn. Am. (exec. council 1963-67), Bibliog. Soc. (Gold medal 1968, London), Bibliog. Soc. Am., of U. Va., of Cambridge, of Oxford. Author books, 1939—; latest being: Principles of Bibliographical Description, 1949; Dramatic Works of Thomas Dekker, 4 vols., 1953-61; On Editing Shakespeare and Elizabethan Dramatists, 1955; Whitman's Manuscripts for 1860 Leaves of Grass, 1955; Textual and Literary Criticism, 1959; Bibliography and Textual Criticism, 1964. Editor: Studies in Bibliography; Papers of Bibliog. Soc. U. Va., 1949—; adv. editor Va. Quar. Rev.; textual editor Centenary Edit. Hawthorne; U. Va. edit. Stephen Crane. Dramatic Works in the Beaumont and Fletcher Canon, 10 vols., 1966—. Contbr. articles to profl. jours. Home: Woodburn Route 8 Charlottesville VA 22901

BOWERS, JOHN Z., physician, educator; b. Catonsville, Md., Aug. 27, 1913; s. John Culler and Adelaide (Schuman) B.; B.S., Gettysburg Coll., 1933, Sc.D., 1958; M.D., U. Md., 1938, Sc.D., 1959; L.H.D., Woman's Med. Coll., 1967; children—John C., Mary I., David W.; m. 2d, Akiko Kobayashi, Apr. 17, 1970. Intern, resident U. Hosp., Balt., 1938-41; dep. dir. AEC, Washington, 1947-50; dean Coll. Medicine, dir. radiobiology lab., med. cons. AEC, U. Utah, Salt Lake City, 1950-55; prof. medicine U. Wis., 1955, dean Med. Sch., 1955- 61; staff mem. Rockefeller Found.; pres. Macy Found., 1965—. Vis. prof. U. Philippines, 1962, Kyoto U. Med. Sch. 1962—. Served as comdr. USNR, 1941-45. Decorated Purple Heart, Legion of Merit (Navy). Alan Gregg travel scholar, 1962. Fellow A.C.P.; mem. A.M.A., Alpha Omega Alpha (pres.). Author: Medical Education in Japan, From Chinese Medicine to Western Medicine, 1965; Doctor on Desima, 1970; Medical Schools for the Modern World, 1970; Western Medical Pioneers in Feudal Japan, 1970. Home: 500 E 77th St New York City NY 10021 Office: 277 Park Av New York City NY 10017

BOWERS, PAUL EDWARD, govt. ofcl.; b. Lima, O., Apr. 10, 1917; s. Lewis Wesley and Nancy Fay (Long) B.; student U. Mich. 1949, Ohio State U., 1952; m. Blodwen Watkins, May 26, 1935; children—Teresa Fern Barnes, Patricia Faye Schultz, Bruce Odell; m. 2d, Dorothy Hornsby, Dec. 28, 1953; children—Paul Edward II, Mark Allen. With United Rubber workers, 1942-60; pres. Union Health Centers, Inc., 1960-62; with Fed. Mediation and Conciliation Service, 1962—, regional dir., 1967—. Mem. President Truman's Adv. Com. Study Nation's Health, 1950. Served with USNR, 1944-45. Recipient Outstanding Service award Fed. Mediation and Conciliation Service, 1965; named hon. citizen Ft. Worth, 1967, Kentucky colonel, 1968. Member Industrial Relations Club St. Louis, Nat. Pilots Assn. Democrat. Conglist. Mason (Shriner). Club: Missouri Athletic (St. Louis). Author: Pension and Insurance Planning 1954. Home: 63 Berry Rd Park Glendale MO 63122 Office: 1520 Market St St Louis MO 63103

BOWERS, RALPH ELMER, lawyer; b. Cleve., July 22, 1910; s. John Elmer and Lauretts (Howe) B.; A.B., U. So. Calif., 1932; LL.B., Harvard, 1935; m. Roberta Thullen, May 28, 1941; children—John Edward, William Ralph, James David, Laurie Ann, Thomas Robert. Admitted to Ill. bar, 1935, since practiced in Chgo.; partner Pope & Ballard, 1937-42; gen. atty. Marshall Field & Co., 1942-46, sec., gen. atty., 1946-54, v.p., sec., gen. atty., 1954—. Mem. Highland Park Civil Service Commn., chmn., 1961-64. Mem. Am., Ill., Chgo. bar assns., Am. Soc. Corp. Secs. (dir. 1955-58, pres. 1957-58), Am. Retail Fedn. (chmn. employee relations com. 1955-58), Delta Sigma Rho, Lambda Epsilon Xi. Clubs: The Law (Chgo.); Biltmore Forest (Ashville, N.C.); Exmoor Country (Highland Park, Ill.). Office: 111 N State St Chicago IL 60690

BOWERS, RAYMOND, educator, physicist; b. London, Eng., July 11, 1927; B.Sc., London U., 1948; D.Phil., Oxford (Eng.) U., 1948; research fellow U. Chgo., 1951-53; married. Came to U.S., 1951, naturalized, 1964. Research physicist Westinghouse Electric Corp., 1954-60; asso. prof. Cornell U., Ithaca, N.Y., 1960—, prof. physics, 1965—, dep. dir. program sci., tech. and soc., 1969—; on leave with Office Sci. and Tech., Exec. Office of President, 1966-67; cons. to industry, 1960—. Fellow Am. Phys. Soc., Phys. Soc. London, A.A.A.S. Office: Clark Hall Cornell Univ Ithaca NY 14850

BOWERS, RAYMOND VICTOR, educator, sociologist; b. Victoria, B.C., Can., June 19, 1907; s. Samuel Victor and Beulah Dodds (Ramsey) B.; student Victoria Coll., 1923-25; A.B., U. Kan., 1927; A.M., Northwestern U., 1930; Ph.D., U. Minn., 1934; m. Virginia Dallam Wallis, June 30, 1933; children—Sally Virginia (Mrs. W.D. Wittliff), Katherine Mary (Mrs. R.L. Arrell). Instr. dept. sociology U. Minn., 1930-34; Social Sci. Research Council post-doctoral fellow Inst. Human Relations, Yale, 1934-35; asst. prof. dept. sociology U. Rochester, 1935-42, acting chmn., 1938-42, chmn., 1942; asst. chief research and statistics div., Nat. Hdqrs. SSS, Washington, 1942-44, chief, 1946-47; dep. exec. dir. com. on human resources Research and Devel. Bd., 1947-48, exec. dir., 1948-49; dir. Human Resources Research Inst. Air U., USAF, Maxwell AFB, Ala., 1949-52; tech. adviser social scis. Air Research and Devel. Command, USAF, 1952-55, dir. Office Social Sci. Programs, Air Force Personnel and Tng. Research Center, 1956-57, tech. dir., 1957-58; prof. sociology and anthropology, head dept., social scis. div. U. Ga., 1958-62; prof., head dept. sociology U. Ariz., Tucson, 1962—. Research leader morale div. U.S. Strategic Bombing Survey, Japan, 1945-46; expert cons. sociol. and pub. opinion surveys G.H.Q., SCAP, Japan, 1946-47. Served as lt. USNR, 1944-46. Recipient Army and Navy commendations, S.S.S. medal. Fellow A.A.A.S., Am. Sociol. Assn.; mem. Sociol. Research Assn., Am. Statis. Assn., Phi Beta Kappa, Delta Tau Delta. Co-Author: ARDC Studies in Personnel and Organizational Effectiveness, 1956. Editor, contbr. Studies in Organizational Effectiveness, 1962, Studies on Behavior in Organizations, 1966. Contbr. to The Uses of Sociology, 1967. Home: 2702 Kiva Pl Tucson, AZ 85715.

BOWERS, RICHARD CHARLES, coll. ofcl.; b. Mt. Pleasant, Ia., May 3, 1927; s. Raymond Paul and Marie (Foster) B.; B.S., U. Mich., 1948; Ph.D., U. Minn., 1953; m. Florence I. Olson, June 17, 1950; children—Lesly Ann, Janet Mary, Robert Paul. Instr., U. Minn., 1953-54; mem. faculty Northwestern U., 1954-65, asso. prof. chemistry, 1960-65, dir. chem. labs., 1962-65; prof., dean Coll. Liberal Arts and Scis., No. Ill. U., DeKalb, 1965-69, v.p., provost, 1969—. Cons.-examiner, commn. colls. and univs. N. Central Assn. Colls. and Secondary Schs., 1968—. Served with USNR, 1944-46. Mem. Am. Chem. Soc., Sigma Xi. Contbr. profl. jours. Home: 1205 University Dr DeKalb IL 60115

BOWERS, RICHARD GEORGE, ins. agt.; b. LeMars, Ia., Mar. 9, 1920; s. Russell S. and Alice (Schneider) B.; B.A., State U. Ia., 1942; m. Alice Rohm, Jan. 9, 1943; children—Richard George, Catherine Alice (Mrs. William P. Woolston), Sarah Rohm (Mrs. David E. Ware). Agt., N.Y. Life Ins. Co., Keokuk, Ia., 1952—; pres. Financial Planning Cons., Inc., 1952—; dir. Hill Dodge Banking Co., Warsaw, Ill., Star Forms, Inc., Bettendorf, Ia. Bd. dirs. Keokuk Community Sch. Bd., YMCA, United Fund. Served to 1st lt., inf., AUS, 1942-46. Named Salesman of Year, Sales Execs. Club, 1965. C.L.U. Mem. Million Dollar Round Table Chgo. (pres.), U. Ia. Alumni Assn. (past dir.), Keokuk C. of C. (past dir.), Nat. Assn. Life Underwriters, Phi Kappa Psi. Episcopalian. Elk. Club: Keokuk Country (past pres.). Home: 1 Mahaska Rd Keokuk IA 52632 Office: 220 N 4th St Keokuk IA 52632

BOWERS, ROBERT S., educator, economist; b. Fairmont, W.Va., Aug. 10, 1911; s. Larkin Bruce and Virginia (Smith) B.; B.A., Kan. Wesleyan U., 1933; M.A., Am. U., 1938; Ph.D., U. Wis., 1951; m. Dorothy Ann Kobussen, Mar. 31, 1951; children—Sook Hee Ann, Robert Bruce. Head dept. econs. Western Mich. U.; Vis. prof. U. Wis., summer 1959. Bd. dirs. Douglass Community Assn., 1956-59. Mem. Am. Econ. Assn., Indsl. Relations Research Assn. Mem. Soc. of Friends. Club: Torch International. Home: 2909 Memory Lane Kalamazoo MI 49007

BOWERS, ROY ANDERSON, coll. dean; b. Racine, Wis., May 11, 1913; s. Sidney and Dagmar (Anderson) B.; B.S., U. Wis., 1936, Ph.D., 1940; m. Harriett Teresa Byer, Aug. 19, 1940; children—Clarke George, Mary Jane. Asst. instr. pharmacy U. Wis., 1937-40; asst. prof. pharmacy U. Toledo, 1940-41; asst. prof. pharmacy U. Kan., 1941-43, asso. prof., 1943-45; prof. pharmacy U. N.M., 1945-51, dean Coll. Pharmacy, 1945-51; prof. pharmacy Rutgers U., New Brunswick, N.J., 1951—, dean Coll. Pharmacy, 1951—. Pharmacist, res. officer USPHS; mem. Am. Council on Pharm. Edn., 1968—. Trustee, pres. Cedar Grove Pub. Library, 1959—; trustee Hosp. and Health Council Met. N.J. Mem. Am. Pharm. Assn. (1st v.p. 1950-51, council mem. 1957-63), Am. Assn. Colls. Pharmacy (pres. 1963-64), N.J., N.M. pharm. assns., Am. Inst. History of Pharmacy, Am. Council on Pharm. Edn., Sigma Xi, Phi Lambda Upsilon, Rho Chi (nat. sec.-treas. 1945-66, nat. v.p. 1954-56, nat. pres. 1956-58, exec. council 1958-60), Delta Sigma Theta (hon.), Rho Pi Phi (hon.), Alpha Chi Sigma, Kappa Psi, Phi Kappa Phi. Roman Catholic. Co-author: The Rho Chi Society, 1955. Mem. bd. authors: Am. Pharmacy (Rufus A. Lyman), 1951, 4th edit. (Lyman, Sprowls), 1955, 5th edit. (J.B. Sprowls), 1960. Home: 11 Fielding Pl Edison NJ 08817

BOWERS, WAYNE ALEXANDER, educator; b. Bilbao, Spain, Mar. 1, 1919; s. Wayne Heyser and Margaret Sturrock (Cameron) B.; came to U.S. 1926; A.B., Oberlin Coll., 1938; Ph.D., Cornell U., 1943; m. Maryellen Severinghaus, Feb. 26, 1944; children—John, Margaret, Ruth, Wayne. Instr. Cornell U., 1943-45; physicist Los Alamos Labs., 1944-46; research asso. Mass. Inst. Tech., 1946-47; asso. prof. physics U. N.C., 1947-55, prof., 1955—; vis. prof. Mass. Inst. Tech., 1968-69. Faculty fellow NSF, 1963-64. Mem. Am. Phys. Soc., Am. Assn. Physics Tchrs., Am. Assn. U. Profs., Am. Fedn. Scientists, Phi Beta Kappa, Sigma Xi. Contbr. articles in field to profl. jours. Home: 714 E Franklin St Chapel Hill NC 27514

BOWERSOCK, DAMAN, banker; b. Copan, Okla., July 18, 1915; s. George M. and Lillian A. (Daman) B.; B.S., Okla. State U., 1937; m. Pearl L. Isham, July 2, 1938; children—Robert D., William D. From messenger to asst. v.p. City Nat. Bank & Trust Co., Oklahoma City, 1937-49; from asst. v.p. to sr. v.p. First Nat. Bank, Kansas City, Mo., 1949-66; pres. First Nat. Bank Albuquerque, 1966—, also dir. Bd. dirs. Albuquerque Indsl. Devel. Service, Albuquerque Indsl. Found.; mem. Gov. N.M. Com. 100; exec. bd. Kit Carson council Boy Scouts Am.; mem. Albuquerque Policy Direction Com. Adv. Bd. Albuquerque United Community Fund. Mem. Am., N.M. bankers assns. Clubs: Albuquerque Country, Petroleum (bd. dirs.) (Albuquerque). Home: 1008 Madison St N E Albuquerque NM 87110 Office: 223 Central Av NW Albuquerque NM 87103

BOWERSOCK, GLEN WARREN, educator; b. Providence, Jan. 12, 1936; s. Donald Curtis and Josephine (Evans) B.; A.B., Harvard, 1957; B.A., Oxford U. (Eng.), 1959, M.A., and D. Phil., 1962. Lectr. ancient history Oxford U., 1960-62, vis. lectr., 1966; instr. Harvard, 1962-64, asst. prof., 1964-67, asso. prof. of the Classics, 1967-69, prof. Greek and Latin, 1969—; cons. Ednl. Services, Inc., 1964; mem. Internat. Colloquium on the Classics in Edn., 1964-66. Rhodes scholar, 1957-60. Mem. Am. Philol. Assn., Archeol. Inst. of Am., Leschetizky Assn. of Am., Soc. for the Promotion of Roman and Hellenic Studies. Author: Augustus and the Greek World, 1965; Pseudo-Xenophon, Constitution of the Athenians, 1968; Greek Sophists in the Roman Empire, 1969. Editor: Philostratus' Life of Apollonius, 1970. Home: 151 Tremont St Boston MA 02111 Office: Dept of Classics Harvard Univ Cambridge MA 02138

BOWERSOCK, JUSTIN DEWITT, III, banker; b. Kansas City, Mo., Dec. 27, 1907; s. Justin Dewitt and Frances (Matteson) B.; A.B., Harvard, 1929; m. Betty Bruce Van Antwerp, Oct. 25, 1930; children—Justin Dewitt IV (dec.), Chiles V., Frances and Caroline (twins). Asst. cashier Fidelity Nat. Bank, Kansas City, Mo., 1929-33; v.p. Union Nat. Bank, Kansas City, 1933-49; exec. v.p. Union Trust Co. of D.C., Washington, 1949-67, pres., 1967-70 chmn. bd., 1970—; dir. Fed. Services Finance Corp., Washington, 1957-67, Group Hospitalization, Inc. 1960-70. Mem. exec. council Washington area Boy Scouts Am., 1960—; mem. exec. com. Fed. City Council, 1969—, com. on banking and monetary policy U.S. C. of C., 1968—. Trustee, V.P. Washington Hosp. Center, 1962—. Served to lt. (j.g.) USNR, 1944-46; PTO. Mem. Am. Bankers Assn. (v.p. D.C. 1957, 62-63, exec. council 1965-68), D.C. Bankers Assn. (pres. 1958-59), Assn. Res. City Bankers. Republican. Episcopalian. Clubs: Chevy Chase (Md.); Metropolitan, Army and Navy, Alfalfa (Washington), Annapolis (Md.) Yacht. Home: 4201 Cathedral Av N W Washington DC 20016 Office: Union Trust Co 15th and H Sts N W Washington DC 20005

BOWERSOX, RALPH BERTRAM, physicist, educator; b. Sand Point, Ida., Sept. 4, 1911; s. Ermin Ralph and Anna (Forst) B.; B.S., U. Chgo., 1933, M.S., 1934, Ph.D., 1938; m. Helen Elizabeth Prosser, Dec. 10, 1938; children—Elizabeth (Mrs. Donald F. Harris), Marian (Mrs. Jerry Wendelin). Asst. prof. Toledo U., 1938- 42; research asso. Harvard, 1942-46; asso. prof. Mich. State U., 1946- 48; research engr. Jet Propulsion Lab., Pasadena, Cal., 1948-59, chief of instrumentation, 1951-59; cons. scientist Lockheed Corp., Palo Alto, Cal., 1959-60; research scientist Martin Co., Denver, 1960-64; prof. physics Colo. Sch. Miners, Golden, 1964—, chmn. dept., 1968—. Fellow Am. Inst. Aero. and Astronautics; mem. Am. Phys. Soc., Am. Assn. Physics Tchrs., Am. Rocket Soc., Phi Beta Kappa, Sigma Xi. Presbyn. (elder). Club: Toastmasters Internat. (past pres.) (Altadena, Cal.). Home: 2483 Coors Dr Golden CO 80401

BOWES, ARTHUR STUTZ, bus. exec.; b. Dec. 7, 1901; s. Julius and Lulie (Stutz) B.; B.S., Purdue U., 1923; m. Jane Mattison, Sept. 4, 1926 (dec.); children—Sally, Arthur; m. 2d, Patricia Kelly Irving, July 10, 1954. Editor, Cement and Engring. News, trade publ., 1924-25; contact man, later v.p. Russell T. Gray Advt. Agy., Chgo., 1925-27; sales mgr. Vortex Mfg. Co., Chgo., 1927-29; dir. Walgreen Co., Chgo., 1929-37; exec. v.p., dir. Universal Paper Products Co., Chgo., 1937-47; pres. Bowes Industries, Inc., 1948-53; chmn. bd. H. M. Byllesby & Co., Chgo., 1959- 64; dir. Owens-Ill., Inc. Mem. Chgo. Pub. Bldg. Commn. Bd. dirs. Hektoen Inst. for Med. Research Cook County Hosp.; trustee U. Chgo. Cancer Research Found. Mem. Chgo. Council Fgn. Relations, Oriental Inst., Pi Kappa Alpha, Sigma Delta Chi. Republican. Clubs: Adventurers, Bob O'Link Country. Home: 209 E Lake Shore Dr Chicago IL 60611

BOWES, CHARLES ALPIN, found. exec.; b. Denver, June 7, 1911; B.S. summa cum laude, Washington and Lee U., 1931; postgrad. Stanford, 1957; m. Elizabeth Quigley Austin, Dec. 30, 1933; children—Charles Austin, Jon Leyshon, Ted Quigley. Reporter, Denver Post, 1934-36, Daily Oklahoman, 1936-39; pub. La Grande (Ore.) Observer, 1939-41; partner Gerth-Pacific, 1941-42; account exec. Ruthrauff & Ryan, 1943-51, Los Angeles mgr., 1951-52; chmn., pres., dir. the Bowes Co., Los Angeles, 1952-71; pres. Living Memls. Found., Los Angeles, 1971—. Served to 1st lt. USMC, 1944-46. Mem. Sales and Marketing Execs., Western States Advt. Agys. Assn. (pres.), Goodwill Industries of So. Cal. (dir.), Sierra Club, Phi Beta Kappa. Presbyn. Club: Jonathan (Los Angeles). Home: 858 San Remo Rd Pasadena CA 91105 Office: 1010 S Flower St Los Angeles CA 90015

BOWES, FREDERICK, Jr., bus. exec.; b. Phila., Jan. 19, 1908; s. Frederick and Edith May (Proctor) B.; A.B., Dartmouth, 1930; student Advanced Mgmt. Program, Harvard, fall 1955; m. Priscilla Herron, Jan. 6, 1940; children—Frederick III, Warren Winslow. Serviceman, salesman Pitney- Bowes, Inc., N.Y.C., Boston, 1930-33, spl. rep., London, Berlin, 1933- 34, Washington, 1934-37, advt. mgr., Stamford, 1939-42, dir. pub. relations and advt., 1945-55, v.p. pub. relations and advt., 1955-59, v.p. charge new internat. div., 1959, v.p. internat. operations, 1959-; asst. to plans bd. Batten, Barton, Durstine & Osborn, Inc., N.Y.C., 1937- 39; dir., internat. bd. dirs. State Nat. Bank Conn.; mem. advt. adv. com. to sec. commerce; mem. joint com. on understanding our econ. system Assn. Nat. Advertisers-Am. Assn. Advt. Agys. Gen. campaign chmn. United Fund of Stamford, Inc., 1956; bd. dirs. Stamford Boys Club. Chief pub. relations officer, N. E., War Prodn. Bd., World War II, also regional dir. war prodn. drive. Mem. Pub. Relations Soc. Am. (past pres., dir.), U.S. C. of C. (pub. relations, advt. coms), Assn. Nat. Advertisers (dir.), Stamford C. of C. (dir.), New Canaan Library (dir.), Citizens' Sch. Council (dir.), The Advt. Council (dir.). Conglist. (deacon; trustee; chmn. bldg. fund campaign). Clubs: The Country (New Canaan, Conn.). Contbr. articles profl. publs. Home: Ramhorne Rd New Canaan CT 06840 Office: Pitney-Bowes Inc Stamford CT 06904

BOWES, HENRY EDWARD, communications exec.; b. Merchantville, N.J., Sept. 7, 1915; s. Henry Joseph and Evaline Sarah (Humphreys) B.; grad. Valley Forge Mil. Acad., 1932; student U.S. Naval Acad., 1934-35; D. in Bus. Adminstrn. (hon.), N.Central Coll.; m. Lauretta Helen Schultz, Jul 17, 1965; children by previous marriage—Henry, Shirley. Asso. Philco Corp., 1936-62, gen. mgr. home radio div., 1955-56, v.p., gen. mgr. TV div., 1956-58, v.p. marketing, 1958-62; v.p., dir. marketing for N.Am., also v.p., dir. govt. relations, Internat. Tel. & Tel. Co., 1962-64, v.p. indsl. marketing-world wide, 1964-66, dir. sales and distbn. ITT System, 1966-67, sr. v.p., 1967-68; pres., chief exec. officer McCall Corp., 1967-68; exec. v.p. Bell & Howell Co., 1969, pres., chief operating officer, 1970—, also dir. Sr. cons. Ency. Britannica, 1968-69. Mem. bd. visitors Valley Forge Mil. Acad.; trustee N. Central Coll., Naperville, Ill. Served from 2d lt. to col. USAAF, World War II. Decorated Legion of Merit; recipient Distinguished Alumni award Valley Forge Mil. Acad. Mem. Valley Forge Mil. Acad. Alumni Assn. (past chmn. bd.). Republican. Episcopalian. Clubs: Congressional Country (Washington); Detroit Boat; Ridgewood Country, Cornell of N.Y.; Union League (N.Y.C.); Skokie Country. Home: 44 Woodley Rd Winnetka IL 60093 Office: 7100 McCormick Rd Chicago IL 60645

BOWHILL, SIDNEY ALLAN, educator; b. Dover, Kent, Eng., Aug. 6, 1927; s. Sidney Allan and Violet (Clarke) B.; B.A., Cambridge (Eng.) U., 1948, M.A., 1950, Ph.D., 1954; m. Margaret M. McLaughlin, Aug. 22, 1959; children—Allan J.C., Amanda M. Came to U.S., 1955, naturalized, 1962. Research engr. Marconi's Wireless Telegraph Co. Ltd., Chelmsford, Essex, Eng., 1953-55; asso. prof. elec. engring. Pa. State U., University Park, 1955-62; prof. elec. engring. U. Ill., Urbana, 1962—. Pres. Aeronomy Corp., Champaign, Ill., 1969—. Chmn., U.S.A. Commn. 3, Internat. Sci. Radio Union, asso. editor Radio Sci., 1964-67, editor, 1968—, vice chmn. Internat. Commn. 3, 1969—; mem. working group 4 Inter-Union Com. Space Research, 1961—, co-chmn. panel interactions neutral and ionized atmospheres, 1965—, convenor, program chmn. Symposium, 9th meeting, Vienna, Austria, 1966, 14th meeting, Seattle, 1971; mem. com. data interchange and data centers Nat. Acad. Scis., 1967—, potential contamination and interference from space expts. 1963—, chmn. panel upper atmospheric phys., com. polar research, 1967-70, mem. Inter-Union Commn. on Solar-Terrestrial Physics, chmn. Working Group II, 1968—; editorial adv. bd. Jour. Atmospheric and Terrestrial Physics, 1965—. Fellow I.E.E.E. (procs. bd. cons., procs. editorial bd. 1965-68) Phys. Soc. London, A.A.A.S., Am. Geophys. Union, Am. Astronom. Soc.; mem. Am. Soc. Engring. Edn., Nat. Acad. Engring., Sigma Xi, Sigma Tau, Eta Kappa Nu. Contbr. numerous articles to profl. jours. Home: 2203 Anderson St Urbana IL 61801

BOWIE, BEN CALHOUN, banker; b. Grandview, Wash., Sept. 21, 1915; s. Samuel D. and Gertrude E. (Calhoun) B.; B.A., U. Ore., 1937; m. June Martin, Oct. 24, 1937; children—Robert W., John M., Scott C. With J. Henry Helser & Co., investment mgrs., Portland, Ore., 1938—, v.p., 1955—; v.p., dir. Helser Securities Co., San Francisco, 1957—; dir. C. & N.W. Ry. Co., 1956—. Served from ensign to lt. (j.g.) USNR, 1943-46. Mem. Theta Chi, Club: Irvington Tennis (Portland). Home: 2611 NE Thompson St Portland OR 97212 Office: 808 S Adler St Portland OR 97205

BOWIE, LESTER, jazz musician on trumpet and flugelhorn; b. Frederick, Md., Oct. 11, 1941; pupil of mem. St. Louis Symphony Orch. Joined Chgo. new jazz movement with Richard Abrams Exptl. Band, 1966; organized own quartet, 1967; recording artist for Delmark, Nessa records. Address: 1443 N Hudson St Chicago IL 60610*

BOWIE, ROBERT RICHARDSON, lawyer, educator; b. Balt., Aug. 24, 1909; s. Clarence Keating and Helen (Richardson) B.; A.B., Princeton, 1931; LL.B., Harvard, 1934; m. Theodosia Chapman, Apr. 15, 1944; children—Robert Richardson, William Chapman. Admitted to Md. bar, 1934; mem. firm Bowie & Burke, Balt., 1934-42; asst. atty. gen. Md., 1941-42; prof. law Harvard, 1945-55, prof. internat. relations, also dir. Center for Internat. Affairs, 1957—. Dir. task force regulatory commn. Com. on Reorgn. Fed. Govt., 1948; gen. counsel, spl. adv. U.S. High Commr. for Germany, 1950-51; dir. policy planning staff Dept. State 1953-55, asst. sec. state for policy planning, 1955-57, counselor, 1966-68. Asst. dir. Md. Legislative Council, 1940-41. Served with AUS, 1942-46, spl. asst. to dep. mil. gov. for Germany, 1945-46. Decorated Legion of Merit with oak leaf cluster. Contbr. articles, studies, reports on law and internat. affairs to profl. jours. Home: 170 Coolidge Hill Cambridge MA 02138 Office: 6 Divinity Av Cambridge MA 02138

BOWIE, THOMAS DONALD, fgn. service officer; b. Duluth, Minn., Sept. 1, 1917; s. William Simpson and Ruth Josephine (Saxine) B.; B.A., Carleton Coll., 1938, M.A., 1940; postgrad. Institut des Hautes Etudes Internationales, U. Paris, France, 1939, Hague Acad. Internat. Law, 1939, Cornell U., 1954-55, U.S. Army War Coll., 1959-60; m. Margit Koren Ramm, Mar. 5, 1949; children—Charles Thomas, Karen Ruth. Instr. internat. relations and French, Carleton Coll., 1940-42; with State Dept., 1942—; divisional asst., attache Am. embassy, Madrid, 1943-45; vice consul Am. Consulate Gen., Marseille, France, 1945-48; vice consul, Rabat, Morocco, 1948-49; 2d sec. Am. embassy, Warsaw, Poland, 1949-51; consul Am. consulate gen., Milan, Italy, 1951-54; with Office Internat. Econ. and Social Affairs, 1955-57; adviser U.S. Delegations to 40th, 49th and 52d Internat. Labor Confs., Geneva; counselor of embassy for polit. affairs, Saigon, Vietnam, 1957-59; labor attache Am. embassy, Paris, France, 1960-62; labor attache Am. embassy, Rome, Italy, 1962—. Home: care Fgn Service Mail Desk Dept State Washington DC 20520 Office: Am Embassy Rome Italy

BOWIE, WALTER C., physiologist; b. Kansas City, Kan., June 29, 1925; s. Robert and Etta Mae (Hill) B.; D.V.M., Kan. State U., 1947; M.S., Cornell U., 1955, Ph.D., 1960; m. Cornelia C. Morris, Aug. 7, 1954; children—Carolyn J. (Mrs. Clovis Guiy), Colleen J. (Mrs. Arthur Lawrence), Sibyl K. Instr. dept. physiology and pharmacology Sch. Vet. Medicine Tuskegee Inst., 1947-50, asst. prof., 1950-55, asso. prof., 1955-60, prof., 1960—, head dept., 1950—; cons. VA Hosp., Tuskegee, Ala.; vis. prof. Howard U., U. Ala. Dir. Tuskegee Fed. Savs. & Loan Assn. Vice-pres., sec., bd. dirs. Tuskegee Inst. Ala. Mem. Am. Vet. Med. Assn. (research sect. officer 1967), Am. Hosp. Assn., Am. Phys. Soc., Ala. Heart Assn., Sigma Xi, Phi Kappa Phi. Baptist. Research comparative cardiovascular dynamics and ruminant physiology. Home: 2009 Patterson St Tuskegee Inst AL 36088

BOWKER, ALBERT HOSMER, univ. chancellor; b. Winchendon, Mass., Sept. 8, 1919; s. Roy C. and Kathleen (Hosmer) B.; B.S., Mass. Inst. Tech., 1941; Ph.D., Columbia, 1949; m. Elizabeth Rempfer, June 14, 1942; children—Paul Albert, Nancy Kathleen, Caroline Anne; m. 2d, Rosedith Sitgreaves, Sept. 29, 1964. Asst. statistician Mass. Inst. Tech., 1941-43; asst. dir. statis. research group Columbia, 1943-45; asst. prof. statistics Stanford, 1947-50, asso. prof., head dept., 1950-53, became prof., head dept., joint head math. dept., 1953, exec. head statistics dept., 1948-59, dean grad. div., 1958-63, prof. math. and statistics, 1953-63, dir. applied math. and statistics labs., 1951-63; chancellor City U. N.Y., 1963-71, U. Cal. at Berkeley, 1971—. Mem. corp. Mass. Inst. Tech.; trustee Inst. for Ednl. Devel., Inst. Internat. Edn., Mt. Sinai Sch. Medicine, Dalton Sch. Mem. Nat. Adv. Council Extension and Continuing Edn. Fellow Am. Statis. Assn. (pres. 1964), Am. Soc. Quality Control, Inst. Math. Statistics (pres. 1961-62), A.A.A.S.; mem. Biometric Soc., Operations Research Soc. Am., Soc. for Indsl. and Applied Math., Sigma Xi (exec. com. 1963-66). Author: (with Henry P. Goode) Sampling Inspection by Variables, 1952; (with Gerald J. Lieberman) Handbook of Industrial Statistics, 1955. Engineering Statistics, 1958; also articles profl. jours. Asso. editor Jour. Am. Statis. Assn., 1949-52. Address: 535 E 80th St New York City NY 10021

BOWKER, JOHN GERALD, banker; b. Westford, Mass., Aug. 2, 1902; s. John Williamson and Mabel Anne (Longbottom) B.; B.S., Tufts U., 1924, L.H.D., 1958; Ed.M., Harvard, 1931; Galton Statist. Lab., U. London (Eng.), 1938-39; m. Doris Cheever Dennett, Aug. 20, 1927; 1 son, John Dennett. Tchr. math. Framingham (Mass.) High Sch., 1924-26; faculty math. Middlebury (Vt.) Coll., 1926—, prof., 1942-52, Baldwin prof., 1952-67, dean faculty, 1953-67, emeritus, 1967—; dir. Middlebury savs. & Loan Assn., 1934—, pres., 1967—. Del., Republican State Conv., 1952. Mem. Am. Math. Soc., Math. Assn. Am., Nat. Council Tchrs. Math. Soc. (Vt. State rep.), Am. Assn. U. Profs., Vt. League Savs. and Loan Assns. (pres. 1949-50), Alpha Tau Omega. Conglist. (past deacon). Mason. Author: (with Llewellyn R. Perkins) Elementary Mathematical Analysis, 1934; (with others) Mathematics of Finance, 1958. Home: 14 Adirondack View Middlebury VT 05753

BOWKETT, GERALD EDSON, newspaper editor; b. Sacramento, Sept. 6, 1926; s. Harry Stephen and Jessie (Fairbrother) B.; B.A., San Francisco State Coll., 1952; postgrad. Georgetown U., 1954; m. Norma Orel Swain, Jan. 1, 1953; children—Amanda Allyn, Laura Anne. Radio wire editor UP, Washington, 1956-57; reporter, columnist Anchorage (Alaska) Daily Times, 1957-64; spl. asst., press sec. to Gov. William A. Egan, 1964-66; pub. Alaska Newsletter, 1966-68; Juneau bur. chief Anchorage Daily News, 1967-68; editor S.E. Alaska Empire (Juneau), 1969—. Served with USMC, 1944-46; PTO. Cited for outstanding news and feature writing, Alaska Press Club, 1962, 64. Mem. Alpha Phi Gamma. Home: 330 W 8th St Juneau AK 99801 Office: 138 Main St Juneau AK 99801

BOWLER, DUANE WILSON, newspaper editor; b. Antelope, Mont., Nov. 20, 1917; s. Burley N. and Maud (Crydermann) B.; B.A. in Journalism cum laude, U. Mont. 1939; m. Edeen Elizabeth Carlson, June 13, 1942; children—Michael H., Bonnie Edeen, Deborah Ellen, Barbara Ann. Reporter, Helena (Mont.) Ind. Record, 1941-60, sports writer, 1941-59, news editor, 1959-60; editor Mont. Health, Helena, 1945-60; mng. editor Billings (Mont.) Gazette, 1960-68, editor, 1968—; chmn. editorial bd. Lee Enterprises Inc. 1970-71. Nat. del. Am. Cancer Soc., Helena, 1954-58, mem. 6th Army adv. com., 1946—. Served with AUS, 1942-43. Mem. Mont. Press Assn., Am. Soc. Newspaper Editors, Billings C. of C., Am. Legion, Sigma Delta Chi. Elk, Rotarian. Home: 3030 Smoky Lane Billings MT 59102 Office: 401 Broadway Billings MT 59013

BOWLER, W. SCANE, financial co. exec.; b. Cleve., July 27, 1925; s. Ralph W. and Mary (Scane) B.; B.A., Dartmouth, 1948; m. Sally Weston-Webb, Dec. 2, 1966; children—William Scott, Lynn F., Collana R., Mary Ann, Donald E. Mng. partner Hopkinson, Burridge, Pearse Co., Cleve., 1949-59; chmn. bd., chief exec. officer Pioneer Western Corp., Clearwater, Fla., 1959—, Western Res. Life Assurance Co., 1959—, Financial Services, Inc., Clearwater, 1959—; dir. Pioneer Fund, Pioneer Enterprises Fund, Pioneer II Fund, Equity Planning Systems, Balanced Programs, Inc., Fund Research & Mgmt., Inc. Mem. exec. bd. Fla. council Boy Scouts Am. Mem. alumni adv. bd. Dartmouth. Served with USNR, 1943-46. Mem. Life Ins. Agy. Mgmt. Assn. Presbyn. Home: 4034 McKay Creek Dr Largo FL 33540 Office: 301 Pierce St Clearwater FL 33516

BOWLES, AUBREY RUSSELL, Jr., lawyer; b. Richmond, Va., May 31, 1896; s. Aubrey Russell and Ida Gertrude (Hockaday) B.; A.B., Richmond Coll., 1915; A.M., Harvard, 1920; LL.B., U. Va., 1923; m. Martha Mary Hoadly, Jan. 15, 1927; children—Mary Hoadly (dec.), Aubrey Russell, III. Admitted to Va. bar, 1922; since practiced in Richmond, asso. firm McGuire, Riely & Eggleston, 1923-32, Bowles, Anderson and Boyd, 1942-57, firm now Bowles and Boyd; pres. Va. Bonded Warehouse Corp., 1942-57; sec., gen. counsel Nolde Bros., Inc. Former mem. exec. com., bd. dirs. Richmond area Community Chest; bd. mgrs. Silver Hill Found. Served as 1st lt., 3d Cav., U.S. Army, AEF, 1917-19. Fellow Am. Bar Found.; mem. Am. Coll. Trial Lawyers, Jud. Council Va., Am. Law Inst., Am. Judicature Soc., Internat. Assn. Ins. Counsel, Fedn. Ins. Counsel, Va. Trial Lawyers Assn., Am. (house of dels. 1957-58), Va. (exec. com. 1949-52), W.Va. (hon.), Richmond bar assns., Va. State Bar (exec. com. and council 1948-57, pres. 1955-56), Inst. Jud. Adminstrn., Inc., Nat. Assn. R.R. Trial Counsel, Nat. Lawyers Club, Raven Soc. (U. Va.), Va. Hist. Soc., Am. Legion, Soc. 40 and 8, Am., Va. power boat assns., Soc. Cin., Family Service Soc. (pres. 1940-43), Meml. Guidance Clinic (past dir.), Assn. Bar City N.Y. (asso.), U. Va. Law Sch. Assn. (council), Judicial Conf. Va., Jud. Conf. U.S. 4th Circuit, Jamestowne Soc., Phi Beta Kappa, Kappa Sigma, Phi Delta Phi. Episcopalian. Clubs: Commonwealth, Downtown, Country of Virginia, Farmington Country; Golden Horseshoe (Williamsburg, Va.). Contbr. articles to profl. publs. Home: 7 Maxwell Rd Richmond, VA 23226. Office: Mutual Bldg Richmond VA 23219

BOWLES, CHESTER, former govt. ofcl.; b. Springfield, Mass. Apr. 5, 1901; s. Charles Allen and Nellie (Harris) B.; student Choate Sch., 1919; B.S., Yale, 1924, LL.D., 1968; LL.D., Howard U., 1955, Oberlin Coll., 1957, R.I. U., 1958, U. Mich., 1961, Bard Coll., 1957; m. Dorothy Stebbins, Feb. 22, 1934; children—Barbara, Chester Jr., Cynthia, Sally, Samuel. With Springfield Republican, 1924-25, George Batten Co., 1925-29; established Benton & Bowles, Inc., N.Y.C., 1929, chmn. bd., 1936-41; Conn. del. Democratic Nat. Conv., 1940, 48, 56; Conn.. elector for Franklin D. Roosevelt, 1940; rationing adminstr. State of Conn., 1942; Conn. dir. OPA, 1942-43, gen. mgr. Washington 1943; price adminstr., 1943-46; dir. Econ. Stblzn. 1946; mem. WPB and Petroleum Council for War, 1943-46; chmn. Econ. Stblzn. Bd., 1946; spl. asst. to sec. gen. UN, 1947-48; gov. Conn., 1949-51; ambassador to India and Nepal, 1951-53; Shaw lectr. Bryn Mawr Coll., 1953-54; Berkeley lectr. U. Cal., 1956; Godkin lectr. Harvard, 1956; Chubb lectr. Yale, 1957; mem. 86th U.S. Congress from 2d Dist. of Conn.; under sec. of state, 1961; Pres.'s spl. rep. for Asian, African and Latin Am. affairs, 1961; ambassador to India, 1963-69. Am. del. UNESCO Conf., Paris, 1946; mem. nat. commn. for UNESCO, 1946-47. Dir. Inst. Internat. Edn., Am. Council Learned Socs., Fund for Peaceful Atomic Development; trustee Fletcher Sch. Law and Diplomacy, Franklin D. Roosevelt Found., Eleanor Roosevelt Meml. Found., Rockefeller Found., Inst. African-Am. Relations. Platform chmn. Dem. Nat. Conv., 1960. Mem. Asia Soc., Conn. Grange. Democrat. Unitarian. Clubs: Essex Yacht, Cruising of Am. Author: Tomorrow Without Fear, 1946; Ambassador's Report, 1954; The New Dimensions of Peace, 1955; American Politics in a Revolutionary World, 1956; Africa's Challenge to America, 1956; Ideas, People, and Peace, 1958; The Coming Political Breakthrough, 1959; The Conscience of a Liberal, 1962; The Makings of a Just Society, 1963; A View from New Delhi, 1969; Promises to Keep—My Years in Public Life, 1971. Home: Hayden's Point Essex CT 06426

BOWLES, EDWARD LINDLEY, cons. engr., educator; b. Westphalia, Mo., Dec. 9, 1897; s. Samuel Addison and Julia (Johnson) B.; B.S., Washington U., 1920; M.S., Mass. Inst. Tech., 1922, D.Sc., Norwich U., 1945; m. Lois Wuerpel, June 17, 1922; childrenEdmund Addison, Frederick Wuerpel. Asst. dept. elec. engring. Mass. Inst. Tech., 1920-21, instr., 1921-25, asst. prof. elec. communications, 1925-27, asso. prof., 1927-37, prof., 1937-, charge communication div. dept. elec. engring., mem. patent com., dir. Round Hill Research Div., cons. prof. elec. communications, 1947-52, cons. prof. Sch. Indsl. Mgmt., 1952-63, prof. emeritus, 1963-. Cons. engr., 1923-, also cons. elec. patent matters; charter mem., sec. microwave sect. Nat. Def. Research Council, 1940-42; cons. sec. war, 1942-47, cons. communications and radar USAAF, 1943, operational and organizational problems, 1944; sci. cons. USAF, 1947-51; sci. warfare adviser weapons evaluation group Office Sec. Def., 1950-52; cons. sec. army, 1951-52; gen. cons. Raytheon Co., Lexington, Mass., 1947-66; pres. Whitin Machine Works, 1965-66; cons., then spl. asst. to pres. Analex Corp., Boston, 1964-67; chmn. bd., pres. Information Transfer Corp., 1968-70; cons., dir. Anderson-Nichols & Co., 1965-68, White Consol. Industries. Chmn. bd. ad hoc adv. com. on VHF-UHF, TV allocations, Senate Com. Interstate and Fgn. Commerce, 1956-58; mem. panel on patents Commerce Tech. Adv. Bd. Army mem. Nat. Acad. Scis., NBC, Research Bd. for Nat. Security 1945. Trustee, mem. exec. com. Bentley Coll.; charter trustee Kodaly Musical Tng. Inst. Served as 2d lt. F.A., U.S. Army, 1918. Decorated D.S.M., Presdl. Medal of Merit; Order Brit. Empire; recipient distinguished alumni citation Washington U., 1955. Registered profl. engr., Mass. Fellow I.E.E.E. (fellowship award I.R.E. 1947), Am. Phys. Soc., Am. Acad. Arts and Scis. (v.p. 1954-56); mem. A.A.A.S., Soc. Promotion Engring. Edn., Operations Research Soc., Sigma Xi. Clubs: St. Botolph (Boston); Cosmos (Washington). Holder numerous patents. Address: 15 Greylock Rd Wellesley Hills, MA 02181.

BOWLES, FRANK HAMILTON, ednl. adminstr.; b. Taihoku, Japan, Nov. 20, 1907; s. Frank Carroll and Sarah D. (Siceloff) B.; student Central Coll.; A.B., Columbia, 1928, M.A., 1930; Litt.D., Wagner Coll., 1949; LL.D., Providence Coll., 1956; L.H.D., Dickinson, 1957; also other hon. degrees; m. Frances Callaway Porcher, 1939; children—Francis Porcher, Courtney Callaway, Mason Banks. Dir. admissions Columbia U., 1934-48; pres. Coll. Entrance Examination Bd., 1948-63; dir. edn. program Ford Found., 1963-66, adviser to pres. Ford Found. in Internat. Edn., 1966—; v.p. Fund for Advancement Edn., 1964-67, pres., 1967—; pres. Fund for Adult Edn., 1965—. Fulbright Nat. Selection Com., 1949-51; con. U.P.R., 1946-56, Internat. study univ. admissions UNESCO-CEEB. Mem. bd. visitors Air U. Chmn. Commn. on Instns. of Higher Edn., Middle States Assn. of Colls. and Secondary Schs., 1947-50; mem. bd. visitors U.S. Mil. Acad., 1958-61, Haile Selassie I U., Addis Ababa, Ethiopa, 1966—; trustee Nat. Scholarship Service and Fund for Negro Students, 1951-56, New Lincoln Sch., 1958-61; mem. adv. com. to study Cath. edn., 1962-65. Served from lt. to lt. comdr. USNR, 1942-45. Mem. Sigma Alpha Epsilon, Phi Delta Kappa. Episcopalian. Clubs: Cosmos, Century, University (N.Y.C.). Author: How to Get Into College, 1958; Access to Higher Education, 1963; Re-founding of the College Board, 1968. Home: Demarest NJ 07627 Office: 477 Madison Av New York City NY 10022

BOWLES, GROVER CLEVELAND, Jr., pharmacist; b. Piedmont, Mo., Feb. 15, 1920; s. Grover Cleveland and Oca (Newton) B.; student S.E. Mo. State Coll., 1938-39; B.S. in Pharmacy, U. Tenn., 1942; D.Sc., Phila. Coll. of Pharmacy and Sci., 1968; m. Mary Lois Van Inwagen, Dec. 23, 1947; childrenRebecca R., Deborah M. Intern hosp. pharmacy U. Mich. Hosp., 1946-47; instr. U. Tenn. Coll. Pharmacy, 1947-48; chief pharmacist Strong Meml. Hosp., also U. Rochester Sch. Medicine and Dentistry, 1948-55; asso. adminstr. Meml. Hosp. Assn., Washington, 1955-56; dir. dept. pharmacy Bapt. Meml. Hosp., Memphis, 1956—; asso. prof. U. Tenn. Coll. Pharmacy, 1959—. Mem. revision com. U.S. Pharmacopeia, 1960-70; mem. Tenn. Hosp. Licensing Bd., 1961-. Bd. dirs. Memphis unit Am. Cancer Soc., Memphis Vis. Nurse Assn. Served with USNR, 1942-46. Mem. Am. Pharm. Assn. (pres. 1965-66, chmn. bd. trustees 1966-67, treas. 1967—), Am. Soc. Hosp. Pharmacists (pres. 1952, Harvey A. K. Whitney lectr. 1962), Tenn. Soc. Hosp. Pharmacists (pres. 1948), A.A.A.S., Phi Delta Chi. Contbg. editor Am. Jour. Hosp. Pharmacy, Modern Hosp. Home: 4997 Warwick Av Memphis TN 38117. Office: 899 Madison Av Memphis TN 38103

BOWLES, HARRY GEORGE, financial exec.; b. Atlantic City, Feb. 22, 1906; s. William Benjamin and Eleanor Louise (Miller) B.; B.A., Detroit Inst. Tech., 1949; m. Margaret Campbell, Dec. 26, 1936; 1 son, John Andrew. With Burroughs Corp., Detroit, 1929-71, plant mgr., 1957-59, corp. controller, 1959-60, v.p. controller, 1960-63, dir., 1963—, v.p. finance, 1963-66, sr. v.p., 1966-71; exec. v.p. finance, dir. Data Trans Mission Co., Vienna, Va., 1971—. Bd. dirs. Detroit Symphony Orch. Mem. Financial Execs. Inst., Nat. Assn. Accountants, Clubs: Oakland Hills Country; Harborview (N.Y.C.); Detroit. Home: 1930 Hillwood Dr Bloomfield Hills MI 48013 Office: 1920 Aline Av Vienna VA 22180

BOWLES, JOHN, drug co. ofcl.; b. Monroe, N.C., Nov. 16, 1916; s. Hargrove and Kelly Bess (Moneyhun) B.; B.S., U. N.C., 1938; D.B.A., Woodbury Coll., 1963; hon. degree Wingate Jr. Coll., 1960; m. Norma Louise Landwehr, Oct. 6, 1950; children—Carol Louise, Kelly Louise, John Hargrove, Normita. With Rexall Drug Co., Los Angeles, 1949-66, v.p., 1953-55, pres., 1955-65, chmn. bd., 1965-66, v.p., dir. Rexall Drug & Chem. Co., 1955-66; dir. Shick Electric Co., Inc., Technicolor, Inc. (vice chmn.), Air Cal., King Industries, Inc., Dick Co., Inc.; trustee Cameron Brown Investment Group. Mem. Pres.'s Com. for Community Relations; mem. headmasters council Harvard; mem. nat. sponsoring com. Duke; mem. pharmacy adv. com. Coll. Pacific; founder Free Enterprise Day; pres. Los Amigos del Pueblo de Los Angeles. Trustee Martin Luther Hosp., U. Cal. at Los Angeles Found., Broadcast Found.; bd. govs. Am. Found. Religion and Psychiatry; bd. regents St. John's Hosp. Served as lt. comdr. USNR, 1941-46. Recipient Horatio Alger award, 1962. Mem. Sales and Marketing Execs. (trustee), Confrerie des Chevaliers du Tastevin (officer comdr.), Master of Foxhounds Assn., Beta Theta Pi. Methodist (steward). Mason. Clubs: Los Angeles Country; Rancheros Vistadores (Santa Barbara); Belvoir Hunt (Eng.). Home: 250 N Delfern Dr West Los Angeles CA 90024 Office: 9500 Wilshire Blvd Beverly Hills CA 90212

BOWLES, LESTER LLEWELLYN, educator; b. Sharpsville, Ind., 1907; s. Edrite M. and Mary (Terrell) B.; student U. Notre Dame, 1933-34; A.B., Franklin Coll., 1934; M.D., Ind. Univ., 1938; m. Miriam Elleman, Sept. 2, 1933; children—Barbara Ann, James Terrell. Research asso. dept. anatomy Med. Coll. Ga., Augusta, 1938-41, asst. prof. microscopic anatomy, 1940-47, asso. prof., 1947-48, prof., 1948—, chmn. dept., 1950-64, head div. microscopic anatomy, 1964-71, instr. psychiatry, 1954. Received Cadaver award for excellence in teaching, 1956, 64, 65; Alumni citation Franklin Coll., 1957. Mem. Am., Ga., County med. assns., Am. Psychiat. Assn., Ga. Acad. Sci., Am. Assn. Anatomists, Alpha Omega Alpha. Mem. Society of Friends. Author: Laboratory Exercises in Histology and Embryology, 1949; also author articles in field. Home: 2903 Sussex Rd Augusta GA 30904

BOWLES, PAUL, composer, author; b. N.Y.C., Dec. 30, 1910; s. Claude Dietz and Rena (Winnewisser) B.; studied with Aaron Copland, N.Y.C., Berlin, 1930-32, with Virgil Thomson, Paris, 1933-34; m. Jane Sydney Auer, Feb. 1938. Guggenheim fellow, 1941; Rockefeller grantee, 1959. Composer mus. scores for My Hearts' in the Highlands, Love's Old Sweet Song, Twelfth Night, Liberty Jones, Roots in the Earth (for Soil Conservation Service, U.S. Dept. Agr.), Watch on the Rhine, Jacobowsky and the Colonel, The Glass Menagerie, Cyrano de Bergerac, Summer and Smoke, In the Summer House, Yerma, Edwin Booth, Sweet Bird of Youth, The Milk Train Doesn't Stop Here Any More; (ballets) Yankee Clipper, Pastorelas, Sentimental Colloquy; (opera) The Wind Remains. Author: The Sheltering Sky; The Delicate Prey; Let It Come Down; The Spider's House; Yallah; The Hours After Noon; A Hundred Camels in the Courtyard, 1962; Their Heads are Green and Their Hands are Blue, 1963; (with Driss ben Hamed Charhadi) (novel) A Life Full of Holes; Up Above the World, 1967; The Time of Friendship; (with Mohammed Mrabet) Love With a Few Hairs, 1968; The Lemon, 1969; M'Hashish, 1969. Home: Itesa 20 Campoamor Tangier Morocco Address: care William Morris Agy 1350 Av of Americas New York City NY 10019

BOWLES, RICHARD SPINK, lawyer; b. Winnipeg, Man., Can., Nov. 16, 1912; s. Manly and Mae (Spink) B.; B.A. cum laude, U. Man., 1933, LL.B. cum laude, 1937, LL.D., 1968, Lincoln Coll., Lincoln (Ill.) U., 1967, U. Winnepeg, 1968; D.C.L., St. John's Coll., 1970; m. Una Frances Arnett, Sept. 14, 1940; children—Sheldon, Kingsley, Maryann, William. Called to Man. bar, 1937; practice with firm W.J. Tupper, 1937-40; practice in Winnipeg, 1940—; sr. partner firm R.S. Bowles and Assos., 1947—. Chmn., Winnipeg Bd. Parks and Recreation, 1956-57; lt. gov. Province of Man., 1965-70. Trustee Man. Law Sch., 1963, 64, 65, 66. Mem. Canadian (council 1955-65), Man. (pres. 1961, past chmn. numerous coms.) bar assns., Law Soc. Man. (pres. 1964-65; life bencher 1965—). Author numerous articles. Address: 310 Edmonton St Winnipeg Manitoba Canada

BOWLES, WALTER DONALD, univ. ofcl.; b. Seattle, Dec. 28, 1923; s. Walter Alexander and Minnie Ellen (Martin) B.; B.A. in Econs., U. Wash., 1949; M.A. in Econs., Columbia, 1952, certificate Soviet economy Russian Inst., 1952, Ph.D., 1958; m. Vincenza Pompea Galasso, Dec. 22, 1955; children—Ellen Maria, Walter Donald. Editor, Research Program on USSR, N.Y.C., 1953-55; fellow Air U., 1955-57; faculty Am. U., Washington, 1957—, prof. econs., chmn. dept., 1964-65, prof. econs., dean Coll. Arts and Scis., 1965-69, prof. econs., v.p. acad. affairs, 1969—. Lectr., dir. seminars in field. Bd. dirs. Nat. Inst. Labor Edn. Served with AUS, 1943-46. Mem. Am., So. econ. assns., Assn. Study Soviet Type Econs., Assn. for Advancement Slavic Studies, Assn. Comparative Econs., Am. Assn. U. Profs., Pi Gamma Mu, Omicron Delta Kappa, Phi Kappa Phi, Omicron Delta Epsilon. Home: 6017 Rossmore Dr Bethesda MD 20014 Office: American Univ Massachusetts and Nebraska Sts NW Washington DC 20016

BOWLEY, ALBERT JOHN, air force officer; b. Ft. Bragg, N.C., Dec. 4, 1921; s. Freeman Wate and Elizabeth (Carpenter) B.; B.S., U.S. Mil. Acad., 1943; grad. Air Force Flying Sch., 1943, Armed Forces Spl. Weapons Project, 1948, Advanced Flying Sch., 1953, Command and Staff Coll., 1955, Air War Coll., 1959; m. Marjorie Rose Marchand, Jan. 10, 1944; children—Robin Mills, Albert John. Commd. 2d lt. U.S. Army, 1943, advanced through grades to maj. gen. USAF, 1969; assigned 306th Bomb Group, ETO, 1944-47, 63d Bomb Squadron, 43d Bomb Group, SAC, 1947-48, operations officer, 1949-51; squadron comdr. 358th Bomb Squadron, 303d Bomb Wing, SAC, 1952-54; chief tng. surveillance br., tng. div. Hdqrs. SAC, 1955-58; dir. operations Hdqrs. 3d. Air Div., SAC, Guam, 1959-61; chief control div. Hdqrs. 15th Air Force, SAC, March AFB, Cal., 1961, dep. dir. operations Hdqrs. 15th Air Force, 1962; dep. exec. to vice chief staff Hdqrs. USAF, 1963, exec. to vice chief staff, 1963-66; comdr. 40th Air Div., Wurtsmith AFB, Mich., 1966-67, 45th Air Div., Loring AFB, Me., 1967-68; dep. dir. J-5, joint staff, Washington, 1968-70, dep. c/s, Hdqrs. MACV, South Vietnam, 1971—. Decorated D.S.M., D.F.C., Air medal with 2 oak leaf clusters, Legion of Merit with oak leaf cluster. Mem. Air. Force Assn., Order Daedalians. Club: Army-Navy Country (chmn. bd. gov.'s 1969-70 Arlington, Va.). Office: HQ MACV APO SF CA 96222

BOWLING, JACK FRANK, artist, silversmith, former naval officer; b. Bonham, Tex., July 5, 1903; s. James Frank and Nanie B. (Sparkman) B.; B.S., U.S. Naval Acad., 1927; grad. U.S. Naval War Coll., 1945; m. Evelyn Renn Fletcher, Jan. 3, 1932; 1 dau., Kathryn R. (Mrs. C. Stuart Perkins, Jr.). Commd. ensign USN, 1927, advanced through grades to rear adm., 1947; staff Adm. King, 1942-43; comdr. Anti-Submarine Task Force, North Atlantic, 1944-45; sank U-248 1945, received surrender U-805, 1945; ret., 1947; profl. artist, metal worker, 1958—; lectr. on silver and silver work. One-man exhbns. include Honolulu Acad. Art, 1935, Lawrence Gallery, Dallas, 1937, Newport Art Assn., 1945, Colombo, Ceylon, 1946, Singapore, 1946, Manila, 1946; group exhbns. include So. Printmakers, 1937, Cal. Printmakers, 1938; exhibited Mpls., 1960, Grace Cathedral, San

Francisco, 1960, Pitts., 1961; represented in permanent collections Honolulu Acad. Art, Library of Congress. Decorated Legion of Merit with V; Recipient 1st award for ecclesiastic arts, Los Angeles, 1959; cash award, San Francisco, 1960, 1st award gold or silver Woodmere Art Gallery, 1962, 63, 67, 68; Best in Show award I.P.A. Exhibit, Washington, 1971. Mem. Woodmere Art Assn., Guild Religious Architects, Stained Glass Assn. Am., Phila. Art Alliance, Am. Craftsmen's Council, Internat. Platform Assn. Episcopalian (vestryman). Clubs: Army-Navy (Washington); Print (Phila.). Address: 1920 Ringgold Pl Philadelphia PA 19146

BOWLING, JAMES CHANDLER, tobacco co. exec.; b. Covington, Ky., Mar. 29, 1928; s. Van Dorn and Belinda (Johnson) B.; B.S., U. Louisville, 1951; m. Ann Jones, Oct. 20, 1951; children—Belinda Ann, Nancy Jo, James, Stephanie. Various positions from campus rep. to v.p. corp. relations Philip Morris, Inc., N.Y.C., then exec. v.p., group v.p., dir. marketing, now asst. to chmn. bd., dir. Chmn. pub. relations Tobacco Inst., Washington, 1958-63. Mem. nat. council Boy Scouts Am., 1961—; mem. alumni admissions adv. bd. U. Louisville; justice of peace, Conn., 1960. Bd. dirs., nat. pres. Keep Am. Beautiful; trustee Berea Coll., Midway Jr. Coll., Low Heywood Sch., King Sch. Served with AUS, World War II; PTO. Recipient Kolodny award as outstanding young exec. in tobacco industry; named U.S. Young Businessman of Year, St. John's U., Outstanding Alumnus, U. Louisville, 1970. Mem. Nat. Assn. Tobacco Distbg. (dir. exec. mgmt. div.), Pub. Relations Soc. Am., N.Y. So. Soc. (trustee), The Kentuckians (sec.), Lambda Chi Alpha. Episcopalian. Clubs: Wee Burn Country; LaSalle. Author: How To Improve Your Personal Relations, 1959. Home: 6 Barnfield Rd Rowayton CT 06853 Office: 100 Park Av New York City NY 10017

BOWLING, JOHN WILLIAM, fgn. service officer; b. Pryor, Okla., Oct. 16, 1920; s. Theodore Cheeseborough and Susan Katharine (Clements) B.; student U. Okla., 1937-40; B.A., George Washington U., 1942; student Nat. War Coll., 1959-60; Ph.D., Am. U. Washington, 1970; m. Mary Ellen Russell, June 11, 1960; children—Theodore Chesebrough, Virginia Ellen. Clk., RFC, 1941-42; entered U.S. Fgn. Service, 1946; assigned Lagos, 1946-48, Karachi, 1949-50, Lahore, 1950-51, Dacca, Pakistan, 1951-52, Kabul, 1952-54, Tehran, 1955-59; dep. dir. Office Greek, Turkish and Iranian Affairs, State Dept., 1962-64; Am. consul gen., Dacca, 1964-66; assigned Fgn. Service Inst., Arlington, Va., 1966—, prof. polit. sci., 1970—. Vis. lectr. U. Va., 1970-71. Served to capt., inf., AUS, 1942-46. Home: 1309 N Lynnbrook Dr Arlington VA Office: Fgn Service Inst Roslyn Arlington VA

BOWLING, WILLIAM GLASGOW, univ. dean; b. St. Louis, May 7, 1902; s. William Walter and Mary Susan (Glasgow) B.; A.B., Washington U., St. Louis, 1924, A.M., 1925; student Harvard, 1930-31; m. Violet Whelen, Aug. 3, 1933; 1 son, Townsend Whelen. Instr., asst. prof., asso. prof. English, Washington U., 1925-70, prof. emeritus, 1970—, asst. to dean, acting dean, dean Univ. Coll., 1925-42, dean Coll. Liberal Arts, 1942-46, dean men, 1942-44, civilian adminstr. pre-profl. unit Army Specialized Tng. Program, Washington U., 1943-44, dean admissions, 1946-65, univ. grand marshal, 1960-68, univ. historian, 1965—. Part time drama critic St. Louis Times, 1929-30. Mem. Am. Assn. Collegiate Registrars and Admissions Officers (hon., book rev. editor quar. jour. Coll. and U., 1955-66), Assn. Coll. Admissions Counselors, N.E.A., Mo. State Tchrs. Assn., Greater St. Louis Council Tchrs. English (pres. 1936-39, exec. sec. 1939-41), Washington U. Assn. Lecture Series (exec. sec. 1940-47), St. Louis Audubon Soc. (dir. 1944—, pres. 1950-52), Phi Delta Theta, Omicron Delta Kappa, Phi Delta Kappa. Republican. Episcopalian. Clubs: University (St. Louis). Contbr. articles to profl. jours. Address: 7408 Washington Av St Louis MO 63130

BOWLS, WOODFORD EUGENE, educator; b. Lewistown, Mo., Jan. 9, 1910; s. Lot Lee and Sarah Elizabeth (English) B.; A.B., U. Cal., 1932, A.M., 1935, Ph.D., 1937; m. Lilian Magrete Beck, May 27, 1935; children—Karen Frances, Kenneth Lanning. Teaching asst. U. Cal., 1932-36; faculty Cal. State Poly. Coll., San Luis Obispo, 1937—, prof. physics, 1945—, head phys. scis. dept., 1943-67, head physics dept., 1967-71. Mem. County Democratic Central Com., 1956-63, vice chmn., 1956-62. Mem. Am. Assn. Physics Tchrs., Am. Phys. Soc., Phi Beta Kappa, Sigma Xi, Gamma Alpha. Mason. Author lab. manual. Contbr. articles to profl. jours. Home: 1935 Hays St San Luis Obispo CA 93401

BOWMAN, A. SMITH, distillery exec.; b. Lexington, Ky., Mar. 26, 1906; s. A. Smith and Katherine L. (DeLong) B.; A.B., Princeton, 1927; M.Arch., Harvard, 1931; m. Kate Hyde Scully, Nov. 17, 1945 (dec.); m. 2d, Mary Walker Lee, Nov. 25, 1960. Pvt. practice architecture, 1931-35; exec. A Smith Bowman Distillery, Sunset Hills, Va., 1935—, now chmn. bd.; dir. Colony Hotel, Jamaica; v.p. Internat. Fueling Co. Dir. Distilled Spirits Inst., 1955—, v.p., 1956-60, treas., 1960—. Pres., mem. exec. com. Fairfax Race Assn.; treas., bd. govs. Fairfax Hunt; mem. exec. bd. Nat. Capital Area council Boy Scouts Am., 1953—, v.p. exec. bd., 1956-66; bd. dirs. United Cerebral Palsy No. Va., 1954-59, United Givers Fund, Nat. Capital Area, 1961—; pres., dir. Bowman Found., 1958—; v.p., bd. dirs. Garfield Hosp., 1956-62; treas., trustee Fairfax Hosp. Assn., 1956-65; trustee D.C. Presbyn. Home, 1961-68; mem. corp. Washington Hosp. Center, 1958—. Served from lt. to lt. comdr., USNR, 1942-46. Recipient Silver Beaver award Boy Scouts Am., 1960. Mem. Hist. Soc. Fairfax County (dir., pres.), Fairfax County C. of C. (dir. 1959-63), Soc. of Cincinnati, S.R., Nat. Steeplechase and Hunt Assn., Am. Legion. Presbyn. (past deacon, past treas., past trustee). Clubs: Metropolitan, Army and Navy, Nat. Press, Princeton, Chevy Chase, City Tavern (gov.), Admiral's (Washington); Princton, Turf and Field (N.Y.C.); Coral Beach and Tennis (Bermuda); Farmington Country (Charlottesville, Va.); Mill Reef (Antigua, W.I.); Rolling Rock (Ligonier, Pa.); Campus (grad. bd. govs.), Nassau (Princeton, N.J.); Springdale Hall (S.C.). Home: Sunset Hills VA 22070

BOWMAN, ALBERT HALL, educator; b. Evanston, Ill., Jan. 16, 1921; s. Francis Brainerd and Gertrude (Bowman) B.; A.B., Trinity Coll., Hartford, Conn., 1947; M.A., Columbia, 1948, Ph.D., 1954; m. Joyce Adair Duschl, June 5, 1948; children—Victoria Joyce, Elizabeth Ann, Catherine Louise. Instr. history N.Y. U., 1948-49; fgn. affairs analyst U.S. Govt., 1951-57; prof. history, chmn. div. social scis. Tenn. Wesleyan Coll., Athens, 1957-62; prof. history, dir. libraries U. Chattanooga, 1962-69; prof. history U. Tenn. at Chattanooga, 1969—. Vis. prof. history L.I.U., summer 1962; Fulbright prof. U. Louvain (Belgium), 1967-68. Served to 1st lt. AUS, 1942-46; mem. N.Y.N.G., 1947-50. Decorated Bronze Star medal, Purple Heart. Mem. Am., Chattanooga hist. assns., Orgn. Am. Historians, Soc. Historians Am. Fgn. Relations, Am. Assn. U. Profs., UN Assn. U.S. (pres. Chattanooga 1963-64), Alpha Delta Phi. Democrat. Episcopalian. Club: Torch. Contbr. profl. and other jours. Editor: The United States and Europe: A Colloquium, 1968. Home: 511 James Blvd Signal Mountain TN 37377 Office: U Tenn at Chattanooga Chattanooga TN 37403

BOWMAN, BARBARA HYDE, educator; b. Mineral Wells, Tex., Aug. 5, 1930; d. John Tom and Cleo (Frost) Bowman; B.S., Baylor U., 1951; M.A., U. Tex., 1955, Ph.D., 1959. Bacteriologist, Tex. Dept. Health, 1954-55; research asso. U. Tex., Austin, 1959-63, prof. human genetics, chmn. dept. Med. Branch, Galveston, 1967—; research asso. Rockefeller Inst., N.Y.C., 1963-65; asst. prof. Rockefeller U., N.Y.C., 1965-67. Mem. genetics study sect. NIH, 1970—. Mem. Am. Soc. Biol. Chemists, Harvey Soc., Am. Soc. Human Genetics (treas. 1970—, bd. dirs. 1970—), Sigma Xi, Editorial bd. Clin. Genetics, 1970—, Tex. Reports on Biology and Medicine, 1967—. Research in human inherited diseases in human protein structure. Home: 3513 Ash Circle Dickinson TX 77539 Office: Dept Human Genetics U Tex Med Branch Galveston TX 77550

BOWMAN, BEN COOK, librarian; b. Los Angeles, Dec. 22, 1912; s. Charles and Frances Rebecca (Cook) B.; B.A., U. Ore., 1937, M.A., 1939; grad. student U. Chgo., 1939-42, B.S. in Library Sci., 1948; m. Marcia Brown, June 1939 (div. 1946); m. 2d, Marion Hatch, May 1951. Grad. asst. English, U. Ore., 1937- 39, U. Ill., 1946; reference librarian Newberry Library, Chgo., 1946-48, head pub. service div., 1948-52, asst. librarian, 1952-61; dir. libraries U. Vt., 1961-66; chief librarian Hunter Coll., N.Y.C., 1966-69; dir. libraries U. Rochester (N.Y.), 1969—. Materials cons. Japan Library Sch. project, 1951-52, Ankara Library Sch. project, 1955. Bd. dirs. Five Asso. U. Libraries, 1969—, Assn. Research Libraries, 1971—. Served with AUS, 1942-46; PTO. Mem. Am., N.Y. library assns. Clubs: Grolier (N.Y.C.); Caxton (Chgo.). Home: 202 Alpine Dr Rochester NY 14618

BOWMAN, BION A., civil engr.; b. Boston; s. Winthrop and Anne Marie Dorothy (Houlen) B.; B.S., Mass. Inst. Tech., 1909; m. Dorothy Hoogs, Dec. 1922; children—Barbara Standish, David Lawrence, Brenda Winthrop. Asst. engr. Boston Transit Commn., 1909-15; engr. Fay, Spofford & Thorndike, cons. engrs., 1915-22, partner, 1922—; dir. Fay, Spofford & Thorndike, Inc., 1956—, charge cos. large civil engring., hwy. projects and sea level canal from New Orleans to Gulf of Mexico project, charge co. offices, N.Y.C., Seattle, New Orleans, Nfld., French Morocco, Alaska; engr. Rockefeller interests, 1927-30; prin. engr., asst. state dir. N.Y., Fed. P.W.A., 1933-39. Registered profl. engr., Conn., La., Ill., Mass., N.Y., N.J., Tex., Wash. Mem. Am. Soc. C.E. (life). Home: 3 Sentry Hill Pl Boston MA 02114 Office: 11 Beacon St Boston MA 02108

BOWMAN, CHARLES HENRY, educator; b. Kentwood, La., Oct. 6, 1911; s. Walter Harvey and Hettie (Rushing) B.; LL.B., Cumberland U., 1935; B.S., U. Ill., 1949, J.D., 1950; m. Ruth Louise Sison, Feb. 27, 1937; children—Mary Virginia, Charles Michael. Admitted to Ala. bar, 1935, Fla. bar, 1936, Ill. bar, 1950; practiced in Marianna, Fla., 1936-37; legal counsel Kelling Nut Co., Chgo., 1937-40; with legal counsel's office U. Ill., 1947-50, acting legal counsel, 1949-50; asst. prof. law U. Ill. Coll. Law, Champaign, 1950- 53, asso. prof., 1953-57, prof., 1957—. Reporter, Joint Com. To Revise Ill. Criminal Code, 1954-64; mem. adv. bd. Effectiveness of Fed. Correctional System Study Project, 1958-63; planning com. Atty. Gen.'s Nat. Bail Conf., 1963-64; legal adviser Ill. Juvenile Officers Assn., 1956-60; mem. adv. com. Ill. Youth Commn., 1962-63; reporter Republican Coordinating Com. Task Force on Crime and Delinquency, 1967-68; chmn. Ill. Supreme Ct. Com. on Discovery in Criminal Cases, 1970—. Bd. dirs. Nat. Safety Council, 1964-67; trustee Carle Found., 1968—. Served with USN, 1928-34, USNR, 1940- 46. Mem. Am. (reporter criminal justice adv. com. on police function 1966-68), Ill., Champaign County bar assns., Am. Law Ins. (adv. com.), Nat. Acad. Scis.-NRC (hwy. research bd. com. on motor vehicle, traffic law), Am. Judicature Soc., Nat. Assn. Def. Lawyers in Criminal Cases, Ill. Acad. Criminology, Fla. Bar, Order of Coif, Phi Delta Phi. Contbr. articles to profl. jours. Home: 604 Eliot Dr Urbana, IL 61801. Office: Coll of Law U Ill Champaign IL 61820

BOWMAN, DAVID LEON, univ. dean; b. Mt. Vernon, N.Y., Jan. 20, 1923; s. Leon C. and Margaret (Bengert) B.; B.A., Colgate U., 1942; M.A., Columbia Tchrs. Coll., 1945, Ed.D., 1954; m. Olive J. Johnson, July 9, 1943; children—James, Lawrence, Nancy, Carol Ann. Tchr. math. Hamilton (N.Y.) High Sch., 1942, Somers (N.Y.) High Sch., 1948-51; tchr. math., sci. and edn. Eau Claire (Wis.) State Coll., 1950-51; research asst. Wis. Bd. Regents of State Colls., 1951-54; dean Sch. Edn., Wis. State U. at Oshkosh, 1954—. Mem. Nat. Commn. Assn. Student Teaching, 1960-66; mem. Wis. Curriculum Guiding Com., 1958. Served with AUS, 1943-45. Mem. Nat., Wis., Northeastern Wis., Oshkosh edn. assns., Assn. Wis. State Univ. Faculties, Wis. Elementary Sch. Prins. Assn., Nat. Soc. Coll. Teaching Edn., Assn. Student Teaching, Assn. Supervision and Curriculum Devel., Kappa Delta Pi, Mu Pi Delta, Phi Delta Kappa. Rotarian. Author: A Study of Two and Four Year Curricular for the Preparation of Elementary School Teachers at Wisconsin State College, 1954; Research and Curriculum Development in Fox River Valley, 1964; Quantitative and Qualitative Effects of Revised Selection and Training Procedures in the Education of Teachers of the Disadvantaged, 1970; An Attack on High Attrition of University Underachievers, 1971. Home: 1517 Pierce Av Oshkosh WI 54901

BOWMAN, DEAN ORLANDO, economist, educator; b. Chalmers, Ind., Sept. 22, 1909; s. Bruce and Aletha G. (Taylor) B.; B.S., Purdue, 1933, M.S., 1934; Ph.D. (Brookings fellow), U. Mich., 1941; m. Fate Thomas, June 8, 1936; 1 dau., Ann Pennington. Regional price exec., dep. regional adminstr. O.P.A., 1946; chief fgn. trade sect., Japan-Korea, econ. affairs div. Dept. State, 1947-48; asst. dir. Office of Industry and Commerce, Dept. Commerce, 1948-50, asst. adminstr. policy coordination N.P.A., 1951-53; coordinator long range planning Crown Zellerbach Corp., 1953-60; v.p. long range planning Autonetics div. N. Am. Rockwell Corp., Anaheim, Cal., 1960-63, v.p. mgmt. systems and planning, 1963-70; dir. mgmt. programs, prof. bus. econs. U. Mich. Grad. Sch. Bus. Adminstrn., Ann Arbor, 1970—. Dir. Newport Nat. Corp. as 2d lt. OSS, AUS, 1943-45. Recipient Gold medal for exceptional service Dept. Commerce, 1953; Distinguished Service award Office Emergency Planning, 1968. Mem. Am., Western econ. assns., Nat. Planning Assn., Nat. Assn. Bus. Economists, Phi Kappa Phi. Author: Public Control of Labor Relations, 1942. Contbr. articles to publs. Home: 1050 Wall St Ann Arbor MI 48105 Office: 3370 MiraLoma Av Anaheim CA

BOWMAN, DONALD EDWIN, educator; b. Orrville, O., Nov. 12, 1908; s. Charles and Minnie (Sheppard) B.; B.A., Adelbert Coll. of Western Res. U., 1933, M.A., 1935, Ph.D., 1937; postdoctoral study Cal. Inst. Tech., 1937, 39; m. Martha Jane Reichenbach, Dec. 25, 1934; childrenAnn Elizabeth, Ray Douglas. Asst. biology Adelbert Coll., 1933-35, asst. biochemistry Western Res. U. Sch. Medicine, 1935-37, instr., 1937-41; asst. prof. biochemistry Ind. U. Sch. Medicine, 1941-45, asso. prof., 1945-52, prof., 1952-, acting chmn. dept. biochemistry and pharmacology, 1956- 58, chmn. dept. biochemistry, 1958-66. Mem. Am. Soc. Biol. Chemists, Soc. Exptl. Biology and Medicine, Am. Chem. Soc., A.A.A.S., Am. Assn. U. Profs., Sigma Xi, Phi Mu Delta, Nu Sigma Nu. Episcopalian. Contbr. articles to profl. jours. Home: 6845 N Delaware St Indianapolis IN 46220

BOWMAN, FRANK PAUL, educator; b. Portland, Ore., June 12, 1927; s. Frank George and Mary Dorothea (Pahl) B.; B.A., Reed Coll., 1949; student Ecole Normale Superieure, 1950-51; M.A., Yale, 1952, Ph.D., 1955. Asst. prof. U. Cal. at Berkeley, 1956-62; asso. prof. Reed Coll., 1962-63; prof. Romance langs. U. Pa., Phila., 1963—. Vis. prof. U. B.C., 1963, Haverford Coll., 1967. Coll., 1967. Served with AUS, 1945-46. Guggenheim fellow, 1968-69. Mem. Modern Lang. Assn., Modern Humanities Research Assn., Assn. Internat. des Etudes Francaises. Democrat. Episcopalian. Author: Prosper Merimee, heroism, pessimism, irony, 1962; Montaigne: Essays, 1965; L'Abbe Constant, visionnaire romantique, 1968. Home: 3932 Delancey St Philadelphia, PA 19104.

BOWMAN, GEORGE ARVENE, former univ. pres.; b. Galion, O., May 11, 1893; s. Walter Scott and Elizabeth (Wirick) B.; A.B., Adelbert Coll., Western Res. U., 1917; A.M., Columbia, 1931; summer student Ohio U., 1912, 13, Ohio State U., 1914, U. Chgo., 1921, 22, Harvard, 1938; LL.D., Bowling Green U., 1945, Western Res. U., 1960, Youngstown U., 1960, Kent State U., 1963, Miami U., 1963; L.H.D., U. Akron, 1960; m. Edith Duncan, July 11, 1923. Tchr. rural sch., South Bloomfield Twp., Morrow County, O., 1911; tchr. prin., supt. sch., Edison Morrow County, O., 1912-14; tchr., prin., Zanesville, O., 1919-23; supt. schs., Chillicothe, O., 1923-29, Marion, O., 1929- 34, Lakewood, O., 1934-41, Youngstown, O., 1941-44; pres. Kent (O.) State U., 1944-63, pres. emeritus, gen. personnel cons., 1963—. Served with engrs. USN, 1917-19. Decorated Atlantic Fleet Service medal. Mem. Ohio Edn. Assn. (past pres.), N.E.A. (v.p. 1944), Soc. for Advancement Edn., A.I.A. (asso.), Ohio Coll. Assn. (pres. 1959-60), Adv. Council on Naval Affairs, Inter-U. Council Ohio (pres. 1952, 58, 62), Ohio Hist. Soc., Kent C. of C. (hon. life), Am. Legion, Horace Mann League, A.A.A.S., Ohio Soc. N.Y., Arnold Air Soc., Pershing Rifles, Common Cause, Phi Delta Kappa, Kappa Delta Pi, Omicron Delta Kappa, Sigma Nu (trustee Ednl. Found.). Rotarian. Club: Akron City. Home: 131 Overlook Dr Kent, OH 44240.

BOWMAN, GEORGE SHEPARD, Jr., marine corps officer; b. Hammond, La., Dec. 24, 1911; s. George Shepard and Marie (Hall) B.; B.S. in Elec. Engring., La. State U., 1936; grad. Nat. War Coll., 1954; m. Velma Elizabeth Roth, Nov. 7, 1959; children—Diane (Mrs. James J. Cunningham), George Shepard III, Denham Warren. Commd. 2d lt. USMC, 1936, designated naval aviator, 1939, advanced through grades to maj. gen., 1965; various assignments U.S. and Pacific, 1936-43; operations officer G-3, MAG-42, Marine Fleet Air Wing, West Coast, 1943-44, group exec. officer, 1944; asst. G-3, Aircraft Fleet Marine Force, Pacific, 1945; operations officer on staff comdr. Naval Air Base, Okinawa, 1945; squadron comdr. MAG-15, Fleet Marine Force Pacific, 1945-46; grad., then instr. aviation sect. Marine Corps Schs., Quantico, Va., 1946-49; asst. head, later head personnel br., div. aviation Hdqrs. USMC, 1949-52; comdg. officer MAG-12, 1st Marine Aircraft Wing, Korea, 1952, group exec. officer, 1952-53, group comdr., 1953; mem. bd. Marine Aviation-Ground Officer Program, 1953; chief staff 2d Marine Wing, Aircraft, Fleet Marine Force, Atlantic, 1954- 56; dir. jr. sch. Marine Corps Schs., Quantico, Va., 1956-58; dep. asst. dir. aviation Hdqrs. USMC, 1958-60; asst. chief staff J-3, on staff comdr. in chief Pacific, 1960-63; asst. wing comdr. 1st Marine Aircraft Wing, 1963- 64, comdg. gen., 1964-66; dep. comdr. Fleet Marine Force, Atlantic, Norfolk, Va., 1966—. Decorated Legion of Merit with combat V and I star, D.F.C., Bronze Star medal with combat V, Air medal. Mem. Nat. Sojurners, Heroes of '76, Nat. Honor Soc., Scabbard and Blade, Delta Kappa Epsilon, Omicron Delta Kappa, Phi Kappa Phi, Theta Nu Epsilon. Episcopalian. Mason (Shriner). Club: Carolina Pines Country (Havelock, N.C.). Home: 415 Dillingham Blvd Naval Station Norfolk VA 23511 Office: Hdqrs Fleet Marine Force Atlantic Norfolk VA 23511

BOWMAN, GILBERT THOMAS, mfg. co. exec.; b. Mt. Clemens, Mich., July 5, 1914; s. Alfred C. and Jane (Connor) B.; B.S. in Chemistry, U. Detroit, 1936; m. Mary Brannigan, May 16, 1940; children—Margaret Ann, Gilbert Thomas, James Francis, Christopher William. With Mich. Consol. Gas Co., 1936-37, Am. Car & Foundry Co., 1937-39; with Rockwell Mfg. Co., Pitts., 1939—, gen. products mgr., 1953-56, asst. v.p., 1956-59, v.p., 1959-60, v.p. internat., 1960-63, v.p. valve and gas products div., 1963-68, exec. v.p., 1968—, also dir.; dir. Allegheny Airlines, Inc. Mem. Am. Soc. M.E., Am., Pacific Coast, Canadian gas assns., Engrs. Club N.Y.C., Engrs. Club San Francisco, Pitts. C. of C. (chmn. world trade council 1961). Roman Catholic. Clubs: Pittsburgh Athletic Assn., Duquesne, Longue Vue (Pitts.). Home: 108 Maple Heights Rd Pittsburgh PA 15232 Office: 400 N Lexington Av Pittsburgh PA 15208

BOWMAN, J. P., asphalt co. exec. Sec., Chevron Asphalt Co., San Francisco. Office: 555 Market St San Francisco CA 94105*

BOWMAN, JAMES HENRY, journalist; b. Chgo., Dec. 29, 1931; s. Paul Clarke and Kathryn (O'Connell) B.; A.B., Loyola U., Chgo., 1955, M.A., 1960, Ph.L., 1957, Th.L., 1964; m. Winifred M. Moore, July 12, 1969. Mem. Soc. of Jesus, 1950-68; ordained priest, 1963; laicized, 1969; asso. editor Ave Maria mag., Notre Dame, Ind., 1968; exec. editor Focus Michiana mag., South Bend, Ind., 1968; religion writer Chgo. Daily News, 1968—; tchr. St. Ignatius High Sch., Chgo., 1957-58, 65-67, Loyola Acad., Wilmette, Ill., 1958-60, Xavier U., Cin., 1967-68. Roman Catholic. Home: 300 S Humphrey Oak Park IL 60302 Office: 401 N Wabash Av Chicago IL 60611

BOWMAN, JOHN WILLIAM, mfg. co. exec.; b. Great Falls, Mont., Aug. 23, 1904; s. Edward Jay and Elizabeth (Galt) B.; Ph.B., Yale, 1926; m. Crete Dillon, June 21, 1928 (dec.); childrenCrete (Mrs. Harvey), John, Timothy (dec.), Diana (Mrs. M. Neely); m. 2d, Beulah Mathew, May 10, 1969. Asst. cashier Daly Bank & Trust Co., Anaconda, Mont., 1926-34; propr. ins., auditing firm, 1934- 35; with Northwestern Steel & Wire Co., Sterling, Ill., 1935-, dir. purchases, 1938-53, v.p., 1953-63, exec. v.p., 1963-; dir. Central Nat. Bank, Sterling. Mem. Ill. C. of C. (dir.), Alpha Delta Phi. Presbyn. Clubs: Union League, University (Chgo.); Yale (N.Y.C.). Home: RFD 3, Hickory Hills Sterling, IL 61081. Office: Northwestern Steel & Wire Co Av B and Wallace St Sterling IL 61081

BOWMAN, JOSEPH MERRELL, Jr., lawyer; b. Valdosta, Ga., June 23, 1931; s. Joseph Merrell and Martha (Stanley) B.; LL.B., Emory U., 1957; m. Mary Isabella Nichols, Dec. 19, 1953; children—Joseph N., Mary B., Henry F. Admitted to Ga. bar, 1958; legislative asst. to Congressman Flynt, Jr., 1958-59; partner Kennedy, Kennedy, Seay & Bowman, Barnesville, Ga., 1959-62; Congl. liaison officer Dept. Labor, 1962-63; dep. asst. to sec. treasury Congl. liaison, 1963-64; asst. to sec. treasury Congl. relations, 1964-67; asst. sec. treas., 1967-69; mem. firm Corcoran, Foley, Youngman & Rowe. Bd. advisers Nat. Bank Washington, 1969—. Mem. bd. visitors Emory U. Served to capt. USAF, 1952-56. Recipient Alexander Hamilton award Treasury Dept., 1967. Mem. Am., Ga., D.C. bar assns., Phi Delta Theta, Phi Delta Phi. Democrat. Methodist. Home: 410 Virginia Av Alexandria VA 22302 Office: 1511 K St NW Washington DC 20220

BOWMAN, JOSEPH SEARLES, oil co. exec.; b. Miami, Ariz., June 13, 1920; s. Joseph Vernol and Catherine (Searles) B.; student U. Cal., 1937-38; S.B., Mass. Inst. Tech., 1941; m. Virginia Reid, Jan. 9, 1943; children—Catherine, Joan, J. Richard, Thomas. Engring. and geol. positions, asst. to pres. Union Sulphur & Oil Corp., 1941-53; head oil and gas dept. Lambert & Co., N.Y., 1953- 54; v.p. Colo. Oil & Gas Corp., Denver, 1954-57, exec. v.p., 1957-64, dir.; pres. Colo. Oil Co., Denver, 1964—; dir. Jayhawk Pipeline Corp. Served to lt. USNR, 1942-46. Mem. Am. Inst. Mining, Metall. and Petroleum Engrs., Am.

Assn. Petroleum Geologists, Ind. Petroleum Assn. Am., Am. Petroleum Inst. Home: 353 Ivy St Denver CO 80220 Office: Denver Club Bldg Denver CO 80202

BOWMAN, KARL MURDOCK, physician; b. Topeka, Nov. 4, 1888; s. Homer Caleb and Isabelle Susanna (Murdock) B.; A.B., Washburn Coll., 1909, D.Sc., 1953; M.D., U. Cal. at Berkeley, 1913, LL.D., also Dr. J. Elliott Royer award, 1964; m. Eliza Abbott Stearns, Aug. 18, 1916 (dec. 1957); children—Richard Stearns, Thomas Elliot, Murdock Stearns, Walter Murdock; m. 2d, Anna Lowrey, July 18, 1959. Intern Children's Hosp., Los Angeles, 1913, Seton Hosp., N.Y.C., 1914, Roosevelt Hosp., N.Y.C. 1915, Bloomingdale Hosp., White Plains, N.Y., 1915-17, 19-21; chief med. officer Boston Psychopathic Hosp., 1921-36; asst. prof. psychiatry Harvard Med. Sch., 1921-36; dir. div. psychiatry Bellevue Hosp., N.Y.C., 1936-41; prof. psychiatry N.Y.U. Coll. Medicine, 1936-41; prof. psychiatry U. Cal. Sch. Medicine, San Francisco, 1941-56, prof. emeritus, 1956—; med. supt. Langley Porter Clinic, San Francisco, 1941-56; vis. prof. U. Philippines Coll. Medicine, 1954-55; dir. div. mental health for Alaska, also supt. Alaska Psychiat. Inst., Anchorage, 1964-67. Sent to China by WHO to assist govt. China in setting up Nat. Psychiat. Inst., Nanking, 1947; cons. USPHS, Office Surgeon Gen., U.S. Army, U.S. Navy, USAF, VA; mem. com. neuropsychiatry NRC, 1944-47; dir. Cal. Sexual Deviation Research, 1950-54; mem. nat. health adv. com. USPHS, 1948-50; mem. profl. adv. com. Office Vocational Rehab., 1944-50; trustee Nat. Com. Mental Hygiene, 1944-47; mem. adv. bd. psychiatry A.R.C., 1938-50. Served as capt., M.C., U.S. Army, World War I; lt. comdr. USNR, 1935-52; ret., 1952. Diplomate in psychiatry Am. Bd. Psychiatry and Neurology (dir. 1942-46, 50-51). Fellow Am. Psychiat. Assn. (life fellow, pres. 1944-46), Physician Philippines (hon.), Am. Coll. Psychiatrists; hon. life mem. Philippine Mental Health Assn.; mem. Cal., San Francisco med. socs., N.Y., Mass. psychiat. socs., A.A.A.S., Boston Soc. Psychiatry and Neurology (sec.-treas. 1933-36), New Eng. Soc. Psychiatry, Assn. Research Nervous and Mental Disease (1st v.p. 1938, 41), Sigma Xi, Phi Delta Theta, Alpha Omega Alpha. Author: Personal Problems for Men and Women, 1931; also numerous articles. Asso. editor Geriatrics, Quar. Jour. Studies on Alcohol, 1942—. Address: 3831 Market St San Francisco CA 94131

BOWMAN, LE ROY EDWARD, author; b. Elgin, Ill., Nov. 21, 1887; s. Frank Edward and Bertha May (Tuck) B.; A.B. with honors, U. Chgo., 1911, postgrad., 1911-12; Ph.D., Columbia, 1954; m. Garda Brown Wise, Sept. 23, 1942; children (by former marriage)—Bruce, Mary Ellen. Dir. receiving and shipping dept. Elgin Butter Co. (Ill.), 1905-07; dir. Greenpoint Neighborhood Assn., Bklyn., 1913- 17; dir. nat. personnnel dept. War Camp Community Service, 1917-18; mem. dept. social sci., Columbia, 1917-31, dir. tng. sch. for community workers, 1920-23, organizer, dir. N.Y.C. Recreation Com., 1919- 27; organizer summer exptl. schs. in various cities on Rosenwald Fund grant under Child Study Assn. Am., 1931-35; organizer discussion project U.S. Dept. Agr., 1935; dir. United Parents Assn. Greater N.Y. (200 parent orgns.), 1935-38; forum leader and dir. S.C. and Vt. state forum demonstrations, U.S. Office Edn., 1938-39; free-lance lectr., 1940-41; supr. bur. adult edn., tng. forum leaders, organizing intercultural community leagues, N.Y. State Edn. Dept., 1942-46, Bklyn. Coll., 1946, advanced steadily, asso. prof., 1954-58. Chmn. Ch. World Service Study Com. to Korea and Hong Kong, 1960. Bd. dirs. Consumer's Coop. Services, N.Y.C., 1925-28; trustee and lectr. Rochdale Inst., 1936-44; bd. dirs. Eastern Coop., Inc., 1948-49. Sec. and editor Nat. Community Center Assn., 1922-30; sec. sect. on community Am. Sociol. Soc., 1924-29; mem. central com. Am. Assn. for Study Group Study Group Work, 1941-43. Mem. Liberal Party, vice chmn. N.Y., 1960—. Recipient honor award N.Y.C. League for Indsl. Democracy, 1962. Author: Wilderness of American Prosperity (Benn), 1929; (with Margaret Lighty) Parenthood in a Democracy (Parents Inst.), 1935; Community Programs for Summer Play Schools (Child Study), 1936; How to Lead Discussion (Woman's Press), 1939; Organization and Leadership of Group Discussions and Forums (N.Y. State Edn. Dept.), 1943; The American Funeral, 1959; Youth and Delinquency, 1960; Reactions to N.Y. City Fair Housing Practices Law, 1960. Home: 110 Remsen St Brooklyn NY 11201

BOWMAN, LINN BRUCE, utility exec.; b. Webster, N.Y., Dec. 14, 1903; s. Henry A. and Birdella (Whiting) B.; B.Chemistry, Cornell U., 1925; m. Martha S. Hawley, Aug. 29, 1925; children—Mary Alice (Mrs. Thomas Leonard), Linda M. With Rochester Gas and Electric Co. (N.Y.), 1925—, v.p. gas and transp., 1956-62, sr. v.p. operations, 1962-65, pres., 1965-67, also dir.; former v.p., dir. Canadea Power Corp., Rochester; past dir. Marine-Midland Trust Co., Rochester. U.S. del. to meeting Econ. Commn. Europe, Geneva, Switzerland, 1957, 8th Internat. Gas Union Conf., Stockholm, Sweden, 1961. Trustee Citizens Pub. Expenditure Survey, 1960—; mem. council Cornell U., 1958—. Mem. Am. (dir.). Canadian, New Eng. gas assns., Internat. Gas Union, Am. Ordnance Assn., Soc. Gas Operators, Soc. Gas Lighting, Rochester Engring. Soc., Inst. Gas Tech. (trustee), Rochester C. of C. (dir.). Rotarian. Home: 3737 Monroe Av Rochester NY 14534

BOWMAN, LLOYD C., corp. exec.; b. Braddock, Pa., 1902. Financial v.p. dir. Thriftimart, Inc., chmn. adv. com. Thriftimart, Inc. Profit Sharing Plan and Trust; sec., treas., dir. Market Equities, Inc.; chmn., dir. Lankershim Center Co. Home: 256 S Swall Dr Beverly Hills, CA 90211. Office: 1837 S Vermont Av Los Angeles CA 90006

BOWMAN, OLIVER AYLSWORTH mfg. exec.; b. Lima, O., Apr. 1, 1932; B.S., U. San Francisco, 1954; M.S., Stanford University, 1956; m. Rosemarie Lois Brown, May 15, 1955; 1 son, Anthony Robinson. Sales rep. Ames-Brockton Fabricated Products, Akron, O., 1956-58, sales mgr. Coshocton, Ohio, 1959-61, gen. manager plant, 1961-68, v.p. sales, 1968--. Instr. bus. Coshocton Jr. College, 1968-69. Mem. Coshocton C. of C. (vice president 1967-68, pres. 1969-70), English Speaking Union, Coshocton Sertoma Club, Nat. Assn. Mfrs., Sales Executives Institute, Phi Beta Kappa, Sigma Chi, Phi Mu. Democrat. Mem. Christian Ch. (lay reader). Mason (32, Shriner). Clubs: Coshocton Country, Coshocton City, Running Deer Country. Home: 2d Av Coshocton OH Office: 3d Av Coshocton OH

BOWMAN, PETER WILLIAM, psychiatrist; b. Hanover City, West Germany, Jan. 30, 1920; s. Herman E. and Dora (Ranck) B.; student Munich U. Med. Sch., 1942-45; M.D., U. Göettingen, 1947; m. Anneliese M. Just, July 5, 1947 (div. July 1958); children—Thomas, J. Christopher, Andrew P., Annette S.; m. 2d, Gerhilde Stahl, Mar. 3, 1961; children—Michelle, Nicole. Intern anatomic pathology U. Med. Center, Göettingen, 1947-48, intern bacteriology, serology, internal medicine, 1948-49; postgrad. trop. medicine U. Inst., Hamburg, 1948; jr. asst. physician psychiatry Danvers State Hosp., Mass., 1950-51; staff Mass. Gen. Hosp., Boston, 1951-52; clin. fellow dept. child psychiatry Harvard, 1951-53; research fellow Walter E. Fernald State Sch., Waltham, Mass., 1952-53; med. supt. Pineland Hosp. and Tng. Center, Pownal, Me., 1953—; psychiatrist Me. Med. Center, Portland, 1955—; adminstrv. cons. State of N.H.; cons. St. Andrew's Hosp., Boothbay Harbor, Me., Harbor Sch. Inc., East Boothbay. Gen. chmn. Internat. Med. Conf. on Mental Retardation, Portland, 1959, v.p., 1961; mem. adv. council Spurwink Sch.; mem. program adv. council sta. WMTW-TV; adv. council Poland Spring Job Corps Center, 1965-69; mem. Pownal Planning Bd. Trustee, Pownal Conservation Bd. Recipient ann. achievement award Am. Psychiat. Assn., 1956, Distinguished Service citation Am. Legion, 1963; nominee Internat. Joseph P. Kennedy award, 1962. Fellow Am. Psychiat. Assn. (chmn. No. New Eng. Dist. br. 1964-66); mem. Group for Advancement Psychiatry, A.M.A., Me. Med. Assn. (chmn. com. on problems long-term patient care and treatment), Cumberland County Med. Soc., Nat. Council State Govs., Am. Orthopsychiat. Assn., Am. Assn. Mental Defiency (chmn. New Eng. region 1959). Co-editor: Proc. 1st Internat. Med. Conf. on Mental Retardation. Home: Saxony Farm Pownal ME 04069

BOWMAN, PHILIP IRVIN, research exec; b. Harrisburg, Pa., Aug. 11, 1909; s. Irvin Philip and Elizabeth (Stehman) B.; A.B., St. John's Coll., Annapolis, Md., 1931; M.A., Princeton, 1933, Ph.D., 1935; postgrad. Columbia, 1941; m. Mary Price Heisley, June 25, 1932 (div. 1964); children—Joan Elizabeth (Mrs. George W. Malone), Richard Philip, Robert Alan, James Lee; m. 2d, Michèle R. Sultan, July 1964. Research chemist Heyden Chem. Corp., 1935- 44; prodn. mgr. Bristol Labs., Inc., 1944, plant mgr., 1945, v.p., 1946- 49, dir., 1947-67, exec. v.p., 1949-58, pres., 1958-64; v.p., dir. Bristol-Myers Co., 1960-66, chmn. internat. operations, 1965-67, sr. v.p. 1966-67; pres. Bio-Marine Research, Inc., Marathon, Fla., 1967—; dir. Carrier Corp. Trustee St. John's Coll. Mem. Am. Chem. Soc. Clubs: University, Anglers (N.Y.C.); Twin Falls (dir. Syracuse). Home: Box 324 Marathon FL 33050 Office: Box 324 Marathon FL 33050

BOWMAN, RALPH, newspaper co. exec.; b. 1922; grad. Darmouth, 1943; M.C.S., Amos Tuck Sch., 1947; C.P.A., N.Y.; married. With Haskins & Sells C.P.A.'s, 1947- 64; with N.Y. Times Co., 1964—, treas., 1967—. Address: 218-229 W 43rd St New York City NY 10036*

BOWMAN, RAYMOND ALBERT, educator; b. Chgo., Apr. 14, 1903; s. Wilhelm F. and Hattie (Howe) B.; B.S. in Edn., Northwestern U., 1928, M.A., 1929; B.D., Garrett Bibl. Inst., 1931; Ph.D., U. Chgo., 1935; m. Marguerite Laidley, Nov. 27, 1924; children—Donna Lee (Mrs. Gunther Mohle), Philip Keith. Faculty, Northwestern U., 1930-34; faculty U. Chgo., 1935-69, mem. Oriental Inst., 1935-69, prof., 1935-69, now emeritus. Mem. Standard Bible Com. Mem. Am. Oriental Soc., Soc. Bibl. Lit. and Exegesis, Am. Assn. U. Profs., Nat. Assn. Hebrew Profs., Soc. Bibl. Lit., Am. Acad. Religion. Mason. Club: Quadrangle (U. Chgo.). Author: Aramaic Ritual Texts from Persepolis; contbg. author Interpreters Bible, 1954. Home: 1314 E 52d St Chicago IL 60615

BOWMAN, RAYMOND TOMLINSON, govt. ofcl.; b. Phila., Dec. 14, 1902; s. Richard Tomlinson and Clara (Victor) B.; B.S., U. Pa., 1925, Ph.D., 1933; m. Edna Cowgill, June 19, 1931; children—Barbara Ann, Carl Cowgill, Marjory Ellen. Instr. econs. Washington and Jefferson Coll., 1925-27, Carnegie Inst. Tech., 1927-28, U. Pa., 1928-34, asst. prof., 1934-45, asso. prof., 1945-49, prof. econs., 1950-57, chmn. dept., 1948-55, chmn. grad. group in econs., 1953-54; former asst. dir. for statis. standards Bur. of Budget, from 1955; asst. dir. research and statistics Pa. Emergency Relief Adminstrn., 1935-36; econ. adviser, statistician Pa. Com. Relief and Assistance, 1936-37; spl. asst. to sec. Pa. Dept. Pub. Assistance, 1937, dep. sec., 1939-42; research asso. Nat. Bur. Econ. Research, 1938-39. Chief staff div. stock piling and transp. WPB, 1942-44; dir. progress reporting Office Contract Settlement, 1944-45; asst. adminstr. research Surplus Property Adminstrn., 1945-46, U.S. rep. UN Statis. Com., 1955—; Mem. UN Com. on Contbns., 1959—; mem. exec. comm. Univs.- Nat. Bur. Econ. Research, 1954—; U.S. del. Conf. European Statisticians, 1955—, Inter-Am. Statis. Conf., Brazil, 1955, Internat. Statis. Inst., Brazil, 1955, 56. Mem. Am. Econ. Assn., Am. Statis. Assn. (pres. 1963), Econometric Soc., Am. Assn., U. Profs., Internat. Assn. Research in Income and Wealth. Club: Cosmos. Author: (with Paul Gemmill), An Economics Question Book, 1931; Contemporary Economic Problems, 1932; A Statistical Study of Profits, 1934; also articles in profl. publs. Office: Executive Office Bldg Washington DC 20503

BOWMAN, ROBERT J., banker; b. Lima, O., Mar. 29, 1925; s. Myron B. and Ethyl (Cramer) B.; student U. N.C., 1944-45; B.A., Bowling Green U., 1946; LL.B., Case Western U., 1948; postgrad. Rutgers U. Sch. Banking, 1961-64; m. Murl E. Franklin, June 15, 1946; children-John L., Thomas C. Admitted to Ohio bar, 1948; practice in Lima, O., 1948-53; sales rep. Universal CIT, Lima, also Grand Rapids, Mich., 1953-56, Old Kent Bank, Grand Rapids, 1956-58; sr. v.p., sr. trust officer Union Bank & Trust, Grand Rapids, 1958-70 dir. Knape & Vogt Mfg. Co., Grand Rapids, Foremost Corp., Grand Rapids. Mem. finance com. United Fund, 1968—. Bd. dirs. Western Mich. Opera Assn. Served with A.C., USNR, 1944-46. Mem. Grand Rapids C. of C. (mem. pollution com. 1969—), Western Mich. Estate Planning Council, Mich., Kent County bar assns., Am. Inst. Banking, Mich. Bankers Assn., Western Mich. Investment Group, Alpha Tau Omega. Clubs: Green Ridge Country (cir., treas. 1965-68), Ski (dir. treas. 1962-69), University Peninsular (Grand Rapids). Home: 410 Glen Oak St NW Grand Rapids MI 49504 Office: Union Bank Bldg Grand Rapids MI 49502

BOWMAN, ROBERT LAURENCE, engring. exec.; b. Akron, O., Oct. 27, 1926; s. Samuel and Esther (Johnson) B.; B.S. in Chemistry, U. Wis., 1951; M.S. in Chem. Engring., Newark Coll. Engring., 1958; m. Marilyn B. Wolfangle, Sept. 10, 1949; children—Robert G., Judith L. With 3M Co., 1951—, supr., Schenectady, 1963-70, mgr. circuit fabrication, St. Paul, 1970—. Jr. Achievement adviser, St. Paul, 1961; bd. dirs. Schenectady Jr. Achievement, 1963-70. Served with AUS, 1944-46. Fellow Am. Soc. Quality Control; mem. Am. Chem. Soc. Lutheran (sec. 1964-67). Author, patentee in field. Home: 2299 Lilac Lane White Bear Lake MN 55110 Office: 3 M Center St St Paul MN 55101

BOWMAN, ROBERT LEWIS, educator; b. nr. Walkertown, N.C., May 3, 1929; s. Chester Lee and Blanche (Lewis) B.; B.A., U. N.C., 1951. Ph.D., 1964; m. Gloria Maready, Dec. 21, 1957; children—David Lewis, Rachel Maready, Amy Carolyn. Staff and field dir. Negro Polit. Participation Study, U. N.C., 1961-62, vis. asso. prof., 1966; instr. Amherst Coll. and Mt. Holyoke Coll., 1962-64; asst. prof. Amherst Coll., 1964-65; asst. prof. U. Va., 1965-68, research asso. Inst. Govt., 1967-68; dir. research Gov.'s Study Commn. on Vocational Rehab. in Va., 1967-68; prof., chmn. dept. polit. sci. Emory U., Atlanta, 1968—; cons. Inst. Pub. Adminstrn., 1969, Model Cities Program, 1969-70, Urban Obs., Atlanta, 1970. Served with AUS, 1952-55. Mem. Am., So. polit. sci. assns., Am. Soc. Pub. Adminstrn., A.A.A.S., Am. Assn. U. Profs., Southwestern Social Sci. Assn. Contbr. articles profl. jours. Home: 522 Princeton Way N E Atlanta GA 30307

BOWMAN, RUSSELL KEITH, educator; b. Poughkeepsie, N.Y., Aug. 27, 1912; s. Harry Gruber and Gertrude Helen (Hoffman) B.; A.B., Columbia, 1934, M.A., 1935, Ph.D., 1940; m. Lillian Marie Milan, Mar. 31, 1934; children—Diane June, Lynn Michele. Instr., then asst. prof. Romance langs. Carleton (Minn.) Coll., 1941- 47; asso. prof., then prof. Romance langs. Carroll Coll., Waukesha, Wis., 1947-56, chmn. dept. modern fgn. langs., 1951-56; prof. Romance langs. Ariz. State U., Tempe, 1956—, chmn. dept. fgn. langs., 1956-65. Mem. Modern Lang. Assn. Am., Rocky Mountain Modern Lang. Assn., Nat. Assn. Standard Medieval Vocabulary, Nat. Fedn. Modern Lang. Tchrs., Am. Assn. Tchrs. French and Spanish, Rocky Mountain Council Latin Am. Studies, Ariz. Coll. Assn., Ariz. Fgn. Lang. Assn., Assn. Latin Am. Studies, Medieval Assn. Pacific. Author: Connections of the Geste des Loherains with Other French Epics and Medieval Genres, 1940. Home: 2014 La Corta Tempe AZ 85282

BOWMAN, SAMUEL LOREN, clergyman; b. Callaway, Va., Oct. 7, 1912; s. Cornelius Daniel and Ellen (Bowman) B.; A.B., Bridgewater Coll., 1934, L.H.D., 1969; B.D., Bethany Theol. Sem., Oak Brook, Ill., 1940, D.D. (hon.), 1952; postgrad. U. Pitts., 1947-48; m. Claire Meaders Andrews, Dec. 23, 1935; children—Barbara Jane (Mrs. Donald R. Miller), Carole Sue (Mrs. Robert P. Dyer). Ordained to ministry in Ch. of the Brethren, 1934; pastor in Melvin Hill, N.C., 1934-37, Marion, Ind., 1937-39, Waynesboro, Va., 1940-45, Meyersdale, Pa., 1945-48. Wenatchee, Wash., 1948-56, Long Beach, Cal., 1956-58; exec. sec. Christian edn. commn. Gen. Bd., Ch. of the Brethren, Elgin, Ill., 1958-68, gen. sec. Ch. of Brethren, 1968—, mem. program bd. div. Christian unity, 1966; rep., mem. exec. com. U.S. Cong. of World Council Chs., 1968—. Bd. Dirs. Wenatchee Community Chest, 1956- 58. Mem. Elgin C. of C. Author: Choosing the Christian Way, 1951. Home: 509 N Melrose Av Elgin IL 60120 Office: 1451 Dundee Av Elgin IL 60120

BOWMAN, VICTOR, business exec.; b. Morrow, O., Mar. 31, 1894; s. Alva C. and Nannie (Hicks) B.; A.B., Twin Valley Coll., 1912; m. Maddah Craven, Jan. 7, 1922. Spl. fgn. rep. Dennison Mfg. Co., 1914-21, traveling in Cuba, P.R., other W.I. Islands, Mexico, Central Am. countries, Argentina, Brazil, other South Am. countries; operated in Hawaii, South Sea Islands, Australia, New Zealand, Africa, Dutch East Indies, Malay States, China, Japan, Philippines, France, Spain, other European countries, domestic dist. sales mgr., N.Y.C., 1921, gen. sales mgr. domestic and fgn. sales, Framingham, Mass., 1922-27; gen. sales mgr. Pacific Mills, N.Y.C., 1927-33; gen. field supr. Schenley Distillers Corp., N.Y.C., 1933; gen. sales mgr. Mohawk Carpet Mills, N.Y. 1933; gen. sales mgr. Mohawk Carpet Mills, N.Y.C., 1933, dir., v.p., Mohawk Import and Export Co., 1940-42; v.p., dir. Am. Steel Export Co., 1942, 1st v.p., exec. v.p., 1943-53, v.p., dir. domestic and fgn. subsidiaries, 1942—. Mem. Spl. Econ. Mission, Dept. State to French North Africa, Middle East and Italy, 1944-45. Treas. Fountain House Found., N.Y.C. Served with Mil. Intelligence to observe pro-German activities in Latin America, 1917-18. Mem. Commerce and Industries Assn. N.Y. (fgn. trade com.), N.Y. State C. of C. (com. on fgn. commerce 1949- 52, now chmn.), Ohio Soc. N.Y., Am. Legion, Soc. for Advancement Mgmt. (mgr. N.Y. chpt.), Marketing Execs. Soc., Taylor Soc., Vet. Corps of Arty. Mil. Soc. War 1812, Alpha Chi Sigma. Clubs: N.Y. Export Managers', Metropolitan (N.Y.C.); Sleepy Hollow Country (Scarborough); Mexico City Country; Circumnavigators; Everglades (Palm Beach, Fla.). Home: 207 Edgemont Dr Allenhurst NJ also Morrow OH 45152 Office: Morrow OH 45152

BOWMAN, WARD SIMON, Jr., educator, economist; b. Everett, Wash., Oct. 29, 1911; s. Ward Simon and Charity E. (Rice) B.; A.B., U. Wash., 1933; M.A. (hon.), Yale, 1959; m. Maxine Beal, Feb. 14, 1937; children—Gary W., George T. Economist, Dept. Justice, 1938-46; research asso. U. Chgo. Law Sch., 1946-56; mem. faculty Yale Law Sch., New Haven, 1956—, prof. law and econs., 1959—. Mem. Am. Econ. Assn. Contbr. articles to profl. jours. Home: 64 Mt View Terrace Hamden CT 06517 Office: Yale Law Sch New Haven CT 06520

BOWMAN, WESLEY ELLSWORTH, ret. illustrative photographer; b. Aberdeen, S.D., Aug. 3, 1898; s. William Samuel and Alice Ott (Claridge) B.; grad. Wayland Acad., Beaver Dam, Wis., 1923; M. Photography, Profl. Photographers Am., 1946, 64; m. Margaret Galloway, Aug. 3, 1926; children—Margaret Alice (Mrs. Wallace E. Brown), David Galloway. Apprentice, Chgo. Comml. Photographic Co., 1924- 28; pres., owner Wesley Bowman Studio, Inc., Chgo., 1928-63, Wesley Bowman Inc., Chgo., 1956-63; pioneer negative-positive system color photography; guest lectr. Winona Sch. Photography, 1956-62; judge internat., nat., state comml. photog. exhbns., 1956-62. Commr., Kenilworth (Ill.) Park Bd., 1974-53; pres. Village Kenilworth, 1953-57; chmn. Kenilworth Plan Commn., 1956-62; mem. dept. information and promotion Episcopal Diocese Chgo. Trustee Wayland Acad.; trustee, treas. Canterbury House of Northwestern U.; chmn. bd. trustees Winona Sch. Photography; chmn. bldg. com. for nat. hdgrs. bldg. Profl. Photographers Am.; mem. adv. bd. Rochester Inst. Tech. Served with U.S. Army, 1917-19; AEF in France. Recipient awards from Art Dirs. Club Chgo., 1944, 52-54, award Affiliated Advt. Agy. Network, 1960; Distinguished Service award Ind. Photog. Assn., 1954, S.W. Photog. Assn., 1957. Mem. Profl. Photographers Am. (dir. exec. bd. 1955-61, sec.- treas. 1962, pres. 1963-64), Chgo. Photog. Guild (pres. 1939-45, dir. 1945-52), Camerascraftsmen Am. Inst. Brit. Photographers. Republican. Episcopalian. Clubs: Kenilworth; Westmoreland Country (Wilmette, Ill.); Dairymans Country (Boulder Junction, Wis.). Home: 640 Kenilworth Terrace Kenilworth IL 60043 also 5639 Natoma Dr Fort Myers FL 33901

BOWMER, ANGUS LIVINGSTON, educator, theatrical producer, dir., cons.; b. Bellingham, Wash., Sept. 25, 1904; s. Charles C. and Flora B.; life teaching certificate Western Wash. Coll. Edn., 1926; B.A., U. Wash., 1930, M.A., 1934; D.F.A., Lewis and Clark Coll., 1960's; hon. degree U. Portland, 1960's; m. Gertrude, Dec. 30. Tchr., adminstr. Wash. pub. schs., 1924-30; from instr. to prof. drama So. Ore. Coll., Ashland, 1931-70; devel. cons.; 1971—; founder Ashland Elizabethan Theatre and Ore. Shakespearean Festival, 1935, producing dir., 1935-71, has produced all the Shakespearean plays in 125 prodns. Served with AUS, 1942-43. Recipient Distinguished Service award U. Ore., 1961; Edith Knight Hill Meml. award for outstanding contbn. to Ore., Portland profl. chpt. Theta Sigma Phi, 1964; Salute, Ore. State Legislature, 1965; award for contbn. to devel. of theater in Northwest, Wash. Arts Council, 1966; Distinguished Service award Ore. State U., 1967; Ford Found. grant for travel and study in Europe, 1960's; indoor theatre named in his honor, 1970. Mem. ANTA, Am. Ednl. Theatre Assn., Northwest Drama Conf. (dir. 1960-63), Internat. Inst. Arts and Letters (life fellow). Home: 1280 Madrone Ashland OR 97520

BOWNES, HUGH HENRY, judge; b. N.Y.C., Mar. 10, 1920; s. Hugh Gray and Margaret (Henry) B.; B.A., Columbia, 1941, LL.B., 1948; m. Irja C. Martikainen, Dec. 30, 1944; children—Barbara Ann, David and Ernest (twins). Admitted to N.H. bar, 1948, since practiced in Laconia; partner firm Nighswander, Lord & Bownes, 1951-66; asso. justice N.H. Superior Ct., 1966-68; U.S. dist. ct. judge, Concord, N.H., 1968—. Mem. Laconia City Council, 1953-57; chmn. Laconia Democratic Com., 1954-57; mayor, Laconia 1963-65; mem. Dem. Nat. Com. from N.H., 1963-66. Chmn., Laconia chpt. A.R.C., 1951-52; pres. bd. Laconia Hosp., Assn., 1963-64. Served to maj. USMCR, 1941-46. Decorated Silver Star. Mem. Am., N.H., Belknap County (pres. 1965—) bar assns., Laconia C. of C. (past pres.). Lion (past pres. Laconia). Home: 4 Poor Richard's Dr Concord NH 03301 Office: Fed Courthouse Concord NH 03301

BOWRA, WILFRED CHARLES, railroad ofcl.; b. Stratford, Ont., Can., Oct. 8, 1910; s. Charles Charlton and Rebecca (Mitchell) B.; student Stratford Collegiate Inst., 1924-28; m. Myrtle Irene Hennick, Apr. 18, 1935; children—Corrine Mae, Judith Anne. With Canadian Nat. Rys., 1928—, gen. supt. motive power and car equipment, Battle Creek, Mich. and Toronto, Can., 1947-55, spl. asst., Toronto, 1955-57, gen. mgr. Great Lakes region, Toronto, 1957-63, v.p. Prarie Region, Winnipeg, 1964-67, system v.p., Montreal, Que., Can., 1967—. Mem. Canadian, Toronto (past pres.) ry. clubs. Club: St. Maurice Fish and Game. Home: 1371 Dumfries Rd Town of Mt Royal Montreal 304 Quebec Canada Office: PO Box 8100 Montreal 3 Quebec Canada

BOWRING, EVA, former govt. ofcl., rancher; b. Nevada, Mo., Jan. 9, 1892; d. John F. and M. Belle (Hinkes) Kelly; m. T. F. Forester, 1911; children—Frank H., James Harold, Jo Donald; m. 2d, Arthur Bowring, Apr. 13, 1928 (dec. 1944). Cattle rancher, operator Bar 99 Ranch, Merriman, Neb., 1928-, registered Hereford breeder; U.S. senator, Neb., 1954; mem. Fed. Bd. Parole, 1956-64. Mem. adv. com. Neb.-S.D. Regional Med. Program 1965—. Trustee Neb. Children's Home Soc. Address: BAR 99 Ranch Merriman, NB

BOWRON, HAROLD ALFRED, Jr., lawyer; b. Birmingham, Ala., Oct. 2, 1927; s. Harold Alfred and Frances (Glenn) B.; B.A., Vanderbilt U., 1952, LL.B., 1955; m. Anne Wakefield Isaacs, June 11, 1955; children—Harold Alfred III, Lucy Glenn, Edward Isaacs, Mark Wakefield, James Alexander. Admitted to Ala. bar; asso. Martin & Blakey and successor firms, Birmingham, 1955-60; partner Martin, Balch, Bingham, Hawthorne & Williams and predecessor firms, Birmingham, 1960—. Served to lt. comdr. USNR, 1946-51. Republican. Presbyn. Home: 2921 Ryecroft Rd Birmingham AL 35223 Office: 600 N 18th St Birmingham AL 35203

BOWRON, RICHARD ANDERSON, utilities exec.; b. Birmingham, Ala., Jan. 18, 1924; s. James Edgar and Mary (Anderson) B.; B.S., U. Ala., 1943; M.B.A., U. Pa., 1948; m. Ruth Womelsdorf Matthews, Dec. 29, 1961; children—Richard Anderson, Mary Anderson, Lee Matthews. With Ala. Power Co., Birmingham, 1948—, asst. sec., 1962; sec. 1963—. Served to 1st lt. AUS, 1943-46, AUS, 1950- 52. Mem. Newcomen Soc. N.Am., Ala. Hist. Assn., Phi Delta Theta. Presbyn. Clubs: Exchange, Mountain Brook. Home: 3629 Springhill Rd Birmingham, AL 35223. Office: Ala Power Co Birmingham AL 35202

BOWS, ALBERT JULIUS, Jr., accountant; b. Chgo., Oct. 5, 1913; s. Albert Julius and Lily (Waldman) B.; B.S.C., Northwestern U., 1934, M.B.A., 1935; m. Helen Johnson, June 22, 1940; children—David, Sally. With Arthur Andersen & Co., C.P.A.'s, 1935—, partner charge Atlanta office, 1959-69, sr. partner, 1971—. Chmn. profl. unity Atlanta United Appeal, 1965. Trustee Atlantic Christian Coll.; adv. com. bus. community relations Emory U.; adv. bd., chmn. youth and bequest and endowment coms., chmn. Salvation Army; mem. exec. com., bd. visitors Emory U., 1971—. Recipient Liberty Bell award Atlanta Bar Assn., 1969, Layman of Yr. award Christian Council Atlanta, 1969, William Booth award Salvation Army, 1971. C.P.A., Ill., Ga. Mem. Am. Inst. C.P.A.'s (chmn. com. auditing procedure 1962-65, chmn. com. relations with SEC and stock exchange, mem. council from Ga. 1965- 66), Ga. Soc. C.P.A.'s (past chmn. Atlanta), Nat. Assn. Accountants, Atlanta (chmn. mag. com. 1965, dir., pres. 1968), Atlanta Jr. (hon. life) chambers commerce, Nat. Alliance Businessmen (dir. Atlanta chpt. 1969—). Mem. Christian Ch. (past treas., elder, deacon). Clubs: Peachtree Golf, Capital City, Commerce (Atlanta). Contbr. articles to profl. jours. Home: 1465 W Wesley Rd NW Atlanta GA 30327 Office: 25 Pryor St NE Atlanta GA 30303

BOWSER, ALPHA LYONS, marine corps officer; b. Crafton, Pa., Aug. 21, 1910; s. Alpha Lyons and Gertrude Elizabeth (Cox) B.; B.S., U.S. Naval Acad., 1932; grad. Nat. War Coll., 1955; m. Mary Health Clapp, Dec. 9, 1936; 1 dau., Joan Alston (Mrs. Dane K. Stoll). Commd. 2d lt. USMC, 1932, advanced through grades to lt. gen., 1965; assigned 3d Marine Div., Bougainville, Guam and Iwo Jima, 1942-45, 1st Marine Div., Korea, 1950-51; mem. SHAPE staff, NATO, Paris, France, 1952-54; comdg. gen. Recruit Tng. Command, San Diego, 1956-58, Marine Corps Base, Twenty Nine Palms, Cal., 1959-60; asst. chief staff G-1 (manpower) Hdqrs. USMC, 1960-63; comdg. gen. Marine Corps Base, Camp Lejeune, N.C., 1963-65; former comdg. gen. Fleet Marine Force Atlantic, Norfolk, Va., from 1965. Mem. nat. council U.S.O. Decorated Legion of Merit with two gold stars, Bronze star with one gold star, Air medal. Club: Army-Navy (Washington).

BOWSER, DAVID GLINES, steel co. exec.; b. Pitts., Feb. 2, 1912; s. John L. and Maude Blanche (Manspeaker) B.; B.S. in Chem. Engring., Ga. Inst. Tech., 1937; postgrad. Carnegie Inst. Tech., 1938-39; grad. Advanced Mgmt. Program, Harvard, 1962; m. Laura O'Day, May 30, 1947; children—Susan Ruth, Timothy D. Gen. mgr. Vanadium Corp. Am., 1945-54; a founder, v.p. Globe Metall. Corp., Beverly, O., 1955-57; gen. mgr. ferro alloy dept. Interlake Iron Corp., 1957-62, v.p., 1962-65; v.p. Interlake Inc., Cleve., 1965—. Mem. Am. Inst. Mining, Metall. and Petroleum Engineers, Am. Iron and Steel Inst. Clubs: Duquesne (Pitts.); Cleveland Athletic. Home: Brecksville OH Office: Interlake Steel Corp Union Commerce Bldg Cleveland OH 44115

BOWSER, LAWRENCE PENDLETON, hosp. adminstr.; b. Winchester, Mass., July 10, 1907; s. William Lawrence and Bessie (Pendleton) B.; B.S., Tufts U., 1930, M.D., 1934; m. Evelyn Lucy Rowlinson, June 19, 1937; children—Eleanor N. (Mrs. Robert Stacy), Lawrence Pendleton. Intern, Salem (Mass.) Hosp., 1934-35; resident Middlesex County Sanatorium, Waltham, Mass., 1935-36; asst. physician, then sr. physician Walter E. Fernald State Sch., Waltham, 1936-52, asst. supt., 1953-60; supt. Belchertown (Mass.) State Sch., 1960—. Spl. agt. Belchertown Bd. Health, 1960—. Diplomate Am. Bd. Psychiatry and Neurology. Fellow Am. Assn. Mental Deficiency; mem. Mass. Med. Soc., New Eng. Psychiat. Soc. Home: State St Belchertown MA 01007 Office: Box 486 Belchertown MA 01007

BOWSHER, CHARLES ARTHUR, accountant; b. Elkhart, Ind., May 30, 1931; s. Matthew A. and Ella M. (West) B.; B.S., U. Ill., 1953; M.B.A., U. Chgo., 1956; m. Mary C. Mahoney, Dec. 14, 1963; children—Kathryn M., Stephen C. Partner, Arthur Andersen & Co., C.P.A.'s, Chgo., 1956-67, Washington office, 1971—; asst. sec. navy financial mgmt., 1967-71. Served with AUS, 1953-55. Recipient Distinguished Pub. Service award U.S. Navy, 1969, 71. C.P.A., Ill. Mem. Am. Inst. C.P.A.'s, Alumni Assn. Grad. Sch. Bus. U. Chgo. (v.p. 1965-67), Pi Kappa Alpha. Clubs: University (Chgo.); Army-Navy, International, Burning Tree (Washington); Home: 2801 New Mexico Av NW Washington DC 20007 Office: 815 Connecticut Av NW Washington DC 20006

BOX, CLOYCE K., constrn. co. exec.; b. Gatesvill, Tex., Aug. 24, 1923; s. R.D. and Zelma Box; B.B.A., W. Tex. State Coll., 1948; student La. Inst. Tech., 1942- 44; LL.B., Baylor U., 1951; m. Fern Virginia Cunningham; children—Don, Gary, Tommy, Douglas. With Detroit Lions Profl. Football Team, 1949-54; pres. Okla. Cement Co., 1959-67; chmn. bd. OKC Corp., Dallas, 1967—, George A. Fuller Co., Dallas, 1966—, also dir.; dir. Citizns Nat. Bank Dallas, Fourth Nat. Bank, Tulsa. Served to capt. USMC, 1942-46, 50-52. Home: PO Box 159 Frisco TX 75034 Office: 1949 N Stemmons Freeway Dallas TX 75207

BOX, CLYDE, air force officer; b. Nevada, Tex., Feb. 3, 1912; s. Michael James and Myrtle (Yeager) B.; student N. Tex. U., 3930-36; grad. Command Class, Ft. Leavenworth, Kan., 1946, Air War Coll., 1949, Nat. War Coll., 1953; m. Martha Ann Hotchkiss, Apr. 9, 1938; children—Martha Ann (Mrs. Crosbie), Jennifer Ra (Mrs. Carrington E. Barrs III). Flying cadet USAAF, 1936, commd. 2d lt., 1937, advanced through grades to maj. gen. USAF, 1962; pilot and operations officer 17th Attack Group, 1937-40, 19th Bomb Group, PTO, 1940-42; dep. chief staff 10th Air Force, India, 1942-43; with gen. staff War Dept., 1944-45; dep. chief staff operations Spl. Weapons Command, 1949-52; comdr. 60th Troop Carrier Wing, Germany, 1955-56, 322d Air Div., France, 1956-59, 464th Troop Carrier Wing, 1959- 60; asst. chief staff J-5, Hdqrs. USSTRICOM, 1961-64; comdr. 6th Allied Tactical Air Force (NATO), Turkey, 1964-67; comdr. 3d Air Force, 1967-68; dep. insp. gen. air staff, 1968—. Decorated Legion of Merit with 4 oak leaf clusters, D.F.C., Air medal with oak leaf cluster, Commendation medal with oak leaf cluster. Recipient Cross of knight comdr. Royal Order Phoenyx. Mem. Order Daedalians. Address: 65 Westover Av Bolling AFB Washington DC 20332

BOX, GEORGE EDWARD PELHAM, educator, statistician; b. Gravesend, Eng., Oct. 18, 1919; s. Harry and Helen (Martin) B.; B.Sc., U. Coll., U. London (Eng.), 1947, Ph.D., 1952, D.Sc., 1961; m. Joan Gunnhild Fisher, Dec. 12, 1959; children—Helen Elizabeth, Harry Christopher. Statistician, head statis. techniques research sect. Imperial Chems. Industry, Blackley, Manchester, Eng., 1948-56; dir. statis. techniques research group Princeton, 1957- 59; prof. statistics U. Wis., Madison, 1960—, holder Ronald Aylmer Fisher chair, 1971—. vis. research prof. U. N.C., 1952-53; Ford Found. vis. prof. Harvard Bus. Sch., 1965-66, U. Essex, Eng., 1970-71; cons. to industry, 1956—. Served with Brit. Army, 1939-45. Decorated Brit. Empire medal. Recipient Profl. Progress award Am. Inst. Chem. Engrs., 1963. Fellow Royal Statis. Soc. (Guy medal 1964), Am. Statis. Assn. (past v.p.), Inst. Math. Statistics, Am. Soc. Quality Control (Shewhart medal 1968), A.A.A.S. v.p.); mem. Internat. Statistics Inst., Biometrics Soc. Author: (with others) Statistical Methods in Research and Production, 1957; Design and Analysis of Industrial Experiments, 1959; Evolutionary Operation: A Statistical Method for Process Improvement; Time Series, Forecasting and Control. Contbr. articles to profl. jours. Home: 3437 Edgehill Pky Madison WI 53705

BOX, JOHN, art dir., film producer; b. London, Eng., Jan. 27, 1920; s. Allan Cyril and Albertha (Storey) B.; grad. London Sch. Architecture, 1947; m. Doris Lee, Apr. 15, 1954. With J. Arthur Rank Orgn., motion pictures, 1948-52; ind. art dir. and prodn. designer for motion pictures, 1952—; prodns. include Inn of the Sixth Happiness, Our Man in Havana, The World of Suzie Wong, Lawrence of Arabia, Doctor Zhivago, A Man for All Seasons, The Looking Galss War, Oliver. Served to maj. British Army, 1939-46. Recipient Acad. awards for color art direction of Lawrence of Arabia, Doctor Zhivago, Oliver, Brit. Film Acad. award for A Man for All Seasons, 1968, Moscow Festival award for prodn. design Oliver, 1969. Asso. mem. Royal Inst. Brit. Architects. Address: William Morris Agency (UK) Ltd Melrose House 4 Savile Row London W 1 England

BOX, JOHN HAROLD, architect; b. Commerce, Tex., Aug. 18, 1929; s. E.O. and Mary Emma (Haynes) B.; B.Arch., U. Tex., Austin, 1950; m. Dorothy Jean Baldwin, Jan. 19, 1952 (div. Jan. 1971); children—Richard B., Kenneth W., Gregory V. Apprentice, O'Neil Ford, architect, San Antonio, 1948; designer Broad & Nelson, architects, Dallas, 1954-56; asso. Harrell & Hamilton, architects, Dallas, 1956-57; partner Pratt, Box, Henderson & Partners, architects, Dallas, 1957—. Prof., chmn. dept. architecture U. Tex., Arlington, 1971—. Prin. works include St. Stephen's Meth. Ch., Dallas, 1962; Great Hall of Apparel Mart, Dallas, 1965; Quadrangle Shopping Center, Dallas, 1965; Garden Center, Dallas, 1970; master plan Griffin Sq., Dallas, 1971. Chmn. design of city task force Goals for Dallas, 1968-70, chmn. Goals Achievement Com., 1970—; chmn. design com. Greater Dallas Planning Council, 1969, v.p. Save Open Space, 1970. Bd. dirs. Dallas Chamber Music Soc., 1960—. Served to lt. C.E. Corps, USNR, 1955. Co-recipient prize Enrico Fermi Meml. Archtl. Competition, 1957, grand prize Homes for Better Living Competition, 1959. Tex. Architecture Found. grantee, 1957. Fellow A.I.A. (pres. Dallas 1967); mem. Tex. Soc. Architects (v.p., commr. edn. and research 1971, design awards 1964-66, 68, 70, 71), Sierra Club, Sigma Nu. Co-author: Prairies Yield, 1962; Goals for Dallas Proposals for Design of City, 1970. Home: 4930 Cedar Springs Dallas TX 75235 Office: 3526 Cedar Springs Dallas TX 75219

BOX, THADIS WAYNE, coll. dean; b. Logan, Utah, May 9, 1929; s. Daniel W. and Mary Madelyn (Hasty) B.; B.S., S.W. Tex. State Coll., 1956; M.S., Tex. A. and M. U., 1957, Ph.D., 1959; m. Virginia Price, July 16, 1954; children—Dennis, Mary, Paul, Emily. Rancher, Burnet, Tex., 1946-51; Welder Wildlife Found. fellow Sinton, Tex. 1956-59; asst. prof. Utah State U., 1959-61, dean Coll. Natural Resources, 1970—; from asso. prof. to prof. Tex. Tech. U., 1962-68; dir. Internat. Center Arid and Semi-Arid Land Studies, 1968-70; cons. FAO, UN, also fgn. govts. and pvt. orgns. Served with AUS, 1951-53. Recipient E. Harris Harbison award for Distinguished Teaching, 1967. Commonwealth Sci. and Indsl. Research Orgn. fellow (Australia), 1968-69. Mem. Soc. Range Mgmt., A.A.A.S., Wildlife Soc., Ecol. Soc., Soil Conservation Soc., World Acad. Arts and Scis., Am. Assn. U. Profs., Sigma Xi. Author articles. Home: 914 River Heights Blvd Logan UT 84321

BOXELL, EARL FRANCIS, lawyer; b. Marion, Ind., Dec. 3, 1894; s. Charles F. and Ida M. (Christman) B.; A.B., U. Mich., 1921, J.D., 1923; m. Mary A. Dotzler, May 27, 1939; children—Earl Francis, Merle A., Charles K., Mary J. Admitted to Ind. bar, 1921, Ohio bar, 1923; practice of law, Toledo, 1923—; mem. firm Boxell, Bebout, Torbet & Baker, 1943—. Candidate for Judge Maumee (O.) Municipal Ct., 1964. Fellow Am. Bar Found., Ohio Bar Found.; mem. Am. Arbitration Assn. (internat. panel arbitrators), Am., Ohio, Toledo (pres. 1960-61) bar assns., Phi Alpha Delta, Delta Sigma Rho. Home: 3217 Glanzman Rd Toledo OH 43614 Office: Toledo Trust Bldg Toledo OH 43604

BOXLEY, ABNEY, corp. exec.; b. Huntington, W. Va., 1904; ed. Va. Mil. Inst. Pres., Blue Ridge Stone Corp., Pounding Mill Quarry Corp., McBain Bldg. Corp., Martinsville Stone Corp.; chmn. bd., pres. Trego Stone Corp.; treas., dir. Downtown Parking Co.; dir. Patrick Henry Hotel Corp., Mchts. Parking, Inc., Colonial Am. Nat. Bank, Roanoke Gas Co.; trustee Eastern Gas & Fuel Assos. Home: 3128 Sommerset St SW Roanoke VA 24014 Office: Box 2459 Boxley Bldg Roanoke VA 24010*

BOY, JOHN BUCKNER, sugar co. exec.; b. Johnson City, Tenn., Mar. 25, 1917; s. David Clark and Elizabeth Kathleen (Jennings) B.; B.S. in Mech. Engring., Ga. Inst. Tech., 1938; m. Nancy Elizabeth Adams, Jan. 29, 1944; childrenElizabeth Kathleen, John Buckner, Howard Lane. With Buckeye Cotton Oil Co., 1938- 41; with U.S. Sugar Corp., 1946—, v.p. adminstrn., 1960-61, exec. v.p., 1961-70, pres., 1970—, also dir. Mem. marketing and research adv. com. Dept. Agr., 1962-. Mem. Hendry County (Fla.) Bd. Pub. Instrn., 1956-60. Served to lt. comdr. USNR, 1941- 46. Mem. Soil and Crop Sci. Soc. Fla., Fla. Farm. Bur., Internat. Soc. Sugar Cane Technologists, Clewiston C. of C., Pi Kappa Phi, Tau Beta Phi, Omicron Delta Kappa. Episcopalian (past vestryman). Elk, Kiwanian (past pres. Clewiston). Club: Clewiston Country. Home: 102 W Circle Dr Clewiston FL 33440 Office: US Sugar Corp Clewiston FL 33440

BOYAN, NORMAN JOHN, educator; b. N.Y.C., Apr. 11, 1922; s. Joseph J. and Emma M. (Pelezare) B.; A.B., Bates Coll., Lewiston, Me., 194; A.M., Harvard, 1947, Ed.D., 1951; m. Priscilla M. Simpson, July 10, 1943; children—Stephen J., Craig S., Corydon J. Instr. U.S. history Dana Hall Sch., Wellesley, Mass., 1946-48; research asso. Lab. Social Relations, Harvard, 1950-52; asst. prin. Mineola (N.Y.) High Sch., 1952-54; prin. Wheatley Sch., East Williston, N.Y., 1954-59; asso. prof. edn., dir. student teaching and internship U. Wis., 1959-61; asso. prof. edn. Stanford, 1961-67; dir. div. ednl. labs. U.S. Office Edn., 1967-68, asso. commr. for research, 1968-69; prof. edn., dean Grad. Sch. Edn., U. Cal. at Santa Barbara, 1969—; cons. numerous U.S. sch. systems, U.S. Govt. and Pacific Trust Terrs. Served with USAAF, 1943-46. Recipient Shankland award for advanced grad. study in ednl. adminstrn., 1950. Mem. Am. Assn. U. Profs., Am. Ednl. Research Assn., Am. Assn. Sch. Adminstrs., Nat. Conf. Profs. Ednl. Adminstrn., Phi Beta Kappa, Phi Delta Kappa. Contbr. articles profl. jours. Editorial bd. Harvard Edn. Rev., 1948-50, Jour. Secondary Edn., 1963-68, Jour. Edn. Research, 1967—, Urban Edn., 1967—. Home: 912 Aleeda Lane Santa Barbara CA 93103

BOYAN, THOMAS ARTHUR, home furnishings co. exec.; b. North Adams, Mass., Sept. 9, 1916; s. Thomas and Lillian (Hawkins) B.; B.A., Dartmouth, 1938; m. Iris Melrose Owens, Aug. 21, 1939; children—Carolyn Ruth, Thomas Arthur, Lawrence Scott. Sales exec. Mohawk Carpet Mills, Inc., Amsterdam, N.Y., 1938-40, dir. indsl. relations, 1945-65; v.p. personnel Mohasco Industries, Inc., Amsterdam, 1965—; v.p., dir. Atlantic Industries, Inc. Bd. dirs. Mohasco Meml. Fund. Served to lt. USNR, 1940-45. Decorated Silver Star medal. Home: 1444 Clifton Park Rd Schenectedy, NY 12309. Office: 57 Lyon St Amsterdam NY 12010

BOYAR, SIDNEY LEON, retail co. exec.; b. Chicago Heights, Ill., Oct. 11, 1913; s. Jacob Leon and Molly (Cohen) Boyarsky; B.S. in Mech. Engring., Purdue U., 1935; m. Selma Ruth Stone, June 30, 1940; children—Janet Lee (Mrs. Melville L. Moses, Jr.), Arthur Kurt, Dorann Lynn (Mrs. Robert Schaffner). With Sears, Roebuck & Co., 1934—, nat. mdse. mgr. Kenmore home laundry appliance div., 1952-65, v.p. factory mgmt. 1965—, also dir.; dir. Armstrong Rubber Co., Chamberlain Mfg. Co., Copolymer Rubber & Chem. Corp., DeSoto, Inc., Globe-Union Inc., Whirlpool Corp., Warwick Electronics, Inc., Sears Bank & Trust Co., Kellwood Co., Signal Delivery Service, Inc. Mem. steering com. Nat. Conf. Christians and Jews, 1960—. Recipient Distinguished Alumni award Purdue U., 1967. Mem. Ill. Mfrs. Assn., Indsl. Mgmt. Assn., Newcomen Soc., Jewish Chautauqua Soc., Jewish Fedn., Sigma Alpha Mu. Jewish religion (trustee temple). Mem. B'nai B'rith. Home: 3150 N Lake Shore Dr Chicago IL 60657 Office: 7401 Skokie Blvd Skokie IL 60076

BOYCE, ALFRED MULLIKIN, entomologist; b. Centreville, Md., May 2, 1901; s. Zell C. and Delia (Sparks) B.; B.S., Cornell U., 1926, M.S., 1927; Ph.D., U. Cal. at Berkeley, 1931; m. Janet Elizabeth Mabry, Aug. 29, 1939; children—Allen W., Karen. Extension specialist entomology Cornell U., 1926-27; with U. Cal. Citrus Expt. Sta., Riverside, 1927-68, jr. entomologist, asst. prof. entomology, asso. prof., prof., head dept. entomology, 1943-52, dir. sta., 1952-68, dean Coll. Agr., 1960-68. Conducted U. Cal. exploration for beneficial insects, countries of Asia, Africa, Europe, 1951; bd. cons. agrl. sci. Rockefeller Found., 1958-64, cons., 1968—. Member A.A.A.S., Entomol. Soc. Am. (pres. 1949), Sigma Xi. Contbr. numerous sci. papers to profl. lit. Home: 266 Frost Ct Riverside CA 93656

BOYCE, BENJAMIN, educator; b. Lansing, Mich., Nov. 26, 1903; s. James Burton and Mabelle Grace (Miles) B.; A.B., U. Mich., 1926; A.M., Harvard, 1927, Ph.D., 1933; m. Dorothy May Green, Apr. 10, 1939. Instr. English, Northwestern U., 1927-30; asst. prof.. English, U..Omaha, 1933-35, prof. and head dept. English, 1935-46; prof. English, U. Neb. 1946- 50; prof. Eng., Duke, Durham, N.C., 1950-68, James B. Duke prof. English, 1968-69, emeritus, 1969—; vis. prof. U. N.C., summer 1940, Harvard, summer 1949. Mem. Modern Lang. Assn., Phi Beta Kappa. Author: Tom Brown of Facetious Memory, 1939; The Theophrastan Character in England to 1642, 1947; The Polemic Character 1640-1661, 1955; The Character Sketches in Pope's Poems, 1962; The Benevolent Man: A Life of Ralph Allen of Bath, 1967. Editor: Adventures of Lindamira, 1948; Prefaces to Fiction, 1952; The Comical Romance, 1968. Mem. editorial com. Studies in English Lit., 1963—, PMLA, 1953-63. Contbr. articles to profl. jours. Home: 1200 Dwire Pl Durham NC 27706

BOYCE, ERNEST F., retail co. exec.; b. Somerville, Mass., 1916; ed. Boston U., Harvard Grad. Sch. Bus. Adminstrn. Formerly v.p., now pres. Colonial Stores, Inc., Atlanta. Home: 5510 Long Island Dr NW Atlanta GA 30327 Office: 2251 N Sylvan Rd East Point GA 30344

BOYCE, EUGENE MAXWELL, educator; b. Polkton, N.C., Nov. 26, 1913; s. John Mason and Margaret Leone (Maxwell) b.; student Rutherford (N.C.) Coll., 1931-32; A.B. in Chemistry, Erskine Coll., 1935; M.A. in Sch. Adminstrn., Emory U., 1939; Ph.D. in Ednl. Adminstrn., George Peabody Coll., Tchrs., 1943; m. Louise Irene McCain, Aug. 14, 1936; children—William Martin, Pauline Maxwell, James Edward. Prin.-tchr. Hannah (S.C.) Sch., 1936-38; dist. sch. supt., Stone Mountain, Ga., 1938-40; prin. Columbus (Ga.) High Sch., 1942-50, Univ. Sch., Fla. State U., 1950-57, asso. dean Sch. Edn., 1957-65, prof. edn., 1953-68; asso. dir. for programs Research and Devel. Center in Ednl. Stimulation, U. Ga., Athens, 1968, dir. center, 1969-70, prof. ednl. adminstrn., 1968—. Temporary faculty mem. spring and summers Ga. Sch. Tech., 1947, Eastern Ill. State Coll., 1948. U. Ga., 1949, Emory U., 1950, Stetson U., 1963; AID adviser to Ministry of Edn., Addis Ababa, Ethiopia, 1965-67; adviser Nigeria Ednl. Research Council, Lagos, 1970-71. Chmn. com. to write curriculum guide for teaching moral and spiritual values in Fla. pub. schs., 1961. Served to lt. (j.g.) USNR, 1944-46; PTO. Gen. Edn. Bd. grantee, 1941-42. Mem. Phi Delta Kappa, Kappa Phi Kappa. Presbyn. (elder, chmn. presbytery coms.). Kiwanian. Home: 330 Beechwood Dr Athens GA 30601

BOYCE, FRANK GORDON, educator; b. Binghamton, N.Y., Apr. 8, 1917; s. Clarence and Ethel (Wilcox) B.; A.B., Colgate U., 1939, A.M., 1948; LL.D., Middlebury Coll., 1962, Cornell Coll., Mt. Vernon, Ia., 1966; L.H.D., Elmira Coll., 1962; m. Joan A. Sweet, Sept. 5, 1941; children—Frank Gordon, Jonathan, Johanna. Reporter, feature writer Binghamton Sun, 1939-41; asst. to pres. Colgate U., 1946-50; pres. Expt. in Internat. Living, Putney, Vt., 1950—, sec. gen., 1956—. First dir. div. pvt. and internat. orgns. Peace Corps, 1961; mem. exec. com. to advise gov. and legislature on devel. Coll. V.I., 1961; pres. Council Student Travel, 1951-55; mem. U.S. commn. for UNESCO, 1965—. Trustee Colgate U., 1963-69, Coll. V.I., 1962—, Am. Students and Artists Center, Paris, 1963-; bd. dirs. Colgate U.

Alumni Corp., 1957-62, pres., 1969—. Served to lt. USNR, 1941-45. Decorated officer's cross Order Merit Fed. Republic Germany, 1964; Legion de O'Higgins award (Chile), 1968; Recipient The Experiment citation, 1970. Mem. Delta Phi Alpha, Alpha Tau Omega. Conglist. Address: The Experiment Way Brattleboro VT 05301

BOYCE, GRAY COWAN, educator; b. San Francisco, Feb. 19, 1899; s. William Thomas and Jessie Irene (Cowan) B.; A.B., U. Cal., 1920, A.M., (teaching fellow), 1921, Ph.D. (Univ. fellow), 1925; postgrad. (George and Martha Derby scholar) Harvard, 1922-23, U. Grenoble, 1925, U. Gand (Ghent), 1925-26. Commn. Relief in Belgium fellow, Belgium, 1925-26; Shreve fellow (Princeton), Germany, Rome, 1934-35; instr. history Princeton, 1926-29, asst. prof., 1929-45; prof. history Northwestern U., Evanston, Ill., 1946-67, prof. emeritus, 1967—, chmn. dept. history, 1948-66; vis. prof. history, Ohio State U., 1938, Columbia, 1942, Stanford, 1962, Dir. Belgian-Am. Ednl. Found., 1960-66. Served in S.A.T.C., U. Cal., 1918; lt., USNR, 1942-44. Fellow Mediaeval Acad. Am.; mem. Am. Hist. Assn., Am. Assn. U. Profs. Democrat. Presbyn. (ruling elder). Clubs: University (Evanston); Cercle des Alumni de la Fondation Universitaire (Brussels). Author books and contbr. articles to jours. Home: 3201 Bayo Vista Av Alameda CA 94501 ☆

BOYCE, IRA FRED, paper co. exec.; b. Brooklyn, Wis., Nov. 22, 1910; s. Fred Remington and Edna (Fairbrother) B.; B.A. in Bus. Adminstrn., U. Wis.; m. Catherine Schneekloth. May 31, 1930; children—Gerald I., William B. With Consol. Papers, Inc., Wisconsin Rapids, Wis., 1942—, asst. to pres., dir., 1950- , v.p., 1958-; dir. Consol. Water Power Co., Preway, Inc. (both Wisconsin Rapids), Nat. Guardian Life Ins. Co., Madison, Wis. Pres., dir. Consolidated's Civic Found., Inc.; trustee Northland Coll., Ashland, Wis. C.P.A., Wis. Home: 711 Third St S Wisconsin Rapids WI Office: PO Box 50 Wisconsin Rapids WI

BOYCE, JOSEPH CANON, physicist, orgn. ofcl.; b. Pitts., Jan. 23, 1903; s. David C. and Mary Losey (Wright) B.; A.B., Princeton, 1922, A.M., 1923; postgrad. U. London, 1923-24, U. Cambridge, 1924-25; Ph.D., Princeton, 1926; m. Emily M. Hughes, June 15, 1934; children—Mary Hughes (Mrs. Nelson A. Gelfman), Emily Jane (Mrs. Thomas E. White), Elizabeth Rogers (Mrs. Sam DePiero), Frances Julia (Mrs. Ronald R. Swann), Katharine Louise (Mrs. Fred J. Hinman). Instr. physics Princeton, 1926-29, research asso., 1929-31; research asso. in physics, Mass. Inst. Tech., 1931-34, asst. prof. physics, 1934-38, asso. prof., 1938-44; prof. physics and chmn. dept. physics, Coll. Engring., N.Y., 1944-50; research asso. Carnegie Instn. Washington, 1939-50; asso. lab. dir. Argonne Nat. Lab., 1950-55; v.p. for acad. affairs, dean grad. sch. Ill. Inst. Tech., 1955-61, v.p. for grad. studies and research, dean grad. sch., 1961-62; staff mem. Office Sci. Personnel, NRC, 1963-70, dep. dir. 1965-68, ret., 1970; Harvard-Mass. Inst. Tech. Eclipse Expdn., Soviet Central Asia, 1936. Tech. aide, sect. chief NDRC, 1941-46. Awarded Presdl. Certificate of Merit, Kings Medal for service in cause of Freedom, Medal of Belgian Fonds National de la Recherche Scientifique, 1952. Fellow Am. Phys. Soc., A.A.A.S., Royal Astron. Soc. (London); mem. Am. Assn. Physics Tchrs., Am. Astron. Soc., Am. Soc. Engring. Edn. Clubs: Cosmos (Washington), Harvard Faculty, Ausable (St. Huberts, N.Y.), Princeton (N.Y.C.); Armour Faculty (Ill. Inst. Tech. hon. life). Editor: New Weapons for Air Warfare, 1947. Contbr. articles to tech. publs. Home: 2500 Que St NW Washington DC 20007

BOYCE, WILLIAM EDWARD, educator, mathematician; b. Tampa, Fla., Dec. 19, 1930; s. Edward G. and Marie (Summers) B.; B.A., Southwestern at Memphis, 1951; M.S., Carnegie Inst. Tech., 1953, Ph.D. in Math., 1955; m. Elsa E. Keitzer, Feb. 19, 1955; children—James E., Carolyn E., Ann C. Research asso. applied math. Brown U., 1955-57; mathematician IBM Corp., 1957; mem. faculty Rensselaer Poly. Inst., Troy, N.Y., 1957—, prof. math., 1963—. Mem. Am. Math. Soc., Soc. Indsl. and Applied Math., Math. Assn. Am., A.A.A.S., Phi Beta Kappa. Author: (with R. C. DiPrima) Elementary Differential Equations and Boundary Value Problems; also research papers. Mng. editor Soc. Indsl. and Applied Math. Rev., 1970—. Home: 215 Brunswick Rd Troy NY 12180

BOYCE-SMITH, JOHN, III, banker; b. N.Y.C., July 25, 1912; s. John and Harriet Mather (Illsley) B.-S.; B.A. in Econs., U. Cal. at Los Angeles, 1934; m. Leola Ellis Wooten, Oct. 15, 1937; children—Tempe Lee (Mrs. John Brooks), John Gifford. Asst. mgr. fgn. dept. Chem. Bank & Trust Co., N.Y.C., 1934-47; asst. v.p. corp. finance Bank of Am., Los Angeles, 1948-51; mgr. accounting and finance Hughes Aircraft Co., 1951-55; treas., controller Calavo Growers of Cal., Vernon, 1955-58; v.p. Cal. Bank, Los Angeles, 1958-59; with First Western Bank & Trust Co., Los Angeles, 1959—, sr. v.p., 1961-63, exec. v.p., 1963-66; v.p., treas. Foremost-McKesson, Inc., 1966—; dir. Provident Enterprises Corp. Bd. dirs. San Francisco Local Devel. Corp., San Francisco Bay Area Social Planning Council, San Francisco region A.R.C. Served to lt. col., F.A., AUS, World War II; ETO. Decorated Bronze Star. Mem. Robert Morris Assos., Theta Delta Chi, Alpha Kappa Psi. Clubs: Joanthan, Los Angeles Yacht (Los Angeles); Stock Exchange, Corinthian Yacht (San Francisco). Home: 2200 Pacific Av San Francisco CA 94115 Office: 1 Pine St San Francisco CA 94104

BOYCHUK, JOSEPH MICHAEL, lawyer, publisher; b. Dunmore, Pa., Oct. 20, 1916; s. Michael Joseph and Amelia Grace (Ropek) B.; A.B., Union Coll., 1939; M.A., U. Pa., 1940; LL.B., Harvard, 1948; m. Audrey Brott, Oct. 15, 1940; children—Nancy Culver, Bruce Lewis; m. 3d, Mabel H. Riley, Sept. 27, 1958. Admitted to N.Y. bar, 1946; partner Brophy, Boychuk & Steinberg, N.Y.C., 1948-69, Hennessy, Boychuk & Steinberg, 1969—; v.p., dir. Springhill Coal Co., 1941-43; chmn. bd. Columbia Features, Inc., 1952—, editor, pres., 1955—; chmn. bd. Columbia Cosmetics Corp., 1963—; v.p. Kensington Indsl. Corp., 1963-66, pres., 1966—, also dir.; chmn. Columbia Books, Inc. Bd. regents Am. Coll. Clin. Pharmacology, 1970—, fellow, 1970. Mem. Am., N.Y. County bar assns., Am. Legion, Acad. Polit. Sci., Phi Sigma Kappa. Club: Overseas Press. Home: Honey Hollow Rd Pound Ridge NY 10576 Office: 36 W 44th St New York City NY 10036

BOYD, ALAN STEPHENSON, transp. exec.; b. Jacksonville, Fla., July 20, 1922; s. Clarence and Elizabeth (Stephenson) B.; student U. Fla., 1939-41; LL.B., U. Va., 1948; m. Flavil Juanita Townsend, Apr. 3, 1943; 1 son, Mark Townsend. Admitted to Va. bar, 1947, Fla. bar, 1948; practiced in Fla. until 1957; gen. counsel Fla. Turnpike Authority, 1955; mem. Fla. R.R. and Pub. Utilities Commn., 1955-59, chmn., 1957-58; mem. CAB, Washington, 1959-65, chmn., 1961-65; under-sec. commerce for transp., 1965-67; sec. dept. transp., 1967-69; pres., dir. I.C.R.R., 1969—. Decorated. Home: 999 Lake Shore Dr Chicago IL 60611 Office: 135 E 11th Pl Chicago IL 60605

BOYD, ALAN WILSON, lawyer; b. Indpls., Mar. 11, 1897; s. John Anderson and Mabel (Conduitt) B.; A.B., U. Mich., 1918, J.D., 1921; m. Dorothy Lee, Oct. 24, 1923; children—Alan C., Thomas L. Admitted to Ind. bar, 1921, U.S. Supreme Ct. bar, 1934; practiced in Indpls., 1921—, mem. firm Noel, Hickam & Boyd, 1923-26, Noel, Hickam, Boyd & Armstrong, 1926-40, Barnes, Hickam, Pantzer & Boyd, 1940—. Mem. Indpls. Bd. Sch. Commrs., 1935-39, pres., 1937; mem. Ind. Bd. Bar Examiners, 1937-42. Served with USMC, 1918- 19. Mem. Am., Ind., Indpls. (pres. 1948) bar assns., Am. Judicature Soc., Am. Law Inst., Bar Assn. 7th Fed. Circuit, Ind. Soc. Chgo., Order of Coif, Delta Upsilon, Phi Delta Phi. Mason. Clubs: Woodstock, Indianapolis Athletic, Contemporary, Lawyers (Indpls); Lawyers (Ann Arbor, Mich.). Home: 4002 N Meridian St Indianapolis IN 46208 Office: Merchants Bank Bldg Indianapolis IN 46204

BOYD, BENJAMIN EARL, corp. exec.; b. Pontiac, Ill., Jan. 21, 1910; s. Benjamin Oliver and Harriet Mae (Capes) B.; student Ill. Wesleyan U., 1927-28; B.S., U. Ill., 1931; m. Ruthmary Virginia Dare, Apr. 22, 1933; children—Julie Dare (Mrs. William S. Bach), Ruthmary (Mrs. Denis M. Robison. Began with Owens-Ill. Glass Co., Columbus, O., 1932, gen. factory mgr. Owens- Corning Fiberglas Corp., Newark, O., 1937-44, gen. factories mgr., 1944- 46, gen. prodn. mgr., 1946, v.p. charge div. mfg., 1946-59, v.p. mfg. for co., 1959-67, sr. v.p., 1967—; dir. Fiberglas Can. Ltd. Named Distinguished Alumnus, U. Ill., 1970. Registered profl. engr., Ohio. Mem. Am. Soc. Heating, Refrigeration and Air-Conditioning Engrs., Am. Soc. M.E., Ohio (adv. council to pres. 1970), Toledo socs. profl. engrs., Am. Inst. Chem. Engrs., Toledo Opera Assn. (trustee), Sigma Chi, Pi Tau Sigma, Sigma Tau. Clubs: Toledo Country (trustee 1948—, pres. 1955, 56), Belmont Country, Toledo (trustee 1968—); Pine Valley (N.J.) Golf; Palmetto Golf (Aiken, S.C.). Home: Eagle Point Colony Rossford, OH 43460. Office: Toledo OH 43601

BOYD, BERNARD HENRY, educator, clergyman; b. Mt. Pleasant, S.C., Nov. 16, 1910; s. Frank T. and Eunice (Beaty) B.; A.B., Presbyn. Coll., 1932; Th.B., M.A., Princeton, 1935; Th.D., Union Theol. Sem., 1946; m. Thelma Hicklin, Aug. 5, 1944; children—Donald Beaty, Karen Elizabeth. Ordained to ministry Presbyn. Ch., 1943; prof. Bible Presbyn. Coll., 1936-46, Davidson Coll., 1946-50; James A. Gray prof. Bibl. lit. U. N.C., 1950—, chmn. dept. of religion, 1952-60, TV lectr.; archaeol. exploration in Israel, summers 1963-70; organizer of expedn. to Lachish, 1966; ednl. dir. Inst. of Mediterranean Studies, 1965-67, archaeol. dir., 1968—; co-dir. U. N.C.-Hebrew U. expdn. to Tell Arad, 1967, Lynn Prickett archaeol. expdn. to Lachish, 1968. Served as chaplain USN, with Marines, 1943-45. Recipient Tanner Meml. award. Mem. Soc. Bibl. Lit. and Exegesis, Am. Acad. Religion, Am. Schs. Oriental Research, Archaeol. Inst. Am., Order Golden Fleece, Blue Key. Pi Kappa Delta. Omicron Delta Kappa. Home: Box 968 313 Country Club Rd Chapel Hill NC 27514

BOYD, CATHERINE EVANGELINE, educator; b. Stoneham, Mass., Feb. 8, 1904; d. Joseph William and Anne (Huestis) Boyd; B.A., Radcliffe Coll., 1926, M.A., 1929, Ph.D., 1934; postgrad. Bryn Mawr Coll., 1927-28, U. Paris, 1926-27, U. Rome, 1935-36. Instr. history U. Colo., 1930-32; Am. Council Learned Socs. research fellow, 1935-36; research asso. Mus. Fine Arts, Boston, 1937-42; lectr. Wells Coll., 1942-43; asso. prof. Cedar Crest Coll., 1943-45, prof. history, 1945-47, chmn. dept., 1943-47; asso. prof. Carleton Coll., Northfield, Minn., 1947-53, prof., 1953-66; vis. prof. U. Wis., Madison, 1966-67, U. Mich., Ann Arbor, 1968; Fulbright research fellow U. Rome, Italy, 1954-55. Pres. Upper Midwest History Conf., 1961-62. Mem. Am. Assn. U. Profs., Mediaeval Acad. Am. Renaissance Soc., Am. Soc. for Italian Hist. Studies, Am. Hist. Assn. (Carnegie award 1951), Phi Beta Kappa. Author: The French Renaissance, 1940; A Cistercian Nunnery in Mediaeval Italy, 1943; Tithes and Parishes in Mediaeval Italy, 1952. Contbr. articles to hist. jours. Home: 385 Massachusetts Av Arlington MA 02174

BOYD, CHARLES ALEXANDER, educator, scientist; b. Snohomish, Wash., Mar. 4, 1917; s. Charles Alexander and Hazel (Gainer) B.; student Mt. Vernon Jr. Coll., 1935-37; B.S., U. Wash., 1939; M.S., Ore. State Coll., 1941; Ph.D., U. WIs., 1948; m. Isabel Withycombe, June 20, 1942; children—Susan, Charles, Elizabeth. Research asso. Allegheny Ballistic Lab., 1942-45; chemist Argonne Nat. Lab., 1946-47; project asso. U. Wis., 1948-50, asst. prof. phys. chemistry, 1950-51; phys. chemist Camp Detrich, 1951- 53; sci. warfare adviser weapons systems evaluation group, Dept. Def., 1953-56, asst. dir. research, 1956-58, dir. research, div. weapons systems evaluation div. Inst. Def. Analyses, 1958-62; chief scientist Aeroprojects, Inc., 1962-65; sr. research asso. Ordnance Research Lab., Pa. State U., 1965-70; tchr. sci. dept. State College (Pa.) Area High Sch., 1970—. Mem. State Coll. Park and Recreation bd. Fellow A.A.A.S.; mem. N.Y. Acad. Scis., Am. Phys. Soc., Operations Research Soc. Am., Faraday Soc., Sigma Xi, Phi Lambda Upsilon, Sigma Pi Sigma, Alpha Chi Sigma. Club: Cosmos (Washington). Home: Box 125A RD 1 Port Matilda, PA 16870. Office: State College Area High School Westerly Pkwy State College PA 16801

BOYD, CLARENCE ELMO, surgeon; b. Leesville, La., Nov. 2, 1911; s. Isaac Clarence and Ada Lee (Stakes) B.; B.A., U. Tex., 1933, M.D., 1935; m. Emma Kittredge Sims, Aug. 13, 1937; children—Charles Elmo, Marjorie Emily (Mrs. James O. Hudson), Frances Ada (Mrs. Thomas H. Thigpen), James E. Boyd. Intern Charity Hosp., New Orleans, 1935-36; resident physician North La. Sanitarium, Shreveport, 1936-37; jr. vis. surgeon Confederate Meml. Hosp., Shreveport, 1937-42, sr. vis. surgeon, 1942—, 1st v.p. vis. staff, 1943-44; pvt. practice, Shreveport, 1937—; founder, 1942, since sr. partner C. E. Boyd Clinic; clin. asst. prof. surgery La. State U. Postgrad. Sch. Medicine, 1957—; founding dir. Doctors' Hosp., Shreveport, 1959, chmn. bd., 1959—, vis. surgeon, 1937—. Founding dir. Shreveport Bank & Trust Co., 1954, chmn. investment com., 1954—, chmn. bd. dirs., 1961—. Bd. dirs. Volunteers Am., 1950-58, chmn. bd., 1955-57; trustee Pub. Affairs Research Council La., 1959—; mem. nat. adv. bd. We, The People, 1964—. Guest speaker Dean's lecture La. State Med. Sch., 1955, 57; hon. col. Gov. La. staff, 1964. Diplomate Internat. Bd. Proctology, Am. Bd. Abdominal Surgeons (a founder); Fellow A.C.S., Internat. Coll. Surgeons, Internat. Acad. Proctology, Southeastern Surg. Congress, Am. Soc. Abdominal Surgeons (a founder, pres. 1966-67, mem. teaching faculty 1962- -, Gold medal 1962); mem. A.M.A. (chmn. surg. sect. 1964, 67, mem. surg. council 1969-71), Assn. Am. Physicians and Surgeons (del. 1960—, chmn. La. membership com. 1950- -), Surg. Assn. La., La. (Ho. of Dels. 1945-59, chmn. pub. policy and legislative com. 1954, chmn. surg. sect. 1957, councilor 1959-66, 1st v.p. 1967-68, chmn. com. on hosps. 1968-71, vice chmn. socio-econs. 1970-71), Shreveport (first chmn. com. medicine and religion 1964-66, Gold medal 1956-57; pres. 1956-57, 1st chmn. med. progress 1957- 59) med. socs., Am. Cancer Soc. (bd. dirs. Caddo br. 1952-59, vice chmn. bd. 1957-58), So. Med. Assn. (asst. councilor 1959-68). Episcopalian (vestryman 1966-69; Gold medal Bible Class 1965). Mason (32), Rotarian (pres. South Shreveport 1940-41; founder, 1942, since chmn. club's student loan fund). Spl. research operative cholangiography. Author numerous articles, producer films in field. Home: 401 Delaware St Shreveport, LA 71104. Office: 6815 Southern Av Shreveport LA 71106

BOYD, CLARENCE EUGENE, Jr., beverage co. exec.; b. Atlanta, Oct. 28, 1915; s. Clarence Eugene and Julia (Dickey) B.; A.B., Emory U., 1936; m. Susan Hippey, Jan. 21, 1939; children—James Eugene, Susan Lowry. With Coca-Cola Co., 1936—, mgr. market research dept., 1959-62, v.p., 1962—, head corporate personnel devel., N.Y.C., 1967—. Mem. Am. Marketing Assn., Am. Statis. Assn. Home: 2662 Battle Overlook NW Atlanta GA 30327 Office: Coca-Cola Co 515 Madison Av New York City NY 10022

BOYD, CROSBY NOYES, newspaper exec.; b. Phila., Jan. 2, 1903; s. George W. and Miranda C. (Noyes) B.; grad. St. George's Sch., Newport, R.I., 1920; A.B., Princeton, 1924; m. Elizabeth Utz, Jan. 2, 1932; children—Elizabeth Noyes, Crosby Noyes, Susan Ann. Asst. advt. mgr. Evening Star Newspaper Co., Washington, 1938-44, asst. sec.- treas., 1941-49, asst. bus. mgr., 1944-49, bus. mgr., treas., 1949-63, exec. v.p., 1955-63, pres., 1963-68, chmn. bd., 1968—; chmn. bd. Washington Star Syndicate, Inc.; dir. Evening Star Broadcasting Co., Nat. Bank Washington. Served to capt. USAAF, 1942-45. Clubs: Metropolitan, Chevy Chase (Washington); Court (Princeton, N.J.). Home: 2801 New Mexico Av NW Washington DC 20007 Office: 225 Virginia Av SE Washington DC 20003

BOYD, DAVID ARMITAGE, Jr., psychiatrist; b. Detroit, Jan. 14, 1906; s. David Armitage and Laura May (Staffin) B.; A.B., U. Mich., 1926, M.S., 1939; M.D., Jefferson Med. Coll., 1930; m. Cathleen Singer, Aug. 29, 1932; 1 son, David IV. Asst. physician Ypsilanti State Hosp., 1932-34; asst. psychiatry U. Mich., 1934-36, asst. prof. psychiatry, 1936-39; prof., head dept. neurology and psychiatry Ind. U., 1939-48; emeritus chmn. sects. psychiatry, child and adolescent psychiatry, clin. psychology, sr. cons. in psychiatry Mayo Clinic, Rochester, 1948—; prof. dept. psychiatry, grad. sch. U. Minn., 1949. Cons. psychiatry and neurology. Diplomate Am. Bd. Psychiatry and Neurology. Fellow Am. Psychiat. Assn.; mem. Central Neuropsychiat. Assn., A.M.A., Sigma Xi. Author articles on psychiatry, neurology. Home: 1140 Plummer Circle Rochester MN 55901

BOYD, DAVID HARTIN, steel mfg. exec.; b. Pitts., Aug. 6, 1914; s. Morton M. and Nettie (McAteer) B.; B.S., Washington and Jefferson Coll., 1936; m. Lois Evelyn Kramer, Sept. 8, 1945; 1 dau., Amy K. With Union Supply div. U.S. Steel Corp., 1936-48, purchasing agt., gen. mdse. mgr., 1948-54, exec. v.p., 1954, pres., 1955-59, pres. Homes div., 1958, asst. to v.p. purchasing U.S. Steel Corp., 1963-64, mgr. purchasing, 1964-66, dir. comml. relations, 1967-69, asst. to v.p. purchasing, 1970—. Mem. Iron and Steel Inst., Phi Delta Theta. Presbyn. (trustee). Clubs: Duquesne (Pitts.), Shannopin Country (Ben Avon Heights, Pa.). Home: 14 Newgate Rd Pittsburgh PA 15202 Office: US Steel Corp 600 Grant St Pittsburgh PA 15230

BOYD, DAVID MILTON, oil products exec.; b. St. Louis, Jan. 5, 1918; s. David M. and Josephine (Drake) B.; B.S., U. Colo., 1941, Chem.E., 1950; m. Louise Vandeventer, June 11, 1941; children—Gwendolyn (Mrs. Kenneth D. Schmidt), David Garrison, Barbara Josephine. With Barratt Chem. Co., 1941-42, Blaw Knox Constrn. Co., 1942-43, Eastern States Petroleum Co., 1943-45, Monsanto Chem. Co., 1945-46, Oak Ridge Nat. Labs., 1946-48; mgr. instl. engring. design and service Universal Oil Products Co., Des Plaines, Ill., 1948—; dir. Intercoastal Paint Co. Recipient Instrument Soc. Am. Sperry award Chgo. Tech. Socs. Council, 1957, Distinguished Engring. Achievement award U. Colo., 1970. Fellow Instrument Soc. Am., Am. Soc. M.E., sr. mem. I.E.E.E.; mem. Am. Inst. Chem. Engrs., Am. Chem. Soc. Presbyn. (elder). Club: Ruth Lake Country Hinsdale, Ill.). Contbr. articles profl. jours. Holder 150 domestic and fgn. patents. Home: 315 Ridge Av Clarendon Hills IL 60514 Office: 30 Algonquin Rd Des Plaines IL 60016

BOYD, DREXELL ALLEN, dentist, educator; b. Marshfield, Mo., Apr. 1, 1910; s. John Barnes and Mable (Allen) B.; student DePauw U., 1928-29; D.D.S., Ind. U., 1934; postgrad. tng. Forsyth Infirmary, 1935, Boston, U. Ia. Hosp., 1936; m. Dorothea Bufler, June 13, 1937. Faculty Ind. U., Indpls., 1937—, asso.. prof. pedodontics, dir. dept., 1937- 48, prof. operative dentistry, 1948—; in dentistry practice, Indpls., 1940-48. Vis. prof. dentistry U. Rio de Janeiro, 1961. Fellow Am. Coll. Dentistry; mem. Internat. Assn. Dental Research, Beta Theta Pi, Delta Sigma Delta. Democrat. Mason. Home: 1050 Collingwood Dr Indianapolis IN 46208

BOYD, EARL NEAL, educator; b. Trinity, Ky., Dec. 20, 1922; s. Samuel Brady and Gladys (Nash) B.; B.S., Eastern Ky. U., 1948; M.S., U. Ky., 1949; Ph.D., Ohio State U., 1952; m. Jeanne Marcia Ruark, Sept. 1, 1948; 1 son, Michael Neal. Asst. prof. dairy sci. U. Ky., 1952-54; research chemist Swift & Co., Chgo., 1954-57; research adminstr. Co-op. State Research Service, Dept. Agr., Washington, 1957-68; head dept. food sci. and tech. Va. Poly. Inst., Blacksburg, 1968-70; asst. dean agr. Va. Poly. Inst. and State U., Blacksburg, 1970—. Served with F.A., CWS, AUS, 1942-46. Mem. Inst. Food Technologists, Am. Dairy Sci. Assn., Am. Legion, Sigma Xi, Gamma Sigma Delta (pres.), Phi Tau Sigma (pres.), Phi Lambda Upsilon. Presbyn. (elder). Home: 813 Mc Bryde Dr Blacksburg VA 24060

BOYD, ELIZABETH MARGARET, educator; b. Liverpool, Eng., July 8, 1908; d. John William and Christianna (Ker) Boyd; B.S. (Vans Dunlop scholar), Edinburgh U., 1930; M.A., Mt. Holyoke Coll., 1933; Ph.D. (Allen Seymour Olmstead scholar), Cornell U., 1946. Asst. zoology Edinburgh U., 1930-31; asst. zoology Mt. Holyoke Coll., South Hadley, Mass., 1931-33, instr. to prof., 1937—, chmn. dept. biol. scis., 1967-70; asst. zoology Mc-Gill U., 1933-37; mem. Cornell Lab. Ornithology; cons. NSF Research Proposals, Reevaluation Instns. Higher Edn. Recipient SUPHS research grants, 1954, 64; fellow Tropical Medicine and Parasitology Central Am. Program, 1964. Fellow A.A.A.S.; mem. Am. Soc. Zoologists, Am. Soc. Parasitologists, Am. Ornithol. Union, Wilson Soc., Nat., Mass. (dir.) audubon socs., Helminothology Soc. Washington, Entomol. Soc. Washington, Wildlife Disease Assn., Sigma Xi. Home: 23 Jewett Lane South Hadley, MA 01075.

BOYD, FISKE, painter, graphic artist; b. Phila., July 5, 1895; s. Peter Keller and Lydia Butler (Fiske) B.; student Pa. Acad. Fine Arts, 1913-16, Art Students League N.Y., 1921-24; m. Clare Mary Constance Shenehon, May 1, 1926; 1 dau., Sheila Shenehon (Mrs. S. A. Hoermann). Paintings and prints exhibited 1923—; represented in collections Met. Mus. Art, Whitney Mus. (N.Y.C.), Philips Meml. Gallery (Washington), Addison Meml. Gallery (Andover, Mass.), Phila. Art Mus., Boston Mus. Fine Arts, Fogg Art Mus. (Cambridge, Mass.), N.Y. Pub. Library, Bklyn. Mus., Gallery Fine Arts (Columbus, O.), Library of Congress, Montclair (N.J.) Art Mus. Served USN, 1917-21. Recipient Boericke prize Phila. Print Club, 1931; Am. Artists Group prize Soc. Am. Graphic Artists, 1947, John Taylor Arms Meml. prize, 1954; Cannon prize N.A.D., 1955; purchase awards Library of Congress, Bklyn. Mus. A.N.A. Mem. Soc. Am. Graphic Artists, Aubugon Artists, Xylon, Boston Printmakers, Phila. Print Club. Address: Plainfield NH 03781

BOYD, FRANCIS VIRGIL, univ. dean; b. Livermore, Ia., Feb. 1, 1922; s. Ernest and Gertrude (Marley) B.; B.A., Ia. State Tchrs. Coll., 1943; M.B.A., Northwestern U., 1948, Ph.D., 1956; m. Mary Celeste Cranny, Nov. 6, 1943; children—Kevin, Therese. Tchr. accounting Northwestern U., 1946-63, asso. dean Sch. Bus., 1963-66; dean Sch. Bus., Loyola U., 1966—; cons., tchr. exec. programs 1956—. Served to lt. (j.g.) USNR, 1943-46. C.P.A., Ill. Mem. Ill. Soc. C.P.A.'s, Econ. Club Chgo., Am. Accounting Assn., Am. Econ. Assn., Beta Gamma Sigma. Author: (with others) Quantitative Controls in Business. Home: 3925 Lyons St Evanston, IL 60203. Office: 820 N Michigan Av Chicago IL 60611

BOYD, GEORGE EDWARD, phys. chemist; b. Evansville, Ind., Sept. 1, 1911; s. Herbert Henry and Mina (Deusner) B.; B.S. with honors, U. Chgo., 1933, Ph.D., 1937; m. Valborg Richter, Feb. 20, 1942; 1 dau., Monica. With U. Chgo., 1937-48, research instr., instr., asst. prof., asso. prof., chief plutonium process devel. Clinton Labs., Oak Ridge, 1943-45; prin. chemist Oak Ridge Nat. Lab., 1945-47, chief chemist, 1947-51, chief research scientist, 1951-55, asst. lab. dir., 1955-70, sr. research adviser, 1970—. Reilly lectr. Notre Dame U., 1954; vis. prof. chemistry Purdue U., 1962. Chmn. com. on awards in chemistry under Fulbright Act, Nat. Acad. Scis.-NRC, 1959-63, Am. Nuclear Soc. rep. to div. chemistry and chem. tech., 1966-69; mem. AEC Mission to Japan, Taiwan, P.I., 1957. Recipient So. Chemist gold medal, 1951. Guggenheim and Fulbright fellow, Leiden, 1952-53. Fellow Am. Nuclear Soc. (chmn. div. isotopes and radiation 1961-62, dir. 1965-66), A.A.A.S.; mem. Am. Phys. Soc., Am. Chem. Soc. (award for nuclear applications in chemistry 1969, chmn. div. colloid and surface chemistry 1952, mem. nat. colloid symposium com. 1958-64, chmn. div. nuclear chemistry and tech. 1966), Phi Beta Kappa, Sigma Xi, Gamma Alpha. Asso. editor Jour. Phys. Chemistry, 1950-54; editorial adv. bd. Analytical Chemistry, 1953-55, Radiochimica Acta, 1963—. Contbr. numerous tech. papers to profl. lit. Home: 504 Delaware Av Oak Ridge TN 37830 Office: Oak Ridge Nat Lab PO Box X Oak Ridge TN 37830

BOYD, GEORGE ROBERT, educator; b. Franklin, Ky., Nov. 26, 1906; s. Ira Hill and Lellie (Stinson) B.; A.B., Western Ky. State Coll., 1931; M.A., U. Ky., 1938, Ph.D., 1943; m. Lucille King, Aug. 3, 1931; 1 dau., Bobbie Lucille (Mrs. J. L. Lubker). Tchr., prin. pub. schs., Ky., 1927-40; acting prin. lab. Sch., Milledgeville, Ga., 1946-47; instr. psychology U. Ga., summer 1947; dean Troy (Ala.) State Coll., 1947-67; acting dir. Lexington Tech. Inst. unit U. Ky. Community Coll. System, 1967-69; edn. adviser, mem. Ohio U. team in South Vietnam, 1969—. Mem. Phi Delta Kappa, Kappa Delta Pi. Rotarian. Home: 1611 Traveller Rd Lexington, KY 40504

BOYD, GORDON, ins. co. exec.; b. Maplewood, N.J., Mar. 14, 1918; s. James and H. Estelle (Boyd) B.; B.S. in Econs., U. Pa., 1940; M.B.A., N.Y. U., 1949; m. Betty Bleakney, Apr. 4, 1941; children—Randall Bleakney, Gordon Reed. Mortgage investments exec. James Boyd, Inc., N.Y.C., 1940-42; with financial div. Socony-Vacuum Oil Co., N.Y.C., 1946; with Mut. Benefit Life Ins. Co., Newark, 1946—, treas., 1956—; dir. Berry Steel Corp., Arsenal Holding Co., Veneered Metals, Inc., Ardmore Products, Inc., Kenilworth Steel Co. Vice pres., Robert Treat council Boy Scouts Am., 1965—. Trustee, chmn. finance com. Overseas Ministries Study Center, Ventnor, N.J., 1960—. Served to lt. USNR, 1942-46. Clubs: Bond (N.J.), Treasurers (N.Y.C.), Money Marketeers (N.Y. U.); Essex (Newark). Home: 34 Dogwood Dr Summit NJ 07901 Office: 520 Broad St Newark NJ 07101

BOYD, HAROLD BUHALTS, orthopaedic surgeon; b. Chattanooga, Dec. 2, 1904; s. Clarence J. and Marie Francis (Buhalts) B.; M.D., Loma Linda (Cal.) University, 1932; m. Jean Frances Stewart, Feb. 23, 1933; children—Heather (Mrs. Charles Lindsay), Julia (Mrs. Orville W. Swarner, Jr.), Jean Frances (Mrs. H. Maynard Lowry). Intern, Los Angeles County Hospital, 1931-32; resident Kern County Hosp., Bakersfield, Cal., 1932-34; fellow in orthopaedic surgery Campbell Clinic, Memphis, 1934-36, partner, 1938—, chief of staff, 1962-70; mem. staff Baptist Meml. Hosp., pres., 1952, Crippled Children's Hosp. Sch.; mem. staff LeBonheur Childrens Hosp.; cons. orthopaedic surgeon John Gaston Hosp. civilian orthopedic cons. for Surg. Gen. U.S. Army to Japan and Korea, 1951; instr. U. of Tenn., 1940-41, asst. prof., 1941, asso. prof. orthopaedic surgery, 1944-59, prof. orthopaedic surgery, head orthopaedic dept., 1959—. Vis. orthopedic prof. Ohio State U., 1961; Camp vis. prof. U. Cal., 1962; F.W. Horner vis. prof. McGill U., 1969. Pres. trustees Campbell Found.; pres., trustee Orthopaedic and Research Edn. Found. 1960-65, pres., 1964-65. Decorated Nat. Order So. Cross, Brazil, 1953. Diplomate Am. Bd. Orthopedic Surgery (mem. bd. 1964-69). Fellow Am. Acad. Orthopaedic Surgeons (pres. 1953), A.C.S. (gov. 1958-61, Tenn. pres. 1965-66), NIH (surg. study sect. 1957-61); mem. A.M.A., Am. Orthopaedic Assn., Westen Surg. Assn., Am. Soc. Surgery of the Hand, Société Internationale de Chirugie Orthopédique et de Traumatologie, Med. and Surg. Assn. of Quito, Bolivian Surg. Soc., Memphis and Shelby County Med. Soc. (pres. 1957); hon. mem. Chilean soc. Orthopaedics and Traumatic Chilean Surg. Soc., la Sociedad Latino Americana de Orthopedia y Traumatologia Venezuelean Soc. Orthopaedic and Traumatic Surgery, Sigma Xi, Alpha Omega Alpha. Contbr. articles to profl. jours. Contbg. author Campbell's Operative Orthopaedics, 1939—. Trustee Jour. Bone and Joint Surgery. Home: 3418 Waynoka Memphis, TN 38111. Office: 869 Madison Av Memphis TN 38103

BOYD, HARPER WHITE, Jr., educator; b. Tampa, Fla., Sept. 14, 1917; s. Harper White and Julia Dade (Dabney) B.; B.A., Beloit Coll., 1938; M.B.A., Northwestern U., 1941, Ph.D., 1952; m. Laurie Ann Brewer, June 6, 1946; children—Harper Dabney (dec.), Lucinda Brewer. Mgr. field research Chgo. Tribune, 1946-48; research dir. Market Research Corp. Am., 1948-52; faculty Northwestern U. Sch. Bus., 1952-62, prof. marketing, chmn. dept., 1958-59, prof. marketing and advt. Sch. Bus. and Sch. Journalism, chmn. marketing dept. Sch. Bus., 1959-62; vis. prof. marketing Stanford Grad. Sch. Bus., 1963-64, prof. marketing, 1964—, Sebastian S. Kresge prof., 1967—; dir. Internat. Center for Advancement Mgmt. Edn., 1967—, dir. continuing edn., 1970—. Dir. Peninsula TV Power, Inc., Instl. Services, Inc., Nat. Dollar Stores. Served to lt. comdr. USNR, 1941-46. Mem. Am. Marketing Assn. (v.p. 1958-59, pres. Chgo. 1951-52, chmn. nat. conf. com., 1953-55, nat. program chmn. 1955), Am. Assn. U. Profs., Phi Beta Kappa, Sigma Chi, Beta Gamma Sigma. Conglist. Author: (with Ralph Westfall) Marketing Research: Text and Cases, 1956, rev., 1964; (with R. Westfall, Richard Clewett) Cases in Marketing Strategy, 1958, rev., 1964; (with Vernon Fryburger, Westfall) Cases in Advertising Management, 1964; (with Steuart Henderson Britt) Marketing Management and Administrative Action, 1963, rev. edit., 1968; also monographs and articles. Editor: (with Westfall, Clewett) Contemporary American Marketing, 1957, rev. 1962; (with Westfall) Cases in Marketing Management, 1961; (with Joseph W. Newman) Advertising Management: Selected Readings, 1965; (with others) Casos en Marketing, 1966, Marketing Management: Cases from the Emerging Countries, 1966; (with Sidney J. Levy) Promotion A Behavioral View; (with Robert T. Davis) Readings in Sales Management, 1970; (with Robert T. Davis) Marketing Management Casebook, 1971. Editorial bd. Jour. Marketing, 1959-70. Home: 796 Cedro Stanford CA 94305

BOYD, HARRY EDWIN, newspaper editor; b. Washington, Kan., June 15, 1904; s. James John and Edwina (Pitcher) B.; B.A., U. Ia., 1929; m. Dorothy Lowrie, June 17, 1925; children—Barbara Rae, James Avery (dec. 1962), John Douglas. Editor, Daily Iowan, Iowa City, 1928-29; with Cedar Rapids (Ia.) Gazette, 1929—, reporter, 1929-30, asso. editor, 1930-40, editor, 1941-71, chmn. editorial bd., 1971—. Mem. Am. Soc. Newspaper Editors, Nat. Conf. Editorial Writers, Phi Beta Kappa, Sigma Delta Chi, Sigma Alpha Epsilon. Republican. Club: Nat. Press (Washington). Author: My America (syndicated newspaper column). Home: 450 Forest Drive SE Cedar Rapids IA 52403 Office: Cedar Rapids Gazette Cedar Rapids IA 52401

BOYD, HOWARD TANEY, gas co. exec.; b. Woodside, Md., June 5, 1909; s. Howard and Mary Violet (Stewart) B.; grad. Georgetown Prep. Sch., Garrett Park, Md.; A.B. magna cum laude, Georgetown U., 1932, J.D., 1935; m. Lucille Belhumeur, June 15, 1935; children—Dennis Brooke, Sharon Ann, Deborah. Admitted D.C. bar, 1934, Tex. bar 1953; sec. to U.S. atty. gen., 1934; spl. atty. U.S. Dept. Justice, 1935; asst. U.S. atty. in and for D.C., 1935-39; formerly prof. Nat. Law Sch., also Washington Coll. Law, Washington; partner firm Hogan & Hartson, Washington, 1939-52; v.p., asst. gen. counsel El Paso Natural Gas Co., 1952-58, dir., 1953—, exec. v.p., 1958-60, pres., 1960-65, chmn. bd., chief exec. officer, 1965—; chmn. bd. Geonuclear Nobel-Paso Products Co.; dir. Armour and Co., Greyhound Corp., Tex. Nat. Commerce Bank. Bd. regents Georgetown U.; bd. councilors Sch. Bus. Adminstrn., U. So. Cal.; adv. council Engring. Found., U. Tex. Research fellows Southwestern Legal Found. Mem. Nat. Petroleum Council, Am. Bar Assn., State Bar Tex., Bar Assn. D.C. (dir. 1950), Am. Gas Assn. (dir.), Ind. Natural Gas Assn. (pres. 1968, dir.), Tex. Research League. Clubs: Barristers, Burning Tree, Chevy Chase, Columbia Country, Metropolitan (Washington); River Oaks Country, Houston Country, Petroleum, Ramada (Houston); Wall Street (N.Y.C.). Home: 6042 Crab Orchard St Houston TX 77027 Office: 2727 Allen Pkwy Houston TX 77019

BOYD, HUGH NEWELL, publisher; b. Rumson, N.J., Aug. 23, 1911; s. William Butler and Ruth (O'Day) B.; student Browning Sch., N.Y.C., 1922-26; grad. Choate Sch., 1930; student Yale, 1930-32; Litt.D., Rutgers U., 1970; m. Jean Maclachlan, 1932 (div. 1946); 1 son, William Maclachlan; m. 2d, Mary Martha Wren. Feb. 10, 1947. Various positions Home News Pub. Co., pubs. Daily Home News, Sunday Home News, New Brunswick, N.J., 1932-42, gen. mgr. newspapers, 1946-55, pub., pres., 1955—; dir. A.P., 1959-68. Adv. council U. Mo. Freedom of Information Center. Mem. bur. pub. relations War Dept., 1942- 43; with OSS, U.S., Eng., France, 1943-45. Recipient citation English Speaking Union, 1957. Mem. N.J. Press Assn. (pres. 1952-53, chmn. freedom of information com. 1953-54), Internat. Press Inst. (Am. chmn. 1968), Am., Newspaper Pubs. Assn., Nat. Editorial Assn. (President's award as chmn. freedom of information com. 1955; Amos award), English Speaking Union U.S. (nat. dir. 1958-66, exec. com. 1964-66), Council Fgn. Relations. Clubs: Nat. Press, Metropolitan (Washington); Nassau, Bedens Brook (Princeton, N.J.); Century Assn.; Yale (N.Y.C.). Home: 141 Hunt Dr Princeton NJ Office: 123 How Lane New Brunswick NJ

BOYD, JACK IRELAND, b. Columbia, Mo., Nov. 12, 1923; s. Alaga H. and Myrtle (Ireland) B.; B.A., Ark. A. and M. Coll., 1942; M.A., U. Chgo., 1947; postgrad. (Rotary Found. fellow), U. Geneva (Switzerland), 1947-48; m. Annelle Butler, Dec. 15, 1951; children—Harrison A. and Harriet A. (twins). Joined ECA, 1948; asst. program officer AID Mission to Jordan, 1956-58; asst. program officer AID Mission to Vietnam, 1958-59, dep. program officer, 1959-62, program officer, 1962; capital projects officer Vietnam desk AID, 1962-64, dep. chief, 1964-65, AID exchange to Dept. Def., 1965-67; sr. loan implementation officer AID, 1968-69; dep. supply officer AID Mission to Pakistan, 1969-70; ret., 1970; research asst. Local Program Planners Inst., U. Ala., 1971—. Served with USAAF, 1943-46. Mem. Nat. Geog. Soc., Sigma Tau Gamma. Episcopalian. Home: PO Box 5961 University AL 35486 Office: Local Program Planners Inst University of Ala University AL 35486

BOYD, JAMES, geologist b. Kanowna, West Australia, Dec. 20, 1904; s. Julian and Mary Innes (Cane) B.; B.S., Cal. Inst. Tech., 1927; M.Sc., Colo. Sch. Mines, 1932, D.Sc., 1934; m. Ruth Ragland Brown, Aug. 17, 1932; children—James Brown, Harry Bruce, Douglas Cane, Hudson. Instr. geology Colo. Sch. Mines, 1929-34, asst. prof. mineralogy, 1934-37, asso. prof. econ. geology, 1938-41, dean faculty, 1946-47; asst. to sec. interior on mineral matters, 1947; dir. Bur. Mines 1947-51, Def. Minerals Adminstrn., 1950-51; exploration mgr. Kennecott Copper Corp., 1951-55, v.p. exploration, 1955-60; pres. Copper Range Co., 1960-70, chmn. bd. dirs., 1970—; dir. Felmont Oil Co., Detroit Edison Co.; geologist U.S. Geol. Survey, 1933-34; cons. geology, mining and geophysics, 1935-40; pres., gen. mgr. Goldcrest Mining Co., 1939-40; dir. engrs. Joint council United Engring. Trustees. Chmn., NSF com. on mineral research, 1952-57; vice chmn. Engrs. Commn. on Air Resources, 1970—; chmn. sec. interior's adv. com. on non-comml. mine safety, 1971—. Served from capt. to col. AUS, 1943-46. Decorated Legion of Merit with oak leaf cluster. Recipient D.S.M., Colo. Sch. Mines, 1949; Distinguished Alumni award Cal. Inst. Tech., 1967. Mem. Mining and Metall. Soc. Am. (pres. 1960-63), Am. Inst. Mining Engrs. (Rand gold medal 1963, pres. 1969), Nat. Acad. Engring., Am. Soc. Econ. Geologists, Geol. Soc. Am., Canadian Inst. Mining and Metallurgy, Soc. Exploration Geophysicists, Acad. Polit. Sci. Clubs: Mining, Union League (N.Y.C.); Cosmos (Washington); Westchester Country. Home: 700 New Hampshire Av NW Washington DC 20037 Office: 630 Fifth Av New York City NY 10020

BOYD, JAMES EMORY, univ. adminstr.; b. Tignall, Ga., July 18, 1906; s. Emory Fortson and Rosa Lee (Wright) B.; A.B., U. Ga., 1927; M.A., Duke (fellow), 1928; Ph.D. (Loomis fellow), Yale 1933; m. Elizabeth Reynolds Cobb, June 2, 1934; children—Betty Cobb, James Fortson. Instr. physics U. Ga., 1928- 30; head math. and sci. dept. West Ga. Coll., 1933-35; asst. prof. physics Ga. Inst. Tech., 1935-37, asso. prof., 1937-42, prof. physics, 1946—, dir. microwave propagation and radar research projects Engring. Expt. Sta., 1946-50, head physics div., 1950-55, dir. research projects in radar, nuclear physics and microwave spectroscopy, asst. dir. (research), 1954-55, asso. sta. dir. 1955-57, dir. Engring. Expt. Sta. 1957-61, pres. Ga. Coll., Carrollton, 1961-71; vice chancellor for acad. devel. U. System Ga., also acting pres. Ga. Inst. Tech., Atlanta, 1971—. Chmn. Carrollton Payroll Devel. Authority, 1965-71; mem. Nuclear Adv. Commn., 1956-64, Ga. Sci. and Tech. Commn., 1964—; dr. Sci. Atlanta, Inc., 1952—; trustee Ga. Tech. Research Inst. 1957—. Served from lt. to comdr. USNR, 1942-46, radar research and development, Bur. Ordnance, Navy Dept., 1942-45, electronics div. Office Chief of Naval Operations, 1945-46; comdg. officer Naval Res. Research Co. 6-1, Atlanta, 1949-57, capt. USNR, 1957—. Mem. A.A.A.S., Am. Phys.Soc., Phi Beta Kappa, Omicron Delta Kappa (hon.), Sigma Xi, Phi Kappa Phi, Gamma Alpha. Episcopalian (dep. gen. conv. 1964, 67, 69, 70.). Rotarian, Kiwanian (hon.). Author sci. articles. Address: 3720 Peachtree Rd Atlanta GA 30319

BOYD, JOHN BALLANTINE, advt. exec.; b. N.Y.C., Nov. 8, 1912; s. Robert W. and Elsie G. (Bushong) B.; Grad. Horace Mann Sch., N.Y.C., 1929; A.B., Princeton, 1933; m. Madelyn Murray, May 21, 1938; 1 son, John M. Reporter Dun & Bradstreet, N.Y.C., 1933-36; copywriter J. Stirling Getchell, Inc., N.Y.C., 1936-38, Detroit, 1938-42; copywriter, also group head Compton Advt., Inc., N.Y.C., 1943-66, creative div. supr., sr. v.p., 1966-70, cons. new bus. and new campaigns, 1970—. Home: 523 75th St Holmes Beach FL 33510 Office: 625 Madison Av New York City NY 10022

BOYD, JOHN DEWEY, former coll. pres.; b. Doloroso, Miss., Sept. 3, 1899; s. John and Elizabeth (Fry) B.; B.S., Alcorn A. and M. Coll., 1931; M.S., U. Ill., 1949; m. Cleopatra Carter, Aug. 14, 1921; 1 dau., Katye (Mrs. H. E. Dockins). Sch. prin., agr. tchr., 1931-47; supt. agr. sch., 1951-57; head dept. agronomy Alcorn A. and M. Coll., Lorman, Miss., 1947-51, pres., 1957-69. Vice pres. State Mut. Savs. and Loan Assn. Del., White House Conf. Edn.; centennial com. Land Grant Coll. Assn. Mem. Phi Beta Sigma, Phi Delta Kappa. Baptist. Mason, Elk. Home: Lorman MS 39096

BOYD, JOSEPH AUBREY, aerospace systems exec.; b. Oscar, Ky., Mar. 25, 1921; s. Joseph Ray and Relda Jane (Myatt) B.; S.B. in Elec. Engring., U. Ky., 1946, M.S., 1949; Ph.D., U. Mich., 1954; m. Edith A. Atkins, May 13, 1942; children—Joseph Barry, Joel Edd. Instr., then asst. prof. elec. engring. U. Ky., 1947-49; faculty U. Mich., 1949-62, prof. elec. engring., 1958- 62, asso. dir., then dir. Willow Run Labs., 1958-60, dir. Inst. Sci. and Tech., 1960-62; exec. v.p. Radiation, Inc., Melbourne, Fla., 1962-63, pres., 1963—; exec. v.p. electronics, dir. Harris Intertype Co., 1967—. Cons. Inst. for Def. Analyses, 1956—, Nat. Security Agy., 1957-62; spl. cons. to Army Combat Surveillance Agy., 1958-62; mem., chmn. adv. group electronic warfare Office Dir. Def. Research, Engring., Def. Dept., 1959-61, cons., 1959—. Sr. mem. I.E.E.E.; mem. Assn. U.S. Army, Armed Forces Communications and Electronics Assn., A.A.A.S., Sigma Xi, Eta Kappa Nu, Tau Beta Pi. Baptist. Contbr. articles to profl. jours. Office: Radiation Inc Melbourne FL 32901

BOYD, JOSEPH DON, state ofcl.; b. Muncie, Ind., Jan. 22, 1926; s. Joseph Corneluis and Waneta May (Barrett) B.; A.B. (Rector scholar), DePauw U., 1948; M.A., Northwestern U., 1950, Ed.D., 1955; m. Cynthia Reiley, Dec. 28, 1957; children—Jane Elizabeth, Craig A., Michael J. Ednl. asst. First Meth. Ch., Anderson, Ind., 1948-49; residence hall counselor Northwestern U., 1949-50, univ. examiner, instr. edn., guidance lab. asst., 1952-54, dean men, asst. prof. edn., 1955-61; exec. dir. Ill. Scholarship Commn., 1961-; residence hall dir., head tennis coach, asst. basketball coach Albion Coll., 1950-52. Mem. Nat. Assn. Adminstrs. State Scholarship Programs, Phi Delta Kappa, Delta Tau Delta, Phi Eta Sigma. Methodist. Rotarian. Home: 1232 Warrington Rd Deerfield IL Office: 730 Waukegan Rd Deerfield IL

BOYD, JULIAN PARKS, historian, educator; b. Converse, S.C., Nov. 3, 1903; s. Robert Jay and Melona (Parks) B.; A.B., Duke, 1925, M.A., 1926, Litt.D., 1951; Litt.D., Franklin and Marshall Coll., 1939, Bucknell U., 1952, Rutgers U., 1956; L.H.D., Washington and Jefferson Coll., 1952, Yale, 1964, Lehigh U., 1966; m. Grace Welch, Dec. 21, 1927; 1 son, Kenneth Miles. Editor Wyo. Hist. and Geol. Soc., Wilkes- Barre, Pa., 1928-32; dir. N.Y. State Hist. Assn., 1932-34; librarian Hist. Soc. of Pa., 1935-40; librarian Princeton, (N.J.), 1940-52, prof. history, 1952—. Hon. cons. in Am. history Library of Congress, 1971—. Mem. bd. Winterthur, Harry S. Truman Library Inst. Mem. Am. Antiquarian Soc., Am. Philos. Soc., Soc. Am. Archivists, N.Y., Mass., Pa., Va. hist. socs., Phi Beta Kappa. Editor: Papers of Thomas Jefferson (to comprise about 50 vols.), 1950- -. Home: RD 1 Titusville NJ 08560 Office: Firestone Library Princeton U Princeton NJ 08540

BOYD, LANDIS LEE, educator, agrl. engr.; b. Orient, Ia., Dec. 1, 1923; s. Harold Everett and Edith Elizabeth (Lauer) B.; B.S. in Agrl. Engring., Ia. State U., 1947, M.S., 1948, Ph.D. in Agrl. Engring. and Engring. Mechanics, 1959; m. Lila Mae Hummel, Sept. 7, -1946; children—Susan Lee, Barbara Edith, Shirley Rae, Carl Steven, Philip Wayne. Sr. research fellow Ia. State Coll., 1947-48, 54-55; from asst. prof. to prof. Cornell U., 1948-64, coordinator grad. instrn., 1958-64; engring. design analyst Allis- Chalmers Mfg. Co., 1962-63; mem. faculty U. Minn., Mpls., 1964—, prof. agrl. engring., head dept., 1964—; vis. scholar Center Study Higher Edn., vis. faculty-in-residence, intern Office V.P. for Research, U. Mich., 1968; cons. FAO, La Molina, Peru, 1964, 69; part-time cons. in field, 1948—; supt. farm bldg. project N.Y. State Fair, 1956, 57. Served with USNR, 1943-45. NATO postdoctoral awardee, 1962; recipient Ia. 4-H Alumni Recognition award, 1968. Registered profl. engr., N.Y., Minn. Mem. Am. Soc. Agrl. Engrs. (grad. paper award 1949, MBMA award 1969, v.p.-regions 1970-73), Am. Soc. Engring. Edn., Sigma Xi, Phi Kappa Phi, Gamma Sigma Delta, Alpha Epsilon, Kappa Sigma. Methodist. Rotarian. Home: 2515 Snelling Curve St Paul MN 55113

BOYD, LINN JOHN, physician, educator; b. Detroit, Mich., Sept. 30, 1895; s. David Armitage and Laura M. (Staffin) B.; M.D., U. Mich., 1918; m. Madeline H. Young, June 8, 1918. In gen. practice, Addison, Mich., 1919-20; asso. prof. medicine Med. Sch. U. Mich., 1920-22, asso. prof. medicine, dir. research labs., 1922-25; in practice, Lansing, Mich., 1925-26; prof. medicine, head dept. pharmacology, N.Y. Med. Coll., 1926-58, clin. prof. medicine, dir. Div. Grad. Studies, 1958-63, cons. Grad. Sch., 1963-70; dir. of medicine, Met. Hosp., 1937-50, also pres. med. board 1940- 50; cons. medicine, U.S. Marine, Sea View Hosp. (S.I.), Otisville Sanatorium (N.Y.), Monmouth Meml. Hosp.; pres. med. bd. Bird S. Coler Meml. Hospital; chmn. med. bd. N.Y. Med. Coll.-Met. Hosp. Center, 1955-58; med. examiner N.Y., 1947-58; dep. chief examiner Nat. Bd. Med. Examiners, 1948-58. Served in U.S. Navy, League Island and Grey's Ferry naval hosps., 1918-19; lt. USNRF. Fellow Am. Coll. Gastroenterology (hon.), Am. Coll. Cardiology, A.C.P.; mem. N.Y. Acad. Medicine, N.Y. Heart Assn., Harvey Soc., Sigma Xi, Alpha Omega Alpha, Alpha Sigma, Alpha Kappa Kappa. Episcopalian. Mason, K.P. Research in lesser known drugs. Author of textbooks on roentgenology of heart and great vessels, also on pharmacology, cardiology and electrocardiography. Home: Palmer House North 611 Palmer Rd Yonkers NY 10701 Office: Flower-Fifth Av Hosp New York City NY 10029

BOYD, LOUISE ARNER, explorer, author; b. San Rafael, Cal., Sept. 16, 1887; d. John Franklin and Louise Cook (Arner) Boyd; ed. Miss Stewart's Sch., San Rafael, Miss Murison's Sch., San Francisco; hon. LL.D., U. Cal., 1939, Mills Coll., 1939. Explorer of East Greenland; explorer polar region, N.E. and West Greenland (Spitzbergen and Franz Josef Land); flew pvt. chartered plane over North Pole, 1955. Decorated Chevalier Legion of Honor (France), St. Olaf of Norway (1st fgn. woman to receive award); awarded Andree plaque by Swedish Anthropol. and Geog. Soc., Cullum gold medal Am. Geog. Soc., medal of King Christian Xth of Denmark; certificate of Appreciation, U.S. Army; made hon. citizen City of San Rafael. Mem. Royal Hort. Soc. (London), Am. Polar Soc. (hon., dir.), Cal. Acad. Sci. (hon.), Am. Soc. Photogrammetry, Am. Geog. Soc. (council), Assn. Pacific Coast Geographers, Brit. Glaciological Soc., Am. Hort. Soc., Soc. Woman Geographers, Cal. Bot. Soc., Nat. League Am. Pen Women, Geog. Soc. Phila. (hon.), Colonial Dames Am., Sigma Delta Epsilon. Republican. Episcopalian. Clubs: San Francisco Garden (hon.); Burlingame (Cal.) Country, Marin Garden (hon.); Colony (N.Y.); Garden of Am. (mem.-at-large). Author: Fiord Region of East Greenland, 1935; Polish Countrysides, 1937; Coast of Northeast Greenland. Contbr. to Geog. Rev. Office: 210 Post St San Francisco CA 94108

BOYD, MALCOLM, clergyman, author; b. Buffalo, June 8, 1923; s. Melville and Beatrice (Lowrie) B.; B.A., U. Ariz., 1944; B.D., Ch. Div. Sch. Pacific, 1954; postgrad. Oxford (Eng.) U., 1955; S.T.M., Union Theol. Sem., N.Y.C., 1956. Pres., TV Producers Assn. Hollywood, Cal., 1950; v.p., gen. mgr. Pickford, Rogers & Boyd, 1949-51; ordained to ministry Episcopal Ch., 1955; rector in Indpls., 1957-59; chaplain Colo. State U., 1959-61, Wayne State U., 1961-65; nat. field rep. Episcopal Soc. Cultural and Racial Unity, 1965-68; resident fellow Calhoun Coll., Yale, 1968—; contbg. editor The Episcopalian,

1964-68; motion picture reviewer Christian Century, 1963-68; corr. Renewal mag., 1965-70; lectr. World Council Chs., Switzerland, 1955, 64; columnist Pitts. Courier, 1962-65; active voter registration Miss., Ala., 1963, 64. Mem. film awards com. Nat. Council Chs., 1965—; program dir. Hollywood Advt. Club, 1949- 50. Mem. P.E.N. Am. Center, Authors Guild, N.A.A.C.P., Episcopal Peace Fellowship. Author: Crisis in Communication, 1957; Are You Running with Me, Jesus?, 1965; Free to Live, Free to Die, 1967; Book of Days, 1968; Human Like Me, Jesus, 1971; (plays) Boy, 1961, Study in Color, 1962, The Community, 1964; As I Live and Breathe: Stages of an Autobiography, 1969; others. Editor: On the Battle Lines, 1964; The Underground Church, 1968. Address: Simon & Schuster 630 Fifth Av New York City NY 10020

BOYD, MAURICE, educator; b. Guthrie, Ky., Apr. 3, 1921; s. Charles Hayden and Lorena (Shelton) B.; A.B., U. Mo., 1943; M.A., U. Mich., 1948, Ph.D., 1951; m. Shirley Mereness, Mar. 5, 1944; children—James, Robert, Jon Christopher, Thomas. Teaching fellow U. Mich., 1949-50; instr. Bradley U., 1950-52, asst. prof., 1952-54, asso. prof., 1954-56, dir. gen. edn., 1953-56; asso. prof. humanities U. Fla., 1956-57, chmn. dept. social sci., 1957- 61, prof. social scis., 1959-64, prof. humanities, 1961-64; prof. history Tex. Christian U., 1964—. Mem. Am., So. hist. assns., N.E.A., Phi Alpha Theta, Pi Sigma Alpha. Author: Cardinal Quiroga: Inquisitor General of Spain, 1955; Eight Tarascan Legends, 1958; American Civilization, 1964; William Knox and Abraham Lincoln, 1966; Contemporary America; Issues and Problems, 1968; Tarascan Myths and Legends, 1969; also hist. articles. Home: 4025 Glenwood Dr Fort Worth TX 76109

BOYD, MAURICE OSWALD, educator; b. Barnsville, Minn., Nov. 1, 1911; s. Edwin Arthur and Frida (Wulfsburg) B.; Mus.B., U. Wis., 1935, M.A., 1936, Ph.D., 1942; student City U., U. Paris, 1945, Acad. Music, Vienna, Austria, 1962-63; m. Eleanor Harriet Ferguson, July 31, 1946; children—William Steven, Susan Anne, Elizabeth Jane. Asst. dir. bands U. Wis., 1935-36; dir. music pub. schs., Edgerton, Wis., 1936-40; instr. music U. Wis., Whitewater, 1940-41, chmn. music dept., 1946-47; chmn. music dept. Oswego Coll. State U. N.Y., 1947—. Bd. dirs. Oswego YMCA, 1951—. Served with AUS, 1942-45. Decorated Purple Heart, Bronze Star, Silver Star. Mem. N.E.A., Music Educator Nat. Conf., N.Y. State Teachers Assn., Phi Mu Sinfonia, Phi Delta Kappa. Lutheran. Rotarian. Home: 316 Washington Blvd Oswego NY 13126

BOYD, OF MERTON, VISCOUNT, ex-cabinet minister U.K.; b. Bournemouth, Eng., Nov. 18, 1904; s. Alan Walter and Florence Ann (Begbie) Lennox-B.; student Christ Ch. Coll., Oxford; m. Patricia Guinness, Dec. 29, 1938; children—Simon, Christopher, Mark. Mem. Parliament for Mid-Bedfordshire, 1931-60; parliamentary sec. to Minister of Labour, 1938-39, Ministry Home Security, 1939, Ministry Food, 1939-40, Ministry Aircraft Prodn., 1943- 45; minister of state for colonial affairs, 1951-52, minister transport, 1952-54; sec. state for colonies, 1954-59; dep. lt. for Bedfordshire, 1954-; Mng. dir. Arthur Guinness Son & Co., Ltd., 1960-; prime warden Goldsmiths' Co., 1964-65; member of court of directors of Royal Exchange, 1962-. Chmn. gov.'s Sherborne Sch. Recipient Messel medal Soc. Chem. Industry, 1966. Created viscount Boyd of Merton, 1960. Privy councillor, 1951. Clubs: Carlton, Pratts (London); Royal Yacht Squadron (Cowes, I.W.). Addresses: Iveagh House Ormond Yard, St James's SW 1, England also Ince Castle Saltash Cornwall, England

BOYD, MYRON FENTON, bishop; b. Shelbyville, Ill., July 19, 1909; s. Edward Pliny and Greta A. (Pierce) B.; A.B., Seattle Pacific Coll., 1932, D.D., 1949; D.Litt., Houghton (N.Y.) Coll., 1957; m. Ruth Elinor Putnam, June 28, 1932; children—Donald E., Darold D., Carolyn E. (Mrs. Dale Martin). Ordained to ministry Free Meth. Ch., 1931; pastor in Tonasket, Wenatchee, Mt. Vernon and Seattle, Wash., 1932-48; dir., speaker Light and Life Hour, Worldwide Radio Ministry, 1945-65; bishop Free Meth. Ch. N. Am., 1964—, chmn. gen. missionary bd., trustee World Gospel Mission Bd. Recipient award for producing best all around nat. religious broadcast Nat. Radio Broadcasters, 1955. Mem. Nat. Holiness Assn. (pres. 1954-58, 68-72), Nat. Assn. Evans. (v.p. 1968-72, pres. 1972—), Nat. Religious Broadcasters (pres. 1954-56). Author: To Tell the World, 1964. Home: 516 School Av Winona Lake IN 46590 Office: 700 College Av Winona Lake IN 46590

BOYD, PHILIP LINNAES, former univ. regent; b. Richmond, Ind., Oct. 8, 1900; s. Linnaes Commer and Mary Thomas (Spencer) B.; A.B., LL.B., Wabash Coll., 1922, LL.D., 1968; postgrad. U. So. Cal. Law Sch., 1926-27; LL.D., U. Cal.; m. Dorothy Burrough Marmon, Mar. 10, 1926. Sec., Palm Springs (Cal.) C. of C., 1928-29; mgr. Palm Springs br. Bank of Am., 1929-32; pres. Deep Canyon Properties, 1950—; dir. Citizens Nat. Trust & Savs. Bank, Riverside, Cal., 1950-58, Security First Nat. Bank, 1958-70. Regent, U. Cal., 1957-70. Mayor, Palm Springs, 1938-42; mem. Cal. Assembly, 1945-49. Chmn., Cal. Republican Central Com., 1950-51. Mem. Phi Delta Phi, Beta Theta Pi. Presbyn. Kiwanian. Home: 4649 9th St Riverside CA 92501 Office: 3900 Market St Riverside CA 92501

BOYD, RALPH E., mfg. co. exec.; b. Orrville, O., 1900. Chmn., dir. Galion Iron Works & Mfg. Co. div. Jeffrey-Galion Inc.; chmn. Galion Mfg. of Can., Ltd.; dir. Jeffrey Co., Gen. Hydraulics Co., Galion (Pty.) Ltd., Jeffrey-Galion Mfg. Co., First Nat. Bank Mansfield. Home: 400 W Southern Av Bucyrus OH 44820 Office: South St Galion OH 44833*

BOYD, RALPH GATES, lawyer; b. Chelmsford, Mass., Oct. 30, 1901; s. Richard Turnbull and Jennie (Gates) B.; A.B. cum laude, Harvard, 1922, LL.B., 1925; m. Dorothy Louise Koch, Apr. 2, 1932; 1 son, Douglas. Admitted to Mass. bar, 1926, since practiced in Boston; asso. firm Dunbar, Nutter & McClennen (now Nutter, McClennen & Fish), 1925-34, partner, 1934-54, own practice, and partner firm Boyd & MacCrelish, 1954-61; partner firm Boyd, MacCrellish & Weeks, 1962—; pres. West Point Mfg. Co., 1950-51, also chmn. bd. dirs. subsidiary and affiliated textile cos.; gen. counsel United-Carr Inc., 1929-65, also dir.; chmn. bd. dirs. Davis- Furber Machine Co.; dir. Roger Boyd, Inc., W. J. Connell Co.; dir., clk. Bankers Service Co. Mem. Beacon Hill Archtl. Com., 1964—. Mem. nat. bd. dirs. Arthritis and Rheumatism Found., also mem. nat. exec. com., trustee gen. counsel Mass. chpt.; trustee, treas. France G. Lee Found. Served as pvt. Jr. Co., S.A.T.C., 1918; maj. to col., U.S. Army, 1941- 46, col., brig. gen. JAGC, U.S. Army Res. 1947-61; ret., 1961. Decorated Legion of Merit, Commendation ribbon, Am., Asiatic, E.T.O. ribbons, Battle star for No. France. Mem. Am. Bar Assn. (chmn. sect. corp., banking and bus. law 1950-51, mem. Ho. of Dels. 1948-52, chmn. com. lawyers in Armed Forces, 1952-53, chmn. com. Mil. Justice, 1953-56; mem. adv. com. to U.S. Mil. Appeals, 1952—; mem. Judge Advs. Assn. (pres. 1947-47, dir. 1946- 57), Mass. State, Boston bar assns., Assn. U.S. Army (pres., dir. Mass. Bay chpt.). Republican. Conglist. Clubs: Union Algonquin, Harvard, Fort Hill, Downtown (Boston); Harvard (N.Y.C.). Author wartime legislation and Army regulations and manuals; also articles. Home: 104 Mt Vernon St Boston MA 02108 Office: 75 Federal St Boston MA 02110

BOYD, RAYMOND G., aluminum co. exec.; b. Des Moines, Feb. 14, 1905; s. William Hamilton and Dora F. (Norris) B.; B.S., U.S. Naval Acad., 1927; m. Elizabeth H. Blake, Dec. 30, 1933; children—James Blake, William Hamilton. Former v.p. Kaiser Aluminum & Chem. Corp. Served from lt. comdr. to comdr., USNR, 1942-45; PTO. Home: 999 Green St San Francisco CA 94133

BOYD, RICHARD FAY, former pub. health adminstr.; b. Kinmundy, Ill., Feb. 21, 1906; s. Mark and Mae (Puffer) B.; student Ill. Coll., Jacksonville, 1924-26; A.B., U. Ill., 1928; M.D., Rush Med. Coll., Chgo., 1935; M.P.H., Harvard, 1938; m. Kathleen Ragan, July 12, 1930. Sci. tchr., prin. Morris (Ill.) High Sch., 1928-31; intern, sr. resident surgery Ill. Central Hosp., Chgo., 1934-35; resident physician Municipal Contagious Disease Hosp., Chgo., 1935-36; gen. med. practice, Cimarron, Kan., 1936-37; asst. dir. child hygiene div. Kan. Bd. Health, 1937-40, dir. div. local health services, 1940-41; sr. med. officer U.S. Dept. Agr., Milw., 1941-42; chief div. local health adminstrn. Ill. Dept. Pub. Health, Springfield, 1942-48; lectr. preventive medicine U. Ill., Northwestern U. Med. Schs., 1942-48; vis. lectr. Harvard Sch. Pub. Health, 1951-53, Columbia Sch. Pub. Health, Administrative Medicine, 1956-58; lectr. Sch. Pub. Health U. Cal. 1953-56; med. officer health and welfare fund U.M.W.A., Washington, May-Dec. 1948; commd. sr. surgeon, USPHS, 1948, med. dir., 1953, chief. Office Med. Programs region II, 1949-50, regional med. dir. region 1, 1951-53, region IX 1953-56, regions I and II, 1956-58; region VII, 1958-70. Pub. health rep. ICA State Dept. Mission to Pakistan, 1952; health adviser Gen. Econ. Survey Mission to Uganda, Internat. Bank Reconstrn. and Devel., 1960. Recipient Meritorious Service medal USPHS. Diplomate Am. Bd. Preventive Medicine (founder, trustee, vice chmn. pub. health). Fellow Am. Coll. Preventive Medicine (v.p. 1964-65), Am. Pub. Health Assn. (sec. health officers sect. 1943-46, chmn. 1946-47, mem. governing council 1943-56); mem. A.M.A., Assn. State Dirs. Local Health Services (sec. 1946-48), Am. Assn. Pub. Health Physicians, U.S.-Mexican Border, Western Br. Ill. (exec. council 1946-48) pub. health assns., Phi Chi, Delta Omega. Contbr. articles to profl. jours. Home: 12436 Pomerado Ct Rancho Bernardo San Diego CA 92128

BOYD, RICHARD HAYS, educator; b. Columbus, Ohio, Aug. 12, 1929; s. Robert E. and Charlotte (Hays) B.; B.Sc., Ohio State U., 1951; Ph.D., Mass. Inst. Tech., 1955; m. Patricia A. Scheible, Sept. 5, 1951; children—David Hays, Elizabeth King. Research chemist E. I. DuPont de Nemours Co., Wilmington, Del., 1955-62; prof. chemistry Utah State U., 1962-67, prof. chem. engring., prof. materials sci. and engring, adj. prof. chemistry, 1967—; cons. phys. chemistry and polymer sci. Troop committeeman Great Salt Lake council Boy Scouts Am., 197—. Mem. Am. Chem. Soc., Am. Phys. Soc., Am. Inst. Chem. Engrs., Faraday Soc., Am. Assn. U. Profs., Phi Beta Kappa, Sigma Xi, Phi Eta Sigma, Phi Kappa Phi, Sigma Chi. Research, articles physical chemistry, polymer sci. Office: Dept Chem Engring U Utah Salt Lake City UT 84112

BOYD, RICHARD MOODY, freight car co. exec.; b. Louisville, Jan. 16, 1915; s. Moody and Nellie Field (Dickinson) B.; A.B., U. Ky., 1936; m. Dale Crowe, May 24, 1941; children—Richard Hart, David Parker. Gen. agt. I.C. R.R., 1936-48; with PPG Industries, Inc., 1949-70, v.p. traffic, transp., 1966- 70; dir. N. Am. Car Corp., Chgo., 1969—, pres., 1970—. Served to col. Transp. Corps. AUS, 1941-46. Mem. nat. Freight Traffic Assn. (pres. 1967), Nat. Indsl. Traffic League (pres. 1960-62), Am. Soc. Traffic and Transp., Nat. Def. Transp. Assn. (v.p. 1965-66), traffic clubs Pitts. (pres. 1965-66), N.Y.C., Am. Legion, Sigma Phi Epsilon. Clubs: Duquesne (Pitts.); Chicago Traffic. Home: 315 Cumnor Rd Kenilworth IL 60043 Office: 77 S Wacker Dr Chicago IL 60606

BOYD, ROBERT NEILSON, educator; b. Chgo., July 18, 1914; s. D'Estraye C. and Alva M. (Haight) B.; B.S., U. Chgo., 1936; Ph.D., U. Cal. at Berkeley, 1939; m. Rosalind Lazarus, Dec. 7, 1961; children—Andrew Neilson, David Llewellyn. Inst., Antioch Coll., Yellow Springs, O., 1939-41, asst. prof., 1941-47; asst. prof., N.Y.U., 1947-54, asso. prof., 1954-63, prof., 1963—. Mem. A.A.A.S., Am. Chem. Soc. (sec. Dayton sect. 1944-45), N.Y. Acad. Sci. (chmn. chemistry sect. 1957-58), Chem. Soc. (London), Sigma Xi, Phi Lambda Upsilon, Phi Delta Theta. Democrat. Author: (with others) Organic Chemistry, 1959. Contbr. articles in field to profl. jours. Home: 3 Washington Sq Village New York City NY 10012

BOYD, ROBERT OSBORN, lawyer; b. Kennewick, Wash., July 29, 1903; s. Daniel and Ethel (Axtell) B.; A.B., Amherst Coll., 1926, M.A. (hon.), 1961; postgrad. George Washington U., 1930-33, LL.B., 1956; m. Jacqueline Zurcher, Dec. 10, 1929; 1 son, Daniel Zurcher. Admitted to Ore. bar, 1933, since practiced in Portland; counsel Ore. Liquor Control Commn., 1939-42; mem. emergency bds. authorized under Railway Labor Act to investigate different disputes affecting several railroads, airlines and their employees, 1948-52; neutral referee Nat. R.R. Adjustment Bd., 1948- 52; mem. Nat. Mediation Booard, 1954-63, chmn. board, 1956-60; arbitrator railroad and indsl. disputes, 1962—. Served with U.S. Coast Guard (TR), 1944-45. Mem. Am. (ho. dels. 1952-54), Ore. (gov. 1946- 49), Fed. (nat. council) bar assns., Nat. Acad. Arbitrators, English Speaking Union (pres. Portland 1953-54), World Affairs Council Ore. (pres. 1952-53), Portland Com. Fgn. Relations (sec. 1947-54), S.A.R. (pres. Ore. 1944), Phi Delta Theta, Delta Theta Phi. Mason. Clubs: University, Multnomah Athletic (Portland); University (Washington). Home: 413 Franklin St Alexandria VA 22314 Office: Bowen Bldg Washington DC 20005

BOYD, ROBERT STEWART, pub. co. exec.; b. N.Y.C., May 17, 1908; s. Robert J. and Esobel (Bole) B.; student bus. adminstrn., Columbia, 1932; student Wesleyan U., Middletown, Conn., 1933; m. Evelyn Allan Power, June 25, 1936; 1 dau., Lee Allan. Traffic rep. Eastern Air Lines, 1933-35; dist. sales mgr. Gen. Foods, Inc., 1935-41; dir. war workers recruiting Mfrs. Assn. Syracuse, N.Y., 1942-44; account exec. Young & Rubicam, 1945-46; advt. mgr. Nat. Biscuit Co., 1947-55; v.p., pub. Curtis Pub. Co., 1956—; now with marketing and sales Good Housekeeping, N.Y.C.; dir. Nat. Analysts, Inc. Pres. Grocery Mfrs. Assn. Syracuse, 1940-41, Advt. Club Syracuse, 1942. Pres. N.Y.C. Youth Devel. Com. Republican campaign mgr. 7th Congl. Dist. N.J., 1951-52; treas. N.J. for Eisenhower, 1951-52; pres. Ridgewood (N.J.) Rep. Club, 1951-52. Trustee, exec. com. Am. Freedom from Hunger Found.; trustee Prospect Hill Sch., Newark. Mem. N.Y. N.G., 1938—. Recipient citations advt. clubs St. Louis, Mpls., Miami, Fla., also Reading, Pa. Mem. Delta Kappa Epsilon. Clubs: Syracuse University; Mendham Golf. Home: Box 201 Meyersville Rd Green Village NJ 07935 Office: 959 8th Av New York City NY 10019

BOYD, ROBERT WRIGHT, Jr., pub. exec.; b. N.Y.C., May 1, 1911; s. Robert W. and Elsie G. (Bushong) B.; A.B., Princeton, 1932; m. Ruth Simpson, June 20, 1939; children—Nancy (Mrs. Richard Moroso), Robert Wright III, James, Richard, Ruth. Began as makeup man for Newsweek mag., 1933-38; with Time Inc., 1938—, asso. editor, 1944-49, sr. editor, 1949-67, editorial prodn. mgr., 1967-71, dir. computer composition, 1971—; pres., dir. Roxmor Realty Corp. Presbyn. Home: 14 Lockwood Av Old Greenwich CT 06870 also Woodland Valley Phoenicia NY 12464 Office: Time and Life Bldg New York City NY 10020

BOYD, ROBIN, architect; b. Melbourne, Australia, Jan. 3, 1919; s. Penleigh and Edith Susan G. (Anderson) B.; student Royal Melbourne Inst. Tech., 1940; D.Litt., U. New Eng.; m. Dorothea P. Madder, Dec. 27, 1941; children—Caroline, Penleigh, Suzy. Dir. homes service Royal Victorian Inst. Architects, Melbourne, 1946-53; partner archtl. firm Grounds, Romberg & Boyd, Melbourne, 1954-62, Romberg & Boyd, Melbourne, 1962—; part-time lectr. design and archtl. history U. Melbourne, 1948-56; vis. Bemis prof. architecture Mass. Inst. Tech., 1956-57. Mem. Nat. Capital Planning Com., Canberra, Melbourne Underground Rail Authority. Trustee, Nat. Gallery Victoria. Recipient gold medal Australian Inst. Architects, 1969. Fellow Royal Soc. Arts, A.I.A. (hon.); mem. Royal Australian Inst. Architects (pres. Victoria 1970-72). Author: The Australian Ugliness, Victorian Modern, Australia's Home: The Walls Around Us; Kenzo Tange; The Puzzle of Architecture; New Directions in Japanese Architecture; Living in Australia. Contbr. articles to profl. jours. Home: 290 Walsh St South Yarra Melbourne 3141 Australia Office: 340 Albert St East Melbourne 3002 Australia

BOYD, SAMUEL MATTHEW, retail stores exec.; b. Uniontown, Pa., Mar. 12, 1908; s. Eli Jacob and Martha (Albright) B.; grad. Inst. Mgmt., Am. U., 1956; m. Mary Kathryn Collins, July 26, 1932; children—Vance Eugene, Maureen Ellen (Mrs. James F. O'Hara), Suzanne Martha (Mrs. Allan Byrne). Salesmgr., Collins Electric Co., Springfield, Mass., 1929-45; pres. New Eng. Service Center, Inc., Springfield, 1945-59, Boyd & Parker, Inc., builders and developers, Springfield, 1948-60, Bailey-Wagner, Inc., retail furniture-appliance stores, Springfield, 1933—; lectr. merchandising Mass. U. extension, 1938—, Internat. Coll., Springfield, 1956—. Mem. Nat. Appliance and Radio-TV Dealers Assn. (pres. 1962-63). Club: Longmeadow (Mass.) Mens (pres. 1956). Home: 699 Shaker Rd Longmeadow MA 01106 Office: 1458 Riverdale St West Springfield MA 01089

BOYD, STEPHEN, actor; b. Belfast, Ireland, July 4, 1928; s. James Alexander and Martha (Boyd) Millar. With Ulster Theatre Group, the summer stock companies and radio in Canada; repertory in U.S., 1952-53; films include Man Who Never Was; Seven Waves Away; Island in the Sun; Seven Thunders; Bravados; Ben Hur; Les Bijouteries de Clair de lune; Woman Obsessed; Best of Everything; The Big Gamble; Lisa; Jumbo, others. Address: care Contemporary-Korman Artists Ltd 132 Lasky Dr Beverly Hills CA 90212*

BOYD, THOMAS ALVIN, research cons.; b. Fairview, O., Oct. 10, 1888; s. William Charles and Amanda (Bell) B.; student Muskingum Coll., 1908-09, Franklin Coll., 1913-14; B. Chem. Engring., Ohio State U., 1918, Chem. Engr., 1938, D.Sc., 1953; D. Engring., U. Detroit, 1952; D.Sc., Wayne State U., 1955; m. Grace Jean Bethel, June 25, 1919; 1 dau., Elinor Jean. Research chemist, research div. Dayton Metal Products Co. (O.), 1918-19; research chemist, asst. head fuel dept. Gen. Motors Research Div. (merger Dayton Metal Products Co. with Gen. Motors Corp.), Dayton, 1919-25, Detroit, 1925-47; research cons., lectr. in field. Recipient Lamme medal for meritorious achievement in engring. Ohio State U., 1939, Thomas Midgley award Detroit sect. Am. Chem. Soc., 1966. Fellow A.A.A.S.; mem. Am. Soc. Testing Materials (dir. 1943-45, v.p. 1945-47, pres. 1947-48), Am. Standards Assn., Am. Chem. Soc., Soc. Automotive Engrs. (Horning Meml. medal 1948), Engrs. Soc. Detroit (dir. 1941-47, pres. 1943-44), Mich. Acad. Arts and Sci., Am. Soc. Engring. Edn., Sigma Xi, Phi Lambda Upsilon, Tau Beta Pi. Presbyn. Clubs: Boat, Torch, Economic (Detroit); Chemists (N.Y.C.). Author: Gasoline—What Everyone Should Know About It, 1925; Research—The Pathfinder of Science and Industry, 1935; Professional Amateur, A Biography of Charles Franklin Kettering, 1957. Editor: Prophet of Progress—Selections frm the Speeches of Charles F. Kettering, 1961. Contbr. articles to profl. jours. Home: 1016 Harvard Rd Grosse Pointe MI 48230

BOYD, THOMAS MUNFORD, lawyer, educator; b. Roanoke, Va., Sept. 25, 1899; s. James and Emma (Munford) B.; B.S., U. Va., 1920, LL.B., 1923; m. Dorothy Pilkington, Sept. 10, 1929; 1 son, Thomas Munford. Admitted to Va. bar, 1923; pvt. practice Charlottesville, 1923-40; judge Juvenile and Domestic Relations Ct. of Charlottesville and Albemarle County, 1925-30; mem. legal staff Nat. Def. Adv. Commn., Office Prodn. Mgmt., W.P.B., Washington, 1940-43; gen. practice Christian, Barton, Parker & Boyd, Richmond, 1943-48, counsel, 1948-70; counsel Paxson, Marshall & Smith, Charlottesville, 1970—; lectr. law, U. Va., 1946- 47, prof. law, 1947-65, Doherty prof. law, 1965-70, prof. emeritus, 1970—; (on leave) chmn. appeals bd. N.P.A., 1951-52; adv. counsel Va. Code Commn., 1953- 58. Pres. Stettinius Fund, Inc., 1947-66; dir., gen. counsel Am. and Fgn. Enterprises, Inc., N.Y.C., 1947—. Vis. prof. Washington and Lee U., 1961-62. Bd. dirs. Va. Soc. for Prevention Blindness. Recipient Thomas Jefferson award U. Va., 1957, Raven award, 1961. Mem. Am. Bar Assn. Jour (adv. com. 1962), Am., Va. bar assns., Am. Judicature Soc., Nat. Fedn. Blind (dir. 1954-62), Order of Coif, Phi Kappa Psi, Phi Delta Phi. Episcopalian. Club: Commonwealth. Author: Burk's Pleading and Practice, 4th edit., 1952; Cases on Virginia Procedure, 1958, rev. edit., 1969. Home: 1309 Rugby Rd Charlottesville VA 22903

BOYD, VIRGIL EDWARD, automobile mfg. co. exec.; b. Benton, Kan., July 8, 1912; s. Vitalis and Bertha (Klemm) B.; grad. Am. Bus. Coll., Omaha, 1931; LL.D., U. Neb., 1969; m. Berniece Nelson, Oct. 13, 1935; children—Sandra K. (Mrs. Robert M. Ireland), Richard N. Accountant, Gen. Motors Acceptance Corp., 1931-37; sales exec. Nash-Kelvinator Corp., 1937-47; owner, operator auto dealerships for Nash and Buick, 1947-54; with Am. Motors Corp., 1954-62; group v.p. sales, dir. Chrysler Corp., 1962-66, pres., 1967—. Named Marketing Exec. of Year, Sales and Marketing Execs. Internat., 1963. Mem. Soc. Automotive Engrs., Sales and Marketing Execs. Detroit (dir.). Home: 376 Dunston Rd Bloomfield Hills MI 48013 Office: 341 Massachusetts Av Detroit MI 48231

BOYD, WILLARD LEE, Jr., coll. pres.; b. St. Paul, Mar. 29, 1927; s. Willard Lee and Frances L. (Collins) B.; B.S.L., U. Minn., 1949, LL.B., 1951; LL.M. (William W. Cook fellow 1951-52), U. Mich., 1952, S.J.D., 1962; m. Susan Kuehn, Aug. 28, 1954; children—Elizabeth Kuehn, Willard Lee III, Thomas Henry. Admitted to Minn. bar, 1951, Ia. bar, 1958; asso. firm Dorsey, Owen, Marquart, Windhorst and West, Mpls., 1952-54; mem. faculty U. Ia. Coll. law, 1954—, prof., 1961—, asso. dean, 1964, v.p. acad. affairs, dean faculties at univ., 1964-69, pres., 1969—. U.S. del. to Spl. Commn. on Succession Hague Conf. on Pvt. Internat. Law, 1970—; mem. Commn. on Arts and Scis. Nat. Assn. Land-Grant Colls. and Univs., 1969—; mem. Commn. on Fed. Relations Am. Council on Edn., 1971—. Vice pres., trustee Ia. Measurement Research Found. Served with USNR, 1945-46. Mem. Am. (past chmn. com. social, labor and indsl. legislation, sect. internat. and comparative law), Ia. bar assns., Am. Assn. UN. Conglist. Contbr. to profl. jours. Home: 508 River St Iowa City IA 52240

BOYD, WILLIAM, Jr., banker; b. Pitts., Mar. 14, 1915; s. William and Catherine (McCutcheon) B.; grad. Phillips Acad., 1933; B.A., Yale, 1937; postgrad. U. Pitts., 1946-50; m. Ann Willets, Nov. 6, 1954; 1 dau., Spencer. With Gulf Oil Corp., Pitts., 1938-54; cons. to pres. Westinghouse Air Brake Co., Pitts., 1954-56; mgmt. cons. W. Boyd, Jr. & Assos., Pitts., 1956-58; v.p. Pitts, Nat. Bank, 1958-68, sr. v.p.,

1968—, mgr. internat. div., 1962—; exec. v.p., dir. Pitts. Internat. Finance Corp. Chmn. Regional Export Expansion Council, 1965-67; mem. Nat. Export Expansion Council, 1965-67, 70-71; mem. adv. bd. fgn. trade com. Export-Import Bank U.S., 1970—. Pres., trustee Pitts. Council for Internat. Visitors. Served with USNR, 1941-46. Decorated Knight Order of Leopold II (Belgium), Mem. C. of C. Greater Pitts., World Trade Council (past chmn.), Bankers Assn. for Fgn. Trade (pres.). Clubs: Allegheny County, Duquesne (Pitts.); India House (N.Y.C.); Seqwanhaka Corinthian (Oyster Bay, L.I.); Royal Ocean Racing (London, Eng.). Home: Woodland Rd Sewickley PA 15143 Office: PO Box 340777 P Pittsburgh PA 15230

BOYD, WILLIAM BEATY, univ. pres.; b. Mt. Pleasant, S.C., Feb. 2, 1923; s. Francis Thomas and Eunice (Beaty) B.; A.B., Presbyn. Coll., Clinton, S.C., 1946; M.A., Emory U., 1947; Ph.D., U. Pa., 1954; LL.D., Alma Coll., 1969; m. Louise Philson, June 25, 1945; children-Marcie, Susan. Faculty, Mich. State U., 1953-58; dean of faculty Alma (Mich.) Coll., 1958-65; dir. honors program Coll. Arts and Scis., Ohio State U., 1965-66; vice chancellor student affairs U. Cal., Berkeley, 1966-68; pres. Central Mich. U., Mt. Pleasant, 1968—. Served with USNR, 1943-46, 51-53. Home: 524 E Bellows St Mount Pleasant MI 48858

BOYD, WILLIAM CLOUSER, educator; b. Dearborn, Mo., Mar. 4, 1903; s. William Oliver and Wilmuth (Clouser) B.; A.B., Harvard, 1925, M.A., 1926; Ph.D., Boston U., 1930; student Sch. Oriental Studies, Cairo, Egypt, 1949-50; m. Lyle A. Gifford, June 9, 1931; 1 dau., Sylvia Lyle. Teaching fellow Boston U. Sch. Medicine, 1926, mem. faculty 1930—, prof. immunochemistry, research, 1948-69, prof. emeritus, 1969—; head dept. biochemistry U.S. Naval Med. Research Inst. No. 3, Cairo, Egypt, 1949-50; research collaborator Brookhaven Nat. Lab., 1956-57; vis. prof. biochemistry and nutrition U. P.R. Med Sch., San Juan, 1970—. Fellow Am. Acad. Arts and Scis.; mem. Am. Assn. Immunologists (pres. 1959-60), Am. Assn. Human Genetics (pres. 1957), Am. Rocket Soc., Sigma Xi. Club: Boston Mycological (pres. 1960). Author: Blood Grouping Technic, 1942; Fundamentals of Immunology, 1943; Genetics and the Race of Man, 1950; (with B.S. Walker and I. Asimov) Biochemistry and Human Metabolism, 1952; (with I. Asimov) Races and People, 1955; Introduction to Immunochemical Specificity, 1962, also textbooks, articles in tech. jours. Home: San Juan PR 00905 Office: 80 E Concord St Boston MA 02118

BOYD, WILLIAM RICHARD, airline exec.; b. Newark, May 13, 1916; s. Samuel and Marion (Suchoy) B.; student U. N.C., 1933-35; m. Katherine Louise Myer, Apr. 24, 1942. Vice pres., gen. mgr. Nationwide Air Transport Service. Miami, Fla., 1947-49; pres., dir., gen. mgr. Frontier Airmotive, Inc., 1950-51; v.p., asst. pres. Resort Airlines, 1951-52; dir. pres., gen. mgr. All Am. Airways, 1952-53; pres., gen. mgr., dir. Riddle Airlines, 1953-55; exec. v.p., gen. mgr., dir. Aerovias Sud Americana, 1955-56; exec. v.p., dir. World Airways, 1956-63; v.p. Continental Air Lines, 1964-68; pres., gen. mgr., dir. Airlift Internat., Inc., Miami, Fla., 1968-70, Holiday Airlines, Inc., Los Angeles, 1970—. Served to flying officer, RAF, 1940-42, to maj. USAAF, 1942-45. Decorated Air medal, D.F.C. (U.S. and Eng.). Home: 9955 Durant Dr Beverly Hills CA 90212 Office: 9841 Airport Blvd Suite 1430 Los Angeles CA 90045

BOYDEN, ALAN ARTHUR, educator; b. Milw., June 16, 1897; s. Arthur and Carrie (Wheeler) B.; A.B., U. Wis., 1921, Ph.D., 1925; m. Mabel Josephine Gregg, Sept. 15, 1923; children—Alan Arthur, Douglas Gregg, Mabel Maxon (Mrs. Thomas Ralph Davenport), Cornelia Wheeler (Mrs. Richard Thum). With Rutgers U., 1925—, New Brunswick, N.J., instr., asst. prof., asso. prof., 1925-44, prof., 1944-62, prof. emeritus, 1962—, acting chmn. dept. zoology, 1947-48, chmn., 1954-59; Fulbright lectr. Queen Mary's Coll. U. London, 1960-61, 67-68; Rose Morgan vis. prof. U. Kan., 1964. Co-founder, chmn. Bur. Biol. Research, 1936- 39; founder, dir. Serological Mus., 1948-62, dir. emeritus, 1971—, editor, 1948—. Served with U.S. Army, 1918. Recipient Distinguished Service citation Beloit Coll., 1970. Am. Cancer Soc. grantee, 1957-58, 58-59, NSF grantee, 1957-59. Fellow A.A.A.S., N.Y. Acad. Scis., N.Y. Zool. Soc.; mem. Soc. Exptl. Biology and Medicine, Am. Soc. Naturalists, Am. Assn. Immunologists, Am. Soc. Zoologists, Soc. Study Evolution, Genetics Soc. Am., Soc. Systematic Zoology, Soc. Study Devel. and Growth, Systematics Assn., English Speaking Union (pres. New Brunswick br. 1960-62), Rockingham Assn. Home: Redwood RD 1 Princeton NJ 08540 Office: Rutgers University New Brunswick NJ 08903

BOYDEN, ALLEN MARSTON, surgeon; b. Brookings, S.D., Oct. 31, 1908; s. Frank Edson and Maude Eva (Hegeman) B.; A.B., U. Ore., 1929; M.D., U. Mich., 1932, M.S. in Surgery, 1936; m. Margery French Davis, Sept. 19, 1936; children—Frank Davis, Allen Moore, Bradley Hunt. Surg. house officer Mass. Gen. Hosp., 1932-34; instr. surgery U. Mich. Med. Sch., 1934-37; practice medicine specializing in surgery, Astoria, Ore., 1937-42; head dept. gen. surgery Portland (Ore.) Clinic, 1948—; clin. instr. U. Ore. Med. Sch., 1946, clin. asso. surgery, 1946-51, asst. clin. prof. surgery, 1951-54, asso. clin. prof. surgery, 1954-66, clin. prof. surgery, 1966—; chief surg. service St. Vincent Hosp., 1955-58, 68-70, chief staff, 1964; mem. exec. com., trustee Ore. Physicians Service, 1954-66, v.p., 1959. Served from capt. to maj., M.C., AUS, 1942-45. Decorated Bronze Star medal. Diplomate Am. Bd. Surgery. Fellow A.M.A., A.C.S. (gov. 1948- 63, vice chmn. bd. govs. 1958-59, 2d v.p. 1960-61); mem. Am., Western, Pacific Coast, North Pacific surg. assns., Internat., Portland (pres. 1958-59) surg. socs., Frederick A. Coller Surg. Soc. (pres. 1955-58), Ore., Multonomah County med. socs. Portland Acad. Medicine (pres. 1965), Phi Beta Kappa, Alpha Omega Alpha, Phi Kappa Phi, Nu Sigma Nu, Kappa Sigma. Republican. Unitarian. Clubs: Racquet, Multnomah Athletic (Portland); Arlington, Flyfishers of Ore. Cons. editor Surgical Gynecology and Obstetrics, 1966—. Home: 4175 SW Greenleaf Dr Portland OR 97221

BOYDEN, DAVID DODGE, musicologist, educator; b. Westport, Conn., Dec. 10, 1910; s. George H. and Louise (Dodge) B.; A.B. magna cum laude, Harvard, 1932, A.M., 1938; postgrad. Columbia, 1935-36, Hartt Coll. Music, Hartford, Conn., 1936-37, Mus.D. (hon.), 1957; student piano with Paranoy, Harold Bauer, viola with Zunsser, Khuner; m. Ruth G. Quimby, Dec. 19, 1938; children—Thomas G., Richard P. Sheldon travelling fellow Harvard, 1932-33; tchr. Avon Old Farms, Avon, Conn., 1933-35; lectr. Mills Coll., 1938-39; instr. music U. Cal. at Berkeley, 1939-43, asst. prof., 1943-49, asso. prof., 1949- 55, prof., 1955—, chmn. dept., 1955-61; vis. prof. Cornell U., summer 1950; lectr. U. Mich., 1951, 56, U. Iowa, 1960. Mem. com. to revise A.B. degree Nat. Assn. Schs. Music, 1956—. Bd. dirs. Oakland Symphony, 1960-71. Guggenheim fellow, 1954-55, 67, 70-71; Fulbright research scholar Oxford U., 1963; humanities research fellow U. Cal., 1966-67. Mem. Am. Musicological Soc. (v.p., 1954-56, 60-62, exec. bd. 1954-62, 65-66), Coll. Music Assn., Internat. Musicological Soc., Royal Mus. Assn., Galpin Soc., Am. Assn. U. Profs., Music Library Assn., Phi Beta Kappa. Democrat. Clubs: California Music Executives (past v.p.); Sierra (San Francisco); Faculty, Kosmos (U. Cal.). Author: A Manual of Counterpoint, 2d edit., 1953; History and Literature of Music, 1948; Introduction to Music, 1956, 2d edit., 1970; The History of Violin Playing, 1965; Catalogue of The Hill Collection of Musical Instruments in The Ashmolean Museum, Oxford, 1969. Editor: Geminiani's The Art of Playing on the Violin (1751), 1952. Contbr. jours., quars., encys. Home: 1208 Shattuck Av Berkeley CA 94709

BOYDEN, LAURANCE ELBRIDGE, Jr., life ins. co. exec.; b. Evanston, Ill., June 17, 1931; s. Laurance E. and Helen (Lorch) B.; B.S. in Bus. Adminstrn. cum laude with honors, Miami U., Oxford, O., 1953; m. Phyllis Ruth Kopcha, May 14, 1955; children—David Laurance, Donald Philip, Patricia Lynn, James Harvey. Brokerage cons., then sr. brokerage cons. Conn. Gen. Life Ins. Co. Chgo., 1957-60; mgr. Continental Assurance Co., Boston, 1960-68; pres., chief exec. officer, dir. Mass. Gen. Life Ins. Co., Boston, 1968—; pres., dir. MGL Equity Sales, Inc.; dir. Harnessed Energies, Inc.; corporator Provident Instn. for Savs. Active United Fund; mem. exec. bd. Norumbega Council Boy Scouts Am. Mem. town council, Wellesley, Mass., 1967—. Served to 1st lt. AUS, 1954-57. Named Outstanding Young Man U.S. Jr. C. of C., 1966. Mem. Mass. Assn. Health Underwriters (charter, past pres.), Boston Life Underwriters, Young Pres.'s Orgn., New Eng. chpt. Estate and Bus. Planning Council, Sigma Alpha Epsilon (v.p. 1952), Delta Sigma Pi (pres. 1952), Alpha Epsilon Rho (v.p. 1951), Beta Gamma Sigma, Omicron Delta Kappa. Republican. Conglist. (deacon). Mason. Clubs: Fort Hill, Federal, Downtown Executives (Boston); Wellesley; Chebeaque Island (Me.) Yacht. Home: 20 Gilson Rd Wellesley Hills MA 02181 Office: 70 Federal St Boston MA 02110

BOYDEN, SIDNEY MILLARD, placement co. exec.; b. Cumberland, Wis., Apr. 4, 1900; s. William J. and Grace (Waterman) B.; B.A., U. Wis., 1923; m. Catherine Barry, Aug. 1, 1923. Personnel dir. Montgomery Ward & Co., Chgo., 1925- 41, Booz, Allen & Hamilton, Chgo., 1941-45; chmn. Boyden Assos., Inc., N.Y.C., 1946-, Boyden Indsl. Services, Inc., N.Y.C., 1954-, Boyden Internat., S.A., Geneva, Switzerland, 1961—, Boyden Far East Ltd., Hong Kong, 1965—, Boyden Latin Am. S.A. de C.V., Mexico City, 1965—, Boyden Australia Ltd., Sydney, 1966—, Boyden Internat. Ltd., London, 1966—. Mem. Phi Delta Theta. Club: Union League (N.Y.C.). Home: 51 Blueberry Lane Darien, CT 06820 Office: 260 Madison Av New York City NY 10016

BOYE, FREDERIC WILLIAM, Jr., army officer; b. Tex., Dec. 16, 1916; B.S., U.S. Mil. Acad., 1939; grad. Command and Gen. Staff Coll., Nat. War Coll. Brit. Staff Coll. Commd. 2d lt. U.S. Army, 1939, advanced through grades to maj. gen.; former chief legislative liason Dept. Army, chief personnel operations Dept. Army. Decorated D.S.M. with oak leaf cluster, Silver Star, Legion of Merit, Bronze Star, Commendation Ribbon with oak leaf cluster. Address: Royal Pines Ladys Island Beaufort SC 29902

BOYE, IBRAHIMA, Senegalese diplomat; b. St. Louis, Senegal (formerly French Africa), Mar. 29, 1924; s. Amadou Abdoulaye and Mareme (Sene) B.; ed. Ecole Speciale Militaire de St. Cyr, Algeria, U. Montpellier (France); license as Bachelor of laws; m. Marie-Anne Cisse, Oct. 1, 1948; children—Lamine, Soukeyna, Mareme, Amadou, Sokhna, Aminata, Tidiane. Practice law, Nimes, France and Montpellier, prior to 1950; French judge in Guinea and Dahomey, also pres. (French) Colonial Ct. Appeal, Dahomey, 1950-55; justice of peace, Abidjan, Ivory Coast, 1955-60; councillor, dir. Ministry Justice Senegalese Govt., 1960-61, atty. gen., 1961—; joined Senegalese Fgn. Service, 1968; ambassador of Senegal to UN, 1968—, also mem. Security Council, pres. Human Rights Commn., 1968—. Speaker 1st Congress African Jurists, Lagos, Nigeria, 1964; travel and research legislative systems U.S., Europe, Far East, other African countries. Named Hon. Citizen Miami Beach, Fla., 1963. Rotarian (pres. 1965-66). Home: 46 E 66th St New York City NY 10021. Office: Senegalese Embassy 51 E 42d St New York City NY 10017

BOYER, BENJAMIN FRANKLIN, educator, lawyer; b. St. Joseph, Mo., Sept. 17, 1904; s. John Sidney and Ruby (Hale) B.; student U. of Va., 1922-24; A.B., U. of Mo., 1926, J.D., 1928; LL.M., Columbia, 1941; LL.D., Waynesburg Coll., 1952, Dickinson Sch. Law, Carlisle, Pa., 1959; m. Marion L. Lehr, Oct. 20, 1928; 1 dau., Judith Ann (dec.). Admitted to Mo. Bar, 1928, U.S. Dist. Ct. for E. Dist. Pa., 1947, Pa. bar, 1950; asst. atty., Mo. State Highway Commn., 1928-33; mem. firm Otto & Boyer, Washington, Mo., 1933-37; faculty Sch. Law, U. of Kansas City, 1937-47, asso. prof. of law, 1937-42, prof. law, 1942-47, asst. to dean, Sch. of Law, 1938-39, chmn. law faculty, 1939-40, dean, Sch. of Law, 1940-47; dean and prof. law, Temple U. Sch. Law, Phila., 1947-65, prof., 1965-69; prof. U. Cal. at Hastings Coll. Law, 1969—. Commd. 2d lt., Inf. Res., U.S. Army, Feb. 1927; apptd. lt. col., in Inf., May 1943; col. 1945; active duty under Res. Commn., 1941-46; instr. Commd. and Gen. Staff Sch. at Fort Leavenworth, Kan., Nov. 1942- Dec. 1945; comdt. Phila. O.R.C. Sch., 1950-51. Recipient Arthur von Briesen medal Nat. Legal Aid and Defender Assn., 1968. Alternate mem. regional enforcement commn. W.S.B., 1952. Bd. curators, Lincoln U. of Mo., Jefferson City, 1939-44; bd. advisers Pa. Tax Inst., 1948-61. Mem. Mo. Supreme Ct. Com. on Civil Procedure, and of sub-com. on Suggestion and Plan, 1939-41; chmn. Personnel (Civil Service) Bd. of Kansas City, 1946-47; mem. Health and Welfare Council Phila., 1964-69, Commn. on Standards and Accreditation of Services for the Blind; mem. Nat. Accreditation Council of Agys. Serving the Blind and Visually Handicapped; mem. Pa. Gov.'s Commn. on Labor Legislation, 1953-54; bd. dirs. Legal Aid Soc. Phila., 1954-69, pres., 1960-69; council mem. Phila. Medico-Legal Inst., 1955-69. Mem. Am., Mo., Pa., Kansas City, Phila., San Francisco bar assns., Nat. Academy of Arbitrators, American Arbitration Assn. (vol. panel), Lawyers Assn. Kansas City, Phi Beta Kappa Associates, Order of Coif, Phi Delta Phi, Alpha Pi Zeta, Sigma Nu, Phi Beta Kappa. Mason (Shriner). Clubs: Germantown Cricket (Phila.); Socialegal, Constitutional, Union League. Editor: (with others) Selected Readings on the Legal Profession, 1962; Materials on Professional Responsibilities of the Legal Profession, 1967. Home: 3801 McMichael St Philadelphia PA 19129 Address: U Cal Hastings Coll of Law 198 McAllister St San Francisco CA 94102

BOYER, CHARLES, actor; b. Figeac, France, Aug. 28, 1899; m. Pat Paterson; 1 son, Michael (dec.). Made stage debut in Paris; appeared on legitimate stage in N.Y.C. and on tour, with First Drama Quartet, in Don Juan in Hell, Lord Pengo, 1962, Man and Boy, 1963; appeared on T.V. in Four Star Playhouse; T.V. series The Rogues, 1964—; appeared in numerous films, including Back Street, Hold Back the Dawn, The Constant Nymph, Gas Light, Cluny Brown, The Happy Time, Thunder in the Ear, Earrings of Madame De, 1954, Around the World in 80 Days, 1956, Fanny, 1961, Is Paris Burning?, 1966, Casino Royale, 1967. Founder, 1940, pres. French Research Found. (non-profit orgn. to provide research and French library facilities); past pres. Beverly Hills chpt. Am. Friends of France, Hollywood chpt. French War Relief. Named chevalier Legion d'Honneur; recipient Della Austria medal for performance in Lord Pengo, 1963. Address: 451 LaClenega Blvd Los Angeles CA 90028

BOYER, DAVID CREIGHTON, stock broker; b. Wilmington, Del., Oct. 1, 1930; s. John Walter and Eva (Hammond) B.; B.A. magna cum laude, Princeton, 1952; m. Lydia Richards, June 3, 1953; children—Margaret Selfridge, Amy Richards, David Creighton. Asst. sec. Wilmington Trust Co., 1956-61; with Laird, Bissell & Meeds, Inc., Wilmington, 1961—, partner, v.p., 1965-69, exec. v.p., 1969-70, pres., 1970—. Pres. Active Young Republicans, New Castle County, 1958. Pres. Tower Hill Sch. Home and Sch. Assn.; bd. dirs. Child Guidance Center, Opportunity Center, Childrens Home. Served to lt. (j.g.) USNR, 1952-56. Baptist. Clubs: Wilmington, Wilmington Country, Vicmead Hunt (Wilmington); Cap and Gown (Princeton, N.J.); Bankers Princeton (N.Y.C.). Home: 2315 Ridgeway Rd Wilmington DE 19805 Office: Laird Bissell & Meeds Inc Bank of Del Bldg Wilmington DE 19899

BOYER, ERNEST LEROY, univ. chancellor; b. Dayton, O., Sept. 13, 1928; s. Clarence and Ethel (Franch) B.; A.B., Greenville Coll., 1950; M.A., U. So. Cal., 1955, Ph.D., 1957, LL.D., 1971; postdoctorate student U. Ia. Hosp., 1960; Litt.D., Chapman Coll., 1971; L.H.D., Dowling Coll., 1971; m. Kathryn Tyson, Aug. 26, 1950; children—Ernest Lerot, Beverly, Craig, Stephen. Mem. faculty Upland (Cal.) Coll., 1951-54, 56-60, asst. prof. speech, chmn. dept., 1953-54, dean instr., prof. speech pathology, 1956-60; teaching asst. U. So. Cal., 1953-55; asst. prof. speech, dir. forensics Loyola U., Los Angeles, 1955-56; dir. commn. to improve edn. tchrs. Western Coll. Assn., 1960-62; dir. Center Coordinated Edn., U. Cal. at Santa Barbara, 1962-65; exec. dean univ. wide activities State U. N.Y., 1965-67, vice chancellor, 1968-70, chancellor, 1970—; vis. fellow Batelle Research Center, Seattle, 1969. Mem. adv. com. Inst. Coll. and Univ. Adminstrs., Am. Council Edn., 1970; gen. chmn. Inst. Man and Sci. Chmn. bd. dirs. Research Found. State U. N.Y.; chmn. trustees State U. Constrn. Fund; bd. dirs. Blue Cross Northeastern N.Y., Saratoga Performing Arts Center, N.Y. Higher Edn. Assistance Corp., Dormitory Authority N.Y. Mem. Am. Speech and Hearing Assn., Pi Kappa Delta, Alpha Kappa Sigma. Mem. Soc. Friends. Club: University (Albany). Home: 40 Marion Av Albany NY 12203

BOYER, FRANCIS, pharm. mfg. co. exec.; b. Penllyn, Pa., June 21, 1893; s. Henry Conover and Nathalie C. (Robinson) B.; grad. Groton Sch., 1912, Harvard, 1912-15, Cambridge (Eng.) U., 1919; LL.D., Hahnemann Med. Coll., 1956, U. Pa., 1961; D.Sc., Trinity Coll., 1961; L.H.D., Jefferson Med. Coll., 1965, Pa. Mil. Coll., 1966, Phila. Coll. Pharmacy and Sci., 1967; m. Marion Angell Godfrey, July 6, 1950; children by previous marriage—Markley Holmes, Mary Robinson (Mrs. Hambro). With circulation dept. Curtis Pub. Co., 1915; with advt. dept. Phila. Pub. Ledger, 1916; with Smith Kline & French Labs., pharm. mfrs., Phila., 1919—, became asst. to pres., 1926, exec. v.p., 1936, pres., 1951, chmn. bd., 1958-66, dir., 1966-70, now chmn. emeritus. Former mem. nat. adv. com. Arthritis and Metabolic Diseases Council. Bd. dirs. Phila. Contributionship, Project Hope, 1958-61; bd. advisers Nat. Fund for Med. Edn.; bd. mgrs. Wistar Inst. Anatomy and Biology; bd. overseers Harvard, 1958-64, mem. overseers com. to visit Peabody Mus. and dept. anthropology, 1966—; pres. Royal Soc. Med. Found., 1967-71; bd. dirs. University City Sci. Center, 1968— Acad. Natural Scis., 1971—; asso. trustee U. Pa., 1960—. Served as 1st lt. F.A., U.S. Army, 1917-19. Fellow Royal Soc. Medicine London (hon.); mem. Pharm. Mfrs. Assn. (dir. 1958-65), Phi Beta Kappa. Clubs: Philadelphia, Harvard (Phila.). Contbr. articles to profl. jours. Home: Mill Creek Rd Ardmore PA 19003 Office: 1500 Spring Garden St Philadelphia PA 19101

BOYER, HAROLD EDWIN, oral surgeon, educator; b. Esterly, Pa., Aug. 9, 1925; s. Floyd and Anna (Snyder) B.; student Lebanon Valley Coll., 1946-48; D.D.S., U. Pa., 1952, M.Sc., 1958; m. E. Kathryn Rhoads, Aug. 11, 1948; children—Bonnie Kay, Brian Keith. Intern U. Pa. Hosp., 1952-53; resident oral surgery Jackson Meml. Hosp., Miami, Fla., 1954-56; faculty U. Louisville Sch. Dentistry, 1956—, chmn. dept. oral surgery, 1957—, prof. oral surgery, 1959—, asso. dean sch., 1966-67, dean elect Sch. Dentistry, 1967-69, dean, 1969—; chief oral surgery Louisville Gen. Hosp. and Childrens Hosp., 1956—; cons. Louisville VA Hosp., USPHS. Served wth inf., AUS, 1943-46. Diplomate Am. Bd. Oral Surgery (dir.). Fellow Am. Coll. Dentists, Internat. Coll. Dentists; mem. Am. Soc. Oral Surgery, Southeastern Soc. Oral Surgeons, Am. Dental Soc. Anesthesiology, Am. Dental Assn., Omicron Kappa Upsilon, Psi Omega. Presbyn. Editorial cons. Jour. Ky. Dental Assn. Contbr. articles to profl. jours. Home: 3106 Townsend Terrace Louisville KY 40222

BOYER, HAROLD WILLIAM, clergyman; b. Melvern, Kan., Sept. 27, 1908; s. William R. and Nellie R. (Lane) B.; student Anderson Coll. and Theol. Sem., 1934-36, D.D. (hon.), 1963; m. Mary T. Tolar, Aug. 21, 1934; 1 dau., Janice M. Ordained to ministry Ch. of God, 1937; pastor, Indpls., 1938-44, St. Louis, 1944-54, First Ch. of God, Springfield, O., 1954—. Chmn. gen. ministerial assembly Ch. of God, 1955-68, mem. exec. com. and council, former mem. ch. service com., com. Christian higher edn., missionary bd. Active juvenile ct., Indpls., 1938- 44; v.p. Met. Ch. Fedn., St. Louis, 1947-53, chmn. reformation commn., 1949; former mem. Weekday Religious Edn. Commn., St. Louis; missionary tour to B.W.I., 1956. Recipient award of honor Anderson Coll. and Theol. Sem. Author: The Way of Love, 1955; The Historic Trace of the Church, 1957; The Apostolic Church and the Apostasy, 1960; Beyond Damascus Road, 1966; Gifts of the Spirit; Thirty Day Discipline Toward Understanding Peace of Mind, 1970. Contbg. editor Christianity. Home: 1754 Maiden Lane Springfield OH 45504 Office: 1201 Maiden Lane Springfield OH 45504

BOYER, JOSEPH HENRY, chemist, educator; b. New Washington, Ind., Jan. 4, 1922; s. Omer C. and Mary (Fairchild) B.; A.B., Hanover Coll., 1942; Ph.D., U. Ill., 1950. Asst. prof., asso. prof. Tulane U., 1953-60; program adminstr. Petroleum Research Fund, Am. Chem. Soc., Washington, 1961-66; prof. chemistry U. Ill., Chgo. Circle Campus, 1966—; cons. Monsanto Chem. Co., 1957-60; research asso. Catholic U., Washington, 1964-66. Served from ensign to lt., USNR, 1943-46. Recipient Alumni award Hanover Coll., 1964. Fellow N.Y. Acad. Sci., A.A.A.S.; mem. Am. Chem. Soc. Republican. Presbyn. Contbr. articles profl. jours. Home: 910 N Lake Shore Dr Chicago IL 60611

BOYER, PERRY FRANCIS, educator; b. Gatesville, Tex., June 5, 1907; s. Perry Franklin and Alice (Davidson) B.; A.B., Baylor U., 1927; M.B.A., U. Tex., 1935, Ph.D., 1940; m. Carra Leon Davis, Apr. 3, 1928; children—Frances Ozelia, Cecelia Ann. High sch. tchr., 1928-34; prin. elementary sch., Mexia, Tex., 1934-37; prin. jr. high sch., Huntsville, Tex., 1937; asst. prof. Tex. State Coll. for Women, 1938-39, asso. prof., 1940-42; tutor U. Tex., 1939- 40; asso. prof. La. State U., 1942-47, asst. dir., bur. bus. research, 1946-47, prof., 1947—, dir. div. research, 1948-69, head dept. bus. finance and statistics, 1961-70. Mem. Assn. U. Burs. Bus. and Econ. Research (pres. 1953-54), Southwestern Social Sci. Assn. (pres. 1954-55), Omicron Delta Kappa, Phi Kappa Phi, Beta Gamma Sigma, Pi Gamma Mu, Alpha Chi, Delta Sigma Pi. Baptist. Rotarian. Editor: La. Bus. Rev., 1946-69. Home: 2053 Hood Av Baton Rouge LA 70808

BOYER, ROBERT ALLEN, educator; b. Hummels Wharf, Pa., Aug. 27, 1916; s. H. Alvin and Jennie (Saurers) B.; A.B. summa cum laude Susquehanna U., 1938; M.A., Syracuse U., 1940; Ph.D., Lehigh U., 1952; m. Eleanor Rae Moyer, June 24, 1939; children—Patty Rae (Mrs. William H. Hinkle), Stephen C. Instr. physics Clarkson Coll. Tech., 1940-41; instr. physics, acting dept. head Muhlenberg Coll., 1941-52, prof. physics, head dept., 1952—; vis. prof. summer grad. sch. Conn. Wesleyan U., 1963-70. Mem. Am. Assn. Physics Tchrs.

(pres. Central Pa. sect. 1956-57), Acoust. Soc. Am., Am. Assn. U. Profs. Lutheran (lay speaker Eastern Pa. Synod 1969-70, v.p. 1958-60, 68, 71). Home: 20 Beverly Dr Allentown PA 18104

BOYER, WILLIS BOOTHE, bus. exec.; b. Pitts., Feb. 3, 1915; s. Pearce F. and Sarah Hester (Boothe) B.; student Mercersburg Acad., 1934-35, Lafayette Coll., 1935- 37, Case Inst. Cleve. Coll., 1937-42; advanced mgmt. tng. Harvard, 1951; D.H.L. (hon.), Lafayette Coll., 1965; m. Esther Greenwood, June 25, 1938; children—Willis Boothe, Jonathan Greenwood, Paul Christopher. With Republic Steel Corp., Cleve., 1937—, asst. to treas., 1946-51, asst. treas., 1951-53, treas., 1953-60, v.p., treas., 1960-63, v.p. finance, 1963, v.p. finance and adminstrn., 1963-66, dir., 1963-66, exec. v.p., 1966-68, pres., 1968—; dir. Sherwin-Williams Co. Nat. City Bank of Cleve., Weatherhead Co., Procter & Gamble Co., Marathon Oil Co. Trustee U. Hosps. of Case Western Res. U.; trustee, v.p. Bluecoats, Inc. Mem. Am. Iron and Steel Inst., Conf. Bd. (vice chmn.), Chi Phi. Clubs: Union, Kirtland Country, Pepper Pike Country, Tavern (Cleve.); Laurel Valley, Rolling Rock (Ligonier, Pa.); Pine Valley Golf (Clementon, N.J.); Augusta (Ga.) National; Links (N.Y.). Home: 22150 McCauley Rd Shaker Heights OH 44122 Office: Republic Bldg P O Box 6778 Cleveland OH 44101

BOYES, JOHN WALLACE, educator, geneticist; b. Sunridge, Ont., Can., Jan. 27, 1907; s. Richard Edward and Orinda Parney Benton (Louden) B.; B.Sc., U. Sask., 1933, M.Sc., 1936; Ph.D., U. Wis., 1939; m. Beatrice Chamberlain Westcott, Aug. 28, 1937; children—Philip Westcott, Barbara Grace (Mrs. Barrie Wilson), Alan Ramsay, Margaret Ruth. Jr. research asst. Nat. Research Council Can., 1939-40; asst. prof. U. Alta., 1940-42; powder foreman Villeray Works, Montreal, Que., Can., 1942-43; research engr. Ont. Paper Co., 1943- 45; mem. faculty McGill U., Montreal, 1945—, chmn. dept. genetics, 1945-69, John and Anne Molson prof. genetics, 1955. Pres. genetics sect. Internat. Union Biol. Scis., 1958-63, Internat. Commn. Genetic Nomenclature, 1963- -; v.p. XI Internat. Congress Genetics, The Hague, 1963. Recipient Silver medal Czechoslovak Acad. Scis., 1965. Mem. Agrl. Inst. Can., Bot. Soc. Am., Am. Genetic Assn., genetics socs. Am. (v.p. 1958), Can. (Eastern dir. 1960-61; mem. editorial bd. jour. 1961-65, pres. 1968-69), Internat. Genetics Fedn. (sec. 1968—), Entomol. Soc. Can., genetical socs. Gt. Britain, Japan (hon.), Yugoslavia (hon.), Internat. Soc. Plant Morchology, Am. Soc. Human Genetics, Genetical Soc. New Zealand, Soc. Study Evolution, Canadian Soc. Cell Biology. Author papers on plant embryology in plumbaginaceae, red clover and wheat, cytology and cytotaxonomy of diptera. Home: 484 Strathcona Av Montreal 217 Quebec Canada

BOYKAN, MARTIN, composer; b. N.Y.C., Apr. 12, 1931; s. Joseph and Matilda (Caspe) B.; A.B. summa cum laude, Harvard, 1951; student U. Zurich (Switzerland), 1951-52; M.Mus., Yale, 1953; m. Constance Berke, June 23, 1963; children—Rachel, Deborah. Asst. prof. music Brandeis U., Waltham, Mass., 1964-67, asso. prof. music, 1967—. Mem. Phi Beta Kappa. Composer: String Quartets, 1949, 65; Flute Sonata, 1950; Violin Duo, 1951; Flute Quintet, 1953; Psalm, 1958; Prelude for Organ, 1959; Chamber Concerto, 1971. Author articles. Home: 155 Sumner St Newton Center MA 02159 Office: Brandeis Univ Waltham MA 02154

BOYKIN, EDWARD MCCALLUM, mgmt. cons.; b. Ft. Worth, July 24, 1913; s. James Edward and Daisy (McCallum) B.; B.S., Carnegie Inst. Tech., 1938; grad. Exec. Program U. Cal. at Los Angeles, 1957; m. Teresa Ibarra, Dec. 24, 1938; children—Noel Edward, Grant McCallum, Craig Alexander. Elec. maintenance supr. San Jose Sugar Co., Prov. de Santa Clara, Cuba, 1932-34; prodn. control and efficiency engr. Beveridge Paper Co., 1938; asst. to supt. distbn. Tex. Electric Service Co., 1938-40; contract relations rep. Metro-Goldwyn Mayer and Paramount for Western Electic Co., 1946-49; mgr. field engring. Hughes Aircraft Co., Culver City, Cal., 1949-53, dir. field service and support div., 1953-56, v.p., mem. policy bd., 1956-69; mgmt. cons., Pacific Palisades, Cal., 1969—. Served to lt. col. USAAF, 1940-45. Mem. I.E.E.E. (sr.), Sigma Xi, Tau Beta Pi, Phi Kappa Phi, Kappa Sigma. Club: Grand Lake (Colo.) Yacht. Address: 14940 Alva Dr Pacific Palisades CA 90272

BOYKIN, ELIZABETH MACRAE, (Mrs. Charles A. Wells), writer, editor; b. Dallas, Feb. 9, 1903; d. Charles Stuart and Kate Pearl (Davis) B.; Ph.B., U. Chgo., 1924; student Chgo. Art Inst., 1925- 26, Columbia Grad. Sch., 1928; m. Charles Arthur Wells; 1 son, Charles Arthur. Reporter, feature and fiction writer for Tex. and Chgo. papers, 1923-28; contbr. articles and fiction to nat. mags.; writer for N.Y. Sun, and author syndicated daily newspaper column, 1935-45; now asst. editor newsletter, Between The Lines, Princeton, N.J. Bd. dirs. George Sch., Friends Jour., Welcome House. Mem. Soc. of Friends. Clubs: N.Y. Newspaper Womans; D.A.R. Home: Echo Farm Washington Crossing PA 18977 Office: 7 Patton Av Princeton NJ 08540

BOYKIN, ROBERT HEATH, banker; b. Carlsbad, N.M., Jan. 10, 1926; s. Calvin Clay and Rubye (Heath) B.; B.B.A., U. Tex., 1950, LL.B., 1953; student Park Coll., 1943-44; spl. courses La. State U., Tex. A. and M. Coll., Am. Mgmt. Assn.; m. Camille Inkman, Nov. 26, 1948; 1 son, Robert Heath. Admitted to Tex. bar, 1952; tabulating supr. Tex. Edn. Agy., 1948-52; with Fed. Res. Bank of Dallas, 1953—, asst. counsel, 1959-61, asst. sec. bd., 1961-65, asst. v.p., asst. sec. bd., 1965-68, v.p., sec. bd., 1968-70, sr. v.p., sec. bd., 1971—. Sec. Conf. Pres.'s of Fed. Res. Banks, 1963-64; instr. negotiable instruments Dallas chpt. Am. Inst. Banking, 1959-61. Served as lt. (j.g.), USNR, 1943-47. Mem. Tex. Bar Assn., Tex. Bankers Assn., Delta Tau Delta, Phi Alpha Delta. Independent. Methodist. Clubs: Lions, Preston Hills Golf (Dallas). Home: 3837 Northwest Pkwy Dallas TX 75225 Office: 400 S Akard St Dallas TX 75222

BOYKIN, SAM MARKS, Jr., iron co. exec.; b. Montgomery, Ala., Feb. 17, 1928; s. Sam Marks and Mary Elizabeth (Julian) B.; B.S., Washington and Lee U., 1949; m. Elesabeth Ingalls, Apr. 4, 1956; children—Robert Ingalls, Sam Marks III. Pres., Indsl. Steel Co., Birmingham, Ala., 1959-62; pres., chmn. bd. Ingalls Iron Works Co., Birmingham, 1962—; dir. Exchange- Security Bank, Birmingham, First State Bank of Decatur (Ala.). Trustee Elesebeth and Barbara Ingalls Found., Eye Found. Hosp., Ingalls Found., St. Vincent's Hosp. Lay Adv. Bd., Birmingham. Mem. Am. Inst. Steel Constrn. (dir.), Steel Plate Fabricators Assn. (dir.), Birmingham C. of C. Clubs: Birmingham Country, Mountain Brook, Club, Relay House, Downtown (Birmingham); Leash (N.Y.C.); Duquesne (Pitts.); Cat Cay (Bahamas). Home: 3805 Forest Glen Dr Birmingham AL 35213 Office: PO Box 2527 Birmingham AL 35202

BOYKIN, SAMUEL, govt. official; b. Montgomery, Ala., July 2, 1905; s. Hamilton Smith and Annie May (Howe) B.; ed. Clason Mil. Acad., 1919-22; B.S., U. Pa., 1926; m. Alice Beard Haight, Oct. 10, 1931; children—Allison (Mrs. James Parsons), Hamilton. Ins. investigator Retail Credit Co., N.Y.C., 1926-28; credit investigator Bank of Am. N.Y.C. 1928-31; credit officer Nat. City Bank of N.Y., 1931-41; asst. to dir. priorities, OPM, Washington, 1941; asst. to Lend Lease Adminstr. and acting dir. Missions Div., Lend Lease and Fgn. Econ. Adminstrn., 1941-44; exec. officer Office Deptl. Adminstrn., State Dept 1944-45, exec. officer and spl. asst. to dir. Office of Spl. Polit. Affairs, 1945, dep. exec. dir. and dir. Control Div., Office Fgn. Liquidation Commn., 1946-47, spl. asst. to asst. sec. of state for adminstrn., 1947-48, dir. Office Controls, 1948-49, dir. Office Consular Affairs, 1949; spl. asst. Office Operating Facilities, 1953; chief division of Biographic Information, 1954; Am. consul gen., Capetown, South Africa, 1957-62; fgn. service insp. Dept. State, 1962-64, dir. profl. placement service, 1964—. Spl. asst. to sec. gen. UN Conf. on Internat. Orgns., San Francisco, Apr.-June 1945; Inter-Am. Conf. on War and Peace, Mexico City, Feb. 1945; Conf. Prep. Commn., UN, London, Eng., Jan.-Feb. 1946, spl. asst. to U.S. rep. to UN, 1945-46. Mem. Fgn. Service Assn. Club: Internat. (Washington). Home: 9139 Sligo Creek Pkwy Silver Spring, MD 20901 Office: Dept of State Washington 25 DC 20525

BOYKIN, WILLIAM ANCRUM, Jr., beverage co. exec.; b. Atlanta, Sept. 29, 1906; s. William Ancrum and Annie (Smith) B.; LL.B., U. Ga., 1927; postgrad. Columbia, 1927-28. Admitted to Ga. bar, 1927; with Coca-Cola Co., Atlanta, 1928-, asst. treas., 1959-63, treas., 1963—; v.p., dir. Coca-Cola Internat. Corp., 1947—. Mem. Am. Bar Assn. Home: 3921 Beechwood Dr NW Atlanta, GA 30327 Office: 310 North Av NW Atlanta GA 30313

BOYKO, EDGAR PAUL, lawyer; b. Vienna, Austria, Oct. 19, 1918; s. Myron David and Florence (Ostiller) B.; student U. Vienna, 1936-38, U. St. Andrew (Scotland), 1936-40; LL.B. with honors, U. Md., 1945; LL.M., George Washington U., 1948; m. Blanche Kohn, Apr. 10, 1940; children—David, Steven. Research and devel. chemist, 1940-43; admitted to Md. bar, 1946, D.C. bar, 1948, Alaska bar, 1953, Cal. bar, 1958; practiced in Balt., 1946, 48-51, Washington, 1948-51, Anchorage, 1953-57; atty. Bur. Land Mgmt., Dept. Interior, 1946-48; br. chief counsel OPS, 1951-52; regional chief counsel Bur. Land Mgmt. Dept. Interior, Alaska, 1952-53; atty. Tidewater Oil Co., world hdqrs., 1958-59; partner firm Richards, Watson & Hemmerling, Los Angeles, 1959-64; sr. partner firm Boyko & Simmons, 1964—, Boyko & Richey, Anchorage, 1968—; atty. gen. State of Alaska, 1967-68, spl. chief trial counsel, 1968—; dir. Beverly Hills Fed. Savs. & Loan Assn.; counsel firm McCracken & Collins, Washington. Alaska rep. Am. Bar Assn. Regional Conf. World Peace Through Law, San Francisco, 1959; del. Cal. State Bar Conf., 1961-63; mem. com. on admiralty rules Dist. Alaska, 1954-57. Charter mem. Operation Statehood, dir., 1953-55. Mem. divisional com. Democratic Party Alaska, 1955-57, del. territorial conv., 1954, 56, chmn. platform com., 1956; chmn. 63d assembly dist. Dem. Council, Cal., 1961-63, chmn. 31st congl. dist. Fellow Alaska Acad. Trial Lawyers; mem. Am., Cal. trial lawyers assns., Am., Md.; D.C., Fed. (v.p. Los Angeles chpt. 1964-66), Alaska, Cal. (trial examiner), Anchorage, Los Angeles bar assns., Am. Arbitration Assn. (nat. panel arbitrators), U. Md., U. George Washington alumni assns., Order of Coif. Unitarian. Clubs: Angeles Mesa Democratic (past pres.), Los Angeles Lawyers (past chmn. civil law and procedure com.), Rotary, Los Angeles Athletic; Alaska Press (past gov.). Office: Suite 910 Global Marine House 811 W 7th St Los Angeles CA 90017 also Tyonek Bldg 428 W 4th Av Anchorage AK 99501 also 1000 Connecticut Av NW Washington DC 20036

BOYLAN, DAVID RAY, educator, chem. engr., b. Belleville, Kan., July 22, 1922; s. David Ray and Mabel (Jones) B.; B.S. in Chem. Engring., U. Kan., 1943; Ph.D., Ia. State U., 1952; m. Juanita R. Sheridan, Mar. 24, 1944; children—Sharon Rae, Gerald Ray, Elizabeth Anne, Lisa Dianne. Instr., U. Kan., 1942-43; project engr. Gen. Chem. Co., Camden, N.J., 1943-47; sr. engr. Am. Cyanamid Co., Elizabeth, N.J., 1947; plant mgr. Arlin Chem. Co., Elizabeth, 1947-48; faculty Ia. State U., Ames, 1948—, prof. chem. engring., 1956—, asso. dir. Engring. Expt. Sta., 1959—, dir. Engring. Research Inst., 1966—. Mem. Am. Chem. Soc., Am. Soc. Engring. Edn., Am. Inst. Chem. Engrs., Sigma Xi, Phi Lambda Upsilon, Sigma Tau, Phi Kappa Phi, Tau Beta Pi. Research in transient behavior and flow of fluids through porous media, unsteady state and fertilizer tech., devel. fused- phosphate fertilizer processes, theoretical and exptl. correlation of filtration; patents and papers in field. Home: 1516 Stafford St Ames IA 50010

BOYLAN, EMMETT B., banker; b. Tarrytown, N.Y., Feb. 16, 1931; s. Patrick Joseph and Jane (Behan) B.; B.S., U. Rochester; m. Sylvia Guzecki, Jan. 18, 1958; 1 dau., Ann Cecelia. Corp. sec., comml. v.p. Marine Midland Trust Co., Rochester. Mem. Robert Morris Assos. Home: 180 Greenvale Dr Rochester NY 14618 Office: 19 Main St Rochester NY 14614

BOYLAN, GEORGE SYLVESTER, Jr., air force officer; b. Wilmington, N.C., Dec. 3, 1919; s. George S. and Lucy (McIntosh) B.; B.S., U. N.C., 1950; postgrad. George Washington U., 1962; m. Louse Worth Washburn, Jan. 25, 1945; children-George Worth, Louise Washburn. Commd. 2d lt. USAAF, 1941, advanced through grades to lt. gen. USAF, 1969; squadron comdr. 8th AF, Eng., 1943-44; with 1st Air Force, Air Def. Command, 1945-48, Hdqrs. USAF, 1950; comdr. 1502 Air Transport Group, 1955-58; Hdqrs., USAF, 1958-64; comdr. U.S. Forces Azores, 1946-65; with Hdqrs. Mil. Airlift Command, 1965-68; dep. chief staff programs and resources Hdqrs. USAF, Washington, 1968—. Decorated D.S.M., Legion of Merit, D.F.C., Air medal. Home: 71 Westover Av Bolling AFB Washington DC 20332 Office: Hdqrs USAF/PR Pentagon Washington DC 20330

BOYLAN, GERALD MICHAEL, cosmetics mfg. co. exec.; b. N.Y.C., Dec. 27, 1936; s. Cornelius J. and Catherine (Trainor) B.; B.B.A., Manhattan Coll., 1959; m. Jacqueline L. Ruark, Aug. 13, 1960; children—Leslie, Paige, Kristen. Sr. auditor Arthur Andersen, Hartford, Conn., 1959-63; corp. accounting mgr. Combustion Engring., Windsor, Conn., 1963-67; accounting dir. Olin Mathieson, New Haven, 1967-68; controller Luhrs div. Bangor Punta, Marlboro, N.J., 1968-70, Alberto Culver, Melrose Park, Ill., 1970—; eve. prof. U. Hartford, 1965-68. Mem. Am. Inst. C.P.A.'s. Home: 1404 Lake Shore Dr Barrington IL 60010 Office: 2525 W Armitage St Melrose Park IL 60160

BOYLAN, J. EDWARD, bank exec. Sr. v.p. Howard Savs. Instn., Newark. Office: 768 Broad St Newark NJ 07101*

BOYLAN, JOHN RICHARD, banker; b. New Rochelle, N.Y., June 25, 1928; s. James Owen and Ethel (King) B.; A.B., Johns Hopkins U., 1950; exchange student, U. Oslo (Norway), 1947; postgrad. Stonier Sch. Banking, 1961; m. Hildegrade W. Scheffler, Apr.14, 1956; children—Cynthia Ann, James Richard. Statistician Reynolds & Co., Phila., 1951-54; with Provident Nat. Bank, Phila., 1954—, sr. v.p., 1968—; dir. The Tatnall Corp., Valley Forge, Pa. Home: Saw Mill Rd Newton Square PA 19073 Office: 1632 Chestnut St Philadelphia PA 19101

BOYLAN, LAURENCE CHARLES, coll. dean; b. Rochester, N.Y., Nov. 26, 1908; s. Frank and Kathryn (Sturdivant) B.; A.B., Allegheny Coll., 1932; M.A., Cornell U., 1946, Ph.D., 1952; m. Elizabeth Eldridge, Apr. 20, 1946. Counselor Guidance Center, Cornell U., 1946-47, instr. student personnel summer schs., 1949-53; dir. student personnel Gloversville (N.Y.) pub. schs., 1947-54; dir. student services Kan. State Tchrs. Coll., Emporia, 1954-57, dean grad. sch., 1957—, also interim pres., 1966-67; cons. to Southwest Minn. State Coll., Marshall, 1965-71. Mem. evaluation, accreditation com. Council Grad. Schs. U.S., 1968-70. Served with Inf., AUS, 1943-45. Decorated Purple Heart. Mem. Am. Psychol. Assn., S.W., Am. psychol. assns., Blue Key, Phi Delta Kappa, Phi Kappa Psi. Conglist. Home: 1402 Exchange Ct Emporia KS 66801

BOYLE, ANDREW JACKSON, former army officer; b. Braddock, Pa., Dec. 11, 1911; s. Elmer Newton and Monica (Shaffer) B.; B.S., U.S. Mil. Acad., 1935; grad. Command and Gen. Staff Coll., 1943, Brit. Staff Coll., 1943, Army War Coll., 1954; postgrad. U. Kan., 1952, Am. U., 1953; m. Elaine White, Sept. 1, 1936; 1 son, Andrew Jackson. Commd. 2d lt. U.S. Army, 1935, advanced through grades to lt. gen., 1965; chief Mil. Assistance Group, Laos, 1961-62; chief operations officer U.S. Army, Pacific, 1962-63; comdg. gen. 25th Inf. Div., 1963-64, Fort Knox, Ky., 1964-65, I Corps, Korea, 1965-67, V Corps Germany, 1967-69; U.S. mil. rep. CENTO, 1969-70, ret., 1970. Mem. nat. council Boy Scouts Am. Decorated D.S.M., Legion of Merit with 4 oak leaf clusters; Norwegian Cross; Croix de Guerre, Order of Leopold (Belgium). Rotarian. Home: Allaway Farm Mitchells VA 22729

BOYLE, ANDREW JOSEPH, univ. prof.; b. Cannanea, Mex., Dec. 21, 1906; s. Andrew Joseph and Rose Theresa (O'Donnell) B.; B.S., U. Notre Dame, 1928, M.S., 1929; Ph.D., 1931; m. Mary Agnes Harris, June 22, 1935; children—Kathleen, Andrew. Asst. in chemistry U. Notre Dame (Ind.), 1928-31, instr., 1931-34, asst. prof., 1934-37, asso. prof., 1937-41, prof. 1941—, acting head dept. of chemistry, 1943-46, administrative head 1946—. Mem. Am. Chem. Soc., Soc. for Metals, Ind. Chem. Soc., Ind. Acad. Sci. Roman Catholic. Home: 1510 McKinley Av South Bend IN 46617 Office: Univ of Notre Dame Notre Dame IN 46556

BOYLE, CHARLES RAYMOND, Jr., banker; b. San Francisco, May 19, 1928; s. Charles Raymond and Myrtle L. (Rude) B.; B.A. in Econs., U. Wash., 1950; m. Nancy J. Lehmann, July 1, 1952; children—Michael Charles, John Howard, Susan Laura. Asst. cashier, v.p. Nat. Bank Commerce, Seattle, 1950-60; v.p., mgr. Bank of Cal., N.A., Burlingame (Cal.) office, 1960-64, sr. v.p., mgr. Portland (Ore.) office, 1964—. Active local United Good Neighbors, Salvation Army Nat. Conf. Christians and Jews. Bd. overseers Lewis and Clark Coll. Clubs: Portland Golf, Arlington, University, Waverley (Portland). Home: 3724 SW 52d Pl Portland OR 97221 Office: 407 SW Broadway Portland OR 97208

BOYLE, EDWARD JAMES, U.S. dist. judge; b. McDonoghbille, La., Oct. 11, 1913; s. Thomas F. and Margaret (Fields) B.; LL.B., Loyola U., New Orleans, 1935; m. Edith Fink, Jan. 29, 1936; children—Edward J., Kathleen A. Admitted to La. bar, 1935; practiced in New Orleans, 1935-66; asst. U.S. atty. Eastern Dist. La., 1942-45; now U.S. judge Eastern Dist. La. Mem. Am., La., Fed., New Orleans bar assns., Am. Judicature Soc., Blue Key (hon.). Democrat. Roman Catholic. Home: 7356 Cameo St New Orleans LA 70124 Office: 400 Royal St New Orleans LA 70130

BOYLE, FRANCIS DENNIS, ret. naval officer; b. Everett, Wash., July 30, 1910; s. Dennis Peter and Louise Anna (Zahler) B.; B.S., U.S. Naval Acad., 1934: postgrad. Armed Forces Staff Coll., 1952; m. Marjorie Felicite Finney, June 24, 1936; childrenDoris (Mrs. J.E. Whitely, Jr.), Patricia Felicite. Commd. ensign USN, 1934, advanced through grades to rear adm., 1963; comdr. U.S.S. Charr, 1944-46; instr. naval history Naval Sch., Newport, R.I., 1946-48; tech. liaison officer Bur. Ordnance, Jet Propulsion Lab., Cal. Inst. Tech., 1949-50; comdr. U.S.S. Bradford, 1950-51; br. head guided missiles research div. Bur. Ordnance, Navy Dept., Washington, 1952, 53- 54; guided missile project supr., tech. dir. Terrier guided missile project, dir. rep. chief Bur. Ordnance, Naval Indsl. Res. Ordnance Plant, Pomona, Cal., 1952-53; officer-in-charge guided missile evaluation unit 1, Operational Devel. Force, Naval Air Sta., San Diego, 1954-56; group comdr. hydrographic survey group II, comdg. officer U.S.S. Tanner, 1956-57; comdr. Naval Ordnance Missile Test Facility, White Sands Proving Ground, N.M., 1958-60; comdg. officer U.S.S. Springfield, 1960-61; asst. dir., spl. asst. to chief naval operations, Washington, 1961-62; comdr. Fleet Tng. Group, San Diego, 1962, Cruiser Destroyer Flotilla 7, 1962-63; dep. dir. Communications Satellite Project Office, Defense Communications Agy., Washington, 1963-66; chief MAAG, Norway, 1966-68. Decorated Navy Cross, Legion of Merit. Mem. Nat. Geog. Soc., Naval Inst., Naval Acad. Alumni Assn. Home: 8 Windsor Rise Monterey CA 93940

BOYLE, HAROLD V. HAL, foreign corr.; b. Kansas City, Mo., Feb. 21, 1911; s. Peter Edward and Margaret (Gavaghan) B.; student Kansas City (Mo.) Junior Coll., 1928-30; B.A. and B.J., U. of Missouri, 1932; m. Mary Frances Young, Nov. 6, 1937. Copy boy, Associated Press, Kansas City office, 1928, corr. for A.P., Columbia, Mo., 1933-35, night editor, St. Louis office, 1935, feature editor, Kansas City office, 1936, reporter and editor, New York City staff, 1937-41, night city editor, N.Y. City, 1942; war corr. for A.P. covering allied campaigns in Mediterranean and European areas 1942—; columnist of daily "Leaves from War Correspondent's Notebook, "pub. by 400 A.P. newspapers; contbr. articles on mil. and journalistic topics to several mags.; now writer of Boyles Column for A.P. Awarded Pulitzer prize for Distinguished Correspondence, 1945; listed by Jr. C. of C. in selection of 10 most outstanding young men, 1945. Mem. Am. Newspaper Guild, Sigma Phi Epsilon, Kappa Tau Alpha. Club: Overseas Press. Home: 110 Waverly Pl New York City NY 10011 Office: A P Cable Desk 50 Rockefeller Plaza New York City NY 10020

BOYLE, JAMES MICHAEL, educator, artist; b. New Castle, Pa., Jan. 30, 1910; s. Michael Augustus and Alice (Troy) B.; B.A., Carnegie Inst. Tech., 1935; M.F.A., U. Colo., 1944; student Inst. Fine Arts, N.Y.U., 1957; m. June Ott, Sept. 2, 1939; children—Kathleen (now Mrs. John G. Champlain), Michael John. From instr. to asst. prof. U. Colo., 1936-46; asso. prof. dept. art U. Wyo., Laramie, 1946-48, prof., 1948—, head dept., 1946—, dir. Art Gallery, 1946—; one-man shows Denver Art Mus., 1946, Joslyn Art Mus., Omaha, 1946, U. Okla., U. Wyo., U. Colo.; exhibited Denver Art Mus. annuals, Joslyn Art Mus. biennials, 1936—, Colorado Springs exhbn. Artists West of Mississippi, 1946-47, D.C. Watercolor Club, 1949, 50, Art U.S.A., 1958, others. Chmn., Wyo. Arts Council, 1967-70, mem., 1971—. Recipient of Edward Yetter landscape award Denver Ann., 1945, first award in oils Joslyn Meml., 1945, Washington Watercolor Club, 1949. Mem. A.I.A., Am. Assn. U. Profs., Artists Equity, Western Assn. Art Schs. and U. Museums (chmn. 1970-71), Delta Phi Delta, Theta Alpha Phi, Democrat. Roman Catholic. Home: 706 S 14th St Laramie WY 82070

BOYLE, JAMES PRESTON, govt. ofcl.; b. Callao, Va., May 15, 1921; s. William Porter and Bertha (Harper) B.; B.C.S., Strayer Coll. Accountancy, 1940; LL.B., Woodrow Wilson Coll. Law, 1950; m. Rosalie Clayton, Dec. 2, 1944; children—Ronald, Gary, Richard, Michael. Admitted to Ga. bar, 1950; with Internal Revenue Service, 1946—, successively internal revenue agt., chief, field audit br., Atlanta, chief audit div., asst. dist. dir., Nashville dist. dir. Richmond (Va.) Dist., 1965—. State coordinator interdepartmental savs. bonds, Va., 1965—. Chmn., Combined Fed. Campaign, 1967. Bd. dirs. Va. Civil Service Interagy. Bd. Served as comdr U.S. Naval Air Corps,

1942-45. C.P.A., Ga. Mem. Richmond Fed. Exec. Assn. (pres. 1968-69). Home: 355 N Mooreland Rd Richmond VA 23229 Office: Fed Bldg Richmond VA 23240

BOYLE, JEROME MICHAEL, clergyman, educator; b. Gary, Ind., Sept. 12, 1911; s. John Charles and Genevieve Marie (O'Boyle) B.; A.B., U. Notre Dame, 1935, A.M., 1936; Ph.D., U. Louvain (Belgium), 1950; student theology Holy Cross Coll., 1941-45. Joined Congregation of Holy Cross, 1939; ordained priest Roman Catholic Ch., 1945; tchr. philosophy U. Notre Dame, 1945-51, prof. philosophy, 1965—, dean liberal arts, 1960-65; prof. philosophy, head dept. U. Portland (Ore.), 1951-65. Mem. Am. Cath. Philos. Assn. Contbr. articles jours. Address: Fisher Hall U Notre Dame Notre Dame IN 46556

BOYLE, JOHN S., county judge; b. Chgo., July 17, 1901; s. Michael and Maria (O'Malley) B.; LL.B., DePaul U., 1926; m. Mary Sullivan, June 9, 1945. Admitted to Ill. bar, 1926, since practiced in Chgo.; asst. corp. counsel, Chgo., 1931-33; asst. states atty. Cook County, 1933-39, states atty., 1948- 52; judge Superior Ct. Cook County, 1960-63; chief justice criminal ct., 1963; chief juge Circuit Ct. Cook County, constl. consolidation of all Cook County cts., 1964—. Alderman, Chgo., 1939-43. Pres. Nat. Conf. Met. Cts., 1965. Del. Democratic Nat. Conv., 1952, 56, 60. Recipient 1st Law award Lincoln Acad. Ill., Distinguished Service award Tau Epsilon Rho, 1966, VIP citation in jurisprudence Catholic Women's Club Ill., 1966; Distinguished Achievement award DePaul U., 1968, Man of Year award Cath. Lawyers Guild Chgo., 1970. Mem. Fed., Am., Ill., Chgo., West Suburban (pres. 1957) bar assns., Phi Alpha Delta. Democrat. Clubs: Executive (dir.), Butterfield Country. Home: 1100 N Euclid Av Oak Park IL 60302 Office: Civic Center Chicago IL 60602

BOYLE, JUNE, state legislator; b. Greeley, Colorado, Sept. 30, 1917; d. Walter J. and Millicent (Williamson) Ott; B.F.A., U. Colo., 1939; grad. student U. Wyo., 1949-52; m. James M. Boyle, Sept. 2, 1939; childrenKathleen (Mrs. John G. Champlain), Michael John. Mem. Wyo. Ho. of Reps. from Albany County, 1963—. Chmn. Albany County Dem. Com., 1960- 62; mem. Nat. Dem. Com. for Wyo., 1964-68. Bd. dirs. Albany County United Fund, 1963-65, S.E. Wyo. Mental Health Center, 1963-. Mem. League Women Voters, Nat. Order Women Legislators, Alpha Phi, Delta Phi Delta. Roman Catholic. Address: 706 S 14th St Laramie, WY 82070

BOYLE, KAY, writer; b. St. Paul, Feb. 19, 1903; d. Howard Peterson and Katherine (Evans) Boyle; student Ohio Mechanics Inst., 1917-19; m. Richard Brault, June 24, 1923 (div.); m. 2d, Laurence Vail, Apr. 2, 1931 (div.); children—Sharon Walsh, Apple-Joan, Kathe, Clover, Faith Carson, Ian Savin; m. 3d, Baron Joseph von Franckenstein (dec. 1963). Mem. faculty San Francisco State Coll. Awarded Guggenheim fellowship, 1934, 61; O. Henry Meml. prize, 1936, 1941. Mem. Nat. Inst. Arts and Letters. Author: A Frenchman Must Die, 1945; Thirty Stories, 1946; "1939," 1947; His Human Majesty, 1949; The Smoking Mountain, 1951; The Seagull on the Step, 1955; Three Short Novels, 1958; The Youngest Camel, 1959; Generation without Farewell, 1960; Collected Poems, 1962; Breaking the Silence, 1962; Nothing Ever Breaks Except the Heart, 1966; Pinky, the Cat, 1967; The Autobiography of Emanuel Carnevali, 1967; Being Geniuses Together, 1968; Pinky in Persia, 1968; Testament For My Students (poems), 1970; The Long Walk at San Francisco State (essays), 1970. Contbr. short stories to mags. Address: care A Watkins 77 Park Av New York City NY 10016

BOYLE, LAWRENCE JOHN, real estate exec.; b. Boston, Aug. 16, 1914; s. Lawrence and Nora (Walsh) B.; student Bentley Sch. Accounting, 1932-34, Northeastern U., 1934-36; m. Priscilla J. Bellows, Nov. 23, 1939; children—Stephen, Kathleen, Kerry. Gen. mgr. Hollywood (Fla.) Beach Hotel, 1938-52; leasee, operator group of hotels, Ill., Minn., S.C., 1952-61; gen. mgr., dir. Caribbean area Hilton Hotel Internat., 1961-65; mgr. dir. Hotel Ambassador East, Hotel Ambassador West, Chgo., 1965-66; pres. Ariz. Biltmore Estates, Inc., Phoenix, 1966—. Served with USAAF, 1942-46. Mem. Hotel Sales Mgmt. Assn. Roman Catholic. Rotarian. Home: 5330 N 32d St Phoenix AZ 85018 Office: PO Box 2290 Phoenix AZ 85002

BOYLE, PHILIP T., lawyer; b. Butte, Mont., May 25, 1910; A.B., U. Cal. at Berkeley, 1932; LL.B., U. Cal., 1935. Admitted to Cal. bar, 1935; now mem. firm Wyckoff, Parker, Boyle & Pope, Watsonville. Mem. Am., Santa Cruz County bar assns., State Bar Cal. Office: 14 Carr St Watsonville CA 95076*

BOYLE, ROBERT PATRICK, lawyer, govt. ofcl.; b. Kansas City, Mo., Nov. 21, 1913; s. Roscoe Virgil and Aletha (Pentecost) B.; B.A., Williams Coll., 1935; LL.B., Harvard, 1938; m. Katherine Warren, Mar. 16, 1940; children—Elizabeth Ann, Carolyn Warren. Admitted to Okla. bar, 1938; with CAA, 1938-58, atty., asst. to gen. counsel, asst. gen. counsel, dep. gen. counsel, gen. counsel, 1953-58; sr. asso. gen. counsel FAA, 1959-63, dep. asst. adminstr. Internat. Aviation Affairs, 1963-68, 70—. Chmn. U.S. delegation legal com. Internat. Civil Aviation Orgn., 1957-60, 62, pres. legal commn. 14th assembly, 1962, U.S. rep. council , 1968-69, chmn. tech. com. extraordinary assembly, Montreal, 1970; chmn. U.S. delegation diplomatic Conf. pvt. air law, Guadalajara, Mexico, 1961, Tokyo, 1963, Guatamala, 1971. Chmn. legal div. Pres.'s Air Coordinating Com.; Served from ensign to lt. USNR, 1943-46. Mem. Am. (chmn. aviation criminal law com. of sect. criminal law 1953-67), Okla., Oklahoma County bar assns., Williams Coll. Alumni Assn. (pres. Washington 1960-61), Theta Delta Chi. Club: National Aviation (Washington). Home: 3929 N 36th St Arlington VA 22207 Office: 800 Independence Av Washington DC 20590

BOYLE, ROBERT WILLIAM, physician, educator; b. St. Paul, Feb. 11, 1908; s. William Henry and Gertrude May (Ritsch) B.; student Hamline U., 1924-26; B.P.E., YMCA Coll., Chgo., 1929, M.P.E., 1937; Ph.B., U. Chgo., 1930; M.A., Coll. City Detroit, 1933, Ph.D., U. Minn., 1936; M.D., U. Ark., 1940; Baruch fellow Mayo Clinic, 1946-47; m. Daphne Jennette Connell, Nov. 26, 1931; children—William Charles, Jeanne Marguerite (Mrs. Leland Hanks) and Georgianna Phyllis (Mrs. Naren-dra Gunaji) (twins). Phys. dir. Eau Claire (Wis.) YMCA, 1930-31; instr. physiology, coach freshman football Coll. City Detroit, 1931-32; teaching fellow physiology U. Minn. Sch. Medicine, 1933-36; asst. prof., and prof., head dept. physiology and pharmacology U. Ark. Sch. Medicine, 1936-44; chief phys. medicine and rehab., later chief profl. services VA Hosp., Ft. Thomas, Ky., 1947-54; prof. phys. medicine and rehab. Med. Coll. Wis., Milw., 1954—, chmn. dept. phys. medicine and rehab., 1965—; dir. dept. phys. medicine and rehab. Milw. County Hosp., 1954—. Chmn. rehab. div. Commn. State Dept., Wis. Med. Soc., 1956-59; exec. com. health services United Community Service, Milw., 1958-60, 62-69; dept. Christian social action Episcopal Diocese Milw., 1960—; cons. VA Center, Wood, Wis., 1954—. Served as capt., M.C., AUS, 1945-46. Diplomate Am. Bd. Phys. Medicine and Rehab. Fellow A.C.P., Am. Coll. Chest Physicians; mem. Am. Acad. Phys. Medicine and Rehab. (gov., pres. 1961-62, sec. 1967—), Mid-Am. Soc. Phys. Medicine and Rehab. (past pres., trustee), Am. Congress Rehab. Medicine, Am. Assn. U. Profs., A.A.A.S., A.M.A. (council sect. phys. medicine and rehab., alternate mem. intersplty. com.), Pan Am. Med. Assn., Internat. Soc. Rehab. Disabled, Nat. Rehab. Assn., Am. Heart Assn., Am. Rheumatism Assn., Am. Geriatrics Soc., Sigma Xi, Phi Beta Pi, Alpha Omicron Alpha. Episcopalian. Contbr. articles to profl. jours., chpt. in book. Home: 8705 Glencoe Circle Wauwatosa WI 53226 Office: 8700 W Wisconsin Av Milwaukee WI 53226

BOYLE, SAMUEL, newspaper editor; b. Lansford, Pa., Nov. 25, 1920; s. Samuel L. and Olive (Bonner) B.; A.B., U. Notre Dame 1942; m. Margaret Grady, Dec. 27, 1947; children—Samuel, Teresa, William, Maureen. With Phila. Bull., 1948- -, asst. mng. editor, 1969—. Served with USNR, 1942-46. Mem. Pa. Soc. Newspaper Editors (past pres.), A.P. Mng. Editors of Pa. (pres. 1969- 70). Home: 1460 Berwyn-Paoli Rd Paoli PA 19301 Office: Phila Bulletin 30th and Market Sts Philadelphia PA 19101

BOYLE, WALTER OTT, retail food chain exec.; b. Louisville, Feb. 8, 1921; s. Lee Roy and Rose (Burton) B.; A.B. in Econs. and Commerce with honors, U. Louisville, 1942; m. Jeannine Fisher, Feb. 4, 1970; children—Gerald C., Margaret L. (Mrs. Roger Keranen), Patricia. With Great Atlantic & Pacific Food Stores, 1945-66; v.p. finance Benner Tea Co., Burlington, Ia., 1967; with Allied Supermarkets, Detroit, 1967—, v.p. finance, 1970—. Served to lt. comdr. USNR, 1942-45, 50-52. Decorated Letter of Commendation. Elk. Home: 16851 Park Dr Livonia MI 48154 Office: 8711 Meadowdale Av Detroit MI 48228

BOYLE, WILLIAM ANTHONY, labor union exec.; b. Bald Butte, Mont., Dec. 1, 1904; s. James P. and Catherine (Mallin) B.; m. Ethel V. Williams, June 3, 1928; 1 dau., Antoinette. Asst. to internat. pres. United Mine Workers Am., 1948-60, internat. v.p., 1960-63, internat. pres., 1963-. Vice chmn. Nat. Coal Policy Conf.; mem. President's Adv. Com. Labor-Mgmt. Policy. Dir., mem. exec. com. National Bank, Washington. Home: 4422 35th St NW Washington DC 20008 Office: 900 15th St NW Washington DC 20005

BOYNE, DAVID HERMAN, educator; b. Marlette, Mich., July 23, 1934; s. Neil Clayton and Elsie May (Weigert) B.; B.S. (Sears Roebuck Found. scholar), Mich. State U., 1957; A.M., U. Chgo., 1960, Ph.D., 1962; m. Linda Jane Balderson, June 29, 1958; children—Leslie Jane, Stephanie Joan. Asst. prof. Mich. State U., 1961-65, asso. prof., dir. Kellogg farmers study program Kellogg Found., 1965-67; prof., chmn. dept. agrl. econs. and rural sociology Ohio State U., Columbus, 1967—. Chmn., Farmhouse Found. Internat. Bd. Trustees. Recipient Outstanding Ph.D. Thesis award Am. Farm Econs. Assn., 1963. Mem. Am. Agrl. Econs. Assn., Am. Econs. Assn., Gamma Sigma Delta, Alpha Zeta. Home: 5950 Litchfield Rd Worthington OH 43085 Office: 2120 Fyffe Rd Columbus OH 43210

BOYNTON, BEN LYNN, ret. physician; b. Chgo., Sept. 3, 1909; s. Melbourne Parker and Hattie (Wells) B.; B.S., U. Chgo., 1932; M.B., Northwestern U., 1936, M.D., 1937; m. Elizabeth Katterjohn, Aug. 19, 1933; children—Lynn William, Irvin Parker, Sylvia Wells, Melbourne Roy, Elizabeth Helen. Intern St. Luke's Hosp., Chgo., 1936-37; instr. phys. therapy U. Wis. Med. Sch., 1937-39; dir. dept. phys. medicine Norfolk (Va.) Gen. Hosp., 1940-42; dir. phys. medicine service Shannon Meml. Hosp., San Angelo, Tex., 1946-47; chief phys. medicine and rehab. div., br. office VA, Dallas, 1947-49; chief phys. medicine and rehab. service VA Hosp., Houston, 1949-52; prof. phys. medicine and rehab. Baylor U. Coll. Medicine, 1949-53; med. dir. Rehab. Inst. Chgo., 1953- 56, chmn. dept., prof. phys. medicine, med. sch. Northwestern U., 1953- 60, dir. phys. medicine and rehab. Oak Forest (Ill.) Hosps., 1957-60; med. dir. Rehab. Center of Summit County, Akron, O., 1960-69; ret., 1970. Served as lt. col., M.C., AUS, 1942-46. Diplomate Am. Bd. Phys. Medicine and Rehab. Fellow Am. Acad. Phys. Medicine and Rehab. (past pres.); mem. A.M.A., Am. Congress Phys. Medicine and Rehab. Methodist. Home: Route 2 Box 535 Shelby MI 49455

BOYNTON, CHARLES F., ret. bishop; b. Geneseo, N.Y., Apr. 19, 1906; s. Charles Homer and Frances (Cogswell) B.; A.B., Williams Coll., 1928, D.D., 1950; S.T.B., Gen. Theology Sem., 1933, S.T.D., 1946; D.D., Trinity Coll., 1958; S.T.D., Hobart Coll., 1960; m. Helen B. Fowler, Apr. 4, 1934 (dec. 1969); children—Carol Louise, Charles Frederic; m. 2d, Dori J. Watson, Sept. 29, 1969. Ordained deacon Protestant Episcopal Ch., 1932, priest, 1933; chaplain Christ Sch., Arden, N.C., 1933-39, St. Francis House, U. Wis., 1939-42; priest in charge St. Andrews, Mayaguez, P.R., 1942-44; coadjutor bishop P.R., 1944-47, diocesan bishop 1947-50; bishop suffragan, N.Y. diocese, 1951-69, ret., 1969. Mem. Beta Theta Pi. Address: 20 Little Pond Rd Milford CT 06460

BOYNTON, ROBERT MERRILL, educator; b. Evanston, Ill., Oct. 28, 1924; s. Merrill Holmes and Eleanor (Matthews) B.; student Antioch Coll., 1942-43, U. Ill., 1943-45; A.B., Amherst Coll., 1948; Ph.D., Brown U., 1952; m. Alice Neiley, Apr. 9, 1947; children—Sherry, Michael, Neiley, Geoffrey. Asst. prof. psychology and optics U. Rochester, N.Y., 1952-57, asso. prof., 1957-61, prof., 1961—, dir. Center for Visual Sci., 1963-71, chmn. dept. psychology, 1971—; guest researcher Nat. Phys. Lab., Teddington, Eng., 1960-61; vis. prof. physiology U. Cal. Med. Center, San Francisco, 1969-70. Served with USNR, 1963-65. Fellow A.A.A.S., Optical Soc. Am. (dir. at large 1966-69), Am. Psychol. Assn. Contbr. articles profl. jours. Home: 94 Dunrovin Lane Rochester NY 14618

BOYNTON, WILLARD HAROLD, govt. ofcl., physician; b. Groveland, Mass., Apr. 9, 1914; s. Willard Rollins and Fronie Elvira (Fletcher) B.; B.S., Mass. State Coll., 1935; M.P.H., Yale, 1938; M.D., Tufts U., 1942; m. Ruth Mary Watt, Dec. 20, 1939; childrenDavid Bruce, Susan Ruth, Willard John, Douglas Robin, Sally Jean. Intern Lynn (Mass.) Hosp., 1942-43; asst. medicine Tufts Med. Sch., also fellow medicine Boston Dispensary, 1943-44; pvt. practice, Bethel, Me., 1944-56; pub. health physician ICA mission to Saigon, Vietnam, 1956-58, chief pub. health division, 1958-63; sr. pub. health officer AID, mission to Lahore, Pakistan, 1963-69; population officer Pakistan, 1965-69, chief field support div. Office Population Tech. Assistance Bur., Washington, 1969-70, dep. dir., 1970—; pres. staff Rumford (Me.) Community Hosp., 1950-51. Diplomate Nat. Bd. Med. Examiners. Mem. Am., Me. (sec.) acads. gen. practice, Am. Pub. Health Assn., A.M.A., Oxford County (Me.) Med. Soc. (pres. 1949- 50), Alpha Omega Alpha (pres. Tufts 1941-42), Delta Omega, Phi Kappa Phi. Home: Monhegan ME Office: AID Dept State Washington DC 20037

BOYSEN, HARRY, obstetrician, gynecologist; b. Harlan, Ia., Aug. 21, 1904; s. Hans and Dorothea (Brodersen) B.; B.S., U. Ia., 1924, M.D., 1928; m. Patricia Dougherty, May 4, 1940; children—Gerald, Patricia Anne (Mrs. Thomas P. Lennon). Intern Highland Hosp., Oakland, Cal., 1928-29; resident obstetrics and gynecology Presbyn. Hosp., Chgo., 1930-32, now mem. staff; pvt. practice, Chgo., 1945—; clin. prof. obstetrics, gynecology U. Ill. Coll. Medicine, 1957—; chmn. div. obstetrics and gynecology Presbyn.-St. Luke's Hosp. Served from lt. comdr. to comdr., M.C., USNR, 1942-45. Diplomate Am. Bd. Obstetrics and Gynecology. Fellow A.C.S.; mem. A.M.A., Chgo. Gynecol. Soc. (pres., 1963-64), Am. Coll. Obstetrics and Gynecology, Phi Kappa Psi, Nu Sigma Nu. Clubs: Obstetrics and Gynecology Travel, Chicago Golf. Home: 237 E Delaware Pl Chicago IL 60611 Office: 720 N Michigan Av Chicago IL 60611

BOYSEN, JOHN THOMAS, banker; b. Cedar Falls, Ia., Jan. 19, 1912; s. Carl Christian and Mary (Mulligan) B.; student Rockhurst Coll., 1946; grad. Rutgers U. Grad. Sch. Banking, 1949; m. Regina C. Cranny, Jan. 2, 1939; children—Patricia C. (Mrs. James E. Zishka), Michael D., Ann Marie. Accountant, Waterloo, Cedar Falls & No. R.R., 1930-34; bank examiner Fed. Res. Bd., 1934-41; with Fed. Res. Bank, Kansas City, Mo., 1941—, 1st v.p., 1966-. Served with AUS, 1942-45. Home: 3705 W 52d Terrace Shawnee Mission, KS 66205 Office: 925 Grand Av Kansas City MO 64198

BOYSON, WILLIAM ANDREW, physician; b. Harrisburg, Pa., Sept. 19, 1894; s. Albert McLean and Margaret Ann (Evans) B.; B.S., Pa. Coll., 1917; M.S., Gettysburg Coll., 1924; M.D., M.H.D., Mahnemann Med. Coll., 1930; m. Marie Elizabeth Bentz, Dec. 4, 1919; children—William Albert, Robert Boyson, John Evans. Civil engr., 1915-17; high sch. tchr. and prin., 1919-25; intern St. Luke's and Childrens Med. Center, Phila., 1930-31; pvt. practice medicine, Mechanicsburg, Pa., 1931—; dir. Am. Found. Homeopathy Postgrad. Sch., 1956—. Pres. Am. Inst. Homeopathy, 1964, trustee, 1964- 67; pres. Pan-Am. Homeopathic Congress, 1960-62; sec. Am. Bd. Homeotherapeutics, 1959—; trustee Am. Found. Homeopathy, 1957-65. Served with AUS, 1917-19; to col., M.C., AUS, World War II, Korea. Mem. Homeopathic Med. Soc. Pa. (pres. 1968-69). Internat. Platform Assn., Am. Fedn. Astrologers, Phi Kappa Psi, Kappa Phi Kappa. Lutheran. Mason (K.T.). Contbr. articles to prof. jours. Address: 309 S Market St Mechanicsburg PA 17055

BOZARTH, HOWARD J., banker; b. Abilene, Tex., Aug. 21, 1906; s. Edgar L. and Ethel (Cannon) B.; student Centre Coll. of Ky., 1924-26; B.S., U. Okla., 1928; m. Zereta Sutton, Nov. 3, 1933; children—Howard J., Betty (Mrs. Rudolph Carl Metzner). With Empire Oil Co., Oklahoma City and Guthrie, Okla., 1928-29; collector Seminole Oil Fields area Comml. Credit Co., 1929-30; with Dun & Bradstreet, 1930; with City Nat. Bank, Oklahoma City, 1930-69, exec. v.p., 1955-58, pres., 1958-69; vice chmn. bd. Fidelity Bank, N.Am., Oklahoma City, 1969—; dir. Oklahoma City br. Fed. Res. Bank of Kansas City. Pres., bd. dirs. Oklahoma County chpt. A.R.C.; bd. dirs. Better Bus. Bur., Salvation Army. Served to lt. (j.g.) USNR, 1943- 46. Mem. Oklahoma City C. of C. (dir.). Episcopalian. Kiwanian. Home: 700 NW 41st St Oklahoma City OK 73118 Office: P O Box 24128 Oklahoma City OK 73124

BOZEMAN, ADDA BRUEMMER, educator, author; b. Geistershof, Latvia, Dec. 17, 1908; d. Leon and Anna (von Kahlen) von Bruemmer; diplomee Ecole Libre des Scis. Politiques, Paris, France, 1934; barrister at law, Middle Temple Inn of Ct., London, Eng., 1936; J.D., So. Methodist U., 1937; postgrad. student Stanford, Hoover Inst.; m. Virgil Bozeman, Mar. 26, 1937 (div. 1947); 1 dau., Anya (Mrs. Mark Taylor); m. 2d, Arne Barkhuus, Feb. 8, 1951. Came to U.S., 1936, naturalized, 1941. With law offices Charles H. Huberich, Berlin, Paris, The Hague and London, 1933-36; asso. prof. history Augustana Coll., 1943-47; prof. internat. history Sarah Lawrence Coll., 1947—; vis. prof. Northwestern U., 1945, N.Y.U., 1948, 49; grad. faculty New Sch. Social Research, 1954, 55, 63; mem. faculty seminar study peace Columbia, 1953—. Research grantee Carnegie Endowment Internat. Peace, 1952, Rockefeller Found., 1960. Mem. Am. Soc. Internat. Law, Am. Polit. Sci. Assn., Am. Hist. Assn., Internat. Studies Assn. Author: Regional Conflicts around Geneva, 1948; Politics and Culture in International History, 1960; The Future of Law in a Multicultural World, 1971; also articles, essays. Home: 24 Beall Circle Bronxville NY 10708

BOZZO, AUGUST RUDOLF, watch co. exec.; b. N.Y.C., Aug. 1, 1919; s. Marcel and Maria (Pagano) B.; student Coll. City N.Y., 1936-39, Columbia, 1948-50; grad. Harvard Advanced Mgmt. Program, 1969; m. Dorothy M. Lenna, Feb. 5, 1944; children—Susan, Dorothea. With Bulova Watch Co., N.Y.C., 1946—, exec. v.p., 1966—; dir. B-C Watch Co., Fujiyoshida, Japan. Bd. dirs. Boys Club, Queens, N.Y., 1964—. Served to maj., inf. AUS, 1941-46; ETO. Decorated Bronze Star, Purple Heart. Mem. Am. Soc. Indsl. Engrs., Am. Mgmt. Assn., Am. Ordnance Assn., Queens C. of C. (bd. dirs.). Roman Catholic. Home: 124 Nyac Av Pelham NY 10803 Office: 630 Fifth Av New York City NY 10020

BRABLEC, CARL, ednl. adminstr.; b. Lenawee County, Mich., Sept. 24, 1908; s. George and Mary (Pribyl) B.; A.B., Eastern Mich. U.; postgrad. (Am. Exchange fellow) Charles U., Prague, 1930-31; M.A., U. Mich., 1940; m. Dorothy M. Kanous, July 11, 1937. Tchr., prin., supt. schs., Britton, Mich., 1932-44; supt. schs., Clarkston, Mich., 1944-47, Roseville, Mich., 1947—. Mem. Mich. Corrections Commn. for Juveniles, 1937-39, Mich. Edn. Finance Commn., 1954-58, Mich. Com. Edn. for Health Care, 1968—. Chmn., Roseville City Charter Commn., 1957-58. Bd. regents U. Mich., 1958-66. Mem. Met. Sch. Adminstrs. Assn. (pres. 1956, 68-69), N.E.A., Assn. Governing Bds. State Univs. (regional dir. Ohio-Mich. 1964-66, finance chmn. Mich. Retirement Coordinating Com. 1970—), Am. Assn. Sch. Adminstrs., Mich. Gun Collectors Assn., Southeast Mich. Council Govts., Kappa Delta Pi, Pi Kappa Delta. Democrat. Methodist. Mason, Rotarian. Home: 18308 Mesle St Roseville MI 48066 Office: 18175 Eleven Mile Rd Roseville MI 48066

BRACE, GERALD WARNER, author, educator; b. Islip, N.Y., Sept. 23, 1901; s. Charles Loring and Louise (Warner) B.; B.A., Amherst Coll., 1922, Litt.D., 1969; M.A., Harvard, 1924, Ph.D., 1930; Litt.D., Southeastern Mass. Technol. Inst., 1965; m. Huldah Laird, Dec. 3, 1927; children—Charles Loring, Gerald Warner, Barbara (Mrs. Ralph Seeley). Instr. Williams Coll., 1924- 26; instr., tutor Harvard, Radcliffe Coll., 1927-30; instr. Dartmouth, 1930-34; instr., asst. prof. Mt. Holyoke Coll., 1934-39; prof. English, Boston U., 1939-68, prof. English emeritus, 1968—; tchr. Cummington Sch., summer 1934, Writers Conf., U. N.H., summer 1953; vis. lectr. Harvard, 1955-56. Mem. Am. Assn. U. Profs., Phi Beta Kappa. Author: The Islands, 1936; The Wayward Pilgrims, 1938; Light on a Mountain, 1941; The Garretson Chronicle, 1947; A Summer's Tale, 1949; The Spire, 1952; Bells Landing, 1955; The Age of the Novel, 1957; The World of Carrick's Cove, 1957; Winter Solstice, 1960; The Wind's Will, 1964; Between Wind and Water, 1966; The Department, 1968; The Stuff of Fiction, 1969. Home: 123 Pinehurst Rd Belmont MA 02178 Office: Boston U Boston MA 02215

BRACE, JOHN WELLS, educator, mathematician; b. Evanston, Ill., Jan. 19, 1926; s. George W. and Marcia (Campbell) B.; B.A., Swarthmore Coll., 1949; M.A., Cornell U., 1951, Ph.D., 1953; m. Patricia A. Demarest, June 16, 1950; children—James, George, Ann, Nancy, Catherine. Mem. faculty math. U. Md., 1953—, prof., 1963—, asso. chmn. dept. math., 1964-66; research asso. U. Cal. at Berkeley, 1959-60. Mem. Woodrow Wilson Fellowship Regional Com., 1962—. Fellow A.A.A.S.; mem. Am. Math. Soc., Math. Assn. Am., Nat. Council Tchrs. Math., Societe Mathematique de France, Indian Math. Soc., Sigma Xi, Phi Kappa Phi, Pi Mu Epsilon. Contbr. numerous articles on functional analysis to profl. publs. Office: Math Dept U Md College Park MD 20742

BRACE, RICHARD MUNTHE, educator; b. Alameda, Cal., Aug. 11, 1915; s. Albert H. and Mabel (Munthe) B.; A.B., U. Cal. at Berkeley, 1936, M.A., 1937, Ph.D. (Taussig traveling fellow in Paris 1939-40), 1940; m. Joan Tilden von Schmidt, June 16, 1939;

children—Geoffrey R., Pamela J. Instr. history U. Me., 1941-43; asst. prof. history Pomona Coll., 1943-45; asso. prof. U. Colo., 1945-47; asso. prof. Northwestern U., 1947-57, prof. history, 1957-65; chmn. dept. history Oakland (Mich.) U., 1965-68; history editor D. Van Nostrand & Co., 1960-68; vis. prof. history U. Cal. at San Diego, 1968-69. Pres. Evanston Sch. World Affairs, 1959. Recipient prize in European history Pacific Hist. Assn., 1945; fellow Am. Council Learned Socs., 1946, Social Sci. Research Council, 1951, 60-61, 65; Fulbright research fellow, Paris, 1954-55; Rockefeller Found. fellow, 1964-65. Mem. Am. Hist. Assn. (Herbert B. Adams prize com. 1959-63), Soc. for French Hist. Studies (v.p. 1968), Société Française d'tude du XVIIE Siècle. Author: Bordeaux and the Gironde 1789-94, 1947; Historical Evolution of Modern France, 1949; The Making of the Modern World, 1955; (with Joan T. Brace) Ordeal in Algeria, 1960; Algerian Voices, 1965; Morocco, Algeria, Tunisia, 1964. Bd. editors Jour. Modern History, 1960-62. Home: 740 Indianwood Rd Lake Orion MI 48035

BRACE, ROBERT DEWITT, banker; b. Boston, Mar. 6, 1930; s. Lloyd D. and Helen (Rhodes) B.; grad. Phillips Acad., 1948; A.B., Dartmouth, 1952; m. Patricia F. Rich, July 24, 1954; children—Martha C., Robert R., Thomas L. With C.H. Sprague & Son, Boston, 1959-67, v.p., 1965-67; with United-Carr, Inc., Boston, 1967-69, treas., 1968-69; pres. dir. Investors Bank & Trust Co., Boston, 1969—; dir. Metal-Tech, Inc., Biddeford, Me., Southworth Machine Co., Portland, Me. Trustee Pine Manor Jr. Coll., Greater Boston YMCA; exec. com. Corp. of Winsor Sch., 1970—. Served to lt. (j.g.) USNR, 1952-54. Mem. Dartmouth Alumni Club Boston (exec. com. 1962—). Clubs: Racquet and Tennis (N.Y.C.); Dedham Country and Pole (Dedham, Mass.) Home: 258 Grove St Westwood MA 02090 Office: Investors Bank & Trust Co 24 Federal St Boston MA 02110

BRACE, WILLIAM FRANCIS, educator; b. Littleton, N.H., Aug. 26, 1926; s. Frank C. and Frances (Dodge) B.; B.S., Mass. Inst. Tech., 1946, Ph.D., 1963; m. Margaret Grant, Sept. 3, 1955; children—Colin W., Nathaniel C., Sarah T. Mem. faculty Mass. Inst. Tech., Cambridge, 1954—, prof. geology, 1965—. Served with USNR, 1944-46. Mem. Am. Acad. Arts and Scis., Nat. Acad. Sci. Author numerous articles in field. Home: 136 Lakeview Av Cambridge MA 02138

BRACELAND, FRANCIS JAMES, psychiatrist; b. Phila., July 22, 1900; s. John J. and Margaret (L'Estrange) B.; A.B., LaSalle Coll., Phila., 1926; M.D., Jefferson Med. Coll., 1930, Litt.D.,1965; Sc.D., LaSalle Coll., Phila., 1941; L.H.D., Canisius Coll., 1956, St. Joseph Coll., West Hartford, 1970; LL.D., Manhattan Coll., 1956; Sc. D., Coll. of Holy Cross, 1956. Catholic U. Am., 1957, Northwestern U., 1957, Trinity Coll., Hartford, 1958; Fairfield U., 1961; Litt.D., U. Hartford, 1964, m. Hope Van Gelder Jenkins, June 1, 1938. Resident physician Jefferson Hosp., Phila., 1930-32; asst. physician Pa. Hosp. for Mental Disease, 1932-35; asst. physician Burgholzli Hosp., Zurich, Switzerland, 1935-36, Nat. Hosp., Queen Square, London, 1936; clin. dir. Pa. Hosp., 1936-37; psychiatrist Inst. of Pa. Hosp., Phila., 1937-41, Phila. Gen. Hosp., 1940-41; cons. in chief St. Joseph's and Babies hosps., 1937-41; instr. psychiatry U. Pa. Med. Sch., 1936-38; asst. prof. psychiatry Grad. Sch. Medicine, U. Pa., 1938-41; dean Sch. Medicine, Loyola U. Chgo., 1941-46; prof. psychiatry Grad. School, U. Minn., 1946-51; cons. psychiatrist Mayo Clinic, Rochester, Minn., 1946-51; psychiatrist in chief Inst. of Living, Hartford, Conn., 1951-65, sr. cons., 1965—; clin. prof. psychiatry Yale, 1951-68, emeritus, 1968—; lectr. psychiatry Harvard, 1960-66, Vice pres. World Psychiat. Assn., 1961-66. Served as catp., M.C., USNR, 1942-46; advanced to rear adm. USNR, 1958, ret. 1962; chief neuro-psychiat. div. Bur. Med. and Surgery, Navy Dept., 1944-46; cons. psychiatrist to Surgeon Gen. U.S. Navy; cons. Spl. Med. Adv. Bd., VA; apptd. Armed Forces Med. Adv. Com., 1949. Chmn. 1957 Nat. Health Forum. Recipient Stritch medal Loyola U., 1965, Laetare medal Notre Dame U., 1962. Diplomate Am. Bd. Psychiatry and Neurology (sec.-treas. 1946-52, pres. 1952). Fellow A.C.P., Coll. Physicians Phila., Am. Psychiat. Assn. (pres. 1957); mem. A.M.A., Assn. for Research in Nervous and Mental Disease (pres. 1957 chmn. bd. trustees 1969—). Royal-Medico Psychol. Assn. (hon.), N.Y. Acad. Scis. (chmn. Salmon com. on psychiatry and mental hygiene 1959—). Editor: Am. Jour. Psychiatry, 1965—; mem. editorial bd. Year Book of Psychiatry and Applied Mental Health, 1968—; mem. internat. editorial bd. World Biennial Book of Psychiatry and Psychotherapy, 1966—; editorial dir Med Insight, 1970—. Address: 200 Retreat Av Hartford CT 06106

BRACEWELL, GEORGE, educator; b. Stonefort, Ill., Oct. 11, 1905; s. James Harvey and Etta (Henshaw) B.; Ed.B., So. Ill. U., Carbondale, 1928; M.A., U. Mich., 1931; Ed.D., Washington U., St. Louis, 1952; m. Mabel Goddard, June 23, 1931; children—Ann (Mrs. Bernard Hoffnar), Stephen George. Tchr. pub. schs., Ill., 1928-31; asst. instr. U. Mich., 1934-35; mem. faculty So. Ill. U., Carbondale, 1931—, prof. edn., 1962—. Chmn. dept. ednl. adminstrn. and supervision, 1960-63. Mem. adv. com. Nat. Rural Youth, 1942—. Mem. N.E.A., Nat. Soc. Study Edn., Assn. Supervision and Curriculum Devel., Comparative Edn. Soc., Ill. Edn. Assn. (pres. So. div. 1945). Methodist (trustee). Author: Handbook for Student Teaching, 1950. Home: 2700 Kent Dr Carbondale IL 62901

BRACEWELL, RONALD NEWBOLD, educator; b. Sydney, Australia, July 22, 1921; s. Cecil Charles and Zilla (McGowan) B.; B.Sc., Sydney U., 1941; B. Engring., 1943, M.Engring., 1948; Ph.D., Cambridge (Eng.) U., 1950; m. Helen Mary Lester Elliott, Feb. 27, 1953; children—Catherine Wendy, Mark Cecil. Came to U.S., 1954. Research officer Commonwealth Sci. and Indsl. Research Orgn., Australia, 1943-46, 50-54; vis. prof. astronomy U. Cal. at Berkeley, 1954-55; mem. faculty Stanford (Cal.), 1955—, now prof. elec. engring. Author: The Fourier Transform and it's Applications, 1965; (with J. L. Pawsey) Radio Astronomy, 1955. Home: 634 Campus Dr Stanford CA 94305

BRACH, PAUL HENRY, artist; b. N.Y.C., Mar. 13, 1924; s. Henry and Amelia (Levine) B.; B.F.A., State U. Ia., 1948; M.F.A., 1949; m. Miriam Schapiro, Sept. 6, 1946; 1 son, Peter. One-man shows include Leo Castelli Gallery, N.Y.C., 1957, 59, Union Coll., Schenectady, 1958, Dwan Gallery, Los Angeles, 1960, Cordier-Warren Gallery, N.Y.C., 1962, Cordier-Ekstrom Gallery, N.Y.C., 1964, Univ. Art Mus., Albuquerque, 1965, Loeb Student Center Gallery, N.Y. U., 1966; group shows include St. Louis City Art Mus. (Purchase prize), 1950, Artists Ann., Stable Gallery, N.Y.C., 1950, 52, 54, 55, Tanager Gallery, N.Y.C., 1954, 55; New Printmaking at Mus. Modern Art, 1954, The Responsive Eye, 1965, The Responsive Eye (graphics), 1966, Traveling Exbhns. Prints of Africa, 1966, Four Younger Americans at Sidney Janis Gallery, N.Y.C., 1956, Classic Spirit in 20th Century Art, 1964, Corcoran Gallery, 1959, Mus. Art R.I., 1959, Richard Brown Baker Collection, 1959, Bus. Boys Am. Art at Whitney Mus., 1960, New Acquisitions, 1963, Friends Collect 1964; Saidenberg Gallery, N.Y.C., 1960, 64th Am. Exbhn. at Art Inst. Chgo., 1961, Toward a New Abstraction at Jewish Mus., N.Y.C., 1963, New Graphics, 1965, Banners at Andre Emmerich Gallery, N.Y.C., 1964, New Directions in Am. Painting at Rose Art Mus., Brandeis U., 1964, Contemporary Am. Painting and Sculpture at U. Ill., 1965, For Eyes and Ears at Cordier-Ekstrom Gallery, 1965, Art in Progress at Finch Coll. Art Mus., 1965, An Environment for Faith at San Francisco Mus. Art, 1965; rep. permanent collections Mus. Modern Art, Whitney Mus. Am. Art, St. Louis Mus., N.Y. Pub. Library, Smith Coll. Mus., Albion (Mich.) Coll., Neb. Art Mus., U. Ariz., U. N.M., N.Y. U., also numerous pvt. collections; tchr. U. Mo., 1949-51, New Sch. Social Research 1952-55, Cooper Union, 1960-62. N.Y. U., 1954-66, Cornell U., 1965-67, Parsons Sch. Design, 1956-67; prof. art, chmn. dept. U. Cal. at San Diego, 1967-69; dean Sch. Art, Inst. Arts, Los Angeles, 1969—. Fellow Tamarind Lithography Workship, Los Angeles, 1964; Am. Fedn. Arts artist-in- residence, Albuquerque, 1965. Served with AUS, 1943-45; ETO. Home: 642 Moreno Av Los Angeles CA 90049

BRACHER, FREDERICK, former educator; b. Monohan, Wash., Mar. 28, 1905; s. George M. and Anna Frederika (Ris) B.; B.S., Ore. State U., 1927; M.A., U. Cal., 1929, Ph.D., 1934; m. Agnes Nuttall, Jan. 10, 1937; children—Katherine, David Frederick Ris. Instr., U. Cal., 1934-35, U. Wis., 1936-37, City Coll. San Francisco, 1937-42; asst. prof. English, Pomona Coll., 1943-47, asso. prof., 1947-52, prof., 1952-70, Arthur M. and Fanny M. Dole prof. English, 1962-70, emeritus, 1970—. Mem. nat. selection com. Woodrow Wilson Nat. Fellowship Found., 1958-68. Mem. Am. Assn. U. Profs., Modern Lang. Assn., Assn. Depts. English (adminstrv. com. 1965-68), Philol. Assn. Pacific Coast (exec. com. 1964-67), Audubon Soc., Sierra Club, Beta Theta Pi. Author: Exercises in the Craft of Writing, 1946; The Novels of James Gould Cozzens, 1959; (with Grant and Duff) Correctness and Precision in Writing, 1938; College Handbook of Composition, 6th edit., 1958; (with Elsbree) Heath's College Handbook of Composition, 7th edit., 1967. Editor: Rev. of Ednl. News, 1958-61. Contbr. articles to profl. publs. Home: 284 Central Av Pacific Grove CA 93950

BRACHET, JEAN LOUIS, educator; b. Brussels, Belgium, Mar. 19, 1909; s. Albert and Marguerite (Guchez) B.; M.D., U. Brussels, 1934; m. Francoise de Barsy, July 23, 1935; children—Etienne, Lise, Philippe. Asst. U. Brussels, 1934-38, charge de cours, 1938-43, prof. 1943—, dir. group moleculor embryology Molecular Embryology Lab., 1970—; vis. prof. U. Pa., 1946. Fgn. asso. Nat. Acad. Scis., Am. Acad. Arts and Scis. Author: Chemical Embryology, 1950; Biochemical Cytology, 1957; Biochemistry of Development, 1962. Spl. research nucleic acids in cell differentiation. Office: U Brussels 67 rue des Chevaux Rhode St Genese Belgium

BRACK, REGINALD KUFELD, Sr., airline exec.; b. Radomissl, Russia, Dec. 28, 1910; s. John and Irma (von Liphart) Kufeld; brought to U.S., 1923; B.A., U. Kan., 1935; m. Edythe Ella Mulveyhill, July 28, 1934; children—Reginald Kufeld, Dennis, Linda. Owner, Mfr. Brack Ins. Agy., 1935-44; pres. Brack Finance Co., (both Great Bend, Kan.), 1935-44; dist. sales mgr. Braniff Internat. Airways, Kansas City, Mo., 1944-45, regional sales mgr., 1945-47, gen. traffic and sales mgr., Dallas, 1947-53, v.p., 1953-60, sr. v.p., 1961—, also dir. Nat. bd. regents Leukemia Soc. Am.; state chmn., mem. nat. exec. com. U.S. Savs. Bond. Decorated Order of Balboa (Panama), Honor Al Merito (Paraguay). Mem. Internat. Air Transport, Newcomen Soc., Phi Gamma Delta. Lutheran. Club: Northwood Country (Dallas). Home: 6043 Walnut Hill Lane Dallas TX 75230 Office: Braniff Bldg Exchange Park Dallas TX 75235

BRACK, WILLIAM DENNIS, photojournalist; b. Great Bend, Kan., Nov. 14, 1939; s. Reginald Kufeld and Edyth (Mulveyhill) B.; B.A., Washington and Lee U., 1962; LL.B., George Washington U., 1965; m. Karen Ruth Kastler, Apr. 10, 1965. Free- lance photojournalist, 1965-; regular contbr. Time mag., also rep. Newsweek, Life Fortune, Bus. Week, Nation's Bus., Pageant, Nat. Observer, others. Mem. White House News Photographers Assn., Phi Gamma Delta. Episcopalian. Club: Nat. Press (Washington). Co-author: The Congressman. Address: 3609 Woodhill Pl Fairfax VA 22030

BRACKEN, ALEXANDER MCKNIGHT, lawyer; b. Toronto, Ont., Can., May 7, 1908; s. Thomas Edward and Margaret (Atcheson) McK.; came to U.S., 1914; student Ball State Tchrs. Coll., Muncie, Ind., 1925-26; LL.D., 1965; A.B., U. Mich., 1929, J.D., 1931; LL.D., Ind. State U., 1969; m. Rosemary Wright Ball, July 14, 1932; children—Frank Alexander, Thomas Ball, Elizabeth (Mrs. J. Fredric Wiese, Jr.), William McKnight, Alexander Elliott. Admitted to Ind. bar, 1931; chmn. bd. Merchants Nat. Bank, Muncie, 1956—; pres., dir. Muncie & Western R.R. Co., 1955—; corporate v.p., dir. and gen. counsel Ball Bros. Co. (now Ball Corp.), 1942-68, vice chmn., dir., 1968-70, chmn. bd., dir., 1970—; dir. Caspers Tin Plate Co., Kent Plastics Corp., Ball Bros. Research Corp. Pres. bd. trustees Ball State U., Muncie; trustee Carleton Coll.; pres., dir. George and Frances Ball Found., 1950—; treas., dir. Ball Bros. Found.; bd. dirs. Ball Meml. Hosp. Assn. Mem. Am., Ind., Delaware County bar assns., Indiana Soc., Newcomen Soc., Beta Theta Pi. Episcopalian (vestryman). Rotarian (past pres. Muncie). Clubs: Columbia (Indpls.); University (Chgo. and N.Y.C.); President's (U. Mich.) Home: 10 Berwyn Rd Muncie IN 47304 Office: 1509 Macedonia Av Muncie IN 47303

BRACKEN, CHARLES HERBERT, banker; b. Corry, Pa., June 5, 1921; s. Olin Williams and Vellah (Morgan) B.; B.S., U. Pa., 1948; student spl. banking courses; m. Barbara E. Barton, June 19, 1948; children—Betsy Louise, Sally Anne, Charles Herbert, Barton William, Douglas Morgan. Successively cashier, v.p., exec. v.p., trust officer, pres., dir. Citizens Nat. Bank, Corry, 1948-64; pres., dir. Marine Nat. Bank, Erie, Pa., 1964—; dir. Pitts. br. Fed. Res. Bank Cleve., Erie County Plastics, Inc., BD Corp.; chmn. bd. dirs. Profl. Computer Assos., Inc. Treas., dir. Erie Indsl. Devel. Corp., 1967; dir. Greater Erie Indsl. Devel. Corp., 1965-70; Trustee Hamot Hosp., 1970—, Erie Community Found., 1970—, Erie Episcopal Diocese, 1969—; bd. govs. Erie unit Shriners Hosp. Crippled Children, 1968—; corporator St. Vincent Hosp., 1965—; adv. bd. Behrend Campus, Titusville Campus, Pa. State U., 1968—, U. Pitts., 1963—, Mercyhurst Coll., 1969—. Served with USAAF, 1942-46; CBI. Mem. Am. Bankers Assn. (exec. council), Sigma Alpha Epsilon. Episcopalian. Mason (Shriner). Clubs: Rotary, University, Erie, Kahkwa (Erie). Home: 920 W Arlington Rd Erie PA 16509 Office: 901 State St Erie PA 16512

BRACKEN, DENIS JAMES, automobile co. exec.; b. Kansas City, Mo., Aug. 16, 1911; s. James J. and Bridget Co. (Conway) B.; m. Rosemary Anne King, Nov. 30, 1933; children—James King, Richard Denis, Bruce Paul. With Ford Motor Co., from 1953, former group v.p. charge steel, assembly and stamping divs., from 1963. Home: 1012 Whittier Rd Grosse Pointe Park MI 48236 Office: Ford Motor Co American Rd Dearborn MI 48121

BRACKEN, EDDIE, actor; b. N.Y.C., Feb. 7, 1920; student Profl. Children's Sch. for Actors, N.Y.C.; m. Connie Nickerson. Vaudeville, night club singer; stage debut in Lottery, 1930; plays include Lady Refuses, Iron Men, So Proudly We Hail, Brother Rat, Too Many Girls, Seven Year Itch; motion picture debut in Life with Henry, 1940, others include Fleet's In, Sweater Girl, Young and Willing, Hail the Conquering Hero, Miracle of Morgan's Creek, Girl from Jones Beach, Two Tickets to Broadway, We're Not Married, Slight Case of Larceny, How to Make a Man, Women's Barracks; actor TV, Masquerade Party, other programs; syndicated columnist Crackin' with Bracken, 1963—. Founder, Trinity Sq. Co., Providence.*

BRACKEN, JAMES LUCAS, newspaper editor; b. Greensburg, Kan., Nov. 20, 1913; s. John Newton and Mary Grace (Lucas) B.; m. Frances Cadzow, Mar. 24, 1943; children—Thomas Robert James, Dorothy Cadzow, Frances Margaret. Corr. Brit. newspaper syndicates, writer agrl. publs., 1933-37; field editor, later exec. editor Pacific N.W. Farm Trio, Spokane, 1937- 42; mng. editor Western Metals mag., Los Angeles, 1946; editorial writer, asst. to mng. editor The Spokesman Rev., Spokane, 1947-49, mng. editor, 1949—. Pres. Spokesman-Rev. Charities, Inc. Republican. Presbyn. Home: 1417 Pinecrest Rd Spokane WA 99203 Office: The Spokesman-Review Spokane WA 99210

BRACKEN, THOMAS EDWIN, govt. ofcl.; b. N.Y.C., Apr. 10, 1907; s. John W. and Elizabeth (Bresnan) B.; A.B., Yale, 1929; LL.B., Nat. U., 1937; m. Leath Parker, 1930; children—Leath Mason (Mrs. Robert Brooks), Parker Donald, Martha Elizabeth; m. Louise Prentiss Tubby, 1963. Analyst, NRA, 1934-35; examiner Seante Commn. on Interstate Com., 1935-37; admitted to Cal. and Fla. bars, 1936; atty. WPA, 1937-39; chief counsel Pub. Bldgs. Adminstrn., 1941; gen. counsel OWI, 1942-44; asst. legal adviser State Dept., 1944- 52; practiced in Pasadena, Cal., 1952-62; assigned rev. and insp. fgn. assistance programs State Dept., 1962—. Mem. Los Angeles Democratic County Com., 1960-62. Bd. Dirs. Pasadena Art Mus., 1958-61. Home: 4921 Seminary Rd Alexandria VA 22311 Office: Dept of State Washington DC 20520

BRACKENRIDGE, JOHN BRUCE, educator, physicist; b. Youngstown, O., Apr. 20, 1927; s. John and Azile (Townson) B.; B.S., Muskingum Coll., 1951; M.S., Brown U., 1954, Ph.D., 1959; m. Mary Ann Rossi, June 19, 1954; children—Norma Lynn, Sandra Virginia, Robert Bruce, John Scot. Asst. prof. physics Muskingum Coll., 1955-59; asso. prof. Lawrence U., 1959-65; prof. physics, 1966—; vis. asso. prof. Brown U., 1956-66. Served with USNR, 1945-46. Mem. Am. Assn. Physics Tchrs., Acoustical Soc. Am. Author: Principles of Physics and Chemistry, 1970. Home: 218 N. Union St Appleton, WI 54911.

BRACKETT, ISAAC PARSONS, univ. adminstr.; b. Flemington, W.Va., Aug. 27, 1916; s. George Sylvester and Maude (Parsons) B.; B.S., Northwestern U., 1938, M.S., 1940, Ph.D., 1947; m. Gwendolyn Bertha Conrad, June 10, 1940; children—George Conrad, Denis Capner, Lee Evans. Instr., Northwestern U., Evanston, Ill., 1940-43, 45-47, asst. prof., 1947-51; research asso. Voice Communication Lab., 1943-45; asso. prof. speech pathology, audiology So. Ill. U., Carbondale, 1951-56, prof., chmn. dept., 1956-70, system v.p., 1970—. Cons. various univs., instns. Mem. Am. Speech and Hearing Assn., Am. Cleft Palate Assn. Contbr. chpt. to book, articles to profl. jours. Home: Route 4 Carbondale IL 62901

BRACKMAN, ROBERT, artist; b. Odessa, Russia; s. Moyssi and Celia B.; ed. common schools, Russia; art edn., Nat. Acad. Design, N.Y.C. 1919-21; m. 2d, Frances Richard Davis, Feb. 15, 1936p children—Roberta Frances, Celia Davis. mem. of faclty Art Students League N.Y., 1933—, Bklyn. Inst. of Art, 1936—; Ford grant artist in residence Norfolk Mus.; art cons. USAF. Represented in permanent collections Met. Mus. N.Y.C. and others. Commd. portraits include J.D. Rockefeller, Jr., for Colonial Williamsburg (Va.), Inc., Dr. Evarts Graham, Washington U., St. Louis, John Foster Dulles for State Dept. Awarded Thomas B. Clarke prize, 1932, Saltus medal, 1941, Andrew Carnegie prize, 1965, Nat. Acad. Design; awarded Atheneum prize, Conn. Acad., 1932, Noel Flagg prize, 1936, 1st prize, 1948, Anonymous prize Art Inst. Chgo., 1929; hon. mention Carnegie Inst. Paintings in U.S., 1949; gold medal Nat. Art Club, 1950; gold medal of honor Allied Artists Am., 1952; 1st prize Laguna Beach Art Festival, 1952; Carol H. Beck gold medal Pa. Acad. Fine Arts, 1958, Salmagundi Club award, 1961; Gold Medal of Honor, Allied Artists of Am., 1966. Academician, Nat. Academy of Design. Mem. Allied Artists Am., Mystic Art Assn. (pres. 1951-52), Audubon Soc. Artists, Am. Water Color Soc., Conn. Acad., Wilmington Acad., New Haven Paint and Clay Club, Internat. Inst. Arts and Letters, Royal Soc. Arts (London). Address: Noank CT 06340 ☆

BRACY, CARL CLUSTER, ednl. assn. exec.; b. Carterville, Ill., Jan. 29, 1912; s. Clyde and Ola (Stephens) C.; A.B., McKendree Coll., 1936, D.D., 1946; Th.M., Iliff Sch. Theology, 1940; LL.D., Ohio Wesleyan U., 1959; L.H.D., Ohio No. U., 1968; m. Ermal E. Hacker, Sept. 29, 1936 (div. 1967); children—Marvin, Carla Elaine, Brenda Sue; m. 2d, Katherine P. Branfield. Ordained to ministry Meth. Ch.; pastor, Donnellson, Ill., 1934-36, Broomfield and Greeley, Colo., 1936-39, Faulkton and Madison, S.D., 1939-45; pres. McKendree Coll., 1945-49; chancellor Neb. Wesleyan U., Lincoln, 1949-54; pres. Mount Union Coll., 1954-67; exec. dir. Ohio Found. Ind. Colls., Columbus, 1968—. Mem. Meth. Gen. Bd. Edn, 1948-54; del. 10th, 11th World Meth. Confs., Oslo, Norway, 1961, London, 1966. Mem. Nat. Assn. Schs. and Colls. Meth. Ch. (pres. 1961-62), Newcomen Soc. N.Am., Blue Key, Pi Kappa Delta, Alpha Psi Omega, Sigma Tau Delta, Pi Gamma Mu, Phi Kappa Phi. Rotaran. Home: 4795 Kingshill Dr Columbus OH 43229 Office: 4601 N High St Columbus OH 43214

BRACY, RAY B., former mayor of Allentown, Pa. Address: 1936 Washington St Allentown PA 18104*

BRADBURN, JAMES RUPERT, bus. cons.; b. Los Angeles, May 31, 1911; s. Rupert H. and Alice (Hamilton) B.; B.S., Cal. Inst. Tech., 1932; M.B.A., Harvard, 1934; m. King Turnbull, Sept. 9, 1939; children—Alice, James, Kenneth. Engr., Gen. Electric Co., 1934-37, Gleason works, Rochester, N.Y., 1937-38, Eastman Kodak Co., 1938-41; exec. engr., v.p. Consol. Electrodynamics Corp., 1945-54; pres., dir. Electro Data Corp., 1954-56, gen. mgr. Electro Data Div. and v.p. Burroughs Corp., 1956-60, v.p. engring. and mfg., 1960-65, also dir.; gen. mgr. electronic data processing div., v.p. RCA Corp., 1965-68, exec. v.p., gen. mgr. information systems, 1968-71; bus. cons., 1971—. Bd. dirs. Boy Scouts Am. Served to maj., ordnance dept. AUS, 1941-45. Mem. I.E.E.E., Harvard Bus. Sch. Assn., Tau Beta Pi, Eta Kappa Nu. Republican. Christian Scientist. Club: Bald Peak (Colony, N.H.). Home: Mirror Lake NH 03853

BRADBURY, CHARLES WILLIAM, Jr., sugar refining co. exec.; b. Newark, Jan. 3, 1923; s. Charles William and Evelyn (Steidler) B.; B.S. in Econs., Wharton Sch., U. Pa., 1943; M.S., Columbia, 1947; m. Elizabeth Kelley, July 12, 1947; children—John, Charles, Laurie. With Am. Sugar Co., 1947—, controller, 1969—. Mem. Stamford (Conn.) Bd. Representatives, 1955-57, Stamford Redistricting Commn., 1964, Stamford Golf Authority, 1965-67. Served to 1st lt. USAAF, 1943-46. Mason. Home: 28 Minivale Rd Stamford CT 06907 Office: 120 Wall St New York City NY 10005

BRADBURY, NORRIS EDWIN, physicist; b. Santa Barbara, Cal., May 30, 1909; s. Edwin Perly and Elvira C. (Norris) B.; B.A., Pomona Coll., 1929, D.Sc., 1951; Ph.D., U. Cal., 1932; LL.D., U. N.M., 1953; D.Sc., Case Inst. Tech., 1956; m. Lois Platt, Aug. 5, 1933; children—James Norris, John Platt, David Edwin. NRC fellow in physics, Mass. Inst. Tech., 1932-34; asst. prof. physics, Stanford, 1934-37, asso. prof., 1937-42, prof. 1942-50; prof. physics U. Cal., 1951-70; dir. Los Alamos Sci. Lab., 1945-70. Served with USNR,

1941-45, capt. Res. Decorated Legion of Merit. Fellow Am. Phys. Soc.; mem. Nat. Acad. Sci. Episcopalian. Contbr. tech. articles to phys. revs., jours. Home: 1451 47th St Los Alamos NM 87544

BRADBURY, RAY DOUGLAS, author; b. Waukegan, Ill., Aug. 22, 1920; s. Leonard Spaulding and Esther Marie (Moberg) B.; student pub. schs.; m. Marguerite Susan McClure, Sept. 27, 1947; children—Susan Marguerite, Ramona, Bettina, Alexandra. First pub. short story, 1941; 51 stories pub. pulp. mags., 1941-45; later stories in Best Am. Short Stories, 1946, 48, 52 and in O. Henry Prize Stories of 1947, 48; Benjamin Franklin award best Am. mag. story, 1953. Author: Dark Carnival, 1947; The Martian Chronicles, 1950; The Illustrated Man, 1951; The Golden Apples of the Sun, 1953; Fahrenheit 451, 1953; The Meadow (a play), 1947; Moby Dick (Screenplay), 1954; Switch on the Night (juvenile), 1955; The October Country, 1955; Dandelion Wine, 1957; A Medicine for Melancholy, 1959; R Is for Rocket (stories), 1962; Something Wicked This Way Comes (novel), 1962; The Anthem Sprinters (plays), 1962; The Machineries of Joy, 1963; The Martian Chronicles (screenplay), 1964; The World of Ray Bradbury (plays), 1965; The Vintage Bradbury (stories), 1965; The Autumn People (illus. stories), 1965; The Wonderful Ice Cream Suit (play), 1965; Tomorrow Midnight (illus. stories), 1966; Twice Twenty-Two (stories), 1966; Leviathan '99 (radio drama), 1966; (screenplays) The Picasso Summer, 1968, The Halloween Tree, 1968; (play), Any Friend of Nicholas Nickleby's is a Friend of Mine, 1968; (stories) I Sing The Body Electric, 1969. Mem. Screen Writers Guild, Sci. Fantasy Writers Am. (pres. pro-tem), Pacific Art Found. (v.p.), Writers Guild Am. (mem. screen writers bd.). Prodns. one act plays Royal Shakespeare Festival Theatre, The Pandemonium Theatre Co., 1963. Home: 10265 Cheviot Dr Los Angeles CA 90064

BRADDOCK, DANIEL MCCOY, fgn. service officer; b. Little Rock, Apr. 5, 1906; s. John Sellers and Katherine (McCoy) B.; A.B. summa cum laude, Kenyon Coll. Grambier O., 1925, M.S., 1926; student Ecole des Sciences Politiques, Paris, 1926-27; m. Marguerite Virginia Lipscomb, July 22, 1929; children—Daniel McCoy, John Lipscomb, Carolyn Anderson, Edward Sellers, Richard Scott. Vice consul, Medan, Sumatra, 1929-31; vice consul, Barcelona, Spain, 1932-34, consul, 1934; 36; 2d sec. of embassy, Caracas, Venezuela, 1937-40; consul, Porto Alegre, Brazil, 1940-43, Bahia, Brazil (including details to consulate at Belem and to embassy at Rio de Janeiro), 1943-45; asst. chief, div. of Brazilian Affairs Dept. of State, 1945, chief, 1946-47, asst. chief Am. Republics Br. Chief, Div. of Comml. Policy, 1947-48; 1st sec. embassy, Madrid, Spain, 1948-49; mem. U.S. delegation to Annecy Trade and Tariffs Conf., 1949; mem. Fgn. Service Selection Bd., 1950; conselor economic affairs, Emmbassy Madrid, 1950, Manila, 1952-54; dep. chmn. U.S. Delegation for Philippine Trade Negotiations, 1954-55; counselor, dept. chief of mission, Rangoon, Burma, 1955-57; minister-counselor, dep. chief of mission, Havana, Cuba, 1957-60, career minister, 1960—; sr. fgn. insp., 1964—; acting dep. asst. sec. state for Inter-Am. affairs, summer 1961; mem. United States delegation to UN Gen. Assembly, 1961—; minister, consul gen., Sao Paulo, Brazil, 1962-67; consul gen., Bombay, India, 1967—; assigned Nat. War Coll., 1951-52. Mem. Am. Fgn. Service Assn., Phi Beta Kappa, Delta Kappa Epsilon. Clubs: Internat, PACOR, Foreign Service (Washington). Office: Bombay State Dept Washington DC 20521

BRADDY, HALDEEN, educator; b. Fairlie, Tex., Jan. 22, 1908; s. John Winfield and Lena Moss (Rountree) B.; B.A., E. Tex. State U., 1928; M.A., U. Tex., 1929; Ph. D., N.Y.U., 1934; m. Virginia Bell, June 19, 1927. Instr. English, N.Y.U., 1929-38, prof. Tex. Christian U., 1938-42; supr. Tex. Tech. U., 1943-44; asso. prof. U. Kan., 1944-45; lectr. Tulane U., 1946, U. So. Cal., 1946; prof. English U. Tex. at El Paso 1946—, research prof. 196364. Served as 1st lt. USAAF, 194243. Grantee Am. Council Learned Socs., 1937. Mem. Tex. Folklore Soc. (pres. 1951-52, program chmn. 1952). Modern Lang. Assn. Westerners, Kappa Sigma, Mem. Christian Ch. Author: Chaucer's Parlement of Foules, 2d edit., 1969; Chaucer and the French Poet Graunson,, 2d edit., 1968; Glorious Incense, The Fullfillment of Edgar Allan Poe, 2d edit., 1968; Cock of the Walk, Legend of Pancho Villa, 1955, 2d edit., 1970; Hamlet's Wounded Name, 1964; Pershing's Mission to Mexico, 1966; Pancho Villa Rides Again, 1967; Mexico and the Old Southwest, 1971; Geoffrey Chaucer, 1971. Rev. editor Jour. Am. Folklore, 1945. Home: 2109 Arizona Av El Paso TX 79930

BRADDY, MINTON VENNER, architect; b. Pinehurst, Ga., May 12, 1920; s. Minton Venner and Lola Ethel (Bagley) B.; B.S. in Architecture, Ga. Inst. Tech., 1942; m. Dorothy Lyde Tarte, June 11, 1947; children—Minton V. III, Victoria Spence. Draftsman, Burge & Stevens, architects, Atlanta, 1946; architect, partner Stevens & Wilkinson, Atlanta, 1946-69, v.p. Stevens & Wilkinson, Architects, Engrs., Planners, Inc., 1969—. Pres. Guy Webb P.T.A., 1956-57, 57-58, North Springs High Sch. P.T.A., 1963-64. Trustee Stevens and Wilkinson Employees' Retirement Trust. Served to lt. USNR, 1942-46. Mem. A.I.A., Sigma Alpha Epsilon. Presbyn. Clubs: City, Cherokee Town & Country (Atlanta). Home: 5160 Peachtree-Dunwoody Rd Atlanta GA 30342 Office: 100 Peachtree St Atlanta GA 30303

BRADEMAS, JOHN, congressman; b. Mishawaka, Ind., Mar. 2, 1927; s. Stephen J. and Beatrice Cenci (Goble) B.; B.A. magna cum laude (Vets. nat. scholar), Harvard, 1949; D.Phil. (Rhodes scholar), Oxford U., Eng., 1954. Legislative asst. to U.S. Senator Pat McNamara; adminstrv. asst. U.S. Rep. Thomas L. Ashley, 1955; exec. asst. to presdl. nominee Stevenson, 1955-56; asst. prof. polit. sci. St. Mary's Coll., Notre Dame, Ind., 1957-58; mem. 86th-92d congresses 3d Dist. Ind., majority floor whip 92d Congress, mem. com. house adminstrn., com. on edn. and labor, chmn. select edn. subcom., subcom. on printing. Bd. visitors John F. Kennedy Sch. Govt.; bd. overseers Harvard; mem. adv. council Coll. Arts and Letters U. Notre Dame; mem. adv. bd. Washington Internships in Edn.; mem. Central Com. World Council Chs., Nat. Hist. Publs. Commn. Trustee St. Mary's Coll. Ednl. Testing Service. Served with USNR, 1945-46. Mem. Am. Legion. Methodist. Mason, Ahepa. Home: 750 Leland Av South Bend IN 41616 Office: Rayburn House Office Bldg Washington DC 20515

BRADEN, CHARLES MCMURRAY, educator; b. Santiago, Chile, June 9, 1918 (parents Am. citizens); s. Charles Samuel and Grace (McMurray) B.; B.S., Northwestern U., 1939; student Chgo. Theol. Sem., 1939-41; M.S., U. Minn., 1950, Ph.D., 1957; m. Geraldine Lucile Rugg, July 31, 1943; children—Margaret, Elizabeth, Charles Arthur, Ann. Instr. math. and mechanics Inst. Tech., U. Minn., 1946-56; mem. faculty Macalester Coll., St. Paul, 1956—, prof. math., 1960—, dir. summer programs, 1968-69, dean faculty, 1969-72. NSF sci. faculty fellow, 1959-60, recipient Thomas Jefferson award Macalester Coll., 1970. Mem. Am. Math. Soc., Math. Assn. Am. Conglist. Home: 80 Arthur Av SE Minneapolis MN 55414 Office: Macalester Coll St Paul MN 55105

BRADEN, EMMETT WADE, lawyer; b. Henderson, Tenn., June 12, 1901; s. William B. and Annie B. (McKinney) B.; B.A., U. Tenn., 1923; LL.B., Yale, 1925. Admitted to Tenn. bar, 1925; practiced in Memphis, 1925—; asso. firm Wilson, Gates & Armstrong, 1925-32; partner firm Armstrong, McCadden, Allen, Braden & Goodman, 1932-66; counsel Armstrong Allen Braden Goodman McBride & Prewitt, 1966—. Served to capt. AUS, 1942-45. Mem. Am., Tenn., Memphis and Shelby County bar assns., Kappa Sigma, Corbey Ct. Clubs: Tennessee, Yale, Summit, Rivermont (Memphis). Home: Sheraton-Peabody Hotel Memphis TN 38103 Office: Commerce Title Bldg Memphis TN 38103

BRADEN, MARGARET MIZE, mem. Republican Nat. Com.; b. Emporia, Kan.; d. Robert Herbert and Margaret Talman (Moore) Mize; B.A., U. Kan.; m. Forrest Clifford Braden, May 15, 1937; children—Barbara Louise, Robert Mize, Forrest Arthur. Pres. Yuma County (Ariz.) Rep. Women, 1956-57; vice chmn. Ariz. Rep. Party, 1960-61; mem. Rep. Nat. Com. for Ariz., 1962—, mem. exec. com., 1969—; chmn. Western States Rep. Conf., 1968, 69. Mem. Yuma County Welfare Bd., 1962—, Yuma County Crime Commn., 1969—, Ariz. Adv. Com. Civil Rights Commn., 1957—; mem. U.S. delegation to Inter-Am. Commn. of Women, Bogota, Colombia, 1970. Bd. dirs. Yuma City-County Library, 1952—, San Pablo Home Youth, Phoenix, Yuma County Econ. Opportunity Council. Mem. Pi Beta Phi. Episcopalian. Address: 700 2d Av Yuma AZ 85364

BRADEN, ROBERT GAYNOR, lawyer; b. Parkersburg, W.Va., Jan. 29, 1914; s. Charles Blaine and Dica (Gaynor) B.; A.B., U. Kan., 1935; LL.B., Harvard, 1938; m. Muriel Louise Coultis, Apr. 4, 1941; children—Roberta (Mrs. Fred Powell), Bruce F. Admitted to Tex. bar, 1938, Kan. bar, 1939; practiced in Wichita, 1939—; partner firm Jochems, Sargent & Blaes, 1946—. Pres. Braden Drilling, Inc., Braden-Deem, Inc. Pres. Wichita Guidance Center, 1962-66. Served with AUS, 1942-46. Mem. Harvard Law Assn. Kan. (pres. 1960—), Ind. Petroleum Assn. Am. (bd. dirs. Kan. 1955-60), Wichita Bar Assn. (bd. dirs. 1958-60). Republican. Methodist. Club: Wichita Country (pres. 1968- 69). Home: 1515 Willow Rd Wichita, KS 67208 Office: Farmers and Bankers Life Bldg Wichita KS 67202

BRADEN, SAMUEL EDWARD, educator; b. Hoihow, Hainan, China, June 6, 1914; s. Samuel Ray and Mary (Altman) B.; A.B., U. Okla., 1932; M.A., U. Wis., 1935, Ph.D., 1941; m. Beth Black, 1937; children—Mary Beth, Stephen, John, David. Instr. to prof. Ind. U., 1937-67, asso. dean Coll. Arts and Sci., 1954-59, v.p., 1959-67; pres. Ill. State U. at Normal, 1967-70; chmn. div. bus. and econs. Ind. U. S.E., 1970—; chmn. Council Internat. Ednl. Exchange (N.Y.), 1967—; exec. dir. Ind. Conf. Higher Edn., 1963-67; sr. economist. Combined Raw Materials Bd., Washington, 1942-43. Fulbright sr. research fellow U.K., 1949-50. Bd. overseers St. Memrad Coll.; chmn. bd. dirs. Council on Internat. Ednl. Exchange. Served from pvt. to 1st lt., USAAF, 1943-46. Mem. Am., Midwest econ. assns., Am. Finance Assn., Phi Beta Kappa. Presbyn. (mem. bd. Christian edn.). Author: (with C.L. Christenson, others) Economics, Principles and Problems, 1946; (with G. A. Steiner, others) Economic Problems of the War. Contbr. ednl. publs. Home: 1714 Crestview Dr New Albany IN 47150 Office: Box 459 Jeffersonville IN 47130

BRADEN, SPRUILLE, diplomat; b. Elkhorn, Mont., Mar. 13, 1894; s. William and Mary (Kimball) B.; Ph.B. in Mining Engring., Yale, 1914; hon. degree U. Buenos Aires, 1938; LL.D., Johns Hopkins, 1939, Clark U., Allbright Coll., 1946; E.D., Mont. Sch. Mines, 1947; m. Maria Humeres del Solar, Sept. 5, 1915 (dec. May 1962); children—Maruja, Laurita Isolina, William II, Patricia, Spruille; m. 2d, Verbena Victoria Williams, May 29, 1964. Miner, 1912, engring. various mining constrn. activities, 1912-20; organized Cohoe Processes, Inc., 1926; reorganized Englishtown Carpet Co. (renamed Monmouth Rug Mills Inc.), 1925-29; organized Rehab. Corp., financing income-producing properties, 1932; numerous assignments as ambassador and spl. rep. U.S. Pres., 1935—; asst. sec. state Am. Republic Affairs, 1946-47. Pres., Americas Found., Colombia Found., Colombian Assn. Mut. Aid. Recipient decorations from many fgn. countries including grand cross Ruben Dario (Nicarague), grand cross Order of Quetzal (Gautemala), grand cross Knightly Order St. Brigitte, grand cross Cuba's Legion of Honor; many citations including Order of Lafayette Freedom award, 1962, gold medal Cubans in Exile, Eloy Alfaro grand cross L.I. U. Democrat. Mem. Inter-Am. Edn. Assn. (hon.), Chevaliers du Tastevin (grand officer), Am. Arbitration Assn. (dir., exec. com.). Clubs: Creek (Locust Valley, L.I.); Metropolitan (pres. N.Y.C.); Nejapa Country (Managua, Nicaragua). Author: Diplomats and Demagogues-the Memoirs of Spruille Braden, 1971. Address: 320 E 72d St New York City NY 10021 ☆

BRADEN, THOMAS WARDELL, newspaperman; b. Greene, Ia., Feb. 22, 1918; s. Thomas Wardell and Louise (Garland) B.; A.B., Dartmouth, 1940; m. Joan E. Ridley, Dec. 18, 1948; children—David, Mary, Joan, Susan, Nancy, Elizabeth, Thomas Wardell III, Nicholas R. Newspaperman; instr. English, Dartmouth, 1946, asst. to pres. and asst. prof., 1947-48; exec. sec. Mus. Modern Art, N.Y.C., 1949; dir. Am. Com. on United Europe, 1950; editor, pub. Blade Tribune, Oceanside, Cal., 1954-68; columnist Los Angeles Times Syndicate, 1968—. Mem. Cal. Bd. Edn., 1959-67, past. pres. Trustee Cal. State Coll., 1961-64, Dartmouth. Served with King's Royal Rifle Corps, Brit. Army, Africa and Italy, 1941-44; trans. to inf., AUS, 1944. Mem. Council Fgn. Relations, Casque and Gauntlet, Sigma Alpha Epsilon. Author: (with Stewart Alsop), Sub-Rosa, 1946; also articles in mags. Home: 101 E Melrose St Chevy Chase MD 20015 Office: 101 E Melrose St Chevy Chase MD 20015

BRADEN, WALDO W., educator; b. Ottumwa, Ia., Mar. 7, 1911; s. Wilburn C. and Stella (Warder) B.; B.A., Penn Coll., 1932; M.A., U. Ia., 1938, Ph.D., 1942; m. Dana Crane, Aug. 18, 1938; 1 dau., Helen Dana. Tchr., Fremont (Ia.) High Sch., 1933-35, Mt. Pleasant High Sch., 1935-38; tchr. speech Ia. Wesleyan Coll., 1938-40, dean students, 1942-46; asso. prof. speech La. State U., Baton Rouge, 1946-51, prof., 1951—, chmn., 1958—; vis. prof. Washington U., summer 1952, Mich. State U., summer 1953, U. Pacific, summer 1965. Mem. Speech Assn. Am. (council 1954—, exec. sec. 1954-57, pres. 1962), So. Speech Assn., Am. Studies Assn., Pi Kappa Delta, Delta Sigma Rho, Tau Kappa Alpha, Omicron Delta Kappa. Methodist. Author: (with Gray) Public Speaking, 1951, rev. edit., 1963; (with Brandenburg) Oral Decision-Making, 1955; (with Gehring) Speech Practices, 1958; Public Speaking: Essentials, 1966. Editor: Speech Methods and Resources, 1961; The Speech Teacher, 1967-69. Contbr. articles to speech, hist. jours. Home: 535 Ursuline Dr Baton Rouge LA 70800

BRADERMAN, EUGENE MAUR, govt. ofcl.; b. Phila., Aug. 27, 1914; s. Samuel and Leah (Weiss) B.; B.S., Temple U., 1935; A.M., U. Ill., 1936, Ph.D., 1938; postgrad. U. Pa., 1938-39; m. Betty Salas, June 20, 1941; 1 dau., Joan. Editor, then dir. Hist. Records Survey Pa., 1939-41; economist Dept. Labor, 1941-42; internat. economist Bd. Econ. Warfare and Fgn. Econ. Administrn., 1942-45; with Dept. Commerce, 1945-65, dir. Far East div., 1950-61, dir. Office Internat. Econ. Programs, 1961-62, dir. Bur. Internat. Commerce, 1962-65, dep. asst. sec. internat. commerce, 1963- 65; dep. asst. sec. state U.S. Dept. State, 1965-71; Am. consul gen. Amsterdam, The Netherlands, 1971—. Chmn. alternate rep. or mem. delegations U.S. numerous internat. confs., also dir. U.S. Trade Missions to Japan, 1956, Philippines, 1960; chmn. U.S. Team on Econ. Relations with Philippines, 1967-70. Recipient gold medal for distinguished achievement in fed. service, 1965. mem. Am. Fgn. Service Assn., Phi Beta Kappa, Pi Gamma Mu, Kappa Phi Kappa. Club: National Press (Washington), Foreign Service. Contbr. articles, reports to profl. lit. Home: 1630 45th St NW Washington DC 20007 Office: Am Consulate Gen Amsterdam The Netherlands

BRADFIELD, JAMES MCCOMB, educator; b. Lebanon, Mo., July 31, 1917; s. James McComb and Emma Katherine (Johnson) B.; A.B., U. Kan., 1938; postgrad. U. Chgo., 1939-40, U. Kansas City, 1940-41; M.A., U. Cal., 1946, Ph.D., 1948; m. Helen Annette Haynes, Jan. 8, 1943; children—Kathleen (Mrs. Frank Norton, Jr.), Christopher, Susan, Robin, Polly. Secondary tchr. Oakland (Cal.) Unified Sch. Dist., 1945-48; prof. edn. Sacramento State Coll., 1948—. Behavioral measurement and research cons.; producer children's TV series Wondertime, KCRA-TV, 1960-62; speaker, writer; dean Stebbins Inst., 1951. Served with USMCR, 1941-45. Mem. Cal. Tchrs. Assn., Sigma Nu, Phi Delta Kappa. Democrat. Unitarian. Author: Measurement and Evaluation in Education, 1957; Secondary School Teaching, 1962. Home: 5892 Callister Av Sacramento CA 95819

BRADFORD, A. LEE, lawyer; b. Accomac County, Va., Apr. 23, 1906; s. G.A. and Rachel (Linton) B.; student William and Mary Coll., 1923-25; J.D., U. Fla., 1929; m. Vivienne Louvet, Aug. 10, 1948; 1 dau., Winifred (Mrs. Thomas Morgan Moore.) Admitted to Fla.. bar, 1929; practiced in Miami, Fla., 1929—; partner firm Dixon, Bradford, Williams, McKay, Kimbrell, 1941—. Chmn. rules com., U.S. Dist. Ct., So. Dist. Fla., 1964-65; alternate del. Jud. Conf., 5th circuit, U.S. Ct. Appeals, 1967-68, 69. Mem. Fla. (continuing legal edn. sect. 1967-68), Dade County, Am. (chmn. trial technique com. 1962-63, aviation com. 1968-69) bar assns., Internat. Acad. Trial Lawyers (dir. 1959), Internat. Assn. Ins. Counsel (chmn. automobile ins. com., chmn. profl. liability and malpractice com. 1959- 60, chmn. open forum 1963-64), Am.. Coll. Trial Lawyers, Phi Alpha Delta. Methodist. Club: Riviera Country (Coral Gables, Fla., pres. 1957- 58). Author: (with Paul A. Carlson) Captain of the Ship, 1960; (with Joseph F. Jennings) Products Liability Against, 1962. Home: 1260 Mendavia Ave Coral Gables FL 33146 Office: 101 Flagler St Miami FL 33131

BRADFORD, ARMISTEAD LUDLOW, newspaperman; b. Washington, July 10, 1901; s. Benjamin Boyland and Nellie (Harvey) B.; student Staunton Mil. Acad., also pvt. tutors; m. Georgette Maricot, June 2, 1923 (dec.); 1 son, Geoge Harvey; m. 2d, Mariana Radovic, Aug. 7, 1954. Reporter, Washington Post, 1918; with various daily newspapers, Washington, Phila., N.Y.C., to 1919; with Washington bur. U.P., 1919-23, covering White House, Dept. State, Congress, mgr., 1923, with various burs. U.S., also N.Y. hdqrs., 1923-24, mgr. bur., Paris, France, 1924-29, assigned N.Y.C., 1930, mgr. bur. Rio de Janeiro, Brazil, 1930-31, Buenos Aires, Argentina, 1931-38, gen. S.Am. mgr., 1938-41, successively radio news mgr., gen. radio mgr., dir. fgn. services, 1941-48, v.p., gen. European mgr. United Press Assns., N.Y.C., 1948—. Mem. Soc. Cincinnati. Office: 19 rue Raynouard Paris 16e France

BRADFORD, DAVID HOLLAND, Jr., chem. co. exec.; b. Sabougla, Miss., Oct. 12, 1917; s. David Holland and Clyde (Leverette) B.; B.S., Miss. State U., 1940; m. Willagene Presley Greene, Feb. 6, 1942; children-Sherrilyn, David Clyde. Chem. engr. research lab. Pure Oil Co., Chgo., 1940-41; mgr. indsl. lubrication dept. Mid-South Oil Co., Memphis, 1946-52; spl. cons., sales mgr., sales and operations mgr. Mid-South Chem. Co., Inc., Memphis, 1949-55, sales and operations mgr., v.p., dir., 1955-62; pres. Mid-South Chem. Co. div. Continental Oil Co., Memphis, 1962-65; pres., chief exec. officer Am. Agrl. Chem. Co., 1965; pres., chief exec. officer Agrico Chem. Co. div. Continental Oil Co., Memphis, 1966-69; group v.p. Allied Chem. Corp., N.Y.C., 1969—, dir., mem. exec. com., 1970—; chmn. bd. Commonwealth Bank, Southhaven, Miss.; pres., chmn. bd. commrs. Whitehaven Utility Dist. (Tenn.); pres., dir. Am. Agrl. Chem. Co., N.Y.C.; v.p., sec.- treas., dir. Agrl. Chems., Inc., Memphis; v.p. Petroleum Chems., Inc., Lake Charles, La., v.p., dir. Admiral Ins. Agy., Whitehaven; dir. First Nat. Bank, Southhaven, Port Terminals, Inc., Memphis. Mem. adv. com. Nat. Plant Foods Inst., 1959-63; pres. Agrl. Ammonia Inst., 1961, dir., 1962-64. Mem. Future Memphis, Inc., 1966-69; mem. President's Council, Southwestern at Memphis, 1967; mem. agri-bus. com. Mid South Fair, 1968; mem. Tenn. exec. com. Radio Free Europe, 1969. Vice pres., bd. dirs. Miss. State U. Devel. Found.; bd. dirs. Mid-South Fair, Memphis. Served with USAAF, 1941-45. Registered profl. engr., Tenn. Presbyn. Kiwanian. Clubs: Whitehaven Country, University, Rivermont, Memphi (Memphis). Home: 236 Oak Ridge Av Summit NJ 07901 Office: 1411 Broadway New York NY 10018

BRADFORD, HAROLD KEITH, mut. funds co. exec.; b. Pennsboro, W.Va., Mar. 22, 1902; s. Bert and Augusta (Bee) B.; A.B., W.Va., U., 1923; postgrad. Harvard Grad Sch. Bus., 1924-25; LL.B., George Washington U., 1930; m. Juanita Fought, June 17, 1926; children—Harold Judith, Susan. Mgr., W.Va. office J.A.W. Inglehart & Co., Clarksburg, W.Va., 1926-32; W.Va. securities commr., 1932-35; group chief SEC., Washington, 1935-40; v.p. Investors Diversified Services, Inc., 1940-60; pres. Investors Stock Fund, Inc., 1949—, chmn. bd., 1961—; pres. Investors Selective Fund, Inc., 1949-71, chmn. bd. 1961—; pres. Investors Mut., Inc., 1949-71, chmn. bd., 1961—; pres. Investors Variable Payment Fund, Inc., 1960-71, chmn. bd., 1961—; pres. IDS New Dimension Fund, IDS Progressive Fund, 1968-71, chmn. bd., 1971—. Pres., Nat. Assn. Securities Commrs., 1935. Mason (Shriner, Jester), Rotarian. Clubs: Minneapolis, Minkahda. Home: 5219 Malibu Dr Minneapolis MN 55436 Office: Roanoke Bldg Minneapolis MN 55402

BRADFORD, HILARY PHARISS, lawyer; b. Rolla, Mo., Oct. 12, 1929; s. Arthur Lenox and Mary (Cleino) B.; A.B summa cum laude, U. Buffalo, 1950, J.D. summa cum laude, 1953; m. Beryl M. Hutchby, Oct. 4, 1958; children—James H.L., Ian Arthur, Jennifer Jean. Admitted to N.Y. bar, 1953, also U.S. Supreme Ct.; practice in Buffalo, 1953—; law asst. to Justices Supreme Ct., Appellate div., 4th Dept., 1953-57; lectr. State U. N.Y. at Buffalo Law Sch., 1954-64; mem. firm Cohen Swados Wright Hanifin & Bradford, Buffalo and Niagara Falls, N.Y., 1959—. Dir. Frontier Bronze Corp., Niagara Falls. Bd. dirs. Travelers Aid Soc. Erie County; trustee Erie County Found. for Children. Mem. Am. Judicature Soc., Phi Beta Kappa. Presbyn. (trustee). Clubs: Buffalo, Niagara. Contbr. articles profl. jours. Home: 152 Doncaster Rd Kenmore NY 14217 Office: 70 Niagara St Buffalo NY 14202

BRADFORD, JAMES COWDON, investment banker; b. Nashville, Nov. 24, 1892; s. Alexander and Leonora (Bisland) B.; student Vanderbilt U., 1909-12; m. Eleanor Avent, May 11, 1926; children—Eleanor, James C. Partner J. C. Bradford & Co.; pres., dir. Life Ins. Investors, Inc.; pres. Life Stock Research Corp. Chmn. Nashville, Elec. Power Bd. First lt. F.A., 1917-19. Episcopalian. Mason (32, Shriner). Clubs: Belle Meade, Cumberland; Memphis Country. Home: Belle Mead Blvd Nashville TN Office: 170 4th Av N Nashville TN

BRADFORD, JOHN ROSS, coll. dean, chem. engr.; b. Amarillo, Tex., Nov. 26, 1922; s. Stanley Ross and Gentiliska (Mehaffie) B.; B.S., Tex. Technol. Coll., 1942, M.S., 1948; Ph.D., Case Inst. Tech.,

1953; m. Betty Vaughn, Sept. 4th, 1954; children—Heather Dru, Penelope Ruth. Chem. engr. research lab. Standard Oil Co. (Ind.), Whiting, Ind., 1942, Pan Am. Refining Corp., Texas City, Tex., 1942; asst. seismologist United Geophys. Co., Lubbock, Tex., 1945; lectr. dept. physics Tex. Technol. U., 1946, now dean engring. and dir. Inst. Sci. and Engring., also Textile Research Center; dir. radioisotopes lab., dept. chemistry chem. engr. Case Inst. Tech., 1948-54; research cons. U.S. Radium Corp., N.Y.C., 1954; cons. indsl. applications radioactive materials; exec. dir. Western Information Network. Mem. U.S. Nat. Commn. to UNESCO. Served as ensign, radar officer. USNR, 1944. Registered profl. engr., Tex., Ohio. Mem. Am. Inst. Chem. Engrs., Am. Chem. Soc., Am. Soc. Testing Materials (nat. sec. com. radioisotopes and radiation effects), Am. Nuclear Soc. Nat., Tex. socs. prof. engrs., Sigma Xi, Phi Kappa Phi, Tau Beta Pi. Alpha Chi Sigma. Baptist. Mason (32, Shriner). Author: Chart of the Isotopes, 1953; also articles to profl. jours. Editor, co-author: Radioisotopes in Industry, 1953; contbg. editor Handbook of Chemistry and Physics. Home: 3112 42d St Lubbock TX 79413

BRADFORD, LARNED G., publisher; b. Bloomington, Ill., Feb. 15, 1911; s. L. G. and Nellie May (Yates) B.; student U. Notre Dame, 1929-30; A.B., Depauw U., 1933; m. Pamela Seabury Cottrell, Nov. 28, 1953; children—William L. G., Kate. Sales mgr. Furnas Ice Cream Co., South Bend, Ind., 1933-39; salesman, advt. mgr. textbook dept. Harcourt, Brace & Co., N.Y.C., 1939-47; exec. editor Little, Brown & Co., Boston, 1948-52, N.Y. editor, mgr. N.Y. office, 1952-55, editor in chief, dir., Boston, 1955-68, sr. editor, 1968—. Mem. Soc. Mayflower Descs., Phi Gamma Delta, Sigma Delta Chi. Clubs: University (N.Y.C.); St. Botolph (Boston). Editor: Battles and Leaders of the Civil War. Home: 758 Summer St Marshfield MA 02050 Office: 34 Beacon St Boston MA 02108

BRADFORD, LELAND POWERS, orgn. devel. cons.; b. Chgo., July 12, 1905; s. Theron Draper and Ivy Blanche (Powers) B.; A.B., U. Ill., 1930, A.M., 1935, Ph.D., 1939; L.H.D. (hon.). Boston U., 1968; m. Martha Irene DeMaeyer, Oct. 12, 1933; 1 son, David Lee. Dir. bur. visual aids U. Ill., 1935-36, instr., 1938-41; state dir. adult edn. WPA, Ill., 1941-43; chief tng. U.S. Immigration and Naturalization Services, 1943-44, FSA, 1944-45; dir. div. adult edn. service N.E.A., Washington 1945-62, exec. sec., dept. adult edn., 1945-50, dir. Nat. Tng. Labs., N.E.A., 1947- 67; exec. dir. Nat. Inst. Applied Behavioral Sci., 1967-70; cons. orgn. devel., 1971—. Mem. nat. com. on study grants in adult edn. Ford Found. Fund for Adult Edn., 1952-54; Fulbright adv. selection com., 1952-56. Mem. Am. Mission Human Relations Tng. Team to Austria, 1954-55, Am. delegation Internat. Conf. on Human Relations in Industry, Rome, Italy, 1956; cons. European Productivity Agy., Paris, 1955; sec. International Com. Adult Edn., World Confederation Orgns. Teaching Profession: del. UNESCO World Conf. Adult Edn., Montreal, Can., 1960. Trustee Lesley Coll. Fellow Am. Psychol. Assn.; mem. Soc. Psychol. Study Social Issues, N.E.A., Am. Sociol. Assn., Nat. Soc. Study Communication, Adult Edn. Assn. (exec. com. 1951-54, coordinator research and tng. 1953-56), N.Y. Acad. Sci., A.A.A.S., Phi Delta Kappa. Clubs: Pinehurst, Kenwood. Editor: Adult Edn. Bull., 1942-50; co-editor: T Group and Laboratory Method. Contbr. articles to ednl. publs. Address: Box 247 Center Lovell ME 04016

BRADFORD, REAGAN HOWARD, med. scientist; b. Lawton, Okla., Dec. 19, 1932; s. James Amos and Pauline (Teague) B.; B.S. in Chemistry, U. Okla., 1953, M.S., 1954, Ph.D., 1957, M.D., 1961; m. Conita Ann Hargraves, Aug. 13, 1953; children—Reagan Howard, James David. Research fellow Okla. Med. Research Found., Oklahoma City, 1957-61; intern VA Hosp., Oklahoma City, 1961-62; asst. head cardiovascular sect., 1969-70, acting head, 1970, head cardiovascular sect., mem. found., 1971—; asst. prof. research medicine U. Okla. Sch. Medicine, Oklahoma City, 1958—, prof. biochemistry and molecular biology, 1969—. Bd. dirs. Okla. Heart Assn., 1965—, 1st v.p., 1971. Eli Lilly Research fellow Okla. U., 1953-54; NSF fellow, 1954-56; grad. fellow Oak Ridge Inst. Nuclear Studies biology div., 1956-57. Mem. Am. Chem. Soc., Am. Physiol. Soc., Council Arteriosclerosis, Am. Fedn. Clin. Research, A.M.A., Phi Beta Kappa, Phi Lambda Upsilon. Research and publs. in bioflavanoids, radiation protective agts., influence of parathyroid hormone on mucopolysaccharide and glycoprotein metabolism, lipid transport and metabolism. Home: 6706 N Woodward St Oklahoma City OK 73116

BRADFORD, RICHARD ROARK, writer; b. Chgo., May 1, 1932; s. Roark and Mary Rose (Sciarra) B.; B.A., Tulane U., 1952; m. Julie Dollard, Sept. 15, 1956; 1 son, Thomas Conway. Staff writer, editor N.M. Tourist Bur., 1956-59, New Orleans C. of C., 1959-61, Zia Co., Los Alamos, 1963-65; research analyst N.M. Dept. Devel., 1967-68; screenwriter Universal Pictures, 1968-70. Served with USMC, 1953-56. Mem. Edouard Manet Soc., Sigma Chi. Club: Quien Sabe (Santa Fe). Author: Red Sky at Morning, 1968. Home: P O Box 1395 Santa Fe NM 87501 Office: care McIntosh and Otis Inc 18 E 41st St New York City NY 10017

BRADFORD, ROBERT D., former refinery exec.; b. Salt Lake City, April 29, 1903; s. Robert H. and Nettie (Davis) B.; B.S., U. Utah, 1924, M.S., 1925; m. Ethel Mays, Feb. 14, 1929; children—Suzanne (Mrs. Fred R. Mason), Robert D. Research chemist Utah Copper Co., 1925, metallurgist Garfield Smelter, Am. Smelting & Refining Co., 1926-28, asst. to gen. mgr. western dept., 1929, ore dept., N.Y.C. office, 1930-35, asst. mgr. southwestern dept., 1936-39, mgr. East Helena plant, 1940-41, southwestern dept., 1942-46, Selby plant, 1947- 48, Utah dept., 1949-50, gen. mgr. western dept., 1951, v.p., 1952-59, exec. v.p., 1959-63, pres., 1963-69, also dir., ret. 1969. Mem. Am. Inst. Mining Metall. Petroleum Engrs., Mining and Metall. Soc. Am., Canadian Inst. Mining and Metallurgy, Sci. Research Soc., Sigma Xi, Theta Tau, Pi Kappa Alpha. Clubs: Mining (N.Y.C.); Westchester Country (Rye, N.Y.); Alta (Salt Lake City). Home: 20 Church St Greenwich CT 06830 Office: 120 Broadway New York City NY 10005

BRADFORD, ROBERT FISKE, former gov. of Mass., lawyer, b. Boston, 1902; A.B., Harvard, 1923, LL.B., 1926, LL.D., 1948. Admitted to Mass. bar 1927; partner firm Palmer & Dodge; dir. Cambridge Trust Co., ITB Mgmt. Corp., Trust Mgmt. Corp.; hon. dir. Olivetti Underwood Corp.; trustee Boston Five Cents Savs. Bank; gov. State of Mass., 1947-49. Treas., Olivetti Found., Inc. Trustee Simmons Coll.; sr. warden King's Chapel. Home: 106 Coolidge Hill Cambridge MA 02138 Office: 28 State St Boston MA 02109

BRADFORD, WILLIAM G., govt. ofcl.; b. Ill., Jan. 6, 1925; A.B., Ind. U., 1948. Sales mgr. various ins. cos., 1950-52; with U.S. Dept. of State, 1952—, adminstrv. officer, Saigon, 1962-64, counsel for adminstrn., Saigon, 1964, chief of mission, Leopoldville, 1964-67, exec. dir. Bur. African Affairs, 1969—. Served with AUS, 1943-46. Office: 6811 Lemon Rd McLean VA 22101*

BRADFORD, WILLIAM LESLIE, pediatrician, educator; b. Sedalia, Mo., June 8, 1898; s. John Asbury and Minnie Jane (Price) B.; A.B., U. Mo., 1921; M.D., Washington U., St. Louis, 1923; m. Lenora Dee Dalton, Oct. 27, 1928; 1 son, William D. Intern St. Louis City Hosp., 1923-24; asst. health officer for Mo., 1924-26; resident pediatrics Strong Meml. Hosp., Rochester, N.Y., 1926-27; fellow bacteriology and pathology U. Rochester Sch. Medicine and Dentistry, 1927-28, instr. pediatrics, 1928-30, asst. prof., 1930-34, asso. prof., 1934-49, asst. dean, 1947-54, prof., 1950—, head dept., 1952-64; Distinguished vis. prof., pediatrics U. Mo., 1965; cons. AEC. Served with U.S. Army, 1918. Recipient gold medal U. Rochester Med. Alumni, 1960; Alumni award, U. Mo; 1965, Washington U., 1970. Mem. Am. Pediatric Soc. (chmn. council), Soc. Pediatric Research (v.p.), Soc. Exptl. Biology and Medicine, Soc. Am. Bacteriologists, Am. Acad. Pediatrics, Am. Pub. Health Assn., A.A.A.S., Alpha Omega Alpha, Sigma Xi, Sigma Nu, Tri Chi, Nu Sigma Nu. Mason. Club: Genesee Valley (Rochester). Contbg. editor various pediatric books, encys. Author articles profl. jours. Editor Pediatrics. Home: 300 Winton Rd S Rochester NY 14610 Office: 260 Crittenden Blvd Rochester NY 14620

BRADLEE, BENJAMIN CROWNINSHIELD, journalist; b. Boston, Aug. 26, 1921; s. Frederick J. and Josephine (deGersdorff) B.; grad. St. Mark's Sch., Southboro, Mass., 1939; A.B., Harvard, 1943; m. Jean Saltonstall, Aug. 8, 1942; 1 son, Benjamin Crowninshield; m. 2d, Antoinette Pinchot, July 6, 1956; children—Dominic, Marina. Reporter, N.H. Sunday News, Manchester, 1946- 48, Washington Post, 1948-51; press attachè embassy, Paris, France, 1951- 53; European corr. Newsweek mag., Paris, 1953-57, reporter, Washington bur., 1957-61, sr. editor, chief bur., 1961-65; mng. editor Washington Post, 1965-68, v.p., exec. editor, 1968—. Served to lt. USNR, 1942-45. Author: That Special Grace, 1964. Home: 4521 Dexter St NW Washington DC 20016 Office: 1150 15th St NW Washington DC 20005

BRADLEY, CHARLES CRANE, educator; b. Chgo., Jan. 11, 1911; s. Harold Carnelius and Mary Josephine (Crane) B.; Ph.B., U. Wis., 1935, Ph.M., 1947, Ph.D., 1950; m. Mary Maynard Riggs, Nov. 28, 1942; children—Charles Crane, Dorothy Maynard. Student, also tchr. Clarence White Sch. Photography, N.Y.C., 1936-39; comml. photographer, also instr. social edn. U. Wis., 1939-41, acting instr. geology, 1946-50; tchr. geology Mont. State Coll., Bozeman, 1950—, dean div. letters and scis., 1957-68, prof. geology, 1968—, coordinator Center Environmental Studies, 1968—. Fellow Geol. Soc. Am.; mem. Am. Geophys. Union, Sigma Xi. Home: 1105 S Tracy Av Bozeman MT 59715

BRADLEY, CHARLES EDWARD, III, investment banker; b. Lawrence, Mass., Aug. 25, 1929; s. Charles Edward and Edmee (Cloutier) B.; B.S., Yale, 1951; M.B.A., N.Y. U., 1957; m. Noel Kimball, Sept. 14, 1957; children—Elizabeth, Charles Edward IV, Leslie, Kimball. With Price Waterhouse & Co., C.P.A.'s, N.Y.C., 1951-52, 56-67, partner, 1965-67, exec. v.p., dir. Laird Inc., 1967—, also subsidiaries; dir. S.S. Pierce Co., Gen. Housewares Co., Triangle Corp. Vice chmn. bd. govs. N.Y. Young Republican Club, 1958-59. Served to lt. (j.g.) USNR, 1953-56. Mem. Am. Inst. C.P.A.'s Clubs: Lunch, Yale (N.Y.C.), Stanwich (Greenwich, Conn.). Home: 31 Indian Spring Trail Darien CT 06823 Office: 140 Broadway New York City NY 10005

BRADLEY, CHARLES HARVEY, corp. exec.; b. Dubuque, Ia., Apr. 20, 1899; s. Charles Harvey and Katherine (Wetherbee) B.; grad. Phillips Andover Acad., 1917; A.B., Yale, 1921; LL.D., Butler U., 1969; m. Carolyn Coffin, Jan. 14, 1922; children—Charles Harvey, Barbara (Mrs. J.W. Walker), Katherine Wetherbee (Mrs. W.B. Moseley). With Fletcher Trust Co., Indpls., 1921-24; cashier subsidiary 16th St. State Bank, 1922-24; sec.-treas. W. J. Holliday & Co., 1927-32, pres., 1932-55, co. became div. Jones & Laughlin Steel Corp., 1955, chmn. adv. bd. warehouse div., Indpls., 1955- 60, dir.; pres. Shorewood Corp., 1960-62; chmn. exec. com., vice chmn. bd. dirs. P.R. Mallory & Co., Inc., Indpls., 1963-64, chmn. bd., 1964-68, now dir.; pres. Monarch Steel Co., Hammond, Ind., 1951-55; dir. P.R. Mallory Internat., Ransburg Electrocoating Corp., Indpls., Jones & Laughlin Steel Corp., Ind. Nat. Bank, Ind. Bell Telephone Co., Ind. Gas Co., I.C. R.R., I.C. Industries. Vice pres. Indpls. Bd. Aviation Commrs.; pres. Indpls. Hosp. Devel. Corp. Chmn. bd. dirs. Community Hosp. Indpls.; mem. alumni bd. Yale; gov. Crown Hill Cemetery. Served with USMC, 1917-18. Mem. Ind. (past pres.), Indpls. (dir.) chambers commerce, Delta Kappa Epsilon. Episcopalian. Clubs: Indianapolis Athletic (dir.), Woodstock, Columbia, University (Indpls.); Chicago. Home: 7801 Spring Mill Rd Indianapolis IN 46260 Office: 3029 E Washington St Indianapolis IN 46206

BRADLEY, CHARLES HARVEY, Jr., pharm. co. exec.; b. Indpls., June 17, 1923; s. Charles Harvey and Carolyn (Coffin) B.; grad. Phillips Acad., 1941; B.A., Yale, 1945, LL.B., 1949; m. Mary Jo Albright, Aug. 26, 1944; children—Sally Albright (Mrs. James S.R. Kothe), Jane Coffin. Admitted to Ind. bar, 1949; asso. firm Thompson, O'Neal & Smith, Indpls., 1949-50, partner 1950-60; with Eli Lilly and Co., Indpls., 1960—, sec., gen. counsel, 1964—; mem. mgmt. bd. Elanco Products Co., Indpls., 1963—. Chmn. allocations com. United Fund Indpls., 1963-65. Bd. dirs. Indpls. Hosp. Devel. Bd., 1961—; bd. dirs. Tudor Hall Sch., Indpls., 1961-68, sec., 1964-65. Served to capt. USMCR, 1943-45, 52-53; PTO, MTO. Decorated Air medal with eight oak leaf clusters, D.F.C. with three oak leaf clusters. Mem. Am., Ind., Indpls. bar assns., Lawyers Club Indpls., Am. Soc. Corp. Secs., Wolf's Head, Delta Kappa Epsilon, Phi Delta Phi. Clubs: Meridian Hills Country, Indianapolis Athletic, University, Dramatic (past pres.), Crooked Stick Country (Indpls.). Home: RR 1 Box 221 Zionsville IN 46077 Office: 307 E McCarty St Indianapolis IN 46206

BRADLEY, CHARLES MACARTHUR, architect and engr. cons.; b. Chgo., Sept. 26, 1918; s. Harold S. and Helen F. (MacArthur) B.; B.A., U. Ill., 1940; m. Joan Daane, July 27, 1947; children—Mary Barbara, Nancy Ann, Sally Joan, William C. Designer, Holabird & Root, Chgo., 1940-41; architect Giffels & Vallet, Inc., Detroit, 1941-43; chief design Army Engr. Corps, Europe, Orient, 1943-46; pres. Bradley & Bradley, Rockford, Ill., 1946—; pres. Caretech. Inc., Bradley Bldg. Corp., Medco Inc. Mem. regional bd. Boy Scouts Am., 1962-71, mem. nat. bd., 1964- 71. Pres. Winnebago County Republicans, 1956. Served with AUS, 1943-46. Decorated Bronze Star; recipient Marconi Sch. Design award A.I.A., 1962, Outstanding Center Sch. Design award Freeport, Ill., 1968, Nat. Pool Design award Evergreen Park, Ill., 1968. Mem. A.I.A. (pres. No. Ill. chpt. 1965-66), Ill. Soc. Architects (v.p. 1971), Rockford Engring. Soc., Ill. Assn. Professions (chmn. edn. com. 1967-68), Phi Kappa Psi. Mason (Shriner). Club: Union League (Chgo.). Author papers. Home: 3203 Landstrom Rd Rockford IL 61103 Office: 924 N Main St Rockford IL 61103

BRADLEY, DAVID RALL, newspaper pub.; b. Toledo. Aug. 4, 1917; s. Henry D. and Alta Katherine (Rall) B.; A.B., U. Wis., 1939; m. Shirley Wyeth, Dec. 27, 1941; children—Margaret, Natalie, Henry, David Rall. Advt. salesman Bridgeport (Conn.) Times-Star, 1939-40, Headley-Reed Co., N.Y.C., 1941, Kelly-Smith Co., Chgo., 1942-43; nat. advt. mgr. News-Press & Gazette, St. Joseph, Mo., 1946, dir., 1947—, sec.-treas., prodn. mgr., 1948-57, pub., 1956—; pres. St. Joseph Indsl. Devel. Co., St. Joseph Cablevision, Windward Pub. Co., Kailua, Hawaii; dir. A.P., Buchanan Hotel Corp., Geeco Mfg. Co., St. Joseph. Mem. Am. Newspaper Pubs. Assn. (dir.), Chi Psi. Presbyn. Mason. Clubs: Country, Benton (St. Joseph). Home: 2916 Frederick Blvd St Joseph MO 64506 Office: 9th and Edmond Sts St Joseph MO 64502

BRADLEY, EARL HALLIDAY, mfg. exec.; b. Seekonk, Mass., June 9, 1908; s. Earl L. and Esther (Halliday) B.; S.B. summa cum laude, Brown U., 1928; m. Helen Roberts Wiggins, Apr. 19, 1930; children—William C., Roberta, Earl H., Richard E. Exptl. engr. Brown & Sharpe Mfg. Co., 1928-32; partner Miner-Bradley Mfg. Co., 1932-36; with B-I-F Industries, Inc., 1935-61, successively shop supt., gen. supt., works mgr., v.p., exec. v.p., 1935-53, pres., 1953-61, dir., 1951-61; pres., dir. B-I-F Industries of Can., Ltd., 1950-61; dir. Proportioneers, Inc., 1941-61; sec. Builders-Pacific Inc., 1942-51, v.p., 1951-53, sec., dir., 1946-61; v.p., dir. Harris Kinsley, Inc., 1949-61; v.p., dir. Builders Iron Foundry, Inc., 1951-53, pres., 1953-61; v.p. N.Y. Air Brake Co., 1961-67, gen. mgr. B-I-F Industries Div. 1961-67; pres. BIF unit Gen. Signal Corp., 1967-70, chmn., 1970—; dir. Worcester Pressed Aluminum Co., Builders- Providence, Inc., Omega Machine Co. Dir. United Fund, 1958-66. Mem. R.I. Manpower Council. Trustee Gordon Sch., 1946-50, pres. 1948-49; trustee Providence Country Day Sch., 1950-57, pres. bd. trustees, 1953-55; trustee Roger Williams Jr. Coll., Brown U., 1963-70. Mem. Greater Providence C. of C. (v.p. 1960-62), Nat. Metal Trades Assn. (pres. R.I. br. 1948-50, 52-53), Sci. Apparatus Makers Assn. (chmn. indsl. relations com., recorder- controller sect. 1952-53, exec. com. 1952-55, 59-68). Conglist. Home: 920 County St Seekonk MA 02771 Office: 345 Harris Av Providence RI

BRADLEY, EDWARD SCULLEY, educator; b. Phila., Jan 4, 1897; s. Stephen Edward and Annette Evelyn (Palmer) B.; A.B., U. Pa., 1919, A.M., 1921, Ph.D., 1925; LL.D., Baylor U., 1950; m. Anna Margaret Cashner, June 11, 1921; children—Deborah Ann (Mrs. Oberholtzer), Alison (Mrs. Wilhelm). Instr. English, U. Pa., 1919-26, asst. prof., 1926-37, asso. prof., 1937-40, prof., 1940-67, vice provost, 1956-63, mem. grad. dept. Am. civilization, asst. dir. Extension Sch., 1932-44, moderator Radio Forum Pub. Opinion, 1943-49. Asst. lit. editor Phila. Record, 1930-31; vis. prof. Duke, 1932, 37, 41, Northwestern U., 1938, U. So. Cal., 1940; lectr. lit. Ogontz Sch., 1926-32, Rosemont Coll., 1930-33; lectr. drama Upton Sch. Drama, Phila., 1930-34; lectr. Am. lit. Bread Loaf Sch. English, Middlebury, Vt., 1945. Sometime mem. bd. Germantown Friends Sch. Apprentices' Library, Friends Hosp. (all Phila.). Trustee Walt Whitman Found. Camden, N.J. Served with USN, 1918-19. Fellow Soc. for Am. Studies; mem. Am. Assn. U. Profs., Modern Lang. Assn. Am. (sec. Am. lit. group 1928-36, chmn. 1937-38), Athenaeum of Phila., Phi Beta Kappa, Delta Sigma Rho, Alpha Chi Rho. Club: Lenape (Phila.). Author: George Henry Boker, Poet and Patriot (biography), 1927; Henry Charles Lea (biography), 1931; (with John A. Stevenson, q.v.) Walt Whitman's Backward Glances, 1947; Whiteman's Leaves of Grass and Selected Prose, 1949; Traubel's With Walt Whitman in Camden, vol. IV, 1953. Editor: The Sonnets of George Henry Boker, 1929; Nydia, A Tragic Play (G.H. Boker), 1929; Glaucus and Other Plays (G.H. Boker), 1940: Gen. editor, contbr. to American Tradition in Lit., 1956, latest revision (3 vols.), 1967. Contbr. English Inst. Annual, The United States, 1865-1900; Collier's Ency., 1948; Chamber's Ency. (London), 1948; Dictionary of Am. Biography; Literary History of the U.S., 1948; Revolt in the Arts; Benjamin Franklin Lectures, 1950; A Time of Harvest; American Literature 1910-60, 1962. Editor: Gen. Mag. and Hist. Chronicle, 1945-56, Mem. adv. editorial bd. American Literature, 1932-34, 1939-43; cons. editor: (with Robert H. Elias) Letters of Theodore Dreiser, 3 vols., 1959; gen. editor (with Gay W. Allen), contbr. Collected Writings of Walt Whitman, 14 vols.; editor: (with Harold W. Blodgett) Reader's Comprehensive Edition of Leaves of Grass, 1965, Leaves of Grass, A Textual Variorum, 3 vols., 1971. Contbr. articles to lit. mags., scholarly jours. Home: 6813 McCallum St Philadelphia PA 19119

BRADLEY, EMMETT HUGHES, corp. exec.; b. Hampton, Va., Dec. 8, 1927; s. Alfred Thomas and Bessie Margaret (Patrick) B.; B.S. in Elec. Engring. summa cum laude, Duke, 1949; M.S. in Elec. Engring., Mass. Inst. Tech., 1950; m. Nancy Eva Harris, Oct. 5, 1957; children—Warren Hughes, Mark Harris, Todd Hamilton. With Melpar, Inc., Falls Church, Va., 1950-62, gen. mgr. spl. products div., 1960-62; v.p., gen. mgr. missile systems div. Atlantic Research Corp., 1962-67, pres., 1967—; chief operating officer Susquehanna Corp., 1968—, exec. v.p., 1970—, also mem. exec. com., dir.; sr. exec. v.p. Pan Am. Sulphur Co., 1970—, mem. exec. com., 1970—, bd. dirs., 1969—; dir. Azufrera Panamericana, S.A., Fertilizantes Fosfatados Mexicanos, S.A. Mem. exec. bd. Nat. Capital area council Boy Scouts Am., 1967-69, Orange Empire area council Boy Scouts Am.; chmn. United Fund Duarte-Bradbury, 1964. Bd. dirs. Orange County Safety Council, 1967; mem. president's adv. council Cal. Bapt. Theol. Sem., 1966-68 now bd. trustees. Mem. Nat. Security Indsl. Assn. (exec. com. 1965-67, v.p. 1968, bd. trustees 1969—), I.E.E.E., Phi Beta Kappa, Sigma Xi, Tau Beta Pi. Author, patentee in field. Home: 5375 Duke St Alexandria, VA 22304. Office: Susquehanna Corp Shirley Hwy at Edsall Rd Alexandria VA 22314

BRADLEY, FRANK R., physician; b. Laclede, Ill. Jan. 1, 1900; s. Strother A. and Mattie (DeMonbrun) B.; M.D., Washington U., St. Louis, 1928; LL.D., Central Coll., 1943; m. Rachel Mayo, July 13, 1918; children—Frances (Mrs. John Alderson), Betty Jane (Mrs. Ray Fuchs), Richard Vernon. Surg. intern, U.S. Vets. Hosp., Jefferson Barracks, Mo., 1928; asst. supt. Barnes Hosp., St. Louis, 1928-39, dir. Barnes and asso. hosps., 1930-62, dir. emeritus, 1962—, dir. Washington U. Clinics, 1945-62, dir. emeritus, 1962—; mem. exec. faculty Wash. U. Sch. Medicine, 1939-62, prof. hosp. adminstrn. and dir. dept. hosp. adminstrn., cons. to Surgeon Gen. Army, 1951—, cons. to Surgeon Gen. Navy, 1954—. Sec. Mo. Selective Service Appeal Bd. 1940-45; mem. health and hosp. adv. com. to mayor of St. Louis 1941-44. Trustee Group Hosp. Service, Inc.; mem. Social Planning Council (exec. com. health and hosp. div. 1942-44, 50-52); mem. St. Louis Hosp. Council, 1938 (pres. 1941, 51). Mem. staff corps emergency med. services Office Civilian Def., 1942-45. Fellow Am. Coll. Hosp. Adminstrs. (regent 1942; pres. 1946-47); mem. Am. Hosp. Assn. (pres. 1954-55; trustee 1949-52; mem. joint commn. on accreditation of hosps. 1953), A.M.A., Am. Protestant Hosp. Assn. (pres. 1960—), Mid-West Hosp. Assn. (trustee), Mo. Hosp. Assn. (pres. 1939, 43), St. Louis Med. Soc. (council 1942-45), Med. Adminstrs. Soc. (nat.), Phi Rho Sigma. Presbyn. Mason. Contbr. to hosp. and sci. periodicals. Home: 7404 Oxford Dr Clayton MO 63105 Office: 4901 Barnes Hosp Plaza St Louis MO 63110

BRADLEY, FREDERICK MOFFAT, lawyer; b. Washington, Dec. 7, 1901; s. Thomas and Mabel W. (Moffat) B.; LL.B., George Washington U., 1923; m. Carolyn Chamberlain, June 2, 1928; children—Carol F. (Mrs. John R. Caswell), Thomas, Frederick M. (dec.). Admitted to D.C., U.S. Supreme Ct. bars; partner Hogan & Hartson, Washington, 1954—; dir., gen. counsel Washington Loan & Trust Co., 1938-54; dir. Riggs Nat. Bank of Washington, 1954-69, now adv. dir.; counsel Renegotiation Bd., U.S. Maritime Commn., 1942-43. Trustee Corcoran Gallery Art, Washington Hosp. Center, Louise Home. Mem. Washington Nat. Monument Soc., Am. Law Inst., Am., D.C. (past chmn. com. on probate law) bar assns., Assn. Bar City N.Y., Newcomen Soc. N.Am., Phi Delta Phi, Delta Tau Delta. Episcopalian. Clubs: Alibi, Chevy Chase (past gov.),

Metropolitan (past gov.), Alfalfa, Lawyers, Barristers (Washington). Home: 1319 30th St Washington DC 20007 Office: 815 Connecticut Av Washington DC 20006

BRADLEY, GENE ELLIOTT, mgmt. exec.; b. Omaha, May 8, 1921; s. Paul and Gladys (Elliott) B.; B.S. in Bus. Adminstrn. (Regents scholar), U. Neb., 1943; m. Mary Ann Sullivan, July 30, 1949; children—David Gerald, Barbara Ann. With Batton, Barton, Durstine & Osborn, San Francisco, 1946-51; with Gen. Electric Co., 1953-69, editor Gen. Electric Forum, 1958-64, mgr. internat. govt. relations, 1965-69; pres. Internat. Mgmt. Assn., 1969-70, Internat. Mgmt. and Devel. Inst., Washington, 1970—. White House cons., 1970-71; spl. asst. to dir. Peace Corps, 1964-65; dir., cons. Atlantic Council of U.S., 1965—, bd. sponsors, 1965—, also author, lectr. nat. security and internat. bus. affairs; Washington v.p. Nat. Strategy Information Center. Trustee Counsel of Ams.; bd. dirs. Am.-Asian Ednl. Exchange. Served to capt. USAAF 1943- 46, 51-53; lt. col. Res. Recipient Mgmt. award Gen. Electric Co., 1963, Cordiner award, 1963; spl. Freedom Leadership award Freedoms Found., 1964. Honor award, 1961; McKinsey award, 1968. Mem. N.A.M., Nat. Fgn. Trade Council, Internat. Mgmt. Assn. (pres. 1969-70), Internat. C. of C. (U.S. council), Am. C. of C. France, Assn. Internat. des Etudiant en Sciences Economique et Commercial (dir.), Fund Multinat. Mgmt. Edn. (dir.), Beta Theta Phi, Beta Gamma Sigma. Club: Wings (N.Y.C.). Author: Building The American-European Market, 1967. Home: 5822 Highland Dr Washington DC 20015 Office: Watergate Office Bldg 2600 Virginia Av NW Washington DC 20037

BRADLEY, GEORGE EDGAR, educator, physicist; b. Indpls., Feb. 21, 1924; s. George Stanley and Alice (Edgar) B.; A.B., Miami (O.), U. 1945; M.S., U. Mich., 1947, Ph.D., 1952; m. Jean Garee, May 31, 1950; 1 son, John William. Mem. faculty Western Mich. U., 1951-, prof. physics, 1958-, chmn. dept., 1964-. Mem. Central States Universities Advisory Board. Active, National Council on Religion in Higher Edn. Served with USNR, 1945-46. NSF fellow Harvard, 1959-60. Mem. Am. Phys. Soc., Phi Beta Kappa, Sigma Xi. Kiwanian. Home: 834 Ellendale St Kalamazoo, MI 49007.

BRADLEY, GEORGE SEYMOUR, lawyer; b. St. Louis, Feb. 20, 1908; s. Harry Seymour and O'Tillie (Lange) B.; A.B., U. Mich., 1930, LL.B., 1932; m. Regina M. Maloney, July 19, 1941. Admitted to Ohio bar, 1932; practiced in Toledo, 1932-42, 46—. Dir. Toledo Tank Co., Brennan Indsl. Truck Co., Seeger Brass Co., Profit Builders, Inc. Mem. Presidential Bd. Inquiry, 1957. Pres., trustee Toledo Legal Aid Soc., Toledo Florence Crittenton Home; sec., trustee Boys Club Toledo. Served to lt. col. AUS, 1942-46. Decorated Bronze Star medal; recipient citation for meritorious service Air Transport Command, 1945, Bronze Keystone award Boys Club Am., 1954. Mem. Am., Toledo (past pres., trustee) bar assns., Nat. Legal Aid Soc. (Ohio rep.), Am. Legion. Presbyn. (elder). Elk. Club: Toledo Exchange. Contbr. articles profl. jours. Home: 4644 Indian Ridge Rd Sylvania OH 43560 Office: 1018 United Savs Bldg 240 Huron St Toledo OH 43604

BRADLEY, GILBERT FRANCIS, banker; b. Miami, Ariz., May 17, 1920; s. Ever and Martha (Piper) B.; grad. LaSalle Extension U., 1942, U. Wash., 1953; Advanced Mgmt. Program, Harvard; m. Marion Bebb, June 21, 1941; children—Larry Paul, Richard Thomas, Steven Ever. With Valley Nat. Bank Ariz., Miami, Globe, Clifton, Nogales, Phoenix, 1937—, now sr. v.p., Tucson; instr. Am. Inst. Banking. Mem. Tucson Airport Authority, 1960—. Served to capt. USAAF, 1942-45. Decorated D.F.C., Air medal with three oak leaf clusters. Mem. Ariz. Bankers Assn. (pres.), Tucson C. of C. (dir.), Better Bus. Bur. (dir.), Tucson Clearing House Assn. (past pres.), Am. Legion, Navy League, Air Force Assn., Beta Gamma Sigma. Mason, Elk, Rotarian. Clubs: Sunshine Cimate (dir.); Tucson Country; Old Pueblo. Home: 5532 E 7th St Tucson AZ 85711 Office: 2 E Congress St Tucson AZ 85702

BRADLEY, HAROLD WHITMAN, educator, state legislator, b. Greenwood, R.I., July 9, 1903; s. Harold and Lillian (Whitman) Bradley; A.B., Pomoma Coll., 1925, A.M., 1926; Ph.D., Stanford U., 1932; m. Elizabeth Forbes, Aug. 28, 1940; 1 dau., Anne; m. 2d, Pearle E. Quinn, Dec. 5, 1947; 1 son, David. Tchr. Burbank High Sch., 1926-27; instr. Santa Barbara State Tchrs. Coll., 1929-30; instr. in history, Stanford, 1930-36; asst. prof., 1936-42, asso. prof., 1942-45; asst. prof. history U. Wash., 1938-39; dean and prof. history, Claremont (Cal.) Grad. Sch., 1945-53, prof. history, 1953-54; prof. history Vanderbilt U., 1954—, chmn. dept., 1954-62. Mem. Tenn. Ho. of Reps. 1964—. Mem. com. on Am. History in Schs. and Colls., 1943. Alternate del. Democratic Nat. Conv., 1952. Recipient Albert J. Beveridge Meml. prize Am. Hist. Assn., 1943. Mem. Am., So. hist. assns., Orgn. Am. Historians, Am. Studies Assn. (president Ky.-Tenn. chpt. 1956-57, nat. council 1972—), Phi Beta Kappa. Democrat (mem. Davidson County exec. com. 1960-62). Methodist. Author: The American Frontier in Hawaii, 1942; the United States 1492-1877, 1972. Mem. bd. editors Pacific Hist. Rev. 1940-54, Miss. Valley Hist. Rev., 1946-49. Contbr. Ency. Brit., Collier's Ency. Yearbook. Home: 212 Craighead Av Nashville TN 37205

BRADLEY, HENRY D., newspaperman; b. Detroit, Mich., Jan. 10, 1893; s. William H. and Bertha W.H. (Schulz) B.; ed. pub. schs.; m. Louise McLendon, Jan 16, 1926; children—David R., Natalie D., Rae Louise. With Toledo Blade (O.), 1906-23; adviser to Lord Beaverbrook, London Express (Eng.), 1923; gen. mgr. Norristown Times-Herald (Pa.), 1924-26; pres., gen. mgr. Times-Star, Bridgeport, Conn., 1927-39; pub. News Press and Gazette, St. Joseph, Mo., 1939-56; pres. News Press and Gazette Co., 1950—; former mem. bd. A.P. Former mem. Mo. Hwy. Commn.; former chmn. Nat. Adv. Com. on Scenic Hwys. and Pkwys. Organized St. Joseph Indsl. Devel. Co., Civic Improvements Assns. Awarded citizenship citation V.F.W., 1949. Mem. Internat. Press Inst., Inter-Am. Press Assn., Bridgeport C. of C. (life), Mo. Acad. Squires, Am. Philatelic Soc., Sigma Delta Chi. Republican. Episcopalian. Mason (33, Shriner, Jester); Internat. Supreme Council, Order of De Molay. Clubs: Country, Benton (St. Joseph). Home: 3026 Douglas St St Joseph MO 64506 Office: 9th and Edmond St St Joseph MO 64501

BRADLEY, HENRY STILES, banker; b. Buffalo, Aug. 25, 1907; s. William Ambrose and Alice (Howard) B.; B.S., Emory U., 1929; student Syracuse U., N.Y. State Bankers Sch. Pub. Relations, Rutgers U. Grad. Sch. Banking; m. Geraldine Annin Case, Jan. 14, 1939; children—Susan Thompson (Mrs. Susan B. Tetreault), Henry Stiles, Alice Case (Mrs. Frank L. Grier II). Vice pres., dir. J.N. Adam & Co., Buffalo, 1940-48, W.A. Case & Son Mfg. Co., Buffalo, 1949-54; v.p. Mfrs. & Traders Trust Co., Buffalo, 1956—. Chmn. supplies disaster com. Buffalo chpt. A.R.C., 1942-45, now treas.; trustee United Fund Buffalo and Erie County. Past pres. adv. bd. Albright Art Gallery; past pres. Buffalo Assn. for the Blind; bd. dirs. Buffalo Philharmonic, Buffalo Fine Arts Acad., Buffalo chpt. National Conf. Christians and Jews; rep. at large Buffalo council Boy Scouts Am.; trustee Family Service Soc., Buffalo Council Social Agys. Mem. Newcomen Soc. N. Am., Council World Affairs (bd. advisers), Buffalo C. of C., Phi Delta Theta. Presbyn. (deacon, trustee, elder). Clubs: Tennis and Squash (past pres.), Mid-Day (past pres.), Saturn (past pres.), Pack (past pres.), Country (Buffalo); Thousand Plus (dir.). Home: 86 Cleveland Av Buffalo NY 14222 Office: 284 Main St Buffalo NY 14202

BRADLEY, HOLBROOK, govt. ofcl.; b. Boothbay Harbor, Me., Sept. 25, 1916; s. Frederick and Ruth (Fletcher) B.; student Columbia U. Bus. Sch., 1938; B.A., Yale, 1940; m. Phoebe Footner, June 6, 1946; children—Elsie (Mrs. Michael Mulcahey), Susan (Mrs. Steven Mork), William H., Phoebe F. Salesman, Gen. Electric Sales, Buffalo, 1940-41; reporter, war corr., writer Balt. Sun, Balt. Evening Sun, 1941-46; Washington Bur. corr. Life mag., 1946-48; joined U.S. fgn. service; information officer Office Mil. Govt. Germany, Berlin, Nurenberg, Munich, 1948-51; rep. Asia Found., Ceylon, 1952-55, Indonesia, 1955-57; dir. Southeast Asia, San Francisco, 1957-60; fgn. service officer USIA, Washington, 1961-64, Seoul, Korea, 1964-67, Saigon, Vietnam, 1967-69, Ankara, Turkey, 1969—. Decorated Purple Heart. Recipient Meritorius Honor award USIA, 1968. Mem. Beta Theta Pi. Club: Cruising America, New York Yacht (N.Y.C.). Home: 812 Dahlia Lane Vero Beach FL 32960 Office: 97 Ataturk Blvd Ankara Turkey

BRADLEY, HOWARD ALFRED, mfg. co. exec.; b. Dover, O., Sept. 25, 1924; s. William O. and Eva (Saffel) B.; B.A., Kenyon Coll., 1948; M.B.A., Harvard, 1950; m. Elaine Marie Thys, Dec. 19, 1952; children—William, Ann, James. Trainee, Ford Motor Co., Dearborn, Mich., 1950, supr., 1951-54, dept. mgr., 1954-56; asst. sec., Houdaille Industries, Inc., Buffalo, 1956-61, sec., 1961-66, former asst. to chmn. and pres., from 1966. Div. chmn. Erie County United Fund, 1960-61, mem. exec. allocations com., 1961—. Dir. Nat. United Health Found, Citizens Com. Intermunicipal Affairs. Bd. dirs. Cerebral Palsy Assn. Western N.Y., Vocational Rehab. Center Western N.Y. Served to lt. USAAF, World War II. Decorated D.F.C. with six oak leaf clusters; recipient certificate Outstanding Service, Kenyon Coll., 1957. Mem. Am. Soc. Corporate Secs., Am. Mgmt. Assn. (past seminar leader), Kenyon Coll. Alumni Assn. Western N.Y. (pres., dir., exec. com.), Buffalo C. of C., Phi Kappa Sigma. Republican. Episcopalian. Home: 166 Sherbrooke St Williamsville NY 14221

BRADLEY, HUGH WILSON, former govt. ofcl.; b. Abbeville, S.C., May 28, 1906; s. William Wideman and Mabel Agnes (Tusten) B.; student U. S.C., 1924-28; m. Amelia Jane Wylie, Apr. 7, 1940; children—Hugh Wilson, James Wylie, Ammelia Jane. Asst. county agt. Agrl. Extension Service, Aiken, S.C., 1934-36; county adminstrv. asst. A.A.A., Columbia, S.C., 1936-38, chief marketing quota sect., 1938-41, field rep. So. div., Columbia, also Washington, 1941-42, chief field div., Columbia, 1946-47; regional rep. Bur. Vets. Reemployment Rights, U.S. Dept. Labor, Raleigh, N.C., 1947-48, dep. dir., Washington, 1948-57, nat. dir., 1957-69, ret. Named Civil Servant of Year, AMVETS, 1962. Served as lt. comdr. USNR, 1942-46. Presbyn. Clubs: Sea Pines Golf; Duffers Unincorporated. Home: 18 Black Skimmer Rd Hitlon Head Island SC 29928

BRADLEY, JAMES T., utilities exec.; b. Lorena, Tex., Nov. 23, 1909; s. James Cleveland and Martha (Fulbright) B.; student Amarillo Coll., Alexander Hamilton Inst.; m. Mildred Pearl Umphres, Aug. 16, 1930; children—Sue (Mrs. James E. Cook), Sallie (Mrs. Wayne Cooper Stephens), Julie (Mrs. Ben Patterson Friend). Treas. Southwestern Pub. Service Co., Dallas. Mem. Randall County Vets. Land Bd. 1963—, Potter-Randall Country Citizens Review Bd., 1964—, Nat. Improved Mail Service Com., 1968—, Potter-Randall Citizens Com., 1969—. Named Boss of Year Am. Bus. Women, 1967. Republican. Methodist. Lion. Office: Mercantile Bank Bldg Dallas TX 75201

BRADLEY, JOHN ANDREW, hosp. adminstr.; b. Hammond, Ind., Aug. 3, 1930; s. Andrew C. and Florence (Wolfe) B.; B.S., Loras Coll., Dubuque, Ia., 1952; M.H.A., St. Louis U., 1955, Ph.D., 1962; m. Judith E. Salmi, June 1, 1955; children—John Michael, Kerry Kathleen, Kelly Ann. Asst. adminstr. Santa Rosa Med. Center, San Antonio, 1958, Incarnate Word Hosp., St. Louis, 1958-60; research asso. St. Louis U., 1958-60; asso. adminstr. Santa Rosa Med. Center, 1961-67, adminstr., 1967-69; v.p., regional exec. dir. Am. Medicorp, Inc., 1969—; adj. prof. grad. program Hosp. adminstrn. Trinity U., 1967—; vis. lectr. Baylor U. Sch. Hosp. Adminstr., 1962—. Mem. health services research study sect. Nat. Center Health Services Research and Devel., Dept. Health, Edn. and Welfare, 1967- 69. Chmn. urban devel. com. San Antonio C. of C., 1967; mem. bd. Econ. Opportunities Devel. Corp., 1966-67; vice chmn. Cath. Youth Orgn. Adv. Bd., Archdiocese San Antonio, 1965-66. Bd. dirs. Cath. Welfare Bur., 1965-66. Patrician Movement, 1964-66, Guadalupe Community Center, 1964-66, San Antonio Neighborhood Youth Orgn., 1965-66, Fedn. Am. Hosps., 1971. Served with AUS, 1953-57. Fellow Am. Coll. Hosp. Adminstrs.; mem. Am., Tex. (v.p. 1969) hosp. assns., Nat. League Nursing, Alamo Hosp. Div., Order Alhambra. Home: 200 Village Circle San Antonio TX 78232 Office: 1800 Northeast Loop 410 San Antonio TX 78217

BRADLEY, JOHN EDMUND, physician, educator; b. Balt. Oct. 31, 1906; s. Charles Edward and Mary (Henry) B.; B.S., Loyola Coll., 1928; M.D., Georgetown U., 1932; postgrad. Harvard, 1933-34; m. Kathryn Davis Strong, Sept. 21, 1933; children—Mark, Marcia. Intern, Mercy Hosp., Balt. 1932-33; instr., asst. prof., asso. prof. pediatrics U. Md. Sch. Medicine, 1934-46, prof., head pediatrics, 1948-66, emeritus prof. pediatrics, 1966—, dir. Pediatrics Permanente Found., 1946-48; practice medicine specializing in pediatrics, Balt., 1935—; chmn. med. bd. St. Gabriel's Home; chief pediatrics Luth. Hosp. Mem. Md. Bd. Health and Mental Hygiene; mem. adv. bd. Childhood Study Center Md.; mem. adv. com. Md. Civil Def.; mem. health council Md. Conf. Social Welfare; mem. Maternal Child and Welfare Med. Care Com.; mem. nat. adv. com. SSS. Bd. dirs. Mental Hygiene Soc. Md.; trustee Hosp. Council. Fellow Am. Acad. Pediatrics; mem. A.M.A., N.Y. Acad. Scis. A.A.A.S., Assn. Med. Writers, So. Med. Assn., Alpha Omega Alpha. Contbr. articles to med. jours. Home: Sintonte and Mirasol Rds Rancho Bernardo San Diego CA 92128 Office: Univ Hosp Baltimore MD 21201

BRADLEY, LEE CARRINGTON, Jr., lawyer; b. Charlottesville, Va., Sept. 27, 1897; s. Lee C. and Eleanor (Lyons) B.; Litt.B., Princeton, 1918; LL.B., Harvard, 1921; m. Mary Allen Northington, Jan. 9, 1929; children—Lee Carrington, Merrill Northington, Mary Earle (Mrs. Murray). Admitted to Ala. bar, 1921, since practiced in Birmingham; partner firm Bradley, Arant, Rose & White, and predecessors, 1921—. Dir., mem. exec. com. Birmingham Trust Nat. Bank; dir. Avondale Mills. Mem. Phi Beta Kappa. Episcopalian. Rotarian. Home: 2844 Carlisle Rd Birmingham AL 35213 Office: Brown Marx Bldg Birmingham, AL 35203.

BRADLEY, MARK EDWARD, Jr., ret. air force officer; b. Clemson, S.C., Dec. 10, 1907; s. Mark and Mary Elizabeth (Morrah) B.; student Clemson A. & M. Coll., 1924-26; B.S., U.S. Mil. Acad., 1930; grad. A.A.C. Advanced Flying Sch., 1931, A.C. Engring. Sch., 1938; m. Alice Cecilia Newman, July 7, 1934; children—Alice Cecilia, Mark Edward. Commd. 2d lt., U.S. Army, 1930, trans. to A.C., 1931, advanced through grades to gen., 1962; fighter pilot, 1931-47; flight test pilot, Air Materiel Command fighter, br. prodn. div., 1942-43; dep. comdr. A.S. Comd. 1st TAC Air Force (provisional), France, 1944-45; chief staff 5th Air Force, Japan, 1945; dep. dir. procurement and indsl. planning U.S.A.A.F., 1948-51, dir. procurement and prodn., 1951-53; asst. chief of staff for materiel, later dep. comdr.-in-chief, chief of staff USAFE, 1953-56; asst. dep. chief of staff for materiel Hdqs. USAF, 1956-59, dep. chief staff for materiel, 1959-62; comdr. Air Force Logistics Command, Wright- Patterson AFB, O., 1962-65; v.p., asst. to pres. Garrett Corp., Los Angeles, 1965-69, sr. exec. v.p., 1969—. Decorated Legion of Merit, Bronze Star medal with oak leaf cluster, Air medal, D.S.M. Home: 30327 Oceanaire Dr Palos Verdes CA 90274 Office: 9851 Sepulveda Blvd Los Angeles CA 90009

BRADLEY, MARVIN R., coop. assn. exec.; b. Lebanon, Ind., Jan. 2, 1914; s. Ira and Ada Fern (Rader) B.; student Purdue U., 1931-32, Walton Sch. Commerce, 1935-41; m. Mable Morris, Aug. 18, 1935; children—Steven R., Kathleen F. Bookkeeper, Indpls. Star, 1933-34; with Ind. Farm Bur. Coop. Assn., Inc., Indpls., 1934—, sec., 1948—, treas., 1964—. Coordinator, Speedway (Ind.) Boy Scouts Am., 1949-50. Mem. Speedway Town Bd., 1956- 59. Mem. Nat. Soc. Accountants for Coops. (past pres.). Mem. Christian Ch. (trustees, deacon, treas.). Mason, Lion (past pres. Speedway). Home: 5735 Elaine St Speedway, IN 46224. Office: 47 S Pennsylvania St Indianapolis IN 46204

BRADLEY, MARY HASTINGS (Mrs. Herbert Edwin Bradley), author; b. Chgo.; d. William and Lina (Rickords) Hastings; B.A., Smith Coll.; m. Herbert Edwin Bradley, June 21, 1910; childrenAlice Hastings (Mrs. Huntington Denton Sheldon), Mary Lee. Fellow Royal Geog. Soc.; mem. Soc. Women Geographers, Phi Kappa Psi. Conglist. Clubs: Casino, Fortnightly, Arts, Contemporary (Chgo.). Author: Favor of Kings, 1912; Palace of Darkened Windows, 1914; Splendid Chance, 1915; Wine of Astonishment, 1919; Fortieth Door, 1919; The Innocent Adventures, 1921; On the Gorilla Trail, 1923; Caravans and Cannibals, 1926; Alice in Jungleland, 1927; Trailing the Tiger, 1929; Alice in Elephantland, 1929; Murder in Room 700, 1931; Road of Desperation, 1932; Old Chicago Stores, 1933; Unconfessed, 1934; The Five Minute Girl, 1935; Pattern of Three, 1937; A Hanging Matter, 1938; Mimi Foster, 1945; Understudy, 1946; Without Witness, 1947; Murder in the Family, 1949; Nice People Poison, 1952 (pub. Eng. 1956, Holland 1957, Die Weise Neggerin, 1960, Une Viellr Touquee 1963); I Passed for White, The Story of Reba Lee, 1955. Accompanied husband on expdn. of Carl E. Akeley of Am. Mus. Natural History, into Belgian Congo for gorillas, 2d trip to Belgian Congo with husband, 1924; 1st expdn. to traverse region west of Lake Edward, in Sumatra and Indochina for tigers, 1935; 3d expdn. to Africa, studying Pygmies and Mangbetou tribes, 1930-31. Spl. corr. Coller's mag., covering Eastern, Far Eastern European and Mediterranean war zones, 1945; South African, Eastern Equatorial expdn., auspices Dept. State, 1951, Research Mexico and C. Am. Home: 5344 Hyde Park Blvd Chicago IL 60615 also Florence WI 54121

BRADLEY, OMAR NELSON, watch co. exec.; b. Clark, Mo., Feb 12, 1893; s. John Smith and Sarah E. (Hubbard) B.; B.S., U.S. Mil. Acad., 1915; grad. Inf. Sch. (advance course), 1925, Command and Gen. Staff Sch., 1929, Army War Coll., 1934; LL.D., U. Mo., Drury Coll., 1946, U. Ill., Harvard, Dartmouth, Northwestern U., N.Y. U., 1947, Princeton, U. Wis., U. Cal., 1948, Columbia, Hamilton Coll., Trinity Coll., 1949, Tex. A. and M. Coll. 1950, Cambridge U. (Eng.) U. Pitts. 1951; Sc.D., St. Johns U., 1946, Lafayette Coll., 1949; Dr. Humanities, Birmingham-So. Coll., 1947, D. Eng., Rensselaer Poly Inst., 1950; Dr. Internat. Law, Pa. Mil. Coll., 1951; Dr. Mil. Sci. Norwich U., 1952; LL.D., U. Akron; m. Mary Quayle, Dec. 28, 1916 (dec. Dec. 1965) 1 dau., Elizabeth; m. 2d, Esther Dora Buhler, Sept. 12, 1966. Commd. 2d lt., inf., U.S. Army, 1915, advanced through grades to gen. 1945, gen. of the army, 1950; comdg. gen. 2d corps, No. Tunisian campaign, 1943, Sicilian campaign, 1943, 1st U.S. Army, Normandy campaign, 1944, 12th Army Group, France, Belgium, Holland, Luxembourg, Germany campaigns, 1944-45; adminstr. vets. affairs, 1945-47; chief of staff, U.S. Army, 1948-49; chmn. U.S. Joint Chiefs Staff, 1949-53; chmn. bd. Bulova Watch, 1958—; U.S. rep. standing group, mil. com. NATO, 1949-53. Decorated D.S.M. with 3 oak leaf clusters, D.S.M. (Navy), Legion of Merit with oak leaf cluster, Silver Star, Bronze Star medal, Knight Comdr. Bath (Gt. Britain), Grand Cross Legion of Honor, Croix de Guerre with palm (France), Order Suvorov, 1st degree, Order Kutuzov (Russia), Grand Cross Couronne de Chene, Croix de Guerre (Luxembourg), Grand Cross Order of Crown, Croix de Guerre with palm (Belgium), Cross of 1939 (Czechoslovakia), Grand Cross Ouissan Alaouite; mem. Order Orange-Nassau (Netherlands). Mem. Christian Ch. Mason. Clubs: Army and Navy, Burning Tree (Washington). Author: A Soldier's Story, 1951. Address: 630 Fifth Av New York City NY 10020

BRADLEY, PAUL LINCOLN, marketing cons.; b. Omaha, June 6, 1918; s. Paul and Gladys (Elliott) B.; B.S., U. So. Cal., 1940; grad. student, U. Cal. at Los Angeles, 1941; m. Virginia Fisher, June 38, 1942; children—Paul F., Carol, Sheri. Corr., Internat. News Service, 1936-39; media dir. Lord & Thomas, Inc., 1940-42; Eastern advt. and pub. relations dir. Lockheed Aircraft Corp., Eastern mgr. Exec. Research, Inc., 1946-50; v.p., gen. mgr. N.Y.C. and West coast offices, mem. central exec. com. Grant Advt., Inc., 1952-58; v.p., mem. plans bd. and marketing services com., dir. sales devel., merchandising and pub. relations services Kenyon & Eckhardt, Inc., N.Y.C., 1958-60; pres., chmn. bd. Paul Bradley, Inc., N.Y.C., 1960—; dir. Vulcan Mfg. Co. Chief of plans and policies of pub. relations and industry matters Office Sec. Air Force, 1950-52, adviser pub. information, recruiting and industry matters, 1952—; cons. N.Y.C. Mayor's Office to N.Y.C. Manpower Utilization Council, N.Y.C. Mayor's Task Force on Youth and Work Bd., Bd. Edn., Depts. Commerce and Pub. Events, Civil Service Commn., Inter-Agy. Com., 1960-68; cons. N.Y. State Narcotic Addiction Control Commn., 1970—, Fgn. Policy Assn.-World Affairs Center; mem. interprofl. council Nat. Strategy Information Center; pres., trustee, mem. exec. com. People-to-People Nat. Council, 1970—. Served as pilot USAAF, 1942-46, 50-52; maj. Res. Mem. Alpha Delta Sigma, Beta Theta Pi. Club: Wings (past dir.) (N.Y.C.). Home: 16941 S Pacific Av Sunset Beach CA 90742 Office: 375 Park Av New York City NY 10022

BRADLEY, PRESTON, clergyman; b. Linden, Mich., Aug. 18, 1888; s. Robert McFarlan and Anna Elizabeth (Warren) B.; student Alma (Mich.) Coll., 1905-06; studied law, Flint, Mich., 1906-09; spl. work U. Mich., 1909-10; D.C.L., Hamilton Coll. of Law, Chgo., LL.D., Lake Forest Coll., 1938; D.D., Meadville Theol. Sch., 1939; D.D., Yankton Coll., 1966; m. Grace Wilkins Thayer, Nov. 25, 1915; m. 2d, June Haslet, June 30, 1952. Student pastor, Grand Blanc, Michigan, 1907-09. Ch. of Providence (Presbyn.), Chgo., 1911-12; withdrew from Presbyn. Ch., July 1, 1912, began preaching independently; founded Peoples Ch., Chgo., July 5, 1912; services at Wilson Av. Theatre, 1913-19, Pantheon Theatre, Sheridan Road, 1919-26; church built own building, costing furnished $750,000, dedicated, Oct. 10, 1926; united with Unitarian Conf., Feb. 9, 1922, accepting full fellowship with Unitarian Church, Feb. 9, 1923; continued as pastor Peoples Church. Bd. Dirs. Chgo. Pub. Library, June 1925—; mem. Ill. State Teachers Coll. and Normal Sch. Bds. Recipient Merit award Ill. Dept. Conservation, 1952; Good Human Relations award Dale Carnegie Club Internat., 1955. Mem. Am. Inst. Chgo., Izaak Walton League of Am. (pres. 1930), Drama League Am., Phi Phi Alpha (Alma), Pi Gamma Mu. Clubs: Chicago Press, City, Adventureres (Chicago); Nat. Arts (N.Y.C.); Authors' (London, Eng.). Author: Courage for Today, 1934; Mastering Fear, 1935; Power from Right Thinking, 1936; Life and You, 1940; New Wealth for You, 1941;

Meditations, 1941; My Daily Strength, 1943; Happiness Through Creative Living, 1955; Along the Way, 1962. Editor: Liberalist. Address: Peoples Church 941 Lawrence Av Chicago IL 60640

BRADLEY, RALPH ALLAN, educator; b. Smith Falls, Ont., Can., Nov. 28, 1923; s. Alva Ogle and Ruby (Minnikin) B.; B.A., Queens U., 1944, M.A., 1946; Ph.D., U. N.C., 1949; m. Marion Edith MacRae, Sept. 6, 1946; children—Ralph Allan, Linda Irene. Came to U.S., 1950, naturalized, 1958. Asst. prof. McGill U., 1949-50; asso. prof., prof. Va. Poly. Inst., 1950-59; prof., head dept. statistics Fla. State U., Tallahassee, 1959—; vis. prof. Rutgers U., 1954; program specialist Ford Found. and U. Cairo, 1966-67. Served to lt., inf., Canadian Army, 1944-45. Recipient Brumbaugh award Am. Soc. Quality Control, 1956, Shelton Horsley Research award Va. Acad. Sci., 1957. Univ. distinguished prof., 1970. Fellow Inst. Math. Statistics (past council mem.), Am. Statis. Assn. (past dir.), A.A.A.S.; mem. Biometric Soc. (council), Internat. Statis. Inst., Enar Biometric Soc. (past pres.), Sigma Xi. Editor: Biometrics, 1957-62. Contbr. articles profl. jours. Home: 2522 Killarney Way Tallahassee FL 32303

BRADLEY, RICHARD EDWIN, univ. dean; b. Omaha, Mar. 9, 1926; s. Louis J. and Betsy (Winterton) B.; student Creighton U., 1946-48; B.S.D., U. Neb., 1950, D.D.S., 1952; M.S., State U. Ia., 1958; m. Doris I. McGowan, June 8, 1946; children—Diane, Karen, David. Instr. State U., Ia., 1957-58; asst. prof. Creighton U., 1958-59; asst. prof., chmn. dept. periodontics U. Neb., 1959-62, asso. prof., 1962-65, prof., 1965-67, asso. dean Coll. Dentistry, 1967-68, dean, 1968—; cons. VA, also VA hosps in Lincoln and Omaha. Served with USNR, 1944-46. Fellow Internat. Coll. Dentists; mem. Am. Dental Assn., Am. Acad. Periodontology, Internat. Assn. Dental Research, Sigma Xi, Omicron Kappa Upsilon. Contbg. editor to Orban's Textbook of Periodontics, 1963—. Home: 1904 S 77th St Lincoln NB 68520

BRADLEY, ROBERT JOSEPH, investment co. ofcl.; b. Leon, Ia., Nov. 30, 1909; s. Harry Joseph and Madge Lulu (Wasson) B.; student U. Mo., 1926-29, Northwestern U., 1929- 30, U. Okla., 1930-31; B.S., Loyola U., Los Angeles, 1931; m. Virginia Klarquist, Apr. 6, 1941; children—Susan Virginia, Karen Virginia. Asst. credit mgr. Union Hardware & Metal, Los Angeles, 1932- 37; sec.-treas. Hawaiian Tuna Packers, Honolulu, 1937-38; accountant oil producing dept. Standard of Cal., San Francisco, 1938-39; charge govt. relations Persian Gulf, Cal. Arabian Standard Oil Co. (now ARAMCO), Dhaharan, Saudi Arabia, 1939-41; charge priority on materials and supplies WPB and Standard of Cal., 1941-42; petroleum economist De Golyer and MacNaughton, Dallas, 1946-49; pres., dir. San Juan Oil Co., Dallas, 1949-52; chmn. bd., chief exec. officer Producing Properties, Inc. Dallas, 1952-63; chmn. Brezor River Oil & Gas Co., Dallas, 1956-60; pres. Haas & Haynie Investment Co., San Francisco, 1964-65; dir., mem. exec. com. 1st Western Nat. Bank & Trust, Los Angeles, 1964-65; pres. Bradley Investment Co., Honolulu; dir., mem. finance com. Halliburton Co.; dir. Fund of Letters, Inc., Los Angeles, Cal. Petroleum economist Sec. Navy, Washington, World War II. Served as lt. comdr. USNR, World War II. Recipient unit citation for radio intelligence USN, World War II. Mem. Am. Inst. Mining, Metall. and Petroleum Engrs. (nat. chmn. com. on petroleum econs. 1948-49), Ind. Petroleum Assn. Am., Am. Petroleum Inst., Mid-Continent Oil and Gas Assn. (dir.), Am. Mus. Natural History, Delta Sigma Phi, Alpha Kappa Psi. Home: 4439 Kahala Av Honolulu HI 96816 Office: PO Box 10399 Honolulu HI 96816

BRADLEY, RONALD CALVIN, investment co. exec.; b. Duluth, Minn., Mar. 17, 1915; s. Ralph Dawson and Celeste (Coleman) B.; B.S. with honors, U. Cal. at Berkeley, 1937; M.B.A. with honors, Harvard, 1939; m. Margot H. Tude, Dec. 31, 1949; children—Margot, Michele. With Emporium, San Francisco, 1939-41, U.S. Steel Corp. of Del., Pitts., 1941-42; v.p. Doherty, Clifford, Steers & Shenfield, advt. agy., N.Y.C., 1946-56; sr. v.p. Ted Bates & Co., N.Y.C., 1956-70; investment analyst, adviser, cons., pres. Bradley Investments, N.Y.C., 1970—. Served from lt. (j.g.) to lt. comdr., USNR, 1942- 46. Mem. Phi Beta Kappa. Christian Scientist (1st reader, treas., trustee). Office: 85 East End Av New York City NY 10028

BRADLEY, STANLEY EDWARD, physician; b. Columbia, S.C., Mar. 24, 1913; s. Stanley and Elizabeth (Crowe) B.; A.B., Johns Hopkins, 1934; M.D., U. Md., 1938; m. Geraldine Powell, July 10, 1936; 1 dau., Jane Elizabeth. Intern U. Hosp., Balt., 1938-40; Commonwealth Fund fellow medicine N.Y.U., 1940-42; asst. clin. vis. physician Bellevue Hosp., 1940-42; instr. medicine Boston U., 1942-45, asst. prof. medicine, 1945-47; asst. vis. physician Evans Meml. Hosp., 1942-47, asst. prof. medicine Columbia, 1947-49, asso. prof. medicine, 1949-59, prof. medicine, 1958-60, Bard prof. medicine, 1960—, chmn. dept. medicine, 1959-70; asso. attending physician Presbyn. Hosp., 1951-59, attending physician, 1959—, dir. med. service, 1959-70, pres. med. bd., 1964-67. Mem. vis. com. med. dept. Brookhaven Nat. Lab., 1965-69; bd. sci. cons. Sloan Kettering Inst., 1962—. Trustee Mt. Desert Island Biol. Lab., 1947-60. Recipient Univ. Prizeman med. medal, 1938; Edward N. Gibbs prize N.Y. Acad. Medicine, 1947. Diplomate Am. Bd. Internal Medicine. Fellow A.C.P.; mem. Harvey Soc., Am. (mem. sci. council founders group, council high blood pressure), N.Y. (pres. 1970—) heart assns., Mass. Med. Soc., Am. Physiol. Soc., Exptl. Biol. and Medicine, Assn. Am. Physicians, Peripatetic Soc., A.A.A.S., Am. Soc. Clin. Investigation (editorial com. Jour. Clin. Investigation 1948-52, editor in chief 1952-57, pres. 1957), Societe de Pathologie Renale (hon.), Interurban Clin. Club, Renal Assn. Great Britain (hon.), Am. Acad. Arts and Scis. Club: Century Assn. Home: 116 Pinehurst Av New York City NY 10033 Office: 622 W 168th St New York City NY 10032

BRADLEY, STERLING GAYLEN, microbiologist, educator; b. Springfield, Mo., Apr. 2, 1932; s. Benn and Lora (Brown) B.; B.A., B.S., S.W. Mo. State Coll., 1950; M.S., Northwestern U., 1952, Ph.D. (NSF fellow), 1954; certificate med. mycology Duke, 1957; m. Lois Evelyn Lee, May 13, 1951; children—Don, Evelyn, John, Phillip. Grad. teaching asst. Northwestern U., Evanston, Ill., 1950-51, Abbott research asst., 1951-52, instr. biology, 1954; instr. dept. bacteriology and immunology U. Minn., 1956-57, asst. prof. dept. bacteriology, 1957-59, asso. prof. dept. microbiology, 1959-63, grad. faculty genetics, 1961-68, prof., 1963-68, chmn. genetics faculty group, 1964; chmn. dept. microbiology Med. Coll. Va., Richmond, 1968—. Mem. bd. sci. counselors NIH, 1968-72, chmn., 1970—; mem. Internat. Com. Bacteriol. Systematics, 1966—, exec. bd., 1970-74. Eli Lilly postdoctoral fellow U. Wis., 1954-55, NSF postdoctoral fellow dept. genetics, 1955-56. Mem. Am. Assn. Immunology, Am. Acad. Microbiology, Am. Soc. Cell Biology, A.A.A.S., Am. Assn. U. Profs., Am. Soc. Microbiology (council), Soc. Gen. Microbiology, Soc. Indsl. Microbiology (past pres.), Am. Inst. Biol. Sci. (past dir.), Mycol. Soc. Am., Soc. for Exptl. Biology and Medicine (past chmn. Minn. chpt.), Genetics Soc. Am., Torrey Bot. Club (life), N.Y. Acad. Scis. (life), Va. Acad. Sci. (council), Sigma Xi. Mem. editorial bd. Proc. Soc. Exptl. Biol. Medicine, 1966—, Conf. on Anti-microbial Agts., 1960; editor Jour. Bacteriology, 1970—. Contbr. articles profl. jours. Home: 3111 Hawthorne Av Richmond VA 23222

BRADLEY, STUART B., lawyer; b. Chgo., Jan. 29, 1907; s. Alexander S. and Laura (Bevans) B.; student Wash. State Coll., 1923-25, U. Chgo., 1927-30, Ph.B., J.D.; m. Patricia Goodhue, Mar. 15, 1935; children—Stuart, Barbara, Carolyn, Laura. Admitted to Ill. bar, 1931; partner firm Bradley, Eaton, Jackman & McGovern, and predecessors, Chgo., 1934—, specializing admiralty, maritime law, 1936—; promoter St. Lawrence Seaway, Calumet-Sag projects. Dir. Deerfield Savs. & Loan Assn., 1951—. Mem. adv. com. on admiralty rules U.S. Supreme Ct., 1960—. Scoutmaster, Boy Scouts Am., 1949-52; chmn. planning bd. North Shore Area Council, 1953. Mem. vis. com. U. Chgo. Law Sch., 1956—; trustee Glencoe Pub. Library. Served capt. to lt. col. AUS, 1943-46. Decorated Bronze Star medal; recipient citation for pub. service U. Chgo., 1955. Mem. Chgo. Assn. Commerce (chmn. harbors and waterways com. 1948-52), Maritime Law Assn., (exec. com. 1954-55, 63-66), Am., Ill., Chgo. (chmn. admiralty com. 1958-59) bar assns., Am. Coll. Trial Lawyers, Phi Delta Phi, Kappa Sigma. Methodist. Clubs: Propeller (pres. Port of Chgo. 1948), Jackson Park Yacht (judge adv.), Law, Legal, Export Managers, Attic, Literary (Chgo.); Skokie Country (Glencoe). Author articles mags., law reviews. Home: 750 Bluff St Glencoe IL 60022 Office: 135 S LaSalle St Chicago IL 60603

BRADLEY, THOMAS A., Jr., transp. co. exec.; b. N.Y.C., Nov. 30, 1916; s. Thomas A. and Irene C. Bradley; B.A., Fordham U., 1939; m.; 3 children. Ins. broker Bradley & Parker, N.Y.C.; with Acme Fast Freight, Inc., N.Y.C., 1940—, v.p., 1949, pres., vice chmn. bd., 1969—. Home: Cedar Swamp Rd Glen Head NY 11545 Office: 156 William St New York City NY 10038

BRADLEY, VAN ALLEN, bibliographer, writer; b. Albertville, Ala., Aug. 24, 1913; s. Van and Lula (Montgomery) B.; student Harding Coll., 1930-32; B.J., U. Mo., 1933; m. Patricia Elaine Thompson, Nov. 5, 1939 (div.); children—Van Allen III, Pamela Star, Susan; m. 2d, Sharon Lee Luedke, Dec. 3, 1966; 1 dau., Gremlyn Angelica. Reporter, Nashville Tennessean, 1934-35; reporter, columnist, chief copy desk Omaha Bee-News, 1935-37; copy editor Chgo. Herald-Examiner, 1937-38; copy editor, asst. picture editor Chgo. Tribune, 1938-42; copy editor, book columnist, chief copy desk Chgo. Sun (now Sun-Times), 1942-48; lit. editor Chgo. Daily News, 1948-71, editorial writer, 1953-60, ret., 1971; pres. Heritage Book Shop, Inc., Chgo., 1964—. Author syndicated rare book column Gold in Your Attic; lectr., tchr. Northwestern U. Medill Sch. Journalism, 1942-54; platform lectr. books, current lit. Founder mem. Lincolnwood (Ill.) Little Theatre, Inc., pres. 1957-58; mem. Lincolnwood Bd. Edn., 1950-60, pres., 1953-60; mem. Citizens Com. for Chgo. Pub. Library; poetry and lit. adv. coms. Ill. Arts Council. Recipient award for meritorious service to letters Chgo. Found. for Lit., 1956. Mem. Soc. Midland Authors (dir., pres. 1955-57), Friends Chgo. Pub. Library (dir.), Friends Lit. (adv. council), Chgo. Press Vets. Assn. Democrat. Mem. Ch. of Christ. Club: Tavern (Chgo.). Author: Music for the Millions, 1957; Gold in Your Attic, 1958; More Gold in Your Attic, 1961; The New Gold in Your Attic, 1968. Editor: How to Predict What People Will Buy, 1957. Contbr. articles to nat. mags.; spl. contbr. World Book Ency. Home: 623 Border Lane Barrington IL 60010 Office: 612 N Michigan Av Chicago IL 60611

BRADLEY, WILLIAM BENJAMIN, physician; b. Macon, Mo., Nov. 9, 1930; s. Ralph Emil and Gladys (White) B.; B.A., U. Mo., 1952, B.S. in Medicine, 1953; M.D., U. Cin., 1955; m. Shirley Rae Custer, Aug. 27, 1955; children—William Custer, Megan Beryl, Ralph Leland, Aaron Benjamin. Intern, St. Louis City Hosp., 1955-56; commd. capt., M.C., U.S. Army, 1956, advanced through grades to maj., 1962; resident gen. pediatrics Wm. Beaumont Gen. Hosp., El Paso, Tex., 1957-59; mem. staff Ireland Army Hosp., Ft. Knox, 1956-57, Madigan Gen. Hosp., Tacoma, 1959-61, Munich Army Med. Center, Germany, 1961-62; ret., 1962; pvt. practice medicine, specializing in pediatrics, Mt. Vernon, Ill., 1962-64; clin. dir., acting supt., supt. Murray Childrens Center, Centralia, Ill., 1964-69; pediatric cons. Mo. Div. Mental Health, 1969; supt. Marshall (Mo.) State Sch. & Hosp., 1969—. Diplomate Am. Bd. Pediatrics. Fellow Am. Acad. Pediatrics. Democrat. Baptist. Kiwanian. Home: 1705 Greenberry Rd Jefferson City MO 65101 Office: Marshall State Sch & Hosp Marshall MO 65340

BRADLEY, WILLIAM BESTEDER, biochemist; b. Clinton, Ia., May 15, 1911; s. William H. and Mary E. (Besteder) B.; B.S., Northwestern U., 1933, M.S., 1936, Ph.D., 1938; m. Alice Wixson, Nov. 30, 1935; children—Jean, Ann, William R. Asst. prof. U. Wyo., 1938-41; council on foods and nutrition A.M.A., 1941-42; dir. labs. Am. Inst. Baking, 1945-49, sci. dir., 1949-64, pres., 1964. Mem. cereal com., food and nutrition bd. NRC. Served with AUS, 1942-45. Mem. Am. Physiol. Soc., Am. Assn. Cereal Chemists (pres. 1957-58). Home: 1046 Elmwood Av Wilmette, IL Office: 400 E Ontario St Chicago IL 60611

BRADLEY, WILLIAM CRANE, educator; b. Madison, Wis., Feb. 22, 1925; s. Harold C. and Josephine (Crane) B.; B.S., U. Wis., 1951; M.S., Stanford, 1953, Ph.D., 1956; m. Alice L. Babcock, Nov. 28, 1958; children—Cameron, Melanie, Mark. Field asst. Conn. Geol. Survey, summer 1950; mem. faculty U. Colo., 1955—, prof. geol. scis., 1968—, chmn. dept., 1968—. Served with inf. AUS, 1943-46. Decorated Silver Star. Fellow Geol. Soc. Am., A.A.A.S.; mem. Colo. Sci. Soc. (pres. 1969), Phi Beta Kappa, Phi Kappa Phi. Home: 2885 16th St Boulder CO 80302

BRADLEY, WILLIAM EARLE, oil co. exec.; b. San Francisco, Nov. 28, 1907; s. William Littell and Bothilde (Lorentzen) B.; B.S. in Chem. Engring., Stanford, 1928; Ph.D. in Chemistry, U. Cal. at Berkeley, 1931; div.; 1 son, James Earle; m. 2d, Katharina Berker, Oct. 14, 1961. With Union Oil Co. Cal., 1931—, mgr. refining research div., 1955-60, dir. research, 1960-61, v.p. research, 1961—. Bd. dirs. Coordinating Research Council, Boys Club, Santa Ana, Cal. Mem. Am. Chem. Soc. (past chmn. div. petroleum chemistry), Am. Soc. Testing Materials, Am. Petroleum Inst. (chmn. research com.), Phi Beta Kappa, Sigma Xi, Alpha Chi Sigma. Home: 1892 Omega Dr Santa Ana CA 92705 Office: Union Oil Co Cal PO Box 76 Brea CA 92621

BRADLEY, WILLIAM T., clergyman; b. Derry, Ireland, Oct. 3, 1911; s. William J. and Veronica (Cowley) B.; student Mt. St. Mary Coll., Emmitsburg, 1929-31; A.B., St. Charles Coll. Sem., Columbus, O., 1933; postgrad. Mt. St. Mary Sem., Norwood, O., 1933-37. Ordained priest Roman Catholic Ch., 1937; archdiocesan supt. schs., Santa Fe, 1944-64; archdiocesan dir. hosps., 1945-64, also archdiocesan dir. charities, 1944—; named Domestic Prelate by Pope Pius XII, 1950; apptd. diocesan consultor, 1951-64; resident chaplain St. Catherine Indian Sch., 1950—. Chaplain N.M. Legislature, Senate and House alternately, 1945-64; del., mem. state com. Mid-Century White House Conf. on Children and Youth; 1st v.p. Catholic Hosp. Assn. U.S. and Can., 1956-57; mem. N.M. Fair Employment Practices Com., 1954-69 (chmn. 1959-69), N.M. Health Com. Sch. Health, 1958, N.M. Bd. Edn. High Sch. Com., 1958. Mem. Nat. Catholic Edn. Assn. (exec. com., supt. dept. 1953-58). K.C. (4). Author articles. Home: St Catherine Indian Sch Santa Fe NM 87501 Office: 223 Cathedral Pl Santa Fe NM 87501

BRADLEY, WILLIAM THOMAS, army officer; b. Rockford, Ill., Feb. 10, 1917; s. Thomas J. and Bessie (Carlson) B.; B.S., U.S. Mil. Acad., 1939; M.S., U. Ill., 1950; student U.S. comd. and Gen. Staff Coll., 1953-54, U.S. Army War Coll., 1956-57; m. June E. Alderman, Aug. 25, 1940; children—Carol (Mrs. Jon Veigel), Janice (Mrs. William Beasley), Marcia (Mrs. David A. Stone), Elizabeth. Commd. 2d lt., U.S. Army, 1939, advanced through grades to maj. gen., 1968, comdr. 339th Engr. Contrn. Batt., New Guinea, PI, 1944-45; mem. faculty U.S. Mil. Acad., 1946-49; dist. engr., Los Angeles, 1960-63; div. engr. Southwest div., 1966-68; dir. constrn. U.S. Mil. Adv. Command, Vietnam, 1968-69; comdg. gen., Ft. Leonard Wood, Mo., 1969—. Vice pres. Ozark council Boy Scouts Am., 1969—. Decorated D.S.M., Legion of Merit, Air medal. Registered profl. engr., Tex. Mem. Soc. Am. Mil. Engrs., Assn. U.S. Army, Am. Soc. Civil Engrs., U.S. Com. on Large Dams. Mem. All-American Lacrosse team, 1938-39. Home: 1 Mackenzie Dr Fort Leonard Wood MO 65473 Office: Hqrs USATCE and Ft Leonard Wood Fort Leonard Wood MO 65473

BRADNER, WILLIAM MURRAY, lawyer; b. LaGrande, Ore., May 2, 1926; s. William Murray and Louise (Reynolds) B.; B.A., Yale, 1949, LL.B., 1954; m. Katherine Gibson, June 19, 1951; children—Shelley, William Matthew, Lucinda. Admitted to N.Y. bar, 1955; law clk. firm Dunnington, Bartholow & Miller, N.Y.C., 1954-55, asso. atty., 1955-58, partner, 1959—. Served to 1st lt. AUS, 1944-46; 1st lt., 1950-52. Mem. Am. Bar Assn., Order of Coif, Phi Beta Kappa, Phi Delta Phi. Republican. Episcopalian. Clubs: Manhattan, Yale (N.Y.C.); Scarsdale Golf. Home: 21 Donellan Rd Scarsdale, NY 10583. Office: 161 E 42d St New York City NY 10017

BRADOCK, MICHAEL, univ. adminstr., pub. relations exec.; b. Belle Vernon, Pa., July 17, 1917; s. Nicholas M. and Pauline (Radish) R.; A.B. magna cum laude, Westminster Coll., New Wilmington, Pa., 1942, Litt.D., 1965; M.S. in Journalism, Northwestern U., 1946; post-grad. Western Res. U., 1950-52; m. Helen A. Hower, Sept. 2, 1944; children—Robert Hower, William Michael. Reporter, Fayette City (Pa.) Jour., 1937-39; corr. for Pa. newspapers, 1937-39; reporter, sports editor Charleroi (Pa.) Daily Mail, 1942; dir. news bur., mem. journalism faculty Westminster Coll., 1942-45; dir. news bur., asst. prof. journalism Kent State U., 1945, asso. prof., dir. pub. relations, 1947-52, prof. journalism, 1952-53; ednl. relations rep. Ford Motor Co., 1953-55, mgr. pub. relations publs. dept., 1955-56, mgr. graphic and information services, 1956-58, mgr. ednl. affairs, 1958-61; dir. univ. relations, prof. journalism U. Mich, 1961—, v.p. univ. relations and devel., prof. journalism, 1969—; vis. prof. journalism U. Wyo., summer 1951; spl. radio-TV reporter covering nat. polit. convs., July 1952; newsman radio sta. WHBC, Canton, O., summer 1946; cons. Ford Found., NSF. Pres. Kent Research Group, 1952; established Inst. Pub. Relations, 1947, exec. sec., 1947- 49, nat. adv. com. Urban Coalition; mem. coll. and univ. lisaison com. USIA; adv. com. Office Advancement Pub. Negro Colls. Trustee Greenhills Sch., Ann Arbor. Recipient Distinguished Service award Kent State U., 1965. Mem. Pub. Relations Soc. Am., Edn. Writers Assn., Assn. Edn. Journalism, Am. Coll. Pub. Relations Assn. (pres. 1968-69), Sigma Delta Chi, Sigma Nu. Presbyn. Rotarian, Clubs: Press, Economic (Detroit); Grizzly Riders Internat. Editor The Coll. Pub., 1955-60. Home: 384 Orchard Hills Dr Ann Arbor MI 48104

BRADSHAW, GEORGE BLAIR, savs. and loan assn. exec.; b. Magrath, Alta., Can., Oct. 5, 1918; s. Frederick John and Mildred Amy (Hillier) B.; B.S. in Mech. Engring., U. Utah, 1939; m. Lillie Anne Young, Aug. 22, 1947; children—Russell, Becky, Jeffrey, Kathy, Dick, Suzanne, Thomas. Loan officer Am. Savs. & Loan Assn., Salt Lake City, 1945-47, dir., 1947—, v.p., 1947-60, pres., gen. mgr., 1960—; dir. Amsal Service Corp., United Bond & Finance Co. Mem. exec. council Salt Lake council Boy Scouts Am., 1970-71. Trustee Am. Savs. and Loan Profit Sharing Pension Trust, Am. Savs. and Loan Pension Trust. Mem. Salt Lake C. of C. (adv. com. 1967-71), Pi Kappa Alpha, Theta Tau. Republican. Mem. Ch. of Jesus Christ of Latter-day Saints (bishop; stake high council). Lion. Home: 1948 Laurelhurst Dr Salt Lake City UT 84108 Office: 63 S Main St Salt Lake City UT 84111

BRADSHAW, JOHN RICHARD JOSEPH, soil conservationist; b. Colorado Springs, Colo., June 19, 1912; s. Raymond Michael and Vera Edna (Stanforth) B.; student Colo. Coll., 1930- 32; B.S., Colo. State U., 1937; certificate in Adminstrv. Leadership, U. Mont., 1961; m. Dorothy A. Jones, Jan. 27, 1934; children—Bridget Sue, Richard Michael. Range specialist U.S. Soil Conservation Service, 1946- 51, asst. state conservationist State of Utah, Salt Lake City, 1951—. Mem. Conservation Edn. Com., 1957—; adviser State Dept. Pub. Instrn., 1957—; mem. coordinating group for devel. state water plan. Fellow Soil Conservation Soc. Am. (nat. pres. 1966, past pres. Utah); mem. Am. Soc. Range Mgmt. (past pres. N.M. chpt.). Mason, Lions (past pres. Richfield, Utah). Home: 1030 E 6th St Salt Lake City UT 84105 Office: Fed Bldg 125 S State St Salt Lake City UT 84111

BRADSHAW, LILLIAN MOORE, librarian; b. Hagerstown, Md., Jan. 10, 1915; d. Harry M. and Mabel E. (Kretzer) Moore; A.B., Western Md. Coll., 1937; B.L.S., Drexel U., 1938; m. William Theodore Bradshaw, May 19, 1946. Asst. adult circulation dept. Utica (N.Y.) Pub. Library, 1938-41, asst. head, 1941- 43; adult librarian Enoch Pratt Free Library, Balt., 1943-44, asst. coordinator work with young adults, 1944-46; br. librarian Dallas Pub. Library, 1946-47, readers adviser, 1947-52, head dept. circulation, 1952- 55, coordinator work with adults, 1955-58, asst. dir., 1958-62, dir., 1962—. Mem. steering com. Nat. Library Week, 1967-70; mem. library edn. adv. com. Tex. Coll. and U. System Coordinating Bd.; mem. adv. com. U. Tex., Dallas; mem. bd. publs. So. Meth. U.; 1970—; mem. adv. bd. Friends of Tex. Libraries, 1963-70; mem. Tex. Gov.'s Commn. on Status of Women; mem. profl. adv. com. Greater Dallas Community Relations Commn.; mem. U.S. com. for Am. Library in Paris, 1970-71; Goals for Dallas, conferee, asst. task force leader, vice chmn. Goals Achievement Com. for Continuing Edn. Named Tex. Librarian of Year, 1961; recipient Distinguished Alumnus award Drexel U. Library Sch., 1970, Titche's Arete award for epitome of excellence in chosen field, 1970. Mem. Assn. Grad. Edn. and Research N. Tex. (adv. council trustee), Am. (dir. adult services div. 1962-65, v.p. adult services div. 1966- 67, pres. adult services div. 1967-68, council 1968-69. chmn. nat. library week com. 1968-69, pres. 1970-71, chmn. Wilson Library Periodical award jury 1968-69, dir. exec. com. pub. relations sect., library adminstrn. div. 1964- 66), Tex. (pres. 1964-65, chmn. pub. libraries div. 1955-56) library assns., Dallas Met. Area Pub. Librarians Assn. (pres. 1968-69), Tex. Municipal League, Nat. Reading Council, Am. Assn. U. Women, Beta Phi Mu. Club: Zonta. Bd. cons. Library Jour., 1962-63. Contbr. articles to profl. jours. Home: 6804 Clayton Av Dallas TX 75214 Office: 1954 Commerce St Dallas TX 75201

BRADSHAW, MELVIN B., ins. co. exec.; b. Peoria, Ill., Nov. 7, 1922; s. Andrew J. and Nancy (Norman) B.; B.S., Bradley U., 1949; postgrad. Advanced Mgmt. Program, Harvard, 1968; m. Marcella Jean Bradshaw, June 17, 1949; children—Beth, Kimberley, Dana, Bruce. With Liberty Mut. Ins. Co., Boston, 1949—, now exec. v.p. Served with USNR, 1941-44. Home: 19 Wildwood Rd Dover MA 02130 Office: 175 Berkeley St Boston MA 02117

BRADSHAW, RALPH HODGINS, coll. pres.; b. Kamsack, Sask., Can., Sept. 16, 1917 (parents Am. citizens); s. Frederick H. and Edith Stella (Hodgins) B.; A.B., Washington U., St. Louis, 1939, M.A., 1941; m. Margaret Pease, Apr. 4, 1942; children—Ralph Hodgins, Robert Frederick, Susan. Instr. English, Washington U., 1941-42; mem. faculty Riverside (Cal.) City Coll., 1946—, v.p., 1959-62, pres., 1963—; on leave as dir. personnel Riverside City schs., 1957-58, dir. secondary edn., 1960-61; supt. Riverside United Fund. Bd. dirs. World Affairs Council Inland So. Cal. Served as officer USNR, 1942-46. Mem. Cal. Jr. Coll. Assn. (chmn. nursing edn. com.), Riverside City Tchrs. Assn. (past pres.), Am. Assn. Sch. Adminstrs., Omicron Delta Kappa, Sigma Phi Epsilon (chpt. pres. 1939). Lutheran. Kiwanian (pres. Uptown Riverside 1956). Home: 2855 McAllister St Riverside CA 92503

BRADSHAW, RICHARD BURNETT, advt. exec.; b. Berkhamstead, Eng., Mar. 4, 1927; s. Sidney Basil and Marjorie (Hewett) B.; B.Sc. in Journalism, U. Ill., 1951; m. Jayne McGraw, June 11, 1955; children—David, Brian, Bruce, Dean, Tracey. With Foote, Cone & Belding, 1951—, research analyst, Chgo., 1951-53, account exec., Chgo., 1953-60, pres. Canadian co., Toronto, 1960-68, sr. v.p., dir. parent co., 1968—, pres. internat. co., Brussels, Belgium, 1969—. Served with Brit. Royal Navy, 1943-46. Home: 12 avenue des Anémones Rhode-Ste-Genèse 1640 Belgium Office: 304 avenue Louise 1050 Brussels Belgium

BRADSHAW, RICHARD ROTHERWOOD, bldg. and constrn. exec.; b. Phila., Sept. 12, 1916; s. Joseph Rotherwood and Rosanna (Jones) B.; B.S., Cal. Inst. Tech., 1939; M.S., U. So. Cal., 1950; m. Audrey Grace Skinn, Oct. 3, 1940; children—Linda M., Barbara A., Vicki L. Pres. Richard R. Bradshaw, Inc., Van Nuys, Cal., 1946—; pres. br. offices San Francisco, Honolulu, Orlando (Fla.), Portland. Recipient Alfred Lindau award Am. Concrete Inst., 1968, many others for structural design. Mem. Am. Soc. C.E., Internat. Assn. Bridges and Structural engring., Am. Seismol. Soc., Cons. Engrs. Assn., Internat. Assn. Thin Shells, Am. Concrete Inst., Am. Arbitration Assn. Contbr. articles tech. jours. Home: 17300 Ballinger St Northridge CA 91324 Office: 14606 Victory Blvd Van Nuys CA 91401

BRADSHAW, THOMAS ALEXANDER, lawyer, life ins. co. exec.; b. Ouray, Colo., Dec. 24, 1905; s. Thomas Y. and Jessie Home (McIntosh) B.; A.B., U. Colo., 1928, LL.B., 1930; m. Dorothy Waite Johnson, Sept. 5, 1936 (dec. Sept. 1959); 1 son, Robert Waite; m. 2d, Dorothy Collins Allen, Sept. 27, 1961. Admitted to Colo. bar, 1930; practiced in Ft. Collins, 1930; atty., counsel Provident Mut. Life Ins. Co., Phila., 1931-1949, pres., 1953-69, chmn. bd., 1969-70, hon. chmn. bd., 1971—, dir. 1949; dir. Phila. Nat. Bank, Western Savs. Fund Soc., Phila. Mem. Phila. United Fund, 1962-63. Mem. Assn. Life Ins. Counsel (pres.), Beta Theta Pi, Phi Delta Phi. Clubs: Union League, Philadelphia Country (Phila.). Home: 828 Morris Av Bryn Mawr PA 19010 Office: 4601 Market St Philadelphia PA 19139

BRADSHAW, THORNTON FREDERICK, oil co. exec.; b. Washington, Aug. 4, 1917; s. Frederick and Julia V. (See) B.; grad. Phillips Exeter Acad., 1936; A.B., Harvard, 1940, M.B.A., 1942, D.C.S., 1950; m. Sally Davis, May 18, 1940; children—Nancy M. (Mrs. Thomas Poor), Priscilla W. (Mrs. Richard Page, Jr.), Johnathan G. Asso. prof. Grad. Sch. Bus. Adminstrn., Harvard, 1942-52; partner Cresap, McCormick & Paget, N.Y.C., 1952-56; v.p., dir. Atlantic Richfield Co. (formerly Atlantic Refining Co.), New York, 1956-62, exec. v.p., 1962-64, pres., 1964—, mem. exec. com., 1966—, also dir.; dir. Atlas Chem. Industries, Inc., First Pa. Banking and Trust Co., Penn Mut. Life Ins. Co., U.S. Plywood-Champion Papers, Inc., Diebold Venture Capital Corp. Bd. dirs. Nat. Indsl. Conf. Bd., Pomfret Sch., Fgn. Policy Assn., Aspen Inst. for Humanistic Studies. Served to lt. (j.g.) USNR, 1943-45. Mem. Harvard Bus. Sch. Assn. (pres. 1966), Am. Petroleum Inst. (dir.). Home: River House 435 E 52d St New York City NY 10022 Office: 717 Fifth Av New York City NY 10022

BRADSHER, CHARLES KILGO, chemist, educator; b. Petersburg, Va., July 13, 1912; s. Arthur Bro Brown and Elizabeth (Muse) B.; A.B., Duke, 1933; A.M., Harvard, 1935, Ph.D. in Organic Chemistry, 1937; m. Dorothy Tideman, June 6, 1938; children—Thorston, Catherine (Mrs. Lawrence D. Dunnagan), Marien (Mrs. Linn Litkenhous). Postdoctoral research fellow U. Ill., 1937-39; faculty Duke, Durham, N.C., 1939—, James B. Duke prof. chemistry, 1965—, chmn. dept., 1965- 70. NRC research fellow, 1941-42; Fulbright lectr. Leiden (Netherlands) U., 1951-52; NSF sr. postdoctoral fellow Fed. Inst. Tech., Zürich, Switzerland, 1959-60. Mem. Am., Royal Netherland chem. socs., A.A.A.S., Chem. Soc. London. Author sci. papers. Home: 118 Pinecrest Rd Durham, NC 27705.

BRADY, BARRETT, ret. advt. exec.; b. Phila., Jan. 28, 1900; s. Cyrus Townsend and Mary Mary (Barrett) B.; A.B., Harvard, 1921; m. Claire Wille, July 1923; children—Cyrus Townsend, Jonathan Barrett; m. 2d, Helen Aislee, Aug. 24, 24, 1940; 1 dau., Barrett. Advt. writer, supr. various N.Y. advt. agys., 1921-43; v.p., copy dir. Warwick & Legler, Inc., N.Y.C., 1944-53; with Kenyon & Eckhardt, Inc., N.Y.C., 1954-61, v.p., copy dir., 1955, sr. v.p., creative dir., 1956-61, mem. exec. com., 1958-61; v.p., creative dir. Compton Advt., Inc., 1961-64. Trustee, Clinton Hall Assn., N.Y.C. Mem. Merc. Library Assn. N.Y.C. (pres. 1948-52, 66-68, dir.), Soc. of Cincinnati, Phi Beta Kappa. Clubs: Harvard (N.Y.C.); Long Island Country; The Mallows, (Quogue, N.Y.). Home: 1192 Park Av New York City, NY 10028.

BRADY, BERNARD VINCENT, lawyer; b. Winneconne, Wis., Feb. 24, 1891; s. Owen W. and Mary (Roddy) B.; student Marquette U. Law Sch., 1910-13; m. Amybelle Halbert, July 27, 1922. Admitted to Wis. bar, 1913, since practiced in Milw.; sr. partner firm Brady, Tyrrell, Cotter & Cutler, 1957—. Dir. Briggs & Stratton Corp., Ladish Co., Ladish Malting Co., Milw. Devel. Group, Inc. Served as 2d lt., ordnance dept., U.S. Army, 1917-19. Mem. Am., Wis., Milw. bar assns. Home: 924 E Juneau St Milwaukee WI 53233 Office: 735 N Water St Milwaukee WI 53202

BRADY, CARROLL PARKER, educator; b. Longford, Kan., Oct. 10, 1906; s. Merrill and Rilla (Parker) B.; A.B., U. Cal. at Los Angeles, 1932, M.A., 1934; Ph.D., U. Chgo., 1938; m. Caroline C.S. Dutton, May 2, 1936. Instr. Tex. Tech. Coll., 1938-39, Los Angeles City Coll., 1939-42; from asst. prof. to prof. math. U.S. Naval Acad., 1942—. Served to comdr. USNR, 1942-46. Mem. Am. Math. Soc., Soc. Indsl. and Applied Mathematics, A.A.A.S. Home: Route 5 Box 287 Annapolis MD 21401

BRADY, FRANK MARTIN, lawyer; b. Bloomington, Ill., Feb. 27, 1927; s. Frank J. and Mary (Walsh) B.; B.A. in Econs., St. Ambrose Coll., 1950; postgrad. Ill. State U., Normal, 1968-69; J.D., Loyola U., Chgo., 1955; m. Paula Downey, Nov. 23, 1950; children—Frank Martin, Mary Paula, Julia Margaret, Daniel Patrick, Anne Cathleen. Admitted to Ill. bar, 1956, Ia. bar, 1955, U.S. Supreme Ct. bar; practice in Bloomington, 1956—; asso. Bach & Bach, 1956-57; asso. Dunn & Dunn, 1957-61; partner Dunn, Dunn, Brady, Goebel, Ulbrich & Hayes and predecessor firms, 1962—; instr. dept. econs. St. Ambrose Coll. Faculty, 1955-56. Vice chmn. exec. com. McLean County Republican Central Com., 1965-66; spl. asst. atty. gen. State of Ill. Served with USNR, 1944-46; PTO. Recipient St. Thomas More award Nat. Council Catholic Men, 1966. Mem. Am., Ill., Ia., McLean County, Cook County, Fed. bar assns., Fedn. Ins. Counsel, Am. Legion, V.F.W., Phi Alpha Delta. K.C., Elk. Home: 1406 E Washington St Bloomington IL 61701 Office: Peoples Bank Bldg Bloomington IL 61701

BRADY, FREDERICK JONATHON, pub. health service physician; b. Canton, Pa., July 1, 1908; s. Clarence Abram and Elizabeth (Abbott) B.; grad. Grand Rapids Jr. Coll., 1927; M.D., U. Mich., 1931; spl. student in tropical medicine Tulane U., Sch. Tropical Medicine P.R., 1939-40; m. Lolita Blakeley, May 19, 1932; children—Robert Eugene, Wilson Carl, Barbara Jane. Intern, Hurley Hosp., Flint, Mich., 1931-32; with USPHS, 1934-61, tropical disease research NIH, 1937-49, med. dir., 1947- -, internat. health rep., 1950-55, asst. chief internat. health div., 1955-57; office chief Bur. States Services, 1957-59; asst. dir. Office Pub. Health, ICA, 1959-61; dir. Pima County Health Dept., Tucson, 1961—. Health survey mission ECA, West Africa, 1949; U.S. alternate to exec. com. Pan Am. San. Orgn., 1950-56, to exec. bd. WHO, 1953-55. Diplomate Am. Bd. Preventive Medicine and Pub. Health. Fellow A.A.A.S., Royal Soc. Tropical Medicine and Hygiene (London); mem. Am. Soc. Tropical Medicine and Hygiene (pres. 1954), A.M.A., Am. Pub. Health Assn., Washington Soc. Tropical Medicine (pres. 1960-61), Theta Kappa Psi. Home: 2530 Santa Lucia Dr Tucson AZ 85715 Office: 151 W Congress Tucson AZ 85701

BRADY, HUGH PICKEN, lumber co. exec.; b. Sitka, Alaska, Feb. 19, 1891; s. John Green and Elizabeth (Patton) B.; grad. Phillips Andover Acad., 1910; B.A., Yale, 1914; postgrad. U. Wash., 1959; m. Mary Somerville Schieffelin, June 22, 1921; 1 dau., Cornelia Schieffelin (Mrs. H.G.A. Meili). Asst. mgr. A.C. Dutton Lumber Co., 1915-22, sec., 1920-22; owner, mgr. Colby Lumber Co., 1924-32; partner Brady & Ketcham Lumber Co., 1924-32; pres. Brady Internat. Lumber, Inc., Seattle, 1933—, now chmn. bd. Exec. com. Yale Alumni Bd., 1952-57, nat. com. chmn., 1955-57, del.-at-large, 1961-66, del., 1967—; chmn. council com. Yale Forestry Sch., 1961-66, mem. com., 1966-69; mem. exec. com. Snoqualmie Nat. Forestry Adv. Council, Sitka Hist. Restoration Assn.; alumni rep. Phillips Andover Acad., 1940- 62. Trustee Wash. Forestry Conf., Keep Wash. Green Assn. Recipient Yale medal, 1952; named Distinguished Zete, 1960; fellow Davenport Coll., Yale, 1961—. Mem. Wash. Conservation Soc. (past pres.), Yale Assn. Western Wash. (pres., chmn.), Forest History Assn. (dir.), Zeta Psi (past nat. pres.), Alpha Delta Tau. Republican. Episcopalian. Clubs: University, Tennis, Washington Athletic, Seattle Yacht; Corinthian Yacht; New York Yacht. Home: 1114 39th Av E Seattle WA 98102 Office: 1910 Fairview Av E Seattle WA 98102

BRADY, JAMES HARRY, indsl. exec., mgmt. cons.; b. Cleveland, Tenn., June 4, 1925; s. Harry Lee and Edith (Rutherford) B.; student Am. U. With Manhattan Engring. Dist., Oak Ridge, 1943-44; Navy reporter, Army and Navy Jour., 1944-45; reporter Yankee Network, Indpls. Star, 1944-45; with Mil. News Service, Washington editor, 1945-47; asso. Army & Navy Pub. Co., Washington Press Service, 1945-48; author columns Inside Washington, Washington Newsletter, bus. columns, reporting events on Capitol Hill, White House, others; promotion mgr. Knoxville (Tenn.) News Sentinel, 1948-49; asst. to pres. Lancaster Engring. Corp., Daffin Mfg. Co., Lancaster, 1949-56; now chmn. Brady Enterprises, Knoxville, Tenn.; mem. exec. com., dir. pub. relations Zimmerman Equipment Co., Inc., Nashville; pres. Motel Mgmt. Inc., Knoxville; merchandising cons. Enterprise Paint Mfg. Co., Chgo., 1954-62, Inertol Co., Inc., Newark. Prepared, issued 1st statis. findings on cost of World War II, 1945; pub. relations asso. Soc. for Advancement Mgmt., 1945, Washington Coll. Law, 1945; officer, dir. several corps. Chmn. exec. com. Serene Manor Med. Center. Mem. White House Corrs. Assn. Republican. Methodist. Kiwanian, Elk, Mason (K.T., Shriner, life). Clubs: National Press, Variety of Am. (Washington); Deane Hill Country, Senators (Knoxville); Lancaster County Riding (Lancaster). Contbr. articles to ednl., sci. jours. Address: 3236 Fairmont Blvd Knoxville TN 37917 also Nat Press Club Washington DC 20004

BRADY, JOSEPH VINCENT, behavioral biologist, educator; b. N.Y.C., Mar. 28, 1922; s. James J. and Mary F. (Michaels) B.; B.S., Fordham U., 1943; Ph.D., U. Chgo., 1951; children—Barbara Ann, Michael Joseph, Kathleen Theresa, Janet Elizabeth, Nancy Marie, Joanne Cecelia, Jennifer Anne; m. Julia Dawson, Oct. 9, 1970. Dep. dir. div. neuropsychiatry Walter Reed Inst. Research, 1951-71; prof. psychology U. Md., 1955-69; prof. behavioral biology Johns Hopkins Sch. Medicine, Balt., 1967—. Cons. Pres.'s Sci. Adv. Com., Merck Inst. for Therapeutic Research. Served from 2d lt. to col. M.C., AUS. Fellow A.A.A.S., Am. Psychol. Assn. (div. pres.), Am. Coll. Neuropsycho-pharmacology; mem. Eastern Psychol. Assn. (pres.). Contbr. articles to profl. jours. Home: 11224 Green Dragon Ct Columbia MD 21043 Office: Johns Hopkins U Sch Medicine Baltimore MD 21205

BRADY, LESLIE SNOWDEN, USIA ofcl.; b. College Corner, O., Dec. 14, 1909; s. Irving O. and Mary I. (Snowden) B.; A.B. Miami U., Oxford, O., 1932, M.A., 1934, LL.D., 1969; Ph.D., N.Y.U., 1943; certificate U. Lyon (France), 1933, Sorbonne, Paris, France, 1936; student Nat. War Coll., 1952-53; m. Mary Eastwood Walser; children—Patricia A., Lynn, Philip S. Instr. Romance langs. Miami U., 1934-38, N.Y.U., 1939-43, Coll. City N.Y., 1939-43; with OWI, N.Y.C., London, Paris, Lyon, 1944-46; assigned Dept. of State, 1946-47; cultural attache, Paris, 1947-51; pub. affairs officer, Saigon, 1951-52, Paris, 1953-55; assigned Operations Coordinating Bd., Washington, 1956-58; counselor for cultural affairs, Moscow, 1959-61; pub. affairs adviser for Europe, Dept. of State, 1961-62; asst. dir. Soviet Union and Eastern Europe, USIA, 1962-64; counselor pub. affairs, Paris, France, 1964-69; spl. cons. USIA, 1969—. Decorated Palmes Académiques (France), chevalier Legion of Honor. Mem. Am. Fgn. Service Assn., Phi Beta Kappa. Club: International (Washington). Co-editor two French text books; past mng. editor French Rev.; asso. editor Symposium. Contbr. articles to profl. jours. Home: 4922 Cumberland Av Chevy Chase MD 20015 Office: Dept of State Washington DC 20525

BRADY, SISTER MARY WILLIAM, educator; b. Fall River, Mass., Mar. 4, 1906; d. John James and Gladys Marie (Davol) B.; B.A., Coll. St. Catherine, 1931; M.A., U. Minn., 1941; Ph.D., U. Chgo., 1947. Faculty dept. English, Coll. St. Catherine, St. Paul, 1937-55, pres., 1955-61, now prof. Pres. Minn. Pvt. Coll. Council, 1957- 58; exec. com. Coll. Fund Assn.; mem. bd. studies Sisters of St. Joseph. Mem. Am. Assn. U. Women, Assn. Am. Colls., Assn. Minn. Colls., N.E.A., Nat. Catholic Edn. Assn., Phi Beta Kappa, Delta Phi Lambda, Pi Delta Phi. Club: University (St. Paul). Address: 2004 Randolph St St Paul MN 55105

BRADY, NORMAN AIKMAN, corp. exec.; b. Hull, Que., Can., Feb. 8, 1919; s. Edward Clarence and Laura (Mullen) B.; student Sir George Williams Coll., Montreal, Que.; B.B.A., M.S. in Hosp. Adminstrn., Northwestern U.; m. M. Pauline McDonald, 1949; 1 son, James Roderick. Hosp. mgr. Queen Mary Vets. Hosp., Montreal, 1949-51, Sunnybrook Hosp., Toronto, Ont., Can., 1951-53; asst. dir. Presbyn. Hosp., Chgo., 1954-56, Presbyn.-St. Luke's Hosp., 1956-59, dir., 1959-62, v.p., 1962-63, exec. v.p., 1963- 66; v.p. Wood & Tower, Inc., Princeton, N.J., 1966-68; pres. Norman A. Brady & Assos., Princeton, N.J., 1968—; also pres. Norman A. Brady, R. Riopelle & Assos., Inc., Montreal, 1969—. Bd. govs. Arthritis and Rheumatism Found. Ill.; bd. dirs. Duncan-Med. YMCA, Chgo. Served as lt. Royal Canadian Navy, 1939-46; Fellow Am. Coll. Hosp. Adminstrs., Inst. Medicine; mem. Am., Ill. (trustee), Am. Protestant hosp. assns., Soc. Med. History Chgo., Assembly Episcopal Hosps. and Chaplains, Assn. Med. Colls., Alpha Delta Mu. Clubs: Economic, Canadian, University, Executives (Chgo.). Home: 156 Hunt Dr Princeton NJ 08540 Office: 228 Alexander St Princeton NJ 08540

BRADY, NYLE C., educator; b. Manassa, Colo., Oct. 25, 1920; s. C. Frank and Sarah D. (Rasmussen) B.; B.S., Brigham Young U., 1941; Ph.D., N.C. State Coll., 1947; m. Martha Cornum, Oct. 11, 1936; children—Robert N., Donald R., Dorothy L., Carol A. Asst. prof. N.C. State Coll., 1947; asst. prof. Cornell U., Ithaca, N.Y., 1947-49, asso. prof., 1949-52, prof., 1952-65, head dept. agronomy, 1955-64, dir. research N.Y. State Coll. Agr., Cornell Agr. Expt. Sta., 1965—, asso. dean N.Y. State Colls. Agr., 1970—. Dir. sci. and edn. Dept. Agr., 1963-65; vis. prof. U. P.I., 1953-55; chmn. agr. bd. Nat. Acad. Sci., 1968-71. Recipient prof. of merit award Cornell U., Coll. Agr., 1953. Fellow A.A.A.S. (v.p. 1966), Am. Soc. Agronomy; mem. Am. Assn. U. Profs., Soil Sci. Soc. Am. (editor-in-chief Procs. 1959-62, pres. 1964), Internat. Soil Sci. Soc., Soil Conservation Soc. Am., Soil Sci. Soc. Philippines, Sigma Xi. Mem. Ch. of Jesus Christ of Latter-day Saints. Author: (with T.L. Lyon, H.O. Buckman) The Nature and Properties of Soils, 1952; (with H.O. Buckman) The Nature and Properties of Soils, 1960. Editor: Advances in Agronomy, 1967. Home: 1025 Highland Rd Ithaca NY 14850

BRADY, RAYMOND JOHN, editor; b. Phila.; s. Raymond John and Meta (Martin) B.; B.S., Fordham Coll., 1948; m. Mary Clark Wilson, Jan. 28, 1955; stepchildren—David Wilson, Mary Beth Wilson. Reporter, Long Branch (N.J.) Daily Record, 1950-53; writer Am. Tel. & Tel. Corp., 1953-54; asso. editor Forbes mag., 1954-55, asst. mng. editor, 1956-61; asso. editor Barrons Weekly, 1955-56; editor Dun's Rev., 1961—; lectr. bus. and finance at univs. Served with USNR, 1943-45. Mem. N.Y. Financial Writers Assn. (bd. govs.), Am. Soc. Mag. Editors. Clubs: Nat. Press, Washington; Overseas Press (N.Y.C.); Monmouth County Hunt. Author articles. Home: 30 E 9th St New York City NY 10003 Office: 466 Lexington Av New York City NY 10017

BRADY, ROBERT FREDERICK, ret. elec. engr.; b. Washington, Jan. 14, 1909; s. John Frederick and Elsie Elinor (Dawson) B.; B.E.E., Catholic U. Am., 1932; LL.B., Columbus U., Washington, 1938, M.P.L., 1939; m. Mary Catherine Spillan, June 28, 1941; children—Robert Frederick, Mary Margaret, Mary Catherine (Mrs. Michael Gazarek), Mary Eileen, Francis Joseph. Admitted to D.C. bar, 1938, U.S. Dist. Ct. bar, Ct. Appeals, D.C., U.S. Patent Office FCC; asso. John B. Brady, Washington, 1932-41; research, devel. staff engr. Office Chief Signal Officer U.S. Army, 1941-61; head electronics sect. NATO Internat. Staff, Paris, France, 1961-65; tech. adviser U.S. Army Materiel Command, Washington, 1965-70; sr. staff officer U.S. Army Advanced Materiel Concepts Agy., 1970-71; cons., 1971. Recipient Exceptional Civilian Service award, 1945, Meritorious Civilian Service award, 1958, 70. Registered profl. engr., D.C. Mem. I.E.E.E. K.C. (past grand knight). Home: 7407 Venice St Falls Church VA 22043

BRADY, RODNEY HOWARD, govt. ofcl.; b. Sandy, Utah, Jan. 31, 1933; s. Kenneth A. and Jessie (Madsen) B.; B.S. in Accounting with high honors, M.B.A. with high honors, U. Utah, 1957; D.Bus. Adminstrn., Harvard, 1966; postrad. U. Cal. at Los Angeles, 1969-70; m. Carolyn Ann Hansen, Oct. 25, 1960; children—Howard Riley, Bruce Ryan. Missionary Ch. of Jesus Christ of Latter-day Saints, Great Britain, 1953-55; teaching asso. Harvard Bus. Sch., Cambridge, Mass., 1957-59; v.p. Mgmt. Systems Corp., Cambridge, 1962-65; v.p. Center Exec. Devel., Cambridge, 1963-64, v.p., dir. Boston, 1964-65; v.p. Tamerand Reef Corp., Christiansted, St. Croix, V.I., 1963-65; v.p., dir. Am. Inst. Execs., N.Y.C., 1963-65; v.p., mem. exec. com. aircraft div. Hughes Tool Co., Culver City, Cal., 1966-70; asst. sec. adminstrn., mgmt. U.S. Dept. Health, Edn. and Welfare, Washington, 1970—, also cons.; bd. dirs. Merit Properties, Los Angeles, 1969-70. Cons. Dept. Def., Dept. State, Dept. Commerce, NASA, Govt. of Can., Govt. of India, and indsl. firms, 1962—. Active Boy Scouts Am., 1952—. Served to 1st lt., USAF, 1959-62. Mem. Am. Mgmt. Assn. (award 1969), Am. Ordnance Assn., Nat. Indsl. Security Assn., U.S. Army Assn., Air Force Assn., Am. Helicopter Soc., Los Angeles C. of C. (tax structure com. 1969-70), Phi Kappa Phi, Tau Kappa Alpha, Beta Gamma Sigma. Club: Harvard (Cambridge, Mass.). Author: An Approach to Equipment Replacement Analysis, 1957; Survey of Management Planning and Control Systems, 1962; The Impact of Computers on Top Management Decision Making in the Aerospace and Defense Industry, 1966; (with others) How to Structure Incentive Contracts—A Programmed Text, 1965. Contbr. articles profl. jours. Office: Dept Health Edn and Welfare 330 Independence Av SW Washington DC 20201

BRADY, SCOTT, (Gerard Kenneth Tierney), actor; b. Bklyn., Sept. 13, 1924; s. Lawrence Hugh and Mary Alice (Crowley) T.; ed. Roosevelt High Sch., Yonkers, N.Y., 1939-42; m. Lisa Tireny, Dec. 24, 1967; children—Timothy Eamon Charles Francis, Terence Michael Anthony Vincent. Films include In this Corner, 1947, 1971. Served with USNR, 1942-45. Roman Catholic. Club: N.Y. Athletic. Address: care William Morris Agy 151 El Camino Blvd Beverly Hills CA 90212

BRADY, T. J., communications co. exec. Controller, v.p. RCA Communications, Inc., N.Y.C. Office: 60 Broad St New York City NY 10004*

BRADY, THOMAS FRANCIS, publicist; b. Keokuk, Ia., Aug. 30, 1915; s. Joseph Lajus and Sara (Barney) B.; B.A., U. Cal. at Los Angeles, 1936; postgrad. U. Paris (France), 1951-52; m. Elizabeth Pallette, Mar. 30, 1946; children—Elizabeth, Thomas Frances. Corr., N.Y. Times, 1942-43, 46-70, assigned North Africa, 1955-62, India, 1962-65, Middle East, 1965-69; dir. Regional Information Centre for Tunisia and Libya, UN Secretariat, 1970—. Served with AUS, 1943, dir. UN Regional Informaton Centre for Tunisia and Libya, UN Secretariat, 1970—. Served with AUS, 1943, with USNR, 1944-46. Address: UN PO Box 863 Tunis Tunisia

BRADY, THOMAS PICKENS, state supreme ct. asso. justice; b. New Orleans, Aug. 6, 1903; s. Thomas and Jane Tullia (Smith) B.; A.B., Yale, 1927; LL.B., U. Miss., 1930; m. LaVerne Holmes, July 23, 1929; children—Thomas Pickens, Bruce Holmes. Instr. sociology U. Miss., 1929- 30; admitted to Miss. bar, 1930; mem. firm Brady, Dean & Hobbs, Brookhaven, 1930-38; judge Circuit Ct., 14th Dist. Miss., 1950-63; asso. justice Miss. Supreme Ct., 1963—. Dir. Brookhaven Bank & Trust Co., 1930—, atty., 1947-50; pres. Brookhaven Investment Co., 1934-44; v.p. Arcade Theater, Inc., 1935; pres., atty. Brookhaven Leader Co., 1942-57; dir., atty. Miss. Compress Co., 1947-61. Commr. pub. safety, dir. Miss. Hwy. Safety Patrol, 1940-43, chmn. hwy. traffic adv. com. to War Dept., 1942-43; awards judge

Freedoms Found., 1966. Nat. Chmn. speakers' bur. States' Rights, Democratic Com., 1948, mem. Dem. Nat. Com., 1960-64; del. Dem. Nat. Conv., 1940, 48, 60; chmn. Miss. Dem. Nominating Com., 1960; mem. exec. com. City of Brookhaven, 1932-53. Bd. dirs. Whitworth Coll., 1962. Recipient Distinguished Service citation Miss. Legislature, 1956. Mem. Miss. State Bar (v.p. 1954-55), Miss. Gun Collectors Assn. (pres. 1957), Am. Newcomen Soc., Abraham Lincoln Assn. Am. Judicature Soc., S.A.R., First Families of Miss., Sons Colonial Govs., U. Miss. Alumni Assn. (dir. 1962-64), Co. Mil. Collectors and Historians, Eta Sigma Phi, Phi Delta Phi, Zeta Psi, Omicron Delta Kappa, Eta Sigma Phi. Baptist. Mason (32, K.T., Shriner). Clubs: New Orleans Athletic, Boston (New Orleans). Author: South at Bay, 1948; Black Monday, 1954. Home: Natchez Rd. Jackson MS 39203 Office: Brady Bldg Brookhaven MS 39601 also State Capitol Jackson MS 39201

BRADY, WILLIAM, writer, physician; b. Canandaigua, N.Y., Mar. 26, 1880; s. Andrew E. and Eleen (Farell) B.; M.D., U. Buffalo, 1901; m. Cora May McGuire, 1904; children—Elizabeth, Helen. Began practice at Buffalo, 1901; writer health column, syndicated in daily and Sunday newspapers throughout U.S. and Can., 1914—; former editor Medical Pickwick; contbr. to med. press. Author: Personal Health; Little Lessons in the Ways of Health; Eighty Year Old Doctor's Secrets of Positive Health, 1961. Home: 265 El Camino Beverly Hills CA 90212

BRADY, WILLIAM HAMPTON, bishop; b. Aquasco, Md., Sept. 7, 1912 s. Henry Bernard and Maude Catherine (Gibbons) B.; student Charlotte Hall Mil. Acad., 1924-28; A.B., U. Md., 1935; student Gen. Theol. Sem., 1938, S.T.D., 1954; D.D., Nashotah Sem., 1953; m. Margaret Lodge Brady, June 4, 1944; children—Mary Margaret, Anne Louise, William Hampton, Bernard Lodge. Ordained deacon, priest, Episcopal Ch., 1938; asst. rector Ch. of Resurrection. N.Y.C., 1938-40; rector St. Paul's Ch., Savannah, Ga., 1940-48, Alton, Ill., 1948-53; bishop-coadjustor Diocese of Fond du Lac, Wis., 1953-56, bishop, 1957—. Home: 75 W Division St Fond du Lac WI 54935 Office: 39 N Sophia St Fond du Lac WI 54935

BRADY, WRAY GRAYSON, coll. dean; b. Benton Harbor, Mich., July 20, 1918; s. Wray Grayson and Mildred (Sauters) B.; B.A., Washington and Jefferson Coll., 1940, M.A., 1942; Ph.D., U. Pitts., 1953; m. Emilie Peterson, Apr. 30, 1943; children—Susan, Wray Gordon. Prof., chmn. dept. math. Washington and Jefferson Coll., 1951-65, U. Bridgeport (Conn.), 1965-69; dean Grad. Sch., dir. research Slippery Rock State Coll., 1969—; prof. NSF Summer Inst., U. Ariz., 1963-67; cons. Bettis Plant, AEC, 1955-60. Served with USNR, 1943-46. Fellow A.A.A.S.; mem. Am. Math. Soc., Math. Assn. Am., N.Y. Acad. Sci., Am. Assn. U. Profs., Nat. Council Tchrs. Math. Democrat. Presbyn. Rotarian. Co-author: Calculus, 1960; Analytic Geometry, 1961. Home: RD 1 Mercer PA 16137 Office: Slippery Rock State Coll Slippery Rock PA 16057

BRAESTRUP, PETER, journalist; b. N.Y.C., June 8, 1929; s. Carl Bjorn and Elsebet (Kampmann) B.; B.A., Yale, 1951; Nieman fellow, Harvard, 1959-60; m. Angelica Hollins, June 27, 1959; children—Angelica Elsebet, Elizabeth Kate, Carl Peter Hollins. Editor weekly Conn. Shore, 1949; contbg. editor, reporter Time mag., 1953-57; asst. news devel. editor N.Y. Herald Tribune, 1957-59; corr. N.Y. Times, 1960-68; chief Saigon bur. Washington Post, 1968-69, staff writer, 1969—. Served to 2d lt. USMCR, 1951-53. Decorated Purple Heart. Mem. Berzelius Soc. Presbyn. Club: Elizabethan (Yale). Contbr. articles to nat. mags. on mil., polit. affairs. Home: P O Box 130 Sabillasville MD 21798 Office: 1515 L St NW Washington DC 20005

BRAGA, GEORGE ATKINSON, sugar mcht.; b. N.Y.C., July 9, 1904; s. Bernardo and Maud (Atkinson) B.; student Cutler Sch., 1919-24, Johns Hopkins, 1924-25; m. Gioia Marconi, August 5, 1954; children—Allegra, Michael. Began with Czarnikow- Rionda Co., 1924, dir., 1933—, v.p., 1942-50, pres., 1950-64, chmn. bd., 1964—; dir. Manati Sugar Co., 1935—, pres., 1950—; v.p., dir. Francisco Sugar Co.; partner Braga Bros.; dir. J. Henry Schroder Banking Corp., Schroder Trust Co. Clubs: Brook, River, Racquet and Tennis, Down Town Assn. (N.Y.C.); Metropolitan (Washington). Home: Alpine NJ 07620 Office: 120 Wall St New York City NY 10005

BRAGA, RUSSELL M., mfg. co. exec.; b. Rochester, Mich., Aug. 10, 1918; s. August F. and Bertha Braga; A.B., U. Mich., M.B.A., 1942, J.D., 1948; m. Jeanne Bourgeois; children—Paula, Lyssa. Controller, Ryerson Steel Co., Chgo., 1951-62; exec. v.p. Standard Pressed Steel Co., Jenkintown, Pa., 1962—. Bd. dirs. Abington Meml. Hosp. Served to lt. USNR, 1942-46. Mem. Am. Soc. C.P.A.'s, Financial Execs. Inst., A.I.M., Mich. Bar Assn, Phi Beta Kappa. Home: 949 Leopard Rd Rydal PA 19046 Office: PO Box 608 Benxson East Jenkintown PA 19046

BRAGARNICK, ROBERT, corp. exec.; b. Milw., June 21, 1919; s. Harry and Elizabeth (Maltz) B.; B.S., U. Pa.; m. Ruth Welander, Sept. 22, 1949; children—Peter Harry, Ellen Lisa. Formerly with Ted Bates, Inc., Dancer-Fitzgerald-Sample. Blow-Beirn-Toiga, Inc., Revlon, Inc.; v.p., dir. Joseph E. Seagram & Sons, Inc., 1957-61; pres. Robert Bragarnick, Inc., marketing counsellors, 1961—. Home: 417 Park Av New York City NY 10022 Office Time-Life Bldg Rockefeller Center New York City NY 10020

BRAGG, DAVID GORDON, physician, educator; b. Portland, Ore., May 1, 1933; s. George Tully and Edith (Lee) B.; A.B. in History, Stanford, 1955; M.D., U. Ore., 1959; m. Marcia Robertson, Aug. 19, 1955; children—Eric Allan, Daniel Robert, James Tully. Intern Phila. Gen. Hosp., 1959-60; resident in radiology Columbia-Presbyn. Med. Center, Coll. Physicians and Surgeons, N.Y.C., 1962-64, chief resident, 1964-65, instr., 1965-66; asst. prof. Cornell U. Med. Coll., N.Y.C., 1966-70, asso. prof., 1970; chmn. diagnostic radiology Meml. Sloan-Kettering Cancer Center, N.Y.C., 1967-70; prof., chmn. dept. radiology U. Utah Med. Center at Salt Lake City, 1970—; cons. Salt Lake City VA Hosp., Meml. Sloan-Kettering Cancer Soc., 1970—. Bd. dirs. Bergen County (N.J.) dist. Girl Scouts Am., 1968-69. Served with AUS, 1960-62. Mem. Am. Coll. Radiology, A.M.A., Am. Gastroent. Soc., Radiol. Soc. N.Am., Roentgen Ray Soc., James Ewing Soc. Contbr. chpts. and numerous articles tech. lit. Home: 4403 Cove Crest Dr Salt Lake City UT 84117

BRAGG, JOHN MACKIE, ins. co. exec.; b. Winnipeg, Man., Can., July 10, 1921; s. George Henry and Jessie (Mackie) B.; B.Comm. U. Man., 1943; m. Joan Ellen Griffin, Dec. 4, 1948; children—David, Ian, Nancy, Linda. Asso. group actuary Great West Life Assurance Co., Winnipeg, 1945-56; with Life Ins. Co. of Ga., Atlanta, Ga., 1956—, v.p., chief actuary, 1959—, dir., 1961—, mem. exec. com., 1966—. Mem. Bd. Mgmt. Downtown Y.M.C.A. of Atlanta. Served with RCAF, World War II. Mem. Soc. Actuaries (v.p. 1970), Am. Life Conv. (chmn. joint actuarial com. 1970—). Presbyn. (deacon 1967—). Home: 3252 Rockingham Dr NW Atlanta GA 30327 Office: Life of Georgia Tower Atlanta GA 30308

BRAGONIER, WENDELL HUGHELL, botanist, educator; b. Ia., Aug. 5, 1910; s. Robert Jacob and Cora M. (Hughell) B.; B.A. U. No. Ia., 1933; postgrad. (fellow) U. Chgo., 1939; M.S., Ia. State U., 1941, Ph.D., 1947; Rockefeller Found. fellow, Mexico, 1945-46; m. M. Alice Dowden, June 18, 1934; children—J. Robert, James W., Mary-Ellen. Tchr., Ia. high schs., 1933-34, 35-39, Tenn. 1934- 35; faculty Ia. State U., 1939-63, fellow, instr., research asso., asst. to dir. Indsl. Sci. Research Inst., asso. dir. Camp Dodge br., 1946-47, asso. prof. botany, 1947-50, prof., head botany, 1950-63; dean Grad. Sch., prof. botany and plant pathology Colo. State U., Ft. Collins, 1963—. Chmn. sci. adv. council Am. Seed Research Found. Mem. A.A.A.S., Bot. Soc. Am., Am. Inst. Biol. Scis., Colo.-Wyo., Ia. acads. sci., Sigma Xi, Phi Kappa Phi, Gamma Sigma Delta. Home: 1100 Ellis St Fort Collins CO 80521

BRAHAM, ROSCOE RILEY, Jr., meterologist, educator; b. Yates City, Ill., Jan. 3, 1921; s. Roscoe Riley and Edith L. (Bowman) B.; B.S. in Geology, Ohio U., 1942; S.M. in Meteorology, U. Chgo., 1948, Ph.D., 1951; m. Mary Ann Moll, Mar. 12, 1943; children—Ruth Ann, Nancy Kay, Richard Riley, Jean Lou. Mem. staff U.S. Weather Bur., 1946-49, acting ofcl. charge thunderstorm project, 1948-49; mem. research staff U. Chgo., 1949-50, 51-54, prof. meteorology, 1954—; mem. faculty N.M. Inst. Tech., 1950-51; prof. meteorology U. Ariz., 1954-56; cons. in field. Served as pilot, weather officer, USAAF, 1942-45. Recipient Losey award Inst. Aero. Scis., 1950; Silver medal Dept. Commerce, 1950. Mem. Am., Royal meterol. socs., Am. Geophys. Union, Phi Beta Kappa, Sigma Xi. Republican. Presbyn. (elder). Author: (with H.R. Byers) The Thunderstorm, 1949; also numerous articles. Discoverer cell circulations in thunderstorm. Home: 57 Longcommon Rd Riverside, IL 60546 Office: Dept Geophys Scis Univ Chgo Chicago IL 60637

BRAHAM, WILLIAM WALTER, lawyer, former judge; b. Youngstown, O., Oct. 28, 1893; s. Robert Renwick and Olive (Wilkin) B.; A.B., Westminster Coll., 1915, LL.D., 1945; LL.B., U. Pitts., 1922; m. Selina Forker Whitla, Jan. 18, 1927 (dec. Oct. 1958); children—Isabel Whitla (Mrs. Norman A. Pedersen, Jr.), William Walter, James Whitla; m. 2d, Ruth McEwen Caldwell, Sept. 10, 1960 (dec. June 1970). Admitted to Pa. bar, 1922; practiced in New Castle, Pa., 1922-36; Judge, Lawrence County, Pa., 1936-38, presiding judge, 1938-56; partner firm Braham Mitsos & McCracken, New Castle, 1963—. Mem. procedural rules com. Supreme Ct. Pa., 1942—; mem. adv. com. law of decedents' estate and trusts Joint State Govt. Commn. Pa. Legislature, 1947—; del. Pa. Constl. Conv., 1967-68. Chmn., Lawrence County chpt. A.R.C., 1932-35; pres. Chautauqua (N.Y.) Instn., 1956-60. Trustee Jameson Meml. Hosp., Western Pa. Conservancy. Recipient Alumni Achievement award Westminster Coll., 1966. Fellow Am. Bar Assn.; mem. Pa. (pres. 1966-67) Bar Assn., Am. Law Inst., Am. Judicature Soc., Inst. Jud. Adminstrn., Pa., Western Pa. hist. socs., Scotch Irish Soc., Sigma Nu, Phi Alpha Delta. Republican. Presbyn. Mason, Rotarian. Clubs: Duqesne (Pitts.); New Castle Country, Lawrence (New Castle). Contbr. articles to hist., legal jours. Home: 126 Hazelcroft Av New Castle PA 16105 Office: 1st Nat Bank Bldg New Castle PA 16101

BRAHANA, THOMAS ROY, educator; b. Champaign, Ill., June 26, 1926; s. Henry Roy and Myrtle Gladys (Van Wart) B.; A.B., U. Ill., 1947; M.S., U. Mich., 1948, Ph.D., 1954; m. Mary Ann Weiss, Dec. 29, 1951; children—Elizabeth, Joan, Patrick, Daniel. Instr. math. Dartmouth, 1953-54; prof. math. U. Ga., 1954—. Mem. Inst. Advanced Study, Princeton, 1957-58. Served with USAF, 1944-45. Mem. Am. Math. Soc., Am. Assn. U. Profs. Presbyn. Home: 163 S Homewood Dr Athens GA 30601

BRAHM, WALTER THOMAS, librarian; b. Massillon, O., Oct. 9, 1910; s. Edward and Lydia (Grill) B.; A.B. (Ohio scholar), Western Res. U., 1932, B.L.S., 1933; m. Estelle Hudson, Feb. 29, 1936; 1 dau., Carolyn. Staff mem. Western Res. U. Library, 1933-35, head pub. service dept., 1936-37; head technology dept. Toledo Pub. Library, 1937-38, asst. librarian 1939-42; librarian State of Ohio, Columbus, 1942-64, State of Conn., Hartford, 1964—. Named Outstanding Librarian of Year, Ohio Library Assn., 1959. Mem. Am., New Eng., Conn. library assns., Spl. Libraries Assn., Am. Assn. State Libraries (pres. 1959-60), Alpha Tau Omega. Lutheran. Mason. Co-author county library surveys Pa., N.J., O. Compiler index to pubs. Western Res. U., 1826-1936, 1937. Home: 96 Wildwood Rd West Simsbury CT 06070 Office: State Library and Supreme Ct Bldg Hartford CT 06103

BRAIDWOOD, ROBERT J., archeologist, educator; b. Detroit, July 29, 1907; s. Walter J. and Rhea (Nimmo) B.; A.B., U. Mich., 1932, A.M., 1933; Ph.D., U. Chgo., 1942; Sc.D., U. Ind., 1971; m. Linda Schreiber, 1937; children—Gretel, Douglas. Archeol. field work, Iraq, Syria, Iran, Turkey, Ill., N.M., 1930—; faculty Oriental Inst., U. Chgo.; 1933—, prof. Old World prehistory, 1954—, faculty U. Chgo., 1940—, prof. dept. anthropology, 1954—. Fellow Am. Acad. Arts and Scis., Nat. Acad. Scis., Am. Philos. Soc.; mem. Am. Anthrop. Assn. (exec. bd. 1962- 64), Internat. Union Pre-and-Protohistoric Scis. (U.S. del. permanent council), Conf. Asian Archaeology and New Delhi (found. mem.); corr. mem. Deutsche Archaologische Institut, Göteborgs Kungl. Vetenskaps och Vitterhets Samhalle, Instituto Italiano di Preistoria e Protostoria, Jysk Arkaeologist Selskab, Österreichsche Akademie de Wissenschaft. Office: Oriental Inst U Chgo Chicago IL 60637

BRAIKOVI CH, ANDREW CHRISTOPHER, ins. co. exec.; b. Galveston, Tex., Nov. 30, 1913; s. Christopher John and Anna (Cihlar) B.; B.S. in Finance, Tex. A. and M. U., 1937; m. Alice Rosalind Krejci, June 2, 1941; 1 son, Ronald John. With Am. Nat. Ins. Co., Galveston, 1937—, v.p., sec., 1967—. Served with AUS, World War II. Fellow Life Offce Mgmt. Assn. Home: 3 Adler Circle Galveston TX 77550 Office: Am Nat Life Ins Co Moody Av and Market St Galveston TX 77550

BRAILOWSKY, ALEXANDER, pianist; b. Kiev, Russia, February 16, 1896; s. Peter and Elizabeth (Raptchinsky) B.; grad. with gold medal, Conservatoire (Kiev), 1911; studied with Theodore Leschetizky in Vienna, 1911-14; m. Felicia Karczmar, Nov. 17, 1931. Made debut in Paris, many tours of European countries; has toured U.S. since 1924, S.Am., C.Am., North Africa, Far East. First to present entire work of Chopin in cyclic form, within framework of 6 recitals, Paris (on Chopin's own piano, played only by Franz Liszt since composer's death), Brussels, Zurich, N.Y.C., Mexico City, Buenos Aires, Montevideo Recipient Order of Knight conferred by late King Albert of Belgium; Order "Pour le Merite", by King Carol of Rumania; knight Leg. of Hon. (France), King Christian X medal (Denmark), Silver medal City of Paris, Scroll of Honor for personal contbn. to humanitarian work behalf world's refugees. Mem. Greek Orthodox Ch. Club: Bohemians (N.Y.C.). Address: care Columbia Artists 165 W 57th St New York City NY 10019

BRAILSFORD, JAMES MONCRIEF, state justice; b. Orangeburg, S.C., July 3, 1910; s. James Moncrief and Mary Elizabeth (Bates) B.; A.B., U.S.C., 1932, LL.B., 1934; m. Louise Rook Tompkins, Nov. 5, 1938 (dec. Aug. 1962); children—James Moncrief, Daniel Tompkins, Amelia Tompkins, Martha Aldrich; m. 2d, Joan Ward Culler, June 19, 1971. Admitted to S.C. bar, 1934; practiced in Orangeburg, 1934-49; circuit Judge S.C., 1949-62; asso. justice Supreme Ct. S.C., 1962—. Mem. S.C. Ho. of Reps., 1939-42, 47-49. Served with AUS, World War II. Mem. Phi Beta Kappa. Address: PO Box 386 Orangeburg SC 29115

BRAIN, GEORGE BERNARD, univ. dean; b. Thorp, Wash., Apr. 25, 1920; s. George and Alice Pearl (Ellison) B.; B.A., Central Wash. State Coll., Ellensburg, 1946, M.A., 1949; Ed.D., Columbia Tchrs. Coll., 1957; postgrad. U. Wash., Wash. State U., Harvard, U. Colo., Stanford; m. Harriet Gardinier, Sept. 28, 1940; children—George Calvin, Marylou. Tchr. math. and sci. Yakima (Wash.) secondary schs., 1946-49; instr. Central Wash. State Coll., 1949-50; elementary sch. prin., Ellensburg, 1950-51; successively elementary sch. prin., asst. supt. schs., supt. schs., Bellevue, Wash., 1951-59; vis. prof. Central Wash. State Coll., 1953, Wash. State U., 1959, U. Md., 1964; supt. schs., Balt., 1960-65; dean Coll. Edn., also dir. summer schs., Wash. State U., Pullman, 1965—. Lectr. Columbia, U. Conn., Harvard, U. Ga., U. Del., Johns Hopkins, Morgan U., U. Okla., Towson State Coll., Stanford, Wash. U. Chmn. Fulbright Group Western European Seminar Comparative Edn., 1959; chmn. ednl. policies commn. N.E.A.; ednl. cons. Office Edn., 1962—; cons. Ednl. Testing Service, Princeton, N.J., 1964-67. Bd. dirs. Md. Acad. Sci., 1960-65. Served with USNR, 1941- 42, USMCR, 1942-46; maj. Res. Recipient Distinguished Service award Wash. State Jr. Assn. Commerce, 1956; named Man of Year, Met. Civic Assn. Balt., 1962; Distinguished Service award in edn. Nat. Conf. Christians and Jews, 1963. Fulbright scholar, 1959. Life mem. Am. Assn. Sch. Adminstrs. (exec. com. 1964-66, pres. 1965), N.E.A.; hon. life mem. Wash. State Assn. Sch. Adminstrs. (pres. 1959), Md. Assn. Sch. Adminstrs., Nat. Congress P.T.A.; mem. Wash. Edn. Assn. (pres. dept. adminstrn. and supervision 1957), A.A.A.S. (exec. com. commn. elementary and secondary sci. 1963-66), Assn. Supervision and Curriculum Devel., Univ. Council Ednl. Adminstrn. Nat. Joint Council Econ. Edn. (exec. com. 1963—), Nat. Conf. Profs. Ednl. Adminstrn., Am. Assn. U. Profs., Internat. Platform Assn., Nat. Council for Edn. in Health Professions, Nat. Acad. Sch. Execs., Nat. Council Fgn. Study League, Exec. Hall Fame, Phi Delta Kappa, Kappa Delta Pi. Presbyn. Rotarian (dir. Balt. 1964- 65). Mem. editorial adv. bd. Scholastics Publs., 1963—, Am. Sch. and Univ., 1960-64, Education, USA, 1964-71; mem. editorial bd. World Book, 1966—, Jour. Tchr. Edn., 1966—. Home: 300 N Spring St Pullman WA 99163

BRAIN, GEORGE MAXWELL, paper co. exec.; b. Toronto, Ont., Can., May 10, 1914; s. George Henry and Emily (Paton) B.; m. Mary Frances Hickey, Nov. 10, 1937; children—Mary Elizabeth, Judith Ann, Eileen Patricia, Linda Jane. With Rolland Paper Co. Ltd., Montreal, Que., Can., 1929-49; with Provincial Paper Ltd., Toronto, 1949-61, v.p., 1961-65, pres., gen. mgr. 1965—; v.p. Abitibi Sales Co. Ltd., 1961-63, pres., gen. mgr., 1963-65; v.p. sales Abitibi Power & Paper Co. Ltd., 1963-65; sr. v.p. Fine Papers Group, Abitibi Paper Co. Ltd., 1965—; dir. Abitibi Containers, Ltd., Abitibi Corp. Bd. dirs. Canadian Arthritis and Rheumatism Soc. Clubs: National, Rosedale Golf (Toronto), Seigniory. Home: 195 Hudson Dr Toronto 7 Ontario Canada Office: 408 University Av Toronto Ontario Canada

BRAINARD, CALVIN H., educator; A.B., Columbia, 1935, M.B.A., 1948; Ph.D., N.Y.U., 1951. Prof. finance and ins., chmn. dept. U. R.I., Kingston. Office: Dept Finance U RI Kingston RI 02881*

BRAINARD, ELLIOTT ESTER, indsl. co. exec.; b. Bklyn., Sept. 27, 1905; s. Howard DeWolfe and Maria Josefina (Yara Ester) B.; grad. cum laude, Sheffield Sci. Sch., Yale U., 1926; m. Lois Forsythe Smith, Oct. 19, 1929; children—Beverly Ann (Mrs. Robert Worlock), Barbara Lynn (Mrs. D. Michael Driskel). With Pub. Service Electric & Gas Co., Newark, 1926-29; asst. sec., asst. treas. Lock Joint Pipe Co., East Orange, N.J., 1929-45, treas., v.p. fgn. sales, 1945-48, v.p. sales, dir., 1948-52; v.p. sales Am. Pipe & Constrn. Co. (name changed to Ameron, Inc. 1970), Los Angeles, 1952-54, v.p. domestic operations, 1954-56, exec. v.p., dir., 1956-64, v.p., 1964-67, group v.p., 1967-70, sr. v.p., 1970—, also dir.; v.p., dir. Am. Pipe & Constrn., Internat., Pipe Linings, Inc.; pres., dir. Etiwanda Steel Producers Inc., dir. Amercoat Corp., Gifford-Hill-Am., Inc. Mem. Tau Beta Pi, Sigma Psi. Clubs: San Gabriel (Cal.) Country; Jonathan (Los Angeles); Irvine Coast Country, Balboa Bay (Newport Beach, Cal.); Pauma Valley Country. Home: 900 Sierra Madre Blvd San Marino CA 91108 Office: Ameron Inc 400 Atlantic Blvd Monterey Park CA 91754

BRAINARD, HARRY GRAY, economist, educator; b. Rochester, N.Y., Aug. 16, 1907; s. Harry Cummings and Anna (Connor) B.; B.S., U. N.C., 1930, M.S., 1931; Ph.D., U. Ill., 1935; m. Elizabeth McEvoy, June 10, 1936. Asst. prof. econs. The Citadel, 1935-37; regional economist WPA, summer 1936; economist Dept. Labor, summer 1937; prof., head dept. econs. So. Ill. U., Carbondale, 1937-46; economist OPA, 1942-45, U.S. Strategic Bombing Survey, War Dept., 1945, research div., Gen. Hdqrs. War Dept., Japan, 1946; prof. econs. U. N.C., Chapel Hill, summer 1946; prof. econs. Mich. State U., East Lansing, 1946—, acting head dept., 1960, 61, acting dir. div. research, acting dir. bur. bus. and econ. research, 1966, econs. cons. AID contract Ministry Edn., Turkey, 1967-69; vis. prof. U. Ariz., 1962; lectr. George Washington U., 1944. Cons. com. appropriations U.S. Ho. of Reps., 1951, 52, Air War Coll., Maxwell AFB, Ala., 1964; econs. cons. Naval War Coll., Newport, R.I., 1965; participant Merrill Center Econs., Southampton, L.I., summer 1957. Mem. quota com. Mich. United Fund, 1956- 67. Mem. Am., Midwest (pres. 1965-66) econs. assns., Am. Assn. U. Profs., Beta Gamma Sigma, Delta Sigma Pi, Delta Upsilon, Delta Phi Epsilon. Democrat. Episcopalian. Author: International Economics and Public Policy, 1954; Economics in Action, 1959. Author chpts. in books, articles in profl. jours. Home: 1854 N Harrison Rd East Lansing MI 48823

BRAINARD, MORGAN B., Jr., ins. co. exec.; b. 1906; grad. Kent (Conn.) Sch.; A.B., Yale. With Aetna Life Affiliated Cos., from 1927, v.p., treas., 1956-57, sr. v.p., treas., from 1957, also dir.; dir. Aetna Casualty Co., Standard Fire Ins. Co., Conn. Bank and Trust Co., Arrow Hart and Hegeman Electric Co., Hartford Courant, Fafnir Bearing Co. Address: 31 Woodland Av Hartford CT 06105*

BRAINARD, PAUL HENRY, musicologist, educator; b. Binghamton, N.Y., Apr. 18, 1928; s. George E. and Frances (Weinhauer) B.; B.A., U. Rochester, 1949, M.A., 1951; postgrad. Heidelberg (Germany) U., 1954; Ph.D., Goettingen (Germany) U., 1960; m. Ingrid Gretia Kahrstedt, Sept. 4, 1953; 1 son, Christopher. Research asst. Deutsches Musikgeschichtliches Archiv, Kassel, Germany, 1960; instr. music Ohio State U., 1960-61; faculty Brandeis U., Waltham, Mass., 1961—, asso. prof. music, 1964—, chmn. Sch. Creative Arts, 1965-68, chmn. dept. music, 1969—; spl. research music history, performance practice. Served with AUS, 1951-53. Mem. Am., Internat. musicol. socs., Gesellschaft fuer Musikforschung, Phi Beta Kappa. Mem. editorial board Neue Bach-Ausgabe, 1964—. Contbr. articles to profl. jours. Home: 37 Princess Rd West Newton, MA 02165 Office: Dept Music Brandeis Univ Waltham MA 02154

BRAINARD, WILLIAM CRITTENDEN, educator, economist; b. Jersey City, July 2, 1935; s. William E. and Eleanor (Holston) B.; B.A., Oberlin Coll., 1957, M.A., Yale, 1959, Ph.D., 1963; m. Ellen Rawlings, Oct. 28, 1958; children—David, Michael, Daniel. Asst. prof. econs. Yale, 1962-66, asso. prof., 1966-69, prof., 1969—; research asso. Brookings Instn., 1965-66; acting dir. Cowles Found., New Haven, 1969-70. Mem. Am. Econ. Assn., Econometric Soc. Contbr. articles profl. jours. Home: 310 McKinley Av New Haven CT 06515

BRAINE, JOHN GERARD, author; b. Bradford, Eng., Apr. 13, 1922; s. Fred and Katherine (Henry) B.; ed. Leeds Sch. Librarianship, 1947-48; m. Helen Wood, Oct. 22, 1955; children—Anthony, Frances, Felicity, Ursula. Asst. Bingley Pub. Library, 1940-49, chief asst., 1949-51; br. librarian Northumberland County Library, 1954-56, West Riding County Library, 1956-57; engaged in writing 1957—. Served with Royal Navy, 1942-43. Asso. Library Assn. Author: Room at the Top, 1957; From the Hand of the Hunter, 1959; Life at the Top, 1962; the Jealous God, 1965; The Crying Game, 1968. Clubs: Authors; Arts theatre, PEN, Bingley Little threatre. Address: 5 Broomcroft Close Pyrford Woking Surrey England

BRAINERD, BYRON, lawyer; b. Whitewater, Kan., July 11, 1915; B.A., J.D., U. Kan. Admitted to Kan. bar, 1939; now mem. firm Weigand, Curfman, Brainerd, Harris & Kaufman, Wichita. Mem. Am., Kan., Wichita bar assns., Fedn. Ins. Counsel. Office: 1st Nat Bank Bldg Wichita KS 67202*

BRAINERD, JOHN G., elec. engr., educator; b. Phila., Aug. 7, 1904; s. John Austin and Mabel (Grist) B.; B.S., U. Pa., 1925, Sc.D., 1934; certificate Mass. Inst. Tech., 1941, 54; m. Carol Paxson, Sept. 6, 1930. Reporter The N.Am., Phila., 1922-25; faculty Moore Sch. Elec. Engring., U. Pa., Phila., 1925—, prof., 1954—, also dir., 1954-70, chmn. div. phys. scis., U. Pa. Grad. Sch., 1942-48; engr., acting state dir. PWA, 1935-37; cons. engr. govt. agencies; project supr. large-scale digital gen. purpose electronic computer, completed 1946. Mem. sci. adv. com. Nat. Bur. Standards, 1959-65; mem. U.S. nat. com., com. experts Internat. Electrotech. Commn. Mem. engring. coll. accreditation com., regional chmn. ECPD. Fellow A.A.A.S., I.E.E.E. (chmn. nat. com. for elec. engring. films, chmn. awards, com., dir.); mem. Soc. for History Technology (v.p.), Engrs.' Joint Council, Am. Assn. U. Profs., Am. Standards Assn. (standards council 1949-51), Sigma Xi, Tau Beta Pi. Clubs: Lenape, Engineers (Phila.). Co-author: Ultra High Frequency Techniques, 1942. Contbr. articles to profl. jours. Home: North Ship Rd Exton PA 19341 Office: 200 S 33d St Philadelphia PA 19104

BRAINERD, LYMAN B., ins. co. exec.; b. Hartford, Conn., Oct. 15, 1906; s. Lyman B. and Lucy M. B.; A.B., Trinity Coll., 1930; m. Judith Pigeon, June 12, 1936; children—Lyman, Judith, Richard. With Hartford Steam Boiler Inspection & Ins. Co., 1930—, spl. agt., 1933-37, supt. agys., 1937-43, v.p., 1943-47, pres., 1947—, also dir.; dir. Boiler Inspection & Ins. Co. of Can., Hartford Nat. Bank & Trust Co., Arrow-Hart & Hegeman Electric Co., Hartford Courant Co. Trustee Trinity Coll. Home: 147 Stoner Dr West Hartford CT 06107 Office: 56 Prospect St Hartford CT 06102

BRAISLIN, GORDON STUART, banker; b. Bklyn., Jan. 13, 1901; s. William C. and Alice (Cameron) B.; A.B., Cornell U., 1923; m. Esther Elizabeth Hamm, July 26, 1935; children—Elizabeth Cameron, Alice Stevenson, Gordon Stuart, William Stevenson. With Prudence Co., Inc., N.Y.C., 1924-30; pres. Realty Assos. Mgmt., Inc., N.Y.C., 1931-38; founder Gordon S. Braislin, Inc., 1938 (merged into Braislin, Porter & Baldwin, Inc., N.Y.C., Bklyn. and Westchester County, N.Y. 1942), pres., 1942-49 (merged into Braislin, Porter & Wheelock, Inc., N.Y.C. 1949), pres., 1949-65; trustee Dime Savs. Bank N.Y., 1946—, chmn. trustees, chief exec. officer, 1965—; dir. Savs. Bank Trust Co.; trustee Savs. Bank Life Ins. Fund. Trustee Bodman Found.; bd. dirs., finance com. Am. Bible Soc.; trustee Bklyn. Inst. Arts and Scis.; pres. N.Y. Eye and Ear infirmary, 1961—; trustee Roosevelt Hosp., 1961—; bd. dirs. Bklyn. Eye and Ear Hosp., 1956-61, Community Blood Council Greater N.Y., 1963—, Downtown Bklyn. Assn., 1965—; mem. operating com. Interch. Center, 1959- ; bd. mgrs. dept. missions Episcopal Diocese N.Y., 1956-60. Mem. Savs. Banks Assn. N.Y. State (dir. 1965—), Bklyn. C. of C. (dir. 1965—), Phi Beta Kappa. Clubs: Union League, University (N.Y.C.); Brooklyn; Quaker Hill Country (Pawling, N.Y.). Home: 230 E 48th St New York City, NY 10017 Office: 9 De Kalb Av Brooklyn NY 11201

BRAISTED, PAUL JUDSON, ret. found. exec.; b. Antrim, N.H., Aug. 25, 1903; s. Rev. William E. and Belle (Porter) B.; Ph.B., Brown U., 1925, LL.D., 1970; M.A., N.Y.U., 1927; Ph.D., Columbia, 1935; L.H.D., Lawrence Coll., 1955; H.H.D., Carleton Coll., 1970; m. Ruth Evelyn Wilder, May 2, 1927; children—Paul W., Donald A., Richard R. Prof., chaplain Judson Coll., Rangoon, Burma, 1930-33; master Mt. Hermon Sch., 1935-37; exec. dir. Student Vol. Movement, 1938-39; field rep., program dir. Edward Hazen Found., Inc., 1940-49, pres., 1949-70, pres. emeritus, trustee, 1970—. Mem. exec. com., internat. com. YMCA; mem. adv. com. Am. Friends Service Com. Trustee Internat. Film Found. Asso. fellow Davenport Coll. of Yale. Mem. Council Fgn. Relations. Mem. Soc. of Friends. Clubs: Cosmos (Washington); Century (N.Y.C.); Pine Orchard (Branford, Conn.). Author: Indian Nationalism and the Christian Colleges, 1937. Home: 26 Colonial Dr North Haven, CT 06473

BRAISTED, PAUL WILDER, educator; b. Ootacamund, India, Apr. 21, 1928 (parents Am. citizens); s. Paul Judson and Ruth (Wilder) B.; Sc.B. in Mech. Engring., Brown, 1948; M.M.E., Syracuse U., 1959; Ph.D., Stanford, 1964; m. Anne E. Miner, May 13, 1950; children—David, Kathleen, Ruth (dec.). with IBM Corp., 1948-56, asso. engr., 1955-56, staff engr., 1956; instr. mech. engring. Syracuse U., 1956-60, asso. prof., 1960-66; asso. prof. U. Mo. at Columbia, 1966-69, prof., 1969—, chmn. dept., 1967—. Chmn. Midwest regional selection com. Danforth Asso. Program, 1968-71. Active P.T.A., 1965—. Ford Found. fellow, 1962, NSF fellow, 1960-61. Mem. Am. Soc. M.E., Am. Soc. Engring. Edn., Soc. Mfg. Engrs., Sigma Xi, Tau Beta Pi, Pi Tau Sigma. Presbyn. (elder). Home: 2309 Fairmont Rd Columbia MO 65201

BRAITHWAITE, EDWARD EUSTACE RICARDO, author; b. Georgetown, Brit. Guiana, June 27, 1921; s. Charles Edwardo and Elizabeth Martha (Greene) B.; student Queen's Coll., Brit. Guiana; B.Sc., Coll. City N.Y., 1940; M.Sc. in Physics, Caius Coll., Cambridge (Eng.) U., 1949. Schoolmaster, London, Eng., 1950-59; charge d'affaires Droit de L'Homme, World Vets. Fedn., Paris, 1960-62; ednl. cons. UNESCO, Paris, 1963-66; permanent rep. of Guyana to UN, 1967-68; ambassador to Venezuela, 1968-69. Recipient Anisfield-Wolf award, 1961. Served with RAF 1941- 45. Mem. P.E.N. (London). Author: To Sir, With Love, 1959 (Ainsfield Wolfflit. award); Moments of Grace, short stories, 1960; A Kind of Homecoming, 1961; Paid Servant, 1962; Choice of Straws, 1967; also book reviews, radio and TV scripts. Home: 133 Rue St Dominique Paris 7e France also 305 E 40th St New York City NY 10017

BRAKELEY, GEORGE ARCHIBALD, Jr., fund-raising counsel; b. Washington, Apr. 18, 1916; s. George Archibald and Lillian (Fay) B.; grad. Chestnut Hill Acad.; B.A., U. Pa., 1938; m. Roxana Byerly, Sept. 7, 1946; children—George Archibald III, Deborah Fay, Joan Keller, Linda Smith. Vice pres., dir. John Price Jones Co., Inc., fund-raising counsel, N.Y.C., 1938-50; v.p. Jones & Brakeley, Inc., advt. and indsl. publicity, 1948-53; pres., treas. John Price Jones Co. (Can.), Ltd., Montreal, 1950-53, became G.A. Brakeley & Co., Ltd., 1954, chmn., 1961—; chmn. G.A. Brakeley, Inc., San Francisco, Brakeley Cos., Inc., Diversified Instl. Cons. Corp., N.Y.C.; pres. G.A. Brakeley & Co., Inc., N.Y.C., 1957-67, chmn., treas., 1967—; dir. Jones Brakeley & Rockwell, Inc. Art. Served to capt., C.E., AUS, World War II. Mem. Am. Assn. Fund-Raising Counsel (dir.), Nat. Soc. Fund Raisers (dir.), Am. Orchid Soc., Atlantic Salmon Assn., Zeta Psi. Episcopalian. Clubs: University (N.Y.C., Chgo., Washington), Ski (N.Y.C.); Montreal Racket, Wee Burn Golf (Darien, Conn.); Racquet (Phila.); Minneapolis; Hartford. Home: 1 Pilgrim Rd Darien CT 06820 Office: 230 Park Av New York City NY 10017

BRAKER, WILLIAM PAUL, ichthyologist; b. Chgo., Nov. 3, 1926; s. William Paul and Minnie (Wassermann) B.; B.S., Northwestern U., 1950; M.S., George Washington U., 1953; student U. Chgo., 1954-58; m. Patricia Reese, Sept. 2, 1950. Mem. staff John G. Shedd Aquarium, Chgo., 1953-, dir., 1964-; asst. sec. Shedd Aquarium Soc., 1960-65, secretary, 1965-. Served with United States Army, 1950-52. Mem. Am. Fisheries Soc., Am. Soc. Icthyologists and Herpetologists, Am. Assn. Zool. Parks and Aquariums. Home: Sunset Rd Matteson, IL 60443 Office: 1200 S Lake Shore Dr Chicago IL 60605

BRAKHAGE, STAN, motion picture producer; b. Kansas City, Mo., Jan. 14, 1933; s. Ludwig and Clara (Dubberstein) B.; student pub. schs.; m. Mary Jane Collom, Dec. 28, 1957; children—Myrrena, Crystal, Neowyn, Bearthm, Rarc. Lectr. colls. U.S., Europe, 1955—; dir. Film-Makers Coop., 1968—; prodns. include Interim, 1953; Unglassed Windows Cast a Terrible Reflection, 1953; Desistfilm, The Extraordinary Child, 1954; In Between, The Way to Shadow Garden, Reflections on Black, The Wonder Ring, 1955; Flesh of Morning, Nightcats, Loving, 1956; Daybreak and Whiteye, 1957; Anticipation of the Night, 1958; Wedlock House, An Intereourse, Window Water Baby Moving, Cat's Cradle, Sirius Remembered, 1959; The Dead, 1960; Thigh Line Lyre Triangular, Films By Stan Brakhage, 1961; Blue Moses, 1962; Oh Life-a Woe Story-The A Test News, Mothlight, 1963; Dog Star Man, 1961-64; The Art of Vision, 1961-65; Three Films, 1965; Fire of Waters, 1965; Black Vision, 1965; Songs, I-XXV, 1964-67, Pasht, 1966; Two: Creeley McClure, 1966; 15 Song Traits, 1966; 23d Psalm Branch, 1967; Scenes from Under Childhood, Song 26, 1967; Lovemaking, The Horseman, The Woman and the Moth, My Mountain Song 27, 1968; Song 28, Song 29, American 30's Song, Window Suite of Children's Songs, Scenes from Under Childhood, 1969; The Weir Falcon Saga, The Machine of Eden, The Animals of Eden and After, Sexual Mediations # 1: Motel, Eyes, 1970; Deus Ex, Western History, Foxfire Childwatch, Angels', Door, 1971. Mem. selection com. Anthology Cinema, 1968-69. Recipient Ind. Film award, 1962. Avon Found. grantee, 1965-69; Rockefeller fellow, 1967-69. Author: Metaphors on Vision, 1963; The Moving Picture Giving and Taking Book, 1966; Scrapbook, 1969; The Brakhage Lectures, vol. 1, 1970, vol. 2, 1971. Home: Box 6 Rollinsville CO 80474

BRAKNIS, LEON VINCENT, transp. co. exec.; b. Pitts., Apr. 6, 1917; s. George A. and Elizabeth (Kapp) B.; ed. Bus. Inst., Detroit Inst. Tech., U. Detroit; m. Evelyn Loretta Miller, Aug. 24, 1940; children—Joyce, Gregory. Accounting clk. Baldwin Rubber Co., Pontiac, Mich., 1936-41; cost insp. USN, 1941-43; supervisory accountant Ernst & Ernst, Detroit, 1943-55; v.p., treas. Am. Metal Products Co., Detroit, 1955-67; v.p., treas. Leaseway Transportation Corp., Cleve., 1967—, also dir.; dir. Lab. Service, Inc. (Detroit). Mem. Am. Inst. C.P.A.'s, Mich. Assn. C.P.A.'s. Clubs: Acacia Country (Cleve.); Plum Hollow Golf (Detroit). Home: 75 Hunting Trail Chagrin Falls OH 44022 Office: 21111 Chagrin Blvd Cleveland OH 44122

BRALEY, ALSON EMMONS, ophthalmologist; b. Lake Mills, Ia., Jan. 9, 1906; s. Harry Jackson and Evelyn (Emmons) B.; M.D., U. Ia., 1931; m. Hazel Deming, June 22, 1931; children—Alson Deming, Janet, William Harry. Intern U. Ia. Hosp., 1931- 32, asst. pathology, 1932-33, 1935-36, instr., 1933-34, 1936-37, resident ophthalmologist, 1934-35, research asso., 1937-39, prof. opthalmology U. Ia., 1950-69, prof. emeritus, 1969—; attending ophthalmologist Receiving Hosp., Detroit, 1939-41; asst. prof. ophthalmology Wayne U., 1939-41, Columbia, 1941-49; prof. ophthalmology, postgrad. sch. medicine N.Y.U., 1949-50; research virus diseases of conjunctiva, antibiotics. Diplomate Am. Bd. Opthalmology. Fellow A.C.S.; mem. A.M.A., Am. Opthal. Soc., Am. Acad. Ophthalmology and Otolaryngology, Assn. Research Opthalmology, A.A.A.S., Sigma Xi, Alpha Omega Alpha. Home: 720 McLean Iowa City IA 52240

BRALLEY, JAMES ALEXANDER, Jr., chem. co. exec.; b. Bath County, Va., Aug. 18, 1916; s. James Alexander and Daisy Elizabeth (Williams) B.; B.S., U. Va., 1936, Ph.D., 1941; m. Rosemary Kearfott, Aug. 17, 1946; children—Sandra Lynn, Patricia, James Alexander II. Asst. chemist div. infectious disease. USPHS, 1939-41; research chemist B.F. Goodrich Co., 1941-46; devel. chemist Rohm & Haas Co., 1946-48, sr. devel. chemist, 1948-56; dir. chem. research A.E. Staley Mfg. Co., Decatur, Ill., 1956-61, v.p. research and devel., 1961-70; v.p. research and devel. Puritan Chem. Co., Atlanta, 1971—. Mem. Jr. Coll. Bd., Ill., 1967—. Mem. Am. Chem. Soc., Am. Oil Chemists Soc., Soc. Chem. Industry (London), Sigma Xi, Alpha Chi Sigma. Contbr. articles to profl. jours. Patentee catalysts for monomer synthesis, various plastic compositions. Home: 5209 Pine Bark Lane Atlanta GA 30338 Office: 916 Ashby St NW Atlanta GA 30318

BRAM, JOSEPH, educator; b. Ekaterinburg, Russia, July 17, 1904; s. Nahum and Sophie (Rosenzweig) B.; Licence ès-Lettres, U. Paris (France), 1930; Ph.D., Columbia, 1941; m. Jean Rhys, June 1946; children—Susan, Elizabeth, Margaret. Came to U.S., 1935, naturalized, 1942. Mem. faculty Queens Coll., N.Y.C., 1941-48; mem. faculty N.Y.U., N.Y.C., 1948—, prof. sociology and anthropology, 1948—. Spl. research Jehovah's Witnesses, Spiritualist cult in P.R., French Canadian separatist movement. Author: An Analysis of Inca Militarism, 1941; Language and Society, 1955. Home: 4 Prospect St Baldwin NY 11510 Office: 9 University Pl New York City NY 10003

BRAMAN, JAMES D'ORMA, former mayor of Seattle; b. Lorimor, Ia., Dec. 23, 1901; s. Jacob Wesley and Susie Mae (Huntzinger) B.; student pub. schs., Bremerton, Wash.; m. Margaret V. Young, Nov. 27, 1920; children—James D'Orma, Robert C. Pres. Braman Millwork Supply Co., 1920-29, Braman Mill & Mfg. Co., Inc., Bremerton, 1929-43, Braman Lumber & Hardware Co., Inc., Seattle, 1946- 56; chmn. bd. Shoreline Savs. & Loan Assn., Seattle, 1952—; mem. Seattle City Council, 1954-64; mayor of Seattle, 1964-69; asst. sec. U.S. Dept. of Trans., 1969-70. Rep. Seattle to Wash. State World's Fair Commn., 1957-62; mem. Seattle Center Adv. Commn.; mem. adv. council U.S. Conf. Mayors; chmn. Puget Sound Governmental Com.; mem. Nat. council, exec. bd. Chief Seattle council Boy Scouts Am. Trustee Pacific Sci. Center Found.; trustee, mem. steering com. Century 21 Corp., 1959-62. Served to comdr. USNR, 1942-46. Recipient Silver Beaver award Boy Scouts Am., 1949. Mem. Nat. League Cities (chmn. com. transp. and communications, mem. exec. bd., Japan-Am. Con. of Mayors and C. of C. Presidents (exec. com.), Seattle C. of C. Republican. Mason, Kiwanian. Home: 10659 Durland St NE Seattle WA 98125 Office: Seattle Municipal Bldg Seattle WA 98104

BRAMBLE, JAMES HENRY, educator; b. Annapolis, Md., Dec. 1, 1930; s. Charles Clinton and Edith (Rinker) B.; A.B., Brown U., 1953; M.A., U. Md., 1955, Ph.D., 1958; m. Mary Epps Boze, June 4, 1955; children—Margot, Tammara, Mary, James. Mathematician, Gen. Electric Co., Cin., 1950-59, Naval Ordnance Lab., White Oak, Md., 1959-60; asst. prof., asso. prof., prof. U. Md., 1960-68; prof. Cornell U., Ithaca, N.Y., 1968—. Mem. Am. Math. Soc., Soc. Indsl. and Applied Math. Mem. editorial bd. Mathematics of Computation, 1969—. Contbr. articles profl. jours. Home: 871 Cayuga Heights Rd Ithaca NY 14850

BRAMBLE, WILLIAM CLARK, educator; b. Balt., Nov. 7, 1907; s. John Howard and Ida (Wisotzki) B.; B.S., Pa. State U., 1929; M.F. (Hooker fellow plant physiology 1930-32), Yale, 1930, Ph.D. 1932; postgrad. (NRC fellow) Swiss Inst. Tech., 1936; m. Anne B. Searle, Sept. 4, 1939 (dec. 1953); children—Anne S., Willa C.; m. 2d, Dorothy Catchpole, Mar. 22, 1955; 1 dau., Elizabeth M. Researcher, Dept. Agr., summers 1928-34, collaborator, 1934-35; instr. botany Carleton Coll., 1932-35; prof. forestry Pa. State U. Sch. Forestry, 1937-56, acting dir. sch., 1956-58; prof. forestry Purdue U., Lafayette, Ind., 1958—, head dept. forestry and conservation, 1958—. Forestry cons. Lehigh Coal and Navigation Co., 1946-58; cons. Escritorio Tecnico de Agricultura, Brazil, summer 1960; mem. Adv. Com. on Conservation in Ind.; mem. adv. com. on agrl. sci. U.S. Dept. Agr., 1962—; mem. NRC, 1970—. Served to capt. USAAF, 1942-45. Mem. Soc. Am. Foresters (council), Ecol. Soc. Am., Am. Forestry Assn., Sigma Xi, Alpha Zeta, Alpha Gamma Rho. Rotarian. Contbr. articles to profl. jours. Home: 200 Lindberg Av West Lafayette IN 47906 Office: Dept Forestry and Conservation Purdue U Lafayette IN 47907

BRAMELD, THEODORE, educator; b. Neillsville, Wis., Jan. 20, 1904; s. Theodore and Minnie (Dangers) B.; B.A., Ripon Coll., Wis., 1926; Ph.D. (fellow), U. Chgo., 1931; Ed.D. (hon.), R.I. Coll., 1959; m. Ona Swanson, July 29, 1949; children—Katherine Alice, Patricia Gene, Kristin Elizabeth. Field sec. Ripon Coll., 1926-28; instr. philosophy L.I. U., 1931-35; asst. prof. Adelphi Coll., 1935-38, asso. prof., 1938-39; asso. prof. ednl. philosophy U. Minn., 1939-45, prof. 1945-47; prof. ednl. philosophy N.Y. U., 1947-58; prof. ednl. philosophy Boston U., 1958-69, prof. emeritus, 1969—. Vis. asso. prof. edn., Columbia, summers 1939, 45; vis. lectr. Sch. for Workers, U. Wis., summers 1944-45, 47; vis. prof. Springfield Coll., 1969-70, U. Hawaii, 1970—; lectr. New Sch. for Social Research, William Alanson White Inst. Psychiatry; vis. lectr. Dartmouth, 1953-54; vis. prof. U. P.R., 1955- 58; vis. specialist Dept. State Japan, Korea, 1962, 63; Fulbright research scholar, Japan, 1964-65; sr. fellow East-West Center, 1971-72. Regional v.p. Am. Edn. Fellowship, 1942-53; sec., treas. Philosophy of Edn. Soc., 1941-47, pres., 1947-48; Am. del. Internat. Conf. New Edn. Fellowship, Australia, 1946; mem. exec. bd. Council for Study Mankind, 1969—. Mem. Am. Fedn. Tchrs., Am. Assn. U. Profs., Am. Philos. Assn., John Dewey Soc., Am. Anthrop. Assn., Am. Ednl. Studies Assn., Phi Delta Kappa. Author: A Philosophic Approach to Communism, 1933; Minority Problems in the Public Schools, 1945; Design for America, 1946; Ends and Means in Education-A Midcentury Appraisal, 1950; Patterns of Educational Philosophy, 1950, rev., 1971; Philosophies of Education in Cultural Perspective, 1955; Toward a Reconstructed Philosophy of Education, 1956; Cultural Foundations of Education-An Interdisciplinary Exploration, 1957; The Remaking of a Culture-Life and Education in Puerto Rico, 1959; Education for the Emerging Age, 1961; Education as Power, 1965; The Use of Explosive Ideas in Education-Culture, Class and Evolution, 1965; Japan: Culture. Education and Change in Two Communities, 1968; The Climactic Decades: Mandate to Education, 1970. Editor, co-author: Workers' Education in the U.S., 1941; Values in American Education, 1964. Address: 1515 Ward Av Honolulu HI 96822

BRAMMELL, P. ROY, ret. coll. dean; b. Ozawkie, Kan., Dec. 11, 1900; s. H.L. and Judith Jane (Harnish) B.; A.B., McPherson Coll., 1923; A.M., U. Mich., 1928; Ph.D., U. Wash., 1930; m. Naomi Metzger, July 8, 1930; children—Naomi Helene, Homer Leon. Tchr. rural school, Kan., 1918-19; tchr. Ozawkie High Sch., 1923-25; prin. 1925-27; asst. specialist in sch. adminstrn. U.S. Office Edn., Washington, 1930-32; asst. prof., U. Conn., 1932-35, asso. prof., 1935-39, dir. summer session, 1936- 38, prof. edn., from 1939, dean Sch. Edn. 1940-60, acting dean Grad. Sch., 1942-45; prof. ednl. adminstrn. and supervision, So. Ill. U., Carbondale, 1960-69, asst. dean Coll. Edn., 1965-67. Vis. prof. edn. U. Colo., 1948-49. Research fellow U. Wash., 1928-30. Mem. Am. Assn. for Higher Edn., Am. Assn. U. Profs., Phi Beta Kappa, Phi Kappa Phi, Phi Delta Kappa. Author: Three Hundred Years of Education in Connecticut, 1935; Your Schools and Mine, 1952; also monographs of report of Nat. Survey of Secondary Edn. Home: 2323 Marlborough Rd Colorado Springs CO 80909

BRAMMER, FOREST EVERT, educator; b. Mabscott, W.Va., July 21, 1913; s. Evert C. and V. Susan (Lilly) B.; A.B., Concord Coll., 1933; B.S., N.C. State U., 1933; postgrad. U. N.C., 1936-37, Johns Hopkins, 1947-48; Ph.D., Case Inst. Tech., 1951; m. Evelyn G. Klitzing, Mar. 7, 1942; childrenRobert, Mary, William, Susan. High sch. tchr., Beaver, W.Va., 1933-36; geophys. engr. Schlumberger Well Surveying Corp., Tex., Ill., Mich., 1937-42; research Johns Hopkins Applied Physics Lab., 1946-48; faculty Case Inst. Tech., 1948-60; prof., chmn. elec. engring. dept. Wayne State U., Detroit, 1960- ; cons. Goodyear Aircraft Corp., 1954-58. Republic Steel Corp., 1958-. Served to capt. Signal Corps, AUS, 1942-46. Mem. I.E.E.E., Am. Soc. Engring. Edn., Sigma Xi, Tau Beta Pi, Eta Kappa Nu. Home: 1312 Devonshire St Grosse Pointe, MI 48230 Office: 667 Merrick St Detroit MI 48202

BRAMSON, BERNARD ALLEN, mining consultant; b. Bklyn., February 27, 1907; s. Samuel and Sara Allen (Senft) B.; B.S., E.M., U. Ariz., 1929; vocational teaching license, N.Y. State Tchrs. Coll., 1932; m. Olga del Solar Grove, Dec. 26, 1936; children—Bernice, Brian, Bernard Allen, Sandra, Ronald. Chemist, assayer, ore buyer Am. Smelting & Refining Co. subsidiary, Coplapo & Chanaral, Chile, 1929-35, charge mineral buying for Japan on West coast of S.A., 1935-39; ore buyer, engr. W.R. Grace & Co., N.Y.C. and La Paz, Bolivia, 1940-45; ore buying and export-import, Rio de Janeiro, 1945-47; charge mineral buying Westinghouse Internat. Co., 1948-51; minerals and petroleum attache for West coast of S.A., U.S. Embassy, Lima, Peru, 1951-55, integrated into career diplomatic service as fgn. service officer, 1955; consul, Johannesburg, Transvaal, Union of South Africa, ret. 1959; tech. adviser Minerals & Chem.-Philip Corp. (N.Y.), 1960; dep. project mgr. UN Minerals Survey (Chile), 1960-63, project mgr., 1963-66; now resident rep. Pan-Am. Devel. Found., Washington, also regional rep. McPhar Geophysics Ltd., Toronto, Can. Cons. Army-Navy Munitions Bd., Washington, charge of preclusive buying of minerals in Spain and Portugal under U.S. Commercial Co., 1942-43. Mem. Instituto de Ingenieros de Minas de Chile, Am. Inst. of Mining and Metall. Engrs., Sociedad de Ingenieros de Peru, Instituto Geofisico de Huancayo (dir.). Clubs: Golf, Country, Cricket and Football (Lima); Jockey del Peru; de Regatas; de la Union, Aero de Chile, Prince of Wales Country (Santiago, Chile). Contbr. to Tungsten (by K.C. Li and C.Y. Wang), 1943; also articles profl. jours. Address: Av Los Leones 1380 Santiago 4 Chile

BRAMSON, DAVID JAY, merchant; b. Chgo., Nov. 1, 1937; s. Leo and Ann (Travis) B.; student U. Colo., 1959; m. Suzan Beth Sloan, Feb. 7, 1963; children—Nancy Lynne, Jeffrey Michael, Max J. Pres. Bramson, Inc., Chgo., 1961—, Weathered, Inc., Chgo., 1961—, J.

Bentley Laurence, Ltd., Chgo., 1966—; partner 715 Farms, Ltd., Fla., 1961—, Gold-Dobrow- Bramson, Fla., 1963—. Harrison & Bramson, Fla., 1963—; owner, mgr. Bramson Enterprizes, Fla., 1963—. Chmn. womens wear trade div. Combined Jewish Appeal, 1965-66, Chgo. Heart Assn., 1966. Mem. Zeta Beta Tau. Clubs: Standard, Bryn Mawr Country (Chgo.). Home: 3750 N Lake Shore Dr Chicago IL 60613 Office: 160 N Michigan Av Chicago IL 60601

BRAMSON, LEO, mcht.; b. Chgo., Jan. 19, 1902; s. David Leo and Jenny Rose (Edelman) B.; student architecture Armour Inst. Tech., 1927-31, sculpture Art Inst. Chgo., 1922-26; m. Ann Travis, Dec. 25, 1928; children—Joan Davida (Mrs. Samuel Kraus), David Jay. Supervising architect Provident State Securities Corp., 1929-31; organized Bramson, Inc., Chgo., 1931, chief exec. officer 1931—; pres. Martha Weathered Shops, Inc., 1954—; partner, organizer 715 Farms, Pahokee, Fla., Sugar Cane Growers Coop. of Fla., Belle Glade; gen. partner Chiglades Farms, Ltd., Belle Glade; sec., treas. Tuscany Devel. Corp., Palm Beach, Fla.; pres. Bueno Farm, Inc., Pahokee, Fla. Guarantor, sponsor Lyric Opera of Chgo. Mem. Chgo. Assn. Commerce, Sigma Alpha Mu. Jewish religion. Kiwanian; mem. B'nai B'rith. Clubs: Standard (Chgo.); Palm Beach (Fla.) Country, Palm Beach Golf and Racquet. Home: 3570 S Ocean Blvd Palm Beach FL 33480 Office: 160 N Michigan Av Chicago IL 60601

BRAMSTEDT, ALVIN OSCAR, broadcasting co. exec.; b. Cosmopolis, Wash., May 9, 1917; s. Oscar and Ruth (Lindgren) B.; grad. Grays Harbor Jr. Coll., 1937; student U. Wash., 1938-39; m. Rosa Lea Bailey, July 16, 1940; children—Susan (Mrs. Robert Meilin), Janet Lea (Mrs. Ivan Felton), Alvin Oscar, Shelley Carol. Radio announcer KXRO, Aberdeen, Wash., 1940; announcer Radio Sta. KFAR, Fairbanks, Alaska, 1940-42, sta. mgr., 1942-55; gen. mgr. Midnight Sun Broadcasting Co., Anchorage, 1953-59; pres., gen. mgr. Midnight Sun Broadcasters, Inc., Anchorage, 1959—; pres., gen. mgr. KENI-TV, Anchorage, 1955—; dir., officer Ketchikan Alaska TV, Inc., Sitka Television, Inc. Alaska state chmn. March of Dimes, 1964; mem. Alaskan Command Adv. Bd.; v.p. Alaska Bus. Council, 1967. State chmn. United Nixon-Agnew Club, 1968; chmn. Alaska Republican Party, 1971. Mem. Alaska Broadcasting Assn. (pres. 1967), Alaska C. of C. (v.p. 1968), Alaska Nippon Kai (pres. 1967—). Home: 2612 Brooke Dr Anchorage AK 99503 Office: PO Box 1160 Anchorage AK 99501

BRAMSTEDT, WILLIAM FREDERICK, found. exec.; b. Manila, Philippines, Aug. 21, 1905; s. William and Sarah (McBride) B.; B.S., U. Cal., 1926 m. Margaret Martin (dec.); children—Eric, Sally; m. 2d, Margaret Weaver, May 27, 1950. Engr. Standard Oil Co., Cal., 1927-28, various positions Richmond refinery, 1928-40; v.p., dir. Standard Oil Co., B.C., Vancouver, 1940-43, Standard Oil Co. of Alaska, 1943-45; supt. Standard Oil Refinery, El Segundo, Cal., 1945; in charge crude oil sales Arabian Am. Oil Co., 1945-47; v.p. Cal.-Tex. Oil Corp., 1947-49, exec. v.p., 1949, pres., 1949-57, chmn. bd. dirs. 1957-63; v.p. Standard Oil Co. of Cal., 1963-70; vice chmn. nat. devel. Asia Found., San Francisco, 1970—. Clubs: Rockefeller Luncheon (N.Y.C.); Pacific Union, Bohemian (San Francisco); Silverado Country (Napa, Cal.). Home: 1250 Jones St San Francisco CA Office: 550 Kearny St San Francisco CA 94104

BRANAM, GEORGE CURTIS, univ. adminstr.; b. Amarillo, Tex., July 15, 1923; s. William C. and Mabel (McNutt) B.; B.A., U. Cal. at Berkeley, 1947, M.A., 1949, Ph.D., 1952. Instr., U. Cal. Far East Command, 1950-52; instr. La. State U., 1952-54; asst. prof. La. State U. at Baton Rouge, 1954-58, asso. prof., New Orleans, 1958-63, prof., 1963—, dir. humanities div., 1958-62, dean Coll. Liberal Arts, 1962-64, dean acad. affairs, 1964-69, vice chancellor acad. affairs, 1969—. Served with AUS, 1943-46. Mem. Modern Lang. Assn., Shakespeare Assn. Am., Am. Assn. U. Profs., Bibliog. Soc. Author: Eighteenth Century Adaptations of Shakespearean Tragedy, 1956. Office: Office of Acad Affairs La State U New Orleans LA 70122

BRANCH, CHARLES BENSON, chem. mfg. co. exec.; b. Omaha, May 23, 1915; s. Karl Stonem and Olava Christina (Larsen) B.; A.B., Western Res. U., 1937; m. Shirley Marie Dasher, Aug. 26, 1939; children—Jaquith Lee, Pamela Jill, Kristi Marie, Gretchen Kit, Andrea Denise, Derek, Timotha Victoria. With Dow Chem. Co., 1937—, v.p., mem. exec. com., 1959-62, exec. v.p., 1962-71, pres., chief exec. officer, chmn. exec. com., 1971—, also dir., mgr. overseas operations, pres. Dow Chem. Internat., S.A., 1959-62; v.p., dir. Saran Yarns Co., 1952-59; chmn. 1st Nat. Bank & Trust Co.; dir. Asahi-Dow Ltd., Tokyo, Dow- Uniquinesa S.A. Mem. plastics adv. com. Princeton, 1956-59. Mem. Mfg. Chem. Assn. (chmn. plastics com. 1954-56), Soc. Plastics Industry, Am. Chem. Soc., Phi Beta Kappa, Lambda Chi Alpha. Home: 4607 Eastman Rd Midland MI 48640 Office: 2030 Bldg Dow Center Midland MI 48640

BRANCH, CHARLES FRANKLIN, physician, hosp. exec.; b. Amherst, Mass., Aug. 14, 1897; s. Charles Franklin and Clara (Greenwood) B.; grad. St. Johnsbury Acad., 1917; M.D., U. Vt., 1923; m. Annie Sargent, April 26, 1924 (div.); 1 dau., Betty Ann; m. 2d, Mary Chapman, June 15, 1948; children—Nicholas, Christopher. Intern and asst. in pathology Boston City Hosp., 1923-25; asst. in pathology, Jefferson Med. Sch., Phila., 1925-26; asst. prof. pathology, Boston U. Sch. Medicine, 1926-28, asso. prof., 1928-32, prof., 1932-47, dean, 1944-47; asso. dir. Evans Meml. of Mass. Meml. Hosp., 1939-44; pathologist Mass. Meml. Hosp., 1926-47; Beverly Hosp., 1928-39, Salem Hosp., 1930-39, Framingham Union Hosp., 1928-30, Cambridge Hosp., 1930; cons. pathologist Beverley Hosp., 1940-47, Salem Hosp., 1940-47, Newton Hosp., 1935-47, Waltham Hosp., 1930-47, Martha's Vineyard Hosp., 1930-47, Cable Meml. Hosp. (Ipswich), 1934-37, Essex Sanatorium, 1933- 47, Brockton Hosp., 1938-47, Leonard Morse Hosp. (Natick), 1944-47; dir. Childrens Med. Center (Childrens Hosp., Infants Hosp., Sharon Sanatorium, House of the Good Samaritan, Wellesley Convalescent Home), 1946-47; asst. dir. A.C.S., Chgo., 1947-50; dir. labs. and chief pathologist Central Me. Gen. Hosp. 1950-67; research cons. Smith, Kline & French Labs., Phila.; county med. examiner, 1957-68; lectr. Me., 1952-67; chief med. examiner State of Me., Augusta, 1968—. Sectional vice chmn. 3d Internat. Cancer Congress, 1939. Mem. cancer control com. Nat. Cancer Council, 1948-60; chmn. cancer control com., Nat. Cancer Inst., 1959-60. Pres. Community Chest, 1958. Sgt. S.A.T.C., 1918; 1st lt. Med. Res., 1927-32; surgeon U.S.P.H.S., emergency hosp. sect., ret. Trustee Boston Med. Library, U. Vt., 1946-49. Recipient Distinguished Citizen award, Bates Coll., 1958, St. Johnsbury Acad., 1959. Evans Meml. European fellow, 1932; fellow in tropical medicine Assn. Am. Med. Colls., 1943. Diplomate Am. Bd. Pathology, 1937. Fellow A.C.S. (sec. cancer com. 1948-50), Mass. Med. Soc., Coll. Am. Pathologists (founding fellow emeritus); mem. A.M.A., Me. Med. Soc. (pres. 1969-70, chmn. com. hosps. and med. edn. 1954-59, mem. council, 1963—), Me. Medicolegal Soc. (past pres. 1961-63); Am. Cancer Soc. (mem. service com.), Suffolk County Dist. Soc., Am. Assn. Pathologists and Bacteriologists, Am. Soc. Clin. Pathology, Am. Assn. Cancer Research, New Eng. Cancer Soc., Am. Soc. Exptl. Pathology, Internat. Assn. Med. Museums, New Eng. Pathol. Soc. (founder and past pres.), Nu Sigma Nu, Delta Mu, Delta Psi. Rotarian. Clubs: Algonquin, Althean (Boston). Contbr. numerous articles on gen. pathology, cancer, med. edn. to med. periodicals. Home: 69 Gamage Av Auburn ME 04210 Office: State House Augusta ME 04330

BRANCH, CHARLES HENRY HARDIN, physician; b. Hopkinsville, Ky., Feb. 14, 1908; s. Charles Henry Hardin and Elisabeth Collins (Reed) B.; A.B., U. Fla., 1928; M.D., Tulane U., 1935; m. Erma Smith, Dec. 11, 1937; children—Robert Hardin, Alan Henry. Intern, So. Pacific Hosp., San Francisco, 1935-36; prof., head dept. psychiatry U. Utah Coll. Medicine, 1948-70; clin. prof. U. So. Cal., 1971—; program chief Mental Health Services, Santa Barbara County, Cal., 1971—. Dir. Am. Bd. Psychiatry and Neurology, sec.-treas., 1961, pres., 1962; mem. nat. adv. mental health council Nat. Inst. Mental Health, 1957-61, spl. cons., 1961—; nat. cons. psychiatry to surgeon gen. USAF, 1959-62; cons. psychiatry and neurology consultants br. Office Surgeon Gen., Dept. Army, 1962—; profl. adv. bd. Internat. Com. against Mental Illness. Fellow A.C.P., Am. Geriatrics Soc., Am. Psychiat. Assn. (council, sec., pres. 1962-63); mem. A.M.A., N.Y. Acad. Scis., Nat. Assn. Mental Health (profl. adv. bd., dirs., pres. research found. 1965-69), A.A.A.S., Pan Am., Cal. med. assns., Utah, Salt Lake County, Santa Barbara County med. socs., Intermountain Psychiat. Assn., Nat. Acad. Religion and Mental Health, Group for Advancement Psychiatry, Acad. Psychoanalysis, Royal Soc. Medicine (affiliate), Sigma Xi. Editorial bd. Behavioral Neuropsychiatry. Home: 935 Arcady Rd Montecito CA 93103 Office: Mental Health Services 4440 Calle Real Santa Barbara CA 93105

BRANCH, CLAUDE RAYMOND, lawyer; b. Providence, Jan. 9, 1886; s. John Baker and Fannie Welles (Mowry) B.; A.B., Brown U., 1907; LL.B. cum laude, Harvard, 1911; m. Hope Shepardson Cary, Feb. 19, 1928 (div.); children—Audrey (Mrs. Stephen Smith), Cecily (Freifrau v. Gemmingen Hornberg), Elizabeth Hilary (Mrs. Harvey Eggeman), Judith (Mrs. John L. Hart, Jr.). Admitted to R.I. bar, 1911, Mass. bar, 1932; third asst. atty. gen. of R.I., 1915-16; mem. Edwards & Angell, 1916-29; pres. Providence & Worcester R.R. Co., 1927-29; spl. asst. to U.S. atty. gen., 1929-32; mem. Choate, Hall & Stewart, Boston, 1932—; dir. Providence Washington Ins. Co., Peoples Trust Co.; trustee Peoples Savs. Bank. Head enforce. div. U.S. Food Adminstrn., R.I. 1917-18. Fellow emeritus Brown U. Fellow Am. Acad. Arts and Scis.; mem. Am. Law Inst., Am., R.I., Boston bar assns., R.I. Hist. Soc. (pres. 1928-29), Phi Beta Kappa (pres. R.I. Alpha 1948-49), Alpha Delta Phi. Republican. Clubs: Hope, Providence Art, Agawam Hunt (Providence); Union (Boston). Home: 64 E Orchard Av Providence RI Office: 20 Washington Pl Providence RI 02903 also 28 State St Boston MA 02109

BRANCH, EDGAR MARQUESS, educator; b. Chgo., Mar. 21, 1913; s. Raymond Sydney and Marian (Marquess) B.; B.A., Beloit Coll., 1934; Beloit Jr. Fgn. fellow U. Coll., U. London (Eng.), 1932-33; M.A., U. Chgo., 1938; postgrad. Brown U., 1934-35; Ph.D., State U. Ia., 1941; m. Mary Josephine Emerson, Apr. 29, 1939; children—Sydney Elizabeth, Robert Marquess, Marian Emerson. Grad. asst. English, State U. Ia., 1938-41; faculty Miami U., Oxford, O., 1941—, prof. English, 1957-64, research prof. English, 1964- -, chmn. dept., 1959-64. Mem. Modern Lang. Assn. Am., Am. Studies Assn. (exec. bd. Ohio-Ind. 1961-62), Nat. Council Tchrs. English, English Assn. Ohio (exec. bd. 1959-60), Coll. English Assn. Ohio, Am. Assn. U. Profs., Western Lit. Assn., Soc. for Study So. Lit., Phi Beta Kappa, Beta Theta Pi. Author: The Literary Apprenticeship of Mark Twain, 1950; A Bibliography of James T. Farrell's Writings, 1921-57, 1959; James T. Farrell, 1963; Clemens of the Call, 1969. Editor: Mark Twain's Letters in the Muscatine Journal, 1942. Contbr. articles to profl. jours. Home: 4810 Bonham Rd Oxford OH 45056

BRANCH, HARLLEE, Jr., pub. utility exec.; b. Atlanta, June 21, 1906; s. Harllee and Bernice (Simpson) B.; A.B., Davidson Coll., 1927, LL.D., 1962; LL.B., Emory U., 1931, LL.D., 1965; L.H.D., Howard Coll. (now Samford U.), 1965; m. Katherine Quintard Hunter, June 8, 1932; children—Harllee III, Katherine B. McKenzie, Barrington Heath, David Stuart. Reporter Atlanta Jour., 1929-31; admitted to bar, 1931; publicity dir. radio sta. WSB, 1930-32; lectr. Emory U., 1931-36, U. Ga. Evening Coll., 1929-34; Atlanta Law Sch., 1936-40; asso. firm Colquitt, MacDougald, Troutman & Arkwright, 1931-35; mem. firm MacDougald, Troutman Sams & Branch, 1936-49; v.p., gen. mgr., dir. Ga. Power Co., 1949-50, pres., 1951-56; pres. So. Co. (parent firm of Ala., Ga., Gulf and Miss. power cos.), 1957-69, chmn. bd., 1969—; chmn. bd. So. Services, Inc.; dir., dep. chmn. Fed. Res. Bank Atlanta, 1953-59; dir. U.S. Steel Corp., So. Ry., Gen. Reins. Corp. and affilliated cos., Gen. Motors Corp. Mem., past vice chmn. Ga. Sci. and Tech. Com. Mem. U.S. Steel Found., Inc.; trustee Emory U., Davidson Coll., Ga. Tech. Research Inst., Columbia Theol. Sem.; hon. trustee Ga. Coll., Milledgeville; mem. Bus. Council; dir. 4H Club Found. Ga., State YMCA Council of Ga., 1939—. Served as lt. (j.g.) USNR, 1944-45. Recipient George Washington honor medal Freedoms Found., 1964, 66, Brotherhood award Nat. Conf. Christians and Jews, 1968. Mem. Ga. Bar Assn., Edison Elec. Inst. (pres. 1955-56, adv. com. dir. 1949-66), U.S. C. of C. (dir. 1958-63), Beta Theta Pi, Omicron Delta Kappa, Phi Delta Phi, Alpha Kappa Psi, Beta Gamma Sigma. Presbyn. (elder). Clubs: Piedmont Driving, Capital City, Peachtree Golf. Commerce (Atlanta); Highlands Country. Home: 3106 Nancy Creek Rd NW Atlanta GA 30327 Office: 64 Perimeter Circle E Atlanta GA 30346

BRANCH, JAMES ELLIOTT, architect, educator; b. Martinsville, Ind., July 6, 1906; s. Emmett Forest and Katherine (Bain) B.; B.S. in Archtl. Engring., U. Ill., 1929, M.S., 1933; m. Mary Eloise Kennedy, Feb. 2, 1928; children—Mary Patricia (Mrs. Robert L. Bundy), James Elliott. Draftsman, architect Ulen & Co., Lebanon, Ind., 1929-31; instr., then asso. prof. architecture U. Ill., 1931-41, 46-50; prof., chmn. dept. architecture and archtl. engring. U. Miami (Fla.), 1950—; pvt. practice, 1930—. Served to col., arty., AUS, 1941-46. Decorated Bronze Star. Registered profl. engr., Ill.; registered architect, Fla. Mem. A.I.A., Am. Assn. Engring. Edn., Assn. Collegiate Schs. Architecture, Fla. Planning and Zoning Assn., Assn. U.S. Army. Ret. Officers Assn., Gargoyle, Scarab, Iron Arrow, Beta Theta Pi, Tau Beta Pi, Sigma Tau. Kiwanian. Clubs: Century (Coral Gables); Coral Reef Yacht (Coconut Grove, Fla.); University of Miami Faculty; Committee of One Hundred (Miami Beach, Fla.). Home: 6000 Montgomery Dr Miami FL 33156 Office: Engring Bldg Univ Miami Coral Gables FL 33124

BRANCH, JUDSON B., ins. co. exec.; With Nat. Life Ins. Co. U.S.A., 1929-34; with Allstate Ins. Cos., Skokie, Ill., 1934—, sr. v.p., 1954-57, pres., chief exec. officer, 1957-66, chmn. bd., chief exec. officer, 1966—, also chmn. finance com., chmn. exec. com.; chmn. Allstate Life Ins. Co., Cross Country Life Ins. Co., Allstate Enterprises, Inc.; pres. bd. La Californiana Cia. Gen. DeSeguros, S.A., Mexico City; chmn. bd. Allstate Internat., S.A., Alstadt Versucherungs- Aktiengesellschaft, Zurich, Switzerland, Allstate Ins. Co. Can.; dir. Sears, Roebuck & Co. Chmn. Nat. Motor Vehicle Adv. Council; mem. citizen's council sta. WTTW. Bd. dirs. Evanston Hosp. Assn., Hosp. Planning Council Met. Chgo.; vice chmn. Automotive Safety Found. Named Marketing Man of Year, Chgo. chpt. Am. Marketing Assn., 1960; Distinguished Service award Fedn. Ins. Counsel, 1966. Clubs: Economic, Chicago, Mid-America, Commercial, Executives, (exec. com.) (Chgo.), Skokie Country. Office: Allstate Plaza Northbrook IL 60062

BRANCH, ROBERT LEE, ednl. adminstr.; b. Portsmouth, O., Dec. 20, 1924; s. Clyde C. and Ethel C. (Oliver) B.; B.S., La. State U., 1949; M.P.H., U. Mich., 1951; Ed. D., U. Cal. at Berkeley, 1967; m. Dorothy Lee Niquette, Apr. 20, 1946; children—Barbara Lee, Theresa Ann. Commd. 2d lt. USAAF, 1945, advanced through grades to lt. col. USAF, 1967; mem. B-29 crew, 1943-46; health educator La. Dept. Health, 1946-52; officer flight, edn. and tng. USAF, 1952-69; prof. aerospace studies, chmn. dept. San Francisco State Coll., 1964-68; staff officer Directorate Personnel Planning, Pentagon, 1968-69; ednl. cons. Westinghouse Learning Corp., 1969-70; dir. ednl. research Sacramento County Office Edn., 1970—. Decorated Air medal, Meritorious Service medal. Mem. Royal Soc. Pub. Health (Eng.), Delta Chi (pres. 1948), Phi Delta Kappa, Delta Omega. Lion. Club: Rancho Cordova (Cal.) (pres. 1959). Home: 2429 Masoni Way Rancho Cordova CA 95670 Office: 6011 Folsom Blvd Sacramento CA 95819

BRANCH, ROGER EDDY, savs. and loan assn. exec.; b. Champlain, N.Y., Aug. 5, 1903; s. William F. and Mary Ellen (Eddy) B.; A.B., Dartmouth, 1924; m. Kathleen Shirley, Dec. 21, 1927. Tchr. pub. schs., Lake Worth, Fla., 1925-28; mgr. Household Finance Corp., Flushing, N.Y., 1929-36; exec. v.p. 1st Fed. Savs. & Loan Assn., Lake Worth, 1937-57, pres., 1957-69, mgr., 1937-69, chmn. bd., 1969—. Rotarian. Home: 1919 N Lakeside Dr Lake Worth FL 33460 Office: 200 Lake Av Lake Worth FL 33460

BRAND, DONALD DILWORTH, educator; b. Chiclayo, Peru, Mar. 6, 1905 (parents U.S. citizens); s. Willis C. and Martha Susan (Dilworth) B.; A.B., U. Cal., 1929, traveling fellow, 1930-31, Ph.D., 1933; m. Joy Morenci Erickson, Sept. 16, 1932; children—Donald Dilworth, Joy Beverly (Mrs. William J. Doughty). Teaching fellow U. Cal., 1931-33, instr., 1934, lectr. geography, 1934; asst. prof. U. N.M., 1934-35, asso. prof., 1935-39, prof. anthrop. geography, 1939-47, head dept. anthropology, 1935-43, 46-47; cultural geographer Smithsonian Inst. Mexico, 1944-46; prof. geography U. Mich., 1947-49; prof. geography U. Tex., Austin, 1949—, organized dept. of geography, 1949, chmn. dept. geography, 1949-60. Fellow A.A.A.S., Am. Geog. Soc., Am. Anthrop. Assn.; mem. Assn. Am. Geographers, Soc. History Discoveries, Assn. Tropical Biology, Latin-Am. Studies Assn., Soc. for Am. Archeology, Soc. Mexicana de Antropologia, Current Anthropology (asso.), Sigma Xi, Phi Kappa Phi. Author: Quiroga, A Mexican Municipio, 1951; Coastal Study of Southwest Mexico, 2 vols., 1957, 58; Coalcoman and Motines del Oro-An Ex-distrito of Michoacán Mexico, 1960; Mexico, Land of Sunshine and Shadow, 1966. Contbr. tech. articles various publs. Home: 1210 Windsor Rd Austin TX 78703

BRAND, GERHARD KARLFRIEDRICH, educator, microbiologist; b. Luebeck, Germany, June 10, 1922; s. Johannes and Kaethe (Hoefer) B.; grad. Katharineum High Sch. and Coll. (Germany), 1940; student U. Hamburg and Kiel (Germany), 1942-49; M.D., U. Hamburg, 1949, diploma tropical medicine, 1954; m. Inge Hoellein, Aug. 19, 1949; children—Juliane, Bettina. Came to U.S., 1957, naturalized, 1964. Asst. prof. Tropical Inst. Hamburg, 1949-52, asso. prof., 1952-55; asso. prof. Free U. West Berlin, 1955-57; prof. dept. microbiology U. Minn., Mpls., 1957—. Vis. prof. U. Merida (Venezuela), 1960; prof., dir. Inst. Microbiology, U. Duesseldorf (Germany), 1966-67. Research grantee USPHS, Am. Cancer Soc., 1957—. Mem. Am. Assn. Immunologists, Soc. Exptl. Biology and Medicine, Transplantation Soc., Tissue Culture Assn., others. Author monographs: (with Inge Brand) Evolution of Cell Cultures, 1962; (with L.C. McLaren) Virus Tropism, 1964. Contbr. articles on cancer research, cell immunology, virology to sci. jours. Home: 3117 W Owasso Blvd St Paul MN 55112 Office: Dept Microbiology U Minn Minneapolis MN 55455

BRAND, IRVING RUBIN, lawyer; b. Mpls., Dec. 23, 1918; s. Harry R. and Ruth (Rubin) B.; B.S., U. Minn., 1941, J.D., 1943; m. Ruth Miller, Dec. 20, 1953; children-Judith D., Johanna M., Jonathan M., Jethra E., Joshua L. Admitted to Minn. bar, 1943, also Supreme Ct. Ill., Supreme Ct. U.S., U.S. Dist. Cts., Cts. of Appeal; practice in Mpls., 1947—; law clk. to Circuit Judge Seth Thomas, U.S. Ct. of Appeals for 8th Circuit, 1943-44; asso. atty. U.S. Dept. Justice, Washington, 1944-45; asso. Swiren, Heineman & Antonow, Chgo., 1945-47; pvt. practice, Mpls., 1947-49; asso. Karlins, Groseman, Karlins & Brand, 1949-51; judge Municipal Ct. Mpls., 1951-55; judge Dist. Ct., 4th Judicial Dist. Minn., 1955-66; partner Maslon, Kaplan, Edelman, Borman, Brand & McNulty, 1966—; professorial lectr. Sch. Dentistry, U. Minn., 1947—, instr. Law Sch., 1953-66, adj. prof., 1966—; chmn. adv. com. to study juvenile traffic offender Legislative Commn. on Juvenile Delinquency, Adult Crime and Correction, 1958-59; mem. Minn. Supreme Ct. adv. com. on rules of civil procedure and appellate practice, 1965—. Mem. adv. com. B'nai B'rith Hillel Found. U. Minn., 1951—, pres., 1952-57; mem. B'nai B'rith Nat. Hillel Commn., 1967—; chmn. Isreal Bonds, Mpls., 1970—. Pres. Twin Cities chpt. Am. Friends of Hebrew U.; past bd. dirs. Jewish Family and Childrens Service Mpls., Mpls. Fedn. Jewish Service; trustee, bd. govs. Mt. Sinai Hosp. Assn.; past adv. bd. Am. Friends of Hebrew U. Mem. Am., Minn. (past com. chmn.), Hennepin County (past sect. chmn.) bar assns., Am. Judicature Soc., Am. Law Inst., Minn. Dist. Judges Assn. (past com. chmn.), Law Alumni Assn. U. Minn. (dir.). Home: 4300 Forest Rd Minneapolis MN 55416 Office: Builders Exchange Bldg Minneapolis MN 55402

BRAND, JOSEPH LYON, lawyer; b. Urbana, O., Aug. 11, 1936; s. Vance and Katherine (Lyon) B.; A.B., U. Mich., 1958; M.A., Ohio State U., 1959; J.D. with honors, George Washington U., 1963; m. Millicent Gaye Howard, June 21, 1958; children-Katherine Elizabeth, Stephanie Lyon, Joseph Howard. Admitted to Ohio and D.C. bars, 1963; practice in Washington, 1963—; partner Brand, Wagner & Dodd, 1963-65; atty. Barco, Cook, Patton & Blow, 1965-67; partner Patton, Blow, Verrill, Brand & Boggs, 1967—; v.p. Internat. Investment Co., 1963-65; v.p., gen. counsel C.R. Williams & Co., Inc., 1968—; v.p., gen. counsel Pacific Basin Travel System Corp., 1968-69; dir. Sugar Plantations Internat., Inc., Hospitality Mgmt. Co., Inc. Mem. George Washington Law Assn. (past v.p.), Washington Fgn. Law Soc., Am., D.C. bar assns., Am. Fgn. Law Assn., Am. Soc. Internat. Law, Order of Coif. Author article. Home: 1701 Putter Lane Reston VA 22070 Office: 1200 17th St NW Washington DC 20036

BRAND, OSCAR, folksinger, author; b. Winnipeg, Man., Can., Feb. 7, 1920; s. Isidore and Beatrice (Shulman) B.; B.A., Bklyn. Coll., 1942; m. Karen Lynn Grossman, June 14, 1970; children—Jeannie, Eric, Anthony. Host, Dept. Health, Edn. and Welfare program World of Folkmusic, 1962—, N.Y.C. (AM-FM) Folksong Festival, 1945—, NET-TV Oscar Brand's American Odyssey, 1970—; star CTV show Lets Sing Out CTV Network Can., 1962-68, The First Look, NBC-TV, N.Y.C., 1965-68, Brand New Scene, CTV Network, Can., 1966; composer, lyricist Joyful Noise, 1966; K*A*P*L*A*N, 1967; composer songs for film The Fox; composer, author; How to Steal an Election, 1968, Bridge of Hope (for Lit. Conf.), 1969; composer In White America, 1965, Celebrate (for N.Y. Presbytery), 1970; pres. Harlequin Prodns., Inc., Gypsy Hill Music, Inc.; trustee Newport Festival Corp. Music adviser nat. bd. YWCA; mem. adv. bd. Sesame Street, President's Com. on Nutrition. Served with M.C., AUS, 1942-45. Recipient Venice, Edinburgh, Valley Forge, Golden Reel, Cannes Festival awards for documentary and ednl. films, 1946—,

Peabody, Scholastic, Freedoms Found., Edison, Emmy nominations awards for radio and TV, 1962—. Mem. N.Y. Folklore Soc. Author: Singing Holidays, 1957; Bawdy Songs 1960; Folksongs for Fun, 1961; Ballad Mongers, 1963. Home: 141 Baker Hill Great Neck NY 11023 Office: NBC-TV 30 Rockefeller Plaza New York City NY 10019

BRAND, PAUL WILSON, surgeon; b. India, July 17, 1914; s. Jesse Mann and Evelyn Constance (Harris) B.; student Univ. Coll. Sch., London, Eng., 1933; M.B., B.S., Univ. Coll. Hosp., London, 1943; m. Margaret Elizabeth Berry, May 29, 1943; children—Christopher W., Jean M., Constance M., Estelle F., Patricia N., Pauline F. Intern Univ. Coll. Hosp., 1943-45, resident, 1944-45; resident Hosp. for Sick Children, London, 1945-46; tchr. orthopaedic surgery Christian Med. Coll., Vellore, India, 1946-64, prof. surgery, 1954-64, also past pres.; chief rehab. br. USPHS Hosp., Carville, La., 1966—; clin. prof. sur. Louisiana State U. Med. Sch., 1964—; spl. research to correct deformity in leprosy, 1947—; chmn. world com. Leprosy rehab. Internat. Soc. Rehab. Disabled, 1962—; Hunterian prof. reconstructive surgery in leprosy Royal Coll. Surgeons, 1952. Recipient Lasker award for dist. services field rehab., 1960, founder's medal Nat. Rehab. Assn., 1967 decorated comdr. Order British Empire. Fellow Royal Coll. Surgeons, Royal Soc. Medicine, Brit. Orthopaedic Assn., A.C.S.; hon. fellow Southeastern Surg. Congress, Am. Soc. Surgery Hand; corr. mem. Am. Soc. Plastic and Reconstructive Surgery. Address: USPHS Hospital Carville LA 70721

BRAND, ROBERT ALLYN, fgn. service officer; b. Norwich, Conn., Nov. 5, 1920; s. Allyn Morgan and Nonie Winifred (King) B.; grad. Norwich Free Acad., 1937; B.A., U. Conn., 1941; m. Josephine S. Moulden, Feb. 2, 1950; children—Nicholas, Susan, Allyn. Fgn. service officer, 1946—, assigned Dept. State, Washington, 1946; 3d sec., vice consul Am. Embassy, Rome, Italy, 1946- 49; vice consul, Munich, 1949-51; 2d sec. consul The Hague, 1951-54; 2d sec., consul, Manila, 1954-56; 1st sec. and consul, 1956-57; officer in charge Philippine Affairs, Dept. of State, 1957-60; assigned Nat. War Coll., 1960-61; 1st sec., U.S. delegation to Orgn. for Econ. Coop. and Devel., Paris, France, 1961-64; counselor Am. embassy, Lagos, Nigeria, 1964-67; minister embassy, Paris, 1967-71, London, 1971—. Served as capt. 1st Inf. Div., AUS, 1942-46. Home: 175 Broadway Norwich CT 06360 Office: Am Embassy Grosvenor Sq London England

BRAND, VANCE, banker, lawyer; b. Urbana, O., Sept. 14, 1906; s. Charles and Louise (Vance) B.; A.B., LL.B., George Washington U.; D.Sc., Universitatis Administrationtio, Monterrey, Mexico; m. Katherine Lyon; children—Louise (Mrs. Katker), Dixie, Joseph, Charles Vance. Admitted to Ohio, D.C., Fed. bars; gen. counsel, sec. Imported Date Assn.; gen. counsel, dir. Champaign Nat. Bank, 1935—, pres., 1950-54; dir. Export- Import Bank, Washington, 1954-59; mem. bd., mng. dir. Devel. Loan Fund, 1959-61; pres. Vance Brand Co., Internat. Investment Co., counsel firm Patton, Blow, Verrill, Brand & Boggs, Washington. Mem., sec. citizens adv. com. U.S. Senate Banking and Currency Com.; sr. adviser Am. delegation Council of Orgn. Am. States, Bogota, Colombia, 1960. Recipient George Washington U. Alumni achievement award in law and internat. finance, 1960. Mem. Champaign County Bar Assn. (pres.). Clubs: Metropolitan, 1925 F Street (Washington); Rolling Rock (Ligonier, Pa.); Country of Fla. (Delray); Urbana (O.) Country. Home: Branlan Woodstock OH 43084 Office: 117 W Court St Urbana OH 43078

BRANDBORG, STEWART MONROE, conservation exec.; b. Lewiston, Ida., Feb. 2, 1925; s. Guy Mathew and Edna (Stevenson) B.; B.S. in Wildlife Tech., U. Mont., 8; M.S. in Forestry, U. Ida., 1951; m. Anna Vee Mather, Aug. 8, 1949; children—Becky Glyde, Daniel Mathew, Betsy Edna, Anna Lisa, Fern. With U.S. Forest Service in Ida., Mont. and Ore., 1942-46; research life history and ecology mountain goat in Mont., Mont. Fish and Game Dept., 1947-48; research fellow Ida. Coop. Wildlife Research Unit, 1949-50; research and mgmt. investigations mountain goat, elk, other big game species Ida. Dept. Fish and Game, 1950-53; asst. conservation dir. Nat. Wildlife Fedn., 1954-60; dir. spl. projects, asso. exec. dir. Wilderness Soc., 1960-63, mem. governing council, 1956—, exec. dir., 1964—. Mem. exec. com. Natural Resources Council Am., 1964—, asst. editor Exec. News Service, 1962-64; bd. dirs. Defenders of Wildlife, 1962—; mem. Com. of 100 on Federal City; mem. com. continuing edn. U. Ida. Forest Devel. and Planning Council; mem. nat. conservation com. U.S. Jr. C. of C., 1958-59. Fellow A.A.A.S.; mem. Wildlife Soc., Soc. Am. Mammalogists, Sierra Club. Club: Cosmos. Home: 14401 Turkey Foot Rd Gaithersburg MD 20760 Office: 729 15th St NW Washington DC 20005

BRANDELL, ROY A., corp. exec.; b. 1913; student Northwestern U.; married. With Wolf & Co., C.P.A.'s, Oklahoma City, until 1962; sec., treas., dir. Scrivner Boogaart Inc., Oklahoma City, 1962—. Address: PO Box 26146 Oklahoma City OK 73126*

BRANDENBURG, DAVID JOHN, educator; b. N.Y.C., June 7, 1920; s. Joseph Franklin and Josephine Rose (Baker) B.; B.S., Bowdoin Coll., 1943; M.A., Columbia, 1947, Ph.D., 1954; m. Millicent Louise Harcourt, June 24, 1944; children—John Gifford, Guy Franklin, Ann Rosemary. Tchr., Riverdale Country Sch., N.Y.C., 1944-46; lectr. history Columbia, 1947-48; mem. faculty Am. U., 1948—, prof. history, 1957—, chmn. dept., 1967—; vis. prof. Wash. State U., summer 1970. Pres. Cathedral Heights-Cleveland Park Citizens Assn., 1964-66. Democratic precinct vice chmn., Clarksburg, Md., 1960. Fulbright research grantee, France, 1959; Washington Eve. Star faculty grantee, 1959. Mem. Am. Hist. Assn., Soc. French Hist. Studies, Agrl. History Soc., Societe d'histoire moderne. Author: Early Modern Times, 2d edit., 1969; also articles. Home: 3613 Norton Pl NW Washington DC 20016

BRANDENBURG, RICHARD GEORGE, educator; b. Oak Park, Ill., Feb. 21, 1935; s. George Arthur and Florence (Ream) B.; B.Mech. Engring., Cornell U., 1958, M.B.A., 1960, Ph.D., 1964; m. Maxine Toby Newman, Dec. 21, 1957; children—Suzanne Linda, Cynthia Anne. Asst. to dean GSIA, Carnegie Inst. Tech., Pitts., 1962-64, asst. dean, asst. prof. indsl. adminstrn., 1964-67; acting dean, asso. prof. indsl. adminstrn. GSIA, Carnegie-Mellon U., Pitts., 1967-68; dean, prof. adminstrn. and policy scis. Sch. Mgmt., State U. N.Y. at Buffalo, 1968—. Mem. bus. adv. com. Black Devel. Found., Buffalo, 1969—. Mem. Operations Research Soc. Am., Am. Soc. Engring. Edn., A.A.A.S., Inst. Mgmt. Scis., Buffalo-Niagara Sales and Marketing Exec. (com. chmn.), Phi Kappa Tau, Beta Gamma Sigma, Phi Kappa Phi, Pi Tau Sigma, Tau Beta Pi. Mem. editorial bd. European Business, 1967—; Cal. Mgmt. Review, 1967—; Am. Assn. Collegiate Schs. of Bus. Bull., 1970—. Mem. editorial adv. bd. Jour. of Bus. Policy, 1970—. Contbr. profl. jours. Home: 85 Briarhill Williamsville NY 14221 Office: Sch of Mgmt 103 Crosby Hall State U NY Buffalo NY 14214

BRANDENBURG, WILLIAM AARON, Jr., coll. pres.; b. Mason City, Ia., Jan. 26, 1910; s. William A. and Alta A. (Penfield) B.; B.S., Kan. State Coll., Pittsburg, 1930, M.S., 1931; Ph.D., U. Colo., 1946; m. Gwendolyn Bloker, 1941; children—Ann Avery (Mrs. William F. Zeman, II), William Aaron III. Tchr. pub. schs., Tulsa, 1932-38; instr. history Ohio State U., 1939-40; dean faculty William Woods coll., Fulton, Mo., 1940-50, N.W. Mo. State Coll., 1950- 56; pres. Wayne (Neb.) State Coll., 1956—. Served to capt. USMCR, 1943- 46. Mem. Marine Corps Res. Officers Assn., Am. Hist. Assn., Kappa Delta Pi, Phi Mu Alpha. Phi Sigma Epsilon (past nat. pres.). Presbyn. Mason (33, Shriner), Rotarian (pres. dist. gov., information counselor). Author publs. in field of polit. philosophy, fgn. lang. instrn. Home: Country Club Rd Wayne NB 68787

BRANDENBURGER, ROY LEE, chem. co. exec.; b. St. Louis, Sept. 6, 1910; s. Lee Emery and Adele (Wichmann) b.; B.S., Washington U., 1933; m. Marie Elise Lungstras, Nov. 29, 1935; children—Don Lee, Robert Lee, Tom Roy. With Ralston- Purina Co., St. Louis, 1934-52, gen. mgr. sanitation-farm supply div., 1946-52; gen. mgr., consumer products div. Monsanto co., 1952—, v.p., 1954—. Bd. govs., trustee San Francisco Bay Area Council; exec. bd. San Francisco Bay Area council Boy Scouts. Mem. Am. Ordnance Assn. (dir. San Francisco), Newcomen Soc. N.Am., Kappa Sigma. Clubs: Old Warson Country (St. Louis); Ranier (Seattle); World Trade (dir.) Pacific-Union (San Francisco); Menlo Country (Redwood City); Sainte Claire (San Jose); Los Angeles Country, California (Los Angeles). Home: 140 Degas Rd Portola Valley CA 94025 Office: 2710 Lafayette Santa Clara CA 95050

BRANDHORST, OTTO WILLIAM, dentist; b. Nashville, Ill., Mar. 29, 1889; s. August and Caroline (Finke) B.; D.D.S., Washington U., St. Louis, 1915; m. Eunice L. Schroeder, June 10, 1916; children—William Schroeder, Helen Caroline. Asst. in dental histology, Washington U. Sch. Dentistry, 1915-18, prof., 1918-30, also prof. orthodontia, 1925-30, dean and prof. orthodontics, 1945-52; exec. sec. Am. Coll. Dentists 1953- 69, sec., 1935-53, pres.-elect, 1969-70, pres., 1970-71; in practice of dentistry, specializing in orthodontics, St. Louis, 1918-53. Mem. task force on med. services in fed. govt. Hoover Commn. Orgn. Exec. Br. Govt., 1953-54; mem. Commn. Survey Dentistry in U.S., 1960-61; cons. on Dental Study Bur. Research and Statis., Social Security Bd. and various divs. USPHS, 1945; mem. dental adv. council Com. Econ. Security, 1934; chmn. pub. dental edn. com. St. Louis Dental Soc. Fellow A.A.A.S.; mem. Am. Dental Assn. (pres. 1952-53; mem. council dental edn. 1949-52; chmn. com. survey of dentistry 1952-61), Am. Assn. Orthodontists, Internat. Assn. Dental Research, Am. Soc. Dentistry for Children (mem. publ., editorial and information com. 1936), Mo. Dental Assn. (chmn. program com., 1929; publ. com. 1930; council 1932-38, pres. elect 1943, pres. 1944), St. Louis Dental Soc. (pres. 1931; program com., 1930-46, econ. com., 1932; sec. Study Club bd., 1939-44), St. Louis Soc. Orthodontists, St. Louis Soc. Dental Sci. (council 1935-44), Am. Assn. Dental Editors (hon., sec. 1932-48), Washington U. Dental Alumni Assn. (chmn. 75th Anniversary Com. Washington U. Sch. Dentistry, 1940-41; alumni rep. Washington U. Dental Jour. 1935-44). Editor: Jour. Mo. Dental Assn., 1932-38; asst. editor Jour. Am. Coll. Dentists, 1935-37, asso. editor, 1938-41. Contbr. dental mags. Lectures. Home: 309 Camelia Dr Webster Groves MO 63119 Office: 4236 Lindell Blvd St Louis MO 63108

BRANDI, FREDERIC H., corp. exec.; m. Juliette Howell, Dec. 15, 1939; children—Clare E., E. Bruce, Frederic R., Julia K., James H. Vice pres. Dillon, Read & Co. Inc., N.Y.C., 1927-52, pres., 1952-62, chmn., 1962-71, now dir.; dir., mem. exec. com. Inmont Corp., Nat. Cash Register Co., Colgate-Palmolive Co., Anchor Hocking Corp., Falconbridge Nickel Mines Ltd.; dir. C.I.T. Financial Corp., Am.-South African Investment Co., Ltd., Farbwerke Hoechst A.G. Bd. dirs. Beekman-Downtown Hosp. Home: 3 E 71st St New York City NY 10021 Office: 46 William St New York City NY 10005

BRANDIN, ALF ELVIN, constrn. and mining co. exec.; b. Newton, Kan., July 1, 1912; s. Oscar E. and Agnes (Larsen) B.; A.B., Stanford, 1936; m. Marie Eck, June 15, 1936; children—Alf R., Jon, Erik, Mark. With Standard Group of Detroit, 1936- 42; bus. mgr. Stanford (Cal.), 1946-49, exec. officer for land devel., 1951-59, 1951-59, v.p. for bus. affairs, 1959-70; sr. v.p. Utah Constrn. & Mining Co., San Francisco, 1970—, also dir.; pres. Richardson-Brandin; dir. Am. Factors, Mut. Explorations Funds, Cal. Financial Corp., Security Savs. & Loan, Saga Adminstrv. Corp., Wattis & Co. Bd. govs. San Francisco Bay Area Council; v.p. Reclamation Dist. 2087 Alameda, Cal. Mem. VIII Olympic Winter Games Organizing Com. Served as comdr. USNR, 1942-45. Mem. Zeta Psi. Elk. Clubs: Stanford Golf; Bohemian; Pauma Valley Country; Silverado Country. Home: 668 Salvatierra St Stanford CA 94305 Office: 550 California St San Francisco CA 94104

BRANDIS, HENRY PARKER, Jr., educator; b. Salisbury, N.C., Feb. 8, 1909; s. Henry Parker and Frank Ross (Dorgan) B.; B.A., U. N.C, 1928, postgrad. Law Sch., 1929; LL.B., Columbia, 1931; LL.D., Catawba Coll., 1951; m. Martha Louise Miller, Mar. 25, 1933; 1 son, Henry Parker III. Admitted to N.Y. bar, 1932, N.C. bar, 1934; asso. dir. Inst. of Govt., Chapel Hill, N.C., 1933- 37; exec. sec. N.C. Tax Classification Commn., 1937-39; chief research div. N.C. Dept. Revenue, 1939-40; asst. prof. U. N.C., Chapel Hill, 1940-41, asso. prof., 1941-47, prof., 1947-65, Graham Kenan prof. law, 1965- dean Law Sch., 1949-64, dir. Law Center, 1969—. Vis. prof. Stanford Law Sch., 1956. Chmn. com. on acad. freedom and tenure Assn. Am. Law Schs., 1956, mem. exec. com., 1961. Spl. asst. to U.S. rep. on UN com. Good Offices to Indonesia, 1947-48; mem. adv. bd. on contract appeals U.S. AEC, 1952- 59. Served to lt. comdr. USNR, 1942-46. Mem. Am. Law Inst., Am., N.C. (v.p. 1952-53) bar assns., Am. Judicature Soc., Assn. Bar City N.Y. (asso.), Am. Assn. U. Profs. Phi Beta Kappa, Phi Delta Phi, Chi Phi. Democrat. Author: 1968 and 1970 Supplements to Stansbury, N.C. Evidence. Home: 1002 Arrowhead Rd Chapel Hill NC 27514

BRANDLY, CARL ALFRED, cons. vet. sci.; b. Fairview, Kan., May 23, 1900; s. Alfred and Bertha (Silberberger) B.; D.V.M., Kan. State Coll., Manhattan, 1923, M.S., 1930; Doctoris Medicina Veterinaria, Deutsche Tierartztliche Hochschule, Hannover, Germany, Deutsche Tierartztliche Hochschule, Hannover, Germany, 1963; m. May Victoria Emmitt, Aug. 23, 1930; children—Charles Thomas, Judith May. Asst. prof. Kan. State Coll., 1927-36; asso. prof., pathologist U. Ill., 1936-39; sr. pathologist U.S. Regional Research Lab., 1939-42; spl. research asso. in charge War Research Project, Harvard Med. Sch., Harvard Med. Sch., 1942-45; prof. vet. sci. and bacteriology U. Wis., 1945-56, chmn. dept. vet. sci., 1946-56; prof. microbiology and vet. pub. health, also dean Coll. Veterinary Medicine, U. Ill., dean Coll. Vet. Medicine, U. Ill., 1956-68; prof. comparative medicine Kan. State U., 1968-70. WHO cons. on S. Am. mission, spring 1958; cons. on S. Am. mission, spring 1958; rep. Am. Vet. Med. Assn. to div. med. scis. NRC, 1959-64; dir. Ill. Center for Zoonoses Research, 1960-68; U.S. del. Internat. Congress Vet. Med. Med. Edn., London; 1960, cons. Communicable Disease Center, USPHS, 1949—; mem. Foot and Mouth Disease Commn., U.S. Mem. Foot and Mouth Disease Commn., U.S. Dept. of Agr., 1953-57; cons. Plum Island Animal Disease Lab., 1957—; cons. U.S. Sec. Def., 1960-64; cons. to surgeon gen. USAF, 1964-66; del. World Vet. Congress, Stockholm, Sweden, 1953, also co-chmn. virology sect.; del. Internat. Microbiol. Congress, Rome, Italy, 1953; mem. U.S. State Dept. Mission to USSR, 1963; mem. U. Ill. Mission to India, 1964; mem. adv. com. on Pub. Health Service Quarantine Activities, 1966-67; mem. White House Conf. on Health, 1965; mem. spl. study commn. Nat. Acad. Scis.-Nat. Research Council, 1964-65; mem. Ill. Bd. Pub. Health Advisers, 1962-68; mem. White House Com. on Fgn. Research and Edn., 1961-62. Mem. NSF Postdoctorate Fellowship Com. in Med. Scis, 1954, 55. Recipient Distinguished Alumnus award Kan. State Coll., 1955, Distinguished Service award Ill. Council Health Professions, 1970. Mem. Am. Bd. also co-chmn. virology sect.; del. Internat. Microbiol. Congress, Rome, Italy, 1953; Mem. U.S. State Dept. Mission to USSR, 1963; mem. U. Ill. Mission to India, 1964; mem. adv. com. on pub. Health Service Quarantine Activities, 1966-67; mem. White House conf. on Health, 1965; mem. spl. study commn. Nat. Acad. Scis.-Nat. Research Council, 1964-65; mem. Ill. Bd. Pub. Health Advisers, 1962-68; mem. White House Com. on Fgn. Research and Edn., 1961-62. Mem. NSF Postdoctorate Fellowship Com. in Med. Scis., 1954, 55. Recipient Distinguished Alumnus award Kan. State Coll., 1955, Distinguished Service award Ill. Council Health Professions, 1970. Mem. Am. Bd. Postdoctorate Fellowship Com. in Med. Scis., 1954, 55. Recipient Distinguished Alumnus award Kan. State Coll., 1955, Distinguished Service award Ill. Council Health Professions, 1970. Mem. Am. Bd. Vet. Pub. Health, A.A.A.S., Am. Acad. Microbiology, Am., Ill. pub. health assns., Am. Med. Writers Assn., Am. (chmn. 1956-57, 12th Internat. Congress prize 1966), Wis. (Recognition of Profl. Distinction award 1956), Ill. (Veterinarian of year 1958) vet. med. assns., N.Y. Acad. Sci., Soc. for Exptl. Profl. Distinction award 1956), Ill. (Veterinarian of Year 1958) vet. med. assns., N.Y. Acad Sci., Soc. for Exptl. Biology and Medicine, Ill. Assn. of Professions, Royal Coll. Vet. Surgeons Britain (hon. asso.), Sigma Xi, Phi Kappa Phi, Alpha Psi, Phi Zeta, Surgeons Britain (hon. asso.), Sigma Xi, Phi Kappa Phi, Alpha Psi, Phi Zeta, Gamma Alpha, Omega Tau Sigma, Scabbard and Blade. Rotarian. Sr. editor: (with E.L. Jungherr) (with E.L. Jungherr) Advances in Veterinary Science, Vols. I-IX, 1953-64, (with C.E. Cornelius) Vols. X-XIV, 1965-70; numerous Vols. X-XIV, 1965-70; numerous articles. Mem. Council Biologic and Therapeutic Agts.; mem. editorial bd. Am. Am. Jour. Vet. Research; asso. editor Cornell Veterinarian, 1942—. Home: 2301 S Lynn St Urbana IL 61801

BRANDO, MARLON, Jr., actor; b. Omaha, Apr. 3, 1924; s. Marlon and Dorothy Pennebaker (Myers) B.; student Shattuck Mil. Acad., 1939-41; m. Anna Kashfi, 1957 (div. 1959); 1 son, Christian. Actor N.Y. plays, including I Remember Mama, Truckline Cafe, Candida, Flag is Born, Eagle Has Two Heads, Streetcar Named Desire; motion pictures include The Men, Streetcar Named Desire, Viva Zapata, Julius Caesar, The Wild One, Desiree, On the Waterfront (Acad. award best picture year 1954), Guys and Dolls, Teahouse of the August Moon, Sayonara, The Young Lions, Fugitive Kind, Mutiny on the Bounty, The Ugly American, Bedtime Story, The Chase, Appaloosa, A Countess from Hong Kong, Reflections in A Golden Eye, Candy; dir. and appeared in One Eyed Jacks. Recipient Acad. award for best actor of year, 1954.

BRANDON, ARTHUR LEON, coll. ofcl.; edn. cons.; b. Philippi, W.Va., May 18, 1898; s. Frank V. and Laura (Zinn) B.; B.A., Broaddus Coll. (now Alderson-Broaddus Coll.), 1927, H.L.D., 1962; M.A., Bucknell U., 1927; LL.D., Okla. Bapt. U., 1936; m. Margaret C. Weddell, Mar. 12, 1923. Prof. journalism and English, Okla. Bapt. U., 1927-29; asst. prof. bus. English, dir. publicity Bucknell U., 1929-33, asst. to pres., dir. pub. relations, 1933-35; exec. asst., asso. dir. Youth Commn. of Am. Council on Edn., 1935-39; dir., pub. relations, asso. prof. journalism U. Tex., 1939-43; dir. spl. services Vanderbilt U., 1943-45; dir. univ. relations, prof. journalism U. Mich., 1946-57, dir. Univ. Devel. Council, 1953- 57; exec. com. Inst. Social Research, Ann Arbor, 1947-57; v.p. univ. relations N.Y.U., 1957-64; mem. publs. council N.Y.U. Press, 1958- 64, chmn. 1960-62; v.p. Alderson-Broaddus Coll., Philippi, 1969—. Chmn. policy bd. Inst. Econ. Affairs, N.Y., 1962-64; com. pub. relations N.Y.C. Council Higher Edn., 1958-64, chmn., 1960-62; pres. Nat. Accreditation Council for Agys. Serving Blind and Visually Handicapped, 1967—; mem. exec. com., bd. dirs. Am. Baptist Assembly, Green Lake, Wis., 1969—; acting dir. collegiate edn. div. Am. Bapt. Bd. Edn., 1966. Nat. chmn. commn. on standards and accreditation services for blind Am. Found. Blind, 1963- 66. Trustee Bucknell U., 1951-56, 63—, adv. com. on econs., bus. adminstrn., 1959—, mem. devel. council, 1961—, devel. cons., 1967-69; cons. Ford Found., 1967-69; trustee Alderson-Broaddus Coll., 1936-40, 66-69, chmn. adv. bd. govs., 1959—, v.p., 1969—. Served as seaman USN, World War I. Recipient Migel medal Am. Found. for Blind, 1969. Mem. Am. Coll. Pub. Relations Assn. (pres. 1944-46, v.p. 1941-44, Distinguished Service award, 1947, Outstanding Achievement award 1957, nat. program chmn. 1960, keynote speaker 1963, Fairbanks award 1965), N.Y.U. Hon. Soc., Phi Kappa Sigma, Sigma Delta Chi. Baptist. Clubs: New York University Faculty, University Press of Mich. (sec. 1946-53). Author: Post-war Problems of American Colleges, 1944; co-author: How Fare American Youth, 1938, Adminstrators in Higher Education, 1962. Contbr. articles to ednl. jours. Home: Alderson-Broaddus Coll Philippi WV 26416 Office: 79 Madison Av New York City NY 10016 also Philippi WV

BRANDON, DONALD WAYNE, educator; b. Portland, Ore., May 14, 1926; s. Elmer Irving and Edna Louise (Plog) B.; student Reed Coll., 1946-48; A.B., U. Cal. at Berkeley, 1949, M.A., 1950, Ph.D., 1954; m. Rosemary Vollmar, June 9, 1948; children—Elisabeth, Margaret, Catherine, Jennifer. Staff writer Portland Oregonian, 1946-48; instr. U. San Francisco, 1953-55; intelligence analyst CIA, 1955-56; cultural officer Am. embassy, Bonn, Germany, 1956-58; faculty U. San Francisco, 1958—, prof. polit. sci., 1966—. Served with AUS, 1944-46; ETO. Decorated Combat Inf. Badge. Mem. Am. Polit. Sci. Assn., Am. Council on Germany. Author: American Foreign Policy-Beyond Utopianism and Realism, 1966. Contbg. editor Worldview, 1970—. Home: 524 Moraga St San Francisco CA 94122

BRANDON, HENRY OSCAR, newspaper editor; b. Mar. 9, 1916; s. Oscar and Ida Brandon; student univs. Lausanne (Switzerland), Prague (Czechoslovakia), London (Eng.). With Sunday Times of London, 1939—, war corr. Africa and Europe, then Paris corr., 1945-46, roving diplomatic corr., 1946-49, Washington corr., 1949—, asso. editor, 1963—. Adviser UN Conf. Freedom Information, 1948. Recipient journalistic awards U. Cal. at Los Angeles, 1957, Lincoln U., Jefferson City, Mo., 1962; Hannen Swaffer award Odham Press, London, 1964, 67. Mem. Overseas Writers, Fgn. Press Assn. Clubs: Nat. Press, Federal City (Washington). Author: As We Are, 1961; In the Red, 1966; Conversations with Henry Brandon, 1966; The Anatomy of Error—The Secret History of the War in Vietnam, 1969. Address: Nat Press Bldg Washington DC 20004

BRANDON, INMAN, lawyer; b. Atlanta, May 14, 1906; s. Morris and Harriet Frances (Inman) B.; B.A. magna cum laude, U. Ga., 1927; LL.B., Yale, 1930; m. Louise Courts Glancy, Nov. 14, 1932; children—Louise (Mrs. Robert Castle), Shane, Christopher Inman. Admitted to Ga. bar, 1930, since practiced in Atlanta; partner firm Hansell, Post, Brandon & Dorsey, and predecessors, 1946—. Dir. First Nat. Bank McDonough, Ga., Phoenix Inc., Merc. Financial Corp., Merc. Industries, Inc.; trustee First Atlanta Realty Fund; sec., dir. McDonough Power Equipment, Inc. Co-chmn. Atlanta Community Chest drive, 1956, chmn. budget com., 1957, pres., 1958; chmn. Atlanta United Appeals, Community Chest-A.R.C., 1959; pres., dir. Family Service Soc. Atlanta, 1960-61, hon. dir., 1963—; co-chmn. joint Tech.- Ga. Devel. Fund drive, 1957-58. Co-finance chmn. Ga. Central Republican Com., 1958-62, hon. finance chmn., 1963. Trustee, sec. bd. U. Ga. Found., 1957-61, chmn. trustees,

1961-70. Served to lt. comdr. USNR, 1942- 45; PTO. Recipient Distinguished Alumni award U. Ga., 1961. Mem. Am., Fed., Ga., Atlanta bar assns., Lawyers Club Atlanta, Nat. Lawyers Club, Am. Judicature Society, Sphinx (honorary member U. of Georgia), Phi Beta Kappa, Phi Kappa Phi, Phi Delta Phi. Lion (charter pres. Buckhead club 1941-42). Clubs: Commerce, Piedmont Driving, River Bend Gun (pres. 1965- 66), Capital City (dir. 1961-63) (Atlanta); Florida Yacht, River (Jacksonville, Fla.); Univ. Yacht (Lake Lanier, Ga.). Home: 3200 Arden Rd NW Atlanta GA 30305 Office: First Nat Bank Tower Atlanta GA 30303

BRANDON, ROBERT WILLIAM, gas co. exec.; b. Elkhart, Ind., Dec. 30, 1919; s. Ernest F. and Tressa (Scott) B.; student Ashland Coll., 1939-41; B.S., Ind. U., 1947; m. Margaret Ort, Feb. 3, 1946; 1 dau., Beth. Accountant, Arthur Andersen & Co., Chgo., 1947-50; with Tex. Gas Transmission Corp., Owensboro, Ky., 1950—, asst. treas., 1955-60, treas., 1963—, v.p., 1969—. Served to capt. AUS, 1942-46. Mem. Ind. Natural Gas Assn., Am. Gas Assn. Methodist. Home: 2015 Sheridan Pl Office: 3800 Frederica St Owensboro KY 42301

BRANDON, WILLIAM HAROLD, ret. air force officer; b. Nashville, July 24, 1917; s. David Gilbert and Leone (Dalton) B.; student Vanderbilt U., 1938-40; B.B.A., U. Tex., 1948; grad. Air Command and Staff Coll., 1948, Air War Coll., 1954; m. Virginia Hope Black, Feb. 14, 1941; children—William Harold, Jack Dalton. Joined USAAF as flying cadet. 1940, commd. 2d lt., 1941, advanced through grades to maj. gen. USAF, 1967; successively bomber pilot, group, wing and div. operations officer World War II; comdr. 1503d Air Transp. Wing, Tokyo, Japan, 1954-57; chief promotions and separations div., dep. chief staff personnel, Hdqrs. USAF, 1959-60; dep. chief staff personnel Hdqrs. Mil. Airlift Command, 1960-63; vice comdr. 22d Air Force, 1963-65; comdr. U.S. Forces, Azores, 1965-67; comdr. 21st Air Force, McGuire AFB, N.J., 1967-69, dep. dir. civil disturbance planning and operation Dept. of Army, 1969-70. Decorated D.S.C., D.S.M., Legion of Merit, with oak leaf cluster, D.F.C. with 1 oak leaf cluster, Air medal with 3 oak leaf clusters, Army Commendation medal, Bronze Star; D.F.C. (Britain); Croix de Guerre with palm (France); Order Mil. Merit 1st class (Portugal). Mem. Order Daedalians, Air Force Hist. Found. Baptist. Mason (Shriner). Home: 402 Candleglo Dr San Antonio TX 78239

BRANDOW, GEORGE ELMER, agrl. economist, educator; b. Roxbury, N.Y., June 8, 1913; s. Floyd E. and Rose (O'Hara) B.; B.S., Cornell U., 1935, Ph.D., 1939; m. Adelaide L. Wade, Aug. 20, 1938. Extension economist Cornell U., 1939-40; asst. prof. Pa. State U., University Park, 1941, asso. prof., 1946, prof., 1947—. Exec. dir. Nat. Commn. on Food Marketing, 1964-66; economist OPA, 1942; tech. adviser Turkish Ministry Agr., 1953; economist Congl. Joint Econ. Com., 1957; mem. Nat. Agrl. Adv. Commn., 1963-64. Served with USNR, 1943-45. Fellow Am. Farm Econ. Assn. (pres. 1962-63), Am. Econ. Assn.; mem. Econometric Soc., Internat. Assn. Agrl. Econs. Author articles. Home: 312 E Mitchell Av State College PA 16801 Office: Pennsylvania State U University Park PA 16802

BRANDOW, GEORGE EVERETT, civil engr.; b. Crookston, Minn., Oct. 27, 1913; s. Harry William and Laura (Ramstad) B.; student U. Cal. at Los Angeles, 1931-34; B.S. in Civil Engring., U. So. Cal., 1936; m. Anita Dunn, July 1, 1938; children—Peter Dunn, Gregg Everett. Structural chief engr. Union Oil Co. Cal., 1943-45; cons. structural engr. Brandow & Johnston, Los Angeles, 1945—. Spl. events chmn. Heart Fund Los Angeles, 1966. Trustee U. So. Cal., 1969-72. Mem. Am. Soc. C.E. (pres. Los Angeles sect. 1956—, nat. dir. 1969), Am. Inst. Cons. Engrs. (pres. 1969), U. So. Cal. Alumni Assn. (pres. engring. alumni 1948-49, chmn. ann. giving 1967-68, pres. 1970-71). Clubs: Jonathan, California (both Los Angeles). Home: 1490 Virginia Rd San Marino CA 91108 Office: 1660 W 3d St Los Angeles CA 90005

BRANDOW, THEODORE, architect; b. Phila., Nov. 18, 1925; s. Ralph and Minnie (Weinstock) B.; B.Arch., U. Pa., 1949; m. Selma Koss, July 22, 1945; children—Jonathan, Rinna, Shanna. Apprentice, Oskar Stonorov, Phila., 1949-52; pvt. practice architecture, Phila., 1952—; cons. urban renewal; vis. speaker sch. system Wellspring Ecumenical Center, Phila., 1966—. Mem. Whitemarsh Valley Fair Housing Council, 1966—. Vice pres. Erdenheim (Pa.) P.T.A., 1956; pack master local Boy Scouts Am. Served with USNR, 1943-46. Recipient award A.I.A., 1957, 61; Nat. Assn. Home Builders awards, 1961, World Traveling Exhibit Art and Architecture, 1949, award Homes for Better Living, 1957, 59; Am. Home mag. state citation, 1957, nat. citation, 1958; spl. award Am. Builder mag., 1959; McCall's Congress for Better Living award, 1959. Mem. A.I.A. Jewish religion (bd. trustees synagogue). Author: Close to Saturday, 1971. Prin. works include houses, apt. buildings, office buildings, churches; works pub. in various magazines, including House and Home, Life, House Beautiful, American Home. Address: 911 Fraser Rd Philadelphia PA 19118

BRANDT, ALLEN DEMMY, engr.; b. Mountville, Pa., Nov. 8, 1908; s. Charles G. and Mary Bella (Demmy) B.; B.S. in Civil Engring. (White, Carnegie scholar), Pa. State Coll., 1931, M.S. in San. Engring., Harvard, 1932, D.Sc. (Rockefeller Found. fellow), 1933; B.S. in Law, LaSalle Extension U., 1954; m. Ella Nora Snavely, June 23, 1933; children—Patricia Ella, Barry Allen, Frederick Thomas. Dir. indsl. hygiene research Wilison Products, Inc., Reading, Pa., 1933-40; chief, engring. sect., indsl. hygiene div. USPHS, Washington, 1940-42; asst. chief indsl. hygiene br. safety and security div. Office Chief of Ordnance, War Dept., Chgo., 1942-45; research fellow, assigned by USPHS to research lab. Am. Soc. Heating and Ventilating Engrs., Cleve., 1945-46; chief indsl. hygiene dept. Bethlehem Steel Co. (Pa.), 1946-60, mgr., indsl. health engring., 1960-67, mgr. environmental quality control, 1967—. Cons. environmental engring. problems; vis. lectr. indsl. hygiene engring. Harvard; chmn. Pa. Air Pollution Commn.; mem. council tech. advisers N.Y. Air Pollution Control Bd.; past chmn. Environmental Engring. Engring. Intersoc. Bd. Past pres. Bethlehem Area council Boy Scouts Am. Recipient certificate of commendation U.S. Army; named adm. Navy Great State of Neb. Registered engr., Pa., Ohio. Fellow A.A.A.S.; mem. Am. Soc. Heating, Refrigerating and Air Conditioning Engrs., Am. Indsl. Hygiene Assn. (past pres., Cummings Meml. award), Am. Standards Assn. (mem. 3 coms. dealing with air sanitation and ventilation), Phi Kappa Phi, Tau Beta Pi, Delta Omega, Chi Epsilon. Republican. Club: Saucon Valley Country. Author: Industrial Health Engineering, 1947; also papers on phases of air sanitation, indsl. hygiene, ventilation chpts. in tech. handbooks. Home: RD 4 Bethlehem PA 18015 Office: Bethlehem Steel Co Bethlehem PA 18016

BRANDT, CAROL, lit. agt.; b. N.Y.C., July 28, 1904; d. Austin and Marion (Stephens) Denny; student Barnard Coll., 1923-24; m. Carl Brandt, May 9, 1931 (dec. Oct. 1957); children—Carl Denny, Victoria Search (dec.); m. 2d, Edmund Pavenstedt, July 28, 1961. Partner Brandt & Brandt, N.Y.C., 1935-57, owner, propr., 1957—; internat. story editor Metro-Goldwyn- Mayer Co., 1945-50. Home: 150 Central Park S New York City NY 10023 Office: 101 Park Av New York City NY 10017

BRANDT, CLARENCE, union ofcl. Pres., Asso. Unions Am. Office: 161 W Wisconsin Av Milwaukee WI 53203*

BRANDT, EDWARD NEWMAN, Jr., physician, educator; b. Oklahoma City, July 3, 1933; s. Edward Newman and Myrtle (Brazil) B.; B.S., U. Okla., 1954; M.D., 1960, Ph.D., 1963; M.S., Okla. State U., 1955; m. Patricia Ann Lawson, Aug. 29, 1953; children-Patrick James, Edward Newman III, Rex Carlin. Intern, Oklahoma City VA Hosp., 1960-61; resident U. Okla. Hosps., 1961; from instr. to prof. preventive medicine and pub. health U. Okla. Med. Center, Oklahoma City, 1961-70, asst. to v.p., prof., chmn. dept. biostatistics Sch. Health, 1967-68, asso. dean Sch. Medicine, asso. dir. Med. Center, 1968- 70; dean Grad. Sch., prof. preventive medicine and community health U. Tex. Med. Br., Galveston, 1970—; chmn. adv. com. Traineeship Program in Biometry, VA; mem. research career award com. Nat. Inst. Gen. Med. Scis., 1968—. Com. chmn. Explorers Post, Boy Scouts Am., 1970—. Recipient Superior Performance award VA Hosp. Oklahoma City, 1961. 19th Ann. Stoneburner lectr. Med. Coll. Va., 1966. Mem. Am. Soc. Clin. Pharmacology and Chemotherapy (dir.), A.A.A.S., Am. Fedn. for Clin. Research, Am. Pub. Health Assn., Am. Statis. Assn., Assn. Am. Med. Colls., Assn. Tchrs. Preventive Medicine, Biometrics Soc., N.Y. Acad. Scis., A.M.A., Tex., Galveston County med. assns., Sigma Xi, Phi Eta Sigma, Alpha Epsilon Delta, Phi Kappa Phi, Phi Sigma, Pi Mu Epsilon, Alpha Omega Alpha. Editor, contbr. Proceedings of Conf. at U. Okla. Med. Center, 1968. Home: 4827 Crockett Blvd Galveston TX 77550

BRANDT, HARRY, motion picture exec.; b. N.Y.C., Feb. 22, 1897. Film salesman World Pictures Corp.; co-founder Times Picture Corp., 1934; co-founder, sec. Film Alliance of U.S., 1939; pres., Brandt Theatre Circuit, N.Y.C.; v.p., dir. of Cornwall Press, Inc.; dir. Am. Book-Stratford Press, Inc., Trans-Lux Corp., Movielab Film Labs., Inc., Fairbanks- Whitney Corp. Nat. chmn. Sixth War Loan Drive. Bd. dirs. Will Rogers Meml. Hosp., Am. Theatre Wing, Theatre Authority. Mem. Motion Picture Pioneers (mem. bd.), Ind. Theatre Owners Assn. (pres., 1933—), Council of Motion Picture Orgns. (exec. com.). Clubs: Lambs, Variety, Lotos. Office: Brandt Theatre Circuit 229 W 42d St New York City NY 10036*

BRANDT, HARRY, educator, mech. engr.; b. Amsterdam, Netherlands, Nov. 14, 1925; s. Friedrich H. and Henny (Rous) B.; came to U.S., 1946, naturalized, 1962; B.S., U. Cal. at Berkeley, 1949, M.S., 1950, Ph.D., 1954; m. Muriel Ruth Harman, Jan. 24, 1953; children—Joyce Estelle, Marilyn Audrey, Robert Alan. Supervising research engr. Chevron Research Co., La Habra, 1954-64; lectr. U. Cal. at Los Angeles, 1962-64; prof. U. Cal. at Davis, 1964—, chmn. dept. mech. engring., 1969—. Mem. N.Y. Acad. Scis., Am. Inst. Aero. and Astronautics, Sigma Xi, Tau Beta Pi. Presbyn. Home: 3309 Middle Golf Dr El Macero CA 95618 Office: Dept Mech Engring U Cal Davis CA 95616

BRANDT, KARL, agrl. economist; b. Essen, Germany, Jan. 9, 1899; s. Maximilian and Wilhelmina (Troschwitz) B.; Dipl. agr., Hohenheim Coll. Agr., 1921; Dr.agr., Coll. Agr., U. Berlin, 1926; Dr.phil. (hon.), U. Heidelberg, 1951; m. Anitta Hewelvon-Lindenfels, Dec. 31, 1932; children—Klaus, Jobst, Goetz, Ralph. Came to U.S., 1933. Dir. Coop. Seed Breeding Assn. Heidesand, Rotenburg, Hannover, Germany, 1921-23; chief appraiser, v.p. Domaenenbank, Berlin, 1925-27; dir. research investigation Berlin milk supply, 1928; dir. survey agrl. market, U.S. and Can., 1929; prof. Coll. Agr., U. Berlin, dir. Inst. Agr. Market Research; mem. bd. exports German Bank of Indsl. Obligations, 1929-33; prof. agrl. econs. New Sch. for Social Research, N.Y.C., 1933-38; vis. research prof. La. State U.; cons. to Fed. Land Bank, New Orleans, adviser Gen. Edn. Bd., 1937-38; prof. agrl. econs. Food Research Inst., Stanford, 1938-61, asso. dir., 1952-61, dir., prof. econ. policy, 1961-64, prof. emeritus, 1964—, sr. research fellow Hoover Instn., 1964—. Mem. Pres.'s Council Econ. Advsers, 1958-61; cons. Rockefeller Found., Ford Found., Thyssen Stiftung, Colombia, 1962-65, Torcuato Di Tella Found., Buenos Aires, Argentina, 1964; mem., editor of report Joint Mission World Bank and FAO to Uruguay, 1950-51; adviser to Belgian Govt., Congo and Ruanda-Urundi, 1955; research adviser Stanford Research Inst., 1938-64, sr. econ. adviser, 1965—; numerous other adv. positions. Trustee Found. for Econ. Edn. Decorated Cross of Merit with star (Fed. Republic of Germany); chevalier Ordre National du Merite (France); Order of Brilliant Star (Fed. Republic of China); recipient William Volker Distinguished service award, 1970. Fellow Am. Agrl. Econ. Assn. (pres. 1955-56), Royal Econ. Soc. (Eng.); mem. Mont Pelerin Soc., Western Agrl. Econ. Soc. (pres. 1943-44), Academie d'Agriculture (France). Clubs: Capitol Hill, Cosmos (Washington); University (Palo Alto, Cal.). Author: Reconstruction of World Agriculture, 1945; The Management of Agriculture and Food in the German Occupied and Other Areas of Fortress Europe, 1953. Contbr. articles to profl. jours, chpts. to books and encys. Home: 221 Kingsley Av Palo Alto CA 94301

BRANDT, LESLIE A., ret. gas utility exec.; b. Norway, Mich., Dec. 2, 1905; s. Arthur and Nora (Hansen) B.; M.B.A., U. Mich., 1931; m. Audney Helen Wickstrom, June 8, 1934. Pub. accountant, 1931-34; with Peoples Gas Light & Coke Co., Chgo., 1934-70, v.p., 1952-57, comptroller, 1957-61, pres., 1961-70. Active United Charities Chgo., Community Fund, C.P.A., Ill. Mem. Am. Gas Assn. (dir.). Mem. Community Ch. Clubs: University, Chicagò, Commerical (Chgo.); North Shore Country. Home: 1240 Westview Rd Glenview IL 60025

BRANDT, MORTIMER STIRLING, art historian; b. N.Y.C., July 26, 1905; s. Gabriel and Rose (Sternberg) B.; student fine arts N.Y. U., 1933-35; m. Hilda Harbidge, April 17, 1937; children—Sandra Brandt (Mrs. W. Bowdoin Davis, Jr.), Pamela Brandt (Mrs. Elliott Averett Denniston). Art historian; lectr., dealer in works of art 15th to 18th Century; v.p. Credit Alliance Corps., Ltd., Toronto, Can., 1927-30; Am. rep. Duits, Ltd., London, Amsterdam, 1936-41. Trustee Nat. Cancer Found., pres., 1952-57, hon. pres., 1957-62; trustee Cancer Care, Inc., pres., 1952-57, hon. pres., 1957-62; trustee Showcase for Disabled, Shaker Mus., Old Chatham, N.Y. Del. Welfare and Health Council, N.Y.C. Mem. Assn. Advancement Am. Art (founding trustee). Clubs: Sunningdale Golf (Berkshire, Eng.); Junior Carlton, American (London, Eng.); Old Chatham Hunt. Home: New Lebanon Center NY 12125

BRANDT, PAUL HENRY, furniture mfr.; b. Ft. Worth, Feb. 15, 1911; s. August H. and Ella Louise (Schmalzried) B.; B.S. in Mech. Engring., Valparaiso U., 1933; m. Evelyn Cleo Mauldin, Apr. 25, 1959; children—Mary Helen, Sheryl Gwen, Jerry Wayne. With A. Brandt Co., Inc., Ft. Worth, 1933—, v.p., gen. mgr., 1937-58, pres., 1958—; chmn. bd. dirs. Aid Assn. Lutherans, Appleton, Wis., Bank of Commerce, Ft. Worth. Trustee mem. exec. com. Ft. Worth United Fund; Fund; chmn. bd. dirs. Valparaiso U. Mem. Nat. Assn. Furniture Mfrs. (pres. 1958-59), Tau Beta Pi. Lutheran. Clubs: Colonial Country, Ft. Worth, Ft. Worth Boat (commodore 1961-63), Shady Oaks Country (Ft. Worth). Home: 2001 Oak Hill Rd Fort Worth TX 76112 Office: 1300 E Berry St Fort Worth TX 76110

BRANDT, RAYMOND PETER, ret. newspaperman; b. Sedalia, Mo., June 6, 1896; s. Jacob and Amelia (Sarman) B.; B.J., U. Mo., 1918; B.A., Lincoln Coll., Oxford, Eng., 1922; m. Adele Harrison, Sept. 11, 1926. Reporter St. Louis Post- Dispatch, 1917, 19 corr. Washington bur., 1923, chief Washington bur., 1934-61, contbg. editor, 1962-67; with Am. Relief Adminstrn., Vienna, Austria, 1920, dist. supr., Vitebsk, Russia, 1922-23. Served to 2d lt. U.S.F.A., 1918-19. Recipient U. Mo. Sch. of Journalism medal for distinguished service in journalism, 1939; winner first Raymond Clapper Meml. award for Washington corr., 1945. Mem. Sigma Chi, Sigma Delta Chi, Kappa Tau Alpha. Independent. Methodist. Clubs: Overseas Writers, Gridiron (pres. 1946), Nat. Press (pres. 1933), Metropolitan (Washington); Burning Tree (Bethesda, Md.); Chevy Chase. Visited Russia 1930, 31, 37, 55, for series of articles for St. Louis Post-Dispatch. Home: 4955 Quebec St Washington DC 20016 Office: 1701 Pennsylvania Av Washington DC 20006

BRANDT, REXFORD ELSON, artist; b. San Diego, Sept. 12, 1914; s. Alfred O. and Ellen D. (Woodward) B.; A.B., U. Cal., 1936; postgrad. Stanford, 1938; m. Joan Malloch Irving, June 22, 1938; children—Joan Dale, Shelley Nora. Dir. Riverside Jr. Coll. Art Center, 1937-41; chief designer South Coast Co., shipbuilders, 1941-44; head Rex Brandt Assos., Corona del Mar, 1944- 52; now head Rex Brandt Sch. Painting; numerous one man shows include Principia Coll., Fleming Mus., Burlington, Vt., So. Meth. U., Long Beach Art Assn., Los Angeles County Mus., Faulkner Gallery Art, Crocker Gallery Art, Sacramento, U. Redlands, and throughout Cal., numerous colls. and univs.; numerous group exhbns. include Am. Water Color Soc., N.Y.C., Phila. Acad. Fine Arts, Golden Gate Internat. Expn., N.Y. Water Color Soc., Cal. Centennial Exhbns., others; invitational exhibits include Corcoran Biennial, Nat. Water Color Survey, Nat. Gallery Art, Riverside Mus., Cal. State Fair, John Herron Art Inst., Scripps Gallery, Pasadena Art Inst., others; represented in permanent collections San Diego Fine Arts Gallery, Crocker Gallery Art, U.S. Treasury Dept., N.A.D., West Tex Mus., Walker Art Mus., San Francisco Mus. Art, Reading Mus., Grinnell Coll., Chico State Coll., Am. Airlines, Philco Corp., Chaffey Art Assn., Ford Motor Co., U.S. Maritime Service, Cal. Water Color Soc., others. Recipient numerous awards, 1934—, including 1st purchase award, San Dimas 2d Ann. Invitational Exhibit, 1946; 2d prize. Laguna Beach Art Gallery, 1948; Brugger award Cal. Water Color Soc., 1952, 1st prize, 1970, prize, Laguna Beach Festival Arts, 1952; 1st award, James D. Phelan awards, de Young Mus., San Francisco, 1953; Adolph and Clara Obrig prize in watercolor N.A.D., 1961; Lena Newcastle Meml. award Am. Watercolor Soc., Saportas award, 1968, Bronze medal, 1970, Morse medal N.A.D., 1968, 70. A.N.A. Mem. Am., Cal. (past pres.) water color socs. Author: Watercolor with Rex Brandt, 1949; Watercolor Technique in Fifteen Lessons, 1954; Watercolor Landscape in Fifteen Lessons, 1953; Composition of Landscape Painting, 1959; Watercolor Landscape, 1963; The Artists Sketchbook and Its Uses, 1966; San Diego, Land of the Sundown Sea, 1969; also articles. Home: 405 Goldenrod Av Corona del Mar CA 95625 Office: 407 Goldenrod Av Corona del Mar CA 95625

BRANDT, RICHARD BOOKER, educator; b. Wilmington, O., Oct. 17, 1910; s. Henry and Clara Belle (Guyatt) B.; A.B., Denison U., 1930; B.A., Cambridge U., 1933; Burney student, Stanton student Trinity Coll., Cambridge, 1933-35; student Tuebingen U., Germany, 1934-35; Ph.D., Yale, 1936; m. Mary Elizabeth Harris, June 19, 1937 (div. Oct. 1968); children—Richard Charles and Karen Elizabeth. Mem. faculty Swarthmore (Pa.) Coll., 1937- 64, successively instr., asst. prof., asso. prof., 1937-52, prof., 1952- 64, chmn. dept. philosophy and religion, McDowell prof., 1957-64; prof., chmn. dept. philosophy U. Mich., Ann Arbor, 1964- -. Guggenheim fellow, 1944-45, fellow Center for Advanced Study in Behavioral Scis., 1969-70; sr. fellow Nat. Endowment for Humanities, 1971-72. Mem. Am. Philos. Assn. (exec. com. Eastern div. 1951-54, v.p. 1965, pres. Western div. 1969-70), Am. Soc. Polit. and Legal Philosophy (pres. 1965-66), Am. Assn. U. Profs., Phi Beta Kappa. Club: N.Y. Philosophy. Author: The Philosophy of Schleiermacher, 1941; Hopi Ethics: A Theoretical Analysis, 1954; Ethical Theory, 1959; Value and Obligation, 1961; also articles in profl. publs. Office: Dept Philosophy U Mich Ann Arbor MI 48104

BRANDT, RICHARD PAUL, communications and entertainment co. exec.; b. N.Y.C., Dec. 6, 1927; s. Harry and Helen (Satenstein) B.; grad. Fieldston Sch., N.Y.C., 1945; B.S. with high honors, Yale, 1948; m. Lois Livingston, Feb. 11, 1951; children—Claudia, David, Matthew, Thomas. With Trans-Lux Theatres Corp., 1950-54, v.p., 1952-54; with Trans-Lux Corp., 1954—, v.p., 1959-62, pres., 1962—, also dir.; v.p., dir. Brant Theatres, 1953—; dir. Am. Book-Stratford Press, Inc., 1962—, exec. com., 1969—. Bd. govs. Ind. Film Importers & Distbrs. Am., 1959-63, bd. dirs., 1959-69; v.p., mem. exec. com. Theatre Owners Am., 1962-65; mem. bill of rights com. Council Motion Picture Orgns., 1962-65; bd. dirs. Film Soc. Lincoln Center, 1968—. Mem. N.Y. State Bus. Adv. Com. on Mgmt. Improvement, 1966-70. Chmn. bd. Univ. Settlement Soc., 1964-66, hon. pres., bd. dirs., 1966—; bd. dirs. Harry Brandt Found., 1959—, Am. Theatre Wing, United Neighborhood Houses, 1968—; bd. dirs., treas. Settlement House Employment Devel.; trustee Am. Film Inst. Mem. Nat. Assn. Theatre Owners (dir. 1965—, exec. com. 1965—), Aspen Soc. Fellows-Aspen Inst. for Humanistic Studies, Phi Beta Kappa, Sigma Xi. Clubs: Yale, Lotos, Variety (N.Y.C.). Home: 5 Rittenhouse Rd Bronxville NY 10708 Office: 625 Madison Av New York City NY 10022

BRANDT, WARREN, artist; b. Greensboro, N.C., Feb. 26, 1918; s. Leon Joseph and Jessie (Wooding) B.; student Pratt Inst., 1935-37; B.F.A., Washington U., St. Louis, 1948; M.F.A., U. N.C., 1953; m. Carolyn Coker, 1943 (div. 1959); 1 dau., Isabella; m. 2d, Grace L. Borgenicht, Dec. 27, 1960. Head dept. art Salem Coll., 1949-50; instr. art Pratt Inst., 1950-52, Guilford Coll., Greensboro, 1952-56; prof., chmn. dept. art U. Miss., 1957-59; prof. chmn. dept. art So. Ill. U., 1959-61; in one-man shows at Nonagon Gallery, N.Y.C., 1959, New Gallery, Provinceton, Mass., 1960, Mich. State U., Oakland, 1961, Am. Gallery, N.Y.C., 1961, Stuttman Gallery, Provincetown, 1962, Grippi Gallery, N.Y.C., 1963, 64, Obelisk Gallery, Washington, 1963, Sachs Gallery, N.Y.C., 1966, 67, 68, 70, U. N.C., 1967, Eyraud-Barnes Galleries, Los Angeles, 1967, Reed Coll., Portland, Ore., 1967, Eastern Ill. U., 1968, Grand Avenue Galleries, Milw., 1969, Mercury Gallery, London, Eng., 1969, Allentown Art Mus., Pa., 1969, Agra Gallery, Washington, 1969, 70; exhibited in group shows at Met. Mus. Watercolor Exhbn., 1952, Am. Fedn. Arts, 1952, Bklyn. Mus. Ann. Print Exhbn., 1949, Pratt Inst., 1970; represented in permanent collections Wash. Gallery Modern Art, Chrysler Mus., Mich. State U., Oakland Mus., So. Ill. U., Rochester Art Mus., N.M. State Mus., N.Y. U., U. N.C., Michener Found. Served to 1st lt. USAAF, 1940-46. Mem. Artists Club. Home: Cobb Rd Water Mill NY Studio: 138 E 95th St New York City NY 10028

BRANDT, WARREN WILLIAM, chemist, univ. pres.; b. Lansing, Mich., July 11, 1923; s. Warren Fisher and Esther Antell (Mortimer) B.; B.S., Mich. State U., 1944, postgrad., 1946; Ph.D., U. Ill., 1949; m. Esther Mae Cass, Mar. 18, 1944; children—Richard Warren, Sherry Ann. Teaching asst. Mich. State U., 1943- 44, 46-47; teaching asst. U. Ill., 1947-48, univ. fellow, 1948-49; instr. Purdue U., 1949-50, asst. prof., 1950-55, asso. prof., 1955-61; head dept. chemistry Kan. State U., Manhattan, 1961-63, asso. dean Coll. Arts and Scis., 1962-63; dean Grad. Sch., Va. Poly. Inst., Blacksburg, 1963-65, v.p., 1963-68, exec. v.p., 1968-69; pres. Va. Commonwealth U., Richmond, 1969—. Guggenheim fellow Oxford U., 1958. Mem. Am. Chem. Soc.

(past sec.-treas., chmn. div. analytical chemistry), A.A.A.S., Phi Lambda Upsilon (nat. treas.), Alpha Chi Sigma, Phi Kappa Phi, Omicron Delta Kappa. Home: 1201 Loch Lomond Ct Richmond VA 23221

BRANDT, WILLY, chancellor of Germany; born in Luebeck, Germany, Dec. 18, 1913; student Latin Sch., Luebeck; student history, U. Oslo; Dr. h.c., U. Pa., Harvard, U. Md.; LL.D., U. Md., 1960; m. Rut Hansen, 1948; children--Peter, Lars, Matthias. Journalist, Norway, Sweden, 1933-45; Journalist Scandinavian newspapers, press cooperator diplomatic rep., Berlin, 1945-47; chief editor Berlin Stadtblatt, 1950-51; mem. Ho. of Reps., Berlin, 1950--, pres. 1955-57; governing mayor, West Berlin, formerly fed. minister fgn. affairs; chancellor Germany, 1969--; mem. Bundestag, 1949-57; pres. German Bundesrat, 1957-58, v.p., 1958-59; pres. Deutscher Staedtetag (Conf. German mayors), 1958-63. Chmn. bd. dirs. Berliner Bank, Rep. in Berlin, directive com. Social Dem. Party, 1948-49, mem. provincial com., Berlin, 1950--, dep. chmn., 1954-58, 1950--, chmn., 1958-63, dep. chmn. Germany, 1962-64, party chmn., 1964--, candidate for chancellorship, 1961, 65. Hon. pres. provincial com. German Red Cross. Chmn. governing bodies Free U., Tech. U. Berlin. Decorated Grosses Verdienstkreuz (Germany); also Star of Uprising 1st Class (Jordan), grand Cross Order of St. Olaf (Norway), grand cross Order of King of Greece; recipient Freedom House award, 1961; recipient of the Nobel Peace prize in 1971. Member of the German Hort. Soc., Bonn German Soc. Fgn. Politics, Soc. Christian-Jewish Coop., Ernest Reuter Soc., German Soc. UN. Max Planck Gesellschaft (senator). Author various publs. Office: Berlin 62 (Schoneberg) John F Kennedy Platz (Rathaus) Berlin Federal Republic of Germany

BRANDWEIN, NAFTALI CHAIM, educator, writer; b. Jerusalem, Israel, June 22, 1921; s. Zusia and Menucha (Adler) B.; tchrs. diploma Mizrachi Tchrs. Coll., Jerusalem, 1941; postgrad. Merkaz Harav Rabbinical Coll., Jerusalem, 1941-47, Hebrew U., Jerusalem, 1950-52; Doctorate, Jewish Theol. Sem. Am., 1962; m. Miriam Kosovsky, Oct. 1, 1952; children—Eran, Lilach. Came to U.S., 1960. Ednl. dir. Meshek Hapoaloth High Sch., Tel Aviv, 1947-50; tchr. Judaic studies Hatichon High Sch., Jerusalem (high sch. of Hebrew U.), 1950-53; ednl. supr. Hebrew Schs. Can., Hebrew Cultural Found., Montreal, Que., 1956-57; lectr. Judaic studies Sir George Williams U., Montreal, 1957-59; tchr. Herzelia High Sch., Montreal, 1953-56; dean Hebrew Tchrs. Tng. Coll., Montreal, 1957-60; instr. modern Hebrew lit. Jewish Theol. Sem. Am., N.Y.C., 1960-63, asst. prof., 1963-66; asso. prof. Brandeis U., Waltham, Mass., 1966-68, B. Rose Cohen prof., 1968—, chmn. Sch. Humanities 1967-70; Mem. com. examiners Coll. Exam. Bd., Princeton, 1967—; reader Cornell U. Press, Ind. U. Press, 1968—; mem. adv. bd. Hadoar, Hebrew weekly, N.Y.C., 1968—. Recipient Louis Lamed prize Hebrew lit., 1960. Mem. Hebrew P.E.N. Club (sec. 1965—), Soc. Fgn. Langs., Assn. Am. U. Profs., Assn. Jewish Profs. Judaic Studies, Soc. Bibl. Lit. Author: Be'chazrot Yerushalayim (short stories), 1958; Be'zel Ha'argaman (poetry), 1964; Meshorer Ha'shkiah, 1964; In the Courtyards of Jerusalem (short stories), 1967; Asher Barash, Selection and Critical Analysis, 1969. Editor (English trans.) A Guest for the Night (S.Y. Agnon), 1968. Contbr. numerous sci. and lit. articles to profl. publs. Home: 32 Nonantum St Newton MA 02158 Office: Brandeis U Waltham MA 02154

BRANDWEN, MAXWELL, lawyer; b. Aug. 28, 1898; s. Herman H. and Nellie (Brandwene) B.; A.B., Harvard, 1917, LL.B., 1921; m. Helen Finney, May 23, 1965. Admitted to N.Y. bar, 1922; practiced in N.Y.C., 1921—; partner firm Szold, Brandwen, Brandwen, Meyers & Altman, 1921—; exec. Nat. Def. Adv. Commn., OPM, WPB, War Shipping Adminstrn., 1940-44. Pres., dir. Amalgamated Bank N.Y.; dir. Amalgamated Life Ins. Co., N.Y.C., Amalgamated Life & Health Ins. Co. Chgo.; chmn. exec. com., dir. Urban Community Ins. Co. Counsel, bd. dirs. Sidney Hillman Found. Mem. N.Y. Bar Assn., N.Y. County Lawyers Assn., Phi Beta Kappa. Editorial cons. Rockefeller Bros. Reports. Contbr. articles to profl. jours. Home: 730 Park Av New York City, NY 10021. Office: 30 Broad St New York City NY 10004

BRANGES, LOUIS DE, educator; b. Paris, France, Aug. 21, 1932 (parents Am. citizens); s. Louis and Diane (McDonald) deB.; B.S., Mass. Inst. Tech., 1953; Ph.D., Cornell U., 1957; m. Carol Lynn Duddy, July 20, 1962. Asst. prof. Lafayette Coll., 1958-59; vis. mem. Inst. for Advanced Study, Princeton, N.J., 1959-60; lectr. Bryn Mawr Coll., 1960-61; mem. Courant Inst. N.Y.U., 1961-62; asso. prof. Purdue U., 1962-63, prof., 1963—. Served to lt. AUS, 1957-58. Alfred P. Sloan Found. fellow 1963-66; Guggenheim Found. fellow, 1967-68. Mem. Am. Math. Soc. Episcopalian. Author (with J. Rovnyak) Square Summable Power Series, 1966; Hilbert Spaces of Entire Functions, 1968. Home: Inverwabash Rt 11 Lafayette IN 47905 Office: Dept Math Purdue U West Lafayette IN 47907

BRANHAM, ROBERT SECOR, banker; b. Anoka, Minn., Nov. 28, 1919; s. Donald S. and Rachel (Johnson) B.; student U. Minn., 1937-39, Sch. Banking of U. Wis., 1952-54; m. Alvina Margaretha Kohl, Sept. 3, 1943. With Stockyards Ins. Agy., South St. Paul, Minn., 1946-50; asst. cashier Stockyards Nat. Bank, South St. Paul, 1950-55; asst. sec., asst. v.p., v.p. N.W. Bancorp., Mpls., 1955-64, sr. v.p., 1967—; pres. Northwestern Nat. Bank, Rochester, Minn., 1964-67; dir. Kahler Corp. (Rochester). Dir. Rochester Meth. Hosp., 1964-67. Served to capt. C.E., AUS, 1942-46. Home: 5801 South Dr Minneapolis MN 55436 Office: Northwestern Bank Bldg Minneapolis MN 55436

BRANIGAN, ALAN GREY, newspaper editor; b. Kearny, N.J., Aug. 5, 1909; s. Joseph and Margaret (Bryce) B.; student Columbia, 1930-31, New Sch. Social Research, 1932; m. Mary Elizabeth Braack, June 22, 1941; children—Margaret (Mrs. Peter E. Marcus), Peter, Alison Elizabeth. Mem. staff Newark News, 1923—, drama critic, 1940-50, music editor and critic, 1955-68, editor Entertainment mag., 1968—, book rev. editor, 1969—; panelist on symphonic radio quiz program sta. WNJR, 1948-51; violinist, violist, cellist, 1930—; founder West Hudson Symphony Soc., 1938. Mem. Amateur Chamber Music Soc. Author travel and cinema articles. Home: 193 Hillside Av Nutley NJ 07110 Office: 215 Market St Newark NJ 07101

BRANIGAN, DUANE ADAMS, univ. ofcl.; b. Eau Claire, Wis., July 29, 1911; s. George E. and Sarah L. (Adams) B.; B.Mus., Oberlin Conservatory, 1934; B.A., Oberlin Coll., 1935; M.Mus., Northwestern U., 1937; artist student of Egon Petri, Zakopane, Poland, 1939, with Daniel Ericourt, 1941; D.Mus., Am. Conservatory Music, Chgo., 1968; m. Imogene Wolfe, Aug. 21, 1940; children—Candy, Craig, Lindsay. Master music Chgo. Latin Sch., 1934-36; teacher piano U. Ill., 1936-46, acting dir. Sch. Music, 1946-47, 1950- 51, dir., 1951-71; concert pianist, soloist with symphony orchs.; organist, choirmaster Emmanuel Episcopal Ch., Champaign, Ill., 1937-51; faculty Lincoln Acad. of Ill. Adviser Ill. Art Council. Bd. dirs. Nat. Council of Arts in Edn. Mem. Nat. Assn. Music Execs. in State Univs., Music Tchrs. Nat. Assn. (pres. 1961-63), Music Educators Nat. Assn., Ill. Music Tchrs. Assn. (pres. 1954-58), Nat. Assn. Schs. of Music (past officer), Pi Kappa Lambda (pres. gen. 1954-58), Phi Mu Alpha, Sigma Phi Epsilon. Episcopalian. Rotarian. Assists wife in Ill. farm interests. Address: 14 Fields E Champaign IL 61820

BRANIGAN, GEORGE FRANCIS, educator; b. Shelby, Neb., July 21, 1903; s. Thomas and Jennie (Fyfe) B.; B.S., U. Neb., 1927; M.S., Kan. State Coll., 1933; postgrad. Ia. State Coll., 1946-48; m. Marion Luella Eimers, June 16, 1928; children—George Eimers, Thomas Lynn, Susan Marion. Instr., asst. prof., asso. prof. machine design Kan. State Coll., Manhattan, 1927- 42; asso. prof. gen. engring. Bradley Poly. Inst., Peoria, Ill., 1942-43, dean engring., prof. civil engring., 1943-46; prof. mech. engring. Ia. State Coll., Ames, 1946-48; dean engring., dir. Engring. Expt. Sta., U. Ark., Fayetteville, 1948-71, prof. gen. engring., parttime, 1971—. Summer positions with Gas Service Co., Kansas City, 1927, U.S. Engr. Office, Kansas City, 1928, Sioux City, 1930, 31, Neb. Hwy. Dept., 1929, 36, 38; bridge designer Republic Co., Kan., 1935, designer Phillips Petroleum Co., Bartlesville, Okla., 1939; designer, Meyer Furnace Co., Peoria, 1945. Mem. Am. Soc. C.E., Am. Soc. Elec. Engrs. (com. on evaluation tech. inst. edn. 1961-63), Am. Assn. U. Profs., Nat. Council Engring. Examiners (pres. 1968-69), Nat. Soc. Profl. Engrs., Ark. Safety Council (dir.), Ark. Soc. Profl. Engrs., (v.p., 1949-51), Fayetteville Safety Council (pres., 1950-52), Ark. Bd. Registration Profl. Engrs. (pres. 1956-57, 62-63, 66-67, 70-71), C. of C., Theta Tau, Tau Beta Pi, Theta Xi (nat. v.p. 1955-59, nat. pres. 1966- 68). Presbyn. Clubs: Fayetteville Country; Ark. Auto (dir. 1964—); U. Neb. N; Current Topics, Rotary (pres. 1955-56). Author: Text on descriptive geometry (mimeographed form used as class text), 1943-45. Contbr. chpt. on civil engring. Ency. Americana, 1961. Home: 1776 Applebury Pl Fayetteville AR 72701

BRANIGAN, ROGER DOUGLAS, former gov. Ind., lawyer; b. Franklin, Ind., July 26, 1902; s. Elba L. and Zula (Francis) B.; A.B., Franklin Coll., 1923, LL.D., 1956; LL.B., Harvard, 1926; LL.D., Butler U.; m. Josephine Mardis, Nov. 2, 1929; children—Roger, Robert M. Admitted to Ind. bar, 1926; dep. pros. atty., Franklin, Ind., 1926-29; counsel Fed. Land Bank and FCA, Louisville, 1930-38, gen. counsel, 1935-38; pvt. practice law, 1938-42, 46-65; gov. State of Ind., 1965-69; practice law, Lafayette, Ind., 1969—. Dir., Nat. Homes Corp., Lafayette Nat. Bank, Gen. Telephone Co. of Ind., Inc., Peerless Wire Goods Co., Duncan Electric Co., Lafayette Life Ins. Co. Past pres. Harrison council Boy Scouts Am.; trustee Franklin Coll., Purdue U. Served to lt. col. AUS 1942-46; chief legal div., transp. corps, 1944-45. Decorated Legion of Merit. Mem. Harvard Law Sch. Assn., Am. Legion, Ind. (pres. 1951-52), Am. (ho. of dels.) bar assns., Am. Coll. Trial Lawyers, C. of C. (past pres.), Am. Law Inst., Indiana Soc. of Chgo. (v.p.), Am. Counsel Assn., Am. Judicature Soc. (dir.), Newcomen Soc., Phi Delta Phi, Phi Delta Theta. Democrat (chmn. Ind. conv. 1948). Mason, Elk. Clubs: Indianapolis Athletic Town and Gown, Press (hon. life) (Indpls.); Sagamore of the Wabash; Legal (hon. life Chgo.); Lawyers (U. Mich). Home: 611 S 7th St Lafayette IN 47901 Office: Life Bldg Lafayette IN

BRANLEY, FRANKLYN MANSFIELD, educator, astronomer; b. New Rochelle, N.Y., June 5, 1915; s. George P. and Louise (Lockwood) B.; student State U. N.Y. at New Paltz, 1933-36; B.S., N.Y.U., 1943; M.A., Columbia, 1947, Ed.D., 1957; m. Margaret Genevieve Lemon, June 26, 1938; children—Sandra Kay (Mrs. Edward C. Bridges), Mary Jane (Mrs. Robert Day). Tchr. pub., pvt. elementary and secondary schs., 1936-54; asso. prof. sci. Jersey City State Coll., 1954-56; asst. astronomer Am. Mus. Hayden Planetarium, 1956-63, astronomer, asst. chmn., coordinator ednl. services, 1963-68, chmn., 1968—. Faculty, Columbia, 1945, N.Y.U., 1962; cons. Ala. State Tchrs. Coll., Troy, 1947, S.W. La. Coll., 1949; adviser Nature and Sci. mag., Natural History mag., Sci. and Children mag.; referee NSF, 1960—. Recipient Edison award for best children's sci. book Thomas A. Edison Found., 1960; named Outstanding Citizen, Newburgh, N.Y., 1965. Mem. Am., Royal astron. socs., Author Guild, Nat. Sci. Tchrs. Assn. Unitarian. Author: The Sun-Star Number One, 1964; The Moon-Earth's Natural Satellite, 1963; The Earth-Planet Number Three, 1966; Mars-Planet Number Four, 1962; A Book of the Milky Way Galaxy, 1965; Exploration of the Moon, 1965; Big Tracks, Little Tracks, 1960; also Books for You series, Exploring Our Universe series. Editor: Let's Read and Find Out series. Home: 4 London Ct Woodcliff Lake, NJ 07680. Office: Am Museum-Hayden Planetarium 81st St and Central Park West New York City NY 10024

BRANN, JAMES LEWIS, Jr., educator, entomologist; b. Norwood, Mass., June 24, 1913; s. James Lewis and Elizabeth (Abel) B.; student Boston U., 1931-33; B.S., Mass State Coll., 1939; Ph.D., Cornell U., 1944; m. Doris Colgate, June 27, 1942; children—Bethany Celia (Mrs. Wesley Kraweic), James Lewis III. Research asst. N.Y. State Agrl. Expt. Sta., Geneva, 1939-40; research fellow entomology Cornell U., 1941-42, asso. prof., 1948-54, prof., 1954—, prof. entomology extension, 1964—; investigator N.Y. State Agr. Expt. Sta., 1942-44, asst. prof., 1944-48; cons. UN and F.A.O. to Israel and Greece, 1959. Active Boy Scouts Am. Mem. Entomol. Soc. Am., Sigma Xi. Club: Adirondack Mountain. Author: (with D.E. W Weidhaas) Handbook of Insecticide Dust Diluents and Carriers, 1955. Patentee for spraying apparatus; research on insect control on fruits and vegetables, devel. more efficient pesticide application equipment. Home: 711 Ellis Hollow Creek Rd Ithaca NY 14850

BRANN, LESTER WILLIAM, Jr., assn. exec.; b. Madison, Wis., Mar. 24, 1925; s. Lester William and Esther (Jacobsen) B.; student Los Angeles City Coll., 1944; J.D., U. Wis., 1950; m. Lois Winter, Sept. 4, 1948; children—Lester William III, Thomas Edwin. Admitted to Wis. bar, 1950; practice in Racine, 1950-57; with Milw. Assn. Commerce, 1957-67, exec. v.p., dir., 1960-67; asst. exec. v.p. Ill. C. of C., 1967-68, exec. v.p., 1968-70, pres., 1970—; exec. v.p., dir. Credit Bur. Milw., Inc., 1960-67. Alderman, Racine, 1953-55. Vice pres., dir. Wis. Indsl. Research Council, 1964-67. Served with AUS, 1943-46. Decorated Purple Heart. Mem. Am., Wis. bar assns., Am. C. of C. Execs. (bd. dirs.), Wis. Law Alumni Assn., Kappa Sigma, Phi Alpha Delta. Clubs: Union League, Economic, Executives, Tower (Chgo.). Home: 337 Forest Rd Hinsdale IL 60521 Office: 20 N Wacker Dr Chicago IL 60606

BRANN, WILLIAM PAUL, univ. adminstr.; b. Swifton, Ark., Apr. 21, 1916; s. Ben S. and Ara A. (Jones) B.; B.A., Ark. State U., 1938; postgrad., Tulane U., 1939; M.A., U. Va., 1942, Ph.D. (Gen. Edn. Bd. fellow), 1946. Asso. prof. econs. U. Ark., Fayetteville, 1942-44, prof. econs., dir. Bur. Bus. Research, 1945-54, dir. Indsl. Research and Extension Center, Little Rock, 1955-57; dir. Miss. Indsl. Research Center, Jackson, 1958-59; cons. in econs. 20th Century Fund, N.Y.C., Com. for Econ. Devel., N.Y.C., bd. regents U. Ariz., Phoenix, Small Bus. Adminstrn., Washington, Ark. Study Commn. on Accelerating Econ. Growth, Little Rock, Memphis State U., Ark. C. of C., 1960-61; asst. to v.p. health affairs U. Ala. Med. Center, Birmingham, 1962-64, v.p. for fiscal affairs, 1965—; dir. Participating Annuity Life Ins. Co., Little Rock. Vice pres. 1st Ark. Capital Credit Bank, Little Rock, 1961-62. Mem. Com. on S.W. Economy Pres.'s Council of Econ. Advisers, 1951—. Mem. Am., So. econ. assns., L.Q.C. Lamar Soc., Pi Gamma Mu, Phi Theta Kappa, Omicron Delta Epsilon. Clubs: Relay House, The Club (Birmingham). Home: 1512 9th Av South Birmingham AL 35205

BRANNAN, ROBERT RUSSEL, fence co. exec.; b. Cleve., May 18, 1926; s. William Forrest and Marjorie (Case) B.; B.S. in Elec. Engring., U. Md., 1950; m. Pauline Hillary Crapster, June 17, 1950; children—Robert Russel, John D., Patricia Ann, Stephen P., Elizabeth J. Salesman Balt. Anchor Post Products Inc., 1950, br. mgr., Atlanta, 1951-53, Birmingham, Ala., 1953-54, asst. sales mgr., Balt., 1954-56, v.p. in charge sales, 1957-70, pres., chief exec. officer, 1970—, also dir.; v.p. Sunshine Mining Co., 1970. Troop chmn. Boy Scouts Am., Balt., 1969; mem. bd. Balt. City Unit Am. Cancer Soc., 1967—. Served with USNR, 1944-46. Mem. Chain Link Fence Mfrs. Inst. (pres. 1969-71), Phi Kappa Phi, Tau Beta Pi, Phi Eta Sigma, Theta Chi. Republican. Presbyn. (trustee). Clubs: Baltimore Country; Roland Run (Ruxton, Md.). Home: 323 Southwind Rd Towson MD 21204 Office: 6500 Eastern Av Baltimore MD 21224

BRANNEN, BARRY, lawyer; b. Tuscon, Feb. 14, 1902; s. Phillip Cornelius and Elizabeth (Barry) B,; A.B., U. Cal. at Berkeley, 1922; LL.B., Harvard, 1925. Admitted to Cal. bar, 1925; practice in Los Angeles, 1930-55, Beverly Hills, 1955—. Served with USNR, 1942-46. Decorated Legion of Merit, Purple Heart; Sovereign Order White Eagle (Yugoslavia); medal of merit V.F.W.; recipient Meritorious Pub. Service Citation U.S. Navy. Mem. Navy League U.S. (v.p. 1956, bd. dirs. 1955, adv. council 1956—). Author: articles. Office: City Nat Bank Bldg Beverly Hills CA 90210

BRANNEN, STEPHEN JOSHUA, educator; b. Glennville, Ga., Oct. 19, 1925; s. Henry Lonnie and Ellen Finer (Guy) B.; student Abraham Baldwin Agrl. Coll., 1948-49; B.S.A., U. Ga., 1950, M.S., 1952; Ph.D., N.C. State U., 1966; m. Ruth Edge, June 8, 1948; children—Rita (Mrs. J.C. Hatcher), Carolyn. Instr. Ga. Dept. Edn., Greensboro, 1950; asst. county agt., Cordele, Ga., 1950-51, Swainsboro, Ga., 1952-53; economist Coop. Extension Service, Athens, Ga., 1953-61; chmn. div. agrl. econs. U. Ga., 1961—; cons. Opekasit, Inc., Albany, Ga., 1954, Agr. Dept., 1965-66, Research Group, Inc., 1968—. Bd. dirs. Univ. Employees Credit Union, 1970—. Served with AUS, 1944-46. Oscar Johnston Found. fellow, 1955-56; recipient Agr. Coll. alumni distinguished faculty award, 1969. Mem. Am. Agrl. Econs. Assn. (chmn. distinguished extension program awards com. 1968-69), Internat. Assn. Agrl. Economist, Ga. Soc. Farm Mgrs. and Rural Appraisers (sec.-treas. 1959-62), Gamma Sigma Delta, Alpha Zeta, Phi Kappa Phi, AGHON, Farmhouse Frat. (faculty adviser 1964-71). Baptist (deacon, chmn. bd., finance com.). Editorial adv. com. Agrl. Policy Rev., 1961—. Contbr. articles profl. jours. Home: 170 Ravenwood Run Athens GA 30601

BRANNEN, TEDDY ROE, Jr., coll. dean; b. Tulsa, Feb. 24, 1924; s. Teddy Roe and Hazel Renelle (Adams) B.; B.S., U. Ark., 1944, M.S., 1947; Ph.D., U. Tex., 1954; m. Betty Mathis, June 1, 1948; children—Michael Sean, David Lance, Brooke, Brent. Faculty U. Ark., Texas A. and M. Coll., U. Tex., 1946-51; economist OPS, 1951-53; econ. analyst Texaco, N.Y.C., 1954; indsl. relations adviser Arabian-Am. Oil Co., 1954-57; lectr. mgmt. U. Fla., 1957-58; dean Sch. Bus. Adminstrn. U. Kansas City, 1958-59, vice chancellor, 1959-60; asst. to pres. for univ. affairs, dir. Inst. Grad. Edn. and Research, Grad. Research Center of S.W., Dallas, 1961-63; prof. mgmt., head dept. finance and gen. bus., also dir. grad. studies in bus. Coll. Bus., Okla. State U., Stillwater, 1963- 65; dean Coll. Bus. Adminstrn. U. Houston, 1965—. Served to lt. (j.g.) USNR, 1943-46. Mem. Am. Acad. Mgmt., Am. Econs. Assn., Am. Acad. Polit. and Social Sci., Southwestern Bus. Adminstrn. Assn. (pres. 1968-69), Beta Gamma Sigma, Omicron Delta Epsilon. Author: (with F.X. Hodgson) Overseas Management, 1965. Home: 11010 Hunters Park Dr Houston TX 77024

BRANNER, ROBERT, educator; b. N.Y.C., Jan. 13, 1927; s. Martin M. and Edith (Fabbrini) B.; B.A., Yale, 1948, Ph.D., 1953; student Ecole des Chartes and Inst. d'art et d'archeologie, Paris, 1950-52; m. Shirley S. Prager, Jan. 25, 1953; 1 son, David P. Asst. prof. U. Kan., 1954-57; faculty Columbia, 1957-69, prof. art history and archaeology, 1966-69, chmn. dept. art history and archaeology, 1968-69; prof. history art Johns Hopkins, Balt., 1969-71; prof. art history and archaeology Columbia, 1971—; dir. excavations Bourges (France) Cathedral, 1950-52. Mem. Nat. Com. History Art, 1969-72. Served with AUS, 1945-46. Fulbright-Hayes grantee, 1950-52; Guggenheim fellow, 1963; recipient Alice Davis Hitchcock award for most distinguished book archtl. history Society Archtl. Historians, 1963; Am. Council Learned Socs. fellow, 1967. Mem. Mediaeval Acad. Am., Coll. Art Assn., Soc. francaise d'archaeologie, Soc. Archtl. Historians (bd. dirs. 1960-63, editor jour. 1964-66), Internat. Center Mediaeval Art, Soc. Nat. des Antiquaires de France. Author: Burgundian Gothic Architecture, 1960; Gothic Architecture, 1961; La Cathedrale de Bourges, 1962; Saint Louis and the Court Style, 1965; Chartes Cathedral, 1969. Home: 21 Claremont Av New York City NY 10027

BRANNON, CLIFTON WOODROW, evangelist, lawyer; b. Fitzgerald, Ga., Apr. 14, 1912; s. George Wesley and Beulah (Green) B.; student Ga. Sch. Tech., 1929-30; LL.B., Woodrow Wilson Coll. Law Atlanta, 1932; LL.D., Burton Coll. and Sem., 1953; m. Ola Ruth Hall, Feb. 16, 1935; children—Beverly Mae, Madlyn Sue, Clifton Woodrow. Admitted to Ga. bar, 1932, Tex. bar, 1946, U.S. Supreme Ct. bar; atty. Home Owners Corp., 1933-35; trial atty. Sinclair Refining Co., 1936-40; gen. counsel, sec. R.G. LeTourneau, Inc., LeTourneau Co. Ga., LeTourneau Co. Miss., Vicksburg, Tex. Casualty Ins. Co., radio stas., KLTI, WLET, LeTourneau Tech. Inst. Tex., 1946-49; gen. counsel, dir. Winona Lake (Ind.) Christian Assembly, Inc., 1940-49; pres. Whosoever Heareth, Inc.; evangelist So. Bapt. Ch., 1949—, Word for World Pubs., Inc. Inc. Bd. dirs. Word for World Crusade. Past pres. Tex. Bapt. Brotherhood Conv. Mem. Am., Tex., Ga. bar assns. Democrat. Mason (32, Shriner), Kiwanian. Editor: Soul Winner's New Testament, 1959. Home: 701 Coleman Dr Longview TX 75601 TX 75601 Office: 626 Electra St Longview TX 75601

BRANNON, PETER ALEXANDER, archivist; b. Seale, Ala., Aug. 30, 1882; s. George Thomas and Stephie (Greene) B.; Ph.G., Ala. Poly. Inst., 1900; m. Frances Frazer, Oct. 5, 1904; children—Carolyn Elizabeth (dec.), Peter A. (dec.), Stephen Frazer. Pharm. chemist, 1900-10; curator Ala. Dept. Archives and History, 1910-41, archivist, 1941-55, dir., 1955—. Mem. com. on state archeol. surveys NRC, 1920-37. Mem. Ala. Conf. Hist. Soc. (sec. 1922—), Montgomery Glass Collectors (a founder), Am. Anthrop. Assn., Early Am. Glass Collectors Club, Ala. Anthrop. Soc. (an organizer 1909, sec. 1909-20, pres. 1920-29, exec. sec. 1932—, trustee), Ala. Library Assn., Ala. (exec. bd.), So. hist. assns., Ala. Acad. Sci., Newcomen soc. (Eng.), S.A.R., Sons Confederate Vets. Democrat. Methodist. K.P., Rotarian. Author: Edward Harris: Friend of Audubon, 1947; Organization Confederate Post Office Dept. at Montgomery, 1960; also other publs. in field. Contbr. Montgomery Advertiser, Arrow Points, others. Editor: Ala. Hist. Quar. Home: 1277 S Lawrence St Montgomery AL 36104 Office: Ala Meml Bldg Montgomery AL 36101

BRANSCOM, RUSSELL KEITH, steel co. exec.; b. Ogallala, Neb., June 24, 1912; s. Arthur J. and Susie (Thornburg) B.; B.S. in Commerce and Bus. Adminstrn., U. Ala., 1935; m. Ruth M. Pazzetti, Apr. 15, 1939; children—Susan (Mrs. Roy E. Buck), Russell Keith, Sar (Mrs. Stephen G. Donches), Timothy, Ben. With Bethlehem Steel

Corp., 1935-71, trainee, various positions to asst. v.p., 1957-61, v.p. indsl. and pub. relations, 1961-71, also dir. Mem. Newcomen Soc. N.Am., Am. Iron and Steel Inst., Nat. Indsl. Conf. Bd., Pa. Soc., N.A.M. (dir.). Clubs: Saucon Valley (Bethlehem, Pa.); University (N.Y.C.). Home: The Towers Bethlehem PA 18018

BRANSCOM, WILLIAM JAMES, banker; b. Roanoke, Va., Nov. 29, 1926; s. George A. and Georgia (Firestone) B.; B.A., Roanoke Coll., 1950; M.B.A., U. Pa., 1952; postgrad. Rutgers U., 1961-63; m. Dorothy Jean Larson, Mar. 24, 1951; children—Dorothy Diane, Georgia Kay, Joel Robert, William Eric. Security analyst First Nat. Exchange Bank Va., Roanoke, 1954-58, asst. cashier, 1958-59, asst. v.p., head investment div., 1959-62, v.p., 1962-64, sr. v.p., 1964—; instr. Am. Inst. Banking Roanoke Coll. Evening Sch. Mem. adv. com. on investment funds Roanoke City Employees Retirement System, 1959—; chmn. Roanoke City Savs. Bonds Com., 1965—. Trustee Evergreen Burial Park. Served with USNR, 1945-46; to lst lt., Q.M.C., AUS, 1952-54. Mem. Roanoke C. of C., Am. Inst. Banking, Sigma Chi, Tau Kappa Alpha. Presbyn. (deacon). Home: Route 1 Box 77 Troutville VA 24175 Office: 201 S Jefferson St Roanoke VA 24010

BRANSCOMB, HARVIE, former univ. chancellor; b. Huntsville, Ala., Dec. 25, 1894; s. Lewis Capers and Nancy (McAdory) B.; B.A., Birmingham-So. Coll., 1914, D.Litt.; Rhodes scholar, Ala., Oxford U., 1914-17, B.A. and M.A.; Ph.D., Columbia, 1924; Guggenheim fellow, 1931-32; LL.D., Southwestern Coll., Columbia, 1954, Brandeis U., 1958, Northwestern U., 1958; D.L.H., Hebrew Union Coll.; L.H.D., So. Methodist U., 1961; m. Margaret Vaughan, June 15, 1921; children—Harvie, Ben Vaughan, Lewis McAdory. Adj. prof. philosophy So. Methodist U., 1919-20, asso. prof. N.T., 1920-21, prof., 1921- 25; prof. N.T., Div. Sch., Duke, 1925-45, dean, 1945-46, dir. libraries, 1934-41, chmn. div. ancient langs. and lits., 1937-44; chancellor Vanderbilt U., 1946-63, chancellor emeritus, 1963—; ednl. cons. Internat. Bank for Reconstrn. and Devel., 1963-64; chmn. U.S. Nat. Commn. for UNESCO, 1963-65; vice chmn. U.S. delegation to UNESCO Gen. Conf., 1964; mem. Nat. Adv. Health Council; chmn. U.S. delegation World Conf. Illiteracy, Teheran, 1965; mem. U.S. delegation WHO, Geneva, 1965, 66; cons. Bur. Ednl. and Cultural Affairs, Dept. State, 1966. Bd. dirs. Colonial Williamsburg (Va.), Gen. Edn. Bd., Cordell Hull Found. for Internat. Edn., Tenn. Bot. Gardens and Fine Arts Center, Belgian-Am. Ednl. Found., Nashville Urban League, Planned Parenthood Assn. Nashville (Tenn.); chmn. Commn. A.L.A. to Brazil, 1945; chmn. U.S. Adv. Commn. for Ednl. Exchange, 1947-51; with commn. for relief in Belgium, 1914-15. Served with U.S. Army, 1918. Recipient Medaille du Roi Albert, Medaille de la Reine (Belgium), Order So. Cross (Brazil). Mem. Soc. Bibl. Lit. and Exegesis, Assn. Am. Rhodes Scholars, A.L.A., Am. Council on Edn. (chmn. commn. on edn. and internat. affairs), Phi Beta Kappa, Sigma Alpha Epsilon. Methodist. Clubs: Belle Meade Country; Century Assn. (N.Y.). Editor: The Am. Oxonian, 1943-46. Author: The Message of Jesus, 1925; Jesus and the Law of Moses, 1930; The Teachings of Jesus, 1931; The Gospel of Mark, 1937; Teaching with Books, 1940. Dir. of Library Project of Assn. Am. Colls., 1937-38. Home: 1620 Chickering Rd Nashville TN 37215

BRANSCOMB, LEWIS CAPERS, Jr., librarian, educator; b. Birmingham, Ala., Aug. 5, 1911; s. Lewis Capers and Minnie Vaughn (McGehee) B.; student Birmingham-So. Coll., 1929-30; A.B., Duke, 1933; A.B. in L.S., U. Mich., 1939, A.M. in L.S., 1941; postgrad. U. Ga., 1940; Ph.D., U. Chgo., 1954; m. Marjorie Berry Stafford, Jan. 15, 1938; children—Lewis Capers, III, Ralph Stafford, Carol Jean, Lawrence McGehee. Clk. Young & Vann Supply Co., Birmingham, 1933-38; order librarian U. Ga., 1939-41; librarian Mercer U., 1941-42; librarian, prof. library sci. U.S.C., 1942-44; asst. dir. pub. service depts., asso. prof. library sci. U. Ill., 1944-48, asso. dir. libraries, prof. library adminstrn., 1948-52; dir. libraries, prof. library adminstrn. Ohio State U., Columbus, 1952-71, prof. Thurber studies, 1971—. Mem. Ohio Commn. to Abolish Capital Punishment, 1960-69. Bd. dirs. Center for Research Libraries, 1953-64, exec. com., 1954-56, chmn. bd., 1961-62, mem. council, 1965-71; chmn. bd. trustees Ohio Coll. Library Center, 1968-70, vice chmn., 1970—; chmn. adv. council on Library Services and Constrn. Act, Ohio, 1967-70; cons. Punjab Agrl. U., India, 1967. Mem. Am. Assn. U. Profs. (sec.-treas. U. Ill. 1947-48, Ohio State U. 1948-52, pres., 1953-54; nat. council, 1952-55), A.L.A. (chmn. nominating com. 1954-55), Assn. Coll. and Research Libraries (dir. 1953-55, v.p. 1957-58, pres. 1958- 59), Ohio (chmn. coll. and univ. sect. 1952-53, chmn. library adminstrn. sect. 1969-70, chmn. local conf. com. 1970), Franklin County library assns., Am. Civil Liberties Union (mem. exec. com. Central Ohio chpt., 1958-60, 64-66), Am. Soc. Information Sci., Beta Phi Mu (mem. exec. council 1955-58), Sigma Alpha Epsilon. Clubs: Torch (dir. 1958-59, pres. 1971-72); Faculty (Columbus). Editor: The Case for Faculty Status for Academic Librarians, 1970. Contbr. articles profl. jours. Home: 3790 Overdale Dr Columbus OH 43220

BRANSCOMB, LEWIS MCADORY, physicist; b. Asheville, N.C., Aug. 17, 1926; s. Bennett Harvie and Margaret (Vaughan) B.; A.B., summa cum laude, Duke, 1945; M.S., Harvard, 1947; Ph.D., 1949; m. Margaret Anne Wells, Oct. 13, 1951; children—Harvie Hammond, Katharine Capers. Instr. physics Harvard, 1950; lectr. physics U. Md., 1950-51; vis. staff mem. Univ. Coll., London, Eng., 1957-58; chief atomic physics sect. Nat. Bur. Standards, Washington, 1954-60, chief atomic physics div., 1960-62; chmn. Joint Inst. Lab. Astrophysics, U. Colo., 1962-65, 68-70; chief lab. astrophysics div. Nat. Bur. Standards, Boulder, Colo., 1962-69; prof. physics U. Colo., 1962-69; dir. Nat. Bur. Standards, 1969—. Mem. commn. 14 Internat. Astron. Union, 1961—; mem. atomic collisions sect. of commn. atomic and molecular physics and spectroscopy Internat. Union Pure and Applied Physics, 1967—; mem. JASON div. Inst. Def. Analyses, 1962-69; chmn. internat. gen. com. Conf. Physics of Electron and Atomic Collisions, 1969-71; U.S. rep. to CODATA com. Internat. Council Sci. Unions, 1970—; mem. President-Elect Nixon's Task Force Space Program, 1968-69; mem.-at-large Def. Sci. Bd., 1969-72; mem. high level policy group sci. and Tech. information Orgn. Econ. Coop. and Devel., 1968-70; mem. President's Sci. Adv. Com., 1965-68, chmn. panel space sci. and tech., 1967-68; mem. standing com. controlled thermonuclear research AEC, 1966-68. Mem. president's bd. visitors U. Okla., 1968—; astronomy vis. com. Harvard bd. overseers, 1969—; mem. President's Com. Nat. Medal Sci., 1970—. Bd. dirs. Am. Nat. Standards Inst., 1969—. Served to lt. (j.g.) USNR, 1945-46. USPHS fellow, 1948-49, Jr. fellow, Harvard Soc. Fellows, 1949-51; recipient Rockefeller Pub. Service award, 1957-58, Gold medal exceptional service Dept. Commerce, 1961, Arthur Flemming award D.C. Jr. C. of C., 1962, Samuel Wesley Stratton award Dept. Commerce, 1966, Career Service award Nat. Civil Service League, 1968. Fellow Am. Phys. Soc. (chmn. div. electron physics 1961-68), A.A.A.S. (dir. 1969—); mem. Nat. Acad. Scis., Washington Acad. Scis. (Outstanding Sci. Achievement award 1959), Internat. Astron. Union, Am. Geophys. Union, Am. Astron. Soc., Internat. Union Geodesy and Geophysics, Phi Beta Kappa, Sigma Xi. Editor Rev. Modern Physics, 1968- -. Address: 405 N St S W Washington DC 20024 Office: Nat Bureau of Standards Washington DC 20234

BRANSCOMBE, GENA, (Mrs. John Ferguson Tenney), composer; b. Picton, Ont., Can., Nov. 4, 1881; d. Henry W. and Sara (Allison) Branscombe; ed. high sch., grad. Chgo. Musical Coll. (gold medalist); studied with Rudolph Ganz, composition, Felix Borowski, and Prof. Engelbert Humperdinck, in Berlin; M.A. (hon.), Whitman Coll., 1932; m. John Ferguson Tenney, Oct. 1910; children—Gena, Vivian Allison, Betty (dec.), Beatrice (dec.). Condr. Branscombe Choral N.Y., MacDowell Chorus Mountain Lakes, N.J.; condr. state chorus N.J., 1940-42; condr. first organized Glee Club, Am. Women's Voluntary Services, 1942-44; condr. Contemporary Club Choral, Newark, 1945. Nat. chmn. Am. music and folksong, Gen. Fedn. Women's Clubs, 1930-35. Mem. MacDowell Colony. Bd. dirs. (hon.) N.Y. Fedn. Music Clubs; dir. Nat. Assn. Am. Composers and Conductors (citation 1967). Recipient citation for achievement Beta Sigma Phi, 1958. Mem. numerous profl. assns., A.S.C.A.P. Composer numerous music items, latest being: American Suite (for Fr. horn), 1959; Old Woman Rain (song), Gift at Parting (song), Across the Blue Aegean Sea (song), 1960; Arms That Have Sheltered Us (Navy hymn), 1961, 91st Psalm (for chorus and orch.), 1962; orch. work Procession performed in N.Y.C., San Francisco, Manila, 1962; choral work Prayer for Song performed in Pitts., 1963; orch. manuscripts displayed at N.Y. Pub. Library, 1963; Pilgrims of Destiny (choral drama), 1964, pub. score and orch. parts in Library of Congress; A Joyful Litany, 1967; Our Canada from Sea to Sea, 1967; Youth of The World (for chorus and orch.); Coventry's Choir, spl. performances, N.Y.C., 1970; Soldier, Soldier, Come From Wars (men's chorus), 1969; I Send My Heart up to Thee (song), 1969; Sleep, Then, Ah Sleep (song), 1969; What Are We Two (song), 1969. Contbr. to Showcase mag. Condr. own compositions in U.S., Can., Eng., 1957. Home: 90 La Salle St New York City NY 10027

BRANSFORD, JOSEPH R., elec. mfg. exec.; b. Lonoke, Ark., Feb. 13, 1907; s. William Nelson Nelson and Lena (Rorie) B.; B.S., U. Ala., 1930; M.S. (Alfred P. Sloan fellow), Mass. Inst. Tech. 1940; m. Madeleine Gloriot, July 14, 1934; children—Paul M., Joan K., Roger C. Joined Western Electric Co., 1928, operating assignments in N.J. and N.Y., 1928-47, personnel dir., 1948, v.p., dir., 1950—, mem. exec. com.; dir. Teletype Corp. Mem. Tau Beta Pi. Clubs: University (N.Y.C.); Canoe Brook Country. Home: 29 Ridge Rd Summit NJ 07901 Office: 195 Broadway New York City NY 10007

BRANSON, ALLEN DOYLE, mfg. exec.; b. Lima, O., Apr. 1, 1932; B.S., U. San Francisco, 1954; M.S., Stanford University, 1956; m. Rosemarie Lois Brown, May 15, 1955; 1 son, Anthony Robinson. Sales rep. Ames-Brockton Fabricated Products, Akron, O., 1956-58, sales mgr. Coshocton, Ohio, 1959-61, gen. manager plant, 1961-68, v.p. sales, 1968--. Instr. bus. Coshocton Jr. College, 1968-69. Secretary Coshocton YMCA, 1960-61; active Boy Scouts of America. Named Man of Year, Coshocton Junior Chamber of Commerce, 1968. Mem. Coshocton C. of C. (vice president 1967-68, pres. 1969-70), English Speaking Union, Coshocton Sertoma Club, Nat. Assn. Mfrs., Sales Executives Institute, Phi Beta Kappa, Sigma Chi, Phi Mu. Democrat. Mem. Christian Ch. (lay leader). Mason (32, Shriner). Clubs: Coshocton Country, Coshocton City, Running Deer Country. Home: 2d Av Coshocton OH Office: 3d Av Coshocton OH

BRANSON, CARL COLTON, geologist, educator; b. Oberlin, O., Sept. 15, 1906; s. Edwin Bayer and Grace Muriel (Colton) B.; B.A., U. Mo., 1926, M.A., 1927; Ph.D., U. Chgo., 1929; m. Ila Irene Freeman, Apr. 4, 1948; children—Derick Edwin, Deborah Elizabeth, David Colton. Instr. geology Wash. State Coll., 1929- 30; instr., asst. prof. Brown U., 1930-40; vis. asst. prof. Northwestern U., 1940-41; asso. prof. U. Ky., 1941-44; research geologist Shell Oil Co., 1944-50; prof. geology U. Okla., Norman, 1950—, dir. 1950—, dir. Sch. Geology, 1955-63, dir. Okla. Geol. Survey, 1954-67, geologist, 1967-1967- -. Fellow Paleontol. Soc. Am., Geol. Soc. Am.; mem. Am. Assn. Petroleum Geologists, A.A.A.S., Soc. Econ. Paleontologists and Mineralogists, Soc. Vertebrate Paleontologists, Oklahoma City, Tulsa, Ardmore geol. socs., Paleontol. Soc. India, Assn. Am. State Geologists (pres. 1962-63), Phi Beta Kappa, Sigma Xi, Sigma Gamma Epsilon, Gamma Alpha, Delta Tau Delta. Author: Bibliographic Index of Permian Invertebrates, 1948; Principles of Geology, 3d ed., 1952. Home: 1117 Berry Circle Norman OK 73069

BRANSON, HERMAN RUSSELL, educator, physicist; b. Pocahontas, Va., Aug. 14, 1914; s. Harry C. and Gertrude (Brown) B.; student U. Pitts., 1932-34; B.S., Va. State Coll., 1936; Ph.D., U. Cin., 1939; Sc.D., Va. State Coll., 1967, U. Cin., 1967, Lincoln U. (Pa.), 1969; m. Corolynne M. Gray, Sept. 4, 1939; children—Corolynne G., Herman E. Instr., Dillard U., New Orleans, 1939-41; faculty Howard U., 1941-68 prof. physics, 1942-68, head dept., 1955-68; pres. Central State U., 1968-70; pres. Lincoln U., 1970—. Dir. Sci. Edn. Assistance Fund, Inc., Smith, Kline & French, 1970. Trustee Carver Found., Bank St. Coll. Edn., Hartwick Coll.; bd. dirs. Nat. Med. Fellowships. Sr. fellow NRC, 1948-49; fellow NSF, 1962-63. Mem. Am. Council Edn. (sec., project dir. ad hoc. com. program Negro colls. 1963), Commn. Coll. Physics, Biophysics Soc. (council), Am. Phys. Soc., A.A.A.S. (mem. council 1971—), Am. Assn. Physics Tchrs., Middle States Assn. Colls. and Secondary Schs. (com. on higher edn.), Nat. Assn. for Equal Opportunity in Edn. (pres. 1970), Sigma Xi. Home: Lincoln U Lincoln University PA 19352

BRANT, HENRY, composer; b. Montreal, Que., Can., Sept. 15, 1913 (parents Am. citizens); s. Saul and Bertha (Dreyfuss) B.; student Juilliard Sch. Music, N.Y.C., 1930-34; m. Patricia Gorman, 1949; children—Piri, Joquin, Linus. Composer documentary films, U.S. Govt., OWI, State Dept., Dept. Agr., 1940—; composer, condr. and arranger various radio network program series for N.B.C., C.B.S., A.B.C. since 1942; member faculty Julliard Sch. of Music, 1947-55, dept. of music Columbia, 1943-53; mem. faculty Bennington (Vt.) Coll., 1957—; condr. local community orch. Composer spatial music in temporal polyphony; ensembles include: Angels & Devils, 1931; Signs and Alarms, 1953; Rural Antiphonies, 1953; Millenium 2, 1954; Encephalograms, 1954; Ceremony, 1954; Galaxies, 1954; Dec., 1954, Grand Universal Circus, 1956; Hieroglyphics, 1957; The Fourth Season, 1957; The Children's Hour, 1958; Mythical Beasts, 1958; The Fire Garden, 1960; Atlantis, 1960; Concerto with Lights, 1961; Barricades, 1961; Headhunt, 1962, Voyage Four (total antiphony, in 83 parts), 1963, Odyssey-Why Not?, 1965, others. Recipient Prix Italia, 1955, Alice M. Ditson award, 1962. Guggenheim fellow, 1946, 55, Inst. Arts and Letters grant, 1955, Copley grantee, 1960, Huber grantee, 1960; Dollard grantee, 1966. Home: New York City NY 10001 Office: Bennington College Bennington VT 05201

BRANT, IRVING NEWTON, editor, writer; b. Walker, Ia., Jan. 17, 1885; s. David and Ruth (Hurd) B.; A.B., U. Ia., 1909; m. Hazeldean Toof, Sept. 3, 1913; children—Ruth (Mrs. Jack Davis), Robin (Mrs. Kenneth Lodewick). Reporter, later mng. editor Iowa City Republican, 1909-14; editor Clinton (Ia.) Herald, 1914-15; asso. editor Des Moines Register and Tribune, 1915-18; editorial writer and editor editorial page St. Louis Star, 1918-23; editor editorial page St. Louis Star-Times, 1930- 38, contbg. editor, 1938-41; editorial writer Chicago Sun, 1941-43, fgn. corr., 1945. Cons. covering personal assistance to Sec. of Interior Ickes and Roosevelt, PWA, 1938-40; dir. Nat. Pub. Ho. Conf., N.Y.C., 1935-44; treas. Emergency Conservation Com., N.Y.C., 1930-62; mem. council Inst. Early Am. History and Culture, 1959-62; mem. adv. bd. James Madison Papers, U. Chgo.; vis. scholar U. Va., 1963-64; vis. prof. history U. Ore., Spring 1966. Mem. Soc. Am. Historians, Overseas Writers, Delta Sigma Phi. Author: Dollars and Sense, 1933; Storm Over the Constitution, 1936; James Madison: The Virginia Revolutionist, (Vol. I), 1941; Road to Peace and Freedom, 1943; The New Poland, 1946; James Madison: The Nationalist, 1780-1787 (Vol. II), 1948; James Madison: Father of the Constitution, 1787-1800 (Vol. III), 1950; James Madison: Secretary of State, 1800-1809, (Vol. IV), 1953; James Madison: The President, 1809-1812 (Vol. V), 1956; James Madison: Commander in Chief, 1812-1836 (Vol. VI), 1961; Friendly Cove (hist. novel), 1963; The Bill of Rights: Its Origin and Meaning, 1965; The Fourth President: A Life of James Madison, 1969. Contbr. sect. The Madison Heritage to book The Great Rights, 1963; James Madison and American Nationalism, 1967; Impeachment: Trials and Errors, 1972. Address: 1575 Ferry St Eugene OR 97401

BRANTLEY, LEE REED, educator; b. Herrin, Ill., Sept. 23, 1906; s. Homer L. and Blanche R. (Reed) B.; A.B., U. Cal. at Los Angeles, 1927; M.S., Cal. Inst. Tech., 1929, Ph.D., 1930; m. Audrey Ryan, June 25, 1930. Instr. physics and chemistry Occidental Coll., Los Angeles, 1930-36, asst. prof. chemistry, 1936-40, asso. asso. prof., 1940-42, prof., from 1942, head dept. chemistry, 1940-62; research fellow physics Cal. Inst. Tech., 1936-42; research asst., cons. chemistry Nat. Def. Research Council Contract, Cal. Inst. Tech., 1942- 44; vis. prof. Lehigh U., 1958-59, prof. chemistry U. Hawaii, Honolulu, 1962-63, vis. prof. chemistry, 1965-66, research prof. edn. Curriculum Research and Devel. Group, 1966—. Dir. contract Office Naval Research on Principles of Adhesion,1949-58, Q.M. Research and Devel. Environmental Protection, 1953-58; dir. Corn Industries Research Found. Adhesion Contract, 1957-59; cons. on protective coatings Nat. Bur. Standards, 1951-53; writer Commn. on Sci. Edn., A.A.A.S. Trustee Alpha Chi Sigma Ednl. Found.; bd. mem. Vol. Com. for Clean Air and Water; chmn. air com. air Oahu chpt. Conservation Council of Hawaii. Served as sr. gas officer Glendale (Cal.) Citizens Def. Corps, 1943-45. Recipient Petroleum Research award for advanced study Am. Chem. Soc., 1958-59. Registered profl. engr., Cal. Fellow Chem. Soc., A.A.A.S.; mem., Pacific S.W. Assn. Chemistry Tchrs. (past pres.), Cal. Acad. Sci., Am. Chem. Soc. (pres. So. Cal. sect. 1947-48, Hawaiian sect. 1949-50, councilor), Electrochem. Soc., Faraday Soc., Nat. Sci. Tchrs. Assn., Am. Inst. Physics, Am. Assn. Physics Tchrs., Hawaii Acad. Sci., Sigma Xi, Alpha Chi Sigma (pres. 1958-60), Kappa Sigma. Rotarian. Contbr. articles to profl. publs. Home: 1095 Spencer St Honolulu, HI 96822.

BRANTLEY, OLIVER WILEY, lawyer; b. Troy, Ala., Oct. 30, 1915; s. James T. and Julia (Wiley) B.; LL.B., U. Ala., 1939; m. Betty Jane Gaston, Jan. 20, 1936; children— Michael Wiley, Elizabeth Ayers (Mrs. William M. Greshan), Grace Lamar (Mrs. William C. Anderson), Oliver Wiley. Admitted to Ala. bar, 1939, since practiced in Troy.; solicitor Pike County, 1947—. Dir. Cotton States Life Ins. Co. Mem. bd. commnrs. Ala. State Bar, 1952; trustee Ala. State Bar Found., 1961—. Bd. dirs. U. Ala. Law Sch. Found., 1966—. Served to lt. (j.g.) USNR, 1943-46. Fellow Am. Coll. Probate Counsel, Am. Coll. Trial Lawyers; mem. Am., Ala., Pike County bar assns., Nat. Assn. R.R. Trial Counsel, Delta Kappa Epsilon, Phi Delta Phi, Farrah Order Jurisprudence. Episcopalian. Home: 216 Flavia Circle Troy AL 36081 Office: 220 S Oak St Troy AL 36081

BRANTLEY, RABUN LEE, ret. assn. exec.; b. Sylvania, Ga., July 12, 1903; s. William Luther and Lillie (Waters) B.; A.B., A.M., Mercer U., 1924; Ph.D., George Peabody Coll., 1928; LL.D., William Carey Coll., 1966; m. Elizabeth Estes, June 22, 1929; children—Rabun (dec.), William Henry, Richard Estes. Prof. English and journalism Bessie Tift Coll., Forsyth, Ga., 1924-39; prof., head English dept. Mary Hardin-Baylor Coll., Belton, Tex., 1939-42; dean, prof. English and journalism U. of Ga. Evening Coll., 1942-45; editor So. Automotive Jour., 1943-45; pres. Va. Intermont Coll., Bristol, Va., 1945-56; v.p. Mercer U., Macon, Ga., 1956-59; exec. sec. edn. commn. So. Bapt. Convention, 1959-70. Vice pres. Ga. Found. for Ind. Colls. Mem. Nat. Council Tchrs. English, So. Assn. Jr. Colls. (pres. 1948), So. Assn. Colls. for Women (pres. 1949), Phi Delta Kappa, Sigma Tau Delta, Kappa Alpha. Kiwanian. Author: Georgia Journalism of the Civil War Period, 1928. Home: 804 S Main St Sylvania GA 30467

BRANTON, JAMES RODNEY, clergyman, educator; b. Hathorn, Miss., May 28, 1906; s. Simon Leon and Martha Eulora (Fortenberry) B.; A.B., Miss. Coll., 1926; Th.M., Southwestern Bapt. Theol. Sem., 1929; postgrad. U. Berlin (Germany), 1930- 1930- 31; Ph.D., U. Chgo., 1934; m. Elizabeth Dana, Aug. 5, 1933; children—Dana Sue, James Rodney, Beth Ella. Ordained to ministry Bapt. Ch., 1926; instr. N.T. interpretation and Greek, Southwestern Bapt. Theol. Sem., 1929-30; teaching and research fellow U. Chgo., 1932-34; instr., acting chmn. classical langs. U. Okla., 1934-36; prof. religion Linfield Coll., 1936-38, Coll. Social Sci., U. Ore., 1938-41; John B. Trevor prof. N.T. interpretation Colgate Rochester (N.Y.) Div. Sch., 1941—; 1941—; lectr., mem. Nat. Christian Mission to Univs., 1939—. Mem. Soc. Bibl. Lit. and Exegesis. Contbr. Interpreter's Dictionary of the Bible, 1956; articles profl. jours. Home: 1760 Jackson Rd Rochester NY 14621

BRANTON, WILEY AUSTIN, lawyer; b. Pine Bluff, Ark., Dec. 13, 1923; s. Leo Andrew and Pauline (Wiley) B.; B.S., Ark. A. M. and N. Coll., 1950; LL.B., U. Ark., 1953; m. Lucille McKee, Feb. 1, 1948; children—Richard, Toni Cheryl, Wylene Anita, Wiley Austin, Beverly Lucille, Debra Elaine. Admitted to Ark. bar, 1952, Ga. bar, 1962, D.C. bar, 1967, also U.S. Supreme Ct., other fed. cts.; practiced in Pine Bluff, 1952-62; dir. voter edn. project So. Regional Council, 1962-65; spl. asst. to atty. gen. of U.S., 1965-67; exec. dir. United Planning Orgn., 1967-69; exec. dir. Council United Civil Rights Leadership, 1963-65; dir. community and social action Alliance for Labor Action, 1969-71; partner firm Dolphin, Branton, Stafford & Webber, Attys., 1971—. Bd. dirs. N.A.A.C.P., Big Bros., Health and Welfare Council, Washington Center for Met. Studies. Served with AUS, 1943-46. Named one of 100 most important young men or women in U.S., Life mag., 1962; one of America's 100 most influential Negroes, Ebony mag., 1963; recipient numerous awards for participation civil rights litigation. Mem. Am., Nat. bar assns., Omega Psi Phi, Sigma Pi Phi. Mason. Home: 825 6th St SW Washington DC 20024 Office: 666 11th St NW Washington DC 20001

BRANTON, WILLIAM COLEMAN, banker, lawyer; b. Greenville, Miss., June 30, 1914; s. William Coleman and Marybelle (Crittenden) B.; B.S. cum laude, Davidson Coll., 1936; J.D., U. Miss., 1939; m. Mary Shaw, Apr. 12, 1947; children—Leslie, Page. Admitted to Miss. bar, 1939, Mo. bar, 1946; practiced in Greenville, 1939-40, Kansas City, Mo., 1946-65; sr. v.p., gen. trust officer City Nat. Bank & Trust Co., Kansas City, Mo., 1965-70; chmn. bd. Plaza Bank & Trust Co., Kansas City, Mo., 1970—; spl. asst. to atty. gen. of Mo. on antitrust matters, 1960-65. Mem. Jackson County (Mo.) Capital Improvements Commn., 1962-65; chmn. bond adv. Commn. Jackson County, 1967-69; mem. Armed Forced Council Kansas City, Mo., 1951—, pres., 1960; bd. dirs. Water Resources Assn., Mo.-Ark. Flood Control Assn.; mem. Greater Kansas City Flood Protection Planning Com. Hon. fellow Harry S. Truman Library Inst.; trustee Elko Charitable Trust and Found., P.B. Francis III Found.; trustee Barstow Sch., Kansas City, Mo., 1956-62, chmn., 1960; v.p., bd. dirs. Kansas City Mus. Sci. and Industry; bd. dirs. Starlight Theatre Assn. Kansas City, Mo., Liberty Meml. Assn., Kansas City, St. Luke's Hosp., Kansas City, Mo.; treas. Mo. Soc. Crippled Children and Adults; bd. dirs.

Jackson County Soc. for Crippled Children and Adults, pres., 1969. Served to col. AUS, 1936-66; PTO. Decorated Legion of Merit, Bronze Star with cluster and combat V, Air medal. Mem. Am., Mo., Kansas City bar assns., Lawyers Assn. Kansas City (v.p., dir. 1962-65), V.F.W., Res. Officers Assn., N.G. Assn. Mo. (pres. 1954), Mil. Order World Wars (comdr. 1964), Blue Key, Phi Beta Kappa, Phi Gamma Delta, Phi Delta Phi, Omicron Delta Kappa. Democrat. Episcopalian (vestry 1967-70). Clubs: Kansas City Country, Carriage, University, Mercury (Kansas City, Mo.). Home: 610 W 57th Terrace Kansas City MO 64113 Office: 118 W 47th St Kansas City MO 64113

BRASCO, FRANK JAMES, congressman; b. Bklyn., Oct. 15, 1932; B.A., Bklyn. Coll.; LL.B., Bklyn. Law Sch. Formerly staff atty. Legal Aid Soc., asst. charge rackets bur. Kings County, N.Y.; mem. 90th-92d congresses from 11th Dist. N.Y. Mem. speakers bur. Kings County Dist. Atty.'s Office. Past athletic dir. Brownsville Boys Club; active Police Kings County Democratic Exec. Com.; mem. exec. com. Young Dems. Kings County. Bd. dirs. Louis Pink Houses Community Center. Served with AUS. Named Young Dem. of Year, 1966. Mem. Old Mill Civic Assn., Kings County Criminal Bar Assn. (dir.), Res. Officers Assn.; Bklyn. Coll., Bklyn. Law Sch. alumni assns., Bklyn. Coll. Athletic Assn. Home: Brooklyn NY 11201 Office: Cannon Office Bldg Washington DC 20510*

BRASFIELD, JOHN ROSS, mining co. exec.; b. Morrisburgh, Ont., Can., 1899; ed. McGill U., 1922. Chmn. bd. Noranda Mines Ltd., Toronto; chmn. bd. Canadian Cooper Refiners, Ltd., Noranada Mfg. Ltd.; dir. Gaspe Copper Mines, Ltd., Eastern & Chartered Trust Co., Bank of Nova Scotia, Placer Devel., Ltd., Kerr Addison Mines, Ltd., Noranda Copper Mills Ltd., Maple Leaf Gardens Ltd. Home: 222 Forest Hill Rd Toronto Ontario Canada Office: Bank of Nova Scotia Bldg Toronto Ontario Canada

BRASFIELD, STEPHEN ARNIM, univ. dean; b. Smithville, Miss., Nov. 28, 1910; s. Alsa Halon and Daira (Towery) B.; B.S., U. So. Miss., 1929; postgrad. Tulane U., 1930-31, Vanderbilt U., 1932-33; M.A., George Peabody Coll., 1932; Ed.D., U. Miss., 1954; m. Alice Hodges, May 20, 1937; children—Mary Alice (Mrs. Windsor P. Thomas), Steven Hodges. Tchr. Spanish, U. So. Miss., 1928-29; tchr. sci., athletic coach Hinds County High Sch. and Jr. Coll., 1929-30; 1929-38; tchr. biology, chmn. sci. dept. Delta Jr. Coll., Moorhead, Miss., 1933- 37; prin. West Point (Miss.) High Sch., 1937-39; supt. Philadelphia (Miss.) City schs., 1939-47; state supr. secondary schs. Miss. Dept. Edn., Jackson, 1947-51, dir. div. instrn., 1951-62; dean faculty Miss. State Coll. for Women, Columbus, 1962—. Exec. sec. E. Central Regional Lit. and Athletic Assn., 1939-47, Miss. Accrediting Commn., 1947-52. Dir. Community chest drive, Philadelphia, 1943. Mem. Am. Assn. Secondary Sch. Prins., So. Assn. Colls. and Schs. (pres. 1962-63; exec. com. 1957-60, 61-64, chmn. secondary commn.), N.E.A., Miss. Edn. Assn., Am., So. assns. acad. deans, Phi Delta Kappa, Delta Pi Epsilon. Democrat. Presbyn. Mason. Clubs: Rotary (pres. Philadelphia 1942); Columbus Exchange. Contbr. articles to ednl. publs., edtor numerous bulls. Home: 1006 College St Columbus, MS 39701.

BRASHARES, CREIGHTON AMBROSE, ret. refractories mfr.; b. Lancaster, O., May 14, 1906; s. William Creighton and Mary (Ambrose) B.; B.Sc., Case Inst. Tech., 1928; m. Merry A. Dennis, July 8, 1933 (dec.); children—Merry Jan (Mrs. C.W. Parker), William Charles, James Creighton; m. 2d, Dorothy K. Saylor, May 24, 1958. Research dept. Harbison-Walker Refractories Co., sales dept., 1935-68, v.p. sales, Pitts., 1955-68, cons., 1968-71. Mem. Am. Inst. Chem. Engrs. (emeritus). Home: 747 N Meadowcroft St Pittsburgh PA 15216

BRASHEARS, EDWIN LAWRENCE, hotel exec.; b. Hannibal, Mo., Jan. 6, 1899; s. George W. and Edna (Williamson) B.; ed. U.S. Naval Acad., 1919; m. Katherine Field, Nov. 23, 1922; children—Edwin Lawrence, Charles Walton. With Nat. Realty and Investment Co. becoming pres.; chmn. bd. The Drake Hotel, Chicago; pres., dir. Drake Oakbrook, Inc.; director Bank of Oakbrook (Illinois), Lake Shore Trust & Savings Bank. Mem. Chgo. Bd. Trade. Commd. lt. comdr., U.S. Navy, June 1942; assigned to Midshipmen's Sch., Abbott Hall, Northwestern U.; retired from naval service, Sept. 1944. Clubs: Chicago, Chicago Yacht, Indian Hill. Home: 502 Hoyt Lane Winnetka IL 60093 Office: The Drake Hotel Lake Shore Dr and Michigan Av Chicago IL 60611

BRASHER, CHARLES ALONZO, physician; b. Roswell, N.M., Apr. 13, 1908; s. Marcellus Hampton and Lulu Julia (Snow) B.; A.B., Hardin-Simmons U., 1927; postgrad. U. Tex., Galveston, 1927-28, Austin, 1928, U. Colo. summer 1931; B.S., U. Mo., 1934; postgrad. U. Mich., summer 1933; M.D., Washington U., St. Louis, 1936; m. Louise Hicks, Sept. 2, 1945; children—Julie B. Hampton, Celynda Celynda Lou (Mrs. Timothy E. Gammon), Charles Thomas. Intern St. Louis City Hosp., 1936-37; practice medicine, Mt. Vernon, Mo., 1939—, specializing chest diseases; staff physician State Hosp., No. 2, St. Joseph, Mo., 1937-38, State Hosp. No. 1, Fulton, Mo., 1938-39; staff physician Mo. State Sanatorium, Mt. Vernon, 1942, asst. supt., 1943, acting supt., 1944, supt., med. dir., 1945—; clin. investigator Tb therapy trials USPHS, 1953—, spl. cons. Tb Program, 1953—, chmn. steering com., clin. investigator for coop. study fungus disease, 1957—; co-investigator coop. lung cancer study research grant NIH, 1964-70. Pres., trustee San-o-Zar Co., Inc. Bd. dirs., chmn. blood program Mt. Vernon chpt. A.R.C.; chmn. bd. dirs. Lawrence County chpt. A.R.C. Fellow Am. Coll. Chest Physicians (past gov., regent emeritus, past ho. chmn. Tb com., past editor bull., past chmn. council on hosps.), Am. Sch. Health Assn. (chmn. Mo. com. on Tb; chmn. com. on preschool child); mem. Am. Thoracic Soc., A.M.A., So., Mo. med. assns., Heart of Am. Tb assn., Ozark Med. Soc. (past pres.), Theta Kappa Phi. Mem. Disciples of Christ Ch. Mason (32, Shriner). Contbr. articles to med. jours. Address: Mo Chest Hosp Mount Vernon MO 65712

BRASS, PHILIP, mfg. co. exec.; b. N.Y.C., 1913; ed. City Coll. N.Y., 1932. Exec. v.p., dir. Faberge, Inc., N.Y.C.; dir. Faberge of Can., Ltd., Parfums Fabergé, S.A., Paris. Home: 165 W 66th St New York City, NY 10023. Office: 1345 Av of the Americas New York City NY 10019

BRASSELL, ALLEN L., corp. exec.; b. Taunton, Mass., Aug. 13, 1905; s. Allen Reid and Eva M. (Welch) B.; grad. Bradford Durfee Tech. Inst., 1925; m. Margaret Ovesen, Mar. 18, 1930; children—Barbara Ann (Mrs. Robert Weber), Marilyn (Mrs. Frederick G. Heath), Robert Allen. With U.S. Testing Co., Inc., Hoboken, N.J., 1925-71, v.p., gen. mgr., 1945-47, pres., 1947-71; pres., dir. Nationwide Consumer Testing Inst., Inc., Hoboken, 1962—; dir., mem. exec. com. Hudson Trust Co., Union City, N.J.; dir. Annin Flag Co., Verona, N.J. Mem. Am. Soc. Testing Materials, Assn. Textile Technologists. Republican. Episcopalian. Club: Essex Fells Country. Contbr. profl. jours. Home: 119 Fells Rd Essex Fells NJ 07021 Office: 1415 Park Av Hoboken NJ 07030

BRASSLER, NORMAN, banker; b. N.Y.C., Aug. 1, 1911; s. Otto and Olga (Kroger) B.; B.S., Princeton, 1933; M.B.A., N.Y. U., 1939; m. Carolyn Morgan, Oct. 15, 1937; children—Carolyn M., N. Morgan. With Chem. Bank, N.Y.C., 1933-38; bond dept. Parrish & Co., N.Y.C., 1938-40; with N.J. Bank & Trust Co., Paterson, 1940—, exec. v.p., 1955-62, chmn. bd., 1962—. Trustee Paterson Gen. Hosp., Paterson Orphan Asylum. Mem. Am. Inst. Banking. Clubs: Upper Montclair (N.J.) Country; Glen Ridge (N.J.) Country; Hamilton (Paterson); Bond of N.J. (Newark). Home: 258 Ridgewood Av Glen Ridge NJ 07028 Office: 657 Main Av Passaic NJ 07055

BRASTED, ROBERT CROCKER, educator; b. Lisbon, N.D., Aug. 26, 1915; s. Alva Jennings and Ada (Crocker) B.; B.S., George Washington U., 1938, M.A., 1939; Ph.D., U. Ill., 1942; m. Corinne Beaudry Mense, Oct. 17, 1942; children—Mary Frances, Barclay Mense, Donald More, Robert Crocker. Asst. in instrn. George Washington U., 1935-39, U. Ill., 1939-42; phys. research chemist Celanese Corp., Cumberland, Md., 1942-43; asst. prof. U. Hawaii, 1943- 47; prof. chemistry, dir. gen. chemistry program U. Minn., Mpls., 1947- -. Operations research chemist Johns Hopkins, 1949; guest prof. Poona U., India, U. Heidelberg, 1961, U. Costa Rica, 1961, Jadavpur U., India, 1964, guest prof., lectr. Taiwan Nat. U., 1970; guest prof., Fulbright lectr. Stuttgart U., 1971; Sanders fellow, 1939, Fulbright fellow, 1961, 71, NSF fellow, 1961; recipient Distinguished Tchr. award Inst. Tech., U. Minn., 1969, Nolte award Council on Liberal Edn. of U. Minn., 1970, medal for teaching excellence Mfg. Chemists Assn., 1971. Mem. Am. Chem. Soc. (chmn. Minn. sect. 1962, chmn. div. chem. edn. 1965, com. on edn. 1968—, com. on nominations and elections 1971—), Minn. Acad. Sci, Sigma Xi, Omicron Delta Kappa, Phi Lambda Upsilon, Alpha Chi Sigma. Conglist. Author: (with Sneed and Maynard) General College Chemistry, 1955; (with others) The Chemistry of Coordination Compounds, 1958; Comprehensive Inorganic Chemistry, 8 vols., 1953-62; (with Conro and Tobias) Laboratory Operations, 1971. Contbr. articles to profl. jours. Home: 1488 Branston St St Paul MN 55108 Office: U Minn Inst Tech Dept Chemistry Minneapolis MN 55455

BRASTOFF, SASCHA, artist; b. Cleve., Oct. 23, 1918; s. Louis and Rebecca (Haimowitz) B.; student Cleve. Sch. Art, 1937-40. Set, costume designer 20th Century- Fox, 1947, including motion pictures Razors Edge, Diamond Horseshoe, If I'm Lucky; v.p., art dir. Sascha Brastoff Prodns., Inc., Los Angeles, 1947—; works in permanent collections Syracuse Mus. Fine Art, Houston Mus. Fine Art, Los Angeles County Mus., Sculpture Center, N.Y.C. Served with USAAF, World War II. Home: 2522 Military Av Los Angeles CA 90054 Office: 246 26th St Santa Monica CA 90402

BRASWELL, ROBERT NEIL, educator, indsl. engr.; b. Boaz, Ala., July 23, 1932; s. Homer Winston and Irene (Wright) B.; B.S., U. Ala., 1957, M.S., 1959; Ph.D., Okla. State U., 1964; m. Wynona Monette Chambers, Apr. 17, 1954; children—John Robert, Jeffrey Monroe. Engr., Hughes Aircraft Co., El Segundo, Cal., 1958; mgr. systems engring. Brown Engring. Co., Inc., Huntsville, Ala. and Cape Canaveral, Fla., 1959-64; resident dir. Genesys, prof. indsl. and systems engring. U. Fla., Daytona Beach, 1964-66; chmn. dept. U. Fla., Gainesville, 1965—. Served with USAF, 1950-53. U.S. Steel Research fellow, 1957-59; recipient edn. award Rotary, Daytona Beach, 1967; named Outstanding Indsl. Engr., Region 4, Am. Inst. Indsl. Engrs., 1967, One of 5 Outstanding Young Men of Fla., Fla. Jr. C. of C., 1967, Alumnus of Year, Snead State Coll., Boaz, 1968. Fellow Am. Inst. Aeros. and Astronautics (asso.), Soc. Logistics Engrs. (nat. dir); mem. Nat. Soc. Profl. Engrs., Am. Inst. Indsl. Engrs. (nat. dir. programs 1964-66, regional v.p. 1968—), Fla. Engring. Soc., Am. Soc. Engring. Edn., Operations Research Soc. Am., Inst. Mgmt. Sci., Sigma Xi, Tau Beta Pi, Omicron Delta Kappa, Sigma Tau, Alpha Pi Mu, Pi Mu Epsilon, Chi Alpha Phi, Phi Theta Kappa. Democrat. Baptist. Rotarian. Contbr. articles profl. jours. Home: 732 NW 40th Terrace Gainesville FL 32601

BRATT, FLOYD CLARENCE, physician; b. Clarence Center, N.Y., Nov. 19, 1903; s. Clarence Almon and Agenes Ruth (Eshelman) B.; B.S., Denison U., 1924; M.D., U. Buffalo, 1928; m. Arline Swift Downey, Oct. 12, 1929 (dec. Aug. 1969); 1 dau., Marilyn (Mrs. R. Bruce Kirkwood). Intern, Buffalo City Hosp., 1928-29; family practice of medicine, Hamburg, N.Y., 1929-31; Rochester, N.Y., 1931—; med. staff Highland Hosp., Park Ave. Hosp., Rochester. Mem. President Eisenhower's People-to- People Com. on Health Professions which sponsored Project HOPE; rep. meeting of World Med. Assn., Copenhagen, 1958; cons., mem. orgn. com. Internat. Conf. on Gen. Practice. Montreal, 1964. Dir. Am. Acad. Gen. Practice Found. Recipient citation for outstanding achievements and services Denison U., 1962. Mem. Am. Geriatrics Assn., Am. (pres. 1961 v.p. chmn. bd. 1959; past mem. congress of dels., past dir., past mem. exec. com.; chmn. com. on internat. affairs 1962-63, rep. to various confs.; N.Y. State (pres. 1952), Rochester (sec., pres.) acads. gen. practice, A.M.A.; World med. assns., Med. Soc. State N.Y. (chmn. subcom. gen. practice of council com. on pub. health and edn. 1950-59; sec. gen. gen practice standing community service 1964), Monroe County Med. Soc., Rochester Acad. Medicine, Rochester Path. Soc., Am. Med. Soc. of Vienna (life), Brit. Coll. Gen. Practice (corr. asso., Nu Sigma Nu. Methodist (trustee emeritus local ch.; trustee Genesee conf.). Mason (Shriner). Clubs: Kiwanis (past lt. gov. N.Y. dist.); Rochester; Monroe Golf. Contbr. articles to profl. publs. Home: 40 Ambassador Dr Rochester NY 14610 Office: 833 South Av Rochester NY 14620

BRATTAIN, WATER HOUSER, physicist; b. Amoy, China, Feb. 10, 1902 (parents Am. citizens); s. Ross R. and Ottilie (Houser) B.; B.S., Whitman Coll., 1924, Ross R. and Ottilie (Houser) B.; B.S., Whitman Coll., 1924, D.Sc., 1955; M.A., U. Ore., 1926; Ph.D., U. Minn., 1929; D.Sc., U. Portland, 1952, Union Coll., 1955, U. Minn., 1957, Gustavus Adolphus Coll., 1963; H.H.D., Hartwick Coll. 1964; m. Keren Gilmore, July 5, 1935; (dec. Apr. 1957); 1 son, William G.; m. 2d, Emma Jane Miller, May 10, 1958. With radio sect. Bur. Standards, 1928-29; with Bell Telephone Labs., Murray Hill, N.J., 1929- 67, research physicist, 1929-67; with div. war research Columbia, 1942- 43; vis. lectr. Harvard, 1952-53; part-time prof. Whitman Coll., Walla Walla, Wash.; specializes in study of semiconductors. Recipient Stuart Ballantine medal Franklin Inst., 1952, John Scott award City of Phila., 1955; recipient (with William Shockley and John Bardeen) Nobel prize in Physics, 1956. Fellow Am. Phys. Soc., A.A.A.S., Am. Acad. Arts and Scis.; mem. Franklin Inst., Nat. Acad. Scis., Phi Beta Kappa, Sigma Xi. Co-inventor of transistor. Address: Whitman Coll Walla Walla WA 99362

BRATTON, HOWARD CALVIN, U.S. judge; b. Clovis, N.M., Feb. 4, 1922; s. Sam Gilbert and Vivian (Rogers) B.; B.A., U. N.M., 1941; LL.B., Yale, 1947. Admitted to N.M. bar, 1948; law clk. U.S. Circuit Ct. Appeals, 1948; mem. firm Grantham & Bratton, Albuquerque, 1949-52; spl. asst. U.S. atty. charge litigation OPS, 1951-52; asso., then partner firm Hervy, Dow & Hinkle, Roswell, N.M., 1952-64; U.S. dist. judge Dist. N.M., 1964- -. Chmn. N.M. Jr. Bar Assn., 1952; pres. Chaves County (N.M.) Bar Assn., 1962; chmn. pub. lands com. N.M. Oil and Gas Assn., 1961-64, pub. lands com. Interstate Oil Compact Commn., 1963-64. Mem. N.M. Commn. Higher Edn., 1962-64, Jud. Conf. of U.S. Com. on operation of jury system, 1966—. Bd. regents U. N.M., 1958-68, pres., 1963-64. Served to capt. AUS, 1942-45. Home: 4250 Aspen Dr NE Albuquerque NM 87110 Office: US Courthouse Albuquerque NM 87103

BRATTON, JAMES HENRY, Jr., lawyer; b. Pulaski, Tenn., Oct. 9, 1931; s. James Henry and Mabel (Shelley) B.; B.A., U. South, 1952, Oxford (Eng.) U., 1954; LL.B., Yale, 1956; m. Alleen Sharp Davis, Oct. 15, 1960; children—Susan Shelley, James Henry III, Margaret Alleen. With antitrust div. Dept. Justice, summer 1955; admitted to Tenn. bar, 1956, Ga. bar, 1957, since practiced in Atlanta; partner firm Gambrell, Russell, Killorin, Wade & Forbes, 1964—. Vis. lectr. U. Ga. Law Sch., 1967; Dir. Encold, Inc., S.R. Devel. Devel. Corp., Leisure Properties, Inc. Mem. Gov.'s Citizens Adv. Council on Environmental Affairs, 1970—. Bd. dirs. Christian Council Met. Atlanta, Protestant Welfare and Social Services, Chs. Home for Bus. Girls. Mem. Am. (standing com. on aero. law 1962—), Ga. (chmn. environmental law sect. 1970—), Atlanta bar assns., Lawyers Club Atlanta, Am. Acad. Polit. and Social Scis., Am. Judicature Soc., Phi Beta Kappa, Phi Delta Phi, Pi Gamma Mu, Gridiron. Democrat. Methodist. Contbr. articles to profl. jours. Home: 63 N Muscogee Av NW Atlanta GA 30305 Office: First Nat Bank Tower Atlanta GA 30303

BRATTON, KARL HENRY, educator, condr.; b. Lawrence, Kan., Jan. 29, 1906; s. Irving and Maud (Hostetter) B.; student U. N.M., 1928; B.Mus., U. Kan. 1931, grad. student, 1932, summer 1940; grad. student U. Mo., 1936, Eastman Sch. Music, summer 1937; M.A., Columbia Tchrs. Coll., 1945; m. Florence Lorree Beamer, June 1, 1932; children—Patricia Lorree (Mrs. I. Stuart Gilman), Sheila Gail. Tchr. voice Baker U., 1932-36; artist, tchr. voice No. Ariz. State Tchrs. Coll., 1932-36; tchr. voice Stephens Coll., 1936- 43; dir. fine arts, head music dept., tchr. voice Coll. Puget Sound, 1944-45; pvt. tchr., N.Y.C., 1939; mem. faculty U. N.H., 1945—, prof. music, 1949—, chmn. dept., 1945—; founder, 1946, since dir. Summer Youth Music Sch.; recitals, oratorio, symphony appearances throughout U.S., 1930-50; produced choral sound tracks for Cinerama Holiday, Whistle at Eaton Falls, Lost Boundaries, also short films; appeared with Boston Pops Orchestra, also radio broadcasts nat. networks; ann. broadcasts Voice Am. to Europe, Latin Am., Far East and Am. Armed Forces Radio and TV Service, 1950—; ann. TV shows New Eng., 1950—. Mem. music adv. bd. Nat. U.S.O., 1942-44; music adviser Tacoma Municipal Recreation Assn., 1944-45; exec. com. N.W. Music Tchrs. Assn., 1944-45. Trustee Tacoma Philharmonic Assn., 1944-45; bd. dirs. Tacoma Civic Music Assn., 1944-45, N.H. Opera League, 1962—. Scholar with Maestro William van Giesen, 1937, 38, 40; winner Western div. Atwater-Kent Contest, 1928, 29, 30; Fedn. Music Clubs prize for Kan., 1935; grad. scholar U. Kan., 1933-34; citation of honor Delta Omicron, 1960. Mem. N.H. Music Tchrs. Assn. (chmn. membership com. 1958-59), Music Tchrs. Nat. Assn. (spl. com. sect., nat. orgn. 1958-59), Assn. New Eng. Music Tchrs. (chmn. sight reading com. 1949), Conf. Arts New Eng. Colls. (chmn. music div. 1950), Am. Assn. U. Profs., Nat. Assn. Music Schs., Music Educators Nat. Conf., New Eng. Music Festival Assn., Nat. Assn. Music Execs. State Univs., Phi Mu Alpha, Sigma Chi. Rotarian. Contbr. profl. jours. Lyricist: Spookie Boogie Hop, 1955; To American Youth, 1955; An Old, Old Man, 1956; Danny Downbeat, 1956; O Lord Don't Leave Me Now, 1957; The Song of my Land, 1958; Let Our Great Song Arise, 1958; Relax!, 1959, Night Time, 1959; Banners of Peace, 1962; Sheila, 1960; Our Land, 1965; Chosen Land, 1965; Our America, 1966; Our America, 1968; It's A Joy to Be an American, 1969; You Have Found America, 1970; elementary music textbook series. Author: (children's fairy tales) Tales of the Magic Mirror, 1949; Tales From Once Upon a Time, 1960; They Came and Left an Echo, 1967. Composer opera librettos. Contbr. to music publs. Home: 12 Thompson Lane Durham NH 03824

BRAU, CHARLES FREDERICK, banker; b. Bklyn., Jan. 4, 1911; s. Charles and Emma G. (Koch) B.; student Am. Inst. Banking, 1927-31, N.Y.U. Sch. Bus. Adminstrn., 1947, Rutgers U. Grad. Sch. Banking, 1949-51; m. Ellen Naekel, Feb. 11, 1937 (dec.); children—Charles A., Jane L. Leonard, George Taylor; m. 2d, Vivian H. Taylor, May 13, 1967. With Kings County Savs. Bank, Bklyn., 1927—, pres., 1960-69 (merged with Union Sq. Savs. Bank, now United Mut. Savs. Bank), chmn. bd., 1969—; mem. Bklyn. adv. bd. Chase Manhattan Bank; past pres. and dir. Instl. Investors Mut. Fund; dir. Savs. Banks Trust Co., Instl. Securities Corp. Dir. Bklyn. A.R.C.; past mem. adv. com. supervision mut. inst. N.Y. State State Banking Dept. Dir. Nassau Council of Chs., House of St. Giles, the Cripple. Mem. Investments Officers of Savs. Bank Assn., Nat. Assn. Accountants, Savs. Banks Assn. (pres. 1969-70), Nat. Assn. Mut. Savs. Banks (dir.). Baptist (trustee). Home: 83 Monroe St Garden City NY 11530 Office: 20 Union Sq New York City NY 10003

BRAUCHER, ROBERT, judge; b. N.Y.C., Feb. 23, 1916; s. Howard S. and Edna Vaughan (Fisher) B.; A.B. with high honors, Haverford Coll., 1936; LL.B. magna cum laude, Harvard, 1939; m. Mary Elizabeth King, Jan. 15, 1942; children—Roberta, William King, Jean, Karen. Admitted to N.Y. bar, 1939, Mass. bar, 1950; asso. firm Hughes, Richards, Hubbard & Ewing, N.Y.C., 1939-41; vis. prof. law, Harvard Law Sch., Cambridge, Mass., 1946-49, prof. law, 1949-71; asso. judge Supreme Jud. Court of Mass., 1971—; Fulbright lectr. Chuo and Tokyo univs., Japan, 1959; vis. prof. law U. Minn., 1968-69. Cons. N.Y. Law Revision Commn.; v.p. Nat. Commn. on Uniform State Laws, 1967-70; Mass. commr. Uniform State Laws, 1954-71; reporter Restatement of Contracts 2d, 1960-71; mem. Mass. Statutory Spl. Com. on Code of Ethics, 1961-62; Mass. Atty. Gen. Adv. Council on Conflict of Interest; chmn. Nat. Commn. on Consumer Finance, 1969-71; chmn. Nat. Inst. for Consumer Justice, 1971—; v.p. Unitarian- Universalist Laymen's League, 1965- 66. Mem. Belmont Sch. Com., 1961-68, chmn., 1966-68. Served to maj. USAAF, 1941-45; CBI, PTO; to lt. col. USAF Res., 1946-55. Decorated Legion of Merit, D.F.C., Air medal. Mem. Atlantic Union Com., Am. Vets. Com., Am., Mass. bar assns., Am. Legion, Am. Law Inst., Phi Beta Kappa. Republican. Unitarian. Author: (with Charles Corker) Introduction to Commercial Law, 1949; Cases on Commercial Law, 1950; Commercial Transactions (4th edit. with Sutherland), 1968; Documents of Title, 2d edit., 1958; (with Fuller) Basic Contract Law 1964. Editor: Harvard Law Rev., 1937-39. Home: 40 Temple St Belmont MA 02178 Office: Supreme Jud Ct Boston MA 02108

BRAUDE, JACOB MORTON, justice; b. Chgo., Dec. 13, 1896; s. Emil and Anna (Kaplan) B.; A.B. cum laude, U. Mich., 1918; postgrad. Northwestern U., 1919; J.D., U. Chgo., 1920; m. Adele Covy Englander, Feb. 22, 1946; children—Ann, Jane (Mrs. David M. Berkson). Admitted to Ill. bar, 1920, since practiced in Chgo.; counsel Nat. Jewelers Bd. Trade, 1927-33; asst. atty. gen. State of Ill., 1933-34; judge Municipal Ct. Chgo., 1934-56; judge Circuit Cts. Ill., Cook County, 1956—, chief justice, 1960-61; presiding judge Chgo. Boys' Ct., 1938-45; asso. dir. finance State of Ill., 1933-34. Mem. Citizens Com. on Parole; bd. dirs. Jewish Children's Bur., Big Bro. Assn. Ill., Juvenile Protective Assn.; pres. Portal House Clinic for Treatment Alcoholics, Chgo. Com. Alcoholism; del.-at-large Chgo. Council Social Agys.; v.p. Chgo. Conf. for Youth; mem. Chgo. adv. bd. Nat. Council Family Relations; adv. bd. World Youth, Nat. Assn. for Gifted Children, St. Leonard's House; citizens com. Loyola U.; chmn. Chgo. div. Am. Jewish Com., chmn. bd. Judge Bishop Bernard J. Sheil Youth of Year Award, 1952—; pres. sponsoring orgn. Am. Boys' Commonwealth, Deborah Boys' Club, Albany Park Boys' Club, Camp Wooster; nat. v.p. Com. for Advancement Am. Judaism, 1954-55. Served as 2d lt. F.A., U. S. Army, 1918. Recipient citation for pub. service U. Chgo. Alumni Assn. 1967, award for meritorious service and understanding of Urban problems Chgo. City Coll. Mem. Internat. Platform Assn., Authors Guild, Authors League, Am., Ill., Chgo. bar assns., Am. Judicature Soc., Chgo. (pres.), Ill. (pres. 1950—) acads. criminology, Soc. Midland Authors, Decalogue Soc., Ill. Soc. Mental Hygiene (v.p.), Mil. Order World Wars, Am. Legion, 40 and 8, Beta Phi. Democrat. Jewish religion. Mason. Clubs: City, Standard (Chgo.). Author: I Like Bad Boys, 1939; Speaker's Ency. of Stories, Quotations and Anecdotes, 1955; Braude's Second Ency. of Stories, Quotations and Anecdotes, 1957; Braude's Handbook of Humor for All Occasions, 1958; New Treasury of Stories for Every Speaking and Writing Occasion, 1959; Speaker's Ency. of Humor, 1961; Lifetime Speaker's Ency., 2 vols., 1962; Quips, Quotes and Anecdotes, 1963; Braude's Treasury of Wit and Humor, 1964; Complete Speaker's and Toastmaster's Library (9 vols), 1965; Complete Speaker's and Writer's Index, 1966; Braude's Handbook of Stories for Toastmasters and Speakers, 1967; Braude's Source Book for Speakers and Writers, 1968; Braude's Guide for Public Speakers and Source Book for Ideas, 1969; The Complete Art of Public Speaking, 1970; Speaker's and Toastmaster's Handbook of Anecdotes by and about Famous Personalities, 1971. Contbr. encys. and mags. Lectr. juvenile delinquency. Died Dec. 24, 1970. Home: 1000 Lake Shore Plaza Chicago IL 60611 Office: Civic Center Chicago IL 60602

BRAUER, FRED GUNTHER, educator; b. Königsberg, Germany, Feb. 3, 1932; s. Richard D. and Isle (Karger) B.; B.A., U. Toronto, 1952; S.M., Mass. Inst. Tech., 1953, Ph.D., 1956; m. Esther Luterman, June 22, 1958; children—David, Deborah, Michael. Came to U.S., 1960. Instr., U. Chgo., 1956-58; lectr., then asst. prof. U. B.C., 1958-60; faculty U. Wis., Madison, 1960—, prof. math., math., 1966—. Mem. Am. Math. Soc., Math. Assn. Am., Canadian Math. Congress, Soc. Indsl. and Applied Math., Sigma Xi. Author: (with J.A. Nohel) Ordinary Differential Equations: A First Course, 1967; Elementary Differential Equations; Principles, Problems, Solutions, 1968; Problems and Solutions in Ordinary Differential Equations, 1968; Qualitative Theory of Ordinary Differential Equations, 1969; (with J.A. Nohel and H. Schneider) Linear Mathematics, 1970. Home: 5113 Coney Weston Pl Madison, WI 53711.

BRAUER, JERALD CARL, ch. historian, educator; b. Fond du Lac, Wis., Sept. 16, 1921; s. Carl L. and Anna Mae (Linde) B.; A.B., Carthage Coll., 1943, LL.D., 1957; B.D., Northwestern Luth. Theol. Sem., 1945; Ph.D., U. Chgo., 1948; D.D., Miami U., Oxford, O., 1956; S.T.D., Ripon Coll., 1961; L.H.D., Gettysburg Coll., 1963; m. Muriel I. Nelson, Mar. 18, 1945; children—Christopher, Marian, Thomas. Ordained to ministry United Lutheran Ch. Am., 1951; instr. ch. history and history Christian thought Union Theol. Sem., N.Y.C., 1948-50; asst. prof. history of Christianity, federated theol. faculty U. Chgo., 1950-54, asso. prof., 1954-59, dean federated theol. faculty, 1955-60, dean div. sch., 1960-70, prof. history of Christianity, 1959-70, Naomi Shenstone Donnelly prof. history of Christianity, 1969—. Mem. bd. theological edn. Luth. Ch. in Am., pres. bd., 1962-68; ofcl. delegated observer World Council Chs. 3d, 4th sessions Vatican Council II; mem. bd. Council on Religion and Internat. Afairs. Bd. dirs. Internat. House, Rockefeller Bros. Theol. Fellowship Program, 1956-70. Mem. Am. Soc. Ch. History (pres. 1960), Renaissance Soc. Am., Midwest Conf. Brit. Hist. Studies. Author: Protestantism in America, 1953; Basic Question for the Christian Scholar, 1954; (with J. Pelikan) The Lutheran Reformation, 1955. Editor: The Future of Religious (Paul Tillich), 1966; My Travel Diary 1936 (Paul Tillich) 1970; Westminster Dictionary of Church History, 1971. gen. editor Essays in Divinity, 8 vols., 1967—, editor vols. 2 and 5. Home: 5620 S Blackstone Av Chicago IL 60637

BRAUER, RALPH WERNER, educator, physiologist; b. Berlin, Germany, June 18, 1921; s. Frederick and A. M. (Doering) B.; came to U.S., 1937, naturalized, 1941; A.B. in Chemistry, Columbia, 1940; M.S. in Biochemistry, U. Rochester, 1941, Ph.D., 1943. Research chemist Distillation Products, Inc., 1943-44; instr. pharmacology Harvard Med. Sch., 1944-47; asst. prof. pharmacology and biochemistry, acting head pharmacology dept. La. State U. Sch. Medicine, 1947-51; head metabolism sect. U.S. Naval Research and Devel. Lab., 1951-52, head pharmacology br., 1952-64, prin. investigator biol. and med. sci. div., chmn. oceanography planning com., 1964-66; dir. Wrightsville Marine Bio-Med. Lab., Wilmington, N.C., 1966—; prof. physiology and pharmacology Duke, 1966-71; prof. marine physiology, head dept. marine bio-med. research U. N.C. at Wilmington, 1971—; vis. prof. physiology U. N.C. at Chapel Hill, 1968—; chief radiol. def. for La., 1950-51; chmn. research com. San Mateo (Cal.) Heart Assn., 1959-65; Mary Scott Newbold lectr. Phila. Coll. Physicians, 1961. Mem. Soc. Exptl. Biology and Medicine (chmn. Pacific Coast sect. 1959-66), N.Y. Acad. Scis., Am. Physiol. Soc., Am. Soc. Pharmacology and Exptl. Therapeutics, A.A.A.S., Radiation Research Soc., Am. Soc. Study Liver Diseases, Am. Soc. Phys. Anthropology, Marine Tech. Soc., Aerospace Med. Assn., Soc. for Underwater Medicine. Editor: Liver Function, 1958; mem. editorial bd. Am. Jour. Physiology, also Jour. Applied Physiology, 1960-66. Author numerous articles in field. Home: Route 3 Box 327A Wilmington NC 28401

BRAUER, RICHARD DAGOBERT, mathematician, educator; b. Berlin, Germany, Feb. 10, 1901; s. Max and Lilly Caroline (Jacob) B.; Ph.D., U. Berlin, 1925; D. Math. (hon.), U. Waterloo, 1968; D.Sc., U. Chgo., 1969; m. Ilse Karger, Sept. 17, 1925; children—George Ulrich, Fred Gunter. Naturalized U.S. citizen, 1954. Privatdozent, U. Koenigsberg (Germany), 1927-33; vis. prof. U. Ky., 1933-34; asst. Inst. for Advanced Study, Princeton, N.J., 1934-35; asst. prof. U. Toronto, 1935-43, asso. prof., 1943-46, prof., 1946- 48; prof. math. U. Mich., 1948-52; prof. math. Harvard, Cambridge, Mass., 1952-66, Perkins prof. math., 1966-71. Vis. prof. Nagoya U., 1959, U. Chgo., 1968-69; Gauss prof. Akademie der Wissenschaften, Göttingen. Fellow John Simon Guggenheim Found., 1941-42. Mem. Royal Soc. Can., Am. Math. Soc. (Cole prize 1949; v.p. 1952- 53, pres. 1957-58), Nat. Acad. Sci., Math. Assn. Am., Am. Acad. Arts and Scis., Canadian Math. Congress, Akademie der Wissenschafter Göttingen (fgn. mem.), Sigma Xi. Home: 15 Franklin St Belmont MA 02178

BRAULT, GERARD JOSEPH, educator; b. Chicopee Falls, Mass., Nov. 7, 1929; s. Philias J. and Aline E. (Rémillard) B.; A.B., Assumption Coll., Worcester, Mass., 1950; A.M. cum laude, Laval U., 1952; Ph.D., U. Pa., 1958; m. Jeanne Lambert Pepin, Jan. 20, 1954; children—Francis Gerard, Anne Marie, Suzanne Eveline. Teaching fellow U. Pa., 1954-56, asso. prof. romance langs., 1961-65, vice dean Grad. Sch., 1962-65; instr. French, Bowdoin Coll., 1957-59, asst. prof., 1959-61; prof. French, Pa. State U., University Park, 1965—, head dept. France, 1965-70; dir. NDEA Summer Insts., Bowdoin Coll., 1961, 62, Assumption Coll., 1964; Fulbright fellow Strasbourg, France, 1956-57; Fulbright research scholar and Guggenheim fellow, Strasbourg, 1968-69. Mem. Catholic Commn. on Cultural Affairs, also Comité de Vie Franco-Américaine. Served with CIC, U.S. Army, 1951- 53. Recipient Palmes académiques French Ministry Edn., 1965. Mem. Société Rencesvals pour l'étude des épopées romanes (pres. Am.-Canadian br.), Am. Assn. Tchrs. French, Internat. Arthurian Soc., Medieval Acad. Am., Modern Lang. Assn. Author: Celestine. A Critical Edition of the First French Translation (1527) of the Spanish Classic La Celestina, 1963; Cours de langue Française destiné aux jeunes Franco-Américains 1963, rev. edits., 1965, 69, Early Blazon, 1971. Contbr. articles profl. jours. Home: 705 Westerly Pkwy State College PA 16801 Office: Burrowes Bldg Pennsylvania State U University Park PA 16802

BRAUN, ARMIN CHARLES JOHN, educator; b. Milw., Sept. 5, 1911; s. Adolph and Ella (Schreiber) B.; B.S., U. Wis., 1934, Ph.D., 1938; predoctoral study European sci. labs., 1936-37. With Rockefeller U., N.Y.C., 1938—, successively fellow, asst., asso., asso. mem., asso. prof., 1938-59, mem. and prof., 1959—, head dept. plant biology, 1955—; mem. sci. panel biology and medicine NSF, 1958-61; mem. sci. adv. bd. Inst. Cancer Research Phila., 1959-65; sci. adv. panel Brookhaven Nat. Lab., 1960-64; mem. adv. com. Aspen Biol. Inst., 1965-68. Served to capt. AUS, 1943-46. Recipient Newcomb Cleveland award, A.A.A.S., 1949. Mem. Am. Acad. Arts and Scis., Nat. Acad. Scis., Harvey Soc. (hon.), Internat. Soc. Developmental Biologists, A.A.A.S., Soc. for Development Biology, Am. Phytopath. Soc., Sigma Xi, Phi Sigma, Alpha Zeta, Delta Theta Sigma. Author numerous sci. papers, books. Home: Ridgeview Rd Princeton NJ 08540 Office: Rockefeller U 66th St and York Av New York City NY 10021

BRAUN, CHESTER VAL, aircraft co. exec.; b. E. Orange, N.J., Feb. 11, 1924; s. Chester S. and Beatrice (Heisler) B.; B.S., U.S. Mil. Acad., 1945; m. Elizabeth Jane Riggins, Oct. 22, 1949; children—Chester Val, Garry Nelson, Commd. 2d lt. USAF, advanced through grades to 1st lt., 1947; resigned, 1950; exptl. test pilot Republic Aviation Corp., 1950-52; from exptl. test pilot to gen. mgr. USAF aircraft McDonnell Aircraft Corp., 1952-66; v.p., group exec. Conductron Corp., 1966-68, pres., 1968-69; v.p., program mgr. F-4 McDonnell Aircraft Corp., 1969—. Home: 4 Sherwyn Lane St. Louis MO 63141. Office: PO Box 516 St Louis MO 63166

BRAUN, GERHARD WINFRIED, aero. research engr.; b. Danzig, Germany, Dec. 23, 1907; s. Hermann Adalbert and Alma Elise (Braun) B.; Ph.D., U. Goettingen, Germany, 1932; diploma engring., Inst. Technol., Danzig, 1932; m. Margaretha W. Reese, Sept. 15, 1932; children—Dietrich, Juergen, Gertrud Lawson, Wolfgang, Ilse. Cons. aerodynamics Air Ministry, Berlin, Germany, 1933-37; chief dynamics aircraft br., Aerodynamics Lab., Aero. Research Center. Braunschweig, Germany, 1937-45; cons. aircraft stability and control Wright Air Development Center, Dayton, O., 1945-53; chief aerodynamics and ballistics br. HADC. Holloman Air Force Base, N.M., 1953-57, tech. dir. ballistic missile directorate, 1957-58, sci. adviser Directorate of Advanced Tech., 1958-62; chief scientist Pacific Missile Range, Point Mugu, Cal., 1962-65; prof. aerospace engring. U. Tenn. Space Inst., Tullahoma, 1965—. Asso. fellow Inst. Aero. Sci.; mem. Am. Rocket Soc. (dir. local chpt.), Wissenschaftliche Gesellschaft fur Luftfahrt. Home: 1004 Greenwood Av Tullahoma TN 37388

BRAUN, JOHN GILBERT, oil refining exec.; b. San Francisco, Jan. 16, 1913; s. Carl Franklin and Winifred Hughes (Gilbert) B.; student U. Cal., 1931-34; m. Ruth Richardson, Oct. 26, 1939; children—Beverly, Pamela. With C. F. Braun & Co., Alhambra, Cal., 1934—, pres., 1954—. Trustee Cal. Inst. Tech. Mem. Am. Soc. M.E.'s, Am. Chem. Soc. Republican. Clubs: California (Los Angeles); Annanadale Golf (Pasadena). Home: 1750 Lombardy Rd Pasadena CA 91106 Office: 1000 S Fremont Av Alhambra CA 91803

BRAUN, KURT, economist; b. Berlin, Germany, Sept. 13, 1899; s. Julius and Paula (Beck) B.; student U. Berlin, 1916-20; J.S.D., Breslau, 1922; m. Helene Schön, Dec. 7, 1930; 1 dau., Suzanne Paula. Came to U.S., 1940, naturalized, 1945. Judge Fed. Dist. Ct., Berlin, 1923; asst. to chief, price calculating dept., Internat. Price Cartel of Incandescent Lamp Mfrs., 1924; admitted to Berlin cts., 1924; lawyer in Labor Law; research asso., U. N.H., 1940-42; mem. staff, Brookings Instn., Washington, 1942-51, CIA, 1951-60, U.S. Dept. of Labor, 1960-67; vis. prof. econs. Howard U. Washington, 1943-69; cons. in fgn. and domestic labor and social matters, 1967—; prin. economist (cons.) U.S. Dept. Labor Statistics, 1945, War Dept. Hdqrs., Indsl. Personnel Div., Labor Branch, 1944-45, WSB, 1951. Mem. Am. Econ. Assn., Indsl. Relations Research Assn. Author: Union-Management Co- operation; Experience in the Clothing Industry, 1947, The Right to Organize and Its Limits, 1950; Labor Disputes and Their Settlement, 1955; Labor Law and Practice in Japan, 1970. Editor, author and contbr. articles and book revs. to German and Am. bulls. and jours. Address: 2904 Argyle Dr Alexandria VA 22305 ☆

BRAUN, LUDWIG, educator; b. Bklyn., May 14, 1926; s. Ludwig and Wetie (Schmidt) B.; B.E.E., Poly. Inst. Bklyn., 1950, M.E.E., 1955, D.E.E., 1959; m. Eva Margaret Taylor, Sept. 7, 1947; children—Barbara Ann, Edith Elizabeth, Anne Catherine, John Ludwig. Elec. engr. Allied Control Co., N.Y.C., 1950-51; head electronics dept. Anton Electronics Labs., Inc., Bklyn., 1951-55; instr. elec. engring. Poly. Inst. Bklyn., 1951-59, asst. prof., 1959-62, asso. prof., 1962-66, prof. elec. and system engring., 1966—. Cons. Vertol dev. Boeing Co., Gen. Electric Co., Ford Found. Served with AUS, 1944-46. Mem. I.E.E.E., Am. Soc. Engring. Edn., N.Y. Acad. Scis., Simulation Council, Sigma Xi, Tau Beta Pi, Eta Kappa Nu. Author: (with E. Mishkin) Adaptive Control Systems, 1961; contbg. author: Signals and Systems in Electrical Engineering, 1962; Perry's Chemical Engineering Handbook, 1962; System Engineering Handbook, 1965. Home: 11 Parsons Dr Dix Hills NY 11746 Office: 333 Jay St Brooklyn NY 11201

BRAUN, MAX HILLARD, lawyer, cosmetic co. exec.; b. East Chicago, Ind., June 5, 1902; s. Abraham L. and Minnie (Pitzele) B.; B.S., U. Chgo., 1925; J.D., John Marshall Law Sch., 1929; m. Bernice Wolf, May 26, 1940; children—Joseph Wolf, Susan Miriam (Mrs. Barry Baer). Admitted to Ill. bar, 1929, since practiced in Chgo.; with law dept. Chgo. Motor Club, 1926-36; sec. Helene Curtis Industries, Inc., Chgo; 1936-71; v.p., sec., dir. Curtis Labs., Inc.; sec., treas., dir. numerous indsl. firms. Mem. Planning Commn., Glencoe, Ill., 1961-64; chmn. Heart Fund. Glencoe, 1960- 63; mem. Community Fund, Glencoe, 1961—. Mem. Order John Marshall, Tau Delta Phi. Home: 475 C Laurel St Highland Park IL Office: 4401 W North Av Chicago IL 60639

BRAUN, THEODORE WILLIAM, pub. relations ofcl.; b. Newark, Dec. 26, 1901; s. Adam and Elizabeth (Bayles) B.; spl. student Harvard Sch. Bus., m. Beatrice Banning, July 3, 1920. Pres., Braun & Co., Los Angeles, 1936- -; ltd. partner Merrill Lynch, Pierce, Fenner & Smith, 1955—. Cons. comdg. gen. Fourth Army, Western Def. Command, 1941-43; dir. tech. information div. A.S.F., 1944; staff mem. Gordon Gray Report to Pres., U.S. fgn. and econ. policy, 1950; mem. spl. com. on reorgn. NSC, 1953; asst. to sec. treas., 1953-54, cons. 1955; mem. adv. com. to sec. def. on gen. mil. tng., 1962; gov. U.S. Postal Service, 1971—. Past pres. Hollywood Bowl Assn. Trustee Harvey Mudd Coll.; bd. dirs. Claremont Coll. Mem. C. of C., Town Hall (past gov., past pres.). Clubs: Metropolitan (Washington, N.Y.C.); Men's Garden of Los Angeles (past pres.), Bel Air Country, California (Los Angeles); Eldorado Country (Palm Desert, Cal.). Home: 537 Perugia Way West Los Angeles CA 90024 Office: 625 S Kingsley Dr Los Angeles CA 90005

BRAUN, WALTER GUSTAV, educator; b. Springfield, Mass., June 23, 1917; s. Gustav Franz and Alma Emma (Voigt) B.; B.Chem. Engring., Cooper Union, 1942; M.S., Pa. State U., 1948, Ph.D., 1955; m. Gloria Jean McCurdy, June 20, 1948; children—Karen Jean, Kenneth Walter. Jr. chemist Tide Water Asso. Oil Co., Bayonne, N.J., 1936-42; research asst. Pa. State U., 1943-47, instr., 1947-56, asso. prof., 1956-64, prof., 1964—, asst. dean engring., 1970—. Fellow Am. Inst. Chemists; mem. Am. Chem. Soc., Am. Inst. Chem. Engrs., Am. Assn. U. Profs., Am. Soc. Engring. Edn., Sigma Xi, Phi Lambda Upsilon, Alpha Chi Sigma. Editor: Technical Data Book - Petroleum Refining, rev. edit., 1971; patentee, publns. in field. Home: 225 Twigs Lane State College PA 16801

BRAUN, WERNER, microbiologist; b. Berlin, Germany, Nov. 16, 1914; s. Simon and Edith (Brach) B.; Ph.D., U. Göttingen, 1936; m. Barbara Melnikow, June 7, 1942; children—Renee, Stephanie, Robin. Came to U.S., 1936, naturalized, 1941. Guest investigator U. Mich., 1936-37; research asso. dept. zoology U. Cal. at Berkeley, 1937-42, asso. dept. vet. sci. Expt. Sta. Coll. Agr., 1942-48; med. bacteriologist, chief variation br. Chem. Corps Biol. Labs., Camp Detrick, Frederick, Md., 1948-55; prof. microbiology Inst. Microbiology, Rutgers U., New Brunswick, N.J., 1955—; cons. U.S. Army Chem. Corps, 1955-68; USPHS, 1956—, U.S. Dept. of Def., 1960- 68, NSF, 1967-70; bd. sci. counselors Nat. Inst. Allergy and Infectious Diseases, NIH, 1966-69, chmn. bd. sci. counselors, 1968-69, vis. scientist, 1970—; I.M. Lewis lectr. U. Tex., 1951; vis. prof. U. P.R. Med. Sch., 1957, 59, 60, 61, 63, 65, 67, 68; NIH research fellow, Israel, Paris, also vis. prof. Hebrew U., Hadassah Med. Sch., Jerusalem, 1962-63; vis. scientist Weizmann Inst., Israel, Pasteur Inst., Paris, Karolinska Inst., Stockholm, 1969-70; O. Stark lectr. Miami U., Oxford, O., 1971. Recipient Barnett Cohen award. Soc. Am. Bacteriologists, 1954; superior accomplishment award Chem. Corps, U.S. Army, 1954. Fellow Am. Acad. of Microbiology (pres. 1968-69), A.A.A.S.; mem. Theobald Smith Soc. (pres. 1957-58), Sci. Research Soc. Am., Am. Soc. Microbiology, Am. Assn. Immunologists, Genetics Soc. Am., Soc. Exptl. Biology and Medicine, Soc. Gen. Microbiology, Sigma Xi, Phi Sigma. Author: Bacterial Genetics, 1953, 2d edit., 1965. Editor several sci. books. Contbr. articles to sci. jours. Home: 72 Mason Dr Princeton NJ 08540 Office: Inst Microbiology Rutgers U New Brunswick NJ 08903

BRAUN, ZEV, motion picture producer; b. Chgo., Oct. 19, 1928; s. Julius and Charlotee (Brandau) B.; student Roosevelt U., Chgo., 1948, Marquette U., 1950, U. Chgo., 1964; m. Joan Marie Wilkes, June 23, 1951; children—Benjamin, Jonathan, Jeremy. Supt., later v.p. sales and dir. Braun-Hobar, injection and compression molding plant, Milw., 1951-55; v.p. sales, dir. W. Braun Co., packaging and design, Chgo., 1955-63, pres. div. Braun Internat., Inc., exports, 1964-65; producer film Goldstein (U.S. rep. Cannes Film Festival, also recipient Prix de la Nouvelle Critique), 1964; exec. producer film The Double-Barrelled Detective Story, 1965, Madron, 1970; chmn. bd. Braun/White Prodns., Chgo., 1966—; pres. Zev Braun Prodns., 1971. Bd. dirs. Little City Found., Palatine, Ill., 1962-63; v.p., dir. Gastro-Intestinal Research Found., U. Chgo., 1964-65; sponsor chpt. U.S. Maccabiah Games Fund, 1965; v.p. City of Hope, 1970—; gen. chmn. Ann. Salute to Med. Research, 1969. Jewish religion. Home: 1 E Schiller St Chicago IL 60610 Office: 300 N Canal St Chicago IL 60606

BRAUND, RUSSELL MEDLAND, steel co. exec.; b. DuBois, Pa., Oct. 7, 1908; s. P. Sidney and Emma L. (Medland) B.; B.S., U. Pitts., 1931; m. Evelyn Jones, Sept. 1, 1932. With U.S. Steel Corp. and subsidiaries, 1937—, comptroller Am. Steel & Wire div., Cleve., 1947-57, v.p. corp., 1957-59, adminstrv. v.p., 1959- -. Mem. Am. Iron and Steel Inst., Controllers Inst. Am., Nat. Assn. Accountants. Clubs: Pittsburgh Field; Canterbury Golf (Cleve.). Home: 204 Glenhaven Lane Pittsburgh PA 15238 Office: 525 William Penn Pl Pittsburgh PA 15230

BRAUNER, ERLING BERNHARDT, educator; b. Ithaca, N.Y., Apr. 16, 1906; s. Olaf M. and Nikolina (Berntsen) B.; B.F.A., Cornell U., 1930, M.F.A., 1933; m. Katherine O. Barton, June 30, 1934; children—Louise (Mrs. William L. Broecker), Nikolina (Mrs. Lee J. Workum, Jr.), Arthur Barton. Faculty Mich. State U., 1935—, prof. art, 1958—, chmn. dept. art, 1962-71, prof. art emeritus, 1971—; exhbns. include St. Paul Gallery, Birmingham Little Gallery, Detroit Inst. Art, S. Bend Art Gallery, Ohio State U., Flint Art Inst., Wooster Coll., Grand Rapids Art Inst., Forum Gallery, Saginaw Art Mus., Ball State Gallery, Bay City Art Gallery, Eastern Ill. U. Chmn. com, visual arts, mem. exec. com. Mich. Council Arts, 1962-70. Served to lt. USNR, 1943-46. Home: 2527 Arrowhead Rd Okemos MI 48864 Office: Art Dept Mich State U East Lansing MI 48823

BRAUNER, JULIUS FREDERICK lawyer; b. Mt. Vernon, N.Y., June 20, 1909; s. Julius F. and Lillian (Moore) B.; A.B., Cornell U., 1931, LL.B., 1932; m. Ruth E. Gordon, Apr. 16, 1938; children—Julius Frederick, Andrea (Mrs. Edward Hein). Admitted Admitted to N.Y. bar, 1932; asso. firm Cravath, deGersdorff, Swaine & Wood (now Cravath, Swaine & Moore), 1932-38; atty. CBS, 1938-42, gen. atty., 1942—, sec., 1947—. Mem. F.C.C., N.Y. State, Am. bar assns., Assn. Bar City N.Y., Am. Arbitration Assn., Assn. Gen. Counsel, Order of Coif, Phi Beta Kappa, Phi Kappa Phi. Home: 30 Circle Rd Scarsdale NY 10583 Office: 51 W 52d St New York City NY 10019

BRAUNSTEIN, BARUCH, rabbi, lectr.; b. New Castle, Pa., Mar. 3, 1906; s. Peter and Esther (Pazer) B.; student Western Res. U., 1922-23; B.Sc., Ohio State U., 1926; M.H.L., Rabbi, Jewish Inst. Religion, 1930; Ph.D., Columbia, 1936; m. Gladys Belmont, June 19, 1928. Rabbi, Beth Sholom Congregation, N.Y.C., 1927-29, religious counselor Columbia, 1929-34; mem. exec. staff Emergency Peace Campaign, 1936; spl. lectr. Am. U. of Beirut, Syria, 1933, also spl. lectr. various other univs. Mem. com. China's Children's Fund, 1939; rabbi Congregation Keneseth Israel, Allentown, 1943-49, Congregation Beth Israel, Atlantic City, 1950-51; lectr. U. Cal. Extension, also various religious sems., Berkeley, Cal. Fellow Nat. Council on Religion in Higher Edn., 1927—; Guggenheim fellow for travel abroad, 1932-33. Mem. Am. Acad. Polit. Sci., Am. Geog. Soc. of N.Y., Am. Hist. Assn., Central Conf. Am. Rabbis. Forum Soc., Delta Sigma Rho. Rotarian. Author: The Chuetas of Majorca, 1936, rev., 1971. Book reviewer Sat. Rev. Lit., Jour. Religion. Contbr. articles to Am. European mags., newspapers. Contbr. Help and Comfort from the Bible.

BRAUNSTEIN, RUBIN, educator; b. N.Y.C., May 6, 1922; s. Benjamin and Beatrice (Brunman) B.; B.S., N.Y. U., 1948; M.S., Syracuse U., 1951, Ph.D., 1954; m. Jacqueline Berkowitz, Oct. 2, 1948; children—Mark Benjamin, David Philip. Research asso. molecular beams Columbia U., 1952-53; mem. research staff solid state physics RCA Labs., Princeton, N.J., 1953-64; asso. prof. physics U. Cal. at Los Angeles, 1964, prof., 1964—; cons. Radio Corp. Am. Labs., 1964—. Served with AUS, 1943-45. Fellow Am. Phys. Soc.; mem. A.A.A.S. Research, publications patentee molecular beams; microwave spectroscopy; solid state physics; quantum electronics. Home: 1107 Vista Grande Dr Pacific Palisades CA 90272 Office: Dept Physics U Cal at Los Angeles Los Angeles CA 90024

BRAUNWALD, EUGENE, physician; b. Aug. 15, 1929; s. William and Clare (Wallach) B.; A.B., N.Y. U., 1949, M.D., 1952; m. Nina Starr, May 23, 1952; children—Karen, Denise, Adrienne. Tng. internal medicine Mt. Sinai, Johns Hopkins hosps., also Columbia, 1952-58; commd. USPHS, 1954, med. dir., 1963; research cardiology and physiology Nat. Heart Inst., 1955-67, chief cardiology dept., 1960-67, clin. dir. inst., 1966-67; lectr. medicine Johns Hopkins, 1962-67; clin. prof. medicine Georgetown U., 1966-67; prof., chmn. dept. medicine U. Cal. at San Diego Sch. Medicine, La Jolla, 1967—. Recipient John Abel award research pharmacology; Arthur Fleming award for outstanding fed. service; Outstanding Service award USPHS, 1967; Nylin award Swedish Med. Soc., 1970; Einthoven medal, 1970. Diplomate Am. Bd. Internal Medicine. Fellow A.C.P., Am. Coll. Cardiology (v.p., gov., trustee); mem. Am. Heart Assn. (v.p., dir. chmn. publs. 1965—), Am. Fedn. for Clin. Research (pres. 1968-70), Soc. Clin. Investigation, Western Soc. for Clin. Research (pres. 1971-72), Am. Physiol. Soc., Am. Pharmacology Soc., Soc. Exptl. Biology and Medicine. Author: Mechanism of Contraction of Heart. Editorial bd. Circulation and Jour. Pharmacology, Jour. Clin. Investigation, Am. Jour. Physiology, Annals Internal Medicine, Circulation Research, Yearbook of Cardiovascular Diseases; editor: Principles of Internal Medicine. contbr. numerous sci. articles. Home: 9702 La Jolla Farms Rd La Jolla CA 92037

BRAUTIGAM, DALE PETER, metal casting co. exec.; b. Jackson, Mich., June 17, 1928; s. Charles Otto and Frances Kathryn (Klee) B.; B.A., Albion Coll., 1952; B.S. in Indsl. Engring., Washington U., 1953; M.B.A., U. N.M., 1965; m. Virginia Anne O'Toole, Sept. 28, 1957; children—Philip Charles, Nora Ellen, Christine Anne. Chief plant engr. Westran Corp., Muskegon, Mich., 1955-62; staff indsl. engr., supr. Sandia Corp., Albuquerque, 1953-55, 62-66; mgr. plant and indsl. engring. Campbell, Wyant & Cannon Foundry Co. a Textron Co., Muskegon, 1966—. Cub Pack com. chmn. Grand Valley council Boy Scouts Am., 1966-70, troop committeeman, 1970—; co-leader Brownie troop Girl Scouts Am., 1966-70, jr. troop committeeman, 1970—; v.p. P.T.A., Spring Lake, 1971—. Served with USN, 1946-48. Recipient Mr. Industry award Indsl. Maintenance and Plant Operation Mag., 1970. Registered profl. engr., Mich. Mem. Am. Inst. Indsl. Engrs. (v.p. N.M. chpt. 1966), Am. Inst. Plant Engrs. (internat. treas. 1970—, nat. dir. 1966-69, regional v.p. 1968-69, chpt. pres. 1961-62), Am. Foundrymens Soc. (vice chmn. Mich. Regional Foundry Conf. 1970, chmn. 1972, chpt. dir. 1968—), Inst. Mgmt. Scis., Alpha Pi Mu, Kappa Mu Epsilon. Roman Catholic. Elk. Contbr. articles profl. jours. Home: Littlefield Lane Spring Lake MI 49456 Office: Henry St Muskegon MI 49444

BRAUTIGAM, KARL A., advt. agy. exec. Sr. v.p. McCann-Erickson, Inc., N.Y.C. Office: 485 Lexington Av New York City NY 10017*

BRAUTIGAN, RICHARD, author. Author: Trout Fishing in America; A Confederate General from Big Sur; All Watched Over by Machines of Loving Grace; Please Plant This Book; In Watermelon Sugar; The Pill Versus the Springhill Mine Disaster; Rommel Drives on Deep into Egypt; The Abortion: An Historical Romance 1966; Revenge of the Lawn. Address: care Sterling Lord Agency 660 Madison Av New York City NY 10021

BRAVERMAN, ROBERT PAUL, editor; b. Chgo., Dec. 6, 1920; s. Leo and Lillian (Karish) B.; student Wash. U., 1950-53; m. Barbara Jean Clark, Apr. 1, 1955; children—Michael Lee, Laura Ann, Jeffrey David. Engr., cons. designer hobby and toy field with L.M. Cox, Santa Ana, Cal., 1966-67, Ideal Toy Co., N.Y.C., 1958-60, Monogram Models, Morton Grove, Ill., 1956-57; free-lance writer, photographer, 1960-68; with Cycle Guide Publs., Los Angeles, 1968—, editor, 1970—. Mem. Am. Motorcycle Assn., Soc. Automotive Engrs., So. Cal. Timing Assn. Author: This is Your Hobby—Slot Racing, 1966; Model Cars, 1967. Home: 6906 Colbath Van Nuys CA 91405 Office: 6675 E 26th St Los Angeles CA 90040

BRAWLEY, HIRAM WILKS BILL, co. exec.; b. Lockhart, S.C., Apr. 12, 1917; s. Wilks Hiram and Bernice (Pendergrass) B.; student U. of South, 1940; m. Hazel Townsend, Sept. 12, 1940; children—Frederica Anne, Carol Lee. Personnel, accounting positions Springs Textile Mills, Chester, S.C., 1940-41; textile cost accountant OPA, 1941, est., directed office, Virgin Islands, 1942; investigator FTC, 1946-49; asst. staff dir. Senate Post Office and Civil-Service Com., 1949-51, staff dir., 1951-60; asst. adminstr. Small Def. Plants Adminstrn., 1951; dep. postmaster gen. U.S., 1961-62; exec. asst. to chmn. Dem. Nat. Com., 1962-66; v.p. nat. and internat. relations Genesco, Inc., Washington, 1966—. Asst. nat. campaign mgr. Adlai Stevenson, 1956; Nat. Dem. campaign coordinator Kennedy for Pres., 1960; past pres. Nat. Capitol Dem. Club: regional campaign mgr. Johnson- Humphrey Campaign, 1964. Served to 2d lt. USAAF, 1943-45. Mem. S.C. Soc. in Washington (past pres.). Democrat. Episcopalian (vestry). Home: 1313 Bishop Lane Alexandria VA 22302 Office: Genesco Inc 1700 Pennsylvania Av Washington DC 20006

BRAWNER, ALEXANDER HARRISON, Jr., banker; b. San Francisco, May 30, 1923; s. Alexander Harrison and Virginia (Lowry) B.; B.A., Princeton, 1947; m. Ann Lowry, June 26, 1948; children—William Harrison, Brandon Lowry, James Coleman, Caroline Ann. With W.P. Fuller & Co., San Francisco, 1947-61, factory rep., Honolulu, 1951-53, internat. mgr., San Francisco, 1953-61; mng. dir. Fuller & Co. S.A., Lausanne, Switzerland, 1961-63; joined Bank Am. N.T. & S.A., 1963, head North Am. div.-Internat. Banking, 1965-70, exec. v.p., chief exec. officer Bank of Am., N.Y.C., 1970—, also dir.; dir. Bamerical Internat. Financial Corp., San Francisco, Investor's Group, Winnipeg, Man., Can., World Banking Corp., Nassau, Bahamas, Corporacion Financiera, Mexico, Arrendadora Comermex, Mexico. Bd. dirs. Internat. Hospitality Center, 1966-69. Trustee Menlo Sch. and Coll. Served with USAAF, 1942-45. Mem. Bankers Assn. Fgn. Trade U.S.-Can. Com. U.S. C. of C. Republican. Episcopalian (vestryman). Clubs: Pacific Union (San Francisco); Burlingame Country (Hillsborough, Cal.); Menlo Circus (Atherton, Cal.), Apawamis (Rye, N.Y.). Home: 5 Chester Dr New York City NY 10580 Office: 41 Broad St New York City NY 10004

BRAWNER, JAMES PAUL, educator; b. Magazine, Ark., Aug. 10, 1902; s. Robert L. and Eva Mae (Thomason) B.; A.B., Washington and Lee U., 1924, A.M., 1925; Ph.D., U. Ill., 1935; m. Kirby Lee Smith, June 21, 1925. Faculty Ark. State Tchrs. Coll., 1925-29; asst., instr. U. Ill., 1929-35; faculty W.Va. U., 1935—, asst. prof. English, 1936-45, asso. prof., 1945-52, chmn. dept., 1949-67, prof. 1952—. Vis. prof. U. Ark., Eastern Mich. State U., Ypsilanti, faculty U. Tng. Center, Florence, Italy, 1945. U.S. cons. Office Edn., Dept. Health, Edn. and Welfare, 1966. Mem. Internat. Assn. U. Profs. English. Modern Lang. Assn., Am. Assn. U. Profs. Nat. Council Tchrs. English, Phi Beta Kappa (nat. council, pres. South Atlantic dist. 1967-70), Phi Kappa Phi, Sigma Upsilon. Author: The Wars of Cyrus, 1942. Author articles on English drama, Am. writers. Home: 311 Laurel St Morgantown WV 26505

BRAWNER, R. BRYAN, church ofcl.; b. Pollard, Ark., Oct. 14, 1907; s. Robert Lee and Mary Florence (Renfro) B.; B.S.E., Ark. State Coll., 1928; M.S.Ed., U. Ark., 1933; LL.B. (hon.), Hendrix Coll., Conway Ark., 1969; m. Eva Chastain, Nov. 16, 1929; 1 dau., Elizabeth Ann. Prin. elementary and high schs., Texarkana, Ark., 1928-38; prin., supt. schs., N. Little Rock, Ark., 1938-51; exec. dir. Highland Park Methodist Ch., Dallas, 1951-68; gen. sec. and treas. council world service and finance United Meth. Ch., 1968—. Chmn. ofcl. bd. 1st Meth. Ch., N. Little Rock 1947-49, trustee 1945-51; chmn. bldg. commn. Ark. Edn. Assn., 1950-51; treas. Highland Park Meth. Ch., 1952-68 exec. dir. master plan study for Dallas ch. Found., 1952, 62-64; organizer, 1st pres. Nat. Assn. Ch. Bus. Adminstrs., 1957; chmn. Dallas dist. Bd. Ch. Extension, 1962-64; mem. N. Tex. Conf. Commn. on World Service and Finance, 1961; mem. finance com. S. Central Jurisdiction, 1964; mem. Council World Service and Finance, 1964-68; chmn. bd. Soc. Religious Orgn. Mgmt., 1969—; mem. bd. Nat. Council Chs., 1969—; trustee United Meth. Ch., 1969—. Sustentation fund mem. So. Meth. U. Named Little Rockian of Year, 1950; recipient Circuit Rider award Greater Dallas Bd. Ch. Extension, 1968; 1st recipient Distinguished Service award in Ch. mgmt. Am. U., 1967 Life mem. Ark. Edn. Assn. (past v.p., pres. elect). Lions Clubs: Union League (Chgo.); University (Evanston). Home: 1550 Asbury Av Evanston IL 60201 Office: 1200 Davis St Evanston IL 60201

BRAXTAN, JOHN THOMAS, mfg. co. exec.; b. Baker, Ore., Sept. 23, 1910; s. Thomas Newby and Mary Ellen (Stout) B.; B.S., Harvard, 1932, M.B.A., 1934; m. Lorraine Wardlaw Thorn, Aug. 24, 1945; children—Thomas Newby III, Sharon Elizabeth. With Bemis Co. Inc., 1934—, mgr. planning, asst. comptroller-sec., 1956-62, sec., 1962—. Served to lt. comdr. USNR, 1942-46. Club: Minneapolis Athletic. Home: 5004 Bruce St Edina, MN 55424. Office: 800 Northstar Center MN 55404

BRAXTON, WILBERT LEO, headmaster; b. Snow Camp, N.C., Apr. 22, 1911; s. John H. and Elvira (Newlin) B.; B.S., Guilford Coll., 1932; M.A., Haverford Coll., 1933; student Stanford, 1942-44, Union Coll., Schenectady, summer 1955, Bryn Mawr Coll., 1959, U. Pa., summer 1960; m. Nina Piper, June 1, 1938; children—Lowell, Nancy (Mrs. George Eager), Jane (Mrs. Jon Little), John. Tchr., Kernersville (N.C.) High Sch., 1933-35, Ramallah Friends Sch., Palestine, 1935-36; tchr. Friends Boarding Sch., Barnesville, O., 1936-42, prin., 1944-47; instr. physics Stanford, 1942-44; nat. high sch. dir. Am. Friends Service Com., 1957-58; mem. faculty William Penn Charter Sch., Phila., 1947—, headmaster, 1968—. Mem. bd., treas. Upper Gwynedd Township Sch.; mem. Phila. Sci. Council, 1948—. Bd. dirs. Am. Friends Service Com., 1966—. Mem. Phila. Sci. Tchrs. Assn. (pres. 1961-62). Mem. Soc. of Friends (clk. 1961-65). Home: 154 E Hancock Rd North Wales PA 19454 Office: 3000 W School House Lane Philadelphia PA 19144

BRAY, CHARLES COLLINS, Jr., clergyman; b. Hinsdale, Ill., Feb. 13, 1928; s. Charles Collins and Celia Jessie (Pickell) B.; B.A., Yale, 1950; B.D., Princeton Theol. Sem., 1957; m. Nancy Eldridge, Sept. 16, 1950; children—Karen Lane, Charles Collins III, Betsy Charnan, Wendy Lynne. Owner, Bray Store Equipment Co., Camden, N.J., 1953-56; ordained to ministry Presbyn. Ch., 1957; minister, Joliet, Ill., 1957-59, Upper Darby, Pa., 1959-64, 3d Presbyn. Ch., Pitts., 1964—. Teaching fellow Princeton Theol. Sem., 1957; tchr. Young Pastors Sch., 1965-66; spl. preaching mission to Alaska, 1961; speaker Chgo. Sunday Eve. Club, 1965. Pres. Presbyn. Inter-racial Council, Phila., 1964. Trustee Presbytery of Phila.; bd. dirs. Pitts. Theol. Sem., Westminister Found. Recipient award preaching excellence Princeton Theol. Sem., 1957. Mem. Am. Engring. Soc., Chi Phi, Omicron Delta Kappa. Republican. Home: 501 Edgerton Pl Pittsburgh, PA 15208. Office: Third Presbyn Ch 5th and S Negley Av Pittsburgh PA 15232

BRAY, DALE FRANK, educator; b. Paw Paw, Mich., Mar. 2, 1922; s. Starr David and Florence Ann (Kelly) B.; student Western Mich. Coll. Edn., 1939-40; B.S., Mich. State U., 1947, M.S., 1949; Ph.D. in Entomology, Rutgers U., 1954; m. Polly Jane Moehlman, June 15, 1947; children—Jane (Mrs. Howard Pyle Robinson), James Dale. Instr. U. Del., Newark, 1949-50, asst. prof., 1950-55, prof., chmn. dept. entomology and applied ecology, 1958—; asso. entomologist Bartlett Tree Research Labs., Stamford, Conn., 1955-58. Served with AUS, 1943-45. Mem. Entomol. Soc. Am., A.A.A.S., Sigma Xi, Phi Kappa Phi, Xi Sigma Pi, Epsilon Sigma Phi, Phi Chi Omega. Democrat. Presbyn. Mason. Home: 91 Ritter Lane Newark DE 19711

BRAY, G.M., business exec.; b. Eng., 1928. Pres., Courtaulds N.Am., Inc., N.Y.C. Home: 2855 Normandy Dr NW Atlanta GA 30305 Office: PO Box 2648 Mobile AL 36601*

BRAY, JOHN RANDOLPH, motion picture producer; b. Addison, Mich., Aug. 25, 1879; s. Rev. Edward A. and Sarah Priscilla (Haire) B.; student Alma (Mich.) Coll., 1895-96; m. Margaret Till, Aug. 25, 1905; 1 son, Paul A. Artist Detroit Evening News, 1901, Bklyn. Daily Eagle, 1903-04; contbr. cartoons to Life, Puck, Judge, McClure Newspaper Syndicate European humorous mags., 1905-13; invented and developed animated motion picture cartoon processes; introduced first animated cartoon in theatres, 1912; patented processes by which animated cartoons are made; organized Bray-Hurd Process Co., 1914, to issue licenses under these patents; put into this co. his three basic patents, and one patent by Earl Hurd covering an improvement; organized chmn. bd. Bray Studios Inc., 1914, to produce animated cartoons in quantity; developed and also introduced animated technical drawing, 1916. During World War I, pioneered use motion pictures to expedite tng. of draft army; made over 100 tng. films for same; have continued prodn. for Navy and Air Force since. Producer tng., ednl., comml. and documentary films. Recipient citation for patriotic civilian service to Dept. of Army, 1956, citation as animation pioneer World Retrospective on Animation, 1967. Republican. Home: 3030 Park Av Bridgeport CT 06604 Office: 630 9th Av New York City NY 10036

BRAY, LESLIE WILLIAM, air force officer; b. Wichita Falls, Tex., May 28, 1921; s. Leslie W. and Elizabeth (Morris) B.; student Arlington (Tex.) State U., 1940-41; B.S., U. Md., 1958; grad. Flying Sch., Foster Field, Tex., 1942, Air War Coll., 1959; m. Marie Harrison, Apr. 17, 1943; children—Julie, Casey. Commd. 2d lt. USAF, 1942, advanced through grades to maj. gen., 1970; assigned to 10th Troop Carrier Group, Fla. and Miss., 1942-44, 4th Combat Cargo Group, CBI, 1945, Troop Carrier Command, N.C. and Tex., 1946-47; various positions SAC, 1947-54, HQ USAF, 1954-58; overseas assignments, 1959-63; various plans and operations orgns. HQ USAF, Washington, 1963-70, dir. doctrine, concepts and objectives DCS/Plans and Operations, 1970—. Decorated Legion of Merit, Air medal with oak leaf cluster, Air Force Commendation medal with oak leaf cluster, Army Commendation medal. Home: 3660 Tallwood Terrace Falls Church VA 22041 Office: HQ USAF (AF/XOD) Washington DC 20330

BRAY, OSCAR S., cons. engr.; b. Dover, N.J., Dec. 21, 1905; s. Oscar S. and Bertha (Janner) B.; B.C.E., U. Cin., 1932; m. Helen L. Shanley, Jan. 11, 1933; children—Helen Margaret (Mrs. William Allen Jeffers Jr.), Mary Elizabeth (Mrs. Edward Peters Womack). Surveyman, D.L. & W. RR, Hoboken, N.J., 1923-27; constrn. supt. Nat. Park Service, Cold Springs, N.Y., 1934-35, field engr., Boston and Salem, Mass., 1936-38, engr., Washington, 1939-40; structural engr., asst. chief structural engr., project mgr. Jackson & Moreland, Boston, 1941-58, pres., chief engr., 1959-68; pres., chief engr. Bray, Backenstoss, Inc. Ltd., Lynnfield, Mass., 1969—; lectr. Northeastern U.; guest lectr. U. Ill. Mem. Lynnfield Planning Bd., 1968—, chmn., 1970. Served with AUS, 1933. Fellow Am. Soc. C.E. (dir. 1964-66 pres. elect 1970-71), Am. Inst. Cons. Engrs., Vt. Soc. Engrs., Tau Beta Pi, Sigma Alpha Epsilon. Republican. Presbyn. Home: 18 Lakeview Dr Lynnfield MA 01940 Office: PO Box 907 Lynnfield MA 01940

BRAY, RICHARD MARVIN, ret. univ. dean; b. Redvale, Colo., June 12, 1915; s. Edgar W. and Mattie Kate (Ensign) B.; B.A., U. Colo., 1938, M.A., 1939; m. Mayfield Sleeth, Oct. 15, 1938; children—Michael Edgar, Mayfield Ruth, Martha Alaetha. Dir. Denver Extension Center, U. Colo., 1939-47, Spokane Center State Coll. of Wash., 1947-54; faculty Am. U., 1954-70, prof. govt., 1958-70, asso. dean faculty, 1957-70, dean Coll. of Continuing Edn., 1964-70. Chmn. organizing com. Washington Center for Met. Studies, 1956-58; supr. Adams- Morgan Demonstration Project, prevention urban blight, 1958-60; chmn. com. on univ. ednl. policy, 1962-63; mem com. of 100 for Federal City, chmn. subcoms. on parks and conservation; chmn. Citizens Council for a Clean Potomac, 1956-58; pres. Adult Edn. Assn. Greater Washington, 1956. Bd. dirs., exec. com. Nat. Inst. Labor Edn. Mem. Assn. U. Evening Colls., Adult Edn. Assn. U.S., Lambda Alpha, Pi Sigma Alpha, Phi Alpha Theta. Democrat. Conglist. Home: 6310 Owen Pl Bethesda MD 20014

BRAY, ROBERT STUART, librarian; b. Cin., Sept. 9, 1915; s. Charles Ayers and Helen Mar (Pollock) B.; B.S., George Washington U., 1941; postgrad. library service Catholic U. Am., 1947-50; m. Virginia Elizabeth Ballard, Oct. 2, 1937; children—Robert Stuart, James Sargent, Paul Charles, Philip Austin. Page, D.C. Library, 1935-40; mem. staff Library of Congress, 1940-44, 46- -, chief div. blind and physically handicapped, 1957—. Mem. adv. bd. Rec. for Blind; chmn. service adv. creditation Council Agys. Serving Blind and Visually Handicapped; chmn. library com. President's Com. Employment Handicapped. Served to lt. (j.g.) USNR, 1944-46. Recipient Migel medal Am. Found. Blind, 1963; Apollo award Am. Optometric Assn., 1968; Francis Joseph Campbell award, 1968. Mem. Assn. Hosp. and Instn. Libraries (pres. 1968), Adult Edn. Assn., Am. Pub. Health Assn., Council Exceptional Children, A.L.A., Nat. Assn. Physically Handicapped, Nat. Braille Assn., Nat. Rehab. Assn., Nat. Soc. Prevention Blindness, Am. Assn. Workers Blind, Am. Assn. Instrs. Blind. Assn. Edn. of Visually Handicapped. Democrat. Episcopalian. Home: 910 Seneca Rd Herndon, VA 22070. Office: 1291 Taylor St NW Washington DC 20542

BRAY, WILLIAM GILMER, congressman; b. Morresville, Ind., June 17, 1903; s. Gilmer and Dorcas M. (Mitchell) B.; LL.B., Ind. U., 1927; LL.D., Vincennes U., m. Esther F. Debra, Aug. 16, 1930; 1 son, Richard D. Admitted to Ind. bar, 1927; pros. atty. 15th Ind. Judicial Dist., Martinsville, 1926-30; pvt. law practice, Martinsville, 1930-41, 46-51; mem. 82d to 92d congresses from 7th, later 6th Ind. Dist. Served from capt. to col., AUS, 1941-46; P.T.O. Decorated Silver Star. Mem. V.F.W., Am. Legion, Tau Kappa Alpha, Acacia. Republican. Mason (33, Shriner), Moose, Kiwanian, Elk, Eagle. Clubs: Columbia; Army-Navy, Capitol Hill (Washington). Author: Russian Frontiers, Muscovy to Khrushchev. Home: 489 N Jefferson St Martinsville IN 46151 Office: House Office Bldg Washington DC 20515

BRAYMAN, HAROLD, pub. relations cons., b. Middleburgh, N.Y., Mar. 10, 1900; s. Channing and Minnie C. (Feeck) B.; A.B., Cornell U., 1920; LL.D., Gettysburg Coll., 1965; m. Martha Witherspoon Wood, Jan. 25, 1930; children—Harold Halliday, Walter Witherspoon. Tchr. English and history Ft. Lee (N.J.) High Sch., 1920-22; reporter Albany (N.Y.) Evening Jour., 1922-24; asst. legislative corr. N.Y. Evening Post, 1924-26, corr., 1926-1928, Washington corr., 1928-33; Washington corr. Phila. Evening Ledger, writer syndicated column, Daily Mirror of Washington, 1934-40; Washington corr. Houston Chronicle and other newspapers, 1940-42; accompanied Alfred E. Smith through 1928 campaign and F.D. Roosevelt through 1932 campaign for N.Y. Evening Post, Phila. Public Ledger and Phila. Evening Ledger; spl. corr. in London, 1925; covered all nat. convs. and nat. polit. campaigns, 1928-40; asst. dir., public relations dept. E.I. du Pont de Nemours & Co., 1942-44, dir., 1944-65; corporate exec. in residence Am. U., 1968. Dir. Nat. Press Bldg. Corp., Continental Am. Life Ins. Co. Bd. visitors sch. pub. relations and communications Boston U., 1951—, chmn., 1961—. Dir. Greater Wilmington Devel. Council; Cornell U. Council, chmn., 1961-63; mem. Cornell Centennial planning com., also chmn. adv. council grad. sch. bus. and pub. adminstrn., 1960-65; adv. council Sch. Bus., Rider Coll. Trustee, Gettysburg Coll., Found. for Pub. Relations Research and Edn., 1956-62, Wilmington Med. Center. Mem. sponsoring com. Pub. Relations Seminar, 1952-61. Recipient citation Pub. Relations Soc. Am., 1963; Golden Plate award Am. Acad. Achievement, 1965. Mem. U.S. C. of C. (com. on taxation 1954-60, com. on govt. operations and expenditures 1964-66), Am. Acad. Achievement (v.p. 1966-70, gov.), Mfg. Chemists Assn. (pub. relations adv. com. 1951-56, chmn. 1951-53). Rotarian. Clubs: University, Cornell (N.Y.C.); Gridiron (pres. 1941), Nat. Press (pres. 1938), Overseas Writers (Washington); Wilmington, Du Pont Country, Wilmington Country (dir.) (Wilmington, Del.). Editor Pub. Relations Jour, 1956. Author: Corporate Management in a World of Politics, 1967; Developing a Philosophy for Business Action, 1969; (with A.O.H. Grier) A History of the Lincoln Club of Delaware, 1970. Home: Greenville Wilmington, DE 19807. Office: Wilmington Trust Bldg Wilmington DE 19801

BRAYMER, MARJORIE ELIZABETH, former educator, editor, author; b. Chgo., Mar. 21, 1911; d. Ernest Story and Luella (Lively) Braymer; B.S. in Edn. with distinction, Ohio State U., 1943; M.A., (Morris fellow) Columbia Tchrs. Coll., 1944; postgrad. Stanford, 1960-61. Manuscript reader N.Y.C. studios motion picture cos., also editorial work for books and mags., 1930-40; tchr. history and English, Sequoia High Sch., Redwood City, Cal., 1945-66; editor Harcourt, Brace & World, Inc. (formerly Harcourt, Brace & Co.), 1953-65, Addison-Wesley Pub. Co., Inc., 1965-67. Recipient Scholastic mag. poetry prize, 1929, Vandewater poetry prize Ohio State U., 1943, Newsmaker of Month award Redwood City C. of C., 1960. Mem. Nat. Ret. Tchrs. Assn., Nat. Conf. Tchrs. English, Archaeol. Inst. Am., Pi Lambda Theta. Conglist. Author: The Walls of Windy Troy (biography of Heinrich Schliemann) (N.Y. Herald Tribune Spring Book Festival award 1960), 1960. Editor: (with Evan Lodge) Olympic edit. Adventurers in Reading, 1957, Laureate edit., 1963. Contbr. articles to profl. jours. Address: 587 Greer Rd Palo Alto CA 94303

BRAZEAL, BRALLSFORD REESE, educator, economist; b. Dublin, Ga., Mar. 8, 1905; s. Reese and Love (Troup) B.; A.B. with honors, Morehouse Coll., 1927; M.A., Columbia, 1928, Ph.D., 1942; m. Ernestine Vivian Erskine, Aug. 2, 1934; children—Ernestine Walton, Aurelia Erskine. Instr. econs. Morehouse Coll., 1928-34, chmn. dept. econs., dean men, 1934-46, acad. dean, prof. econs., 1946—; dir. Mut. Fed. Savs. & Loan Assn. of Atlanta; former mem. adv. committee Center for the Study of Liberal Edn. for Adults; mem. exec. council Highlander Research and Edn. Center. Mem. Fulton Co. Commn. Employment Opportunity, nat. council community services to internat. visitors U.S. Dept. State; exec. com. Project Opportunity, So. Assn. Colls. and Univs.; dir., chmn. social sci. selection com. & So. Fellowships Funds. Social Sci. Research Council fellow, 1932-33,

Rosenwald Fund fellow, 1938-39, 46; Hazen Found. asso., 1940-45; recipient European study-travel grant, 1955. Mem. Nat. Assn. Collegiate Deans and Registrars (pres. 1947-48), Assn. Am. Bapt. Ednl. Instns. (v.p. 1954-56), Am. Conf. Acad. Deans (mem. exec. com.), Assn. Colls. and Secondary Schs. (chmn. commn. on colls. and univs. 1956, pres. 1957), Morehouse Nat. Alumni Assn. (chmn. exec. com.). Am. Economics Assn., Am. Acad. Polit. and Social Sci., So. Sociol. Soc., Am. Civil Liberties Union (adv. council academic freedom), N.A.A.C.P. Nat. Council Chs. (com. on labor mgmt.) Conf. Academic Deans Southern States, Southern Regional Council (dir.), Phi Beta Kappa. Omega Psi Phi, Sigma Pi Phi, Delta Sigma Rho. Democrat. Baptist. Author: The Brotherhood of Sleeping Car Porters: Its Origin and Development, 1946. Author chpt. Desegregation and the Negro College (Yearbook Jour. Negro Edn., 1958; Studies of Negro Voting in Eight Rural Counties of Georgia and one of South Carolina, 1960. Home: 193 Ashby St SW Atlanta GA 30303

BRAZELL, REID, petroleum co. exec.; b. Lamont, Okla., July 17, 1905; s. Edmund and Pearl (Tebow) B.; A.B., U. Okla., 1927; LL.D., Alma Coll., 1968; m. Ruby Hines, July 8, 1929; 1 son, James Reid. Asst. supt. Continental Oil Co., Artesia, N.M., 1927-30; gen. mgr. Allegheny-Arrow Oil Co., Canton, O., 1930-36; refining supt. Leonard Refineries, Inc., Alma, Mich., 1936, v.p., gen. mgr., dir., 1937, pres., dir., 1942-70, chmn. bd., chief exec. officer, 1970—; chmn. bd., chief exec. officer Total Petroleum (N.Am.) Ltd., Calgary, Alta., Can., 1970—; dir. Bank of Alma; former pub. interest dir. Fed. Home Loan Bank Indpls. Dir. 5th World Petroleum Congress, mem. Com. on Michigan's Econ. Future, Sci. Adv. Bd.; Mich. indsl. ambassador, chmn. petroleum industries coms., Dist. 2, World War II; dir. refining Petroleum Adminstrn. for Def., 1951; mem. Mil. Petroleum Adv. Bd., Nat. Petroleum Council. Trustee Citizens Research Council of Mich.; past chmn. bd. trustees Alma College; mem. indsl. com. U. Mich. Engrng. Labs. Mem. Am. Petroleum Inst. (dir.), Nat. Petroleum Assn. (trustee), Nat. Petroleum Refiners Assn. (past pres.), Am. Acad. Transp. (trustee), Western Petroleum Refiners Assn. (pres. 1955-57), Alpha Chi Sigma. Mason (32), Elk. Clubs: Detroit Athletic, Pine River Country (Alma); Crystal Downs Country (Frankfort, Mich.). Home: 7 Crystal Downs Frankfort MI 49635 Office: E Superior St Alma MI 48801

BRAZELTON, THOMAS BERRY, physician; b. Waco, Tex., May 10, 1918; s. Thomas Berry and Pauline (Battle) B.; A.B., Princeton, 1940; M.D., Columbia Coll. Phys. & Surg., 1943; m. Christina Lowell, Dec. 3, 1949; children—Catherine Bowles, Pauline Battle, Christina Lowell, Thomas Berry III. Intern Roosevelt Hosp., N.Y.C., 1944; resident Mass. Gen. Hosp., Boston, 1945-47, Children's Hosp., Boston, 1947; resident child psychiatry Putnam Children's Center, Roxbury, Mass., 1947-50; practice medicine, specializing in pediatrics, Cambridge, Mass., 1950—; instr. pediatrics Harvard Med. Sch., 1951—, also Mass. Gen. and Children's Hosp.; researcher in child devel. Putnam Children's Center, also Center for Cognitive Studies, Harvard, 1968—; sch. physician, Shady Hill Sch., 1966—, Cambridge Nursery Sch., 1967—. Served with USNR, 1944-45. Clubs: Badminton & Tennis (Cambridge); Barnstable (Mass.) Yacht. Author: Infants and Mothers Individual Differences in Development, 1969 (Child Study Assn. annual award 1970); contbr. articles to Redbook mag., profl. jours. Home: 23 Hawthorn St Cambridge MA 02138

BRAZELTON, WILLIAM THOMAS, engring, educator; b. Danville, Ill., Jan. 22, 1921; s. Edwin Thomas and Gertrude Ann (Carson) B.; student Ill. Inst. Tech., 1939-41; B.S. in Chem. Engrng., Northwestern U., 1943, M.S., 1948, Ph.D., 1952; m. Marilyn Dorothy Brown, Sept. 23, 1943; children—William Thomas, Nancy Ann. Chem. engr. Central Process Corp., 1942-43; instr. chem. engrng. Northwestern U., 1947-51, asst. prof., 1951-53, asso. prof., 1953-63, prof., 1963—, chmn. dept., 1955-56, asst. dean Technol. Inst., 1960-61, asso. dean, 1961—. Engrng. and ednl. cons., 1949—. Mem. Prospect Heights (Ill.) Bd. Edn., 1957-61. Mem. Am. Inst. Chem. Engrs. (chmn. Chgo. sect. 1966-67), Am. Chem. Soc., Am. Soc. Engrng. Edn. (chmn. Ill.-Ind. sect. 1963-64), Sigma Xi, Tau Beta Pi, Phi Lambda Epsilon, Alpha Chi Sigma, Triangle. Home: 10 E Willow Rd Prospect Heights, IL 60070. Office: Technol Inst Northwestern U Evanston IL 60201

BRAZIER, MARY A. B., neurophysiologist; b. Eng.; B.Sc., Ph.D., D. Sc., U. London; 1 son, Oliver G. Prof. anatomy and physiology Brain Research Inst., U. Cal. at Los Angeles. Fellow Am. Acad. Arts and Scis.; mem. Am. Physiol. Soc., Am. (past pres.), English electroencephalographic socs., Am. Neurol. Assn., Am. Acad. Neurology, Am. Assn. Anatomy, Internat. Fedn. of Electroencephalographic Socs. (hon. pres.), affiliate Royal Soc. Medicine (London). Author: Electrical Activity of the Nervous System; A History of the Electrical Activity of the Brain. Mem. editorial bd. Jour. Electroencephalography and Clin. Neurophysiology, Jour. History Behavioral Scis. Contbr. articles to profl. jours. Address: Brain Research Inst U Cal Los Angeles CA 90024

BRAZZEL, JAMES ROLAND, educator; b. Hico, La., May 2, 1921; s. Lee and Benson (Campbell) B.; B.S., La. State U., 1951, M.S., 1953; Ph.D., Tex. A. & M. Coll., 1956; m. Allie B. Fowler, Jan. 28, 1941; 1 dau., Carolyn Ann. Research asso. La. State U., 1953, asst. prof., 1955-57; asso. prof. dept. entomology Tex. A. & M. Coll., 1957-60, prof., 1961-62; prof., head dept. entomology Miss. State U., 1963-68; chief staff officer Plant Pest Control div. ARS, U.S. Dept. Agr., 1968—. Served with AUS, 1942-45; with USAF, 1946-50. Mem. Entomol. Soc. Am., Am. Inst. Biol. Scis., Sigma Xi. Contbr. articles field cotton insects to profl. jours. Home: 10801 Ashfield Rd Adelphi MD 20705 Office: Consumer and Marketing Service Independence and 14th Sts Washington DC 20250

BRCIN, JOHN DAVID, sculptor; b. Gracac, Yugoslavia, Aug. 15, 1899; s. David and Milica (Kesich) B.; pres. edn., gymnasium, Gracac; came to U.S., 1913; student Valparaiso U., 1916-17; B.F.A., Art Inst., Chgo., 1946; M.A., Ohio State U., 1930; m. Blanche Elizabeth Moore, June 14, 1923. Instr. modeling and drawing Mpls. Sch. Art, 1922-23; head of sculpture dept. Layton Sch. Art, Milw., 1923-24; instr. modeling Rockford (Ill.) Coll., 1934-36. Prin. works: Mark Twain (owned by City of Chgo.); Caroline (owned by Witte Meml. Mus., San Antonio); portrait bust of Judge Elbert H. Gary for Gary Commercial Club; meml. tablet to Newton, Mann, 1st Unitarian Ch. of Omaha; Rudulph Hering Medal for Am. Soc. C.E.; meml. tablet to Benjamin Franklin Lounsbury, Washington Blvd. Hosp., Chgo.; sculpture for Joslyn Meml. Art Mus., Omaha, (home of Symphony Orch. of Omaha); monument to Cyrus Hall McCormick, campus of Washington and Lee U.; monument to Gov. Henry Horner, Grant Park, Chgo.; Stephen Decatur Monument for Decatur, Ill., heroic portrait bust of Stephen Decatur for U.S. Naval Acad., Annapolis; bust of Mark Twain for North Central Coll., Naperville, Ill.; exhibited at N.A.D., Pa. Acad. Fine Arts, Art Inst. Chgo., Detroit Inst. Arts, Mus. Fine Arts, Houston, Cal. Palace of Legion of Honor, Bklyn. Mus., Albright Art Gallery, Buffalo, Dayton Art Inst., White Meml. Mus., San Antonio, John Herron Art Inst., Indpls., Milw. Art Inst.; represented in permanent collections U. Ill., Roosevelt U., Pioneer Mus. Art, Stockton, Cal., Evansville (Ind.) Mus. Arts, various pub. schs. Bryan Lathrop European traveling fellow Art Inst., Chgo., 1920, certificate of merit, 1922, Mrs. John C. Shaffer prize, 1923, William M. R. French meml. gold medal, 1926 Municipal Art League portrait prize, 1945; Catherine Barker Spaulding prize, Hoosier Salon, Hickox prize, 1936; Mem. Nat. Sculpture Soc. Club: Cliff Dwellers. Author: The Sculpture of John David Brcin, 1967. Address: 4 East Ohio St Chicago IL 60611

BREAK, GEORGE FARRINGTON, economist, educator; b. London, Ont., Can., June 10, 1920; s. Thomas Howard and Florence (Farrington) B.; B. Commerce, U. Toronto, 1942; Ph.D., U. Cal. at Berkeley, 1951; m. Helen Dean Schnacke, July 31, 1948. Came to U.S., 1945, naturalized, 1951. Instr. Pomona Coll., Claremont, Cal., 1949-51; faculty U. Cal. at Berkeley, 1951—, prof. econs., 1963—, chmn. dept., 1969—. Mem. sr. staff Brookings Instn., 1962—, cons. to govt., 1963—. Served with RCAF, 1942-45. Author: Intergovernmental Fiscal Relations in the United States, 1967; The Economic Impact of Federal Loan Insurance, 1961; (with E.R. Rolph) Public Finance, 1961; Federal Lending and Economic Stability, 1965; Agenda for Local Tax Reform, 1970. Home: 1844 Yosemite Rd Berkeley, CA 94707.

BREAM, HERBERT, editor, author; b. Detroit, Dec. 10, 1907; s. Walter Joseph and Eva R. (Dumas) B.; A.B., U. Mich., 1929; m. Dorothy Skeman, Oct. 6, 1934; children—Judith Ann, Martha Elizabeth. Reporter, asst. bur. mgr. U.P.I. Assns., N.Y.C., Detroit; reporter, columnist, feature writer, asst. city editor, picture editor Detroit Times, 1933-43; news bur. chief, Detroit, for Time, Life, Fortune mags., 1943-44, asso. editor Life mag., N.Y.C., 1944, asst. editor nat. affairs, 1953—, staff writer, 1953-62. Lectr. mystery writing Columbia, N.Y. U.; cons. Gen. Motors Corp., 1966. Fellow Internat. Inst. Arts and Letters; mem. Baker St. Irregulars, Mystery Writers Am. (nat. pres.), Crime Writers Assn., Authors League N.Y. Clubs: Players (N.Y.C.); Scarsdale Golf. Author: Wilders Walk Away, 1948; The Darker the Night, 1949; Hardly a Man is Now Alive, 1950; How to Stop Smoking, 1951; The Clock Strikes Thirteen, 1952; A Matter of Fact, 1956. Editor: The Mystery Writer's Handbook, 1956; The Traces of Brillhart, 1959; The Life Treasury of American Folklore, 1961; The Music of Life, 1962; The Only Diet That Works, 1963; The Traces of Merrilee, 1966. Contbr. fiction to mags., articles to profl. publs. Home: 500 E 77th St New York City, NY 10021; also 9-39 Vessup Bay Saint Thomas VI 00801

BREAM, JULIAN, guitarist; b. London, Eng., July 15, 1933; s. Henry G. Bream; ed. Royal Coll. Music. First recital, 1946; London debut, 1950, U.S. debut, 1958; concerts in Continental Europe; frequent radio, TV appearances; recording artist for RCA Victor, including Malcolm Arnold's Guitar Concerto written for Bream. Decorated Order Brit. Empire. Research in Elizabethan lute music. Address: care Basil Douglas Ltd 8 St George's Terrace London NW1 England*

BREATHITT, EDWARD THOMPSON, ex-gov. Ky.; b. Hopkinsville, Ky., Nov. 26, 1924; s. E.T. and Mary Jo (Wallace) B.; B.S., U. Ky., 1948, LL.B., 1950; m. Frances Holleman, Dec. 20, 1948; children—Mary Fran, Linda, Susan, Edward Thompson III. Admitted to Ky. bar, 1950; mem. firm Trimble, Soyars & Breathitt, Hopkinsville, 1952-63; gov. Ky., 1963-67. Mem. Ky. Ho. of Reps. from Christian County, 1952- 58; personnel commnr. State of Ky., 1959-60. Chmn., Inst. Rural Am.; fed. rep. So. Interstate Nuclear Bd.; mem. Gov. Ky. Commn. Mental Health, 1955-59, Ky. Pub. Service Commn., 1961-62; state chmn. Heart Fund Drive, 1969-70. Pres., Ky. Young Democratic Clubs, 1952. Served with USAAF, 1942-45. Mem. Ky. Jr. C. of C., Omicron Delta Kappa, Sigma Alpha Epsilon. Office: Planters Bank Bldg Hopkinsville KY 44240

BREAZEALE, HOPKINS PAYNE, lawyer; b. Natchitoches, La., Oct. 16, 1886; s. Hopkins Payne and Cammila (Lachs) B.; A.B., La. Northeastern Coll., 1905; LL.B., Yale, 1910; m. Nita Sims, Nov. 22, 1916; children—Hopkins Payne, Nita Sims (Mrs. Maurice J. Wilson), Robert P. Sch. tchr., 1905-07; admitted to La. bar, 1911, since practiced in Baton Rouge; senior mem. Breazeale, Sachse & Wilson; U.S. referee in bankruptcy, 1919-45; city atty., Baton Rouge, 1924-45; dir., atty. Fidelity Nat. Bank; mem. Jud. Council 5th Circuit Ct. of Appeals 1945—. Mem. exec. com. Baton Rouge Community Chest and United Givers, Pub. Affairs Research Council La.; dir. La. Heart Assn., Inc. Mem., sec. bd. appeals SSS No. 2, 1940- 47. Served as capt. 358th inf. 90th Div., A.U.S., World War I; officer in charge Civil Affairs Pelm, Germany, 1918; participated in Preny, St. Mehielf, St. Mihiel, Meuse Argonne offensives. Decorated For Gallantry in Action. Mem. Am., Baton Rouge (pres. 1935-36), La. State (pres. 1931- 32) bar assns., Nat. Assn. of Rr. Trial Counsel, Am. Judicature Soc., Am. Legion (charter mem. Nicholson post; dept. judge adv. La. dept.), Baton Rouge C. of C. (past pres.), La. Golf Assn. (past pres.), Am. Counsel Assn., Baton Rouge Community Concerts. Baton Rouge Symphony Soc., Newcomen Soc., Selden Soc., U.S. C. of C. (counsellor 1940-49), La. Law Inst., Phi Delta Pi. Episcopalian (vestryman). Mason, Elk (past exalted ruler). Clubs: Baton Rouge Country (past pres.), City (Baton Rouge); Boston, Avoca (New Orleans). Author: Revenue Laws of Louisiana (with Porter), 1912; History-358th Combat Infantry, 90th Division, World War I. Home: 2255 Oleander St Baton Rouge LA 70806 Office: Fidelity Nat Bank Bldg Baton Rouge LA 70101

BREAZEALE, JAMES LLOYD, II, banker; b. Meridian, Miss., Feb. 1, 1935; s. James Lloyd and Charlene (Hewlett) B.; B.A., Southwestern at Memphis, 1959; m. Peggy Wilkes, Apr. 22, 1962; children—Synthia Allison, James Lloyd. With Nat. Bank Commerce, Memphis, 1965—, cashier, 1969—. Served with USAF, 1959-65. Presbyn. Club: Memphis Exchange. Home: 4852 Boeingshire St Memphis TN 38116 Office: 45 South St Memphis TN 38101

BREAZEALE, JOHN BALLARD, physicist, educator; b. Brandon, Miss., Jan. 1, 1926; s. John Bridges and Jessie (Owen) B.; B.S. Millsaps Coll., 1947; M.S., U. Ala., 1951; Ph.D., U. Va., 1955; m. Wilma Ruth Myers, Sept. 23, 1949; children—Susan Elizabeth, Barbara June, Rachel Annette. Tchr., Grenada (Miss.) City Schs., 1947-48; instr. Hinds County Jr. Coll., Raymond, Miss., 1948-50; instr., asst. prof. Va. Mil. Inst., Lexington, 1951-53; research physicist Bill Jack Sci. Instrument Co., Solana Beach, Cal., 1955-58; sr. physicist U. Va. Ordnance Research Lab., 1958-59; asso. prof. physics Wichita (Kan.) State U., 1959-61, prof., head physics dept., 1961-66, dean Grad. Sch., 1966-70, academic v.p., 1969—. Served with USNR, 1943-45. Mem. A.A.A.S., Phi Beta Kappa, Sigma Xi. Home: 225 S Ridgewood St Wichita KS 67218 Office: 185 Fairmount St Wichita KS 67208

BREAZILE, JAMES EDWARD, educator, veterinarian; b. Rockport, Mo., Dec. 31, 1934; s. Benjamin F. and Ruth B. (Knezick) B.; B.S., D.V.M., U. Mo., 1958; Ph.D., U. Minn., 1963; m. Joan P. Vazzano, June 15, 1957; children—Felicia Diane, Kevin James, Gregory Thomas. Pvt. practice vet. medicine, Pilot Grove, Mo., 1958-60; asst. prof., then asso. prof. physiology Okla. State U., 1963-67; mem. faculty U. Mo. at Columbia, 1967—, prof., chmn. dept. vet. anatomy, 1969—; cons. neurology vet. clinics, 1963—. Mayor of Pilot Grove, 1959-60. Recipient Blue Key award Okla. State U., 1966, Caduceus award, 1967. Mem. Am. Assn. Anatomists, Am. Assn. Vet. Anatomists, World Assn. Vet. Anatomists, Conf. Research Workers in Animal Diseases, Am. Vet. Med. Assn., Mo., Intermountain vet. med. assns., U. Mo. Vet. House, Sigma Xi, Gamma Sigma Delta, Phi Zeta, Alpha Psi. Club: Cajal. Author articles in field. Home: 3401 Valencia St Columbia MO 65201

BREBBIA, JOHN HENRY, lawyer; b. Boston, Feb. 16, 1932; s. Joseph Dante and Gertrude (Hogan) B.; A.B., Stonehill Coll., 1953; LL.B., Boston Coll., 1956; m. Patricia Mary Burke, Jan. 9, 1967. Admitted to Mass. bar, 1957, D.C. bar, 1965; pvt. practice, Boston, 1960-61; trial atty. Bur. Restraint of Trade, FTC, 1961-63; asso. firm Davies, Richberg. Tydings, Landa & Duff, Washington, 1965-67; partner firm Alston, Miller & Gaines, Washington and Atlanta, 1967—. Dir., v.p., gen. counsel First Western Financial Corp., Las Vegas, 1966-67, 69—, pres., dir., 1969—; dir. First Western Savs. & Loan Assn., Las Vegas, 1966—. Mem. campaign staff Senator Robert F. Kennedy, 1964. Served to capt. AUS, 1957-60. Mem. Am., Fed. bar assns., Bar Assn. D.C. Home: 3232 Klingle Rd N W Washington DC 10008 Office: 1776 K St N W Washington DC 20006

BRECHER, GEORGE, educator, physician, b. Olomouc, Czechoslovakia, Nov. 5, 1913; s. Gideon and Else (Ziegler) B. (parents U.S. citizens); student U. Gottingen, 1931-33, U. Zurich, 1935-36; M.D., U. Prague, 1938; D.T.M.H., London Sch. Hygiene and Tropical Medicine, 1940; m. Otti Demian, Dec. 22, 1938; 1 dau., Eva Anne (Mrs. Alan Baker); m. 2d, Eva Buchwald, Oct. 16, 1959; stepchildren—Manuel Buchwald, Miguel Buchwald, Monica Buchwald (Mrs. Stephen S. Lamont), Claudio Buchwald. Intern Louth Infirmary, Lincolnshire, Eng., 1941, Anlaby, Rd. Hosp., Hull, Eng., 1942; fellow Mayo Clinic, Rochester, Minn., 1942-43, Nat. Insts. Health, 1946-47; sr. asst. surgeon to med. dir. USPHS, 1947-66; chief hematology sect. clin. pathology dept. Nat. Insts. Health, 1953-66, dep. chief clin. pathology dept., 1959-66; prof., chmn. div., later dept. clin. pathology and lab. medicine U. Cal. Med. Sch., 1966—; cons. Nat. Insts. Health, Ft. Miley VA Hosp., Irwin Meml. Blood Bank. Served as capt.M.C., AUS, 1944-46. Recipient distinguished service medal USPHS, 1968. Mem. Acad. Clin. Lab. Physicians and Scientists (pres. 1970), Assn. Am. Physicians, Am. Soc. Exptl. Pathology, Am. Soc. Hematology (v.p. 1971), Am. Soc. Clin. Pathology, Am. Assn. Pathologists and Bacteriologists, German Soc. Hematology, Internat. Soc. Hematology, N.Y. Acad. Sci., Radiation Research Soc., Soc. Exptl.Biology and Medicine, Cal. Soc. Pathologists, Transplantation Soc., A.M.A., Western Assn. Physicians, San Francisco Med. Soc. Home: 319 Yale Av Berkeley CA 94708 Office: Univ Cal Med Center San Francisco CA 94122

BRECHER, GERHARD ADOLF, physician, educator; b. Goldap, Germany, June 14, 1909; s. Otto Ernst and Hedwing (Wulst) B.; student U. Hamburg, 1928-29, Ph.D., 1932; M.A., Duke, 1930; postgrad. U. Prague, 1932-34, U. Berlin, 1934-35; M.D., U. Kiel, 1937; m. Eleanor Baker, Apr. 23, 1941; children—Armin G., M. Herbert, Elisabeth E. Came to U.S., 1948, naturalized, 1955. Instr. physiology U. Kiel, 1937-38; intern U. Cal. Hosp., San Francisco, 1938- 41; asst. resident Orange Meml. Hosp., Orlando, Fla., 1939-40; resident Brewster Hosp., Jacksonville, Fla., 1940-41; sr. instr. physiology U. Prague, 1941-45; asst. prof. Western Res. U., 1948-54, asso. prof., 1954- 55; prof., dir. Inst. Research in Vision, Ohio State U., Columbus, 1955- 57; prof. physiology Emory U., Atlanta, 1957-66, chmn. dept., 1957-66, chief clin. physiology, dept. internal medicine, 1966; med. cons. Gen. Electric Co., Cleve., 1954—, Tuskegee Inst. Sch. Vet. Medicine, 1963-67; distinguished prof. U. Okla. Med. Center, Oklahoma City, 1967—. Fellow Am. Coll. Cardiology; mem. Am. Physiol. Soc., Assn. for Research in Ophthalmology, Am. Heart Assn. Am. Soc. physiology (distinguished mem. circulation group), Am. Illuminating Soc. Author: Venous Return, 1956; (with P.M. Galletti) Heart Lung Bypass, 1962. Contbr. numerous articles to sci. publs. Home: 7708 Rumsey Rd Oklahoma City OK 73132

BRECHER, MELVIN, architect; b. Bklyn., June 13, 1924; s. Abraham and Mary (Weiner) B.; B.A., M.Arch., Harvard, 1950; m. Anita Borowitz, June 10, 1945; children—Leah, Alan. With Constantine A. Pertzoff, Cambridge, Mass., 1948-52, Bellante & Clauss, Phila., 1952-53; partner, founder Geddes Brecher Qualls Cunningham, Phila., 1953—. Chmn. Nat. Com. on Adminstrv. Office Practice, 1971—. Trustee Phila. Architects Charitable Trust. Served with USAAF, 1943-45. Decorated Air medal with silver oak leaf cluster. Mem. A.I.A. (recipient accolade Phila. chpt. 1970, also dir. chpt.), Pa. Soc. Architects (dir.). Home: 35 Rittenhouse Rd Broomall PA 19008 Office: 2410 Pine St Philadelphia PA 19103

BRECHT, EDWARD ARMOND Jr., educator; b. Minnesota Lake, Minn., June 30, 1911; s. Edward Armond and Randina (Halgrimson) B.; B.S., U. Minn., 1933, M.S., 1934, Ph.D., 1939; m. Mary Louise Ramsay, Aug. 10, 1942 (dec. Sept. 1964). Part-time clk. City Drug Store, Minnesota Lake, 1918-36; licensed pharmacist River Road Pharmacy, Mpls. 1936-39; instr. pharmacy U. N.C., Sch. Pharmacy, 1939-41, asst. prof., 1941-43, asso. prof., 1943-46, prof. pharmacy, 1946-66, dean Sch. Pharmacy, 1950-65; prof. pharmacy N.E. La. U., Monroe, 1966—. Sec., N.C. Pharm. Research Found., 1946-66; chmn. subcom. on solid preparations for internal use Com. on Nat. Formulary 1944-50, subcom. inorganic compounds and aliphatics, 1950-56, subcom. on pharm. preparations, 1956-60. Mem. Am., Minn., N.C., La., 5th Dist. (sec.-treas. 1969-71, pres. 1971-72) pharm. assns., Am. Chem. Soc., Nat. Assn. Retail Druggists, Sigma Xi, Phi Delta Chi, Rho Chi (nat. pres. 1958-60), Phi Lambda Upsilon. Clubs: Torch (pres. Durham-Chapel Hill chpt. 1962-63); Faculty (pres. 1955-56). Co-author: (with 21 collaborators) Am. Pharm. 1945, 6th edit., 1966; (with 3 collaborators) Scoville's Art of Compounding, 9th edit., 1957. Home: Box 4722 Monroe LA 71201

BRECHT, GEORGE, artist; ed. New Sch. for Social Research. Exhibited one-man shows Reuben Gallery, N.Y.C., 1959, Fischbach Gallery, N.Y.C., 1965, Galleria Schwarz, Milan, Italy, 1967, 69, Gallerie Zwirner, Cologne, 1969; exhibited in group shows including Stedelijk Mus., Amsterdam, Netherlands, Moderna Museet, Stockholm, Sweden, Louisiana Mus., Copenhagen, Denmark, 1961, Mus. Modern Art, 1961, Washington Gallery Modern Art, 1963, Solomon R. Guggenheim Mus., N.Y.C., 1965, Galleria Schwarz, Milan, 1967. Performances include: Gossoon, Reuben Gallery, 1960; Yam Day, Hardware Poets Playhouse, N.Y., 1963; Fluxus Concerts, N.Y.C., 1964; Musikfestival, Galerie Block, Berlin, Germany, 1966; sets and music for James Waring Dance Co., N.Y.C. Home: 83 Ladbroke Grove London W 11 England

BRECK, ALLEN DUPONT, educator; b. Denver, May 21, 1914; s. Chesney Yales and Isabelle E. (Lee) B.; A.B., U. Denver, 1936; M.A., U. Colo., 1939, Ph.D., 1950; m. Alice Rose Wolfe, Sept. 7, 1944; 1 dau., Anne Rose (Mrs. Vance T. Peterson). Tchr., Denver Pub. Schs., 1936-42; faculty U. Denver, 1946—, prof. history, chmn. dept., 1960—. Danforth lectr. various dists., 1959-61. Mem. commn. coll. student Am. Council Edn., 1958-61; regional program chmn. Danforth Assos., 1960-63, mem. nat. adv. bd., 1961-63; mem. Gov. Colo. Com. on Ednl. Standards, 1962-65; v.p. Colo. Com. on Social Studies, 1964—. Served with F.A., AUS, 1942-46. Fellow Royal Hist. Soc.; mem. Am., Great Britain, Western hist. assns., Medieval Acad. Am., Far Western Slavic Conf. Ecclesiastical History Soc. Gt. Britain, Assn. Am. Archivists, Rocky Mountain Social Sci. Assn. (pres. 1962-63), English Speaking Union (v.p. Denver 1963-64), Rocky

Mountain Medieval and Renaissance Assn. (pres. 1968), Phi Beta Kappa, Phi Alpha Theta, Lambda Chi Alpha, Omicron Delta Kappa. Episcopalian (historiographer Diocese Colo.). Author: A Centennial History of the Jews of Colorado, 1960; Johannis Wyclyf Tractatus de Trinitate, 1962; Episcopal Church in Colorado, 1860-1960, 1963; William Gray Evans, Western Businessman, 1964; John Evans of Denver, 1971. Editor: Internat. Colloquim I; Physical Sci., History, Philosophy, 1968, II Biological Science, History, Natural Philosophy, 1971. Contbr. articles to profl. jours. Home: 2060 S St Paul St Denver CO 80210

BRECK, LUTHER ADAMS, Jr., mail order co. exec.; b. London, Eng., Mar. 25, 1912 (parents Am. citizens); s. Luther and Marguerite (Jones) B.; A.B., Harvard, 1934; m. Clara Taft, Mar. 25, 1937; children—Margaret Reeves (Mrs. Franz Euler III), Sarah Adams. With Breck's of Boston, 1935—, pres., 1947-64, chmn. bd., 1964—; chmn. Sonolite Corp., Gloucester, Mass., 1966—; dir. Boston Industries, Inc., First Bank & Trust Co. Wellesley (Mass.). Home: 33 Allen Rd Wellesley Hills MA 02181 Office: One Washington St Wellesley Hills MA 02181

BRECKENRIDGE, ADAM CARLYLE, educator; b. Turney, Mo., July 10, 1916; s. Adam Carlisle and Mabel Ruth (Sheldon) B.; A.B., N.W. Mo. State Coll., 1936; M.A., U. Mo., 1938; Ph.D., Princeton, 1942; m. Marion S. Nickerson, Apr. 13, 1963; 1 step-son, Thomas S. Nickerson. Instr., Christian Coll., Columbia, Mo., 1940; instr. to asso. prof. polit. sci. U. Neb., Lincoln, 1946-55, chmn. dept., 1953-55, prof. polit. sci., 1955—, dean faculties, 1955-66, vice chancellor, 1962-68. Vis. prof. Pa. State U., summers 1948, 49. Mem. City-County Planning Commn., Lincoln, 1965—. Served from ensign to lt. comdr. USNR, 1942-46, 50-52; capt. Res. Mem. Am. Polit. Sci. Assn., Am. Soc. Pub. Adminstrn., Nat. Municipal League, Neb. Hist. Soc., Pi Sigma Alpha (nat. exec. council 1960-64). Author: One House for Two, 1957; The Right to Privacy, 1970; Congress Against the Court, 1970. Editor: (with L.W. Lancaster) Readings in American State Government, 1950. Home: 1545 E Manor Dr Lincoln NB 68506

BRECKENRIDGE, JAMES DOUGLAS, educator; b. N.Y.C., Aug. 8, 1926; s. Clarence E. and Erna (Gritschke) B.; A.B., Cornell U., 1945; M.F.A., Princeton, 1949, Ph.D., 1957; m. Dorte Ulrich, Jan. 8, 1964; children—Alexander D., Susanne U. Curator Corcoran Gallery Art, Washington, 1952-55, Balt. Mus. Art, 1955-60; research fellow Am. Council Learned Socs., 1959-60; vis. asso. prof. U. Pitts., 1960-61; asso. prof. dept. art Northwestern U., 1961-66, prof., 1966—, chmn. dept., 1964—; art critic Chicago's Am., 1962-64. Sr. fellow Nat. Endowment for Humanities, 1970-71. Fellow Am. Numis. Soc., Royal Soc. Arts; mem. Coll. Art Assn. Am. (dir.), Am. Inst. Archeology, Soc. Archtl. Historians, Mediaeval Acad. Am. Author: Numismatic Iconography of Justinian 11, 1959; Likeness, 1969. Home: 2420 Harrison St Evanston IL 60201

BRECKENRIDGE, JOHN B., pharm. co. exec.; b. Plattsburg, Mo., Sept. 15, 1917; s. Charles Adam and Aldyth (Kirk) B.; A.B., William Jewell Coll., 1939; LL.B., Duke, 1942; postgrad. Harvard, 1943-44; m. Eleanor Woolston Stone, May 3, 1952; children—John Cabell, Stephen Kirk, Alan Stone. Admitted to N.Y. bar, 1946; practiced in N.Y.C., 1946-53; asso. counsel Mudge, Stern, Baldwin & Todd, 1946-53; asst. to pres. Bristol Brass Corp. (Conn.), 1953-59; sec. Mead Johnson & Co., Evansville, Ind., 1959-62, v.p., sec., 1962—. Bd. dirs. N.Y.C. Young Men's Bd. Trade, 1949-53, chmn., 1950; incorporator, chmn. Effective Citizens Orgn., 1954-55. Served to lt. comdr. USNR, 1944-46. Mem. Am. Bar Assn., Sigma Nu. Republican. Methodist. Clubs: Evansville Country; Evansville Petroleum. Home: 22 Johnson Pl Evansville IN 47714 Office: 2404 W Pennsylvania St Evansville IN 47721

BRECKENRIDGE, WALTER JOHN, ret. educator; b. Brooklyn, Ia., Mar. 22, 1903; s. Robert James and Bessie (Lang) B.; B.A., U. Ia., 1926; M.A., U. Minn., 1934, Ph.D., 1941; m. Dorothy Shogren, July 26, 1933; children—Betsy Jean, Thomas Robert, Barbara Ann. Preparator Minn. Mus. Natural History, U. Minn., 1926-33, asso. curator, 1933-36, curator, 1936-46, dir., 1946-70. Fellow A.A.A.S.; mem. Am. Assn. Univ. Profs., Am. Ornithol. Union, Wilson Ornithol. Soc. (pres. 1952-54), Am. Soc. Mammalogists, Minn. Acad. Sci. (pres. 1946- 47), Minn. Ornithologists Union (pres. 1945-46), Phi Beta Kappa, Sigma Xi, Gamma Alpha, Phi Gamma Delta. Conglist. Author: Reptiles and Amphibians of Minnesota, 1944. Home: 8840 West River Rd N Minneapolis MN 55444

BRECKINRIDG E, JOHN BAYNE, lawyer, state govt. ofcl.; b. Washington, Nov. 29, 1913; s. Dr. Scott Dudley and Gertrude (Ashby-Bayne) B.; A.B., U. Ky., 1937, LL.B., 1939; m. Helen Congleton; children—Knight, John Bayne. Admitted to Ky. bar, 1940; atty. anti-trust div. Dept. of Justice, 1940-41; pvt. practice of law, 1946—; mem. Ky. Ho. of Reps., 1956-59; atty. gen. Ky., 1960-64, 68-; corp. counsel City Lexington (Ky.), 1964. Del. to White House Conf. on Children and Youth, 1960; mem. adv. com. state ofcls. AEC; past chmn. So. Interstate Nuclear Bd.; chmn. Ky. Adv. Com. Nuclear Energy, 1960-66; bd. trustees Frontier Nursing Service; commr. Nat. Conf. Commns. on Uniform State Laws, 1960-64; mem. Ky. Constitution Revison Com., 1960- 62; past mem. Ky. Atomic Energy and Space Authority, 1964—; counsel Ky. Citizens for Child Welfare, 1956-59. Bd. dirs. Ky. Welfare Assn., v.p., 1962-63; chmn. So. Interstate Nuclear Bd.; vice chmn. Ky. Social Welfare Found.; chmn. Ky. Sci. and Tech. Adv. Council, 1966-68; mem. Ky. Commn. on Children and Youth, 1966—; v.p., mem. operating bd. officers and exec. com. United Cerebral Palsy Assn., Inc., past asst. v.p. So. region, past pres. United Cerebral Palsy of Ky., United Cerebral Palsy of Bluegrass. Del. Democratic Nat. Conv., mem. rules com., Los Angeles, 1960. Served from 1st lt. to col., AUS, 1941-46; chief projects and indsl. licensing div. Bd. Econ. Warfare, 1941-42, asst. chief internat. div. USAFIME Hdqrs., comdg. officer Mil. Liaison Hdqrs., Albania. Mem. Am. Council for Community (past mem. exec. com., dir.), Am., Ky., Fayette County bar assns., Am. Judicature Soc. (dir. Ky.), Ky. Hist. Soc. (pres. 1962-64), Atlantic Union Com. (pres. Ky. chpt. mem. council), Civil War Round Table, Kappa Alpha (pres. Theta chpt. 1936-37). Democrat. Contbr. articles to legal jours. Home: 1100 Fincastle Rd Lexington KY 40502 Office: Atty Gen's Office New Capitol Frankfort KY

BREDEHOFT, LAMBERT WILLIAM, banker; b. Fairmont, Okla., Apr. 4, 1912; s. William D. and Dina S. (Beermann) B.; B.S., Northwestern U., 1933; m. Helen V. Pierce, 1941; children—Carl, Paul, William. With Harris Trust and Savs. Bank, Chgo., 1934—, sr. v.p., 1967—. Served to lt. USNR, 1943-45. Mem. Chgo. Council Fgn. Relations, Chgo. Assn. Commerce and Industry, Robert Morris Assos., Phi Beta Kappa. Clubs: University (Chgo.); Inverness Golf (Palatine, Ill.). Home: 2260 Longacres Lane Palatine, IL 60067. Office: 111 W Monroe St Chicago, IL 60690.

BREDELL, HAROLD HOLMES, lawyer; b. Indianapolis, June 18, 1907; s. Jesse Bailey and Flora E. (Glasscock) B.; A.B., Butler U., 1929; LL.B., Harvard, 1932; m. Victoria Schreiber, Apr. 20, 1939; children—Harold H., Philip K. Admitted to Ind. bar, 1932, since practiced in Indianapolis, mem. firm Bredell, Martin & McTurnan, 1947—. Pres. Vernon Fire & Casualty Ins. Co., Vernon Gen. Ins. Co.; dir. Bobbs-Merrill Pub. Co.; pres., chmn. Vernon Financial Corp., Insurance Investment Corporation; chmn. First Nat. Bank, N. Vernon, Ind. Lectr. Ind. Law Sch., 1938-40. Served as lt., USNR, 1944-46. Mem. Am. (treas., mem. bd. govs., 1949-59, bd. dirs. endowment 1959—, treas. 1959-65, v.p. 1969-71, pres. endowment 1971—), Ind., Indianapolis bar assns., C. of C., Ind. Soc. Chgo., Ind. Harvard Law Assn. Republican. Episcopalian. Clubs: Lawyers, Athletic, Harvard, Columbia (Indpls.); Highland Country. Contbr. legal jours. Home: 5038 Allisonville Rd Indianapolis IN 46205 Office: Ind Nat Bank Tower Indianapolis IN 46204

BREDEMEIER, LORENZ FRIEDRICH, conservationist; b. Mayberry, Neb., Apr. 2, 1911; s. Friedrich Wilhelm and Louisa (Gottula) B.; B.S., U. Neb., 1934, M.S., 1938; m. Audrey White, June 25, 1938; children—Linda Kay (Mrs. Boyd Holloway), Lana Loumeda (Mrs. Richard H. McWilliams), Brenda Jean (Mrs. John L. Meister). Asst. agr. agt. Neb. Agr. Extension, Lincoln, 1934-36, adminstrv. asst., 1936-38; jr. agronomist Soil Conservation Service, U.S. Dept. Agr., Centerville, Ia., 1938-39, Coydon, Ia., 1939-41, soil conservationist, Auburn, Neb., 1941-42, work unit conservationist, Hebron, Neb., 1942-44, O'Neill, Neb., 1944-48, Valentine, Neb., 1948-49, dist. conservationist, Valentine, 1949-51, range conservationist, Valentine, 1951-52, North Platte, Neb., 1952-63, Milw., 1963-64, resource devel. specialist, Madison, Wis., 1964-69, range conservationist, Ft. Worth, 1969—. Recipient Superior Accomplishment award U.S. Dept. Agr., 1948, Outstanding Performance award, 1962, Neb. Range Mgmt. award, 1965, Neb. Centennial Grassland award, 1966. Mem. Am. Soc. Range Mgmt. (pres.), Ecol. Soc. Am., Soil Conservation Soc. Am., Am. Inst. Biol. Scis., Alpha Zeta, Gamma Sigma Delta, Alpha Gamma Rho. Methodist. Mason (Shriner), Lion. Contbr. articles profl. jours. Home: 4332 Selkirk Dr W Fort Worth TX 76109 Office: PO Box 11222 Fort Worth TX 76110

BREDENBERG, PAUL ARNOLD, educator; b. Schenectady, Oct. 24, 1923; s. Alfred Jr. and Cora Edith (Felton) B.; student U. Pitts., 1940-43; B.A., U. Pa., 1947; Ph.D., Yale, 1951; m. Gladys Marie Ellis, June 21, 1947; children—Alfred Roy, Jeffrey Ellis. Asst. prof. philosophy N.C. State U., 1950-57, asso. prof., 1957-63, prof., 1963—. Sec. Wake County chpt. Am. Civil Liberties Union, 1970—. Served with USNR, 1943-46. Ford Found. Faculty fellow, 1955-56. Mem. Am. Assn. U. Profs., Am. Philos. Assn., N.C. Philos. Soc. (pres. 1964-67), Phi Kappa Phi. Democrat. Unitarian-Universalist. Club: Raleigh (N.C.) Racquet. Home: 1600 Crump Rd Raleigh NC 27606

BREDER, CHARLES MARCUS, Jr., biologist; b. Jersey City, June 25, 1897; s. Charles Marcus and Albertine Louise (Agthe) B.; D.Sc. (hon.), Newark U.; m. Ruth B. Demarest, Nov. 18, 1918; children—Charles Marcus III, Richard Frederick; m. 2d, Ethel Lear Snyder, Apr. 17, 1933; m. 3d, Priscilla Rasquin, Jan. 3, 1967. With U.S. Bur. Fisheries, 1919-21; aquarist N.Y. Aquarium, 1921-25, research asso., 1925-33, asst. dir., 1933-37, acting dir., 1937-40, dir., 1940-43, research asso., 1944—; curator, chmn. dept. fishes and aauatic biology Am. Mus. Natural History, 1944-65, dept. ichthyology, 1960-65, curator emeritus, 1965—. Participant numerous sci. expdns. including Marsh Darien (Panama), 1924, Mexican Cave expdn., 1940, Fla. tarpon lab., 1938-42; Ecuador for OSRD, 1942; NRC Commn., utilization marine shore resources, 1943; Lerner Marine Lab., Bimini, Bahamas, 1947-57; research asso. Am. Mus. Nat. History, 1926-43, Bingham Oceanographic Found., Yale, 1933-57; vis. prof. N.Y. U., 1941-52. Mem. adv. bd. Mote Marine Lab., 1958-66, bd. dirs., research asso., 1967—. Fellow N.Y. Zool. Soc., A.A.A.S., N.Y. Acad. Sci. (A. Cressy Morrison prize 1925); mem. Am. Fisheries Soc., Am. Soc. Ichthyologists and Herpetologists (pres. 1932, gov. 1932—), Am. Soc. Zoologists, Chgo. Acad. Scis. (hon. life). Author: Fishes of the Atlantic Const., 1929. Contbr. to numerous tech. jours. Home: R F D 1 Box 452 Englewood FL 33533 Office: Mote Marine Lab Sarasota FL 33581

BREDICEANU, MIHAI, orch. condr.; b. Brasov, Romania, June 14, 1920; s. Tiberius and Eugenia (Mazzucchi) B.; student music Bucharest Conservatory; law degree Bucharest U.; m. Dina Cocea, Dec. 24, 1958. Came to U.S., 1969. Condr. Bucharest Opera, 1946—; permanent condr. Bucharest Philharmonic Orch., 1958—; gen. dir. Bucharest Opera, 1959-67; prin. guest condr., music adviser Syracuse (N.Y.) Symphony Orch., 1969—. Condr. various orchs., U.S., France, USSR, West and East Germany, Austria, Czechoslovakia, Brazil, Peru, Greece, Belgium, Poland, 1955—. Pres., European Music Research Center, Foundation Dragon, Paris, France, 1970—. Recipient Geroges Enescu Competition prize; named Laureate of Bucharest Internat. Festival of Youth, 1953; artist emeritus Republic of Romania. Patentee Programed System for Complex Poly-Tempi Music and Ballet Performances; composer chamber and symphonic works and ballet music; recs. for Romanian Electrecord Co. Home: 1662 James St Syracuse NY 13203 Office: 730 Fifth Av New York City NY

BREDO, WILLIAM, economist; b. Calgary, Alta., Can., Feb. 7, 1912; s. Jacob Henry and Barbara (Murschel) B.; B.A., U. Alta., 1942; M.S., Ia. State U., 1943; M.A., Harvard, 1946, Ph.D., 1948; m. Doris Genevieve Burgeson, Mar. 18, 1943; 1 son, Eric Robert. Came to U.S., 1942, naturalized, 1946. Asst. to pres. United Mine Workers Am. Dist. 18, Calgary, 1938-39; labor economist Dominion Dept. Labor, Ottawa, Ont., 1943-44; agrl. economist Bur. Agr. Econs., U.S. Dept. Agr., Washington, 1944-45, sect. chief, 1950-52; asst. agrl. economist U. N.H., 1946- 47; exec. sec. New Eng. Research Council on Marketing and Food Supply, Boston, 1948-50; sr. economist Stanford Research Inst., Menlo Park, Cal., 1952—. Dir. Internat. Devel. Center, 1962—, dir. devel. econs. and agr. industries program, 1967-71; research and econ. adviser to govts., internat. agencies, Ford Found. Mem. Southeast Asia Devel. Adv. Group; exec. com. World Assn. Indsl. and Tech. Research Orgns., 1970—. Recipient awards Am. Farm Econ. Assn., D.C. chpt. Am. Marketing Assn., 1952. Mem. Western Econ. Assn., Am. Farm Econ. Assn., Econometric Soc., Fgn. Policy Assn. Office: Stanford Research Inst Menlo Park CA 94025

BREE, GERMAINE, educator; b. France, Oct. 2, 1907; d. Walter and Lois Marguerite (Andrault) B.; Licence, U. Paris, 1930, Diplome d'Etudes Supérieures 1931, Agregation, 1932; postgrad. Bryn Mawr Coll., 1931-32; D.Litt., Smith Coll., 1960, Mt. Holyoke, 1963, Allegheny Coll., 1963, Duke, 1964, Oberlin, 1966, Dickenson U., 1968, Brown U., 1971; L.H.D., Wilson Coll., 1960; LL.D., Middlebury Coll., 1965, U. Mich., 1970 (all hon.). Came to U.S., 1936, naturalized, 1952. Tchr., Algeria, 1932-36; from lectr. to prof. Bryn Mawr Coll., 1936-53; faculty French summer sch. Middlebury Coll., 1937, 40, 41, 46; chmn. dept. French, Washington Sq. Coll., 1953-60; head Romance lang. dept., grad. sch. arts and sci. N.Y. U., 1954-58, head dept. Romance langs. and Russian, 1958-60; prof. U. Wis. Inst. for Research in Humanities, Madison, 1960—. Mem. Am. Council Learned Socs. Adv. Bd. Served with French Army, 1943-45. Decorated Bronze Star medal; chevalier Legion of Honor (France). Mem. Modern Lang. Assn., Am. Assn. Tchrs. French, Société des Professeurs Francais, Am. Assn. U. Profs., P.E.N., Am. Philos. Soc., Alliance Francaise, Nat. Council Humanities. Author: Camus; Proust; Gide An Age of Fiction; (with Micheline Dufau) Voix d'aujourd'hui, 1964; The World of Marcel Proust, 1966; (with Al Kroft) Twentieth Century French Drama, 1969; Defeat and Beyond, An Anthology of French Wartime Writing (1940-1945), 1970; others. Contbr. articles to profl. publs., book revs. to N.Y. Times, Saturday Rev. Lit. Home: 3819 Monona Dr Madison WI 53714

BREECH, ERNEST ROBERT, industrialist; b. Lebanon, Mo., Feb. 24, 1897; s. Joseph F.E. and Martha (Atchley) B.; student Drury Coll., Springfield, Mo., 1915-17, Walton School Commerce, 1918-21; C.P.A., U. Ill., 1921; LL.D., Drury Coll., U. Mo., U. Detroit, U. Mich.; D.Sc. in Bus. Adminstrn. (hon.), Bowling Green (O.) State U.; m. Thelma Rowden, Nov. 11, 1917; children—Ernest Robert, William Howard. Accountant, Fairbanks, Morse & Co., Chgo., 1917- 20; auditor Adams & Westlake, Chgo., 1920-22; comptroller Yellow Cab Mfg. Co., Chgo., 1923-29; dir. Yellow Truck & Coach Mfg. Co., Chgo., 1927-33; gen. asst. treas. Gen. Motors Corp., N.Y.C., 1929-33, group exec., 1935-39; pres. N.Am. Aviation, 1933-35, chmn. 1933-42, v.p. charge household appliance div., aviation subsidiaries, mem. adminstrn. com., 1939-42; pres. Bendix Aviation Corp., 1942-46; exec. v.p. Ford Motor Co., 1946-55; chmn. bd., alternate chief exec. officer, 1955-60, chmn. finance com., 1960-61, dir. 1946-67; chmn. Trans-World Airlines, 1961-69, hon. chmn., dir. emeritus, 1969—; dir. One William St. Fund, Inc., Dart Industries, Inc.; Lehman Corp. Mem. Business Council, 1954-59, vice chmn., 1957-58, hon. mem., 1967—. Chmn. Central Aircraft Council, Detroit, 1942-45. Mem. Anglo-Am. Council on Productivity, 1948. Trustee Drury Coll. Republican Mason (33). Clubs: Bloomfield Hills Country (Birmingham, Mich.); Recess, Athletic (Detroit); Wequetonsing (Mich.) Golf; Paradise Valley (Scottsdale, Ariz.). Office: 12723 Telegraph Rd Detroit MI 48239

BREECHER, CHARLES HERMAN, govt. ofcl.; b. Vienna, Austria, July 26, 1916; s. Siegfried and Elisabeth (Friedlaender) B.; came to U.S., 1939, naturalized, 1942; Absolutorium law, U. Vienna, 1938; student De Paul U., Chgo., 1940-41; C.P.A. tng. diploma, La Salle Extension U., 1954, LL.B., 1957; m. Renee Senel, Nov. 19, 1946. Accountant for realty co., 1940-42; auditor U.S. Mil. Govt., 1946-47, asst. comptroller, 1947-49; transport attache U.S. High Commn. for Germany, 1950-53; div. chief, attache Am. Embassy, Bonn, Germany, 1954-57; program officer U.S. Operations Mission, Tunis, 1957-59; chief N. African div. ICA, Washington, 1959-60; chief program staff Africa-Europe, ICA, Washington, 1960-62; spl. asst. for NATO econ. affairs, 1962-66; dir. Office Devel. Planning Far East, AID, Washington, 1966—. Home: 1654 32d St Washington, DC 20007. Office: Dept State Bldg Washington DC 20510

BREED, CLARA ESTELLE, ret. city librarian; b. Ft. Dodge, Ia., Mar. 19, 1906; d. Reuben Leonard and Estelle (Potter) Breed; A.B., Pomona Coll., 1927, B.S. in L.S., Western Res. U., 1928. Children's librarian East San Diego br. Pub. Library, San Diego, 1928-29, supervising librarian children's dept., 1929-45, acting city librarian, 1945-1946, city librarian 1946-70. Mem. Cal. Pub. Library Devel., Bd. 1963-66. Named Woman of the Year, Women's Service Clubs, 1955; recipient Lay Citizens award for contbn. to edn. Phi Delta Kappa, 1958. Mem. Am. (vice chmn. sect. for library work with children, div. libraries for children and young people, 1941-42, acting chmn., 1942, council 1944-48, 52-56, mem. adv. com. for studies in pub. library services to children of adminstrn. div. 1958-65, v.p. Pub. Library Assn. 1961-62, pres. 1962-63), Cal. (v.p. so. dist. 1950, pres. 1950-51, 2d v.p. 1951-52, pres. pub. libraries sect. 1956, mem. publs. com. 1959-62, pres. Palomar dist. 1962; v.p. 1965, mem. exec. com. 1968, council 1968-69) library assns., Pub. Library Execs. So. Cal. (pres. 1959). Club: Altrusa (pres. 1959-60, San Diego). Contbr. to library and gen. mags. Home: 4215 Trias St San Diego CA 92103 Office: Public Library San Diego CA 92101

BREED, NATHANIEL PRESTON, banker; b. Lynn, Mass., Apr. 24, 1908; s. Nathaniel Pope and Effie Watson (Thomson) B.; grad. Phillips Acad., Andover, Mass., 1925; A.B., Harvard, 1929, M.B.A. magna cum laude, 1932; postgrad. N.Y.U., 1934-35; m. Elaine Silsby Cammett, Nov. 14, 1936; children—Nathaniel Preston, Elizabeth Pope. Treas. Provident Instn. for Savs., Boston, 1949-56, incorporator, 1954—; sr. v.p. State Street Bank and Trust Co., Boston, 1956—; dir. Boston Mut. Life Ins. Co., Rose Run Co., Sr. Living, Inc.; trustee Lomas & Nettleton Mortgage Investors, Dallas. Bd. dirs. Grimes-King Found., Nat. Found. for Elderly, Inc. Recipient Joint Army-Navy certificate of appreciation, 1947. Mem. Greater Boston Real Estate Bd. (dir.). Home: 25 Somerset St Belmont, MA 02178. Office: 225 Franklin St Boston MA 02101

BREED, WILLIAM CONSTABLE, Jr., lawyer; b. N.Y.C., Feb. 13, 1904; s. William Constable and Emma (Ryder) B.; student St. Paul's Sch.; A.B., Princeton, 1927; LL.B., Harvard, 1930; m. Ellen Whitman, June 29, 1928 (dec. Oct. 1957); children—Ellen B. (Mrs. F.F. Staniford, Jr.), Jane B. (Mrs. Peter E. Fleming, Jr.), William Constable III; m. 2d, Helen S. Croll, Sept. 25, 1965. Admitted to N.Y. bar, 1931; asso. firm Breed, Abbott & Morgan, N.Y.C., 1930-37, partner firm, 1937-67, counsel firm, 1967—. Chmn. bd. dirs. Manhattan Eye, Ear and Throat Hosp.; bd. dirs., chmn. bd. Nat. Multiple Sclerosis Soc. Mem. Am., N.Y. State bar assns., Assn. Bar City N.Y., N.Y. County Lawyers Assn., Am. Jud. Soc. Home: 135 E 66th St New York City NY 10021 Office: 1 Chase Manhattan Plaza New York City NY 10005

BREEDEN, EDWARD LEBBAEUS, Jr., lawyer, state senator; b. Norfolk, Va., Jan. 28, 1905; s. Edward L. and Cora Lee (McCloud) B.; student Hampden-Sydney Coll., George Washington U. Law Sch.; m. Willie Holland, Sept. 8, 1928 (dec.); children—Billye-Lee (Mrs. John Stokes Adams, III), Edward Lebbaeus III; m. 2d, Virginia Hurt Sneed, April 16, 1966. Admitted to Va. bar, 1927; mem. Va. State Ho. of Dels., 1936-44, Va. Senate, 1944—; sec.- treas., gen. counsel Elizabeth River Tunnel Commn.; chmn. bd. 1st Va. Bank of Tidewater; dir. 1st Va. Life Ins. Co., 1st Va. Bankshares Corp., Arlington Mortgage Co., Trust Co. of 1st Va. Pres., Hunter Found. Mem. bd. Gen. Hosp., Norfolk. Mem. Va. Adv. Legislative Council, 1944, chmn., 1946; mem. Va. Gov.'s Adv. Bd. on Budget, 1968—. Trustee Jamestown Found., Williamsburg, Va. Mem. Am., Va., Norfolk-Portsmouth bar assns., Kappa Sigma. Presbyn. (elder). Clubs: Virginia, Yacht and Country, Princess Anne Country, Harbor (Norfolk); Commonwealth (Richmond). Home: 923 Graydon Av Norfolk VA 23507 Office: Va Nat Bank Bldg Norfolk VA 23510

BREEDEN, JOHN ROBERT, banker; b. Berkeley, Cal., Feb. 11, 1918; s. Vic E. and Willo C. (Edwards) B.; A.B., U. Cal. at Berkeley, 1939; m. Jane E. Jackson, Aug. 16, 1941; children—Ann (Mrs. John F. Maher), John Robert, William E. With Am. Trust Co., San Francisco, 1946-60, asst. v.p., 1956-58, v.p., 1958-65; bank merged with Wells Fargo Bank, San Francisco, 1960, sr. v.p., 1965-67, exec. v.p., 1967—. Served with USAAF, 1940-46; col. Res. Mem. Res. Cities Bankers Assn., Cal. Bankers Assn. (dir., pres.), Delta Upsilon. Clubs: Pacific-Union (San Francisco); Pauma Valley (Cal.) Country; Los Angeles Country, California, Stock Exchange (Los Angeles). Home: 535 S Orange Grove Blvd Pasadena CA 91105 Office: 415 W 5th St Los Angeles CA 90054

BREEDEN, ROBERT HANCOCK, state govt. ofcl.; b. Vicksburg, Miss., May 20, 1908; s. Roscoe and Zula (Hancock) B.; A.B. in Journalism, Okla. U., 1929; m. Marion Miller, Jan. 5, 1931; children—Carolyn (Mrs. George McLellan), Nancy (Mrs. R.G.

Vaughn). Publisher newspapers in Cleveland and Pawnee, Okla., 1931-62. Russelville, Charleston, Paris and Greenwood, Ark., 1937—; gen. mgr. Grand River Dam Authority, 1963-65; dir. Indsl. Devel. and Park Dept. Okla., 1965-71; area dir. Fed. Housing and Urban Devel. for State of Okla., 1971—. Mem. Okla. Senate from Pawnee County, 1957-63. Mem. Sigma Delta Chi, Alpha Delta Sigma, Alpha Sigma Phi. Home: 3622 N W 42d St Oklahoma City OK 73112 Office: 301 N Hudson St Oklahoma City OK

BREEDIS, CHARLES, educator; b. Morrisville, Pa., Aug. 7, 1911; s. Anthony and Ottilia (Kallenberg) B.; A.B., N.Y. U., 1938; M.D., Cornell U., 1942; m. Marjorie Alberta Andresen, Feb. 17, 1968; stepchildren—Richard G., Elizabeth A., Diane P., Patricia M., Stephen A., Peter J., John K. (all McManus). Intern, Grasslands Hosp., Valhalla, N.Y., 1943; instr. U. Pa. Sch. Medicine, Phila., 1946-50, asst. prof., 1951-55, asso. prof., 1955-59, prof. pathology, 1959—, chmn. grad. group pathology, 1965—, dir. pathology Div. Grad. Medicine, 1968—. Mem. pathology study sect. USPHS, 1962-66. Served with M.C., AUS, 1944-46. Cancer research grantee USPHS, 1952—. Mem. Am. Assn. Cancer Research, Am. Assn. Pathologists and Bacteriologists, Am. Soc. for Cell Biology, Am. Soc. for Exptl. Pathology, Am. Assn. U. Profs., A.A.A.S., N.Y. Acad. Scis., Franklin Inst., Sigma Xi. Contbr. articles on growth and cancer to profl. jours. Home: 3 Hilldale Circle Lansdowne PA 19050 Office: U Pa Sch Medicine Dept Pathology 36th St and Hamilton Walk Philadelphia PA 19104

BREEN, F. GLENN, banker; b. Chgo., Nov. 14, 1912; s. Frank J. and Ella C. (Burke) B.; Ph.B., U. Chgo., 1935; m. Dorothy I. Otto, Mar. 20, 1937; children—Barbara Jean, F. Glenn. Vice pres., mgr. Standard Fire Ins. Co. of N.J. (merger with Reliance Ins. Co. 1962), Trenton, 1943-51, pres., 1951-62, v.p., 1962-68; pres. Trenton Sav. Fund Soc., 1968—, also bd. mgrs.; dir. N.J. Nat. Bank, Port of Reading R.R., Phila. Home: Evergreen Rd Morrisville PA 19067 Office: 123 E State St Trenton NJ 08608

BREEN, JOHN FRANCIS, banker; b. Memphis, Feb. 6, 1929; s. John Francis and Eleanor (Cousins) B.; B.S. cum laude, Memphis State U., 1957, M.A., 1961; postgrad. La. State U., 1961; m. Gloria Fransioli, Nov. 27, 1957 (div. 1970); children—John Francis III, Lynne, James; m. 2d, Barbara G. Steenberg, 1971. With Memphis br. Fed. Res. Bank of St. Louis, 1957-62, asst. cashier, 1959-62, cashier Little Rock br., 1962-65, v.p., mgr. Little Rock br., 1965—; mem. faculty evening div. Memphis State U., 1959-60. Sect. chmn. United Fund, 1968-70. Bd. dirs. Opportunities Industrialization Center, Inc. Served with inf. U.S. Army, 1948-49, 53-55. Recipient Frank K. Houston award Tenn. Bankers Assn., 1958. Mem. Am., Ark. bankers assns., So. Econ. Assn., Robert Morris Assos., Little Rock C. of C., Sigma Phi Epsilon. Roman Catholic. Rotarian. Home: 2003 Clapboard Hill Rd Little Rock AR 72207 Office: 325 W Capitol Av Little Rock AR 72203

BREEN, JOHN RICHARD, govt. ofcl.; b. Metheun, Mass., Nov. 19, 1934; s. John H. and Grace (Graf) B.; A.B., Merrimack Coll., 1956; M.P.A., Syracuse U., 1957; m. Edith Anne Howard, Dec. 20, 1959; children—Kathryn M., Joanna. Exec. trainee Office Sec. Def., 1957, budget analyst, 1957, budget and systems analyst, 1962-63; dir. Latin Am. programs AID, 1963-68; country dir. for Central Am., State Dept., 1968—. Past v.p. Fairfax County Fedn. Citizens Assn. Served to lt. (j.g.) USNR, 1958-62. Home: 4117 Whispering Lane Annandale VA 22003 Office: Dir Central Am Affairs State Dept Washington DC 20525

BREEN, JOSEPH B., lawyer; b. N.Y.C., June 28, 1930; s. Joseph A. and Catherine (McTigue) B.; B.A., Holy Cross Coll., 1952; LL.B., Fordham U., 1958; postgrad. N.Y. U. Law Sch., 1958-62; m. Christine O'Connell, Dec. 27, 1952; children—Christine, Stephen, Regis, Joseph, Deidru, Sean. Mem. firm Emmett, Marvin & Martin, 1962—. Dir. Hundoin Oayne & Co., Inc., Huntoon Paige & Co., Inc. Bd. dir. Children's Rehab. Inst., Rechestown, Md. Served to capt. USMCR, 1952-54. Mem. N.Y. State Bar Assn. (past pres.). Democrat. Roman Catholic. Home: Todd Rd Katonah NY 10536 Office: 48 Wall St New York City NY 10005

BREEN, LEONARD ZACHARY, sociologist; educator; b. Chgo., Sept. 26, 1922; s. Joseph A. and Jennie (Nelson) B.; B.S., Ill. Inst. Tech., 1949; M.A., U. Chgo., 1950, Ph.D., 1956; m. Mildred A. Steinberg, June 25, 1946; children—Jeni Ann, Martha Gail, Richard Joseph. Sr. study dir. Chgo. Community Inventory, 1949-51; asst. prof. polit., social sci. Ill. Inst. Tech., Chgo., 1951-55; asst. prof. sociology U. Chgo., 1955-57; asso. prof. Purdue U., Lafayette, Ind., 1957-63, prof., 1963—, head dept. sociology, 1967—; asst. dean grad. sch., 1966-67. Vis. prof. sociology Indian Inst. Tech., Kanpur, U.P., India, 1964-66, U. Essex, Colchester, Eng., 1971; cons. Ind. State Commn. on Aging, Aged, 1966—. Served with USAAF, 1942-46. Fellow Am. Sociol. Assn., The Gerontol. Soc.; mem. Inst. Comparative Sociology, Am. Anthropol. Assn. Author articles, chpts. on gerontology to profl. mags., books. Home: 164 Creighton Rd West Lafayette IN 47906

BREEN, MARY FRANCES, librarian; b. Albany, N.Y., Dec. 24, 1914; d. Gerald and Norine (McGaughan) Breen; B.S., N.Y. Coll. Tchrs., Albany, 1936; Ed.M., U. Buffalo, 1949, Ed.D., 1954. Mem. staff Albany Pub. Library, also substitute Albany pub. schs., 1936-41; librarian N.Y. State Tng. Sch. for Girls, Hudson, 1941-44; asst. librarian N.Y. State Coll. Tchrs., Buffalo, 1944-55; librarian State U. Coll. at Plattsburgh, N.Y., 1955-70, dir. libraries, 1970—. Mem. Am., N.Y. State, Catholic library assns., Am. Assn. U. Profs., N.Y. State Tchrs. Assn., Am. Assn. U. Women, Pi Lambda Theta, Delta Kappa Gamma. Home: 24 S Catherine St Plattsburgh NY 12901

BREEN, WILLIAM JOHN, Jr., former yacht broker; b. Boston, Sept. 23, 1904; s. William John and Frances Carrie (Boileau) B.; student Worcester Poly. Inst., 1927; m. Parker Goodwin, Mar. 16, 1946. With N.W. Ayer & Son, Inc., Phila., 1929-40, Gen. Aniline & Film Corp., N.Y., 1941-42; account exec. Young & Rubicam, Inc., N.Y.C., 1943-46; account exec. Sherman & Marquette, Inc., N.Y.C., 1947-51; v.p. mgmt. account supr., mgr. account service div., vice chmn. plans rev. bd. McCann-Erickson, Inc., N.Y.C., 1952-59; sr. v.p., mgmt. account supr. Lennen & Newell, Inc., N.Y.C., 1959-60; pres. William J. Breen, Inc., Ft. Lauderdale, Fla., yacht brokers, 1961-71; partner Brenn-Fisher & Assos. Clubs: Seawanhaka Corinthian Yacht (Oyster Bay, N.Y.); Coral Reef Yacht (Miami). Home: 524 Orton Av Fort Lauderdale FL Office: 2190 S E 17th St Fort Lauderdale FL Died Apr. 30, 1971.

BREES, EUGENE WILSON, former govt. ofcl.; b. Richmond, Ind., July 22, 1914; s. Perry Samuel and Maude (Doyle) B.; LL.B., Southeastern U., 1939; m. Betty Jo Johnston, May 29, 1947; children—Eugene Wilson II, Mildred J., Virginia J. Clk., USPHS, Washington, 1935-40; with Social Security Adminstrn., 1940—, claims adjudicator, Washington, 1940-42, claims supr., Phila., 1946, asst. office chief, Birmingham, Ala., 1949-52, policy cons., chief Payment Center, dep. dir. Bur. Retirement and Survivors Ins., Balt., 1959-71. Served to col. AUS, 1942-46. Recipient Superior Service award Dept. Health, Edn. and Welfare, 1963, Commr.'s citation Social Security Adminstrn., 1971. Mem. Judge Adv. Gen.'s Assn. Methodist. Home: 4831 S Kachina Dr Tempe AZ 85282

BREESE, GERALD WILLIAM, educator; b. Horseheads, N.Y., June 4, 1912; s. Bert Minard and Leona (Goodrich) B.; A.B., Ohio Wesleyan U., 1935; B.D., Yale, 1938; Ph.D. (Marshall Field fellow), U. Chgo., 1947; m. Alice Janette Bailey, July 4, 1937; children—Adele Embree, James Bert, Dana Sue Bailey, Brinda Sue Bailey. Asst. prof. sociology, dean men Pacific U., Forest Grove, Ore., 1939-41; research planner Chgo. Plan commn., 1942; instr. urban sociology Shrivenham Am. U., Eng., 1945, U. Chgo., 1947; sec. com. on housing research Social Sci. Research Council, 1947-49; asst. prof. sociology Princeton, 1949-51, asso. prof., 1951-59, prof., 1950—, dir. bur. urban research, 1950-66. Fulbright prof. Am. U., Cairo, Egypt, 1954-55; coordinator Ford Found., Delhi Regional Master Plan Cons. Team, New Delhi, India, 1957-58; vis. lectr. U. Natal, South Africa, summer 1963; vis. fellow Inst. Advanced Studies Australian Nat. U., 1966. Mem. N. J. Resources Com., 1950-57. Served with AUS, 1942-45. Recipient Demobilization award Social Sci. Research Council, 1946-47. Mem. Am. Inst. Planners, Am., Eastern sociol. socs., Population Assn. Am., Phi Beta Kappa. Author: Daytime Population of Central Business District of Chicago, 1949; Industrial Land Use in Burlington County, N.J., 1951; An Approach to Urban Planning, 1953; Regional Analysis Trenton-Camden Area, 1954; Industrial Site Selection, 1954; Accelerated Urban Growth in a Metropolitan Fringe Area, 1954; Urbanization in Old and New Countries, 1964; Urbanization in Newly Developing Countries, 1966; Impact of Large Installations on Nearby Areas, 1966, rev., 1968. Editor, contbr. The City in Newly Developing Countries, 1968. Home: 195 Russell Rd Princeton NJ 08540

BREESE, MELVIN WILSON, physician; b. Miller, S.D., July 13, 1914; s. Orville V. and Ruth (Wilson) B., B.S., Ore. State U., 1936; M.D., U. Ore, 1943; m. Elizabeth J. Beaty, Oct. 31, 1937; children—Shelby L. (Mrs. Thomas Ballen), Mark W., Sheila L. (Mrs. Greg Anderson), Kirk W., Craig E. intern Emanuel Hosp., Portland, Ore., 1943-44; resident, U. Ore. Med. Sch. Hosp., 1944-47; practice medicine, specializing in obstectrics and gynecology, Portland, 1947—; asso. clin. prof. obstetrics and gynecology U. Ore. Med. Sch., 1947—. Served to capt., M.C., U.S. Army, 1953-54, 65-66. Mem. A.M.A. (council med. edn.), Ore Med. Assn. (council med. edn., past pres.), Multnomah County Med. Soc. (past pres.), Am. Coll. Obstetrics and Gynecology, Pacific Cost, Pacific N.W., Ore., Portland obset. and gyncol. socs. ‡

BREESKIN, ADELYN DOHME, art mus. dir.; b. Balt., July 19, 1896; d. Alfred R.L. and Emmie (Blumner) Dohme; grad. Sch. Fine Arts, Crafts and Decorative Design, Boston, 1918; L.D., Goucher Coll., Balt., 1958; D.F.A., Washington Coll., 1961, Wheaton Coll., 1964, Hood Coll., 1966, Morgan State Coll., 1966; m. Elias Breeskin, Apr. 12, 1920; children—Jean (Mrs. Clayton Timbrell), Dorothy (Mrs. Sanuel E. Brown, Jr.), Gloria (Mrs. Cornelius Peck). Asst. print dept. Met. Mus., N.Y.C., 1918-20; with Balt. Mus. Art 1930—, acting dir., 1942-47, dir., 1947-62; dir. Washington Gallery Modern Arts, 1962-64; also curator graphic art lectr. U.S.A. and abroad; now spl. cons. and curator 20th Century painting and sculpture. Nat. Collection of Fine Arts, Smithsonian Instn., Washington. Decorated Star of Solidarity by Italian Govt., 1954; recipient Distinguished Service award U. Md., 1962. U.S. Commr. Am. Pavilion, Venice Exhbn., 1960. Mem. Assn. Art Mus. Dirs. (sec.-treas. 1953-56, pres. 1956-57), Internat. Graphic Arts Soc. (mem. Am. jury of selection, 1955-65), Print Council Am. (sec. 1956—). Author: Catalogue Raisonne, Graphic Works of Mary Cassatt, 1949; Catalogue Raisonne of Paintings, Pastels, Watercolors and Drawings by Mary Cassatt, 1970. Home: 1254 31st NW Washington DC 20007 Office: Nat Collection Fine Arts 8th and G Sts Washington DC 20560

BREEZE, WILLIAM HANCOCK, life ins. co. exec.; b. Cin., Nov. 25, 1923; s. William Talbot and Nancy (Hancock) B.; student Berea Coll., 1943; A.B., Centre Coll., 1945; M.A., U. Ky., 1948; m. Joanne Robertson Watson, Oct. 8, 1949; 1 dau., Nancy Louise. Actuary Ohio Nat. Life Ins. Co., Cin., 1948-65, asst. to pres., 1965-67, sr. v.p., 1967—, also dir.; dir. ON Funds, Inc. Served with USNR, 1943-46. Fellow Soc. Actuaries, Am. Acad. Actuaries. Home: 1363 Suncrest Dr Cincinnati OH 45208 Office: PO Box 237 Cincinnati OH 45201

BREGER, WILLIAM N., educator, architect; b. N.Y.C., Aug. 1, 1922; s. S.A. and B. (Kalvar) B.; B.Arch., Harvard, 1945; M.A. in Philosophy, N.Y. U., 1954. Asst. to Walter Gropius, Cambridge, Mass., 1944-46; tchr. N.Y. Sch. Interior Design, 1945—; prof. architecture, former chmn. dept. archtl. design Pratt Inst., 1946—; lectr. Columbia Sch. Pub. Health and Hosp. Adminstrn., 1964—. practice architecture with S. Salzman, 1947-55; architect William N. Breger Assos., 1955—. Trustee, dir. N.Y. Sch. Interior Design, 1960—. Served with AUS, 1942-44. Recipient 3d Art Inst., 1954, Bklyn. Mus., 1955, others. Served with AUS, 1942-43. Recipient Langford Warren prize, 1944, 3d prize Jefferson Nat. Meml. Competition (with C. Herbostel and G. Lewis), St. Louis, 1947; 1st prize House and Garden mag., 1950; 1st prize Carson Pirie Scott Chicago Loop design, 1954; hon. mention hosp. design Rubberoid Competitio, 1958; 1st prize Allegheny Sq. competition (with J. Terjesen and W. Winter), Pitts., 1964; hon. mention Fremont Civic Center Master Plan, 1966, numerous others. Mem. A.I.A. (Nat. Honor award 1968). Author article. Mem. editorial bd. Ency. Philosophy, 1967. Home: 193 W 10th St New York City NY 10014 Office: 12 E 53d St New York City NY 10022

BREGMAN, JACOB ISRAEL, environmentalist; b. Hartford, Conn., Sept. 17, 1923; s. Aaron and Jennie (Katzoff) B.; B.S., Providence Coll., 1943; M.S., Poly. Inst. Bklyn., 1948, Ph.D., 1951; m. Mona Madan, June 27, 1948; children—Janet, Marcia, Barbara. Research chemist Fels & Co., 1947-48; head phys. chem. labs. Nalco Chem. Co., Chgo., 1950-59; supr. phys. chemistry research sect. Armour Research Found., Chgo., 1959-63; asst. dir. chemistry research Ill. Inst. Tech. Research Inst., Chgo., 1963-65, dir. chem. scis., 1965-67; dep. asst. sec. U.S. Dept. Interior, 1967-69; pres. Wapora Inc., 1969—. Chmn. N.E. Ill. Met. Area Air Pollution Control Bd., 1962-63; chmn. Ill. Air Pollution Control Bd., 1963-67; chmn. adv. bd. on saline water conversion NATO Parliamentarians Conf., 1963; chmn. Water Resources Research Council, 1964-67. Mem. plan commn., Park Forest, Ill., 1956-58, trustee, 1958-62. Served with AUS, 1943-46; ETO. Fellow Am. Inst. Chemists; mem. Am. Chem. Soc., N.Y. Acad. Scis., Sigma Xi, Phi Lambda Upsilon. Author: Corrosion Inhibitors, 1963; Surface Effects in Detection, 1965; The Pollution Paradox, 1966. Contbr. articles profl. jours. Home: 5630 Old Chester Rd Bethesda MD 60014 Office: 1725 DeSalles St Washington DC 20036

BREHM, CARL THEODORE, educator; b. Rockwell City, Ia., Feb. 9, 1925; s. Carl Theodore and Charlotte (Williams) B.; B.A., Drake U., 1949. M.A., 1951; Ph.D., Ind. U., 1958; m. Lois Elaine Williams, May 30, 1948; children—Barbara Ann, Susan Kay. Jr. financial economist Fed. Res. Bank, Cleve., 1953-55; instr. Mich. State U., 1955-58, asst. prof., 1958-63; asso. prof. Kenyon Coll., Gambier, O., 1963-68, prof., 1968—, chmn. econs. dept., 1965—; lectr. econ. edn. Ohio U., 1967-70, Akron U., 1970—. Mem. com. on econ. edn. Mt. Vernon Pub. Sch., 1966—. Served with AUS, 1943-46. Decorated Bronze Star medal with oak leaf cluster. Mem. Am. Assn. U. Profs. (pres. Kenyon chpt.), Am., Midwest econs. assns., A.A.A.S., Internat. Peace Research Soc. Author: Introduction to Economics, 1970. Contbr. chpt. to Structure of American Industry, 1961. Home: Box 269 Gambier OH 43022

BREHM, KARL FRANZ, hotel exec.; b. St. Louis, Mar. 9, 1914; s. Karl and Elizabeth (Gaham) B.; B.S. in Elec. Engring., Washington U., St. Louis, 1936; m. Virginia Setzekorn, Mar. 9, 1946; children—Karlton, Terry, Camella, Colleen. Operator indsl. cafeterias, Chattanooga, 1943-45; credit mgr. Jefferson Hotel, St. Louis, 1945-47, night mgr., 1947-54, exec. asst. gen. mgr., 1954-55, asst. gen. mgr., 1955-61; gen. mgr. Sheraton Hotel, also Sherwyn Hotel, Louisville, 1961-65, Sheraton Motor Inn, Phila., 1965-66, Ramada Inn, Palm Springs, Cal., 1966-68; pres., owner Brehm's Restaurant & Lounge, Inc., Overland, Mo., 1968—; gen mgr. Sunset Country Club, St. Louis County, Mo. Chmn. Louisville central area Tourists and Conv. Com., 1961—; commr. Ky. Tourist Commn., 1962—. Mem. Ky. Conservation Com., 1962—. Recipient Civilian Certificate of Appreciation, Army Dept., 1958, U.S. Army Recruiting Service, 1957; named Ky. col., 1961. Mem. Louisville C. of C. (committeeman conv. and visitors com.) Ky., Am., Phila., Palm Springs hotel and motel assns., Louisville Hotel Assn. (pres.), U.S. Coast Guard Aux., C. of C. Overland. Clubs: Yacht (Louisville); Optimists (Overland). Home 12679 Grandin Lane Bridgeton MO 63042 Office: 9210 Lackland Rd Overland MO 63114

BREHM, WILLIAM KEITH, corp. exec.; b. Dearborn, Mich., Mar. 29, 1929; s. Walter E. and Lucille (Hankinson) B.; B.S. in Math., U. Mich., 1950, M.S., 1952; m. Delores Soderquist, June 28, 1952; children—Eric William, Lisa Karen. Research asso. U. Mich. Engring. Research Inst., 1950-52; design specialist Gen. Dynamics-Convair, San Diego, 1952-57; chief operations analysis Convair- Astronautics, San Diego, 1958-59; exec. staff asst. to v.p. planning Gen. Dynamics-Convair, 1960-62; corp. dir. devel. planning N.Am. Aviation, Los Angeles, 1962-64; dir. land forces programs Office Sec. Def., 1964-67; dep. asst. sec. def., 1967-68; asst. sec. army, 1968-71; v.p. corporate devel. Dart Industries, Inc., Los Angeles, 1971—. Mem. Operations Research Soc. Am. Home: 3144 Corda Dr Los Angeles CA 90049 Office: 8480 Beverly Blvd Los Angeles CA 90048

BREIDENSTINE, AARON GIBBLE, educator; b. Lebanon County, Pa., Dec. 22, 1902; s. John Dohner and Leah Meyer (Gibble) B.; B.S. Elizabethtown Coll., 1927, D.Litt., 1966; M.Ed., Temple U., 1934, Ed.D., 1936; m. Ella Elizabeth Steffy, June 16, 1927; children—Elma Jane, Glenn S. Tchr. Prescott (Pa.) Sch., 1925-27; tchr. and prin. East Lampeter High Sch., 1927-37; prof. secondary edn. and psychology Elizabethtown Coll., 1937-38; adminstrv. dean Hershey Jr. Coll., 1938-47; mem. faculty Franklin and Marshall Coll. 1947-55, dean, 1947-55; dean acad. affairs Millersville (Pa.) State Coll., 1955-66; dep. supt. pub. instrn., Pa., 1966-68; adminstrv. coordinator Brethren Colls. Abroad, 1969—. Recipient Phi Delta Kappa Gold medal for Thesis, The Educational Achievement of Pupils in Differentiated and Undifferentiated Groups, 1936. Mem. N.E.A., State Edn. Assn., Phi Delta Kappa. Mem. Ch. Brethren (past pres. nat. council, moderator 1969-70, mem. hymnal com.; nat. moderator 1970). Lectr. ednl. and religious subjects. Home: 715 Pleasure Rd Lancaster PA 17601

BREIDENTHAL, JOHN W., banker; b. Kansas City, Kan., Nov. 4, 1911; s. Willard J. and Mary (Gray) B.; student U. Kan., Kansas City Law Sch.; m. Mary Ruth Pyle, Feb. 11, 1939; children—Julie (Mrs. Henry C. Gold), Nancy, Mary Ann (Mrs. Scott A. Nordheimer), Susan Jane. With Riverview State Bank, 1933-38, 40-42, chmn. bd., 1957-62; asst. cashier Victory State Bank, 1938-40, now dir.; vice chmn. bd., chmn. exec. com. Security Nat. Bank, Kansas City, Kan., 1962-66, chmn. bd., 1966—; adv. dir. Turner State Bank; dir. Victory State Bank, Fort Riley Nat. Bank, ERC Corp., Employers Reins. Corp., Gas Service Co., Kan. Bankers Surety Co., Kan. & Mo. Ry. & Terminal Co., Ortmeyer Lumber Co., Wyandotte Hotel Co. Chmn. Greater Kansas City Flood Protection Planning Commn.; chmn. dist. 5, Water Resources Assn. Mem. Pres.'s Adv. Com. on Mo.-Ark. Basins Flood Control and Conservation; mem. adv. council Kansas City FAA. Trustee Midwest Research Inst., Ottawa U.; bd. dirs. Central Indsl. Dist. Assn., Civic Council Greater Kansas City, 1st v.p., exec. bd. Agrl. Hall Fame. Served to maj., cav., AUS, 1941-46. PTO; brig. gen. Kan. N.G. Mem. Am. Royal Assn. (exec. com.), Assn. U.S. Army, N.G. Assn. U.S., Newcomen Soc., Mil. Order World Wars, 35th Div. Assn. (exec. com.), Am. Legion. Rotarian. Clubs: Kansas City (Kan.); Ft Leavenworth (Kan.) Officer's Open Mess; Richards-Gebaur Officers; Terrace; Victory Hills Golf and Country; Garden of the Gods (Colorado Springs). Home: 1508 N 21st St Kansas City, KS 66102. Office: 655 Minnesota Av Kansas City KS 66117

BREIG, ROBERT EDWARD, drug chain exec.; b. Vandergrift, Pa., Apr. 27, 1909; s. George F. and Clara E. (McKenzie) B.; student Georgetown U., 1927-29, Duquesne U., 1929-30; m. Elva Louise McCasland, Feb. 12, 1937; children—Barbara (Mrs. Frederick M. Haney), Robert Edward. Cost analyst U.S. Steel Corp., Vandergrift, 1937-43; supr. cost accounting Elliott Co., Jeanette, Pa., 1943-46; br. accountant Am. Home Foods, Inc., Pitts., Hamilton, O., 1946-48; supr. accounting Gray Drug Stores, Inc., Cleve., 1948-54, asst. treas., 1954-62, treas., 1962-68, v.p., 1968—. Mem. Nat. Assn. Chain Drug Stores (vice chmn. methods and control conf. 1965-66, chmn. 1967-68). Home: 2981 Essex Rd Cleveland Heights OH 44118 Office: 666 Euclid Bldg Cleveland OH 44114

BREINES, SIMON, architect; b. Bklyn., Apr. 4, 1906, s. Louis and Anna (Backrack) B.; B.Arch. Pratt Inst., 1941; m. Nettie Weissman, 1935; children—Paul, Joseph. Partner, Pomerance & Breines, N.Y.C., architect for pub. bldgs. including Bronx Municipal Hosp. Center, Grand Concourse Pub. Library, Bronx, N.Y.C., Lexington Sch. for Deaf., Rose F. Kennedy Research Center, New Campus, State U. N.Y. at Brockport. Cons. Housing Assistance Adminstrn.; adviser Gen. Services Adminstrn. Bd. dirs. Fine Arts Fedn. of N.Y. Mem. Citizens Union, Community Service Soc., Parks Assn. (all N.Y.C.); architect mem. Art Commn. City N.Y., 1971—. Arnold W. Brunner scholar N.Y. chpt. A.I.A., 1947, 66. Recipient Bard award City Club N.Y. 1967. Fellow A.I.A. (honor award 1967). author: (with John Dean) The Book of Houses, 1946. Home: 8 Horseguard Lane Scarsdale NY 10583

BREININ, GOODWIN M. physician; b. N.Y.C., Dec. 10, 1918; s. Louis and Mary (Mirsky) B.; B.S., U. Fla., 1939; A.M., Emory U., 1940, M.D. 1943; m. Rose-Helen Kopelman, June 22, 1947; children—Bartley James, Constance. Intern, U.S. Marine Hosp., Stapleton, N.Y., 1944; resident ophthalmology N.Y. U.-Bellevue Med. Center, 1947-51, sr. Heed fellow ophthalmology, 1954, Daniel B. Kirby prof. research ophthalmology, 1958, Daniel B. Kirby prof., chmn. dept. ophthalmology, 1959—; dir. eye service Bellevue and U. Hosps., N.Y.C., 1959—; chmn. vision research tng. com. Nat. Insts. Neurol. Diseases and Blindness, 1963-64; chief cons. Manhattan VA Hosp.: cons. Manhattan Eye, Ear and Throat Hosp., USPHS Hosp., Stapleton, French Hosp., St. Vincent's Hosp., N.Y. Eye and Ear Infirmary, Lenox Hills Hosp., St. Clare's Hosp., surg. gen. USPHS. Mem. various adv. coms. relating to field, mem. med. adv. bd. Nat.

Council to Combat Blindness. Served as capt., M.C., AUS, 1944-46. Recipient Knapp Medal for contbn. ophthalmology A.M.A., 1957; Edward Lorenzo Holmes citation and award for contbns. to med. sci. Inst. Medicine Chgo., 1959, Gifford lectr. and award Chgo. Ophthal. Soc., 1970, Heed Ophthalmic Found. award, 1968. Diplomate Am. Bd. Ophthalmology (dir.). Fellow Am. Acad. Ophthalmology Otolaryngology, A.C.S., N.Y. Acad. Medicine (sec. sect. ophthalmology 1962-63, chmn. sect. 1967-68); mem. A.M.A. (sec. sect. on ophthalmology 1966-69, chmn. 1970—), Research Ophthalmology, Am., N.Y. ophthal. socs., Harvey Soc., A.A.A.S., Am. Commn. for Optics and Visual Physiology (chmn. 1970—), Am. Orthoptic Council, Pan. Am. Assn. Ophthalmology, Nat. Soc. Prevention Blindness, Sigma Xi, Alpha Omega Alpha. Clubs: Lotos (New York City): Cosmos (Washington). Author: The Electrophysiology of Extraocular Muscle, 1962. Mem. editorial bd. Archives of Ophthalmology, Investigative Ophthalmology. Also papers. Home: 912 Fifth Av New York City NY 10021 Office: 550 1st Av New York City NY 10016

BREININ, RAYMOND, painter, sculptor; b. Vitebsk, Russia, Nov. 30, 1910; student Chgo. Acad. Fine Arts, Uri Penn. Exhibited paintings Met. Mus. Art., Mus. Modern Art, Bklyn. Mus., Art Inst. Chgo., Phillips Meml. Gallery, Washington, Boston Mus. Fine Arts, Fogg Mus. Art, San Francisco Mus. Art, San Diego Fine Arts Soc., Newark Mus. Art, Cranbrook Acad. Art, Williams Coll., John Herron Art Inst., U. Ill., Am. Acad. Arts and Letters. U.S. State Dept., Ency. Brit., Capehart Coll., Eli Lilly Co., Nat. Gallery, Scotland, Munson-Williams-Proctor Inst.; executed costumes, settings Ballet Theatre's Undertow, murals Winnetka (Ill.) High Sch., State Hosp., Elgin, Ill., U.S. P.O., Wilmette, Ill., Pump Room in Ambassador East Hotel. Chgo., Jade and Emerald rooms Sherman Hotel. Chgo. Recipient prizes Art Inst. Chgo., Met. Mus. Art, Pa. Acad. Fine Arts, U. Ill., Eccles. Art Guild, others. Artist-in-residence So. Ill. U.; instr. art U. Minn., Breinin Sch. Art, Chgo.; instr. painting and drawing Art Students League, N.Y.C., N.A.D. Mem. N.A.D. Home: 121 Inwood Rd Scarsdale NY 10583

BREINING, NELSON H., ins. exec.; b. Newark, 1907; s. John and Nell (Buntele) B.; student Am. Inst. Banking, 1925-26, Newark Coll., 1927-28; m. Helen Ulisnik, June 20, 1930; children—Beverly (Mrs. Donald Nichols), Nelson D., Constance G. (Mrs. Kenneth Grant). Vice pres., sec., dir. Reins. Corp. N.Y., 1935—. Republican, Methodist. Kiwanian. Home: 446 Carpenter Pl Union NJ 07083 Office: 99 John St New York City NY 10007

BREISACH, ERNST, prof. Western Mich. U. Author: Introduction to Modern Existentialism, 1966; Caterina Sforza, 1967. Home: Dept of History Western Mich Univ Kalamazoo MI 49001

BREIT, GREGORY, physicist; b. Russia, July 14, 1899; s. Alfred and Alexandra (Smirnova) B.; came to U.S., 1915, naturalized, 1918; A.B., Johns Hopkins, 1918, A.M., 1920, PH.D., 1921; D.Sc. (hon.), U. Wis., 1954; m. Marjorie MacDill, Dec. 30, 1927. Nat. Research fellow U. Leiden, Holland, 1921-22, Harvard, 1922-23; asst. prof. physics Minn. U., 1923-24; math. physicist dept. terrestrial magnetism Carnegie Inst., Washington, 1924-29; prof. physics, N.Y. U., 1929- 34, U. Wis., 1934-47; prof. physics Yale, 1947-58, Donner prof. 1958-68; Distinguished prof. physics State U. N.Y., Buffalo, 1968—. Research asso. Carnegie Inst., Washington, 1929-44; vis. mem. Inst. for Advanced Study, Princeton, N.J., 1935-36; resident Technische Hochschule, Zurich, Switzerland, 1928. War work; degaussing Naval Ordnance Lab., Washington Navy Yard, 1940- 41; sect. mem. OSRD, NDRC 1940-42; coordinator fast neutron project Met. Lab., U. Chgo., 1942; Radiation Lab. Johns Hopkins, 1942-43; Aberdeen Proving Ground, Md., 1943-45. Recipient Franklin medal Franklin Inst. Phila., 1964; Nat. Medal of Sci., 1967; Tom Bonner prize Am. Phys. Soc., 1969. Fellow Am. Phys. Soc. (Tom Bonner prize, 1969), I.E.E.E., Phys. Soc. (London), A.A.A.S., Am. Acad. Arts and Scis., Washington Acad. Sci., Geophys. Union; mem. Nat. Acad. Sci., Phi Beta Kappa, Sigma Xi. Contbr. articles to profl. jours. Home: Dept Physics State U New York Buffalo NY 14214

BREITEL, CHARLES D. judge; b. N.Y.C., Dec. 12, 1908; s. Herman L. and Regina D. (Zuckerberg) B.; A.B., U. Mich. 1929; LL.B., Columbia, 1932; LL.D., L.I. U., 1953; m. Jeanne S. Hollander, April 9, 1927; children—Eleanor H. (Mrs. William D. Zabel), Sharon H. (dec.), Vivian H. Admitted to N.Y. bar, 1933; asso. Moers & Roseshein, 1933; asso. Engelhard, Pollask, Pitcher, Stern & Clarke, 1934-35; def. asst. dist. atty., staff Thomas E. Dewey, 1935-37, spl. rackets investigations; asst. dist. atty., 1938-41; chief Indictment Bur., 1941; asso. with Dewey, pvt. law practice, 1942; counsel to Gov. Dewey, 1943-50; apptd. justice state supreme ct. Dewey, 1950; asso. justice Appellate Div., First Dept., 1952-66; judge Ct. Appeals State N.Y., 1967—. Adj. prof. Columbia Sch. Law, 1963-69, also mem. bd. visitors. Mem. Pres.'s Commn. on Law Enforcement and Adminstrn. Justice, 1965-67; mem. Fed. Commn. on Internat. Rules Jud. Procedure, 1958-66, N.Y. State Post War Pub. Works Planning Commn., Joint Legislative Com. on Interstate Cooperation (adminstr.); mem. Gov's Com. on State Ednl. program, Commn. on Municipal Revenues and Reduction of Taxes. Mem. exec. com. N.Y. chpt. Am. Jewish Com. also mem. nat. bd. govs.; vis. com. Vanderbilt U. Law Sch., Sch. Criminal Justice State U. N.Y. Mem. Am. Law Inst. (council), Inst. Jud. Adminstrn., Lawyer's Club, Assn. Bar City N.Y., N.Y. County Lawyers Assn., Am., N.Y. State bar assns., Columbia Law Sch. Alumni Assn. (past pres.), Phi Delta Phi. Mem. B'nai B'rith. Clubs: Century (N.Y.C.); University (Albany, N.Y.). Home: 146 Central Park W New York City NY 10023 Office: Ct of Appeals Eagle St Albany NY 12207 also 74 Trinity Pl New York City NY 10006

BREITENBACH, EDWARD VICTOR, transp. cons.; b. Bostinin, Russia, Oct. 12, 1896; s. Richard and Bertha (Mueller) B.; came to U.S., 1901; student Nat. U. Law Sch., Washington; m. 2d, Anna Mae Perry, Apr. 10, 1951; 1 son, Edward Darwin. Accountant, C.M.St.P. & P. Ry., Chgo., 1913-18, U.S. R.R. Adminstrn., Washington, 1919-25; accountant ICC, Chgo., 1925-28, sect. chief accounts, Washington, 1935-42; transp. specialist Burroughs Adding Machine Co., Detroit, 1928-35; dir. adminstrn. Iranian Hwy. Transport System, Teheran, 1943-45; chief R.R. br. U.S. Mil. Govt., Berlin, Germany, 1945-48; chief, bur. finance, U.S. Maritime Commn., Washington, 1948-49; transport cons. Civil Transport Tokyo, Japan, 1949-52; adviser Japanese Nat. Rys., Tokyo, 1960-61; part-time cons. World Bank, 1964. Served with USNRF, 1918-19. Home: 460 Horizons W Boynton Beach FL 33435

BREITENBACH, HAROLD EUGENE, state judge; b. Washington, Ia., May 28, 1903; s. Eugene L. and Christina (Frank) B.; B.A., Grinnell Coll., 1925, LL.D., 1965; LL.B. (Charles E. Perkins scholar) Harvard, 1930; m. Harriet Gail Allen, Aug. 4, 1928; children—Constance Jean (Mrs. Edwin B. McCornack), Eugene Allen, Carolyn Gail (Mrs. William P. Hickey). Admitted to Cal. bar, 1931; practiced in Los Angeles, 1931-52; mem. bd. Cal. Youth Authority, 1952-57, Cal. Bd. Corrections, 1952-57; judge Superior Ct. Cal. for County Los Angeles, 1957—; presiding judge Juvenile Ct. Los Angeles County, 1961-65; chief enforcement atty, OPA, So. Cal. and Ariz., 1944-46; part-time prof. law Southwestern U., 1931-42, Loyola U., Los Angeles, 1943-44; judge appellate dept. Superior Ct. Los Angeles County, 1964-66. Pres. Mental Hygiene Soc. So. Cal., 1948; chmn. bd. Los Angeles Downtown YMCA, 1944-46; v.p., dir. Los Angeles Jr. C. of C., 1937-39; v.p. Los Angeles Area council Boy Scouts Am., 1937-41; mem. Bd. Met. Recreation and Youth Services Council Los Angeles, 1946-66; mem. Permanent Jud. Commn. United Presbyn. Ch. U.S.A., 1961-67, moderator, 1965-66, mem. Gen. Council Synod of So. Cal., 1967—, Trustee Presbytery Los Angeles, 1946-52, 57-60, Legal Aid Found. Los Angeles County, 1937—, Sch. Theology, Claremount, Cal., 1964—; bd. dirs. UN Assn. Los Angeles, 1957-67, Big Bros. Greater Los Angeles, 1955-60; bd. overseers Grinnell Coll., 1960-67. Recipient Alumni award Grinnell Coll., 1958. Mem. Am. Bar Assn. (chmn. sect. criminal law 1969- 70), Ia. Assn. So. Cal. (pres 1961), Nat. Council Juvenile Ct. Judges (exec. com. 1963-64), Phi Beta Kappa. Presbyn. (ruling elder). Mason (Shriner), Lion (past pres. Los Angeles Host Club). Clubs: Lake Arrowhead (Cal.), Yacht (commodore 1953, staff commodore 1953—); Los Angeles Athletic. Editor-in-chief Los Angeles Bar Assn. Bull., 1952; chmn. editorial bd. Cal. Bar Jour., 1955. Home: 1539 Princes Dr Glendale CA 91207 Office: Superior Court County Court House Los Angeles CA 90012

BREITENSTEIN, JEAN SALA, judge; b. Keokuk, Ia., July 18, 1900; s. George J. and Ida M. (Sala) B.; A.B., U. Colo., 1922, LL.B., 1924, LL.D., 1965; LL.D., U. Denver, 1960; m. Helen Collamore Thomas, July 8, 1925; children—Eleanore Thomas, Peter Frederick. Admitted to Colo. bar, 1924; asst. atty. gen. Colo., 1925-29; asst. U.S. dist atty. Colo., 1930- 33; pvt. practice law, Denver, 1933-54; atty. State Colo., interstate water matters, 1940-54; U.S. dist. judge Colo., 1954-57; U.S. circuit judge 10th Circuit, Denver, 1957-70, sr. circuit judge, 1970—., Mem. Am., Colo., Denver bar assns., Phi Beta Kappa, Order of Coif. Republican. Episcopalian. Mason (33). Clubs: Law, Denver Country, Denver (Denver); University. Home: 1201 Williams St Denver CO 80218 Office: US Ct House Denver CO 80202

BREITHAUPT, ERWIN MILLARD, educator; b. Columbus, O., Nov. 12, 1920; s. Erwin Millard and Lillian (Cox) B.; B.F.A., Miami U., Oxford, O., 1942; M.A., Ohio State U., 1947, Ph.D., 1954; m. Eleanor Ruth Averill, June 8, 1946; 1 dau., Bonnie. Asso. prof. U. Ga., 1947-62; prof. art, chmn. dept. Ripon (Wis.) Coll., 1962—. Asso. dir. Upward Bound, 1964-68. Mem. exec. com. Fond du Lac County Democratic Party, 1968—. Served with AUS, 1942-46. Rockefeller fellow, 1951-52. Mem. Coll. Art Assn., Am. Assn. U. Profs., So. Soc. Philosophy and Psychology. Exhibns. in perception and art Chgo. Mdse. Mart, also Mus. Modern Art. Home: 844 Ransom St Ripon WI 54971

BREITHUT, RICHARD COMMANDER, former fgn. service officer; b. N.Y.C., Mar. 18, 1910; s. Frederick Ernst and Edith Kingsmill (Commander) B.; B.S., Harvard, 1931; M.A., Columbia, 1933; m. Ulla Nilson Strand, May 5, 1950; 1 step-dau., Kristina Strand (Mrs. Ronald E. Miller). Instr., Western Res. U., Cleve., 1934- 39; economist bd. govs. Fed. Res. System, 1939-41; with U.S. Treasury Dept., 1941-42; with U.S. Dept. State, 1945—, economist, U.S. Treasury rep. Scandinavian area, dep. to U.S. rep. on NATO def. finance and econ. com., adviser U.S. NATO delegation, 1945- 54, adviser Office Internat. Trade and Resources, 1954-56; dep. spl. asst. to sec. state for disarmament and atomic energy, 1957-59; exec. asst. to sec. gen. Central Treaty Orgn., 1959-61; econ. counselor Am. embassy, Karachi, Pakistan, 1961-66, Tel Aviv, Israel, 1966-70; fgn. service officer, 1955-70. Served from 1st lt. to lt. col. USAAF, 1942-45. Decorated Legion of Merit. Mem. Fgn. Service Assn. Clubs: Sind, Karachi (Pakistan) Yacht: Caesarea Golf and Country (Israel); Dacor House (Washington); Butler Country; HVP (Pitts.). Home: 121 Larchwood Dr Butler PA 16001

BREITLING, SISTER MARIE, hosp. adminstr.; b. Algiers, La., Aug. 30, 1917; d. Norman Edward and Mary (Reid) B.; R.N., Hotel Dieu Sch. Nursing, New Orleans, 1942; B.S., La. State U., 1950; M.H.A., St. Louis U., 1955. Mem. Daughters of Charity of St. Vincent de Paul, 1942; hosp. nursing supr. and instr., 1943-53; adminstr. Seton Hosp., Austin, Tex., 1955-58, St. Joseph Hosp., Chgo., 1958-60, O'Connor Hosp., San Jose, Cal., 1960-62, St. Joseph (Mo.) Hosp., 1962-68, St. Paul Hosp., Dallas, 1968—. Dir. Blue-Cross-Blue Shield, 1969—. Mem. adv. bd. Dallas Ind. Sch. System, 1968—, Southwestern Med. Sch. Found., 1968—; pres. bd. trustees Seton Hosp., Austin, Tex., 1970—. Fellow Am. Coll. Hosp. Adminstrs.; mem. Nat. League Nursing, Am. Hosp. Financial Mgmt. Assn., Am. Heart Assn., Am., Cath. hosps. assns. Contbr. articles profl. jours. Address: 5909 Harry Hines Blvd Dallas TX 75235

BREITMEYER, ELEANOR AMELIA, author; b. Detroit, Apr. 16, 1926; d. Martin and Elizabeth (Goetz) Breitmeyer; B.A., U. Mich., 1948. With Northville (Mich.) Record, 1948- 52; with Detroit News, 1952—, club editor, 1958-62, society editor, 1963—. Recipient Mayor Detroit award, 1962; Headliner of Year award, 1965; Quota Club award, 1962. Mem. Detroit Press Club, Theta Sigma Phi (past pres.). Home: 9530 Faust St Detroit MI 48228 Office: 615 W Lafayette St Detroit MI 48231

BREITWEISER, ROBERT ALLEN, ret. air force officer; b. St. Joseph, Mo., Apr. 23, 1916; s. Edgar Allen and Fern (Fish) B.; student Colo. Sch. Mines, 1932-34; B.S., U.S. Mil. Acad., 1938; grad. Air War Coll., 1950, Nat. War Coll., 1955; m. Eleanor Stevenson, June 18, 1938; children—Robert Allen, William S. Commd. 2d lt., C.E., U.S. Army, 1938, advanced through grades to lt. gen. USAF, 1967; attached 68th Composite Wing, 14th Air Force, China, World WAr II; various command and staff assignments to 1958; dir. intelligence Joint Staff, Washington, 1958-61; asst. chief staff intelligence Hdqrs. USAF, Washington, 1961-63; comdr. USAF, So. Command, 1963-66; comdt. Air War Coll., 1967-67; comdr. in chief, Alaska, 1967-69; ret. 1969. Decorated D.S.M., Legion Merit, Bronze Star medal, Air medal, Distinguished Unit citation; Order of Yun Hui (China); Order of Condor of Andes (Bolivia); Royal Order Sword (Sweden); Grand Star Mil. Merit (Chile): Order Aero. Merit (Brazil). Mem. Air Force Assn., Order Daedalians. Home: PO Box 2454 New Bern NC 28560

BREITWIESER, CHARLES JOHN, corp. exec., engr.; b. Colorado Springs, Colo., Sept. 23, 1910; s. Joseph Valentine and Ruth (Fowler) B.; B.S. in E.E., U. N.D., 1930, D.Sc. (hon.), 1949; student Chgo. Central Sta. Inst., 1930- 31; M.S., Cal. Inst. Tech., 1933; m. Irene Louise Kellman, May 29, 1943; children—Diane Louise, Janice Lynn. Instr. engring. and math. U. N.D., 1931; elec. engr., Pub. Service of No. Ill., 1930-31; engr. United Sound Products Corp., Los Angeles, 1933-34; cons. engr. and mfg. comml. research, Pasadena, Cal., 1934-37; formed C.J. Breitwieser & Co., 1935, co. merged with Bropar Engring. Co. of Los Angeles, forming Caldo Corp. of which became chief engr. and v.p., 1937, sec.- treas. Conducto-Therm. Corp. Los Angeles, 1939; cons. engr. DeForest Labs. and chief engr. DeForest Research; with Consol.-Vultee Aircraft Mfg. Co., chief engring. labs. and electronics, 1940- 50; v.p. engring., gen. mgr. research and devel. div. Lear, Inc., Santa Monica, Cal., 1954-57; v.p., gen. mgr. Learcal div. Lear, Inc., 1955-57; pres. Metrolog Corp., a subsidiary of Air Logistics Corp. 1958- 60, v.p. engring. and customer relations Air Logistics Corp., 1958-60; pres., chmn. bd. Dominion Devel. Corp., 1960—; exec. v.p., gen. mgr. Cubic Corp., San Diego, 1961—, dir.; dir. Swan Electronics Corp., U.S. Elevator Corp.; dir. engring. P.R. Mallory & Co., Indpls. 1950-54; cons. engr. Los Angeles Police and Fire depts., 1932- 35. Cons. to Research and Devel. Bd. Fellow Inst. Radio Engrs.; mem. Am. Inst. E.E. (mem. com. on electronics), A.A.A.S., American Physics Soc., Nat. Aircraft Standards Com., Sigma Xi, Phi Delta Gamma. Author papers in field. Patentee. Home: 617 Ridgeline Pl Solana Beach CA 92075 Office: Cubic Corp 9233 Balboa Av San Diego CA 92123

BREKKA, THOMAS THORWALD, aerospace co. exec.; b. Bklyn., Sept. 14, 1928; s. Thorwald T. and Edna (Brennan) B.; B.S. in Accounting, Fordham U., 1950, LL.D., 1959; m. Patricia Ann Flynn, Aug. 4, 1952; children—Patricia, Thomas, Rosemary, Kathleen, Michael, Christine, Richard, Kevin, Maureen, Susan. Statistician, W. R. Grace & Co., 1950-51; financial asst. Grace Nat. Bank, also asst. v.p. Marine Midland Grace Trust Co., N.Y.C., 1955-66; mgr. financial planning Rohr Corp., Chula Vista, Cal., 1966-67, treas., 1967-70, chief financial officer, 1970—. Mem. Am. Bar Assn., N.Y. Soc. Security Analysts. Nat. Assn. Accountants. Financial Execs. Inst. Catholic. Clubs: Cuyamaca; Kona Kai (San Diego). Home: 2671 Palomino Circle La Jolla CA 92037 Office: Rohr Corp Foot of H St Chula Vista CA 92012

BREL, JACQUES, singer; b. Brussels, Belgium, Apr. 8, 1929; m.; children—Chantal, France, Isabelle. Worked in father's corrugated carton factory, 1948-53; singer-writer 1948—; debut at Theater of the Three Donkeys, Paris, 1953, then appeared at l'Ecluse, Patachou, Olympia; toured with Sydney Bechet in provinces and N. Africa, 1955; singing tours in Paris at Alhambra, 1957, Olympia, 1958, 61, 64, 66, Bobino, 1959, USSR, 1965; radio performances in The Idiot, Lettres d'amour, also serial En attendant Madeleine; cinema performances Les Risques du metizr, 1967, la Bande à Bonnot, 1968; theatre performances L'Hemme de la Mancha, Brussels and Paris, 1968; appeared in 4 films, France; prin. songs include: Ne me quitte pas, les Bourgeois, Mathilde, le Moribord, les Bonbons, Amsterdam, Jacky, Mon Enfance, Fils de, Les Vieux Amants, Quand on a que L'Amour, others. Address: Tavel et Marpuani 35 rue Marbeuf Paris 8e France*

BREM, THOMAS HAMILTON, physician; b. C.Z., 1910; M.D., Johns Hopkins, 1937. Intern, Johns Hopkins Hosp., Balt., 1937-38; asst. pathology Stanford, 1938-39; resident physician Los Angeles County Gen. Hosp., 1939-41, now mem. attending staff; cons. VA Hosp., Long Beach, Cal.; physician-in-chief Los Angeles County Hosp.; prof., head dept. medicine U. So. Cal. Served to capt. AUS, 1942-45. Diplomate Am. Bd. Internal Medicine (chmn. bd. 1963-65). Fellow A.C.P.; mem. A.M.A., Assn. Am. Physicians, Alpha Omega Alpha. Address: 2025 Zonal Av Los Angeles CA 90033

BREMBECK, COLE SPEICHER, educator; b. Urbana, Ind., May 22, 1917; s. Paul and Hulda (Speicher) B.; Ph.B., U. Wis., 1939, Ph.D., 1951; M.A., Bucknell U., 1941; m. Helen Simpson, June 28, 1941; children Elizabeth Ann, Mark. Instr. English, Lehigh U., 1941-43; asst. to pres. Manchester Coll., 1945-49; asso. prof. Pa. State U., 1950-51; supt. schs., North Muskegon, Mich., 1951- 54, Livonia, Mich. 1954-55; chmn. dept. tchr. edn., chmn. founds. of edn. dept. Mich. State U., 1955-59, prof., 1955—; chmn. All-Univ. secondary sch. com., dir. Center for Study Higher Edn., prof. edn., 1960-61; now director Inst. Internat. Studies in Edn., also asso. dean Coll. Edn. Cons. community devel., Govt. Pakistan, 1956, 58, 59-60; cons. East-West Center., U. Hawaii, 1962-68; cons. ednl. planning Republic of Korea, 1968—. Mem. Comparative and Internat. Edn. Soc., Am. Ednl. Studies Assn., Soc. Internat. Devel. Author: Discovery of Teaching; Social Foundations of Education. Co-author: Education for the Development of Nations. Home: 3655 Meridian Rd Okemos MI 48864

BREMBECK, WINSTON LAMONT, educator; b. Urbana, Ind., Sept. 28, 1912; s. Paul John and Hulda (Speicher) B.; B.A. magna cum laude, Manchester Coll., N. Manchester, Ind., 1936; M.A., U. Wis., 1938, Ph.D., 1947; m. Neva Gloyd, June 20, 1940. Instr., Westmar Coll., LeMars, Ia., 1936-39; tutor Bklyn. Coll., 1939-42; mem. faculty U. Wis., 1947—, prof. communication and pub. 1960—; 1960-; cons. in communications and persuasion to business, profl. and religious groups, 1947—. Served with AUS, 1943-46. Recipient A.T. Weaver Outstanding Tchr. award Wis. Speech Assn., 1970. Mem. Speech Assn. Am. (exec. com. 1966-68), Central States (pres. 1965-66), Wis. (pres. 1949-50) speech assns., Internat. Platform Assn., Am. Assn. U. Profs., Delta Sigma Rho, Tau Kappa Alpha, Phi Kappa Phi. Republican. Methodist. Author: (with W.S. Howell) Persuasiona Means of Social Control, 1952; also articles. Home: 3206 Leyton Lane Madison, WI 53713.

BREMENT, MARSHALL, fgn. service officer; b. N.Y.C., Jan. 10, 1932; s. Isidore and Haya (Glauberman) B.; B.A., U. N.Y., 1952; M.A., U. Md., 1955; N.I.P.A. fellow Stanford, 1966-67; m. Joan Bernstein, May 2, 1953; children—Diana, Mark, Gabriel. Joined U.S. Fgn. Service 1956; staff asst. State Dept. asst. sec. Far East, 1956-57; assigned Chinese lang. tng. 1958-60; consul polit. sect. Am. Consulate Gen., Hong Kong, 1960-63; Russian lang. tng., 1963-64; polit. sect. Am. embassy Moscow, 1964-66; chief polit. sect. Am. embassy Singapore, 1967-70; counsellor pub. affairs Am. embassy Djakarta, 1970—. Served with USAF, 1952-54. Fellow N.I.P.A., mem. Nat. Inst. Pub. Affairs, Am. Fgn. Service Assn., Phi Kappa Phi. Home: Brawidjaja III I Kebajoran Djakarta Indonesia Office: U S Embassy APO San Francisco CA 96356

BREMERMANN, HANS JOACHIM, educator; b. Bremen, Germany, Sept. 14, 1926; s. Bernhard and Berta (Wicke) B.; Staatsexamen, Ph.D., U. Münster (Germany), 1951; m. Maria Isabel Lopez Perez-Ojeda, May 16, 1954. Came to U.S., 1952, naturalized, 1965. Instr. math. U. Münster, 1952; research asso. Stanford, 1952-53, vis. asst. prof. math., 1953-54; asst. prof. math. U. Münster, 1954-55; mem. Inst. Advanced Studies, Princeton, 1955-57, 58-59; mem. faculty U. Cal. at Berkeley, 1959—, prof., 1966—, vice chmn. exec. com., grad. group biophysics and med. physics, 1966-68, vice chmn. dept. math., 1961-62, 68; asst. prof. U. Wash., 1957-58; vis. prof. U. Tex., Austin, 1966. Mem. biophys. tng. grant com. NIH, 1966-70. Research fellow Harvard, 1953. Mem. Am., Austrian, German math. socs., German Soc. Applied Math. and Mathanics, Biophys. Soc. Author: Distributions, Complex Variables and Fourier Transforms, 1965; also articles. Editorial bd. Biophys. Jour.; asso. editor Math. Bioscis., Applicable Analysis. Home: 1873 San Ramon Av Berkeley CA 94707

BREMSER, GEORGE, Jr., co. exec.; b. Newark, May 26, 1928; s. George and Virginia (Christian) B.; B.A., Yale, 1949; postgrad. U. Miami, 1959; M.B.A., N.Y. U., 1962; m. Marie Sundman, June 21, 1952; children—Christian Frederick II, Priscilla Suzanne, Martha Anne, Sarah Elizabeth. Sales trainee Pitts. Plate Glass, South Bend, Ind., 1949-50; with McCann-Erickson, Inc., N.Y.C., 1952-61, asst. gen. mgr., Bogota, Colombia, 1955, gen. mgr., 1955-57, account supr., N.Y.C., 1958, v.p., mgr., Miami, Fla., 1959-61; asso. product mgr. Maxwell House div. Gen. Foods Corp., White Plains, N.Y., 1961-62, product mgr., 1962-63, advt., merchandising mgr., 1963- 64, marketing dir. internat. div., 1964, area dir. internat. div., 1965- 66, asst. gen. mgr. internat. div., 1966-67, v.p., gen. mgr. Gen. Foods Europe 1967, pres., Gen. Foods Internat., 1967-71, group v.p. Gen. Foods Corp, 1970-71; pres., dir., chief exec. officer Texstar Corp., Grand Prairie, Tex., 1971—; dir. Butler Aviation Internat., Inc.

Chmn., Citizens Com. for Conservation, New Canaan, Conn.; treas. Yale Alumni Chorus, N.Y.C., 1961-62. County committeeman 1st dist. Democratic party, Ridgewood, N.J., 1962-63; mem. Town Council New Canaan, 1970—. Served to 2d lt. USMCR, 1950-52; capt. Res. Mem. Phi Beta Kappa, Beta Gamma Sigma, Beta Theta Pi. Conglist. Clubs: Yale (N.Y.C.); New Canaan Field, New Canaan Winter; Block Island. Home: 5 Jennifer Lane New Canaan CT 06840 Office: 802 Av J E Grand Prairie TX 75050

BRENAN, RALPH BETTS, business exec.; b. St. John, N.B., Nov. 20, 1901; s. Frederick Betts and Mabel Ella (Engall) B.; student pub. schs., St. John; m. Gertrude Edna Hunt, Oct. 17, 1927; children—Ralph Betts, Diana Hunt. With T.H. Estabrooks Co., Ltd., 1922-49, pres., 1938-49; mng. dir. G. E. Barbour Co., Ltd., 1949-58, pres., 1958—; v.p., dir. Fraser Cos. Ltd.; dir. Adm. Beatty Hotel Co., Fundy Broadcasting Co., Bank of Montreal, Crush Internat., Zeller's, Ltd. Clubs: Union, Cliff (St. John); Mt. Royal (Montreal Que.). Home: Rothesay New Brunswick Canada Office: St John New Brunswick Canada

BRENDEL, ALFRED, pianist; b. Wiesenberg, Jan. 5, 1913; s. Albert B. and Ida (Wieltschnig) B.; State Diploma with excellence, Vienna Acad. Music, 1947; studied with S. Dezelic, Zagreb, 1937-43, L.V. Kaan, Graz, Austria, 1943-47, Edwin Fischer, Lucerne, Paul Baumgartner, Basel, Switzerland, Eduard Steurmann, Salzburg; m. Iris Heymann-Gonzala, December 22, 1960; one daughter, Doris. Gave his first piano recital, Graz, Austria, 1948; tours with Vienna Chamber Orch. 1951, Vienna Symphony, 1954; concerts many European countries, four Latin Am. tours; debut with Vienna Philharmonic, Salzburg Festival, 1960, soloist Salzburg Festival, 1960-69, Edinburgh Festival, 1970; 1st appearance with Berlin Philharmonic, 1961; several appearances Vienna Festival; Australian tours, 1963, 66, 69; regular tours N. Am. 1963—; debut Los Angeles Philharmonic; N.Y. appearances Hunter Coll., 1963, 64, 71, Philharmonic Hall, Phila. Orch., 1965, N.Y. Philharmonic, 1971; numerous recordings works of Beethoven, Liszt, other classical music. Recipient Grand Prix du Disque, Paris, Grand Prix du Discophiles, 1965. Home: 11 Ungargasse Vienna 3, Austria Office: care Colbert Artists Mgmt 850 7th Av New York City NY 10019

BRENDEL, OTTO JOHANNES, educator; b. Nuremberg, Germany, Oct. 10, 1901; s. Randolf and Mathilde (Gareis) B.; Ph.D., U. Heidelberg (Germany), 1928; m. Maria Weigert, Feb. 9, 1929; 1 dau., Cornelia (Mrs. Lukas Foss). Came to U.S., 1938, naturalized, 1943. Docent, Erlangen U., 1931; vis. asst. prof. Washington U., St. Louis, 1939; asso. prof., then prof. Ind. U., 1941, 45-56; prof. art history and archaeology Columbia, 1956—. Fellow German Archaeol. Inst., Am. Acad. Rome; mem. Archaeol. Inst. Am., Coll. Art Assn., Renaissance Soc. Am. Spl. research Greek, Etruscan and Roman art and archaeology, ancient religion classical survivals in Renaissance and later art. Home: 315 Riverside Dr New York City NY 10025

BRENDLER, HERBERT, surgeon; b. N.Y.C., Jan 20, 1914; s. Charles and Frances (Glaser) B.; A.B., Columbia, 1934; M.D., N.Y.U., 1938; m. Virginia Palmer Burgess, Nov. 27, 1942 (dec. 1952); children—Charles Burgess, Anne Clark, Robert Alston; m. 2d, Sarah Burwell Childs, Jan. 20, 1959; children—Katherine Burwell, Jane Childs, Elizabeth Dudley. Surg. tng. Bellevue, Sydenham and N.Y. Postgrad. hosps., 1938-42; urology tng. Johns Hopkins Hosp., 1945-49; attending urologist, prof. urology N.Y.U.-Bellevue Med. Center, 1946-53; attending urologist Bronx VA Hosp., 1950-55; cons. Norwalk (Conn.) Hosp., 1961—; urologist-in-chief, head dept., Mt. Sinai Hosp., N.Y.C., 1963—; prof. urology, chmn. dept. Mt. Sinai Sch. Medicine, 1966—; asso. clin. prof. Columbia Coll. Phys. and Surg., 1964-67. Vis. scientist Imperial Cancer Research Fund, London, Eng., 1963; chmn. com. coop. study prostatic cancer, USPHS, 1956-63. Mem. citizens adv. com. Pelham (N.Y.) Bd. Edn., 1957-60; asst. commr. Pelham Little League, 1954-61. Served with M.C. USNR, 1942-45. Recipient Career Scientist award N.Y.C. Health Research Council, 1961. Mem. A.M.A., A.C.S., Am. Urol. Assn. (treas. N.Y. sect. 1966-67, pres. elect 1968—), Am. Assn. Cancer Research, Endocrine Soc., Soc. Internat. D'Urologie, Johns Hopkins Med. and Surg. Assn., Urol. Investigators Forum, Am. Assn. Genito-Urinary Surgeons. Author articles med. jours. Home: 305 Pelhamdale Av Pelham NY 10803 Office: 11 E 100th St New York City NY 10029

BRENDTRO, LARRY KAY, educator, psychologist; b. Sioux Falls, S.D., July 26, 1940; s. A. Kenneth and Bernice (Matz) B.; B.A., Augustana Coll., 1961; M.S., S.D. State U., 1962; Ph.D., U. Mich., 1965. Prin. Crippled Children's Hosp. and Sch., Sioux Falls, 1962-63; psychologist Hawthorn Center, Northville, Mich., 1964-65; instr. ednl. psychology U. Mich., 1965-66; dir. grad. programs emotional disturbance U. Ill., 1966-67; co-dir. pub. sch. research project for behaviorally disordered children, Urbana, Ill., 1966-67; pres. Starr Commonwealth for Boys, Albion, Mich., 1967—; cons. in field, 1966. Cons. U.S. Office Edn., 1967—. Mem. Council Exceptional Children, Council Children with Behavioral Disorders. Lutheran. Co-author: The Other 23 Hours, 1969. Address: Starr Commonwealth for Boys Albion, MI 49224.

BRENEMAN, WILLIAM RAYMOND, educator; b. Indpls., June 3, 1907; s. William Trytle and Minnie Nell (Stephenson) B.; A.B., Ind. Central Coll., 1930, LL.D., 1962; Ph.D., Ind. U., 1934; m. Mary Alice Petty, Sept. 13, 1930; children—William Louis, Raymond Bruce, Miriam Eilene. NRC fellow U. Wis., 1934-35; instr. zoology Miami U., Oxford O., 1935-36; mem. faculty Ind. U., 1936—, Waterman prof. zoology, 1962—, chmn. dept. zoology, 1966-68; spl. research avian endocrinology. Recipient Lieber award for distinguished teaching Ind. U., 1955. Fellow Ind. Acad. Sci.; mem. A.A.A.S., Am. Soc. Zoologists, Poultry Sci. Assn., World Poultry Congress, N.Y. Acad. Scis., Sigma Xi. Methodist. Author: Animal Form and Function, 1954; also research articles. Home: 3500 Bradley St Rural Route 12 Bloomington IN 47401

BRENER, BERNARD JOSEPH, educator; b. N.Y.C., Jan. 20, 1925; s. Reuben and Irene (Schoenbrun) B.; B.A., N.Y. U., 1947, M.A., 1950, Ph.D., 1958. Instr., L.I. U., 1950-58, Bklyn. Poly. Inst., 1955-60; lectr. Hofstra Coll., 1956; mem. faculty L.I. U., 1958—, prof. German, 1963—, chmn. dept. modern langs., 1962—. Served with AUS, 1942-45. Mem. Am. Assn. Tchrs. German (treas. Met. chpt.), Modern Lang. Assn., Thomas Mann Gesellschaft. Home: 25 Minetta Lane New York City NY 10012 Office: Long Island Univ Brooklyn NY 11201

BRENGEL, F. L., instrument co. exec.; b. Hicksville, N.Y., Mar. 31, 1923; s. Henry C. and Anna C. (Jones) B.; M.E., Stevens Inst. Tech., 1944; m. Joan E. Files, Dec. 4, 1948; children—Douglas A., Edith Ann, Kenneth F. Test engr. Fairchild Aviation Co., 1946-47; sales engr. Permutit Co., 1947-48; with Johnson Service Co., 1948—, exec. v.p., 1965-67, pres., 1967-; dir. First Wis. Bankshares Corp. Mem. Am. Soc. Heating, Refrigerating and Air-Conditioning Engrs., Milw. Assn. Commerce and Industry (bd. dirs.), Am. Legion. Mason, Rotarian. Clubs: Milwaukee Athletic, Milwaukee, Town (Milw.). Home: 7836 N Club Circle Milwaukee, WI 53217. Office: 507 E Michigan St Milwaukee WI 53202

BRENIZER, ADDISON GORGAS, Jr., surgeon; b. Charlotte, N.C., Dec. 3, 1915; s. Addison Gorgas and Mary (Harding) B.; grad. McCallie Sch., 1932; student Davidson Coll., 1932- 34; A.B., Princeton, 1936; M.D., Harvard, 1940; m. Meredith Marshall, Jan. 1, 1942; children—Meredith, Leigh (Mrs. William C.C. Barnes), David, Nancy, William. Practice in Charlotte; chief surg. service Charlotte Meml. Hosp. Dir. First Union Nat. Bank. Served to maj., M.C., AUS, 1944-48; PTO. Mem. A.C.S., So., N.C. surg. assns., Alpha Omega Alpha. Contbr. med. jours. Home: 1333 Queens Rd Charlotte NC 28207 Office: 1012 Kings Dr Charlotte NC 28207

BRENKERT, KARL, Jr., mech. engr., univ. dean; b. Detroit, June 29, 1921; s. Karl and June Garland (Young) B.; B.S. in Mech. Engring., U. Mich., 1944; M.S. in Engring. Mechanics, Stanford, 1952, Ph.D. in Engring. Mechanics, 1955; m. Elizabeth Scott, June 2, 1945; children—Gail (Mrs. James Victor Rackley), Karl III, Pamela Karen, Scott Jeffrey, Eric Randolph. With RCA, 1944-47; owner, mgr. T.E.K. Industries, Inc., also Bracey Corp., 1947-49; mem. faculty Sch. Engring., U. Utah, 1949-50, Stanford, 1950- 54; asst. prof. U. Ala., 1954-56; asso. prof. Mich. State U., 1956-60; prof., asst. dean Auburn U., 1960-63; dean Sch. Engring., U. Miss., 1964—. Program dir., div. instl. programs NSF, 1963-64; mem. research adminstrv. com. Engring. Coll. Research Council, 1964—; cons. NSF, 1964-68. evaluation cons. Engrs. Council Profl. Devel., 1962-69. Mem. bd. dirs. Lafayette County Red Cross. Registered prof. engineer, Ala., Miss. Mem. Am. Inst. Aero. and Astronautics, Am. Soc. Mech. Engrs., American Soc. C.E., A.A.A.S., Nat. Soc. Profl. Engrs., Am. Soc. for Engring. Edn., Miss. Cattlemen's Assn., Sigma Xi, Pi Tau Sigma, Omicron Delta Kappa, Tau Beta Pi, Alpha Tau Omega. Author: Elementary Theoretical Fluid Mechanics, 1960. Club: Oxford Country. Contbr. Applied Mechanics Revs., 1960-67. Home: 107 Colonial Rd Oxford, MS 38655. Office: Sch Engring Univ Mississippi University MS 38677

BRENNAN, ANDREW PETER, dept. store exec.; b. Chgo., May 3, 1916; s. Andrew Peter and Florence Mary (LeBeau) B.; student Ariz. State Coll., Northwestern U.; m. Virginia J. McCann, May 16, 1942; 1 dau., Vandy (Mrs. Gerald Nies). Regional and co. exec. Montgomery Ward & Co., Chgo., 1945-55; v.p. charge operations Top Value Enterprises, Dayton, O., 1955-61; exec. v.p., gen. mgr., dir. E.F. MacDonald Stamp Co., Dayton, 1961-62; v.p. May Dept. Stores Co., St. Louis, 1962—, chmn. bd. Eagle Stamp Co., 1962—; dir. Jefferson Bank & Trust Co. Served with USAAF, World War II. Decorated Air medal with 4 clusters. Mem. St. Louis C. of C. Clubs: Forest Hills Country, Mo. Athletic, St. Louis Camera. Home: 541 Fox Ridge Rd Frontenac MO 63131 Office: 3100 Market St St Louis MO 63103

BRENNAN, DONALD GEORGE, nat. security affairs researcher; b. Waterbury, Conn., Apr. 9, 1926; s. George J. and Jessie (Griswold) B.; B.S., Mass. Inst. Tech., 1955, Ph.D. (Gerard Swope fellow), 1959; m. Katie Sheldon, Oct. 11, 1969. Chief engr. radio sta. WWCO, Waterbury, Conn., 1947-49; mem. staff Crystal Research Lab., Hartford, Conn., also instr. Ward Sch. Electronics, U. Hartford, 1949-51; mem. staff Lincoln Lab., Mass. Inst. Tech., 1953-59, group leader, 1959-62; research asso. math. Mass. Inst. Tech., 1959-61; pres. Hudson Inst., Croton-on-Hudson, N.Y., 1962-64, mem. staff, 1964—; cons. Dept. Def., State Dept., Arms Control and Disarmament Agy., Exec. Office Pres. Mem. President's Nat. Citizens' Commn. Internat. Coop. Year, 1965. Served with AUS, 1944-47. Mem. I.E.E.E., Inst. Strategic Studies, Am. Math. Soc., Council on Fgn. Relations, Mass. Inst. Tech. Faculty Club, Sigma Xi. Co- author, editor: Arms Control, Disarmament and National Security, 1961. Editor Arms Control and Nat-Security Jour. Home: 105 Deer Track Lane Irvington NY 10533

BRENNAN, EDWARD THOMAS, fgn. service officer; b. Toorak, Australia, Feb. 28, 1921; s. William Rowley and Katherine Angela (Donovan) B.; came to U.S., 1922, naturalized, 1924; B.S. in Fgn. Service, Georgetown U., 1949; m. Denise Helen Meier, Dec. 31, 1945; children—Kevin, Denise, Edward Thomas, Peter. Joined U.S. Fgn. Service, 1941; assigned State Dept., 1941-42, charge diplomatic courier operations for Latin Am., South Pacific and No. Europe, 1947-50, chief couriers, 1952-53, officer charge European region, Paris, France, 1953-54, Frankfort am/Main, Germany, 1954-56; assigned Am. embassy, Manila, Philippines, 1957-59, Tunis, Tunisia, 1959-63; dep. chief mission, counselor Am. embassy, Bangui, Central African Republic, 1963-66; assigned Nat. War Coll., Washington, 1966-67; spl. asst. Internat. affairs div. plans and operations USAF, 1967-68, asst. dep. dir. plans for policy, 1968-69, dir. Office Multilateral Policy and Programs, Dept. State, 1969-71, U.S. consul gen. Am. embassy, Thessaloniki, Greece, 1971—. Alternate del. U.S. delegation to 16th Gen. Conf., UNESCO, Paris, 1970. Served as aviator USNR, 1942-47, 50-52. Recipient Exceptional Civilian Service commendation Dept. of Air Force, 1970; Superior Service award Dept. state, 1971, Mem. Am. Fgn. Service Assn., U.S. Naval Inst., Georgetown U. Alumni Assn. Home: 18 High St Beverly Farms MA 01915 also 9104 Kirkdale Rd Bethesda MD 20034 Office: Am Consulate Gen Thessaloniki Greece

BRENNAN, FRANCIS EDWIN, pub. cons.; b. Maywood, Ill., July 14, 1910; s. Frank E. and Gertrude A. (Nickelsen) B.; student exptl. coll. U. Wis., 1927-28, Chgo. Art Inst., 1928-31; m. Elizabeth Reid Dewson, Dec. 16, 1938; children—Elizabeth Chandler, Julia Sheridan; m. 2d, Frances Margaret Myers, July 24, 1946; children—Christopher, Richard Lee. Asst. art dir. Conde Nast Publs., 1933; art dir. Brit. Vogue, London, 1934, House and Garden, 1935-37; asso. art dir. Life mag., 1937; art dir. Fortune mag., 1938-42; art adviser to editor-in-chief Time-Life-Fortune, N.Y.C., 1947-61; v.p. McCann- Erickson, N.Y.C., 1961-62; spl. asst. to pres. McCall Corp., N.Y.C., 1966-68; art adviser Newsweek mag. Washington Post Co., 1969—. Picture editor Life's Picture History of World War II, 1950. Served with AUS, World War II. Decorated chevalier Legion of Honor, chevalier Orde du Merite Comml. (France). Mem. Am. Fedn. Arts (sec.). Clubs: Century Assn., Coffee House (N.Y.C.). Home: 40 E 62d St New York City NY 10021

BRENNAN, FRANCIS PATRICK, banker; b. Sommerville, Mass., Jan. 9, 1917; s. John Joseph and Bridget (Sullivan) B.; A.B. cum laude , Boston Coll., 1939; postgrad. Bentley Coll. Accounting and Finance, 1941; m. Mary J. Gilhooly, July 23, 1949; children-Mary Ann, Eileen, John, Thomas. Loan officer Reconstrn. Finance Corp., Boston, 1941-42, 46-53; exec. v.p. Mass. Bus. Devel. Corp., Boston, 1954-61, now dir.; pres. Union Warren Savs. Bank, Boston, 1961- -; dir. Mut. Savs. Central Fund, Inc., Johnston Mut. Fund, Inc., Federal St. Capital Corp. Bd. advisers Stonehill Coll., 1968—; mem. corp. Walter E. Fernald Sch., 1964—. Mem. Winchester (Mass.) Town Meeting, 1970. Bd. dirs. Mass. Taxpayers Found., Boston Municipal Research Bur., Com. for Central Bus. Dist. Served to 2d lt. AUS, 1942-45; ETO Decorated Bronze Star, Mem. Savs. Banks Assn. Mass. (v.p. 1970—), Nat. Assn. Mut. Savs. Banks (dir.), Mortgage Bankers Assn. Am. (Washington com.). Home: 36 Central St Winchester MA 01890 Office: 216 Tremont St Boston MA 02116

BRENNAN, FRANCIS W., brewery exec.; b. Newark, Nov. 18, 1919: s. William J. and B. Agnes (McDermott) B.; A.B., Princeton, 1940; LL.B., Harvard, 1947; m. Betty Kirkwood, Feb. 19, 1944; children—Judith, Francis K., Robert. Admitted to N.J. bar, 1947; asso. firm Pitney, Hardin & Ward, Newark, 1947-53; gen. counsel Cal. Oil Co., Perth Amboy, N.J., 1953-54; v.p. legal, sec. P. Ballatine & Sons, Newark, 1954-71; v.p., sec., gen. counsel Rheingold Breweries, Inc., Bklyn., 1971—; sec. Boston Celtics Basketball Club; 1968-69; mem. adv. bd. First Nat. State Bank N.J., Newark. Commr., Essex County (N.J.) Park Commn., 1958—, pres., 1963-65, 70-71. Chmn. trustees Boys Clubs Newark, 1966-69. Served to capt. USAAF, World War II. Mem. Am., N.J., Essex County bar assns. Home: 4 Winding Way North Caldwell NJ 07006 Office: 36 Forrest St Brooklyn NY 11206

BRENNAN, HAROLD JAMES, writer, critic; b. Indpls., Oct. 25, 1903; s. William Henry and Jane (Grass) B.; A.B. (Tiffany Found. fellow 1932), Carnegie Inst. Tech., 1932, M.A., 1942; student Harvard, 1934-35; Inst. Internat. Edn. scholar, U. Paris (France), 1938; m. Novelda Reine Noderer, June 8, 1933; children—Jennifer (Mrs. Roberts French), James, Julie (Mrs. Fletcher R. Silker), Kelley. Prof. art at Westminster Coll., New Wilmington, Pa., 1934-43, chmn. div. arts, 1946-48; dir. Sch. Am. Craftsmen, Alfred U., 1948-50; dir. Sch. Am. Craftsmen, Rochester Inst. Tech., 1950-54, chmn. div. arts, 1954-56, dean Coll. Fine and Applied Arts, 1956-70, dean emeritus, 1970—; now writer, critic; lectr. fine and applied arts Assn. Am. Coll., 1934-43. Mem. Webster (N.Y.) Bd. Edn., 1953—; chmn. civic devel. com. Arts Council Rochester, 1958—. Pres. Webster Council Chs., 1954. Trustee Rochester Mus. Arts and Scis. Served to capt. AUS, 1944-46. Mem. Nat. Art Edn. Assn., Am. Indsl. Arts Assn., Delta Tau Delta, Tau Sigma Delta, Phi Kappa Phi. Mason. Contbr. articles profl. jours. Home: 920 Lake Rd Webster NY 14580

BRENNAN, JAMES B., U.S. atty.; B.S., U. Notre Dame; LL.B., Marquette U. Admitted to bar, 1952; now U.S. atty. Eastern Dist. Wis. Address: 2813 N 87th St Milwaukee WI 53233*

BRENNAN, JAMES G., physicist; b. Hazelton, Pa., Aug. 30, 1927; s. Thomas H. and Helen (Gallagher) B.; B.S., U. Scranton, 1948; M.S., Ph.D., U. Wis.; m. Anne Searls, July 28, 1951; children—Thomas, Sean, Kathleen, James, Theodore. Mem. Faculty Cath. U., 1952—, now prof. physics, chmn. dept.; cons. Naval Orinance Lab., 1955; liason scientist Office Naval Research, London, 1965-66. Faculty rep. Cath. U. bd. trustees, 1968—. Mem. Am. Phys. Soc., Washington Philos. Soc. Roman Cath. Club: Cosmos (Washington). Author articles theoretical nuclear physics. Home: 8910 Sudbury Rd Silver Spring MD 20012 Office: Keane Physics Bldg Michigan Av NE Washington DC 20012

BRENNAN, JAMES THOMAS, educator, radiologist; b. St. Louis, Jan. 12, 1916; s. James Thomas and Ellen Loretta (Hayes) B.; B.A. in Philosophy, U. Ill., 1939; M.D., U. 10 children—Martha Ellen, James Thomas. Commd. 1st lt., M.C., AUS, 1943, advanced through grades to col. U.S. Army, 1959; intern St. Mary's Group Hosps., St. Louis, 1943; engaged in radiation hazard control and radiobiology research, Los Alamos Labs., 1948-52; chief biophysics dept. Walter Reed Army Inst. Research, 1952-54; resident radiology Walter Reed Army Hosp., 1954-57; cons. radiol. def. to chief surgeon U.S. Army, Europe, 1957-60; chief radiation therapy Walter Reed Gen. Hosp., 1960-61; dir. Armed Forces Radiobiology Research Inst., 1961-66; ret., 1966; vis. lectr. radiology U. Pa. Med. Sch., Phila., 1966-67, Matthew J. Wilson prof. research radiology, 1967—; cons. in field, 1965—. Decorated Bronze Star. Diplomate Am. Bd. Radiology. Mem. Radiol. Soc. N. Am., A.M.A., Am. Assn. U. Profs., A.A.A.S. Home: 3940 Delancey St Philadelphia PA 19104

BRENNAN, JOHN E., bank exec. Auditor, Albany (N.Y.) Savs. Bank. Office: Box 70 20 N Pearl St Albany NY 12201*

BRENNAN, JOHN WESTON, lawyer; b. St. Louis, Sept. 16, 1903; s. Jesse Ketchum and Mary (Sharpe) B.; B.S., U.S. Naval Acad., 1925; LL.B., N.Y.U., 1940; m. Eleanor Janet Hirst, June 25, 1929; children—John Weston, Nancy Janet, James Keen. Salesman Am. Colortype Co., N.Y.C., 1927-31; sales promotion Continental Baking Co., 1931-33; exec. sec. Code Authority, Advt. Specialty Industry, 1933-37, also sec. Advt. specialty Nat. Assn.; asst. bus. counsel Group of Calendar Mfrs., 1937-42; admitted to N.J. bar, 1940; joined U.S. Pipe & foundry Co., Burlington, N.J., co. counsel 1946—, sec. 1950—, treasurer, 1953, v.p., 1959-64, adminstrv. v.p., 1964—. dir. Served as ensign, USN, 1925-27 and World War II; asst. prof. naval science and tactics U. Pa., 1942-43; navigator U.S.S. Sargent Bay, 1944-45; lt. comdr., USNR (ret.). Home: Gosnold Rd Box 427 East Orleans MA 02643

BRENNAN, JOSEPH BENJAMIN, lawyer; b. Savannah, Ga., Aug. 17, 1903; s. Patrick and Margaret (Dowling) B.; A.B., Georgetown U., 1925; LL.B., Harvard, 1928; m. Catherine Ginn, May 30, 1931; children—Helen Ginn (Mrs. William E. Gilbert), John Charles. Admitted to Ga. bar, 1928, D.C. bar, 1937; 4 1928—, & Tuttle, 1928-31; partner firm Sutherland, Asbill & Brennan, and predecessors, Atlanta, 1931—. Hon. bd. dirs. Atlanta chpt. A.R.C. Mem. Am., Ga., Atlanta bar assns., Georgetown U. Alumni Assn. (John Carroll award 1956; pres. 1954-56). Democrat. Roman Catholic. Clubs: Piedmont Driving, Atlanta Athletic, Lawyers, Commerce (Atlanta); University (Washington); Oglethorpe (Savannah). Home: 2507 Dellwood Dr NW Atlanta, GA 30305. Office: First Nat Bank Bldg Atlanta GA 30303

BRENNAN, JOSEPH CANTWELL, banker; b. Roslyn, N.Y., Sept. 26, 1910; s. Joseph P. and Evangeline (Walsh) B.; student LaSalle Mil. Acad., 1929; Ph.B., Georgetown U., 1933; m. Anne C. Patterson, Sept. 7, 1935; 1 dau., Constance C. With Mfrs. Trust Co., 1933-45, asst. sec., 1940-45; asst. treas. Bankers Trust Co., 1946-49, asst. v.p., 1949-51, v.p., 1951-52; v.p., asst. to pres. Emigrant Savs. Bank, N.Y.C., 1953-56, pres. 1957-67, chmn. bd., 1967—, also trustee; dir. Savs. Banks Trust Co., Scranton Lehigh Coal Co., Floral Park, N.Y., Diamond Internat. Corp.; real estate and mortgage adv. bd. Mfrs. Hanover Trust Co. Mem. adv. council Am. Inst. of Banking. Mem. adv. council Pace Coll.; mem. Cardinals Com. of the Laity. Bd. dirs. Cath. Youth Orgn., N.Y.C., United Hosp. Fund N.Y. Mission Immaculate Virgin; trustee Coll. Mount St. Vincent, Riverdale, N.Y., Savs. Banks Life Ins. Fund. Served as lt. comdr. USNR, 1942-46. Mem. Savs. Banks Assn. N.Y. State (dir.). Knight of Malta. Club: Union League. Home: 200 E 66th St New York City NY 10021 Office: 5 E 42d St New York City NY 10017

BRENNAN, JOSEPH GERARD, educator; b. Boston, Nov. 2, 1910; s. Joseph and Nora (Sheridan) B.; A.B., Boston Coll., 1933; A.M., Harvard, 1935; Ph.D., Columbia, 1942; m. Mary Jean McLeod, June 7, 1938; children—Peter, Colin, Mario, Ainslie, Nicholas, Patrick. Instr., then asso. prof. philosophy Coll. New Rochelle (N.Y.), 1937-47; faculty Barnard Coll., 1947—, prof. philosophy, 1962—, chmn. dept., 1953-65; lectr. Hofstra U., 1949—; vis. lectr. Sarah Lawrence Coll., 1965-66. Founding trustee Levittown (N.Y.) Pub. Library, 1950-54; trustee Bethpage (N.Y.) Pub. Library, 1956- -. Served to lt. USNR, 1943-46; comdr. Res. Mem. Am. Philos. Assn., Am. Metaphys. Soc., Authors Guild, Phi Beta Kappa. Author: Thomas Mann's World, 1942; The Meaning of Philosophy, 1953; A Handbook of Logic, 1957; Three Philosophical Novelists, 1964. Home: 8 Sylvia Rd Bethpage Plainview PO NY 11803 Office: Barnard Coll Columbia Univ New York City NY 10027

BRENNAN, JOSEPH TUREENE, II, lawyer; b. Milw., Sept. 29, 1899; s. Bernard A. and Mary A. (Flynn) B.; student Johns Hopkins, 1917-19, Catholic U., 1919-21; LL.B., U. Md., 1922; m. Florence McGarry, Oct. 1., 1927; children—Joseph Turenne III. Anthony Ladd. Admitted to Md. bar, 1922, since practiced in Balt.; mem. firm Niles, Barton & Wilmer, and predecessors., 1935—. Sec., dir. Samuel Kirk & Son, Balt., 1963-67. Trustee Oldfields Sch., 1961—, chmn., 1964-68; bd. dirs. Balt. Equitable Soc., 1968—. Mem. Am., Md., Baltimore County bar assns., Kappa Alpha. Democrat. Roman Catholic. Clubs: Elkridge Maryland, Wednesday (Balt.). Home: 1908 Ruxton Rd Ruxton, MD 21204. Office: 929 N Howard St Baltimore MD 21201

BRENNAN, LEO F., banker. Comptroller, Bank of Del., Wilmington. Office: 300 Delaware Av Wilmington DE 19899*

BRENNAN, MATTHEW J., conservationist; b. Litchfield, Conn., July 12, 1917; s. Patrick S. and Jane (Bannon) B.; A.B., Brown U., 1939; A.M., Columbia, 1946; grad. dipl. meteorology Mass. Inst. Tech., 1943; Ed.D., Columbia Tchrs. Coll., 1949; m. Muriel Trebay, Sept. 3, 1943; 1 dau., Patti Jo. Instr. biology Manhattan Coll., 1946-49; asst. prof. biology Jersey City State Coll., 1949-55; prof. biology Fitchburg State Coll., 1955-57; chief scientist Ellsworth Sta., Antarctica, 1957-59; splst. sci. U.S. Office Edn., 1959- 60; chief conservation edn. U.S. Forest Service, 1960-63; dir. Pinchot Inst. for Conservation Studies, 1963-70; dir. Brentree Environmental Center, 1970—, UNESCO Conservation Curriculum Project for Venezuela, 1970—; dir. NSF Summer Insts. Rutgers U., 1957, 1959. Mt. Brennan in Antarctica named for him. Nat. bd. dirs. Girls Scouts U.S.A. Mem. Am. Forestry Assn. (dir. 1968-70, hon. v.p. 1964). Author: The World of Living Things, 1964; The Earth, Its Living Things, 1970. Editor: People and Their Environment, 8 vols., 1969. Home: Brentree Environmental Center Milford PA 18337

BRENNAN, MAYNARD JAMES, educator; b. St. Marys, Pa., Feb. 24, 1921; s. Alfred P. and Julia (Caskey) B.; B.A., St. Vincent Coll., Latrobe, Pa., 1944, M.A. in Philosophy, 1946; M.A. in English, U. Wis., 1948; Ph.D. in English, U. Mich., 1953; m. L. Carole Zippi, Aug. 28, 1970. Joined Order St. Benedict, 1942, ordained priest Roman Cath. Ch., 1947; mem. faculty St. Vincent Coll., 1947-68, chmn. dept. English, 1955-63, chaplain, 1958-62, pres., 1963-68; prof. English, Monmouth Coll., West Long Branch, N.J. 1970—. Recipient 1st prize in graphics Am. Inst. Indsl. Artists. Mem. Nat. Honor Soc., Modern Lang. Assn., Am. Benedictine Acad., Nat. Conf. Coll. Tchrs. English, Phi Kappa Phi, Delta Epsilon Sigma. Author: Compact Handbook of College Composition, 2d edit., 1971; also articles . Editor: Catholic Accent, 1962-64. Home: 364 Westwood Av Long Branch NJ 07740

BRENNAN, MICHAEL JOSEPH, univ. dean; b. Chgo., Aug. 29, 1928; s. Michael J. and Nora (McHugh) B.; B.S., DePaul U., 1952; M.A., U. Chgo., 1954, Ph.D., 1956; m. Isabel Bernice Thomas, Dec. 4, 1954; children—Mark Etienne, Moira Sioban, Keelin Marta. Mem. faculty Brown U., 1956—, prof. econs., 1964—, dean 3 1966—. 1966— Served with AUS, 1946-48. Danforth Teaching fellow, 1957; Ford Found. Faculty Research prof., 1960. Mem. Am. Econ. Assn., Econometric Soc., Assn. Grad. Schs., (sec-treas. 1969—), Council Grad. Schs. Club: University (Providence). Author: Preface to Econometrics, 1960; Theory of Economic Statics, 1965; Patterns of Market Behavior, 1965; The Economics of Age, 1967. Home: 44 Oriole Av Providence, RI 02906.

BRENNAN, PAUL JOSEPH, educator, civil engr.; b. Auburn, N.Y., June 29, 1920; s. William Henry and Hannah Frances (Murphy) B.; B.Arch. Engring. cum laude, U. Detroit, 1943; M.Eng. in Civil Engring., Yale, 1944, D.Eng., 1951; m. Virginia Ann Burns, Sept. 8, 1951; children—Patricia Ann, Margaret Mary, Maureen Ellen, William Henry II, Elizabeth Ann, Kathleen Ann, John Robert, Nancy Eileen, Virginia Ann, Mary Eileen. Asst. instrn. Yale, 1946-48, asst. prof. civil engring., 1948-53; prof. civil engring. U. Del., 1953- 58, chmn. dept., 1953-57, chmn. dept. civil engring. and engring. mechanics, 1957-58; prof. civil engring., chmn. dept. Syracuse U., 1958- -; civil engring. cons. Chmn. planning bd. Town of Onondaga. Served to lt. (j.g.) USNR, 1944-46. Registered profl. engr. Mem. Yale Engring. Assn., N.Y. Acad. Scis., Am. Soc. Engrs., Am. Concrete Inst., Sigma Xi, Tau Beta Pi, Phi Kappa Phi, Alpha Sigma Nu. Author numerous publs. Home: 4243 Wolf Hollow Rd Syracuse NY 13219

BRENNAN, THOMAS PAUL, business exec., lawyer; b. Pitts., Aug. 7, 1928; s. Thomas Paul and Mary (Danahey) B.; B.A., U. Pitts., 1952, LL.B., 1955, J.D., 1968; m. Margaret Jane Stavar, July 28, 1956; 1 dau., Mary Kay. Admitted to Pa. bar, 1956, to Minn. bar, 1970; law clk. to Allegheny County judge, 1955-56; atty. Duquesne Light Co., Pitts., 1956-57; atty. to gen. counsel Crucible Steel Corp., Pitts., 1957-69; asso. gen. counsel Allis Chalmers Mfg. Co., Milw., 1969-70; v.p., gen. counsel, sec. Internat. Multifoods Corp., Mpls., 1970—. Served with USNR, 1946-48. Mem. Am., Minn., Hennepin County, Allegheny County bar assns., Am. Soc. Corporate Secs. Home: 7012 Mark Terrace Dr Edina MN 55435 Office: Investors Bldg Minneapolis MN 55402

BRENNAN, WALTER ANDREW, actor; b. Lynn, Mass., July 25, 1894; s. William John and Margaret Elizabeth (Flanagan) B.; grad. Rindge Tech. Sch., Cambridge, Mass., 1915; A.F.D. (hon.), Morris Harvey College; LL.D., Stonehill Coll., 1968; m. Ruth Caroline Wells; children—Arthur Wells, Walter Andrew, Ruth Caroline. Motion picture actor, 1924—; more recent pictures include: Surrender, Best of the Badmen, Across the Great Divide, 1950; Return of the Texan, Lure of the Wilderness, 1951; Sea of Lost Ships, Drum across the River, The Far Country, 1953; Four Guns to the Border, Bad Day at Black Rock, 1954; At Gunpoint, Come Next Spring, Glory, Good Bye My Lady, 1955; The Proud Ones, Tammy, 1956; The Way to the Gold, God is My Partner, 1957; Rio Bravo, 1958; How the West Was Won, 1963; Those Calloways, 1965; The Knomobile; 1966; The Family Band, 1967; Support Your Local Sheriff, 1968; The Over The Hill Gang, 1969; appeared TV series The Real McCoys, The Tycoon, Guns of Will Sonnett, now appearing in TV series To Rome With Love. Served with 101st F.A., U.S. Army, 1917-19; with A.E.F., 19 mos. Recipient acad. awards as best supporting actor, Come and Get It, 1936, Kentucky, 1938, The Westerner, 1940; Freedoms Found. award, 1965; Horatio Alger award, 1966; Western Heritage Nat. Cowboy Hall of Fame award, 1967; elected to Cowboy Hall of Fame, 1970. Has appeared as guest on TV. Address: Moorpark CA 93021 ☆

BRENNAN, WILLIAM JAMES, mfg. co. exec.; b. Tomah, Wis., Mar. 22, 1915; s. William James and Kathryn Mary (Costello) B.; student Marquette U., 1934-36; B.S.M.E., U. Wis., 1938; M.S. in Aero. Engring., Chrysler Inst. Engring., 1940; m. Doris Mary Thomas, May 8, 1943; children—Jeffrey, Gregory, Timothy. Automobile devel. engr. Chrysler Corp., 1938-41; design engr. Consol. Aircraft, 1941; chief engr. Lockheed Aircraft, 1941-45; chief engr. Menasco Mfg. Co., 1945-48; project engr. Wright Aero. Corp., 1948; design engr. successively to pres. Rocketdyne div. N. Am. Rockwell, Canoga Park, Cal., 1948—. Recipient NASA Achievement award, 1969. Mem. Am. Inst. Aeros. and Astronautics, Am. Mgmt. Assn., Am. Ordnance Assn. Home: 5440 Corbin Tarzana CA 91356 Office: 6633 Canoga Canoga Park CA 91304

BRENNAN, WILLIAM JOSEPH, Jr., justice; b. Newark, Apr. 25, 1906; s. William J. and Agnes (McDermott) B.; B.S., U. Pa., 1928; LL.B., Harvard, 1931; LL.D., U. Notre Dame, 1968; m. Marjorie Leonard, May 5, 1928; children—William Joseph, Hugh Leonard, Nancy. Admitted to N.J. bar, 1931, practiced Newark, 1931-49, mem. Pitney, Hardin, Ward & Brennan; superior ct. judge, 1949-50; appellate div. judge, 1950-52; justice Supreme Ct. N.J., 1952-56; asso. justice U.S. Supreme Ct., 1956—. Served with gen. staff corps AUS, World War II. Decorated Legion of Merit. Address: Supreme Ct US Washington DC 20543

BRENNAN, WILLIAM R., lawyer; b. Veteran, Alta., Can., Augl 17, 1922; B.A., U. Alta., 1949, LL.B., 1950. Admitted to Alta. bar, 1951; partner firm Fenerty, McGillivray, Robertson, Prowse, Brennan, Fraser, Bell & Code, Calgary, Alta. Mem. Canadian, Calgary bar assns., Law Soc. Alta. Office: Guinness House Calgary 2 Alberta Canada*

BRENNEN, JOHN HENRY, business exec.; b. Bklyn., Feb. 14, 1911; s. John H. and Hortense M. (Buchanan) B.; student Iona Prep. Sch., 1924-28; A.B., Georgetown U., 1932; m. Alexandra Diana Kirckl, Jan. 28, 1939; children—John Henry, Michael. Mgr. leased dept. Whelan Studios, 1932-33; with credit dept. Guaranty Trust Co., 1934-37; salesman Cannon Mills, Inc., 1937-48, sales mgr., 1948-57, v.p., 1952—, charge marketing variety chains and jr. dept. stores, 1957-62, charge marketing towels, 1962—. Served as maj. USAAF, World War II. Mem. Georgetown U. Alumni Assn. Club: Whippoorwill Golf (Armonk, N.Y.). Home: 1 Hudson Hudson Harbour Edgewater, NJ 07020. Office: Cannon Mills Inc 1271 Av of Americas New York City NY 10020

BRENNEN, WILLIAM STUART, banker; b. Pitts., May 15, 1924; s. William M. and Irene (MacFarland) B.; B.S., U.S. Merchant Marine Acad., 1944; A.B., Columbia, 1947, LL.B., 1949; m. Justine Bright, Dec. 15, 1951; children—Stephen, Robert. Admitted to N.Y. bar, 1949; with firm Dow & Symmers, 1949-51, N.Y. State Banking Dept., 1951-53; 1st dep. supt. banks N.Y. State, 1959-63; with Greenwich Savs. Bank, N.Y.C., 1963—, pres., 1969—, also trustee. Bd. dirs. Broadway Assn. Republican. Episcopalian. Home: 441 E 20th St New York City NY 10010 Office: 1356 Broadway New York City NY 10018

BRENNER, CHARLES, educator, psychoanalyst; b. Boston, Nov. 18, 1913; s. Samuel and Ann (Aronie) B.; A.B. in Chemistry cum laude, Harvard, 1931, M.D., 1935; m. Erma Brandt, Sept. 8, 1935; children—Elsa (Mrs. Roger David Cohen), Lucy Jane. Intern, Peter Bent Brigham Hosp., Boston, 1935-37; jr. physician Boston Psychopathic Hosp., 1937-38; resident neurology Boston City Hosp., 1938-39; instr. neurology Harvard Med. Sch., 1939-44, Columbia Coll. Physicians and Surgeons, 1945-50; asso. clin. prof. psychiatry Yale Med. Sch., 1950-68, lectr. in psychiatry, 1968—; staff physician cons. Boston City Hosp., 1939-44, Cambridge (Mass.) City Hosp., 1941-44, Montefiore Hosp., N.Y.C., 1945-50. Life fellow Am. Psychiat. Assn.; mem. Am. (pres. 1967-68), Internat. psychoanalytic assns. N.Y. (pres. 1960-62), N.J. psychoanalytic socs., A.M.A., Mass., N.Y. med. socs. Author: An Elementary Textbook of Psychoanalysis, 1955. Contbr. articles to profl. jours., chpts. to books. Home: 30 Rugby Lane Scarsdale NY 10583 Office: 1040 Park Av New York City NY 10028

BRENNER, DANIEL, architect; b. N.Y.C., Apr. 13, 1917; s. Samuel and Yetta (Grubman) B.; B.Arch., Columbia, 1939; M.S., Ill. Inst. Tech., 1949; m. Rachael Bracken Orner, July 30, 1949; children—Ariel, Jonathan. Partner, Brenner & Turck, 1957-61; partner Brenner-Danforth-Rockwell, Chgo., 1961—; prof. dept. architecture Ill. Inst. Tech. Mem. A.I.A.-Am. Bar Assn. Joint Com. Design of Courtrooms and Courtroom Facilities. Chmn. Fedn. for an Open Lakefront. Trustee Mus. Contemporary Art, Chgo., Chgo. Sch. Architecture Found. Served with Signal Corps Intelligence, AUS, 1943-46. Recipient A.I.A. citations for design excellence. Fellow A.I.A.; mem. Arts Club Chgo. Important works include Maremont Bldg., Graham Found. Hdqrs., Nat. Design Center, Old Stock Exchange Bldg., Mus. Contemporary Art, J.B. Speed Art Mus. Addition, Louisville. Home: 5128 Hyde Park Blvd Chicago IL 60615 Office: 646 N Michigan Av Chicago IL 60611

BRENNER, DANIEL LEON, lawyer; b. Kansas City, Mo., Sept. 9, 1904; s. Adolph and Tillie (Brenner) B.; A.B., U. Mo., 1925; J.D., U. Mich., 1927. Admitted to Mo. bar, 1926; with Borders & Borders, 1927; mem. Roach, Brenner & Wimmell, Kansas City, 1947-51; sr. mem. Brenner, Van Valkenburgh & Wimmell, 1951-59, Brenner, Ewing, Lockwood & O'Neal; judge circuit ct., Jackson County, Mo., 1943-44. Mem. nat. council Am. Jewish Distbn. Com.; nat. panel Am. Arbitration Assn., 1964—; nat. commr. B'nai B'rith Hillel Founds.; pres. Kansas City Jewish Welfare Fedn. and Council. Trustee U. Mo. Hillel Found. (charter), Leo N. Levi Meml. Hosp., Bellefarie, Rockhurst Coll.; bd. dirs., v.p., counsel Community Chest Greater Kansas City; bd. dirs., counsel United Funds campaign; bd. dirs., v.p. Heart of Am. United campaign; bd. dirs. Nat. Conf. Christians and Jews, Jewish Vocational Service Bur. Recipient Brotherhood citation Nat. Conf. Christians and Jews, 1956; citation State of Israel, 1961; Man of Year award Jewish Theol. Sem. Am., 1967. Mem. Legion of Honor Order de Molay, Am., Kansas City bar assns., Mo. Bar, Am. Judicature Soc. Jewish religion (bd. dirs. synagogue). Mason; mem. B'nai B'rith (dist. pres. grand lodge 1950-51, v.p. supreme lodge). Club: Oakwood Country (Kansas City). Contbr. articles to legal jours. Home: 311 E 70th St Kansas City MO 64113 Office: Lathrop Bldg Kansas City MO 64106

BRENNER, EDWARD JOHN, lawyer; b. Wisconsin Rapids, Wis., June 26, 1923; s. Edward Charles and Lillian (Hephner) B.; B.S. in Chem. Engring., U. Wis., 1947, M.S., 1948, J.D., 1950; m. Jane Segrest, June 1, 1951; children—Beverly, Douglas, Carolyn, Mary. Admitted to Wis. bar, 1950, D.C. bar, 1970; chem. engr. Esso Standard Oil Co., 1950-53; with Esso Research and Engring. Co., 1953-64, asst. dir. legal div., 1960-64; U.S. commr. patents, 1964-69; v.p., asst. to pres. Gen. Instrument Corp., 1969-70; sr. partner law firm Brenner, O'Brien & Guay, Arlington, Va., 1970—. Served with AUS, 1944-46. Mem. Am., Wis., Va. bar assns., Bar Assn. D.C., Am., N.J. patent law assns., Am. Chem. Soc. Home: 1304 Forestwood Dr McLean VA 22101 Office: 2001 Jefferson Davis Hwy Arlington VA 22202

BRENNER, ELLIOTT HERBERT, architect; b. Detroit, Aug. 6, 1930; s. Morton H. and Bluma S. (Sachse) B.; B.A., U. Cal., Berkeley, 1953; m. Lois J. Freedberg, Mar. 13, 1957; children—Suzanne, Marianne, Michael. Chief designer Paul R. Williams, Los Angeles, 1955-59; prin. E.H. Brenner, Architect, Lafayette, Ind., 1959—; dir. Pantek Corp.; vis. lectr. Sch. Architecture, Ball State U. Bd. dirs. Lafayette Art Assn., Wabash Center for Mentally Retarded. Served with USNR, Korean War. Decorated Comdg. Officer commendation; recipient Distinguished Service award Lafayette Jr. C. of C., 1965; named Outstanding Young Man of Year, Ind. Jr. C. of C., 1965. Mem. A.I.A., Bldg. Research Inst., Am. Assn. U. Profs. Important works include Residence for Mr. & Mrs. E.A. Freedberg, 1961, Orthodontic Office for Dr. Paul Draper (ISA-AIA Honor award), 1962, Offices, Fennig & Weir, 1964, St. Thomas Aquinas Ch. Addition (Cardinal Lercaro Gold medal 1964, N.Am. Liturgical Conf. award 1964, Spaeth Found. First award 1964, ISA-AIA Honor award 1965), 1964, Residence for Dr. & Mrs. E.C. Stuntz (ISA-AIA Merit award 1965), 1964, Offices, IBM, Lafayette, 1965, Fowler-Benton County Library Addition (ISA-AIA Merit award 1965), 1965, Lab. Bldg., Purdue Research Found., 1965, Residence for Dr. Mary Endres (ISA-AIA Merit award 1968, House & Home First Hon. Mention 1969), 1966, J.M. Foster Co. Shop and Office (ISA-AIA Merit award 1968), 1967, Redeemer Luth. Ch. Classroom Addition, 1967, Wabash Center for the Mentally Retarded, 1968, Dewey Hall, Geriatric Care Center, 1970, Pantek System Devel. (HUD Operation Breakthrough winner 1970), 1969. Home: 3601 Cypress St Lafayette IN 47904 Office: 101 N 4th St Lafayette IN 47901

BRENNER, HOWARD, educator; b. N.Y.C., Mar. 16, 1929; s. Max and Margaret (Wechsler) B.; B.Chem. Engring., Pratt Inst., 1950; M.Chem. Engring., N.Y.U., 1954, Eng.Sc. D., 1957; m. Lorraine Feldman, June 17, 1951; children—Leslie K., Joyce M., Suzanne A. Faculty, N.Y.U., 1955—, instr., 1955-57, asst. prof., 1957-61, asso. prof., 1961-65, prof. chem. engring., 1965-66; prof. chem. engring. Carnegie-Mellon U., Pitts., 1966—. Cons., Dorr-Oliver, Inc., 1959-65, Pulp and Paper Inst. Can., 1962-66. Recipient 11th Ann. Honor Scroll indsl. and engring. chemistry div. Am. Chem. Soc., 1961. Mem. A.A.A.S., N.Y. Acad. Sci., Am. Inst. Chem. Engrs., Sigma Xi, Tau Beta Pi. Author: (with John Happel) Low Reynolds Number Hydrodynamics, 1965. Contbr. articles profl. jours. Home: 1301 Folkstone Dr Pittsburgh PA 15243

BRENNER, JOSEPH DONALD, mfg. co. exec.; b. Carlisle, Pa., Mar. 1, 1917; s. Clyde E. and Pearl T. (Hastings) B.; Ph.B., Dickinson Coll., 1939; M.B.A., Harvard, 1941; m. Jane B. Wimett, June 24, 1944; children—Margaret E. (Mrs. Richard Bushey), Joseph Donald, Nancy E., Katherine H. Mfg. mgr. AMP, Inc., Harrisburg, Pa., 1947-50, chief engr., asst. div. mgr., 1950-55, div. mgr. automatic machine div., 1955-58; operations mgr., 1958-61, v.p. mfg. divs., 1961-67, corporate v.p. mfg., 1967-71, pres., 1971—; dir. Farmers Trust Co., Carlisle. Bd. dirs. Carlisle Hosp., Carlisle YMCA. Served to lt. USNR, 1944-46. Mem. Phi Kappa Sigma. Presbyn. Home: 246 Conway St Carlisle PA 17013 Office: Eisenhower Blvd Box 3608 Harrisburg PA 17105

BRENNER, MELVIN ARTHUR, airlines exec.; b. N.Y.C., Dec. 15, 1919; s. Harry and Ruth (Simon) B.; B.B.A., Coll. City N.Y., 1939; postgrad. Am. U., 1943-47; m. Margaret Lindblom, Aug. 30, 1941; children—Paul Richard, Thomas Craig. Economist, Nat. Resources Planning Bd., 1941-43; asst. to vice chmn. CAB, 1944-46; chief air transport sect. Dept. Commerce, 1946-47; transport specialist Bur. of Budget, 1947-53; aviation adviser to under sec. of commerce, 1953-55; with Am. Airlines, 1955-69, vice pres. schedules and market devel., 1959-69; v.p. marketing, planning TWA, 1969—. Clubs: Burning Tree Country; Wings (N.Y.C.). Home: Byfield Lane Greenwich CT 06830 Office: 633 3d Av New York City NY 10017

BRENNER, ROBERT, govt. ofcl.; b. Atlantic City, N.J., May 20, 1922; s. Samuel and Jennie (Erien) B.; B.S. in Mech. Engring., U. Pa., 1943; M.S. in Engring., U. Cal. at Los Angeles, 1949, Ph.D., 1962; m. Esther Fairmont, Dec. 18, 1955; children—Richard Aaron, Ruth Andrea, Sharon Lynn. Designer, Lockheed Aircraft Co., 1943-44; plant engr. Am. Can Co., 1946-48; mem. faculty U. Cal. at Los Angeles, 1949-66; cons. Dept. Commerce, 1966; dep. dir. Nat. Hwy. Safety Bur., Dept. Transp., 1966—, acting dir., 1969-70; chief scientist Nat. Hwy. Traffic Safety Adminstrn. Dept. Transp., 1971—; cons. in field. Mem. exec. com. Regional Plan Assn. S. Cal., 1965-66; mem. accident prevention panel NIH, 1962-64; sec. hwy. safety com. Hwy. Research Bd., 1960-65; mem. com. traffic safety Dept. Health, Edn. and Welfare, 1967. U.S. del. to CCMS NATO Rd. Safety Pilot Study, 1969—. Served with AUS, 1944-46; USA, 1950-53. Named Cal. Hwy. Safety Man of Year, 1967. Registered profl. engr., Cal. Mem. Soc. Automotive Engrs. (tech. bd. 1970-73), Am. Pub. Health Assn., Sigma Xi, Tau Beta Pi. Author articles in field. Home: 4 Carnegie Ct Rockville MD 20850 Office: Nat Highway Traffic Safety Adminstrn Dept Transportation Washington DC 20591

BRENT, ANDREW JACKSON, lawyer; b. Richmond, Va., Nov. 25, 1918; s. Andrew Jackson and Gussie Millhiser (Reinhardt) B.; LL.B., U. Va., 1941; m. Virginia Armistead McGuire, Nov. 1, 1941; children—Virginia Armistead, Roberta Harper, Elizabeth Marshall McGuire, Andrew Mason, Maria Meade. Admitted to Va. bar, 1940; practice in Richmond, 1946—; partner Christian, Barton, Parker, Epps & Brent, 1949—. vice pres., gen. counsel Security Fed. Savs. & Loan Assn.; gen. counsel, sec., dir. Media Gen., Inc.; chmn., dir. Central Va. Ednl. TV Crop., 1968—; sec., dir. Evening News Pub. Co. of N.J., Garden State Paper Co., Inc., Southeast Media, Inc., Piedmont Pub. Co., Inc., Winston-Salem, N.C.; dir. So. Title Ins. Co. Pres., dir. Richmond Area Community Council, 1963-66; gen. counsel, sec. Richmond Met. Authority; chmn., Va. Adv. Council for Ednl. TV; sec., visitor Virginia Commonwealth Univ. Bd. dirs. Richmond Eye Hosp.; trustee Richmond Meml. Hosp., Collegiate Schs., Richmond Profl. Inst. Found., Mary Baldwin Coll. Served to lt. comdr. USNR, 1941-46. Recipient Annual Good Govt. award Richmond First Club, 1965. Mem. Am., Va., Richmond bar assns., Am. Judicature Soc., S.A.R., Richmond C. of C. (past pres., dir.), Omicron Delta Kappa, Phi Alpha Delta, Phi Kappa Psi, Pi Delta Epsilon. Democrat. Episcopalian (warden, vestryman). Clubs: Commonwealth, Country of Virginia, Downtown (past pres., dir.). Home: Highland Rd Richmond VA 23229 Office: Mut Bldg Richmond VA 23219

BRENT, JOHN ELFORD, mfg. co. exec.; b. Brantford, Ont., Can., Sept. 26, 1908; s. John Elford and Rosa Mae (Walker) B.; B.A. in Bus. Adminstrn., U. Western Ont., 1931; LL.D., Waterloo Luth. U., 1966; m. Paula Mary Tillmann, Sept. 24, 1938; children—William, Susan, Peter, Paul, with IBM Co., Ltd., Totonto, 1931-49, 62—, pres., dir. 1 1962-69. chmn., chief exec. officer, dir., 1969—; v.p., dir. IBM World Trade Corp. N.Y.C. 1950—; dir. Sci. Research Assos. (Can.) Ltd., Dominion Ins. Corp., Toronto-Dominion Bank, IBM Information Services Ltd., London, Eng., Nat. Life Assurance Co. Can., Toronto, Connaught Biologics Ltd.; adv. bd. internat. bus. Chem. Bank. Vice pres., dir. U. Western Ont. Found., N.Y., adv. com. Sch. Bus. Adminstrn.; v.p. bd. dirs. Toronto Symphony Orch. Assn.; bd. govs. U. Toronto; v.p., trustee Toronto Western Hosp.; trustee United Community Fund Greater Toronto; bd. dirs. Canadian Council Christians and Jews, Canadian Exec. Service Overseas. Mem. Internat. C. of C. (dir. Canadian council), Canadian C. of C. (dir.) Canadian Mfrs. Assn. (exec. council), Canadian Export Assn., Newcomen Soc. N. Am. Clubs: Engineers, Mt. Royal (Montreal); Seigniory (Montebello, Que.); Canadian (Toronto, N.Y.C.); Granite, Toronto, Rosedale Golf, York, Empire of Canada (Toronto); Lyford Cay (Bahamas); Caledon Mountain Trout (Inglewood, Ont.). Home: 61 Old Forest Hill Rd Toronto 199 Ontario Canada Office: 1150 Ellington Av E Don Mills Ontario Canada

BRENT, MORGAN MCKENZIE, educator, biologist; b. Evanston, Ill., Jan. 31, 1923; s. Cyril E. and Adelaide (Post) B.; student Ill. Coll., 1941-42; B.S., Northwestern U., 1948, M.S., 1949, Ph.D., 1953; m. Frances H. Martin, Aug. 1, 1955; children—Morgan T., Victoria, Elizabeth. Research zoologist U. Cal. at Berkeley, 1953-54; instr.

microbiology Jefferson Med. Coll., Phila., 1954-57; faculty Bowling Green State (O.) U., 1957—, prof. biology, 1965—, chmn. dept., 1964-67. Trustee Bowling Green Meml. Soc. Served with AUS, 1943-46. Fellow Ohio Acad. Sci.; mem. A.A.A.S., Soc. Protozoologists, Am. Micros. Soc., Sigma Xi. Club: Bowling Green Faculty (pres. 1964-65). Home: 924 Lyn Rd Bowling Green OH 43402

BRENT, ROBERT LEONARD, physician, educator; b. Rochester, N.Y., Oct. 6, 1927; s. Charles and Rose (Katz) B.; A.B., U. Rochester, 1948, M.D. with honors, 1953, Ph.D., 1955; m. Lillian H. Hoffman, Aug. 21, 1949; children—David A., James R., Lawrence H., Deborah A. Fellow Nat. Found., Strong Meml. Hosp., 1953-54; intern pediatrics Mass. Gen. Hosp., Boston, 1954-55; chief radiation biology Walter Reed Army Inst. Research, 1955-57; faculty Jefferson Med. Coll., 1955—, prof. radiology 1962—, also prof. pediatrics, chmn. dept. and dir. Stein Research Center. Mem. med. adv. bd. Nat. Found., FDA. Served AUS, 1955-57. Travelling fellow Royal Soc. Medicine, 1971-72; vis. fellow FitzWilliam Coll., Cambridge, 1971-72. Recipient Richie meml. prize U. Rochester Med. Sch., 1953; Lindback Found. award for distinguished teaching, 1968. Mem. Teratology Soc. (pres. 1967-68), A.A.A.S., Radiation Research Soc., Am. Soc. Exptl. Pathology, Soc. Pediatric Research, Am. Pediatrics Soc., Am. Acad. Pediatrics, Soc. Exptl. Biology and Medicine, Phila. Coll. Physicians, Phila. Pediatric Soc., Am. Assn. Immunology, Sigma Xi, Alpha Omega Alpha. Home: 949 Irvin Rd Huntingdon Valley PA 19006 Office: 920 Chancellor St Philadelphia PA 19107

BRENTANO, ALAN, advt. agy. exec.; b. Evansville, Ind., 1911; grad. U. Ill., 1932. Pres., chief exec. officer, dir. Keller Crescent Co., Evansville; dir. Old Nat. Bank Evansville, Sunbeam Plastics Corp. Trustee U. Evansville. Home: 3120 E Balckford Av Evansville IN 47714 Office: PO Box 3 Evansville IN 47706*

BRENTLINGER, WILLIAM BROCK, coll. dean; b. Flora, Ill., Aug. 21, 1926; s. Arthur Kenneth and Frances (Maxwell) B.; student Washington U., 1946-47; A.B., Greenville Coll., 1950; M.A., Ind. State U., 1951; Ph.D., U. Ill., 1959; m. Barbara Jean Weir, Dec. 29, 1946; children—Gregory, Gary, Rebecca Anne, Garth, Barbara Sue, Geoffrey. Instr. speech Greenville Coll., 1951-59, chmn. dept., 1959-62, dean of coll., 1962-69; dean Sch. of Fine Arts of Lamar State Coll. Tech., Beaumont, Tex., 1969—; cons. higher edn. Bd. dirs. Beaumont Symphony Orch., 1969—, Beamont Music Commn., 1970—. Served with USNR, 1944-46. Recipient tchr. study award, Danforth Found., 1957. Mem. Speech Communication Assn. Am., Tex. Speech Assn., Tex. Assn. Coll. Tchrs., Phi Kappa Phi. Baptist. Club: Rotary Beaumont). Home: 6530 Salem Circle Beaumont TX 77706

BRERETON, HARMAR, lawyer, photog. co. exec.; b. Diamond Point on Lake George, N.Y., May 31, 1909; s. Denny and Mary (Whiteside) B.; grad. Taft Sch., 1927; Ph.B., Yale, 1931, LL.B., 1934; m. Eleanor Collins, July 7, 1934; children—Constance (Mrs. Francis E. Volz), Linda (Mrs. H.K. Wirts), Harmar D., Derek P. Admitted to N.Y. bar, 1935; with law firm Sullivan & Cromwell, N.Y.C., 1934-41; with Eastman Kodak Co., 1941—, asst. sec., 1946-57, v.p., gen. counsel, 1957—, dir.; dir. Security Trust Co. of Rochester, mem. finance com. Hon. mem. Allendale Sch. Bd. chmn. Taft Sch. Bd. dirs., treas. Highland Hosp.; past pres. trustees Rochester Travelers Aid Soc.; bd. dirs. Rochester Better Living. Fellow Am. Bar Assn.; mem. N.Y. State, Rochester bar assns., N.A.M. (past chmn. renegotiation subcom.), Rochester C. of C., Assn. Gen. Counsel Am. (pres. 1968-70), Rochester Yale Assn. (past pres.). Episcopalian (treas.). Club: Rochester Country. Home: 42 Knollwood Dr Rochester NY 14618 Office: 343 State St Rochester NY 14608

BRESIN, MILLARD, architect; b. Bklyn., Mar. 14, 1925; s. Charles and Gussie (Roffwarg) B.; B. Arch. magna cum laude, Cath. U. Am., 1949; m. Florence Becker, June 19, 1948; children—Howard, Michael, Barry. Chief draftsman C. M. Spindler Assos., Bklyn., 1949-55, partner, 1956; partner firm Haus & Bresin, Queens, N.Y., 1956-64; owner, architect Millard Bresin, Queens, N.Y., 1964—. Mem. Queens Planning Bd., 1968—. Served with AUS, World War II. Decorated Silver Star Mem. A.I.A. (pres. Queens 1967-68), N.Y. State Assn. Architects (dir. 1969-70), Architects' Council N.Y.C. (sec. 1970-71), N.Y. Soc. Architects. K.P. Home: 3421 Oceanside Rd Oceanside NY 11572 Office: 3760 82d St Jackson Heights NY 11372

BRESKY, OTTO, milling co. exec.; b. Mpls., 1889; ed. Dartmouth. Chmn., chief exec. officer, also dir. Seaboard Allied Milling Corp., Seaboard Flour Corp. Home: 52 Hammondswood Rd Newton MA 02167 Office: 200 Boylston St Newton MA 02167*

BRESLER, BORIS, educator; b. Harbin, China, Oct. 18, 1918; s. Samuel and Hena (Gonopolsky) B.; came to U.S., 1937, naturalized, 1943; B.S., U. Cal. at Berkeley, 1941; M.S., Cal. Inst. Tech., 1946; m. Joy Bloom, July 5, 1946; 1 dau., Deborah. Structural designer Kaiser Shipyards, 1941-43; stress analyst Convair Co., 1943-45; mem. faculty U. Cal. at Berkeley, 1946—, prof. civil engring., 1958—, asst. dean Coll. Engring., 1956-59, chmn. div. structural engring. and structural mechanics, 1963-64, dir. structural materials lab., 1963-65; cons. engr., Berkeley, 1946—. NSF postdoctoral fellow, 1961; Guggenheim fellow, 1962; State of the Art of Civil Engring. award, 1968. Mem. Am. Soc. C.E., Am. Concrete Inst. (Wason medal for research 1959), Internat Assn. Bridge and Structural Engring., Structural Engring. Assn., Reinforced Concrete Research Council. Author: (with T.Y. Lin) Design of Steel Structures, 1959, 2d edit., 1968; also articles. Home: 329 Rugby Av Berkeley CA 94708

BRESLIN, JIMMY, newspaperman; b. Jamaica, L.I., N.Y., Oct. 17, 1930; s. James Earl and Frances (Curtin) B.; student L.I. U., 1947-50; m. Rosemary Dattolico, Dec. 26, 1954; children—James and Kevin (twins), Rosemary, Patrick. Syndicated columnist N.Y. Herald-Tribune, Paris Tribune, others; contbr. articles nat. mags.; TV actor nationwide programs and commercials. Recipient award for nat. reporting Sigma Delta Chi, 1964, Meyer Barger award for local reporting, 1964, N.Y. Reporters Assn. award reporting, 1964. Mem. Screen Actors Guild, A.F.T.R.A., N.Y. Boxing Writers Assn. Author: Sunny Jim; Can't Anybody Here Play This Game?, 1963; Gang That Couldn't Shoot Straight, 1969. Home: 848 Hayes St Baldwin Harbor NY 11510 Office: care Sterling Lord Lit Agency 75 E 55th St New York City NY 10022

BRESLOW, LESTER, physician; b. Bismarck, N.D., Mar. 17, 1915; s. Joseph and Mayme (Danziger) B.; A.B., U. Minn., 1935, M.D., 1938, M.P.H., 1941; children—Norman, Jack, Stephen. Intern USPHS Hosp., Stapleton, N.Y., 1938-40; dist. health officer Minn. Dept. Health, 1941-43; chief bur. chronic diseases Cal. Dept. Pub. Health, Berkeley, 1946-60, chief div. preventive medicine, 1960-65, dir. dept., 1965-68. Lecturer U. Cal. Sch. of Pub. Health (Berkeley and Los Angeles) 1950-68, prof. of health services adminstrn., 1968—, chmn. dept. preventive medicine and social medicine, 1969—. Chmn. adv. com. on research etiology Am. Cancer Soc.; dir. study President's Commn. Health Needs of Nation, 1952. Served to capt. AUS, 1943-45. Decorated Bronze Star. Recipient Lasker award Cal. Dept. Pub. Health. Diplomate Am. Bd. Preventive Medicine and Pub. Health. Fellow Am. Coll. Preventive Medicine, A.C.P.; mem. A.A.A.S., Am. Heart Assn. (fellow epidemiology sect.), Am. Pub. Health Assn. (past pres.), Pub. Health Cancer Assn. (past pres.), Am. Epidemiological Soc., Internat. Epidemiological Assn. (past pres.), Am. Cancer Soc. (nat. dir., Cal. dir.). Author Med. publs. Editorial cons. Jour. Chronic Diseases, Jour. Med. Care. Home: 10926 Verano Rd Los Angeles CA 90024

BRESLOW, RONALD CHARLES, educator, chemist; b. Rahway, N.J., Mar. 14, 1931; son Alexander E. and Gladys (Fellows) B.; A.B. summa cum laude, Harvard, 1952, M.A., 1953, Ph.D., 1955; m. Esther Greenberg, Sept. 7, 1955; children—Stephanie. Karen. NRC fellow Cambridge (Eng.) U., 1955-56; mem. faculty Columbia, 1956—, prof. chemistry, 1962-66, S.L. Mitchell prof., 1966—; cons. to industry 1958—; editor Benjamin, Inc., 1962—. Mem. medicinal chemistry panel NIH, 1964—. Fellow Am. Acad. Arts and Scis.; mem. Nat. Acad. Scis., Am. Chem. Soc. (Pure Chemistry award 1966, Baeheland medal 1969; chmn. div. organic chemistry 1970), Phi Beta Kappa (first marshall 1952), Phi Lambda Upsilon (Fresenius award, 1966, Mark van Doren award 1969). Author: Organic Reaction Mechanisms, 1965, 2d edit., 1969; also articles. Mem. editorial bd. Organic Syntheses, 1964—. Home: 275 Broad Av Englewood, NJ 07631. Office: Dept Chemistry Columbia Univ New York City NY 10027

BRESNAHAN, WILLIAM ALMAN, trade assn. exec.; b. Washington, July 5, 1915; s. William Lloyd and Vivien (Whelan) B.; m. Lillian Anita Springmann, Jan. 8, 1937; children—William Byron, Daniel Alman, Patricia Erin. With A.P., Washington, 1935-37; editor Am. Trucking Assns., Inc., Washington, 1938- 43, research dir., 1944-53, dir. interstate cooperation, 1954-56, asst. mng. dir., 1961-64, mng. dir., 1964-70, pres., 1970—; gen. mgr. Nat. Automobile Transporters Assn., Washington, 1957-60. Home: 10110 Chickadee Lane Adelphi Forest, MD 20783. Office: Am Trucking Assn Inc 1616 P St NW Washington DC 20036

BRESNICK, EDWARD, educator; b. Jersey City, Sept. 7, 1930; s. Frank and Tillie (Lobel) B.; B.S. magna cum laude, St. Peter's Coll., Jersey City, 1952; M.S., Fordham U., 1954, Ph.D., 1958; m. Etta Krupitsky, Jan. 20, 1957; children—Eric Lawson, Emery Hilliard. Research asso. U. Tex., 1957-58; research biochemist Wellcome Research Labs., 1958-59, sr. research biochemist, 1959-61; mem. faculty Baylor U. Coll. Medicine, 1961—, prof. pharmacology, 1968-71; prof., chmn. dept. cell and molecular biology Med. Coll. Ga., 1971—. Mem. pharmacology, toxicology rev. panel Nat. Insts. Gen. Med. Sci., 1968—. Recipient Lederle Med. Faculty award, 1966-69. Mem. Am. Chem. Soc., A.A.A.S., Biochem. Soc., Am. Assn. Cancer Research, Am. Soc. Cell Biology, Am. Soc. Pharmacology and Exptl. Therapeutics, Am. Soc. Biol. Chemists, Sigma Xi, Phi Lambda Upsilon. Author: Functional Dynamics of the Cell, 1968; also articles. Home: 305 Kennelworth Pl Augusta GA 30904

BRESS, DAVID GERALD, lawyer, educator; b. N.Y.C., June 7, 1908; s. Abraham and Elizabeth (Geto) B.; B.S., U. Va., 1928; LL.B., Harvard, 1931; m. Flora M. Lyon, Sept. 20, 1941; children—Pamela Lyon, David Gerald. Admitted to D.C. bar, 1931, since practiced in Washington; mem. firm Ginsburg, Feldman & Bress, 1969—; U.S. atty. for D.C., 1965-69; faculty Washington Coll. Law, Am. U., 1932-52; prof. law Georgetown U. Law Sch., Washington, 1953-61, U. Va. Law Sch., 1963-64. Mem. adv. bd. dirs. Riggs Nat. Bank. Bd. dirs. Columbia Hosp., Police Boys Club; v.p. Nat. Capitol Area council Boy Scouts Am. Served as comdr. USNR, 1941-45. Fellow Am. Coll. Trial Lawyers, Am. Bar Found.; mem. Am. Bar Assn. (ho. of dels. 1957-64, chmn. com. on uniform rules evidence fed. cts. 1958-59, 64—), Bar Assn. D.C. (pres. 1957-58), Am. Jewish Com. (past pres. Washington chpt.), Criminal Law Inst. (dir. 1966—), Am. Jud. Soc., (dir. 1966-68), Phi Beta Kappa. Jewish religion (past pres. congregation). Home: 3126 Ellicott St Washington DC Office: 1700 Pennsylvania Av NW Washington DC 20006

BRESS, HYMAN, violinist; b. Cape Town, S. Africa, June 30, 1931; s. Mendel and Dora (Nachman) B.; grad. Curtis Inst. Music, Phila., 1946; m. Patricia Bagrit, July 7, 1960; 1 dau., Reda. Tours of U.S. and Europe, 1958—; artist on long playing records with Royal Philharmonic, London, Eng., Vienna (Austria) Symphony, English Chamber Orch., Montreal, (Can.) Symphonia; performed numerous contemporary works for first time; innovator audio-visual realization known on tour as score on screen. Recipient Concert Artists Guild award, 1956, Jascha Heifetz award, Tanglewood, Mass., 1957. Composer violin pieces, author articles in field. Address: 3172 Van Horne Av Montreal Quebec Canada

BRESSLER, BERNARD, lawyer; b. N.Y.C., Jan. 23, 1928; s. Morris and Masha (Roitman) B.; B.A., Rutgers U., 1949; LL.B. summa cum laude, Harvard, 1952; m. Teresa Stern, June 25, 1950; children—Lisa, Jeanette. Admitted to N.Y. bar, 1953; atty. firm Greenman, Shea, Sandomire & Zimet, N.Y.C., 1952-60; partner Bressler, Meislin, Tauber & Bressler, N.Y.C., 1960—. Sec., dir. Am. R.D.M. Corp., Plenum Pub. Corp., Tad's Enterprises, Inc. (all N.Y.C.); dir. Electro-Catheder Corp. (N.J.). Campaign dir. Summit (N.J.) United Jewish Appeal, 1957-60. Chmn. Summit Democrat Club, 1957. Trustee Summit Civic Found., 1958-65. Served with USNR, 1945-46. Jewish religion (v.p. Temple). Author: (with others) Tax Annotations Nichols Ency. Forms, 1954-59. Editor: (with B. Meislin) New York Lawyers Manual, 1954. Home: 101 Kent Pl Blvd Summit NJ 07901 Office: 90 Broad St New York City NY 10004

BRESSLER, CHARLES, tenor; b. Kingston, Pa., Apr. 1, 1926; s. Herbert Clair and Verna (Snyder) B.; grad. Juilliard Sch. Music, 1950, postgrad. diploma, 1951. Mem. N.Y. Pro Musica, 1950-63; soloist with orchs. including N.Y. Philharmonic, Chgo., Boston, San Francisco, Oakland, Mpls., Cin. symphonies; ann. tours of Europe; faculty Mannes Coll. Music, 1966—; rec. artist Decca, Columbia, Cambridge, Project 3, Nonesuch; appeared with Santa Fe Opera, Washington Opera Soc. Served with USNR, 1944-46, 51- 52. Recipient Best Male Singer award for role in The Play of Daniel, Nat. Festival of Paris, 1960. Office: Mannes Coll Music 157 E 74th St New York City NY 10021

BRESSLER, MARVIN, educator; b. N.Y.C., Apr. 10, 1923; s. George and Clara (Kitzis) B.; B.S., Temple U., 1947; A.M. in Sociology, U. Pa., 1948, Ph.D., 1952; m. Nancy Rosner, Feb. 1, 1944; children—Jan Darcy, Amy Gwen. Asst. prof. sociology U. Pa., 1953-57; asso. prof. sociology N.Y.U., 1957-60, prof., chmn. dept. ednl. sociology, 1961-63; prof. sociology Princeton, 1963—, chmn. dept. sociology, 1970—. Author: (with R. D. Lambert) Indian Students on American Campus, 1956; Tax-Supported Medical Institutional Care for the Needy and Medically Needy, 1957; (with M. Tumin) Quality and Equality in Education, 1967, Evaluating the Effectiveness of Educational Systems, 1969. Home: 123 Maclean Circle Princeton NJ 08540

BRESSLER, RICHARD MAIN, airline exec.; b. Wayne, Neb., Oct. 8, 1930; s. John T. and Helen (Main) B.; grad. Lake Forest (Ill.) Acad., 1946-48; B.A., Dartmouth, 1952; m. Carol Gregory Leighton, Sept. 20, 1952; children—Kristin M., Alan L. With Gen. Electric Co., 1952-68; v.p., treas. Am. Airlines Inc., 1968—. Home: Bailiwick Rd Greenwich, CT 06830. Office: 633 3d Av New York City NY 10017

BRETALL, ROBERT WALTER, educator; b. Hinckley, Ill., Feb. 8, 1913; s. Walter Herbert and Ora Jane (Bastian) B.; A.B., Princeton, 1935, A.M., 1937, Ph.D. (Chancellor Green fellow), 1938; postgrad. U. Chgo., 1939-42, 53-54, Union Theol. Sem., 1942-43, 52-54, Columbia, 1952-54, Cambridge U., 1962-63; m. Patricia Hodgkinson, Aug. 30, 1954. Philosophy, music editor Am. Educator Ency., 1945-47; grad. asst. in philosophy Northwestern U., 1945-46; asst. prof. philosophy and humanities U. Ariz., Tucson, 1947-52, asso. prof., 1954-64, prof., 1964—; lectr. philosophy Wagner Coll., N.Y.C., 1952-53; vis. prof. philosophy Wash. State U., 1967-68; cons. Princeton U. Press, Macmillan Co., Northwestern U. Press. Mem. exec. bd. So. br. Ariz. Civil Liberties Union, 1966—, chmn. ch.-state com., 1966-67, chmn. acad. freedom com., 1967-69. Democratic precinct committeman Pima County, Ariz., 1970—. Corr. sec., bd. dirs. Ariz. Friends Music. Ford Found. Faculty fellow, 1953-54. Mem. Am. Assn. U. Profs. (past pres. U. Ariz. chpt.), Am. Acad. Religion, Am. Philos. Assn., Princeton Grad. Alumni Assn., Phi Beta Kappa. Democrat. Episcopalian. Author: A Kierkegaard Anthology, 1946. Editor: (with Charles W. Kegley) The Theology of Paul Tillich, 1952; Reinhold Niebuhr: His Religious, Social and Political Thought, 1956; The Empirical Theology of Henry Nelson Wieman, 1963. Home: 4720 Camino Luz Tucson AZ 85718

BRETSCHER, WILLY, Swiss editor; b. 1897. Journalist, NEUES Winterthurer Tagblatt, 1914; editor Neue Zürcher Zeitung, 1917, Berlin corr., 1925-29, chief editor, 1933-67. Patron Liberal Internat.; mem. Nat. council, 1951-67, pres. fgn. affairs com., 1953-54, 62-63. Pres. Swiss Winston Churchill Found., 1966, Swiss Assn. Fgn. Affairs, 1968. Author books. Address: Freiestrasse 29 8032 Zurich, Switzerland.

BRETSCHNEIDER, CHARLES LEROY, educator, oceanographer; b. Red Owl, S.D., Nov. 9, 1920; s. Charles and Jennie (Seifert) B.; B.S. in Physics, Hillsdale Coll., 1947; M.S. in Civil Engring., U. Cal. at Berkeley, 1950; Ph.D., Tex. A. and M. Coll., 1959; m. Yveline Kerr, June 1, 1948; children—Eric Charles, Anne Denise. Mem. faculty Hillsdale (Mich.) Coll., 1946-48, U. Cal. at Berkeley, 1950-51, Tex. A. and M. Research Found., College Station, 1951-56; mem. beach erosion bd. C.E., U.S. Army, Washington, 1956-61; dir. Washington office Nat. Engring. Sci. Co., 1961-64, v.p. Eastern operations, McLean, Va., 1964-66; prof. civil engring. and phys. oceanography, chmn. ocean engring. U. Hawaii, 1966—; cons. engr. various offshore operations; lectr. various instns. Registered profl. engr., Tex., D.C. Mem. Am. Soc. C.E., Am. Geophys. Union, Am. Meteorol. Soc., Permanent Internat. Assn. Navigation Congresses (life), Marine Tech. Soc. (v.p. 1964-67), Soc. Naval Architects and Marine Engrs., Am. Soc. Engring. Edn., Am. Soc. Oceanographers, Sigma Xi. Contbr. articles profl. jours. Home: 4096 Blackpoint Rd Honolulu HI 96816

BRETT, JEREMY, actor; b. Warwickshire, Eng.; student London Central Sch. Speech and Drama. Appeared in stock prodns. with Manchester (Eng.) Library Theatre; now mem. Old Vic Company; appeared in London in The Edwardians, Mr. Fox of Venice, The Kitchen, Variations on a Theme, also Hamlet; appeared as Dunois in St. Joan and in The Workhouse Donkey at Chichester (Eng.) Festival, 1964; Broadway appearances include Troilus and Cressida, 1957, Macbeth, 1957, The Deputy, 1964; appeared as Freddy in film My Fair Lady, 1965; TV appearances include The Picture of Dorian Gray, Three Roads to Rome.*

BRETT, WILLIAM JOHN, educator, physiologist; b. Chgo., Mar. 23, 1923; s. Richard and Emily (Salter) B.; B.S., No. Ill. U., 1949; M.S., Miami U., Oxford, O., 1950; Ph.D., Northwestern U., 1953; m. Lorraine E. Petrie, Sept. 11, 1948; 1 son, Edward R. Instr., Loyola U., Chgo., summer 1953; from asst. prof. to prof. biology, acting chmn. dept. Millsaps Coll., 1953-56; mem. faculty Ind. State U., 1956—, prof. life scis., 1959—, chmn. dept., 1964-67. Served with USAAF, 1943-46. Recipient research prize Assn. S.E. Biologists, 1954. Mem. Am. Inst. Biol. Scientists, Am. Soc. Zoologists, Animal Behavior Soc., Ind. Acad. Sci., Sigma Xi. Author: Laboratory Manual for Cell Biology, 1967. Home: 2321 S 10th St Terre Haute IN 47802

BRETTHOLLE, FRANK MARSH, food co. exec.; b. Carnegie, Pa., May 4, 1917; s. Frank William and Sarah Atkinson (Marsh) B.; B.B.A., Westminster Coll., 1939; M.B.A., U. Chgo., 1941; m. Thelma Evans, Nov. 4, 1950; children—Frank Evans, Sarah Ann. Asso. prof. bus. adminstrn. Westminster Coll., 1942-46, bus. mgr., treas., 1944-46; asst. to pres. Welch Coal Co., Clarksburg, W. Va., 1947- 48; with H.J. Heinz Co., Pitts., 1948—, comptroller, 1959—, v.p., 1962-64, sr. v.p., 1964-71, v.p., controller, 1971—. Mem. Financial Execs. Inst., Nat. Soc. Bus. Budgeting, Sigma Phi Epsilon. Mason, Elk. Club: University, Chartiers Country, Duquesne (Pitts). Home: 23 Winthrop Rd Rosslyn Farms Carnegie PA 15106 Office: HJ Heinz Co Box 57 Pittsburgh PA 15230

BRETTING, RALPH CHRISTOPHER, utility co. exec.; b. Ashland, Wis., Sept. 8, 1923; s. Ralph Christopher and Prudentia (McDermott) B.; student Northwestern U., 1941-42; B.S. in Engring., U.S. Naval Acad., 1945; Advanced Mgmt. Program, Harvard, 1968; m. Elizabeth Fabac, Oct. 9, 1948; children—George C., Patricia A. Owner, mgr. weekly newspaper, Muskegon Heights, Mich., 1947-48; with Consumers Power Co., 1948—, v.p., 1965—. Served with USN, 1945-47. Mem. Am. Gas Assn. (indsl. relations com.), Edison Electric Inst. (indsl. relations com.). Republican. Episcopalian. Mason (Shriner), Elk. Home: 1305 W Franklin St Jackson MI 49203 Office: 212 W Michigan Av Jackson MI 49201

BRETTSCHNEIDER, BERTRAM DONALD, educator; b. Bklyn., May 7, 1924; s. Joseph and Fannie (Cohn) B.; B.A., Tulane U., 1947, M.A., 1948; M.A., Columbia, 1951; Ph.D., N.Y.U., 1956; m. Rita Roberta Fischman, June 25, 1950; children—Jane Ann, Joseph Michael. Grad. asst. psychology Tulane U., 1947-48; instr. philosophy Ft. Trumbull br. U. Conn., 1949-50; elementary sch. tchr., Valley Stream, N.Y., 1951-54; mem. faculty Hofstra Coll., 1954—, asso. prof. philosophy edn., 1954-59, asso. dean coll., 1959-63, prof. philosophy, 1963—, fellow in philosophy New Coll. of Hosftra U., 1967—; visiting asso. prof., N.Y.U., 1959-62. Served with AUS, 1943-46. Mem. Am. Soc. Aesthetics, Soc. Phenomenology and Existential Philosophy, Middle Atlantic States Philosophy of Edn. Soc. (exec. com. 1959-61), Eastern Deans Assn., Philosophy Edn. Soc., Am. Philos. Assn., Phi Delta Kappa, Kappa Delta Pi. Author: The Philosophy of Samuel Alexander: Idealism in Space, Time and Deity, 1963; (with Charles J. Calitr.) The Goliath Head, 1972). Home: 6 Lendale Pl Huntington NY 11743 Office: New College of Hofstra Univ Hempstead NY 11552

BRETT-SMITH, JOHN RALPH BRETT, publisher; b. Oxford, Eng., Aug. 23, 1917; s. Herbert Francis Brett and Helena (Yates) Brett-S.; grad. Rugby Sch., Eng., 1936; B.A., Christ Church, Oxford, Eng., 1939, M.A., 1945; Henry fellow Harvard, 1947-48; m. Catharine Hill, Apr. 19, 1952; children—Sarah Catharine, Helena Mary, John. With Oxford Univ. Press, London, Eng., 1946—, v.p., N.Y.C., 1955- 58, pres., 1958—. Served from pvt. to maj., Brit. Army, 1939-46; attached Combined Chiefs of Staff, Washington, 1945-46.

Clubs: Grolier, Century; Vincents (Oxford, Eng.). Home: 211 Prospect Av Princeton NJ 08540 Office: 200 Madison Av New York City NY 10016

BRETZ, THURMAN WILBUR, glass co. exec.; b. Lucas, Kan., Aug. 12, 1934; s. W. Kermit and Meta (Shockley) B.; A.B., Harvard, 1956, LL.B., 1959; m. Joanne Wakefield Morgens, July 11, 1959; children—Anne Elizabeth, Matthew Howard. With Owens-Corning Fiberglas Corp., Toledo, 1960—, asst. treas., 1968-69, treas., 1969—; dir. First Nat. Bank of Toledo. Trustee Toledo Symphony Orch.; trustee, chmn. finance com. Med. Coll. of Ohio, Toledo. Home: 85 Locust St Perrysburg OH 43551 Office: Fiberglas Tower Toledo OH 43601

BREUER, CARL A., steel co. exec.; b. Pitts., Dec. 22, 1911; s. Andrew J. and Emma M. (Becker) B.; B.S. in Mgmt. Engring., Carnegie Inst. Tech., 1933; m. Dolores Marcella Ogden, Oct. 28, 1933; children—Carol Ann (Mrs. William K. Saber), Douglas A., Bruce B. With Am. Rolling Mill., Butler, Pa., 1933-36, William B. Scaife Co., Oakmont, Pa., 1936- 37, H.H. Robertson Co., Ambridge, Pa., 1937-38; with Pitts. Steel Co. (now Wheeling-Pitts. Steel Co.), 1938—, v.p., 1957-68, exec. v.p., 1968—. Trustee Charlerio-Monessen Hosp., N. Charleroi, Pa., 1958—. Mem. Am. Iron and Steel Inst., Am. Petroleum Inst. Mason, Elk. Home: 106 Orchard Av Belle Vernon PA 15012 Office: Wheeling-Pitts Steel Co Gateway 4 Pittsburgh PA 15222

BREUER, DELMAR WALLACE, educator; b. St. James, Mo., June 21, 1925; s. Oscar B. and Ida May (Johnson) B.; B.S. in Aero. Engring., Ia. State Coll., 1947; M.S. in C.E., Mo. Sch. Mines, 1950; Ph.D., Ohio State U., 1961; m. Ethelen Paschal, July 31, 1949; children—Deborah Diane, Theresa Lea. Instr. mechanics Mo. Sch. Mines, 1947-50; stress analyst N. Am. Aviation Co., 1950-51; mem. faculty Air Force Inst. Tech., 1951—, prof., head dept. mechs., 1961—. Served with USNR, 1943-46. Asso. fellow Am. Inst. Aero. and Astronautics; mem. Am. Soc. Engring. Edn., Soc. Exptl. Stress Analysis, Sigma Xi, Tau Beta Pi.‡

BREUER, MANFRED, educator; b. Trier, Germany, May 15, 1929; s. Hans Peter Josef and Maria (Nettersheim) B.; student U. Mainz, 1950-51, U. Bonn, 1951-58; m. Mechthild Elisabeth Richter, Oct. 18, 1963; children—Adelheid, Annette, Sebastian. Came to U.S., 1966. Vis. asst. prof. U. Cal. at Berkeley, 1961-63; dozent U. Bonn (Germany), 1964-65; vis. asso. prof. U. Cal. at Berkeley, 1965-66; prof. math. U. Kan., 1966—. Research Fredholm and vector bundle theory relative to von Neumann algebras. Home: 2409 Manchester Rd Lawrence KS 66044

BREUER, MARCEL LAJOS, architect; b. Pécs, Hungary, May 22, 1902; s. Jacques and Franciska (Kan.) B.; grad. Magyar Kir, Föreáliskola, Pécs, Hungary, 1920; M.A., Bauhaus, Weimer, Germany, 1924; Dr. Govt. Hungary (hon.), 1968; Dr. Arts, Harvard, 1970; D.F.A. (hon.), Pratt Inst., 1969; m. Martha Erps, Aug. 14, 1926; m. 2d, Constance Leighton, Mar. 30, 1940. Master of Bauhaus, Dessau, Germany, 1925-28; architect Berlin, 1928-31; archtl. commns. and travel in Spain, Morocco, Switzerland, Germany, Hungary, Greece and Eng., 1931-35; architect, London, 1935- 37; asso. prof. Harvard U. archtl. dept., 1937—; partner Walter Gropius & Marcel Breuer, Cambridge, Mass., 1937-42. Recipient Medal of Honor N.Y. chpt. A.I.A., 1965; Washington award Am. Hungarian Studies Found., 1967, Thomas Jefferson Found. medal U. Va., 1968, 1st Internat. prize La Rinascente's "Compasso d'Oro" for indsl. 1957. Fellow A.I.A. (gold medal, 1968), Am. Acad. Arts and Scis.; mem. Nat. Inst. Arts and Letters (v.p. 1968). Clubs: Harvard, Century (N.Y.C.). Author: Sun and Shadow, Marcel Breuer, 1921-1961; Marcel Breuer: New Buildings and Projects. Contbr. jours. Travelled in Japan, Pakistan, Italy, Colombia, Venezuela, Argentina, Haiti. Home: 628 West Rd New Canaan CT 06840 Office: 635 Madison Av New York City NY 10022 also 48 Rue Chapon Paris France

BREUL, FRANK RENNELL, educator; b. Bridgeport, Conn., May 10, 1916; s. Alvin C. and Mildred (Rennell) B.; A.B., Amherst Coll., 1938; A.M., U. Chgo., 1941; Ph.D., McGill U., 1951; m. Gertrude L. Kirsten, June 7, 1947; 1 dau., Nancy. Lectr., McGill U., 1949-51; asso. prof. social welfare U. Wash., 1951- 56; mem. faculty U. Chgo., 1956—, prof. social welfare, 1960—, asso. dean Sch. Social Service Adminstrn., 1966-70. Served to maj., F.A., AUS, 1941-46. Decorated Bronze Star medal. Mem. Nat. Assn. Social Work, Nat. Conf. Social Welfare. Episcopalian. Home: 5801 S Dorchester Av Chicago IL 60637

BREUNIG, LEROY CLINTON, educator; b. Indpls., Mar. 29, 1915; s. LeRoy Clinton and Lydia (Latham) B.; A.B., DePauw U., 1936; student U. Bordeaux (France), 1937; M.A., Cornell U., 1938, Ph.D., 1941; m. Herse Lukia Niskos, Dec. 13, 1945; 1 stepdau., Maria Hellé. Instr. French, Cornell U., 1939-41; instr., asst. prof. Romance langs. Harvard, 1946-53; asso. prof., prof. French, Barbard Coll., Columbia, 1953—, chmn. dept., 1953-70, dean faculty, 1970—. Served to lt. comdr. USNR, 1942-46. Decorated officer Palmes Acad.; Guggenheim fellow, 1960-61; Fulbright fellow, 1960-61, 66. Mem. Modern Lang. Assn., Am. Assn. Tchrs. French, Phi Beta Kappa, Delta Kappa Epsilon. Author: (with others) Forme et Fond, 1964; Guillaume Apollinaire, 1970. Editor (Guillaume Apollinaire) Chroniques d'art, 1960; (Guillaume Apollinaire) Les Peintres cubistes, 1965. Editorial bd. Romanic Rev. Home: 90 Morningside Dr New York City NY 10027

BREUNINGER, LEWIS TALMAGE, mem. Republican Nat. Finance Com., real estate exec.; b. Washington, July 23, 1893; s. Lewis Eugene and Sadie I. (Love) B.; A.B., Johns Hopkins, 1913; LL.B., George Washington U., 1916; LL.D., Southeastern U., 1956; m. Marie L. Ashford, June 28, 1919 (dec. 1959); 1 son, Lewis Talmage. Admitted to D.C. bar, 1916; practice in D.C.; pres. L.E. Breuninger & Sons, Inc., builders and realtors, Washington, 1929—; dir. Nat. Savs. & Trust Co., Dist. Title Co. (both Washington). Active Rep. Party, 1944—; chmn. D.C. Rep. Finance Com., 1944-60; vice chmn. Rep. Nat. Finance Com., 1956—; exec. vice chmn. 1957 Inaugural Com.; mem. Rep. Nat. Com. for D.C., 1960- 68. Pres. Washington Real Estate Bd., 1944-45, Washington Met. Home Builders Assn., 1956. Pres. Washington Met. YMCA, 1954-56, bd. dirs., 1940—; Am. dir. Benjamin Franklin Found., coop. with City of Berlin, Germany; bd. dirs. Central Union Mission, Washington. Mem. Am., D.C. bar assns. Kiwanian (pres. Washington 1934). Clubs: Metropolitan, Nat. Press, Capitol Hill (bd. govs.), Congressional Country. Army and Navy (Washington); George Town. Home: 2701 Foxhall Rd NW Washington DC 20007 Office: 1825 F St N W Washington DC 20006

BREUSCH, ROBERT HERMANN, educator; b. Freiburg, Germany, Apr. 2, 1907; s. Friedrich and Luise (Stehle) B.; student univs. Freiburg, Bonn and Berlin (Germany), 1925- 30; Ph.D. in Math., U. Freiburg, 1932; M.A. (hon.), Amherst Coll., 1954; m. Kate Dreyfuss, July 25, 1936. Came to U.S., 1939, naturalized, 1945. Asst. math. U. Freiburg (Germany), 1930-32; tchr. Schula Birklehof, Hinterzarten, Germany, 1932-36; tchr. math. and physics U. Santa Maria, Valparaiso, Chile, 1936-39, Shady Hill Sch., Cambridge, Mass., 1940-43; mem. faculty Amherst (Mass.) Coll., 1943—, prof. math., 1954—, chmn. dept., 1963-68. Ford Found. lectr. U. Medellin (Colombia), 1964; vis. prof. U. Waikato (N.Z.), 1969-70. Mem. Math. Assn. Am. (lectr. 1965-66), Am. Math. Soc., Am. Assn. U. Profs. Contbr. articles prime number theory. Home: 19 Dana Pl Amherst MA 01002

BREVIG, PER ANDREAS, musician; b. Berg by Halden, Norway, Sept. 7, 1936; s. Knut and Aslaug (Maarud) B.; Mus.B., Juilliard Sch., 1968, Mus.M., 1969, D.Mus. Arts, 1971; studied trombone under Palmer Traulsen, Copenhagen, 1958; conducting in Holland and Sweden, 1962-64, with Leopold Stokowski, 1966-67; m. Berit Lillian Johannessen, June 27, 1959; children—Kjetil, Berit Elizabeth, Ingrid Lillian. Numerous premiers, solo performances, Scandinavia, Germany, Czechoslovakia, P.R., U.S.; mem. Bergen (Norway) Symphony Orch., 1957-65; 1st trombone Am. Symphony Orch., 1965-68; 1st trombone Met. Opera Orch., 1968—; mem. trombone faculty, brass chamber music dept. Juilliard Sch., 1966—; faculty Aspen Music Festival, 1970—. Served with Norwegian Army. Recipient prize XIV Internat. Music Competition, Prague, Czechoslovakia, 1962, Henry B. Cabot award Boston Symphony Orch., 1966; S. Koussevitzky fellow Tanglewood Music Festival. Author: Avant-Garde Techniques in Solo Trombone Music; Problems of Notations and Execution. Office: Juilliard Sch Lincoln Center Plaza New York City NY 10023

BREVIK, J. ALBERT, broadcasting co. exec.; b. Seattle, Aug. 1, 1920; s. Anton Christian and Olga Elise (Setter) B.; B.A., U. Wash., 1947, M.A., 1951; m. Norma Jacquelin Ringman, June 26, 1953; children—Jay Christian, Jon Henry. Guidance counselor music dept. U. Wash., Seattle, 1947-52, entertainment dir. athletic dept., 1947-52; vocal music educator Clover Park High Sch., Tacoma, Wash., 1952-54; television coordinator Pierce County Schs., Tacoma, 1954-59; dir. television edn., gen. mgr. KPEC-TV, Clover Park Schs., Tacoma, 1959—. Asso. faculty dept. edn. U. Puget Sound, 1955-69; dir. Norwegian Male Chorus, Seattle, 1946-48, Clarion Chorus, Seattle, 1947-52; free-lance radio musician, Seattle, 1938-52; entertainment dir. BC Lions, profl. football club, Vancouver, Can., 1954-55; ednl. television cons. B.C., Can., 1960-61. Mem. Fir Tree, Phi Mu Alpha Synfonia, Phi Delta Kappa. Lutheran (v.p., dir. 1959-69). Kiwanian (pres. 1963, dir., 1955-71). Clubs: Tacoma Yacht, Day Island Yacht, Firecrest Golf (Tacoma). Home: 1920 Day Island Blvd W Tacoma WA 98466 Office: 4400 Steilacomm Bldg SW Tacoma WA 98499

BREW, JOHN OTIS, educator, archeologist; b. Malden, Mass., Mar. 28, 1906; s. Michael Parker and Edith (Fryer) B.; A.B. in Fine Arts, Dartmouth Coll., 1928; student Harvard Grad. Sch. of Arts and Scis., 1928-31; Ph.D., Harvard, 1941; LL.D. in Internat. Relations, U. Liberia, 1970; m. Evelyn Ruth Nimmo, June 11, 1939; children—Alan Parker, Lindsay Edward. Fellow archeology U. Chgo. Expdn., 1930; with Harvard U. Peabody Mus., 1930—, asst. dir. 1930-48, sci. dir. Claflin-Emerson expdn., 1931, dir. Southeastern Utah Expdn., 1931-33, asst. to dir. Harvard Irish Expdn., 1934, dir. Awatovi Expdn., field seasons 1935-39, mem. staff Harvard dept. anthropology, 1937—, asst. curator Southwest Am. Archeology, 1941-45, curator No. Am. Archeology, 1945-48, dir. 1948-67, engaged archeol. reconnaissance for mus., N.M. and Ariz., 1946-47, Peabody Prof. of Am. archeology and ethnology, 1949—, mem. bd. syndics. Mem. Mass. Hist. Commn.; chmn. adv. com. Pre-Columbian Art, Dumbarton Oaks, 1963—; chmn. UNESCO comm. for Monuments, artistic and historic sites and archaeol. excavations; mem. adv. bd. Nat. Parks Service, 1952-58; bd. dirs. Human Relations Area Files, chmn. bd., 1954-57; vice chmn. spl. com. Natural Survey of Historic Sites and Bldgs., 1958—; chmn. U.S. Nat. Com. for Preservation of Monuments of Nubia. Trustee, Children's Mus., Boston, Mus. Navajo Ceremonial Art, pres.; trustee Santa Fe, Fruitlands and the Wayside Museums, Donations for Edn. in Liberia, v.p. 1958—, Plimouth Plantation, Inc. Recipient Viking Fund medal for anthropology, 1947. Fellow Am. Acad. Arts and Scis.; mem. Nat. Council for Preservation of Historic Sites, Bldgs. and Monuments (charter mem., chmn. Com. for Recovery of Archaeol. Remains, Nat. Research Council (mem. Div. of Anthropology and Psychology 1949-54, pres. 1954), Soc. Am. Archaeology (council 1944-46; pres. 1949-50), Internat. Inst. for Conservation Mus. Objects, Internat. African Inst. (exec. council), Mass. Archaeol. Soc. (exec. council 1941- 44, trustee 1949-52), Tree Ring Soc., Soc. Applied Archaeology Am. Assn. Mus. (council 1956-60), Colonial Soc. Mass., Acad. Am. Francisco Hist. (corr. mem.), S.W. Mus. (hon.), Los Angeles, No. Ariz. Soc. Hist. Sci. and Art, Am. Antiquarian Soc., Mass. Hist. Soc., German Archeol. Inst. Clubs: Harvard Faculty (pres. 1951-55), Odd Volumes (pres. 1964-69); Cosmos (Washington). Contbr. articles to jours. and papers of Peabody Mus. Address: Peabody Mus Archaeology and Ethnology Harvard U Cambridge MA 02138

BREWER, ALBERT PRESTON, former gov. of Ala.; b. Bethel Springs, Tenn., Oct. 26, 1928; s. Dan A. and Clara (Yarber) B.; A.B., U. Ala., 1952, LL.B., 1952; LL.D., L.H.D., Jacksonville State U.; LL.D., Samford U.; m. Martha Farmer, Jan. 31, 1951; children—Rebecca Ann, Beverly Alison. Admitted to Ala. bar, 1952, since practiced in Decatur; mem. Ala. Ho. of Reps., 1955-66, speaker, 1963-66; lt. gov. of Ala., 1966-68, gov., 1968-71. Chmn. Decatur City Planning Commn., 1956-63; mem. exec. com. Nat. Gov.'s Conf.; vice chmn. So. Gov.'s Conf.; chmn. Appalachian Regional Commn., 1970. Mem. Ala. Democratic Exec. Com., 1964—. Named Outstanding Young Man of Decatur, Decatur Jr. C. of C., 1963, One of Four outstanding Young Men of Ala., Ala. Jr. C. of C., 1963, Outstanding Mem. Ala. Ho. of Reps., 1963. Mem. Am., Ala. bar assns., Am. Legion, Phi Alpha Delta, Delta Sigma Phi. Baptist. Mason (Shriner). Home: Montgomery AL Office: Montgomery AL

BREWER, CHARLES MOULTON, lawyer; b. Washington, June 9, 1931; s. Charles M and Monemia (Moulton) B.; B.A., U. Md., 1953; J.D. George Washington U., 1957; m. Lavon Brown, June 14, 1958; children-Charles Robert, Lisa Ann, John Brian. Admitted to Ariz. bar, 1959, since practiced in Phoenix; law clk. to Chief Justice Ariz. Supreme Ct. Levi S. Udall, 1958-59; pvt. practice, 1959—. Served to capt. USAF, 1954-56. Mem. Am., Ariz., Maricopa County bar assns., Am. Judicature Soc., Am., Cal. trial lawyers assns., Am. Bd. Trial Advs. Contbr. articles profl. jours. Home: 7105 N Wilder Rd Phoenix AZ 85021 Office: Luhrs Bldg Phoenix AZ 85003

BREWER, CURTIS CLAUDE, banker; b. Bonlee, N.C., Aug. 20, 1922; s. Curtis Claude and Mebel (Lambee) B.; B.S. in Commerce, U. N.C., 1943; m. Gladys Ross Smith, June 20, 1942; children—Curtis Claude III, Constance Susan, Ted LeRoy, Barry Dwight. With N.C. Nat Bank, Greensboro, 1943-44; with First Union Nat. Bank N.C., Charlotte, and predecessors, 1945—, exec. v.p., 1955—; pres. Siler City Devel. Corp. (N.C.), 1960—; v.p., dir. Piedmont Cattle Credit Co., Siler City, 1959—. Pres. Chatham Hosp., Siler City, 1959- 61. Bd. dirs. Junior Achievement. Served with Transp. Corps, AUS, World War II. Methodist. Mason (Shriner). Clubs: Democratic Men's, Charlotte Execs., Myers Park Country (Charlotte). Home: 4112 Arbor Way Charlotte, NC 28201.

BREWER, EDMUND LEONARD, govt. ofcl.; b. St. Thomas, V.I., July 23, 1899; s. Charles Augustus and Augusta Altagracia (Risse) B.; student Sacred Heart Convent, St. Thomas; m. Nina Jean Parker, Apr. 20, 1928. Hotel exec., N.Y.C., 1927-40; lessee, mgr. Bluebeard's Castle Hotel, 1940-50; U.S. commr. Carribbean Commn., 1956-58; Royal Norwegian consul Consul of The Netherlands, 1949—. Chmn. St. Thomas Park Authority, 1946—, Devel. Bd., 1950-52. Decorated Knight Order of St. Olav, Knight Order of Orange Nassau. Mem. St. Thomas C. of C. (pres. 1942, 49, 56, 57). Home: Blackbeard's Charlotte Amalie St Thomas VI 00801

BREWER, EDWARD EUGENE, tire and rubber co. exec.; b. Findlay, O., July 19, 1925; s. William B. and Edna (Hurrell) B.; B.S. in Mech. Engring., Purdue U., 1949; m. Joyce K. Josephson, Feb. 7, 1948; children—Stephen, Rebecca, Mary, Sara, Debra. With Cooper Tire & Rubber Co., Findlay, 1949-56, v.p., 1956-70, exec. v.p., 1970—. Pres. bd. trustees Findlay Coll. Mem. Am. Soc. M.E. (sec. rubber and plastic div.). Home: 857 S Main St Findlay OH 45840 Office: Cooper Tire & Rubber Co Lima and Western Avs Findlay OH 45840

BREWER, GENE CEDRIC, wood and paper products exec.; b. Satsop, Wash., Oct. 17, 1913; s. Edgar Leon and Mary Alice (Nesbitt) B.; B.S., U. Ore., 1934; m. Helen B. Hendry, Dec. 29, 1934; children—David, Robert, Beth. Supt. U.S. Plywood Corp., Orangeburg, S.C., 1937-45, asst. mgr., 1946-49; gen. mgr. Plywood, Inc., 1949-51, pres., 1951-54; v.p. West Coast operations U.S. Plywood Corp., 1954-58, pres., 1958; pres. U.S. Plywood-Champion Papers, 1969; pres., dir., mem. exec. com. S.W. Forest Industries, Inc., Phoenix, 1970—; dir. Apache Ry. Co., Carolina Pacific Plywood, Inc.; Allen Homes, Inc., Home Capital Funds. Bd. dirs. Phoenix Art Mus. Home: 2323 N Central St Phoenix AZ 85004 Office: 3443 N Central St Phoenix AZ 85011

BREWER, HAROLD REID, educator, physicist; b. College Park, Ga., Aug. 1, 1924; s. William Irvin and Mary (Reid) B.; B.S., Ga. Inst. Tech., 1949; Ph.D., U. N.C., 1956; m. Vivian Eleanor Rasmussen, Oct. 7, 1955; children—Jefferson Drew, Peter Nielsen, William Irvin. Instr. physics Ga. Inst. Tech., 1950-51, research physicist engring. expt. sta., 1951-54, asso. prof. physics, 1956-65, prof., 1965—. Served with USNR, 1942-45. Decorated D.F.C., Air Medal. Mem. Am. Phys. Soc., Sigma Xi. Home: 3896 Parkcrest Dr Atlanta GA 30319

BREWER, JOHN ISAAC, physician; b. Milford, Ill., Oct. 3, 1903; s. John H. and Edna (Ishler) B.; student Bradley U., 1921-24; S.B., U. of Chgo., 1925, Ph.D., 1935; M.D., Rush Med., 1928; m. Ruth Russell, June 2, 1928; 1 son, John Vernon. Intern St. Luke's Hosp., Chgo., 1928-29; resident gynecology and obstetrics St. Luke's Hosp., 1929-30; pvt. practice splty., Chgo., 1930—. Instr. Northwestern U. Med. Sch., 1930-36, asst. prof., 1938- 42, asso. prof., 1942-47, prof. gynecology and obstetrics, 1948—; chief dept. gynecology and obstetrics Passavant Hosp., Chgo. Served as lt. col., med. dept., U.S. Army Air Forces, 1942-45. Decorated Legion of Merit. Diplomate, dir. Am. Bd. Obstetrics and Gynecology. Fellow A.C.S. (regent); mem. Am. Coll. Obstetricians and Gynecologists (pres.), Am. Gynecology Society (pres. 1964-65), Am. Assn. of Obstetricians and Gynecologists, (pres. 1968-69), Am. Assn. Anatomists, A.M.A., Central Assn. Obstetrics and Gynecology (pres.), Chgo. Gynecol. Soc. (pres.), Chgo. Path. Soc., Chgo., Ill. med. Socs., Alpha Delta Phi, Sigma Xi, Nu Sigma Nu. Clubs: Lake Shore, Flossmoor Country. Author: Gynecology, 1950; Textbook of Gynecology, 1953; Textbook of Gynecology, 1958; Textbook of Gynecology, 1961, 67. Editor in chief Am. Jour. Obstetrics and Gynecology. Contbr. sci. publs. Home: 860 Lake Shore Dr Chicago IL 60611 Office: 707 N Fairbanks Ct Chicago IL 60611

BREWER, JOHN WITHROW, educator; b. Boston, Mar. 26, 1904; s. Daniel Chauncey and Genevieve (Withrow) B.; A.B. maxima cum laude, Princeton, 1926, M.A., 1930, Ph.D., 1932; student Harvard Law Sch., 1926-28; m. Thelma Lillian Martin, Aug. 22, 1943. Instr. polit. sci. George Washington U., 1933-34, asso. prof. internat. law, 1939-46, prof., 1946—, head dept. polit. sci., 1946-63; instr. Dartmouth, 1934-35; asst. prof. polit. sci. Conn. State Coll., 1935-38, asso. prof., 1938-39. Vis. prof. U. So. Cal., 1950—. Served with AUS, 1942-46. Decorated Legion of Merit. Mem. Am. Soc. Internat. Law, Am. Polit. Sci. Assn., Phi Beta Kappa. Home: 3710 N Roberts Lane Arlington VA 22207 Office: Dept Polit Sci George Washington U Washington DC 20006

BREWER, LEO, educator; b. St. Louis, June 13, 1919; s. Abraham and Hannah (Resnik) B.; B.S., Cal. Inst. Tech., 1940; Ph.D., U. Cal. at Berkeley, 1943; m. Rose Strugo, Aug. 22, 1945; children—Beth A., Roger M., Gail L. Mem. faculty U. Cal. at Berkeley, 1946—, prof. phys. chemistry, 1955—, research asso. Lawrence Berkeley Lab., 1943-61, head inorganic materials div., 1961—, asso. dir. lab., 1967—. Huffman Meml. lectr. Calorimetry Conf., 1967; Coover lectr., 1967; Robert W. Williams lectr. Mass. Inst. Tech., 1963; Henry Werner lectr. U. Kan., 1963; O.M. Smith lectr. Okla. State U., 1964; G.N. Lewis lectr. U. Cal., 1964, faculty lectr., 1966 corn products lectr. Pa. State U., 1970; mem. rev. com. reactor chem. div. Oak Ridge Nat. Lab., research asso. Manhattan Dist., 1943-45; sec. gas subcom. high temperature commn. Internat. Union Pure and Applied Chemistry, 1957-60; chmn. materials adv. bd. Com. Investigation Application Plasma Phenomena, 1959-60. Great Western Dow fellow, 1942; Guggenheim fellow, 1950; recipient Ernest Orlando Lawrence Meml. award, 1961 Palladium medal, 1971. Mem. Nat. Acad. Scis. (exec. com. Office Critical Tables 1961-66), Am. Assn. U. Profs., A.A.A.S., Am. Chem. Soc. (Leo H. Baekeland award 1953), Am. Electrochem. Soc. (lectr. 1970), Am. Plant Life Soc., Am. Civil Liberties Union, Cobletz Soc., Combustion Inst., Faraday Soc., Fedn. Am. Scientists, Cal. Assn. Chemistry Tchrs., Internat. Plansee Soc. Power Metallurgy, Am. Phys. Soc., Nat. Park Assn., Sigma Xi, Alpha Chi Sigma, Tau Beta Pi. Author: (with others) Thermodynamics, 1961. Asso. editor Jour. Chem. Physics, 1959-63; editorial adv. bd. Jour. Physics and Chemistry Solids, Progress Inoganic Chemistry, Jour. Chem. Thermodynamics, Jour. High Temperature Sci. Home: 15 Vista del Orinda Orinda CA 94563 Office: Dept Chemistry Univ California Berkeley CA 94720

BREWER, MARION CAREY, coll. pres.; b. Lynchburg, Va., July 8, 1927; s. James Allen and Esther Goode (Leftwich) B.; B.A., Lynchburg Coll., 1949; student Am. U., 1951; M.P.A., Harvard, 1952, Ph.D., 1956; m. Betty Ann Brighton, Sept. 3, 1949; children—Mary Elizabeth, Robert Allen, Ruth Ann, Catherine Lee. Analyst with legislative reference service Library of Congress, 1949-56; sr. def. specialist mil. operations subcom. Ho. of Reps., 1956-60; mem. staff joint com. atomic energy U.S. Congress, 1960-61; various positions Office Emergency Planning, Exec. Office of Pres., 1961-64; pres. Lynchburg Coll. 1964—; lectr. Am. U., 1954-56. Mem. Bd. Higher Edn., also mem. Gen. Bd., Christian Ch. (Disciples of Christ); mem. Pres.'s Civil Def. Adv. Council, 1970—. Bd. dirs. Regional Ednl. Lab. for Carolinas and Va. Served with USNR, 1945- 46. Littauer fellow Harvard, 1951-53. Mem. Am. Polit. Sci. Assn., Am. Soc. Pub. Adminstrs. Mem. Christian Ch. (elder). Author: Civil Defense in the United States, 1951; Implications of a National Service Program, 1952; Science and Defense, 1956; also numerous articles. Home: 3806 Faculty Dr Lynchburg VA 24501

BREWER, MELVIN DUANE, ednl. counsellor; b. Rochester, Pa., Mar. 6, 1913; s. Percy McPherson and Ida Viola (Noss) B.; student Geneva Coll., Beaver Falls, Pa., 1931-32; A.B., Washington and

Jefferson Coll., 1937; m. Lila Margarett Scott, Nov. 28, 1940; children—Melvin Duane (dec.), Barbara Jo (Mrs. John T. Davis), Margaret Scott. Served successively as alumni sec. dean freshmen, dir. admissions Washington and Jefferson Coll., 1937-44, asst. to pres., 1946-48; mem. staff Marts & Lundy, Inc., N.Y.C., 1948—, v.p., sec., 1961-69, exec. v.p., treas., 1969-71, pres., 1971—, also dir. Trustee, Washington and Jefferson Coll. (life); mem. exec. com. Nat. Soc. Prevention Blindness. Served to lt. (s.g.) USNR, 1944-46, bd. dirs. Bartlett Arboretum Assn., The Fedn. Thantology. Mem. Am. Assn. Fund Raising Counsel, Phi Kappa Psi. Republican. Presbyn. Club: Union League (N.Y.C.). Contbr. articles ednl. adminstrn., fund raising. Home: 42 Pinnacle Rock Rd Stamford CT 06903 Office: 521 Fifth Av New York City NY 10017

BREWER, OLIVER GORDON, Jr., corp. exec.; b. Winston-Salem, N.C., Dec. 8, 1936; s. Oliver Gordon and Lula Irene (Masencup) B.; B.A., Guilford Coll., 1960; postgrad. Dartmouth; m. Gail Olt, Aug. 29, 1959; children—Nancy Lynne, Oliver Gordon III. With Phila. Nat. Bank, 1963-70, regional v.p., 1969-70; treas. Alco Standard Corp., Valley Forge, Pa., 1970—. Mem. Pa. Golf Assn. (exec. com.), Pa. Soc. Methodist. Clubs: Huntingdon Valley (Pa.) Country; Pine Valley (Pa.) Golf. Home: 3645 Holt Lane Huntingdon Valley PA 19006 Office: Alco Standard Corp Valley Forge PA 19481

BREWER, ORLANDO SWIFT, ret. investment banker; b. Oneida, N.Y., Feb. 13, 1898; s. James Edward and Clarissa (Swift) B.; B.S., Hobart Coll., 1920; m. Margaret Elizabeth Doran, Sept. 9, 1922; children—Constance Anne, Prudence Pomeroy (Mrs. Peter Bancroft Read), James Edward. Salesman Estabrook & Co., 1920-23; partner Phelps, Fenn & Co., N.Y.C., 1924-68. Home: Newfane VT Office: 39 Broadway New York City NY 10006

BREWER, ROBERT PALMER, editor; b. Henderson, N.C., Dec. 13, 1915; s. Charles Stephen and Eva (Hart) B.; B.J., U. N.C., 1939; m. Percye Venable Burwell, Sept. 27, 1946; children—Robert Palmer Jr., Catharine Spottswood, Donna Morton. Reporter Washington Daily News, 1939-40; commd. ensign U.S. Navy, 1942, advanced through grades to comdr., 1966, asso. prof. naval history Duke, 1949-51; editor Approach, 1954-57; instr. U.S. Naval Postgrad. Sch., 1959-62; sea and shore navy assignments, including conventional and jet carrier sqdns., 1962-66; ret., 1966; editor U.S. Naval Inst. Proceedings, Annapolis, Md., 1966—. Mem. Am. Aviation Hist. Soc., U.S. Naval Inst. Baptist. Home: Rt 4 1160 River Bay Rd Annapolis MD 21401 Office: US Naval Inst Annapolis MD 21402

BREWER, ROY MARTIN, labor union ofcl.; b. Cairo, Neb., Aug. 9, 1909; s. Martin M. and Lottie B. (Woodworth) B.; student pub. schs.; m. Alyce J. Auhl, July 9, 1929; children—Roy Martin, Ramona Rae, Motion picture projectionist, 1926-33: pres. Neb. State Fedn. Labor, 1933-34, 1937-43; N.R.A. labor compliance officer, Neb., 1934-37; chief plant community facilities div. W.P.B., 1943-45; Internat. rep. Internat. Alliance Theat. Stage Employees, 1945-53, mgr. prodn. devel., 1965—; mgr. bd. operations Allied Artists Prodns., 1953, asst. v.p., studio mgr., Hollywood, Cal., 1966-67, Allied Artists Pictures Corp.; pres. Hollywood Film Council, AFL, 1947—, also Fortune; dir. indsl. relations Technicolor, Inc., 1969—. Mem. Permanent Charities Com. (pres. 1949-50), Los Angeles Welfare Council, Motion Picture Industry Council (pres. 1950). Contbr. labor publs. Home: 4230 Jubilo Dr Taryana CA 90038 Office: 6311 Romaine St Hollywood CA 90038

BREWER, SEBERT, soft drink co. exec.; b. Chgo., Aug. 4, 1906; s. Loren Hadley and Edna (Sebert) B.; grad. McCallie Sch., Chattanooga, 1924; B.B.A., U. Chattanooga, 1928; m. Sara Stephenson, Dec. 31, 1930; children—Sara Harvey (Mrs. Richard Vail), Sebert. With Coca-Cola Bottling Co. (Thomas), Inc., Chattanooga, 1925—, v .p., 1943-60, pres., 1960-67, chmn. bd., 1967—, also dir.; pres., dir. Coca-Cola Bottling Co., Meadville, Pa., 1939—; dir. Coca-Cola Bottling Co. of Memphis, Provident Life & Accident Ins. Co., Chattanooga, Am. Nat. Bank & Trust Co., Chattanooga. Past chmn. bd. trustees Baroness Erlanger Hosp.; past pres. Chattanooga Symphony, Heart Assn., Salvation Army, Council Community Forces, Allied Arts Fund; bd. dirs. Big Bros., Area Beautification Com.; trustee Chattanooga Art Assn., Benwood Found., U. Chattanooga Found., First Presbyn. Ch. Fund,Tenn. Hosp. Edn. and Research Found., Tenn. Mid-South Regional Program. Mem. Chattanooga C. of C. (dir.), Blue Key, Delta Chi, Sigma Chi, Phi Gamma Mu, Alpha Soc. Presbyn. (deacon). Clubs: Mountain City, Chattanooga Golf and Country (past pres.) (Chattanooga). Home: 212 Lindsay St Chattanooga TN 37403 Office: Am Nat Bank Bldg Chattanooga TN 37402

BREWER, THOMAS BOWMAN, coll. dean; b. Fort Worth, July 22, 1932; s. Earl Johnson and Maurine (Bowman) B.; B.A., U. Tex., 1954, M.A., 1957; Ph.D., U. Pa., 1962; m. Betty Jean Walling, Aug. 4, 1951; children—Diane, Susan, Thomas Bowman. Instr., St. Stephen's Episcopal Sch., Austin, Tex., 1955-56, S.W. Tex. State Coll., San Marcos, 1956-57; from instr. to asso. prof. N. Tex. State U., Denton, 1959-66; asst. prof. U. Ky., 1966-67; asso. prof. Ia. State U., 1967-68; prof. history, chmn. dept. U. Toledo, 1968-71; dean Tex. Christian U. Coll. Arts and Scis., Fort Worth, 1971—. Mem. Am. Hist. Assn., Orgn. Am. Historians, Econ. History Assn., Bus. History Assn., Labor History Assn., So., Western hist. assns. Editor: Views of American Economic Growth, 2 vols., 1966; The Robber Barons, 1969. Gen. editor: Railroads of America Series, 1967—. Home: 4808 Barkridge Trail Fort Worth TX 76109

BREWER, WAYNE BURDETTE, rubber co. exec.; b. Findlay, O., Sept. 6, 1923; s. William B. and Edna (Hurrel) B.; B.S. in Chem. Engring., Purdue U., 1944; m. Leola E. Karpuleon, June 27, 1946; children—Sharon, Larry, Nancy, Patricia, Michael, David. With Cooper Tire & Rubber Co., Findlay, 1946—, exec. v.p., 1958-60, pres., 1960—, also dir. Served to lt. (j.g.) USNR, 1943- 46. Recipient distinghished service award Findlay Jr. C. of C. Mem. Am. Chem. Soc., Catalyst Soc. (Purdue), Tau Beta Pi, Phi Lambda Upsilon, Omega Chi Epsilon. Mason, Kiwanian. Home: 1003 S Main St Findlay OH 45840 Office: Cooper Tire & Rubber Co Lima & Western Avs Findlay OH 45840

BREWER, WILLIAM CONANT, Jr., lawyer; b. Bklyn., July 17, 1922; s. William Conant and Jeannette (Nostrand) B.; grad. Phillips Acad., Andover, Mass., 1938-39; A.B., Williams Coll., 1943; LL.B., Harvard, 1949; m. Ann Arnot Wickes, Dec. 18, 1948; children—Gale Arnot, Anita Warren, William Conant III. Admitted to Mass. bar; gen. counsel Mut. Boiler & Machinery Ins. Co., Waltham, Mass., 1949-52; partner firm Peabody, Koufman & Brewer, Boston, 1952-65, Hill & Barlow, Boston, 1966—; instr. Boston Coll. Law Sch., 1964—. Dir. Guilford Industries, Inc., Computer Systems for Medicine, Inc. Chmn. personnel bd., Manchester, Mass., 1960-62, selectman, 1962-63. Bd. govs. Beverly (Mass.) Hosp., 1964—. Served to 2d lt. AUS, 1942-44. Mem. Am. Bar. Assn., Am. Soc. Internat. Law. Clubs: Sommerset, New York Yacht; Cruising of Am. (rear commodore 1966-67). Home: Nortons Point Manchester MA 01944 Office: 225 Franklin St Boston MA 02110

BREWER, WILLIAM DODD, ambassador; b. Middletown, Conn., Apr. 4, 1922; s. Arnold and Cornelia (Dodd) B.; grad. cum laude Taft Sch., 1940; B.A. with honors, Williams Coll., 1944; M.A., Fletcher Sch. Law and Diplomacy, 1947; m. Alice Van Ess, Jan. 22, 1949; children—John, Daniel, Priscilla. Staff OWI, 1944, Am. Field Service, 1944-45; instr. Williams Coll., 1946, Bowdoin Coll., 1947; with U.S. Fgn. Service, 1947—, assigned Beirut, Lebanon, 1947-49, Jidda, Saudia Arabia, 1949-51, Damascus, Syria, 1952- 55, Kuwait, Persian Gulf, 1955-57; staff Office Near Eastern Affairs, Dept. State, 1957-58, officer charge UAR-Sudan affairs, 1958-61; detailed to Dept. State Sr. Seminar in Fgn. Policy, 1961-62; dep. chief mission, Kabul, Afghanistan, 1962-65; mem. policy planning council Dept. State, 1965-66, country dir. Arabian Peninsula states, 1966-70; ambassador to Mauritius, Port Louis, Mauritius, 1970—. Recipient Arthur S. Flemming award, 1959. Mem. Theta Delta Chi. Episcopalian (vestryman). Address: Port Louis care of Dept State Washington DC 20521

BREWER, WILLIAM DONALD, govt. ofcl.; b. Nashtown, Ky., Mar. 19, 1912; s. Craig Allen and Martha (Cropper) B.; student pub. schs.; m. Lena Catherine Hickerson, Oct. 14, 1932; 1 son, William David. With P.O. Dept., Wallingsford, Ky., 1933, 37-43; postal insp. Cin. div. Postal Service, 1943-46, 53-54, asst. decentralization officer, asst. to asst. postmaster gen. Bur. Operations, 1954, acting regional operations mgr., regional operations mgr., Denver, 1955, regional operations dir., Denver, 1958-61; exec. asst. to pres. Western Bancorp., Los Angeles, 1961-62; exec. v.p. O.K. Tire & Rubber, Inc., nationwide distbr. automobile tires, Littleton, Colo., 1963-64, pres., 1964-68; exec. asst. to mgmt. Ashland Oil & Refining Co., 1968-70; mem. ICC, Washington, 1971—; dir. Rose Mfg. Co., First Nat. Bank Englewood (Colo.); chmn. bd. O.K. Tire Stores, Can., Ltd., 1964-68; pres. Arapahoe Advt. Agy., Littleton, 1965-68. Asst. vice chmn. nat. finance com. Nixon for Pres., 1968; exec. chmn. Republican Nat. Finance Com., 1968—. Trustee Ezra M. Bell Estate. Mem. Fed. Postal Employees Assn. (dir.), Denver Fed. Bus. Assn. (pres.), Am. Soc. Pub. Adminstrn. (v.p.), Am. Mgmt. Assn., N.A.M. (vice chmn. money-credit-capital formation com. 1967—). Methodist. Mason, Rotarian. Home: 9011 Old Dominion Dr McLean VA 22101 Office: ICC 12th and Constitution Av Washington DC 20423

BREWER, WILLIS RALPH, coll. dean; b. Zell, S.D., June 8, 1919; s. Willis E. and Mathilda Irene (Heider) B.; B.S., S.D. State Coll., 1942; Ph.D., Ohio State U., 1948; m. Myrdas Joyce Parrott, June 6, 1942; children—Susan Joyce, Willis Ralph. Asst. prof. pharmacy U. Utah, 1948-49; asso. prof. pharmocognosy, head dept. U. Ariz., 1949-52, dean Coll. Pharmacy, 1952—, dir. scholarships and awards, 1957-70. Cons. and mem. rev. com. on constrn. colls. of pharmacy div. hosp. and med. facilities, Bur. State Services USPHS, 1964-66; pres. So. Ariz. Council on Alcoholism, 1969-71; chmn. U. Ariz. Com. Alcoholism and Drug Abuse, 1969—. Tucson Council Chs., 1962, Ariz. Ecumenical Council of Chs., 1971. Served from ensign to lt. (j.g.), USNR, World War II. Registered pharmacist, S.D., Ohio, Utah, Ariz. Pres. Mem. Am. Pharm. Assn., Am. Assn. Colls. of Pharmacy (exec. com. 1963), Blue Key, Am. Coll. Apothecaries, Sigma Xi, Kappa Alpha, Kappa Psi, Rho Chi, Phi Kappa Phi. Contbr. articles sci. publs. Home: 6901 Acoma Pl Tucson AZ 85715

BREWIN, ROGER CHARLES, III, fgn. service officer; b. Phila., Nov. 9, 1925; s. Roger Charles, Jr. and Bessie (Carpenter) B.; B.A., Miami U., Oxford, O., 1948; M.A., Soc. Advanced Internat. Studies, 1950; student Stanford, 1960-61; m. Mary Eleanor Tolleson, Mar. 26, 1955; children—Barbara Ann, Roger Charles IV. Joined U.S. Fgn. Service, 1951; assigned Zurich, Bombay, Washington, La Paz, 1951-69; dep. chief mission, Asuncion, Paraguay, 1969—. Served with AUS, 1944-46. Mem. Am. Fgn. Service Assn., Sigma Nu. Episcopalian. Home: 1239 Calle Espana Asuncion Paraguay Office: American Embassy Asuncion Paraguay

BREWSTER, DANIEL BAUGH, lawyer, former U.S. Senator; b. Balt., Nov. 23, 1923; s. Daniel Baugh and Ottolie Young (Wickes) B.; grad. St. Paul's Sch., 1942; student Princeton, 1942, Johns Hopkins, 1946; LL.B., U. Md., 1949; m. Anne Bullitt, Apr. 29, 1967. Admitted to Md. bar, 1949; mem. Md. Ho. of Dels., 1950-58; mem. 86th- 87th Congresses, 2d Dist. Md.; mem. U.S. Senate from Md., 1963-69, mem. armed services, commerce, post office, civil services coms. Served from pvt. to col. USMCR, 1942-44: PTO. Decorated Purple Heart with gold star, Bronze Star medal. Mem. V.F.W., D.A.V. Democrat. Episcopalian. Home: Golf Course Rd W Owings Mills MD 21117

BREWSTER, DOROTHY, author, ret. educator; b. St. Louis; d. William Morris and Lillie May (Higbee) Brewster; A.B., Barnard Coll., 1906; A.M., Columbia, 1907, Ph.D., 1913. Asst., Barnard Coll., 1908-11; reader Bryn Mawr (Pa.) Coll., 1914-15; instr. English, Columbia, 1915-23, asst. prof., 1923-44, asso. prof., 1944-50, ret. Fellow Internat. Inst. Arts and Letters; mem. Modern Lang. Assn. Am., Phi Beta Kappa. Author: Aaron Hill-Poet, Dramatist, Projector, 1913; East- West Passage, 1954; Virginia Woolf's London, 1959; (with A. Burrell) Dead Reckonings in Fiction, 1924, Adventure or Experience, 1930, Modern Fiction 1934, Modern World Fiction, 1951; Virginia Woolf, 1962; Doris Lessing, 1965; William Brewster of the Mayflower: Portrait of a Pilgram, 1970. Editor: A Book of Modern Short Stories, 1928; A Book of Contemporary Short Stories, 1937. Home: 310 Riverside Dr New York City NY 10025

BREWSTER, FRANCIS ANTHONY, lawyer; b. Foochow, China, Jan. 28, 1929 (parents Am. citizens); s. Francis Thoburn and Eva (Melby) B.; B.S., U. Wis., 1950, LL.B., 1955; m. Joan L. Heller, Aug. 5, 1950; children—Sara E., Julia L., Anne N., Ellen H., Rebecca J. Admitted to Wis. bar, 1955; counsel Scott Paper Co., Phila., 1955-56, employee relations counsel, 1957, div. personnel mgr. Detroit div., 1958-60; counsel mfg. and services div. RCA, Camden, N.J., 1961; practice law, Madison, Wis., 1961—; partner firm Murphy, Huiskamp, Stolper, Brewster & Desmond, Madison, 1966—. Dir. Nat. Guardian Life Ins. Co., Madison, 1966—, Am. Gas Co. Wis., Inc., 1969-70; dir., interim exec. v.p. AGC Industries, Inc., Omaha, 1970; lectr. labor law Law Sch., U. Wis., 1962-65, lectr. law and bus. Sch. of Commerce, 1969—. Chmn. personnel bd. City of Madison, 1970—. Bd. dirs. Dane County Chpt. A.R.C., 1965—, Madison Symphony Inc., 1968—. Served to lt. USMC, 1950- 52. Recipient Certificate of Merit, Inst. Labor and Indsl. Relations, U. Mich.-Wayne State U., 1959. Mem. Am., Dane County (past sec. and program chmn.) bar assns., State Bar of Wis., Interfraternity Alumni Council U. Wis. (pres. 1968—), Delta Upsilon (pres. Wis.). Republican. Presbyn. (elder). Kiwanian (Madison pres. 1969). Contbr. articles to profl. jours. Home: 3818 Cherokee Dr Madison WI 53711 Office: 2 E Gilman St Madison WI 53703

BREWSTER, JAMES HENRY, educator; b. Ft. Collins, Colo., Aug. 21, 1922; s. Oswald Cammann and Elizabeth (Booraem) B.; A.B., Cornell U., 1942; Ph.D., U. Ill., 1948; m. Christine Barbara Germain, Jan. 23, 1954; children—Christine Carolyn, Mary Elizabeth, Barbara Anne. Chemist, Atlantic Refining Co., Phila., 1942-43; postdoctoral fellow U. Chgo., 1948-49; instr. Purdue U., 1949-50, asst. prof., 1950-55, asso. prof., 1955-60, prof., 1960—. Served with Am. Field Service, 1943-45. Mem. Am. Chem. Soc., Chem. Soc. (London, Eng.), A.A.A.S., Am. Assn. U. Profs., Phi Beta Kappa, Sigma Xi, Phi Lambda Upsilon. Democrat. Unitarian. Research mechanism reductions; stereochemistry Stevens rearrangement; epoxide ring opening; relation optical rotation and constitution; absolute configurations cycloalkylidenes and spiranes. Home: 334 Hollowood Dr West Lafayette IN 47906 Office: Dept Chemistry Purdue U Lafayette IN 47907

BREWSTER, JOHN E., oil co. exec.; b. 1924; married. Surveyor, Standard Oil Co. Ind., 1949-50; mgr. Pan Am. So. Corp., 1951-56; mgr. Ind. Oil Purchasing Co., 1957-59; with Commonwealth Oil Refining Co. Inc., 1959—, exec. v.p., chief operating officer, 1967—, also dir. Address: Pan Am Bldg 200 Park Av New York City NY 10017*

BREWSTER, KINGMAN, Jr., univ. pres.; b. Longmeadow, Mass., June 17, 1919; s. Kingman and Florence (Besse) B.; A.B., Yale, 1941; LL.B., Harvard, 1948; LL.D., Am. Internat. Coll., 1961, Butler U., U. Bridgeport, Columbia, Harvard, Trinity Coll., Princeton, 1964, U. Pa., St. Lawrence U., Case Inst. Tech., Williams Coll., 1965, Amherst Coll., Brown U., 1967, Boston Coll., George Washington U., 1968, Dartmouth, Dickinson Coll., Johns Hopkins, Mich. State U., 1969, Carleton Coll., U. Mass., 1970, Wesleyan U., 1971; m. Mary Louise Phillips, Nov. 30, 1942; children—Constance, Kingman III, Deborah, Alden, Riley. Chmn., Yale Daily News, 1940-41; spl. asst. to coordinator Inter-Am. affairs, 1941; research asso. dept. econs. Mass. Inst. Tech., 1949-50; asst. prof. law Harvard, 1950-53, prof. law, 1953-61; prof., provost Yale, 1961-63, pres., 1963, Asst. gen. counsel Office U.S. Spl. Rep. in Europe, 1948-49; cons. Pres.'s Materials Policy Commn., 1951, Mut. Security Agy., 1952; mem. Pres.' Commn. on Law Enforcement and Adminstrn. Justice, 1965, on Selective Service, 1966; chmn. Nat. Policy Panel UN, 1968. Mem. corp. Belmont Hill Sch.; pres. bd. dirs. Buckingham Soc.; bd. dirs. Nat. Ednl. TV. Served as lt. AC, USNR, 1942-46. Mem. Mass. Bar Assn., Am. Council Learned Socs. (dir.), Am. Acad. Arts and Scis., Council Fgn. Relations. Clubs: Tavern (Boston); Vineyard Haven (Mass.) Yacht: Graduates (New Haven); Yale (N.Y.C.), Century Assn. (N.Y.C.). Author: Anti-trust and American Business Abroad, 1959; (with M. Katz) Law of International Transactions and Relations, 1960. Home: 43 Hillhouse Av New Haven CT 06511

BREWSTER, LEO, judge; b. Fort Worth, Oct. 16, 1903; s. C. B. and Mary (Thomas) B.; LL.B., U. Tex., 1926; m. Lois Rice, Mar. 21, 1928; children—Gayle (Mrs. Ben Rollert, Jr.), Sarah (Mrs. Richard Griffith). Admitted to Tex. bar, 1926, since practiced in Fort Worth; 1st asst. dist. atty., Tarrant County, Tex., 1935-39; now U.S. dist. judge No. Dist. Tex. Fellow Am. Coll. Trial Lawyers; mem. Fort Worth Jr. C. of C. (pres. 1932), Am. (mem. Ho. of Dels. 1958-62), Fort Worth (v.p. 1951, pres. 1952) bar assns., State Bar of Tex. (dir. 1952-57, chmn., pres. 1958- 59). Clubs: Fort Worth, Ridglea Country (Fort Worth). Home: 1700 Ridgmar Blvd Fort Worth TX 76116 Office: U S Courthouse Fort Worth TX 76102

BREWSTER, OLIVER H., mfg. co. exec.; b. Cranston, R.I., 1904; ed. Worcester Poly. Inst., 1926. Pres., dir. Phillips Electronics & Pharm. Industries Corp., 1964— (name changed to Pepi, Inc.); pres. Phillips Roxane, Inc.; chmn. bd. Thompson-Hayward Chem. Co. Home: Hawthorne Rd Essex Fells NJ 07021 Office: 691 Central Av Murray Hill NJ

BREWSTER, RAYMOND, editor; b. Ironton, O., May 27, 1906; s. John Wesley and Margaret May (Maccklin) B.; A.B., Marshall Coll., D. Lit. (hon.); m. Esther Christine McCormick, Feb. 6., 1932; children— Timothy Drake, John Macklin. Asso. with Huntington (W.Va.) Publishing Co., 1927—, now v.p., exec. editor, dir.; editor-in-chief, Herald Dispatch, Huntington, 1938—. Mem. W. Va. Bd. Edn., 1941, 46; apptd. mem. reconstituted Bd. Edn., 1947, pres., 1947—; mem. exec. com., Huntington and Tri-State councils Boy Scouts Am.; past pres. bd. Family Service; W. Va. mem. of Nat. Econ. Council; bd. dirs. Huntington Y.M.C.A. Mem. A.P. Mng. Editors, Am. Soc. Newspapers Editors, Nat. Conf. Editorial Writers, W. Va. Newspaper Council, So. Newspaper Pubs. Assn., W.Va. C. of C. (exec. com.), Order of the South, Kappa Alpha, Sigma Delta Chi, Omicron Delta Kappa. Republican. Methodist. Elk, Rotarian (dir.). Home: 1016 Euclid Pl Huntington WV 25701 Office: Huntington Publishing Co Huntington WV 25704

BREWSTER, ROBERT CHARLES, fgn. service officer; b. Beatrice, Neb., May 31, 1921; s. Charles Lee and Lillian Aseneth (French) B.; student Grinnell Coll., 1939-41; A.B., U. Wash., 1943; student U. Mexico, summer 1946, George Washington U., summer 1947, Columbia, 1946-48; m. Mary Virginia Blackman, Feb. 22, 1951. Fgn. affairs analyst State Dept., 1948-49; fgn. service officer, 1949—; 3d sec. Am. embassy, Mamagua, Nicaragua, 1949-51, 2d sec., 1951- 52; vice consul Am. consulate gen., Stuttgart, Germany, 1952-55; policy briefing officer ICA, 1956-57; staff asst. to under sec. of state for econ. affairs, 1958, spl. asst., 1959; spl. asst. to under sec. of state, 1959-60; assigned Nat. War Coll., 1960-61; fgn. service insp., 1961-63; counselor American embassy, Asuncion, 1964-66; dep. exec. dir. Bur. European Affairs, Washington, 1966-67, exec. dir., 1967-69; dep. exec. sec. Dept. State, 1969-71, dep. dir. gen. fgn. service, dir. personnel, 1971—. Served to lt. (j.g.) USNR, 1943. Mem. Am. Fgn. Service Assn. Home: 2528 Queen Anne's Lane NW Washington DC 20037 Office: Dept of State Washington DC 20520

BREWSTER, SEWARD BLANCHARD, utility exec.; b. Newton, Mass., Nov. 6, 1927; s. William Russell and Leona M. (Wright) B.; grad. Kimball Union Acad., 1944; A.B., Dartmouth, 1950; LL.B., Harvard, 1955; m. Carol V. Whitham, June 11, 1955; children—Benjamin S., Seth W., William T. Instr. Deerfield Acad., 1950-52; admitted to Mass. bar, 1956, Me. bar, 1962; asso. Mirick, O'Connell, DeMallie & Logee, Worcester, Mass., 1955-61; asst. gen. counsel Central Me. Power Co., Augusta, 1961-68, gen. counsel, sec., 1968—; sec. Me. Yankee Atomic Power Co., Me. Elec. Power Co., Inc., Kennebec Water Power Co. Dir. Kennebec Valley YMCA. Served with AUS, 1946-47. Mem. Am., Me., Kennebec County bar assns. Independent. Club: Kiwanis (Augusta). Home: Pond Rd Manchester ME 04351 Office: 9 Green St Augusta ME 04330

BREWSTER, WILLIAM SOUTHER, machinery co. exec.; b. Plymouth, Mass., Apr. 15, 1917; s. Ellis W. and Ellen (Hatch) B.; B.S., Mass. Inst. Tech., 1939; grad. Advanced Mgmt. Program, Harvard, 1959; m. Lucile Christmas, June 2, 1945; children—Bartlett C., Ellen S. With USM Corp., Boston, 1939-40, 46—, v.p., dir., 1958-61, pres., 1961, mem. exec. com., 1960—, chmn., chief exec. officer, 1968—; dir. 1st Nat. Bank Boston, Liberty Mut., Internat. Paper Co.; trustee Charlestown Savs. Bank. Mem. Mass. Natural Resources Bd.; mem. The Bus. Council, Nat. Indsl. Pollution Control Council, mem. gen. mfg. sub-council. Bd. govs. Plimoth Plantation, Plymouth, 1955—. Bd. dirs. New Eng. Aquarium; trustee Boston Mus. Sci. Served to lt. col., Ordnance Dept., AUS, 1940- 46. Mem. Machinery and Allied Products Inst., Nat. Indsl. Conf. Bd., Internat. C. of C. (trustee U.S. council), Mayflower Descs. Clubs: Algonquin, Union Commercial (Boston). Home: Wellsbrook Plymouth MA 02360 Office: 140 Federal St Boston MA 02107

BREWTON, CHARLES SIDNEY, Jr., govt. ofcl.; b. Larkinsville, Ala., Nov. 9, 1913; s. Charles Spurgeon and Ora (Smith) B.; student Birmingham-So. Coll., 1932-35; LL.B., J.D., U. Ala., 1938; m. Jewell Wann, Oct. 12, 1940; children—Carol Ann, Charles Sidney III. Admitted to Ala. bar, 1938; partner firm Brewton & Jones, Scottsboro, Ala., 1938-40; spl. asst. to U.S. atty. gen., 1940- 43; staff dir. U.S. Senate Com. Expenditure in Exec. Depts., 1943-44; adminstrv. asst. to U.S. Senator Lister Hill, 1943-56; asso. dir. law and legislation Joint Commn. Mental Illness and Health, Cambridge, Mass., 1956-59; gen. counsel Senate Com. Small Bus., 1959-61; asst. dir. Office Emergency Planning, Exec. Office of Pres., 1961-69; gen. counsel Joint Com. on Def. Prodn., Washington, 1969—. Chmn. com. arrangements Nat. Conf. Nat. Def. Exec. Res., 1965. Asst. campaign mgr. presdl. nominee Adlai E. Stevenson, 1952, 56; asst. to chmn. Presdl. Inaugural Com., 1965. Mem. Assn. Senate Adminstrv. Assts. and Exec. Secs. (past pres.), Nat. Grange, Sigma Alpha Epsilon. Clubs: President's, Nat. Capitol Democratic. Author: (with others) Action for Mental Health, 1961. Home: 2206 Belle Haven Rd Alexandria, VA 22307. Office: Senate Office Bldg Washington DC 20510

BREYER, HENRY W., Jr., corp. exec.; b. Phila., Aug. 15, 1904; s. Henry W. and Edith (Scott) B.; student Penn. State Coll.; m. Margaret McKee, Oct. 24, 1929; 1 son, Henry W. 3d. Pres., Breyer Corp.; dir. Breyer Ice Cream Co. (Phila.), Nat. Dairy Products Corp. Pres., Breyer Found. Home: 726 Williamson Rd Bryn Mawr PA 19010 Office: 1600 Locust St Philadelphia PA 19103

BREYFOGLE, PETER NICHOLAS, mfg. exec.; b. Barcelona, Spain, Sept. 24, 1935; s. Robert Joshua and Elsie (McLaughlin) B.; student Winchester Coll., 1949-54; B.Eng., Cambridge U., 1957; M.B.A., Harvard, 1959; m. Josephine Mary King, Dec. 11, 1965; 1 son, Nicholas Brenton. Financial analyst Massey-Ferguson, Ltd., Toronto, Ont., Can., 1959-61, plans and controls coordinator, Coventry, 1961-64; gen. financial analysis mgr., Toronto, 1964; plans and controls coordinator MF, Inc./MF Industries, Toronto, 1964-65, comptroller, Toronto-Des Moines, 1965-69; comptroller MF, Ltd., Toronto, 1969—. Mem. Financial Execs. Inst. Clubs: Royal Canadian Yacht, Badminton and Racquet (Toronto); Sunningdale Golf (Berkshire, Eng.). Home: 161 Roxborough Dr Toronto 5 Ontario Canada Office: 200 University Av Toronto 1 Ontario Canada

BREYMANN, WALTER NORMAN, educator; b. Freeport, Ill., Apr. 29, 1919; s. Charles William and Ragnilda (Lee) B.; B.S. in Edn., U. Ill., 1941, M.A. in History, 1947; Ph.D. in History, 1950; m. Irmundine Nienhaus McDonald, Aug. 12, 1950. Prof. history, chmn. div. social scis. So. State Coll., Magnolia, Ark., 1950-56; asso. prof. history, chmn. dept. Drake U., 1956-61, prof., chmn. dept., 1961—; spl. research Latin Am. history, age discovery and exploration, also modern Mexico. Served with AUS, 1942-45. Mem. Conf. Latin Am. History, Am. Hist. Assn., Am. Assn. U. Profs. Author articles. Home: 4512 Beaver Crest Dr Des Moines IA 50310

BREZHNEV, LEONID ILYICH, Soviet party ofcl.; b. Dnieprodzerzhinsk, Ukraine, Dec. 19, 1906; grad. sch. land planning and reclamation, 1927, Metall. Inst. Dnieprodzerzhinsk, 1935. Land surveyor Land Dept. Kursk, dir. dist. agrl. dept., dir. regional agrl. dept., dep. chmn. dist. exec. com., dep. chmn. agrl. and metall. dept. Sverdlov region, 1927-30; dep. chief Ural Regional Land Dept.; joined Communist Party Soviet Union (CPSU), 1931; dir. tech. sch., vice chmn. Metall. Inst., dir. city exec. com. Communist Party in Ukraine, 1935-39, sec., 1939-41, 1st sec., 1947-50; polit. work with army, 1941-46; 1st sec. Zaporozhye (Ukraine) Regional Party Com., 1946-47; 1st sec. Central Com. Communist Party Moldavia, 1950-52; mem. Central Com., 1952; sec. Central Com., CPSU, 1952-53, 1956-60, 66; vice chmn. Central Polit. Dept. Soviet Army and Navy, 1953-54; 2d sec. Central Com., Communist Party Kazakhstan, 1954, 1st sec., 1955-56; gen. sec. Presidium Supreme Soviet USSR, 1960-66; candidate mem. Presidium, Central Com. CPSU, 1957-66; mem. Poliburo, 1966—; dep. to Supreme Soviet of 3d to 7th convocations, mem. Presidium 9th Supreme Soviet of USSR. Decorated 4 Orders of Lenin; 2 Orders of the Red Banner; Order of Patriotic War, 1st class; 2d class Order of Bogdan Khmelnitski; Order of the Red Star; other medals of USSR; named Hero of Soviet Union, Hero of Socialist Labour, 1961. Address: Central Committee CPSU Moscow USSR

BRIAN, HARRY FINDLEY, advt. exec.; b. Lancaster, Pa., Mar. 29, 1914; s. Harry Zellers and Emma Moriah (Findley) B.; B.S., Ursinus Coll., 1935; student U.S. Coast Guard Acad., 1943; m. Margaret Paxson, Aug. 17, 1940; children—Bonnie, Penny, Terry. Copywriter M.T. Garvin Co., Lancaster, Pa., 1936-37; copywriter Foltz-Wessinger, Inc., Lancaster, 1937-40; v.p. J.G. Kuester, York, Pa., 1940-42; copywriter Vansant Dugdale Co., Inc. Advt., Balt., 1942-48, copychief, 1948, v.p., 1949, creative dir., 1956-64, sr. v.p., 1964-67, pres., chief exec. officer, 1967—; prof. advt. Johns Hopkins, 1950-71. Served to lt. (j.g.) USCGR, 1943-46. Mem. Am. Assn. Advt. Agys. (bd. dirs. 1970-72), Balt. Asso. Commerce. Methodist. Clubs: Roland Run; Center. Home: Box 13 Riderwood MD 21139 Office: Vansant Dugdale 1 N Charles St Baltimore MD 21201

BRIAN, PIERRE LEONCE THIBAUT, educator; b. New Orleans, July 8, 1930; s. Alexis Morgan and Evelyn (Thibaut) B.; B.S., La. State U., 1951; Sc.D., Mass. Inst. Tech., 1956; m. Geraldine Lou Earl, Aug. 23, 1952; children—Evelyn Ann, Richard Earl, James Edward. Mem. faculty Mass. Inst. Tech., 1955—, prof. chem. engring., 1966—; cons. to industry, 1957—. Mem. exec. council Episcopal Diocese Mass., 1966-69. Mem. Am. Inst. Chem. Engring., Am. Chem. Soc., Sigma Xi, Tau Beta Pi, Phi Lambda Upsilon, Pi Mu Epsilon. Author articles, chpt. in book on applied chem. kinetics, heat and mass transfer, numerical math., cystalization. Home: Lindsay Pond Rd Concord MA 01742 Office: Dept Chem Engring Mass Inst Tech Cambridge MA 02139

BRICCETTI, THOMAS BERNARD, orch. condr.; b. Mt. Kisco, N.Y., Jan. 14, 1936; s. Thomas Bernard and Joan Therese (Filardi) B.; student Dr. Jean Dansereau, 1948-60, Dr. Richard Lert, 1963-64, U. Rochester Eastman Sch. Music, 1953-54, Columbia Grad. Sch. Fine Arts, 1954-55; m. Eleanor Ruth Child, Sept. 19, 1966; children—Katherine Anne, David Clark. Pianist, composer, 1955-62; apptd. mus. dir. Pinellas County Youth Symphony, Fla., 1962-68, St. Petersburg (Fla.) Philharmonic Orch., 1963-68, St. Petersburg Civic Opera Co., 1964-68; asso. condr. Indpls. Symphony Orch., 1968—; mus. dir. Ft. Wayne (Ind.) Philharmonic Orch., 1970—. Recipient Prix de Rome for mus. composition Italian Govt., 1958-59. Ford Found. fellow, 1961-62; YADDO grantee, 1963; named Outstanding Young Man Fla. Jr. C. of C., 1967-68, Profl. Artist of Year Indpls., 1970. Mem. A.S.C.A.P., Phi Mu Alpha Sinfonia. Commd. by Nat. Endowment for Arts Commn. to compose Violin Concerto, 1967; 18 pub. compositions. Home: 4466 N Pennsylvania Indianapolis IN 46205

BRICE, ASHBEL GREEN, publishing co. exec.; b. York, S.C., July 21, 1915; s. John Steele and Claudia Wilkie (Moore) B.; A.B., Columbia, 1936, M.A., 1937; postgrad. Duke, 1937-39. Instr. dept. English, Duke, Durham, N.C., 1939-45, North Tex. State Tchrs. Coll., 1940, Coll. City N.Y., summers 1937-42; joined Duke U. Press, 1945, asst. editor, 1945-47, editor, asso. dir., 1947-51, dir., editor, 1951—. Mem. Assn. Am. U. Presses (dir. 1965-66). Democrat. Presbyn. Home: 813 Vickers Av Durham NC 27701 Office: Duke U Press Durham NC 27701

BRICE, CAROL, concert singer; b. Indianapolis, Ind., April 16, 1918; d. John and Ella (Hawkins) Brice; grad. Palmer Memorial Inst., High Sch., Sedalia, N.C., 1933. Jr. Coll., 1935; Mus.B., Talladega (Ala.) Coll., 1939; Juilliard Grad. Sch., 1944; m. Neil Scott, Dec. 24, 1942; 2 children. Awarded fellowship to Juilliard Grad. Sch. in voice for five consecutive years; pupil of Francis Rogers, 1939-44; 11st prof appearance. The Chaplet, New York City, 1941; chosen to sing on program celebrating third inauguration of Pres. Roosevelt, 1940; soloist St. George's Episcopal Ch., N.Y. City, 1939-43; made N.Y. Town Hall debut, 1944; appeared with Kansas City Symphony, 1944; Pittsburgh Symphony, 1945-46; Boston Symphony, Tanglewood, 1946; appeared with Boston Symphony, Boston and New York, 1947, with Boston Symphony, San Francisco Symphony, 1948. First Negro recipient Walter Naumberg award, 1943. Mem. Alpha Kappa Alpha. Conglist. Recording: (with Pittsburgh Symphony Orchestra under baton of Fritz Reiner) Leider Eines Fahrenden Gesellen, Gustav Mahler, and El Amor Brujo, Manuel De Falla, for Columbia, 1946; Sacred Arias of Back (Daniel Saidenburg and orchestra); A Carol Brice Recital Album (accompanied by Jonathan Brice).

BRICHTA, IRA, advt. exec.; b. Chgo., Dec. 12, 1925; s. Jacob Morris and Beck (Friedman) B.; student Roosevelt U., 1946-48, Inst. Design, 1949; m. Vivian Gollin, Apr. 11, 1948; children—Carol Marcie, William Joseph. Marketing mgr. Philco Corp., Chgo., Phila., 1948-58; regional dir. McCann Erickson Co., N.Y.C., 1958-60; pres. Herbert Baker Advt., Inc., Chgo., 1960—. Served with AUS, 1943-46. Decorated Bronze Star medal. Mem. Internat. Food Service Mfrs. Assn., Food Service Marketing Assn. Jewish religion (trustee congregation). Home: 1126 Lincoln Av S Highland Park IL 60035 Office: 875 N Michigan Av Chicago IL 60611

BRICK, JOHN, investment banker; b. N.Y.C., Oct. 27, 1904; s. Patrick and Catherine (Culloty) B.; m. Helen E. Kelly, Nov. 24, 1938; children—John, Robert, Nancy A. With Kidder, Peabody & Co., investment bankers, N.Y.C., 1922- 52; with Paine, Webber, Jackson & Curtis, investment bankers, N.Y.C., 1953—, partner, 1955—. Mem. Council Borough Tenafly N.J. until 1959. Home: 465 Knickerbocker Rd Tenafly NJ 07670 Office: 140 Broadway New York City NY 10005

BRICK, MAURICE J., banker; b. N.Y.C., 1914; B.A., Manhattan Coll., 1937; grad. Rutgers U. Grad. Sch. Banking. Pres., chief adminstrv. officer, dir., N.J. Bank Nat. Assn., Clifton; exec. dir. Gov. Paterson Towers Sr. Citizens Housing Corp.; dir. Villiers Realty Corp., N.J. Bus. Devel. Corp. Chmn. N.J. Bank Scholarship Bd.; financial cons. Archdiocese of Newark, Eparchy of Passaic, Diocese of Paterson; mem. Diocesan Hosp. Commn. Trustee St. Joseph's Hosp., Paterson, Felician Coll., Lodi, N.J.; chmn. bd. trustees John Marshall Inst. Law and Taxation; pres.'s council Manhattan Coll., Riverdale, N.Y. Master Knight Sovereign Mil. Order Knights of Malta. Clubs: Ridgewood Country, Upper Montclair Country, Pennington, Hamilton. Author: Say Please and Collect, 1955. Home: 330 Concord Dr Fairway Knolls Maywood NJ 07607 Point of Americas 2100 S Ocean Lane Ft Lauderdale FL 33316 Office: 129 Market St Paterson NJ 07505

BRICKBAUER, CHARLES GUSTAV, architect; b. Plymouth, Wis., Apr. 11, 1930; s. Arthur John and Arlone (Des Ermia) B.; student U. Wis., 1948, U. Hawaii, 1949; B.Arch., Yale, 1954. With Philip Johnson, Harrirson & Abramovitz, architects, N.Y.C., 1958-61; pvt. practice architecture, Rome, Italy, 1961-63; partner Peterson & Brickbauer, Balt., 1965—. Recipient Rome prize in architecture, 1955-58. Fellow Am. Acad. Rome. Editor: Perspecta, 1952-55. Important works include Sun Life Bldg., Charles Center, Balt.‡

BRICKEN, CARL ERNEST, composer; b. Shelbyville, Ky., Dec. 28, 1898; s. Bird E. and Lillie M. (Martin) B.; A.B., Yale U., 1922; studied composition under Scalero and piano under Leopold and Bert, David Mannes Sch.; studied under Cortot (Paris) and Weisse (Vienna); m. Dorothy Moran, Dec. 17, 1927; children—Anne. C. Alexander. Tchr. of piano, David Mannes Sch., 1925-29; tchr. theory Inst. of Mus. Art, 1929-30; chmn. music dept. U. Chgo., 1931-38; dir. Sch. Music, U. Wis., 1938-44; mus. dir. and conductor Seattle Symphony, 1944-48; prof. theory and composer in residence Sweet Briar Coll., also chmn. dept. music, now prof. emeritus. Awarded Pulitzer prize, 1929; Guggenheim fellowship, 1930-31. Mem. Am. Assn. U. Profs., Am. Musicological Soc., Am. Composers Alliance. Methodist. Rotarian. Clubs: Elizabethan (Yale). Composer of two ballads for baritone, Edward, Lord Randall, Songs from Emily Dickinson; miscellaneous songs; Daniel Boone (legend for orch.); The Prairie Years; 2d Sonata for Violin and Piano; Making of a River (music for film); Symphony No. 1, d minor, Symphony No. 2, f minor; Symphony No. 3, a Maj., The Travelled Sea (for women's voices); Sonata for Violin and Piano; Piano Sonatas Nos. 1 and 2; incidental music to the Trojan Woman; For the Time Being (Christmas oratorio); others. Home: Sweet Briar VA ☆ also Mendhan, NJ☆27

BRICKER, CLARK EUGENE, educator; b. Shrewsbury, Pa., June 17, 1918; s. Melvin Eugene and Mabel (Trout) B.; B.A., Gettysburg Coll., 1939; M.S., Haverford Coll., 1940; M.A., Princeton, 1941, Ph.D., 1944; m. Anna Margaret Walker, Dec. 25, 1942; children—Susan, David, Bruce. Research chemist Heyden Chem. Corp., Garfield, N.J., 1943-46; asst. prof. Johns Hopkins, 1946-48; asst. prof. Princeton, 1948-51, asso. prof., 1951-60, prof. chemistry, 1960-61; dean, prof. chemistry Coll. of Wooster, 1961-63; prof. chemistry U. Kan., 1963—. Adv. panel Nat. Bur. Standards; adv. bd. Analytical Chemistry, 1959-62. Vol. fireman, Princeton, 1948-61. Mem. Am. Chem. Soc. (past pres., councilor Princeton), Phi Beta Kappa, Sigma Xi (pres. Princeton 1960-61), Omicron Delta Kappa. Republican. Presbyn. (past deacon, elder). Mason. Author: (with H.H. Willard, N.H. Furman) Elements of Quantitative Analysis, 1956; Foundations of Chemistry; A Laboratory Manual, 1966; College Chemistry; A Laboratory Manual, 1967. Contbr. sci. articles to profl. jours. Home: 1812 21st St Terrace Lawrence KS 66044

BRICKER, EUGENE MURON, physician; b. Carbondale, Ill., Aug. 1, 1908; s. George Sylvester and Flora Elizabeth (Tripp) B.; student So. Ill. Tchrs. Coll., 1927-30; M.D., Washington U., St. Louis, 1934; m. Margaret Jones, Aug. 31, 1937; children—David Caroll, Robert Stephen, Cynthia Jean. Intern, resident Barnes Hosp., St. Louis, 1934-38; chief surgeon Ellis Fishel State Cancer Hosp., Columbia, Mo., 1939-42; pvt. practice gen. surgery, St. Louis, 1946—; mem. staff St. Lukes, Barnes and allied hosps.; asso. prof. clin. surgery Washington U. Sch. Medicine, 1947-67, prof. clin. surgery, since 1966. Bd. govs. Washington U., 1964—. Served to col., M.C., AUS, World War II; ETO. Decorated Legion of Merit; recipient Amory prize Am. Acad. Arts and Sci. Diplomate Am. Bd. Surgery (mem. bd. 1960-66, chmn. 1965-66). Mem. A.C.S. (bd. govs. 1963, 2d v.p. 1967-68), A.M.A., Am. (first v.p. 1966-67), Central So. (v.p. 1968), assns., Soc. Internat. de Chirurgie, Soc. Pelvic Surgeons, Soc. Univ. Surgeons (pres. 1952), Southwestern Surg. Congress (pres. 1963), Soc. Surgery Alimentary Tract. Home: 43 Briarcliff Saint Louis MO 63124 Office: Queeny Tower Barnes Hosp Plaza St Louis MO 63110

BRICKER, JOHN WILLIAM, lawyer; b. Madison County, O., Sept. 6, 1893; s. Lemuel Spencer and Laura (King) B.; A.B., Ohio State U., 1916, LL.B., 1920, LL.D., 1939; m. Harriet Day, Sept. 4, 1920; 1 son, John Day. Admitted to Ohio bar, 1917; solicitor Grandview Heights, O., 1920-28; asst. atty. gen. Ohio, 1923-27; mem. Pub. Utilities Commn., 1929-32; atty. gen., 1933-37; mem. firm Bricker, Evatt, Barton & Eckler; dir. Republic Steel Corp., Buckeye Internat., Inc., Galbreath First Mortgage Investments, Buckeye Fed. Savs. & Loan Assn. Gov. Ohio, 1939-45. Republican candidate for vice pres. U.S., 1944; mem. U.S. Senate from Ohio, 1946-58. Served to 1st lt. U.S. Army, World War I. Mem. Am., Ohio, Columbus bar assns., Am. Legion, Order of Coif, Delta Chi, Delta Sigma Rho. Republican. Mem. Community Ch. Mason (33, Shriner), Rotarian. Clubs: Faculty (Ohio State U.), Torch, Athletic, Kit-Kat, University. Home: 2407 Tremont Rd Columbus OH 43221 Office: 100 E Broad St Columbus OH 43215

BRICKER, NEAL SHELDON, educator, physician; b. Denver, Apr. 18, 1927; s. Eli D. and Rose (Quiat) B.; B.A., U. Colo., 1946, M.D., 1949; m. Miriam Thalenberg, June 24, 1951; children—Dale, Cary, Susan. Intern, resident Bellevue Hosp., N.Y.C., 1949-52; sr. asst. resident Peter Bent Brigham Hosp., Boston, 1954-55, asso. dir. cardio-renal lab., 1955-56; instr. Harvard, 1955-56; fellow Howard Hughes Med. Inst., 1955-56; asst. prof. Washington U., 1956-62, asso. prof., 1962-65, prof., 1965—, dir. renal div., 1956—. Mem. sci. adv. bd. Nat. Kidney Disease Found:, 1962, chmn. research and fellowship grants com., 1964, mem. exec. com., 1964; mem. med. adv. bd., mem. program com. Council on Circulation Am. Heart Assn., 1962—; cons. NIH, 1964, chmn. gen. medicine study sect., 1966-68, chmn. renal disease and urology tng. grants com., 1969; vis. investigator Inst. Biol. Chemistry, Copenhagen, Denmark, 1960-61. Served with USNR, 1944-45, U.S. Army, 1952-54. Recipient Gold-Headed Cane award U. Colo., 1949, USPHS Research Career award, 1964. Diplomate Am. Bd. Internat. Medicine, Fellow A.C.P.; mem. A.M.A., Am. Fedn. for Clin. Research, Central Soc. Clin. Research (council 1970—), Assn. Am. Physicians, Am. Soc. for Clin. Investigation (mem. editorial com. Jour.), Internat. Soc. Nephrology (exec. com. 1966—, v.p. 1966-69, treas., 1969—), Am. Soc. Nephrology (past pres.), Am. Physiol. Soc., Soc. for Exptl. Biology and Medicine, Sigma Xi, Alpha Omega Alpha. Asso. editor Jour. Lab. and Clin. Medicine, 1961-67; editorial bd. Physiol. Revs., 1970—. Contbr. articles profl. jours., chpts. to books, Home: 7246 Wydown Blvd St Louis MO 63105

BRICKER, SEYMOUR MURRAY, lawyer; b. N.Y.C., May 19, 1924; s. Harry and May (Glick) B.; student U. Okla., 1943-44; A.B., U. Cal., Los Angeles, 1947; LL.B., U. So. Cal., 1950; m. Darlene M. Mohilef, July 29, 1951; children-Andrea Helene, Phillip Alan, Julie Ellen. Admitted to Cal. bar, 1951; practice in Beverly Hills, 1956—; atty. Cal. Judicial Council, 1951-52; with legal dept. Universal Pictures, 1952-56; partner Cohen & Bricker, 1956-68; partner Kaplan, Livingston, Goodwin, Berkowitz & Selvin, 1968—. Asst. sec. Dena Pictures, Inc. Served with inf., AUS, 1943-46. Mem.Am. Bar Assn. (past chmn. copyright div.), Los Angeles Copyright Soc. (past pres.), Order of Coif. Home: 524 Loring Av Los Angeles CA 90024 Office: 450 N Roxbury Beverly Hills CA

BRICKETT, MOODY, lawyer, former U.S. atty.; b. Haverhill, Mass., Oct. 18, 1918; s. Caleb Thorndyke and Mary Alice (Ring) B.; student Boston U., 1937-38, Dickinson Coll., 1942; LL.B., Mont. State U., 1951; m. Beverly Eileen Lockhart, Mar. 18, 1947; children—Stephen Mark, Laura Elleen, Rebecca Jean, Janis Rachel. With First Nat. Stores, Boston, 1937-39, Bethlehem Steel Co., Quincy, Mass., 1940-41, Boston Navy Yard, 1941-42; admitted to Mont. bar, 1951; 1st asst. atty. gen. Mont., 1951-57; pvt. practice, Great Falls, Mont., 1958-61. Former U.S. atty. for Mont., 1961. Bd. dirs. Mont. Hosp. Service Assn. Served to capt. USAAF, 1942-46. Decorated D.F.C., Air medal with 3 clusters. Mem. Mont., Am. bar assns. Home: 2930 Elizabeth Warren Av Butte MT 59701

BRICKFIELD, CYRIL FRANCIS, lawyer; b. Bklyn., Jan. 30, 1919; M.S., LL.M., S.J.D., George Washington U.; LL.B., Fordham U.; m. Ann Jacobsen, Aug. 4, 1951; children—Anne Irene, Edmund Cyril. Admitted to N.Y. bar, 1948, D.C. bar, 1952; with firm Brickfield & Brickfield, Bklyn., 1948-49; law clk. to chief judge N.Y. Ct. Appeals, 1949-51; counsel judiciary com. U.S. Ho. of Reps., 1951-61; gen. counsel VA, 1961-63; chief benefits dir. VA, 1963-65, dep. adminstr., 1965-67; exec. dir. NRTA/AARD, 1967-69; pvt. practice law, 1969—. Del., U.S. Internat. Treaty Convs. on Patents, Trademarks, Copywrights, 1958-61. Trustee Suburban Hosp., Bethesda, Md. Served to capt., pilot, USAAF, World War II: ETO. Decorated Air medal with 9 oak leaf clusters. Mem. Am., Fed. (pres. 1968, chmn. gen. counsels com., jud. selection com., pres. D.C. chpt.; del. Am. Bar Assn.), Bklyn. bar assns., Delta Theta Phi. K.C. Club: Bethesda Country (pres. 1967, 69) Author govt. reports. Home: 17 Savannah Ct Bethesda MD 20034

BRICKHOUSE, JOHN B., (Jack), radio, TV sports mgr.; b. Peoria, Ill., Jan. 24, 1916; s. John William and Daisy (James) B.; student Bradley U., Peoria; m. Nelda Teach, Aug. 7, 1939; 1 dau., Jean. Comml., sports announcer Sta. WMBD, Peoria, 1934-40; with WGN, Chgo., 1940-43, 44—, mgr. sports WGN and WGN TV, 1948—; v.p., mgr. sports WGN Continental Broadcasting Co., 1970—; free lance, comml. announcer, Chgo., 1945, sports announcer, 1947, N.Y. Giants baseball announcer, N.Y.C., 1946. Broadcaster radio and/or TV play-by-play World Series, All Star Baseball Game, All Star Football game, Rose Bowl, Orange bowl, Chgo. Cubs, Chgo. White Sox games, Golden Gloves, Louis-Charles and Walcott-Charles fight, Rep. and Dem. nat. convs., Roosevelt Inauguration (1945), Chicago Bears football games, Chgo. Bulls basketball games, Inaugural Ball, Papal audience. Bd. dirs. Chgo. Boys Clubs, City of Hope, Chgo. Wesley Meml. Hosp.; trustee St. Procopius Coll. Served as pvt. USMCR, 1943-44. Recipient numerous Emmy awards, bronze medallions for World Series coverage Look mag., 1954, 59; Man of Year award City of Hope, 1966; Communications award Lincoln Acad., 1968; named Best Sports Announcer, Am. Coll. Radio Arts and Scis.; Nat. Sportscasters and Sportswriters award as outstanding sportscaster of year in Ill. (5 times), Acor award Am. Coll. Radio Arts, Nat. Sportswriters and Broadcasters awards, many others. Mem. Western Golf Assn. (dir.), Acad. Television Arts and Scis. (past pres., gov. Chgo. chpt.). Writer for Chgo. Today, Chgo. Tribune, Ency. Brit. Yearbook, others; pub. Jack Brickhouse's Major League Baseball Record Book, 21 edits. Home: 1100 Locust Rd Wilmette IL 60091 Office: WGN Continental Broadcasting Co 2501 W Bradley Pl Chicago IL 60618

BRICKLEY, RICHARD AGAR, surgeon; b. Bluffton, Ind., Aug. 15, 1925; s. Harry Dwight and Ina (Agar) B.; student Ind. U., 1943-44; B.S., B.M., Northwestern U., 1947, M.D., 1948; m. Suzanne Slusser, Nov. 28, 1964; children—Dinah M., Sarah Jane, Richard Agar II, Laura Jean, Andrew John. Intern Cook County Hosp., Chgo., 1947-49, surg. resident, 1955-56; gen. practice Bluffton, Ind., 1949-50; surg. preceptorship with Drs. Gatch and Owen, Indpls., 1950-51, 54; pvt. practice medicine, specializing in surgery, Indpls., 1957—; chmn. gen. surgery div. Meth. Hosp., Indpls., 1962-66, Winona Meml. Hosp. Indpls., 1971—. Served with M.C., USAF, 1951-53. Diplomate Am. Bd. Surgery. Fellow A.C.S.; mem. Am., Ind.,

Aerospace med. assns., Beta Theta Pi, Nu Sigma Nu. Home: 4530 Crooked Creek Ridge Dr Indianapolis IN 46208 Office: 3266 N Meridian St Indianapolis IN 46208

BRICKMAN, MORRIE, newspaper cartoonist; b. Chgo., July 24, 1917; s. Samuel David and Rose (Wilson) B.; student Art Inst. Chgo., 1934, Am. Acad. Art, 1935; m. Shirley Kronenthal, Oct. 13, 1945; children—Harriet Esther, Paul Martin. Syndicated cartoon Do It Yourself, 1954-59, Blue Chips, 1960-67, The Small Society, 1966—. Served with AUS, World War II. Mem. Nat. Cartoonist Soc., Newspaper Comics Council. Club: Chicago Press. Author: Do it Yourself, 1955; Don't Do It Yourself, 1957; This Little Pigeon Went to Market, 1965. ‡

BRICKWEDDE, FERDINAND GRAFT, physicist; b. Balt., Mar. 26, 1903; s. Ferdinand Henry and Virginia (Graft) B.; A.B., Johns Hopkins, 1922, M.A., 1924, Ph.D., 1925; m. Marion Langhorne Howard, July 28, 1934; children—Marion Virginia (dec.), Ruth (Mrs. Lance Cooper), Langhorne Virginia. Research asso. Nat. Bur. Standards, Washington, 1925-26, chief low temperature lab., 1926-46, chief thermodynamics sect., 1946-52, chief, heat and power div. 1946-56, cons. to dir. 1957-62; prof. physics U. Md., 1942-56; dean Coll. Chemistry and Physics, prof. chemistry and physics Pa. State U., 1956-63, Evan Pugh research prof. physics, 1963- 68, Evan Pugh research prof. physics emeritus, 1968—, on leave of absence U. Cal. radiation lab., Libermore, 1952-53. Initiated NBS- AEC Cryogenic Engrng. Lab., Boulder, Colo., headed group designed liquefaction plant; cons. Los Alamos Sci. Lab., 1948—; part-time prof. U. Md., 1942-57; mem. NRC div. math. and phys. scis., 1944-47, mem. exec. com., 1945; mem. Commn. 1 for cryophysics and crycengrng. in Internat. Inst. Refrigeration, 1957—, also v.p. Commn. 1, mem. U.S. nat. com., 1957-63; chmn. com. on Physics Abstracts Am. Inst. Physics, 1959-67; mem. adv. com. on thermonetry Internat. Com. Weights and Measures, 1958—, chmn. 2 internat. working groups thermometry, 1962-67, pres. adv. com. 1965-68. Am. del. Internat. Union Pure and Applied Physics, Amsterdam, 1948, 10th Internat. Congress on Refrigeration, Copenhagen, 1959, 11th Congress, Munich, 1963. Recipient Hillebrand prize Chem. Soc. Washington, 1940; Washington Acad. award, 1941. Co- discover a heavy isotope of hydrogen, deuterium. Mem. Am. Phys. Soc. (mem. council 1940-43, treas. div. chem. physics 1952-58, bd. editors for Phys. Rev. 1952-54), Am. Chem. Soc., A.A.A.S., Wash. Acad. Scis. (v.p. 1939), Acoustical Soc. Am., Am. Assn. Physics Tchrs., Philos. Soc. Washington (pres. 1939), Am. Inst. Physics, Sigma Xi (pres D.C. prof. chpt. 1950- 51). Mason. Club: Cosmos (Washington). Contbr. articles in fields physics and phys. chemistry. Home: 630 W Fairmount Av State College PA 16801 Office: Osmond Lab Pa State U University Park PA 16802 ☆

BRICO, ANTONIA, conductor; b. June 26, 1902; B.A., U. Cal., 1923; grad. Berlin (Germany) State Acad. Music, Master Sch. of Conducting, 1929; pupil Dr. Karl Muck and Sigismond Stojowski, 1925-30; Doc. Mus. (hon.), Mills Coll. 1933. Began as concert pianist, 1919; mus. coach Bayreuth Wagner Festival 1929; condr. Berlin Philharmonic Orch., 1930, Los Angeles Symphony Orch., Hollywood Bowl, San Francisco Symphony Orch. and in Berkeley (Cal.) Greek Theater, 1930, Hamburg Philharmonic Orch., also orchs. in Riga, Latvia and Warsaw, Poland, 1931; Musicians' Symphony Orch. at Met. Opera House, N.Y.C., summer concerts White Plains, N.Y., 1933; Detroit and Buffalo Symphony orchs., New York Civic Orch., 1934, Nat. Symphony Orch., Washington, 1935; Brico Symphony Orch., N.Y.; Fed. Orch. Concerts, New York World's Fair, 1939; organizer, 1935. and condr. New York Women's Symphony Orch.; conducted in Finland, Sept. 1946, spl. Sibelius concert, Helsinki, Dec. 8, 1946; London Philharmonic Orch., Royal Albert Hall, No. 1946, piano and conducting tour, Yugoslavia, Dec., 1946, New York Philharmonic, Lewisohn Stadium, 1938. Organizer and condr. Brico Symphony Orch., 1939; founder Bach. Soc. of Denver; condr. in Finland, Vienna, Salzburg (Mozarteum Orch.), Frankfurt-am-Main, Boise Symphony Orch., 1956-58, Boise (Idaho) Civic Symphony, 1957—, Boulder (Colo.) Philharmonic Orch, also Denver Community Symphony, Greater Denver Opera Assn.; lectr., guest condr., Denver; tchr. of conducting classes and piano; operatic coach. Address: 959 S Pennsylvania St Denver CO

BRIDENBAUGH, CARL, historian, writer; b. Phila., Aug. 10, 1903; s. Charles Herbert and Mabel (Corbin) B.; B.S., Dartmouth Coll., 1925, Litt.D., 1958; student U. Pa., 1925-27; A.M., Harvard, 1930, Ph.D., 1936; A.M., Brown U., 1963; m. Jessica Hill, Sept. 8, 1931 (dec. 1943); m. 2d, Roberta Haines Herriott, June 17, 1944. Master Meadowbrook (Pa.) Sch., 1925-26, Episcopal Acad., Overbrook, Pa., 1926-27; instr. English and history Mass. Inst. Tech., 1927-29, 30-34, asst. prof. history, 1934-38; asso. prof. history Brown U., Providence, 1938-42, Univ. prof., 1962-68; lectr. history Coll. William and Mary, 1945- 46; dir. Inst. Early Am. History and Culture, Williamsburg, Va., 1945- 50; Margaret Byrne prof. Am. history U. Cal. at Berkeley, 1950-62; specialist U.S. State Dept., India, 1956. Mem. Hist. Am. Bldgs. Survey, 1957-62; cons. Am. civilization to U.S. Nat. Commn. for UNESCO, 1957-60. Commd. lt., USNR, 1942, lt. comdr., 1946. Fellow Center for Advanced Study in Behavioral Scis., 1965-66; Guggenheim fellow, 1958, 62, 68. Fellow Royal Hist. Soc., Am. Acad. Arts and Scis.; mem. Am. Philos. Soc., Am. Antiquarian Soc., Am. Hist. Assn. (pres. 1962.), Colonial Soc. Mass., Mass. Hist. Soc., Phi Beta Kappa. Club: Providence Art. Editor: N.B. Tucker, The Partisan Leader, 1933; P. M'Robert, Tour Through North America, 1935; Gentleman's Progress, 1948. Author: Cities in the Wilderness, 1938; (with Jessica Bridenbaugh) Rebels and Gentlemen, 1942; Peter Harrison, 1949; Seat of Empire, 1950; Colonial Craftsman, 1950; Myths and Realties, 1952; Cities in Revolt, 1955; Mitre and Sceptre, 1962; Vexed and Troubled Englishmen, 1590-1640, 1968; (with Roberta Bridenbough) No Peace Beyond the Line, 1971. Bd. editors N.E. Quarterly. Contbr. articles to revs. and newspapers. Home: 364 Benefit St Providnce RI 02903

BRIDGE, ANN, (Lady O'Malley), author; b. Shenley, Herts, Eng., Sept. 11, 1889; d. James Harris and Marie (Day) Sanders; diploma social sci. and adminstrn. London Sch. Econs., 1913; m. Sir Owen O'Malley, Oct. 25, 1913; children—Jane, John Patrick, Grania (Mrs. Paul Willert). Sec. Charity Orgn. Soc., Chelsea, Soho, Whitechapel (London), 1911-13; central pres. Wives Fellowship, 1923-25; mem. prize com. Femina-Vie Heureuse, 1935-39. Brit. Red Cross rep., Hungary, 1940-44; active Polish Red Cross, 1944-45; relief work in France. Fellow Soc. Antiquaries of Scotland, Royal Hort. Soc., Wine and Food Soc. Author: Peking Picnic (Atlantic Monthly prize), 1932; The Ginger Griffin (Brit. Book Soc., choice), 1934; Illyrian Spring (Brit. Book Soc. choice), 1935; The Song in the House, (short stories), 1936; Enchanter's Night Shade (Brit. Book Soc. choice), 1937; Four-Part Setting, 1939; Frontier Passage, 1942; Singing Waters (Brit. Book Soc. and Lit. Guild choice), 1945; And Then You Came, 1948; The House at Kilmartin (juvenile), 1950; The Dark Moment (Lit. Guild choice), 1951; A Place to Stand, 1953; A Family of Two Worlds (autobiography), 1955; The Light-Hearted Quest, 1956; (with Susan Lowndes) The Selective Traveller in Portugal, 1949; The Portuguese Escape (Lit. Guild choice), 1958; The Numbered Account, 1959; The Tightening String, 1962; The Dangerous Islands, 1963; Emergency in The Pyrenees, 1964; The Episode at Toledo, 1966; Facts and Fictions (Literary Recollections), 1968; The Malady in Madeira, 1969; Moments of Knowing, 1971. Home: 27 Charlbury Rd Oxford England Office: care McGraw-Hill Book Co Inc 330 W 42d St New York City NY 10036

BRIDGEMAN, HARRY MORRIS, research adminstr.; b. Great Falls, Mont., Apr. 23, 1918; s. Harry S. and Anita (Swanson) B.; student San Bernadino (Cal.) Valley Coll., 1934-36; B.A., U. Cal. at Berkeley, 1939; m. Ida M. Petersen, June 1, 1940; children—Carole A., Patricia M., Susan C. With Bur. Labor Statistics, 1940-41, war plans div. Office Chief Army Ordnance, 1941-42, San Francisco Ordnance Dist., 1942, War Assets Adminstrn., 1946-48; with Stanford Research Inst., 1949-69, mgr. econ. research So. Cal. labs., 1956-57, dir. naval warfare research center, 1957-61, past dir. transp. research, team leader econ. study of Honduras, 1962, Bolivia, 1967-68; v.p. Westwood Research, Inc., 1969—. Served from ensign to lt. USNR 1942-46; Mem. Inst. Aero. Scis., A.I.M., Operations Research Soc. Am., Sci. Resarch Soc. Am., Naval Order U.S. Club; Commonwealth (San Francisco). Prin. author: A Ten Year Highway Program for Honduras; The Economic Development of Bolivia. also author classified publs.; contbr. to Development of Australia. Home: 416 Chaucer St Palo Alto CA 94301 Office: 750 Welch Rd Palo Alto CA 94304

BRIDGEMAN, MAURICE RICHARD, petroleum co. exec.; b. Jan. 26, 1904; s. 1st Viscount Bridgeman and Caroline Beatrix (Parker); student Trinity Coll., Cambridge (Eng.) U.; m. Diana Mary Erica Wilson, Feb. 23, 1933; four daus. With Anglo-Persian Oil Co., 1926; mng. dir. Brit. Petroleum Co., 1956-69, chmn. 1960-69; Indsl. Reorgn. Corp., 1969-71. Petroleum adviser Ministry Econ. Warfare, 1939; asst. sec. petroleum dept., also joint sec. Oil Control Bd., 1940; temporarily loaned as petroleum adviser Govt. India, 1942; prin. asst. sec. petroleum div. Ministry Fuel and Power, 1944-46; mem. adv. council Middle East Trade, 195863. Created knight, 1964; comdr. Brit. Empire, 1946; knight of St. John, 1961; knight grand cross Italian Republic. 1966; hon. fellow Fitzwilliam Coll., Cambridge U., 1967; grand officer Order Orange Nassau, 1968; decorated 2d class Order Homayun (Iran), 1968; recipient Cadman Meml. medal, 1969. Mem. Middle East Assn. (pres.). Club: White's (London). Home: The Glebe House, Selham, Petworth, Sussex, England. Office: 10 Kylestrome House Ebury St London SW 1 England

BRIDGEN, CLARENCE J., investment banker; b. Toronto, Ont., Can., 1898. Partner Paine, Webber, Jackson & Curtis, Chgo. Home: care Chgo Athletic Club 12 S Michigan Av Chicago, IL 60601. Office: 209 S LaSalle St Chicago IL 60604

BRIDGER, GROVER LEON, chem. engr.; b. Memphis, July 11, 1911; s. Grover Cleveland and May (Beckham) B.; B.S., Rice Inst., 1933, A.M., 1935; Ph.D., Ia. State Coll., 1938; m. Elizabeth Lou Everett, Aug. 2, 1941; children—Carolyn A., Susan E., Ellen E., Elizabeth L. Engaged in plant operations and research Shell Petroleum Corp., Houston, 1933-35; grad. asst., instr. chem. engring. Ia. State Coll., Ames, 1935-38, head dept. chem. and mining engring., also in charge chem. engring. divs. Engring. Expt. Sta. and Ames Lab. of AEC, 1947-55; instr. chem. engring. Rice Inst., 1938-39; project leader and chief of process devel. div. TVA, Wilson Dam, Ala., 1939-47; prof. chem. engring. Ga. Inst. Tech., Atlanta, 1964—, dir. Sch. Chem. Engring., 1968—. Cons. chem. engr., 1947—; dir. agrl. chem. research Davison Chem. Co. Balt., 1955-57, W.R. Grace & Co., 1957-64; cons. on devel. of recently discovered phosphate deposits in So. Rhodesia (visited area in 1948, 50); Smith-Mundt appointee to N.Z. to survey fertilizer prodn. problems summer 1951. Registered profl. engr., Ia., Ga., Md. Mem. Am. Soc. Engring. Edn., Fertilizer Soc., Am. Inst. Chem. Engrs., Am. Chem. Soc., Sigma Xi, Tau Beta Pi, Phi Kappa Phi, Phi Lambda Upsilon. Baptist. Author: Development of Processes for Production of Concentrated Superphosphate, TVA Chem. Engring. Report No. 5 (book- length bull.), 1949. Contbr. articles tech. jours. Patentee in field. Home: 5585 Lake Forrest Dr NW Atlanta GA 30342

BRIDGES, FRANK GORDON Jr., lawyer; b. Pine Bluff, Ark., Aug. 24, 1906; s. Frank Gordon and Vive (Walker) B.; B.A., Vanderbilt U., 1928, LL.B., 1930; m. Anna L. Young; children—Frank Gordon III, Rhea B. (Mrs. J. William Sanders), Lunsford W. Admitted to Ark. bar, 1929; practice in Pine Bluff, 1930—; partner firm Bridges, Young, Matthews & Davis, 1930—. Dir. Nat. Bank Commerce, Ark. Oak Flooring Co. Served to lt. comdr. USNR, 1943-45. Mem. Am., Ark., Jefferson County bar assns. Home: 3515 Elm St Pine Bluff AR 71601 Office: 15 E 8th Av Pine Bluff AR 71601

BRIDGES, HAROLD, oil co. exec.; b. Dronfield, Eng., Mar. 14, 1916; s. George H. and Alice (Allen) B.; B.S., U. Durham (Eng.), 1937; m. Shirley May Cresswell, June 26, 1943; children—Margaret Enid (Mrs. A. Perrelet), Jennifer Shirley (Mrs. Michael Phillips), John H.C. Various positions with Shell Group, New Guinea, India, Australia, Indonesia, U.S., Pakistan, Netherlands, Ecuador, Colombia, Venezuela, Persian Gulf, Nigeria, Can.; now exec. v.p., chief operating officer Shell Oil Co., N.Y.C. Served with Royal Australian Air Force, 1942-44. Home: Lombardy Hotel 115 E 56th St New York City NY 10022 Office: 50 W 50th St New York City NY 10020

BRIDGES, HARRY, (Alfred Renton Bridges), union ofcl.; b. Melbourne, Australia, July 28, 1901; s. Alfred Ernest and Julia (Dorgan) B.; ed. St. Brennan's Parochial Sch., Melbourne, m. Agnes Brown, Dec., 1923; 1 dau. Jacqueline; m. 2d, Nancy Berdico; children—Julie Ellen, Robert Alfred; m. 3d, Noriko Sawada; 1 dau., Katherine. Joined Internat. Longshoremen's Assn., 1920, again in 1935; leader strike against Pacific Coast shipowners, 1934; pres. Pacific Coast dist. Internat. Longshoremen's Assn.; organizer Maritime Fedn. of Pacific, 1935, later pres. Dist. Council 2; joined Internat. Longshoremen's and Warehousemen's Union, 1937, now pres.; writer column On the Beam, appearing in The Dispatcher, 1943—; apptd. commr. San Francisco Port Commn., 1970—. Mem. San Francisco Port Authority, 1970—. Author: (pamphlet) Women in War, 1943. Address: 150 Golden Gate Av San Francisco CA 94102

BRIDGES, HENRY LEE, state ofcl.; b. Franklin County, N.C., June 10, 1907; s. John Joseph and Ida Loraine (Carroll) B.; A.B., Mars Hill Jr. Coll., 1929; B.A., Wake Forest Coll., 1931; postgrad in law, 1932-33; m. Clarice Hines, Dec. 12, 1936; children—Joseph Henry, George Hines. Atty. at law; dep. clk. Superior Ct. Guilford County, 1935-40, 41-42, 45-46; auditor State of N.C., Raleigh, 1947—. Sec., treas. Guilford County Democratic Exec. Com., 1933-40. Trustee Wake Forest U., 1949-52, 55-58, 60-63, 65-68, Southeastern Bapt. Theol. Sem., 1968—. Served with AUS, 1940-41, 42-45. Mem. Nat. Assn. State Auditors, Comptrollers and Treasurers (exec. dir. 1958-69), Am. Legion, 40 and 8. Baptist (deacon). Mason (K.T., Shriner), Lion. Home: 2618 Grant Av Raleigh NC 27608 Office: Box 870 Raleigh NC 27602

BRIDGES, LLOYD, actor; b. San Leandro, Cal., Jan. 15; s. Lloyd and Harriet (Brown) B.; student U. Cal. at Los Angeles; m. Dorothy Bridges; children—Beau, Jeff, Lucinda. Appeared in stock cos., coll. dramatic prodns.; Broadway appearance in Oh Men Oh Women; motion pictures: Walk in the Sun; High Noon, Home of the Brave, White Tower, The Goddess, The Rainmaker; TV series The Sea Hunt, The Lloyd Bridges Show, The Loner, McCloud, San Francisco Internat. NBC, 1970—. Office: care William Morris Agy 1740 Broadway New York City NY 10019

BRIDGES, ROBERT LYSLE, lawyer; b. Altus, Ark., May 12, 1909; s. Joseph Manning and Jeffa Alice (Morrison) B.; A.B., U. Cal., 1930, LL.B., 1933; m. Alice Marian Rodenberger, June 10, 1930; children—David Manning, James Robert, Linda Lee. Admitted to Cal. bar, 1933, U.S. Supreme Ct., 1938; practiced in San Francisco, 1933—; asso. firm Thelen & Marrin, 1933-39, partner firm, 1939—, firm name Thelen, Marrin, Johnson & Bridges, 1941—; Dir., Trans Mt. Oil Pipe Line Co., Vancouver, B.C., Can., Alpac Constrn. & Surveys, Ltd., Vancouver; v.p., dir. Canadian Indsl. Corp., Toronto, Ont., Can.; dir., gen. counsel Bechtel Corp., San Francisco; dir. Indsl. Indemnity Co., San Francisco, Hendy Internat. Co., Los Angeles, Wells Fargo Bank, San Francisco, Calabasas Enterprises, Inc., Los Angeles, Wells Fargo & Co., Crum and Forster, N.Y.C., Mountain Pacific Pipeline Ltd., Vancouver. Mem. Am., Cal., San Francisco bar assns. Republican. Clubs: Links (N.Y.C.); Commonwealth of Cal., World Trade, Pacific Union, Stock Exchange (San Francisco); Claremont Country (Oakland); California (Los Angeles). Home: 3972 Happy Valley Rd Lafayette CA 94549 Office: 111 Sutter St San Francisco CA 94104

BRIDGES, SAMUEL WILLARD, Jr., textile co. exec.; b. Newton, Mass., July 11, 1930; s. Samuel Willard and Dorothy McGlennon (Denike) B.; A.B., Harvard, 1952; m. Jane Seymour Mortenson, June 21, 1952; children—Samuel Willard III, Adam M. Mfg. and sales positions Top Co., Boston, 1954-70, dir., treas., asst. sec., 1970—. Mem. Carlisle (Mass.) Conservation Commn., 1969-70. Bd. dirs. Emerson Hosp., Concord, Mass. Served to lt. (j.g.) USNR, 1952-54. Mem. Carlisle Colonial Minute Men. Clubs: Kittansett (Marion, Mass.); Concord Country; Spee (Cambridge, Mass.). Home: 187 West St Carlisle MA 01741 Office: 470 Atlantic Av Boston MA 02210

BRIDGES, WILLIAM ANDREW, author; b. Franklin, Ind., Jan. 27, 1901; s. Harry and Katherine (Vaught) B., A.B., Franklin Coll., 1923, Litt.D., 1952; m. Lynn Vandivier, July 31, 1924 (dec. 1949); m. 2d, Lucille Hedges, 1962 (dec. 1968); m. 3d, Nana Hedges Marts, 1969. Reporter European edit. Chgo. Tribune, Paris, 1923-25, Riviera edit., Nice, 1924; reporter Franklin Star, 1925; rewrite desk, Paris (France) Times, 1926-28, N.Y. Sun, 1929-34; editor, curator of publs. N.Y. Zool. Soc., 1935-66. Mem. Phi Delta Theta. Democrat. Bapt. Author: True Zoo Stories; Wild Animals of the World, 1948; Zoo Babies, 1953; Zoo Expeditions, 1953; Zoo Pets, 1955; Zoo Doctor, 1957; Zoo Celebrities, 1959; (with Lee S. Crandall) A Zoo Man's Notebook, 1966; The Bronx Zoo Book of Wild Animals, 1968; The New York Aquarium Book of the Water World, 1970; Zoo Careers, 1971. Contbr. publs. Home: 85 Brook Manor Lane Pleasantville NY 10570 Office: N Y Zoöl Park New York City NY 10460 ☆

BRIDGES, WILLIAM EMERY, educator; b. Boston, Nov. 24, 1933; s. Ronald and Helen (Emery) B.; A.B., Harvard, 1955; A.M., Columbia, 1956; Ph.D., Brown U., 1963; m. Ramonda Kump, Dec. 27, 1959; children—Anne, Sarah, Margaret. Dir. admissions Pine Manor Jr. Coll., Chestnut Hill, Mass., 1958-60, head English dept., 1962-66; Aurelia Henry Reinhardt asso. prof. Am. lit. Mills Coll., Oakland, Cal., 1966—, dir. Center Innovative Studies, 1970—, dir. summer workshop for coll. tchrs., 1970. Served with AUS, 1956- 58. Author articles in field. Home: 28 Valenica Rd Orinda CA 94563 Office: Mills Coll Oakland CA 94613

BRIDGEWATER, ERLE HENRY, lawyer; b. Chauncey, O., Mar. 27, 1919; s. Benjamin Erle and Ruth Brown (England) B.; B.S., Ohio State U., 1939, J.D., 1946; m. Virginia McQuade, May 7, 1941; children—Erle Stephen, Gregory, Bradley Scott. Admitted to Ohio bar, 1946, since practiced in Athens. Mem. bd. grievances and discipline Supreme Ct. of Ohio, 1969—; spl. counsel Ohio U.; dir. Beasley Industries, Inc. Mem. citizens adv. com. Ohio Library Bd. pres. bd. United Appeal Athens, 1963, trustee, 1959-64; mem. Athens Bd. Edn., 1960-64. Fellow Ohio State Bar Found. Served AUS, World War II; brig. gen. Ohio N.G., ret. Decorated Bronze Star medal with oak leaf cluster, Presidential Meritorious Service medal. Fellow Am. Coll. Probate Counsel; mem. Am., Ohio (mem. exec. com., chmn. spl. probate court com., past pres.), Athens County bar assns., Am. Judicature Soc., Am. Law Inst., Inst. Jud. Adminstrn., Ohio N.G. Assn. (pres. 1961), Order of Coif, Am. Legion, Pi Kappa Alpha. Mem. Christian Ch. Mason. Home: 19 Roosevelt Dr Athens OH 45701

BRIDGFORTH, RICHARD BASKERVILLE, Jr., tobacco co. exec.; b. Kenbridge, Va., Jan. 3, 1925; s. Richard Baskerville and Elizabeth (Cunningham) B.; student Va. Mil. Inst., 1942-43, Cornell U., 1943-44, U. Va., 1946-48; m. Nancy Dunton Dickinson, June 12, 1948; children—Richard Baskerville III, Andrew D., Robert M., Nancy H., John C. With Internat. Planters Corp., Richmond, Va., 1949-58, v.p., dir., 1956-58; pres., dir. G.R. Garrett Co., Rocky Mount, N.C., 1958-61; v.p. Dibrell Bros., Inc., Danville, N.C., 1961-68, dir., 1962—, pres., 1968—; dir. Carolina Leaf Tobacco Co., Greenville, N.C.,, Security Bank & Trust Co., Danville, Va. Commonwealth Bankshares, Richmond. Dir. bd. assos. Averett Coll., Danville; bd. dirs. YMCA. Served with USMCR, 1943-45. Mem. Leaf Tobacco Exporters Assn. (chmn. exec. com.), Tobacco Assn. U.S. (exec. com.). Home: 172 Brocton Pl Danville VA 24541 Office: 512 Bridge St Danville VA 24541

BRIDGMAN, ANNA JOSEPHINE, biologist, educator; b. Gainesville, Ga., Sept. 26, 1906; A.B., Agnes Scott Coll., 1927; M.A., U. Va., 1935; Ph.D. in Zoology, U. N.C., 1947. Tchr. pub. schs., N.C., 1927-30, Va., 1930-35; asso. prof. biology Flora Macdonald Coll., 1935-40; prof. Limestone Coll., 1942-49; asso. prof. biology Agnes Scott Coll., Decatur, Ga., 1949-52, prof., 1952—, chmn. dept., 1952-71; with NACA, 1931. Corporate mem. Woods Hole Biol. Lab. Mem. A.A.A.S., Am. Soc. Zoologists, Am. Soc. Protozoologists, Phi Beta Kappa, Sigma Xi. Research in radiation on ciliates, excystment in fresh water ciliates. Address: Dept of Biology Agens Scott Coll Decatur GA 30030

BRIDGMAN, CHARLES SIMMONS, educator, psychologist; b. Rochester, N.Y., Jan. 24, 1913; s. George A. and Eleanor (Simmons) B.; A.B., Union Coll., 1934; M.S., Brown U., 1936; Ph.D., U. Rochester, 1938; B.S., Ohio State U., 1940; m. Marjorie Deninger, July 22, 1938; children—Charles P., George J., Katherine A., Joan C. From instr. to asso. prof. physiol. optics Ohio State U., 1938-48; prof. psychology U. Wis., Madison, 1953—, chmn. dept. psychology U. Wis. Extension, 1950—, and Center System, 1950-71. Mem. Am. Psychol. Assn., Psychonomic Soc., Am. Optical Soc., Am. Acad. Optometry. Spl. research in vision, test theory, applications indsl. psychology. Home: 3417 Crestwood Dr Madison WI 53705

BRIDGMAN, WILBUR BENJAMIN, educator, chemist; b. New Wilmington, Pa., Jan. 28, 1913; s. Benjamin Williams and Lida (Manley) B.; B.Ed., Eau Claire (Wis.) State Tchrs. Coll., 1933; Ph.D., U. Wis., 1937; m. Viola Maude Kongsgaard, Sept. 1, 1937; children—Robert Benjamin, Mary Catherine. Successively grad. asst., instr., research fellow U. Wis., 1934-43; mem. faculty Worcester Poly

Inst., 1943—, prof. chemistry, 1959—. Mem. A.A.A.S., New Eng. Assn. Chemistry Tchrs., Am. Chem. Soc., Sigma Xi, Phi Lambda Upsilon. Home: 113 Hillcroft Av Worcester, MA 01606.

BRIDGWOOD, JOHN B., banker; b. N.Y.C., 1903; grad. N.Y.U., 1925. Formerly v.p. Chase Nat. Bank of N.Y. (now merged Chase Manhattan Bank), now exec. v.p.; dir. U.S. Fidelity & Guaranty Co., Gen. Aniline & Film Corp., Western Md. Ry. Co.; trustee Central Savs. Bank, N.Y.C. Bd. dirs. Rockefeller Center, Inc., Andrew Freeman Home; treas., trustee Leonard Wood Meml. Mem. Nat. Indsl. Conf. Bd., N.Y. C. of C. Home: 34-27 79th St Jackson Heights NY 11372 Office: 1 Chase Manhattan Plaza New York City NY 10015

BRIDSTON, PAUL JOSEPH, banker, ex-govt. ofcl.; b. Grand Forks, N.D., May 28, 1928; s. Joseph B. and Anna (Sophia) B.; B.A. in Internat. History magna cum laude, Yale, 1950; M.B.A., Stanford, 1952; m. Peggy C. Cullen, Aug. 26, 1955; children—Peter Cullen, Rebecca, Sarah. Prof. corp. finance Sch. Bus., U. N.D., 1956-59; sec.-treas. First Fed. Savs. & Loan Assn., Grand Forks, 1955-61, pres., chmn. bd., 1961—; pres. J. B. Bridston Ins. Co., Inc., 1963—, Cullen Ins. Co., Inc., 1964—; chief housing guaranties program for Latin Am., AID, Washington 1964-65, cons., 1965, asst. insp. gen. of Fgn. Assistance, 1970; lectr. internat. bus. U. N.D., 1967—. Pres. Grand Forks United Fund, 1961-62, Grand Forks YMCA, 1959-60, Grand Forks U.S.O., 1963; nat. asso. Boys Clubs Am., 1963-69; chmn. internat. devel. com. U.S. League, 1968, 69. Bd. dirs. Tyrone Guthrie Theatre, Mpls., 1963-69. Served with USNR, 1952-55. Mem. N.D. Savs. and Loan League (dir. 1961), Am. Legion (chmn. oratory com.), Yale, Stanford alumni assns., Yale Glee Club Assos. Lutheran. Elk. Clubs: Federal City (Washington, Dist. Columbia); Grand Forks Country. Author articles. Home: 401 Reeves Dr Grand Forks ND 58201 Office: 201 S 4th St Grand Forks ND 58201

BRIEF, HENRY, assn. exec.; b. Bklyn., Feb. 18, 1924; s. Jacob and Clara (Tannenbaum) B.; B.B.A., City Coll. N.Y., 1948; m. Rosalie Menchin, Apr. 16, 1950; children—Andrew S., Judith M. Feature writer Overseas News Agy., 1948-50; news editor radio sta. WEOK, Poughkeepsie, N.Y., 1951-52; radio-TV-high fidelity editor Home Furnishings Daily, 1952-60; exec. dir. Recording Industry Assn. Am., Inc., N.Y.C., 1960—. Mem. Exec. com. Nat. Music Council. Home: Bellmore NY 11710 Office: 1 E 57th St New York City NY 10022

BRIEGLEB, PHILIP ANTHES, cons. forestry; b. St. Clair, Mo., July 23, 1906; s. Charles Ferdinand and Emma (Anthes) B.; student Drury Coll., 1924-26, U. Minn., 1926; B.S. magna cum laude in Forestry, Syracuse U., 1929, M.Forestry, 1930; m. Ione Wedemeyer, Apr. 13, 1935; children—Kathryn, Gretchen. Forester, Pacific N.W. Forest Expt. Sta., 1929-43, chief div. forest mgmt. research, 1946-51, dir. sta., Portland, Ore., 1963-71; forester Northeastern Forest Expt. Sta., 1944-46; dir. Central States Forest Expt. Sta., Columbus, O., 1951-53, So. Forest Expt. Sta., New Orleans, 1954-63; lectr. U. Cal. at Berkeley, 1942. Mem. Chilean Forestry Mission, 1944; U.S. rep. 7th Brit. Commonwealth Forestry Conf., 1957. Bd. dirs. Ore. Mus. Sci. and Industry; mem. Western Forestry Center, hon. v.p., 1967—. Recipient Superior Service award USDA, 1960. Fellow A.A.A.S., Soc. Am. Foresters (council 1956-57, 58-59, pres. 1964-65); mem. Am. Forestry Assn. (hon. v.p. 1964—), Phi Kappa Phi. Alpha Xi Sigma, Lambda Chi Alpha. Episcopalian. Clubs: Mazama, Multnomah Athletic (Portland); Irvington. Address: 4217 S W Agate Lane Portland OR 97201

BRIELAND, DONALD, educator; b. Peacer, Minn., Jan. 15, 1924; s. Martin L. and Gene (Medhus) B.; B.A., Carleton Coll., 1943; M.A., Northwestern U., 1945; Ph.D., U. Minn., 1949; m. Christine Grant, Aug. 6, 1945; children—Elizabeth, Joan. Asst. prof. Grinnell (Ia.) Coll., 1947-49; research asso., asst. prof. U. Minn., 1949-54; exec. dir. Elizabeth McCormick Fund, Chgo., 1954-61; dir. Ill. Dept. Children and Family Service, 1961-65; prof., dir. U. Chgo. Social Service Center, 1965-70, asso. dean Sch. Social Service Adminstrn., 1968-70; prof., dir. research U. Ill. Jane Addams Grad. Sch. Social Work, Urbana, 1970—; cons. in field, 1954—. Chmn. research com. Child Welfare League, 1968—; exec. officer Commn. Services to Children, 1961-63. Fellow Am. Psychol. Assn., (pres. div. 22 1971—), A.A.A.S., Am. Social Assn.; mem. Nat. Assn. Social Workers (dir. 1969—), Am. Pub. Health Assn., Ill. Welfare Assn. (pres. 1963-65), Nat. Conf. Social Welfare (sec. 1967-68). Episcopalian. Contbr. articles, monographs in field. Home: 55 Chestnut Ct Champaign IL 61820 Office: 1207 W Oregon Urbana IL 61801

BRIER, ROYCE, author, columnist; b. River Falls, Wis., Apr. 18, 1894; s. Warren Judson and Marion (Royce) B.; student U. Wash., 1914-15; m. Monica Doonan, Oct. 14, 1926 (dec. Feb. 1949); children—Susan and Judith (twin daus.); m. 2d, Crystal Smith, July 1, 1949 (dec. Nov. 1970); 1 son, Royce. Short story writer, 1920-25; studied in Orient, Middle East and Europe, 1925, Europe and Middle East, 1936; reporter San Francisco Chronicle, 1926-36, interpretive news columnist since 1937, dir. of editorials, 1942-53. Awarded Pulitzer prize for reporting, 1934; lit. gold medal Commonwelath Club of Cal., 1947. Author: Crusade, 1931; Reach for the Moon, 1934; Boy in Blue (Civil War), 1937; Last Boat from Beyrouth, 1943; Western World (history), 1946. Home: San Anselmo CA 94960 Office: The Chronicle San Francisco CA 94103

BRIER, WARREN JUDSON, coll. dean; b. Seattle, Apr. 25, 1931; s. Howard Maxwell and Grace (Kielstad) B.; B.A., U. Wash., 1953; M.S., Columbia, 1954; Ph.D., U. Ia., 1957; m. Genie Kurack, Sept. 6, 1953; children—Lynn Diane, Karin Lee. Copyreader, Seattle Times, 1953; reporter Seattle Post-Intelligencer, 1956-57; newsman A.P., Seattle, Los Angeles, N.Y. and Helena, Mont., summers, 1959, 61-64, 66, 70; asst. prof. San Diego State Coll. (Cal.), 1959-60, U. So. Cal., 1960-62; asso. prof. U. Mont., 1962-67, prof., 1967—, dean Sch. Journalism, 1968—. Served to 1st lt. USAF, 1957-59. Mem. Assn. for Edn. in Journalism, Sigma Delta Chi, Beta Theta Pi, Kappa Tau Alpha. Author: The Frightful Punishment, 1969; (with Howard C. Heyn) Writing for Newspapers and News Services, 1969. Co-editor: A Century of Montana Journalism, 1971; also contb. jours. Home: 3711 Bellecrest Dr Missoula MT 59801

BRIERLEY, RICHARD GREER, mfg. exec.; b. Kearney, N.J., July 1, 1915; s. Josiah Richards and Castella Sophia (Parker) B.; B.A., Dartmouth, 1936, M.C.S., 1937; Harvard student Advanced Mgmt. Program, 1955; m. Margaret Jean LaLone, Aug. 24, 1940; children—Linda Jean, Sandra Greer, Martha Gail, Ruth Ann. With Armstrong Cork Co., Lancaster, Pa., 1937-41, Thomas B. Keen Co., N.Y.C., 1941-42; staff Sovben div. Archer-Daniels-Midland Co., Mpls., 1942-52, asst. v.p., 1948-53, asst. v.p. charge operations W.J. Small div., 1953-56, v.p., mgr. alfalfa div., 1956-58. asst. to pres., 1957-58; exec. v.p. Arthcer-Daniels-Midland Co., Mpls., 1958-61, dir., 1957-61, cons., 1961—; exec. v.p., sec. Drackett Co., Cin., 1966-68; pres. Bristol-Myers Can. Ltd., 1968-69; v.p. corporate devel. Bristol-Myers Co., 1969-70; pres. Stearns & Foster Co., Cin., 1970—; dir. G.T. Schieldahl Co. Mem. soy food adv. com. War Food Adminstrn., World War II; vice chmn. exec. bd. Soya Food Research Council, 1949-52; mem. linseed crushers industry adv. com. U.S. Dept. Agr.; cons. Chief Food and Agr. Group Bipartite Control Office, Frankfurt, Germany. 1948; cons. German sec. agr., Frankfurt. 1950. Mem. exec. bd. Dan Beard council Boy Scouts Am. Mem. Soy Flour Assn. (past pres.), Am. Dehydrators Assn. Clubs: Camargo, Racquet; Bankers, Union League (N.Y.C.). Home: 5381 Kugler Mill Rd Cincinnati OH 45236 Office: Stearns & Foster Co Cincinnati OH 45215

BRIESE, FRANKLIN, ins. co. exec.; b. Plainview, Minn., Dec. 25, 1905; s. Adolph E. and Amanda (Hostettler) B.; LL.B., U. Minn., 1928; m. Dorothy D. Vine, Aug. 20, 1929; children—Franklin W., Gretchen (Mrs. David B. Calvit). Admitted to Minn. bar, 1928; with Minn. Mut. Life Ins. Co., St. Paul, 1928—, exec. v.p., 1962-66, pres., 1966-67, chmn. bd., pres., 1968-70, chmn. bd., 1970—, also trustee, chmn. exec. com.; dir. Northwestern Nat. Bank, St. Paul Hilton Hotel Co., Minn. Fed. Savs. & Loan Assn. (all St. Paul), First Midwest Capital Corp., Title Ins. Co. Minn. (both Mpls.), Cameron Brown Investment Group, Raleigh, N.C. Mem. Gov. Minn. Investment Adv. Com., 1960—. Pres., Greater St. Paul Community Chest and Council, 1960; 1st v.p. Greater St. Paul Area United Fund, 1961-65; bd. dirs. North Star Research and Devel. Inst., Bush Found.; trustee, treas., chmn. investment com. Charles T. Miller Meml. Hosp., St. Paul. Mem. Am. Life Conv. (past chmn. financial sect., mem. exec. com.), Life Ins. Assn. Am., Soc. Securities Analysts, Mortgage Bankers Assn. Am. (bd. govs. 1963—, exec. com. 1963-65, 67, treas. 1971—), U. Minn. Alumni Assn. (mem. bd., mem. exec. com.). Rotarian. Clubs: Gyro (pres. 1940), Town and Country (pres. 1965), St. Paul Athletic, Minnesota, Pool and Yacht (St. Paul). Home: 803 Ridge St St Paul MN 55116 Office: 345 Cedar St St Paul MN 55101

BRIGANCE, THOMAS FRANKLIN, designer; b. Waco, Tex., Feb. 4, 1913; s. John and Annie (Wolfe) B.; grad. Waco Jr. Coll.; student Nat. Acad. Design, McDowell Sch. Costume Design, Parson Sch. Design, N.Y.C., Sorbonne French Sch., Atelier de la Grande Chaumiere, Paris, France. Worked with various dressmakers, Paris; staff Jaeger, London; designer Lord & Taylor, N.Y.C., 1935-37, exclusive designer, 1937-49; designer, Charles Nudelman, Inc., 1949-50, Sportsmaker, Inc., Frank Gallant, Inc.; now with Touraine, Co., Inc. Served with 13th A.I.C., USAAF., 1941-44. Received Am. Fashion Critics award, 1953. Address: 122 E 78th St New York City NY 10021

BRIGGS, AUSTIN EUGENE, artist; b. Humboldt, Minn., Sept. 8, 1908; s. Harry and Ethel (Davison) B.; student Wicker Art Sch., Detroit, 1924-26, Art Students League, N.Y.C., 1927-28, Harvey Dunn classes in illustration, 1945; m. Ellen Jeannette Weber, May 12, 1927; children—Austin Eugene, Lorna (Mrs. Sherwood Harris). Illustrator for Henry Ford's Dearborn Independent, 1925-27, also nat. mags.; one of founders, mem. faculty Famous Artists Schs., Westport, Conn., 1950—; paintings in permanent collections including Bruce Barton scuptures include Bernard Meadows, Alexander Calder, Leonard Baskins. Mem. Westport Artists Group (pres. 1952-53), Soc. Illustrators. Recipient numerous awards including gold medals from Soc. Illustrators, Art Dirs. Club; named to Hall of Fame, Soc. Illustrators, 1969. Club: New York Art Directors (judge 33d annual exhbn. 1954, recipient medal, 1951, award of distinctive merit, 1953, 54, 63, 64, 66, 67-69). Author articles in pop. mags. Address: Chestnut Woods Rd West Reading CT 06896

BRIGGS, CHARLES AUGUSTUS II, banker; b. N.Y.C., Aug. 1, 1909; s. Alanson Tuttle and Maud (Miller) B.; A.B., Dartmouth Coll., 1931; grad. Grad. Sch. Banking, 1953; m. Mary Jean Nicholson, Jan. 15, 1937; children-Betsy Hallett (Mrs. Murray), Deborah Ann (Mrs. Edson), Ellen Dobbs (Mrs. Martin). With Guaranty Co. of N.Y., 1931-32; v.p., dir. Fiduciary Council, Inc., 1932-48; v.p. Fiduciary Mgmt., Inc., 1944-48; v.p., sr. trust officer County Trust Co., White Plains, N.Y., 1948-66, sr. v.p., trust officer, 1966—; dir. Am. Water Works Co., Port Chester Water Co. Mem. N.Y. State Bankers Assn. (past chmn. investment com. trust div., past exec. com. trust div.), Bank Pub. Relations and Marketing Assn. (past chmn. trust div.), Newcomen Soc. N.Am. Clubs: Economic (N.Y.C.); Dartmouth (past gov.) (Westchester, N.Y.), Eastward Ho Country (past gov.) (Chatham, Mass.); Ardsley Curling. Home: 300 Martine Av White Plains NY 10601 also Shore Rd Chatham MA 02633 Office: 55 Church St White Plains NY 10602

BRIGGS, CHARLES WILLIAM, lawyer; b. Cairo, Ia., July 30, 1887; s. Edward Samuel and Lucy Maria (Weaver) B.; A.B., U. Ia., 1909; LL.B., Harvard, 1913; m. Lois Ione Johnson, June 3, 1922; children—Warren Marshall, Edward Samuel, Charles William. Admitted to Ia. bar, 1912, Minn. bar, 1919; practicing lawyer, Wapello, Ia., 1913-17, pros. atty., 1914-17; mem. firm Briggs and Morgan, and predecessor firms, St. Paul, 1919—; counsel Weyerhaeuser Co., 1940—; dir., mem. exec. com. First Trust Co. St. Paul. Chmn. exec. com. Timber Industries Com. on Timber Valuation and Taxation. Served as capt., Inf., U.S. Army, World War I; AEF in France; lt. col. Inf. Res., 1932-46. Mem. Minn., Am. bar assns., Am. Judicature Soc., Am. Interprofl. Inst., Am. Polit. Sci. Assn., N.A.M. (tax revision com. tax sect.), Am. Soc. Internat. Law, Fgn. Policy Assn., Delta Sigma Rho. Republican. Conglist. Mason. Clubs: Minnesota, Athletic, Informal (St. Paul). Contbr. profl. jours. Home: 1905 Summit Av St Paul MN 55105 Office: First Nat Bank Bldg St Paul MN 55101

BRIGGS, DAVID GARRISON, govt. ofcl.; b. Ashaway, R.I., Jan. 19, 1920; s. Ralph Maxon and Frances Heard (Babcock) B.; B.A. in Journalism, U. Wis., 1942; student Nat. War Coll., 1963-64; m. Yvonne Armande Haré, Aug. 20, 1947; children—Jean Ellen, Anne Babcock, David Garrison. Reporter, New York and Paris Post, Paris, 1945-46; fgn. corr. Reuters Ltd., Paris, London and Washington, 1946-49; editor, corr. United Press, Washington, 1949-52; press attache Am. embassy, Belgrade, 1952-54; information officer USIA, Paris, 1954-57, Calcutta, 1957-59, Ankara, 1959-63, Saigon, 1964-66; counselor, dep. pub. affairs officer Am. embassy, New Delhi, 1966-71; chief nat. security adv. staff USIA, 1971—. Vol., Am. Field Service, Brit. 8th Army, 1942-44, French 1st Army, 1944-45. Mem. Am. Fgn. Service Assn., Am. Numis. Soc., Am. Numis. Assn., Numis. Soc. India, Oriental Numis. Soc., Soc. Ancient Numis. Club: Delhi Polo. Author: Action Amid Ruins, 1945. Home: 122 Grafton St Chevy Chase MD 20015 Office: 1750 Pennsylvania Av NW Washington DC 20547

BRIGGS, ELLIS O., writer, former U.S. ambassador; b. Watertown, Mass., December 1, 1899; s. James and Lucy (Hill) B.; A.B., Dartmouth, 1921, LL.D., 1955, Bowdoin Coll., 1959, Colby Coll., 1965, Ricker Coll., 1965, Nasson Coll., 1966; m. Lucy Barnard, May 26, 1928; children—Lucy, Everett. Instr. Robert Coll., Constantinople, 1921-23; contbr. articles mags., 1923-25; joined Fgn. Service, 1925, after jr. service Peru, Liberia, Cuba, Chile and Washington, apptd. ambassador 1945-62, to Dominican Republic, 1944, to Czechoslovakia, 1949, to Korea, 1952, to Peru, 1955, to Brazil, 1956, to Greece, 1959, Spain, 1961; minister- counselor, Chungking, China, 1945; dir. Office Am. Republics Affairs, 1945-47, vis. prof. U.S.C. Inst. Internat. Relations, 1965. Recipient Medal Freedom for meritorious services as ambassador to Korea, 1955; Annual award The Americas Found., 1966. Clubs: Metropolitan, Chevy Chase (Washington); University, Brook, Century (N.Y.C.). Author: Shots Heard Round the World, 1957; Farewell to Foggy Bottom, 1964; Anatomy of Diplomacy, 1968; also numerous mag. articles. Home: 3 Pleasant St Hanover NH 03755 Office: Topsfield ME 04490

BRIGGS, ERNEST, artist; b. San Diego, Dec. 24, 1923; s. Ernest and Emma (Docili) B.; student Cal. Sch. Fine Art, San Francisco, 1947-50; m. Anne Arnold, Aug. 7, 1961. Exhibited one man shows at Metart Gallery, San Francisco, 1949, Stable Gallery, N.Y.C., 1954, 55, San Francisco Art Assn. Gallery, 1956, Howard Wise Gallery, N.Y.C., 1960, 62, 63; exhibited group shows at Jewish Mus., N.Y.C., 1967, Yale Art Gallery, 1968; rep. perm. colls. at Carnegie Inst., Pitts., Mich. State U., Rockefeller Inst., N.Y.C., Whitney Mus. Am. Art, N.Y.C., San Francisco Mus. Art; faculty U. Fla., 1958, Pratt Inst., 1961-, Yale, 1968. Served with USAAF. 1943-46; CBI. Home: 128 W 23d St New York City, NY 10011.

BRIGGS, FRANK P., newspaper co. exec.; govt. ofcl.; b. Armstrong, Mo., Feb. 25, 1894; s. Thomas H. and Susan Almira (Pyle) B.; student Central Coll., Fayette, Mo., 1911-14; B.J., U. Mo., 1915; m. Catherine Allen Shull, May 28, 1916; children—Thomas Frank, Eugene Allen, Darlene Ruth, Betty Barbara, Dorothy Catherine. Editor, Fayette (Mo.) Democrat-Leader, 1915; city editor Moberly (Mo.) Monitor-Index, 1916-17; editor Trenton (Mo.) Times, 1917-18, city editor, 1919; night editor Shawnee (Okla.) Morning News, 1919-23; editor and owner Macon (Mo.) Chronicle-Herald, 1942—. Asst. sec. Interior, Fish and Wildlife, 1961-65. Mayor, Macon, Mo., 1930-33; mem. Mo. State Senate, 1933-45, pres. 1941-45; apptd. U.S. Senator from Mo., Jan. 18, 1945, to fill unexpired term of Harry S. Truman. Mem. Mo. Conservation Commn., 1947-61, Internat. Commn. for N. Atlantic Fisheries, 1961-65. Recipient Distinguished Pub. Service award U. Mo. Sch. Journalism, 1958. Mem. Sigma Delta Chi. Mason (grand master Mo. 1957-58), Elk, Rotarian. Club: National Press (Washington). Office: Briggs Bldg Macon MO 63552

BRIGGS, GEORGE MCSPADDEN, educator; b. Grantsburg, Wis., Feb. 21, 1919; s. George McSpadden and Mary Etta (McNelly) B.; B.S. in Biochemistry, U. Wis., 1940, M.S., 1941, Ph.D., 1944; m. Eleanor Reese, June 21, 1941; children—Catherine, Marilyn, Nancy. Asso. prof. poultry nutrition, then prof. U. Md., 1945-47; asso. prof. poultry nutrition U. Minn., 1947-51; chief nutrition unit Nat. Inst. Arthritis and Metabolic Diseases, NIH, Bethesda, Md., 1951-58, exec. sec. biochemistry and phasmacology tng. com. NIH div. gen. med. scis., 1958-60; chmn. dept. nutritional scis. U. Cal. at Berkeley, 1960-70, prof. nutrition and biochemist Agr. Expt. Sta., 1960—. Spl. research vitamin B 12, unidentified growth factors, vitamin B complex, guinea pig nutrition; sci. adv. bd. Nutrition Found., 1961—; chmn. U.S. Nat. Com. Internat. Union Nutritional Scis., 1971—; chmn. Cal. Nuitrition Council, 1970-71. Recipient Borden award in poultry sci., 1957. Fellow A.A.A.S., Am. Pub. Health Assn.; mem. Soc. for Nutrition Edn. (pres. 1968-69), Am. Inst. Nutrition (pres. 1967-68), Am. Soc. Biol. Chemists, Am. Chem. Soc., Poultry Sci. Assn., Am. Dietetic Assn., Am. Soc. Animal Sci., Am. Home Econs. Assn., Sigma Xi, Phi Kappa Phi. Author: (with Bogert and Calloway) Nutrition and Physical Fitness, 1966. Exec. editor Jour. Nutrition Edn., 1969—. Author numerous articles in field. Home: 877 Revere Rd Lafayette CA 94549 Office: U Cal Dept Nutritional Scis Berkeley CA 94720

BRIGGS, HAROLD MELVIN, corp. exec.; b. Shelbyville, Mich., Apr. 6, 1904; s. Wallace E. and Eva M. (Dowell) B.; B.S., U.S. Naval Acad., 1927; M.E., U.S. Naval Postgrad. Sch., 1936; student Harvard Advanced Mgmt. Program, 1948; m. Helen J. Fadden, Mar. 26, 1949; 1 dau., Helen J. Commnd. ensign USN, 1927, advanced through grades to rear adm., 1955; naval aide White House, 1940- 41; prodn. officer Bur. Ordnance, 1941-43; exec. U.S.S. St. Louis, 1943- 44; staff comdr.-in-chief Atlantic Fleet, 1944-46; comdr. U.S.S. Pocono, 1946-48; comptroller Naval Gun Factory, 1949-51; staff comdr. Naval Forces Far East, sec. UN mil. armistice negotiating group, 1951-52; comdr. Destroyer Squdn. 12, 1952-53; chief of staff comdr. Amphibious Force Atlantic Fleet, 1953-55; dep. comdt. (Navy) Armed Forces Staff Coll., 1955-57; comdr. Middle East Force, 1957-58; dir. Pan Am. affairs Naval Missions and Adv. Groups div. Office Chief Naval Operations, Washington, 1958-61; pres., chief exec. Washington Technol. Assos., Inc., 1961—. Mem. sci. bur., indsl. council Washington Bd. Trade. Decorated Silver Star medal, Legion of Merit with 3 gold stars, Bronze Star medal with oak leaf cluster; Order Eulchi (Korea); Order Naval Merit (Brazil); Cross Naval Merit (Peru); Order Abdon Calderon (Ecuador); Order San Carlos, Order of Almirante Padilla (Colombia); Grand Order Naval Merit (Venezuela); Spl. Order Naval Merit (Mexico); Distinguished Service medal (Chile). Registered profl. engr., D.C. Mem. Am. Soc. Naval Engrs., Am. Ordnance Assn., Mil. Order Carabao, Naval Acad. Alumni Assn., Harvard Grad. Sch. Bus. Adminstrn. Assn., Navy League U.S., Nat Rocket Club, Advanced Mgmt. Assn. N.Y., Am. Mgmt. Assn., Rockville, Montgomery County chambers commerce. Rotarian. Club: Army and Navy (Washington). Home: 4721 Tilden St Washington DC 20016 Office: 979 Rollins Av Rockville MD 20852

BRIGGS, HERBERT SPENCER, assn. exec.; b. N.Y.C., Feb. 9, 1910; s. Arthur Vanderbilt and Frances (Cleary) B.; A.B., Coll. City N.Y., 1929; m. Erena von Grek, Aug. 7, 1953; children—Natasha, Thomas, Edward George. Personnel research N.Y. and Queens Electric Light and Power Co., 1929-34, job and wage analyst-in-charge, 1934-42; personnel research Consol. Edison Co. N.Y., Inc., 1946-47; sr. research specialist employee remuneration The Conf. Bd., Inc., N.Y.C., 1947-52, asst. sec., 1953, sec., 1953—. Served to lt. col. USAAF, 1942-46. Mem. Delta Sigma Phi. Republican. Episcopalian. Author: Wage Payment Systems, 1948; Evaluating Managerial Positions, 1951. Home: 4555 Henry Hudson Pky New York City NY 10471 Office: 845 3d Av New York City NY 10022

BRIGGS, HERBERT WHITTAKER, univ. prof.; b. Wilmington, Del., May 14, 1900; s. Frederic Foyé and Eleanore Ashton (Lewis) B.; A.B., W. Va. U., 1921; Ph.D., Johns Hopkins U., 1925; student Acad. of Internat. Law, The Hague, summers, 1925-27, 29; m. Virginia Elizabeth Yoder, Dec. 22, 1937; children—Sarah Ashton, Deborah Anne, Jeffrey Peter, Lucinda Moseley. Instr. polit. sci., Johns Hopkins U., 1925-26; C.R.B. fellow in internat. law Brussels, Belgium, 1926-27; mem. research staff Foreign Policy Assn. N.Y.C., 1927-28; acting asso. prof. polit. sci., Oberlin Coll., 1928-29; asst. prof. govt., Cornell, 1929-37, prof., 1937- 47; prof. internat. law, Cornell U., 1947—, chmn. dept. govt., 1946-51; lectr. Academy of Internat. Law, The Hague, summer 1958; guest lectr., Turkish Inst. Internat. Law, Univs. of Instanbul, Ankara and Turkish Gen. Staff War Academy, Apr. 1947. Fulbright lectr. in Internat. Law, U. of Copenhagen Law Faculty, Denmark, 1952, 53; lectr. U.S. Naval War Coll., 1955, 56, 58. Mem. Internat. Law Commn. of UN, 1962-66. Member l'Institut de Droit Internat., Am. Soc. of Internat. Law, (pres. 1959- 60), bd. editors Am. Jour. Internat. Law, 1939—, editor-in-chief, 1955-62. Author: The Doctrine of Continuous Voyage, 1926; The Law of Nations, 1938. The Progressive Development of International Law, 1947; The International Law Commission, 1965. Home: 117 Cayuga Park Rd Ithaca NY 10471 Office: Cornell Univ Law Sch Ithaca NY 14850

BRIGGS, HILTON MARSHALL, coll. pres.; b. Cairo, Ia., Jan. 9, 1913; s. John Weaver and Ethel Gladys (Marshall) B.; B.S., Ia. State Coll., 1933; M.S., N.D. State U., 1935, Sc.D. (hon.), 1963; Ph.D., Cornell U., 1938; m. Lillian Thorbjorg Dinusson, June 16, 1935; children—Dinus Marshall, Janice Sue. Grad. asst. N.D. Agrl. Coll., 1934-35, Cornell U., 1935-36; asst. prof. Okla. State U., 1936-41, asso. prof., 1941-45, prof., 1945-50, asso. dean agr., asso. dir. Agrl. Expt. Sta., 1949-50; dean agr., dir. Wyo. Agrl. Expt. Sta. 1950-58; pres. S.D. State Coll., Brookings, 1958—. Mem. com. on animal nutrition NRC, 1951-57. Trustee Midwestern Ednl. Television, Inc. Recipient Nat. 4-H Club Alumni Achievement award, 1959; Builder of Men award Farm House Frat., 1960. Fellow A.A.A.S.; mem. Am. Soc. Animal Prodn. (sec. 1947-50, v.p. 1951, pres. 1952, bus. mgr. Jour. Animal Sci. 1948-50), Assn. So. Agrl. Workers (sec. animal husbandry sect. 1947-48, chmn. 1948-49), Commn. Colls. and Univs. N. Central Assn., Inst. Internat. Edn., Nat. Inst. Animal Agr., Upper Midwest Research and Devel. Council, Am. Southdown Breeders Assn. (dir.), Alpha Zeta, Gamma Sigma Delta, Phi Kappa Phi, Sigma Xi. Methodist. Club: Continental Dorset (exec. com. 1943-48, pres. 1948). Author: Modern Breeds of Livestock, 1949, rev. edits., 1958, 69; cattle sect. World Book Ency., 1956 edit., rev. 1964; feeds sect. Ency. Chem. Tech., 1951 edit., rev. 1965. Specialist in determining quantity, quality of protein required by sheep and cattle. Home: 929 10th St Brookings SD 57006

BRIGGS, JAMES L., mfg. co. exec.; b. 1916; grad. Mill Hill Sch., 1934, Law Soc. Law Sch., 1936; married. With Aluminum Co. Can., 1947-48, John C. Paige & Co., 1948-50, Appleton & Co., Inc., 1950-52, Drake Am. Corp., 1952-54; with Am. Standard, Inc., 1954—, exec. v..p., 1968—. Address: 40 W 40th St New York City NY 10018*

BRIGGS, JOHN FRANCIS, physician; b. St. Paul, Dec. 3, 1904; s. Charles H. and Mary (Rowan) B.; M.D., U. Minn., 1928; m. Myrtle Paulson, Aug. 17, 1936. Gen. practice medicine, 1929-36, specializing in internal medicine, 1937- -; asso. prof. clin. medicine U. Minn., 1940-62, clin. prof. 1962—. Diplomate Am. Bd. Internal Medicine. Mem. Am. (past chmn. sect. diseases of chest), Minn. med. assns., Am. Thoracic Soc., Am. (past pres.), Internat. colls. chest physicians, A.C.P., Am. Trudeau Soc., Am., Minn. (corporate mem.) heart assns., Minn. Tb and Health Assn. (dir.), Ramsey County Med. Soc., Am. Diabetes Assn., Am. Therapeutic Assn., Alpha Omega Alpha. Editor: Geriatrics; mem. editorial bd. Postgrad. Medicine. Home: 193 Maria Av St Paul MN 55106 Office: Lowry Med Arts Bldg St Paul MN 55102

BRIGGS, JOHN GURNEY, Jr., music critic and editor; b. High Point, N.C., Feb. 17, 1916; s. John Gurney and Hazel Irene (Harmon) B.; student U. N.C., 1932-35; grad. Curtis Inst. Music, 1938; m. Elizabeth Balée Westmoreland, Dec. 23, 1938; children—Robert Ragan, Mary Curtis. Music editor NBC, 1938-40; music critic N.Y. Post, 1940-49; editor Etude music mag., 1949-52; music critic N.Y. Times, 1952-60; sr. writer Smith, Kline & French Labs., 1961-70; writer Camden (N.J.) Courier- Post, 1970—; program annotator Phila. Orch., 1963—. Served with AUS, 1943-46. Mem. Athenaeum of Phila., Phila. Art Alliance, Pa. Hort. Soc. Episcopalian. Author: The Collector's Tchaikovsky, 1959; Leonard Bernstein: The Man, His Work and His World, 1961; The Collector's Beethoven, 1962; Requiem for a Yellow Brick Brewery, 1969. Contbr. articles and short stories to mags. Home: 318 N Bowman Av Merion PA 19066 Office: Courier-Post Camden NJ 08101

BRIGGS, LLOYD ARNOLD, investment co. exec.; b. Ortonville, Minn., Apr. 15, 1916; s. Leslie Arnold and Cynthia Estelle (Brown) B.; B.B.A., U. Minn., 1939; m. Ruth Helyn Zotter, Dec. 11, 1943. With Procter & Gamble Co., 1939, Hardware Mut. Casualty Co., 1939-40; spl. agt. FBI, 1940-45; with Addressograph- Multigraph Co., 1946-48; with Am. Photocopy Equipment Co., Evanston, Ill., 1948-63, exec. v.p., 1956-63, also dir.; v.p. Bell & Howell Co., and pres. Bus. Equipment Group, 1964-67; pres. Dempster Investment Co., 1967—; pres. Ditto, Inc.; dir. Stover Water Softener Co., Nat. Bank North Evanston, Pulaski Road Corp., Chgo., B.K. Elliott Corp., Pitts., Computer Copies Corp., N.Y.C. U.S. cons. to Van Der Grinten N.S., Venlo, Holland. Mem. Soc. Former Spl. Agts. FBI, Delta Upsilon. Clubs: Executives, Mid-Am. (Chgo.); North Shore Country (Glenview, Ill.); Bob O'Link Golf (Highland Park, Ill.). Home: 1420 Sheridan Rd Winnetka IL 60091 Office: 540 Frontage Rd Northfield IL 60093

BRIGGS, LLOYD GIMLICH, mfg. co. exec.; b. Ashaway, R.I., Nov. 7, 1910; s. Asa Lloyd and Mildred Pauline (Gimlich) B.; A.B., Brown U., 1931; M.B.A., N.Y.U., 1940; m. Virginia Macrae Briggs, June 30, 1940; children—Jonathan A., Lydia (Mrs. John G. Poole), Caroline (Mrs. Corliss K. Wells). Mem. staff Loomis, Suffern & Fernald C.P.A.s, N.Y.C., 1937-40, Harris & Gifford, Providence, 1940-42; asst. treas. Orkil, Inc., Hartford, Conn., 1942-46; with Albany (N.Y.) Internat. Corp., 1946—, chief accountant, 1946-52, asst. treas., 1952-56, treas., 1956—; pres., dir. West End Fed. Savs. & Loan Assn., Albany, 1948—. Trustee Village Altamont, N.Y., 1947-51, mayor, 1953-57. Bd. govs., exec. v.p. Child's Hosp., Albany, C.P.A., N.Y. Mem. Am. Inst. C.P.A.'s, Financial Execs. Inst. (dir. 1966-69). Club: Albany Country. Home: 151 Main St Altamont NY 12009 Office: 1373 Broadway Albany NY 12201

BRIGGS, MAURICE MORGAN, dept. store exec.; Lawrence, Kan., Nov. 8, 1909; s. Edward Maurice and Edith (Morgan) B.; A.B., U. Ill., 1931, J.D., 1933; m. Miriam Massey, May 4, 1937 (dec. Dec. 1970); 1 dau., Katharine Massey (Mrs. Myron E. Gire, Jr.). Admitted to Ill. bar, 1933, also U.S. Supreme Ct. bar; practiced Chgo., 1933-41; with real estate dept. Montgomery Ward & Co., Chgo., 1941-43; mgr. real estate Aldens, Inc., Chgo., 1946-49; with city mortgage dept. Equitable Life Assurance Soc. U.S., Chgo., 1949- 51; with Federated Dept. Stores, Inc., Cin., 1952-67, operating v.p. real estate, 1958-62, v.p. real estate, 1962-67; pres., dir. Allmor Devel. Corp. 1960-67; prof. real estate Coll. Bus. and Pub. Adminstrn., U. Ariz., 1967—. Served to lt. USNR, 1943-46, 51-52. Mem. Urban Land Institute. Internat. Council Shopping Centers, Zeta Psi, Phi Delta Phi. Club: Skyline Country (Tucson). Home: 6202 N Campbell Av Tucson, AZ 85718.

BRIGGS, MORTON WINFIELD, educator; b. Millbrook, N.Y., Mar. 11, 1915; s. Anthony Joseph and Verlina (Reardon) B.; Diplme d'Etudes Francaises, U. Paris (France), 1936; B.A., Cornell U., Ithaca, N.Y., 1937; M.A., Harvard, 1938, Ph.D. in Romance Langs., 1944; m. Kathryn Minor Ivey, June 26, 1941; children—Christopher Reardon, Anthony Kirk, Katherine Minor. Asst. d'anglais Lycée Descartes, Tours, France, 1937-38; teaching fellow French, tutor Romance langs. Harvard, 1940-43; faculty Wesleyan U., Middletown, Conn., 1943—, prof. Romance langs., 1956—, acting chmn. master arts in teaching program, 1964-66, 68-69, dir. honors coll., 1966—. Dir. Sweet Briar Coll. Jr. Year in France, 1962-63; chmn. Fgn. Lang. Adv. Com. Conn., 1963—. Pres. bd. Middletown United Fund, 1966. Bd. dirs. Middlesex chpt. A.R.C., 1961—, chmn., 1965-67. Mem. Am. Assn. Tchrs. French (nat. exec. council 1949—), Modern Lang. Assn., Am. Assn. U. Profs., Phi Beta Kappa. Phi Kappa Phi. Episcopalian (vestryman 1952-55, 64-67, warden 1968—). Rotarian (dir. 1967—). Mng. editor French Rev., 1968—, advt. mgr., 1949—. Home: 145 Mt Vernon St Middletown CT 06457

BRIGGS, PAUL WARREN, supt. schs.; b. Mayville, Mich., Nov. 23, 1912; s. Arthur Eugene and Lydia (Miller) B.; A.B., Western Mich. U., 1934; M.A., Mich. State U., 1943; postgrad. Columbia, 1956; Ed.D., Baldwin-Wallace Coll., 1964, Central State U., 1965, Cleve. State U., 1966; L.H.D., Case Inst. Tech., 1966; m. Arvilla Moran, June 18, 1933; children—Betty Ann (Mrs. Loren Smith), James A. Tchr., prin. Brown City (Mich.) High Sch., 1934-40; tchr. Bay City (Mich.) Central High Sch., 1940-42, vice prin., 1942-43, prin., 1943-53; supt. schs., Bay City, 1953-57, Parma Pub. Schs., 1957-64, Cleve. Pub. Schs., 1964—. Mem. summer sch. staff Mich. State U., 1947-50; lectr. edn. U. Mich., 1952, Columbia, 1965, Ohio State U., 1963; adj. prof. Cleve. State U. Bd. mgrs. Cleve. Met. YMCA, 1964—; mem. exec. bd. Greater Cleve. council Boy Scouts Am., 1960—; mem. exec. com. Nat. Urban Coalition; hon. life mem. Nat. P.T.A. Bd. dirs. Greater Cleveland Gowth Assn. Mem. Nat., Ohio (life) edn. assns.; Am., Ohio assns. schs. adminstrs., Mich. High Sch. Athletic Assn. (exec. com. 1949-53). Rotarian (past pres. Bay City), Mason (33, Shriner). Adv. bd. Education 1954-58. Home: 11625 Edgewater Dr Cleveland OH 44102 Office: 1380 E 6th St Cleveland OH 44114

BRIGGS, ROBERT LEROY, unvi. ofcl.; b. Tulsa, Nov. 9, 1916; s. Thomas LeRoy and Ethel (Williams) B.; B.Mus., U. Kan., 1938, M.Mus., 1939, Ph.D., 1951; m. Joan Rae Norton, May 26, 1944; children—Tom, Jan. Supr. Fredonia (Kan.) schs., 1939-41; dir. instl. music Haskell Inst., Lawrence, Kan., 1946-48; asst. instr. music U. Kan., 1946-48, Inst. Music Edn., summer 1948; asso. prof. music edn. Fla. State U., 1948-57; dean Coll. Fine Arts and Profl. Arts, U. Tulsa, 1957-69; dir. Sch. Music, U. Houston, 1969—. Past mem. bd. dirs. Tulsa Philharmonic Soc.; bd. dirs. Tulsa Opera Co.; past v.p. Arts Council of Tulsa; past pres. Tulsa Civic Music Assn. Former mem. Okla. Tchr. Edn. Adv. Council, Okla. Curriculum Improvement Commn. Served to 1st lt. USMCR, 1942-45. Mem. Southwestern Music Tchrs. Assn. (past pres., 1st v.p.), Nat. Assn. Schs. Music (rec. sec.), Tex. Assn. Music Schs. (exec. com.), Tex. Music Educators Assn., Houston C. of C. (cultural affairs com.), Okla. Music Edn. Assn. (past pres.), Phi Mu Alpha (past nat. 2d v.p.), Pi Kappa Lambda, Phi Delta Kappa, Kappa Delta Pi. Presbyn. Rotarian. Contbr. articles to profl. jours. Home: 10622 Sugar Hill Dr Houston TX 77042

BRIGGS, ROBERT PETER, state ofcl.; b. Monroe, Mich., Apr. 3, 1903; s. Robert Douglas and Rose (Pierce) B.; A.B., U. Mich., 1925, M.B.A., 1928; m. Maxine Corliss, Dec. 22, 1925; children—Ruth Terrilyn, Peter Alan. Faculty bus. adminstrn. Kan. Wesleyan U., 1925-27; instr. econs. U. Mich., 1927- 35, asst. prof. econs. and accounting, 1935-40, asso. prof., 1940-44, prof. accounting, v.p., 1945-51; v.p., dir. Consumer Power Co., Jackson, Mich., 1951-52, exec. v.p. 1952-68, now dir., asst. to pres. Standard Steel Spring Co., 1944-45; jr. accountant, sr. accountant, partner Paton & Ross, F.E. Ross & Co. & Briggs & Iceman, Ann Arbor, Mich., 1927-45; dir., dep. chmn., chmn. Fed. Res. Bank of Chgo., 1956-64; commr. Mich. Financial Instns. Bur., Lansing, 1968—. Chief gen. office div. Detroit Ordnance Dist., War Dept., 1941-44. Regent, U. Mich., 1964-68. C.P.A., Mich. Mem. Mich. C. of C. (past pres.), Am. Inst. Accountants. Presbyn. Home: Box 758 Elk Rapids MI 49629 Office: Financial Instn Bur Sta B Lansing MI 48913

BRIGGS, ROBERT WILLIAM, biologist, educator; b. Watertown, Mass., Dec. 10, 1911; s. Robin John and Bridget (McGonigle) B.; B.S., Boston U., 1934; Ph.D., Harvard, 1938; m. Janet Elizabeth Bloch, Sept. 27, 1940; children—Evan William, Alexander Bloch, Meredith. Research fellow McGill U., Montreal, Que., Can., 1938-42; mem. Inst. Cancer Research, Phila., 1942-56; prof. biology Ind. U., Bloomington, 1956-63, research prof., 1963—, chmn. dept., 1969—. Mem. Am. Soc. Naturalists, Genetics Soc. Am., Am. Soc. Zoologists, Nat. Acad. Scis., Am. Acad. Arts and Scis., Soc. Study Devel. and Growth. Home: 1900 Atwater Av Bloomington IN 47401 Office: Dept Zoology Univ Ind Bloomington IN 47401

BRIGGS, RODNEY ARTHUR, univ. adminstr.; b. Madison, Wis., Mar. 18, 1923; s. George McSpadden and Mary Etta (McNelly) B.; student Oshkosh (Wis.) State Coll., 1941-42; B.S. in Agronomy, U. Wis., 1948; Ph.D. in Field Crops, Rutgers U., 1953; m. Helen Kathleen Ryall, June 1, 1944; children—Carolyn, Kathleen, David, Andrew, Amy. Extension asso. farm crops Rutgers U., New Brunswick, N.J., 1949-50, 52- 53; mem. faculty U. Minn., 1953—, supt. W. Central Sch. and Expt. Sta., Morris, Minn., 1959-60, prof. agronomy, dean U. Minn., administrv. head, provost Morris Campus, 1960-69, 71—; on leave of absence Ford Found. as asso. dir., dir. research Internat. Inst. Tropical Agr., Ibadan, Nigeria, 1969-71. bd. dirs. Channel 10 ETV, Appleton, Minn. Chmn. Nat. Silage Evaluation Com., 1957; sec. Minn. Corp Improvement Assn., 1954-57; columnist crops and soils Minn. Farmer mag., 1954-59; judge grain and forage Minn. State Fair, 1954-6l; mem. Gov.'s Commn. Law Enforcement, 1967-69; adv. com. State Planning Agy., 1968-69, Minn. Interinstnl. TV, 1967—. Bd. dirs. Rural Banking School, 1967—. Served with inf. AUS, 1942-46, 50-52. Recipient Staff award U. Minn., 1959, Spl. award U. Minn. at Morris, 1961; commendation Soil Conservation Soc. Am., 1965. Mem. Am. Soc. Agronomy, Corp Sci. Soc. Am., Soil Conservation Soc. Am., N.E.A., Minn. Adult Edn. Assn., Am. Civil Liberties Union (dir. Minn.), Sigma Xi, Alpha Gamma Rho. Republican. Conglist. Address: 1015 Univ Minn Minneapolis MN 56267

BRIGGS, RONALD LEE, lawyer; b. Murphysboro, Ill., Apr. 19, 1937; s. Myron S. and Pauline (McDaniel) B.; student So. Ill. U., 1955-57; J.D., U. Ariz., 1961; m. Bonnie Hirons, June 26, 1960; children—Michael Lee, Martin Lee. Admitted to Ariz. bar, 1961, Ill. bar, 1970; practiced in Casa Grande, Ariz., 1961-70, Carbondale Ill., 1970—; dep. Pinal County atty., Florence, 1963-67; spl. counsel Ariz. Ho. of Reps., 1964; dir. Neighborhood Youth Corps, Pinal County, 1965; partner law firm Stanfield, McCarville, Coxon & Briggs, 1967-70; city atty., Carbondale 1970—; tchr. bus. law Central Ariz. Coll.; dir. Ariz. Job Colls., Inc.. Carbondale Indsl. Corp. Republican Party precinct committeeman, 1962-64; gen. counsel Pinal County Rep. Com., 1965-70. Bd. dirs. Easter Seal Soc. Ariz., 1962-65; trustee Casa Grande (Ariz.) Elementary Sch. Dist., 1968-70. Fellow, group study exchange program Rotary Internat., 1967. Mem. Am., Ariz., Ill., Jackson County, Pinal County (Pres., 1965) bar assns. Presbyn. (elder). Elk. Home: 105 S Lark Lane Carbondale IL 62901 Office: 222 E Main St Carbondale IL 62901

BRIGGS, WALLACE NEAL, educator; b. Meridian, Miss., Mar. 1, 1914; s. Wallace R. and Mary (Neal) B.; A.B., U. Ky., 1937, M.A., 1945; student Yale, 1953-54, Sorbonne, 1939-40; m. Olive Terrill, June 24, 1942. Tchr., Univ. Sch., Lexington, Ky., 1940-43; dir. Guignol Theatre, U. Ky., Lexington, 1943—, prof. theatre arts, 1962—, chmn. dept., 1966. Dir., The Stephen Foster Story, Bardstown, Ky., 1964; pres. Lexington Childrens Theatre, 1970-71. Bd. dirs. Ky. Living Arts Center, 1970—. Served with AUS, 1942-43. Recipient Outstanding Tchr. award U. Ky., 1968, great tchr. award, 1971. Mem. Am. Ednl. Theatre Assn. Southeastern Theatre Assn., Ky. Speech Assn., Omicron Delta Kappa, Phi Delta Kappa, Phi Kappa Tau. Author articles. Home: 3013 Windermere Rd Lexington KY 40502

BRIGGS, WILLIAM EGBERT, coll. dean; b. Sioux City, Ia., Mar. 26, 1925; s. Egbert Estabrook and Berenice (Reynolds) B.; B.A., Morningside Coll., 1948, D.Sc., 1968; M.A., U. Colo., 1949, Ph.D., 1953; m. Muriel Mae Lambert, Aug. 29, 1947; children—William L., Roger P., Barbara E., Lindsey A. Asst. instr. Morningside Coll., 1947; math. tchr. Elwood (Ia.) High Sch., 1948, Baseline Jr. High Sch., Boulder, Colo, 1954-55; research asso. U. Colo., 1953-54, faculty, 1955—, prof. math., 1964—, dean Coll. Arts and Scis., 1964—. NSF faculty fellow, hon. research asso. Univ. Coll., London, Eng., 1961-62; mem. Region XIII Selection com. Woodrow Wilson Found. Fellowship Program; bd. dirs. Edn. Projects Inc., 1966—; chmn. math. adv. com. Colo. Dept. Edn., 1964-66. Bd. dirs. Colo. Conglist. Conf., 1953-56, Colo. Conf. United Ch. Christ, 1963-68. Served to 1st lt. AUS, 1943-46. Mem. Math. Assn. Am. (gov. 1963-66), Am. Math. Soc., Council Colls. Arts and Scis. (dir. 1969—), Am. Assn. U. Profs., London Math. Soc., Sigma Xi. Author: (with others) Analytic Geometry, 1963; also articles. Home: 1440 Sierra Dr Boulder, CO 80302.

BRIGGS, WILLIAM PAUL, found. exec.; b. Washington, May 29, 1903; s. James Smith and Effie Evelyn (Hutchinson) B.; Ph.G., George Washington U., 1924, B.S., 1927; M.S., U. Md., 1931; Sc.D. (hon.), Phila. Coll. Pharm. and Sci., 1947; LL.D., Temple U., 1951; L.H.D., Northeastern U., 1963; Ed.D., Ohio No. U., 1965; m. Lois Evelyn Shipman, June 29, 1927. Faculty, George Washington U., 1927-46, dean Sch. Pharmacy, 1934-46; dir. Pharmacy Service VA 1946-47; head pharm. sect. Bur. Med. and Surgery, U.S. Navy, 1948-51; cons. to chief med. dir. VA; exec. dir. Am. Found. for Pharm. Edn., Washington, 1951—. Treas. U.S. Pharmacopeia, 1940—. Served as comdr., bur. medicine and surgery USNR, 1942-45. Recipient Remington honor medal, 1957. Mem. Am. Pharm. Assn., Theta Delta Chi, Kappa Psi (hon.). Home: 4600 Connecticut Av Washington DC 20008 Office: Am Found for Pharm Edn Washington DC 20005

BRIGHAM, NELSON ALLEN, educator; b. Holyoke, Mass., Nov. 6, 1915; s. Nelson Elisha and Bertha May (Wheeler) B.; B.S., Rutgers U., 1937, M.S., 1938; Ph.D., U. Pa., 1948. Asst. instr. math. U. Pa., 1938-41; asst. prof. math. Pa. State Center, Swarthmore, 1947-48, U. Md., 1948-51; mathematician Applied Physics Lab., Johns Hopkins, 1951-56; sr. scientist Avco Corp., 1956-59; head math. sect. Baird-Atomic, Cambridge, Mass., 1959-60; mem. staff Lincoln Lab., Mass. Inst. Tech., 1960-62; mathematician Mitre Corp., Bedford, Mass., 1962-64; asso. prof. Southeastern Mass. Tech. Inst., Fall River, 1965; prof., head dept. math. and astronomy Butler U., 1965- 70; prof., chmn. math. dept. Bradley U., Peoria, Ill., 1970—. Served to lt. comdr. USNR, 1941-46. Decorated Bronze Star medal. Mem. Am. Math. Soc., Math. Assn. Am., Soc. Indsl. and Applied Math., A.A.A.S., Am. Assn. U. Profs., Sci. Research Soc. Am., Phi Beta Kappa, Sigma Xi. Phi Kappa Phi, Kappa Mu Epsilon. Contbr. articles to profl. jours. Home: 753 W Wonderview Dr Dunlap IL 61525 Office: Dept of Math Bradley University Peoria IL 61606

BRIGHAM, THOMAS MYRON, educator; b. Rochester, N.Y., Feb. 4, 1924; s. Charles Dana and Beatrice (McNaught) B.; student U. Cin., 1941-43, The Citadel, 1943-44, Vanderbilt U., 1944, Colo. State Coll., summer 1946; A.B., San Francisco State Coll., 1948; M.S.W., U. Cal. at Berkeley, 1944; m. Aimee Eugenia Doucette, May 13, 1944; children—Pamela Susan (Mrs. Paul Schramm), Peter Eugene, Timothy James, Corinne Anne. Boys work dir. community program Central YMCA, San Francisco, 1947-50; group program dir. Internat. Inst. San Francisco, 1950-53; faculty Fresno (Cal.) State Coll., 1953—, prof. social work, chmn. dept., 1964—, dir. div. social work. 1965, dean Sch. Social Work, 1968-71; UN adviser, Philippines, 1971—. Cons. in field, 1955—; UN adviser. Indonesia, 1961-62. Vice foreman Fresno County Grand Jury, 1963-64. Bd. dirs. Internat. Inst., Fresno Community Council, Cal. Center Community Devel., Rehab. Enterprises, North Av. Community Center, Citizens Com. on Alcoholism. Served with AUS, 1943-46. Licentiate mem. Royal Soc. Health (Eng.); mem. Council Social Work Edn., Nat. Assn. Social Workers. Am. Assn. U. Profs., Internat. Soc. Community Devel. Author papers in field. Home: 4838 E Brown Av Fresno CA 93703

BRIGHOUSE, GILBERT, educator; b. Hornsea, East Yorks. Eng., May 29, 1906; s. Charles Davidson and Sarah Jessie (Piper) B.; first came to U.S., 1923, naturalized. 1940; student Hymer's Coll., Eng., 1919-23. Univ. Ore.. 1925-27; Ph.B., U. of Chgo., 1930. M.S., 1934; Ph.D., U. of Ia.,1936; m. Helen G. Williams, Aug. 29, 1928 (dec. 1949); children— Beverly Jean, Shirley Ann. Nancy Jo; m.2d, Janice Pheatt, June 29, 1951; children—Jeb, Geralda, Ann. Instr. U. of Ill. 1936-38; asso. prof. psychology Occidental Coll., 1938-42, prof. psychology since 1942, chmn. dept., 1938-55, dir. grad. studies, 1950-55; lectr. psychology Cal. Inst. Tech., 1940-47; sci. cons. U.S. Dept. of Commerce Mission to Germany, specialist on psychology of physically handicapped, 1946-47; clin. psychologist San Marino (Cal.) Pub. Schs., 1945-56. Glendale Guidance and Counseling Service. 1950-54; research asso. Lockheed Aircraft, 1944-45; cons. psychologist to various industries. Fellow Am. Psychol. Assn. (council rep.); mem. So. Cal. Psychol. Assn. (past pres.), Academy Magical Arts, Sigma Xi, Psi Chi, Theta Xi. Clubs: Twilight (Pasadena); Alamitos Bay Yacht; University Personnel. Author (monographs); The Physically Handicapped in Industry. 1946: The Physically Handicapped in German Industry, 1947. Contbr. psychol. publs. Home: 1039 Laguna Rd Pasadena, CA 91105.

BRIGHT, EDGAR ALLEN GORDON, banker; b. New Orleans, May 15, 1895; s. Edgar H. and Ella (Mehle) B.; Ph.B., Yale U. Sheffield Sci. Sch., 1916; m. Ethel Fox, Nov. 29, 1927; children—Edgar Allen Gordon. Jane (Mrs. Maunsel W. Hickey). Partner, Tullis, Craig & Bright, cotton mchts., New Orleans, 1923-56; ltd. partner Merrill Lynch, Pierce, Fenner & Smith, 1957-59, non-voting stockholder, 1959—; chmn. bd. Standard Mortgage Corp., New Orleans, 1964—; pres. AVRICO, 1970—; dir. Maison Blanche, 1921—, Royal St. Louis, Inc., 1958—, Urban Corp., 1970—, Kal-Graphic, Inc., Lawyers Title Co. La. Pres. New Orleans Cotton Exchange, 1948-50. Pres. bd. commrs. Port of New Orleans. 1956-57. Bd. dirs. Tennis Patrons Assn. Greater New Orleans. 1960-64, United Fund Greater New Orleans. 1960-61. Yale Alumni Assn. La., 1924-29, 47-54, Cottage Sch. for Deaf Children, 1958-70; v.p. Information Council Am., 1964—; treas. New Orleans Community Chest. 1965—. Pres. bd. trustees Metairie Park Country Day Sch., 1940-42; bd. dirs. Internat. House, 1965-69. Internat. Trade Mart, 1966—. New Orleans Speech and Hearing Center, 1963-67. Flint-Goodridge Hosp., 1958—, Cultural Attractions Fund, 1964-66. Served to 1st lt., F.A., U.S. Army, 1917-19: AEF in France; served to lt. col. AUS, 1942-45: PTO. Named Rex King of Mardi Gras, 1956; recipient Times- Picayune Loving Cup, 1966. Home: 421 Andubon St New Orleans LA 70118 Office: Baronne Bldg New Orleans LA 70112

BRIGHT, HAROLD ELIAS, banker; b. Reading, Pa., June 5, 1901; s. Albert R. and Celesa F. (Daniels) B.; B.S., U. Pa. Wharton Sch., 1923; m. Dorothy Mauger, Oct. 18, 1933. With Reading (Pa.) Nat. Bank & Trust Co., 1923-33, Farmers & Penn Nat. Bank, Reading, 1933-34; asst. trust officer Am. Bank & Trust Co. Pa., Reading, 1935-40, trust officer, 1940-50, v.p., 1950-56, sr. v.p., 1956-66, exec. v.p., trust officer, 1966-68, pres., sr. trust officer, 1968-69, chmn. trust investment and adminstrv. policy com., also sr. trust officer, 1969—; dir. of sec. Provident Fed. Savs. & Loan Assn., Reading. Trustee, treas. Reading Mus. Found.; bd. dirs. Reading Symphony Orch.; trustee Reading Police Pension Fund; trustee, mem. finance com. Community Gen. Hosp. Mem. Am. Bankers Assn. Home: 1408 Monroe Av Wyomissing PA 19610 Office: PO Box 1102 Reading PA 19603

BRIGHT, HAROLD FREDERICK, univ. administr.; b. Smethport, Pa., Aug. 6, 1913; s. Stanley and Florence K. (Dunn) B.; A.B., Lake Forest Coll., 1937; M.S., U. Rochester, 1944; Ph.D., U. Tex., 1952; m. Elizabeth Korhumel, Mar. 23, 1938; children—Stanley Joseph, Beverly Ann (Mrs. Stephen M. White). Chmn. dept. math. San Angelo (Tex.) Coll., 1941-43, registrar, dir. guidance, 1945-49; asst. prof. math. Denison U., 1943-44, U. Rochester, 1944-45; asso. dir. research Am. Assn. Jr. Colls., 1949-52; specialist operations research and Synthesis Gen. Electric Co., 1957-58; dep. dir. Human Resources Office, George Washington U., Washington, 1952-56, chmn. dept. statistics, 1958-64, dir. Computer Center, 1963-65, asso. dean faculties, 1964-66, v.p. acad. affairs, 1966—, provost, 1969—; cons. in fields, 1956—. Mem. A.A.A.S., Am. Soc. Quality Control, Am. Statis. Assn., Am. Psychol. Assn., Inst. Math. Statistics, Math. Assn. Am., Royal Statis. Soc., Assn. Instl. Research, Sigma Xi, Sigma Pi Sigma. Republican. Episcopalian. Club: Cosmos (Washington). Home: 314 Branch Circle SE Vienna, VA 22180. Office: George Washington Univ Washington DC 20006

BRIGHT, HORACE O., stock broker; b. Cambridge, Mass. Aug. 1, 1895; s. Elmer H. and Mary (Bill) B.; grad. Brown and Nichols Sch., 1913; A.B., Harvard, 1917. With Elmer H. Bright & Co., Boston, 1919-58, partner, 1925-58; ltd. partner Tucker Anthony & R. L. Day, Boston, 1958—; dir. Meuthuen Internat. Mills, Tamco; trustee Holmes Real Estate trust. Mem. N.Y., Boston stock exchanges; gov. Boston Stock Exchange, 1930-66. Treas. Cambridge Civic Assn., 1953-54. Chmn. trustees Boys and Girls Camps, Charlestown, Mass., 1962—; trustee Mount Auburn Hosp., 1955-60, Browne and Nichols Sch., 1966—. Served to 1st lt., inf., U.S. Army, 1917-19: AEF in France. Decorated D.S.C. Home: 165 Brattle St Cambridge MA 02334 Office: 74 State St Boston MA 02109

BRIGHT, JAMES RIESER, educator; b. Pitts., Apr. 28, 1917; s. Jacob and Clara Balthaser (Rieser) B.; B.S. in Indsl. Engring., Lehigh U., 1939; M.S., Columbia, 1950; m. Mary Elizabeth Powell, Nov. 25, 1946; children—Clara Rieser, James Powell, Steven Waller. Test engr. Gen. Electric Co., 1939-40, comml. engr. Internat. Gen. Electric Co., 1940; asst. editor Product Engring., McGraw-Hill, 1945-48, mng. editor, 1948-50, chief editor Modern Material Handling, 1950-54; faculty Harvard Grad. Sch. Bus. Adminstrn., 1954-69, prof., 1960-69; ind. cons.; distinguished vis. prof. U. Tex., Austin, 1968-69, prof., asso. dean Grad. Sch. Bus., 1969—; pres. Indsl. Mgmt. Center, 1954—. Served from 2d lt. to lt. col., Ordnance Corps, AUS, 1940-45. Decorated Bronze Star medal. Mem. Am. Soc. M.E. Author: Automation and Management, 1958; Research Development and Technological Innovation, 1964. Editor: Technological Forecasting for Industry and Government, 1968. Home: 1100 Red Bud Trail Austin TX 78746 Office: Grad Sch Bus Univ Tex Austin TX 78746

BRIGHT, JOHN, clergyman, educator; b. Chattanooga, Sept. 25, 1908; s. John and Elizabeth (Nall) B.; A.B., Presbyn. Coll., Clinton, S.C., 1928, D.D., 1947; B.D., Union Theol. Sem., Richmond, Va., 1931, Th.M., 1933; Ph.D., Johns Hopkins, 1940; m. Carrie Lena McMullen, July 28, 1938; children—Charles Crawford, Robert Nall. Ordained to ministry Presbyn. Ch., 1935; pastor, Durham, N.C., 1936-37, Balt., 1937-40; Cyrus H. McCormick prof. Hebrew, interpretation O.T., Union Theol. Sem., Richmond, Va., 1940—. Served as capt., Chaplain Corps, AUS, 1943- 46: ETO. Mem. Soc. Bibl. Lit. and Exegesis, Am. Oriental Soc., Am. Theol. Soc., Bibl. Colloquium, Pi Kappa Phi. Author: The Kingdom of God, 1953; Early Israel in Recent History Writing; A Study in Method, 1956; A History of Israel, 1959; Jeremiah (The Anchor Bible), 1965; The Authority of the Old Testament, 1967. Contbr. to The Interpreter's Bible; Peake's Commentary on the Bible, 1962; articles to theol. publs. Home: 1204 Confederate Av Richmond VA 23227

BRIGHT, MYRON H., judge; b. Eveleth, Minn., Mar. 5, 1919; s. Morris and Lena A. (Levine) B.; B.S.L., U. Minn., 1941, LL.B., 1947; m. Frances Louise Reisler, Dec. 26, 1947; children—Dinah Ann, Joshua Robert. Admitted to N.D. and Minn. bars; asso. firm Wattam, Vogel & Vogel., Fargo, N.D., 1947-68, partner, 1949-68; judge 8th U.S. Circuit Ct. Appeals, Fargo, 1968—. Bd. dirs. Fargo United Fund, 1965. Chmn. Cass County Democratic Com., 1958-60. Served to capt. AUS, 1942-46: CBI. Mem. Am., N.D. bar assns., Am. Legion, V.F.W. Jewish religion (pres. congregation 1959-62, president's award 1965). Elk. Home: 906 21st Av S Fargo ND 58102 Office: Federal Bldg US Post Office PO Box 2707 Fargo ND 58102

BRIGHT, RINEHART SENSING, mfg. exec.; b. Plaindealing, La., May 21, 1912; s. Robert E. and Nell (Sensing) B.; student Union U., 1930-31; B.S. in Mech. Engring., U. Tenn., 1936; M.S. in Automotive Engring., Chrysler Inst., 1940; m. Anne Mary Magee, Sept. 30, 1942. Instr. mech. engring. U. Tenn., 1936-38; student engr. Chrysler Inst. Engring., 1938-41; mgr. assembly and test Dodge Chgo. plant Chrysler Corp., 1942-45, asst. resident engr. Chrysler div., 1946. supt. engine assembly, 1947-51, mgr. New Orleans Tank Engine plant, 1951-53. mgr. Indpls. plant, 1953-54, v.p. Dodge div., 1954-55, gen. mgr. supply div. Chrysler Corp., 1955, group exec., engine and transmission group, 1956. v.p. corp., dir., V.P. 1956—, operations staff. Mem. Soc. Automotive Engrs., Am. Soc. Tool Engrs., Am. Ordnance Assn., Sigma Alpha Epsilon. Club: Orchard Lake (Mich.) Country. Home: Cranbrook Ct Bloomfield Hills MI 48013 341 Massachusetts Av Detroit MI 48203

BRIGHT, WILLARD MEAD, mfg. exec.; b. N.Y.C., Mar. 26, 1914; s. William Van Horn and Bernice Hartwell (Reynolds) B.; B.S., U. Toledo, 1936, M.S., 1937; postgrad. U. Pitts., 1937-38; A.M., Harvard, 1941, Ph.D., 1942; m. Martha Norris Land, May 15, 1944; 1 son, Willard Mead. Research chemist Kendall Co., Boston, Chgo., 1942-52, asst. lab. dir. Bauer & Black div., 1944-48; lab. dir. Theodore Clark Lab. div., Cambridge, Mass., 1948-52, pres., chief exec. officer, Boston, 1970—; asst. research dir. Lever Bros. Co., 1952-54, research dir., 1954-60, v.p. research and devel., 1960-64, dir., 1962-64; chmn. bd. W. H. Norris Lumber Co., Houston, 1957-64; treas. Border Lumber Co., Weslaco, Tex., 1957-64; v.p., dir. R.J. Reynolds Tobacco Co., 1964-68; sr. v.p., pres. profl. products group, dir. Warner-Lambert Pharm. Co., 1968-70, 1st Nat. Bank Boston, 1970—. Mem. adv. com. on patents U.S. Dept. Commerce, 1966-69. Recipient Gold T award U. Toledo, 1960. Mem. N.A.M. (research com., dir.), Am. Chem. Soc., A.A.A.S., N.Y. Acad. Scis., Assn. Research Dirs., Indsl. Research Inst. (pres. 1967-68), Dirs. Indsl. Research, Corn Refiners Assn. (trustee 1965-68), Am. Found. for Pharm. Edn., Nat. Planning Assn., Phi Kappa Phi. Clubs: University, Chemists (N.Y.C.); The Country (Brookline, Mass.); Forsyth Country (Winston-Salem, N.C.). Home: 31 Lime St Boston MA 02108 Office: 225 Franklin St Boston MA 02110

BRIGHTMAN, EMERSON ELIOT, chain store exec.; b. Roxbury, Mass., Jan. 21, 1916; s. Harold W. and Florence (Pennington) B.; B.A., Dartmouth, 1937; M.B.A., Harvard, 1939; m. Janet A. Altreuter, Jan. 4, 1947; children—Joan, Linda, Robert. With R. H. Macy's, N.Y.C., 1939-40. Bloomingdale's, N.Y.C., 1940-41, Pratt's Fresh Frozen Foods, N.Y.C., 1946-47; with Grand Union Co., East Paterson, N.J., 1947—, sr. v.p., 1967-68, exec. v.p., 1968- -, also dir. Served to capt., Q.M.C., AUS, 1941-46. Mem. Nat. Assn. Food Chains, A.I.M., Supermarket Inst. (treas.). Home: 32 Windermere Rd Upper Montclair NJ 07043 Office: 100 Broadway East Paterson NJ 07407

BRIGHTMAN, ROBERT LLOYD, importer, textile co. exec.; b. Rockville Center, N.Y., July 17, 1920; s. Harold Warren and Florence (Pennington) B.; grad. cum laude, Montclair Acad., 1936, cum laude Phillips Exeter Acad., 1937; B.A., Princeton, 1941; m. Marion Altreuter, Oct. 31, 1942; children—Richard Warren, Shelley Anne, Susan Boyd. With A. Johnson & Co., Inc., N.Y.C., 1946-48; with Johaneson, Wales & Sparre, Inc., N.Y.C., 1948-67, v.p., 1952-64, pres., 1964-67; v.p. Grangesberg Am. Corp., N.Y.C., 1967-68; pres. R.L. Brightman Co., Upper Montclair, N.J., 1967—; dir. purchases West Point-Pepperell, N.Y.C., 1968—. Mem. Nat. Council Am. Importers, Inc., 1954-69, dir., 1956-69, v.p., 1959-61, pres., 1961-63, sr. councillor, 1963-69; mem. nat. panel arbitrators Am. Arbitration Assn., 1958—. Served with USNR, 1942-46. Mem. Swedish C. of C. of U.S.A. (dir. 1965—). Home: 118 Cooper Av Upper Montclair NJ 07043 Office: 111 W 40th St New York City NY 10018

BRIGNONE, CARLOS SANTIAGO, Argentine govt. ofcl.; b. Oliva, Córdoba. Argentina, Oct. 30, 1918; s. Carlos Antonio and Dolores (Lola) Cuquego Brignone; Contador Publico, Buenos Aires U., 1941; M. Pub. Adminstrn., Harvard, 1944; m. Nélida Elena Castelli, Aug. 1, 1942; children—Carlos Alberto, Jorge Luis, Ana Maria, Eduardo Santiago. With Banco Central de la Republica Argentina, 1936-46; ministerio de hacienda, Argentina, 1947-56, adviser, 1957; sub- dir. Nacional de Estadística y Censos, 1950-56; prof. current econ. problems Escula Superior de Economía, Buenos Aires, 1956-57; adviser joint com. econ. devel. UN-Argentina, 1956; mem. census subcom. Inter-Am. commn. for Improvement Nat. Statistics, 1957-58; adviser Pres. of Argentina, 1958; exec. dir. Internat. Bank for Reconstrn. and Devel.; dir. Internat. Finance Corp. 1958-64; financial counsellor Argentine embassy Washington, 1961-64; financial adviser Argentine govt., 1964-66; 1st v.p. Central Bank of Argentina, 1967-68; exec. dir. for Argentina and Peru, Inter-Am. Devel. Bank, 1968-71. Mem. Econometric Soc. Co-editor Mercurio, Weekly, Buenos Aires, 1956-57. Home: 4501 Connecticut Av NW Washington DC 20008 Office: 808 17th St NW Washington DC 20577

BRIGUET, LOUIS JOSEPH, savs. and loan exec.; b. St. Paul, Mar. 6, 1915; s. A. Peter and Amelia (Gay) B.; student parochial and pub. schs., St. Paul; m. Alvene M. Vannelli, Nov. 25, 1942; children—A Peter II, Dennis L., Richard J., Kathleen M. Bus. systems salesman Remington-Rand Co., 1937-38; asst. mgr. Commerce Acceptance Co., 1938-41; br. and dist. mgr. U-CIT Credit Corp., 1945-49; gen. mgr. Danielson Enterprises, South St. Paul, Minn., 1949-56; exec. v.p., sec. United Fed. Savs., South St. Paul, 1956-68, pres., 1969—; pres., dir. Gopher Mining & Refining Co., Bismarck, N.D., 1958—. Mem. adv. com. South St. Paul United Fund, 1963-66, pres., 1961-62; mem. exec. bd. Indianhead council Boy Scouts Am. Trustee St. Paul chpt. A.R.C., Minn. Community Research Council, Automobile Workers Health and Welfare Fund. Served to capt. AUS, 1941- 45. Recipient Community Service award United Fund S. St. Paul, 1962. Mem. U.S., Minn., Twin City (pres. 1963) savs. and loan leagues, Nat. Real Estate Bd., Soc. Residential Appraisers, South St. Paul C. of C. (pres. 1964, Community Service award 1964). Republican. Roman Catholic (trustee). Kiwanian (past treas., dir. S. St. Paul). Home: Route 1 South St Paul MN 55411 Office: 224-28 N Concord St South St Paul MN 55075

BRIL, JACQUES L., criminologist; b. N.Y.C., Sept. 17, 1906; s. Issac L. and Masha (Ravid) B.; ed. Western Mil. Acad., Alton, Ill., Flint (Mich.) Jr. Coll., U. Mich., Washington and Lee Coll.; m. Ethel Wittcoff, June 7, 1936 (dec. 1962); children—Ira Lawrence, Marsha Susan. Began as criminologist, 1929; founded firm Jacques L. Bril, criminology cons. and investigators, N.Y.C., 1931; cons. to dist. attys. Kings and Westchester counties (N.Y.), Somerset County, N.J., atty. gen. N.J., Police Dept., City of Yonkers; collaborated with Father Summers, prof. psychology Fordham U., in devel. of pathometer (lie detector), 1936; authority in field of sci. detection of deception; invented Brilograf and devised technique known as Bril deception test; inventor of listening-in and rec. devices; installed lie detection lab. N.J. State Hosp., Trenton; sec.-treas. 2170 Broadway Corp.; dir. Blue Bell Holdings and Rolling Gardens Corp., Benjamin Franklin Hotel, Smithtown Spa, B & B Farms, Inc. Spl. dep. commr. pub. safety, Yonkers, N.Y.; dep. chief police, Smithtown, L.I.; spl. dep. sheriff, Dade County, Fla. Mem. nat. bd. Am. Orgn. Rehab. through Tng. Fedn., pres. Greater Miami chpt. Mem. Nat. Sheriffs Assn., Am. Inst. Criminal Law and Criminology, Internat. Assn. for Identification (life), Am. Radio Relay League, Nat. Aero. Assn., U.S. Civil Air Patrol, Internat. Assn. Chiefs of Police (life), N.Y. State Assn. Chiefs Police, Nat. Guard Assn. of U.S. Vets Assn., 2d Regiment Ofcrs. Assn., Internat. Assn. Lions Clubs. First lt., comdg. officer communication sect. New York Guard, Capt. 22d Regt. Regimental Intelligence officer; maj.-monitoring officer C.A.P.; lt. col., dir. communications N.E. region U.S. for Aux. USAF. Address: 222 W 77th St New York City NY 10024 and Box 4322 Miami Beach FL 33141

BRILEY, CLIFTON BEVERLY, mayor of Nashville; b. Nashville, Jan. 11, 1914; s. Clifton Weaver and Willie Whithorne (Vaughan) B.; student Sch. Engring., Vanderbilt U., 1929-31; LL.B., Cumberland U., 1932; m. Dorothy Gordon, July 3, 1934; childrenClifton Beverly, Diane (Mrs. P. R. Easterly). Admitted to Tenn. bar, 1932; practiced in Nashville, 1932-50; judge Davidson County, 1950- 63; mayor Met. Nashville and Davidson County, 1963-. Mem. Fed. Hosp. Council; cons. U.S. Civil Service Commn., U.S. Dept. Housing and Urban Devel.; exec. bd. U.S. Conf. Mayors; cons. Md. Constn. Commn.; mem. Pres.' Adv. Commn. on Intergovtl. Relations. Democratic candidate for Tenn. Senate, 1946. Served with USNR, World War II; PTO. Mem. Nat. League Cities (exec. bd., pres. 1969—), Nat. Assn. Counties (exec. bd., past pres.). Home: 1406 Winding Way Nashville TN 37216 Office: Mayor's Office City Hall Nashville TN 37201

BRILEY, JOHN MARSHALL, lawyer, industrialist; b. Monmouth, Ill., Jan. 10, 1905; s. Lewis Henry and Mary Frances (Ryan) B.; A.B., Monmouth Coll., 1927; LL.B., Harvard, 1930; LL.D., Miami (O.) U., Toledo U., Akron U.; m. Dorothy Louise DeWolf, Sept. 8, 1931; children—Suzanne (Mrs. René H. M. Gimbrère), Millicent, John Marshall, Michael Marshall. Admitted to N.Y. bar, 1931, Ohio bar, 1952; asso. firm Shearman & Sterling, N.Y.C., 1930-51, partner, 1941-51; sr. v.p. Owens-Corning Fiberglass Corp., 1957-70, v.p., gen. counsel, 1952- 66; dir. Fed. Prison Industries; chmn. Hotel Pierre, N.Y.C. Ohio chmn. Crusade Freedom, 1959-61. Mem. of the Toledo Bd. Community Relations. Mem. Toledo Port Commn.; chmn. Presdl. Task Force on Prisoner Rehab., 1969-70. Candidate U.S. Senate from Ohio, 1962. Exec. com. Ohio Republican Finance Com., 1947—, state chmn., 1961; del.-at-large Rep. Nat. Conv., 1960, 64; mem. Rep. Nat. Finance Com., 1963—. Trustee, Sec. Toledo Soc. Crippled Children; dir. Jr. Achievement Northwestern Ohio. Chmn. Ohio bd. regents; Sisters of Mercy Provincial bd. regents (vice chmn.); chmn. bd. trustees Mercy Hosp. Decorated Sovereign Mil. Order Knights of Malta. Mem. Internat., Am., N.Y. State, N.Y.C., Ohio bar assns., Internat. Econ. Policy Assn., Am. Enterprise Assn. (trustee), Ohio C. of C. (dir.), Tau Kappa Alpha, Alpha Tau Omega. Roman Catholic. Moose. Clubs: Toledo, Toledo Country, Carranor Hunt and Polo Auto, Belmont Country (Toledo); Harvard, Links (N.Y.C.); Internat. (Washington). Home: Riverwood West River Rd Perrysburg OH 44454 Office: Fiberglas Tower Toledo OH 43604 also 399 Park Av New York City NY 10022

BRILL, DANIEL HERBERT, economist; b. N.Y.C., Apr. 23, 1918; s. Nathaniel M. and Etta (Hasinsky) B.; B.A., N.Y. U., 1936; M.A., Columbia, 1937; student Am. U., 1938-39; m. Charlotte Lobel, Sept. 8, 1940; children—Nicky, Edward. Economist, Bur. Labor Statistics, Washington, 1937-39, 40-43, 46-47; economist to bd. govs. Fed. Res. System, 1947-63, dir. research, 1964-69; Chief economist Fed. Open Market Com., 1965-69, sr. adviser to bd., 1967-69. sr. v.p. Comml. Credit Co., Balt., 1969—. Recipient Rockefeller Pub. Service award, 1954. Club: Cosmos (Washington). Home: 121 Delford Av Silver Spring MD 20904 Office: 300 St Paul Pl Baltimore MD 21202

BRILL, HENRY, psychiatrist, hosp. supt.; b. Bridgeport, Conn., Oct. 3, 1906; s. August Michael and Gussie (Kissel) B.; B.A., Yale, 1928, M.D., 1932; m. Wenonah Beale, Apr. 17, 1948; children—Michael Henry, Jean Malcolm; 1 dau. by previous marriage, Helen Elizabeth (Mrs. Charles Broxmeyer). Intern, resident Pilgrim State Hosp., West Brentwood, N.Y., 1932-38, clin. dir. hosp., 1942-50, dir., 1958—; from instr. to clin. prof. Albany (N.Y.) Med. Coll., 1952-54; professorial lectr. State U. Med. Center at Syracuse, lectr. history psychiatry Columbia Med. Sch., 1957—; dir. Craig Colony, Sonyea, N.Y., 1950-52. From asst. to 1st dep. commnr. N.Y. State Dept. Mental Hygiene, 1952-64; adminstr. N.Y. State Mental Hygiene Research Program, 1952-64; charge narcotic treatment program N.Y. State, 1958-64; vice chmn. N.Y. State Narcotic Addiction Control Commn., 1966-68; chmn. com. clin. drug. evaluation Nat. Inst. Mental Health, 1960-65, com. drug dependence NRC, 1959—; mem. expert panel drug dependence WHO, 1968—; chmn. com. hallicinogenic drugs FDA-Nat. Inst. Mental Health, 1960-70; mem. com. sedatives, stimulating and hallucinogenic drugs Dept. Justice, 1969—; chmn. methadone evaluation com. Columbia Sch. Pub. Health, 1966—; chmn. Narcotic Addiction Control Commn. Suffolk County, N.Y., 1968—; FDA Methadone Com., Fellow Am. Psychiat. Assn. (council 1964-68, chmn. com. nomenclature and statistics 1960); mem. A.M.A. (chmn. com. drug dependence and alcoholism), Am. Coll. Neuropsychopharmacology (pres. 1969), Internat. Coll. Psychopharmacology (past pres.), Eastern Psychiat. Research Assn., Am. Psychopath. Assn. (v.p. 1970.) Home: Box 22 West Brentwood NY 11717 Office: Pilgrim State Hosp West Brentwood NY 11717

BRILL, JOSEPH EUGENE, lawyer; b. Warsaw, Poland, Sept. 16, 1903; s. Max and Renie (Silber) B.; came to U.S., Jan., 1904, naturalized, 1917; ed. Coll. Arts and Scis., N.Y. U., 1921-24; LL.B., Fordham U., 1928; m. Doris Wright Sutton; children—Elizabeth, Victoria, Maxine, Walter. Admitted to N.Y. bar, 1930, and began practice N.Y.C.; asso. with Bainbridge Colby, N.Y.C., 1930-31; asst. U.S. atty., So. Dist. of N.Y., 1931-34; spl. asst. U.S. atty. gen., N.Y.C., 1934-37; mem. firm Brower, Brill & Tompkins, N.Y.C., 1937-38; asst. dist. atty. for N.Y. County by apptmt. of Thomas E. Dewey, 1938; spl. asst. to U.S. atty. gen. in charge Wage and Hour Unit, Dept. of Justice, 1938- 40; mem. firm Brower, Brill & Tompkins, name now Brower, Brill & Gaugel, N.Y.C. Commd. 1st. lt. U.S. Army Air Corps, 1942, capt., 1943, lt. col., adj. gen. troop carrier command. Decorated Bronze Star Medal, Army Commendation Ribbon, also Conspicuous Service Medal. Fellow Am. Coll. Trial Lawyers, Am. Acad. Matrimonial Lawyers; mem. Nat. Assn. Def. Lawyers in Criminal Cases, Am. Bar Assn. N.Y. County Lawyers Assn. Jewish religion. Mason. K.P. Home: 300 E 74th St New York City NY 10021 also Margaretville NY 12455 Office: 233 Broadway New York City NY 10007

BRILL, NORMAN QUINTUS, physician; b. N.Y.C., Aug. 2, 1911; s. Louis and Ella (Applebaum) B.; B.S., Coll. City N.Y., 1930; M.D., N.Y. U., 1934; m. Doris R. Corcoran, Jan. 21, 1937 (dec. 1968); children—James C., Peter L., Mary C.; m. 2d, Alice F. Jennings, May 2, 1970. Practice medicine, specializing in neurology and psychiatry, N.Y.C., 1939-41; pvt. practice, cons. Walter Reed Gen. Hosp., 1946-53; prof., chmn. dept. neurology Georgetown U. Med. Sch., 1946-49; chief research br. neurology and psychiatry div. VA central office, 1946-49; prof. psychiatry U. Cal. Med. Sch., Los Angeles, 1953—, chmn. dept. 1953-67; med. supt. Neuropsychiat. Inst., U. Cal. Med. Center, 1953-67; sr. cons. psychiatry Brentwood VA Hosp., Los Angeles, 1953—; cons. VA, 1966-70, U.S. Navy Neuropsychiat. Research Unit, 1966-70; cons. in psychiatry USAF, 1962—. Bd. regents Nat. Library Medicine, 1961-65. Served from capt. to lt. col., M.C., AUS, 1941-46. Decorated Legion of Merit. Fellow Am. Psychiat. Assn. (com. med. edn., council professions and assns.), Soc. Med. Cons. Armed Forces (com. psychiatry), Am. Psychoanalytic Assn., Am. Coll. Psychiatrists; mem. A.M.A. (former mem. mental health council), A.A.A.S., Internat. Assn. Social Psychiatry, Am. Assn. U. Profs., Navy League, Sigma Xi. Alpha Omega Alpha. Author: Psychiatry in Medicine, 1962; (with other) Treatment of Psychiatric Outpatients, 1967. Contbg. author Comprehensive Textbook of Psychiatry, 1967; Neuropsychiatry in World War II; I. Zone of Interior, 1966. Chmn. adv. editorial bd. History of Neuropsychiatry, Med. Dept. U.S. Army, in World War II, 1967; mem. adv. bd. Internat. Jour. Social Psychiatry. Home: 6911 Oakwood Av Los Angeles CA 90036

BRILLIANT, RICHARD, educator; b. Boston, Nov. 20, 1929; s. Frank and Pauline (Apt) B.; B.A. magna cum laude, Yale, 1951, Ph.D., 1960; LL.B., Harvard, 1954; m. Eleanor Luria, June 24, 1951; children—Stephanie, Livia, Franca, Myron. From asst. prof. to prof., chmn. dept. art history U. Pa., 1962-70; prof. Columbia, 1970—; vis. Mellon prof. fine arts U. Pitts., 1971; admitted to Mass. bar. Fulbright grantee, Rome, 1957-59; fellow Am. Acad. in Rome, 1960-62; Guggenheim fellow, 1967-68; Nat. Endowment for Humanities sr. fellow, 1972-73. Mem. Mas. Bar Assn. Archaeol. Inst. Am., Coll. Art Assn., Am. Numismatic Soc., Soc. Bib. Lit., Hellenic Soc., Phi Beta Kappa. Democrat. Author: Gesture and Rank in Roman Art, 1963; Arch of Septimius Severus in the Roman Forum, 1967. Home: 10 Wayside Lane Scarsdale NY 10583 Office: Dept Art History Columbia Univ New York City NY 10027

BRIM, KENNETH MILLIKAN, lawyer; b. Mt. Airy, N.C., Jan. 21, 1898; s. Thomas L. and Laura (Payne) B.; student Trinity Park Sch., Durham, N.C., 1914-16; A.B., Duke, 1920, student law sch., 1920-21; m. Doris Overton, June 9, 1923 (dec. Apr. 1967); 1 dau., Doris (Mrs. David Schenck). Admitted to N.C. bar, 1921, pvt. practice, Greensboro, 1921-44; mem. firm McLendon. Brim. Holderness & Brooks and predecessors, Greensboro, 1944—, referee bankruptcy, 1929-44; master chancery, 1930-44; dir., gen. counsel Piedmont Natural Gas Co.; gen. counsel Fed. Home Loan Bank of Greensboro. 1955. Chmn. nat. council Duke, 1951, trustee, 1952—, mem. exec. com. bd. trustees, 1962—. Mem. Am., N.C. bar assns., Duke U. Alumni Assn. (pres. 1954), Mchts. and Mfrs. Club, Order of Coif, Pi

Kappa Phi. Republican. Methodist. Rotarian. Home: 106 Sunset Dr Greensboro NC 27408 Office: 440 W Market St Greensboro NC 27402

BRIM, ORVILLE GILBERT, Jr., sociologist, found. exec., b. Elmira, N.Y., Apr. 7, 1923; s. Orville G(ilbert) and Helen (Whittier) B.; B.A., Yale, 1947, M.A., 1949, Ph.D. in Sociology, 1951; m. Kathleen J. Vigneron, May 30, 1944; children—John G., Scott W., Margaret L., Sarah M. Instr. sociology U. Wis., 1952-53, asst. prof., 1953-55; lectr. grad. faculty N.Y. U., 1955-59; sociologist Russell Sage Found., N.Y.C., 1957-64, asst. sec., 1959-64, pres., 1964—. Chmn. bd. dirs. Automation Engrng. Lab., 1959-67; dir. Consumer Behavior, Inc., 1957-61. Mem. enviroment panel U.S. Office Edn., 1962-64, chmn., 1963-64; mem. drug research bd. Nat. Acad. Scis., 1964-66; mem. mental health tng. com. Nat. Inst. Mental Health, 1959-62; chmn. commn. social scis. NSF; nat. adv. food and drug council Dept. Health. Edn. and Welfare; mem. adv. com. Population Council, Smith-Richardson Found. Bd. dirs. Greenwich Hosp. Served as 1st lt. USAAF, 1943-46. Fellow Am. Sociol. Assn., Am. Psychol. Assn., A.A.A.S., Eastern Sociol. Soc. (pres.); mem. Social Sci. Research Council (past com. socialization and social structure). Soc. Research Child Devel. Clubs: Century, Cosmos, Yale (N.Y.C.). Author: Sociology and the Field of Education, 1958; Education for Child Rearing, 1959; Personality and Decision Processes, 1962; Intelligence, Perspectives 1965, 66; Socialization after Childhood: Two Essays, 1966; American Beliefs and Attitudes Toward Intelligence, 1969; The Dying Patient, 1970. Cons. editor Child Development, 1958-61; Merrill-Palmer Quar., 1962-63; Sociology of Education, 1963—; Sociometry, 1957- 62. Home: 172 Shore Rd Old Greenwich CT 06830 Office: Russell Sage Found 230 Park Av New York City NY 10017

BRIMBLE, ALAN, museum exec.; b. Langwith, Eng., June 5, 1930; s. Arthur George and May (Emery) B.; B.A. with honors, Edmund Hall, Oxford (Eng.) U., 1952, M.A., 1958; fellow Chartered Inst. Secretaries. Came to U.S., 1967. Asst. sec. Crompton Parkinson Ltd., London, 1960-62; music and arts programmes organizer BBC TV, 1962-67; sec., controller City Art Museum, St. Louis, 1969—. Mem. Citizens Com. Met. St. Louis Zoo-Museum Dist., 1970-71. Bd. dirs. Internat. Inst., St. Louis, 1970—. Served with RAF, 1948-49. Mem. Am. Assn. Museums, Am. Mgmt. Assn. Home: 412 Union Blvd St Louis MO 63108 Office: City Art Museum St Louis MO 63110

BRIMMER, ANDREW FELTON, educator, govt. ofcl.; b. Newellton, La., Sept. 13, 1926; s. Andrew and Vellar (Davis) B.; B.A., U. Wash., 1950, M.A., 1951; postgrad. (Fulbright fellow) U. Bombay (India), 1951-52; Ph.D., Harvard, 1957; LL.D., Neb. Wesleyan U., Marquette U., 1968, L.I.U., 1969, Oberlin Coll., 1969, Tufts U., 1970, Colgate U., 1970, Atlanta U., 1970; m. Doris Millicent Scott, July 10, 1953; 1 dau., Esther Diane. Economist, Fed. Res. Bank, N.Y.C., 1955-58; asst. prof. Mich. State U., 1958-61, Wharton Sch. Finance and Commerce, U. Pa., 1961-66; dep. asst. sec. Dept. Commerce, Washington, 1963-65, asst. sec. for econ. affairs, 1965-66; mem. Fed. Res. Bd., 1966- -. Mem. Fed. Res. Central Banking Mission to Sudan, 1957; cons. SEC, 1962-63. Trustee Taukegee Inst., Negro Student Fund, Salk Inst. for Biol. Studies; bd. overseers Harvard; adv. com. Grad. Sch. Bus., Atlanta U. Served with AUS, 1945-46. Named Govt. Man of Year, Nat. Bus. League, 1963; recipient Arthur S. Flemming award, 1966; Ruswurm award, 1966; Capital Press Club award, 1966, Golden Plate Award Am. Acad. Achievement, 1967. Fellow Am. Acad. Arts and Scis.; mem. Am. Econ. Assn., Am. Finance Assn., Assn. for Study Negro Life and History (pres. 1970—), Council on Fgn. Relations. Author: Survey of Mutual Funds Investors. 1963; Life Insurance Companies in Capital Market. 1962. Contbr. articles to profl. jours. Office: Bd Govs Fed Res System 20th and Constitution Av NW Washington DC 20551

BRINAS, AMADO R., banker; b. Manila, P.I., Feb. 25, 1913; s. Antonino and Esperanza (del Rosario) B.; LL.B., U. P.I., 1936; LL.M., U. Santo Tomas, 1938; B.C.S., Jose Rizal Coll., 1941; A.M., Columbia, 1952; m. Mercedes Evangelista, Jan. 29, 1942; children—Percival, Cynthia (Mrs. Solomon Carpio), Amanda. Clk., computer Bur. Lands, Manila, 1935-36; law clk., income tax examiner Bur. Internal Revenue, 1937-39; with Dept. Finance P.I., 1939-55, chief tech. staff, 1950-55; asst. to monetary bd., dir. exchange control dept. Central Bank P.I., Manila, 1955-59, dep. gov., 1962—; professorial lectr., later head dept. taxation and tariff U. of East, Manila, 1950-62; prof. Ateneo Grad. Sch. Bus., Manila, 1964. Campaign chmn. for advance solicitation for fund drives Community Chest P.I. Nat. Red Cross, P.I. Anti-TB Soc., P.I. Cancer Soc., and others. Named Distinguished alumnus Jose Rizal Coll., Manila, 1965. Mem. P.I. Tax Inst., Bankers Club Manila. Home: 67 Horseshoe Dr Quezon City Philippine Island Office: Central Bank PI Aduana St Manila Philippine Islands

BRINCKERHOFF, CHARLES M., engr.; b. Mpls., Mar. 15, 1901; s. William and Marybelle (Sharp) B.; B.A., Columbia, 1922, Met.E., Sch. Mines, 1925; m. Florence Andreen, Oct. 11, 1926; 1 dau., Carol (Mrs. Koetzman). With Phelps-Dodge Corp., Ariz, Inspiration Consol. Copper Co., Andes Copper Mining Co., 1925-48; gen. mgr. Chile Exploration Co., 1948-56; v.p. Andes Copper Mining Co., Chile Exploration Co., 1956-57, exec. v.p., 1957-58; pres., dir. Anaconda Co., 1958, vice chmn. bd., chief exec. officer, 1964-65, chmn. bd., chief exec. officer, 1965-69, chmn. exec. com., cons., 1969—, also dir.; chmn. bd., dir., pres., subsidiary and affiliated cos.; dir. ACF Industries. Inc. Served with U.S. Army, World War I. Decorated Bernardo O'Higgins Order of Merit (Chile); recipient George Vincent Wendell medal Columbia, also Egleston medal; Gold medal Chilean Mining Soc. Mem. Internat. C. of C. (trustee U.S. council), Mining and Metall. Soc. Am., Pan Am. Soc. U.S., Am. Inst. Mining, Metall. and Petroleum Engrs. (Saunders medal), Holland Soc. of N.Y. (trustee 1967—, Gold medal), Sigma Xi. Presbyn. (trustee). Clubs: University, Mining (N.Y.C.); Union (Santiago, Chile). Contbr. articles to profl. jours. Home: 784 Park Av New York City NY 10021 Office: 25 Broadway New York City NY 10004

BRIND, CHARLES ALBERT, lawyer; b. Albany, N.Y., Sept. 16, 1897; s. Charles Albert and Mary Eleanor (Gordon) B.; A.B., Union Coll., 1919, J.D., 1968; LL.B., Albany Law Sch., 1922; LL.D., Keuka Coll., 1941; L.H.D., N.Y. Inst. Tech., 1970, m. Laura Stuart Hutchison, June 9, 1923; children—Charles Albert, III (dec.), David Hutchison, Nancy Virginia (Mrs. William L. Wallace). Admitted to N.Y. bar. 1922, U.S. bar, 1952; claim dept. United Traction Co., 1920-23; asso. atty. N.Y. Dept. Edn., Albany, 1923-33, prin. atty., dir. div. of law, 1933-40; gen. counsel State Dept. Edn., State U. N.Y., 1940-68, also N.Y. State Bd. Regents, N.Y. State Tchrs. Retirement System, 1940-68, Dormitory Authority State of N.Y.; v.p., dir., George R. Cooley, Inc., investments; past pres. Northeastern N.Y. Med. Service, Inc. Lectr. State U. N.Y. at Albany, Union Coll., Hofstra Coll., Cornell U., N.Y. State Law Tchrs. Coll., Columbia, Syracuse U. Trustee Philatelic Found. Past pres. Assn. of State Civil Service Employees. Mem. Legislative Commn. on Extension Civil Service to Local Units of Govt.; pres. Asso. Hosp. Service Capitol Dist. of N.Y. (Blue Cross); bd. govs. Albany Med. Center; mem. Council of Sch. Supts. (Cities and Villages); bd. visitors Union U. Sch. Nurses. Bd. dirs. Albany Tng. Sch. for Practical Nurses; Served with R.O.T.C., 1918. Mem. Alumni Assn. Delta Chi (v.p.), Albany County Bar Assn., N.Y. State Tchrs. Assn., Delta Chi, Phi Beta Kappa (past pres. Upper Hudson chpt.). Presbyn. (trustee). Mason. Club: Ft. Orange Stamp (past pres.). Author: (with A.K. Getman) Story of State Government (N.Y.), 1942. Editor: State Employee, 1935-42. Contbr. articles to ednl. jours. Home: 30 N Pine Av Elsmere NY 12054 Office: Dormitory Authority State of NY Normanskill Blvd Elsmere NY 12054

BRINEGAR, CLAUDE STOUT, oil co. exec.; b. Rockport, Cal., Dec. 16, 1926; s. Claude Leroy and Lyle (Rawies) Stout; B.A. in Econs., Stanford 1950, M.S. in Math. Statistics, 1951, Ph.D. in Econs., 1954; m. Elva Jackson, July 1, 1950; children—Claudia, Meredith, Thomas. Research asst. Food Research Inst., Stanford, Cal., 1950-53; econ. cons. Emporium-Capwell Corp., San Francisco, 1950-53; with Union Oil Co. Cal., 1953—, mgr. econs. and corp. planning, 1962-65, v.p. econs. and corp. planning, 1965-66, pres. div. Pure Oil Co., 1965-68; pres. Pure Transp. Co., 1966—, Union 76 div., Los Angeles, 1968—, also sr. v.p., mem. exec. com., dir., 1968—; dir. Internat. Speedway Corp., Daytona Beach, Fla. Extension instr. U. Cal. at Los Angeles, 1955-60, Cal. Inst. Tech., 1957, Whittier Coll., 1956. Bd. dirs. Los Angeles County Mental Health Assn., 1964-65. Served with USAAF, 1945-47. Mem. Young Presidents Orgn., Am. Statis. Assn., Am. Petroleum Inst. (dir.), Phi Beta Kappa, Sigma Xi. Clubs: California (Los Angeles); Mid-America (Chgo.). Contbr. articles to profl. jours. Home: 15 Georgett Rd Rolling Hills CA 90274 Office: Union Oil Center Los Angeles CA 98017

BRINEGAR, DAVID FRANKLIN, newspaper editor b. Rulo, Neb., Sept. 2, 1910; s. Thomas P. and Rebecca Way (Marsh) B.; student U. Ariz., 1927-30, Phoenix Coll., 1941; m. Lorette Cooper, Oct. 2, 1937; 1 dau., Becky Lorette. Reporter, Ariz. Daily Star, Tucson, also Ariz. Republic, Phoenix, 1926-42; mng. editor Ariz. Times, Phoenix, 1946-47, capitol reporter, columnist, 1947-48; engaged as pub. relations counsel, 1948-56; asso. editor Ariz. Daily Star, 1956-61, exec. editor, 1961-. Active local A.R.C., United Community Campaign. Served with AUS, 1942-46. Mem. Delta Chi. Democrat. Presbyn. Clubs: Ariz. Press (pres. 1948) (Phoenix); Tucson Press. Contbr. articles to mags. Home: 6532 E Speedway Blvd Tucson AZ 85710 Office: 208 N Stone Av Tucson AZ 85701

BRINEGAR, WILLARD CLOUSE, physician; b. Luverne, Ia., Mar. 24, 1913; s. George Henry and Cora (Clouse) B.; B.Ed., Ill. State U., 1933; B.Sc., U. Neb., 1935, M.D., 1937; m. Rosa Wordeman, Aug. 28, 1936; children—Willard Charles, David Jonathan Frederick. Intern Columbia Hosp., Milw., 1937- 39; resident Gardner (Mass.) State Hosp., 1939-41, Norfolk (Neb.) State Hosp., 1941-42; asst. supt., then supt. N.H. State Hosp., Concord, 1942- 47; supt. Mental Health Inst., Cheroke, Ia., 1948-69, dir. dept. med. genetics, dir. residency program in psychiatry, 1949-69; med. dir. N.E. Mental Health Clinic, Norfolk, Va., 1969—; cons. Sioux Valley Meml. Hosp., Cherokee. Chmn. Ia. Bd. Eugenics, 1953-69. Recipient SSS medal, 1945. Mem. A.M.A., Am. Psychiat. Assn., Ia. Neuropsychiat. Soc. (past pres.), Cherokee County Med. Soc. (past pres.), Inter-Univ. Forum for Educators in Community Policy. Mason (32, Shriner). Contbr. articles to profl. jours. Address: PO Box 1209 Norfolk NB 68701

BRINER, DREW CORNELIUS, ins. co. exec.; b. Phil., July 16, 1910; s. Andrew Cornelius and Rosanna (Austin) B.; student U. Pitts., 1930-31; m. Hildegarde J. Weingand, Feb. 5, 1947; children—Andrea Kathleen, Marica Ruth. Br. mgr., gen. adjuster Gen. Adjustment Bur., Inc., N.Y.C., 1929-56; mgr. Winchester Assos., N.Y.C., 1956-57; v.p. Nat. Union Ins. Co., Pitts., 1958-68, Lexington Ins. Co., Boston, 1965-68; regional adjuster Gen. Adjustment Bur., 1968- -. Mem. Loss Execs. Assn. (pres. 1965, exec. com. 1966—), Ins. Club Pitts. Club: Drug and Chemical (N.Y.C.). Home: 616 Scrubgrass Rd Pittsburgh PA 15216. Office: Greentree Rd Pittsburgh PA 15220

BRINER, LEWIS ANDREW, clergyman, educator; b. Lewistown, Pa., Nov. 28, 1917; s. Lewis Edward and Ruth Lydia (Stine) B.; A.B. magna cum laude, Albright Coll., 1939; B.D. (Monroe scholar 1943), Oberlin Coll., 1943; student Union Theol. Sem., N.Y.C., 1946-47; D.D., Coe Coll., 1959; m. Mildred Rosine Woodward, May 31, 1942; children—Janet Lynd, Karen (dec.). Ordained to ministry Presbyn. Ch., 1943; pastor in Md., N.Y., Pa., 1943-58; teaching fellow Oberlin (O.) Coll., 1942-43; vis. lectr. Beaver (Pa.) Coll., 1950- 58; sec. gen. div. vocation and ministry Bd. Christian Edn., United Presbyn. Ch., 1959-61; dean of chapel, Lane prof. pastoral theology and liturgics McCormick Theol. Sem., Chgo., 1961-70; co-pastor First Presbyn. Ch., Kalamazoo, 1970—. Vice pres. Ministry Studies Bd., 1960-61; exec. com. dept. ministry Nat. Council Chs., 1959- 61; bd. dirs., exec. com. Greater Phila. Councils Chs., 1955-58; chmn. religious activities United Fund Greater Phila., 1958; exec. sec. Joint Com. 9 on Christian Edn. Program in Colls., 1959-61; mem. council theol. edn. United Presbyn. Ch., 1959-61; cons., dir. office of worship United Presbyn. Ch. U.S.; mem. Theol. Faculties Union Chgo., 1961—; mem. nat. adv. com. on worship and music Presbyn. Chs. in U.S.A., 1970—, intersynodical com. Student Christian Movement Middle Atlantic Region, 1955-59. Bd. dirs. Westminster Found. of U. Pa., 1954-57. Served to lt. comdr., chaplain corps, USNR, 1945-46. Mem. Am. Assn. Sem. Profs. in Practical Fields, Societas Liturgica. Author articles. Home: 2509 Frederick Av Kalamazoo MI 49001

BRINGS, LAWRENCE MARTIN, publisher; b. St. Paul, Sept. 29, 1897; s. Lee Brings and Bertha (Haugen) B.; A.B., Gustavus Adolphus Coll., 1920, A.M., 1925; m. Ethel Mattson, Aug. 26, 1921 (dec.); 1 son, Keith; m. 2d, Nettie A. Johnson, Jan. 9, 1961. High sch. tchr., 1920- 21; head dept. speech No. State Tchrs. Coll., Aberdeen, S.D., 1921- 23; instr. speech U. Minn., 1923-26; pres., dir. dept. oratory Mpls. Sch. Music, Oratory and Dramatic Art, 1923-25; prof. speech Luther Theol. Sem., St. Paul, 1923-46, Northwestern Theol. Sem., Mpls., 1925- 49; founder, pres. Northwestern Coll. Speech Arts, Mpls., 1926-51; pres. Northwestern Press, 1926—, T. S. Denison & Co., 1944—. Brings Press, 1951—, Denison Yearbook Co., 1952—; lectr., dramatic reader. Pres. Minn. Protestant Found., Central Luth. Ch. Found.; trustee Union City Mission of Mpls., Goodwill Industries Mpls., Minn. Council of Chs., Mpls. United Hosp. Fund, Count Folke Bernadotte Meml. Found. Served in U.S. Army, World War I. Mem. USCG League, Internat. Platform Assn., Nat. Assn. Tchrs. Speech, Nat. Thespian Dramatic Soc. (hon.), Citizens League of Mpls., Mpls. Civic Council, Am. Legion, Phi Kappa Delta, Phi Beta (hon.). Republican. Lutheran. Mason (32, Shriner), Rotarian. Clubs: Minneapolis Auto, Compiler, editor numerous books, most recent being Minnesota Heritage, 1960; One-Act Dramas and Contest Plays, 1962; Rehearsal-less Skits and Plays, 1963; Gay Nineties Melodramas, 1963; Golden Book of Christmas Plays, 1963; What God Hath Wrought, 1969. Home: 4350 Brookside Ct Minneapolis MN 55431 Office: 5100 W 82d St Minneapolis MN 54431

BRINIG, MYRON, author; b. Mpls.; s. Maurice and Rebecca (Coin) B.; student N.Y. U. and Columbia, 1917-21. Author: Singermann, 1929; Wide Open Town, 1931; This Man Is My Brother, 1932; The Flutter of an Eyelid, 1933; Out of Life, 1934; Sun Sets in the West. 1935; The Sisters, 1937; May Flavin, 1938; Anne Minton's Life. 1939; All of Their Lives. 1941; The Family Way, 1942; The Gamble Takes a Wife, 1943; You and I, 1945; Hour of Nightfall, 1947; No Marriages in Paradise, 1949; Footsteps on the Stair, 1950; The Sadness in Lexington Avenue, 1951; Street of the Three Friends, 1953; The Looking-Glass Heart, 1958.

BRINK, CAROL RYRIE, author; b. Moscow, Ida., Dec. 28, 1895; d. Alexander Ryrie and Henrietta (Watkins) Ryrie; student Portland Acad. 1912-14, U. Ida., 1914-17, D.Litt., 1965; B.A., U. Cal., 1918; m. Raymond W. Brink, July 12, 1918; children—David Ryrie, Nora Caroline. Began writing stories for children about 1925. Awarded Newberry medal for year's most distinguished contbn. to juvenile lit., 1935; ann. award So. Cal. Council Lit. Children, 1966. Mem. Nat. League Am. Pen Women, Cal. Writers Guild, Phi Beta Kappa, Theta Sigma Phi, Gamma Phi Beta. Presbyn. Club: Faculty Women's Author: Caddie Woodlawn, 1935 (Newbery Medal, 1935); Harps in the Wind (adult biography), 1947; Stopover (novel), 1951; Family Grandstand (Jr. Lit. Guild selection), 1952; The Highly Trained Dogs of Prof. Petit (Children's Book Club selection), 1953; The Headland (award Friends Am. Writers), 1955; Family Sabbatical (Jr. Lit. Guild selection), 1956; Strangers in the Forest, The Pink Motel, 1959; The Twin Cities, 1961; Chteau Saint Barnabé, 1962; Snow in the River (McKnight Family Lit. Fund award 1966; prize Nat. League Am. Pen Women), 1964; Andy Buckram's Tin Men (Jr. Lit. Guild selection), 1966; Winter Cottage, 1968; Two Are Better Than One, 1968. Editor: Best Short Stories for Children, 1935; Best Short Stories for Boys and Girls, 1936, 37, 38, 39. Contbr. stories and verse for children to pop. mags. Home: 6036 Bellevue Av La Jolla CA 92037

BRINK, CHARLES BERNARD, govt. ofcl.; b. Kansas City, July 31, 1910; s. Vincent Bernard and Anne Rae (Linder) B.; A.B., U. Mo., 1932; M.Sc., Western Res. U., 1936, certificate in psychiat. social work, 1937; m. Dorothy Mary Reid, Apr. 21, 1934; children—Sarah Anne, David Vincent, Nancy Patricia, Steven Charles. Exec. dir. Family Service Soc., Lansing, Mich., 1943-44, 46-48; lectr. Mich. State Coll., 1946-48; exec. dir. Family Service Soc. of St. Louis County, Clayton, Mo., 1948-51; dean Sch. Social Work, Wayne State U., Detroit, 1951-63; dean Sch. Social Work, U. Wash., Seattle, 1963-71; dep. sec. Wash. Dept. Social and Health Services, Seattle, 1971—. Mem. social work adv. com. VA; bd. dirs., v.p. Council on Social Work Edn.; mem. Gov.'s Com. on Pub. Assistance. Served as 1st lt., M.C., AUS, 1944-46. Mem. Nat. Assn. Social Workers, Alpha Kappa Delta, Delta Upsilon. Home: 10652 Exeter NE Seattle WA 98125

BRINK, DAVID LIDDELL, educator; b. St. Paul, July 7, 1917; s. Morse Chapin and Naneen (Blanchard) B.; B.S., U. Minn., 1939, Ph.D., 1949; m. Annie Mary Gould, May 22, 1943; children—Nancy Margaret (Mrs. Paul E. Darley), David Liddell, Patricia Anne. Research chemist Salvo Chem. Corp., Rothschild, Wis., 1943-45; group leader lignin research Mead Corp., 1949-53; chief chem. sect. Weyerhauser Co., 1954-57; forest products chemist, lectr. wood chemistry U. Cal. at Berkeley, 1958-66, prof. forestry and forest products chemist, 1966—. Served with USNR, 1945-47. Mem. Am. Chem. Soc., T.A.P.P.I. (chmn. Golden Gate sect. 1963-64, chmn. wood chemistry com. 1964-70), Forest Products Research Soc. (chmn. No. Cal. sect. 1962- 63), Sigma Xi, Xi Sigma Pi, Alpha Zeta, Gamma Sigma Delta, Gamma Alpha. Home: 1068 Woodside Rd Berkeley CA 94708 Office: 1301 S 64th St Richmond CA 94804

BRINK, FRANK, Jr., biophysicist, educator; b. Easton, Pa., Nov. 4, 1910; s. Frank and Lydia (Wilhelm) B.; B.S., Pa. State Coll., 1934; M.S., Cal. Inst. Tech., 1935; Ph.D., U. Pa., 1939; m. Marjory Gaylord, May 1, 1939; children—Patricia, David Warner. Research asst. Johnson Research Found., U. Pa., 1937-38, research fellow, 1938-40, Lalor Found. fellow, 1939-40, lectr. biophysics 1941-46, asst. prof., 1946-49; instr. physiology Cornell Med. Coll., N.Y.C., 1940-41; asso. prof. biophysics Johns Hopkins, 1949-53, prof., biophysicist Rockefeller U., N.Y.C., 1953—, dean grad. studies, 1958—. Divisional com. biol. and med. sci. NSF, 1953- 59; chmn. Pres.'s com. for Nat. Medal Sci., 1963, 64. Mem. Nat. Acad. Scis. (editorial bd. procs. 1970—), Biophys. Soc., A.A.A.S., Am. Acad. Arts and Scis., Soc. Gen. Physiology, Am. Physiol. Soc. Editor Biophys. Jour., 1960-63. Home: Box 443 RD 1 Pleasant Valley Rd Titusville NJ 08560 Office: Rockefeller U 66th St and York Av New York City NY 10021

BRINK, ROYAL ALEXANDER, educator; b. Woodstock, Ont., Can., Sept. 16, 1897; s. Royal Wilson and Elizabeth Ann (Cuthbert) B.; B.S.A., Ont. Agrl. Coll., 1919; M.S., U. Ill., 1921; D.Sc., Harvard, 1923; postgrad. (NRC fellow) Institut f. Vererbungsforschung, Berlin, U. Birmingham, 1925- 26, Cal. Inst. Tech., 1939-39; m. Edith Margaret Whitelaw, Dec. 27, 1922 (dec. May 1962); children—Andrew Whitelaw, Margaret Alexandra; m. 2d, Joyce Hickling, Oct. 19, 1963. Came to U.S., 1920, naturalized, 1933. Chemist, Western Can. Flour Mills, Winnipeg, Man., Can., 1919-20; Emerson fellow in biology Harvard, 1921-22; asst. prof. of genetics U. Wis., 1922-27, asso. prof., 1929-31, prof., 1931-68, emeritus prof. genetics, 1968—, chmn. dept. 1939-51. Haight Travelling fellow U. Wis., 1960-61; NSF Sr. Postdoctorate fellow, 1966-67. Fellow A.A.A.S.; mem. Am. Genetics Assn., Genetics Soc. Am. (pres. 1957), Bot. Soc. Am., Am. Acad. Arts and Scis., Am. Soc. Naturalists (pres. 1963). Nat. Acad. Scis., Wis. Acad. of Scis., Arts and Letters, Sigma Xi (pres. Wis. chpt. 1940-41), Phi Sigma, Phi Eta. Club: University. Editor: Heritage from Mendel, 1967; mng. editor Genetics, 1952-56. Contbr. numerous research papers to biol. jours. Home: 4237 Manitou Way Madison WI 53711

BRINK, WILLIAM PAUL, clergyman; b. Chgo., Sept. 21, 1916; s. Paul W. and Cora (Wagenaar) B.; B.A., Calvin Coll., 1938; B.Th., Calvin Sem., 1941; m. Alta Mae Ibershof, July 25, 1941; children—Paul William, Esther Jean (Mrs. Cornelius A. Leugs), John H., Daniel Jay, Stephen Robert. Ordained to ministry Christian Ref. Ch., 1941; pastor, Goshen, Ind., 1941-44, Chgo., 1944-48, Grand Rapids, Mich., 1948-53, Holland, Mich., 1953-64, 2d Christian Ref. Ch., Fremont, Mich., 1964-70; stated clk. Christian Ref. Ch., 1970—. Pres. Young Calvinist Fedn. N. Am., 1958-70, Gen. Synod Christian Reformed Ch., 1966-69. Author: Author: Learning Doctrine from the Bible, 1965. Address: 5305 Queensbury St SE Grand Rapids MI 49508

BRINKER, JOHN HENRY, Jr., indsl. equipment co. exec.; b. Cleve., May 31, 1914; s. John Henry and Marion (Crawford) B.; A.B., U. Rochester, 1936; M.B.A. with high distinction, Harvard, 1947; m. Virginia Grosvenor Bryant, Feb. 10, 1940; children—Ann Grosvenor, Lynn Crawford, John Henry. Sales engr. Pfaulder Co., Rochester, N.Y., 1937-42; gen. sales mgr., dir. marketing A.O. Smith Corp., Milw., 1947-55, gen. mgr. Permaglas div,, 1955-59, v.p. corp., 1957, v.p., Chgo., 1964—; exec. v.p., dir. J.I. Case Co., Racine, Wis., 1959-60; exec. v.p. Cherry Burrell Corp., 1960-64; pres. Glascote Products, Inc., Cleve., 1964-65. Chmn. fund appeal St. Mary's Hosp., 1956. Trustee U. Rochester; bd. dirs. YMCA. Served from ensign to lt. comdr. USNR, 1942-46. Mem. Ill. C. of C. Presbyn. Rotarian. Clubs: Chicago; Knollwood; Union League (N.Y.C.). Home: 1185 Wilson Dr Lake Forest IL 60045 Office: 8501 W Higgins Rd Chicago IL 60631

BRINKER, RUSSELL CHARLES, educator; b. Easton, Pa., Dec. 7, 1908; s. Edgar Walter and Emily Matilda (Arnold) B.; B.S., Lafayette Coll., 1929; M.S., U. Minn., 1933, C.E., 1939; postgrad. Worcester Poly. Inst., 1937, Columbia, 1944; m. Ruth Meta Thomas, June 20, 1933 (dec. July 1964); m. 2d, Mildred Letellier, Nov. 23, 1966. Detailer, Am. Bridge Co., 1929-30; instr. U. Minn., 1930-35, asst. prof. structural engring., 1940-41, asso. prof. civil engring., 1945-47; instr. U. Hawaii, 1935-36, asst. prof. engring., 1937-40, prof. civil engring., 1966- 67; exchange tchr. civil engring. Worcester Poly. Inst., 1936-37; asso. prof. U. So. Cal., 1947- 50; prof. civil engring. Va. Poly. Inst., 1950-57, head dept., 1951-57; editorial dir. engring. books Ronald Press Co., 1957- 58; prof. civil engring. Tex. Western Coll., 1958-61, N.M. State U., 1961-69, prof., head civil engring. dept., 1962-66, vis. prof., 1969—. Served from lt. (j.g.) to rear adm., CEC, USNR, 1941-57. Decorated Bronze Star medal with combat V. Mem. Am. Soc. C.E., Am. Congress Surveying and Mapping, Am. Soc. Photogrammetry, Am. Soc. for Engring. Edn., Sigma Xi, Chi Epsilon, Tau Beta Pi. Author: Elementary Surveying, 1961, 5th edit., 1969; 4300 Review Questions for Surveyors, 1970; (with Austin) Noteforms for Surveying Measurements, 1957; (with others) 1301 Review Problems from EIT and Engineering Registration Examinations, 1960, rev. as 1777 Review Problems from EIT and Engineering Registration Examinations. 1967, Cons. editor civil engring. series Internat. Textbook Co., 1959—. Contbr. tech articles to mags. Home: 10432 Tropicana Circle Sun City AZ 85351

BRINKER, WADE OBERLIN, veterinarian, educator; b. Fulton, O., Oct. 11, 1912; s. Frank Leroy and Elma (Oberlin) B.; D.V.M., Kan. State Coll., 1939; M.S., Mich. State U., 1947; m. Eleanor Bayles, May 29, 1939; children—Gerald, Judith, Jack. With Coll. Vet. Medicine, Mich. State U., East Lansing, 1939—, prof., head dept. surgery and medicine, 1957-67, prof. dept. small animal surgery and medicine, 1967—. Served from 1st lt. to capt., Vet. Corps, AUS, 1941-46. Recipient Distinguished Service award; 1959, Centennial award for distinguished service Kan. State U., 1963; Distinguished Faculty award Mich. State U., 1969. Mem. Am. (award 1959), Mich. (pres. 1954-55) vet. med. assn., Conf. Research Workers N.A., Am. Coll. Vet. Surgeons (pres. 1968-69), Sigma Xi, Phi Kappa Phi, Phi Zeta. Author: (with others) Canine Surgery, 1952, rev., 1965. Home: 5009 N Okemos Rd East Lansing MI 48823

BRINKER, WALTER EVANS, army officer; b. Mt. Pleasant, Pa., Jan. 29, 1917; s. Walter B. and Ruth (Evans) B.; student U. Ia., 1934-35; B.S., U.S. Mil. Acad., 1939; M.B.A. (Baker scholar), Harvard, 1950; m. Agnes Marie Kane, Jan. 13, 1943; children—Walter Evans, Nicole (Mrs. Wm. A. Schnarr), Ann (Mrs. Richard Dreher), Marie, Mylene. Commd. 2d lt. U.S. Army, 1939, advanced through grades to maj. gen., 1967; comdr. F.A. Bn., Alaska, 1943, Europe, 1944- 47; War Dept. gen. staff, 1947-48; asst. prof., asso. prof. econs. and internat. relations U.S. Mil. Acad., 1950-53; asst. to chief of staff SHAPE, Paris, France, 1954-57; staff, faculty U.S. Army Arty. and Missle Sch., 1958-59; dir. dept. tactics and combined arms Ft. Sill, Okla., 1959-60; comdr. 52d Arty. Group, 1960-61; Dept. Army staff, personnel, chief of distbn. div., 1961-62; J-1 exec. Office Joint Chiefs Staff, 1962; asst. dir. Army Budget operations, 1963-65; comdg. gen. 1 Corps Group, Arty. Cp. St. Barbara, Korea, 1965-66; comptroller U.S. Army Europe, Heidelberg, Germany, 1966-67, dir. plans, programs and budget, personnel Dept. Army staff, 1967-68, asst. dep. chief of staff for personnel, 1968-70. Pres., dir. USAA Fund Mgmt. Co.; v.p., dir. USAA Capital Growth Fund, 1970—; v.p. USAA Life Ins. Co. Decorated D.S.M., Legion of Merit, Bronze Star medal. Mem. Phi Gamma Delta. Clubs: Century, Harvard Business School (Boston). Home: 10102 Sunflower Lane San Antonio TX 78213 Office: 4119 Broadway San Antonio TX 78215

BRINKERHOFF, DERICKSEN MORGAN, educator; b. Phila., Oct. 4, 1921; s. Robert Joris and Marion (Butler) B.; grad. Taft Sch., 1939; A.B., Williams Coll., 1943; M.A., Yale, 1947; postgrad. U. Zurich, 1948-49; Ph.D., Harvard, 1958; m. Mary Dean Weston, Dec. 20, 1946; children—Derick W., Elizabeth, Jonathan D., Caroline. Teaching fellow Harvard, 1949-50; instr. Brown U., 1952-55; asso. prof., head history dept. R.I. Sch. Design, 1955-59, chmn. div. liberal arts, 1956-59; asso. prof. Pa. State U., 1961-62, Tyler Sch. Art, Temple U., Phila., 1962-65; chmn. dept. art U. Cal. at Riverside, 1965-71, prof., 1967—. Trustee Riverside Art Assn., 1968—. Served with AUS, World War II. Summer fellow Belgian Am. Ednl. Found., 1959; sr. fellow classical studies Am. Acad. in Rome, 1959-61; grantee Am. Philos. Soc., 1960-61. Mem. Am. Numismatic Soc. (¾ 0 prize seminar 1952), Am. Research Center Egypt, Archaeol. Inst. Am., Art Historians So. Cal., Coll. Art Assn. Am., Internat. Assn. Classical Archaeology, Los Angeles County Mus. Art, Soc. Promotion Roman Studies. Author articles, monograph. Home: 4985 Chicago Av Riverside CA 92507

BRINKHOUS, KENNETH MERLE, pathologist; b. Clayton County, Ia., May 29, 1908; s. William and Ida (Voss) B.; student U.S. Mil. Acad., 1925; A.B., State U. Ia., 1929, M.D., 1932; D. Sc., U. Chgo., 1967; m. Frances E. Benton, Sept. 5, 1936; children—William Kenneth, John Robert. Asst. in pathology State U. Ia., 1932-33, instr., 1933-35, asso. in pathology, 1935-37, asst. prof., 1937-45, asso. prof., 1945-46; prof. pathology U. N.C., Chapel Hill, 1946-62, alumni distinguished prof., 1962—. Mem. hematology study bd. NIH, USPHS, 1948-52, chmn. 1959-62, chmn. pathology study section, 1957-59, National Advisory Heart Council, 1969- -; mem. bd. editors Jour. Lab. and Clin. Medicine, 1948-53, Proc. Soc. Exptl. Biology and Medicine, 1950-53, Blood, 1950-65. Mem. panel on blood coagulation NRC, 1951-62, chmn., 1954-62; chmn. med. adv. com. Hemophilia Found., 1954—; mem. Nat. Bd. Med. Examiners, 1957-59; mem. sci. adv. bd. Armed Forces Inst. Pathology, 1957—, chmn., 1964-65; mem. sci. adv. bd. Nat. A.R.C., 1965—; sec. gen. Internat. Com. Hemostasis and Thrombosis, 1965—, Served from capt. to lt. col. M.C., U.S. Army, 1941-46; col., Med. Res. Corps, 1946—. Co-recipient Ward Burdick award Am. Soc. Clin. Pathologists, 1940, recipient same, 1963; recipient O. Max Gardner award, 1961; N.C. award, 1969; Internat. Heart Research award, 1969, Fellow A.A.A.S., Med. Soc. N.C., Coll. Am. Pathologists; mem. Assn. Am. Physicians, Internat. Soc. Hematology, Internat. Acad. Pathology, A.A.A., Am. Assn. Pathologists and Bacteriologists, (sec., treas. 1968- -), Am. Soc. Clin. Pathologists, Am. Soc. Exptl. Pathology (pres. 1965- 66), Fedn. Am. Socs. Exptl. Biology (pres. 1966-67), Univs. Asso. Research and Edn. Pathology (pres. 1964-68). Central Soc. Clin. Research, Soc. Exptl. Biol. and Medicine, Am. Assn. U. Profs., Phi Beta Kappa, Sigma Xi, Phi Lambda Upsilon, Alpha Omega Alpha, Phi Chi. Bd. editors Thrombosis et Diathesis Haemorrhagica, 1961—. Home: Chapel Hill NC 27514

BRINKLEY, DAVID, news commentator; b. Wilmington, N.C., July 10, 1920; s. William Graham and Mary (West) B.; m. Ann Fischer, Oct. 11, 1946; children—Alan, Joel, John. Reporter, Wilmington (N.C.) Star-News, 1938-41; reporter, bur. mgr. United Press Assns., various so. cities, 1941-43; news writer, broadcaster radio and TV, NBC, Washington, 1943—, Washington corr., 1951—. Recipient duPont award, Peabody award, Sch. Bell award, other journalism awards. Club: Cosmos (Washington). Office: 4001 Nebraska Av NW Washington DC 20016

BRINKLEY, HOMER LEE, co-ops. exec.; b. Linneus, Mo., Mar. 26, 1898; s. Floyd O. and Maude Emily (Howe) B.; B.S., La. State U., 1919, postgrad., 1922; m. Alice May Brogan, Sept. 5, 1925 (dec.); 1 son, Homer (dec.); m. 2d, Dorothy Fowler Munster, Nov. 27, 1965. Mgr. cotton livestock farms, La., 1919-21; instr. agr. La. State U., 1922; state supr. La. State U., farm trainees war VA, 1923; county agt. Calcasieu Parish, La., 1924-28; gen. mgr. Am. Rice Growers Coop. Assn. and Exchange (covering rice belt La., Tex., Ark.), Lake Charles, La., 1928- 52; exec. v.p. Nat. Council Farmer Coops., 1952—. Dir. Security Nat. Bank, Falls Church, Va., chmn. audit com. Former dir. Central Bank for Co-ops., FCA, Washington; past trustee, mem. exec. com. Am. Inst. Cooperation, Washington; cons. Am. delegation Conf. on Internatl. Orgn., San Francisco; mem. U.S. delegation 3d Inter-Am. Conf. on Agr., Caracas, Venezuela, 1945; del. White House Conf. on Conservation, 1962; chmn. Agrl. Internat. People-to-People Program, 1962; mem. U.S. Food for Peace Council, 1962; adv. com. World Food Congress, 1963; past mem. govtl. adv. coms. Dir. Found. for Am. Agr. pres. Nat. Council Farmer co-ops., exec. com., chmn. labor-mgmt. com., 1944-45; past pres. La. Council Farmer Coops.; past mem. fgn. agrl. trade policy com. U.S. Dept. Agr.; bd. suprs. La. State U., 1940-54, Citzens League S.W. La. (former pres.); mem. U.S. delegation FAO, Geneva, 1957, Rome, 1953; del. Internat. Fedn. Agr. Producers, Rome, 1953, chmn. N.Am. regional conf. 1962; chief Presdl. Fgn. Agrl. Trade Mission Asia, 1954; mem. Dept. Agr. nat. com. on agrl. research, policy, 1952-57, Pres.'s Spl. Com. on Civilian Nat. Honors, 1956; adviser U.S. delegation to Gen. Agreement on Trade and Tariffs, Geneva, 1956, 61-62; adv. com. on rural rehab. Dept. Agr., 1961-64; exec. com. U.S. Freedom from Hunger Found., 1961-65; mem. com. on co-ops. AID. Served 2d lt. U.S. Army, 1918; capt. La. N.G., ORC, 1925-35. Mem. Am. Legion, Lambda Chi Alpha, Alpha Zeta. Methodist. Club: Metropolitan (Washington). Home: Malbrook Falls Church VA 22044 Office: 6551 Brooks Pl Falls Church VA 22044

BRINKLEY, JACK THOMAS, congressman; b. Faceville, Ga., Dec. 22, 1930; s. Lonnie Elester and Pauline (Spearman) B.; student Young Harris Coll., 1947-49, Okla. A. and M. Coll., 1952; LL.B. cum laude, U. Ga., 1959; m. Alma Lois Kite, May 29, 1955; children—Jack Thomas, Fred Alen II. Sch. tchr., Ga., 1949-51; admitted to Ga. bar, 1958; asso. firm Young, Hollis & Moseley, Columbus, Ga., 1959-61; partner firm Coffin & Brinkley, Columbus, 1961- 66; mem. Ga. Ho. of Reps., 1965-66; mem. 90th-92d congresses from 3d dist. Ga. Fund raising chmn. Muscogee-Chattahoochee chpt. Nat. Found., 1966, Ga. vol. chmn., 1968. Served to 1st lt. USAF, 1951-56. Mem. Ga., Columbus bar assns., Younger Lawyers Club of Columbus (pres. 1963-64), Am. Legion, Blue Key, Gideons. Democrat. Baptist. Mason. Home: 4108 Appalachian Way Columbus, GA 31907. Office: Cannon House Office Bldg Washington DC 20515

BRINKLEY, WILLIAM CLARK, author; b. Custer, Okla., Sept. 10, 1917; s. Daniel Squire and Ruth (Clark) B.; student William Jewell Coll., 1936-37; B.A., U. Okla., 1940; spl. student Yale Drama Sch., 1961-62. Reporter. Daily Oklahoman, Oklahoma City, 1940-41, Washington Post, 1941-42, 49-51; successively corr., asst. editor, staff writer Life mag., 1951-58. Served to lt. USNR. 1942-46. Mem. Phi Beta Kappa. Clubs: Nat. Press (Washington); Overseas Press (N.Y.C.). Author: Quicksand, 1948; Don't Go Near the Water, 1956; The Fun House, 1961; The Two Susans, 1962; The Ninety and Nine, 1966. Address: 1200 Nolana Av McAllen TX 78501

BRINKMAN, GABRIEL RICHARD, educator; b. Indpls., Dec. 3, 1924; s. John Henry and Mary Frances (Bartsch) B.; A.B., Our Lady of Angels Sem., Cleve., 1947; student St. Joseph Sem., Teutopolis, Ill., 1947-51; B.S., Quincy (Ill.) Coll., 1952; M.A., Cath. U. Am., 1954, Ph.D., 1957. Joined Order of Friars Minor, 1943, ordained priest Roman Catholic Ch., 1951; instr. philosophy Our Lady of Angels Sem., 1955-57; asso. prof. sociology Quincy Coll., 1957-63, prof., 1970—, chaplain, 1958-60, pres., 1963-70. Mem. adv. bd. Adams County chpt. A.R.C. Mem. Am., Am. Cath. sociol. socs., Am. Correctional Assn., Am. Acad. Polit. and Social Sci. Address: Quincy Coll Quincy IL 62301

BRINKMANN, HEINRICH WILHELM, educator; b. Hannover, Germany, Nov. 29, 1898; s. Christian and Elizabeth (Heimsoth) B.; A.B., Stanford, 1920; A.M., Harvard, 1923, Ph.D., 1925; postgrad. U. Goettingen, 1923-24; m. Elizabeth Kellogg, June 18, 1932; 1 dau., Betsy Jane. Instr., asst. prof. Harvard, 1925-33; asso. prof. math. Swarthmore (Pa.) Coll., 1933-43, prof. 1948-69, chmn. math. dept., 1952—, Edward Hicks Magill prof. math., 1957-65, Albert L. and Edna Pownall Buffington prof. math., 1965-69, prof. emeritus, 1969—. Mem. Am. Math. Soc., Math. Assn. Am. (gov. 1954-57), Am. Assn. U. Profs., Sigma Xi. Home: Wallingford Arms Wallingford PA 19086

BRINNER, HAROLD ALLAN, chem. co. exec.; b. St. Louis, Mar. 31, 1917; s. Robert and Claire (Setzekorn) B.; B.S., B.A., Washington U., St. Louis, 1938; m. Alita Mattick, Mar. 1, 1941; children—Richard A. and Roger E. (twins). Mgr., Price Waterhouse & Co., C.P.A.'s, St. Louis, 1949-54; with Malinckrodt Chem. Works, St. Louis, 1954—, treas., 1957, v.p., 1961, also dir., now sr. v.p., treas.; dir. Mallinckrodt Chem. Works Ltd., Montreal, Can., Labs. Rey-Mol, S.A. de C.V., Tialpam, Mexico. Bd. dirs. Asso. Industries Mo., 1966—. Served as ensign USNR, 1945-46. Mem. Financial Execs. Inst. Home: 11549 Clayton Rd St Louis MO 63131 Office: 3600 N 2d St St Louis MO 63160

BRINNER, HOWARD J., ry. exec.; b. 1914; married. With Norfolk & Western Ry., Roanoke, Va., 1951—, comptroller, 1966—. Served with USNR, World War II. Office: 8 N Jefferson St Roanoke VA 24011*

BRINNER, WILLIAM MICHAEL, educator; b. Alameda, Cal., Oct. 6, 1924; s. Fred and Sadie (Weiser) B.; B.A., U. Cal. at Berkeley, 1948, M.A., 1950, Ph.D., 1956; m. Lisa Johanna Kraus, Sept. 23, 1951; children—Benjamin Elon, Leyla Anat, Rafael Jonathan. Faculty U. Cal. at Berkeley, 1956—, prof. Near Eastern langs., 1964—, chmn. dept., 1965-70. Bd. dirs. Near Eastern Lang. and Area Center, 1965- 70, Center Arabic Study Abroad, 1967-70. Lectr. Harvard, spring 1961; mem. exec. com. Am. Research Center Egypt, 1968—, Am. Inst. Iranian Studies, 1968-70; mem. joint com. Near and Middle East. Am. Council Learned Socs. Social Sci. Research Council, 1966-70, chmn., 1968-69; cons. U.S. Office Edn., 1965-68. Research fellow Harvard U. Center Middle Eastern Studies, fall 1960; grantee Near Eastern studies Am. Council Learned Socs.-Social Sci. Research Council, 1961-62; Guggenheim fellow, 1965-66; Fulbright-Hays Faculty research award, 1970-71. Mem. Medieval Acad. Am., Am. Oriental Soc., (dir. 1967—), Middle East Studies Assn. (dir. 1967-68, pres. 1970), Am. Assn. Tchrs. Arabic (chmn. 1967-68). Author: Advanced Arabic Readers, vol. I and II, 1961-62; Chronicle of Damascus 1389-1397, 2 vols., 1963; Sutro Library Hebraica: A Handlist, 1967. Mem. adv. bd. Internat. Jour. Middle East Studies, 1968—. Home: 753 Santa Barbara Rd Berkeley CA 94707

BRINNIN, JOHN MALCOLM, author; b. Halifax, N.S., Can., Sept. 13, 1916 (parents Am. citizens); s. John Thomas and Frances (Malcolm) B.; B.A., U. Mich., 1941; postgrad. Harvard, 1941-42. Dir., Poetry Center, N.Y.C., 1949-56; prof. English, Boston U. Recipient Gold medal for distinguished service to poetry Poetry Soc. Am., 1955; award Nat. Inst. Arts and Letters, 1968. Author: (poetry) The Garden is Political, 1942, The Lincoln Lyrics, 1942, No Arch, No Triumph, 1945. The Sorrows of Cold Stone, 1951, Skin Diving in the Virgins, 1970; (biography) Dylan Thomas in America, 1955, The Third Rose: Gertrude Stein and Her World, 1959; Arthur, The Dolphin Who Didn't See Venice; William Carlos Williams; The Selected Poems of John Malcolm Brinnin, 1965. Editor: (with Kimon Friar) Modern Poetry: American and British, 1951; A Casebook on Dylan Thomas, 1960; The Poems of Emily Dickinson, 1960 (with Bill Read) The Modern Poets; An American-British Anthology; Selected Operas and Plays of Gertrude Stein, 1970. Home: King Caesar Rd Duxbury MA 02332 Office: Boston U Commonwealth Av Boston MA 02215

BRINSFIELD, SHIRLEY DELONAS, mfg. co. exec.; b. Seattle, Nov. 6, 1922; s. Elzie Delonas and Sylvia Ann (McGuire) B.; B.A., U. Wash., 1949; LL.B. (editor Law Rev. 1951-52), Columbia, 1952; m. Sumiko Itoi, Sept. 5, 1948; children—Shawn Delonas, Mark Taylor. Admitted to N.Y. bar, 1953; with T. Roland Berner, atty., N.Y.C., 1952-56, Frederick P. Glick, atty, N.Y.C., 1956-60; v.p. Technograph Printed Electronics, Winston-Salem, N.C., 1960; spl. asst. to chmn. and pres. Curtiss-Wright Corp., 1960-65, gen. counsel 1961-63, gen. mgr. electronics div., 1963-65, adminstrv. v.p., 1965-67, exec. v.p., 1967-70; dir. Lynch Corp., 1965—, pres., 1968-70; dir. Dorr-Oliver, Inc., 1968—, Stamford, Conn., chmn. exec. com., 1968—, pres., 1969—, chief exec. officer, 1971—; dir. United Jersey Banks, Peoples Trust of N.J. Bd. overseers Fairleigh Dickinson U. Served with USAAF, 1942-45. Mem. Assn. Bar City N.Y., N.Y. County Lawyers Assn., N.Y. Patent Law Assn., Assn. U.S. Army, Phi Beta Kappa. Home: 39 Moeser Pl Old Tappan NJ 07675 Office: 77 Havemeyer Lane Stamford CT 06904

BRINTON, JAMES E., univ. dean; b.; Fessenden, N.D., Mar. 21, 1916; s. Charles MacKay and Elizabeth (Mueller) B.; B.S. in Journalism, U. Ore., 1939; A.M. in Journalism, Stanford, 1952, Ph.D. in Mass Communication, 1956; m. Thelma Maxine Gillette, June 7, 1941; children—Ann Louise (Mrs. George Rice III), David James, Mary Catherine. Reporter, then mng. editor Bend (Ore.) Bull., 1939-48; editor Bend Pilot, 1949-51; asso. prof. journalism Stanford, 1956-65; dean Sch. Journalism, U. Colo., Boulder, 1965—. Served with AUS, 1943-46; ETO. Mem. Assn. Edn. Journalism, Am. Assn. Schs. and Depts. Journalism, Phi Beta Kappa, Sigma Delta Chi, Alpha Delta Sigma. Co-author: The Newspaper and Its Public; also articles. Home: 2270 Bluebell Av Boulder CO 80302

BRINTON, SAMUEL JERVIS, Jr., banker; b. Ardmore, Pa., Aug. 15, 1923; s. Samuel Jervis and Edith V. (Ketcham) B.; B.A., Williams Coll., 1948; M.B.A., N.Y. U., 1953; grad. Stonier Grad. Sch. Banking and Trusts, 1959; m. Helen Marguerite Baker, Aug. 12, 1943; children—Samuel Jervis III, Patricia Carr, James Christopher. With Nat. Newark & Essex Bank, sr. trust officer, 1964—, sr. v.p., 1969—; dir. Art Wire & Stamping Co., Bio-Med. Scis., Inc. Pres. Newark Jr. C. of C., 1952-53, Upper N.J. chpt. Nat. Multiple Sclerosis Soc., 1961-63; treas. Child Service Assn. Newark, 1959—; mem. adv. bd. Babies Hosp., Newark, 1964—. Trustee Boys' Clubs Newark, 1961—, Fannie E. Rippel Found., 1967—. Kessler Inst., 1967—; Marcus L. Ward Home, 1968—. Served with AUS, 1943-46. Mem. Williams Alumni Assn. (pres. No. N.J. chpt. 1961-63), Delta Upsilon. Republican. Clubs: Morris County Golf (Convent, N.J.); Essex (Newark). Home: Normandy Pky Convent Station NJ 07961 Office: 744 Broad St Newark NJ 07102

BRIODY, GEORGE MICHAEL, Jr., savs. and loan assn. exec.; b. Chgo., May 6, 1927; s. George Michael and Evelyn L. (Vincent) B.; B.A. cum laude, Notre Dame U., 1950; J.D., DePaul U., 1955; grad. Sch. Savs. and Loan, 1959; m. Alice L. Woods, June 9, 1956; children—George Michael III, Margaret Frances, Patricia Louise, James Everest. With Fairfield Savs. & Loan Assn., Chgo., 1950—, sr. exec. v.p., 1955-65, pres., 1966—; admitted to Ill. bar. 1955. Served with AUS, 1945-46. Mem. Am., Ill, Chgo. bar assns., Chgo. C. of C., Delta Theta Phi. Kiwanian, Lion. Home: 1307 Bonnie Glen Lane Glenview IL 60025 Office: 1601 Milwaukee Av Chicago IL 60647

BRISBIN, ALBERT WARD, govt. ofcl.; b. Dayton, Tex., Dec. 7, 1910; s. Arthur Wesley and Annie Laurie (Simmons) B.; student U. Tex., Austin, 1929-32; m. Roberta Winslow, July 14, 1931; children—A. Winslow, Anthony B. Adminstrv. positions Nat. Youth Adminstrn., Waco, Tex., 1936-42; supervisory adminstrv. officer VA, San Antonio, 1945-56; mgmt. positions Internal Revenue Service, Washington, 1956-61, asst. to dep. commr., 1961-66, asst. commr. planning and research, 1966—. Served to maj. AUS, 1942-45; ETO. Decorated Bronze Star medal, Purple Heart; recipient Meritorious Service award Treasury Dept., 1965. Mem. Am. Soc. Pub. Adminstrn., Tax Inst. Am., Fedn. Tax Adminstrs. (trustee). Home: 1362 4th St SW Washington DC 20024 Office: 1111 Constitution Av Washington DC 20224

BRISCO, MILO MARTIN, oil co. exec.; b. Maud, Okla., Nov. 7, 1912; s. John Marion and Mattie (Moss) B.; student U. Okla., 1930-32, 33-34, 40; m. Lucile Frances Solomon, Nov. 1, 1940; children—Susan Blair (Mrs. Thomas A. Larson), Martha Frances (Mrs. William E. Dee III). With Tropical Oil Co., 1935- 46, Andian Nat. Corp., 1946-48, Internat. Petroleum (Co.) Ltd., 1948-57; exec. v.p., dir. Internat. Petroleum Co. Ltd., 1957-61, pres., dir., 1961-66; pres. Andian Nat. Corp., 1955-57, Esso Colombiana, 1955- 57; v.p., dir. Standard Oil Co. (N.J.), 1966-68, exec. v.p., dir. 1968- 69, now pres., dir.; dir. 1st Nat. City Bank, 1st Nat. City Corp. Dir. Internat. Exec. Service Corps. 1966—. Pres. United Fund Dade County (Fla.), 1965; chmn. 1970 fund drive N.Y. Urban Coalition, Inc. Bd. dirs. Econ. Devel. Council of N.Y.C., Council for Financial Aid to Edn., Inc. Trustee, U. Miami (Fla.), 1967—. Mem. Am. Inst. Mining, Metall. and Petroleum Engrs., Am. Petroleum Inst. (dir. 1969—), Council on Fgn. Relations, Brookings Instn., Phi Delta Theta. Episcopalian. Clubs: Sleepy Hollow Country (Scarborough-on-Hudson, N.Y.); Winged Foot Golf (Mamaroneck, N.Y.); Economic (N.Y.C.); Presidents'. Home: 60 Sutton Pl South New York City NY 10022 Office: 30 Rockefeller Plaza New York City NY 10020

BRISCOE, BIRDSALL, architect; b. Harrisburg, Tex., June 10, 1876; s. Andrew Birdsall and Annie Frances (Payne) B.; student San Antonio Acad., Tex. A. and M. Coll., U. Tex.; m. Ruth Dillman, 1927. Specializing in residences. Served to maj., inf., U.S. Army, World War I. Fellow A.I.A. Author: (fiction) In the Face of the Sun, 1935, Spurs from San Isidro, 1951. Contbr. tech. articles, short stories to nat. mags. Home: 2317 Claremont Lane Houston TX 77019

BRISCOE, MARTHA BROWN HIGLEY, former coll. trustee, civic worker; b. Boulder, Colo., Sept. 23, 1909; d. Alden and Martha (Chadbourne) Brown; A.B., Vassar Coll., 1931; M.A., Radcliffe Coll., 1937; m. John D. Briscoe, June 23, 1934; children—John A., Alden F. Alumna trustee Vassar Coll., 1963-71; bd. regents U. Hartford (Conn.), 1963-66. Sec. League Women Voters, Cambridge, Mass., 1936-39, bd. dirs., Sallisbury, Conn., 1946-50, Conn., 1948-52, pres. Conn., 1953- 57, mem. nat. bd., 1958-60, 62-64, 1st v.p., 1960-62, trustee ednl. fund, 1960-62, trustee overseas edn. fund, 1958-64, pres., 1964-70; mem. Housatonic Regional High Sch. Bd., 1946-55,

Salisbury Bd. Edn., 1950-53, Gov. Conn. Com. Full Employment, 1948, Conn. Flood Recovery Com., 1955, Conn. 3d Merc. Minimum Wage Bd., 1950, Conn. Personnel Appeal Bd., 1957—; chmn. 6th Beauty Shop Wage Bd. Conn., 1957; mem. edn. com. President's Commn. Status Women, 1963. Bd. dirs. Asso. Alumnae Vassar Coll., 1950-53. Mem. Am. Civil Liberties Union, N.A.A.C.P., Fgn. Policy Assn. Democrat. Club: Vassar (pres. Northwestern Conn. 1957-58). Address: Silent Meadow Farm Lakeville CT 06039

BRISCOE, RALPH OWEN, communications co. exec.; b. Trenton, Mich., Nov. 15, 1927; B.A., Kenyon Coll., 1950; M.B.A., Harvard, 1952; m. Joan Trefry, Aug. 24, 1952; children—Ralph Owen, Donald, Stephen, Linda, Lisa. Financial staff Ford Motor Co., 1953-56, Curtiss-Wright Corp., 1956-57; with CBS, Inc., N.Y.C., 1958—, controller, 1963-65, v.p. finance, 1965-69, group pres., 1969—. Served with USAF, 1952-53. Home: 5 Suncliff Dr Tarrytown, NY 10591. Office: 51 W 52d St New York City NY 10019

BRISSON, FREDERICK, theatrical producer; b. Copenhagen, Denmark, Mar. 1917; s. Carl Brisson; student Rossall Coll., Fleetwood, Eng.; m. Rosalind Russell. Asso. Producer Gaumont-British, Eng.; prod. motion pictures in Eng., Two Hearts in Three-Quarter Time, Prince of Arcadia; exec. Joyce-Selznick Agy., Hollywood; talent agy. rep. Brit. and Am. talent, Eng.; jr. partner Vincent Agy., Hollywood; producer Broadway plays Pajama Game, Damn Damn Yankees, New Girl in Town, The Gazebo, The Pleasure of His Company, Five Finger Exercise, Under the Yum Yum Tree, The Caretaker, First Love, Alfie, Generation, The Flip Side, Coco; producer films including The Velvet Velvet Touch, Never Wave at a Wac, The Girl Rush, Pajama Game, Five Finger Exercise, Under the Yum Yum Tree, Damn Yankees, Generation, Mrs. Pollifax -Spy. Spl. cons. to sec. of war WW II, also lt. col. AAC, chief office radio propaganda. Decorated Legion of Merit; King Christian X medal (Denmark); recipient N.Y. Drama Critics award for Five Finger Exercise; Perry awards for Pajama Game, Damn Yankees. Club: Racquet and Tennis (N.Y.C.). Office: Brisson Prodns Inc 745 Fifth Av New York City NY 10022

BRISTOL, BENJAMIN HIEL, banker; b. Naugatuck, Conn., June 19, 1896; s. Edgar H. and May C. (Rexford) B.; student Worcester Acad., 1914-15; B.S., Mass. Inst. Tech., 1918; m. Lida C. Brannon, June 24, 1933; children—Edgar H., Eleanor C., William L. With Foxboro Co., 1919—, pres., dir., 1944-62. chmn. bd., 1962-67; with Foxboro Nat. Bank, 1938—, v.p., 1942-63, pres., 1963-67, now chmn. bd., dir.; dir. Sentry Co. Trustee, Worcester Acad., Mass. Meml. Hosp.; trustee, former pres. bd. trustees Norwood Hosp. Served with USN, 1918-19. Mem. Sci. Apparatus Makers Am., Instrument Soc. Am. (hon.). Home: 28 Union St Foxboro MA 02035

BRISTOL, JAMES DAVID, mgr. profl. baseball club; b. Macon, Ga., June 23, 1933; s. Thomas Bruce and Aline (Edwards) B.; m. Betty Jean Greenwood, May 31, 1952; children—James Milchael, Laura Kathryn. With Cin. Reds Baseball Club, 1951, mgr. farm system, 1957-66, mgr. Reds, 1966; now mgr. Milw. Brewers Baseball Club. Served with AUS, 1953-55. Methodist. Mason. Home: Box 204 Andrews NC 28901 Office: Milw Brewers Baseball Club Milwaukee County Stadium S 44th St off Bluemound Rd Milwaukee WI

BRISTOL, LEE HASTINGS, Jr., ch. orgn. exec.; b. Bklyn., Apr. 9, 1923; s. Lee Hastings and Elizabeth (Wigton) B.; A.B., Hamilton Coll., 1947; postgrad. Grad. Inst. Internat. Studies, Geneva, Switzerland, U. Geneva, also Conservatoire de Musique, Geneva, 1947-48; L.T.C.L., Trinity Coll. Music, London, 1947; HH.D., Los Angeles Conservatory, 1955; Litt.D., Webber Coll., 1957; Mus.D., Dickinson Coll., 1957; LL.D., Mo. Valley U., 1961, Findlay Coll., 1961; Mus.D., Combs Coll. Music, 1965; L.HD., Hobart and William Smith colls., 1965, Temple U., 1966; Ped D., Ricker Coll., 1968; LL.D., Hamilton Coll., 1968; m. Louise Wells, May 20, 1950; children—Elizabeth, Henry Platt, Sara, Lee Hastings III. Asst. to pres. Bristol-Myers Co., N.Y.C., 1948-49, home research staff, dir. products div., 1951, asst. advt. mgr., 1951-52, advt. mgr., 1952-56, dir. pub. relations, 1957-62; stage mgr. TV prodn. dept. NBC, 1949-50; trainee Doherty, Clifford, Steers & Shenfield, Inc., advt., 1950-51; pres. Westminster Choir Coll., Princeton, N.J., 1962-69; vice chmn., exec. sec. Joint Commn. on Ch. Music of Episcopal Ch., 1969—. Dir. Laymen's Movement for a Christian World, Rye, N.Y., 1949-58, pres., 1954-55; faculty mem. Creative Problem- Solving Inst., State U. N.Y. at Buffalo, 1956-69; chmn. Greater N.Y. campaign Assn. for Help Retarded Children, N.Y.C., 1957-59, hon. chmn., 1959-60; co-chmn. nat. campaign Am. Nurses Found., 1960-61; hon. faculty U.S. Army Mgmt. Sch., Ft. Belvoir, Va., 1960-61; dir. Atlantic Corp., Newark, 1961—. Mem. regional pub. relations adv. com. YMCA, 1959—. Trustee All Saints' Ch., Bay Head, N.J., 1947—, Creative Edn. Found., Buffalo, 1955-70; (pres. 1960-68); bd. dirs. N.Y. Philharmonic Symphony Orch.; trustee Berkeley Div. Sch., New Haven, 1956-62, 65-70, Westminster Choir Coll., 1957-70, Miss Mason's Sch., 1958-69, Princeton Pub. Library, 1960-61, Princeton Chamber Orch., 1964-66; bd. advisers Edward W. Root Art Center, Hamilton Coll., Clinton, N.Y., 1958—; Presser Found., 1969— , Diocese of N.J. Music Commn., 1969, Hamilton Coll., 1971, Union Theol. Sem., 1971—, John Jay and Eliza Watson Found., 1969—, Lillia Babbitt Hyde Found., 1970—. Recipient Outstanding Civilian Service award Dept. Army, 1962, Bishop of N.J. Medal of Honor, 1966, Partner in Edn. award Salem Coll., Man of the Year award Greater Princeton C. of C., 1969. Mem. Hymn Soc. Am. (exec. com. 1948—), Am. Guild Organists (nat. council 1964—), Am. Bible Soc. (trustee 1968—), N.J. Hist. Soc. (trustee 1968—), Pilgrims of U.S., Pub. Relations Soc. Am., Royal Coll. Organists, Royal Sch. of Church Music, Phi Beta Kappa, Sigma Phi, Alpha Delta Sigma. Episcopalian (lay reader 1943—, vice chmn. laymen's work Province II, 1959-64). Clubs: Century Assn., University (N.Y.C.); Nassau (Princeton, N.J.); Essex (Newark); Bay Head (N.J.) Yacht; Manasquan River Golf (Brielle, N.J.); Bedins Brook (Skillman, N.J.). Author: Hymns for Children and Grown-ups, 1952; Seed for a Song, 1958; Developing the Corporate Image, 1960. Composer anthems, sacred music, collections of songs. Contbr. articles and music profl. jours. Home: 210 Mercer St Princeton NJ 08540

BRISTOL, MORRIS CORNELIUS, lawyer, piano mfg. co. exec.; b. Cin., July 14, 1903; s. Morris Nutting and Mary (McCloskey) B.; LL.B., U. Cin., 1926; m. Margaret Petersen, May 30, 1928; 1 dau., Nancy Jane (Mrs. Thomas G. Parker). Admitted to Ohio bar, 1926, Ill. bar, 1942; practiced in Cin., 1926-36; mem. firm Harmon, Colston, Goldsmith and Hoadly, Cin., 1936-41; corporate counsel Wurlitzer Co., Chgo., 1941-45, v.p., gen. counsel, 1945-65, sr. v.p., gen. counsel, 1965—; dir. L.E. Myers Co. Mem. Am., Ohio, Chgo. bar assns. Club: Union League (Chgo.). Home: 1033 Bristol Rd New Richmond OH 45157 Office: 105 W Adams St Chicago IL 60603

BRISTOL, NORMAN, food co. exec.; b. Bronx, N.Y., June 14, 1924; s. Lawrence and Bell (Allchin) B.; grad. Phillips Exeter Acad., 1939-41; A.B., Yale, 1944; student Columbia Law Sch., 1947-49; m. Doreen Kingan, Mar. 28, 1953; children—Charles L., Norman, Alexander, Barnaby. Admitted to N.Y. bar, 1950, Mich. bar, 1954; with firm Root, Ballantine, Harlan, Bushby & Palmer, N.Y.C., 1949-53; with Kellogg Co., Battle Creek, Mich., 1954—, asst. gen. counsel, 1958-64, sec., 1960—, gen. counsel, 1964—, v.p., 1968—. Mem. Gull Lake Community Schs. Bd. Edn., 1963-70, pres., 1965-67. Served to lt. (j.g.) USNR, 1943-46. Mem. Am. Bar Assn., State Bar Mich. Home: Route 1 Hickory Corners MI 49060 Office: 235 Porter St Battle Creek MI 49017

BRISTOL, REXFORD ALLYN, automation co. exec.; b. Naugatuck, Conn., June 25, 1903; s. Bennet B. and Gertrude (Rexford) B.; B.A., Amherst Coll., 1924; S.B., Mass. Inst. Tech., 1926; D.C.S., Suffolk U., 1951; m. Margaret E. Chickering, Sept. 15, 1926; children—Betsy B., Margaret A. and Barbara A. (twins). Engaged in mfg., 1926-30, engring., 1930-40, engring. and sales, 1940—; with Foxboro Co. (Mass.), 1926—, treas. 1943-57, exec. v.p., 1958-62, pres., 1962—, chmn. bd., 1968-71, chmn. exec. com., 1971—; pres. Foxboro Nat. Bank, 1945-63, v.p., 1963- 68; chmn. bd., 1968—; dir. Arkwright Boston Ins. Co., New Eng. Mchts. Bank, Sentry Co., Foxboro. Mem. Mass. Adv. Council on Vocational and Tech. Edn. Trustee Suffolk U.; chmn. bd. Mass. Taxpayers Found., 1966-69; past pres., trustee Retina Found., Adm. Richard E. Byrd Polar Center, Found. for Instrumentation Edn. and Research, Dean Jr. Coll.; mem. corp. Northeastern U., Mus. Sci. Wentworth Inst., Boston. Recipient Silver Beaver award Boy Scouts Am. Mem. Elec. Mfrs. Club. Instrument Soc. Am., Mass. Taxpayers Assn. Taxpayers Assn. (chmn.), Chi Psi. Clubs: Algonquin, University (Boston). Home: 19 Water St Foxboro MA 02035 Office: Foxboro Co Foxboro MA 02035

BRISTOW, DAVID IAN, lawyer; b. Toronto, Can., May 19, 1931; s. Horace George and Elizabeth (Bourne) B.; B.A., U. Toronto, 1953; LL.B., Osgoode Hall, Toronto, 1957; m. Suzanne Snow, Sept. 9, 1959; children—Timothy Charles, Julie Anne. Called to Ont. bar, 1957, since practiced in Toronto; mem. firm Shibley, Righton, McCutcheon, 1969—; apptd. Queen's counsel; tchr. Osgoode Hall Law Sch., 1967—. Dir. Ajax Engring. Ltd., Marley Canadian Ltd. Mem. Advocates Soc., Country of York Bar Assn., Canadian Bar Assn., Phi Delta Phi. Club: Lawyers (Toronto). Co-author: Mechanics Liens in Canada, 1962; also articles. Home: 88 Blythwood Rd Toronto Ontario Canada Office: 401 Bay St Toronto Ontario Canada

BRISTOW, GWEN, author; b. Marion, S.C., Sept. 16, 1903; d. Louis Judson and Caroline Cornelia (Winkler) Bristow; A.B., Judson Coll.; student Anderson Coll. and Sch. of Journalism, Columbia U.; m. Bruce Manning, Jan. 14, 1929 (dec.). Newspaper reporter, 10 yrs. Author: Invisible Host, 1930: Gutenberg Murders, 1931; Two and Two Make Twenty-two, 1932 (all 3 titles with Bruce Manning); Deep Summer 1937, Handsome Road, 1938, This Side of Glory, 1940 (with background chpts. pub. as Plantation Trilogy, 1962); Tomorrow Is Forever, 1943; Jubilee Trail, 1950; Celia Garth, 1959; Calico Palace, 1970. Home: Box 144 Encino CA 91316 Office: care Brandt and Brandt 101 Park Av New York City NY 10017

BRITAIN, RADIE, composer; b. Amarillo, Tex., Mar. 17, 1903; d. Edgar Charles and Katie (Ford) Britain; student U. Chgo., 1920-21; B.M., Am. Conservatory, Chgo., 1924; D.Mus., Mus. Arts Conservatory, 1958; m. Ted Morton; 1 dau., Lerae. Composer orchestral, piano and vocal music, debut as composer, Munich, Germany, 1925; represented by string quartet at White House. Awarded nat. prizes for orchestral and vocal compositions; Internat. prize Heroic Poem for Orchestra. Awarded Juilliard Publ. prize, 1945; first Nat. prize for We Believe, and for Suite for Strings; award merit Nat. League Am. Pen Women, 1957; Internat. award for Nisan for chorus and orch. Delta Omicron; Achievement award A.S.C.A.P. Mem. Tex. Composers Guild (life), A.S.C.A.P., A.S.C.A.P., League of Am. Penwomen; hon. mem. Gamma Chpt. S.A.I., Tex. Fed. of Music Clubs; life hon. mem. Tex. Music Tchrs. Assn. Democrat. Club: Etude (life hon. mem.), Schubert (Los Angeles); Philharmonic (Amarillo, Tex.). Home: 1945 N Curson St Hollywood CA 90028

BRITE, RALPH WATKINS, lawyer; b. San Antonio, June 27, 1917; s. Tom S. and Nora (McConnell) B.; B.S., S.W. Tex. Coll., 1937; LL.B., U. Tex., 1942; m. Thelma Errington, Mar. 31, 1961. Admitted to Tex. bar, 1942, since practiced in San Antonio; partner firm Bobbitt, Brite, Bobbitt & Allen, 1949—; city atty. San Antonio, 1954. Served to capt. USAAF, World War II. Decorated D.F.C., Bronze Star. Mem. State Bar Tex. (pres. 1968-69), San Antonio Bar Assn. (pres. 1953). Club: San Antonio Exchange (pres. 1969). Home: 2611 Hopeton St San Antonio, TX 78370. Office: 2000 Alamo Nat Bldg San Antonio TX 78205

BRITSCH, CARL CONRAD, architect; b. Archbold, O., Apr. 12, 1889; s. Hans George and Anna (Kutzli) B.; B.A., Carnegie Inst. Tech., 1916; m. Leone F. Northway, June 4, 1920; children—Virginia Marie (Mrs. R. J. Hollister), James Arthur. Pvt. practice of architecture, Toledo, 1923-27; partner Britsch & Munger, 1927-55, Britsch, Macelwane & Assos., Toledo, 1955—; projects include numerous schs., chs., hosps., coll. bldgs. for Bowling Green State U., Ohio No. U., Nat. Am. Legion hdqrs., Washington. Chmn. Downtown Toledo Planning Com. Served with U.S. Army, World War I. Recipient 1st prize in drawing, six 1st prizes in water color, art shows in N.W. Ohio. Fellow A.I.A. (pres. Toledo 1944-45); mem. Architects Soc. Ohio (pres. 1951-52), Church Archtl. Guild Am., Toledo Fedn. Art Socs. (pres. 1952-53). Toledo C. of C., Am. Legion. Methodist. Mason (32). Clubs: Torch, Lions. Author: (hist. novel) The Sound of the Hammer, 1963; also articles on travel, architecture. Home: 3528 Woodley Rd Toledo OH 43606 Office: 2446 Sylvania Av Toledo OH 43613

BRITSCH, RALPH ADAM, educator; b. Ephraim, Utah, Jan. 30, 1912; s. Edwin Adam and Clara (Breinholt) B.; A.B. magna cum laude, Brigham Young U., 1933, M.A., 1951; student U. Wis., 1938, U. Okla., 1950-51, U. So. Cal., 1961; m. Florence Todd, Dec. 18, 1936; children—Todd A., R. Lanier, Charlotte (Mrs. David Hamblin), Merlene (Mrs. Timothy Roberts), Royden E. Instr., Gunnison (Utah) High Sch., 1933-35, Provo (Utah) High Sch., 1936-38; mem. faculty Brigham Young U., 1938—, prof. English and humanities, 1962—; chmn. dept. English, 1957-60, acting dean Coll. Humanities and Social Scis., 1962-64, chmn. dept. humanities and comparative lit., 1967—. Recipient Maeser Distinguished Teaching award 1971. Mem. Am. Soc. for Aesthetics, Am. Comparative Lit. Assn., Rocky Mountain Modern Lang. Assn.; Nat. Council Tchrs. English. Bishop Ch. of Jesus Christ of Latter-day Saints ward, 1952-60, mem. presidency stake, 1961-68. Democrat. Co-author: The Arts in Perspective, 1971. Editor: A Humanities Reader, 1965; co-editor: Literature as Art: A Reader, 1971. Home: 465 S 650th E Orem UT 84057 Office: Brigham Young Univ Provo UT 84601

BRITT, DONALD ALLEN, brewing co. exec.; b. Madison, Wis., June 14, 1934; s. William C. and Eleanor (Harmining) B.; B.A., U. Wis., 1956; m. Ruth L. Schmidt, Nov. 11, 1956; children—Thomas, Cathie, Suzanne, Jennifer. Adminstrv. services mgr. Arthur Andersen & Co., Milw., 1959-67; dir. systems and computing Joseph Schlitz Brewing Co., Milw., 1968-69, controller, 1970—. Treas., dir. Luth. Social Services of Wis. and Upper Mich. Served with USAF, 1956-59. Mem. Am. Inst. C.P.A.'s, Wis. Soc. C.P.A.'s. Home: 8409 Jackson Park Blvd Wauwatosa WI 53226 Office: 235 Galena St Milwaukee WI 53201

BRITT, HARRY MAX, Jr., oil co. exec.; b. Amarillo, Tex., Feb. 6, 1918; s. Harry Max and Kate Ann (Dykeman) B.; B.S. in Mining Engring., Tex. Western U., 1941; m. Alice Wanita Walker, June 22, 1940; children—Harry Wayne, Elizabeth Ann, Robert Max. With Sinclair-Prairie Oil Co., 1941-42; with Diamond Shamrock Oil & Gas Corp. (formerly Shamrock Oil and Gas Corp.), 1946—, chief geologist, 1954-63, v.p. charge geology, 1963—. Served with USMCR, 1942-46. Mem. Am. Assn. Petroleum Geologists, Soc. Econ. Palentologists and Mineralogists, Sigma Gamma Epsilon. Home: Tawney St Amarillo TX 79106 Office: Box 631 First Nat Bank Bldg Amarillo TX 79105

BRITT, JAMES THOMAS, lawyer; b. Kansas City, Mo., Feb. 27, 1904; s. Aylett T. and Katherine B. (Henderson) B.; LL.B., Washington U., St. Louis, 1926; m. Ruth E. Burgin, Sept. 18, 1930; children—Thomas Burgin, Robert McCammon. Admitted to Mo. bar, 1926, since practiced in Kansas City; sr. partner firm Spencer, Fane, Britt & Browne, 1951-; instr. Real Estate Bd. Inst., 1945-66. Mem. bd. visitors Jackson County, Mo., 1948-53; bar com. 16th Jud. Circuit Mo., 1942-49; legal adviser local SS, 1939—; counsel Children's Cardiac Center, Kansas City, Mo., 1946-70, Sec., dir. Commonwealth Theatres, Inc., Indsl. Land & Airport Properties, Inc., Lida Investment Co., Lida Hotel Operating Co.; v.p., dir. K.C. Airtel Co., Independent Elec. Company. Chmn. Recreation Adv. Com. Kansas City, 1955-62; chmn. citizens adv. bd. City-County Office of Aging. Co- founder, dir. Nat. Council on Alcoholism, Kansas City, area pres., 1966- 67, exec. v.p., 1967- 68; bd. dirs. Kansas City Social Health Agy.; mem. Gov.'s Com. on Alcoholism for Mo. Mem. Am., Mo., Kansas City bar assns., Lawyers Assn. Kansas City. Kappa Alpha, Phi Delta Phi. Clubs: Kansas City, Rotary. Contbr. articles legal jours. Home: 409 W 58th Terrace Kansas City, MO 64113. Office: Power & Light Bldg Kansas City MO 64105

BRITT, LAURENCE VINCENT, clergyman, educator; b. San Francisco, Apr. 30, 1912; s. Laurence and Alice L. (Boyle) B.; A.B., U. Detroit, 1933; M.A., Loyola U., 1939; S.T.L., West Baden Coll., Ind., 1944; Ph.D., U. Minn., 1954. Joined Soc. of Jesus, 1933, ordained priest Roman Catholic Ch., 1943; tchr. St. Ignatius High Sch., Cleve., 1937-40, Loyola U., 1943; dean freshmen Loyola U., Chgo., 1946-47, dean Coll. Arts and Scis., 1954-56; dean Coll. Arts and Scis., U. Detroit, 1956-59, pres., 1960-66; prof. edn., dir. acad. counselling John Carroll U., Cleve., 1966-67, dean Coll. Arts and Scis., 1967—. Mem. bd. visitors U.S. Army Transp. Sch. Mem. N.E.A., Assn. Am. Colls., Jesuit, Nat. Cath. ednl. assns., Assn. Cath. Colls. Mich., Mich. Assn. Colls. and Univs. (pres. 1965-66), Alpha Kappa Psi, Phi Delta Kappa, Alpha Sigma Nu, Alpha Delta Gamma. Address: John Carroll U University Heights Cleveland OH 44118

BRITT, MAURICE, lt. gov. Ark.; b. Carlisle, Ark., June 29, 1919; s. Maurice Lee and Virgie (Oliver) B.; B.A. in Journalism, U. Ark., 1941, student law, 1945- 46; m. Pat A. Allbright; children—Andrea (Mrs. Bernie Tomlinson), Nancy Lea, Mike, Timmy, Patty. Mem. Detroit Lions Profl. Football Team, 1941; v.p., sales mgr. Mitchel Mfg. Co., Inc., Fort Smith, Ark., 1946-66; lt. gov. Ark., 1967—. Past pres. Sebastian County chpt. A.R.C.; past head indsl. sect. Fort Smith Community Chest; past chmn. USO fund drive. Served to capt. AUS, 1941-45: ETO. Decorated Congl. Medal of Honor, D.S.C., Silver Star medal, Purple Heart, Bronze Star medal with 3 oak leaf clusters, Combat Inf. Badge; Brit. Mil. cross; Italian cross of valor. Mem. Disabled Am. Vets., Am. Legion, V.F.W., Blue Key, Phi Eta Sigma, Sigma Chi. Republican. Baptist. Home: 4805 Crestwood Dr Little Rock AR 72207

BRITT, ROLAND W., telephone co. exec.; b. Madison, Wis., 1922; B.A. in Accounting, U. Wis., 1943; married. With Arthur Andersen & Co., C.P.A.'s, 1943-49; v.p., dir. Gen. Telephone Co. Ill., 1949-67; pres., chief exec. officer Gen. Telephone Co. Pa., Erie, 1967—, also dir.; pres., dir. York Tel & Tel. Co., Princeton Telephone Co.; v.p., dir. Bethel & Mt. Aetna Tel & Tel. Co.; dir. Wattsburg Telephone Corp. Home: 221 W 39th St Erie PA 16508 Office: 150 W 10th St Erie PA 16512*

BRITT, RUSSELL WILLIAM, utility co. exec.; b. Madison, Wis., Mar. 28, 1926; s. William Charles and Eleanor (Harmening) B.; B.S. in Elec. Engring., U. Wis., 1946, B.B.A. in Accounting, 1948; m. Jean A. Swanton, Feb. 9, 1952; children—William Swanton, Lynette Ann. With Wis. Electric Power Co., Milw., 1948—, methods analyst, 1948-54, asst. controller, 1960-62, controller, 1962—. treas., 1969—; pres., dir. Employers Mut. Savs. Bldg. & Loan Assn. Treas., dir. St. John's Home for Aging. Served to lt. USNR, 1943-46, 52-54. Mem. Financial Execs. Inst. (dir. 1968—), Wis. Alumni Assn. Milw. (dir. 1965—). Home: 8148 Milwaukee Av Wauwatosa WI 53213 Office: 231 W Michigan St Milwaukee WI 53201

BRITT, STEUART HENDERSON, educator, marketing cons.; b. Fulton, Mo.; s. A. T. and Katherine (Henderson) B.; student Washington U., Columbia schs. law; A.B., Washington U., 1931, M.A. in Psychology, 1932; Ph.D. in Psychology (Inst. Human Relations fellow), Yale, 1935; m. Marion M. Hansell, June 1, 1936. Admitted to Mo. bar, 1929, also N.Y. bar, U.S. Supreme Ct. bar; research asst. Columbia Inst. Ednl. Research, 1935- 36; asst. prof. psychology George Washington U., prof. psychology Mount Vernon Sem., Washington, 1936-42; civilian wartime work, Washington, 1941-43. exec. dir. Office Psychol. Personnel, NRC, sec. Emergency Com. in Psychology, exec. sec. Com. on Wartime Requirements for Specialized Personnel; expert cons. Nat. Resources Planning Bd. and War Manpower Commn.; exec. positions McCann- Erickson, N.Y.C., 1945-51; v.p. Needham, Louis & Brorby, Inc., Chgo., 1951-56; adminstrv. v.p. Earle Ludgin & Co., Chgo., 1956- 57; prof. marketing Grad. Sch. Mgmt., Medill Sch. Journalism, Northwestern U., Evanston, Ill., 1957—. Cons. several bus. firms, —; Westinghouse Ann. Sci. Talent Search, 1942-60; cons. editor McGraw-Hill series advt. and marketing, 1951-64; producer ann. Advt. Age Creative Workshop, 1958-70. Served from lt. to lt. comdr. USNR, 1943-45, comdr.-in-chief Hdqrs. U.S. Fleet. Recipient Alumni citation Washington U., 1959; mem. Hall of Fame in Distbn., 1963. Diplomate Indsl. Psychology. Fellow A.A.A.S., Am. Psychol. Assn. (pres. div. consumer psychology 1963-64), Am. Sociol. Assn., Am. Acad. Advt.; mem. Am. Marketing Assn. Roman Catholic. Clubs: Cosmos (Washington); Yale (N.Y.C.); University (Chgo., Evanston); Kenilworth. Author, editor several books including: Social Psychology of Modern Life, 1941, rev. 1949; (with I. Graeber) Jews in a Gentile World, 1942; Selected Readings in Social Psychology, 1950; (with D.B. Lucas) Advertising Psychology and Research, 1950; The Spenders, 1960 (Spanish edit. 1961); (with D.B. Lucas) Measuring Advertising Effectiveness, 1963; (with Harper W. Boyd, Jr.) Marketing Management and Administrative Action, 1963; Consumer Behavior and the Behavioral Sciences, 1966; Do Advertising Agencies Train Trainees?, 1968; Consumer Behavior in Theory and in Action , 1970; Psychological Experiments in Consumer Behavior, 1970; numerous articles. Bd. editors Jour. Marketing, 1947-57, editor, 1957-67. Home: 211 Greenleaf Av Wilmette IL 60091 Office: Grad Sch Mgmts Northwestern U Evanston IL 60201

BRITTAIN, ALFRED III, banker; b. Evanston, Ill., July 22, 1922; s. Alfred, Jr. and Sibyl (Collins) B.; grad. Phillips Exeter Acad., 1941; B.A., Yale, 1945; m. Beatrice Memhard, Dec. 18, 1948;

children—Stephen M., Linda C. With Bankers Trust Co., N.Y.C., 1947—, pres., 1966—, also dir., mem. exec. com., now chmn.; dir. Bankers Trust N.Y. Corp., Philip Morris, Inc., Collins & Aikman Corp., Bancom Devel. Corp. Trustee Carnegie Endowment for Internat. Peace, Phillips Exeter Acad., Rosemary Hall Found.; bd. dirs. Marshall H. and Nellie Alworth Meml. Fund. Served with USAAF, 1942-46. Home: Cognewaugh Rd Cos Cob CT 06807 Office: 280 Park Av New York City NY 10017

BRITTAIN, JOHN OLIVER, educator; b. Pitts., Feb. 15, 1920; s. Joseph and Mabel (Morgan) B.; B.S., Pa. State U., 1943, Ph.D., 1951; m. Lois Miller, Apr. 20, 1945; children—Douglas, John Oliver, Susan, Lisa. Research asst. Research Labs., Aluminum Co. of Am., New Kensington, Pa., 1943-44; instr. metallurgy Pa. State U., 1947-48; prin. metallurgist Battelle Meml. Inst., Columbus, O., 1950-51; research asso. sci. staff Columbia, 1951- 55; prof. material sci. dept. Northwestern U., 1955—, chmn. materials sci. dept., 1968—; materials cons. Johnson Service Co., Milw., 1964-66, Universal Oil Products Co., Des Plaines, 1968—, Amphenol Corp., 1968, USAF Materials Lab., 1968. Served to 1st lt. AUS, 1944-46. Internat. Nickel Co. fellow, 1949-50. Mem. Am. Soc. Metals, Am. Inst. Mining and Metall. Engrs., Am. Phys. Soc., Am. Assn. U. Profs., Sigma Xi, Tau Beta Pi, Alpha Chi Sigma, Alpha Sigma Mu. Home: 2710 Crawford St Evanston IL 60201

BRITTEN, EDWARD BENJAMIN, composer; b. Lowestoft, Eng., Nov. 22, 1913; s. Robert Victor and Edith Rhoda (Hockey) B.; student Gresham's Sch., Holt and Royal Coll. of Music, London, Eng. Engaged in work on documentary films, 1934-35; free lance composer for films, radio and theater, 1934—; came to U.S., 1939; returned to Eng., 1942; concert tour U.S. with tenor Peter Pears, 1949. Decorated Companion of Honour. Order of Merit; recipient Aspen award, 1964. Mem. Ch. of England. Composer. Orchestra: Sinfonietta; Soirees Musicales and Matinees Musicales (2 suites after Rossini); Mont Juic (with Lennox Berkeley); Canadian Carnival; Sinfonia da Requiem; Young Person's Guide to the Orchestra, string orchestra; Simple Symphony; Variations on a Theme by Frank Bridge; Prelude and Fugue; chamber music: Phantasy; Suite; Six Metamorphoses after Ovid; String Quartets Nos. 1 and 2, Lachrymae; Golden Sonata; organ: Prelude and Fugue on a Theme of Vittoria, Missa Brevis; concerti: Piano Concerto; Violin Concerto; Diversion; Scottish Ballad; Cello Symphony; piano: Holiday Diary; Introduction and Rondo alla Burlesca; Mazurka Elegiaca; chorus: A Boy Was Born; Our Hunting Fathers (text W.H. Auden); Ballad of Heroes; Hymn to St. Cecilia; Ceremony of Carols; Rejoice In the Lamb (text Christopher Smart); Festival Te Deum; Saint Nicolas Cantata; Spring Symphony; Five Flower Songs; I Lov'd A Lass; Lifi Boy; Advance Democracy; Ballad of Little Musgrave; A Wedding Anthem; Cantata Academica; War Requiem; A Hymn of St. Columba; Cantata Misercordium; vocal: Friday Afternoons; On This Island; Les Illuminations, (text Rimbaud); Seven Sonnets of Michelangelo; Holy Sonnets of John Donne; Canticle I (Text Francis Quarles); Canticle II (text from Chester Miracle play); Canticle III (Still Falls the Rain-E. Sitwell), 1954; Nocturne; Serenade; The Birds. Fish in the Unruffled Lakes; Under the Abject Willow; Mother Comfort; Charm of Lullabies; 3 Vols. of Folk Song arrangements (Brit. Isles and France); realisations of Purcells vocal and instrumental works; operas: Peter Grimes (polled 1st choice in Metropolitan Opera Broadcasts, 1948); Rape of Lucretia; Beggar's Opera (after Gay); Albert Herring; Let's Make An Opera (The Little Sweep); Billy Budd; Gloriana (presented for Coronation of Queen Elizabeth, 1953); The Turn of the Screw, 1954; The Prince of the Pagodas (3 act ballet); Noye's Fludde (opera), 1958; A Midsummer Night's Dream, 1960; Notturno (piano), 1963; Nocturnal (guitar), 1964; Curlew River (opera), 1964; Suite for Cello Solo, 1965; Gemini Variations, 1965; Songs and Proverbs by William Blake, 1965; Voices for Today, 1965; The Poet's Echo, 1965; The Burning Fiery Furnace (opera), 1966; the Golden Vanity, 1966; the Building of the House (overture), 1967; Second Suite for Cello, 1967; the Prodigal Son (opera), 1968; Children's Crusade, 1969; Suite for Harp, 1969; Owen Wingrave (opera), 1970. Home: The Red House Aldeburgh Suffolk England

BRITTEN, MILTON REESE, editor; b. Wilkes-Barre, Pa., Dec. 17, 1924; s. Isaac Milton and Marguerite (Reese) B.; B.A., with honors, Yale, 1949; m. Virginia Butler, Nov. 11, 1951; children—Ann George, Jonathan B., Martha, Anthony. Reporter, Memphis Press-Scimitar, 1949-56, Washington corr. Memphis Press-Scimitar, also Knoxville News-Sentinel, 1956-63; night editor Scripps-Howard Newspaper Alliance, Washington, 1963-66, asst. mng. editor, 1966—. Served with AUS, 1942-45; ETO. Recipient Christopher award, 1953. Mem. Phi Beta Kappa. Author: (with Andrew Tully) The Foreign Aid Story: Where Did Your Money Go?, 1964. Home: 10000 Belhaven Rd Bethesda MD 20015 Office: 1013 13th St Washington DC 20005

BRITTENHAM, RAYMOND LEE, communications co. exec.; b. Moscow, Russia, Feb. 8, 1916 (parents U.S. citizens); s. Edward Arthur and Marietta (Wemple) B.; A.B., Principia Coll., Elsah, Ill., 1936; LL.B., Harvard, 1940; student Kaiser Wilhelm U., Berlin, Germany, 1937; m. Mary Ann Stanard, Nov. 3, 1956; children—Edward C., Carol. Admitted to Ill. bar, 1940, N.Y. bar, 1946; with firm Pope & Ballard, Chgo., 1940-42, Mitchell Carroll, N.Y.C., 1947-56; asst. gen. counsel Internat. Tel. & Tel. Corp., and subsidiaries, 1957-62, v.p., gen. counsel, 1962-68, sr. v.p. law, counsel, 1968—, dir., 1965—. Sec. U.S. sect. Internat. Fiscal Assn., 1950- 57; bd. dirs. Nat. Fgn. Trade Council, 1961—. Served to maj. AUS, 1942-46. Decorated Bronze Star medal; Croix de Guerre (France and Belgium); chevalier Ordre de Leopold (Belgium). Mem. Am. Bar Assn., Council Fgn. Relations. Club: University (N.Y.C.). Home: 925 Park Av New York City NY 10028 Office: 320 Park Av New York City NY 10022

BRITTIN, NORMAN AYLSWORTH, educator; b. Syracuse, N.Y., Sept. 9, 1906; s. Lewis J. and Grace (Aylsworth) B.; A.B., Syracuse U., 1927, A.M., 1930; postgrad. U. Cal., 1934-37; Ph.D., U. Wash., 1947; m. Florence Sykes Mellor, Mar. 1, 1929 (dec.); children—Geoffrey Mellor, Anthony Norman; m. 2d, Ruth Harris Lowe, June 3, 1951. Asso. character edn. U. So. Cal., 1931-34; instr. U. Utah, 1937-45, asst. prof. English 1947; acting instr. English, U. Wash., 1945-46; vis. asst. prof. humanities U. Chgo., 1947-48; asso. prof. to prof. English, Auburn U., 1948-62, Hollifield prof. English literature, 1966—; lectr., prof. English, U. P.R., 1962-66; Fulbright lectr., Spain, 1968-69; vis. prof. English, U. So. Cal., summer 1967. Recipient Warshaw award for the humanities Western Humanities Rev., 1952; Folger library fellow, summer 1965; faculty fellow Fund Advancement Edn., 1952-53. Mem. Am. Assn. Univ. Profs. (pres. local chpt. 1956-57), Modern Lang. Assn. Am., S. Atlantic Modern Lang. Assn., Shakespeare Assn. Am., Renaissance Soc. Am., Nat. Council Tchrs. of English. Author: A Writing Apprenticeship, 1963; Edna St. Vincent Millay, 1967; Writing Description and Narration, 1969; A Reading Apprenticeship: Literature, 1971; Thomas Middleton, in press. Co-editor So. Humanities Rev., 1966—. Contbr. articles, poems and reviews to periodicals. Home: PO Box 550 Auburn AL 36830

BRITTIN, WESLEY EMIL, physicist, educator; b. Phila., Apr. 21, 1917; s. Wesley and Anna (Vogel) B.; B.S. in Chem. Engring., U. Colo., 1942; M.S. in Physics, 1945; M.A., Princeton, 1948; Ph.D., U. Alaska, 1957; m. Donna Katherine Doherty, Jan. 18, 1941; 1 dau., Bonnie Anne; m. 2d, Janine Halpern; children—Anne, Elizabeth, Phillip Halpern, Alex Halpern. Mem. faculty U. Colo., Boulder, 1944—, prof. physics, 1959—, chmn. dept. 1958—, acting dean Grad. School, spring 1968. Fellow, Joint Inst. Lab. Astrophysics, 1962—. Fellow Am. Phys. Soc.; mem. Sigma Xi. Home: 2425 Vassar Dr Boulder CO

BRITTINGHAM, RUSSELL, farmer, former glass co. exec.; b. Orange, N.J., Dec. 29, 1904; s. Russell and Ellen (Bradbury) B.; student Sheffield Sci. Sch., Yale, 1922-25; m. Margaret Van Nostrand, July 13, 1929. Salesman, Automotive Splty., 1926-33; with Crowell Collier Pub. Co., 1933-41, Hearst Mags., Inc., 1941-44; asst. to dir. research Corning Glass Works, 1944-46, mgr. tech. products div., 1946-56, mgr. consumer products div., 1948-51, v.p., 1954-57, dir. purchases, 1956-57; pres. Pittsburgh, Corning Corp., 1957-67, chmn. bd., 1967-70; chmn. bd. Pitts. Corning van Belgie, 1963-70; farmer, 1970—. Home: RD 3 Ligonier PA 15658

BRITTON, ALLEN PERDUE, educator, musician; b. Elgin, Ill., May 25, 1914; s. Walter Allen and Mary (Perdue) B.; B.Sc., U. Ill., 1937, M.A., 1939; Ph.D., U. Mich., 1950; m. Veronica Fern Wallace, Aug. 30, 1938. Tchr. music and English, Griffith (Ind.) pub. schs., 1938-41; instr. music and English, Eastern Ill. U., 1941-43; prof. music U. Mich., Ann Arbor, 1949—, asso. dean Sch. Music, 1960-69, dean, 1969—. Bd. dirs. Mus. Youth Internat., 1965—; cons. Youth for Understanding, 1967; mem. overseas tours screening com. U.S.O., 1962—; arts and humanities panel U.S. Office Edn., 1964—. Served with AUS, 1943-46. Mem. Am. Musicol. Soc. (council 1964-66), Am. Studies Assn., Internat. Folk Music Council, Music Educators Nat. Conf. (pres. 1960- 62), Internat. Soc. Music Edn., Phi Mu Alpha (dir. 1962-67), Phi Eta Sigma, Phi Kappa Phi, Pi Kappa Lambda, Phi Delta Kappa. Editor Jour. Research Music Edn., 1953—; gen. editor Foundations of Music Education, textbook series, 1964—. Author numerous revs., articles. Home: 1475 Warrington Dr Ann Arbor MI 48103

BRITTON, ANDREW CYRIL, cigarette mfr.; b. Richmond, Va., Oct. 21, 1908; s. Andrew L. and Hattie L. (Jenkins) B.; student bus. adminstrn. U. Richmond, 1925-28; B.S., Va. Poly. Inst., 1932, M.S. in Chem. Engring., 1933; student Advanced Mgmt. Program, Harvard, 1953; m. Lillian W. Hargrove, Dec. 30, 1937; 1 dau., Diane L. Chemist, Albermarle Paper Co., Richmond, Va., 1933-34; with Philip Morris, Inc., Richmond, 1934—, beginning as chemist, successively foreman, factory supt., factory mgr., factories mgr., gen. factories mgr., 1934-57, v.p., 1957—, dir. overseas div., 1955—. Served as 1st lt. USCGR, 1932-40. Mem. Am. Soc. Quality Control, Am. Chem. Soc., Central Va. Engrs. Club. Methodist. Clubs: Rotary, Hermitage Country, Commonwealth (Richmond); Pendennis (Louisville) Home: 3813 Dover Rd Richmond VA 23221 Office: 4001 Commerce Rd Richmond VA 23224

BRITTON, ARLINGTON ALBERT, Jr., steel co. exec.; b. Reading, Pa., July 12, 1909; s. Arlington Albert and Mary (Eck) B.; evening student U. Pa.; m. Sara K. Daniels, Apr. 30, 1936; children—Sara E., Nancy K. Bookkeeper, Reading Trust Co. (Pa.), 1927-29; with sales dept. Reading Foundry & Supply Co., 1929-33; with Carpenter Steel Co., Reading, 1933—, v.p. operations, 1953-68, sr. v.p., 1968—. also dir.; v.p., dir. United Fund Berks County (Pa.), 1960-63. Mem. Am. Iron and Steel Inst., Ass. Iron and Steel Engrs. Mason. Home: 106 E 37th St Reiffton Reading PA 19606 Office: 101 W Bern St Reading PA 19601

BRITTON, JAMES JUDSON, assn. exec.; b. Montgomery, Ala., July 23, 1913; s. William Brown and Ruth (Abbott) B.; student U. Ala., 1932-34; LL.B., Jones Law U., Montgomery, 1936; m. Dorothy Bennett, Feb. 4, 1939; children—Karen (Mrs. John B. Johnson), Nancy A. With Interstate Oil Co., 1937-43, 47-50; exec. dir. Ala. Petroleum Council, 1950-66; exec. v.p. Ala. C. of C., 1966-. Exec. v.p. Guatamala-Ala. Partners in Alliance, 1967—. Served with AUS, 1943-46, 51-52. Recipient Outstanding Service award Petroleum Industry, 1965. Mem. Council State Chambers Commerce, U.S. C. of C., Am. Judicature Soc., Ala. Hist. Soc., English Speaking Union, Newcomen Soc., Ala. U. Alumni Assn., The Thirteen, Pi Kappa Alpha. Episcopalian. Rotarian (dir. Mongomery 1970). Home: 1222 Augusta St Montgomery AL 36111 Office: 468 S Perry St Montgomery AL 36104

BRITTON, JOHN DOYLE, educator; b. Los Angeles, Mar. 6, 1930; s. John Joseph and Dorothy (Dearing) B.; B.S., U. Cal. at Los Angeles, 1951; Ph.D., Cal. Inst. Tech., Tech., 1955; m. Judith Gavin VanValkenburg, Oct. 27, 1962; children—Jennifer, David, Mary Katherine. Asst. prof. U. Minn., Mpls., 1955-60, asso. prof., 1960-65, prof., 1965—. NSF sr. postdoctoral fellow, 1963-64. Mem. Am. Crystallographic Assn., Am. Chem. Soc., Sigma Xi. Contbr. articles to profl. jours. Office: Dept Chemistry U Minn Minneapolis MN 55455

BRITTON, LESTER GEORGE, lawyer; b. Box Butte County, Neb., Aug. 23, 1899; s. William J. and Lena (Martz) B.; A.B., U. Neb., 1921; J.D., U. Chgo., 1924; m. Hazel Marguerite Stellman, Aug. 13, 1927; children—Georgia Jean (Mrs. Arnold Moritz), Barbara Anne (Mrs. Chester K. Lacy), William L. Admitted to Ill. bar, 1925; asso., then partner firm Schiff, Hardin, Waite, Dorschel & Britton, and predecessors, Chgo., 1924—; dir. Cedar St. Corp., Deringer Mfg. Co. Trustee, mem. exec. com. Seabury-Western Theol. Sem. Mem. Am., Ill., Chgo. bar assns., Am. Judicature Soc., Phi Beta Kappa, Delta Chi. Republican. Episcopalian. Club: Union League (Chgo.). Home: 70 E Cedar St Chicago IL 60611 Office: 231 S LaSalle St Chicago IL 60604

BRITTON, ROBERT EUGENE, advt. agy. exec.; b. Brainerd, Minn., Dec. 10, 1924; s. Fred Lawrence and Clara (Grondin) B.; B. Aero Engring., U. Minn., 1945, B.A. in Journalism and Advt., 1950, M.A. in Communications and Marketing Research, 1951; m. Elizabeth Timmerman; children—Debra, Richard, Michael, Robert. Tech. editor Mpls. Honeywell Co., 1946-49, operations research dir. Aero. div., 1952-57; research and advt. Gen. Mills, Inc., Mpls., 1952-57; sr. v.p., Midwestern regional dir. MacManus, John & Adams, Inc., Chgo., now exec. v.p., Bloomfield Hills, Mich. Bd. regents Nat. Nat. Center Communications Scis. Served with USNR, 1943-46. Mem. Am. Marketing Assn., Am. Assn. Advt. Agys., Chgo. Federated Advt. Club. Clubs: Executives (Chgo.); Bloomfield Hills Country, Bloomfield Open Hunt. Home: 1128 Chesterfield Birmingham MI 48009 Office: Woodward Av and Long Lake Rd Bloomfield Hills MI 48013

BRITTON, WILLARD P., pub. co. exec.; b. Mitchell, S.D., May 28, 1923; s. Clarence B. and Bessie (Price) B.; B.A., U. Wash., 1949; m. Dorothy Lorraine Hanlon, Apr. 27, 1946; children—Leslie Diane, Linda Gail. Staff accountant Haskins & Sells, Seattle, 1949-55; controller, treas. Northwest Publications, Inc., St. Paul, Minn., 1955—; dir. Boulder Pub. Inc., Boulder, Colo., Twin Cities Newspaper Service Inc., St. Paul. Treas. March of Dimes, 1957-58. Mem. Inst. Newspaper Controllers and Finance Officers (dir. 1958-59), Tax Execs. Inst., Financial Execs. Inst., Phi Beta Kappa, Alpha Kappa Psi. Home: 3097 Sandy Hook Dr St Paul MN 55113 Office: 55 E 4th St St Paul MN 55101

BRITZ, HARLAND MARSHALL, lawyer; b. Toledo, July 2, 1931; s. Morris J. and Lillian (Pintis) B.; B.A., U. Mich., 1953, M.A., 1956, LL.B., 1956; m. Nancy Gould, Oct. 12, 1962. Admitted to Ohio bar, 1956, since practiced in Toledo; partner Fuhrman, Gertner, Britz & Barkan, 1964—; asst. U.S. atty., 1961-63; instr. English dept. U. Toledo, 1964. Sec. Lucas County Democratic Central Com., 1966—; alternate del. Dem. Nat. Conv., 1968. Bd. dirs. Jewish Welfare Fedn. Toledo, Interfaith Housing, Inc. Recipient trophy Am. Civil Liberties Union of N.W. Ohio, 1970. Mem. Toledo and N.W. Ohio Civil Liberties Union (chmn. legal com.). Home: 4751 W Central Av Toledo OH 43615 Office: Spitzer Bldg Toledo OH 43604

BRIXEY, JOHN CLARK, educator; b. Mounds, Okla., June 28, 1904; s. Albin Monroe and Ethel Lillian (Buchanan) B.; B.A., U. Okla., 1924, M.A., 1925; Ph.D., U. Chgo., 1936; m. Dorothea B. Morrison, Dec. 26, 1926; children—John Clark, Dorothy Jane (Mrs. George W. Ingels). Mem. faculty U. Okla., 1925—, prof. math., 1947—; cons. prof. biostatistics and epidemiology U. Okla. Med. Center, 1960—. Recipient award excellence teaching U. Okla., 1956. Mem. Am. Math. Soc., Math. Assn. Am. (bd. govs. 1951-52, sec. Okla.-Ark. sect. 1939-51), Phi Beta Kappa, Sigma Xi. Democrat. Mem. Disciples of Christ Ch. (elder). Co-author: Modern Trigonometry, 1955; Fundamentals of College Mathematics, rev. edit., 1961. Home: 927 S Pickard St Norman OK 73069

BRIZEL, LOUIS L., business exec.; s. Victor and Cilia (Bass) B.; student spl. courses; m. Rosita Schar, Apr. 16, 1935; children—Victor L., Patricia Ann (Mrs. Robert Lehr). Pres., treas. U.S. Hat and Mills, Inc., N.Y.C.; pres. Brizel Leather Corp., N.Y.C., Roberts, Cushman & Co., N.Y.C., U.S. Ribbon Mills, Inc., Williamsport, Pa., and Anniston, Ala., West Indies Trading Co.; dir. 900 Fifth Av. Corp., N.Y.C., Kranz-Nectow, Inc., Boston; pres., dir. Sci. Dyers, Ltd., Anniston, Ala. Founder, dir. United Jewish Appeal; founder Albert Einstein Coll. Medicine. Republican. Jewish religion. Mason. Clubs: Lotos, N.Y. University (N.Y.C.); Elmwood Country (White Plains, N.Y.). Home: 900 Fifth Av New York City, NY 10021. Office: 665 Broadway New York City NY 10012

BRIZZOLARA, RALPH DOMINIC, steel co. exec.; b. Chgo., Oct. 28, 1895; s. Charles Anthony and Louise Mary (Segale) B.; ed. pub. schs., Chgo.; m. Florence M. Hurley, Sept. 19, 1925; children—Robert F., Charles A., Nancy (Mrs. Lorenz). Editing engr. Western Electric Co., Chgo., 1915-17; engr. Am. Steam Conveyor Corp., 1917-18, Am. Steel Foundries, Chgo., 1919—, asst. chief engr., 1928-31, chief engr., 1931-43, v.p., 1943-61; sec. dir. Chgo. Bears Football Club, Inc., 1933—, acting pres., 1942-45, dir.; dir. Danly Machine Spltys., Onsrud Machine Co.; chmn. bd., dir. Poor & Co., 1962-65, chief exec. officer, 1962-64. Trustee Barat Coll. until 1970. Served with USNR, 1918-19; cons. to chief of ordnance, Dept. Army, 1950. Fellow Am. Soc. M.E. Clubs: Tavern, Chicago, Chicago Athletic Assn. Home: 100 Bellevue Pl Chicago IL 60611

BROAD, ELI, bldg. co. exec.; b. N.Y.C., June 6, 1933; s. Leon and Rebecca (Jacobson) B.; B.A. cum laude in Bus. Adminstrn., Mich. State U., 1954; m. Edythe Lois Lawson, Dec. 19, 1954; children—Jeffrey Alan, Gary Steven. Accountant, Goldman & Golman, C.P.A.'s, Detroit, 1954-55, Albert K. Lubin, C.P.A., 1955-56; asst. prof. Detroit Inst. Tech., 1956-57; co-founder Kaufman & Broad, Inc., Detroit, Chgo., N.Y., N.J., Los Angeles, San Francisco, Toronto, and Paris, 1957, pres., 1958-68, chmn., 1968—. Dir. devel. bd. Mich. State U.; mem. Nat. Indsl. Pollution Control Council. Del., Democratic Nat. Conv., 1968. Trustee, City of Hope, Pitzer Coll., Clarence C.P.A., Mich. Recipient Man of Year award City of Hope, 1965; Golden Plate award Am. Acad. Achievement, 1971. Mem. Beta Alpha Psi. Club: Presidents (Mich. State U.). Home: 121 N Rockingham Av Los Angeles CA 90049 Office: 10801 National Blvd Los Angeles CA 90064

BROADBENT, SAM ROBERT, mgmt. cons.; b. St. Louis, Sept. 23, 1898; s. Samuel and Hermine (Karberg) B.; B.S. in Forestry, U. Mo., 1920; M.F., Yale, 1922; m. G. Isabelle Jackson, Dec. 18, 1926. With Laurentide Pulp & Paper Co., 1921; with U.S. Forestry Service, 1922-39, alternate chief div. operations, 1937-39; with Bur. of Budget, 1939-68, chief commerce and transp. div., 1965-68. Cons. Hoover Commn. Reorgn. Fed. Govt., 1948. Served with U.S. Army, 1918. Recipient Commendation for Outstanding Service during tornado at Gainesville, Ga., 1936; Citation of Merit, Nat. Civil Service League. Mem. Soc. Am. Foresters (sr.), Am. Forestry Assn. (asst. treas. 1962-70), Kappa Sigma. Club: Cosmos (pres. 1960, treas. 1962-71). Address: 4201 Cathedral Av NW Washington DC 20016

BROADBENT, SMITH DUDLEY, Jr., agriculturist; b. Cadiz, Ky., Feb. 8, 1914; s. Smith Dudley and Anna (Hopson) B.; B.S., U. Ky., 1934, M.S., 1935; m. Mildred Holmes, Dec. 22, 1934; children—Sarah Holmes, Smith III, Robert K., Anne Bennett. Owner Broadbent Hybrids, Cadiz. 1937—; pres. Ky. Seed Stocks, Inc., 1948-51; chmn. Fed. Res. Bank, Louisville, 1953-55; dep. chmn. bd. dirs. Fed. Res. Bank St. Louis, 1965—; exec. com. West Ky. Produce, Inc.; pres. Broadbent-Bingham Food Products, Louisville, Cardinal Circle, Inc.; dir. South Central Bell Telephone Co., Birmingham, West Ky. Liquid Fertilizer, Inc., Cedar Bluff Stone Co., Cedar Bluff Land Co., Life Ins. Co. of Ky. Pres. Ky. State Fair Bd., Thomas P. Cooper Found., 1953-59; bd. dirs. Ky. YMCA, Pennyrile Rural Electrification, Trigg County Hosp., Ky. Econ. Devel. Assn. Ky.'s Western Waterlands, Inc., Ky. Mountain Laurel Festival; mem. exec. com. bd. trustees U. Ky., exec. com. alumni bd., 1958—; trustee Ky. Wesleyan Meth. Coll., Methodist Hosp., Henderson. Mem. Nat. Tobacco Adv. Com. Recipient Man of Yr. award for Ky., Progressive Farmer mag., 1956; Distinguished Service awards Ky. Farm Bur., 1964, Ky. Seed Improvement Assn., 1964. Mem. Ky. Farm Bur. Fedn. (past pres.), Ky. Seed Improvement Assn. (pres.), Ky. Lake Assn. (pres.), Ky. Agrl. Council (dir. past pres.), Ky. C. of C. (past pres.), West Ky. Ducks Unlimited (pres.), West Ky. Prodns. Assn. (dir.), Between Lakes Nat. Recreational Assn. (pres.). Trigg County Farm Bur. (dir.). Methodist (lay leader, Louisville conf., dir. gen. bd. lay activity). Lion. Club: Pendennis (Louisville). Home: Cadiz KY 42211

BROADBENT, THOMAS RAY, surgeon; b. Heber, Utah, Aug. 4, 1921; s. Charles N. and Sarah Jane (Wood) B.; B.A., Brigham Young U., 1943; M.D., Duke, 1946; m. Edith Stovall, June 3, 1950; children—Kenneth Ray, Stephanie, Catherine, Lisa Anne. Intern, Duke U. Hosp., 1947, gen. surgery residency, 1948- 50, plastic surgery residency, 1950-52; instr. surgery Duke, 1951-52; asso. clin. prof. U. Utah Sch. Med., 1955; active staff Primary Children's Hosp., Salt Lake City; active staff W.H. Groves Latter-Day Saints Hosp., Salt Lake City, also dir. residency program, dept. plastic surgery, 1957—; trainee Natl. Cancer Inst., 1950-52. Sec. gen. 3d Internat. Congress Plastic Surgery, 1963. Served to 1st lt. AUS, World War II. Recipient prize on original research Found. Am. Soc. Plastic and Reconstructive Surgery, 1958; Distinguished Service award Brigham Young U., 1969. Diplomate Am. Bd. Surgery, Am. Bd. Plastic Surgery (examiner). Fellow A.C.S., I.C.S. (vice regent 1959-60); mem. A.M.A., Utah Med. Assn., Cal. Soc. Plastic Surgery, Am. Soc. Plastic and Reconstructive

Surgery (gen. sec. 1958-63, pres. 1968-69, asso. editor jour. 1964-70), Internat. Confedn. Plastic Surgeons (exec. com. 1964—). Am. Assn. Plastic Surgery, Salt Lake Surg. Soc. (pres. 1968-69), Alpha Omega Alpha. Mormon. Home: 2635 St Mary's Way Salt Lake City UT 48108 Office: 508 E South Temple Salt Lake City UT 84102

BROADDUS, LUTHER, III, publishing co. exec.; b. Berryville, Va., May 9, 1932; s. Luther and Sally (Williams) B.; B.S. in Agr., Va. Pol. Inst., 1954; m. Jean Cook, Oct. 11, 1952; children—Harry Lee, Frank, Lucia B., Laura Jean, Linda Lou. County agrl. agt. Culpeper, Va., 1954-56; mgr. sales Tripplett Milling Co., Culpeper, 1956-57; pres. Seal Kote of Roanoke (Va.), Inc., 1957; county agrl. agt. Whiteville, N.C., 1957-58; editor Miss. Farmer, Jackson, 1962-63; editor N.C. Farm and Ranch mag., Raleigh, 1963-64; founder pres., pub. Specialized Agrl. Publs., Inc., Raleigh, 1964—; pres. So. Planter Pub. Co., Inc., 1970—. Home: Rte 2 Box 74 Pittsboro NC 27312 Office: 11 S Boylan Av Raleigh NC 27603

BROADDUS, THOMAS NASH, textile co. exec.; b. Richmond, Va., Oct. 18, 1918; s. Thomas Nash and Louise (Eubank) B.; student U. Richmond, 1939; m. Betty Kirk Steel, Mar. 22, 1941; children—Thomas Nash III, Kirk Beverley, Elizabeth Louise; m. 2d, Suzy M. Hansen, Nov. 28, 1969; 1 son, Christopher C. North. With E. I. du Pont de Nemours & Co., Inc., 1946-65; pres., chief exec. Duplan Corp., N.Y.C., 1965—. Served to comdr. USNR, 1940-46, 51-52. Mem. Phi Kappa Sigma. Episcopalian (vestryman, treas.). Office: 1440 Broadway New York City NY 10018

BROADHEAD, DAKEN K., record mfr.; b. Nephi, Utah, Apr. 17, 1905; s. Samuel D. and Alice Anne (Carter) B.; grad. Utah State Agrl. Coll., 1928; m. Olene Smith, May 7, 1934; children—Jon D., David K., Bruce V., Samuel M., Stephen R. Pres., Allied Record Co., 1945—; chmn. bd. Campus Marketing Corp.; dir. Manhattan Refrigerating & Union Cold Storage Co.; chmn. bd. advisers KBIG AM-FM; exec. asst. to sec. of agr., 1953. Vice pres., sec. bd. trustees San Marino Unified Sch. Dist.; mem. nat. adv. bd. Brigham Young U. Sch. of Bus., Ettie Lee Homes, Utah Symphony; mem. adv. com. Los Angeles council Boy Scouts Am. Mem. Mchts. and Mfrs. Assn. (dir.), Los Angeles (dir.), Hollywood (hon. dir., past pres.) chambers commerce, Newcomen Soc. N.Am., Republican Assos., Pi Delta Epsilon, Sigma Nu, Alpha Kappa Psi. Rotarian. Home: 1520 Charlton Rd San Marino, CA 91108. Office: 2423 E 57th St Los Angeles CA 90058

BROADHEAD, JAMES LOWELL, metals co. exec.; b. New Rochelle, N.Y., Nov. 28, 1935; s. Clarence James and Mabel Roseader (Bowser) B.; B.M.E., Cornell U., 1958; LL.B., Columbia, 1963; m. Sharon Ann Rulon, May 6, 1967; children—Jeffrey Thorton, Kristen Ann. Admitted to N.Y. bar, 1963; mech. engr. sales dept. Ingersoll- Rand Co., 1958-59; with Debevoise, Plimpton, Lyons & Gates, N.Y.C., 1963-68; with St. Joe Minerals Corp., N.Y.C., 1968—, sec., 1970—; dir. Legal Systems, Inc., N.Y.C. Served with AUS, 1960-61. Mem. Am. Soc. Corporate Secs. (treas. N.Y. regional group 1971-72), Am., N.Y. State bar assns., Assn. Bar City N.Y. Home: 17 Royle Rd Darien CT 06820 Office: 250 Park Av New York City NY 10017

BROADMAN, ARTHUR R., corp. exec.; b. 1915; engring. degree Yale. With Tenneco Chems., Inc., and predecessor, 1940—, v.p., 1953-67, sr. v.p., 1967—, also dir.; dir. subsidiary Tenneco Mfg. Co.; v.p. Tenneco Inc., 1968—. Address: 280 Park Av New York City NY 10017

BROADNAX, MADISON, govt. ofcl.; b. Swords, Ga., Feb. 9, 1916; s. Asbury and Rosa A. (Ingram) B.; B.S., W.Va. State Coll., 1940; M.S., Mich. State Coll., 1942; postgrad., W.Va. U., 1955-57, Cornell U., 1968-69; m. Ruth Elaine Mitchell, Aug. 15, 1942. Farm mgr. State of W.Va., Lakin, 1942-43; agrl. extension agt. W.Va. State Coll., Institute, 46-49, with div. Dept. Agr., 1949-58; agrl. extension adviser AID, State Dept., Sudan, Khartoum, 1958-65, chief, agrl. research extension tng., Korea, 1965-68, dep. chief rural devel. div. U.S. Mission to Korea, 1969-70, dep. dir. Office Agr. and Fisheries, Tech. Assistance Bur., Washington, 1970—; prof. agr. and biol. scis. W.Va. State Coll., 1949-58. Served with USAAF, 1943-46. Recipient Achievement placque Korean Edn. and Research Inst., 1968-70. Mem. Rural Sociol. Soc., Am. Legion (dept. vice comdr. W.Va. 1949-50), Cornell Adult Edn. Assn., Beta Kappa Chi, Kappa Alpha Psi. Episcopalian. Mason (Shriner). Home: 2100 Washington Av Silver Spring MD 20910 Office: AID 21st and Virginia Av NW Washington DC 20523

BROADY, KNUTE OSCAR, educator; b. Pitzer, Ia., May 8, 1898; s. George Augustus and Mary (Brown) B.; B.S., Washburn Coll., 1920; M.A., U. Chgo., 1927; Ph.D., Tchrs. Coll., Columbia, 1930; m. Lois Thelma Pedersen, Dec. 28, 1932; children—Karen Margaret, Paula Marie, Merritt Pedersen, Teacher rural sch., Plains, Kan., 1916-17; sci. tchr., Lincoln (Kan.) High Sch., 1920-22, prin., 1922-24; supt. pub. schs., Sylvan Grove, Kan., 1924-26; asso. prof. sch. adminstrn. U. Neb., 1928-31, prof., 1931-41, prof. sch. adminstrn., dir. univ. extension, 1941-60, dir. univ. extension, head Center for Continuing Edn., 1959-63; prof. edn. U. Ala., 1964-68; acting pres. Stillman Coll., Tuscaloosa, 1965-67; chmn. div. edn. Lane Coll., Jackson, Tenn., 1968—. Sec. Internat. Conf. Corr. Edn., 1938, pres. 1948; mem. survey staff Wash. Ednl. Survey, 1946, D.C. Ednl. Survey, 1948; mem. U.S. Nat. Commn. UNESCO; vis. expert cons. Edn. Div., U.S. Forces, Austria, 1947, F.O.A., Turkey, 1954, ECA, Jamaica, 1961, AID, Venezuela, 1963, 71. Served as pvt. U.S. Army, 1917. Mem. Am. Assn. U. Profs., Phi Delta Kappa. Presbyn. Author: (with M.A. Stoneman and A. D. Brainard) Construction, Modernization, Renovation and Repair of Twelve Grade School Plants, 1949; (with others) Your Life Plans and The Armed Forces, 1955. Home: 53 Beechwood Dr Jackson TN 38301

BROBECK, JOHN RAYMOND, educator; b. Steamboat Springs, Colo., Apr. 12, 1914; s. James Alexander and Ella (Johnson) B.; B.S., Wheaton Coll., 1936, LL.D., 1960; M.S., Northwestern U., 1937, Ph.D., 1939; M.D., Yale, 1943; m. Dorothy Winifred Kellogg, Aug. 24, 1940; children—Stephen James, Priscilla Kimball, Elizabeth Martha, John Thomas. Instr. physiology Yale, 1943-45, asst. prof., 1945-48, asso. prof. physiology, 1948-52; prof. physiology, chmn. dept. U. Pa., Phila., 1952-70, Herbert C. Rorer prof. med. scis., 1970—. Sci. research adv. bd. Nat. Assn. Retarded Children. Fellow Am. Acad. Arts and Scis.; mem. Am. Physiol. Soc., Am. Inst. Nutrition, Am. Soc. Clin. Investigation, Phila. Coll. Physicians, Sigma Xi, Alpha Omega Alpha. Editor Yale Jour. Biology and Medicine, 1949-52; chmn. editorial bd. Physiol. Revs., 1963—. Home: 224 Vassar Av Swarthmore PA 19081 Office: U Pa Philadelphia PA 19104

BROBSTON, WILLIAM ALLEN, cement co. exec.; b. Nazareth, Pa., Jan. 11, 1913; s. Joseph and Alma (Spear) B.; B.S. in Econs., Wharton Sch., U. Pa., 1937; m. Catherine Louisa Porter, Sept. 6, 1937; children—Catherine Louisa (Mrs. L. Kirk Payne), Sarah Joanne (Mrs. Anthony L. Harriman), Mary Carolyn (Mrs. Peter Koch), William Allen. Eastern sales mgr. Lehigh Portland Cement Co., 1937-61; v.p. marketing Atlantic Cement Co., 1962-66; v.p. marketing Alpha Portland Cement Co., Easton, Pa., 1967-68, pres., 1968- -, also dir.; dir. Easton Nat. Bank and Trust Co., Slattery Assos., Inc., N.Y.C. Clubs: N.Y. Athletic, Marco Polo (N.Y.C.); Forest Lake (Hawley, Pa.); Pomfret, Country of Northampton County (Easton). Home: 227 E Lafayette St Easton PA 18042 Office: 15 S 3d St Easton PA 18042

BROCATO, JOSEPH V., banker; b. Merigold, Miss., Nov. 11, 1923; s. Joseph and Concetta (Marsiglia) B.; B.B.A., Loyola U. of South, New Orleans, 1949; student Grad. Sch., U. Bufalo, 1952-54; m. Mary Green, Feb. 5, 1949; children—Barbara, Kathleen, Peggy Ann, Joseph V., Robert, John, Annette, Mary, Patricia, Michael. With Firestone Tire & Rubber Co., 1948; with Mfrs. & Traders Trust Co., Buffalo, 1948—, exec. v.p., 1968—. Financial chmn., mem. bd. sta. WNED-TV, Buffalo, Greater Niagara council Boy Scouts Am. Bd. dirs. Villa Maria Coll., Buffalo; trustee Buffalo United Fund. Served with USNR, 1943-46. Home: 4720 Main St Synder NY 14226 Office: 1 M & T Plaza Buffalo NY 14240

BROCHES, ARON, internat. orgn. ofcl.; b. Amsterdam, Netherlands, Mar. 22, 1914; s. Abraham and Chaja (Person) B.; LL.M., U. Amsterdam, 1936, LL.D., 1939; LL.B., Fordham U., 1942; m. Catherina J. Pothast, May 2, 1939; children—Ida Alexandra (Mrs. Richard P.. Calabro), Paul Elias. Legal adviser Netherlands embassy, also Netherlands Econ. Mission, Washington and N.Y.C., 1942-46; with Internat. Bank Reconstrn. and Devel., 1946—, gen. counsel, 1959—. Mem. President's Council, 1965—; sec. gen. Internat. Centre for Settlement Investment Disputes, 1967—. Sec. Netherlands del. UN Monetary and Financial Conf., Bretton Woods, N.H., 1944; sec., legal adviser Netherlands Delegation inaugural meeting bd. govs. Internat. Monetary Fund and Internat. Bank Reconstrn. and Devel., Savannah, Ga., 1946; chief Internat. Bank gen. survey mission to Nigeria, 1953-54. Clubs: Society De Witte (The Hague); Cosmos (Washington). Author legal articles, Netherlands, U.S. and internat. publs. Home: 2600 Tilden Pl NW Washington DC 20008 Office: 1818 H St N W Washington DC 20433

BROCHIN, MURRY DAVID, lawyer; b. Hackensack, N.J., June 11, 1930; s. Samuel Z. and Anna (Levy) B.; B.A., Yale, 1952, postgrad. Law Sch., 1952-55; m. Leona Nelkin, Sept. 20, 1959; children-James Lewis, Nathaniel Edward, Esther Elizabeth. Admitted to N.J. bar, 1956; practice in Newark, 1960—; law sec. to Justice Nathan L. Jacobs, N.J. Supreme Ct., 1955-56; asso. Isreal B. Green, 1956-59; N.J. dep. atty. gen., 1959-60; asso. partner Lowenstein, Sandler, Brochin, Kohl & Fisher, 1960—. Trustee Newark Legal Services Project; mem. exec. com., trustee Jewish Ednl. Assn. Essex County. Mem. Am., N.J., Essex County bar assns., Phi Beta Kappa. Democrat. Jewish religion. Home: 62 Sagamore Rd Millburn NJ 07041 Office: 744 Broad St Newark NJ

BROCK, ALICE MAY, restaurateur, author; b. 1941; m. Ray Brock (div.). `Formerly tchr. in Stockbridge, Mass.; propr. restaurant, Stockbridge, 1966-67. Author: Alice's Restaurant Cookbook, 1969. Address: Stockbridge MA 01262*

BROCK, CLAUDE LOUIS, pub. relations dir.; b. Milltown, Ind., June 23, 1939; s. Claude Alex and Laura (Wilson) B.; student U. Ky., 1957-60, Bellarmine Coll., Louisville, 1961-65; m. Bobbye Dene Black, Jan. 25, 1958; children—Elizabeth Ann. Cluade Franklin. Advt. mgr. Spencer Magner, Taylorsville, Ky., 1960-61; owner B & B Printing & Pub. Co., Eminence, Ky., 1960-64; advt. mgr., editorial asst. Shelby Sentinel, Shelbyville, Ky., also partner Matthews-Brock Printing Co., 1964-66; gen. mgr. Newspapers, Inc., Shelbyville, 1966-67; editor Rural Kentuckian mag., Louisville, 1967-70; asst. sales promotion and pub. relations mgr. Stitzel-Weller Distillery, Louisville, 1970—; pub. relations dir. Tombstone Junction Scenic R.R. and Western Town, Whitley City, Ky.; owner Tombstone Junction Epitaph and Printing Mus.; pub. relations dir. Ky. Coop. Council, 1968-70. Sec. Henry County Indsl. Devel. Found., 1962-64; sec.-treas. Henry County Fair Assn., 1962-64. Dir. Ky. com. Inst. Internat. Edn., U. Louisville, 1970—. Recipient award for editing best rural coop. news publs. in nation Nat. Council Farm Coops., 1969. Mem. Farm Press and Radio Assn. Ky. Home: 322 N Main St Eminence KY 40019 Office: Fitzgerald Rd Louisville KY 40216

BROCK, DONALD CAMPBELL, former bookbinding co. exec.; b. Chgo., June 8, 1898; s. Archibald J. and Maud (Campbell) B.; grad. Shieffield Sci. Sch., Yale, 1920; m. Marjorie Farwell, 1924; 1 dau., Nancy Jean. Now dir. W. A. Krueger Co. Mem. adv. com. Book Pub. and Mfg. Industry, WPB, 1942. Served in naval aviation, World War I. Home: 180 DeWindt Rd Winnetka IL 60093

BROCK, GLEN PORTER, ry. exec.; b. Alden, Ia., Nov. 22, 1896; s. Loren Ellsworth and Mabel Mabel L. (Porter) B.; B.Sc., U. Ill., 1922; LL.D., Ill. Wesleyan U., 1959; m. Esther Goodwin, May 27, 1922; children—Paul Warrington, Glen Porter, Jr. Various positions. I.C.R.R., 1912-22; with G.,M. & N. R.R., 1922—, v.p., gen. mgr. merged G., M. & N. R.R., Mobile and Ohio R.R. and Alton R.R. (now G., M. & O. R.R. Co.), 1940-47; pres., dir. G., M. & O.R.R., 1957—, dir., 1947; pres., dir. New Orleans Gt. No. Ry. Co.; pres., dir. G., M. & O. Land Co.; dir. Gulf Transport Co., Protective Life Ins. Co. (Birmingham), Home Savs. & Loan Assn., Mchts. Nat. Bank (Mobile); alternate dir. Kansas City Terminal Ry. Co. Mem. Ala. Docks Adv. Bd., 1959-63; bd. dirs. Mobile Area Found. for Higher Edn., 1961- 63; mem. Mobile County Bd. Dept. Pensions and Security; chmn. bd. trustees United Fund Mobile County, Inc.; mem. bd. So. States Indsl. Council; chmn. founders com. Mobile Bapt. Coll.; mem. fund raising com. Florence Crittenton Home; mem. adv. council Ala. Civil War Centennial Commn.; mem. Army Adv. Com. Mobile; adv. com. to bd. dirs. Mobile Mental Health Assn.; adv. bd. Mobile County Hosp., Providence Hosp.; trustee Mobile Heart Assn., Ill. Wesleyan U.; chmn. bd. trustees Mobile County United Fund; dir. A.R.C., Mobile Assn. Blind; mem. adv. com. U. Ala. Center, Mobile, Friends of Mobile Library. Mem. Water Works Bd., Mobile. Served in U.S. Army, 1918. Named Mobilian of Year, 1960. Mem. Am. Legion, Mobile C. of C. (pres. 1950-52, indsl., adv. com.), Nat. Freight Traffic Assn., So. States Indsl. Council, Am. Royal Assn. (gov.), Pi Kappa Phi, Beta Gamma Sigma. Methodist (chmn. stewards). Mason (Shriner), Rotarian (2d v.p. 1961-62). Clubs: Lakewood Golf, Athelstan, Country, Isle Dauphine, Seamen's (trustee) (Mobile). Home: 2008 Dauphin Way Mobile AL 36605 Office: Gulf Mobile & Ohio R R Bldg Mobile AL 36601

BROCK, HORACE RHEA, educator; b. Leggett, Tex., Aug. 26, 1927; s. Hobby B. and Winona (Epperson) B.; B.S., Sam Houston State U., 1946, B.B.A., 1951, M.A., 1951; Ph.D., U. Tex., 1954; m. Frances Euline Williams, May 24, 1955; children—Alan Howard, Mary Ann, Charles. Prof. U. Ark., 1954-55; prof. North Tex. State U., 1955—, chmn. dept. acctg., 1966—; adviser AID, Istanbul, Turkey, 1967-69; cons. taxation and financial reporting. Served with USAF, 1946-49. Mem. Am. Inst. C.P.A.s, Tex. Soc. C.P.A.s, Nat. Assn. Accountants, Beta Gamma Sigma. Author: Introduction to Taxation, 1969; Cost Accounting, 1970; College Accounting, 1969; Intermediate and Advanced Accounting, 1966; Accounting for Oil and Gas Producers, 1960. Home: 1900 Westridge St Denton TX 76201

BROCK, IGNATIUS WADSWORTH, educator; b. Asheville, N.C., July 29, 1901; s. Ignatius W. and Ora Levicy (Koonce) B.; Ph.B., Emory U., 1927, A.M., 1930; Ph.D., (Dept. fellow 1936-37, Univ. fellow 1937-38, Markham Meml. grad. fellow 1938), U. Wis., 1938; certificate Inst. Touraine (France), 1928; postgrad. Duke U., Berea Coll., U. N.C.; m. Mary Will Weaver, Apr. 3, 1926; children—Hugh Wadsworth, Susan Koonce. Staff, Howard Photog. Studios, Asheville; prin. Roswell (Ga.) High Sch., 1925-26; asst. Romance lang. Emory U., Atlanta, 1926-27, instr., 1927-40, asst. prof., 1940-43, asso. prof., 1943-45, prof. Romance langs., 1945-69, emeritus, 1969—, registrar, 1948-69, asst. to pres., 1953-57. Mem. Phi Beta Kappa, Kappa Phi Kappa, Phi Sigma Iota. Democrat (independent). Methodist. Asso. editor Emory U. Quar. Contbr. articles to various lang. jours. Researcher in bibliography, 16th Century lit. and history. Home: 1908 N Decatur Rd NE Atlanta GA 30307

BROCK, JAMES DANIEL, airline exec.; b. Montgomery County, Ala., Feb. 19, 1916; s. Alexander Franklin and Rebecca Bookhart (Lamar) B.; student Tulane U., 1936-37; m. Alice Ferguson Jones, Jan. 8, 1948; childrenJames Daniel, Alice Timoxena, Franklin Laurens. Vice pres. TACA Internat. Airlines and TACA Corp., 1953-59, Frontier Airlines, 1959-62, Nat. Airlines, Miami Fla., 1962-. Hon. consul Guatemala in Denver, 1960-62. Served to capt. USAAF, 1941-45. Bd. dirs. Lighthouse for Blind, Miami Mem. Caribbean Air Transp. Assn. (pres. 1956-59) Am. Soc. Travel Agts., Nat. Orgn. Travel Orgns. (dir.) Air Traffic Conf. Am. (pres. 1970), Discover Am. Travel Orgns. (dir.), Phi Delta Theta Methodist Clubs: Riviera Country; Nat. Aviation; Internat. House (bd. dirs. 1955-59) (New Orleans); Aviation Executives, Biscayne Bay Yacht (Miami, Fla.). Home: 4107 Santa Maria Coral Gables FL 33146 Office: P O Box 2055 AMF Miami, FL 33159.

BROCK, JAMES SIDNEY, lawyer; b. Newbury, Vt., Sept. 2, 1913; s. Frank Nelson and Louise (Johnson) B.; B.S., Middlebury Coll., 1935; LL.B., St. Lawrence U., 1942; m. Gladys H. Linton, Sept. 14, 1940; children—Linda L. (Mrs. Christopher Scoggins), Richard L., Elizabeth A. Admitted to N.Y. bar, 1942, Vt. bar, 1947; practiced in N.Y.C., 1942-47, Montpelier, Vt., 1947—; claims adjuster Liberty Mut. Ins. Co., 1935-42; asso. LeBoeuf & Lamb, 1942-46; pvt. practice, Montpelier, 1947-50; atty. Nat. Life Ins. Co., 1950-56, asst. counsel, 1956-63, gen. counsel, 1963—, v.p., gen. counsel, 1968-70, sr. v.p., gen. counsel, 1970—. Bd. dirs. Central Vt. Med. Center, Inc.; trustee Wood Art Gallery. Mem. Assn. Life Ins. Co., Am., Vt. (bd. mgrs.) bar assns., Associated Industries Vt. (dir.). Republican. Conglist. Elk. Home: 9 Jordan St Montpelier VT 05602 Office: Nat Life Dr Montpelier VT 05602

BROCK, JAMES WILSON, educator; b. Greensfork, Ind., May 23, 1919; s. Virgil Prentiss and Blanche (Kerr) B.; A.B., Manchester Coll., 1941; M.A., Northwestern U., 1942, Ph.D., 1950; m. Martha Faught, June, 1942 (div. Mar. 1956); m. 2d, Patricia Anne Clemons, Mar. 16, 1956 (div. Nov. 1967); children—Lisa Anne, Tamsen Lee, Julie Michele; m. 3d, Marjorie Mellor, Feb. 1, 1969. Faculty, Albion (Mich.) Coll., 1946-56; asst. prof. communication skills Mich. State U., East Lansing, 1955-56; asst. prof. speech U. Mich., Ann Arbor, 1956-57; asso. prof. drama Fla. State U., Tallahassee, 1957-58; prof. drama, chmn. dept. San Fernando Valley State Coll., Northridge, Cal., 1958—. Mng. dir. Plymouth (Mass.) Drama Festival, 1956-58; dir. Wingspread Theatre, Colon, Mich., 1955. Served with USAAF, 1942-45; MTO. Decorated Bronze Star. Ch. Soc. for Coll. Work fellow, 1964-65; San Fernando Valley State Coll. Found. grantee, 1964, 66, 67. Mem. Nat. Theatre Conf., Am. Ednl. Theatre Assn. (coll. v.p. So. Cal. dist. 1963-64), Theta Alpha Phi (nat. sec.-treas. 1952-57), Delta Sigma Rho, Tau Kappa Alpha. Author: Modern Chancel Drama (Baker's Plays), 1964. Home: 19119 Nordhoff St Northridge CA 91324

BROCK, JEFFRY VANSTONE, Canadian naval officer; b. Vancouver, B.C., Can., Aug. 29, 1913; s. Eustace Alexander and Margaret Rhoebe (Jukes) B.; ed., St. John's Coll., Winnipeg, Man., U. Man.; m. Patricia Elizabeth Folkes, Mar. 11, 1950; children—Jeffrey Patrick Alexander, Constance Alexandra, William Ranulf Augustus D'Aquillan. Formerly with Great West Life Assurance Co., then Western mgr. Cockfield, Brown & Co.; commd. 1st lt. Royal Canadian Naval Vol. Res., 1934, advanced through grades to rear adm. Royal Canadian Navy, 1961; served afloat in N. Atlantic, W. and N. Africa, Italy, E. Mediterranean, World War II; comdr. H.M.S. Ontario, 1945-47; dir. naval plans, Ottawa, Can., 1948-50; comdr. Canadian Destroyers Far East, 1950- 51; naval mem. directing staff Nat. Def. Coll. Can., 1951-53; naval mem. Canadian Joint Staff, London, also naval adviser high commr. Can., 1953- 57; sr. Canadian officer afloat, Atlantic, 1957-58; asst. chief naval staff air and warfare, also mem. Naval Bd., Ottawa, 1958-61; vice chief naval staff, permanent mem. joint Bd. Def. Can. and U.S., 1961-63; Canadian maritime comdr. Atlantic, also flag officer Atlantic Coast and NATO comdr. Canadian Atlantic Area, 1963—. Pres., chief exec. officer Scotia Marinas, Ltd., Can., 1969—. Decorated D.S.C., Distinguished Service Order, Legion of Merit. Mem. P.C. Assn. Nova Scotia (v.p.). Mem. Anglican Ch. Home: Chester House Chester Nova Scotia Canada

BROCK, MARIANNE, educator; b. Winnipeg, Can., Oct. 9, 1908; d. Stanley and Edith (Codd) Brock; B.A., McGill U., 1928; B.A., Oxford (Eng.) U., 1930, M.A., 1935; Ph.D., Bryn Mawr Coll., 1944. Mem. faculty Mt. Holyoke Coll., 1930, 38- -, now prof. English; scholar, fellow Bryn Mawr Coll., 1933-36; instr. U. Colo., 1938. Office: Dept of English Mt Holyoke Coll South Hadley MA 01075

BROCK, PAUL WARRINGTON, lawyer; b. Mobile, Ala., Feb. 23, 1918; s. Glenn Porter and Esther (Goodwin) B.; student Ala. Poly. Inst., 1944; B.S., U. Ala., 1948, J.D., 1950; m. Grace Leigh Blasingame, Sept. 4, 1948 (dec., June 1960); children-Paul W., Bette Leigh, Valerie Grace; m. 2d Louise Morris Shearer, July 6, 1962; children-Louise Shearer, Richard Goodwin. Admitted to Ala. bar, 1950; practice in Mobile, 1953—; mem. firm Hand, Arendall & Bedsole, 1953-56, Hand, Arendall, Bedsole, Greaves & Johnston, 1956—; faculty continuing legal edn. program Ala. Bar Assn. Served to 2d lt. USAF, 1952-53. Recipient Nat. Balfour award Sigma Chi, 1946-47. Mem. Am., Ala., Mobile bar assns., Internat. Assn. Ins. Counsel, Ala. Def. Lawyers Assn. (past pres.), Def. Research Inst. (regional v.p.,), Fedn. Ins. Counsel, Nat. Assn. R.R. Trial Counsel, Omicron Delta Kappa, Beta Gamma Sigma. Republican. Episcopalian. Home: 1970 Oak Knoll Circle Mobile AL 36607 Office: P O Box 123 Mobile AL 36601

BROCK, POPE FURMAN, lawyer; b. Avalon, Ga., Oct. 13, 1888; s. William Thomas and Eliza Jane (Keeling) B.; A.B., U. Ga., 1911, LL.B., 1913; LL.D., Piedmont Coll., Oglethorpe U., 1956; m. Alice Matthews, Mar. 30, 1921; children—Pope F., Mary Jane. Part time instr. history dept. U. Ga., 1911-14; admitted to Ga. bar, 1913, practiced in Macon, 1914-32; mem. firm Brock, Sparks & Russell, 1920-32, mem. Spalding, MacDougald, Sibley & Brock, Atlanta, 1935, Spalding, Sibley, Troutman & Brock, 1936- 42; gen. counsel Coca-Cola Co., Atlanta, 1942-54, ret., continues in adv. capacity; chmn. bd. dirs. Fulton Nat. Bank of Atlanta; dir. Georgia Marble Co., Piedmont Securities Co. Chmn. Local Govt. Commn. Atlanta and Fulton County, Ga., 1966. Bd. regents U. System Ga., 1943-49, chmn. bd., 1947-49; trustee Oglethorpe U., 1944-59, chmn. bd. trustees, 1956-59; trustee Univ. Center in Ga. Mem. task force on water resources and power devel. 2d Hoover Commn. on Govt. Reorganization. Mem. Am., Ga., Atlanta bar assns., Am. Judicature

Soc., U. Ga. Alumni Soc. (pres. 1931-32), Atlanta Hist. Soc., Nat. Council Juvenile Ct. Judges and Nat. Juvenile Ct. Found. (asso.), Phi Beta Kappa Assos., Phi Beta Kappa. Club: Piedmont Driving. Home: 2629 Arden Rd N W Atlanta GA 30327 Office: 310 North Av N W Atlanta GA 30313

BROCK, RAYMOND EUGENE, pub. co. exec.; b. Blackwell, Okla., Oct. 17, 1926; s. Clarence Eugene and Ester Ann (McGuire) B.; student U. So. Cal., 1945-50; m. Joann Maureen Learnihan, Apr. 9, 1955; children—Maureen Louise, Sara Elaine, Katherine Anne. Asso. editor Hot Rod mag., Los Angeles, 1953-57, tech. editor, 1957-63, pub., 1963; v.p. Petersen Automotive Group, 1969—. Served with USNR, 1944-45. Home: 7969 Mulholland Dr Los Angeles CA 90046 Office: 8490 Sunset Blvd Los Angeles CA 90069

BROCK, SARAH PRATT, assn. ofcl., writer; b. West Chester, Pa., Oct. 4, 1905; d. Maurice Baldwin and Beulah (Darlington) Pratt; A.B., Swarthmore Coll., 1927; postgrad. Bryn Mawr Coll., 1928, Columbia, summer 1927; m. Lynmar Brock, June 18, 1932; children—Lynmar, Barbara (Mrs. Donald A. Kidder), Charles Nonnater II. Tchr. elementary edn. Friends' Central Sch., Phila., 1927-33, U. Pa. summer sch., 1932. Mem. Nat. League Am. Pen Women, 1947—, pres. Phila. br., 1952-54, Pa., 1960-62, nat. v.p., 1956- 58, mem. nat. bd. and nat. chmnships, 1954-64, nat. pres. 1964-66; mem. Delaware County Coll. Women's Club, 1936-38, Manoa P.T.A., 1941-44, Manoa Community Library, 1943-45, Delaware County Writers' Club, 1946- 48, Phila. Regional Writers' Conf., 1956; co-founder Friends of Caleb Pusey House, Inc., 1960, 1st pres., 1960; 1st v.p. Haverford Twp. Civic Council, 1945, Haverford Twp. League Women Voters, 1942, St. Davids Christian Writers' Conf. 1963-65; dist. dir. United Fund, 1943-45, 58- 62; bd. mgrs. Friends Jour., 1959-64. Recipient Lit Brothers award community service, 1961; Distinguished Service award Clearwater br., 1965; named Ark. traveler, 1965; recipient keys to Tampa, Fla., Baltimore, St. Louis, Tulsa, Knoxville, Nashville, Birmingham, Ala., Little Rock and San Diego; named Pa. Mother of Tear, 1970. Life mem. Phila. Regional Writers' Conf. (bd. (dirs.); mem. D.A.R., Colonial Dames, Daus. Am. Colonists (regent chpt.), Founders and Patriots Am. (pres. 1967-70), Huguenot Soc., Welcome Soc., Internat. Platform Assn., League Women Voters, Chester County (bd. dirs., program chmn.), Delaware County (bd. dirs., editor Bulletin) hist. socs., Hist. Delaware County (bd. dirs.), St. Davids Christian Writers' Conf. (bd. dirs.), Nat. Soc. Arts and Letters, Kappa Kappa Gamma. Republican. Mem. Soc. Friends (past clk.). Author: William Penn Project, 1944; Friends' Religious Education Series, 1942-43; (with Sophie H. Drinker) Historical Research Booklet, 1963; also features articles, poems, juveniles. Home: Hunters' Hill Valley Rd Newtown Square PA 19073 Office: 420 E Erie Av Philadelphia PA 19134

BROCK, WILLIAM EMERSON, III, U.S. senator; b. Chattanooga, Nov. 23, 1930; s. William Emerson Jr. and Myra (Kruesi) B.; grad. McCallie Sch., 1949; B.S., Washington and Lee U., 1953; m. Laura Handly, Jan. 11, 1957; children—William Emerson IV, Oscar, Laura, John. With Brock Candy Co., Chattanooga, 1956-63; mem. 88th-91st congresses from 3d Dist. Tenn.; mem. U.S. Senate from Tenn., 1970—. Served as lt. (j.g.) USNR, 1953-56; Mem. Sigma Alpha Epsilon. Republican. Presbyn. Home: Dogwood Dr Lookout Mountain TN 37350 also 10837 Stanmore Dr Potomac MD 20850 Office: Senate Office Bldg Washington DC 20525

BROCK, WILLIAM EMERSON, Jr., candy mfr.; b. Clarksville, Tenn., Nov. 5, 1903; s. William Emerson and Miriam (Acree) B.; grad. McCallie Sch., Chattanooga, 1921; Washington and Lee U., 1925; student Babson's Inst., Babson Park, Mass.; L.H.D. (hon.), U. Chattanooga, 1969; m. Myra Krusi, Apr. 5, 1928; children—William Emerson III, Paul Kruesi, Frank Acree. Chmn. bd. Brock Candy Co., Chattanooga, pres. Century Co., Chattanooga; dir. Hamilton Nat. Bank, Provident Life & Accident Ins. Co. (both Chattanooga). Past chmn. confectionary industry div. Com. Econ. Devel. Chmn. organizing com. United Fund Greater Chattanooga, also mem. exec. com. Chmn. trustees U. Chattanooga; trustee McCallie Sch., Dr. E. Stabley Jones Found.; mem. adv. bd. Chattanooga Salvation Army. Recipient Liberty Bell award Chattanooga Bar Assn., 1965; Man of Year award Chattanooga Kiwanis Club, 1966. Mem. Nat. Confectionary Assn. (past v.p., dir.), Sigma Chi. Presbyn. (elder, tchr.) Clubs: Mountain City, Lookout Mountain, Fairland (Chattanooga). Home: 213 W Watkins St Lookout Mountain TN 37350 Office: 1113 Chestnut St Chattanooga TN 37402

BROCK, WILLIAM MEGRUE, banker; b. Cin., Aug. 24, 1884; s. J. Harry and Virginia E. (Megrue) B.; ed. pub. schs., Cin. With Gem City Savs. Assn., Dayton, O., 1904—, chmn. bd., 1965—; pres. Home Av. R.R. Co., Dayton, 1940—; dir. Dayton Power & Light Co., 1947—; bd. dirs., vice chmn. bd. FHLB, Cin., 1936-56. Mem. local Draft Bd., World War II; pres. Dayton Better Bus. Bur., 1925. Pres. Dayton Art Inst., 1942. Recipient SSS medal, 1945. Mem. U.S. Savs. and Loan League (pres. 1945), Ohio Bldg. Assn. League (pres. 1935). Republican. Methodist. Home: 922 E Schantz Av Dayton OH 45419 Office: 6 N Main St Dayton OH 45402

BROCKEL, HARRY CHARLES, educator; b. Chgo., Sept. 18, 1908; s. Thomas J. and Margaret (Strachan) B.; student U. Wis., Marquette U., 1926-31; m. Ella M. Searth, Nov. 4, 1936; 1 dau., Leslie Jeanne. Various positions City Milw. Bd. Harbor Commrs., 1926-36, sec., 1936-42, municipal port dir., 1942-68; faculty U. Wis., Milw., 1969—. Vice chmn. Wis. Deep Waterways Commn., 1945-69, Gt. Lakes Commn.; chmn. Wis. Gov.'s com. St. Lawrence Seaway Project, 1952—; adv. bd. St. Lawrence Seaway Devel. Corp., 1954-69; chmn. Gt. Lakes Compact Commn. Wis.; adv. bd. Gt. Lakes Pilotage Adminstrn.; fed. port controller Gt. Lakes-St. Lawrence Seaway Ports; mem. export expansion council Dept. Commerce. Mem. adv. council on naval affairs World Affairs Council. Trustee Gt. Lakes Found. Recipient good govt. award Milw. Jr. C. of C., 1951, Distinguished Pub. Service award Milw. Assn. Commerce, 1954, Nat. Pub. Service award Fraternal Order Eagles, 1954, Pere Marquette award Marquette U., 1956; Distinguished Engring. Service award U. Wis., 1958; award Cosmopolitan Club, 1959, Milw. Found., 1960. Mem. Am. Assn. Port Authorities (pres. 1949, dir.), Gt. Lakes Harbors Assn., Nat. Rivers and Harbor Congress (dir.), Am. Soc. Mil. Engrs., USCG League, USCG Aux., Am. Soc. for Pub. Adminstrn. (pres. Milw. chpt.), Navy League U.S., Gt. Lakes Model Shipbuilders Guild, Internat. Assn. Shipmasters, Civil War Round Table, Assn. Municipal Engrs., Alpha Kappa Psi (hon.). Mason. Clubs: Milwaukee Athletic, Executives, Milwaukee Traffic, Milwaukee Transportation, Milwaukee Yacht, Port of Milwaukee Propeller, World Trade (Milw.); Propeller U.S. (nat. v.p. 1951); Chicago Traffic. Author: The Milwaukee River, 1968; co-author: Transportation Century. Contbr. articles to jours. Home: 2742 N 95th St Milwaukee WI 53222

BROCKELBANK, WILLIAM JOHN, lawyer; b. Ont., Can., Mar. 13, 1895; s. William and Mary (Hunter) B.; student Pickering Coll., Newmarket, Ont., 1913-15; A.B., Haverford Coll., 1919; LL.B., Harvard, 1923; Lincoln's Inn, Barrister at Law, 1928; Docteur en Droit, U. Paris, 1934; m. Mary Chambers, July 29, 1922 (div. 1937); 1 dau., Frank Leslie; m. 2d, Naomi Lorene Campbell, July 8, 1939 (div. 1941); m. 3d, Esther Norie, Aug. 17, 1945. Admitted to Ida. bar, 1944; asso. prof. law U. Ala., 1923-24; lectr. law U. Pitts., 1924-25; sec. Internat. Corp. Co., Paris, France, 1925-28; prof. law U. Ala., 1928-31; practiced law, Paris, 1934-35, U. Kan., 1935-40; practiced law Vancouver, B.C., 1940-42; lectr. govt. U. B.C., 1941-42; vis. prof. law U. Kansas City, 1942-43; asso. prof. law U. Ida., 1943-45, prof. law, 1946-66, prof. law emeritus, 1966—. Vis. prof. law at U. Auckland (New Zealand), 1967, U. P.R., 1954-55, 62-63; spl. lectr. on law for Dept. State, Haiti, 1958-59. Uniform Laws Commr. for Ida., 1947—. Served with A.R.C., 1918-19. Decorated officier l'ordre des Palmes Academiques (France). Mem. Am. Assn. U. Profs., Order of Coif, Phi Beta Kappa, Phi Delta Phi. Democrat. Unitarian. Mason. Author: Interstate Enforcement of Family Support, 1960; The Community Property Law of Idaho, 1963. Contbr. to law revs. Home: 203 S Polk St Moscow ID 83843

BROCKENBROUGH, HENRY WATKINS, banker; b. Richmond, Va., Aug. 28, 1923; s. Benjamin Willard and Kathleen Reading (Watkins) B.; B.A. cum laude, Hampden-Sydney Coll., 1944; Ll.B., U. Va., 1948; grad. Stonier Grad. Sch. Banking, Rutgers U., 1957; m. Mary Lane Williams, Oct. 30, 1948; children—Henry Watkins, Rebecca Lane, John Reading, Willson Williams. Admitted to Va. bar, 1949; with State-Planters Bank, Richmond, Va., 1948—, v.p., trust officer, 1963- 67, sr. v.p., trust officer, 1967—. Past pres. Estate Planning Council Richmond. Vice pres., bd. dirs. St. Giles Endowment Fund. Served to lt. (j.g.) USNR, 1943-46. Mem. Va. Bankers Assn. (chmn. trust com. 1970-71), Richmond, Va. chambers commerce, Navy League, Va. State Bar, Lambda Chi Alpha, Delta Theta Phi. Presbyn. (elder, past chmn. bd. deacons). Club: Richmond Downtown. Home: 802 Horsepen Rd Richmond VA 23229 Office: 900 E Main St Richmond VA 23214

BROCKETT, ERNEST DELWIN, oil exec.; b. Itasca, Tex., Apr. 16, 1913; s. Ernest Delwin and Janet (Baines) B.; B.S., Tex. A. and M. Coll., 1934; m. Frances Maxine Sammons, Mar. 7, 1936; children—Belmont Sammons, Janet. Various positions Gulf Oil Corp., Crane, Tex., 1934-36, then prodn. engr., Odessa, Tex., 1936-40, asst. chief engr., Fort Worth, 1945-48, asst. supt. prodn., Ft. Worth, 1948-49, staff engr. prodn. dept., 1949-52, v.p., mgr. Houston prodn. div., 1955-57, adminstrv. v.p. prodn. dept., Pitts., 1957-58, exec. v.p., 1960, dir., 1960—, pres., 1960-65, chmn. bd., chief exec. officer, 1965—, also chmn. bd. subsidiary firms; asst. to pres., then Eastern dist. mgr. Mene Grande Oil Co., Caracas, Venezuela, 1952-55; pres., chief exec. officer Brit. Am. Oil Co., Ltd., Toronto (now Gulf Oil Can. Ltd.), 1958-60; dir. Bank N.S., Mellon Nat. Bank and Trust Co., Aluminum Co. Am., ADELA Investment Co. S.A. Mem. Internat. Urban Transp. Conf. Com., Pitts. Urban Transit Council, Regional Indsl. Devel. Corp. South-western Pa.; chmn. Nat. Petroleum Council; mem. citizens sponsoring com. Allegheny Conf. on Community Devel. Trustee, Carnegie-Mellon U. Served from 1st lt. to col. AUS, 1940-45. Decorated Silver Star medal with cluster, Legion of Merit, Bronze Star medal with cluster, Air Medal (U.S.); Distinguished Service Order (Britain). Mem. Am. Inst. Mining, Metall. and Petroleum Engrs., Am. Petroleum Inst., Pa. Economy League. Clubs: Longue Vue (Verona, Pa.); Duquesne, Pittsburgh Athletic Assn. (Pitts.); Houston. Office: Gulf Bldg Pittsburgh PA 15230

BROCKETT, ROGER WARE, educator, system theorist; b. Wadsworth, O., Oct. 22, 1938; s. Roger L. and Grace (Patch) B.; B.S., Case Western Res. U., 1960, M.S., 1962, Ph.D., 1964; M.A., Harvard, 1969; m. Carolann C. Riske, Aug. 20, 1960; children—Mark William, Douglas Matthew. Postdoctoral fellow, asst. prof. Mass. Inst. Tech., 1963-67, asso. prof., 1967-69; prof. applied math. Harvard, Cambridge, Mass., 1969—. Recipient Donald P. Eckman award, 1967. Sr. postdoctoral fellow SRC Eng., 1969. Mem. Sigma Xi, Tau Beta Pi, Sigma Nu. Author: Finite Dimensional Linear Systems, 1970. Home: 5 Blinn Rd Lexington MA 02173 Office: Pierce Hall Harvard Cambridge MA 02138

BROCKETT, WILLIAM ALDEN, coll. pres.; b. Chgo., Feb. 22, 1914; s. Clarence Lewis and Rosina (Miller) B.; B.S., U.S. Naval Acad., 1934; student U.S. Naval Postgrad. Sch., 1940-42; M.S., Mass. Inst. Tech., 1943; student grad. mgmt. courses U. Pitts., 1955, Harvard Bus. Sch., 1960; m. Juana Elizabeth Sutton, May 3, 1939; children—William Alden, Cynthia Ann. Commd. ensign U.S. Navy, 1934, advanced through grades to rear adm., 1961; assigned battleships and cruisers, 1934-38, river gunboats Luzon and Oahu, Yangtze Patrol, 1938-40; chief engr. U.S.S. New Orleans, 1943-45; designated engring. specialist, 1945; instr. U.S. Naval Acad., 1947-51; material officer battleships and cruisers, Atlantic Fleet, 1951-54; assigned David Taylor Model Basin, 1954-56; dir. machinery div. Bur. Ships, 1956-58; prodn. officer Long Beach Naval Shipyard, 1958-60; comdr. Boston Naval Shipyard, 1960-62; asst. chief Bur. Ships, 1962-63, chief, 1963-66; pres. Webb Inst. Naval Architecture, Glen Cove, N.Y., 1966 —. Decorated Legion of Merit. Mem. Soc. Naval Architects and Marine Engrs., Am. Soc. M.E., Am. Soc. Naval Engrs. (pres. 1963), Am. Soc. Engring. Edn. Co-author: Elements of Applied Thermodynamics, 1949. Address: Webb Inst Naval Architecture Glen Cove, NY 11542.

BROCKEY, HAROLD, dept. store exec.; children—Mrs. Joel Goldberg, Mrs. Lewis Kravitz. Pres., dir. Rich's Inc., Atlanta; dir. Nat. Bank of Ga. Bd. dirs. Met. Atlanta Community Services, United Appeal. Mem. Nat. Retail Assn. (v.p.). Rotarian. Home: 3201 Ridgewood Rd N W Atlanta GA 30327 Office: Broad Alabama Forsyth and Hunter Sts Atlanta GA 30303

BROCKHAUS, HERMAN HENRY, educator; b. Antigo, Wis., May 20, 1907; s. Henry Herman and Rose (Jenewein) B.; B.A., N. Central Coll., 1929; M.A., U. Wis., 1937, Ph.D., 1949; m. Lorraine Ann Fergot, Dec. 25, 1930. Tchr. speech and English, New London (Wis.) High Sch., 1929-38; prof. speech Pacific U., 1938-41; instr. Oberlin Coll., 1941-42; faculty U. Wis., 1947—, prof. speech, 1956—, chmn. univ. extension dept. speech, 1947-70, chmn. univ. center system dept. speech, 1964-66. Served with M.C., AUS, 1942-45. Mem. Wis. High Sch. Forensic Assn. (exec. sec. 1965—), Nat. Univ. Extension Assn., Am. Assn. U. Profs., Speech Com. Assn., Central States, Wis. speech assns., Alpha Psi Omega, Delta Sigma Rho, Tau Kappa Alpha, Phi Delta Kappa, Pi Kappa Delta. Contbr. profl. jours. Home: 3914 Priscilla Lane Madison WI 53705

BROCKMANN, LOUIS ORVAL, educator; b. Seymour, Wis., May 3, 1905; s. Henry and Emma (Dorrow) B.; B.A., U. Wis., 1928, M.A., 1929, Ph.D., 1945; postgrad. Colo. State Coll., summers 1934, 37; m. Marion O. Danielson, June 9, 1941. Personnel work Wis. Telephone Co., 1929-30; asst. prin., dir. vocational guidance and tng. Fergus County High Sch., Lewistown, Mont., 1930-44; grad. asst. U. Wis., 1942-43; asst. prof. edn., psychology Mont. State Coll., 1944- 46, dir. counseling and testing service, 1944-47, asso. prof., 1946-47, prof., head dept. edn., psychology, dir. summer quarter, 1947-51; pres. No. Mont. Coll., 1951-63; prof. counselor preparation Cal. State Coll., Fullerton, 1963—, mem. grad. council, 1965-67. Recorder Nat. Conf. Improvement of Teaching, 1948, cons. 1950; chmn. adv. com. guidance Mont. Dept. Pub. Instrn., 1943-46; vice chmn. Statewide Guidance Services Com., 1947-50. Chmn. exec. council U. Mont., 1953-55, 61-62. Montana Inst. Arts fellow, 1968. Mem. Mont. Edn. Assn. (dist. pres. 1938, v.p. 1946-48), N.E.A., Am. Personnel and Guidance Assn., Nat Vocational Guidance Assn., Assn. Sch. Counselors, Am. Vocational Assn., N.W. Assn. Jr. Colls. (pres. 1958), N.W. Assn. Secondary and Higher Schs. (research com. 1957-61), Phi Kappa Phi, Phi Delta Kappa. Kiwanian (dist. gov. 1941, chmn. Mont. dist. com. vocational guidance 1936, Legion of Honor 1966). Author: (with others) A Basic Test for Guidance Workers, 1947; (with Hollis Allen) Occupational Curricular Needs Orange County Junior Colleges, 1966; (with J. Hugo Aronson) The Galloping Swede, 1970. Also articles ednl. jours. Editor Guidance Page, Mont. Edn. Jour., 1946-48. Home: 527 N Lincoln Av Fullerton CA 92631

BROCKMANN, ROBERT JOHN, investment co. exec.; b. N.Y.C., Feb. 22, 1927; s. Herman L. and Matilda (Schroeder) B.; A.B., Columbia, 1948, M.S., 1949; m. Marilyn Frechette, Nov. 24, 1949; children—R. John, Mary Elise, Ann Louise, Paul Herman, Jane Elizabeth, Susan V., Peter. Mgr., Arthur Andersen & Co., N.Y.C., 1949-57; treas. Minerals & Chems. Phillipp Corp., Menlo Park, N.J., 1957-62; exec. v.p. Wallace & Tiernan, Inc., Belleville, N.J., 1962-69, also treas., dir.; exec. v.p. Am. Investment Co., St. Louis, 1970—, also dir.; dir. Republic Investment Corp. Served with U.S. Mcht. Marine, 1945-46. C.P.A., N.Y. Mem. Am. Inst. C.P.A.'s, N.Y. Soc. C.P.A.'s, Financial Execs. Inst. Clubs: Glen Ridge Country, University (N.Y.C.). Home: 11106 Hermitage Hill Frontenac MO 63131 Office: 825 Maryland Av St Louis MO 63105

BROCKUNIER, SAMUEL HUGH, historian, educator; b. Wheeling, W. Va., Nov. 17, 1903; s. Samuel Hugh And Clare (Reed) B.; A.B., Harvard, 1926, M.A., 1928, Ph.D., 1937; M.A., Wesleyan U., 1945; m. Eloise Marcy, July 8, 1933; 1 son, Nicholas. Editorial staff Boston Globe, 1926-27; with Wesleyan U., Middletown, Conn., 1930—, successively instr. history, asst. and asso. prof., prof., 1944—, William F. Armstrong prof. history, 1949—. Vis. lectr. Am. history Amherst Coll., 1935-36, Conn. Coll. for Women, 1941-42; vis. prof. Northwestern U., 1946, Yale, 1947-48. Polit. adviser to Sen. Brian McMahon, 1944; del. Dem. State Conv., 1944. Mem. Am., Miss. Valley hist. assns., Am. Assn. U. Profs., Social Sci. Research Council (sec. com. historiography 1948-54), Phi Beta Kappa. Democrat. Episcopalian. Author: The Irrepressible Democrat. Roger Williams, 1940, The United States, 1947; The Making of American Democracy, 1950, rev. edit. 1962 (both with Billington and Loewenberg); (with others) The Social Sciences in Historical Study, 1954. Editor Connecticut in Transition (R.J. Purcell), 1963. Contbr. to Dictionary of American Biography, New Century Cyclopedia of Names, Encyclopedia Italiana, Hist. jours. Home: 390 Pine St Middletown CT 06457 Office: Dept History Wesleyan Univ Middletown CT 06457

BROCKWAY, BRIAN GEORGE, univ. dean; b. Grand Rapids, Mich., Aug. 31, 1933; s. George Raymond and Marie (Pettit) B.; student U. Notre Dame, 1951-52; B.S., Northwestern U., 1957; J.D., Georgetown U., 1961, LL.M., 1963; m. Elizabeth Ann Martens, July 12, 1958; children—Matthew, Marie, Gregory. Admitted to Va. bar, 1961; prof. comml. law Lehigh U., 1963-67, chmn. dept. finance, marketing and law, 1967-69; vis. prof. law U. Detroit, 1969, dean Sch. Law, 1969—. Served as cpl. AUS, 1952-54. Mem. Am., Va. bar assns., Bus. Law Assn., Blue Key, Omicron Delta Kappa, Beta Gamma Sigma. Home: 15115 Windmill Pointe Grosse Pointe Park MI 48230 Office: 651 E Jefferson St Detroit MI 48226

BROCKWAY, DUNCAN, librarian; b. Manchester, N.H., July 23, 1932; s. Walter Priest and Eleanor (Duncan) B.; B.A., St. John's Coll., Annapolis, Md., 1953; student Harvard Div. Sch., 1953-55; B.D., Princeton Theol. Sch., 1956; M.A. in L.S., Rutgers U., 1960; m. Lois Simpson, Jan. 19, 1957; children—Peter, Andrew, Ellen, Catherine. Ordained to ministry Presbyn. Ch., 1956; pastor in Windham, N.H., 1956-58; order librarian Speer Library, Princeton Theol. Sem., 1958-62; pastor in Frenchtown, N.J., 1962-65; with Case Meml. Library, Hartland Sem. Found., 1965—, librarian, 1967—. Sec. W. Hartford Fire Dept., 1966—; mem. Hartland Bd. Edn., 1970-71. Mem. Am., Conn. library assns., Am. Theol. Library Assns. Democratic. Home: Box 23 West Hartland CT 06091 Office: 55 Elizabeth St Hartford CT 06105

BROCKWAY, GEORGE POND, publisher; b. Portland, Me., Oct. 11, 1915; s. Walter B. and Elizabeth E. (Priest) B.; A.B., Williams Coll., 1936; postgrad. Yale, 1937; m. Lucile M. Hunt, Sept. 2, 1939; children—Susan, David, Nancy, Carol, Sally, Douglas, Laura, Andrew. With McGraw-Hill Book Co., 1937-42, W. W. Norton and Co., Inc., N.Y.C., 1942—, dir., 1948—, editor, 1949—, pres., 1958—. Served with AUS, 1944-46. Mem. Phi Beta Kappa. Clubs: Coffee House; Publishers Lunch; Century Assn. Author: (with Lucile H. Brockway) Greece, a Classical Tour with Extras, 1966; contbg. author What Happens in Book Publishing, 1957. Home: 63 Brevoort Rd Chappaqua NY 10514 Office: 55 Fifth Av New York City NY 10003

BROCKWAY, LAWRENCE OLIN, educator, chemist; b. Topeka, Kan., Sept. 23, 1907; s. Paul Lemon and Kate (Weed) B.; B.S., U. Neb., 1929, M.S., 1930; Ph.D., Calif. Inst. Tech., 1933, research fellow, 1933-37; Guggenheim fellow Oxford, Royal Inst., 1937-38; m. Hazel Klein, Sept. 30, 1932; 1 dau., Doris Marie. Asst., asso. prof. U. Mich., 1938-45, prof. 1945-. Recipient award in pure chemistry Am. Chem. Soc., 1940. Mem. Am. Chem. Soc.,A.A.A.S., Am. Assn. U. Profs., Am. Crystallographic Assn., Electron Microscope Soc. Am. Home: 2665 Geddes Rd Ann Arbor, MI 48104.

BROCKWAY, RICHARD CRANE, ins. orgn. exec.; b. Rochester N.Y., Feb. 18, 1908; s. Guy H. and Anna Anna (Crane) B.; B.S. in Econs., Wharton Sch., U. Pa., 1931; m. Constance Delinni, Apr. 16, 1934; children—Carla (Mrs. Charles M. Rodstrom), Joanna C. (Mrs. Gerald S. Padnessa). With WPA, 1935-37; with div. employment N.Y. State Dept. Labor, 1938-58, asst. exec. dir., 1948-54, exec. dir., 1954-58; with War Manpower Commn., N.Y.C., 1941-46; exec. dir. Mass. Hosp. Service, Inc. (Blue Cross), Boston, 1959-65; pres. Nat. Health and Welfare Retirement Assn., Inc., N.Y.C., 1966—. Cons. U.S. Dept. Labor. Mem. Nat. Commn. Community Health Services Task Force on Financing; mem. adv. bd. Booth Meml. Hosp., Boston; mem. council on Blue Cross and finance Am. Hosp. Assn.; bd. govs., chmn. exec. com. Blue Cross Assn., Chgo.; research on unemployment ins. N.Y. State Legislature. Mem. Am. Hosp. Assn., Am. Pub. Health Assn., Nat. Assembly for Social Planning and Welfare (council). Club: Union (Boston). Home: 40 E 10th St New York City, NY 10003. Office: 360 Park Av S New York City NY 10010

BRODA, FREDERICK MARTIN, ins. co. exec.; b. Canton, O., Jan. 14, 1895; s. Frederick and Katherine (Slusser) B.; A.B., Western Res. U., 1917; m. Amy A. Ash, Mar. 17, 1951. Pres., treas. Webb-Broda & Co., Inc., gen. ins. and surety bonds, Canton, 1921—. Mem. Stark County Rep. Exec. Com.; del. 16th Congl. Dist., Rep. Nat. Conv., 1952. Trustee Kent State U., 1958-69; mem. Inter-Univ. Council for State Supported Univs., Ohio, 1964-69. Served to 1st lt., inf., U.S. Army, World War I. Recipient Man of Year award Canton C. of C., 1962. Mem. Stark County Hist. Soc. (trustee, past pres.), Ohio (trustee), Canton (pres. 1931-32) chambers commerce, Am. Legion, Delta Upsilon. Baptist. Mason. Club: Canton (pres.). Home: 1700 Harvard Av N W Canton OH 44703 Office: First National Bank Bldg Canton OH 44702

BRODBECK, MAY, educator; b. Newark, July 26, 1917; d. Louis and Etta (Bragar) Schachter; B.A., N.Y.U., 1941; M.A., U. Ia., 1945, Ph.D., 1947. Mem. faculty U. Minn., 1947—, prof. philosophy, 1959—, chmn. dept., 1967-70; vis. lectr. Cambridge (Eng.) U., 1970; vis. prof. U. Md., 1964. NSF research grantee, 1966-68; Fulbright research scholar, Italy, 1962-63; Social Sci. Research Council faculty fellow, 1955-58. Mem. Am. Philos. Assn. (sec.-treas. 1955-57, v.p. Western div. 1970-71), Philosophy Sci. Assn., Am. Assn. U. Profs. Editor: Readings in the Philosophy of the Social Sciences; co-editor: Readings in the Philosophy of Science, 1953; editorial bd. Philosophy of Sci., 1959—. Author: American Non-Fiction, 1900-1950, 1952; also articles. Home: 2180 Folwell St St Paul MN 55108 Office: Dept Philosophy Univ Minn Minneapolis MN 55455

BRODE, ROBERT B., physicist; b. Walla Walla, Wash., June, 12, 1900; s. Howard Stidham and Martha Catherine (Bigham) B.; B.S., Whitman Coll., 1921, D.Sc., 1954; Ph.D., Cal. Inst. Tech., 1924; postgrad. (Rhodes scholar), Oxford (Eng.) U. 1924-25, (Internat. Edn. Bd. fellow) Göttingen (Germany) U., 1925-26, (NRC fellow) Princeton, 1926-27; LL.D., U. Cal. at Berkeley, 1970; m. Bernice Hedley Bidwell, Sept. 16, 1926; children—William (dec.), John Howard. Asso. physicist U.S. Bur. Standards, 1924; asst. prof. physics U. Cal. at Berkeley, 1927-30, asso. prof., 1930-32, prof., 1932-67, prof. emeritus, 1967—. Vis. prof. Mass. Inst. Tech., 1932; Guggenheim fellow London and Cambridge, 1934-35; physicist dept. terrestrial magnetism Carnegie Inst., 1941, sect. T., applied physics lab. OSRD, Johns Hopkins, 1942-43, supervising research and devel. on proximity fuse and fire control equipment; group leader Los Alamos Atomic Bomb Lab., 1943-46, Harvard, summer 1948; Fulbright award, Manchester, 1951-52; mem. physics div. NRC, 1951-57; v.p. Internat. Union Pure and Applied Physics, 1954-60, U.S. del. Internat. Council Sci. Unions, Norway, 1955, Washington, 1958; asso. dir. NSF, 1958-59; mem. bd. fgn. scholarships Dept. State, 1963-66. Fellow Am. Phys. Soc., A.A.A.S. (v.p. 1949, pres. Pacific div. 1956); mem. Am. Assn. Physics Teachers, Am. Assn. U. Profs. (2d v.p. 1960-61), Am. Assn. Rhodes Scholars, Am. Acad. Arts and Scis., Nat. Acad. Scis., Phi Beta Kappa, Sigma Xi. Contbr. articles to profl. publs. Home: 1471 Greenwood Terrace Berkeley CA 94708

BRODE, WALLACE REED, sci. cons.; b. Walla Walla, Wash., June 12, 1900; s. Howard Stidham and Martha Catherine (Bigham) B.; B.S., Whitman Coll., 1921, D.Sc., 1955; M.S., U. Ill., 1922, Ph.D., 1925; D.Sc., Ohio State U., 1958, Ohio Weslyan U., 1962; D.Textile Sci., Phila. Coll. Textiles and Sci., 1970; m. Ione Sundstrom, Mar. 19, 1941. Grad. asst. dept. chemistry U. Ill., 1922, asst., 1922-24; asst. and asso. chemist U.S. Nat. Bur. Standards, 1924-25, asso. dir., 1947-58; Guggenheim Meml. Found. fellow, Leipzig, Zurich, Liverpool, 1926-28; asst. prof. chemistry Ohio State U., 1928-32, asso. prof., 1932-39, prof., 1939-48; mem. London mission of liaison office OSRD, 1944-45, head Paris office, 1944-45, Alsos Mission, 1944-45; head sci. dept. U.S. Naval Ordnance Test Station, Inyokern, Cal., 1945-47, mem. adv. bd., 1948-58; mem. phys. div. NRC, 1947-54, chemistry div., 1954-60, 69-71. Sci. adviser to sec. of state, 1958-60; sci. cons., 1960—; fgn. sec. Am. Chem. Soc., 1965-67; co-chmn. People-to-People Com. for Scientists and Engrs., 1957- 58, 64—; mem. Pres.'s Com. Sci. and Engrs., 1957; cons. to Pres.'s Sci. Adv. Com., 1958-60; mem. Sci. Manpower Commn., 1960—; mem. adv. bd. Desert Research Inst., U. Nev., 1964-69; dir. Barnes Engrng. Co., 1960—; Am. del. Internat. Union Pure and Applied Chemistry, Zurich, Switzerland. 1936, 55, N.Y.C., 1951, Paris, France, 1957, Internat. Council Sci. Unions, Washington, 1958; mem. Harvard-M.I.T. eclipse of sun expdns. Siberia, 1936; Marburg lectr. Am. Soc. for Testing and Materials, 1950. Bd. overseers Whitman Coll., 1954—. Mem. Ann. Assay Commn. for U.S. Mint., 1952. Served with U.S. Army, 1918. Recipient Presdl. certificate of merit, 1945; medal Soc. for Applied Spectroscopy, 1958; Exceptional Service medal Dept. Commerce. 1958; Priestley medal Am. Chem. Soc., 1960. Fellow Am. Phys. Soc.; mem. Soc. Applied Spectroscopy (hon.), Am. Chem. Soc. (councilor, chmn. sec. Columbus sect., nat. dir. 1951-60, 68-70, pres. 1969), Optical Soc. Am. (pres. 1960, dir. 1951-60), Am. Inst. Physics (gov. 1948-52, 60-63), Sci. Research Soc. Am. (gov. 1950-58, 60-63, chmn. 1954-57), Am. Assn. U. Profs., Sci. Service (dir., treas. 1958—), Nat. Acad. Scis., A.A.A.S. (dir. 1953-60, pres. 1958, chmn. bd. 1959), Phi Beta Kappa, Sigma Xi (nat. lectr. 1952, nat. pres. 1961-62), Phi Lambda Upsilon (hon.), Sigma Pi Sigma (hon.), Alpha Chi Sigma, Gamma Alpha, Alpha Epsilon Delta. Club: Cosmos (Washington). Author: Chem. Spectroscopy, 1939, 2d edit., 1943; (with others) Lab Outlines for Organic Chemistry, 1940, 4th edit., 1955; (with Gilman) Organic Chemistry, 1938; Scott's Standard Method of Analysis (with Furman), 1939; Advances in Enzymology (with Nord and Werkman), 1944; Applications of Instruments in Chemistry (with Burk and Grummitt) 1945; Physical Methods in Chemical Analysis (with Berl and Corning), 1960; (with others) Science in Progress, 1956; Roger Adams Symposium, 1955. Editor Science in Progress, vols. 12- 16, 1962-67; Jour. Optical Soc. Am., 1950-60. Home: 3900 Connecticut Av NW Washington DC 20008

BRODEN, EDWIN RAUCH, ret. business exec.; b. Cleve., July 20, 1904; s. Edwin Herbert and Helen (Rauch) B.; student Carnegie Inst. Tech., 1922-26, 33-36; m. Estelle Frances Gill, Oct. 18, 1935 (div.); children—Gretchen (Mrs. George L. Bartholomew), Ronald Edwin; m. 2d, Helen Lee Trumpy, Apr. 16, 1966. Indsl. engr., cons. United Natural Gas Co., Oil City, Pa., 1931-36; asst. chief engr. Blaw-Knox Co., Pitts., 1936-41, asst. div. mgr., 1941-44, div. mgr., 1944-47; v.p. in charge operations Carborundum Co., Niagara Falls. N.Y., 1947-51, exec. v.p., 1951-55; exec. v.p. SKF Industries, Inc., Phila., 1955-56, pres., 1956-68, chmn. bd., 1957-70. Mem. Commonwealth of Pa. Planning Bd.; past pres. Jr. Achievement Del. Valley; life trustee Carnegie Mellon U. Mem. Am. Soc. Corporate Execs., Mfrs. Assn. Greater Phila. (past pres., Am. Mgmt. Assn., Am. Ordnance Assn., Am. Soc. Testing Materials, Am. Iron and Steel Inst., Am. Welding Soc., Am. Soc. M.E., Anti-Friction Bearing Mfrs. Assn., Inc. (past pres.), Engrng. Soc. Western Pa., Soc. Automotive Engrs., Sigma Nu. Presbyn. Clubs: Annapolis Yacht, Key Largo Anglers, Lafayetta, Union League (Phila.); Duquesne (Pitts.); Engineers, Philadelphia Country (Phila.): N.Y. Yacht; Delray Beach, Ocean Reef Yacht. Home: 191 Apts Bala-Cynwyd PA 19004 Office: SKF Industries Inc Philadelphia PA 19132

BRODERICK, CARROLL JOSEPH, banker; b. Balt., Oct. 1, 1905; s. John William and Katherine (McKew) B.; student Balt. City Coll., 1922-26, Balt. Coll. Commerce, 1930- 34; m. Agnes Marie Daily. Apr. 8, 1940; 1 son, John Carroll. With O'Neil and Co., Balt., 1920-21, Savs. Bank Balt., 1921, was sr. v.p., treas., 1965; instr. accounting Balt. Coll. Commerce Eve. Sch., 1950- -. Served to lt. comdr. USNR, 1941-46. Home: 302 Taplow Rd Baltimore MD 21212 Office: 1 E Baltimore St Baltimore MD 21203

BRODERICK, EDWIN B., bishop; b. Bronx, N.Y.C., Jan. 16, 1917; s. Patrick J. and Margaret Margaret (O'Donnell) B.; A.B., St. Joseph's Coll., Yonkers, N.Y., 1938; Ph.D. in English, Fordham U., 1951; L.H.D., L.I. U., 1968. Ordained priest Roman Catholic Ch., 1942; tchr. Cardinal Hayes High Sch., 1943-47; asst. pastor St. Patrick's Cathedral, N.Y.C., 1947; dir. radio-TV, Archdiocese N.Y., also sec. to Cardinal Spellman, 1954-64; pres. St. Joseph's Sem. and Coll., Yonkers, 1964-68; consecrated bishop, 1967; appointed bishop of Albany, N.Y., 1969—; conclavist Papal election, 1958. Decorated grand knight Grand Cross Holy Sepulchre. Mem. Modern Lang. Assn., Met. Opera Club. Author: Your Child and Television, 1954; Your Place in Television, 1953. Home: 35 Pine Tree Lane Albany NY 12208 Office: 465 State St Albany NY 12206

BRODERICK, FAY LEONE, mem. Democratic Nat. Com.; b. Gardiner, Me., June 3, 1933; m. Richard Richard H. H. Broderick, Dec. 24, 1957; children—Michael, Richard, Paul. Former profl. profl. singer; photographer Lincoln News. Mem. Lincoln (Me.) Dem. Town Com.; mem. Nat. Dem. Com. for Me., 1964—, Penobscot County Dem. Com.; del. Dem. Nat. Conv., 1968, chmn. permanent orgn. com.; past mem. Me. Dem. Com.; del. Dem. state convs.; mem. Me. Commn. on Party Structure and Del. Selection. Episcopalian. Address: Address: Transalpine Rd Lincoln ME 04457

BRODERICK, FRANCIS LYONS, historian, univ. chancellor; b. N.Y.C., Sept. 13, 1922; s. Joseph Aloysius and Mary (Lyons) B.; grad. Phillips Acad., Andover, Mass., 1939; A.B. with high honors, Princeton, 1943; M.A. in History, Harvard, 1947, Ph.D. in History Am. Civilization, 1955; m. Barbara Baldridge, June 12, 1950; children—Thomas, Joseph, James, Ann. Instr. history Princeton, 1945-46, State U. Ia., 1948-50, Phillips Exeter Acad., 1951-63; dir. Peace Corps, Ghana, 1964-66; dean Lawrence and Downer Colls., also Gordon R. Clapp prof. Am. studies Lawrence U., Appleton, Wis., 1966-68; chancellor U. Mass., Boston, 1968—. Served to 1st lt. USAAF, 1943-45. Woodrow Wilson fellow, 1945-46. Mem. Am. Cath. Hist. Assn. (pres. 1968). Author: W.E.B. DuBois: Negro Leader in a Time of Crisis, 1959; Right Reverend New Dealer: John A Ryan, 1963; The Origins of the Constitution, 1964; (with August Meier) Negro Protest Thought in the Twentieth Century, 1966; Reconstruction and the American Negro, 1969. Editor: (John Tracy Ellis) The Life of James Cardinal Gibbons (Nat. Cath. Book award 1964), 1963. Home: 23 Appleton St Boston MA 02116

BRODERICK, HENRY, business exec.; b. Mpls., Oct. 12, 1880; s. Lawrence and Mary (Cronin) B.; student pub. schs., Mpls.; m. Mary Barclay, Oct. 1901 (dec.). Founder, Henry Broderick, Inc., 1911, pres., 1911—; pres., dir. Henry Broderick Investment Co.; pres. Realty & Leasehold Co., Boston Drug Co.; sec. 1941 Corp.; dir. Seattle 1st Nat. Bank, New World Life Ins. Co., Seattle Baseball Club; trustee J.C. Silverton Trust. Mem. Prison Parole Bd., 1929-33. Trustee Seattle U. Republican. Roman Catholic. Clubs: Rainier Tennis, Washington Athletic, Press, Harbor. Author: The Shoveler, 1932; The Commandment Breakers of Walla Walla, 1933; Early Seattle Profiles. Home: 1717 39th Av Seattle WA 98122 Office: Second and Cherry Sts Seattle WA 98104

BRODERICK, JOHN P., former public relations and advt. cons.; b. Breckenridge, Minn., June 3, 1904; s. Edward J. and Sarah Elizabeth (Carr) B.; A.B., U. Minn., 1926; m. Lucille Kern, July 1, 1938; children—John Patrick, Stephanie. Editorial asst. Northwestern Miller, 1927-29; reporter Wall Street Jour., 1929-35, editor, 1935-42; v.p., dir. Doremus & Co., 1942-52; partner Broderick & Coleman, financial pub. relations, N.Y.C., 1953-65; v.p., dir. Albert Frank-Guenther Law, Inc., advt.-pub. relations agy., 1966-71. Lectr. English, Columbia, 1956-57. Mem. N.Y. Financial Writers Assn. (charter). Pub. Relations Soc. Am. (charter), Cath. Inst. of Press, Soc. Silurians, N.Y. Soc. Security Analysts, Zeta Psi, Sigma Delta Chi. Roman Catholic. Clubs: National Press (Washington); Overseas Press, Deadline (N.Y.C.); Bankers Am. Home: Sun City AZ 85351

BRODERICK, RAYMOND JOSEPH, judge lawyer; b. Phila., May 29, 1914; s. Patrick J. and Catharine (Burns) B.; A.B. magna cum laude, U. Notre Dame, 1935; J.D. (editor law rev. 1936-38), U. Pa., 1938; L.H.D., Pa. Coll. Podiatric Medicine, 1968; m. Marjorie Beacom, Oct. 2, 1945; children—Patrick J., Timothy B., Tara M., Deirdre C., Brian X. Admitted to Pa. bar, 1938, since practiced in Phila.; sr. partner Broderick, Schubert & Fitz-Patrick, 1962—; lt. gov. Pa., 1966-71; U.S. dist. ct. judge, Phila., 1971—. Dir.. civil def. Plymouth Twp., Pa., 1948-51; commr. Plymouth Twp., 1952-54; chmn. Adminstrn. Task Force for Constl. Revision, 1966, Preparatory Com. Pa. Constl. Conv., 1967; pres. Pa. Constl. Conv., 1967-68; chmn. nat. conf. Lt. Gov.'s Conf., 1969-70. Chmn. Phila. Republican Policy Com., 1965-66, exec. com., 1967-69; vice chmn., del. Pa. delegation Rep. Nat. Conv., 1968. Bd. mgrs. Youth Study Center, Phila., 1966-69; chmn. lawyers div. Cath. Charities, 1966. Served to lt. comdr. USNR, 1942-46. Mem. Am., Pa., Phila. (chmn. arbitration com. 1963, com. of censors, fee disputes com. 1960-61) bar assns., Am., Pa., Phila, trial lawyers assns., Notre Dame Law Assn., Socialegal Club, St. Thomas More Soc., Constl. Club, Friendly Sons of St. Patrick. Clubs: Whitemarsh Valley Country, Overbrook Farms, Notre Dame (Phila.): Seaview Country (Absecon, N.J.). Home: 6408 Church Rd Overbrook Philadelphia PA 19151 Office: 1330 Two Penn Center Plaza Philadelphia PA 19102

BRODERICK, VINCENT LYONS, lawyer; b. N.Y.C., Apr. 26, 1920; s. Joseph A. and Mary Rose (Lyons) B.; grad. Phillips Acad., Andover, Mass., 1937; A.B., Princeton, 1941; LL.B., Harvard, 1948; m. Sally Brine, Apr. 15, 1950; children—Kathleen, Vincent, Mary, Ellen, Joan, Justin. Admitted to N.Y. bar, 1948; with firm Root, Barrett, Cohen, Knapp & Smith, N.Y.C., 1948-54; dep. commnr. charge legal matters N.Y.C. Police Dept., 1954-56; gen. counsel Nat. Assn. Investment Cos., N.Y.C., 1956-61; chief asst. U.S. atty. So. dist. N.Y., 1961-62, 62-64, U.S. atty. 1962; police commnr., N.Y.C., 1965-66; mem. firm Phillips, Nizer, Benjamin, Krim & Ballon, 1966-71, Forsyth, Decker, Murray & Broderick, 1971—. Trustee East River Savs. Bank. Treas., bd. dirs. Met. Applied Research Council; pres. bd. Brotherhood-In-Action. Bd. overseers Center for N.Y.C. Affairs, New Sch. Mem. Am., N.Y. Bar assns., Bar Assn. City N.Y., N.Y. assns. chiefs police, N.Y. County Lawyers Assn., Catholic Lawyers Guild. Home: 1424 Park Lane Pelham Manor NY 10803 Office: 51 W 51st St New York City NY 10019

BRODERSON, ROBERT MAURICE, painter; b. West Haven, Conn., July 6, 1920; s. Hans and Ruby (Meeker) B.; A.B., Duke, 1950; M.F.A., State U. Ia., 1952; m. Doris Gertrude Hunt, June 15, 1924; children—Robert Edward, Penne Jac, Robin Jai, Catherine Viviano. Exhbns. including Whitney Mus., Mus. Modern Art, Nat. Acad. Arts and Letters; represented in pub. and pvt. collections; tchr. art Duke, 1952-64. Served with USAAF, 1942-45: ETO. Guggenheim fellow, 1964. Address: 315 Broadway New York City NY 10007

BRODEY, WARREN MORTIMER, ecologist; b. Toronto, Ont., Can., Jan. 25, 1924; s. Abraham and Blanche (Levy) B.; M.D., U. Toronto, 1947; m. Jane Tolson, Nov. 15, 1956 (div. Dec. 1970); children—John, Kim, Lisa, Benjamin, Ivan. Came to U.S., 1947, naturalized, 1954. Intern, Lincoln Hosp., N.Y.C., 1947-48; resident psychiatry Sch. Medicine Boston U., 1948-51; fellow Judge Baker Youth Guidance Center, 1951-53; practice medicine, specializing in psychiatry, Boston, 1950-59, Washington, 1959- 64; asst. dir. Worcester (Mass.) Youth Guidance Center, 1953-56; research psychiatrist family study sect. Nat. Inst. Mental Health clin. center, 1956-59; faculty, research asso. Washington Sch. Psychiatry, 1959-65; asst. prof. Georgetown U., 1959-64; research affiliate Research Lab. Electronics, cognitive information processing group Mass. Inst. Tech., 1964-67; dir. M.I.T. Upward Bound program, 1966-68; candidate Wash. Psychiat. Analytic Inst., 1959-64; cons. Pilot Sch. For Blind Children, Washington, 1959; asso., ecologist Environmental Ecology Lab., Inc., Boston, 1968-70; ecologist, inventor Ecology Tool & Toy Co., Milford, N.H., 1970—. Cons. NASA Electronics Research Center Instrumentation and Computer Labs., 1965. Diplomate Am. Bd. Psychiatry and Neurology. Mem. Am. Acad. Child Psychiatry, Am. Soc. Cybernetics (charter). Author: Changing The Family, 1968. Contbr. articles to profl. jours. Address: Armory Rd Milford NH 03055

BRODHEAD, GEORGE MILTON, lawyer; b. Phila., May 23, 1904; s. George M. and Clara (Chaplain) B.; A.B., Wesleyan U., Middletown, Conn., 1926; LL.B., U. Pa., 1930; m. Pauline W. Hand, Sept. 13, 1934; children—Anne Foster (Mrs. William Draper Lewis III), Richard Chaplain. Tchr., Choate Sch., 1926-27; admitted to Pa. bar, 1930, since practiced in Phila.; asso. Rawle & Henderson, 1930-43, partner, 1943—; dir. Eastern Ill. Water Co., Mchts. Warehouse Co. Bd. dirs. Barra Found., Claneil Found., Stephen Watchorn Found., Germantown Boys Club, Tabor Home for Children, Preachers Aid Soc., 1937- 70. Mem. Pa. Soc. S.R. (v.p.), Mil. Order Loyal Legion, Netherlands Soc. Phila., Soc. War 1812, Colonial Soc. Pa., Am., Pa., Phila. bar assns., Maritime Soc. U.S., Soc. Colonial Wars, Holland Soc. of N.Y., Phi Beta Kappa, Psi Upsilon, Phi Delta Phi. Methodist. Clubs: Cricket, Union League (pres. 1969-70), Lawyers' (pres. 1967-68) (Phila.). Home: 228 W Willow Grove Av Philadelphia PA 19118 Office: Packard Bldg Philadelphia PA 19102

BRODIE, BERNARD, educator, author; b. Chgo., May 20, 1910; s. Max and Esther (Bloch) B.; Ph.B., U. Chgo., 1932, Ph.D., 1940; m. Fawn McKay, Aug. 28, 1936; children—Richard M., Bruce R., Pamela B. Instr., Dartmouth, 1941-43; asso. prof., dir. grad. studies internat. relations Yale, 1945-51; sr. staff mem. RAND Corp., 1951-66; prof. U. Cal. at Los Angeles, 1966—. Vis. prof. Nat. War Coll., 1946, bd. cons., 1955-57; tech. expert UN Conf., San Francisco, 1945. Bd. dirs. Found. Research Psychoanalysis, Los Angeles, 1965-68. Served to lt. USNR, 1943-45. Recipient Gold medal Argentine Naval War Coll., 1948. Fellow Inst. Advanced Study, Princeton, 1940-41; Carnegie reflective year fellow, Paris, 1960-61. Author: Sea Power in the Machine Age, 2d edit., 1943; A Guide to Naval Strategy, 5th edit., 1965; The Absolute Weapon, 1946; Strategy in the Missile Age, 2d edit., 1965; (with Fawn M. Brodie) From Cross-Bow to H-Bomb, 1962; La Guerre Nucleaire, 1965; Escalation and the Nuclear Option, 1966. Home: 619 Resolano Dr Pacific Palisades CA 90272 Office: Dept Polit Sci Univ Cal Los Angeles CA 90024

BRODIE, BERNARD BERYL, pharmacologist; b. Liverpool, Eng., Aug. 7, 1909; s. Samuel and Esther (Ginsburg) B.; B.S., McGill U., 1931; Ph.D., N.Y.U., 1935; Ph.D. (hon.), U. Paris (France), 1963; D.Sc., Phila. Coll. Pharmacy and Sci., 1965, U. Barcelona, 1967, N.Y. Med. Coll., 1970, U. Louvain (Belgium), 1971; M.D. (hon.), Karolinska Inst., 1968; m. Anne Lois Smith, Aug. 30, 1950. Asst. prof. pharmacology N.Y.U. Med. Sch., 1943- 47, asso. prof. biochemistry, 1947-50; chief lab. chem. pharmacology Nat. Heart Inst., 1950-70, ret., 1970; sr. cons. Hoffmann-LaRoche Inc., 1971—; prof. pharmacology Pa. State U. Coll. Medicine, 1971—. Vis. prof. George Washington U. Med. Sch., 1950—; cons. Nat. Heart and Lung Inst., NIH, Bethesda, Md., 1971—. Served with Canadian Army, 1926-28. Recipient Distinguished Service award Dept. Health, Edn. and Welfare, 1958; Shionogi Commemoration lectr., Japan, 1962; Karl Beyer award, 1962; Julius Sturmer Meml. lectr., 1962; Torald Sollmann award, Am. Pharmacology Soc., 1963; Distinguished Achievement award Modern Medicine med. jour., 1964; Albert Lasker award for basic med. research, 1967; Carl Wilhelm Scheele lectr. Royal Pharm. Inst., Stockholm, 1967; Nat. Medal of Sci., 1968; Claude Bernard prof. U. Montreal, 1969; Schmiede-Plakette, German Pharmacological Soc., 1969; Oscar B. Hunter Meml. award Am. Pharm. Soc., 1970; Paul Lamson lectr. Vanderbilt U., 1971; Rosemary Cass Meml. lectr. U. Dundee (Scotland), 1971. Mem. Nat. Acad. Scis., Internat. Pharm. Soc., Am. Coll. Neuropsychopharmacology (pres. 1965), Am. Soc. Biol. Chemists, Am. Soc. Pharmacology and Exptl. Therapeutics, Harvey Soc., N.Y., Washington acads. scis., Royal Soc. Medicine. Author: Metabolic Factors Controlling Duration of Drug Action, 1963; Drug Enzyme Interactions, 1964. Founder, U.S. editor Life Sciences, Internat. Jour. Neuropharmacology; Editor, co-founder Pharmacology. Contbr. to Handbook Exptl. Pharmacology, also numerous articles in field. Home: 4977 Battery Lane Bethesda MD 20014 Office: Nat Heart and Lung Inst Nat Institute Health Bethesda MD 20015

BRODIE, GANDY, artist; b. N.Y.C., May 20, 1924; s. Max and Minnie (Tau) B.; m. Jocelyn Levine, Jan. 25, 1955; 1 son, Shane. One-man show Krasner Gallery, N.Y.C.; exhbns. include Kootz Gallery, N.Y.C., Durlacher Gallery, N.Y.C., Saidenberg Gallery, N.Y.C., represented in permanent collections Mus. Modern Art, Whitney Mus., Jewish Mus., N.Y.C., Park Av. Synagogue, N.Y.C., Phillips Collection, Washington, Balt. Mus. Art, Chrysler Mus., Provincetown, Mass., Mass. Inst. Tech., Sarah Lawrence Coll., Gloria Vanderbilt Mus. (purchase fund), Longview Found. (Purchase award 1960, 61), Mint Mus., Charlotte, N.C.; art faculty New Sch. Social Research, 1967; artist-in-residence Hollins Coll., 1968; vis. scholar Wash. State Colls., 1968-69; asso. prof. Gandie Brodie Sch. Fine Arts, Carnegie Mellon U., Newfane, Vt. Winner Mark Twain Contest, 1958; recipient Ingram Merrill Found. award, 1962; Nat. Arts Council award, 1968; Guggenheim fellow, 1968-69. Home: West Townshend VT Office: 32 Gansevoort St New York City NY 10014

BRODIE, HENRY, fgn. service officer; b. Ottawa, Ont., Can., May 13, 1913; s. Samuel and Etta (Guinsburg) B.; B.Sc., N.Y. U., 1937, M.A., 1940, Ph.D., 1942; m. Elizabeth Kaufman, Sept. 23, 1939; children—Paula, Mark, Julie. Came to U.S., 1933, naturalized, 1942. Econs. instr., N.Y.C., 1941-42; econ. officer Am. embassy, London, 1943-44; econ. adviser Office Intelligence Research, Dept. State, 1948-56; 1st sec. Am. embassy, Manila, 1956-58, counselor, 1958-60; mem. policy planning staff Dept. State, 1960-71, dir. Office Internat. Resources, 1961-66; minister econ. affairs U.S. Mission, Geneva, Switzerland, 1966-71; sr. econ. adviser Officer Environmental Affairs, 1971—. Served lt. (j.g.) USNR, 1944-46. Mem. Am. Econ. Assn. Contbr. articles to profl. jours.; chpt. contbg. author chpt. South Asia in the World Today (Phillips Talbot), 1950; Principles of Political Geography (Weigert and others), 1957. Address: care Dept of State Washington DC 20520

BRODKIN, HERBERT HARRISON, TV producer; b. N.Y.C., Nov. 9, 1912; s. Adolph and Rose (Hutner) B.; B.A., U. Mich., 1934; M.F.A. in Drama, Yale, 1940; m. Patricia Montgomery, June 25, 1941; childrenLucinda Day, Brigit Ann. Producer TV prodns. Motorola Hour, 1953-54, Elgin Hour, 1954-55, Goodyear Playhouse 1955-56, Alcoa Hour, 1955-56, Studio One, 1957, Playhouse 90, 1958-60, The Defenders, 1961-66, The Nurses, 1962-66; pres. Plautus Prodns. (now called Titus Prodns., Inc.), N.Y.C. 1961—; producer feature films for Paramount Pictures Corp., 1964—, including Mr. Sebastian, 1967. Served to maj AUS, 1941-46. Home: 171 W 12th St New York City NY 10011 Office: 211 E 51st St New York City NY 10022

BRODL, RAYMOND FRANK, lumber co. exec.; b. Cicero, Ill. June 1, 1924; s. Edward C. and Lillian (Cerny) B.; student Norwich U., Northfield, Vt., 1943, Ill. Coll., 1946-48; LL.B., Loyola U., Chgo., 1951; m. Ethel Jean Johnson, Aug. 15, 1953; children—Mark Raymond, Pamela Jean, Susan Marie. Admitted to Ill. bar, 1951; atty. law office Joseph A. Ricker, Chgo., 1951-58, Brunswick Corp., Chgo., 1958-62; sec., gen. atty. Edward Hines Lumber Co., Chgo., 1962—. Democratic candidate for local jud. office, 1953, 57. Served with AUS, 1943-46. Mem. Am., Ill., Chgo. bar assns., Am. Soc. Corporate Secs. Home: 366 W Lance Dr Des Plaines IL 60016 Office: 200 S Michigan Av Chicago IL 60604

BRODMAN, ESTELLE, educator, librarian; b. N.Y.C., June 1, 1914; d. Henry and Nettie (Sameth) Brodman; A.B., Cornell U., 1935; B.S., Columbia, 1936, M.S., 1943, Ph.D., 1954; post-doctoral study U. Cal., Los Angeles, 1959, U. N.M., 1960. Asst. librarian Cornell U. Sch. Nursing Library, N.Y.C., 1936-37; asst. med. librarian Columbia Libraries, N.Y.C., 1937-49; asst. librarian for reference services Nat. Library Medicine, Washington, 1949-61; librarian, asso. prof. med. history Washington U. Sch. Medicine, St. Louis, 1961-64, librarian, prof. med. history, 1964—. Documentation expert UN Tech. Assistance program UN, Central Family Planning Inst., New Delhi, 1967-68, WHO, New Delhi, 1970. Mem. Pres.'s Commn. Instr., Columbia, 1946-52, Cath. U. Am., 1957, Keio U., Tokyo, Japan, 1962, U. Mo., 1971; cons. Am. Hosp. Assn. Mem. Am., Med. (recipient spl. award 1957, pres. 1964-65) library assns., Spl. Libraries Assn. (dir. 1949-52), Bibliog. Soc. Am., Am. Assn. History Medicine. Author: Development of Medical Bibliography, 1954; Bibliographical Lists for Medical Libraries, 1950. Editor: Bull. Med. Library Assn., 1947-47. Home: 4464 W Pine Blvd St Louis MO 63108

BRODNEY, KENNETH, sci. journalist NBC News, N.Y.C. Address: 412 W 20th St New York City NY 10011*

BRODSKY, NATHAN, govt. ofcl.; b. Phila., Sept. 22, 1916; s. Alfred and Pauline (Sennett) B.; B.S. with honors, Temple U., 1937; postgrad. U. Pa., 1938-40; Ph.D. in Econs., Am. U., 1959; m. Margaret Sara McStay, Dec. 27, 1946; children—James Alfred, David Arthur, Barbara Ann. Social worker Pa. Dept. Pub. Assistance, 1937-40; successively chief Brit. Dominions and India br. and chief procurement coordination br. UNRRA, 1946-48; chief policy div. office of distbn., dep. chief office of distbn., dep. vice-chmn. for supply mgmt. Munitions Bd., 1948-52; dep. dir. Def. Supply Mgmt. Agy., 1952-53; asst. dir. cataloging, standardization and inspection Dept. Def., 1954-57; dir. research and spl. projects Office Sec. Def., 1957-66, dir. edn. programs and mgmt. tng., 1966, acting dep. asst. sec. def. for edn., 1968-70; comdg. officer Moblzn. detachment, 1961-63, chmn. Def. Logistics Mgmt. Tng. Bd., 1963-66, chmn. Def. Logistics Research Conf., 1965. Vis. lectr.; cons. intergovtl. relations subcom. U.S. Ho. of Reps., 1949-52; mem. Interagy. Council on Internat. Ednl. and Cultural Affairs, 1966—; mem. Fed. Interagy. Com. Edn., 1968—; assisted Hoover Commn. Task Force on Fed. Supply, 1948. Served as 2d lt. to col., AUS, 1941-46. Decorated Bronze Star medal; recipient Civilian Meritorious Service medal Sec. of State, 1970. Mem. Am. Econ. Assn., Acad. Polit. Sci., Am. Polit. Sci. Assn., Inst. Mgmt. Sci., Washington Operations Research Council. Contbr. articles in bus. and econ. jours. Home: 2840 Lorcom Lane Arlington VA 22207 Office: The Pentagon Washington DC 20301

BRODSKY, SAMUEL, lawyer; b. Kansas City, Mo., June 12, 1912; s. Abraham and Anne (Brodsky) B.; B.A., U. Tulsa, 1933; LL.B., Harvard, 1936; m. Margery J. Bach, Oct. 17, 1944; children—Joan E., Alice E. Admitted to N.Y. bar, 1937, since practiced in N.Y.C.; law clk. to Fed. Circuit Ct. Judge Julian W. Mack, 1936-37; asst. U.S. atty. So. Dist. N.Y., 1937-43, 46, charge civil div., 1942-43, 46; partner Aranow, Brodsky, Bohlinger, Benetar, Einhorn & Dann, 1947—; lectr. taxation N.Y. U. Law Sch., 1953, 56-64; lectr. Inst. on Fed. Taxation, N.Y. U., Practicing Law Inst., Trustee N.Y. Fedn. Reform Synagogues. Served to lt. USNR, 1943-46. Mem. Am., Fed., N.Y. State (past chmn. tax sect.) bar assns., Assn. Bar City N.Y., N.Y. County Lawyers Assn. Jewish religion (v.p., trustee synagogue). Contbr. articles profl. jours. Home: 1155 Park Av New York City NY 10028 Office: 469 Fifth Av New York City NY 10017

BRODWATER, WILLIAM WESLEY, stock exchange exec.; b. Magnolia, N.J., Sept. 9, 1906; s. Isaac Barr and Clara (Morris) B.; student U. Pa. Wharton Sch., 1946; m. Florence I. Irwin, May 29, 1930; children—William Wesley, Ronald Barr, Michael Irwin. With Phila.-Balt.-Washington Stock Exchange, 1946—, asst. to pres., 1963-65, v.p., chief examiner, 1965-71, v.p., 1971—. Lutheran (councilman 1965—). Rotarian. Club: Forum (Phila.). Home: S-815 Cooper River Plaza Pennsauken NJ 08109 Office: Phila-Balt-Washington Stock Exchange 17th St Exchange Pl Philadelphia PA 19102

BRODY, ARTHUR, indsl. co. exec.; b. Newark, June 30, 1920; s. Samuel A. and Ruth (Marder) B.; student Columbia, 1939-42; m. Sophie Mark, Mar. 5, 1944; children—Janice (Mrs. Mark Rosenberg), Donald. Organizer, operator Library Service, 1940-42; exec. buyer L. Bamberger & Co., Newark, 1942-43; pres., chmn. Bro-Dart Industries, Williamsport, Pa., 1946—. Mem. at large Robert Treat council Boy Scouts Am.; mem. adv. panel study on libraries and industry Nat. Adv. Com. on Libraries; past pres. Friends of N.J. Libraries. Trustee Newark Symphony Hall. Served with AUS, 1943-46. Mem. A.L.A., N.E.A., Nat. Book Com. (nat. bd.). Mason (Shriner). Patentee in field. Home: 605 Mountain Av South Orange NJ 07079 Office: 1609 Memorial Av Williamsport PA 17701

BRODY, CARL, former beverage co. exec.; b. 1923; B.B.A., Coll. City N.Y., 1944; LL.B., N.Y. U., 1948. Tax accountant Haskins & Sells, C.P.A.'s, 1951-63; with Canada Dry Corp., 1963-71, treas., 1967-71. C.P.A. Address: 100 Park Av New York City NY 10017*

BRODY, CLARK LOUIS, Jr., clarinetist; b. Three Rivers, Mich., June 9, 1914; s. Clark L. and Margaret E. (York) B.; B.A., Mich. State Coll., 1934; Mus.B., U. Rochester, 1936, Mus.B. in Clarinet, 1937; m. Florence Chaikin, Feb. 19, 1946; 1 son, Robert David. Solo clarinetist CBS Symphony Orch., 1941-51, also Columbia, RCA Victor rec. orchs.; soloist chamber music groups including New Friends of Music, Gordon Quartet, Paganini Quartet; with Budapest String Quartet, Library of Congress, 1952, Juilliard Quartet, 1966; solo clarinetist Chgo. Symphony Orch., 1951—. Home: 1621 Colfax St Evanston IL 60201 Office: care Chicago Symphony Orchestra 220 S Michigan Av Chicago IL 60604

BRODY, EUGENE BLOOR, psychiatrist, educator; b. Columbia, Mo., June 17, 1921; s. Samuel and Sophie (Dubos) B.; A.B., M.A., U. Mo., 1941; M.D., Harvard, 1944; grad. N.Y. Psychoanalytic Inst., 1957; m. Marian Holen, Sept. 23, 1944; children—Julie Anne, James Clarke, John Holen. Resident, Yale Med. Sch., 1944-46, 48-49, from instr. to asso. prof., 1949-57; prof. psychiatry U. Md. Sch. Medicine, Balt., 1957—, chmn. dept., also dir. Inst., Psychiatry and Behavior, 1959- -. Vis. prof. U. Brazil, 1968; mem. adv. bd. Inst. Social Psychiatry, U. San Marcos, 1968-70; mem. nat. profl. adv. bd. psychiatry, psychology, neurology service VA, 1963-67; cons. Pan Am. Health Orgn., 1965—, Inst. Psychiatry and Fgn. Affairs, 1971—; program dir. Interam. Mental Health Studies Program, 1967-69; mem. exec. bd. World Fedn. Mental Health, 1969—. Chmn. adv. bd. Balt. chpt. Internat. Students Council, A.R.C., 1964-67. Bd. dirs. Md. Partners of Alliance for Progress, 1965-66, Nat. Assn. Mental Health, 1964- 66, mem. profl. adv. bd., 1967—. Served to capt., M.C., AUS, 1946-48. Fellow Am. Psychiat. Assn. (chmn. com. transcultural psychiatry 1966-68, rep. interam. council 1965—, trustee 1968-71), Am. Coll. Psychiatrists (charter); mem. Am., Internat. psychoanalytic assns., Peruvian Psychiat. Assn. (hon.), Peruvian Assn. Psychiatry, Neurology and Neurosurgery (hon.). Author: Psychiatric Patients in Latin American Metropolis. Editor: (with F.C. Redlich) Psychotherapy with Schizophrenics, 1952; (with R. Monroe and G. Klee) Psychiatric Epidemiology and Mental Health Planning, 1967; Minority Group Adolescents in the United States, 1968; Behavior in New Environments, 1970; cons. editor Jour. Nervous and Mental Disease, 1959—, editor in chief, 1967—; adv. editor Tice Med. Ency., 1967—; editorial bd. Psychiatry Digest, 1967-71, Mental Hygiene, 1968—. Contbr. articles to profl. jours. Home: 2007 Skyline Rd Ruxton MD 21204 Office: 645 W Redwood St Baltimore MD 21201

BRODY, J. K., mfg. co. exec.; b. Bridgeport, Conn., 1923; A.B., Yale, 1932, LL.B., 1949. Exec. v.p., dir. Evans Products Co., Portland, Ore.; sec., dir. Aloha Lumber Co.; v.p. Capp-Homes, Inc., Moore's Super Stores, Inc., Rand Acceptance Corp., U.S. Ry. Equipment Co.; v.p., dir. Evans Products Co. Ltd., Williamson Veneer Co. Home: 2425 S W 19th Av Portland, OR 97201. Office: 1121 S W Salmon St Portland, OR 97205.

BRODY, MARTIN, food service co. exec.; b. Newark, Aug. 8, 1921; s. Leo and Renee (Kransdorf) B.; B.A., Mich. State U., 1943; m. Florence Gropper, Nov. 22, 1946; children—Marc, Renee. Pres. Indsl. Feeding Co., Newark, 1951- 61; pres., dir. A.M. Capital Corp., N.Y.C., 1961—; chmn. bd., dir. Waldorf System Inc., Boston, 1963-66, Restaurant Assos., Inc., N.Y.C., 1964-66; chmn. bd., pres. Restaurant Assos. Industries Inc., 1966—; dir. Caldor, Inc., Dollar Savs. Bank. Bd. dirs. MacCauley Spl. Fund; trustee Child Care and Guidance Assn. Essex County, Opportunity Workshop Essex County. Served to capt. AUS, 1943-45. Mem. Young Pres. Orgn. (treas. N.J.). Club: Greenbrook Country (North Caldwell, Caldwell, N.J.). Home: 30 Kean Rd Short Hills NJ 07078 Office: 1540 Broadway New York City NY 10036

BRODY, ROBERT DAVID, investment trust exec.; b. Chgo., Dec. 27, 1925; s. Maurice S. and Eleanor (Perlman) B.; B.S., U. Denver, 1948, M.S., 1953, M.P.A., 1953; m. Paulette L. Glow, Mar. 23, 1961. Pres., Am. Growth Fund, Inc., Denver, 1958—; pres. Investment Research Corp., 1960—, Am. Growth Fund Sponsors, Inc., 1963—. Vice pres., treas. Jewish Community Centers Denver, 1962-65; chmn. equal opportunity com. Denver chpt. Am. Jewish Com., 1968—. Trustee, Am. Med. Center, Denver, 1971—. Mem. Phi Sigma Delta, Zeta Beta Tau. Home: 1155 Ash St Denver CO 80220 Office: 650 17th St Denver CO 80202

BRODY, SIDNEY FRANKLIN, investment co. exec.; b. Des Moines, Nov. 15, 1915; s. Abraham and Lena (Freedman) B.; B.S., Harvard, 1937; m. Frances W. Lasker, Aug. 14, 1942; children—Christopher W., Susan L. Pres. Brody Investment Co., Beverly Hills, Cal., 1954—; dir. Security Pacific Nat. Bank, Los Angeles, Am. Electric, Inc. Trustee Los Angeles County Mus. Art, 1959—, pres., 1966-70, chmn. trustees, 1970—; bd. dirs. Los Angeles Civic Light Opera Assn., 1963—; bd. regents St. John's Hosp., 1964—; trustee Thacher Sch., 1963—, Cal. Community Found., 1969—; mem. vis. com. Harvard Grad. Sch. Edn., 1965—. Served to lt. col. USAAF, 1941-45: PTO, ETO. Decorated Bronze Star medal with oak leaf cluster; Croix de Guerre (France); Fleur de Guerre (Belgium). Home: 360 S Mapleton Dr Los Angeles CA 90024 Office: 9477 Brighton Way Beverly Hills CA 90210

BRODY, THEODORE MEYER, educator, pharmacologist; b. Newark, May 10, 1920; s. Samuel and Lena (Hammer) B.; B.S., Rutgers U., 1943; M.S., U. Ill., 1949, Ph.D., 1952; m. Ethel Vivian Drelich, Sept. 7, 1947; children—Steven Lewis, Debra Jane, Laura Kate, Elizabeth. Mem. faculty U. Mich. Med. Sch., Ann Arbor, 1952-66; prof. pharmacology, chmn. dept., Coll. Med., Mich. State U., East Lansing, 1966—; cons. in field. Served with AUS, 1943-46. Mem. Soc. Pharmacology and Exptl. Therapeutics (John Jacob Abel award 1955, chmn. membership com. 1965, chmn. Abel award com. 1966, mem. council 1969-72, sec.-treas. 1970). Internat. Soc. Biochem. Pharmacology, Soc. Toxicology, Sigma Xi, Rho Chi, Phi Kappa Phi. Mem. editorial bd. Jour. Pharmacology and Exptl. Therapeutics, 1965—. Home: 842 Longfellow St East Lansing MI 48823 Office: Dept of Pharmacology Mich State Univ East Lansing MI 48823

BROEG, BOB, (Robert William), sports editor; b. St. Louis, Mar. 18, 1918; s. Robert Michael and Alice (Wiley) B.; B.Journalism, U. Mo., 1941; m. Dorothy Carr, June 19, 1943. With A.P., Columbia, Mo., 1939-40, Jefferson City, Mo., 1941, Boston, 1941-42; reporter St. Louis Star-Times, 1942; staff sports dept. St. Louis Post-Dispatch, 1945—, sports editor, 1958—. Served with USMCR, 1942-45. Recipient Nat. Sportscasters, Sportswriters awards, Mo., 1962-65, 67; Journalism medal U. Mo., 1971. Mem. Baseball Writers Assn. Am. (pres. 1958), Kappa Tau Alpha, Sigma Delta Chi, Sigma Phi Epsilon, Omicron Delta Kappa. Author: Don't Bring That Up!, 1946; Stan Musial: The Man's Own Story, 1964; Super Stars of Baseball, 1971; also numerous articles. Home: 30 Plaza Sq St Louis MO 63103 Office: Pulitzer Pub Co St Louis MO 63101

BROEHL, WAYNE GOTTLIEB, Jr., educator; b. Peoria, Ill., Aug. 11, 1922; s. Wayne G. and Dimple (Rush) B.; B.S., U. Ill., 1946; M.B.A., U. Chgo., 1950; D.Sc. in Bus. Adminstrn., Ind. U., 1954; M.A. (hon.), Dartmouth, 1958; m. Jean Kirby, Aug. 4, 1944; children—David Robert, James Richard, Michael Kirby. Staff labor relations dept. Western Electric Co., 1946-48, asst. prof., asst. dean Coll. Commerce, Bradley U., 1948-51; faculty lectr. Sch. Bus., Ind. U., 1951-54; prof. bus. Amos Tuck Sch. Bus., Dartmouth, 1954—; vis. prof. bus. history U. Coll., Dublin, Ireland, 1960-61; vis. prof. U. Buenos Aires, 1962. Mem. Am. Econ. Assn., Am. Hist. Assn., Econ. History Assn., Acad. Mgmt., Beta Gamma Sigma, Beta Theta Pi. Author: Trucks, Trouble and Triumph, 1954; Precision Valley, 1959; The Molly Maguires, 1964; The International Basic Economy Corporation, 1968. Co-author: Administering the Going Concern, 1962; Business Research and Report Writing, 1965; Hospital Policy; Process and Action, 1966. Home: 6 Kingsford Rd Hanover NH 03755

BROEK, JAN OTTO MARIUS, geographer; b. Utrecht, Netherlands, Dec. 8, 1904; s. Jan and Geertruida Elizabeth Juliana (van Zwicht) B.; came to U.S., 1936, naturalized, 1942; student U. Utrecht, 1924-29, Ph.D., 1932; fellow Rockefeller Found., 1929-31; postgrad. London Sch. Econs., 1929, U. Cal. at Berkeley, 1930-31; m. Orletta Ruth Heineck, May 25, 1931; children—Orietta Marianne (Janna) (Mrs. John M. Leffingwell), Gertrude Juliana (Mrs. G.A. Williams), Jan Maarten. With Netherlands Inst. Housing and Town Planning, Amsterdam, 1929, Netherlands Rys., Utrecht, 1933-36; vis. lectr. univs. Ia., Ohio, Cal., 1936-37; asst., then asso. prof. geography U. Cal. at Berkeley, 1937-46; prof. geography, dir. Social Geography Inst., U. Utrecht, 1946-48; prof. U. Minn., 1948-70, chmn. dept. geography, 1948- 57. Vis. prof., adviser U. Indonesia, Batavia, 1947; Fulbright vis. prof. U. Malaya, Singapore, 1954-55; hon. research asso. U. Coll., London, 1961-62; vis. prof. U. Cal. at Berkeley, 1970-71; cons. geog. br. M.I. Service, 1943; spl. asst. to chief Far Eastern div., Research and Analysis Br., OSS, 1945. Recipient Research award Am. Council Learned Socs.-Social Sci. Research Council, 1961-62. Fellow Am. Geog. Soc.; mem. Alexander Maconochie Found. (hon.), Assn. Am. Geographers (pres. 1960-61), Royal Netherlands Geog. Soc. (corr. mem.), Netherlands Soc. Econ. and Social Geography, S.E. Asia Inst., Inst. Pacific Relations, El Instituto de la Producion (U. Buenos Aires, corr. mem.). Club: Campus. Author: The Santa Clara Valley, California, 1932; The Economic Development of the Netherlands Indies, 1942; Geography, its Scope and Spirit, 1965; Compass of Geography, 1966; (with J.W. Webb) A Geography of Mankind, 1968. Adv. editor Terrae Incognitae, Annals Soc. for History of Discoveries, 1967- -. Contbr. numerous articles to profl. jours. Address: 235 Southampton Av Berkeley CA 94707

BROEKER, BERNARD DREHER, steel co. exec.; b. Natoma, Kan., May 10, 1909; s. Felix and Ruth (Dreher) B.; A.B., U. Notre Dame, 1930; LL.B. cum laude, Harvard, 1933; m. Katherine Oostdyke, Apr. 15, 1934 (dec. 1960); children—Katherine Anne (Mrs. A. Haigh Cundey), Bernard D.; m. 2d, Frances W. Mills, Sept. 30, 1961. Admitted to N.Y. bar, 1934; asso. Cravath, de Gersdorff, Swaine & Wood, N.Y.C., 1933-40; atty. Bethlehem Steel Co. (Pa.). 1940- 53; asst. sec. Bethlehem Steel Corp. (Del.), 1953-57, sec., dir., 1957- 65, asst. v.p. 1961-65, gen. counsel, 1963-70, vice chmn. finance com., 1965-67, chmn. finance com., 1967-70, dir., 1967—, exec. v.p., 1970—. Mem. Am. Judicature Soc., Am. Bar Assn., Am. Law Inst., Am. Iron and Steel Inst. Home: 501 E Macada Rd Bethlehem PA 18017 Office: 701 E 3d St Bethlehem PA 18015

BROEMAN, CHARLES WILLIAM, lawyer; b. Cin., Jan. 16, 1890; s. Frank and Mary (Meyers) B.; A.B., U. Cin., 1911; LL.B., Cin. Law Sch., 1913; m. Ina Warner, June 15, 1915; children—Dwight Warner, Betty (Mrs. Thomas Jos. Klinedinst). Admitted to Ohio bar, 1913, practiced in Cin.; pres. Charels W. Broeman Co., Cin., 1930—; dir. Hennegan Co., Brockamp Bldg. Materials Co., Tresler Oil Co. Mem. Cin. Bar Assn. Clubs: Queen City, Bankers (Cin.), Home: 2401 Ingleside Av Cincinnati OH 45206 Office: First Nat Bank Bldg Cincinnati OH 45202

BROERSMA, SYBRAND, educator; b. Harlingen, Netherlands, Sept. 20, 1919; s. Jacob and Johanna (Zwanenburg) B.; B.A. in Physics, Leiden U., 1939, M.A., 1941; Ph.D. cum laude in Physics, Delft Inst. Tech., 1947. Came to U.S., 1947, naturalized, 1957. Research asso. Columbia, 1947; instr. U. Toronto, 1948; prof. physics U. Indonesia, Bandung, 1949-51; asst. prof. physics Northwestern U., 1952-58; prof. physics U. Okla., 1959—; adj. prof. materials research U. Tex. at Dallas, 1967-70. Internat. exchange fellow Northwestern U., 1947; NSF grantee, 1956-68, Fellow Okla. Acad. Sci.; mem. Netherlands Phys. Soc., Am. Phys. Soc., Am. Assn. U. Profs., Sigma Xi. Author: Magnetic Measurements on Organic Compounds, 1947; Elementary Physics Laboratory Manual, 1963; also articles. Home: 520 Fleetwood Norman OK 73069

BROFSKY, HOWARD, educator; b. N.Y.C., May 2, 1927; s. Barney and Frances (Reich) B.; Ph.D., N.Y. U., 1963; m. Miriam Kley, June 30, 1953; children—Alexander, Natasha. Mem. faculty U. Chgo., 1960-67; asso. prof. Queens Coll., Flushing, N.Y., 1967-68, chmn. dept. music, 1968—, prof., 1970—; spl. editor music Harper & Row, 1969—. Served with AUS, 1946-48. Fulbright grantee, 1953-54; Research grantee U. Bologna (Italy). Mem. Am. Musicological Soc. (Council 1971-73), Phi Beta Kappa. Author: (with Jeanne S. Bamberger) The Art of Listening: Developing Musical Perception, 1969; also articles. Home: 186 Riverside Dr New York City NY 10024 Office: Dept Music Queens Coll Flushing NY 11367

BROFSKY, MIRIAM, artist; b. Can., June 30, 1929; ed. Bklyn. Coll., Art Students League, New York City, also Ossip Zadkine, Paris, France; m. Howard Brofsky; 1 child. Group exhbns. include U. Chicago, 1963, Chicago Art Inst., 1961, 62, Exp. des Ateliers Zadkine, Paris, 1955, exp des Jeunes Sculpteurs, Paris, 1955; rep. pvt. collections. Home: 5821 Dorchester Av Chicago, IL 60637.*

BROGAN, SIR DENIS WILLIAM, educator; Glasgow, Scotland, Aug. 11, 1900; s. Denis and Elizabeth (Toner) B.; m. Olwen Kendall, Aug. 20, 1931; children—Denis Hugh Vercingetorix, Patrick William Kendall, Brian Joseph, Olwen Elizabeth. Lectr., London Sch. Econs; hon. fellow Corpus Christi Coll., Oxford U., also Peterhouse, Cambridge; prof. polit. sci. Cambridge (Eng.) U., 1939-67, prof. emeritus, 1967—. Decorated Legion of Honor; comdr. Order of Orange Nassau; created knight. Mem. Institut de France, Brit. Acad., Am. Philos. Soc., Mass. Hist. soc. Clubs: Reform (London); Lotos (N.Y.C.); Nat. Press (Washington). Author: The Free State, 1945: French Personalities and Problems, American Themes, Politics in America, 1954; The French Nation, 1957; American Aspects, 1964. Home: 1 Hedgerley Close Cambridge England

BROGAN, HOWARD OAKLEY, educator; s. Jesse and Anne (Braga) B.; B.A., Grinnell Coll., 1936; M.A., U. Ia., 1938; Ph.D., Yale, 1941; m. Isabel Brower, Apr. 2, 1938; children—Patrick Alan, Jesse William, Pamela Ann. Grad. asst. U. Ia., 1936-37; instr. Ill. Coll., Jacksonville, 1937-39; asst. prof. The Citadel, Charleston, S.C., 1942-44; lectr. Princeton, 1944-46; asso. prof. Franklin and Marshall Coll., 1946-47, Syracuse U., 1947-53; prof. English, Bowling Green State U., 1953-62, chmn. dept., 1955-62; Commonwealth prof. U. Mass., Amherst, 1962—, head dept. English, 1962-67; Sterling research fellow Yale, 1941-42, Carnegie intern gen. edn. 1952-53. Mem. Am. Assn. U. Profs., Coll. English Assn., Internat. Assn. U. Profs. of English, Nat. Council Tchrs. of English, N.E.A., Modern Lang. Assn., Phi Beta Kappa. Home: 10 Dana St Amherst MA 01002

BROGAN, JOHN CHRISTOPHER, hotelier; b. Lansing, Mich., Mar. 7, 1933; s. Harold C. and Laura (Taylor) B.; B.S., Mich. State U., 1955; m. Mary Louise Heck, Feb. 27, 1965. Mgmt. tng. Waldorf Astoria Hotel, N.Y.C., 1955-58; front officer mgr. Boston Statler Hilton Hotel, 1957-59; asst. gen. mgr. Sheraton Hotels in Hawaii, 1960-61; gen. mgr. French Lick (Ind.) Sheraton Hotel, 1962-66, Sheraton Schroeder Hotel, Milw., 1967-68, Royal Hawaiian Hotel, Honolulu, 1968-70; v.p., gen. mgr. Sheraton Waikiki Hotel, Honolulu, 1970—. Served with inf. AUS, 1956-57. Mem. Psi Upsilon. Roman Catholic. Home: Sheraton Waikiki Hotel Honolulu HI 96815

BROGAN, JOHN JOSEPH, mfg. co. exec.; b. Chgo., Jan. 9, 1916; s. John Joseph and Mabel (McCarthy) B.; m. Anne Mullin, Apr. 26, 1943; children—John Patrick, Anne (Mrs. Richard E. Segerson), Thomas Joseph, James Edward, Sheila Mary. With Jefferson Electric Co., 1937-55, gen. sales mgr., 1954-55; with Pneumo Dynamics Corp., 1955-, v.p., 1958-61, exec. v.p., 1961-69; now pres., dir.; pres., dir. Claud S. Gordon Co., Richmond, Ill., 1962- -; dir. Cone Ltd., Staffordshire, Eng., LaTouraine Coffe Co., Boston, Midwestern Nat. Life Ins. Co., Cleve., Midwest Bank & Trust Co. Trustee Pneumo Dynamics Found., 77th St. Trust, Claud S. Gordon Co. Profit Sharing and Savs. Trust. Gen. campaign chmn. Cath. Charities Corp., also trustee, 1st v.p.; mem. adv. bd. Cath. Charities Bur., St. Alexius Hosp., Better Home for Cleve. Found; bd. dirs. Pharmadale Village for

Children. Served to maj., AUS, 1942-46. Mem. Am. Ordnance Assn., Soc. Automotive Engrs., Aerospace Industries Assn., Nat. Aero. Assn., Am. Assn. Indsl. Mgmt., Helicopter Soc., Nat. Machine Tool Builders Assn., Grinding Wheel Inst., Abrasive Grain Assn., Sci. Apparatus Makers Assn. (past chmn. indsl. instrument sect.) Navy League, Clubs: Cleve. Athletic, Mid-day, Skating (Cleve.); Shaker Heights (O.) Country: Wings (N.Y.C.); Chatham (Mass.) Yacht (past commodore), Eastward Ho! Country, Country, Stage Harbor Yacht (Chatham, Mass.); Chicago Athletic Assn. Home: 2489 Coventry Rd Cleveland Heights OH 44118 Office: 3781 E 77th St Cleveland OH 44105

BROGDEN, WILFRED JOHN, psychologist; b. Sydney, Australia, May 6, 1912; s. John and Elsie May (Taylor) B.; came to U.S., 1914, naturalized, 1926; student So. Meth. U., 1929-32; A.B., U. Ill., 1933, Ph.D., 1936; NRC fellow Johns Hopkins Sch. Medicine, 1936-37; m. Elinor Taylor Davis, Sept. 8, 1935; children—Penelope, Ann. Research asst. in psychiatry Johns Hopkins Sch. Medicine, 1937-39; asst. prof. psychology U. Wis., 1939-43, asso. prof., 1944-46, prof. psychology, 1946—, asst. dean Grad. Sch., 1947, asso. dean, 1951-58. Vis. lectr. U. Rochester, summer 1942, Harvard, summer 1946. Active research applied psychology panel NDRC, 1942-45 (awarded presdl. certificate of appreciation, 1947); expert cons. to sec. nat. def., 1947-54; mem. sub-panel on sensory functions Research and Dev. Bd., 1947-48, chmn., 1948, mem. panel on human engring. and psychophysiology, 1948-54; mem. div. anthropology and psychology NRC, 1948-52, chmn. com. fellowship selection procedures. Mem. profl. adv. com. on human resources USAF, 1948-50. Fellow A.A.A.S., Am. Psychol. Assn. (pres. div. physiology and comparative psychology 1949; sec. div. theoretical and exptl. psychology 1948); mem. Am. Assn. U. Profs., Psychonomics Soc. (organizing com. 1960; governing bd. 1960-63, chmn. 1962), Soc. Exptl. Psychology, Midwestern Psychology Assn., Sigma Xi. Contbr. articles to sci. jours. Home: 1429 Vilas Av Madison WI 53711

BROGDON, BYRON GILLIAM, educator, physician; b. Ft. Smith, Ark., Jan. 22, 1929; s. Paul Preston and Lela (Gilliam) B.; B.S., U. Ark., 1951, B.S., 1951, M.D., 1952; m. Jane Bricker Kittleman, Mar. 23, 1951; 1 son, David Pope. Intern Univ. Hosp., Little Rock, 1952-53, resident, 1953-55; resident N.C. Baptist Hosp., Winston-Salem, 1955-56; asst. prof. radiology U. Fla., 1960-63; asso. prof. radiology Johns Hopkins U., 1963-67, radiologist-in-charge Div. Diagnostic Radiology, 1963-67; prof., chmn. dept. radiology U. N.M. Sch. Medicine, 1967—, asst. dean Sch. Medicine, 1969—; med. dir. Bernalillo County Med. Center, 1968—. Served to maj. USAF, 1953-60. Diplomate Am. Bd. Radiology. Fellow Am. Coll. Radiology; mem. A.M.A., Radiol. Soc. North Am., Am. Roentgen Ray Soc., Soc. Pediatric Radiology, Assn. U. Radiologists, Soc. So. Radiol. Conf. Home: 4708 Westridge Pl NE Albuquerque NM 87111

BROGGI, DANTE, elec. mfg. co. exec.; b. Barre, Vt., Mar. 18, 1900; s. Angelo and Josephine (Stella) B.; B.S. cum laude, Coll. City N.Y., 1920; m. Charlotte V. Green, Dec. 20, 1935; 1 dau., Dantia Charlotte (Mrs. Thomas F. Quirk).. With Neptune Meter Co., N.Y.C., 1920-58, pres., 1950-58; v.p., treas., dir. mem. exec. com. Am. Meter Co. subsidiary Singer Co., Phila., 1958—; dir. Gen. Precision Equipment Co., Tarrytown, N.J. Office: 13500 Philmont Av Philadelphia PA 19116

BROGGINI, ADRIAN JOSEPH, engring. and constrn. co. exec.; b. Lakewood, O., Oct. 16, 1912; s. Andrew and Letitia (Sinton) B.; B.S. in Chem. Engring., U. Mich., 1934; m. Virginia Reutter, Aug. 15, 1934; children—Carol Ann (Mrs. Anthony B. Catlin), Judith Elin (Mrs. D.L. Gunner), Adrienne Joan. With E.B. Badger & Sons Co., Boston, 1936-50, v.p., 1948-50; with Stone & Webster Engring. Co., Boston, 1950-53; with Badger Co., Inc., 1953—, pres., chief exec. officer, treas., dir., 1957-68, chmn., dir., 1971—; dir. Harvard Trust Co., Cambridge, Badger Ltd., London, Eng., Badger N.V., The Hague, United Engrs. and Constructors, Phila. Registered profl. engr., Mass. Mem. Nat., Fla. engring. socs., Am. Petroleum Inst., Am. Inst. Chem. Engrs., Tau Beta Pi. Clubs: Brae Burn Country (Newton, Mass.); Hague Country (Holland); University, Chemists (N.Y.C.); Algonquin (Boston); Lost Tree Country (North Palm Beach, Fla.). Home: 126 Woodlawn Av Wellesley Hills MA 02181 Office: Cambridge Gateway One Broadway Cambridge MA 02142

BROKAW, AUGUSTUS VAN LLEW, stockbroker; b. St. Louis, Oct. 20, 1899; s. Augustus Van L. and Julia (Crawford) B.; B.S., Washington U., 1922; m. Elizabeth Cabell Gray, Nov. 25, 1931; children—Augustus Van Liew, Elizabeth Cabell. Registered rep. I.M. Simon & Co., 1926-34; partner Friedman, Brokaw & Samish and successor firms, 1934-53; partner G.H. Walker & Co., St. Louis, 1954—, ltd. partner, 1967—. Gov., Midwest Stock Exchange, 1952-55. Bd. dirs. Jr. Achievement Miss. Valley, 1955-57, sec., 1957-58; mem. Majors Bond Issue-Screening Com., 1966. Mem. Beta Theta Pi. Republican. Episcopalian. Clubs: Press, University (St. Louis). Home: 5363 Waterman Av St Louis MO 63112 Office: 503 Locust St St Louis MO 63103

BROKER, THOMAS OERTER, educator; b. Bklyn., Mar. 22, 1915; s. Thomas and Elsie (Oerter) B.; B.A., Wesleyan U., Middletown, Conn., 1936; J.D., Cornell U., 1939; M.A., Tufts U., 1969; m. Evelyn Froetscher, Jan. 16, 1942; children—Thomas Richard, Stephen Paul. Admitted to N.Y. bar, 1939, N.J. bar, 1941, Ohio bar, 1949, Va. bar, 1965; with firm McCarter English & Studer, Newark, 1939-41; with Lehigh Valley R.R. Co., 1941-48, asst. gen. counsel, 1947-48; with N.Y., C. & St. L. R.R., 1948-64, v.p., gen. counsel, 1961-64; gen. counsel N. & W. Ry. Co., 1964-68; asst. prof. polit. sci. Va. Western Community Coll., Roanoke, 1969-70, asso. prof. law and govt., 1970—. Served to capt. AUS, 1942-46; ETO Mem. Assn. ICC Practitioners (nat. pres. 1965-66), Am. Soc. Traffic and Transp., Am., Va., Roanoke, Cleve. bar assns., Phi Beta Kappa, Chi Psi, Phi Delta Phi. Republican. Unitarian (past pres.). Home: 1616 Blair Rd S W Roanoke VA 24015 Office: 3098 Colonial Av S W Roanoke VA 24015

BROMAGE, ARTHUR WATSON, educator; b. East Windsor, Conn., Feb. 27, 1904; s. William George and Emma Irene (Bower) B.; B.S., Wesleyan U., 1925, A.M., Harvard, 1926, Ph.D., 1928; m. Mary Cogan, July 5, 1928; 1 dau., Susanna Sarah (Mrs. John Paterson). Asst. in govt. Harvard, 1926-28, instr., 1928-29; instr. U. Mich., Ann Arbor, 1928, asst. prof. polit. sci., 1929-31, asso. prof., 1931-38, prof., 1938—, chmn. dept. polit. sci., 1961-64. Cons. Mich. Commn. of Inquiry into County, Twp. and Sch. Dist. Govt., 1931-33; mem. Nat. Municipal League Com. on County Govt. 1932-42; leader roundtable on local govt. Va. Inst. Pub. Affairs, 1936; sec. Mich. Commn. on Reform and Modernization Govt., 1938-39; chmn. exec. bd. Ann Arbor Citizens Council, 1942-43; mem. city council Ann Arbor, 1949-53; Mich. Commn. on Inter-govtl. Relations, 1954-55; adv. mem. Mich. Legislative Interim Com. on Intergovtl. Relations, 1954-55; mem. Mich. Commn. on Annexation, 1962-63, Mich. Commn. on Local Govt., 1970- 71. Mem. exec. com. Coll. Lit., Sci. and Arts, U. Mich., 1948-49, 67-70; v.p. Midwest Conf. Polit. Scientists, 1963-64. Served to lt. col. AUS, 1943-45. Mem. Am. Polit. Sci. Assn. (exec. council 1944-46), Am. Soc. Pub. Adminstrn., Nat. (council 1953-60), Mich. (v.p. 1952, hon. life) municipal leagues, Internat. City Mgrs. Assn. (hon.), Mich. Acad. Scis., Arts and Letters, Inst. Pub. Adminstrn. (exec. com. 1947-64), Survey Research Center U. Mich. (exec. com. 1947-52), Delta Sigma Rho, Phi Beta Kappa, Phi Kappa Phi. Club: University (Ann Arbor). Author: American County Government, 1933; (with T.H. Reed), Organization and Cost of County and Township Government, 1933; State Government and Administration in the United States, 1936; Manager Plan Abandonments, 1940; Introduction to Municipal Government and Administration, 1950; On the City Council, 1950; A Councilman Speaks, 1951; Councilman at Work, 1954; Political Representation in Metropolitan Agencies, 1962; Urban Policy Making: The Council-Manager Partnership, 1970. Contbr. articles to to jours. Home: 2300 Vinewood Blvd Ann Arbor MI 48104

BROMAN, KEITH LEROY, educator; b. Randolph, Wis., July 13, 1922; s. Oscar Rudolph and H. Marie (Carlson) B.; student Ind. U., 1940-43; student Berea Coll., 1944; M.B.A., Harvard, 1947; Ph.D., U. Neb., 1954; m. Ruth Jane DuBois, Oct. 27, 1944; children—Rebecca Ann (Mrs. Phillip Cross), Lisa Marie. With Sears Roebuck & Co., South Bend, Ind., 1940-42, Bendix Aviation, South Bend, 1942-43; tchr. Ohio U., 1947-51, U. Neb., 1951-54, U. Wis., 1954-55; prof. finance, chmn. dept. U. Neb., 1955—; cons. investment edn. and practice. Served with USNR 1943-46; comdr. Res. Ford Found. summer fellow, 1959. Mem. Am. Finance Assn., Am. Accounting Assn., Midwest Bus. Adminstrn. Assn., Beta Gamma Sigma, Delta Sigma Pi. Home: 3540 Calvert St Lincoln NB 68506

BROMBERG, BEN GEORGE, aero. engr.; b. N.Y.C., Feb. 14, 1915; s. Louis and Anne (Steinhouse) B.; B.S. (Sylvanus Reed fellow), N.Y. U., 1936, M.S., 1937; Sc.D. (Consol. Vultee fellow), Mass. Inst. Tech., 1947; m. Pauline Riggs, May 10, 1941; 1 son, Jeffrey. Chief tech. engr. research Consol. Vultee Aircraft Corp., 1939-45; research asso., instr. lab. Mass. Inst. Tech., 1945-47; chief engr. missile div. McDonnell Aircraft Corp., St. Louis, 1947-59, v.p., 1959-68; v.p., gen. mgr. McDonnell-Douglas Astronautics Co., Eastern div. McDonnell Douglas Corp., 1968—, also dir. Instr. servomechanisms Washington U., 1951; space sci. research and devel. com. St. Louis U., 1962—; vis. com. dept. aeros. and astronautics Mass. Inst. Tech., 1962—; mem. Berg Sci. Found., St. Charles High Sch. Bd. dirs. McDonnell scholarship Found. Recipient Alumni Achievement award N.Y. U., 1970-71. Fellow Brit. Interplanetary Soc., Am. Inst. Aeros. and Astronautics; mem. Aerospace Industries Assn. (missile and space council), Navy League U.S., I.E.E.E. (sr.), Am. Phys. Soc., Engring. Council Profl. Devel. (coll. accreditation. bd.), Sigma Xi. Club: Nat. Space. Contbr. papers to profl. lit. Home: 523 Tregaron Pl Frontenac MO 63131 Office: Box 516 St Louis MO 63166

BROMBERG, HENRI LOUIE, Jr., lawyer; b. Dallas, Jan. 15, 1911; s. Henri Louie and Felice (Fechenbach) B.; A.B., U. Tex., Austin, 1932; J.D., Northwestern U., 1935; m. Janice Mayer, Apr. 12, 1936; 1 son, Henri Louie III. Admitted to Tex. bar, 1935, since practiced in Dallas; partner Johnson, Bromberg, Leeds & Riggs and predecessor firm, 1935—. Dir. Northpark Nat. Bank of Dallas, Peoples Am. Bank of Atlanta, Dallas Market Center Co. Nat. vice chmn. Joint Def. Appeal Nat. Council, 1957-58; mem. nat. bd. Nat. Conf. Christians and Jews, 1959-62, co-chmn. Dallas chpt., 1960-68; chmn. Dallas chpt. Am. Jewish Com., 1951, dir., 1951-; mem. Gov.'s Com. for White House Conf. on Children and Youth, 1960; del. White House Conf. on Internat. Coopertion, 1965. Bd. dirs. West Dallas Social Center, 1953-58, pres., 1955; bd. dirs. Jewish Welfare Fedn. Dallas, 1947 -61, pres., 1956-58; bd. dirs. Tex. Psychiat. Found., 1955-62, v.p., 1959-62; sec., bd. dirs. Urban League Greater Dallas, 1967—, Dallas Grand Opera Assn., 1946—; bd. dirs. Dallas County Assn. for Blind, 1952-60, Council Social Agys. Dallas, 1958-65, Dallas County Community Action Com., 1965-70, Council Jewish Fedns. and Welfare Funds, 1958-60; bd. visitors So.Meth. U. Law Sch., 1965—; bd. govs. Hebrew Union Coll.-Jewish Inst. Religion; 1968—, mem. exec. com., 1970—; vice chmn. Nat. Cabinet Reform Jewish Appeal, 1970. Served to lt. col. USAAF, 1942-46. Recipient Brotherhood award Nat. Conf. Christians and Jews, 1970; Co-recipient Human Relations award Am. Jewish Com., 1970. Mem. Am. Judicature Soc., Archeol. Inst. Am., Dallas Art Assn., Am., Tex., Dallas bar assns., Confrerie Des Chevaliers Du Tastevin. Jewish religion (past pres., dir. 1950— temple). Clubs: Columbian (past pres., dir.), Dallas, City, Commonwealth (Dallas). Home: 4842 Brookview Dr Dallas, TX 75220. Office: 211 N Ervay St Dallas TX 75201

BROMBERGER, SYLVAIN, educator, philosopher; b. Antwerp, Belgium, July 7, 1924; s. Jacques and Esther (Helman) B.; A.B., Columbia, 1948; Ph.D., Harvard, 1961; m. Nancy Alice Lilienthal, Aug. 7, 1949; children—Allen Richard, Daniel Martin. Instr., Princeton, 1954-57, lectr., 1957-60; asso. prof. U. Chgo., 1961- 66; mem. faculty Mass. Inst. Tech., 1966—, prof. philosophy, 1967—. Served with AUS, 1943-46. Santayana fellow Harvard, 1957-58; recipient Quantrell prize U. Chgo., 1964. Mem. Am. Philos, Assn., Am. Assn. U. Profs. Mem. adv. bd. Philos. Forum; cons. editor Metaphilosophy. Home: 146 Beaumont Av Newtonville MA 02160 Office: Mass Inst Tech Cambridge MA 02139

BROMBERT, VICTOR HENRI, educator; b. Berlin, Germany, Nov. 11, 1923; s. Jacques and Vera B.; came to U.S., 1941, naturalized, 1943; B.A., Yale, 1948, M.A., 1949, Ph.D., 1953; postgrad. U. Rome, 1950-51; m. Beth Anne Archer, June 18, 1950; children—Lauren Nora, Marc Alexis. Faculty, Yale, New Haven, 1951- -, asso. prof., 1958-61, prof., 1961—, Benjamin F. Barge prof. Romance lits., 1969—, chmn. dept. romance langs., lit., 1964—. Summer prof. Middlebury Coll., 1951-53, Institut d'Etudes Francaises, Avignon, 1962, 64, U. Colo., 1965; Christian Gauss Seminar in criticism Princeton, 1964; lectr. Alliance Francaise, humanities U. Kan., 1966. Mem. Fulbright screening com., 1965. Served with M.I., AUS, 1943-45. Am. Council Learned Socs. grantee, 1966; Fulbright fellow, 1950-51; Guggenheim fellow, 1954-55, 70. Mem. Modern Lang. Assn., Am. Assn. Tchrs. French, Assn. Internationale des Etudes Francaises, Phi Beta Kappa. Club: Elizabethan. Author: The Criticism of T.S. Eliot, 1949; Stendhal et la Voie Oblique, 1954; The Intellectual Hero, 1961; The Novels of Flaubert, 1966; Stendhal; Fiction and the Themes of Freedom, 1968; Flaubert par lui-mme, 1971. Editor: Stendhal: A Collection of Critical Essays, 1962; The Hero in Literature, 1969. Contbg. author The World of Lawrence Durrell, 1962; Ideas in the Drama 1964. Contbr. articles to periodicals. Home: 115 W Park Av New Haven CT 06511

BROME, ROBERT HARRISON, banker; b. Basin, Wyo., June 28, 1911; s. Charles L. and Margaret (Kennedy) B.; A.B., Whitman Coll., 1933, LL.D., 1970; LL.B., Columbia, 1936; m. Mary E. Reed, Aug. 28, 1937; children—Thomas R., Robert H. Admitted to N.Y. bar, 1936, Wyo. bar, 1946; asst. counsel, asst. sec. Fed. Res. Bank of N.Y., 1936-46, 48-50; resident counsel Bankers Trust Co., N.Y.C., 1950- 62, sec., 1955-66, gen. counsel, 1962-66, sr. v.p., gen. counsel, 1966- 68, sr. v.p., sec., 1968—; v.p., sec. Bankers Internat. Corp., 1962-70, also dir.; sec., gen. counsel BT N.Y. Corp., 1966-68, sr. v.p., 1968—; dir. First Trust Co. of Albany, Ball Co., Inc., Sackman-Gilliland Corp., B.T. Advisors, Inc. Overseer, Whitman Coll. Mem. Am. Bar Assn., Am. Bankers Assn., Phi Beta Kappa. Clubs: Tuxedo, University (N.Y.C.); Blackmeadow (Chester, N.Y.); Fort Orange (Albany); National Lawyers (Washington). Home: 175 Beechwood Rd Ridgewood NJ 07450 Office: 280 Park Av New York City NY 10017

BROMILOW, FRANK, coll. dean; b. Lancashire, Eng., May 13, 1916; s. Peter and Jane (Gregory) B.; came to U.S., 1923, naturalized, 1929; B.S. in Civil Engring., U. Pitts., 1937, M.S., 1939; student Carnegie Inst. Tech., 1941-42; m. Dorothy O'Neill, June 10, 1941; children—Margaret, Neil, Mary. Instr., then asst. prof. civil engring. U. Pitts., 1937-46; chief engr. Plasteel Product Co., Washington, Pa., 1946-48; asso. prof. civil engring. U. Fla., 1948-51; head dept. civil engring. N.M. State U., University Park, 1951- 61, dean Coll. Engring., dir. Engring. Expt. Sta., 1961—. Mem. N.M. Bd. Registration Profl. Engrs. Registered profl. engr., N.M., Pa. Mem. Nat., N.M. (past bd. dirs.) socs. profl. engrs., Am. Soc. Engring. Edn. (council, chmn. civil engring. div.), Am. Soc. C.E., Am. Concrete Inst., Sigma Xi, Sigma Tau, Lambda Chi Alpha, Chi Epsilon, Phi Kappa Phi. Rotarian. Home: 2029 Crescent Dr Las Cruces NM 88001 Office: NM State U University Park NM 88001

BROMLEY, BRUCE, lawyer; b. Pontiac, Mich., Mar. 20, 1893; s. Peter Brewater and Sarah Suydam (Ditmas) B.; A.B., U. Mich., 1914, LL.D. (hon.), 1949; LL.B., Harvard, 1917; LL.D. (hon.), Union U., Schenectady, 1958; m. Esther Baldwin, May 10, 1922; children—Stephen Baldwin, Peter Brewster, Bruce (dec.), Sarah Suydam (Mrs. Cory B. Kilvert). Admitted to N.Y. bar, 1920; asso. firm Cravath, Swaine & Moore, N.Y.C., 1923-26, partner, 1926-49, 50—; asso. judge N.Y. State Ct. Appeals, 1949; Sterling lectr. Yale Law Sch., 1933-38, 46-47; dir. IBM Corp., 1958—. Mem. Lawyers Com. for Civil Rights Under Law, 1963—, N.Y.C. Mayor's Bd. Ethics, 1961—, Nat. Com. Study Antitrust Laws, 1953—. Fellow Am. Coll. Trial Lawyers; mem. Am., N.Y. bar assns., Met. Trial Lawyers Assn. Home: 10 Gracie Sq New York City NY 10028 Office: 1 Chase Manhattan Plaza New York City NY 10005

BROMLEY, DAVID ALLAN, educator, physicist; b. Westmeath, Ont., Can., May 4, 1926; s. Milton Escourt and Susan Anne (Anderson) B.; B.Sc. in Engring. Physics, Queen's U., Kingston, Ont., 1948, M.Sc. in Physics, 1950; Ph.D. in Nuclear Physics, U. Rochester, 1952; M.A. (hon.), Yale, 1961; m. Patricia Jane Brassor, Aug. 30, 1949; children—David John, Karen Lynn. Operating engr. Hydro Electric Power Commn. Ont., 1947-48; research officer NRC Can., 1948, mem.-at-large, mem. exec. com. div. phys. scis., 1970—; instr., then asst. prof. physics U. Rochester, 1952-55; sr. research officer, sect. head Atomic Energy Can. Ltd., 1955-60; asso. prof. physics, asso. dir. heavy ion accelerator lab. Yale, 1960-61, prof. physics, dir. A.W. Wright Nuclear Structure lab., 1961—, chmn. physics dept., 1970—. Dir. United Nuclear Corp., Labcore, Inc., Extrion Corp.; cons. Brookhaven and Oak Ridge Nat. Labs., Bell Telephone Labs., IBM. Mem. panel nuclear structure research NSF, 1961—; mem. panel nuclear physics Nat. Acad. Scis., 1964, chmn. com. on nuclear sci., 1966—, chmn. physics survey, 1969—; mem. U.S. nat. com. Internat. Union Pure and Applied Physics, 1969—. Recipeint medal Gov. Gen. Can., 1948; NRC fellow 1952; fellow Branford Coll., 1961—. Fellow Am. Phys. Soc. (vice chmn. organizing com. div. nuclear physics, mem. council 1967-71); mem. Canadian Assn. Physicists, Sigma Xi (pres. Yale 1962-63). Co-editor: Procs. Kingston Internat. Conf. on Nuclear Structure, 1960; Facets of Physics, 1970. Asso. editor Phys. Rev., 1963—, Nuclear News, 1964—, Annals of Physics, 1968—, Am. Scientist, 1969—, IL Nuovo Cimento, 1970—; cons. editor Acad. Paperbacks in Physics, 1961-67, McGraw Hill Series in Fundamentals of Physics, 1967—. Home: 35 Tokeneke Dr Hamden CT 06518 Office: Wright Nuclear Structure Lab 260 Witney Av New Haven CT 06520

BROMLEY, WILLARD SCHARFF, assn. exec.; b. Pa., 1909; s. Edward and Mary (Walbridge) B.; grad. Pa. State Coll., 1931; M.S., Yale, 1939; m. Frieda L. Hilgner, Aug. 21, 1931; children—Mary, Barbara, Sylvia, Dorothy, Bruce, Alan, Cynthia. Ranger, supt. Civilian Conservation Corps, 1932-36; asst. forester U.S. Forest Service, 1936-39; faculty dept. forestry, U. Mich., 1939-41; forester Cleve. Cliffs Iron Co., 1941-45; forest cons., Ironwood, Mich., 1945-49, pulpwood prodn., 1946-49; dir. Timber Producers Assn. Mich. and Wis., 1947-49; exec. v.p. Am. Pulpwood Assn. N.Y.C., 1966- -. Industry adviser to employee delegation Timber Industry Conf. of ILO, Geneva, 1958. Mem. Soc. Am. Foresters. Home: New Rochelle NY 10801 Office: 605 3d Av New York City NY 10016

BROMMEL, BERNARD JOSEPH, educator; b. Des Moines, Aug. 13, 1930; s. Wilbur B. and Nellie (Hanrahan) B.; B.A., Ia. No. U., 1950; M.A., U. Ia., 1955; Ph.D., Ind. U., 1963; m. Wilma Funkhouser, Sept. 4, 1950; children—Michaela Ann, Brian, Debra, Brent, Bradley, Blair. Tchr. speech, theatre and history Rowley (Ia.) Consol. High Sch., 1950-54; tchr. English and speech Keokuk (Ia.) Sr. High Sch. and Community Coll., 1954-59; asso. prof. speech and theatre Ind. State U., 1959-67; prof.; Chmn. speech and theatre radio-TV dept. U. N.D., 1967-71; prof. speech and communication Northeastern State Coll., Chgo., 1971—. Bd. dirs. Eugene V. Debs Found. Danforth fellow, summers 1960, 61. Mem. Ind. Speech Assn. (exec. com. 1964-66), Am. Assn. U. Profs. (pres. Ind. 1966), Central States Speech Assn. (chmn. adv. council 1969-72), Speech Communication Assn. Am., Internat. Communication Assn., Am. Ednl. Theatre Assn., Nat. Assn. Ednl. Broadcasters, Delta Sigma Rho, Tau Kappa Alpha, Phi Delta Kappa. Home: 906 Columbia Rd Grand Forks ND 58201 Office: U ND Grand Forks ND 58201

BROMSEN, MAURY AUSTIN, bibliographer, historian; b. N.Y.C., Apr. 25, 1919; s. Herman and Rose (Elsenberg) B.; B.S., Coll. City N.Y., 1939; M.A., U. Cal. at Berkeley, 1941; student U.S. Govt. (exchange fellow) U. Chile, 1942; M.A. (Woodbury Lowery Travelling fellow, also Social Sci. Research Council fellow 1946-48), Harvard, 1945, postgrad. in history, 1945- 50. Vis. lectr. Am. history Cath. U., Santiago, Chile, 1942; instr. history Coll. City N.Y., 1943-44; vis. prof. U. Chile, Santiago, 1947; editor, sect. chief dept. cultural affairs Pan. Am. Union, Washington, 1950-53, exec. sec. Medina Centenial Celebration, Washington, 1952; founding editor Inter-Am. Rev. Bibliography, 1950-54, adv. editor, U.S. rep., 1956—; founder, dir. Maury A. Bromsen Assos., Inc., Boston, 1954—, pres., treas., 1963—. Named knight comdr. Orden al Mérito Bernardo O'Higgins (Chile). Mem. Am. Hist. Assn., A.L.A., Bibliog. Soc. Am., Manuscript Soc. (charter), Conf. on Latin Am. History, Academia Nacional de la Historia (Buenos Aires), Latin Am. Studies Assn., Sociedad de Historia Argentina (corr.), Pan Am. Soc. New Eng. (patron), Bibliog. Soc. U. Va., Harvard, Iowa (patron) library assos., Va. (life), Fla., Mo., Del., N.Y. hist. socs., Bell, Ky., Miami, Clements, Yale library assos., Sociedad Chilena de Historia Georgrafía, Filson Club, Phi Beta Kappa. Club: Harvard (Boston). Editor: José Toribio Medina, Humanist of the Americas: an Appraisal, 1960. Research and publs. in history and bibliography of Ams. Established Medina and Harrisse rare book collections U. Fla. Library, 1958, 63. Address: 195 Commonwealth Av Boston MA 02116

BROMWELL, JAMES EDWARD, lawyer; b. Cedar Rapids, Ia., Mar. 26, 1920; s. Maxwell Thomas and Olive Marguerite (MacDuff) B.; B.A., U. Ia., 1942, J.D., 1951; M.B.A., Harvard, 1947; m. Dorothy Bennett, Sept. 10, 1946; children—Maxwell Thomas II, Helen Kirk (Mrs. John R. Dent), Catharine MacDuff, James Edward. Admitted to Ia. bar, 1951, since practiced in Cedar Rapids; asst. atty. Linn County, 1956-59; owner, operator farm nr. Cedar Rapids; now engaged in law practice, Cedar Rapids; mem. firm of Nazette and Bromwell. Mem. 87th and 88th Congresses, 2d Dist. Ia.; mem. com.

judiciary, com. vets. affairs. Served to capt. AUS, 1942-46: ETO. Mem. Am., Ia., Linn County bar assns., Am. Legion, Phi Kappa Psi, Phi Delta Phi, Omicron Delta Kappa. Mason, Elk. Clubs: Capitol Hill (Washington); Kiwanis. Home: 1920 Ridgeway Dr SE Cedar Rapids IA also RFD 2 Center Point IA 52213 Office: 200 1st St SW Cedar Rapids IA 52404

BROMWICH, ELROY WILLIAM, tool co. exec.; b. St. Louis, Oct. 21, 1899; s. George and Pauline (Binder) B.; m. Mary Fearing, Apr. 21, 1919; children—Jane (Mrs. Russell Grass), Jean (Mrs. Earl Provost), June (Mrs. Donald Domermuth). Pres. Tools & Supplies, Inc., St. Louis, 1932—. Clubs: Missouri Athletic (St. Louis); Glen Echo Country (Normandy, Mo.); Noonday. Home: 4548 Nadine Ct St Louis MO 63121 Office: 3131 Olive St St Louis MO 63103

BRON, ELEANOR, actress; b. Stanmore, Middlesex, Eng.; d. Sydney and Fagah Bron; B.A. in French and German, Newnham Coll. Cambridge U. With The Establishment Group, London, Chgo., Washington, N.Y.C., various theatre cos. including Bristol Old Vic; roles include Hedda Gabler, Jean Brodie; films include Help, Alfie, Bedazzled, Two for the Road, Thank You All Very Much, Women in Love; roles TV series; writer, performer Where Was Spring?, BBC-TV, 1969—. Office: c/o David White 34 Berkeley House Hay Hill London W1 England

BRONEER, OSCAR THEODORE, archaeologist, Greek scholar; b. Backebo, Sweden, Dec. 28, 1894; s. Otto and Johanna Sofia (Pettersson) Johnson; A.B., Augustana Coll., 1922; A.M., U. Cal., 1923, Ph.D., 1931; postgrad. Am. Acad., Rome, Italy, summer 1924, Am. Sch. Classical Studies, Athens, Greece, 1924-27; m. Verna Pauline Anderson, Sept. 1, 1927 (dec. Jan. 1948); children—Paul Theodore, Jon Winroth; m. 2d, Lula R. Logan, June 27, 1955. Came to U.S., 1913, naturalized, 1939. Instr. archaeology Am. Sch. Classical Studies, Athens, 1927-30, asst. prof., 1930-35, asso. prof., 1935-40, prof. 1940-52, acting dir., 1947-48, hon. prof. archaeology, 1952—; on spl. assignment Dept. State, 1952-53; field dir. U. Chgo. excavations at Isthmia, 1952-60; vis. lectr. in Greek, Johns Hopkins, 1942-43; tech. asst. Office Fgn. Relief and Rehab. Operations, 1943-44; exec. v.p. Greek War Relief Assn., Inc., 1944-46; on spl. relief mission to Greece, 1945; Sather lectr. U. Cal.; vis. prof. archeology U. Chgo., 1948-49, prof., 1949-60, prof. emeritus, 1960—; Norton lectr. Archael. Inst. Am., 1960-61; vis. prof. U. Cal. at Los Angeles, 1964, Stanford, 1965, Condr. excavations Corinth. Athens, others. Decorated comdr. Royal Order Phoenix of Greece, 1962; hon. citizen of Ancient Corinth, Greece. Mem. Archaeol. Inst. Am. (Norton lectr. 1960-61, Gold medal for distinguished archaeol. achievement 1969), German Archaeol. Inst., Greek Archaeol. Soc. (hon. counselor), Swedish Acad. History and Antiquities, Soc. Promotion of Byzantine and Modern Greek Studies. Clubs: Yacht and Country (Tampa, Fla.); Quadrangle (Chicago); Phi Beta Kappa. Author books and articles; The South Stoa and Its Roman Successors, 1955; Isthmia I, Temple of Poseidon 1971. Home: 4607 Bayshore Blvd Tampa FL 33611 also Ancient Corinth Greece

BRONER, ROBERT, artist, educator; b. Detroit, Mar. 10, 1922; s. Abraham and Ida (Opperman) B.; B.F.A., Wayne State U., 1945, M.A., 1946; student U. Cal. at Los Angeles, 1946-47; pupil of Stuart Davis, 1949-50, S.W. Hayter, 1949-51; m. Esther Masserman, Jan. 18, 1948; children—Sari, Adam, Jeremy, Nahama. Asso. prof. humanistic studies Monteith Coll., Wayne State U., 1965—; one man exhbns. include Wellons Gallery, N.Y.C., 1955, Phila. Art Alliance, 1956, Werbe and Garelick Detroit Galleries, 1953, 57, 61, Mich. State U., 1957, Drake Gallery, Carmel, Cal., 1960, Feingarten Gallery, Los Angeles, 1961, Ohio State U. Galleries, 1969, The J.L. Hudson Gallery, 1971; numerous group exhbns. U.S. and abroad, 1951—; represented in perm. colls. Art Inst. Chgo., Bklyn. Mus., Cin. Mus., Detroit Inst. Arts, Boston Pub. Library, Met. Mus. Art, Guggenheim Mus., Los Angeles County Mus., Fogg Mus., Harvard, Mus. Modern Art, Nat. Gallery, Washington, N.Y. Pub. Library, Phila. Mus., Smithsonian Inst., Walker Art Center, also pvt. collections. Mem. Mich. Assn. Printmakers (pres. 1958), Drawing and Print Club Detroit Inst. Arts (bd. dirs.), Met. Ednl. and Cultural Activities Assn., Soc. Am. Graphic Artists, Brit. Printmakers Council, Phila. Print Club. Home: 18244 Parkside St Detroit MI 48221

BRONFENBRENNER, MARTIN, economist, educator; b. Pitts., Dec. 2, 1914; s. Jacques Jacob and Martha (Ornstein) B.; A.B., Washington U., St. Louis, 1934; Ph.D., U. Chgo., 1939; postgrad. Northwestern U. Law Sch.; m. Teruko Okuaki, Nov. 13, 1951; children—Kenneth, June. Asst., U. Chgo., 1937-38; faculty Central YMCA Coll., Chgo., 1938-40; economist U.S. Treasury, 1940-41; financial economist Fed. Res. Bank, Chgo., 1941-42, 46-47; asso. prof. U. Wis., 1947-54, prof., 1954-57; prof. econs. Mich. State U., 1957-58, U. Minn., Mpls., 1958-62; prof. econs. Grad. Sch. Indsl. Adminstrn., Carnegie- Mellon U., Pitts., 1962-71, chmn. dept. econ., 1966-71, Kenan prof. econs. Duke, Durham, N.C., 1971—. Vis. fellow Behavioral Scis. Center, Stanford, Cal., 1966-67, Fulbright lectr., Japan, 1962-63. Fiscal economist SCAP, Tokyo, Japan, 1949-50; economist UN Econ. Commn. for Asia and Far East, Bangkok, Thailand, 1952. Served as officer USNR, 1943-46. Mem. Am. Econ. Assn., Am. Assn. U. Profs., Econometric Soc., Assn. for Asian Studies, Phi Beta Kappa. Author: Academic Encounter, 1961; Income Distribution Theory, 1971. Contbr. numerous articles to profl. jours. Home: 2915 Friendship Rd Durham NC 22705

BRONFMAN, CHARLES ROSNER, distilling co. exec.; b. Montreal, Que., Can., June 27, 1931; s. Samuel and Saidye (Rosner) B.; student Trinity Coll., Port Hope, Ont., McGill U., 1948-51; m. Barbara Baerwald, May 7, 1962; children—Stephen Rosner, Ellen Jane. With Distillers Corp. Ltd. and subsidiary cos., Montreal, 1951—, v.p., dir. Distillers Corp.-Seagrams Ltd., 1958—; nat. sales mgr. Thomas Adams Distillers Ltd. (subsidiary Ho. Seagrams Ltd.), Montreal, 1954-57, v.p. House of Seagram Ltd., 1955-58, pres., 1958—; pres. Cemp Investments Ltd.; chmn., dir. Supersol Ltd., Israel; chmn. Montreal Baseball Club Ltd.; dir. Bank Montreal, Canadian Pacific Airlines. Chmn. exec. com. Allied Jewish Community Services Montreal. Bd. dirs. Que. div. Canadian Council Christians and Jews; life gov. Jewish Gen. Hosp., Montreal; gov. Montreal YMHA-YWHA. Mem. Young Presidents Orgn., Montreal Bd. Trade, LaJeune Chambre de Montreal (gov.), Gen. Council Industry Province Que. Mem. Jewish religion. Clubs: Elm Ridge Golf and Country, Montefiore, Mount Royal, Saint-Denis, Mount Royal Tennis, Hillside Tennis, Montreal Amateur Athletic Assn., Greystone Curling (Montreal); Hollywood Golf (Deal, N.J.). Home: 78 Summit Crescent Westmount Montreal 217 Quebec Canada Office: 1430 Peel St Montreal 110 Quebec Canada

BRONFMAN, EDGAR MILES, distillery exec.; b. Montreal, Can., June 20, 1929; s. Samuel and Saidye (Rosner) B.; student Williams Coll., 1946-49; B.A., McGill U., 1951; m. Ann Margaret Loeb, Jan. 10, 1953; children—Samuel II, Edgar Miles, Holly Dorothy, Matthew, Adam Rodgers. Came to the U.S., 1935. Accounting, prodn. tng. Distillers Corp., Ltd. subsidiary Distillers Corp. Seagrams Ltd., 1951-53, asst. to pres., 1953-55; v.p., dir. Distillers Corp. and Seagrams, Ltd., Montreal, 1955, treas., 1956—; chmn. adminstrn. com. Jos. E. Seagram & Sons, Inc., N.Y.C., 1955—, pres., dir., 1957—; dir. Cleve. Container Corp., Empire Trust Co., Rheingold Corporation. Bd. dirs. N.Y. Philharmonic Soc., United Cerebral Palsy Assn., Police Athletic League; trustee Mt. Sinai Hosp., Com. Econ. Devel., Council Econ. Edn., John F. Kennedy Center for Performing Arts, Samuel Bronfman Found. Mem. Am. Arbitration Assn. (dir.), Park Av. Assn., Hundred Year Assn. N.Y., Fedn. Jewish Philanthropies, Nat. Indsl. Conf. Bd., Delta Phi. Home: 60 Lincoln Av Port Chester NY 10918 Office: 375 Park Av New York City NY 10022

BRONHEIM, DAVID, corp. ofcl.; b. N.Y.C., Apr. 28, 1932; s. Nathan and Malvina (Mermelstein) B.; B.A., U. Mich., 1953; LL.B., cum laude, Harvard, 1956; m. Helen Allentuck, Jan. 20, 1957; children—Jeffrey, Elizabeth. Admitted to D.C. bar, 1956; atty.-adviser to U.S. Tax Ct. Judge Raum, 1956-58; atty. legal dept. Internat. Bank Reconstrn. and Devel., 1958-60; with AID, and predecessor, 1960—, asst. gen. counsel Bur. Latin Am., 1963- 65, dep. U.S. coordinator Alliance for Progress, 1965-67; dir. Center for Inter-Am. Relations, 1967-70, Dreyfus Corp., 1971—. Author article. Home: 38 W 7th St New York City NY 10003 Office: 767 Fifth Av New York City NY 10022

BRONK, DETLEV W., scientist, educator; b. N.Y.C., Aug. 13, 1897; s. Mitchell and Marie (Wulf) B., A.B., Swarthmore Coll., 1920; postgrad. U. Pa., 1921; M.S., U. Mich., 1922, Ph.D., 1926; recipient over 55 hon. degrees from univs. and colls.; m. Helen A. Ramsey, Sept. 10, 1921; children—John Everton Ramsey, Adrian, Mitchell Herbert. Mem. univ. faculties, 1921-49; pres. Johns Hopkins, 1949-53; pres. Rockefeller U., N.Y.C., 1953-68, pres. emeritus, 1968—. Coordinator research Air Surgeons Office. Hdqrs. Army Air Forces, 1942-46. Has held 12 endowed named lectureships, 1938—; dir. Johnson Research Found., U. Pa., 1929-49; chmn. NRC, 1946-50; pres. Nat. Acad. Scis., 1950-62; chmn. bd. NSF, 1956-64; mem. Pres.'s Sci. Adv. Com., 1956-63; cons.-at-large, 1963—; chmn. Panel on Internat. Sci., 1957-63; vice chmn. N.Y. State Sci. and Tech. Found., 1965-68, chmn., 1968—; pres. N.Y. Hall of Sci.; mem. Inter-Am. com. on sci. and tech. OAS, 1969—. Trustee Atoms for Peace Awards, Renssalaer Poly. Inst. (chmn. bd. 1966-71), Tulane U., U. Pa., Bucknell U., Marine Biol. Lab., Johns Hopkins, Population Council, Protein Found., Rockefeller Bros. Fund, Sloan-Kettering Inst. Served as ensign U.S. Naval Aviation Corps, 1918-19. Decorated officer Brit. Empire; recipient award for exceptional civilian service, 1946, Longacre award Aero. Med. Assn., 1948, Priestley award Dickinson Coll., 1956; Gold medal Internat. Ben Franklin Soc., 1958; medal Soc. Promoting Internat. Sci. Relationships, 1959, Gold medal Holland Soc., 1961, George Washington award Hungarian-Am. Soc., 1962, Franklin medal Franklin Inst., 1962; Presdl. Medal of Freedom, 1964; Pub. Welfare medal Nat. Acad. Scis., 1964; Nat. Sci. medal, 1969. Fellow A.A.A.S. (pres. 1952), mem. or hon. mem. many Am., fgn. prof. socs. (sometime officer several). Baptist. Clubs: N.Y. Yacht, University, Century, Lotos (N.Y.C.); Rittenhouse (Phila.); Maryland (Balt.); Seal Harbour Yacht; Cosmos (Washington); Athenaeum (London, Eng.). Home: 25 Sutton Pl S New York City NY 10022 also Hill House Farm Media PA 19063 Office: Rockefeller University New York City NY 10021

BRONNER, EDWIN BLAINE, educator; b. Yorba Linda, Cal., Sept. 2, 1920; s. Blaine Garretson and Nellie Elizabeth (Garretson) B.; A.B., Whittier Coll., 1941; M.A., Haverford Coll., 1947, Ph.D., U. Pa., 1952; m. Marian Phillips Taylor, Mar. 9, 1946; children—Margaret G., Judith S. Sylvia T., Virginia H. Faculty, Temple U., 1947-62, asso. prof. history, 1959-62; vis. prof. Whittier Coll., 1961; prof. history, curator Quaker Collection, Haverford (Pa.) Coll., 1962—, librarian, 1969—. Mem. cons. council Conf. Peace Research in History, 1964-67; mem. Montgomery County (Pa.) Assistance, 1961-64; with Am. Friends Service Com., 1943-46, chmn. internat. centers com., 1961-65, bd. dirs., 1967—, vice chmn. Am. sect. Friends World Com. Consultation, 1962-68, chmn., 1968—, chmn. planning com. 4th Friends World Conf. 1965-67. Mem. Am., Pa. (mem. council) hist. assns., Am. Assn. U. Profs., Orgn. Am. Historians, Hist. Soc. Pa., Friends Hist. Assn. (bd. dirs., pres. 1970—), Friends Hist. Soc. (Eng., pres. 1970). Author: Thomas Earle as a Reformer, 1948; William Penn's Holy Experiment, 1962. Contbr. articles to profl. jours. Editor: Sharing Our Quaker Faith, 1959; American Quakers Today, 1966; An English View of American Quakerism , 1970. Mem. adv. bd. Am. Jour. Legal History, 1957—. Home: 4 College Lane Haverford PA 19041

BRONNER, FREDERICK LIDELL, educator; b. Richfield Springs, N.Y., Feb. 2, 1901; s. Frederick and Grace Aurelia (Lidell) B.; B.S., Union Coll., Schenectady, 1923; M.A., Harvard, 1925, Ph.D., 1937; m. Julia Voorhees, Feb. 7, 1922; children—Frederick V., Elizabeth, Louise. Faculty, Union Coll., 1923-66, prof. history, 1944-66, John Bigelow prof., 1961-66, sec. coll., 1942- 66, chmn. social studies, 1937-40; faculty Wake Forest Coll., Winston-Salem, 1966—, exchange prof. St. Andrews U., Scotland, 1958-59. Vis. prof. U. Rochester, summer 1938, prof. Albany Grad. Program Pub. Adminstrn., 1961. Mem. Am., N.Y. hist. assns., Am. Assn. U. Profs., Phi Beta Kappa, Delta Upsilon, Episcopalian. Club: Strathkiness Curling. Home: Home: 1C Wake Forest Apts Winston-Salem NC 27106

BRONOWSKI, JACOB, mathematician; b. Poland, Jan. 18, 1908; s. Abraham and Celia (Flatto) B.; M.A., Jesus Coll., Cambridge (Eng.) U., 1930, Ph.D., 1933; m. Rita Coblentz, Feb. 17, 1941; children—Lisa Anne, Judith Jill, Nicole Ruth, Clare Beth Alice. Came to U.S., 1964. Sr. lectr. Univ. Coll., Hull, Eng., 1934-42; sr. scientist Ministry Home Security, 1942-45; asst. dir. Ministry Works, 1946-50; dir. Coal Research Establishment, Nat. Coal Bd., 1950-59, dir. gen. process devel., 1959-63; fellow, trustee, dir. council for biology in human affairs Salk Inst. Biol. Studies, San Diego, 1964—. Carnegie vis. prof. Mass. Inst. Tech., 1953-54; lectr. man and nature Am. Mus. Natural History, 1965; Eastman Meml. vis. prof. U. Rochester, 1965; Condon lectr. Ore. State U., 1967; Silliman lectr. Yale, 1967; Bampton lectr. Columbia, 1969; Mellon lectr., Washington, 1969. Sci. dep., joint target group, Washington, also Brit. chiefs staff mission to Japan, 1945-46; head projects UNESCO, 1947-48. Hon. fellow Jesus Coll., Cambridge U., 1967. Fellow Royal Soc. Lit., World Acad. Art and Sci.; fgn. hon. mem. Am. Acad. Arts and Scis. (Blashfield address 1966); mem. Soc. Vis. Scientists. Author: The Poet's Defence, 1939, 66; William Blake, A Man Without a Mask, 1944; The Common Sense of Science, 1951; The Face of Violence, 1954, 67; Science and Human Values, 1958; Selections from William Blake, 1958; (with Bruce Mazlish) The Western Intellectual Tradition, 1960; Insight, 1964; The Abacus and The Rose; A New Dialogue on Two World Systems, 1965; William Blake and The Age of Revolution, 1965; The Identity of Man, 1965; Nature and Knowledge, 1969. Home: 9438 La Jolla Farms Rd La Jolla CA 92037 Office: PO Box 1809 San Diego CA 92112

BRONSEN, ALEXANDER NATHANIEL, mfg. co. exec.; b. London, Eng., July 14, 1909; s. Alexander and Sonia (Gustafson) B.; student Weybridge Park Coll., 1929; B.Sc., U. Danzig, 1934; m. Maria de Varady, Dec. 30, 1942. Exec. v.p. Crescent Corp., N.Y.C., 1964—; dir. several other companies. Address: 270 Park Av New York City NY 10017

BRONSON, BERTRAND HARRIS, educator; b. Lawrenceville, N.J., June 22, 1902; s. Thomas Bertrand and Isabel (Harris) B.; A.B., U. Mich., 1921, L.H.D., 1970; M.A., Harvard, 1922; postgrad. (Rhodes scholar) Oriel Coll., Oxford U., 1922-25, B.A. 1st class, 1924, M.A., 1929; Ph.D., Yale, 1927; Docteur ès Lettres honoris causa, U. Laval, Que., Can. 1961, L.H.D., U. Chgo., 1968; LL.D., U. Cal., 1971; m. Mildred Sumner Kinsley, June 25, 1927. Instr. U. Mich., 1925-26; instr. U. Cal. at Berkeley, 1927, asst. prof., 1929, asso. prof., 1938, prof., 1945-70, prof. emeritus, 1970—. Vis. prof. Yale, 1945; Alexander lectr. U. Toronto, 1958-59. Guggenheim Fellow, 1943, 1944, 1948. Recipient Am. Council of Learned Societies award, 1959; Medal of Honor, Rice U., 1962; Wilbur Cross medal Yale, 1970. Fellow Brit. Acad. (corr.), Am. Acad. Arts and Scis.; mem. Modern Lang. Assn. Am., Philol. Assn. Pacific Coast, Am. Musicol. Soc., Cal., Am. folklore socs., Internat. Folk Music Council, Oxford Soc., Phi Beta Kappa; Beta Theta Pi. Clubs: Faculty; Arts (Berkeley). Author: Joseph Ritson, Scholar-at-Arms, 1938; Johnson Agonistes and Other Essays, 1946; In Search of Chaucer, 1960; Facets of the Enlightenment, 1968; The Ballad As Song, 1969; essays on 18th century topics, Chaucer, folk-songs. Editor That Immortal Garland, 1941; Samuel Johnson: Selected Prose and Poetry, 1952; Johnson & Boswell in Major British Writers, 1954; Samuel Johnson: Rasselas, Poems & Selected Prose, 1958, 3d edit., 1971; The Traditional Tunes of the Child Ballads, vol. 1, 1959, vol. 2, 1962, vol. 3, 1966. Home: 927 Oxford St Berkeley CA 94707

BRONSON, EDWARD DUERDIN, lawyer; b. Los Angeles, May, 6, 1893; s. E.D. and Mabel (Knox) B.; A.B., U. Cal., 1917; m. Martha Slade Duke, Dec. 22, 1924; children—Edward D., Eugenia (Mrs. John K. Kramer), Carolyn (Mrs. Kenneth Wherry); m. 2d, Margaret N. Eickhoff, Mar. 13, 1956. Admitted to Cal. bar, 1922; mem. Bronson, Bronson & McKinnon, San Francisco, 1922—. Bd. govs. Def. Research Inst., 1961-67, San Francisco Legal Aid Soc., San Francisco adv. bd. Salvation Army. Served to lt., U.S. Army, 1917-19. Fellow Am. Coll. Trial Lawyers (regent 1951-56, pres. 1953-54), Am. Judicature Soc., Am. Bar Found.; mem. Am. Legion (past post comdr.), Am., San Francisco bar assns., State Bar Cal. (gov. 1950-53, v.p. 1952-53), Internat. Assn. Ins. Counsel, Phi Gamma Delta. Clubs: Family, Olympic, Merchants Exchange, Balboa, Lawyers. Home: 2219 Pacific Av San Francisco CA 94109 Office: 555 California St San Francisco CA 94104

BRONSON, OSWALD PERRY, educator, clergyman; b. Sanford, Fla., July 19, 1927; s. Uriah Perry and Flora (Hollingshed) B.; B.D., Gammon Theol. Sem., 1959; Ph.D., Northwestern U., 1965; m. Helen Carolyn Williams, June 8, 1952; children—Josephine Suzette, Flora Helen, Oswald Perry. Ordained to ministry Methodist Ch., 1957; pastor in Fla., Ga. and Rock River Conf., Chgo., 1950-66; v.p. Interdenominational Theol. Center, Atlanta, 1966-68, pres., 1968—. Chmn. Ga. Conf. Bd. Edn. United Methodists. Trustee Carrie Steel Pitts Home, Atlanta, Hinton Rural Life Center; bd. dirs. Wesley Community Center, Atlanta; chmn. bd. mgrs. Ga. Pastors' Sch. Crusade scholar, 1957-64. Mem. Ga. Assn. Pastoral Care (bd. govs.), Am. Assn. Theol. Schs. (v.p. 1968-70), Religious Edn. Assn. (past pres.), Mid-Atlantic Assn. Profs. Religious Edn., N.A.A.C.P. Theta Phi, Alpha Kappa Mu. Home: 3360 Laren Lane SW Atlanta GA 30331

BRONSON, ROY A., lawyer; b. Los Angeles, July 20, 1889; s. Edward and Mabel S. (Knox) B.; A.B., U. Santa Clara, 1912, A.M., 1913, LL.B., 1914; m. Clarisse Caspers, Feb. 16, 1916 (div.); children—Jean (Mrs. John E. Miller), Margery (Mrs. Stephen S. Townsend), Claire (Mrs. Van S. Trefethen); m. 2d, Lola Jones Rankin, Oct. 8, 1949. Admitted to Cal. bar, 1914, since practiced in San Francisco; founder, sr. partner firm Bronson, Bronson & McKinnon, 1927—; dir. Parr Indsl. Corp. Bd. dirs. Fairbairn Found. Pres. Cal. Safety Council, 1949. Pres. adv. bd. Mary's Help Hosp. Fellow Am. Bar Found.; mem. Internat., Am. (ho. of dels. 1952-58, 62-63, chmn. traffic ct. program), San Francisco (past pres.) bar assns., Am. Judicature Soc., Am. Law Inst., Western States Bar Conf. (past pres.). Republican. Roman Catholic. Clubs: Bohemian, Commercial, World Trade, San Francisco. Home: 2455 Jackson St San Francisco CA 94115 Office: 555 California St San Francisco CA 94111

BRONSON, WILLIAM HOWARD, publisher, lawyer, radio and TV exec.; b. Dadeville, Ala., July 10, 1912; s. George A. and Meige (Berkstresser) B.; student at the Alabama Poly. Inst., 1929-30; B.A., U. Ala., 1933; grad. study Harvard, 1933-34; LL.B., La. State U., 1938, J.D., 1968; m. Lillian Francez, July 9, 1935; children—William H., and Susan Francez (now Mrs. E.S. Croft III). Admitted to La. bar, 1938, practiced in Shreveport, 1938-40; with firm Tucker, Bronson & Martin, 1940- 52; pres., pub., dir. Shreveport Times; pres., dir. Monroe (La.) News Star, Monroe Morning World, radio stas. KWKH, Shreveport, Radio Broadcasting, Inc., Shreveport, Louisiana, also the Tri State Broadcasting System, Inc., Shreveport, 1952—; pres. Newspaper Prodn. Co. (agts. Shreveport Times, Shreveport Jour.), 1953—; chmn. bd., dir. Ark. TV Co., Inc. (TV sta. KTHV, Little Rock), 1952—; dir., mem. exec. com. of bd. dirs. Kansas City So. Ry.; dir., mem. exec. com. Kansas City So. Industries, Inc., La. & Ark. Ry.; dir. Shreveport Engraving Co., Inc. Mem., Trustee Shreveport Obs., 1963-65; exec. com., dir. organizer Council Better La., 1962—; pres. bd. trustees Southfield Sch., 1949-50; mem., vice chmn. La. Coordinating Council for Higher Edn., 1969—; trustee S.W. Research Inst., San Antonio, La. Council Econ. Edn., Pub. Affairs Research Council La.; dir. La. State Fair Assn. Mem. Nat. Planning Assn. (nat. council). Shreveport C. of C. (dir.; 1st v.p. 1959), Newcomen Soc., Sigma Delta Chi. Episcopalian (former vestryman). Clubs: Shreveport (dir.), Shreveport Country (pres. 1958); Boston (New Orleans); Fairway Farm Hunt (San Augustine, Tex.); Press (Dallas). Home: 6024 E Ridge Dr Shreveport LA 71106 Office: care Shreveport Times PO Box 222 222 Lake St Shreveport LA 71102

BRONSTEIN, AARON JACOB, lawyer; b. Balt., May 6, 1905; s. Max S. and Rose (Lebow) B.; A.B., Harvard, 1925, LL.B., 1928; m. Gertrud Nagels, July 5, 1930 (dec. May 1942); m. 2d, Jeanette F. Lyons, Apr. 23, 1944; 1 dau., Judith R. (Mrs. Arnold D. Rubin). Admitted to Mass. bar, 1928, U.S. Supreme Ct. bar; practice in Boston, 1928—; partner firm Schneider, Bronstein, Wolbarsht & Deutsch, 1944-69, Brown, Rudnick, Freed & Gesmer, 1969—. Sec. Am. Biltrite Rubber Co., Inc., Chelsea, Mass., 1954—, dir., 1959—. Pres. New Eng. div. Am. Jewish Congress, 1955-59, Jewish Community Fedn. Greater Lynn (Mass.), 1962-67, Jewish Community Council Boston, 1959-61, New Eng. Zionist Region, 1949-51; mem. nat. com. Am. Israel Pub. Affairs Com., 1959—; mem. Nat. Council Join Distbn. Council, 1954—. Trustee, Am. Biltrite Rubber Charitable Trust. Mem. Am., Mass., Boston bar assns. Clubs: New Century (Boston); Harvard Varsity, Harvard Glee Club Found. Home: 28 Atlantic Av Swampscott MA 01907 Office: 85 Devonshire St Boston MA 02109

BRONSTEIN, DANIEL J., educator; b. N.Y.C., Dec. 11, 1908; s. Anatole and Liza (Wegman) B.; B.S., Coll. City N.Y., 1928; M.A., Harvard, 1930, Ph.D., 1933; m. Gertrude Paley, 1930 (dec. 1940); m. 2d, Betty R. Grossman, Sept. 29, 1940; 1 dau., Gene (Mrs. John J. Hayden, III). Instr. philosophy Coll. City N.Y., 1932-42, asst. prof., 1942-49, asso. prof., 1949-53, prof., 1953—, chmn. dept., 1953-59, 62-63. Carnegie fellow Inst. Mediaeval Studies, U. Toronto, 1930;

Ford Found. fellow, 1951-52. Mem. Am. Philos. Assn., Am. Assn. U. Profs., (chpt. pres. 1966), Mind Assn., Phi Beta Kappa. Co-author: Basic Problems of Philosophy, 3d edit., 1964; Approaches to the Philosophy of Religion, 1954. Editor: Essential Works of Descartes, 1961, rev. edit., 1966. Contbr. to books, articles to profl. jours. Home: 536 Ogden Av West Englewood NJ 07666 Office: The City U New York City NY 10031

BRONSTETTER, W. EDGAR, lawyer; b. Montreal, Que., Can., Oct. 11, 1914; B.A., Loyola Coll., 1937; B.C.L., McGill U., 1941. Admitted to Que. bar, 1942; now partner firm Duquet, MacKay, Weldon, Bronstetter, Willis & Johnston, Montreal; lectr. civil procedure McGill Faculty of Law, 1951-57. Dir. Internat. Shoe Machine Corp. Can. Mem. Canadian Bar Assn. Office: Royal Bank Canada Bldg Montreal 113 Quebec Canada*

BRONSTON, CHARLES BENJAMIN, electronics co. exec.; b. Plainfield, N.J., July 13, 1924; s. Harry Edgar and Yetta (Cohen) B.; A.B., Harvard, 1948; student Rutgers U. Sch. Bus., 1964-65; m. Judith Margaretten, Dec. 20, 1949; children—Beth, Jan, Deborah, Susan, Ruth. Vice pres. Bronston Hat Co., Plainfield, 1948-58, 63-65; sec. Service Poly-Pak Inc., N.Y.C., 1958-63; pres. Byer-Rolnick Casual Headwear Co., Plainfield, 1965-67 dist. dir. R.J. Carroll Assos., Inc., 1967-69; personnel mgr. Quindar Electronics, Inc., Springfield, N.J., 1970—. Served with USAAF, 1943-46. Address: 15 N Wickom Dr Westfield NJ 07090

BRONSTON, SAMUEL, movie producer; b. Russia; ed. Sorbonne, Paris. Film distbr., Paris; former prodn. exec. Columbia Studios, Hollywood, films include: Martin Eden, City Without Men; organized Samuel Bronston Pictures, Inc.; exec. prod. Jack London, A Walk in the Sun; prod. series color documentaries Vatican; prod. TV series, Capt. Grief, with Guild Films; prod. John Paul Jones, 1959; now pres. Samuel Bronston Prodns., Inc.; pres. Samuel Bronston Studios, Madrid, Spain; prod. King of Kings, El Cid, 1960, 55 Days to Peking, 1962, the Fall of the Roman Empire, 1963, Circus World, 1964. Recipient Meritorious Service pub. citation, USN, Condor award for El Cid, Soc. Pan-Am. Culture, 1962, Golden Globe for El Cid, Hollywood Fgn. Press Assn., 1962; decorated Italian Order of Merit; Grand Cross of Merit, Knights of Holy Sepulchre; Order of Gt. Cross, Isabel la Catolica. Address: Avenida de Burgos 5 Madrid 16 Spain

BRONSTON, WALTER ESHELL, mfg. co. exec.; b. Wichita, Kan., Aug. 17, 1903; s. Eshell and Diana (Levitt) B.; B.B.A., N.Y.U., 1925; m. Flora Lehmann, Dec. 27, 1924. Pres., Novo Corp. (formerly Indsl. Enterprises, Inc.), N.Y.C., 1955-61, chmn., 1961—. Home: 7 Normandy Lane Scarsdale NY 10583 Office: 733 3d Av New York City NY 10017

BRONWELL, ARTHUR B., educator; b. Chgo., Aug. 18, 1909; s. Arthur F. and Lulu M. Bronwell; B.S., Ill. Inst. Tech., 1933, M.S., 1936; M.B.A., Northwestern U., 1947; grad. engr. U. Mich., summers 1939-40; LL.D., Northeastern U., 1955; D.Eng., Wayne U., 1958; m. Virginia R. White, Aug. 2, 1941; children—James Arthur, Susan Virginia. Instr. Northwestern U., 1937-40; asst. prof. elec. engring., 1940-43, asso. prof., 1943-47, prof., 1947-54; exec. sec. Am. Soc. for Engring. Edn., 1945-55; pres. Worcester Poly. Inst., 1955-62; dean engring. U. Conn., Storrs, 1962-70, now prof.; engring. cons. Motorola Co., 1941-45; spl. project engr. Bell Telephone Labs., N.Y.C., summer 1941; mem. bd. Jamesbury Corp., Worcester Five Cents Savs. Bank; NSF research microwaves, 1952; U.S. del. to UNESO Conf. on Engring. Edn., Paris, 1967, Pan Am. Engrs. Conf., San Juan, 1968, World Congress Engrs. and Architects, Israel, 1970, Internat. Congress European Tech. Forecasting Assn., 1971. Organized and supervised Army Signal Corps Officers Sch., Northwestern U., 1942-43; dir. radar research, 1943-45. Mem. adv. com. Nat. Sci. Found.; mem. bd. Worcester Acad., Worcester Pub. Library, Worcester Orch. Soc., Worcester Council Chs.; mem. numerous coms. Engrs. Joint Council and Engrs. Council for Profl. Devel., other profl. socs. Adviser on edn. U.S. Dept. Defense; mem. U.S. Mission to Japan, 1951. Recipient Distinguished Alumni citation Ill. Inst. Tech. Fellow I.E.E.E.; mem. Am. Soc. Engring. Edn., Am. Econ. Assn., Nat. Electronics Conf. (pres. 1947), Council Fgn. Relations, Sigma Xi, Eta Kappa Nu, Tau Beta Pi. Author: (with R.E. Beam) Theory and Application of Microwaves, 1947; Advanced Mathematics in Physics and Engineering, 1955; Science and Technology In the World of the Future, 1970. Editor Jour. Engring. Edn., 1947-52; also numerous tech. articles. Patentee in field of color TV. Home: Hillyndale Rd Storrs CT 06268

BROOK, ALAN JOHN, educator; b. Newcastle-upon-Tyne, Eng., Mar. 5, 1923; s. John and Annie (Rogers) B.; B.Sc., U. Durham, 1942, Ph.D., 1949; D.Sc., U. Edinburgh, 1960; m. Rosemarie Grant Simpson, Apr. 28, 1949; children—Erica, Cathro, Mark. Came to U.S., 1964. Lectr. botany U. Khartoum, Sudan, 1949-52; sr. sci. officer Freshwater Fisheries Lab., Scotland, 1952-58; lectr. botany U. Edinburgh, Scotland, 1958-64; prof., head, dept. ecology U. Minn., 1964—; cons. Environmental Protection Agy., 1969—. Exec. sec. 10th Internat. Bot. Congress, 1964. Bd. dirs. Minn. Freshwater Biol. Research Found. Served to flight lt. RAF, 1942-46. Fellow Royal Soc. Edinburgh; mem. Internat. Soc. Pure and Applied Limnology, Phycol. Soc. Am. Author: The Living Plant, 1964; also articles. Home: 1908 Linner Rd Wayzata MN 55391

BROOK, ALEXANDER, artist; b. Brooklyn, N.Y., July 14, 1898; s. Onufri and Eudoxia (Gelescu) B.; student Art Students League, 1915-19; m. Peggy Bacon, May 4, 1920 (div. 1940); children—Belinda, Alexander Bacon; m. 2d, Gina Knee, Dec. 22, 1944. Awards: Logan medal and purchase prize ($ 2,500), Chgo. Art Inst. 1929; 2d prize, Lehman award, 29th annual, Carnegie Inst., Pitts., 1930; Temple gold medal, 126th annual Pa. Acad. Fine Arts, Philadelphia, 1931; fellowship in painting, Guggenheim Found., N.Y.C., 1931; 1st prize, Los Angeles Mus, 1934; gold medal Am. Sect. Internat. Expn., Paris, 1937; 1st prize and special merit of award 17th Annual Expn. of Advertising Art, N.Y. City, 1937; 1st prize, Am. painting, Worcester, Mass., 1938; medal of award, Art Assn., San Francisco, 1938; 1st prize 38th Annual, Carnegie Inst., 1939; Beck gold medal Pa. Acad., 1948; Benjamin Altman 2d prize N.A.D., 1957, 60. Represented permanently Metropolitan Mus., N.Y. City; Brooklyn (N.Y.) Mus.; Art Inst. Chgo.; Carnegie Inst., Pitts.; U. of Neb.; William Nelson Gallery Kansas City, Mo.; Wadsworth Atheneum, Hartford, Conn.; Mus. Modern Art, N.Y.C.; Newark (N.J.) Mus., Boston (Mass.) Mus.; Toledo Mus., Toledo, O., Ann Arbor (Mich.) State U.; De Young Mus., San Francisco Mus.; Corcoran Gallery, Washington, D.C.; Albright Gallery, Buffalo, N.Y.; City Art Mus., St. Louis, Mo.; Whitney Mus. of Am. Art, N.Y. City; Univ. of Nebraska, Lincoln. Mem. Nat. Inst. Arts and Letters, N.A.D. (gold medal, 1950). Home: Sag Harbor NY 11963 Office: 36 E 61 St New York City NY 10021

BROOK, HERBERT CECIL, lawyer; b. Stronghurst, Ill., Feb. 11, 1910; s. John C. and Maud (Simonson) B.; A.B., Northwestern U. 1932; J.D., U. Chgo., 1936; m. Jane C. Lord, Oct. 17, 1942; children—John L., David M., Susan J. Admitted to Ill. bar, 1936, since practiced in Chgo.; partner Lord, Bissell & Brook, and predecessors, 1948—; Ill. atty.-in-fact for underwriters Lloyd's of London, 1961—. Life regent Northwestern U., 1970—; pres. Village of Hinsdale (Ill.), 1969—. Served as ensign USNR, 1941-42; to capt. USMCR, 1943-45: PTO. Mem. Am., Ill., Chgo. bar assns., Internat. Assn. Ins. Counsel, Law Club Chgo., Execs. Club: Chgo., Order of Coif, Phi Beta Kappa. Contbr. articles to profl. jours. Home: 222 E 3d St Hinsdale IL 60521 Office: 135 S LaSalle St Chicago IL 60603

BROOK, PETER, theatre and film dir.; b. London, Eng., Mar. 21, 1925; s. Simon and Ida (Jolson) B.; student Magdalen Coll., Oxford U., 1942-45; m. Natasha Parry, Nov. 3, 1951; 2 children. Dir. plays in London, Stratford-on-Avon, Paris and N.Y.C. including Love's Labour's Lost, 1946, Romeo and Juliet, 1947, Ring Around the Moon, 1950, Measure for Measure, 1950; dir. prodns. Covent Garden Opera House, London, 1948- 49, Faust at Met. Opera, N.Y.C., 1953, House of Flowers, N.Y.C., 1955, Titus Andronicus, Stratford, 1955, View From the Bridge, London, 1956, Paris, 1958, Cat on a Hot Tin Roof, Paris, 1956, Tempest, Stratford, 1957, Eugene Onegin, Met. Opera, 1957, The Visit, London, N.Y.C., 1957, Irma La Douce, London, 1958, also N.Y.C., The Fighting Cock, N.Y.C., 1959, Le Balcon, Paris, 1960, King Lear, Stratford and London, 1963, The Physicists, 1964, Marat Sade, London, 1965, U.S., 1966, Oedipus, 1968, A Midsummer Night's Dream, Stratford-on-Avon, 1970, N.Y.C., 1971; European tour, 1957; dir. films The Beggars Opera, Eng., 1952, Moderato Cantabile, France, 1960, Lord of the Flies, 1963, Marat Sade, 1967; dir. Internat. Centre of Theatre Research, Paris, 1970-71. Address: care PL Representation Ltd 33 Sloane St London S W 1 England

BROOKBY, HARRY DUDLEY, oil co. exec.; b. Chgo., Aug. 21, 1916; s. Harry Esmond and Edith Mabel (French) B.; B.S. in Geology, Northwestern U., 1938; m. Wannajean England, May 30, 1941; children—Harry England, Bruce Kimball, Robert Greer. With Phillips Petroleum Co., 1938-42, 45—, mgr. exploration and prodn. div. internat. dept., 1959-62, mgr. exploration and prodn. dept., 1962-63, v.p. exploration and prodn. dept., 1963-68. v.p., chmn. operating com., 1968—. Served to lt. USNR, 1942-45. Mem. Am. Assn. Petroleum Geologists, Am. Assn. Petroleum Landmen, Tulsa Geol. Soc., Delta Tau Delta. Presbyn. Rotarian. Clubs: Hillcrest Country; N Men's Letterman (Northwestern U.). Home: 1443 Valley Bartlesville OK 74003 Office: Phillips Petroleum Co Bartlesville OK 74003

BROOKE OF CUMNOR, LORD HENRY, former Brit. cabinet minister; b. Apr. 9, 1903; s. L. Leslie and Sybil Diana (Brooke) B.; student Balliol Coll., Oxford U.; m. Barbara Mathews, 1933; 2 sons, 2 daus. Mem. Parliament for West Lewisham, 1938-45, Hampstead, 1950-66; minister housing and local govt., minister for Welsh affairs, 1957-61, chief sec. to Treasury, paymaster gen., 1961-62; home sec., 1962-64; Privy councellor, 1955. Dep. chmn. So. Ry. Co., 1946-48. Mem. Central Housing Adv. Com., 1944-54; mem. London County Council, 1945-55, Hampstead Borough Council, 1936-57; financial sec. to Treasury, 1954-57. Mem. governing bodies Marlborough Coll., Charterhouse Sch. Created peer, 1966; companion of Honor, 1966. Mem. Conservative Party. Home: The Glebe House Mildenhall Marlborough Wilts England

BROOKE, DAVID STOPFORD, dir. art gallery; b. Walton-on-Thames, Eng., Sept. 18, 1931; s. Somerset Stopford and Marguerite Louise (Thomas) B.; came to U.S., 1954; B.A., Harvard, 1958, A.M., 1963; m. Dixie Ann Cortner, June 6, 1959; children—Peter, Nicholas. Asst. to dir. Smith Coll. Mus. Art, Northampton, Mass., 1963-64; chief curator Art Gallery Ont., Toronto, 1965-68; dir. Currier Gallery Art, Manchester, N.H., 1968—. Mem. Am. Assn. Art Mus. Dirs. Contbr. articles to profl. publs. Office: 192 Orange St Manchester NH 03104

BROOKE, DWIGHT, lawyer; b. West Liberty, Ia., Sept. 12, 1907; s. Robert and Mayme (Ditmars) B.; student Grinnell Coll., 1925-28; LL.B., State U. Ia., 1931; m. Margaret Lemley, June 6, 1930; children—Elizabeth, Philip. Admitted to Ia. bar, 1931, since practiced in Des Moines; mem. firm Kelly , Shuttleworth & McManus, 1931-35, Holliday & Brooke, 1935-37; atty. Bankers Life Co., 1937-38, asst. counsel, 1938-47, gen. counsel, 1947—, v.p., 1951—. Served to lt. USNR, 1944-46. Mem. Am., Ia., Polk County bar assns., Assn. Life Ins. Counsel, Am. Life Conv. (legal sect.), Order of Coif. Clubs: Des Moines, Law. Contbr. articles to profl. jours. Home: 126 51st St Des Moines IA 50312 Office: 711 High St Des Moines IA 50307

BROOKE, EDGAR DUFFIELD, former fgn. service officer, bank exec.; b. Roanoke, Va., July 22, 1906; s. Edgar S. and Mary F. (Rucker) B.; B.A. with honors, U. Va., 1928, postgrad. Grad. Sch., 1928-29; m. Frances V. Lea, Oct. 3, 1936; children—Robert T., Lawrence L., Julia H. Sales mgr. Duplex Envelope Co., Richmond, Va., 1929-43; corr. Time and Life mags., 1946-47; free lance writer, 1947-48; news eidtor State Dept., 1948-49, unit chief Office Pub. Affairs, 1949-51; dir. publs. and reports Office Pub. Information, Nat. Prodn. Authority, 1951; fgn. resources editor Pres.'s Materials Policy Commn., 1952; cons., then statistics and reports officer Office Def. Moblzn., 1952-54; press attache Am. embassy, London, Eng., 1954-57; pub. affairs officer Am. embassy, Beirut, Lebanon, 1957-61; asst. dep. dir. (media content) USIA, 1961-65, insp. gen. USIA, 1965-69; counselor for pub. affairs Am. embassy, Brussels, Belgium, 1969-70; pub. relations officer First Nat. City Bank, London, Eng., 1970—. Served from lt. (j.g.) to lt. comdr. USNR, 1943-46. Recipient Superior honor award USIA, 1967. Mem. Soc. Cin. Club: Propeller (pres. Beirut 1961). Contbr. articles, short stories to Colliers, America, This Week, Nation, Time, N.Y. Times Book Rev., Sat.Eve.Post, Reader's Digest included anthologies. Office: 34 Moorgate London EC 2 England

BROOKE, EDWARD WILLIAM, U.S. senator; born Washington, Oct. 26, 1919; s. Edward W. and Helen (Seldon) B.; B.S., Howard U., 1940; LL.B. (editor Law Rev.), Boston U., 1948; LL.M., 1949; m. Remigia Ferrari Scacco, June 7, 1947; children—Remi, Edwina. Admitted to Mass. bar, 1948; chmn. Boston Finance com., 1961-62; atty. gen. state of Mass., 1963-66; mem. v.s. senate from Mass., 1967—. Chmn. Boston Opera Co. Served to capt. inf., AUS, World War II; ETO. Decorated Bronze Star; recipient Distinguished Service award Amvets, 1952; Spingarn medal from Mass., 1967- N.A.A.C.P., 1967. Fellow Am. Bar Found., Am. Acad. Arts and Scis. Home: 535 Beacon St Newton Center MA 12159 Office: Old Senate Office Bldg Washington DC 20510

BROOKE, F. DIXON, railroad ofcl.; b. Birmingham, Ala., Aug. 13, 1919; s. Robert Thomas and Gamaliel (Dixon) B.; grad. McCallie Sch.; B.S. in Commerce, U. Va., 1941; m. Sybil Vogtle, Aug. 26, 1941; children—Gayle Dixon, Robert T. (dec.), F. Dixon, Sybil V., William Wade. Gen. mgr., dir. Lamar Advt. Co., Baton Rouge, 1945-58; asst. v.p. sales, asst. pres. De-Bardeleben Coal Corp., Birmingham, Ala., 1958-61; asst. to pres. L. & N. R.R., 1961-63, resident v.p., Birmingham, 1963—. Bd. dirs. Birmingham Symphony Assn., Birmingham chpt. A.R.C., Birmingham Centennial Corp. Served to lt. comdr. USNR, 1941-45. Mem. Birmingham C. of C. (pres. dir.). Home: 3500 Pine Ridge Rd Birmingham AL 35213 Office: 1825 Morris Av Birmingham AL 35203

BROOKE, FRANICS JOHN, 3d, univ. ofcl.; b. Charleston, W.Va., Mar. 4, 1929; s. Francis John, Jr. and Elizabeth (Baird) B.; B.A., Hampden-Sydney Coll., 1949; M.A., U. Chgo., 1951; Ph.D., U. N.C., 1954; m. Helen Holmes Morgan, Dec. 20, 1958; children—Francis John, Haynes Morgan, David Tucker. Instr. German, Roanoke (Va.) Coll., summers 1950-52; teaching fellow, then part-time instr. German, U. N.C., 1951-54; faculty U. Va., 1956-65, asso. prof. German, 1962-65, asst. dean Coll. Arts and Scis., 1959-62, acting chmn. dept. modern langs., 1962-63; exec. dean, prof. German, Centre Coll. Ky., Danville, 1965-68; v.p. acad. affairs, prof. German, Va. Commonwealth U., Richmond, 1968—. Vice chmn. So. Humanities Conf., 1965. Served with AUS, 1954-56. Grantee Old Dominion Found., 1960; Ellis L. Phillips Found. intern acad. adminstrn., Cornell U., 1963-64. Mem. Am. Assn. Tchrs. German (pres. South Atlantic chpt. 1965- 67), Modern Lang. Assn. (exec. com. South Atlantic chpt. 1963-66), Omicron Delta Kappa. Presbyn. Office: 901 W Franklin St Richmond VA 23220

BROOKE, G. CLYMER, former mfg. exec.; b. Ardmore, Pa., Oct. 29, 1905; s. George Clymer and Rhoda F. (Morris) B.; student St. Paul's Sch., Concord, N.H., 1918-24; Ph.B., Yale, 1928; m. Madeline R. Blackburn, Mar. 30, 1932; children—George C., Morris R. With Birdsboro Corp. (Pa.), 1931-70, beginning as sales rep., successively asst. to v.p., asst. sec., asst. to pres., v.p., exec. v.p., pres., chmn. bd., 1954-70. Clubs: Racquet, Wyomissing, Reading (Pa.) Country. Home: Ocean Reef Club 17 Bay Ridge Rd Key Largo FL 33037

BROOKE, JOHN, tea co. exec.; b. Golders Green, London, Eng., Mar. 7, 1912; s. Gerald and Winifred (Storr) B.; grad. Bedales Sch., Hampshire, Eng., 1930; m. Bridget May, Dec. 4, 1936; children—Sarah, Peter, Andrew. With Brooke Bond Liebig Ltd., London, 1930—, dir., 1937—, chmn., 1952—. Served with RAF, 1942-46. Home: Rowmore Leigh Hill Rd Cobham Surrey England Office: 35 Cannon St London EC4 England

BROOKER, JAMES K., lawyer; b. Cass City, Mich., Aug. 12, 1902; LL.B., U. Mich., 1925. Admitted to Mich. bar, 1925; now mem. firm Smith & Brooker, Bay City. Fellow Am. Coll. Trial Lawyers; mem. Bay County Bar Assn., Phi Alpha Delta. Office: Phoenix Bldg Bay City MI 48706*

BROOKER, MARVIN ADEL, educator b. Bell, Fla., Sept. 8, 1903; s. Hampton B. and Eula (Roberts) B.; B.S.A., U. Fla., 1926, M.S.A., 1927; Ph.D., Cornell U., Ithaca, N.Y., 1931; m. Eddie Sue Colson, Dec. 29, 1926 (dec. Oct. 1957); children—Marvin Adel, Ralph, Sue; m. 2d, Edith B. Hendrix, Aug. 11, 1958. Asso. agrl. economist agrl. expt. sta. U. Fla., Gainesville, 1931-34, prof. agrl. econs. Coll. Agr., 1947—, asst. dean, 1955-56, dean, 1956-69, also head acad. devel. program; chief statistician FCA, Columbia, S.C., 1934-39, dir. research, New Orleans, 1941-46, comptroller, 1946; v.p., sec. Columbia Bank for Coops., 1939-41; exec. sec. Price Decontrol Bd., Washington, 1946-47. Bd. govs. Agr. Hall of Fame. Mem. Am. Farm Econ. Assn., Social Sci. Research Council (agrl. fellow 1929- 30), Sigma Xi, Alpha Zeta, Phi Kappa Phi, Gamma Sigma Delta, Sigma Phi Epsilon. Mem. Ch. of Christ. Author numerous articles on agrl. econs. Home: 2244 NW 6th Pl Gainesville FL 32601

BROOKER, ROBERT ELTON, corp. exec.; b. Cleve., July 18, 1905; s. Robert and Isadora (Roberts) B.; B.S., U. So. Cal., 1927, LL.D., 1969; m. Sally Burton Smith, Mar. 13, 1933; children—Robert Elton, Thomas Kimball. With So. Cal. Edison Co. 1928-34, Firestone Tire & Rubber Co., 1934-44, Sears, Reobuck & Co., Chgo., 1944-58; pres., dir. Whirlpool Corp., 1958-61; pres., dir. Montgomery Ward & Co., 1961- 66, chmn. bd., chief exec. officer, dir., 1966-70, chmn. exec. com., dir., 1970—; chmn., chief exec. officer, dir. Marcor Inc., 1968-70, chmn. exec. com., dir., 1970—; dir. Container Corp., Ampex Corp. Trustee U. So. Cal., U. Chgo., Ill. Inst. Tech. Mem. Sigma Nu, Chi Epsilon, Tau Beta Pi. Clubs: Economic, Chicago, Indian Hill, Old Elm. Commerical, Mid- America. Home: 68 Locust Rd Winnetka IL 60093 Office: 619 W Chicago Av Chicago IL 60607

BROOKES, CHARLES ERWIN, chem. co. exec.; b. Orange, N.J., Feb. 27, 1925; s. Charles Edward and Helen (Timberlake) B.; grad. St. Mark's Sch., Southborough, Mass., 1943; B.S. in Chem. Engring., Yale, 1949; m. Joan Barry, July 28, 1951; children—Stephen B., Wendy, John Lincoln. With W.R. Grace & Co., 1952—, formerly v.p., gen. mgr. organic chems. div. Dewey & Almy Chem. div., Cambridge, Mass., now pres. Davison Chem. div., Balt., 1967—; chmn. bd. Davison Chem. Co., Ltd., Valleyfield, Que., Can.; dir. Union Trust Co. Md., Balt. Commr. Balt. Econ. Devel. Comm. Trustee S. Balt. Gen. Hosp., Chesapeake Bay Found. Served with AUS, 1943-45; ETO. Decorated Combat Infantryman's badge, Bronze Star medal. Mem. Am. Chem. Soc., Sigma Xi, Tau Beta Pi, Chi Phi. Clubs: Concord (Mass.) Country, Yale (N.Y.C.), Mayland, Center (Balt.), Gibson Island (Md.). Home: 212 Edgevale Rd Baltimore MD 21210 Office: 101 N Charles St Baltimore MD 21203

BROOKFIELD, DUTTON, clothing mfr.; b. Kansas City, Dec. 31, 1917; s. Arthur D. and Elizabeth (Blish) B.; B.S., U. Mo., 1939; m. Betty Bell, Nov. 16, 1940; children—Karen Ann, Arthur Dutton II, Charles R., Betty Bell. Pres. Unitog Co., Kansas City, 1953—; dir. Northwestern Mutual Life Ins. Co., Milw., mem. exec. com., 1971—; dir. First Nat. Bank (Kansas City), Southwestern Bell Telephone Co. (St. Louis), Starlight Theatre; rancher Lee's Summit, Mo. Mem. Bd. Police Commrs., Kansas City, 1957-61; dir., v.p. Kansas City (Mo.) Crime Commn., 1964; dir. United Funds, Inc., Kansas City, 1964; dir. Civic Council Greater Kansas City, Am. Royal Assn.; chmn. Jackson County Sports Complex Authority. Nat. chmn. U. Mo. Devel. Fund, 1968-71; chmn. athletic council U. Mo., 1952-55; vice chmn. trustees U. Mo. at Kansas City, 1962; trustee Midwest Research Inst., 1955—; trustee Barstow Sch., pres. bd. 1958. Mem. N.A.M. (dir.), Nat. Assn. Uniform Mfrs. (dir. 1965), U. Mo. Gen. Alumni Assn. (pres. 1955-56). Republican. Presbyn. Clubs: Kansas City, Kansas City Country, Rotary (pres. 1954-55) (Kansas City); River, Carriage. Home: 310 W 49th St Kansas City MO 64112 Office: 1004 Baltimore Av Kansas City MO 64105

BROOKHART, JOHN MILLS, physiologist, educator; b. Cleve., Dec. 1, 1913; s. Leslie Shellabarger and Anna Rose (Mills) B.; B.S., U. Mich., 1935, M.S., 1936, Ph.D., 1939; m. Anna Louise Simon, Aug. 26, 1939; children—Cornella Mills, Constance Lee, John Howard. Instr., asst. prof. physiology Loyola U. Sch. Medicine, 1940-46; asst. prof. physiology U. Ill. Coll. Medicine 1946; asst. prof. neurology Northwestern U., Med. Sch., 1947-49; asso. prof. physiology U. Ore. Med. Sch., Portland, 1949-51, prof., head dept. physiology, 1952—. Cons. OSRD, 1945; spl. cons. USPHS, 1951—; mem. adv. com. on physiology Office Naval Research, 1960-62; bd. sci. counselors USPHS, 1961-65, mem. physiology tng. com., 1963-67, chmn. physiology tng. com., 1966-67; mem. physiology exam. com. Nat. Bd. Med. Examiners, 1959-62. Fulbright scholar, 1956-57. Fellow Am. Acad. Arts and Scis.; mem. Ore. Neuropsychiat. Soc., Portland Acad. Med., Am. Physiol. Soc. (council 1960, pres. 1965-66), A.A.A.S., Soc. Exptl. Biology and Medicine, Internat. Brain Research Orgn., Academia delle Science dell'Institute di Bologna, Sigma Xi, Alpha Omega Alpha, Delta Phi. Bd. editors Jour. Neurophysiology, 1960-64, editor in chief, 1964—; bd. editors Ann. Rev. Physiology, 1958-61. Home: 3126 NE 39th Portland OR 97212

BROOKING, GEORGE EDWARD, Jr., lawyer, pollution control co. exec.; b. Ky., July 14, 1925; s. George Edward and Ollie (Clark) B.; A.B., U. Ky., 1949; LL.B., Harvard, 1952, grad. Advanced Mgmt. Program, 1962; m. Ruth Bradlee Dumaine, Sept. 19, 1953; children—Frederic, Jonathan, Elizabeth, Anne. Admitted to Fed. bar, 1952; asst. counsel Office Gen. Counsel, Dept. Navy, Washington, 1952-54, asst. European counsel, London, Eng., 1954-56; asso. firm McKinsey & Co., Inc., Washington, 1956-58; with Amoskeag Co., Boston, 1958-66; pres., chmn. exec. com. Fanny Farmer Candy Shops Inc., 1966-70; pres., dir. Rollins-Purle, Inc., Wilmington, Del., 1970—; v.p., dir. Rollins Internat.; dir. Shawmut Assn., Boston, Fed. St. Capital Corp., Boston. Mem. spl. adv. com. on pub. opinion Dept. State. Clubs: Metropolitan (N.Y.C.); Idle Hour Country (Lexington, Ky.); Country (Brookline, Mass.). Home: 1608 Barley Mill Rd Wilmington DE 19807 Office: 3208 Concord Pike Wilmington DE 19803

BROOKMEYER, BOB ROBERT, composer, trombonist; b. Kansas City, Kan., Dec. 19, 1929; student piano Kansas City Conservatory, clarinet, trombone; pianist Tex Beneke's band, 1951; pianist with Ray McKinley, Louis Prima, Claude Thornhill, Jerry Wald, Terry Gibbs; with Stan Getz quartette, 1953, Gerry Mulligan quartet, 1954, also appeared Paris Jazz Festival, 1954; toured France and Italy with Mulligan sextet, 1956, with quartette, Eng., 1957, with big band, 1960, with Jimmy Guiffre trio, 1957-58; free lance, N.Y.C., 1959; appeared in motion picture film Jazz ona Summer's Day; now with Gerry Mulligan Quartet and Big Band; own quintet with Clark Terry; free-lance recording and arranging. White House performance, 1964; now appearing with and arranging for Thad Jones-Mel Lewis Jazz Band. Recipient Downbeat Critics poll New Star award on trombone, 1953. Address: 244 W. 48th St New York City, NY 10036.

BROOKNER, LESTER I., ednl. adminstr.; b. N.Y.C., Jan. 13, 1925; s. Nathan and Rose (Greenberg) B.; student Cornell U., 1942-44; B.S., N.Y.U., 1948, M.A., 1951, Ph.D., 1966; m. Elaine Farber, Oct. 20, 1946; children—Andrew, Howard, Steve. Tchr., Julia Ward Howe Jr. High Sch., N.Y.C., 1952-54; tchr., audio visual dir. Central High Sch., Valley Stream, N.Y., 1954-56; mem. adminstrn. and faculty N.Y.U., both N.Y.C. and Ankara, Turkey, 1949-52, 55—, budget dir., asst. exec. v.p., 1967-70, vice chancellor for adminstrn., 1970—, asso. prof. bus. edn., 1967—. Trustee Angew Found., N.Y.C. Served to ensign USNR, 1943-46. Mem. Delta Pi Epsilon, Pi Omega Pi. Club: New York University (N.Y.C.). Home: 109 Wooleys Lane Great Neck NY 11023 Office: New York Univ Washington Sq New York City NY 10003

BROOKS, ALLISON COCHRAN, air force officer; b. Pitts., June 26, 1917; s. Allison Cochran and Deidamia (Allaben) B.; B.S., U. Cal., 1938; m. Geraldine Nordell, June 11, 1942; children—James C., Kris M., John S. Commd. 2d lt. USAAF, 1940, advanced through grades to maj. gen. USAF, 1970; with 8th Air Force, Eng., 1943-45; operations and command assignments bombers and fighters Tactical Air Command, 1945-47; instr. Army Command and Gen. Staff Coll., 1948-51, Air War Coll., 1951-52; staff and command assignments Mil. Airlift Command, Europe and U.S., 1952-63; dep. comdr. 2d Air Div. RVN, 1964-65; comdr. Aerospace Rescue and Recovery Service, 1965-70; dep. dir. Office Dep. Asst. Sec. of Def., Washington, 1970—. Decorated D.S.M., Legion of Merit with oak leaf cluster, D.F.C. with 2 oak leaf clusters, Soldiers medal, B.S.M., Air Medal with 7 oak leaf clusters. Home: 1600 S Joyce St Arlington VA 22202 Office: ODASD(IS)/OASD (A) The Pentagon Washington DC 20301

BROOKS, ANGIE, UN official; b. Montserrado County, Liberia, 1928; law degrees from several Am. univs.; grad. student London U., also Liberia U. Mem. Liberian delegation to UN, 1954—; former pres. UN Gen. Assembly. Address: Protocol and Liaison Div UN New York City NY 10017*

BROOKS, ARTHUR OAKLEY, investment banker; b. Boston, Sept. 12, 1911; s. J. Arthur and Mary T. E.(Oakley) B.; grad. magna cum laude, Groton (Mass.) Sch., 1929; A.B., Harvard, 1933; m. Barbara Connick, Jan. 10, 1942; children—Pamela (Mrs. Stevenson), Arthur Oakley, Peter Connick, Candace Anne. With Chase Nat. Bank, N.Y.C., 1933-34, Mfrs. Trust Co., N.Y.C., 1934-41; with Wood, Struthers & Winthrop, Inc., and predecessor, N.Y.C., 1945—, gen. partner, 1953-69, vice chmn., 1969—; pres., dir. DeVegh Mut. Fund, Inc., 1964—; v.p., dir. Pine St. Fund, 1949—; dir. Medusa Portland Cement Co.; dir., mem. exec. com. Delteo Internat. Treas., mem. exec. com. N.Y. State Communities Aid Assn.; chmn. Mental Health Assn. N.Y. and Bronx counties. Served to lt. comdr. USNR, 1941-45. Home: 1220 Park Av New York City NY 10028 Office: 20 Exchange Pl New York City NY 10005

BROOKS, CHARLES LLEWELLYN, air force officer; b. St. Louis, May 14, 1921; s. Llewellyn Albert and Pauline (Lemaitre) B.; D.C., Ratledge Chiropractic Coll., Los Angeles, 1942; student Coe Coll., 1951-54; B.B.A., U. Pitts., 1962; grad. Air Force Mgmt. Course, Air Force Inst. Tech., 1959; grad. with honors Acad. Instrs. Course, Air U., 1967; m. Julia May Curtis, Jan. 8, 1949; children—Michael Curtis, Wendy Sue. Commd. 2d lt. USAAF, 1943, advanced through grades to col. USAF, 1963; communications officer USAAF, 1943-44; comdr. Arctic Search and Rescue Squadron, 1944-46; asst. prof. air sci. and tactics Coe Coll., 1950-54; comdr. Decatur (Ill.) Air Res. Center, 1956-58; dir. manpower and orgn. Hdqrs. 26th Air Div., 1960-62, Hdqrs. 13th Air Force, 1962-64; chief manpower requirements Hdqrs. Air Def. Command, 1964-67; prof. aerospace studies Va. Poly. Inst., 1967- 70; comdt. for Southwestern U.S. and Hawaii, Air Force R.O.T.C., Maxwell AFB, Ala., 1970—. Mem. sec. air force appeal and grievance com. Air Def. Command, 1965- 67; mem. Arctic Roster Project, 1947. Drive leader Decatur YMCA, 1957; publicity chmn. Decatur chpt. A.R.C., 1956-58; chmn. Blacksburg Civic Commn., 1968; pres. Monument (Colo.) P.T.A., 1966; bd. govs. Decatur Crippled Childrens Assn., 1966, U.S. Pony Club, Air Acad., 1967. Decorated Meritorious Service medal. Mem. Tau Kappa Epsilon. Kiwanian. Contbr. articles to lit. Home: 434 East Dr Maxwell AFB AL 36113

BROOKS, CHARLES MATTOON, Jr., educator; b. East Orange, N.J., Aug. 21, 1908; s. Charles Mattoon and Grace May (Barlow) B.; student U. Ill., 1926-27; B.F.A., Yale, 1931, M.F.A., 1934. Asst. prof. architecture Tex. A. and M. Coll., 1934-37, Scripps Coll., 1937-42; Myra Goodwin Plantz prof. art and architecture Lawrence U., Appleton, Wis., 1946—; dir. John Nelson Bergstrom Art Center, Neenah, Wis. Served to lt. comdr. USNR, 1942-45. Recipient First medal, Fontainebleau prize, 1932; medallist design competitions Beaux Arts Inst. Ford Found. fellow, 1952-53. Mem. Soc. Archtl. Historians, Phi Gamma Delta. Republican. Conglist. Author: Texas Missions, Their Romance and Architecture, 1936; Vincent van Gogh, a Bibliography, 1942. Home: Cotuit Cape Cod MA 02635 Office: Lawrence U Appleton MI 54511

BROOKS, CLEANTH, educator; b. Murray, Ky., Oct. 16, 1906; s. Cleanth and Bessie Lee (Witherspoon) B.; A.B., Vanderbilt U., 1928; A.M., Tulane U., 1929; Rhodes scholar, La. and Exeter, Oxford, 1929-32, B.A. (honors), 1931, B.Litt., 1932; D.Litt., Upsala Coll., 1963, U. Ky., 1963, U. Exeter, 1966, Washington and Lee U., 1968, Tulane U., 1969; L.H.D., St. Louis U., 1968; m. Edith Amy Blanchard, Sept. 12, 1934. Prof. English, La. State U., 1932-47; mng. editor (with R.P. Warren), So. Rev., Baton Rouge, 1935-41, editor (with R.P. Warren), 1941-42; vis. prof. U. Tex., summer 1941, U. So. Cal., 1953; fellow Library of Congress, 1951-62; cultural attache Am. embassy, London, Eng., 1964-66; now Gray prof. rhetoric Yale U., New Haven. Guggenheim fellow, 1953, 60. Mem. Modern Lang. Assn. Am., Am. Assn. U. Profs., Am. Acad. Arts and Scis., Nat. Inst. Arts and Letters, Phi Beta Kappa. Democrat. Episcopalian. Clubs: Yale (N.Y. U.); Athenaeum, Savile (London). Author books including: Modern Poetry and the Tradition, 1939; The Well Wrought Urn, 1947; (with R.P. Warren), Understanding Poetry, 1938; Modern Rhetoric, 1950; (with W.K. Wimsatt, Jr.) Literary Criticism: A Short History, 1957; The Hidden God, 1963; William Faulkner; The Yoknapatawpha Country, 1963. Gen. editor (with David N. Smith), The Percy Letters, 10 vols., projected 1942—. Editor The Correspondence of Thomas Percy and Richard Farmer, 1946. Mem. adv. com. for Boswell Papers, 1950. Contbr. articles, revs. to lit. mags., jours. Home: Northford CT 06778 Office: 1315 Davenport Coll Yale New Haven CT 06520

BROOKS, CONLEY, lumber co. exec.; b. St. Paul, Sept. 16, 1921; s. Edward and Markell (Conley) B.; grad. St. Paul Acad., 1940; B.A., Yale, 1966; m. Marney Brown, Mar. 18, 1944; children—Conley, Marlow, Sarah, Stephen, Markell. With Fla. div. Brooks-Scanlon, Inc., 1946-52, v.p., then exec. v.p., pres., now chmn. bd., chief exec. officer, Mpls., 1952—, also dir.; dir. Northwestern Nat. Life Ins. Co., 1st Nat. Bank Mpls. Chmn., dir. Abbott-Northwestern Hosp. Corp., Mpls. Served from pvt. to lt. USAAF, 1942- 46. Mem. Chi Psi. Clubs: Minneapolis; Union League (Chgo.); Woodhill. Home: 2 Spring Hill Rd Long Lake MN 55356 Office: 127 S 10th St Minneapolis MN 55403

BROOKS, DAVID BARRY, mineral economist; b. Easton, Mass., Feb. 15, 1934; s. Abraham and Mae (Fox) B.; S.B. in Geology, Mass. Inst. Tech., 1955; M.S. in Geology, Cal. Inst. Tech., 1956; Ph.D. in Econs., U. Colo., 1963; m. Toby Judith Haftka, Sept. 11, 1955; children—Michael Jan, Naomi Sara. Geologist, U.S. Geol. Survey, 1956-59; summer instr. U. Colo. Econs. Inst., 1960-61; research asso. Resources for the Future, Washington, 1961-66; asst. prof. econs. Berea Coll., 1966-67; chief div. mineral econs. Bur. Mines, Dept. Interior, 1967-70; chief Mineral Research div. Can. Dept. Energy, Mines and Resources, 1970—. Cons., Center Appalachian Studies and Devel., W.Va. U., 1966-68. Chmn. No. Va. chpt. Congress Racial Equality, 1963-65; mem. Commn. to Study the Orgn. of Peace, 1966—, mem. drafting com. ann. reports, 1966, 69; sec. Fed. Employees for a Democratic Soc. Served with AUS, 1957. Mem. Am. Econ. Assn., Am. Inst. Mining, Metall. and Petroleum Engrs. (sec. treas. council econs. 1967-69). Author: Supply and Competition in Minor Metals, 1965; Low-Grade and Nonconventional Sources of Manganese, 1966; Peaceful Use of Nuclear Explosives: Some Economic Aspects, 1969; also monographs on environmental problems of mining. Home: 2832-G Cedarwood Dr Ottawa 8 Ontario Canada Office: Dept of Energy Mines and Resources Ottawa Ontario Canada

BROOKS, DAVID WILLIAM, farmer coop. exec.; b. Royston, Ga., Sept. 11, 1901; s. David William and Letty Jane (Tabor) B.; B.S. in Agr., U. Ga., 1922, M.S., 1923; LL.D., Emory U., 1964; m. Ruth McMurray, Aug. 7, 1930; children—David William, Nancy Ruth. Tchr. agronomy div. U. Ga., 1922-25; field supr. Ga. Cotton Growers Coop. Assn., 1925-33; gen. mgr. Gold Kist Inc. (formerly named Cotton Producers Assn.), Atlanta, 1933-68, chmn. bd. dirs., 1968—; pres. Cotton States Life & Health Ins. Co., 1955-59, chmn. bd., 1959—; chmn. bd. Cotton States Mut. Ins. Co., pres., 1947-59; dir. Ga. So. & Fla. Ry. Co., 1963—. Dir. Am. Cotton Coop. Assn., Atlanta, 1940—; dir. Nat. Council Farmers Coops., Washington, 1938-68, mem. exec. com., 1944-63, pres., 1951-52; mem. cotton adv. com. Dept. Agr., 1947-50; mem. Textiles Industry Adv. Com. of Army-Navy Munitions Bd., 1947-51; industry adv. Internat. Cotton Adv. Com., Washington, 1950; mem. nat. adv. bd. Moblzn. Policy, 1951-52; mem. Nat. Agrl. Adv. Commn., 1953-56; mem. Benson's Cotton Export Adv. Com., 1953-56, chmn., 1953; mem. nat. cotton adv. com. U.S. Dept. Agr., 1961-63; dir. Found. for Am. Agr., 1960—; mem. Nat. Agrl. Adv. Commn., 1964-65; dir. Agrl. Mission, 1959-67; dir. Coop. Fertilizers Internat., Chgo., 1968—; mem. Agribus. Industry Adv. Com., Washington, 1968-70. Trustee Am. Inst. Cooperation (Wash.), 1944, v.p. Ga. Coop. Council, Athens, 1940-47, chmn., 1951-52; trustee Reinhardt Coll., Waleska, Ga., Emory U., Atlanta, Wesleyan Coll., Macon, Ga.; chmn. Emory U. Com. of One Hundred, 1958—; bd. govs. Agrl. Hall of Fame, 1958—. Selected Man of Year in Agr. for Ga., Progresseve Farmer, 1950, Southwide Man of Year in Agr., 1966. Mem. N.Y. (adv. com. 1948-68), New Orleans (adv. com.) cotton exchanges, Nat. Cotton Council (adv. com., v.p. 1958-69), Nat. Peanut Council, Farmers Chem. Assn. (chmn. bd.), Nat. Council Chs. (governing board 1960—), Nat. Planning Assn. (agrl. com. 1946-63), Alpha Zeta, Phi Kappa Phi. Methodist (steward, bd. mgrs., exec. com. bd. missions). Mason, Kiwanian. Home: 2374 Dellwood Dr PO Box 2210 Atlanta, GA 30301.

BROOKS, DEAN KENT, hosp. supt., physician; b. Colony, Kan., July 22, 1916; s. Robert Stewart and Myrtle (Balyeat) B.; B.S. in Medicine, U. Kan., 1940, M.D., 1942; D.Sc., Ch. Div. Sch. of Pacific, 1964; m. Ulista Jean Moser, Mar. 8, 1941; children—Denise (Mrs. Charles Hiber), India (Mrs. James P. Civey), Ulista Jean. Intern Akron (O.) City Hosp., 1942-43; staff physician VA Hosp., American Lake, Wash., 1946-47; mem. staff Ore. State Hosp., Salem, 1947-54, supt., 1955—; chmn. med. adv. bd. VA Hosp., Rosenburg, Ore., 1970—. Cons. psychiatrist Hillcrest Sch. Girls, Salem, 1951-54, Ore Liquor Control Commn., 1954-56. Pres. Salem Symphony Soc., 1955-56; mem. Nat. P.E. Ch. Joint Commn. Study Church's Ministry of Healing, 1961-70, Nat. P.E. Ch. Joint Commn. on Soc. and Alcohol, 1955-61; del. gen. conv. Nat. P.E. Ch., 1955, 58, 61, 64. Trustee Ch. Div. Sch. of Pacific, 1955-65. Served to capt., M.C., USNR, World War II: PTO. Fellow Am. Psychiat. Assn. (pres. Ore. dist. br. 1969-70); mem. Assn. Med. Supts. of Mental Hosps. (nat. pres. 1970-71), Marion-Polk County Med. Soc., Phi Beta Pi. Republican. Episcopalian (sr. warden). Mason. Home: 2440 NE Greenway Dr Salem OR 97310 Office: Oregon State Hosp Station A Salem OR 97310

BROOKS, DONALD MARC, designer; b. N.Y.C., Jan. 10, 1928; s. Harry and Miriam (Goodwin) B.; student Fine Arts Sch., Syracuse U., 1947-49, Parsons Sch. Design, N.Y.C., 1949-50. Vice pres. Donald Brooks, Inc., mfg. better ready to wear; designer musical prodn. No Strings, 1962, prin. designs in Prints, tweeds; designer Barefoot in the Park, Fade Out, Fade In, Third Day, Flora the Red Menace, The Cardinal, costumes for On a Clear Day You Can See Forever, Star, Promises, Promises. Recipient Nat. Cotton award, 1962; Coty award, 1962, 67; N.Y. Drama Critics award, 1963. Office: 550 7th Av New York City NY 10001

BROOKS, EARL, educator, personnel exec.; b. Bloomdale, O., Mar. 7, 1914; s. George Allen and Etta (Turley) B.; A.B., B.S. in Edn., State U., Bowling Green, O., 1935; A.M., Am. U., 1938; m. Mary Clauder, May 10, 1941; children—Susan, James. Personnel asst. U.S. Labor Dept., 1937-39; tng. officer U.S. Forest Service, 1939-41; tng. dir. USAAF, 1941-43; dir. personnel Nat. Housing Agy, 1946-47; prof. indsl. and labor relations Cornell U. and asst. dean. N.Y. State Sch. of Indsl. and Labor Relations, 1947-59, Cornell Univ. Prof. adminstrn. Grad. Sch. Bus. and Pub. Adminstrn., Ithaca, N.Y., 1959—. Arbitrator of labor disputes, 1948—; cons. personnel administrn. and supervisory devel., 1940—. Served with USNR, 1943-46. Author: In-Service Training of Federal Employees, 1938; Training Plans and Procedures, 1943; Facts and Figures for Collective Bargaining, 1950; Financial Reports in Collective Bargaining, 1950; What Successful Executives Do, 1955. Contbr. articles in field. Address: Cornell Univ Ithaca NY 14850

BROOKS, EDWARD HALE, ex-assn. dir.; b. New Hampshire, Apr. 25, 1893; s. Edward Waite and Mary Frances (Hale) B.; B.S. in Civil Engring., Norwich (Vermont) University, 1916, Master Miltary Science, LL.D. (honorary); graduate Field Artillery Sch., 1922, Command and Gen. Staff Sch., 1934, Army War Coll., 1937; Doctor Mil. Sc., Pa. Mil. Coll.; m. Beatrice Leavitt, Nov. 29, 1917; children—Elizabeth Allen (Mrs. R. Potter Campbell, Jr.), Maj. Edward Hale, Jr., A.C. (dec.). Served as capt. 1st Vt. Cav., 1915-16; commd. 2d lt., cav., U.S. Army, Aug. 1917 and advanced through grades to lt. gen., 1948; participated in Second Battle of Marne, Aisne-Marne, San Mihiel and Meuse-Argonne offensives; with Army of Occupation, Nov. 1918- July 1919, transferred to F.A., 1920; served in Philippines, 1926-28; chief, statistics branch, War Dept. Gen. Staff, 1939-41; artillery officer, Armored Force, 1941-42; comdg. gen. 11th Armored Div., Aug. 1942-Mar. 1944, 2d Armored Div., England, Normandy, Belgium Mar. 1944- Sept. 1944, comdg. gen. V Corps, Luxembourg, Germany Sept. 1944-Oct. 1944, comdg. gen. VI Corps, France, Germany, Austria Oct. 1944-May 1945; accepted surrender of German 19th Army, Innsbruck, Austria, May 5, 1945; later dep. comdg. gen. 3d Army, Atlanta; comdg. gen. Antilles Dept., San Juan, Puerto Rico; comdg. gen., U.S. Army Caribbean. Asst. chief of staff, G-1, Personnel, Dept. Army, Wash.; comdg. gen. 2d Army, Ft. Meade, Md. 1951-53; exec. dir., Assn. Mil. Coll. and Sch. U.S., 1953-64. Corporator, New Hampshire Savings Bank. Exec. bd. Daniel Webster council Boy Scouts Am. Decorated D.S.C., D.S.M. with oak leaf cluster. Legion of Merit with oak leaf cluster. Silver Star with oak leaf cluster, Bronze Star, Victory Medal with five bars, European Theater with five stars (U.S.), officer Legion of Honor, Croix de Guerre with two palms (France); grand officer Netherlands Order Orange-Nassau; Mil. Order 1st Class, Army Republic of Chile; officer Order of the Crown, Croix de Guerre with Palm (Belgium); Abdon Calderon, 1st class, Republic of Ecuador. Mem. Soc. of Cincinnati, Assn. U.S. Army (council trustees 1959-65). Home: 4 Vernon St Concord NH 03301

BROOKS, EDWIN BICKFORD, petroleum co. exec.; b. Akron, O., Sept. 21, 1914; s. Edwin Hinchman and Mae (Bickford) B.; B.A., Dartmouth, 1936, M.C.S., Amos Tuck Sch. Bus. Adminstrn., 1937; m. Ruth Louise Daugherty, Jan. 28, 1939; children—Susan (Mrs. Peter D. Pockel), Sarah (Mrs. John H. Foehl), Stephanie (Mrs. Donald M. Elliman, Jr.), Edwin. Pres., dir. Binney & Smith Internat., Inc., N.Y.C., 1949- 57; dir. Binney & Smith Inc., 1950-55; gen. sales mgr. pigment div. Columbian Carbon Co., N.Y.C., 1955-58, v.p., dir., 1958-63, exec. v.p., 1963-64, pres., 1964-70; chmn. bd. Columbian Continental Europa S.p.a., 1959-70, Cities Service Chems. Ltd.; group v.p. Cities Service Co., N.Y.C., 1970—, also dir. Served to 2d lt. USMCR, 1936-40; to lt. USNR, 1943-46. Mem. Mfg. Chemist Assn. (dir.). Clubs: Union, Sky, Bankers (N.Y.C.); Edgartown Yacht; Portage Country (Akron). Home: 251 E 61st St New York City NY 10021 Office: 60 Wall St New York City NY 10005

BROOKS, ELMER LEROY, educator; b. Rush Spring, Okla., May 16, 1917; s. Sankey and Ethel (McCoy) B.; B.A., Central State Coll., 1941; M.A., Okla. U., 1948; Ph.D., Harvard, 1954; m. Catherine Eleanor Sweeney, Jan. 2, 1952; children—Paul, Christopher, Jeffrey. Tchr. pub. schs., Okla., 1937-40; with U.S. Post Office Dept., Washington, 1941-42; instr. Panhandle Agrl. and Mech. Coll., 1948-49; with Germain Machinery Co., 1953; instr. Duke, 1953-56; asst. prof. Eastern Ill. U., 1956-60, asso. prof., 1960-64, prof., 1966-69; prof. English, Ind. State U., Terre Haute, 1969—; lectr. U. Cal. at Los Angeles, 1963-64. Served with USNR, 1942-46. Mem. Ill. Assn. Tchrs. English (past leader Eastern dist., 1st v.p., 1966-67, pres. 1967-68), Ill. Edn. Assn., Nat. Council Tchrs. English, (dir. 1967), Conf. Coll. Composition and Communication. Democrat. Author: (with R.G. Richardson and Agnes Voris) Correlated Grammar and Composition, 1962; In Lieu of Wit, 1967. Contbr. articles profl. jours. 1504 S 6th Terre Haute IN 47802 Office: Dept English Ind State U Terre Haute IN 47809

BROOKS, ERNEST, Jr., found. exec.; b. N.Y.C., Dec. 5, 1907; s. Ernest and Jeanne L. (Marion) B.; grad. St. Mark's Sch., 1926; B.A., Yale, 1931; LL.B., Harvard, 1933; m. Mary Caroline Schoyer, June 23, 1934; children—Joan (Mrs. John R. McLane III), Peter Preston, Howard Turner, Ernest III. Admitted to N.Y. bar, 1934; asso. firm Breed, Abbott & Morgan, N.Y.C., 1933-42; officer Old Dominion Found., N.Y.C., 1948-69, trustee, 1951-69, pres., 1956-69; officer Bollingen Found., N.Y.C., 1947-69, trustee, 1948- 69, v.p., sec. treas., 1956-69; cons. Andrew W. Mellon Found., 1969-71; trustee Anne S. Richardson Fund, Nat. Humanities Faculty, 1969—; bd. dirs. Nat. Audubon Soc., 1957-63, sec., 1959-60, v.p., 1969—; trustee Conservation Found., 1956—, New Canaan (Conn.) Country Sch., 1955-64, Putney Sch., 1965-71, Stanford Mus. and Nature Center, 1971—; bd. govs. Nature Conservancy, 1954- 61, 69—. Fellow Berkeley Coll., Yale Served with OSS, 1943-46. Mem. Scroll and Key, Phi Beta Kappa. Clubs: Country (New Canaan); Century Assn. (N.Y.C.). Home: 152 Marvin Ridge Rd New Canaan CT 06840

BROOKS, EUGENE HOWARD, machinery mfg. co. exec.; b. Olive Branch, Miss., Dec. 10, 1901; s. Howard Wilbur and Lillie (Reynolds) B.; student U. Cal., 1921-23; m. Evelyn Elizabeth Payne, Sept. 9, 1927; children—Evelyn Elizabeth (Mrs. Frank Wallace Bromberg), Gene Adele (Mrs. James C. Wilson). With Continental Gin Co., Birmingham, Ala., 1923- 59, exec. v.p., 1956-1958, dir., 1956-59, pres., chief exec. officer, 1958-59; pres., chief exec. officer, dir. Hardwicke-Ette Co., 1959-71, vice chmn. of bd. treas., dir., 1971—. v.p., dir. Continental Gin Service Co., 1950-58. Mem. Navy League U.S., Am. Ordnance Assn. Presbyn. Clubs: Oil and Industry, Woodlawn Country (Sherman, Tex.); Tanglewood-on-the-Lake (Pottsboro, Tex.). Home: 1701 Shields Dr Sherman TX 75090 Office: 301 E Houston St Sherman TX 75090

BROOKS, EUGENE TATUM, architect, urban planner; b. Carthage, Tex., Nov. 2, 1935; s. Clayton Lee and Parthenia (Tatum) B.; A.A., Los Angeles City Coll., 1954; B.Arch., U. So. Cal., 1964; m. Emily Marie Beaird, Feb. 20, 1959 (div. Jan. 1966); 1 dau., Ellen Marie. Asst. prof. environmental design Cal. Poly. State Coll., Pomona, Cal., 1969-70; asst. prof. U. Cal. at Los Angeles, 1971—. Mem. Mayor's Environmental Mgmt. Com., Los Angeles, 1969. Mem. A.I.A., Am. Inst. Planners. Projects have included community plan for Watts, Los Angeles, 1965—, master plan for Calabassas Park, Cal., 1964, Charles R. Drew Postgrad. Med. Sch. in assn. with Martin Luther King Jr. Gen. Hosp., Watts. Address: 1673 E 108th St Los Angeles CA 90059

BROOKS, EVANS BARTLETT, graphic arts co. exec.; b. New Albany, Ind., Jan. 28, 1900; s. William Wilson and Bertha (Evans) B.; student bus. adminstrn. Louisville YMCA Extension and Ind. U. Extension; m. Margaret Marby, Mar. 6, 1926; children—Marcia

Jayne (Mrs. C. Dean Browne), Sandra Lee (Mrs. Robert C. Jordan). Vice pres. Del. Engraving Co., Muncie, Ind., 1926-30, Ditzel-Brooks Co., Dayton, O.; 1931-32; v.p.-sec. Wayne Colorplate Co. Ohio, Dayton, 1932-37, pres., treas., 1937—; v.p., treas. Brooks Investment Co., Dayton, 1953—; dir., chmn. bd. Third Nat. Bank & Trust Co., Dayton, Charter mem. Dayton Area Progress Council, 1961; chmn. Montgomery County Bldg. Commn.; founder mem., 1st pres. All-Dayton Com., 1945-47; past chmn. Montgomery County chpt. A.R.C.; chmn. bldg. com. Air Force Mus.; past pres. Dayton Philharmonic Assn. Trustee Dayton and Montgomery County Pub. Library (past pres.); trustee Dayton Art Inst., pres., 1951-53; trustee U. Dayton. Mem. Am. Photoengravers Assn. (past pres.), Photo-Engravers Research Inst. (dir., past pres.), Dayton Printing Industry Assn. (past pres.), Dayton C. of C. (past pres., dir.), Research and Engring. Council Graphic Arts (dir.), Newcomen Soc. Presbyn. (past pres. Ohio Bd. Home Missions, ch. elder). Mason, Rotarian. Clubs: Tavern (Chgo.); Moraine Country, Engineers, Bicycle, Racquet, Dayton City. Home: 4365 Delco Dell Rd Dayton OH 45429 Office: 34 N Main St Dayton OH 45402

BROOKS, FORREST EDMUND, cons. engr.; b. Kansas City, 1890; s. John Bryns and Jennie Priday (Cadle) B.; B.S. in Elec. Engring, Case Inst. Tech., 1912; m. Ruth Hetzel, Apr. 30, 1923; children—Mary Jane, Forrest Edmund, Ruth Lee. With N.Y. Telephone Co., N.Y.C., 1912-55, successively engr., engr. plant extension, chief engr., 1912-50, v.p., 1950-55; cons. engr., 1955- -; directed survey of transit facilities N.Y. Met. area conducted by Met. Rapid Transit Commn. and Port N.Y. Authority. With Office Civilian Def., World War II; mem. group under Fed. contract (project East River) to study Civil Def., 1951, 52. Served to maj. Signal Corps, U.S. Army, 1917-19; col. N.Y. N.G., 1941-54. Recipient citation in communications mgmt. Case Inst. Tech., 1953. Licensed profl. engr., N.Y. Fellow I.E.E.E.; mem. Am. Inst. Cons. Engrs., N.Y. C. of C., Commerce and Industry Assn. N.Y., Ohio Soc. N.Y., Eta Kappa Nu (past nat. pres.), Sigma Nu. Episcopalian. Clubs: EngineerS (trustee, mem. bd. mgmt.), N.Y. Railroad, Railroad-Machinery (N.Y.C.); Scarsdale (N.Y), Golf; Skytop (Pa.). Home: 6 Brookline Rd Scarsdale NY 10583 Office: 330 Madison Av New York City NY 10017

BROOKS, FOSTER LINDSEY, educator; b. Carrollton, O., Sept. 4, 1908; s. Thomas Howard and Bronta (Herron) B.; A.B., Mt. Union Coll., 1929; Ph.D., Ohio State U., 1934. Tchr. math., physics Carrollton High Sch., 1933-35; instr. through prof. math. Kent (O.) State U., 1935—; with Operations Research Group USN, 1942-45, staff Research, Devel. Bd., 1948, Weapons Systems Evaluation Group, 1948-49; vis. instr. N.Tex. State U., summers 1936, 37, 39, 40; cons. Dept. Def., Goodyear Aerospace Co., United Electro Dynamics, Inc. Recipient Presidential certificate of merit, 1947. Mem. Am. Math. Soc., Math. Assn. Am. (sec.-treas. Ohio sect.), Operations Research Soc. Am., Soc. Indsl. and Applied Math., Photog. Soc. Am., Sigma Xi, Phi Kappa Tau. Republican. Methodist. Kiwanian. Home: 1741 Dollar Lake Dr Kent OH 44240

BROOKS, GEORGE DANIEL, ins. exec.; b. Martin Tenn., Oct. 13, 1907; s. George Martin and Mayme (Mathis) B.; student Vanderbilt U., 1924-28; m. Julia Evans Clements, Apr. 23, 1929; children—Frances Moore (Mrs. Michael Corzine), Julia Clements (Mrs. Clarke T. Reed). Employed Caldwell & Co., Investment bankers, Nashville, Tennessee, 1928-30; Third National Bank, Nashville, Tenn., 1930-31; joined Nat. Life & Accident Ins. Co., Nashville, 1931, mgr. investment dept., 4 1939—, v.p., 1950-59, treas., 1953-59, financial v.p., 1959-63, senior v.p., chmn. finance com., 1963-64, exec. v.p. 1964- 65, pres., 1965-67, chairman of the board of directors, 1967—, also dir.; chmn. bd., dir. WSM, Inc., Nashville; trustee U.S. Trust Co. N.Y. Financial adviser of Old Woman's Home, Nashville; past. dir. United Givers Fund, Nashville, Vanderbilt U. Devel. Found.; adv. bd. Jr. League Nashville; bd. dirs. Nashville YMCA. Served as lt. comdr. USNR, 1942-45. Decorated Letter of Commendation, Commendation medal (Navy). Mem. Mortgage Bankers Assn. Am. (past gov.), Vanderbilt U. Alumni Assn. (past pres.), Sigma Nu. Ind. Democrat. Presbyn. Clubs: Cumberland, Belle Meade Country (past pres.) (Nashville); National Golf (Augusta, Ga.); Links (N.Y.C.). Home: Clarendon Av Nashville, TN 37205. Office: National Life Center Nashville TN 37203

BROOKS, GEORGE WILLIAM, coll. dean; b. Macon, Ga., June 7, 1918; s. John William and Lois (Henderson) B.; B.S., Ind. U., 1941, M.S., 1942, Ed.D., 1955; LL.B., LaSalle Extension U., 1947; m. Fannie E. Crafton, May 25, 1945; 1 son, George W. (dec.). Instr., Voorhees Jr. Coll., 1942-43; asst. prof. social studies Prairie View A. and M. Coll. of Tex., 1943-53; prof. social studies and edn. S.C. State Coll., Orangeburg, 1955-59, chmn. dept. social studies, 1959-60, dean Sch. Grad. Studies, 1960—. Mem. council on coop. coll. projects TVA, 1963—. Mem. Am. Assn. Sch. Adminstrs., N.E.A., Nat. Council for Social Studies, S.C. Psychol. Assn., Palmetto Edn. Assn. (parliamentarian ho. of dels. 1959—), Kappa Alpha Psi, Phi Delta Kappa, Phi Alpha Theta. Mason (Shriner). Home: SC State Coll Sch Grad Studies Orangeburg SC 29115

BROOKS, GEORGE WILSON, educator, physician; b. Warren, Vt., Feb. 11, 1920; s. Henry W. and Lena (LaMorder) B.; B.S., U. N.H., 1941; M.D., U. Vt., 1944; m. Jean Duncan, Mar. 5, 1943; children—Jeanie (Mrs. Brian Martin), Prudence (Mrs. Prudence Dowers), George Peter, James. Rotating intern Mary Fletcher Hosp., Burlington, Vt., 1944-45; resident psychiatry Vt. State Hosp., Waterbury, 1947-49, asst. physician, 1949-51, sr. psychiatrist, 1953-56, dir. research and staff edn., 1957-61, asst. supt., 1961-68, acting supt., 1968, supt., 1968—; exchange resident N.H. State Hosp., Concord, 1952; Smith, Kline & French Found. fellow Mass. Mental Health Center, Boston, 1956-57; instr. clin. psychiatry U. Vt. Coll. Medicine, Burlington, 1953-57, asst. prof., 1957-63, asso. prof., 1963-70, prof., 1970—. Served as capt., M.C., AUS, 1945-47. Recipient citation for meritorious service President's Com. on Employment Physically Handicapped, 1959, citation for orgn. and devel. services in rehab. of hospitalized mentally ill Nat. Rehab. Assn., 1963. Diplomate Am. Bd. Psychiatry and Neurology. Fellow Am. Psychiat. Assn. (chmn. com. on rehab. 1961), A.C.P.; mem. A.M.A., Vt. Med. Assn., Washington County Med. Soc., Nat. Rehab. Assn., Vt. Psychiat. Assn., New Eng. Soc. Psychiatry, Med. Supts. Med. Hosps., Vt. Assn. Mental Health, Group Without-A-Name. Contbr. articles profl. jours. Home: 83 S Main St Waterbury VT 05676

BROOKS, GWENDOLYN, author; b. Topeka, June 7, 1917; d. David Anderson and Keziah Corinne (Wims) Brooks; grad. Wilson Jr. Coll., Chgo., 1936; L.H.D., Columbia Coll., 1964; m. Henry L. Blakely, Sept. 17, 1939; children—Henry L., Nora. Instr. poetry Columbia Coll., Chgo., Northeastern Ill. State Coll., Chgo. Mem. Ill. Arts Council. Named One of 10 Women of Year, Mademoiselle mag., 1945; recipient award for creative writing Am. Acad. Arts and Letters, 1946, Guggenheim fellow for creative writing, 1946, 47; Pulitzer prize for poetry, 1950; Anisfield-Wolf award, 1969; named Poet Laureate of Ill., 1969. Mem. Soc. Midland Authors. Author: A Street in Bronzeville (poetry), 1945; Annie Allen (poetry), 1949; Maud Martha (novel), 1953; Bronzeville Boys and Girls (for children), 1956; The Bean Eaters (poetry), 1960; Selected Poems, 1963; In the Mecca, 1968; Riot, 1969; Family Pictures, 1970; Aloneness, 1971. Editor mag. The Black Position. Home: 7428 S Evans Av Chicago IL 60619

BROOKS, HARVEY, educator, physicist; b. Cleve., Aug. 5, 1915; s. Chester Kingsley and Elizabeth Freeman (Brown) B.; student Hawken Sch., Cleve., Hill Sch., Pottstown, Pa.; A.B., Yale, 1937; postgrad. Cambridge (Eng.) U., 1937-38; Ph.D., Harvard, 1940; D.Sc., Kenyon Coll., Harvard, 1963, Yale, 1962; Brown U., 1964; m. Helen Gordon Lathrop, Oct. 20, 1945; children—Alice Lathrop, Katharine Gordon, Kingsley Chapin, Rosalind Hickox. Mem. Soc. of Fellows Harvard, 1940-41, research asso. Underwater Sound Lab., 1942-45; asst. dir., prof. engring. research Ordnance Research Lab., Pa. State Coll., 1945-46; research asso., asso. lab. head Knolls Atomic Power Lab., Gen. Electric Co., 1946-50; Gordon McKay prof. applied physics Harvard, 1950—, dean engring. and applied physics, 1957—. Dir. Raytheon Co.; mem. com. on underseas warfare NRC, 1948-65; mem. U.S. Pres.'s Sci. Adv. Com., 1959-64; mem. naval research adv. com. Nat. Sci. Bd. Trustee Woods Hole Oceanographic Instn., Case Western Res. U.; mem. Council on Library Resource. Recipient Ernest Orlando Lawrence award, 1960. Fellow Am. Phys. Soc., Am. Nuclear Soc.; mem. Nat. Acad. Scis., Am. Philos. Soc., Acoustical Soc. Am., Am. Acad. Arts and Scis., Phi Beta Kappa, Sigma Xi. Editor-in-chief Jour. Physics and Chemistry of Solids. Home: 46 Brewster St Cambridge MA 02138

BROOKS, HENRY LUESING, U.S. circuit judge; b. Louisville, Dec. 9, 1905; s. Horace G. and Amelia (Luesing) B.; A.B., U. Wis., 1927; J.D., U. Louisville, 1929; m. Christine Clarke, Oct. 29, 1930; children—Henry Luesing, Peggy C. (Mrs. Robert B. Beale, III), Thomas C. Admitted to Ky. bar, 1928; practiced in Louisville, 1929-54; judge Jefferson Circuit Ct., 1946-48; faculty Jefferson Sch. Law, 1948-52; U.S. dist. judge, Louisville, 1954-69; U.S. circuit judge 6th Circuit, Cin., 1969- -. Mem. Ky. Bd. Bar Commrs., 1950-54. Served as lt. USNR, 1943-46. Mem. Louisville Bar Assn. (pres. 1949), Sigma Chi, Phi Delta Phi. Mason (32, Shriner). Home: 21 Belnap Beach Prospect KY 40054 Office: US Court House Louisville KY 40202

BROOKS, JACK BASCOM, congressman; b. Crowley, La., Dec. 18, 1922; s. Edward Chachere and Grace Marie (Pipes) B.; A.A., Lamar Jr. Coll., Beaumont, Tex., 1939- 41; B.J., U. Tex., 1943, J.D., 1949; m. Charlotte Collins, Dec. 15, 1960; children—Jack Edward, Katherine Inez. Admitted to Tex. bar, 1949; mem. Tex. Legislature, 1946-50, author Lamar Coll. bill, 1949; mem. 83-89th congresses from 2d Dist. Tex., mem. 90th-92d congresses from 9th Dist. Tex. Served from pvt. to lst lt. USMCR, 1942-46; now col. Res. Mem. Am. Bar Assn., State Bar Tex., Am. Legion, V.F.W., Sigma Delta Chi. Home: 1029 East Dr Beaumont TX 77706 Office: Rayburn House Office Bldg Washington DC 20515 also Fed Building Beaumont TX and Fed Bldg Galveston TX 77550

BROOKS, JAMES, artist; b. St. Louis, Oct. 18, 1906; s. William Roldolphus and Abigail (Williamson) B.; student So. Meth. U., 1923-25, Art Students League, 1927-31; studied with Wallace Harrison, 1945; m. Charlotte Park, Dec. 22, 1947. Instr. Pratt Inst., N.Y.C., 1947-59; faculty Columbia, 1947- 48, Queens Coll., N.Y.C., 1966-69, New Coll., 1966, U. Pa., Phila., 1971; vis. critic advanced painting Yale, New Haven, 1955-56, 57-59; vis. artist New Coll., Sarasota, Fla., 1965—; one-man shows Peridot Gallery, N.Y.C., 1950-53. Borgenicht Gallery, N.Y.C., 1954. Stable Gallery, N.Y.C., 1957, 59, Kootz Gallery, N.Y.C., 1961, 63, 64 Phila. Art Alliance, 1966; Martha Jackson Gallery, 1968, 71, Berenson Gallery, Miami, Fla., 1969; exhibited Retrospective Exhbn. at Whitney Mus., N.Y.C., 1963-64; artist in residence Am. Acad., Rome, 1963; exhibited Rose Art Mus., Brandeis U., Walker Art Center, Mpls., U. Cal. at Los Angeles, Balt. Mus., Mus. Modern Art, Washington, 1963, Whitney Mus., Modern, Bklyn., Met., Guggenheim museums, Art Inst. Chgo., numerous others, also Tokyo, Sao Paulo, Basle, Milan, London, Berlin, Brussels, Paris, Barcelona, 1958; executed murals Little Falls (N.J.) Post Office, Woodside (L.I.) Library, LaGuardia Airport. Recipient prizes Pitts. Internat., 1952, Art Inst. Chgo., 1957, 62. Guggenheim fellow, 1967-68. Club: Century (N.Y.C.). Home: 128 Neck Path Springs East Hampton NY 11937

BROOKS, JAMES ELWOOD, educator; b. Salem, Ind., May 31, 1925; s. Elwood Edwin and Helen Mary (May) B.; A.B., DePauw U., 1948; M.S., Northwestern U., 1950; Ph.D., U. Wash., 1954; m. Eleanore June Nystrom, June 18, 1949; children—Nancy, Kathryn, Carolyn. Research asso. Ill. Geol. Survey, 1950; geologist Gulf Oil Corp., Salt Lake City, summers 1951-53; instr. geol. scis. So. Meth. U., Dallas, 1952-55, asst. prof., 1955-59, asso. prof., 1959-62, prof., 1962—, chmn. dept., 1961-70, asso. provost univ., 1970—. Cons. geologist firm DeGolyer & MacNaughton, Dallas, 1954-59. Bd. dirs. Inst. Study Earth and Man, Inst. for Underwater Research, Dallas. Served with USNR, 1943-46. Fellow Geol. Soc. Am., A.A.A.S., Tex. Acad. Sci.; mem. Sigma Xi, Phi Eta Sigma, Sigma Phi. Contbr. articles to profl. jours. Home: 7055 Arboreal Dr Dallas TX 75231

BROOKS, JAMES EUGENE, coll. pres.; b. Forest, Wash., Oct. 10, 1925; s. James Edmon and Nellie (Cecelia) B.; B.A. in Edn., Central Wash. State Coll., Ellensburg, 1949; M.A. in Geography, U. Wash., 1952, Ph.D. in Geography, 1957; m. Lillian Janell Literal, Sept. 19, 1947; children—Carol, Marla, Ronda, Brian, Kenneth. Instr. geography Central Wash. State Coll., spring 1952; instr., then asst. prof. Eastern Wash. State Coll., 1953-58; asst. prof. Portland State Coll., 1958-59, asst. to pres., 1959-61; pres. Central Wash. State Coll., 1961—. Home: 211 E 10th St Ellensburg WA 98926

BROOKS, JAMES L., TV writer, producer; b. Bklyn., May 9, 1940; s. Edward M. and Dorothy Helen (Sheinheit) B.; student N.Y.U., 1958-60; m. Marianne Catherine Morrissey, July 7, 1964; 1 dau., Amy Lorraine. Writer, CBS News, N.Y.C., 1964-66; writer- producer documentaries Wolper Prodns., Los Angeles, 1966-67; exec. story editor/creator TV series Room 222, 1968-69; exec. producer/creator TV series Mary Tyler Moore Show, 1970; writer/producer Thursday's Game, 1971—; guest lectr. Stanford Grad. Sch. Communications. Recipient Emmy award for creation of Room 222, 1969, for comedy writing Mary Tyler Moore Show, 1970. Mem. Writers' Guild Am., TV Acad. Arts and Scis. Home: 20552 Pacific Coast Hwy Malibu CA Office: 4024 Radford Av Studio City CA 91604

BROOKS, JOHN, writer; b. N.Y.C., Dec. 5, 1920; s. John Nixon and Bessie (Lyon) B.; A.B., Princeton, 1942; m. Anne Curtis Brown, Mar. 6, 1948 (div. 1952); m. 2d, Rae Alexander Everlitt, Aug. 15, 1953; children—Carolyn, John Alexander. Contbg. editor Time mag., 1945-47; staff contbr. New Yorker mag., 1949—. Served with AUS 1942-45; ETO, Mem. Authors Guild Am. (treas. 1964-71, v.p. 1971—), P.E.N. (v.p. 1962-66). Clubs: Coffee House, Century Assn. (N.Y.C.). Author: The Big Wheel, 1949; A Pride of Lions, 1954; The Man Who Broke Things, 1958; The Seven Fat Years, 1958; The Fate of the Edsel, 1963; The Great Leap, 1966; Business Adventure, 1969; Once in Golconda, 1969; also articles in revs. Editor: The One and the Many, 1962. Home: 41 Barrow St New York City NY 10014 Office: New Yorker Mag 25 W 43d St New York City NY 10036

BROOKS, JOHN EDWARD, coll. pres.; b. Boston, July 13, 1923; s. John Edward and Mildred (McCoy) B.; B.S. in Physics, Coll. Holy Cross, 1949; postgrad. in geophysics, Pa. State U., 1949-50; M.A. in Philosophy, Boston Coll., 1954, M.S. in Geophysics, 1959; S.T.D. in Dogmatic Theology, Gregorian U., Rome, Italy, 1963. Joined Soc. of Jesus, 1950, ordained priest Roman Catholic Ch., 1959; mem. faculty, adminstrn. Coll. Holy Cross, Worcester, Mass., 1954-56, 63—, asso. prof. theology, 1967—, pres. Coll., 1970—. Mem. N.A.A.C.P., Worcester, 1969—, Cambridge-Southbridge Neighborhood Council, 1968-70; subcom. Human Rights Com. Worcester, 1968—; planning council of urban affairs com. Community Services Greater Worcester, Inc., 1969—, also chmn. a subcom. Bd. dirs. Worcester Jr. Ballet, Main South area Worcester Community Action Council, Inc.; trustee St. Peter's Coll., Jersey City, N.J. Served with AUS, 1942-46. Mem. The Liturgical Conf., Catholic Theol. Soc. Am., Coll. Theology Soc., Religious Edn. Assn., Soc. Sci. Study Religion, Am. Acad. Religion, Ch. Soc. for Coll. Work, Jesuit Theol. Assn. Home: College Holy Cross Loyola Hall Worcester MA 01610

BROOKS, JOHN GAUNT, mfg. exec.; b. Chgo., Jan. 9, 1913; s. Overton and Emmilgene (Wortsman) B.; student Northwestern U., 1931-36; m. Ann Malcolm, Oct. 30, 1941; children—William Blair, Robert Malcolm. With Commonwealth Edison, 1930- 36, Zenith Radio Corp., 1936-42, Majestic Radio Corp., 1946-47; with Ekco Products Co., 1947-54, v.p., 1950-54; pres., dir. Siegler Corp., Los Angeles, 1954-62; chmn. bd., chief exec. officer Lear Siegler, Inc., Santa Monica, Cal., 1962—, pres., 1964—; dir. Gen. Telephone Co. So. Cal., So. Cal. Edison Co., United Cal. Bank. Campaign chmn. Los Angeles County Heart Assn., 1969; vice chmn. Nat. UN Day, 1968; chmn. U.S. Indsl. Payroll Savs. campaign Greater Los Angeles Met. Area, 1970, 7l; mem. exec. bd. Crescent Bay council Boy Scouts Am., 1970—; gov. Henrotin Hosp., Chgo.; regent St. John's Hosp., Santa Monica; asso. Cal. Inst. Tech.; founding friend Harvey Mudd Coll. Trustee City of Hope; trustee U. So. Cal., 1966—, vice chmn., 1970—; trustee Cal. Council Econ. Edn. Served to capt. USAAF, 1942-46. Mem. U. So., Cal. Assos., U.S. C. of C. (chmn. sci. and tech. com. 1968-69, marine resource adv. panel). Clubs: Los Angeles Country, Bel Air Country (Los Angeles); The California. Died Jan. 15, 1971. Home: 671 Siena Way Los Angeles CA 90024 Office: 3171 S Bundy Dr Santa Monica CA 90406

BROOKS, JOHN HERON, investment banker; b. Pitts., Sept. 21, 1918; s. Joseph J. and Martha (Heron) B.; grad. Choate Sch., 1936; A.B., Yale, 1940; m. Susan White, Jan. 11, 1941; childrenJohn H., James B., Joseph J., Susan E. With Putnam, Coffin & Burr, Hartford, Conn., 1946-, partner, 1954-. Bd. govs. Am. Stock Exchange, 1964-; treas., bd. govs. Assn. Stock Exchange Firms, 1959-65. Treas. Conn. Humane Soc. Home: 38 Orchard Rd West Hartford, CT 06117. Office: 6 Central Row, Hartford, CT 06103.

BROOKS, JOHN ROBINSON, educator, physician; b. Cambridge, Mass., Nov. 15, 1918; s. Arthur Hendricks and Caroline Elizabeth (Harrington) B.; M.D., Harvard, 1943; m. Dorothy Kalbfleisch, Sept. 9, 1944; children—David C., Stephen H., Nancy, Geoffrey H. Intern, Roosevelt Hosp., N.Y.C., 1944; resident Peter Bent Brigham Hosp., Boston, 1951; surgeon Harvard Med. Sch., 1960—; prof. surgery Peter Bent Brigham Hosp., Harvard, 1970—; chief surgery Harvard Health Services, 1962—. Head drs. sect. United Fund, 1969. Trustee Noble and Greenough Sch. Served to capt. AUS, 1946. Author: Endocrine Tissue Transplantation, 1960. Editor: Harvard Med. Alumni Bull., 1956-68. Contbr. articles to profl. jours. Home: 29 Webster Rd Weston MA 02193 Office: 721 Huntington Av Boston MA 02115

BROOKS, JOHN WOOD, chemical mfr.; b. N.Y.C., Oct. 9, 1917; s. J. Arthur and Mary TenEyck (Oakley) B.; grad. Groton Sch., 1935; A.B., Harvard, 1939; m. Margaret O. Magoun, July 19, 1958; children—Sylvia B., John W., Laurence O., Anne Strong, Mary Strong, Selina Strong. Various sales, sales exec. positions in fibers industry, 1939-53; v.p., gen. sales mgr. Spring Mills, Inc., 1953-54; gen. mdse. mgr., fibers div. Celanese Corp., N.Y.C., 1955, dir. marketing fibers div., 1955-56, v.p., gen. mgr. fibers div., 1956- 59, exec. v.p. domestic operations, 1960-61, exec. v.p. operations, 1961-65, pres., 1965—, chief exec. officer, 1968—, chmn., 1971—, also dir.; pres. Celanese Fibers Co., 1959-60; dir. ACF Industries, Inc., Bankers Trust Corp. Mem. adv. com. Internat. Bus. Problems, State Dept. Bd. dirs. Fashion Inst. Tech. Clubs: Bedford (N.Y.) Golf and Tennis; University, Links, Economic, Union. Home: 363 Cantitoe Rd Bedford Hills NY 10507 Office: 522 Fifth Av New York City NY 10036

BROOKS, JOHN WOOLSON, architect; b. Mt. Pleasant, Ia., Aug. 29, 1897 s. Gilbert Ernest and Miriam (Woolson) B.; B.S. in Architecture, U. Pa., 1920; m. Marguerite Palcho, June 22, 1920; children—Miriam, Julia. With Brooks, Borg & Skiles, and predecessor firm, Des Moines, 1912—, now partner; bldgs. designed include Windsor Terrace Apts., Mercy Hosp., Des Moines, Meml. Union, Ia. State Coll. Dir. Ia. Savs & Loan Assn. Bd. dirs. Edmundson Art Found. Mem. Ia. Bd. Archtl. Examiners, 1947-62. Registered profl. engr. and architect. Former Fellow A.I.A. (mem. jury fellows 1960-62, pres. Ia. chpt. 1939); mem. Sigma Xi, Tau Sigma Delta, Kappa Sigma. Republican. Contbr. profl. jours. Patentee color index device. Home: 3405 Wakonda Ct Des Moines IA 50321 Office: 815 Hubbell Bldg Des Moines IA 50309

BROOKS, KEITH, educator; b. Tigerton, Wis., May 14, 1923; s. Oscar Derby and Henrietta (Mierswa) B.; B.S., U. Wis., 1949, M.A., 1949; Ph.D., Ohio State U., 1955; m. Laquata Sue Walters, Dec. 29, 1951; children—Todd Randall, Craig William. Mem. faculty Eastern Ky. State U., Richmond, 1949-53; mem. faculty Ohio State U., 1953—, prof., chmn. dept. speech communication, 1968—; communications cons. Procter & Gamble, Ohio Bell Telephone, Eastern R.R. Assn., Shaw U., Raleigh, N.C. Served with USNR, 1945-46. Mem. Speech Communication Assn. (chmn. interpretation div., vice chmn., sec.), Central States Speech Assn. (editor Jour. 1958-61), Am. Ednl. Theatre Assn. (dir. 1958-60). Author: (with Bahm and Okey) Literature for Listening, 1968, The Communicative Art of Oral Interpretation, 1967; The Communicative Arts and Sciences of Speech, 1967; (with Dietrich) Practical Speaking, 1959. Home: 3732 Romnay Rd Columbus OH 43220

BROOKS, KENNETH THOMAS HARLING, educator; b. Parkman, Me., Dec. 25, 1916; s. Walter Edward and Alice (Harling) B.; A.B., U. N.H., 1946; Ed.M., Boston U., 1948, Ed.D., 1950; m. Dena Alice Webber, Mar. 19, 1943; children—Barbara Alice, Linda Harling, Laurie Jean, Keith Thomas. Tchr., prin. schs. in Me., 1937-46; headmaster Austin-Cate Acad., Center Stafford, N.H., 1946-47, now trustee; teaching fellow, lectr. edn. Boston U., 1948-50; asst. dir. profl. edn., dir. admissions So. Conn. State Coll., New Haven, 1950-59; dean instrn. Gorham (Me.) State Tchrs. Coll., 1959-60, pres., 1960-70, Univ. prof., 1970—. Mem. bd. corporators Me. Savings Bank. Bd. dirs. Greater Portland (Me.) United Community Services, Pine Tree council Boy Scouts Am.; trustee Baxter Pub. Library, Gorham, Me. Recipient Champion of Free Enterprise award. Mem. N.E.A., Am. Assn. Sch. Adminstrs., Com. Fgn. Relations, Phi Delta Kappa, Pi Gamma Mu. Mason, Rotarian. Contbr. articles to profl. jours. Home: 37 College Av Gorham ME 04038

BROOKS, LAURA JEAN JARRETT (M Gary Brooks), former educator; b. Pitts., Apr. 23; d. Ewing and Alcinda V. (Conaway) Jarrett; A.B., Mt. Holyoke Coll., 1915; A.M., U. Okla., 1928; postgrad. Cambridge (Eng.) U., 1930; L.H.D., Cornell Coll., Am. U.; LL.D., LaGrange Coll.; Litt.D., Ill. Wesleyan U.; m. Frank Gary Brooks, Dec. 26, 1918 (dec. Mar. 1955); 1 dau. Cornelia (Mrs. David

I. Hull). Faculty dept. English lit. Oklahoma City U., 1920-36; instr., asst. prof. English lit. Cornell Coll., 1939-47. Nat. pres., Meth. Women, 1948-56; mem. gen. bd. Nat. Council Chs. of Christ in U.S., 1950-56; mem. central com. World Council Chs., 1954-61; speaker, del. World Meth. Council, Oxford, Eng., 1951. Bd. regents State Instns. Higher Edn., Ia., 1953-57. Mem. Chi Delta Phi, Beta Beta Beta (nat. sec.—treas. 1955-67). Mng. editor Bios. Nat. biol. jours., 1955-67. Home: 3650-C Colegrove St San Mateo CA 94403

BROOKS, LAURANCE WADDILL, lawyer; b. Baton Rouge, June 22, 1900; s. Claude Morley and Pennie (Overton) B.; B.A., La. State U., 1920, LL.B., 1922, J.D., 1968; m. Neveda Stokes, Aug. 12, 1925; children—Neveda Merlyn (Mrs. William A. Norfolk), Laurance Waddill. Admitted to La. bar, 1922, U.S. Supreme Ct., 1946, other fed. cts.; practiced in Baton Rouge, 1922—; counsel firm Taylor, Porter, Brooks & Phillips, and predecessors, 1925—; spl. asst. to atty. gen. La.; dir. emeritus La. Nat. Bank of Baton Rouge. Dir. Baton Rouge Port Devel. Assn., 1948-50, Council Better La., 1963—; mem. Pub. Affairs Research Council La., 1964—. La. Civil Service League, 1964—. Asst. clk. La. Ho. of Reps., 1920-26; asst. sec. La. Senate, 1928. Mem. La. State U. Found., 1964—. Served as 2d lt., inf., U.S. Army, World War I. Fellow Am. Coll. Trial Lawyers; mem. Am., La. (chmn. ins. sect. 1955, legislative com. 1956-58; gov. 1963-65), Baton Rouge (pres. 1950), Internat. (patron 1963—) bar assns., Internat. Assn. Ins. Counsel, La. State Law Inst. Council (dir. 1964—), Baton Rouge C. of C. (pres. 1954), Mil. Order World Wars, Am. Legion, La. Def. Council, Kappa Alpha, Phi Delta Phi, Sigma Delta Chi. Democrat. Episcopalian (past sr. warden). Mason, Elk (past exalted ruler Baton Rouge). Clubs: Knife and Fork (charter, 1st pres. 1951), Baton Rouge Country City (Baton Rouge); Boston (New Orleans). Home: 1820 Country Club Dr Baton Rouge LA 70808 Office: Louisiana Nat Bank Bldg Baton Rouge LA 70801

BROOKS, LIONEL B., business exec. Pres., Eastern Co., Westwood, Mass. Office: 26 Dartmouth St Westwood MA 02090*

BROOKS, LORIMER PAGE, patent lawyer; b. Swampscott, Mass., May 11, 1917; s. William Lorimer and Maud (Page) B.; B.S. in Elec. Engring. with honors, Northeastern U., 1939; J.D., Fordham U., 1940-41, 45-48; student N.Y.U., Law Sch., 1951; m. Arlene M. Cook, Nov. 9, 1941; children—Lorraine E. (Mrs. Gilbert P. Wood), Rosalind P. (Mrs. Steven Barbour). Admitted to N.Y. bar, 1948; patent agt. Internat. Tel. & Tel. Corp., 1939-41, patent atty., 1945-50; patent atty. Ward, Crosby & Neal, N.Y.C., 1950-54; partner firm Ward, McElhannon, Brooks & Fitzpatrick, N.Y.C., 1954-71, Brooks, Haidt & Haffner, 1971—. Vice pres. Drum Fire Inc. Sec. Westchester Park Citizens Assn., 1950-52, pres., 1952-54. Dir. Westchester County Cerebral Palsy Assn., 1962-64. Mem. Young Men's Republican Club Eastchester, 1952-56; candidate for Rep. village commiteeman, Tuckahoe, N.Y., 1954. Served with AUS, 1941-45. Mem. Am. Bar Assn., Westchester County Bar Assn., N.Y. Patent Law Assn. (bd. govs. 1961-64, chmn. subcom. practice and procedure in cts. 1961-62), I.E.E.E., Aircraft Owners and Pilots Assn., N.Y. State Pilots Assn., Fordham Law Alumni Assn., Tau Beta Pi. Holder patents. Home: 6 Hyatt Rd Briarcliff Manor NY 10510 Office: 99 Park Av New York City NY 10016

BROOKS, MARJORY, univ. dean; b. Amarillo, Tex.; d. Henry F. and Ethel (Land) Brooks; B.S., Miss. State Coll. for Women, 1943; M.S., U. Ida., 1951; Ph.D., Ohio State U., 1963. Lab. analyst E.I. duPont de Nemours & Co., Millington, Tenn., 1943-44; chemist Cities Service Refining Corp., Lake Charles, La., 1944-47; tchr. high sch. sci. and math., Wash., Ida., Miss., 1947-57; instr. Wash. State U. Coll. Home Econs., Pullman, 1957-60; prof., dir. Sch. Home Econs., head home econs. research Mont. State U., Bozeman, 1963-67; dean Coll. Home Econs., U. Md., 1967—. Mem. Mont. Vocational Edn. Adv. Council, Mont. State U. Peace Corps Adv. Council, Univ. Honors Council, Mont. Gov.'s Commn. on Status of Women. Fellow A.A.A.S.; mem. Am., Mont. home econs. assns., Am. Psychol. Assn., N.E.A., Nat. (exec. bd. 1970-73), Pacific N.W. (co-dir. Mont. 1964-65) councils family relations, Nat. Council Adminstrs. Home Econs. (exec. bd. 1968-71), Beta Beta Beta, Gamma Sigma Epsilon, Kappa Delta Pi, Phi Upsilon Omicron, Omicron Nu, Sigma Xi. Contbr. articles profl. jours. Home: 4 W Indian Spring Dr Silver Spring MD 20901 Office: U Md Coll Home Econs College Park MD 20742

BROOKS, MARY THOMAS, dir. U.S. Mint; b. Colby, Kan.; d. John and Florence Jessie (Johnson) Thomas; student Mills Coll., 1926-27; B.A., U. Ida., 1929; m. Arthur J. Peavey, Jr., July 28, 1930 (dec.); children—John Thomas Peavey, Betty Anne Peavey (Mrs. Gordon Eccles); m. 2d, C. Wayland Brooks, May 8, 1946 (dec.). Formerly bus. mgr. Mills Coll.; mem. Ida. Senate, 1964-69; chmn. agr. and livestock com., mem. fish, game and recreation com., local govt. affairs com., state affairs com.; mem. Republican Nat. Com.. 1957-63, asst. chmn., 1965-69; dir. U.S. Mint, 1969—. Bd. dirs. Immigrants Service League, Ill., 1957-64, Children's Home and Aid Soc., 1957-64, Lighthouse for Blind, 1959-64. Mem. Am. Assn. U. Women, Am. Legion Aux., Arden Shore Assn., Kappa Kappa Gamma. Home: Watergate W 2700 Virginia Av Washington DC 20037 Office: Dept of Treasury Washington DC 20220

BROOKS, MAURICE GRAHAM, educator; b. French Creek, W.Va., June 16, 1900; s. Fred Ernest and Hettie Grace (Coburn) B.; student W.Va. Wesleyan Coll., 1918-21; A.B., W. Va. U., 1923; M.S., 1935; postgrad. U. Mich., 1939-41; m. Ruth Anna Brown, Dec. 23, 1931; 1 son, Fred Carson. Agt., W.Va. State 4-H Club, 1923-26; asst. prin. Upshur County High Sch., Buckhannon, W.Va., 1926-34; instr. biology W. Va. U., Morgantown, 1935-38, prof. Wildlife mgmt., 1938—, also forester W. Va. Agrl. Exptl. Sta. Tchr. U. Va., summer 1938, U. Minn., summer 1941; chmn. W.Va. Biol. Survey, 1936-46. Mem. W.Va. Conservation Commn., 1945-54; dir. W. Va. Conservation Sch., 1945—; chmn. com. recreation W.Va. Planning Bd., 193845. Fellow A.A.A.S., Am. Ornithologists Union; mem. Wilson Ornithol. Club (pres. 1950-52), Soc. Am. Foresters, Wildlife Soc., Phi Beta Kappa, Sigma Xi, Alpha Zeta. Author: The Appalachians; The Life of The Mountains; also Univ. bulls. Home: Route 4 Box 69 Morgantown WV 26505

BROOKS, MAX GIERHART, banker; b. Oberlin, Kan., May 28, 1916; s. Elwood M. and Laura (Gierhart) B.; student Wichita Bus. Coll., 1934-35; m. Josephine C. Gallacher, Aug. 2, 1939; children—Gary Evan, Philip Micael, Judith Ann, Elwood M. With FHA, 1935-37; asst. nat. bank examiner U.S. Treasury Dept., 1937-43; chmn. Central Bank & Trust Co., Denver; Mullins Broadcasting Co., 1st State Bank, Idaho Springs, Colo., Citizens State Bank, Norcatur, Kan., First Nat. Bank, Meeker, Colo., D.H. Baldwin Co. Dir. Denver Community Chest; past pres. Denver Conv. and Visitors Bur. Served as staff sgt., finance dept., AUS, 1943-45. Mem. Am. Legion, 40 and 8. Roman Catholic. Kiwanian. Home: 4600 Montview Blvd Denver CO 80207 Office: 15th and Arapahoe Sts Denver CO 80217

BROOKS, MEL, playwright, sketch writer. Author sketch Of Fathers and Sons in New Faces of 1952, 1952; co-author book for musical Shinbone Alley, 1957, All American, 1962; writer for TV series Your Show of Shows, also Caesar's Hour; recordings include The 2000 Year Old Man, 2000 and One Years, Address: care Capitol Records 1750 N Vine St Hollywood CA 90028*

BROOKS, PAUL, publisher; b. N.Y.C., Feb. 16, 1909; s. Ernest and Jeanne L. (Marion) B.; grad. St. Mark's Sch., 1927; A.B. cum laude, Harvard, 1931; m. Susan Anderson Moller, June 24, 1931; children—Elizabeth Sweetser (Mrs. John W. Harris), Douglas (dec.), Samuel Jameson, Susan (Mrs. John D. Morris), Kate. With Houghton Mifflin Co., Boston, 1931—, editorial reader, asst. editor, mng. editor, editor-in-chief gen. book dept., dir., 1943-69, v.p. co., 1968-69, editorial adviser, 1969—. Served as chief book sect. for ETO, OWI, 1945. Dir. Mass. Audubon Soc., 1943-47. Recipient Sarah Chapman Francis medal Garden Club Am. Fellow Am. Acad. Arts and Scis.; mem. Sierra Club (v.p. 1968—, dir.), Phi Beta Kappa. Clubs: St. Botolph, Tavern, Examiner, Saturday (Boston); Century (N.Y.C.). Author: Roadless Area (John Burroughs Assn. medal 1965), 1964; The Pursuit of Wilderness, 1971; also mag. articles. Home: Lincoln MA 01773 Office: 2 Park St Boston MA 02107

BROOKS, PHILIP COOLIDGE, archivist, library dir. b. Washington, Jan. 14, 1906; s. Franklin E. and Sara (Coolidge) B.; B.A., U. Mich, 1928; M.A., U. Cal., 1930. Ph.D., 1933; m. Dorothy H. Holland, Feb. 12, 1938; 1 son, Philip Coolidge. Teaching and traveling fellow U. Cal., 1929-33; teaching asst. George Washington U., 1933-34; bibliographer Am. Hist. Assn. 1933-35; exam., staff officer, chief archivist records br. Nat. Archives, 1935-48, 50-53; records officer Nat. Security Resources Bd., 1948-50; chief fed. records center Gen. Services Adminstrn. San Francisco, 1953-57; dir. Harry S. Truman Library, Gen. Services Adminstrn., 1957—; sec. Harry S. Truman Library Inst., 1957—. Vis. lectr. U. Panama, 1954; records mgmt. adviser Republic Panama, ICA, 1954-55. Mem. adv. bd. Nat. Trust for Historic Preservation. Recipient Distinguished Service award Gen. Services Adminstrn., 1967. Fellow Soc. Am. Archivists (sec. 1936-42, pres. 1949-51); mem. Am. Hist. Assn., Am. Assn. State and Local History, Internat. Council Archives, Jackson County Hist. Soc. (v.p. 1960—). Orgn. Am. Historians, Methodist. Author: Diplomacy and the Borderlands, 1939, 70; Public Records Management, 1949, rev. 1961, El Manejo de Archivos y Documentos, 1955; Research in Arhives, 1969. Contbr. articles, revs. to hist., archival jours. Home: 1332 W Truman Rd Independence MO 64050 Office: Harry S Truman Library Independence MO 64050

BROOKS, R. FRANK, mortgage co. exec.; b. Haddam Neck, Conn., July 10, 1897; s. Sidney and Etta (Forbes) B.; ed. pub. schs., Conn.; m. Leontine Kent, July 19, 1919; children—Donald Kent, Philip R., Jane (Mrs. Stephen Hart), Ralph F., William Collier; m. 2d, Grace Macdonald, Dec. 26, 1947. Pres. Brooks, Harvey & Co.; pres., dir. Orlando Central Park, Inc., Haddam Holdings; trustee Title Guarantee Co. Bd. dirs. N.Y. Conv. and Visitors Bur., Downtown-Lower Manhattan Assn. Trustee Flower and Fifth Av. Hosp., N.Y. Med. Coll.; bd. dirs. Fedn. Protestant Welfare Agencies, N.Y.C., Graham Home Children. Clubs: Union, Metropolitan (bd. govs.), Fifth Av., Racquet and Tennis, Deepdale (N.Y.C.). Home: 605 Park Av New York City NY 10021 Office: 41 E 42d St New York City NY 10017

BROOKS, RICHARD, writer, dir.; b. Phila., May 18, 1912; student Temple U.; m. Jean Simmons. Formerly radio writer, narrator, commentator NBC; now author screenplays for motion pictures. Author: (screen plays) Swell Guy, White Savage, Brute Force; (original screen plays) To The Victor, Crossfire; (collaborator screen plays) Key Largo, Mystery Street, Storm Warning; (dir. author screen plays) Deadline, U.S.A., Battle Circus, Last Hunt, Something of Value, The Brothers Karamazov, Cat On a Hot Tin Roof, Elmer Gantry (Acad. award for screen play 1961), Sweet Bird of Youth; (dir.) Take the High Ground, Flame and the Flesh, Catered Affair; (dir. collaborator screen plays) Last Time I Saw Paris, Blackboard Jungle; (producer, dir., writer) Lord Jim; (dir., writer) In Cold Blood, The Professionals (novels) Brick Fox. Hole, Boiling Point, The Producer. Address: care Metro-Goldwyn-Mayer 10202 Washington Blvd Culver City CA 90230*

BROOKS, RICHARD ALBERT EDWARD, educator; b. Karachi, Pakistan, May 14, 1904; s. Septimus Hawkins and Adelaide (Kearns) B.; student Philander Smith Coll., Naini Tal, United Provinces, India, 1920-21; A.B., Wesleyan U., 1926, M.A. (Olin Fellow), 1927; Ph.D. (Univ. fellow, 1929-30), Yale, 1936; m. Edith Margaret Hill, Sept. 24, 1926 (dec. Sept. 1966); children—Joan E. (Mrs. John D. Gindele), Judith Anne (Mrs. Judith B. Fitzhugh); m. 2d, Harriet Helen Ogsbury, June 30, 1967. Instr. English Wesleyan University, 1927-29, F. B. Weeks vis. prof. English, 1952-53; asst. in English, Yale, 1930-32, instr., 1932-33; faculty Vassar College, 1933—, successively instructor, assistant prof., asso. prof., prof., 1933-69, emeritus, 1969—. faculty fellow, 1939-40 and 1961-62, Mary Conover Mellon House fellow, 1954-59, chmn. English dept., 1958-60, Henry Noble McCracken prof. English, 1963—. Instr. Naval Pre-Flight Sch., summer 1944, Biarritz Am. U., 1945-46. Active Am. Friends Service Com., 1955-59. Trustee Poughkeepsie Day Sch., 1944-45, 46-47. Modern Lang. Assn. Am., Am. Assn. U. Profs., Phi Beta Kappa. Club: Knickerbocker (N.Y.C.). Author; Thomas Carlyle's Journey to Germany, Autumn 1858, 1940. Editor; The Diary MacCracken) Ben Johnson's Sad Shepherd: Completed by Alan Porter, 1944. Home: 130-A Heritage Village Southbury CT 06488 also 155 E 47th St New York City NY 10017

BROOKS, RICHARD BOYNTON, coll. dean; b. Springfield, Mass., Nov. 17, 1908; s. Walter C. and Beulah (Boynton) B.; B.Phys. Edn., Springfield Coll., 1930, M.A., U. Pa., 1942; Ed.D., U. Va., 1959; m. Virginia Rose Dove, Feb. 17, 1944; children—Carter D., Leila Kay (Mrs. William J. Odle). Instr. psychology Colby Coll., Waterville, Me., 1946-47; dir. counseling Coll. William and Mary, Williamsburg, Va., 1947-57, dean Sch. Edn., 1968—; faculty Longwood Coll., Farmville, Va., 1957-64, prof. edn., 1962-64, dean coll., 1964-68. Served to capt. AUS, 1942-46. Mem. Am. Psychol. Assn., Va. Edn. Assn. Conglist. Home: Box CQ Williamsburg VA 23185

BROOKS, RICHARD M., sugar co. exec.; b. 1928; B.S., Yale; M.B.A., U. Cal. at Berkeley; C.L.U.; married. With Mut. of N.Y. until 1957; with Cal. and Hawaiian Sugar Co., 1957—, v.p. finance and corporate devel., treas., 1967—. Address: 1 California St San Francisco CA 94106

BROOKS, ROBERT ANGUS, mus. ofcl.; b. Calcutta, India, Oct. 16, 1920 (parents U.S. citizens); s. Milton and Mabel (Spence) B.; A.B. summa cum laude, Harvard, 1940, M.A., 1941, Ph.D., 1949; m. Jane S. Kochmann, Jan 2, 1943; children—Allison Spence, Roger Angus, Camilla Jane. Jr. fellow Soc. Fellows, Harvard, 1942, 46-48, instr., 1949-51; research asso., v.p., dir. Harbridge House, Inc., Boston, 1951-65, pres., 1969-71; asst. sec. of army for installations and logistics, 1965-69; dep. under sec. Smithsonian Instn., 1971—. Mem. Cambridge Civic Assn., Nat. Adv. Council on Minority Bus. Enterprise, 1969-71. Served to capt. USAAF, 1942-46; PTO. Mem. Am. Philol. Assn., Phi Beta Kappa. Episcopalian. Club: Harvard (Boston). Home: 111 Lakeview Av Cambridge MA 02138

BROOKS, ROBERT GILES, univ. adminstr.; b. Bloomington, Ill., July 25, 1917; s. James Stokley and Lillie (Cobb) B.; B.Ed., Ill. State U., 1939; M.A., U. Ill., 1942, Ph.D., 1951; m. Joanne Hellstrom, Dec. 26, 1952; children—Robert Giles, James Emmett, Alison. Tchr. Princeville High Sch., 1939-42; teaching asst. U. Ill., 1942-43, counseling bur., 1946-51; prof. English, chmn. lang. and literature N.M. Western U., 1951-55; dean of coll. Franklin Coll., 1955-61; v.p. acad. affairs Sam Houston State U., 1961—. Served to sgt., AUS, 1943-46; ETO. Mem. Sigma Tau Delta, Kappa Delta Pi, Beta Beta Beta. Republican. Episcopalian. Mason. Home: 1609 Av R Huntsville TX 77340

BROOKS, ROBERT MAX, architect; b. Malvern, Ark., Dec. 23, 1906; s. Robert Johnson and Margaret Ann (Orr) B.; B.Arch., U. Tex., 1933; M.S., Mass. Inst. Tech., 1936; m. Marietta Moody, June 29, 1935; children—Carole Louise (Mrs. James S. Doherty), Robert Johnson II. Mem. firm Brooks & Barr, Graeber & White, 1942—; pres. East Side Investment Co., Austin, 1949-61, Brazos Tenth St. Co., 1956-59; sec.-treas. Central Bldg., Inc., 1950-61, pres., 1961—. Cons. architect U. Tex., 1962-67. Projects include design and preparation bldg. plans Am. embassy, Mexico City, new Dept. Labor bldg., Washington; prin. works in Austin, Perry-Brooks Office Bldg., Am. Nat. Bank Bldg., U.S. Fed. Office Bldg. and P.O., Lyndon B. Johnson Library. Vice chmn. archtl. adv. commn. for devel. area Tex. State Capitol, 1958-62; commr. Austin Housing Authority, 1961-70; pres. Tex. Archtl. Found., 1960; mem. Sec. Interior's Potomac River Task Force. Mem. Ednl. Council, Mass. Inst. Tech. Served to lt. C.E. Corps, USNR, 1942-45. Medary scholar, 1934, Fellow A.I.A. (scholarship medal 1934, bd.); mem. Tex. Soc. Architects (pres. 1956, bd.), Sociadad de Arquitectos Mexicanos (hon., listed Libro de Honor), Pi Kappa Alpha. Home: 1500 W 24th St Austin TX 78703 Office: Perry-Brooks Bldg Austin TX 78701

BROOKS, ROBERT ROMANO RAVI, educator; b. Rome, Italy (of Am. parents), Dec. 5, 1905; s. James and Rubina Anna Gaillanza (Ravi) B.; Ph.B., Wesleyan U., 1926; B.A. (Rhodes scholar 1926-29), Oxford U., 1928; Ph.D., Yale, 1935; m. Mary Elizabeth Storer, May 31, 1929; children—Patricia (Mrs. William V. Skidmore, Jr.), Robin Bruce Stirling, Jonathan Storer. Instr. econs. Wesleyan U., 1929-32; instr. indsl. relations Yale, 1931-37; dean New Haven Workers Sch., 1935-37; instr. Bryn Mawr Summer Sch. for Women Workers, 1936; asst. prof. econs. Williams Coll., 1937-45, dean and Orrin Sage prof. econs., 1945-63, 68-71, prof. emeritus, 1971—, dir. grad. tng. Center Devel. Econs., 1959-63; apptd. cultural attache U.S. embassy, New Delhi, India, 1963- 68; chmn. bd. dirs. U.S. Ednl. Found., New Delhi, 1963-68; instr. labor relations U. Cal., 1940. Labor adv. WPB, 1940-41; dir. labor office OPA, 1942-44, sr. exec. officer, 1944-45, dep. adminstr. for information, 1945-46; cons. OPS, 1950; mem. New Eng. Wage Stblzn. Enforcement Commn., 1950-51. Initiator Faculty Children's Tuition Exchange Plan, 1947; exec. dir. Tuition Exchange, Inc., 1954—; mem. Williamstown Capital Outlay Com., 1951-54; chmn. Williamstown Bicentennial Hist. Com., 1953; mem. Williamstown Finance Com., 1969-70; moderator Williamstown Town Meeting, 1970—. Trustee Bennington Coll.; bd. dirs. Mass. higher Edn. Assistance Corp. Recipient President's Certificate of Merit, 1947. Mem. Phi Beta Kappa. Democrat. Author: When Labor Organizes, 1937; Unions of Their Own Choosing, 1938; As Steel Goes, 1940; Williamstown, The First Town Hundred Years, 1953; Love in a Pasture, 1968. Editor Am. Review, New Delhi, 1963-68; Exploration and Research, Stone Age Painting in India, 1971—. Home: Bee Hill Rd Williamstown MA 02167

BROOKS, ROZANNE MARIE, sociologist, educator; b. Williamsport, Pa., Oct. 20, 1922; ward of Donald Parish Brooks; B.A. in Journalism, Pa. State U., 1944, Ph.D., in Sociology, 1957; M.A., U. Mo., 1951. Instr. sociology and journalism Mesa Coll., Grand Junction, Colo., 1950-52; instr. sociology Pa. State U., 1952-56; faculty State U. N.Y. Coll. at Cortland, 1956—, prof. sociology, 1963—, chmn. dept., 1963—, coordinating chmn. social scis., 1966-68. Vis. prof. Kirkland Coll., Clinton, N.Y., 1968-69. State U. N.Y. faculty research fellow, 1959, 66, 67; State U. N.Y. grantee, 1967; fellow N.Y. State Dept. Edn.-Cornell Latin Am. Seminar fellow, Peru, 1963, 64, 65. Mem. Am., Eastern, Upstate (pres. 1966-67) sociol. socs., Am. Acad. Social and Polit. Sci., Soc. Study Social Problems, Am. Assn. U. Profs., Faculty Assn. State U. N.Y. (sec. 1967-69), Theta Sigma Phi, Kappa Delta Pi. Author: Instructor's Manual for Green's Sociology, 5th edit., 1968; also articles. Home: R D 4 Cortland, NY 13045.

BROOKS, SETH ROGERS, clergyman; b. N.Y.C., June 21, 1901; s. John I. and Sarah Collwell (Spencer) B.; B.S., St. Lawrence U., 1922, D.D. (hon.), 1936; B.D., St. Lawrence Theol. Sem., 1924; D.D., Miami U., 1955; m. Corinne H. Hellstrom, Oct. 14, 1925. Ordained to ministry Universalist Ch., 1924; pastor in Little Falls, N.Y., 1924-28, Malden, Mass., 1928-39, Nat. Meml. Ch., Washington, 1939—; chaplain Harvard Summer Sch., 1940-41, resident preacher Harvard Coll., 1946, 1947. Mem. budget com. D.C. Community Chest, 1942-45; adv. bd. Alcoholic Clinic, 1948, Gen. Commn. on Army and Navy Chaplains, 1940-46; chmn. D.C. com. on youth participation, dir. homemakers service 1960 White House Conf. on Children and Youth. Trustee St. Lawrence U., 1935-45. Recipient Nat. Interfraternity Conf. gold medal award, 1966. Interfraternity service award, Lambda Chi Alpha, 1968; Freedoms Found. medal, 1967. Mem. Nat. Conf. Christians and Jews (chmn. clergy com.), Lend a Hand Soc. (dir.), Planned Parenthood Assn. (dir.), Alumni Council St. Lawrence U. (chmn. Alumni Fund), Washington Fedn. Chs. (dir.), Universalist Retirement Soc. (pres.), Com. on Religious Life in Nations Capital (chmn. 1943, 1944), Pilgrim Pastors Union (past pres.), Washington Ministerial Union (pres. 1954-55), Beta Theta Pi (gen. sec., trustee 1950-60, pres. 1960-66), Tau Kappa Alpha. Mason. Clubs: Cosmos, Interchurch. Author: Universalism in Faith and Deed; In Beta's Broad Domain, 1967. Home: 1661 Crescent Pl Washington DC 20009 Office 1810 16th St Washington DC 20009

BROOKS, THEODORE WILLIAM, banker; b. Billorica, Mass., June 30, 1918; s. William O. and Mabelle (Baker) B.; B.A., Williams Coll., 1940; m. Patricia Hubbard, Oct. 12, 1946; 1 son, John W. With Chase Manhattan Bank, N.Y.C., 1940—, sr. v.p., 1965—; dir. Raybestos-Manhattan, Inc. Served with USNR, 1941-46. Home: 92 Sherwood Dr Southport CT 06490 Office: 1 Chase Manhattan Plaza New York City NY 10015

BROOKS, THOMAS JOSEPH, Jr., educator, researcher; b. Starkville, Miss., May 23, 1916; s. Thomas Joseph and Lelia Adeline (Perkins) B.; B.S., U. Fla., 1937; M.S., U. Tenn., 1939; Ph.D., U. N.C., 1942; M.D., Bowman Gray Sch. Medicine, 1945; m. Mary Alice Pollard, Dec. 30, 1941; children—Thomas Joseph III, Michael Pollard, Mary Browning, Melinda Anne. Teaching fellow zoology U. Tenn., 1937-39, U. N.C. Sch. Medicine, Div. Pub. Health, 1939-42; dir. parasitology dept. Bowman Gray Sch. Medicine, parasitologist N.C. Bapt. Hosp., 1942-45, interne, 1945-46; asso. prof. pharmacology U. Miss., Jackson, 1947-48, prof. preventive medicine, chmn. dept., 1953—, cons. tropical medicine U. Hosp., 1955—, asst. dean Sch. Medicine, 1957—. Vis. prof. preventive medicine U. Costa Rica, San Jose, 1962- 63, Keio U., Tokyo, 1968; vis. prof. pub. health Kyoto (Japan) U., 1968-69; med. dir. U. Hosp., Fla. State U., 1948-52; cons. tropical medicine VA Hosp., Jackson, 1955—; UN cons. med.

edn., India, 1966. Mem. bd. examiners Am. Bd. Microbiology, 1967—. Served with USNR, 1953-54. Assn. Am. Med. Colls. grantee for study tropical diseases Tulane U. Sch. Tropical Medicine, 1943; Assn. Am. Med. Colls. travel grantee, Latin Am., 1944, Rockefeller Found. travel grantee, 1952; fellow China Med. Bd. N.Y. (P.R. and Haiti), 1956; La. State U. fellow in tropical medicine, 1960; Alan Gregg fellow in med. edn., Japan, S.E. Asia, 1968. Mem. Am. Pub. Health Assn. (com. on infectious disease), Am. Soc. Tropical Medicine and Hygiene, Assn. Am. Med. Colls. (chmn. com. student aspects internat. med. edn. 1961-65, mem. various coms.), Sigma Xi, Omicron Delta Kappa, Phi Delta Kappa, Kappa Kappa Psi. Author: Essentials of Medical Parasitology, 1963. Mem. editorial com. Control of Communicable Disease in Man, 11th edit., 1970. Contbr. articles to profl. jours. Home: 750 Lenox Dr Jackson MS 39211

BROOKS, VERNON BERNARD, scientist, educator; b. Berlin, Germany, May 10, 1923; s. Martin and Margarete (Hahlo) B.; B.A., U. Toronto, 1946, Ph.D., 1952; M.Sc., U. Chgo., 1948; m. Nancy Fraser, June 29, 1950; children—Martin Fraser, Janet Mary, Nora Vivian. Lectr., asst. prof. McGill U., Montreal, Que., Can., 1950-56; asst. prof., asso. prof. Rockefeller Inst., N.Y.C., 1956-64; prof. physiology N.Y. Med. Coll 1964-71, chmn. dept., 1964-69; prof., chmn. dept. physiology U. Western Ont., London, Can., 1971—. Vis. fellow Australian Nat. U., Canberra, 1954-55; spl. research brain mechanisms in motor control. Mem. Am. (editorial bd. jour. 1962-65, editor sect. neurobiology 1969-71), Canadian (asso. editor 1969—) physiol. socs., Assn. Research Nervous and Mental Diseases, Internat. Brain Research Orgn., Can. Assn. U. Profs., A.A.A.S., Sigma Xi, Unitarian. Home: 42 Hampton Circle London Ontario Canada

BROOKS, WILLIAM F., editor and writer; b. Kansas City, Mo., Nov. 2, 1902; s. James Lucian and Willa May (McCully) B.; student U. Mo., 1920; m. Louise Daly, July 10, 1944; 1 son, William F. Newspaper work Sedalia (Mo.) Capital, 1917; worked various newspapers in Middle West, including Kansas City Star, 1920-26; joined A.P., 1926, served in Washington and N.Y.C. as exec. editor feature service, 1926-30, exec. asst. to gen mgr., 1930-33, exec. news editor, 1933-37; mng. dir. The Asso. Press of Great Britain, London, 1937-40; advt. agy. bus., N.Y.C., 1940-41; exec. editor Forbeds mag., 1941-42; dir. news and spl. events, also dir. internat. relations, NBC, 1942-46, v.p., 1946-50, chief pub. relations officer, 1950-52; corp. cons., 1953-59; pres. William F. Brooks & Assos., Inc., N.Y.C., 1959-61; editorial staff N.Y. Daily News, 1961—. Presbyn. Clubs: Press (Washington); Dutch Treat, Overseas Press (N.Y.C.); Savage (London, Eng.). Author: Radio News Writing, 1948. Home: 230 E 48th St New York City NY 10017 Office: 220 E 42d St New York City NY 10017

BROOM, H.N., educator; B.S., Sam Houston State Coll.; M.B.A., Ph.D., U. Tex. Prof., chmn. dept. mgmt. and statistics Hankamer Sch. Bus., Baylor U., Waco, Tex. Office: Hankamer Sch Bus Baylor U Waco TX

BROOM, LEONARD, educator; b. Boston, Nov. 8, 1911; B.S., Boston U., 1933, A.M., 1934; Ph.D., Duke, 1937; m. Gretchan Noel Cooke, Aug. 31, 1940; children—Karl Cooke, Dorothy Howard (Mrs. Russell Kent Darroch). Vis. instr. Clemson Coll., 1937-38; instr. sociology Kent State U., 1938-41; asst. prof. sociology U. Cal. at Los Angeles, 1941-48, asso. prof., 1948-53, prof., 1953-59, chmn. dept. anthropology and sociology, 1952-57; prof., chmn. dept. sociology U. Tex., 1959-66, Ashbel Smith prof. sociology, 1963-71; vis. prof. Inst. Advanced Studies, Australian Nat. U., Canberra, 1964-65, 69-70, prof., 1971—. Fulbright research fellow B.W.I., 1950-51; faculty fellow Fund for Advancement Edn., 1953-54; hon. fellow Australian Nat. U., 1958; Guggenheim fellow, 1958; fellow Center for Advanced Study in Behavioral Scis., 1962-63. Fellow Am. Anthrop. Assn., Royal Anthrop. Inst., Am. Sociol. Assn. (v.p. 1962-63); mem. Inst. Internat. des Civilisations Differentes, Pacific Sociol. Soc. (pres. 1951), Sociol. Research Assn., Population Assn. Am. Author: (with Ruth Riemer), Removal and Return, 1949; (with Frank G. Speck) Cherokee Dance and Drama, 1951; (with Philip Selznick Sociology, 1955, 4th edit., 1968; (with John Kitsuse), The Managed Casualty, 1956; (with Norval Glenn) Transformation of the Negro American, 1965, 67. Editor Am. Sociol. Rev., 1955-57. Contbr. articles to profl. jours. Address: Dept Sociology Inst Advanced Studies Australian Nat University Canberra ACT 2600 Australia

BROOM, WILLIAM WESCOTT, newspaper editor; b. Dieterich, Ill., July 12, 1924; s. Albert M. and Wilhelmina (Martens) B.; B.S. in Journalism, U. Ill., 1948; m. Adeline Birdsall Smith, Mar. 30, 1957; children—William Wescott, Timothy Caleb. Mng. editor Momence (Ill.) Progress-Reporter, 1948-49; reporter El Paso (Tex.) Herald-Post, 1950-52; pub. relations with S.P. Ry., 1952-54; feature writer San Jose (Cal.) Mercury, 1954-55; Washington corr. Ridder Publs. Inc., 1955-65; editor Long Beach (Cal.) Ind. and Press-Telegram, 1965-70, chief Washington bur. Ridder Publs., 1970—. Mem. adv. bd. Cal. State Coll., Long Beach, 1966-70; exec. bd. Long Beach council Boy Scouts Am. Served with AUS, 1943-46. Recipient Best Column award Ill. Press Assn., 1948. Clubs: National Press, Federal City (Washington); International City (Long Beach); Chevy Chase. Home: 1114 Spring Hill Rd McLean VA 22101 Office: 1325 E St NW Washington DC 20004

BROOMELL, G. LUPTON, instrument mfg. co. exec.; b. Phila., Feb. 2, 1916; s. George Lupton and Anna (Pettit) B.; B.S. in Elec. Engring., Swarthmore Coll., 1937; m. Elizabeth Dobson, Aug. 27, 1938; children—Louise (Mrs. John Harris), Barbara, (Mrs. Thomas Dickson), Margery (Mrs. John Swanson), John. Formerly v.p. systems, sr. v.p. mfg., Leeds & Northrup Co., now exec. v.p. operations, also dir.; dir. market area II bd. 1st Pa. Banking & Trust Co.; dir. Phila. Mfrs. Mut. Ins. Co. Pres. North Penn United Fund; chmn. Lower Gwynedd Zoning Bd. Bd. mgrs. Swarthmore Coll. Registered profl. engr. Mem. instrument Soc. Am., I.E.E.E., Sci. Apparatus Makers Assn., Franklin Inst., Mfrs. Assn. Delaware Valley (1st v.p.), Pa. (councilor, dir.), North Penn (pres. 1967) chambers commerce. Mem. Soc. of Friends. Club: Penllyn. Patentee in field. Home: Gwynedd Valley PA 19437 Office: Leeds & Northrup Co North Wales PA 19454

BROOMFIELD, WILLIAM S., congressman; b. Royal Oak, Mich., Apr. 28, 1922; s. S.C. and Fern Broomfield; student Mich. State U.; m. Jane Thompson, 1951; children—Susan, Nancy, Barbara. Mem. 85th to 92d congresses from 18th Dist. Mich. Prin. del. to Gen. Assembly of UN, 1967-68; dist. del. NATO Parliamentarians Conf., 1960; mem. delegation to Can.-U.S. Interparliamentary Group; Congl. adviser to U.S. delegation to Geneva Disarmament Conf., 1970. Mem. Mich. Ho. of Reps., 1948-54, Mich. Senate, 1954-56. Mem. Am. Legion. Republican. Presbyn. Mason, Odd Fellow, Optimist, Lion. Home: S Lafayette St Royal Oak MI 48067 Office: Rayburn House Office Bldg Washington DC 20515

BROPHY, BRIGID, author; b. London, Eng., June 12, 1929; d. John and Charis Weare (Grundy) Brophy; student U. Oxford; m. Michael Levey, June 12, 1954; 1 dau., Katharine Jane. Author: Hackenfeller's Ape, 1953; The King of a Rainy Country, 1956; Black Ship to Hell, 1962; Flesh, 1962; The Finishing Touch, 1963; The Snow Ball, 1964; Mozart the Dramatist, 1964; Don't Never Forget, 1966; The Burglar (play), 1967; co-author Fifty Works of English and American Literature We Could Do Without, 1967; Black and White: A Portrait of Aubrey Beardsley, 1968; In Transit, 1969; also numerous articles. Address: 185 Old Brompton Rd London SW 5 England

BROPHY, FRANCIS L., chem. co. exec.; b. 1925; B.S., St. Joseph's Coll., 1950; married. Bookkeeper, Columbia Boiler Co., 1950-52; tax mgr. Price Waterhouse & Co., 1952-62; asst. tax. mgr. tax dept. Philco Corp., 1962-64; mgr. corporate taxes Nat. Distillers & Chem. Corp., N.Y.C., 1964-67, asst. comptroller, 1967-69, comptroller, 1969-71, v.p., comptroller, 1971—. Served with USNR, 1943-46. C.P.A. Office: Nat Distillers Bldg New York City NY 10016

BROPHY, FRANK CULLEN, banker, rancher, b. Bisbee, Ariz., Nov. 16, 1894; s. William Henry and Ellen (Goodbody) B.; grad. Phillips Acad., Andover, 1913; A.B., Yale, 1917; m. Sallie Ropes Blake, May 3, 1919; children—Alice Blake (Mrs. John T. McChesney), William H., Anthony Blake, Sallie Cullen (Mrs. George J.W. Goodman), Frank C., Mary Kathleen, James M.R. Dir. Ariz. Central Bank, Flagstaff, No. Ariz. Securities Co., Los Angeles, 1923-27; dir., exec. v.p. Phoenix Nat. Bank, Phoenix Savs. Bank & Trust Co., 1923-30; dir., pres. Bank of Douglas (Ariz.), 1935-55, chmn. of Douglas, Phoenix, 1955-59; pres. Phoenix Date Co., 1927-55, Gen. Grocery Co., 1941-58, Gen. Sales Co., 1943-58, PM Sales Co., 1957—, Libbey Fruit Packing Co.; owner, operator Babacomari Ranch, Elgin, Ariz., 1937—, El Fresnal Ranch, Auga Prieta, Sonora, Mexico, 1942-48. Mem. nat. council John Birch Soc., 1961—. Trustee St. Joseph's Hosp., Barrows Neur. Inst., 1952-68, Brophy Coll. Prep. Dir. Am. Inst. for Fgn. Trade, 1946- 55. Founder Maricopa County Taxpayers Assn.; mem. Ariz. State Fair Commn., 1938-40; chmn. Ariz. Racing Commn., 1949-53, mem., 1970—; Ariz. Semicentennial Com., 1960. Mem. adv. bd. for Am. 1955; nat. bd. Campaign for 48 States, 1956. Decorated comdr. Sovereign Order of St. John of Jerusalem, Knights of Malta. Clubs: University (Seattle); Athletic (Los Angeles); Old Pueblo (Tucson); Phoenix Country. Author: Arizona Sketch Book. Contbr. articles to Commonweal, Cath. World, Ariz. Hwys. Home: 7601 N Central Av Phoenix AZ 85020 Office: PO Box 9338 Phoenix AZ 85020

BROPHY, GERALD B., ret. lawyer; b. Yonkers, N.Y., Nov. 12, 1901 s. Patrick F. and Mary E. (Renahan) B.; A.B., Columbia, 1924, LL.B., 1926. Admitted to N.Y. State bar, 1927, Cal. bar, 1957; asso. firm Chadbourne, Parke, Whiteside, Wolff & Brophy and predecessors, N.Y.C., 1926-34, partner, 1934-55; dir. N. Am. Aviation, Inc., Los Angeles, 1940-42, 46-61, gen. counsel, v.p., 1955, sr. v.p., 1958-61, sr. counsel, 1961-66; dir. Oppenheim Collins & Co., Inc., 1935-42, Gen. Aniline & Film Corp., 1948-53. Spl. cons. to U.S. sec. of State, 1950-51. U.S. rep. Internat. Civil Aviation Orgn., Montreal, 1945-46; chief, U.S. delegation North Atlantic Air Conf., Dublin (Eire), 1946; cons. to U.S. delegation Gen. Assembly of Internat. Civil Aviation Orgn., 1947; mem. adv. council Congressional Aviation Policy Bd., 1948. Served as maj., later col., USAAF, 1942-45; col., USAF Res., 1945-53. Decorated Legion of Merit. Mem. Bar Assn. City of N.Y., Am., N.Y. State bar assns., Psi Upsilon, Phi Delta Phi. Roman Catholic. Clubs: University (N.Y.C.); Army and Navy (Washington). Home: Hotel Gramatan Pondfield Rd Bronxville NY 01708

BROPHY, GERALD PATRICK, geologist, educator; b. Kansas City, Mo., Sept. 11, 1926; s. William Edward and Dorothy (Johnson) B.; A.B., Columbia, 1951, M.A., 1953, Ph.D., 1954; M.A., Amherst Coll., 1968; m. Joanne Young, Mar. 29, 1951; children—William Michael, James Gerald, Thomas Andrew. Instr., Amherst (Mass.) Coll., 1954-56, asst. prof., 1956-62, asso. prof., 1962-67, prof., 1967—; research prof. U. Baghdad, Iraq, 1965-66; curator Pratt Mus. Geology; cons. numerous mining cos. Served to lt. (j.g.) USNR, 1943- 46. Fellow Geol. Soc. Am., Am. Soc. Phys. Chemists; mem. Mineral. Soc. Am., Mineral. Soc. Can., Sigma Xi, Phi Kappa Psi. Roman Catholic. Rotarian. Contbr. articles profl. jours. Home: 70 Red Gate Lane Amherst MA 01002

BROPHY, JAMES DAVID, Jr., educator; b. Mt. Vernon, N.Y., Oct. 5, 1926; s. James David and Mildred (Stall) B.; student Mass. Inst. Tech., 1944-45; B.A., Amherst Coll., 1949; M.A., Columbia, 1950, Ph.D., 1965; postgrad. U. Dijon, 1950-51; m. Elizabeth Bergen, Mar. 26, 1951; children—Sheila, David, Katharine, Elizabeth, James Mark. Instr. English, Iona Coll., New Rochelle, N.Y., 1951-58, asst. prof., 1958-64, asso. prof., 1964-68, prof., chmn. dept., 1968—. Served with USNR, 1945-46. Fulbright fellow, France, 1950-51; N.Y. State scholar in internat. studies, 1965; recipient Pro Operis medal Iona Coll., 1971. Mem. Modern Lang. Assn., Northeastern Modern Lang. Assn. Author: Edith Sitwell, 1968; W.H. Auden, 1970. Editor: The Achievement of Galileo, 1962; Aspects of Modern Irish Literature, 1972. Home: 35 Crystal St Harrison NY 10528 also Ocean View Dr Southampton NY 11968 Office: Iona Coll New Rochelle NY 10801

BROPHY, JAMES JOHN, physicist, univ. ofcl.; b. Chgo., June 6, 1926; s. James J. and Ella Helen (Nerad) B.; B.S. in Elec. Engring., Ill. Inst. Tech., 1947, M.S. in Physics, 1949, Ph.D. in Physics, 1951; m. Muriel Ann Johnson, Aug. 26, 1949; children—James J., John R., Thomas C. Research physicist Armour Research Found. of Ill. Inst. Tech., 1951-53, supr. solid states physics, 1953- 56, asst. dir. physics div., 1956-61, dir. tech. devel. of Found., 1961- 63, v.p. for tech. dvel., 1963-66, acad. v.p., 1967—. Fellow Am. Phys. Soc.; mem. Sigma Xi. Author: Semiconductor Devices, 1965; Basic Electronics for Scientists, 1966; co-author Electronic Processes in Materials, 1963. Co-editor: Organic Semi-conductors. Contbr. articles profl. jours. Patentee on semiconductors, magnetic devices. Home: 4901 Lawn Av Western Springs IL 60558 Office: 10 W 35th St Chicago IL 60616

BROPHY, JOSEPH THOMAS, ins. co. exec.; b. N.Y.C., Oct. 25, 1933; s. Joseph R. and Mary (Mitchell) B.; B.S. cum laude, Fordham U., 1957; m. Carole A. Johnson, June 8, 1957; children—Thomas J., David W., Patricia J., Marueen A., Kathleen M. Mathematician, Vitro Labs., West Orange, N.J., 1957; dir. mgmt. information systems Prudential Ins. Co., Newark, 1957-67; v.p. Huggins & Co., cons. actuaries and mgmt. cons., Phila., 1967-68; cons. actuary Palisades Life Ins. Co., 1968—; v.p., chief actuary Bankers Nat. Life Ins. Co., 1968—; cons. in field, 1967—. Trustee OEO Waron Poverty Program, Franklin Twp., N.J. 1965-66. Served with USMCR, 1949- 50, AUS, 1952-54. Fellow Soc. Actuaries; mem. Am. Acad. Actuaries, N.Y. Actuaries Club. Club: Cedar Hill (Somerset, N.J.). Home: 7 Grier Rd Somerset NJ 08873 Office: Littleton Rd Parsippany NJ 07054

BROPHY, THEODORE F., telephone co. exec.; b. N.Y.C., Apr. 4, 1923; s. Frederick H. and Muriel W. (Osborne) B.; grad. Kent Sch., 1941; A.B., Yale, 1944; LL.B., Harvard, 1949; m. Sallie M. Showwalter, Sept. 16, 1950; children—Stephen F., Anne R. Admitted to N.Y. bar; asso. with firm Room, Balantine, Harlan, Bushby & Palmer, N.Y.C., 1949-55; gen. counsel Lummus Co., 1955- 58; counsel Gen. Telephone Co., N.Y.C., 1958-59, v.p., gen. counsel, 1959—; exec. v.p., gen. counsel Gen. Telephone Service Corp.; v.p., gen. counsel Gen. Telephone & Electronics Corp., 1959—; v.p., gen. counsel, dir. Gen. Telephone & Electronics Lab., Inc.; now exec. v.p., gen. counsel Gen. Telephone and Electronics Corp. Bd. trustees General Telephone & Electronics Found. Served to lt. (s.g.) USNR, 1944-46. Mem. Am., N.Y. State bar assns., Am. Fgn. Law Assn., Assn. Bar City N.Y., Fed. Communications Bar Assn. Home: Rocky Craig Rd Cos Cob CT 06807 Office: 730 3d Av New York City NY 10017

BROQUIST, HARRY PEARSON, educator, biochemist; b. Chgo., Jan. 23, 1919; s. Eric A. and Olive (Pearson) B.; B.S., Beloit (Wis.) Coll., 1940; M.S., U. Wis., 1941, Ph.D., 1949; m. Marion E. Englof, July 25, 1942; children—Alan H., Lynn M. Biochemist, Lederle Labs., Pearl River, N.Y., 1941-46, group leader microbiology, 1949-58; prof. biochemistry U. Ill. at Urbana, 1958-69; prof. biochemistry Vanderbilt U., Nashville, 1969—; cons. NIH, NASA. Recipient Borden award in nutrition, 1969. NSF fellow, 1965-66. Mem. Am. Soc. Biol. Chemistry, Am. Inst. Nutrition,, Am. Chem. Soc., A.A.A.S. Contbr. articles profl. jours., chpts. to books. Patentee in field. Home: 4629 Benton Smith Rd Nashville TN 37215

BRORBY, MELVIN, advt. exec.; b. Decorah, Ia., Sept. 20, 1894; s. Martin J. and Louise (Wimmer) B.; student Oxford U., 1919; A.B., U. Wis., 1920; student U. Strasbourg, 1920, The Sorbonne, 1920-21, Free Sch. Polit. Scis., Paris, 1921-22; m. Rowena Williams, Jan. 1, 1927; children—Harry, Virginia (Mrs. Wesley Horner). Vice pres. Needham, Harper & Steers, Inc., (formerly known as Needham, Louis & Brorby, Inc.), advt. agy., Chgo., 1925—, now sr. v.p. Gov. life memb. Art Inst. Chgo.; mem. citizens coms. U. Chgo., U. Ill., mem. Orchestral Assn.; mem. bd. dirs. of Nat. Outdoor Advt. Bur. Sponsor Nat. Soc. Crippled Children and Adults; mem. Stevenson Com.; trustee, v.p. Johnson Found. Mem. Soc. of Contemporary Am. Art (past pres.), Inst. Internat. Edn. (trustee; mem. midwest adv. com.), Am. Assn. Advt. Agys. (past chmn.), Art Club Chgo., Oxford Soc. (past br. sec.), Chgo. Council Fgn. Relations (dir. past pres.), N.Y. Council Fgn. Relations, Phi Beta Kappa, Phi Gamma Delta, Artus. Clubs: Tavern, Arts, Lake Shore (past pres.), Mid-America (Chgo.), Century (N.Y.C.); Flossmoor (Ill.) Country. Home: 1320 N State Pkwy Chicago IL 60610 also 2775 Lake Shore Av Holland MI 49423 Office: 401 N Michigan Av Chicago IL 60611

BROSH, ZVI, Israeli diplomat; b. Berlin, Germany, July 6, 1922; s. Paul and Edith (Friedlaender) Boroschek; student Beit Hakerem Secondary Sch., Jerusalem, 1936-40; m. Dorit Lilian Audrey Goldston, Oct. 26, 1948; children—Edward Oded, Liora Shlomit. Asst. controller news Palestine Broadcasting Service, 1946-50; dir. Israel Armed Forces Radio, 1950-54; asst. to chief edn. officer Israel Army, 1954-60; joined Israel Fgn. Service, 1960; press counselor Israel Govt. Mission, Cologne, Germany, 1960-63; dep. dir. information div. Israel Fgn. Ministry, 1963-64, acting dir. internat. coop. div., 1965-66; charge d'affaires, Colombo, Ceylon, 1966-68; ambassador to Burma, also non-resident ambassador Maldive Republic and minister Colombo, 1968-70; minister information Israeli embassy, Washington, 1970—. Mem. Israel Govt. Survey Mission on TV (U.S., Can., U.K., France), 1953; mem. Israel del. congress edn. ministers UNESCO, Teheran, Iran, 1965; chmn. staff com. Israel Fgn. Ministry, Jerusalem, 1965-66; mil. commentator Israel Broadcasting Service, 1955-58, polit. commentator, 1963-65. Bd. dirs. Agrl. Research Center, Rehouot, Israel, 1965-66, Internat. Training Center for Community Services, Haifa, 1965-66. Served with Royal Navy (Gt. Britain), 1942-46, to lt. col. Israel Army, 1948, 50-60. Home: 5914 Onondaga Rd Bethesda MD 20016 Office: 1621 22d St NW Washington DC 20008

BROSHOUS, CHARLES RUSSELL, army officer; b. Atchison, Kan., Feb. 6, 1908; s. Walter Everett and Stella May (Robinson) B.; B.S., U.S. Mil. Acad., 1933; M.S., U. Cal. at Berkeley, 1938; m. Barbara Blood, May 24, 1937; chilren—Charles Russell, Barbara Blood. Commd. 2d lt. U.S. Army, 1933, advanced through grades to col., 1943; various assignments, U.S., 1933-42; dep. comdr., chief staff South Base Sects. Communications, ETO, 1942-44; chief staff Advance Sect. Communications Zone, ETO, 1944-45; dep. chief staff Communications Zone, ETO, 1945-46; faculty U.S. Mill Acad., West Point, N.Y., 1946—, prof., head earth, space and graphic scis. dept., 1961—, also dir. acad. expansion planning group. Decorated D.S.M., Legion of Merit with oak leaf cluster. Mem. Am. Soc. Engring. Edn. Home: Quarters 89 West Point NY 10996

BROSIN, HENRY WALTER, educator, psychiatrist; b. Blackwood, Va., July 6, 1904; s. Martin and Marie (Danowski) B.; A.B., U. Wis., 1927, M.D., 1933; postgrad. (Commonwealth Fund fellow in Psychiatry) U. Colo., 1934-37, (Rockefeller fellow) Inst. Psychoanalysis, Chgo., 1937-40; m. Ruth Hatfield, 1949; 1 son, Lloyd Wisdom. Rotating intern Cin. Gen. Hosp., 1933-34; fellow Colo. Psychopathic Hosp., Denver, 1934-37; staff div. psychiatry U. Chgo., 1937-41, prof., head div. 1946; dir. Western Psychiat. Inst. and Clinics, 1951-69; psychiat. cons. Office Surgeon Gen., Washington, 1944-64; prof., chmn. dept. psychiatry U. Pitts. 1951-69; prof. psychiatry U. Ariz. Coll. Medicine, Tucson, 1969—. Mem. Social Sci. Research Council; fellow Center Advanced Study Behavioral Scis., 1956-66; mem. div. med. scis. Nat. Acad. Sci., NRC, 1958-68, mem. naval med. research com. Served as col. M.C., AUS, 1941-46. Decorated Legion of Merit; recipient Distinguished Service award U. Chgo. Sch. Medicine, 1952; Med. Alumni citation U. Wis., 1962; Col. Wm. S. Porter award Assn. Mil. Surgeons U.S., 1967. Diplomate Am. Bd. Psychiatry and Neurology (pres. 1961). Fellow Am. Acad. Arts and Scis., Rorschach Inst., A.C.P., Am. Psychiat. Assn. (councillor 1948-51, pres. 1967-68); mem. A.M.A., Phila. (v.p. 1960-61), Chgo. psychoanalytic assn., A.A.A.S., Am. Psychol. Assn., Am. Coll. Psychiatrists (pres. 1970-71), Am. Soc. Research Psychosomatic Problems (councillor), Assn. Research Nervous and Mental Diseases, Pitts. Neuropsychiat. Soc., Pitts. Psychoanalytic Inst. and Soc., Allegheny County Med. Soc., Group Advancement Psychiatry (pres. 1961-63), Nat. Assn. Mental Health, Soc. Biol. Psychiatry, Royal Psychol. Assn. (hon), Sigma Xi, Alpha Omega Alpha. Club: Cosmos. Asso. edit. Am. Jour. Psychiatry, 1965—. Contbr. articles to profl. jours. Home: 240 Sierra Vista Dr Tucson AZ 85719

BROSIO, MANLIO, Italian diplomat, NATO ofcl.; b. Turin, Italy, July 10, 1897; s. Edoardo and Fortunata (Curadelli) B.; Law Degree, Turin U., 1920; m. Clotilde Brosio, Oct. 1, 1936. Practice law, Turin, 1922-43; mem. Liberal Party, central sec. Liberal Revolution movement, 1922-25, sec.-gen. Party, 1944-45; mem. underground Nat. Liberation Com., 1943-44; minister without portfolio, Bonomi Govt., 1944; v.p. Council of Ministers, Parri Govt., 1945; minister def., 1845-46, ambassador to Moscow, 1947-51, to London, 1952-54, to U.S., 1955-61, to France 1961-64; sec. gen. NATO 1964-71. Served with Alpini Corps. Italian Army, 1916-19. Contbr. articles profl. jours. Home: Corso Umberto 29 bis Torino Italy

BROSIUS, WILLIAM BRINTON, banker; b. Avondale, Pa., May 29, 1902; s. J. Howard and Alice (Brintoñ) B.; A.B., Swarthmore Coll., 1922; m. Anna S. Roberts, Apr. 27, 1927; children—William Brinton, Anne S. Cashier Nat. Bank of Malvern, Pa., 1926-34, Berwyn (Pa.) Nat. Bank 1934-39; cashier Nat. Bank of Chester County & Trust Co., West Chester, Pa., 1939-46, pres., 1946-69, chmn. bd., 1969-70; vice chmn. S.E. Nat. Bank of Pa., Chester, 1970—. Mem. Chester County Planning Commn., 1960—. Bd. dirs. Chester County Hosp. Home: 18 Bodine Rd Berwyn PA 19312 Office: 17 N High St West Chester PA 19380

BROSKI, GERALD STEPHEN, metal products co. exec.; b. Grand Rapids, Mich., Dec. 23, 1933; s. Floyd Leonard and Margaret Bell (Tolhurst) B.; B.A., Mich. State U., 1955; m. Suzanne Marie Maher, May 3, 1958; children—Michael, Lisa Ann, Kurt. With Seidman & Seidman, C.P.A.'s, Grand Rapids, 1957-63; with Rockford Products Corp. (Ill.), 1963—, treas., 1967—. Bd. dirs. St. Anthony Hosp., 1967—, sec., 1969—; bd. dirs. No. Ill. Blood Bank, 1970—, v.p., 1971—; bd. dirs. Rockford Credit Bur., treas., 1970—. Served to 1st lt. AUS, 1955-57. C.P.A., Mich. Mem. Am. Inst. C.P.A.'s, Nat. Assn. Accountants, Rockford Area C. of C. (treas., dir.). Club: Forest Hills Country (Rockford). Home: 1721 Parkview Rockford IL 61107 Office: 707 Harrison Rockford IL 61101

BROSNAN, JOHN FRANCIS, lawyer; b. N.Y. City, May 23, 1890; s. Michael L. and Nora B. (Cotter) B.; student De LaSalle Inst., 1904-09; B.S. in C.E., Manhattan Coll., 1911, M.A., 1913, hon. LL.D., 1935, Fordham, 1949; LL.B., N.Y.U., 1914, J.D., 1914, LL.D., 1958; D.C.L., St. Johns U., 1952; LL.D., Cath. U. Am., 1955, Iona College, 1958, Union College, 1959, LeMoyne College, 1959, Canisius College, 1959, Nat. U. Of Ireland, 1960; D.C.S., Pace Coll., 1957; Pd.D., St. Bonaventure U. 1957; m. Irene V. Bannin, June 30, 1923; children—John Patrick, Mary Ellen (Rev. Sister Mary Ellen), Vincent Michael. Admitted to the New York bar, 1915, District of Columbia bar, 1966; legal sec. to Hon. John P. Cohalan, 1915-21, law asst. to surrogates Cohalan and Foley, 1922-23; mem. firm Mudge, Rose, Guthrie, Alexander and predecessors, N.Y.C., 1928-69; counsel firm Cusack & Stiles, N.Y.C., 1970—. Apptd. by Gov., mem. N.Y. State Temporary Commn. Against Discrimination, 1944, adv. bd. Prevailing Rate Wages on Pub. Works, 1946. Trustee State U., 1948, Moreland commr. investigating harness racing, 1953; elected regent Univ. State of N.Y., 1949, vice chancellor of regents, 1957, chancellor, 1957-61. Trustee Roger Williams Straus Memorial Found., Catholic Charities, Archdiocese of N.Y. Mem. Cardinal's Com. Laity for Catholic Charities; mem. bds. Servants of Relief for Incurable Cancer, Marquette League for Cath. Indian Missions, Health and Hosp. Council N.Y., St. Vincent's Hosp., N.Y.C., N.Y. Foundling Hosp., William Nelson Cromwell Found.; sr. trustee Manhattan College, chairman, 1967-70. Chmn. N.Y. Brotherhood Week of Nat. Conf. Christians and Jews, 1958. Served as pvt. U.S. Army, World War I. Decorated Bros. Christian Schs. (affiliated mem.), Knight of Malta (bd. founders), knight Grand Cross Holy Sepulchre; recipient medal Manhattan Coll., 1938, medal St. De LaSalle, 1951; medal Am. Irish Hist. Soc. 1958; medal N.Y. Acad. Pub. Edn., 1958, George Washington Honor medal Freedoms Found. at Valley Forge, 1961, LaSallian medal of Bros. of Christian Schs., Manhattan Coll., 1967. Fellow Am. Bar Found.; mem. Am. Judicature Soc., N.Y. County Lawyers Assn. (past.pres.), Am. N.Y. State bar assns., Soc. Med. Jurisprudence, Assn. of Bar of City of N.Y., U.S. Catholic Hist. Soc. Catholic Lawyers Guilds, Am. Irish Hist. Soc. (council), Manhattan Coll. Alumni Soc. (past pres., Medal of Honor 1960), Blessed Sacrament Conf. of St. Vincent de Paul Soc. (past pres.), Xavier Alumni Sodality (past pres.), Soc. Friendly Sons of St. Patrick (past pres.), Delta Chi. K.C. (hon. life; Charles Carroll Gen. Assembly award 1960). Club: City Midday (N.Y.C.). Home: 945 Fifth Av New York City NY 10021 Office: 61 Broadway New York City NY 10006

BROSNAN, THOMAS JOSEPH, power co. exec.; b. Washington, Apr. 7, 1905; s. John D. and Margaret (Hanlon) B.; B.S. in Elec. Engring., Catholic U. Am., 1925; m. Jean Swindeman, Nov. 3, 1931; children—Thomas Joseph, Jean A. (Mrs. George F. Leger), John Houston. With Westinghouse Electric Co., 1925-30, gen. engr., 1926-30; distbn. engr. Buffalo Niagra Electric Power Corp., 1930-50; chief engr. Western div. Niagara Mohawk Power Corp., Syracuse, N.Y., 1950-63, v.p., asst. chief engr., 1963-66, v.p., chief engr., 1966—, also dir.; v.p., chief engr. Canadian Niagara Power Co., Ltd., 1966—; v.p., dir. St. Lawrence Power Co. Former pres., dir. Cerebral Palsy Assn. Western N.Y.; past trustee United Fund Erie County. Fellow I.E.E.E. (past chmn. Niagara Frontier sect., past chmn. transmission and distbn. com.), Edison Electric Inst. (past. chmn. transmission and distbn. com.; exec. com. engring. and operating div.), Conf. Internationale des Grands Reseaux Electriques, Am. Assn. Engring. Edn., N.E. Power Coordination Council (past chmn. system design coordinating com.), Atomic Indsl. Forum, Am. Standards Assn. Clubs: Century; Buffalo Yacht. Home: 138 Edgemere Lane Fayetteville NY 13066 Office: 300 Erie Blvd Syracuse NY 13202

BROSS, JOHN ADAMS, govt. ofcl.; b. Chgo., Jan. 17, 1911; s. Mason and Isabel Foster (Adams) B.; student Chgo. Latin Sch., Groton Sch.; A.B., Harvard, 1933, LL.B., 1936; m. Priscilla Prince, June 1936; children—Wendy, John, Justine; m. 2d. Joanne Bass, Oct. 28. 1947; 1 son, Peter F. Admitted to N.Y. bar, 1938, practiced, N.Y.C., 1936-42; 46-49, asso. firm Parker & Duryee, N.Y.C., mem. firm, 1941—; asst. gen. counsel U.S. High Commr. to Germany, 1949-51; U.S. govt. cons. fgn. affairs, 1951-57, 60—; adviser, coordinator Am. embassy, Bonn, Germany, 1957-63, dep. to dir. of central intelligence for programs evaluation, 1963—. Staff mem. task force on nat. mil. establishment, Hoover Commn., 1948. Served from 2d lt. to col., USAAF, 1942-46. Decorated Legion of Merit, Bronze Star; Order Brit. Empire; King Christian X Medal of Liberty. Mem. Assn. Bar City N.Y. (chmn. com. state legislation 1946-49), Council on Fgn. Relations N.Y. Clubs: River, Harvard (N.Y.C.). Home: 4501 Crest Lane McLean VA 22101

BROSSMAN, WALTER ROBERT, coll. cons.; b. N.Y.C., Nov. 24, 1920; s. Walter Werner and Mabel Adams (Kelly) B.; A.B., Allegheny Coll., 1942; m. Susan J. Bertrand, Sept. 23, 1951 (dec. 1958); children—Bruce W., Nancy J.; m. 2d, Virginia Kerlin, Nov. 22, 1959; chilren—Robert Kerlin, Ann Baldwin, Beth Allison. Reporter, sports editor Tribune Newspapers, Meadville, Pa., 1942-44; dir. publicity Allegheny Coll., 1946-47; dir. pub. information Cornell U., 1947-56; v.p. Colo. Coll., 1956-69; cons., 1969—. Cons., Assn. Governing Bds. of Univs. and Colls., others; asso. cons. Frantzreb and Pray Assos., Inc., N.Y.C. Served in USNR, 1944-46. Mem. Am. Coll. Pub. Relations Assn., Sigma Delta Chi, Phi Sigma Iota, Phi Delta Theta. Mem. United Ch. of Christ (dir. Colo. conf. 1967-70). Clubs: Broadmoor Golf, Winter Night. Home: 1508 Wood Av Colorado Springs CO 80907

BROSTRON, CURTIS, chief police St. Louis; b. Winesap, Tenn., Feb. 5, 1905; s. Emil and Ellen (Owensbey) B.; grad. FBI Nat. Acad.; m. Virginia Korkoian, May 27, 1950; 1 son by prev. marriage, Curtis Charles. Mem. St. Louis Police Dept., 1929-52, 60—, chief police, 1960—; guest lectr. FBI Nat. Acad., So. Police Inst.; v.p. St. Regis Paper Co., and predecessor, 1952-60; dir. Conservation Fed. Savs. and Loan Assn. Mem. U.S. Atty. Gen.'s Adv. Com. Law Enforcement, U.S. Atty. Gen.'s adv. Com. Riot Control. Pub. rep. corp. bd. Blue Cross Hosp. Service. Mem. Internat. Assn. Chiefs Police (1st v.p.), Mo. Peace Officers Assn. (pres. 1962), Profl. Investigators Council (pres. 1960). Mason (32, Shriner). Home: 714 Lookout Dr St Louis MO 63137 Office: 1200 Clark Av St Louis MO 63103

BROTHERS, DWIGHT STANLEY, economist, educator; b. Sterling, Kan., May 3, 1929; s. Irving Samuel and Blanche (Leonard) B.; B.A., Colo. Coll., 1951; postgrad. U. Bristol (Eng.), 1951-52; M.A., Princeton, 1954, Ph.D., 1957; m. Sue Carolyn Coker, Sept. 17, 1952; children—Leslie Ann, Dwight Douglas, Bruce Colin. Instr. dept. econs., Woodrow Wilson Sch. Pub. and Internat. Affairs, Princeton, 1954-56; faculty Rice U., 1956-67, prof. econs., 1964-67; vis. prof. Grad. Sch. Bus. Adminstrn., research asso. Center Internat. Affairs, Harvard, Cambridge, Mass., 1965-67; faculty Grad. Sch. Bus. Adminstrn., asso. dir. devel. adv. service, 1967—. Vis. prof. Brookings Instn., 1961-63; program adviser econ. devel. and mgmt. for Eastern and So. Africa, Ford Found., 1970—; cons. industry, govt. Mem. internat. tech. coop. and assistance panel Pres.'s Sci. Adv. Com., 1966-68. Mem. Am. Econ. Assn. Author: (with Leopoldo Solis) Mexican Financial Development, 1966. Home: Fairhaven Hill Concord MA 01742 Office: 1737 Cambridge St Cambridge MA 02138

BROTHERS, JOYCE DIANE, (Mrs. Milton Brothers), psychologist; b. N.Y.C.; d. Morris K. and Estelle (Rapoport) Bauer; B.S., Cornell U., 1947; M.A., Columbia, 1950, Ph.D., 1953; L.H.D. (hon.), Franklin Pierce Coll.; m. Milton Brothers, July 4, 1949; 1 dau., Lisa Robin. Asst. psychology Columbia, 1948-52; instr. Hunter Coll., 1948-52; research project on leadership UNESCO, 1949; co-host TV program Sports Showcase, 1956; appearances TV program Dr. Joyce Brothers, 1958-63, Consult Dr. Brothers, 1960-66, Ask Dr. Brothers, 1965—; columnist N. Am. Newspaper Alliance, 1961—, Bell-McClure Syndicate, 1963—, Good Housekeeping mag., 1962—; appearances radio sta. WNBC, 1966-70, radio program Emphasis, 1966—, Monitor, 1967- -, WMCA, 1970—, ABC Reports, 1966-67; news analyst Metro Media-TV; spl. feature writer Hearst papers, U.P.I.; $64,000 winner TV program $64,000 Question, 1956; winner $70,000 TV program $64,000 Challenge, 1957. Co-chmn. sports com. Lighthouse for Blind; door- to-door chmn. Jewish Fedn. Philanthropies, N.Y.C.; mem. fund raising com. Olympic Fund; mem. People-to-People Program. Recipient Mennen Baby Found. award, 1959, Newhouse Newspaper award, 1959; Am. Acad. Achievement award; Am. Parkinson Disease Assn. award, 1971. Mem. Sigma Xi. Home: 305 E 86th St New York City NY 10028 Office: NBC 30 Rockefeller Plaza New York City NY 10020

BROTHERS, LEROY ARGLUS, former ret. provost univ. b. Wilmington, N.C., Mar. 6, 1904; s. Joseph Arglus and Mita Catherine (Miller) B.; B.S. in Civil Engring., N.C. State Coll., 1925, C.E., 1931, D.Sc. (hon.), 1957; m. Alice Stephenson, Mar. 23, 1932; foster children—Margaret Ann Stephenson (Mrs. Henry S. Raub), Robert Stephenson. Various positions in constrn., surveying and design of structures and hwys., 1925-26; from instr. to asso. prof. civil engring. Drexel U., Phila., 1927-45, dean Coll. Engring. and Sci., 1958-69, v.p. for acad. affairs, 1969, provost, 1969-70. Cons. Hdqrs. USAF; research phys. damage to bldg. and machine structurers NDRC, 1942-43; target and weapons analysis 8th Air Force targets, Brit.-Am. Research Unit, Princes Risborough, Eng., 1943; operations analysis USAAF, 1944-45; chief analysis br., phys. damage div. U.S. Strategic Bombing Survey, Japan, 1945-46; dir. operations analysis program Hdqrs. USAF, Washington, 1946-58. Decorated Bronze Star medal with cluster. Recipient Exceptional Civilian Service award Dept. Air Force, 1958; named Engr. of Year by engring. and tech. socs. of Phila., 1963. Fellow Soc. C.E.; mem. Am. Soc. for Engring. Edn., Operations Research Soc. Am. (pres. 1955-56), Phi Kappa Phi, Tau Beta Pi, Chi Epsilon, Pi Tau Sigma, Theta Chi. Home: 1040 Great Springs Rd Rosemont PA 19010

BROTJE, ROBERT JOHN, Jr., mfg. co. exec.; b. Toledo, Apr. 18, 1920; s. Robert John and Martha (Wolf) B.; B.B.A., U. Toledo, 1942; m. Eileen Marie Wernert, June 6, 1942; children—Susan Lizabeth, Bradford John, Julie Louise. With Konopak & Dalton, C.P.A.'s, Toledo, 1946-57; tax mgr. Champion Spark Plug Co., Toledo, 1957-64, controller, 1964—. Served to lt. (j.g.) USNR, 1943-45. C.P.A., Ohio. Mem. Am. Inst. C.P.A.'s, Ohio Soc. C.P.A.'s, Financial Execs. Inst. Home: 4246 Tejon Rd Toledo, OH 43623. Office: 900 Upton Av Toledo OH 43607

BROTT, BORIS, orch. condr.; b. Montreal, Que., Can., Mar. 14, 1944; s. Alexander and Lotte (Goetzel) B.; student Conservatoire de Musique, Montreal, 1958-61, also McGill U.; studied with Pierre Monteux, Igor Markevitch and Leonard Bernstein. Founder, Philharmonic Youth Orch. of Montreal, 1959; asst. condr. Toronto Symphony, 1963-65; prin. condr. No. Sinfonia, Gt. Britain, 1964-68; asst. condr. New York Philharmonic under Leonard Bernstein, 1968-69; music dir. Hamilton (Ont.) Philharmonic, 1969—; music dir. Lakehead U. and Lakehead Symphony, Thunder Bay, Ont., 1967—; music cons. Kitchener-Waterloo Symphony, 1969; music dir. Regina (Sask.) Symphony, 1971—; guest condr. L'Orchestre des concerts Colonne, Paris, RIA, Rome and Milan Philharmonia, Royal Philharmonic, BBC Symphony, Liverpool Philharmonic and BBC No. in Britain, Vancouver, Montreal, Toronto, Winnipeg, N.Y.C., Ottawa, Calgary, N.A.C., Quebec, Atlantic, Los Angeles philharmonics, RIAS in Berlin and Berlin Philharmonic; recordings for MACE Records, New York; writer-host- condr. series: Music from Bach to Rock-CBC (winner Ohio State award), Mods Make Music-CBC Radio, Music, Why Bother-CBC-TV, Hear-out-CBC Radio (winner Ohio State award), 2 13 program TV series for ITV-Gt. Britain; currently doing Brott to You-22 program series for CBC Radio AM and FM coast to coast network; also TV spls. on CHCH-TV. Dir. J.K.T. Pub. Relations, Ltd., Eng. Recipient Jr. C. of C. Man of Year award Thunder Bay and Province Ont., 1969, Gold medal Dimitri Mitropoulos Internat. Conductors Competition, 1968, Pan Am. Conductors prize, 1958, 2d prize Liverpool Philharmonic Competition, 1961. Club: Royal Hamilton Yacht. Home: 1 Turner Av Hamilton Ontario Canada Office: 795 Main St W Hamilton Ontario Canada

BROTZEN, FRANZ RICHARD, educator; b. Berlin, Germany, July 4, 1915; s. Georg and Lena (Paculty) B.; came to U.S., 1941, naturalized, 1943; B.S. in Metall. Engring., Case Inst. Tech., 1950, M.S., 1953, Ph.D., 1954; m. Frances B. Ridgway, Jan. 31, 1950; children—Franz Ridgway, Julie Ridgway. Salesman, A. Quimica Bayer Ltd., Rio de Janeiro, Brazil, 1934-40; engr. J. Magnus e Cla. Ltda., Rio de Janeiro, 1940-41, A.G. McKee & Co. Cleve., 1941- 42; mfrs. rep. R.G. LeTourneau, Inc., Longview, Tex., 1947-48; research metallurgist U.S. Bur. Mines, 1950-51; research asso. Case Inst. Tech., 1951-54; faculty Rice U., Houston, 1954—, prof. materials sci., 1959—, dean engring., 1962-66. Cons. Naval Research Lab., 1955-57; vis. lectr. U. Brazil. 1963, 65; vis. prof. Eidgenössische Technische Hochschule, Zurich, 1966-67. Bd. dirs. Contemporary Arts Assn., Houston, 1960-63, chmn. bd., 1963-64. Served to 1st lt., inf. AUS, 1942-46. Guggenheim fellow, 1960-61. Mem. Am. Inst. Mining, Metall. and Petroleum Engrs., Am. Phys. Soc., Am. Soc. Metals, Am. Soc. Engring. Edn., Sigma Xi, Tau Beta Pi. Home: 3612 Overbrook Dr Houston TX 77027

BROTZMAN, DONALD GLENN, lawyer, congressman; b. Logan County, Colo., June 28, 1922; s. Harry and Priscilla Ruth (Kittle) B.; B.B.S., LL.B., U. Colo., 1949; m. Louise Love Reed, Apr. 9, 1944; children—Kathleen Love, Donald Glenn. Admitted to Colo. bar, 1949, since practiced in Boulder; mem. Colo. Ho. of Reps., 1950-52, Colo. Senate, 1952-56; U.S. atty. Dist. Colo., 1959-61; mem. 88th, 90th-92d congresses from 2d Dist. Colo., now mem. ways and means com. Mem. Colo. Crime Commn., 1952-56; commr. Uniform State Laws from Colo., 1954—. Colo. chmn. Eastern Seal and Colo. Highlander Boys Club drives, 1958; Colo. chmn. Youth in Govt. program, YMCA, 1958-62. Republican candidate for gov. of Colo., 1956; chmn. Rep. Task Force on Transp. Served to lst lt., inf. AUS, 1942-46; PTO. Selected by Colo. press as Outstanding Freshman Mem. of House, 1951, as Outstanding Freshman Senator, 1953; recipient Distinguished Service award Colo. Jr. C. of C., 1954. Mem. Am., Fed., Colo., Boulder County bar assns., Am. Legion, V.F.W., Res. Officers Assn., Boulder C. of C., Beta Theta Pi, Phi Delta Phi (past magister). Methodist (trustee). Mason, Elk, Rotarian (dir. Boulder). Home: 735 Highland St Boulder CO 80302 Office: Cannon House Office Bldg Washington DC 20515

BROUDY, HARRY SAMUEL, educator; b. Filipows, Poland, July 27, 1905; s. Michael and Mollie (Wyzanski) B.; came to U.S., 1912, naturalized, 1936; student Mass. Inst. Tech., 1924-25; A.B., Boston U., 1929; M.A., Harvard, 1933. Ph.D., 1935; H.H.D., Oakland U., 1969; m. Dorothy L. Hogarth, Aug. 15, 1947; 1 son, Richard M. Reporter, Milford (Mass.) Daily News, 1925-26, 29-32; supr. dept. edn. Commonwealth Mass., 1936-37; prof. psychology and philosophy N. Adams (Mass.) State Tchrs. Coll., 1937-49, Framingham (Mass.) State Tchrs. Coll., 1949-57; prof. philosophy of edn. U. Ill., Champaign, 1957—; Jennings scholar lectr., 1965; Boyd H. Bode lectr. Ohio State U., 1960; 1st annual Cornell U. Sch. Edn. lectr., 1962. Mem. adv. bd. tchr. examinations Ednl. Testing Service, 1968-71; mem. com. evaluate criteria accreditation tchr. tng. instns. Am. Assn. Colls. Tchr. Edn., 1966-69; mem. com. preparation books of readings Am. Ednl. Research Assn., 1965. Fellow Center Advanced Study Behavioral Scis., 1967-68. Mem. Am. Philos. Soc., Am. Psychol. Assn., A.A.A.S., Am. Metaphys. Soc., John Dewey Soc., Nat. Soc. Coll. Tchrs. Edn., Am. Ednl. Research Assn., Philosophy Edn. Soc. (pres. 1953), Assn. Realistic Soc. (pres. 1955), Am. Assn. U. Profs. (pres. U. Ill. chpt. 1966-67), Phi Beta Kappa, Phi Kappa Phi, Kappa Delta Pi. Club: Harvard (Chgo.). Author: Building a Philosophy of Education, 2d edit. 1961 (trans. into Korean and Spanish); Paradox and Promise, 1961; (with others) Psychology for General Education, 1956; (with others) Democracy and Excellance in American Secondary Education, 1964: (with others) Exemplars of Teaching Methods, 1965; (with others) Philosophy of Education; An Organization of Topics and Selected Sources, 1967; also articles. Editor: Educational Forum, 1964—; mem. editorial bd. Jour. Aesthetic Edn. Home: 1411 S Prospect St Champaign, IL 61820 Office: Education Bldg Univ Ill Urbana, IL.

BROUGH, KENNETH JAMES, educator, librarian; b. Scotch Grove, Ia., Aug. 22, 1906; s. Rev. R.A. and Sarah (Metcalf) B.; A.B., Grinnell Coll., 1927; A.M., U. Colo., 1931; B.L.S., Columbia, 1942; Ph.D., Stanford, 1949; m. Ruth Bloomer, May 22, 1933. Tchr. Portales (N.M.) High Sch., 1927-34; librarian, dir. instrn. Eastern N.M. U., 1934-43; asst. reference librarian Stanford, 1946-49; prof. bibliography, librarian San Francisco State Coll. 1949—. Mem. N.M. Library Planning Com., 1940-42, N.M. Library Commn., 1946. Served as exec. officer 54th A.A.A. replacement tng. bn., U.S. Army, 1943-46. Mem. A.L.A., N.E.A., N.M. (pres. 1935-36), Cal. library assns., Phi Beta Kappa. Phi Delta Kappa. Presbyn. Mason. Author: Scholar's Workshop, 1953. Contbr. articles to profl. jours. Home: 2364 S Court Palo Alto CA 94301 Office: San Francisco State College San Francisco CA 94132

BROUGHAM, ROYAL, newspaperman; b. St. Louis, Sept. 17, 1894; s. Hervert David and and Mattie (Brewer) B.; ed. pub. schs.; Litt.D., Biola Coll., LaMirada, Cal.; m. Alice Swanson, Apr. 14, 1915 (dec.); 1 dau., Alice May. Reporter Post-Intelligencer, Seattle, 1911, mng. editor, 1925, now asso. editor. Founder Royal Brougham Found. Mem. Sigma Delta Chi. Clubs: Rotary, Washington Athletic, Seattle Yacht. Home: 2633 42d Av W Seattle WA 98199

BROUGHTON, JOHN GERARD, geologist; b. Rome, N.Y., Oct. 16, 1914; s. Judson Lee and Grace E. (Johnson) B.; A.B., U. Rochester, 1936, M.S., 1938; Ph.D., Johns Hopkins, 1940; m. Katherine Braman Oster, June 22, 1940; children—Karen Joan, Susan Lee. Field asst. U.S. Geol. Survey, 1936, jr. geologist, 1941-43; grad. asst. U. Rochester, 1937-38, Johns Hopkins, 1938-40; instr. dept. geology Syracuse U., 1940-42; asst. state geologist, N.Y., 1942-44, acting state geologist, 1944-49, sr. geologist, 1947-49, state geologist and principal scientist N.Y. State Sci. Service, 1949-68; asst. commr. for State Mus. and Sci. Service, N.Y. State Dept. Edn., 1968—, asso. commr. for cultural edn., 1970—. Hon. fellow Rochester Mus. of Arts and Scis. Fellow Geol. Soc. Am.; mem. Appalachian Geol. Soc., Am. State Geologists (hon.), Am. Assn. Museums (councillor, v.p.). Albany Inst. History and Art (trustee), N.Y. Mus. Assn. (v.p. 1970—), Sigma Xi. Unitarian. Home: 42 Dove St Albany NY 12202 Office: NY State Education Bldg Albany NY 12226

BROUGHTON, THOMAS ROBERT SHANNON, educator; b. Corbetton, Ont., Can., Feb. 17, 1900; s. Thomas and Margaret Jane (Shannon) B.; B.A., U. Toronto, 1921, M.A., 1922, LL.D., 1971; postgrad. U. Chgo., 1922, 23, 25; Ph.D. (Rogers fellowship 1925-26, 27-28), Johns Hopkins, 1928, LL.D., 1969; m. Annie Leigh Hobson, Sept. 4, 1931; children—Margaret Shannon (Mrs. T.A. Tenney), Thomas Alan Broughton. Teaching fellow Victoria Coll., 1921-23; instr. Greek, Amherst Coll., 1926-27; asso. Latin, Bryn Mawr Coll., 1928-30, asso. prof., 1930- 37, prof., 1937-65, sec. faculty, 1954-64; Paddison prof. classics U. N.C. at Chapel Hill, 1965- 70, emeritus, 1970—. Vis. prof. Johns Hopkins U., 1938-40; prof. in charge Sch. Classical Studies, Am. Acad. in Rome, 1959-61; dir. Am. office, L'Année Philologique, 1965-68; ann. mem. Inst. for Advanced Studies, Princeton, 1971-72. Guggenheim Meml. fellow, 1945-46, Fulbright research grant, Italy, 1951-52. Asso. trustee U. Pa., 1955-59. Recipient Gov.-Gen.'s Gold medal, Toronto, 1921; award of merit, Am. Philol. Assn., 1953, Lindback award for distinguished teaching Bryn Mawr Coll., 1964. Fellow Am. Acad. Arts and Scis.; corr. fellow Brit. Acad.; mem. Am. Philos. Soc., Internat. Fedn. Socs. Classical Studies (v.p. 1959-69). Soc. Promotion Hellenic Studies, Soc. Promotion Roman Studies (hon.) Classical Assn. Middle West and South, Am. Philol. Assn. (pres. 1954), Archaeol. Inst. Am. (hon. v.p. 1953-58), Author: Romanization of Africa Proconsularis, 1929; Roman Asia Minor, 1938; Index to the Economic Survey of Ancient Rome (with others), 1940; Magistrates of the Roman Republic (2 vols.), 1951-52. Mem. editorial bd. Am. Hist. Rev., 1953-58, Historia; editor Mommsen, Provinces of the Roman Empire; The European Provinces, 1968. Contbr. monographs, articles, revs. in field. Home: 1111 Roosevelt Dr Chapel Hill NC 27514

BROUILLETTE, THEODORE ROLAND, ret. dept. store exec.; b. Tower, Minn., Feb. 26, 1908; s. Treffle Joseph and Florence Mary (Schneider) B.; grad. Ely Jr. Coll., 1928; student U. Mich., 1928-29; B.A.E., U. Minn., 1931; m. Lucille Noah, May 3, 1931; children—Theodore Roland, Jean Treffle. Vice pres. L.S. Donaldson Co., Mpls., 1936-43, pres., 1943-48; v.p., dir., Allied Stores Corp., N.Y.C., 1948-68; chmn. bd., chief exec. officer Donaldson's, Mpls., 1961-68; bus. cons., 1968—; chmn., dir. Bishop & Mahoney, Inc., Mpls., 1966—; dir., mem. exec. com. Kodiak Inc.; dir. chmn. adv. com. KOL, Inc., St. Paul; dir. No. Potteries Inc., Newark, Lawndale Industries Inc., Aurora, Ill. Mem. Twin Cities Area Met. Transit Commn. Clubs: Minikahda; Union League (N.Y.C.); Minneapolis. Home: 2928 Dean Blvd Minneapolis MN 55416 Office: Midwest Plaza Bldg Minneapolis MN 55402

BROULLIRE, JOHN MERLIN, govt. ofcl.; b. Iron Mountain, Mich., July 2, 1917; s. Peter Joseph and Minnie (Grossbusch) B.; student U. Mich., 1936-38; B.B.A., U. Tex., 1941; m. Mary Theresa Sullivan, Feb. 19, 1950; children—John Christopher, Joseph Michael, Mary Patricia, James Mark, Frances, Marie. Financial analyst SEC, 1941-55; regional supr. FHLB, 1955-66; dep. dir. Fed. Savs. & Loan Ins. Corp., 1966—; cons. AID, El Salvador, 1963-64; mem. savs. and loan thesis rev. bd. Grad. Sch., U. Ind., 1967. Mem. Beta Alpha Psi, Delta Sigma Pi, Beta Gamma Sigma. Club: Univ. Mich. Alumni (Washington). Home: 4004 Underwood St Hyattsville MD 80782 Office: 101 Indiana Av NW Washington DC 20552

BROUN, MAURICE, naturalist; b. N.Y.C., Aug. 27, 1906; s. Jacob and Rebecca Broun; ed. pub. schs.; D.Sc., Muhlenberg Coll., 1952; m. Irma Knowles Penniman, Jan. 15, 1934. Ornithol. work with Edward H. Forbush, 1927-29; pioneer devel. Pleasant Valley Sanctuary, Lenox, Mass., 1929-31; research asso. Austin Ornithol. Research Sta., South Wellfleet, Mass., 1931- 34; established nature trails near Rutland, Vt., summers 1939-42, also sanctuaries and nature trails in five other states; curator Hawk Mountain Sanctuary, Kempton, Pa., 1934-66. Served with USNR, 1943-45; PTO. Recipient Certificate of Merit award Am. Motors-Nash Conservation Assn., 1953; Conservation award Am. Motors Corp., 1965. Fellow Delaware Valley Ornithol. Club: hon. mem. Rochester Acad. Sci.; elective mem. Am. Ornithologists Union; mem. Am. Fern Soc., Wilson Ornithol. Soc. Author: Index to North American Ferns, 1938; Hawks Aloft, The Story of Hawk Mountain, 1949; also ann. newsletter Hawk Mountain Sanctuary Assn., 1939-66. Contbr. to Birds of Massachusetts and Other New England States, 3 vols., 1927-20; also numerous other books and profl. jours. Home: Strawberry Hill Farm Route 1, New Ringgold, PA17960.

BROURMAN, JACQUES, conductor; b. Pitts., Apr. 23, 1931; s. Mair and Rose (Hineck) B.; student Carnegie Inst. Tech., 1940-53, Julliard Sch. Music, 1953-54; m. Audrey Breier, Dec. 29, 1956; children—Ronn Michael, Paul David. Violinist, Houston Symphony, 1954-56; asst. condr. New Orleans Symphony, 1956-58; condr. Boise (Ida.) Philharmonic, 1960-67; condr. Charlotte (N.C.) Symphony, 1967—. Dir. Sun Valley (Ida.) Music Camp. Address: 827 East Blvd Charlotte NC 28203

BROUSE, ROBERT CORNELIUS, lawyer; b. Akron, O., June 19, 1913; s. Edwin Walter and Helen (Fouts) B.; A.B., Princeton, 1935; J.D., U. Mich., 1938; m. Martha Ake, July 9, 1938; children—Susannah (Mrs. John L. Feudner III), Martha (Mrs. Jerome J. Joondeph). Admitted to Ohio bar, 1938; with Brouse, McDowell, Bierce, Roetzel & Hunsicker and predecessor firms, Akron, 1938—, partner, 1949—; chmn. bd. Permanent Fed. Savs. and Loan Assn., Akron, 1963—; mem. exec. com. Summit Nat. Life Ins. Co., 1962—. Pres. bd. Western Res. Acad., Hudson, O., 1966—, Childrens Hosp. of Akron, 1950-51. Trustee, Akron Community Trust, Sunnyslope Found. Served to lt. USNR, 1942-46. Mem. Am., Ohio, Akron bar assns., Phi Delta Phi (pres. Kent chpt. 1938). Republican. Clubs: Akron City (pres. 1963), Portage Country (Akron); Union (Cleve.). Home: 520 Ridgecrest Rd Akron OH 44303 Office: First Nat Tower Akron OH 44308

BROUSSARD , JOSEPH OTTO, III, architect; b. Abbeville, La., Jan. 3, 1938; s. Joseph Otto and Dorothy (Kennon) B.; B.Arch., U. Southwestern La., 1963; m. Sidney Prejean, Dec. 17, 1960; children—Kent, Kelly, Russ. Architect firm Tolson & Hamilton, Opelousas, La., 1963-65; architect, prin., owner Laudun & Broussard, Franklin, La., 1965-69; architect Hamilton, Meyer & Assos., Opelousas, La., 1969—. Mem. A.I.A. (sec. Coastal chpt. 1965-68, v.p. 1968-69), La. Architects Assn., Am. Forestry Assn., Constrn. Specification Inst., Theta Xi. Blue Key. Kiwanian. Home: 357 W Vine St Opelousas LA 70570 Office: 461 Bertheaud St Opelousas LA 70570

BROUWENSTYN, GRE, opera singer; b. den Helder, Holland, Aug. 26, 1915; pvt. study music and singing; m. A. C. van Swol, May 24, 1956; 1 son, Jan Paul. Appearances with Amsterdam Opera, 1946, later Stuttgart, Bayreuth, London, Madrid, Barcelona, Lisbon, Glyndebourne, Buenos Aires, Chicago, Rome, Florence, Venice, Vienna, San Francisco, Los Angeles operas. Decorated Order Orange Nassau (Netherlands). Club: Amsterdam Golf and Country. Home: Rossini Laan 3 Hilversum, Holland.

BROUWER, LUITZEN EGBERTUS JAN, petroleum co. exec.; b. July 1, 1910; studied mining engring., Delft; m. Maria F. Rueb, 1938. With Royal Dutch/Shell Group, 1931—; beginning as geologist in Germany, Indonesia and Egypt, assignments in U.S.A. and Netherlands, 1946-51, coordinator exploration and prodn., 1951; gen. mng. dir. Iranian Oil Exploration & Producing Co., Iranian Oil Refining Co., 1954; mng. dir. Royal Dutch Petroleum Co., 1956; pres., 1965—, dir., 1971—; prin. dir. Shell Petroleum N.V. (formerly B.P.M.): mng. dir. Shell Petroleum Co. Ltd., 1956-71, dir., 1971—; chmn. Shell Can.; dir. Shell Petroleum N.V. Decorated Knight Order of Netherlands Lion; officer Order of Orange Nassau. Home: Dorpsstraat 9 Warmond Netherlands Office: Royal Dutch Petroleum Co Carel van Bylandtlaan 30 The Hague Netherlands

BROW, LEE HENRY, c. of c. exec.; b. Saranac Lake, N.Y., Mar. 22, 1890; s. Henry W. and Carrie (Wilkins) B.; student pub. schs., Saranac Lake; m. Grace Evelyn Nugent, July 23, 1921 (div.); 1 dau., Elizabeth (Mrs. John P. Pappas). Asst. gen. sec. Holyoke (Mass.) YMCA, 1912-20; mng. sec. Westfield C. of C., 1920-24; mng. sec. Portsmouth (N.H.) C. of C., 1924-28; personal counsellor Wm. L. Fletcher, Inc., 1928-42; pvt. practice personal counsellor, 1942-49; personnel mgr. R.H. Hinkley Co., Boston, 1949-59; mem. staff Boston YMCA, 1959-64; exec. v.p., dir. Mass. C. of C., Boston, 1964—. Justice of Peace, 1967-68. Mem. Gov.'s Com. on Tourism, 1968-69, Gov.'s Com. on World Trade, 1969-70, Gov.'s Com. on Port of Boston, 1968-69. Kiwanian (pres.). Club: Adirondack Shillelagh (founder). Home: 440 Tremont St Boston MA 02109 Office: 126 State St Boston MA 02116

BROWDER, FELIX EARL, mathematician, educator; b. Moscow, USSR, July 31, 1927 (father Am. citizen) B.; s. Earl and Raissa (Berkmann) B.; S.B., Mass. Inst. Tech., 1946; Ph.D., Princeton, 1948; m. Eva Tislowitz, Oct. 5, 1949; children—Thomas, William. C.L.E. Moore instr. math. Mass. Inst. Tech., 1948-5l, vis. asso. prof., 1961-62; instr. math. Boston U., 1951-53; asst. prof. Brandeis U., 1955- 56; from asst. prof. to prof. math. Yale, 1956-63; prof. math. U. Chgo., 1963—; vis. mem. Inst. Advanced Study, Princeton, 1953-54, 63-64, Served with AUS, 1953-55. Guggenheim fellow, 1953-54, 66-67; Sloan Found. fellow, 1959-63; NSF sr. postdoctoral fellow, 1957-58. Fellow Am. Acad. Arts and Scis.; mem. Am. Math. Soc. (editor bull. 1959-68, mng. editor 1964-68, council mem. 1969—), Math. Assn. Am. Home: 5505 S Kimbark Av Chicago, IL 60637.

BROWDER, OLIN LORRAINE, Jr., legal educator; b. Urbana, Ill., Dec. 19, 1913; s. Olin Lorraine and Nellie (Taylor) B.; A.B., U. Ill., 1935, LL.B., 1937; S.J.D., U. Mich., 1941; m. Edna Olive Forsythe, Sept. 9, 1939; children—Ann (Mrs. William Sorensen), Catherine (Mrs. Robert Demeritt), John. Admitted to Ill. bar, 1939; practiced in Chgo., 1938-39; asst. prof. bus. law U. Ala., 1939- 41; asst. prof. law U. Tenn., 1941-42; mem. legal dept. TVA, 1942-43; spl. agt. FBI, 1943-45; prof. law U. Okla., 1946-53, U. Mich., Ann Arbor, 1953—. Mem. Am. Bar Assn., Order of Phi Beta Kappa, Beta Theta Phi, Phi Alpha Delta, Phi Kappa Phi. Author: (with others) American Law of Property, 1953; (with R. V. Wellman) Family Property Settlements, 1965; (with R. A. Cunningham and J. R. Julin) Basic Property Law, 1966. Home: 1520 Edinborough Rd Ann Arbor MI 48104

BROWDER, ROBERT PAUL, historian, educator, b. Spokane, Wash., Jan. 25, 1921; s. Paul McCroskey and Helen Elizabeth (Hungate) B.; A.B., Stanford, 1942, M.A., 1947; M.A. (Austin fellow, Rockefeller fellow Slavic studies 1947-50), Harvard, 1949, Ph.D., 1951; m. Rosemary Meininger, June 1, 1946 (div. 1970); children—Kathleen Hale, Ann Elizabeth, Judith Lee. Instr. history Stanford, 1951, vis. asst. prof., 1954-55; faculty U. Colo., 1951- 65, prof. history, 1960-65, chmn. dept., 1960-63, acting dean Grad. Sch., 1962-64, dir. Center for Slavic and East European Studies, 1964- 65; prof., head dept. history Kan. State U., 1965-69; prof., head dept. history U. Ariz., Tucson, 1969—. Research asso. Hoover Instn. War, Revolution and Peace, 1956-59. Served to lt. USNR, 1942-46. Mem. Am. Hist. Assn., Am. Assn. Advancement Slavic Studies, Conf. Slavic and East European Studies, Far West Slavic Conf., Rocky Mountain Sci. Assn. Author: The Origins of Soviet-American Diplomacy, 1953, 2d, edit., 1966; (with others) Russian Thought and Politics, 1957; (with A.F. Kerensky) The Russian Provisional Government 1917, 3 vols., 1961; (with others) Soviet Foreign Policy and World Communism, 1965; also articles. Office: Dept of History Univ Ariz Tuscon AZ 85721

BROWDER, ROBERT WILLIAM, lawyer; b. El Paso, Tex., May 14, 1933; s. Robert Warren and Mary Browder; B.S., U. Ariz., 1955, J.D., 1958; m. Charlene Jane Cobb, Sept. 17, 1954; 1 dau., Rebecca. Admitted to Ariz. bar, 1958; partner firm Browder, Gillenwater & Daughton, Phoenix, 1967—. Mem. State Bar Ariz. (bd. govs. 1965-71, pres. 1970-71), Maricopa County Bar Assn. (pres. 1966), Order of Coif, Phi Alpha Delta, Phi Kappa Phi. Republican. Home: 6149 E Indian Bend Scottsdale AZ 85251 Office: 3003 N Central Av Phoenix AZ 85201

BROWDER, WALTER GORDON, educator; b. Petersburg, Va., June 9, 1914; s. Samuel W. and Cassie Anne (Tudor) B.; A.B., U. Va., 1936; A.M., U. N.C., 1941, Ph.D., 1943; m. Alice Frances Jarman, June 6, 1940; children—David Gordon, Thomas Martin, James Lewis. Research asso. U. Tex., 1939-41, instr. sociology, 1941-43; asst. prof. sociology U. Fla., 1946-48; prof. sociology, chmn. dept. U. Mont., Missoula, 1948-67, prof., dir. Inst. for Social Sci. Research, 1966-70. Mem. planning com. mental retardation Mont. Bd. Health; mem. regional adv. council Gov.'s Crime Control Commn.; mem. Mont. Commn. Crime and Delinquency. Served with AUS, 1943-45. Fellow Am. Sociol. Assn.; mem. A.A.A.S., Am. Correctional Assn., Am. Assn. U. Profs. Population Assn. Am., Mont. Acad. Sci., Alpha Kappa Delta, Pi Gamma Mu. Kiwanian. Author: Use of City Directories in Urban Population Research, 1942; Family Mobility in Dallas, Texas, 1943; Family Mobility in Houston, Texas, 1943; Pattern of Internal Migration in Texas, 1944; Population and Income in Montana, 1953. Home: 2309 Cloverdale Dr Missoula MT 59801

BROWDER, WILLIAM, mathematician, educator; b. N.Y.C. Jan. 6, 1934; s. Earl and Raissa (Berkmann) B.; B.S., Mass. Inst. Tech., 1954; Ph.D., Princeton, 1958; m. Nancy O'Brien, Jan. 30, 1960; children—Julia, Risa, Daniel. Instr., U. Rochester, 1957-58; from instr. to asso. prof. math. Cornell U., 1958- 63; prof. math. Princeton (N.J.), 1964—, chmn. dept., 1971—. Home: 21 Maple St Princeton NJ 08540

BROWDER, WILLIAM BAYARD, corp. exec., lawyer; b. Urbana, Ill., Sept. 6, 1916; s. Olin Lorraine and Nellie Sheldon (Taylor) B.; A.B., U. Ill., 1938, J.D., 1941; m. Mary Bain Lehmann, Sept. 6, 1942; children—David Sheldon, Wendy Elisabeth (Mrs. John A. Drees), Amy Spence. Admitted to Ill. bar, 1941; atty. IC. R.R., 1941-47; atty. Union Tank Car Co., Chgo., 1948—, sec., 1952—, dir., 1954—, gen. counsel, 1956—; v.p., 1965—; v.p., gen. counsel, sec., dir. Trans Union Corp., 1969—; sec., dir. products Tank Line of Can., Ltd.; dir. Procor, Ltd. Bd. dirs. Mid. Am. Chpt. A.R.C., 1964- 66, Wilmette Pu. Library, 1964-67. Mem. Citizens Com. To Study Police-Community Relations; pres. Chgo. Crime Commn., 1965-67. Pres. Wilmette United Fund, 1962; chmn. bd. trustees YMCA-U. Ill.; trustee Chgo. Wesley Meml. Hosp.; mem. U. Ill. Found. Mem. Am. Petroleum Inst., Am. Soc. Corporate Secs., Assn. Interstate Commerce Practitioners, Am., Ill., Chgo. bar assns., Chgo. Law Club, Order of Coif, Phi Beta Kappa, Phi Eta Sigma, Beta Theta Pi, Phi Alpha Delta. Methodist (trustee Wesley Found., U. Ill. 1964-68). Clubs: Union League, Traffic, Mid Day (Chgo.); Westmoreland Country. Home: 1442 Lake Av Wilmette IL 60091

BROWER, CHARLES HENDRICKSON, ret. business exec.; b. Asbury Park, N.J., Nov. 13, 1901; s. Charles Hendrick and Mary Amelia (Hendrickson) B.; B.Sc., Rutgers U., 1925, LL.D., 1966; L.H.D., Pace Coll., 1962; LL.D., Monmouth Coll; 1967; m. Mary Elizabeth Nelson, July 8, 1930; children—Brock Hendrickson, Charles Nelson, Anne Clayton (Mrs. James Culver). Tchr., Bound Brook (N.J.) High Sch., 1925-26; writer Batten, Barton, Durstine, Osborn, N.Y.C., 1928-46, v.p., dir., 1940-46, exec. v.p. charge creative services, 1946, mem. exec. com., 1951, gen. mgr., vice chmn. exec. com. 1957, pres., 1957-64, chmn. exec. com., 1957—, chmn. bd., 1964-71. Mem. Westfield (N.J.) Bd. Edn. 1945-48. Chmn., United Community Campaigns and Community Chests of Am., 1965. Chmn. bd. govs., life trustee Rutgers U. Mem. Alpha Chi Rho. Republican. Epsicopalian. Clubs: University (N.Y.); Manasquan River Country. Home: 914 Cole Dr Brielle NJ 08730 Office: 383 Madison Av New York City NY 10017

BROWER, DANIEL, psychologist; b. Bklyn., Mar. 27, 1916; s. William and Edith (Korant) B.; A.B., N.Y.U., 1940, M.A., 1942, Ph.D., 1946; student Columbia, 1940-42, New Sch. for Social Research, 1942-45; m. Judith L. Fagen, Dec. 20, 1942 (div.); 1 son, William Charles. Lectr. psychology N.Y.U., 1943-52; asst. prof. City U. N.Y., 1946-50; asst. med. psychology N.Y.U., Bellevue Med. Center, 1945-46; lectr. Pratt Inst. Tech., 1948-49; asso. prof. dept. psychology Montclair (N.J.) State Coll., 1958-67, prof. psychology, chmn. dept., 1967—; practice clin. and child psychology, Montclair, 1946—. Cons. Bellevue Psychiat. Hosp., Essex County Hosp. and Guidance Clinic, St. Barnabas Hosp., Montclair Guidance Center, Kingston Av. Hosp. Served with USAAF, 1942-43. Diplomate Am. Bd. Clin. Psychology. Fellow Am. Psychol. Assn., A.A.A.S., Projective Soc.; mem. Sigma Xi, Psi Chi. Contbr. articles prof. jours., books. Home: 295 Claremont Av Montclair NJ 07042

BROWER, DAVID ROSS, conservationist; b. Berkeley, Cal. July 1, 1912; s. Ross J. and Mary Grace (Barlow) B.; student U. Cal., 1930-31; D.Sc., Hobart and William Smith Colls., 1967; D.H.L., Claremont Colls. Grad. Sch., 1971; m. Anne Hus, May 1, 1943; children—Kenneth David, Robert Irish, Barbara Ann, John Stewart. Editor U. Cal. Press, 1941-52; exec. dir. Sierra Club, 1952-69; dir. John Muir Inst. for Environmental Studies, 1969—; pres. (founder) Friends of the Earth, 1969—. Principal activist in conservation campaigns; saving Dinosaue Nat. Monument, 1952- 56; initiating Nat. Outdoor Recreation Resources Rev., 1956-58; Wilderness Act, 1952-64; North Cascades Nat. Park, 1955-68; Redwood Nat. Park, 1963-68; saving Grand Canyon, 1952-68. Founder, Trustees for Conservation, 1954 (sec., 1960-61, 64-65, past v.p., trustee); founder Sierra Club Found., 1960; dir. Citizens Côm. Natural Resources, 1955—; mem. Natural Resources Council Am. (chmn. 1955-57); dir. North Cascades Conservation Council, 1957—, Ore. Cascades Council, 1960-63, Kern Plateau Assn., 1959—, Rachel Carson Trust for Living Environment, 1967; founder League Conservation Voters, 1969, Les Amis de la Terre, 1970. Hon. mem. Nat. Parks Assn., The Mountaineers. First lt. with 10th Mountain Div., Infantry, AUS, 1943-45; maj. Infantry-Res., ret. Decorated Bronze Star; recipient awards Cal. Conservation Council, 1953, Nat. Parks Assn., 1956, Carey-Thomas award, 1964, Paul Bartsch award, Audubon Naturalist Soc. of Central Atlantic States, 1967. Clubs: Sierra (editorial bd. 1935-69, dir. 1941-43, 46-53, exec. dir. 1952-69), Am. Alpine (western v.p. 1955-58). Motion pictures: Sky-Land Trails of the Kings, 1940; Skis to the Sky-Land, 1942; Wilderness River Trail (writer script, 1953); Two Yosemites, 1955; Wilderness Alps of Stehekin, 1958. Editor: Manual of Ski Mountaineering, 1942, rev. 46, 47, 61, 69; Sierra Club Handbook, 1947, 51, 55, 57, 60, 64; Remount Blue, 1948; Going Light, 1951; The Meaning of Wilderness to Science, 1960; This is the American Earth, 1960; Wilderness; America's Living Heritage, 1961; These We Inherit; The Parklands of America, 1962; The Place No One Knew; Glen Canyon on the Colorado, 1963; Time and the River Flowing; Grand Canyon, 1964; Gentle Wilderness; The Sierra Nevada, 1964; Wildlands in our Civilization, 1964; Sierra Club Wilderness Handbook, 1964; Not Man Apart, 1965; The Wild Cascades. Forgotten Parklands, 1965; Everest; The West Ridge, 1965; Summer Island; Penobscot Country, 1966; Glacier Bay; The Land and the Silence, 1967; Central Park Country; A Tune Within Us, 1968; Galapagos; The Flow of Wildness, 2 vols., 1968; Return to the Alps, 1970; Eryri, the Mountains of Longing, 1971; Maui: The Last Hawaiian Place, 1970; Earth and the Great Weather: The Brooks Range, 1971; The Primal Alliance, Earth and Ocean, 1971; A Sense of Place: The Artist and the American Land, 1971. Contbr. articles nat. mags., profl. pubs. Contbr. to U.S. Army mountain manuals, instruction, 1943-45; 1st ascent, Shiprock, N.M., 1939; many first ascents, Sierra Nevada, 1933-41. Home: 40 Stevenson Av Berkeley CA 94708 Office: 451 Pacific Av San Francisco CA 94133

BROWER, REUBEN ARTHUR, educator; b. Lanesboro, Pa., May 5, 1908; s. Arthur and Hannah Adeline (Taylor) B.; B.A. summa cum laude, Amherst Coll., 1930, Litt.D., 1964; B.A., Cambridge U., 1932, M.A., 1936; Ph.D., Harvard, 1936; D. Litt., Amherst Coll., 1964; m. Helen Porter, Sept. 12, 1934; children—Jonathan, Richard, Ellen. Tutor English and classics Harvard, Cambridge, Mass., 1932-36, instr. English, 1936-39, prof., 1953—, master Adams House, 1954—; asst. prof. Greek and English Amherst Coll., 1939-44, asso. prof., 1944-48, class of 1880 prof. Greek and English, 1948-53. Faculty Bread Loaf Sch. Eng., summers 1940, 41 47, 5l; vis. prof., Fulbright fellow Oxford U., 1968-69; Martin Classical lectr. Oberlin Coll., 1970. Trustee, Radcliffe Coll., 1963—, English Inst., 1969—. Guggenheim fellow, 1956-57, 65-66; fellow Center Advanced study Behavioral Scis., 1961-62; Mem. Classical Assn. N.E., Soc. Fellows of Harvard (sr. fellow), Club of Odd Volumes, Modern Lang. Assn., Am. Assn. U. Profs., Acad. Arts and Scis., Phi Beta Kappa (Christian Gauss award 1960). Club: Century Assn. (N.Y.C.). Author: The Fields of Light, 1951; Alexander Pope; The Poetry of Allusion, 1959; The Poetry of Robert Frost (Explicator award 1963, 1964). Editor: On Translation (hon. mention Harvard Faculty prize), 1959; (with R. Poirer) In Defense of Reading, 1962; John Dryden, 1962; Jane Austen; Mansfield Park, 1965; Shakespeare; Coriolanus, 1966; (with W.H. Bond) Pope's Iliad, 1965; Forms of Lyric, 1970; Harvard English Studies, II, 1971. Contbr. to various books; articles in mags., learned jours. Home: 1 Hay Rd Belmont MA 02178 Office: Harvard MA 02138

BROWMAN, LUDVIG GUSTAV, educator; b. Dekalb, Ill., Apr. 23, 1904; s. Andrew H. and Anne Elizabeth (Valsas) B.; B.S., U. Chgo., 1928, Ph.D., 1935; m. Audra Arnold, Mar. 25, 1933; children—Andrew, Audra, David, Catherine. Research embryologist Tex. Agrl. Expt. Sta., 1935-36; instr. Johns Hopkins, summer 1937; instr. U. Mont., Missoula, 1937-41, asst. prof., 1941-43, asso. prof., 1943-46, prof. 1946—; chmn. dept. zoology, 1949-56. Bd. nat. dirs. Credit Union N.Am. Vice pres. bd. trustees Missoula Community Hosp. Fellow A.A.A.S.; mem. Am. Assn. Anatomists, Genetics Soc. Am., Am. Soc. Zoology, Soc. Exptl. Biol. and Medicine, Soc. Biol. Rhythm, Soc. Devel. and Growth, Sigma Xi. Home: 664 S 6th St E Missoula MT 59801

BROWN, A. L., savs. and loan assn. exec. Exec. v.p. Miami Beach Fed. Savs. and Loan Assn. Office: 401 Lincoln Rd Miami Beach FL 33139*

BROWN, A. THEODORE, educator. Prof. history U. Wis. at Milw. Office: Dept History U Wis at Milw Milwaukee WI 53201*

BROWN, AARON, educator; b. Pensacola, Fla., Dec. 1, 1906; s. Aaron and Alice (Lowe) B.; A.B., Talladega Coll., 1928, A.M., Atlanta U., 1933; Ph.D. (Gen. Edn. Bd. fellow, Rosenwald Found. fellow), U. Chgo., 1943; Litt.D., Lane Coll., Jackson, Tenn., 1954; LL.D., Livingstone Coll., Salisbury, N.C., 1965; Ed.D., Daniel Payne Coll., 1970; m. Martha Ivory, July 10, 1930; children—Marjorie (Mrs. Edward Walton), Chlotele (Mrs. Henry Hopkins), Karl I. Prof. sci. Le Moyne Coll., Memphis, 1928-32; prin. Moultric (Ga.) High Sch., 1933-35; dean State Tchrs. Coll., Forsyth, Ga., 1935; supr. schs., Athens, Ga., 1935-39; dean Ft. Valley (Ga.) State Coll., 1939-41; pres. Albany (Ga.) State Coll., 1943-54; project dir. Phelps-Stokes Fund, N.Y.C., 1954-65; spl. asst. to provost for urban edn. opportunities L.I.U., Bklyn. Center, 1965-69, prof. edn., 1965—, asst. to pres., 1969-; ednl. cons., 1950—. Mem. N.Y.C. Bd. Edn., 1962-69; charter mem., bd. dirs. Nat. Com. for Econ. Edn. Trustee Interdenominational Theol. Center, Atlanta, 1962-68. Recipient Silver medal Treasury Dept., 1945; Gold plaque Albany Movement, 1964, Ga. Tchrs. Assn., 1954: Alumni citation U. Chgo., 1963. Life mem. N.E.A., U. Chgo. Alumni Assn.; mem. Sigma Pi Phi, Alpha Phi Alpha, Phi Delta Kappa. Democrat. Methodist. Mason (33, Shriner), Elk. Author: An Evaluation of the Secondary Schools for Negroes in the South, 1944; The Albany Negro, 1945; Ladders to Improvement, 1963. Home: 1468 President St Brooklyn NY 11213

BROWN, ALBERT EDMOND, ret. labor union exec.; b. Nome, Alaska, Jan. 17, 1907; s. Charlie and Eliza Emerett (Taff) B.; ed. pub. schs., Alaska and Wash.; m. Boma Elleyne Bigelow, June 21, 1935; 1 dau., Elleyne Marie (Mrs. Clarence Lamar Jolly). With Fibreboard Products, Inc., Port Angeles, Wash., 1930-44; sec. Port Angeles Central Labor Council, 1931-44; bus. agt. Retail Clks. Internat. Protective Assn., 1932-44; internat. rep. Internat. Brotherhood Paper Makers, 1944-48, 5th v.p., 1948-50, 4th v.p., 1950-57; merged to become United Papermakers and Paperworkers, 1957, v.p., 1957- 61, gen. v.p., 1961-62, sec.-treas., 1962-70. Active Safety program, also cond. negotiations W. Coast Pulp and Paper Industry U.S. and Can.; mem. labor conf. Nat. Safety Council, 1956—, chmn., 1959-60, bd. dirs., 1957- 61. Recipient citation for accident prevention gov. Wash., 1951; placque Nat. Safety Council, 1960. Elk. Home: 7180 Valley View Dr Los Verdes Estates Gladstone OR

BROWN, ALBERT LINWOOD, econ. cons. co. exec.; b. Lowell, Ariz., Aug. 7, 1922; s. Albert and Elizabeth (Schwab) B.; B.S., U. Ariz., 1947, M.S. (fellow botany 1947- 48), 1948; postgrad. (Princeton fellow pub. affairs) Princeton, 1964-65; m. Virginia Louise Walter, July 3, 1943. Asst. range ecologist USDA/BPR, Woodward, Okla., 1948; instr., asst. range ecologist U. Ariz. and Ariz. Agr. Expt. Sta., 1948-52; range mgmt. expert FAO, UN, Mexico, 1953-55; livestock adviser ICA, Colombia, 1955-57, dep. chief agrl. div., 1957- 59; chief agrl. div. ICA and AID, Honduras, 1959-61; chief agrl. div. AID, Guatemala, 1961-64; chief rural devel. br. Latin Am. Regional Bur., AID, Washington, 1965-66, asst. dir., acting dir. Office Instnl. Devel., Bur. for Latin Am., 1966-67, dir., 1967-68; chief agrl. and rural devel. office AID, Rio de Janeiro, 1968-69; sr. cons. Am. Tech. Assistance Corp., Washington, 1969-70, v.p. internat., 1970—. Served as 1st lt. USAAF, 1942-46; CBI. Mem. Am. Fgn. Service Assn., Soc. for Internat. Devel., Sigma Xi, Alpha Zeta. Home: 3262 Aberfoyle Pl NW Washington DC 20015 Office: 1725 I St NW Washington DC 20006

BROWN, ALBERT WARREN, coll. pres.; b. LaFargeville, N.Y., Nov. 2, 1921; s. Nicholas Haggerman and Edith Elizabeth (Haller) B.; A.B., Syracuse U., 1949, D. Social Sci., 1952; m. Marjorie Anne Higley, Sept. 1, 1946; children—Brewster, Solye, Nelson, Shauna, Sheryl. Faculty, Eastern Ill. U., 1952-58; prof. geography, head dept. Eastern Mich. U., 1958-60, dean Coll. Arts and Scis., 1960-65; pres. State U. Coll. at Brockport, N.Y., 1965—. Mem. Phi Beta Kappa. Episcopalian. Home: 230 Holley St Brockport NY 14420

BROWN, ALEXANDER, (Sandy), clarinetist; b. Izatnagar, India, Feb. 25, 1929. Own band in Eng., 1946—; occasional solo work with Humphrey Lyttelton, Chris Barber; recording artist for Tempo, PyeNixa, Columbia Records. Address: CBS Records 28 Theobalds Rd London WC 1 England*

BROWN, ALEXANDER JOSEPH, Jr., govt. ofcl.; b. Chgo., Sept. 7, 1905; s. Alexander Joseph and Rose Ann (Wilson) B.; LL.B., Loyola U., Chgo., 1930; m. Helen Joan Savage, Dec. 27, 1939; children—Paul Kevin, Alexander Joseph III. Admitted to Ill. bar, 1932, U.S. Supreme Ct. bar, 1960; spl. referee Dept. Labor, 1935-38; pvt. practice, Chgo., 1935-41; with SEC, 1941—, asst. adminstr. Washington regional office, 1958-62, regional adminstr., Washington, 1962—. Mem. Am., Fed. bar assns. Club: Nat. Lawyers (Washington). Home: 3937 Garrison St N W Washington DC 20016 Office: Room 300 Tower 3 Ballston Center 4015 Wilson Blvd Arlington VA 22203

BROWN, ALICE COOKE, educator; b. Westfield, Mass., Apr. 13, 1913; d. William Alfred and Kate (Gault) Cooke; A.B., Middlebury Coll., 1935; M.A., N.Y.U., 1939, Ph.D., 1948; postgrad. (fellow) Columbia, 1940; m. John Hull Brown, June 30, 1947. Tchr., Rutherford (N.J.) High Sch., 1937-45; tchr. history and English, Fairleigh Dickinson Coll., 1945; dean freshman women, dir. admissions Middlebury Coll., 1945-47; prof., chmn. dept. history and govt. U. Hartford, 1953-63, dean women Hillyer Coll., 1953-62, univ. archivist, 1962-63; faculty Green Mountain Coll., Poultney, Vt., 1963—, prof. history, 1967—; chmn. social scis. div., 1966—. Moderator TV series As We Were, WNBC-TV, 1959, Americana, 1960; exhibited oil paintings group shows, Bridport, Goshen, Vergennes, Chaffee Art Gallery, Rutland, Poultney, Vt., U. Hartford, Green Mountain Coll. Mem. evaluation com. social studies Conn. Dept. Edn., 1959-63; overseer Old Sturbridge Village, 1966—; mem. Mayor of Hartford Commn. Civil War Centennial; mem. U.S. com. for UN Internat. Children's Emergency Fund. Mem. Am. Assn. U. Women (past pres. Vt. div.; chmn. mass media and edn. com. Conn. div. 1958- 60), Soc. for Preservation Indian Lore, Inc., Assn. Higher Edn., N.E.A., U. Hartford Womens Assn., New Eng. Polit. Sci. Assn., League Women Voters, Am. Soc. Pub. Adminstrn. (exec. bd.), Conn. Antiquarian and Landmark Soc., Vt., Conn. hist. socs., So. Vt. Art Center, Hartford Civil War Round Table (bd. govs.), Service Bur. Women's Orgns., Soc. Descs. Founders Hartford, Soc. Founders Norwich (Conn.), Vt. Acad. Arts and Scis. (v.p. 1967-69, trustee), Vt. Council on Arts, Sigma Kappa, Delta Gamma, Pi Lambda Theta. Clubs: Soroptimist (past pres. Hartford, del. nat. conv. N.Y.C. 1956); Faculty Women's. Author: History of the University of Hartford, 1959; Connecticut's Role in the Civil War, 1959; Connecticut's Roots, 1963; Mrs. Lincoln's Closest Friend, 1963; Early American Herb Recipes, 1966; Vermont's Role in American Art; also radio and TV scripts; articles in field. Home: Sky Ranch in Goshen RFD 3 Brandon VT 05733

BROWN, ALLAN HARVEY, biologist, educator; b. Newark, Sept. 14, 1917; s. Harvey Winfield and Emma Cecil (Abbott) B.; B.S., U. Md., 1939; M.S., U. Rochester, 1940, Ph.D., 1944; m. Helen Somers, June 14, 1941; children—Bonnie, Kenneth Allan, Janice. Grad. asst. U. Rochester, 1939-42, research asst. physiology Sch. Medicine and Dentistry, 1942-44; staff Radiation Lab., Mass. Inst. Tech., 1944-45; research asso. chem. dept. Fels Fund, U. Chgo., 1945-47; asst. prof. botany U. Minn., 1947-48, asso. prof., 1948- 51, prof., 1951-63, chmn. dept., 1957-60; chmn. dept. biology U. Pa., Phila., 1963-68, prof. biology, 1963—. Mem. Pa. Gov.'s Sci. Adv. Com., 1965-70; chmn. life scis. com. Space Sci. Bd., 1962-68. Trustee Biol. Abstracts, 1965-71, pres. bd., 1970. Guggenheim fellow, 1956-57. Mem. Am. Soc. Plant Physiologists, Bot. Soc. Am., Soc. Gen. Physiologists, Japanese Soc. Plant Physiologists, Internat. Acad. Astronautics (corr.), Sigma Xi, Alpha Zeta, Phi Kappa Phi. Editor: Plant Physiology, 1957-62. Contbr. articles to profl. jours. Research in plant physiology. Home: 1329 Vallee Dr Woodbury NJ 08096 Office: University of Pa Philadelphia PA 19104

BROWN, ALLEN WEBSTER, bishop; b. La Fargeville, N.Y., July 22, 1908; s. Nicholas H. and Edith (Haller) B.; B.A., Syracuse U., 1930; Th.B., Phila. Div. Sch., 1934, Th.M., 1937, D.D., 1955; m. Helen Belshaw, July 5, 1930; children—Allen Webster, Raymond Dutson, Reed Haller, Elizabeth E. Ordained deacon and priest Episcopal Ch., 1934; rector St. Johns Ch., Richfield Springs, N.Y., 1934-40, St. Mark's Ch., Malone, N.Y., 1940-42, Christ Ch., Hudson, N.Y., 1942-53; dean All Sts. Cathedral, Albany, N.Y., 1953-59; suffragan bishop Diocese of Albany, 1959-61, bishop, 1961—. Mem. house depts. Episcopal Ch., 1943, 46, 49, 52, 55; mem. Archbishop's Anglican Orthodox Internation Commn., 1968-70; mem. exec. council Episcopal Ch., 1970—. Mem. Mayor's Adv. Council, Hudson, 1952-53, mem. Chancellor's Panel on Univ. Purposes, 1970—. Trustee St. Agnes Sch., Child's Hosp., St. Margaret's Home, Housae Sch., St. Francis Homes, Nelson House. Mem. N.A.A.C.P. (life), Elka Assn. Clubs: University, Fort Orange. Editor: The Anglican, 1945-47. Home: 62 S Swan St Albany NY 12210 Office: 62 S Swan St Albany NY 12210

BROWN, ALVA BERTRAND, gas and electric co. exec.; b. Vandalia, Ill., July 29, 1899; s. William Henry and Mary I. (Shelton) B.; B.S. in Elec. Engring., Mont. State Coll., 1923; LL.D., Evansville Coll., 1957; m. Lorna LaVyrne Hanson, June 28, 1925; 1 dau., Joyce D. (Mrs. Stephen M. Hill). Student engr. Westinghouse Electric Mfg. Co., 1923-24; test engr. Ohio Edison Co., 1924-26; with So. Ind. Gas and Electric Co., Evansville, 1926—, v.p., 1949-53, pres., 1953-68, chmn., 1965—; dir. CrediThrift Financial Corp., Ind.-Ky. Electric Corp., Internat. Steel Co.; mem. exec. com. Nat. City Bank; dir. Ohio Valley Electric Corp. Trustee East Central Nuclear Group; bd. dirs. Evansville's Future, Inc., Evansville Indsl. Found., Evansville Mus. Arts and Scis.; trustee mem. exec. com. Evansville Coll. Recipient Civic award Evansville Rotary Club, 1956, Spl. Civic award Mayor of Evansville, 1956. Registered profl. engr., Ind. Mem. Evansville C. of C. Nat., Ind. (Engr. of Year award 1952) socs. profl. engrs. Lutheran. Mason (33, Shriner). Clubs: Evansville Country, Petroleum, Exchange, Scientec (Evansville). Home: 5420 Lincoln Av Evansville IN 47715 Office: 20-24 NW 4th St Evansville IN 47708

BROWN, ANN CURPHEY, ch. ofcl.; b. Abilene, Kan., Sept. 23, 1901; d. William Charles and Edith Catherine (Kean) Curphey; student Kan. Wesleyan U., 1921-22, L.H.D., 1966; B.A. in Sociology, U. Denver, 1924; postgrad Iliff Sch. Technology, Denver, 1956; LL.D., Alaska Methodist U., 1967; m. Porter Brown, Sept. 1, 1926; 1 dau., Sally (Mrs. Robert B. Geis). Dir. religious edn. First Methodist Ch., Salina, Kan., 1924-26; treas. woman's div. Christian Service Bd. Missions, Meth. Ch., 1958-60, gen. sec., 1960-64; gen. sec. Bd. Missions United Meth. Ch., 1964-69, mem. Commn. to Restructure Bds. and Agys., 1969—; mem. gen. bd. Nat. Council Chs. Pres. Woman's Home Missionary Soc., N.W. Kan. Conf., 1918. Mem. Gov. Kan. Com. for White House Conf. Children and Youth, 1940. Nat. v.p. U.S.O., 1941-50; mem. nat. bd. YWCA, 1942-54. Author: (with Sally B. Geis) Handbook for Group Leaders, 1952. Address: 2512 S University Blvd Denver, CO 80210.

BROWN, ARNOLD KAYWOOD, Jr., mfg. co. exec.; b. Providence, May 2, 1933; s. Arnold Kaywood and Alva (Jefferds) B.; grad. Phillips Exeter Acad., 1951; B.A. cum laude, Harvard, 1955; m. Edith Helen Chinlund, June 18, 1955; children—Lynne C., Cynthia D. With Fram Corp., 1960—, exec. v.p., dir., 1968—; dir. Fram Filters, Ltd., Canadian Fram, Ltd., Fram Can., Ltd., Fram (N.Z.), Ltd., Martha's Vineyard Shipyard, Inc. Served to 1st Lt. U.S. Army, 1955-60. Mem. Nat. Audubon Soc., Internat. Oceanographic Soc., Marine Hist. Assn. Conglist. (deacon). Clubs: Vineyard Haven (Mass.) Yacht; University (Providence). Home: 79 Middle Hwy Barrington RI 02806 Office: Fram Corp Providence RI 02916

BROWN, ARTHUR, educator; b. N.Y.C., Feb. 12, 1922; s. Samuel S. and Ida (Hoffman) B.; B.A., Bklyn. Coll., 1943; postgrad. fellow U. Ky., 1946-47; Ph.D., U. Chgo., 1950; sr. postdoctoral fellow U. Geneva (Switzerland), 1964; m. Elaine Belaief, Dec. 24, 1947; children—Karen A., Kenneth M., Stephen S., David P. Research asso. U. Chgo., 1951; instr. microbiology State U.N.Y., 1951-55; br. chief virology biology lab. Ft. Detrick, Frederick, Md., 1955-69; head dept. microbiology, prof. U. Tenn., 1969—; vis. prof. Georgetown U., 1967-68, George Washington U., 1957-69, U. Md., 1957-59; mem. tng. grants com. NIH, 1969—; cons. spl. virus cancer program Nat. Cancer Inst., AEC. Bd. dirs. YMCA, Frederick, Md., 1959-61. Served to 1st lt. USAAF, 1943-46. Diplomate Am. Bd. Microbiology. Fellow Am. Acad. Microbiology; mem. Am. Soc. Microbiology, Soc. Gen. Exptl. Biology and Medicine, Am. Assn. Immunologists, A.A.A.S. Jewish religion (dir. synagogue, pres. congregation). Mason. Contbr. articles profl. jours. Home: 7012 Sheffield Dr Knoxville TN 37919

BROWN, ARTHUR BARTON, educator; b. Boston, Feb. 10, 1905; s. George and Elizabeth (Goldberg) B.; B.A. summa cum laude, Harvard, 1925, M.A., 1926, Ph.D., 1929; m. Ruth Levison, Aug. 18, 1935; 1 son, Alan R. Instr., Harvard, part time 1928, 29; Nat. Research fellow Princeton, 1929-30; instr. to asst. prof. Columbia, 1930-38; asst. prof. math. Queens Coll., City U. N.Y., 1938-48, asso. prof., 1945-55, prof., 1955—. Bd. trustees Reece Sch., N.Y.C. Mem. Am. Math. Soc., Math. Assn. Am., Soc. Indsl. and Applied Math., Inst. Math. Statistics. Contbr. articles to math. publs. Home: 155-01 90th Av Jamaica NY 11432

BROWN, ARTHUR HUNTINGDON, Canadian govt. ofcl.; b. Huntingdon, Que., Can., Dec. 15, 1895; s. S. and Florence (Dalgleish) B.; student U. Toronto, 1913-15, Wetmore Hall Law Sch., Regina, Sask., Can., 1919-22; m. Regina Margaret Milliken, July 28, 1926; chidren—Robert Ronald, Alice Jean, James Harold. Admitted to Sask. bar, 1922, practiced in Sask., 1921-29; sec.-treas., legal adviser Canadian Farm Loan Bd., Ottawa, Ont., 1929-39; mem., chmn. Dependents' Allowance Bd., Ottawa, 1939-42; mem. dependents' bd. trustees Dept. Nat. Def., 1942-45; chief exec. officer, legal adviser Dept. Labor, 1943, asst. dep. minister labor, 1951-53, dep. minister labor, 1953-60; vice chmn. Wartime Labor Relations Bd., 1945-48; chmn. Canadian Labor Relations Bd., 1963—; Canadian govt. rep. governing body ILO, Geneva, 1953-57, chmn. 1955-56; chmn. Can. Labour Relations Bd., Ottawa. Served with F.A., Canadian Army, World War I. Decorated Order Brit. Empire, 1943. Mem. United Ch. of Can. Home: 15 Allan Pl Ottawa Ontario Canada Office: 340 Laurier Av W Ottawa Ontario Canada

BROWN, ARTHUR THOMAS, architect; b. Tarkio, Mo., May 6, 1900; s. John Vallance and Ada (Moore) B.; B.S., Tarkio Coll., 1923; B.Arch., Ohio State U., 1927; scholar Lake Forest Found. Architecture and Landscape Arch., 1927; m. Margaret Caroline Munn, Dec. 23, 1927; children—Gordon Vallance, Arthur Thomas. Draftsman, office David Adler, Chgo., 1928-32; with Century of Progress Expn., Chgo., 1932-34, Richard A. Morse, Tucson, 1936-39; partner Richard A. Morse, 1939-42; pvt. practice architecture, Tucson, 1942-70; partner Gordon V. Brown, 1970—. Dir. Tucson Fine Arts Assn., 1948-52. Recipient mention for Rosenberg House, Progressive Architecture awards, 1946, award of merit A.I.A., 1949, Western Mountain Dist. awards for Winsor House, Ariz. Biltmore Motor Hotel, 1st Christian Ch., A.I.A., 1953, 54; Smith Meml. Chapel exhibited Pan Am. Congress of Architects, Lima, Peru, 1947; Alumni citation Tarkio Coll., 1958; Distinguished Alumnus award Ohio State U., 1960. Fellow A.I.A. (mem. nat. com. on sch. bldgs. 1948-50, pres. Ariz. chpt. 1946); mem. Palette and Brush Club, Tucson Watercolor Guild, Tucson Gem and Mineral Soc. Presbyn. Rotarian. Contbr. archtl. books and mags. Patentee prefabricated cylinder house, method of producing a shell roof structure, open wall door frame, Modular Mobile. Home: 740 N Country Club Rd Tucson AZ 85716 Office: 726 N Country Club Rd Tucson AZ 85716

BROWN, ARTHUR WAYNE, coll. pres.; b. Sheshequin, Pa., Apr. 20, 1917; s. Arthur L. and Helen E. (Laclair) B.; A.B., U. Scranton, 1937; M.A., Cornell U., 1938; Ph.D., Syracuse U., 1950; m. Dorothy C. Johnston, Sept. 17, 1938; children— Anne (Mrs. Allan Root), Margaret (Mrs. Frank O'Neill), Michael, Patricia (Mrs. Eugene Crabbe), Thomas, Arthur, Mary, Deborah. Prof. English, Utica Coll. of Syracuse U., 1955-63; prof. English, chmn. dept., dir. Inst. Humanities, Adelphi U., 1963-65, pres., 1965-67; dean faculties, dean Grad. Sch., Fordham U., 1967-68, v.p. for acad. affairs, 1968-69; pres. Marygrove Coll., Detroit, 1969—. Westchester dir. 1st Nat. City Bank. Sec., Catholic Commn. on Intellectual and Cultural Affairs, 1970—; exec. com. Mich. Colls. Found. Bd. dirs. Catholic Charities, Utica, 1960-62, United Fund, L.I.; chmn. bd. dirs. St. Elizabeth Sch. Nursing, Utica, 1961-62; trustee Molloy Coll., L.I.; bd. govs. St. Paul's Sch., Garden City, 1968-69. Am. Council Learned Societies grantee, 1961-62. Mem. Am. Assn. U. Profs., Modern Lang. Assn., Newcomen Soc. N.Am. Clubs: Detroit Golf, Detroit Economic. Author: Always Young for Liberty. 1956; William Ellery Channing, 1960; Margaret Fuller, 1964. Co- editor: (series) Great American Thinkers, 1964. Home: 8827 Marygrove Dr Detroit MI 48221

BROWN, AUBREY J., agrl. economist; b. Hemple, Mo., July 3, 1913; s. Aubrey Samuel and Della Florence (Holmes) B.; B.S., U. Ill., 1935, M.S., 1938, Ph.D., 1946; m. Helen Margaret Molloy, Sept. 1, 1935; children—Margaret Ann (Mrs. Roger Huston), Aubrey Charles, Paula Louise. Asst. U. Ill., 1935- 38; former mem. faculty U. Ky., prof. agrl. marketing, head dept. markets and rural finance, 1946-52, head dept. Agrl. Econs., trustee, 1957-63. Mem. Nat. Tobacco Industry Adv. Council, Ky. Gov.'s Agrl. Adv. Com., Agrl. com. Agrl. and Indsl. Devel. Bd. Mem. Am. Farm Econ. Assn. (chmn. agrl. marketing com. 1948-50; mem. editorial council 1949-55; v.p. 1958-59), Am. Assn. U. Profs., Am. Bankers Assn. (mem. Ky. agrl. council and com. 1959—), Ky. C. of C. (agrl. com.), Burley and Dark Leaf Tobacco Export Assn. (dir.), Ky. Farm Bur. Fedn. (resolutions com.), Ky. Bankers Assn. (agrl. com.), Sigma Xi, Lambda Chi Alpha, Gamma Sigma Delta, Omicron Delta Kappa. Author: Agrl. Expt. Sta. bulls. Home: 119 Dantzler Ct Lexington KY 40503

BROWN, AUBREY NEBLETT, Jr., clergyman, editor; b. Hillsboro, Tex., May 6, 1908; s. Aubrey Neblett and Virginia Rose (Sims) B.; A.B., Davidson Coll., 1929; B.D., Union Theol. Sem., Va., 1932; Litt.D., Southwestern at Memphis, 1950; D.D., Maryville Coll., 1961; m. Sarah Dumond Hill, Oct. 4, 1932; children—Aubrey Neblett III, Zaida English (Mrs. Douglas Robb Paden), Julia Haywood (Mrs. Edward Townsend Diehl), Virginia Sims (Mrs. Rod E. Ashworth), Eleanor Berkeley (Mrs. Milton Byrum Bigger), William Hill, Ernest Thompson, Katherine Purdie. Ordained to ministry Presbyn. Ch., 1932; pastor Presbyn. chs., Ronceverte, W. Va., 1932-38, Montgomery, W.Va., 1938-43; editor Presbyn. Outlook, Richmond, Va. 1943- -, Going-to-Coll. Handbook, 1946—. Moderator Presbyn. Ch. of U.S., Synod of W.Va., 1946. Pres., Richmond Council Human Relations, 1957-59, Va. Council Human Relations, 1963-65; chmn. Va. Adv. Com. to U.S. Commn. on Civil Rights, 1966-67; pres. Richmond Area chpt. UN Assn. U.S.A., 1967-69. Recipient Editorial citation Asso. Ch. Press, 1952, Torch of Liberty award Va. B'nai B'rith, 1966. Mem. Omicron Delta Kappa. Democrat. Club: Internat. Torch. Home: 3213 Brook Rd Richmond VA 23227 Office: 512 E Main St Richmond VA 23219

BROWN, BAILEY, U.S. judge; b. 1917; A.B., U. Mich.; LL.B., Harvard. Admitted to bar, 1941; now chief U.S. judge Western Dist. Tenn. Mem. Am. Bar Assn. Address: U S District Court Memphis TN 38103

BROWN, BEN HILL, Jr., cons.; b. Spartanburg, S.C., Feb. 8, 1914; s. Ben Hill and Clara Twitty (Colock) B.; A.B., Wofford College, 1935; J.D., George Washington U., 1939; diploma in res. Northwestern U., 1969-70; m. Barbara B. Burt, Mar. 3, 1940 (div.); children—Ben Hill III, Barbara Middleton, Clara Colcock, Hardy Burt; m. 2d, Naomi Huber, June 27, 1970. Admitted So. Car. bar, 1939, practiced in Spartanburg, South Carolina, 1939-41; asst. to legal adviser Dept. of State, 1946-49, dep. asst. sec. for Congl. Relations, 1949-55; assigned Nat. War Coll., 1955-56; fgn. service officer, 1956—; dir. U.S. Operations Mission to Iraq, 1956-58, U.S. Operations Mission to Libya, 1959-60; consul general Turkey, Istanbul, 1960-64; U.S. ambassador to Liberia, 1964-69; ret., 1970; pvt. cons., 1971—. Attended the Gen. Assembly U.N. as adviser, 1947, mem. survey mission to Germany, 1948, mem. U.S. del. to Intergovtl. Conf. to draft agreement establishing Internat. Authority for the Ruhr, 1948; vice chmn. U.S. delegation to UN Conf. on Trade and Devel., 1964. Called active duty as res. officer, 1941; served mil. govt. Italy, Supreme Hdqrs., Allied Expeditionary Forces, in England, France and Germany; dep. chief, acting chief legal br., Office Mil. Govt. (U.S. Zone), Germany, 1945-46; inactive duty as lt. col., Judge Adv. Gen. Dept., 1946. Decorated Legion of Merit, Bronze Star Medal, Am. Defense and Am. Theater ribbons, European Theater ribbon with 4 battle stars, Victory and Army of Occupation medals. Mem. Spartanburg Bar Assn., Phi Delta Phi, Kappa Alpha Order, Pi Kappa Delta, Chi Beta Phi, Sigma Upsilon, Blue Key. Episcopalian. Mason. Home: 539 S Fairfax St Alexandria VA 22314

BROWN, BERNARD J., former U.S. atty.; b. 1919; grad. Providence Coll.; LL.B., Dickinson Coll., Carlisle, Pa. Admitted to bar, 1948; former U.S. atty. Middle Dist. Pa. Mem. Am. Bar Assn.*

BROWN, BERNARD LOREN, financial exec.; b. Galva, Ill., Nov. 5, 1919; s. S. W. and Hettie (Lapan) B.; B.S., U. Cal. at Los Angeles, 1943; m. Pauline Kahler, June 30, 1940; children—Sharon (Mrs. B. Z. Moore), Lawrence, Richard. With Douglas Aircraft Co., Santa Monica, Cal., 1940-62, finance mgr., 1955- 59, treas., 1959-62; treas. Ling-Temco-Vought, Inc., Dallas, 1962-67, v.p., treas., 1967—. Served with USNR, 1944-46. Home: 5707 Meletio Lane Dallas TX 75230 Office: PO Box 5003 1600 Pacific St Dallas TX 75222

BROWN, BERTRAM S., govt. ofcl.; b. Bklyn., Jan. 28, 1931; s. David and Jean (Gubkin) B.; M.D., Cornell U., 1956; M.P.H., Harvard, 1960; m. Joy Gilman, June 17, 1952; children—Dale, Laurie, Wendy, Tracy. Intern pediatrics Yale Sch. Medicine, 1956-57; resident, psychiatry teaching fellow Boston Psychopathic Hosp., Harvard Med. Sch., also Mass. Mental Health Center, 1957-60; with Nat. Inst. Mental Health, Washington, 1960—, dep. dir., 1967-70, dir., 1970—; asst. clin. prof. psychiatry George Washington U. Sch. Medicine, 1962-71, clin. prof. psychiatry, 1971—. Dep. spl. asst. and cons. to Pres. for Mental Retardation, 1963-66; mem. President's Com. Adminstrn. Law Enforcement and Justice, 1966-67; mem. tech. adv. panel Maurice Falk Med. Fund, Pitts., 1963-70; mem. adv. bd. Parents Without Partners, Washington, 1966-; spl. asst. to sec. Dept. Health, Edn. and Welfare for drug abuse prevention, 1970—. Recipient Commendation medal USPHS, 1967. Diplomate Am. Bd. Psychiatry and Neurology. Fellow Council Nat. and Internat. Affairs, Am. Psychiat. Assn., A.M.A.; mem. Am. Pub. Health Assn., Am. Assn. Mental Deficiency, Am. Sociol. Assn., Med. Assn. Mental Health, Phi Beta Kappa, Alpha Omega Alpha, Delta Omega. Editorial adv. com. Social Psychology of Mental Health (with H. Wechsler, L. F. Solomon, B.M. Kramer), 1966, Research, profl. publs., spl. reports (with others) mental health, therapy, preventive medicine, community health programs. Bd. editors PHS World. Home: 7817 Greentwig Rd Bethesda MD 20034 Office: 5600 Fishers Lane Rockville MD 20852

BROWN, BOB MARION, physicist, educator; b. Asherton, Tex., Mar. 25, 1922; s. Allie Marion and Martha Lee (McCarley) B.; B.S., Southwestern U., 1942; Ph.D., Cornell U., 1952; m. Mary Elizabeth Feagin, June 23, 1946; childrenAlan Marion, Robert Feagin, Craig McCarley. Research scientist research lab. Gen. Electric Co., 1952-53; mem. faculty Southwestern U., 1953-61, prof., head dept. physics, 1953-61, chmn. physics dept., since 1967-; research scientist Def. Research Lab., U. Tex., 1955-61; sr. physicist Tracor, Inc., Austin, Tex., 1961-. Served with AUS, 1944-46. Recipient award for excellence in teaching Scarborough Found. of Southwestern U., 1959. Mem. Am. Assn. Physics Tchrs., Am. Phys. Soc., Am. Acoustical Soc., Am. Assn. U. Profs. (pres. Southwestern U. chpt. 1960). Author articles, tech. papers electromagnetic wave scattering and propagation, acoustic propagation and scattering, signal processing. Home: 1230 Austin Av Georgetown, TX 78626. Office: Tracor Inc 6500 Tracor Lane Austin, TX 78721.

BROWN, BRENDAN F., jurist and legal educator; b. Sioux City, Ia., Oct. 19, 1898; s. Matthew Francis and Bertha Isabella (Brady) B.; A.B., Creighton U., Omaha, Neb., 1921, LL.B., 1924; LL.M., Cath. U. of Am., 1925, J.U.B. and J.U.L., 1926, J.U.D., 1927; Ph. D. in Law, Oxford, 1932; spl. law research student, Harvard, 1937-38; unmarried. Admitted to Neb. bar, 1924, D.C. bar, 1925, U.S. Supreme Ct., U.S. Ct. of Claims and U.S. Ct. of Customs and Patent Appeals, 1939; with firm Root, Clark, Buckner and Ballantine, N.Y. C., summer 1939, Smart and Von Sneidern, part time 1940-41; spl. research work as spl. asst. to atty. gen. Dept. of Justice, 1946; chief of opinions and regulations sect. Post Office Dept., 1948; instr. in English, history and Latin, Creighton U., 1931- 23; instr. in law Cath. U. of Am., 1926-27 and 1932-40, asso. prof. and acting dean, 1942-46, prof. of law 1946-54, dean 1949-54; prof. of law, Loyola U. of So., New Orleans, 1954-; legal adviser law firm Urciolo, Miller, Platshen & Urciolo, Washington. Chancellor to Bostwell Inst. New Orleans; dir. Legal Inst., Regional Offices, VA; gen. reporter 6th Internat. Congress of Comparative Law, Hamburg, Germany, 1962. Jud. econs. chief prosecution Internat. Mil. Tribunal for Far East, war crimes trial, Tokyo, Japan, 1946-48. Recipient Creighton U. Alumnus of Year award, 1963; Distinguished Alumnus Outstanding Achievement award in field of law Catholic U. of Am. 1963, Mem. Internat, Assn. for Philosophy Law and Social Philosophy (Am. sect.), Canadian Inter- American Research Inst. (corr.), Inter-Am., Fed. (dist. v.p., mem. nat. council), Am., Neb., D.C., La., New Orleans bar assns., Bar City N.Y., Am., La. law insts., Riccobono Seminar Roman Law Am. (past sec.), Assn. Am. Law Schs. (chmn. Round Table council jurisprudence 1956-57), Canon Law Soc. of Am. (past v.p.), St. Thomas More Soc. of Am. (pres.), Am. Soc. Internat. Law, Internat. Law Assn., Am. Assn. U. Prof., Am. Soc. for Legal History (v.p. 1956-57), Catholic Assn. for Internat. Peace, Am. Cath. Hist. Assn., Am. Cath. Philos. Assn., U.N. League of Lawyers (former mem. exec. com. U.S. div.), Oxford (Catholic Assn., St. Catherine Soc. Oxford, England), mem. Am. Legion, Krewe of Virgilians, Alpha Pi Omicron (hon.), Alpha Simga Nu, Delta Sigma Rho, Gamma Eta Gamma, Blue Key, Alpha Delta Gamma. K.C. Clubs: Harvard, Nat. Lawyers (Washington); Round Table (New Orleans). Author: The Natural Law Reader, 1960; Crimes Against International Law (with Joseph B. Keenan), 1950. Contbr. numerous articles to law bulls. and publs., also many book reviews. Address: 5211 New Hampshire Av NW Washington DC also 8010 Freret St New Orleans LA ☆

BROWN, BRUCE ALAN, motion picture producer; b. San Francisco, Dec. 1, 1937; s. Dana Earl and Myrna (Severin) B.; ed. pub. schs., Cal.; m. Patricia Hunter, June 15, 1959; childrenDana, Wade, Nancy. Film prodns. include; (90 minute lectures) Slippery When Wet, 1959, Surf Crazy, 1960, Barefoot Adventure, 1961, Surfing Hollow Days, 1962, Water-Logged, 1963; (feature length) The Endless Summer (Bell Ringer award Scholastic mag. 1966, Picture of month award Boxoffice mag. 1967), 1964; (TV) Holiday, 1959, True Adventure, 1961-62, Wanderlust, 1962, Islands in the Sun, 1963, The Surfing Set, 1966, also sports specials; producer promotional films, commercials, also stock footage; frequent TV guest appearances. Served with USNR, 1955-58. Office: 24633 Del Prado Dana Point, CA 92629.

BROWN, BRUCE K., mgmt. cons.; b. Columbus., O. May 4, 1899; s. B. Frank and Anna S. (Lotspiech) B.; B.S., U. Ill., 1918, M.S., 1920; m. Antoinette Turner, July 19, 1919; children—Janet, Bruce K. With Burgess Labs., Madison, Wis., 1920-23, Comml. Solvents Corp., Terre Haute, Ind., 1923-27; admitted to Ill. bar, 1937, Ind. bar, 1925, D.C. bar, 1937, U.S. Supreme Ct. bar, 1930; practiced patent law, N.Y.C., 1923-29; with Standard Oil Co. of Ind., Chgo., 1929-41; gen. mgr. research and devel. 1938-41, v.p., dir., 1945-49; pres. Pan-Am. So. Corp., 1949-56; pres., chief exec. officer Petroleum Chems., Inc., 1956-60; bus. cons.; former chmn. bd., chmn. exec. com., dir. Murphy Corp., El Dorado; dir. Ingram Corp., New Orleans. asst. dep. petroleum coordinator, Washington, 1941-45, chmn. mil. petroleum adv. bd., 1947-50; mem. Nat. Petroleum Council; dep. adminstr. Petroleum Adminstrn. for Def., Washington, 1950-52. Trustee Dillard U. Served as 2d lt., inf., U.S. Army, 1918. Republican. Methodist. Mason. Clubs: Pickwick, Plimsoll (New Orleans). Author: A Survey of Nitrocellulose Lacquers, 1926; Oil Men in Washington, 1965; Committee Structures, 1965. Home: 1550 2d St New Orleans LA 70130 Office: 2828 Internat Trade Mart New Orleans LA 70130

BROWN, BRUCE MCCLAVE, librarian; b. N.Y.C., June 11, 1917; s. Earl Bigelow and Maude (McClave) B.; A.B., Middlebury Coll., 1938; M.A., N.Y.U., 1946; B.S. in L.S., Columbia, 1947; m. Helen Brown, June 27, 1941; children—Duncan, Laurie, Deborah. Engaged in advt. and printing, 1940-45; reference librarian Free Pub. Library, Englewood, N.J., 1947-48; mem. staff Colgate U. Library, Hamilton, N.Y., 1948—, acting librarian, 1959-60, librarian, 1960—. Sec.-treas. Central N.Y. Reference & Resources Council. Mem. Am. (publs. com. coll. and research libraries assn. 1960-63). N.Y. State (pres. coll. and univ. sect. 1962-63, mem. scholarship com. 1965-69, chmn. 1966-68, 1st v.p. 1970, pres. 1971); library assns., Electric Railroaders Assn., Assn. Coll. and Research Libraries (com. non-western resources), Am. Assn. U. Profs. Socialist. Unitarian. Home: RD 2 Earlville Rd Hamilton NY 13346

BROWN, BUCK, cartoonist; b. Morrison, Tenn., Feb. 3, 1936; s. Michael Fate and Doris (Lemings) B.; A.A., Wilson Jr. Coll., Chgo., 1962; B.F.A., U. Ill., 1966; m. Mary Ellen Steverson, Dec. 24, 1965; children—Robert, Tracy Elizabeth. Bus driver Chgo. Transit Authority, 1958-63; cartoonist, works appearing Playboy, Esquire, True, Cavalier, Rudder, Tuesday, Rogue mags., 1961—; founder, pres. Fat Chance Prodns., Ltd. Mem. Vice Pres.'s Task Force on Youth Motivation, 1968-70. Served with USAF, 1955-58. Named one of 10 outstanding young men, Chgo. Jr. C. of C., 1970. Mem. Mag. Cartoonists Guild.‡

BROWN, BYRON WILLIAM, Jr., biostatistician, educator; b. Chgo., Apr. 21, 1930; s. Byron William and Ruth (Munson) B.; B.A. in Math., U. Minn., 1952, M.S. in Statistics, 1955, Ph.D. in Biostatistics, 1959; m. Janet Louise Hyde, July 30, 1949; children—Byron William III, Eric Paul, Alan Thomas, Nancy Ellen, Mark Andrew, Lisa Anne. Asst. prof. biostatistics, La. State U. Med. Sch., New Orleans, 1956-57; lectr., asst. prof., asso. prof. biostatistics Sch. Pub. Health, U. Minn., 1957-65, prof., head biostatistics, 1965-68; prof., head biostatistics Stanford, 1968—; cons. FDA, VA, NIH, NASA. Served with USAF, 1949. Fellow Am. Statis. Assn. (sect. pres., asso. editor Jour.); mem. Biometrics Soc., Am. Pub. Health Assn., Am. Heart Assn., Phi Beta Kappa, Sigma Xi. Democrat. Lutheran. Contbr. articles profl. jours. Home: 981 Cottrell St Stanford CA 94305

BROWN, CALVIN SMITH, educator; b. Oxford, Miss., Sept. 27, 1909; s. Calvin Smith and I. Maud (Morrow) B.; B.A., U. Miss., 1928; M.A., U. Cin., 1929; (Rhodes scholar 1930-33), Oxford (Eng.) U., 1932; Ph.D., U. Wis., 1934; m. Irene M. Hughes, Aug. 18, 1934; 1 son, Calvin Hugh. Instr. English and German, Phillips Exeter Acad., 1934-35; asso. prof. English, Memphis State Coll., 1935-38; asst. prof. U. Ga., Athens, 1938-40, asso. prof., 1940-46, prof., 1946-57, Found. prof. English and comparative lit., 1957—, head comparative lit. dept., 1968—; lectr. U. Miss., summers 1937, 38; acting head dept. comparative lit. U. Wis., 1941, 42. Research analyst (cryptanalytic) U.S. Mil. Intelligence, Arlington, Va., 1942-46. Am. Council Learned Socs. Faculty Study fellowship, 1951-52. Mem. Am. (adv. bd. 1968—), Internat. comparative lit. assns., Am. Musicol. Soc., Am. Soc. Aesthetics, Modern Lang. Assn., S. Atlantic Modern Lang. Assn. (exec. com. 1960-61). Author: Music and Literature, 1949; Repetition in Zola's Novels, 1952; Tones Into Words, 1953; also articles. Editor: Masterworks of World Literature, 1947, 55, 70; Reader's Companion to World Literature, 1956. Home: 145 Milledge Terrace Athens GA 30601

BROWN, CAMERON, ins. co. exec.; b. Chgo., Sept. 29, 1914; s. George Frederic and Irene (Larmon) B.; A.B., U. Ill., 1937; m. Dorothea Fruechtenicht, May 10, 1947 (div. Feb. 1965); children—Reid L., Deborah Sue; m. 2d, Jean McGrew, Dec. 22, 1965; 1 dau., Sophia Lyn. Vice pres. R. B. Jones & Sons, Inc., 1938-41; v.p. Geo. F. Brown & Sons, Inc., Chgo., 1947, exec. v.p., 1950-53, pres., dir., 1953-64, chmn., chief exec. officer, dir., 1964—; pres., dir. Interstate Nat. Corp., 1968—, chmn., 1970—; pres. Brown & Hawley, Inc., 1962—; chmn., pres., chief exec. officer, dir. Nat. Student Marketing Corp., 1970—; v.p., dir. Interstate Fire & Casualty Co., 1952—, exec. v.p., 1953-56, pres., 1956—; pres., dir. Chgo. Ins. Co., 1957—, Interstate Reins. Corp., 1961—, Interstate Life Assurance Co., 1963—; chmn. exec. com. Higham, Neilson, Whitridge & Reid, Inc., 1962—. Underwriting mem. Lloyd's of London, 1971—; sec., dir. Ill. Ins. Information Service, 1967—. Pres. Chgo. area Planned Parenthood Assn., 1969-72. Trustee U. Chgo. Cancer Research Found.; mem. John Evans Club, Northwestern U., U. Ill. Pres.'s Club, U. Ill. Found. Served from 2d lt. to lt. col. Gen. Staff Corps, AUS, 1941-45. Decorated Bronze Star medal with oak leaf cluster. Mem. Am. Mgmt. Assn., Commerce and Industry Assn., Lloyd's Brokers Assn. (chmn. 1959-60), Nat. Assn. Ind. Insurers (bd. govs.), Newcomen Soc., Internat. Wine and Food Soc. (Chgo.), Surplus Line Brokers Assn. (chmn. 1954), Confrerie des Chevaliers du Tastevin (comdr.), Psi Upsilon. Clubs: Chicago, Attic, Executive (dir., 1st v.p. 1970-71), Economic, Mid-America, Racquet, Arts, Casino (Chgo.); Army-Navy Country (Washington); Winter, Shoreacres, Onwentsia (Lake Forest, Ill.); Pine Valley Golf (Clementon, N.J.); India House, University (N.Y.C.). Contbg. author: Property and Liability Handbook, 1965. Home: 600 S Ridge Rd Lake Forest IL 60045 Office: 175 W Jackson Blvd Chicago IL 60604

BROWN, CAROLYN RICE, (Mrs. Earle Brown), dancer, choreographer; b. Fitchburg, Mass., Sept. 26, 1927; d. James Parker and Marion (Stevens) Rice; B.A. cum laude (Wheaton scholar), Wheaton Coll., 1950; postgrad. Juilliard Sch. Music, 1952-53; studied dance with Marion Rice, Margaret Craske, Anthony Tudor, Merce Cunningham; m. Earle Brown, June 28, 1950. Leading soloist Merce Cunningham Dance Co., N.Y.C., 1953—; with resident dance co. Bklyn. Acad. Music, 1968—; performances throughout U.S., Can., Europe, Mexico, S. Am., India, Thailand, Japan; duo tours to Europe, 1958, 60, world tour, 1964; Europe tours summer, fall 1966; TV performances in U.S., Europe, Can.; tchr. Merce Cunningham Studio, 1954—, Conn. Coll. Sch. Dance, 1958-61, U. Cal. at Los Angeles, 1963, Walker Art Center, Mpls., 1967, U. Colo., 1968; performed in John Cage's Theatre Piece, 1960, in Robert Rauschenberg's Pelican, 1963; choreographer Balloon for First N.Y. Theatre Rally, 1965, Car Lot for Manhattan Festival Ballet, 1967 (Jersey Jour. award for best choreography 1967-68), West Country for Juilliard Dance Ensemble, 1970. Bd. dirs. Paper Bag Players, 1965-66, Found. for Performance Arts, 1967—. Recipient Dance Mag. award, 1970, 100th Anniversary Distinguished Service award Wheaton Coll., 1970. Mem. Phi Beta Kappa. Contbr. articles to Ballet Rev., Dance Perspectives. Office: Cunningham Dance Found Inc 463 West St New York City NY 10014

BROWN, CECIL, TV-radio news commentator, educator, lectr.; b. New Brighton, Pa., Sept. 14, 1907; s. Maurice I. and Jennie (Broida) B.; student Western Res. U., 1925-27; B.S., Ohio State U., 1929; Litt. D. (hon.), Union Coll. m. Martha Leaine Kohn, July 20, 1938. Sailed as seaman to S. Am., Russia, West Africa; wrote stories of experience, pub. in Youngstown (O.) Vindicator, 1928-29; reporter for United Press, Los Angeles, 1931-32; editor Prescott (Ariz.) Jor.-Miner, 1933; staff Pitts. Press, 1934-36, Newark Ledger, 1936-37, free lance writer, Europe, North Africa, 1937-38; with Internat. News Service, 1938-39; news broadcast for CBS, Rome, 1940-41, Yugoslavia, Cairo, Singapore, 1941-42, Australia, N.Y.C., 1942-58; news commentator over MBS, 1944-57; news commentator ABC, 1957-58; Far East bur. chief NBC, 1958-62, TV-radio news commentator, Los Angeles, 1962-64; dir. news and pub. affairs, commentator Community TV of So. Cal., KCET-28, Los Angeles, 1964-67; TV cons. Ency. Brit., 1967-68; prof. communications and internat. affairs Cal. State Poly. Coll., Pomona, 1967—. Expelled from Italy Apr. 1, 1941, by Italian govt. for continued hostile attitude toward Fascism. Survivor of sinking by Japanese bombers of Prince of Wales and Repulse, South China Sea, Dec. 10, 1941. Recipient awards for distinguished radio news reporting from abroad during 1941 from Sigma Delta Chi, Overseas Press Club, Nat. Council for Edn. by Radio, Nat. Headliners Club, George Foster Peabody Award, Motion Picture Daily's award, winner World-Telegram poll for outstanding single broadcast of 1942, Alfred I. Dupont award for best TV news commentary, 1965; awards for commentary A.P., 1965, 66. Club: Overseas Press (past pres.). Author: Suez to Singapore, 1942; Introduction to ltd. edits. Club edit. Carlyle's The French Revolution, 1956; chpt. on Japan in Memo to J.F.K. Contbr. to mags. Home: 10450 Wilshire Blvd Los Angeles CA 90024

BROWN, CECIL M., author; b. Bolton, N.C., July 3, 1943; s. Cecil and Dorothy Brown; B.A., Columbia, 1966; M.A., U. Chgo., 1967. Tchr. English, U. Ill. U. Cal. At Berkeley. Merrit Coll., Oakland, Cal., prod. own plays Merritt Coll.. Author books including Life and Loves of Mister Jiveass Nigger, 1970. Address: 1856 Dwight Way Berkeley CA 94703

BROWN, CHARLES ARTHUR, lawyer; b. Greenwood, Miss., Sept. 30, 1929; s. Charles and Lois (Finch) B.; student Henderson State Tchrs. Coll., Arkadelphia, Ark., 1947-49; LL.B., U. Ark., 1953; m. Jennifer Sue Carter, June 2, 1957; children—Chryl Adele, Krista Lynne, Charles Carter. Admitted to Ark. bar, 1953; practice in Little Rock, 1956—; asso. Patten & Brown, 1956-60, partner, 1960—; instr. Ark. Law Sch., 1956-67; spl. instr. bus. law Little Rock U., 1965-67. Asso. legal counsel U.S. Jaycees, 1964-65, mem. exec. com., 1964- 66, gen. counsel, 1965-66. Pres. Leawood Property Owners Assn., 1966-68; mem. Little Rock Sch. Bd., 1968—. Served with AUS, 1954-55. Recipient Distinguished Service award Little Rock Jaycees, 1966, Boss of Year award Greater Little Rock Jaycees, 1970. Mem. Am., Ark., Pulaski County bar assns., Am. Ark. trial lawyers assns., Little Rock C. of C. (past dir.). Mason (Shriner). Home: 7713 Leawood Blvd Little Rock AR 72205 Office: Nat Investors Bldg Little Rock AR 72201

BROWN, CHARLES EARL, lawyer; b. Columbus, O., June 6, 1919; s. Anderson and Ruth (Keeran) B.; A.B., Ohio Wesleyan U., 1941; J.D., U. Mich., 1949; m. Mary Elizabeth Hiett, May 23, 1959; children—Douglas Charles, Rebecca Ruth. Admitted to Ohio bar, 1949, since practiced in Toledo; pvt. practice, 1949-50; asso. Zachman, Boxell, Bebout & Torbet, 1950-53; partner Boxell, Bebout, Torbet & Baker and predecessor firm, 1953—. Pres., dir. Maumee Fabrics Co.; sec., dir. Herman Bros., Inc. Chmn. steering and exec. coms. Auto Trim Wholesalers sect. Automotive Service Industry Assn., 1960-68. Republican county chmn. adv. com., 1969-70, mem. exec. com. Served to capt. AUS, 1941-46; col. Res. Decorated Bronze star medal; recipient John J. Pershing award U.S. Army Command and Gen. Staff Coll., 1963, certificate of achievement XX U.S. Army Corps, 1966. Mem. Am., Ohio (bd. govs. real property sect.), Toledo (mem. exec. com.) bar assns., Toledo Area C. of C. (past trustee, com. chmn.), Res. Officers Assn., Assn. U.S. Army, Phi Beta Kappa. Conglist. (past chmn. trustees). Mason (32). Home: 3716 Grantley Rd Toledo OH 43613 Office: Toledo Trust Bldg Toledo OH 43604

BROWN, CHARLES LEE, telephone co. exec.; b. Richmond, Va., Aug. 23, 1921; s. Charles Lee and Mary (McNamara) B.; B.S. in Elec. Engring., U. Va., 1943; m. Ann Lee Saunders, July 25, 1959; 1 son, Charles A. With Am. Tel. & Tel. Co., and affiliates, 1946—, v.p., gen. mgr. Ill. Bell Telephone Co., 1963-65, v.p. operations, dir., 1965-69, pres. 1969—, also dir.; dir. Harris Trust and Savs. Bank, Inland Steel Corp. Chmn. governing bd. Ill. Council on Econ. Edn., chmn. Ill. Citizens for Clean Water; mem. adv. council Northwestern U. Assos.; mem. bus. adv. council Chgo. Urban League; mem. citizens bd. U. Chgo.; mem. Merit Employment Steering Com.; mem. sponsoring bd. United Settlement Appeal; mem. Com. for Econ. and Cultural Devel. of Chgo. Bd. dirs. Better Bus. Bur. Met. Chgo., 1963-70, Crusade of Mercy, 1968; citizens bd. U. Chgo.; sponsoring bd. Travelers Aid Soc., Chgo.; bd. dirs. Businessmen's Tng. Consortium, Lake Forest Hosp.; mem. adv. bd. Met. Chgo; past dir. Community Fund Chgo.; trustee Loyola U., Chgo.; nat. trustee Lake Forest Coll.; bd. dirs. Chgo. Central Area Com.; trustee Chgo. Ednl. TV Assn., Mus. Sci. and Industry. Served with USNR, 1943-46. Mem. Delta Upsilon, Theta Tau, Omicron Delta Kappa. Presbyn. Clubs: Chicago, Economic, Mid-America (governing bd.), Chicago Athletic Assn., Commercial, Old Elm, Onwentsia, Wayfarers 66 N Mayflower Rd Lake Forest IL 60045 Office: 225 W Randolph St Chicago IL 60606

BROWN, CHARLES LEONARD, educator; b. Ranger, Tex., June 30, 1920; s. Charles C. and Maxine (Seed) B.; B.S. in Mech. Engring., Rice Inst., 1940; M.S., Purdue U., 1943, Ph.D., 1949; m. Elizabeth Eleanor Baird, Feb. 24, 1945; children—Lynn Manice, Margaret Lee. Mem. faculty Purdue U., 1940—, prof. mech. engring., 1957—. Mem. Am. Soc. M.E., Am. Soc. Engring. Edn., Sigma Xi, Pi Tau Sigma, Tau Beta Pi. Author: Basic Thermodynamics, 1951.‡

BROWN, CHARLES PERSHING, army officer; b. McAlester, Okla., Jan. 11, 1918; s. Samuel Franklin and Minerva (Price) B.; B.S., U. Okla., 1940; M.B.A., N.Y. U., 1948; grad. Command and Gen. Staff Coll., 1953, Army War Coll., 1957; m. Evelyn Jean Brandon, Jan. 4, 1942; children—Patricia Lynn, Charles Michael. Commd. 2d lt. U.S. Army, 1940, advanced through grades to maj. gen., 1961; comdg. officer 694th F.A. Battalion, PTO, 1944-45; asst. chief staff operations XIV Corps Arty., Philippines and Japan, 1945-46; chief land staff Allied Forces No. Europe, U.S. Army element SHAPE, Oslo, Norway, 1953-56; comdg. officer 214th and 52d Arty. Groups, Ft. Sill, Okla., 1959-60; dir. programs and budget div. Office Dep. Chief Staff Mil. Operations 1962-63; asst. div. condr. 1st Cav. Div., Korea, 1963-64; dir. army budget Office Comptroller Army, 1966-67; comdg. gen. U.S. Army Arty. and Missile Command, also comdt. U.S. Army Arty. and Missile Sch., Ft. Sill, 1967—. Decorated Legion of Merit with oak leaf cluster, Bronze Star, Army Commendation medal with oak leaf cluster. Mem. Nat. Sojourners, Phi Eta Sigma, Beta Gamma Sigma. Mason. Home: 422 Hamilton Rd Fort Sill OK 73503 Office: McNair Hall Fort Sill OK 73503

BROWN, CHARLES PUGH, Jr., banker; b. Troy, Ala., May 3, 1934; s. Charles Pugh and Mary (Wood) B.; B.A., Harvard, 1956; m. Elizabeth Ely Butler, Apr. 27, 1957; children—Peter McDowell, Elizabeth Ely. Securities analyst trainee Stone & Webster Securities Corp., Boston, 1956-57; securities analyst, asst. sec. Conn. Bank & Trust Co., Hartford, 1957-64; financial planning v.p. 1st Pa. Banking & Trust Co., Phila., 1964—; v.p. sales Vestaur Corp. Commr., Tredyffrin Twp. Planning Commn., 1969—. Mem. Phila. Estate Planning Council. Office: 15th and Chestnut Sts Philadelphia PA 19101

BROWN, CHARLES SAVILLE, pharm. mfr.; b. Orange County, Va., Oct. 1, 1920; s. Clarence Blair and Keith Woodson (Saville) B.; B.S., Va. Poly. Inst., 1941; Ph.D., U. Wis., 1946; student Lake Forest Coll., 1950-54, Harvard, 1956; m. Millicent Courtenay Phinney, June 8, 1946; children—Keith Carter, Charles Saville, Robert Allen. Began career as process control engr. with Nat. Aniline div. Allied Chem. & Dye Corp., Buffalo, 1941; successively asst. dept. mgr., dept. mgr., advisor to v.p. charge prodn., supt. pharm. mfg. Abbott Labs., North Chicago, Ill., 1944-59, supt. prodn., 1959-60, v.p. in charge of prodn. 1960-61, v.p. in charge of U.S. and Canadian operations, 1961-64, v.p. pharm. operations, 1964- 65, exec. v. pres., 1965—, also dir. of co.; dir. Am. Nat. Bank & Trust Co., Waukegan, Ill. Mem. Am. Management Assn., A.A.A.S., Am. Inst. Chem. Engring., Am. Chem. Soc., Ill., Waukegan-North Chicago C.'s of C., Sigma Xi, Phi Kappa Phi, Omicron Delta Kappa, Tau Beta Pi, Phi Lambda Upsilon, Alpha Chi Sigma. Methodist. Home: 421 Tiffany Dr Waukegan IL 60085 Office: 1400 N Sheridan Rd North Chicago IL 60064

BROWN, CHARLES THOMAS, educator; b. Braddock, Pa., Mar. 22, 1912; s. Charles W. and Mabel A. (Losey) B.; student Geneva (Pa.) Coll., 1930-32; B.B.A., Westminister (Pa.) Coll., 1934; M.A., U. Wis., 1940, Ph.D., 1949; m. Martha P. Clark, Sept. 19, 1936; children—Judith A. (Mrs. James T. Harris), Charles H. Asst. prof. speech Fla. So. Coll., 1940-44, 46-47; prof. communication Western Mich. U., Kalamazoo, 1948—, dir. Center for Communication Research, 1958—, chmn. dept. communication arts and scis., 1966—. Served to lt. USNR, 1944-46; PTO. Recipient Distinguished Faculty award Alumni Assn. Western Mich. U., 1967. Mem. Speech Communication Assn. Am., Internat. Soc. for Study Communication, Internat. Soc. for Study Symbols, Central States, Mich. speech assns. Author: Introduction to Speech, 1955; (with Charles van Riper) Speech and Man, 1966. Asso. editor: Jour. of Communication, 1967—. Contbr. articles profl. jours. Home: 1828 Hillsdale St Kalamazoo MI 49007

BROWN, CHESTER EDWARD, mfg. co. exec.; b. Louisville, Mar. 13, 1914; s. Edward J. and Johanna (Hartlauf) B.; B.S. in Chem. Engring., U. Louisville, 1936, M.S. in Chem. Engring., 1937; m. Ann Sedler, Nov. 16, 1940; children— Edward, Joanne, William, Catherine, Linda. With Hiram Walker Inc., 1937-39, Seagram Distillers Co., 1939-43; sr. engr. Smith, Hinchman and Grylls, architects and engrs., Detroit, 1946-49; with Koppers Co., Inc., Pitts., 1949-64, v.p., gen. mgr. tar products div., 1961-62, v.p., asst. gen. mgr. plastics div., 1962-64, v.p., gen. mgr., 1964-65; pres. Sinclair-Koppers Co., 1965—. Served with USNR, 1943-46. 46. Mem. Am. Wood Preservers Assn., Am. Inst. Chem. Engrs., A.I.M., Soc. Plastic Industry, Pitts. C. of C. Clubs: Duquesne (Pitts.); Oakmont Country. Home: 860 11th St Oakmont PA 15139 Office: Sinclair-Koppers Co Inc Koppers Bldg Pittsburgh PA 14 15219

BROWN, CHESTER MELVILLE, chem. co. exec.; b. Cape Girardeau, Mo., Nov. 24, 1907; s. Edward Eugene and Emma I. (Caudle) B.; student Southeast Mo. State Coll., 1925-27, U. Mo.,

1927-29; m. Nelda Juanita Prather, June 11, 1937; children—Stewart Dean, Stephen Mel, Phyllis Irene. With Allied Chem. Corp., 1929—, trainee, successively supt., prodn. mgr., dir. sales, v.p., 1929-57, pres. Gen. Chem. div., 1957, pres. Nat. Aniline div., 1958-59, pres. co., 1959-69, also chief exec. officer, 1962-69. chmn. bd. dirs., 1962-69, dir., 1959—; dir. Nat. State Bank, Elizabeth, N.J. Trustee Wells Coll., Aurora, N.Y. Mem. Am. Ordnance Assn., Synthetic Organic Chem. Mfrs. Assn., Mfg. Chemists Assn. (dir.). Presbyn. (trustee). Home: 860 Gate Way Hillside NJ 07205 Office: 375 Park Av New York City NY 10022

BROWN, CLAIR ALAN, ret. botanist, educator; b. Port Allegany, Pa., Aug. 16, 1903; s. Charles Melvin and Jennie Henrietta (Burrows) B.; B.S. cum laude, N.Y. State Coll. Forestry, 1925; A.M., U. Mich., 1926, Ph.D., 1934; m. (Bertha) Maude Nichols, Sept. 4, 1926 (dec. Apr. 1962); children—Dorcas Ellin, Sarah Janet (dec.); m. 2d, Clara Douglas, July 1963. Tech. asst. to N.Y. state botanist, summers 1924-26; herbarium asst. U. Mich., 1925-26, research asst., 1929-31; instr. botany La. State U., Baton Rouge, 1926-29, asst. prof., 1931-35, asso. prof., 1935-44, prof., 1944-70; bot. cons. oil, paper and lumber industries. Photographer Soil Erosion Service, summer 1934. Guggenheim fellowship for study Europe, summer 1952, Edmund Niles Huyck fellow, summers 1958-59; NSF Advanced Biology, San Jose, Costa Rica, summer 1961-62. Mem. Bot. Soc. Am., Torrey Bot. Club, La. Acad. Scis. (pres. 1942-44) So. Weed Conf. (pres. 1948-49), Am. Soc. Plant Taxonomists, Internat. Assn. Plant Taxonomy, Bot. Soc. Lund, Ecol. Soc. Am., Am. Fern Soc. (pres. 1960-61), Sigma Xi, Phi Sigma. Episcopalian. Author: Ferns and Flowering Plants of Isle Royale, Michigan 1937; (with D.C. Correll), Ferns and Fern Allies of Louisiana, 1942; Louisiana Trees and Shrubs, 1945, Commercial Trees of Louisiana, 1959, Vegetation of the Outer Banks of North Carolina, 1959; Palynological Techniques, 1960; Mississippi Trees, 1966. Editorial bd. Ecology, 1964-66. Home: 1180 Stanford Av Baton Rouge LA 70808

BROWN, CLARENCE FLEETWOOD, educator; b. Anderson, S.C., May 31, 1929; s. C. F. and Mildred (Cunningham) B.; B.A., Duke, 1950; M.A., U. Mich., 1955; Ph.D., Harvard, 1962; m. Jacqueline Duquesne, July 6, 1956; children—Katherine Olivia, Christopher Duquesne. Prof. Russian lit. Princeton, 1959-71, prof. comparative lit., 1971—. Mem. exec. com. Nat. Translation Center; mem. jury Nat. Book Award, 1968. Served with U.S. Army, 1951-54. Mem. Modern Lang. Assn., Am. Assn. Advancement Slavic Studies, Am. Assn. Tchrs. of Slavic and East European Langs., Comparative Lit. Assn. Author: The Prose of Osip Mandelstam, 1965. Creator comic strip Ollie. Home: 142 Moore St Princeton NJ 08540

BROWN, CLAUDE, author; b. N.Y.C., Feb. 23, 1937; s. Henry Lee and Ossie (Brock) B.; student Howard U., 1961-65; m. Helen Jones, Sept. 9, 1961. Writer plays, performed by Am. Afro-Negro Theater Guild, 1960-61. Mem. Harlem Improvement Project Group. Methodist. Author: Manchild in the Promised Land, 1965. Home: 2736 8th Av New York City, NY 10039.

BROWN, CLAUDE HAROLD, educator b. Galatia, Kan., Sept. 25, 1905; s. John W. and Millie E. (Lynge) B.; student Kan. State U., 1923-24, 28-29; B.S. Ed., Kan. State Coll., Pittsburg, 1931, M.S., 1934; Ph.D., Kan. U., 1940; postgrad. Colo. State Coll. Edn., summer 1935; m. Bernadine K. Reagan, May 31, 1931; 1 dau., Marilyn Jo (Mrs. Thomas A. Giltner). Tchr. pub. schs., Kan., 1926-38, U. Kan., 1938-40; faculty Western Ill. State U., Macomb, 1940-43; faculty Central Mo. State Coll., Warrensburg, 1943—, prof. math., chmn. div. sci. and math., 1947—, dean Sch. Arts and Scis., 1969—. Mem. Trails Regional Library Bd., 1957-65, pres., 1963-65. Mem. A.A.A.S., Nat. Council Tchrs. Math., Math. Assn. Am., Phi Delta Kappa, Kappa Mu Epsilon, Rotarian (pres. Warrensburg 1957). Author: The Teaching of Secondary Mathematics, 1953. Home: 402 Hillcrest Dr Warrensburg, MO 64093.

BROWN, CLAYTON A., transp. co. exec. Comptroller, Pub. Service Coordinated Transport. Office: 180 Boyden Av Maplewood NJ 07040*

BROWN, CLIFFORD EUGENE, investment co. exec.; b. Pitts., June 1, 1924; s. Frank E. and Mary (Joyce) B.; B.S., Duquesne U., 1947; M.B.A., St. Louis U., 1957; C.P.A., Pa., 1951; m. Carol L. Rueckel, Dec. 26, 1960; children—Stephen, Matthew, Margaret. With Bachrach Sanderbeck & Co., C.P.A.'s, Pitts., 1947-51; mem. econs. faculty Loyola Coll., Balt., 1957-58; exec. v.p. Federated Research Corp., Pitts., 1958-65, pres., 1965—, also dir.; v.p., dir. Empire Fund, Inc., 2d Empire Fund, Inc., Gen. Exchange Fund, Inc., Presdl. Exchange Fund, Inc., 2d Presdl. Exchange Fund, Inc., 3d Empire Fund, Inc., 4th Empire Fund, Inc., Luth. Brotherhood Fund, Inc., Boston Found. Fund, Inc., 5th Empire Found, Inc., 6th Empire Fund, Inc., 5th Presdl. Fund, Inc., Federated Dual-Exchange Fund, Inc., Pension Capital Growth Fund, Inc., Mut. Fund for Investing in U.S. Govt. Securities, Inc.; dir. Federated Investors, Inc. Mem. president's adv. bd. Mt. Mercy Coll., Pitts. Served with Am. Field Service, 1945. Mem. Am. Inst. C.P.A.'s, N.Y. Soc. Security Analysts. Roman Catholic. Home: 906 Amberson Av Pittsburgh PA 15232 Office: 421 7th Av Pittsburgh PA 15219

BROWN, COLON, bldg. materials mfg. co exec.; b. Scooba, Miss., Mar. 17, 1910; s. Lannie Paschal and Mary Florence (Bethany) B.; B.S., U. Miss., 1933; LL.D., U. Tampa, 1966; m. Margaret Ann Massey, Apr. 12, 1935; 1 son, John Colon. With U.S. Gypsum Co., 1934-37, dept. supt., St. Joseph, Mo., 1936-37; with Nat. Gypsum Co., 1937—, dir. subsidiaries in U.S. and Can., 1952-55, gen. mgr. Pacific Coast subsidiary Wesco Waterpaint, Inc., 1955-59, asst. to pres., 1959-60, v.p. charge corp. devel., 1960-64, vice chmn. bd., 1964, chmn. bd., chief exec. officer, dir. Nat. Gypsum Co., 1965—, pres. Bldg. Products div., 1966-69; dir. Mfrs. & Traders Trust Co., Buffalo; trustee Buffalo Savs. Bank. Bd. dirs. Buffalo Fine Arts Acad. Mem. Buffalo C. of C., Newcomen Soc. N. Am., Canisius Coll. Bus. Council. Presbyn. (trustee). Mason (32). Clubs: Buffalo (dir., past pres.), Buffalo Country, Cherry Hill, Ltd. Home: Campanile Apts 925 Delaware Av Buffalo NY 14209 Office: 325 Delaware Av Buffalo NY 14202

BROWN, COURTNEY C., univ. adminstr.; b. St. Louis, Oct. 15, 1904; s. Alexander Hanks and Joan (MacCallum) B.; student Stanton Mil. Acad., 1918-22; B.S., Dartmouth, 1926; Ph.D., Columbia, 1940; LL.D., Miami U., Oxford, O., 1959; D.B.A., U. Sherbrooke (Que., Can.), 1967; m. Marjorie Warren Lawbaugh, Nov. 26, 1930; children—Joanne B. Finney, Roxanne B. McDowell, Courtney Warren. Investment work N.Y. Stock Exchange firms, Bankers Trust Co., 1926-35; instr., lectr. Columbia, 1937-41; asso. dir. research Chase Nat. Bank, 1941-42; v.p. CCC, Dept. of Agr., 1942-43; dep. dir. Equipment Bur., WPB, 1943-44, also chief Div. War Supply and Resources, Dept. State, 1943-45; vice chmn. Pres.'s Famine Emergency Com., 1946; chmn. Gov.'s Com. on Minimum Wage in N.Y. State; economist, asst. to chmn. bd. Standard Oil Co. (N.J.), 1946-54; dir. Esso Standard Oil Co., 1952-54; dean Grad. Sch. Bus., Columbia, N.Y.C., 1954-69, v.p. for bus., 1955-57, George E. Warren prof. bus. policy, 1963—; editor Columbia Jour. World Bus. Dir. Borden Co., CBS, Am. Electric Power Co., U.P.R.R. Asso. Dry Goods Corp., Uris Bldgs. Corp.; West Side adv. bd. Chem. Bank N.Y. Trust Co. Mem. Pres.'s Commn. on Internat. Trade and Investment Policy, 1970-71. Mem. bd. pub. govs. N.Y. Stock Exchange, 1959-62. Exec. dir. Am. Assembly, 1955-56, chmn. bd. trustees 1969—; mem. bd. Council for Financial Aid to Edn., Internat. Exec. Service Corps. Conglist. Clubs: Scarsdale (N.Y.) Golf; Century Assn. Author: Liquidity and Instability, 1940; contbr. to Contemporary Economic Problems and Trends, 1941; Symbols and Values, 1954; Political Economy of American Foreign Policy, 1955, The Director Looks at His Job, 1957; Journey Toward Understanding, 1958; The Creative Interface, 1968. Editor: World Business, Promise and Problems, 1970. Home: 4 Kent Rd Scarsdale NY 18503

BROWN, DARWIN CHARLES, lawyer; b. Albany, California, July 13, 1912; s. Charles Thomas and Jennie Gertrude (Needham) B.; A.B., U. of Cal. 1934, J.D., 1937; M.B.A. with high distinction, Harvard, 1939 (class marshal and commencement speaker); m. Elizabeth Mary Reed, June 2, 1937; 1 son, Darwin Charles; m. 2d, Marianthe Caraber, Nov. 6, 1943. Began practice law, 1937; administrative asst. Am. Republics Aviation Div. Defense Supplies Corp., 1941; sec. Civil Aeronautics Bd., 1941-43; chief, Office Air Transport Information, 1943. atty. Victor div. RCA, 1943-51; partner firm Ginsburg, Leventhal & Brown 1952-57, Ginsburg, Leventhal, Brown & Morrisson, 1957-61, Ginsburg, Leventhal & Brown, 1961-62, Brown & Orleans, 1962, Brown, Orleans & Isakov, 1963, Brown & Isakov, 1963—, specializing in adminstrn. practice and internat. bus. law. Asso. law Temple U. Sch. Law, 1945. Admitted to U.S. Supreme Ct. bar, U.S. Ct. Mil. Appeals bar, U.S. Ct. Claims bar, U.S. Ct. Appeals br, U.S. Treasury ICC., Served with U.S. Army, 1943. Recipient Wisdom award of honor Wisdom Soc., 1970. Fellow Internat. Acad. Law and Sci.; mem. Am., Fed., FCC, Inter Am., Cal. bar assns., Assn. Bar City N.Y., N.Y. County Lawyers Assn., Am. Judicature Soc., Internat. Platform Assn., World Peace Through Law Center, Am., Indian, Washington socs. internat. law, Soc. Internat. Devel., A.A.A.S., Art Alliance (Phila.) Mason. Clubs: Harvard (N.Y.C., Washington); Commonwealth (San Francisco); Nat. Lawyers, Harvard Business School, Nat. Communications (Washington); Wig and Pen (London, Eng.); Dambusters (Nairobi, Kenya). Office: Barr Bldg 910 17th St NW Washington DC 20006 ☆

BROWN, DAVID, motion picture exec., pub. co. exec.; b. N.Y.C., July 28, 1916; S. Edward Fisher and Lillian (Baren) B.; A.B., Stanford, 1936; M.S., Columbia, 1937; m. Liberty LeGacy, Apr. 15, 1940 (div. 1951); 1 son, Bruce LeGacy; m. 2d, Wayne Clark, May 25, 1951 (div. 1957); m. 3d, Helen Gurley, Sept. 25, 1959. Apprentice, San Francisco News, also Wall St. Jour., 1936; night editor, asst. drama critic Fairchild Publs., 1937-39; editorial dir. Milk Research Council, 1939-40; asso. editor Street & Smith Publs., 1940-43; asso. editor, exec. editor, editor-in-chief Liberty mag., 1943-49; editorial dir. Nat. Edn. Campaign, A.M.A., 1949; asso. editor, mng. editor Cosmopolitan mag., 1949-52; mng. editor, story editor, head scenario dept. 20th Century-Fox Film Corp. Studios, Beverly Hills, Cal., 1952-56, mem. studio exec. com., 1956-60, producer, 1960-62, also exec. story editor, head scenario dept.; editorial v.p. New Am. Library World Lit., Inc., 1963-64; v.p., dir. story operation 20th Century Fox Film Corp., 1964-69, exec. v.p. creative operations, 1969-70, dir., 1968-70. Final judge, best short story pub. in mags., ann. Benjamin Franklin Mag. awards, 1955-58. Served as 1st lt., M.I., AUS, World War II. Mem. Acad. Motion Picture Scis. Clubs: Players, Overseas Press (N.Y.C.); Nat. Press (Washington). Author stories and articles pub. Am. mag., Collier's, Harper's, Readers Digest, Am. Mercury, Sat. Eve. Post, Sat. Rev. Lit., Cosmopolitan, others. Editor: I Can Tell It Now, 1964, How I Got That Story, 1967. Contbr. to Journalists in Action, 1963. Home: 605 Park Av New York City, NY 10021. Office: 444 W 56th St New York City, NY 10019.

BROWN, DAVID EDWARD, physician, educator; b. Indpls., July 9, 1909; s. Edward A. and Elizabeth (Kitzmiller) B.; A.B., Stanford, 1932, M.D., 1936; m. Mary Rebekah Van Nuys, July 15, 1939; children—Douglas, Robekah Van Nuys. Intern, Alameda County Hosp., Oakland Cal., 1935-36; resident Presbyn. Hosp., Chgo., 1938-39; practice medicine, specializing in otolaryngology, Indpls., 1939—; mem. staff Ind. U. Med. Center, St. Vincent's, Methodist, Community hosps., Marion County Gen. Hosp.; prof. otolaryngology Ind. U. Med. Sch., 1962—, chmn. otorhinolaryngology, 1962—. Fellow Am. Acad. Opthamology and Otolaryngology; mem. Ind. Acad. Ophthalmology and Otolaryngology, Indpls. Opthal. and Otolaryn. Soc., Am. Triological Soc. Home: 7344 Lakeside Dr Indianapolis, IN 46278. Office: 1944 N Capitol Av Indianapolis IN 46202

BROWN, DAVID GRANT, univ. adminstr.; b. Chgo., Feb. 19, 1936; s. Wendell J. and Margaret (James) B.; A.B., Denison U., 1958; M.A., Princeton, 1960, Ph.D., 1961; m. Eleanor Rosene, Aug. 16, 1958; children—Alison, Dirksen. Research asst. Indsl. Relations Center, Princeton, summers 1959-60; asst. prof., asso. prof. econs., dir. academic labor market study, gen. coll. adviser U. N.C., 1961-66; faculty St. Augustines Coll., N.C. Coll., 1961-66; Am. Council on Edn. intern in academics adminstrn. U. Minn., 1966-67; provost, v.p. academic affairs Drake U., 1967-70; exec. v.p., provost Miami U., Oxford, O., 1970—. Recipient U. N.C. Research Council grants, 1961-63, Tanner award, 1965, Research grants Dept. Labor, 1964, NSF, 1965, U.S. Office Edn., 1965; Harold Dodds fellow, 1960-61. Mem. Am. Assn. U. Profs., Am., So. econs. assns., Indsl. Relations Research Assn., Ohio Civil Liberties Union, Blue Key, Phi Beta Kappa, Omicron Delta Kappa. Author: The Market for College Teachers, 1965; The Mobile Professors, 1967. Contbr. articles profl. jours. Home: Robin Ct Oxford OH 45056

BROWN, DAVID HENRY, educator, biol. chemist; b. Ely, Nev., June 17, 1921; s. E. Bryce and Verna (Cryst) B.; B.S., Cal. Inst. Tech., 1942, Ph.D., 1948; m. Barbara A. Illingworth, Nov. 24, 1951; children—Philip, Christopher, Emily. Research asst. Cal. Inst. Tech., NDRC, 1942-45; co-dir. field analytical lab. div. 9 NDRC-Dugway Proving Ground, Chem. Warfare Service, Bushnell, Fla., 1944-45; Frasch Found. postdoctoral fellow plant biochemistry div. biology Cal. Inst. Tech., 1947-48; Merck fellow biol. chemistry Washington U. Sch. Medicine, St. Louis, 1948-50, faculty, 1950—, prof. biol. chemistry, 1962—. Mem. A.A.A.S., Am. Soc. Biol. Chemists, Biochem. Soc. (Eng.), Sigma Xi. Research, publs. on enzymatic processes in carbohydrate metabolism in mammalian tissues. Home: 6440 Cecil Av Clayton MO 63105 Office: Washington U Sch Medicine St Louis MO 63110

BROWN, DAVID SPRINGER, educator; b. Bangor, Me., Dec. 27, 1915; s. Lyle Lincoln and Myra Jane (Springer) B.; A.B., U. Me., 1936; Ph.D., Syracuse U., 1955; m. Evelyn Lovett, May 1, 1943 (dec. 1967); children—David Springer, Christopher, Robert, Adele; m. 2d, Anne Elizon, 1968. Newspaper reporter Bangor Daily News, 1931-36; teaching asst. Syracuse U., 1937-40; with Dept. Agr., 1940, 42, N.Y. State Dept. Edn., 1941, CAA, 1946-48; Air Coordinating Com., 1948-50, ECA, 1950-52; exec. sec. pub. adv. bd. Mut. Security Agy., 1952-53; asst. exec. dir. Com. Nat. Trade Policy, 1953-54; asso. prof. pub. adminstrn. George Washington U., Washington, 1954-57, prof., 1957-69, prof. mgmt., 1969—, dir. USAF adv. mgmt. program, 1954-61; vis. prof. Royal Coll. Sci. and Tech., Glasgow, Scotland, 1958. Pres. Leadership Resources Inc., Washington, 1970—. Sec. U.S. delegation Internat. Civil Aviation Orgn., Montreal, Que., Can., 1950; mem. U.S. delegation Internat. Inst. Adminstrv. Scis., Brussels, Belgium, 1958; adv. com. tng. Internal Revenue Service, 1959-60; dep. chief U. So. Cal. Party in Pub. Adminstrn. Lahore, Pakistan, 1961-62. Mem. Am. Polit. Sci. Assn., Am. Soc. for Pub. Adminstrn., Soc. Personnel Adminstrn., Am. Assn. U. Profs., Acad. Mgmt. Author: Federal Contributions To Management, 1971 and articles, monographs. Home: 319 S St Asaph St Alexandria VA 22314 Office: George Washington U Washington DC 20006

BROWN, DELMER MYERS, historian, educator; b. Harrisonville, Mo., Nov. 20, 1909; s. Ren E. and Mary Margaret (Myers) B.; B.A., Stanford, 1932, M.A., 1940, Ph.D., 1946; m. Mary Nelson Logan, Aug. 30, 1934; children—Charlotte Logan, Delmer Ren. Lectr. English, Dai Shi Koto Gakko, Kanazawa, Japan, 1932-38; faculty U. Cal. at Berkeley, 1946—, prof. history, 1956—, chmn. dept., 1958-62. Cons. U.S. Army in Japan, summer 1948; lectr. U. Colo., summer 1950; rep. Asia Found., Hong Kong, 1953-54, Tokyo, 1954-55; lectr. Colo. State U., summer, 1965; vis. prof. Internat. Christian U., Tokyo, 1967-69. Fulbright research fellow, Japan, 1959-60; East-West Center research fellow, Hawaii, 1964. Served as officer USNR, 1941-45. Mem. Am. Hist. Assn., Assn. Asian Studies. Author: Money Economy in Medieval Japan, 1951; Nationalism in Japan, 1955. Co-translator: Studies in Shinto Thought, 1965. Home: 1560 Euclid Av Berkeley CA 94708

BROWN, DONALD ATHERTON, ret. telephone co. exec.; b. Medford, Mass., Dec. 15, 1905; s. Edward Newton and Mabel (Atherton) B.; B.S., Bowdoin Coll., 1927; m. Adele Sadler, Mar. 12, 1927; children—Cynthia (Mrs. John H. Gillmore), Judith (Mrs. Gene B. Fechner), David G. Asst. sec. Stone and Webster Service Corp., Boston, 1928-30; statistician Gulf States Utilities Co., Baton Rouge, 1930-38, ins. dir., 1938-42; asst. supt. Royal-Eagle-Globe indemnity Co., N.Y.C., 1942-44; field mgr. Standard Research Consultants, N.Y.C., 1944-49; v.p., sec., treas., dir. Gen. Telephone System. N.E. Cos., Johnstown, N.Y., 1949-62; sec., treas. Gen. Telephone of Fla., Tampa, 1962-70. Former vice chmn., dir. Johnstown (N.Y.) chpt. A.R.C., 1956-62; mem. adv. bd. Fulton County Salvation Army; trustee Johnstown Meml. Day Assn. Mem. Ind. Telephone Pioneer Assn., Am. Soc. Ins. Mgmt., Gloversville C. of C. (dir.), Am. Soc. Corp. Secs., Beta Theta Pi. Presbyn. (past trustee, elder). Mason, Kiwanian. Home: 207 S West Shore Blvd Tampa FL 33609

BROWN, DONALD ROBERT, educator; b. Albany, N.Y., Mar. 5, 1925; s. J. Edward and Natile (Roseberg) B.; A.B., Harvard, 1948; M.A., U. Cal. at Berkeley, 1951, Ph.D., 1951; m. June Gole, Aug. 14, 1945; children— Peter Douglas, Thomas Matthew, Jacob Noah. Mem. faculty Bryn Mawr Coll., 1951—; prof. psychology, 1963—; sr. research cons. Mellon Found., Vassar Coll., 1953-63; part-time vis. prof. Swarthmore Coll., U. Pa., also U. Cal. at Berkeley, 1953-63; fellow Center Advanced Study Behavioral Scis., 1960-61; prof. psychology, sr. research scientist, Center Research Learning and Teaching, U. Mich., 1963—; cons. Peace Corps., 1965-71; hon. research fellow Univ. Coll., London, Eng., 1970-71. Served with AUS, 1943-46; ETO, Mem. Am. Psychol. Assn., Soc. Psychol. Study Social Issues, A.A.A.S., Am. Assn. U. Profs., Sigma Xi, Psi Chi. Author: articles, chpt. in books. Editor, Changing Role and Status of Soviet Women, 1967. Home: 1015 Ferdon Rd Ann Arbor MI 48104

BROWN, DONALD RUSSELL, educator; b. Wilder, Vt., Feb. 1, 1931; s. Raymond Harold andd Eleanor (Kibbey) B.; A.B., U. Vt., 1953; M.A., Harvard, 1957, Ph.D., 1960; m. Dalphia Rae Hall, Aug. 30, 1952; children—Jennifer Ray, Stephen Charles. Instr. to asst. prof. govt. Harvard, 1960-66, exec. sec. gen. edn., 1961-66; prof. polit. sci. Bennington Coll., 1966—, acting dean studies, 1967-68, dean of faculty, 1970—. Served with AUS, 1953-55. Mem. Vt. Hist. Soc. (trustee), Phi Beta Kappa. Home: RD 1 Box 28 Shaftsbury VT 05262 Office: Bennington College Bennington VT 05201

BROWN, DONALD SPENCER, fgn. service officer; b. Queens Village, N.Y., Apr. 2, 1928; s. Lewis Philip and Elizabeth Amy (Crossley) B.; student Cornell U., 1945-46; B.A., Antioch Coll., 1952; m. Micheline Charbonnel, Dec. 23, 1950; children—Alain B., Dean M., Christopher L. Planning asst. Ethiopia and Iran econ. program FOA, 1952-54; asst. program officer USOM to Iran, 1954-56, to Libya, 1956-58; program officer USOM to Somali Republic, 1958-61; program officer AID mission to Sudan, 1961-63; dep. exec. sec. AID, Washington, 1964-65, exec. sec., 1965, AID affairs officer, Algeria, 1966-67, dep. dir. mission to Congo, 1967-70. Served to 2d lt. AUS, 1946-48. Mem. Am. Fgn. Service Assn. Home: 5909 Cranston Rd Washington DC 20016

BROWN, DOUGLASS VINCENT, economist, educator; b. Wilkes Barre, Pa., May 16, 1904; s. George Henry and Frederica (Reinert) B.; A.B., Harvard, 1925, A.M., 1926, Ph.D., 1932; m. Mary A. Nuss, Dec. 2, 1933; children—Deborah, Constance. Instr., tutor econ. Harvard, 1927-33; as. prof. med. econ. Harvard Med. Sch., 1933-38; asst. prof., asso. prof. and prof. indsl. relations Mass. Inst. Tech., Cambridge, 1938-46, Alfred P. Sloan prof. indsl. mgmt, 1946—. Various positions with adv. commn. to Council of Nat. Def. and OPM, 1940-41; staff mem. Harriman-Beaverbrook Mission to Russia, 1941; cons. to War Dept., 1942-43; pub. mem. Nat. War Labor Bd., Region I, 1943-45. Fellow Am. Acad. Arts and Sci.; mem. Am. Econ. Assn., Indsl. Relations Research Assn., Nat. Acad. Arbitrators. Co-author: (with others) Economics of the Recovery Program, 1934; (with others) Industrial Wage Rates, Labor Costs, and Price Policies, Temporary National Economic Committee, Monograph 5, 1940. Home: 46 Griggs Rd Brookline MA 02146 Office: Mass Institute of Technology Cambridge MA 02139

BROWN, DUGALD E.S. physiologist; b. St. Thomas, Ont., Can., July 9, 1901; s. Edmund Shepard and Florence Louise (Smith) B.; student St. Thomas Collegiate Inst., 1914-18; A.B., M.Sc., U. Mich., 1919-24; postgrad. Harvard Med. Coll., 1924-25; Ph.D., Cornell U., 1933; m. Edith Showers, 1927; children—Dugald Edmund Sinclair, Nancy Van Metre. Came to U.S., naturalized, 1965. Asst. zoology U. Mich., 1922-24, chmn. dept. zoology U. Mich., 1949-66, prof. zoology, 1949-68, prof. emeritus zoology, 1968—, teaching fellow physiology Harvard Med. Coll., 1924-25; instr. biology N.Y.U., 1925-28, asst. prof. gen. physiology, 1928-30, instr. physiology Med. Coll., 1930-31, asst. physiology, 1931-39, appointed to grad. faculty, 1936, prof. physiology Dental Coll., 1940-47; dir. Bermuda Biol. Sta. for Research Inc., N.Y., 1946-49, pres. 1949-54. Trustee, Marine Biol. Lab., Woods Hole, Mass., 1940; exec. com., 1941-42. Has been successful in use of high hydrostatic pressures as a tool in analysis of nature and velocity of processes in living cells. Recipient (with Frank Harris Johnson and Douglas A. Marsland) ann. A.A.A.S. $1000 prize, 1941. Fellow N.Y. Acad. Scis.; mem. Am. Soc. Gen. Physiologists (council), Am. Physiol. Soc., Am. Soc. Zoologists, Harvey Soc., Sigma Xi. Author numerous sci. articles on action of pressure and temperature on biol. processes, muscular contraction, protoplasmic gels, bioluminescence; high pressure equipment for work on biol. systems. Home: 38 Whitman Rd Woods Hole MA 02543

BROWN, DYKE, (Franklin Moore), sch. dir., lawyer; b. San Francisco, Apr. 16, 1915; s. Frank Arthur and Dorothy Gary (Moore) B.; A.B., U. Cal., 1936; B.A. (Rhodes scholar), Oxford (Eng.) U., 1938, M.A., 1942; J.D., Yale, 1941; m. Catherine Louise Whiteley,

Sept. 14, 1940; children—Patricia, Susan, Christopher Admitted to Cal. bar, 1941; asst. dean Yale Law Sch., 1941-42; practiced in San Francisco, 1946-54, partner firm Cooley, Crowley & Gaither, San Francisco, 1950-54; asst. dir. study Ford Found., 1948-49, v.p., 1953-62; dir. Athenian Sch., Danville, Cal., 1963—. Served as lt. USNR, 1942-45. Mem. Am. Bar Assn., Am. Law Inst., Am. Polit. Sci. Assn., Council Fgn. Relations, Phi Beta Kappa. Club: University (N.Y.C.) Address: Athenian Sch 2100 Mt Diablo Scenic Blvd Danville CA 94526

BROWN, E. ALLEN, educator; A.B., M.A., Ph.D., U. N.C. Prof. English, chmn. dept. English Va. Commonwealth U., Richmond. Office: Dept English Va Commonwealth U Richmond VA 23220*

BROWN, EARLE, composer, conductor; b. Lunenburg, Mass., Dec. 26, 1926; s. Earle Appleton and Grace (Freeman) B.; student Northeastern U., 1944-45; grad. Schillinger Sch. Music, Boston, 1950; pvt. student of Roslyn B. Henning and Kenneth McKillop; Mus.D. (hon.), Peabody Conservatory, 1970; m. Carolyn Rice, June 28, 1950. Tchr., Schillinger System Mus. Composition, Denver, 1950-52; asso. Project Music Magnetic Tape, N.Y.C., 1952-54; faculty Conservatory of City Cologne (Germany), 1966; dir. Contemporary Sound Series for Time-Mainstream Records, Inc., 1960; W. Alton Jones chair composition Peabody Conservatory, 1968-70, 71-72; composer in residence Artists Program, West Berlin, 1970-71; condr. own works at N.Y. Philharmonic, 1964, Rome Radio Orch., 1962, Domaine Mus., Paris, France, 1963. Internat. Chamber Ensemble, Darmstadt, Germany, 1964, Munich (Germany) Radio Orch., 1963, Cologne (Germany) Radio Orch., 1963, Contemporary Chamber Ensemble, N.Y.C., 1963; works performed in Paris, Venice, Zagreb, Cologne, Munich, Hamburg, Prague, Rome, Helsinki, The Hague, Vienna, Bremen, Buenos Aires, Tokyo, Stockholm, Madrid, Berlin, throughout U.S.; recipient commns. from Domaine Mus., 1958, City Darmstadt, 1961, Rome Radio Orch., 1962, Found. Performance Arts, 1963. Radio Diffusion Francaise, 1963, Bremen Radio, 1964, Sudwestfunk, Baden-Baden, 1964, Donaueschingen, Germany, 1965. Served with USAAF, 1945-47. Guggenheim Fellow, 1965. Mem. Broadcast Music Inc. Composer: Perspectives, 1952; Folio and Four Systems, 1952-54; Indices, 1954; Pentathis, 1958; Available Forms I and II, 1961-62; Times Five, 1963; From Here, 1963; Calder Piece, 1963-66; String Quartet, 1965; Corroboree, 1964; Nine Rarebits, 1965; Modules I and II, 1966; Brass Mass, 1968; others.

BROWN, EARL IVAN, II, engring. educator; b. Carrollton, Ga., Feb. 15, 1917; s. Ralph S. and Gertrude (Chandler) B.; B.S., Va. Mil. Inst., 1940; M.S., N.C. State U., 1949; Ph.D., Tex. U., 1953; m. Anna Mercer Taylor, June 30, 1941; children—Ralph Edward, Elizabeth Anne (Mrs. Jacques R. Houyoux), Earl Ivan III. Jr. engr. TVA, 1940-41; asst. engr. C.C.C. and St.L. Ry, Indpls., 1941-42; cons. structural engr., 1946—; instr. N.C. State U., 1946-49; asst. prof. Ga. Inst. Tech., 1949-53; prof., chmn. dept. civil engring., also asst. dean engring. Auburn U., 1954-60; J. A. Jones prof., chmn. dept. civil engring. Duke, Durham, N.C., 1960—; vis. prof. U. Liverpool (Eng.), 1966-67; spl. research torsional characteristics reinforced concrete, crackering characteristics prestressed concrete. Chmn. bd. dirs. Lee County chpt. A.R.C., 1957-60. Served to maj. AUS, 1942-46. Fellow Am. Soc. C.E. (pres. N.C. 1965); mem. Am. Rd. Builders Assn. (dir. edn. div. 1961-64, 66-69), Durham Engring. Club (pres. 1964). Republican. Methodist (Sunday Sch. tchr.). Author articles in field. Home: 1631 Marion Av Durham, NC 27705.

BROWN, EARL THOMAS, optical co. exec.; b. Can., Jan. 10, 1915 (parents Am. citizens); s. Fred N. and Mabel (Mason) B.; came to U.S., 1916; student New Eng. Sch. Accounting, 1932-34; m. Dorothy C. Simpson, June 21, 1941; children—Judith D., Nancy J. With Am. Optical Co., 1937—, controller, 1958—. Home: 5 Hickory Rd Southboro MA 01772 Office: Pleasant St Connector Framingham MA 01701

BROWN, EDGAR CARY, educator; b. Bakersfield, Cal., Apr. 14, 1916; s. Verne Brainard and Ruth (Cary) B.; B.S., U. Cal., Berkeley, 1937; Ph.D., Harvard, 1948; m. Tomlin Edwards, May 28, 1937 (div.); childrenRebecca, Gretchen; m. 2nd. Margaret Durham, June 6, 1969. Teaching fellow U. Cal. at Berkeley, 1937-39; economist U.S. WPB, 1940-41; teaching fellow Harvard, 1941-42; economist U.S. Treasury Dept., 1942-47; prof. econs. Mass. Inst. Tech., 1947-, head dept., 1965-; vis. prof. econs. Yale, 1953- 54, U. Chgo., 1963-64; cons. economist U.S. Treasury Dept., Council Econ. Advisers, Dept. Health, Edn. and Welfare, also cons. Brookings Institution. Guggenheim fellow, 1957, Ford Found. Faculty Research fellow, 1956-57. Mem. Nat. Tax Assn., Am. Econ. Assn., Royal Econ. Soc., Internat. Inst. Pub. Finance, Am. Acad. Arts and Scis., Phi Beta Kappa, Beta Gamma Sigma. Author: Financing Defense, 1951; Depreciation Adjustments for Price Changes, 1952; Studies in Economic Stabilization, 1967. Acting editor; Nat. Tax Jour., 1958-59. Home: 163 Valley Rd Concord, MA 01742. Office: E52-373A Memorial Dr Cambridge, MA 02139.

BROWN, EDGAR HENRY, Jr., educator, mathematician; b. Chgo., Dec. 27, 1926; s. Edgar Henry and Viola (Offen) B.; B.S., U. Wis., 1949; M.S., Wash. State U., 1951; Ph.D., Mass. Inst. Tech., 1954; m. Gail Hamilton, June 13, 1954; children—Jessica, Nicholas. Instr., Washington U., St. Louis, 1954-55, U. Chgo., 1955-57; Office Naval Res. fellow Brown U., 1957-58; faculty Brandeis U., 1958—, prof. math., 1963—. Served with USNR, 1944-46. NSF fellow, 1962- 63; Guggenheim fellow, 1965-66, Mem. Am. Math. Soc. Home: 32 Fisher Av Newton, MA 02161. Office: Math Dept Brandeis Univ Waltham MA 02154

BROWN, EDITH PETRIE, physician; b. Conneaut Lake, Pa., June 7, 1900; d. William and Hattie Elnina (Shontz) Petrie; B.S. with honors, Westminster Coll., New Wilmington, Pa., 1923, H.H.D., 1963; M.D. with distinction, George Washington U., 1927; m. William H. Brown, Sept. 13, 1928; children—Margaret Elizabeth (Mrs. Margaret Ackerman), William Stanley. Intern Grace Hosp., Detroit, 1927-28; pediatric resident Children's Hosp., Washington, 1929; asst. physician Rochester (Minn.) State Hosp., 1929; resident physician Sunny Acres Tb Sanatorium, Warrensville, O., 1929-31; gen. practice of medicine, Bedford, O., 1937-63; sec. staff Bedford Municipal Hosp., 1945-51, chief staff, 1954-60; vice chief staff Woman's Hosp., Cleve., 1947-48, 55-56; exec. com. Bedford Community Hosp. Corp., 1957-63; physician, field rep. Joint Commn. on Accreditation Hosps., 1964-68; staff mem. Sage Meml. Hosp., Ganado, Ariz., 1968-69, Pima County Hosp., So. Ariz. Mental Health Center, 1969-70, Carl Hayden Community Hosp., 1970; measles immunization adminstr. in Kenya, 1971; staff Christian Meml. Hosp., Sialkote, Pakistan, 1971—. Mem. corp. Cleve. Center on Alcoholism; hon. mem. governing bd. Woman's Hosp., Cleve. Fellow Acad. Psychosomatic Medicine; mem. Assn. Am. Physicians and Surgeons, Am. Physicians Art Assn., A.M.A., Am. Med. Women's Assn. (br. pres. 1943-44, nat. pres. 1962, founder, pres. Tucson br. 1970), Am., Ariz. acads. gen. practice, George Washington U. Med. Soc., Am. Heart Assn., Cleve. Acad. Medicine, Ohio Med. Assn., Christian Med. Soc., World Med. Assn., Bedford Hist. Soc., Nat. Council on Alcoholism, United World Federalists, Internat. Soc. Christian Endeavor, Nat. Resuscitation Soc., Cleve. Mus. Art, Cleve. Health Mus. Presbyn. Club: Zonta Internat. Contbr. articles to med. journals. Home: 835 E Copper St Tucson AZ 85719

BROWN, EDMOND, physicist, educator; b. Bklyn., July 22, 1924; s. Irving and Rose (Schrieber) B.; student Coll. City N.Y., 1940-43; B.S., U. Ill., 1948; Ph.D., Cornell U., 1954; m. Lucille Wernick, Apr. 14, 1946; children—Adrienne, Margaret, Gail. Asst. prof. Rensselaer Poly. Inst., Troy, N.Y., 1954-59, asso. prof. 1959-65, prof. 1965—. Vis. prof. State U. N.Y., Albany, 1967-68; cons. Atomics Internat. div. N.Am. Aviation Corp., summer 1960; vis. scientist Thomas J. Watson Research Center, IBM Corp., 1969. Served with AUS, 1943-46; PTO. Fellow Am. Phys. Soc.; mem. Fedn. Am. Scientists, Am. Assn. U. Profs., Sigma Xi, Sigma Pi Sigma, Tau Beta Pi. Home: 1157 Highland Park Rd Schenectady NY 12309 Office: Physics Dept Rensselaer Poly Inst Troy NY 12181

BROWN, EDMUND GERALD "PAT", ex-gov. Cal.; b. San Francisco, Apr. 21, 1905; s. Edmund Joseph and Ida (Schuckman) B.; LL.B., San Francisco Law School, 1927; LL.D., U. of San Francisco, 1959, U. San Diego, 1961, U. Santa Clara, 1961; D.C.L., California College Medicine, Los Angeles, 1964; m. Bernice Layne, Oct. 30, 1930; children—Barbara (Mrs. Philip Corwin), and Cynthia (Mrs. Steven Goldberg), Edmund Gerald, Kathleen. Admitted to Calif. bar, 1927, practiced San Francisco, 1927-43; dist. atty. city and co. San Francisco, 1943-47, 1947-50; atty. gen. Cal., 1951-58; gov. of Cal., 1959-66. Del. from Cal. Democratic National Conv., 1940, 44, 48, 52, 56, 60, 64. Mem. Golden Gate Bridge and Hwy. Dist., 1942-. Chmn. San Francisco Coordinating Council, 1947. Mem. Dist. Attys' Assn. Cal. (pres. 1950-51), San Francisco. Western Assn. Atty. General (past pres.), Nat. Assn. Attys. Gen. (mem. exec. bd.), Am. bar assns., N.Y. Bd. of Trade (v.p.), Am. coll. Trial Lawyers (fellow). Roman Catholic. Democrat. Elk. Clubs: Native Sons Golden West, Commonwealth Comml., Olympic, Jonathan (San Francisco).

BROWN, EDMUND RANDOLPH, publishing co. exec.; b. Everett, Mass., Sept. 2, 1888; s. Joseph and Mary Somers (Hosmer) B.; A.B., Harvard, 1909; m. Alice Needham Very, June 22, 1916; children—Rosalye, Edmund Hosmer, Charlotte (Mrs. Cedric Jackson), Cynthia, Martha (Mrs. Robert Bragg). Pres. Four Seas Co., Boston, 1909-30, Burce, Humphries, Inc., Boston 1930-64, The Branden Press, Inc., Boston, 1964—; treas Lit. Publs. Found, Inc. Mem. Harvard Music Assn. Club: Sharon Chess. Editor: Internat. Pocket Library, 1930—, Poetry Jour., 1910-30, Poet Lore, 1930—, The World in Books, 1960—. Home: 10 Edge Hill Sharon MA 02067 Office: 221 Columbus Av Boston MA 02116

BROWN, EDWARD JAMES, dept. store exec.; b. Boston, Aug. 9, 1907; s. George and Libbie (Goldberg) B.; B.A., Harvard, 1929, M.B.A., 1931; div.; children—Barbara Ann, Patricia Bette. Buyer, Bloomingdales, N.Y.C., 1931- 34; asst. to pres. Gimbels, Pitts., 1934-38; div. mdse. mgr. Arnold Constable, N.Y.C., 1938-41; from mdse. mgr. to exec. head Saks 34th St., N.Y.C., also v.p. Saks & Co., 1941-65; adminstrv. v.p. Gimbel Bros., Inc., N.Y.C., 1965—. Bd. dirs. Broadway Assn., 1957—, Westside Assn. Commerce, 1961—, N.Y. Bd. Trade, 1965—; v.p. N.Y. State Council Retail Merchants, 1966—. Mem. Mayor N.Y.C. Youth Bd., 1961—; bus. adv. council Boy Scouts Am., 1960—. Recipient Humanitarian award Am. Med. Center, Denver, 1959; Good Scout award Boy Scouts Am., 1961; Service award United Jewish Appeal, 1947. Mem. Am. Retail Fedn. (dir., v.p.), Nat. Retail Mchts. Assn., Tau Epsilon Phi. Clubs: Harvard Business School (N.Y.C.); Beach Point (Mamaroneck, N.Y.). Home: 715 Park Av New York City, NY 10021 Office: Gimbels Corporate Office 1275 Broadway New York City NY 10001 10001

BROWN, EDWARD JAMES, educator; b. Chgo., July 12, 1909; s. Edward James and Marie (O'Neill) B.; A.B., U. Chgo., 1933, A.M., 1946; Ph.D., Columbia, 1950; m. Catherine Stillman Cossum, Oct. 7, 1941; 1 dau., Meredith Ann (Mrs. Gerald Frazee Craig). From instr. Russian to prof. Brown U., 1947-65, chmn. dept. Slavic langs., 1960-65; prof. Russian, chmn. dept. Slavic langs. and lits. Ind. U., Bloomington, 1965-69; prof. Slavic langs. Stanford (Cal.), 1969—. Mem. Am. Com. Slavists, 1958; del. IV Internat. Congress Slavists, 1958; cons. Fgn. Area Fellowship Program, 1964-66; cons. grants Am. Council Learned Socs., 1964-71; mem. Joint Com. Slavic Studies, 1964-65, 67-71; exec. com. Inter-Univ. Com. Travel Grants, 1965-67. Served with USAAF, 1943-45. Rockefeller fellow, 1946; Am. Council Learned Socs. fellow, 1946-47; Howard fellow, 1955-56; exchange prof. to USSR, Am. Council Learned Socs.-Acad. Scis. Program, fall 1963. Mem. Modern Lang. Assn., Am. Assn. Tchrs. Slavic and Eastern European Langs. (pres. 1966), Am. Assn. Advancement Slavic Studies (pres. 1967-70), Phi Beta Kappa. Author: The Proletarian Episode in Russian Literature, 1953, reissued, 1971; Russian Literature Since the Revolution, 1963, rev., 1969; Stankevich and His Moscow Circle, 1966. Home: 801 Tolman Dr Stanford CA 94305

BROWN, EDWARD MAURICE, lawyer, business exec.; b. Watertown, N.Y., Aug. 22, 1909; s. Ernest E. and Eunice (Lewis) B.; A.B. magna cum laude, Miami U., 1931; J.D., Harvard, 1934; m. Anne Amos, Oct. 2, 1937; children—Edward Dustin, Ernest Amos. Admitted to Ohio bar, 1934, U.S. Supreme Ct., 1941, N.Y. bar, 1948, asso. firm Nichols, Wood, Marx & Ginter, 1934-47; asst. to pres. McCall Corp., N.Y.C., 1947-49, v.p., asst. sec., 1949-51, v.p., sec. 1951-57, dir., 1953-57; treas. Sperry Gyroscope Co. div. Sperry Rand Corp. 1958-59, v.p., treas, 1959-60, v.p. adminstr., 1960-65, v.p., Sperry Group, 1965-68; asst. treas. Sperry Rand Corp., 1958-68; group exec. of Teledyne, Inc., 1968—. Trustee Village of Pelham Manor, N.Y., 1961-65, village mayor, 1965-67. Bd. govs. Human Resources Center; trustee Abilities, Inc. Served as lt. comdr., USNR, 1942-45. Member N.Y. County Lawyers Assn., Am. Bar Assn., Phi Beta Kappa, Phi Eta Sigma, Phi Sigma, Beta Theta Pi. Republican. Episcopalian. Home: 400 Pelham Manor Rd Pelham Manor NY 10803 Office: Box 372 Pelham NY

BROWN, EDWARD P., lawyer; b. Springfield, Mass., July 29, 1900; s. Edward Manning and Elizabeth (Pettinger) B.; grad. Hartford Conservatory Music, 1919; LL.B., Boston U., 1921; m. Kathryn Allen, June 7, 1924; 1 son, Timothy Manning. Asso. firm Ropes, Gray, Boyden & Perkins, 1921-35; partner firm Ely, Bartlett, Brown & Proctor, 1935—; asst. sec. Packaging Industries Ltd., Inc.; dir. Environment Research & Electronics, Inc., Howard Food Cos., Inc., Candy Snacks Corp., Modern Biscuit Corp., Dragone Cheese Mfg. Co., Inc., Environmental Cleaning Services, Inc.; gen. counsel Crosby-Yacht Bldg. & Storage Co., Inc.; dir., clk. Hildreth| Baker, Inc., Rogers Foam Corp. Trustee Bentley Coll. Accounting and Finance. Served with U.S. Army, 1918. Mem. Am., N.Y. Boston bar assns., Am. Guild Organists (colleague), Delta Theta Phi. Republican. Conglist. Clubs: Algonquin, Down Town, (Boston); Wianno, Wianno Yacht (Cape Cod) Home: 27 Chestnut St Boston MA 02108 Office: 225 Franklin St Boston MA 02110

BROWN, EDWARD STICKNEY, Jr., educator; b. El Paso, June 3, 1912; s. Edward Stickney and Elizabeth (Hunt) B; A.B., Dartmouth, 1934, C.E., 1935; S.M. in San. Engring., Harvard, 1937; m. Barbara Beetle, Sept. 4, 1937; children—Helen Elizabeth, Robert Alan. Instr., Thayer Sch. Engring., Dartmouth, Hanover, N.H., 1937-41, asst. prof., 1941-45, prof. civil engring., 1945—. Sr. san. engr. N.H. Dept. Health, 1947—; with Western Electric Co. Alaska, 1956-57. Health officer, selectman, cons, engr. Town of Hanover, 1960—. Mem. Am. Soc. C.E., Am. Soc. Engring. Edn., New Eng. Sewer Works Assn., New Eng., N.H. water works assns. Home: 13 N Balch St Hanover NH 03755

BROWN, EDWIN LEWIS, Jr., lawyer; b. Parker, S.D., Mar. 15, 1903; s. Edwin Lewis and Lucy, Elizabeth (Lowenberg) B.; J.D., U. Neb., 1926; m. Faye Hulbert, May 8, 1926; children—Betty Lou (Mrs. Philip Trainer), Lewis Charles. Admitted to Neb. bar, 1926, Ill. bar, 1933, U.S. Supreme Ct. bar, 1960; practiced in Chgo., 1933—; partner firm Brown, Stine, Cook, Hanson, 1950—. Mem. wills and bequests com. Shriners Crippled Childrens Hosp., Chgo. Mem. Am., Ill., Chgo. bar assns., Nat. Conf. Lawyers and Collection Agys., Law Inst., Comml. Law League Am. (pres. 1963-64), Comml. Law Found (treas.), Phi Alpha Delta. Republican. Presbyn. Mason (32, K.T., Shriner). Clubs: Union League (Chgo.); Westmoreland Country (Wilmette, Ill.). Home: 2617 Hurd Av Evanston IL 60201 Office: 135 S LaSalle St Chicago IL 60603

BROWN, EDWIN WILSON, Jr., physician, educator; b. Youngstown, O., Mar. 6, 1926; s. Edwin Wilson and Doris (McClellan) B.; student Carnegie Inst. Tech., 1943, Houghton Coll., 1946- 47, Amherst Coll., 1943-44; M.D., Harvard, 1953, M.P.H. (Nat. Found. fellow), 1957; m. Patricia Ann Currier, Aug. 9, 1952; children—Edwin Wilson III, John Currier, Wende Patricia. Research fellow U. Buffalo, 1953-54; intern E. J. Meyer Meml. Hosp., Buffalo, 1954-55; resident pub. health Va. Dept. Health, 1955-56; tchr. medicine, specializing in preventive medicine, Boston, 1958-61, Hyderabad, India, 1961-63; asso. med. dir. People-to-People Health Found., Washington, 1965-66; dir. internat. activities Ind., U., also dir. div. internat. affairs Ind. U.- Purdue U., Indpls., 1966—; field dir. Harvard Epidemiological Project, Egedesminde, Greenland, 1956-57; asst. prof. preventive medicine Sch. Medicine Tufts U., 1958-61; dep. chief staff Boston Dispensary 1961; vis. prof. preventive medicine Osmania Med. Coll., Hyderabad, India, 1961-63; asst. dir. div. internat. med. edn., dir. AAMC-AID project internat. med. edn. Assn. Am. Med. Colls., Evanston, 1963-65; exec. sec. Study Group on Childhood Accidents, Boston, 1959-61; research asso. Sch. Pub. Health Harvard, 1959-60; cons. Boston City Health Dept., 1959-60; chmn. bd. dirs. Med. Assistance Programs, Inc. Bd. dirs. Paul Carlson Found. Campus Teams. Served with AUS, 1944-46; ETO, Fellow Am. Pub. Health Assn.; mem. Assn. Tchrs. Preventive Medicine, Indian Assn. Advancement Med. Edn., Mass. Med. Soc., Sigma Xi. Contbr. articles to profl. jours. Home: 5420 N Meridian St Indianapolis IN 46208

BROWN, ELI HUSTON, III, lawyer; b. Frankfort, Ky., Nov. 5, 1906; s. Eli Huston and Rose McKnight (Crittenden) B.; B.A., Princeton, 1929; LL.B., Harvard, 1933; LL.D., U. Louisville, 1967; m. Mavin Hamilton, Apr. 27, 1935 (dec. 1967); children—Mavin Hamilton, Eli Huston, IV. Admitted to Ky. bar, 1934; atty. Fed. Land Bank, Louisville, 1934-35; 2d asst. U.S. atty., Western Dist. Ky., 1935-37, 1st asst., 1937-38, U.S. dist. atty., 1938-45; now sr. partner Brown, Todd & Heyburn. Dir. Liberty Nat. Bank & Trust Co. Chmn. of com. Ky. Center Performing Arts; mem. Louisville and Jefferson County Air Bd., 1971—. Trustee U. Louisville, 1948-70, acting pres., 1950-51, chmn. bd. trustees, 1949-51, 62-66. Mem. Am., Ky., Louisville bar assns. Democrat. Episcopalian. Clubs: Century, Harvard-Princeton (N.Y.C.); Wynn-Stay; Louisville Country; River Valley. Home: 485 Lightfoot Rd Louisville KY 40207 Office: Citizens-Fidelity Bldg 300 S 5th St Louisville KY 40202

BROWN, ELIZABETH ANN, fgn. service officer; b. Portland, Ore., Aug. 15, 1918; d. Edwin Keith and Grace Viola (Foss) Brown; A.B., Reed Coll., 1940; postgrad. (teaching fellow) Wash. State Coll., 1940-41; A.M., Columbia, 1943. Exec. asst. to chmn. 12th region WLB, Seattle, 1943-45; internat. affairs officer Dept. State, 1946-56; joined U.S. Fgn. Service, 1956, assigned Office UN Polit. Affairs, Dept. State, 1956-60; 1st sec. Am. embassy, Bonn, Germany, 1960-63; dep. dir. Office UN Polit. Affairs, 1963-65, dir., 1965-69; mem. State Dept. Sr. Seminar in Fgn. Policy, 1969-70; counselor for polit. affairs Am. embassy, Athens, Greece, 1970—. Adviser U.S. delegation UN Gen. Assembly, 1946-50, 53, 55, 57-59, 64-65. Recipient 7th ann. Fed. Woman's award, 1967. Mem. Am. Fgn. Service Assn., Phi Beta Kappa. Home: 4848 Reservoir Rd NW Washington DC 20007 Office: Dept State Washington DC 20520

BROWN, EMILY CLARK, economist; b. Mpls., Oct. 15, 1895; d. Edward J. and Mary (Fullerton) Brown A.B., Carleton Coll., 1917; M.A., U. Chgo., 1923, Ph.D., 1927. Research asst. United Typothetae of Am., 1920-25; Social Sci. Research Council fello 1927-28; asst. prof. Wellesley Coll., 1929-32; asst. prof. Vassar Coll., 1932-33, asso. prof., 1933-39, prof., 1939-61, chmn. dept., 1950-54; operating analyst NLRB, 1942-44. Mem. Am. Econ. Assn., Indsl. Relations Research Assn., Am. Assn. U. Profs., Am. Assn. for Study of Soviet-Type Economics. Author: Book and Job Printing in Chicago, 1931; From the Wagner Act to Taft-Hartley (with Harry A. Millis), 1950; Soviet Trade Unions and Labor Relations, 1966. Home: 4327 Abbott Av Minneapolis MN 55410

BROWN, EPHRAIM TAYLOR, Jr., lawyer; b. Birmingham, Ala., Aug. 31, 1920; s. Ephraim Taylor and Lida (Otts) B.; A.B., Princeton, 1941; LL.B., Cornell U., 1943; m. Clara DeBardeleben Ebaugh, Oct. 21, 1949; children—Ephraim Taylor III, Clara DeBardeleben, Lida Otts. Admitted to Ala. bar, 1943, since practiced in Birmingham; asso. Cabaniss, Johnston, Gardner & Clark, 1943-52, partner, 1952—. Chmn. spl. com. on Revision Probate Laws Ala., 1967; counsel Jr. League Birmingham; chmn. bd. bar examiners Ala. State Bar. Bd. dirs. Childrens Fresh Air Farm. Fellow Am. Coll. Probate Counsel; mem. Am., Ala. (past sect. chmn.), Birmingham bar assns., Ala. Law Inst. (mem. counsel) Sigma Alpha Epsilon. Presbyn. (elder, deacon). Club: Birmingham Country. Home: 3105 Sterling Rd Birmingham AL 35213 Office: First Nat Bldg Birmingham AL 35203

BROWN, ERIC REEDER, immunologist, educator; b. Cortland, N.Y., Mar. 16, 1925; s. Harold McDaniel and Helen (Seitz) B.; B.A., Syracuse U., 1949, M.S., 1951; Ph. D. (Nat. Cancer Inst. Fellow), U. Kan., 1957; D.Sc., Quincy Coll., 1966; m. 2d, Chloe Cassandra Ledbetter, May 11, 1961; children— Eric Reeder Carl F., Christopher H.A., Amy Elizabeth French; children by previous marriage—Eric Reeder III, Christine Virginia, Dianne Mary, Daniel K. Instr. U. Ill. Med. Sch., 1957-58; asst. prof. U. Ala., 1958-60, U. Minn. Sch. Medicine, 1960-61; sr. research asso. Hektoen Inst., Chgo., 1961—; asso. prof. Northwestern U. Med. Sch., 1964-68; chmn. dept. microbiology Chgo. Med. Sch., 1967—; cons. Newport Pharms., Inc., U. Ill.; med. adviser to Ill. dir. SSS; Am. Cancer Soc. fellow, 1960-63; Leukemia Soc., scholar, 1965—. Served with USCGR, 1942-46; to maj. USAF, 1951-55; maj. Res. Fellow Am. Inst. Chemists, Am. Acad. Microbiology, Chgo. Inst. Medicine; mem. Royal Soc. Medicine, Histochem. Soc., Internat. Soc. Lymphology, Am. Assn. U. Profs., Am. Mus. Natural History, Med. Mycol. Soc. of Ams., Soc. Exptl. Biology and Medicine, Res. Officers Assn., Sigma Xi, Psi Chi, Phi Sigma. Contbr. articles to profl. jours. Research on virus etiology of cancer and leukemia. Home: 3740 Candlewood Dr Downers Grove IL 60615 Office: 2020 W Ogden Av Chicago IL 60612

BROWN, ERNEST JOSEPH, educator; b. Lake Providence, La., May 30, 1906; s. John Ernest and Pearl (Fisher) B.; A.B., Princeton, 1927; LL.B., Harvard, 1931. Admitted to N.Y. bar, 1934; practiced in Buffalo, 1934-41; prof. law, U. of Buffalo Law Sch., 1937-42, Harvard Law Sch., 1946-71; with tax div. U.S. Dept. Justice, Washington, 1970—; mem. legal staff A.A.A., 1933, WPB, 1942, hearing commr. N.P.A., 1952. Served to capt. AUS, 1942-45; CBI. Fellow Am. Acad. Arts and Scis.; mem. Am., N.Y. bar assns. Editor: (with Freund, Sutherland and Howe) Constitutional Law, Cases and Other Problems. Home: 4201 S 31st St Arlington VA 22206 Office: Tax Div US Dept of Justice Washington DC

BROWN, ESTHER LUCILE, author, lectr.; b. Manchester, N.H.; d. Charles Wesley and Nellie (Morse) Brown; B.A. with spl. honors, U. N.H. 1920; Ph.D. in Social Anthropology, Yale, 1929; LL.D. (hon.), Skidmore Coll., 1950. Asst. prof. social sci. U. N.H., 1926-29; research asso. Russell Sage Found., N.Y.C., 1930-45, dir. dept. studies in profession, 1945-48, exec. program planning and direction, 1948-63; writer, lectr., cons. vis. prof. U. Wis. at Madison, 1970. Cons. for WHO, 1952-53. Social Sci. Research Council fellow in France, 1929-30. Hon. life mem. Nat. League for Nursing; mem. Am. Sociol. Assn., Soc. Applied Anthropology. Author: The Professional Engineer, 1935; Social Work as a Profession, 4th edit, 1942; Nursing as a Profession, 2d edit, 1940; Physicians and Medical Care, 1934; Lawyers and the Promotion of Justice, 1938; Lawyers, Law Schools and the Public Service, 1948; Nursing for the Future, 6th edit., 1953; (with Milton Greenblatt and Richard H. York), From Custodial to Therapeutic Patient Care in Mental Hospitals, 1955; Newer Dimensions of Patient Care; Part I, The Use of Physical and Social Environment of the Hospital for Therapeutic Purposes, 1961; Part II, Improving Staff Motivation and Competence in the General Hospital, 1962; Part III, Patients as People, 1964; Newer Dimensions of Patient Care, vol. 1, 1965; Nursing Reconsidered: A Study of Change, 1970; also numerous articles. Address: 1980 Washington St San Francisco CA 94109

BROWN, ETHAN ALLAN, physician; b. London, Eng., Mar. 16, 1905; s. Edward Arnold and Marie (Riegarowska) B.; student Balliol Coll., Oxford, 1928-29; student internat medicine U. London, 1930-35; M.R.C.S., England, L.R.C.P., London, 1935; m. Helen Alice Flaherty, Sept. 14, 1949. Demonstrator biology, asst. lectr. St. Mary's Hosp. Med. Sch., U. London, 1932-35; fellow medicine Lahey Clinic, 1935-36, staff allergy sect. dept. internal medicine, 1936-38; pvt. practice medicine, 1938—; physician-in- chief allergy sect. Boston Dispensary unit N.E. Med. Center, 1938-58; lectr. allergy Tufts Coll. Med. Sch., 1939-46, instr. medicine, 1946-47, asst. prof. pediatrics, 1951-58, cons. allergy dept. clin. labs., 1953- 58. Bd dirs., Asthma Research Found., Salvation Army; trustee Allergy Found. Am. Recipient Wallace Meml. prize and medal in bacteriology, 1934. Malcolm Morris prize in dermatology, 1935, Proxime Accessit Cheadle gold medal in medicine, Proxime Accessit Agnes Cope prize in clin. medicine, 1935, Miss. Valley Med. Writers Assn. gold medal, 1958. Fellow Am. Soc. Clin. Hypnosis, Am. Med. Writers Assn., Internat. Assn. Allergology (founders group), Am. Coll. Allergists (founder's group, pres. 1956-57), Am. Acad. Allergy, Mass. Med. Soc., A.M.A., A.A.A.S., Am. Acad. Chest Physicians, Am. Acad. Tb Physicians (past pres.), Acad. Psychosomatic Medicine (founder's group; pres. 1956-57), Am. Geriatrics Soc., Acad. Internat. of Medicine, Royal Soc. Medicine; mem. Am. Assn. Immunologists, Brit. Assn. Immunologists, Royal Coll. Physicians, N.Y. Acad. Scis., Soc. Investigative Dermatology, Am. Psychosomatic Soc., Am. Assn. Mycol. Investigation, Brit. Allergy Soc., Am. Bd. Clin. Immunology (founder), Am. Assn. Clin. Immunology and Allergy (founder), Internat. Soc. Comprehensive Medicine, Royal Coll. Surgeons, Soc. Clin. Hypnosis, World Med. Assn. Editor in chief; Annals of Allergy, 1942-65, Rev. of Allergy, 1946—. Editor: Folia Clinica Internacional, 1952—, Antibiotic Medicine, 1954-62, Current Med. Digest, 1951—, Clin. Physiology, 1959—, Am. Bd. Clin. Medicine, 1965—. Address: 75 Bay State Rd Boston, MA 02215.

BROWN, EVERETT AUSTIN, interior color and design cons.; b. Remmington, Ind., Apr. 3, 1913; s. Luther and Zoe Lee (Blackwell) B.; ed. pub. schs., Ind.; m. Martha Isabel Wilson, Jan. 11, 1934; children—Marcia, Zoe Lee. With home furnishing sects. Marshall Field & Co., Chgo., 1934-37, interior design sect., 1939-44; with Stower's Furniture Co., Houston, 1937-39; color and design coordinator Grand Rapids Furniture Makers Guild (Mich.), 1944-50; propr. Everett Brown Assos., N.Y.C. and San Francisco, 1950-67; pres. Everett Brown Assos., Inc., N.Y.C., 1967—. Bd. advisers Pavilion Am. Interiors, also design com. House Good Taste, N.Y. World's Fair, 1964; color and design cons. to various cos. Fellow Am. Inst. Interior Designers (nat. bd. 1955-57, chmn. nat. bd. 1963-66, bd. govs. No. Cal. chpt. 1954-61, 66, chmn. internat. design awards com. 1963-66, gov. N.Y. chpt. 1967—), Color Assn. U.S. Home: 15 W 55th St New York City NY 10019 Office: 225 E 57th St New York City NY 10022

BROWN, FIELDING, educator, physicist; b. Berlin, N.H., Jan. 2, 1924; s. William Robinson and Hildreth (Smith) B.; B.A., Williams Coll., 1947, M.A., 1949; Ph.D., Princeton, 1953; m. Eleanor Reier, Oct. 26, 1944; children—Angela (Mrs. Kris Parnicky), Elizabeth, Marcia. Lucinda. Research physicist Sprague Electric Co., N. Adams, Mass., 1952-59; mem. faculty Williams Coll., 1959—, prof. physics, 1967—, dir. Bronfman Sci. Center, 1965-67; vis. prof. Grad. Sch. Physics, U. Tokyo, 1965-66; vis. scientist Frances Bitter Nat. Manet Lab., Mass. Inst. Tech., 1968—, Lincoln Lab., 1961-62; cons. solid state physics Arthur D. Little, Inc., Cambridge, Mass., 1959-61. Served to 1st lt. AUS, 1943-46. Research grantee NSF, 1960-62, U.S. Army, 1962-65, USAF, 1966-71. Mem. Am. Phys. Soc., Kappa Alpha. Home: 85 Park St Williamstown MA 01267

BROWN, FIRMAN HEWITT, Jr., educator, theatrical dir.; b. Bradenton, Fla., Sept. 30, 1926; s. Firman Hewitt and Eunice (DeVane) B.; student U. Fla., 1944; B.A. in Journalism, U. Mont., 1949, M.A., 1953; postgrad. Columbia, 1954; Ph.D. in Speech, U. Wis., 1963; m. Margery Arlene Hunter, Mar. 21, 1953; children—Sarah Hunter, Blakely DeVane. Reporter, Havre (Mont.) Daily News, 1950-51; dir. pub. service, instr. No. Mont. Coll., Havre, 1951- 54; vis. lectr. U. Mont., 1956-57, prof., chmn. dept. drama, 1957-69; prof., chmn. dept. drama Ithaca (N.Y.) Coll., 1969—. Producer-dir.-owner Bigfork (Mont.) Summer Playhouse, 1960-67; founder, dir. Mont. Repertory Theatre Co., Missoula, 1967-69; co-founder, dir. Ithaca Summer Repertory Theatre, 1970—; columnist On Stage, Sunday Missoulian, 1965-68; guest lectr., 1961—. Mem. Mont. Arts Council, 1967-69. Nat. Theatre Conf., 1965—; bd. dirs. Rocky Mountain Theater Conf., 1967-69. Served with USNR, 1944-46. Recipient 1st Arts Mgmt. Career Service award for outstanding contbn. to theatre over past decade, 1969. Mem. Am. Ednl. Theatre Assn., Am. Soc. Theatre Research, Mont. Inst. Arts (certificate of merit 1966). Democrat. Spl. research Mont. Theatre history. Home: Box 522 Ithaca NY 14850

BROWN, FOSTER SARGENT, former univ. pres.; b. Leyden, N.Y., Sept. 18, 1908; s. Wallace Duane and Ruth Belle (Jackson) B.; B.S., St. Lawrence U., 1930, M.A., 1935, LL.D., 1961; Ed. D., Columbia, 1950; L.H.D., Clarkson Coll. Tech., 1965; m. Catherine Pickard, June 27, 1936; children—Ruth Jackson, Susan Houghton, Wallace David, Celia Elizabeth, Irving Foster. Teaching prin. Coeymans (N.Y.) Union Sch., 1930-35; supervising prin. Roeliff Jansen Central Sch., Hillsdale, N.Y., 1935-43; supt. schs., Suffern, N.Y., 1943-51; dean State U. Tchrs. Coll., Cortland, N.Y., 1951-52; pres. State U. Tchrs. Coll., Oswego, N.Y., 1952-63; pres. St. Lawrence U., 1963-70, now emeritus. Dir. St. Lawrence County Nat. Bank. Mem. adv. bd. St. Lawrence Seaway Devel. Corp.; mem. State Adv. Council on Employment and Unemployment Ins. Bd. dirs. St. Lawrence U. Inn Corp., bd. govs. St. Lawrence County Labs.; North County Reference and Research Resources Council; trustee emeritus St. Lawrence U. Mem. St. Lawrence County Hist. Assn., Phi Delta Kappa, Sigma Alpha Epsilon. Presbyn. Rotarian. Contbr. to ednl. jours. Home: 208 Proctor Av Ogdensburg NY 13669

BROWN, FRANCES RAYMOND, educator; b. N.Y.C., Jan. 2, 1908; d. Barnum and Marion R. (Brown) Brown; A.B., Wells Coll., 1929; M.A., U. Chgo., 1930; postgrad. U. Chgo., Johns Hopkins, St. Hugh's Coll. (Eng.), U. N.C.; tchrs. certificate in voice Peabody Conservatory Mus., Balt., 1936; postgrad. (scholar) Harvard Jr. Coll. Workshop, 1942; Ed.D., Harvard, 1958. Instr., Ind. State Tchrs. Coll., 1931, Hannah More Acad., Reisterstown, Md., 1931-33, Balt. City night schs., 1934-36; head. English dept., instr. Arlington Hall Jr. Coll., 1936-42; dean Mary Lyon Jr. Coll., 1942-43; dean Chevy Chase Jr. Coll., 1944-47, pres., 1947-51, also instr., 1944-51; acad. dean Pine Manor Jr. Coll., 1953-56; dean residence and student affairs Radcliffe Coll., 1957-63; dean residence for women grad. students Harvard, 1958-63; prof. English, Longwood Coll., Farmville, Va., 1963—, asso. dean students, 1963-70. Editorial asst. A.R.C., 1943- 44; exec. dir. central br. YWCA, Balt., 1951-53; adv. com. Reid Hall, Inc., Paris, N.Y.C., 1954-56. Mem. Nat. Council Tchrs. English, Nat. Assn. Women Deans and Counselors (sec. jr. coll. sect. 1955-57), Nat. Assn. Prins. Schs. Girls, N.E.A., Assn. Ind. Schs. Md. (pres. 1949-50), Am. Assn. Jr. Colls., Middle Atlantic (pres. elect, 1951), Mass. assns. deans, Am. Assn. U. Women, Delta Kappa Gamma, Alpha Lambda Delta. Episcopalian. Home: 711 High St Farmville VA 23901

BROWN, FRANCIS, editor, writer; b. Amherst, Mass., Dec. 31, 1903; s. Ernest G. and Jessie A. (Scott) B.; B.S., Dartmouth, 1925; Litt.D., 1952; A.M., Columbia, 1927, Ph.D., 1931; m. Mary Elizabeth Adden, June 8, 1940; children—Victoria Allen, Francis Scott. Instr. Dartmouth, 1926-29; asso. editor Current History mag. N.Y.C., 1930-36; mem. Sunday staff N.Y. Times, 1936-45; sr. editor Time mag., 1945-49; editor N.Y. Times Book Rev., 1949-70. Trustee Barlow Sch., Amenia, N.Y. Decorated Order Bernardo O'Higgins (Chile), 1948. Mem. Mass. Hist Soc., Phi Beta Kappa. Club: Century Assn. (N.Y.C.). Author: Joseph Hawley, Colonial Radical, 1931; Edmund Niles Huyck; The Story of a Liberal, 1936; The War in Maps, 1942; Raymond of the Times, 1951; Highlights of Modern Literature, 1954; Opinions and Perspectives, 1964; Page 2, 1969; A Dartmouth Reader, 1969. Home: 165 West St Amherst MA 01002

BROWN, FRANCIS C., pub. utility exec.; b. Sherwood, Ore., Apr. 7, 1907; s. Braxton and May (Driskell) B.; student U. Ore., nights 1928-30. With Pacific Power & Light Co., Portland, Ore., 1928-70, treas., 1964-70. Mem. Portland C. of C., N.W. Electric Light and Power Assn., Financial Execs. Inst. Club: University (Portland). Home: 9035 SW 91st Av Portland OR 97223

BROWN, FRANK ARTHUR, Jr., biologist, educator; b. Beverly, Mass., Aug. 30, 1908; s. Frank Arthur and Arletta Esten (Robinson) B.; A.B., Bowdoin Coll., 1929; M.A., Harvard, Ph.D., 1934; m. Jennie Wentworth Pettegrove, June 24, 1934; children—Charlotte, Frank Arthur, III, Marilyn Diane. Austin Teaching fellow Harvard, 1929-32, teaching asst. in zoology, 1932-34; instr. U. Ill., 1934-37; asst. prof. zoology Northwestern U., Evanston, Ill., 1937-40, asso. prof., 1940-46, prof., 1946—, chmn. dept. biol. scis., 1949-56, Morrison prof. biology, 1956—; Instr. Mt. Desert Biology Lab., summer, 1940; vis. prof. U. Chgo., summer, 1941; nat. lectr. Sigma Xi, 1968; asso. and book rev. editor Physiol. Zoology, 1942—; in charge dept. invertebrate zoology Marine Biol. Lab., Woods Hole, Mass., 1945-49. Trustee Marine Biol. Lab., 1946—, John G. Shedd Aquarium, 1969—. Fellow A.A.A.S., Animal Behavior Soc.; mem. Am. Assn. U. Profs., Am. Soc. Zoologists (v.p. 1954), Am. Soc. Limnology and Oceanography, Am. Physiol. Soc., Soc. Study Growth and Devel., Ill. Acad. Sci., Soc. Extpl. Biology and Medicine, Am. Inst. Biol. Scis., Am. Soc. Naturalists (v.p. 1956), Soc. Gen. Physiologists (pres. 1955), Ecol. Soc. Am., Am. Soc. Plant Physiologists, Am. Geophys, Union, Soc. for Biol. Rhythms, Internat. Soc. for Biometeorology, Sigma Xi, Gamma Alpha, Phi Sigma, Delta Upsilon. Conglist. Club: Harvard (Chgo.). Author: Selected Invertebrate Types, 1950; Comparative Animal Physiology, 1950, 61; Biological Clocks, 1962; The Biological Clock: Two Views, 1970. Contbr. articles to profl. jours. Home: 906 Greenleaf Av Wilmette IL 60091 Office: Northwestern University Evanston IL 60201

BROWN, FRANK EDWARD, archeologist; b. La Grange, Ill., May 24, 1908; s. Philip Sidney and Rose Louise (Swain) B.; A.B., Carleton Coll., 1929; postgrad (fellow) Am. Acad., Rome, 1931-33; Ph.D., Yale, 1938; Litt.D., Carleton Coll., 1968; m. Jaquelin Goddard, July 21, 1935. Asst. dir. Yale Excavations, Dura-Europos, 1932-35, dir., 1935-37, research asst., asst. prof. Yale, 1938-42, prof. classics, 1952-63, master Jonathan Edwards Coll., 1953- 56; gen. rep. O.W.I., Syria, Lebanon, 1942-45; dir. gen. antiquities, Republic of Syria, 1945-47; prof. in charge, dir. excavations Am. Acad., Rome, 1947-52, 63-66, 69—, dir. acad., 1965-69. Mem. Internat. Fedn. Socs. Classical Studies (v.p.), Internat. Assn. Classical Archaeology (v.p.). Archeol. Inst. Am. (exec. com.), Am. Schs. Oriental Research (sec.), Am. Philol. Assn., Am. Oriental Soc., Instituto di Studi Etruschi ed Italici, German Archaeol. Institute, Pontif. Academy of Archaeology. Club: Century Assn. Editor and contbr. to: Excavations at Dura-Europos (vols. 6-9), 1936-52; Fasti Archeologici (vols. 1-5), 1946-52; Pubs. of the Am. Acad. in Rome, 1951- 60; Roman Architecture, 1962. Home: Via Giacomo Medici 11 Rome Italy 00153

BROWN, FRANK H., govt. official; b. Orange, N.J., Dec. 12, 1902; s. William F. and Margaret (Byrne) B.; LL.B., New Jersey Law Sch., 1925; m. Grace Lauterette, June 26, 1935; children—Maureen, Judith Ann, Francis. Admitted to N.J. bar, 1928, and practiced in N.J., 1928-42; arbitrator U.S. Conciliation Service, 1942-46; regional dir. Federal Mediation and Conciliation Service, Region one (N.Y. and N.J. 6 New Eng. states), since 1948; asso. judge Orange Police Court, 1935-39. Mem. Orange Bar Assn. Home: 6 Manor Rd Livingston NJ 07039 Office: 26 Federal Plaza New York City NY 10007

BROWN, FRANK NEWTON MITHERY, aeronautical engr.; b. near Jamestown, N.D., Sept. 16, 1902; s. Newton Mithey and Minnie Dennis (Lee.) B.; B.S.E., U. of Mich., 1928, M.S.E., 1932; m. Ruth Hodge Lee, Jan. 19, 1922 (dec.); m. 2d, Mari Wilson Fichtel, May 5, 1945 (dec.) ; m. 3d, Marie Meyer Lee, March 30, 1968. Aeronautical engr., Ford Motor Co., 1928; asst. prof. aeronautical engring. U. Mich., 1938-30; tech. editor, U.S. Army Air Corps, 1931- 33; research engr. attached to U.S.S. Macon, 1933-35; head dept. aeronautical engring. U. Notre Dame, 1935-64, professor of aerospace engineering, 1964-69, prof. emeritus, 1969—; consultant to the Minister of Edn., China, 1943; cons. and research engr., Johns Hopkins, Applied Physics Lab. on Supersonic Wind Tunnel, 1945-46. Recipient Distinquished Alumnus, University of Michigan; Citation of Honor, Indiana Technical College. Asso. Fellow Institute Aero. Scis.; mem. S.A.R., Sigma Xi, Iota Alpha, Tau Beta Pi. Repub. Author: The Brown Navigator, 1943; See The Wind Blow, 1971. Inventor of a photographic space time recorder, capacity pick-up for torsional vibration investigations and various flow visualization devices. Home: 636 Ostemo Pl South Bend IN 46617 Office: University of Notre Dame Notre Dame IN 46556

BROWN, FRED, educator, clin. psychologist; b. Pressburg, Austro-Hungary, May 18, 1905; s. Max and Ethel (Wolkowitz) B.; brought to U.S., 1908, naturalized, 1916; B.A., Ohio State U., 1929, M.A., 1930, Ph.D., 1933; m. Minerva B. Lehrman, Apr. 10, 1938; children—Janet, Daniel. Instr., Ohio State U., 1930-33; chief psychologist Alfred Willson Childrens Center, Columbus, O., 1934-36; asst. prof., dir. psychol. edn. clinic Pa. State Coll., 1937-38; chief psychologist Mpls. Pub. Schs., 1939-43; adj. prof. psychology N.Y.U., 1946-51; chief psychologist, div. psychology Inst. Psychiatry, Mt. Sinai Hosp., N.Y.C., 1946—; prof. psychiatry Mt. Sinai Med. Sch., 1966—; diagnostic cons. VA, 1959—; cons. St. Lukes Hosp. Secondary Sch. Research Project, 1964-70, Air Force Acad., 1967-70. Sec. Mental Health Film Bd., 1964—; mem. scholarship bd. Robert Louis Steven Sch., N.Y.C. Served from 1st lt. to maj., USAAF, 1943-46. Fellow Am. Psychol. Assn., Am. Psychosomatic Soc., Soc. Projective Techniques, N.Y. State, Eastern psychol. assns., N.Y. Soc. Projective Techniques (past pres.). Editorial bd. Psychosomatic Medicine, 1958—. Home: 1200 Fifth Av New York City NY 10029 Office: 1440 Madison Av New York City NY 10029

BROWN, FRED, hotel cons.; b. Coleman County, Tex., Dec. 11, 1902; s. S. E. and Eugenia (Canady) B.; B.A., Abilene Christian Coll., 1923; m. Elnora Dulaney, Jan. 31, 1926. Mgr., Baker Hotel, Mineral Wells, Tex., 1938-43, 49-54, vice pres. Eastland Nat. Bank (Tex.), 1943-49; gen. mgr. Crazy Water Hotel, Mineral Wells, 1954-57; resident mgr., dir. sales and pub. relations Hotel Adolphus, Dallas, 1957-63; gen. mgr. Inn of Six Flags, Arlington, Tex., 1963-65; owner Fred Brown, hotel cons., Dallas, 1965—; exec. v.p. Ind. Innkeepers Internat. Dallas, 1966-68; pres. Innkeepers Mgmt. & Services, Inc., Florence Miller Cosmetics, Inc., 1968—. Bd. dirs. Tex. Found., Tex. Good Roads Assn., Tex. Law Enforcement Found.; trustee Presbyn. Village Dallas. Mem. Dallas, Ft. Worth, E. Tex., W. Tex. c.'s of c., Tex. Farm Bur., Tex. Mfrs. Assn., Dallas Hotel Assn., Tex., Am. hotel and motel assns. Democrat. Presbyn. (elder). Clubs: Lakewood Country, Imperial, King's (Dallas). Home: 2511 Wedglea Dr Dallas TX 75211 Office: Adolphus Tower Dallas TX 75202

BROWN, FRED ELMORE, investment exec.; b. Muskogee, Okla., July 20, 1913; s. Fred E. and Alice (Washington) B.; B.S., U. Okla., 1934; M.B.A., Harvard, 1936; m. Margaret Ann Gillham, Nov. 15, 1941; 1 son, Frederick Elmore. With J. & W. Seligman & Co., 1936—, partner, 1955—; pres., chmn., chief exec. officer Tri-Continental Corp., Broad Street Investing Corp., Nat. Investors Corp., Union Capital Fund, Inc., Whitehall Fund, Inc., Union Service Corp., Union Data Service Center, Inc.; dir. Transatlantic, Reinsurance Co., Am. Internat. Group, Inc., Am. Internat. Life Assurance Co., Commerce and Industry Ins. Co., Ins. Co. State of Pa., Mut. Benefit Life Ins. Co. Am. Home Assurance Co. Trustee College Retirement Equities Fund, Morristown (N.J.) Meml. Hosp., Thomas Gilcrease Inst. Am. History and Art, Vassar Coll.; adv. com. Center for Study Financial Instns., Law Sch., also Wharton Sch. Finance, U. Pa. Served from 2d lt. to lt. col. OQMG, AUS, 1942-46. Decorated Legion of Merit. Mem. Assn. Closed-End Investment Co. (gov.), Investment Co. Inst. (gov.), N.Y. Soc. Security Analysts, Beta Theta Pi, Delta Sigma Pi, Beta Gamma Sigma. Episcopalian. Clubs: Lake Placid; Morristown; Downtown Assn.; Somerset Hills Country. Home: Van Beuren Rd Morristown NJ 07960 Office: 65 Broadway New Yok City NY 10006

BROWN, FREDERICK CALVIN, physicist, educator; b. Seattle, July 6, 1924; s. Fred Charles and Rose (Mueller) B.; B.S., Harvard, 1945, M.S., 1947, Ph.D., 1950; m. Joan Schauble, Aug. 9, 1952; children—Susan, Gail, Derek. Physicist, Systems Research Lab., Harvard (NDRC), 1945-46; staff physicist Naval Research Lab., Washington, 1950; physicist Applied Physics Lab., U. Wash., 1950-51; asst. prof. Reed Coll., Portland Ore., 1951-55; asst. prof. U. Ill., Urbana, 1955-58, asso. prof., 1958-61, prof. 1961—, asso. Center for Advanced Study, 1969—. NSF Sr. Postdoctoral fellow Clarendon Lab., Oxford, 1964-65. Fellow Am. Phys. Soc. Author: (with W.A. Benjamiin) The Physics of Solids-Ionic Crystals, Lattice Vibrations and Imperfections, 1967. Contbr. articles profl. jours. Home: 1014 W Clark St Champaign IL 61820 Office: Physics Dept U Ill Urbana IL 61801

BROWN, FREDERICK NATHAN, Jr., architect; b. Providence, Dec. 9, 1899; s. Frederick Nathan and Mary Woodhull (Coombs) B.; student R.I. Sch. Design, 1916-19, Brown Prep. Sch., Phila., 1919-20, U. Pa., 1920-23; m. Helen May Brakenwagen, June 28, 1924; children—Helen Mary (Mrs. Ralph Vernon Boyens), Frederick Nathan III. Architect, Jackson, Robertson & Adams, 1923-31; gen. practice architecture, Providence, 1931-41; architect War Dept., 1942-46; asso. architect Charles A. Maguire & Assos., Boston, Providence, 1946-54; specifications writer Perry, Shaw, Hepburn & Dean, Boston, 1954-66; head dept. graphics New Eng. Tech. Inst. of R.I., 1966—, drafting instr., 1966—. Mem. A.I.A. (asso. editor R.I. chpt.), Constrn. Specification Inst., U. Pa. Gen. Alumni Soc., Boston Philatelic Soc., R.I. Philatelic Soc. Conglist. Mason. Office: 99 Melbourne Rd Warwick RI 02886

BROWN, FREDRIC, novelist; b. Cin., Oct. 29, 1906; s. Karl Lewis and Emma Amelia (Graham) B.; student pub. schs., Cin.; m. Elizabeth Charlier, Oct. 11, 1948; children (by previous marriage)—James Ross, Linn Lewis. Author: The Fabulous Clipjoint (winner Edgar Allen Poe award Mystery Writers of Am., Inc., 1947), 1947; The Dead Ringer, 1948; Murder Can Be Fun, 1948; The Bloody Moonlight, 1949; What Mad Universe, 1949; The Screaming Mimi, 1949; Compliments of a Fiend, 1950; Here Comes a Candle, 1950; Night of the Jabberwock, 1950; Death Has Many Doors, 1951; The Far Cry, 1951; Space On My Hands, 1951; We All Killed Grandma, 1952; The Deep End, 1952; Mostly Murder, 1953; The Lights in the Sky Are Stars, 1953; His Name Was Death, 1954; Angels and Spaceships, 1954; The Wench Is Dead, 1955; Martians, Go Home, 1955; The Lenient Beast, 1956; One for The Road, 1958; The Office, 1958; Honeymoon in Hell, 1958; The Late Lamented, 1959; The Mind Thing, 1963; Nightmares and Geezenstacks, 1961; The Murderers, 1961; The Five Day Nightmare, 1962; The Shaggy Dog and Other Murders, 1963; Daymares, 1968. Mem. Mystery Writers of Am. Home: 622 E Seneca St Tucson AZ 85705

BROWN, GARRY ELDRIDGE, congressman; b. Schoolcraft, Mich., Aug. 12, 1923; s. E. Lakin and Blanche (Jackson) B.; B.A., Kalamazoo Coll., 1951; LL.B., George Washington U., 1954; L.H.D., Lawrence Inst. Tech., 1964; Frances E. Wilkins, Sept. 10, 1955; children—Frances E., Mollie E., Amelia L., Abigail V. Admitted to Mich. bar, 1954; partner firm Ford, Kriekard, Brown and Staton, Kalamazoo, 1954-67; commr. So. div. U.S. Dist. Ct. Western Dist. Mich., 1957-62; mem. Mich. Senate, 1962-66; mem. 90th-92d congresses from 3d Dist. Mich. Del. Mich. Constl. Conv., 1961-62. Served to 2d inf., AUS, 1946-47; PTO. Mem. Am., Mich., Kalamazoo

County bar assns., Schoolcraft Jr. C. of C. (chmn. bd.), Am. Legion. Republican. Elk. Home: 321 W Eliza St Schoolcraft MI 49087 Office: Longworth House Office Bldg Washington DC 20515

BROWN, GENE MONTE, educator, biochemist; b. Pioneer, Mo., Jan. 21, 1926; s. John Arthur and Leah (Hart) B.; student Coll. of Ida., 1943-44; B.S., Colo. A. and M. Coll., 1949; M.S. (Wis. Alumni Research Fond. fellow), U. Wis., 1950, Ph.D., 1953; m. Shirley Lewis, June 14, 1954; children—James Lewis, Lindsey Arthur, Holly Ann. Research scientist U. Tex., Austin, 1951-54; instr. dept. biology Mass. Inst. Tech., 1954-56, asst. prof., 1956-61, asso. prof., 1961-67, prof., 1967—, exec. officer dept. biology, 1967—; cons. NSF, 1964-67; mem. panel NSF Grad. Fellowship Program, 1968—, chmn. biochemistry sect., 1970—. Served with USAAF, 1944-45. Mem. Am. Soc. Biol. Chemists, Am. Chem. Soc., Sigma Xi, Phi Kappa Phi. Editorial bd. Jour. Biol. Chemistry, 1969—. Home: 30 Jennie Dugan Rd Concord MA 01742 Office: 77 Massachusetts Av Cambridge MA 02139

BROWN, GEORGE ALFRED, British govt. ofcl.; b. London, Eng., Sept. 2, 1914; s. George Brown; m. Sophie Levine; 2 daus. Jr. clk. London's financial dist.; fur salesman John Lewis Partnership Ltd., 1931-36; organizer Transport and Gen. Workers' Union, 1936-44; mem. parliament for Belper, 1945—, joint Parliamentary sec. to Ministry Agr. and Fisheries, 1947; vice chmn. def. com., 1960—, mem. exec. com. Western European Union, 1960—; minister of works, 1951; mem. Privy Council, Labour Party, 1951, mem. parliamentary com., 1955—, opposition spokesman on def., 1956—, on home affairs, 1961—, dep. leader, 1960, v. chmn., 1960—, chmn. orgn. subcom., 1960-63, chmn. home policy subcom., 1963—; fgn. Sec., 1966-68; productivity counsellor Courtaulds Ltd., part-time, 1968—. Mem. Nat. Youth Adv. Council; Brit. rep. Council of Europe's Consultative Assembly, 1951-53, 60; indsl. adviser Daily Mirror, London, 1953—. Bd. govs. Repton Sch. Home: 77 Court Lane London SE 22 England Office: House Commons London SW1 England

BROWN, GEORGE BOSWORTH, chemist, educator; b. Birmingham, Ala., Apr., 18, 1914; s. Edwin and Phyllis (Bosworth) B.; B.S., Ill. Wesleyan U., 1934, D.Sc., 1959; M.S., U. Ill., 1938, Ph.D., 1938; m. Katherine Matthews, May 4, 1940. Fellow to asst. prof. biochemistry Cornell U. Med. Coll., 1938-46, asso. prof., 1946- 51; asso. Sloan-Kettering Inst. Cancer Research of Cornell U., 1946-48, mem., 1948—, v.p., 1968—; prof. biochemistry Sloan-Kettering div. Cornell U. Med. Coll., 1951—, head protein div., 1946-61, biol. chemistry dir., 1961—. Cons. on panels of USPHS, 1949-54, 64-68, NRC, 1949-51, 54-56, Am. Cancer Soc., 1956-59, NSF, 1959-60, Cancer Chemotherapy Nat. Service Center, 1959-60. Traveling fellow Rockefeller Found., 1949; Fulbright fellow, Australia, 1965. Mem. Am. Soc. Biol. Chemistry, Biochem. Soc. (London), Am. Chem. Soc. (chmn. N.Y. sect. 1966), Harvey Soc., A.A.A.S. (mem. at large council Gordon research confs. 1954-56, trustee confs., 1956-59, 71—, chmn. bd. trustees 1958- 59), Am. Assn. Cancer Research, Sigma Xi, Phi Kappa Phi. Mem. editorial bd. Jour. Biol. Chemistry, 1954-59, 61-66, Biochem. Preparations, 1956-69 (editor Vol. 10, 1963), Jour. Am. Chem. Soc., 1958-63. Contbr. articles to profl. jours. Home: 800 Grove St Mamaroneck NY 10543 Office: Sloan-Kettering Inst for Cancer Research 145 Boston Post Rd Rye NY 10580

BROWN, GEORGE CAMERON, paper mfg. co. exec.; b. Woodstock, Ont., Can. Aug. 7, 1916; s. George H. and Myrtle Olive (Paisley) B.; B. Engring. in Elec. Engring., McGill U., 1940; m. Margaret E. Barrett, Sept. 1941; 1 dau., Diane. Various positions Bell Telephone Co. of Can., 1933-39, constrn. and testing outside plant, plant engring., 1940-42, plant engr., 1945-46; project engr. Barrett Co., Ltd., 1946-48; elec. engr., asst. elec. supt. Riverbend mill Price Bros. & Co., Ltd., 1949-51, project engr. Chute des Georges hydroelectric devel. Shipshaw River, 1951-53, asst. mgr. paper div., 1953-55, mgr. paper div., 1955-58, v.p. charge mfg., 1959, v.p., gen. mgr., 1960-65, v.p. paper and allied products, 1965—; dir. Price Kraft & Paperboard Corp., Montreal, Price (Newfoundland) Pulp & Paper Ltd., J. C. Wilson, Ltd. Served with RCAF, 1942-45. Mem. Corp. Profl. Engrs. Que., Engring. Inst. Can., Canadian Pulp and Paper Assn., T.A.P.P.I. Home: 1380LeblancAv Quebec 6 Quebec Office: 65 St Anne St Quebec Canada

BROWN, GEORGE DAVID, architect; b. N.Y.C., Dec. 3, 1906; s. George David and Mary (Russell) B.; A.B., Columbia, 1928, B. Arch., 1931, M.S., 1932. Pvt. practice architecture, N.Y.C., 1949—; housing cons. Mut. Life Ins. Co., 1945-48; exec. dir. N.Y. State Div. Housing, 1939-43; cons. West Side Urban Renewal, 1956-57, Brookings Instn., 1958, N.Y.C., Housing and Redevel. Bd., 1958-59; works include Trinity Sch. and housing, staff housing Bard Haven of Columbia and U. Rochester. Mem. Cardinal's Com. of Laity for Cath. Charities; mem. exec. com. Citizens Housing and Planning Council N.Y. Mem. Bd. Higher Edn., 1965-70; asso. rent dir. O.P.A., N.Y.C., 1944-45. Fellow A.I.A. Clubs: New York Athletic; Wykagyl Country (New Rochelle, N.Y.), St. David's Golf (Wayne, Pa.). Home: 340 E 64th St New York City NY 10021 Office: 250 W 57th St New York City NY 10019

BROWN, GEORGE EDWARD, Jr., former congressman; b. Holtville, Cal., Mar. 6, 1920; s. George Edward and Bird Alma (Kilgore) B.; B.A., U. Cal. at Los Angeles, 1946, grad. fellow Fund Adult Edn., 1954; m. Rowena Somerindyke. Mgmt. cons., Cal., 1957-61; v.p. Monarch Savs. & Loan Assn., Los Angeles, 1960-68; mem. Cal. Assembly from 45th Dist., 1959-62; mem. the 88th-91st congresses from 29th Dist. of Cal. Mem. Cal. Gov.'s Adv. Com. on Housing Problems, 1961-62, Mayor Los Angeles Labor-Mgmt. Com., 1961-62. Councilman, Monterey Park, Cal., 1954-58, mayor, 1955-56. Served to 2d lt., inf., AUS, World War II. Mem. Am. Legion, Monterey Park and Lincoln Heights C. of C., Urban League, AFL-CIO, Internat. Brotherhood Elec. Workers, Friends Com. Legislation, Audit Edn. Assn. Democrat. Methodist. Mem. Soc. of Friends. Kiwanian. Home: Monterey Park CA 93940 Office: Cannon House Office Bldg Washington DC 20525

BROWN, GEORGE EVANS, ret. air force officer; b. Salt Lake City, Aug. 1, 1918; s. Alma Edwin and Lucille (Evans) B.; B.S., U. Utah, 1939; M.B.A. with distinction, Harvard, 1953; grad. Indsl. Coll. Armed Forces, 1961; m. Marjorie Ann Warner, Apr. 22, 1944; 1 dau., Beverly Jean. Commd. 2d lt. U.S. Army Air Force, 1940, advanced through grades to maj. gen., 1968; various assignments Air Tng. Command, 1940-45; comdr. B-29 squadron, 1946-47; dep. comptroller Far East Air Materiel Command, Japan, 1947-49, Wright Air Devel. Center, O., 1950-51; comptroller Air U., Maxwell AFB, Ala., 1953- 57; dep. comptroller Air Def. Command, Colorado Springs, Colo., 1957-60; comptroller 17th Air Force, Ramstein, Germany, 1961-62; dep. comptroller USAF, Europe, Wiesbaden, Germany, 1962-63; comptroller Air Def. Command, Colorado Springs, 1963-64; dir. accounting and finance Hdqrs. U.S. Air Force, 1964-67; auditor gen. USAF, 1967-70. Decorated D.S.M., Legion of Merit. Home: 19425 Old Fort Lane PO Box Y Monument CO 80132

BROWN, GEORGE H., Jr., banker; b. Phila., Dec. 17, 1905; s. George Henry and Mary J. (Pole) B.; m. Helen M. Fountain, Sept. 12, 1931; 1 dau., Barbara (Mrs. Barbara B. Gray). With Girard Trust Bank, Phila., 1923—, beginning as clk., successively asst. real estate officer, real estate officer, asst. v.p., v.p., sr. v.p., 1923-55, exec. v.p., 1955-59, pres., chief exec. officer, 1959-66, chmn., 1966-70, dir., 1970—. Home: 327 Spring Mill Rd Villanova PA 19085 Office: Girard Trust Bank Bldg Broad and Chestnut Sts Philadelphia PA 19101

BROWN, GEORGE HAROLD, radio engr.; b. North Milwaukee, Wis., Oct. 14, 1908; s. James Clifford and Ida Louise (Siegert) B.; B.S., U. Wis., 1930, M.S., 1931, Ph.D., 1933, E.E., 1942; D. Engring, U.R.I., 1968; m. Julia Elizabeth Ward, Dec. 26, 1932; children—James Ward, George H. With RCA, 1933-37, 38—, successively research engr., Camden, Princeton, N.J., dir. Systems Research Lab., chief engr. Comml. Electronic Products div., Camden, chief engr. indsl. electronic products, 1933-59, v.p. engring., 1959-61, v.p. research and engring., 1961-65, exec. v.p. research and engring., 1965-68, exec. v.p. patents and licensing, 1968—, also dir.; dir. RCA Communications, Inc., RCA Internat., Ltd., Trane Co., 1st Nat. Bank of Hamilton Square; cons. engr., 1937-38. Exec. bd. George Washington council Boy Scouts Am. Bd. govs. Hamilton Hosp. Recipient DeForest Audion award, 1968, Fellow I.E.E.E. (Edison medal 1967), A.A.A.S.; mem. Nat. Acad. Engring., Am. Mgmt. Assn. (dir.), Sigma Xi, Eta Kappa Nu (eminent mem.). Author: (with R.A. Bierwirth and C.N. Hoyler) Radio Frequency Heating, 1947; also articles in sci. jours. Patentee in field. Home: 117 Hunt Dr Princeton NJ 08540 Office: RCA Princeton NJ 08540

BROWN, GEORGE HAY, govt. ofcl.; b. Denver, Feb. 4, 1910; s. Orville G. and Clara Amsden (Topping) B.; A.B., Oberlin Coll., 1929; M.B.A., Harvard, 1931; Ph.D., U. Chgo., 1945; m. Catherine Smith, June 11, 1932 (dec. May 1962); one dau., Ann. Divisional sales mgr. Mallinckrodt Chem. Works, St. Louis, 1931-38; instr. marketing U. Chgo., 1938-41, asst. prof., 1941-42, asso. prof. 1942-44, prof., 1945-54, dir. bus. problems bur., 1942-46, dir. devel. for social sci., bus. and social service adminstrn., 1947-49; mgr. marketing research Ford. div. Ford Motor Co., 1954-60, dir. marketing research, marketing staff, 1960-69; exec. com. nat. marketing adv. com. U.S. Dept Commerce, 1964-69, dir. Census Bur., 1969—. Trustee Found. for Research on Human Behavior, Ann Arbor, 1962-69, Marketing Sci. Inst., Phila., 1963-69, Advt. Research Found., 1967-69. Fellow Am. Psychol. Assn., Am. Statis. Assn.; mem. Am. Econ. Assn., Am. Marketing Assn. (nat. pres. 1951-52), Population Assn. Am., Delta Sigma Pi, Beta Gamma Sigma. Club: Cosmos (Washington). Author: The International Economic Position of New Zealand, Journal of Business Monograph, 1946; (with Jenck and Peterson) Readings in Marketing and Price Policy, 1951. Editor: Marketing Series, Henry Holt & Co., 1950-55. Contbr. to econ. jours. Home: 2510 Virginia Av Washington DC 20037 Office: Bureau of Census Dept of Commerce Washington DC

BROWN, GEORGE M., lawyer; b. Boston, Jan. 1, 1908; s. Harry and Ethel (Little) B.; A.B., Ohio U., 1927-31; LL.B., Western Res. U., 1934; m. Ruth Louise Fowler, July 9, 1932; children—Don P., George M., Richard H. Football coach, also instr. theory courses Western Res. U., 1931-39; admitted to Ohio bar, 1934; asst. to Judge Harry L. Eastman, Juvenile Ct. Cuyahoga County, O., 1934-35; practiced in Cleve., 1934—; sr. partner firm Roudebush, Adrion, Brown, Corlett, Ulrich, 1950—. Football ofcl. coll. and profl. games, 1933-52. Dir. SAE Steels, Inc., Roach-Reid Co., Neale-Phypers Co., Hostels Inc., Drop Dies & Forgings, Inc., Roach-Reid Co., Am. Stamping Co., Haberacker Optical Co., Mercury Optics, Inc. Mem. Cuyahoga County Republican Exec. Com., 1947. Trustee, Christian Residences Found. Elected to Hall of Fame, Ohio U., 1970. Mem. Am., Ohio, Cleve. bar assns., Nat. Council Juvenile Ct. Judges (asso.), Ohio U. Alumni Assn. (trustee 1956-59, pres. 1946; Certificate of Merit 1953), Beta Theta Pi (nat. officer 1938-52), Omicron Delta Kappa. Conglist (trustee 1965-70). Clubs: Cleveland Athletic (dir. 1947, 53, pres. 1956); Shaker Heights Country (dir. 1959—, pres. 1959, sec., 1962—). Home: 17101 Drexmore Rd Shaker Heights OH 44120 Office: Williamson Bldg Euclid Av Cleveland OH 44114

BROWN, GEORGE RUFUS, engr.; b. Belton, Tex., May 12, 1898; s. Riney Louis and Lucy Wilson (King) B.; student Rice U.; C.E., Colo. Sch. Mines; m. Alice Pratt, Nov. 25, 1925; children—Nancy Nelson (Mrs. Alfred Walter Negley), Alice Maconda (Mrs. Ralph Sturges O'Connor), Isabel Anne King (Mrs. Wallace Wilson). Former chmn. bd. Tex. Eastern Transmission Corp., Brown & Root, Inc.; dir. Internat. Tel. & Tel. Corp., Halliburton Co., Southland Paper Mills, Inc., La. Land & Exploration Co., 1st City Nat. Bank, Houston. Former chmn. bd. trustees William M. Rice U. Episcopalian. Home: 3363 Inwood Dr Houston TX 77019 Office: 4100 Clinton Dr PO Box 3 Houston TX 77001

BROWN, GEORGE SCRATCHLEY, air force officer; b. Montclair, N.J., Aug. 17, 1918; s. Thoburn Kay and Frances (Scratchley) B.; student U. Mo., 1936-37; B.S., U.S. Mil. Acad., 1941; grad. Nat. War Coll., 1957; m. Alice Colhoun, May 19, 1942; children—Dudley K., Daniel W., Susanah B. Commd. 2d lt. U.S. Army Air Force, 1941, advanced through grades to gen., 1968; comdr. 62d Troop Carrier Group, Washington, 1950-51, 56th Fighter Interceptor Wing, Air Def. Command, Mich., 1951-52, 1952, 3525th Pilot Tng. Wing, Ariz., 1953-56, Eastern Transport Air Force, McGuire AFB, N.J., 1963-64, Joint Task Force 2, Sandia Base, N.M., 1964-66; dir. operations 5th Air Force, Korea, 1952-53; exec. to chief staff USAF, 1957-59; mil. asst. to sec. def., 1959-63; asst. to chmn. Joint Chiefs Staff, Washington, 1966-68; comdr. 7th Air Force PACAF, Saigon, 1968-70; comdr. Air Force Systems Command, Andrews AFB, Md., 1970—. Decorated D.S.C., Silver Star, Legion of Merit with two oak leaf clusters, D.F.C. with oak leaf cluster, Bronze Star medal, Air medal with three oak leaf clusters, D.S.M. with oak leaf cluster, Air Force Distinguished Service Order, D.F.C. (Brit.); Croix de Guerre with palm (France); Mil. Service medal with silver star. Office: Air Force Systems Command Andrews AFB MD 20331

BROWN, GEORGE WILBUR, electric co. exec.; b. Tipton, Ind., July 6, 1904; s. George W. and Inez (Riddle) B.; student Wooster Coll., 1921; B.S. in Elec. Engring., Ohio State U., 1926; m. Ruth Virginia Beall, Sept. 17, 1930. With Wagner Elec. Co., St. Louis, 1926-71, pres., chief exec. officer, 1959-66, chmn. bd., 1966-71, also dir.; dir. First Nat. Bank of St. Louis, St. Louis, Mo. Bd. dirs. St. Louis area council Boy Scouts Am., trustee David Rankin, Jr. Sch. Mech. Trades; Lindenwood Coll. Mem. N.A.M. (chmn. bd. 1969), Tau Beta Pi, Eta Kappa Nu. Presbyn. Clubs: Bellerive Country, Bogey, Missouri Athletic, Noon-day, St. Louis, (St. Louis). Home: 9 Cricklewood Pl St Louis MO 63131 Office: 6400 Plymouth Av St Louis MO 63133

BROWN, GERALD ALTON, govt. ofcl.; b. Olustee, Okla., Aug. 13, 1914; s. Clarence Luther and Florence Mae (Guy) B.; student Amarillo Coll., 1931-33; B.A., W. Tex. State Coll., 1935; M.A., U. Tex., 1938; postgrad. U. N.C., 1939-42; m. Mary May Harrison, Apr. 6, 1939; children—Barbara Lynne, Carol Alison. Tchr. social sci. Canyon (Tex.) High Sch., 1935-38; instr. econs. and polit. sci. Amarillo Jr. Coll., 1938-39; instr. econs. U. N.C., 1939- 42; field examiner NLRB, Atlanta and Chgo., 1942-43, examiner charge sub-regional office, Memphis, 1945-47, regional dir. 20th Region, San Francisco, 1947-61, mem. NLRB, Washington, 1961—. Served from pvt. to capt., USAAF, 1943-45. Named Exec. of Year, San Francisco Fed. Bus. Assn., 1957. Mem. Unitarian Laymen's League (regional v.p. 1958-59). Unitarian (pres. bd. trustees) Club: Commonwealth of Cal. Home: 6500 Marjory Lane Bethesda MD 20034 Office: 1717 Pennsylvania Av NW Washington DC 20570

BROWN, GILES TYLER, educator, lectr.; b. Marshall, Mich., Apr. 21, 1916; s. A. Watson and Ettroile (Kent) B.; A.B., San Diego State Coll., 1937; M.A., U. Cal., Berkeley, 1941; Ph.D., Claremont Grad. Sch., 1948; student seminar U. Edinburgh, Scotland, 1949; m. Crysta Beth Cosner, Nov. 21, 1951. Tchr., counselor, Binet intelligence tester San Diego City Schs., 1937-46; dir. social sci. project, chmn.. social sci. div. Orange Coast Coll., Newport Beach, Cal., 1948-60; prof. history, chmn. social sci. div. Cal. State Coll., Fullerton, 1961-66, also chmn. history dept., dean grad. studies, 1967—; pub. lectr. nat., internat. affairs, 1951—; also cons. gerontology. State adv. com. overseas program Cal. State Colls. Trustee World Affairs Council Orange County. Served from ensign to lt., USNR, 1942-46. Recipient Pacific History award Pacific Coast br. Am. Hist. Assn., 1950; named Outstanding Prof. Cal. State Coll., 1966, Hon. Citizen of Orange County, 1969. Mem. A.A.A.S., Internat. Platform Assn. (past western pres., nat. bd. dirs.), Am. Scandinavian Found., S.A.R., Phi Delta Kappa, Phi Alpha Theta. Baptist. Mason. Author: Ships That Sail No More, 1966. Contbr. to Help in Troubled Times, 1962; also Ency. Brit. Contbr. articles, book reviews profl. jours. Home: 413 Catalina Dr Newport Beach CA 92660 Office: Cal State Coll 800 N State College Blvd Fullerton CA 92631

BROWN, GLADYS LILLIAN HAMILTON (Junie Brown), journalist; b. Long Beach, Cal., May 21, 1940; d. Horton Bryan and Gladys (Beauford) Hamilton; B.A. in English and Edn., Winthrop Coll., Rock Hill, S.C., 1957-61; M.A. in Am. Lit., U. S.C., 1970; m. Arnold Kolah Brown, Aug. 26, 1967. Tchr. English high sch., N. Augusta, S.C., 1961-62; edn. writer, reporter Augusta (Ga.) Chronicle, 1962-64; reporter Atlanta Times, 1964; reporter, asst. state editor The State, Columbia, S.C., 1965-67; reporter Atlanta Jour., 1967—, edn. editor, 1968—. Community ambassador representing Augusta to Pistoia, Italy, summer 1963. Recipient 1st pl., 3d pl., hon. mentions women's div. awards S.C. Press Assn., 1966, Ga. Sch. Bell award, 1971. Mem. Nat. Assn. Press Women, Kappa Delta Pi. Methodist. Home: 3044 Margaret Mitchell Ct NW Atlanta GA 30327 Office: 10 Forsyth St Atlanta GA 30303

BROWN, GLENN HALSTEAD, chemist, educator; b. Logan, O., Sept. 10, 1915; s. James E. and Nancy J. (Mohler) B.; B.S., Ohio U., 1939; M.S., Ohio State U., 1941; Ph.D., Ia. State U., 1951; m. Jessie Adock, May 27, 1943; children—Larry H., Nancy K., Donald S., Barbara J. Asst. prof. U. Miss., 1941-46, 49-50; instr. Ia. State U., 1946-49; asst. prof. U. Vt., 1950-52; asso. prof. U. Cin., 1952-60; with Kent (O.) State U., 1960—, prof. chemistry, head dept., 1960-65, dir. Liquid Crystal Inst., 1965—, dean for research, 1963-69, Regents prof., 1968—; spl. research X-ray structural studies liquids, concentrated salt solutions, photochromism, liquid crystals, electrochemistry solutions. Fellow Ohio Acad. Sci. (pres. 1960); mem. Am. Chem. Soc. (chmn. Akron sect. 1965, chmn. regional meeting planning com. 1966-68), Am. Inst. Chemists (chmn. Ohio 1969-71), Am. Crystallographic Assn., A.A.A.S., N.Y. Acad. Scis., Sigma Xi, Alpha Chi Sigma, Phi Lambda Upsilon. Methodist. Author: (with F.A. Anderson) Fundamentals of Chemistry, 1944; (with Wollett and Fogelsong) Laboratory Manual for Organic Chemistry, 1944; Record Book for Quantitative Analysis, 1954; (with E. M. Sallee) Quantitative Chemistry, 1963; (with others) Liquid Crystals, 1967; (with others) Review of the Structure and Properties of Liquid Crystals. Editor: Liquid Crystals 2, Parts I and II, 1969; Photochromism, 1971; co-editor: Jour. Molecular Crystals and Liquid Crystals, 1968—; also articles. Home: 470 Harvey Av Kent OH 44240

BROWN, GLENN MAX, mfg. exec.; b. Napoleon, O., Nov. 19, 1905; s. James Max and Maude (McNulty) B.; student Toledo U.; m. Marie Kuehnl, Nov. 24, 1926; children—Carol (Mrs. Donald R. Lewellen), Marilyn (Mrs. R. E. Croasdaile, Jr.), Pro. Production mgr., industrial engr. Logan Gear Co. and subsidiary Bingham Stamping & Tool Co., 1928-38; asst. to pres., then v.p. Ryerson & Haynes, Inc., Jackson Mich., 1938-42, pres., gen. mgr., 1942-53; pres., gen. mgr. Aspro Inc. (formerly Automatic Steel Products, Inc.), 1953-70, chmn. exec. com., dir., 1970—; dir. Hayes-Albion Corp., Jackson, Mich., 1st Nat. Bank, Canton, O. Asst. chmn. integration com. Ammunition Container Program for Army Ordnance, World War II. Mem. Soc. Automotive Engrs. Rep. Meth. Mason (32, Shriner). Clubs: Canton, Congress Lake (Canton); Toledo. Home: 3725 Eaton Rd NW Canton OH 44708

BROWN, GORDON STANLEY, educator; b. Drummoyne, New South Wales, Australia, Aug. 30, 1907; s. Herbert C. and Alice A. (Schofield) B.; came to U.S., 1929, naturalized, 1939; S.B. in Elec. Engring., Mass. Inst. Tech., 1931, S.M., 1934, Sc.D., 1938; D. Engring., Purdue U., 1958; D.Sc., Dartmouth, 1964; D.Engring., Stevens Inst. Tech., 1968, So. Meth. U., 1968; D.Eng. Tech., Tech. U. Denmark, 1965; m. Jean Alfred, Aug. 23, 1935; children—Sydney E., Stanley A. Engr., Victorian Electricity Commn., Australia, 1935-39; research asst., Mass. Inst. Tech., Cambridge, 1931-32, instr. elec. engring., 1932-39, asst. prof., 1939-41, asso. prof., 1941-46, dir. Servomechanisms Lab., 1941-52, prof. 1946—, asso. head dept. elec. engring., chmn. faculty, 1951-52, head dept. elec. engring., 1952-59, dean engring., 1959-68, Jackson prof. engring., 1968—. Vis. Mackay professor U. Cal. at Berkeley, 1956; J. I. Carroll fellow, Sydney U., Australia, 1958; dir. Allegheny Ludlum Industries, Gillette Co., Rogers Corp., Leeds & Northrup. Bd. overseers Thayer Sch., Dartmouth, 1957-65, 70—. Mem. Pres.'s Com. on Nat. Medal of Sci., 1962-65; mem. Commn. Engring. Edn., cons. NDRC, 1942- 45, Sperry Gyroscope, 1941-45, War Dept. on fire-control, 1941-45; Participant in conf. on automatic control, Royal Coll. Aero., Cranfield, Eng., 1951; mem. adv. council elec. engring. dept. Princeton, 1957-62. Recipient Naval Ordnance Devel. award, 1946; Certificate of Merit, 1948; George Westinghouse award, 1952; Lamme medal Am. Soc. Engring. Edn., 1959; Elec. Engring. Edn. medal I.E.E.E., 1959. Fellow I.E.E.E. (dir.-at-large 1958-60, 65-66), Am. Acad. Scis.; mem. Nat. Acad. Engring., Am. Soc. Engring. Edn., Sigma Xi, Tau Beta Pi, Eta Kappa Nu (eminent mem.). Author: (with D.P. Campbell) Principles of Servomechanisms, 1948; contbr. sci. articles. Home: 329 Heath Bridge Rd Concord MA 01742 Office: Mass Inst Tech Cambridge MA 02139

BROWN, GRANT A., chem. co. exec. Gen. counsel Amoco Chems. Corp., Chgo. Office: 130 E Randolph Dr Chicago IL 60601*

BROWN, GROVER CLEVELAND, air force officer; b. Jefferson County, Miss., Dec. 28, 1912; s. Grover Cleveland and Dora (O'Quinn) B.; A.B., U. Tex., 1935; grad. Air War Coll., 1949; m. Marguerite Lockhardt, Aug. 2, 1942; children—Byron C., Keri L., Stephen L., Michael C. Commd. 2d lt. USAAF, 1940, advanced through grades to maj. gen. USAF, 1966; various assignments, U.S. and ETO, 1940-45; assigned Hdqrs. USAAF, 1945-48; faculty, then dep. acad. dir. Air War Coll., 1948-53; intelligence officer Hdqrs. FEAF, Japan, then comdg. officer 4th Fighter Wing, 1953-56; mem.

staff, then dir. directorate targets, asst. chief staff intelligence Hdqrs. USAF; attache, London, Eng., 1959-62; comdr. Seattle Air Def. Sector, McChord AFB, 1962-64; asst. chief staff intelligence Staff Comdr. in Chief Pacific, 1964-67; asst. dir. prodn. Def. Intelligence Agy., Dept. Def. 1967-70; ret., 1970. Decorated D.S.M., Legion of Merit with oak leaf cluster, D.F.C., Bronze Star, Air medal with 4 oak leaf clusters, Army Commendation ribbon with oak cluster, numerous unit and area ribbons; Croix de Guerre with palm (France). Mem. Air Force Hist. Found., Order Daedalians, Alpha Sigma Phi. Home: Fayette MS 39069

BROWN, H. TEMPLETON, lawyer; b. St. Joseph, Mo., Feb. 5, 1902; s. Robert A. and Mary (Guitar) B.; grad. Phillips Andover Acad., 1919; A.B., Yale, 1923; LL.B., Harvard, 1926; m. Jessie McLaren Hosmer, Oct. 27, 1928; children—H. Templeton, Jessie Grace. Admitted to Mo. bar, 1926, Ill. bar, 1942, Supreme Ct. U.S., U.S. Dist. Ct. D.C., 1970; partner Brown Douglas & Brown, St. Joseph, 1926-42; partner Mayyer, Brown & Platt and predecessor firms, Chgo., 1942—. Dir. UAL, Inc., United Air Lines, Inc., Scott, Foresman & Co., South-Western Pub. Co., A.M. Castle & Co. Bd. dirs. United Air Lines Found., Passavant Meml. Hosp., Chgo., Northwestern U.-McGraw Med. Center, Mem. Northwestern U. Assos., Chgo. Zool. Soc., Am., Ill., Chgo. bar assns., Am. Bar Found., Am. Judicature Soc., Am. Soc. Internat. Law, Am. Coll. Trial Lawyers, Bar Assn. 7th Fed. Circuit, Beta Theta Pi. Republican. Episcopalian. Clubs: Indian Hill Country, Onwentsia Country, Old Elm Country, Chicago, Commonwealth, Commercial (Chgo.); Benton (St. Joseph). Home: 1010 Hubbard Lane Winnetka IL 60093 Office: 231 S LaSalle St Chicago IL 60604

BROWN, HAMILTON, architect; b. Alameda, Cal., Mar. 23, 1908; s. Herbert Hamilton and Florence Emma (Sharon) B.; student U. Cal. at Berkeley, 1926-28; B.S. in Architecture, Mass. Inst. Tech., 1932; diploma architecture, Ecole des Beaux Arts, Fontainebleau, France, 1931; m. Carol Wilson Crow, Dec. 22, 1965; children—Peter Hoyt, Christopher James. Practicing architect, Houston, 1937-68; now partner firm Carham Design Assos., Carmel, Cal.; dir. Sharlands Corp.; prin. works include First Christian Ch., Med. Center Nat. Bank, Adams Petroleum Center, Jr. League of Houston (all in Houston). Mem. vis. com. Nat. Archtl. Accrediting Bd., 1955—. Pres. Arts Council Harris County, 1953, bd. dirs., 1959-66; pres. Neighborhood Improvement Council Houston, 1957, bd. dirs., 1958-64; program com. Mus. Fine Arts, Houston, 1959-62; founding mem. Houston Friends of Byzantine Inst., 1945-62; chmn. bd. Ballet found. for Houston, 1961, 66; bd. dirs. Riverside Gen. Hosp., 1966, Monterey Peninsula Mus. Art, 1971—; mem. Mayor's Com. on Old Market Sq., 1962. Served to lt. comdr. USNR, World War II. Recipient 2d award Ch. Archtl. Guild Am., 1952, hon. mention, 1955; award of merit Tex. Soc. Architects, 1949, 52, 59, 64; hon. mention Houston chpt. A.I.A., 1949-52, 55, 58, 60, gold medal, 1958. Fellow A.I.A. (pres. Houston 1948, dir. Monterey Bay chpt. 1971); mem. Tex. Soc. Architects (v.p. 1948), Houston C. of C. (chmn. Downtown Beautification Com. 1962), Nat. Trust for Hist. Preservation, Soc. Archtl. Historians, Beta Theta Pi. Protestant Episcopalian. Works pub. numerous mags., also photog. exhibits. Address: PO Box 4915 Carmel CA 93921

BROWN, HARLAN CRAIG, librarian; b. Cleve., Jan. 26, 1906; s. Edgar Dwight and Harriet J. (Weakley) B.; A.B., U. Minn., 1930, B.S., 1931; A.M., U. Mich., 1935; m. Helen Abel, June 16, 1936. Asst. librarian S.D. State Coll., 1931-34; gen. service asst. U. Mich. Library, 1935-36; circulation librarian N.C. State Coll., 1936-39, librarian State Coll. Agr. and Engring., 1939-64; asso. dir. D.H. Hill Library, N.C. State U. at Raleigh, 1964-71, dir. emeritus, 1971—. Served to capt. AUS, 1942-46; maj. Res. ret. Mem. S.D. (v.p. 1933-34), N.C. (v.p. 1946-48, pres. 1949-51), Southeastern, Am. library assns., Phi Kappa Phi. Democrat. Unitarian. Home: 3217 Merriman Av Raleigh NC 27607

BROWN, HAROLD, univ. pres.; b. N.Y.C., Sept., 19, 1927; s. Abraham Howard and Gertrude (Cohen) B.; A.B., Columbia, 1945, A.M., 1946, Ph.D. in Physics (Lydig fellow 1948-49), 1949; D.Eng., Stevens Inst. Tech., 1964; LL.D., L.I. U., 1966, Gettysburg Coll., 1967, Occidental Coll., 1969, U. Cal., 1969; m. Colene Dunning McDowell, Oct. 29, 1953; children—Deborah Ruth, Ellen Dunning. Research scientist Columbia, 1945-50, lectr. physics, 1947-48; lectr. physics Stevens Inst. Tech., 1949-50; research scientist Radiation Lab., U. Cal. at Berkeley, 1951-52, lectr. physics, 1951-52, group leader Radiation Lab. at Livermore, 1952-61; dir. def. research and engring. Dept. Def., 1961-65; sec. of air force, 1965-69; pres. Cal. Inst. Tech., Pasadena, 1969—. Dir. Schroders Ltd., 1970—. Mem. Polaris Steering Com., 1956-58; cons., mem. Air Force Sci. Adv. Bd., 1956-61; mem. sci. Adv. Com. Ballistic Missiles to Sec. Def., 1958-61; cons., mem. President's Sci. Adv. Com., 1958-61; sr. sci. adviser Conf. Discontinuance Nuclear Tests, 1958-59. Trustee Harvard Sch., Los Angeles, 1971—. Recipient medal of excellence Columbia U., 1963; named One of 10 Outstanding Young Men of 1961, U.S. Jr. C. of C. Mem. Nat. Acad. Engring., Am. Phys. Soc., N.Y. Acad. Scis., Am. Acad. Arts and Scis., Phi Beta Kappa, Sigma Xi. Clubs: Cosmos (Washington); One Hundred (Los Angeles); Bohemian (San Francisco); University (N.Y.); Athenaeum (London). Home: 415 S Hill Av Pasadena CA 91106

BROWN, HAROLD WILLIAM, prof. of parasitology; b. Muskegon, Mich., Jan. 16, 1902; s. Clarence and Florence (Henderson) B.; A.B., Kalamazoo Coll., 1924; M.S., Kan. State Coll., 1925; Sc.D., Johns Hopkins, 1928; M.D., Vanderbilt U., 1933; student London (England) Sch. Trop. Medicine and Hygience, 1934- 35; Dr. Pub. Health, Harvard, 1936; LL.D. (hon.), U. Puerto Rico, 1954; m. Nell Cardwell, Oct. 1, 1933; children—William Cardwell, David Henderson. Research asso. (Panama, 1926, Costa Rica, 1932), Vanderbilt Medical Sch., 1927-34; traveling fellow, Gen. Edn. Bd., 1934- 36; past asst. surgeon, USPHS, 1936-37; prof. pub. health, N.C. Univ., 1937-43, dean sch. pub. health, 1941-43; prof. preventive medicine and pub. health, Duke U. Med. Sch., 1938-43; prof. parasitology, since 1943, acting dir. Sch. of Pub. Health. Columbia University since 1947, dir. School of Public Health 1951-55; vis. lecturer, Duke Univ., 1944-45; vis. lecturer tropical diseases, Yale U., 1945; vis. prof. Nat. Taiwan U., Formosa, 1953, 57, 58, 60, 62, 63, 64, 66, Airlangga U. Med. Sch., 1962, 64, U. Ky. Med. Sch., 1962, Univ. Colo. Medical Sch., 1965; spl. asst. to chancellor charge med. affairs. Univ. of P.R., 1949-53; cons. in tropical diseases, Vets. Adminstrn.; cons. in parasitology, Presbyn. Hosp., N.Y.; cons. in tropical medicine, Secretary of War, 1943-46. Member med. bd. Am. Leprosy Mission. Mem. Am. Acad. Tropical Medicine, Panama Hookworm Expdn., Soc. Parasitology, Pub. Health Assn., Helminth Soc., Nat. Malaria Soc. (V.P. 1942). Am. Soc. Tropical Medicine (v.p. 1944), Am. Epidemiological Soc., Nat. Research Council (mem. subcom. tropical medicine). Sigma Xi, Delta Omega, Alpha Omega Alpha. Author: articles on tropical diseases. Home: 42 Appleton Place Dobbs Ferry NY 10522 Office: 600 W 168th St New York City NY 10032

BROWN, HARRISON SCOTT, chemist, educator; b. Sheridan, Wyo., Sept. 26, 1917; s. Harrison H. and Agatha (Scott) B.; B.S., U. Cal., 1938, LL.D., 1970; Ph.D., Johns Hopkins, 1941; LL.D., U. Alta., 1961; Sc.D., Rutgers U., 1964, Amherst Coll., 1966, Cambridge U., 1969; m. Rudd Owen, Nov. 11, 1949; 1 son, Eric Scott. Instr. chemistry Johns Hopkins, 1941-42; asst. dir. chemistry Clinton Labs., Oak Ridge, 1943-46; research asso. plutonium project U. Chgo., 1942-43; asst. prof. Inst. for Nuclear Studies, 1946-48, asso. prof. 1948-51; prof. geochemistry, Cal. Inst. Tech., 1951—, prof. sci. and govt., 1967—. Trustee Charles F. Kettering Found., Resources for Future. Recipient Lasker Found. award. Mem. Nat. Acad. Scis. (fgn. sec.), Am. Chem. Soc. (received award in pure chemistry, 1952), Geol. Soc. Am., A.A.A.S. (ann. award, 1947), Am. Geophys. Union, Phi Beta Kappa, Sigma Xi. Author: Must Destruction Be Our Destiny?, 1946; The Challenge of Man's Future, 1954, The Next Hundred Years, 1957; The Cassiopeia Affair, 1968. Editor-at-large Saturday Rev. Home: 623 E California Blvd Pasadena CA 91106 Office: Cal Inst Tech Pasadena CA 91109

BROWN, HARRY JOE, motion picture dir.-producer; b. Pitts., Sept. 22, 1893; s. Nathan and Anna Brown; student U. Mich., 1909-10; LL.B., U. Syracuse, 1915; m. Dorothy Gray, Sept. 1, 1953; 1 son, Harry Joe. Stage and screen actor, dir., producer Warner Bros., Paramount Pictures, Pathe, R.K.O.; pres. Federal TV Prodns., Producers Actors Corp., 1944—, Murphy Brown Prodns., Sage Prodns. Served as capt., inf., AUS, World War I. Mem. Am. Picture Alliance, Motion Picture Arts and Scis. Elk. Clubs: Masquers (pres. 1954-58), Friars (dir.) Hollywood); Pioneers, Lambs (N.Y.C.); Tamarisk Country; Hillcrest Country; Variety. Home: 622 N Roxbury Dr Beverly Hills CA 90210 Office: Columbia Studios Hollywood CA

BROWN, HARRY JOHN, symphony condr.; b. Chgo., June 6, 1924; s. Harry Louis and Libushka (Bartusek) B.; Mus.B., Eastman Sch. Music, 1945; M.A., U. Chgo., 1947. Conductor, Tri-City Symphony Orch., Davenport, Ia., 1949-54; asso. condr. Boston Pops Tours, 1954-57; music dir. Manhattan Concert Orch., N.Y.C., 1957—; guest condr. Voice of Firestone, 1962-63; music dir. condr. Milw. Symphony Orch., 1960-68; guest condr. symphonies in Chgo., Balt., Miami, Boston, Nurnberg (Germany), Munich, Germany, Vienna, Austria. Prof., State U. N.Y. Coll. Fredonia, 1968—. Served with AUS, 1942-45. Recipient N.Y. Philharmonic award for tone poem Arizona 1942; Pere Marquette award, Marquette U., 1968; Mt. Mary Coll. Medal for Distinctive Civic Service, 1968. Hon. mem. Delta Omicron, Phi Mu Alpha Sinfonia. Home: Temple Rd Dunkirk NY 14048 also 9464 Bay Dr Surfside FL 33154

BROWN, HARRY MATTHEW, univ. dean; b. Newark, O., Jan. 24, 1921; s. Marlin Alexander and Elizabeth (Cahill) B.; Th.B., Malone Coll., 1945; B.A., Baldwin-Wallace Coll., 1946; M.A., Western Reserve U., 1948, Ph.D., 1955; m. Jeanette Karen Brown, Aug. 25, 1951; children—Michele, Inga, Karren, Kit. Instr. English, Baldwin-Wallace Coll., 1946-50; teaching fellow Western Res. U., 1950-53; asst. prof. Shepherd Coll., 1953-56; asso. prof. La. Poly. Inst., 1956-63; asso. prof. Cal. State Poly. Coll., 1963-66; prof. English, Midwestern U., 1966—, dean 1968—. Author: A Workbook for Writers, 4th edit., 1970; co-author: Readings for College Writers, 2d edit., 1967; Patterns in Poetry, 1968; What the Poem Means, 1970; The Contemporary College Writer, 1971. Home: Rt 1 Box 74A Wichita Falls TX 76301

BROWN, HARRY PETER MCNAB, Jr., author; b. Portland, Me., Apr. 30, 1917; s. Harry McNab and Bessie Maude (Hiles) B.; student Harvard, 1940; m. 3d, June Jollie de Baun, Dec. 30, 1959; one son, Jared Jollie Clark Brown. With Time mag., 1939, New Yorker mag., 1939-40; attached to Yank, Army newspaper, N.Y.C., 1942. Served with AUS, 1941-45. Recipient Young Poets' prize, 1935; Lloyd McKim Garrison award Harvard, 1937, Shelley award, 1939; award Commonwealth Club, Cal., 1949; Acad. award for best screenplay, 1952. Mem. Acad. Motion Picture Arts and Scis., Nat. Rifle Assn. (life), Writers Guild of Am., also mem. Authors Guild. Author: The End of a Decade, 1941; The Poem of Bunker Hill, 1941; The Violent, 1943; A Walk in the Sun, 1944; Poems, 1941-44 (Eng.), 1945; Artie Greengroin, 1945; A Sound of Hunting, 1946; The Beast in His Hunger, 1948; The Stars in their Courses, 1960; A Quiet Place to Work, 1968; also numerous film scripts. Home: Apartado 114 Guanaluato Gto Mexico Office: care of Robert Lescher 159 E 64th St New York City NY 10021

BROWN, HARRY S., publ., map co. exec.; b. Pitts., Mar. 12, 1933; s. Harry S. and Florence (Archer) E.; B.S. in Finance, Pa. State U., 1958; M.B.A., U. Pitts., 1964; m. Nancy Jane May, June 21, 1958; children—Bonnie Jane, Charles Lawrence, Sallie Anne. With Pitts. Nat. Bank, 1958-65, asst. cashier, 1963-65; with Hygrade Food Products Corp., Detroit, 1965-69, v.p., treas., 1967-69; treas. Rand McNally & Co., Chgo., 1969—; dir. Hubbard/McNally Co. Served with USNR, 1951-54. Mem. Am. Mgmt. Assn., Financial Execs. Inst., Alpha Sigma Phi, Delta Sigma Pi, Beta Gamma Sigma. Club: Glenview (Ill.). Author chpt. in The Bankers Handbook. Home: 649 Glendale Dr Glenview IL 60025 Office: PO Box 7600 Chicago IL 60680

BROWN, HELEN GURLEY, author, editor; b. Green Forest, Ark., Feb. 18, 1922; d. Ira M. and Cleo (Sisco) Gurley; student Tex. State Coll. for Women, 1939-41, Woodbury Coll., 1942; m. David Brown, Sept. 25, 1959. Exec. sec. Music Corp. Am., 1942-45, William Morris Agy., 1945-47; copywriter Foote, Cone & Belding, advt. agy., Los Angeles, 1948-58; advt. writer, account exec. Kenyon & Eckhardt, advt. agy., Hollywood, Cal., 1958-62; editor-in-chief Cosmopolitan mag., 1965—. Recipient Francis Holmes Achievement award for outstanding work in advt., 1956-59. Mem. Authors' League Am., A.F.T.R.A., Eta Upsilon Gamma. Author: Sex and the Single Girl, 1962; Sex and the Office, 1965; Outrageous Opinions, 1966; Helen Gurley Brown's Single Girl's Cook Book, 1969, Sex and the New Single Girl, 1970. Home: 605 Park Av New York City NY 10021 Office: Hearst Corp 959 8th Av New York City NY 10019

BROWN, HELEN MARGARET, librarian; b. Troy, N.Y., July 17, 1912; d. Edwin Nelson and Margaret Jane (Walker) Brown; A.B., Vassar Coll., 1933; B.S., Columbia, 1934, M.S., 1942. Mem. library staff Vassar Coll., 1934-44; librarian MacMurray Coll., Jacksonville, Ill., 1944-47, Skidmore Coll., Saratoga Springs, N.Y., 1947-53, Wellesley (Mass.) Coll., 1953—. Mem. A.L.A. (council 1961—), Assn. Coll. and Research Libraries, (pres.), Am. Assn. U. Profs., Am. Assn. U. Women. Club: Vassar (Boston). Contbr. articles to profl. jours. Address: Fiske House Wellesley Coll Wellesley MA 02181

BROWN, HENRY RUSSELL, surgeon; b. St. Paul, Aug. 29, 1903; s. William Henry and Anna (Herr) B.; B.S., U. Minn., 1924, B.M., 1926, M.D., 1927; m. Mary Ruth Carroll, Mar 1, 1924; children—Russell T., Carroll (Mrs. Richard H. Guddal), Virginia (Mrs. Gerald E. Tracy), Constance (Mrs. Earl R. Kinsman), Patti (Mrs. James T. Hanson), James W., Mary (Mrs. Jack R. Cunningham). Resident physician and surgeon Charles T. Miller Hosp., St. Paul, 1927; practice surgery Bartron Clinic, Watertown, S.D., 1928-35, Brown Clinic, Watertown, 1935—; mem. surg. staff Bartron Hosp., 1928-35; staff mem., chief surgery, past chief staff Meml. Hosp., Watertown, 1935—, St. Ann Hosp., Watertown, 1950—; med. dir. Brown Clinic, 1935—; clin. asso. teaching staff U. S.D. Med. Sch., 1948-68; supt. Codington County Bd. Health, 1936—. Bd. dirs. S.D. Med. Sch. Endowment Fund, 1950-62; bd. dirs. S.D. Blue Shield Plan, 1958—, pres., 1964-69; mem. profl. relations bd. Nat. Assn. Blue Shield Plans, 1966-70. Del. S.D. Republican Conv., 1964, 66, 68, 70; del. Rep. Nat. Conv., 1968. Mem. Devel. commn. U. S.D., 1948-54. Diplomate Am. Bd. Abdominal Surgery. Fellow Am. (pres. S.D. 1958), Internat. (vice regent S.D. 1952—) colls. surgeons; mem. Am. (ho. of dels. 1946-54, chmn. com. lay-sponsored vol. health plans 1950-58, chmn. com. miscellaneous and unclassified plans 1954-59, chmn. com. prepayment plans, 1963-69, mem. adv. com. to bd. trustees 1953), S.D. (pres. 1948) med. assns., Watertown Med. Soc. (pres. 1937), S.D. Pub. Health Assn. (pres. 1936), North Central Med. Conf. (pres. 1952), St. Paul Surg. Soc., Pan-Pacific Surg. Assn., Watertown C. of C. (pres. 1941), Greater S.D. Assn., Internat. Platform Assn., Med. Soc. Pan Am. Drs. Club (pres. 1970), Phi Rho Sigma. Roman Catholic. K.C. (4), Elk, Rotarian (pres. Watertown 1936). Author numerous papers in field. Home: 820 N Broadway Watertown SD 57201 Office: 506 1st Av S E Watertown SD 57201

BROWN, HENRY STANLEY, union ofcl.; b. Pitts., Oct. 24, 1920; s. Stanley J. and Sophie Brown; student San Antonio Coll., 1950-51, St. Mary's U., 1952, Harvard, 1956; m. Sophie E. Wegman, Sept. 30, 1939; children—Henry Stanley, Gerald, Sophie. Bus. mgr. Plumbers and Pipefitters Local 142, San Antonio, 1946- 53; 59-61; edn. dir. Tex. Fedn. Labor, 1953-59; pres. Tex. AFL-CIO, Austin, 1961-71. Labor rep. savs. bond com. U.S. Dept. Treasury; mem. adv. com. Tex. Employment Commn.; mem. Regional Manpower Com.; mem. Tex. Emergency Resources Planning Com.; mem. Nat. Labor-Mgmt. Panel, 1965-68; mem. Regional Labor-Mgmt. Manpower Com.; mem. adv. com. Tex. Occupational Safety Bd., 1967—; Nat. Adv. Council Vocational Edn., 1969. Served with AUS. Mem. Tex. Fedn. Labor (past v.p.), Tex. Pipe Trades Assn. (past pres.), Tex. Bldg. and Constrn. Trades Council (past exec. sec.), San Antonio Bldg. Trades Council (past v.p.) Roman Catholic. Home: 1411 Sunshine Dr San Antonio TX 78228 Office: PO Box 208 Waco TX

BROWN, HERBERT CHARLES, educator; b. London, Eng., May 22, 1912; s. Charles and Pearl (Stine) B.; brought to U.S., 1914; Asso. Sci., Wright Jr. Coll., Chicago, 1935; B.S., U. Chgo., 1936, Ph.D., 1938, D.Sc., 1968; m. Sarah Baylen, Feb. 6, 1937; 1 son, Charles Allan. Asst. chemistry U. Chgo., 1936-38; Eli Lilly post-doctorate research fellow, 1938-39; instr., 1939-43; asst. prof. chemistry Wayne U., 1943- 46, asso. prof., 1946-47; prof. inorganic chemistry, Purdue U., 1947-59, Richard B. Wetherill prof. chemistry 1959, Richard B. Wetherill research prof., 1969—; vis. prof. U. Cal. at Los Angeles, 1951, Ohio State U., 1952, U. Mexico, 1954, U. Cal. at Berkeley, 1957, U. Colo., 1958, U. Heidelberg, 1963, State U. N.Y. at Stonybrook, 1966, U. Cal. at Santa Barbara, 1967, Hebrew U., Jerusalem, 1969; Harrison Howe lectr., 1953; Friend E. Clark lectr., 1953 Freud-McCormack lecturer, 1954; Centenary lecturer (England), 1955, Thomas W. Talley lecturer, 1956, Falk-Plaut lecturer, 1957, Julius Stieglitz lecturer, 1958, Max Tishler lecturer, 1958, Kekule-Couper Centenary lectr., 1958; E. C. Franklin lectr., 1960, Ira Remsen lectr., 1961, Edgar Fahs Smith lecturer, 1962; Seydel-Wooley lectr., 1966; Baker lectr., 1969; chem. cons. to indsl. corps. Served as co-dir. war research projects U. of Chgo. for U.S. Army, Nat. Defense Research Com., Manhattan Project, 1940-43. Recipient Purdue Sigma Xi research award, 1951; Nichols medal, 1959; award Am. Chem. Soc., 1960, S.O.C.M.A. medal, 1960; H. N. McCoy award, 1965; Linus Pauling medal, 1968; Nat. Medal of Sci., 1969; Roger Adams medal, 1971. Fellow Chem. Soc. (London), A.A.A.S.; mem. Am. Acad. Arts and Scis., Nat. Acad. Scis., Am. Chem. Soc. (chmn. Purdue sect. 1955-56), Ind. Acad. Sci., Sigma Xi, Alpha Chi Sigma, Phi Lambda Upsilon (hon.). Author: Hydroboration, 1962. Contbr. articles to chem. jours.; awarded patents (with others) on preparation of borohydrides, diborane; synthesis of aliphatic derivatives; research in phys., organic, inorganic chemistry relating chem. behavior to molecular structure; selective reductions; hydroboration; chemistry of organoboranes. Home: 1840 Garden St West Lafayette IN 47906

BROWN, HERBERT JOSEPH, banker; b. Oakland, Cal., Jan. 27, 1914; s. Harry Lewis and Yetta (Jacobson) B.; student San Francisco State Coll., 1932-33, Pacific Coast Sch. Banking, 1961-64; m. Beatrice Brenner, June 4, 1939; 1 son, Richard David. With Levi Strauss & Co., 1930-36, Bank of Am., 1936-46; with First Nat. Bank Nev., Reno, 1946—, v.p., br. mgr., 1967—. Pres. Better Bus. Bur. No. Nev., 1966, bd. dirs., 1964-70, hon. bd. dirs., 1970—. Pres. Community Welfare Reno, 1969-70, bd. dirs., 1960—; treas. Vis. Homemaker and Home Aide Service Washoe County, 1962-68, pres., 1969-70, bd. dirs., 1962—; treas. United Jewish Appeal Reno, 1955—. Bd. dirs. Nat. Jewish Welfare Bd., Nat. Conf. Christians and Jews. Served as glider pilot, flight officer AUS, 1942-45. Mem. Am. Inst. Banking (past pres. Sierra Nev. chpt.). Jewish religion (pres. congregation 1952-54, 68-71, treas. 1954-68). Lion (treas. Reno 1966-67), Elk. Home: 1200 W 12th St Reno NV 89503 Office: PO Box 461 Reno NV 89504

BROWN, HERBERT L., Jr., editor, govt. ofcl.; b. Cin., Jan. 15, 1913; s. Herbert L. and Jeanette (Kahn) B.; B.A., U. Cin., 1934; M.A., Harvard, 1935; Rhodes scholar, Oxford U., Eng., 1935-37; m. Ada Estelle Alpaugh, July 21, 1937; children—Herbert Northcott, Carolyn (Mrs. Steven Robert Sears). Mem. editorial staff Cin. Enquirer, 1937-42; staff editor, mng. editor, editor Changing Times, Kiplinger Mag., 1946-64; v.p., dir. Kiplinger Washington Editors, 1959-64; dir. Office Publs., Dept. Commerce, Washington, 1964—; dir. Inter-Ocean Corp., Cin. Mem. Arlington County (Va.) Bd., 1957-61, chmn., 1960. Trustee Antioch Coll., 1963-66; trustee Orthopaedic Hosp. Served from lt. (j.g.) to lt. comdr., USNR, 1942-46. Mem. Phi Beta Kappa. Home: 2710 S Hayes St Arlington VA 22202 Office: Dept Commerce Washington DC 20230

BROWN, HERBERT LYCETT, Jr., engr.; b. Dallas, Sept. 17, 1932; s. Herbert L. and Rubye (Tatum) B.; B.S., So. Meth. U., 1955, M.S., 1961; m. Edwina Lynn Millican, Dec. 19, 1954; 1 son, Herbert L. III. Research engr. Temco Aircraft, Dallas, 1954; design engr. Tex. Instruments, Dallas, 1957-60, project engr., 1960—. Served with USAF, 1955-57. Registered profl. engr., Tex. Mem. Am. Soc. M.E., Alpha Tau Omega. Methodist. Patentee in field. Home: 4808 Willow Lane Dallas TX 75214 Office: 13500 N Central Express Dallas TX 75222

BROWN, HERBERT ROSS, univ. prof., editor; b. Allentown, Pa., Feb. 9, 1902; s. Guy Paul and Jeannie (Miller) B.; B.Sc., Lafayette, Coll., 1924, Litt.D., 1949; L.H.D., L.H.D., Bucknell U., 1950; A.M., Harvard, 1928; Ph.D., Columbia, 1929; Litt. D., Bowdoin Coll., 1963; LL.D., U. Me., 1965; m. Ruth Raker, Aug. 21, 1929. Instr. English, Lafayette Coll., 1924-25; instr. Bowdoin Coll., Brunswick, Me., 1925-29, asst. prof., 1929-33, asso. prof., 1933-39, prof. 1939, Edward Little Prof. Rhetoric and Oratory, 1949—; vis. prof. Am. lit., Duke U. 1940. Columbia, 1941, 1945-46, U. Minn., 1947, U. Maine, 1958; vis. prof. Bread Loaf Sch. English, 1948-56, Harvard, 1968; Am. specialist, India, 1968; mng. editor New Eng. Quar., 1944—; trustee Zeta Psi Ednl. Found., N. Yarmouth Acad., 1945—, U. Me., also Brunswick and Topsham Water District. Moderator, Brunswick. Recipient Duke U. Centennial Award in Am. literary history, 1940, N.E. Soc. of N.Y. award in Edn. and Lit., 1958. Fellow Am. Acad. Arts and Scis.; mem. Me. Bd. Edn. (past chmn.), Colonial Soc. (Mass. corr.), Phi Beta Kappa, Zeta Psi. Clubs: Tavern (Boston); Odd Volumes, century (N.Y.C.); Cumberland. Author: The Sentimental Novel in America, 1940; Sills of Bowdoin, 1963. Editor: Nathaniel

Hawthorne's, The Snow Image, 1933; Hannah Fosters, The Coquette, 1939; The Heritage of American Literature (with L. Richardson and G. Orians); Autocrat of the Breakfast Table, 1958; The Power of Sympathy (by William Brown), 1961. Contbr. articles to American Literature, Modern Lang. Notes, Dictionary of World Lit., Dictionary of Notable American Women, Ency. Brit. Home: 32 College St Brunswick ME 04011

BROWN, HOMER R., geologist, state ofcl.; b. Terre Haute, Ind., Dec. 14, 1921; s. Homer R. and Ruth (Schuster) B.; student Ind. State U., 1940; B.A. in Geology, Ind. U., 1949; m. Virginia Lee Bingman, Dec. 28, 1942; children—Robert Paul, Richard Bingman. Asst. dir. div. oil and gas Ind. Dept. Natural Resources, 1950-53, dir. div., 1953—; mem. regulatory and secondary recovery coms. Interstate Oil Compact Commn., 1950—, ofcl. rep. from Ind.; chmn. Ind. Secondary, Recovery and Pressure Maintenance Com., 1951—. Served with USAAF, World War II. Mem. Am. Assn. Petroleum Geologists, Ind.-Ky. Geol. Soc., Sigma Gamma Epsilon. Mem. Christian Ch. (deacon). Home: 2810 E 67 St Indianapolis IN 46220 Office: State Office Bldg Indianapolis IN 46204

BROWN, HORACE BRIGHTBERRY, Jr., coll. dean; b. Holly Springs, Miss., Aug. 19, 1908; s. Horace Brightberry and Aileen May (Blackburn) B.; B.S., U. Miss., 1931; M.B.A., Northwestern U., 1932, Ph.D., 1941; m. Dorothy Pittman Seale, Dec. 26, 1932; 1 son, Horace Jacquelin. Instr. econs. U. Miss., 1932-37, asst. prof., 1937-38, asso. prof. econs., dir. News Bureau, 1938-40, acting dean Sch. Commerce and Bus. Adminstrn., prof. econ., 1941-42, dean Sch. of Commerce and Bus. Adminstrn., prof. econ., 1942-49, rep. of armed services, 1942-44, dir. mgmt. courses in engring., sci., mgmt. war tng. program, 1941-45, chmn. geog. div. of army specialist tng. program, 1942-44, dir. vets. edn., 1944-45; dean Coll. Bus. Adminstrn. U. Okla., Norman, 1949—, v.p. for bus. and finance, 1960-68. Vis. prof. bus. adminstrn. Grad. Sch., Harvard, 1955-56. Dir. Norman Saving & Loan Assn., Friendly Nat. Bank, Oklahoma City. Pres. Nat. Council on Profl. Edn. for Bus., 1956; joint council ednl. advisers Am. Coll. Life Underwriters, Am. Inst. Property and Liability Underwriters, 1955-65; mem. edn.-industry adv. council Lincoln Ednl. Found., 1955—. Chmn. price panel Lafayette County Price and Rationing Bd., 1942-46; cons. to controller gen. of U.S. in recruitment and tng., 1955-64. Fellowship in econs. U. Miss., 1930-31, in marketing, Northwestern Marketing Assn. Mem. Econ. Assn., Southwestern Social Sci. Assn., Am. Assn. Collegiate Schs. of Bus. (pres. 1955), Oxford (Miss.) C. of C. (dir., v.p.), Alpha Sigma Phi, Delta Sigma Pi. Omicron Delta Kappa, Beta Gamma Sigma. Republican. Methodist (steward). Rotarian. Club: University Faculty (U. Okla.). Contbr. revs. and articles to profl. jours. and bus. papers. Home: 316 Merkle Dr Norman OK 73069

BROWN, HORACE GARFIELD, lawyer; b. Clayton, N.J., Dec. 3, 1902; s. Garfield and Ada (Ingersoll) B.; student U. Ky., 1922; LL.B., Temple U., 1928; m. Kathryn E. Moody Black, Dec. 1, 1945; stepchildren—Daniel D. Black, Murray D. Black, Judith A. Black (Mrs. Peter W. Kaiser), children—Horace M., Allan B., Maureen (Mrs. Theodore K. Hutz). Admitted to N.J. bar, 1928, since practiced in Camden; partner firm Brown, Connery, Kulp, Wille, Purnell & Greene, 1957—. Trustee Underwood Meml. Hosp., Woodbury, N.J. Fellow Am. Coll. Trial Lawyers; mem. Am., Inter-Am., Internat., N.J. State (trustee 1955-63), Gloucester County (pres. 1949), Camden County bar assns., Internat. Acad. Trial Lawyers (dir. 1958-63, 66-70, dean 1970—), Am. Judicature Soc., Internat. Soc. Barristers (dir. 1966—). Presbyn. Club: Tavistock Country (Haddonfield, N.J.). Home: 1223 Cooper River Plaza S Pennsauken NJ 08109 Office: 518 Market St Camden NJ 08102

BROWN, HOWARD ALEXANDER, surgeon; b. Stockton, Cal., Apr. 1, 1904; s. Alexander and Mattie Laura (Close) B.; A.B., U. Cal., 1924, M.D., 1928; m. Dorothy Elizabeth Farran, June 11, 1929; children—Howard A., Barton A., Andrea A. Neurosurg. Resident U. Cal. Hosp., 1928-30; instr. surgery, U. Cal. Med. Sch., 1930-35, asst. clin. prof. surgery, 1935-41, asso. clin. prof. of neurosurgery, 1941-55, clin. prof., 1955—; vis. neurosurgeon San Francisco Hosp., U. Cal. Hosp., 1930-48; chief neurosurg. service Franklin Hosp., 1939-61, chief of staff, 1955-59; cons. neurosurgery Mt. Zion Hosp. Diplomate Am. Bd. Neurol. Surgery (mem. bd. 1950-56). Fellow A.C.S.; mem. Am. Acad. Neurol. Surg. (pres. 1947-48), Harvey Cushing Soc. (v.p., 1948- 49), pres. 1957-58), Soc. Neurol. Surgeons, San Francisco County Med. Soc., A.M.A., Cal. Med. Assn., Cal. Acad. Medicine, San Francisco Neurol. Soc., Internat. Surg. Soc., Western Neurosurg. Soc. (pres. 1958), Pacific Coast Surg. Assn., Sigma Chi, Nu Sigma Nu. Republican. Contbr. articles on neurosurgery to sci. jours. Home: 2240 Hyde St San Francisco CA 94109 Office: 2001 Union St San Francisco CA 94123

BROWN, HOWARD JAMES, clergyman; b. St. Louis, Aug. 6, 1907; s. John C. and Mary (O'Hara) B.; B.A., Ohio Wesleyan U., 1929; D.D., 1952; B.D., Garret Theol. Sem., 1932; m. Helen Janney, June 18, 1931; children—Jacelyn (Mrs. Robert Dininny), Patricia (Mrs. Kenneth Kropp), H. James. Ordained to ministry Methodist Ch., 1932; minister in Ft. Wayne, Ind., 1934-41, Goshen, Ind., 1941-43, Richmond, Ind., 1941-49, Ch. of Savior, Cleveland Heights, O., 1949—. Dean Ind. Sch. of Prophets, 1947-48, Ohio Area Meth. Pastor's Sch., 1956-61, Coll. Preachers Ohio East Area, 1965—; pres. Cleve. Council Chs., 1960-62; sec. gen. Commn. Pub. Relations and Meth. Information, 1964—; del. World Meth. Conf., 1951, 61. Trustee Ohio Wesleyan U., 1958—. Mem. Phi Kappa Tau, Omicron Delta Kappa, Theta Alpha Phi. Mason (33), Rotarian. Home: 2510 Arlington Rd Cleveland Heights OH 44118 Office: 2537 Lee Rd Cleveland Heights OH 44118

BROWN, HOWARD JUNIAH, physician; b. Peoria, Ill., Apr. 15, 1924; s. Frank Howard and Frances (Timmons) B.; B.A., Hiram (O.) Coll., 1945; M.D., Western Res. U., 1948. Intern, Univ. Hosp., Cleve., 1949-50; resident Jennings Meml. Hosp., Detroit, 1950-51, Detroit Receiving Hosp., 1952-54; staff physician UAW- CIO, Clinic, Detroit, 1951-52; dir. profl. services Health Ins. Plan Greater N.Y., 1954-61; med. dir. Gouverneur ambulatory care unit Beth Israel Med. Center, N.Y.C., 1961-66; health services adminstr. N.Y.C., 1966-68; asso. attending 1st div. Bellevue Hosp., N.Y.C., 1954-63; instr. medicine Columbia Coll. Phys. & Surg., 1956-63, lectr. Sch. Pub. Health and Adminstrv. Medicine, 1966—; asso. prof. clin. medicine N.Y.C. Sch. Medicine, 1964-66, vis. lectr. Sch. Pub. Adminstrn., 1964—; asso. attending medicine Beth Israel Hosp., 1956-69; asso. prof. community medicine Mt. Sinai Hosp. Sch., 1966-68, Albert Einstein Coll. Medicine, 1968-70; lectr. Yale Coll. Medicine, 1968—; dir. community medicine Miseri Cordia, Fordham hosps., 1968-70; prof. pub. adminstrn., prof. preventive medicine N.Y. U., 1970—. Mem. adv. bd. Regional Med. Programs, Borough Pres. Tech. Adv. B.D. Served with AUS, 1943-44. Recipient citation N.Y. state Optometric Assn., dept. dentistry Beth Israel Hosp., Beth Israel Med. Center, 1966, Apollo award Am. Optometric Assn., 1965. Diplomate Am. Bd. Internal Medicine. Fellow Am. Pub. Health Assn., N.Y. Acad. Medicine; mem. Pub. Health Assn. N.Y.C. (Merit award 1965). Contbr. profl. jours. Home: 225 W 11th St New York City NY 10014 Office: 4 Washington Sq N New York City NY 10003

BROWN, HOWARD MAYER, educator; b. Los Angeles, Apr. 13, 1930; s. Alfred R. and Florence (Mayer) B.; B.A. magna cum laude, Harvard, 1951, M.A., 1954, Ph.D., 1958. Instr. music Wellesley Coll., 1958-60; asst. prof., asso. prof., prof. music U. Chgo., 1960—, chmn. dept., 1970—; Walter Naumburg Travelling fellow Harvard, 1951-53; Guggenheim fellow, 1963-64; curator Smithsonian Instn., 1965; Villa I Tatti fellow, Florence, 1969-70. Mem. Am. Musicol. Soc. (past v.p.), Phi Beta Kappa. Author: Music in the French Secular Theater, 1400-1550, 1963; Theatrical Chausons, 1963; Instrumental Music Printed Before 1600, 1965. Contbr. articles profl. jours. Home: 1415 E 54th St Chicago IL 60615

BROWN, HUBERT RAP GEROLD, chmn. Student Non-Violent Coordinating Com., 1967—. Address: 300 Fifth Av New York City NY 10001*

BROWN, HUGH AUCHINCLOSS, elec engr., author; widower; children—Samuel C., Hugh Auchincloss. Pres., Columbia U.'s Grand Army of the 49th St Era. Mem. A.A.A.S. Author: Cataclysms of the Earth. Home: 115 Prospect Av Douglaston NY 11363 Office: care Twayne Publishers Inc 31 Union Sq W New York City NY 10003

BROWN, HUGH B., clergyman; b. Granger, Utah, Oct. 24, 1883; s. Homer Manley and Lydia J. (Brown) B.; student pub. schs., Salt Lake City; legal edn. and tng., mil tng., Alta., Can.; m. Zina Young Card, June 17, 1908; children—Zina Lydia (Mrs. Guardello Brown), Zola Grace (Mrs. Waldo G. Hodson), LaJune (Mrs. Jerry Hay), Mary Myrtice (Mrs. Edwin R. Firmage), Hugh Card (dec.), Charles Manley, Margaret Alberta (Mrs. Clinton Jorgensen), Carol Rae (Mrs. Douglas Bunker). Latter Day Saints missionary to Gt. Britain, 1904- 06, officers tng. sch., 1910-14; pres. Latter Day Saints Stake, Lethbridge, Alta., 1921-27, Salt Lake City, 1928-36; pres. Brit. Mission, 1937-40, 44-46; prof. Brigham Young U., 1946-50; asst. Council of Twelve, 1953-58; ordained an apostle, 1958, now member of first presidency. Former barrister, solicitor, Alta., 1921-27; practice of law, Salt Lake City, 1927-53; gen. mgr. Richland Oil Devel. Co. of Can., Ltd., 1950-53. Author: Rational Faith, 1949; Eternal Quest, 1956; You and Your Marriage, 1960; Continuing the Quest, 1961; The Abundant Life, 1965. Home: 1002 Douglas St Salt Lake City UT 84105 Office: 47 E South Temple St Salt Lake City UT 84111

BROWN, IVAN WILLARD, Jr., thoracic surgeon, educator; b. Newfane, N.Y., July 6, 1915; s. Ivan Willard and Agnes E. (Clarke) B.; student U. Rochester, 1933-36; B.S., Duke, 1940, M.D., 1940; m. Madeline Davis, Dec. 28, 1939; children—Sandra E. (Mrs. James E. Ling), Diane E., Ivan Willard III. Instr. physiology Duke Sch. Medicine, 1939-40; intern asst. resident pathology Duke U. Hosp., 1940-42, sr. asst. resident surgeon, 1945-48, resident gen. and thoracic surgery, 1952-54; mem. faculty Duke Sch. Medicine, 1940-71, prof. surgery, 1960-66, James B. Duke distinguished prof., 1966-71; thoracic and cardiovascular surgeon Watson Clinic, Lakeland, Fla., 1968—; attending staff Lakeland (Fla.) Gen. Hosp. Exec. com., div. med. scis. Nat. Acad. Scis.-NRC, 1965-71; mem. surg. study sect. NIH, 1966-69. Dir. Ward Labs., Inc. Served to capt., M.C., AUS, 1942-45. Markle scholar med. sci., 1948-53; recipient First Research award Glycerine Producers Assn., 1952. Mem. Am., So. surg. assns., Am. Assn. Thoracic Surgeons, Soc. Thoracic Surgery, Soc. Univ. Surgeons, Soc. Vascular Surgery, Am. Soc. Clin. Investigation, Internat. Cardiovascular Soc., Am., Internat. socs. hematology, Soc. Exptl. Biology and Medicine, Underwater Med. Soc., Halsted Soc., A.C.S., Aerospace Med. Assn., Phi Beta Kappa, Sigma Xi, Alpha Omega Alpha, Theta Delta Chi, Alpha Kappa Kappa. Episcopalian. Author papers hypothermia, cardiac surgery, hyperbaric. Editor: Hyperbaric Medicine, 1966. Address: 1600 Lakeland Hills Blvd Lakeland FL 33802

BROWN, J. MARSHALL, state ofcl.; b. 1924; m. Ellen McInniss; 1 child. Pres. Marshall Brown Ins. Agy., Inc.; Democratic nat. committeeman La.; mem. La. legislature, 1952-60; campaign mgr., chmn. finance com. Gov. John J. McKeiten; pres. La. bd. edn., 1962—; La. campaign mgr. Lyndon Johnson, 1964. Mem. Pres.'s Club, Nat. Capital Dem. Club. Club: Plimson (New Orleans). Home: 225 Baronne St New Orleans LA 70112 Office: State Capitol Baton Rouge LA 70804*

BROWN, JACK EDWARD lawyer; b. Omaha, Mar. 15, 1927; s. Joseph J. and Mary (Radinsky) B.; B.S., Northwestern U., 1949; LL.B., Harvard, 1952; m. Suzanne J. Goldman, Aug. 27, 1950; children-Charles Wilson, Abigal Victoria, James Robinson, Amanda Jane. Admitted to N.Y. bar, 1954. Ariz. bar, 1959; practiced in N.Y.C., 1953-59. Phoenix, 1959—; law clk. Charles E. Wyzanski, U.S. Dist. Ct. judge, Dist. Mass., 1952-53; asso. firm Cravath, Swaine & Moore, 1953-59; law clk. Charles C. Bernstein, Ariz. Supreme Ct. Justice, 1959; asso. firm Evans, Kitchel & Jenckes, 1959-60; sr. partner Brown, Vlassis & Bain and predecessor firms, 1960—; instr., asst. dir. Northwestern U Nat. High Sch. Inst. 1949-50; instr. Tufts Coll., 1949-50. Dir. Scottsdale Pub., Inc. Campaign aide Senator Robert F. Kennedy, 1968; chmn. Democratic Party Maricopa County Legislative Candidates Com., 1970. Pres. Phoenix Jewish Community Center; bd. dirs. Ariz. Region Nat. Conf. Christians and Jews; bd. dirs., mem. exec. com. of bd. Legal Aid Service to Navajo Indians. Served to 2d lt., inf., AUS, 1945-47. Mem. Assn. Bar City N.Y., Am., Ariz. Maricopa County bar assns., Am. Arbitaation Assn. (nat. panel arbitrators). Home: 6032 N 2d Av Phoenix AZ 85013 Office: 222 N Central Av Phoenix AZ 85004

BROWN, JACK LEONDUS, sewer pipe co. eexec.; b. Huntington, W.Va., Sept 16, 1913; s. Wyatt Thornton and Lillian Vivian (Williams) B.; ed. pub. schs.; m. Lillian Louise Matchett, Jan. 5, 1935; children—Marjorie (Mrs. Bauman Hyde), Sally (Mrs. Alan C. Good), Jack Leondus. With Am. Vitrified Products Co., 1935- 66, v.p., 1959-63, pres., 1963-66; gen. mgr. Superior Concrete Pipe Corp., Cleveland, Ohio, 1966—. Trustee Ohio Turnpike Commn. Mem. Clay Sewer Pipe Assn. (v.p.), Nat. Clay Pipe Inst. (bd. dirs.), Am. Concrete Pipe Assn. (past dir.). Baptist. Club: Acacia Country (Lyndhurst, O.). Home: 2685 Wicklow Rd Shaker Heights OH 44120

BROWN, JAMES, IV, found. exec.; b. Connellsville, Pa., Feb. 3, 1907; s. James and Emma (McCune) B.; B.S., Haverford Coll., 1930; Ph.D., U. Chgo., 1939. With Pa. Dept. Pub. Assistance, 1932-36; faculty U. Chgo., 1939-49, dean pre- professional students, 1942-49; exec. dir. Chgo. Community Trust, 1949- -. Bd. dirs. Community Fund Chgo., George M. Pullman Ednl. Found., Field Found., Welfare Council of Met. Chgo.; trustee Ill. Children's Home and Aid Soc.; hon. governing life mem. Art Inst. Chgo. Fellow Royal Hort. Soc.; mem. Sons and Daus. Pioneer Rivermen. Republican. Presbyn. Clubs: Wayfarers, University, Casino, Commercial (Chicago). Home: 190 E Pearson St Chicago IL 60611 Office: 10 S LaSalle St Chicago IL 60603

BROWN, JAMES ANDREW, constrn. co. exec.; b. Columbia, Tenn., Aug. 19, 1914; s. Charles Allen and Martha (Crawford) B.; B.S., U.S. Naval Acad., 1936; M.S., Mass. Inst. Tech., 1941; m. Frances Adelaide Jones, June 7, 1941; children—James Andrew, Martha Janet. Commd. ensign U.S. Navy, 1936, advanced through grades to rear adm., 1963; jr. officer in U.S.S. W.Va., 1936-38; asst. hull supt. charge new constrn. Boston Naval Shipyard, 1942-45; mem. staff Comdr. Service Force Pacific, 1945-47; with Bur. Ships, Navy Dept., 1947-50, project officer destroyer types, 1950- 51, head hull design, 1955-59, asst. chief design, shipbldg. and fleet maintenance, 1963-65; prof. naval architecture Mass. Inst. Tech., 1951-54; comdg. officer ship repair facility Subic Bay, P.I., 1954-55; planning officer N.Y. Naval Shipyard, 1959, prodn. officer, 1959-61; supr. shipbldg. U.S. Navy, Camden, N.J., 1961-63; comdr. Norfolk Naval Shipyard, also supr. shipbldg. 5th Naval Dist., Portsmouth, Va., 1965-70; ret. 1970; prodn. mgr. J.L. Smith Constrn. Co., Portsmouth, 1970—. Pres., Tidewater Fed. Exec. Agy., 1968; exec. bd. Inter Agy. Bd. Examiners Civil Service for Va., 1968-70. Decorated Legion of Merit. Registered profl. engr., Va. Mem. Soc. Naval Engrs. (council 1959), Naval Inst., Naval Architects and Marine Engrs. (council 1968-69, chmn. Hampton Roads sect. 1969—, v.p. 1969—), Am. Philatelic Soc., World Affairs Council Greater Hampton Roads (v.p. 1969-70, pres. 1971), Portsmouth C. of C. (dir., chmn. urban affairs com.), Sigma Xi. Home: 351 Middle St Portsmouth VA 23704

BROWN, JAMES BARRETT, plastic surgeon; b. Hannibal, Mo., Sept. 20, 1899; s. Albert Sydney and Evelyn (Segsworth) B.; M.D., Washington U., 1923, D.Sc., 1970; m. Bertha Phillips, Sept. 30, 1946; children—Jane Hamilton, Frances Reith; (by prev. marriage)—James Barrett, Charles Sydney. Interne and asst. resident surgical service, Barnes and Childrens' Hospital, 1923-25; engaged in pvt. practice plastic surgery, Saint Louis, Mo., 1925-71; prof. clin. surgery, Sch. Medicine, Washington Univ., 1948-71; prof. maxillo-facial surgery, Sch. of Dentistry 1936-71; mem. surg. staff. Barnes, St. Louis Children's St. Luke's, Jewish, Deaconess and DePaul hosps., St. Louis Mo. Consultant surgeon, Shriners. Barnard Free Skin & Cancer, Ellis Fischel State Cancer Hosps., and others; cons. surgeon M.P. & Frisco R.R.; cons. plastic surg. USAF; consultant Los Alamos Medical Center. Served as colonel, M.C., U.S. Army, 1942-1946; chief consultant plastic surgery, E.T.O., 1942-43; chief plastic surgeon, Valley Forge Gen. Hosp. Hosp., 1943-45; sr. cons. plastic surgery U.S. Army, 1945-46; sr. civilian cons. plastic surg., U.S. Army, Office Surgeon Gen.; chief cons. plastic surg., U.S. Vets. Adminstrn. Decorated Legion of Merit; Am. Design Award, Lord & Taylor, 1944; Alumni Citation, Washington U., 1955; Modern Medicine award, 1968. Diplomate Am. Bd. Surgery (founders group), Am. Bd. Plastic Surgery (founders group). Fellow A.C.S. (v.p. 1959-60), Am. Assn. Plastic Surgeons (hon.; pres. 1954); mem. Am., Southern, Western (v.p. 1955, pres. 1958), Central surg. assns., Am. Assn. Surg. Trauma, Assn. Mil. Surgs., Am. Soc. Plastic and Reconstructive Surgery, Internat. Soc. Surgeons (Brussels), Assn. of Medical Consultants, World War II, Surgeons' and Halsted clubs, Am. Soc. Surgery Hands, Soc. Head and Neck Surgeons, Phi Delta Theta, Nu Sigma Nu, Alpha Omega Alpha. Presbyterian. Clubs: Grolier (New York City); University (St. Louis). Co- author: Skin Grafting, 1958; Plastic Surgery of the Nose, 1951; Neck Dissections, 1957; Surgery of Face, Mouth and Jaws, 1954; Post-Mortem Homografts, 1960; (with Dr. Thomas Zaydon) Early Treatment Facial Injuries, 1964; other books on plastic surgery. Editorial bd. Excerpta Medica, Amsterdam; and others. Contbr. chpts. textbooks and articles in surg. jours. and other sci. publs. Died Mar. 18, 1971.

BROWN, JAMES BRIGGS, bus. forms co. exec.; b. Sterling, Ill., Oct. 10, 1922; s. Lloyd H. and Marguerite (Briggs) B.; B.A., Carleton Coll., 1943; J.D., Northwestern U., 1949; m. Lois Dorothy Brenner, June 13, 1946; children—Bradford James, Todd Wells. Admitted to Ill. bar, 1949; atty. Pabst Brewing Co., Chgo., 1949-51; atty., asst. sec. Miehle-Printing Press & Mfg. Co., 1951-57; asst. sec. Miehle-Goss-Dester, Inc., Chgo., 1957-62, sec., counsel, 1962-70; Sec., counsel UARCO, Inc., Barrington, Ill., 1970—. Bd. dirs. Joseph S. Duncan YMCA, Chgo., 1964—. Served to lt. comdr. USNR, 1943-46, 52-53. Mem. Am., Chgo. bar assns., Phi Delta Phi. Clubs: Legal, Economic, Tavern (Chgo.). Home: 355 Birch St Winnetka IL 60093 Office: West County Line Rd Barrington IL 60010

BROWN, JAMES DOUGLAS, economist, ret. univ. ofcl.; b. Somerville, N.J., Aug. 11, 1898; s. James and Ella M. (Lane) B.; A.B., Princeton, 1920, A.M., 1921, Ph.D., 1928; Litt.D., Rutgers U., 1947; L.H.D., Kenyon Coll., 1954; LL.D., Union Coll., 1955; Ped.D., Franklin and Marshall Coll., 1966; m. Dorothy Andrews, June 18, 1923; children—Martha Jane, Dorothy Andrews James Douglas, Elizabeth Andrews (dec.). Instr. Princeton, 1921-23, 26- 27, dir. indsl. relations sect., 1926-55, asst. prof. econs., 1927- 34, prof. econs., 1934-67, dean faculty, 1946-67, provost, 1966-67, dean of faculty and provost emeritus, 1967—; instr. N.Y. U., 1923- 25; vis. asst. prof. U. Pa., 1932-33. Served on many N.J. and Federal commns. and adv. coms., including devel. and revisions of fed. social security program, N.J. unemployment ins. law and formulation of nat. manpower policies, 1930—; cons. NSRB, 1950-53; mem. sci. adv. bd. Chief of Staff USAF, 1950-54; mem. com. specialized personnel ODM, 1951, mem. mobilization program adv. com. 1955-58; cons. to sec. of labor, 1954-55; mem. Fed. adv. council on Social Security Financing, 1957-59, Fed. Adv. Council on Social Security 1963-64; mem. adv. com. to sec. health, edn. and welfare on revision Nat. Def. Edn. Act, 1960-61; mem. adv. com. on research Social Security Adminstrn., 1961; mem. commn. on acad. affairs Am. Council Edn., 1962- 66, adv. com. Inst. College and Univ. Adminstrs., 1966-68; mem. Fed. Adv. Council on Social Security, 1969-71; cons. to Office of Spl. Internat. Programs NSF, 1960-64; research adv. bd. Com. Econ. Devel., 1967—. Dir. McGraw-Hill, Inc., Mem. bd. pensions United Presbyn. Ch. in U.S.A., 1969—. Trustee U. Rochester. Served with 167th Inf., 42d Div., AEF, U.S. Army. World War I. Fellow Am. Acad. Arts and Scis.; mem. Assn. Am. Colls. (chmn. commn. on faculty and staff benefits 1960-63), Indsl. Relations Research Assn. (pres. 1952), Am. Econ. Assn., N.J. Assn. Colls. and Univs. (pres. 1952-53), Phi Beta Kappa. Presbyn. Author: (with Eleanor Davis) The Labor Banking Movement in U.S., 1929; The Liberal University, 1969; The Genesis of Social Security in America, 1969; also articles on indsl. relations, social ins. and higher edn. Joint author or editor of reports on indsl. relations, pub. by indsl. relations sect., Princeton, 1926-55. Home: 6 Edgehill St Princeton NJ 08540

BROWN, JAMES DOUGLAS, lawyer; b. Ozark, Ala., Feb. 14, 1912; s. W.A. and Pearl (Hicks) B.; student Southwestern U., 1929, Auburn U., 1930-32; J.D., U. Ala., 1935; postgrad. Georgetown U., 1936; m. Kathryne Parker, Nov. 1, 1944; children—Kathryne, Patricia, Clementine. Admitted to Ala. bar, 1935; practice in Athens, 1936-38, Ozark, 1938—. Pres., dir. Ozark Broadcasting Corp., 1953—; dir. Comml. Bank of Ozark; pres., owner Douglas Brown Ins. Agy., Inc.; owner Brown Real Estate Co.; pres. Brown Devel. Co., Enterprise, Ala.; dir. Enterprise Motel Co. Chmn. Ala. Adv. Com. Civil Rights, 1959-60. Mem. Ala. Senate, 1942-46; mayor of Ozark, 1948-60, 64-68. Chmn. Dale County Hosp. Assn., 1964—; pres. Mental Retardation Bd. Served with USAAF, 1943-44. Mem. Am., Ala. bar assns., Assn. ICC Practitioners, Law Sci. Acad., Am. Judicature Soc., Farrah Law Soc., Kappa Alpha, Phi Alpha Delta. Democrat. Presbyn. (elder). Mason (Shriner). Rotarian. Club: Ozark Country. Home: 737 E Broad St Ozark Al 36360 Office: 35 S Court Sq Ozark AL 36360

BROWN, JAMES E., banker; b. 1919; student City Coll. Law and Finance, St. Louis; m. With Merc. Trust Co., 1945-52; asst. cashier Am. Fletcher Nat. Bank, 1952-54; with Mercantile Trust Co. N.A., 1954—, sr. v.p., dir., dir. sales and marketing, 1966—; exec. v.p. Merc.

Bancorp., Inc. Bd. dirs. Better Bus. Bur., Downtown St. Louis Inc. Served with AUS, 1951-52; mem. Res. Address: 721 Locust St St Louis MO 63166

BROWN, JAMES GRADY, educator; b. Winona, Miss., Feb. 27, 1920; s. John James and Lovenia (Bridges) B.; A.B., George Washington U., 1948, M.A., 1949; Ed.D., U. Md., 1961; m. Vivian Harris, Jan. 21, 1966. Bus. edn. tchr., also prin. Balt. city schs., 1948-57; instr. bus. adminstrn. U. Md., 1957- 61; asst. dean adminstrn., asso. prof. bus. adminstrn. George Washington U., 1961-66; prof., chmn. dept. bus. edn. Central Mich. U., 1966-77; prof. bus., head dept. Miss. State Coll. for Women, 1967-69; prof. bus. edn. Ga. State U., Atlanta, 1969-71; prof., head dept. bus. Miss. State Coll. for Women, Columbus, 1971—. Pres. Eastebern Bus. Assn., 1963. Served with USAAF, 1941-45. Mem. Nat. Bus. Edn. Assn. (exec. bd. 1960- 63), Nat. Office Mgmt. Assn. (v.p., exec. bd. Washington chpt. 1961- 63), N.E.A., Am. Bus. Communication Assn., Phi Delta Kappa. Home: Route 6 Box 232-C Columbus MS 39701

BROWN, JAMES ISAAC, educator; b. Tarkio, Mo., Dec. 15, 1908; s. John Vallance and Ada (Moore) B.; B.A., Tarkio Coll., 1930; M.A., U. Chgo., 1933; Ph.D., U. Colo., 1949; m. Ruth Bernice Sam, Sept. 19, 1942; children—Katherine Ada, Susan Phyllis. Instr. English, Monmouth Coll., 1933-34; faculty U. Minn., 1934—, successively instr., asst. prof., asso. prof., 1934-54, prof. rhetoric, 1954—, acting chief rhetoric, 1947-48. Vis. lectr. U. Colo., summers 1950, 52, 54, U. Utah, summer 1955; staff mem. Effective Communication in Industry Course, summer 1954, 55, instituted. Reading Efficiency Program in Industry, summers 1957, 58; conf. leader Mgmt. Clinic, Hot Springs, Va., 1956; courses ednl. TV, Through Eye and Ear, Efficient Reading, Advanced Efficient Reading and Words, Words, Words; tapes Putting Words to Work, for U.S. Dept. Edn.; communications cons. Minn. Mining & Mfg. and Caterpillar Tractor Cos., 1964. Served with AUS, 1943-45; ETO. Recipient Tarkio Coll. Student Assn. Hall of Fame Award, 1965. Mem. Internat. Platform Assn., Nat. Council Tchrs. English, Nat. Soc. Study Communication (exec. sec. 1951; chmn. com. on reading comprehension 1951- 63, pres.), Internat. Reading Assn., Conf. Coll. Composition and Communication, Speech Assn. Am., Am. Assn. U. Profs., Am. Council Edn., Phi Delta Kappa. Methodist (pres. bd. trustees 1960, lay leader 1961-63). Author: Efficient Reading, 1952; (with G. Robert Carlsen) Brown-Carlsen Listening Comprehension Test, 1954; Lex-o-Gram, 1954; (with Eugene S. Wright) Minnesota Efficient Reading Tachistolide Series, Minnesota Clerical Training Tachistoslide Series and Minnesota Timing Series, 1955; Revision of Nelson Denny Reading Test, 1960; (with Rachel Salisbury) Building a Better Vocabulary, 1959; Explorations in College Reading, 1959; Exercise Manual for Explorations in College Reading, 1959; Efficient Reading, rev. edit., 1962; (with George Sanderlin), Effective Writing and Reading, 1962; Pyramid, 1963; Programmed Vocabulary (TV edit., coll. edit. and high sch. edn.), 1964; Guide to Effective Reading, 1966; (with O.M. Haugh) College English Placement Test, 1969; Acceleread System, 1970; also the visual-linguistic basic reading series, 1966—; Acceleread, 1970. Mem. adv. bd., cons. ednl. edit. Reader's Digest, 1957—; editoral counsellor U. Seven Seas, 1960—. Home: 1269 N Cleveland Av St Paul MN 55108

BROWN, JAMES JOSEPH, corp. exec.; b. N.Y.C., Apr. 4, 1928; s. Peter J. and Mary (O'Neil) B.; B.S., Fordham U., 1952; C.P.A., N.Y.; m. Mary E. McKeon, Dec. 30, 1961; children—Patricia, James, Carolyn, Denise. Accountant, Touche, Ross, Bailey & Smart, C.P.A.'s, N.Y.C., 1952-54; sr. accountant Price Waterhouse & Co., C.P.A.'s, Caracas, Venezuela and N.Y.C., 1954-63; mgr. internal audit Litton Industries, 1963-65; sr. v.p., dir. Walter Kidde & Co., Inc., 1965—. Named Alumni Man of Year, Fordham U. Coll. Bus. Adminstrn., 1971. Served with AUS, 1946-48. Home: 441 Weymouth Dr Wyckoff NJ 07481 Office: 9 Brighton Rd Clifton NJ 07014

BROWN, JAMES MONROE, III museum dir.; b. Bklyn., Oct. 7, 1917; s. James Monroe and Helen (Adriance) B.; B.A., Amherst Coll., 1939, M.A. (hon.), 1954; M.A., Harvard, 1946; m. Alice De Wolf Doggett, Nov. 16, 1946; children— Barbara Allison, Amy, Elizabeth. Asst. to dir. Inst. Contemporary Art, Boston, 1942, asst. dir., 1946-48; asst. to dir. Dumbarton Oaks Research Library and Collection, Washington, 1946; dir. William A. Farnsworth Art Mus., Rockland, Me., 1948-51; dir. Corning Glass Center (N.Y.), 1951-63; dir. div. pub. affairs Corning Glass Works, 1956-58, dir. mgmt. devel., 1958-61; pres. Corning Glass Works Found.; dir. Oakland (Cal.) Mus., 1963-68, Norton Simon, Inc. Mus. Art, Fullerton, Cal., 1968-69, Va. Mus. Fine Arts, Richmond, 1969—. Served with USNR, 1942-45. Mem. Am. Assn. Museums (pres. 1970—), Internat. Council Museums, Am. Fedn. Arts. Rotarian. Clubs: Harvard, Grolier (N.Y.C.): Rotunda, Deep Run Hunt, Forum (Richmond). Address: Blvd and Grove Richmond VA 23219

BROWN, JAMES ROBERT, diversified mfg. co. exec.; b. Morgantown, W.Va., Nov. 13, 1917; s. Matthew Alexander and Elizabeth M. (Williams) B.; student Westminster Coll., 1935-37; B.S. in Mgmt. Engring, Carnegie-Mellon U., 1940; m. Margaret Jane Davis, Sept. 21, 1940; children—Rebecca (Mrs. James Milton Black), Judith (Mrs. Jack Alan Barkley). With U.S. Steel Corp., 1940-53; With Spang & Co., Butler, Pa., 1953—, exec. v.p., 1962-68, pres., 1968—; pres. Spang Industries, Inc., Butler, 1968—, also dir.; dir. Spang Stores, Inc. Bd. dirs. Butler (Pa.) YMCA, Butler County United Fund. Registered profl. engr., O. Mem. Assn. Iron and Steel Engrs., Am. Soc. M.E., Newcomet Soc. in N.Am. Republican. Presbyn. (ruling elder). Elk. Club: Butler Country. Home: 108 Forest Mere Circle Butler PA 16001 Office: 120 Etna St Butler PA 16001

BROWN, JAMES ROBERT, mfg. co. exec.; b. Sullivan, Ind., Oct. 21, 1913; s. James Rolla and Sarah (Holsen) B.; B.S., Northwestern U., 1935; m. Marianne Kirkland, June 20, 1936; children—Sally (Mrs. John H. Frahm), Bonnie (Mrs. James M. Rock), Meredith (Mrs. Steven G. Brestin). With West Bend Co. (Wis.), 1935—, sec., 1949-52. v.p. adminstrn., 1952-59, pres., 1959—; dir. Dart Industries, 1st Nat. Bank of West Bend. Pres. West Bend Sch. Bd., 1945-48. Bd. dirs. West Bend Library, 1938-47; regent Northwestern U., 1958-64; trustee Lawrence U., 1967—. Mem. N.A.M. (dir. 1967-70), Aluminum Wares Assn. (past pres.), Outboard Motor Mfrs. Assn. (past pres.), Nat. Assn. Engine and Boat Mfrs. (past dir.), Wis. Mfrs. Assn. (past pres., dir.), Wis. Taxpayers Alliance (pres., dir.). Rotarian. Home: 668 Highland View Dr West Bend WI 53095 Office: 400 W Washington St West Bend WI 53095

BROWN, JAMES SEAY, engring. educator; b. Franklin, Ky., Feb. 8, 1920; s. William Seay and Mary Rose (Dinning) B.; B.S., Tenn. Poly. Inst., 1941; M.S., U. Ill., 1950; m. Virginia Lee Fritts, July 25, 1941; children—James Seay, Rebekah Dinning. Faculty Tenn. Poly. Inst., 1941-44, 46—, prof. mech. engring., 1952—, dean Sch. Engring., Cookeville, 1961—. Served to lt. (j.g.) USNR, 1944-46; PTO. Registered profl. engr., Tenn. Mem. Am. Soc. Engring. Edn. (v.p. Southeastern sect. 1960-61, nat. council 1961- 63), Am. Soc. M.E., N.E.A., Nat. Soc. Profl. Engrs., Am. Legion, Sigma Xi, Tau Beta Pi, Phi Kappa Phi, Pi Tau Sigma. Baptist (deacon). Rotarian Rotarian. (pres. Cookeville 1959-60). Home: 1496 Barnes St Cookeville, TN 38501.

BROWN, JAMES THOMAS, lawyer, banker; b. near Richmond, Va., Oct. 15, 1885; s. Thomas A. and Virginia Ann (Elliott) B.; LL.B., U. of Miss., 1912; m. Lucia Jane Lampton, June 28, 1916 (dec. Nov. 1959); m. 2d, Jennie Bullard Runge, Jan. 12, 1961. Admitted Miss. bar, 1912, practiced in Jackson, 1912-40; mem. firm Flowers, Brown & Hester; pres. Capital Nat. Bank, 1933 (consol. with Jackson-State Nat. Bank to become First Nat. Bank of Jackson, 1949, pres., 1949-53, chmn., 1953—; chmn. adv. bd. Tylertown Bank Br. First Nat. Bank Jackson (Miss.); counsel Miss. Banking Dept., 1917-37, Miss. Bankers Assn. since 1937. Served as mem. Miss. State Legislature, 1940-48. Mem. adv. council, Fed. Reserve System, rep. 6th Fed. Reserve Dist., 1946-51. Member Am. and Miss. (pres. 1956-57) bankers assos., Am. and Miss. bar assns., U.S.C. of C. (finance dept. com.). Democrat. Methodist. Author: Banks and Banking- Brown Compilation of Banking Laws, 1925; Handbook of Banking Law, 1951. Home: Woodland Hills Jackson MS 39206 Office: First Nat Bank of Jackson 248 E Capitol St PO Box 291 Jackson MS 39201

BROWN, JAMES VINCENT, oil exec.; b. Lawrence, Mass., Feb. 6, 1896; s. Fred H. and Mary Ann (Guilfoyle) B.; grad. McIntosh Comml. Sch., 1921, Bentley Coll. Accounting and Finance, 1924; student St. Bonaventure Coll.; m. Jeanie Small Murray Eaton, Sept. 22, 1925; children—Martha (Mrs. John L. Murphy), Florence (Mrs. James J. Vaughn, Jr.), Harriett (Mrs. Lynton E. Gilbreath), James Webster, Vincent Murray, Elizabeth Anne (Mrs. Borland Bardell). Accountant, office mgr. Murray Bros. Co., Lawrence, 1919-24; instr. accounting McIntosh Comml. Sch., 1924; agt. U.S. Internal Revenue, Washington, Pitts., Bradford, Pa., 1924- 29; pub. accountant, tax specialist, Bradford, 1929-52; comptroller Healey Petroleum Corp., Bradford, 1929-41; petroleum specialist U.S. Tariff Commn., 1941-42; petroleum econs. analyst Ind. Petroleum Assn. Am., Washington, 1942-46, chmn. cost. com., mem. tax policy com. supply and demand com. of assn., dir., 1953; partner, mgr. Healey Ins. Agy., Bradford, 1941-45; exec. sec., treas. Nat. Petroleum Council, Washington, 1947-62; pres., dir. Brown Realty Corp. 1938—, Ella Oil Corp., 1940-48, Le Suer Oil Corp., 1940-48; treas., dir. Terminal Bldg. Corp, 1930-62, Moody, Karl & Wintermantel Inc., 1938-45; dir. Haas Dobson, Inc., participant in Allegheny Land & Mineral Co., oil and gas production, W.Va., 1959—. Sec.-treas. nat. crude oil industry adv. com. OPA, 1945-46; mem. requirements panel and domestic civilian demand com. Mil. Petroleum Adv. Bd. 1947-51. City treas., Bradford, 1930-31; town commr., Bethany Beach, Del., 1960-62. Trustee, corporator Bentley Coll., 1964—. Mem. bd. govs. Port St. Lucie (Fla.) Country Club Home and Plan Owner's Assn., 1964-70. Served as cpl. A.A.F., 1918. Fellow Baker Vanguard Soc., Bentley Coll.; mem. Am. Petroleum Inst., Ind. Petroleum Assn. Am., Interstate oil Compact Commn. (vice chmn. econ. adv. com. 1946-50), Mid-Continent Oil and Gas Assn. (econ. adv. subcom. to depletion com.), Internat. Platform Assn., St. Andrews Soc. of Fla., Omega Beta Omega (charter). Clubs: National Press (Washington); Ocean Beach; St. Lucie Country. Author articles to profl. jours. Home: St Lucie Country Club Port St Lucie, FL 33450. Office: Commonwealth Bldg 1625 K St Washington DC 20006

BROWN, JAMES WILLIAM RAYMOND, lawyer; b. Ruthven, Ia., Oct. 31, 1916; s. William H. and Mary (Donahoe) B.; B.A., U. Ia., 1940, J.D., 1942; m. Mary P. Pattavina, May 5, 1945; children—James R., Kathryn Ann, Mary Patricia, Thomas R., Therese M., William C. Admitted to Neb. Bar, 1946; practiced in Washington, 1942, Omaha, 1946—; asso. Covington, Burling, Rublee, Acheson & Shorb, 1942; asso. Fitzgerald & Smith, 1946-50, partner, 1950-51; partner Fitzgerald, Hamer, Brown & Leahy, 1951-63; partner Fitzgerald, Brown, Leahy, 1951- 63; partner Fitzgerald, Brown, Leahy, McGill & Strom, 1963—; lectr. fed. tax insts. sponsored by U. Neb., Creighton U., U. Ia., Neb. State Bar Assn. Dir. Dutton-Lainson Co., Airlite Plastics Co., Brand Hydraulics, Inc., Vaughn Insulation Co. Mem. Neb. Bar Commn., 1968—; mem. Neb. Constl. Revision Commn., 1969—. Served with CIC, AUS, 1942- 46. Mem. Am., Neb. bar assns., Order of Coif, Phi Beta Kappa. Rotarian. Home: 693 J E George Blvd Omaha NB 68132 Office: 1000 Woodmen Tower Omaha NB 68102

BROWN, JAMES WILSON, educator; b. Hanford, Wash., Sept. 18, 1913; s. Harrison and Sophia Estelle (Tuttle) B.; student U. Wash., 1931-32; B.A., Central Wash. Coll., 1935; M.A., U. Chgo., Ph.D., 1947; m. Winifred Louise Weersing, Dec. 31, 1940; children—Martha Lee, Pamela Jean, Gregory James. Marine radio operator, 1930-31; gen. edn. bd. fellow motion picture project Am. Council Edn., 1940; state supr. teaching materials Va. Dept. Edn., Richmond, 1941-42, 1945-46; asst. prof. edn. Syracuse U., 1947-48: supr. Univ. Film Center, U. Wash, 1948-53; information specialist U.S. Dept. State OSR, Paris, 1951-52; prof. edn., dean grad. studies and research San Jose State Coll., 1953—; dir. Fruitland Grove, Inc., Covina, Cal., Calico Hills, Inc., San Marcos, Cal. Adv. bd. ednl. policies commn. N.E.A.; mem. adv. panels Far West Regional Lab. for Research and Devel., also Stanford U. Center for Research and Devel. in Teaching. Served to lt. comdr. USNR, 1942- 45; ETO. Mem. N.E.A. (v.p. 1950-51, pres. dept. audio- visual instrn. 1952-53), Cal. Ednl. Research Assn., Western Assn. Grad. Schs. (chmn. 1963-64), Phi Delta Kappa. Author: Virginia Plan for Audio-Visual Education, 1947; co-author: A-V Instruction: Materials and Methods, A-V Instructional Materials Manual, College Teaching: Perspectives and Guidelines, New Media in Higher Education, 1963, Going to College in California, 1965, New Media and College Teaching, 1968, AV Instruction, Media and Methods, 1969, College Teaching: A Systematic Approach, 1971. Home: 1678 Sweetbriar Dr San Jose CA 95125

BROWN, JAMES WRIGHT, JR., consultant; b. Chicago, Jan. 1, 1902; s. James Wright and Sarah (Wilson) B.; ed. Bordentown (N.J.) Military Acad.; U. of Mo. Sch. of Journalism; m. Thelma Ann Pitz, Mar. 25, 1925 (dec.); 1 dau., Matil; 2nd m. Sally Jeanette Brown, Nov. 8, 1930; childrenAnne Elizabeth, Jane Wright. Cons. Editor & Publisher Co. Mem. Sigma Chi, Sigma Delta Chi. Episcopalian. Mason (past master). Home: 9701 Fields Rd Gaithersburg, MD 20760.

BROWN, JESSE EDWARD, radio mfr.; b. Greenport, N.Y., Sept. 11, 1902; s. Willis H. and Lottie Buckley (Horton) B.; student Sch. Elec. Engring., Cornell U., 1920-24; m. Eudora Smith, July 21, 1925, Staff radio div. U.S. Dept. Commerce, Fed. Radio Commn., FCC, 1924-37; with Zenith Radio Corp., Chgo., 1937—, asst. v.p., chief engr., 1942-58, v.p., 1958—. Fellow I.E.E.E.. Republican. Episcopalian. Clubs: Radio Engineers, Racquet (Chgo.); Skokie (Ill.) Country; Lake Zurich (Ill.) Golf. Home: 631 Drexel Av Glencoe IL 60022 also Cottage Plantation St Francisville LA 70775 Office: 6001 W Dickens Av Chicago IL 60639

BROWN, JIM, former profl. football player, film actor; b. Feb. 17, 1936; s. Swinton and Theresa Brown; grad. Syracuse U.; m. Sue Jones, 1958; children—Kim and Kevin (twins), Jim. Fullback for Cleve. Brown Profl. Football Team, 1957-65; now film actor. Recipient numerous Nat. Football League awards including Player of Year, 1958, 63; named to every all-star team, 1963; holder rushing mark and greatest distance gained in one season. Address: care Phil Gersh Agy 232 N Canon Dr Beverly Hills CA 90210*

BROWN, JOE EVAN, actor; b. Holgate, O., July 28, 1892; s. Matthias and Anna (Evans) B.; ed. pub. schs.; m. Kathryn Frances McGraw, Dec. 24, 1915; childrenDon Evan, Joe LeRoy, Mary Elizabeth Ann, Kathryn Frances. Began as circus acrobat, 1902; with burlesque and vaudeville, 1916-19, with musical comedies, 1919-27, including "Listen Lester," "Greenwich Village Follies," "Capt. Jinks," etc.; in motion pictures since 1927, leading roles in "Crooks Can't Win," 1st silent picture, "Painted Faces," 1st talking picture, etc.; movie Some Like It Hot, 1959. Member of the Actors Equity Assn.; hon. mem. Los Angeles High Sch. Alumni Assn., Blue "C" S Soc. (U. of Calif.) Episcopalian. Mason (Shriner), Elk. Clubs: Masquers (Hollywood); Mayfair (Los Angeles); Beach (Santa Monica); Lambs (New York). Home: 1004 N Bundy Dr Los Angeles CA 90049

BROWN, JOE LEROY, baseball exec.; b. N.Y.C., Sept. 1, 1918; s. Joseph Evan and Kathryn (McGraw) B.; grad. Mercersburg Acad., 1937; student U. Cal. at Los Angeles, 1937-40; m. Virginia Lee Newport, Sept. 24, 1940; children—Cynthia Lee, Don Evan. Bus. mgr. Lubbock (Tex.) Baseball Club, 1939-40; pres. Waterloo (Ia.) Baseball Club, 1941; publicity dir. Hollywood (Cal.) Baseball Club, 1946-47; spl. sports publicity Allied Artists Studio, 1948; gen. mgr. Zanesville (O.) Baseball Club, 1949, Waco (Tex.) Baseball Club, 1950; gen. mgr. New Orleans Baseball Club, 1951, pres., gen. mgr., 1952-54; scouting coordinator Pitts. Pirates, 1955, gen. mgr., 1956—. Served from pvt. to capt. USAAF, 1942-46. Mem. Zeta Psi. Clubs: Duquesne, St. Clair Country, Pittsburgh Athletic. Home: 190 Crestvue Manor Dr Pittsburgh PA 15228 Office: Forbes Field Pittsburgh PA 15213

BROWN, JOE ROBERT, physician, educator; b. Mt. Pleasant, Ia., Nov. 24, 1911; s. James Smith and Olive (Smith) B.; B.A., U. Ia., 1933, M.D., 1937; M.S. in Neurology and Psychiatry (fellow), Mayo Grad. Sch., U. Minn., 1943; m. Rebecca Frisbee, Aug. 14, 1937; children—Hugh Frisbee, Carolyn Emily, Stephen Robert. Intern Presbyn. Hosp., Chgo., 1937-38; faculty Mayo Grad. Sch., U. Minn., Rochester, 1949—, asso. prof. neurology, 1949-63, prof., 1963—, dir. neurologic edn., 1966—; clin. asst. prof. U. Minn., 1946- 48, clin. asso. prof., 1948-49; chief neurology service VA Hosp., also asst. chief neurology U. Minn. Hosps., Mpls., 1946-49; cons. Mayo Clinic, Rochester, 1949-53, head sect. neurology, 1953-66, sr. cons., 1966—. Cons. VA, 1949—; from mem. to chmn. neurol. sci. research tng. com. Nat. Inst. Neurologic Diseases and Blindness, 1957-61; mem. com. perinatal research collaborative program NIH, 1965-66; mem. med. adv. bd. Nat. Multiple Sclerosis Soc., 1959—, chmn., 1971—; mem. med. adv. bd. Ability Bldg. Center Rochester, 1954-60. Pres. Minn. Council Liberal Chs., 1956-58, mem. Rochester Art Center Bd., 1959-65, Rochester Com. for Mpls. Symphony, 1954-58. Served from capt. to maj. MC, AUS, 1943-46; PTO Diplomate Am. Bd. of Neurology. Mem. Am. Acad. Neurology (v.p. 1967-68, pres. 1971—, trustee), Am. Neurol. Assn., Assn. for Research in Nervous and Mental Disease, Central Neuropsychiat. Assn. (pres. 1966-67), A.M.A., Minn. Soc. Neurol. Scis., Assn. U. Profs. Neurology, Acad. Aphasic (chmn. 1968-69). Unitarian-Universalist (Pres. 1953, 66, trustee). Editorial bd. Neurology, 1957—. Research and publs. speech and lang. disorders. Home: 2303 Crestlane SW Rochester MN 55901 Office: 200 1st St SW Rochester MN 55901

BROWN, JOHN ANTHONY, Jr., coll. pres.; b. Harrisburg, Pa., July 15, 1918; s. John Anthony and Agnes (Smith) B.; A.B., Temple U., 1943; M.A., U. Chgo., 1945; LL.D., Westminster Coll., 1962; L.H.D., Ursinus Coll., 1962; LL.D. Tarkio (Mo.) Coll., 1967; Litt.D., Rider Coll., 1969; m. Franceline Harrison, 1943; children—Barbara, John Anthony III, Philip, David. Prodn. editor Time, Inc., 1943-48; asst. prof. polit. sci. Temple U., 1948-54, dean of men, 1952-55, asst. to pres., 1955-60; v.p. pub. affairs and finance Occidental Coll., 1960-63; v.p. plans and resources George Washington U., 1963-64, v.p., dean faculties, 1964-66; pres. Lindenwood Coll., 1966- -. Cons. higher edn. N.Y. State Legislature, 1964; cons. Acad. Ednl. Devel., 1965- 65; mem. ednl. evaluation team in Brazil, AID, 1964; cons. Ford Found., Bogota, Colombia, 1965; pres. Ind. Colls. and Univs. of Mo., Seven Colls. Consortium of Mo.; exec. com. Mo. Colls. Fund, Mo. Assn. Colls. and Univs.; adv. com. on higher edn. Midwestern Council State Govts.; bd. dirs. Nat. Council Ind. Colls. and Univs.; adv. com. on accreditation and instnl. eligibility U.S. Office of Edn., 1971—; writer, broadcaster CBS radio series Governments of Man, 1959-63; host TV series Q.E.D. Capital, 1964-65, Washington Profile, 1965-66. Bd. dirs. Fed. Union, Washington. DuBois fellow polit. sci. Princeton, 1947-48; Fund for Advancement Edn. Faculty Fellow, 1951-52. Mem. Am. Assn. U. Profs., Am. Polit. Sci. Assn., Am. Alumni Council. Club: University (Washington); University (St. Louis). Home: President's House Lindenwood Coll St Charles MO 63301

BROWN, JOHN CARTER, art mus. dir.; b. Providence, Oct. 8, 1934; s. John Nicholas and Anne (Kinsolving) B.; student Groton Sch., 1946-51, Stowe (Eng.) Sch., 1951- 52; A.B., summa cum laude, Harvard, 1956, M.B.A., 1958; student Munich (Germany) U., 1958, with Bernard Berenson in Florence, Italy, 1958-59, mus. tng. course, Ecole du Louvre, Paris, France, 1959, Netherlands Inst. Art History, 1960; M.A., Inst. Fine Arts, N.Y. U., 1962; LL.D., Brown U., 1970. Asst. to dir. Nat. Gallery Art, Washington, 1961-63, asst. dir., 1964-68, dep. dir., 1968-69, dir., 1969—. Alternate mem. Citizens Stamp Adv. Com., 1961-69, mem., 1969—. Bd. dirs. Asso. Harvard Alumni, 1964-67, Com. Internat. Non-Theatrical Events, 1967-70; trustee Hope Found., N. Y. U. Inst. Fine Arts; trustee Am. Fedn. Arts, also chmn. exhbn. com., 1966—; bd. overseers Boston Symphony Orch.; mem. assos. John Carter Brown Library; mem. vis. com's. library, fine arts dept. Harvard; ednl. com. R.I. Sch. Design; bd. Nat. Humanities Faculty; bd. advisers to pres. U.S. Naval War Coll. Mem. Am. Assn. Museums, Coll. Art Assn., Internat. Council Museums, Assn. Art Mus. Dirs., Asso. Council of Arts, Nat. Trust Historic Preservation (trustee 1969—), Soc. Archtl. Historians, Phi Beta Kappa. Episcopalian. Clubs: N.Y. Yacht, Cruising Am., Century, Knickerbocker (N.Y.C.); 1925 F Street, Harvard, Federal City (Washington); Ida Lewis Yacht (Newport); Severn Sailing Assn. (Annapolis). Author-dir. films: The American Vision, 1965; Conquerors of the Wilderness, 1966; America in Transition, 1966. Home: 6 Kalorama Circle Washington DC 20007 Office: Nat Gallery of Art Washington DC 20565

BROWN, JOHN ELWARD, Jr., univ. pres.; b. Siloam Springs, Ark.; s. John Elward and Juanita (Arrington) B.; B.S., John Brown U., 1943; LL.D., Biola Bible Coll., 1952, Tex. Wesleyan Coll., 1954; m. Ella Caroline Trahin, Nov. 23, 1941; children—Karen Jean, John Elward III, Melinda Suzanne. Vice pres. John Brown U., 1946-48, pres., 1948—; pres., mem. bd. radio sta. KUOA, Siloam Springs, Ark., KOME, Tulsa, KGER, Long Beach Cal. Mem. Northwest Ark. council Boy Scouts Am. Pres. Brown Mil. Acad., San Diego, Cal., Brown Sch. for Girls, Glendora, Cal., So. Cal. Mil. Acad., Long Beach. Mem. Siloam Springs C. of C. (pres.). Mason (K.T., 32), Rotarian. Address: John Brown University Siloam Springs AR 72761

BROWN, JOHN FRANKLIN, gas pipeline co. exec.; b. Hannibal, Mo., Nov. 9, 1932; s. William K. and Clara (Hamann) B.; B.S., Washington U., 1953; J.D., St. Louis U., 1971; m. Lois M. McCorkell, Feb. 14, 1953; children—Lynneece, John F., Renee, Jeffrey. With Miss. River Fuel Corp., 1955—, treas. subsidiary Miss. River

Transmission Corp., St. Louis, 1967—, v.p., 1971—. Served to sgt. Finance Corps, AUS, 1953-55. Home: 101 Little Hill Ct Ballwin MO 63011 Office: 9900 Clayton Rd St Louis MO 63124

BROWN, JOHN GILBERT NEWTON, pub.; b. London, Eng., July 7, 1916; s. John and Molly (Purchas) B.; student Lancing Coll. of Eng., 1930-34; M.A. in Zoology, Hertford Coll., Oxford, 1937; m. Virginia Braddell, May 22, 1946; children—Julia Ann, Olivia, John. Mgr. Bombay office Oxford Univ. Press, 1937-40, London, Eng., 1946-49, sales mgr., 1949-55, dep. pub., 1955, pub., 1956- -; vice chmn. bd. Oxford U. Press, Inc., N.Y.C. Served as 2d lt., 5th Field Regt. Royal Arty., Brit. Army, 1940-41; Japanese prisoner war, 1942-45. Decorated comdr. Order Brit. Empire. Mem. Pubs. Assn. London (pres. 1963-65, mem. council), Pubs. Assn. U.K. (pres. 1963). Home: 3 Alma Terrace Allen St London W.8, England. Office: Oxford U Press Ely House 37 Dover St London W 1 England

BROWN, JOHN LACKEY, educator; b. Ilion, N.Y., Apr. 19, 1914; s. Leslie Beecher and Katherine-Anne (Lackey) B.; A.B., Hamilton Coll., 1935; postgrad. Ecole des Chartres, Paris, 1935-38; Ph.D., Catholic U. Am., 1939; m. Simone- Yvette L'Evesque, Aug. 25, 1941; children—Michel-Simon, John- Halit. Instr., Catholic U. Am., 1939-41; asst. chief fgn. lang. publ. sect. OWI, 1942-43; corr. in Paris, N.Y. Times Sunday edit., 1945-48; European editor Houghton Mifflin Pub. Co., 1945-48; chief information div. Marshall Plan, France, 1948-49; chief regional services U.S. Information Service, Am. embassy, Paris, 1949-54; cultural attache Am. embassy, Brussels, 1954-58, Rome, Italy, 1958-62, Am. embassy, Mexico City, 1964-69; prof. comparative lit. Catholic U., Washington, Barry Bingham Distinguished vis. prof. humanities U. Louisville, 1966. Fellow Center for Advanced Studies, Wesleyan U., Middletown, Conn. Served with the OSS, AUS, 1943-45. Decorated comdr. Chevaliers du Tastevin (Burgundy). Mem. Fondation Universitaire of Brussels, Syndicat des Critiques (Paris), PEN Club, Phi Beta Kappa, Psi Upsilon. Club: Cosmos (Washington). Author: Jean Bodin, 1939; Panorama de la Litterature Contemporaine aux Etats Unis (Grand Prix de la Critique), 1954; Hemingway, 1961; Il Gigantesco Teatro: Saggi Europei e Americani 1963; Dialogos transatlanticas, 1966. Editor: So You're Going to Paris, 1947; Discovering Belgium, 1958. Translator works André Maurois, André Malraux, Georges Sion, others. Contbr. articles Am., European periodicals. Home: 3024 Tilden St NW Washington DC 20008

BROWN, JOHN MARSHALL, psychologist, educator; b. Manasquan, N.J., Aug. 27, 1924; s. John Marshall Jr. and Ella Beatrice (VanSickle) B.; B.S., Pa. State U., 1947, Ph.D., 1951; m. Harriet Cox, Jan. 29, 1949; children—Wayne Marshall, Jeffrey Paul, Lynn Cheryl. Grad. asst. Pa. State U., 1947-50; asso. Psychol. Corp., N.Y.C., 1947-50; asst. then asso. prof. Bucknell U., 1950-54; faculty Lafayette Coll., Easton, Pa., prof., 1960—, head dept. psychology, 1958—. Psychol. cons., 1950—. Mem. Easton Area Joint Sch. Bd., 1959-70, Forks Twp. Sch. Bd., 1959-70; mem. bd. Northampton County Prison, 1960—, chmn. 1966—; mem. Northampton County Mental Health/Mental Retardation Bd., 1967-71, chmn., 1970-71. Served with USAAF 1943-45. Fellow Am., Eastern, Pa. (pres. 1966-67, bd. exams. for certification of psychologists 1967-71) psychol. assns. , A.A.A.S.; mem. Lehigh Valley Psychol. Assn. (past pres.), Am. Assn. U. Profs., Psi Chi, Pi Gamma Mu, Alpha Chi Rho. Presbyn. (deacon 1956-69). Editor, maj. author Applied Psychology, 1966. Home: 401 Dogwood Terrace Easton PA 18042

BROWN, JOHN ROBERT, judge; b. Funk, Neb., Dec. 10, 1909; s. E. E. and Elvira (Carney) B.; A.B., U. Neb., 1930, LL.D., 1965; J.D., U. Mich., 1932, LL.D., 1959; m. Mary Lou Murray, May 30, 1936; 1 son, John R. Admitted to Tex. bar, 1932, practiced in Houston and Galveston, mem. Royston & Rayzor, 1932-55; judge 5th Circuit, U.S. Ct. Appeals, 1955—, serving as chief judge, 1967—. Republican, chmn. Harris County, Tex., 1953-55. Served from lt. to maj. Transp. Corps, USAAF, 1942- 46. Mem. Am., Tex., Houston bar assns., Am. Judicature Soc., Am. Law Inst., Maritime Law Assn. U.S., Assn. ICC Practitioners, Order of Coif, Phi Delta Phi, Sigma Chi. Presbyn. (elder). Clubs: Houston, Houston Country; Boston (New Orleans). Home: 3209 Ela Lee Lane Houston TX 77019 Office: US Courthouse Houston TX 77002

BROWN, JOHN ROWLAND, Jr., research exec.; b. Mansfield, O., Mar. 4, 1912; s. John Rowland and Mary Ethel (Sloane) B.; A.B., Oberlin Coll., 1933, M.A., 1935; Sc.D., Mass. Inst. Tech., 1938; m. Elizabeth Watermulder, June 5, 1938; children—Joanne Elizabeth, John Edward, Mary Marcella. Instr. Mass. Inst. Tech., 1938; asst. dir. Esso Labs., Standard Oil Devel. Co., Elizabeth N.J., 1938-46; tech. dir. Prophylactic Brush Co., Florence, Mass., 1946-49; v.p., dir. research Lambert Pharmacal Co., St. Louis, 1949-53; v.p. research and devel. Spencer Chem. Co., Kansas City, Mo., 1953-57; v.p. research and devel. Colgate-Palmolive Co., N.Y.C., 1957—, also dir. Trustee Oberlin Coll., 1963—, Newark State Coll., 1967—. Mem. Am. Chem. Soc., Am. Inst. Chem. Engrs., Indsl. Research Inst., A.A.A.S., Phi Beta Kappa, Sigma Xi. Clubs: Chemists, University (N.Y.C.), Short Hills (N.J.), Baltusrol Golf. Home: 19 Western Dr Short Hills NJ 07078 Office: 909 River Rd Piscataway NJ 08854

BROWN, JOHN THOMAS, lawyer; b. Christiansburg, O., Jan. 23, 1931; s. Harry Leroy and Henrietta (Wolfram) B.; student Heidelberg Coll., 1948-50, Syracuse U., 1950-51; LL.B., Ohio State U., 1958; m. Joan Helen Franks, Dec. 2, 1950; children—James R., John M., Jeffrey A. Admitted to Ohio bar, 1958, since practiced in Mansfield; partner Gongwer, Murray, Brown & Bemiller, 1958- -. Mem. Mansfield City Planning Commn., 1968—; mem. Mansfield Zoning Bd. of Appeals, 1968—; mem. Selective Service Local Bd. 103, 1968—. Pres. Mansfield Park Commn. Served with USAF, 1950-54. Mem. Ohio (del.), Richland County (com. chmn.) bar assns., N. Central Ohio Assn. Claimsmen (past pres.), Ohio Def. Assn. Ins. Attys. Mason, Elk, Kiwanian (pres. Mansfield club 1970-71). Office: 70 Park Av W Mansfield OH 44901

BROWN, JOHN TRUMAN, utilities exec.; b. Pitts., July 31, 1913; s. Samuel T. and Nelle (Herron) B.; A.B., U. Pitts., 1935, LL.B., 1938; m. Jannette Guenther, Sept. 26, 1943. Admitted to Pa. bar, 1938; practice of law, Pitts., 1938- 50; gen. counsel Equitable Gas Co., Pitts., 1951-52, v.p., gen. counsel, 1953-56, exec. v.p., 1957-66, pres., 1966—. Home: Grandview Dr N Pittsburgh PA 15215 Office: 420 Blvd of the Allies Pittsburgh PA 15219

BROWN, JOHN WELCH, physician; b. Fairfield, Ia., Feb. 15, 1911; s. Harold Lewis and Luella Bell (Welch) B.; A.B., U. Cal., 1931, M.D., 1935; m. Evelyn Karen Munk, Sept. 4, 1938; 1 son, John Christian. Intern San Francisco Hosp., 1934- 35; asst. resident medicine U. Cal. Hosp., San Francisco, 1935-36; from asst. medicine to asst. prof. U. Cal., 1935-46; research fellow Harvard, Boston City Hosp., 1936-38; prof. dir. and chmn. dept. preventive medicine and student health U. Wis., 1946-54; cons. U.S. Navy Tng. Center, Great Lakes, Ill., 1950-55; pub. health officer Cal. Dept. Pub. Health, 1956—; cons. Naval Biol. Lab. (Naval Med. Research Unit No. 1), Berkeley, Oakland; lectr. medicine U. Cal. Med. Sch., 1958—; vis. prof. preventive medicine, Fulbright- Smith Mundt lectr. Teheran U. Sch. Medicine, 1959-60; cons. med. edn. AID, Bangkok, Thailand, 1961-63; prof., acting dean Pub. Health Coll., Haile Selassie U., Gondar, Ethiopia, 1967-68. Served from 1st lt. to maj. M.C., AUS, 1935- 45; lt. col. Res. ret. Diplomate Am. Bd. Internal Medicine, Am. Bd. Gen. Preventive Medicine. Fellow A.C.P., A.A.A.S., Am. Pub. Health Assn.; mem. A.M.A., Am. Coll. Health Assn. (pres. 1955-56), Am. Fedn. Clin. Research (sr., charter mem.), Am. Soc. Clin., Investigation, Central (emeritus), Western (charter mem., emeritus), socs. clin. research, Soc. for Exptl. Biology and Medicine, Nat. Bd. Med. Examiners (com. on pub. health and preventive medicine), Western Assn. Physicians (charter), Assn. Tchrs. Preventive Medicine, Central Interurban Clin. Club, Sigma Xi, Alpha Omega Alpha, Sigma Sigma (hon). Author papers on med. topics. Home: 5779 Gloria Dr Sacramento CA 95822 Office: 744 P St Sacramento CA 95814

BROWN, JOHN WILLIAM, lt. gov. Ohio; b. Athens, O., Dec. 28, 1913; s. James A. and Daisy (Foster) B.; grad. high sch.; m. Violet A. Helman; 1 dau., Rosalie (Mrs. Grant N. Angelus). With Ohio Hwy. Patrol, 1941; mayor City of Medina (O.), 1950- 53; lt. gov. State of Ohio, 1953-57, 62—; gov. Ohio, 1957; mem. Ohio Ho. Reps., 1959-60, Ohio Senate, 1961-62; pres., dir. Investors Heritage Life Ins. Co. of Ohio, Columbus. Mem. Medina Vol. Fire Dept., 1953—. Served with USCGR, World War II; comdr. Res. Mem. Am. Legion, V.F.W., Pi Kappa Alpha. Mason (32, Shriner). Home: 401 Baxter St Medina OH 44256

BROWN, JOSEPH ALLEN, lawyer, corp. exec.; b. Worcester, Mass., Sept. 18, 1926; s. Joseph A. and Anna G. (Moynihan) B.; B.S., Franklin and Marshall Coll., 1948; J.D., Georgetown U., 1951; m. Joan E. Auchter, June 11, 1949; children—Margaret, Jeanne, Joseph Allen, Theresa, Timothy, Michael, Richard. Admitted to D.C. bar, 1951; atty. Workmen's Compensation Appeals Bd., U.S. Dept. Labor, 1951-53; patent atty. B.E. Shlesinger, Washington and Rochester, N.Y., 1953-55; patent atty.. New Holland div. Sperry Rand Corp., New Holland, Pa., 1955-64, patent counsel, 1964-67, gen. counsel, asst. sec., 1967—. Chmn. Eastern dist. Lancaster County council Boy Scouts Am., 1965-66, mem. bd., 1966—. Mem. Lancaster County Citizens for Kennedy. Served with USNR, 1944-46. Mem. Am., Canadian farm and indsl. equipment insts., Am. Bar Assn., Am., Phila. patent law assns. Roman Catholic. Home: 1360 Hunter Dr Lancaster PA 17601 Office: Sperry Rand Corp New Holland PA 17557

BROWN, JOSEPH DAVID, mfg. co. exec.; b. N.Y.C., Sept. 27, 1905; s. Menno and Pauline (Buckner) B.; E.E., Bklyn. Poly. Inst., 1926; m. Marion Fenton, June 7, 1931; children—Toni (Mrs. Jack Porter, Jr.), Kenneth M. Pres. Poloron Products, Inc., New Rochelle, N.Y., 1930—. Bd. dirs. United Fund of Westchester, 1969—. Pres. Eastchester (N.Y.) Union Free Sch. Dist 1, 1961-68. Trustee Bklyn. Poly. Inst.; asso. Pace Coll. Recipient Most Distinguished Alumnus award Bklyn. Poly. Inst., 1971. Mem. Am. Bus. Congress (pres. 1942-49), Cal. Ridge Assn. (pres. 1957-59), Tau Beta Pi. Home: 209 Red Fox Rd Stamford CT 06903 Office: 165 Huguenot St New Rochelle NY 10801

BROWN, JOSEPH GORDON, coll. dean; b. Terre Haute, Ind., Aug. 25, 1927; s. Joseph H. and Helen (Gordon) B.; student U. Ky., 1946-47; B.S., East Tenn. State U., 1950; M.S., U. Tenn., 1957; m. Margaret Ann Grindstaff, Dec. 29, 1949; children—Sheridan Lynn, Karen Sue, Michael Gordon. Prin., Bassel Sch., Alcoa, Tenn., 1950-51, Springbrook Sch., Alcoa, 1951-57; dean men, dir. student activities Emory and Henry Coll., Emory, Va., 1957-60, dean men, asso. prof. edn., 1960-64; dean men Va. Poly. Inst., Blacksburg, 1964-68, dean for student services, 1968—. Pres. Blacksburg Community Fedn. Served with USNR, 1945-46. Mem. N.E.A., Nat. (commns. on profl. relations and financial aids), Va. (past pres.) assns. student personnel adminstrs., So. Assn. Colls. and Schs., Phi Delta Kappa, Phi Eta Sigma, Pi Delta Epsilon. Methodist. Rotarian. Contbr. to Interfraternity Council Research Bull., 1960. Home: 1418 Locust Av Blacksburg VA 24060

BROWN, JOSIAH, educator, physician; b. Centerfield, Utah, Dec. 19, 1932; s. Nathan and Sophie (Lederman) B.; A.B., U. Cal. at Los Angeles, 1944, M.D., at San Francisco, 1947; m. Pearl Holen, Oct. 21, 1944; children—Jeffrey Josiah, Celia Lynn, Todd Evan. Intern San Francisco City and County Hosp., 1947- 48; jr. resident Mallory Inst. Pathology, Boston City Hosp., 1948-49; resident medicine Cin. Gen. Hosp., 1949-51; mem. faculty U. Cal. Sch. Medicine at Los Angeles, 1956—, prof., chief div. endocrinology, 1966- -, chmn. ednl. policy and curriculum com., 1968-70. Served with USPHS, 1951-53. Hon. fellow Courtauld Inst. Biochemistry, Middlesex Hosp. Med. Sch., 1964-65. Mem. Am. Soc. Clin. Investigation, A.A.A.S., Endocrine Soc., Diabetes Assn. So. Cal. Author: (with C.M. Pearson) Clinical Uses of Adrenal Steroids, 1962. Home: 1673 Pandora Av Los Angeles CA 90024

BROWN, KATHARINE KENNEDY, former mem. Republican Nat. Com.; b. Dayton, O.; d. Grafton Claggett and Louise (Achey) Kennedy; ed. pub. schs., Dayton, (O.) student Dana Hall, 1906-08; m. Kleon Thaw Brown, Apr. 20, 1921. Vice pres. Ohio Yellow Cab Co., Dayton. Founder pres. Jr. League, Dayton, 1920-22, 1926-28; v.p. Assn. Jr. Leagues Am., 1926-28; organizer, 1st pres. Army-Navy Officer Club, Dayton 1943. Mem. Montgomery County (O.) Rep. Exec. Com., 1920-21, 1926—; mem. Rep. State Com., 1928—; Rep. nat. committeewoman, 1932-68, v. chmn. Rep. Nat. Com., 1944-52 (co-dir. western div., 1936; mem. exec. com., 1942-52); del. at large from Ohio to Rep. Nat. Conv., 1932, 44, 48, 52, 56, 60, 64, 68; pres. Ohio Fedn. Rep. Women's Orgns., 1940—; adv. bd. Nat. Fedn. Women's Rep. Clubs of Am.; mem. strategy com. for Senator Robert A. Taft in presdl. campaigns, 1948 and 1952. Trustee Wilberforce U., 1961-67; chmn. for Montgomery county of Ohioana Library. Recipient award Nat. Fedn. Rep. Women, 1963. Mem. D.A.R. (regent Jonathan Dayton chpt., 1970—), Colonial Dames Am. (chmn. Dayton circle), Dist. League of Rep. Women (Washington). Presbyn. Clubs: Capitol Hill (Washington); Moraine Country (Dayton). Author (pamphlets): What You Want To Know About the Great Game of Politics, 1941; Outline for Precinct and Ward Organization, 1936; The Rudiments of Political Organization, 1960. Home: Duncarrick Keowee and Webster Sts Dayton OH 45402

BROWN, KEITH SPALDING, former mem. Republican Nat. Com.; b. Hinsdale, Ill., June 15, 1913; s. William Bruce and Sara Morgan (Gardner) B.; grad. cum laude, Phillips Acad., 1931; B.A., Yale, 1935; m. Katherine Noyes McLennan, July 3, 1937; children—Keith Spalding, Julia (Mrs. Parker D. Perry, Jr.), Katherine M. (Mrs. James R. Davis), Stephen G. With Procter & Gamble Co., 1935-37; prodn. supr. Lyon Metal Products Co., Aurora, Ill., 1937-39; mem. staff Booz, Fry, Allen & Hamilton, mgmt. consultants, Chgo., 1939-42; owner, operator Santa Rita Ranch, cattle, Tucson, 1946-70; v.p., dir., mem. investment com. Selective Life Ins. Co., 1958-65; v.p., treas., mem. exec. com., dir. Southwestern Research & Gen. Investment Co., 1965; chmn. bd. Am. Atomics Corp., also dir.; dir. So. Ariz. Bank. Mem. Ariz. Ho. of Reps. from Pima County, 1955-58; vice chmn. Ariz. Rep. Com., 1959-60, chmn., 1963-65; mem. Rep. Nat. Com. for Ariz., 1963-65, mem. 1964-65; del., vice chmn. Ariz. delegation Rep. Nat. Conv., 1964, del. at large, 1968. Mem. Continental Pub. Sch. Bd., 1947-65, pres., 1959-65. Mem. Am. Nat. Cattlemens Assn., Atomic Indsl. Forum, Alpha Delta Phi. Home: 3200 N Swan Rd Tucson AZ 85716 Office: 425 S Plumer St Tucson AZ 85719

BROWN, KENNETH HAROLD, lawyer; b. Montreal, Que., Can., Apr. 12, 1908; s. Ernest and Ruby (Kirkus) B.; B.A., McGill U., 1929; B.A., B.C.L., Oxford U., 1932; m. Agnes Morton, Aug. 8, 1934; children—Micaela Margaret (Mrs. William S. Wilson), Alan Geoffrey Lloyd. Called to bar, Eng., 1932, Que., 1933, created Queen's counsel, 1947; practiced in Montreal, 1933—; mem. firm Lafleur & Brown and predecessor firms, 1933—. Dir. Montreal Trust Co., Montreal Life Ins. Co., Dominion Equity Investments, Ltd., Dubonnet, Inc., Canadian Stebbins Engring. & Mfg. Co., Ltd. Bd. govs. McGill U. Served to lt. col. Canadian Army, 1941-45. Decorated Order Brit. Empire. Mem. Canadian Bar Assn., Psi Upsilon. Home: 4717 Roslyn Av Montreal Quebec 247 Canada Office: 800 Victoria Sq Montreal Quebec 115 Canada

BROWN, KENT LOUIS, surgeon; b. Westfield, N.Y., 1916; M.D., U. Buffalo, 1942; m. Elizabeth Myers; children—Karen, Kent Louis, David, Garry. Rotating intern, St. Luke's Hosp., Cleve., 1942-43, asst. resident surgery, 1946-49, chief resident surgeon, 1949-50, now mem. active staff; active staff St. Vincent Charity Hosp.; courtesy staff Woman's Gen. Hosp., Hillcrest Hosp., Euclid Gen. Hosp., Cleve. Trustee Cleve. Med. Library. Served as lt., M.C., USNR, 1943-46. Diplomate Am. Bd. Surgery. Fellow A.C.S. (trauma com.); mem. A.M.A., Am. Assn. Surgery of Trauma. Kiwanian (past pres.). Clubs: Aesculapian Soc. Cleve.; Innominatum Soc.; Pasteur; Medical Arts; Union. Author: Medical Problems and the Law. Contbr. numerous articles to profl. jours. Home: 18600 S Woodland Rd Shaker Heights OH 44122 Office: 3461 Warrensville Center Rd Cleveland OH 44122

BROWN, L. DAVID, clergyman; b. Fargo, N.D., Feb. 16, 1926; s. John Nicolai and Ada Amelia (Johnson) B.; B.A., U. Minn., 1948; C.T.H., Luther Theol. Sem., St. Paul, 1951; m. Virginia Ann Allen, Sept. 6, 1950; children—Patricia Anne, Julia Louise, Claudia Ruth. Ordained to ministry Lutheran Ch., 1951; pastor in New Ulm, Minn., 1951-55; asso. dir. youth activities Evang. Luth. Ch., 1955-59; exec. dir. youth activities Am. Luth. Ch., 1959-69; editor Arena One Mag., 1967-69; instnl. relations coordinator, tng. of tchr. trainers program U. Minn., 1969-70; exec. dir. Am. Freedom from Hunger Found., Washington; tchr. Augusburg Coll., Mpls., 1961, 66. Mem. youth com. World Council Chs., 1962—; chmn. youth com. Luth. World Fedn., 1965—; mem. exec. com. Nat. Luth. Campus Ministry, 1966—. Mem. Gov. Minn. Com. Corrections, 1965-67. Served with USNR, 1943-46. Author articles, booklets. Home: 3158 Cedar Grove Dr Fairfax VA 22030

BROWN, LAURIE MARK, educator, physicist; b. Bklyn., Apr. 10, 1923; s. William and Elvira (Fleischman) B.; A.B., Cornell U., 1943, Ph.D., 1951; m. Judith Kobrin, Dec. 27, 1942 (dec. May 1963); children—Joanna Lisa, Julie Elena; m. 2d, Brigitte Winzeler, June 6, 1969. Mem. faculty physics Northwestern U., Evanston, Ill., 1950—, prof., 1961—. Mem. Inst. for Advanced Study (NSF fellow), Princeton, 1952-53; cons. Argonne Nat. Lab., 1960-70; vis. prof., Vienna, 1966, Rome, 1967. Fulbright research scholar, Italy, 1958-60. Fellow Am. Phys. Soc. A.A.A.S. Contbr. articles profl. jours. Home: 807 Milburn St Evanston IL 60201

BROWN, LEO CYRIL, clergyman, economist, educator; b. Stanberry, Mo., Apr. 28, 1900; s. Edward P. and Mary (Wallace) B.; A.B., St. Louis U., 1926, A.M., 1928, S.T.L., 1935; A.M., Harvard, 1938, Ph.D., 1940; LL.D. (honoris causa), Loyola U., Chgo., 1970. Entered Jesuit Order, 1921; priest, Roman Cath. Ch., 1934; Wertheim fellow Harvard, summer, 1940; instr. econs. Regis Coll., Denver, 1940-41; asst. in econs. St. Louis U., 1930-35, instr. 1942-43, asst. prof., 1943-45, asso. prof., 1945-49, prof. econs., 1949—, dir. labor sch., 1942-47, acting regent sch. law, 1948-49, dir. Inst. Social Order, 1947-62; research asso. Cambridge (Mass.) Center of Social Studies, 1965-68. Arbitrator of permanent umpire labor agreements 1942—; pub. mem. War Labor Bd. VII, 1943-45; public mem. WSB VII, 1945, IX 1951-52; mem. Atomic Energy Labor-Mgmt. Relations Panel, 1953- 68, chmn. of panel, 1968—. Trustee St. Louis U., 1949, 54, 56-64, council regents, deans, 1944-63; trustee Marquette U. Mem. Nat. Acad. Arbitrators (nat. pres. 1960), Am., Cath. (pres.'1949) econ. assns. Author: Union Policies in the Leather Industry, 1947; Impact of New Labor Law on Union-Management Relations, 1948. Editor social sci. area Cath. Ency., 1963-65. Home: 221 N Grand St St Louis MO 63103

BROWN, LEON, architect, educator; b. Blackville, S.C., Sept. 25, 1907; s. Isador and Sadie (Cohen) B.; student Cornell U., 1924-25; B.S. in Architecture, Ga. Inst. Tech., 1929; M.Arch., U. Pa., 1933; m. Marguerite Kahn, Aug. 30, 1944; 1 son, Warren Lee. Designer-draftsman R. B. Okie, Phila., 1929-31; jr. partner Thalheimer & Weitz, Phila., 1934-42; propr. Leon Brown, architect, Washington, 1946-50; partner Brown & Wright, architects, Washington, 1950-68, Brown, Wright & Mano, architects, 1968-71; prof. architecture Howard U., Washington, 1947—. Mem. Washington Bldg. Congress, 1958—; chmn. D.C. Bd. Appeals and Rev., Licenses and Insp., 1956-60; mem. bd. Washington Planning and Housing Assn., 1958-70; mem. urban renewal planning com. Washington Urban League, 1960-65; nat. panel arbitrators Am. Arbitration Assn., 1959—; sec. D.C. Bd. Registration Architects, 1964-67, pres., 1967-69. Treas. D.C. Com. Job Opportunities, 1956-60; co- chmn. D.C. Nat. Conf. Christians and Jews, 1966—, bd. govs., 1967, bd. Wash. chpt. 1968; pres. Forest Hills Citizens Assn., 1965-68. Mem. com. planning and housing Democratic Central Com., 1963—. Bd. dirs. N.W. Settlement House, 1952—. Served to capt., C.E., AUS, 1942-46. Recipient Meritorious Pub. Service award Mil. Dist. Washington, 1946. Fellow A.I.A. (pres. Washington met. chpt. 1956-58; Coll. Fellows); mem. Assn. Coll. Sch. Architecture, Zeta Beta Tau. Jewish religion. Club: Cosmos (Washington). Author: (with others) R. Brognard Okie, Architect of Philadelphia, 1955; also articles. Home: 4158 Linnean Av NW Washington DC 20008 Office: 1640 Wisconsin Av NW Washington DC 20007

BROWN, LEONARD CARLTON, educator; b. Mineral Springs, Ark., Mar. 26, 1915; s. Leonidas C. and Willie (Graves) B.; A.B., Henderson State Coll., Ark., 1937; M.A., Fla. State U., 1952; Ph.D., Ohio State U., 1955; m. Hazel Elizabeth Weatherly, Aug. 27, 1938; 1 dau., Jo Carol. Research asso. Ohio State U., 1955-57, asst. prof., 1957-59, asso. prof., 1959-64, prof. physics, 1964—. Served with USAAF, 1943-46. Mem. Am. Phys. Soc., Am. Assn. Physics Tchrs., Sigma Xi, Sigma Pi Sigma. Home: 2170 Lane Rd Columbus OH 43220

BROWN, LEON CARL, educator; b. Mayfield, Ky., Apr. 22, 1928; s. Leon Carl and Gwendolyn (Travis) B.; B.A., Vanderbilt U., 1950; postgrad. U. Va., 1950-51, London Sch. Econs., 1951-52; Ph.D., Harvard, 1962; m. Anne Winchester Stokes, Aug. 29, 1953; children—Elizabeth Boone, Joseph Winchester, Jefferson Travis. U.S. fgn. service officer, Beirut, Lebanon, 1954-55, Khartoum, Sudan, 1956-58; asst. prof. Middle Eastern studies Harvard, 1962-66; asso. prof. Near Eastern history and civilization Princeton, 1966-70, prof., 1970—, chmn. dept. Near Eastern studies and dir. program Near Eastern studies, 1969—. Served with USAAF, 1945-46. Author: (with C.A. Micaud and C.H. Moore) Tunisia: the Politics of Modernization, 1964. Editor: State and Society in Independent North Africa, 1966. Translator with commentary: The Surest Path: the Political Treatise of a 19th Century Muslim Statesman, 1967. Home: 191 Hartley Av Princeton NJ 08540

BROWN, LES, (Lester Louis), journalist; b. Indiana Harbor, Ind., Dec. 20, 1928; s. Irving H. and Helen (Feigenbaum) B.; B.A. in English, Roosevelt U., Chgo., 1950; student Loyola U., Chgo., 1950; m. Jean Rosalie Slaymaker, June 12, 1959; children—Jessica, Joshua, Rebecca. Entertainment industry reporter, reviewer theatrical events Chgo. bur. Variety, 1953-55; asso. editor Downbeat mag., 1955; co-founder, operator folk music cabaret The Gate of Horn, Chgo., 1956; bur. mgr. Chgo., Variety, 1957-65; editor radio-TV dept., N.Y.C., 1965—; lectr. creative writing and entertainment industries Columbia Coll., Chgo., 1959-62. Served with AUS, 1951-53. Author: (lyrics) Abilene, 1956; Television: The Business Behind The Box, 1971; also articles. Home: 131 N Chatsworth Av Larchmont NY 10538 Office: 154 W 46th St New York City NY 10036

BROWN, LESTER RUSSELL, former govt. ofcl.; b. Bridgeton, N.J., Mar. 28, 1934; s. Calvin C. and Delia (Smith) B.; B.S. in Agrl. Sci., Rutgers U., 1955; M.A. in Econs., U. Md., 1959; M.P.A., Harvard, 1962; m. Shirley Ann Woolington, June 12, 1960; children—Brian, Brenda. With Dept. of Agr., 1959-69, adminstr. internat. agr. devel. service, 1966-69; sr. fellow Overseas Devel. Council, 1969—. Faculty mem. Salzburg Seminar in Am. Studies, summer 1971. Recipient Superior Service award Dept. Agr., 1965; Arthur S. Flemming award, 1965; named one of 10 outstanding young men in Am., U.S. Jr. C. of C., 1966. Mem. Am. Farm Econs. Assn., Soc. Internat. Devel., Internat. Assn. Agrl. Economists, Am. Acad. Arts and Scis. (working group on year 2000), Am. Econs. Assn., Council of Fgn. Relations, Zero Population Growth, Common Cause, World Future Soc., Amateur Athletics Union. Club: Cosmos. Author: Man, Land and Food, 1963; Increasing World Food Output, 1965; Seeds of Change, 1970; also articles. Home: 8716 Preston Pl Chevy Chase MD 20015 Office: 1717 Massachusetts Av NW Washington DC 20005

BROWN, LEWIS DEAN, U.S. ambassador; b. N.Y.C., Aug. 21, 1920; s. Lewis Philip and Elizabeth Amy (Crossley) B.; B.A., Wesleyan U., 1942; m. June Vereker Farquhar, 1947; 1 son, Michael. With Dept. of State, 1946—, beginning as vice consul, Leopoldville, Belgian Congo, successively vice consul, St. John, N.B., Can., 2d sec. Am. Embassy, Ottawa, Can., Canadian desk officer, staff asst. to asst. sec. of state for European affairs, 1946-65, 1st sec. Am. Embassy, Paris, France, 1955-58, officer-in-charge French- Iberian affairs, 1958-61, dep. dir. Western European affairs, 1961-62; at Imperial Def. Coll., London, Eng., 1962-63, counselor Am. Embassy, Rabat, Morocco, 1963-66; ambassador to Senegal and Gambia, 1967-70; ambassador to Jordan, 1970—. Served as lt., inf. AUS, 1942-46. Home: 3030 Cambridge Pl Washington DC 20007 Office: State Dept Washington DC 20525

BROWN, LINDSEY A., govt. ofcl.; b. Windsor, Colo., July 19, 1906; s. Harry J. and Eva L. Brown; student Colo. Agrl. Coll., 1925-28; B.S., U. Neb., 1930, M.S., 1931; Ph.D., Pa. State U., 1934; m. E. Grace Ackerman, June 2, 1929; children—Harlan J., Donna L. (now Mrs. William Spaar), Barbara A. (now Mrs. Ronald Brown). Asso. prof. Colo. Agrl. Coll., 1936-41; irrigation planner U.S., 1941-46; agr. and water resource adv. planner, administrator of the foreign aid program to Japan, Okinawa, Colombia, Egypt, Ceylon, Ecuador, Turkey, also Libya, also at Saudi Arabia, 1946—. Recipient citations from govts. Japan and Colombia. Mem. Soil Sci. Soc. Am., Sigma Xi, Phi Delta Phi, Gamma Sigma Delta. Author articles profl. jours., bulls. Address: care PO Box 558 Riyadh Saudi Arabia

BROWN, LOUIS M., lawyer; b. Los Angeles, Sept. 5, 1909; s. Emil and Anna Brown; A.B. cum laude, U. So. Cal., 1930; J.D., Harvard, 1933; m. Hermione Kopp, 1937; children—Lawrence David, Marshall Joseph, Harold Arthur. Admitted to Cal. bar, 1933, U.S. Supreme Ct. bar, 1944; practiced in Los Angeles, 1933-35; with Emil Brown & Co., Dura Steel Products Co. (both Los Angeles), 1936-41; counsel RFC, Washington, 1942-44; partner firm Pacht, Warne, Ross and Bernhard, Los Angeles, also Beverly Hills, Cal., 1944- 47; partner firm Irell & Manella, Los Angeles, 1947-69, counsel, 1969—. Lectr. in law Southwestern U. Law Sch., Los Angeles, 1939-41, U. Cal. at Los Angeles, 1944-46; lectr. in law U. So. Cal., 1950-51, lectr., adj. prof. law, 1960—, mem. planning com., Tax Inst., 1948-69; mem. nat. panel arbitrators Am. Arbitration Assn., 1956-63. Mem. com. Jewish Personnel Relations Bur., Community Relations Com., 1950-60; founder, adminstr. Emil Brown Fund Preventive Law Prize Awards, 1963—, Mock Law Office Competition, 1968—. pres. Friends of Beverly Hills Pub. Library, 1960. Fellow Am. Bar Found.; mem. Am. (chmn. standing com. legal assistance for servicemen 1969—), Beverly Hills (pres. 1961), Los Angeles County (chmn. prepaid legal services com. 1970—), San Francisco bar assns., State Bar Cal., Am. Judicature Soc., Am. Bus. Law Assn., Town Hall Los Angeles, Order of Coif. Jewish religion. Mason; mem. B'nai B'rith. Club: Harvard Southern Cal. Author: Preventive Law, 1950; How to Negotiate a Successful Contract, 1955; also case books, articles profl. jours. Editor: Major Tax Problems, 3 vols., 1948-51. Mem. Am. Community Symphony Orch. European Tour, 1968. Home: 606 N Palm Dr Beverly Hills CA 90210 Office: Gateway East Bldg Century City Los Angeles CA 90067

BROWN, LOY THIETJE, naval med. officer; b. Omaha, Nov. 7, 1919; s. Frank Arthur and Winona (Thietje) B.; A.B., U. Omaha, 1944; M.D., U. Neb., 1945; m. Ann Marie Friedrich, Oct. 28, 1950; children—Jeanne Ann, Mary Jane. Commd. lt. (j.g.), M.C., U.S. Navy, 1945, advanced through grades to capt., 1961; intern U.S. Naval Hosp., St. Albans, N.Y., 1945-46, U.S. Naval Hosp., Chelsea, Mass., 1947; resident radiology U.S. Naval Hosp., Bethesda, Md., 1951-53; fellow radiology Mayo Found., 1953-54; radiologist U.S. Naval Hosp., Bainbridge Md., 1954-56, Portsmouth, Va., 1956-59; chief radiology U.S. Naval Hosp., Great Lakes, Ill., 1959-61, U.S. Naval Hosp., Nat. Naval Med. Center, Bethesda, Md., 1961-68; exec. officer U.S. Naval Hosp., Portsmouth, Va., 1968-69; comdg. officer U.S. Naval Hosp., Phila., 1969—. Diplomate Am. Bd. Radiology. Fellow Am. Coll. Radiology. Home: Qtrs A US Naval Hosp Philadelphia PA 19145 Office: Comdg Officer US Naval Hosp Philadelphia PA 19145

BROWN, LUTHER, ednl. adminstr.; b. Swain County, N.C., Mar. 9, 1912; s. John Henry and Hannah Vian (Wilson) B.; B.S., Northeastern State Coll., Tahlequah, Okla., 1935; M.S., Okla. State U., 1938; Ph.D., George Peabody Coll., 1953; m. Marie Lucille Haber, Mar. 9, 1945; 1 dau., Cathryn Ann. Elementary and secondary sch. tchr. and adminstr., Dewey, Okla., 1935- 42; dir. tchr. edn. and placement service Northeastern State Coll., 1946- 55; pres. Northwestern State Coll., 1955-56; prof., dir. audiovisual edn. and curriculum materials St. Cloud (Minn.) State Coll., 1956-58, dean bur. learning resources services (audiovisual, curriculum materials, coll. and campus sch. libraries), chmn. dept. library and audiovisual edn., 1958—. Mem. audio-visual adv. com. Minn. Dept. Edn.; mem. Citizens Com. on Pub. Edn., State Feasibility Study on Ednl. TV: cons. West Central Materials Center, East-West Twin City Suburban Audiovisual Group, Anoka Materials Center, Central Minn. Regional Materials Center; mem. Minn. Commn. on Pub. Edn. Served with USNR, 1942-46. Recipient Scout Leaders key Boy Scouts Am., 1942, Silver Beaver award, 1955. Mem. Nat., Okla. (life), Minn. edn. assns., Sch. Library Assn., Am. (life), Minn. library assns., Nat. Soc. Study Edn., Assn. Higher Edn., Div. Audio-Visual Instrn. Midwest Acad. Librarians, Audio-Visual Coordinators Assn. Minn. (past pres., dir.), St. Cloud C. of C., Future Farmers Am. (hon.), Phi Delta Kappa (past chpt. pres.), Alpha Phi Omega (hon.), Rho Theta Sigma. Kiwanian (past pres.). Clubs: Executives, Discussion. Address: State Coll St Cloud MN 56301

BROWN, MADISON BALDWIN, assn. exec.; b. Burlington, Vt., Apr. 28, 1911 s. Thomas Stephen and Jessie (Baldwin) B.; M.D., U. Vt., 1936; m. Vernon Kimball, July 12, 1958; children—Thomas Stephen II, George Hayden. Intern Mary Hitchcock Meml. Hosp., Hanover, N.H., 1936-37; gen. practice medicine, Laconia, Lebanon, N.H., 1937-40; asst. dir. Roosevelt Hosp., N.Y.C., 1940-42, 45-47; 1st asst. dir. Johns Hopkins Hosp., 1947-49; exec. v.p., med. dir. Roosevelt Hosp., 1949-53, Hahnemann Med. Coll. and Hosp., Phila., 1953-56; asst. dir. Am. Hosp. Assn., Chgo., 1956-57, asso. dir., 1957-68, dep. dir., 1968—. Mem. spl. med. adv. group VA, 1965-71, chmn., 1969-71; com. vital and health statistics USPHS; vice chmn. Commn. on Fgn. Med. Grads., 1970-71; co-sec. Spl. Com. on Provision Health Services, 1969-70. Trustee Commn. Profl. and Hosp. Activities Inc., Ann Arbor, Mich., pres., 1969-71; trustee Ednl. Council Fgn. Med. Grads, 1961-68; prin. investigator project dir. Collaborative Research in Hosp. Planning, USPHS, 1959-64. Served with M.C., AUS, 1942-45. Decorated Bronze Star; recipient Trustees award, 1966, Honor award, 1971 (both Am. Hosp. Assn.). Fellow Am. Coll. Hosp. Adminstrs.; mem. Hosp. Med. Adminstrs. Corr. Club, Soc. Med. Adminstrs. (pres. 1965-66), A.M.A., Med. Adminstrs. Conf., Am. Pub. Health Assn., Royal Soc. Health, Inst. Medicine Chgo. Home: 615 Chatham Rd Glenview IL 60025 Office: 840 N Lake Shore Dr Chicago IL 60611

BROWN, MARCIA, author, artist; b. Rochester, N.Y., July 13, 1918; s. Clarence Edward and Adelaide Elizabeth (Zimber) Brown; student Woodstock Sch. Painting, summers 1938, 39; student painting New Sch. Social Research, Art Students League, B.A., N.Y. State Coll. Tchrs., 1940. Tchr. English, dramatics Cornwall (N.Y.) High Sch., 1940-43; library asst. N.Y. Pub. Library, 1943-49; tchr. puppetry extra-mural dept. U. Coll. West Indies, Jamaica, B.W.I., 1953; woodcut prints exhibited Bklyn. Mus., Peridot Gallery, Hacker Gallery, Library Congress, Carnegie Inst., Phila. Print Club; prints in permanent collection Library of Congress, N.Y. Pub. Library, pvt. collections; writer, illustrator picture books for children. Life fellow Internat. Inst. Arts and Letters, 1961. Mem. Authors Guild, Print Council of Am., Art Students League. Illustrator: The Trail of Courage (by Virginia Watson), 1948; The Steadfast Tin Soldier (by Hans Christian Andersen), 1953; Anansi (by Philip Sherlock), 1954; The Three Billy Goats Gruff (by Asbjornsen and Moe), 1957; Peter Piper's Alphabet, 1959; The Wild Swans (by Hans Christian Andersen), 1963; Giselle, 1970. Author and also illustrator of the following: The Little Carousel, 1946; Stone Soup, 1947; HenryFisherman, 1949; Dick Whittington and His Cat (retold), 1950; Skipper John's Cook, 1951; The Flying Carpet (retold), 1956; Felice, 1958; Tamarindo!, 1960; Once a Mouse (retold), 1961 (winner Caldecott award 1962); Backbone of the King, 1966; The Neighbors, 1967; The Būn (retold), 1972. Translator, illustrator: Puss in Boots, 1952; Cinderella (by Charles Perrault) (winner Caldecott award), 1954; How, Hippo! (honor book Book World Spring Book Festival), 1969. Travel in Europe, 1956- 57, lived Venice, Italy, winter 1958-59, 61-62. Home: PO Box 113 West Redding CT 06896

BROWN, MARCUS ALLAN, consumer finance co. exec.; b. St. Louis, Feb. 11, 1914; s. John Esai and Esther (Shurman) B.; J.D., Washington U., 1937; m. Charlotte Emily Myer, Jan. 15, 1939; 1 dau., Pauline Emily. Admitted to Mo. bar, 1937; practiced in St. Louis, 1937-40; with Aetna Finance Co., Mpls., Cleve., Detroit, Norfolk, Va., 1940-42; atty. VA, St. Louis, 1946-51; operations v.p., house counsel ITT Aetna Corp. and predecessor corps., St. Louis, 1951—. Served to lt. USNR, 1942-45; PTO. Mem. Law Forum, Nat. Consumer Finance Assn., Conf. Personal Finance Law. Jewish religion. Home: 4 Granada Way Ladue MO 63124 Office: 212 S Central Av St Louis MO 63105

BROWN, MARION FULLER, mem. Republican Nat. Com.; b. Kansas City, Mo., May 14, 1917; d. Charles T. and Marion (Morean) Thompson; B.S., Smith Coll., 1938; m. 2d, Brooks Brown, Jr., 1967; children by previous marriage—Alexandra (Mrs. O. Kelly Anderson, Jr.), Martha (Mrs. Geoffrey Clark), Henry Weld Fuller, Emily Anne Fuller. Mem. Me. legislature from York County, 1966—. Dir. Strawberry Bank. Mem. women's com. York (Me.) Hosp., mem. York Planning Bd.; mem. Nat. Hwy. Beautification Commn., 1971—. Mem. town, county and state Rep. coms., 1952—; sec. Me. Rep. Com., 1962-66; mem. Rep. Nat. Com. for Me., 1966—. Vice pres., trustee Pine Tree Soc. for Crippled Children. Mem. Piscataqua (pres. 1960-61), York garden clubs. Ram's Head Farm York ME 03980

BROWN, MARION, JR., jazz saxophonist; b. Atlanta, Sept. 8 1935; also studied sax, clarinet, oboe in high sch., coll. Started playing with Atlanta teen-age group, then in army band; with Johnny Hodges, Atlanta, 1957, later with Archie Shepp, N.Y.C., Jazz Composer Guild Orch., 1964; formed own group, Newark, 1965; appeared in original prodn. LeRoi Jones' The Dutchman. Address: 224 E 21st St New York City, NY 10010.*

BROWN, MARTIN, broadcasting exec.; b. Bklyn., Apr. 4, 1925; s. Abraham and Lena (Korenberg) B.; B.A., George Washington U., 1949. With Price Waterhouse & Co., C.P.A.'s, Washington, 1949-54, audit mgr., N.Y.C., 1954-59; asst. treas. Am. Broadcasting Companies, Inc., 1959-60, treas., 1960- 69, v.p., asst. treas. ABC div., N.Y.C., 1959-61, v.p., treas., 1961-69. Served as flight officer with the USAAF, 1943- 46. C.P.A., D.C., N.Y. State. Mem. Am. Inst. C.P.A.'s, Financial Execs. Inst., Newcomen Soc., Phi Sigma Delta. Office: 1330 Av of the Americas New York City NY 10019

BROWN, MARY-AGNES, lawyer; b. Washington, D.C., Feb. 13, 1902; d. Homer John and Agnes Rogers (Jack) Brown; A.B., George Washington U., 1924, LL.B., 1932, S.J.D., 1942; postgrad. Cornell U., 1930, Cath. U., 1931, U. Mexico, 1941; m. Gordon Lewis Groover, May 28, 1952. Stenographer, Bur. War Risk Ins., 1919; exec. sec. to med. dir. U.S. Vets., Bur., 1921-31; admitted to D.C. bar, 1932, bar U.S. Supreme Ct., 1935; atty. solicitor's office VA, 1931-41; Organizer and first chmn. women's junior bar sect. Am. Bar Assn., D.C., 1935-36; pres. Women's Bar Assn., D.C., 1941-42; del. Fed. Bar Assn. to 2d Internat. Congress on Comparative and Internat. Law, The Hague, 1937, Am. Bar. Assn. to 1st meeting Inter-Am. Bar Assn., Havana, 1941. pvt. WAAC, 1942, advanced through grades to lt. col. WAC, 1944; bn. adj. 3d tng. regt.; pub. relations officer, hdqrs. 3d Service Command, Balt.; spl. duty, Washington; staff dir. hdqrs. 8th Service Command, Dallas, 1942-43; dept. exec., Washington, 1943; staff dir. Southwest Pacific Area, 1944-45; detailed to staff adminstr. vet. affairs. Gen. Omar N. Bradley as adviser on matters affecting women vets., 1945- 1946; chief legislative projects div. office for Va., Va. 1946-48; mem. U.S. Bd. Vets. Appeals, 1949- 59. Recipient certificate distinction George Washington U., 1943; Legion of Merit. Mem. Am., Fed., D.C., Women's D.C. bar assns., Nat. Assn. Women Lawyers, Am. Assn. U. Women, Colonial Dames, 17th Century, George Washington Law Assn., Nat. Lawyers Club, Sarasota Art Assn., Sigma Kappa, Phi Delta Delta, Pi Delta Epsilon, Pi Delta Gamma. Co-editor: Fed. Laws Relating to Vets. of Wars of U.S. (annotated), Senate Document 131, 72d Congress, 1932, supplement 1937. Address: 2809 Blaine Dr Chevy Chase, MD 20015.

BROWN, MATTHEW, lawyer; b. N.Y.C., Mar. 26, 1905; s. Jack Goddard and Pauline (Roth) B.; B.S., N.Y. U., 1925; LL.B., Harvard, 1928; m. Edna Goodrich, Nov. 8, 1932; children—Patricia, Ronald (dec.). Admitted to Mass. bar, 1928, Supreme Ct. bar; practice in Boston, 1928—; sr. partner firm Brown, Rudnuck, Freed & Gesmer, 1961—; spl. justice Boston Municipal Ct., 1962- -. Dir. Norfolk County Trust Co., Winde-McCormick Lumber Co. Gen. chmn. Combined Jewish Philanthropies fund raising drive, Boston, 1953, hon. trustee, 1954—, pres., 1970—; mem. adminstrv. com. Jewish Community Council Met. Boston, 1952—; chmn. Boston chpt. Am. Jewish Com., 1949-51; hon. chmn., 1951—, pres. New Eng. region, 1967-70. Alternate del. Republican Nat. Conv., 1952; mem. bd. selectmen Brookline, Mass., 1953-63, chmn., 1961- 63. Trustee Beth Israel Hosp., Boston, 1963—; past bd. dirs. Brookline Forum. Mem. Am., Fed., Mass., Boston, (council 1964—) bar assns., Pi Lamba Phi. Club: Belmont (Mass.) Country (past v.p.). Author: A Manual on Conditional Sales Contracts, Chattel Mortgages and Trust Receipts. Home: 419 Clinton Rd Brookline MA 02146 Office: 85 Devonshire St Boston MA 02109

BROWN, MELVIN F., corp. exec.; b. Carlinville, Ill., June 4, 1935; s. Ben and Selma (Frommel) B.; A.B., Washington U., 1957, J.D., 1961; m. Jacqueline Sue Hirsch, Sept. 2, 1962; children—Benjamin Andrew, Mark Steven. Admitted to Mo. bar, 1961; pvt. practice, St. Louis, 1961-62; asst. to gen. counsel Union Elec. Co., St. Louis, 1962-65; sec., atty. ITT Aetna Corp., St. Louis, 1965—. Dir. Civic Employment Corp., 1970—; mem. Interracial Conf. Bus. Opportunities, 1969—. Mem. Mo. Commn. Democratic Party Constn. By-laws and Party Structure, 1969-70, Mo. Dem. Platform Com., 1966, 68. Chmn. St. Louis chpt. Am. Jewish Com., 1968—. Served to capt. AUS, 1957-64; mem. Res. Hon. col. Mo. Gov.'s staff. Mem. Bar Assn. Met. St. Louis (pres. young lawyers sect. 1965-66), Mo. Bar Assn. Home: 7449 Oxford Dr St Louis MO 63105 Office: 212 S Central Av St Louis MO 63105

BROWN, MICHAEL ANDREW, mfg. co. exec.; b. Phila., Dec. 28, 1916; s. Michael A. and Katharine (Gallagher) B.; B.S. in Econs., Wharton Sch., U. Pa., 1938; m. Mercia Schipfer, June 10, 1938; children—Michael Andrew III, Katherine Claire (Mrs. Colin Hopkins), Mercia (Mrs. James Howard), Eleanor. Began career as asso. editor Modern Plastics mag., 1938-39; pub. relations supr. Monsanto Chem. Co., 1940-46; pres. Impression Molding, Inc., N. Wilbraham, Mass., 1946-47; editor Plastics mag., 1948; sales promotion mgr. Libbey-Owens-Ford Glass Co., 1948-52; with Rayonier, Inc., 1952—, gen. mgr. sales, 1955-61, v.p., 1961—; pres., dir. Rayonier Lumber Sales, Inc., 1955—, Nihon Rayonier Kabushiki Kaisha, 1956—; v.p., dir. Rayonier Industries Ltd., 1960—; v.p. Rayonier Export Corp., 1955—; dir. Rayonier Can. Sales Ltd., B.C. Pulp & Paper Co. Ltd. Author: (with John Sasso) Plastics in Practice, 1945; also articles. Home: 432 Field Point Rd Greenwich CT 06830 Office: Rayonier Inc 161 E 42d St New York City NY 10017

BROWN, MILTON PEERS, educator; b. Yonkers, N.Y., Jan. 19, 1919; s. George Edwin and Linda Miriam (Schneider) B.; S.B. cum laude, Harvard, 1940, M.B.A., 1942; m. Joan Hawley, Aug. 25, 1945; children—Susan, Janet, Pamela. Mem. faculty Harvard Bus. Sch., 1942—, prof. bus. adminstrn., 1958—, Lincoln Filene prof. retailing, 1963—; mgmt. cons., 1950—. Dir. Gen. Real Estate Shares, Detroit, Allied Stores Corp., Collins & Aikman Co. (both N.Y.C.), Dunkin Donuts, Quincy, Mass., LTM Corp., Boston, Savogran Co., Norwood. Mem. adv. com. Navy Resale System Office. Pres., bd. dirs. Harvard Coop. Soc. Trustee Beaver Country Day Sch., Chestnut Hill, until 1970. Mem. Am. Marketing Assn., Nat. Retail Mchts. Assn. (dir.). Author: Operating Results of Multi-Unit Department Stores, 1961; Problems in Marketing, 3d edit., 1968; co-author Strategy Problems in Mass Retailing and Wholesaling. Home: 141 Cherry Brook Rd Weston MA 02193 Office: Morgan Hall Harvard Business Sch Soldiers Field Boston MA 02163

BROWN, MILTON WOLF, art historian, educator; b. Newark, July 3, 1911; s. Samuel and Celia (Harriton) B.; B.A., N.Y.U., 1932, M.A., 1935, Ph.D., Inst. Fine Arts, 1949; postgrad. Courtauld Inst., summer 1934, U. Brussels, summer 1937, Harvard, 1938-39; m. Blanche R. Levine, July 15, 1938. Instr. art dept. Bklyn. Coll., 1946-49, asst. prof., 1949-56, asso. prof., 1956-60, prof., 1960-70, chmn. dept. art, 1964—; exec. officer doctoral program in art history City U. N.Y., 1971—. Mem. adv. bd. Archives Am. Art, 1967—. Served with AUS, 1943-46; ETO. Decorated Bronze Star medal. Mem. Coll. Art Assn. Am., Inst. Fine Arts Alumni Assn. (chmn.). Author: Painting of the French Revolution, 1937; American Painting from the Armory Show to the Depression, 1955; The Story of the Armory Show, 1963. Mem. editorial bd. Coll. Art Bull.; contbg. editor Ency. Painting, 1955. Home: 15 W 70th St New York City NY 10023 Office: Grad Center City U NY 33 W 42d St New York City NY 10036

BROWN, MONTREVILLE JAY, lawyer; b. Morris, Minn., June 13, 1884; s. Calvin Luther and Annette (Marlow) B.; A.B., U. Minn., 1907, LL.B., 1909; married Minnie Stinchfield, Nov. 19, 1910; children—Alice Katherine (Mrs. Raymond Brown), Louise (Mrs. Robert James Christianson), Margaret Annette (Mrs. Conley Brooks), Joanne (Mrs. Theodore Douglas Wright). Admitted to Minn. bar, 1909; practiced in Bemidji, 1909-18; city atty., 1917-18; asst. atty. gen. Minn., 1918-23, also mem. State Securities Commn., 1918-21; instr. Minn. Coll. Law, 1921-31; mem. Oppenheimer, Hodgson, Brown, Wolff and Leach, St. Paul, 1923—; counsel Mpls. St. Paul Met. Airports Commn., 1944—; spl. counsel City of Mpls., 1948-60. Mem. Draft Bd., Beltrami County, World War I; appeal agt. Draft Bd. 3, Ramsey County, World War II. Mem. Am., Minn., Ramsey County bar assns., Alpha Delta Phi, Phi Delta Phi. Conglist. Mason (grand master Minn. 1933). Club: Athletic (St. Paul). Home: 740 River Dr St Paul MN 55116 Office: First Nat Bank Bldg St Paul MN 55101

BROWN, MOREAU DELANO, banker; b. N.Y.C., Mar. 30, 1905; s. Thatcher Magoun and Caro Lord (Noyes) B.; student St. Paul's Sch., Concord, N.H., 1917-22; B.A., Yale, 1926; m. Alice Cordelia Barbour, Oct. 8, 1927; children—Alice Cordelia, Moreau Delano. With Brown Bros. & Co. and successors Brown Bros. Harriman & Co., 1928—, clk., N.Y.C., 1928-34, Phila., 1934, mgr. Phila., 1935-39, partner, 1939—; sec., dir. Beaver Mgmt. Corp.; dir. Leeds & Northrup Co., Phila. Reins. Corp., Fidelity Mut. Life Ins. Co., Magee Carpet Co., Colonial Assurance Co., Tolethorpe Corp., SKF Industries, Inc. (Phila.); bd. mgrs. Western Savs. Fund Soc. of Phila.; mem. Phila-Balt.- Washington Stock Exchange. Chmn. bd. trustees Moore Coll. Art, Phila., Robert Coll. Am. Coll. for Girls, Istanbul; dir., vice chmn. Southeastern Pa. chpt. A.R.C., dir., v.p. Phila. Maritime Mus.; bd. dirs. Union Theol. Sem. N.Y.C., Children's Aid Soc. of Pa., Grenfell Assn. of Am., Community Services of Pa.; trustee mem. exec. com. United Fund of Phila. Area. Mem. Wolf's Head Soc. Phi Beta Kappa, Alpha Delta Phi. Clubs: Philadelphia, Racquet, Yale (Phila.); Merion Cricket (Haverford); Edgartown Yacht; Corinthian Yacht; New Bedford Yacht; N.Y. Yacht. Home: North Rose Lane Haverford PA 19041 Office: 1531 Walnut St Philadelphia PA 19102

BROWN, MORGAN CORNELIUS, sociologist, educator; b. Macon, Ga., July 26, 1916; s. Morgan Cornelius and Ida (Moore) B.; B.A., Paine Coll., 1937; M.A., Ohio State U., 1950, Ph.D., 1954; m. Anne Boles, Sept. 7, 1946; children—Morgan Cornelius III, Andrea Elaine. Guidance dir., Brunswick, Ga., 1938-40; vocational counsellor Fed. Civil Service, Ft. Dix, N.J., 1946-47; research sec. Urban League, Columbus, O., 1948-50; from asst. prof. to prof. sociology So. U. and A. and M. Coll., Baton Rouge, 1954-68, chmn. dept. sociology, 1960-68; post-doctoral research Harvard, Cambridge, 1968-69; prof. sociology Bridgewater (Mass.) State Coll., 1969—, chmn. dept., 1970—. Served to 1st lt. AUS, 1942-45. Trustee Miss. Indsl. Coll., Holly Springs, Miss. Mem. Am., So. sociol. socs., Population Assn. Am., Am. Anthrop. Assn., Alpha Kappa Delta, Pi Gamma Mu, Psi Chi. Methodist. Contbr. articles to sociology jours. Home: 1462 Centre St Newton MA 02159

BROWN, MYRTLE IRENE, nursing educator; b. East Peoria, Ill., Feb. 1, 1915; d. Clifford Richard and Sarah (Scoville) Brown; B.A., Eureka Coll., 1939; B.S., U. Minn., 1942, M.S., 1947; Ph.D., N.Y. U., 1961. Instr. supr. pediatric nursing Mont. State Coll., Great Falls, 1939-41; instr., supr. pediatric nursing U. Minn., 1942-46, instr. advanced pediatric nursing, 1947-49; nursing cons. maternal and child health team WHO, India, 1949- 50; pub. health staff nurse Wayne County Health Dept., Eloise, Mich., 1950-52; asst. prof. maternal and child health Johns Hopkins, Balt., 1952-55; instr., then asso. prof. introductory epidemiology, sr. clin. nursing maternal and children's nursing, N.Y. U., 1955-61; research cons. Am. Nurses' Found. N.Y.C., 1961-64; asso. prof. community health and med. practice U. Mo. Sch. Medicine, Columbia, 1964-67, asso. prof. Sch. Nursing, 1966-67; dean prof. Sch. Nursing, Duke, 1967-70; prof., curriculum coordinator Coll. Nursing, U. S.C., Columbia, 1970—. Mem. Trained Nurse Assn. India (life), Am. Sociol. Assn., Am. Pub. Health Assn., Am., S.C. nurses assns., Nat., N.C. leagues nursing, Kappa Delta Pi, Alpha Kappa Delta, Sigma Theta Tau. Home: 5400 Lake Shore Dr Columbia SC 29206

BROWN, NESTOR MELLOY, foods co. exec.; b. Akron, O., Nov. 15, 1914; s. Ellsworth Grant and Emma Elizabeth (Rector) B.; B.S. in Mech. Engring., U. Akron, 1939; m. Virginia Wallace Zinkhann, Dec. 23, 1939; children—Jane, Victoria Ann, Rebecca Ellen. Indsl. engr. Am. Hard Rubber, Akron, 1939-40; indsl. engr. Nat. Screw & Mfg. Co., Cleve., 1940-42; asst. supt. Defiance Pressed Steel Co., Marion, O., 1942-44; asst. supt. Omar Mills, Inc., Omaha, 1944-45; v.p. prodn. Taylor Reed Corp., Glenbrook, Conn., 1945-50; sr. v.p. Welch Foods Inc., Westfield, N.Y., 1964-67, exec. v.p., 1967—, also dir. Mem. Industry Group Can Standard Sizes, 1970—. Mem. Concord Grape Assn. (pres. 1966), N.Y. State Canners and Freezers Assn. (pres. 1968), Am. Mgmt. Assn., Grocery Mfrs. Presbyn. Clubs: Lakeview Country (North East, Pa.); University (Erie, Pa.); Cleveland Playhouse. Home: 9950 E Lake Rd North East PA 16428 Office: Main and Portage Sts Westfield NY 14787

BROWN, NICHOLAS COMLY, coll. ofcl.; b. Harrisburg, Pa., Aug. 17, 1920; s. Arthur Edward and Mabel Warner (Stoddard) B.; grad. Harrisburg Acad., 1938; B.A., Ohio Wesleyan U., 1942; M.A., Yale, 1948, Ph.D., 1952; m. Mary Esther Kirkpatrick, Sept. 12, 1942; children—Nicholas Kirkpatrick, Susan Stoddard, Barbara Ann, Catherine Comly. Instr. math. Cheshire (Conn.) Acad., 1946-49; instr. English, New Haven YMCA Jr. Coll., 1950-51; teaching asst. edn. Yale, 1951-52; dean men, registrar Emory and Henry Coll., 1952-55; staff asso. Am. Council Edn., Washington, 1955-62; dean univ. U. Evansville, 1962-67, v.p. for acad. affairs, 1967-69; v.p. for acad. affairs Millersville State Coll., 1969—. Cons. President's Com. on Edn. Beyond High Sch., 1956; mem. adv. com. nat. orgns. U.S. Office Edn., 1957-58; adv. com. for jr. colls., colls. and univs. Dept. Labor, 1961-62. Bd. dirs. U.S. Book Exchange, 1959-62. Mem. Va. Assn. Collegiate Registrars and Admission Officers (pres. 1953-54), Phi Beta Kappa, Phi Kappa Phi, Blue Key, Omicron Delta Kappa, Delta Sigma Rho, Pi Mu Epsilon, Kappa Mu Epsilon, Sigma Alpha Epsilon. Methodist. Editor: The Study of Religion in the Public Schools: An Appraisal, 1958; Higher Education: Incentives and Obstacles, 1960; Orientation to College LearningA Reappraisal, 1961. Home: 2107 Clover Hill Rd Lancaster PA 17603

BROWN, NICHOLAS ELMER, lawyer; b. Rochester, N.Y., Sept. 26, 1906; s. Nicholas J. and Matie (Welch) B.; A.B., U. Rochester, 1928; LL.B., Harvard, 1931; m. Betty Cunningham, Aug. 19, 1933 (div. Apr. 1954); children—Nicholas Barry, Susan (Mrs. Robert C. Melech); m. 2d, Jean Stubbs, Mar. 13, 1958. Admitted to N.Y. State Bar, 1932; practiced in Rochester , 1931—; partner firm Harris, Beach and Wilcox, Rochester, 1942—. Pres. Rochester Gen. Hosp., 1965-66. Mem. Am., N.Y. State bar assns., U. Rochester Asso. Alumni (past pres.), Psi Upsilon. Home: 21 Fieldstone Terrace Rochester, NY 14610. Office: 2 State St Rochester NY 14614

BROWN, NORMAN JAMES, steel co. exec. b. Brantford Ont., Can., Dec. 27, 1911; s. William Dickson and Jean (Watson) B.; grad. Advanced Mgmt. Program, Harvard, 1947; m. Beatrice Welsh, Oct. 20, 1939; 1 son, Dennis. Accountant, Waterous, Ltd., Brantford, 1930-35; clk. Steel Co. of Can., Ltd., 1936-40, chief clk., works accountant, asst. comptroller, 1940- 56, comptroller, 1956-59, v.p., comptroller, 1959—. Active United Appeal. Mem. Nat. Office Mgmt. Assn., Financial Execs. Inst. Mem. United Ch. Home: 36 Eden Brook Hill Islington Ontario Canada Office: Steel Co of Canada Ltd Toronto-Dominion Center Toronto Ontario Canada

BROWN, NORMAN OLIVER, educator; b. El Oro, Mexico, Sept. 25, 1913; s. Norman C. and Marcarita Brown; B.A., Balliol Coll., Oxford U., 1936; Ph.D., U. Wis., 1942; m. Elizabeth Potter, Oct. 1, 1938; children—Stephen R., Thomas N., Rebecca M., Susan E. Prof. langs. Neb. Western U., 1942-43; with OSS, 1943-46; mem. faculty classics Wesleyan U., Middletown, Conn., as J.A. Seney prof. Greek; Wilson prof. Classics, U. Rochester. Commonwealth Fund fellow, 1936-38; Ford Found. teaching fellow, 1953-54; Guggenheim fellow, 1958-59. Author: Hermes the Thief, 1947; Hesiod's Theogeny, 1953; Life Against Death, 1959; Love's Body, 1966. Address: Univ Rochester Rochester NY 14627

BROWN, OSCAR, Jr., writer, entertainer; b. Chgo., Oct. 10, 1926; s. Oscar Cicero and Helen Clark (Lawrence) B.; student pub. schs., Chgo.; m. Irene Hebert, Dec. 26, 1948 (div. Nov. 1953); children—David, Donna; m. 2d, Maxine Fleming, Jan. 15, 1954; children—Joan, Iantha, Oscar, Margaret. Writer book, music and lyrics Kicks & Co., Chgo., 1961; appeared in Village Vanguard, 1961, Apollo Theater, 1961, Carnegie Hall, 1962, Blue Angel, 1962, Hungry I, 1962, Crescendo, 1962, Berns, Stockholm, 1963, Waldorf Astoria, 1963, Cool Elephant, London, Eng., 1965; one-man shows Prince Charles Theater, London, 1963, Music Box Theater, Los Angeles, 1964, Gramercy Arts Theater, N.Y.C., 1965; producer, dir. Joy '66, at Happy Medium Theater, Summer in the City, at Harper Theater; producer, dir. Alley Theater. Mem. Author's League Am. Composer: Brown Baby, 1960; Work Song, 1960; Dat Dere, 1960; The Snake, 1963; Muffled Drums, 1965. Address: 111 N Wood St Chicago IL 60612

BROWN, OTIS, state ofcl.; b. Brunswick, Va., Sept. 11, 1934; s. George Washington and Ruth (Lafoon) B.; B.A., U. Richmond, 1956; M.S., Fla. State U., 1959; m. Frances Young, Mar. 20, 1957; 1 son, Jeffrey Alan. Asst. field sec. League of Va. Counties, Charlottesville, Va., 1959-62; asst. county exec., county exec. County Albemarle, Va., 1962-66; dir. Va. Dept. Welfare and Instns., Richmond, Va., 1966—. Served to capt. AUS. Club: Sertoma Home. Home: 3303 Archdale Rd Richmond VA 23235 Office: 429 S Belvidere St Richmond VA 23220

BROWN, PATRICIA LAVERNE, educator; b. Chgo., Mar. 10, 1942; d. Edward H. and Anna Mae (Martin) Brown; A.B., Loyola U., Chgo., 1964, M.A., 1969. Copywriter, Callaghan & Co., Chgo., 1964-65; staff writer Charles A. Davis & Assos., 1965-66; pub. information officer Chgo. Com. on Urban Opportunity, 1966-69; inst. Malcom X Community Coll., Chgo., 1969—; speech and drama coach, sec.-treas., bus. mgr. Kuumba Workshop; Midwest area coordinator Communications Council, Congress of African People. Mem. Welfare Pub. Relations Forum, 1967-69. Mem. Nat. Assn. for Community Devel., Inst. of Black World, African Heritage Studies Assn., Modern Lang. Assn., Kappa Beta Gamma (past editor nat. mag.). Editor: To Gwen with Love, 1970. Home: 7959 S Jeffery Blvd Chicago IL 60617 Office: 1900 W Van Buren St Chicago IL 60612

BROWN, PAUL, paper co. exec.; b. Phila., Mar. 3, 1910; s. Robert W. and Virginia (Bailey) B.; grad. Advanced Mgmt. Program, Harvard, 1955; m. Jenette Pageler, Oct. 5, 1938; 1 son, Robert Neal. With Scott Paper Co., 1931—, sales dir., 1953-60, v.p. sales, 1960-63, v.p. sales devel, 1963—. Adv. bd. food distbn. course Mich. State U., 1958—. Served to maj. USAAF, World War II. Mem. Harvard, Alumni Assn. Clubs: Rolling Green Country (dir.) (Springfield, Pa.), Pine Valley Golf. Home: 109 E Country Club Lane Wallingford PA 19086 Office: Scott Paper Co Internat Airport Philadelphia PA 19113

BROWN, PAUL BRADLEY, architect; b. Lake City, Minn., Apr. 20, 1912; s. Clark William and Belle (Patton) B.; A.B., Oberlin Coll. 1933; B.Arch., U. Mich., 1936; m. Betty V. Padou, Dec. 29, 1945. children—Barry, Bennett, Bradley. Draftsman Hugh Keyes, Architet, Detroit, 1936-37; designer I. M. Lewis, Architect, Detroit, 1937-39; designer Harley Ellington Assos. Inc., Detroit, 1939-48, project architect, 1948-55, prin., 1955—. Pres. Birmingham (Mich.) Planning Commn., 1956-58; pres. Forum for Detroit Area Met. Goals, 1962-67. Served with USNR, 1943-45. Fellow A.I.A. (pres. Detroit chpt. 1961-63); mem. Mich. Soc. Architects (dir. 1964-65), Engring. Soc. Detroit. Home: 2785 Ayrshire Dr Bloomfield Hills MI 48013 Office: 26111 Evergreen Rd Southfield MI 48075

BROWN, PAUL EDGAR, lawyer; b. Canton, O., June 24, 1909; s. Harry J. and Ina G. (McGranahan) B.; B.S., Kent State U., 1935; LL.B., William McKinley Sch. Law, 1942; m. Pauline B. Kinsey, July 30, 1932; children-Bette I. (Mrs. T. Tim Solon), Paul B. Tchr., prin. pub. schs. Carroll, Stark and Summit Counties, O., 1927-45; admitted to Ohio bar, 1945, since practiced in Massillon; asso. Brown, Roesch, Netzly & Reichel and predecessor firm, 1953—. Mem. Massillon Bd. Edn., 1947-55. Candidate for common pleas judge Stark County, 1958. Pres. Massillon Sch. Dist. Library, Family Service Soc. and Childrens Bur. Massillon; trustee Massillon Salvation Army, Welfare Fedn. Western Stark County; mem. adv. bd. trustees Massillon Sch. Nursing. Mem. Am., Ohio, Stark County (pres.) bar assns., Am. Judicature Soc. Mem. Christian Ch. (elder). Mason (K.T., Shriner); mem. Order Eastern Star. Home: 1231 Lincoln Way East Massillon OH 44646 Office: First Nat Bank Bldg Massillon OH 44646

BROWN, PAUL HOWARD, mgmt. cons.; b. Commerce, Ga., July 3, 1906; s. John Glenn and Carrie H. (Holcomb) B.; student U. Ga., 1927-28; m. Mildred Chesnutt, June 6, 1935; children—Beverly Louise (Mrs. Paul F. Goree, Jr.), Virginia Elaine (Mrs. Harold W. Lochner, Jr.). Cost accountant Morse Bros. Lumber Co., 1926-30, office mgr., sales mgr., 1930-35; br. mgr. Seaboard Finance Corp., 1935-38; br. mgr. Gen. Finance Corp., Evanston, Ill., 1938, successively regional mgr., v.p., Orlando, Fla., 1938-62, exec. v.p., 1962-63, chmn., chief exec. officer, 1963-70; mgmt. cons., 1970—; pres. Brown Bros. Farms, Inc.; v.p. C.N.A. Financial Corp. Methodist. Clubs: Orlando Country, University (Orlando). Home: 803 Lake Davis Dr Orlando FL 32806

BROWN, PAUL MARVIN, Jr., oil refining co. exec.; b. Amite, La., Nov. 5, 1893; s. Paul Marvin and Mary Alice (Perry) B.; A.B., Centenary Coll., 1916, LL.D., 1966; A.M., So. Meth. U., 1917; m. Willie Eleanor Cavett, July 30, 1918; children—Eleanor (Mrs. Greve), Charles Ellis. Instr. classical langs. Centenary Coll., 1917-18; asst. cashier Am. Nat. Bank, Shreveport, La., 1919-25, cashier, 1925-30; cashier Continental Am. Bank and Trust Co., Shreveport, 1930-35; pres. gen. mgr. Bayon State Oil Corp., Shreveport, 1935—; became receiver Comml. Nat. Bank Shreveport, 1936, resigned; pres. Ida Gasoline Co., Inc., 1957—, Uni Prodn. Co., Inc., 1966—; chmn. bd. La. Bank and Trust Co., 1956—; pres. Caddo Light Aggregate Co., Inc., 1959—. Pres. Better Bus. Bur., Shreveport, 1963-64; treas., dir. Gulf South Research Inst., 1965—; mem. La. Commn. Higher Edn. Facilities; pres. Pub. Affairs Research Council of La., 1962-63. Mem. La. Civil Service Commn., 1941-48, 52-56, (chmn. 1947-48, 52-56). Trustee Centenary Coll. (treas. 1933-41; chmn., 1941-65). Served with U.S. Army, 1918-19; AEF. Mem. Kappa Alpha. Democrat. Methodist. Mason (K.T.). Clubs: Rotary (dist. gov. 1964-65), Shreveport. Home: 302 Linden St Shreveport LA 71104 Office: Louisiana Bank Bldg Shreveport LA 71101

BROWN, PAUL W., atty. gen. Ohio; b. Cleve., Jan. 14, 1915; s. William and Mary (Foster) B.; A.B., Ohio State U., 1937, J.D., 1939; m. Helen Page; children—Susan, Julie, Barbara, Mary Jeffrey, Molly, Daniel. Admitted to Ohio bar, 1939, U.S. Supreme Ct. bar; practiced in Youngstown, O., 1939- 40, 46-60; faculty, asst. to pres. Youngstown U.; judge 7th Dis. Appeals of Ohio, 1960-64, Ohio Supreme Ct., Columbus, 1964-69; atty. gen. state of Ohio, Columbus, 1969—. Del., Republican Nat. Conf., 1948. Served with AUS, 1941-45. Decorated Purple Heart, Silver Star. Mem. Ohio, Mahoning County bar assns., Inst. Jud. Adminstrn., Am. Legion, D.A.V., 1st Armored Div. Assn., Mil. Order Purple Heart. Mason. Home: 2396 Wimbledon Dr Columbus OH 43220 Office: State House Annex Columbus OH 43215

BROWN, PETER CAMPBELL, lawyer; b. August 12, 1913; s. Peter P. and Ellen (Campbell) B.; A.B., Fordham Coll., 1935, LL.B., 1938; LL.D., St. Bonaventure U., New York, 1951; m. Joan Gallagher, June 8, 1943; children—Peter Campbell, Patricia, Thomas, Michael, Robert. Admitted N.Y. State bar, 1938; practiced in Bklyn., 1938-41; asst. U.S. atty. for Eastern Dist. of N.Y. (Brooklyn), 1946; 1st. asst. criminal div., Dept. of Justice, 1947-48; exec. asst. to atty. gen. of U.S., 1948, spl. asst. to atty. gen. 1949-50; mem. subversive activities control bd. (under the Internal Security Act of 1950), 1950-53, chmn., 1952-53; commr. of investigation N.Y.C., 1954-55; corp. counsel City of N.Y., 1955-58; pvt. practice law as mem. firm Manning, Hollinger & Shea, 1958-65, firm Brown, Carlino & Emmanuel, 1965—. Dir. Thomas Pub. Co., Fedn. Bank & Trust Co. Bd., dirs. St. Mary's Coll., South Bend, Ind. From pvt. to maj., U.S. Army, 1942-45; ETO. Decorated: 6 Battle Stars on European African Middle Eastern ribbon, Fourragere of Belgium for Battle of Ardennes (The Bulge); named Knight Holy Sepulchre, Knight Malta. Fellow Am. Coll. Trial Lawyers, Bar Supreme Ct. U.S., Fed. District Courts, U.S. Court Appeals, Am., N.Y. State bar assns., V.F.W., Legion, Catholic Lawyers Guild, Assn. Bar City of N.Y., St. Patrick Soc. Bklyn. (past pres., dir.), Friendly Sons St. Patrick City N.Y., Fordham College Alumni Assn. (past pres.). Democrat. Roman Catholic. Clubs: Lawyers, Montauk (Bklyn.); Manhattan, New York Athletic, Pinnacle (N.Y.C.), Army-Navy (Washington); Pelham Country; Westchester Country (Rye, N.Y.). Home: 29 Witherbee Av Pelham Manor NY 10803 Office: 90 Park Av New York City NY 10016

BROWN, PHILIP BRANSFIELD, lawyer; b. Middletown, Conn., Mar. 30, 1924; s. Philip Joseph and Elizabeth Pauline (Bransfield) B.; B.A. (Olin scholar), Wesleyan U., Middletown, 1944; LL.B. (bd. editors Law Jour.), Yale, 1946; m. Elinor Merrill Kenney, Feb. 7, 1959; children—Elizabeth, Sarah, Marcia, Admitted to Conn. bar, 1946, D.C. bar, 1947, U.S. Supreme Ct., 1950; asso., then partner firm Cox, Langford, Stoddard & Cutler, Washington, 1946-62; partner firm Cox, Langford & Brown, 1962—. Pres. bd. trustees Wesleyan U.; trustee, sec. Meridian House Found.; bd. dirs. Madeira Sch., Greenway, Va. Mem. Am., D.C. bar assns., Yale Law Sch. Assn. (pres. Washington 1956-57, mem. nat. exec. com. 1957-58), Phi Beta Kappa. Clubs: Metropolitan, Nat. Capital Democratic (Washington). Home: 2425 Kalorama Rd NW Washington, DC 20008. Office: 1521 New Hampshire Av NW Washington, DC 20036.

BROWN, R. HARPER, packaging co. exec.; b. Oak Park, Ill., Apr. 22, 1923; s. Arthur E. and Edith (Watters) B.; A.B., Brown U., 1945; M.B.A., Harvard, 1947; m. Anne Richardson, Oct. 8, 1949; children—Carol, Margaret, Nancy, Linda. With Container Corp. Am., 1947—, v.p., 1965-67, sr. v.p., 1967—, also dir.; dir. Meyercord Co. Trustee Brown U. Served to lt. (j.g.) USNR, World War II. Mem. Ill. St. Andrews Soc., Alpha Delta Phi. Clubs: University (Chgo.); Exmoor Country (Highland Park, Ill.); Whitford Country (Exton, Pa.). Home; 965 Castlegate Ct Lake Forest, IL 60045. Office: 1 First National Plaza Chicago IL 60603

BROWN, RALPH MANNING, Jr., ins. co. exec.; b. Elizabeth, N.J., July 1, 1915; s. Ralph Manning and Anna Alethea (Rankin) B.; grad. Gilman Sch., 1932; A.B., Princeton, 1936; m. Margrette Burnham, Oct. 6, 1950; children—Anne Alethea, Ralph Manning. With Gen. Motors Acceptance Corp., 1936-51; asst. v.p. N.Y. Life Ins. Co., N.Y.C., 1951-53, 2d v.p., 1953-55, v.p., 1955-62, exec. v.p., 1962- 69, now pres., chief exec. officer, dir.; dir. Gt. Atlantic & Pacific Tea Co., La. Land & Exploration Co., Avon Products, Inc., Morgan Guaranty Trust Co., Union Camp Corp., Union Carbide Corp. Trustee Princeton. Clubs: University, Links (N.Y.C.); Pretty Brook Tennis (Princeton). Home: 50 Westcott Rd Princeton NJ 08540 Office: 51 Madison Av New York City NY 10010

BROWN, RALPH SHARP, Jr., educator; b. Federalsburg, Md., Apr. 1, 1913; s. Ralph Sharp and Ruth (Elliott) B.; grad. Phillips Exeter Acad., 1931; B.A., Yale, 1935, LL.B., 1939; m. Elizabeth Mills, Mar. 6, 1943; children—Lauren, Valerie, Lila. Admitted to N.Y. bar, 1941; with Yale Law Sch., New Haven, 1946—, prof. law, 1953—, exec. dir. Walter E. Meyer Research Inst. Law, 1958-65, trustee, 1966—, asso. dean Law Sch., 1965-70. Selectman of Guilford, 1953-57. Served as lt. USNR, 1942-46. Mem. Am. Civil Liberties Union (dir. 1954—), Am. Assn. U. Profs. (pres. 1968-70), Phi Beta Kappa. Author: Loyalty and Security (Harvard U. Henderson Meml. prize), 1958; also articles in profl. jours. and periodicals. Home: Old Quarry Guilford CT 06437 Office: Yale U New Haven CT 06520

BROWN, RAY EVERETT, univ. administr., educator; b. Union, S.C., Sept. 26, 1913; s. Rev. William Thomas and Fan (Casey) B.; student Gardner Webb Coll., 1932-34; S.B., U. of N.C., 1937; M.B.A., U. of Chicago, 1943; L.H.D., Wake Forest U., 1958; m. Mary Norvell Witherspoon, Nov. 26, 1937; children—Margaret Witherspoon, Mary Norvell, Barbara Casey. County mgr. Cleveland County, N.C., 1937-40; supt. Shelby (N.C.) Hosp., 1940-42; supt. N.C. Baptist Hosp. (Winston- Salem) and pro. hosp. administrn. Bowman-Gray Sch. of Medicine, Wake Forest U., 1943-45; supt. U. Chgo. Clinics and Hosps., 1945-61; v.p. for adminstrn. U. Chgo., 1961-64, asso. prof. sch. of bus. 1947-53, prof. 1953-64; asso. dir., grad. program in hosp. adminstrn., 1947-51, dir., 1951-62; prof. adminstrn., dir. grad. program in hosp. adminstrn. Duke, 1964-67; prof. adminstrn. Harvard, 1967-70, exec. v.p. affiliated hosps., 1967-70; prof. mgmt. Northwestern U., Chgo., 1970—, exec. v.p. Med. Center, 1970—. Mem. exec. com. White House Conference on Health, 1965; trustee U. Chicago Settlement 1945-54, pres., 1952-54; cons. surgeon-gen. USAF, 1957-63, surgeon-gen. U.S. Army, 1964-70; trustee Home for Destitute Crippled Children, 1950; dir. Chgo. Welfare Council, 1953-59. Mem. Nat. Joint Commn. Accreditation Hosps., 1955-61; chmn. Nat. Joint Council Health Care of Aged, 1960-61; chmn. Nat. Task Force Health Facilities, 1963-66; mem. Nat. Commn. To Study Medicine, 1967-68; mem. com. on med. edn. A.M.A., 1967—. Bd. dirs. Blue Cross Plan of Chgo., 1960-64, 70—, Community Fund Chgo., 1959-64 (exec. com. 1961-64), Health Information Found., 1961-68. Recipient Gold Medal award Am. Assn. for Hosp. Planning, 1963. Fellow Royal Coll. Health (Eng.), Am. Pub. Health Assn., Am. Coll. Hosp. Adminstrs. (bd. regents 1952-61, pres. 1959-60, Gold Medal award 1969); mem. Am. Hosp. Assn. (pres. 1955-56, trustee 1954-57, ho. of dels. 1954-57, 59-62, Distinguished Service award 1963), A.I.M., Assn. U. Program in Hosp. Adminstrn. (pres. 1966-67), Chgo. Hosp. Council (pres. 1952-53, trustee 1950-63), Ill. Hosp. Assn. (trustee 1953-60, pres. 1958-59, recipient Distinguished Service award 1962), U. Hosps. Exec. Council, U. Chgo. Gen. Alumni Assn. (bd. dirs. 1947-57), Phi Beta Kappa, Beta Gamma Sigma, Baptist. Club: Economics (Chgo.). Author: Hospitals Visualized (with others), 1952; Criteria for Student Selection, 1958, Graduate Education for Hospital Administration, 1959; Judgment in Administration, 1966; also articles on mgmt. and hosps. to profl. jours. Mem. editorial bd. Hosp. Mgmt., 1951—, Med. World News, 1967—, Modern Hosp. Mag., 1958—, Med. Edn., 1968—. Home: 1212 N Lake Shore Dr Chicago IL 60611

BROWN, RAYMOND RUSSELL, educator; b. Alberta, Can., Dec. 23, 1926; s. William Fred and Anna Elizabeth (Wilson) B.; B.S., U. Alta., 1948, M.S., 1950; Ph.D., U. Wis., 1953; m. Eleanor Jane Springer, Dec. 27, 1952; children—Laura Jane, Jeffrey Frederick, Douglas Edward. Came to U.S., 1950, naturalized, 1956. Instr. chemistry U. Alta., 1948-50; prof. cancer research U. Wis. Med. Sch., Madison, 1955—. Mem. Am. Assn. Cancer Research, Am. Chem. Soc., Am. Soc. Biol. Chemists. Contbr. articles, revs. to research publs. Home: 2817 Van Hise Av Madison WI 53705

BROWN, REYNOLD FREDRICK, educator, physician; b. Homestead, Pa., Dec. 26, 1916; s. Joseph H. and Jeanne (Fredrick) B.; A.B., U. Cal., 1944, M.D., 1947; m. Edwina Lee Vandivert, Sept. 14, 1941; 1 dau., Patricia Lynn. Intern U. Cal. Hosp., San Francisco, 1947-48; clin. prof. radiology U. Cal. Med. Sch. at San Francisco, 1968—, asst. to chancellor environmental health and safety, 1965—, clin. prof. preventive medicine, 1968—, radiation safety officer, 1956—; chief med. examiner N.Y. Life Ins. Co.; cons. Cal. Dept. Health, Dept. Health, Edn. and Welfare, AEC. Mem. Radiol. Soc.

N.A. (pres. 1970), Cal. (pres. 1969), San Francisco (pres. 1969) radiol. socs. Home: 1482 Paseo Nogales Alamo CA 94507 Office: Univ California San Francisco CA 94122

BROWN, RICHARD FARGO, found. exec.; b. N.Y.C., Sept. 20, 1916; s. Percy Melville and Hazel (Wyatte) B.; A.B., Bucknell U., 1940; postgrad. N.Y.U., 1940-42; M.A., Harvard, 1948, Ph.D., 1952; m. Polly Story, Dec. 19, 1941; 1 son, Michael Fargo; m. 2d, Jane Hoag, 1968; 1 son, Richard B. Teaching fellow Harvard, 1947-49, vis. prof. fine arts, 1954; research scholar, lectr. Frick Collection, N.Y.C., 1949-54; chief curator Los Angeles County Mus., 1955-62; dir. Los Angeles County Mus. Art, 1962-66, also trustee; head dept. art County Los Angeles, 1961-66; dir. Kimbell Art Found., Ft. Worth, 1966—. Trustee Mus. Western Art, Ft. Worth. Mem. Cal. Arts Commn. Served with USNR, 1942-46. Decorated Order Arts and Letters (France). Bacon-Rich travelling fellow Harvard, 1949. Mem. Coll. Art Assn. Am. (pres., dir.), Am. Assn. Art Mus. Dirs. (sec.-treas., exec. com., pres. 1970-71), Am. Assn. Museums (council), Western Assn. Museums (pres.), Phi Beta Kappa. Home: 4001 Edgehill Rd Fort Worth TX 76116 Office: Kimbell Art Found Ft Worth Club Bldg Fort Worth TX 76102

BROWN, RICHARD KETTEL, mathematician, educator; b. Long Branch, N.J., Feb. 3, 1928; s. George Borden and Florence (Kettel) B.; B.S., Muhlenberg Coll., 1948; M.S., Rutgers U., 1950, Ph.D., 1952; m. Veronica Augusta Kasten, Sept. 3, 1955; children—Blake Kettel, Amie Kasten. Adj. lectr., then asst. prof. Rutgers U., 1955-58; research mathematician U.S. Army Electronics Lab., Ft. Monmouth, N.J., 1958-60, 61-65, David Sarnoff Labs., Princeton, N.J., 1960-61; prof., chmn. math. dept. Kent. (O.) State U., 1965—. Served with AUS, 1953-55. Mem. Am. Math. Soc., Math. Assn. Am., Sigma Xi. Mem. United Ch. Christ. Contbr. articles to profl. jours. Home: 5790 Horning Rd Kent, OH 44240.

BROWN, RICHARD LEE, lawyer; b. Ft. Worth, Dec. 7, 1925; s. Marvin H. and Janie (McIntosh) B.; student Rice U., 1942-43; LL.B., U. Tex., 1949; LL.M., George Washington U., 1954; m. Elizabeth McPherson, Nov. 19, 1949; children—Beverly Elizabeth, Leigh Ann. Admitted to Tex. bar, 1949; practice in Ft. Worth, 1956—; asst. dist. atty., Tarrant County, 1949- 50; spl. atty. Chief Counsel's Office, Internal Revenue Service, Washington, 1953-56; partner Friedman & Brown, 1956-60; partner Stone, Parker, Snakard & Brown, 1961-66; partner Stone, Tilley, Parker, Snakard, Law & Brown, 1967—. Dir. Riverside State Bank, Ft. Worth. Chmn. bd., chmn. competition Van Cliburn Internat. Piano Competition, 1966-69. Served with AUS, 1944-46, U.S. Army, 1950-53. Decorated Bronze Star medal. Fellow Tex. Bar Found.; mem. Am., Tex., Ft. Worth-Tarrant County bar assns., Newcomen Soc. N.Am. Office: Ft Worth Nat Bank Bldg Fort Worth TX 76102

BROWN, RICHARD LELAND, educator; A.B., Amherst Coll., 1934; A.M., Wesleyan U., Middletown, Conn., 1936; Ph.D., Mass. Inst. Tech., 1942. Asst. physics Wesleyan U., 1934-37; teaching fellow Mass. Inst. Tech., 1937-40, mem. research staff, 1941-47; prof. physics Allegheny Coll., Meadville, Pa., 1947—, now William S. Twining prof. physics. Address: 211 Meadow St Meadville PA 16335

BROWN, RICHARD MAXWELL, educator, historian; b. Mobridge, S.D., July 26, 1927; s. John Floyd and Norma (McClary) B.; B.A., Reed Coll., 1952; A.M., Harvard, 1955, Ph.D., 1959; m. Estella Dee Cutler, Jan. 25, 1951; children-Brooks Richard, Laura Jean. Research fellow Harvard Center Study History Liberty in Am., 1959-60; asst. prof., then asso. prof. Rutgers U., 1960-67; vis. prof. Columbia, 1967; prof. History Coll. William and Mary, 1967—; cons. Nat. Commn. Causes and Prevention of Violence, 1968-69. Mem. council Inst. Early Am. History and Culture, 1969—. Served with AUS, 1946-48. Mem. Am., So., Western hist. assns., Orgn. Am. Historians, Am. Assn. U. Profs., Phi Beta Kappa. Democrat. Unitarian. Author: The South Carolina Regulators, 1963; American Violence, 1970; (with Alison G. Olson) Anglo- American Political Relations 1675-1775, 1970; also articles. Bd. editors William and Mary Quar., 1969-70. Home: 106 Spring Rd Williamsburg VA 23185

BROWN, RICHARD P., ret. corp. exec.; b. Phila., Sept. 27, 1884; s. Edward and Fannie (Harding) B.; student Wm. Penn Charter Sch., (hon.) D. Eng., Drexel Inst. Tech.; m. Edith Gillette, Oct. 5, 1918 (dec. 1957); children—Anita (Mrs. Anita Brown Wilson), Richard P., Jr. Organized Brown Instrument Co., Phila., 1910, pres., 1910-35, chmn. bd. dirs. 1935-48, when co. became div. of Mpls.-Honeywell Regulator Co., was v.p., dir. div., now. dir. emeritus. Patentee on measuring, signaling and automatically controlling temperature, pressure and elevator positioning. Apptd. by Gov. George H. Earle mem. of com. to investigate alleged disfranchisement of electors in Phila., 1938; apptd. by Gov. Arthur H. James to organize new Dept. of Commerce, State of Pa., and served as sec. of commerce, 1939-41; chmn. Pa. State Planning Bd., Pa. Commn. on Interstate Cooperation, Pa. World's Fair Commn., Anthracite Emergency Com.; mem. Interstate Commn. on the Del. River Basin Commn. To Report on Living Conditions of Negro Urban Population, 1939-41; regional cons. Dist. No. 4, Def. Plant Corp., Washington, 1942-43; mem. Def. Workers Transp. Com., 1942; dep. dir. in charge pdn., WPB, Region 3, 1943-44; industry mem. W.L.B., Region 3, 1945; industry Wage Stblzn. Bd., Region 3, 1946, chmn. joint airport zoning bd. Phila. and Del. County, 1948-53; mem. U.S. Assay Commn., 1954- -. Dir. Germantown Hosp., Phila.; trustee Drexel Inst. Tech., 1943-58, vice chmn., 1945-56, chmn., 1956-58, hon. chmn., 1958—. Fellow Am. Soc. M.E.; mem. Sci. Apparatus Makers Assn. Am. (pres. 1933-34), I.E.E.E., Franklin Inst., Instrument Soc. Am. (hon.). Republican (del. to nat. conv., 1940; chmn. Eisenhower Citizens Com., Phila. 1952, 54). Episcopalian. Clubs: Union League, Phila. Country, Cricket (Phila.); Eastward-Ho Country (Chatham, Mass.). Home: 3830 Oak Rd Philadelphia, PA 19129. Office: 1100 Two Girard Plaza Philadelphia PA 19102

BROWN, RICHARD PARKE, corp. exec.; b. Wichita, Kan., Feb. 25, 1912; s. John Wesley and Golda Leona (Dodds) B.; A.B., Washburn Coll., 1934; B.D., Colgate-Rochester Div. Sch., 1938; M.A., Cornell, 1939; m. Marcie Geraldine Williams, Aug. 20, 1932; children—Barbara Christine (Mrs. R.N. Page), Suzanne Louise (Mrs. Henry). Dir. personnel relations Mesta Machine Co., 1946-51, dir. indsl. relations, 1954-63, v.p. finance, 1963-68, exec. v.p., 1968- -, also dir.; dir. O. Hommel Co., Asko Industries, Inc., Italmesta (Rome), Forsyth Engring. and Machine Corp. Adv. mem. Pan-Am. Internat. Monetary Fund. Dir. Community Fund, Pitts. Fellow Soc. Advancement Mgmt. (dir., past pres. Pitts.); mem. Am. Mgmt. Assn., Pitts. Personnel Assn. (dir., past pres.), Pa. Assn. for Blind, psychol. Services Pitts. (pres., dir.), Fgn. Policy Assn., Indsl. Relations Research Assn., Sigma Alpha Epsilon. Clubs: University, Cornell (Pitts), Duquesne, University (Washington). Author: The Development of Public Sentiment Against Child Labor, 1910-35; The Development of Industrial Democracy, 1900-40; The Human Factor in Industry; articles in field. Home: 5870 Aylesboro Av Pittsburgh, PA 15217. Office: PO Box 1466 Pittsburgh PA 15230

BROWN, RICHARD ROLLAND, govt. ofcl.; b. Littleton, Colo., Jan. 6, 1902; s. Clarence Edward and Clara Alice (Bivins) B.; A.B., U. Denver, 1926, A.M., 1927; LL.D., Coll. of South Jersey, 1938; m. Sarah Marian Armstrong, Aug. 20, 1927; children—Laurel Jean, Richard Bolland. Tchr., boys' advisor, Byers Jr. High Sch., Denver, 1927-35; state dir. Nat. Youth Adminstrn., 1935, dep. exec. dir., Washington, 1936-38; asst. dir., Am. Youth Commn. of Am. Council on Edn., 1938-39; asst. chief of distbn. Surplus Marketing Adminstrn., U.S. Dept. Agr., 1939-41; asst. chief apprenticeship div. U.S. Dept. Labor, 1941-42; dir. Div. Adminstrn., Nat. War Labor Bd., 1942-43; dir., Central Adminstrv. Services, Exec. Office of Pres., Office Emergency Mgmt., 1943- 44; asst. chief, Bur. of Areas, UNRRA, 1944-46, Bur. Services, 1946-47; dep. dir. gen. and chief exec. officer UNRRA, 1947-48, western hemisphere rep., prep. commn. IRO of UN, 1947; spl. rep. of UNRRA dir. gen., Prague Czechoslovakia, 1946, Tirana, Albania, 1946; dir. exec. staff, econ. area Dept. of State, 1949, gen. mgr. U.S. High Commn. Germany, 1951, dir. Office of Field Coordination, U.S. Escapee Program, Frankfurt, Germany, 1952-58; dir. Office of Refugee and Migration Affairs, 1958-63; spl. asst. to asst. sec. Dept. State, 1963-67, cons. to sec. of state, 1967—. Decorated Order of White Lion (Czechoslovakia), 1947, officer Cross Polonia Restituta (Poland), 1948. Mem. N.E.A., Am. Pub. Welfare Assn., Scarab, Kappa Delta Phi, Phi Delta Kappa. Democrat. Presbyn. Author: The Reflecting Pool, 1937; The King's First Gift, 1940. Contbr. articles on youth, edn. methods, tng., counseling to edn. jours. and numerous articles on world conditions to nat. jours. Home: 3303 Upland Terrace Washington DC 20015 Office: Dept of State Washington DC 20520

BROWN, ROBERT, actor; appeared in N.Y. prodns. Skipper Next to God, Barefoot in Athens, Come of Age, The Dark is Light Enough, The Tempest, King John, Two Gentlemen of Verona, The Private Ear and the Public Eye, Ulysses in Nighttown, Portrait of the Artist, The Deputy; toured in The Circle, Member of the Wedding, The Corn is Green; co-dir. Theatre Group prodn. Ladies of Hanover Tower; performer on TV programs. Address: care Gen Artists Corp 9025 Wilshire Blvd Beverly Hills CA 90211*

BROWN, ROBERT A., corp. exec.; b. Rensselaer, Ind., May 14, 1918; s. Frank and Kathryn Morgan) B.; B.S., Ind. U., 1947; m. Marcella June Jones, June 29, 1944; children—Michael, James. Auditor, Peat, Marwick, Mitchell & Co., Chgo., 1947-51; controller Borg-Warner Internat. Corp., Chgo., 1951-52, treas., v.p. 1952-64, pres., 1964-67, chmn. 1964—; v.p. mgmt., services Borg Warner Corp., 1967—. Served with USAAF, 1941-45. Elk, Moose. Clubs: Internat. Trade Ill. Athletic. Home: 2206 Linden Dr Valparaiso, IN 46383. Office: 200 S Michigan Av Chicago IL 60604

BROWN, ROBERT ARTHUR, Jr., oil exec.; b. Calgary, Alberta, Can., Mar. 20, 1914; s. Robert Arthur and Christine (McLaughlin) B.; grad. U. Alberta, 1936; m. Genevieve Mary Sulphur, Feb. 18, 1950; children—Pamela Mary, Lois Lorraine, Carolyn Genevieve. Pres., mng. dir. Home Oil Co. Ltd.; pres., dir. United Oils, Ltd., Calgary; dir. Trans-Can. Pipe Lines Ltd., Crown Trust Co., Canadian Nat. Rys., Air Can. Home: 2211 7th St SW Calgary Alberta Canada Office: 304 6th Av SW Calgary Alberta Canada

BROWN, ROBERT BAIRD, bus. cons.; b. Yonkers, N.Y., June 5, 1906; s. Marshall Stewart and Margaret (Baird) B.; A.B., Cornell U., 1927, A.M., 1928; m. Matilda Serly Peary, Jan. 12, 1940; 1 dau., Beverly Jean. Asst. in history Cornell U., 1927; with Gimbel Brothers, N.Y.C., 1929; advt. copywriter, Daniel Starch & Staff, N.Y.C., 1929-30; account exec., Pedlar & Ryan, Inc., N.Y.C., 1930-35; advt. mgr., Bristol-Myers Co., N.Y.C., 1936-45, dir. advt., 1946-47, asst. v.p., 1940-45, v.p., 1946- 50, exec. v.p., 1958-65, pres. products div., 1950-57, also dir.; pres. Controlled Circulation Audit, Inc., 1944-46; vice chmn. and treas. Cooperative Analysis of Broadcasting, Inc., 1944-46; dir. Dole Co., 1965-70; asst. to dean Coll. Bus. Adminstrn., U. Hawaii, Honolulu, 1965-68; pub. Honolulu Mag., 1968-71; bus. cons., 1971—. Dir. Honolulu Symphony Soc., Honolulu Community Theatre, Hawaii Heart Assn. Chmn. bd. Assn. Nat. Advertisers, Inc., 1947-48; dir. Advertising Research Found., 1948-52. Mem. Toilet Goods Assn. (dir.), Market Research Council, Proprietary Assn. (pres. 1958-60), Phi Beta Kappa, Zeta Psi, Phi Kappa Phi. Clubs: River (N.Y.C.); Pacific, Outrigger Canoe. Home: 4999 Kahala Av Honolulu HI 96816 Office: 1000 Bishop St Honolulu HI 96813

BROWN, ROBERT CLARENCE, Jr., patent lawyer; b. Evanston, Ill., Sept. 7, 1906; s. R. Clarence and Ella (Pierce) B.; B.S., Northwestern U., 1926, J.D., 1928, M.S., 1929; m. Alice Haas, June 15, 1931; children—Lawrence Haas, Warren Pierce, Ronald Owen. Admitted to Ill. bar, 1929, pvt. practice patent law, Chgo., 1929—; partner firm Mann, Brown, McWilliams and Bradway, 1950—; v.p. Internat. Research and Devel. Co., 1949-66. Cons. dir. tech. devel. div. WPB, 1942-43; chmn. Assn. Def. Com. of Chicago Tech. Socs.; pres. North Shore Area council Boy Scouts Am., 1949-51, exec. com. region 7, 1953—, hon. life mem. exec. com., 1968—, vice chmn., 1962-64; past chmn. adv. council Northwestern U. Technol. Inst.; trustee Northwestern U. Alumni Assn. (pres. 1963-64), Tau Beta Pi, Delta Mem. Am., Chgo. bar assns., Chgo Patent Law Assn. (pres. 1961), Northwestern University Alumni Assn. (pres. 1963-64), Tau Beta Pi, Delta Tau Delta, Phi Alpha Delta. Republican. Presbyn. Clubs: Northwestern University, Physics, Union League (Chgo.); Exmoor Country (Highland Park, Ill.); University (Evanston, Ill.). Home: 201 Michigan Av Highwood IL 60040 Office: 53 W Jackson Blvd Chicago IL 60604

BROWN, ROBERT DIXON, chemist, educator; b. Banks, Ala., Nov. 13, 1902; s. Charles Kane and Minnie Lee (Barr); diploma Troy State Tchrs. Coll., 1924; B.S., U. Ala., 1926, M.S., 1928; Ph.D. (teaching fellow), Stanford, 1933; m. Sarah Natalie Thornton, Dec. 29, 1928 (dec. Feb. 1967); 1 son, Robert Dixon; m. 2d, Lillian Fay Brown, Jan. 20, 1968. Prin. Florala (Ala.) Jr. High Sch., 1924-25; tchr. sci. Montgomery County High Sch., 1926-27, 28- 31; instr. chemistry San Mateo (Cal.) Jr. Coll., 1933-35; vis. instr. Stephens Coll., 1935-36; instr. chemistry and physics Cal. Poly. Inst., 1936-37; prof. chemistry and math. Livingston (Ala.) State Tchrs. Coll., 1937-42; prof. chemistry U. Ala., Tuscaloosa, 1946-71, dean sch. chemistry, 1952-65, dean emeritus, 1971; sr. chemist Oak Ridge Nat. Lab., 1951-52. Served as maj. AUS, 1942-46, 50-51. Mem. Am. Chem. Soc., Sigma Xi, Gamma Sigma Epsilon. Home: 1608 First Av Tuscaloosa AL 35401

BROWN, ROBERT EUGENE, mag. publisher; b. Lynn, Mass., Sept. 2, 1923; s. James Edward and Sara May (Taylor) B.; grad. Tilton (N.H.) Jr. Coll., 1942; m. Elizabeth Whitcomb; children (by previous marriage)—Robert Eugene, Barrett Benton, Scott McFarlane. With R. Wallace & Sons, silversmiths, Wallingford, Conn., 1946-50; with Hearst Mags., Inc., N.Y.C., 1950—, pub. Bride and Home mag., 1958-60, pub. Cosmopolitan mag., 1960-62, advt. dir. Harper's, asso. pub. Town and Country mag., 1963—; advt. mgr. Teen Mag. Served with AUS, 1942-46. Home: 121 E 48th St New York City NY 10022 Office: 551 Fifth Av New York City NY 10022

BROWN, ROBERT GRATTAN, banker; b. Memphis, June 21, 1906; s. Robert Grattan and Anne (Clarke) B.; student Southwestern at Memphis, 1925-27; LL.B., U. Memphis, 1930; m. Eleanor R. Crenshaw, Nov. 17, 1928; children—Eleanor (Mrs. Robert H. Weaver), Robert Grattan III. Admitted to Tenn. bar, 1930; clk. Bank of Commerce & Trust Co., Memphis, 1927-33; with Nat. Bank of Commerce, Memphis, 1933—, sr. v.p., chmn. trust com., 1969—; pres., dir. Frederick Smith Enterprise Co., Inc.; dir. Sharvania Oil & Grease Corp. First v.p., dir. U. Tenn. Memphis Med. Units Found. Mem. Kappa Sigma. Rotarian. Clubs: Memphis Country, Petroleum, University (Memphis). Home: 305 N Garland St Memphis TN 38104 Office: 45 S 2d St Memphis TN 38101

BROWN, ROBERT GUY, educator; B.A., U. R.I., 1949; M.A., U. N.C. at Chapel Hill, 1951, Ph.D., 1960. Prof. sociology, chmn. dept. George Washington U., Washington. Office: Dept Sociology George Washington U Washington DC 20006*

BROWN, ROBERT HAROLD, educator, geographer; b. Rochester, N.Y., Sept. 16, 1921; s. Harold Cecil and Marion (Johnson) B.; B.S., U. Minn., 1948, M.A., 1949; Ph.D., U. Chgo., 1957; m. Helene Adeline Zukey, Sept. 1, 1945; children—Suzanne Odette, Kurtis Johnson, Mem. faculty St. Cloud (Minn.) State Coll., 1949- 64; prof. geography, chmn. dept. U. Wyo., 1964—. Mem. Assn. Am. Geographers, Nat. Council Geog. Edn., Regional Sci. Assn., Phi Delta Kappa. Author: Political Areal Functional Organization, 1957; (with Phillip Tideman) Atlas of Minnesota Occupancy, 3d edit. 1969; Wyoming Occupance Atlas, 1970. Home: 1303 Mitchell St Laramie WY 82070

BROWN, ROBERT HENRY, coll. pres.; b. Sioux Falls, S.D., Aug. 27, 1915; s. Harry James and Isabelle Lee (Ross) B.; B.A., Union Coll., Lincoln, Neb., 1940; M.S., U. Neb., 1942; Ph.D., U. Wash., 1950; m. Ruth Frances Miller, May 26, 1942; children—Rebecca Sue, Judith Ann. Asst. instr. physics U. Neb., 1940-42; research engr. Sylvania Products Co., 1942-45; head sci. dept. Canadian Union Coll., Lacobe, Alta., 1945-47; instr. physics U. Wash., 1948-49; faculty Walla Walla Coll., 1947-70, prof. physics, 1954-70, v.p., 1961-70; pres., prof. physics Union Coll., Lincoln, Neb., 1970—. Mem. Am. Assn. Physics Tchrs., Am. Phys. Soc., Am. Geophys. Union, Sigma Xi. Rotarian. Home: 4840 Bancroft St Lincoln NB 68506

BROWN, ROBERT HORATIO, orthopedic surgeon; b. Dedham, Mass., Aug. 30, 1917; s. Walter Horatio and Harriet (Crocker) B.; B.S., Tufts U., 1940; M.D., Harvard, 1943; m. Virginia Fales Lane, Dec. 26, 1943; children—Edith Persis, Robert Horatio, Betsy. Intern, surg. resident Mass. Gen. Hosp., 1944-45; surg. resident Cushing VA Hosp., 1946-47; orthopedic resident USN, Duke, 1952-56; commd. lt. (j.g.) USN, 1945; ret., 1946; commd. lt. USN, 1950, advanced through grades to capt., 1959; chief orthopedic service U.S. Naval Hosp., Nat. Naval Med. Center, Bethesda, Md., 1964-70; gen. practice medicine, Sharon, Mass., 1947-50; course dir. orthopedic pathology Armed Forces Inst. Pathology, 1963-64; asst. clin. prof. orthopaedic surgery George Washington U. Sch. Medicine, 1968-70; attending orthopedic surgeon Eastern Me. Med. Center, 1970—, St. Joseph's Hosp., Bangor, Me., 1970—. Navy liaison mem. musculoskeletal com. NRC, 1965-70, surg. study group B. NIH, 1968-70. Diplomate Am. Bd. Orthopedic Surgery. Fellow A.C.S. (mem. com. on trauma), Am. Assn. for Surgery Trauma; mem. A.M.A., Mass. Med. Soc., Am. Acad. Orthopedic Surgeons, Assn. Mil. Surgeons U.S., Soc. Med. Cons. to Armed Forces, Me. Med. Assn., Phi Beta Kappa. Home: MRC-Box 45 Bangor ME 04401 Office: 35 2d St Bangor ME 04401

BROWN, ROBERT HOWARD, mut. funds exec.; b. Los Angeles, Jan. 9, 1925; s. Robert Howard and Margaret M. (Harris) B.; student Occidental Coll., 1943, U. So. Cal., 1949-51; m. Jane M. Mountford, July 29, 1945; children—Robert Howard III, Linda Lee. Partner Brown, Bechard & Co., investments, Norfolk, Va., 1957-59; Mid-west dist. mgr. Broad Street Sales Corp., 1959-61, pres., dir., 1961-65; v.p., nat. sales mgr., dir. Keystone Co., Boston, 1965- 68; v.p. Keystone Provident Life Ins. Co., Kelly & Morey, Inc., 1968—; v.p. New Eng. Financial Services, Inc. (marketing div. of Integrated Resources). Served to lt. USNR, 1943-56. Decorated D.F.C., Air medal (3). Mem. Phi Gamma Delta. Club: Columbine Country. Home: Box 609 Bolton Landing NY 12814 Office: 295 Madison Av New York City NY 10017

BROWN, ROBERT LEE, physician, educator; b. Franklin, Pa., Feb. 26, 1908; s. Robert E. and Amy (Lee) B.; A.B., U. Mich., 1929; M.D., Harvard, 1933; m. Alice Johnston, Sept. 26, 1940; children—David W., Jean A., Anne K. Clin. fellow, resident surgeon Meml. Hosp., N.Y.C., 1935-38; instr. surgery U. Rochester Sch. Medicine, 1939-42, asso. surgery, 1947-52; asso. surgery Emory U. Sch. Medicine, Atlanta, 1952-54, asst. prof., 1954-57, asso. prof., 1957-66, prof., 1966—; dir. Robert Winship Clinic, Emory U., 1958-66, Emory U. Clinic, 1966—. Diplomate Am. Bd. Surgery. Fellow A.C.S.; mem. A.M.A., Am. Cancer Soc. (exec. bd. Ga., nat. dir.), Am. Radium Soc., James Ewing Soc., Ga. Med. Assn., Fulton County Med. Soc. Presbyn. Home: 321 Robin Hood Rd NE Atlanta GA 30309

BROWN, ROBERT MCAFEE, clergyman, educator; b. Carthage, Ill., May 28, 1920; s. George William and Ruth Myrtle (McAfee) B.; B.A., Amherst Coll., 1943, D.D., 1958; B.D., Union Theol. Sem., N.Y.C., 1945; Ph.D., Columbia, 1951; postgrad. Mansfield Coll., Oxford (Eng.) U., 1949-50, St. Mary's Coll., 1959, St. Andrews (Scotland) U., 1959-60; Litt.D., U. San Francisco, 1964; L.H.D., Lewis and Clark College, 1964; LL.D., U. Notre Dame, 1965, Boston Coll., 1965; m. Sydney Thompson Brown, June 21, 1944; children—Peter Thomson, Mark McAfee, Alison McAfee, Thomas Seabury. Ordained to ministry Presbyn. Ch., 1944; asst. chaplain Amherst Coll., 1946-48; prof. religion, chmn. dept. Macalester Coll., St. Paul, 1951- 53; faculty Union Theol. Sem., N.Y.C., 1953-62; prof. religion Stanford (Cal.), 1962—. Served as chaplain USNR, 1945-46. Mem. Am. Theol. Soc., Soc. Theol. Discussion, Phi Beta Kappa. Author: P. T. Forsyth: Prophet for Today, 1952; The Bible Speaks to You, 1955; The Significance of the Church, 1956; (with Gustave Weigel) An American Dialogue, 1960; The Spirit of Protestantism, 1961; Observer in Rome: A Protestant Report on the Vatican Council, 1964; The Collected Writings of St. Hereticus, 1964. Gen. editor: The Layman's Theological Library, 12 volumes, 1956-58. Translator: (deDietrich) God's Unfolding Purpose, 1960; (Casalis) Portrait of Karl Barth, 1963; (Dumas) Dietrich Bonhoeffer: Theologian of Reality, 1971. Editor: (with David Scott) The Challenge to Reunion, 1963; The Spirit of Protestantism, 1965; The Ecumenical Revolution, 1967; (with others) Vietnam: Crisis of Conscience, 1967. Contbr. books, mem. editorial bd. various mags. and jours. Home: 837 Cedro Way Stanford CA 94305

BROWN, ROBERT MINGE, lawyer; b. Mobile, Oct. 16, 1911; s. Collier Harrison Minge, Jr. and Madie (Diggett) B.; A.B., Stanford U., 1931; B.C.L. (Rhodes scholar), Oriel Coll., Oxford (Eng.) U., 1934; m. Gloria Frances Gillingham, May 29, 1935; children—Douglas Minge, Harrison Minge. Admitted to Cal. bar, 1935, since practiced San Francisco; partner firm McCutchen, Doyle, Brown & Enersen, and predecessors, 1946—. Chmn. bd. Cal. Water Service Co., 1961—; dir. San Jose Water Works Co., Hawlett-Packard Co., Greyhound Corp. Trustee Stanford U. Served with USNR, 1942-46. Mem. Am., Cal., San Francisco bar assns., Phi Beta Kappa. Clubs: Bohemian, Pacific-Union (San Francisco); Burlingame (Cal.) Country. Home: 943 Hayne Rd Hillsborough CA 94010 Office: 601 California St San Francisco CA 94108

BROWN, ROBERT MONTGOMERY, architect; b. Phila., June 22, 1908; s. Clarence Montgomery and Luella (Conwell) B.; grad. Hotchkiss Sch., Lakeville, Conn., 1926; A.B., Princeton, 1930; B.Arch., N.Y. U., 1933; m. Ysobel Rush McClain, Feb. 24, 1948; 1 adopted dau., Diana McFarlain (Mrs. William M. Samuels). Propr. own firm in Phila., 1938-67, in Toms River, N.J., 1967—; prin. works include comml. bldgs.; co-designer Phila. Eve. Bull. bldg., 1952. Served with USNR, 1942-45. Decorated Bronze Star medal. Address: Trebosy Haines Rd Toms River NJ 08753

BROWN, ROBERT ORVILLE, lawyer; b. Duncan, Okla., Feb. 26, 1908; s. Robert Henry and Annie (Cund) B.; student Kemper Mil. Acad., 1926-27; A.B., LL.B., U. Okla., 1932; m. Frances Virginia Johnson, July 29, 1933; children—Ann Kinser, Sally North. Admitted to Okla. bar, 1932; with legal dept. Halliburton Co., Duncan, Okla., 1932—, gen. counsel, 1946—, v.p., 1954—, sr. v.p., sec., 1969—; sr. v.p., gen. counsel, dir. Halliburton Services div., 1967-69, dir., 1969—. Mem. Am., Okla., Stephens County bar assns., Am. Soc. Corporate Secs., N.A.M. Baptist. Elk. Home: 2102 Country Club Terrace Duncan OK 73533 Office: Box 1431 Duncan OK 73533

BROWN, ROBERT RAYMOND, bishop; b. Garden City, Kan., June 16, 1910; s. Joseph L. and Madeleine R. S. (Wells) B.; B.A., St. Mary's U., 1933; M.Div., Va. Theol. Sem., 1937, D.D., 1956; D.D., U. of South, 1956; m. Warwick Rust, Nov. 3, 1937; children—Anne W., Robert L., Katherine W. Ordained priest Episcopal Ch., 1937; priest-in-charge St. Albans Ch., Harlingen, Tex., 1937-40, All Saints Ch., San Benito, Tex., 1937-40; asst. rector, Houston, 1940-41; rector, Waco, Tex., 1941-47, Richmond, Va., 1947-55; consecrated bishop, 1955; bishop co-adjutor Diocese of Ark., 1955-56, bishop, 1956-70; rector St. Thaddeus Ch., Chattanooga, 1970—. Chmn. Commn. on Evangelism of Episcopal Ch. Regent U. of South; trustee All Saints Jr. Coll., Vicksburg, Miss., Theol. Sem. of Southwest, Astin, Tex. Author: Miracle of the Cross, 1954; Friendly Enemies, 1955; Bigger than Little Rock, 1958; Alive Again, 1964. Home: 4524 Murray Hill Dr Chattanooga TN 37416 Office: 4300 Locksley Lane Chattanooga TN 37416

BROWN, ROBERT UTTING, editor; b. Yonkers, N.Y., Oct. 20, 1912; s. James Wright and Sarah A. (Wilson) B.; B.A., Dartmouth, 1934; student Empire State Sch. Printing, Ithaca, N.Y., 1935; m. Susan C. Steele, May 21, 1938; children—Robin (Mrs. Richard M. Woods), Elizabeth (Mrs. W.I. Phillips, Jr.). Reporter Trenton (N.J.) Times, 1935; reporter United Press, Phila., 1935; reporter, apprentice editorial writer Auburn (N.Y.) Citizen-Advertiser, 1935-36; reporter Editor & Pub., N.Y.C., 1936-39, news editor, 1939-47, mng. editor, 1942-43, exec. editor, 1943-44, editor, 1944—, dir., sec., 1940—, v.p., editor, 1947-52, pres. 1952—. Mem. Inter-Am. Press Assn. (chmn. exec. com. 1963-69), Am. Soc. Newspaper Editors, Sigma Delta Chi (pres. 1953- 54). Presbyn. Clubs: Nat. Press (Washington), N.Y. Athletic, Union League, Dutch Treat (N.Y.C.); Bedford Golf and Tennis. Home: Wood Rd Mt Kisco NY 10549 Office: 850 3d Av New York City NY 10020

BROWN, ROBERT WALLACE, educator; b. Portland, Ore., May 20, 1925; s. Bert and Stella (Conway) B.; B.S., Pacific U., 1950; M.S., Ore. State U., 1952, Ph.D., 1958; m. Doris Arrilda Burroughs, Sept. 4, 1948; children—Robert Wallace, Janice Dianne. Mathematician, Nat. Bur. Standards, Corona, Cal., 1952-54, Boeing Co., Seattle, 1958-66; vis. asso. prof. Ore State U., Corvallis, 1966-67; prof. math., dept. head U. Alaska, College, 1967—. Served with USNR, 1942-45. Mem. Math. Assn. Am., Am. Math Soc., A.A.A.S., Sigma Xi. Pi Mu Epsilon, Sigma Pi Sigma. Contbg. author Error in Digital Computers, 1965. Home: G 5-447 College AK 99701 Office: Dept Math U Alaska College AK 99701

BROWN, ROBERT WALLACE, banker; b. Los Angeles, Feb. 27, 1925; s. Atlas M. and Gladys (Brewster) B.; B.S. in Finance, U. So. Cal., 1948; m. Jacqueline Dee, Jan. 18, 1947; children—David, Eric, Christopher. Examiner FDIC, 1948-51; comml. loan officer Wells Fargo Bank, 1951-56; financial v.p. Booth Leasing Corp., San Francisco, 1956; v.p. United Cal. Bank, Los Angeles, 1956-61; pres. Robert W. Brown & Assos., Los Angeles, 1961-63; pres. Bank of Los Angeles, 1963-66; exec. v.p. First Western Bank, Los Angeles, 1966—, also chief adminstrv. officer, dir., mem. exec. com.; dir. Sutter Hill Co. Bd. dirs. Glendale Community Hosp., Los Angeles area council Boy Scouts Am. Mem. Robert Morris Assos., Cal. Bankers Assn., Los Angeles C. of C. Clubs: California, Stock Exchange (Los Angeles); Oakmont Country (Glendale). Home: 1345 Imperial Dr Glendale CA 91207 Office: 548 S Spring St Los Angeles CA 90013

BROWN, ROBERT WAYNE, physician, educator; b. Atwood, Kan., June 27, 1923; s. Paul D. and Florence (Sawer) B.; B.A., U. Colo., 1949; M.D., Kan. U., 1955; m. Julia L. Potochnick, Dec. 15, 1945; children—Sandra S., Craig. Intern Kan. U. Med. Center, 1955-56, resident, 1956-59; practice medicine specializing in internal medicine, Kansas City, Kan., 1959—; mem. faculty Kan. U., 1959-61; chief med. service Kansas City (Kan.) VA Hosp., 1961-64, cons., 1964—; asst. prof. endocrinology and metabolism Kan. U. Med. Center, 1965-68, prof. internal medicine, 1969—; dir. Kan. Regional Med. Program, Kansas City, 1968—; cons. Kansas City Sch. Dentistry, VISTA, USAF. Served to 1st lt. USAAF, 1943-46. Fellow A.C.P.; mem. Am. Pub. Health Assn., Am. Fedn. Clin. Research, Phi Beta Pi, Alpha Omega Alpha. Home: 10322 Wenonga Lane Leawood KS 66206 Office: 3909 Eaton St Kansas City KS 66103

BROWN, ROBERT WELLS, advt. exec.; b. Newton, Mass., Aug. 9, 1921; s. John Franklin and Gladys Brigham (Lobdell) B.; B.A. in Internat. Relations, Yale, 1944; m. Louise Blair Stewart, Feb. 2, 1944; children—Stewart Jason, Margaret Wells, John Franklin III. With Compton Advt., Inc., N.Y.C., 1958—, sr. v.p. mgmt., 1969—. Served with USNR, World War II. Decorated Purple Heart. Mem. St. Andrew's Soc., Alpha Sigma Phi. Republican. Presbyn. Home: Orchard Hill Lane Greenwich CT 06830 Office: 625 Madison Av New York City NY 10022

BROWN, ROBERT WOODROW, newspaper editor; b. Covington County, Miss., Jan. 3, 1912; s. Emmett Lige and Alma Louise (Garner) B.; grad. high sch.; Nieman fellow Harvard, 1951-52; m. Sarah Elizabeth Wood, Feb. 6, 1936; 1 dau., Barbara. Reporter, Hattiesburg (Miss.) American, 1930-32; mng. editor Greenville (Miss.) Delta Star, 1936-38; staff corr. United Press, New Orleans, 1938; reporter, city editor Times-Picayune and New Orleans States, 1938-42; asst. city editor Washington Daily News, 1942-43; news supr. NBC, 1943-45; exec. editor Internat. News Service, 1945-47; news editor ABC, 1947-48; editor Columbus (Ga.) Ledger, 1948-57; information officer fgn. service USIA, New Delhi, India, 1957-58; asso. editor St. Petersburg (Fla.) Times, 1958-63; mng. editor Delta Democrat-Times, Greenville, 1963; editor Rock Hill (S.C.) Evening Herald, 1964-68; mng. editor Augusta (Ga.) Chronicle, 1968—; lectr. Am. press freedom, India and Iceland, 1954. Recipient Pulitzer prize for disinterested meritorious pub. service, 1955. Mem. Am. Soc. Newspaper Editors, So. Assn. Nieman Fellows, Inc., Sigma Delta Chi. Methodist. Contbr. articles for Parade mag., Editor and Pub. mag., others. Office: Augusta Chronicle Augusta GA 30902

BROWN, ROBINSON S., Jr., distilling co. exec.; b. Louisville, 1917. Exec. v.p., dir. Brown-Forman Distillers Corp., also chmn.; dir. Martin Sweets Co., Jack Daniel Distillery. Home: PO Box 312 Harrods Creek KY 40027 Office: 850 Dixie Hwy Louisville KY 40210*

BROWN, RODGERS N., food chain exec.; b. Columbia, Tenn., Jan. 3, 1911; s. William Albert and Bessie Belle Brown; grad. Inst. Mgmt., Northwestern U.; m. Mary Elizabeth Cook, Apr. 1, 1934; children—Mary Elizabeth (Mrs. James B. Green), Patricia Diane (Mrs. Louis P. Mattis), Deborah Cook. With Kroger Co., 1928-57, v.p., dir. subsidiary Wesco Foods Co., 1951-57; pres., dir. Mohican Co., 1957-59; v.p., dir. Nat. Food Stores La., Inc., 1961- -; v.p. Nat. Tea Co., 1965—, regional v.p., 1967-69. Active local Community Chest, 1950, 59, 60, 64. Home: 45 Farnham Pl Metairie LA 70005

BROWN, ROGER WILLIAM, psychologist, educator; b. Detroit, Apr. 14, 1925; s. Frank Herbert and Muriel Louise (Graham) B.; A.B., U. Mich., 1948, Ph.D., 1952; M.A. (hon.), Harvard, 1962; D. Univ. (hon.), U. York (Eng.). Asst. prof. psychology Harvard, Cambridge, Mass., 1952-57, prof. social psychology, 1962—, chmn. dept. social relations, 1967-70; asso. prof. psychology Mass. Inst. Tech., Cambridge, 1957-61, prof. social psychology, 1961-62. Chmn. behavioral scis. study sect. NIH, 1961- 63. Mem. Am., New Eng. (pres. 1965-66), Eastern (pres. 1971-72) psychol. assns., Linguistic Soc. Am., Am. Acad. Arts and Scis. Author: Words and Things, 1958; (with others) New Directions in Psychology, 1962; The Acquisition of Language, 1964; Social Psychology, 1965; Psycholinguistics, 1970. Home: 100 Memorial Dr Cambridge MA 02142

BROWN, RONALD FREDERICK, chemist, educator; b. Washington, Apr. 14, 1910; s. Virgil Lee and Laura Lee (Hoover) B.; B.S., U. Md., 1932; A.M., Harvard, 1937, Ph.D., 1939; m. Allie M. Sandridge, Mar. 24, 1935; children—Karen A., Stephen M. Instr. Harvard, 1939-40, Purdue U., 1940-42; asst. prof. U. So. Cal., Los Angeles, 1942-48, asso. prof., 1948-55, prof., 1955—, head dept. chemistry, 1953-56, 1958- 63. Vis. research asso. Cal. Inst. Tech., 1963-64; responsible investigator OSRDCMR, 1943-45. Sr. Fulbright research fellow Imperial Coll., U. London, 1956-57. Fellow A.A.A.S.; mem. Am. Chem. Soc., Chem. Soc. London, Am. Assn. U. Profs., Sigma Xi, Phi Kappa Phi, Phi Lambda Upsilon, Alpha Chi Sigma. Author tech. articles. Home; 3827 S Ridgeley Dr Los Angeles, CA 90008.

BROWN, ROWLAND CHAUNCEY WIDRIG, mfg. co. exec.; b. Detroit, Oct. 11, 1923; s. Rowland Chauncey and Rhea (Widrig) B.; B.S. cum laude, Harvard, 1947, LL.B., 1950; m. Kathleen Heather Savre, May 18, 1946; children—Stephanie Anne, Geoffrey Rowland, Kathleen Heather. Admitted to D.C. bar, 1951; counsel Econ. Stblzn. Agy., 1950-52; staff counsel Small Bus. Adminstrn., 1954; counsel Machinery and Allied Products Inst., Washington, 1955-59; with Dorr Oliver, Stanford, Conn., 1959-70, pres. 1968-70; pres., chief exec. officer Buckeye Internat., Inc., Columbus, O., 1970—. Served to maj. USMCR, 1942-46, 51-53. Decorated Air medal (3), Purple Heart; Korean Republic citation. Mem. Am., Inter-Am. bar assns., Harvard Engring. Soc. Clubs: Harvard (N.Y.C.); Columbus Athletic, University, Sciota Country, Hoover Yacht (Columbus, O.). Home: 2711 Edington Rd Upper Arlington OH 43221 Office: 100 E Broad St Columbus OH 43215

BROWN, RUSSELL RICHARDS, chmn. bd., chief exec. officer Am. Distilling Co., New York City. Home: Greenwich CT 06830 Office: 150 E 42d St New York City, NY 10017.

BROWN, RUSSELL SALATHIEL, clergyman; b. London, Ky., Aug. 31, 1892; s. Bartlett and Alice (Carr) B.; A.B., Western Res. U., 1933; B.D., Wilberforce Coll., 1915; m. Floy Smith, June 24, 1915 (dec.); children—Alice Elaine, Russell Charles Shelton; m. 2d, Sallie Dee Holderness, Mar. 27, 1955. Ordained to ministry A.M.E. Ch., 1915; pastor various chs., Atlanta, Cleve., Denver, St. Louis; pastor St. Paul A.M.E. Ch., 1940-52; supt. St. Louis- Booneville dist. A.M.E. Ch., 1949-52; pastor Coppin A.M.E. Ch., Chicago, 1952-56, gen. sec., 1956—; sec. gen. Conf. A.M.E. Ch., 1946—. Former mem. City Council, Cleve.; mem. City Plan Commn., St. Louis. Bd. dirs. Urban League. Mem. Sigma Pi Phi, Alpha Phi Alpha. Mason. Home: 8348 S Vernon Av Chicago IL 60619

BROWN, RUSSELL WILFRID, educator; b. Gray, La., Jan. 17, 1905; s. John Daniel and Lizzie Elna (Saulsby) B.; B.S., Howard U., 1926; postgrad. U. Chgo., 1927-29; M.S., Ia. State U., 1932, Ph.D., 1936; LL.D., Tuskegee Inst., 1971; m. Mildred Marguerite McConnell, Oct. 31, 1932, Faculty Tuskegee Inst. (Ala.) 1936-70, prof. bacteriology, 1943-70; chmn. div. natural scis., 1942-46, dir. Carver Research Found., 1944-57, dean research, 1957-62, v.p., dean grad program, 1962-68, v.p., 1962-70; distinguished prof. microbiology sch. med. scis., U. Nev., Reno, 1970—. Research fellow Ia. State U., 1933- 36, research asst., 1942-43; sr. postdoctoral fellow NSF, Yale Sch. Medicine, 1956-57; spl. research mammalian cell and tissue culture and virus host cell relationships. Mem. council Oak Ridge Asso. Univs., 1951-62, bd. dirs., 1962-68; trustee Carver Research Found., 1957-70; bd. dirs. So. Fellowships Fund; trustee Stillman Coll., 1964—, chmn., 1969—. Recipient Alumni Merit award Ia. State U., 1951; Alumni Distinguished Postgrad. Achievement Sci. award Howard U., 1955. Fellow Am. Inst. Chemists; mem. Am. Soc. Microbiology (pres. S.E. br. 1961-62), A.A.A.S., Nat. Inst. Sci. (pres. 1949-50), Tissue Culture Assn., Am. Soc. Cell Biology, Am. Acad. Microbiology, Scabbard and Blade, Phi Beta Kappa, Sigma Xi, Phi Kappa Phi, Beta Kappa Chi, Alpha Phi Alpha. Contbr. articles to profl. jours. Home: PO Box 8097 University Station Reno NV 89507

BROWN, SAMUEL CARSON, ednl. authority exec.; b. Evanston, Ill., Oct. 28, 1911; s. Hugh Auchincloss and Sarah Pirie (Briggs) B.; grad. St. Paul's Sch., Garden City, N.Y., 1929; student Williams Coll., 1929-31, Am. Inst. Banking, 1931-34; m. Imogene Ellen Peelle, June 24, 1939; children—Samuel Carson, Andrew Peelle, Susan Wilson. With Fifth Avenue Bank, N.Y.C., 1931-37, Orvis Bros. & Co., N.Y.C., 1937-40; with S. S. Pierce Co., Boston, 1940-68, v.p., 1954-63, exec. v.p., treas., 1963-68; v.p. Williams Coll., Williamstown, Mass., 1968-71; exec. dir. Health and Ednl. Facilities Authority, Boston, 1971—. Dir. Arvida Corp., Mass. Investors Growth Stock Fund, Eastern Utilities Assos., Inc., Mass. Investors Trust, Mass. Income Devel. Fund, Mass. Capital Devel. Fund, Pierce Co., Inc. Served to lt. comdr. USNR, 1943-45. Mem. Zeta Psi. Conglist. Clubs: Union (Boston); Country (Brookline, Mass.). Home: 59 Moulton Rd Duxbury MA 02332

BROWN, SAMUEL PRESTON, cons. engr., indsl. and transp. cons.; b. Orange, N.J., May 16, 1913; s. Samuel Percy and Elizabeth (Sloan) B.; B.S., Mass. Inst. Tech., 1935; m. Helen Marie Cook, Oct. 27, 1934; children—Donald Kendrick, Joan Catherine. Cons. engr. Research Corp., N.Y.C., 1936-38; sales engr. Delehanty Inst. and Def. Mfg. Co., N.Y.C., 1938-41; with Coverdale & Colpitts, cons. engrs., N.Y.C., 1945—, partner, 1952—; chmn. bd. Coverdale & Colpitts, Inc., 1970—; dir. Gaspesia Pulp & Paper Ltd., Chandler, Que., Can., Bklyn. Union Gas Co., Kaiser Steel Corp., Oakland, Cal., Catawba Newsprint Co. (S.C.). Bd. dirs. Nat. Indsl. Conf. Bd. Served to maj. USAAF, 1942-45. Decorated Legion of Merit. Mem. Am. Inst. Cons. Engrs. (pres. 1965, counsellor 1962-68), Am. Soc. M.E., Theta Delta Chi. Clubs: Wings, City Midday (N.Y.C.); Canoe Brook Country (Summit, N.J.). Home: 32 Cayuga Way Short Hills NJ 07078 Office: 140 Broadway New York City NY 10005

BROWN, SAMUEL ROBBINS, Jr., naval officer; b. Chgo., May 6, 1913; s. Samuel Robbins and Rebecca (Atkinson) B.; B.S., U.S. Naval Acad., 1934; grad. Nat. War Coll., 1957; m. Anne Banning Macfarland, June 11, 1940; children—Eleanor Banning (Mrs. Reid A. Dunn), Marion Townsend, Robin Anne, Elizabeth Macfarland, Fellow Am. Soc. Commd. ensign U.S. Navy, 1934, designated naval aviator, 1937, advanced through grades to rear adm., 1961; served in U.S.S. Marblehead, 1934-36, U.S.S. Yorktown, 1938-40, U.S.S. New Orleans, 1940-42, U.S.S. Interpid, 1944-45, U.S.S. ShangriLa, 1946; assigned staff Chief Naval Air Basic Tng., 1947-48: comdr. Carrier Div. 6, 1948-50, Naval Air Forces Atlantic, 1958-59; comdr. Bombing Squadron 82, 1944, Carrier Air Group 14, 1945, Composite Squadron 11, 1952-54, U.S.S. Orca, 1957-58, U.S.S. Forrestal, 1959-60, Naval Air Sta., Whidbey Island, 1950, Carrier Div. 4, 1963-64; asst. chief naval operations (fleet operations and readiness), Washington, 1964—. Decorated D.F.C., Air medal. Home: 5155 37th Rd N Arlington VA 22207. Office: Office Chief Naval Operations The Pentagon Washington DC 20350

BROWN, SANBORN CONNER, physicist; b. Beirut, Lebanon, Jan. 19, 1913 (parents Am. citizens); s. Julius Arthur and Helen Elizabeth (Conner) B.; A.B., Dartmouth, 1935, A.M., 1937; Ph.D. (Kramer fellow 1937-38), Mass. Inst. Tech., 1944; m. Lois L. Wright, June 21, 1940; children—Peter M., Stanley W., Prudence E. Asst. physics Dartmouth, 1935-37; teaching fellow Mass. Inst. Tech., 1938-41, instr. physics, 1941-45, asst. prof., 1945-49, asso. prof., 1949-62, prof., 1962—, asso. dean Grad. Sch., 1963- -. Dir. Metcom. Inc., Salem, Mass. Mem. Sch. Com., Lexington, Mass., 1958-64, chmn., 1961-64; tech. adviser U.S. del. 2d UN Internat. Conf. on Peaceful Uses Atomic Energy, Geneva, 1958; U.S. del. Internat. Atomic Energy Agy. Conf. on Plasma Physics and Controlled Thermonuclear Fusion, Salzburg, Austria, 1961; mem. U.S. nat. com., Internat. Union Pure and Applied Physics, 1960-66, vice chmn., 1968—, sec. plasma sub-commn. on atomic and molecular physics and spectroscopy, 1966-69, vice chmn. physics edn., 1960-66, sec. commn. on plasma physics, 1969—; mem. research adv. com. on fluid mechanics NASA, 1963-65; mem. com. internat. exchange of persons Conf. Bd. Asso. Research Councils, 1965-67. Recipient Distinguished Service citation Am. Assn. Physics Tchrs., 1962. John Simon Guggenheim Meml. fellow, 1968-69. Fellow Am. Acad. Arts and Scis. (chmn. Rumford Com. 1955-58, chmn. com. on ednl. activities 1957-61, sec. 1964-67), Am. Phys. Soc. (chmn. div. electron physics 1951-52), A.A.A.S. (committeeman-at-large physics sect. 1963-65, council 1965-66); mem. Am. Assn. physics Tchrs. (treas. 1955- 62, commn. on coll. physics; chmn. com. internat. edn. physics, 1962-66), History Sci. Soc., Nat. Sci. Tchrs. Assn., Royal Instn. Gt. Britain, Phi Beta Kappa, Sigma Xi (nat. lectr.). Author: Basic Data of Plasma Physics, 1959, 2d rev. edit., 1967; Elementary Processes in Extraordinary, 1962; Introduction to Electrical Discharges in Gases, 1966; Benjamin Thompson-Count Rumford (Count Rumford on the Nature of Heat, 1967. Co-editor; International Education in Physics, 1960; Why Teach Physics?, 1964; The Education of a physicist, 1966; editor Electrons, Ions, and Waves (Selected Works of William Phelps (Allis), 1967; Collected Works of Count Rumford, Vol. I, The Nature of Heat, 1968, Vol. II, Practical Applications of Heat, 1969, Vol. III, Devices and Techniques, 1969, Vol. IV, Light and Armament, 1970, Vol. V, Public Institutions, 1970. Contbr. profl. jours. Home: 37 Maple St Lexington, MA 02173.

BROWN, SPENCER WHARTON, geneticist, educator; b. Vermillion, S.D., Nov. 26, 1918; s. J. Maughs and Lillian (James) B.; B.A., U. Minn., 1938; postgrad. U. Mo., 1938-41; Ph.D., U. Cal. at Berkeley, 1942; m. Roberta Marie Schuknecht, Jan. 6, 1939 (div., 1958). Asst. prof. botany U. Ga., 1943-45; asso. in genetics U. Cal. at Berkeley, 1945-46, instr., 1946-48, asst. prof., 1948-54, asso. prof., 1954-60, prof. genetics, 1960—. Guggenheim fellow, 1956- 57. Mem. Am. Soc. Naturalists, Genetics Soc. Am. (sec.-gen. XIII Internat. Congress Genetics), Bot. Soc. Am., Am. Assn. U. Profs., Phi Beta Kappa, Sigma Xi. Contbr. articles to profl. jours.

BROWN, STANLEY MELVIN, lawyer; b. Derry, N.H., May 29, 1916; s. Norman Chandler and Ethel (Hodgkins) B.; A.B., Dartmouth, 1939; J.D., Cornell U., 1942; m. Thalia May Ryder, Nov. 10, 1942; 1 son, Kenneth Chad. Admitted to N.Y. bar, 1942, N.H. bar, 1945; partner firm McLane, Carleton, Graf, Greene & Brown, Manchester, N.H., 1945—. Pres., dir. Loch Lyndon, Inc.; dir. Lyons Iron Works; clk. J.C. Pitman & Sons Co., Inc., Kearsarge Real Corp., Lewin Forests, Inc., Pitco Realty Corp. Exec. councillor Jr. Bar Conf., 1948-49, chmn. legislative drafting com., 1950- 51. Del. N.H. Constl. Conv., 1948; mem. N.H. Senate from 9th dist., 1951- 53; del. Republican Nat. Conf., 1952, Served to lt. USNR, 1942-45; PTO. Sr. fellow Dartmouth, 1939; recipient Churchill award, 1936. Mem. Am. (state del. 1967-70, gov. 1969—), N.H. (pres. 1968-69), Manchester bar assns., Internat. Soc. Barristers, Order of Coif, Phi Beta Kappa. Bus. mgr. Cornell Law Quar., 1941-42. Home: Main St Bradford NH Office: 40 Stark St Manchester NH 03101

BROWN, STEPHEN, physician, educator; b. Northampton, Mass., May 5, 1907; s. Edward W. and Laura (Hall) B.; A.B., Amherst Coll., 1928; M.D., Yale, 1932; m. Elsa M. Parshley, Dec. 17, 1940; children—Anne, Stephen, Laurie, Edward, Nancy. Intern internal medicine New Haven Hosp., 1932-33, pediatrics Babies Hosp., N.Y.C., 1933-35, 45-46; practice medicine, Northampton, Mass., 1935-42, specializing in pediatrics, 1946-53; asso. coll. physician Amherst Coll., 1936-49, coll. physician, 1949—, Pharmley Billings prof. hygiene, 1953—. Pres. Children's Aid Assn. Hampshire County, 1955-58. Served as capt. (flight) surgeon), USAAF, 1942-46. Mem. A.M.A., Mass. Med. Soc., Chi Psi. Home: 58 Woodside Av Amherst MA 01002

BROWN, STERLING ELLIOTT, paper co. exec.; b. Pitts., Dec. 10, 1908; s. Harry Gregg and Mary Agnes (Colmer) B.; B.A., Pa. State U., 1931; m. Helen Bennett Ralston, Oct. 29, 1934 (dec. June 1962); children—Sterling Elliott, John Ralston, Susan (Mrs. Mark Benninghofen); m. 2d, Mary Ann Menzer, Aug. 31, 1963. Sales mgr. Interstate Cordage & Paper Co., Pitts., 1931-36; exec. v.p. Caldwell Sites Co., Roanoke, Va., 1936-39; asst. gen. sales mgr. Crossett Paper Mills (Ark.), 1939-40; with Champion Papers, Inc., 1940- -, v.p., sales, 1962—; pres. Champion Paper Spltys., Inc., 1959-62. Mem. Chi Phi. Club: Marco Island Country. Home: 1792 Wavecrest Ct Marco Island FL 33937

BROWN, STERLING WADE, clergyman, educator; b. Cookville, Tex., Dec. 28, 1907; s. Charles A. and Pludie (Bready) B.; A.B., Tex. Christian U., 1930, B.D., 1932; Ph.D., U. Chgo., 1936; LL.D., Eureka Coll., 1965, Tex. Christian U., 1966; m. Mary Jeanne Murray, Sept. 8, 1938; children—Charlene Ann, Vicki Sue. Ordained to ministry Disciples of Christ Ch., 1928; prof. religion U. Okla., 1936-40; chmn. dept. religion Drake U., 1940-43; dir. Vassar Intergroup Workshop, Poughkeepsie, N.Y., 1945-46; field supr. Nat. Conf. Christians and Jews, St. Louis, Chgo., 1943-45, asst. to pres., N.Y. City, 1945-47, gen. dir., N.Y.C., 1949-53, exec. v.p., 1953-65, pres., 1965—. Mem.

staff Mil. Govt., Germany 1947-49. Mem. Alpha Tau Omega. Republican. Author: Changing Functions of Disciple Colleges, 1936; Developing Christian Personality, 1944; Primer on Intergroup Relations, 1946. Home: Old Mill Rd Weston CT 06880 Office: 43 W 57th St New York City NY 10019

BROWN, STUART GERRY, educator, writer; b. Buffalo, Apr. 13, 1912; s. Charles H. and Edith (Brown) B.; A.B., Amherst, 1934; Ph.D., Princeton, 1937; m. Katharine duB. Franchot, Sept. 15, 1934 (div. 1940); 1 dau. Antoinette Franchot; m. 2d. Mildred Kraus, Aug. 22, 1941; children—Stuart Gerry, Thomas Stuart. Instr. English U. Wis., 1937-40; asso. prof. English, Grinnell Coll., 1940-43, dir. Army Specialized Tng., 1942-44, prof. English and philosophy, 1943-47; prof. citizenship and Am. Culture, Maxwell Grad. Sch. Citizenship and Pub. Affairs, Syracuse U., 1947-58, Maxwell prof. Am. civilization, 1958-65; vis. prof. East West Center, U. Hawaii, Honolulu, 1961-62, 64-65, prof. Am. studies, 1965—. Peace Corps tng. cons., 1963—. Bd. overseers Mauna Olu Coll., 1968—. Mem. Am. Studies Assn. (exec. council 1956-59), Delta Upsilon. Democrat. Author: (with C. Peltier and R. Farnen) Government in Our Republic, 4th edit.; 1972; Memo for Overseas Americans, 1960; The First Republicans, 1954; Conscience in Politics, 1961; Jefferson, 1963; Adlai E. Stevenson, 1965; The American Presidency, 1966; (with others) Government in the United States, 1967; Hamilton, 1967; The Presidency on Trial, 1971. Editor: (with W. Thomas) Reading Poems, 1941; We Hold These Truths, 2d edit., 1948; The Social Philosophy of Josiah Royce, 1950; (with Wright Thomas), Reading Prose, 1952; The Religious Philosophy of Josiah Royce, 1952; The Autobiography of James Monroe, 1959; (with H. Bragdon and S. McCutchen) Frame of Government, 1962; Revolution: Confederation and Constitution, 1971. Contbr. to ednl. revs. and jours. Home: 4706 Kahala Av Honolulu HI 96816

BROWN, STUART MACDONALD, Jr., coll. ofcl. b. Concord, N.C., Mar. 14, 1916; s. Stuart MacDonald and Maud (Reynolds) B.; B.S., Cornell U., 1937, Ph.D., 1942; m. Catherine Hemphill, June 21, 1941; children—James, Deborah, Margaret, Peter. Instr. zoology Mass. State Coll., spring 1938; asst. philosophy Cornell U., Ithaca, N.Y., 1940-42, instr., 1942-43, spring 1946, asst. prof., 1947-49, asso. prof., 1949-56, prof., 1956-70, chmn. dept., 1953-63, dean Coll. Arts and Scis., 1964-68, v.p. for acad. affairs, 1968-70; prof. philosophy, v.p. for acad. affairs U. Hawaii, Honolulu, 1970—. Served with AUS, 1943-46. Rockefeller post-war fellow in philosophy, 1947-48; Guggenheim fellow, 1957-58. Mem. Am. Philos. Assn., Am. Soc. Polit. and Legal Philosophy, Acad. Polit. Sci. Mng. editor The Philos. Rev., 1950-54, 59-62. Home: 119 Niuiki Circle Honolulu HI 96821

BROWN, T. DAWSON, banker; b. Providence, 1891; former pres., Indsl. Nat. Bank, Providence, now exec. v.p., dir.; 1st v.p., dir. Indsl. Trust Co.; dir. Providence Gas Co., Nicholson File Co., Am. Bleached Goods Co., Inc., Ponemah Mills, Sayles Finishing Plants, Inc., Sayles Biltmore Bleacheries, Inc. Home: 15 Bond Rd East Providence RI 02914 Office: 111 Westminster St Providence RI 02903

BROWN, TED WILLIAM, state ofcl.; b. Springfield, O., Apr. 19, 1906; s. George A. and Mabel (Rohnemus) B.; student Wittenberg Coll., 1924-25; m. Florence Mitchell, Apr. 19, 1926; children—Marilyn Ann (Mrs. Bruning), Barbara Lou (Mrs. Larkins), Sherrie Lucille (Mrs. Rogers). Owner of retail bus., Springfield, 1926-32; Clark Co. recorder, Springfield, 1932-36; adminstrv. position Ohio Bur. Motor Vehicles, 1937-42; sec. Trade Assn., State of Ohio, 1943-46; owner, operator bus., Columbus, O., 1947-50; sec. State of Ohio, 1951—. Sec. Sinking Fund, State Ohio, 1951—, World War II Bonus Commn., State Ohio, 1951—, also the Korean Bonus Commn., 1957—. Recipient Am. Heritage Found. award, 1953, 57, 61, Wittenberg U. Alumni Assn. citation, 1969, Am. Credo award Freedoms Found. at Valley Forge, 1970. Mem. State Employees Credit Union (v.p.). Ohio Assn. Co. Recorders (past pres.), Jr. Order United Am. Mechanics, Nat. Assn. Secs. State (past pres.), Springfield C. of C. (charter mem. bd. dirs.), Kappa Phi (pres.). Republican. Methodist. Mason (Shriner), K.P. Compiler: Laws of Ohio; Federal, State and County Roster; Ohio Election Statistics; Ohio Capitols; Ohio Election Laws. Home: 6036 Dublin Rd Dublin OH 43017 Office: State House Columbus OH 43215

BROWN, THATCHER MAGOUN, Jr., investment banker; b. Plainfield, N.J., June 28, 1908; s. Thatcher Magoun and Caro (Noyes) B.; grad. Lawrenceville Sch., 1926; B.A., Yale, 1930; m. Virginia Storm, Oct. 6, 1933 (dec. Aug. 1949); children—Thatcher Magoun III, Frederick Storm, Mary Magoun (Mrs. Herrick Jackson), Marian Adams; m. 2d, Marian Batcheller, Mar. 15, 1951. With fgn. dept. Clark Dodge & Co., N.Y.C., 1930-40; sr. v.p., dir., mem. exec. com., head fgn. dept. G.H. Walker & Co., Inc., N.Y.C., 1940—; trustee, mem. exec. com. N.Y. Bank for Savs. Treas., trustee, mem. exec. com. Columbia Presbyn. Hosp.; trustee, treas. Community Service Soc.; trustee, mem. exec. com. Provident Loan Soc.; asst. treas. Union Settlement; field dir. charge Paris office A.R.C., World War II. Presbyn (elder). Home: 42 Forest Av Rye NY 10580 Office: GH Walker & Co 45 Wall St New York City NY 10005

BROWN, THEODORE DANA, banker; b. Denver, Jan. 8, 1922; s. Dana W. and Lillian (Bullis) B.; A.B., U. Denver, 1943; LL.B., Harvard, 1948; m. Barbara Towne, Oct. 3, 1943; children—Pamela (Mrs. Eric Sankey), Carolyn. Asst. trust officer Internat. Trust Co., Denver, 1948-51; v.p., trust officer Security State Bank of Sterling, Colo., 1952-54, exec. v.p., 1954-62, pres., 1962-70, chmn. bd., 1970—, also dir.; chmn. bd., dir. Farmers State Bank, Yuma, Colo., 1963—; exec. v.p., dir. First Nat. Bank of Denver, 1970—; dir. Denver br. Fed. Res. Bank of Kansas City, 1965-70, Pub. Service Co. of Colo., Sterling Colo. Beef Co., First Nat. Bancorporation, Inc. Trustee Graland Country Day Sch., Denver. Served with Supply Corps, USNR, 1943-45. Home: 6300 Greenbriar Dr Englewood CO 80110 Office: 621 17th St Denver CO 80202

BROWN, THEODORE DAVID, govt. ofcl.; b. Oregon City, Ore., Apr. 23, 1908; s. William Carlton and Marian Delight (Bill) B.; student U. Ore., 1938-40, U. Cal. at Berkeley, 1952, Nat. FBI Acad., 1950; Nat. FBI Acad., 1950, Johns Hopkins, 1961; m. Lita Huebner, Oct. 24, 1954; 1 son, Douglas A. From patrolman to chief of police, Eugene, Ore., 1937-55; dir. pub. safety Island of Guam, 1955-56; chief pub. safety adviser for AID, Liberia, 1956-57, Greece, 1957-58, Libya, 1958-61, El Salvador, 1962; dir. Police Acad., Panama, 1962-64, Brazil, 1967-71; chief Latin Am. br. Office pub. safety, Washington, 1964-67; dep. dir. Pub. Safety Directorate, Saigon, Vietnam, 1971—. Home: 282 Woodlane Dr Springfield OR 97477 Office: CORDS/PSD APO San Francisco CA 96243

BROWN, THEODORE LAWRENCE, educator, chemist; b. Green Bay, Wis., Oct. 15, 1928; s. Lawrence A. and Martha E. (Kedinger) B.; B.S. in Chemistry, Ill. Inst. Tech., 1950; Ph.D., Mich State U., 1956; m. Audrey Catherine Brockman, Jan. 6, 1951; children—Mary Margaret, Karen Anne, Jennifer Gerarda, Philip Matthew, Andrew Lawrence. Faculty U. Ill., Urbana, 1956—, prof. chemistry, 1965—. Cons. editor C.E. Merrill Books, Inc., 1964. Served with USNR, 1950-53. Sloan research fellow, 1962-66; NSF sr. postdoctoral fellow, 1964-65. Fellow Chem. Soc. London; mem. Am. Chem. Soc., A.A.A.S., Sigma Xi, Alpha Chi Sigma. Author: (with R.S. Drago) Experiments in General Chemistry. 3d edit., 1970; General Chemistry, 2d edit., 1968; Energy and the Environment, 1971. Asso. editor Inorganic Chemistry, 1969—; mem. editorial adv. bd. Chem. Revs., Jour. Organometallic Chemistry, Progress in Inorganic Chemistry, Jour. Molecular Structure; also articles. Home: 1511 Alma Dr Champaign IL 61820 Office: Noyes Lab Univ Ill Urbana IL 61801

BROWN, THOMAS ELZIE, Democratic nat. committeeman; b. Lampasas, Tex., Sept. 18, 1900; s. Thomas P. and Hattie L. (Hughes) B.; grad. high sch.; m. Anna C. Bowers, June 10, 1923; 1 son, Thomas Elzie, Pres. Brown Pipe & Supply of Artesia, Inc. (N.M.), 1951—. Democratic precinct committeeman, 1950-52; vice chmn. Eddy County (N.M.) Dem. Central Com., 1952-54; chmn. Dem. Central Com. N.M., 1954-56; Dem. nat. committeeman for N.M., 1956—. Member governing bd. Permian Basin Writer's Collection. Bd. dirs. N.M. Boys Ranch, Baptist Found. N.M., 1955-70, Coll. Artesia. Mem. Southeastern N.M. Agrl. Research Assn. Baptist (deacon). Mason (32), Rotarian (pres. 1964-65). Home: Box 68 Artesia NM 88210 Office: 701 S 1st St Artesia NM 88210

BROWN, THOMAS MCPHERSON, physician, educator; b. Washington, June 29, 1906; s. Thomas Janney and Elsie (Palmer) B.; A.B., Swarthmore Coll., 1929; M.D., Johns Hopkins, 1933; m. Olive H. Young, July 6, 1937; 1 dau., Gael McPherson. Successively intern, asst. resident, chief resident medicine Johns Hopkins Hosp., 1933-37, 39-40; research rheumatic fever Rockefeller Inst. Hosp., N.Y.C., 1937-39; from asso. medicine to asst. clin. prof. medicine Johns Hopkins, 1939-46; chief medicine VA Hosp., Washington, 1946-48; Eugene Meyer prof. medicine, chmn. dept. medicine, also dir. arthritis research unit George Washington U., 1948-70, prof. medicine, 1948—, co-dir. Rehab. Research and Tng. Center, 1965-70; also chief of medicine George Washington U. Hosp., 1948-70; dir. Arthritis Inst. Nat. Orthopaedic and Rehab. Hosp. Vice pres. Eugene and Agnes Meyer Found.; bd. dirs. Sidwell Friends Sch. Served to lt. col., M.C., AUS, 1942-45. Recipient Ivy medal Swarthmore Coll., 1929, Joshua Lippincott fellow, 1929; Dennison Strong fellow Johns Hopkins, 1929-33. Fellow A.C.P.; mem. Soc. Clinical Investigation, Am. Clinical and Climatological Society, Southern Soc. Clinical Research, Phi Beta Kappa, Sigma Xi, Alpha Omega Alpha, Phi Kappa Psi. Mem. Soc. of Friends. Author articles in gen. clin. medicine, infectious and tropical diseases. Basic research on PPLO microorganisms, also author related concept of mechanism rheumatoid arthritis and rheumatic diseases. Home: 814 26th Pl S Arlington VA 22202 Office: 2455 Army-Navy Dr South Arlington VA 22206

BROWN, TIMOTHY, judge; b. Madison, Wis., Feb. 24, 1889; s. Frederic M. and Annie H. (Storer) B.; A.B., U. Wis., 1911; LL.B., Harvard, 1914; m. Margaret S. Titchener, 1921 (dec. 1936); 1 son, Timothy; m. 2d, Louise Coxon, July 16, 1936. Admitted to Wis. bar, 1914, practiced in Madison, 1914-49; ct. commr. Dane County, 1926-49; exec. counsel to Govs. Goodland and Rennebohm of Wis., 1945, 1947-49; commr. Pub. Service Commn. of Wis., 1939; justice Wis. Supreme Ct. 1949-64, chief justice, 1962-64, resident judge, 1964—. Served to lt. (j.g.) USN, 1917-19. Mem. Am., Wis. bar assns., Am. Legion, V.F.W., Order of Coif, Beta Theta Pi. Club: Mendota Yacht. Home: 655 Farwell Dr Madison WI 53704

BROWN, TRUESDELL SPARHAWK, educator; b. Phila., Mar. 21, 1906; s. Carleton and Emily (Truesdell) B.; student Haverford Coll., 1922-23; A.B., Harvard, 1928, A.M., 1929; postgrad. Die Univ., Innsbruck, 1932-33; Ph.D., Columbia, 1947; m. Ruth Anna Edgar; children—Priscilla Jane (Mrs. Arthur P. Collins), Edgar Newton, Truesdell Sparkhawk. Tchr. ancient history U. Colo., 1929-32, 33-37, U. Tex., 1940-47; faculty U. Cal. at Los Angeles, 1947—, prof., 1956—, chmn. dept. history, 1959-62. Fulbright Research fellow, Greece, 1950; Guggenheim fellow, Eng., 1954-55. Mem. Am. Hist. Assn. Democrat. Unitarian. Author: Onesicritus: A Study in Hellenistic Historiography, 1949; Timaeus of Tauromenium, 1958. Editor: Ancient Greece, 1964; joint sr. editor (with W.K. Pritchett) Cal. Studies in Classical Antiquity, 1967-70; also articles. Home: 3816 Rambla Orienta Malibu CA 90265 Office: History Dept Univ of California Los Angeles CA 90024

BROWN, VICTOR LEE, clergyman; b. Cardston, Alta., Can., July 31, 1914; s. Gerald S. and Maggie (Lee) B.; student Latter-Day Saints Bus. Coll., U. Utah; spl. studies U. Cal. at Berkeley; m. Lois A. Kjar, Nov. 13, 1936; children—Victor Lee, Gerald E., Joanne K., Patricia L., Stephen M. With United Air Lines, 1940-61, successively supr., reservations mgr., Washington, Chgo., chief payload control, Denver, mgr. space control, 1956-60, asst. to dir. reservations, Chgo., 1960-61; dir. Beneficial Life Ins. Co.; presiding bishopric Ch. of Jesus Christ of Latter-Day Saints. 1961—; v.p., dir., exec. com. Murdock Travel, Inc.; chmn. exec. com. Deseret Mut. Benefits Assn.; mem. Deseret Dir., News bd. Deseret News Pub. Co.; exec. com. Hotel Utah. Second vice chmn. bd. trustees Health Services Corp. of Ch. of Jesus Christ of Latter-Day Saints, vice chmn. gen. scouting com. Mem. adv. com. Coll. Bus. Brigham Young U. Bd. dirs. Terracor, Am. Ranches and Recreation; mem. Utah Symphony Bd. Mem. Newcomen Soc. N.Am., Beta Gamma Sigma. Home: 1653 Orchard Dr Salt Lake City UT 84106 Office: 47 E South Temple St Salt Lake City UT 84111

BROWN, VINCENT MURRAY, lawyer, oil industry exec.; b. Bradford, Pennsylvania, Aug. 24, 1930; s. James Vincent and Jeanie Small (Murray) B.; A.B. cum laude, Georgetown U., 1952, M.A., 1954, J.D., 1957, LL.M., 1960; m. Mary Beatrice Mark, December 27, 1950; children—James Vincent, Vincent Mark, Lauretta Jean, William Thomas. Admitted to D.C. and Md. bars, 1957; pvt. practice law, Washington, 1957—; asso. firm Brown, Williams & Esparolini, 1959-62; with Nat. Petroleum Council, Washington, 1951—, asst. sec.-treas., 1961-62, sec.-treas., 1963-69, exec. dir., 1970—, also sec. com. impact oil exports from Soviet bloc, 1962, sec. com. on U.S. energy outlook, 1970—; sec. Terminal Bldg. Corp., Bradford, 1961—; sec.-treas. Brown Realty Corp., Bradford, 1954-67; 1st v.p., dir. Tidewater Broadcasting, Inc., 1966—. Mem. 75th anniversary com. City Takoma Park, Md., 1958. Sec. Nat. Petroleum Council's Com. on Petroleum Resources Under the Ocean Floor, 1969. Dir. St. Aidan Sch., Washington, 1963-68, pres., 1965-67. Served with USMCR, 1948-50. Mem. Assn. Petroleum Writers, Am. Bar Assn., Am. Petroleum Inst., Ind. Petroleum Assn. Am., Takoma-Langley Jr. C. of C. (pres. 1958-59, 1960-62), Internat. Law Assn. (Am. br. 1968—), Am. Inst. Mining, Metallurgical and Petroleum Engrs., Delta Theta Phi, Phi Alpha Theta. Republican. Roman Cath. Club: Nat. Lawyers (Washington). Home: 3700 Northampton St NW Washington DC 20015 Office: 1625 K St NW Washington DC 20006

BROWN, VINCENT WILLIAM, fgn. service officer; b. San Francisco, Sept. 27, 1924; s. Samuel Vincent and Ivah Wilhelmina (Jacobson) B.; B.S., U. Cal. at Los Angeles, 1949; student Inst. Devel. Programming, Sch. Advanced Internat. Studies, Johns Hopkins, 1956; m. Francoise S.G. Durand, Apr. 12, 1954; children—Christopher Michel Lance, Gregory Vincent, Valerie Francoise. Tech. asst. specialist U.S. delegations to regional orgns. in Paris for ECA, MSA, FOA, ICA, 1950-57; asst. program officer USOM, Tunis, 1957-59; orgn. and program cons. Asian Productivity Orgn., Tokyo, 1960; internat. coop. officer charge Libyan affairs, also officer charge Nigerian affairs AID, 1961-62; asst. dir. AID mission to Congo, 1963-64; asst. dir. devel. policy AID Mission to Korea, 1964-67; fellow Center Internat. Affairs, Harvard, 1967-68; dep. dir. AID Mission to Pakistan, 1968—. Decorated Order Civil Merit (Korea). Mem. Sigma Alpha Epsilon, Phi Mu Alpha. Home: 470 4th Av San Francisco CA 94118 Office: American Embassy Islamabad Pakistan

BROWN, VIRGINIA MAE, govt. ofcl.; b. Pliny, W.Va., Nov. 13, 1923; d. Felix M. and Hester (Crandall) Brown; A.B., W.Va. U., 1945, J.D., 1947; m. James Vernon Brown, Apr. 8, 1955; children—Victoria Anne, Pamela Kay. Admitted to W.Va. bar, 1947; law clk. atty. gen. W.Va., 1947-49; exec. sec. W.Va. Jud. Council, 1949-52; asst. atty. gen. W.Va., 1952-61; counsel to Gov. of W.Va., 1961; commr. ins. W.Va., 1961-62; mem. W.Va. Pub. Service Commn., 1962-64; mem. ICC, 1964—, vice chmn., 1968, chmn. 1969. Home: 19104 Mills Choice Rd Montgomery Village Gaithersburg MD 20760 Office: Interstate Commerce Commn 12th and Constitution Av Washington DC 20423

BROWN, W. SHELBURNE, coll. pres.; A.B., Pasadena Coll., 1940, M.A., 1942, D.D., 1960; Ed.D., U. So. Cal., 1969. Pastor in Carson City, Nev., Banning, Cal. and Alhambra, Cal., 1942-54; dist. supt. Los Angeles, Ch. of Nazarene, 1952-64: pres. Pasadena Coll., 1964- -. Address: Pasadena Coll Howard at Bresee Sts Pasadena CA 91104

BROWN, WALSTON SHEPARD, lawyer; b. Darien, Conn., Jan. 20, 1908; s. Clarence Shepard and Alma Mary (Mitchell) B.; A.B., Leland Stanford, 1930; student L'Ecole Libre des Science Politiques, Paris, 1931-32; LL.B., Harvard, 1935; m. Ellen F. Regan, August 13, 1955. Admitted to D.C. bar, 1936; atty. various govt. depts., 1935-40; asst. gen. counsel U.S. Maritime Commn., also mem. various adv. coms. on drafting and adminstrn. mem. various adv. coms. on drafting and adminstrn. reconversion and contract termination legislation, 1940-45; practiced in N.Y.C., 1945—; partner firm Willkie Farr & Gallagher, and predecessors. Dir. Internat. Products Corp., Am. Sumatra Corp., Gap Instrument Corp. Mem. Newcomen Soc. N. Am., Assn. Bar City of N.Y., Am. Bar Assn., S.R., Phi Beta Kappa. Unitarian. Clubs: Metropolitan (Washington); University, Wall Street., River (N.Y.C.). Home: 136 E 64th St New York City NY 10021 Office: 1 Chase Manhattan Plaza New York City NY 10005

BROWN, WALTER HAROLD, Jr., lawyer; b. Johnson City, Tenn., May 20, 1910; s. Walter H. and Constance (Malone) B.; B.A., Birmingham-So. Coll., 1931; LL.B., Columbia, 1934; m. Phyllis Elizabeth Barnard, June 6, 1935; children—Walter Barnard, Phyllis Deborah (Mrs. George J. Pillorgé). Admitted to N.Y. bar, 1934, since practiced in N.Y.C.; partner firm Willkie, Farr & Gallagher, and predecessors, 1943—. Dir. Internat. Minerals and Metals Corp.; gen. counsel Seaboard Coast Line R.R. Co., 1965-70; reorgn. mgr. M.P. R.R. Co., 1956. Trustee Finch Jr. Coll., 1943-53. Fellow Am. Bar Found.; mem. Am., N.Y. State bar assns., N.Y. C. of C., Sigma Alpha Epsilon, Omicron Delta Kappa. Clubs: Wall Street (N.Y.C.); Port Washington (N.Y.) Yacht. Home: 100 Ivy Way Port Washington NY 11050 Office: 1 Chase Manhattan Plaza New York City NY 10005

BROWN, WALTER LINDSEY, lawyer; b. Williamson, W.Va., Feb. 14, 1903; s. Douglas W. and Mary Glidden (Williams) B.; B.S., U. Va., 1924, LL.B., 1926; B.A. (Rhodes Scholar), U. Oxford, 1928; m. Dorothy Anne Rardin, Nov. 17, 1932; children—Helen Lee (Mrs. James R. Billingsley), Walter Rardin. Asso. firm Fitzpatrick, Brown & Davis, Huntington, W.Va., 1928-36, partner, 1936-41; v.p., gen. counsel and dir. Western Electric Co. and subsidiaries, 1941-64: v.p., dir. Tolten Corp.; dir. Cities Service Co. Pres., trustee Henry L. and Grace Doherty Charitable Found., U. Va. Law School Found.; trustee U. Va. Endowment Fund. Mem. Am. Bar Assn. (com. on profl. ethics and grievances, 1937-44; special committee on law lists, 1944-45), New York, W.Va. bar assns., Assn. Bar City of N.Y., Council on Foreign Relations, Phi Beta Kappa Assos., U. of Va. Law School Assn. (pres. 1959-61), Phi Beta Kappa, Delta Phi, Phi Delta Phi. Democrat. Presbyn. Clubs: University; Farmington (Charlottesville, Va.); Wee Burn (Darien, Conn.). Home: 5 South Trail Darien CT 06820

BROWN, WAYNE SAMUEL, educator; b. Provo, Utah, Mar. 19, 1928; s. Cleveland W. and Wilmirth (Brown) B.; B.M.E., U. Utah, 1951; M.S., U. Tenn., 1953; Ph.D., Stanford, 1960; m. Joyce Fechser, Mar. 4, 1948; children—Karen, Diane, Gary Wayne, Don Reed, Janet. Engr., Oak Ridge Nat. Lab., 1951-53; asst. prof. mech. engring. U. Utah, 1953-57; acting asst. prof. mech. engring. Stanford, 1957-59; engring. mgr. Utah Research and Devel. Corp., Salt Lake City, 1959-64; prof., chmn. mech. engring. dept. U. Utah, 1964-70, dir. Inst. for Biomed. Engring., 1970—, asso. dean Coll. Engring., 1971—; co-founder, cons. Kenway Engring, Bountiful, Utah, Terra Tek, Inc., Salt Lake City; chmn. bd. dirs. AAA Sprinkler Inc., Salt Lake City. Mem. Utah Nuclear Energy Commn., 1971—. Served with USMCR, 1946-47. Mem. Am. Soc. M.E., Soc. Exptl. Stress Analysis, Internat. Assn. Dental Research, Internat. Soc. Rock Mechanics. Mem. Ch. Jesus Christ of Latter-day Saints (bishop 1965-68). Home: 1931 E Millbrook Dr Salt Lake City UT 84106

BROWN, WENDELL JAMES, assn. ofcl.; b. Des Moines, Aug. 7, 1913; s. Velora O. and Mamie (Durham) B.; ed. pub. schs., Ia.; m. Vivian Rose Young, Jan. 18, 1935; children—Wendell J., Beverly Marie, Loren Dennis. Partner, Master Tire & Supply Co., 1935-48, Master Sales Co., 1948—; v.p., dir. Graymills Corp. Nat. v.p. United Cerebral Palsy Assn., 1955-59, pres., 1960-64; vice chmn. United Cerebral Palsy Research Found. Recipient citation plaques United Cerebral Palsy Assn. Baptist. Mason, (Shriner), Kiwanian. Club: Des Moines Golf and Country. Address: 2300 Ashworth Rd West Des Moines IA 50265

BROWN, WESLEY ERNEST, U.S. judge; b. Hutchinson, Kan., June 22, 1907; s. Morrison H.H. and Julia (Wesley) B.; student Kan. U., 1925-28; LL.B., Kansas City Law Sch., 1933; m. Mary A. Miller, Nov. 30, 1934; children—Wesley Miller, Mary Loy (Mrs. John K. Wiley). Admitted to Kan. bar, 1933, Mo. bar, 1933; practiced in Hutchinson, 1933-58; county atty. Reno County, Kan., 1935-39; referee in bankruptcy U.S. Dist. Ct. Kan., 1958-62, judge, 1962—, now chief judge. Dir. Nat. Assn. Referees in Bankruptcy, 1959-62; mem. Jud. Conf., U.S. Bankruptcy Adminstrn., 1963-70. Served with USNR, 1944-46. Mem. Am., Kan. (exec. council 1950-62, pres. 1964-65), Reno County (pres. 1947), Wichita bar assns., S.W. Bar Kan., Delta Theta Phi. Home: 316 St James Wichita KS 67206 Office: Federal Bldg Wichita KS 67201

BROWN, WILFRED JACOBS, former r.r. exec.; b. Plymouth, Mass., Aug. 10, 1893; s. Wilfred Gardner and Stella Clinton (Jacobs) B.; grad. Plymouth High Sch., 1911; Phillips Acad., Andover, Mass., 1913; A.B., Harvard, 1917; postgrad. Harvard Sch. Bus. Adminstrn., summer 1929; m. Gertrude Dudley Danforth, Oct. 10, 1917; children—Wilfred Jacobs, Beverly Danforth. Supercargo, U.S. Shipping Bd., 1919; successively shipping clk., asst. purchasing agt., sec. to pres., asst. to pres. The Cuba R.R. Co., The Cuba Co., Compania Cuba NA, 1919-24; asst. to pres., Consol. R.R.s of Cuba, The Cuba R.R. Co., 1924-38; v.p., dir. Consol. Railroads of Cuba. Cuba R.R. Co., Cuba No. Rys. Co., 1938-41, pres., dir., 1941-48; chmn. bd. Consol. R.R.'s of Cuba; pres., dir. Cuba R.R. Co.; Cuba North Ry. Co. 1948-54, ret. 1954; pres., dir. Expresos de Cuba, S.A., 1943-53, Omnibus Consolidados de Cuba, Omnibus La Mambisa S.A., Omnibus La Criolla S.A. 1943-54, Cuba Co., Compania Cubana,

1948-54; trustee Ryder Home Corp. Chmn. adv., finance com. Plymouth, 1959-60, Vall is New York, for mem. Planning Bd., Town Meeting, 1960-68. Bd. dirs. Jordan Hosp. Served from seaman to lt. (j.g.). USNRF, 1917-19. Mem. Pilgrim Soc. (trustee, sec. 1957-68), Mass Soc. Mayflower Descs., Plymouth Plantatiion, Inc., Kappa Sigma. Mason. Club: Old Colony. Home: 66 Allerton St Plymouth, MA 02360.

BROWN, WILLARD WALKER, research corp. exec.; b. Cleve., June 11, 1915; s. Fayette and Geraldine (Walker) B.; B.A., Yale, 1938, LL.B., 1941; m. Louise Ingalls, 1947; children—Willard Walker, David, Alice, Barbara. Admitted to Ohio bar, 1941; with Jones, Day, Cockley & Reavis, Cleve., 1941-51; dir. moblzn. Cleve. Graphite Bronze Co., 1951; asst. to pres. Clevite Corp., Cleve., 1952-53, dir., marketing, 1954, v.p. marketing, 1954-55, pres. Cleve. Graphite Bronze Co. div., 1955-60, v.p. bearing group Clevite Corp., 1960-62; pres. Univ. Circle Research Center Corp.; dir. ARDAC/u.s.a., Inc., Cleve. Trust Co., Ferro Corp., Va. Hot Springs, Inc., Sci. Resources Corp. Pres. Cleve. Opera Assn. Bd. dirs. Am. Inst. Strategy; trustee U. Hosps.; chmn. bd. trustees, acting pres. Nat. Recreation and Park Assn., bd. overseers Case Western Res. U. Served to maj. USAF, 1941-46. Decorated D.F.C., Bronze Star, Air medal. Mem. Ohio, Cleve. bar assns. Home: Fairmount Blvd Chagrin Falls OH 44022 Office: Union Commerce Bldg Cleveland OH 44115

BROWN, WILLARD WALKER, research corp. exec.; b. Cleve., June 11, 1915; s. Fayette and Geraldine (Walker) B.; B.A., Yale, 1938, LL.B., 1941; m. Louise Ingalls, 1947; children—Willard Walker, David, Alice, Barbara. Admitted to Ohio bar, 1941; with Jones, Day, Cockley & Reavis, Cleve., 1941-51; dir. moblzn. Cleve. Graphite Bronze Co., 1951; asst. to pres. Clevite Corp., Cleve., 1952-53, dir., marketing, 1954, v.p. marketing, 1954-55, pres. Cleve. Graphite Bronze Co. div., 1955-60, v.p. bearing group Clevite Corp., 1960-62; pres. Univ. Circle Research Center Corp.; dir. ARDAC/u.s.a., Inc., Cleve. Trust Co., Ferro Corp., Va. Hot Springs, Inc., Sci. Resources Corp. Pres. Cleve. Opera Assn. Bd. dirs. Am. Inst. Strategy; trustee U. Hosps.; chmn. bd. trustees, acting pres. Nat. Recreation and Park Assn., bd. overseers Case Western Res. U. Served to maj. USAF, 1941-46. Decorated D.F.C., Bronze Star, Air medal. Mem. Ohio, Cleve. bar assns. Home: Fairmount Blvd Chagrin Falls OH 44022 Office: Union Commerce Bldg Cleveland OH 44115

BROWN, WILLET HENRY, broadcasting exec.; b. Detroit, July 28, 1905; s. Joel E. and Gertrude (Ransom) B.; m. Betty Jane Rhodes, Sept. 29, 1948; 1 dau., Laurie Kim; children by previous marriage—Patricia, Michael, Peter. Asst. gen. mgr. Don Lee Inc., 1932-33; exec. v.p. Don Lee Broadcasting System, Hollywood, 1933, 48; pres. Thomas S. Lee Enterprises, Inc., 1947-50, Don Lee Broadcasting System, 1949-58; founder, dir. MBS; v.p., dir. RKO Teleradio Pictures, Inc., 1958; stockholder, dir. San Francisco-Oakland TV, Inc. operating KTVU, Oakland, 1958-63; pres. Pacific States Investment Corp., 1948—, Laurie Leasing Corp., Don Lee Motors Corporation, Hillcrest Motor Co.; owner, pres. KGB, Inc., operating KGB-AM and KBKB-FM, San Diego, Cal., 1962—; cons. RKO Gen., Inc. Clubs: Los Angeles Yacht, University, Newport Harbor Yacht, Balboa Bay, Bel Air Country; St. Francis Yacht (San Francisco). Holder of television patent. Home: 10693 Chalon Rd W Los Angeles CA 90024 Office: 9200 Wilshire Blvd Beverly Hills CA 90212

BROWN, WILLIAM DONALD, banker; b. N.Y.C., Apr. 29, 1920; s. William Henry and Ella (Robertson) B.; B.A., Dartmouth, 1941; m. Rose Marie Elliott, May 26, 1951; children—Jeffrey Donald, Joshua Douglas. With J. Henry Schroder Banking Corp., N.Y.C., 1946-69, sr. v.p., 1965-69; sr. v.p. in charge Far East, Middle East, Africa, Chem. Bank, N.Y.C., 1969—; trustee Prudential Savs. Bank, N.Y.C. Served to lt. comdr. USNR, 1941-45. Mem. St. Andrews Soc. Clubs: Wee Burn Country (Darien); India House (N.Y.C.). Home: 101 Inwood Rd Darien CT 06820 Office: 20 Pine St New York City NY 10008

BROWN, WILLIAM F., editor; b. Chgo., Nov. 5, 1903; s. Thomas J. and Ellen (Walsh) B.; ed. St. Mark's Parochial Sch., St. Patrick's High Sch., and DePaul U.; m. Vonne Ellen Windchy, June 14, 1941; children—Ellen Catherine, Barbara Ann, William F. With the Am. Field, 1922—; stenographer, registrar, 1924, field trial reporter, 1925, asst. editor, 1927, bus. mgr., 1931, editor, 1940, pres. of the Am. Field Pub. Co., weekly, 1943—. Roman Catholic. Author: The FIeld Trial Primer, 1934; A. F. Hochwalt Biography, 1940; How to Train Hunting Dogs, 1942; Rod and Gun Calendar, 1944; Retriever Gun Dogs, 1945; Field Trials, 1947; National Field Trial Champions, 1956-66, 1966. Section on Dogs, Ency. Americana. Contbr. articles to various publs. Home: 1315 Park Av River Forest IL 60305 Office: 222 W Adams St Chicago IL 60606

BROWN, WILLIAM FRANKLIN, oil co. exec.; b. Norman, Ark., Sept. 27, 1917; s. William Franklin and Mary Virginia (Nutt) B.; B.S., U. Tulsa, 1943, M.S. (Ethyl Corp. fellow), 1944; M.S. (Sloan fellow), Mass. Inst. Tech., 1951; m. Ethel Marion Foster, Dec. 26, 1943. With Continental Oil Co., 1943—, dep. mng. dir. Continental Oil Co. Ltd., London Eng., 1963-65, chmn., mng. dir., 1965-70, v.p. mfg. and marketing Eastern Hemisphere Petroleum Div., 1971—. 35 Timber Mill Rd Stamford CT 06903 Office: Continental Oil Co 9 Rockefeller Plaza New York City NY 10020

BROWN, WILLIAM FULLER, educator; b. Lyon Mountain, N.Y., Sept. 21, 1904; s. William Fuller and Mary Emily (Williams) B.; A.B., Cornell, 1925; Ph.D., Columbia, 1937; m. Nancy Shannon Johnson, Aug. 17, 1936; 1 son, Eric Ramsay. Tchr. Carolina Acad., Raleigh, N.C., 1925-27; lectr. Columbia, 1928-38; asst. prof. Princeton, 1938-43; contract employee Naval Ordnance Lab., Washington, 1941-43, sr. physicist, 1943-45; research physicist Sun Oil Co., Newtown Square, Pa., 1946-55; sr. research physicist Minn. Mining & Mfg. Co., 1955-57; prof. elec. engring. U. Minn., Mpls., 1957—. Research on magnetism, electricity, elasticity, applied theoretical physics, numerical calculation and statistics; guest prof. Max-Planck-Institut für Metallforschung, Stuttgart, 1963-64. Mem. adv. com. on ferromagnetism Office Naval Research, 1949-55. Recipient Meritorious Civilian Service award Dept. of Navy. Fulbright scholar Weizmann Inst. Sci., Rehovot, Israel, 1962. Fellow A.A.A.S., Am. Phys. Soc., N.Y. Acad. Scis. (A. Cressy Morrison award, 1967), I.E.E.E.; mem. Am. Soc. Information Sci., Am. Assn. Physics Tchrs. (Coulomb's law com. 1944-50), Philos. Soc. Washington, Internat. Soc. Gen. Semantics, Operations Research Soc. Am., Inst. Math. Statistics, Soc. Natural Philosophy, Phi Beta Kappa, Sigma Xi, Tau Beta Pi, Phi Kappa Phi. Author: Magnetostatic Principles in Ferromagnetism, 1962; Micromagnetics, 1963; Magnetoelastic Interactions, 1966. Contbr. Handbook of Physics (E.U. Condon, editor); Ency. of Physics (S. Fluegge, editor). Translator Soviet Physics JETP. Contbr. articles to sci. jours. Home: 2033 Fremont Av St Paul MN 55119 Office: Dept Elec Engring U Minn Minneapolis MN 55455

BROWN, WILLIAM HENRY, metals co. exec.; b. Iron Mountain, Mich., May 3, 1911; s. William E. and Nellie M. (Shields) B.; B.S., Western Mich. U., 1939; m. Valerie M. Platteter, Jan. 25, 1912; children—William Edward, Laurel Kay. With Hoskins Mfg. Co., Detroit, 1939—, now pres. and chmn. bd. dirs.; pres. Hoskins Alloys Can. Td., Toronto, 1955—, also dir. Club: Plum Hollow Golf (Detroit). Home: 14539 Stahelin St Detroit MI 48223 Office: 4445 Lawton Av Detroit MI 48208

BROWN, WILLIAM HILL, III, govt. ofcl.; b. Phila., Jan. 19, 1928; s. William Hill, Jr. and Ethel (Washington) B.; B.S., Temple U., 1952; J.D., U. Pa., 1955; m. Sonya M. Brown, Aug. 29, 1953; 1 dau., Michele Denise. Admitted to Pa. bar, 1955, since practiced in Phila.; mem. firm Norris, Schmidt, Green, Harris & Higginbotham, 1959-63; partner, mng. partner Norris, Brown & Hall, 1963- 68; chief of frauds Phila. Dist. Atty.'s Office, 1968, dep. dist. atty., 1968; mem. Equal Employment Opportunity Commn., Washington, 1968- 69, chmn., 1969—; regional atty. Alpha Phi Alpha Fraternity, Inc., 1957- 60, gen. counsel, 1960-63. Dir. First Pa. Banking & Trust Co. Mem. 3d Circuit Jud. Conf. Pres. bd. Singing City; bd. dirs. Mercy Douglass Hosp., Big Bros. Served with USAF, 1946-48. Recipient award of recognition Alpha Phi Alpha, 1969. Mem. Am., Fed., Pa., Phila. bar assns., Am. Arbitration Assn., Am. Trial Lawyers Assn. Home: 4701 Willard Av Chevy Chase MD 20015 Office: 1800 G St NW Washington DC 20506

BROWN, WILLIAM J., pub. co. exec.; b. Youngstown, O., 1913. Pres., treas., pub., gen. mgr. Vindicator Printing Co., Youngstown. Pres., gen. mgr. WFMJ Broadcasting Co.; dir. Dollar Savs. & Trust Co., Home Savs. & Loan Co. Trustee Youngstown Hosp. Assn., Youngstown State U. Home: 302 Broadman Poland Rd Youngstown OH 44501 Office: Vindicator Sq Youngstown OH 44501*

BROWN, WILLIAM L., banker; b. Hendersonville, N.C., Feb. 1, 1922; s. William W. and Sarah (Maxwell) B.; student Mars Hill Coll., Newberry Coll.; M.B.A., Harvard, 1947; m. Helen Presbrey, June 1947; children—Kathryn H., Richard P., Steven J., Melissa M. With First Nat. Bank Boston, 1949—, now pres., dir.; dir. Stone & Webster, Inc., N.Y.C., Standard Internat. Corp., Andover, Mass. Vice pres., mem. exec. com., trustee Children's Hosp. Med. Center, Boston. Served to lt. USNR, World War II. Home: 80 Black Oak Rd Weston MA 02193 Office: 67 Milk St Boston MA 02106

BROWN, WILLIAM LEE LYONS, Jr., distilling co. exec.; b. Louisville, Aug. 22, 1936; s. William Lee Lyons and Sara (Shallenberger) B.; B.A., U. Va., 1958; B.S., Am. Inst. Fgn. Trade, 1960; m. Alice Cary Farmer, June 13, 1959; children—William Lee Lyons III, Alice Cary, Stuart Randolph. Sales rep. Ariz., Brown-Forman Distillers Corp., Phoenix, 1959-61, v.p., Louisville, 1965-68, sr. v.p., 1968—; asst. v.p. Jos. Garneau Co. import div. Brown-Forman, N.Y.C., 1961-62, v.p., Paris, France, 1962-65; dir. Brown-Forman Distillers Corp., First Nat. Bank of Louisville, Ky. Trust Co., First Ky. Co., Jack Daniel Distillery. Bd. dirs. Internat. Center U. Louisville, Shakertown, Inc., Pleasant Hill, Ky. bd. govs. J.B. Speed Art Mus., Louisville. Served to 1st lt. U.S. Army, 1958-59. Decorated Commandeur d'Honneur, Commanderie du Bontemps de Medoc et des Graves. Mem. Soc. Sons Colonial Wars. Republican. Episcopalian. Clubs: Travellers (Paris); Fishers Island (N.Y.) Country; River Valley, Wynn Stay, Pendennis, Louisville Country (Louisville); Fifth Avenue, University (N.Y.C.). Home: Fincastle Prospect KY 40059 Office: 850 Dixie Hwy Louisville KY 40210

BROWN, WILLIAM OSCAR, oil co. exec.; b. Lincoln, Neb., Mar. 14, 1909; s. James Arthur and Ida (Dibble) B.; A.B., Neb. Wesleyan U., 1930; J.D., U. Neb., 1933; grad. student Columbia, 1948; m. M. Mildred Farnsworth, Aug. 15, 1931 (dec. 1961); children—William Oscar, Richard Arthur, Steven Rogers, Patricia (Mrs. Keith A. Larsen); m. 2d, Gertrude Harris Wood, Nov. 25, 1964; stepchildren—Barbara (Mrs. John M. Sutton), Pamela. Admitted to Neb. bar, 1933; with firm Brown & Brown, Lincoln, 1933-42; investigator Civil Service Commn., VA, CIA, 1942-48; asst. mgr. land dept. Columbian Carbon Co., 1948-63, asst. corp. sec., 1967-68, corp. sec., 1968—; corp. sec. Cities Service Oil Co., Tulsa, 1963—; corp. sec. Coltexo Corp., Cities Service Tulsa Inc., Petgas Co., Hydrocarbon Prodn. Co., Cities, Service Pipeline Co., Badger Pipe Line Co., Cities Service Fractionators, Inc.; dir. Petgas Co. Corp.; sec. Can. Cities Ltd. Commr., v.p. Hutchinson River council Boy Scouts Am., 1948-63, mem. exec. bd. Indian Nations council, 1969—; conf. lay leader N.Y. Conf. Methodist Ch., 1960-63, dir. Meth. Mens Work, Okla. Conf., 1964-68; bd. dirs. Tulsa Goodwill Industries, Inc. Recipient Silver Beaver award Boy Scouts Am., 1958. Mem. Mid-Continent Oil & Gas Assn., Am. Petroleum Inst., Tulsa Assn. Petroleum Landmen, Am. Soc. Corporate Secs. Pi Kappa Delta, Blue Key. Home: 5811 E 53d St Tulsa OK 74135 Office: PO Box 300 Tulsa OK 74102

BROWN, WILLIAM RUSSELL, lawyer; b. Holly Springs, Miss., July 5, 1914; s. Horace Brightberry and Aileen (Blackburn) B.; B.B.A., U. Tex., 1937, LL.B., 1937; m. Ruth Cunningham, Apr. 19, 1941; children—Betsy (Mrs. Thomas M. Smith III), Virginia, Russell. Admitted to Tex. bar, 1937, since practiced in Houston; partner firm Baker & Botts, and predecessors, 1948—; gen. counsel, dir Houston Lighting & Power Co. Served to lt. USNR, 1943-45. Decorated Bronze Star. Fellow Tex. Bar Found.; mem. Am., Tex., Houston bar assns., Newcomen Soc., Chancellors, Friar Soc., Order of Coif, Delta Tau Delta, Beta Gamma Sigma. Clubs: Houston, Houston Country. Democrat. Episcopalian. Home: 5816 Bayou Glen Houston, TX 77027. Office: One Shell Plaza Houston TX 77002

BROWN, WILLIAM SELSOR, ret. architect; b. Washington Court House, O., July 29, 1909; s. Harrison Foster and Florence E. (Selsor) B.; B.Arch., Ohio State U., 1932; M.Sc., Columbia, 1935; m. Sara Louise Ervin, Aug. 3, 1935; children—Nancy Davis, Peter Harrison, David Selsor. Schermerhorn traveling fellow Columbia, 1939; partner Skidmore, Owings & Merrill, N.Y.C., 1949-69; partner charge Terrace Plaza Hotel, Cin., Lever House, N.Y.C., Mfrs. Trust Co., N.Y.C., Istanbul Hilton Hotel, Town of Oak Ridge (Tenn.), Conn. Gen. Life Ins. Co., Hartford, Am. Republic Ins. Bldg., Des Moines, Union Carbide Bldg., N.Y.C. Former chmn. Archtl. Bd. Review, Rye, N.Y. Mem. A.I.A., Sigma Chi, Tau Sigma Delta. Clubs: University (N.Y.C.); Sankaty Head Golf (Nantucket, Mass.). Home: Main St PO Box 161 Siasconset MA 02564

BROWN, WILMORE KENDALL, advt. co. exec.; b. Detroit, May 23, 1927; s. Herbert H. and Faye (Daniels) B.; B.A., U. Mich., 1950; m. Marilyn J. Weihe, Nov. 3, 1951; children—Barbara Joan, Claudia Lynn, Cynthia Ann. V.P. McCann- Erickson, Inc., N.Y.C., 1954-64; exec. v.p. Gaynor & Ducas, Inc., N.Y.C., 1964-66, Zlowe Co., N.Y.C., 1966-68; pres. W. Kendall Brown & Co., 1968—. Served with M.I., AUS, 1945-47. Home: 58 Huckleberry Hill Rd New Canaan CT 06840

BROWN, WINTHROP GILMAN, govt. ofcl.; b. Seal Harbor, Me., July 12, 1907; s. William Adams and Helen Gilman (Noyes) B.; ed. St. Paul's Sch., Concord, N.H.; B.A., Yale, 1929, LL.B., 1932; m. Peggy Ann Bell, Dec. 28, 1946; children—Winthrop, Julia, Anne. Clk., Platt, Taylor and Walker, N.Y.C., 1932-38; mem. firm Bleakley, Platt & Walker, 1938-41; in office of gen. counsel Lend Lease Adminstrn., Washington, 1941; exec. officer Harriman Mission, U.S. embassy, London, 1941-43, U.S. Lend-Lease Mission to India, 1943, Mission for Econ. Affairs, U.S. embassy, London, 1943-45, acting chief, 1945; chief Div. Comml. Policy, Dept. State, Washington, 1945-48; acting dir. Office Internat. Trade Policy, 1947-48; dir., 1948-50, dir. Office Internat. Materials Policy, 1950-52; dep. to minister for econ. affairs U.S. embassy, London, 1952-55, minister, econ. affairs, dir. U.S. operations mission, 1955-57; minister-counsellor, dep. chief mission Am. embassy, New Delhi, India, 1957-60; U.S. ambassador to Laos, 1960-62; dep. commandant for fgn. affairs Nat. War Coll., Washington, 1962-64; U.S. ambassador to Korea, 1964-67; dep. asst. sec. state for East Asian and Pacific affairs State Dept., 1968—. Recipient President's Medal for Distinguished Fed. Civilian Service, 1963. Mem. Soc. Scroll and Key, Zeta Psi. Club: Chevy Chase (Washington). Home: 2435 Tracy Pl NW Washington DC 20008 Office: Dept State Washington DC 20520

BROWN, WOOD, lawyer; b. Ruston, La., Oct. 26, 1905; s. Samuel Wood and Mary Gertrude (Mayfield) B.; A.B., Davidson Coll., 1926; LL.B., Tulane U., 1930; J.S.D., Yale, 1931; m. Martha Hyland, Feb. 14, 1933; children—Wood, Claiborne Hyland (dec.), Peter Howard. Admitted to La. bar, 1930; asso. firm Spencer, Phelps, Dunbar & Marks, New Orleans, 1931-41; partner firm Montgomery, Barnett, Brown & Read, and predecessor, 1942—; lectr. law sch. Tulane U., 1934—, prof., 1941-65, prof. emeritus, 1965—; mem. bd. adv. editors Tulane Law Rev. Chmn. bd. Supervisors Elections for New Orleans, 1940-48; pres. Bur. Govtl. Research of New Orleans, 1950-52, mem. Civil Service Commn., 1953-58. Past Pres. So. area YMCA, past pres., dir. New Orleans; dir. Protestant Home for Aged; pres. New Orleans Community Chest, 1962-65, bd. dirs., 1965-69; trustee Pub. Affairs Research Council La.; trustee So. Eye Bank, Gulf States Eye Surgery Found.; mem. exec. bd. New Orleans council Boy Scouts Am. Research fellow Southwestern Legal Found. Mem. Am. Law Inst., Am., La., New Orleans (past v.p.) bar assns., Am. Assn. Ins. Counsel, New Orleans C. of C., Order of Coif, Sigma Chi, Phi Delta Phi. Presbyn. Club: Boston. Home: 619 Chartres St New Orleans LA 70130 Office: Nat Bank of Commerce Bldg New Orleans LA 70112

BROWN, WYLIE D., banker. Vice pres., cashier Nat. Bank Commerce, San Antonio, Tex. Office: Soledad Martin and Pecan Sts San Antonio TX 78205*

BROWNE, ALAN KINGSTON, banker; b. Alameda, Cal., Nov. 12, 1909; s. Ralph Stuart and Etta E. (Bouve) B.; student U. Cal., 1929; m. Elisabeth Leone Henrotte, Feb. 7, 1942. With Bankamerica Co., 1929-41, successively clk., mgr. municipal bond dept., asst. v.p.; with Bank of Am. Nat. Trust & Savs. Assn., 1941- , successively asst. cashier, asst., v.p., mgr. municipal bond dept., 1941-52, v.p., 1952-65, sr. v.p., 1965—, head investments, 1964; pres., dir. San Francisco Stadium, Inc. Mem. San Francisco Symphony Found., San Francisco Mus. Art; v.p. Cal. County Govt. Edn. Found.; bond screening com. City and County of San Francisco; first v.p. Nat. Municipal League. Chmn. bd., past pres. Friends of San Francisco Pub. Library; chmn. adv. board on financing San Francisco Bay Area Rapid Transit Dist.; dir. Adminstrv. Bldg. Corp. Served to maj. AUS, 1942-46. Mem. San Francisco C. of C. (past pres.; chmn. sr. council), Municipal Finance Officers Assn. U.S. and Can. (asso.), Municipal Forum N.Y., Air Force Assn., Assn. U.S. Army, Cal. Alumni Assn., Cal. Hist. Soc., Def. Orientation Conf. Assn., Friends Bancroft Library, Investment Bankers Assn. Am. (past gov.), S.A.R., Phi Kappa Sigma. Clubs: Bond, Olympic, Merchants Exchange, Pacific Union, Commonwealth, Stock Exchange (San Francisco), Federal City (Washington), Wall Street (N.Y.C.). Home: 307 Bridge Rd Hillsborough, CA 94010. Office: Bank of America Center San Francisco CA 94120

BROWNE, ALLAN ROLAND, lawyer; b. El Paso, Tex., Nov. 18, 1900; s. Cecil W. and Anne (Welsh) B.; A.B., Harvard, 1922; LL.B., U. Mo., Kansas City, 1925; grad. Command and Gen. Staff Coll., Ft. Leavenworth, Kan.; m. Blanche Longan, June 27, 1925; children—Virginia (Mrs. Robert Mount), Carol (Mrs. Horace Hearne); m. 2d, Phoebe Mosman Harrington, July 5, 1958. Admitted to Mo. bar, 1923, Hawaii bar, 1956, Kan. bar, 1962, U.S. Supreme Ct. bar, Ct. Appeals, Dist. Ct.; practiced in Kansas City, Mo., 1927-42, 56—; served from capt. to col., U.S. Army, 1942-56; asst. judge adv. gen. for Pacific Ocean area, 1945-46; judge adv. 8th Army, Japan, 1946-49; presiding officer Bd. Review, Washington, 1949-53; judge adv. U.S. Army Pacific, 1953-56; ret., 1956; mem. firm Ennis, Browne, Martin and Tapp, 1956—. Mem. Am., Kansas City (pres. 1962-63, chmn. grievance com.) bar assns., Mo. Assn. Trial Attys. (v.p. 1970), Mo. Bar, Inst. Mil. Law, Alumni Assn. Sch. Law U. Mo. at Kansas City (pres. 1967), Delta Theta Phi, Alpha Sigma Phi. Presbyn. Home: 6545 Overbrook Rd Shawnee Mission KS 66208 Office: Profl Bldg Kansas City MO 64106

BROWNE, BENJAMIN PATTERSON, coll. chancellor; b. Wiscasset, Me., Jan. 25, 1893; s. Benjamin Randall and Lena Evelyn (Patterson) B.; student Harvard, summer 1924, Boston U., summers 1926, 27, Sch. Theology, 1928-30, Andover-Newton Sem., 1930-32; D.D., Eastern Baptist Theol. Sem., Overbrook, Pa., 1947, William Jewell Coll., 1962; L.H.D., Hillsdale Coll., No. Bapt. Theol. Sem., 1963; Litt.D., Ottawa U., 1961; Ed.D., Judson Coll., 1967; m. Rachel Eunice Sprague, Apr. 3, 1915; children—Rachel Sprague (Mrs. Robert F. Simpson), Priscilla Alden (Mrs. W. Henry Harper), Benjamin Judson, Marcia Carol. Ordained to ministry Baptist Ch., 1912; pastor Corliss St. Ch., Bath, Me., 1912-16, Essex St. Ch., Bangor, Me., 1916-21, 1st Baptist Ch., Rockland, Me., 1921-28 (pres. Me. United Baptists Ministers Conf., 1926), 1st Baptist Ch., Winchester, Mass., 1928-32, 2nd Baptist Ch., Holyoke, Mass., 1932-41 (pres. No. Baptists Ednl. Soc., 1941-42); dir. promotion Mass. Baptist Conv. hdqrs. Tremont Temple, Boston, 1941-44; exec. sec. Pa. Baptist Conv., Phila., 1944-47; editorial exec. Christian publs. of Bd. of Edn. and Pubsl. Am. Bapt. Conv., Phila., 1947—, pres. Am. Bapt. Conv., 1962-63, also pres. Asso. Ch. Press; pres. No. Bapt. Theol. Sem., 1959-64; pres. Judson Coll., Elgin, Ill., 1962-66, chancellor, 1967—; pres. Christian Writers Conf., 1948; exec. dir. Nat Christian Author's Guild. Trustee David C. Cook Found., 1967—, Lincoln Acad. Republican. Mason. Club: Holyoke. Author: Let There Be Light, 1956; The Writers Conference Comes to You, 1956; Techniques of Christian Writing, 1959; Signal Flares, 1960; Gateway to Morning, 1961; Tales of Baptist Daring, 1962; (booklets) Meaning of Church Membership, 1944, Martyrs of Christ, 1945, Magnificent Men, 1946. Compiler and editor: Christian Journalism for Today, 1952. Staff editor Mass. Baptist Bull., 1941-44, editor The Penn Baptist 1944-47, The Baptist Leader, 1947. Home: 1349 Tyler Lane Elgin IL 60120

BROWNE, BURTON, advertising exec.; b. Harbor Beach, Mich., July 14, 1905; s. Burton Fulmer and Grace Greenwood (Winches) B.; ed. Jackson, Michigan High Sch. and Chicago Acad. Fine Arts; D.Sc. (hon.), Hollywood U., 1950; m. Jeneva Louise McCrum, Mar. 1, 1929 (div.); children—Belinda, Candis. Owner art studio, artist and illustrator, 1926; art editor Quigley Publs.; editor mag., Retail Furniture Selling, later publisher; copy chief R. J. A. McLaughlin Advertising Agency; adv. mgr. Silver-Marshall Mfg. Co., Howard Radio Co.; partner Ford, Browne & Matthews Advt. Agency; sr. partner Burton Browne Advt.; pres. Gaslight Clubs, Aero Phonograph Needle Company, Milline Publishing Co.; retired temporarily to pub. annual book, Best Nat. Advt. of Year; pres. Browne & Hastin mfrs. reps.; pres. Burton Browne Prodns. (films). Served as officer USNR. Recipient citation from Navy for Civilian

Activities, World War II. Mem. Am. Radio Relay League. Home: 22 W Schiller St Chicago IL 60610 winter: 717 Ponte Vedra Blvd Ponte Vedra FL 32802 Office: 664 N Michigan Blvd Chicago IL 60611

BROWNE, CLEMENT GEORGE, mgmt. cons.; b. Vienna, Austria, Feb. 17, 1930; s. Herman H. and M. Steffy (Hermann) B.; came to U.S., 1940, naturalized, 1946; B.A., Syracuse U., 1951; M.S., Columbia, 1955; m. Gisela Helene Pluskat, Mar. 22, 1954; children—Bruce Clement, Eric Clement (dec.), Cordelia Gisela. With Procter & Gamble Co., 1955-62, asst. brand mgr., 1960-62; with Andrew Jergens Co., Cin., 1962—, marketing dir. Europe, 1965-68; exec. v.p. Andrews Jergens Co. Ltd., 1968-71; partner marketing services firm, Toronto, Can., 1971—; dir. Jergens Italiana, S.P.A. Served to 1st lt. USAF, 1951-53. Home: PH 6 50 Prince Arthur Av Toronto 5 Ontario Canada

BROWNE, CORNELIUS PAYNE, educator; b. Madison, Wis., Oct. 30, 1923; s. Frederick Lincoln and Vera (Payne) B.; B.A., U. Wis., 1946, Ph.D., 1951; m. Cynthia Cochrane, July 6, 1957; children—Margaret, Cornelius. Research asso. Mass. Inst. Tech. at Cambridge, 1951-56; prof. physics U. Notre Dame, 1956—; cons. Argonne Nat. Lab., Los Alamos Nat. Lab. Served with USNR, 1944-45. Mem. Sigma Xi (pres. 1969-70), Phi Beta Kappa, Theta Delta Chi. Episcopalian (chpt. mem. 1968-70). Club: Eagle Lake (Mich.). Yacht. Contbr. articles profl. jours. Research in nuclear reactions and excitation levels Browne-Buechner broad-range magnetic spectrograph. Home: 1616 Dorwood Dr South Bend IN 46617 Office: Physics Dept U Notre Dame Notre Dame IN 46556

BROWNE, DONALD EDWARD, bus. exec.; b. Los Angeles, Dec. 23, 1909; s. Henry Lawrence and Florence Christine (Sankey) B.; A.B., U. Cal., 1930; m. Evelyn Martin, July 12, 1936; children—Katrine E., Victoria. Staff, Pacific Nat. Bank, San Francisco, 1931-34; with Chevrolet div. Gen. Motors Corp., Oakland, Cal., 1934-35; accounting and office mgmt. Henry J. Kaiser Co. & Affiliates, 1935-46; comptroller Kaiser Aluminum & Chem. Corp. & Subsidiaries, 1946-50, v.p., treas., 1950-56; v.p., treas. Kaiser Industries Corp., 1957—. Home: 12050 Tartan Way Oakland CA 94619 Office: 300 Lakeside Dr Oakland CA 94612

BROWNE, DUDLEY E., business exec.; b. Los Angeles, 1912; grad. U. Cal. at Los Angeles; m. Helen Currer, 1947; children—Barbara Anne, Lindsay Dudley, Mark Alan. Former comptroller, v.p. finance, v.p. finance and adminstrn. Lockheed Aircraft Corp., now dir., sr. v.p.; dir. Lockheed Aircraft Corp. of Can., Ltd., Lockheed Air Terminal, Inc., Lockheed Aircraft Internat., Inc., Lockheed Western Export Co., Lockheed Electronics Co., Inc., Tel Autograph Corp.; mem. central trust com. United Cal. Bank. Mem. investment co. Childrens Hosp. Bd. dirs. Hosp. of Good Samaritan, YMCA of Los Angeles; past pres. Financial Execs. Research Found.; chmn. bd. trustees Buckley Sch. Mem. Cal. Taxpayers Assn. (past pres.), Financial Execs. Inst. (past nat. pres.), Am. Inst. C.P.A.'s, Nat. Assn. Accountants, Cal. Soc. C.P.A.'s, Am. Accounting Assn. Home: 504 N Beverly Glen Blvd Los Angeles CA 90024 Office: Lockheed Aircraft Corp PO Box 551 Burbank CA 91503

BROWNE, FRANCIS CEDRIC, patent lawyer; b. Cleve., Jan. 22, 1915; s. William Henry and Anna Loretta (Ginley) B.; student Ohio State U.; 1935; A.B., U. Akron, 1936; J.D., Cleve. State U., 1942; postgrad. George Washington U., 1942, 50; m. Elizabeth Ann Cullen, July 3, 1937; children—Richard C., James F., Barbara Ann, Martha Louise, David F. Admitted to D.C., Md. bars; patent lawyer, Washington, 1945—; partner firm Browne, Beveridge & DeGrandi, and predecessor; patent solicitor Indsl. Rayon Corp., Cleve., 1938-41; pres. Bain Internat., Inc., 1964—, Capsyn, Inc., 1966—. Served as patent atty., USAF, 1945; col. Judge Adv. Gen. Dept., USAF res. ret. Mem. Am., Fed., Inter-Am., D.C., Md. bar assns., John Carroll Soc., Am. Patent Law Assn., Internat. Assn. for Protection Indsl. Property (Am. group pres. 1964-68, exec. com. 1964—), Canadian Patent and Trademark Inst., Am. Chem. Soc., U.S. Trademark Assn., Thomas More Soc. (treas. 1961—), Catholic War Vets., Inter- Am. Assn. Indsl. Property (hon. pres. 1964—), Chartered Inst. Patent Agts. (Gt. Britain), Delta Theta Phi, Phi Delta Theta (pres. Washington alumni 1962-63), Omicron Delta Kappa, Pi Kappa Delta. K.C. (4th). Clubs: N.Y. Athletic; Nat. Lawyers (gov., sec. 1959—), Patent Lawyers, Army Navy Country, Internat., Cosmos, Capitol Hill (Washington). Home: 4936 Western Av Chevy Chase MD 20016 Office: Fed Bar Bldg West Washington DC 20006 also 50 Lincoln's Inn Fields London WC2 England

BROWNE, GLENN GORDON, b. Park City, Utah, Dec. 17, 1917; s. Joseph Stacy and Emily (Gordon) B.; student U. Cal. at Berkeley, 1934-36; m. Barbara Ann Jameyson, Sept. 5, 1948; children—Linda Louise, Daniel Glenn. Asst. v.p., regional mgr. Fed. Land Bank, Berkeley, Cal., 1936-58; asst. dir. program and econ. policy, chief investment and finance div. AID, Dept. State, Seoul, Korea, 1959-64; dep. gov., dir. land bank service FCA, Washington, 1964-68; fiscal agt. Fiscal Agy., Farm Credit Banks of U.S., N.Y.C., 1968—. Spl. cons. U.S. Dept. State, South Vietnam, spl. cons. on credit and banking to Thai Govt., 1966, 68; U.S. cons. to 6th Far East Workshop on Agr. Credit and Coops., Bangkok. Mem. S.E. Asia Devel. Adv. Group. Served with USNR, 1942-45. Named Ky. Col. Clubs: Bond, Darien Boat, Bankers of Am. Home: 8 Silver Lakes Dr Darien CT 06820 Office: 1 Chase Manhattan Plaza New York City NY 10005

BROWNE, HARRY L., lawyer; b. South Bend, Ind., July 27, 1911; s. Alex and Lena (Godfried) B.; B.S., Ind. U., 1934, J.D., 1936; postgrad. labor law, Columbus U., Washington, 1939; m. Helen Lieberman, Apr. 16, 1942; 1 son, Douglas F. Admitted to Ind. bar, 1936, Mo. bar, 1948, U.S. Supreme Ct. bar; pvt. practice, South Bend, 1936-38; atty. NLRB, 1938-49, regional atty. 6th region, 1948-49; practiced in Kansas City, Mo., 1949—; mem. firm Spencer, Fane, Britt & Browne, 1951—. Labor adv. chmn. Starlight Theatre Assn., Kansas City, Mo.; chmn. Kansas City Personnel Appeal Bd. Bd. dirs. Menorah Hosp., Kansas City, Planned Parenthood, Greater Kansas City Sports Commn.; bd. govs., trustee Kansas City Philharmonic Assn.; hon. trustee Rockhurst Coll., Kansas City U., Kansas City Conservatory; hon. fellow Truman Library Inst. Served to lt. USNR, 1942-45; PTO. Mem. Am. (co-chmn. com. on relations between lawyers and agys. and depts. in field labor law, mem. com. on practice and procedure under Nat. Labor Relations Act), Kansas City (chmn. labor com. 1960-63) bar assns., Mo. Bar (chmn. labor com. 1957-61), Am. Judicature Soc., Lawyers Assn. Kansas City, Kansas City C. of C., Nat. Retail Merchants Assn., Am. Retail Fedn. Rotarian (past dir., sec.-treas., pres. 1970-71 Kansas City). Contbr. articles to profl. jours. Home: 1220 W 69th Terrace Kansas City MO 64106 Office: Power & Light Bldg 106 W 14th St Kansas City MO 64106

BROWNE, JAMES CLAYTON, educator; scientist; b. Conway, Ark., Jan. 16, 1935; s. Walter Everett and Louise (James) B.; B.A., Hendrix Coll., 1956; Ph.D., U. Tex., 1960; m. Gayle Carleton Moseley, July 11, 1959; children—Clayton, Duncan, Valerie. Asst. prof. physics U. Tex., 1960-64, prof., 1968—; NSF postdoctoral fellow Queen's U., Belfast, Ireland, 1964-65, prof., dir. computer lab., 1965-68; cons. Nat. Sci. Found., Sandia Research Labs., Geophysics Corp. Am.; sec., dir. Information Research Assos., Inc. Fellow Brit. Computer Soc., Am. Phys. Soc.; mem. Soc. Indsl. and Applied Mathematics, Assn. Computing Machinery, A.A.A.S., Sigma Xi. Contbr. articles sci. jours. Home: 3410 Mt Barker St Austin TX 78731

BROWNE, JAMES ROLL, educator; b. Dayton, O., Mar. 22, 1904; s. Walter Wilson and Mabel (Roll) B.; B.S., U.S. Naval Acad., 1926; M.A., U. Cin., 1934; Ph.D., U. Chgo., 1940; m. Elizabeth Thomas, Dec. 26, 1939; children—Thomas, Julia. Commd. ensign U.S. Navy, 1926; resigned, 1929; engr. diesel div. Cooper- Bessemer Corp., Grove City, Pa., 1929-31; instr. Ohio Mil. Inst., Cin., 1931-36; teaching fellow U. Mich., 1937-38; former mem. faculty Kenyon Coll., prof. Romance langs., Archer M. Huntington prof. Spanish lang. and lit. Served to comdr. USNR, 1941-46. Grantee Fund Advancement Edn., 1952-53. Mem. Modern Lang. Assn., Am. Assn. Tchrs. Spanish and Portuguese. Contbr. profl. jours. Editor. Studies of the Spanish Speaking World, 1950. Home: Box 106 Gambler OH 43022

BROWNE, JOHN SYMONDS LYON, physician, educator; b. London, Eng., Apr. 13, 1904; s. William Lyon and Ellen Winifred (Nealor) B.; A.B., McGill U., 1925, B.Sc., 1929, M.D.C.M., 1929, Ph.D., 1932; LL.D., Queen's U., 1953. Royal Soc. Can. travelling fellow U. Gottingen, U. Graz, and U. Coll., London, 1932-33; lectr. medicine and pathol. chemistry McGill U., Montreal, Que., Can., 1933, asst. prof. medicine, 1938, asso. prof. medicine, 1945-47, prof. medicine, chmn. dept., 1947-55, prof., chmn. dept. investigative medicine, 1955-69, emeritus prof., 1971—, prof. exptl. medicine McGill Royal Victoria Hosp., 1933, physician, 1941-66, asst. dir., 1940, acting dir. Univ. Clinic, 1942-44, dir., 1947-55, now cons. in medicine; Charles Mickle fellow U. Toronto, 1963. Recipient Can. medal, 1967. Fellow Royal Soc. Can., Royal Coll. Physicians Can., A.C.P.; mem. Can., Am. physiol. socs., Soc. Expt. Biology and Medicine, Montreal Physiol. Soc. (past pres.), Endocrine Soc. (pres. 1948), Brit. Endocrinology Soc., Canadian Med. Assn., Montreal Medico-Chirurg. Soc. (pres. 1949), Am. Soc. Clin. Investigation (pres. 1947), Assn. Am. Physicians, Am. Clin. and Climatological Assn. Contbr. articles to med. jours. Home: 900 Sherbrooke St W Montreal 110 Quebec Canada Office: Strathcoma Medical Bldg McGill Univ 3640 University St Montreal 112 Quebec Canada

BROWNE, JOSEPH BUSHEY, banker; b. Balt., Apr. 20, 1907; s. Joseph George and Florence (Bushey) B.; student Balt. City Coll., Johns Hopkins, U. Balt. With Union Trust Co. of Md., Balt., 1928—, beginning as clk., successively auditor. br. mgr., asst. v.p., v.p., 1928-59, pres., chmn. bd., also dir.; dir. Nat. Sash Weight Corp.; treas., dir. Industrial Corp. Served from 1st lt. to col., USAAF, 1943-46. Decorated Air medal, Presidential citation. Home: 1 Goodale Rd Baltimore MD 21212 Office: Union Trust Co Baltimore and St Paul Sts Baltimore MD 21203

BROWNE, KENNETH ALTON, educator; b. Edgar, Neb., Sept. 1, 1906; s. George Nathan Richard and Lucretia Garfield (Warren) B.; A.B., Hastings Coll., 1928; A.M., Stanford, 1931; Ph.D. (Harrison fellow), U. Pa., 1941; LL.D., Doane Coll., 1949; m. Maria Dorothea Bauer, Aug. 24, 1931. High sch. prin., Callaway, Neb., 1929-30, Fullerton, Neb., 1931-34; dir. publicity, instr. journalism and edn., Hastings Coll., 1934-39, registrar, dir. publs., prof. edn. and journalism, 1940-44; asst. to dir. coll. dept. Presbyn. Bd. Christian Edn., Phila., 1938-39; dean, dir. admissions Doane Coll, Crete, Neb., 1944-49; dean Univ., Ill. Wesleyan U., Bloomington, 1949-51; dean instrn., Md. State Tchrs. Coll., Towson, 1951-63, acting pres., 1959-60; dean instrn. Wayne (Neb.) State Coll., 1963-65; prof. edn., chmn. higher edn. Okla. State U., Stillwater, 1965-66; coordinator tchr. edn. Md. Dept. Edn., Balt., 1966—. Sec., Md. Tchr. Edn. Adv. Council. Chmn. Lutheran Campus Christian Ministry Com. for Md. and Del. Mem. Md. Tchrs. Assn., N.E.A., Phi Delta Kappa, Lutheran. Mason. Home: 414 Range Rd Baltimore MD 21204

BROWNE, LAWRENCE J., bank exec. Auditor, Queens County Savs. Bank, Flushing, N.Y. Office: 38-25 Main St Flushing NY 11352*

BROWNE, MALCOLM WILDE, journalist; b. N.Y.C., Apr. 17, 1931; s. Douglas Granzow and Dorothy Rutledge (Wilde) B.; student Swarthmore Coll., 1948-50, N.Y. U., 1950-52; m. Huynh thi Le Lieu, July 18, 1966. Cons. chemist, tech. writer, 1952-56; newsman, copy editor Middletown (N.Y.) Daily Record, 1958-60; with Balt. bur. A.P., 1960-61, chief corr. for Viet Nam, 1961-65; Saigon corr. ABC, 1965-66; freelance writer and corr., N.Y.C., 1966-68; New York Times corr. in Buenos Aires, 1968-71, in S. Asia, 1971—. Press officer Saigon U.S.O., 1963-68. Served with AUS, 1956-58. Recipient 1st prize World Press Photo award The Hague, 1963, Pulitzer prize fgn. corr., 1964, Overseas Press Club award, 1964, Sigma Delta Chi award, 1964, Louis M. Lyons award, 1964, Nat. Headliners Club award, 1964; A.P. Mng. Editors award, 1964; Edward R. Murrow Meml. fellow, Council on Fgn. Relations, 1966-67. Clubs: Overseas Press (N.Y.C.); Nat. Press (Washington). Author: The New Face of War, 1965; also numerous articles. Address: care of Fgn News Desk NY Times 229 W 43d St New York City NY 10036

BROWNE, MILLARD CHILD, editor; b. Sprague, Wash., Feb. 7, 1915; s. Clarence Swain and Irma Josephine (Child) B.; A.B., Stanford, 1936, M.A., 1939; postgrad. (Nieman fellow) Harvard, 1942-43; m. Jane Sweet, Aug. 25, 1939; children—Katherine Anne (Mrs. Samuel Kunkle), Millard Warren, Jeffrey Child, Barbara Jane. Reporter, Columnist, editorial writer Cal. newspapers, Santa Paula Chronicle, Santa Ana Jour., Sacramento Union, 1936-42; asso. editor Sacramento Union, 1943-44; editorial writer Buffalo Evening News, 1944—, chief editorial writer, 1953-66, editorial page editor, 1966—. Mem. Clarence (N.Y.) Sch. Bd., 1953-65. Recipient Freemdoms Found. citation for editorial writing, 1953, 54, 55, 57, 69. Mem. Nat. Conf. Editorial Writers (pres. 1962-63), Am. Soc. Newspaper Editors, Sigma Delta Chi, Sigma Alpha Epsilon. Unitarian. Home: 41 Meadowstream Dr Snyder NY 14226 Off ce: 218 Main St Buffalo NY 14202

BROWNE, MORGAN TREW, editor; b. Chestertown, Md., Nov. 22, 1919; s. Morgan and Mary Groome (Trew) B.; student Balt. City Coll., 1934-37, Johns Hopkins, 1937-40; m. Ann Elizabeth Riley, Feb. 14, 1949; children—Elizabeth, Morgan. Mgr. Sci. Book Club, Religious Book Club, 1945-46; mng. editor Tide mag., 1946-49, 1949-53, editor, 1953-50, also gen. mgr.; exec. v.p., also gen. mgr.; exec. v.p., editorial dir. Bill Communications. Dir. periodicals N.A.M., 1949-51. Home: Eaton's Neck Rd Northport NY 11768 Office: 630 3d Av New York City NY 10017

BROWNE, SAMUEL STANHOPE STRYKER, educator; b. Wynnewood, Pa., Nov. 13, 1904; s. Thomas Beaver and Sarah Stryker (Albert) B.; A.B., Princeton, 1926; B.Litt., Oxford, 1929; A.M., Harvard, 1940, Ph.D., 1944; m. Florence Jeanette Reynolds, May 17, 1930 (dec. 1966); children—Stanhope Stryker, Ann DeBaun; m. 2d, Ruth Huntington Johnston, Dec. 16, 1967. Instr., Colo. Coll., Colorado Springs, 1930-34, asst. prof., 1934-43, asso. prof., 1943-47; asso. prof. U. Cin., 1947-65, prof. philosophy, 1965—. Mem. Am. Philos. Assn., Am. Assn. U. Profs. Author: A Pragmatist Theory of Truth and Reality, 1930, Fundamentals of Deductive Logic, 1964. Home: 1003 Dana Av Cincinnati OH 45229

BROWNE, SECOR DELAHAY, govt. ofcl.; b. Chgo., July 22, 1916; s. Aldis Jerome and Elizabeth (Cunningham) B.; A.B., Harvard, 1938; m. Mary Denise Giles, Aug. 23, 1945; children—Patrick R., Giles C. Engr. draftsman Kroeschell Engring. Co., Chgo., 1938-39; engr. salesman Barber-Colman Co., Rockford, Ill., 1939-42, mgr. aircraft prodn., 1946-51; with Clifford Mfg. Co., Waltham, Mass., 1951-55; pres., chmn. bd. Browne & Shaw Co., 1955-69. Browne & Shaw Research Corp., 1963-68; asso. prof. Mass. Inst. Tech., 1958-69; v.p. Bolt, Beranek and Newman, Inc., Cambridge, Mass., 1968-69; asst. sec. for research and tech. Dept. Transp., 1969; chmn. CAB, 1969—. Mem. Lincoln (Mass.) Republican Town Com., 1962-68. Served to maj. USAAF, 1942-46. Decorated Bronze Star. Mem. Soc. Automotive Engrs., Am. Heating, Ventilating and Refrigerating Engrs., Am. Helicopter Soc. Roman Cath. Clubs: Harvard, St. Botolph (Harvard); Wings (N.Y.C.); Nat. Aviation (Washington); Kittery Point Yacht (Kittery, Me.). Author articles. Home: Trapelo Rd Lincoln, MA 01773. Office: 4201 Cathedral Av NW Washington DC 20016*

BROWNE, SYD, artist; b. Bklyn., Aug. 21, 1907; s. William David and Lillian Isabel (Danforth) B.; student Pratt Inst., 1927-29. Art Student's League, 1930- 32; m. Sandra James, July 28, 1934, Exhibited at N.A.D., Corcoran Gallery, Pa. Acad., Chgo., Internat. Water Color Show, Butler Art Inst., Met. Mus., ann. shows Am. Water Color Soc., Audubon Artists; one-man exhbn. Grand Central Art Galleries; works in permanent collections S.I. Inst., New Britain Mus., Library Congress, N.Y. Pub. Library, Pvt. collections; art instr. Newark Sch. Fine and Indsl. Art, 1947-50. Served with C.E., AUS, World War II. Recipient Mischa Lempert Meml. prize Salmagundi Club, also Shaw and Hill meml. prizes; Emy Herzfield prize Audubon Artists; William Church Osborne and Joseph Grumbacher prizes Am. Water Color Soc.; bronze medal of honor Allied Artists; Thomas Saltz prize, Washington; Herman Wick meml. prize Salmagundi Club, 1956; Stanton and Katherine Woodman prize Ogunquit Art Center, 1960, 64; hon. mention Ann. Black and White Exhbn., Salmagundi Club, 1962; Council Am. Artists prize, 1967. Mem. N.A.D., Am. Water Color Soc., Audubon Artists. Club: Salmagundi. Home: Winter Harbor ME 04693

BROWNE, VINCENT J., ednl. adminstr.; b. Washington, July 21, 1917; A.B., Howard U., 1938; A.M., Harvard, 1941, Ph.D. in Govt., 1946; married, 1943; one child. Research asst. Carnegie Corp., 1939-40; instr. polit. sci. Howard U., Washington, 1941-42, asst. prof., 1946-50, asso. prof., 1950-61, asst. to pres., 1955-64, dir. affairs scholars program, 1964-67, dir. civil rights document project, also Fund For Advanced Edn., 1968-70, dean Coll. Liberal Arts, 1970—; spl. asst. field relations Fed. Civil Def. Adminstrn., 1951-53. Cons. Fed. Civil Def. Adminstrn. 1954-55, Pres.'s Commn. Vet. Benefits, 1955-56. Served with AUS, 1941-46. Mem. Soc. Pub Adminstrn., Polit. Sci. Assn. Contbr. articles to profl. publs. Address: 3915 24th St NE Washington DC 20018*

BROWNE, WILLIAM HERMAN, business forms mfg. co. exec.; b. Havelock, Ont., Can., Mar. 25, 1901; s. Johnson and Augusta (Hicks) B.; B Commerce, Queen's U., Kingston, Ont., 1923; m. Phyllis Margaret Mary McManus, Feb. 23, 1925. Cashier, Brit. Am. Oil Co. Ltd., 1923-25; tech. service Goodyear Tire & Rubber Co. Can. Ltd., 1925; with Moore Corp. Ltd., Toronto, Ont., 1925—, sec., 1935-55, exec. v.p., sec., 1955-59, exec. v.p., 1959-62, pres., 1962-68, chmn. bd. dirs., 1968—, also dir.; pres., dir. subsidiaries. Mem. Wartime Labour Relations Bd., Ottawa, 1944-45. Bd. dirs. Canadian Mental Health Assn.; trustee Queens U. Mem. Royal Canadian Inst., Toronto Bd. Trade Mem. United Ch. Can. Mason. Clubs: University, York, Granite, National, York Downs Golf (past pres.) (Toronto); Niagara (Niagara Falls, N.Y.). Home: 239 Strathallan Wood Toronto 12 Ontario Canada Office: 330 University Av Toronto 1 Ontario Canada

BROWNELL, ELIZABETH HYDE, civic leader; b. Greenwich, Conn., Sept. 25, 1904; d. Fritz Carlton and Harriet (Baker) Hyde; grad. Emma Willard Sch., 1922; A.B., Vassar Coll., 1926; m. Kenneth C. Brownell, Feb. 12, 1927 (dec. Aug. 1958); children—Kenneth H., Ann (Mrs. J.E. Thomas), Jonathan. Bd. dirs. Internat. Social Service, Inc., 1967-69; mem. Greenwich Bd. Pub. Welfare, 1940-44, sec., 1940-41, vice chmn., 1942-43, chmn., 1943-44. Mem. Greenwich Republican Town Meeting, 1928-48. Bd. dirs., trustee Greenwich Hosp., 1933—; trustee Vassar Coll., 1955-66, Rosemary Hall, 1967—. Mem. Community Ch. (bd.). Club: Hortulus (founder 1930) (Greenwich). Address: Pecksland Rd Greenwich CT 06830

BROWNELL, GEORGE ABBOTT, lawyer; b. N.Y.C., May 13, 1898; s. George Francis and Anne (Abbott) B.; A.B., Harvard, 1919, A.M., 1920, LL.B., 1922; m. Katharine Gray Dodge, June 8, 1946. Admitted to N.Y. bar, 1922, since practiced in N.Y.; mem. firm Davis, Polk & Wardwell, and predecessors, 1922-30, partner firm, 1930—. Trustee Bklyn. Savs. Bank. Served from pvt. to 2d lt., F.A., U.S. Army, 1918, from lt. col. to brig. gen., USAAF, 1942-45; brig. gen., O.R.C. 1947. Personal rep. Pres. U.S., rank of Minister to India. Middle East, 1946, Mexico, 1948; spl. asst. to sec. air force, 1950; cons. to State Dept., 1946-57. Trustee Army Relief Society, Seeing Eye, Inc., Leake and Watts Childrens Home (chmn.), Lenox Hill Hosp., N.Y. U. Medical Center; bd. overseers Harvard, 1960-66; bd. dirs. Legal Aid Soc., N.Y.C., Pub. Health Research Inst. of N.Y.C. Decorated Order of So. Cross (Brazil). D.S.M. (U.S.), Selective Service medal; recipient William Nelson Cromwell medal N.Y. County Lawyers Assn., 1968. Mem. Am. Bar Found., Am. N.Y. State bar assns., N.Y. County Lawyers Assn., Bar Assn. N.Y.C. (v.p. 1968-70, Am. Law Inst., Council Fgn. Relations. Clubs: Century, University, Links, Harvard (pres. 1955-57), Down Town Assn., Anglers (N.Y.C.); Metropolitan (Washington); Delphic (Cambridge, Mass.); The Pilgrims, Home: 119 E 78th St New York City NY 10021 Office: 1 Chase Manhattan Plaza New York City NY 10005

BROWNELL, HERBERT, former atty. gen. of U.S.; b. Peru, Neb., Feb. 20, 1904; s. Herbert and May A. (Miller) B.; A.B., U. Neb., 1924, LL.D.; L.B., Sch. Law, Yale, 1927; m. Doris A. McCarter, June 16, 1934; children—Joan, Ann, Thomas McCarter, James Barker. Admitted to N.Y. bar, 1927; with Root, Clark, Buckner & Ballantine, 1927-29, Lord, Day & Lord, 1929-53, 57—; atty. gen. of U.S., 1953-57, U.S. mem. Permanent Hague Ct. of Arbitration; chmn. Inst. Ct. Mgmt. Bd. dirs. Childrens Village; trustee Boys Clubs of Am. Mem. Am. Judicature Soc., Am., N.Y. State bar assns., Assn. Bar City New York, Pilgrims Soc., Order of Coif, Phi Beta Kappa, Sigma Delta Chi, Delta Upsilon, Phi Delta Phi. Republican. Methodist. Clubs: Century Assn., Downtown Assn. (N.Y.C.). Office: 25 Broadway New York City NY 10004

BROWNELL, JAMES GARLAND, editor; b. Valparaiso, Ind., July 29, 1933; s. Walter Ezra and Floy Gladys (Binyon) B.; B.A. in Polit. Sci., Ind. U., 1955; diploma, Internat. Grad. Sch. for English Speaking Students, U. Stockholm (Sweden), 1956; postgrad., Valparaiso U. Law Sch., 1959-60. With Scholastic Mags., Inc., N.Y.C. 1961—, asst. to asso. editor Sr. Scholastic, 1961-64, mng. editor World Week mag., 1964-66, mng. editor Sr. Scholastic, 1966-68, editor Jr. Scholastic, 1968—. Served to 1st lt. AUS, 1957-59. Home: Kent Hollow Rd RFD 1 New Preston CT 06777 Office: 50 W 44th St New York City NY 10036

BROWNELL, JOHN ARNOLD, univ. adminstr.; b. Whittier, Cal., Sept. 26, 1924; s. Benjamin E. and Anna (Arnold) B.; B.A., Whitter Coll., 1947, M.A., 1948; Ed.D., Stanford, 1952; m. Rena Topping, Feb. 28, 1946; children—Ann Elizabeth, William Alan, Robert Benjamin. Tchr., Punahou Sch., Honolulu, 1948-50; tchr.-counsellor Whittier High Sch., 1951-54; asst. prof. Cal. State Coll. at Long Beach, 1954-58; asso. prof. Claremont (Cal.) Grad. Sch., 1958-65, prof., 1965-66; vis. prof. Internat. Christian U., Tokyo, 1964- 65; prof. edn., researchers, asso. dir. Hawaii Curriculum Center, U. Hawaii, 1966-68, dep. chancellor acad. affairs, East-West Center, 1968- -. Chmn. com. Coop. English in Japan, 1967—; bd. dirs. Nat. Council Tchrs. English, 1960-64; mem. Hawaii Adv. Council Title III, Elementary Secondary Edn. Act, 1968—, chmn., 1970—; cons. curriculum theory and design IBM Corp., 1963-64; project dir. feasibility study Pacific region ednl. lab. U.S. Office Edn., 1966—; v.p. Pacific States Student Presidents Assn., 1947-48. Bd. dirs. Orange Coast YMCA, 1957-58; chmn. bd. Christian edn. Bay Shore Community Ch., 1957-58; moderator Claremont Congl. Ch., 1960-62, mem. exec. com., 1962- 64. Phi Delta Kappa grantee, 1967-68; Harold Benjamin fellow Kappa Delta Pi, 1964-65. Mem. Am. Assn. U. Profs., Am. Ednl. Research Assn., Nat. Council Research English, Internat. House (Tokyo), Phi Delta Kappa. Author: (with A.R. King) The Curriculum and the Disciplines of KNowledge, 1966; Japan's Second Language, 1967; also articles. Home: 5243 Poola St Honolulu HI 96821

BROWNELL, LLOYD EARL, educator, chem. engr.; b. Potsdam, N.Y., Nov. 8, 1915; s. Earl Harvey and Ida (Kenyon) B.; B.Chem. Engring., Clarkson Coll., 1937, B.Mech. Engring. cum laude, 1939; M.S. in Chem. Engring., U. Mich., 1942, Ph.D. in Chem. Engring., 1947; m. Janet Doris Emmons, Aug. 14, 1938; children—Gary Gene, Stephen Bruce, John Charls, Pamela Sue, Carol Cam. Jr. engr. Gen. Chem. Co., Markus Hook, Pa., summer 1937; design engr. Baker Perkins Inc., Saginaw, Mich., 1939-40; research engr. Engring. Research Inst., U. Mich., 1940-42, mem. faculty, 1942—, prof. chem. engring., 1953—, prof. chem. and nuclear engring., 1951-59, dir. Fission Products Lab., 1951-59, dir. AEC Insts., 1961-68, on leave as cons. U.S. Army on ballistics Atlantic Richfield Hanford Co., Richland, Wash.; cons. to industry, 1947—. Mem. U.S. delegation UN Conf. Peaceful Uses of Atomic Energy, Geneva, Switzerland, 1955; mem. adv. bd. irradiated food nat. Acad. Scls.-NRC, 1959-62. Fellow Am. Inst. Chemists; mem. Am. Chem. Soc., A.A.A.S., Am. Inst. Chem. Engrs., Am. Nuclear Soc. (charter), N.Y. Acad. Sci., Inst. Food Tech., Am. Soc. Refrigeration Engrs., Sigma Xi, Tau Beta Pi, Phi Lambda Upsilon. Author: (with others) Design of Process Equipment Vessels, 1959; Radiation Uses in Industry and Science, 1961. Home: 1118 McMurray St Richland WA 99352

BROWNELL, PHILIP CURTIS, lawyer; b. Lincoln, Neb., Nov. 12, 1911; s. Herbert and May (Miller) B.; B.A., U. Neb., 1933; LL.B., Yale, 1936; m. Leola Schill, July 10, 1936; children—David, Mary. Admitted to N.Y. bar, 1936, N.C. bar, 1948, D.C. bar, 1944, U.S. Supreme Ct. bar, 1937; practiced in N.Y.C., 1937-41; atty. various govt. agys., including gen. counsel WLB, Wage Stabilization Bd., Washington, 1941-46; counsel, corp. officer Ecusta Paper Corp., Pisgah Forest, N.C., 1947-56; v.p. Olin Mathieson Chem. Corp. (now Olin Corp.), Pisgah Forest, 1958-63, v.p., gen. mgr., Packaging div., 1963-64, group v.p., 1964-69; mgr. Ecusta Paper and Film operations, Pisgah Forest, 1959-63; bd. mgrs. Ashville office Wachovia Bank and Trust Co. Mem. N.C. Gov.'s Study Commn. on Pub. Sch. System, 1967-68. Chmn. bd. dirs. U. N.C. at Asheville Found., Inc.; trustee Ashville-Biltmore Coll. Mem. Order of Coif, Phi Beta Kappa. Home: 7 Park Rd Asheville NC 28803

BROWNELL, SAMUEL MILLER, educator; b. Peru, Neb., Apr. 3, 1900; s. Herbert and May (Miller) B.; A.B., U. Neb., 1921, LL.D., 1963; A.M., Yale, 1924, Ph.D., 1926; B.L., Shurtleff Coll., 1954; Ed. D., Tufts Coll., 1954; LL.D., U. Denver, 1954, Harding Coll., 1955, Central Coll., 1955, U. S.D., 1955. High Point Coll., 1956, Wayne State U., 1959, U. Neb., 1963, Mich. State U., 1963; Ph.D., Bradley U., 1955; Ed.D., Western Mich. U., 1956; L.H.D., Doane Coll., 1966; m. Esther Delzell, June 23, 1927; children—Richard, Dorothy (Mrs. Bryce Templeton), Jane (Mrs. K. Check), Ruth (Mrs. Thomas Green). Prin., Demonstration High Sch., State Tchrs. Coll., Peru, 1921-23; asst. prof. edn. N.Y. State Coll. for Tchrs., 1926-27; supt. schs., Grosse Pointe, Mich., 1927-38; vis. prof. ednl. adminstrn., Yale, 1937-38, prof. ednl. adminstrn. Grad. Sch., 1938-53; pres. New Haven State Tchrs. Coll., 1947-53; U.S. commr. edn., 1953-56; supt. pub. schs., Detroit, 1956-66; part-time prof. urban ednl. adminstrn. Yale, 1966- -; part-time prof. edn. U. Conn., 1966-70; lectr. U. Wis., 1927, 39, Cornell U., 1930, 41, Harvard, 1931- 35, U. So. Calif., 1940, 49, 56, 59, U. Mich., 1942, 44. Vice chmn. U.S. delegation UNESCO, Montevideo, Uruguay, 1954, U.S. rep. Conf. Ministers of Edn. of Ams., Lima, Peru, 1956; chmn. U.S. delegation Internat. Conf. on Edn., Geneva, Switzerland, 1960. Mem. Mayflower Soc., Phi Beta Kappa, Phi Delta Kappa, Kappa Phi Kappa. Author: Progress in Educational Administration, 1935; Urban Education, 1962. Contbr. articles to profl. jours., and author numerous sch. surveys. Travel in S. Am., European countries, Can. Home: 311 St Ronan St New Haven CT 06511

BROWNFIELD, LYMAN, lawyer; b. Uniontown, Pa., June 7, 1913; s. William Watson and Fay (Shipman) B.; B.A., Mt. Union Coll., Alliance, O., 1934; LL.B., Duke, 1937; m. Alice Bowman, June 24, 1939; children—Diana, Candace. Admitted to Ohio bar, 1937, D.C. bar, 1961; law clk. Vorys, Sater, Seymour & Pease, 1937-42; partner Brownfield, Kosydar, Bally & Sturtz, and predecessors, Columbus, 1946—; gen. counsel FHA, 1959, HHFA, 1959-61. Sec. Claycraft Co., Columbus. Trustee, past pres. Legal Aid Soc. Columbus; trustee Mt. Union Coll. Vice chmn. Urban Renewal Commn. of Columbus, 1961-66. Served from pvt. to capt., judge adv. gen. dept., AUS, 1942-46. Mem. Fed., Am., Ohio, Columbus bar assns., Nat. Lawyers Club, Phi Kappa Tau. Republican. Methodist. Clubs: Columbus Country, University (Columbus). Home: 185 S Drexel Av Columbus OH 43209 Office: 88 E Broad St Columbus OH 43215

BROWNING, ARTHUR MONTCALM, ins. co. exec.; b. Grafton, W.Va., Sept. 4, 1908; s. William L. and Hattie L. (Corpening) B.; A.B., Dartmouth, 1930; LL.B., Harvard, 1933; m. Martha P. Reed, Sept. 1, 1934, children—Reed St. Clair, Simms C., Sandra M. Clk., Equitable Life Assurance Soc., 1934-36, legal asst. president's staff, 1936-39, asst. counsel, 1939-49, asso. group underwriter, 1949, mgr. group casualty coverages, 1949-50; admitted to N.Y. state bar, 1938; exec. asst. N.Y. Life Ins. Co., 1950-51, asst. v.p., 1951-55, 2d v.p., 1955, v.p. charge group ins., 1955-61, v.p. charge group adminstrn., 1961-62, v.p. charge group sales and adminstrn., 1962-63, v.p., 1963—. Mem. central com. Health Ins. Council, 1957-62, chmn., 1960-61, chmn. N.Y. State com., 1965—, mem. exec. com., 1969—, chmn. state council's dept., 1969-71; mem. adv. com. Nat. Health Survey, 1957-61; adviser Nat. Center Health Statistics, 1965—; N.Y. State coordinator community health action planning Health Ins. Council, 1967—; mem. N.Y.C. Mayor's Orgn. Task Force for Comprehensive Health Planning, 1968-70; mem. health task force N.Y.C. Urban Coalition, 1969—. Del. White House Conf. on Aging, 1961, 71. Bd. dirs. Greater N.Y. Safety Council, 1960—; trustee L.I. Health and Hosp. Planning Council, 1969—. Mem. Am. Pub. Health Assn., Am. Judicature Soc., Assn. Life Ins. Counsel, N.Y. State Bar Assn., Health Ins. Assn. Am. (N.Y. legislative chmn. 1968—), Gamma Delta Chi, Phi Kappa Sigma, Gamma Delta Epsilon. Conglist. Contbr. author: Group Insurance Handbook, Principles of Risk Management. Home: 96 N Woods Rd Manhasset NY 11030 Office: NY Life Ins Co 51 Madison Av New York City NY 10010

BROWNING, CHAUNCEY HOYT, judge; b. Logan, W.Va., May 15, 1903; s. Ballard Preston and Mary Ellen (Curry) B.; A.B., W.Va. U., 1924, LL.B., 1927; m. Evelyn Mahone, Chauncey Hoyt. Admitted to W.Va. bar, 1927; asst. pros. atty. Logan Co., W.Va., 1927-28, pros. atty., 1944-52; atty. City of Logan, W.Va., 1930- 32; sec. W.Va. Workmen's Compensation Commn., 1933-44; atty. gen. W.Va., 1952, judge Supreme Ct. Appeals 1952—. Mem. W.Va. Bar Assn., Kappa Sigma. Democrat. Methodist. Moose, Rotarian. Home: 3901 Kanawha Av SE Charleston WV 25304 Office: State Capitol Charleston WV 25305

BROWNING, COLLEEN, painter; b. County Cork, Eire, May 16, 1929; d. Langley and Violet (Cairnes) Browning; student Farnham Sch. Art, 1942, Salisbury Sch. Art, 1943-44, Slade Sch. Art, 1945-46; m. Geoffrey Wagner, June 14, 1949. Came to U.S., 1949, naturalized, 1956. One-man exhbns. include Edwin Hewitt Gallery, N.Y.C. 1951, 54, 57, Robert Isaacson Gallery, N.Y.C., 1960, 62, Jacques Seligmann Gallery, N.Y.C., 1965, 67, Lehigh U., 1966, Kennedy Galleries, N.Y.C., 1968, 72; group exbns. include Whitney Mus., 1951, 53, 56, 57, 63, Art Inst. Chgo., 1954, Walker Art Center, 1954, Butler Art Inst., 1953, 54, 55, 56, 58, 60, Newark Mus., 1965, Pa. Acad. Art, 1962, Fedn. Arts, 1964, Nat. Inst. Arts and Letters, 1954, 55, 56, Carnegie Internat., 1952, Rochester Meml. Art Gallery, 1950, Contemporary U.S. Art at Los Angeles County Fair, 1956, Columbia Mus., 1957, N.A.D., 1953, 57, Stanford, 1956; represented permanent collections San Francisco Palace Legion of Honor, Detroit Art Inst., Butler Mus., Milw. Art Center, N.A.D., U. Miami. Rochester Meml. Art Gallery, Columbia (S.C.) mus. Art; lectr. art City Coll. N.Y., 1960—. Recipient Turck Rienfeld award, 1959, 66; recipient prizes N.A.D., 1953, 57, Stanford U., 1956. Butler Art Inst., 1955, 56, 60, Los Angeles County Fair, 1956, Columbia (S.C.), 1957. Edwin Austen Abbey fellow, 1944; MacDowell fellow, 1956; Tupperware fellow, 1954.

BROWNING, ELMER ROSS, coll. dean; b. Logan, W.Va., Apr. 17, 1904; s. Samuel Scott and Roxie Bell (Hicks) B.; B.S., Bowling Green Coll. Commerce, 1925; B.A., Marshall U., 1932; M.E., Duke, 1936; D.E., Colo. State Coll., 1942; m. Reva Marie Boggess, Aug. 5, 1932; 1 son, Robert Ross. High sch. prin. W.Va. pub. high schs., 1925-36; dean Sch. Bus., East Carolina Coll., 1936-68; acting dean Sch. Bus. Marshall U., Huntington, W.Va., 1968—. vis. prof. Woman's Coll. U. N.C., 1946, U. Mont., 1950; prof. Shrivenham Am. U., Eng., 1945, Blarritz Am. U., France, 1946. Bd. mgrs. Planters Nat. Bank & Trust Co. Mem. coop. research com. N.C. Coll. Conf.; chmn. bus. edn. div. State Conf. on Tchr. Edn.; ednl. counsellor A.I.M. Served with AUS, 1945-46. Mem. Phi Delta Kappa, Pi Omega Pi, Delta Sigma Pi, Beta Gamma Sigma. Rotarian (past pres.). Home: 1601 E 1st St Greenville NC 27834

BROWNING, GEORGE MONROE, agronomist; b. Verona, Mo., Dec. 4, 1908; s. David Sherman and Etta Dell (Nance) B.; B.S. in Agr., U. Mo., 1932; M.S., W.Va. U., 1934, Ph.D., 1938; m. Velma Alice Calhoun, Sept. 5, 1931; 1 son, David Richard, Grad, asst. W.Va. U., 1932-34; soil scientist, then asso. soil scientist Dept. Agr., 1934-41; sr. soil scientist in Iowa, 1942-48; asst. dir. Ia. Agr. Expt. Sta. and Extension Service, Ia. State U., 1950-51, asso. dir. Ia. Agr. and Home Econs. Expt. Station, 1951-66, prof. agronomy; regional dir. Assn. N. Central Agr. Expt. Sta., 1967—. Mem. Soil Conservation Society of Am. (pres. 1963-64), Ia. Acad. Sci., Am. Soc. Agronomy, Soil Sci. Soc. Am., Sigma Xi, Gamma Sigma Delta, Phi Lambda Upsilon, Alpha Zeta. Home: 1013 Murray Dr Ames IA 50010

BROWNING, HENRY PRENTICE, banker; b. Montclair, N.J., Apr. 23, 1911; s. Henry P. and Ida Stewart (Bartow) B.; grad. Amherst Coll., 1933, Rutgers U. Sch. Banking, 1949; m. Nancy Jane Littell, Oct. 7, 1939; children—Penny (Mrs. Russell Fortune III), Nancy, Henry Prentice. With Winthrop, Mitchell & Co., Chgo., 1933-34; financial cons. E. M. Stark, Chgo., 1934- 40; asst. cashier Continental Ill. Nat. Bank & Trust Co., Chgo., 1944, 2d v.p., 1946; v.p. Worcester County Trust Co. (Mass.), 1948-56; exec. v.p. Am. Fletcher Nat. Bank & Trust Co., Indpls., 1956-57, pres., dir., 1957-69; vice chmn. Nat. Bank N.Am., N.Y.C., 1969-70; pres., chief exec. officer Exchange Bancorp., Inc., Tampa, Fla., 1970-71; dir. Arvin Industries, Inc., Columbus, Ind. Served as lt. USNR, 1944-46. Episcopalian. Home: 72 Martinique Av Tampa FL 33606

BROWNING, JAMES ALEXANDER, inventor, engring. co. exec.; b. Great Neck, N.Y., Feb. 24, 1922; s. James Herbert and Willa Bullett (Alexander) B.; A.B., Dartmouth, 1944; M.S. in Engring., Stanford, 1949; M. Marian Lucille Barkdull, June 16, 1949; children—William A., Joel B., James H. Faculty Thayer Sch., Dartmouth, 1949-66; prof. mech. engring., 1960-62, adj. prof. engring., 1962-66; chmn. bd. Thermal Dynamics Corp., Lebanon, N.H., 1958- 68; pres. Browning Engring. Corp., Hanover, N.H., 1960—; cons. high temperature research and applications, 1951—. Mem. Am. Soc. M.E., Am. Rocket Soc., Am. Welding Soc., Phi Beta Kappa, Sigma Alpha Epsilon. Inventor miniature rocket devices for indsl. use, also plasmaarc apparatus. Patentee. Home: 35 Rope Ferry Rd Hanover NH 03755

BROWNING, JAMES FRANKLIN, music orgn. exec.; b. Tonawanda, N.Y., Feb. 19, 1923; s. Charles Oscar and Gertrude (Keller) B.; student La. State U., 1943, U. Buffalo, 1948- 49; pvt. study music, 1942—. Regional dir. Civic Concert Services, N.Y. C., 1954-57; asst. mgr. Pitts. Symphony Orch., 1957-59; adminstr. Met. Opera Nat. Council, N.Y.C. 1959-62; spl. rep. to chmn. John F. Kennedy Center Performing Arts, 1962-63; gen. mgr. Am. Music Center, N.Y.C., 1963—; exec. sec. Nat. Music Council, N.Y.C., 1965—. Tech. cons. N.Y. State Council of Arts, 1963—; sec. Pioneer Editions, N.Y.C., 1965-67; mem. exec. com. Nat. Council Arts and Govt., N.Y.C., 1964—; treas. Arlington (Va.) Opera Theatre, 1962-63; bd. dirs. U.S. Inst. Theatre Tech., 1960-62; U.S. rep. Internat. Music Council Congress, Rotterdam, Holland, 1966, Internat. Rostrum Composers, Paris, France, 1966; adv. bd. Musicians Club Am., 1969—. Served with USAAF, 1943-46. Life mem. N.A.A.C.P.; mem. Contemporary Music Soc. (dir. 1968—); life hon. profl. mem. Phi Mu Alpha. Contbr. to publs. in field. Editor: Music Today Newsletter, 1963—, Nat. Council Music Bull., 1965—; mem. adv. council Music Jour., 1964—. Home: 114 W 70th St New York City, NY 10023. Office: 2109 Broadway New York City NY 10023

BROWNING, JAMES ROBERT, U.S. judge; b. Belt, Mont., Oct. 1, 1918; s. Nicholas Henry and Minnie Sally (Foley) B.; LL.B. with honors, Mont. State U., 1941; m. Marie Rose Chapell, Aug. 14, 1941. Admitted to Mont. bar, 1941, D.C. bar, 1950, U.S. Supreme Ct. bar, 1952; spl. atty. antitrust div. Dept. Justice, 1941-46, chief N.W. regional office, 1948-49, asst. chief gen. litigation sect. antitrust div., 1949-51, 1st asst. civil div., 1951-52, exec. asst. to atty. gen. U.S., 1952-53, chief Exec. Office for U.S. Attys., 1953; pvt. practice, Washington, 1953-58; lectr. N.Y.U. Sch. Law, 1953, Georgetown U. Law Center, 1957-58; clk. Supreme Ct. U.S., 1958-61; judge U.S. Ct. Appeals 9th Circuit, 1961—. Mem. Am. Law Inst., Am., Mont., Fed. bar assns., Am. Judicature Soc., Am. Soc. Legal History (adv. bd. jour.). Office: US Court of Appeals and Post Office Bldg San Francisco CA 94101

BROWNING, JOHN, concert pianist; b. Denver, May 23, 1933; s. John S. and Esther Alice (Green) B.; student Occidental Coll., Los Angeles, 1951-53, Juilliard Sch. Music, 1953-56; student Josef and Rosina Lhevinne, Dalies Frantz, Lee Pattison. Debut, Denver, 1943; recitals in Carnegie Hall, N.Y.C., Orchestra Hall, Chgo., other U.S. cities; concert appearances with N.Y. Philharmonic, Phila., Los Angeles Philharmonic, Cleve. orch., Nat. Symphony of Washington, Pitts., San Francisco, Toronto, Montreal symphonies, also Brussells Philharmonic, London Symphony, London Philharmonia, Residentie. Orch. of The Hague, others; tours of Europe, Near East, Can., Mexico. Recipient Steinway Centennial award, 1954, Edgar M. Leventritt award, 1955, Gold medal Concours Musical Internat., Reine Elisabeth, Belgium, 1956. Address: 250 W 57th St New York City NY 10019

BROWNING, JOHN VAL, sporting goods co. exec.; b. Rocour, Belgium, June 30, 1925; s. Val Allen and Ann (Chaffin) B.; came to U.S., 1935; ed. Mass. Inst. Tech.; m. Carol Conroy, Aug. 5, 1967; 1 son, John Allen. With J.M. & M. S. Browning Co., 1947-51; with Browning Arms Co., Ogden, Utah, 1951—, now pres., dir.; pres. Browning Industries, Inc.; adviser First Security Bank Utah, Ogden. Belgium consul for Intermountain region 1969. Nat. trustee Ducks Unltd. Served with USNR, 1944-46. Home: Route 4 Box 649 Ogden UT 84402 Office: Route 1 Morgan UT 84050

BROWNING, NORMA LEE, (Mrs. Russell Joyner Ogg), journalist; b. Spickard, Mo., Nov. 24, 1914; d. Howard R. and Grace (Kennedy) Browning; A.B., B.J., U. Mo., 1937; M.A. in English, Radcliffe Coll., 1938; m. Russell Joyner Ogg, June 12, 1938. Reporter, Los Angeles Herald-Express, 1942-43; with Chgo. Tribune, 1944—, Hollywood columnist, 1966—. Vis. lectr. creative writing, editorial cons., mem. nat. adv. bd. Interlochen Arts Acad. Recipient E.S. Beck award Chgo Tribune. Mem. Theta Sigma Phi, Kappa Tau Alpha. Author: City Girl in the Country, 1955; Joe Maddy of Interlochen, 1963; (with W. Clement Stone) The Other Side of the Mind, 1965; The Psychic World of Peter Hurkos, 1970. Contbr. articles to nat. mags. Address: 226 Morongo Rd Palm Springs CA 92262

BROWNING, RALPH LESLIE, cement co. exec.; b. Buffalo, Apr. 18, 1915; s. Leslie E. and Bertha L. (Rea) B.; A.B., Colgate U., 1937; m. Nancy B. Crane, Sept. 6, 1940; children—Peter Crane, Richard Leslie, Pamela. With Lehigh Portland Cement Co., Allentown, Pa., 1937—, asst. v.p., 1951-52, v.p., asst. gen. sales mgr., 1952-55, v.p. of sales 1955-59, exec. v.p., 1959—, also dir.; dir. Fall City Concrete Co., Louisville, Acme Concrete Co., Miami. Fla. Bd. dirs. Swain Country Day Sch. Served as lt. (j.g.) Supply Corps, USNR, 1944-46. Mem. Kappa Delta Rho. Republican. Episcopalian. Clubs: Lehigh Country, Livingston (Allentown); Ponte Vedra (Fla.). Home: Saucon Valley Rd RD 4 Allentown PA 18015 Office: 718 Hamilton St Allentown PA 18105

BROWNING, ROBERT HAMILTON, medical educator; b. Oberlin, O., Apr. 7, 1903; s. Charles H. and Julia (Hotchkiss) B.; A.B., Oberlin Coll., 1923; M.D., Western Res. U., 1927; m. 2d, Margaret G. Rose, Aug. 26, 1958; children by previous marriage—Thomas B. (dec.), Peter, Charles H., Rufus P., Nora (Mrs. Philip Stephens), Martha. Intern Cleve. City Hosp., 1927-28, resident in medicine, 1928-29; resident Trudeau Sanatorium, Saranae Lake, N.Y., 1930; dir. Sunny Acres Hosp., Cleve., 1931-48; dir. coll. health service Oberlin Coll., 1948-51; asst. prof. medicine Western Res. U., 1937-50; prof. medicine Ohio State U. Coll. Medicine, 1951—; dir. Ohio Tb Hosp., Columbus, 1951-66; attending physician Ohio State U. Hosps., 1966—; cons. in pulmonary diseases VA, 1955—, USPHS, 1956—, Wright-Patterson AFB, 1960—. Diplomate Am. Bd. Internal Medicine. Fellow A.C.P.; mem. Am. Thoracic Soc., Nat. Tb and Respiratory Disease Assn. (bd. dirs.), Alpha Omega Alpha. Home: 2138 Cheshire Rd Columbus OH 43221

BROWNING, ROBERT MASTERS, mgmt. cons.; b. Stratford, N.J., June 30, 1912; s. M. Corbit and Florence I. (Masters) B.; grad. Germantown Friends Sch., 1930; B.A., Swarthmore Coll., 1934; LL.D. (honorary), Lebanon Valley College, 1965; m. Margaret Helms, June 12, 1937; children—Deborah (Mrs. Edward Phillip LeVeen, III), Elizabeth (Mrs. Michael Fitzgerald Thiel), Lucy (Mrs. James Hay Wallace), Margaret. With Gen. Electric Co., 1934-45; with Booz. Allen & Hamilton, Inc., 1945—, partner, 1948-61, v.p., 1962—; dir. Standard Pressed Steel Co. Mem. Mary Hitchcock Hosp. Corp. Chmn. bd. mgrs. Swarthmore Coll.; trustee Germantown Hosp. Mem. Newcomen Soc., Pa. Soc., Inst. Mgmt. Consultants (founder), World Affairs Council Phila., Delta Upsilon. Mem. Soc. Friends. Clubs: Union League (Phila.); Lake Sunapee (N.H.) Yacht; Woodstock (Vt.) Country. Home: Pomfret VT 05068 RD 2 South Royalton VT 05068 Office: 245 Park Av New York City NY 10017

BROWNING, SAM GRIFFIN, ins. co. exec.; b. Hattiesburg, Miss., July 17, 1907; ed. La. State U. With La. Rating and Fire and Prevention Bur., 1926-36; with Fidelity and Guaranty Ins. Corp., La. and Ark., 1936-52, sec., 1943-52 (co. merged with U.S. Fidelity and Guaranty Co., 1952), v.p., dir. fire, marine and multi-peril depts., 1955-60, exec. v.p., 1960—; v.p. Fidelity & Guaranty Ins. Underwriters, Inc.; dir. Fidelity Ins. Co. Can., Thomas Jefferson Life Ins. Co., N.Y., Del Mar Co., Balt.; dir., mem. exec. com. Union Trust Co., Balt. Home: RFD Crownsville MD Office: US Fidelity and Guaranty Co Calvert and Redwood Sts Baltimore MD 21203

BROWNING, VAL ALLEN, firearms co. exec.; b. Ogden, Utah, Aug. 20, 1895; s. John Moses and Rachel Teressa (Child) B.; student Cornell U., 1914-17; D.Sc., Weber State Coll., Ogden, 1967; m. Ann Chaffin, Aug. 9, 1924; children—John Val, Carol (Mrs. Edmund W. Dumke), Bruce W., Judith Ann (Mrs. Leon L. Jones). With Browning Arms Co., Ogden, 1927—, pres., 1935- 62, chmn. bd., 1962—, also dir.; dir. First Security Corp., Amalgamated Sugar Co., Utah Constrn. & Mining Co. Served with U.S. Army, World War I. Decorated chevalier de l'Ordre de Leopold, officier l'Ordre de Leopold, II (Belgium). Home: 1515 Beverly Dr Ogden UT 84403 Office: RFD 1 Morgan UT 84050

BROWNLEE, JERRY L., food co. exec.; b. Lawrence, Kan., July 17, 1931; s. William Oscar and Laverne (Sanders) B.; A.B., U. Kan., 1953, M.P.A., 1956; m. Marjorie Woodson, June 24, 1955; children—Laura, Jerald Michael, Susan, John. With research and budget dept. City of Kansas City (Mo.), 1954-59, dir. dept., 1958-59; asst. to city mgr. City of Ft. Worth, 1959-63, city mgr., 1963-67; sr. v.p. Kimbell Inc., 1967—. Vice chmn. Tex. Water Quality Bd. Named Outstanding Young Texan, 1963, also Ft. Worth's Outstanding Young Man, 1964; recipient certificate of merit Municipal Finance Officers Assn., 1961, Achievement award Municipal Adv. Council Tex. Mem. Nat. Municipal League, Phi Beta Kappa, Beta Theta Pi. Home 3609 Kimberly Lane Fort Worth TX 76133

BROWNLEE, OSWALD HARVEY, educator, economist; b. Moccasin, Mont., Apr. 14, 1917; s. William and Sarah (Fyffe) B.; B.S., Mont. State Coll., 1938; M.A., U. Wis., 1939; Ph.D., Ia. State U.,

1945; m. Lela McDonald, June 11, 1939; children— Barbara (Mrs. Gregory Greer), Richard. Prof. econs. Ia. State Coll., 1943- 47, Carnegie Inst. Tech., 1947-48, U. Chgo., 1948-50; prof. econs. faculty U. Minn., 1950—; economist ICA mission to Chile, 1956-57; vis. prof. econs. Cath. U. Chile, 1967-69; vis. scholar Office Comptroller of Currency, 1965; cons. in field, 1947—. Farm Found. fellow, 1941-42; Ford faculty fellow, 1958. Mem. Am. Econ. Assn., Econometric Soc., Phi Kappa Phi. Author: Economics of Public Finance, 1954; (with J.A. Buttrick) Producer, Consumer and Social Choice, 1968; also articles. Home: 1943 East River Rd Minneapolis MN 55414

BROWNLEE, THOMAS MARSHALL, assn. exec.; b. Omaha, Oct. 11, 1926; s. John Templeton and Reed (Marshall) B.; B.S. in Bus. Adminstrn., U. Neb., 1950; m. Olive Ann Gettman, Sept. 13, 1950; children—Linda Sue, Thomas John, Curtis Marshall, Reed Ann. Asst. mgr. Daytona Beach (Fla.) C. of C., 1950, Tampa (Fla.) C. of C., 1952-53; exec. mgr. Tallahassee C. of C., 1953- 58; exec. v.p. Greater Columbia (S.C.) C. of C., 1959-63, Winston-Salem (N.C.) C. of C., 1963-64, Orlando Area (Fla.) C. of C., 1964—. Dir. Central Fla. Fair. Bd. dirs. Chamber Inst., U. Ga. Served with USNR, 1944-46; as 1st lt. AUS, 1951-52. Mem. Am. (pres. 1966- 68, dir. So. Assn.), S.C., Fla. (pres.) chambers commerce execs. assns. Presbyn. (deacon). Rotarian. Clubs: Country of Orlando; University; Citrus; Cypress Creek. Contbr. articles to profl. jours. Home: 1101 W Princeton Orlando FL 32802 Office: PO Box 1913 Orlando FL 32802

BROWNLEE, WILSON ELLIOT, food co. exec.; b. Rochester, Minn., Oct. 14, 1906; s. Harry and Ella (Ringland) B.; B.S., U. Minn., 1928, M.S., 1929; m. Pearl Woodings, June 15, 1934; 1 son, Wilson Elliot. With Sunshine Biscuits, Inc., 1929-, v.p. milling div., 1936-47, asst. v.p. co., 1957-59, v.p. mfg., 1959-65, pres., 1965-68, chmn. bd., 1968—, also dir.; dir. Am. Tobacco Co. Trustee, mem. food industries adv. com. Nutrition Found. Mem. Am. Chem. Soc., Inst. Food Technologists, Am. Assn. Cereal Chemists, Grocery Mfrs. Am. (dir.), Biscuit and Crackers Mfg. Assn. (dir.). Conglist. Clubs: Union League, Pinnacle (N.Y.C.). Home: 31 Bellows Lane Manhasset NY 11030 Office: 245 Park Av New York City NY 10017

BROWNLEY, FLOYD IRVING, Jr., educator; b. Atlanta, Jan. 1, 1918; s. Floyd Irving and Ruth (Ballentine) B.; B.S., Wofford Coll., 1939; M.S., Va. Poly. Inst., 1942; Ph.D., Fla. State U., 1951; D.Sc., Wofford Coll., 1966. m. Martine Newlin Watson, July 23, 1943; children—Tina, Karen. Chemist, Hercules Powder Co., Radford, Va., 1946; instr. Clemson (S.C.) U. 1941, asst. prof. chemistry, 1947-52, asso. prof., 1952-53, prof., head dept. chemistry and geology, 1953—, dean grad. school, 1966—, dir. univ. research, 1967-69; vice chancellor U. Tenn., Chattanooga, 1969—. Sr. postdoctoral fellow in Europe, Organization European Econ. Coop., 1962. Served from ensign to lt. (j.g.), USNR, 1942-46. Mem. Am. Chem. Soc., Am. Water Works Assn., A.A.A.S., Alpha Chi Sigma, Pi Kappa Phi, Phi Kappa Phi. Kiwanian (pres. 1958-59). Home: 311 Dawn St Signal Mountain TN 37377 Office: University of Tenn Chattanooga TN

BROWNSON, JACQUES CALMON, architect; b. Aurora, Ill., Aug. 3, 1923; s. Clyde Arthur and Iva Kline (Felter) B.; B.S. in Architecture, Ill. Inst. Tech., 1948, M.S., 1954; m. Doris L. Curry, 1946; children—Joel C., Lorre J., Daniel J. Instr., asst. prof. architecture Ill. Inst. Tech., 1949-59; prof. architecture, chmn. dept. U. Mich., 1966-68; chief design C.F. Murphy Assos., Chgo., 1959-61; project architect, chief designer Chgo. Civic Center Architects, 1961-68; mng. architect Pub. Bldg. Commn. Chgo., 1968—. Recipient award for Geneva House, Archtl. Record mag., 1956; Design award for steel framed factory Progressive Architecture mag., 1957. Mem. A.I.A. Prin. works include Conteintal Center Bldg., Hektoen Inst. Med. Research, Chgo. Civic Center. Home: 3 W Burton Pl Chicago IL 60610 Office: Pub Bldg Commn Civic Center Chicago IL 60602

BROWNSON, ROBERT HENRY, med. edn. research; b. Evanston, Ill., Mar. 14, 1925; s. Walter Converse and Martha Virginia (White) B.; B.S., John Carroll U., 1948; M.S., George Washington U., 1950, Ph.D., 1953; m. Carol Ann Priestaf, June 15, 1957; children—Michael R., Patrick S., Barbara L., Timothy T. Instr. anatomy U. So. Cal. Med. Sch., 1952-54; asst. prof. anatomy Med. Coll. Va., 1954-62, asso. prof., 1962-66, prof., 1966-68, prof., chmn. dept., 1967-68; vis. prof. postdoctoral NIH fellow Donner Lab., Lawrence Radiation Lab., U. Cal. at Berkeley, 1964-65; prof., vice chmn. dept. human anatomy U. Cal. at Davis Sch. Medicine, 1968-70, prof., vice chmn. dept. human anatomy, 1971—. Comdt.'s rep. ensign program for med. student's 12th Naval Dist., U. Cal. at Davis, 1969—. Active Boy Scouts Am. Served with USNR, 1943- 46. Mem. Am. Assn. Anatomists, Am. Assn. Neuropathologists, Am. Acad. Neurology, Radiation Research Soc., Sigma Xi, Phi Chi. Author articles in field. Home: 2927 Country Club Circle El Macero CA 95618 Office: Dept Human Anatomy Univ Cal Sch Medicine Davis CA 95616

BROWNSTEIN, PHILIP NATHAN, lawyer; b. Ober, Ind., Feb. 14, 1917; s. Max and Anna (Katz) B.; student George Washington U., 1937-38; LL.B., Columbus U., Washington, 1940, LL.M., 1941; m. Esther Savelle, Sept. 4, 1938; 1 son, Michael. With FHA, 1935-44 commr., 1963-66; admitted to D.C. bar, 1940; with VA, 1946-63, dir. loan guaranty service, 1956-61, chief benefits dir., 1961-63; asst. sec. mortgage credit Dept. Housing and Urban Devel., 1966-69; partner firm Brownstein Zeidman and Schomer. Mem. President's Task Force on Low Income Housing, 1969. Served with USMCR, 1944-46. Recipient Exceptional Service award VA, 1960, Top Performer in Housing award House and Home, 1964; Career Service award Nat. Civil Service League, 1967. Home: 560 N St SW Washington DC 20024 Office: 1025 Connecticut Av NW Washington DC 20036

BROWNSWORD, RAYMOND ARTHUR, banker; b. Akron, O., Mar. 23, 1909; s. Arthur and Mabel (Crisp) B.; U. Akron, 1930; grad. Rutgers U. Grad. Sch. Banking, 1953; m. Ethel Alice Sturgil, June 21, 1934. With Akron Nat. Bank and Trust Co. and predecessor, 1924—, pres., gen. adminstrv. officer, 1964—, also dir. Vice pres. Summit County Heart Assn.; mem. Akron Area Progress Bd.; treas. Ohio Heart Assn. Bd. dirs. Akron Jr. Achievement, Akron Gen. Hosp., Akron Clinic; bd. dirs., exec. com. Summit chpt. A.R.C.; mem. adv. bd. Tech. and Community Coll., Akron U. Served with AUS, World War II. Mem. Akron Area C. of C. (sec.). Kiwanian, Mason (Shriner). Clubs: City, Portgage Country (Akron). Home: 3063 Stanely Rd Akron OH 44313 Office: 1 Cascade Plaza PO Box 351 Akron OH 44309

BROWNYER, NELSON R., corp. exec.; b. Bay City, Mich., July 10, 1900; s. Raymond W. and Emma (Nye) B.; m. Betty Mier, Nov. 1930; children—Bob, Grace (Mrs. Hawkins), Kathryn (Mrs Esling). Vice pres., cons. Rockwell-Standard Corp. now automatic adviser Rockwell-Standard div. N. Am.-Rockwell Corp. Mem. Soc. Automotive Engrs. Clubs: Bloomfield Hills Country; Biltmore Forest Country. Home: 3731 Peabody Dr Birmingham MI 48010 Office: Birmingham MI 48012

BROXON, JAMES WILLIAM, physicist; educator; b. Jefferson Twp., Whitley County, Ind., July 12, 1897; s. William Chester and Victoria Ann (Gillespie) B.; A.B., Wabash Coll., 1919; M.A., U. Minn., 1920, Ph.D., 1926; m. Vera Maude Peacock, Dec. 16, 1922 (dec. Jan. 1954); children—William David, Patricia Jane. Asst. in physics, instr. German, Wabash Coll., 1917-18, instr. math., 1918-19; teaching fellow in physics U. Minn., 1919-22, instr. in physics, summer 1921; instr. physics U. Colo., Boulder, 1922-23, asst. prof., 1923-27, asso. prof., 1927-29, prof., 1929-63, prof. physics emeritus, 1963—, chmn. dept. physics, 1954-56. Instr. physics Yale, 1924-25; research asso. Metall. Lab., U. Chgo., (on leave), 1943-44. Recipient Robert L. Stearns award Assn. Alumni U. Colo., 1964. Fellow Am. Phys. Soc., mem. Am. Assn. Physics Tchrs., Am. Soc. Engring. Edn., Am. Geophys. Union, Colo.-Wyo. Acad. Sci. (pres. 1952-53), Am. Assn. U. Profs. (past pres. U. Colo. chpt.), Phi Beta Kappa (past pres. U. Colo. chpt.), Sigma Xi (past Pres. U. Colo. chpt.), Sigma Pi Sigma, Lambda Chi Alpha. Mason. Clubs: Town and Gown. Author: (textbook) Mechanics, 1960. Contbr. articles on cosmic rays, ions in gases to profl. jours. Derived law of sunspot magnetic fields. Home: 945 14th St Boulder CO 80302

BROYARD, ANATOLE, writer. Former lectr. sociology and lit., N.Y. U.; lectr. creative writing Columbia; faculty New Sch. for Social Research, N.Y.C. Author short stories; contbr. articles on popular culture to jours., textbooks, anthologies. Home: 151 E 62d St New York City NY Office: care New Sch for Social Research 66 W 12th St New York City NY 10011*

BROYHILL, JAMES EDGAR, furniture mfr., mem. Republican Nat. Com.; b. Wilkes County, N.C., May 5, 1892; s. Isaac and Margaret (Parsons) B.; student Appalachian Tng. Sch., Boone, N.C., 1913-17; m. Satie L. Hunt, June 21, 1921; children—Allene (Mrs. William E. Stevens Jr.), Paul, James T., Bettie (now Mrs. William A. Gortner). With Lenoir Furniture Corp., 1919; organized Lenoir Chair Co., 1926; exec. head Broyhill Furniture Factories, Lenoir Furniture Corp., Lenoir Veneer Co., Nat. Veneer Co., Harper Furniture Co., Lenoir Furniture Forwarding Co., Lenoir, Whitmel, N.C., Lenoir Chair Co. 5, Taylorsville, N.C., Conover Furniture Co., Conover, N.C., Otis L. Broyhill Furniture Co., Marion, N.C.; dir. Wachovia Bank & Trust Co. (Charlotte, N.C.), C. & N.- W. Ry.; mem. adv. bd. Am. Mut. Liability Ins. Co. (Charlotte). Bd. govs. Am. Furniture Mart, Chgo. Mem. Rep. Nat. Com., 1948—; del. Rep. Nat. Conv., 7 times. Trustee Wake Forest Coll., Southeastern Bapt. Theol. Sem.; bd. dirs. Caldwell Meml. Hosp., Lenoir. With U.S. Army, World War I. Recipient Man of Year plaque by bd. govs. Am. Furniture Mart, 1946, Free Enterprise award, 1961; James T. Ryan Award So. Furniture Mfrs. Assn., 1967. Pres. So. Furniture Mfrs. Assn., 1943-46. Baptist. Mason (Shriner), K.P. (past chancellor). Clubs: Charlotte Country, Charlotte City, Quail Hollow (Charlotte); Sedgefield (N.C.) Country; Boone (N.C.) Golf; Biltmore (N.C.); Forest Country; Mimosa Golf (Morganton, N.C.); Blowing Rock (N.C.) Golf; Lenoir (N.C.); Golf, Lenoir Country. Home: Wilkesboro Rd Lenoir NC 28645 Office: Broyhill Furniture Industries Broyhill Park Lenoir NC 28645

BROYHILL, JAMES THOMAS, congressman; b. Lenoir, N.C., Aug. 19, 1927; s. James Edgar and Satie (Hunt) B.; B.S., U. N.C., 1950; m. Louise Robbins, June 2, 1951; children—Marilyn L., James Edgar II, Philip R. Partner, Broyhill Furniture Factories, Lenoir, 1948- 62; mem. 88th-92d Congresses, 9th and 10th Dists. N.C. Recipient Young Man of Year award City of Lenoir, 1957. Republican. Baptist (Sunday sch. tchr.). Mason (Shriner), Moose. Home: Hill Haven Dr Lenoir NC 28645 Office: House Office Bldg Washington DC 20515

BROYHILL, JOEL THOMAS, congressman; b. Hopewell, Va., Nov. 4, 1919; s. Marvin Talmage and Nellie Magdalene (Brewer) B.; student Fork Union (Va.) Mil. Acad., George Washington U.; m. Jane Marshall Bragg, May 17, 1942; children—Nancy, Jane-Anne, Jeanne Marrie. Partner, gen. mgr. M.T. Broyhill & Sons, 1945- 52; mem. 83d-92d Congresses, 10th Dist. Va. Active numerous local civic orgns. Chmn. Arlington County Planning Commn. Served as capt. 106th Inf. Div., U.S. Army, World War II. Mem. Va. State, Arlington Co. (past pres., bd. dirs.) C.'s of C., Izaak Walton League, Am. Legion, Reserve Officers Assn. U.S., V.F.W., D.A.V., Kappa Alpha Alumni Assn. Republican. Lutheran (past mem. ch. council). Mason, Elk, Moose, Eagle. Club: Optimist (bd. dirs., past pres., sec.). Home: 4845 Old Dominion Dr Arlington VA 22207 Office: House of Reps Washington DC 21515

BROYLES, JOHN FRANKLIN, univ. football coach; b. Decatur, Ga., Dec. 26, 1924; s. O.T. Broyles; student Ga. Inst. Tech.; m. Barbara Day; children—Jack, Hank, Dan, Tommy, Betsy and Linda (twins). Mem. staff Ga. Inst. Tech., 1951-57; head football coach U. Mo., 1957-58, U. Ark., 1958—. Past mem. staff Coll. All-Star Game, also All-Am. Games; head coach West team Copper Bowl Game, 1958. Served with USNR, World War II. Named to All-Star Eastern Conf. squad, 1944, 46; named Player-of-Year, 1944; named to Ga. Inst. Tech. Hall of Fame; Coach of Year in Tex., 1960. Home: 1525 Hope St Fayetteville AR 72701

BROZ, JOSSIP, premier of Yugoslavia; see Tito, Marshall.

BROZEK, JOSEF, scientist, educator; b. Melnik, Bohemia, Aug. 14, 1913; s. Josef Francis and Filomena (Sourek) B.; Ph.D., Charles U., Prague, Czechoslovakia, 1937; m. Eunice Magnuson, Mar. 23, 1945; children—Josef, Margaret, Peter. Came to U.S., 1939, naturalized, 1945. Teaching asst., librarian dept. philosophy Charles U., 1936-37; psychotechnologist Bata Shoe Co., Zlin, Czechoslovkia, 1937-39; jr. psychologist lab. physiol. hygiene, Sch. Pub. Health, U. Minn., 1941-43, asso. scientist, 1943-44, asst. prof., 1944-49, asso. prof., 1949-56, prof., 1956-59; prof. psychology, chmn. dept. Lehigh U., Bethlehem, Pa., 1959-63, research prof., 1963—; dir. Summer Inst. Hist. Psychology U. N.H., 1968, Lehigh U., 1971. Sec. com. nutritional anthropometry, food and nutrition NRC, 1950-55; orgn. chmn. Symposium on Adjustment to Aging, 15th Internat. Congress Applied Psychology, 1964, Kyoto Symposium on Anthrop. Aspects of Growth, 1968; adviser nutrition WHO, 1964-68. Mem. Am. Psychol. Assn., History of Sci. Soc., Pavlovian Soc., Am. Physiol. Soc. Co-author: The Biology of Human Starvation, 1950, Origins of Psychometry, 1970. Editor, contbr.: Symposium on Nutrition and Behavior, 1957; Body Measurements and Human Nutrition, 1956; Performance CapacityA Symposium, 1961; Techniques for Measuring Body Composition, 1961; Soviet Studies on Nutrition and Higher Nervous Activity, 1962; Body Composition, 1963; Human Body Composition, 1965; The Biology of Human Variation, 1966; Physical Growth and Body Composition, 1970; book review editor Human Biology, 1954-65; editorial cons. Slavic lits. Contemporary Psychology, 1960-71. Home: 265 E Market St Bethlehem PA 18105

BROZEN, YALE, economist, educator; b. Kansas City, Mo., July 6, 1917; s. Oscar and Sarah (Sholtz) B.; B.S., 1941; m. Lee Parsons, Apr. 26, 1962; children—Yale, II, Reed. Asst. prof. social sci. U. Fla., 1940-41; asst. prof. econs. Ill. Inst. Tech., 1941-44, asso. prof., 1944-46; asso. prof. econs. U. Minn., 1946-47, vis. prof. econs., 1948; prof. econs. Northwestern U., Evanston, Ill., 1947-57, dir. Research Transp. Center, 1957-59; prof. econs. U. Chgo., 1957—, dir. research mgmt. program Grad. Sch. Bus., 1959-67. Cons. State Dept., 1956-63; vis. prof. econs., Sao Paulo, Brazil, 1954, Rikkyo U., Tokyo, 1964, U. Va., 1965, Grad. Inst. Internat. Studies, 1969; research asso. Social Sci. Research Council, 1949; cons. pub. utility econs. Cook County State's Atty's Office, 1950; dir. econ. tng. Am. Tel. & Tel. Co., 1951; cons. President's Materials Policy Commn., 1951, Anti-Trust Div., Dept. Justice, 1952, NSF, 1954-55, Nat. Assn. Mfrs., 1954-55, Loewi & Co., 1969. Dir., Univ. Nat. Bank, West Burton Place Corp. Trustee Center for Ind. Action. Civilian tng. adminstr. Signal Corps, U.S. Army, 1942-43. Mem. Am. Econ. Assn., Mont Pelerin Soc., Phi Beta Kappa, Delta Sigma Pi. Clubs: Quadrangle, Technology (Chgo.). Author: Workbook for Economics, 1946; Textbook for Economics, Vol. I, 1948. Address: U Chgo Chicago IL 60637

BROZMAN, ROBERT F., ins. co. exec. Pres., treas. Century Acceptance Corp. Office: 1003 Walnut St Kansas City MO 64106*

BRUBAKER, CARL H., Jr., educator; b. Passaic, N.J., July 13, 1925; s. Carl H. and Lillian (Rochow) B.; B.S., Franklin and Marshall Coll., 1949; Ph.D., Mass. Inst. Tech., 1952; m. Mary Ellen Fiske, June 26, 1949; 1 son, Peter. Asst. prof. Mich. State U., 1952-58, asso. prof., 1958-61, prof., 1961—; research asso. Mass. Inst. Tech., 1952, summer 1955, Argonne Nat. Lab., summer 1957; Smith-Mundt-Fulbright lectr. radiochemistry U. Chile, 1958; asst. editor Jour. American Chem. Soc., 1964-69, asso. editor, 1969-70. Served with AUS, 1943-46. Mem. Am. Chem. Soc. (council 1971—), Chem. Soc. (London), Sigma Xi, Phi Beta Kappa. Research transition element compounds in molecular oxygen transport; molecular nitrogen fixation and hydrogenation catalysis. Home: 4466 Tacoma Blvd Okemos MI 48864 Office: Dept Chemistry Mich State U East Lansing MI 48823

BRUBAKER, CARROLL HARPER, ret. electronics co. exec.; b. Pasadena. Cal., Mar. 26, 1921; s. Ezra Leroy and Louise Elizabeth (Whitmer) B.; student Citrus Coll., Azusa, Cal., 1939-40, Cal. Inst. Tech., 1941-43; L.H.D., U. Redlands, 1966; m. Agnes Marie Hanes, Aug. 23, 1941; children—David Charles, Thomas Harper. Chief indsl. engr. Consol. Vultee Aircraft Co., 1940-45; partner, officer mgmt. cons. co., 1946-47; chief engr. Joyce Shoe Co., 1947-51; with Hughes Aircraft Co., 1951-68, v.p. group exec. ground systems, 1958-65, sr. v.p. group systems group, 1965-66, sr. v.p., ground systems group exec., 1966-67; pres. Meva Corp., 1963-68, Powder Cities Constrn. Co., 1965-68. Trustee Covina Valley (Cal.) Unified Sch. Dist., 1954-67, pres. 1962-67; mem. spl. com. Cal. Trustees Assn. Sch. Finance and Constrn., 1955-57; mem. exec. com. Los Angeles Trustees Assn., 1955-57; mem. bd., exec. com., pres. Orange County council Cal. Industry Edn. Council, 1963-64. Served with AUS, 1945-46. Recipient Alumni Achievement award Citrus Coll., 1964. Mem. Am. Mgmt. Assn., Navy League, Am. Soc. Naval Engrs., Assn. U.S. Army. Home: 3128 Virginia Av West Covina CA 91791

BRUBAKER, CHARLES EDWARD, clergyman; b. Birmingham, Ala., Dec. 22, 1917; s. Lauren E. and Nora (Drake) B.; B.A., Maryville (Tenn.) Coll., 1938, D.D., 1956; Th.B., Princeton, 1941; postgrad. Union Theol. Sem., N.Y.C., 1941- 43, 46-48; m. Doris Jane King, Sept. 14, 1946; children—Wendy, Scott, Lynn, Laurie. Ordained to ministry Presbyn. Ch., 1941; asst. pastor, New Rochelle, N.Y., 1941-43; pastor Central Presbyn. Ch., also dir. Westminster Found., Fayetteville, Ark., 1948-53; pastor Tabernacle Presbyn. Ch., Phila., also dir. Westminster Found. Phila., 1953-60; pastor First Presbyn. Ch., Englewood, N.J., 1960-69, Wichita, Kan., 1969—. Brit. Am. exchange minister, summer 1963. Chmn. Dept. Chaplains and Service Personnel, United Presbyn. Ch., 1961-69, chmn. Gen. Commn. Chaplains and Armed Forces Personnel, 1969-71. Trustee Princeton Theol. Sem., 1960-63. Maryville Coll., 1958—. Served as chaplain USNR, 1943-46; PTO. Decorated Bronze Star. Mem. Theta Alpha Phi, Pi Kappa Tau. Address: 525 N Broadway Wichita KS 67214

BRUBAKER, LAUREN EDGAR, educator; clergyman; b. Birmingham, Ala., Oct. 8, 1941; s. Lauren Edgar and Nora (Drake) B.; A.B., Birmingham So. Coll., 1935; Th.M., Princeton Theol. Sem., 1938, postgrad., 1946-47; S.T.M., Union Theol. Sem., N.Y., 1943, Th.D., 1944; m. Leonte Soye, June 6, 1944; children—Lauren Eugene, Edward Soye. Ordained to ministry Presbyn. Ch., 1938; asst. pastor in Parkersburg, Va., 1938-41; instr. Union Theol. Sem., 1941-43; grad. asst. Princeton Theol. Sem., 1946-47; prof. philosophy and religion, chaplain Parsons Coll., Fairfield, Ia., 1947-49; asso. prof. U. S.C. at Columbia, 1949-58, prof., 1958—, chmn. dept. religion, 1949—, chaplain, 1949—. Dir. S.C. Council Human Relations, 1966-69. Exec. committeman Columbia and Richland County Democratic Party, 1950-60. Served to maj., AUS, 1943-46. Mem. Inst. Religion (dir. 1960-63), S.C. Acad. Religion (founder 1968, pres. 1968), Am. Acad. Religion (pres. 1960), Presbyn. Edn. Assn. South, Columbia Ministers Assn. (past sec.), Am. Assn. U. Profs. (past officer), Nat. Assn. Coll. and U. Pastors, Soc. Bibl. Lit. (past officer), Omicron Delta Kappa (faculty adviser 1968-71), Pi Gamma Mu, Phi Kappa Phi, Tau Kappa Alpha. Club: Executive of Columbia (pres. 1960-61). Contbr. articles profl. jours. Research teaching religion in accredited colls. and univs. Home: 9 Churchill Circle Columbia SC 29206

BRUBECK, DAVID WARREN, musician; b. Concord, Cal., Dec. 6, 1920; s. Howard and Elizabeth (Ivey) B.; B.A., U. Pacific, 1942; Ph.D. (hon.), U. Pacific and Fairfield U.; postgrad. Mills Coll., 1946-49; m. Iola Whitlock, Sept. 21, 1942; children—Michael, David Darius, Christopher, Catherine, Daniel, Matthew. Pianist dance bands and small jazz trio 3 D's, 1946-49; formed trio, 1950, with bookings throughout U.S. in jazz night clubs; formed Dave Brubeck Quartet, 1951; leader with Gerry Mulligan Quartet; has made concert tours at U.S. Colls., festival, etc., 1953—, 3 month tour Europe and Middle East for U.S. State Dept.; tour Europe and Australia; European tour as soloist with Cin. Symphony, 1969; affiliated with Columbia Record Co. and Decca. Mem. adv. com. for Hopkins Center at Dartmouth. Recipient Editor's Choice, Metronome mag., 1952, first place in popularity poll, 1953- 55; 1st place in critics poll, Downbeat mag., 1953, cover story Time mag., 1954; named one of Cal.'s 5 outstanding young men, 1957; winner jazz polls conducted by Downbeat, Melody Maker, Cashbox, Billboard, Playboy mags., 1962. Fellow Internat. Inst. Arts and Scis; mem. Broadcast Music, Inc., Phi Mu Alpha. Composer oratorio The Light in the Wilderness; (cantatas) The Gates of Justice, Truth; (symphony) Elementals; and over 100 jazz compositions. Home: 221 Millstone Rd Wilton CT 06897 Office: care of Sutton Artists Inc 505 Park Av New York City NY 10022

BRUCE, CAROL, actress; b. Great Neck, L.I., N.Y., Nov. 15, 1919; d. Harry and Beatrice (Cohen) Levy; student pub. schs.; m. Milton Nathanson, June 17, 1943 (div. May 1961); 1 dau., Julie. Broadway debut in Irving Berlin's La. Purchase, 1940; other Broadway appearances include Priorities of 1943, Julie in revival of Showboat (Donaldson award), 1946, Along Fifth Avenue, 1949, A Family Affair, 1962, Do I Hear a Waltz?, 1965; appeared on weekly radio shows Ben Bernie, 1940, Al Jolson, 1942-45, Carton of Cheer program, 1942-45; films include This Woman Is Mine, Keep 'Em Flying, Behind the Eight Ball (all 1941); appeared in numerous summer theatre roles, 1948-52, 55-61; made nat. tour in Pal Joey, 1953, London debut, 1954; frequent TV appearances, recordings include Showboat, The Fabulous Carol Bruce, Do I Hear a Waltz?. Home: 211 E 53d St New York City NY 10022 Office: care Gen Artists Corp 640 Fifth Av New York City NY 10019

BRUCE, DAVID K. E., govt. ofcl.; b. Balt., Feb. 12, 1898; s. William Cabell and Louise Este (Fisher) B.; student Princeton, U. Va., U. Md.; m. Ailsa Mellon; 1 dau., Audrey (dec.); m. Evangeline Bell;

children—Alexandra, David, Nicholas. Admitted to Md. bar, 1921, practiced in Balt., 1921-25; vice consul U.S. Fgn. Service, Rome, 1926- 28; engaged in bus. and farming, 1928-40; chief rep. in Gt. Britain for A.R.C., 1940; with OSS, 1941- 45, dir., ETO, 1943-45; asst. sec. of commerce, 1947-48; chief ECA Mission to France, 1948-49; U.S. ambassador to France, 1949-52; under sec. of state, 1952-53; apptd. spl. U.S. observer at interim com. of European Def. Community, 1953; spl. Am. rep. to European High Authority for Coal and Steel, 1953-54; ambassador to fed. Republic Germany, 1957-59, to Great Britain, 1961-69; U.S. rep. to Vietnam Peace Talks, Paris, 1970-71. Mem. Md. Ho. of Dels., 1924-26, Va. Ho. Dels., 1939-42. Served with U.S. Army, 1917-20, 42- 45. Awarded mil. decorations by U.S., Gt. Britain, France, Poland, Norway, Denmark, Czechoslovakia. Democrat. Episcopalian. Author: Revolution to Reconstruction, 1938. Home: 1405 34th St NW Washington DC 20007

BRUCE, DONALD CHARLES, Australian diplomat; b. Melbourne, Australia, Apr. 29, 1921; s. Alexander Coad and Ethel (Redfern) B.; diploma chem. engring. Royal Melbourne Inst. Tech., 1942, postgrad., 1943; m. Pauline Sheppard, Feb. 10, 1950; children—Andrew Alexander, Margot Helen, Jeanie Christine, Ian Clement. Engr., Dept. Munitions Australia, 1939-45; engr. Dept. of Supply Australia, 1945-59; student Royal Australian Air Force Staff Coll., 1960; def. supply attache Washington, 1962-65; asst. sec. prodn. planning Dept. Supply, 1966-68; counsellor supply Australian embassy, Washington, 1969—. Asso. mem. Royal Australian Chem. Inst. Clubs: University, Nat. Aviation, Washington Golf and Country (Washington). Home: 1616 S Lynn St Arlington VA 22202 Office: 1601 Massachusetts Av Washington DC 20036

BRUCE, DOUGLAS IAN WALLACE, elec. appliance mfg. co. exec.; b. Toronto, Ont., Can., Nov. 7, 1916; s. William Wallace and Florence (Lamport) B.; B.A., U. Toronto, 1938; grad. Osgoode Hall Law Sch., Toronto, 1947; m. Beverley Kirk Hughes, July 16, 1949; children—Heather, John, Jane, Barbara. Called to Ont. bar, 1947, apptd. Queen's counsel, 1968; mem. firm Smith, Rae, Greer & Cartwright, Toronto, 1947-51; with Westinghouse Can. Ltd. (formerly Canadian Westinghouse Co., Ltd.), Hamilton, Ont., 1951—, sec., 1962—, v.p., sec., 1968—. Chmn. Canadian Nat. Inst. Blind, Hamilton, 1967-68. Mem. corp. Trinity Coll., Toronto. Served to lt. comdr. Royal Canadian Naval Vol. Res., 1939-45. Mem. Canadian Bar Assn., Hamilton Law Assn., Assn. Canadian Gen. Counsel, Canadian Mfrs. Assn., Am. Soc. Corp. Secretaries, John Howard Soc. (pres. Hamilton 1967-68), Alpha Delta Phi. Presbyn. Office: 286 Sanford Av N Hamilton 23 Ontario Canada

BRUCE, FRASER WALLACE, aluminum co. exec.; b. Newmarket, Ont., Can., Dec. 1, 1903; B.A.Sc. in Mech. Engring., U. Toronto, 1927. With Aluminum Co. Can. Ltd., 1927—, v.p., gen. sales mgr., 1946-52, pres., dir., 1957—; mng. dir. Alcan Industries Ltd., London, Eng., 1952-57; v.p., dir. Alcan Aluminium Ltd., 1959-68, exec. v.p. smelting, 1968—; dir. Alcan Aluminum Ltd., Nat. Trust Co. Ltd.; chmn. bd. Canadian Exec. Service Overseas. Clubs: St. James's, Mt. Royal (Montreal); Rideau (Ottawa); University (Toronto). Office: 1321 Sherbrooke St W Montreal 109 Quebec Canada

BRUCE, GORDON MURPHY, ophthalmic surgeon; b. Shelburne, N.S., Can., July 4, 1901; s. Alfred D. and Mary (Murphy) B.; student Acadia U., 1918-19, Columbia, 1919-20; B.A., Dalhousie U., 1925, M.D., 1925; D. Ophth., Oxford U., 1928; Sc.D. in Medicine, Columbia, 1934; m. Daisy K. Hallett, Nov. 9, 1929; children—Roger G., Barbara. Came to U.S., 1926, naturalized, 1932. Intern, 1925-26; resident Knapp Meml. Eye Hosp., N.Y.C., 1926-28; faculty Coll. Physicians and Surgeons, Columbia, N.Y.C., 1928—, prof. clin. ophthalmology, 1947-67, prof. emeritus, 1967—, spl. lectr., 1967—; mem. staff opthalmology Columbia Presbyn. Med. Center, N.Y.C., 1928-68, surgeon, 1938-68; mem. staff Vanderbilt Clinic, N.Y.C., 1928-68, ophthalmologist, 1936-68, chief, 1938-42; surgeon Inst. Ophthalmology, N.Y.C., 1938-67, cons., 1967—; chief ophthalmology St. Albans Naval Hosp., 1945-46; cons. Ophthalmology Englewood Hosp., 1957—, Yonkers Gen. Hosp., 1967—; cons. ophthalmologist surgeon gen. U.S. Navy; mem. med. adv. com. VA, 1964-69, cons. ophthalmologist, 1964—. Served from lt. comdr. to capt., M.C., USNR, 1942-45; rear adm. ret. 1948. Decorated Silver Star, Gold Star. Diplomate Am. Bd. Ophthalmology (chmn. 1958-60, cons. 1962-65). Fellow A.C.S., N.Y. Acad. Medicine (trustee); mem. Am. (editor trans. 1950-59), N.Y. State, N.Y.C. (past chmn.) opthal. socs., Am. Acad. Ophthalmology and Otolaryngology, A.M.A. (vice chmn. ophthal. sect.), A.A.A.S., Assn. Research Ophthalmology, Nat. Med. Found. Eye Care (charter), N.Y. State, N.Y. County med. socs., Nat. Soc. Prevention Blindness, 3d Marine Div. Assn., Arista Honor Soc. (hon.), Phi Rho Sigma, Alpha Omega Alpha (hon.). Republican. Episcopalian. Club: Skytop (Pa.). Author numerous med. articles and revs. Home: 1 Horizon Rd Ft Lee NJ 07024

BRUCE, HOMER LINDSEY, lawyer; b. Blanco, Tex., Aug. 24, 1892; s. William Herschel and Lillie Ora (Hart) B.; B.A., U., Tex., 1913; B.A. (Rhodes scholar), Oxford U., Eng., 1915, M.A., 1919; m. Anna Clare Chrisman, Aug. 18, 1917 (dec. 1959) children—Homer Lindsey, Robert Chrisman (dec.), Caroline (Mrs. Peter B. Vanderhoef); m. 2d, Dorothy Murie Blue, Mar. 24, 1964. Admitted to Tex. bar, 1920, since practiced in Houston; sr. partner firm Baker and Botts, 1920—, Miranda, Santamarina & Steta, Mexico City. Dir. Imperial Sugar Co. Served as capt. U.S. Army, World War I, AEF in France; lt. col. Res. Mem. Am., Houston bar assns., State Bar Tex., Am. Judicature Soc., Am. Camellia Soc., Beta Theta Pi. Clubs: Friars; Houston Country, Houston, International Panorama Golf, Conroe. Home: 3965 Del Monte Dr Houston TX 77019 Office: 1 Shell Plaza Houston TX 77002

BRUCE, IMON ELBA, coll. pres.; b. Blevins, Ark., Dec. 9, 1910; s. Jewell Joseph and Ada Lee (Wortham) B.; B.A., Henderson State Tchrs. Coll., 1932; M.S., La. State U., 1937; D.Ed., Ind. U., 1952; m. Catherine Coles, Dec. 24, 1938; children—Catherine Jane, Carolyn Louise, Elizabeth Ann. Tchr. math. and sci. Hope (Ark.) High Sch., 1932-33; tchr. math and sci. Fordyce (Ark.) High Sch., 1933-36; supt. schs., Fordyce, 1937-49; teaching fellow math. La. State U., 1936-37; dir. student teaching Ark. State Tchrs. Coll., Conway, 1949-53; supt. schs., Hot Springs, Ark., 1953-59; pres. So. State Coll., Magnolia, Ark., 1959—; summer vis. lectr. Ind. U., 1955, U. Ark., 1956, 57, U. N.M., 1958. Bd. dirs. So. Extrusions, Inc. Bd. dirs. S. Ark. Indsl. Devel. Council Mem. Nat., Ark. edn. assns., Am., Ark. (past pres.) assns. sch. adminstrs., Am. Ednl. Research Assn., Magnolia C. of C. (past pres.). Phi Delta Kappa. Methodist (steward). Rotarian. Home: So State Coll Magnolia AR 71753

BRUCE, JAMES, ret. bus. exec.; b. Balt., Dec. 23, 1892; s. William Cabell and Louise Este (Fisher) B.; Litt.B., Princeton, 1914; LL.B., U. Md., 1916; m. Ellen McHenry Keyser, May 24, 1919; children—Ellen McHenry, Louise Este. Mem. 1st Plattsburg Camp Com., 1915; pvt. to maj., U.S. F.A., 2d Div. Staff lst Army, 1917-18; mil. aide to Pres. Wilson at Treaty Versailles; asst. mil. attaché Italy, 1919; financial adviser to bd. dirs. Home Owners Loan Corp., Wash., 1933-34; ambassador to Argentina, 1947-49; 1st dir. Mut. Defense Assistance Program, 1949-50; v.p. Nat. Park Bank, N.Y.C., 1925-29; mem. governing bd. Chase Nat. Bank, N.Y.C., 1929-31; pres. Balt. Trust Co., 1931-33; v.p., dir., mem. exec. com. Nat. Dairy Products Corp., 1937-58. Decorated Order of Merit (Italian Republic); Croix de Guerre (France). Mem. Am. Legion. V.F.W., English-Speaking Union, Pilgrims, Council Fgn. Relations. Democrat, Episcopalian. Mason (Shriner, 32), Moose. Clubs: Maryland (Balt.); Brook, Links Golf (N.Y.C.); 1925 F St. (Washington); Turf and Field, Ends of the Earth. Author: Those Perplexing Argentines. Home: 825 Fifth Av New York City NY 10021

BRUCE, JAMES WILLIAM, fuel co. exec.; b. Dorchester, Mass., Feb. 21, 1921; s. William B. and Isabella (McMillan) B.; certificate Bentley Coll. Accounting and Finance, 1946; B.A., Northeastern U., 1951; grad. Advanced Mgmt. Program, Harvard, 1963; m. Margaret C. Hoffman, July 20, 1945; children—William B., Robert E., Laurie C. With Eastern Gas & Fuel Asso., Boston, 1940—, treas., 1966—, v.p., 1970—; treas. Boston Gas Co., 1964-66; dir. U.S. Mut. Liability Ins. Co. Bd. dirs., mem. exec. com., asst. treas. Boston council Boy Scouts Am. Mem. New Eng. Gas Assn., financial Execs. Inst., Mass. Soc. C.P.A.'s. Club: Treasurer's (Boston). Home: 30 Sutton Rd Needham MA 02192 Office: Prudential Tower Boston MA 02199

BRUCE, JOHN GREGORY, ret. judge; b. Edinburg, Ind., Feb. 16, 1897; s. John and Nancy (Moore) B.; A.B., Transylvania U., 1921; LL.B. cum laude, U. Ky., 1924; m. Zilpha Foster, Aug. 19, 1930; children—William Gregory, John Foster, Charles Moore. Admitted to Ky. bar, 1923, Dist. Cts., 1924, Circuit Ct. Appeals, 1925, U.S. Supreme Ct. bar, 1934; atty. Fordson Coal Co., 1924-31; practiced in Pineville, Ky., 1931-34; atty. appeals sect. Bur. War Risk Litigation, Dept. Justice, Washington, 1934-36, chief trial sect., 1936-43, asst. chief, chief frauds sect., claims div., 1943-52; judge U.S. Tax Ct., 1952-67. Presdl. elector, Ky., 1932. Served with USN, 1918-19. Mem. Am., Fed., Ky., D.C. bar assns., Order of Coif, Phi Alpha Delta, Phi Kappa Tau. Mem. Christian Ch. Mason (K.T.). Clubs: Nat. Lawyers (Washington); Kenwood Golf and Country (Bethesda). Home: 5524 Pembroke Rd Bethesda MD 20034

BRUCE, LOUIS ROOKS, lawyer; b. Onondaga Indian Reservation, N.Y., Dec. 30, 1906; s. Louis R. and Nellie (Rooks) B.; B.A., Syracuse U., 1930; m. Anna Jennings Wikoff, Nov. 19, 1930; children—Charles Wikoff, Katherine (Mrs. William H. Huxtable), Donald Kenneth. Owner, operator dairy farm, Richfield Springs, N.Y., 1930-34; N.Y. State dir. Indian projects NYA, 1935-42; edn. and youth dir. Dairymen's League Coop. Assn., 1946-55; v.p. Compton Advt., N.Y.C., 1955-59; with FHA, also N.Y. State Housing Authority, 1959-69; commnr. Indian Affairs, 1969—. Dir. Yale Broadcasting Co. Founder, past exec. dir. Nat. Congress Indian Affairs; founder, mem. bd. Arrow, Inc. Recipient Freedom's Found. award, 1949, Liberty Bell award Otsego County (N.Y.) Bar Assn., 1970. Mem. Assn. Am. Indian Affairs, Indian Council Five (Achievement award), N.Y. State Village Indian Assns., Mid Eastern Coops., Farm Bur. Fedn., Nat. Grange, Syracuse U. Alumni Assn. (Achievement award 1970), Zeta Psi (pres. 1962-64), Sigma Delta Chi. Methodist (trustee, lay leader). Rotarian. Mason. Home: RD 1 Richfield Springs NY 13439 also 4200 Cathedral Av NW Washington DC 20016 Office: 1951 Constitution Av NW Washington DC 20242

BRUCE, OTHO BEALL, banker; b. Decatur, Ga., May 31, 1914; s. Rufus Chester and Vivian (Beall) B.; B.S., Samford U., Birmingham, Ala., 1936; m. Mary Frances McCarty, Jan. 22, 1944; children—Robert Otho, William Beall. Dist. mgr. B.F. Goodrich Co., Jacksonville, Fla., 1936-57; v.p. Fla. Nat. Bank, Jacksonville, 1957-61; dir. indsl. div. Fla. Devel. Commn., Tallahassee, 1961-64; sr. v.p. First Nat. Bank, Miami, Fla., 1964—; chmn. bd. Southeast Bank of Dadeland (Fla.), 1971—; adv. com. Fla. Small Bus. Adminstrn.; dir. Fla. Industries Expn. Mem. steering com. Fla. Legislative Council Com. Rds. and Hwys.; mem. citizens bd. U. Miami; mem. S.Fla. Export Expansion Council of U.S. Dept. Commerce; adv. bd. Center for Theoretical Studies; mem. sea grant bd. U. Miami; trustee Museum of Sci. Served to lt. comdr. USNR, 1940-45. Mem. Fla. Bankers Assn. (com. chmn.), Fla. State (dir., chmn. indsl. devel. com.), Miami (chmn. indsl. devel. com.), Dade County (dir.) chambers commerce, Am., So. indsl. devel. councils, Econ. Soc. S. Fla. (chmn.), N.A.M., Marine Tech. Soc., Nat. Oceanography Assn., Air Pollution Control Assn. (finance chmn.), Navy League U.S., Clubs: Miami, Ocean Reef, Kings Bay Yacht and Country (Miami). Home: 7695 SW 133d St Miami FL 33156 Office: P O Box 2500 Miami FL 33101 also P O Drawer H Kendall Branch Miami FL 33156

BRUCE, ROBERT HALL, univ. dean; b. Columbus, O., July 28, 1906; s. Charles A. and Jeannette (Hall) B.; A.B., Ohio State U., 1928, Ph.D., 1932; A.M., U. Cal., 1930; m. Huldah Means, Aug. 20, 1932; children—Robert Keady, Margaret Jean, Virginia Anne. Teaching fellow psychology U. Cal., 1928-30; instr. psychology Ohio State U., 1930-33; head dept. psychology U. Wyo., Laramie, 1933-49, dean Grad. Sch., 1946—; chief grad. fellowship sect. U.S. Office Edn., 1960-61. Mem. com. on dental tng. NIH, 1933-36; cons. U.S. Office Edn., NSF; mem. exec. com. Council Grad. Schools in U.S., 1962-64; mem. commn. on colls. and univs. North Central Assn., 1964-67; mem. Nat. Adv. Dental Research Council, 1966-70; chmn. of Western Assn. Grad. Schs., 1962-63, Commn. on Grad. Edn., Land-Grant Colls. and State Univs., 1969-71. Served with USNR, 1941-44. Recipient Centennial award Ohio State U., 1970. Fellow Am. Psychol. Assn., A.A.A.S.; mem. Colo.-Wyo. Acad. Sci. (v.p. 1948-49, trustee research found.), Phi Beta Kappa, Sigma Xi, Beta Theta Pi, Phi Kappa Phi. Presbyn. Contbr. articles to psychology and ednl. jours. Home: 1303 Park Av Laramie WY 82070

BRUCE, ROBERT KEADY, librarian; b. Laramie, Wyo., May 12, 1935; s. Robert Hall and Huldah (Means) B.; B.A., U. Wyo., 1957, M.A., 1959; postgrad. Rutgers U., 1959- 63, M.L.S., 1960; m. Lin McLaughlin, Aug. 23, 1959; children—Rob McLaughlin, Marylin, David Murray, Scott Michael. Grad. asst. history dept. U. Wyo., 1957-58; reference asst. Rutgers U. Library, New Brunswick, N.J., 1959-62, research asst. Grad. Sch. Library Sci, 1960-61, teaching asst., 1961-63; librarian Fort Lewis Coll., Durango, Colo., 1963-66; library adv. AID, Kabul (Afghanistan) U., 1966-69; head librarian Gorham (Me.) State Coll. Library, 1968-69; librarian Carleton Coll., Northfield, Minn., 1969—. Participant, Internat. Assn. Tech. U. Libraries triennial working session, Haifa, Israel, 1967. Colonial Dames of Am. scholar, 1956-57. Mem. Am., Minn., Colo. (pres. coll. and univ. sect. 1967-68), Mt. Plains library assns., Omicron Delta Kappa, Phi Alpha Theta, Sigma Nu. Contbr. articles profl. jours. Home: 411 Winona St Northfield MN 55057

BRUCE, WILLIAM CONRAD, ret. publishing co. exec.; b. Milw., Jan. 17, 1882; s. William George and Monica (Moehring) B.; A.B., Marquette U., 1901, M.A., 1905, LL.D., 1956; LL.D., Mt. Mary Coll., 1954. Editorial asst. Am. Sch. Bd. Jour., 1902-10, asst. editor, 1910-52, editor, 1952-67; v.p., mng. editor Bruce Pub. Co., Milw., 1914-52, pres., 1952-60, chmn. bd., 1961-68; chmn. Am. State Bank, Milw., 1959- 61. Sec. bd. govs. Mt. Mary Coll., Milw., 1941-63; mem. lay bd. advisers Misericordia Hosp., Milw., 1952-60. Mem. Nat. Council Schoolhouse Constrn. (hon. mem., sec., 1922-37). Home: 9205 Jackson Park Blvd Wauwatosa, WI 53226

BRUCH, HILDE, psychiatrist, psychoanalyst, author, educator; b. Germany; d. Hirsch and Adele (Rath) Bruch; M.D., U. Freiburg, 1929; 1 adopted nephew, Herbert. Came to U.S., 1934, naturalized, 1940. Pediat. tng. Leipzig U. Clinic; pediatrician Babies Hosp., N.Y.C., 1934-53; psychiat. tng. Johns Hopkins, 1941-43; psychoanalytic tng. Washington Balt. Inst., 1941-45; asso. psychoanalyst Psychoanalytic Clinic for Tng. and Research, Columbia, 1947-64, clin. prof. psychiatry Coll. Physicians and Surgeons, 1953-58, clin. prof., 1958-64, attending psychiatrist N.Y. State Psychiat. Inst., 1954-64, dir. children's psychiat. service, 1953-55, psychotherapeutic supr., 1955-64; pvt. practice psychoanalysis and child psychiatry, N.Y.C., until 1964; prof. psychiatry Baylor U. Coll. Medicine, 1964—. Wartime work on food habits for NRC. Diplomate Am. Bd. Pediatrics, Am. Bd. Child Psychiatry. Fellow Am. Psychiat. Assn., Internat., Am. psychoanalytic assns. Author: Don't Be Afraid of Your Child, 1952; The Importance of Overweight, 1957; Studies in Schizophrenia, 1959; Eating Disorders, 1971. Contbr. articles to profl. jours. Home: 1600 Holcombe Blvd Houston TX 77025

BRUCHEY, STUART WEEMS, educator; b. Washington, Aug. 6, 1917; s. Walter Latrobe and Nellie (Richardson) B.; A.B., Johns Hopkins, 1943, M.A., 1946, Ph.D., 1955; m. Eleanor Stephens Small, June 16, 1956; 1 son, Stuart Andrew. Instr., Dickinson Coll., 1956-57; asst. prof. Northwestern U., 1957-59; asst. prof. Mich. State U., 1959-60, asso. prof., 1960-64, prof., 1964-67; prof. Columbia, N.Y.C., 1967-68, Allan Nevins prof. Am. econ. history, 1968—; faculty fellow Social Sci. Research Council, 1963-64; fellow Center for Recent Am. History, Johns Hopkins, 1965; mem. Council on Research Econ. History, 1966—. Mem. adv. bd. Bus. History Rev., 1962- 65. Mem. Am. Hist. Assn., Am. Econ. Assn., Am. Assn. U. Profs. Democrat. Author: Robert Oliver, Merchant of Baltimore, 1783-1819, 1957; The Roots of American Economic Growth, 1607-1861, 1965; The Colonial Merchant, 1966; Cotton and the Growth of the American Economy, 1967; (with others) The Changing Economic Order, 1968. Contbr. sect. to Ency. Brit. 1963. Home: 460 Riverside Dr New York City NY 10027

BRUCHHAUSEN, WALTER, judge; b. Bklyn., May 29, 1892; s. Hugo and Anne (Dietrich) B.; LL.B., N.Y. U., 1912; m. Lois Thayer, June 12, 1943; 1 dau., Alice. Admitted to N.Y. bar, 1919, since practiced in N.Y.C.; mem. Firm Duncan & Bruchhausen, 1919-42, Cadwalader, Wickersham & Taft, 1942—; U.S. dist., judge, 1953—; chief judge U.S. Dist. Ct. for Eastern Dist. of N.Y., 1959- 62, now sr. judge. Mem. N.Y. State Jud. Council, 1950-53. Trustee Poly. Prep. Sch. Mem. Bklyn. Bar Assn. (past pres.), Brooklyn Heights Assn. (past pres.). Home: Brooklyn NY Office: US Court Brooklyn NY 11201

BRUCK, RICHARD HUBERT, mathamatician, educator; b. Pembroke, Ont., Can., Dec. 26, 1914; s. Joseph Hubert and Hellise (Workman) B.; B.A., U. Toronto, 1937, M.A. fellow in math. 1937-40), 1938, Ph.D., 1940; m. Helen Olive Glorine Troop, June 29, 1940. Came to U.S., 1940, naturalized, 1948. Instr. math. U. Ala., 1940-42; faculty U. Wis., Madison, 1942—, prof. math., 1952—, research prof. math., 1967—; Fulbright lectr., Canberra, Australia, 1963; summer research lectr. Canadian Math. Congress, Saskatoon, 1963; cons. to industry, 1961—. Decorated officier l'Ordre de Mérite du Grand-Duché de Luxembourg. Guggenheim fellow and research fellow U. Wis., 1946-47, Frankfurt/Main, Germany, Oxford, Eng., 1959-60, U. N.C., 1963-64. Mem. Math. Assn. Am. (Chauvenet prize 1956), Am. Math. Soc. (asso. sec. 1945-48, asst. editor bull. 1945-47, editor proc. 1955-57), Canadian Congress, London Math. Soc., Am. Assn. U. Profs., Institut Grand-Ducal de Luxembourg (hon. Section de Sciences). Asso. editor Jour. of Algebra, 1963—. Home: 6342 Inner Dr Madison WI 53705

BRUCKENSTEIN, STANLEY, chemist, educator; b. Bklyn., Nov. 1, 1927; s. Max and Rose (Kaltoon) B.; B.S., Poly. Inst. Bklyn., 1950; Ph.D., U. Minn., 1954; m. Pearl Yavel, Sept. 10, 1950; children—Barbara, David A., Lisa S. Faculty, U. Minn., 1954-68, prof. chemistry, 1965-68, chief div. analytical chemistry, 1962-68; prof. chemistry State U. N.Y. at Buffalo, 1968—. Sci. adviser Mpls. dist. FDA, 1966-68; cons. chemistry dept. Argonne Nat. Lab., 1962-70; cons. to industry, 1966—; mem. com. examiners Grad. Record Examinations, 1968—; asso. mem. commn. V5 and V6, Internat. Union Pure and Applied Chemistry, 1966—; Nat. Acad. Sci. exchange visitor with USSR Acad. Scis., Moscow, 1964-65. Served with USNR, 1945-46. Mem. Am. Chem. Soc., A.A.A.S., Am. Assn. U. Profs., Electrochem. Soc., Sigma Xi. Author: (with others) Quantitative Chemical Analysis, 4th edit., 1969. Co-editor: (English transl.) Electrochemical Kinetics, 1967. Mem. adv. bd. Talanta, 1965-68, Analytical Chemistry, 1958-68, also articles. Home: 115 Foxpoint West Williamsville NY 14221 Office: Chemistry Dept State Univ NY Buffalo NY 14214

BRUCKER, GENE ADAM, historian, educator; b. Cropsey, Ill., Oct. 15, 1924; s. Walter C. and Alberta (Koehler) B.; B.A., U. Ill., 1947, M.A., 1948; B.Litt., Oxford (Eng.) U., 1950; Ph.D., Princeton, 1954; m. Patricia Chantrill, Sept. 24, 1949; children—Mark, Francesca, Gwendolyn; m. 2d, Marion Skinner, Feb. 27, 1971. Faculty U. Cal. at Berkeley, 1954—, prof. history, 1964—; fellow Inst. for Advanced Study, Princeton, 1968-69. Served with AUS, 1943-46. Rhodes scholar, 1948-50; Fulbright scholar, Italy, 1952-54; Guggenheim fellow, 1960-61; Am. Council Learned Socs. fellow, 1964-65. Mem. Am. Hist. Assn., Renaissance Soc. Am., Medieval Acad. Am., Am. Assn. U. Profs. Author: Florentine Politics and Society, 1343-1378, 1962; Renaissance Florence, 1969. Office: Dept of History University of Cal Berkeley CA 94720

BRUCKER, HERBERT, writer, editor; b. Passaic, N.J., Oct. 4, 1898; s. Carl and Adele (Balthasar) B.; A.B., Williams Coll., 1921, LL.D., 1964; B. Litt., Columbia, 1924, L.H.D., 1963; Pulitzer traveling scholar, 1924; L.H.D., Colby Coll., 1960; D. Litt., U. Hartford, 1965; m. Sydney Seabury Cook, Feb. 6, 1926 (dec. Apr. 1950); children—Christopher, Sydney (Mrs. James Sowles), Thomas; m. 2d, Mrs. Elizabeth Spock Dominick, Aug. 10, 1951; 2 stepsons—William F., Anthony Dominick. Reporter, Springfield (Mass.) Union, 1923, World, N.Y.C., 1925-26; mem. editorial staff World's Work, 1926-27, Rev. of Revs., 1927-32; asst. to dean Columbia Sch. Journalism, 1932-44, asst. prof. journalism, 1933-35, asso. prof., 1935-42, prof., 1942-44; chief media div., asso. chief Bur. Overseas Publs., OWI, 1942-43; asso. editor Hartford Courant, 1944-47, editor, 1947-66; dir. profl. journalism fellowships Stanford, 1966-69; syndicated newspaper columnist, 1968—. Served with USN, 1918. Recipient John Peter Zenger award U. Ariz., 1959. Mem Am. Soc. Newspaper Editors (pres. 1963-64), Am. Council Edn. for Journalism (pres. 1959-63), Chi Psi, Sigma Delta Chi. Episcopalian. Author: The Changing American Newspaper, 1937; Freedom of Information, 1949; Journalist: Eyewitness to History, 1962. Address: Box 127 Rural Route 2 Windsor VT 05089

BRUCKNER, DON, journalist; Rhodes scholar, Oxford (Eng.) U. Formerly labor writer Chgo. Sun-Times, also Brit. Press rep. TV program Press Internat.; now nat. reporter and columnist Los Angeles Times. Address: care Los Angeles Times 1301 Av Americas New York City NY 10019

BRUDE, CHARLES JULIUS, meat packing co. exec.; b. N.Y.C., May 30, 1918; s. Charles Julius and Clare (Deysher) B.; student N.Y. U., 1938-41; B.A., Northwestern U., 1949; m. Garleydene L. Robinson, Nov. 14, 1945. With J. Henry Schroder Banking Corp., N.Y.C., 1936-39; with credit dept. Cudahy Co., N.Y.C., 1939-41, asst. treas., Chgo., 1946-50, Omaha, 1950-61, treas., 1961-65, treas., Phoenix, 1965-66, v.p., treas., 1966—. Bd. dirs. YMCA. Served to lt. USNR, 1941-46. Mem. Financial Execs. Inst., Financial Analysts Soc., Phoenix, Ohaha jr. chambers commerce. Mason. Club: Moon Valley Country. Home: 8512 N 10th Av Phoenix AZ 85021 Office: 100 W Clarendon St Phoenix AZ 85013

BRUDER, CHARLES FREDERIC, III, diversified industry exec.; b. Englewood, N.J., Oct. 11, 1906; s. Charles Frederic and Edith M. (Gardner) B.; B.S., Dartmouth, 1928; m. Nona M. Stout, June 23, 1934 (div. June 1967); children—Rosalind Ann, Charles Frederic IV; m. 2d, Ingrid Rasp, May 1968. With Harris Forbes & Co., dir.; v.p. corporate relations Singer Co.; dir. Thomas & Betts Co. Home: 53 E 64th St New York City NY 10021 Office: 30 Rockefeller Plaza New York City NY 10020

BRUDER, THOMAS A., business exec.; b. Phila., Jan. 15, 1904; s. Michael A. and Ella T. (Wagner) B.; student Pierce Sch. Bus. Adminstrn.; m. Mary A. Stitt, June 13, 1934; children—Thomas A., Mary Ann, Patricia, Michael, James, Janet. Pres. M.A. Bruder & Sons, Inc., also dir.; pres. Lambert Realty Co., Phila. Club: Union League (Phila.). Home: West Rolling Rd Springfield Delaware County PA 19064 Office: 52d and Grays Av Philadelphia PA 19143

BRUDEVOLD, FINN, educator, dentist; b. Glovik, Norway, June 12, 1910; s. Peder and Ingrid (Haugom) B.; came to U.S., 1939, naturalized, 1949; D.D.S., U. Minn., 1940; M.S. in Dental Sci., U. Rochester, 1954; A.M. (hon.), Harvard, 1958; Doctoral (hon.), U. Oslo (Norway), 1965; Dr. Odont. h.c., U. Umea (Sweden), 1969; m. Esther Asher, June 27, 1941; children—Anne, Catherine, Christine. Instr. dental pathology Tufts Coll. Dental Sch., 1942, instr. clin. dentistry, 1945-46, asst. prof. prosthodontia, 1946-48, asst. prof. clin. dentistry, 1948-49; asst. prof. dental research U. Rochester, 1949-58; dir. dental research Eastman Dental Dispensary, Rochester, 1949-58; chief dental medicine Forsyth Dental Infirmary, also prof. dentistry Harvard Sch. Dental Medicine. Mem. dental study section NIH, 1955-69. Served as capt. Norwegian Army, 1942- 45. Recipient H. Trendley Dean award for fluoride research, 1969. Mem. Am. Dental Assn., Internat. Assn. Dental Research (recipient award for basic research in oral therapeutics 1966), Sigma Xi, Omicron Kappa Upsilon; corr. mem. European Orgn. for Research Flourine and Dental Caries Prevention, Norwegian Dental Assn. Home: 284 Woodward St Waban MA 02168 Office: 140 The Fenway Boston MA 02215

BRUECKHEIMER, WILLIAM ROGERS, educator; b. Gary, Ind., Aug. 19, 1921; s. Albert Gustav and Lucille (Schwartz) B.; student Wabash Coll., 1941-42; M.A. in Social Sci., U. Chgo., 1949; M.A. in Geography, U. Mich., 1952, Ph.D., 1953; m. Mary Ellen Roe, Nov. 7, 1942; children—William Rogers, David Rogers, Suzanne Rogers. Instr. geography Fla. State U., 1949-51; teaching fellow, instr. geography U. Mich., 1951-53; asst. prof., then asso. prof. geography So. State Coll., Magnolia, Ark., 1953-55; faculty Western Mich. U., Kalamazoo, 1955-64, prof. geography and geology, head dept., 1958-64; prof., head dept. geography Fla. State U., Tallahassee, 1964—, dir. London (Eng.) Study Center, 1971-72. Mem. Fla. Gov.'s Resource Use Edn. Com. Fellow in bus. Found. Econ. Edn., summer 1955. Served with AUS, 1942-46; ETO. Mem. Assn. Am. Geographers (chmn. East Lakes div. 1957-58), Mich. Schoolmasters Club (chmn. geography sect. 1958-59), Am. Assn. U. Profs., Nat. Council Geog. Edn., Fla. Soc. Geographers, Leon County Soc. Geographers and Anthropologists. Club: Exchange. Contbr. articles to profl. jours. Home: 1210 Waverly Rd Tallahassee FL 32303

BRUECKNER, KEITH ALLAN, educator, theoretical physicist; b. Mpls., Mar. 19, 1924; s. Leo John and Agnes (Holland) B.; B.A., U. Minn., 1945; M.A., 1947; Ph.D., U. Cal. at Berkeley, 1950; m. Elsa Dekking, Aug. 12, 1960; children—Jan Keith, Anthony Leo, Leslie. Prof. physics U. Pa., 1956-59; prof. physics U. Cal. at San Diego, 1959—, chmn. dept. physics, 1959-61, dean letters and sci., 1963-65, dean grad. studies, 1965, dir. Inst. Pure and Applied Phys. Scis., 1965-69; v.p., dir. research Inst. Def. Analysis, Washington, 1961-62 (on leave); cons. AEC, 1953—. Served with USAAF, 1943- 46. Recipient Dannie Heineman prize for math. physics, 1963. Fellow Am. Phys. Soc., Am. Acad. Arts and Scis.; mem. Nat. Acad. Scis., Am. Inst. Aeros. and Astronautics. Cons. editor Pure and Applied Physics series. Home: 7723 Ludington Pl La Jolla, CA 92037.

BRUEN, HOWARD GERALD, physician; b. Youngtown, Ohio, June 6, 1905; s. Alexander H. and Fanny (Bergstein) B.; A.B., Columbia, 1925, M.S., 1934, D.M.S., 1935; M.D., Johns Hopkins, 1929; m. Dorothy Conner, June 10, 1937; children—Stephen, Nancy (Mrs. Howard Noyes), James. Intern Boston City Hosp., 1929-31; asst. resident Presbyn. Hosp., N.Y.C., 1932-34, chief med. resident, 1934-35, attending physician, 1961—; chief cardiology, cardiac, Bethesda Naval Med. Center and 3rd Naval Dist., 1942-46; chief Vanderbilt Cardiac Clin., N.Y.C., 1946—, asso. attending physician, 1946-61; clin. prof. Medicine Columbia, N.Y.C., 1962-68, clin. prof. 1968—. Served to comdr. USNR, 1942-46, Markle fellow medicine, 1935-37. Diplomate Am. Bd. Internal Medicine. Fellow Am. Heart Assn., Council of Clin. Cardiology; mem. A.M.A., Soc. Med. Con.'s to Armed Services, N.Y. County Med. Soc., N.Y. Acad. Medicine, N.Y. Acad. Sci. Contbr. articles on cardiology to profl. jours. Home: 4551 Livingston Av New York City NY 10471 Office: 903 Park Av New York City NY 10021

BRUENING, JOSEPH M., indsl. distbr.; b. Cin., Jan. 1, 1896; s. George M. and Catherine (HaugFr) B.; student pub. schs., Ohio; m. Eva L. Black, July 19, 1924. Service mgr. Standard Parts Co., 1920-22; pres. Ohio Ball Bearing Co., 1922-52, Bearings, Inc., Cleve., 1952—. Bd. dirs. Cath. Charities Corp. Knight of St. Gregory, local unit Am. Cancer Soc.; trustee Cleve. Zool. Soc. Mem. Cleve. C. of C., Bluecoats, Inc. Rotarian. Clubs: Shaker Heights Country, Rockwell Springs Trout, Cleve. Playhouse, Athletic. Home: 16201 Parkland Dr Shaker Heights OH 44120 Office: 3634 Euclid Av Cleveland OH 44115

BRUERE, RICHARD TREAT, educator; b. N.Y.C., Dec. 28, 1907; s. Henry and Jane (Munroe) B.; A.B., Harvard, 1928, Ph.D., 1936; m. Carol Whitcomb, Dec. 28, 1937. Instr. Latin, U. Chgo., 1937-41, asst. prof. 1941-49, asso. prof. 1949-54, prof., dir. Latin studies dept. classics, 1954—. Served to comdr. USNR, 1942-46. Mem. Am. Philol. Soc. Home: 5760 Blackstone Av Chicago, IL 60637.

BRUES, ALICE MOSSIE, educator, phys. anthropologist; b. Boston, Oct. 9, 1913; d. Charles Thomas and Beirne (Barrett) Brues; A.B., Bryn Mawr Coll., 1933; Ph.D., Radcliffe Coll., 1940. Faculty, U. Okla. Sch. Medicine, 1946-65, prof., 1960-65; vis. prof. anthropology U. Colo., Boulder, 1965-66, prof., 1966—, chmn. dept. anthropology, 1969-71; curator Stovall Mus., Norman, Okla., 1956-65; asso. curator U. Colo. Mus., 1966—. Fellow Am. Anthrop. Assn.; mem. Am. Assn. Phys. Anthropologists (v.p. 1966-68, pres. 1971—), A.A.A.S., N.Y. Acad. Sci., Am. Soc. Human Genetics, Soc. Study Evolution, Phi Beta Kappa, Sigma Xi. Asso. editor: Am. Jour. Phys. Anthropology, 1962-66. Contbr. articles profl. jours. Home: 4325 Prado Dr Boulder CO 80303

BRUES, AUSTIN MOORE, physician; b. Milw., Apr. 25, 1906; s. Charles Thomas and Beirne (Barrett) B.; A.B., Harvard, 1926, M.D., 1930; m. Mildred Carter, June 1, 1930; children—Roger Austin, Nancy Carter, Charles Thomas. Med. resident Collis P. Huntington Meml. Hosp., Boston, 1930-31, responsible investigator OSRD, 1941-44; sr. biologist Metall. Lab., Manhattan Engrs. Dist., Chgo., 1944-46; asso. prof. medicine U. Chgo., 1945-52, prof., 1952—, mem. Inst. Radiobiology and Biophysics, 1945-54; sr. biologist, dir. biol. and med. research Argonne Nat. Lab., AEC, 1946-62, sr. biologist, 1962-71. med. cons., 1971—. Served as expert to Sec. of War in study of atomic bomb casualties in Japan, 1946-47; mem. com. on atomic casualties NRC; mem. U.S. delegation to UN Sci. Com. on Atomic Radiation, 1957—; mem. sci. adv. bd. Armed Forces Inst. Pathology, 1950-60, Internat. Commn. on Radiol. Protection, 1957—; expert cons. WHO, 1962—; mem. research adv. council Am. Cancer Soc., 1969—. Mem. A.A.A.S., Am. Assn. for Cancer Research (dir., 1946—, pres. 1954-55), Am. Physiol. Soc., Am. Assn. Anatomists, Am. Clin. and Climatol. Soc., Soc. Cell Biol., Soc. for Exptl. Biology and Medicine, Soc. Clin. Investigation, Central Soc. for Clin. Research, Radiation Research Soc. (council 1952- -, pres. 1955-56). Clubs: Quadrangle, Literary (Chgo.); Harvard (Boston). Editor: Low Level Irradiation, 1959; Aging and Levels of Biological Organization, 1965. Contbr. articles to med., sci. jours. Home: 4907 Lee Av Downers Grove IL 60515 Office: Argonne Nat Lab Argonne IL 60439

BRUESTLE, BEAUMONT, educator, writer; b. Phila., Dec. 23, 1905; s. Adolph and Florence (Schrader) B.; A.B., U. Pa., 1927, A.M., 1930, Ph.D., 1932. Faculty English dept. U. Pa., 1927-31, Temple U., 1931-45; actor profl. theatre, N.Y.C., 1945-47; faculty dept. speech and English, U. Tulsa, 1947-70, chmn. dept., 1953-70; actor, dir., writer ednl., community and profl. theatre; lectr. theatre and opera. Mem. Broadway Theatre League Tulsa (pres. 1959-65, chmn. bd. 1965—), Internat. Platform Assn., Theta Alpha Phi. Author: (poetry) Storm Signals, 1931, Things of Earth, 1935; (children's play) The Wonderful Tang, 1952; (mus. comedy) The Gusher, 1958, The Name Is Jones, 1959; (mus. play) Lola, 1963; (comedy) Love, Art and Anthony Thorndyke, 1963; (mus. comedy) Know-It-All, 1965; That Fair Affair (mus. comedy), 1966; But Don't Gild Lily (mus. comedy, 1968); (mus. comedy) Young B.F., 1970; (new adapation from Norwegian of Henrik Ibsen) Peer Gynt, 1970; also author book revs. in So. Speech Jour.; opera reviews in Giffith Park News, Los Angeles; articles in The Cue (theatre mag.), Tulsa World, Okla. editor Players Mag., 1959-63. Home: 2149 Panorama Terrace Los Angeles CA 90039

BRUGGEMAN, JOSEPH ANTHONY, lawyer; b. Ft. Wayne Ind., Dec. 28, 1906; s. Henry Otto and Helen (Trentman) B.; grad. Phillips Exeter Acad., 1924; A.B., Harvard, 1928, LL.B., 1931; m. Marie Cellard, Apr. 1, 1946; children—Henry, Patrick, Joseph, Jack, Frederick, Marie, Ann. Admitted to Ind. bar, 1931, since practiced in Ft. Wayne; asso., partner Barrett, Barrett & McNagny, 1931- -. Chmn. bd. Holsum Bakery Co., Ft. Wayne, Holsum Bakery Co. of Lima, O., Bedford Bakery Corp.; dir. Old Fort Industries, Inc. Served to capt., Q.M.C., AUS, 1943-46. Mem. Am., Fed., Ind., Allen County, 7th Circuit bar assns., Am. Judicature Soc., Internat. Soc. Labor Law and Social Legislation. Home: 4202 N Washington Rd Fort Wayne IN 46804 Office: Lincoln Bank Tower Fort Wayne IN 46802

BRUGH, ALBERT G., banker. Sr. v.p. Battle Creek office Mich. Nat. Bank. Office: 1 W Michigan Av Battle Creek MI 49016*

BRUGLER, MERCER, diversified industry exec.; b. Phila., Nov. 25, 1904; s. Elmer G. and Virginia (MacDonald) B.; grad. U. Rochester, 1925, student Bus. Sch., Harvard, 1926; m. Bernie Whitham, Oct. 4, 1927; 1 son, John Whitham. With financial office U. Rochester (N.Y.), 1926; with Pfaudler Co., Rochester, 1926-59, credit mgr., asst. to pres. 1926-29, asst. sec., asst. treas., 1929-31, asst. to chmn. bd., asst. sec., asst. treas., 1931-36, asst., gen. mgr. and v.p., 1936-39, v.p., gen. mgr., 1939-45, pres., 1945-59; chmn. bd., chmn. exec. com. Pfaudler- Permutit, Inc., 1959-65; vice chmn. bd. Ritter Pfaudler Corp., 1965-67; dir., exec. com. Sybron Corp., 1967—; dir. McCurdy & Co., B. Forman Co., Lincoln First Banks, Inc., Xerox Corp., mem. adv. bd. Lincoln Rochester Trust Co.; trustee Rochester Savs. Bank. Trustee U. Rochester, dir. bond drives in Rochester, Rochester Community Chest; mem. men's bd. St. Mary's Hosp.; bd. dirs. Met. Rochester Found., Inc.; chmn. exec. com., trustee U. Rochester; trustee Rochester Area Ednl. Television Assn. Mem. Rochester C. of C. (pres. 1949; trustee), Rochester Assn. Credit Men (past pres.). Rochester Engring. Soc., Phi Beta Kappa, Theta Delta Chi. Presbyn. Clubs: Country, University (Rochester). Home: 12 Creekdale Lane Rochester NY 14618 Office: 1100 Midtown Tower Rochester NY 14604

BRUHN, ERIK BELTON EVERS, dancer; b. Copenhagen, Denmark, Oct. 3, 1928; s. Ernest Emil and Ellen (Evers) B.; student Royal Danish Ballet Royal Theatre, Copenhagen. Made debut with Danish Ballet, 1946, premiere danseur, 1949, 58-61; guest artist Met. Ballet, London, 1947-49, Am. Nat. Ballet Theatre, 1949, 51, 53, permanent mem., 1953-58, N.Y.C. ballet, 1959, Am. ballet, 1960; quest Bolchai Ballet, Moscow, 1961, also Danish ballet, 1961—; ballet dir. Royal Opera, Stockholm, Sweden; partner with Jeanmarie in movie Hans Christian Andersen. 1952; has appeared as partner with Alicia Markova, Alicia Alonso, Nora Kayo, Mary Ellen Moylan, Mia Salvenska, Rosella Hightower. Tours with Ballet Theatre Europe, North Africa. Chef Stockholm Operaens Ballet, 1967. Named Ridder of Danebrog by King Denmark, 1968; recipient Narslav Nifinsky prize Paris, France, 1968. Mem. Royal Danish Ballet Union, Equity (London), Am. Guild Mus. Artists, Screen Actors Guild. Choreographer; Concetette (Morton Gould), 1953. Address: Stockholm Operaen Stockholm Sverige Sweden

BRUHN, JOACHIM, coll. dean; b. Kiel, Germany, Aug. 28, 1927; s. Johannes and Gertrud (Timm) B.; diploma, U. Kiel, 1949, Ph.D., 1953; postgrad. U. Zurich, 1949-50, U. Oxford, 1950-52, St. Anthony's Coll., Oxford, 1953-55, Brown U., 1955-57, Inst. in Higher Edn. Claremont U. Center, 1969-70; m. Marsha Soldineer, Aug. 22, 1959; children—Elisa, Dietrich, Erika, Christa. Came to U.S., 1955, naturalized, 1963. Instr. German, British pub. schs., 1953-55; asst. instr. German, Brown U., 1956-57; instr. German, U. Md., 1957-58; instr., modern langs. Denison U., 1958- 59; instr., asst. prof. German, lectr. edn. U. Mich., 1959-65; vis. asso. prof. German, Duke, 1965-66; prof. German, head dept. fgn. langs. Va. Poly. Inst., Blackburg, 1966-70, chmn. Univ. Com. on Internat. Edn.; dean studies Richmond Coll. City U. N.Y., 1970—; cons. pubs., Indsl. Relations, 1967—; Expt. in Internat. Living program leader in Germany, 1966. Bd. mem. Campus YMCA, Blacksburg Chamber Music Soc., Blacksburg Art Assn. Brown U. fellow, also U. Mich. research fellow, U.S. Govt. fellow in higher edn. Mem. Modern Lang. Assn. (life), Am. Assn. Tchrs. German (pres. Va. chpt. 1968-70), Linguistic Soc. Am., N.E.A. (life), Am. Assn. U. Profs., Am. Assn. Higher Edn. (life), Modern Humanities Research Assn., Am. Council on Teaching Fgn. Langs., Internat. Assn. Germanic Studies, Nat. Carl Schurz Assn., German-Am. Soc., German Shakespeare Soc., Mich. Acad. Sci., Arts and Letters, Central States Modern Lang. Tchrs. Assn. (exec. sec. Mich. chpt. 1962-65), Met. Mus. Art, Mus. Modern Art, Whitney Mus. Am. Art, N.Y. Cultural Center, Mus. Natural History, S.I. Mus., Richmond Hist. Soc., S.I. Zool. Soc., Delta Phi Alpha. Club: Cosmopolitan. Contbr. articles to profl. jours. Home: 2 Silver Beech Rd Emerson Hill Staten Island NY 10304

BRUHN, JOHN GLYNDON, educator; b. Norfolk, Neb., Apr. 27, 1934; s. John Franz and Margaret Constance (Treiber) B.; B.A., U. Neb., 1956, M.A., 1958; Ph.D., Yale, 1961. Research sociologist Grace-New Haven Hosp., 1960-61, U. Edinburgh (Scotland), 1961-62; mem. faculty U. Okla. Med. Center, 1962—, prof., chmn. dept. human ecology, 1969—; cons. in field. Bd. dirs. Okla. Sci. and Arts Found., Okla. Health and Welfare Assn. Served with AUS, 1957-58. Commonwealth Fund-Yale fellow, 1958-60; USPHS fellow, 1960-61; Fulbright fellow, 1961-62; recipient Career Devel. award Nat. Heart Inst., 1968-69. Fellow Am. Sociol. Assn., Am. Pub. Health Assn., Am. Heart Assn., Royal Soc. Health; mem. Am. Psychosomatic Soc., Assn. Am. Med. Colls., Assn. Tchrs. Preventive Medicine, N.Y. Acad. Sci., Sigma Xi, Alpha Kappa Delta, Kappa Sigma. Home: 4208 N Drexel St Oklahoma City OK 73112

BRUINS, PAUL FASTENAU, chem. engr., educator; b. Albert Lea, Minn., Dec. 22, 1905; s. Henry Martin and Lillian (Fastenau) B.; B.S., Central Coll., Pella, Ia., 1926; D. Sc., 1960; M.S., Ia. State U., 1927, Ph.D., 1930; m. 2d, Bess L. Collins, Aug. 11, 1946; children—Barbara (Mrs. Robert Henninges), Janna, Ruth (Mrs. Lyle Prince), Lillian (Mrs. Cather Boyd), Cynthia. Instr., Ia. State U., 1927-30; chem. engr. A.O. Smith Corp., 1930-32, Geuder, Paeschke & Frey Co., Milw., 1932-34, Fulton Co., Milw., 1934-35; faculty Bklyn. Poly. Inst., 1935—, prof. chem. engring., 1946—. Cons. plastics engring. and tech., 1935—. Mem. Soc. Plastics Engrs. (chmn. nat. edn. com. 1966-68), Soc. Plastics Industry, Am. Inst. Chem. Engrs., Am. Chem. Soc., Electrochem. Soc., Sigma Xi, Phi Lambda Upsilon, Tau Beta Pi, Omega Chi Epsilon, Alpha Chi Sigma. Mem. Community Ch. (chmn. council 1967-69). Editor Plasticizer Technology, Plastics for Electrical Insulation, Epoxy Resin Technology, Polyurethane Technology, New Polymeric Materials, Silicone Technology, Polyblends and Composites. Home: 7 Shore Rd Douglaston NY 11363 Office: 333 Jay St Brooklyn NY 11201

BRUINSMA, HENRY ALLEN, educator; b. Prospect Part, N.J., July 29, 1916; s. Henry John and Anna (Wierenga) A.; Mus.B., U. Mich., 1937, Mus. M., 1938, Ph.D., 1949; student Harvard, 1940, 42, U. Utrecht, 1947-48; m. Grace Lois Hekman, June 7, 1939; childrenBruce Henry, James Allen. Dir. summer opera U. Mich., 1938, 39; asst. prof. music, dir. undergrad. studies Duke, 1938- 43; prof. music Calvin Coll., 1946-55; vis. prof. U. Mich., 1953-54; chmn. dept. music Ariz. State U., 1955-56, 64-, dean Coll. of Fine Arts, 1965-; chmn. dept. music So. Ill. U., 1956-59; dir. Sch. Music, Ohio State U., 1959-64, mem. pres. univ. permanent Planning com.; specialty Reformation music; lectr. U. for Presidents, 1963; v.p. String Teaching Research & Devel., Inc., 1962—. Mem. citizen's adv. com., Grand Rapids (Mich.) pub. schs., 1952-55; nat. chmn. com. ch. music Christian Reformed Ch., 1952-60. Mem. Arix. Council on Arts and Humanities, Phoneix Arts Council; bd. dirs. Phoenix Symphony Orch. Served with AUS, 1943-45. Distinguished Alumnus Award, U. Mich., 1968. Travelling F. Am. Council Learned Societies, 1947-48. Mem. Nat. Fedn. Music Clubs (chmn. crusade for strings), Music Tchrs. Nat. Assn. (chmn. coll. music com.), Nat. Assn. Schs. Music, chms. liason com.; grad. commn. 1963—), Coll). Music Assn. (chmn. liaison com.), Am. Musicol. Soc., Music Educators Nat. Conf., Ohio Music Tchrs. Assn. (chmn. Central Dist. 1962-), Vereeniging voor Nederlandsche Muziekgeschiedenis, International Council on Fine Arts Deans, Phi Kappa Phi, Phi Delta Kappa, Phi Mu Alpha, Pi Kappa Lambda, Phi Sigma Kappa. Rotarian. Composer orchestral and choral compositions; author numerous articles in field. Home: 5608 N Quail Run Rd Scottsdale AZ 85251

BRUMAN, HENRY JOHN, educator; b. Berlin, Germany, Mar. 25, 1913; s. William A. and Anna Berta Else (Fromme) B.; came to U.S., 1922, naturalized, 1930; student Cal. Inst. Tech., 1930-31, Universidad Nacional de Mexico, Escuela de Verano, 1934; A.B. in Chemistry, U. Cal. at Los Angeles, 1935; Ph.D. in Geography, U. Cal. at Berkeley, 1940. Teaching asst. geography U. Cal. at Berkeley, 1936-38, instr. extension div., 1939-40; instr., then asst. prof. Pa. State Coll., 1940-44; cultural geographer Smithsonian Instn. and M project, 1944-45; faculty geography U. Cal. at Los Angeles, 1945—, prof., 1955—, chmn. dept., 1957-61; coordinator U. Cal. at Los Angeles-Colombia U. projects, 1958- 61, U. Cal. at Los Angeles-Brazil U. Projects, 1961-66, acting dir. Center of Latin Am. Studies, 1962-63, asso. dir. U. Cal. Latin Am. Center, 1963-65. Mem. Nat. Acad. Scis.-NRC adv. com. on geography to State Dept., 1961-65; dir. NDEA lang. and area program in Latin Am. Studies, 1962-65, dir. U. Cal. Study Center, Göttingen, 1966-68; vis. prof. Philosophische Fakultät, Georg- August-Universität, Göttingen, 1966-68; research in S.Am. for geography br. Office Naval Research, 1951-52; coop. research with Intergovtl. Com. for European Migration in Switzerland, Italy, Netherlands, Germany, Brazil, 1955-56; organized ednl. exchanges univs. in Colombia, 1958-60; reconnaissance field trip, Galápagos Islands, 1959. Recipient Alexander von Humboldt Gold medal Fed. Republic of Germany, 1971; Fulbright-Hays travel grantee to Portugal, 1963. Field fellow in Mexico and C.Am., Social Sci. Research Council, 1938-39. Mem. Assn. Am. Geographers, Am., Los Angeles geog. socs., Assn. Pacific Coast Geographers, Cal. Geography Council, Am. Assn. U. Profs., A.A.A.S., Sociedad Colombiana de Geógrafos Bogotá (hon.), Sigma Xi, Pi Gamma Mu. Home: 969 Hilgard Av Los Angeles CA 90024

BRUMBAUGH, DAVID EMMERT, lumber co. exec.; b. Martinsburg, Pa., Oct. 8, 1894; s. Moses R. and Sarah Florence (Stuard) B.; ed. pub. schs., North Woodbury Twp., Pa., Summer normal school, Martinsburg, Pa., and Internat. Corr. Schs., Scranton, Pa.; D.C.S. (hon.), Franklin and Marshall Coll.; m. Carolyn L. Acker, Oct. 29, 1919; children—D. Robert, Sumner E., Carol and Carolyn (twins). Engaged in banking bus., Claysburg, Pa., 1914—, now pres.; partner Queen Lumber Co., 1921—; established D. Emmert Brumbaugh Ins. Agy., 1920; chmn. bd. Central Pa. Nat. Bank; dir. Penn State Mut. Ins. Co., Johnstown; mem. 78th Congress from 23d Pa. Dist., 79th Congress, 22d Pa. Dist.; sec. of banking Commonwealth of Pa., 1947-52; former state senator Pa., 30th Dist. Chmn. Blair County S.S.S. Bd. No. 1, Hollidaysburg, Pa., 1941-43; chmn. Blair Co. chpt. A.R.C. 1934-62, now mem. exec. com. Trustee Pa. Indsl Sch., Huntingdon, Pa., Cedar Crest Coll., Altoona Hosp. Served as pvt. 33d Div., U.S. Army, World War I. Citation from Hood Coll., Frederick, Md. Mem. of V.F.W., Am. Legion, 40 and 8, Pa. Soc. of N.Y. Mason (32, Shriner, Jester). Republican. Clubs: Union League (Phila.); Blairmont Country (Hollidaysburg); Bedford Springs Country (Bedford). Address: Claysburg PA 16625

BRUMBAUGH, DAVID WILLIS, mag. exec.; b. Roanoke, Va., May 20, 1908; s. Marshall Frantz and Anna Lee (Willis) B.; A.B., Roanoke Coll., 1929; M.B.A., Harvard Grad. Bus. Sch., 1931; m. Dorothy Seay, Oct. 13, 1934 (dec. Aug. 1956); children—David Willis, Ann Seay; m. 2d, Juanita Cooley, January 28, 1958. Certified pub. accountant Haskins & Sells, 1931-33; with Time, Inc., 1933—, became sec., 1939, v.p., 1945-60, exec. v.p., treas., dir., 1960—; mem. adv. bd. Mfr.-Hanover Trust Co. Bd. dirs. Asso. Hosp. Service N.Y.; trustee Roanoke Coll. C.P.A., N.Y. Mem. Mag. Pubs. Assn. (chmn.). Baptist. Clubs: Internat. (Washington); Harvard, River, Scardale Golf, Siwanoy Country, Pine Valley Golf, Hemisphere, Treasurers, Shenorock Shore, 200, Country of N.C., Pinehurst Country, Tin-Whistlers. Home: 39 Hampton Rd Scarsdale NY 10583 also Linden Rd Pinehurst NC 28374 Office: Time & Life Bldg Rockefeller Center Bldg Rockefeller Center New York City NY 10020

BRUMBAUGH, GRANVILLE MARTIN, lawyer; b. St. Louis, Mar. 10, 1901; s. Noah J. and Rosa (Flory) B.; E.E., Lehigh U., 1922; LL.B., George Washington, 1925; m. Sophia Waldman, June 19, 1926; children—Mary Ann (Mrs. James Grant Hellmuth; dec.), Granville Martin, John. Asst. examiner U.S. Patent Office, 1922-25; admitted to N.Y. bar, 1927; asso. Redding, Greeley, O'Shea & Campbell, 1925-34; partner Hoguet, Neary & Campbell, N.Y.C., 1934-46, successor firm Campbell, Brumbaugh, Free & Graves (now Brumbaugh, Graves, Donohue & Raymond), 1946—. Mem. bd. finance, Westport, Conn., 1947-48, town meeting rep., 1949—. Mem. Am. Bar Assn., Am. Patent Law Assn., N.Y. Patent Law Assn. (pres. 1953-54), Assn. Bar City N.Y., Phi Delta Phi, Phi Delta Theta. Clubs: Downtown Assn. (N.Y.C.); Country (Fairfield, Conn.). Home: 7 Crooked Mile Rd Westport CT 06880 Office: 90 Broad St New York City NY 10004

BRUMBAUGH, ROBERT SHERRICK, educator; b. Oregon, Ill., Dec. 2, 1918; s. Aaron John and Marjorie Ruth (Sherrick) B.; A.B., U. Chgo., 1938, M.A., 1938, Ph.D., 1942; m. Ada Zarbell Steele, June 5, 1940; children—Robert Conrad, Susan Zarbell Steels, June 5, 1940; children—Robert Conrad, Susan Christianna, Joanna Pauline. Faculty Bowdoin Coll., 1946-49, Ind. U., 1949-52; faculty Yale, New Haven, 1951—, prof. philosophy, 1961—. Research fellow Am. Sch. Classical Studies, Athens, Greece, 1962-63; Morse fellow, 1954-55. Mem. Metaphys. Soc. Am. (councillor 1961-65), Am. Philos. Assn., Soc. Ancient Greek Philosophy, Am. Assn. U. Profs., Phi Beta Kappa. Author: (with N.P. Stallknecht) The Spirit of Western Philosophy, 1950; Plato's Mathematical Imagination, 1953; (with N.P. Stallknecht) The Compass of Philosophy, 1954; Plato on the One, 1960; Plato for the Modern Age, 1961; (with Nathaniel Lawrence) Philosophers on Education, 1963; The Philosophers of Greece, 1964; Ancient Greek Gadgets and Machines, 1966. Co-editor: Plato Manuscripts: A Catalogue of the Plato Microfilm Project, Yale University Libraries, parts I and II, 1962. Contbr. jours., encys. Home: 150 Ridgewood Av Hamden, CT 06517 Office: Saybrook College Yale Univ New Haven CT 06520

BRUMBLAY, RAY ULYSSES, educator, chemist; b. Azusa, Cal., Feb. 8, 1912; s. Joseph E. and Cora (Reed) B.; A.B., Ind. U., 1934; M.S., U. Wis., 1936, Ph.D., 1938; m. Lolita Dorothy Roska, Aug. 16, 1941; children—Lynn L. (Mrs. Robert D. Falconer), Raymond S., Jean M. (Mrs. Clemence C. Richau), Robert J., Laurie E. Instr., Ind. U. Calumet Center, 1938-43; from instr. to prof. chemistry U. Wis.-Milw., 1946-69, chmn. dept., 1957-64; prof. chemistry U. Wis., Marathon County Center, 1969—; cons. Bradley Washfountain Co., 1950—. Served with AUS, 1943-46. Mem. Am. Chem. Soc., Sigma Xi. Conglist. Author: Quantitative Analysis, 1960; Qualitative Analysis, 1964; A First Course in Quantitative Analysis, 1970. Home: 1407 Steuben St Wausau WI 54401

BRUMBY, PAUL RICHARD SYLVESTER, fgn. service officer; b. St. Louis, Aug. 12, 1911; s. William Vanderhorst and Katherine (Aylward) B.; student Notre Dame U., 1931-32; LL.B., St. Louis U., 1936; certificate in marketing Harvard Bus. Sch., summer 1961; m. Ruth E. Heath, Jan. 8, 1939; children—Paul George, Jacquelynn Heath, William Vanderhorst, Ruth Aylward. Admitted to Mo. bar, 1936; practiced in St. Louis, 1936-43; legal adviser Dept. of Army, Japan, 1946-52; legal officer Am. embassy, Tokyo, 1952-55; econ. officer Am. embassy, Tel Aviv, 1956-58; 1st sec., consul diplomatic service, 1958; fgn. affairs officer Internat. Orgn. Affairs, Dept. State, Washington, 1958-60; fgn. affairs adviser Dept. Commerce, Washington, 1960-62; 1st sec. Am. embassy, London, Eng., 1962—. Served from lt. (j.g.) to lt. comdr., USNR, 1943-46. Mem. Am., Fed., Mo. bar assns., Delta Theta Phi. Club: Internat. Sportsmens (London). Home: 1 Abbey Rd London NW 8 England Office: American Embassy London England

BRUMDER, WILLIAM G., ret. banker; b. Milw., Dec. 12, 1901; s. William C. and Thekla (Uihlein) B.; student Hotchkiss Sch., 1918-20; B.S., Princeton, 1924; M.B.A., Harvard, 1926; m. June Ellen Johnston, Apr. 28, 1934; children—June Ellen, William Charles, Valerie P., H. Christopher J., Cecelie A., Christina E. With Mchts. & Farmers Bank, 1928-29; with Wis. Bankshares Corp. (now First Wis. Bankshares Corp.), 1930—, pres., 1954-68, dir., 1954—; asst. cashier First Wis. Nat. Bank of Milw., 1932-35, asst. v.p., 1935-36, v.p., 1936-49, sr. v.p., 1949-50, dir., 1941—, chmn. bd., 1950-66, pres., 1954-62; dir. Joseph Schlitz Brewing Co., First Wis. Trust Co., Waukesha Cutting Tools. Mem. Am. Bankers Assn., Am. Inst. Banking, Assn. Res. City Bankers, C. of C. U.S., Def. Orientation Conf. Assn., Navy League U.S., World Affairs Council Milw., Newcomen Soc. Eng., Aspen Inst. Humanistic Studies, Milwaukee County Hist. Soc., Milw. U. Sch. Alumni Assn. Clubs: Harvard, Town, Milwaukee, Milwaukee Country, Princeton, University, Wisconsin, Milwaukee; Country of Fla. (Delray Beach). Home: 8265 North River Rd Milwaukee WI 53217 Office: 743 N Water St Milwaukee WI 53202

BRUMER, MILTON, civil engr.; b. Phila., Jan. 21, 1902; s. Lewis and Nellie (Strilkofski) B.; M.E., Rensselaer Poly. Inst., 1923, D. Eng., 1970; M.S. (U.S. Bur. Mines fellow), U. Ala., 1924; m. Mary Stein, Jan. 24, 1926; children—Barbara Lee, Carolyn Faith. Asst. engr. Port N.Y. Authority, 1925-38; chief engr. tunnel design Pa. Turnpike Commn., Harrisburg, 1938-40; prin. engr. O.H. Ammann & Ammann & Whitney, N.Y.C., 1940—; became partner Ammann & Whitney, 1949; now pres. Ammann & Whitney, Inc., Ammann & Whitney Internat., Ltd.; chief engr., prel.-final design Ammann & Whitney portions N.J. Turnpike, 1949-51, N.Y. Thruway, 1951-53, N.J. Garden State Parkway, 1952-53, Ohio Turnpike, 1952-55. Milw. Expressway, 1951-57, Conn. Turnpike, 1954-58; partner charge Ammann & Whitney design Walt Whitman Bridge, Phila., 1952-58; design, supervision constrn. Throgs Neck Bridge, N.Y., 1957-61, Verrazano-Narrows Bridge, N.Y., longest suspension span in world, 1959-65. Recipient Engr. of Year award Met. sect. Am. Soc. C.E., 1965. Registered profl. engr., Conn., N.J., N.Y., Pa., Ohio, Cal. Fellow Am. Soc. C.E., N.Y. Acad. Scis.; mem. Nat. Acad. Engring., Am. Concrete Inst., Am. Inst. Cons. Engrs., Am. Bridge Tunnel and Turnpike Assn., Hwy. Research Bd. (supporting), Sigma Xi. Home: 3333 C Henry Hudson Pkwy Riverdale NY 10463 Office: 111 8th Av New York City NY 10011

BRUMFIELD, RICHARD MANOAH, mfg. exec.; b. Princeton, Ind., Oct. 21, 1909; s. John A. and Myrtle (Smith) B.; B.S., Purdue U., 1931; m. Martha Boren, Dec. 23, 1935; children—Ann, Alice. Engr., Hansen Mfg. Co., Princeton, 1931-33; sec.-treas. Potter & Brumfield Mfg. Co., Princeton, 1933-47, pres., 1947- 66, became subsidiary AMF, Inc., N.Y.C., 1954, group exec. elec. products group, 1959-62, chmn. Potter & Brumfield div., 1966—; dir. AMF, Inc., AMP Inc., Gibson County Bank, Gibson County Perpetual Bldg. & Loan Assn., Hurst Tool & Mfg. Co., Princeton Hardware and Plating Co., Universal Sci. Co., Old Nat. Bank Evansville, Internat. Steel. Active fund drives. Trustee Purdue U., 1963—. Mem. Princeton C. of C., Scabbard and Blade, Lambda Chi Alpha, Pi Tau Sigma. Presbyn. Mason (Shriner), Elk. Home: Petersburg Rd Princeton IN 47570 Office: Potter & Brumfield Princeton IN 47570

BRUMFIELD, WILLIAM ANDREW, Jr., physician; b. Halifax County, Va., Apr. 14, 1905; s. Dr. William A. and Effie Flournoy (Thornton) B.; B.S., Va. Polytech. Inst., 1926; M.D., U. of Va., 1930, M.S., 1934; M.P.H., Johns Hopkins, 1935; m. Elizabeth Mitchell Fagg, Oct. 7, 1930; 1 dau., Katherine Thornton. Instr. bacteriology and pathology, Ind. U., 1930-31; resident and instr. dermatology and syphilology U. Va. Hosp., 1931-33; med. cons. venereal diseases control, N.Y. State Dept. Health, 1935-36, dir. div. syphilis control, 1936-47; dep. commr. health State N.Y., 1947-53; prof. and chmn. dept. preventive medicine N.Y. State U. Sch. of Medicine at Syracuse, 1953-56; mem. pub. health research study sect. Nat. Insts. Health, 1957-60; asso. prof. pub. health practice, sch. hygiene and adminstrv. med., Columbia, 1956—; commr. health, Westchester County, N.Y. Served as maj. to col. M.C., AUS, 1942-46; venereal disease survey, Central Africa, Middle East, and China, Burma, India theatres; mem. pub. health br., G5, Sup. Hq. A.E.F., E.T.O., 1943-46; col. M.C. Res. Decorated C.R.; recipient Certificate of Honor, A.M.A. exhibit on epidemiology of syphilis, 1935. Pres. N.Y. State Ann. Health Conf. 1948—; chmn. civilian collaboration sect. Veneral Disease Control br., SGO, 1942; chmn. med. sect. Sup. Hq. Mission to Norway, 1944; cons. venereal disease control Mil. Govt., Germany, 1945-46. Mem. subcom. on veneral disease NRC, 1946-50; mem. N.Y. State Mental Hygiene Council; mem. Nat. Adv. Com. on Local Health Depts. Diplomate Am. Bd. of Preventive Medicine. Fellow A.M.A.; mem. Am. Pub. Health Assn., Am. Epidemiol. Soc., Nat. Conf. Cardiovasular Diseases (chmn. com. on case finding and epidemiology, 1950) State N.Y. (mem. ho. dels.), West Chester County (pres. 1967-68) med. socs., Sigma Xi, Alpha Omega Alpha. Author articles on epidemiology, with special emphasis on epidemiology of syphilis. Home: 8 Vermont Av White Plains NY 10606 Office: County Office Bldg White Plains NY 10601

BRUMLEY, LLOYD E., business exec.; b. 1928; B.S., Miami U., 1955; married. Comml. mgr. Arthur Andersen & Co., Cleve., 1955-68; asst. controller Pneumo Dynamics Corp., Cleve., 1968-69, controller, 1969—. Served with AUS, 1948-51. Office: 3781 E 77th St Cleveland OH 44105*

BRUMLEY, WILLIAM M., Jr., oil co. exec.; b. 1928; B.S., Okla. State U., 1950; married. With Arthur Andersen Y Co., C.P.A.'s, 1951-56, Zapata Petroleum Corp., 1956-63; with Pennzoil Co., 1963-68, treas., 1964-67, v.p., controller, 1967-68; v.p., controller Pennzoil United Inc., Houston, 1968—; v.p. Pennzoil Offshore Gas Operators Inc. Office: 900 Southwest Tower Houston TX 77002*

BRUMM, JOSEPH DANIEL, dept. store exec.; b. St. Louis, Aug. 8, 1916; s. Edward and Henrietta (Knehans) B.; certificate in commerce St. Louis U., 1939; m. Virginia Crady, July 13, 1940; children—Gregg Edward, Eric Joseph. With Bemis Bros. Bag Co., 1934-41; with Stix, Baer & Fuller Co., St. Louis, 1941-69, sec.-treas., 1957-69, exec. v.p., 1961-69, also dir.; financial v.p., treas., dir. Rich's, Inc., Atlanta, 1969—; mem. adv. bd. Liberty Mut. Ins. Co. Bd. dirs. Atlanta chpt. Nat. Found. March of Dimes, Boy Scouts Am., Atlanta, Heart Assn., Atlanta, Salvation Army, Atlanta. Mem. Financial Execs. Inst. Clubs: Capital City, Old Warson Country, Mo. Athletic, Commerce. Home: 510 King Rd NW Atlanta GA 30305

BRUMMETT, MARVIN KIGHT, lawyer; b. Claude, Tex., Dec. 7, 1913; s. William Andrew and Mae (Kight) Wilson; B.S., Okla. State U., 1934; LL.B., U. Tex., 1937; m. Fanella Clift, Aug. 17, 1940; children—Marla (Mrs. Marla Sinclair), Jay C. Admitted to Tex. bar, 1937; asso. Simpson, Dorenfield & Fullingim, Amarillo, Tex., 1937-38; lawyer Halliburton Co., Duncan, Okla., 1938-69, asso. gen. counsel, 1946-69, sec., 1953-69, v.p., 1959- 67, sr. v.p., 1967-69, trustee Halliburton Employees' Benefit Fund, 1949-69, chmn. bd trustees, 1962-69; pres., dir. Life Ins. Co. of S.W., Dallas, 1964-69; dir. Investors Trust Co., Duncan, Okla., Security Nat. Bank and Trust Co., Duncan, J & M Steel Co., Fort Worth. Mem. Am., Okla., Dallas bar assns., State Bar Tex., Am. Soc. Corporate Secs. (v.p. 1968-69), Sigma Phi Epsilon. Home: 7216 Glendora Av PO Box 30245 Dallas TX 75230

BRUN, ALICE, govt. ofcl.; b. Copenhagen, Denmark, Feb. 25, 1904; d. Alf Harald and Dagmar (Hage) Brun; Master's degree in Polit. Economy, Copenhagen U., 1930. Joined Danish Finance Ministry, 1932; personal sec. to minister finance, 1945-46, head sect. in budget div., 1946; exec. dir. for Denmark, Finland, Iceland, Norway and Sweden Internat. Bank Reconstrn. and Devel., 1962-64; with Ministry of Finance, Denmark, 1964—. Mem. Danish Govt. Com. Tech. Assistance to Developing Countries, 1951-62, 64- 68. Decorated knight Danebrog 1st Class. Mem. Danish Assn. U. Women (pres. 1958-62), Internat. Fedn. U. Women (hon. treas. 1965-68), Scandinavian Adminstrv. Soc. (bd. 1948—). Home: Overgadlden o/v 52 DK 1415 Copenhagen K Denmark Office: Finansministeriet Christiansborg Slotsplads 1 Copenhagen K Denmark

BRUN, EDMOND ANTOINE, educator; b. St. Cannat (B du R), France, Dec. 31, 1898; s. Antoine Marius and Marie (Villecrose) B.; B.Sc., U. Marseille, 1921, M.S. (fellowship nat. competitive test), 1923; D. Scis., Paris, 1934; m. 1923. Prof. spl. courses Lycée Nice, 1925-30, Parisian Lycée, 1930-42; lectr., then prof. fluid mechanics Faculté des Sciences de Paris, 1942-70, hon. prof., 1970—; dir. Laboratoire d'Aerothermique, 1942- 70, hon., 1970—, prof. Ecole Nationale Superieure de l'Aéronautique, 1942-70. Mem. Armed Forces, 1917-19. Decorated officer Legion of Honor; comdr. Military Merit (Brazil); comdr. Palmes Académiques, Laureate Acad. Scis. Fellow Royal Aero. Soc., Am. Inst. Aeros. and Astronautics (hon.), Am. Astronautical Soc., fgn. asso. Nat. Acad. Scis., Internat. Astronautics Acad. (v.p.), Société Francaise d'Astronautique (pres. 1960-62), Internat. Astronautical Fedn. (pres. 1960-62), Société Francaise des Thermiciens (pres. 1964- 65). Sociét é Mét éorologique de France (pres. 1959), Sociét é des Ingénieurs Civils de France (pres. 1969); mem. Acad. Scis. Author articles and books on aerodynamic heating convection, icing of aircraft, fluid mechanics. Home: 8 pl Commerce Paris XV France Office: 4 ter route des Gardes 92-Meudon France

BRUN, HERBERT, composer, educator; b. Berlin, Germany, 1918; student composition with Stefan Wolpe, Jerusalem Conservatory Music, Columbia; m. Marianne Kortner; children—Michael, Stefan. Faculty U. Ill. Sch. Music, Urbana, 1963—; research in computer composition. Composer: Mobile for Orchestra; Sonoriferous Loops; Gestures for Eleven; Non-Sequitur VI; Gesto for Piccolo and Piano; Trio for Flute, Double Bass, Percussion; Trio Trumpet, Trombone, Percussion; Futility 1964; Mutatis Mutandis: Computer- Graphics for Interpreters; Infraudibles; Nonet; also scores for theatre. Address: 1209 W University Av Champaign IL 61820

BRUNDAGE, AVERY, engr., amateur sportsman; b. Detroit, Sept. 28, 1887; s. Charles and Amelia (Lloyd) B.; B.S. in C.E., U. Ill., 1909; LL.D. and M.P.E. (hon.), Springfield Coll.; m. Elizabeth Dunlap, 1927. Pres. Avery Brundage Co., builders, 1915-47; chmn. Roanoke Real Estate Co., 1932—; pres. Roanoke Hotel Corp., 1939-45; chmn. bd. Susquehanna Corp., 1957-59. Pres. U.S. Olympic Assn. and Com., 1929-53; v.p. Comite Internationale Olympique, 1945-52, pres., 1952—; first pres. Comite Deportivo Pan-Am., 1940. Vice pres. Internat. Amateur Athletic Fedn., 1930-52; past pres. Amateur Athletic Union of U.S. (pres. seven terms). Collector of Oriental art; trustee Art Inst. Chgo. Recipient Olympic Order of Germany, 1936, Olympic Order of Finland, 1952, spl. award from Northwestern U., 1951, Commander's Cross with Star of Order of St. Olav of Norway, 1952; Comdr. Order of Merit of Italian Republic; Legion of Honor, France; Das Grosse Verdienst Kreuz Mit Stern, Germany; Golden Cross of Merit, Finland; Grand Officer, Order of Vasa, Sweden; Sport Medal, first class, Iran; Comdr. de l'Ordre Nat. du Cedre, Lebanon; Cavaliere Grand Ufficale dell' ordine Equestre de Sant' Agata, San Marino; Excelentisimo Senor Don de Santa Barbara, Cal.; also recipient first Medal of Merit, City Chgo.; 1st John Perry Bowditch Meml. for outstanding service Key to City and Hon. Citizen of San Francisco, Tokyo, Seoul; 1st Order of Sacred Treasure (Japan); Order Cultural Merit (Republic of Korea); Comdr. L'Ordre du Merite Sportif (France); LaCondecoracion Nacional de la Orden Mexicana del Aguila Azteca, Mexico, 1962, Grand Cross Civil Merit (Spain); comdr. Order of Merit, Congo (Brazzaville), Order of Lincoln from the State of Ill.; Order of Lion (Finland); Order of Leopold II (Belgium); Order of White Elephant (Thailand); Grand Cordon of Brilliant Star (Republic of China). Mem. Sigma Xi, Tau Beta Pi, Sigma Alpha Epsilon. Clubs: Chicago Athletic, Chicago Engineers; Montecito Country (past pres.). Amateur all-around champion of America, 1914, 16, 18. Author numerous articles on amateur sport. Office: 10 N La Salle St Chicago IL 60602

BRUNDAGE, CHARLES EDWIN, former investment counsel; b. East Orange, N.J., May 20, 1895; s. John Norman and Martha Elizabeth (Riker) B.; A.B., Dartmouth, 1916, M.C.S., 1917; postgrad. (fellow) Carnegie Inst. Tech., 1917, Ecole des Hautes Etudes Sociales, Paris, France, 1919; m. Edna Thompson, May 25, 1922; children—Robert Peter, June, John Edwin. Asst. personnel mgr. Celluloid Co., Newark, 1919-21; examiner Fed. Res. Bank of N.Y., Washington, 1921-22, Guaranty Co. of N.Y., 1922-23; asso., gen. partner Scudder, Stevens & Clark, 1923-31; gen. partner firm of Brundage, Story & Rose, 1932—; dir. Fluid Dynamics, Inc., Hanover Twp., N.J.; trustee Union Dime Savs. Bank, N.Y.C. Chmn. bd. trustees Canaan (N.H.) Coll. Served with 15th Engrs., U.S. Army, 1917-19. Mem. Investment Counsel Assn. Am., Phi Beta Kappa. Clubs: Bankers of Am., Weavers; Shongum. Dartmouth (N.Y.C.); Morristown (N.J.). Contbr. articles to profl. jours. Home: Mount Freedom Rd Dover NJ 07801

BRUNDAGE, HOWARD DENTON, advt. agy. exec.; b. Newark, Nov. 9, 1923; s. Edgar Ray and Salome (Denton) B.; B.A., Dartmouth, 1944; postgrad. Harvard Bus. Sch., 1944-45; m. Nancy Williams, Oct. 20, 1945; children—Louise, Peter, Joanne, Geraldine. With Morgan Stanley & Co., 1945-50; asst. sec. Hanover Bank, 1950-52; with J.H. Whitney & Co., 1952-58; partner, 1958, 1960-62; v.p., sec., treas. Plymouth Rock Publs., Inc., 1958-60; dir., chmn. Herald Tribune, 1958-59; exec. v.p. finance J. Walter Thompson Co., 1962—, also dir.; dir. Phoenix Assurance Co., London Guarantee & Accident Co., N.Y.C., Faber Coe & Gregg, Inc., N.Y.C., Smith Barney Equity Fund. Former trustee, treas. Montainside Hosp., Montclair. Home: 120 Lloyd Rd Montclair NJ 07042 Office: 420 Lexington Av New York City NY 10017

BRUNDAGE, JAMES ARTHUR, historian, educator; b. Lincoln, Neb., Feb. 5, 1929; s. Frank L. and Anna (Morrissey) B.; B.A., U. Neb., 1950, M.A., 1951; Ph.D., Fordham U., 1955; m. Marie T. McDonald, Aug. 23, 1952; children—James Arthur, Marie G., Gregory C., David B., Thomas T., Ann Kristin. Instr., Fordham U., 1953-57; asst. prof. U. Wis. Milw., 1957-60, asso. prof., 1960-65, prof., 1965—; Catedratico visitante U. Madrid, 1967-68; postdoctoral research at Cambridge U., Paris, Munich, Innsbruck, Rome and Madrid. Corporate sec., bd. dirs. Newman Club of Archdiocese of Wis., Inc. Guggenheim fellow, 1964-65; Fulbright grant to Spain, 1967-68. Mem. Am., Am. Catholic (past mem. exec. council) hist. assns., Mediaeval Acad. Am., Am. Assn. U. Profs. (past chpt. pres.). Democrat. Author: The Chronicle of Henry of Livonia, 1961; The Crusades: A Documentary Survey, 1962; Medieval Canon Law and the Crusader, 1969. Contbr. articles profl. jours. Home: 3314 N Downer Av Milwaukee WI 53211

BRUNDAGE, JOHN DENTON, ins. co. exec.; b. Newark, Mar. 28, 1919; s. Edgar Ray and Salome (Denton) B.; A.B., Princeton, 1941; m. Ann Lounsbury, Nov. 29, 1941; children—Elizabeth Ann, Susan, Patricia, John. Agy. asst. Bankers Nat. Life Ins. Co., Montclair, N.J., 1945-46, asst. to pres., 1953-54, adminstrv. v.p., 1955- 57, exec. v.p., 1957-58, pres., dir., 1958—; sales promotion mgr. Mut. Benefit Life Ins. Co., Newark, 1946-47, regional supt. agys., 1948- 50, dir. agys., 1950-52, agy. mgr., N.Y.C., 1952-53; chmn., dir. Palisades Life Ins. Co., New City, N.Y.; dir. Am. Nat. Bank & Trust, Annin & Co. Chmn., Montclair Urban Coalition, 1969-70. Chmn. bd. Am. Heart Assn., 1962-65; trustee N.J. Coll. Fund Assn. Served from ensign to lt. comdr., USNR, 1940-45. Recipient Gold Heart award Am. Heart Assn., 1965, Citizens award for distinguished community service N.J. Acad. Medicine, 1964. C.L.U. Fellow Life Office Mgmt. Assn. (dir.); mem. Life Ins. Assn. Am., Nat. Assn. Life Underwriters, Am. Coll. Life Underwriters. Club: Princeton: Short Hills (N.J.). Home: 50 Stewart Rd Short Hills NJ 07078 Office: 1599 Littleton Rd Parsippany NJ 07054

BRUNDAGE, PERCIVAL FLACK, consultant; b. Amsterdam, N.Y., Apr. 2, 1892; s. William Milton and Charlotte (Flack) B.; A.B. cum laude, Harvard, 1914; D.Sc., N.Y. U. Partner Price Waterhouse & Co., N.Y.C., 1930-54, cons., 1958—; pres., dir. 56 Pine St. Inc., N.Y.C., 1944-54; dep. dir. Bur. of Budget, 1954-56, dir., 1956-58, cons., 1958-60. Dir. Montclair Community Chest 1950-54; dir. Nat. Bur. Econ. Research, 1942-67, pres., 1954, hon. dir., 1967—; chmn. Unitarian Devel. Fund Campaign, 1959-62. Dir., treas. People to People Health Found., Inc., Atlantic Council U.S.; treas. Internat. Movement for Atlantic Union. C.P.A., N.Y., N.J., Mass. Mem. Internat. Assn. Liberal Christianity (pres. 1952-55), Fed. Union, Inc. (dir. Unitarian Service Com. (dir. 1949-54), Am. Unitarian Assn. (dir. 1942-48), N.Y. C. of C. (chmn. exec. com. 1952- 54), Am. Inst. Accountants (pres. 1848-49), Council Fgn. Relations, Fgn. Policy Assn., UN Assn., Washington Inst. Fgn. Affairs. Clubs: Century Assn., Harvard (N.Y.C.); Hillsboro (Florida); Gulf Stream Golf (Florida); Chevy Chase (Md.); Metropolitan, City Tavern Assn. (Washington). Home: 969 Hillsboro Mile Pompano Beach FL 33362 also 2601 Woodley Pl NW Washington DC 20008

BRUNELL, ALBERT A., corp. exec.; b. Worcester, Mass., 1923. Treas., dir. A.A. Brunell Electroplating Corp.; pres., dir. Precision Chrome & Ginished Corp. Home: 14 Lincoln Av Paxton MA 01612 Office: 41 Sutton Lane Worchester MA 01603*

BRUNELL, ARTHUR B., electroplating co. exec.; b. Worcester, Mass., 1920; Chmn., pres., advt. mgr. A.A. Brunell Electroplating Corp., Worcester; treas., dir. Precision Chrome & Finishing Corp. Home: 3 Coombs Rd Worcester MA 01602 Office: 41 Sutton Lane Worcester MA 01603*

BRUNENKANT, EDWARD JAMES, govt. ofcl.; b. Cleve., Nov. 15, 1921; s. Edward J. and Margaret Lura (Miller) B.; student U. Mich., 1939-40, Case Inst. Tech., 1940-41, Northwestern U., 1941-42; LL.B., George Washington U., 1957; m. Evelyne Jeanette Lodwock, Oct. 28, 1946; children—Edward James, Jon Lodwick, Jennifer, Robert. Field editor Pit and Quarry mag., Chgo., 1946-49; asst. exec. sec. Nat. Agrl. Limestone Assn., Washington, 1949-50; bus. analyst OPS, 1950-52; chief indsl. information br., div. information service AEC, Washington, 1953-60, dir. div. tech. information, 1969—, also chmn. tech. information panel, chmn. adv. com. tech. information. Mem. panel sci. and tech. information Internat. Atomic Energy Agy.; com. sci. information Fed. Council Sci. and Tech. Bd. govs. sci. information exchange Smithsonian Instn. Served with AUS, 1942-46. Mem. Va. Bar Assn., Phi Kappa Psi. Home: 11808 Beekman Pl Potomac MD 20854 Office: Div Tech Information AEC Washington DC 20545

BRUNER, DORSEY WILLIAM, educator, vet. microbiologist; b. Windber, Pa., Dec. 25, 1906; s. William W. and Laura (Harner) B.; B.A., Albright Coll., 1929; Ph.D., Cornell U., 1933, D.V.M., 1937; m. Beatrice D.E. Christman, Aug. 25, 1940. Tchr., Middleburg (Pa.) High Sch., 1929-30; instr. bacteriology Cornell U., 1931-37; bacteriologist dept. animal pathology U. KY., 1937- 49; mem. faculty Cornell U., 1949—, prof., chmn. dept. vet. microbiology, 1965—. Chmn. bacteriology and mycology study sect. NIH, 1962-66; mem. tng. grant com. Nat. Inst. Allergy and Infectious Disease, 1968—. Served with AUS, 1942-46. Decorated Bronze Star; recipient citation outstanding work sci. Albright Coll., 1949. Diplomate Am. Bd. Microbiology, Am. Coll. Vet. Microbiology. Mem. Am., N.Y. State vet. med. socs., Res. Officers Assn., Sigma Xi, Pi Tau Beta, Pi Gamma Mu, Phi Zeta, Phi Kappa Phi. Sr. author Hagan's Infectious Diseases of Domestic Animals. Contbr. numerous articles in field. Editor Cornell Veterinarian, 1951—. Home: 1365 Taughannock Blvd RD 3 Ithaca NY 14850

BRUNER, JEROME SEYMOUR, psychologist; b. N.Y.C., Oct. 1, 1915; s. Herman and Rose (Glücksmann) B.; A.B., Duke, 1937; A.M., Harvard, 1939, Ph.D., 1941; D.Litt., Lesley Coll., 1964, Duke, 1969, No. Mich U., 1969; D.Sc. Northwestern U., 1965, U. Sheffield, 1970; LL.D., Temple U., 1965, U. Cin., 1966, U.N.B., 1969; m. Katherine Frost, Nov. 10, 1940 (div. 1956); children—Whitley, Jane; m. 2d, Blanche Marshall McLane, Jan. 16, 1960. Pub. opinion and intelligence on war problems U.S. Army, OWI, U.S., France, 1941-44; lectr., asso. prof. psychology specializing in attitudes, perception, cognition and devel. Harvard, Cambridge, Mass., 1944- 52, prof. psychology, 1952-72, dir. Center for Cognitive Studies, 1951- 52, 61-72, master Currier House, Harvard-Radcliffe Coll., 1970-71; Watts prof. psychology, dept. exptl. psychology U. Oxford (Eng.), 1972—. Lectr. Salzburg Seminar, 1952; adviser on ednl., psychol. problems to UN, White House, Nat. Acad. Sci., NIH, U.S. Office Edn., State Dept. , Edn. Devel. Center, Time-Life-Fortune; Harvard Bacon prof. U. Aix-en-Provence, France, 1965. Guggenheim fellow Cambridge U., 1955. Fellow Am. Psychol. Assn. (recipient Distinguished Sci. Contbn. award 1962, pres. 1964-65), A.A.A.S., Am. Acad. Arts and Sciences, Swiss Psychol. Soc. (fgn. hon.), Nat. Acad. Edn. (founding), Officier de l'Instruction Publique (hon.) (France), Puerto Rican Acad. Arts and Scis. (hon.). Clubs: Manchester Yacht; Boston Badminton and Tennis; Harvard of N.Y.; Cosmos. Author: Mandate from the People, 1944; (with Smith and White) Opinions and Personality, 1956; (with Goodnow and Austin) A Study of Thinking, 1956; Process of Education, 1960; On Knowing , 1962; Toward a Theory of Instruction, 1966; (with Olver and Greenfield) Studies in Cognitive Growth, 1966; Processes of Cognitive Growth; Infancy, 1968; The Relevance of Education, 1971. Contbr. articles to tech. profl. jours. Dept of Experimental Psychology Univ of Oxford Oxford England

BRUNER, WILLIAM WALLACE, banker; b. Orangeburg, S.C., Nov. 6, 1920; s. Robert Raysor and Bessie (Livingston) R.; children—William W., Thomas W., James L. Accountant, J. W. Hunt & Co., C.P.A.'s, Columbia, S.C., 1945-48; with First Nat. Bank S.C., Columbia, 1948—, sr. v.p., 1961-64, pres., 1964—, also dir.; dir. Palmetto State Life Ins. Co., Columbia, Columbia Coca- Cola Bottling Co. S.C. Treas., United Fund Columbia, 1958-59, bd. dirs., 1956- 58, chmn. large firms div., 1965, bd. dirs. treas., 1956-57; chmn. chpt. A.R.C., 1958-60, nat. fund vice chmn., 1960-61, bd. visitors Columbia Coll.; vice chmn. bd. trustees Spartanburg (S.C.) Jr. Coll.; trustee Benedict Coll., Columbia. Treas. S.C. Soc. Crippled Children and Adults, 1967-70, v.p., 1970-71. Served to lt. comdr. USNR, 1941-45. C.P.A., S.C. Mem. Am. Inst. C.P.A.'s, S.C. Assn. C.P.A.'s, Columbia C. of C. (treas. 1961, v.p. 1962), Urban League Columbia (treas., dir.), Am. (adv. com. on fed. legislation 1966-71), S.C. (v.p. 1967-68, pres. 1970-71) bankers assns., Phi Beta Kappa, Beta Gamma Sigma, Sigma Nu. Methodist. Office: 1208 Washington St Columbia SC 29202

BRUNET, BARRIE KIRK, motion picture co. exec.; b. Scobey, Mont., Mar. 4, 1925; s. Alfred L. and E. Fay (Richardson) B.; B.A., U. Wash., 1949; m. Barbara Walker, July 19, 1952; children—Dennis, Douglas, Craig. Auditor, accountant, mgr. adminstrv. services Arthur Andersen & Co., Seattle and Los Angeles, 1949-58; studio controller, corporate controller Metro-Goldwyn-Mayer, Inc., Los Angeles and N.Y.C., 1958—. Served with AUS, 1943-46. C.P.A., Wash. Mem. Motion Picture Controllers Assn. (pres. 1964-65), Nat. Assn. Accountants (asso. dir. Los Angeles chpt. 1960), Phi Beta Kappa, Beta Gamma Sigma, Beta Alpha Psi. Methodist. Home: 6615 Holt Av Los Angeles CA 90056 Office: 10202 W Washington Blvd Culver City CA 90230

BRUNET, MEADE, ret. mfg. co. exec.; b. Petersburg, Va., June 21, 1894; s. Robert Edward and Sally (Minson) B.; B.E., Union Coll., 1916. LL.D., 1966; m. Edyth Redman, Oct. 2, 1925; children—Sally (Mrs. K. H. Beyan), Stuart. Engaged as prodn. clerk, Gen. Electric Co., Schenectady, N.Y., 1915-16, Sperry Gyroscope Co., 1916-17; comml. engr. Gen. Electric, Public Utility Dept., 1919-22; with Radio Corp. of Am., 1922-66, dist. mgr., Chgo., 1923-25, asst. gen. sales mgr. in charge merchandising, 1925-28, v.p. Radio Victor 1928-29, sales mgr. R.C.A. radiotron 1929-32, v.p. mfg. R.C.A., Washington rep., 1939-45, mgr. engring. products dept. R.C.A. Victor Div. 1945-46, v.p. Radio Corp. of Am., 1946-66, mng. dir. RCA Internat. Div., 1946-57. Dir. Nat. Fgn. Trade Council, 1946-67, Pan Am. Soc.; chmn. Bus. Council Internat. Understanding, 1957-60; nat. adv. com. Sch. of World Bus. of San Francisco State Coll.; mem. adv. bd. Internat. and Comparative Law Center; chmn. bd. trustees Union Coll., Schenectady, 1963-69, acting pres., 1966; past trustee U.S. Inter Am. Council, Far East Council; adviser internat. bus. program Rutgers Grad. Sch. Bus. Adminstrn.; gov. Union U., Albany, 1956-69. Former mem. bus. and industry adv. com. Orgn. for European Cooperation and Devel. Past mem. N.J. Republican Finance Com. Served as 1st lt. 56th Engrs. World War I, mil. combat service with French VIII Army and 1st Am. Army AEF. Decorated Officer Cruzeiro do Sul (Brazil), Order El Merito (Chile). Fellow Radio Club Am.; mem. Internat. C. of C. (exec. com., trustee U.S. council), Arbitration Assn., N.A.M. (chmn. internat. econs. affairs com. 1962-63, dir.), I.E.E.E. (life), Acad. Polit. Sci., Am. Sigma Phi, Sigma Xi, Tau Beta Pi. Clubs: University (N.Y.C.); Army and Navy (Washington); Somerset Hills (Bernardsville, N.J.); Radio Pioneers (life). Author: History of the 56th Engineers in First World War. Home: Millsdale Farm Mendham NJ 07945

BRUNGART, ROBERT RAYMOND, fgn. service officer; b. Detroit, Nov. 2, 1925; s. Raymond Jacob and Della Irene (Anderson) B.; B.S., Georgetown U., 1949; student U. Cal. at Berkeley, 1955-56; m. Elizabeth Anne Johnson, June 26, 1946; children—William Raymond, Ralph Walter, Karen Louise. Economist, ECA, Washington, 1950, ECA mission to Germany, Frankfort, 1951-52, Bonn, 1952- 53, Berlin, 1954-55; intelligence research analyst State Dept., 1956- 58; economist, 2d sec. Am. embassy, U.S. mission to NATO and OECD, 1958-63; asst. chief, gen. comml. policy div. State Dept., 1963-65, chief general comml. policy div., 1965-67; trade adviser U.S. Mission to OECD, Paris, France; econ. counselor Am. embassy, Ankara, 1971—. Mem. Am. Econ. Assn., Am. Fgn. Service Assn. Unitarian. Office: Am Embassy Ankara Turkey

BRUNHILD, GORDON, economist, educator; b. Chgo., May 2, 1928; s. Morris and Rosalind (Gordon) B.; student U. Ill., 1946-47; B.S., U. So. Cal., 1949, M.B.A., 1951, Ph.D., 1957; m. Lieba Golda Fruchter, Feb. 4, 1951; children—Victoria Joanne, Maurice Michael, Steven Richard, Robert Morris. Instr., Loyola U., Los Angeles, 1954-57; lectr. U. So. Cal., 1956-57; asst. prof. So. Ill. U., 1957-60; asso. prof. econs. U.So. Fla., Tampa, 1960-67, prof. econs., 1967—, prof. finance, 1968—. Exec. dir. Fla. Council Econ. Edn., 1965-66; acting chief div. program analysis Office Program Planning and Evaluation, Small Bus. Adminstrn., 1966-67; vis. prof. econs. dept. U. Cal. at Los Angeles, summer 1970. Ford Found. regional fellow U. Va., summer 1962. Mem. Am. Assn. U. Profs., Am. So. finance assns., Am., So. econ. assn. Club: Tampa Torch (pres. 1971). Mem. editorial bd. Bus. Perspectives, 1969—. Contbr. articles to profl. jours. Home: 501 Riviera Dr Tampa FL 33606

BRUNING, EDWIN COPE, office equipment co. exec.; b. White Plains, N.Y., May 18, 1930; s. Paul Jacob and Vashti (Cope) B.; grad. Deerfield Acad., 1948; B.A., Amherst Coll., 1952; M.B.A., Harvard, 1956; m. Joan Apgar, Oct. 5, 1958; children—Edwin J., James, Jonathan. Exec. v.p. Charles Bruning Co. div. Addressograph-Multigraph Corp., Mt. Prospect, Ill., 1963—; dir. Addressograph-Multigraph Corp. Bd. dirs. Suburban Community Chest Council, Chgo., N.W. Suburban YMCA; trustee Beloit Coll. Mem. Phi. Alpha Psi. Clubs: Mid-America (Chgo.); Inverness Golf. Home: 1900 Tweed Rd Inverness Palatine IL 60067 Office: 1800 Central Rd Mt Prospect IL 60056

BRUNING, PAUL JACOB, mfg. exec. b. N.Y.C., May 12, 1901; s. Charles and Eugenie (Naffz) B.; A.B., U. Wis., 1924; m. Vashti Cope, Aug. 20, 1927; children—Edwin C., Carolyn E. (Mrs. A. E. Jellison), Paul C. With Charles Bruning Co., Inc., Mt. Prospect, Ill., 1924-63, br. mgr., 1927-30, v.p., 1930-37, pres., 1937-54, chmn., 1954-60, vice chmn., 1960-63. Trustee Gunnery Sch., Washington, Conn., 1957—, Center for Information on Am., Washington, Conn., 1960—, New Milford (Conn.) Hosp., 1961—. Mem. Internat. Assn. Blue Print and Allied Industries (v.p., dir. 1934-36), Sci. Apparatus Makers Am. (dir. 1937-39), Delta Sigma Phi. Republican. Conglist. Clubs: University (N.Y.C.); Washington (Conn.) Club: U.S. Seniors' Golf Assn. Home: Old North Rd Washington CT 06793

BRUNING, WALTER HENRY, food chain exec.; b. N.Y.C., Apr. 1, 1904; s. Charles and Minna (Bunger) B.; student N.Y. U., 1923-26, Acad. Advanced Traffic, 1943-46; m. Gertrude Goossen, June 10, 1927; 1 dau., Joan M. (Mrs. Harold B. Schell). With Gristede Bros., Inc., 1928-69, clk. and store mgr., asst. mgr. produce div., traffic mgr., corp. sec., 1928-61, v.p., sec., dir., 1961-69, chmn. bd., 1965-69; chmn. bd. Charles & Co., 1965-69; trustee Dollar Savs. Bank, N.Y. City. Mem. transp. research adv. com. U.S. Dept. Agr., 1956-63, chmn., 1961-62. Home: 183 A Sterling Ct Lakewood NJ 08701

BRUNINGS, KARL JOHN, chemist, research dir.; b. Balt., Dec. 4, 1913; s. Johann Karl and Eleanor Marie (Meyrahl) B.; student U. Heidelberg (Germany), 1935-36; Ph.D., Johns Hopkins, 1939; grad. Harvard Bus. Sch. Advanced Mgmt. Program, 1960; m. Helen Medcalf; children—Frieda, Laura. Chemist, Eastman Kodak Co., 1939- 41; research fellow, instr. Johns Hopkins, 1941-44, asso. prof., 1946-48; asst. prof. N.Y. U., 1944-46; dir. chem. research and devel. Chas. Pfizer & Co., Inc., 1948-61, adminstrv. dir. research, 1961-62; pres. Geigy Research div. Geigy Chem. Corp., 1962-68; sr. v.p., dir. medicinal research Geigy Pharms. div. Geigy Chem. Corp., 1968-71; sr. v.p. pharm. research and devel. CIBA-Geigy Corp., Ardsley, N.Y., 1971—; Rennebohm lectr., 1965, chmn. 1st Internat. Pharmacology Meeting, Stockholm. Bd. dirs. Westchester div. Am. Cancer Soc. Mem. Pharm. Mfrs. Assn. (chmn. subcom. 1965-67), A.A.A.S. (chmn. medicinal chem. sect.), Am. Chem. Soc. (corp. asso., dir. N.Y. sect.), Indsl. Research Inst. (chmn. tellers com., bd. editors Research Mgmt.) , Soc. Chem. Industry (hon. sec. 1959, exec. com. 1960-63), Assn. Research Dirs., Am. Inst. Chemists. Club: Scarsdale Golf. Contbr. articles to profl. jours. Home: 3 Harcourt Rd Scarsdale NY 10583 Office: Saw Mill River Rd Ardsley NY 10502

BRUNINI, EDMUND LAWRENCE, lawyer; b. Vicksburg, Miss., May 8, 1911; s. John and Blanche (Stein) B.; B.A., Georgetown U., 1831; LL.B., U. Miss., 1934; m. Mary Elizabeth Hickman, Sept. 19, 1935; children—Mary Bea, Tessie, Edmund Lawrence. Admitted to Miss. bar, 1934; practice in Jackson, 1945—; partner firm Brunini, Everett, Grantham & Quin, 1938—. Dir. First Miss. Corp., First Nat. Bank Jackson, First Capital Corp. chmn., Gov.'s Emergency Council, 1969—; pub. mem. Legislative Resources Com. Miss., 1957-58; adminstrv. bd. Mercy Hosp., 1956-58; col., a.d.c. staff gov. Miss., 1952-56; Bd. dirs. Miss. A. and I. Bd. Decorated knight St. Gregory, 1951; 1st class order Stella Della Solidaniete (Italy). Fellow Am. Coll. Trial lawyers; mem. Am., Miss. (v.p. 1938), Hinds County bar assns., Am. Judicature Soc., Vicksburg C. of C. (pres. 1941), Mid Continent Oil and Gas Assn. (pres. Miss.-Ala. div. 1954-55), Ind. Petroleum Assn. Am., Newcomen Soc. Am., Jackson C. of C. (pres. 1970- 71). K.C. Clubs: Petroleum, Jackson Country (pres. 1966), Capitol City (pres. Jackson 1967); Vicksburg Country. Home: 4060 Boxwood Circle Jackson MS 39211 Office: First Nat Bank Bldg Jackson MS

BRUNINI, JOSEPH BERNARD, bishop; b. Vicksburg, Miss., July 24, 1909; s. John and Blanch (Stein) B.; A.B., Georgetown U., 1930, LL.D., 1957; S.T.D., North Am. Coll., Rome, 1933; J.C.D., Cath. U., Washington, 1937. Ordained priest Roman Cath. Ch., 1933; rector Cathedral, Natchez, Miss., 1943-44; chancellor Natchez Diocese, 1941-49; pastor St. Peter's Co-Cathedral, Jackson, Miss., 1949-62; vicar gen. of Diocese, 1951-66, aux. bishop Natchez-Jackson Diocese, 1957-66, apostolic adminstr., 1966-67, bishop, 1967—. Recipient John Carroll award Georgetown U. Mem. Cath. Hosp. Assn. U.S. and Can. (past pres.), Fed. Hosp. Council, Am. Hosp. Assn. (trustee), K.C. (4). Home: 123 N West St Office: Box 2248 Jackson MS 39205

BRUNIS, GEORGE, (George Brunies), jazz trombonist; b. New Orleans, Feb. 6, 1902; s. Henry and Elizabeth (Lotz) B.; m. Chloris Wyckoff. At age 6 played alto horn with Papa Laine's Street Parade Band at the Mardi Gras; studied trombone with brother, Henry Brunies; in 1918 went to Chgo. and played jazz on showboats, ' J.S. ' , ' Predident ' , etc., between Davenport, Ia. and St. Louis, with nucleus of future New Orleans Rhythem Kings. The NORK, which included, in addition to Brunis, Paul Mares, trpt., Leon Rappolo, clar., Jack Pettis, sax, Elmer Schoebel, pianist and composer, Arnold Loyocano and later Steve Brown, bass, and Frank Snyder, drums; was organized in Chgo., 1921, for a long engagement at Mike Fritzel's Friar's Inn. The NORK, one of the first great dixieland bands in the North, influenced Frank Teschemacher, Bud Freeman, and the ' Austin High Gang ' , in the development of the Chgo. Jazz Style. Known as ' King of the Tailgate Trombone ' , Brunis subsequently played with Ted Lewis and Eddie Condon for many years, and more recently with bands in Chgo., including his own: retaining his mellow vocal tone and hard-driving Chgo. style in disregard of the many shifting trends of jazz and periods of apathy to it. Home: 5536 N Sheridan Rd Chicago, IL 60640.

BRUNK, CHARLOTTE, motion picture and theatrical writer. Travel and book editor Des Moines Register and Tribune; asst. editor Picture mag. Address: 715 Locust St Des Moines IA 50309*

BRUNN, DAVID JOSEPH, ret. furniture corp. exec.; b. Hazelton, Pa., July 7, 1907; s. Joseph and Lucia (DiAngelis) B.; B.S., Lafayette Coll., 1928; grad. Exec. Program U. N.C., 1964; m. Margaret E. Birdsall, July 7, 1935; children—Susan R. (Mrs. John David Puett), Barbara E. (Mrs. Robert D. Hughes III). Salesman, W & J Sloane, N.Y.C., 1928-37, buyer, 1937-40, gen. mdse. mgr., 1941-45, v.p., gen. mgr., 1945- 52, bd. dirs., 1945-52; with Drexel Furniture Co. (N.C.), 1952-67, eastern sales mgr., 1952-55, v.p., dir. marketing, dir., 1955-64, pres., 1965-67; exec. v.p. marketing, bd. dirs. Drexel Enterprises, Inc., 1964- 65, v.p. marketing, 1965-67. Cons., House Beautiful mag., Home Furniture Council. Mem. adv. bd. Pavilion Am. Interiors, N.Y.C. World's Fair, 1964-65; mem. U.S. Trade Mission to Europe, 1964. Mem. N.Y.C. Mission Soc., past pres. Big Bro.; mem. adv. council Appalachian State U., 1970—. Mem. Forest Products Research Soc., Newcomen Soc., So. Furniture Mfrs. Assn. (dir.), Furniture Factories Marketing Assn. (sec-treas. 1965-68), Phi Kappa Tau. Club: University (N.Y.C.). Home: 377 Tenney Circle Chapel Hill NC 27514

BRUNN, HERBERT THEODORE, corp. exec.; b. Bklyn., Nov. 22, 1912; s. Arthur and Pauline (Schwarze) B.; B.S., Lehigh U., 1934; LL.B., Cornell U., 1937; m. Marion R. Blenderman, Oct. 21, 1939; children—Richard, Joan. Admitted to N.Y. bar, 1937; asso. Chadbourne, Wallace Parke & Whiteside, N.Y.C., 1937- 39; spl. agt. FBI, 1939-41; atty. RCA, N.Y.C., 1941-52, asst. gen. atty. mfg. and service divs., 1952-57, v.p. corp., 1957-61, div. v.p. R.C.A. Internat. Operations 1961-67, div. v.p., regional dir. Europe, Africa and Middle East, 1967-70, v.p. corp., consumer affairs, N.Y.C., 1970—. Served as lt. USNR, 1943- 46. Mem. Am. Bar. Assn., Bar Assn. City N.Y., Phi Beta Kappa. Home: 72 Pondfield Rd W Bronxville NY 10708 Office: 30 Rockefeller Plaza New York City NY 10020

BRUNNER, EDMUND DE SCHWEINITZ, sociologist; b. Bethlehem, Pa., Nov. 4, 1889; s. Franklin Henry and Nina (de Schweinitz) B.; B.A., Moravian Coll., 1909, M.A., 1912, Ph.D., 1914, L.H.D., 1935; B.D., Moravian Theol. Sem., 1911; LL.D., U. Natal, S. Africa; m. Mary Vogler, Dec. 16, 1912 (dec.); children—Edmund de Schweinitz, Wilfred Robert; m. 2d, Lousene Rousseau, Nov. 6, 1948. Ordained to ministry Moravian Ch., 1911; pastor, Coopersburg, Pa., 1911- 14, 1st Ch., Easton, 1914-18; rural sec. Com. on War Indsl. Communities, 1918-19; dir. Town and County Survey Dept., Interch. World Movement, 1919- 20; dir. Town and Country Surveys, Inst. Social and Religious Research, 1921-33; asso. in rural edn. Columbia Tchrs. Coll. 1926-31, prof., 1931- 55, grad. faculty polit. sci., 1940-63, chmn. Bur. Applied Social Research, 1951-63; lectr. Western Conn. State Coll., 1957-67; lectr. New Zealand and Australia state univs., 1937; collaborator Bur. Agrl. Econs., U.S. Dept. Agr., 1936-54; adviser Extension Service, 1942- 51; cons. Inst. Social Research, U. Natal, 1954. Mem. Am., Rural (pres. 1945), sociol. socs., Am. Philatelic Soc., Am. Philatelic Congress, Fgn. Policy Assn. Author, co-author numerous books, including: Village Communities, 1927; Rural Korea, 1928; (with J.H. Kolb), Rural Social Trends, 1933; (with Irving Lorge) Rural Trends in Depression Years, 1937; American Society: Urban and Rural Patterns, (with W.C. Hallenbeck), 1955; 22 vols. of Town and Country Studies; Rural America and the Extension Service (with Hsin Yang), 1949; Growth of a Science: A History of Rural Sociological Research, 1957; (with Sloane Wayland) The Educational Characteristics of the American People, 1958; (with others) An Overview of Adult Education Research, 1859; As Now Remembered, 1968. Home: 10 High Ridge Rd Wilton CT 06897

BRUNNER, ENDRE KOPPERL, physician, hosp. adminstr.; b. Debrecen, Hungary, Dec. 4, 1900; s. Lajos and Gabrielle (Kopperl) B.; student U. Ala. Med. Sch., 1922-23; M.D., N.Y. U., 1926; m. Eleanor Carroll, July 10, 1937; children—Endrea, John Stephen. Came to U.S., 1920, naturalized, 1928. Intern, Tuxedo Park Meml., Bellevue hosps., N.Y.C., 1925-28; chief gynecology clin. N.Y. U. Coll. Medicine, 1929-48, instr., asst. prof. obstetrics and gynec., 1930-50, lectr. hygiene Washington Sq. Coll.; pvt. practice gynecology and obstetrics, N.Y.C., 1929-41; clin. dir. Halloran VA Hosp., N.Y.C., 1947-51; chief med. officer VA Center, Me., 1951-52; dir. profl. services VA Hosp., Boston, 1952-54; mgr. VA Hosp., Manchester, N.H., 1954-55, VA Hosp., Bronx, N.Y.C., 1956-57; adv. bd., vis. lectr. Columbia Sch. Pub. Health and Adminstrv. Medicine, 1956-65; hosp. adminstrn. adviser ICA, U.S. Operations Mission, Asuncion, Paraguay, 1958-60; acting dir. Servicio Cooperativo Interamericano de Salud Publica, Paraguay, 1960-61; dir. S.C.I.S.P., chief health div. U.S. AID, La Paz, Bolivia, 1961-63; pub. health adviser Africa Bur. AID, Dept. State, Washington, 1963-64; chief of staff U.S. VA Hosp., Providence, 1964-65; supt. Rutland Heights Hosp., Commonwealth Mass., 1965—. Preceptor hosp. adminstrn. Northeastern U., 1966-68; hon. prof. medicine U. San Andres, La Paz. Served from lt. comdr. to comdr. USNR, 1941-47. Diplomate Am. Bd. Obstetrics and Gynecology. Fellow N.Y. Acad. Medicine, Am. Coll. Hosp. Adminstrs; mem. A.M.A., Mass., Worcester Dist. med. socs., Mass. Hosp. Assn. (Worcester area council), New Eng. Hosp. Assembly, Alpha Omega Alpha, Phi Beta Pi. Calvinist. Club: New York University. Author: Dirección del Hospital Moderno, 1960. Contbr. articles to profl. jours. Address: Rutland Heights Hosp Rutland MA 01543

BRUNNER, HENRY SHERMAN, ret. educator; b. Reading, Pa., Mar. 12, 1898; s. Harry Keely and Emma Benz (Sherman) B.; B.S. in agronomy, Pa. State U., 1920, M.S. in Agrl. Edn., 1935; Ph.D., Ohio State U., 1943; m. Vivian Erica Jenkin, Sept. 1, 1928 (dec. 1948); children—Gay (Mrs. Maynard L. Hill), Robin (Mrs. Joseph L. Leitzinger); m. 2d, Helen Payne Seashore, Oct. 19, 1952. Owner, operator farm, Berks Co., Pa., 1920-30; tchr., supr. vocational agr. Oley Twp. High Sch., Berks Co., Pa., 1930-34; instr. agrl. edn. Pa. State U., 1934-37, asso. prof., head dept. agrl. edn., 1937-39, prof., head dept., 1939-59, prof. emeritus agrl. edn., 1959—; specialist for agrl. colls. Div. Ednl. Orgn. and Adminstrn., U.S. Office Edn., Washington, 1959-65; cons. Center for Research and Leadership Devel., Ohio State U., 1966-67; vis. prof. U. Me., summers 1950, 54, 69, Colo. State U., summers 1949-63, U. Ariz., 1966, 69, Auburn U.,

1967-68; spl. editor Nat. Agrl. Edn. mag., 1947-51, chmn. mng. editing bd., 1950-51. U.S. del. Com. on Edn. for Food and Agr., OECD, Paris, 1962-63, spl. agrl. edn. Near-East Found., Iran, 1970-71. Chmn. N. Atlantic Region Commn. on Research in Agrl. Edn., 1951-53. Mem. nat. adv. com. The Danforth Found., 1950-54; Am. bd. trustees Lingnan U.; chmn. Penn-State-in- China, 1949-53. Served as 2d lt. inf., U.S. Army, 1917-18; expert cons. in agrl. edn. to H.I.C.O.G., E.C.A., Frankfurt, 1950; exchange prof., Dept. State, Bremen, Germany, 1955. Awarded hon. Am. Farmer degree, Future Farmers Am., 1950; award Honor, Wisdom Soc. for Advancement in Edn., 1969; Distinguished Service award Ohio State U., 1970. Mem. Am. Vocational Assn. (com. on research in agrl. edn., 1949-53, chmn. 1952-56), Pa. Vocational Assn. (sec., treas. 1945-51), N.E.A., Pa. Edn. Assn., Penn State Christian Assn. (dir. 1938, chmn. 1942-48), Phi Kappa Phi, Alpha Zeta, Gamma Sigma Delta, Alpha Tau Alpha, Delta Theta Sigma, Kappa Gamma Psi, Sigma Chi, Scabbard and Blade. Author: Criteria for Evaluating Programs of Preparation for Teachers of Vocational Agriculture, 1945; This We Believein Teacher Education in Agriculture, 1957; Federal Programs Affecting Agricultural Education, 1961; Land-Grant Colleges and Universities, 1862- 1962, 1962; also bulls. Violinist, dir. Theatre and Symphony orchestra, 1920-30; organizer Pa. State F.F.A. Band, 1937, dir., 1937-49, Nat. F.F.A. Band, dir., 1947-61. Home: 2420 Sonoita Pl Tucson AZ 85712

BRUNNER, JAY ROBERT, educator; b. Royersford, Pa., Sept. 17, 1918; s. Howard S. and Nora (Fox) B.; B.S., in Dairy Mfg., Pa. State U., 1940; M.S., U. Cal. at Davis, 1942; Ph.D., Mich. State U., 1952; m. Jeane Adams, June 19, 1947; children—Tom, Barbara, Kathy. Faculty Mich. State U., 1946—, prof. food sci., 1959—. Served to lt. USNR, 1942-46. Recipient Borden award in dairy chemistry Am. Chem. Soc., 1964. Mem. Am. Inst. Food Technologists, Am. Chem. Soc., Am. Dairy Sci. Assn., Sigma Xi, Alpha Gamma Rho. Mason. Home: 3940 N Zimmer Rd Williamston, MI 48895 Office: Dept Food Science and Human Nutrition Mich State U East Lansing MI 48823

BRUNNER, JOHN WILSON, educator; b. Phila., Oct. 5, 1924; s. Harry Leroy and Viola (Batman) B.; B.A., Ursinus Coll., 1949; Ph.D., Columbia U., 1957; m. Ingrid Arvide, July 2, 1953; children—Karin A., Kirstin E., Inge L., Erika E., Bjoern E. Intelligence officer OSS-CIA, China, 1944-47; lectr. German, Columbia, 1950-52, 1954-55; prof. German, head fgn. lang. dept. Muhlenberg Coll., 1954, 1955—. Served with AUS, 1943-46. Mem. Am. Assn. Tchrs. German (exec. com. Central Pa. 1970—), Modern Lang. Assn., Linguistic Soc. Am., Am. Oriental Soc., Am. Assn. U. Profs., Chinese Lang. Tchrs. Assn., Pa. Modern Lang. Assn. Author: The Natur-Geist Polarity in Hermann Hesse, 1968. Home: 328 N 26th St Allentown PA 18104

BRUNNER, PAUL A., elec. co. exec.; b. Antwerp, Belgium, July 11, 1935; s. Sigmund S. and Henriette (Weisslitz) B.; B.B.A., U. Buenos Aires, 1957; postgrad. Syracuse U., 1967; m. Elizabeth Phillips, Nov. 2, 1963; 1 dau., Pamela. Came to U.S., 1959, naturalized, 1965. Internatl auditor Ford Motor Co., Buenos Aires, Argentina, 1957-58; with Lybrand, Ross Bros. & Montgomery, N.Y.C., 1959-66; v.p. finance, treas. Crouse-Hinds Co., Syracuse, N.Y., 1966—. C.P.A., D.C., N.Y. Mem. Am. Inst. C.P.A.'s N.Y. State Soc. C.P.A.'s. Home: 5215 Winterton Dr Fayetteville NY Office: Crouse Hinds Co Wolf and 7th Morth Sts Syracuse NY 13201

BRUNO, HAROLD ROBINSON, Jr., journalist; b. Chgo., Oct. 25, 1928; s. Harold Robinson and Tallulah (Kandel) B.; B.S. in Journalism, U. Ill., 1950; m. Margaret E. Christian, Nov. 12, 1959; children—Harold Robinson III, Daniel John. Sports editor DeKalb (Ill.) Chronicle, 1950; reporter City News Bur. Chgo., 1953-54, Chgo.'s Am., 1954-60; with Newsweek, 1960—, Chgo. bur. chief, 1963-66, news editor, N.Y.C., 1966-71, chief polit. corr., Washington, 1971—. Lectr., Adult Ednl. Council Chgo., 1961—. Mem. Port Chester Vol. Fire Dept., Bethesda-Chevy Chase Rescue Squad. Served to 1st lt. AUS, 1951-53. Fulbright scholar, India, 1956. Mem. Chgo. Newspaper Reporters Assn., Inst. Internat. Edn., Sigma Delta Chi, Tau Delta Phi. Jewish religion. Contbr. articles to various publs. Home: 3414 Cummings Lane Chevy Chase MD 20015 Office: 1750 Pennsylvania Av Washington DC 20006

BRUNO, HARRY A., ret. public relations counsel; b. London, England, Feb. 7, 1893; s. Henry A. and Annie (Thompson) B.; ed. Action County Sch., Portland Coll., London, Eng., Montclair (N.J.) High Sch.; m. Nydia de Sosnowska, Jan. 18, 1930. Came to U.S., 1907, naturalized, 1928. Advt. mgr. Montclair (N.J.) Herald, 1914-15, Am. Press, N.Y., 1916-17; local sales mgr., N.Y. City Car Adv. Co., 1919; publicity dept., Mfrs. Aircraft Assn., 1920; sales and advt. mgr., Aeromarine Airways, Inc., 1921-22, v.p., 1923; partner H. A. Bruno, R. R. Blythe and Associates public relations, 1923-34; owner, H. A. Bruno and Associates, 1934—; pres. H. A. Bruno and Associates, Inc., 1953-68, chmn., 1968-69; asst. to head of div. of contract distribution, O.P.M., dir. of Defense Specials for WPB, Washington 1941-42. Has acted as personal representative for Adm. R. E. Byrd, Col. Charles A. Lindbergh, Wiley Post, Harold Gatty, Dr. Hugo Eckener, Lincoln Ellsworth, Jacqueline Cochran. Gov., Flight Safety Found. Served with the Royal Flying Corps., Can., 1917. Received Glidden trophy N.Y. Aero Club, 1921. diploma d'honneur, Ligue Internationale des Aviateurs, 1930; McGough Memorial Award A.S. Post 501, Am. Legion, 1950; Cross of Lorraine (France), 1951; Nat. Aero Assn.'s Elder Statesman of Aviation award, 1962. Chmn. Pub. Relations Adv. Com. to USAF, 1949- 54. Recipient Gen. William Mitchell medal Aviation Writers Assn., 1951; Exceptional Service Award, USAF, 1953, Hap Arnold award Gen. Arnold chpt. Air Force Assn., 1968. Founder mem. Airplane Owners and Pilots Assn.; mem. Aviation Space Writers, Air Force Assn., Navy League, Silurians, Am. Legion, Quiet Birdmen Early Birds, Internat. Assn. Chiefs of Police (asso.), Air Force Hist. Soc (trustee), Broadcast Pioneers. Democrat. Baptist. Clubs: Wings (founder), N.Y. Athletic (life), Lotos (pres. 1951-62, hon. pres. 1962-67, pres. emeritus 1968—), Sales Executives (founder), Nat. Press., Gypsy Trail; Adventurers (pres. 1948), N.Y. Yacht (N.Y.C.); Overseas Press; Sky. Author: Wings Over America, 1942. Contbr. articles to mags. Home: Green Chimneys 4 Fairview Av Montauk NY 11954

BRUNO, JOANNA, soprano. Former apprentice artist; made European debut in 1969 at Spoleto Festival as Monica in Menotti's The Medium, 1969, repeated role in 1970; made debut with Santa Fe Opera in 1970 as Anne Trulove in The Rake's Progress; made debut as Mimi in La Boheme with Netherlands Opera, 1970, engaged to appear with them again in 1971-72 season; sang world premiere performances with N.Y.C. Opera of Menotti's The Most Important Man, 1971. Address: c/o Santa Fe Opera Taos Hwy Santa Fe NM*

BRUNO, LOUIS, state govt. ofcl., educator; b. Roslyn, Wash., July 10, 1907; s. Emil and Rose (Bevilacqua) B.; B.A., Wash. State U., 1927; M.A., U. Wash., 1940; LL.D., Seattle Pacific Coll., 1964; m. Mary Stark, Jan. 3, 1931; children—Mary Louise (Mrs. Edwin Closs), James Louis. Elementary sch. tchr. in Wash., 1928, high sch. tchr., 1928-30, high sch. prin., 1930-41; supr. secondary edn. Wash. State Dept. Edn., 1945-47; supt. schs., Pullman, 1947-61; vis. staff mem. Sch. Finance, Wash. State U., summers 1948-60; supt. pub. instrn. Wash. State, 1961—. Pres. Wash. Bd. Edn.; chmn. Wash. Library Commn.; mem. Wash. Bd. Natural Resources. Served to lt. col. USAAF, World War II. Mem. Council Chief State Sch. Officers, Am. Assn. Sch. Adminstrs., Wash., Inland Empire (past pres.) edn. assns., Pullman C. of C., Am. Legion, Phi Kappa Phi, Phi Delta Kappa. Conglist. Mason, Kiwanian (lt. gov.). Home: 2922 S Boundary St Olympia WA 98501 Office: Old Capitol Bldg Olympia WA 98501

BRUNO, REXFORD EVANS, airlines exec.; b. Urbana, Ill., Nov. 26, 1916; s. Harry Leland and Alta Bell (Graham) B.; B.S. in Accounting, U. Ill., 1940; m. Ella Mae Beaird, Aug. 6, 1939; children—Barbara Ann (Mrs. David B. Headley), Susan Kay, Sally Lee. With United Air Lines, Chgo., 1940—, accountant, supr. property accounting, instr. and supt. procedures, regional mgr. accounting, San Francisco, asst. to v.p. finance and property, comptroller, 1952-57, comptroller and asst. sec., 1957-61, v.p., treas., 1961-67, v.p. finance, 1967-70, sr. v.p. finance and property, 1970—, also dir.; dir. Roosevelt Nat. Investment Co., Roosevelt Nat. Life Ins. Co. Am., 1st Nat. Bank of Western Springs, Countryside Bank; pres., dir. Algonquin Realty, Inc., Linneman Corp.; incorporator, dir. Roosevelt Nat. Investment Co.; partner Countryside Devel. Co. Pres., dir. United Air Lines Found.; pres. Airline Finance and Accounting Conf., 1958; mem. businessman's adv. bd. U. Ill.; adv. bd. West Suburban Family Counseling Service. Bd. dirs. Northwest Suburban YMCA, Des Plaines, Ill. Mem. Financial Execs. Inst. (pres. 1964, gen. chmn. Midwest conf. 1967, nat. dir., exec. com.), U. Ill. Commerce Alumni Assn. (pres. 1964-66, dir.), Alpha Kappa Psi. Kiwanian (pres. Western Springs 1958). Club: La Grange Country (gov. treas. 1968-70, v.p.). Home: 4916 Woodland Av Western Springs IL 60558 Office: PO Box 66100 Chicago IL 60666

BRUNOT, RICHARD L., business exec.; b. 1932; B.S., Ind. U., 1954; married. Staff mgr. Arthur Andersen & Co., 1956-60, mgr., 1960-64; accounting supr. Chgo. Bridge & Iron Co., Oak Brook, Ill., 1964-68, asst. controller, 1968-69, controller, 1969—. Served with AUS, 1954-56. Office: 901 W 22d St Oak Brook IL 60521

BRUNS, CARL HERBERT, banker; b. N.Y.C., July 10, 1906; s. Charles H. and Wilma A. (Meyer) B.; student Am. Inst. Banking, N.Y.C., 1926-29, Columbia, 1929-30, Practicing Law Inst., N.Y.C., 1940-45; m. Beatrice Marjorie Schauf, Apr. 30, 1930; children—Caryl (Mrs. William D. Hutchens), Joan (Mrs. Jerome C. Silvey). Trust officer N.Y. Trust Co., N.Y.C., 1928-57; vice chmn., dir. First Nat. Bank Miami (Fla.), S.E. Bancorp., Inc., Miami; chmn. bd. S.E. Financial Consultants, Inc.; dir. S.E. Data Processing, Inc., S.E. Properties, Inc., S.E. Services, Inc., Am. Bankers Ins. Co. Fla., Financial Carriers, Inc., S.E. Mortgage Co. (all Miami). Mem. Am., Fla. bankers assns., Greater Miami C. of C., Econ. Soc. So. Fla. (dir.), Assn. Res. City Bankers. Lutheran. Clubs: Aviation Executives, Miami (Florida), Riviera (Coral Gables, Florida). Home: 3420 Druango St Coral Gables FL 33134 Office: P O Box 2500 Miami FL 33101

BRUNS, HENRY GERARD, business exec.; b. N.Y.C., Mar. 14, 1904; s. August and Anne (Grieme) B.; grad. Speyer Sch., N.Y.C., 1918; m. Mildred Scott, June 30, 1956; children—Priscilla (Mrs. Peter H. Searl), Elizabeth. Sr. partner H.G. Bruns & Co., N.Y.C., 1939-52, T.L. Watson & Co., N.Y.C., 1952-69; chmn. bd. Norfolk So. Ry. Co., 1956—, also dir.; chmn. bd., dir. Durham & So. R.R. Co., 1956—, Norfolk So. Indsl. Devel. Co., 1958—. Clubs: Downtown Athletic, City-Midday, Stock Exchange Luncheon (N.Y.C.); Montclair Golf. Home: 96 Lewellyn Rd Montclair NJ 07042 Office: 25 Broad St New York City NY 10004

BRUNS, LESLIE AUGUST, railroad ofcl.; b. St. Louis, Apr. 26, 1908; s. Benjamin H. and Hattie (Engler) B.; student St. Louis U. Sch. Commerce and Finance, evenings 1945-47; m. Grace Giese, Oct. 8, 1931; children—Kenneth A., Richard C. With M.P. R.R., 1929—, asst. treas., 1960-61, treas., 1961—; treas. Tex. & Pacific Ry. Co. and subsidiaries; treas. C&EI R.R., 1968—. Sec.-treas. treasury div. Midwest group Assn. Am. R.R.'s, 1962-63, chmn., 1963-64, mem. adv. com., com. collection transp. charges, sec.-treas. treasury div., 1963-67, vice chmn. div., 1967-68, chmn., 1968-69. Home: 1648 Monticello Dr St Louis County MO 63138 Office: Missouri Pacific R R Co 210 N 13th St St Louis MO 63103

BRUNS, WILLIAM HENRY, fgn. service officer; b. Washington, Feb. 19, 1916; s. Henry Frederick and Mary (Thompson) B.; B.S. in Fgn. Service, Georgetown U., 1938; student Yale, 1948-49; m. Patricia Blake Thompson, Aug. 4, 1944; children—Barbara, Kathleen, Henry, Deborah, Beverly, Rosemary. Vice consul fgn. service auxilliary, Panama, 1941-43, Lagos, 1943-44; joined U.S. Fgn. Service, 1947; vice consul, Seoul, 1947-48; 3d sec., Tokyo, 1949-51, 2d sec., 1954-55; prin. officer, Nagoya, 1951-54; assigned Washington, 1955-60; 1st sec., Manila, Philippines, 1960-63, Tokyo, 1963-64; polit. officer, Okinawa, 1966-68; dep. chief mission, Singapore, 1968—. Served with AUS, 1944-47. Home: 145 San Benito Way San Francisco CA 94127 Office: care Dept of State Washington DC 20525

BRUNSCHWIG, ROGER E., mfg. co. exec.; b. Argenteuil, France, July 14, 1891; s. Achille and Blanche (Picard) B.; student French Mil. Sch.; Baccalauret of Arts, French schs.; m. Zelina Comegys, June 25, 1938. Partner, Brunschwig & Fils, mfrs. in France of decorative fabrics, N.Y.C., 1925—; pres. Brunschwig & Fils, Inc. Pres., Union of French Facial Wounded. Served with French Army, 1909-21; with Free French Forces, 1940-46; col. inf. Army Res. Decorated grand cross Legion of Honor, Croix de Guerre (2) (France); Croix de Guerre (Belgium); Legion of Merit, Bronze Star medal (U.S.). Author: Historical Studies of the French Revolution and Empire Periods. Home: 447 E 57th St New York City NY 10022 also Old Chatham NY also Paris France Office: Brunschwig & Fils Inc 410 E 62d St New York City NY 10021 also 979 3d Av New York City NY 10022

BRUNSON, JOEL GARRETT, physician, educator; b. Greenville, S.C., Apr. 22, 1923; s. James Edwin and Leila (Ballenger) B.; student Furman U., 1940-43, Miss. State Coll., 1943; M.D., U. Buffalo, 1950. Intern U. Ala. Med. Center, 1950-51; resident pathology U. Minn. Hosps., 1951-55; Am. Cancer Soc. fellow U. Minn., 1952-55, instr. pathology Med. Sch., 1955-57, sr. research fellow USPHS, also asst. prof. pathology, 1957-59; prof. pathology, chmn. dept. U. Miss. Med. Center, 1959—; cons. VA Hosp., Jackson, Miss.; cons. pathology a study sect. USPHS; mem. instnl. grants com. VA, instnl. research programs evaluation com. Diplomate Am. Bd. Med. Examiners, Am. Bd. Pathology. Mem. Am. Assn. Pathologists and Bacteriologists, Internat. Acad. Pathology, Am. Soc. Exptl. Pathology, Am. Nuclear Soc., A.A.A.S., Soc. Research Reticuloendothelial System, Nat. Assn. Standard Med. Vocabulary, Pan Am. Med. Assn., Cryobiology Soc., N.Y. Acad. Scis., Miss. Assn. Pathologists, Am. Heart Assn., Am. Assn. Pathology Chmn. (v.p.), Sigma Xi, Nu Sigma Nu. Contbr. articles to med. jours. Mem. editorial bd. Am. Jour. Pathology. Home: R F D 2 Terry MS 39170 Office: Univ Med Center Jackson MS 39201

BRUNSTING, LOUIS ALBERT, physician, educator; b. Grand Rapids, Mich., July 7, 1900; s. Albert L. and Kate (Bolt) B.; student Calvin Coll., 1917-18, Grand Rapids Jr. Coll., 1918-19; M.D., U. Mich., 1924; M.Sc., Mayo Found. U., 1929; m. Lena J. Pleune, 1923 (dec. Nov. 1967); children—Anna Lea (Mrs. Franklin Earnest, III), Louis Albert, Carl David, Linda Jane; m. 2d, Kathryn Chabot, Sept. 28, 1969. High sch. sci. tchr., Grandville, Mich., 1919-20, gen. practitioner, Nashville, Mich., 1925- 26; staff cons. dermatology and syphilology Mayo Clinic, 1930—; prof. dermatology and syphilology Mayo Found., U. Minn. Grad. Sch., 1950-65; pvt. practice as cons. in dermatology, 1965—. Civilian cons. indsl. dermatosea USPHS, 1947-53. Mem. Minn. Bd. Parks and Recreation, 1940-47. Served with inf. SATC, U.S. Army, 1918. Diplomate Am. Bd. Dermatology. Mem. A.M.A. (residency rev. com. on dermatology and syphilology), Am. Dermatology Assn. (sec. 1948-53, pres. 1953-54), Minn., Chgo. (pres. 1956), dermatol. socs., Soc. Investigative Dermatology, Am Acad. Dermatology (rep. Am. Bd. Dermatology 1958-61), Minn. Med. Assn. (chmn. com. on syphilis and social diseases), Sigma Xi, Phi Chi; hon. mem. Austrian, German, Yugoslav. Brazilian, Polish, Venezuelan dermatol. socs., , Brit. Assn. Dermatology, Royal Soc. Medicine; corr. mem. Swedish, Dutch, French dermatol. socs., dermatol. socs. of Israel, Argentina, Norway, Denmark. Presbyn. Mem. adv. panel on dermatology U.S. Pharmacopoeia. Contbr. articles to profl. jours. Home: 2459 N Sonoita Pl Tucson, AZ 85716 Office: 601 N Wilmot Rd Tucson AZ 85711

BRUNT, HARRY HERMAN, Jr., psychiatrist; b. Phila., Jan. 22, 1921; s. Harry Herman and Ann (Zurbrugg) B.; B.S. with honors, Va. Poly. Inst., 1942; M.D., U. Pa., 1945; m. Zoe M. Bower, July 2, 1944; children—Marianne, Margaret, Jane. Intern, Lankenau Hosp., 1946; resident psychiatry Trenton (N.J.) State Hosp., VA Hosp., Coatesville, 1948-52; practice medicine specializing in psychiatry, Trenton, 1952, Princeton, N.J., 1952-54, Hammonton, N.J., 1954-69, Long Branch, N.J., 1969—; acting asst. clin. dir. Trenton State Hosp., 1952; asst. supt. N.J. Neuropsychiat. Inst. Princeton, 1952-54; med. dir. Ancora State Hosp., 1954-69; dir. dept. psychiatry Monmouth Med. Center and Pollak Clinic, Long Branch, 1969—; instr. psychiatry Jefferson Med. Coll., 1952-66, U. Pa., 1953- 65; adj. asso. prof. psychiatry Temple Med. Sch., 1968—; asso. prof. psychiatry Hahneman Med. Coll., 1970—. Cons. bur. family services Dept. Health, Edn. and Welfare Dept. Trustee Haven Beach Assn. Served to capt. M.C., AUS, 1946-48. Diplomate Am. Bd. Psychiatry and Neurology. Fellow A.C.P., Am. Psychiat. Assn. (chmn. future planning com. Assembly Dist. Brs., mem. policy com. area III 1968, recorder 1969, speaker 1971), A.A.A.S., Am. Geriatric Soc.; mem. A.M.A., N.J., Monmouth County med. soc., N.J. Neuropsychiat. Assn. (past pres.), Alpha Kappa Kappa, Phi Kappa Phi. Club: Chanel. Home: 3404 Hurley Pond Rd Wall NJ 07719 Office: Monmouth Med Center Long Branch NJ 07740

BRUNTON, PAUL EDWARD, diversified industry exec.; b. Decatur, Ind., July 8, 1922; s. John Harrison and Jessie (Holthouse) B.; B.S. in Finance, St. Joseph's Coll., Ind., 1944; m. Margaret Alice Rice, July 10, 1945; children—Patricia Ann, David John, Thomas Edward, Mary Josephine, Elizabeth Alice, Daniel William. Staff accountant Haskins & Sells, C.P.A.'s, Chgo. and Mpls., 1946-48, Runking Keun & Co., C.P.A.'s, Chgo. and Mpls., 1946-48; sr. accountant Reinking Kein and Co., C.P.A.'s. Ft. Wayne, Ind., 1948-53; controller, sec. Ft. Wayne Builders Supply Co., 1953-54; with Internat. Tel.&Tel. Co., 1954-61, controller Farnsworth Electronics, 1954-57, asst. controller ITT Fed. div., 1958-61, dir. finance and adminstrn. ITT Kellogg div., 1961; with Litton Industries, Inc., 1961—, v.p. guidance and control systems div., Woodland Hills, Cal., 1961-66, v.p. adminstrn. Ingalls Shipbuilding div., Pascagoula. Miss., 1966, v.p. finance bus. equipment group, 1967, corp. controller, Beverly Hills, Cal., 1967-70, pres. Louis Allis Co., Milw., 1970—. Served as lt. (j.g.) USNR, World War II. Mem. Financial Execs. Inst., Am. Inst. C.P.A.'s, Cal., Ind. socs. C.P.A.'s. Address: 5202 Woodbudge Lane Greenfield WI 53221

BRUNZELL, GEORGE MANCE, utilities cons.; b. Reynolds, Ida., Mar. 16, 1909; s. Oscal F. and Laura (Winchester) B.; B.S. in Elec. Engring., U. Ida., 1936; D.Sc., 1970; m.; children—John, Dawn (Mrs. Gregory Holt), Jennifer (Mrs. William Platts), Diane, Laura. With Spokane div. Wash. Water Power Co., 1936—, elec. engr., supt., div. mgr., asst. to pres., 1936-58, exec. v.p. 1958-60, pres., chief exec. officer, 1960-71, also dir., now cons.; v.p., dir. Wash. Irrigation & Devel. Co., Limestone Co., Spokane Indsl. Park, Inc.; pres., dir. Water Improvement Co.; pres., chmn. Wash. Underground Gas Storage Co., Inc.; pres., dir. Devel. Assos. Mem. engring. adv. bd. Wash. State U., Whitworth Coll., Assoc. Industries Inland Empire; dir. Assn. Wash. Bus.; adv. bd. U. Ida. Coll. Engring. Fellow I.E.E.E.; mem. Nat., Wash. socs. profl. engrs., N.A.M., N.W. Electric Light and Power Assn. (past pres.), N.W. Sci. Assn. (hon. trustee), Delta Tau Delta. Conglist. Mason (Shriner), Lion, Elk, Eagle. Clubs: Spokane Country, Spokane; Wash. Athletic. Home: 429 W 33d Av Spokane WA 99206 Office: P O Box 1445 Spokane WA 99210

BRUSH, BROCK EDWIN, physician; b. Amherstburg, Ont., Can., July 4, 1911; s. Frank and Ida (Bratt) B.; came to U.S., 1936, naturalized, 1941; A.B., M.D., U. Western Ont., 1936; M.Sc., Wayne U., 1938; m. Mary Ellen Burnett, Aug. 1, 1940; 1 dau., Cynthia B. Intern Providence Hosp., Detroit, 1936-37; instr. physiology Wayne U., 1937; resident gen. surgery Henry Ford Hosp., Detroit, 1938-43, surgeon-in-chief 1st surg. div., 1946—; past pres., chmn. med. and sci. com. Mich. Cancer Found., chmn. bd. dirs. Trustee Boys Clubs of Metropolitan Detroit, Metropolitan Detroit Committee. Mem. A.C.S., Am., Central, Western, Pan Pacific, Detroit Surg. assns., Royal Soc. Medicine, Am. Thyroid Assn., Acad. Surgery (past pres.), Detroit Acad. Medicine (past pres.), Wayne County Med. Soc. (Past pres.), Am. Geriatric Soc. (past pres.), Canadian Physiol. Society, Detroit Historical Society, Alpha Omega Alpha, Alpha Kappa Alpha. Episcopalian. Mason. (33). Clubs: Economic (Detroit); Dearborn Country. Associate editors Detroit Medical News. Home: 22313 Cherryhill Dr Dearborn MI 48124 Office: Henry Ford Hosp Detroit MI 48202

BRUSH, CAREY WENTWORTH, coll. adminstr.; b. Tisbury, Mass., Sept. 25, 1920; s. Bartlett W.W. and Zelda (Goodwin) B.; B.S., State Tchrs. Coll., Bridgewater, Mass., 1941; M.A., Columbia, 1949, Ph.D., 1961; m. Margaret Eloise Marks, Apr. 8, 1946; children—Bartlett M., Elizabeth W. Tchr., Gallup (N.M.) Pub. Schs., 1949-50; instr. State Tchrs. Coll., Oneonta, N.Y., 1951; chmn. social sci. dept. Cortland (N.Y.) Pub. Schs., 1951-57; prof. history, acting v.p. acad. affairs State U. Coll. at Oneonta, 1958—. Mem. Bd. Edn., Oneonta, 1968-69. Served with USAAF, 1942-46. Tchrs. Coll. fellow, 1957-58. Mem. Am. Hist. Assn., Orgn. Am. Historians, Nat. Council Social Studies, Middle States Assn. Colls. and Secondary Schs. (mem. accreditation team), Nat. Council Accreditation Tchr. Edn. (mem. accreditation team). Author: In Honor and Good Faith: A History of the State University College at Oneonta, New York, 1965. Home: 18 Ford Av Oneonta NY 13820

BRUSH, CYRUS EUGENE, mfg. exec.; b. Verona, Pa., 1910; s. Hudson D. and Fronie (Young) B.; A.B., Cornell, 1932, LL.B., 1934; m. Georgianna Orebaugh, Jan. 9, 1941; children—Michael G., Jonathan Y., Georgianna, Cyrus R., Anthony Stewart. Sec. Am. Brake Shoe Co., N.Y.C., 1948-54, v.p., sec., treas., 1958-61. Served with USNR, 1941-45, lt. comdr. Res., 1945. Mem. Fed. Bar Assn., Assn. Bar City N.Y., Nat. Lawyers Club. Republican. Episcopalian. Clubs: Cornell, University (N.Y.C.). Home: Redding Ridge Redding CT

BRUSH, DAVID MALCOLM, food co. exec.; b. Greenwich, Conn., Nov. 4, 1919; s. Graham M. and Marjorie G. (Smith) B.; B.A., Yale, 1941; M.B.A., Harvard, 1947; m. Dorothea Randolph Berkeley, Dec. 28, 1957; children—Peter C., Alison G., Lee K., Marjorie G.; stepchildren—Judith W. Oliver, Dorothea R. Clarke, Robert T., Stuart N. Houk. Vice pres., treas. Seatrain Lines, Inc., N.Y.C., 1947-58; v.p., treas. Gen. Foods Corp., White Plains, N.Y., 1959—. Served to lt. USNR, 1942-46. Home: Winfield Lane New Canaan CT Office: 250 North St White Plains NY 10625

BRUSH, DONALD J., banker; b. Grinnell, Ia., Dec. 17, 1939; s. J. Basil and Mabel (Kenner) B.; B.S. in Accounting, St. Ambrose Coll., 1964; m. Kathryn L. Beran, Oct. 12, 1963; children-Steven James, David Paul, Susan Marie. Staff accountant Peat, Marwick, Mitchell & Co., Des Moines, 1964-67; auditor Ia.-Des Moines Nat. Bank, Des Moines, 1967—. Mem. Plan and Zoning Commn. City of Urbandale, Ia., 1969—. Mem. Inst. Internal Auditor (organizer, charter mem. Ia. Chpt.; treas. 1970-71), Nat. Assn. Accountants, Bank Adminstrn. Inst., Jaycees (state dir., 1967-69), Am. Inst. Banking, C. of C. Club: Serra Internat. (Des Moines). Home: 4320 64th St Urbandale IA 50322 Office: Ia Des Moines Nat Bank 6th and Walnut St Des Moines IA 50306

BRUSH, EDWARD NEWCOMB, educator; b. Rochester, N.Y., July 11, 1904; s. George Robert and Josephine (Taylor) B.; A.B., U. Vt., 1925; A.M., Harvard, 1926, Ph.D., 1932; m. Lillian Maynard Hatfield, Sept. 6, 1933; children—Stephen George, Mary Josephine Anne. Interne in psychology. Boston Psychopathic Hosp., 1926-27, psychologist, 1927-28; instr. in psychology, U. Me., 1928-29, asst. prof., 1929-30, asso. prof., 1931-46, prof. psychology, 1946-70, prof. emeritus, 1970—, dean of grad. study, 1946-62; lectr. in psychology Bates Coll., 1970-71. Served as capt., Adj. Gen.'s Dept., AUS, 1942-46; maj. Med. Service Corps, U.S. Army Res., 1947-55, lt. col., 1955—. Mem. Am., Me. (pres. 1958-59) psychol. assns., New Eng. Conf. on Grad. Edn. (v.p., 1950- 51, pres., 1951-52), Phi Beta Kappa, Sigma Xi. Phi Kappa Phi. Home: Ledge Hill Orono ME 04473

BRUSH, GERALD F., stock broker; b. San Franciscoo, Aug. 17, 1921; s. Spencer and Anne (Fenwick) B.; B.A., U. Cal., 1943; m. Nancy Miller, Sept. 8, 1943; children-Spencer Miller, Gerald F., Nancy Gertrude, Anne Simmons. With Brush, Slocumb & Co., Inc., San Francisco, 1945—, pres., 1968—. Bd. govs. Pacific Coast Stock Exchange, 1962-64. Mem. Investment Bankers Assn. (chmn. Cal. group 1966-67, nat. bd. govs). Assn. Stock Exchange Firms (bd. govs.) Republican. Clubs: San Francisco Golf; Pacific Union; Bohemian; Cypress Point. Home: 68 Lincoln Av Piedmonnt CA 94611 Office: 465 California St San Francisco CA 94104

BRUSH, ROBERT MURRAY, hotel exec.; b. Denver, July 1, 1913; s. Roy Arthur and Adele (Twitchell) B.; B.S., Cornell U., 1934; m. Marjorie C. Culver, Oct. 12, 1945; children-Richard L., John T., Robert Murray (dec.) and Frederick Culver. From steward to manager at the Basin Harbor Club (Vt.), 1934-39; asst. to pres. Hosts, Inc., Springfield, Mass., 1940-42; gen. mgr. Wayland Manor, Providence, 1946-47, Sheraton-Biltmore, 1947- 48; v.p. Sheraton Corp. Am., Boston, 1956-59, sr. v.p., 1959-69; v.p. TravaLodge Internat., Inc., El Cajon, Cal., 1969—. Vice pres. Cultural Found. Boston. Served from lt. to maj. USAAF, 1942-46. Mem. N.E. Hotel Assn., Cornell Soc. Hotelmen (pres. 1951), C. of C., New Eng. Council (past dir.), Am. Hotel and Motel Assn. (chmn. student affiliate activities 1967-68), Sigma Nu. Club: Loma Santa Fe County. Home: PO Box 1174 Rancho Santa Fe CA 92067 Office: PO Box 308 El Cajon CA 92022

BRUSHWOOD, JOHN STUBBS, educator; b. Glenns, Va., Jan. 23, 1920; s. John Benson and Evelyn (Stubbs) B.; B.A., Randolph-Macon Coll., 1940; M.A., U. Va., 1942; Ph.D., Columbia, 1950; m. Carolyn Darrach Norton, May 19, 1945; children—David Benson, Paul Darrach. Instr. Romance langs. Va. Poly. Inst., 1942-44; from instr. to prof. Spanish, U. Mo. at Columbia, 1946- 67; Roy A. Roberts prof. Latin Am. Lit. U. Kan., 1967—; reviewer Latin Am. books Kansas City Star, 1967—. Fellow Fund Advancement Edn., 1951- 52; grantee Am. Philos. Soc., 1957, Am. Council Learned Socs., 1961, Social Sci. Research Council, 1971. mem. Midwest Modern Lang. Assn. (pres. 1962-63), Modern Lang. Assn. Am. (chmn. Spanish 7, 1966), Inst. Internacional de Literatura Iberomericana, Latin Am. Studies Assn., Am. Assn. Tchrs. Spanish and Portuguese, Am. Assn. U. Profs. Author: The Romantic Novel in Mexico, 1954; (with Jose Rojas Garciduenas) Breve historia de la novela mexicana, 1959; Mexico in Its Novel, 1966; Enrique Gonzalez Martinez, 1969; Los ricos en la prosa mexicana, 1970; also articles. Translator: (with Carolyn Brushwood) The Precipice (by Sergio Galindo), 1969. Home: 2813 Maine Ct Lawrence KS 66044

BRUSILOW, ANSHEL, orch. condr.; b. Phila., Aug. 14, 1928; s. Leon and Dora (Epstein) B.; grad. Curtis Inst. Music, 1943; artist's diploma Phila. Mus. Acad., 1947; m. Marilyn Rae Dow, Dec. 23, 1951; children—David, Jennie, Melinda. Concertmaster, asst. condr. New Orleans Symphony, 1954-55; asso. concertmaster Cleve. Orch., 1955-59; concertmaster Phila. Orch., 1959-66; founder, condr. Phila. Chamber Orch., 1961-65, Chamber Symphony Phila., 1966-68: exec. dir., condr. Dallas Symphony Orch., 1970—. Host TV program Portraits in Music, Sta. WRCV, 1961-63. Bd. dirs. Ednl. TV Council. Named Outstanding Young Man of Year, Phila. C. of C., 1963. Home: 4545 Laren Lane Dallas TX 75234 Office: Dallas Symphony Orch PO Box 8472 Dallas TX 75205

BRUSKI, GEORGE, dept. store exec.; b. Paris, France, 1888; ed. John Marshall Law Sch., 1914. Treas. Goldblatt Bros., Inc. Home: 777 N Michigan Av Chicago IL 60611 Office: 333 S State St Chicago IL 60604*

BRUSON, HERMAN ALEXANDER, chemist; b. Middletown, O., July 20, 1901; s. Samuel J. and Rebecca (Arnovitz) B.; B.Sc., Mass. Inst. Tech., 1923; D. Sc., Fed. Poly. Inst., Zurich, Switzerland, 1925; m. Virginia Haber, Mar. 30, 1929; children—Rita, Dorothy, Barbara. Sect. editor Chem. Abstracts, 1937-60; asso. prof. organic chemistry Temple U., 1939-48; Priestly lectr. Pa. State Coll., 1944; with Olin Mathieson Chem. Corp., New Haven, 1952-66, v.p. research chem. div., 1960-66, chem. cons., 1966—. chem. research specializing petroleum-based chems. U.S. rep. to OECD Plastics Com., 1967. Recipient Pioneer award in creative chemistry N.A.M., 1965. Mem. Société de Chimie Industrielle, Am., (chmn. New Haven 1953), Brit. chem. socs., A.A.A.S., Am. Inst. Chemists (award), Chemists Club N.Y. Club: Graduate (New Haven). Author: Cvancethylation, chpt. in Organic Reactions, 1949. Contbr. articles to profl. jours. Holder numerous U.S., fgn. patents. Home: 98 Ansonia Rd Woodbridge CT 06525

BRUSS, JOHN ANDREW, oil co. exec.; b. Milw., Oct. 6, 1920; s. John H. and Selina (Beck) B.; m. Mary M. Marek, June 12, 1948; children—John P., Michael S. Accountant, Anchor Gasoline Corp., 1948-52; with Clark Oil & Refining Corp., 1951—. treas., Milw., 1966—, v.p., 1970—. Bd. dirs. Milw. Credit Bur. Served with USAAF, 1942-45. Home: 3320 Vista Granada New Berlin WI 53151 Office: 8530 W National Av Milwaukee WI 53227

BRUSSEL-SMITH, BERNARD, artist; b. N.Y.C., Mar. 1, 1914; s. Raymond and Belle (Epstein) B.- S.; student Penn Acad. Fine Arts, 1931-36; m. Mildred Cornfeld, Sept. 25, 1937; 1 son, Peter. Art dir. Geyer Publs., 1939-42; head advt. dept. Chance-Voight Aircraft Co., 1942-44; art dir. Noyes & Sproul, 1944-45; free lance wood engraver, 1945—; instr. Cooper Union, Bklyn. Mus., Phila. Mus. Sch. Art, N.A.D., Coll. City N.Y. Prints included in collections Library of Congress, Carnegie Inst., N.Y. Pub. Library, U. Ill., Phila. Mus., Smithsonian Instn. Co-founder Bedford Art Center, 1965. Recipient Frank Hartley Anderson award, 1948, Am. Artist Group award, 1948, John Taylor Arms Meml. prize, 1970; asso. Nat. Acad., 1952. Clubs: Art Directors, Type Directors, Dutch Treat. Home: 328 Cherry St Bedford Hills NY 10507

BRUST, PAUL CHRISTOPHER, architect: b. Milw., July 18, 1905; s. Peter J. and Olga (Greulich) B.; student Marquette U., 1924-25; B.S. in Architecture, U. Notre Dame, 1928; postgrad. Columbia, 1928-29; m. Mary McGinn, May 18, 1936 (dec. 1960); children—Barbara, Peter, Charlotte, Daniel, Richard, William, Janet, Marian; m. 2d, Ruth Garnt, Oct. 22, 1962. With Fed. Architect's Office, Treasury Dept., 1933-35, FHA, 1935-36, Office of Peter Brust 1936-43, C.E., Milw., 1943-46; partner firm Brust & Brust, Milw., 1946—. Mem. St. Jude Parish Bd. Edn., 1966-69. Bd. dirs. Cath. Information Center. Milw., 1962—. Recipient Nat. Sch. of Month award for Alexander Hamilton High Sch., Milw. Mem. A.I.A. Wis. Architects Assn., Friends of Art of Milw. Art Center, St. Vincent de Paul Soc., Holy Name Soc. (past pres.), Archdiocesan Council Cath. Men (past pres.), Milw. Assn. Commerce. K.C. (4). Prin. works include hosps., schs., instl. bldgs., comml. projects, also bldgs. for city, county, state and fed. govt. Clubs: Milwaukee Athletic, Serra (Milw.); Lake Beulah (Wis.) Yacht (past commodore). Home: 622 N 77th St Milwaukee WI 53213 Office: 1212 W Wisconsin Av Milwaukee WI 53233

BRUSTEIN, ROBERT SANFORD, univ. adminstr., author; b. N.Y.C., Apr. 21, 1927; s. Max and Blanche (Haft) B.; B.A., Amherst Coll., 1948; postgrad Yale Drama Sch., 1948-49; M.A., Columbia, 1950, Ph.D., 1957; postgrad. U. Nottingham (Eng.) 1953-55; LL.D., Lawrence U., m. Norma Ofstrock, Mar. 25, 1962; children—Phillip Cates (stepson), Daniel Anton. Instr. English, Cornell U., 1955-56; instr. drama Vassar Coll., 1956-57; faculty Columbia, 1957-66, prof. English and comparative lit., 1965-66; dean Yale Sch. Drama, artistic dir. Yale Repertory Theatre, New Haven, 1966—; drama critic New Republic, 1959—. Served with U.S. Mcht. Marine, 1945-47. Recipient George Jean Nathan award dramatic criticism, 1962, George Polk Meml. award outstanding criticism, 1965. Fulbright fellow, 1953-55, Guggenheim fellow, 1961-62, Ford Found. fellow, 1964-65. Author: The Theatre of Revolt: Studies in the Modern Drama, 1964; Seasons of Discontent: Dramatic Opinions 1959-65, 1965; The Third Theatre, 1969; Revolution as theatre! Notes on the New Radical Style, 1971. Contbr. numerous articles to profl. jours. Editor: The Plays and Prose of Strindberg. 1964. Home: 10 St Ronan Terrace New Haven CT 06511

BRUTON, HENRY JACKSON, educator, economist; b. Dallas, Aug. 30, 1921; s. Guss and Mary (Clark) B.; A.B., U. Tex., 1943; Ph.D., Harvard, 1952; m. Mary Frances Barnes, Apr. 21, 1959. Prof. econs. Yale, 1952-58; prof. econs. Williams Coll., Williamstown, Mass., 1962—; econ. cons. in Iran, 1958-60, Pakistan, 1960-61, Malaysia, 1970-71; vis. prof. econs. U. Bombay, 1961-62, U. Chile, 1965-66. Served with AUS, 1943-46; ETO. Author: Inflation in a Growing Economy, 1963; Principles of Development Economics, 1965; Productividad en America Latina, 1968. Contbr. articles profl. jours. Home: 300 Syndicate Rd Williamstown MA 01267

BRUTON, JAMES DEWITT, Jr., judge; b. Magazine, Ark., Feb. 2, 1908; s. James David and Pattie Lee (Bruton) B.; J.D., U. Fla., 1931; m. Quintilla Geer, June 11, 1932. Admitted to Fla. bar, 1931, practiced at Plant City, 1931-61; asst. criminal court solicitor, Tampa, 1934-37; elected to Fla. Ho. of Reps., 1935-36; municipal judge. Plant City, 1937-57; corp. and civil lawyer, 1931-61; probate judge, Tampa, 1961-64; circuit judge 13th Jud. Circuit Fla., 1964—; founder, owner Bruton's Audubon Acres Bird Sanctuary, Plant City, 1952—; dir. Tampa Abstract and Title Ins. Co., Hillsboro Bank, Plant City, Fla. Bd. dirs. Children's Home, Tampa, 1947-67, Tampa Mental Health Assn., 1962-68, Inter-Profl. Family Council, Inc., Tampa chpt. A.R.C., 1967-68; bd. dirs., life mem. Tampa Humane Soc. Mem. Fla. State Bd. Law Examiners, 1950-54; chmn. bd. editors Fla. Bar Jour., 1950-52. Fellow Am. Coll. Probate Counsel (jud. fellow 1961), Am. Bar Found. (life fellow 1961); mem. Fla. Municipal Judges Assn. (pres. 1956-57), C. of C. (dir.), Plant City Civic Music Assn. (pres. 1949), Tampa Symphony Soc. (dir. 1952), Jr. C. of C. (pres. 1940), Fla. County Judges Assn. (v.p. 1962), U. Fla. Alumni Assn. (v.p. 1948), Am. (ho. of dels. 1951-58), Fla. (state chmn. com. on integration, gov. 1949-50, chmn. com. Am. citizenship 1952-53, chmn. com. on co-operation with Am. Bar Assn. 1956-59, chmn. com. on world peace through law 1959-63), Tampa bar assns., Fla. Bar (del. to Am. Bar Assn. Conf. on World Peace 1959, chmn. com. on memls. 1962—), Seldon Soc. London, Am. Judicature Soc. (dir. 1953-58), Audubon Soc. (life), Am. Ornithologists' Union (life), Fla. Cattle Assn., Fla. Hist. Soc. (dir. 1967-68). Chi Phi. Democrat. Methodist. Elk, Kiwanian (past lt. gov.; bd. dirs. Plant City club). Clubs: Tampa Executives (pres. 1951-52, dir. 1948-55), Tampa Bird, University (Tampa). Home: 910 Roux St Plant City FL 33566 Office: Courthouse Tampa FL 33602

BRUTON, PAUL WESLEY, educator; b. Woodland, Cal., Aug. 1, 1903; s. Philip and Nancy (Gilstrap) B.; A.B., U. Cal., 1929, LL.B., 1929; J.S.D., Yale, 1930; m. Margaret Perry, Sept. 2, 1931; children—Margaret Jane (Mrs. Duane R. Batista), David, Laura (Mrs. L. Clausen). Sterling fellow law Yale, 1929-30, instr. law, 1930-32; asso. prof. law Duke, 1932-35; atty., office chief counsel Bur. Internal Revenue, Washington, 1935-37; vis. asso. prof. law, U. Pa., Phila., 1937-38, asso. prof., 1938-39, prof., 1939—, Ferdinand Wakeman Hubbell prof. law, 1964-69, Algernon Sidney Biddle prof. law, 1969—; admitted to Cal. bar, 1930, Pa. bar, 1943, Supreme Ct. U.S., 1935; asso. firm Ballard, Spahr, Andrews & Ingersoll, Phila., 1943-44; tax cons. law firm MacCoy, Evans & Lewis, Phila., 1953-62. Vis. prof. Stanford, 1941, 52, U. Tex., 1947, McGill U., 1961, spl. asst., gen. counsel A.A.A., 1934; chief price atty. Phila. OPA, 1942-43. Chmn., Phila. Tax Rev. Bd., 1953-59: mem. Task Force on Revision Pa. Tax Law. Mem. Pa., Am. bar assns., Cal. State Bar, Juristic Soc. Phila., Phi Beta Kappa, Pi Sigma Alpha, Delta Sigma Rho, Order of Coif. Democrat. Mem. Soc. of Friends. Club: Franklin Inn. Editor: Cases on Federal Taxation, 1954; (with Edward L. Barrett and John Honnold) Cases and Materials on Constitutional Law, 1959, 3d edit., 1968. Home: 429 Montgomery Av Haverford PA 19041 Office: 3400 Chestnut St Philadelphia PA 19104

BRUTON, THOMAS WADE, ret. govt. ofcl.; b. Capelsie, N.C., Sept. 10, 1902; s. David Dudley and Susan Eleanor (Wade) B.; A.B., Va. Mil. Inst., 1925; student Duke Law Sch., 1925-27; m. Marion Sheppard Piatt, Feb. 1, 1928 (dec. Feb. 1960); m. 2d, Elizabeth Nelms Flournoy, December, 1964. Admitted to N.C. bar, 1927; practice law, 1927-29; mem. N.C. Ho. of Reps. from Montgomery County, 1929-31; practice law, 1931-33; asst. atty. gen. N.C., 1933-60, atty. gen., 1960-68. Served to lt. col. AUS, World War II; mem. N.C. N.G., 1947-62, col., 1955, ret. brig. gen., 1962. Decorated Bronze Star medal, N.C. Distinguished Service medal N.C. N.G. Mem. N.C. Bar Assn., Order of Coif, Kappa Sigma. Democrat. Methodist. Home: 5005 North Hills Dr Raleigh NC 27609

BRUYN, HENRY BICKER, physician; b. Bklyn., Jan. 24, 1918; s. Henry Bicker and Mary Janet (Retter) B.; B.A., Amherst Coll., 1940; M.D., Yale, 1943; m. Marion Helen Burkhardt, Sept. 19, 1942; children—Martha Elizabeth, Barbara Jane, Charles DeWitt, Jonathan Henry. Intern pediatrics New Haven Hosp., 1943-44; resident Buffalo Children's Hosp., 1944-45; fellow infectious disease U. Cal. Med. Sch., San Francisco, 1946-47, mem. faculty, 1948—, asso. prof. medicine, pediatrics, 1956-69, clin. prof. medicine, pediatrics, 1969—; chief isolation service San Francisco Gen. Hosp., 1950-59, chief pediatrics, 1954-59; lectr. Sch. Pub. Health U. Cal. at Berkeley, 1960—, dir. student health service, 1959—; cons. U.S. Naval Hosp., U.S. Army Hosp., Children's Hosp. East Bay. Cons. Cal. viral and rickettsial disease lab., bur. maternal and child health Office Dir. Pub. Health, City and County San Francisco; mem. med. service com. Alameda County Council Social Planning, 1962-64; med. cons. Morrison Center Rehab., 1954-58, Elizabeth Kenney Found., San Francisco, 1950-52, Drug Abuse Rehab., Bridge Over Troubled Waters, Inc.; dir. Berkeley Med. Instrument Co. Alumni fund chmn. N.Cal. sect. Yale Med. Sch. Bd. dirs. Alameda County Suicide Prevention, Carmel Valley Manor, Alameda County Council Alcoholism, 1960-70; trustee, mem. ch. council Arlington Community Ch. Served to lt. comdr. M.C., USNR, 1945-46, 53-54. Mem. A.M.A., Royal Soc. Health, Am. Pub. Health Assn., Am. (pres. 1965-66), Pacific Coast (pres. 1968-69) coll. health assns., Am. Fed. Clin. Research (pres. 1969-70), Western Soc. Clin. Research, Am. Acad. Pediatrics (chmn. pub. health com. No. Cal. sect.), Cal. Fedn. Pediatric Socs., Delta Tau Delta, Nu Sigma Nu. Co-author: Handbook of Pediatrics, 9th edit., 1971; Handbook of Medical Treatment, 1971; Current Diagnosis and Therapy, 1971; Practice of Pediatrics, 1963, Contbr. articles to profl. jours. Home: 26 Sunset Dr Kensington CA 94707 Office: Cowell Meml Hosp U Cal Berkeley CA 94720

BRYAN, ALBERT HUGHES, physician; b. Rocky Ford, Colo., Oct. 20, 1904; s. Albert Hugh and Alma (Haworth) B.; B.S., Harvard, 1927, M.D., 1931; m. Barbara Fenlason, June 27, 1927; 1 son, Hugh; m. 2d, Rebecca A. Broach, Sept. 7, 1966. Intern, Royal Victoria Hosp., Montreal, Que., Can., 1931-32; resident, 1932-33; research fellow medicine Harvard Med. Sch., 1933-34; instr. U. Chgo., 1934-40, asst. prof. medicine, 1940-43; surgeon USPHS, chief nutrition sect., health div. UNRRA, Washington, 1943-45, dept. dir. health, 1945-46, released as sr. surgeon, 1946; prof. pub. health nutrition U. N.C. Sch. Pub. Health, Chapel Hill, 1946-69, prof. emeritus, 1970—. Diplomate Am. Bd. Preventive Medicine and Pub. Health Assn. Mem. Central Soc. Clin. Research. Home: 406 Long Leaf Dr Chapel Hill NC 27514

BRYAN, ALBERT VICKERS, judge; b. Alexandria, Va., July 23, 1899; s. Albert and Marion (Beach) B.; LL.B., U. Va., 1921; m. Marie Gasson, Dec. 1, 1923; children—Albert Vickers, Henry Gasson. Admitted to Va. bar, 1920, practiced in Alexandria, 1921-47; city atty., Alexandria, 1926-28, commonwealth's atty., 1928-47; U.S. dist. judge Eastern Dist. Va., 1947-61; U.S. circuit judge, 1961—. Mem. State Bd. Corrections, Va., 1943- 45, mem. Bd. Law Examiners, 1944-47. Bd. visitors U. Va., 1956-64, rector, 1960-64. Mem. Am., Va. bar assns., Am. Law Inst., Phi Beta Kappa, Phi Kappa Sigma, Phi Delta Phi, Omicron Delta Kappa, Raven Soc. Home: 2826 King St Alexandria PA 16611 Office: U S Court House Alexandria PA 16611

BRYAN, ARTHUR, pottery co. exec.; b. Stoke-on-Trent, Staffordshire, Eng., Mar. 4, 1923; s. William Woodall and Isobel Alan (Tweedle) B.; m. Betty Ratford, Mar. 17, 1947; children—Lawrence, Linda. With Josiah Wedgwood & Sons, Ltd., Barlaston, Staffordshire, 1947—, successively trainee, salesman, London mgr. gen. mgr. Wedgwood Rooms, Ltd. and gen. sales mgr. co., 1959-60, dir., 1962—; pres., dir. Josiah Wedgwood & Sons, Inc. of Am., 1960-62; mng. dir. Wedgwood Ltd., 1963—, chmn., 1968—; dir. Josiah Wedgwood & Sons (Can.) Ltd., Josiah Wedgwood & Sons (Australia) Pty. Ltd. Chmn. Stoke-on-Trent local employment com., 1967. Bd. govs. Stoke-on-Trent Coll. Art, 1967—. Served with RAF Vol. Res., 1941-45. Fellow Royal Soc. Arts, Inst. Marketing, Brit. Inst. Mgmt.; mem. Brit. Pottery Mfrs. Fedn. (pres. 1970-71). Home: Parkfields Cottage Tittensor Stoke-on-Trent England Office: Wedgwood Ltd Barlaston Stoke on Trent Staffordshire England

BRYAN, CLARENCE PROCTOR, savs. assn. exec.; b. Hillsdale, Mich., June 28, 1910; s. Stanley I. and Betsy D. (Proctor) B.; A.B., Ohio U., 1932, M.A., 1933; LL.B., Cleve. Marshall Law Sch., 1939; m. Kathleen Conaway Bryan, Nov. 10, 1934; children—Nancy (Mrs. Ronald Fischer), William Reid, Betsy (Mrs. Kenneth Hegyes). With Cuyahoga Savs. Assn., Cleve., 1935—, pres., mng. officer, 1953—; dir. Fed. Home Loan Bank of Cin.; mem. Fed. Savs. & Loan Adv. Council. Trustee Real Property Inventory of Cleve., Fed. of Realty Interests, Building Owners and Mgrs. Assn.; trustee, treas. The Cleve. Internat. Program for Youth Leaders and Social Workers, Inc.; trustee, past pres. Greater Cleve. Neighborhood Centers Assn.; trustee Community Housing Corp., Cleve. Council on World Affairs. Mem. U.S. (exec. com., chmn. com. on capital stock assns., former chmn. com. on urban renewal), Ohio (exec. com., past pres.), Cuyahoga County (past pres.) savs. and loan leagues. Clubs: Shaker Heights Country; Cleve. Athletic. Home: 2901 Southington Rd Shaker Heights OH 44120 Office: 1 Erieview Plaza Cleveland OH 44114

BRYAN, COLGAN HOBSON, educator; b. Trenton, S.C., Oct. 7, 1909; s. John William and Mary (Hobson) B.; B.S. in Elec. Engring., U. S.C., 1932; M.Ed., Duke, 1940; M.S. in Aero. Engring., Ga. Inst. Tech., 1948; m. Sara Lucille Turbeville, June 18, 1938; 1 son, Colgan Hobson. Faculty U. Ala., 1942—, prof. aerospace engring., 1948—, chmn. dept., 1952—; research scientist NASA, 1962; on leave with U. Tenn. Space Inst., 1968-69; cons. to industry, 1941—. Mem. Ala. Aero. Commn., 1944-48. Registered profl. engr., Ala. Asso. fellow Am. Inst. Aero. and Astronautics; mem. Am. Soc. M.E., Am. Soc. Engring. Edn., Am. Ordnance Assn., Am. Assn. U. Profs., Nat., Ala. socs. profl. engrs., N.E.A., Ala. Edn. Assn. Episcopalian. Kiwanian (pres. Tuscaloosa 1966; recipient Service award 1966). Research projects in theoretical and applied aerodynamics. Home: 39 E Cherokee Hills Tuscaloosa AL 35401 Office: P O Box 1461 University AL 35486

BRYAN, COURTLANDT DIXON BARNES, author; b. N.Y.C., Apr. 22, 1936; s. Joseph III and Katharine (Barnes) O'Hara; B.; grad. Berkshire Sch., 1954; B.A. in English, Yale, 1958; m. Phoebe Miller, Dec. 28, 1961 (div. Sept 1966); children— J. St. George III, Lansing Becket; m. 2d, Judith Snyder, Dec. 21, 1967; 1 dau., Amanda Barnes. Writer-in-residence Colo. State U., winter 1967; vis. lectr. writers workshop U. Ia., 1967-69; editor Monocle mag., 1961—; spl. cons. editorial matters Yale, 1970. Served with AUS, 1958-60, 61-62. Club: Yale. Author: P.S. Wilkinson (Harper prize novel), 1965; The Great Dethriffe, 1970; also short stories, criticism, articles, polit. satire, introductions; rep. anthologies; narration Swedish film, The Face of War, 1963. Home: 56 Union St Guilford CT 06437 Office: care Brandt & Brandt 101 Park Av New York City NY 10022

BRYAN, DAVID TENNANT, newspaper pub.; b. Richmond, Va., Aug. 3, 1906; s. John Stewart and Anne Eliza (Tennant) B.; student U. of Va., 1925-28; m. Mary Harkness Davidson, May 11, 1932; children—Mary Tennant, John Stewart, Florence (Mrs. H.W. Robertson III). Chmn. dir. Media Gen., Inc.; publisher Richmond Times-Dispatch and Richmond News Leader; chmn. Tribune Co., Tampa, Fla.; dir. So. Ry.; dir., v.p. A.P. Mem. Adv. bd. Hoover Instn. trustee, v.p. Richmond Meml. Hosp.; trustee Va. Union U., Episcopal High Sch., Alexandria. Active duty U.S.N.R., 1942-46. Mem. Am. Newspaper Pubs. Assn. (pres. 1958-60); Soc. of Cincinnati, S.A.R., S.R. Soc. Colonial Wars, Sigma Delta Chi. Clubs: Commonwealth, Country of Va. (Richmond). Farmington Country (Charlottesville); St. Anthony, Union (N.Y.C.): Nat Press (Washington); Bohemian (San Francisco). Home Amthill Rd Richmond VA 23226 Office: 333 E Grace St Richmond VA 23213

BRYAN, FRED E., educator; b. Uledi, Pa., Apr. 7, 1908; s. James Edward and Lilliam (Marks) B.; B.S., California (Pa.) State Coll., 1932; M.A., Columbia Tchrs. Coll., 1936; D.Ed., U. Pitts., 1952; m. Elizabeth Nancy Murray, Apr. 4, 1931; 1 son, F. Murray. Elementary tchr. and prin., Pa., 1926-32; secondary sch. tchr., Pa., 1932-39; engaged in ins. bus., 1940-41; secondary sch. prin., Pa., 1942-46; supr. curriculum Uniontown, Pa., 1946-50, supt. schs., 1950-58; supt. schools, Harrisburg, Pa., 1958- 64; pres. Mansfield (Pa.) State Coll., 1964-68; exec. sec. Tri-State Area Sch. Study Council, also prof. edn. U. Pitts., 1968—. Dir. Harrisburg (Pa.) Area Center Higher Edn., 1960-63; pres. S. Central Ednl. TV Broadcasting Corp., 1963-64. Pres. Uniontown YMCA, 1955-56, Fayette County (Pa.) Tb Soc., 1952-58, Uniontown Community Concert Assn., 1950-58. Bd. dirs. Harrisburg Community Theatre, 1959-60; bd. mgrs. Harrisburg Hosp., 1959-63. Recipient Central Pa. Brotherhood award, 1962. Mem. Pa. Assn. Sch. Dists. of Second Class (pres. 1962-63), Am. Assn. Sch. Adminstrs. (adviser, Pa. adv. com. 1960-64), N.E.A. (life), Air Force Assn., Internat. Platform Assn., Phi Delta Kappa (pres. Gamma Rho chpt. 1960-61), Phi Sigma Pi, Delta Psi Omega. Presbyn. (elder). Rotarian, Mason. Home: 26 Beach Farm Rd Pennsboro Manor Wormleysburg (Harrisburg) PA 17043

BRYAN, FREDERICK VAN PELT, judge; b. Bklyn., Apr. 27, 1904; s. Frederick J. and Mary Elizabeth (van Pelt) B.; A.B., Columbia, 1925, LL.B., 1928; m. Denise Frances Farquharson, Apr. 4, 1945; children—Antonia Denise, Neville Johanna Farguharson. Admitted to N.Y. bar, 1929; asso. firm Spence, Hopkins & Walser, N.Y.C., 1928-33; asst. corp. counsel, City N.Y., 1933-37, 1st asst. corp. counsel, 1938-42; mem. firm Saxe, Bacon, O'Shea & Bryan, N.Y.C., 1946- 56; mem. State Commn. to Study Orgnl. Structure Govt. City N.Y., 1953- 54; counsel Temporary Commn. Cts. of State N.Y., 1954-56; U.S. dist. judge So. Dist. N.Y., 1956—. Rep. candidate for Congress, 18th Congl. Dist. N.Y., 1946; chmn. N.Y. State Eisenhower Clubs, 1952. Bd. dirs. Child Care Center, 1940-69, Windham Child Care, 1969—; trustee Columbia, 1967—, Buxton Sch., Brit. Am. Ednl. Found. Served with USAAF, 1942-45, col.; dep. chief staff 2d Air Div., 8th Air Force, col. Res. ret. Decorated Legion of Merit (U.S.); Officer Brit. Empire (Gt. Britain); Croix de Guerre with palm (France). Fellow Am. Coll. Trial Lawyers; mem. Columbia U. Alumni Fedn. (pres. 1951-55), Am., N.Y. State bar associations, Assn. Bar City N.Y., American Judicature Society (dir. 1968—), The Pilgrims, Inst. Jud. Adminstrn., Am. Law Inst., Phi Delta Phi, Delta Upsilon. Presbyn. Clubs: Century. Columbia University (N.Y.C.). Home: 426 E 89th St New York City NY 10028 Office: US Courthouse Foley Sq New York City NY 10007

BRYAN, GEORGE GREGORY, mining engr.; b. Carthage, Mo., Oct. 28, 1909; s. George Gregory and Nellie (James) B.; B.S., S.D. Sch. Mines, 1934; M.S., U. Utah, 1935; m. Gertrude I. Simkins, June 14, 1934; children—Barbara A. (Mrs. Miguel Zuniga), Margaret E. (Mrs. Robert Viers), Mary G. (Mrs. Jerry Robertson), Marcia S. (Mrs. John Verba), Robert E. Various postions, U.S. and S.A., 1935-41; foreman, TVA, 1941-42; supt. Metals Res. Co., Cuba, 1942-43; gen. supt. Chonta Mercury Mine, Peru, 1943-44; mgr. Abangerez Gold Mines, S.A., Costa Rica, 1944-47; pvt. mine operator, cons., Costa Rica, 1947-54; mining engr. Nat. Lead Co., N.Y.C., 1954-58; prodn. mgr. Nat. Lead Co., S.A., Argentina, 1958-64, also dir.; gen. mgr. Sedren, S.A., Haiti, 1964-66; with Behre Dolbear & Co., N.Y.C., 1966—, sr. mem., v.p., treas., 1967—. Mem. Am. Inst. Mining Engrs., Mining and Metall. Soc., Mining Club N.Y.C. Club: Explorers (N.Y.C.). Home: 8 Seymour Pl E Armonk NY 10504 Office: 299 Park Av New York City NY 10017

BRYAN, GORDON KEY, educator; b. Cleburne, Tex., Dec. 20, 1906; s. Benjamin Franklin and Myrtle (Young) B.; B.A., U. Tex., 1929, M.A., 1930; Ph.D. (Sloan Found. fellow, Gen. Edn. Bd. fellow), U. Cal. at Los Angeles, 1949; m. Lake Cummings, Aug. 18, 1929; 1 dau., Lynda Lake (Mrs. John W. Yount). High sch. tchr., Tex., 1930-37; instr. Miss. State U., 1937-38, asst. prof., 1938-42, asso. prof., 1942-49, prof. polit. sci., 1949—, acting head dept., 1942-45, head dept., 1963—; vis. prof. polit. sci. Vanderbilt U., 1955; edn. supr. engring., sci. Mgmt. War Tng. Program, 1942-44; cons. on govt., taxation Miss. Econ. Council, 1950—. Recipient Golden Triangle award Miss. State U. YMCA, 1957. Mem. Am., Miss. (pres. 1970-71), So., Western, Southwestern polit. sci. assns., Southwestern Social Sci. Assn., Blue Key, Phi Beta Kappa, Phi Kappa Phi, Pi Sigma Alpha, Lambda Chi Alpha. Presbyn. (elder). Rotarian. Contbr. articles profl. jours. Home: 27 Lakewood Dr Sheeley Hills Starkville MS 39762 Office: P O Box 114 State College MS 39762

BRYAN, JACK YEAMAN, author, photographer; b. Peoria, Ill., Sept. 24, 1907; s. James Yeaman and Regina (Gibson) B.; student U. Chgo., 1925-27; B.A. with high distinction, U. Ariz., 1932, M.A., 1933; postgrad. (fellow philosophy), Duke, 1933-35; Ph.D., U. Ia., 1939; m. Margaret Gardner, June 21, 1934; children—Joel Yeaman, Guy Kelsey, Donna Gardner, Kirsten Stuart. Research analyst Fed. Emergency Relief Adminstrn., Washington, 1935-36; from instr. English to prof., head dept. journalism U. Md., 1936-48; pub. relations adviser OCD, 1942-43; dir. pub. relations Welfare Fedn. Cleve., 1943-45; pub. information officer UNRRA, 1945-46; cultural attache Am. embassy, Manila, Philippines, 1948-51; chief program planning Internat. Exchange Service, State Dept., 1951-53; pub. affairs officer USIS, Bombay, India, 1953-54, Bangalore, India. 1954-55; cultural affairs officer embassy, Cairo, Egypt, 1956, Tehran, Iran, 1956-58; cultural attache, chief cultural affairs officer embassy, Karachi, Pakistan, 1958-63; chief personnel officer for Africa, USIA, 1964-65; officer in charge Project AIM, U.S. Dept. State, Washington, 1965, officer-in-charge spl. recruitment program Bur. Edn. and Cultural Affairs, 1965-67; chief cultural affairs adviser USIA, 1968; ret., 1968. Photog. exhibits one man shows, Pakistan, 1961-62, U.S., 1964, 66, perspectives Eastward on tour U.S., 1968-71. Chmn. publs. bd. U. Md., 1964-48; chmn. bd. dirs. U.S. Ednl. Founds, Philippines., 1949-51, Pakistan, 1958-63; exec. dir. Iran Am. Soc. in Tehran, 1956-58; founder, exec. dir. Pakistan-Am. Cultural Center, 1959-60, 62-63. Recipient ann. prize for best fiction Tex. Inst. Letters, 1964, Summerfield Roberts award, 1964. Mem. Tex. Inst. Letters, Nat., Tex. hist. assns., Am. Mus. Natural History, Arts Council Pakistan, Iran Am. Soc. U.S., Am. Fgn. Service Assn., Nat Parks and Conservation Assn., Phi Delta Theta, Delta Sigma Rho, Pi Kappa Phi, Phi Gamma Mu. Club: Sind (Karachi). Author: (novel) Come to the Bower, 1963. Contbr. short stories, articles, photographs to numerous mags. Home: 3594 Ramona Dr Riverside CA 92506; also 4107 Van Buren St University Park MD 20742

BRYAN, JAMES EDMUND, librarian; b. Easton, Pa., July 11, 1909; s. William Whitely and Florence (Shimer) B.; B.S., Lafayette Coll., 1931; B.L.S., Drexel Inst. Tech., 1932; M.A., Am. U., 1937; Litt. D., Rutgers U., 1964; m. Helen Elizabeth Lamb, July 2, 1938; children—James Edmund, Arthur Lamb. Library asst. Pub. Library, Washington, 1932-36; librarian Pub. Library, Easton, 1936- 38; head adult lending dept. Carnegie Library of Pitts., 1938-43; asst. dir. Newark Pub. Library, 1943-58, dir., 1958—. Chmn. Middle Atlantic States Regional Library Conf., 1949; chmn. adv. bd. Grad. Sch. Library Service, Rutgers U. Recipient 70th Anniversary Alumni citation Drexel Inst. Tech., 1961. Mem. A.L.A. (council, exec. bd. 1961-64, pres. 1962- 63), Pub. Library Assn. (pres. 1959-60), N.J. Library Assn. (pres. 1952- 54), Delta Upsilon, Beta Phi Mu. Democrat. Presbyn. Kiwanian. Cons. on library bldgs. Contbr. to profl. periodicals. Home: 666 Highland Av Newark NJ 07104 Office: 5 Washington St Newark NJ 07101

BRYAN, JAMES EDWARD, cons., adminstr. sci. societies; b. Asbury Park, N.J., Apr. 6, 1906; s. Joseph Harker and Irene (Dobbins) B.; Ph.B., Wesleyan U., Conn., 1927; m. Lucile Marvin Elder, Dec. 1, 1928 (div. 1970): children—Faith Elder Faith Elder (Mrs. Hedley V. Tingley), June Harker (Mrs. Samuel R. Boorujy, Jr.). Lay mgr. Am. Inst. Homeopathy, N.Y.C., 1929-31; exec. sec. Westchester County (N.Y.) Med. Soc., mng. editor Westchester Med. Bull., 1933- 44; exec. sec. N.Y. County Med. Soc., also mng. editor N.Y. Medicine, 1944-47; exec. officer Med. Soc. N.J., 1947-50; adminstr. Med.-Surg. Plan N.J., 1950-55: med. adminstrn. cons., 1955—; exec. sec. Nat. Med. Found Eye Care, 1956-63; research asso. administrv. medicine Columbia Sch. Pub. Health and Administrv. Medicine, 1956-63; exec. sec. Am. Fedn. Clin. Research, 1958-70, Am. Med. Writers Assn., 1962-66; exec. dir. Am. Soc. Information Sci., 1964-70, Nat. Investor Relations Inst., 1969—; dir. Washington office Nat. Assn. Blue Shield Plans, 1963-70; pres. Med. Soc. Execs. Assn., 1950. Professorial lectr. George Washington U. Med. Sch., 1969—; lectr. community medicine and internat. health Georgetown U. Sch. Medicine. Pres., Westchester Tb and Health Assn., 1940-41, Tb and Health Assn. So. Fairfield County, Conn., 1963-64. Trustee N.J. Soc. Crippled Children and Adults, 1948-56, v.p., 1955-56. Fellow Am. Med. Writers Assn., A.A.A.S.; mem. Nat. Assn. Sci. Writers, Assn. Am. Med. Colls., Washington Assn. N.J., Am. Soc. for Information Sci. (hon. life). Club: National Press (Washington). Author: Public Relations in Medical Practice, 1954; The Role of the Family Physician in America's Developing Medical Care Program, 1968, Contbr. articles to profl. jours. Home: 1255 New Hampshire Av NW Washington DC 20036 Office: 2011 Eye St NW Washington DC 20006

BRYAN, JOHN EDWARD, editor; b. Cleve., Nov. 24, 1913; s. Charles F. and Rose (Matt) B.; student Adelbert Coll., 1931-34, Western Res. U.; m. Allane Hoyt Horner, Nov. 25, 1933; children—John C., Nancy; m. 2d, Helen Urban, Jan. 6, 1944. Promotion and pub. relations dir. Gen. Outdoor Advt. Co., 1934-40; estate analyst Conn. Gen. Life Ins. Co., 1940-41; asst. promotion dir. Cleve. Press, 1942; editor lamp publ. Gen. Electric Co., 1943-45; financial editor Cleveland Plain Dealer, 1945—. Mem. Cleve. Soc. Sec. Analysts, Nat. Security Traders Assn., Soc. Am. Bus. Writers, Alpha Delta Phi, Sigma Delta Chi. Club: Mid-Day. Contbr. articles mags. Home: 22420 Edgecliff Dr Euclid OH 44123 Office: 1801 Superior Av Cleveland OH 44114

BRYAN, JOSEPH, III, writer; b. Richmond, Va., Apr. 30, 1904; s. Joseph St. George and Emily Page (Kemp) B.; grad. Episcopal High Sch., A.B., Princeton, 1927; m. 1930, div. 1954; children—St. George II (dec. 1969), Joan (Mrs. Peter Gates), Courtlandt D. B.; m. 2d, Jacqueline de la Grandière, 1960. Reporter and editorial writer Richmond News Leader, also Chgo. Jour., 1928-31; asso. editor Parade, Cleve., 1931-32; mng. editor Town & Country, 1933-36; asso. editor Sat. Eve. Post, 1937-40; freelance writer, 1940—. Trustee and fellow Va. Mus. Fine Arts. Spl. asst. to sec. USAF, 1952-53. Served as lt. U.S. Field Arty. Res., 1927-37; lt. comdr. USNR, 1942-53; col. USAFR, 1953-62. Recipient Distinguished Pub. Service award USN. Mem. Va. Hist. Soc., Soc. Cincinnati, Soc. Colonial Wars. Episcopalian. Clubs: Commonwealth (Richmond); Buck's (London, Eng.); Ivy (Princeton); Racquet and Tennis (N.Y.C.); 1925 F St. (Washington). Author: (with Philip Reed) Mission Beyond Darkness, 1945; (with Admiral Halsey) Admiral Halsey's Story, 1947; Aircraft Carrier, 1954; The World's Greatest Showman, 1956; The Sword Over the Mantel, 1960. Home: Brook Hill Richmond VA 23227

BRYAN, JOSEPH MCKINLEY, ins. co. exec.; b. Elyria, O., Feb. 11, 1896; s. Bart and Caroline (Ebert) B.; ed. Mount Hermon Sch.; LL.D., Belmont (N.C.) Abbey Coll.; m. Kathleen Marshall Price, Nov. 1927; children—Kay (Mrs. Bryan Edwards), Nancy Ann (Mrs. D. McLauchlin Faircloth), Joseph McKinley. Mem. N.Y. Cotton Exchange, 1923-31; with Jefferson Standard Life Ins. Co., 1931-61, now dir., mem. exec. com.; chmn. bd., dir. Jefferson Standard Broadcasting Co., owners and operators stas. WBT, WBTV, Charlotte; hon. chmn., dir. exec. com. Pilot Life Ins. Co.; pres., dir. Carolina Apt. Hotel Corp., Raleigh, N.C. Chmn. financial sect. Am. Life Conv., 1948-49, pres., 1955-56. Chmn. N.C. Bd. Elections, 1960-61. Bd. govs., Shriner's Hosp. for Crippled Children, Greenville. Served with U.S. Army, World War I; AEF. Mem. Southeastern Shrine Assn. (past pres.), Sigma Chi. Mason (Shriner). Clubs: Rotary, Bath and Tennis, Everglades, Merchant and Manufacturers, Greensboro Country, Sedgefield Country, Starmount Country (Greensboro); Rolling Rock (Ligonier, Pa.); Nat. Golf (Augusta, Ga.); Metropolitan (Washington); City (Charlotte, N.C.); Lyford Cay (Nassau, Bahamas). Home: 711 Sunset Dr Greensboro NC 27408 Office: P O Box 21008 Greensboro NC 27420

BRYAN, JOSEPH SHEPARD, Jr., lawyer, retail grocery exec.; b. Wilson, N.C., Nov. 8, 1922; s. Joseph Shepard and Anna (Cavenaugh) B.; student Campbell Coll., 1939-40, U. N.C., 1940-41; B.S. in Engring., U.S. Naval Acad., 1944; LL.B., Harvard, 1950; m. Mary Ann Shands, Aug. 10, 1950; children—Ann Shands, Frances Evans, Mary Courtney, Helen Harris, Joseph Shepard, III. Admitted to N.C. bar, 1950, Fla. bar, 1955; asst. research prof. publ. law and govt., asst. dir. Inst. Govt., U. N.C. at Chapel Hill, 1950-54; asst. sec., head legal dept. Winn-Dixie Stores, Inc., Jacksonville, Fla., 1954- 61; sec. Winn-Dixie Stores, Inc., Jacksonville, Fla., 1961—, v.p., 1966- -, gen. counsel, 1961—. Sec. Jacksonville Symphony Assn., 1966—; trustee Bartram Sch., Jacksonville, 1961—, pres., 1965-66; trustee Jacksonville Art Mus., 1967—. Served to lt. USNR, 1944-47; PTO; 1951-52; Korea. Mem. Jacksonville Area C. of C., Am., N.C., Fla., Jacksonville bar assns., Am. Soc. Corporate Secretaries, Democrat. Presbyn. Clubs: Deerwood, Timuguana Country (Jacksonville); Ponte Vedra (Ponte Vedra Beach); St. Johns Dinner, Menianak (Jacksonville). Home: 4823 Apache Av Jacksonville FL 32210 Office: 5050 Edgewood Ct Jacksonville FL 32203

BRYAN, JULIEN, documentary film maker; b. Titusville, Pa., May 23, 1899; A.B., Princeton, 1921; B.D., Union Theol. Sem., 1926; m. Marian Knighton, Dec. 25, 1936; 1 son, Samuel Knighton. After completing theol. studies, served as dir. boys work, Bklyn. YMCA several years; toured Russia, 1930, on return, gave lectures while operating film; lectured with Burton Holmes 1933; has photographed Russia, Japan, China, Turkey, Poland (notably the bombardment and fall of Warsaw in film, "Slege"), Finland, Nazi Germany (for The March of Time), Afghanistan, The South American countries and Mexico; observer for UNRRA, western Russia, 1946-47; produced over 30 U.S. documentaries for U.S. Dept. State for use fgn. countries; exec. dir. Internat. Film Found., 1945-71. Documentary films Japan 1957, Russia, Middle East, 1958. Presbyn. Clubs: University, Overseas Press, Coffee House, Explorers, Circumnavigators, Dutch Treat, Princeton (N.Y.C.); Adventurers (Chgo.). Author and photographer: Ambulance 464, Siege, Warsaw, 1960; recent films include: Japan, 1957; Russia, 1958; Middle East, 1959; South America, 1960; Tropical Africa, 1961, Amazon Family, 1961, Yugoslavia, 1962, Turkey, 1962, Africans All, 1963, Ancient Egyptian, 1964, Poland, 1965, Israel, 1965; African Village Life (Mali), 1967; Ancient Peruvian (with Sam Bryan), 1968; Mountain Peoples of Central Asia, 1968; First Americans, 1969; Ancient Africans (with Sam Bryan). Home: 200 Boulder Trail Bronxville NY 10708 Office: 475 Fifth Av New York City NY 10017

BRYAN, LESLIE AULLS, transp. economist; b. Bath, N.Y., Feb. 23, 1900; s. Daniel Beach and Anna (Aulls) B.; B.S., Syracuse U., 1923, M.S., 1924, J.D., 1939; Ph.D., Am. U., 1930; m. Gertrude Catherine Gelder, Aug. 22, 1931; children—Leslie A., George G. Prof. bus. adminstrn. Southwestern Coll., Winfield, Kan., 1924-25; asst. coach of track Syracuse U., 1925-42, dir. of athletics, 1934-37. also instr., 1925-28, asst. prof. transp., 1928-31, asso. prof., 1931-39, prof., 1939-45. Franklin prof. transp., 1945-46; also pres. Seneca Flying Sch., Syracuse, N.Y., 1943-46; dir. Inst. Aviation, prof. mgmt. U. Ill. 1946-68, emeritus, 1968—; aviation adv. bd. Norwich U., 1954-59; mem. Pres. Kennedy's Task Force on Aviation Goals, 1961; U. Ill. faculty rep. Intercollegiate Conf. (Big Ten), 1959-68, dir. athletics, 1965-66. Bd. dirs. Nat. Found. For Asthmatic Children, 1956-65. Served as lt., inf. and Air Corps, U.S. Army, 1917-19; overseas, 1918-19; col. USAF Res. ret. Dir. aviation, State of N.Y., 1945. Pres. Eastern Intercoll. Boxing Assn., 1936-38, N.Y. State Aviation Council, 1944-46, Traffic Club of Syracuse. 1942. Transp. cons. Nat. Resources Planning Bd., 1942-44; aviation cons., New Standard Endv., 1947—, mem. net. Aerospace ednl. adv. com. Civil Air Patrol; mem. bd. aero. advisors State of Ill., 1949-69 tech. assistance bd. Link Found., 1953-71; adv. com. FCDA, 1957-60; chmn. Gen. Aviation Facilities Planning Group, 1957-58; adv. com. Washington Internat. Airport, 1958-62; cons. Fed. Aviation Agy., 1959-62; mem. adv. bd. Air Tng. Command, 1964, cons., 1965-69. Pres. Arrowhead council Boy Scouts Am., 1954-60, mem. at large nat. council, 1960—, regional exec. bd., 1959—. Awarded Sec. War Commdn., 1946; Arents Medal, 1955; Brewer Trophy, 1953; Sigma Delta Chi award, 1955; Air Power Award, 1956; Silver Beaver award Boy Scouts Am., 1957, Silver Antelope, 1959; Tissandier diploma Fedn. Aeronautique Internat., 1958; distinguished service award Am. Assn. Airport Execs. 1959; Continental Air Command certificate of recognition, 1960, Nat. Aero Assn. certificate of recognition, 1966, FAA distinguished pub. service award, 1965, Elder Statesman of Aviation, 1966, Distinguished Alumni award Am. U., 1969, Letterman of Distinction award Syracuse U., 1969, Patriots medal S.A.R., 1968. Fellow U. Aviation Assn. (pres., 1948-49: Wheatley award 1955); mem. Am. Soc. Traffic and Transp. (bd. examiners 1948-60), Nat. Aerospace Edn. Council (pres. 1952-53, 64-66, dir. 1953-54, 59-64, 66-67), National Aero Association (v.p. 1953-56, 60-61, 65-66, dir. 1950- 52, 54-55, 57-59, 62-64), Civil Air Patrol (Distinguished Service award 1954), Am. Assn. Airport Execs. (v.p. 1953-55; pres. 1955-56, dir. edn. 1952-68, hon. life mem.), Am. Inst. Aeros. and Astronautics, Acad. Mgmt., Assn. ICC Practitioners, Aerospace Writers Assn., Newcomen Soc. No. Am., Scabbard and Blade. Arnold Air Soc., Pershing Rifles, Sigma Alpha Tau, Alpha Eta Rho, Phi Gamma Mu, Zeta Psi, Phi Delta Phi, Phi Kappa Alpha, Alpha Kappa Psi, Phi Kappa Phi, Alpha Phi Omega, Kappa Phi Kappa, Alpha Delta Sigma, Delta Nu Alpha, Tau Omega, Beta Gamma Sigma. Author: Principles of Water Transportation, 1939; Aviation Study Manual (with others), 1949; Air Transportation, 1949; Fundamentals of Aviation and Space Technology, rev. 1968; Traffic Management in Industry, 1953; also monographs and articles. Adv. editor Nat. Air Rev., 1948-50; editorial adviser (aeros.) Holt. Rinehart & Winston. Inc., 1960- 64; bd. editors Air Affairs, 1949-51; cons. Our Wonderful World, 1954- 55; contbr. World Book Ency., 1952—, Compton's Pictured Ency., 1959—, McGraw Hill Ency. of Sci. and Tech., 1959—. cons. editor Above and Beyond Ency., 1967—. Home: 1016 W John St Champaign IL 61820

BRYAN, R. L., savs. and loan assn. exec. Pres., Des Moines Savs. and Loan Assn. Office: 210 6th Av Des Moines IA 50309*

BRYAN, RAY JAMES, educator; b. Bavaria, Kan., Sept. 16, 1909; s. James Clarence and Alice Amna (Fultz) B.; B.S., Kan. State Coll., 1933, M.S., 1937; Ph.D., U. Neb., 1940; m. Helen Marie Horner, June 16, 1934; children—Robert Ray, Joe Charles, James Lee. Tchr. pub. schs., Kan., 1930-38; grad. asst. U. Neb., 1938-40; dir. tchr. edn. Kan. Wesleyan U., 1940-41; head dept. edn., dir. Campus Sch., Neb. State Tchrs. Coll., 1941-44. dean, 1944-46; asso. prof., dir. tchr. placement Ia. State U., 1946-50, head department education, 1950—. Fellow Ia. Acad. Sci.; mem. Ia. (pres. 1959-60), Nat. edn. assns. , Am. Ednl. Research Assn., Am., Ia. vocational assns., Nat. Soc. Study Edn., Phi Delta Kappa, Gamma Sigma Delta, Phi Kappa Phi, Acacia. Methodist. Home: 918 Garfield St Ames IA 50010

BRYAN, ROBERT FESSLER, investment analyst; b. New Castle, Pa., Jan 19, 1913; s. Harry A. and Nell (Fessler) B.; A.B. summa cum laude, Oberlin Coll., 1934; Ph.D., Yale, 1939; m. Elaine A. Norwood, Sept. 7, 1940; children—Diane Elaine (Mrs. James M. Lyon), and Barbara Norwood (Mrs. Michael C. Bowen); m. 2d, Dorothy Darr MacKenzie, Aug. 11, 1961. Instr. econs. Yale, 1935-36, 37- 39, Princeton. 1936-37: economist Lionel D. Edie & Co., Inc., N.Y.C., 1939-40, asst. v.p., 1943-45, v.p. 1946-48: price exec., rubber br. OPA, 1941-42: economist Goodyear Aircraft Corp., Akron, O., 1943; with J.H. Whitney & Co., N.Y.C., 1948-50. partner, 1951-59: financial v.p., treas., dir. Whitney Communications Corp., 1959-69; dir. Edie Growth Fund; partner Whitcom Investment Co., 1967-69. Mem. exec. com. Yale Graduate Sch. Council; trustee Oberlin Coll., 1960-70. Mem. Am. Mgmt. Assn (finance council 1952-55), Phi Beta Kappa. Clubs: Ocean, Delray Dunes Golf (Delray Beach, Fla.); Apawamis (Rye, N.Y.): Economic, Board Room (N.Y.C.). Home: 600 Purchase St Rye NY 10580 also 6823 N Ocean Blvd Delray Beach FL 33444 Office: 100 Park Av New York City NY 10017

BRYAN, ROBERT SEDGWICK, educator; b. South River, N.J., July 14, 1925; s. Wilbur Aaron and Mazie Tremaine (Brown) B.; student Lafayette Coll., 1946-48; B.A., U. Va., 1950, M.A., 1952, Ph.D., 1956; m. Geraldine Parker Jones, Aug. 29, 1948; children—Robert Sedgwick, Sherwood Parker, William Samuel. Prof. philosophy, chmn. dept. Thiel Coll., Greenville, Pa., 1958-65; asso. prof., dep. chmn. dept. Wright State U., Dayton, O., 1965-66; prof., head dept. philosophy and religion N.C. State U., Raleigh, 1966—. Served with USNR, 1943-45. DuPont fellow, 1950-52. Mem. Am. Philos. Assn., N.C. Philos. Soc., So. Soc. Philosophy and Psychology, Raven Soc., Phi Beta Kappa. Home: 2301 Tyson St Raleigh NC 27609

BRYAN, W. CARROLL, banker. Chmn. bd. Bank N.C., N.A. Office: 235 New River Dr Jacksonville NC 28540*

BRYAN, WILLIAM WELLINGTON, ret. petroleum co. exec.; b. Petersburg, Va., Nov. 26, 1905; s. Willie Wellington and Susie Logan (Northington) B.; grad. Advanced Mgmt. Program, Harvard, 1946; m. Georgia Chaffin Hudson, Aug. 1, 1927; children—William Wellington, Robert Hudson. With Standard Oil Co. (N.J.), 1923-56; v.p. marketing, dir. Carter Oil Co., 1956-60; pres. Esso Standard Oil Co., 1960-61; v.p., dir. Humble Oil & Refining Co., 1961-70; ret., 1970. Bd. dirs. United Fund, Family Service; mem. exec. bd. Boy Scouts Am.; mem. exec. com. Welfare Planning Assn. Mem. Am. Petroleum Inst., Am. Soc. Corporate Execs., Petroleum Club Houston. Mason. Clubs: Houston, River Oaks Country (Houston). Home: 5625 Briar Dr Houston TX 77027

BRYAN, WILLIAM WHITELEY, librarian; b. Easton, Pa., Dec. 31, 1911; s. William Whiteley and Florence C. (Shimer) B.; B.S., Lafayette Coll., 1935; B.S. in L.S., Drexel Inst. Tech., 1936; postgrad. Columbia, also U. Pitts.; m. Elizabeth Overton, Aug. 24, 1940; children—Anne Dickerson, Richard W. Br. asst. Bklyn. Pub. Library, 1936-40; asst. librarian Lafayette Coll., 1940-44; asst. to dir. Carnegie Library, Pitts., 1946-48; librarian Scranton (Pa.) Pub. Library, 1948-55; dir. Peoria (Ill.) Pub. Library, 1955—, Ill. Valley Library System, 1966-70. Served with AUS, 1945-46. Mem. Am. (council 1965-69), Pa. (pres. 1952-53), Ill. (pres. 1962-63; Library citation 1964) library assns. Home: 1523 E Marietta St Peoria Heights IL 61614 Office: 107 N E Monroe St Peoria IL 61602

BRYAN, WRIGHT, ret. univ. adminstr., former editor; b. Atlanta, Aug. 6, 1905; s. Arthur Buist and Inez (Sledge) B.; B.S., Clemson Coll., 1926, Litt.D., 1956; U. Mo. Sch. Journalism, 1926-27; LL.D., Coll. of Wooster, 1958; m. Ellen Hillyer Newell, Oct. 12, 1932; children—Ellen Newell (Mrs. N. Bryan Tozzer), Mary Lane (Mrs. John K. Sullivan), William Wright. Reporter, 1924, sports editor, 1926, Greenville (S.C.) Piedmont; with Atlanta Jour., 1927-53, successively reporter, city editor, mng. editor, asso. editor and mng. editor, editor, 1945-53; editor Cleve. Plain Dealer, 1954-63; v.p. devel. Clemson (S.C.) U., 1964-70; war corr. for Atlanta Jour. and NBC, 1943-45; captured by German army, Sept. 12, 1944, liberated Jan. 22, 1945. Chmn. Ga., Press. Inst., 1942, Atlanta chpt. A.R.C., 1950-51; pres. Atlanta Rotary Club, 1953; first v.p. Welfare Fedn. of Cleveland, 1960-61. Bd. overseers, bd. dirs. Sweet Briar College. Recipient Medal of Freedom for services as war corr. Mem. Am. Soc. Newspaper Editors (pres. 1953); Clemson Alumni Assn. (pres. 1958), Sigma Delta Chi, 1958), Sigma Delta Chi, Phi Kappa Psi. Methodist. Clubs: Capital City, Piedmont Driving, Nine O'Clocks (Atlanta); Overseas Press (N.Y.C.); Poinsett (Greensville, S.C.). Home: 100 Wyatt Av Clemson SC 29631

BRYANS, HENRY BUSSELL, cons. engr.; b. Phila., Mar. 26, 1886; s. Henry M. and Ella (Lonergan) B.; A.B., Central High School, Phila., 1903; B.S. in mech. engring., U. of Pa., 1907; m. Ada Matilda Trinkle, May 1, 1911; children—Henry Trinkle, Robert Trinkle. Began as engr. United Gas Improvement Co., 1907; gen. supt. Phila. Suburban-Counties Gas & Electric Co., 1927-28, asst. gen. mgr. Phila. Electric Co., 1928-29, v.p. in charge operations, 1929-38, exec. v.p., 1938-47, dir., 1940-52, pres., 1947-52; v.p., dir. United Engrs. & Constructors, Inc., 1952-55; dir. mem. exec. com. Bellevue-Stratford Hotel; dir. Baldwin Securities Corp.; mem. bd. mgrs. emeritus Western Sav. Fund Soc. of Phila. Mem. electrical utility Def. Adv. Council, 1950-51. Life trustee past chmn., mem. finance, investment and devel. coms., exec. bd. U. Pa. Fellow Royal Soc. Arts, Manufactures and Commerce; mem. Am. Standards Assn. (past pres.), Am. Soc. M.E., I.E.E.E., Franklin Inst. (bd. mgrs., past chmn., mem. finance com., past mem. exec. com.), Pa. Elec. Assn. (past pres.), Elec. Assn. Phila. (past pres.), Hist. Soc. Pa., Newcomen Soc., Pa. Soc. N.Y. Republican. Presbyterian. Mason. Clubs: Engineers, Union League (past pres.), Midday (Phila.); Penn., Sunday Breakfast. Home: 515 Lynmere Rd Bryn Mawr PA 19010 Office: 101 S Broad St Philadelphia PA 19107

BRYANS, ROBERT E., banker. Pres., First Nat. Bank Casper (Wyo.). Office: 1st and Wolcott Sts Casper WY 82601*

BRYANT, ANITA JANE, (Mrs. Robert Einar Green), entertainer; b. Barnsdall, Okla., Mar. 25, 1940; d. Warren Gene and Lenora (Cate) Bryant; student Northwestern U., Chgo., 1959; m. Robert Einar Green, June 25, 1960; children—Robert Einar, Gloria Lynn, William Bryant and Barbara Elisabet (twins). Miss. Okla. and runner-up in Miss Am. contest, 1959; guest star Bob Hope's Christmas Tours, 1960-67; sang Star Spangled Banner for Democratic and Republican Nat. Convs., 1968; numerous White House performances, 1964-69; numerous Billy Graham Evangelistic Crusades, 1965—; performed at Orange Bowl and Super Bowl games, 1970-71; television, recording artist, author, 1971—; spokeswoman for Coca-Cola Co., 1963-67, State of Fla. Citrus Industry, 1968—, Friedrich Air Conditioning Co., 1969—. Mem. U.S.O. Nat. Council, 1961-66; bd. mem. Womens U.S.O. of N.Y., 1965—; hon. chmn. Freedoms Found. at Valley Forge, 1969-70; hon. chmn. First Found. for One Nation Under God, 1969—; mem. Am. Orchid Soc., 1970—, Friends of Art Soc., 1970—; com. mem. Project Survival, 1970—; film narrator Drugs Are Like That, 1970; hon. chmn. Mental Health Assn. Fla., 1970—. Recipient U.S.O. 25th Ann. Silver Medallion award, 1966, V.F.W. Gold medal and citation award, 1966, Leadership award Freedoms Found. at Valley Forge, 1969, Woman of Year award, 1970; nominated for Grammy award for best religious recording of How Great Thou Art, 1968; named to Okla. Hall of Fame, 1966. Mem. U. Tampa Alumni Assn. (hon.), Fla. Future Bus. Leader of Am. Author: Mine Eyes Have Seen the Glory, 1970; Amazing Grace, 1971. Most recent Sacred recording Abide With Me, 1971. Address: 4682 North Bay Rd Miami Beach FL 33140

BRYANT, BILLY FINNEY, educator; b. McKenzie, Tenn., Nov. 29, 1922; s. Robert Picard and Ray Ona (Pace) B.; B.S., U. S.C., 1945; M.A., Peabody Coll., 1948; Ph.D., Vanderbilt U., 1954; m. Mary Nelle Park, Aug. 28, 1946; children—Robert, David, Elizabeth. Mem. faculty Vanderbilt U., 1948—, asst. prof. math., 1954-60, asso. prof., 1960-66, prof., 1966—, chmn. dept., 1970—. Served with USNR, 1942-46. Ford Found. Faculty fellow Princeton, 1955-56; NSF Faculty fellow U. Cal. at Berkeley, 1967-68. Mem. Am. Math. Soc., Math. Assn. Am. (sec.-treas. Southeastern sect.). Research publs. in topology. Home: 6020 Sherwood Dr Nashville TN 37212

BRYANT, CECIL FARRIS, former gov. Fla., lawyer; b. Ocala, Fla., July 26, 1914; s. Charles Cecil and Lela (Farris) B.; student Emory U., 1931-32; B.S., U. Fla., 1935; J.D., Harvard, 1938; LL.D., Rollins Coll., Fla. State U., Fla. Atlantic U., Fla. So. Coll.; m. Julia Burnett, Sept. 18, 1940; children—Julie Lovett, Cecilia Ann, Allison Adair. Admitted to Fla. bar, 1938; pvt. practice, Ocala, 1940-60; mem. firm Green, Bryant & Simons, 1946- 60; gov. Fla., 1961-65; partner firm Bryant, Freeman, Richardson & Watson, attys., Jacksonville, Fla., 1965-70; mem. firm Bryant, Dickens, Rumph, Franson & Miller, 1970—. Chmn. bd. Eagle Nat. Life Ins. Co.; pres. Nat. Life Fla. Corp., Voyager Life Ins. Co. Dir. Office Emergency Planning, Exec. Office Pres., 1966-67; chmn. Fla. Citizenship Clearing House, 1953-54; mem. Nat. Security Council, 1966-67; chmn. adv. Commn. on Intergovtl. Relations, 1966-69. Mem. Fla. Ho. of Reps., 1942, 46-56, speaker, 1953-54; del. Democratic Nat. Conv., 1952, alternate del., 1960, chmn. Fla. delegation, 1964, del., 1968. Trustee Fla. So. Coll., Jacksonville U. Served from ensign to lt. USNR, 1942-46. Recipient Gold Key distinguished service award Fla. Jr. C. of C., 1948, 50, nat. distinguished service award U.S. Jr. C. of C., 1948. Mem. Am. Bar Assn., Am. Legion, V.F.W., Marion County C. of C. (pres. 1950), Fla. Jr. C. of C. (v.p. 1948), Fla. Bar, Alpha Kappa Psi, Alpha Tau Omega, Phi Delta Phi, Kappa Delta Phi. Methodist (trustee Fla. conf. 1954-64). Mason (Shriner), Elk (exalted ruler 1948), Rotarian (local pres. 1948). Co-author: Government and Politics of Florida. Home: 1870 Challen Av Jacksonville FL 32205 Office: Box 2918 Jacksonville FL 32203

BRYANT, DANIEL PENNINGTON, van and storage co. exec.; b. Waukegan, Ill., Sept. 28, 1908; s. Daniel and Emma (Dempcy) B.; A.B., Stanford, 1931, J.D., 1934; m. Noel Walster, Dec. 25, 1932; children—Rachel, Dan W., David W. Admitted to Cal. bar, 1934; mem. firm Chase, Barnes & Chase, Los Angeles, 1934-43; v.p., sec. Bekins Moving & Storage Co., Los Angeles, 1943-45, gen. mgr., 1945-57, pres., 1957-68, chmn. bd., chief exec. officer, 1968-; chmn. bd. chief exec. officer The Bekins Co., 1968—; dir. Bank of Am. Nat. Trust & Savs. Assn., Pacific Tel & Tel. Co., Pacific Lighting Co., Olga Co. Bd. dirs. Greater Los Angeles Urban Coalition; trustee Occidental Coll., Los Angeles, Com. Econ. Devel.; regent ct. of honor Forest Lawn Meml. Park, Glendale, Cal.; mem. corp. Conf. Bd. Mem. Nat. Furniture Warehousemen's Assn. (past pres.), Mchts. and Mfrs. Assn. Los Angeles (past pres.,dir.), Los Angeles C. of C. (dir. past pres.,). Conglist. Clubs: California, Bohemian, Lincoln (past pres.). Home: 625 Burleigh Dr Pasadena CA 91105 Office: 1335 S Figueroa St Los Angeles CA 90015

BRYANT, DAVID LOGAN, ret. coll. dean; b. Sallisaw, Okla., Oct. 4, 1907; s. Julian Lytle and Lelia Mattie (Logan) B.; B.S. in Bus. Adminstrn., U. So. Cal., 1929, Ed.D., 1951; M.A. in Econs., Stanford U., 1933; m. Marjorie Lenore Hull, Sept. 10, 1929 (dec.); children—Marcia Lenore (Mrs. William L. Tyra), Penelope Anne (Mrs. Robert L. Turk); m. 2d, Wilma Hastings, July 18, 1968. Asst. prof. bus. and econs. U. Puget Sound, 1929-31; grad. teching asst. econs. Stanford, 1931-33; procedural analyst, budget analyst, orgn. and methods cons. U.S. Govt., 1933-42, 46- 47; lectr. personnel adminstrn. and pub. adminstrn. U. So. Cal., 1947- 48; asso. prof. bus. Los Angeles State Coll., 1948-49; faculty Long Beach (Cal.) State Coll., 1949-69, dean students, 1949-51, exec. dean coll., 1951-69, also sec.-treas. coll. found. and sec. coll. adv. bd.; ednl. cons. So. Cal. regional office State Farm Mut. Ins. Co., 1955-64. Chmn. bd. Forty-Niner Shops, Inc., 1949-66. Pres. Community Welfare Council Long Beach, 1955-57. Adv. bd. Long Beach Children's Theatre 1956—; bd. dirs. Long Beach Community Chest, 1955- 57, Long Beach Area council Boy Scouts Am., 1953-56; Long Beach Travelers Aid Soc., 1967, bd. dirs. Long Beach YMCA, 1963-68, sec., 1967-68. Served to lt. col. AUS, 1942-46. Mem. Navy League U.S., Alpha Phi Omega, Phi Kappa Tau (Alumni award 1957), Phi Kappa Phi, Alpha Kappa Psi, Beta Gamma Sigma, Phi Delta Kappa, Delta Phi Epsilon, Pi Delta Epsilon, Epsilon Pi Tau. Methodist (trustee). Mason (33, Shriner, K.T.). Rotarian (sec.-treas. 1965-66). Club: Long Beach Dinner (pres. 1957-58). Home: 31158 Flying Cloud Dr Laguna Niguel CA 92677

BRYANT, DONALD CROSS, educator; b. N.Y.C., Sept. 17, 1905; s. William Ashbrook and Rebecca Louise (Cross) B.; A.B., Cornell, 1927, A.M., 1930, Ph.D., 1937; m. Mary Mildred Osborne, June 25, 1932. Tchr. history and math. Ardsley (N.Y.) High Sch., 1927-29; instr. English, N.Y. State Coll. for Tchrs., 1929-37; asst. prof. English, Washington U., 1937-43, asso. prof., 1943-48, prof., 1948-50, prof. speech and English, 1950-58, chmn. dept. English, 1956- 58, dir. div. speech, 1948-58; prof. speech U. Ia., 1958- -, also research prof., spring 1962; lectr. cons. U. So. Cal., May 1966, vis. prof. speech, summer 1956; vis. prof. speech U. Wash., summer 1969; vis. scholar U. Center Va., 1971. Mem. Am. Assn. U. Profs., Modern Lang. Assn. Am., Speech Communication Assn. Am. (2d v.p. 1968, 1st v.p. 1969, pres. 1970), Phi Beta Kappa, Phi Kappa Phi, Delta Sigma Rho. Author: Edmund Burke and his Literary Friends, 1939; Papers in Rhetoric (ed.), 1940; (with K.R. Wallace) Fundamentals of Public Speaking, 1947-68; (with K.R. Wallace) Oral Communication, 1948-62; (with O.G. Brockett and S.L. Becker) Bibliographical Guide to Research in Speech and Drama, 1963. Editor and contbr. The Rhetorical Idiom, 1958; Papers in Rhetoric and Poetic, 1965; joint editor: History and Criticism of American Public Address, 1955; editor, joint compiler: Select British Speeches, 1967; editor Ancient Greek and Roman Rhetoricians: A Biographical Dictionary, 1968. Editor Quar. Jour. Speech, 1957-59. Contbr. to jours. Home: 903 Highwood St Iowa City IA 52240

BRYANT, DONALD H., banker; b. Eaton, O., Mar. 27, 1919; s. Virgil L. and Marquerite (Marker) B.; B.S. in Bus., Miami U., Oxford, O., 1941; grad. Grad. Sch. Banking, U. Wis., 1968; m. Bettijane Pees, Oct. 31, 1942; children—Pamela Jane, William R. With Winters Nat. Bank, Dayton, O., 1946—, dir. banking offices adminstrn., 1968—. Served to maj. USMCR, World War II and Korea. Decorated Bronze Star. Mem. Phi Kappa Tau. Home: 149 Winding Ridge Dr Dayton OH 45415 Office: 40 N Main St Dayton OH 45402

BRYANT, DOUGLAS WALLACE, librarian; b. Visalia, Cal., June 20, 1913; s. Albert George and Ethel (Wallace) B.; student U. Munich (Germany), 1932-33; A.B., Stanford, 1935; A.M. in L.S., U. Mich., 1938; m. Rene Leilani Kuhn, Apr. 6, 1953; 1 dau., Heather Corbally. Translator, Hoover Inst. Library, Stanford, 1934-35; asst. curator printed books William L. Clements Library, U. Mich., 1936-37; sr. reference asst., tech. dept. Detroit Pub. Library, 1938-41, asst. chief Burton Hist. Collection, 1941-42; asst. librarian U. Cal. at Berkeley, 1946-49; dir. libraries, attache Am. embassy, USIS, London, 1949-52; adminstrv. asst. librarian Harvard Coll. Library, 1952- 55, asso. dir. Harvard U. Library, 1955-64, univ. librarian Harvard, 1964—. Mem. U.S. nat. commn. for UNESCO, 1953-55; v.p. Internat. Fedn. Library Assns., 1952-58, Am. del. to meetings of council, 1950-55, 57-58; v.p. Internat. Fedn. for Documentation, 1956- 58; cons. Ford Found., Ankara, Turkey, on establishment Inst. Librarianship, U. Ankara, 1954; cons. Rockefeller Found., London, 1956; lectr., cons. Japanese univ. libraries, 1963; cons. Inst. Am. Studies, Free U., Berlin, 1964-66, London Sch. Econs., 1965-66. Chmn. bd. dirs. Center Research Libraries, 1969-70. Served to lt. comdr. USNR, World War II; head tech. data br. Bur. Aeros., Navy Dept., Washington. Fellow Am. Acad. Arts and Scis.; mem. A.L.A. (chmn. internat. relations com. 1952-55, chmn. coordinating com. on Slavic and East European library resources 1959-61, chmn. Assn. Research Libraries Com. on preservation research library materials 1960-68, pres. 1969-70), Mass. Hist. Soc., Am. Antiquarian Soc. Clubs: Harvard (N.Y.); Odd Volumes (Boston). Home: 35 Woodland Rd Lexington MA 02173 Office: Harvard U Library Cambridge MA 02138

BRYANT, EDWARD ALBERT, dir. art gallery; b. Lenoir, N.C., July 23, 1928; s. Edmond Henry and Shelton Emmaline (Robbins) B.; A.B., U. N.C., 1950, M.A., 1955; postgrad. U. Italiana per Stranieri, Perugia, 1954, U. di Pisa (Italy), 1954-55, U. di Ravenna (Italy), 1955, N.C. State Coll., 1956, Columbia U., 1958; m. Tamara Thompson, May 28, 1965; 1 son, Adam Edmond. Fellow, Bklyn. Mus., 1957-58; European study grant for research contemporary Italian drawings, 1958-59; gen. curator Wadsworth Atheneum, Hartford, Conn., 1959-61; asso. curator Whitney Mus. Am. Art, N.Y.C., 1961-65; dir. U. Ky. Art Gallery, Lexington, 1965-68; dir. Picker Gallery: asso. prof. Colgate U.; exhbns. include African sculpture Bklyn. Mus., 1958, contemporary Italian drawings and collage Am. Fedn. Arts, 1959; Jack Tworkov Retrospective Exhbn., Whitney Mus., 1964; A Decade of New Talent, Am. Fedn. Arts, 1964: Graphics 1968; U. Ky., 1969; Larry Zox Colgate U.; cons. Ky. Arts Commn., 1967-68. Fulbright fellow, 1954-55; spl. research grant Colgate U., 1969-70. Author: Painting, 1958; Jack Tworkov, 1964; 32 Drawings by Robert Broderson, 1964. Co-author: African Sculpture, 1958; Forty Artists Under Forty (with Lloyd Goodrich), 1962. Home: Box 54 Poolville NY 13432 Office: Picker Gallery Dana Creative Arts Center Colgate U Hamilton NY 13346

BRYANT, EMMONS, investment banker; b. Elizabeth, N.J., 1910; s. Emmons Bryant and Dorothy (Lyon) B.: grad. Amherst Coll., 1932; m. Mary Esther Stilwell, Sept. 11, 1937; children—Penelope (Mrs. Hale H. Carey), Mary E., Barbara Ann. Vice chairman board Blair & Company, Granbery Marache, Inc., 1953—: director Overhead Door Corporation, Hartford City, Indiana, Echlin Mfg. Co. (Branford, Conn.), Dulany Industries (N.Y.C.), World Wide Helicopters (Nassau), Laboratory for Electronics (Boston). Trustee Williston Acad., Easthampton, Mass. Home: 1172 Park Av New York City NY 10028 Office: 20 Broad St New York City NY 10005

BRYANT, FRANK LEONARD, machinery co. exec.; b. Weymouth, Mass., Mar. 6, 1914; s. Frank M. and Helen (Sulis) B.; A.B., Dartmouth, 1935; m. Ada Laurie, 1937; children—Jane, Leonard, Robert, Richard and Laurie (twins). Chemist, supt., then works mgr., Hooker Chem. Corp., 1935-57, v.p. prodn., 1957-59, v.p., gen. mgr. phosphorus div., 1959, v.p. research 1959-60, exec. v.p., 1960-61, pres., dir., 1961-62, chmn. bd., 1963-70; pres., dir. Natvar Corp., Woodbridge, N.J., 1971—; dir. Natvar-Indael, Mexico City, Mexico, Dilectrix Corp., Farmingdale, N.Y., Marine Midland Grace Trust Co. of New York. Mem. Mfg. Chemists Assn. (chmn. bd. 1969-70). Clubs: University (N.Y.); Nassau; Colonia Country. Home: 108 Hunt Dr Princeton NJ 08540 Office: 211 Randolph Av Woodbridge NJ

BRYANT, GORDON WHITMAN, retailing co. exec.; b. Boston, Mar. 8, 1906; s. Herbert Alonzo and Grace (Hurlburt) B.; B.S., Bowdoin Coll., 1928; M.B.A., Harvard, 1930; m. Marjorie Helen Smith, Sept. 12, 1931; children—Cynthia Hyde (Mrs. Allan H. McCue), Judith Hurlburt (Mrs. Robert T. Hale), Gordon Whitman. Advt. mgr., then salesman F.A. Foster & Co., Inc., Boston, 1931- 46; dept. supr. Personal Bookshops, Inc., Boston, 1941-43; pres., treas., dir. Charles E. Lauriat Co. Inc., Boston, 1946—; pres., treas., dir. Lauriat's Northshore Inc., 1958—, Lauriat's Southshore Inc., 1961—, Lauriat's Burlington. Inc., 1968—; dir. De Wolfe & Fiske Co., Boston, 1959—; trustee Braintree Savs. Bank (Mass.), 1950—, bd. investment, 1967—, v.p., 1967—. First v.p. Am. Booksellers Assn., 1965-69; mem. gov. council Retail Trade Bd. Boston, 1960—, pres., 1965-67; bd. dirs. Greater Boston C. of C., 1965-67, Com. for Central Bus. Dist., 1965-70. Sec. Braintree Taxpayers Assn., 1937-38, Braintree Finance Com., 1943-44; chmn. Braintree Sch. Com., 1948-51, Braintree Pub. Library, 1959-61. Mem. Beta Theta Pi (pres. New Eng. area 1962-63). Clubs: Rotary (bd. dirs. 1951), Bowdoin, Harvard Business School (Boston). Home: 175 West St Braintree MA 02184 Office: 50 Franklin St Boston MA 02107

BRYANT, HARLAN, coll. pres.; b. Moberly, Mo., May 25, 1910; s. Fred E. and Frances I. (Mowry) B.; B.S., S.W. Mo. State Coll., 1933; A.M., also Ed.D., U. Mo.; m. Adelaide E. Tarleton, Nov. 28, 1930; children—Robert E., Mary Frances. Tchr. high sch., Camdenton, Mo., 1933-34; prin. high sch., Clever, Mo., 1934-38, Eldon, 1938-41; prin. Jr.-Sr. High Sch., Nevada, Mo., 1941-42; asst. prof. edn., U. Tulsa, 1946-47; dean Joplin Jr. Coll., 1947-49; prof. edn. U. Okla., 1949-54; dean Coll. Edn., U. Wyo., 1954-62; pres. Western State Coll. Colo., Gunnison, 1962—. Served as lt. USNR, 1942-45. Recipient Okla. Found. award for extraordinary excellence teaching and counseling. Mem. N.E.A., Wyo. Edn. Assn., Nat. Assn. Secondary Sch. Prins., Am. Assn. Sch. Adminstrs., C. of C., Phi Delta Kappa, Kappa Delta Pi. Methodist. Rotarian. Address: Western State Coll of Colo Gunnison CO 81230

BRYANT, JACK WALSWORTH, librarian; b. Los Angeles, Jan. 8, 1926; s. Roy C. and Cora (Walsworth) B.; B.S., U. Cal. at Los Angeles, 1951; M.S. in L.S., U. So. Cal., 1952; certificat de civilization Francaise, U. Paris (France), 1950; m. Jean Calhoun Bacon, Oct. 11, 1958; children—Charles Walsworth, David Calhoun. Asst. to librarian Hoover Library, Stanford, 1954-57; adminstrv. asst. Enoch Pratt Free Library, Balt., 1957-60; dir. Crandall Library, Glens Falls, N.Y., 1960-62, Greenwich (Conn.) Library, 1962-66, Worcester (Mass.) Pub. Library, 1966-70, Wilmington Inst. and New Castle County Free Library, Wilmington, Del., 1970—; cons., lectr. in field, 1961—; lectr. Simmons Coll., Boston, 1969. Film adviser Wing Prodns., Bedford, Mass., 1964-69. Served with AUS, 1944-46. Mem. Am., Conn., Mass., New Eng., N.Y., Del., Pa. library assns., Library Pub. Relations Council. Rotarian. Author: Suburban Service, 1964; also articles. Home: 2315 W 17th St Wilmington DE 19801

BRYANT, JAMES CLUTE, oral surgeon, bank exec.; b. Mpls., Apr. 22, 1894; s. John Clute and Ada (O'Brien) B.; D.D.S., U. Minn., 1920; m. Edith MacDonald, Nov. 30, 1923; children—John, Susan (Mrs. Tom Buchman), Judith (Mrs. John Suess), Diane (Mrs. Doug Holcombe), Daniel. Dir. dept. oral surgery Glen Lake Sanatorium, Oak Terrace, Minn., 1920-63. Dir. First Nat. Bank Hopkins (Minn.). Served with inf., U.S. Army, World War I. Recipient awards sci. and health exhibits Am. Dental Assn., 1941, 47. Fellow Royal Soc. Health; mem. Am., Minn., Mpls. Dist. dental assns., S.A.R., S.R., Baronial Order Magna Carta, Minn. Territorial Pioneers, Am. Legion, Am. Geneal. Soc., Detroit Soc. Geneal. Research, Am., Minn. Tb. assns., Descendants Knights Garter, Order of Crown of Charlemagne in U.S.A. Republican. Mason (Shriner). Clubs: Minneapolis Athletic, Rotary, 6 O'Clock, Lafayette, University. Address: 32 Sabal Island Dr Ocean Ridge Delray Beach FL 33444.

BRYANT, JAMES WILLIAM, ednl. adminstr.; b. Richland, Ga., June 26, 1916; s. Ed and Tabitha (Thomas) B.; B.S., Tuskegee Inst., 1938; M.B.A., Wharton Sch., U. Pa., 1951; LL.D., Fla. Meml. Coll., 1969; m. Lois F. Thompson, Aug. 24, 1938; children—James William, Bertina Adele, Edward Henry. Application and enrollment clk. Tuskegee, 1938-41; chief accountant Johnson C. Smith U., 1941-42; dir. Booker T. Washington Bus. Coll., 1942-43; bus. mgr. Fla. Normal Coll., St. Augustine, 1943-45; from cashier to auditor Tuskegee Inst., 1945-53; bus. mgr. Tex. Coll., Tyler, 1953-56; cons. spl. services United Negro Coll. Fund, also asst. bus. mgr. Hampton Inst., 1956-57; bus. mgr. Hampton Inst., 1957-65; exec. v.p. United Negro Coll. Fund, 1965-67; project specialist Ford Found., 1967-69, program adviser, 1969-70, cons., 1971—; v.p. for univ. relations and devel. Howard U., 1971—. Dir. Peoples Bldg. and Loan Assn., Hampton, Va., 1957-65, Hampton Inst. Employees Fed. Credit Union, 1956-65; sec.-treas. Granger Cts., Inc., Hampton, 1959-63. Trustee, mem. finance com. Dixie Hosp., Hampton, 1960-65; v.p. New Bay Shore Corp., 1962-65, Armstrong League of Hampton Workers, 1963-65; trustee Weaver Orphan Home, Hampton, 1959-65, Common Fund, 1970—; trustee finance com. Coll. Entrance Exam. Bd., 1970; bd. dirs.

Moton Meml. Found., 1969—. Mem. Am. (sec. 1962-63, v.p. 1963, pres. 1964-65, mem. exec. com. 1965-66), Eastern, Nat. (sec. 1962-65) assns. coll. and univs. bus. officers, Coll. and Univ. Personnel Assn., Peninsula C. of C., Omega Psi Phi, Sigma Pi Phi. Mason. Author: Survey of Black American Doctorates. Home: 651 Suffern Rd Teaneck NJ 07666 Office: 2400 6th St NW Washington DC 20001

BRYANT, JOSEPH ALLEN, Jr., educator; b. Glasgow, Ky.; Nov. 26, 1919; s. Joseph Allen and Florence (Rogers) B.; A.B., Western Ky. U., 1940; M.A., Vanderbilt U., 1941; Ph.D., Yale, 1948; m. Mary Virginia Woodruff, Dec. 28, 1946; children—Joseph Allen, Garnett Woodruff. Instr. U. Ky., 1946; asso. prof. Vanderbilt U., 1948-56, U. South, Sewanee, Tenn., 1956-59, Duke, 1959- 61; prof. chmn. English dept. U. N.C., 1961-68; Fulbright lectr. U. Nantes (France), 1965-66; prof; chmn. English dept., Syracuse U., 1968- -. Served with USNR, 1942-46. Ford fellow, 1952-53; Sewanee Review fellow, 1958-59. Mem. Modern Lang. Assn. Am., Renaissance Soc. Am., Shakespeare Assn. Am. Democrat. Episcopalian. Author: Hippolyta's View: Some Christian Aspects of Shakespeare's Plays, 1961; Eudora Welty, 1968. Contbr. articles and reviews to profl. jours. Home: 100 Enfield Pl Syracuse NY 13214

BRYANT, MARGARET M., ret. educator; b. Trenton, S.C., Dec. 3, 1900; d. John Lee and Harriet (Yonce) Bryant; A.B., Winthrop (S.C.) Coll. for Women, 1921, H.L.D., 1968; student U. Va., 1922; A.M., Columbia, 1925, Ph.D., 1931; scholarship, Linguistic Inst., U. Mich., summer 1939, U. Wis., summers 1943-44, Inst. Gen. Semantics, N.Y. U., 1945, Folklore Inst., Ind. U., 1946; Litt. D., Cedar Crest Coll., 1966. Prin. pub., pvt. schs., S.C., Kan., W.Va., N.Y., 1921-25; faculty Chowan Coll., N.C., 1925-26, Hunter Coll., 1926-33; instr. to prof. Bklyn. Coll., City U. N.Y., Bklyn. Coll., City U. N.Y. day session 1930-71, evening session, 1931-38, departmental rep. English dept., evening session 1937-40, acting chmn. English dept., 1940-41, chmn., 1941-44, asst. prof. to prof. Grad. Sch., 1937-71; vis. prof., univs. of Vt., Ark., Utah, Colo., New Sch. Social Research, 1947-50; vis. prof. Columbia 1952-53, adj. prof., fall, 1955-56; vis. lectr. univs. Uppsala and Stockholm, Handelshögskolan, 1950-51; vis. prof. Rutgers U., summer 1962, with commn. on English Inst. Recipient gold medal for conspicuous service Columbia, 1941, Mary Mildred Sullivan award, Winthrop Coll., 1956. Mem. N.Y. Council Tchrs. English, Coll. Council English in Central Atlantic States, Modern Lang. Assn., Nat. Council Tchrs. English, Am. Dialect Soc., Am. Name Soc. (pres. 1958-59), Internat. Assn. U. Profs. English, Philol. Soc. Eng., Internat. Folk Music Council, Am., N.Y. folklore socs., Linguistic Soc. Am., Am. Soc. Geolinguistics, Am. Assn. U. Profs., Internat. Linguistic Soc. (v.p. 1969—), Am. Assn. U. Women (pres. N.Y.C. 1955-59, recipient Founders' Day citation 1962, 66, Woman of Achievement award N.Y.C. br. 1969), Internat. Fedn. U. Women, N.Y. Coll. English Assn., Modern Humanities Research Assn., Coll. English Assn., English Inst., Philol. Soc. Eng., Internat. Soc. for Gen. Semantics, Phi Beta Kappa, Phi Kappa Phi. Author: English in the Law Courts, 1930, 2d edit., 1962; A Functional English Grammar, 1945; Proverbs and How to Collect Them, 1945; Modern English and Its Heritage, 1948, 2d edit., 1962; Introduction to R.H. Thornton's An American Glossary, 2d edit. (3 vols.), 1962; co-author: Psychology of English, 1940, 2d edit., 1962; English at Work (4 vols.), 1953. Editor: Current American Usage, 1962. Contbr. to periodicals. Home: 222 Hicks St Brooklyn NY 11201 ☆

BRYANT, MARVIN PIERCE, educator; b. Boise, Ida., July 4, 1925; s. Melvin Berry and Emma Louise (Bucklin) B.; diploma Boise Jr. Coll., 1947; B.S., Wash. State U., 1949, M.S., 1950; postgrad. Cornell U., 1950; Ph.D., U. Md., 1955; m. Margaret Amelia Betebenner, June 30, 1946; children—Margaret (Mrs. Richard Ricker), Lyman, Susan Jean, Katherine Claire, Robert Marvin, Steven Edward. Research bacteriologist U.S. Dept. Agr., Beltsville, Md., 1951-62; leader rumen microbiology investigations, 1962-64; asso. prof. bacteriology U. Ill., Urbana, 1964-66, prof. microbiology, 1966—; cons. on anaerobic bacteria. Served with USAAF, 1944-45. Recipient Superior Service award Dept. Agr., 1959. Fellow A.A.A.S.; mem. Am. Soc. for Microbiology, Soc. for Gen. Microbiology, Am. Dairy Sci. Assn., Phi Beta Kappa, Sigma Xi, Phi Kappa Phi. Editor Applied Microbiology, 1969-71, editor-in-chief, 1971—. Isolation and characterization of anaerobic bacteria of gastro-intestinal tract and methanogenic fermentations and research on their ecology and metabolism. Home: 1003 S Orchard St Urbana IL 61801

BRYANT, PAUL CARLTON JEFFERSON, organist, actor; b. Long Branch, N.J., Sept. 22, 1933; s. Maxwell and Jean (Odom) B.; grad. high sch.; m. Shirley Jeanne Harris, Oct. 25, 1957; children—Paul Carlton Jefferson, Angela Gene. Appeared in numerous motion pictures including Kitty, 1944, Green Pastures, 1937, Star Spangle Rhythm, 1943, Tales of Manhattan, 1942, Foxes of Harrow, Lady of New Orleans, 1941, Stormy Weather, I Married An Angel, Kiss The Boys Goodbye, 1941, Tarzen's Secret Treasure, 1940, Cabin in the Sky, Yankee Doodle Dandy, 1942, Saratoga Trunk, 1945, Thank Your Lucky Stars, 1943, Arabian Nights, 1943, Crazy House, 1941, Bachelors Daughter, Is Everbody Happy, The Senator Was Indiscreet, The Old Grouch, 1942, The Jackie Robinson Story, The Underdog, Knickerbocker Holiday, 1943; appeared at Chit Chat Sugar Hill, Las Vegas, Ruben's Supper Club, Las Vegas, numerous others in Las Vegas, Los Angeles; rec. artist. Served with USAF, 1951-55. Mem. A.S.C.A.P., Prof. John A. Gray's Conservatory Music, Willie Covan Dance Acad., Screen Actors Guild, Hollywood Theatrical Tng. Studios, Prodn. Corp. Am., Am. Fedn. Musicians, Internat. Platform Assn. Composer: Searchin, 1960; Churchin, 1961; My Three, 1964; Sister Lovie, 1964; Why Me, 1964; Funky Mountain, 1963; Walrus Whiskers, 1963. Home: 3923 Gibralter Av Los Angeles CA 90008

BRYANT, PAUL WILLIAM, univ. football coach, athletic dir.; b. Kingsland, Ark., Sept. 11, 1913; s. Wilson Monroe and Ida (Kilgore) B.; B.S., U. Ala., 1939; m. Mary Harmon Black, Aug. 3, 1934; children—Mae Martin (Mrs. John Tyson), Paul William. Asst. football coach U. Ala., 1936-40, Vanderbilt U., 1940-41; head football coach U. Md., 1945, U. Ky., 1946- 53, Tex. A. and M. Coll., 1954-57, U. Ala., 1958—; head coach Sugar Bowl games, 1951, 62,64,67, Orange Bowl, 1950, 63, 65, 66, Cotton Bowl, 1952, 1967, Blue Bonnet Game, 1960, 70, Gator Bowl, 1957, 1968, Liberty Bowl Game, 1959, 69, Great Lakes Bowl Game, 1947. Dir. First Nat. Bank, Cotton States Life Ins. Co., R.L. Zeigler Co., Inc. (all Tuscaloosa). Active local YMCA, United Fund, Heart Fund, Tb Seal drive. Trustee Am. Football Coaches Assn., Pop Warner Hall of Fame. Served to lt. comdr. USNR, 1941-45. Recipient Legion of Honor award Tex. Upsilon chpt. Sigma Nu, 1956, Ann. award Louisville Optimist Club, 1950, Meritorious Service plaque Ky. Press Assn., 1951, plaque D.C. chpt. U. Ala. Alumni Assn., 1962, Outstanding Citizen Ky. award Ky. Press Assn., 1950, Silver Anniversary award Sports Illustrated mag., 1960, Outstanding Achievement in Coll. Football award Dapper Dan Club, Pitts., 1962, Worlds No. 1 Coach award Birmingham (Ala.) Downtown Action Com., 1965; named to Ark. Hall of Fame, 1965; named hon. col. Ala. Militia, 1963, Ark. traveler, 1959, hon. Texan, 1954, adm. Tex. Navy, 1954, adm. of Lake Martin, Ky., 1962, Ky. Col., 1950, coach of year in South West Conf., 1956, in South East Conf., 1961, 64, coach of year Coach and Athletic mag., 1955, 56, 60, 61, 64; coach of year Am. Football Coaches Assn., 1961, Dist. III coach of year medallion, 1964; U. Ala. athletic dormitory named Paul Bryant Hall, 1965. Mem. Jasons, Sigma Nu, Omicron Delta Kappa. Methodist (steward). Clubs: A (U. Ala.); Athletic Letterman's. Author: Building a Championship Football Team, 1960. Office: Box K University AL 35486

BRYANT, ROBERT RALPH, labor union and ins. exec.; b. El Paso, Tex., July 10, 1920; s. William Thomas and Eva (Smith) B.; student Tex. A. and M. Coll., 1937-39, Tex. Coll. Mines, 1939-40; m. Barbara Nelle Skinner, Feb. 2, 1942; children—Robert Ralph, Harry Thomas. Mem. Brotherhood of Locomotive Firemen and Enginemen, 1941—, Tex. legislative chmn., 1954-62, gen. sec., treas., 1962—. Mem Fed. Golden Spike Centennial Celebration Commn., 1967-69; pres. Nat. Fraternal Congress Am., 1970—. Mem. exec. com. Democratic Organizing Com. Tex., 1955-56; mem. exec. com. Democrats of Tex., 1956-60; del.-at-large Dem. Nat. Conv., 1956. Served with AUS, 1946-47. Methodist. Mason (Shriner). Home: 26404 Rechner Dr Westlake OH 44145 Office: 666 Euclid Av Cleveland OH 44114

BRYANT, RUTH ALYNE, banker; b. Memphis, Jan. 12, 1924; d. James Walter and Leola (Edgar) Bryant; student Southwestern Coll., Memphis, 1941-43. Clk. Fed. Res. Bank of St. Louis, Memphis Br., 1943-47, exec. sec., 1947-68, asst. cashier, 1968-69, asst. v.p., 1969—. Mem. Am. Inst. Banking (nat. women's com., 1962-63; pres. Memphis chpt., 1968-69), Tenn. Bankers Assn. (award 1957), Nat. Assn. Bank Women (editor Woman Banker, 1959-62, v.p. so. region 1967-68; v.p. 1969-70, pres. 1970-71), Memphis Employers Merit Employment Assn. (adv. bd. 1971—), Quota Internat. Home: 4344 E Faronia Sq Memphis TN 38116 Office: Fed Res Bank of St Louis 170 Jefferson Av Memphis TN 38101

BRYANT, WILLIAM ALTON, educator, univ. adminstr.; b. Sanford, Miss., Oct. 24, 1907; s. Willis Allen and Zetta (Knapp) B.; A.B., U. Miss., 1929, M.A., 1939; Ph.D., Vanderbilt U., 1941; m. Willie Hume Branham, Dec. 21, 1931; children—William Alton, Alfred Hume, David Leland, Mary Elizabeth. Tchr., Seminary (Miss.) High Sch., 1930-31; instr. Branham and Hughes Mil. Acad., Spring Hill, Tenn., 1931-32, Battle Ground Acad., Franklin, 1932-36, University (Miss.) High Sch., 1936-39; teaching fellow Vanderbilt U., 1939-41; asst. prof. English, U. Miss., 1941-45, asso. prof., 1945-46, prof. English, 1946—, acting dir. and dir. summer session, 1942-47, acting registrar, 1944- 45, instl. adviser for vets., 1945-46, chmn. dept. English, 1947-54, asst. to chancellor, 1952-53, acting dean univ., 1953-54, provost, 1954-60, vice chancellor, 1960—. Mem. N.E.A., Modern Lang. Assn. Am., So. Lit. Festival Assn. (pres. 1948-49), Scribblers, Omicron Delta Kappa. Democrat. Presbyn. Author: Conceptions of America and Americans by the English Romantic Poets: 1790-1850 (Vanderbilt Univ. Summaries of Theses), 1945. Address: Box 128 University MS 38677.

BRYANT, WILLIAM B., U.S. dist. judge; b. Wetumpka, Ala., Sept. 18, 1911; s. Benson and Alberta Bryant; A.B., Howard U., 1932, LL.B., 1936; m. Astaire A. Gonzalez, Aug. 25, 1934; childrenAstaire, William B. Asst. U.S. atty for D.C., 1951-54; partner firm Houston, Bryant & Garder, 1954-65; U.S. dist. Judge for D.C., 1965—; prof. law Howard U. Sch. Law, 1965—. Served with AUS, 1943-47. Mem. Am. Bar Assn. Home: 3725 17th St N E Washington MA 20018 Office: U S Court House Washington MA 20001

BRYANT, WILLIAM JUNIOR, archaeol. found. exec.; b. Springfield, Vt., May 4, 1904; s. William LeRoy and Blanche (Brown) B.; grad. Phillips Exeter Acad., 1921; B.A., Dartmouth, 1925; m. Frances Hazelton, May 29, 1926; 1 son, Bruce Hazelton. With Bryant Chucking Grinder Co., Springfield, 1925-59, pres., 1946-58; founder William L. Bryant Found., conducting excavations Fla., Carribean and Spain, also publs. in Am. and Spanish, 1950—; founder Centro Arqueologico Hispano-Americano de Los Baleares. Trustee Eaglebrook Sch., Deerfield, Mass., 1946-51, 55-60, Calvin Coolidge Meml. Found., 1964—; mem. exec. com. Friends of Dartmouth Library, 1953—; mem. visitors com. classical dept. Museum Fine Arts, Boston, 1960—. Mem. Am. Inst. Archaeology, Fla. Anthrop. Soc., Real Sociedad Arqueologica Tarraconense, Am. Forestry Assn., Boston Anthenaeum, Sigma Alpha Epsilon. Clubs: Union (Boston); Dartmouth (N.Y.C.). Author: Flames of Life, 1961; The Magic of Spain, 1967, others; also book revs., articles. Patentee machine tools and measurement. Home: R F D South Woodstock VT 05071 Office: R F D 1 Springfield VT 05156

BRYCE, MAYO, coll. pres.; b. Walhalla, N.D., Aug. 13, 1914; s. James Henry and Lois (Mayo) B.; A.B., San Jose State Coll., 1937; M.A., Columbia Tchrs. Coll., 1941, Ed.D., 1948; m. Corinne Howe, Aug. 5, 1945; children—David King, Mark Adams. Instr. art Santa Clara (Cal.) High Sch., 1937-41; head art dept. U. Ala., 1941-42; field dir. A.R.C., 1942-45; prof. art and edn. San Francisco State Coll., 1948-58; specialist edn. for fine arts U.S. Office Edn., 1958-61; dean Coll. Fine and Applied Arts, No. Ill. U., DeKalb, 1961-64; pres. Moore Coll. Art, Phila., 1964—. Head delegation Commn. on Fine Arts in Edn., USSR, 1960; pres. Pacific Arts Assn., 1956-58. Mem. Nat. Council Arts in Edn. (dir.-at-large), Nat. Art Edn. Assn., Internat. Soc. Edn. Through Art, Phila. Art Alliance (dir.), Phi Delta Kappa, Kappa Delta Pi, Delta Epsilon. Club: Franklin Inn (Phila.). Home: 2220 Walnut St Philadelphia PA 19103 Office: Moore Coll of Art 20th and Race Sts Philadelphia PA 19103

BRYMER, JACK, clarinettist; b. S. Shields, Eng., Jan. 27, 1915; s. John and Mary (Dixon) B.; music tchrs. diploma, Goldsmiths Coll., London U., 1935; m. Joan Richardson; 1 son. Schoolmaster, 1935-40; prin. clarinettist Royal Philharmonic Orch., 1947- 63, BBC Symphony Orch., 1968-; mem. London Baroque Ensemble, 1948, Wigmore Ensemble, 1949, Prometheus Ensemble, 1952; dir. London Wind soloists, 1960—; prof. clarinet Royal Acad. Music, 1950-58, Royal Mil. Sch. Music, 1968—; broadcast talks in field, lectr. films in series We Make Music. Served with RAF, 1940-45. Decorated officer Order Brit. Empire, 1960. Recs. of complete wind works of Mozart, Beethoven, Haydn and J.C. Bach. Home: Underwood Ballards Farm Rd South Croydon Surry England Office: BBC Broadcasting House Portland Pl London W 1 England

BRYNER, CHARLES LESLIE, educator; b. Dunbar, Pa., Oct. 15, 1914; s. John Henry and Sarah Elizabeth (Hardy) B.; B.S. in Math., Waynesburg Coll., 1940; M.S. in Biology, W.Va. U., 1948, Ph.D. in Botany, 1957; m. Anna Marie Wilson, Aug. 24, 1947; children—Lisbeth Ann, Charles Leslie. Supervising prin. Dunbar Borough Pub. Schs., 1940-42; asst. prof. math., biology Waynesburg (Pa.) Coll., 1945-46, prof. biology, 1957—, chmn. div. sci., 1958-71, dean men, 1952-58, asso. acad. v.p., 1959. Served with USNR, 1942-46. Mem. A.A.A.S., Am. Inst. Biol. Scis., Pa., W.Va. acads. sci., So. Appalachian Bot. Club. Democrat. Methodist. Home: RD 3 Waynesburg PA 15370

BRYNILDSSEN, YNGVAR, corp. exec.; b. Fredrikstad, Norway, May 19, 1905; s. Bjarne and Margit (Bramer) B.; brought to U.S., 1907, naturalized, 1911; student Northwestern, 1930; m. Alletta Elizabeth Mathison, Apr. 27, 1926; children—Joy Mathilda (Mrs. L. F. Draper, Junior), Jack Peter. Began as bank examiner for State of Ill., 1930-33; examiner R.F.C., 1933- 36; exec. v.p. Home Fed. Savs & Loan Assn., Chgo., 1936-39; v.p. Gen. Mortgage Investments, Inc., 1940-42; asst. treas. Stewart-Warner Corp., 1945-47; v.p., dir. finance Best Build Co. of Ill., Chgo., 1947-51, 53- -; chmn. bd. pres. Guardian Savs & Loan Assn., 1964—; deputy adminstr. Small Def. Plants Adminstrn., Washington, 1952, adminstr., 1953; v.p., dir. Community Savs. & Loan Assn., Chgo.; dir.-at-large Fed. Home Loan Bank, Chgo. Mem. bd. Tb Inst. Chgo. and Cook County, pres., 1966-67; trustee Ill. Masonic Med. Center, 1970—. Served as lt. comdr. USNR, 1942-45. Mem. Am. Legion. Mason (32, Shriner: past potentate Medinah Temple). Home: 923 Michigan Av Evanston IL 60202 Office: 3335 N Ashland Av Chicago IL 60657

BRYNNER, YUL, actor; b. Sakhalin (Island), Japan, July 11, 1920; ed. chiefly in France including at the Sorbonne; m. Virginia Gilmore, Sept. 6, 1944; 1 son, Yul II. Came to U.S., 1940. Connected with entertainment field since early yrs.; made debut in circus and on legitimate stage in Paris; first appeared on U.S. stage, 1940, in Shakespearean role with Michael Chekov company; debut on Broadway stage in Lute Song. 1946, later on tour throughout U.S. in same prodn.; appeared abroad in Dark Eyes, 1947-48, also as entertainer in Paris night clubs; actor, producer, dir. TV show for NBC, 1948; became TV dir. CBS programs; on legitimate stage in The King and I. 1951-54, star of the play, 1952-54, also on tour, 1954; in film prodns. as Rameses in The Ten Commandments, 1955, as the king in The King and I, 1956; co-star with Ingrid Bergmen in Anastasia, 1956; new pictures The Buccaneer, Brothers Karamazov, 1958; Journey, Sound and the Fury, 1959; Solomon and Sheba. 1959: Once More With Feeling, Magnificent Seven, 1960; Cast a Giant Shadow, 1966; Triple Cross, 1967; The Long Duel, 1967; The Double Man, 1968; others. Recipient Donaldson award, 1946, Nat. Bd. Rev. Motion Pictures award for best performance, in The King and I, 1956. Acad. Award in Motion Pictures, 1957. Served as radio announcer and commentator (in French), OWI, 1942-46. Author: Bring Forth the Children, 1960. Office: 18 Place de la Madeleine Paris 8e France

BRYNYCH, ZBYNEK, film producer and dir.; b. Karlovy Vary, June 13, 1927; s. Josef and Anna (Heinlova) B.; grad. Acad. Films, Prague, Czechoslovakia, 1948; m. Milena le Breux, May 3, 1963. Films include Suburban Romance, 1958; Five From Millions, 1959; Carambolage, 1960; The Place, 1962; The Fifth Horseman is Fear, 1963; Transit Karlovy Vary, 1965; I'm the Justness, 1968; Dialog, 1968; Franz Kafka; America, 1969. Named Laureat of Price of State, Czechoslovakia, 1963, Deserved Artist of Nation, 1968. Mem. Assn. Filmworkers Czechoslovakia. Address: 2 Nove Zamecke schody Prague 1 Czechoslovakia

BRYSON, ARTHUR EARL, Jr., engring. educator; b. Evanston, Ill., Oct. 7, 1925; s. Arthur Earl and Helen Elizabeth (Decker) B.; student Haverford Coll., 1942-44; B.S., Ia. State U., 1946; M.S., Cal. Inst. Tech., 1949, Ph.d. in Aero., 1951; M.A. (hon.), Harvard. 1956; m. Helen Marie Layton, Aug. 31, 1946; children—Thomas Layton, Stephen Decker, Janet Elizabeth, Susan Mary. With Container Corp. Am., 1947-48, United Aircraft Corp., 1948; research asst. aero. Cal. Inst. Tech., 1949-50; mem. tech. staff Hughes Research & Devel. Labs., 1950-53; mem. faculty Harvard, 1953-68, Gordon McKay prof. mech. engring., 1961-68, chmn. dept. applied mechanics, 1969-71, Stanford, 1969-71, chmn. dept. aeronautics and astronautics, 1971—; Hunsaker prof. Mass. Inst. Tech., 1965-66. Mem. planning bd. Town of Lexington, Mass., 1961-66. Mem. nat. com. Fluid Mechanics Films, 1961-68. Served as ensign USNR, 1944-46. Mem. Am. Acad. Arts and Scis., Am. Inst. Aeros. and Astronautics (asso. editor Jour. 1963-65, bd. dirs. 1965-68, Pendray Award 1968; fellow), Am. Soc. Engring. Edn. (Westinghouse award 1969), Nat. Acad. Engring., Sigma Xi, Tau Beta Pi. Conglist. Book (with Y.C. Ho) Applied Optimal Control, 1969. Home: 761 Mayfield Av Stanford CA 94305

BRYSON, BRADY OLIVER, lawyer; b. Overton, Nev., Mar. 14, 1915; s. Samuel Oliver and Emma (Brady) B.; A.B., Western Md. Coll., 1935; LL.B., Columbia, 1938; m. Mary Elizabeth Brown, Nov. 1, 1938; children—Linda Bryson (Mrs. Jonathan Flaccus), David Brady, John Alan, Timothy Sean. Admitted to D.C. bar, 1938, Pa. bar, 1942, N.Y. bar, 1946, Md. bar, 1952; practice in Washington, 1943-47, N.Y.C., 1948-54, Phila., 1955—; mem. firm Alvord & Alvord, 1943-47: mem. firm Chapman, Bryson, Walsh & O'Connell, 1948-54; mem. firm Morgan, Lewis & Bockius, 1955—. Dir. Bulletin Co., Phila., Curtis Pub. Co., Phila., Polymer Corp., Reading, Pa., Rolle Mfg. Co., Lansdale, Pa., Devel. Co. Am., Westminster, Md. Trustee Louis L. Stott Found., Reading. Served to lt. (j.g.) USNR, 1944-46. Mem. Am., N.Y. State, Pa., Phila. bar assns., Masters of Foxhounds Assn. Am., Green Spring Valley Hounds, Elkridge-Harford Hounds. Clubs: Midday, Racquet (Phila.). Home: Box 868 Westminster MD 21157 Office: 123 S Broad St Philadelphia PA 19109

BRYSON, GENE E., advt. agy. exec. Sr. v.p., mgr. McCann-Erickson, Inc., Los Angeles. Office: 3325 Wilshire Blvd Los Angeles CA 90005*

BRYSON, REID ALLEN, educator; b. Detroit, June 7, 1920; s. William Riley and Elma (Turner) B.; A.B., Denison U., 1941, D.Sc. (honoris causa), 1971; postgrad. U. Wis., 1941, 46; Ph.D., U. Chgo., 1948; m. Frances Edith Wiliamson, June, 13, 1942; children—Anne, William, Robert, Thomas. Asst. prof. meterology and geology U. Wis., 1946-48, asst. prof. meteorology, 1948-50, asso. prof., 1950-56, chmn. dept., 1948-50, 52-54, prof., 1957—, dir. Inst. for Environmental Studies, 1970—; prof. U. Ariz., 1956-57. Mem. various coms. Nat. Acad. Sci.-NRC, 1958—, mem. remote sensing com., 1964-67, mem. com. on mil. geography, 1966-69. Trustee Univ. Corp. for Atmospheric Research. Cited by Denison U., 1966. Fellow Am. Meterol. Soc.; mem. Wis. Phenological Soc. (past pres.), Soc. Am. Archaeology, Assn. Am. Geographers, Am. Geophys. Union, Am. Soc. for Limnology and Oceanography, Phi Beta Kappa, Sigma Xi, Phi Kappa Phi (hon.). Author: Atlas of 500 mb Wind Characteristics for the Northern Hemisphere, 1958; Atlas of Five-Day Normal Sea-Level Pressure Charts for the Northern Hemisphere, 1958; Atlas of 300 mb Wind Characteristics, 1959; also numerous articles. Application of climatic methods and information to cultural changes among Gt. Plains Indians climatic modification in India; meterol. methods in limnology and geography; interdisciplinary environmental studies. Home: 11 Rosewood Circle Madison WI 53711

BRYSON, VERNON, biologist; b. Detroit, Sept. 17, 1913; s. Lyman Lloyd and Hope (Mersereau) B.; A.B., U. Calif., 1934; A.M., Columbia, 1936, Ph.D., 1944; m. Jean Herreshoff, Aug. 25, 1935; children—Constance Herreshoff, David Lyman, Stephen, Susan Mersereau. Asst. dept. of zoology, Columbia, 1937-42; research asso., dept. of genetics, Carnegie Inst. of Washington, Cold Spring Harbor, N.Y., 1942-43; research biologist The Biol. Lab., Cold Spring Harbor, N.Y., 1943-55; research Chemical Corps, Office Naval Research AEC, Nat. Tb Assn.; lectr. Columbia, 1953-55, State U. N.Y., 1955-56, Adelphi Coll., 1956, Douglass Coll., (Rutgers), 1958-59; program dir. genetic and development biology, Nat. Sci. Found., 1955-56, cons., 1956-59; prof. microbiology Rutgers U., 1956—, asso. dir. Inst. of Microbiology, 1956-58. Recipient Newberry prize, Columbia, 1939. Fellow N.Y. Acad. Sci., A.A.A.S., Am. Acad. Microbiology; mem. Theobald Smith Society, Society for Study Evolution, Radiation Research Society, Am. Assn. U. Profs., Society for General Microbiology (Gt. Britain), Genetics Soc. Am., Am. Soc. Microbiologists, Am. Soc. Cell Biology, Tissue Culture Assn., Conf. Biol. Editors, L.I. Biol Assn. (trustee 1956—), Am. Type Culture

Collection (chmn.), Soc. Exptl. Biology and Medicine, Soc. Naturalists, Sigma Xi. Author articles in field. Editor: The American Naturalist, 1960-65. Home: 44 South Dr East Brunswick NJ 08816 ☆

BRZANA, STANISLAUS JOSEPH, bishop; b. Buffalo, July 1, 1917; s. Frank and Catherine (Mikosz) B.; B.A., St. Bonaventure Coll., 1938, M.A., 1946; S.T.D., Gregorian U., Rome, Italy, 1953. Ordained priest Roman Cath. Ch., 1941; assigned Buffalo Missionary Apostolate, 1941; asst. St. Joseph's Ch., Gowanda, N.Y., 1942, SS Peter & Paul, Jamestown, N.Y., 1943, 46; dir. Cath. Information Center, Buffalo, also weekend asst. Transfiguration Ch., 1949, asst., 1953; vice officialis of Tribunal of Diocese of Buffalo, in charge Tribunal Office, 1954-64, weekend asst. Our Lady of Grace Parish, Woodlawn, N.Y., 1956, adminstr., 1957; appt. Officialis Tribunal, Diocese of Buffalo, St. Adalbert's Parish, Buffalo, 1958; adminstr. Resurrection Parish, Cheektowaga, N.Y., 1959, Queen Peace Parish, Buffalo, 1959, pastor, 1961-1968; domestic prelate, 1959-64; aux. bishop Diocese Buffalo, 1964-68; bishop Diocese Ogdensburg, N.Y., 1968—; Mem. Diocesan Commn. on Sacred Liturgy, Music and Art, 1964; vicar Gen. Diocese of Buffalo, 1966-68. Home: 624 Washington St Ogdensburg NY 13669

BRZEZINSKI, ZBIGNIEW, govt. ofcl.; author; b. Warsaw, Poland, Mar. 28, 1928; s. Tadeusz and Leonia (Roman) B.; came to Can., 1938, naturalized, 1958; B.A. with 1st class honors in Econs. and Polit. Sci., McGill U., 1949; M.A. in Polit. Sci., Harvard, 1950, Ph.D., 1953; m. Emilie Ann Benes, June 11, 1955; children—Ian, Mark, Mika. inst. of govt. and research fellow Russian Research Center, Harvard, 1953-56; asst. prof. govt., research asso. Russian Research Center and Center Internat. Affairs, Harvard, 1956-60; asso. prof. pub. law and govt. Columbia, 1960-62, prof., 1962—, dir. Research Inst. Communist Affairs, 1962—, mem. faculty Russian Inst., 1960—; cons. State Dept., also RAND Corp., 1962—; mem. policy planning council Dept. of State. Mem. joint com. contemporary China, Social Sci. Research Council, 1961-62; guest lectr. numerous pvt. and govt. instns., 1953—; participant internat. confs., 1955—. Mem. hon. steering com. Young Citizens for Johnson, 1964—. Guggenheim fellow, 1960; Ford fellow, 1970; named one of ten outstanding young men U.S. Jr. Co. of C., 1963. Fellow Am. Acad. Arts and Scis.; mem. N.A.A.C.P., Council Fgn. Relations. Club: Federal City (Washington). Author: The Permanent Purge- -Politics in Soviet Totalitarianism, 1956; The Soviet Bloc—Unity and Conflict, 1960; Ideology and Power in Soviet Politics, 1962; Alternative to Partition, 1965; Between Two Ages, 1970; co-author: Totalitarian Dictatorship and Autocracy, 1957; also numerous articles. Editor, contbr.: Political Controls in the Soviet Army, 1954; Africa and the Communist World, 1963; Political Power: USA/USSR, 1964 (German edit. 1966); Alternative to Partition: For A Broader Conception of America's Role In Europe, 1965 (German edit. 1966, Polish edit. 1966); Dilemmas Of Change In Soviet Politics, 1969; Dilemmi Internationazionali In Un-epoca. Teonetronica, 1969. Columnist, Newsweek, 1970—. Home: 40 Brayton St Englewood NJ 07631 Office: Research Inst on Communist Affairs Columbia U 420 W 118th St New York City NY 10027

BUA-IAM, PONG, diplomat of Thailand; b. Ayudhya, Thailand, May 24, 1925; s. Moon and Phaew (Ratanavihok) B.-I.; LL.B., U. Moral and Polit. Scis., Bangkok, 1950; m. Yurawongsa Angsumalee, Apr. 3, 1951; children—Pruthidej, Pisnu, Bhandhuprem. Mem. Thai Ministry of Fgn. Affairs, 1945—; attache Royal Thai Embassy, Paris, 1951-55; chief consular sect. Ministry Fgn. Affairs, 1955-61; 2d sec. Royal Thai Embassy, Phnom-Penh, 1961-62, Vientiane, 1962-66, 1st sec., 1966-67; chief legal div. Ministry Fgn. Affairs, 1967-70; 1st sec. Royal Thai embassy, Washington, 1970—. Decorated comdr. Most Noble Order of Crown of Thailand. Home: 5910 Ryland Dr Bethesda MD 20034 Office: 2300 Kalorama Rd NW Washington DC 20008

BUBB, HENRY AGNEW, savs. and loan assn. exec.; b. Williamsport, Pa., Mar. 26, 1907; s. Harry A. and Marjorie (Wheeler) B.; student U. Kan., 1924-27; D.B.A. in Bus., Washburn U.; m. Elizabeth Black, June 26, 1929; 1 dau., Barbara Elizabeth (Mrs. John C. Dicus). Chmn. bd. Elizabeth (Mrs. John C. Dicus). Chmn. bd. Capitol Fed. Savs. and Loan Assn., Topeka, Mortgage Guaranty Ins. Corp. of Milw., MGIC Financial Corp., Milw., MGIC Investment Corp., Milw., Comml. Loan Ins. Corp., Milw.; vice chmn. N.Y. Guaranty Corp., N.Y.C., former chmn. Fed. Home Loan Bank of Corp., Milw., Comml. Loan Ins. Corp., Milw.; vice chmn. N.Y. Guaranty Corp., N.Y.C.; former chmn. Fed. Home Loan Bank of Topeka; dir. CIC Leasing Corp. of Buffalo, Columbian Title and Trust Co., Security Co., Security Benefit Life Ins. Co. Past pres. Mid-West Savings and Loan Conf.; past trustee Am. Savs. and Loan Inst.; mem. adv. com. of savs. and loan bus. Treasury Dept.; mem. task force Fed. Home Loan Bank Bd., Washington. Mem., chmn. bd. regents State of Kan.; chmn. Kan. Edn. Commn. Former dir. Shawnee County A.R.C.: former chmn. numerous charitable drives; chmn., mem. war loan and victory fund coms.; past vice chmn., mem. Topeka Planning Bd.; past chmn. Topeka Housing and Planning Com.; mem. Fiscal Adv. Bd. Topeka; chmn. United Fund; bd. regents Washburn U. Past nat. chmn. Young regents Washburn U. Past nat. chmn. Young Republicans. Bd. trustees Kan. U. Endowment Assn.; mem. Kan. Research Found. Recipient award Treasury Dept., 1946; Distinguished Service citation University of Kansas. Mem. U.S. (past chmn. legislative com., legislative cons., exec. com., past pres.), Kan. (past pres.) savs. and loan leagues, Internat. Union Savs. and Loan Assns. (v.p. exec. bd.), U.S., Kan. (past dir., v.p.), Topeka (past (past pres., dir.) chambers commerce, Kan. U. Alumni Assn. (past nat. pres.), S.A.R., 35th Div. Assn., Sigma Chi (past pres. alumni chpt.), Alpha Kappa Psi. Episcopalian (past warden). Mason (33 Shriner, past potentate, Jester), Elk, Rotarian. Clubs: Topeka Press, Topeka Country (past pres., dir.) (Topeka); Kansas City, The Cabiri; Garden of the Gods (Colorado Springs, Colo.) Home: 2701 Fairway Dr Topeka KS 66611 Topeka KS 66611 Office: 700 Kansas Av Topeka KS 66603

BUBIER, ROBERT HARVEY, city ofcl.; b. Hartford, Conn., June 12, 1927; s. Sylvester Breed and Ruth (Harvey) B.; A.B. in Journalism, U. Miami, 1951; m. Rosemary Theresa Brogan, July 26, 1951; children—Debra Ruth, Michelle. Personnel technician City of Ft. Lauderdale (Fla.), 1956-59, acting dir. recreation, also asst. city mgr., 1961-62, city mgr., 1963—. Dir. Civil Def., Ft. Lauderdale, 1964—. Bd. dirs. United Fund, YMCA, Swimming Hall of Fame. Served with USNR, 1943-46, USAF, 1951-53, 61-62. Recipient Good Govt. award Ft. Lauderdale Jr. C. of C., 1967. Mem. Internat. City Mgrs. Assn., Fla. (dir.), Broward Co. (pres.) leagues of municipalities, Am. Legion, Sigma Delta Chi, Sigma Chi. Episcopalian (vestryman). Rotarian, Elk. Home: 300 Lido Dr Fort Lauderdale FL 33301 Office: 100 N Andrews Av Fort Lauderdale FL 33302

BUCHAN, GEORGE COLIN, medical educator; b. Seattle, Aug. 30, 1927; s. George Bruce and Edith (Warren) B.; student U. Wash., 1944-46, 47-48, 52-54; M.D., McGill U., 1958; m. Elisabeth Louise Lehman, Mar. 3, 1962; children—Melissa Jane, Elizabeth Louise. Intern St. Luke's Hosp., Cleve., 1958-59; resident, fellow U. Wash., Seattle, 1960-65; asst. prof. pathology Med. Sch., U. Ore., Portland, 1965-67, prof., head div. neuropathology, 1968—; cons. pathology Portland VA Hosp., 1969—. Served with M.C., AUS, 1946-47. Mem. Am. Assn. Neuropathologists. Home: 7305 SW 87th St Portland OR 97233

BUCHAN, LESLIE JAMES, educator; b. Clarion, Ia., Mar. 27, 1901; s. James and Fannie Luzetta B.; B.S., U. Ill., 1922, M.S. 1923, Ph.D., 1943; LL.D., Korea U., 1962; m. Bliss Seymour, Apr. 19, 1924; children-Bliss Seymour, Margaret Leslie. Instr. in accounting U. of Ill., 1922-24; accounting methods dept., Southwestern Bell Telephone Co., St. Louis, 1924-25; successively jr. and sr. accountant and partner Graham, Ramsey & Selden, C.P.A.'s, Miami, Fla., 1925-30; prof. accounting Tulane U., New Orleans, 1930-39, dean. Coll. Commerce and Business Adminstrn., 1939-49, asst. to pres. Tulane U. in finance adminstrn., 1944-47; dean Sch. of Bus., Pub. Adminstrn., Washington U., 1949-51, acting dean and dean faculties, 1950-51, vice chancellor, dean faculties, 1951-53, Distinguished Service prof. adminstrn., 1953—. Dir. R.D. Irwin, Inc. Trustee Am. Coll. Life Underwriters, 1963—. Served in S.A.T.C., 1918. C.P.A., Ill., La. Mem. Am. Assn. Collegiate Schs. Bus. (sec.-treas. 1943-47, pres. 1947-48), Am. Inst. Accountants (com. on acct. procedure 1940, 41), Am. Accounting Assn. (v.p. 1940; editorial bd. Accounting Rev. 1943-46), Am. Econ. Assn., Nat. Assn. Cost Accountants (dir. in charge publs. New Orleans chpt. 1939-47), New Orleans Assn. Commerce (mem. nat. legislation com. 1940), Am. Arbitration Assn. (mem. nat. panel arbitrators 1944), La. Small Business Adv., Bd, to the Gov. (mem. 1944-45), Beta Alpha Psi, Sigma Alpha Epsilon, Beta Gamma Sigma (nat. pres. 1963-), Omicron Delta Kappa. Home: 636 Jefferson St Hillsboro IL 62049.

BUCHANAN, ALBERT BROWN, clergyman; b. Milroy, Pa., Oct. 24, 1916; s. Blair G. and Helen Spengler (Brown) B.; B.A., Oberlin Coll., 1938; S.T.B., Union Theol. Sem., 1942; grad. student Columbia, 1950-52; m. Barbara Hall Masten, Feb. 13, 1943; children—Ann Blair, Constance Hall, Mark Landrum. Ordained to ministry Episcopal Ch., 1953; asst. prof. religion and history Western civilization Hobart Coll., 1946-47; chmn. dept. religion Northfield Schs., E. Northfield, Mass., 1947-50; asst. minister St. Bartholomew's Episcopal Ch., N.Y.C., 1952-59; rector Calvary Episcopal Ch., N.Y.C., 1959—; lectr. religious studies Spence Sch., N.Y.C., 1953-65. Dean Manhattan conv. Episcopal Ch., 1962-67; fellow Coll. Preachers, Nat. Cathedral, Washington, 1960-61. Bd. mgrs. Episcopal Diocese N.Y., 1962-67; bd. dirs. Union Theol. Sem., 1963- -, City Mission Soc. N.Y., 1954-71, Fedn. Protestant Welfare Agencies, N.Y.C., 1962—, Community Council Greater N.Y., 1961-64. Served to maj. AUS, 1942-46; ETO. Decorated Bronze Star with Oak leaf cluster; Croix de Guerre with silver star (France). Mem. Soc. Cum Laude, Alumni Assn. Union Theol. Sem. (pres. 1965-67), Gramercy Park Assn. (v.p. 1964—), Delta Sigma Rho. Home: 61 Gramercy Park New York City NY 10010

BUCHANAN, ARCHIBALD C., ret. judge; b. Tazewell, Va., Jan. 7, 1890; s. A. Beauregard and Nannie E. (Chapman) B.; A.B., Hampden-Sydney Coll., 1910; LL.B., Washington and Lee U., 1914, LL.D., 1949; m. Ollie McCall, Dec. 18, 1915; children—Sara (Mrs. Herbert Silvers, dec.), Archibald C. Admitted to Va. bar, 1914; gen. practice state and fed. courts, 1915-27; mem. law partnership, Chapman, Peery and Buchanan, Tazewell, Va., judge 22d jud. circuit of Va., 1927-46 justice Supreme Ct. Appeals of Va., 1946-69; mayor, Tazewell, Va., 1917-21; commr. of accounts, Tazewell County, 1919-27; mem. Jud. Council Va., 1928-32; com. (chmn.) of judges to fix salaries of trial justices of Va. and their clerks, 1942-46; com. of Judiciary of Va. State Bar, 1941-46. Recipient Algernon Sydney Sullivan Medallion, 1950. Trustee Hampden-Sydney Coll., 1928-69, Mary Baldwin Coll., Staunton, Va., 1948-62. Mem. Am. Bar Assn., Va. Historic Soc., Va. Bar Assn., Pi Kappa Alpha, Phi Delta Phi, Phi Beta Kappa. Democrat. Presbyn. (elder). Clubs: Tazewell County Country, Rotary, Commonwealth. Home: Tazewell VA 24651

BUCHANAN, DANIEL HARVEY, educator; b. New Haven, Sept. 18, 1923; s. James and Kathryn (Dolan) B.; B.A., Yale, 1945, M.A., 1948, Ph.D., 1953; m. Penelope Minturn Draper, Dec. 28, 1949. War relief work in France and Germany with Am. Friends Service Com., 1944-47; with Quaker UN Relief Program, Gaza, Palestine, 1949; mem. faculty Case Inst. Tech., 1952-67, prof. history, head dept. humanities and social studies, 1962-67; asso. dean humanities, head div. interdisciplinary studies Case Western Res. U., 1967-71, dean humanities, fine arts, 1971—; cons. Ohio Arts Council, 1966—. Pres. Cleve. Soc. Contemporary Art, 1965—. Mem. bd. Hathaway Brown Sch. Fulbright fellow Italian Inst. Hist. Studies, Naples, 1949-51. Mem. Am. Hist. Assn., Ohio Acad. History. Mem. Soc. Friends. Club: Elizabethan (Yale). Contbr. profl. jours. Home: Battles Rd Gates Mills OH 44040 Office: Crawford Hall Case Western Res U Cleveland OH 44106

BUCHANAN, DEWITT WHEELER, Jr., coal mine exec.; b. Chgo., Dec. 16, 1916; s. D.W. and Helen (Stoppenbach) B.; B.S., Princeton, 1938; m. Katherine L. Hamilton, Apr. 27, 1940; children—K. Reed, DeWitt Wheeler, III, Kenneth Hamilton. Pres., Old Ben Coal Corp., Chgo.; dir. A., W. & W. Ry., Standard Oil Co. (Ohio), Portec, Inc. Served to lt. USNR. Office: 10 S Riverside Plaza Chicago IL 60606

BUCHANAN, DOUGLAS N., educator, neurologist; b. Scotland, Jan. 14, 1901; s. Andrew Dick and Mary (Nisbet) B.; M.A., B.Sc., M.B., Ch.B., U. Glasgow (Scotland), 1925; postgrad. Trinity Coll., Cambridge (Eng.) U., 1925-30, U. Paris, 1924, 31; M.D. (hon.). U. San Carlos de Guatemala, 1956; m. Marian Anderson, 1930. Formerly mem. faculty staff Nat. Hosp. Nervous Diseases, London, Eng; mem. faculty Med. Sch., U. Chgo., 1932—, prof. neurology 1940—; neurologist U. Chgo. Hosps., 1932—; attending and cons. neurologist Children's Meml. Hosp., Chgo., 1935—. Cons. neurologist D.R.G., NIH, Washington, 1964-68, chmn., 1968-71. Mem. Am. Neurol. Assn., Am. Pediatric Soc., Chgo. Neurol. Soc. (pres. 1956). Home: 5344 Hyde Park Blvd Chicago IL 60615 Office: 950 E 59th St Chicago IL 60637

BUCHANAN, G. CAMERON, lawyer; b. Ontario Can., Oct. 12, 1906; s. Robert G. and Mary (Henry) B.; ed. Wayne State U.; LL.B., Detroit Coll. Law, 1930; m. Helen G. Mansfield, Aug. 12, 1933; children—Cameron F., Dean M. Admitted to Mich. bar, 1930, since practiced in Detroit; sr. mem. firm Alexander, Buchanan & Conklin. Chmn. lawyers div. United Found. Detroit, 1963. Trustee Detroit Coll. Law, 1955—, v.p., 1958—. Fellow Am. Coll. Trial Lawyers; mem. Detroit Bar Assn. (dir. 1957-33, pres. 1962-63), Internat. Assn. Ins. Counsel (exec. com.), Am. Bar Assn., State Bar Mich. Mason. Clubs: Detroit Athletic, Detroit; Birmingham (Mich.) Country. Home: 31055 Woodside Dr Franklin MI 48025 Office: 2217 First Nat Bldg Detroit MI 48226

BUCHANAN, JAMES MCGILL, Jr., economist, educator; b. Murfreesboro, Tenn., Oct. 2, 1919; s. James McGill and Lila (Scott) B.; B.S., Middle Tenn. State Coll., 1940; M.A., U. Tenn., 1941; Ph.D. (fellow So. Regional Program Pub. Adminstrn.), U. Chgo., 1948; m. Anne Bakke, Oct. 5, 1945. Prof. econs. U. Tenn., 1950-51; prof. econs. Fla. State U., 1951-54, prof., chmn. dept., 1954-56; prof. econs. U. Va., 1956-62, Paul G. McIntyre prof. econs., 1962-68, chmn. dept., 1956-62; prof. econs. U. Cal., Los Angeles, 1968-69; univ. prof. econs. Va. Polytech. Inst., 1969- -; dir. Center for Publ. Choice, 1969—; Fulbright research scholar, Italy, 1955-56; Ford Faculty research fellow, 1959-60; Fulbright vis. prof. Cambridge U., 1961-62. Served as lt. USNR, 1941-46. Decorated Bronze Star medal. Mem. Am. (exec. com. 1966-69, v.p. 1971), So. (pres. 1963) econ. assns., Royal Econ. Soc. Author: (with C.L. Allen and M.R. Colberg) Prices, Income and Public Policy, 1954; Public Principles of Public Debt, 1958; The Public Finances, 1960; Fiscal Theory and Political Economy, 1960: (with G. Tullock) The Calculus of Consent, 1962: Public Finance in Democratic Process, 1966; The Demand and Supply of Public Goods, 1968; Cost and Choice, 1969; (with N. Devleloglov) Academia in Anarchy, 1970. Contbr. profl. jours. Home: 504 South Gate Dr Blacksburg VA 24060

BUCHANAN, JESSE EVERETT, civil engr.; b. nr. Algona, Ia., Apr. 22, 1904; s. Sophus and Jessie Ann (Samuelson) B.; B.S., U. Ida., 1927, M.S., 1929, C.E., 1936, L.H.D., 1951, Sc.D. 1953; m. Leah Rachel Tuttle, June 10, 1929; children—Nancy Tuttle, John Austin. Instr. civil engring., testing engr. U. Ida., Ida. Bur. Hwys., 1927-29, asst. prof., testing engr., 1929-36, dean Coll. Engring., dir. engring. Expt. Sta., prof. civil engring., 1938-42, pres., 1946-54; research engr. Asphalt Inst., 1936-38, pres., 1954-69, cons., 1969—. Mem. Ida. Bd. Engring. Examiners, 1939-48; sec. Automotive Safety Found., Washington, 1956-69. Served to lt. col. C.E., AUS, 1942-46; CBI. Decorated Legion of Merit. Mem. Nat., Ida., Md. socs., profl. engrs., Am. Soc. C.E., Am. Rd. Builders Assn., Newcomen Soc., Phi Beta Kappa, Sigma Xi, Tau Beta Pi, Sigma Tau. Home: 1110 Kathryn Rd Silver Spring MD 20904 Office: Asphalt Inst College Park MD 20740

BUCHANAN, JOHN DONALD, Jr., ins. co. exec.; b. St. Joseph, Mo., June 5, 1914; s. John Donald and Florence (Holman) B.; student Grinell Coll., 1932-33, Creighton U., 1933- 37; C.L.U., 1952; m. Jo Janet Dodds, Sept. 7, 1940; children—Margaret Susan (Mrs. Stephen Davies), Jo Janet, Nancy Dodds. Sec. to Bishop Oxnam of Methodist Ch., 1936-39; with WPB and War Assets Adminstrn., 1942-47; with Prudential Ins. Co. Am., 1947—, v.p., 1963-65, sr. v.p., charge S. Central home office, Jacksonville, Fla., 1965—. Mem. Fla. Council One Hundred, Jacksonville-Duval Area Planning Bd. Bd. dirs. Jr. Achievement. United Fund, YMCA, Jacksonville; mem. Jacksonville bd. Nat. Conf. Christians and Jews. Mem. Jacksonville Area (pres. elect), Fla. (dir.) chamber commerce. Clubs: River (pres.) University, Deerwood Country, Ponte Vedra, St. Johns Dinner (dir.), Baymeadows Golf (Jacksonville). Home: 8123 Summit Ridge Lane Jacksonville FL 32216 Office: 841 Prudential Dr Jacksonville FL 32201

BUCHANAN, JOHN GRIER, lawyer; b. Allegheny (now Pitts.), Pa., July 24, 1888; s. John Jenkins and Ellen (Grier) B.; student Shady Side Acad., Pittsburgh, 1902-05; A.B., Princeton, 1909; LL.B., Harvard, 1912; LL.D., U. Pitts., 1954, Waynesburg Coll., 1959; m. Charity A. Packer, Nov. 14, 1916 (dec. Mar. 1950); children—John Grier (dec.), Gibson Packer, James Junkin; m. 2d, Olive Elizabeth McDougall, Dec. 28, 1959. Admitted to Pa. bar, 1912, U.S. Supreme Court, 1918; asso. firm Gordon & Smith 1912-16, partner firm Ingersoll, Rodewald Kyle & Buerger, and Predecessors, 1916- -; prof. law U. Pitts., 1914-37. Served as 1st lt. San. Corps. Nat. Army, Feb.-Sept. 1918; capt. U.S. Army, staff Judge Adv. Gen., 1918-19; maj., Judge Adv., O.R.C., 1919-24. Trustee Princeton, Princeton Theol. Sem., Shady Side Acad., Holmes House; corporator, past mem. bd. mgrs. Allegheny Cemetery; bd. dirs. Pitts. History Found.; vice chmn. overseers com. to visit Harvard Law Sch. Mem. procedural rules com. Supreme Ct. Pa., 1937-45. Named Man of Year in Law, Jr. C. of C. Pitts., 1957. Fellow Am. Bar Found. (Fifty-Year award 1969), Am. Coll. Trial Lawyers; mem. Internat. Law Assn. (exec. com. Am. br.), Am. Law Inst. (com. on conflict of laws 1923-34, mem. council 1938—, exec. com. past 2d vice pres.), Am. Judicature Soc. (v.p. 1939-41, Am. (v.p. Pa. 1931-32; mem. house dels. 1937-38, 1940, 46, 48; chmn. com. on judiciary 1946-49), Pa. (pres. 1945-46), Allegheny Co. (pres. 1940-41) bar assns., Assn. Bar City of N.Y., Harvard Law Sch. Assn. (pres. 1949-51), Fgn. Policy Assn. (chmn. Pitts. br. 1934-36), Phi Beta Kappa Assos., Phi Beta Kappa (pres. assn. Western Pa. 1946-54). Republican. Presbyn. Clubs: Harvard-Yale-Princeton (pres. 1940-41), Duquesne, University, Pittsburgh Golf, Law (Pittsburgh); Cosmos (Washington); Terrace (Princeton); Princeton (New York). Contbr. to law jours. Home: 620 Amberson Av Pittsburgh PA 15232 Office: Oliver Bldg Pittsburgh PA 15222

BUCHANAN, JOHN HALL, Jr., congressman; b. Paris, Tenn., Mar. 19, 1928; s. John Hall and Ruby (Lowrey) B.; A.B., Howard Coll., 1949; postgrad. U. Va., 1950-51; Th.B., So. Baptist Theol. Sem., 1957; LL.D., Samford U., 1967; m. Elizabeth Moore, May 9, 1961; children—Elizabeth Jakes, Lynn Lowrey. Ordained to ministry Baptist Ch., 1952; pastor in Glasgow, Va., 1952-53, Hartsville, Tenn., 1955-56, Birmingham, Ala., 1957-62; minister edn. Southside Bapt. Ch., Birmingham, 1953-54; speaker, lectr. in Ala., also interim and supply pastor, 1962-64; mem. 89th-92d congresses 6th Dist. Ala. Chmn. Jefferson County Republican Party, 1964—; pres. Rep. Workshops Ala., 1963-64; mem. exec. com., dir. finance Ala. Rep. Party, 1963-64. Served with USNR, 1945-46. Mem. Pi Kappa Alpha. Mason, Kiwanian. Home: 120 Crestview Dr Birmingham AL 35213 Office: Longworth House Office Bldg Washington DC 20515

BUCHANAN, JOHN MACHLIN, educator; b. Winamac, Ind., Sept. 29, 1917; s. Harry James and Eunice Blanche (Miller) B.; A.B., De Pauw U., 1938; M.S., U. Mich., 1939, D.Sc., 1961; Ph.D., Harvard, 1943; m. Elsa Nilsby, Dec. 11, 1948; children—Claire Louise, Stephen James, Lisa Renne, Peter Nilsson. Instr. dept. physiol. chemistry Sch. Medicine U. Pa., 1943-46, asst. prof., 1946-49, asso. prof., 1949-50, prof., 1950-53; NRC fellow Med. Nobel Inst., Stockholm, 1946-48; prof., head div. biochemistry dept. biology Mass. Inst. Tech., 1953-67, Wilson prof. biochemistry, 1967—; lectr. Harvey Soc., 1958. Civilian with Nat. Def. Research Com., 1943; mem. subcom. blood and related substances NRC, 1951-55, mem. med. fellowship bd., 1954—; fellow Guggenheim Meml. Found., 1964-65, leave of absence to Salk Inst. Biol. Studies, LaJolla, Cal. Mem. Am. Soc. Biol. Chemists, Am. Chem. Soc. (Eli Lilly award in biol. chemistry 1951), Am. Acad. Sci., Internat. Union Biochemists (mem. nat. com.), Nat. Acad. Scis., Sigma Xi. Mem. editorial bd. Jour. Biol. Chemistry, 1961-67, Jour. Am. Chemistry Soc., 1961-68, Physiol. Revs., 1957-60, 65—. Home: 56 Meriam St Lexington MA 02173

BUCHANAN, JOHN MURDOCH, ret. univ. chancellor; b. Steveston, B.C., July 21, 1897; s. Donald and Christie Ann (Morrison) B.; B.A., U. B.C., 1917; m. Mildred Abercrombie, Mar. 14, 1925; 1 son, 1 dau. Fishing bus., Steveston, B.C., 1917-20; with firm of auditors, 1920-21, Cedar's Ltd., lumber mfrs., 1921-27; with British Columbia Packers, Ltd., 1928-64, sec.-treas., 1932, gen. mgr., 1935, v.p., gen. mgr., 1941, pres., 1946-56 chmn. bd., 1956- 58, chmn. bd., pres., 1958-64; dir. Mac Millan & Bloedel. Ltd., B.C. Packers Ltd.; adv. com. Erie Mortgage Corp.; chancellor U. B.C., Vancouver, 1966-69. Mem. United Ch. of Can. Clubs: Vancouver, Faculty, University of Vancouver (hon.). Home: 2095 Beach Av Vancouver 5 British Columbia Canada

BUCHANAN, JOHN ROBERT, physician, educator; b. Newark, Mar. 8, 1928; s. John Hamilton and Elsie (Castles) B.; A.B. cum laude, Amherst Coll., 1950; M.D., Cornell U., 1954; student Inst. Arthritis and Metabolic Diseases, USPHS, 1956-57, 60- 61; m. Susan Townsend Carver, Oct. 27, 1962; children—Ross, Allyn. Intern, asst. resident physician N.Y. Hosp., N.Y.C., 1954-58, physician to outpatients, 1956-57, 60-62, asst. attending physician, 1962—, asso. dir. welfare med. care project, 1961-64; vis. asst. physician Rockefeller

Inst. Hosp., N.Y.C., 1960-61; asso. vis. physician Bellevue Hosp., N.Y.C., 1965-68; instr. medicine Cornell U., 1961-63, asst. prof. medicine, 1963-67, asst. dir. comprehensive care and teaching program, 1961-64, asst. to chmn. dept. medicine, 1964-65, asso. dean Med. Coll., 1965-69, dean; 1969—, clin. asso. prof. medicine, 1967-69, asso. prof., 1969-71, prof., 1971—. Mem. com. on sci. policy Sloan-Kettering Inst., 1969—. Bd. dirs. Pub. Health Research Inst. of N.Y.C., 1969—; trustee China Med. Bd. of N.Y., Inc., 1970; bd. mgrs. Meml. Hosp., 1969—. Capt. AUS, 1958-60. Diplomate Am. Bd. Internal Medicine, Nat. Bd. Med. Examiners. Fellow A.C.P., mem. Harvey Soc., N.Y. State, N.Y. County med. socs., N.Y. Acad. Scis., Assn. Med. Colls., N.Y. Acad. Medicine, Royal Soc. for Promotion Health, Sigma Xi. Home: 10 Dellwood Circle Bronxville NY 10708 Office: 1300 York Av New York City NY 10021

BUCHANAN, LILIAN BARKER, librarian; b. Charleston, W.Va., Sept. 24, 1896; d. John Quenton and Mamie Deborah (Keeney) Barker; B.S., Western Carolina Coll., 1934; M.S., Columbia, 1938; m. Corsey Candler Buchanan, May 10, 1920; 1 son, John Osborne. Head primary dept. Sylva (N.C.) Collegiate Inst., 1919-21; tchr. English, Sylva High Sch., 1926-27; librarian Western Carolina U., 1930—. Founder, Pub. Library, Sylva, N.C., 1928. Edna M. Sanderson fellow Columbia Library Sch., 1942-43. Mem. N.C. Library Assn. (chmn. coll. and univ. library div. 1957). Club: Twentieth Century of Sylva (1st pres. 1925-27). A founder Smoky Mountain Nat. Park. Home: Dillsboro NC 28725

BUCHANAN, MARK TWAIN, agrl. scientist; b. Van Buren, Mo., June 6, 1915; s. Charles Rock and Lenora Forstelle (Rodgers) B.; B.S., U. Mo., 1937; Ph.D., Cornell, 1940; m. Laura Lou Maxwell, Dec. 18, 1937; children—Thomas Mark, Linda Lee, Charles Robert. Grad. asst. Cornell U., 1937-40; with Wash. State U., 1940-69, beginning as asst. agriculturalist, successively extension marketing specialist, research and tchr. agrl. econs., chmn. dept. agrl. econs., vice dir. Inst. Agrl. Scis., dir. Agrl. Expt. Stas., prof. agr., chief adviser Wash. State U. field party to U. Punjab, Pakistan, 1940-58, campus coordinator Pakistan Project, 1958- 63; dir. aat large Western Assn. Agrl. Expt. Stas., 1967—. Mem. governing bd. Agrl. Research Inst., Nat. Acad. Scis.-NRC, 1965-67; mem. exec. com. Nat. Assn. State Univs. and Land-Grant Colls., 1964-65; mem. ad hoc joint com. U.S. Dept. Agr.-SAES Relations, 1968. Gen. Motors fellow Cornell U.; Found. Econ. Edn. fellow, 1951. Mem. Am., Western farm econ. assns., A.A.A.S., Sigma Xi, Alpha Zeta, Gamma Sigma Delta, Alpha Phi Sigma, Phi Eta Sigma, Phi Kappa Phi. Club: Commonwealth (San Francisco). Home: 1945 Berkeley Way Berkeley CA 94704

BUCHANAN, PATRICK JOSEPH, govt. ofcl.; b. Washington, Nov. 2, 1938; s. William Baldwin and Catherine E. (Crum) B.; A.B. in English, Georgetown U., 1961; M.S. in Journalism, Columbia, 1962; m. Shelley Ann Scarney, May 8, 1971. Editorial writer St. Louis Globe Democrat, 1962-64, asst. editorial editor, 1964-66; exec. asst. to Richard M. Nixon, 1966-69; spl. asst. to Pres. Nixon, 1969—. Mem. President's Commn. White House Fellowships. Home: 2500 Virginia Av NW Washington DC 20037 Office: The White House Washington DC 20008

BUCHANAN, PAUL HYDE, Jr., state judge; b. Indpls., Jan. 6, 1918; s. Paul Hyde and Ruth (Geiger) B.; B.A., Swarthmore Coll., 1939; LL.B., U. Denver, 1948; fellow U. Cin., 1940; m. Betty Kerbox, June 24, 1950; children—Brian Kerbox, Bruce Warren, Lucinda. Admitted to Ind. bar, 1948; pvt. practice law, Indpls., 1949-55; partner firm Cook, Bose & Buchanan (name changed in 1957 to Cook, Bose, Buchanan & Evans and in 1963 to Bose, Buchanan, McKinney & Evans), Indpls., 1955—, mng. partner, 1957—; judge Ind. Appellate Ct., 1971—. Served to lt. (j.g.) USNR, 1940-44. Mem. Indpls. (pres. 1968), Am. (house of dels. 1968-69), Ind. State (mem. house of dels. 1964—, bd. mgrs. 1969) bar assns., Indpls. Jr. C. of C. (pres. 1952), Phi Delta Theta, Phi Delta Phi. Methodist (chmn. trustees 1969-70, dir. weekday religious edn. sr. citizens center 1967—). Club: Contemporary (pres. 1969—) (Indpls.). Contbr. articles to legal jours., author law column. Home: 5936 Stafford Rd Indianapolis IN 46208 Office: State House Indianapolis IN 46204

BUCHANAN, PERCY WILSON, educator; b. Takamatsu, Japan, of missionary parents, Sept. 7, 1900; s. Walter McSimon and Mary Atlee (Wilson) B.; Certificate of Graduation, dept. music, Maryville (Tenn.) Coll., 1921, A.B., 1922; B.D., Union Theol. Sem. 1925; A.M., Princeton, 1932, Ph.D., 1947; m. Clara Mildred Browning, June 23, 1921; children—Dorothy June (Mrs. Forrest Leon Duncan), Donal Browning. Ordained to ministry Presbyn. Ch., 1925; commd. missionary, 1925, head music dept. Kinjo Coll., Nagoya, Japan, 1925-40; linguistic research in Mongolia for Am. Philosophic Soc., summers 1937, 38, 39; instr. Japanese lang., Princeton, 1941; head Intelligence Lang. Sch., Washington, 1942-45; head, counter intelligence tng. div., Tokyo, Japan, 1945-46; vis. prof. Far Eastern history U. Colo., 1947-48; dir. Inst. Asiatic Affairs, U. Okla., 1948—, also prof. history. Served with Tank Corps, U.S. Army, World War I. Awarded Congl. citation, World War II. Mem. Am. Oriental Soc., Conf. on Asian Affairs (permanent sec.), Am. Hist. Soc., Far Eastern Assn., Asiatic Soc. Japan. Author: Glossary of Japanese Business Terms, 1945; (with others) A History of the Far East, 1958. Composer: Simon Peter, 1937. Home: 1118 E Idaho St Norman OK 73069☆

BUCHANAN, PHILIP FOSTER, univ. ofcl.; b. Kenney, Ill., Nov. 2, 1920; s. Ralph Lester and Helen (Foster) B.; B.S., Wis. State Coll., 1947; M.S., U. Wis., 1948, Ph.D., 1967; m. Helen Ann Hegy, Aug. 28, 1948; children—Peter, Pamela, David, Cheryl. Tchr. Ann Arbor (Mich.) High Sch., 1948-51, adminstrv. asst., 1951-54; mng. editor Menomonee Falls (Wis.) News, 1954-55; dir. pub. information Ann Arbor pub. schs., 1955-57; dir. pub. relations Wis. State U., 1957—. Mem. exec. bd. Blackhawk Council Boy Scouts Am., 1971, dist. commr. Mound dist., 1971. Served with USAAF, 1943-45. Mem. Am. Assn. U. Profs., Phi Delta Kappa. Home: 260 W Cedar St Platteville WI 53818

BUCHANAN, ROBERT NORMAN, Jr., physician; b. Hendersonville, Tenn., Mar. 13, 1911; s. Robert Norman and Margaret Jane (Terry) B.; A.B., Vanderbilt U., 1931, M.D., 1934; m. Rachelle Blackman, Sept. 15, 1945; children—Robert Norman, John Blackman, Jane Blackman, Alexander Blackman. Intern Vanderbilt U. Hosp., 1934-35, City Hosp. Cleve., 1934; resident Mass. Gen. Hosp., 1939-41; individual practice gen. medicine, Lebanon, Tenn., 1936-39; individual practice dermatology, Nashville, 1939—; mem. staff Vanderbilt U. Hosp., VA Hosp., Nashville, Park View Hosp., Nashville; cons. staff St. Thomas Hosp., Hasville, Nashville Meml. Hosp., Madison Meml. Hosp. (Tenn.), also VA, AEC. Served to lt. col. AUS, 1942-46. Diplomate Am. Bd. Dermatology nd Syphilology. Mem. Nashville Acad. Medicine, Tenn., So., Am. med. assns., Am. Dermatol. Assn., Am. Acad. Dermatology and Syphilology, Alpha Omega Alpha, Alpha Kappa Alpha. Rotarian. Club: Belle Meade Country. Contbr. articles med. jours. Home: 1111 Belle Meade Blvd Nashville TN 37205 Office: 1905 Hayes St Nashville TN 37203

BUCHANAN, SAM A., mfg. co. exec.; b. Nashville, Mar. 8, 1914; s. Samuel Albert and Etta (Johnson) B.; LL.B., YMCA Law Sch., Nashville, 1941; m. Ann Campbell, Nov. 8, 1941; children—Sam A. III, Ann C. Admitted to Tenn. bar, 1941; with Genesco, Inc., 1935—, now v.p., group dir. mfg., distbg. outer apparel, also dir., gov., exec. and operating coms. Trustee Scarritt Coll., Nashville. Methodist (steward, chmn. personnel com. and youth div.). Clubs: Exchange Hillwood Country, Bluegrass Country (Nashville). Home: 709 Darden Pl Nashville TN 37205 Office: 111 7th Av Nashville TN 37203

BUCHANAN, WALLACE DAVIS, radiologist; b. Burnettsville, Ind., June 6, 1907; s. James J. and Fanny (Davis) B.; B.S., Ind. U., 1930, M.D., 1933; m. Ione Hamilton, Sept. 15, 1928; children—Jane (Mrs. Paul F. Arnold), Sally Kay (Mrs. David A. Giordano). Intern Indpls. City Hosp., 1933; pvt. practice gen. medicine, Bremen, Ind., 1934-42; resident physician radiology Wesley Meml. Hosp., Chgo., 1946-47; pvt. practice radiology, South Bend, Ind., 1947—; mem. staff St. Joseph Hosp., South Bend, St. Joseph Hosp., Mishawaka, Ind.; pres. bd. mgr. St. Joseph County Tb Hosp., 1963—. Bd. dirs. South Bend Symphony Orch., St. Joseph County Scholarship Fund; hon. trustee St. Joseph County Tb League. Served with USNR, 1942- 46. Fellow Am. Coll. Radiology (bd. chancellors 1961—, chmn. bd. 1964- 65, pres. 1965-66); mem. Am. Roentgen Ray Soc., Ind. (pres. 1960), Chgo. (non resident) roentgen socs., Am. Soc. Therapeutic Radiologists, St. Joseph County Med. Soc. (pres. 1956), Am., Ind. med. assns., Detroit Roentgen Ray and Radium Soc., Radiol. Soc. N. Am., Lambda Chi Alpha, Phi Chi. Presbyn. (elder). Mason (Shriner). Club: South Bend Country (dir. 1966). Home: 1326 E Wayne St N South Bend IN 46615 Office: 919 E Jefferson Blvd South Bend IN 46622

BUCHANAN, WESLEY EVANS, builder, developer; b. Washington, Oct. 6, 1917; s. J. Wesley and Rosalyn (Evans) B.; B.S., Wharton Sch. of U. Pa., 1940; m. Mary Clifton LaForce, Mar. 12, 1941; children—Robert Evans, Dorothy Elaine, Hope Louise (Mrs. Lance Alan Wilmarth), Jane Adele (Mrs. William Gurley). With W. Evans Buchanan Cos., 1940—, pres., 1960—; v.p., dir. County Fed. Savs. & Loan Assn., Rockville, Md., 1957—. Bd. dirs. Nat. Council Good Cities, 1964-65; mem. housing and urban devel. adv. com. AID, 1964-65; mem. performance concept in bldg. com. Bldg. Research Adv. Bd., Nat. Acad. Scis., 1965; mem. com. vol. home mortgage credit program HHFA, 1963; mem. home improvement adv. com. FHA, 1959-60; pub. mem. Geneva (Switzerland) Conf. Housing, Bldg. and Planning Com., Econ. Commn. for Europe, 1963; trustee Nat. Housing Center, 1964-65; mem. nat. adv. council Urban America; mem. adv. bd. AID; Housing and Urban Devel., 1971. cons. Project Rehab. Pres. Montgomery County Boys Baseball Assn., 1956; mem. Pres.'s Nat. Tax Revision Com., 1963. Bd. govs. Nat. Cathedral Sch., 1960-66. Mem. Nat. Assn. Home Builders (pres. 1963), Home Builders Assn. Met. Washington (pres. 1958), real estate bds. D.C., Md. Presbyn. (past vice chmn. trustees). Clubs: Columbia Country (Chevy Chase, Md.); Touchdown, University, Nat. Democratic (Washington). Home: 9616 Hawick Lane Kensington MD 20795 Office: 8720 Georgia Av Silver Spring MD 20910

BUCHANAN, WILEY THOMAS, Jr., diplomat, govt. ofcl., corp. exec.; b. Myrtle Hill, Van Zandt County, Tex., Jan. 4, 1914; s. Wiley T. and Lilla A. (Youngblood) B.; student So. Meth. U., George Washington U.; LL.D., Alam Coll.; H.H.D., Dickinson Coll.; m. Ruth Elizabeth Hale, Apr. 12, 1940; children—Bonnie Ruth (Mrs. C.T. Matheson), Diane Dow, Wiley Thomas III. Sec.-treas. Nat. Agrol Co., 1942-50; v.p. Berks Parachute Co., Reading, Pa., 1943-46; bd. dirs. Nat. Savs. & Trust Bank, Washington, Mut. Broadcasting Corp., L'Enfant Plaza Corp. Exec. sec. machine tool br., tech. intelligence investigating com., Joint Chiefs of Staff, World War 11; head metal cutting tool dept. NPA, 1950-52; minister to Luxembourg, 1953-55, ambassador, 1955-57; chief protocol U.S. with rank of ambassador, 1957-61. Bd. dirs. D.C. Symphony Orch., Fed. City Council; nat. adv. bd. Boy Scouts Am.; trustee of Johns Hopkins Sch. Advanced Internat. Studies, George Washington U., Landon Sch. for Boys, Bethesda, Md. Decorated by govts. of Belgium, Luxembourg, Denmark, P.I., Thailand; comdr. Legion of Honor (France), Knight Comdr. of Merit (Germany). Methodist. Clubs: Everglades (Palm Beach, Fla.); Metropolitan, 1925 F Street (Washington); Chevy Chase (Md.); Dallas Country, Brook Hollow Country (Dallas); Grand Ducal Golf (Luxembourg); Travelers (Paris); Reading Room, Spouting Rock Beach, Clambake (Newport, R.I.). Author: Red Carpet at the White House, 1964. Home: Under Oak 4220 Nebraska Av Washington DC 20016 (summer) Beaulieu Newport RI 02840 (winter) Round Hill Montego Bay Jamaica British West Indies Office: 1100 New Hampshire Av NW Washington DC 20037

BUCHANAN, WILLIAM, educator; b. Richmond, Va., Dec. 25, 1918; s. Daniel Littleton and Cora (Briggs) B.; A.B., Washington and Lee U., 1941, M.A., 1941; M.A., Princeton, 1953, Ph.D., 1955; m. Vivian Landrum, Aug. 8, 1946; children—James Landrum, David Briggs, Mary Warrington. Instr. English, Roanoke Coll., 1946-47; asso. dir. Bicentennial of Washington and Lee, 1947-49; asst. prof. govt. Miss. State U., 1952-55; exec. dir. Woodrow Wilson Centennial Commn. Va., 1956; asst. prof. polit. sci. U. So. Cal., 1956—58, asso. prof., 1958-62; vis. research prof. legislative process U. Cal. at Berkeley, 1959-60; prof. polit. sci. U. Tenn., 1962-66; prof., head dept. polit. sci. Washington and Lee U., Lexington, Va., 1966—. Mem. council Interuniv. Consortium Polit. Research, 1964-66. Bd. dirs. Clinch-Powell River Valley Assn., 1965-66. Served to lt. comdr. USNR, 1942-46. Mem. Am. Polit. Sci. Assn. (past council), Am. Assn. U. Profs., Phi Beta Kappa, Omicron Delta Kappa. Democrat. Methodist. Author: (with Hadley Cantril) How Nations See Each Other, 1953; Legislative Partisanship; The Deviant Case of California, 1963; Understanding Political Variables, 1969. Mem. editorial bd. Western Polit. Quar., 1963-64. Contbr. articles to profl. jours. Home: 618 Ross Rd Lexington VA 24450

BUCHANAN, WILLIAM EUGENE, wire works corp. exec.; b. Appleton, Wis., Jan. 11, 1903; s. Gustavus E. and Josephine (Pond) B.; B.S., Dartmouth, 1924, M.A. (hon.), 1962; M.B.A., Harvard, 1926; M.A. (hon.), Lawrence Coll., 1959; m. Josephine Breneman, Jan. 3, 1931; children—Charles, William, Jean, Robert. Chmn. bd., dir. Appleton Wire Works Corp., Outagamie Corp., Appleton, Albany Internat. Corp. (N.Y.); v.p., dir. 1st Nat. Bank, Appleton; mem. exec. com., dir. Allis-Chalmers Mfg. Co., Employers Mut. Liability Ins. Co., Wausau, Wis., Employers Mut. Fire Ins. Co., Wausau; dir. Menasha Corp., Am. Can Co., Breneman, Inc., Cin.; trustee, mem. exec. com. Northwestern Mut. Life Ins. Co., Milw. Trustee Lawrence U., Appleton, Dartmouth Coll. Republican. Conglist. Home: 345 Lake Rd Menasha WI 54952 Office: Appleton Wire Works Corp Appleton WI 54911

BUCHEN, IRVING H., educator; b. N.Y.C., Sept. 6, 1930; s. Morris and Lucille (Hochberg) B; B.A., N.Y. U., 1952, M.A., 1955; Ph.D., Johns Hopkins, 1960; m. Dorothy Leiter, Dec. 26, 1955; children—Nedda Aleen, Mishael. Prof. English, Farleigh Dickenson U., Madison, N.J., 1960—; cons. Western Electric, 1969—, Am. Camping Assn., 1970—. Mem. Northeast Modern Lang. Assn. (v.p.). Author: Isaac Bashevis Singer and the Eternal Past, 1968; The Perverse Imagination, 1970; also articles. Home: 24 Tralee Rd Hazlet NJ 07730 Office: 285 Madison Av Madison NJ 07730

BUCHENHOLZ, JANE JACOBS, ednl. exec.; b. Bklyn., Oct. 28, 1918; d. Joseph and Sofia (Frucht) Jacobs; A.B. magna cum laude, Hunter Coll., 1942; postgrad. psychology, New Sch. Social Research, 1947-48; m. Bruce Buchenholz, Feb. 22, 1942 (div. 1962); children—Nancy Jan, Susan Jay. Successively tchr. math., control chemist, plant pathologist, 1942-46; remedial reading tchr. Reading Clinic, N.Y. U., 1946-49; spl. tchr. emotionally disturbed children, 1948-49; pianist, accompanist modern dance classes, 1955-61; dir. Nat. Roosevelt Day Dinner, Ams. for Democratic Action, 1961- 66, nat. sec., 1963-67, mem. nat. bd., nat. exec. com., 1963—, recipient Chpt. Chairmen's award, 1963; dir. devel. New Sch. Social Research, 1968—, New Lincoln Sch., 1971—; exec. dir. radio sta. WMCA, Call for Action, 1962-64; research cons. voter registration Nat. Council Negro Women, 1964; spl. cons. systems and inventory control Crown Fabrics div. Bangor Punta Industries, 1966-68. Mem. nat. bd. Com. for Sane Nuclear Policy, 1966- 68; mem. nat. adv. council Nat. Conf. for New Politics, 1966-67; exec. dir. Broadway For Peace, 1968; mem. nat. council, nat. exec. com. Nat. Emergency Civil Liberties Com., 1969—. Sec.- treas. fgn. policy council N.Y. Democrats, 1966—; alt. del. 19th congl. dist. N.P. to Dem. Nat. Conv., 1968; dist. leader 65th Assembly Dist. Dem. Party, N.Y.C. Mem. Phi Beta Kappa, Phi Sigma. Home: 205 West End Av New York City NY 10023 Office: New Sch Social Research 66 W 12th St New York City NY 10011 also New Lincoln Sch 31 Central Park N New York City NY 10026

BUCHER, CHARLES AUGUSTUS, educator; b. Conesus, N.Y., Oct. 2, 1912; s. Grover C. and Elizabeth (Barr) B.; B.A., Ohio Wesleyan U., 1937; M.A., Columbia, 1941; Ed.D., N.Y. U., 1948; post-grad. Yale, 1948-49; m. Jacqueline N. Dubois, Aug. 24, 1941; children—Diana, Richard, Nancy, Gerald. Tchr. pub. schs. N.Y., 1937-41; asst. prof. New Haven State Coll., 1946-50; prof. edn. N.Y. U., 1950—; editor Appleton-Century-Croft, N.Y.C. Am. Specialist U.S. State Dept., 1962; del. Pres. Eisenhower's White House Conf. on Youth Fitness, 1956. Trustee, chmn. scholarship com. Coll. Scholarship Plan, Inc., 1959- . Recipient Sch. Bell award, 1960. Served to capt., USAAF, 1941-46. Fellow A.A.H.P.E.R., Am. Coll. Sports Medicine, Am. Sch. Health Assn.; mem. N.E.A. Author: Methods and Materials in Physical Education and Recreation, 1954; Ad-Edn. Assn. Foundations of Physical Education rev. edit., 1968; Methods & Materials ministration of School Health and Physical Education Programs, rev. edit., 1967; Physical Education in Modern Elementary School, rev., 1971; College Ahead, rev. edit., 1961; Athletics in Schools and Colleges, 1965; Foundations of Modern Health, 1967; Guiding Your Child toward College, 1967; Physical Education for Life, 1969; Dimensions of Physical Education, 1969; Administration of Health and Physical Education Programs, 1971; Administrative Dimensions of Health and Physical Education Programs, 1971. also numerous articles. Home: 3 The Knoll Armonk, NY 10504. Office: N Y University New York City NY 10003

BUCHER, ROBERT MONROE, govt. ofcl.; b. Phila., May 28, 1920; s. Jonas W. and Ellen K. (Drager) B.; student U. Pa., 1941; M.D., Temple U., 1944, M.S. in Surgery, 1950; m. Elizabeth Ann Matlack, Mar. 23, 1946; children—Elizabeth Ann, Robert David, Barbara Jean. Intern, Temple U. Med. Center, 1944-45, resident surgery, 1945-46, 48-50, instr. surgery, 1950-54, asso. surgery, 1954- 57, asst. prof. surgery, 1957-60, asso. dean Med. Sch., 1958-59, dean, 1959-69, asso. prof. surgery, 1960—; dep. dir. Bur. Health Manpower Edn., NIH, Bethesda, Md., 1969-71; dean Coll. Medicine, U. South Ala., Mobile, 1971—; asst. vis. surgeon Phila. Gen. Hosp., 1950-59; attending surgeon gen. and thoracic VA Hosp., Phila., 1953-59. Trustee Magee Meml. Hosp. Convalescents, Phila. Diplomate Am. Bd. Surgery, Am. Bd. Thoracic Surgery. Fellow A.C.S.; mem. A.M.A., Pa., Phila., acads. surgery, Babcock Surg. Soc., Phi Chi, Alpha Omega Alpha. Republican. Presbyn. Author articles. Home: 745 Westmoreland Dr E Mobile AL 36609

BUCHHAUSER, ANDREW WILLIAM, educator, musician; b. Chgo., Feb. 8, 1910; s. Andrew J. and Anna Martha (Kilian) B.; Mus.B., U. Ariz., 1937, Mus.M., 1938; student Eastman Sch. Music, U. Rochester, 1949-50; m. Betty Mary Urech, Oct. 25, 1943; children—Andrea, David, John, Peter, Ann, James. Faculty Sch. Music, U. Ariz., 1938—, prof. music, 1953—, dir. Sch. Music, 1957—; organist, choir dir. Lake View Presbyn. Ch., Chgo., 1928-34; organist St. Johns Luth. Ch., Evanston, Ill., 1930-31, St. Thomas Episcopal Ch., Rochester, 1949-50, 1st Congl. Ch., Tucson, 1937-42, St. Philips-in-the-Hills Ch., Tucson, 1946-60; soloist Tucson Symphony Orchestra, Northwestern U. Orchestra, Springfield (Mo.) Symphony. Served with AUS, 1943-46. Mem. Ariz. Soc. Composers (past pres.), Am. Guild Organists (dean So. Ariz.), Music Educators Nat. Conf., Ariz. Music Educators Assn., Music Tchrs. Nat. Assn., Ariz. Music Tchrs. Assn., Nat. Assn. Music Tchrs. State Univs., Phi Mu Alpha. Composer: Piano Concerto, 1937; Suite for Piano and Orchestra, 1938; Sonato for Cello, 1940; Sinfonietta for Orchestra, 1950; Sonata for Two Pianos, 1952; others. Home: 2400 E Kleindale Rd Tucson AZ 85719

BUCHHEIM, ROBERT WILLIAM, aero. engr.; b. Highland, Ill., Jan. 22, 1925; s. William C. and Irene (Klaus) B.; student La. Poly. Inst., 1943-44, Ga. Inst. Tech., 1944-45; B.Engring., Yale, 1946, M.Engring., 1948, Ph.D., 1953; m. Helen M. Drega, Sept. 22, 1947; children—Robert K., Linda S. Instr., Yale, 1946-49; project engr. N. Am. Aviation Co., 1949-54; head aero-astronautics dept. RAND Corp., 1954-63, mem. research council, 1964-67; chief scientist USAF, 1963-64; exec. dir. research and engring. N.Am. Rockwell Corp., 1967-68; became asso. provost, prof. engring. mgmt. Vanderbilt U., Nashville, 1968-69; exec. v.p. Southwestern Research Corp., Phoenix, 1969-70, pres., 1970—; dir. Southwestern Research & Gen. Investment Co. Mem. space tech. panel Pres.'s Sci. Adv. Com., 1961-67; mem. com. on undersea warfare Nat. Acad. Scis., 1969—; mem. Nat. UN Day Com., 1971. Served with USMCR, 1943-46. Recipient Exceptional Civilian Service award USAF, 1964. Fellow Yale Engring. Assn.; mem. Am. Inst. Aeros. and Astronautics (tech. com. on mgmt. 1967-69), Nat. Conf. Adminstrn. Research (program chmn. 1965, conf. chmn. 1967), A.A.A.S., Am. Assn. Engring. Edn., Air Force Assn., N.Y. Acad. Scis., Sigma Xi. Club: Cosmos. Author: Space Handbook, 1958. Home: 312 E State Av Phoenix AZ 85020

BUCHHEISTER, CARL WILLIAM, conservationist; b. Balt., Jan. 20, 1901; s. George Albrecht and Mary Hermine (Koch) B.; B.A., Johns Hopkins, 1923, postgrad. Latin and Greek, 1923-25; LL.D., Pace Coll.; H.H.D., Bowdoin Coll.; m. Harriet Nettleton Gillilan, Dec. 26, 1924; children—Harriet Ann (Mrs. Louis C. Reggio), Mary Carol (Mrs. Robert L. Massonneau), Elizabeth Clare (Mrs. Thomas C. Shortell). Tchr. Lation, Park Sch., Balt., 1925-26, Lawrence Sch., Hewlett, L.I., N.Y., 1927-36; founder, dir. Camp Mocassin, pvt. boys' camp, Lochmere, N.H., 1926-34; dir. Audubon Camp of Maine for tchrs., adult leaders, Medomak, Me., 1936-57; exec. dir. Mass. Audubon Soc., 1936-39, asst. dir. dir. Mass. Audubon Soc., 1936-39, asst. dir. Nat. Audubon Soc., 1940-44, sr. v.p., 1944-59, pres., 1959-67, pres. emeritus, 1967—. Pres., Edward Ball Wildlife Found., Nat. Audubon Soc. Greenwich; pres. Alice Rich Northrop Assn., 1950-60, now hon. pres. Bd. dirs. Chewonki Found., Inc., Can. Audubon Soc., 1960-67. Mem. Nat. Parks Assn. (director), American Forestry Assn. (hon. v.p. 1963), Am. Ornithologists' Union, Wilson Ornithol. Club, N.Y. Zool. Soc., Linnaean Soc. N.Y., Johns-Hopkins

Alumni Assn. (pres. N.Y., N.J., Conn. 1958-60), Omicron Delta Kappa. Clubs: Century Assn., Johns Hopkins (N.Y.C.). Home: Tallahassee FL 32302

BUCHHOLZ, HAROLD W., food mfg. co. exec.; b. 1910; married. Chmn. bd., dir. Welch Foods Inc., Westfield, N.Y., 1967—. Pres., dir. Nat. Grape Coop. Assn. Inc., 1954—. Office: Welch Foods Inc Westfield NY 14787*

BUCHHOLZ, HORST WERNER, actor; b. Berlin, Germany, Dec. 4, 1933; ed. pub. schs., Berlin; studied acting with Marlise Ludwig; m. Miriam Bru, Dec. 7, 1958. Became extra at Metropol Theatre, Berlin, 1947; played 1st solo part in Emil and the Detectives at age 14; made film debut in Marianne, My Youthful Love, 1955, later appeared in European films: No Star in the Sky, Regine, Teen- Age Wolf Pack, Ruler Without a Crown, Robinson Must Not Die, The Confessions of Felix Krull, Monpti Destination Love, Wet Asphalt, Resurrection, The Death Ship; made debut in English-lang. films with Tiger Bay, 1959; Broadway debut in Cheri, 1959; later films include; Fanny, The Rebel, One, Two, Three, Nine Hours to Rama, The Empty Canvas, others. Recipient Nat. Film prize, 1956; Bambi prize as most popular German actor, Film-Revue mag., 1957, 58. Address: care of Agentur MacKeben Douglasstr 2-4 Berlin 33 West Germany

BUCHI, GEORGE HERMANN, educator, chemist; b. Switzerland, Aug. 1, 1921; s. George J. and Martha (Mueller) B.; D.Sc., Fed. Inst. Tech., Zurich, Switzerland, 1947; m. Anne Westfall Barkman, Aug. 20, 1955. Came to U.S., 1948, naturalized, 1955. Mem. faculty Mass. Inst. Tech., 1951—, prof. chemistry, 1958—. Mem. Nat. Acad. Sci., Am. (Fritzsche award 1958), Swiss (Ruzicka award 1958) chem. socs. Home: 100 Memorial Dr Cambridge, MA 02142.

BUCHLER, JUSTUS, educator; b. N.Y.C., Mar. 27, 1914; s. Samuel and Ida (Frost) B.; B.S.S., Coll. City N.Y., 1934; M.A., Columbia, 1935, Ph.D., 1939; m. Evelyn Urban Shirk, Feb. 20, 1943; 1 dau. Katherine Urban. Lectr. philosophy Columbia, 1937-42; instr. philosophy Bklyn. Coll., 1938-43; faculty Columbia, 1942-71, prof. philosophy 1956-71, Johnsonian prof. 1959-71, chmn. dept. philosophy, 1964-67, chmn. Contemporary Civilization program in coll., 1950-56; distinguished prof. philosophy State U. N.Y. at Stoney Brook, 1971—. Mem. Am. Philos. Assn., Am. Civil Liberties Union (vice chmn. nat. acad. freedom com. 1958-64). Author: Charles Peirce's Empiricism, 1939; (with J.H. Randall Jr.) Philosophy: An Introduction, 1942; (with others) The Philosophy of Bertrand Russell, 1944; Toward a General Theory of Human Judgment, 1951; (with others) Studies in the Philosophy of Charles Sanders Peirce, 1952; (with others) A History of Columbia College on Morningside, 1954; Nature and Judgment, 1955; The Concept of Method, 1961. Editor: (with B. Schwartz) The Obiter Scripta of George Santayana, 1936; The Philosophy of Peirce: Selected Writings, 1940; (with Randall and Shirk) Readings in Philosophy, 1946; Metaphysics of Natural Complexes, 1966; Introduction to Contemporary Civilization in the West, 2 vols., 1946; Chapters in Western Civilization, 1948. Home: 3 Homestead Av Garden City NY 11530 Office: Physics Bldg State U NY Stony Brook NY 11790

BUCHSBAUM, DAVID A., educator, mathematician; b. N.Y.C., Nov. 6, 1929; s. Joseph and Kate (Havel) B.; A.B., Columbia, 1949, Ph.D., 1954; m. Betty Ellen Sanders, Oct. 5, 1949; children—Helen, Susan, Marion. Instr. Princeton, 1953-54. NSF postdoctoral fellow, 1954-55; instr. U. Chgo., 1955-56; asst. prof., then asso. prof. Brown U., 1956-60; mem. faculty Brandeis U., 1960—, prof. math., 1963—. Guggenheim fellow, 1965-66. Mem. Am. Math. Soc. (editor transactions 1967—). Editor Jour. of Algebra, 1964—. Author research papers. Home: 3 Victoria Circle Newton Centre MA 02159 Office: Brandeis Univ Waltham MA 02154

BUCHWALD, ART, columnist; b. Mt. Vernon, N.Y., Oct. 20, 1925; s. Joseph and Helen (Kleinberger) B.; student U. So. Cal., 1945-48; m. Anne McGarry, Oct. 11, 1952; children—Joel, Connie, Jennifer. Syndicated columnist, newspapers throughout world; columnist Los Angeles Times Syndicate. Served as sgt. USMCR, 1942-45. Clubs: Anglo-American Press (Paris); Nat. Press (Washington). Author: Paris After Dark, 1950; Art Buchwald's Paris, 1954; The Brave Coward, 1957; A Gift From the Boys; More Caviar: Un Cadeau Pour Le Patronn (Prix de la Bonne Humeur, 1958); Don't Forget to Write, 1960; Art Buchwald's Secret List to Paris, 1963; How Much Is That in Dollars?, 1961; Is It Safe to Drink the Water?, 1962; I Chose Capitol Punishment, 1963; And Then I Told the President, 1965; Son of the Great Society, 1966; Have I Ever Lied To You, 1968; The Establishment Is Alive and Well in Washington, 1969; Counting Sheep, 1970; Getting High in Government Circles, 1971. Office: 1750 Pennsylvania Av N W Washington DC 20006

BUCK, ALFRED ANDREAS, physician, epidemiologist; b. Hamburg, Germany, Mar. 9, 1921; s. Heino C. and Antonie (Schwarz) B.; M.D. in Pharmacology, U. Hamburg, 1945; M.P.H., Johns Hopkins, 1959, D.P.H., 1961; m. Kay I. Amann, Sept. 21, 1962; children—Suzanne Karen, Alfred Andreas. Came to U.S., 1958, naturalized, 1967. Med. resident Univ. Hosp., Hamburg, 1945-52; physician, cons. Gen. Govt. Hosp., Makassar, Celebes, Indonesia, 1952- 55; head physician Red Cross Hosp., Pusan, Korea, 1955-58; mem. faculty Johns Hopkins, 1963—, prof. epidemiology and internat. health, 1967—, dir. div. bacteriology and mycology, Sch. Hygiene, 1967—, also research dir., geog. epidemiology group; cons. AID, Ethiopia, 1962-64; West and Central Africa, 1971; mem. sr. staff WHO, Geneva, 1971—. Bd. dirs. Timonium Heights Residents Assn. Fellow Am. Pub. Health Assn.; mem. Am. Soc. Tropical Medicine, A.A.A.S., Am. Assn. U. Profs., Tropical Medicine Assn. D.C. Lutheran. Contbr. books and numerous articles in field. Home: 117 Old Padonia Rd Cockeysville MD 21030 Office: 615 N Wolfe St Baltimore MD 21205

BUCK, BENJAMIN ANTON, coll. dean; b. Fairchild, Wis., Dec. 13, 1925; s. Paul F. and Clara M. (Wacker) B.; B.A., Lawrence Coll., 1946; M.A., U. Minn., 1950, Ph.D., 1963; m. Dorothy Jean Schult, June 15, 1947; children—Barbara Jean, Beverly Jane. Instr., Morristown (Minn.) High Sch., 1945-47, Osseo (Minn.) High Sch., 1947-50; elementary sch. prin. Watertown (Minn.) schs., 1950-52; high sch. prin. Morgan (Minn.) pub. schs., 1952-54; supt. schs., Welcome, Minn., 1954-56; prof. edn. Mankato (Minn.) State Coll., 1956—, dean edn., 1970—. Served with USNR, World War II. Recipient Herman Erb award in German, Lawrence Coll., 1945. Mem. Nat., Minn. edn. assns., Assn. Higher Edn., Phi Delta Kappa. Lutheran. Kiwanian. Home: 907 Carney Av Mankato MN 56001

BUCK, CHARLES A., banker. Sr. v.p., trustee Soc. for Savs., Hartford, Conn. Office: 31 Pratt St Hartford CT 06101*

BUCK, CHARLES HENRY, title ins. exec.; b. Balt., Oct. 18, 1889; s. Charles Henry and Roselia (Robinson) B.; LL.B., U. Md., 1911; m. Adele C. Strauss, June 1, 1914; children—Charles Henry, Frederick R., Adele (Mrs. John A. Ware). Abstractor Title Guarantee & Trust Co., 1911; admitted to Md. bar, 1911; examiner, city solicitor's office, Balt., 1912; title examiner Md. Title Guarantee Co., 1913, active charge mgmt., 1918—, pres., dir., 1929-60, chairman board and chief executive officer, 1960-62, chairman of the board, since 1962 (co. merged to form Title Guarantee Co. 1960); v.p. Equitable Trust Co., 1921-40; v.p. Md. Title Securities Corp., 1931-33, pres., 1933-40; dir., mem. exec. com. U.S. Fidelity & Guaranty Co., Maryland National Bank; mem. finance com. U.S. Fidelty & Guaranty Co.; dir. Lyric Co., Fidelity & Guaranty Life Ins. Co., Tower Bldg. Co. (Balt.), Dover Perpetual Bldg. & Loan Assn. Mem. bd., v.p., finance com. Church Home and Hosp.; chmn. exec. com. Greater Balt. Com., Inc., 1957—, chmn. New Revenue Commn., Balt., 1958; pres. Balt. Real Estate Board, 1932. Mem. Mayor's com. to rep. Balt. at Md. Legislature, 1941, 43 sessions; chairman State Aviation Commission, 1944-46; member Mayor's Alcoholism Task Force Committee, past chairman Dem. candidate for mayor City Balt., 1939. Mem. Md., Balt. bar assns., Am. Title Assn. (chmn. title ins. sect. 1940-41, pres. 1941-42), Maryland Historical Society. Episcopalian. Rotarian. Clubs: Baltimore Country (pres. 1963), Center Advertising (Balt.). Home: 105 Cross Keys Rd Baltimore MD 21212 Office: Title Bldg St Paul and Lexington Sts Baltimore MD 21202

BUCK, CHARLES HENRY, Jr., clergyman; b. Balt., July 1, 1915; s. Charles Henry and Adele C. (Strauss) B.; A.B., Johns Hopkins, 1935, Ph.D., 1938; B.D., Episcopal Theol. Sch., 1941; m. Elizabeth Rose Richards, Aug. 30, 1944 (dec. 1952); children—Charles Henry III, William Richards, Richard Robinson; m. 2d, Elizabeth de la Roche Greenleaf, Aug. 1, 1957. Ordained to ministry Episcopal Ch., 1941; rector Severn Parish, Md., 1941-42; from instr. to prof. N.T., Episcopal Theol. Sch., 1945-53; dean St. Paul's Cathedral, Boston, 1953—. Served as chaplain USNR, 1942-45. Author: A Chronology of the Plays of Plautus, 1941; (with Greer Taylor) Saint Paul: A Study of the Development of his Thought, 1969. Home: 53 Powell St Brookline MA 02146 Office: 138 Tremont St Boston MA 02111

BUCK, CLAYTON DOUGLASS, Jr., architect; b. Phila., Mar. 26, 1923; s. Clayton Douglass and Alice H. (duPont) B.; B.A., Williams Coll., 1946; M.F.A., Princeton, 1952; m. Mary Biddle Sinclair, Oct. 4, 1947; children—David Douglass, John Clayton, Alice Sinclair, Mary Hewes. With V. & S. Homsey, architects, Wilmington, Del., 1952-56; former partner Fletcher & Buck, architects, Wilmington; now pvt. practice architecture. Commnr. Del. Human Relations Commn., 1962—; pres. Wilmington Soc. Fine Arts, 1960-68, New Castle County Council, 1968—. Bd. dirs. Brittingham Arts Found.; trustee Hampton Inst., Nat. Conf. Christians and Jews. Mem. A.I.A. Club: Torch. Address: Box 3659 Wilmington DE 19807

BUCK, ERVIN OSCAR, banker; b. Stamps, Ark., Apr. 20, 1904; s. Thomas Ervin and Willy Maud (Hawley) B.; B.S. in Indsl. Edn., Tex. A. and M. Coll., 1926; m. Nina Marie Bohn, Oct. 8, 1941. Geologist, Gulf Oil Corp., 1926-31; dist. engr. Tex. R.R. Commn., 1931-33; chmn. Conroe Operators Assn., 1933-35; cons. geologist and petroleum engr., 1935-41; dir. prodn., dist. 3, Petroleum Adminstrn. War, 1941-43; mgr. Rowan Drilling Co., Ft. Worth, 1943-47; with Tex. Nat. Bank Commerce, Houston, 1948—, sr. v.p., exec. asst. to chmn. bd., 1961-66, adv. dir., 1965-66, vice chmn. bd., dir., 1966-69, adv. dir., tech. adviser petroleum, 1969—; dir. First Nat. Bank, Stafford, Tex., Real Eight Co., Inc., Melbourne, Fla. Mem. adv. bd. Houston Salvation Army. Bd. dirs. St. Joseph Hosp. Found., Houston; Mem. Houston C. of C., Houston Geol. Soc., Am. Assn. Petroleum Geologists, Clubs: Houston, Petroleum (Houston); Sugar Creek Country (Sugar Land, Tex.); Fort Bend Country (Stafford). Home: 411 W Alkire Dr Sugar Land, TX 77478. Office: Gulf Bldg 712 Main St Houston TX 77002

BUCK, GEORGE H., business exec., cons. engr.; b. Eliot, Me., Dec. 22, 1894; s. A.O. and Sophie (Simpson) B.; B.S., U. Pa., 1918; m. Loretto Reavey, Sept. 10, 1927; 1 son, George H. Partner Buck, Seifert & Jost, Englewood Cliffs, N.J., 1936—; pres., dir. Hackensack Water Co., Weehawken, N.J., Spring Valley (N.Y.) Water Co., Inc.; dir. Hudson Trust Co. Served as pvt. C.A.C., 1917. Mem. Delta Kappa Epsilon. Episcopalian. Clubs: Downtown Assn. (N.Y.C.); Cosmos (Washington). Office: P O Box 1218 429 Sylvan Av Englewood Cliffs NJ 07632

BUCK, HARRY LAMBERT, elec. supplies mfr.; b. Phila., 1911; s. Henry L. and Sarah G. (Simmington) B.; B.S. Elec. Engring., Drexel Inst. Tech., 1934, D.Engring. (hon.), 1965; m. Mary Esther Oman, Oct. 18, 1935; children—Harry Lambert, Richard S., Thomas A. With I-T-E Imperial Corp., Phila., 1935—, treas., 1946-55, v.p., gen. mgr., 1955-60, exec. v.p., 1960-67, chmn. exec. com., 1967-70, pres., 1967-68, vice chmn. bd., 1968—; dir. Imperial Eastman Corp., Chgo., Componcontrol Corp., Chgo., Bio-Logics Inc., Salt Lake City. Bd. dirs. Goodwill Industries of Phila.; bd. dirs. S.E. Pa. Devel. Fund; trustee Hahnemann Med. Coll. and Hosp., Drexel U. Mem. Am. Mgmt. Assn., I.E.E.E., Nat. Elec. Mfrs. Assn. (gov.), Franklin Inst. Pa., Newcomen Soc. N.Am. Club: Union League (Phila.). Home: 911 Morris Av Bryn Mawr PA 19010 Office: 1900 Hamilton St Philadelphia PA 19130

BUCK, HUGH QUINN, lawyer; b. Pecos, Tex., Apr. 30, 1909; s. John A. and Mazie D. (Wilson) B.; grad. Tex. Christian U., alternate nominee for Rhodes scholar, 1930; student Harvard Sch. Law, U. Tex. Law Sch.; m. Bobbie Sue Whitten. June 20, 1935; children—Bobbie Sue, John. Admitted Tex. bar, counsel RFC, Washington, 1934; gen. counsel Keswick Corp., Balt., 1935; Tex. counsel Transcontinental Gas Pipe Line Corp.; counsel Houston Natural Gas Corp.; pvt. practice law, Houston, 1936-39; asst. atty. gen. Tex., 1939-40; spl. counsel cities of Houston and El Paso, 1941-42; partner Gresham, McCorquodale, Martin & Buck, Houston, 1942-45, sr. partner Fulbright, Crooker, Freeman, Bates & Jaworski, 1945—. Dir. Bank of S.W., Western Nat. Bank. Trustee Tex. Wesleyan Coll., Ft. Worth, Baylor Coll. Medicine. Mem. Am. Bar Assn. Am. Soc. Corporate Secs., Delta Theta Phi. Clubs: The Houston, Coronado, River Oaks Country (Houston). Home: 2701 Westheimer Houston TX 77006 Office: Bank of the Southwest Bldg Houston TX 77006

BUCK, J. MAHLON, Jr., drug co. exec.; b. Bryn Mawr, Pa., 1925; grad. Princeton, 1946. Chmn., The Drug House, Inc., Phila.; dir. Drug Distbn. Data, Inc. Home: 121 Rose Lane Haverford PA 19041 Office: 1011 W Butler St Philadelphia PA 19101*

BUCK, JOHN BONNER, biologist; b. Hartford, Conn., Sept. 26, 1912; s. George Sumner and Carrie Elizabeth (Bonner) B.; A.B., Johns Hopkins, 1933, Ph.D., 1936; m. Elisabeth Tennent Mast, Dec. 22, 1939; children—Peter, Susan, Judith, Alan. Asst. zoology Johns Hopkins, 1933-36; NRC fellow Cal. Inst. Tech., 1936-37; research asso. Carnegie Instn., 1937-39; asst. prof. zoology U. Rochester, 1939-45; physiologist NIH, 1945—, chief lab. phys. biology, 1962—; mem. Johns Hopkins expdns. to Jamaica, 1936, 41, 62; vis. prof. U. Wash., 1951, Cal. Inst. Tech., 1953; guest Cambridge (Eng.) U., 1963-64; instr. Marine Biol. Lab., Woods Hole, Mass., 1942- 44, 57-59, trustee, 1959—; spl. research chromosome structure, insect respiration, firefly physiology. Leader Alpha Helix Expdn. to New Guinea, 1969. Mem. NRC, 1957-59, 71—. Mem. Soc. Gen. Physiologists (sec. 1953-55, pres. 1960), Am. Soc. Zoologists (v.p. 1956). Contbr. articles in field. Mem. editorial bd. Biol. Bull., 1957-60, 65-68, Jour. Morphology, 1964-68. Home: 4505 Saul Rd Kensington MD 20795 Office: Nat Insts Health Bethesda MD 20014

BUCK, JOHN PETER, automotive co. exec.; b. Mason City, Ia., July 20, 1915; s. A. O. and Estella (Goss) B.; student DePauw U., 1933-34, Dakota Wesleyan U., 1936, Ill. Inst. Tech., 1942-48; M.B.A., U. chgo., 1950; m. Alice Zimmer, Aug. 28, 1938; childrenJeffrey, Brian, Bradley, Barbara. Parts and service mgr. Mitchell Motor Co. (S.D.), 1935-37, 39-40, Jansen Chevrolet Co., Madison, S.D., 1938; clk. Govt. Auditing Office, Brookings, S.D., 1938- 39; with Maremont Corp., Chgo., 1940-, pres., gen. mgr. automotive div., 1963-67, pres. international div., since 1967—. Active local Boy Scouts Am. Bd. dirs. Harvey (Ill.) YMCA, 1950-56; trustee Ingall's Meml. Hosp., Harvey, 1950-. Mem. Soc. Automotive Engrs. Clubs: Mid-America (Chgo.); Flossmoor (Ill.) Country. Home: 19020 Kedzie Av Homewood IL 60430 Office: 168 N Michigan Av Chicago, IL 60601.

BUCK, JUNIOR C., financial cons.; b. Chgo., Jan. 3, 1900; s. George Clyde and Maude A. (Blickley) B.; grad. U. Minn., 1923, Harvard Bus. Sch., 1925; m. Helen Wheeler, 1933 (dec. 1938); m. 2d, Florence Simpson, Nov. 19, 1941; children—Sheldon W., G. Clyde, Leslie Simpson. With Associated Dry Goods Corp., 1924-70, with Lord & Taylor div., 1924-26, Powers div., 1926-33, pres. Hahne & Co. div., 1933—, dir. corp., Wilmington, 1946—, chmn. bd., chief exec. officer, until 1970; dir. 1st Nat. State Bank of N.J., C. F. Mueller Co., Jersey City. Trustee Marcus L. Ward Home, Endicott Jr. Coll., Beverly, Mass. Served as sgt., U.S. Army, A.E.F., 1918-19. Mem. Delta Kappa Epsilon. Presbyn. (trustee). Clubs: Montclair (N.J.) Golf; Orange Lawn Tennis (South Orange, N.J.); Harvard, Princeton (N.Y.C.); Essex (Newark); Forest Lake (Hawley, Pa.). Home: 44 Eagle Rock Way Montclair NJ 07042 Office: 44 Eagle Rock Way Montclair NJ 07042

BUCK, LEE ALBERT, life ins. co. exec.; b. Jonesboro, Ark., July 28, 1923; s. Lee A. and Annie (Ballew) B.; B.A. with honors, U. Mich., 1947, M.A. in Colonial Am. History, 1948; C.L.U., 1960; m. Audrey Ruth McMurphy, Feb. 26, 1945; children—Melody Anne, Merrilee Ruth, Bonnie Sue, Lisa Carol. With N.Y. Life Ins. Co., 1949—, dir. agys., 1962-63, 2d v.p., 1963-64, v.p. agys., 1964-66, regional v.p. charge Southeastern U.S., 1966-67, v.p. marketing, N.Y.C., 1967—. Chmn. comml. div. Akron (O.) United Fund, 1957; chmn orgn. and extension commn. Greater N.Y. councils Boy Scouts Am. Nat. trustee Life Underwriter Tng. Council. Served to lt. USNR, 1942-46, 50-52. Mem. Nat. Assn. Life Underwriters, Am. Assn. C.L.U.'s, Life Ins. Agy. Mgmt. Assn. (vice chmn. exec. devel. com.), Sales Execs. Club N.Y., Sales and Marketing Execs. Internat., Sales Promotion Exec. Assn. Methodist (youth leader). Home: 126 Huckleberry Hill Rd New Canaan, CT 06840. Office: 51 Madison Av New York City NY 10010

BUCK, PAUL HERMAN, ret. educator; b. Columbus, O., Aug. 25, 1899; s. Henry John and Adele (Kreppelt) B.; A.B., Ohio State U., 1921, A.M., 1922; A.M., Harvard, 1924, Ph.D., 1930; LL.D., Coe Coll., 1946, Ohio State U., 1946, Colby Coll., 1952, Brown U., 1953; Litt.D., Harvard, 1946, Princeton, 1947; L.H.D., Western Res. U., 1956; Sheldon Traveling fellow, London and Paris, 1925-26; m. Sally Burwell Betts, Dec. 21, 1927. Instr. history, Harvard U., 1926-36, asst. prof., 1936-39, asso. prof., 1939-42, prof., 1942-69, dean faculty, 1942-53, provost, 1945-53, dir. univ. libraries, 1955-64, Carl H. Pforzheimer univ. prof., 1958, Univ. prof. Am. history, 1965-69, univ. prof. emeritus, 1969—. Mem. adminstrv. com., Dumbarton Oaks, 1944-53, chmn., 1952-53; mem. civilian adv. com. USN, 1945-47; bd. dirs. Center for Advanced Study in Behavioral Scis., 1952-69, chmn., 1960-69; chmn. Role of Edn. in Am. History, 1957-69; mem. com. on financing higher edn. and research Rockefeller Found., 1949-53. Trustee High Altitude Obs., Boulder, Colo., 1952, Smith Coll., 1952-62, Harvard Yen Ching Inst., 1945-53, Teachers Ins. and Annuity Co., 1954-58, Ednl. Testing Service 1956-58. Recipient Pulitzer prize in history, 1938; Ohioana Career medal, 1957; decorated chevalier Legion Honor (France); comdr. Order Phoenix (Greece). Mem. Am. Hist. Assn., Mass. Hist. Soc., Miss. Valley, So. hist. assns., Am. Agrl. Soc., Phi Beta Kappa, Kappa Sigma. Episcopalian. Clubs: Odd Volumes, Tavern, Harvard (Boston); Harvard (N.Y.); Faculty (Cambridge). Author: The Road to Reunion, 1937; Libraries and Universities, 1964. Co-author: General Education in a Free Society, 1945; Nature and Needs of Higher Education, 1953. Editor: The Social Sciences at Harvard, 1965. Bd. editors, Jour. So. History, 1941-47. Contbr. to hist. jours. and Dictionary Am. Biography. Home: 989 Memorial Dr Cambridge MA 02138

BUCK, PEARL SYDENSTRICKER (Mrs. Richard J. Walsh), author; b. Hillsboro, W.Va., June 26, 1892; d. Absalom and Caroline (Stulting) Sydenstricker; A.B., Randolph-Macon Woman's Coll., Lynchburg, Va., 1914; M.A., Cornell U., 1926; M.A., Yale, 1933; Litt.D., W.Va. University, 1940, St. Lawrence University, 1942; LL.D., Howard University, 1942; L.H.D. (hon.), Lincoln U., 1953, Women's Med. Coll. Pa., 1954, U. Pitts., 1960, Bethany Coll., 1963; Mus.D. (hon.), Combs Coll. Music, Phila., 1962; H.H.D. (hon.), W.Va. State Coll., 1963; L.H.D., Bethany Coll., 1963, Hahnemann Hosp., 1966; Litt.D., Del. Valley Coll., 1965; LL.D., Muhlenberg College, Pennsylvania, 1966; L.H.D., Rutgers University, New Brunswick, 1969; m. John Lossing Buck, May 13, 1917; children—Carol, Janice; m. 2d, Richard J. Walsh, June 11, 1935 (dec. May 1960); adopted children—Richard, John, Edgar Sydenstricker, Jean C., Henriette, Mary Chieko, Johanna Michiko, Theresa. Tchr. University of Nanking (China), 1921-31, Southeastern U., Nanking, 1925- 27, Chung Yank U., Nanking, China, 1928-30. Bd. dirs. Weather Engring. Corp. of Am. Chmn. bd. Welcome House, Inc., 1956—. Awarded Pulitzer prize, 1932; William Dean Howells medal, 1935; Nobel award in literature, 1938; Skinner award Women's National Book Assn., 1960; Pa. Award for Excellence, Gov.'s Com. 1000,000 Pensylvanians, 1968; Phila. Club Advt. Women award, 1969; ELA award in Lit., 1969. Mem. American Academy of Arts and Letters, National Institute of Arts and Letters, Phi Beta Kappa, Kappa Delta. Club: Cosmopolitan (New York). Author: East Wind-West Wind, 1930; The Young Revolutionist, 1931; The Good Earth (awarded Pulitzer prize), 1931; Sons, 1932; The First Wife and Other Stories, 1933; All Men Are Brothers (translation of the Chinese classic Shui Hu Chuan), 1933; The Mother, 1934; A House Divided, 1935; House of Earth, 1935; The Exile, 1936; Fighting Angel, 1936; This Proud Heart, 1938; The Patriot, 1939; The Chinese Novel, 1939; Other Gods, 1940; Stories for Little Children, 1940; Today and Forever, 1941; Of Men and Women, 1941; Dragon Seed, 1942; American Unity and Asia, 1942; The Chinese Children Next Door, 1942; What America Means to Me, 1943; The Water-Buffalo Children, 1943; The Promise, 1943; The Dragon Fish, 1944; (with James Yen) Tell the People, 1945; Yu-Lan, Flying Boy of China, 1945; Portrait of a Marriage, 1945; (with Masha Scott) Talk about Russia, 1945; Pavilion of Women, 1946; (with Erna von Pustau) How It Happens, 1946; Far and Near, 1947; The Big Wave, 1948; Peony, 1948; (with E. S. Robeson) American Argument, 1949; Kinfolk, 1949; One Bright Day, 1950; The Child Who Never Grew, 1950; God's Men, 1951; The Hidden Flower, 1952; Come My Beloved, 1953; My Several Worlds, 1954; The Beech Tree, 1955; Imperial Woman, 1956; Letter From Peking, 1957; Christmas Miniature, 1957; American Triptych, 1958; (with Carlos P. Romulo) Friend to Friend, 1958; Command The Morning, 1959; Christmas Miniature, 1959; The Christmas Ghost, 1960; Fourteen Stories, 1961; A Bridge for Passing, 1962; The Living Reed, 1963; Welcome Child, 1963; The Joy of Children, 1964; The Big Fight, 1965; (with Gweneth Zarfoss) The Gifts they Bring, 1965; Death in the Castle, 1965; (with Theodore F.

Harris) For Spacious Skies, 1966; The Time is Noon, 1967; Matthew, Mark, Luke and John, 1967; To My Daughters, With Love, 1967; The New Year, 1968; The Three Daughters of Madame Liang, 1969; The Good Deed and Other Stories of Asia, Past and Present, 1970. Address: Route 1 Box 164 Perkasie PA

BUCK, PHILIP WALLENSTEIN, educator; b. Rapid City, S.D., May 29, 1900; s. Joseph P. and Helen M. (Bangs) B.; A.B., U. Ida., 1923; B.A., Oxford Univ., Eng., 1926; Ph.D., U. Calif., 1933, m. Barbara Jacobs, June 24, 1926; children—Priscilla, Olwen Margaret, Constance Eleanor. Asst. prof. history and govt., Mills Coll., Oakland, Calif., 1926-34; instr. polit. sci., Stanford U., 1934-35, asst. prof., 1935-37, asso. prof., 1937-41, became prof. polit. sci., 1941, now emeritus; prof. polit. sci. Cal. State Coll., 1966-70, now prof. emeritus; summer faculty U. Ore., 1938, 39, U. of Calif., 1943; faculty Salzburg Seminar in Am. Studies, 1952; vis. prof. polit. sci. Pa. State Univ., 1965-66. Ford Foundation Research Grant on British Political careers, 1955-56. Mem. Am. Polit. Sci. Assn., Phi Beta Kappa, Phi Gamma Delta. Author: The Politics of Mercantilism, 1942; (with John W. Masland) The Governments of Foreign Powers, 1947, rev. edit., 1950; Amateurs and Professionals in British Politics, 1918-59, 1963. Co-editor, contbr. (with Martin B. Travis, Jr.) The Control of Foreign Relations, 1957. Office: Cal State Coll 1000 E Victoria St Dominguez Hills CA 90247

BUCK, R. CREIGHTON, educator, mathematician; b. Cin., Aug. 30, 1920; s. Robert Jirah and Martha (Creighton) B.; B.A., U. Cin., 1941, M.A., 1942; Ph.D., Harvard, 1947; m. Ellen Fedder, Dec. 28, 1944; children—Nancy Elizabeth, Donald Paul. Mem. Harvard Soc. Fellows, 1942-43, 45-47; asst. prof. Brown U., 1947-50; asso. prof. U. Wis., 1950-54, prof., 1954—, chmn. dept., 1964-68. Mem. project FOCUS, Inst. Def. Analyses, 1959-60; chmn. Com. Undergrad. Program, 1959-63; mem. film panel Com. Ednl. Media, 1963-66; mem. programmed learning panel Sch. Math. Study Group, 1960-64; mem. U.S. Commn. Math. Instrn., 1963-67; exec. com. div. math. NRC, 1963-65; math. panel Nat. Security Agy. Sci. Adv. Bd., 1963—. Guggenheim fellow, 1958-59. Mem. Am. Math. Soc. (council 1959-63, 64-70, exec. com. 1960-64, editor proc. 1964-67), Math. Assn. Am. (editor monographs 1957-60, bd. govs. 1960-63, vis. lectr. 1962-63), Lutheran Acad. Scholarship, Phi Beta Kappa, Sigma Xi. Republican. Author: Advanced Calculus, 2d edit., 1965: (with R.P. Boas), Polynomial Expansions 1958, also articles. Editor: Studies in Modern Analysis, 1962; Modern Analysis Series, 1962- 0. Home: 3601 Sunset Dr Madison, WI 53705.

BUCK, RAYMOND ELLIOTT, lawyer, ins. exec.; b. Ft. Worth, July 13, 1894; s. Raymond H. and Eula E. (Blackmore) B.; student Tex. Christian U., 1911-13; LL.B., U. Tex., 1917; m. Katherine Camp, Dec. 8, 1921; children—Raymond Elliott Buck (deceased), Katherine Camp Buck (Mrs. McDermott). Admitted to Tex. bar, 1919, since in general practice as mem. firm Buck & Buck; city atty., Ft. Worth, 1920-22; gen. counsel, dir. So. Air Transport, 1928-30; pres. Midway Airport Corp., 1948—; asso. gen. counsel Am. Airlines, Inc., 1929—; dir., gen. counsel Trinity Life Ins. Co., 1934-35; dir., gen. counsel Comml. Standard Ins. Co., 1935-43, chmn., gen. counsel, 1943—, pres., 1952—; chmn., past pres., gen. counsel, chmn. exec. com. Comml. Standard Fire & Marine Co., 1952—, Comml. Standard Life Ins. Co., 1955—, Comml. Standard Title Ins. Co., 1958—; owner, operator Raymond E. Buck Ranch & Cattle Co., 1938—; asso. gen. counsel Convair, div. Gen. Dynamics Corp., 1941—; pres. Rucco Homes, Inc., 1950—, Tarrant Land Co., 1954—; v.p., dir. Geyser Corp., 1964—; dir., sec., mem. exec. com. Ft. Worth Air Terminal, Inc., 1948—; dir. Continental Nat. Bank, Fort Worth. vice chmn. bd., mem. exec. com., 1967—. Active mem. internat. bd. electors Ins. Hall of Fame, 1962-65; co-chmn. U. Tex. Internat. Ins. Seminar; bd. govs. Internat. Invitational Ins. Seminar, 1965-66; mem. ins. adv. council and planning commn. U. Tex., 1962—, U. Tex. Council Bus. Adminstrn. Foundation, 1964—. Mem. Tex. Gov.'s Post War Planning Com. on Taxes and Aviation, 1944- 47; mem. Texas War Bonds Com., 1942-45; dir. Ft. Worth Better Bus. Bur., 1957—; bd. dirs. Tex. Technol. Coll. Found., 1956- . Chmn. Young Democrats Tex., 1931-35; finance chmn. Tex. Democratic Party, 1942; Tex. chmn. Jefferson Day Dinner, 1941-42; chmn. Tex. Dem. Conv., 1956; mem. Dem. Adv. Council, 1955. Lay council St. Joseph's Hosp.; citizens council Scott and White Meml. Hosp.; sponsoring com. Nat. Jewish Hosp. at Denver. Served as capt., inf., U.S. Army, 1917-19; AEF in France. Mem. Am., Tex. bar assns., First Officers Tng. Camp Assn. (pres. 1952-53), Tex. U. Alumni Assn. of Ft. Worth (pres. 1925), Ft. Worth C. of C. (dir. 1957—, pres. 1962-63), Tex. Christian U. Ex-Student Assn. (pres. 1949-50), Am. Assn. UN (pres. Ft. Worth 1964—). Clubs: Fort Worth (gov. 1946-57, dir., exec. com.), Town River Crest Country, Ridglea Country, Admirals (Ft. Worth). Home: 1500 Alta Dr Fort Worth TX 76107 Office: 6421 Camp Bowie Blvd Fort Worth TX 76116

BUCK, RICHARD DAVID, conservator mus. objects; b. Middletown, N.Y., Feb. 3, 1903; s. Louis I. and Florence (Huxtable) B.; B.S., Harvard, 1926, A.M., 1934; m. Robina Hirsch, June 1, 1939; children—Christopher D., Jeremy R. Asst., tutor Harvard, 1928-31; instr. Wheaton Coll., Norton, Mass., 1931-33; staff dept. conservation Fogg Mus. of Art, Harvard, 1937-52, conservator, 1947- 52, lectr. fine arts, 1951-52; dir. Intermuseum Lab., Oberlin, O., 1952—; sec. treas. Intermuseum Conservation Assn., 1952—; adviser on conservation (on leave of absence from Harvard) Nat. Gallery, London, 1949-50; lectr. fine arts Oberlin Coll., 1958; dir. ICA Tng. Program, 1970—. Fellow Internat. Inst. Conservation Historic and Artistic Works (council mem.). Office: Intermuseum Lab Allen Art Bldg Oberlin OH 44074

BUCK, RICHARD JOSEPH, broker; b. Bethlehem, Pa., June 27, 1902; s. Charles Austin and Josephine Martha (Rankey) B.; student Lehigh U., 1924, Harvard Bus. Sch., 1926; m. Rosamond Farrell, Mar. 3, 1930; children—James Farrell, Rosamond Farrell (Mrs. G. Ruppert Vernon), Richard J., Barbara Farrell (Mrs. George Moss), Josephine Farrell, Constance Farrell. Dir., chmn. finance com. Harsco Corp., Harrisburg, Pa. Home: 1105 Park Av New York City NY 10028

BUCK, ROBERT FOLLETTE, banker, lawyer; b. Superior, Neb., June 7, 1917; s. Samuel Rea and Faye (Follette) B.; B.A., U. Wash., 1938, LL.B., 1942; children—Carolyn (Mrs. Robert G. Norman), Vincent Templin; m. 2d, Barbara J. Carlson, Apr. 29, 1963. Admitted to Wash. bar, 1946, D.C. bar, 1960; practice in Wash. State, 1946-59; pres. Orcas Power & Light Co., Eastsound, Wash., 1947-54; regional dir. Small Bus. Adminstrn., Seattle, 1954-59, dep. adminstr., Washington, D.C., 1959-61; v.p. Nat. Bank Commerce, Seattle, 1961-66, sr. v.p., 1966—; dir. Internat. Bank Commerce, Seattle, Overseas Pvt. Investment Corp., Washington, Nat. Bank Commerce, N.Y.; pros. atty. San Juan County, Wash., 1947-54. Pres. Pacific Northwest Trade Assn., 1969-70. Trustee Assn. Wash. Business, 1968—. Greater Seattle, Inc., 1966—; v.p. Seattle Municipal League, 1966- 67, trustee, 1964—; trustee Seattle Area Indsl. Council, 1961—, chmn., 1964- 66; trustee, pres. Wash. State Internat. Trade Fair, 1967-69. Served with USNR, 1942-46; PTO. Decorated Bronze Star. Mem. Seattle C. of C. (trustee 1965-66, v.p. 1968-69), Phi Gamma Delta, Phi Delta Phi. Mason (32). Clubs: Wash. Athletic, Rainer (Seattle). Home: 1611 Roanoke Way Mercer Island WA 98040 Office: P O Box 3966 Seattle WA 98124

BUCK, THOMAS RANDOLPH, transp. co. exec.; b. Washington, Feb. 5, 1930; s. James Charles Francis and Mary Elizabeth (Marshall) B.; B.A. summa cum laude, Am. U., 1951; LL.B., U. Va., 1954; m. Alice Armistead James, June 20, 1953; children—Kathryn James, Thomas Randolph, Douglas Marshall, David Andrew; m. 2d, Sunny Clark, Sept. 15, 1971. Admitted to Va. bar, 1954; asst. gen. atty. Seaboard Air Line R.R. Co., 1958-63; sec., gen. counsel Am. Comml. Lines. Inc., Houston; asst. gen. atty. Tex. Gas Transmission Corp.; dir. Am. Comml. Barge Line Co., Jeffboat Inc., Terminal Transp. Co., Bauer Dredging Co., Inc. Served to capt. USMCR, 1954-58. Mem. Assn. ICC Practioners (nat. v.p., mem. exec. com.), Am., Va., Ky. bar assns., Maritime Law Assn. U.S., Am. Judicature Soc., Omicron Delta Kappa, Alpha Sigma Phi, Delta Theta Phi. Kiwanian. Club: Propeller of U.S. Home: 809 Brookhollow Dr Port Lavaca TX 77979 Office: 106 S Commerce St Port Lavaca TX 77979

BUCK, WILLIAM DAVID, ret. labor union exec.; b. St. Louis, Aug. 8, 1902; s. William Thomas and Anna Marie (Leahy) B.; student Labor Sch., St. Louis U., 1943; m. Kathleen M. Harty, Mar. 17, 1922; children—William Thomas, James Terrence. With Scullin Steel Co., St. Louis, 1916-19, 22-26, M.P. R.R. Co., 1919-22, St. Louis Underwriters Salvage Corps, 1926-30; capt. St. Louis Fire Dept., 1930-56; mem. Internat. Assn. Fire Fighters, 1930—, sec.-treas., 1956-57, internat. pres., 1957-68, mem. gen. bd. AFL-CIO. 1958-68, exec. bd. community services com., 1958-68, exec. bd. maritime trades dept., 1959-68, pres. emeritus, 1968—. Del. St. Louis Central Trades and Labor Union, 1935-56; mem. legislative com. Mo. AFL-CIO Labor Council, 1948-56; adv. com. firemanship tng. U. Mo., 1946- 56; adv. council fire prevention D.C. Commrs., 1958—; nat. fire def. adv. com. OCDM, 1958—; mem. Pres.'s Conf. Occupational Safety, 1959- 68, Captive Nations Week Com., 1960-68, White House Conf. Aging, 1960-68; exploratory com. application water Western Actuarial Bur. Chgo., 1966—, Joint Civilian Orientation Conf. U.S. Dept. Def. Bd. dirs. Muscular Dystrophy Assn. Am., 1959-68, United Community Funds and Councils Am., 1959-68; nat. labor council City of Hope Nat. Med. Center, 1958—. Mem. Nat. Fire Protection Assn. (vice chmn. fire service tng. com.), Internat. Municipal Signal Assn., Holy Name Soc. Democrat. Catholic. K.C. Clubs: Touchdown (Washington); Terre Du Lac Country (Bonne Terre, Mo.). Home: St. Francois Rd and Mount Carmel Terre DuLac Bonne Terre, MO 63628.

BUCKALEW, MARSHALL, coll. pres.; b. Jackson County, W.Va., Nov. 29, 1912; s. Floyd Wesley and Dorothy Iva (Sayre) B.; student W.Va. Wesleyan Coll., 1932-33; M.A., W.Va. U., 1941; A.B., Morris Harvey Coll., 1938; J.D., Harvard, 1948; m. Mary Ennelle Hoover, Nov. 15, 1944; children—Ronald William, James Leonard, Marsha Jean. Mem. faculty Morris Harvey Coll., Charleston, W.Va., 1938—, prof. bus. adminstrn., 1949—, trustee, 1957—, v.p. coll., 1951- 64, dir. devel., 1957-64, pres., 1964—; admitted to W.Va. bar, 1948. Mem., past pres. W.Va. Found. Ind. Colls., W.Va. Assn. Colls. and Univs. Mem. gen. council Presbyn. Ch. U.S., 1967—, chmn., 1969-71; mem. Charleston Hosp. Facilities Survey Com., 1960-61, Citizens Adv. Com. Housing, 1941-42, W.Va. Com. Constl. Revision, 1957-64, Gov. W.Va. Com. Physically Handicapped, 1957-58, Citizens Adv. Com. on Community Improvement, 1962-69; mem. Buckskin council Boy Scouts Am., 1958—; mem. fair practices com. W.Va. Hosp. Assn., 1970—; v.p. Creative Arts Festival W.Va., 1958-60. Bd. dirs. local A.R.C., 1953-56, Kanawha Welfare Council, 1952-62, United Fund Kanawha County, 1956-61, Charleston Gen. Hosp. and Sch. Nursing. Served to lt. comdr. USNR, 1942-45. Decorated Commendation ribbon. Mem. W.Va., Kanawha County bar assns., Nat., W.Va. edn. assns., W.Va. Hist. Soc., W.Va. Assn. Higher Edn. Rotarian. Club: Anvil. Author: The Life of M.P. Shawkey. Home: 2122 Kanawha Av S E Charleston WV 25304

BUCKE, EMORY STEVENS, clergyman, editor; b. Williamsport, Pa., Nov. 18, 1913; s. Jacob Edward Ambrose and Linnie Mae Coulter; B.A., American U., 1935, D.D., 1948; S.T.B., Boston U., 1938; LL.D., Claflin Coll., 1950; m. Barbara Burns, Nov. 5,1938; children—Charles Wesley, Susan. Ordained to ministry Meth. Ch., 1938, pastor Oxford. Mass., 1938-42, Hyde Park, Mass., 1942-44; ed. Meth. weekly Zions Herald, 1944-53; coll. editor Abingdon Press, 1953- 56, editor in chief, 1956—, also book editor Meth. Ch., 1956—. Protestant del. to Yugoslavia, summer 1947; del. N.E. Conf., World Meth. Council, 1947, Meth. Gep. Conf., 1952. Chmn. alumni bd. govs. Am. U., 1969—. Trustee, Christian Com. for Israel. Recipient St. George's Medal, Phila., for Church History, 1966; named Distinguished Alumnus, Boston U., 1964, Am. U., 1970. Clubs: Torch, Sertoma: Authors (London, Eng.); Mockus (Boston). Gen. editor: The History of American Methodism, 1964; bd. editors Interpreter's Dictionary of the Bible, 4 vols., 1962; editor The Book of Discipline of the United Meth. Ch. Home: 2009 Castleman Dr Nashville TN 37214 Office: 201 8th Av S Nashville TN 37203

BUCKELS, MARVIN WAYNE, savs. and loan exec.; b. Sterling, Colo., Feb. 11, 1929; s. Harvey and Myrl (Tarr) B.; B.A., U. Denver, 1951; M.S., U. Wis., 1952; m. Doris Torrance, Aug. 1, 1959; children—Lisa K., Devon Carol. Trainee, Beatrice Foods, Denver, 1952-53, mgr. sales devel., 1953-54, sales mgr., 1954-55; loan counselor Midland Fed. Savs. & Loan Assn., Denver, 1955-56, asst. treas., 1956-58, treas., 1958-60, v.p. and treas., 1960-62, exec. v.p., 1962—. Vice chmn. Colo. Bd. for Community Colls. and Occupational Edn., 1967—; vice chmn. Colo. Bd. Vocational Edn., 1967; chmn. task force on employment Met. Denver Urban Coalition, 1970; pres. Adult Edn. Met. Denver, 1970; bd. dirs. Denver Opportunity, 1965-68. Served with U.S. Army, 1946-48. Mem. U.S., Colo. (legislative com.) savs. and loan leagues, Am. Savs. and Loan Inst. (past pres. Denver chpt.), Controllers Soc. (past pres. Denver chpt., nat. gov.), Systems and Procedures Assn. (past pres. Denver chpt.), Adminstrv. Mgmt. Soc. (past pres. Denver chpt.), Denver C. of C. (past chmn. spl. task force studying sch. bond issue, loaned exec. Nat. Alliance Businessmen's Program), Phi Beta Kappa. Democrat. Home: 3003 S Columbine St Denver CO 80210 Office: 444 17th St Denver CO 80202

BUCKHOUT, CLAY, former publishing exec.; b. N.Y.C., June 13, 1910; s. Frank C. and Mary (Cotter) B.; B.A., Fordham U., 1932; m. Martha Morgan, June 16, 1932; children—Annette (Mrs. Jerome K. Chase), Constance (Mrs. George Poillon). Sales work with Gen. Air Express, 1933-34; br. mgr. McDonnell Co., brokerage, 1934-37; v.p., advt. mgr. Balsa Wood Co., 1938-39; asst. to gen. mgr. Life mag., 1939-44, advt. mgr., 1944-48, advt. dir., 1948-57; v.p. Time, Inc., N.Y.C., 1957-70; sr. v.p. Am. Assn. Advt. Agys., Washington. Pub. Army-Navy Jour. of Recognition, 1948-61, other recognition manuals, World War II. Mem. nat. metric adv. panel Dept. Commerce, 1969-71, commerce adv. information com., 1970—. Recipient achievement award Fordham Alumni Assn., 1957. Mem. Advt. Council (dir.), Sales and Marketing Execs. Internat. (dir.). Clubs: Round Hill (Greenwich, Conn.); Talbot County Country, Chesapeake Bay Yacht (Easton, Md.); Georgetown, Federal City (Washington). Home: Mount Pleasant Farm St Michaels MD 21663

BUCKINGHAM, ALFRED OLIVER, advt. exec.; b. Symmes, O., Feb. 1, 1897; s. Harry Montford and Luella (Humphrey) B.; student U. Cin.; m. Doris Rogers, Mar. 16, 1920 (dec. Mar. 1946); children—Alfred Oliver, Harry Montford, Anne Peabody, William Rogers; m. 2d, Mary Houdinski, May 23, 1946. With Cluett, Peabody & Co., Inc., advt., 1919—, successively order clk., Cin., salesman in Ind., asst. mgr. in San Francisco, salesman, Cal., credit man and mgr., Los Angeles, mgr., advt. mgr., Troy, N.Y., advt. dir., N.Y.C., 1919-36, became v.p. charge advt. and market research, 1936, dir., 1930; mng. dir. United Kingdom and continental Europe offices Young & Rubicam, Inc., London, 1952-61, became sr. v.p., N.Y.C., 1961; now chmn. bd. Adjunct-to-Mgmt., Inc., N.Y.C.; dir. Cluett, Peabody & Co. of Can., Ltd., Franc-Strohmenger & Cowan. Bd. dirs. Brand Names Found. Served with U.S. Army, AEF. Mem. Delta Tau Delta, Alpha Delta Sigma. Mason. Clubs: Advertising (N.Y.); Bath (London); Turf and Field (N.Y.C.). Address: 2 Tudor City Pl New York City, NY 10017.

BUCKINGHAM, DAVID RANDALL, ret. dept. store exec.; b. Washington, Nov. 12, 1903; s. David E. and Roberta (Randall) B.; student George Washington U., 1922-24, Babson Coll., 1925; m. Dorothy R. Bierer, Apr. 14, 1936; children—Thomas R., James B. With Woodward & Lothrop Inc., Washington, 1925-68, sec., 1946-68, treas., 1957- 68, sr. v.p., 1966-68, also dir.; dir. Nat. Bank of Washington. Bd. dirs. YMCA Met. Washington; pres. Episcopal Home for Children, Washington, 1948-53; treas., trustee Goodwill Industries, Washington, 1950-60. Mem. Sigma Alpha Epsilon. Episcopalian (sr. warden 1958-65). Mason. Home: 3108 Hawthorne St N W Washington DC 20008

BUCKINGHAM, JERRY, physician. Adminstr., Univ. Hosp., N.Y.C. Office: Univ Hosp 560 1st Av New York City NY 10016*

BUCKINGHAM, JOHN HERBERT, educator, chemist; b. Caputa, S.D., Oct. 5, 1912; s. George and Ida (Jensen) B.: B.S. in Chem. Engring., S.D. Sch. Mines and Tech., 1934; Ph.D. in Phys. Chemistry, Ohio State U., 1940; m. Betty Irene Windomaker, Sept. 5, 1940; 1 dau., Barbara-Jo. Instr., Hiram Coll., 1940; asso. prof. chemistry N.D. State U., 1940-41; prof. chemistry Colo. Sch. Mines, 1941-43; mem. faculty Miami U., Oxford, O., 1943—, prof. chemistry, 1953—, chmn. dept., 1959—. Pres., dir. Miami Valley Isotope Service, Inc., 1954—. Mem. A.A.A.S., Am. Chem. Soc., Am. Assn. U. Profs., Ohio Acad. Sci., Kappa Sigma, Gamma Alpha, Sigma Tau. Kiwanian. Home: 1220 Tollgate Dr Oxford OH 45056

BUCKINGHAM, LISLE MARION, lawyer; b. Monroeville, O., July 20, 1895; s. Jesse and Bretna (Latham) B.; A.B., Western Res. U., 1917, LL.B., 1919; m. Mildred Heter, Oct. 9, 1920 (dec. Sept. 1951); m. 2d, Ruth Heter, Feb. 25, 1959. Admitted to Ohio bar, 1919 and since practiced trial law and served as corporated counsel, Akron; sr. partner firm Buckingham, Doolittle & Burroughs, 1942—; asst. county prosecutor, 1922; gen. counsel Ohio Motor Trucking Assn. Assn. of Motor Carries of Ohio, 1951; dir. 1st Nat. Bank, Roadway Express, many other corps. Trial counsel for entire rubber industry in hearings at Washington and before War Labor Bd., 1943- 45; chief counsel in Big 4 Negotiations for Firestone, B. F. Goodrich, Goodyear and U.S. Rubber Cos., 1946-47. Trustee Community Chest (chmn. drive 1933). Y.M.C.A. Peoples Hosp., Summit County Tb Assn.; pres. Akron Community Trusts; trustee U. Akron, pres. devel. found.; gov. Western Res. U., 1947-69; mem. Ohio State Bar Examiners, 1938-43, chmn. 1943. Mem. Am., Ohio, Akron (pres. 1931) bar assns., Akron C. of C. (pres. 1935), Phi Beta Kappa, Delta Upsilon, Order of Coif, Phi Delta Phi, Delta Sigma Rho. Presbyn. (trustee). Mason. Club: Rotary (trustee). Home: 474 N Portage Path Akron OH 44303 Office: Cascade Bldg Akron OH 44308

BUCKINGHAM, ROB ROY, editor; b. Concordia, Kan., June 29, 1920; s. Alfred Roy and Mary Jane (Denman) B.; student U. Chgo., 1939-41, m. Helen A. Rolfe-Rogers, Sept. 28, 1946 (div. 1962); m. 2d, Patricia Lee Malloy, Aug. 24, 1962; children—Mallory Alexandra, Rob Roy. With United Press, Mexico City, 1943, Chgo. Daily News, 1944; with U.P., 1945-59, European continental editor, London, Eng., 1951-59; asst. editor-mgr. N.Y. Times News Service, 1960-61, editor, gen. mgr., 1962—. Served with USNR, 1941-42. Clubs: N.Y. Athletic, Overseas Press (N.Y.C.) Office: 229 W 43d St New York City NY 10036

BUCKLER, WILLIAM EARL, univ. adminstr.; b. Loretto, Ky., Oct. 10, 1924; s. William Oscar and Mary (Hiestand) B.; B.A., U. Ky., 1944, M.A., 1946; Ph.D., U. Ill., 1949. With U. London (Eng.) and British Mus. auspices Fulbright Com. and U. Ill., 1949-51; fellow Fund Advancement Edn. at U. Chgo., Columbia, St. John's Coll., 1951-52; instr. U. Ill., 1951; mem. faculty N.Y.U., 1953—, prof. English, 1961—, dean Washington Sq. Coll. Arts and Sciences, 1962-69, vice chancellor academic planning, 1969-70; spl. research 19th Century English lit. Mem. Modern Lang. Assn. Am., Nat. Council Tchrs. English, Century Assn., Phi Beta Kappa. Home: 2 Horatio St New York City NY 10014 Office: 100 Washington Sq New York City NY 10003

BUCKLEY, ALFRED, fuel oil, heating equipment and dental supplies exec.; b. Providence, Dec. 24, 1890; s. Alfred and Margaret (Gray) B.; student pub. schs.; m. Helen Agnes Searles, Apr. 2, 1934; children—Cyril H., Alfred David L., Carter Y., Richard B. Pres., treas. Buckley & Scott, Inc., Providence; pres. Smith-Holden, Inc.; dir. Indsl. Nat. Bank. Bd. dirs. Home for Aged. Episcopalian. Home: 11 Intervale Rd Providence RI 02906 Office: 101 Corliss St Providence RI 02904

BUCKLEY, CHARLES EDWARD, museum dir.; b. South Hadley Center, Mass., Apr. 29, 1919; s. William Bertram and Alice (Nicholl) B.; B.F.A., Art Inst. Chgo., 1940; M.A., Harvard, 1948. Keeper, W.A. Clark Collection, Corcoran Gallery Art, 1949-51; gen. curator Wadsworth Atheneum, Hartford, Conn., 1951-55; dir. Currier Gallery Art, 1955-64, City Art Mus., St. Louis, 1964—; lectr. Art Inst. Chgo., Nat. Gallery Art, Old Sturbrudge Village, Henry Ford Mus., Detroit Inst. Arts, Colonial Williamsburg, others; mem. juries for Chgo. Art Inst., Corcoran Gallery Art, Boston Arts Festival, others; teaching fellow fine arts Harvard, 1948-49; tchr. Loomis Sch., Windsor, Conn., 1953-54, Hartford Coll., 1953-54; spl. research 17th to 20th century Am. art, 18th century Am. decorative art, 20th century European and Am. painting and sculpture, 18th century English painting. Pres. League N.H. Arts and Crafts, 1959-64; trustee N.H. Hist. Soc., 1959-64, Hartford Art Sch., 1954-55. Served with AUS, World War II; ETO. Mem. Assn. Art Mus. Dirs. (sec.-treas.), Soc. Archtl. Historians, Am. Assn. Museums (v.p.), Coll. Art Assn. (dir.). Author articles, mus. bulls., also introductions to catalogues. Home: 665 S Skinker Blvd St. Louis, MO 63105. Office: City Art Museum St Louis MO 63105

BUCKLEY, EDMOND COLLINS, aero. engr.; b. Fitchburg, Mass., July 5, 1904; s. Dennis F. and Elizabeth (Bassidy) B.; E.E., Rensselaer Polytech. Inst., 1927; m. Mary L. Austin, Nov. 30, 1920; children—Douglas M., Kathleen M. Engr., Conn. Light & Power Co., 1927-29, Los Angeles water dept., 1928-30; elec. engr., 1930-43; chief instrument research div. NACA Langley Research Center, 1943- 59; asst. dir. space flight operations NASA, 1959-61, dir. tracking and data acquisition, 1961—. Vice chmn. space flight ground environment panel Aeros. and Astronautics Coordinating Bd. Mem. Instrument Soc. Am. Home: 3501 Glenmoor Dr Chevy Chase MD 20015 Office: 1512 H St NW Washington DC 20005

BUCKLEY, EMERSON, music dir., condr.; b. N.Y.C., Apr. 14, 1916; s. Wendell and Minnie (Buckley) B.; B.A., Columbia, 1936; L.H.D., U. Denver, 1959; m. Mary Henderson, May 27, 1948; children—Robert Allen, Richard Edward. Music dir. Columbia Grand Opera, 1936-38, Palm Beach (Fla.) Symphony and Chorus, 1938-41, N.Y.C. Symphony, 1941-42, San Carlo Opera, 1943-45, WOR-MBS, N.Y.C., 1945-54, Marquis de Cuevas Ballet, 1950, Mendelssohn Glee Club, N.Y.C., 1954-63, P.R. Opera Festival, 1954-58, Symphony of the Air, also Empire State Mus. Festival, 1955, Tagarazuka Dance Theatre, also Greek Theatre, Los Angeles, 1958, Chautauqua Festival, N.Y., 1960; music dir. Miami (Fla.) Opera Guild, 1950—, Central City (Colo.) Opera, 1956—; music dir., condr. Ft. Lauderdale Symphony, 1963—; music dir. Seattle Opera, 1964—; condr. N.Y.C. Opera, 1955—, Duluth (Minn.), New Orleans and Balt. Operas, 1970—. Guest appearances with various orchs., including Toronto (Ont., Can.) Philharmonic, Mpls. Symphony, Miami Symphony; mem. faculty U. Denver, 1956, Columbia, 1957-58, Manhattan Sch. Music, 1958-70, Temple U., 1970, N.C. Sch. Arts, 1971; dir. world premiers of Am. operas including The Ballad of Baby Doe, 1956, Gallantry, 1958, He Who Gets Slapped, 1959, The Crucible, 1961, Gentlemen Be Seated, 1963, Lady from Colorado, 1964; recordings for M-G-M, Columbia, Composers Records Inc., Heliodor. Recipient Fox prize Columbia Coll., 1936, Alice M. Ditson Conductor's award, 1964, Colo. Ambassadors Sash, 1965, Gold Chair award Central City Opera, 1965, Am. Patroit award Fla., 1971; chevalier Order Arts and Letters (France), 1970. Mem. Nat. Assn. Am. Composers and Condrs. Mason (Shriner). Home: 2271 N E 61st Ct Imperial Point Fort Lauderdale FL 33308 Office: 450 E Las Olas Blvd Fort Lauderdale FL 33301

BUCKLEY, FRANK WILSON, educator; b. Prentiss, Miss., Oct. 7, 1914; s. Frank Wylie and Otto (Watts) B.; B.A., La. Coll., 1936; LL.B., Vanderbilt U., 1954; M.A., Fla. State U., 1955; Ph.D., So. Ill. U., 1966; m. Vonnie Verette Crouch, Dec. 22, 1940; children—Charles Ray, Ronald L., Mary Carole. Mng. editor Daily News, Mt. Pleasant, Tex., 1936-37; reporter-photographer Daily Town Talk, Alexandria, La., 1937-40; telegraph editor Morning Free Press, Easton, Pa., 1940-41, Mobile Register, 1941; copy editor Buffalo Eve. News, 1941-42; editor, pub. Carroll County Democrat, Huntingdon, Tenn., 1945-46; mgr. security brokerage office, Alexandria, La., 1947-49; grad. asst. journalism Fla. State U., 1949-50; copy editor, editor financial sect. Nashville Tennessean, 1950-55; admitted to Miss. bar, 1954; prof., head dept. journalism U. So. Miss., 1955-64, asso. prof. journalism, 1966-67; lectr. journalism So. Ill. U., 1964-65; chmn. dept. journalism, S.W. Tex. State U., San Marcos, 1967—, asso. prof., 1967-70, prof., 1970—. Pres. Buckley Newspapers, Inc., pubs. The News-Bay Springs, Miss., The Reformer, Raleigh, Miss., The Signal, Taylorville, Miss. Served from ensign to lt. (s.g.), naval aviator, USNR, 1943-46; lt. Res. 1945-54. Mem. Am., Miss. bar assns., Assn. for Edn. in Journalism, American Assn. Journalism Sch. Adminstrs. Democrat. Baptist (deacon). Address: 111 Nichols St San Marcos TX 78666

BUCKLEY, IRVING MELVYN, transp. co. exec.; b. N.Y.C., June 3, 1920; s. David and Rose (Zinn) B.; student Coll. City N.Y., 1938-40; m. Helen Chalk, Sept. 7, 1947; children—Richard Elliott, Steven Harvey. With Trans Caribbean Airways, 1945—, treas., exec. v.p., 1947—, also dir.; officer, dir. subsidiaries D.C. Transit System, Inc., Transp. Communications Am., T.C.A. Broadcasting, Inc., El Diario-La Prensa. Mem. Washington Bd. Trade. Mem. Nat. Commn. Playgrounds for Young Am., 1964—; mem. transp. div. United Jewish Appeal. Served with AUS, 1942-45. Recipient citation Govt. Virgin Islands; citation Teritorio Insular Di Aruba, Antilles Neerlandes. Mem. Air Transp. Assn. Clubs: Wings, Friars (N.Y.C.); Nat. Aviation (Washington). Home: 1335 Club Dr Hewlett Harbor NY 11557 Office: 714 Fifth Av New York City NY 10019

BUCKLEY, JAMES BUCHANAN, mfg. exec.; b. Atlantic City, N.J., Apr. 18, 1915; s. William Howard and Kathleen J. (McShane) B.; grad. Portsmouth Priory Sch., 1934; B.S., Yale, 1938; m. Jean Russell, Nov. 30, 1940; children—Barbara J., J. Russell, William H., Karen M. With Superior Meter Co., Bklyn., 1938-42; with Revere Copper & Brass, Inc., New Bedford, Mass., 1942—, in various mill depts. and engring., 1942-48, asst. works mgr., 1948-52, asst. gen. mgr., 1952-53, now exec. vice pres., dir.; dir. Baystate Corp., New Bedford Gas and Edison Light Co.; trustee, clk. New Bedford Instn. for Savs. Area chmn. Mass. Econ. Stablzn. Bd. Bd. dirs. (pres. 1963-64) United Fund of Greater New Bedford, (past pres.) Jr. Achievement of Greater New Bedford, Asso. Industries of Mass., Boston; trustee St. Lukes Hosp., New Bedford, Millicent Library, Fairhaven, Mass. Clubs: Yale (Boston); Wamsutta, Country (New Bedford). Home: 6 Fort St Fairhaven MA 02719 Office: 24 N Front St New Bedford MA 02740

BUCKLEY, JAMES LANE, U.S. senator; b. N.Y.C., Mar. 9, 1923; s. William Frank and Aloise (Steiner) B.; B.A., Yale, 1943, LL.B., 1949; m. Ann Frances Cooley, May 22, 1953; children—Peter Pierce, James Wiggin, Priscilla Langford, William Frank, David Lane, Andrew Thurston. Admitted to N.Y. bar, 1949; asso. firm Wiggin & Dana, N.Y.C., 1949-53; v.p., dir. Catawba Corp., 1953-70; U.S. senator from N.Y., 1971—. Candidate for U.S. senator from N.Y., 1968; campaign mgr. William F. Buckley for mayor N.Y.C., 1965. Served to lt. (j.g.) USNR, 1943-46. Office: Old Senate Office Bldg Washington DC 20510

BUCKLEY, JEROME HAMILTON, educator; b. Toronto, Ont., Can., Aug. 30, 1917; s. James Ora and Madeline Isabelle (Morgan) B.; B.A., U. Toronto, 1939; A.M., Harvard, 1940, Ph.D., 1942; m. Elizabeth Jane Adams, June 19, 1943; children—Nicholas, Victoria, Eleanor. Came to U.S., 1939, naturalized, 1948. Successively instr., asst. prof., asso. prof., prof. English, U. Wis., 1942-54; Guggenheim fellow, 1946- 47; vis. asso. prof. Columbia, 1952-53, prof., 1954-61; prof. Harvard, 1961—; summer vis. prof. various univs.; Guggenheim fellow, 1963-64. Recipient Christian Gauss award Phi Beta Kappa, 1952. Mem. Internat. Assn. U. Profs. English, Modern Lang. Assn., Tennyson Soc. Episcopalian. Author: William Ernest Henley, 1945; The Victorian Temper, 1951; Tennyson, the Growth of a Poet, 1960; The Triumph of Time, 1966. Editor: Poems of Tennyson, 1958; Victorian Poets and Prose Writers, 1966; The Pre-Raphaelites, 1968. Co-editor: Twelve Hundred Years, 1949; Poetry of the Victorian Period, 1965; Masters of British Literature, 1962. Home: 191 Common St Belmont MA 02178 Office: Widener Library 245 Harvard U Cambridge MA 02138

BUCKLEY, JOHN BEECHER, lawyer; b. N.Y.C., Aug. 31, 1923; s. John B. and Emily (Enstrom) B.; B.A., Rutgers U., 1950, LL.B. cum laude, 1950; LL.M., N.Y. U., 1951; m. Ruth N. Eck, Aug. 15, 1947; children—John B., Beverly P., Alison M. Denis E. Admitted to N.Y. bar, 1953, Ind. bar, 1959; instr. law N.Y. U., 1951-53; trial atty. and spl. assignments as spl. asst. to Atty. Gen. U.S. Dept. Justice, 1953-57; with Miles Labs., Inc., Elkhart, Ind., 1957- -, now group v.p., dir.; dir. Corn-Refiners Assn.; lectr. Served to capt., USAAF, 1943- 46. Mem. Am., Elkhart City bar assns., Elkhart City C. of C. Contbr. to law reviews and jours. Home: 4101 Winding Waters Lane Elkhart IN 46514 Office: 1127 Myrtle St Elkhart IN 46514

BUCKLEY, JOHN LEE, Jr., food co. exec.; b. Balt., July 7, 1916; s. John Lee and Marie (Freburger) B.; student Balt. Poly. Inst., 1930-34; B.S. in Econs., Wharton Sch. U. Pa., 1938; m. Rita M. Scanlan, Sept. 30, 1939; children—Barbara Lee (Mrs. Harry R. Kleinben), Susan Scanlan (Mrs. Thomas F. Mullan III), Patricia Marie, Karen Rita. Accountant, Consol. Gas & Electric Co. Balt., 1938-41; accountant Ernst & Ernst, Balt., 1941-45, 46-47; controller McCormick & Co., Inc., Balt., 1947—, v.p., 1969—, also dir., mem. Jr. Bd. Execs., chmn., 1951-52; dir. Ampacco, Inc., Balt., treas., 1954—. Treas., mem. exec. com. Cath. Youth Orgn. Retreat House and Summer Day Camp, Balt., 1961—. Trustee Bon Secours Hosp., Balt., mem. finance com., 1971—. Served as lt. (j.g.) USNR, 1945-46. C.P.A., Md. Mem. Financial Execs. Inst. (pres. Balt. chpt. 1965-66). Am. Inst. Accountants, Md. Assn. C.P.A.'s, Md. Acad. Scis. (exec. com., controller 1968—), Am. Mgmt. Assn., Pa. Alumni Club Balt., Am. Legion (chmn. post scholarship com. 1953—), Oriole Advs., Kappa Sigma. Democrat. Roman Catholic (chmn. ch. finance com. 1968—, mem. adv. bd. 1968—). Home: 5600 N Charles St Baltimore MD 21210 Office: 11350 McCormick Rd Hunt Valley MD 21030

BUCKLEY, JOHN WILLIAM, petroleum co. exec.; b. N.Y.C., June 22, 1920; s. William F. and Aloise (Steiner) B.; B.A., Yale, 1942; m. Ann B. Harding, Nov. 1949 (dec.); children—Mary, Aloise, John M. Engaged in exploratory and producing aspects of oil, Venezuela, Can., other countries; pres., dir. Can. So. Petroleum, Ltd., 1954—; pres., dir. United Canso Oil & Gas Ltd., Pantepec Internat., Inc.; dir. Pancoastal Petroleum Co., C.A. Served from pvt. to 1st. lt., AUS, 1942-46; N. Africa France. Clubs: Camp Fire of America; Racquet and Tennis, Union League (N.Y.C.). Roman Catholic. Home: Lakeville CT 06039 Office: Sharon CT 06069 also 103 E 37th St New York City NY 10016

BUCKLEY, JOSEPH, clergyman; b. St. Paul, Sept. 3, 1905; s. James Augustine and Mary (Magner) B.; student Marist Coll., Washington, 1925-27; S.T.D., Angelico U., Rome, Italy, 1931; M.A. in Philosophy, U. Notre Dame, 1947. Joined Soc. of Mary, 1925, ordained priest Roman Catholic Ch., 1931; prof. theology and philosophy Marist Coll., 1931-34, Notre Dame Sem., New Orleans, 1934-41, 46-52, 58-59; lectr. U. Notre Dame, 1946, summers 1949, 50-51; founding pastor St. Pius X Parish, Beford, O., 1952-58; provincial Washington Province, Soc. of Mary, 1959-61, 70—, superior gen., 1961-69. Voting mem. Vatican Ecumenical Council II and First Synod Bishops, 1967. Served to maj. Chaplain Corps, AUS, 1942-46. Decorated Bronze Star. Mem. Am. Philos. Assn., Am. Cath. Theol. Soc., Am. Legion (chaplain La. 1950-51, Ohio 1953-54, Italy-Greece 1969-70). Author: Man's Last End, 1949; Christian Design for Sex, 1952; Purity, Modesty, Marriage, 1960. Translator (from French to English): The Three Stages of Spiritual Life, 3 vols., 1956. Home: 480 Northfield Rd Bedford OH 44146 Office: 220 Taylor St NE Washington DC 20017

BUCKLEY, JOSEPH PAUL, pharmacologist; b. Bridgeport, Conn., Jan. 12, 1924; B.S., U. Conn., 1949; M.S., Purdue U., 1951, Ph.D., 1952; m. Shirley Elizabeth Jane Shipman, Aug. 16, 1947. Asst. prof. pharmacology U. Pitts., 1952-55, asso. prof., 1955-58, prof., head dept. pharmacology, 1958—, asso. dean Sch. Pharmacy, 1969—; staff pharmacologist St. John's Gen. Hosp., Pitts., Western Pa. Hosp.; cons. pharmacologist Eaton Labs., Norwich, N.Y., A.H. Robins & Co., Inc., Richmond, Va. Served as 2d lt. USAAF, 1943-45. Decorated Air medal with clusters; Am. Found. Pharm. Edn. fellow, 1950-52; recipient award Angiology Research Found., 1965, award Am. Pharm. Assn., 1966. Registered pharmacist, Conn., 1949- -. Mem. Acad. Pharm. Scis. (chmn. sect. pharmacology and bio-chemistry 1965-67, v.p. 1969-70), Am. Soc. Pharm. and Exptl. Therapeutics, Am. Pharm. Assn., A.A.A.S. (sec. sect pharm. scis. 1961-67, chmn. sect., v.p. 1969), N.Y. Acad. Sci., Sigma Xi, Rho Chi, Phi Sigma, Phi Lambda Upsilon, Kappa Psi (grand council dep.). Presbyn. Contbr. articles profl. jours. Cons. editor Jour. Behavioral Pharmacology. Home: 1264 Arrowood Dr Pittsburgh PA 15243 Office: Salk Hall Terrace St Pittsburgh PA 15243

BUCKLEY, PRISCILLA LANGFORD, mag. exec.; b. N.Y.C., Oct. 17, 1921; d. William Frank and Aloise (Steiner) Buckley; B.A., Smith Coll., 1943. Copy girl, sports writer U.P., N.Y.C., 1944, radio rewrite, 1944-47, corr., Paris, France, 1954- 57; news editor radio sta. WACA, Camden, S.C., 1947-48; reports officer CIA, Washington, 1951-53; with Nat. Review mag., N.Y.C., 1957—, mng. editor, 1959—. Club: Overseas Press (N.Y.C.). Home: Great Elm, Sharon, CT 06069. Office: National Review 150 E 35th St New York City NY 10016

BUCKLEY, ROBERT JOSEPH, machine tool mfg. co. exec.; b. N.Y.C., Mar. 16, 1924; s. Thomas William and Catherine Alberta (Nolan) B.; B.A. with distinction, Wesleyan U., Middletown, Conn., 1950; J.D., Cornell U., 1953; m. Polly Dee, June 18, 1948; children—Robert Joseph, John Nolan, Peter Thomas, Claire Dee, Brian Edwin, Mark Charles, Christopher Lawrence, and Paul Gerard. Asst. plant engr. Nat. Cash Register Co., 1951-52; supr. N.Y. State Law Revision Commn., 1952-53, admitted to N.Y. bar, 1954; with Gen. Electric Co., 1953-61, mgr. union relations, Schenectady, 1959-61; with Baldwin-Lima-Hamilton Corp., 1961-68, gen. mgr. Standard Steel div., 1962-68, v.p. corp., 1962-68; exec. v.p. Ingersoll Milling Machine Co., Rockford, Ill., 1968-70, pres., 1970—. Bd. dirs. St. Anthonys Hosp., Rockford. Served with inf. AUS, 1942-46. Decorated Purple Heart. Mem. Am. Iron and Steel Inst., N.Y. State Bar Assn., Pa. Mfrs. Assn., Am. Ordnance Assn., Transp. Assn. Am., Machinery and Allied Products Inst. (mfg. council). Newcomen Soc. Club: Cornell N.Y. Athletic, Overseas Press (N.Y.C.). Home: 924 Ridgewood Rd Rockford IL 61107 Office: 707 Fulton St Rockford IL 61103

BUCKLEY, ROBERT WILLIAM, mfg. co. exec.; b. Boston, Dec. 28, 1905; s. Joseph William and Mary Ellen (Dimes) B.; Ph.B., Brown U., 1927; student Harvard Grad. Sch. Bus. Adminstrn., 1929; m. Marion Hedley, June 29, 1935; children—Robert William, Arthur Hedley, Marion Susan. With Dancer-Fitzgerald-Sample, advt., 1946-47, Benton & Bowles, advt., 1948-49; with Ludlow Typograph Co., Chgo., 1950—, v.p., 1961-64, pres., 1964—, also dir.; treas. NPEA Exhibits, Incorporated. Chairman parents committee Monmouth College. President board of edn. Freemont (Ill.) Township Sch. Dist 79, 1955. Republican candidate for Ill. Ho. of Reps., 1964. Mem. Nat. Printing Equipment Assn. (dir.), Brown U. Asso. Alumni (regional v.p.). Club: Brown Univ. (Chgo.); Onwentsia (Lake Forest, Ill.); Everglades (Palm Beach, Fla.). Home: Pine Knoll Libertyville IL 60048 Office: 2032 Clybourn Av Chicago IL 60614

BUCKLEY, TIM, composer, vocalist; b. Washington, Feb. 14, 1947; s. Tim and Elaine (Scalia) B. Recorded Tim Buckley, Hello and Goodbye, Happy Sad, 1966-; composer (with others) mus. score for film Changes; concert performances include Royal Albert Hall, London, Eng., 1968, appearance with N.Y. Philharmonic, 1969. Lyricist. Contbr. anthologies, poetry books. Address: care of Herb Cohen 150 W 55th St New York City, NY 10019.

BUCKLEY, WILLIAM ELMHIRST, publisher; b. Rahway, N.J., Oct. 6, 1913; s. John A. and Margaret Elsie (Elmhirst) B.; student U. Pa., 1932-34; m. Virginia Smith, Aug. 2, 1941; children—Carolyn E. (Mrs. Carolyn B. Meyer), William E. Jr. exec. Quinn & Boden Co., Inc., book mfrs., Rahway, N.J., 1935-42, Doubleday & Co., N.Y.C., 1945-49; with Henry Holt & Co., N.Y.C., 1949- 58, v.p., dir., 1951-58; v.p. sales World Pub. Co., Cleve., 1958-60; v.p. book div. McCall Corp., N.Y.C., 1960-62; v.p. Curtis Pub. Co., N.Y.C., 1962-68, dir. book div., 1962-68; asst. to pres. Cowles Communications, Inc., 1968—; chmn. Cowles Book Co., 1968—; chmn., pres. Cambridge Book Co., subsidiaries Cowles Communications Inc., 1968—. Served to lt. comdr. USNR, 1942-45. Mem. Phi Delta Theta. Clubs: Dutch Treat (N.Y.C.); Lawrence (N.Y.) Beach; Ocean of Florida (Delray Beach). Home: 480 Park Av New York City NY 10022 Office: 488 Madison Av New York City NY 10022

BUCKLEY, WILLIAM FRANK, Jr., mag. editor, author; b. N.Y.C., Nov. 24, 1925; s. William Frank and Aloise (Steiner) B.; student U. Mexico, 1943; B.A., Yale, 1950; L.H.D., Seton Hall U., 1966, Niagara U., 1967, Mt. St. Mary's Coll., 1969; LL.D., St. Peter's Coll., 1969, Syracuse U., 1969, Ursinus Coll., 1969, Lehigh U., 1970; D.Sc., Curry Coll, 1970; m. Patricia Taylor, July 6, 1950; 1 son, Christopher T. Asso. editor Am. Mercury, 1952; editor-in-chief Nat. Rev., N.Y.C., 1955—. Mem. USIA Adv. Commn., 1969—. Served to 2d lt., inf. AUS, 1944-46. Clubs: New York Yacht, Overseas Press (N.Y.C.): National Press (Washington). Author: God and Man at Yale, 1951; (with L. Brent Bozell) McCarthy and His Enemies 1954; Up From Liberalism, 1959: Rumbles Left and Right, 1963; The Unmaking of a Mayor, 1966; The Jeweler's Eye, 1968, The Governor Listeth, 1970. Editor: The Committee and Its Critics, 1962, Odyssey of a Friend, 1970; Did You Ever See a Dream Walking?, 1970. Contbr. to Ocean Racing, 1959, The Intellectuals, 1950, What is Conservatism? 1964; Dialogues in Americanism, 1964; Violence in the Streets, 1968, The Beatles Book, 1968, Spectrum of Catholic Attitudes, 1969, Great Ideas Today Annual, 1970; also periodicals. Host weekly show Firing Line, 1966—; syndicated columnist, 1962—. Office: 150 E 35th St New York City NY 10016

BUCKLLIN, DONALD HARTWELL, educator; b. Providence, Feb. 25, 1922; s. Harold Stephen and Hazel (Hartwell) B.; A.B. Brown U., 1943; M.A., Amherst Coll., 1948; postgrad. Harvard, 1952-53; m. Hope Lamprey Cone, Sept. 1946; children—William Hartwell, Anne Cone, Stephen Loomis. Research fellow biology Harvard, 1952-53; asst. prof. biology Coll. William and Mary, 1953-54; asst. prof. zoology, U. Wis., Madison, 1964-69, asso. prof., 1959-65, prof. zoology 1965-70. Asst. biologist Va. Fisherie Lab., summer 1954; dir. NSF Academic Year Inst., 1959-61, cons. Madison Center BSCS, 1960—, writing conf., summer 1960, 61,62; coordinating tchr. film series Am. Inst. Biol. Scis., 1961, 67- 68, CUEBS, 1967-68. Active Brown U. Alumni Fund. Served to lt. USNR, 1943-46. Mem. A.A.A.S., Am. Soc. Zoologists, Soc. for Study of Devel. and Growth, Am. Inst. Biol. Scis., N.A.B.T. Author: (with T. Weis) Readings in Growth and Differentiation, 1963; Syllabus for Experimental Course in General Zoology, 1964. Contbg. author to biol. surcebooks, lab. manuals. Home: 222 Frigate Dr Madison WI 53705

BUCKMAN, KARL EMMET, educator; b. Muscatine, Ia., Dec. 25, 1906; s. John Buck and Sarah (Creese) B.; A.B. in Polit. Sci., Fresno State Coll., 1942; grad. student, Stanford, 1944; M.A. in Polit. Econs., Claremont U., 1952. Prof. polit. sci. Fresno State Coll., 1942—, chmn. dept., 1964—. Spl. cons. Cal. Bd. Edn. on Jr. High Texts in Govt., 1965. Dep. Chmn., Fresno County Grand Jury, 1956; chmn. com. reorgn. Nursing Home Fresno County, 1957; chmn. Fresno Redevel. Agy., 1956-66. Mem. Am., No. Cal. (presdl. citation 1964, pres. 1960) polit. sci. assns., Western Assn. Slavic Studies, Blue Key, Pi Gamma Mu, Kappa Delta Rho. Republican. Home: 3536 N Poplar St Fresno CA 93704

BUCKMAN, THOMAS RICHARD, educator, found. exec.; b. Reno, May 3, 1923; s. Thomas Eli and Georgia Christina (Damm) B.; B.A., U. Pacific, 1947; certificate U. Stockholm, 1951; M.A. (fellow Scandinavian studies), U. Minn., 1952, B.L.S. (H.W. Wilson scholar), 1953; m. Gunhild Margareta Malmkjell, May 1, 1948; children—Anne Christina, Carol Erica. Clk., Permit Office for Germany, Allied High Commn., Stockholm, Sweden, 1949-50; sr. clk. U. Minn. Library, 1952-53; asst. reference librarian Ore. State U. Library. 1953-54; King Gustav V fellow in Sweden, Am. Scandinavia Found., 1954-55; asst. librarian Modesto (Cal.) Jr. Coll. Library, 1955-56; head acquisitions dept. U. Kan. Library, 1956-60, asso. dir., 1960-61, dir. libraries, 1961-68, lectr. in Scandinavian, 1958-61; prof. bibliography, univ. librarian Northwestern U., Evanston, Ill., 1968-71; pres. Found. Center, 1971—; dir. internat. relations office A.L.A., 1966-67. Mem. Gov. Kan. Com. Library Service, 1963-64; mem. Kan. State Library Adv. Commn. 1963-67; mem. master plan com. Ill. Bd. Higher Edn., 1968-69. Served with USNR, 1943-46. Guggenheim fellow, 1964-65. Fellow Linnean Soc. London; mem. A.L.A. (chmn. internat. relations adv. com. for liaison with Japanese Libraries 1967-71), Kan. Library Assn., (chmn. intellectual freedom com., pres. 1967-68), Assn. Research Libraries (pres. 1971-72), Bibliog. Soc. Am., Soc. Advancement Scandinavian Study (sec.-treas. 1959-69), Am. Civil Liberties Union, Am. Assn. U. Profs., Am. Soc. Information Sci. Clubs: Caxton, Arts (Chgo.) ; Rockefeller Luncheon (N.Y.). Editor, translator: Modern Theatre: Seven Plays and an Essay (by Pär Lagerkvist), 1966. Editor: Bibliography and Natural History, 1966; University and Research Libraries in Japan and the United States, 1972. Contbr. articles to profl. jours. Home: 3 Pine Dr Port Washington NY 11050

BUCKNAM, JAMES ROMEO, newspaper editor; b. Livermore Falls, Me., Apr. 26, 1911; s. Howard Leland and Rose Alma (Deshenes) B.; student U. N.H., 1930-33; m. Adrienne Meteyer, Aug. 6, 1934, (div. Dec. 1965); children-Beverly Anne (Mrs. Louis F. Marcou), Howard V., James L., Nancy R. (Mrs. Charles E. Murphy); m. 2d, Cecilr LeBlanc, Jan. 14, 1967. Reporter-editor Berlin (N.H.) Reporter, 1933-43; deskman Manchester (N.H.) Union Leader, 1943-49, night editor, 1949-62, mng. editor, 1962-69, exec. editor, 1969—. Mem. Gov.'s Traffic Safety Commn. 1963-65; chmn. N.H. Traffic Safety Comn., 1965—; mem. bd. rev. Boy Scouts Am., 1968—; mem. Joint Hosp. Commn., Manchester, 1969—. Vice pres. Our Lady of Mercy Hosp.; pres., bd. govs., mem. adv. bd. Notre Dame hosp. Served with USMCR, World War II; PTO. Mem. Am. Legion, V.F.W., Marine Corps Combat Corrs. Assn., Marine Corps Res. Officers Assn. Home: 34 Albin Rd Bow NH 03301 Office: 35 Amherst St Manchester NH 03105

BUCKNELL, EARL FAY, ins. exec.; b. Colon, Mich., Feb. 23, 1905; s. Orlie Fay and Nellie (Louder) B.; A.B., U. Mich., 1926; m. Wave Pauline DeBolt, June 16, 1928; children—Robert Irving, Pauline Faye. Actuarial dept. The Maccabees, Detroit, 1926-27; asst. actuary New World Life Ins. Co., Spokane, Wash., 1928-30; actuarial dept. Bankers Life Co., Des Moines, 1930-31, supr. actuarial dept., 1931-34, asst. actuary, 1934- 45, asso. actuary, 1945-46, v.p., actuary, 1946-56, v.p. 1956-60, exec. v.p. 1960-61, pres., 1961-68, chmn. bd., 1968-71. Mem. adv. bd. Mercy Hosp., Des Moines. Fellow Soc. Actuaries. Club: Des Moines, Wakonda. Home: 1906 Willomere Des Moines IA 50315 Office: 711 High St Des Moines IA 50307

BUCKNER, ELMER LA MAR, ins. exec., state legislator; b. Provo, Utah, Apr. 27, 1922; s. Elmer R. and Altis LaVern (Maxfield) B.; B.S., Brigham Young U., 1946; m. Melba Hale, Oct. 3, 1945; children—Lynda, Brent, Terry, Kathy, David. Partner Buckner Ins. Counselors, Ogden, Utah, 1947-62, co. inc., pres., 1962—; dir. Zion's

Coop. Merc. Instn.; mem. Utah Ho. of Reps., 1965-67, Utah Senate, 1967—, asst. majority leader, 1971—. Bd. govs. A.R.C., 1956-62; gen. bd. Young Men's Mut. Improvement Assn., Ch. of Jesus Christ of Latter Day Saints, 1957-58, bishop of Ogden 55th Ward, 1958-63; 2d counselor Weber Heights Stake presidency, 1963-68; pres. Weber State Coll. Stake, 1968—. Former dir. Citizens Co. for Hoover Report; mem. Com. on Religion in Am. Life Inc.; former mem. adv. com. FOA. Mem. exec. com. Am. Nat. Red. Cross, 1961-62; v.p. Lake Bonneville council Boy Scouts Am., 1968-69, pres., 1970, recipient Silver Beaver award, 1967. Mem. bd. alumni Brigham Young U., 1959-63, pres., 1961-62; v.p. Ogden area United Fund, 1962, pres. No. Utah United Fund, 1963; chmn. Utah Cancer Crusade, 1970; v.p. Utah Cancer Soc., 1971. Utah del. Republican Nat. Conv., Chgo., 1960, chmn. Weber County Rep. Party, 1960-64; elected Utah state Rep. elector, Rep. State Conv., 1964. Served as 1st lt. USAAF, World War II; 23 missions. C.L.U. Mem. U.S. (dir. 1955-56), U.S. Jr. (pres. 1954-55), Utah Jr. (pres. 1952-53), Ogden (dir. civic affairs com.), Ogden Jr. (pres. 1950) chambers commerce, Jr. Chamber Internat. (treas. 1956), Weber Coll. Alumni Assn. (pres. 1958-59), Sigma Gamma Chi (internat. pres. 1967-69). Kiwanian pres. Ogden 1967). Home: 1550 Country Hills Dr Ogden UT 84403 Office: 1180 28th St Ogden UT 84403

BUCKNER, GEORGE WALKER, Jr., church official; b. Pike County, Mo., Oct. 1, 1893; s. George Walker (clergyman) and Anna (Griffth) B.; student Culver-Stockton Coll., 1911, Southport (Eng.) Univ. Sch., 1912-13, Langenburg (Germany) Gymnasium Schule, 1913; A.B., Culver-Stockton Coll., 1914, A.M., 1915; A.M., Central Wesleyan Coll., 1916; D.D., Hastings Coll., 1925; LL.D., Culver-Stockton College, 1940; D.Litt. from Atlantic Christian Coll., 1953; m. Winifred Magee, August 24, 1915; children—Susan (Mrs. Philip Jackson), Julia Anna (Mrs. Raymond Wheeler), Georgia Winifred (Mrs. Dorlaque). Ordained minister Disciples of Christ, 1915; filled pastorates of churches at Mokane, La Monte and Lee's Summit, Mo., 1916-21; pastor First Christian Church, Hastings, Neb., 1921-27; also prof. Biblical lit. Hastings Coll., 1922-24, prof. sociology, 1926-27; pastor Central Ch. of Christ, Grand Rapids, Mich., 1927-35; editor of World Call, internat. mag. of Disciples of Christ, 1935-61; internat. commissioner Council of Christian Unity (Disciples of Christ), 1961—; interim minister St. Paul's Christian Ch., Raleigh, 1964-65, 67; grad. lectr. Phillips U., 1940; lecturer, Union Sem., P.R., 1947. Exec. sec. Council on Christian Unity, 1941-61; mem. exec. com. Fed. Council Chs. of Christ in America, 1940-50; mem. Am. Com. World Council of Chs., 1944-48; mem. dept. internat. affairs of Nat. Council Chs.; mem. bd. Ecumenical Inst., Switzerland, 1948—; del. to World Conf. on Faith and Order Edinburgh, and to World Conf. on Church, Community and State, Oxford, 1937; del. to World Missionary Conf., Madras, India, 1938; fraternal del. to Conference of Churches of Christ in Great Britain and Ireland, 1945; delegate to the Assembly World Council of Chs., 1948, 1954. adviser, 1961; mem. Central Com., World Council Chs., 1948-61, founding; on ecumenical, editoral mission to the Middle East and Asia, 1961-62; com. Christian U. in Japan; delivered Earle Lecture Pacific Sch. of Religion. 1949, Cuthrell Lectures Atlantic Christian Lecture Pacific Sch. of Religion, 1949, Cuthrell Lectures Atlantic Coll., 1952; mem. commn. on social action N.C. Council Chs. mem. Protestant Catholic Editorial Study Mission to Israel, 1970; mem. nat. adv. com. Am.-Israel Cultural Found.; spl. rep. Lexington Theol. Sem., 1968—. Recipient citation Nat. and World Council Chs., 1960. Clubs: Indianapolis Athletic, Wranglers, Asso. Ch. Press (past pres.); overseas member of Authors Club of London, Eng. Author: Concerns of a World Church, 1943; The Winds of God, 1947. Contbr. religious and sociol. articles; lectr. Staff corr. The Christian Century, 1939-61. Address: Glenn Heights Chapel Hill NC 27514

BUCKNER, HUBBARD GEORGE, cons.; b. Erlanger, Ky., Oct. 13, 1905; s. Hubbard G. and Etheline (Buckner) B.; B.A., Centre Coll., Danville, Ky., 1928; m. Kate Tebbs Helm, Sept. 22, 1934; children—Hubbard Taylor, John Alexander. Pres. Louisville Pub. Warehouse Co., 1949-50; with First Nat. Bank Louisville, 1950-70, sr. v.p., 1963-70, past dir.; gen. bus. cons., Louisville, 1971—; dir. First Ky. Co., Brinly-Hardy Co., Reliance Universal Inc., H.J. Scheirich Co., Star Hill Distilling Co., Mchts. Ice & Cold Storage Co. Trustee Centre Coll. Mem. Soc. Colonial Wars, Beta Theta Pi. Clubs: Pendennis (pres., dir. 1963-65), Louisville Country, Filson (Louisville). Home: 191 Bow Lane Louisville KY 40207 Office: 595 Starks Bldg Louisville KY 40201

BUCKNER, ROBERT HENRY, writer, producer; b. Crewe, Va., May 28, 1906; s. Robert Henry and Inez (James) B.; grad. U. Va., 1927; U. Edinburgh, Scotland; m. Mary Duckett Doyle, Dec. 8, 1937; children—Sharon, Robert Henry. Newspaper corr., Europe, 1927-29; with Alfred A. Knopf, Inc., also Doubleday, Doran, N.Y.C., 1929-30; advt. exec., N.Y.C., 1930-33; writer New Yorker, Esquire, Atlantic Monthly, Colliers, Cosmopolitan, others, 1933-36; writer, producer Warner Bros. Studios, Hollywood, Cal., 1936-46, Universal-Internat. Pictures, 1946—; writer, producer pictures Yankee Doodle Dandy, Life With Father, Dodge City, Mission to Moscow, Rogues Regiment, Desert Song, God is My Co-Pilot, Gentleman Jim, Devotion, Sword in the Desert, Deported, Bright Victory, To Paris With Love, Prize of Gold, Love Me Tender, others; writer TV series Hong Kong, 1960—. Recipient O'Brien award for best Am. short story, 1936; Screen Writers Guild Meltzer award for best screenplay, 1952. Author: (novels) Sigrid and the Sergeant, 1957; Tiger by the Tail, 1960. Starfire, 1960. Mem. Pi Kappa Alpha. Home: Calle Canal 16 San Miguel De Allende Gto Mexico

BUCKNER, WALKER GENTRY, investment banker; b. Harvey, Ill., Sept. 2, 1907; s. Samuel G. and Bina (Glascock) B.; A.B., U. Mo., 1929; student Harvard, 1930; M.B.A., U. Pa., 1931; m. Helen M. Watson, Sept. 9, 1940 (div. 1970); children—Thomas W., Walker Gentry, Mary B. Loud, Elizabeth Bina. With trust dept. Summit Trust Co. (N.J.), 1931-35, Riter & Co., N.Y.C., 1935-41, Hemphill, Noyes & Co., N.Y.C., 1941-53; partner Reynolds & Co., N.Y.C., 1953-56; partner Buckner & Co. of N.Y.C., 1956-70; pres. Walker Buckner & Co., Inc., 1970—. Sec., chmn. adv. bd. Salvation Army N.Y.C., Trustee Ednl. Broadcasting Corp.; bd. dirs. Met. Opera Assn. Mem. Sigma Nu. Clubs: University, Downtown Assn., Links, Pinnacle (N.Y.C.); Blind Brook (Purchase, N.Y.); Gulf Stream (Fla.) Golf.

BUCKS, CHARLES ALAN, airline exec.; b. Lubbock, Tex., Dec. 14, 1927; s. Charles Henry and Nell (Lattimore) B.; student Tex. Technol. Coll., 1947-48, Amarillo Jr. Coll., 1948-49; m. Joyce Laverne Turner, Aug. 19, 1949; children—Jimmy Charles, David Alan, Robert Doyle, Dawne Alyce. With Continental Air Lines, Inc., 1948—, gen. sales mgr., 1958-61, v.p. field sales, 1961-65, v.p. sales, Los Angeles, 1965-66, v.p. sales and service, 1966-69, sr. v.p., 1969—, also dir. Pres. One Shot Antelope Hunt, Lander, Wyo., 1968; 2d v.p., dir. African First Shotters. Trustee Continental Found., Denver; bd. dirs. Mustang Sanctuary Found. Served with USNR, 1945-46; PTO. Recipient Distinguished Alumnus award Tex. Tech. U., 1971. Mem. Conquistadores del Ciel. (bd. dirs.), So. Cal. Safari Club (bd. dirs.). Pacific Area Travel Assn. Democrat. Presbyn. Club: Lakeside Country (Hollywood, Cal.). Home: 17101 Strawberry Dr Encino CA 91316 Office: Los Angeles Internat Airport Los Angeles CA 90009

BUCKSON, DAVID P., atty. gen. Del.; b. Townsend, Del., July 25, 1920; grad. U. Del., 1941; LL.B., Dickinson Sch. Law, 1948; five chidren. Admitted to Del. bar, 1949; engaged in practice law in Dover and Middletown; judge Ct. Common Pleas, Kent County, 1956; lt. gov. Del., 1957-60; interim gov. Del., 1960-61; atty. gen. Del., 1963—. Dir. Wilmington Trust Co. Served to maj. AUS, 1941-46. Mem. Del. Bar Assn. (v.p.), V.F.W., Sigma Nu. Methodist (sec., treas.). Rotarian, Mason. Clubs: Maple Dale Country; Vicmead Hunt. Home: RFD 3 Beach Haven Dr Doverr DE 19901 Office: Office Atty Gen State Capitol Dover DE 19901

BUCKWALTER, WILLIAM ROY, educator, economist; b. Phila., May 28, 1906; s. Elmer M. and Mary L. (Arters) B.; B.S., U. Pa., 1929, M.A., 1932, Ph.D., 1940; m. Marie E. Mallon, Dec. 30, 1931; children—Bernadine (Mrs. R. J. McConnell), Barbara. Instr. Upper Darby (Pa.) High Sch., 1929-40; instr. mgmt. Temple U., 1940-43, asst. prof., 1943-46, asso. prof., 1946-47, prof., 1947—, acting dean School of Business Adminstration. Economist Nat. War Labor Bd., 1942-43, pub. mem. disputes bd., 1943-45; impartial chmn. Full-Fashioned Hosiery Industry, 1944, Phila. Ladies Dress Industry, 1954-56; mem. arbitration panel Fed. Mediation and Conciliation Service. Mem. Am. Arbitration Assn. (mem. arbitration panel), Indsl. Relations Assn. Philadelphia, National Academy of Arbitrators, C. of C., Indsl. Relations Research Assn., Pi Gamma Mu, Beta Gamma Sigma. Methodist. Contbr. articles profl. jours. Home: 404 Haverford Av Narberth PA 19072 Office: Temple University Philadelphia PA 19122

BUCY, CHARLES WILLIAM, govt. official; b. Westfield, Mass., Sept. 25, 1902; s. Charles Gilbert and Sarah Elizabeth (Kerwin) B.; certificate of fgn. service, Georgetown U., 1923; LL.B., Fordham U., 1926; m. Emilie Marie Kolipinski, Sept. 4, 1926; children—Charles Andrew, Donald Louis, Karen Marie. Admitted to New York bar, 1926; practiced law, New York City, 1927-37; Office of Solicitor, U.S. Dept. of Agr., 1937-52, asso. solicitor, 1946-59, asst. gen. counsel Office Gen. Counsel, 1959—. Chmn. Com. on Adminstrv. Procedure Act, U.S. Dept. Agr.; mem. Pres.' Adminstrv. Conf. of U.S., 1961-62; chmn. com. on reports and statistics Pres.' Adminstrv. Conf. U.S., 1961-62; vice chmn. rule making com. Statutory Adminstrv. Conf. U.S., 1968—. Served War Food Adminstrn., World War II. Mem. Fed., Am. bar associations. Roman Catholic. K.C. (state adv., state dep. Md. 1949-52). Clubs: Nat. Lawyers (Washington); Bethesda Country. Home: 4618 Langdrum Lane Chevy Chase MD 20015 Office: US Dept Agr South Bldg Washington DC 20515

BUCY, PAUL C., neurol. surgeon; b. Hubbard, Ia., Nov. 13, 1904; s. Isaac and Lillian (Clancy) B.; B.S., State U., Ia., 1925, M.S., 1927, M.D., 1927; M.D., U. Thessaloniki, 1970; Dr. h.c. U. Utrecht, 1971; m. Evelyn Richards, June 12, 1927; children—Paul Craig, James Gordon. Intern Henry Ford Hosp., Detroit, 1927-28; resident, instr. neurosurgery U. Chgo., 1928-30, instr., 1930-33, asst. prof., 1933- 38, asso. prof. in charge neurosurgery, 1938-41; prof. neurology and neurol. surgery, U. Ill., 1941-54; prof. surgery, med. school Northwestern U., 1954—, in charge neurosurgery, 1964—; traveling fellow to Eng. and Germany, 1930-31; research asst., Yale U., 1933; attending neurologist and neurol. surgeon Ill. Neuropsychiat. Inst. and Research and Ednl. Hosps., U. Ill., 1941-54; attending neurol. surgeon, v.p. bd. trustees Chgo. Meml. Hosp., 1941-54, chief of staff, 1943-54; attending neurol. surgeon charge dept. neurol. surgery Chgo. Wesley Meml. Hosp., 1954—; cons. neurol. surgeon Evangel. Hosp., Engelwood Hosp., Woodlawn Hosp.; editorial bd. Jour. of Neuro-Surgery, 1951-58, chairman, 1957-61, dir. publs., 1961—; Gorgas lectr. U. Ala., 1944; John Black Johnston lectr. U. Minn., 1949; Commonwealth vis. prof. U. Louisville, 1950; George A. Ball vis. prof. Ind. U., 1953; vis. hon. prof. U. Minas Gerais, Brazil, 1954; Fedor Krause lectr. German Neurosurg. Soc. (recipient Fedor Krause medal), 1961, 62; J.H. Jackson meml. lectr. Montreal Neurol. Inst., 1965; W. P. Van Wagenen lectr. U. Rochester, 1965; vis. lectr. Free U. Berlin, 1963; vis. prof., lectr. Creigton U., 1966; vis. prof. Med. Coll. Ga., 1966, U. Wis., 1968, Harvard, 1969; Fulbright vis. prof. U. Utrecht, 1969; also other lectrs. Adv. council NIH, 1961-65; member program projects com. Nat. Inst. Neurol. Disease and Blindness, 1965-66; chmn. Nat. Com. on Research in Neurol. Disorders, 1969—; chmn. med. adv. com. Nat. Paraplegic Found. Recipient Certificate of Accomplishment, State U. Ia., 1947: Distinguished Service Award, Med. Alumni. U. Chgo., 1955; Distinguished Achievement award, Modern Medicine mag., Speedy award Paralyzed Vets. Am., 1969. Diplomate Am. Bd. Psychiatry and Neurol., Am. Bd. Neurol. Surgery (dir. 1940-48, sec.-treas. 1943- , 47, residency review com.-A.M.A. 1963-69). Fellow A.C.S., Am. Surg. Assn; mem. Am. Neurol. Assn. (v.p. 1954- 55, pres.-elect 1970-71), Soc. Neurol. Surgeons (pres. 1959-60), Harvey Cushing Soc. (pres. 1951-52, dir. publs. 1959—), Am. Physiol. Soc., A.M.A. (sec. 1936-39. chmn. sect. on nervous and mental dis.), Chgo. Neurol. Soc. (pres. 1947-48), Chgo. Path. Soc., Inst. Medicine Chgo., Chgo. Med. Soc. (mem. council 1948- 52), Ill. State Med. Soc., Central Neuropsychiat. Assn., Soc. Exptl. Biology and Medicine, Chgo. Surg. Soc. (v.p. 1955- 56). Soc. Biol. Psychiatry, World Fedn. Neuro-Surg. Socs. (pres. 1957-61), 2d Internat. Congress Neurol. Surg. (pres. 1957-61), Phi Chi, Delta Sigma Rho, Alpha Omega Alpha, Sigma Xi; hon. mem. various fgn. profl. socs. including Soc. Brit. Neurol. Surgeons. Clubs: University, Literary (pres.) (Chgo.). Author: Intercranial Tumors of Infancy and Childhood (with P. Bailey and D. N. Buchanon, 1939; The Precentral Motor Cortex, 1944, 49; Neurology (with R. R. Grinker and A. L. Sahs), 1959; also publs. sci. jours.; sects. of books on various phases nervous system. Home: 505 Lake Shore Dr Chicago IL 60611 Office: 251 E Chicago Av Chicago IL 60611

BUDD, GEORGE FITCH, coll. pres.; b. Oswego, N.Y., July 2, 1915; s. George Francis and Mary Ellen (Carter) B.; B.S., Buffalo State Tchrs. Coll., 1942; M.A., Columbia Tchrs. Coll., 1944, Ed.D., 1951; m. Laura A. Schmelzer, Dec. 23, 1942; children—John Carter, George Thomas, Catherine Elizabeth. Tchr., Monticello (N.Y.) pub. schs., 1939-41; adminstr. asst. Horace Mann Sch., N.Y.C., 1943-44; instr. edn. Cortland (N.Y.) State Tchrs. Coll., 1944-45; dir. tchr. edn. and certification Wash. State Dept. Edn., 1946-47; dir. field services Oneonta (N.Y.) State Tchrs. Coll., 1947-51; pres. St. Cloud (Minn.) State Coll., 1951-65, also chmn. bd. dirs. Coll. Found.; pres. Kan. State Coll. of Pittsburg, 1965-. Breeder, shower Morgan Horses; bd. govs. Am. Royal Live Stock and Horse Show; sec. North Central Morgan Horse Assn., 1959—; dir. Nat. Morgan Horse Club, Inc., City Nat. Bank of Pittsburg. Adv. Com. on U. Relations AID; adv. council grad. edn. U.S. Office Edn., Dept. HEW. Mem. exec. bd. Central Minn. council Boy Scouts Am. Chmn. bd. dirs. Alexandria-St. Cloud Performing Arts Found.; trustee Midwestern Ednl. TV; dir. North Star Research and Devel. Inst. Served with USAAF, 1942-43. Mem. Minn. Citizens Com. Pub. Edn., Minn. Edn. Assn., Nat. Council for Accreditation of Tchr. Edn. (co-chmn. visitation and appraisal com.), Assn. Minn. Colls. (pres.), St. Cloud (pres. 1955-56), Pittsburg chambers commerce, Nat., N.Y. State (exec. com., pres. so. zone) ednl. assns., Am. Assn. State Colls. and Univs. (pres.), Assn. Supervision and Curriculum Devel., Assn. Student Teaching., Am. Assn. Colls. Teaching Edn. (pub. relations com.), Family Service Soc., Phi Delta Kappa. Presbyn. (trustee). Rotarian (pres. Pittsburg). Home: 515 E Ford St Pittsburg, KS 66762.

BUDD, JOHN M., railroad exec.; b. Nov. 1907; s. Ralph and Georgia (Marshall) B.; B.S., Yale, 1930, grad. work, 1 yr. Began as chainman, G.N. Ry., summer 1926, asst. to elec. engr., 1930-31, asst. trainmaster, div. supt., various locations, 1933-42, asst. gen. mgr., lines east of Williston, N.D., 1945-47, v.p. operating dept., 1949-51, pres., 1951-70; chmn., chief exec. officer Burlington No. Inc., 1970-71, chmn. finance com., 1971—; pres. Chgo. and Eastern Ill. R.R., 1947-49. Served as lt. col. Mil. Ry. Service, Africa, Italy, France and Germany, AUS, 1942-45. Office: 176 E 5th St St Paul MN 55101

BUDD, JOSEPH LINCOLN, mem. Republican. Nat. Com.; b. Salt Lake City, May 31, 1911; s. John C. and Lucille (McGinnis) B.; student Wyo. U., 1929-30, Utah State U., 1932- 34; m. Ruth Francis Peterson, Dec. 27, 1936; children—Betty Louis (Mrs. Frank C. Fear), Mary Kaye (Mrs. Stanley Flitner), Nancy Ruth. Partner, mgr. Budd Hereford Ranch, nr. Big Piney, Wyo., 1934—; mem. Wyo. Ho. of Reps., 1951-63, minority floor leader, 1959, speaker, 1961; mem. Republican Nat. Com. for Wyo. Dir. Pacific Atlantic Life Ins. Co. Mem. Interstate Streams Commn.; member Wyoming Game and Fish Commission; pres. Wyo. Reclamation Assn., 1943-45; chairman trustees Big Piney Schs. Dir. Wyo. Safety Found. Mem. Wyo. Stock Growers Assn. (exec. com. 2d v.p. 1970-71), Am. Hereford Assn. (dir., v.p.), Am. Cattlemen's Assn. (2d v.p.), S.A.R. Presbyn. Mason (Shriner), Elk, Lion (past pres. Big Piney). Home: P O Box 340 Big Piney WY 83113

BUDD, PHILIP JOSEPH, govt. ofcl.; b. St. Louis, May 26, 1919; s. Vincent and Sophia (Kaiszo) Budrewicz; student St. Louis U., 1947-48, George Washington U., 1951- 52; m. Crystal C. Knox, Nov. 8, 1945; children—Stephen, Janet, Jeffrey, Thomas. With VA, 1940—, various positions, St. Louis, 1940-50, trans. to Washington, 1950, asst. chief systems and procedures div. Office Systems and Evaluation, Dept. Ins., 1954-57, chief evaluation staff, 1957, exec. asst. to adminstr. vets. affairs, 1957-60, chief ins. dir. VA, 1960-63, chief data mgmt. dir., 1963—. Served to 2d lt. AUS, 1942-46; lt. col. Res. Recipient Outstanding Performance award VA, 1959, 60, 64-70, Exceptional Service award, 1960; Presdl. Nat. award for Economy Achievement, 1964. Mem. Am. Legion, Res. Officers Assn., Data Processing Mgmt. Assn., Internat. Systems Mgmt. Assn. Home: 5424 Backlick Rd Springfield VA 22151 Office: VA Washington DC 20420

BUDD, RICHARD DONALD, psychiatrist; b. Detroit, Sept. 21, 1923; s. Sigmond Ziegfried and Helen (Wesley) B.; M.D., Wayne State U., 1948; m. Barbara Jean Renton, Jan. 21, 1950; children—Mary Aldeen, Cynthia Lynn, Deborah Ann, Laurie Jean. Intern Grace Hosp., Detroit, 1945-49; fellow Menninger Found. Sch. Psychiatry, 1949-52; asst. chief of service Topeka (Kan.) State Hosp., 1952-53; chief of service, asst. clin. dir. Northville (Mich.) State Hosp., 1953-57, med. supt., 1968—; pvt. practice psychiatry, 1957-68. Mem. Livonia (Mich.) Youth Symphony Soc. Served with AUS, 1943-44. Diplomate Am. Bd. Psychiatry and Neurology. Mem. Am., Northville psychol. assns., Mich. Assn. Hosp. Physicians. Home: 17730 Fairfield Av Livonia MI 48152 Office: 41001 W Seven Mile Rd Northville MI 48167

BUDD, WILBERT H., corp. exec.; b. Ann Arbor, Mich., 1913; ed. U. Mich., 1935. Exec. v.p., dir. CTS Corp.; dir. Chgo. Telephone of Cal., Inc. Home: 1929 Rainbow Bend Blvd Elkhart, IN 46514. Office: 1142 W Beardsley Av Elkhart IN 46514

BUDENHOLZER, ROLAND ANTHONY, educator, mech. engr.; b. St. Charles, Mo., Nov. 24, 1912; s. Joseph P. and Mary (Willey) B.; B.S. in Mech. Engring., N.M. State U., 1935; M.S. in Mech. Engring., Cal. Inst. Tech., 1937, Ph.D., 1939; m. Florence C. Christiansen, Nov. 28, 1941; children—Francis Edward, John Christopher, Robert Joseph. Grad. asst. Cal. Inst. Tech., 1935-39; research fellow Am. Petroleum Inst., 1939-40; faculty Ill. Inst. Tech., 1940—, prof. mech. engring., 1947-; resident research asso. Argonne Nat. Lab., summer 1961; cons. IIT Research Inst., 1946—; dir. Midwest Power Conf., 1949-52, Am. Power Conf., 1952—; rep. Am. Power Conf. to World Power Conf., 1965—. Recipient George Westinghouse gold medal American Society of Mechanical Engineers, 1968. Fellow Am. Soc. M.E. (sec., exec. com. power div., 1967-68, chmn. 1970-71); mem. Am. Soc. Engring. Edn., Nat. Soc. Profl. Engrs., Western Soc. Engrs. (dir. 1969—), Am. Assn. U. Profs. (pres. Ill. Inst. Tech. chpt. 1963-64), Sigma Xi (pres. Ill. Inst. Tech. chpt. 1948-49), Tau Beta Pi, Pi Tau Sigma, Tau Kappa Epsilon, Triangle. Club: Armour Faculty. Author handbooks, contbr. to encys., profl. jours. Home: 306 Harris Av Clarendon Hills, IL 60514. Office: Ill Inst Tech Chicago IL 60616

BUDENZ, LOUIS FRANCIS, ret. educator, journalist; b. Indianapolis, Ind., July 17, 1891; s. Henry Joseph and Mary Gertrude (Sullivan) B.; student St. Xavier's Coll., Cin.; St. Mary's Coll.; LL.B., Indpls. Law School Indpls., 1912; D.Polit. Sci., Providence Coll., 1971; m. Margaret D. Rodgers; children—Julia, Josephine (Mrs. Donald A. Palermo), Justine, Joanna. Asso. editor The Carpenter, organ of United Brotherhood of Carpenters and Joiners, 1912-13; asst. dir. Central Bur. of Central Verein, St. Louis, Mo., 1913-14; sec. St. Louis Civic League, 1914-19; franchise expert, Fed. Electric Rys. Commn., 1920; publicity dir. Am. Civil Liberties Union, 1920-21; editor The Labor Age, 1921-31; organizer for special situation, A.F. of L. unions, 1927-34; leading strikes on Kenosha, Wis., 1928, Nazareth, Pa., 1929, Paterson Silk, 1930, Toledo Auto Lite, 1934; tried 21 times in labor disputes and acquitted 21 times; labor editor, The Daily Worker, 1935-37; editor Midwest Daily Record, Chicago, 1937-40; pres. and mng. editor The Daily Worker, 1940-45; prof. econ., Notre Dame U., 1945-46; prof. econ. Fordham U., 1946-56, ret.; adviser on Communist research to Cardinal Cushing, 1959-63; prof. Seton Hall U., 1952; witness for govt. in numerous Communist trials; columnist Nat. Cath Welfare Conf. News Service, 1948-63. Mem. Am. Econ. Assn., Am. Acad. Polit. and Social Science, Acad. Polit. Sci. Roman Catholic. Author: This Is My Story, 1946; Men Without Faces, 1950; The Cry is Peace, 1952; The Techniques of Communism (textbook), 1953; Ex-Red (in newspaper syndicated series), 1954; The Bolshevik Invasion of the West, 1965. Contbr. articles to nat. mags. Home: 196 Allston Av Newport RI 02840

BUDGE, ALEXANDER GROW, bus. exec.; b. Grand Forks, N.D., Dec. 4, 1891; s. William and Minnie L. (Grow) B.; A.B., Leland Stanford, 1912; m. Ruth E. Whithed, May 11, 1920; children—William, Alexander Grow, Ruth H., Hamilton W. Engr., Charles C. Moore & Co., engrs., San Francisco, 1912-20; became successively engr., asst. sec., sec., Castle & Cooke, Inc., Honolulu, 1920-36, pres., 1936-59; chmn. bd., dir. Castle & Cooke, Inc., 1959; v.p., dir. Dole Co.; dir. Waialua Sugar Co., Kohala Sugar Co., Bumble Bee Seafoods. Clubs: Pacific Union, Burlingame Country, Merchants Exchange (San Francisco); Pacific Honolulu. Office: Merchant St Honolulu HI 96813

BUDGE, HAMER HAROLD, former govt. ofcl., financial exec.; b. Pocatello, Ida., Nov. 21, 1910; s. Alfred and Ella (Hoge) B.; student Coll. of Ida., 1928-29, 29-30; A.B., Stanford, 1933; LL.B., U. Ida., 1936; m. Jeanne Keithly, Aug. 30, 1941; 1 dau., Kathleen. Admitted to Ida. bar, 1936; practiced in Boise, 1936-42, 46- 51; mem. Ida. Legislature, 1939, 41, 49, majority floor leader; mem. 82d- 86th Congresses, 2d Dist. Ida.; mem. SEC, 1964-70, chmn., 1969-70; now pres. Investors Diversified Service, Inc. Mem. Lincoln Day Banquet

Assn. Mem. bd. Salvation Army. Served with USNR, 1942-45; lt. comdr. Res. Mem. Am., Ida. bar assns., Ida. C. of C., Sigma Alpha Epsilon. Republican. Mem. Ch. of Jesus Christ of Latter Day Saints. Elk. Home: Boise ID 83707

BUDIANSKY, BERNARD, educator; b. N.Y.C., Mar. 8, 1925; s. Louis and Rose (Chaplick) B.; B. Civil Engring., City Coll. N.Y., 1944; Sc.M., Brown U., 1948, Ph.D., 1950; m. Nancy Cromer, Dec. 21, 1952; children—Michael, Stephen. With NACA, Langley Field, Va., 1944-55, head structural mechanics br., 1952- 55: faculty Harvard, 1955—, Gordon McKay prof. structural mechanics, 1961—. Cons. AVCO Corp., 1958-70, Arthur D. Little Co., 1960- 70, Gen. Motors Research Labs., 1963—. Mem. research adv. com. on aircraft structures NASA, 1966-71; mem. U.S. Nat. Com. on Theoretical and Applied Mechanics, 1970—. Guggenheim fellow Tech. U. Denmark, 1961. Mem. Am. Acad. Arts and Scis., Am. Inst. Aeros. and Astronautics (asso. editor Jour. 1963-66), Am. Soc. M.E., Am. Soc. C.E., Sigma Xi, Tau Beta Pi. Bd. editors Jour. Math. and Physics, 1961-68; cons. editor Addison-Wesley Pub. Co., 1962—. Author tech. reports. Home: 11 DeMar Rd Lexington MA 02173 Office: Pierce Hall Harvard Cambridge MA 02138

BUDINA, ADOLPH OTTO, architect; b. O'Fallon, Ill., Feb. 25, 1891; s. Gustav W. and Sophia (Tiedemann) B.; B.Sc., U. Ill., 1914; m. Edna McCray Darrow, July 17, 1917; children—Margaret Jane (Mrs. John J. Zenner, Jr.), Barbara McCray (Mrs. William R. L. Smith, III). Draftsman Holabird & Roche, Chgo., 1916, Louis H. Sullivan, Chgo., 1917; office mgr. John Eberson, Chgo. and N.Y.C., 1919-30; pvt. practice architecture, 1930-54, mem. Budiana, Freeman & Beckwith, architects and engrs., Richmond, Va. Mem. Va. Bd. Exam. and Certification of Architects, Profl. Engrs. and Land Surveyors, 1947-52, pres., 1952. Sec.-treas. Va. Found. Archtl. Edn., 1955-57. Fellow A.I.A.; mem. Alpha Rho Chi. Presbyn. Home: 6903 Park Av Richmond VA 23226 Office: 1004 N Thompson St Richmond VA 23230

BUDINGER, FRANCIS JOSEPH, ret. ins. co. exec.; b. Chgo., Feb. 14, 1899; s. John Peter and Margaret (Birong) B.; student Kan. U.; m. Margaret L. Kennedy, June 21, 1924; children—Ann Wagener, Jane Silverman, Tom, Sheila Pigott, Gina Martin, Susan Rubenstein, Charles Budinger, John Budinger, Margie O'Connor. Agt. Franklin Life Ins. Co., Chgo., 1923-29, gen. agt. Chgo. area, 1929- 43, regional sales dir. Chgo. area, 1943-59, exec. v.p., 1959-61, pres., 1961-64, vice chmn. bd., 1964-69, now hon. dir.; dir. Springfield Marine Bank. Mem. Springfield Met. Expn. Authority. Bd. dirs., 1st v.p. United Community Services; bd. dirs., pres. Springfield Orchestra Assn.; chmn. bd. trustees Springfield Coll., vice chmn. lay adv. bd.; dir. lay adv. bd. St. John's Hosp. Served with SATC, 1918. C.L.U. Mem. Am. Soc. C.L.U. (past pres. Chgo.), Phi Kappa. Roman Catholic. K.C. Clubs: Union League (Chgo.); Illini Country, Sangamo (Springfield). Rotary Internat. (gov. Chgo. No. Ill. dist. 1943- 44); Tavern (Chgo.). Home: 1631 Leland Av Springfield IL 62704

BUDINGTON, WILLIAM STONE, librarian; b. Oberlin, O., July 3, 1919; s. Robert Allyn and Mabel (Stone) B.; B.A., Williams Coll., 1940; B.S. in L.S., Columbia, 1941, M.S., 1951; B.S. in Elec. Engring., Va. Poly. Inst., 1946. Reference librarian Norwich U., 1941-42; librarian, engring. and phys. scis. Columbia, 1947-52; asso. librarian John Crerar Library, Chgo., 1952-65, librarian, 1965-69, exec. dir., librarian, 1969—. Served with AUS, 1942-46. Fellow A.A.A.S.; mem. A.L.A., Am. Soc. Information Sci., Spl. Libraries Assn. (pres. 1964-65), Am. Soc. Engring. Edn., Med. Library Assn., Phi Beta Kappa, Tau Beta Pi, Eta Kappa Nu. Club: Caxton. Home: 1350 Lake Shore Dr Chicago IL 60610 Office: 35 W 33d St Chicago IL 60616

BUDLONG, JOHN POST REYNOLDS, publishing co. exec.; b. Anthony, R.I., Aug. 11, 1921; s. Frederick Reed and Mary Bissell (Reynolds) B.; A.B. magna cum laude, Harvard, 1948; m. Ramona Lee Evans, Jan. 6, 1945; children—Sean Page, Granville Duke, Samuel Sewall. Owner insulating materials bus., 1940-41; war work, 1941-42; mgr. importations dept. Macmillan Co., 1948-51, trade sales mgr., 1951- 55, dir. trade (gen. pub.) dept., 1955-59, also dir.; gen. mgr. trade book div. McGraw-Hill Co., 1959-61, v.p., 1961—, gen. mgr. gen. book div., 1962-63; exec. v.p., dir. New Am. Library, Inc., 1964-65, pres., 1965-67; corporate v.p. Am. Mgmt. Assn., 1967—; trustee Seabury Press, Hackley Sch. Trustee Village of Irvington, 1959-63. Served as 1st lt. USAAF, 1942-46. Mem. Phi Beta Kappa. Club: Ardsley Country. Home: Airdrie Cottage Irvington-on-Hudson NY 10533

BUDNEY, ARTHUR VINCENT, singer; b. Hamtramck, Mich., Jan. 24, 1922; s. Frank and Helen (Palkowski) B.; student Wayne U., 1945, Chgo. Conservatory Music, 1948; m. Ingrid Hallberg, Mar. 2, 1945 (div.); m. 2d, Joan McMillen, May 25, 1957. Soloist Wayne U. Choir, 1945; debut as Herald in Lohengrin, Met. Opera Co., 1952; now in Germany on engagement with major opera houses. Received award for best voice in state Ill. Opera Guild, 1949; winner Arthur Godfrey Talent Show, 1951; winner Met. Opera auditions of the air, 1952. Address care Metropolitan Opera Assn 39th St and Broadway New York City NY 10023

BUDNICK, JOSEPH IGNATIUS, educator; b. Jersey City, July 9, 1929; B.S., St. Peters Coll., 1951; Ph.D. in Physics (Socony Vacuum fellow), Rutgers U., 1955. Asst. physics lab, Rutgers U., 1951-52, atomic and nuclear lab., 1952-53; project physicist Superconductivity Research Center IBM Corp., N.Y.C., 1955, instr. gen. edn., 1957-58; from asso. prof. physics to prof., chmn. Physics Dept. Fordham U., Bronx, N.Y., 1958—. Mem. A.A.A.S. Office: Dept Physics Fordham U Bronx NY 10485*

BUDO, HALIM, Albanian diplomat; b. 1913. Dep. minister fgn. affairs, 1958-61; former permanent rep. Albanian to UN.*

BUECHE, ARTHUR MAYNARD, mfg. co. research exec.; b. Flushing, Mich., Nov. 14, 1920; s. Bernard Paul and Margaret (Rekart) B.; A.S., Flint (Mich.) Jr. Coll., 1941; B.S. in Chemistry, U. Mich., 1943; student Ohio State U., 1943; Ph.D., Cornell U., 1947; m. Margaret Louisa Bassler, Dec. 27, 1945; children—Kristine L., Arthur J., Margaret K., Elizabeth M. Research asso. Cornell U., 1947-50; with Gen. Electric Co., 1950—, mgr. chemistry research dept., 1961-65; v.p. research and devel., Schenectady, 1965—; trustee Schenectady Savs. Bank. Mem.-at-large NRC, 1966; mem. chemistry vis. com. Harvard U. Councilor exec. com. Gordon Research Confs., 1960, chmn. bd. trustees, 1966; trustee Albany Med. Coll.; council Coll. Engring., Cornell U., also univ. council; bd. mgrs. Ellis Hosp.; bd. dirs. Sunnyview Hosp. and Rehab. Center; mem. metal properties council Engring. Found., 1966; Registered profl. engr., N.Y. Fellow Am. Phys. Soc. (chmn. exec. com. div. high polymer physics 1953); mem. Am. Chem. Soc. (chmn. div. polymer chemistry 1963, bd. dirs. 1966), A.A.A.S., Indsl. Research Inst. (dir.), Dirs. Indsl. Research, Empire State C. of C. (dir.), Nat. Acad. Scis., Sigma Xi, Alpha Chi Sigma, Gamma Alpha, Phi Kappa Phi, Phi Lambda Upsilon. Clubs: Mohawk Golf, Mohawk (Schenectady); Susquehanna Valley Country (Sunbury, Pa.). Patentee polymer field. Home: 1065 Avon Rd Schenectady NY 12308 Office: PO Box 8 Schenectady NY 12301

BUECHNER, CARL FREDERICK, clergyman, author; b. N.Y.C., July 11, 1926; s. Carl Frederick and Katherine (Kuhn) B.; grad. Lawrenceville Sch., 1943; A.B., Princeton, 1947; B.D., Union Theol. Sem., 1958: m. Judith Friedrike Merck, Apr. 7, 1956; children—Katherine, Dinah, Sharman. Tchr. English, Lawrenceville Sch., 1948-53: tchr. creative writing, summer sessions N.Y.U., 1954-55; chmn. dept. religion Phillips Exeter Acad., 1958-60, sch. minister, 1960-67; ordained to ministry United Presbyn. Ch. U.S.A., 1958; William Belden Noble lectr. Harvard, 1969, Russell lectr. Tufts, 1971. Trustee Barlow Sch., 1965-71. Served with AUS, 1944-46. Recipient Irene Glascock Meml. intercollegiate poetry award, 1947; O'Henry prize for story The Tiger, 1955; Richard and Hinda Rosenthal award for the Return of Ansel Gibbs, 1958. Mem. Nat. Council Chs. (com. on lit. 1954- 57), Council for Religion in Independent Schs. (regional chmn. 1959-63), Found. for Arts, Religion and Culture, Presbytery No. New Eng., P.E.N., Author's Guild. Club: Century Assn. Author: A Long Day's Dying. 1950; The Seasons' Difference, 1952; The Return of Ansel Gibbs, 1958; The Final Beast, 1965; The Magnificent Defeat, 1966; The Hungering Dark, 1969; The Entrance to Porlock, 1970; The Alphabet of Grace, 1970; Lion Country, 1971. Office: care Atheneum 122 E 42d St New York City NY 10017

BUECHNER, THOMAS SCHARMAN, found. exec.; b. N.Y.C., Sept. 25, 1926; s. Thomas Scharman and Anne (Lines) B.; grad. Lawrenceville, 1944; student Princeton, 1945, Ecole des Beaux Arts, Fontainebleau, 1946, Paris, 1947, Art Students League, 1946, 48, Institut voor Pictologie, Amsterdam, 1947; m. Mary C. Hawkins, Sept. 15, 1949; children—Barbara Lines, Thomas Scharman III, Matthew Jones. With Compania de Fomento, San Juan, P.R., 1946; asst. display mgr. Met. Mus. Art, N.Y.C., 1949-51; tchr., mus. dir. Corning (N.Y.) Mus. of Glass, 1951-60, pres., 1971—; head art dept. Corning Community Coll., 1958-60; dir. Bklyn. Mus., 1960-71; Pres. Corning Glass Works Found., 1971—; v.p. Steuben Glass, Inc.; dir. Corning Glass Works Internat. Mem. Portraits, Inc.; chmn. devel. council Bklyn. Inst. Arts and Scis. Trustee Van Dantzig Meml. Found. Cadet, Naval Air Corps, 1945-46. Mem. Assn. Art Mus. Dirs. Episcopalian (vestry). Club: Century (N.Y.C.). Author: Glass Vessels in Dutch Painting of the 17th Century, 1952; Life and Work of Frederick Carder, 1952; Guide to the Collections of the Corning Museum of Glass, 1955; Guide to Collections of Brooklyn Museum, 1967; Norman Rockwell, Artist Illustrator, 1960. Home: Corning NY 14830 Office: Corning NY 14830 also 717 Fifth Av New York City NY 10022

BUECHNER, WILLIAM WEBER, physicist, educator; b. Vallejo, Cal., May 12, 1914; s. William Robert and Edna Blanche (Weber) B.; student Pomona Coll., 1930-31; S.B., Mass. Inst. Tech., 1935, Ph.D., 1939; Dr. Honoris Causa, Nat. U. Mexico, 1954; m. Christina MacLeod, June 20, 1939. Teaching fellow physics Mass. Inst. Tech., 1936-39, research asso., 1939-42, asst. prof., 1942-51, asso. prof., 1951-56, prof., 1956—, head dept. physics, 1961-67; vis. prof. at Nat. U. Mexico, 1952, 55, 56, 58; vis. prof. at Indian Univs. (U.S. State Dept., India Wheat Loan Program), 1957, Catholic Univ., Rio de Janeiro, 1959; member committee on Nuclear masses Internat. Union Pure and Applied Physics, 1958—; mem. nuclear physics panel Nat. Acad. Scis., 1965; dir. High Voltage Engring. Corp., 1954—. Bd. dirs. Boston Council for Internat. Visitors. Recipient Naval Ordnance Devel. award, 1946; Charles B. Dudley gold medal Am. Soc. Testing Materials, 1949; prof. Extraordinary, Nat. U. Mexico, 1952—. Fellow Am. Acad. Arts and Scis., Am. Phys. Soc. (organizing com. div. nuclear physics 1966); mem. Am. Assn. Physics Tchrs., Mexican Soc. Physics, Sigma Xi. Mem. editorial bd. Physics Today, 1952-56. Contbr. profl. jours. Home; 351 Mystic St Arlington MA 02174

BUEDING, ERNEST, educator, biochemist; b. Frankfurt am Main, Germany, Aug. 19, 1910; s. Frederick and Katia (Margoulieff) B.; B.A., Goethe Coll., Frankfurt, 1928; M.D., U. Paris (France), 1936; m. Raya Palzeff, Apr. 3, 1940; 1 son, Robert. Came to U.S., 1939, naturalized, 1944. Fellow Pasteur Inst., Paris, 1933-35; asst. biochemistry U. Istanbul (Turkey), 1936-38; research fellow Coll. Medicine, N.Y.U., 1939-44; asst. prof. pharmacology, then asso. prof. Western Res. U. Med. Sch., 1944-54; prof. pharmacology, chmn. dept. Sch. Medicine, La. State U., 1954-60; prof. pathobiology Sch. Hygiene and Pub. Health, Johns Hopkins, 1960—, prof. pharmacology and exptl. therapeutics, 1966—; vis. Fulbright prof. U. Oxford (Eng.), 1959, Guggenheim fellow Oxford, summer 1963. Investigator, OSRD, 1941-45; mem. bd. Nat. Vitamin Found., 1949-52; mem. commn. parasitology Armed Forces Epidemiological Bd., 1953—; mem. study sect. tropical medicine and parasitology NIH, 1956-60; mem. panel metabolic biology NSF, 1962-65; cons. WHO, 1961, 63, mem. expert com. schistosomiasis, 1959, 62, expert adv. panel parasitic diseases, 1963—; mem. parasitic diseases panel U.S.-Japan Coop. Med. Sci. Program, 1965-71. Founder Cleve. Chamber Music Soc., 1949, pres., 1953-54; founder New Orleans Friends Music, 1955, counselor, 1955-60; chmn. Johns Hopkins Chamber Music Com., 1965—. Fellow A.A.A.S.; mem. Am. Soc. Biol. Chemists, Am. Soc. Pharmacology and Exptl. Therapeutics, Am. Chem. Soc., Brit. Biochem. Soc., Brit. Pharmacol. Soc. (asso.), Phi Beta Kappa (hon.), Brazilian Soc. Tropical Medicine (hon.). Contbr. articles to profl. jours., revs., also chpts. in books. Mem. editorial bd. Exptl. Parasitology, 1952-63, Biochem. Pharmacology, 1958-68, Molecular Pharmacol., 1969—, The Johns Hopkins Mag., 1971—. Home: 4001 Roundtop Rd Baltimore MD 21218

BUEGE, WILLIAM ALBERT, clergyman; b. Milw., Oct. 7, 1912; s. William and Martha (Fabian) B.; student Concordia Coll., Milw., 1932; student Concordia Sem., St. Louis, 1936, D.D., 1961; m. Gladys Apel, June 29, 1938; children—William, Karen Jean. Ordained to ministry Lutheran Ch., 1938; asst. pastor in Milw., 1936-38; pastor in Carthage, Mo., 1938-41, St. Joseph, Mo., 1941-43, Christ Luth. Ch., Mpls., from 1946; later dean chapel and preacher to univ. Valparaiso (Ind.) U.; pastor Luth. Ch. of Resurrection, Sappington, Mo., 1967—. Chmn. bd. of mission to deaf Luth. Ch. Mo. Synod, 1947-57, v.p. Minn. dist., 1957-60, bd. dirs., 1960-71. Bd. dirs. Valparaiso U., 1960—; bd. control Concordia Sem., St. Louis, 1971—. Served as chaplain AUS, 1943-45; PTO. Author: Preaching with Power, 1959; The Cross of Christ, 1963; The Lord's Men; also pamphlets, theol. articles. Home: 9907 Sappington Rd St Louis MO 63128

BUEHLER, ALBERT CARL, mfg. exec.; b. Chicago, June 20, 1897; s. Carl and Rose (Stupp) B.; student U. of Illinois, 1919; m. Fern Davis; children—Carl, Barbara, Bert, Rose. With Victor Comptometer Corporation, Chgo., 1920—, pres., 1932-64, chairman and chief executive officer, 1964—. Mem. Kappa Sigma. Clubs: Athletic, Chicago (Chicago); Barrington Hills Country (Barrington, Ill.). Home: 66 S Brinker Rd Barrington IL 60010 Office: 3900 N Rockwell St Chicago IL 60618

BUEHLER, JOHN L., corp. exec.; m. Bessie Ryan, June 9, 1935; children—Patricia, Mary, Louis C. II, William L. Partner Ind. Gear Works, 1933-49, pres., gen. mgr., 1949-60; chmn. bd., pres. Buehler Corp., 1960, 69, chmn., chief exec. officer, 1969—; dir. Circle Leasing Corp. Past co-chmn. United Fund Greater Indpls.; Ind. chmn. Nat. Found., March of Dimes, 1964-70; v.p. finance com. Latin Am., Boy Scouts Internat., 1968—, pres., 1958-68, mem. Nat. council Boy Scouts Am., hon. life mem. bd. dirs. Central Ind. council, recipient Silver Beaver award Boy Scouts Am. Pres. Buehler Found; bd. dirs. Fall Creek Pkwy. YMCA. Mem. Am. Helicopter Assn. (chmn. bd., pres. 1965-67), Conf. Bd. (exec. council), Am. Gear Mfrs. Assn. (past pres.), Asso. Employers Ind. (dir.), Am. Inst. Aeros. and Astronautics (tech. com.), Am. Soc. Metals, Am. Soc. Tool Engrs. Republican. Mason (Shriner). Clubs: Union League (Chgo.); Hundred, Indpls. Sailing (past commodore); Indianapolis Athletic; Columbia; Meridian Hills Country; Rod and Reel (Miami Beach). Home: 6477 N Chester Av Indianapolis IN 46220 Office: 9000 Precision Dr Indianapolis IN 46236

BUEHNER, CARL WILLIAM, ch. authority, mfg. exec.; b. Stuttgart, Germany, Dec. 27, 1898; s. Carl Frederick and Anna Bertha (Geigle) B.; brought to U.S., 1901; grad. Granite High Sch.; m. Lucile Thurman, Aug. 2, 1922; children—Ruth (Mrs. Jos. M. McPhie), June (Mrs. Jack Ferrin), Marilyn (Mrs. John C. Riches), Carl Thurman. Missionary Ch. Latter-day Saints, to Eastern states, 1919-21, now gen. authority of the church; pres. Utah Fur Farm, Inc.; v.p. Otto Buehner Co.; v.p. Buehner Block Co., Mineral Fertilizer Co., Western Travel, Inc.; pres. Brookfield Products Co.; dir., sec. Sunset Lawn Memorial Corp.; res. Beehive State Bank; v.p. dir. Sunset Life Ins. Co. Utah rep. Bus. Adv. Com. to Sec. Commerce, 1951-54. Pres. Gt. Salt Lake council Boy Scouts Am. Author: Do Unto Others. Home: 1564 Cherokee Circle Salt Lake City UT 84108 Office: 5200 S Main St Salt Lake City UT 84107

BUEHRIG, EDWARD HENRY, educator; b. Minier, Ill., Oct. 4, 1910; s. Edward S. and Emma (Kuhfuss) B.; Ph.B., U. Chgo., 1932, M.A., 1934, Ph.D., 1942; m. Margaret E. Masters, June 18, 1935; children—Edward M., Robert M. Instr. polit. sci. Ind. U., Bloomington, 1934-62, prof., 1962—, acting chmn. dept., 1966- 67; officer Dept. State, 1944-46; faculty Nat. War Coll., 1951; with Brookings Instn., 1952; vis. prof. Am. U., Beirut, 1957-58. Vis. mem. Inst. for Advanced Study, Princeton, N.J., 1948. Recipient Smith-Mundt award, 1957-58, Social Sci. Research Council grant, 1965-66. Mem. Am. Polit. Sci. Assn., Am. Soc. Internat. Law. Author: Woodrow Wilson and the Balance of Power, 1955; The UN and the Palestinian Refugees, 1971. Editor: Wilson's Foreign Policy in Perspective, 1957; Essays in Political Science, 1966. Contbr. articles profl. jours. Home: 1301 Maxwell Lane Bloomington IN 47401

BUEK, CHARLES WELLES, banker; b. Glenbrook, Conn., Oct. 27, 1911; s. Thomas C. and Katharine (Welles) B.; grad. Phillips Acad., Andover, Mass.; A.B., Yale, 1933; m. Marjorie Ann Pinckney, Apr. 19, 1941; children—Ann Pinckney, Thomas Welles. With U.S. Trust Co. of N.Y., 1933—, successively analyst, asst. sec., asst. v.p., 1933-51, v.p., 1953-58, exec. v.p., 1958-59, 1st v.p., 1959-62, pres., 1962-71, chief exec. officer, 1971—, trustee, 1959—; dir. Gen. Reins. Corp., Equitable Life Ins. Soc. of U.S.; mem. investment com. Royal-Globe Ins. Group. Pres. bd. trustees, nat. bd. YMCA; trustee N.Y. U., N.Y.C. Served as maj. USAAF, 1942-46. Mem. Am. Bankers Assn. (pres. trust div. 1968-69). Home: 15 Driftway Lane Darien CT 06820 Office: 45 Wall St New York City NY 10005

BUEL, JACK, educator; b. Pasadena, Cal., July 16, 1905; A.B., U. Cal., 1929, Ph.D., 1935; married; 2 children. Asst. in psychology U. Cal., 1932-37, tech. asst. Inst. Child Welfare, 1932-35; research asst., instr. Wesleyan U., 1937-40, asst. prof., 1940-42; asso. prof., U. Wyo., 1946; commd. 2d lt. USAF, 1942, advanced through grades to col.; aviation psychologist Sch. Aviation Medicine, 1942-46, chief dept. psychology, 1947-48, dep. for research, 1948-49, research adviser, 1949-50; spl. asst., project officer, surgeon gen. Aeromed. Center, U.S. Air Force, 1951-54, dir. utilization planning, Personnel and Tng. Research Center, 1954, skill components research lab. Lackland AFB, 1954-56, operator lab. Randolph AFB, 1956-57, asst. project officer aerospace med. center Air U., Brooks AFB, 1957-59, spl. asst. to comdr., chief airman proficiency test br. Personnel Lab., Lackland AFB, 1959-60; ret., 1960; prof. psychology Trinity (Tex.) U., 1960-62; prin. scientist human factors, space and information systems N.Am. Aviation, Inc., 1962-64; personnel analyst, mil. personnel center, U.S. Air Force, Randolph AFB, Tex., 1965-67; prof. psychology and human engring. St. Mary's Coll., 1967-68; prof., chmn. dept. psychology Tulane U., New Orleans, 1968—. Cons. Research and Devel. Bd., 1950. Fellow Am. Psychol. Assn.; mem. A.A.A.S. Office: Dept Psychology Tulane U New Orleans LA 70118*

BUELL, ELLIOTT LYNDON, educator; b. Syracuse, N.Y., Nov. 5, 1916; s. Harold Douglass and H. Marie (Billings) B.; A.B., Syracuse U., 1938; Ph.D., Mass. Inst. Tech., 1941; m. Doris Mildred Perry, June 12, 1943; children—Carolyn Joan, Paul Elliott. Grad. asst. math. Mass. Inst. Tech., 1938-41; instr. math. Northwestern U., 1941-44, mathematician, head analog div., tech. dir. aerial measurements lab., 1944-57; prof. math. Worcester (Mass.) Polytech. Inst., 1957—, dir. computation facility, 1959-67, head math. dept., 1960-68; lectr. engring. math. Northwestern U., 1952-57. Mem. Am. Math. Soc., Math. Assn. Am., Assn. Computing Machinery, Am. Soc. Engring. Edn. Episcopalian. Home: 2 St Paul Dr Worcester, MA 01602.

BUELL, JAMES HAMILTON, mfg. co. exec.; b. Milw., June 24, 1925; s. Theodore W. and Bernice (Anderson) B.; student Lawrence Coll., 1944-45; B.S. in Accounting, Marquette U., 1947; m. Jessie E. Hankins, May 1, 1948; children—James Hamilton II, William Lee, Janice Elizabeth, Bonnie Louise. Sr. accountant Ernst & Ernst, C.P.A.'s Mpls., 1947-55; with Doughby Industies, Inc., New Richmond, Ind., 1955—, 1st v.p. indsl. group, 1964- 66, pres., 1966—, also dir.; dir. Doughboy Ltd., Doughboy Pty., Ltd., Combustion Products Corp., Energy Transmission Corp. Served with USNR, 1943-46. C.P.A., Minn. Mem. Beta Alpha Psi, Sigma Phi Epsilon. Mem. United Protestant Ch. (past mem. bd., tchr. Sunday sch.). Club: Toastmasters (pres. New Richmond 1960). Home: 265 Greaton Rd New Richmond WI 54017 Office: 215 N Main Av New Richmond WI 54017

BUELL, MURRAY F., educator; b. New Haven, Oct. 6, 1905; s. Charles E. and Elinor (Fife) B.; B.A., Cornell U., 1930; M.A., U. Minn., 1934, Ph.D., 1935; m. Helen Foot, Dec. 22, 1902; children—Peter F., Honor M. Teaching asst. U. Minn., 1931-35; instr. N.C. State Coll., 1935-37, asst. prof., 1938-46; asst. prof. Rutgers U., 1946-48, asso. prof., 1948-56, prof., 1956-71, prof. emeritus, 1971—; vis. prof. U. Minn., 1971. Dir. Hutcheson Meml. Forest. Mem. Torrey Bot. Club (pres. 1954, editor Bull. 1963-69), N.J. Acad. Sci. (pres. 1963-65), Ecol. Soc. Am. (pres. 1961-62 Eminent Ecologist citation 1970), Bot. Soc. Am., Soc. Am. Foresters, Sigma Xi. Office: care Rutgers State U New Brunswick NJ 08903

BUELL, ROSS, banker; b. San Francisco, Apr. 8, 1911; s. Ross Philip and Bernice (Carlton) B.; grad. Am. Inst. Banking, 1933; m. Jane Seeley Perry, Feb. 26, 1971; children—Barbara, Carla. With Wells Fargo Bank, San Francisco, 1930-53, as officer charge customer relations; supt. U.S. Mint, San Francisco, 1935-55; v.p. in charge of pub. and govtl. affairs Wells Fargo, 1955—. Served as capt. Cal. N.G. Mason. Clubs: Commercial, Press and Union League (San Francisco); Capitol Hill (Washington). Office: Wells Fargo Bank 464 California St San Francisco CA 94104

BUELL, TEMPLE HOYNE, architect, engr.; b. Chgo., Sept. 9, 1895; s. Charles Clinton and Modrea (Hoyne) B. grad. Lake Forest Acad., 1912; B.S., U. Ill., 1916; M.S., Columbia, 1917; m. Virginia Bennett Crocker Tyng Vroman, Feb. 9, 1963; children—Callae Mackey (Mrs. E. Atwill Gilman), Temple Hoyne, Beverly Milne (Mrs. John More), Marjorie Daphne (Mrs. Carl Groos), Marianne Crocker (Mrs. Marianne Crocker Ploch). Founder, pres. Buell & Co., architects & engrs., Denver, 1923—, Buell Devel. Corp., 1949—; chmn. bd. Kings County Devel. Co. Chmn. Cherry Hills Planning Commn., 1937—, Arapahoe County Planning Commn., 1939—, Tri-County Planning Commn. and Upper Plate Valley Planning Commn., 1940-42. Trustee Temple Hoyne Buell Found. Donated endowment to Colo. Woman's Coll. (Temple Buell Coll. Trust) (name changed to Temple Buell Coll.), 1967. Served to 1st lt. U.S. Army, 1917-19. Registered architect, Colo., N.M., Tex., Wyo., Neb., Utah. Mem. A.I.A., Colo. Soc. Engrs., Soc. Mil. Engrs., Nat. Council Archtl. Registration Bd. Mason (32, Shriner, K.T., Jester). Clubs: University (Chgo.); Denver, Country, City (Denver); Cherry Hills Country; Columbine Country; Metropolitan (N.Y.C.); Camp Fire of Am.; El Paso, Cheyenne Mountain Country (Colorado Springs, Colo.). Spl. works include univ. bldgs. secondary and elementary schs., municipal, state and fed. bldgs., shopping centers, others. Home: 106 S University Blvd Denver CO 80209 Office: Buell Bldg 14th and Stout St Denver CO 80202

BUELL, VICTOR PAUL, educator, mgmt. cons.; b. McAlester, Okla., Oct. 18, 1914; s. Victor Paul and Genevieve (Keller) B.; A.B., Pa. State U., 1938; grad. Advanced Mgmt. Program, Harvard, 1943; m. Virginia Stevens, May 16, 1942; children—Elizabeth Wilson (Mrs. John Barrow), Nancy Trimble (Mrs. Dieter Tamms), Victor Paul III. Mgr. market research, mgr. operations Real Silk Hosiery Mills, Inc., Indpls., 1938-51; marketing cons. McKinsey & Co., N.Y.C., 1952-55; mgr. marketing div. Hoover Co., North Canton, O., 1955-59; v.p. marketing Archer Daniels Midland Co., Mpls., 1959-64; corporate v.p. marketing Am. Standard, Inc., N.Y.C., 1964-70; asso. prof. marketing Sch. Bus. Adminstrn., U. Mass., Andover, also dir. mgmt. devel. programs, 1970—. Dir. Glasrock Products Co., Atlanta, Ga. Cons. to bus., publs. and assns. Bd. dirs. Hennepin County United Fund, vice chmn. indsl. campaign; trustee Grad. Sch. Sales Mgmt. and Marketing, Syracuse U. Served from pvt. to maj. Q.M.C., AUS, 1941-45. Mem. Am. Marketing Assn. (dir. 1957-59, chmn. nat. co. membership com. 1957-58, nat. v.p. 1960- 61, pres. 1968-69; editorial bd. Jour. Marketing), Home Mfrs. Assn. (dir.), Am. Mgmt. Assn. (mem. nat. planning council), N.A.M. (marketing com.), Canton Sales Execs. Club (dir. 1956-58, v.p. 1958-59), Sales and Marketing Execs. Internat., Assn. Nat. Advertisers (dir.). Episcopalian (vestryman). Clubs: Union League (N.Y.C.); Faculty (U. Mass.); Hickory Ridge Country (Amherst). Author: Marketing Management in Action, 1966. Contbg. author: Effective Marketing Action, 1958; The Marketing Job, 1961; Handbook of Business Administration, 1966; also articles in mags., marketing jours. Editor-in- chief Handbook of Modern Marketing, 1970. Editorial bd. Indsl. Marketing mag. Speaker before mgmt., marketing groups, seminars. Home: 235 Heatherstone Rd Amherst MA 01002

BUELL, VIRGINIA, (Mrs. Temple Hoyne Buell), civic worker; b. Denver; d. Horace Wilson and Mrs. (Riche) Bennett; ed. Spence Sch., N.Y.C.; m. Temple H. Buell, Feb. 9, 1963. Charter mem. Colo. Woman's Coll. Library Assos.; donor (with husband) endowment Colo. Woman's Coll. (name changed to Temple Buell Coll.), 1967. Clubs: River, Regency (N.Y.C.). Address: 106 S University Blvd Denver CO 80209*

BUELL, WAYNE HERBERT, coll. pres.; b. Lewis, Ind., July 2, 1913; s. Clifford and Grace Edith (Miller) B.; B.Chem. Engring, Lawrence Inst. Tech., 1936, D.Engring. (hon.), 1958; M.S., Wayne State U., 1951; m. Vita Schaefer, Oct. 21, 1939. Instr. math. and chemistry Lawrence Inst. Tech., Southfield, Mich., 1936-44, prof. chemistry, 1946-48; dir. research Aristo Corp., Detroit, 1944-46, v.p., dir. research, 1948-51, exec. v.p., dir., 1951-64; pres. Lawrence Inst. Tech., 1964—. Pres. Russell Lawrence Found., 1960-62. Recipient award sci. merit Am. Foundrymen's Soc., 1970. Mem. Am. Chem. Soc., Am. Foundrymen's Assn. Author papers in field. Home: 21320 W 10 Mile Rd Southfield MI 48075

BUELOW, FREDERICK HENRY, educator; b. Minot, N.D., Mar. 13, 1929; s. Albert Wilhelm Gustav and Frieda Alvina Adele (Hass) B.; B.S., N.D. Agrl. Coll., 1951; M.S.E., Purdue U., 1952; Ph.D., Mich. State U., 1956; m. Selma Lois Iona Eia, July 21, 1954; children—David Frederick, Diane Louise, Darci Jo, Darin Martin. Faculty agrl. engring. Mich. State U., 1956-66, prof., 1965-66; prof., chmn. dept. agrl. engring. U. Wis.-Madison, 1966—. Served to lt. USAAF, 1952-54. NSF grantee, 1963, 69, 70. Mem. Am. Soc. Agrl. Engrs. (Jour. Paper award 1957), Am. Soc. for Engring. Edn., Sigma Xi, Gamma Sigma Delta. Lutheran. Home: 6401 Landfall Dr Madison WI 53705

BUELOW, GEORGE JOHN, educator; b. Chgo., Mar. 31, 1929; s. George J. and Florence (Cook) B.; Mus.B., Chgo. Mus. Coll., 1950, Mus.M., 1951; postgrad. U. Hamburg, Germany, 1953-54; Ph.D., N.Y.U., 61. Instr. music history Chgo. Conservatory, 1959-61; asso. prof. musicology U. Cal., Riverside, 1961-68; prof., chmn. dept. music U. Ky., 1968-69; prof., chmn. music depts. Rutgers U., 1969—; Am. editor ACTA Musicologica, 1967—; editor Coll. Music Soc.'s Symposium, 1970—. Fulbright scholar Germany, 1954-55; Guggenheim fellow, 1967. Mem. Am., Internat. musicol. socs., Coll. Music Soc., Music Library Assn. Author: Thorough-bass Accompaniment According to J.D. Heinichen, 1966; Johann Mattheson's Opera, Cleopatra, in Das Erbe Deutscher Musik, 1971. Contbr. articles profl. jours. Home: 105 Drake Rd Somerset NJ 08873 Office: Rutgers U Dept Music New Brunswick NJ 08903

BUERGER, DAVID BERNARD, lawyer; b. Phila., Dec. 1, 1909; s. Charles B. and Ada (Fischel) B.; A.B., U. Pitts., 1928, A.M., 1929; LL.B., Columbia, 1932, J.D., 1969; m. Anne M. Fortun, June 30, 1946; 1 son, David C. Admitted to Pa. bar, 1932, since practiced in Pitts.; partner firm Buchanan, Ingersoll, Rodewald, Kyle & Buerger, and predecessors, 1947—; lectr. taxation and corp. law Com. Continuing Legal Edn., Am. Law Inst., 1951—. Vice pres., dir. Pitts. Stage, Inc., Tapatco Industries, Ltd., Jersey City Investment Co., Don Irwin, Inc., R. Munroe & Sons Mfg. Co., Fourteen Bell Corp., gen. counsel Magee Womens Hosp., Hunt Found., Allegheny Acad., Hampton Civic Assn., Roy A. Hunt Found.; trustee Helen Clay Frick Found. Pres. Hampton Civic Assn., 1956-57. Fellow Am. Bar Found.; mem. Am. Law Inst., Am. Arbitration Assn., Am. Judicature Soc., Am. Bar Assn., Sigma Alpha Mu, Omicron Delta Kappa, Delta Sigma Rho. Home: 3000 McCully Rd Allsion Park PA 15101 Office: Oliver Bldg Pittsburgh PA 15222

BUERGER, JOSEF HENRY, Jr., steel co. exec.; b. Beaver, Pa., Aug. 19, 1917; s. Josef Henry and Julia St. Clair (McDonald) B.; A.B., Princeton, 1940; m. Barbara McNally, Feb. 4, 1940; children—Josef Henry III, Lisa M. With U.S. Steel Co., 1940-42; sales mgr. steel and tubes div. U.S. Pipe & Foundry Co., 1945-59; v.p. marketing Yuba Consol. Industries, 1959-60; gen. sales mgr. Crucible Steel Co., 1963, v.p. sales, 1964-69; gen. sales mgr. Shenango Co., 1969- 70, v.p., 1970—. Served with AUS, 1942-45. Mem. Am. Ordnance Assn. Clubs: Tiger Inn (Princeton, N.J.); Field, Duquesne (Pitts.); Seaview Country (Absecon, N.J.); Columbus (O.) Country. Home: 344 Walnut Cliffs Dr Columbus OH 43213 Office: 611 Marion Rd Columbus OH 43207

BUERGER, MARTIN JULIAN, crystallographer, mineralogist; b. Detroit, Apr. 8, 1903; s. Martin John and Julie Emma (Weber) B.; S.B., Mass. Inst. Tech., 1925, S.M., 1927, Ph.D., 1929; Dr. (hon.), U. Bern (Switzerland), 1958; m. Lila Mae MacAskill, July 5, 1938; children—Marla Christine, Julie Margaret, Laura Pauline, Janet Elizabeth, Dorothy Ruth, Patricia Anne. Asst. prof. mineralogy and petrog. Mass. Inst. Tech., 1929-35, asso. prof., 1935-37, asso. prof. mineralogy and crystallography, 1937-44, prof., 1944-56, inst. prof., 1956-68, inst. prof. emeritus, 1968—, chmn. faculty, 1954-56; dir. Sch. for Advanced Study, 1956-63; Univ. prof. U. Conn., 1968—; vis. prof. crystallography U. Rio de Janiero (Brazil), 1948, U. Chile, 1962, U. Minn., 1970; dir. Inst. Advanced Christian Studies, 1967—. Roebling medallist Mineral. Soc. Am., 1958. Fellow Mineral. Soc. Am. (pres. 1947), Geol. Soc. Am. (v.p. 1948, Arthur L. Day medalist 1951); mem. German Mineral. Soc. (hon.), Am. Crystallog. Assn. (pres. 1939-46, 48, Fankuchen award 1971) Nat. Acad. Scis., Real Sociedad Espaola de Historia Natural (hon.); fgn. mem. acads. sci. Lincei, Torino, Italy, Brazil, Bavaria and Austria (corr. mem.). Conglist. Author: Optical Identification of Crystalline Substances, 1939; X-Ray Cystallography, 1942; Elementary Crystallography, 1956; The Power Method in X-Ray Crystallography, 1958; Vector Space and its Application in Crystal-Structure Investigation, 1959; Crystal-Structure Analysis, 1960; The Precession Method in X-Ray Crystallography, 1964; Contemporary Crystallography, 1970; Introduction to Crystal Geometry, 1971; 200 sci. jour. articles. Patentee ceramic bodies of close tolerance and various tech. instruments. Co-editor: Zeitschrift für Kristallographie, 1953—; Internat. Tables for Crystallography, 1946—. Home: Weston Rd Lincoln MA 01773 Office: 77 Massachusetts Av Cambridge MA 02139

BUERKI, ROBIN CARL, med. adminstr., hosp. cons.; b. Black Earth, Wis., July 25, 1892; s. Otto C. and Katherine Ann (Kuntz) B.; B.S., U. Wis., 1915; M.D., U. Pa., 1917, D.Sc. (hon.), 1951; m. Louise Matthews, Oct. 6, 1918; 1 son, Robin Carl. Chief resident physician Univ. Hosp., U. Pa., 1917-18; in practice, Boise, Ida., and Burn, Ore., 1920-23; prof. hosp. adminstrn. U. Wis. and supt. State of Wis. Gen. Hosp., U. Wis., 1923-41; also supt. Wis. Orthopedic Hosp. for Children, 1931-41, chmn., exec. sec. Med. Sch., 1935-41; dir. study of commn. on grad. med. edn., 1938-40; dean Grad. Sch. Medicine, U. Pa., also dir. hosps., 1941-48, v.p. charge med. affairs, 1948-51; exec. dir. Henry Ford Hosp., Detroit, 1951-64, 68-71; spl. lectr. Columbia U. Sch. Pub. Health, 1946-49. Mem. Adv. Bd. Med. Specialties, 1934—, pres., 1947-50; mem. Fed. Hosp. Council, 1946-50; mem. numerous adv. coms. to govtl. agencies, assns., hosps.; mem. Albert and Mary Lasker Found. Com. on Awards of Nat. Com. for Mental health, Inc., 1948; chmn. com. on edn. and publ. Nat. Found. for Infantile Paralysis, 1948-58; Trustee, mem. exec. com. Mich. Hosp. Service, v.p., 1954-61; bd. dirs. mem. sci. adv. com. United Health Founds., Inc., 1962-65; Nat. Found. med. adv. com. task force on comprehensive health care Nat. Commn. on Community Health Services, 1963-66; mem. hosp. constrn. adv. council VA, 1963-68; chmn. Conf. on Group Practice, 1967. Served to 1st lt. M.C., U.S. Army, 1918-19; spl. cons. surgeon gen. U.S. Army, 1953—. Recipient Wis. Hosp. Assn. Award of Merit, 1942; Am. Hosp. Assn. Award of Merit, 1947, Tri-State Hosp. Assn. Award of Merit, 1948; Silver award, City of France Chevaliers du Tastevin, Chateau du Clos de Vougeot en Bourgogne; 1st Gold Medal award Am. Coll. Hosp. Adminstrs., 1964. Mem. Founders Group Am. Bd. Preventive Medicine and Pub. Health. Founding fellow Am. Coll. Hosp. Adminstrs. (pres. 1938-39, bd. regents 1953-59); mem. A.M.A., state and local med. assns., Am. Hosp. Assn. (pres. 1935, chmn. council govt. relations 1957-59, 60-61), Internat. Hosp. Fedn. (bd. mgmt.), Inter-Am. Hosp. Assn. (chmn. 1955-60), state and local hosp. assns., various spl. med. groups. Clubs: Detroit (Detroit); Grosse Point (Mich.). Mem. editorial bd. Modern Hosp. Home: 205 Lake Shore Rd Grosse Pointe Farms MI 48236 ☆

BUERKLE, JACK VINCENT, educator, sociologist; b. W. Frankfort, Ill., Aug. 9, 1923; s. Henry Adam and Clemence (Henderson) B.; B.A., U. Ill., 1948, M.A., 1949; Ph.D., U. Ia., 1954; m. Martha Louise Edwards, June 1946; children-Stephen Vincent, Malanie Lake. Asst. prof. Lake Forest Coll., 1954-55, Yale, 1955-60; mem. faculty Temple U., 1960—, prof. sociology, chmn. dept., 1963—; vis. prof. sociology, chmn. dept., 1963—; vis. prof. Der Wirtschaftschochschule, Mannheim, W. Germany, 1966-67. Mem. Am. Sociol. Assn., Am. Physol. Assn., Eastern Sociol. Soc., Institut International de Sociologie, Sigma Xi. Club: Corinthian Yacht of Cape May (N.J.) (commodore), Author articles in field. Home: 526 Revere Rd Merion Station PA 19066 Office: Dept Sociology Temple Univ Philadelphia PA 19122

BUESCHER, ALFRED JOSEPH, editorial polit. cartoonist; b. Cleve., Feb. 21, 1903; s. John F. and Elizabeth (Blickhan) B.; student Cleve. Sch. Art, 1920; m. Ruth Helen Blackmore, June 18, 1924; childrenAlfred J., Joan Marie (Mrs. Dan Roach), Robert Richard. With Cleve. News, 1921-22; with Central Press Assn. 1922, chief editorial cartoonist, 1964—. Recipient award for best editorial cartoon Newspaper Guild, 1932. Catholic. Home: 3399 Seaton Rd Cleveland Heights, OH 44118. Office: 1380 Dodge Ct Cleveland, OH 44114.

BUESCHER, FRED E., corp. exec.; b. Cleve., Oct. 10, 1912; s. Fred Henry and Anna (Olosh) B.; B.A., Wittenberg U., 1934; B.C.S., Western Res. U., 1939; m. Evelyn Marie Schumacher, Oct. 3, 1942; children—Stephen Lee, Carol Ann. Gen. accountant Glidden Co., Cleve., 1934-38; mem. bus. service dept. Toledo Pub. Library, 1939-41; sec., personnel dir. Parker-Hannifin Corp., Cleve., 1941—. Bd. dirs. Jr. Achievement Greater Cleve., 1962-65. Served Served with AUS, 1942-46. Mem. Am. Assn. Indsl. Mgrs. (past pres. dir.), Am. Soc. Corporate Secs. Home: 1703 Overbrook Rd Lyndhurst, OH 44124. Office: 17325 Euclid Av Cleveland OH 44112

BUESSEM, NIELS CHRISTIAN, pub. co. exec.; b. Berlin, Germany, Feb. 5, 1934; s. Wilhelm R. and Gritta (Hennig) B.; came to U.S., 1948, naturalized, 1957; B.A., Pa. State U., 1958; student U. Munich (Germany), 1955-56, Sorbonne (Paris), 1956; m. Janet Evans, June 18, 1960; children—Christopher, William. Editorial dir. Charles E. Merrill, pub., Columbus, O., 1959-61; exec. editor Harcourt, Brace, Jovanovich, N.Y., 1961-69; pres. Gune & Stratton, Inc., N.Y.C., 1969—. Served with USAF, 1961-62. Mem. Internat. Group Sci., Tech. and Med. Pubs., Am. Assn. Med. Book Pubs., Sigma Nu. Democrat. Home: 42 Lounsbury Rd Croton-on-Hudson NY 10520 Office: 111 Fifth Av New York City NY 10003

BUESSER, FREDERICK GUSTAVUS, Jr., lawyer; b. Detroit, Mar. 3, 1916; s. Frederick G. and Lela (Carpenter) B.; A.B., U. Mich., 1937, LL.B., 1940; m. Betty Ronal, Jan. 2, 1939; children—Frederick Gustavus III, William Ronal, Anne Alexander (Mrs. Edward Reynolds). Admitted to Mich. bar, 1940, practiced in Detroit, 1940-44, 46-48; mem. firm Chase, Goodenough & Buesser, Detroit, 1948-66, Buesser, Buesser, Snyder & Blank, 1966—; columnist The Detroit Lawyer, 1949—; counsel Wayne County Med. Soc.; dir. Detroit Pistons. Bar commr. State Bar Mich., 1964- -, now pres. Trustee Detroit Country Day Sch., 1942-70; trustee Mich. Delta Found., 1948—, pres., 1951-53; dir. U. Mich. Alumni Interfrat. Council, 1953-58, pres., 1956-58. Served from pvt. to 1st. lt. 770 Mil. Police Bn., AUS, 1944-46. Fellow Am. Bar Assn., Am. Coll. Trial Lawyers; mem. Mich., Detroit (dir. 1953-59, 1st v.p. 1957, pres. 1958-59) bar assns., Am. Judicature Soc., Lambda Sigma, Delta Tau Delta, Phi Delta Phi. Episcopalian (asst. chancellor Mich. diocese, chmn. bishop's com., sr. warden). Clubs: Thomas M. Cooley, Detroit Athletic, Huron River Hunting Fishing, University of Michigan (gov. 1956-60), Detroit (Detroit). Home: 2450 Bradway Blvd Birmingham MI 48010 Office: Penobscot Bldg Detroit MI 48226

BUETER, ARNOLD GERHARD, govt. ofcl.; b. N.Y.C., July 31, 1917; s. Frederick W. and Johanna (Mertins) B.; B.B.A. cum laude, Coll. City N.Y., 1939; M.B.A., George Washington U., 1965; m. Mary Eleanor Minzler, Aug. 22, 1945; 1 dau., Christine E. Rudy. Sr. accountant Seidman & Seidman, C.P.A.'s, N.Y.C., 1939-43; with auditor gen. USAF, 1946-59, dist. dir., Chgo., 1954-59; asso. dir. accounting and finance USAF, Washington, 1959-65; dep. comptroller USAF, 1965—; lectr. bus. adminstrn. Univ. Coll., U. Md., 1962—. Served with USAAF, 1943-46. C.P.A., N.Y. Mem. Am. Inst. C.P.A.'s, Am. Accounting Assn., Am. Soc. Mil. Comptrollers, Fed. Govt. Accountants Assn. (Meritorious Civilian Service award 1965, Exceptional Civilian Service award 1971), Beta Gamma Sigma. Lutheran (treas. 1966—). Home: 3412 Fiddler Green Falls Church VA 22044 Office: AFAAC The Pentagon Washington DC 20330

BUETOW, ARMIN P., corp. exec.; b. 1909; ed. U. Minn. Sch. Bus., 1933; married. With Richardson, Buetow & Morgan, cons., 1947-51; exec. v.p., controller Magnecord, Inc., 1951-54; pres. Continental Outdoor Advt. Co., 1954-59; cons., 1959-60; formerly v.p., treas. Hoerner Waldorf Corp.; dir. Roseville State Bank. Address: 737 Amber Dr St Paul MN 55114*

BUETTNER, KONRAD JOHANNES KARL, educator; b. Westendorf, Germany, Oct. 6, 1903; s. Johannes Samuel and Elisabeth (Kreuser) B.; student U. Erlangen, 1922, Hannover, 1924; Ph.D., U. Gottingen, 1926; m. Lucie S. Fischer, Aug. 19, 1933; 1 son, Michael. Came to U.S., 1947, naturalized, 1955. Research meterologisches Observatorium, Potsdam, 1927-33; head phsycis prof. Inst. Bioclimatology, U. Kiel, 1931-47; research sci. Sch. Aviation Medicine, USAF, 1947-52; asso. prof. U. Washington, 1953-56, prof. atmospheric sciences, 1956-70; lecturer dermatology, 1963-70; cons. Boeing Co., Seattle, Rand Corp., Santa Monica, California. Mem. Am. Meteorol. Soc. (award work on bioclimatology), Am. Geophys. Union, Am. Physiol. Soc., Internat. Soc. Bioclimatology, Internat. Sci. Inst. (sci. council). Author: Physikalische Bioklimatologie. Inventor aluminum coated fire protection suit, 1943. Died Nov. 14, 1970.

BUETTNER-JANUSCH, JOHN, educator anthropologist, geneticist; b. Chgo., Dec. 7, 1924; s. Frederick William nd Gertrude (Buettner) J.; Ph.B., U. Chgo., 1948, S.B., 1949, A.M., 1953; Ph.D., U. Mich., 1957; m. Vina Mallowitz, Sept. 22, 1950. Instr., research asst. U. Utah, 1953-55; instr. Wayne U., 1956; research asst. U. Mich., 1956-58; asst. prof. Yale, 1958-62, asso. prof., 1962-65; mem. faculty Duke, 1965—, prof. anatomy, anthropology and zoology, 1967—. Mem. A.A.A.S., Am. Assn. Phys. Anthropologists, Am. Soc. Human Genetics, Internat. Primatological Soc., Am. Anthrop. Assn. Author: Origins of Man, 1966; also articles. Research on human and nonhuman primate evolution by study hemoglobin molecule primates, population distbn. human biochem. traits. Home: 1528 Hermitage Ct Durham NC 27707

BUFF, CONRAD, artist; b. Speicher, Switzerland, Jan. 15, 1886; s. Conrad and Anna (Bruderer) B.; student Sch. Arts and Crafts, St. Gallen, Switzerland, 1900-03, pvt. art sch., Munich, Germany, 1903; m. Mary Marsh, July 7, 1922; children—Conrad, David Marsh. Came to U.S., 1905, naturalized, 1933. Represented by lithographs in permanent collections of Brit. Mus., London, Met. Mus., N.Y.C., also murals. Recipient purchase prize Los Angeles Mus., 18th Annual Exhbn. of Paintings and Sculpture, for painting "Westward," 1937; second award in painting L.A. Municipal Exhbn., 1948. Mem. Am. Artists Group, Co-author, illustrator of "Dancing Cloud" on Navajo Indians, 1936; "Kobi" on Switzerland, 1939; "Dash and Dart," 1942; Big Tree, 1946; Peter's Pinto, 1949; The Apple and The Arrow, 1951; Magic Maize, 1953; Hurry Skurry and Flurry, 1955; Hah-Nee, 1956; Elf Owl, 1958; Trix & Vix, 1960; Forest Folk, 1962; Kemi (Friends of Library award U. Cal. at Irvine 1968), 1966; The Colorado; River of Mystery, 1968. Home: 517-B Calle Aragon Laguna Hills CA 92653 ☆

BUFFALO, HARVEY ALEXANDER, corp. exec.; b. Lonoke County, Ark., Nov. 21, 1909; s. Harrison Arthur and Millie (Johnson) B.; student Ark. A. and M. Coll., U. Mo.; B.S., Ark. State Coll., 1932; grad. student U. Wis., 1936; m. Suzan Elaine McCabe, May 14, 1938; children—Harvey Alexander, Robin B. Sci. instr., Hamburg, Ark., 1932-33. Monticello, Ark., 1933-34; constrn. supr., Monticello, Ark., 1933-34; entered goverment service, 1934, various positions U.S. Dept. Agriculture, 1934-42; associate director, sec. Housing Expediter, 1946-47; fgn. service officer, 1947- 60; attache Am. legation, Budapest, Hungary, 1947-49, Am. embassy, Paris, 1949-50, Cairo, Egypt, 1950-54; attache, 1st sec. Am. embassy, Rio de Janeiro, Brazil, 1954-56; cons. Dept. State, 1956-60; v.p., exec. sec. James S. Kemper & Co., 1960-61; pres., dir. Lloyd Sul Americano Ins., Co., also Lloyd Indsl. Sul Americano Ins. Co., Brazil, 1961—; gen. rep. Am. Motorists Ins. Co. in Brazil, 1961—; mgr., partner Kemperco Representac oẽs E Administracaõ Ltda.; dir. Frigorifico Central do Brasil Ltda., Saõ Paulo, Victor Juntas Ltda, Brazil. Served from capt. to lt. col., C.E., AUS, 1942-45; overseas. Decorated Bronze Star medal. Mem. Am. C. of C. (Rio de Janeiro and Saõ Paulo), Am. Soc. (Rio de Janeiro and Saõ Paulo), Lambda Delta Lambda, Alpha Chi. Clubs: Tower (Chgo.); Army-Navy Country (Washington); American, Gavea Golf and Country, dos Seguradores, Jockey Brasileiro, Half-Way House, Federal (Rio de Janeiro); Anglo-Am. (Saõ Paulo); President's Assn. (N.Y.). Home: Rua Timóteo da Costa 623 Rio de Janeiro Brazil Office: 20 N Wacker Dr Chicago IL 60606 also Rua Debret 79 Rio de Janeiro Brazil

BUFFET, BERNARD, artist; b. Paris, France, July 10, 1928; student Lycée Carnot, Ecole Nationale Supériure des Beaux-Arts (Paris); m. Annabel May Schwab de Lure, Dec. 12, 1958; 2 daus., Virginie, Daniele. Painter, illustrator, exhibited, 1948—; ann. one-man show Galerie Drouant-David, Galerie Visconti, Paris; exhibited Musée nationale d'Art Moderne, Musée de Grenoble, Lefevra Gallery, London, 1961, 63, 65, prin. cities throughout world; represented Soc. Salon d'Automne, Salon des Jeunes Peintres, Salon des Truileries, Salon de maj, others. One of two representatives of France, Venice Biennale, 1956. Recipient French Critics' award, 1948; voted outstanding painter of today, 1956. Illustrator 3 vols.; Rocherche de la Puerté (Jean Gion). Address: Chateau de la Vallee Saint Cast Cotes du Nord France*

BUFFETT, WARREN EDWARD, investor; b. Omaha, Aug. 30, 1930; s. Howard Homan and Leila (Stahl) B.; student U. Pa., 1947-49; B.S., U. Neb., 1950; M.S., Columbia, 1951; m. Susan Thompson, Apr.

19, 1952; children—Susan, Howard, Peter. Investment salesman Buffett-Falk & Co., Omaha, 1951-54; security analyst Graham-Newman Corp., N.Y.C., 1954-56; gen. partner Buffett Partnership, Ltd., Omaha, 1956-69; chmn. bd. Berkshire, Hathaway, Inc., Diversified Retailing Corp., Nat. Indemnity Co., Nat. Fire & Marine Ins. Co., Sun Newspapers Co., Cornhusker Casualty Co., Asso. Retail Stores, Inc.; dir. Blue Chip Stamps, Omaha Nat. Bank, Omaha Nat. Corp., Ill. Nat. Bank & Trust Co.; trustee Gen. Growth Properties; pres., dir. Reins. Corp. Neb. Gov. Boys Clubs Omaha, 1962—; trustee Grinnell Coll., 1968—. Home: 5505 Farnam St Omaha NB 68132 Office: 1440 Kiewit Plaza Omaha NB 68131

BUFFINGTON, ALBERT FRANKLIN, educator; b. Pillow, Pa., July 11, 1905; s. John N. and Lizzie (Hepler) B.; A.B., Bucknell U., 1928; student U. Berlin (Germany), 1926; A.M., Harvard, 1932, Ph.D., 1937; m. Dorothy Lorine Harris, June 20, 1932; children—Albert Franklin, Lorine Harris. Head German dept. Central High Sch., Scranton, Pa., 1928-30; instr. German, Harvard, 1930-37; from instr. to asso. prof. langs. U. N.H., 1937-45; mem. faculty Pa. State U., 1945—, prof. German, 1948-65, emeritus, 1965—, acting head dept., 1964-65; prof. German, Ariz. State U., 1965—; weekly broadcasts in Pennsylvania German radio sta. WKOK, 1946-59; lectr. for USIS in Rheinpfalz, Germany, 1961. Mem. Modern Lang. Assn. (chmn. comparative lit. group 1951-52), Pa. German Soc. (bd. dirs., publs. com. 1948-65), Pa. German Folklore Soc. (bd. dirs., publs. com. 1948-65), Am. Assn. Tchrs. German. Author: (with W. E. Boyer and D. Yoder) Songs Along the Mahantongo; Pennsylvania Dutch Folksongs, rev. edit., 1964; (with P. A. Barba) A Pennsylvania German Grammar, rev. edit., 1965; The Reichard Collection of Early Pennsylvania German Plays, 1962; "Dutchified German" Spirituals, 1965. Home: 407 E Geneya Dr Tempe AZ 85281

BUFFINGTON, ALBERT LANG, walnut co. exec.; b. Birmingham, Ala., July 14, 1924; s. A. W. and Ellen (McLean) B.; B.A., Stanford, 1947, M.B.A., 1949; m. Ruth Maxwell, Dec. 8, 1945; children—Dale, Lee, Lynn. Line supr., indsl. engr. Proctor & Gamble Mfg. Co., Long Beach, Cal., 1949-53; cons. Booz, Allen & Hamilton, Los Angeles, 1953-55; product mgr., asst. gen. mgr., pres., gen. mgr. Diamond Walnut Growers, Inc., Stockton, Cal., 1955—. Pres. DFA of Cal.; mem. Walnut Control Bd. Bd. dirs. Calicopters of Stockton. Served to 1st lt. USAAF, 1942-45, USAF, 1950-52. Mem. Consol. Agrl. Industries (sec.-treas.), Nat. Council Farmer Coops., Cal., Greater Stockton chambers commerce. Club: Commonwealth (San Francisco). Home: 7221 Alexandria Pl Stockton CA 95207 Office: PO Box 1727 Stockton CA 95201

BUFFINGTON, RALPH MELDRIM, architect; b. White Sulphur, Ga., Feb. 7, 1907; s. Marion Cook and Frances Louvinia (Moss) B.; B.S. in Architecture, Ga. Inst. Tech., 1928; scholar pvt. study, Europe, 1929-30, also Ecole Speciale d'Architecture & Travel, 1958. Practice architecture, Houston, 1939-42, 1946-66; asso. Buffington & McAllister, Houston, 1966—. Cons. Bapt. fgn. mission projects, Hawaii, Hong Kong, Taiwan, Thailand, P.I., Indonesia, Mexico. Served with AUS, 1942-45; PTO. Recipient Outstanding Service Commendation Houston C. of C., 1962, also various archtl. awards. Registered profl. architect, Tex., Ga., Cal., Hawaii, Conn. Mem. A.I.A., Tex. Soc. Architects, Nat. Geog. Soc. Nat. Council Archtl. Registration Bds. Democrat. Baptist. Club: Old Capitol (Houston). Prin. archtl. works include Chinese Bapt. Temple Evangelistic, 8 Houston schs., Houston, Taipeh Bapt. Sem., Taiwan, schs., instns. and residences. Author: Buffington Family in America, 1965. Home: 1710 Welch St Houston TX 77006

BUFFUM, WILLIAM BURNSIDE, govt. ofcl.; b. Binghamton, N.Y., Sept. 10, 1921; s. Frederic Francis and Lucy (Davis) B.; B.Ed., Oneonta State Teachers Coll., 1943; M.Litt., U. Pitts., 1949; student Oxford U., 1946, Harvard U., 1952-53; m. Alma Emma Bauman, Sept. 25, 1944; children—Karen (Mrs. Joseph Clarkson), Diane, Andrea. Instr. U. Pitts., 1946-49; vice-consul U.S. Dept. State, Stuttgart, 1946-49; polit. officer, Bonn, 1953-58; dir. polit. affairs Bur. Internat. Orgn. Affairs, Washington, 1959-67, dep. asst. sec., 1965-67; dep. U.S. rep. to UN, 1967-70; U.S. ambassador to Lebanon, 1970—. Served with AUS, 1943-46. Mem. Sigma Chi Sigma. Home: Beirut Dept State Washington DC 20521

BUFORD, CURTIS DONALD, railroad car leasing co. exec.; b. Sioux City, Ia., July 6, 1920; s. Charles Homer and Bess (Thomas) B.; B.S., Mass. Inst. Tech., 1942; m. Barbara Anderson, Apr. 29, 1947; children—Nancy Joanne, Jerome Donald, Roberta Jane, William Warwick, Ruth Elizabeth, John Anderson. With N.Y.C. Railroad, 1946-59; v.p. operation and maintenance Assn. Am. Railroads, 1959-64; exec. v.p. P. & L.E. R.R., 1964, pres., 1965-69, past dir.; now pres. Trailer Train Co. Served to capt. AUS, 1942-46; PTO, ETO. Mem. Am. Soc. M.E., Ry. Systems and Mgmt. Assn., Newcomen Soc. N.Am., Nat. Def. Transp. Assn., Transp. Assn. Am. (dir.). Republican. Clubs: Duquesne; Chicago; Aronimink Golf (Phila.). Home: 228 Raleigh Rd Kenilworth IL 60043 Office: 300 S Wacker Dr Chicago IL 60606

BUFORD, DON ALVIN, profl. baseball player; b. Linden, Tex., Feb. 2, 1937; s. Leon and Sedalia (Williams) B.; student Los Angeles City Coll., 1955-56, U. So. Cal., 1957-59; m. Alescia R. Jackson, Sept. 30, 1961; children—Don, Daryl, Damon. Profl. baseball player Chgo. White Sox, 1960-67; outfielder Balt. Orioles, 1968—. Named most valuable player of Internat. League, 1963, Minor League Player of Year, Sporting News, 1963; set Balt. Oriole record of 109 walks, 1970. Mem. Kappa Alpha Psi. Home: 15412 Valley Vista Blvd Sherman Oaks CA 91403 Office: Memorial Stadium Baltimore MD 21212

BUFORD, JACK WILLIAM, ore mining, shipping exec.; b. Topeka, July 22, 1912; s. Charles Homer and Bess (Thomas) B., B.C.E., U. Wash., 1933; M.S., Harvard, 1934; m. Helen Louise Malott, Dec. 27, 1934; children—Anne, Thomas. Various positions operating dept. Pa. R.R., 1934-50; coordinator Canadian development M.A. Hanna Co., 1950-53; v.p. Hanna Coal & Ore Corp., 1953; v.p. fgn. operations Hanna Mining Co., 1962-69, sr. v.p. internat. operations, 1970—. Served as lt. col. Transp. Corps, AUS, 1941-46. Mem. Cleve. C. of C., Candian Inst. Mining and Metallurgy, Am. Inst. Mining Engrs., Am. Iron and Steel Inst., Am. Mining Congress, Am. Mgmt. Assn. Clubs: Cleveland Yacht, Cleveland Athletic, Mid-Day, Clevelander, Union (Cleve.); Lakewood Country; Westwood Country. Home: 18800 N Valley Dr Fairview Park OH 44126 Office: 100 Erieview Plaza Cleveland OH 44114

BUFORD, JOSEPH C., educator; B.Ed., M.S.Ed., Ill. State U.; Ph.D., U. Cal. at Los Angeles. m. Zola Harvey. Now prof. geography, chmn. dept. Bowling Green State U. Col. U.S. Army Res.; sr. instr. 1st U.S. Army Instr. Tng. Sch., mem. cons. faculty Command and Gen. Staff Coll., Ft. Leavenworth, Kan. Mem. Assn. Am. Geographers (chmn. East Lakes div.). Address: Dept Geography Bowling State U Bowling Green OH 43402

BUGAS, JOHN STEPHEN, business exec.; b. Rock Springs, Wyo., Apr. 26, 1908; s. Andrew P. and P. and Nell (Ladamus) B.; J.D., U. Wyo., 1934, LL.D., 1946; m. Margaret Stowe McCarty, Aug. 13, 1938; children—Helen Patricia, Margaret Jane, Elizabeth Diane, John Stephen, Jr. Admitted to Wyo. bar, 1934, with law office Walton & Kerr, Cheyenne, 1934-35; spl. agt. FBI, Washington, 1935, Los Angeles, 1935-36, Omaha, 1936, spl. agt. in charge, Juneau, Alaska, 1936-37, Birmingham, Ala., 1937-38, Detroit, 1938- 1937-38, Detroit, 1938- 43; indsl. relations exec. Ford Motor Co., 1944-59, v.p. indsl. relations 1946-59, v.p. internat. group, 1957-65, v.p., cons., dir., 1965-68, also mem. exec. and operating coms.; dir. One William Street Fund, Inc., Standard Oil Co. (Ind.), Kelsey-Hayes Co. Bd. dirs. dirs. Boy's Clubs Detroit, Boys' Clubs Am. Clubs: Detroit, Yondotega Detroit Athletic; Bloomfield Hills (Mich.) Country; Country of Fla. (Par, Fla.). Home: Bloomfield Hills MI 48013 Office: 16025 Northland Dr Southfield MI 48075

BUGBEE, GEORGE, hosp. adminstrn. tng. cons.; b. Waukesha, Wis., Sept. 2, 1904; s. Benjamin C. and Edith A. (Puffer) B.; student Carroll Coll., Waukesha, Wis., 1922-23; A.B., U. Mich., 1926; m. Karin Sederholm, Oct. 16, 1931. With bus. dept. U. Mich., 1926, resigned as asst. dir. U. Mich. Hosp., 1938; commr. City Hosp., Cleve., 1938-42; exec. dir. Am. Hosp. Assn., Chgo., 1943-54; pres. Health Information Found., 1954-62; dir. Center Health Adminstrn. Studies and grad. program hosp. adminstrn. U. Chgo., 1962-70; cons. health adminstrn. studies, 1970—. Health Fellow Am. Coll. Hosp. Adminstrs., Am. Pub. Health Assn. Home: Genesee Depot WI 53127 Office: 1 Dupont Circle Washington DC 20036

BUGBEE, HENRY GREENWOOD, educator, philosopher; b. N.Y.C., Feb. 19, 1915; s. Henry Greenwood and Della (Searles) B.; A.B., Princeton, 1936; Ph.D., U. Cal. at Berkeley, 1947; m. Daphne Eaches, Dec. 24, 1949; children—Ann (Mrs. John Berkley), Joan, Bruce, Henry Greenwood III, Barbara. Asst. prof. philosophy U. Nev., 1946-47, Stanford, 1947-48, Harvard, 1948-53; asso. prof. Chatham Coll., 1953-57, chmn. dept., 1953-57; prof. U. Mont., Missoula, 1957-61, Pa. State U., 1961-67; prof. philosophy, chmn. dept. U. Mont., 1967—; Danforth lectr. arts program, 1964-67. Served to lt. USNR, 1942-46. George Santayana fellow philosophy Harvard, 1953-54; research fellow, 1961. Mem. Am. Assn. U. Profs. (pres. Chatham Coll. 1955-57), Am. Philos. Assn. Author: The Inward Morning, 1958. Home: Route 6 Missoula, MT 59801.

BUGBEE, PERCY, ret. assn. exec.; b. Marblehead, Mass., Sept. 5, 1898; s. James McKellar and Marion (White) B.; B.S., Mass. Inst. Tech., 1920; m. Wilhelmina Ross, May 28, 1921; children—Richard, Alan, Margery. With Nat. Fire Protection Assn., 1921—, cons. Internat. City Mgrs. Assn. gen. mgr., 1939- 68, hon. chmn. bd., 1968—; Pres. World Conf. Fire Protection Assns., 1966. Mem. adv. bd. fire protection U.S. War Dept.; chmn. Provost Marshal Gen.'s Adv. Council on Fire Protection; chmn. U.S. Office of Civilian Def. Indsl. Protection Com.; cons. U.S. Office Civilian Def., World War II; chmn. Nat. Fire Prevention Week Com.; mem. Nat. Commn. on Fire Prevention and Control, 1970—. Hon. mem. Brit. Instn. Fire Engrs, Pacific Coast, Can., Internat. assns. fire chiefs, Dominion Fire Prevention Assn., French Nat. Soc. des Sapeurs-Pompiers, Internat. Assn. Fire Fighters, Australian Fire Protection Assn., Fire Marshals Sect. NFPA, Maritime Fire Chiefs Assn., Internat. Fire Chiefs Assn. Asia, Mass. Fire Chiefs Club, Memphis Fire Dept., N.J. Fire Chiefs Assn., R.I. Fire Chiefs Assn., Soc. Fire Protection Engrs.; Hon. Citizen of State of Tex., Washington Fire Dept.; hon. state fire marshal, Ga., 1956. Gold medal Swedish Fire Prevention Assn., Halsingborg, 1955; recipient Standards Engrs. Soc.-Am. Soc. Testing and Materials award, 1966. Mem. New Eng. Assn. Fire Chiefs, Paris Fire Brigade, Am. Soc. Assn. Execs. Republican. Unitarian. Mem. Alumni Council, Mass. Inst. Tech. Club: Winchester Country. Traveled in U.S., Can. and Europe. Contbr. to fire protection assns. publs.; author ann. survey of fire protection in U.S. for Municipal Year Book. Home: 22 Symmes Rd Winchester MA 01890 Office: 60 Batterymarch St Boston MA 02110

BUGELSKI, BERGEN RICHARD, psychologist, educator; b. Johnstown, Pa., Apr. 3, 1913; s. Ignatius J. and Stefania (Florek) B.; student Alliance Coll., 1930-32; B.A., U. Buffalo, 1934, M.A., 1935; Ph.D., Yale, 1938; m. Sadie Locurto, Dec. 29, 1937; children—Victoria (Mrs. Gerald L. Stearns), Catherine. Faculty, Antioch Coll., 1937-39, U. Toledo, 1939-42; asst. prof. U. Buffalo, 1946- -; cons. psychologist Cornell Aero. Lab., 1950-60. Served to lt. USNR, 1943-46. Named Distinguished prof. State U. N.Y. at Buffalo, 1969. Mem. Eastern Psychol. Assn. (pres. 1970). Author: Introduction to the Principles of Psychology, 1960; The Psychology of Learning, 1956; The Psychology of Learning Applied to Teaching, 1964. Home: 2525 N Forest Rd Getzville NY 14068 Office: Dept Psychology State U NY Buffalo NY 14214

BUGG, JAMES LUCKIN, Jr., univ. pres.; b. Farmville, Va., July 25, 1920; s. James Luckin and Clair (Woodruff) B.; A.B., Hampden-Sydney Coll., 1941; M.A., U. Va., 1942, Ph.D., 1950; m. Anne Barrington Hunter, June 26, 1956; children— Anne Barrington, James Luckin, III. Instr. history George Washington U., summer 1948; faculty U. Mo., Columbia, 1949-69, prof. history, 1960-63, chmn. dept., 1959-62, dean faculty St. Louis, 1963-65, chancellor, 1965-69; pres. Old Dominion U., Norfolk, Va., 1969—. Mem. Nat. Commn. Coll. work, Episcopal Ch., 1964-69, now chmn. div. coll. work and mem. dept. ministry Diocese of So. Va., chmn. higher edn., 1965-69; mem. region XI selection com. Woodrow Wilson Scholarship Found., 1959-69; mem. adv. council Va. Commn. on Higher Edn. Bd. dirs. Central Midwestern Regional Edn. Labs., 1966-69, St. Louis Higher Edn. Coordinating Council, 1963-69, Norfolk Symphony Soc., Tide Water Better Bus. Bur. Served with USAAF, 1942-46. Mem. Am., So. hist. assns., Orgn. Am. Historians, Am. Acad. Polit. and Social Scis., Phi Beta Kappa, Omicron Delta Kappa, Lambda Chi Alpha. Kiwanian. Author articles. Editor: Jacksonian Democracy; Myth or Reality, 1962. Home: 5000 Edgewater Dr Norfolk VA 23508

BUGG, WILLIAM JOHN, hosp. dir.; b. Wingham, Ont., Can., Jan. 25, 1912; s. James Herbert and Margaret (Galbraith) B.; M.D., U. Western Ont., 1938; m. Blanche Mary Godin, June 16, 1941; children—William John Jr., James Allan, Stephen Charles, Judith Maryln (Mrs. George Douglas Keenan). Intern Foote Meml. Hosp., Jackson, Mich., 1938-39; resident surgeon Victoria Hosp., London, Ont., Can., 1939-40; pvt. practice medicine, Mitchell, Ont., Can., 1940-41; surgeon Westminster Hosp., London, Ont., Can., 1941-52, adminstr., 1952-62, hosp. dir., 1962—; mem. council med. faculty U. Western Ont. Med. Sch., also mem. adv. bd. dental faculty. Mem., chmn. London Hosp. Planning Council, 1967-69. Served to capt. Canadian Army, World War II. Mem. Can. Council Hosp. Adminstrs., Assn. Can. Med. Colls., Assn. Can. Teaching Hosp. Adminstrs., Can. Legion (dir. 1948-60), Royal Coll. Physicians and Surgeons of Can., Can. Ont. hosp. assns. Address: Westminster Hosp Box 5701 London Ontario Canada

BUGGE, WILLIAM ADAIR, civil engr.; b. Hadlock, Wash., July 10, 1900; s. Samuel and Amelia (Bishop) B.; C.E., State Coll. Wash., 1922; m. Evelyn Bernice Bishop, Aug. 9, 1930; 1 son, William Adair. Engr., Jefferson Co., Wash., 1930-44; dist. engr. Asphalt Inst., 1944-48; mng. engr. Pacific Coast div. Asphalt Inst., 1948-49; dir. hwys. State of Wash. 1949-63; project dir. Parsons Brinckerhoff-Tudor-Bechtel, constrn. engrs. San Francisco Bay Area Rapid Transit, 1963—. Chmn., Bldg. Industry Conf. Bd., San Francisco, 1970. Registered engr., Wash., Ore., Cal. Mem. bd. cons. Eno Found.; vis. com. Coll. Engring., U. Wash. Recipient Bartlett award 1960, Thomas H. McDonald award 1961, Top 10 Constrn. Men award, 1961. Fellow Am. Soc. C.E. (past chmn. tech. council on urban transp., past chmn. exec. com. hwy. div., chmn. coordinating com. on transp. engring., past pres. San Francisco chpt.); mem. N.W. Soc. Hwy. Engrs. (past pres.), Inst. Traffice Engrs. (affiliate), Am. Pub. Works Assn., Western Assn. State Hwy. Ofcls. (past pres.), Am. Soc. Mil. Engrs., Nat. Soc. Profl. Engrs., Hwy. Research Bd. (past chmn.), Am. Road Builders' Assn. (past v.p. western sect.), Am. Assn. State Hwy. Ofcls. (pres. 1956-57, exec. com. 1958-63), Nat. Acad. Scis. (exec. com. hwy. research 1957-63). Elk, Mason. Home: 3441 Tice Creek Dr No 11 Walnut Creek CA 94595 Office: 814 Mission St San Francisco CA 94103

BUGGERT, ROBERT WILLIAM, musician, educator; b. Chgo., July 25, 1918; B.Mus., Vandercook Sch. Music, Chgo., 1938; M. Mus.Edn., U. Mich., 1947; Ph.D., 1956; m. Helen Woodward, May 12, 1946; children—Barbara Helen, Richard Woodward. Mem. Oak Park-River Forest (Ill.) Symphony Orch., 1935-39; instr. percussion Vandercook Sch. Music, 1938-39; supr. music Anson (Tex.) pub. schs., 1939-40; instr. percussion Roy C. Knapp Sch. Percussion, Chgo., 1940-41; teaching fellow percussion U. Mich., 1946-48, grad. fellow, 1951-52; asso. prof. music, head grad. music studies U. Wichita, 1948-51, 52-59; timpanist Wichita Symphony Orch., 1948-51, 52-59; condr. U. Wichita Percussion Ensemble, 1952-59; dir. Sch. Music, U. Okla., 1959-61; exec. v.p. Norman Youth Orch. Assn., 1959—; prof. music No. Ill. U., DeKalb, 1964—, asso. dean grad. sch., 1967-69, asst. to dean Coll. Fine and Applied Arts, acting dean, 1970-71, dean, 1971—; chmn. div. music Sch. Fine and Applied Arts, Boston U., 1961-63; head dept. applied music, condr. concert band and percussion ensemble Amherst Summer Music Center, Raymond, Me., 1963; mem. faculty New Eng. Conservatory Music, 1963. Served with AUS, 1944-46. Mem. Am. Music Center (asso. composer), Am. Musicol. Soc., Music Educators Nat. Conf., Music Tchrs. Nat. Assn. (chmn. musicology S.W. div.), Nat. Assn. Coll. Wind and Percussion Instrs. (chmn. composition contest 1958-60), Pi Kappa Lambda, Phi Mu Alpha, Kappa Kappa Psi. Methodist (steward). Lion. Composer: Percussion Methods, Solos and Ensembles, 1937—; Introduction and Fugue for Piano and Percussion, 1957; Toccata No. 1 for Percussion, 1968, Short Overture for Percussion, Dialogue for Solo Percussion and Piano, Fanfare, Song, and March for Solo Percussion and Piano, Didiption I and II, others. Percussion editor The Instrumentalist, 1956-59. Author; Teaching Techniques for the Percussions, 1960, also articles. Editor: Contemporary Percussion Library. Home: 1712 Judy Lane Dekalb IL 60115

BUGGS, CHARLES WESLEY, educator, microbiologist; b. Brunswick, Ga., Aug. 6, 1906; s. John Wesley and Leonora Victoria (Clark) B.; A.B., Morehouse Coll., Atlanta, 1928; M.S. (Rosenwald scholar 1931-34), U. Minn., 1932, Ph.D. (Shevlin fellow medicine 1933), 1934; m. Maggie Lee Bennett, Dec. 27, 1927; 1 dau., Margaret Leonora. Prof. biology, chmn. div. scis. Dillard U., 1934- 43, 49-56; from instr. to asso. prof. bacteriology Sch. Medicine, Wayne U., 1943-49; prof. microbiology Sch. Medicine, Howard U., 1956-71, chmn. dept., 1958-70; program dir. Faculty Allied Health Scis. Charles R. Drew Postgrad. Med. Sch., Los Angeles, 1969—; vis. prof. microbiology U. Cal. at Los Angeles and U. So. Cal., 1969—; spl. research resistance bacteria to antibiotics. Fellow Washington Acad. Scis., Am. Acad. Microbiology; mem. A.A.A.S., Am. Soc. Microbiology, N.Y. Acad. Scis., Soc. Exptl. Biology and Medicine, Am. Pub. Health Assn., Assn. Am. Med. Colls., Social Hygiene Soc. Met. Washington (dir. 1965—), Am. Assn. Dental Schs., Assn. Schs. Allied Health Professions, Sigma Xi, Alpha Phi Alpha, Sigma Pi Phi. Author: Premedical Education for Negroes, 1949. Home: 4123 Don Luis Dr Los Angeles CA 90008

BUGHER, ROBERT DEAN, assn. exec.; b. Lafayette, Ind., Oct. 17, 1925; s. Walter Earl and Lillie Victoria (Feldner) B.; student Millsaps Coll., 1943, Miami U., Oxford, O., 1944; B.S. in Civil Engring., Purdue U., 1948; M.P.A., U. Mich., 1951; m. Patricia Jean McConnell, Sept. 7, 1945; children—Vickie Leigh, Robert James. Staff engr. Mich. Municipal League, 1948-53; mgr. Municipal Purchasing Service, 1951-53; sec.-treas. Mich. Municipal Utilities Assn., 1951-53; asst. dir. Am. Pub. Works Assn., 1953-58, exec. dir., 1958—. Lectr., Internat. Seminar on Exestics, Athens, Greece, 1970. Mem. steering com. Keep Am. Beautiful, Inc.; chmn. Nat. Conf. on Solid Waste Disposal Sites, Washington, 1971. Bd. dirs. Govtl. Affairs Inst., Pub. Adminstrn. Service, Chgo.; trustee Nat. Acad. Code Adminstrs. Served from pvt. to 2d lt. USMCR, 1943-45. Mem. Am. Soc. C.E., Am. Soc. Assn. Execs., Am. Soc. Pub. Adminstrn., Am. Road Builders Assn., Internat. Union Local Authorities (v.p. U.S. sect. 1968-70), Internat. Solid Wastes and Pub. Cleaning Assn. (v.p. 1968-70), Sigma Alpha Epsilon. Baptist. Editor pub. works sect. Municipal yearbook, Internat. City Mgmt. Assn., 1953-58; cons. editor Municipal Pub. Works Adminstrn., 1957. Home: 418 Indiana St Park Forest IL 60466 Office: 1313 E 60th St Chicago IL 60637

BUGLIARELLO, GEORGE, univ. dean; b. Trieste, Italy, May 20, 1927; s. Federico and Spera (Gefter-Wondrich) B.; came to U.S., 1951, naturalized, 1964; Dr. Ing. summa cum laude, U. Padua (Italy), 1951; M.S. in Civil Engring., U. Minn., 1954; Sc.D., Mass. Inst. Tech., 1959; m. Virginia Upton Harding, Jan. 23, 1960; children-Federico David, Nicholas Luigi. Research engr. U. Padua, 1951; from research asst. to research asso. Mass. Inst. Tech., 1956-59; mem. faculty Carnegie-Mellon U., 1959-69, prof. biotech. and civil engring. 1956-69, chmn. biotechnologt program, 1964-69; dean engring. U. Ill. at Chgo. Circle, 1969—. Dir. Metasystems, Inc., 1968- -. Mem. bd. hydraulic cons. U.S. Waterways Expt. Sta., 1968—; sci. adv. panel Armed Forces Explosive Safety Bd., 1968-69; biomed. tng. engring. com. NIH, 1966-70; commn. edn. Nat. Acad. Engrngg., 1970—, chmn. com. ednl. systems, 1970—. NATO sr. fellow U. Berlin, 1968. Mem. Am. Soc. C.E. (exec. com. engring. mechanics div. 1968—, chmn. interdivisional task com. civil engring. in medicine and health care delivery 1969—; Huber research prize 1967), Internat. Assn. Hydraulic Research (chmn. task com. computer langs. 1969—), Internat. Soc. Hemorheology (sec. 1966-69). Author papers in field. Editor: Bioengineering-An Engineering Book, 1967; Biorheology, 1968—; asso. editor Am. Jour. Cybernetics. Home: 808 Sheridan Rd Evanston IL 60202 Office: Seo Bldg Box 4348 Chicago IL 60680

BUHLER, CHARLOTTE, (Mrs. Karl Buhler), clin. psychologist; b. Berlin, Germany, Dec. 20, 1893; d. Hermann and Rose (Kristeller) Malachowski; ed. univs. Freiburg, Berlin, Munich (Germany); Ph.D., U. Munich, 1918; postgrad. U. Vienna, 1923; Columbia, 1924-25; m. Karl Bühler, Apr. 4, 1916; children—Ingeborg (Mrs. Alf-Jorgen Aas), Rolf D. Came to U.S., 1940, naturalized, 1945. Privat dozent Sch. Tech., Dresden, Germany, 1920-23; privat dozent U. Vienna (Austria), 1923-29, asso. prof., 1929-38; prof. U. Oslo (Norway), 1938-40, St. Catherine Coll., St. Paul, 1940-41; guest prof. Clark U., 1941-43; chief clin. psychologist Mpls. Gen. Hosp., 1943-45, Los Angeles County Gen. Hosp., 1945-53; asst. clin. prof. psychiatry U. So. Cal. Med. Sch., 1950-58; now emeritus; individual practice, Beverly Hills, Cal., 1950—; dir. Child Guidance Clinics, Vienna, 1930-38, London, 1930- 35, Oslo, 1938-40, Worcester, Mass, 1941-43. Recipient Hon. medal City of Vienna, 1964; Outstanding award Group Psychotherapy Assn. So. Cal., 1958. Diplomate in clin. psychology Am. Bd. Examiners in Profl. Psychology. Fellow Am.

Psychol. Assn., Soc. for Projective Techniques, Am. Orthopsychiat. Assn.; mem. Psychologists for Advancement in Psychotherapy (dir.), Am. Assn. for Humanistic Psychology (dir. 1961—, pres. 1966-67), Am. Assn. for Psychotherapy, Am. Assn. for Gerontology, Los Angeles Soc. Practicing Psychologists, Am., So. Cal. (pres. 1958-59) group psychotherapy assns. Author: Childhood and Adolescence, 1928, 4th edit., 1967; The First Year of Life, 1930; The Human Course of Life as a Psychological Problem, 1933, 2d edit., 1959; From Birth to Maturity, 1935; Childhood Problems and the Teacher, 1952; Values in Psychotherapy, 1962; Psychologie im Leben unserer Zeit (Psychology in the Life of Our Time), 1962, 5th edit., 1967; The Human Course of Life in its Goal Aspects, 1968; Psychology for Contemporary Living, 1968; also articles in profl. jours. Home: 999 N Doheny Dr Los Angeles CA 90069 Office: 436 N Roxbury Dr Beverly Hills CA 90210

BUHLER, CURT FERDINAND, historian, librarian; b. N.Y.C., July 11, 1905; s. Conrad and Martha (Warburg) B.; A.B., Yale, 1927; Ph.D., Trinity Coll., U. Dublin, 1930, Litt. D., 1947; postgrad. U. Munich, 1931-33; m. Frances Lynham, Apr. 28, 1939 (dec. Nov. 1966); 1 son (by previous marriage), Conrad Alexander; m. 3d, Lucy Jane Ford, July 10, 1971. Staff printed books Pierpont Morgan Library, 1934-48, keeper printed books, 1948-66, research fellow for texts, 1967—; Rosenbach fellow U. Pa., 1947-58-59, Guggenheim fellow, 1965. Del. Union Académique Internationale, Brussels, 1957—; vis. fellow All Souls Coll., Oxford, 1969. Fellow Medieval Acad., Am. Acad. Arts and Scis., Gutenberg Gesellschaft; mem. Am. Philos. Soc. (com. on library), Bibliog. Soc. Am. (pres. 1952-54), Am. Council Learned Socs. (sec. 1960—), Early English Text Soc., Modern Lang. Assn. (exec. council 1956-60), Bibliog. Soc. Eng. (treas. U.S. 1949-64), Renaissance Soc. Am. (pres. 1961-63), Ligue Internationale de la Librarie Ancienne (hon.), Union Academique Internat. (dir. 1968-71), Dante Soc. Am. (com. on hon. mems.), Phi Beta Kappa. Clubs: Century Assn., Grolier (N.Y.C.); Cosmos (Washington); Devonshire (London); Royal Dublin, University (Dublin); Gutenberg Gesellschaft (Mainz). Author: The Sources of the Court of Sapience, 1932; The Dicts and Sayings of the Philosophers, 1941; The Bible, Manuscripts and Printed Bibles from the Fourth to the Nineteenth Century, 1947; (with Selmer) The Melk Salbenkrämerspiel, 1948; Fifteenth Century Books and the Twentieth Century, 1952; The University and the Press in Fifteenth Century Bologna, 1958; William Caxton and His Critics, 1960; The Fifteenth Century Book, 1960; Neue Kunst und neue Welt, der Buchdruck und Amerika, 1963; The History of Tom Thumbe, 1964; The Epistle of Othea, 1970; also articles, essays to learned publs. Home: 200 E 66th St New York City NY 10021 Office: 33 E 36th St New York City NY 10016

BUHLER, JEAN EMIL, naval architect; b. Hazleton, Pa., Oct. 7, 1917; s. Emil and Jeannette Marguerite (Voyer) B.; grad. Hill Sch., 1936; student Stevens Inst. Tech., 1936-39; B.S., U. Mich., 1941; m. Phyllis Hugh Arthur, May 20, 1955; 1 son, Phillip Arthur. Prin. naval architect Miami Shipbldg. Corp., 1939-45, 48-60; naval architect Burgess Co., 1945-48; naval architect, test pilot Marine Systems Corp., also N. Am. Hydrofoils, Inc., Miami, N.Y.C. and Chgo., 1960-64; hydrofoil designer and pilot, naval architect J.B. Hargrave, Naval Architects, Inc., W. Palm Beach, Fla., 1964—. Mem. Soc. Naal Architects and Marine Engrs. (past chmn. S.E. sect.), Internat. Oceanographic Found., Chi Phi. Club: Biscayne Bay Yacht (past commodore). (Miami, Fla.) Home: 508 Caligula Av Coral Gables FL 33146 Office: 205 1/2 6th St West Palm Beach FL 33401

BUHLER, JOHN EMBICH, coll. dean; b. Marion, Ind., June 28, 1908; s. Jesse Thurman and Ethel Claire (Pillars) B.; D.D.S., Ind. U., 1935; m. Ruth Zike, Jan. 24, 1940; children—Karen Ann (Mrs. Lawrence Douglas Wilkerson), and John Embich. Intern, Ind. U. Med. Center and Dental Sch., 1935-36, instr. clin. dentistry and oral histology-pathology, 1936-37, instr. clin. oral surgery and oral histology, 1937-42; asso. prof. clin. oral surgery Temple U., 1942-48, sec. to faculty, prof., chmn. dept. oral diagnosis, 1947-48; dean Emory U. Sch. Dentistry, Atlanta, 1948-61; exec. v.p. Hanau Engring. Co., Inc., Buffalo, 1961-64; dean Coll. Dental Medicine, Med. U. S.C., 1964—; cons. dental div. Office Surgeon Gen., Dept. Army, 1954-61; cons. to chief dental officer USPHS, 1945-48, dental dir. Res. Dir. Fund for Dental Edn., 1954-61. Fellow Am. Coll. Dentists; mem. Am. Assn. Dental Schs. (sec. 1946-50, pres. 1954-55, exec. com. 1946-55), Am. Dental Assn. (council on dental edn. 1955-61), Ga., S.C. dental assns., A.A.A.S., Omicron Kappa Upsilon, Delta Sigma Delta. Episcopalian. Home: 2 Johnson Rd The Crescent Charleston SC 29407 Office: 80 Barre St Charleston SC 29401

BUHLER, NELSON, lawyer; b. Columbus, Ga., 1915; B.A., Columbia, 1936; LL.B., N.Y.U., 1940; grad. Command and Gen. Staff Coll., Ft. Leavenworth, Kan., 1945; m.; children—Nelson Jay, Millary S. Admitted to N.Y. bar, 1940, since practiced in N.Y.C.; with firm Buhler, King & Buhler, and predecessor, 1936—, partner, 1946—; war crimes prosecutor on legal staff Gen. Douglas MacArthur. Pub., CATALYST for Environmental Quality; pres. C & S Publs., Inc. Past treas., dir. Lambs Found.; v.p., dir. Joseph S. Buhler Found.; trustee Taraknath Das Found., Belle W. Baruch Found.; mem. legacy devel. com. Columbia Coll.; mem. library com. Wheaton Coll., Norton, Mass.; chmn. found. relations com. Island Center of St. Croix, V.I.; trustee Gene Tunney and Mary Lauder Tunney Found.; mem. legacy com. Morris Animal Found.; mem. adv. com. Boy Scouts Am., Stamford, Conn. Served to capt., Judge Adv., Gen. Office, AUS, 1942-46; PTO. Clubs: Rotary, Lambs (past mem. council, past chmn. law com.) (N.Y.C.). Address: 274 Madison Av New York City, NY 10016.

BUHLMAN, F.C., corp. exec.; b. Monroe, Wis., Sept. 30, 1924; s. Christ and Mary (Jacobs) B.; student U. So. Cal., 1946-49; m. Charleen M. Wold, Feb. 9, 1968; children by previous marriage—Cristina R., Craig A. Auditor, Ernst & Ernst, C.P.A.'s, Los Angeles, 1952-53; with Whittaker Corp., Los Angeles, 1953—, treas., 1963—. Served as navigator USAAF, 1943-46, USAF, 1950—52. Mem. Cal. Soc. C.P.A.'s. Address: 10880 Wilshire Blvd Los Angeles CA 90024*

BUHNER, JOHN COLIN, univ. adminstr.; b. Seymour, Ind., May 18, 1920; s. John H. and Marietta (Sawyer) B.; A.B. magna cum laude, Franklin (Ind.) Coll., 1942; M.A. in Polit. Sci., Ind. U., 1949, Ph.D., 1963; m. Betty Bevis, Mar. 27, 1942; children—Carol, John Colin, Byron. Editorial asst. Commonwealth Life Ins. Co., Louisville, 1945-46; grad. asst. Ind. U., 1946-48, 51-52, asst. dir., instr. govt. Calumet Center, 1948-51, dir., instr. govt. Gary Center, 1952-59, instr. govt. Indpls. Center, 1959-61, dir., instr. govt. Gary Center, 1961-63, dir., asst. dean div. univ. extension, also asst. prof. govt. N.W. campus, 1963-66, dean, asso. prof. govt. N.W. campus, 1966-68, dean, acting chancellor Ind. U. N.W., 1968-69; vice chancellor, dean faculties Ind. U.-Purdue U. at Indpls., 1969—. Recipient Distinguished Alumnus citation Franklin Coll., 1958; named Outstanding Prof., N.W. Campus Ind. U., 1964; recipient Outstanding Civic Service award I.U. Gents, 1968. Presbyn. (elder). Rotarian. Author articles in field. Address: Indiana U Purdue U at Indianapolis Indianapolis IN 46205

BUHSE, HOWARD EDWARD, investment banker; b. Prairie du Chien, Wis., June 4, 1906; s. Maximilian E. and Caroline (Grelle) B.; LL.B., U. Minn., 1929; m. Virginia Dixon, Sept. 30, 1933; children—Howard, Joan, Deborah. With Hornblower & Weeks (now Hornblower & Weeks, Hemphill, Noyes), investment bankers, N.Y.C., 1929—, partner, 1943—, now chmn. bd. of directing partners, 1970—; dir., mem. exec. com. Nat. Aviation; dir. Ceco Corp., Amsted Industries Inc., EDP Resources, Inc., Columbia Pictures Industries, Hanover Planning, Hornblower Growth Fund, Hornblower Equity Fund. Chmn. Chgo. Assn. Stock Exchange Firms, 1948; chmn. bd. govs. Nat. Assn. Securities Dealers, Inc., 1951; gov. N.Y. Stock Exchange, 1961-67. Mem. Winnetka Bd. Edn., 1952-58, pres., 1957-58. Trustee Manhattanville Coll. Mem. Knights Malta, Sigma Phi Epsilon, Phi Alpha Delta. Clubs: Metropolitan, Recess, Bond (pres. 1969) (N.Y.C.); Chicago; Home: 29 Middle River Rd Danbury CT 06810 Office: 8 Hanover St New York City NY 10004

BUIE, BENNETT FRANK, geologist, educator; b. Patrick, S.C., Jan. 9, 1910; s. Daniel Franklin and Mary Julia (Smith) B.; B.S., U. S.C., 1930; M.S. (research fellow 1930-32), Lehigh U., 1932; M.A., Harvard, 1934, Ph.D., 1939; grad. Command and Gen. Staff Coll.; m. Susanna Townsend Peirce, Aug. 9, 1938; children—Susanna (Mrs. Susanna Matthews), Julia (Mrs. Geog von Steinitz), Carolyn (Mrs. Voldoray Erdener), Margaret (Mrs. J. Duncan Keppie). Asst. in geology Harvard, 1932-37, resident adviser, proctor, 1935- 37; mem. Shaler Meml. Expdn., summers 1933-35; geologist subsidiaries Seaboard Oil Co. in Iran and Afghanistan, 1937-38, subsidiaries Standard Oil Co. Cal. in Brit. India and Tex., 1939-42; prof. geology U.S.C., also geologist S.C. Devel. Bd., 1946-56; chief geologist Resources Devel. Corp., Iran, 1952; geologist U.S. Geol. Survey, 1953-57; prof. geology Fla. State U., 1956—, chmn. dept., 1956-64; cons. geologist J. M. Huber Corp. Continuing pres. class 1930 U.S.C. Served to maj. C.E., AUS, 1943-45; col. Res. ret. Decorated Bronze Star medal; Order Red Star (USSR): Fulbright fellowship, Iran, 1951. Fellow Geol. Soc. Am., A.A.A.S. Mineral. Soc. Am.; mem. Soc. Econ. Geologists (life), Am. Inst. Mining, Metall. and Petroleum Engrs. (mem. exec. com. indsl. minerals div., Am. Assn. Petroleum Geologists, Geol. Soc. Washington, Carolina Geol. Soc. (pres. 1958), Société Géologique de France, Sigma Xi, Omicron Delta Kappa. Episcopalian. Author articles in field. Home: 1510 High Rd Tallahassee FL 32304

BUIE, LOUIS ARTHUR, Sr., surgeon; b. Kingstree, S.C., July 30, 1890; s. Wilson Robert and Mable (Benjamin) B.; A.B., U. S.C. 1911, D.Sc., 1949; M.D., U. Md., 1915; m. Zelma Jones, Aug. 19, 1920; children—Nancy Louise, Louis Arthur. Resident in surgery Univ. Hosp., Balt., 1915; in charge Kernan Hosp., Balt., 1916; chief of dept. proctology Mayo Clinic, 1919-53, sr. cons., 1953- 55; fellow Mayo Found., U. Minn., 1917, instr. surgery, 1920, asso. prof. surgery, 1921, prof. surgery (proctology), 1935- 55, prof. emeritus U. Minn. Med. Sch., 1955—; emeritus mem. Mayo Clinic Staff, Rochester, Minn., 1955—. Nat. cons. to surgeon gen. USAF, 1956-58. Served as 1st lt. Med. Corps, U.S. Army, Base Hosp. No. 102, attached to 4th and 6th Italian armies, No. Italy, 1918-19; received la Croce al Merito di Guerra, Italian Govt., 1934. Mem. Gov.'s Adv. Council on Health, Phys. Edn. and Recreation, 1945-47. mem. Nat. Joint Com. on Phys. Fitness (A.M.A. and FSA), 1944-45. Mem. central certifying com. Am. Bd. Surgery, 1936-49; mem. Am. Bd. Proctology (pres. 1934-35; chmn. bd. 1934-37; sec. 1949-53); sec. emeritus Adv. Bd. for Med. Specialties, 1957—. Fellow A.C.S.; mem. Am. Proctologic Soc. (pres. 1928, 34-35). Minn. Med. Assn. (pres. 1947). A.M.A. (mem. jud. council 1945-60), The Nat. Found. (mem. com. on fellowships 1954-62), A.A.A.S., Med. Library Assn.; has been active in state, local and spl. med. socs. and assns., Sigma Xi, Phi Beta Kappa, Nu Sigma Nu. Author: numerous med. books and articles, primarily in field of proctology. Editor-in- chief emeritus: Diseases of Colon and Rectum, 1957. Home: 720 10th Av SW Rochester MN 55901 Office: 102-110 2d Av SW Rochester MN 55901 ☆

BUKATY, RAYMOND MARTIN, aviation co. exec.; b. Kansas City, Kan., Jan. 30, 1920; s. Anthony and Elizabeth (Rost) B.; B.S. in Mech. Engring., Kan. State U., 1941; M.B.A., Harvard, 1950; m. Felicia Zapolsky, Nov. 25, 1954; children—Robin F., Raymond M. Dir. marketing G.A.F. Corp., N.Y.C., 1954-58; v.p. electronics and controls div. AVCO, Cin., 1958-60; v.p., gen. mgr. data systems div. Autonetics, Anaheim, Cal., 1961-70; pres. Pacific Airmotive Corp., Burbank, Cal., 1970—. Served to lt. col. AUS, 1941-45. Decorated Bronze Star medal. Mem. Am. Soc. M.E., I.E.E.E., Harvard Bus. Sch. Assn. Club: Harvard (N.Y.C.). Home: 2800 Anacapa Pl Fullerton CA 92632 Office: 2940 N Hollywood Way Burbank CA 91503

BUKETOFF, IGOR, orchestral condr.; b. Hartford, Conn., May 29, 1915; s. Constantin and Millitza (Lebedeff) B.; student U. Kan., 1931-32; B.S., Juilliard Inst. Mus. Art, 1935, M.S., 1941; student Juilliard Grad. Sch., 1939-42; Mus.D. (hon.), Los Angeles Conservatory Music and Art, 1949; m. Margaret Elizabeth Smith, Sept. 18, 1941; 1 dau., Barbara Elizabeth. Mem. faculty Juilliard Sch., 1935-45, Chautauqua Sch. Music, summers 1941-47, Columbia, 1943-47; condr. Broadway co. Menotti's operas, The Medium, The Telephone, tours Am. and Europe, 1947-48; condr. Ft. Wayne Philharmonic Orch., 1948-66; condr. young people's concerts N.Y. Philharmonic Orch., 1948-53, mus. dir., 1950-53; asso. prof. music Butler U., 1953-63; composer choral works; guest condr. Oslo Philharmonic, 1957, Danish State Radio Orch., 1959, Lisbon Radio Orch., 1969, Hague Philharmonic, 1970, Prague Symphony, 1971, Kansas City Philharmonic, Chautauqua, Chgo., Denver, Hartford, Houston, Indpls., Minn., San Diego, symphony orchs., Royal Philharmonic Orch. (London) 1968, Orquestra Sinfonica Nacional, Rio de Janeiro, Brazil, 1969; mus. dir., condr. St. Paul Opera Assn., 1968—; mus. dir. Iceland State Symphony, 1964-65; dir. contemporary composers project Inst. Internat. Edn., 1967-70. Founder, chmn. World Music Bank, 1959—. Alice M. Ditson grantee 1956; Rockfeller Found. grantee for establishment of World Music Bank, 1959; recipient Alice M. Ditson Ann. award, 1967. Bd. dirs. Am. Symphony Orchestra League, 1959-62. Contbr. chpt. on Russian Music, Music in Middle Ages. Recs. with Oslo Philharmonic and Iceland Symphony Orch., London Symphony, Royal Philharmonic, New Philharmonia. Home: 500 E 85th St New York City NY 10028

BUKSBAUM, DAVID EUGENE, TV producer; b. Bklyn., Mar. 1, 1935; s. Lewis and Claire (Weldon) B.; student U. Miami (Fla.); m. Susan Ravitch, July 10, 1966; 1 dau., Jennifer Louise. With CBS, 1957-67; with Pub. Broadcast Lab., Nat. Ednl. TV, 1967-. Mem. Dirs. Guild Am. Club: Friars (N.Y.C.).‡

BULAND, GEORGE LEONARD, lawyer; b. Greenwood, Wis., Apr. 6, 1897; s. George L. and Bertha E. (Mason) B.; A.B., Reed Coll., 1916; LL.B., Columbia, 1919; m. Anne D. Shea, Sept. 10, 1924; children—Nan (Mrs. Peter Koerner), George. Editor, Columbia Law Rev., 1917-19; practiced in Portland, Ore., 1919-30; partner firm Dey, Hampson & Nelsen, 1923-30; lectr. Northwestern Coll. Law, 1926-30; pres. Kalama State Bank (Wash.), 1923-30; editor Ore. Law Rev., 1927-30; asst. gen. counsel S.P. Co., N.Y.C., 1930-44, eastern gen. counsel, 1944-45, asso. gen. counsel, 1945-47, gen. counsel, 1948-50, v.p., gen. counsel, 1951-63; dir. Pacific Fruit Express Co., 1935-44 (pres. 1943- 44); St. Louis Southwestern Ry. Co.; dir., exec. com. So. Pacific Co., various subsidiaries, 1953-69; counsel Severson, Werson, Berke & Melchior, 1963—. Melchior, 1963—. Hon. trustee Reed Coll., Portland; bd. visitors Stanford Law Sch. Served in USN, 1918. Mem. Am., Ore. bar assns., State Bar Cal., C. of C. Clubs: Commonwealth, Family, Pacific Union (San Francisco); Menlo Country (pres.) (Redwood City). Author publs. in field. Home: 75 Crescent Dr Palo Alto, CA 94301. Office: 433 California St San Francisco CA 94104

BULATKIN, ELEANOR WEBSTER, (Mrs. Iliya Fomich Bulatkin), educator; b. Balt., Sept. 2, 1913; d. Silas Rodney and Anna May (Rich) Webster; certificate, Md. Inst. Fine and Applied Arts, 1934; M.A., Johns Hopkins, 1951, Ph.D., 1952; m. Iliya Fomich Bulatkin, Sept. 27, 1946. Asst. prof. French and Spanish, U. Md., 1948-61; asso. prof. Ohio State U., 1961-64, prof., 1964—, chmn. dept. Romance langs., 1966—. Univ. fellow Johns Hopkins, 1946-48; U. Md. grantee, 1956, Ohio State U. grantee, 1965; Fulbright lectr., Colombia, 1960-61. Mem. Modern Lang. Assn., Am. Assn. Depts. Fgn. Langs. (exec. com. 1971—), Modern Humanities Research Assn., Medieval Acad., Linguistic Soc. Am., Am. Assn. U. Profs., Midwest Modern Lang. Assn. Author: Structural Arithmetic Metaphor in the Oxford Roland, 1971; also articles. Home: 1369 La Rochelle Dr Columbus OH 43221

BULBULIAN, ARTHUR H., med. museum dir.; b. Talas, Turkey, Dec. 20, 1900; s. Hagop C. and Naomi (Iynejian) B.; came to U.S., 1920, naturalized, 1931; B.S., Middlebury Coll., 1925, M.S., 1926, D.Sc.(hon.); D.D.S., U. Minn., 1931; m. Wilhelmine M. Wilson, Sept. 9, 1944; children—Naomi, Josephine, Rachel. Asst. Mus. Natural History, U. Ia., 1927-28; instr. Coll. Dentistry, U. Minn., 1931-32; with Mayo Found., Rochester, Min., 1933—, asso. prof. med. edn. Mayo Grad. Sch. Medicine; dir. Mayo Found. Mus. of Hygiene and Medicine, 1935—, mem. staff Mayo Clinic, 1935—; clin. prof. maxillofacial prosthetics U. Minn. Sch. Dentistry, 1966—; spl. cons. U. Minn. Hosps., Mpls.; prepared Mayo Found. exhibit Hall of Science, A Century of Progress, Chgo., 1932-33. Mem. Nat. Resources Planning Bd., 1942-44 (mem. com. on conservation culture resources). Recipient Billing's Gold medal A.M.A., 1955, 58, 64, Am. Acad. of Achievement golden plate award, 1965, Award of Merit, Am. Assn. Inhalation Therapy, 1960, Andrew Ackerman award, 1964. Fellow Am. Coll. Dentists; mem. Am. Dental Assn., Assn. Med. Illustrators, Am. Acad. Maxillofacial Prosthetics (pres. 1956-58, dir. 1953—, editor jour.), Sigma Xi. Author: Facial Prosthesis (textbook), 1945; co-author (with Dry, Edwards et al), Atlas on Congenital Anomalies of the Heart and Great Vessels, 1948; articles on medical mus. techniques and facial prosthetic methods. Co-inventor (with Lovelace and Boothby), BLB Oxygen Mask for oxygen therapy and high altitude flying; designer A-14 oxygen mask used by USAAF during World War II. Home: 22 Skyline Rochester MN 55901 Office: Mayo Clinic Rochester MN 55901

BULEN, LAWRENCE KEITH, lawyer, mem. Republican Nat. Com.; b. Pendleton, Ind., Dec. 31, 1926; s. Lawrence and Ople (Benefiel) B.; A.B., Ind. U., 1949, J.D., 1952; m. N. Carole Guillot; children—Leslie, Lisa. Admitted to Ind. bar, 1952, since practiced in Indpls.; mem. firm Bulen & Castor, 1952—; chmn. Marion County Republican Com., 1966—, 11th Dist. Rep. Com., 1966-68; mem. Rep. state Com., 1966—; mem. Rep. Nat. Com. from Ind., 1968—; mem. Rep. Nat. Exec. Com., 1968—; del. Nat. Conv., 1968; chmn. Ind. Nat. Inaugural Com., 1968; Mem. Ind. Legislature, 1960-64; mem. steering com. Rep. Nat. Med-West Conf., 1969—. U.S. del. ECOSOC, UN, Geneva, Switzerland, 1970. Served with USAAF, 1945-46. Mem. Indpls. Laywer Assn. (past pres.). Home: 700 N Alabama St Indianapolis IN 46204 Office: 1 Indiana Sq Indianapolis IN 46204

BULEY, HILTON CLIFFORD, coll. pres.; b. Waverly, N.Y., Dec. 25, 1903; s. Joseph Myron and Nora Belle (McCutcheon) B.; B.S., Hobart Coll., 1927; M.A., Cornell, 1934; Ed.D., Columbia, 1947; grad. study Cortland State Tchrs. Coll., 1928, Syracuse U., 1939-40; L.H.D., Hobart Coll., 1963; m. Arline Besse, Aug. 30, 1930; children—Hilton M., David R. Tchr. sci., athletic coach, Brewster, N.Y., 1927-30, Milw. Country Day Sch., 1930-34; supervising prin. Spencer Central Sch. 1934-38, Vestal Central Sch., N.Y. State, 1938-42; supt. schs., Gloversville, N.Y. and Bound Brook, N.J., 1942-48; commr. edn., State N.H., 1948-54; pres. So. Conn. State Coll., 1954—; lectr.; cons. Commn. Tchr. Edn. and Profl. Standards, 1950. Past pres. Community Chest; mem. dist. council Boy Scouts Am. Dir. N.H. Council Tchr. Edn., N.H. League Arts and Crafts; cons. N.H. Bd. Nursing Edn., N.H. Jackson Meml. Found. for Cancer Research; state coordinator edn. N.H. Civil Def.; trustee Community Libraries; hon. mem. bd. dirs. New Haven Opera Soc. Recipient State citation for outstanding service to citizenship edn., V.F.W., state citation for exceptional service to pub. edn., N.H., Wisdom award of honor Wisdom Soc., 1969, First medal of excellence Hobart Coll. Alumni Assn., 1970. Mem. Conn. Com. on Edn. of Gifted. Mem. Conn. Accreditation Council. Mem. N.E.A., Am. Assn. Sch. Adminstrs., N.H. State Tchrs. Assn., N.E. Supts. Assn., Am. Assn. State Colls. and Univs. (dir., treas., pres. 1971), Nat. Chief State Sch. Officers U.S., Nat. Soc. for Study Edn., Conn. Edn. Assn., Am. Assn. Coll. for Tchr. Edn., (chmn. com. on TV and tchr. edn.; citation exceptional service and studies in new media of instrn.), Greater New Haven C. of C. (dir.), Phi Delta Kappa, Phi Phi Delta. Chimera, Kappa Delta Phi. Conglist. Rotarian (dist. gov.). Author profl. publs., articles profl. jours. Home: Old Lane Rd Cheshire CT 06410 Office: 501 Crescent St New Haven CT 06515

BULGANIN, NIKOLAI ALEKSANDROVICH former premier of USSR; b. Nizhni-Novgorod (now Gorky), 1895. Mem. bd. Goselectrotest, 1923-27; dir. Moscow Elect. Works, 1927; mayor of Moscow, 1931; chmn. Council of People's Commissars, RSFSR, 1937; dep. chmn. Council of People's Commissars USSR, chmn. Gosbank, 1938-41; full gen. of the army, 1944, Marshall, 1947; dept. People's Commissar for Defense, 1944; minister of Armed Forces, 1947; dept. chmn. Council of Ministers of USSR, 1949-55; premier of USSR, 1955-58; mem. Politburo (now Presidium), Central Com. Community Party of Soviet Union, 1948-61. Address: Ministry Social Security RSFSR 14 Shabolovka Moscow USSR*

BULGER, PAUL GRUTZNER, educator; b. Lake Luzerne, N.Y., July 25, 1913; s. John Michael and Nellie May (Grützner) B.; B.S., N.Y. State Coll. for Tchrs., 1936, M.S., 1941; Ed.D., Columbia, 1951; L.H.D., Canisius Coll., 1967; m. Marion Mleczek, Aug. 18, 1938; children—Cynthia Anne, John Lawrence. High sch. tchr., Coeymans, N.Y., 1936; dir. tchr. placement, coll. instr. N.Y. State Coll. for Tchrs., Albany, 1936-42, asst. prin. Milne Sch., 1940-43, dir. men's residence hall, 1941-43, coordinator field services and pub. relations, 1947-48; exec. asst. office field relations and placement Columbia Tchrs. Coll., 1946-47, asst. provost, asso. prof. edn., 1948-54, provost, prof. edn., 1955-59; pres. State U. Coll., Buffalo, 1959-67; asso. commr. higher and profl. edn. State of N.Y., Albany, 1967-68; prof. higher edn. State U. Albany, 1968—. Trustee Erie County Savs. Bank. Ednl. cons. Dept. State, S. Vietnam, 1966; mem. N.Y. State Exams. Bd.; exec. dir. N.Y. State Temp. Commn. on Youth Edn. in Conservation, 1969-72; v.p. bd. trustees Santiago (Chile) Coll., ednl. cons. 1962; ednl. cons. U. Conception, 1961; cons. on adminstrn. U. Chile, 1958, also mem. Inst. Orgn. and Adminstrn. Faculty Econs., U. Chile; cons. to Kenya, Uganda, Tanganyika; U.S. Dept. of State Am. Specialist grant, 1960; cons. State Dept. AID to presdl. com. on ednl. planning, Chile, 1963;

cons. on edn. West German Govt., State Dept. AID on edn., Indonesia, 1964. Second v.p. N.Y. State Congress Parents and Tchrs.; bd. dirs. Jr. Achievement of Niagara Frontier, Inc.; trustee Siena Coll., Loudonville, N.Y.; mem. adv. com. Edna G. Dyett Sch. for Practical Nursing, Millard Fillmore Hosp., Buffalo; hon. mem. Buffalo Fine Arts Acad. Mem. N.E.A. (pres. assn. for higher edn. 1957-58), Am. Assn. U. Profs., Student Personnel Assn. Tchr. Edn., N.Y. State Tchr. Assn., Am. Council Edn. (mem. com. equality opportunity higher edn., mem. Peace Corps com.), Am. Assn. Colls. for Tchr. Edn. (spl. study commn. 1962), Buffalo Area C. of C. (dir.). Contbr. articles profl. publs. Home: Lake Shore Park Watervliet NY 12189

BULGRIN, VERNON CARL, chemist, educator; b. Cuyahoga Falls, O., May 10, 1923; s. Otto Paul and Nina Bertha (Smith) B.; B.S., U. Akron, 1948; Ph.D., Ia. State Coll., 1953; m. Dorothy Ann Littig, Aug. 28, 1954; children—Thomas Frederick, Anne Louise. Instr. chemistry U. Wyo., Laramie, 1953-56, asst. prof., 1956-58, asso. prof., 1958-62, prof., 1962—, acting head dept. chemistry, 1961-62, head dept. chemistry, 1962-67. Fellow A.A.A.S.; mem. Am. Chem. Soc. Home: 716 S 24th St Laramie WY 82070

BULKELEY, JOHN DUNCAN, naval officer; b. N.Y.C., Aug. 19, 1911; s. Frederick Fisk and Elizabeth (MacCuaig) B.; B.S., U.S. Naval Acad., 1933; m. H. Alice Wood, Nov. 10, 1938; children—Joan (Mrs. Herbert Stade), John, Peter, Regina, Diana. Commd. ensign U.S. Navy, 1934, advanced through grades to rear adm., 1963; served in PT boats, PTO, also Normandy invasion, World War II; comdr. Guantanamo Naval Base, 1963-66, Cruiser Destroyer Flotilla 8, 1966-67; pres. U.S. Navy Bd. Inspection and Survey, 1967—. Decorated Medal of Honor, Navy Cross, D.S.C. (2), Silver Star (2), Legion of Merit (2). Home: 10706 Lorain Av Silver Spring MD 20390 Office: Bd Inspection and Survey Navy Dept Washington DC 20370

BULKLEY, EDWIN MUHLENBERG, Jr., investment broker; b. Englewood, N.J., Sept. 13, 1903; s. Edwin Muhlenberg and Lucy (Kidder) B.; student Hill Sch., Choate Sch., Occidental Coll.; m. Marianne Dodge, 1924 (div. 1941); 1 dau., Joan (Mrs. Edward B. deSelding); m. Maud Oberman, Nov. 9, 1969. With Spencer Trask & Co., N.Y.C., 1924—, partner, 1937-68. Clubs: Gulf Stream Golf, Bath and Tennis, Yacht (Delray Beach, Fla.); Oyster Harbors (Osterville, Mass.); Wianno (Mass.). Home: 50 East Rd Delray Beach FL 33444 also 451 Wianno Av Osterville MA 02655 Office: 60 Broad St New York City NY 10004

BULKLEY, JAMES STEWART, lawyer; b. Rocky Hill, Conn., Aug. 4, 1909; s. George Grant and Caroline Augusta (Griswold) B.; grad. Phillips Andover Acad., 1927; Ph.B., Yale, 1931; LL.B., Harvard, 1934; m. Eleanor F. Young, June 12, 1937; children—Martha keyes (Mrs. Robert F. Hostetter, Jr.), Deborah Church (Mrs. David B. Anderson), Judith Eleanor. Admitted to Mass. bar, 1934; since practiced law, Springfield; now partner Bulkley, Richardson, Ryan & Burbank; asst. city solicitor Springfield, 1936-37; v.p., gen. counsel, dir. Monarch Capital Corp.; gen. counsel, dir. Monarch Life Ins. Co.; dir. Valley Bank & Trust Co., Springfield, Springfield Life Ins. Co. Mem. Mass. Gov.'s Council, 1943-44. Mem. Republican State com., 1945-46. Trustee Northampton Comml. Coll. Mem. Am., Mass., Hampden County bar assns., Assn. Life Ins. Counsel, Springfield Library and Museums Assn. (pres.), Beta Theta Pi. Conglist. Clubs: Colony (Springfield); Longmeadow (Mass.) Country. Home: 432 Long Hill St Springfield MA 01108 Office: 83 State St Springfield MA 01109

BULL, ALVIN FRED, farm mag. editor; b. Ottumwa, Ia., Apr. 13, 1925; s. Fred Raymond and Mary S. (Carris) B.; m. Joyce Elaine Edgar, Aug. 5, 1950 (dec. Jan. 1963); children—Debra Elaine, Randall Fred; m. 2d, Carol Jean Schad, May 9, 1964. Agronomist, Spencer Chem. Co., Ames, Ia., 1950-57; asso. editor Am. Soc. Agronomy, Madison, Wis., 1951-53; field editor Wallaces Farmer, Des Moines, 1953-58, mng. editor, 1958-68, editor, 1968—. Mem. Nat. Farm Inst. com., 1957—, chmn., 1970—. Mem. Ia. adv. council Title III, Elementary and Secondary Edn. Act, 1969—, adv. com. Gt. Plains Sch. Dist. Orgn. Project, 1967-68, Gov.'s Ednl. Adv. Com., 1969-71. Served with USNR, 1945-46. Recipient Profl. Writers award Am. Seed Trade Assn., 1962, Leadership and Service award Ia. Soil Conservation Com., 1968. Fellow Soil Conservation Soc. Am.; mem. Am. Agrl. Editors Assn., Phi Kappa Phi, Alpha Zeta, Gamma Sigma Delta, Farmhouse. Acting editor Jour. Soil and Water Conservation, 1956-57, chmn. editorial bd., 1964—. Home: 3312 47th St Des Moines IA 50310 Office: Wallaces Farmer 1912 Grand Av Des Moines IA 50305

BULL, FRED WARREN, educator; b. Erwin, Tenn., Aug. 30, 1912; s. Fred and Mary (Kirk) B.; B.Sc. in Chem. Engring., Va. Poly. Inst., 1933, M.S., 1934, B.Sc. in Ceramics Engring., 1938, Ph.D., 1953; m. Charlcie Virginia Smith, Apr. 3, 1934; children—Mary Anne, Susan Lynn. Service and sales engr. Mead Corp., Lynchburg, Va., 1934-38; tech. service Donald Hagar, cons. engr., Zanesville, O., 1938-40; instr. chem. engring. Va. Poly. Inst., 1940-43, asst. prof., 1943-46, asso. prof., 1946-54, prof., head dept. chem. engring., 1954-63, dir. Engring. Expt. Sta., 1963-65, dean Grad. Sch., 1965—. Registered profl. engr., Va. Mem. Sigma Xi, Tau Beta Pi, Phi Lambda Upsilon, Phi Kappa Phi, Keromas. Home: 617 N Main St Blacksburg VA 24060

BULL, GERALD VINCENT, research co. exec.; b. Northbay, Ont., Can., Mar. 9, 1928; s. George L.T. and Gertrude (LaBrosse) B.; B.A., U. Toronto, 1948, M.A., 1949, Ph.D., 1951; m. Noemie Louise Gilbert, July 3, 1954; children—Philip, Michel, Richard, Stephen, Robert, Cathy, Jane. Research scientist Govt. of Can., Quebec, P.Q., 1951-61; prof. engring. scis. McGill U., 1961-64, dir. Space Research Inst., 1964-69; pres., tech. dir. Space Research Corp., North Troy, Vt., 1969—; prof. aerospace grad. studies Norwich U., Northfield, Vt. Mem. acad. adv. bd. Bishops U., Lennoxville, Que. Fellow Canadian Aeros. and Aerospace Inst. (McCurdy award 1967); mem. N.Y. Acad. Scis., Am. Inst. Aeros. and Astronautics, A.A.A.S., Am. Geophys. Union, Nat. Space Club. Contbr. articles profl. jours. Home: 1195 E Main St Newport VT 05855 Office: PO Box 281 North Troy VT 05859

BULL, HENRIK HELKAND, architect; b. N.Y.C., July 13, 1929; s. John and Sonja (Geelmuyden) B.; B.Arch., Mass. Inst. Tech., 1952; m. Barbara Alpaugh, June 9, 1956; children—Peter, Nina. With Mario Corbett, San Francisco, 1954-55, Goetz & Hansen, San Francisco, 1955-56; pvt. practice architecture, 1956-68; partner Bull, Field, Volkmann, Stockwell, San Francisco, 1968—; works include restoration Columbus Tower, San Francisco, Christ Ch. Parish Hall, Sausalito, Cal., Sunset mag. Discovery House, Tahoe Tavern Condominiums, Tahoe City, Snowmass Villas, Aspen, Colo., Northstar Master Plan; vis. lectr. Syracuse U., 1963, U. Cal. Extension, 1964. Mem. adv. com. San Francisco Urban Design Study, 1970-71. Dir. Golden Gate chpt. Children's Home Soc., 1969; dir. French- Am. Bilingual Sch., 1970-71. Served as 1st lt. USAF, 1952-54. Fellow A.I.A. (pres. N. Cal. chpt. 1968). Democrat. Home: 477 Arlington Av Berkeley CA 94707 Office: 350 Pacific Av San Francisco CA 94111

BULL, IRVING HORTON, lawyer; b. Middletown, N.Y., July 7, 1905; s. Irving Crawford and Mable (Horton) B.; grad. Taft Sch., 1924; A.B., Yale, 1928; LL.B., Harvard, 1931; LL.M., Columbia, 1932; m. Elizabeth Schofield Magnuson, Sept. 14, 1935; children—Barkley Horton, James Horton, Melinda (Mrs. John Barret), Prudence (Mrs. Brendon Smith). With Lybrand, Ross Bros. & Montgomery, accountants, 1932-35; admitted to N.Y. bar, 1933; with firm Dunnington, Bartholow & Miller, N.Y.C., 1936—, partner, 1938—. Mem. Am., N.Y. State bar assns., Assn. Bar City N.Y. Clubs: Union, Cloud, Yale (N.Y.C.). Home: 19 Sky Meadow Dr Stamford CT 06903 also 196 E 75th St New York City NY 10021 Office: 161 E 42d St New York City NY 10017

BULL, MASON, lawyer; b. Redfield, S.D., Mar. 7, 1903; s. Roy Taylor and Ida (Mason) B.; A.B., Harvard, 1924; J.D., Northwestern U., 1929; m. Kathryn M. Doyle, June 3, 1933; children—Mason, Jane Ann (Mrs. David B. Weihaupt), David, Nicholas. Admitted to Ill. bar, 1929; mem. firm Bull, Ludens & Potter, Morrison, 1935—; mem. law dept. C.M., St.P. & P. R.R. Co., 1929- 35; master-in-chancery Whiteside County Circuit Ct., 1940-65. Fellow Am. Coll. Trial Lawyers, Am. Bar Found.; mem. Am., Ill. (gov. 1957-63, 1st v.p. 1961-62, pres. 1962-63), Whiteside County bar assns., Am. Judicature Soc., Am. Law Inst. Republican. Conglist. Home: 644 Genesee Av Morrison IL 61270 Office: 212 N Genesee St Morrison IL 61270

BULL, RICHARD GORDON, paint co. exec.; b. Cleve., Mar. 14, 1915; s. Clarence Garfield and Lena (Black) B.; B.S., Harvard, 1937; m. Virginia Gates, Dec. 30, 1939; children-Richard, Katherine. With Sherwin-Williams Co., 1938—, v.p., dir. marketing, Cleve., 1966-69, exec. v.p. marketing, 1969—. Mem. Nat. (dir., mem. exec. com.), N.Y. (past pres.) paint, varnish and laquer assns. Home: 3201 Fox Hollow Dr Pepper Pike OH 44124 Office: 1901 Prospect Av N W Cleveland OH 44113

BULL, RICHARD SUTTON, Jr., paper co. exec.; b. Chgo., Jan. 21, 1926; s. Richard Sutton and Sara (Smith) B.; grad. Phillips Acad., 1944; student Ill. State Normal U., 1944, 46, Columbia, 1944-45; B.A., Yale, 1948, J.D., 1951; LL.M. (Food Law Inst. fellow), N.Y. U., 1952; postgrad. U. Chgo., 1954-69; m. Lois Karna Werme, July 19, 1950; children—Lois Karna, Sara Annette, Richard Sutton III, Harry Calvin, Mary Ellen Frantz. Instr. econs. Stone Coll., New Haven, 1950-51; admitted to Ill. bar, 1953, also U.S. Supreme Ct.; atty. Swift & Co., 1952-57; with Bradner Central Co., Chgo., 1957—, pres., 1965-66, pres., chmn. bd., 1966—; v.p., dir. Eastern Central Co., Cranbury, N.J.; sec., treas., dir. Clearview Farms Corp., Hinsdale, Ill.; gen. counsel Morris Co., Park Ridge, Ill.; dir. Sangamon Co., Taylorville, Ill. Mem. Maercker Sch. Bd., Hinsdale, Ill., 1956-59; mem. Hinsdale Community House Council, 1955-58; bd. dirs. Hinsdale Community Chest, 1955-58, treas., 1956-57; mem. Chgo. Crime Commn., 1969—; mem. Hinsdale Community Caucus, 1965-68; mem. alumni fund com. N.Y. U. Law Center, 1964—; regional agt. Andover Alumni Fund, 1963-69. Bd. dirs. John Howard Assn., Duncan Med. Center, YMCA. Served with USNR, 1944-46. Mem. Am. Mgmt. Assn., Am., Chgo. bar assns., Am. Arbitration Assn. (nat. panel arbitrators), Chgo. Assn. Commerce and Industry, Newcomen Soc., Ill. C. of C. Elk. Clubs: Morey's Assn. (New Haven); Paper (dir., past pres.), Yale, Ill. Athletic, Executives (Chgo.); Johnson's Slough Yacht, Salt Creek (Hinsdale); Oak Brook Polo; Khyble Bay Yacht. Home: 4 Countryside Ct Hinsdale IL 60521 Office: 333 S Desplaines St Chicago IL 60606

BULLARD, CHARLES WINSTON, educator; b. Richmond Hill, N.Y., Dec. 31, 1914; s. Charles Pearly and Jean (Jardine) B.; A.B., Ohio U., 1940, M.A., 1948; Ph.D., U. Ia., 1954; m. Trudie I. Kissner, Dec. 25, 1940; children—Winston Perry, Spencer Douglas, Sunny Charlene. Asst. dean of men Ohio U., 1946-48; asst. prof. economics U. N.D., 1948-56, asso. prof., 1956-69, prof., 1969—, chmn. dept., 1961—. Served with USNR, 1941-46. Ford Found. fellow U. Minn., 1958. Mem. N.D. Council Econ. Edn. (exec. dir. 1968—), Am., Midwest econ. assns., Am. Assn. U. Profs. Home: 103 Conklin Av Grand Forks ND 58201

BULLARD, EDWARD CLARKE, ret. business exec.; b. Bridgeport, Conn., Mar. 13, 1896; s. Dudley Brewster and Alice Anna (Clarke) Bullard; student Curtis Sch., Brookfield Centre, Conn., 1906-10, Univ. Sch., Bridgeport, 1910-14; Ph.B., Yale, 1917; m. Ruth Leslie Johnson, June 28, 1920; children—Brewster Leslie, David Edward. Asso. with The Bullard Co., mfrs. machine tools, Bridgeport, 1919—; dir. Rolock, Inc., Conn. Nat. Bank of Bridgeport. Served in Ordnance Dept., U.S. Army, World War I. Mem. Am. Soc. M.E., S.A.R., Sigma Xi, Phi Sigma Kappa. Conglist. Mason. Home: 413 Mill Hill Terrace Southport CT 06490

BULLARD, EDWARD CRISP, physicist; b. Norwich, Norfolk, Eng., Sept. 21, 1907; s. Edward John and Eleanor Howes (Crisp) B.; B.A., Cambridge U., 1929, Ph.D., 1932, Sc.D., 1948; m. Margaret Thomas, July 25, 1931; children—Belinda, Emily, Henrietta, Polly. Demonstrator in geodesy Cambridge U., 1931-35, reader in exptl. geophysics, 1944-48; research fellow Royal Soc., 1935-43; exptl. officer Brit. Admiralty, 1939-45; prof. physics Toronto U., 1948- 49; dir. Nat. Phys. Lab., Teddington, Middlesex, Eng., 1950-56; fellow Caius Coll., Cambridge, 1956-57, fellow Clare Coll., 1957-60, asst. dir. research Cambridge U., 1956-60, reader in geophysics, 1960- 64, prof. geophysics, 1964—; prof. Inst. Geophysics and Planetary Physics, U. Cal. at San Diego; fellow Churchill Coll., Cambridge, 1960- -; dir. IBM (U.K.). Created knight, 1953; recipient Day medal Geol. Soc. Am., 1959; Agassiz medal Nat. Acad. Sci., 1965; gold medal Royal Astron. Soc., 1965; Wollaston medal Geol. Soc. London, 1967; Vetlesan Prize, 1968. Mem. Geophys. Union, Royal Sooc. London (Hughes medal 1953), Royal Astron. Soc., The Phys. Soc. (Chree medal 1956), Cambridge Philos. Soc., Geol. Soc., London, Geol. Soc. Am., Am. Acad. Arts and Scis., U.S. Nat. Acad. Sci. (fgn. asso.); fgn. mem. Philos. Soc. Home: 19 Clarkson Rd Cambridge England Office: Madingley Rise Madingley Rd Cambridge England

BULLARD, EDWARD PAYSON III, mfg. exec., inventor; b. Stratford, Conn., June 8, 1910; s. Edward Payson and Mary E. (Deacon) B.; grad. Phillips Exeter Acad., 1928; B.A., Yale, 1932; student Harvard Sch. Bus. Adminstrn., 1932-33; m. Jane Alling, Mar. 3, 1934; childrenEdward Payson Jr., Mary Jane (Mrs. John A. S. McGlennon), Daniel Alling. With The Bullard Company, Bridgeport, Conn., 1933-51, 57-, successively asst. chief engr., v.p. charge mfg., v.p. and asst. gen. mgr., 1933-51, dir., 1938—, pres., gen. mgr., 1957—, also chief exec. officer, 1959—, br. plant mgr., then chief prodn. engring. Pratt & Whitney Aircraft, div. United Aircraft Corp., 1951-57; trustee Peoples Savs. Bank of Bridgeport; director Kerite Company, Conn. Nat. Bank. Mem. U.S. Strategic Bombing Survey, Germany, 1945. Dir. YMCA, Bridgeport. Holder 39 machine tool patents. Home: Cherry Lane Fairfield CT 06430 Office: The Bullard Co Bridgeport CT 06603

BULLARD, LOREN J., publishing co. exec.; b. Clve., Aug. 6, 1922; s. Loren J. and Florence N. (Burval) B.; student Cleve. Coll., 1940-42, Heidelberg Coll., 1943; M.B.A. Western Res. U., 1947; m. Geraldine B. Zupp, Feb. 14, 1948; children—Lauren Jay Burnette, Timothy Charles, Jerrie Kendall. Asst. research metallurgist Chase Brass & Copper Co., Cleve., 1942, 46; sales engr. Viking Mfg. Corp., Cleve., also Dayton, O., 1946-47; with L.J. Bullard Co., Cleve., 1947-60, v.p., 1955-57, pres., 1957-60; v.p. How & Why Bldg. Corp., Cleve., 1951-60; pres., founder Shore Advt., Inc., Mentor, O., 1956-60; sales mgr. Field Enterprises Ednl. Corp., Chgo., 1961-64, gen. sales mgr., 1965, v.p., gen. sales mgr., 1965-69, mem. adv. com., 1964—, exec. v.p., dir. U.S. and Canadian sales, 1969—. Home: 1076 Old Barn Lane Lake Forest IL 60045 Office: 510 Merchandise Mart Plaza Chicago IL 60654

BULLARD, ROBERT WINSLOW, physiologist, educator; b. Waltham, Mass., June 13, 1929; s. Alvan Henry and Florence (Dennison) B.; B.S., Springfield (Mass.) Coll., 1951; M.A., U. Mass., 1953; Ph.D., U. Rochester, 1956; m. Marlene Verbridge, Aug. 17, 1957; children—Kristen Ann, Carolyn Joan, Alicia Brooke. Asst. prof. physiology Ind. U., Bloomington, 1956-62, asso. prof., 1962-64, prof., chmn. dept. anatomy and physiology, 1964—; vis. prof. epidemiology Yale, vis. fellow John B. Pierce Found. Lab., 1969-70. Dir. Sage Heights, Inc. Mem. physiol. com. Nat. Bd. Med. Examiners, 1969—; mem. USPHS applied physiol. study sect. Mem. Am. Phys. Soc., A.A.A.S., Hibernation Information Exchange, Soc. Gen. Physiologists, Sigma Xi. Mem. editorial bd. Am. Jour. Physiology, 1964-70; Jour. Applied Physiology, 1964-70. Contbr. articles to profl. jours. Home: 3601 Hollywood Dr Bloomington IN 47401

BULLARD, TODD HUPP, educator; b. Wheeling, W.Va., May 31, 1931; s. Luther Todd and Virginia (Netting) B.; student Bethany (W.Va.) Coll., 1949-50; B.A., W.Liberty (W.Va.) State Coll., 1953; M.A., W.Va. U., 1956; Ph.D., U. Pitts., 1964; m. Ella J. Rickey, June 6, 1953; children—Todd Whittam, Katharine Anne, Alice Elizabeth, Janice, James. Dir. edn. W.Va. State Penitentiary, Moundsville, 1953; research asst. Bur. Govt. Research, W.Va. U., 1956- 57; asst. dir. W.Va. League Municipalities, 1956-57; asst. prof. polit. sci., dir. Falk program practical politics Bethany Coll., 1959-60; sr. research analyst Bur. Govt. Research, W.Va. U., 1960-61, dir. Parkersburg br., 1961-63, acad. dean Potomac State Coll. of univ., Keyser, 1963-64, pres., 1964-70; provost, v.p. acad. affairs Rochester (N.Y.) Inst. Tech., 1970—; vis. prof. higher edn. U. Mich., 1968-69. Chmn. task force for study br., Jr. and Community Colls. in W.Va., 1965-66; mem. survey team study Am. Sch. Tangier, Morocco, 1965. Mem. exec. com. Mineral County United Fund, 1966-70. Served with AUS, 1953-55. Mem. Am. Assn. Jr. Colls. (commn. instrn. 1966-69), N. Central Assn. Colls. and Secondary Schs. (commn. colls. and univs. 1966-70), Am. Polit. Sci. Assn., W.Va. Assn. Coll. and Univ. Pres., Pi Sigma Alpha. Author: (with E. R. Elkins) Manual of West Virgina Municipal Goverment, 1957; Labor and The Legislature, 1965. Home: 68 N Country Club Dr Rochester NY 14618

BULLARD, WILLIS CLARE, lawyer, corp. exec.; b. Toledo, June 15, 1916; s. Clare N. and Anna (Davidson) B.; A.B., Western Mich. U., 1939; J.D., U. Mich., 1942; m. Virginia Gilmore, June 29, 1941 (div. Oct. 1970); children—Willis Clare, David G., Jonathan K.; m. 2d, Leota Carroll, Nov. 28, 1970. Admitted to Mich. bar, 1942; asso. Dyer, Meek, Ruegsegger & Bullard and predecessor firms, Detroit, 1942-53, sr. partner, 1953—. Sec., dir. Kelly Services, Inc., 1952—; chmn. bd. McGregor-Mich. Corp., 1961—, Down River Casting Co., 1956—; pres. Mill Supply & Machine Co., 1960—; sec., dir. Dawson Carbide Industries, Inc.; dir. Gorham Tool Co., Inst. Temporary Services. Mem. Nat. Def. Exec. Res., Dept. Commerce, 1962—. Mem. exec. com. United Republican Fund Mich., 1969—. Mem. Am., Mich., Detroit bar assns., Nat. Assn. R.R. Trial Counsel, Assn. ICC Practitioners, Nat. Tech. Services Assn. (dir.), Delta Theta Phi. Clubs: Copper (N.Y.C.); Detroit, Propeller (Detroit); Lochmoor Country, U. Mich. (pres. 1958-59) (Grosse Pointe, Mich.). Author: Equal Employment Opportunity Laws and The Temporary Contract Service, 1968. Home: 150 E Long Lake Rd Bloomfield Hills MI 48013 Office: 1 Woodward Av Detroit MI 48226

BULLEN, KEITH EDWARD, applied mathematician, educator; b. Auckland, New Zealand, June 29, 1906; s. George Sherrar and Maud (Burfoot) B.; M.A., U. New Zealand, 1928, B.Sc., 1930; M.A., U. Melbourne (Australia), 1945; Ph.D., U. Cambridge (Eng.), 1937, Sc.D., 1946; D.Sc., U. Auckland, 1963; m. Florence Mary Pressley, May 15, 1935; children—John Edward, Anne. Master, Auckland Grammar Sch., 1926-27; lectr. math. Auckland U., 1928-39; sr. lectr. math. Melbourne U., 1940- 45; prof. applied math. U. Sydney (Australia), 1946—; spl. lectr. math. physics Hull (Eng.) U. Coll., 1933; Einstein Meml. lectr. Australian Inst. Physics, 1959, Harricks lectr., 1963. Pres. Internat. Assn. Seismology and Physics Earth's Interior, 1954-57; v.p. Internat. Sci. Com. Antarctic Research, 1958-62, Internat. Union Geodesy and Geophysics, 1963-67; chmn. Australian nat. com. for I.G.Y., 1955-60. Sr. Univ. scholar pure and aplied math. U. New Zealand, 1925; Strathcona exhibitioner St. John's Coll., Cambridge U., 1932-33; Lyle medallist Australian Nat. Research Council, 1951; Found. fellow Australian Acad. Sci., 1953; Walter Burfitt prizeman Royal Soc. New South Wales, 1953, Hector medalist, Royal Soc. New Zealand, 1952; Flinders lectr., medallist Australian Acad. Sci., 1969; Pontifical Academician, 1968. Fellow Royal Soc. London, Am. Geophys. Union (William Bowie medallist 1961); corr. Geol. Soc. Am. (Arthur Day medallist 1963); fgn. hon. mem. Am. Acad. Arts and Scis.; fgn. asso. Nat. Acad. Sci.; hon. fellow Royal Soc. New Zealand; fgn. and commonwealth mem. Geol. Soc. London. Author books, articles, chpts. in field. Office: Dept Applied Math Univ Sydney Sydney NSW 2006 Australia

BULLEN, RICHARD HATCH, corp. exec.; b. Logan, Utah, May 9, 1919; s. Asa and Georgia Vivian (Hatch) B.; B.S., Utah State U., 1941, LL.D., 1965; M.B.A., Harvard, 1943; m. Annabelle Smith, June 19, 1942 (div. 1965); children—Richard Hatch, Steven Asa, Thomas Kenneth; m. 2d, Anne-Marie deLeur, Aug. 16, 1965. With IBM Corp., 1946—, exec. asst. to pres., 1955-56, dir. orgn., 1956-61, treas., 1961-63, v.p., 1963-64, v.p., group exec., 1964- 67, sr. v.p., mgmt. com., 1967—; dir. Upjohn Co. Trustee Lenox Hill Hosp. Served to 1st lt. Q.M.C., AUS, 1943-46. Mem. Sigma Chi. Clubs: Harvard, Racquet and Tennis (N.Y.C.). Home: 1050 Fifth Av New York City NY 10028 Office: Armonk NY 10504

BULLER, CECIL, (Mrs. Cecil T. Murphy), artist; b. Montreal, Can.; d. Frank and Lily Elizabeth (Langlois) Buller; student art, Art Assn., Montreal; London Co. Council Sch. (under Noel Rook), London; Acad. Ranson (under Maurice Denis), Paris, France; m. John J. A. Murphy, 1917; 1 son, Dr. Sean Buller. Came to U.S., 1920. Work executed in oil and wood engraving; regular exhibitor Nat. Acad. of Design, Am. Soc. of Etchers, Gravers, Lithographers and Wood Cutters; represented in permanent collections of Brit. Mus., London, Nat. Gallery of Can., Montreal Mus. Fine Arts, La Bibliotheque Nationale, Paris, N.Y. Pub. Library, Library of Congress, Washington, Royal Albert Meml. Mus., Exeter. Awarded 2d purchase prize, Library of Congress, 1945; Audubon Artists prize, 1947; Nat. Acad. Design prize (graphic art sect.), 1949, Audubon Artists gold medal, 1953. Asso. mem. Nat. Acad. Design. Mem. Soc. Am. Graphic Arts, Audubon Artists Soc. Address: 3421 Drummond St Montreal Quebec Canada

BULLERJAHN, EDUARD HENRI, architect; b. Mile., Mar. 9, 1920; s. Adolph David and Hazel Roselle (te Selle) B.; student U. Wis., 1937-39; B. Arch., Mass. Inst. Tech., 1943; diploma Royal Acad. Fine Arts, Stockholm, Sweden, 1957; m. Julianna S. Bullerjahn, 1951;

children—Stephen R., John te Selle, George S. Designer, Perry Shaw and Hepburn, Boston, 1948, Edward Durrell Stone, N.Y.C., 1951-54; partner Robert Hegardt, N.Y.C., 1954-57; individual practice architecture, Marion, Mass., 1957-61; partner Andrew Hepburn, Boston, 1961-67; ind. practice Bullerjahn Assos., Boston, 1967—; cons. in field. Mem. Marion Planning Bd., 1960-61. Bd. dirs. Boston Children's Theatre, Cambridge Sch. Ballet. Served to lt. USNR, 1943-46. Fellow Swedish Am. Found., 1946. Recipient King Gustav V Gold Medal Architecture, Stockholm, 1948; Rotch travelling scholar, 1949. Mem. A.I.A. Clubs: Royal Swedish Yacht; Eastern Yacht, Somerset (Boston); Brit. Officers New Eng. Home: 27 Chestnut St Boston MA 02108 Office: 27 Chestnut St Boston MA 02108

BULLION, BRUCE THOMAS, lawyer; b. Little Rock, Ark., Feb. 13, 1914; s. Bruce Thomas and Jessie (Rice) B.; LL.B., U. Ark., 1938; m. Mary Fletcher Ford, Sept. 28, 1940; childrenMary Ellis (Mrs. Gus B. Walton, Jr.), Bruce Thomas. Admitted to Ark. bar, 1938; chief atty. Ark. Revenue Dept., 1946-48; pvt. practice, Little Rock, 1948-; partner firm Warren & Bullion, 1948-. Served to capt. USAAF, 1942-46. Mem. Am., Ark. (pres. 1964-65), Pulaski County bar assns. Presby. (clk. of session). Author articles. Home: 5411 Edgewood Rd Little Rock, AR 72202. Office: Tower Bldg Little Rock, AR 72201.

BULLIS, HAROLD EDMUND, assn. consultant; b. Manlius, N.Y., July 24, 1888; s. George E. and Ida H. (Wood) B.; M.E., Cornell U., 1909; LL.D., Philippine Women's University, 1960; m. Miriam Payne, July 14, 1923; children—Edmund Payne, Carolyn. Engaged in C. of C. organization and publicity work, 1910-17; editor Am. Chamber Commerce Journal, Manila, P.I., and pres. Philippine Publicity Service, 1920-22; sent by Gov. Gen. Leonard Wood on spl. mission to rulers of Indo-China, Siam, Federated Malay States, Straits Settlements, Dutch Indies, Borneo, 1922-23; in charge mission to U.S. of Premier Herriot of France, Chinese High. Commn., 1923-24, and Pulaski mission from Poland, 1929; chief of Organized Reserve Sect., Gen. Staff, U.S. Army, 1924-27; exec. officer Nat. Com. for Mental Hygiene, 1930-42; now cons. Del. Soc. Mental Hygiene; spl. cons. USPHS; cons. Philippine Govt., Philippine Womens U., 1954; round-the-world lectr. tour as cons. on mental health education World Fedn. Mental Health, 1960. Nat. vice pres. Americans for the Competitive Enterprise System. Secretary of Committee for Research in Dementia Praecox. Served from capt. to lt. col., arty., U.S. Army, World War I, as col., claims div., AUS, World War II. Decorated Legion of Merit, Bronze Star Medal, Commendation Ribbon with two oak-leaf clusters, also eight fgn. decorations; named Man of Yr., Del. C. of C., 1963. Fellow Royal Geog. Soc.; mem. Founders and Patriots Am., S.A.R., A.A.A.S., Am. Legion, and several fgn. socs. Republican. Mason (33). Rotarian. Clubs: Explorers, Circumnavigators, Army and Navy, Nat. Press (Washington); Manila (P.I.) Polo. Author several books, including: Human Relations in Action. Home: 418 Shipley Rd Wilmington DE 19809 ☆

BULLIS, WILLIAM FRANCIS, educator; b. Washington, Oct. 22, 1901; s. William John and Cynthia DeLay (Rowley) B.; B.S., U.S. Naval Acad., 1924; M.A., George Washington U.; m. Lois Elizabeth Hoover, Nov. 27, 1929; children—William Clark, Lawrence Hoover, Starr B. Phillips, Faith Sebring. Founder Bullis Sch., Potomac, Md., 1930, prin., 1930—. Served as 2d lt. U.S. Army, 1924-26; lt. comdr. to comdr., USNR, 1940-45, now comdr. U.S. Naval Res., ret. Mem. Mil. Order World Wars, Am. Legion, Washington Bd. Trade, Washington Naval Acad. Alumni Assn. Clubs: Congressional Country, Chesapeake Yacht, Fed. Schoolmen's, Touchdown, Columbia Country, Potomac Hunt, Army and Navy (Washington); Lions (past pres.), Rotary. Home: 9125 River Rd Potomac MD 20854

BULLITT, JOHN CHRISTIAN, lawyer; b. Phila., June 6, 1925; s. Orville H. and Susan B. (Ingersoll) B.; B.A., Harvard, 1950; LL.B., U. Pa., 1953; m. Lelia M. Wardwell, Nov. 20, 1954; children—Thomas W., Clarissa W. Admitted to N.Y. bar, 1956; asso. Shearman & Sterling, N.Y.C., 1953-60; dep. asst. sec. internat. affairs U.S. Treasury, Washington, 1961-62, asst. sec. internat. affairs, 1962-64; U.S. exec. dir. Internat. Bank Reconstrn. and Devel., 1962-65; dir. N.J. Office Econ. Opportunity, 1964-67; asst. adminstr. for Far East Asia AID Dept. State, 1967-69; partner Shearman & Sterling. Organized book air lift to Moscow to re-open Book-mobile, Am. Nat. Exhb., 1959. Trustee Bank St. Coll. Edn. Served with inf., AUS, World War II. Home: R D 1 Princeton NJ 08540 Office: 53 Wall St New York City NY 10005

BULLITT, JOHN MARSHALL, educator; b. Seattle, July 9, 1921; s. Keith Logan and Dorothy (Terry) B.; A.B., Harvard, 1943, Ph.D., 1950; m. Sarah Cowles, Aug. 11, 1948 (div.); children—Elizabeth, Margaret, Sarah, John; m. 2d, Sandra Merrihue, June 27, 1969; 1 son, Daniel Edmund, 1 stepson, Jeffrey Merrihue. Mem. faculty English dept. Harvard, 1946—, asso. prof., 1956-62, prof., 1962—, master Quincy House, 1957-66; regional dir. Peace Corps, Bolivia, 1966-68. Served from pvt. to capt., inf. AUS, 1943-46. Mem. Modern Lang. Assn. Author: Jonathan Swift and the Anatomy of Satire, 1953. Co-editor: Samuel Johnson, The Idler and the Adventurer, 1963. Home: 19 Garfield St Watertown MA 02172

BULLITT, ORVILLE HORWITZ, banker; b. Cape May, N.J., July 30, 1894; s. William C. and Louisa G. (Horwitz) B.; B.S., U. Pa., 1915, L.H.D., 1970; m. Susan B. Ingersoll, Nov. 15, 1916. Partner W.H. Newbold's Son & Co., 1926-43; former pres., dir. Beaver Coal Co.; now pres., dir. Beaver Mgmt. Corp.; formerly dir. Fidelity Bank, Westmoreland Coal Co., Va. Coal & Iron Co., Stonega Coal & Coke Co., Central Pa. Nat. Bank; formerly trustee Phila. Saving Fund Soc., Penn Mut. Life Ins. Co. Founder, pres., dir. Asso. Hosp. Service, Phila.; life trustee U. Pa.; pres., chmn. bd. Phila. Orch. Assn., 1938-68, dir., 1938—; pres., mgr. Hosp. of Univ. Pa., 1931-61; trustee Phila. Mus. Art; treas., dir. Fairmont Park Art Assn.; dir. Acad. Music, Phila. Participant Univ. Museum discovery Sybaris. Author: Search for Sybaris, 1969. Home: Ft Washington PA 19034 Office: 1517 Locust St Philadelphia PA 19102

BULLITT, STIMSON, lawyer; b. Seattle, June 16, 1919; s. Alexander Scott and Dorothy (Stimson) B.; student Yale, 1937-41, U. Wash., 1946-48; m. Katharine Squire Muller, Nov. 27, 1954; children—Ashley, Scott, Jill, (by previous marriage)—Dorothy Churchill, Benjamin Logan, Margaret Muller. Admitted to Wash., 1949; partner firm Riddell, Williams, Voorhees, Ivie & Bullitt, Seattle, 1958—. Pres. King Broadcasting Co., Seattle, 1961—. Guest lectr. U. Cal. at Berkeley, 1959. Mem. King County (Wash.) Charter Commn., 1950-52; nominee U.S. Ho. of Reps. Democratic Party, 1952; del. at large Dem. Nat. Conv., 1956. Served with USNR, 1941-45. Decorated Purple Heart. Author: To Be A Politician, 2d edit., 1961. Home: 1125 Harvard Av E Seattle WA 98102 Office: 320 Aurora Av N Seattle WA 98109

BULLOCK, ALAN LOUIS CHARLES, univ. adminstr., historian; b. Dec. 13, 1914; s. Frank Allen Bullock; M.A. with 1st class honours in classics, (scholar), Wadham Coll., Oxford U., 1936, 1st class honours in Modern History, 1938, D.Litt., 1969; hon. Dr. Univ., Aix-Marseilles (France); m. Hilda Yates; 3 sons, 1 dau. With European service, then diplomatic corr. BBC, 1940-45; fellow, dean, tutor modern history New Coll., 1945-52; censor St. Catherine's Soc., Oxford U., 1952-62, master St. Catherine's Coll., 1960—, vice chancellor Oxford, 1969—. Chmn. research com. R.I.I.A.; chmn. Nat. Adv. Council Tng. and Supply Tchrs., 1963; chmn. Schs. Council, 1966-69; mem. Arts Council Great Britain, 1961-64; mem. Adv. Council on Pub. Records, 1965—. Trustee The Observer. Hon. fellow Merton Coll., Wadham Coll., Linacre Coll. Decorated chevalier Legion of Honor. Fellow Brit. Acad.; mem. Internat. Assn. Cultural Freedom (chmn.). Author: Hitler, A Study in Tyranny, rev. edit., 1962; The Liberal Tradition, 1956; The Life and Times of Ernest Bevia, Vol. 1, 1960, Vol. II, 1967; The Twentieth Century, 1971. Gen. editor: (with F. W. Deakin) The Oxford History of Modern Europe. Address: Master's Lodgings St Catherine's Coll Oxford England

BULLOCK, E. DOROTHY DANN, assn. ofcl.; b. Horseheads, N.Y., Apr. 7, 1906; d. Frederick O. and Mary B. (Mosher) Dann; B.S., Cornell U., 1928; student Mansfield State Coll., 1936-38: student Chautauqua Instn. 1944-53; Mus. D., Elizabethtown Coll., 1968; L.H.D., Susquehanna U., 1968; m. Charles Arthur Bullock, Aug. 7, 1928 (dec. 1966); children—Charles Arthur, Donna Mary (Mrs. Harry K. Ziel). Pres., mgr. Cornell U. Women's Glee Club, 1926-28; bd. dirs. Pa. Fedn. Music Clubs, 1935—, finance chmn., 1935-44, 2d v.p., 1938-42, 1st v.p., 1942- 44, pres., 1944-48, parliamentarian, 1952-58, 68—, Am. music chmn., 1964-68; bd. dirs., exec. com. Nat. Fedn. Music Clubs, 1947—, recording sec., 1947-51, chmn. council state and dist. presidents, 1951-55, chmn. Chautauqua Fedn. Weekend, 1950. chmn. conv., N.Y.C., 1953, chmn. budget, 1955-59, chmn. screening scholarships, awards and contests, 1957-59, v.p., 1955-59, pres., 1959-63, chmn. Am. music dept. and Parade Am. Music, 196367; chmn. Award Program for Ednl. Instns. on Performance and Promotion Am. Music, 1963-67; pres.'s council Pa. Fedn. Music Clubs, 1964-68; vice chmn. MacDowell in Hall of Fame; asst. observer to UN, 1953-55. Mem. com. on music UNESCO; pres. Chautauqua Women's Club, 1967—, Canton Improvement Assn., 1967-69; mem. adv. com. on the arts Kennedy Center for Performing Arts, state chmn., mem. exec. com.; mem. Nat. Creative Arts com. for Better Broadcasts; vice chmn. Found. Advancement Mus. Arts of Nat. Fedn. Music Club; mem. sponsoring bd. Nat. Assn. for Advancement of Native Am. Composers and Musicians; friend Am. Symphony Orch. League; mem. Nat. Com. on Music in Recreations; organizer Williamsport and Leroy (Pa.) music clubs; pres. Canton (Pa.) Beethoven Club, 1934-37, Canton Mendelssohn Club, 1944-46; founder Canton Eve. Musicales. Bd. dirs. Music for the Blind. Named Musician of the Year 1962 by Mich. State U.; recipient Community Leader of Am. award, 1969; citation for Distinguished leadership and Service to musical life state and nation, Mansfield State Coll., 1968. Mem. Nat. Music Council (v.p. 1959-63), Internat. Platform Assn., Gen. Fedn. Women's Clubs (county chmn.), Am. Legion Aux. (dist. chmn. music), Nat. Assn. Am. Composers and conductors, Nat. Grass Roots Opera found. (vice chmn.), Internat. String Congress (adminstrv. adv. bd.), Nat. Council on Arts and Govt., Pa. Music Tchrs. Assn. (hon. and charter mem. Am. Assn. U. Women, Guy Maier Assn. (hon. life mem.), Grange, Sedowa, Sigma Alpha Iota (hon. life mem.). Republican. Presbyn. (soloist). Mem. Order Eastern Star (dist. dep. grand matron). Address: 121 South Av W Canton PA 17724

BULLOCK, HENRY MORTON, minister, editor; b. Chgo., Dec. 6, 1902; s. Hugh Morton and Alma Pauline (Smith) B.; Ph.B., Emory U., 1924, B.D., 1925; B.D., Yale, 1927, Ph.D., 1932; m. Julia Sargent, Aug. 16, 1937; 1 son, David Morton. Ordained to ministry Methodist Ch., 1927; pastor Union City, Ga., 1924-25, Concord Park Ch., Orlando, Fla., 1925-26, Cheshire, Conn., 1927-28, Bayshore Ch., Tampa, Fla., 1928-29; prof. of English Bible, Blackburn Coll., Carlinville, Ill., 1929-35; prof., and head dept. religion Millsaps Coll., Jackson, Miss., 1935-42; vis. prof., Scarritt Coll., Nashville, 1939; pastor Jefferson St. Meth. Ch., Natchez, Miss., 1942-45, First Meth . Ch., Gulfport, Miss., 1945-49, Capitol Street Meth. Ch., Jackson, 1949-52; editor of church sch. publs. Meth. Church, Nashville, 1953-. Chmn. bd. ministerial tng. Miss. Meth Conf., 1940-44, 48- 52; mem. gen. bd. Nat. Council Chs. of Christ, 1954-66, mem. exec. bd. dept. ednl. devel., 1964—. Trustee Scarritt Coll., 1964-70. Mem. Phi Beta Kappa, Omicron Delta Kappa, Tau Kappa Alpha. Author: A History of Emory University, 1936, The Divine Fatherhood, 1945. Editor: (with Edward C. Peterson) Young Readers Bible, 1965. Contbr. to ednl. and religious publs. Home: 2145 Chickering Lane Nashville TN 37215 Office: 210 8th Av S Nashville TN 37202

BULLOCK, H. RIDGELY, lawyer, mfg. co. exec.; b. N.Y.C., June 16, 1934; s. H.R. and Marian (Batterman) B.; B.A., Colby Coll., 1955; LL.B., U. Va., 1967; m. Sylvia Ann Vandervlis, Apr. 23, 1934; children-James William, Sylvia Marian, David Duncan Ridgely. Theatrical producer, N.Y.C., 1955-64; admitted to Va. bar, 1967, N.Y. bar, 1970; asso. Mudge, Rose, Guthrie & Alexander, N.Y.C., 1967-70, partner, 1970—; sec. UMC Industries, Inc., St. Louis, 1969-70, exec. v.p., 1970, pres., 1970—, also dir.; chmn. bd. Eastern Air Devices, Inc., N.Y.C.; dir. First Washington Securities Corp., Trend Exploration, Ltd., Denver. Served to capt. USAF, 1956-59. Mem. Am., N.Y. State bar assns., Va. State Bar. Home: 1155 Park Av New York NY 10005 Office: 72 Wall St New York NY 10005 also 20 Broad St New York NY 10005

BULLOCK, MRS. HUGH, (Marie Leontine Graves), civic leader; b. Paris, France, June 30, 1911; d. William Leon and Florence Christmas (Eno) Graves; grad. student Sorbonne, Paris, also Columbia, 1933-37, Julliard Sch. Music, 1937; mem. Tchrs. Astronomy Course, Hayden Planetarium, 1952-53; m. Hugh Bullock, Apr. 5, 1933; children—Florence Eno (Mrs. Allan Block), Fair Alice Seymour (Mrs. Peter H. McCormick). Founder of Acad. Am. Poets, 1934, pres., 1939—; bd. dirs. Edward MacDowell Assn.; bd. dirs., exec. com. Theodore Roosevelt Assn.; ex-officio mem. pres. adv. com. on arts John F. Kennedy Center Performing Arts, 1960—. Dir. Calvin Bullock, Ltd. Chmn. belles lettres com. Office Cultural Affairs, City of N.Y., 1964. Mem. vis. com. dept. astronomy Harvard Coll., 1968—. Council fellows Pierpont Morgan Library, 1969-71. Recipient King's medal for service in cause of freedom; Distinguished Service award National Inst. Arts and Letters, 1963. Mem. Nat. Soc. Colonial Dames, Poetry Soc. Am. (exec. bd. 1938-39), Nat. Inst. Social Sci. (gold medal 1961), Hroswitha Club, English Speaking Union. Episcopalian. Clubs: Colony (bd. govs. 1968—), River (N.Y.C.); Sulgrave (Washington). Address: 1030 Fifth Av New York City NY 10028

BULLOCK, HUGH, investment banker; b. Denver, June 2, 1898; s. Calvin and Alice Katherine (Mallory) B.; grad. Hotchkiss Sch., 1917; B.A., Williams Coll., 1921, LL.D., 1957; L.H.D., Hamilton Coll., 1954; m. Marie Leontine Graves, Apr. 5, 1933; children—Florence Eno, Fair Alice (Mrs. Peter Hamilton McCormick). Investment banker, 1921—; chmn. bd., chief exec. officer of Calvin Bullock, Ltd.; pres., dir. Bullock Fund, Ltd., Canadian Investment Fund, Ltd., Carriers and Gen. Corp., Dividend Shares, Inc., Canadian-Fund, Inc.; chmn., dir. Nation- Wide Securities Co. Mem. Marshall Scholarship Regional Com., 1955-58; life trustee, mem. exec. com. Williams Coll.; trustee Roosevelt Hosp.; adv. council Grad. Sch. Bus., Columbia, 1958. Served as 2d lt., inf., World War I; lt. col. World War II. Civilian aide to sec. Army, for First Army Area, 1952-53. Decorated Knight Comdr. Order Brit. Empire; Knight of grace Order of St. John of Jerusalem (v.p. Am. soc.), Knight comdr. Royal Order George I (Greece); recipient U.S. Army certificate of appreciation, 1953; James C. Rogerson Cup for Service, Loyalty, Achievement, Williams Coll., 1961; Exceptional Service award Dept. of Air Force, 1961. Benjamin Franklin fellow of the Royal Soc. of Arts; mem. France-Am. Soc., Mil. Order Fgn. Wars in U.S., Am. Legion, Pilgrims of U.S. (chmn., pres.), St. George's Soc., New Eng. Soc., English-Speaking Union, Fgn. Policy Assn., Acad. Polit. Sci., Investment Bankers Assn. Am. (gov. 1953-55), Am. Geog. Soc., Am. Mus. Natural History, Assn. Ex-members Squadron A (gov. 1945-50), Calvin Bullock Forum (pres.), Council on Fgn. Relations, Nat. Inst. Social Scis. (pres. 1950-53), Newcomen Soc., Acad. Am. Poets (dir.), Ends of the Earth, Gargoyle Alumni Assn., Kappa Alpha. Episcopalian. Clubs: Chevy Chase, Metropolitan (Washington); Racquet and Tennis, Recess (gov.), N.Y. Yacht, Bond, Century Assn., River, Williams, Church, Union (N.Y.C.); West Side Tennis (Forest Hills, N.Y.); Denver Country, Mount Royal (Montreal); Edgartown (Mass.) Yacht (commodore), Edgartown Reading Room; White's (London). Author: The Story of Investment Companies, 1959. Home: 1030 Fifth Av New York City NY 10028 Address: 1 Wall St New York City NY 10005

BULLOCK, JOHN MCDONELL, banker; b. Cin., June 21, 1932; s. John R. and Marion (McDonell) B.; student U. Ky., 1950-51; B.A., U. Mich., 1954; LL.B., U. Va., 1959; m. Ann Gibson Vaughan, Dec. 28, 1956; children-Lynn A., John R. II, Amy V. Admitted to Ohio bar, 1959; asso. firm Taft, Stettinius & Hollister, Cin.; 1959-67, partner, 1967-69; sr. v.p. First Nat. Bank Cin., 1969—; asst. sec.-treas., dir., mem. exec. com. Cin. Terminal Warehouses, Inc.; dir. Clopay Corp., Inner-Tank Lining Corp. Trustee, mem. exec. com. Children's Hosp., cin.; trustee, sec. Cin. Symphony Orch.; trustee Hamilton County Community Mental Health and Mental Retardation Bd., 1968- -, chmn., 1968-70; trustee Health Planning Assn. Central Ohio River Valley, Providence Hosp., St. Francis Hosp., St. Mary Hosp. Mem. Am., Ohio, Cin. bar assns., Ohio Bankers Assn., Robert Morris Assos., Delta Tau Delta. Clubs: Queen City, Gyro (Cin.); Ryland Lakes Country (Covington, Ky.). Home: 6749 Wetheridge Dr Cincinnati OH 45230 Office: P O Box 1038 Cincinnati OH 45201

BULLOCK, JOHN RICE, lawyer; b. Covington Ky., July 16, 1906; s. John R. and Harriet (Dulaney) B.; A.B., U. Ky., 1928; LL.B., Yale, 1930; LL.D., U. Cin., 1963; m. Marion McDonell, 1937; children—Arden Marion (Mrs. William H. P. Robertson), John McDonell. Admitted to Ky. bar, 1930, Ohio bar, 1931; asso. firm Taft, Stettinius & Hollister, 1930—, partner, 1936—; sec., dir. Coca-Cola Bottling Corp. and subsidiaries; pres., dir. Cin. Terminal Warhouses, Inc.; dir. 1st Nat. Bank of Cin., also various corps. Trustee Bethesda Hosp., trustee Cin. Symphony Orch., pres. 1957-61; v.p., cin. Inst. Fine Arts; chmn. United Fine Arts Fund, Cin., 1952; chmn., pres. Community Chest and Council of Cin. Area, Inc., 1966-67; chmn. Cincinnatians United for Good Schools, 1967-68. Mem. U. Ky. Alumni Assn. (pres. 1948), Am., Ohio, Cin. (pres. 1969) bar assns., Phi Beta Kappa, Delta Tau Delta. Republican. Episcopalian. Clubs: Cincinnati Country, Queen City, Optimists, Commercial (Cin.) Ryland Lakes Country. Recess, Commonwealth, Gyro. Home: 2496 Grandin Rd Cincinnati OH 45208 Office: Dixie Terminal Bldg Cincinnati OH 45202

BULLOCK, KENNETH C., educator; b. Pleasant Grove, Utah, Sept. 8, 1918; s. Irving and Cora M. (Carlson) B.; B.S., Brigham Young U., 1940, M.A., 1942; Ph.D., U. Wis., 1949; m. Annie Alena Gardiner, Sept. 8, 1938; children—Kenneth G., Virginia, Mary A., Sherilyn. Research asst. U. Wis., 1942-43, 48-49; instr. geology Brigham Young U., 1943-48, asst. prof., 1948-52, asso. prof. geology, 1952-57, prof., 1957—, chmn. dept., 1956-62; field geologist U.S. Mining, Smelting & Refining Co., summers 1947-48, Interstate Brick Co., summers 1949-50; geol. engr. Columbia-Geneva Steel Co., summers, 1951-52, Columbia Iron Mining Co., 1953-54, 60. Served from ensign to lt. (j.g.), USNR, 1944-46. Fellow Geol. Soc. Am.; mem. Am. Inst. Mining and Metall. Engrs., Mineral. Soc. Am., Nat. Assn. Geology Tchrs., Geology Tchrs., Utah Acad. Arts, Sci. and Letters, Utah Geol. Assn., Sigma Xi, Sigma Gamma Gamma Epsilon. Author: Principles of Optical Mineralogy, 1955; Geology of Lake Mountain, Utah, 1961; Minerals and Mineral Localities of Utah, 1960; Minerals of Utah, 1967; Iron Deposits of Utah, 1971; co-author Uranium, Where It Is and How To Find It, 1954. Home: 1035 N 900 E Provo UT 84601

BULLOCK, MAURICE RANDOLPH, lawyer; b. Colorado City, Tex., Aug. 20, 1913; s. Jesse H. and Georgia (White) B.; LL.B., U. Tex., 1936; m. Wilda Marie Frost, Nov. 25, 1939; children—Dan Randolph, Sara Virginia. Admitted to Tex. bar, 1936, mem. firm Silliman & Bullock, Ft. Stockton, Tex., 1936-39; Pecos County atty., 1939-43; pvt. practice law, Ft. Stockton, 1946—; partner firm Bullock, Kerr & Scott, Ft. Stockton, 1963-65; now partner firm Bullock & Scott, Midland, Tex. Past chmn. State Securities Bd. Tex.; Texas adv. com. to Civil Rights Commn., 1960-62; bd. executors Permian Basin Petroleum Mus., Library and Hall of Fame. Dir., mem. exec. com. Tex. Law Enforcement Found., 1964—; past pres. Midland Symphony Assn., Midland-Odessa Symphony and Chorale, Inc. Served as chmn. 1958 Tex. Dem. Conv. Served as spl. agt. Security Intelligence Corps, AUS, 1943-46. Fellow Am., Tex. bar founds.; mem. Am. (house of dels. 1958-62), Trans-Pecos (pres. 1964-65), Midland County bar assns., State Bar Tex. (pres. 1955-56) Southwestern Legal Found., Tex. Trial Lawyers Assn., Am. Judicature Soc. (past dir.), Permian Basin Petroleum Assn. (dir.), Ft. Stockton Hist. Soc. (dir.), Big Bend Trail Assn. (past v.p.), Pecos Country (past pres.), West Tex. (past v.p.) chambers commerce, Order of Coif. Democrat. Methodist. Lectr. on oil and gas and securities law. Home: 3200 Racquet Club Dr Midland TX 79701 Office: Midland Nat Bank Bldg Midland TX 79701

BULLOCK, ROBERT OLIVER, aerodynamics engr.; b. Chgo., Apr. 16, 1913; s. Oliver and Olga (Neef) B.; B.S., Purdue U., 1934; m. Frances Fay DeGaris, Feb. 19, 1943; children—Charles H., Stephen E. Engr. Panama Canal, 1934-39; supr. Nat. Adv. Com. Aeros., Hampton, Va., 1939-43, sect. head, br. chief, asst. div. chief, Cleve., 1943-57; project engr., chief aerodynamics AiResearch Mfg. Co. Ariz., Scottsdale, 1957—; instr. Case U., 1945; cons. A.E.C., 1954-57. Dir. Scottsdale Players, 1959-62, pres., 1961-62; committeeman Boy Scouts Am., 1956-63. Asso. fellow Am. Inst. Aeros. and Astronautics (Robert H. Goddard award 1967); mem. Am. Soc. M.E., Episcopalian. Editor: NASA Handbook on Design of Axial-Flow Compressors, rev. edit., 1965. Developer design techniques used for turbomachinery in aircraft. Home: 6017 N Invergordon Dr Scottsdale AZ 85253 Office: 402 S 36th St Phoenix AZ 85034

BULLOCK, THEODORE HOLMES, biologist, educator; b. Nanking, China, May 16, 1915 (parents U.S. citizens); s. Amasa Archibald and Ruth (Beckwith) B.; student Pasadena Jr. Coll., 1932-34; A.B., U. Cal. at Berkeley, 1936, Ph.D., 1940; Sterling fellow zoology Yale, 1940-41, Rockefeller fellow exptl. neurology, 1941-42; m. Martha Runquist, May 30, 1937; children—Elsie Christine, Stephen Holmes. Research asso. Yale U. Sch. Medicine, 1942- 43, instr. neuroanatomy, 1943-44; instr. Marine Biol. Lab., Woods Hole, Mass., 1944-46, head invertebrate zoology, 1955-57, trustee, 1955-57; asst. prof. anatomy U. Mo., 1944-46; asst. prof. zoology U. Cal. at Los Angeles, 1946, asso. prof., 1948, prof., 1955-66; Brain Research Inst., U. Cal. at Los Angeles, 1960-66; prof. neuroscis. Med. Sch., U. Cal. at San Diego, 1966—. Fulbright scholar Stazione Zoologica, Naples,

1950-51; fellow Center Advanced Study in Behavioral Scis., Palo Alto, 1959-60. Mem. AEC 2d Resurvey of Bikini Expdn., 1948. Fellow A.A.A.S.; mem. Am. Soc. Zoologists (chmn. comparative physiology div. 1961, pres. 1965), Am. Physiol. Soc., Soc. Gen. Physiologists, Am. Acad. Arts and Scis., Nat. Acad. Scis., Am. Philos. Soc., Phi Beta Kappa, Sigma Xi. Author (with G.A. Horridge) Structure and Function in the Nervous Systems of Invertebrates, 2 volumes, 1965. Home: 7281 Rue Michael La Jolla CA 92037

BULMAN, JAMES CORNELIUS, state judge; b. Greenfield, Mass., July 24, 1911; s. James Henry and Mary (Shea) B.; B.S., U. Mass., 1933; LL.B., Fordham U., 1940; m. Marian B. McLaughlin, Mar. 23, 1935; children—Georgia (Mrs. Douglas K. Goss), James Cornelius, Sarah Shea. Spl. agt. FBI, 1942-46; admitted to N.Y. bar, 1946, R.I. bar, 1947; trial lawyer firm Boss, Conlan, Keenan, Bulman & Rice, Providence, 1947-64; judge R.I. Superior Ct., 1964—. Mem. Am., R.I. (pres. 1963-64) bar assns., Nat. Conf. Bar Presidents, Inst. Jud. Adminstrn., Nat. Conf. State Trial Judges. Home: 53 Washington St Newport RI 02840 Office: Providence County Courthouse Providence RI 02908

BULMAN, JOHN NOEL THOMPSON, lithographer; b. Winnipeg, Manitoba, Can., Dec. 25, 1900; s. William John and Lily (Thompson) B.; grad. Royal Mil. Coll., Kingston, Ont.; m. Ruth Odell Antliff, June 3, 1925; children—Ruth Elizabeth (Mrs. George Frederick Bondar), William John Antliff, Nancy Jean (Mrs. Antony Kingsmill Stephens). Apprentice plate maker Lithographic Trade, 1920-25; supt. Bulman Bros., Ltd., 1925-30, sales mgr., 1934-38, pres., gen. mgr., chmn. board; dir. Norfield-Bulman Ltd., Winnipeg, Bulloch's Ltd., Cable Ltd., Wawanesa Mut. Ins. Co., Wawanesa Mutual Life Ins. Co., Western Business Forms, Ltd. Mem. bd. regents United Coll. Past pres. Canadian Mfrs. Assn., Manitoba div. Canadian Red Cross Soc. Mem. United Church of Can. Rotarian (past pres.). Clubs: Manitoba; National Travel (N.Y.C.). Home: 967 McMillan Av Winnipeg 9 Manitoba Canada

BULOFF, JOSEPH, actor; b. Wilno, Lithuania; s. Benjamin and Sarah (Buloff); ed. abroad; m. Luba Kadison, 1925; 1 dau., Barbara. Actor, dir. in Yiddish and English; appeared in over 200 plays on stage, 25 on Broadway, 10 off Broadway; appeared in more than 200 live and tape television shows, 18 movies; appeared in Poland, Vienna, Paris, London, Roumania, Buenos Aires, Brazil, Uruguay, S. Africa, Israel, U.S. Address: 40 W 67th St New York City NY 10023

BULOVIC, BOZDAR, gum co. exec.; b. Chgo., June 29, 1922; s. Nicholas and Rose (Radoja) B.; B.S., U.S. Merchant Marine Acad., 1946; B.S., Northwestern U., 1949; m. Ann Rogulic, Dec. 21, 1946; 1 son, Mark. With Wm. Wrigley Jr. Co., Chgo., 1949-, supr. factory operations, 1960-62, v.p., 1962-. Served with U.S. Merchant Marine, 1944-46. Mem. Tau Beta Pi. Home: 332 Gatesby Rd Riverside IL 60546 Office: 410 N Michigan Av Chicago IL 60611

BULSHEFSKI, VERONICA, naval nursing officer; b. Ashley, Pa., Feb. 2, 1916; d. George and Roseann (Matthews) Bulshefski; diploma nursing U. Pa. Hosp. Sch. Nursing, 1937; B.S. in Nursing Service Adminstrn., Ind. U., 1956; M.S. in Mgmt., U.S. Naval Postgrad. Sch., 1962. Apptd. Nurse Corps. U.S. Navy, 1940, advanced through grades to capt., 1965; assigned naval hosps., Pearl Harbor and Aiea Heights, Hawaii, World War II; chief nursing services naval hosps., Beaufort, N.C., 1956-57, Guam, 1958-59, Jacksonville, Fla., 1959-61, Pensacola, Fla., 1962-64, Oakland, California, 1964-66; former dir. Navy Nurse Corps. Mem. Am. Nurses Assn., Ind. U. Alumni Assn., Assn. Mil. Surgeons U.S., Pi Lambda Theta. Home: 17 Grandview Av Wilkes-Barre PA 18702

BULTMAN, FRITZ, painter, sculptor; b. New Orleans, Apr. 4, 1919; s. Anthony F. and Pauline (Angele) B.; student New Orleans Arts and Crafts Sch., Munich (Germany) Prep. Sch., New Bauhaus, Chgo., Hans Hofmann Sch. Fine Arts, N.Y.C.; m. Jeanne Lawson, Dec. 24, 1943; children—Anthony Frederick IV, Johann. Tchr., Grad. Art Sch., Hunter Coll., 1959-63, Sch. Edn., Pratt Inst., 1958-59, 62-63; cons., artist-in-residence in fine arts Provincetown Fine Arts Work Center, Provincetown, Mass., 1968-72; exhbns. include Hugo Gallery, N.Y.C., 1947-50, Kootz Gallery, N.Y.C., 1951-53; one-man shows include Stable Gallery, N.Y.C., 1958, Martha Jackson Gallery, N.Y.C., 1959, Delgado Mus., New Orleans, 1959, Mayer Gallery, N.Y.C., 1960, Stadler Gallery, Paris, France, 1960-63, Tibor de Nagy Gallery, N.Y.C., 1963-65, Arts Club, Chgo., 1965. Vice pres. Bultman Mortuary Co., New Orleans, 1954—. Mem. Tougaloo (Miss.) Coll. Art Com. Italian Govt. scholar, 1950-51; Fulbright fellow in France, 1964-65; recipient Sculpture award Am. Show, Art Inst. Chgo., 1964. Home: 176 E 95th St New York City NY 10028 Office: 3338 St Charles Av New Orleans LA 70215

BULTMANN, RUDOLF KARL, theologian; b. Wiefelstede, Germany, Aug. 20, 1884; s. Arthur and Helene (Stern) B.; ed. univs. Tübingen, Berlin, Marburg (all Germany); D.Theol., U. Marburg, 1920, Dr. phil. h.c., 1959; D.D., U. St. Andrews, 1935; D.S. Th., Syracuse U., 1959; m. Helene Feldmann, Aug. 6, 1917; children—Antje (Mrs. R. Lemke), Gesine (Mrs. Malte Diesselhorst). Heilke. Instr. N.T. sci. U. Marburg, 1912-16; asst. prof. N.T. sci. U. Breslau (Germany), 1916-20; prof. U. Giessen (Germany), 1920-21, U. Marburg, 1921-51, now emeritus. Mem. Soc. Bibl. Lit. and Exegesis (hon.). acads. Oslo, Heidelberg Göttingen (corr.). Academia Goethena (corr. Sao Paulo, Brazil). Evangelical religion. Author; Jesus, 1926; Glauben und Verstehen, Vol. I, 1933, Vol. II, 1954, Vol. III, 1960, Vol. IV, 1965; Das Evangelium des Johannes, 1941; Primitive Christianity in Its Contemporary Setting, 1956 (German edit. 1949) Jesus Christ and Mythology, 1958; (with others, edited by H.W. Bartsch) Kerygma and Myth, 1961; History and Eschatology; The Presence of Eternity, 1962; (with Karl Kundsin) Form Criticism, 1962; History of the Synoptic Tradition, 1963 (German edit. 1921); Existence and Faith; Theology of the New Testament, 2 vols. (German edit. 1953); This World and the Beyond; (with others) Translating Theology into the Modern Age; Die Drei Johannesbriefe, 1969. Address: Calvin St 14 Marburg on the Lahn Germany

BUMBRY, GRACE ANN, mezzo soprano; b. St. Louis, Jan. 4, 1937; d. Benjamin and Melzia (Walker) Bumbry; student Boston U., 1954-55, Music Acad. West, 1956-59; studied with Lotte Lehmann, Northwestern U., also fgn. countries; H.H.D. (hon.); m. Andreas Jaeckel, July 5, 1963. Operatic debut Paris Opera, 1960; concert and operatic appearances in Europe, Japan, Bayreuth, Germany and U.S., also command performance The White House; performed Met. Opera, N.Y.C., Royal Opera House Covent Garden, London, La Scala Milan, Vienna Stateopera, Teatro Colon Buenos Aires; recs. for Deutsche Grammophon, Angel, London and RCA. Recipient John Hay Whitney award, 1959. Mem. Zeta Phi Beta, Sigma Alpha Iota. Home: Villa Arasio Lugano-Montagnola Switzerland Office: care Met Opera Assn Lincoln Center Plaza New York City NY

BUMGARNER, JOHN CARSON, Sr., oil co. exec.; b. Tulsa, Feb. 5, 1908; s. Aaron Alvin and Lottie Esther (Turkington) B.; student U. Tulsa, 1925-26; B.S., U. Ill., 1929; m. Susan Elizabeth Nall, Nov. 6, 1937; children—Betty Sue, John Carson. Staff accountant Haskins & Sells, C.P.A.'s, Tulsa, 1929-40; sec.-treas. Lawson Petroleum Co., Tulsa, 1940-42, v.p., 1942-44; sec.-treas. Wood River Oil & Refining Co., Inc., Wichita, Kan., 1944-54; controller Mid- Continent Petroleum Corp., Tulsa, 1954-55, D-X Sunray Oil Co., 1955- 58, Sunray DX Oil Co., Tulsa, 1958-68; asst. controller Sun Oil Co. DX Div., 1968-70, mgr. gen. accounting Sun Oil Co., 1970—. C.P.A., Tex. Mem. Financial Execs. Inst. (past pres. Okla.), Nat. Assn. Accountants (past pres. Wichita), Am. Inst. C.P.A.'s, Am. Petroleum Inst. Presbyn. Home: 3714 S Delaware Pl Tulsa OK 74105 Office: Sun Bldg Tulsa OK 74120

BUMGARNER, RAY QUINCY, hosp. supt.; b. Wauneta, Kan., Nov. 8, 1902; s. Walter A. and Emma (Goode) B.; student Marquette U., 1922-23, U. Wis. at Milw., 1940-41; m. Thelma E. Leyden, Oct. 16, 1945; 1 son, Ray Quincy. Engaged in pvt. business, 1923-40; bus. adminstr. Milw. County instns., 1940-46; with VA, 1946—, dir. VA Center, Dayton, O., 1959—. Pres. Met. Hosp. Fedn., Dayton, 1967; chmn. adv. com. hosp. facilities Dayton Hosp. Planning Council, 1968; mem. exec. com., interagy bd. U.S. Civil Service Examiner So. Ohio, 1968; chmn. Fed. Exec. Assn., 1968. Served to capt. AUS, 1943- 46. Decorated Army Commendation medal; recipient awards D.A.V., Am. Legion, V.F.W. Fellow Am. Coll. Hosp. Adminstrs. Club: Walnut Grove Country (Dayton). Home: 4100 W 3d St Dayton, OH 45428. Office: 4100 W 3d St Dayton OH 45428

BUMKE, JAOCHIM, educator; b. Berlin, Germany, Mar. 31, 1929; s. Erich and Irmgard (Gunther) B.; student U. Heidelberg (Germany), 1947-50, U. Hamburg (Germany), 1950-52, U. Paris (France), 1952-53; Ph.D., U. Heidelberg, 1953; m. Sylvia Meyer-Wolde, July 15, 1954; children—Ulrike, Christian. Came to U.S., 1958. Asst., then privatdozent U. Heidelberg, 1954-58; asst. prof. Johns Hopkins, 1958-61; faculty Harvard, 1961-65, prof. German, 1964-65; prof. Free U. Berlin, 1965- 69, U. Cologne (Germany), 1969—. Mem. Internat. Arthurian Soc., Deutscher Germanistenverband, Kleist Gesellschaft. Author: Wolframs Willehalm, 1959; Wolfram von Eschenbach, 1964; Studien zum Ritterbegriff im 12 und 13 Jahrhundert, 1964; Die romanisch-deutschen Literaturbeziehungen in Mittelalter, 1967; Die Wolfram von Eschenbach-Forschung seit 1945, 1970. Home: Kölnstrasse 52 Niederzier 5161 Germany

BUMP, BOARDMAN, investment mgr.; b. Pittsfield, Mass., Dec. 8, 1908; s. Charles Henry and Esther Elizabeth (Boardman) B.; A.B. magna cum laude, Amherst Coll., 1930; M.B.A., Harvard, 1932; m. Eleanor Myrick, June 28, 1933; children—Carolyn (Mrs. John B. Marsh), Daniel Boardman, Susan (Mrs. Pavel Van#86cura), and Jonathan. Asst. purchasing agt. Mt. Holyoke Coll., 1932- 34, comptroller, 1934-51, asst. treas., 1939-42, treas., 1942—, v.p., 1951-54, trustee, 1955—; partner Morrison & Bump, 1955, Morrison, Bump & Morse, 1956—; trustee Home Savs. Bank (Boston); dir. Liberty Mut. Ins. Co., Liberty Mut. Fire Ins. Co., Diversification Fund, Inc. Boston Fund, Inc., Exchange Fund of Boston, Liberty Life Assurance Co. of Boston, Vance Sanders Spl. Fund, Inc., Depositors Fund of Boston, Inc., Capital Exchange Fund, Inc., Leverage Fund of Boston, Inc., Fiduciary Exchange Fund, Inc., Boston Common Stock Fund, Inc., 2d Fiduciary Exchange Fund, Inc. Mem. Eastern Assn. Coll. and U. Bus. Officers (sec.-treas. 1941-48, pres. 1949), Phi Beta Kappa. Club: Harvard of Boston. Home: 6 Linden St Wellesley MA 02181 Office: 24 Milk St Boston MA 02109

BUMP, MORRISON MCKEIVY, chem. co. exec.; b. N.Y.C., Feb. 27, 1919; s. Milan R. and Mary (Morrison) B.; grad. Phillips Acad., 1937; student Yale, 1938-39; m. Helen Frances Kelley, Oct. 26, 1940; children—Cynthia Coburn (Mrs. Neusbaum), Barbara Morrison, Morrison, Lawrence Winslow. With Union Paste Co., Boston, 1939-59, territorial sales, sales mgmt., 1940-58, pres., 1956-59; chmn. So. Adhesives Corp., Richmond, Va., 1955-59; dir. marketing United Carbon Co., Houston, 1959-62, also exec. v.p., dir. United Carbon Co., Inc., 1959-62; now with Ashland Oil, Inc., v.p. Ashland Chem. Co. div., exec. asst. to mgmt.; dir. subsidiaries Cobia Boats, Inc., Modern Fiberglass, Inc., Polaris Plastics, Inc., Tri State Plastic Molding Co., Inc., Kyova Pipe Co.; dir. United Rubber & Chem. Corp., United Carbon France S.A., Carbon Black Export Inc., United Producing Corp., 1959-62. Lectr., Am. Mgmt. Assn., N.Y.C. Mem. sch. bd., Duxbury, Mass., 1950-54, chmn., 1954-56. Mem. Internat. Inst. Synthetic Rubber Producers (dir. 1960-62), Sales Execs. Club N.Y., Am. Mgmt. Assn. (planning council). Clubs: Bellefonte Country, Ashland Boat (Ashland). Home: 616 Amanda Furnace Dr Ashland KY 41101 Office: care Ashland Oil Inc Ashland KY 41101

BUMP, W. NELSON, ch. found. exec.; b. Syracuse, N.Y., Apr. 21, 1906; s. Fred and Caroline Decker (Haughwout) B.; grad. Hotchkiss Sch., 1924; grad. engrng. sch. Harvard, 1928; m. Catharine Richardson, Oct. 14, 1939; children—Lucile, William, Frederick, Catharine. With Am. Airlines, Boston, N.Y., 1929-60, regional v.p., 1944-60; pres. Products Internat., Inc., 1962-63; exec. v.p. Episcopal Ch. Found., 1963—. Bd. dirs. U.S.O., Nat. Travelers Aid Assn., Antique Auto Museum of Mass.; trustee Marlboro Coll. Home: Ferris Hill Rd Office: 815 2d Av New York City NY 10017

BUMPERS, DALE LEON, gov. of Ark.; b. Charleston, Ark., Aug. 12, 1925; s. William Rufus and Lattie (Jones) B.; student U. Ark., 1943, 46-48; J.D., Northwestern U., 1951; m. Betty Lou Flanagan, Sept. 4, 1949; children—Dale Brent, William Mark, Margaret Brooke. Pres. Charleston Hardware and Furniture Co., 1951-66; admitted to Ark. bar, 1952; pvt. practice, Charleston, 1952-70; operator Angus cattle farm, 1966-70; gov. of Ark., 1970—. Pres. Charleston Sch. Bd., 1969-70. Served with USMC, 1943-46. Mem. Charleston C. of C. (pres.). Methodist. Home: Charleston AR 72933 Office: State Capitol Little Rock AR 72201

BUNCE, STANLEY CHALMERS, educator, chemist; b. Bayonne, N.J., Aug. 21, 1917; s. Arthur Chalmers and Elizabeth (Sticht) B.; B.S. in Chemistry, Lehigh U., 1938, M.A., 1942; Ph.D. in Chemistry, Rensselaer Poly. Inst., 1951; m. Lillis Adelle Jackson, Oct. 2, 1943; children—Gale Elizabeth (Mrs. Andrew Schmidt), Judith Preston (Mrs. Ralph Turner), James Arthur. Secondary sch. tchr. Hershey (Pa.) Indsl. Sch., 1939-41, Bound Brook (N.J.) High Sch., 1941-43; research chemist Johns-Manville Corp., 1943-46; mem. faculty Rensselaer Poly. Inst., Troy, N.Y., 1946- -, prof. chemistry, 1958—, asst. chmn. dept., 1967—. Fellow A.A.A.S.; mem. Am. Chem. Soc. (chmn. Eastern N.Y. sect. 1961), Fedn. Am. Scientists, Sigma Xi, Phi Lambda Upsilon. Author: (with others) Principles of Chemistry, 1966; An Approach to Physical Science, 1967; also research publs. Home: Taconic Lake Rd Grafton NY 12082 Office: Dept Chemistry Rensselaer Poly Inst Troy NY 12181

BUNCE, WILLIAM KENNETH, fgn. service officer; b. Gallipolis, O., Aug. 31, 1907; s. Thurman D. and Elma (Coughenour) B.; A.B., Otterbein Coll., 1930, H.L.D. (hon.), 1946; M.A., Ohio State U., 1933, Ph.D., 1939; M.A., Columbia, 1944; m. Alice Shively, June 13, 1933; children—Sylvia (Mrs. William Duvall, Jr.), Julia E. (Mrs. Donald Elfving), Peter W., Michael R. Tchr., Westerville (Ohio) High Sch., 1931-33; teaching asst. history Ohio State U., 1934-36; lectr. Matsuyama (Japan) Higher Sch., 1936-39; prof. history, head dept. social sci. N.M. State Tchrs. Coll., 1939-40; Prof. history, chmn. dept. Otterbein Coll., 1940-41, dean coll., 1941-43; chief religious and cultural resources div. hdqrs. SCAP, Tokyo, Japan, 1945-52; chief program planning staff U.S. Information Service, Am. embassy, Tokyo, 1952-54, acting pub. affairs officer, 1954-55; assigned Nat. War Coll., 1955-56; dir. U.S. Information Service, India, also counselor of embassy for pub. affairs, New Delhi, 1956-61; asst. dir. for Far East, USIA, Washington, 1961-65; counselor for pub. affairs, Seoul, Korea, 1965-68, spl. asst. for polit. and mil. affairs, 1968-69, cultural affairs adviser, 1969—. Served to lt. comdr. USNR, 1943-46. Decorated Legion of Merit. Editor, contbr.: Religions in Japan, 1955. Home: 3217 Old Dominion Blvd Alexandria VA 22305 Office: USIA 1776 Pennsylvania Av Washington DC 20547

BUNCH, FRANKLIN SWOPE, architect; b. Madison, Ind., Jan. 4, 1913; s. Walker Franklin and Susan Beatrice (Swope) B.; B.S. in Arch., U. Fla., 1934; m. Virginia Aurelia Boggs, June 8, 1937; children—Franklin Swope, Dean Boggs. Draftsman, designer, architect and constrn. supr. various Fla. architects, 1934-41; archtl. engr. U.S. Engrs. Dist. Office, Jacksonville, Fla., 1942-43, Jacksonville Naval Air Sta., 1944-45; partner Kemp, Bunch & Jackson, Architects, Inc., Jacksonville, 1946-69, sr. v.p., 1970—, projects include S. Central Home Office Prudential Ins. Co. Am., Jacksonville, gen. offices Seaboard Coast Line R.R., Jacksonville, Jacksonville Civic Auditorium, Fla. State Prison, Raiford Hdqrs. Bldg. State Rd. Dept., Tallahassee. Pres. Fla. Bd. Architecture, 1959-61; mem. com. on exams. Nat. Council Archtl. Registration Bds., 1961-62; pres. bldg. code adv. bd., Jacksonville, 1949-68; mem. examining com. Jacksonville, 1949—; chmn. bldg. codes adjustment bd. Jacksonville Consol. Govt.; mem. housing com. Jacksonville Council on Aging, 1962. Pres. Little Theatre of Jacksonville, 1952-53. Fellow A.I.A.; mem. Fla. Assn. Architects (pres. 1947-48), Jacksonville Symphony Assn., Jacksonville Jr. (chmn. luncheon club 1938), Jacksonville Area (chmn. city, county, state affairs com. 1963, chmn. fed. assistance 1949-68) chambers commerce, Phi Kappa Tau. Meth. (past chmn. ofcl. bd.). Clubs: San Jose Country (sec. 1964, gov. 1964-67), Ye Mystic Revellors, River (Jacksonville). Home: 4300 Gadsden Ct Jacksonville FL 32207 Office: Coast Line Bldg Jacksonville FL 32202

BUNCH, MARION E., psychologist; b. Rochester, Ky., Dec. 5, 1902; s. Marion Estel and Montie (Taylor) B.; A.B., U. Ky. 1925: A.M., Washington U., 1926; Ph.D., U. Chicago, 1934; m. Alice Pardon, Sept. 18, 1926; 1 son, Rob R. Mem. faculty Washington U., St. Louis 1926-48, prof. psychology, chmn. dept., 1949; prof. psychology Ill., 1948-49. Mem. Am., Midwestern (pres. 1961-62), Mo. (pres. 1950-51) psychol. assns., So. Soc. for Philosophy and Psychology (pres. 1955-56), A.A.A.S. Home: 4521 Pershing Av St Louis MO 63108

BUNCHMAN, HERBERT HARRY, business exec.; b. Joppa, Ill., Feb. 6, 1906; s. Arthur D. and Katherine (Brenningmeyer) B.; B.S., U. Ill., 1928; m. Mary Halleran, June 26, 1936; children—Herbert Harry II, John D., Mary Jo. With Crane Co., Chgo., 1946-56, treas., 1948-52, dir., 1951-56, v.p., 1952-56; sec., treas. Plough, Inc., Memphis, 1956-68; pres. Gen. Investments Co., 1959—. Mem. Investment Anaysts Soc., Financial Execs. Inst., Nat. Assn. Accountants, Newcomen Soc. Clubs: Executives; Chicago Athletic Assn. Home: 4410 Normandy Av Memphis, TN 38117.

BUNDY, FREDERICK MCGEORGE, banker; b. Grand Rapids, Mich., Jan 4, 1900; s. McGeorge and Mary Goodhue (Hollister) B.; grad. Berkshire Sch.; A.B., Yale, 1921; M.B.A., Harvard Bus. Sch., 1923; m. Anita Hollister, Nov. 10, 1928; children—Frederick McGeorge, Patty Hollister (Mrs. David B. Wray), Samuel Swift, David Hollister. With Gorton Corp., Inc., 1923-67, v.p., 1937-46, treas., 1943-46, pres., 1946- 58, chmn. bd., 1958-67; pres. Cape Ann Bank & Trust Co., 1958-70, chmn. bd., 1970—. Pres. trustees Addison Gilbert Hosp., Gloucester, 1950-52, life trustee. Served as 2d lt. F.A., U.S. Army, 1918. Mem. North Atlantic Fillet Council (pres. 1956-59), Nat. Fisheries Inst. (pres. 1953), C. of C. (pres. 1940-44), Phi Beta Kappa. Clubs: Country (Brookline, Mass.); Essex County (Manchester, Mass.); Yale (pres. 1944- 46) (Boston). Home: 102 Bridge St Manchester MA 01944

BUNDY, HARVEY HOLLISTER, food co. exec.; b. Cambridge, Mass., May 1, 1916; s. Harvey Hollister and Katherine Lawrence (Putnam) B.; B.A., Yale, 1938; M.B.A., Harvard, 1940; m. Edith Southerland Wright, May 29, 1943; children—Harvey Hollister III, Harriet Southerland (Mrs. William T. Burgin), Peter Putnam, Rodman Richards. Accountant, Lybrand Ross Bros. & Montgomery, C.P.A.'s Boston, 1940-41; with Gorton Corp., Gloucester, Mass., 1946—, treas., 1948—, financial v.p., 1958-69, exec. v.p., 1969—, also dir.; dir. Cape Ann Bank & Trust Co., Point Chehalis Packers Inc., Blue Water Sea Foods, Ltd. , Gorton-Pew, Ltd., Can. Agincourt Foods Ltd. (Can.), Canapro Ltd. (Magdalen Islands), Gloucester Peruvian S.A. (Peru). Trans World Seafood, Inc., N.Y.C. Mem. Manchester (Mass.) Sch. Com., 1948-54, chmn., 1951-53, pres. Internat. Friendship Hospitality Trips, Inc.; chief agt. Class of '38, Yale Alumni Fund, 1967—; mem. com. to visit applied math., math. and statistics, bd. overseers Harvard Coll., 1970—. Bd. dirs. Internat. Friendship League; trustee Addison Gilbert Hosp., Gloucester. Served to maj. AUS, 1941-46. C.P.A., Mass. Mem. Nat. Fisheries Inst. (dir. 1955—, pres. 1961-62, chmn. bd. 1962-63), Am. Inst. Accountants, Mass. Soc. C.P.A.'s. Home: Smith's Point Manchester MA 01944 Office: 327 Main St Gloucester MA 01930

BUNDY, JEAN DAVIS, educator: b. Seattle, Sept. 21, 1924, s. Leo Wesley and Edna (Torgerson) B.; B.A., Wash. State U., 1950; M.A., U. Wis., 1952, Ph.D., 1957; student U. Dijon, U. Paris (France), 1953-55; M.A., Colby Coll., 1964; m. Ann Hemenway Becker, Aug. 17, 1957; 8 children—Christopher Davis, Alison Fairchild, Lisa Lanham, Nicholas Bennett. From instr. to asso. prof. U. Tex., 1957-63; prof. French, Colby Coll., 1963-69, Dana prof. French lit., 1969—, chmn. dept., 1963—. Cons. Ednl. Testing Service, Coll. Entrance Exam. Bd. Served with inf. AUS, 1943-46. Decorated Bronze Star; Fulbright scholar 1953-55, 67-68. Mem. Am. Assn. U. Profs., Modern Lang. Assn., Am. Assn. Tchrs. French, Internat. des Etudes Francaises, Phi Beta Kappa, Phi Kappa Phi, Sigma Kappa Phi. Editor: Three French Comedies, 1965. Address: Route 1 Box 40 Waterville ME 04901

BUNDY, MCGEORGE, found. exec.; b. Boston, Mar. 30, 1919; s. Harvey Hollister and Katharine Lawrence (Putnam) B.; A.B., Yale, 1940; m. Mary Buckminster Lothrop, June 10, 1950; children—Stephen, Andrew, William, James. Polit. analyst Council Fgn. Relations, 1948-49; vis. lectr. Harvard, 1949-51, asso. prof. govt., 1951-54, dean faculty arts and scis., 1953-61, prof., 1954-61; spl. asst. to the President for nat. security, 1961-66; pres. Ford Found., 1966—. Mem. Am. Polit. Sci. Assn., Phi Beta Kappa. Author: On Active Service (with Stimson), 1948; The Strength of Government, 1968. Editor: Pattern of Responsibility, 1952. Home: 1040 Fifth Av New York City, NY 10028. Office: 320 E 43d St New York City NY 10017

BUNDY, MERLE, physician; b. Salem, Ind., Apr. 23, 1918; s. Trestle Merle and Reba (Zink) B.; A.B., Ind. U., 1939, M.D., 1942; M.P.H., U. Mich., 1946; (postgrad.) N.Y.U., 1956; m. Marjorie Davis, Nov. 8, 1941; children—Karen (Mrs. Edmund Truelove), Pamela (Mrs. Brian Bestafka). Intern U.S. Marine Hosp., Seattle, 1942-43, resident surgery, 1943; chief tuberculosis control Ind. State Bd. Health, 1946-51; chief tuberculosis control and med. services Pitts. Dept. Health, 1951-54; works physician Jones & Laughlin Steel Corp., Pitts.,

1954-58; asst. med. dir. U.S. Steel Corp., Pitts., 1958-61, med. dir., 1961—; clin. asst. prof. occupational medicine U. Pitts. Mem. gov.'s com. peneumoconiosis and residency adv. com. Pa. Dept. Health, 1968—; mem. coal mine health research adv. council Dept. HEW, 1970—; dir. Western Pa. Comprehensive Health Plan Agy., 1969—, Occupational Health Inst., 1969—. Adv. bd. John J. Kane Hosp., 1968—; dir. Health Research and Services Found., 1967—. Served with USPHS, 1942-47. Named Man of Year, Pitts. Newspaper Guild, 1954. Mem. Tb League Pitts. (dir.), Am. Cancer Soc. (dir.), Indsl. Med. Assn. (pres. 1970), Am. Acad. Occupational Medicine, Am. Pub. Health Assn., Am. Acad. Preventive Medicine, Allegheny County Med. Soc., A.M.A., Pa. Med. Soc., Am. Coll. Chest Physicians. Home: 2290 Country Club Dr Pittsburgh PA 15241 Office: 600 Grant St Pittsburgh PA 15230

BUNDY, WILLIAM PUTNAM, writer; b. Washington, Sept. 24, 1917; s. Harvey Hollister and Katharine Lawrence (Putnam) B.; A.B., Yale, 1939, M.A. (hon.), 1961; M.A., Harvard, 1940, LL.B., 1947; m. Mary Acheson, Jan. 30, 1943; children—Michael, Carol, Christopher. Admitted to D.C. bar, 1947; with firm Covington & Burling, Washington, 1947-51; with CIA, 1951-61; staff dir. President's Commn. Nat. Goals, 1960; dep. asst. sec. def. internat. security affairs, 1961-63; asst. sec. def. internat. security affairs, 1963-64; asst. sec. state te for East Asian and Pacific affairs, 1964-69; vis. prof., research asso. Center Internat. Studies, Mass. Inst. Tech., 1969—. Fellow Yale U. Corp.; trustee Am. Assembly, N.Y. Mem. Council Fgn. Relations (bd. dirs.), Harvard Law Sch. Assn. D.C. (pres. 1961). Democrat. Home: 108 Brattle St Cambridge MA 02138 Office: 30 Wadsworth St Cambridge MA 02142

BUNGE, ELDO FREDERICK, educator; b. Linton, N.D., Feb. 10, 1908; s. John G. and Caroline (Schneider) B.; A.B., Luther Coll., Decorah, Ia., 1931; A.M., State Univ. Ia., 1932; Ph.D., Univ. of Ia, 1940; m. Evelyn Nay, 1931; children—Jeanine, Joanne. Teacher of English, Iowa Falls (Ia.) High Sch., 1932-34; instr. Ellsworth Jr. Coll., Iowa Falls, 1934-38; asso. prof. English Augustana Coll., Rock Island, Ill., 1938-43; prof. English and head, dept. English Washburn Univ., Topeka, Kan., 1946—. Active YMCA. Lt. cmdr. USNR since 1945; active duty as armed guard officer on S.S. Livingston Roe, 1943-44; exec. officer V 12, N.R.O.T.C. Unit, Univ. of Wis., 1944-46; in active status since 1946. Mem. Nat. Council Tchrs. of English, Modern Lang. Assn. Lutheran. Club: Fortnightly. Contbr. articles profl. jours. Home: 2405 W 19th St Topeka KS 66604

BUNGE, MARIO AUGUSTO, educator, physicist, philosopher; b. Buenos Aires, Argentina, Sept. 21, 1919; s. Augusto and Marie (Müser) B.; doctorate physico-math. scis., U. Nat. de La Plata, 1952; m. Marta Irene Cavallo, Feb. 5, 1959; 1 son, Eric Russell; children by previous marriage—Carlos A., Mario A.J. Instr. theoretical physics U. Buenos Aires, 1946-52; prof. theoretical physics univs. Buenos Aires and La Plata, 1956-59; prof. philosophy U. Buenos Aires, 1957-62; vis. prof. philosophy U. Pa., 1960-61, U. Tex., 1963; vis. prof. physics and philosophy Temple U., 1963-64, U. Del., 1964-65; prof. philosophy McGill U., 1966—. Founder, sec. gen. Universidad Obrera Argentina, 1938-42; assessor Internat. Union History and Philosophy of Sci., 1969—. Fellow Conselho de Pesquisas Físicas, Brazil, 1953, Fundación E. Santamarina, Argentina, 1954, Alexander von Humboldt-Stiftung, 1965-66. Guggenheim fellow, 1972-73. Mem. Acad. Internat. de Philosophie des Sci., Inst. Internat. de Philosophie, Assn. Ríoplatense de Lógica y Filosofía Cientifica (pres. 1959-63). Author: Causality, 1959; Metascientific Queries, 1959; La cinemática del electrón relativista, 1960; Intuition and Science, 1962; The Myth of Simplicity, 1963; Foundations of Physics, 1967; Scientific Research, 2 vols., 1967; also numerous articles. Editor: Studies in the Foundations, Methodology and Philosophy of Science, 1967—; Library of Exact Philosophy, 1970—; mem. editorial bd. Internat. Jour. Theoretical Physics, Folia Humanistica. Home: 4444 Sherbrooke W 608 Montreal 215 Quebec Canada

BUNGE, WALTER RICHARD, publishing co. exec.; b. Fond du Lac, Wis., June 19, 1911; s. Richard H. and Dorothea (Wagner) B.; M.Accounting, Madison (Wis.) Coll.; m. Gertrude Clara Wendland, June 29, 1932; children—Walter Richard, Carol W. (Mrs. James D. Newman), Margaret Ruth. Engaged as pub. accountant, Milw., 1941-42; mgr. budgets Allis-Chalmers Mfg. Co., 1942-54, Inland Steel Co., 1955-61; dir. financial planning Hughes Aircraft Co., 1961- 62; dir. financial operations Jos. Schlitz Brewing Co., 1962-66, controller, 1966-68; v.p., treas., dir. Zerand Corp., 1968-70; tchr. U. Wis. Grad. Sch., 1955-56; chmn. bd. Northwestern Pub. House, Milw., 1951-56, mgr., 1971—; cons. publishing, 1952—. Corp. mem. United Community Service Greater Milw., 1952-65, mem. gen. budget com., chmn. budget com. for property, 1952-56; pres. Wis. Lutheran Synod Found., 1965—. C.P.A., Wis. Fellow Budget Execs. Inst. (pres. 1951-52; Neil Dennen award 1962), Wis. Soc. C.P.A.'s (sec. 1949-51), Beta Alpha Psi (life). Republican. Author: Managerial Budgeting for Profit Improvement, 1968. Contbr. to Managerial Budgeting, 1964. Home: 3158 N 104 St Wauwatosa WI 53222

BUNGER, WILLIAM BOONE, educator, chemist; b. Alta Vista, Kan., Feb. 14, 1917; s. Harry T. and Lila (Beagel) B.; B.S., Washburn Coll., 1940; M.S., Kan. State U., 1941, Ph.D., 1949; m. Ida Margaret Chitwood, May 29, 1941; s. dau., Jane Margaret (Mrs. Richard E. Winn). Chemist, Hill Packing Co., Topeka, 1939, Hercules Powder Co., 1941-45; instr. chemistry Kan. State U., 1947-49; asst. prof., then asso. prof. Auburn U., 1949-64; prof. chemistry, chmn. dept. Ind. State U., Terre Haute, 1965—; vis. prof. Oak Ridge Nat. Lab., 1951, 53, Ala. State Chem. Lab., 1955, Humble Oil and Refining Co., 1957. Mem. A.A.A.S., Am. Chem. Soc. (chmn. Auburn sect. 1953-54), Ind. Acad. Sci., Sigma Xi, Phi Lambda Upsilon. Author: (with others) Organic Solvents, 3d edit., 1971. Home: 3327 Poplar St Terre Haute, IN 47803.

BUNKE, HARVEY CHARLES, educator; b. Oshkosh, Wis., Nov. 7, 1922; s. Harvey and Charlotte (Zahn) B.; B.S., U. Ill., 1947, M.S., 1949, Ph.D., 1951; m. Margaret Carlsten, May 29, 1947; children—Charles Martin, Richard Carlsten, Anna Christine. Prof., Coll. Bus., State U. Ia., 1953-63, prof. pub. policy, 1963, chmn. dept. econs., 1964-65; pres. Western Wash. State Coll., 1965- 67; dir. undergrad. studies, Ind. U., Bloomington, 1967-69, coordinator overseas projects Bus. Sch., 1967—, asso. dean academic affairs, 1969—. Served with USAAF, 1941-44. Rotarian. Author: The Liberal Dilemma, 1964; American Economic History, 1969. Home: 3526 Park Lane Bloomington IN 47401

BUNKER, BRUCE FREEMAN, lawyer; b. Porterville, Cal., Dec. 10, 1924; s. Beulan Freeman and Clara (Williams) B.; A.A., Porterville Jr. Coll., 1946; J.D., U. So. Cal., 1950; m. Betty Monroe, June 11, 1949; children—Suzanne Margaret, Carolyn Ruth, Robin Anne. Admitted to Cal. bar, 1951, since practiced in Bakersfield; dep. dist. atty., 1952-55; partner firm Wagy, Bunker & Hislop, 1959—. Sec., dir. San Joaquin TV Transmission Co., 1964- -. Pres. Kern County council Camp Fire Girls, 1967-69; mem. adv. com. Bakersfield Nursing Program, 1964—. Served with AUS, 1943-46. Mem. State Bar Cal. (exec. com., conf. dels., chmn. 1968-69, mem. disciplinary bd. 1970—), Am., Kern County (past pres.) bar assns., Internat. Foot Printers Assn., Phi Alpha Delta. Methodist (trustee). Clubs: Exchange (past pres.), Stockdale Country (Bakersfield). Home: 2511 Kent Dr Bakersfield CA 93306 Office: 2821 H St P O Box 2428 Bakersfield CA 93303

BUNKER, EDMUND CASON, broadcasting exec.; b. Balboa, C.Z., Sept. 24, 1915; s. Edmund C. and Geneva (Read) B.; B.S., Coll. of Charleston, 1936; postgrad. U. S.C. Law Sch., 1939-42; m. Katherine Aubrey Gooding; children— Katherine B. Emory, Virginia Forsyth. Radio announcer, writer, 1934-38, radio sales, 1938-42; exec. Avery-Knodel Corp., 1946-48; sales exec. ABC Network, 1948-49; account exec. CBS-TV Network, 1949-52, gen. sales mgr. CBS-TV Pacific Coast Network, 1952-54, gen. mgr. CBS-TV Milw., 1954-56 v.p., dir. sta. relations CBS-TV Network, 1956-58, v.p., gen. mgr. sales, 1958-59; v.p. CBS, Inc., 1959-61; exec. v.p. Froedert Div., Basic Products Corp., Milw., 1961-62; pres. Radio Advt. Bur., N.Y.C., 1962-65; v.p., dir. broadcast Foote, Cone & Belding, 1965-66; sr. v.p. Interpub., Inc., 1966-68; pres., gen. mgr. radio sta. KFI, Earle C. Anthony, Inc., 1968—. Bd. dirs. Radio Advt. Bur., John Tracy Clinic. Served from ensign to lt. USNR, 1941-45. Mem. Greater Los Angeles Press Club, Mayflower Soc. Clubs: Shenorock, Washington Press, Canadian, Bel-Air Country. Home: 1159 Calle Vista Dr Beverly Hills, CA 90210. Office: 141 N Vermont Av Los Angeles CA 90004

BUNKER, ELLSWORTH, ambassador; b. Yonkers, N.Y., May 11, 1894; s. George R. and Jean Polhemus (Cobb) B.; A.B., Yale, 1916, LL.D., 1959; LL.D., Mt. Holyoke Coll., 1962, Windham Coll., 1963; m. Harriet Allen Butler, Apr. 24, 1920 (dec.); children—Ellen (Mrs. Fernando Gentil), John Birkbeck, Samuel Emmet; m. 2d, Carol C. Laise, Jan. 3, 1967. Dir. Nat. Sugar Refining Co., 1927-66, pres. 1940, chmn. bd., 1948-51; dir. Centennial Ins. Co.; trustee Atlantic Mut. Ins. Co.; U.S. ambassador to Argentina, 1951, Italy, 1952-53, India, 1956-61, also Nepal, 1956-59; mediator Dutch- Indonesian dispute over W. New Guinea, 1962; cons. to sec. of state, 1963; U.S. rep. on council OAS, 1964-66; ambassador-at-large, 1966-67; ambassador to Viet-Nam, 1967—; pres. Am. Nat. Red Cross, 1953-56. Dir. or trustee Hampton Inst., Inst. for Internat. Social Research, Asia Found., Expt. in Internat. Living (hon.), Vt. Council on World Affairs (hon. pres.), Fgn. Policy Assn., New Sch. for Social Research (hon.), Bur. Social Sci. Research. Decorated Grand Cross Knight Republic of Italy, Presdl. Medal of Freedom with Spl. Distinction, 1963, 68. Mem. Council on Fgn. Relations, Am. Acad. Arts and Scis. Home: Putney VT 05346 Office: American Embassy Saigon Republic of Viet-Nam

BUNKER, GEORGE MAVERICK, company exec.; b. Chgo., Jan. 2, 1908; s. Gerald DeForest and Helen Louise (Blanchard) B.; B.S., Mass. Inst. Tech., 1931; m. Natalie Keeney, 1959; 1 son, Gerald E. Began career with Campbell Soup Co., Chicago, 1931-34; indsl. engr. Wilson & Company, 1934-36; partner A. T. Kearney & Co., management engrs., 1936-1942; v.p. mfg. The Kroger Co., Cin., 1942-49; pres., gen. mgr., dir. Trailmobile, Inc., 1949-52; pres., gen. mgr., dir. The Martin Co., Balt., 1952-59, chmn. bd., 1952-61; pres., dir. Martin-Marietta Corp., N.Y.C.; chmn. exec. com., dir. Bunker-Ramo Corp.; dir. Am. Security & Trust Co., Bulova Watch Co., Nuclear Corp. Am., Fla. Capital Corp., Washington Senators. Dir. Fed. City Council, Washington. Clubs: M.I.T., Wings (N.Y.C.); Nat. Aviation, Burning Tree, 1925 F St., Columbia Country, Carlton, Metropolitan (Washington). Home: 4940 Indian Lane NW Washington DC 20016 Office: 277 Park Av New York City NY 10017 also 815 Connecticut Av N W Washington DC 20006

BUNKER, JOHN PHILIP, educator, physician; b. Boston, Feb. 13, 1920; s. Philip H. and Emily L. (Glover) B.; B.A., Harvard, 1942, M.D., 1945; m. Mary Franklin Bush, Aug. 12, 1944; children—Jane Williams (Mrs. Henry Mason Morfit, Jr.), Katherine Ford, John Philip, Emily Lane. Intern Mass. Gen. Hosp., Boston, 1945-46, resident, 1949-50; resident George Washington Hosp. Washington, 1948-49; instr. anesthesia Harvard Med. Sch., 1950-52, asso., 1952-55, asst. clin. prof., 1955-60; prof. Stanford Med. Sch., 1960—. Chmn. nat. halothane study NRC, 1963-68. Served to lt. (j.g.), M.C., USNR, 1946-47. Mem. A.M.A., Am. Soc. Anesthesiologists, Am. Soc. for Pharmacology and Exptl. Therapeutics, Assn. U. Anesthetists. Editor: Education in Anesthesiology. Home: 722 Mayfield Av Stanford CA 94305

BUNKLEY, JOEL WILLIAM, Jr., educator; b. Washington, Nov. 12, 1916; s. Joel William and Sally (Williams) B.; A.B., Coll. William and Mary, 1938; LL.B., U. Miss., 1946; postgrad. Yale, 1950; m. Rubye Barnes, May 16, 1942; 1 son, Joel William III. With U.S. Dept. Commerce, 1938-40; admitted to Miss. bar, 1946; prof. law, dean U. Miss. Sch. Law, 1946—. Commr. on Uniform State Laws, 1969—. Served to lt. comdr. USNR, 1941-45. Mem. Miss. State Bar, Am. Bar Assn., Phi Delta Phi, Omicron Delta Kappa. Episcopalian. Rotarian. Author: Divorce and Separation in Mississippi, 1957. Home: Box 132 University MS 38677

BUNN, EDWARD BERNARD, clergyman, educator; b. Balt., Mar. 25, 1896; s. Sebastian Philip and Philomena (Fortmann) B.; A.B., Loyola Coll., Balt., 1917; student St. Andrew-on-Hudson, M.A., 1921; Woodstock Coll., Md., 1921-30; Ph.D., Gregorian U., Rome, Italy, 1930; hon. LL.D., Fordham U., 1938, Brandeis U., 1958, Notre Dame U., Wheeling Coll., Seattle U., Boston Coll., Coll. Holy Cross, 1964, Nat. U. Ireland, 1965, Gannon Coll., Erie, Pa., 1965; L.H.D, Am. U., 1964, St. Joseph's Coll., 1965, Georgetown U., 1968; Ed.D., Catholic U. Am., 1968; Litt.D., George Washington U., 1964. Entered Soc. of Jesus, 1917; ordained priest Roman Cath. Ch., 1929. Asst. prof. Eng. lit. Fordham U., 1923-26; dean of boys Bklyn. Prep. Sch., 1930-31; asso. prof. systematic and adolescent psychology Canisius Coll., Buffalo, 1931-34; asso. prof. systematic and adolescent psychology and asst. dir. Child and Adolescent Guidance Clinic, Fordham U., 1934-38; pres. Loyola Coll., Balt., 1938-47; regional dir. studies of colls. and univs. of Md. province, 1944-52; became pres. university, 1952, chancellor, 1964—; regional dir. studies Md. province Soc. Jesus. Former chmn. panel Regional War Labor Bd., Md. Ednl. Conf. Postwar Orgn. Trustee Loyola U., Balt., chmn. emeritus bd. trustees Consortium Univs. Wash. Met. Area. Decorated Comdr.'s Cross Order Merit (Germany); Order of Merit Rank of Grand Cross (Peru); Grand Gold Badge of Honor (Austria). Mem. Jesuit Edn. Assn. (mem. exec. com.), Nat. Cath. Ednl. Assn., Assn. for Higher Edn., N.E.A., Assn. Am. Colls., Am. Council on Edn., Newcomen Soc. Club: Cosmos (Washington). Author, producer of pageants, Spirit of Canossa, Civilization. Address: Georgetown University, Washington, DC 20007.

BUNN, GEORGE, educator; b. St. Paul, May 26, 1925; s. Charles and Harriet (Foster) B.; B.S. in Elec. Engring., U. Wis., 1946; LL.B., Columbia, 1950; m. Fralia S. Hancock, July 9, 1949; children—Peggy Joan, Peter Wilson, Matthew George. Admitted to D.C. bar, 1950, Wis. bar, 1969, also U.S. Supreme Ct. bar; atty. Gen. Counsel's Office, AEC, 1950-51; asso., then partner firm Arnold, Fortas & Porter, Washington, 1951-61; mem. staff preparedness subcom. U.S. Senate, 1957; counsel to President's adviser on disarmament, 1961; gen. counsel U.S. Arms Control and Disarmament Agy., 1961-69; vis. prof., prof. Law Sch., U. Wis., Madison, 1969—. Mem. U.S. delegation 18 Nation Disarmament Conf., 1962-66, dep. chmn. U.S. delegation, 1966-67; mem. U.S. delegation UN Disarmament Commn., 1965; U.S. rep. Western 4 Jurists Group, 1963-66; alternate U.S. rep. with rank of ambassador 18 Nation Disarmament Conf., 1968. Mem. com. on campus tensions Am. Council on Edn., 1969-70. Candidate D.C. Dem. Central Com., also candidate D.C. delegation Dem. Nat. Conv., 1960. Served with USNR, 1943-46. Mem. Fed., Wis. bar assns., Am. Soc. Internat. Law. Home: 1902 Capital Av Madison WI 53705

BUNN, GEORGE P., Jr., corp. exec.; b. Atchison, Kan., Oct. 17, 1917; s. George P. and Helen (Eastham) B.; student Carlton Coll., 1935-36; B.S. in Mech. Engring., U. Kan., 1940; m. Alberta Grace Jones, June 19, 1941; children—Linda Louise, Marcia Beth, George P. III. Jr. exptl. engr. Clark Bros. Co., 1940-42; sr. gas engr. Shell Oil Co., 1942-50; exec. asst. to v.p. Columbian Carbon Co., Houston, 1950-57 gen. mgr. mid-continent area Houston, 1957-59, v.p. oil and gas operations, N.Y.C., 1959-62; v.p., dir. Cities Service Oil Co., 1962—; v.p. Cities Service Co., N.Y., 1965- -; pres. Cities Service Internat., Brussels, Belgium, 1965—. Mem. Natural Gas Processors Assn., Ind. Natural Gas Assn., Mid-Continent Oil and Gas Assn., Beta Theta Pi, Theta Tau. Presbyn. Clubs: Union League (N.Y.C.); Tulsa. Home: 161 Av Winston Churchill Brussels Belgium Office: Cities Service Bldg Bartlesville OK 74003

BUNN, GEORGE WALLACE, Jr., banker; b. Springfield, Ill., Jan. 28, 1890; s. George Wallace and Ada (Richardson) B.; Litt. B., Princeton, 1912; L.H.D., Blackburn Coll., 1956; m. Melinda Jones, Oct. 9, 1920; children—Sally, George Wallace, Linda. Reporter N.Y. Sun, 1912-14; with John W. Bunn and Co., wholesale grocers, 1919-28; with Springfield Marine Bank, 1928—, pres. now chmn. bd.; dir. Capitol Grocery Co., Ill. Nat. Ins. Co. Served as 1st lt., 333 Machine Gun Bn., 1917-19. Pres. Springfield War Fund Council, 1942-46, Springfield Park Bd., 1932-33, Springfield Pub. Library Bd., 1939-42; trustee Lawrenceville (N.J.) Sch., Blackburn Coll., Carlinville, Ill. Mem. Abraham Lincoln Hist. Assn. (pres.). Republican. Presbyn. Clubs: Sangamo, Ill. Country (Springfield); University (Chicago); Princeton (N.Y.). Home: 1630 W Laurel St Springfield IL 62704 Office: Springfield Marine Bank Springfield IL 62701

BUNN, JOHN FRANKLIN, Jr., investment banker; b. Phila., Dec. 5, 1896; s. John Franklin and Clara C. (Stolpp) B.; student U. Pa., 1920; m. Emma D. Irwin, Sept. 22, 1956; children—Elsie R. Edith S.M., Jacquelyn (Mrs. John C. Gwynn). With Harris Forbes & Co., N.Y.C., 1920-30, Chase Harris Forbes & Co., N.Y.C., 1930-33; with Bioren & Co., mems. N.Y. Stock Exchange, Phila., 1933-69, sr. partner, 1950—; dir., pres. Eastern Gas & Water Investment Co. and subsidiaries; dir. Hamburg Broom Works, Duquesne Natural Gas Co., Ky.-Ohio Gas Co., Southwestern Va. Gas Co. Mem. N.Y. Stock Exchange. Pres., dir. Childrens Cruise Playground Assn., Phila. Served to 2d lt., inf., U.S. Army, 1917-18. Mem. Nat. Assn. Security Dealers (gov.). Republican. Episcopalian. Clubs: Bankers (N.Y.C.); Union League (Phila.); Hillsborough (Pompano Beach, Fla.); Westmoreland (Wilkes-Barre, Pa.); Huntingdon Valley Country (Abington, Pa.); Bald Peak Colony (Melvin Village, N.H.). Home: 1603 Harris Rd Chestnut Hill Philadelphia PA 19118 Office: 2 Penn Center Philadelphia PA 19102

BUNN, KENNETH RODNEY, artist; b. Denver, June 1, 1935; s. Robert Miles and Lucille (Hostick) B.; ed. U. Utah. Exhbtd. group shows Nat. Sculpture Soc., N.Y.C., 1969-70, Nat. Acad. Design, N.Y.C., 1970, Soc. Animal Artists Traveling Show, 1970; rep. pvt. collections. Recipient Nat. Sculpture Soc. Bronze medal, 1969; Nat. Acad. Design Barnett award, 1970. Fellow Nat. Sculpture Soc.; mem. Soc. Animal Artists. Home: Elizabeth CO 80107 Office: 2496 W 2d Av Denver CO 80223

BUNN, RONALD FREEZE, educator; b. Jonesboro, Ark., Aug. 11, 1929; s. S. Neal and Velma (Freeze) B.; B.A., Southwestern at Memphis, 1951; M.A., Duke, 1953, Ph.D., 1956; postgrad. Universitat zu Koln, 1954-55; m. Rita E. Hess, Mar. 29, 1955; children—Robin Gail, Katharine Sue, Lisabeth Joann. Instr., U. Tex., Austin, 1956-59, asst. prof., 1960-64; asso. prof. La. State U., Baton Rouge, 1964-67; asso. prof. U Houston, 1967-69, prof., dean Grad. Sch., 1969—; cons. Council of Grad. Sch. Bd. dirs. S.W. Center for Urban Research, Houston, Univs. Anti-War Fund. Mem. So. (mem. exec. council), Southwestern (past v.p.) polit. sci. assns., Phi Beta Kappa, Omicron Delta Kappa. Author: Politics and Civil Liberties in Europe, 1967; German Politics and the Spiegel Affair: A Case Study of the Bonn System, 1968. Contbr. articles profl. jours. Home: PO Box 220M Route 2 Cypress TX 77429 Office: Grad Sch U Houston Houston TX 77004

BUNN, WILLARD, Jr., banker; b. Springfield, Ill., Oct. 27, 1913; s. Willard and Ruth (Regan) B.; A.A., Springfield Jr. Coll., 1934; student U. Wis., 1935; m. Jane Huntington Hatcher, Oct. 11, 1939; children—Ada Octavia (Mrs. Peter Casper), Willard III, Robert H. With Springfield Marine Bank, 1935—, pres., 1961—, also dir.; dir. Ill. Bell Telephone Co., Ill. Nat. Ins. Co., Sangamo Electric Co., Bunn-O-Matic Corp.; v.p., dir. Bunn Capitol Co. Mem. lay adv. bd. St. John's Hosp., Springfield; lay trustee Springfield Jr. Coll. Mem. Psi Upsilon. Republican. Roman Catholic. Home: 2101 Willemoore Av Springfield IL 62704 Office: 114 S 6th St Springfield IL 62701

BUNNEL, KEITH DWIGHT, mfg. co. exec.; b. Colony, Kan., July 10, 1923; s. Lloyd H. and Ruby (Lewis) B.; B.A. in Bus. Adminstrn., U. Kan., 1946; m. Joan Stewart, June 21, 1946; children—Diane, David. Adminstrv. mgr. Internat. Minerals & Chem. Corp., Chgo., 1946-62; exec. v.p., then pres. O. Hommel Co., Pitts., 1962-66; asst. to v.p., then v.p. finance Westinghouse Air Brake Co., Pitts., 1966-68, v.p., group exec. transp., 1968—. Mem. Financial Execs. Inst. Presbyn. Home: 164 Warwick Dr Pittsburgh PA 15241 Office: 3 Gateway Center Pittsburgh PA 15222

BUNNELL, C. STERLING, banker; b. Loraine, O., 1901; s. Sterling Haight and Rebecca (Lapham) B.; Ph.B., Yale, 1924; m. Naneen Burnap, Feb. 18, 1946; 1 dau., Shirley (Mrs. Peter Fitzhugh Dawson). With First Nat. City Bank, N.Y.C., 1930—, sr. v.p., 1958—, chmn. credit policy com., dir., 1959-66; chmn. Del. Separater Co., Siemens Inc.; dir. Munich Mgmt. Corp., Siemens Overseas Investments Ltd., Inspiration Consol. Copper Co., B.A.S.F.-Wyandotte, Inc. Pres., Miriam Osborn Meml. Home Assn., Rye, N.Y. Mem. Council Fgn. Relations Inc., Kingsley Trust Assn., Pilgrims U.S., Winthrop Trust Assn., English Speaking Union (N.Y. br.). Clubs: Knickerbocker, University (N.Y.C.). Home: Cornwall CT 06753 Office: 399 Park Av New York City NY 10022

BUNNELLE, ROBERT ELLSWORTH, newspaper pub.; b. Urbana, O., Aug. 21, 1903; s. Elmer Ellsworth and Olivemay (Colbert) B.; student Wittenberg Coll., 1921-23, Northwestern U., 1924; m. Margaret Elizabeth Harrison, Oct. 30, 1926 (dec.); m. 2d, Frances McKay Peace, August 23, 1962. Reporter Lynchburg (Va.) News, Asheville (N.C.) Times, also mng. editor Bristol (Va.) Bull., 1925-31; with A.P., 1931-54, beginning as editor, Atlanta, successively chief of bur., mng. exec., London, Eng., chief bur., Can., 1931-49, gen. exec., N.Y.C., 1949-54; pub. Asheville Citizen-Times, 1954—, pres., 1958—; dir. 1st Union Nat. Bank of N.C.; v.p., dir. Multimedia, Inc. Mem. 6th Dist. Adv. Council Naval Affairs; mem. N.C. Hwy. Commn., 1957-61; pres. Greater Asheville Council, Council, 1962-64. Trustee Meml. Mission Hosp., 1968-69. Mem. N.C. Press Assn. (pres.

1962-63), Am. Corrs. Assn. (pres. London 1943-44), Parliamentary Press Gallery Assn. (dir. 1950-51). Asheville C. of C. (pres. 1967), Phi Kappa Psi. Clubs: Biltmore Forest Country, Mountain City (pres. 1959), City (Asheville); Sphinx. (Raleigh); Nat. Press (Washington); Overseas Press (N.Y.C.); Greenville (S.C.) Country; Southern Cross (Little Cayman Island, N.W.I.). Home: Lower Waverly Plantation Pawleys Island SC 29585 Office: 14 O'Henry Av Asheville NC 28801

BUNNETT, JOSEPH FREDERICK, educator, chemist; b. Portland, Ore., Nov. 26, 1921; s. Joseph and Louise Helen (Boulan) B.; B.A., Reed Coll., 1942; Ph.D., U. Rochester, 1945; Fulbright scholar Univ. Coll., London Eng., 1949-50; Guggenheim fellow, Fulbright scholar U. Munich (Germany), 1960-61; m. Sara Anne Telfer, Aug. 22, 1942; children—Alfred Boulan, David Telfer, Peter Sylvester. Mem. faculty Reed Coll., 1946-52, U. N.C., 1952-58; mem. faculty Brown U., 1958-66, prof. chemistry, 1959-66, chmn. dept., 1961-64; prof. chemistry U. Cal. at Santa Cruz, 1966—. Erskine vis. fellow U. Canterbury, New Zealand, 1967. Trustee Reed Coll. Mem. Am. Acad. Arts and Scis., A.A.A.S., Am. Chem. Soc. (editor jour. Accounts of Chem. Research), Chem. Soc. (London), Gesellschaft Deutscher Chemiker. Contbr. papers in field. Home: 608 Arroyo Seco Santa Cruz CA 95060

BUNSHAFT, GORDON, architect; b. Buffalo, May 9, 1909; s. David and Yetta (Bunshaft) B.; B. Arch., Mass. Inst. Tech., 1933, M.Arch. (fellow), 1935; D.F.A. (hon.), U. Buffalo, 1962; m. Nina Elizabeth Wayler, Dec. 2, 1943. Rotch travelling fellow, 1935-37; chief designer Skidmore, Owings & Merrill, 1937-42, partner, N.Y.C., Chgo., San Francisco and Portland, Ore., 1949- -; partner charge design Lever House, Fifth Av. br. Mfrs. Trust Co. (both N.Y.C.), Conn. Gen. Life Ins. Co. (Hartford), H.J. Heinz Co., Ltd. (Hayes Park, Middlesex, Eng.), Banque Lambert (Brussels, Belgium), Beinecke Rare Book and Manuscript Library, Yale (New Haven). Reynolds Metals Co. Bldg. (Richmond, Va.), Albright-Knox Art Gallery (Buffalo), Lyndon Baines Johnson Library and East Campus Library and Research Bldg. U. Tex. at Austin, Joseph H. Hirshhorn Mus. and Sculpture Garden (Washington), Am. Can Co. (Greenwich, Conn.). Vis. com. Sch. Architecture, Mass. Inst. Tech., 1940-42, Harvard, 1954-60, Yale, 1959-62; mem. President's Commn. on Fine Arts, 1963—, Mem. internat. council Mus. Modern Art. Served As maj. C.E., AUS, 1942-46. Recipient Mass. Inst. Tech. and Rotch travelling fellowships for study Europe and N. Africa, 1935-37; Brunner award Nat. Inst. Arts and Letters, 1955; medal of honor N.Y. chpt. A.I.A., 1961; Chancellor's medal U. Buffalo, 1969, Academician N.A.D. Fellow A.I.A. mem. Nat. Inst. Arts and Letters, Municipal Art Soc. N.Y., Buffalo Fine Arts Acad. (hon.). Club: Architectural League (N.Y.C.). Home: 200 E 66th St New York City NY 10021 Office: 400 Park Av New York City NY 10022

BUNT, FREDERICK BENJAMIN, Jr., coll. adminstr.; b. Flushing, N.Y., Aug. 15, 1926 s. Frederick Benjamin and Mildred (Jahoda) B.; B.S., Queens Coll., 1950; M.S., State U. Coll. at New Paltz, 1955; Ed.D., Columbia chrs. Coll., 1964; m. Catherine Johnson, July 9, 1955; children—Cathleen, Cynthia, Patricia. Grade sch. tchr., Merrick, N.Y., 1950-55; asso. prof. dir. student teaching State U. Coll. at New Paltz, 1955-65; dir. student teaching Nat. Coll. Edn., Evanston, Ill., 1965-66; dean Sch. Edn., Pace Coll., N.Y.C., 1966—. Served with USNR, 1944-46. Recipient N.Y. State Regents War Service scholarship, 1957. Mem. N.Y. Assn. Student Teaching (exec. com. 1964-65, 67-69), Kappa Delta Pi (past pres. Northeastern Ill. alumni chpt.). Home: 1 Howard St New Paltz NY 12561 Office: Pace Coll Plaza New York City NY 10038

BUNTEN, HUGH, lawyer, corp. exec.; b. Ransom, Kan., Dec. 14, 1915; s. Peter Wiley and Dordy (Ford) B; A.B., Baker U., 1936; J.D., Northwestern U., 1939, postgrad., 1948-50; m. Ruth Elizabeth Ross, Mar. 23, 1940; children—Hugh Harwood, Ruth Joy. Admitted to Ill. bar, 1939; atty. Nat. Tea Co., 1939- 42; atty. Butler Bros., 1945-49; atty. Signode Corp., 1949-50, atty., asst. sec., 1950-55, sec., atty., 1955—, v.p., 1961—. also dir.; sec., atty. Paslode Co., Signode Internat., Signode Overseas Co., Signode Internat., Ltd. Mem. Chgo. Crime Commn. Served as lt. USNR, 1942-45. Mem. Am. Soc. Corporate Secs., Ill. Mfrs. Assn., Chgo. Assn. Commerce and Industry. Republican. Methodist. Mason. Home: 1123 Hull Terrace Evanston IL 60202 Office: 2600 N Western Av Chicago IL 60647

BUNTEN, WILLIAM ANDREW, surgeon; b. Pawnee City, Neb., Aug. 22 1898; s. William Muir and Mary M. (Milligan) B.; student Grinnell Coll., 1916-18; B.Sc., U. Neb., 1920, M.D., 1922; fellow surgery Mayo Clinic, 1927-29; m. Elsa Louise Boesel, July 17, 1923; children—John A., William Andrew. Intern Univ. Hosp., Omaha, 1922-23, house surgeon, 1922; gen. practice, Worland, Wyo., 1923-27; chief subdiv. neurosurgery Grace Hosp., Detroit, 1929-30; cons. neurosurgery Providence and Woman's Hosp., Detroit, 1929-30; propr. Bunten Clinic, Cheyenne, Wyo., 1932-58; pres. staff Meml. Hosp., Cheyenne, 1943; surgeon U.P. R.R. 1938-48, dist. surgeon Employees Hosp. Assn., 1948—; chief staff DePaul Hosp., Cheyenne, 1962, chief surgery, 1959-61, mem. exec. com., 1956-66. Mem. med. adv. bd. Wyo. SSS, 1940-45. Fellow Internat. Coll. Surgeons (regent for Wyo.), A.M.A. (del. 1952-56, pres. conf. presidents, 1952, bd. dirs. grass roots conf. 1947- 52, mem. joint commn. on accreditation hosps. 1956-65, mem. council med. edn. 1954-64; v.p. 1965-66), Wyo. (pres. 1945), Laramie County (pres. 1938) med. socs.; sr. fellow Southwest Surg. Congress; mem. Am., Western assns. ry. surgeons, World Med. Assn. (chmn. Wyo.), Phi Rho Sigma. Presbyn. (elder). Rotarian. Contbr. numerous articles in field. Home: 320 W 4th Av Cheyenne WY 82001 Office: VP Dispensary 15th and Warren Av Cheyenne WY 82001

BUNTIN, THOMAS EUGENE, Jr., lawyer; b. Dothan, Ala., Apr. 29, 1929; s. Thomas Eugene and Eleanor (Neely) B.; LL.B., U. Ala., 1955; m. Mabel Hodges, Sept. 5, 1950 (div., 1963); children—Elizabeth, Thomas Eugene III, Ellen; m. 2d Zelma Penton, Sept. 21, 1963; children—Catherine, Rosemary, Charles Douglas. Salesman, Norhtcutt Gen. Tire Co., Dothan, 1949; exec. trainee Wilson & Co., meat packers, Dothan, 1950; admitted to Ala. bar, 1955, since practiced in Dothan; partner Buntin & Buntin, 1955-58; pvt. practice, 1958-67; sr. partner Buntin & White, Dir. Poplar Head Co., F & G Farms, Ramada Inn of Dothan. Chmn. March of Dimes, 1956; mem. Dothan Indsl. Devel. Bd., 1966- -. Served with inf. A.U.S., 1950-52. Recipient certificate of appreciation from Pres. Nixon for 10 years service as govt. appeal agt. for local Selective Service System, 1969—, awards for scholastic achievement Bur. Nat. Affairs and Sigma Delta Kappa, 1955, award for outstanding student in Wills, 1955. Mem. Am., Ala., Houston County (past pres.) bar assns., Ala. Trial Lawyers Assn., Def. Research Inst., Am. Judicature Soc., Farrah Law Soc., Ala. Law Inst., Dothan C. of C. (past dir.), Dothan Jr. C. of C. (past pres.), Sigma Nu, Phi Alpha Delta. Presbyn. (deacon). Elk. Club: Dothan Country. Home: 1524 Choctaw St Dothan AL 36301 Office: 313 N Foster St Dothan AL 36301

BUNTING, CYRENUS GARRITT, finance co. exec.; b. Ann Arbor, Mich., Apr. 10, 1914; s. Russel W. and Mattie (Janes) B.; A.B., U. Mich., 1934, J.D., 1937; m. Helen Jean Talbot, Apr. 19, 1941; children—Gregory T., Kirk R. Admitted to Mich. bar, 1937; practice in Detroit, 1937-42; procurement specialist U.S. Army, 1942-43; with Fenestra Inc., 1946-59, sec.-treas., 1951-59; mgmt. cons., Detroit, 1960-61; treas. Studebaker Corp., South Bend, Ind., 1961- 64; v.p. Assos. Enterprises Co.; treas. Assos. Corp. N.Am., 1965-70, v.p. finance, 1970—. Pres. Detroit Assn. Credit Men, 1955-56; bd. dirs. Mich. Mfrs. Assn., 1957-59. Served to lt. (j.g.) USNR, 1943- 46; PTO. Mem. Tax Execs. Inst. (pres. Detroit 1955-56), Mich. Bar Assn. Home: 18150 Inwood Rd South Bend IN 46614 Office: 1700 Mishawaka Av South Bend IN 46624

BUNTING, GEORGE LLOYD, cosmetics and toiletries co. exec.; b. Balt., Oct. 14, 1909; s. George Avery and Nellie (Bowen) B.; grad. Staunton Mil. Acad., 1928; student Washington Coll., Balt. Bus. Coll., U. Balt., m. Dorothy Williams, Sept. 6, 1933; children—Dorothy Ellen (Mrs. Dorothy B. Duffy), Mary Catherine (Sister Mary Lloyd), George Lloyd, Jr. With Noxzema Chem. Co. (now Noxell Corp.), Balt., 1932—, pres., 1949-63, chmn. bd., 1963. Dir. Proprietary Assn., Greater Balt. Com. Served with U.S. Army, 1944-45. Clubs: Baltimore Country; Hunt Valley Golf; Tamarac (Fla.). Home: Valley Rd Brooklandville, MD 21022. Office: 11050 York Rd Baltimore MD 21203

BUNTING, JAMES FREDERICK, retired assn. exec.; b. Little Falls, N.Y., Aug. 17, 1906; s. James and Lula E. (Cheney) B., B.A., Syracuse U., 1927; M.A., Yale, 1943; H.L.D. (hon.), George Williams Coll., 1963; m. Emma Lee Morgan, Mar. 31, 1931; children—Margaret Jamison (Mrs. William D. Comings, Jr.), Elizabeth Cheney (Mrs. Thomas O. Barnett, Jr.). Mem. staff YMCA Rochester, N.Y., 1927-39, New Haven, 1939-44; gen. sec. YMCA. Schenectady, 1944-50, Newark, 1950-60, Washington, 1960-64, Nat. Council and Nat. Bd. YMCAs U.S., 1964-71, retired, 1971. Recipient George Arents Pioneer medal Syracuse U., 1966. Home: 356 Wyoming Av Millburn NJ 07041

BUNTING, JAMES WHITNEY, coll. pres., cons.; b. Phila., Nov. 23, 1913; s. George Miller Lewis and Helen Elizabeth (Whitney) B.; B.S., U. Pa., 1934, M.A., 1936, M.B.A., 1937, Ph.D., 1946; postgrad. U. Louisville, 1938-39; m. Mildred Eleanor Griscom, Oct. 14, 1939; 1 dau., Helen Whitney. Economist, Pa. State Planning Bd., Harrisburg, 1934-35; gen. freight agt. Preston Trucking Co. (Md.), 1935-36; instr. econs., marketing, finance Jr. Coll. Commerce, New Haven, 1937-39, coll. dean, 1949-50; asst. prof. bus. adminstrn. Hanover (Ind.) Coll., 1939-42, also dir. pub. relations; prof. applied econs. Hobart Coll., Geneva, N.Y., 1945-49, asso. and acting dean, 1946-48, dir. indsl. community program, 1947-48; asst. treas. Market Basket Corp., Geneva, 1948-49; prof. econs., chmn. dept. U. Ga., Atlanta, 1950-51, prof. econs., Athens, 1951-52, dir. bur. bus. research 1951-52; exec. v.p. Oglethorpe U., 1952, pres. 1953-55; prof. finance N.Y. U., 1957-60; cons. higher edn. and research Gen. Electric Co., 1955-62; dean Coll. U. Ga., Bus. Adminstrn., 1962-68; pres. Ga. Coll., Milledgeville, 1968—. Cons. Exchange Bank of Milledgeville; consultation utility costs Ga. Pub. Service Commn.; economist WPB, Washington, 1942. Pres., Citizens Com. for Rye Pub. Schs.; vice chmn. Atlanta Regional Export Expansion Council, 1971—; chmn. com. on pub. affairs Am. Assn. State Colls. and Univs., 1970—. Served as lt. Supply Corps, USNR, 1942-45. Life fellow Internat. Inst. Arts and Letters; mem. Nat. Invest in Am. Com. (pres. nat. council, bd. govs., eastern regional chmn., mem. exec. com.), Am. Econ. Assn., Am. Geog. Soc., Am. Marketing Assn., Am. Acad. Polit. and Social Sci., Nat. Sales Execs., So. Econ. Soc., Gamma Omicron Tau, Delta Sigma Pi, Delta Chi, Beta Gamma Sigma, Phi Kappa Phi. Rotarian. Clubs: Advertising (N.Y.C.); Milledgeville Country. Author: Effective Retail Selling, 1953; Ethics for Modern Business Practice, 1953; Higher Education, A Twenty Year Look Ahead, 1957; Your Share in America's Prosperity, 1960. Author, editor; Bus. Leaders in People's Capitalism, 1959. Editor: Atlanta Econ. Rev., 1950-51; Ga. Bus., 1951-52; contbg. econs. editor Elec. South, 1952-70. Contbr. articles to profl. jours. Home: The Mansion Milledgeville GA 31061

BUNTING, JOHN RICHARD, Jr., banker; b. Phila., June 29, 1925; s. John Richard and Dorothy (McNair) B.; B.S., Temple U., 1950, M.A., 1952; m. Jame Anne Shuttleworth, June 29, 1946; children—Robin Anne, John Richard III. Economist, v.p. Fed. Res. Bank, Phila., 1950-64; economist, v.p., exec. v.p. First Pa. Banking & Trust Co., Phila., 1964-68, pres. and chief exec. officer, 1968—; dir. Fidelity Mut. Life Ins. Co., City Stores, Inc. Finance chmn. Citizens for Arlen Specter mayoral candidate Phila., 1967. Bd. dirs. Girl Scouts Am., Phila., Magee Meml. Hosp.; trustee Drexel Inst. Tech., Beaver Coll., Presyn.-U. Pa. Med. Center. Served with AUS, 1944-46. Recipient 2d ann. John Wanamaker award. Mem. Nat. Assn. Bus. Economists, Pa. C. of C. (dir.), Greater Phila. C. of C. (dir.). Presbyn. Clubs: Manufacturers Country (Oreland, Pa.); Seaview Country (Absecon, N.J.). Author: The Hidden Face of Free Enterprise, 1964. Home: 909 Meeting House Rd Jenkintown PA 19046 Office: SE Corner 15th and Chestnut Sts Philadelphia PA 19101

BUNTING, MARY INGRAHAM, coll. pres.; b. Bklyn., July 10, 1910; d. Henry A. and Mary T. (Shotwell) Ingraham; B.A., Vassar Coll., 1931; M.A., U. Wis., 1932, Ph.D., 1934; m. Henry Bunting, June 22, 1937 (dec.); children—Mary, Charles, William, John. Instr. biology Bennington Coll., 1936-37; instr. physiology, hygiene Goucher Coll., 1937-38; research asst. dept. bacteriology Yale, 1938-40, 48-52, lectr., 1953-55; lectr. dept. botany Wellesley Coll., 1946-47; dean Douglass Coll., Rutgers U., 1955-59; pres. Radcliffe Coll., Cambridge, Mass., 1960—, on leave with AEC, 1964-65. Bd. dirs. Kaiser Found. Hosps., Kaiser Found. Health Plan. Mem. Nat. Sci. Bd., 1965-70, NSF, 1965-70. Mem. Am. Acad. Arts and Scis., Phi Beta Kappa, Sigma Xi. Home: 76 Brattle St Cambridge MA 02138

BUNTON, CLIFFORD ALLEN, educator, chemist; b. Chesterfield, Eng., Jan. 4, 1920; s. Arthur and Edith (Kirk) B.; B.Sc., Univ. Coll., London, 1941, Ph.D., 1945; m. Ethel Clayton, July 28, 1945; children—Julia Margaret, Claire Jennifer, Came to U.S., 1963. Successively asst. lectr., lectr., reader Univ. Coll., 1944-63; prof. chemistry U. Cal. at Santa Barbara, 1963—, chmn. dept., 1967—. Commonwealth Fund fellow U. Columbia, 1948-49; Brit. Council vis. lectr., Chile and Argentina, 1960; vis. prof. U. Cal. at Los Angeles, 1961, U. Toronto, 1962; Mem. policy com. U. Chile-U. Cal. Coop. Program. Mem. Am. Chem. Soc., Chem. Soc. (London). Contbr. profl. jours. Home; 935 Cocopah Dr Santa Barbara, CA 93105.

BUNTON, GEORGE WALLACE, astronomer; b. Covington, Ky., Nov. 16, 1910; s. George Walter and Ina (Case) B.; A.B., U. Cal. at Los Angeles, 1940; postgrad. U. So. Cal., 1941-42; m. Marie Evelyn Jardine, Mar. 30, 1930; 1 dau., Bette Joe (Mrs. Roland P. Michaelis). Technician, planetarium lectr. Griffith Obs., Los Angeles, 1938-51; instr. astronomy U. So. Cal., 1945-46, Golden Gate Coll., San Francisco, 1953-60; mgr. Alexander F. Morrison Planetarium, curator dept. astronomy Cal. Acad. Scis., 1951-61; staff astronomer, mgr. Hawaii Sci. Center, Bishop Mus.; instr. astronomy U. Hawaii, 1963-66. Mem. Astron. Soc. of Pacific, A.A.A.S., Am. Assn. Museums. Home: 130 Ohana St Kailua HI 96734 Office: Bishop Mus Honolulu HI

BUNUEL, LUIS, film dir.; b. Calanda, Spain, Feb. 22, 1900. Films include: Un Chien Andalou, 1929; L'Age d' Or, 1930; Land without Bread, 1936; Los Olvidados, 1950; The Adventures of Robinson Crusoe, 1953; The Criminal Life of Archibald de la Cruz, 1955; La Mort en ce Jardin (Evil Eden), 1956; Nazarin, 1958; Le Fievre monte a El Pao, La Jeune Fille, 1959; The Republic of Sin, 1960; The Young One, 1960; Viridiana, 1961 (prize Cannes Festival); Island of Shame, 1961; El Angel Exterminador, 1962; Diary of A Chambermaid, 1965; Simon of the Desert (prize Venice Festival), 1965; Belle de Jour (Golden Lion St. Mark Venice Film Festival 1967), 1967; The Milky Way, 1969; Tristana, 1970. Address: care of Telimex Division del Norte 2462 Mexico City Mexico*

BUNZEL, JOHN HARVEY, coll. pres.; b. N.Y.C., Apr. 15, 1924; s. Ernest Everett and Hariett (Harvey) B.; grad. Kent Sch., 1942; A.B. magna cum laude, Princeton, 1948; M.A., Columbia, 1949; Ph.D. in Polit. Sci., U. Cal. at Berkeley, 1954; m. Barbara Bovyer, May 11, 1963; children by previous marriage—Cameron, Reed. Instr., San Francisco State Coll., 1953- 56, Mich. State U., 1956-57; asst. prof. Stanford, 1957-63; mem. faculty San Francisco State Coll., 1963-70, prof. polit. sci., chmn. dept., 1967- 70; vis. scholar Center For Advanced Study in Behavioral Scis., Stanford, Cal., 1969-70; pres. San Jose State Coll., 1970—. Mem. Atty. Gen. Cal. Adv. Com. Equal Rights, 1959-60; bd. dirs. Mich. Citizenship Clearing House 1956-57, No. Cal. Citizenship Clearing House, 1958-61. Del. to Democratic Nat. Conv., 1968. Served with AUS, 1943-46. Mem. Am., Western, No. Cal. (pres. 1962; Ann. Presdl. award for outstanding service in the field of polit. sci., 1969) polit. sci. assns. Democrat. Author: The American Small Businessman, 1962; Issues of American Public Policy, 2d edit., 1964; Anti-Politics in America, 1967. Home: 1519 Escondido Way Belmont CA 94002 Office: San Jose State Coll San Jose CA 95114

BUONICONTO, PASQUALE, physician; b. Springfield, Mass., Oct. 27, 1908; s. Antonio and Crestina (Amato) B.; B.S., Yale, 1929; M.D., Royal U., Naples, Italy, 1935; children—Phyllis (Mrs. Patrick Doyle), Mark Buoniconto. Intern St.Luc's Hosp., Montreal, Que., Can., 1935-38; practice medicine, specializing in psychiatry, Danvers, Mass., 1938-39; staff physician Danvers State Hosp., 1939-49; sr. physician in charge Summer St. Dept., Worcester (Mass.) State Hosp., 1949-53; asst. supt. Walter E. Fernald State Sch., Waverly, Mass., 1953-54; supt. Del. Colony, Stockley, 1954-55; med. supt. Wayne County Child Devel. Center, Northville, Mich., 1955—. Fellow Am. Psychiat. Assn., Am. Assn. on Mental Deficiency (councilor, past chmn. Gt. Lakes Region VI); mem. A.M.A., Am. Acad. on Mental Retardation, Assn. Supts., Pub. Residential Facilities for Mentally Retarded, Mass. Med. Soc., Assn. Med. Supts. Mental Hosps. K.C., Rotarian. Address: 16000 Sheldon Rd Northville MI 48167

BURACK, BENJAMIN, educator; b. Chgo., Apr. 28, 1914; s. Hyman and Ida (Glasser) B.; student Chgo. City Jr. Colls., 1931-33; B.S., Ill. Inst. Tech., 1936; M.A., Northwestern U., 1938, Ph.D., 1940. Instr., Chgo. City Jr. Colls., 1940-41; asst. prof. Roosevelt U., Chgo., 1946-47, asso. prof., 1947-56, prof., 1956—. Served to capt. AUS, 1941-46. Fellow Am. Psychol. Assn., A.A.A.S.; mem. Chgo. Psychol. Assn. (past pres.). Asst. editor: The Internat. Psychologist, 1968-69. Contbr. articles profl. jours. Inventor Elec. Logic Machine, 1936, King Square Game, 1955. Home: 2617 W Fitch Av Chicago, IL 60645.

BURACK, ELMER HOWARD, educator; b. Chgo., Oct. 21, 1927; s. Charles H. and Rose (Taerbaum) B.; B.S., U. Ill., 1950; M.S., Ill. Inst. Tech., 1956; Ph.D., Northwestern U., 1964; m. Ruth A. Goldsmith, Feb. 15, 1953; children-Charles Michael, Robert Jay, Alan Jeffrey. Prodn. supt. Richardson Co., Melrose Park, Ill., 1953-55; prodn. control mgr. Fed. Tool Corp., Lincolnwood, Ill., 1955-59; Booz, Allen & Hamilton, mgmt. cons., Chgo., 1959-60; lectr., asso. prof., prof. mgmt., acting chmn. dept. bus. and econs. Ill. Inst. Tech., Chgo., 1960—. Project dir. tech. and automation research study Dept. Labor, 1965-68. Vice pres., chmn. Bd. Edn. Beth El Religious Sch., Highland Park, Ill., 1967-69. Served with USAAF, 1946-47. Mem. Acad. Mgmt. (pres. elect Midwest div.), Inst. Mgmt. Sci., Indsl. Relations Assn. Chgo. (dir.). Mem. B'nai B'rith (past pres. Highland Park). Mem. editorial bd. Acad. of Mgmt. Jour., 1969—, Business Perspectives, 1970- -. Contbr. articles profl. jours. Home: 2755 Marl Oak Dr Highland Park IL 60035 Office: Ill Inst Tech 31st and Dearborn Sts Chicago IL 60616

BURANDT, GUS JOSEPH, assn. exec.; b. Covington, La., Mar. 9, 1919; s. Gustave Traugott and Cecile (Cantrelle) B.; B.S. in Bus. Adminstrn., La. State U., 1966; m. Mary Josephine Schuerger, Oct. 2, 1944; children—Jane Elizabeth, (Mrs. John Pfingsten), Marianna Cara. Partner Barksdale Motel, Bossier City, La., 1945-70, owner, 1970—; v.p. La. Motel Assn., 1964, pres., 1965-66; v.p. Motel Assn. Am., 1967-69, pres., 1970—. Pres. La. Tri Tron Co., Bossier City, La., 1968—. Vice pres. Shreveport Humane Soc., 1950; vice chmn. Community Chest, Bossier City, 1954. Served to maj. AUS, 1941-44; ETO. Decorated Silver Star medal; named to Hall Fame Motels, Hospitality mag., 1970. Mem. Am., La. Motel assns., Am. Legion. Roman Catholic K.C. Home: 4740 N Market St Shreveport LA 71107 Office: 2450 Barksdale Blvd Bossier City LA 71010

BURBAGE, THOMAS L., mfg. co. exec.; b. N.C., 1905. Former sec. Black & Decker Mfg. Co. Home: 11 Cedar Av Towson MD 21204*

BURBANK, BURR GAMALIEL, educator; b. Whiting, Ind., Aug. 24, 1912; A.B., San Jose State Coll., 1934; Ph.D. in Physics, Stanford, 1946; married, 1940. Tchr. high schs., Cal., 1939-42; instr. physics and engrng. Stockton Jr. Coll., 1942-47; asst. prof. physics San Francisco State Coll., 1947-51, asst. prof. phys. sci., 1947-51, asso. prof., 1941-58, prof., 1958—, chmn. physics dept., 1961—; asst. prof. Coll. of Pacific, 1945-47. Office: San Francisco State Coll San Francisco CA 94132*

BURBANK, NELSON STONE, investment banker; b. Winchester, Mass., Sept. 16, 1920; s. Willis H. and Vivian (Casson) B.; student Boston U., 1946-47; m. Rita B. Healey, Feb. 12, 1950; children—Peter N., Nelson Stone, Jane Vivian. Registered rep. Vance, Sanders & Co., Inc., Boston, 1946-53; pres. Burbank & Co., Inc., Boston, 1953—; trustee Reading Savs. Bank. Bd. govs. Boston Stock Exchange, 1965—, vice chmn., 1968-71, chmn., 1971—. Bd. dirs. Reading (Mass.) chpt. A.R.C., 1963—, now vice chmn.; trustee Pike Sch., Andover, Mass. Served with AUS, 1942-45. Decorated D.F.C., Air medals. Home: 24 Juniper Circle Reading MA 01867 Office: 75 Federal St Boston MA 02110

BURBANK, REGINALD, physician; b. Pittsfield, Mass., July 26, 1888; s. Charles Henry and Jennie Halford (Brooks) B.; grad. Phillips Acad., Andover, Mass., 1908; A.M., Trinity Coll., Hartford, 1911; M.D., Cornell, 1915; m. Marion B. Powers, Dec. 2, 1916; children—Marion (Mrs. John Walker McNeely), Jeanne, Margaret (Mrs. Arthur Curtis Welch), Reginald (dec.); m. 2d, Kathryn Poole Muse, July 26, 1943 (dec. May 1970). Asst. surgeon N.Y. Orthopedic Hosp., 1916-26; chief arthritis clinic Cornell Med. Coll., 1917-19; instr. arthritis, chief arthritis clinic Bellevue Med. Coll., 1917-26; cons. on arthritis Bklyn. Hosp., 1926-46; dir. arthritis clinic St. Clare's Hosp., 1940-56, also asso. attending; practice of medicine limited to gout, arthritis, allied rheumatoid diseases. Fellow N.Y. Acad. Medicine; affiliate Royal Soc. Medicine; mem. Am. Soc. for Study Arthritis (founding mem., chmn. 12 years), Pan Am. Med. Assn., Am. Soc. Microbiology, N.Y. County Med. Soc., N.Y. State Med. Soc.,

Royal Soc. Health. Presbyn. Mason. Clubs: Union, Pilgrims. Contbr. numerous monographs to sci. jours. Home: 6 E 78th St New York City NY 10021

BURBANK, ROLAND WAINWRIGHT, ednl. cons.; b. Syracuse, N.Y., Mar. 30, 1910; s. William Roland and Henrietta (Cole) B.; student McGill U., 1932; B.A., Dartmouth, 1933, M.S., 1934; postgrad. Plymouth (N.H.) Coll., 1964; m. Constance Christie Wilson, Sept. 17, 1932. Sci. master Proctor Acad., Andover, N.H., 1934-55, asst. headmaster, 1953-55; headmaster Cardigan Mountain Sch., Canaan, N.H., 1955-63, Manilus (N.Y.), Sch., 1964-68; bus. mgr. New (N.H.) Hampton Sch., 1968-70; ednl. cons., 1970—. Pres. Canaan St. Improvement Soc., 1959-60; chmn. Canaan Planning Bd., 1959-63. Pres. N.H. Unitarian Assn., 1940-42, exec. treas., 1942-48; v.p., dir. Am. Unitarian Assn., 1944-48; presiding officer Council Liberal Chs., 1959-61. Mem. corp. Proctor Acad. Mem. New Eng. Assn. Chemistry Tchrs., No. New Eng. Assn. Ind. Schs. (pres. 1961-62), Newcomen Soc., Camp Dirs. Round Table (chmn. 1963), Nat. Assn. Secondary Sch. Prins. Club: Dartmouth (pres. Hanover Area 1964). Home: Wolfeboro NH 03894

BURBANK, WILBUR SWETT, geologist, b. Amesbury, Mass., Mar. 30, 1898; s. Wilbur Augustus and Emma Elizabeth (Swett) B.; S.B., Mass. Inst. Tech., 1919, S.M. 1920, post grad., 1924-25; m. Beryl Frances Loughlin, Apr. 1, 1933; children—John Francis, Phillip Augustus. With U.S. Geol. Survey, 1920—, successively mineral resource investigations, gen. geologic mapping, Republic of Haiti, geologic mapping, Mont., studies copper deposits of Mich., fed. and state coop. study geology and mineral resources of Colo., 1926-39, mineral investigations Republic of Haiti, Dominican Republic, strategic mineral investigation minor metal resources of U.S., research volcanism and mineralizing processes ancient volcanic areas, San Juan Mountains, Colo., adminstrv. com. work geologic programs, 1920-58, field research ancient volcanic processes in relation geochemistry, thermodynamics of mineralizing processes, 1958—. Soc. Econ. Geologists rep. earth scis. div. NRC, 1934-36, exec. com. div. earth scis., 1955- 58. Recpient Distinguished Service award Dept. Interior, 1958. Mem. Am. Geophys. Union (v.p. volcanology 1935-38. pres. 1947-50, sec. tectonophysics sect. 1947-53), Soc. Econ. Geologists, Geol. Soc. Am., Mineral. Soc. Am., Geochem. Soc., No. New Eng. Acad. Scis., Colo. Sci. Soc., Geol. Soc. Washington. Unitarian. Clubs: Cosmos, Petrologists (Washington). Contbr. numerous tech. articles profl. publs. Home: 9 Bayberry Lane, Exeter, NH 03833. Office: US Geological Survey Washington DC 20242

BURBIDGE, ELEANOR MARGARET PEACHEY (Mrs. Geoffrey Burbidge), astronomer; b. Davenport, Eng.; d. Stanley John and Marjorie (Stott) Peachey; B.Sc., Ph.D., U. London; Sc.D. (hon.), Smith Coll., 1963, U. Sussex, 1970; m. Geoffrey Burbidge, Apr. 2, 1948; 1 dau., Sarah. Came to U.S., 1955. Mem. staff U. London Obs., 1948-51; research fellow Yerkes Obs., U. Chgo., 1951-53, Cal. Inst. Tech., Pasadena, 1955-57; Shirley Farr fellow Yerkes Obs., 1957-59, asso. prof., 1959-62; mem. Enrico Perth Inst. for Nuclear Studies, 1957-62; prof. astronomy dept. physics U. Cal. at San Diego, 1964—. Recipient (with husband) Warner prize in Astronomy, 1959; hon. fellow Girton Coll., Cambridge. Fellow Royal Soc., Royal Astron. Soc.; mem. Am. Astron. Soc., Internat. Astron. Union (pres. commn. 28, 1970—). Author: (with G. Burbidge) Quasi-Stellar Objects, 1967. Editor Observatory mag., 1948-51; editorial bd. Astronomy and Astrophysics, 1969—.

BURCH, CHARLES, educator; b. Erie, Pa., Jan. 15, 1919; B.S., Slippery Rock State Coll.; M.S., Ph.D., Cornell U.; Married, 1946; three children. Asst., Cornell U., 1947-51; prof. biology Cal. State Coll., Long Beach, 1951-64; asso. prof. Hartwick Coll., Oneonta, N.Y., from 1964; now prof. biology, chmn. dept. Wells Coll., Aurora, N.Y. Served to capt. USAAF, 1941-45. Mem. A.A.A.S., Soc. Study Evolution, Internat. Soc. Plant Morphology. Office: Dept Biology Wells Coll Aurora NY 13026*

BURCH, DEAN, former chmn. Republican Nat. Com; b. Enid, Okla., Dec. 20, 1927; s. Bert Alexander and Leola (Atkisson) B.; LL.B., U. Ariz., 1953; m. Patricial Meeks, July 7, 1961; children—Shelly, Dean, Dianne. Admitted to Ariz. bar, 1953; asst. atty. gen., Ariz., 1953-54; adminstrv. asst. to Sen. Barry Goldwater, 1955-59; mem. firm. Dunseath, Stubbs & Burch, Tucson, 1959-69; chmn. Fed. Communications Commn., Washington, 1969—; dep. dir. Goldwater for President Com., 1963-64; chmn. Rep. Nat. Com., 1964-65; mgr. Goldwater for Senate Campaign 1968. Mem. Ariz. Bd. Regents, 1969-70. Served with AUS, 1946-48. Mem. Phi Delta Theta, Blue Key. Home: 5000 Westpath Terrace Washington DC 20016 Office: Fed Communications Commn 1919 M St NW Washington DC 20554

BURCH, FRANCIS BOUCHER, lawyer, state ofcl.; b. Balt., Nov. 26, 1918; s. Louis Claude and Constance (Boucher) B.; Ph.B. summa cum laude (scholarship 1937-41), Loyola Coll., Balt., 1941; LL.B., Yale, 1943; m. Mary Patricia Howe, Apr. 12, 1947; children—Francis Boucher, Catherine Howe, Richard Claude, Constance Boucher, Edwin Howe, Robert Stuart, Mary Patricia. Admitted to Md. bar, 1943, also U.S. Supreme Ct.; mem. firm Allen Burch and Baker, Balt., 1945—; pres. Balt. Civil Service Commn., 1960-61; mem. Balt. Bd. Estimates, 1961-63; city solicitor, Balt., 1961-63; ins. commnr. Md., 1965-66; atty gen. Md., 1966—; instr. bus. law Loyola Coll., Evening Sch., 1945-57. Chmn. bd. Lauderdale '70, Inc., Ft. Lauderdale, Fla., 1964-68. Mem. bd. Balt. Credit Union, 1961-63; mem. Pension Study Com. Balt., 1962; chmn. Mayor Balt. Com. Scholarship Program, 1961, Mayor Balt. Com. Mass. Transit, 1961; mem. Standard Salary Bd. Md., 196O-61, Mayor Balt. Com. Conflict of Interest, 1960. Chmn. Md. Cancer Crusade, 1967; nat. chmn. Constl. Prayer Found., 1963-66; pres. Balt. Safety Council, 1963-65, chmn. exec. com., 1965-67, v.p., 1958-62 lay chmn. Papal Volunteers Com. Latin Am., Archdiocese Balt., 1962-65; vice chmn. Alumni div. Loyola Coll. Devel. Program, 1957; chmn. Md. Catholic Lawyers Retreat, 1957-59; pres. Reciprocity Club Balt., 1956-57, bd. dirs., 1954-59. Bd. dirs. Legal Aid Bur. Balt., 1954, Goodwill Industries Balt., 1959-65, 1959-65; trustee Camp Fire Girls Balt., 1960—. Served with USCGR, 1944-45. Recipient Spiritum award Cardinal Gibbons High Sch., Balt., 1966; Man of Year award Hibernian Soc. Md., 1967; Pub. Servant award Md. Cath. War Vets., 1967; Humanitarian award Nu Beta Epsilon, 1967; Nat. Jewish Hosp. award, 1969; Alumnus of Year award Loyola Coll., 1970. Mem. Am., Med., Balt. bar assns., Am. Arbitration Assn. (mem. panel 1954—), Nat. Assn. Atty. Gens. (pres. 1970-71, mem. exec. com. 1969—), So. Md. Soc., Hibernian Soc. Md., St. Thomas Soc. (pres. Md. 1962-63), St. Georges Soc. Md. Clubs: Paint and Powder (bd. govs. 1957-63), Balt. Country, Center (Balt.); Tri-State Anglers (Md.-Del.-Va.). Author: On Calling of a Constitutional Convention, 1950. Home: 207 Chancery Rd Baltimore MD 21218 Office: One S Calvert Bldg Baltimore MD 21202

BURCH, FRANK HAZE, lawyer; b. Phoenix, Nov. 16, 1919; s. William Hazelton and Dora (Murr) B.; A.A., Phoenix Coll., 1948; J.D., U. Ariz., 1950; m. Mary Jane Lester, Apr. 17, 1949; children-Lewiis Terris, Frank Haze II, Claudia Susan, Carter Allan, Vicki Louise. Admitted to Ariz. bar, 1951, since practiced in Phoenix; partner firm Burch, Cracchiolo, Levie & Guyer, 1970—; cons. Ariz. Planning Assn.; cons., spl. counsel City of Scottsdale, Ariz. Bd. dirs. Law Soc. of Ariz. State U., 1968—; pres. Lawyers Club Phoenix, 1968. Adv. bd. Phoenix Salvation Army; trustee Phoenix Union High Sch. Dist., 1950-65. Served with USNR, World War II. Mem. State Bar Ariz., Am., Maricopa County bar assns., Am. Soc. Planning Ofcls., Internat. Assn. Ins. Counsel, Def. Research Inst., Southwestern Legal Found., Am. Kennel Club. Home: 36 N Country Club Dr Phoenix AZ 85014 Office: 2333 N Central Av Phoenix AZ 85004

BURCH, GEORGE E., physician; b. Edgard, La., 1910; s.George Edward and Lottie Edith (Monroe) B.; M.D., Tulane, 1933, B.S., 1935; m. Vivian Ann Gerard, Sept. 16, 1932; children—Vivian Anna, Janet Vivian, George Edward III, Bryan George. Intern Charity Hosp., New Orleans, 1933-34; asst. dept. medicine Tulane U., New Orleans, 1934-35, instr. 1935-42, asst. prof., 1942-43, asso. prof. 1943-47, prof., chmn. dept., 1947—; asst. Rockefeller Inst. Hosp., 1939-41, Commonwealth fund fellow, 1939-41; asst. vis. physician Charity Hosp., 1934-36, vis. physician, 1936-44, sr. vis. physician, 1944-47, cons., physician-in-chief Tulane unit, 1947—. Mem. exptl. adv. com. cardiovascular diseases WHO, 1960—. Served as capt. La. N.G., 1936-40; capt. Med. Res. Corp, U.S. Army, Tulane Unit Base Hosp. No. 23, 1940-42. Diplomate (emeritus) Am. Bd. Internal Medicine. Master A.C.P., Am. Coll. Clin. Pharmacology and Chemotherapy, Am. Coll. Cardiology (pres. 1968); mem. Assn. U. Cardiologists (founder), Assn. Am. Physicians, Am. Heart Assn., A.M.A., Am. Soc. for Clin. Investigation, A.A.A.S., Harvey Society, Am. Fedn. Clin. Research, Central, So. socs. for clin. research, N.Y. Acad. Medicine, So. Med. Assn., Soc. for Exptl. Biology and Medicine, Am. Therapeutic Soc., Royal Soc. Medicine, Editor Am. Heart Jour., 1959—. Address: Tulane U Sch Medicine 1430 Tulane Av New Orleans LA 70112

BURCH, JAMES CHARLIE HORTON, educator; b. Durham, N.C., May 4, 1907; s. Charles Hill and Vella Lee (Horton) B.; A.B., Duke, 1928, A.M., 1929, Ph.D., 1933; m. Kathleen Smith, Oct. 24, 1945; children—Nancy Jane, James Charlie Horton, Susan Kathleen. Instr. English, Duke, 1935-36; asst. prof. English, Ga. Inst. Tech., 1945-50; mem. faculty Ga. State U., 1950—, prof. English, 1955—, head dept., 1951-52, dean sch. Arts and Scis., 1951-67. Served with AUS, 1942-45. Mem. S. Atlantic Modern Lang. Assn., Ga. Edn. Assn., Phi Eta Sigma. Baptist (deacon). Home: 1468 Ragley Hall Rd NE Atlanta GA 30319

BURCH, LUCIUS EDWARD, Jr., lawyer; b. Nashville, Jan. 25, 1912; s. Lucius Edward and Sarah (Cooper) B.; B.A., Vanderbilt U., 1934, LL.B., 1936; m. Elsie Caldwell, Dec. 27, 1935; children—Sarah Polk (Mrs. John F. Gratz, Jr.), Elsie Caldwell (Mrs. Jonathan Donald), Edith Montague (Mrs. Burch Caywood), Lucia Newell (Mrs. John H. Pritchard, Jr.). Admitted to Tenn. bar, 1936, since practiced in Memphis; sr. partner firm Burch, Porter & Johnson, 1947—. Dir. Memphis Aero Corp., Mid-South Quick Freeze Co., Lincoln Am. Life Ins. Co., City Finance Co. Bd. dirs. Memphis Civic Research Com., 1947- 67; chmn. com. to study and effect charter reform municipal govt., Memphis, 1964; founder, charter mem. Memphis Com. Community Relations, 1958-59, pres., 1959; chmn. Tenn. Game and Fish Commn., 1949-55, Memphis Manpower Com., 1968-69; pres. Tenn. Conservation League, 1955-56; chmn. riot com. Memphis Com. Community Relations, 1966; mem. Nat. Council Atlantic Union, 1949—; adv. com. Internat. Movement Atlantic Union, 1961—; mem. devel. council Vanderbilt U. Law Sch., 1968—; adv. com. internship program U. Miss. Law Sch., 1969. Del. Democratic Nat. Conv., 1952; mem. Tenn. Dem. Exec. Com., 1962. Trustee Edmund J. Meeman Found., LeMoyne-Owen Coll.; bd. govs. Assn. Advancement Aging Research, 1968-; bd. dirs. Memphis Sunshine Home, 1940-. Recipient Cartter-Patten award Tenn. Conservation League, 1956; certificate of merit Memphis Urban League, 1952. Fellow Am. Coll. Trial Lawyers; mem. Am., Tenn. (gov. 1958), Memphis and Shelby County (dir. 1962-63) bar assns., Tenn. Acad. Sci. (hon. life), Gerontol. Soc., Tenn., West Tenn. hist. socs. Clubs: Memphis Country Memphis Hunt and Polo, Tennessee, Wolf River Soc. (founder, 1st pres.) (Memphis). Author articles. Home: Whiteacre Farm Collierville, TN 38017. Office: 128 N Court Av PO Box 26 Memphis TN 38101

BURCH, LYNDON WALKUP, design engr., inventor; b. Grand Rapids, Mich., Feb. 9, 1899; s. Thomas Walkup and Grace Burch; student Curtiss Sch. Aviation, Buffalo, 1917, U. Cal., 1920; m. Isabella Keys, June 1919 (div. 1926); children— Hadley K., Marilyn K. (Mrs. Harry Kindle); m. 2d, Sarah C. Wells, Aug. 17, 1946. Test engr. Packard Motor Car Co., 1925-30; design engr., sales engr. Wilcolator Co., Newark, 1930-41; tank proof officer Aberdeen Proving Ground, also project engr. Tank Automotive Center, Detroit, 1942-43; project officer USAAF, Wright Field Equipment Lab., 1943-44, asst. chief personal flight equipment lab., 1944-45; organizer, v.p., sales mgr. Control Products, Inc., Harrison, N.J., 1946-54; engring. and sales cons. metals and controls div. Tex. Instruments, Inc., Attleboro, Mass., 1954-60; pvt. practice, Boston, 196O-. Fellow Acad. Applied Science; mem. Soc. Automotive Engrs. Inventor of automotive and aircraft circuit breaker, aircraft and tank fire detector systems, basic electromechanical sine switch element, thermostat for temperature control indsl., domestic and aircraft devices, new design for elec. contactors for all types of elec. switching; designer switch elements used in Mercury projects, Mariner, Telstar and all Apollo projects for critical control functions. Address: 3 River St Pl Boston MA 02108.

BURCH, ROBERT DALE, lawyer; b. Washington, Jan. 30, 1928; s. Dallas Stockwell and Hepsy (Berry) B.; student Va. Mil. Inst., 1945-46; B.S., U. Cal. at Berkeley, 1950, LL.B., 1953; m. Joann D. Hansen, Dec. 9, 1966; children—Berkeley, Robert Brett. Admitted to Cal. bar, 1954, since practiced in Beverly Hills; partner firm Gibson, Dunn & Crutcher, 1961—; lectr. U. So. Cal. Inst. Fed. Taxation, 1960-62, 65; guest lectr. U. Cal. Law Sch., 1959. Mem. Beverly Hills Estate Planning Council. Bd. dirs. charitable founds. Served with AUS, 1945-46. Mem. Am. Law Inst., Beverly Hills Bar Assn. (bd. govs., probate and trust com.), Law Trust, Tax and Ins. Council (past czar), Los Angeles World Affairs Council, Beverly Hills C. of C. Contbr. profl. jours. Home: 1301 Delresto Dr Beverly Hills CA 90210 Office: 9601 Wilshire Blvd Beverly Hills CA 90210

BURCH, WENDEL, editor; b. Bloomington, Ind., Aug. 26, 1908; s. Audry Richard and Ethel (Williams) B.; m. LaVerne Blundell, July 6, 1933; children—Robert (dec.), Richard Norman, Barbara Julene. Formerly mem. staff San Francisco News, Los Angeles Herald, Santa Monica (Cal.) Sun; with U.P.I., 1931—, assigned N.Y.C., 1940—, now dir. internat. services. Mem. Delta Upsilon. Episcopalian (vestryman). Club: West Side Tennis (Forest Hills). Home: 111-16 65th Av Forest Hills NY 11375 Office: UPI 220 E 42d St New York City NY 10017*

BURCHAM, LESTER ARTHUR, retail merchandising exec.; b. Lancaster, O., April 26, 1913; s. Arthur L. and Estella (Grannan) B.; student pub. schs. Lancaster; m. Zora M. Gray, Apr. 20, 1935; 1 son, James Edward. Dist. mgr. F. W. Woolworth Co., 1931-58, v.p., 1958-62, exec. v.p., 1962- 64, pres., 1965-69, chmn. bd., chief exec. officer, 1970—, dir. Kinney Shoe Corp., F. W. Woolworth Ltd., Can., F. W. Woolworth Co. (Mexico), F. W. Woolworth Co. Ltd. (Eng.), Richman Bros. Co., Western Electric Co. Bd. dirs. United Fund Greater N.Y. Mem. Nat. Retail Merchants Assn. (dir.). Clubs: Economic (N.Y.); Scarsdale Country; Greenwich Country; Indian Harbor Yacht. Home: Baldwin Farms South Greenwich CT 06830 Office: 233 Broadway New York City NY 10007

BURCHAM, PAUL BAKER, educator; b. Fayette, Mo., Feb. 22, 1916; s. Frank E. and Bula (Richardson) B.; B.A., Central Coll., 1935; M.A., Northwestern U., 1938, Ph.D., 1941; postgrad. U. Chgo., 1942; m. Helen Kennard Spencer, Dec. 27, 1941; children—Jane, Ann. Instr., asst. prof., asso. prof. U. Mo., Columbia, 1946-54, prof., 1954—, chmn. dept. math., 1948-66. Served to capt. USAAF, 1942-46. Mem. Am. Math. Soc., Math. Assn. Am. Author: (with Ewing and Betz) Differential Equations with Applications, 1954. Home: 401 Westmount St Columbia MO 65201

BURCHARD, CHARLES, coll. dean; b. N.Y.C., June 27, 1914; s. Carl and Mary (Jahn) B.; B.Arch., Mass. Inst. Tech., 1938; M.Arch. (Nelson Robinson fellow 1940-41), Harvard, 1940; m. Helen Schwob, Aug. 7, 1943; children—Linda Sue, Thomas Kirk, Peter. Asst. prof. architecture Harvard, 1946-53; Fulbright sr. fellow, vis. lectr. Archtl. Assn., Sch. Architecture, London, Eng., 1950-51; pvt. practice, Cambridge, Mass., 1946-53; sr. partner firm A.M. Kinney Assos., Cin., 1953-63, cons. 1964-68; dean Coll. Architecture, Va. Poly. Inst. and State U., 1964- -, Univ. prof., 1970—; cons. A.M. Kinney Assos., 1964-68, D.C. Redevel. Land Agy., 1966—, Study Profession Landscape Architecture, 1969—; prin. archtl. Works include Agoos residence, East Andover, N.H., 1948, Thompson Cadillac Agy., Cin., 1953, Hilltop and Clovernook elementary schs., Heinold Jr. High Sch., Aiken High Sch. (all Cin.), 1955-62, Miles Research Lab., Elkhart, Ind., 1961, U.S. Post Office Annex, Cin., 1963, Crosley Tower & Brodie Engring. & Sci. Complex, U. Cin., 1963. Trustee Roanoke Fine Arts Center. Recipient award Progressive Architecture mag., 1954, Am. Assn. Sch. Adminstrs., 1955, 56, 59 60, Sch. Exec. mag., 1955, 56. Fellow A.I.A. (nat edn. and research com. 1967-69, dir. Va., exec. com.; commr. for edn.; council on licensing and edn. 1969—); mem. Archtl. Assn. (London), Va. Assn. Professions (edn. com.), Assn. Collegiate Schs. Architecture (treas. 1967-69, pres. 1969-71, dir.), Tau Sigma Delta, Alpha Rho Chi. Home: 1610 Greenwood Dr Blacksburg VA 24060

BURCHARD, JOHN ELY, archtl. historian, critic and cons., b. Marshall, Minn., Dec. 8, 1898; s. James Clark and Sidonie (Schupp) B.; U. Minn. Coll. Liberal Arts, 1915-17, Coll. Medicine, 1917; S.B. in Archtl. Engring., Mass. Inst. Tech., 1923, S.M., 1925; L.H.D. (hon.), Union Coll., 1953; D. Architecture (hon.) U. Mich., 1956; m. Marjorie Walker Gaines, Sept. 7, 1926; children—John Ely, Jr., Marshall Gaines. With Bemis Industries, Inc., Boston, dir. research, devel. and patents, 1928-38, v.p., 1933-38; prof. and dir. Albert Farwell Bemis Found., Mass. Inst. Tech., 1938-48, became dean sch. humanities and social sci., 1948, now dean emeritus, lectr.; Canadian Hazen lectr., 1953; Lowell Inst. lectr. Boston Mus. Fine Arts, 1955; vis. prof. U. Cal., 1954, 55, 64-68, acting head dept. design, 1965-66, acting dean Coll. Environmental Design, 1966-67; Mellon vis. prof. environmental design 1967-68; sr. lectr. Mass. Inst. Tech., 1968-71; Thomas Jefferson vis. prof. U. Va., 1969; cons. on aesthetics Bay Area Rapid Transit Dist., lectr., Iran, Pakistan, India, 1962; studied new German architecture as guest of Fed. Republic, 1963; cons. Graham Found. for Advanced Studies in Fine Arts, 1955-60. Mem. adv. bd. Aspen Inst. Humanistic Studies, 1961-65, seminar moderator, 1956-65. Exec. officer various def. coms. NRC, 1940-44; various posts OSRD, 1940-46, ending as chief div. 2 and dep. chief Office Field Services; chmn. coms. on amphibious nav. and demolition OSRD, 1944-46; mem. Am. delegation to France and Norway on higher edn., 1957; mem. panel on sci., engring. Pres.'s Sci. Adv. Com., 1958-59; mem. Kawana (Tokyo) Conf. on Sci. and Modern Civilization, 1960. Mem. adv. bd. U.S. Mcht. Marine Acad., Kings Point, N.Y., 1953-60, chmn., 1956-57; mem. Yale Council Com. on Library, 1949- 58, Princeton U. adv. council of library, 1949-55; trustee Mt. Holyoke Coll., 1951-61, mem. exec. com., 1953-61; mem. com. to visit grad. sch. design Harvard, 1953-59; trustee Boston Mus. Fine Arts, 1957-60. Recipient Presdl. medal for Merit, 1948; U. Minn. outstanding achievement award, 1960; Thomas Jefferson Meml. medal Architecture, 1969; decorated officier de l' Ordre des Arts et des Lettres (France). Fellow Am. Acad. Arts and Scis. (pres. 1954-57, bd. editors Daedalus 1958—); mem. A.I.A. (hon.), Chi Psi, Tau Beta Pi. Club: Examiner (Boston). Author: (with others) The Evolving House, 3 vols., 1933-36; (with Oscar Handlin) The Historian and the City, 1963; (with A. Bush-Brown) The Architecture of America, 1961; The Voice of the Phoenix, Post-war Architecture in Germany, 1966. Editor, annotator: Mid-Century; The Social Implications of Scientific Progress, 1950. Contbr. chpts. to Planning the University Library Building, 1949, Religious Faith and World Culture, 1951, The Individual and Liberal Education, 1952, The Metropolis in Modern Life, 1954, Symbols and Society, 1954, Brain Power Quest, 1957, The Metropolitan Enigma, 1967. Cons. editor Archtl. Record, 1957-61. Home: 56 Mt Vernon St Boston MA 02108 Office: Mass Inst of Technology Cambridge MA 02139

BURCHARD, WALDO WADSWORTH, sociologist, educator; b. Satanta, Kan., Nov. 28, 1916; s. Charles and Jennie Grace (Swink) B.; A.B., U. Cal. at Berkeley, 1949, M.A., 1951, Ph.D., 1953; m. Rachael Caroline Ballenger, May 24, 1945; children—Gina Michel, Petrea Celeste, Stuart Gregory, Margot Theresa. Instr. sociology U. Denver, 1952-53, U. Kan., 1953-55; asst. prof. sociology Hollins Coll., 1955-58; asso. prof. No. Ill. U., 1958-61, prof., 1961—, head dept. social scis., 1959-61, head dept. sociology and anthropology, 1961-68. Cons. sociology Nat. Assn. Standard Med. Vocabulary. Served with USMC, 1942-46. Fellow Am. Sociol. Assn; mem. Midwest (chmn. publs. com.), So., Ohio Valley (past exec. com.) sociol. socs., Soc. Sci. Study Religion, Ill. Sociol. Assn. (hon. Past pres., chmn. publs. com., ex officio dir.), Assn. Sociology Religion. Contbr. articles profl. jours. Home: 907 Sharon Dr DeKalb IL 60115

BURCHELL, HOWARD BERTRAM, physician, educator; b. Athens, Ont., Can., Nov. 28, 1907; s. James Edward and Edith (Milligan) B.; M.D., U. Toronto, 1932; Ph.D., U. Minn., 1939; m. Margaret Helmholz, Aug. 12, 1942; children—Susan, Judith, Cynthia, Rebecca. Came to U.S., 1934, naturalized, 1939. Prof. medicine Mayo Found., U. Minn., 1941-67; prof. medicine U. Minn., 1968—; cons. cardiologist Mayo Clinic, Rochester, Minn., 1941-68. Mem. sci. adv. bd. Chief Staff USAF, 1950-54; mem. Nat. Adv. Heart Council, 1958-62. Served with USAAF, 1942-46. Mem. Am. Physiol. Soc., Assn. Am. Physicians, Am. Heart Assn. (Gold Heart award 1970), A.M.A., Aero. Med. Assn. Editor-in-chief: Circulation, 1966-70. Home: 260 Woodlawn Av St Paul MN 55105

BURCHELL, JOHN SAMUEL, utility exec.; b. Dover, N.J., Aug. 4, 1915; s. John S. and Elvira (Clark) B.; certificate accounting, Rutgers U. Coll., 1947; m. Norma S. Scadden, Sept. 25, 1943; 1 son, Robert C. With N.J. Power & Light Co., Morristown, 1935—, comptroller, 1963—; comptroller Jersey Central Power & Light Co., 1963—. Vol. fireman; mem. exec. com. United Fund, 1965-67. Mem. Nat. Assn. Accountants. Methodist (trustee, treas. ch.). Home: 57 Conger St Dover NJ 07801 Office: Madison Av Morristown NJ 07960

BURCHENAL, JOSEPH HOLLAND, physician; b. Milford, Del., Dec. 21, 1912; s. Caleb E. and Mary E. (Holland) B.; grad. Phillips Exeter Acad., 1930; student Princeton, 1930- 33; M.D., U. Pa., 1937; m. Margaret Pembroke Thom, Oct. 15, 1938; m. 2d, Joan Barclay Riley, Mar. 20, 1948; children—Mary Holland, Elizabeth Payne, Joan Littlefield, Barbara Fahys, Caleb Wells, David Holland, Joseph Emory Barclay. Rotating intern Union Meml. Hosp., Balt., 1937-38; resident pediatrics N.Y. Hosp., also research pathology Cornell U., 1938-39; asst. resident medicine Boston City Hosp., 1940-42; spl. fellow medicine Meml. Hosp., N.Y.C., 1946-49, asst. attending physician, 1949-52, attending physician, 1952—, chief chemotherapy service, 1952- 64, asso. med. dir. for clin. investigation, 1964-66, director of clinical investigation, 1966—; research fellow medicine Harvard, 1940-42; asso. Sloan-Kettering Inst., 1948-52, mem., 1952—, vice president, 1964—; assistant prof. clin. med. Cornell U., 1949-50, asst. prof. med., 1950-51, asso. prof., 1951-52, prof. Sloan-Kettering div., 1952-55; professor medicine Cornell U. Medical Coll., 1955—; spl. cons. clin. panel Cancer Chemotherapy Nat. Service Center, 1955-64; spl. cons. pub. health service, hematology study sect. Nat. Inst. Health, 1955-58; cons. Am. Cancer Soc., 1958-64; chmn. U.S. nat. com. Internat. Union Against Cancer, 1960-63, chmn. chemotherapy panel of research commn., 1962-66; chmn. WHO expert com. on cancer chemotherapy, 1961, mem. WHO expert adv. panel on cancer, 1961—; cons. in oncology Stamford (Conn.), St. Albans (N.Y.) Naval hosps. Mem. Rep. Town Meeting, Darien, Conn., 1957—; Recipient Alfred P. Sloan Cancer Research award, 1963. Served M.C., AUS, 1942-45. Diplomate Am. Bd. Internal Medicine. Mem. Am. Soc. Clin. Investigation, Soc. Exptl. Biology and Medicine, American Association for Cancer Research (v.p. 1964-65, pres. 1965-66), European, Internat., Am. socs. hematology, Am. Soc. Tropical Medicine, Soc. Study Blood, Am. Fedn. Clin. Research, N.Y. Acad. Scis., Harvey Soc., Am. Soc. Pediatric Research (rep. to div. med. scis. NRC 1955-58), A.M.A., A.C.P., med. socs. County N.Y., State N.Y., Am. Inst. Nutrition, Academia Nacional de Medicina de Buenos Aires (corr.), Czechoslovak Med. Soc. (corr.), Brazilian Nat. Acad. Medicine (corr.). Home: Juniper Rd Noroton CT 06820 Office: 444 E 68th St New York City NY 10021

BURCHILL, GEORGE PERCIVAL, Canadian politician; b. Nelson-Miramichi, N.B., Nov. 3, 1889; s. John Percival and Eliza (Wilkinson) B.; B.Sc., U. N.B.; m. Jean Gordon Garden, Oct. 23, 1916; 1 son, John Garden. Pres., dir. George Burchill & Sons, Nelson-Miramichi; pres., chmn. bd. dirs. N.B. Telephone Co., 1930-65; dir. Montreal Trust Co., 1953-69; senator of Can., 1945—. Pres. N.B. Boy Scouts, 1960-62. Mason. Home: Nelson-Miramichi New Brunswick Canada

BURCHINAL, DAVID ARTHUR, air force officer; b. Washington, Pa., Apr. 17, 1915; s. Warren Sturgis and Florence (Iseman) B.; grad. Blair Acad., 1934; A.B., Brown U., 1938; m. Jean Kingsland Fales, Mar. 23, 1940 (div. June 1968); children—Wendy Clarke, David Kent; m. 2d, Kathryn Kellogg, July 29, 1968. Commd. 2d lt. USAAF, 1940, advanced through grades to gen. USAF, 1966; first air attache to Can., 1943-44; dep. A-3 and A-3, 20th Air Force, Guam, 1944- 45; mem. U.S. Strategic Bombing Survey, Japan, 1945-46; faculty Air War Coll., 1946-49; chief program analysis Hdqrs. USAF, 1949-51; sec. Air Force Council, 1951-53; comdr. 40th and 43d bomb wings, 1954-55; chief staff 8th Air Force, 1955-58; dep. dir. operations. Joint Chiefs of Staff, 1958-60; dir. plans Hdqrs. USAF, 1960-62, dep. chief staff plans and operations, 1963-64, dir. Joint Staff, Joint Chiefs Staff, 1964-66, dep. comdr. in chief U.S. European Command, 1966—. Active Boy Scouts Am. Decorated D.S.M., Silver Star, Legion of Merit, D.F.C., Air medal, Commendation ribbon; French Legion Honor. Mem. Council Fgn. Relations, Daedalions, V.F.W., Res. Officers Assn., Phi Beta Kappa. Clubs: Army and Navy, Burning Tree. Home: Stuttgart Germany Office: Dep Comdr in Chief US European Command APO New York City NY 09128

BURCK, ARTHUR ALBERT, business orgn. ofcl.; b. Mpls., June 8, 1913; s. Herman J. and Emma (Wirth) B.; B.S., U. Minn., 1935, LL.B., 1937; LL.D., U. Cin., 1969; m. Rutilia Poli-Sandri, June 2, 1945; children—Stephan W. (dec.), Adriana, Jeffrey L., Christopher C. Admitted to N.Y. bar, 1938; asso. Carter, Ledyard & Millburn, N.Y.C., 1937-39, Simons, Schur & Straus, N.Y.C., 1953-54; with SEC, 1939-53; head corp. reorgn. dept. Fahnestock & Co., N.Y.C., 1954-56; partner McClellan & Burck, negotiators bus.-mergers, acquisitions, N.Y.C., 1957- 58; pres. McClellan & Burck, Inc., N.Y.C., 1958-62; partner Arthur Burck & Co., planners, negotiators bus. mergers, acquisitions, corporate reorgans., 1963—; pres. Arthur Burck & Co., Inc., 1968—. Trustee Wagner Coll., S.I., 1955-61, mem. devel. council, 1961-67, vice chmn., 1966-67; trustee S.I. Acad., 1965-67; chmn. pres. bd. trustees Graham-Eckes Sch., Palm Beach, Fla., 1971—. Served to maj. AUS, 1942-47. Decorated Bronze Star medal; recipient SEC citation, 1952. Clubs: Richmond Country (S.I.); Ocean (Palm Beach, Fla.). Home: Villa Pompano 240 El Vedado Way Palm Beach FL 33480 Office: 37 Wall St New York City NY 10005

BURCK, JACOB, editorial cartoonist, painter; b. Poland, Jan. 10, 1904; s. Abraham and Rebecca (Lev) B.; student Cleve. Sch. Art, Art Students' League of N.Y.; studied portrait painting with Albert Sterner, N.Y.C., 1924-26; pupil Boardman Robinson; m. Esther Kriger, Jan. 12, 1933; children—Joseph, Conrad. Exhibited Cleve. Mus. Art, 1924, Whitney Mus. Am. Art, Mus. Modern Art; exhbn. murals Fine Arts Bldg., N.Y.C., Archtl. League, Chgo. Art Inst.; creator daily editorial cartoon Chgo. Sun-Times. Recipient Pulitzer prize, 1941, profl. journalistic frat. award Sigma Delta Chi, 1942; Birmingham Mus. Art 1st prize editorial cartooning, 1958. Member Sigma Delta Chi. Home: 921 Castlewood Terrace Chicago IL 60640 Office: Chgo Sun-Times Sun Times Plaza Chicago IL 60611

BURCKEL, CHRISTIAN EHRENFRIED, cons., publisher, analyst; b. Hamburg, Germany, Feb. 28, 1898; s. Christian O. and Clara E. (Husing) B.; brought to U.S. 1905; B.C.E., Ohio State U., 1922; M.A. Western Res. U., 1928; Ph.D.Tchrs. Coll. Columbia, 1941; m. Rutheda Fae Slemmons, Mar. 17, 1923. Asst. to san. engr. City of Cleve. 1922-23; tchr. Cleve. Pub. Schs., 1924-29, supt. sch., 1929; tchr. Lincoln Sch., Tchrs. Coll., Columbia, 1930-36; pub. The Mount Vernon (N.Y.) News and The Pelham News, 1937-38. Coll. Blue Book, 1939-66; dir. guidance Stamford, Conn. High Sch., 1939-40; cons. edn. and typography, 1940; special advisor Col. James L. Jackson, Tech. Data sect. USAAF, 1942-44; owner, dir. Christian E. Burckel and Assos., 1944-70; edn. editor The Bell-McClure Syndicate, 1964—; cons. mgmt. Pa. R.R., Gen. Electric, Internat. Harvester. Ward Leonard Electric Co., USAAF, Dept. Navy, Corps of Engrs., Goodyear, 1944-70, U.S. Army, 1918-19. Mem. N.E.A. (life), Am. Personnel and Guidance Assn. (life); Am. Mil. Engrs., Tech. Pubs. Assn. (pres.), Graphic Arts Industry Am. (research and engrng. council), Nat. Assn. Mfrs., U.S. C. of C., Triangle, Am. Legion, Phi Delta Kappa. Mason (32). Clubs: Engineers, National Republican, Lions, Mens Faculty (Columbia U.). Home: 100 Rockledge Rd Bronxville NY 10708 Office: 35 Washington St Yonkers NY 10707

BURCKHALTER, JOSEPH HAROLD, educator; b. Columbia, S.C., Oct. 9, 1912; s. Edward Wilson and Elizabeth (Strain) B.; B.S., U. S.C., 1934; M.S., U. Ill., 1939; Ph.D., U. Mich., 1942; m. Virginia Feikert, July 10, 1943; children—David Liggett, Robert Edward, Jane Ellen. Sr. research chemist Parke, Davis & Co., Detroit, 1942-47; Asso. prof. medicinal chem. U. Kan., Lawrence, 1947-50, prof., chmn., 1950-60; prof. medicinal chem. U. Mich., 1960—, chmn., 1967—; cons. Nat. Cancer Inst., 1957-60, 67—, mem. adv. com. cancer chemotherapy, 1969-72. Mem. Am. Chem. Soc. (chmn. div. medicinal chem. 1962, local sect. Kan. 1957), Chem. Soc. (London), Am. Pharm. Assn. (Research Achievement award, 1962), Phi Beta Kappa. Home: 2101 Melrose Av Ann Arbor MI 48104

BURD, JAMES E., merchandising exec.; b. Chgo., 1914. Exec. v.p., dir. Spiegel, Inc., Chgo.; v.p., dir. Beneficial Corp.; dir. Randolph Computer Corp., District Nat. Bank of Chgo. Home: 6336 N Kilpatrick Chicago IL 60646 Office: 2511 W 23d St Chicago IL 60608

BURD, LAURENCE HULL, newspaperman; b. Kansas City, Mo., Feb. 26, 1915; s. J. Laurence and Vera (Hull) B.; B.S., Northwestern U., 1936; m. Mary June Miller, July 29, 1939; children—Laurence, David, Stephen, Sally. Reporter Chgo. Tribune, 1937-63, mem. Washington bur., 1942-63, White House corr., 1947- 63; former Washington news editor Los Angeles Times. Mem. White House Corrs. Assn. (pres. 1955-56). Methodist. Clubs: Nat. Press (Washington); Bethesda (Md.) Country. Home: 5721 Bradley Blvd Bethesda MD 20014

BURD, VAN AKIN, educator; b. Miami, Fla., Apr. 19, 1914; s. Melvin S. and Elizabeth (Van Akin) B.; B.A., U. Chgo., 1936; M.A., Stanford, 1941; Ph.D., U. Mich., 1951; m. Julia Ella Robinson, June 18, 1943; 1 dau., Joyce Ellen (Mrs. Garland F. Hicks). Tchr. English, pub. schs., Flint, Mich., 1936-40; tchr. Menlo Sch. and Jr. Coll., Menlo Park, Cal., 1941-42; teaching fellow U. Mich., 1946-51; prof. English, State U. N.Y. Coll. at Cortland, 1951—, chmn. English dept., 1959-60, 61-63, 65-68, dir. arts and scis., 1963-64. Served to lt. comdr. USNR, 1942-46. Grantee Am. Philos. Soc., 1960, 65, 68, Research Found. State U. N.Y., 1955, 65, 67, 68, 70, Am. Council Learned Socs., 1968; Am. Council Learned Socs. fellow, 1960- 61. Mem. Modern Lang. Assn., Nat. Council Tchrs. English, Am. Assn. U. Profs., Thoreau Soc., Victorian Soc. Gt. Britain. Author: The Winnington Letters: The Correspondence of John Ruskin with M.A. Bell and the Children at Winnington Hall, 1969. Contbr. articles profl. jours. Home: 22 Forrest Av Cortland NY 13045

BURDELL, EDWIN SHARP, ednl. consultant; b. Columbus, Ohio, Feb. 2, 1898; s. William Frederick and Jennie Nottingham (Kelsey) B.; student Asheville (N.C.) School, 1911-15, Chaucey Hall Sch., Boston, 1915-16, Mass. Inst. Tech., 1916-20, Harvard Grad. Sch. Bus. Adminstrn., 1920-21; A.M., Ohio State U., 1929, Ph.D., 1934, D.L. (hon.), 1954; Litt.D. (hon.), Pratt Institute, 1960; m. Emma Metthea Mathiasen, Apr. 2, 1927; children—Karla Kelsey (Mrs. A. Basaran), Mary Matthea (Mrs. Edward Webb Keane). Banking, 1922-24; traveling and writing in Europe, Mexico, Central America, 1924-27; grad. study and teaching, Ohio State U., 1928-34; mem. Ohio Commn. on Unemployment Insurance, 1932; dir. Sch. for Unemployed, Ohio State U., 1932; state adminstr, for Emergency Edn. in Ohio, 1933-34; prof. of sociology and dir. summer sch., Mass. Inst. Tech., 1934-38, dean of humanities, 1937-38; dir. Cooper Union for Advancement Sci. and Art, N.Y., 1938-51, pres., 1951-60. pres. emeritus, 1960—; pres. Middle East Tech. U., Ankara, Turkey. 1960-62; cons. Cranbrook Found., Bloomfield Hills, Mich., 1962—; dean Rollins Coll., Winter Park, Fla., 1963-66. Co-chmn. Canada-United States Commn. on Edn, 1958-60; dir. Regional Plan Assn., 1957-60. Chmn. A.I.A. Commn. for Survey Edn. and Registration, 1949-54. Bd.. dirs. Central Fla. Red Cross. 1963—; trustee Winter Park Meml. Hosp., 1969—. Served as 2d lt., inf., AUS, World War I. Decorated King Christian X Medal of Liberation; Knight Cross of the Dannebrog (Danish), 1951. Vice chmn. Zoning Bd., Columbus, O., 1923-34; chmn. Municipal Housing Board, Columbus, 1933-34; mem. Mass. Bd. Prison Industries, 1935-38; chmn. com. on housing Community Service Soc., 1948, trustee 1942; trustee Am.-Scandinavian Found.; mem. USCG Acad. adv. com., 1956-60. Capt. USCG Res., 1960—. Fellow Am. Sociol. Soc.; mem. A.I.A. (hon.), Am. Inst. of Interior Designers (hon.), Am. Inst. Planners, Am. Soc. Nat. Recreation and Parks Assn. (bd. dirs. lay div.), Sigma Chi, Phi Beta Kappa. Episcopalian. Clubs: Century (N.Y.C.); University (Winter Park, Fla.). Contbr. to jours. Home: 521 Dommerich Dr Maitland FL 32751

BURDEN, WILLIAM ARMISTEAD MOALE, financier; b. N.Y.C., Apr. 8, 1906; s. William A. M. and Florence Vanderbilt (Twombly) B.; A.B. cum laude, Harvard, 1927; D.Sc., Clarkson Coll. Tech., 1953; LL.D., Fairleigh Dickinson U., 1965, Johns Hopkins U., 1970; m. Margaret Livingston Partridge, Feb. 16, 1931; children—William A. M. (dec.), Robert Livingston, Hamilton Twombly, Ordway Partridge. Analyst aviation securities Brown Bros., Harriman & Co., N.Y.C., 1928-32; charge of aviation research Scudder, Stevens & Clark, N.Y.C., 1932-39; v.p., dir. Nat. Aviation Corp., aviation investment trust, N.Y.C., 1939-41; v.p. Def. Supplies Corp. (subsidiary RFC), 1941-42; spl. aviation asst. Sec. of Commerce, 1942-43; mem. NACA, 1942-47, asst. Sec. Commerce for Air, 1943-47; U.S. del. Civil Aviation Conf., 1944; chmn. U.S. delegation interim assembly Provisional Internat. Civil Aviation Orgn., 1946; aviation cons. Smith Barney & Co., Inc., 1947-49; partner William A.M. Burden & Co., 1949—; spl. asst. for research and devel. to Sec. of Air Force, 1950-52; mem. Nat. Aeros. and Space Council, 1958-59; U.S. ambassador to Belgium, 1959-61; mem. U.S. Citizens Commn. for NATO, 1961-62; dir. Am. Metal Climax, CBS, Inc., Mfrs. Hanover Trust Co. (hon.). Chmn. bd. Inst. for Def. Analyses, 1961—; trustee, past pres., chmn. Mus. Modern Art; gov. Soc. of N.Y. Hosp., 1950—; trustee Columbia, 1956—, Fgn. Service Edn. Found., French Inst. in U.S. Regent Smithsonian Instn., 1962—; bd. dirs. Atlantic council U.S., 1961—; bd. govs. Atlantic Inst., 1964—. Decorated comdr. Cruzeiro do Sul (Brazil), comdr.'s cross Order of Merit (Fed. Republic Germany), grand official El Sol del Peru (Peru), grand officer French Legion of Honor, comdr.'s cross Order of Merit (Italy), grand cordon Order of Leopold (Belgium), asso. comdr. (Bro.) Order of St. John. Mem. Council Fgn. Relations (dir.), Am. Inst. Aeros. and Astronautics, France-Am. Soc. (pres.), Confrerie des Chevaliers du Tastevin. Clubs: Somerset (Boston, Mass.); The Brook, Racquet and Tennis, River, Links, Century, Downtown Assn. (N.Y.C.); Metropolitan, Chevy Chase Cosmos (Washington); Buck's and White's (London); Travelers (Paris). Author: The Struggle for Airways in Latin America, 1943. Address: 630 Fifth Av New York City NY 10020

BURDEN, WILLIAM DOUGLAS, naturalist; b. Troy, N.Y., Sept. 24, 1898; s.James Abercrombie and Florence Adele (Sloane) B.; A.B., Harvard, 1922; M.A., Columbia, 1926; grad. Naval Aviation Tng. School, 1918; m. Katharine Curtin White, Aug. 1924 (divorced 1939); children—Wendy (Mrs. Edw. Morgan), William Douglas, Andrew White; m. 2d, Elizabeth Chace Gammack, Jan. 26, 1940; 1 son, Christopher; m. 3d, Jeanne Wight Booth, Apr. 26, 1971. Began in diamond mine, Brazil, 1921; collecting expdn. Far East, Am. Mus. Natural History, 1922-23, exploration, Nicaragua, 1924, led expdn. to capture dragon lizards of Komodo, 1926, started dept. exptl. biology, later animal behavior, 1928; producer Red Indian documentary film The Silent Enemy, 1928-29; pres., dir. Burden Pictures, Inc., 1928-31; v.p., dir. Beacon Films, 1931-35; pres., dir. Marineland, Inc., 1937-61; chmn. bd. Surluga Gold Mines, Ltd., 1962-68, hon. chmb., 1968—. Trustee Am. Mus. Natural History, 1926-61, asso. benefactor, 1927—, now hon. trustee; trustee N.Y. Zool. Soc., 1938-41; Chmn. bd., trustee Vt. Wild Land Found.; mem. sci. com. Human Betterment Assn. Am.; mem. governing bd. Marineland Research Lab. Mem. Gov.'s Scenery Preservation Commn., 1970—; chmn. bd. Vt. Wildlife Found., 1966—. Cons. OSS, Wright Field, Dayton, O., 1944; responsible investigator com. med. research Office Sci. Research and Devel., 1945, assigned Joint Target Group, War Dept. Mem. Sigma Xi. Clubs: Boone and Crockett, River, Amateur Ski, Harvard Travellers Club, Somerset Hills, Chevy Chase, Explorers. Author: Dragon Lizards of Komodo, 1927; Look to the Wilderness, 1960; various articles nat. mags. Home: Charlotte VT Office: Charlotte VT

BURDETSKY, BEN, govt. ofcl.; b. Phila., July 15, 1928; s. Morris and Rebecca (singer) B.; B.S. in Edn., Temple U., 1950, M.S. in Psychology, 1958; Ph.D. in Bus. Adminstrn., Am. U., 1968; m. Irene Lusky, Feb. 9, 1958; childrenJune, Andrew, Marjorie, Matthew, Abbe. Tchr., Phila. schs., 1954-55; with U.S. Bur. Employment Security, 1955-61; chief data systems Dept. Labor, 1961-66; dir. adminstrv. mgmt. Bur. Labor Statistics, 1966- 67, acting commnr., 1968-69, dep. commnr., 1967-; part-time tchr. grad. program Sch. Bus. Adminstrn., Am. U., 1963-. Served with USAF, 1950-54. Mem. Indsl. Relations Research Assn., Am. Statis. Assn., Internat. Assn. Personnel in Employment Security. Home: 4619 N Dittmar Rd Arlington, VA 22207. Office: 441 G St NW Washington DC 20212

BURDETT, ALLEN MITCHELL, Jr., army officer; b. Washington, Aug. 25, 1921; s. Allen Mitchell and Margaret (Briscoe) B.; B.S., U.S. Mil. Acad., 1943; grad. Inf. Sch., 1951, Command and Gen. Staff Coll., 1953, Armed Forces Staff Coll., Norfolk, Va., 1955; Army War Coll., 1959; M.A., George Washington U., 1965; m. Antoinette Salley, Apr. 19, 1948; children—Allen Mitchell III, William M., Margaret B., Douglas N. Commd. 2d lt. U.S. Army, 1943, advanced through grades to maj. gen., 1970; asst. prof. mil. sci. and tactics Ga. Inst. Tech., 1947-50; S3 and bn. exec. officer 508th Airborne Regtl. Combat Team, 1951-52; inf. bn. comdr., regtl. exec. officer 31st Inf., 7th Inf. Div., 1953-54; G1 and G2, 7th Inf. Div., 1954; army rep. Office of Comdt. USAF Acad., 1955-58; dir. Combat Devels. Office, dep. asst. comdt. Army Aviation Sch., 1960-62; exec. officer to asst. sec. army, 1962-65; comdg. officer 11th Aviation Group, 1st Cav. Div., 1965-66; mil. asst. Office Dir. Def. Research and Engring., 1966-68; asst. div. comdr. 101st Airborne Div., 1968-69; comdg. gen. 1st Aviation Brigade, 1969-70; dir. Army Aviation, Office Asst. Chief of Staff for Force Devel., Dept. Army, 1970; comdg. gen. U.S. Army Aviation Center and comdt. U.S. Army Aviation Sch., Ft. Rucker, Ala., 1970—. Mem. exec. bd. Ala.-Fla. council Boy Scouts Am. Decorated D.S.M., Silver Star with oak leaf cluster, Legion of Merit with oak leaf cluster, D.F.C. with oak leaf cluster, Bronze Star with V and 2 oak leaf clusters, Air medal with 24 oak leaf clusters, Army Commendation medal, Air Force Commendation medal, Purple Heart, Combat Inf. badge, Vietnamese Gallantry Cross with palm. Mem. Am. Helicopter Soc. (v.p. S.E. region), Army Aviation Assn. Am. (mem. at large nat. exec. bd.), Assn. Grads U.S. Mil. Acad., Assn. U.S. Army, Soc. of the Cincinnati. Home: 45 Red Cloud Rd Fort Rucker AL 36360 Office: Office Comdg Gen US Army Aviation Center Fort Rucker AL 36360

BURDETT, CHARLES FRED, ret. coll. pres.; b. Woburn, Mass., Apr. 3, 1904; s. Fred H. and Sadie (Hayward) B.; A.B., Amherst Coll., 1929; student bus. adminstrn., Harvard, 1929-30; m. Dorothy E. Leibensperger, June 26, 1930; children— Charles, Mary Ann, Sara May, Caroline. Treas. Burdett Coll., Boston and Lynn, Mass., 1929-35, pres., 1935-70. Mem. Woburn Hist. Commn., 1971—. Bd. dirs., past pres. Woburn YMCA; pres. Frederika Home, 1957—, Mass. New Church Union, 1970—. Mem. Bus. Edn. Research Assos. (sec. 1947-59, pres. 1959-61), Mass. Assn. Pvt. Bus. Schs. (pres. 1962-64), New Eng. Bus. College Assn. (pres. 1965-66), Woburn C. of C., Swedenborgian. Clubs: Rushlight (pres. 1959-60); Harvard; Back Bay Exchange (Boston). Home: 605 Main St Woburn MA 01801

BURDETT, ROBERT JAMES, lawyer; b. Chgo., July 5, 1907; s. James Henderson and Josephine Amanda (Pettett) B.; student Centre Coll. Ky., 1925-26, U. Ill., 1926-28; LL.B., Chgo.-Kent Coll. Law, 1930, M.L., 1931; m. Bernice Lohmeyer, Aug. 30, 1930; children—Virginia Ann (Mrs. Everett Moore, Jr.), Joan Elizabeth (Mrs. Walter Cejner), Robert James, John William. Admitted to Ill. bar, 1930, U.S. Supreme Ct., 1951; partner firm Bishop and Burdett, Chgo., 1941-69; gen. counsel Anchor Coupling Co. Inc., Libertyville, Ill., 1956—, dir., asst. sec., 1962—; atty. Village South Chicago Heights, 1939—; Ill. asst. atty. gen. charge appeals, 1949-52. Dir., sec., counsel Central State Inst. Addiction Programs, 1965—; pres. Schizophrenia Found. Ill., 1967—; dir., counsel Oasis, Midwest Center Human Potential, 1967—, sec., 1970—; counsel Ch. of the Awakening, 1963—, dir., 1969—. Mem. Am., Ill., Chgo. bar assns. Clubs: Law, Union League (Chgo.); Flossmoor (Ill.) Country. Home: 17834 Howe Av Homewood IL 60430 Office: 105 W Adams St Chicago IL 60603

BURDETT, WILLIAM CARTER, fgn. service officer; b. Knoxville, Tenn., Oct. 25, 1918; s. William Carter and Elizabeth Hardwick (Burke) B.; A.B., Princeton, 1941; m. Marlys Maxine Hanson, March 10, 1956. Clerk Dept. State, 1941; v. consul, Guayaquil, Ecuador, 1942-44, Basra, Iraq, 1946-47; v. consul, Jerusalem, 1948, consul, 1948-50, acting U.S. rep. security council truce commn. for Palestine; consul, Tabriz, Iran, 1950-52; 1st sec. Am. Embassy, Tehran, Iran, 1952; U.S. Liaison Officer, Khartoum, Sudan, 1952- 53; officer in charge Egyptian and Sudan affairs, 1953-55; dep. dir. Office Near Eastern Affairs, 1955; spl. asst. Bur. Near Eastern, South Asian and African Affairs, 1956-57; 1st sec. Am. Embassy, London, 1957- 60; dir. Office Brit. and No. European Affairs, 1960-61, acting dep. asst. sec. for European affairs, 1961-62, dep. asst. sec. for European affairs, 1962-64; fgn. service inspector, 1964-66; student Senior Seminar in Foreign Policy, 1966; minister-counselor Am. embassy, Ankara, 1967-70; career minister, 1969; ambassador to Malawi, 1970—. Served with U.S. Marine Corps, 1944-45. Recipient Meritorious Service award. State Department, 1954. Home: 171 Callaway St Macon GA 31204 Office: Dept of State Washington DC 20520

BURDETT, WINSTON, fgn. corr., radio reporter; b. Buffalo, Dec. 12, 1913; grad. magna cum laude, Harvard, 1933; grad. study Columbia; m. Lea Schiavi (dec. 1942); m. 2d, Georgina Nathan, July 1945; children—Christina Sandra, Richard Michael. Formerly associated with the Brooklyn Eagle; then reporter, columnist The Sound Track, asso. editor Sunday supplement The Trend, roving corr., covering World War II; Scandinavian corr. Transradio Press; fgn. corr. CBS, broadcaster to U.S. over CBS on daily roundup of news from fgn. capitols; chief of Rome Bur. CBS. Home: Via Cassia 15 Rome Italy Office: Plazza Grazioli 5 Rome Italy

BURDETTE, FRANKLIN L., educator; b. Huntington, W.Va., Dec. 7, 1911; s. Frank Lee and Laura (Buckner) B.; A.B. summa cum laude, Marshall Coll., 1934; A.M., U. Neb., 1935; postgrad. U. N.C., 1935-36, U. Chgo., 1936; A.M., Princeton, 1937, Ph.D., 1938; LL.D., Marshall Coll., 1959; m. Evelyn Spruill Page, June 28, 1938; children—Franklin Page, Joseph Bryan. Instr. politics Princeton U., 1936-37, 1938-39, fellow, 1937-38; research asso. Princeton Local Govt. Survey, 1939-4O; mem. faculty Butler U., 1940-46; asso. prof. govt. and politics U. Md., 1946-47, prof., 1947—, head dept., 1950-54, dir. bur. govtl. research, 1956—, on leave as head of overseas book program and related cultural activities U.S. Govt., 1954- 56; exec. sec. Nat. Found. Edn. Am. Citizenship, 1940-46, editor publs., 1946-50; editor polit. sci. series D. Van Nostrand Co., 1948—; bd. dirs. Operations and Policy Research, Inc. Mem. bd. editors Am. Polit. Sci. Rev., 1948-49; lectr. polit. sci. Am. U., 1948-49. Trustee Westminster Choir Coll., Princeton, N.J.; bd. dirs. Council on Islamic Affairs, 1957-60; chmn. Md. Gov.'s Commn. on Reapportionment of Legislature, 1962-64; mem. Md. State Constl. Conv. Commn., 1965-67; del. Md. Constl. Conv., 1967-68. Sec., mem. bd. trustees Inst. for Am. Univs., U. Aix-Marseille, France, 1958—; trustee Montgomery Coll., 1969—. Mem. ednl. bd. YMCA evening high sch., Indpls., 1941-46; mem. bd. Ind. Merit Assn., 1941-46; mem. Ind. War History Commn., 1943-46; sec. Indpls. br. Fgn. Policy Assn., 1944-46. Mem. Am. Soc. Internat. Law, Am. Hist. Assn., Am. Polit. Sci. Assn. (pres. Washington chpt. 1950-51, mem. nat. council 1962-64), Middle States Council for Social Studies (pres. 1953-54), Am. Soc. Pub. Administrn. (ofcl. observer Baghdad Pact in Iraq 1957, pres. Md. chpt. 1958-59), Nat. Civil Service League (mem. council), Nat. Municipal League, S.A.R. (v.p. gen. nat. soc. 1933-38; sec. W.Va. Soc. 1930-38; sec. Ind. soc. 1943-46). So. Polit. Sci. Assn. (v.p. 1952), Assn. Coll. Honor Socs. (pres 1969-71), Kappa Delta Pi, Phi Alpha Theta, Phi Kappa Phi, Pi Sigma Alpha (nat. sec., treas. 1946-48, nat. pres. 1956-58, nat. dir. 1960—). Baptist. Mason. Author: Filibustering in the Senate, 1940; Political Parties: An American Way, 1945; Lobbyists in Action, 1950; Election Practices in Maryland, 1950; The Republican Party: A Short History, 1968. Editor: Education for Citizen Responsibilities, 1942; biog. directory of Am. Polit. Sci. Assn., 1945-48, 61. Co- Editor hist. monographs on religion and Am. Instn., 1947-49; chmn. bd. editors World Affairs, 1965—; adv. editor Ency. Americana, 1968—. Contbr. articles on polit. subjects to publs. Home: 5201 Wilson Lane Bethesda MD 20014. Office: Bur Govtl Research Research U Md College Park MD 20742

BURDETTE, WALTER JAMES, surgeon, educator; b. Hillsboro, Tex., Feb. 5, 1915; s. James S. and Ovazene (Weatherred) B.; A.B., Baylor U., 1935; A.M., U. Tex., 1936, Ph.D., 1938; M.D., Yale, 1942; m. Kathryn Lynch, Apr. 9, 1947; children— Susan, William J. Intern Johns Hopkins Hosp., 1942-43; Harvey Cushing fellow surgery Yale, 1943-44, asst. resident surgery New Haven Hosp., 1944-46; instr., asst., asso. prof. surgery La. State U., 1946-55; vis. surgeon Charity Hosp. of La., 1946-55; cons. Touro Infirmary and So. Baptist Hosp., 1952-55, Oak Ridge Inst. Nuclear Studies Hosp., 1953- 59; vis. investigator Chester Beatty Inst. Cancer Research and Royal Cancer Hosp., London, 1953, Max Planck Institut Fuer Biochemie, Tuebingen, Germany, summer 1955; prof., chmn. dept. surgery U. Mo., 1955-56; prof. clin. surgery St. Louis U. Sch. Medicine, 1956-57; prof., head dept. surgery U. Utah, 1957-65; dir. lab. clin. biology, surgeon-in-chief Salt Lake Gen. Hosp., 1957-65; chief surg. cons. VA Hosps., Salt Lake City, 1957-65; prof. surgery, asso. dir. U. Tex-M. D. Anderson Hosp., and Tumor Inst., Houston, 1965—; prof. surgery U. Tex. Sch. Medicine at Houston, 1971—; cons. Hermann Hosp., Center Pavilion Hosp., 1970—; Gibson lecturer advanced surgery Oxford U. 1966; vis. prof. U. Oxford, spring 1965, Official U. Congo, summer 1968. Chmn. genetics study sect. mem. morphology study sect. NIH; cons. Nat. Cancer Inst., mem. Nat. Adv. Cancer Council, National Advisory Heart Council, Surgeon General's Committee on Smoking and Health; chmn. U.S.A. nat. com. Internat. Union Against Cancer; mem. transplantation com. Nat. Acad. Scis.; chmn. working Cadre on cancer large intestine Nat. Cancer Inst. Rockefeller travel fellow, summer 1957. Diplomate Am. Bd. Surgery, Am. Bd. Thoracic Surgery. Fellow A.C.S.; mem. Soc. Surgery Alimentary Tract, Am. Assn. Cancer Research (dir.), Am. Cancer Soc. (chmn. research adv. council, member council on analysis and projection), Am. Surg. Assn., Soc. Clin. Surgery (treas.), Soc. U. Surgeons, A.M.A., Soc. Exptl. Biology and Medicine, Genetics Soc. Am., A.A.A.S., Western Soc. Clin. Research, Am. Assn. Thoracic Surgery, Transplantation Soc., N.Y. Acad. Sci., Soc. Am. Naturalists, New Orleans, St. Louis, Salt Lake City, Houston surg. socs., Tex. Med. Soc., Harris County Med. Soc., So., Western surg. assns., So. Thoracic Surg. Soc., others, Soc. Internat. di Chirurg, Sigma Xi, Alpha Omega Alpha. Editor: Etiology, Treatment of Leukemia, 1958; Methodology in Human Genetics, 1962; Methodology in Mammalian Genetics, 1962; Methodology in Basic Genetics, 1963; Primary Hepatoma, 1965; Carcinoma of the Alimentary Tract, 1965; Viruses Inducing Cancer, 1966; Carcinoma of the Colon and Antecedent Epithelium, 1970; Planning and Analysis of Clinical Studies, 1970. Mem. editorial bd. Cancer Research. Contbr. articles med. and sci. jours. Home: 239 Chimney Rock Rd Houston TX 77024

BURDICK ALGER ERNEST coll. ofcl.; b. Milw., Dec. 9, 1911; s. Ernest Frank and Addie (Phillips) B.; B.A., U. Wis., 1943; M.A. 1936; student Columbia, 1937-38; Ph.D., George Peabody Coll. 1951; m. Anne Gray, Aug 15, 1937; children— Charles Gray, Grad. asst. U. Wis., 1935-36; instr. geography Ark. State Tchrs. Coll., 1937, asst. prof. social studies 1938- 47, prof. head dept. geography 1947, asst. dean, 1952-54 dean 1954-70, v.p., 1970—. Instr. geology and geography N.W. Mo. State Tchrs. Coll., Maryville, 1938; vis. prof. geography Hendrix Coll., Conway, Ark., 1950- -. Fellow Am. Geog. Soc., mem. Assn. Am. Geographers, Nat. Council Geography Tchrs. (state coordinator), Ark. Council Geography (pres.), Am. Am. Meteorol. Soc., Nat. Council Social Studies, Conway C. of C., Phi Delta Kappa. Contbr. articles to profl. jours. Home: 222 Mitchell St Conway AR 72032

BURDICK, ALLAN BERNARD, geneticist; b. Cin., Aug. 16, 1920; s. Theodore Allan and Rachel C. (Mullen) B.; B.S., Ia. State U., 1945, M.S., 1947; Ph.D., U. Cal., at Berkeley, 1949; m. Sally Ann Cummins, Feb. 17, 1943; children—Michael Allan, Nancy Cecilia, Stephen Franklin, Lindy Lou. Asst. prof. genetics U. Ark., 1949-52; asst. prof. Purdue U., 1952-54, assoc. prof., 1954-59, prof. genetics, 1959-63; prof., asso. dean sci. Am. U., Beirut, Lebanon, 1963-66; prof., chmn. biology dept. Adelphi U., Garden City, N.Y., 1966- 69; prof., chmn. dept. genetics U. Mo., Columbia, 1969—; dir., co- founder Tomato Genetics Coop., 1950-62; cons. Pahlavi U., Shiraz, Iran, 1965-66, Jordanian Ministry Edn., 1964-65. Mem. Com. Edn. Women in Sci., 1962. Bd. dirs. Ecumenical Center, Columbia, Mo., 1970—. Served to maj. USAAF, 1942-46. Recipient medallion of H.I.M., Shah of Iran, 1966; Guggenheim fellow, 1959-60; Fulbright research scholar, Kyoto U., 1959-60. Fellow A.A.A.S.; mem. Genetics Soc. Am., Am. Soc. Naturalists, Am. Assn. U. Profs., Am. Inst. Biol. Scis., Sigma Xi, Sigma Phi Epsilon (bd. dirs. Mo. Alpha Corp. 1970—). Episcopalian (vestryman 1954-62, warden 1957, lay reader 1951—). Contbr. articles profl. jours. Established single gene heterosis for lethal gene, 1959, that minor genes have higher mutation rates than major genes, 1958-59. Home: 2412 W Rollins Rd Columbia MO 65201

BURDICK, BENJAMIN LOVELL, lawyer; b. Stillwater, Okla., Jan. 4, 1919; s. Cary Lovell and Cora (Chaney) B.; A.B., U. Okla., 1940; LL.B., Yale, 1947; m. Tracey June Spencer, June 11, 1946; children-Tracey Ann (Mrs. Richard Linn Cowan Virtue, Jr.). Carol Lynn, Susan Cary. Admitted to Okla. bar, 1948, since practiced in Oklahoma City; mem. firm Crowe, Dunlevy, Thweatt, Swinford, Johnson & Burdick. Pres. Okla. Found. for Disabled Adults, 1963. Oklahoma City council Camp Fire Girls, 1964. Bd. dirs. Okla. chpt. Arthritis Found.; bd. mgmt. Central br. Oklahoma City YMCA. Served from 2d lt. to lt. col., F.A., AUS, 1940-46. Fellow Am. Coll. Trial Lawyers; mem. Internat. Assn. Ins. Counsel, Fedn. Ins. Counsel, Am., Okla., Oklahoma County bar assns., Phi Beta Kappa, Sigma Chi, Phi Delta Phi. Democrat. Presbyn. (elder). Clubs: Petroleum, Oklahoma City Golf and Country, (Oklahoma City).

BURDICK, CHARLES LALOR, chem. engr.; b. Denver, Apr. 14, 1892; s. Frank Austin and Anna (Lalor) B.; B.S., Drake U., 1911, LL.D., 1970; B.S. Mass. Inst. Tech., 1913, M.S., 1914; postgrad. Kaiser Wilhelm Inst., Berlin, and Univ. Coll., London, 1914-16; Ph.D., U. Basel, Switzerland, 1915; D.Sc., U. Del., 1955; m. Alison Ward, 1938; children—Lalor, Cynthia. Research asso. in chemistry, Mass Inst. Tech. and Cal. Inst. of Technology, 1916-17; metall. engr. Guggenheim Bros., N.Y. and Chile, 1919-24; v.p. and cons. engr. Anglo-Chilean Consol. Nitrate Corp., 1924-28; with E. I. du Pont de Nemours, 1929-57, in various positions as asst. chem. dir., ammonia dept., spl. asst. to pres. chmn. bds. in Mex. of DuPont S.A., and Cia. Mexicana de Explosives. Mem. Scientific adv. com. Henry Francis du Pont Winterthur Mus.; mem. exec. com. Internat. Planned Parenthood Fedn., 1962-68. Pres. Christiana Found.; exec. dir., trustee Lalor Found., Wilmington; founding trustee U. Del. Research Found.; trustee Del. Acad. Medicine; bd. dirs. Planned Parenthood-World Population, 1961-67. Served as 1st lt. Ordnance div., U.S. Army, 1917-18. Fellow A.A.A.S., fgn. Fellow Royal Hort. Soc. (Eng.); mem. N.Y. Acad. Sci. (life), Am. Inst. Chem. Engrs., Am. Chem. Soc., Am. Fertility Soc., Am. Assn. Planned Parenthood Physicians (asso.), Am. Eugenics Soc., Am. Inst. Biol. Scis., (Soc.) for Study Reprodn. (charter), Soc. Study Fertility (Eng.), Phi Beta Kappa. Clubs: Wilmington Vicmead, Greenville Country. Home: 4400 Lancaster Pike Wilmington DE 19805 Office: du Pont Bldg Wilmington DE 19898

BURDICK, DEAN LANPHERE, advt. exec.; b. Little Genesee, N.Y., June 12 1920; s. Herman R. and Mary A. (Lanphere) B.; A.B., U. Mich., 1943; m. Onilee L. Shaner, Aug 28, 1942; children—Dean Lanphere, Kathryn L. Mng. editors. publs., Corning Glass Works, 1945-48; copy head advt. dept. Abbott Labs., 1948- 52; exec. v.p. creative head William Douglas McAdams, Inc., 1952-56; pres. Burdick & Becker, Inc., pharm. advt., N.Y.C., 1956-61; pres. Dean L. Burdick Assos., Inc., 1961—. Mem. Pharm. Advt. Club, Inc., N.Y.C. Conglist. Clubs: Woodway Country (Darien, Conn.); Canadian (N.Y.C.). Home: Hickory Lane New Canaan CT 06840 Office: 655 Madison Av New York City NY 10021

BURDICK, LEONARD WALLACE, lawyer; b. Homer, N.Y., Apr. 26, 1900; s. William E. and Cara (Babcock) B.; student Colgate U., 1918-20; LL.B., Cornell U., 1923 m. Ruth M. Balcom, May 12, 1925; 1 dau., Carol (Mrs. Harold R. Roffmann, Jr.). Admitted to N.Y. bar, 1924, Cal. bar, 1929; practice in Utica, 1931, mem. firm Evans Burdick, Severn & Jones, 1937—; U.S. appeal agt. local draft bd., 1942-43. Past dir. Utica Drop Forge & Tool Corp., Internat. Heater Co. Past trustee Faxton Hosp., Utica. Mem. Order of Coif, Phi Delta Theta, Delta Theta Phi. Presbyn. Club: Fort Schuyler (past bd. mgrs.) (Utica). Home: 51 Arlington Terrace Utica NY 13501 Office: Mayro Bldg Utica NY 13501

BURDICK, QUENTIN NORTHROP, U.S. senator; b. Munich, N.D., June 19, 1908; s. Usher Lloyd and Emma (Robertson) B.; B.A., U. Minn., 1930, LL.B., 1932; m. Marietta Janecky, Mar. 18, 1933 (dec. Mar. 1958); children—Jonathan, Jan, Mary, Jennifer, Jessica. Admitted to N.D. bar, 1932, practiced in Fargo, 1932- 58; mem. 86th Congress, N.D. at large; U.S. senator, from N.D., 1960—. Candidate for lt. gov., 1942, for gov., 1946, for U.S. sentor, 1956. Mem. Sigma Nu. Democrat. Conglist. Mason, Elk, Eagle. Home: 310 10th Av S Fargo ND 58102 also 305 C St NE Washington DC 20002 Office: Senate Office Bldg Washington DC 20525

BURDING, WARREN NEWCOMB, business exec.; b. Salem, Mass, Mar. 20 1907; s. William A. and Hattie A. (Newcomb) B.; B.S., Dartmouth Coll., 1928; m. Alice H. Dart, June 22, 1935 (dec. 1963); children—Barbara, William, Margaret; m. 2d, Hazel S. Hackett, 1965. Employed Standard Brands, Inc., 1928, v.p., 1944; pres. Good Luck Products div. Lever Bros. Co., 1949-53, marketing v.p. Lever div. 1953-59, dir. co., 1956—, exec. v.p., 1959-68, exec. v.p. operations, 1968—, chmn. exec. com., 1969—. Mem. Delta Tau Delta. Clubs: University Siwanoy Country; Country of Fla.; Everglades. Home: 31 Ridge Croft Rd Bronxville NY 10708 Office: 390 Park Av New York NY 10022

BURDITT, JOHN FREDERIC, mfg. co. exec.; b. Newton, Mass., Apr. 4, 1918; s. Frederic McGregor and Florence Lovejoy (Willey) B.; student Browne and Nichols Sch., Cambridge, Mass.; B.A., Yale 1940; m. Jane Spaulding Nye, Sept. 6, 1947; children—Faraday Nye, Frederic McGregor, John Carver, Timothy Nye Benjamin Ames. With Chem. Bank & Trust Co., N.Y.C., 1945-48; with ACF Industries, Inc., N.Y.C., now chmn., chief exec. officer; dir. Polymer Corp., Seaboard Surety Co., N.Y.C.; mem. midtown adv. com. Chase Manhattan Bank, N.Y.C. Trustee Clarkson Coll. Tech., Potsdam, N.Y. Served to lt. comdr. USNR, 1941-46. Clubs: Economic, Treasurer's, Pinnacle, Board Room (N.Y.C.); Bedford Golf and Tennis (N.Y.). Home: Bedford Center Rd Bedford Hills NY 10507 Office: 750 3d Av New York City NY 10017

BURES, CHARLES EDWIN, educator; b. Cedar Rapids, Ia., Mar. 7, 1910; s. Frank Joseph and Olga (Janda) B.; B.A., Grinnell Coll., 1933; postgrad. Columbia, 1933-34; M.A., U. Ia., 1936, Ph.D., 1938; m. Helen Elizabeth Bonde, June 1, 1948. Prof. philosophy and psychology Coll. Ida., 1938-42; with N.Am. Aviation, Inc., 1943-45; lectr. U. So. Cal., 1947-48, instr. U. Ore., 1948-49; asst. prof. Cal. Inst. Tech., Pasadena, 1949-53, asso. prof., 1953-69, prof., 1969—. Fellow A.A.A.S.; mem. Am. Philos. Assn., Am. Math. Soc., Am. Psychol. Assn. Philosophy Sci. Assn., Assn. for Symbolic Logic, Nat. Audubon Soc., Sierra Club, Phi Beta Kappa. Home: 564-C S Marengo Av Pasadena CA 91101

BURFORD, CYRUS EDGAR, retired urologist; b. Girard Ill., Aug. 20, 1876; s. Giles McKenzie and Elizabeth Ellen (Hamilton) B.; Ph.B., LL.D., Central Coll., Fayette, Mo., 1899; M.D. Marion Simms Beaumont Med. Coll., St. Louis U., 1902, Zeugnis, U. Vienna, 1912; m. Katherine Lloyd Humber, June 15, 1899 (dec.); children—Ada Margaret (Mrs. George Osburn Cutter), Edgar H. (dec.) Intern St. Louis City Hosp., 1902-03; instr. St. Louis U. Med. Sch., asst. to Dr. Bransford Lewis, urologist, 1904-10; postgrad. work European clinics, 1912; prof., dir. urology dept. St. Louis U., 1922—, now emeritus; urologist Columbia (Mo.) State Cancer, Firmin DesLoge, St. Mary's, St. Luke's, Mo. Baptist, Bethesda Gen., Jewish hosps. Shriners Hosp. Crippled Children: now ret. Pres. bd. curators Central Coll. (chmn. emeritus). Diplomate Am. Bd. Urology. Fellow A.C.S., Am. Assn. Genito-Urinary Surgeons (past pres.); mem. Am. Urol. Assn. (past pres.), St. Louis Med. Soc. (past pres.), Mo. Med. Assn. (past pres.) St. Louis Surg. Soc. (past pres.). St. Louis Urol. Assn. (past pres.), Sigma Alpha Epsilon, Phi Beta Pi, Alpha Omega Alpha. Mason (32). Clubs: Contemporary of St. Louis (bd. dirs.), University, Glen Echo Country, Automobile of Mo. (dir.). Contbr. chpt. to Christopher's Surgery. Author papers on kidney and bladder surgery. Home: 6655 Waterman Av St Louis MO 63130

BURFORD, MORTIMER GILBERT, educator; b. Brooklyn, Oct. 27 1910; s. Mortimer Gilbert and Leila Lowe (Howell) B.: B.A., Wesleyan U., 1932; M.A., Princeton, 1933, Class of 1860 fellow in exptl. sci., 1934-35, Ph.D., 1935; m. Beatrice Mary Guelf, June 20, 1934. Instr. analytical chemistry Cornell U., 1935- 36, summer session, 1936; instr. chemistry Wesleyan U., Conn., 1936-39, asst. prof., 1939-45, asso. prof., 1945-47, Beach prof. chemistry, 1947, E. B. Nye prof. chemistry, 1951—. asso. provost, 1969—, incorporator, dir. U. Research Inst. Conn., 1964—. Research chemist Nat. Def. Research Com., 1941-45; cons. chemist State Water Commn., 1942—, N.E. Interstate Water Pollution Control Commn., 1950—; mem. adv. com. to coordinator of lab. services Pub. Health Services Br., Office Civil Def.; examiner Conn. Merit System. Faculty fellow. Fund for Advancement Edn., 1955-56; mem. region II reviewing com. Woodrow Wilson Nat. Fellowships, 1958-68, chmn. 1964-68. Fellow A.A.A.S., Am. Chem. Soc. (past chmn. Conn. Valley sect., mem. nat. vis. scientist program 1958-68), Am. Inst. Chemists; mem. Am. Assn. U. Profs. (pres. Conn. conf. 1963- 64), History of Sci. Soc. (chmn. Conn. sect. 1953-55), Sigma Xi, Phi Beta Kappa, Sigma Chi. Clubs: Rotary, Faculty. Contbr. papers on analytical chemistry and indsl. trade waste pollution. Home: Meeting House Rd Haddam CT 06438

BURFORD, SAMUEL POUNDERS, lawyer; b. Mt. Pleasant, Tex., Oct. 1, 1911; s. Joseph Milton and Florence (Pounders) B.; B.A., So. Methodist U., 1933, LL.B., 1936; m. Nable Isabel Rife, Dec. 28, 1935; children—Nancy Lee (Mrs. Donald J. Needham), Samuel Ponders. Admitted to Tex. bar, 1936, since practiced in Dallas; mem. firm Burford, Ryburn & Ford, 1942—; instr. dental jurisprudence Baylor Dental Coll. Pres., dir. Lone Star Water Co., Paris and Mt. Pleasant R. R. Co.; dir. Tex. Water Co., Kansas City Suburban Water Co. Co-chmn. attys. div. United Fund Dallas, 1964-65. Alderman, mayor pro-tem. Highland Park, Tex., 1960-66; mayor Town of Highland Park, 1966-70. Served with USNR, 1942-44. Fellow Am. Coll. of Trial Lawyers; mem. Am., Tex., Dallas bar assns. Rotarian. Clubs: Dallas Country (past pres.), Chaparral, Cipango, Terpischorean (Dallas). Home: 4209 Versailles Av Dallas TX 75205 Office: 1511 Fidelity Union Life Bldg Dallas TX 75201

BURG, ANTON BEHME, educator, chemist; b. Dallas City, Ill., Oct. 18, 1904; s. Frank Winchester and Sadie Hornby (Quinton) B.; B.S., U. Chgo., 1927, M.S., 1928, Ph.D., 1931. Instr. Chemistry U. Chgo., 1931-39; asst. prof. chemistry U. So. Cal., 1939-42, asso. prof., 1942- 43, prof., 1943—, head dept. chemistry, 1940-50. Ofcl. investigator Div. 10, Nat. Def. Research Com., 1941-45, War Dept., 1945-46, Navy Dept., 1946—, Air Force, 1955-62. Mem. panel inorganic chemistry Office Naval Research, 1948-51, chmn., 1949-51; cons. Nat. Bur. Standards, 1951-53; mem. adv. panel for chemistry NSF, 1956-59; mem. com. on inorganic chemistry NRC, 1959—. Awarded OSRD certificate of Merit; War-Navy certificate of Appreciation; Univ. Assos. award for creative scholarship. Fellow A.A.A.S.; mem. Am. Assn. U. Profs. (chpt. pres. 1948-49), Am. Chem. Soc. (councilor 1944, 46, chmn. So. Cal. sect. 1954, councilor So. Cal. sect. 1958-63, 65-70; Tolman medal award So. Cal. sect. 1961, award for distinguished service in advancement inorganic chemistry 1969), Phi Beta Kappa (del. 25th triennial conf., chpt. pres. 1958) Sigma Xi (chpt. pres. 1963-64), Phi Lambda Upsilon (faculty adviser Psi chpt. 1961-64). Author on boron chemistry for Ency. Brit.; also articles profl. jours. Contbr. Jour. Am. Chem. Soc., 1931—. Editorial adv. bd. Jour. Inorganic and Nuclear Chemistry, 1955—, Inorganic Nuclear Chem. Letters, 1965—, Inorganic Macromolecules Revs., 1969—; Phosphorus, 1971—. Former Western Conf. Amateur Athletic Union nat. champion in running high jump. Home: 459 W 38th St Los Angeles CA 90037

BURG, GEORGE ROSCOE, journalist; b. New Lexington, O., Apr. 1, 1916; s. Roscoe E. and Erie (Kreider) B.; B.S. in Journalism, Ohio State U., 1938, B.S. in Edn., 1939; m. Mary Vesta Ford, Oct. 31, 1941; children—George F., Mary Jane. Sch. tchr., Pike Twp. High Sch., Madison County, O., 1939-40; engaged in newspaper work, 1948—; mng. editor Kansas City (Mo.) Star, 1967—. Served with AUS, 1940-48. Mem. Kansas City C. of C., Mil. Order World Wars, Tau Kappa Epsilon. Methodist. Elk. Club: Kansas City Press. Home: 4926 W 78th Terrace Prairie Village KS 66208 Office: 1729 Grand Av Kansas City MO 64108

BURGARD, JOHN WILLIAMS, tobacco co. exec.; b. Louisville, Aug. 13, 1910; s. Louis Charles and Roberta (Williams) B.; B.S., Va. Mil. Inst., 1931; m. Gloria Lewis, Nov. 30, 1946; children—John Williams, Lewis Alexander. With Brown & Williamson Tobacco Co., Louisville, 1932—, now sr. exec. v.p., dir. Served to col. USAAF, World War II. Decorated Legion of Merit, Army and Navy Commendation medal; recipient Human Relations award Am. Jewish Com., 1967, Alpha Delta Sigma Golden Fifty award, 1963. Mem. Advt. Council (dir.), Assn. Nat. Advertisers (past dir.). Clubs: Louisville Country, Pendennis (Louisville). Home: 514 Club Lane Louisville KY 40207 Office: 1600 W Hill St Louisville KY 40210

BURGE, DAVID RUSSELL, concert pianist, composer; b. Evanston, Ill., Mar. 25, 1930; s. Russell David and Sylvia (Swensen) B.; Mus.B., Northwestern U., 1951, Mus.M., 1952; D.Mus. Arts, artists diploma, Eastman Sch. Music, 1956; student Cherubini Consevatory, Florence, Italy, 1956-57; m. Betty Lou Child, Sept. 30, 1957; (div.); 1 son, Christopher; m. 2d, Patricia Ann Keeney, Dec. 23, 1961; 1 son, Russell David. Instr. piano Northwestern U., 1949-52; first major postarmistice concert, Seoul, Korea, 1953; toured Korea, 1953-54, Europe, 1956-57, U.S.A., annually 1960—; New York debut playing all-modern program, 1961; asso. prof. music, composer-pianist in resident Whitman Coll., 1957-62, dir. MacDowell Hall Concert Series at coll., 1959-62; organist Ch. of Christ Scientist, Walla Walla, 1958-62; asst. prof. music U. Colo., 1962-64, asso. prof., 1964-68, prof., 1968—; rec. artist Mercury, Advance Records, Candide Records, Turnabout Records; mus. dir. Boulder Philharmonic Orch., 1965—; founder, dir. New Music Ensemble, dir. Festival Contemporary Music, U. Colo. Served with AUS, 1952-54; Korea. Decorated by U.S. Army for cultural relations work in Korea, 1954; Fulbright fellow in Italy, 1956-57. Mem. Am. Musicol. Soc., Internat. Webern Soc. (charter), Am. Soc. Univ. Composers (a founder; nat. chmn. 1970—), Pi Kappa Lambda. Composer: four piano sonatas, 1948-58, 59, 61; string quartet, 1950; woodwind quartet, 1955; piano concerto, 1956; piano quintet, 1958; Variation on a Well- Known Tune for orchestra, 1958; viola concerto, 1959; violin sonatina, 1960; Serenade for violin and orchestra, 1960; musical comedy, Popoff, 1961; opera, Intervals, 1961; Trio (violin, cello, piano), 1962; Eclipse (piano), 1963; Souces (flute-piano), 1964; Sources II (violin-celeste-piano), 1965; Eclipse II (piano), 1966; Sources III (clarinet-percussion), 1967; A Song of Sixpence (soprano-piano), 1967; Aeolian Music (flute-clarinet-violin-cello-piano-tape), 1968; Sources IV (piano), 1969; String Quartet, 1969; Twone in Sunshine, an Entertainment for Theater, 1969; ... that no one knew (violin- orch.), 1969; also songs, anthems. Contbr. articles. Home: 6766 N 63d St Longmont CO 80501

BURGE, HENRY CHARLES, architect; b. Peyton, Somerset, Eng., May 28, 1911; s. Charles Henry and Gladys (Chedgey) B.; came to U.S., 1923, naturalized, 1930; B.Arch., U. So. Cal., 1935; m. Doris Greener, Jan. 12, 1932; children—Charles Henry, Evilaura (Mrs. Lawrence Linker-Hus), William Temple. With Clifford A. Truesdell,

1927-32, Samuel Lunden, 1934, Meyer & Holler, 1935-40, Risly & Gould, 1944-45; layout artist Walt Disney Prodns., Burbank, Cal., 1943-44; with Douglas Aircraft Interiors, Los Angeles, 1944; with U. So. Cal., 1945-62, acting dean, 1962-63; with Burge-Roach and successor firm Urban Architects, Montebello, Cal., 1945—, pres., 1969—; dir. Atlantic Savs. & Loan Assn., Los Angeles; cons. Cal. Bd. Architecture, Los Angeles Civil Service. Dir. La Canada Youth House. Recipient nat. better neighborhood award Nat. Assn. Home Builders, 1951, many A.I.A. and A.R.A. awards. Fellow A.I.A., A.R.A.; mem. Pasadena Fine Arts Club, Montebello C. of C. Home: 2161 E Lemon Heights Dr Santa Ana CA 92705 Office: 869 N Garfield Montebello CA 90640

BURGE, WILLIAM LEW, business information exec.; b. Atlanta, June 27, 1918; s. William Frederick and Leona (Payne) B.; ed. Ga. State Coll. Bus. Adminstrn., 1937-42; m. Willette Richey, Feb. 27, 1937; children—Judith (Mrs. Judith Cathcart), William Roger. With Retail Credit Co., 1936—, br. mgr., Greensboro, N.C., 194951, div. mgr., Pitts., 1951-58, v.p., Atlanta, 1959-65, exec. v.p., 1964-65, pres., 1965—, chief exec. officer, 1967—, also dir.; chmn. Retail Credit Co. affiliates; dir. First Nat. Bank Atlanta, Nat. Service Industries. Gen. chmn. United Appeal, Atlanta, 1961; active United Negro Coll. Fund; regional chmn. Nat. Alliance of Businessmen, 1969-70. Trustee Shorter Coll., YMCA; chmn. bd. regents Univ. System Ga. Served to lt. AUS, World War II. Named Atlanta's Young Man of Year, 1948, one of Atlanta's Leaders of Tomorrow, Time mag., 1952. Mem. Am. Mgmt. Assn., Atlanta C. of C. (pres. 1966), Jr. C. of C. (pres. 1947-48). Kiwanian. Home: 3659 Northside Dr NW Atlanta GA 30305 Office: 1600 Peachtree St NW Atlanta GA 30309

BURGEE, JOHN HENRY, architect; b. Chgo., Aug. 28, 1933; s. Joseph Zeno and Helen (Dooley) B.; B. Arch., U. Notre Dame, 1956; m. Gwendolyn Mary Henson, June 30, 1956; 1 son, John Gerard. Supt. constrn. Holabird & Root & Burgee, Chgo., 1955-56; project mgr. Naess & Murphy, Chgo., 1958-61; adminstr. design, project architect C. F. Murphy Assos., Chgo., 1961-65, asso. partner, 1965-67, partner, 1967; asso. Philip Johnson, Architects, N.Y.C., 1967-68; partner Philip Johnson & John Burgee, N.Y.C., 1968—. Chmn. bldg. material sect. Met. Crusade of Mercy, Chgo., 1966-67; pres. Chgo. Nr. N. Montessori Sch. Bd., 1962-63. Pres. German-Am. Club, Bad Kreuznach, Germany, 1957-58. Served with U.S. Army, 1956-58. Mem. A.I.A. Clubs: Am. Yacht; Shenorock; Bronxville Field. Home: 1 Willow Rd Bronxville NY 10708 Office: 375 Park Av New York City NY 10022

BURGER, ALFRED, chemist; b. Vienna, Austria, Sept. 6, 1905; Ph.D., U. Vienna, 1928; D.Sc., Phila. Coll. Pharmacy and Sci., 1971; m. Frances Page Morrison, Aug. 1, 1936; 1 dau., Frances Page. Came to U.S., 1929, naturalized, 1937. Research chemist Hoffman-LaRoche Co., 1928-29; research asso. Drug Addiction Lab., NRC, U. Va., 1929-38, asst. prof. chemistry U. Va., 1938-46, asso. prof., 1946-52, prof., 1952-70, emeritus, 1970—, chmn. chemistry dept., 1962-63; vis. prof. N.M. Highlands U., 1962, U. Cal., 1963, U. Tenn., 1970, U. Ala., 1970; Renenbom lectr. U. Wis., 1962; spl. NIH research fellow biochemistry U. Hawaii, 1965; Hartung lectr. U. N.C., 1966. Chmn. Gordon Research Conf. on Medicinal Chemistry, 1959; mem. study sect. pharmacology and exptl. therapeutics, USPHS, 1956-60, mem. study sect. on medicinal chemistry, 1960-64; mem. Cancer Chemotherapy Chem. Panel, 1956-60; mem. rev. panel Nat. Inst. Mental Health, 1967-71; cons. Smith Kline & French Labs., 1943—, Am. Tobacco Co., 1951-63, Philip Morris Inc., 1967—. Recipient Pasteur medal Pasteur Inst., Paris, France, 1953; Distinguished Service award Va. sect. Am. Chem. Soc., 1961; Am. Pharm. Assn. Found. award in medicinal chemistry, 1967. Mem. Am. Chem. Soc. (chmn. div. medicinal chemistry 1954), Am. Soc. Pharmacology and Exptl. Therapeutics, A.A.A.S., Sigma Xi, Alpha Chi Sigma, Rho Chi (hon.). Author: Medicinal Chemistry, 1951, 3d edit., 1969. Contbr. articles to profl. jours. Editor Jour. Medicinal Chemistry, 1959—; Medicinal Research. Home: 1310 Blue Ridge Rd Charlottesville VA 22903

BURGER, ANDRIES PETRUS JACOBUS, banker; b. Clanwilliam, South Africa, Oct. 1, 1924; s. Petrus Johannes and Elizabeth (Olivier) B.; B.Comm., Stellenbosch U.; m. Letty Jones, Oct. 8, 1949; children—Petrus Johannes, Philip Cornelius. Co-founder Trust Bank of Africa Ltd., Cape Town, asst. gen. mgr., 1954-59, gen. mgr., 1959-68, mng. dir., 1968—; dep. chmn. Trust Accepting Bank, Trust Finance Corp., Trust Bldg. Soc., Trust Bank Growth Group, South Africa Met. Life Assurance Co.; dir. Angra Pequena Fishing Corp. Ltd. Mem. Soc. Banking Insts. (past chmn.). Office: 112 Adderly St Capetown Republic of South Africa*

BURGER, CHESTER, mgmt. cons.; b. Bklyn., Jan. 10, 1921; s. Benjamin W. and Terese (Felleman) B.; B.A., Bklyn. Coll., 1946; m. Hannah Kaufman, Jan. 30, 1948; children—Jeffrey Allen, Todd Oliver, Amy Louise, m. 2d, Ninki Hart, Jan. 9, 1959 (dec. Jan. 1969); m. 3d, Elisabeth Miller, Sept. 2, 1971. With CBS Radio, 1941-42; visualizer CBS TV News, 1946-48, asst. news editor CBS-TV, 1948-50, news editor, 1950-52, film assignment editor, 1952-53, nat. newsfilm mgr., 1953; writer- producer Omnibus program for Ford Found., 1954-55; cons. Life mag., 1955, pub. relations dept. Am. Tel. & Tel. Co., 1955—; pub. relations counsel, asst. to pres. Ruder and Finn, Inc., 1955-57, v.p. charge plans, 1957-60; pres. Communications Counselors, pub. relations div. Interpublic, Inc., N.Y.C., 1960-62; pres. Echelons Office Temporaries, Inc. and asso. cos., 1963-65; pres. Chester Burger & Co., Inc., mgmt. and pub. relations cons., 1965—; cons. Coca-Cola Export Corp.; guest lectr. New Sch. for Social Research, 1967—, U. Mich. Grad. Sch. Bus. Adminstrn., 1969—, N.Y. U. Div. Bus. and Mgmt., 1970—, Dalhousie U., 1970; author, lectr. pub. relations role in mgmt. Dir. N.Y. Interracial Council for Bus. Opportunity, 1965-68; chmn. pub. relations com., mem. exec. com., trustee Nat. Urban League; pub. relations chmn. Young Pres.' Orgn., 1962-63; mem. adv. com. Black Exec. Exchange Program; 1st v.p. Nat. Urban League Devel. Found., Inc.; dir. N.Y. Diabetes Assn., 1964-67. Served with AUS, 1942-46. Mem. Internat., Am. (dir. N.Y. chpt. 1959-60, Eastern v.p. 1960-61, nat. dir. 1959-60) pub. relations assns., Pub. Relations Soc. Am. (dir. 1961-63), Am. Mgmt. Assn. Author: Survival in the Executive Jungle, 1964; Executives Under Fire, 1966; Executive Etiquette, 1969; also articles. Editor: Mike and Screen Press Directory, 1953, 54, 55. Contbg. editor Quar. Rev. Pub. Relations (name now Pub. Relations Quar.), 1959—, Popular Photography mag., 1967-68. Home: 33 W 67th St New York City NY 10023 Office: 275 Madison Av New York City NY 10016

BURGER, EDMUND GANES, architect; b. Yerington, Nev., Mar. 28, 1930; s. Edmund Ganes and Rose Catherine (Kobe) B.; B.M.E., U. Santa Clara, 1951; B.Arch., U. Pa., 1959; m. Shirley May Pratini, Jan. 21, 1968; 1 dau., Jane Lee. Engr., Gen. Electric Co., 1951-52; design engr. U. Cal. Radiation Lab., 1952-57; architect Wurster, Bernardi & Emmons, San Francisco, 1960-63; founder Burger & Coplans, Inc., Architects, San Francisco, 1964, pres., 1964—; guest lectr. U. Cal., Berkeley. Recipient citation for excellence in community architecture A.I.A., 1969, award of merit A.I.A. Homes for Better Living, 1970, Holiday award for a beautiful Am., 1970, Honor award 4th Biennial HUD awards for design excellence, 1970. Important works include Acorn Housing Project, Oakland, Cal., Crescent Village Housing Project, Suisun City, Cal. Home: 1331 Oxford St Berkeley CA 94709 Office: West Wind Basin 15th Av Oakland CA 94606

BURGER, JAMES WENDELL, biologist, educator; b. Phila., Mar. 1, 1910; s. Mark Leopold and Gertrude Leah (Shirey) B.; student Albright Coll., 1927- 29; A.B., Haverford Coll., 1931; A.M., Lehigh U., 1933; Ph.D., Princeton, 1936; m. Ruth H. Hollenbach, June 26, 1937; children—James Mark, Judith Ruth. Mem. faculty Trinity Coll., Hartford, Conn., 1936—, prof. biology, 1952—, chmn. dept., 1952-69, J. Pierpont Morgan prof., 1952—; mng. dir. Mt. Desert Island Biol. Lab., 1948-51, sec., 1951-61, trustee, 1948—, v.p., 1963-67; commr. Conn. Geol. and Natural History Survey, 1960—; spl. research vertebrate physiology and vertebrate reproductive cycles. Chmn. com. Sch. Nursing, Hartford Hosp., 1943-67, bd. dirs. hosp., 1956—. Fellow A.A.A.S.; mem. Am. Soc. Zoologists, Phi Beta Kappa, Sigma Xi. Contbr. articles profl. jours. Home: 21 Glenbrook Rd West Hartford CT 06107

BURGER, JOSEPH CHARLES, ret. marine officer; b. Washington, May 11, 1902; s. Clarence Walter and Mary Decker (Sedgwick) B.; A.B., U. Md., 1925; m. Frances Fooks Freeny, Dec. 22, 1928; children—Joseph Charles (USMC), Eleanor Sedgwick. Commd. 2d lt. USMC, 1925, advanced through grades to lt. gen., 1959; assigned ships Atlantic and Pacific fleets, also stationed in China, Cuba, Hawaii; participated operations Guadalcanal, Bougainville, other South Pacific areas, World War II; chief staff Fleet Marine Force, Pacific, 1950-51; a.d.c. 1st Marine Div., Korea, 1953; dir. Marine Corps Res., 1954—; comdg. gen. USMC Recruit Deport, Parris Island, 1956, Marine Corps Base, Camp Lejeune, 1952, 2d Marine Div., 1957-59; comdg. gen. Fleet Marine Force, Atlantic, 1959-61; ret. Decorated D.S.M. (Navy), Bronze Star medal, Letter of Commendation; Order Mil. Merit, Ulchi with gold star (Korea). Mem. Kappa Alpha. Clubs: Army and Navy (Washington); Army and Navy Country. Home: 1009 Chumley Rd Virginia Beach VA 23151

BURGER, WARREN EARL, Chief Justice U.S.; b. St. Paul, Sept. 17, 1907; s. Charles Joseph and Katharine (Schnittger) B.; student U. Minn., 1925-27; LL.B. magna cum laude, St. Paul Coll. Law, 1931; m. Elvera Stromberg, Nov. 8, 1933; children—Wade Allan, Margaret Elizabeth. Admitted to Minn. bar, 1931; partner firm Faricy, Burger, Moore & Costello (and predecessor firms), 1935-53; faculty Mitchell Coll. Law, 1931-48; asst. atty. gen. U.S., 1953-56; judge U.S. Ct. Appeals, Washington, 1956-69; Chief Justice U.S., 1969—; lectr. Am. and European law schs. Office: Supreme Ct Bldg Washington DC 20543

BURGESS, ANTHONY, author; b. Manchester, Eng., Feb. 25, 1917; s. Joseph and Elizabeth (Wilson) B.; B.A. with honours, Manchester U., 1940; m. Llewela Isherwood Jones, Jan. 23, 1942 (dec. 1968); m. 2d, Liliana Macellari, 1968. Lectr., schoolmaster, 1946-54; edn. officer in Malaya and Borneo, 1954-59; composer, 1933—; play producer, 1947—; jazz pianist, 1941—. Served with British Army, 1940-46. Author: The Right to an Answer, 1961; Devil of a State, 1962; The Wanting Seed, 1963; A Clockwork Orange, 1963; Honey for the Bears, 1964; Nothing Like the Sun, 1964; The Long Day Wanes, 1965; Language Made Plain, 1965; Re Joyce, 1965; The Doctor is Sick, 1965; Tremor of Intent, 1966; The Novel Now, 1967; Enderby, 1968; Urgent Copy, 1969; Shakespeare, 1970; MF, 1971; Cyrano de Bergerac-a version for the modern stage, 1971. Address: Piazza Padella Bracciano Rome Italy

BURGESS, C. J., savs. and loan assn. exec. Exec. v.p. Sarasota Fed. Savs. and Loan Assn. Office: PO Box 2199 1718 Main St Sarasota FL 33578*97

BURGESS, CARTER L., bus. exec.; b. Roanoke, Va., Dec. 31, 1916; B.A., Va. Mil. Inst.; m. May Gardner Smith; children—Jane (Mrs. James L. Wiley, Jr.), Mary, Nan, Sue, Beth, Carter L. Asst. to the pres. Trans World Airline, Washington, 1946- 47; asst. to pres., dir. adminstrn. Gen. Aniline & Film Corp., N.Y.C., 1947-53; asst. to pres. Univ. S.C., 1953-54; asst. sec. Dept. of Def., for manpower, 1954-57, cons. for UN, Dept. of State, ODM, Def., White House, and U.S. Senate; pres., dir. Trans World Airlines, Inc., 1957; pres., dir. Am. Machine & Foundry Co., 1958, former chmn. bd., chief exec. officer; former U.S. ambassador to Argentina; chmn., dir. Nat. Corp. for Housing Partnerships; dir. Am. Airlines, Inc., Ford Motor Co., Morgan Guaranty, J.P. Morgan, SKF. Served from 2d lt. to col., sec. Gen. Staff SHAEF, AUS, 1941-45. Decorated Legion of Merit; L'Ordre de Leopold with palm, Croix le Guerre with palm (Belgium); Order Brit. Empire; Legion of Honor, Croix de Guerre with palm (France); U.S. Dept. Def. and Army highest civilian awards. Home: 25 Beechtree Lane Pelham Manor NY 10803 Office: 1133 15th St NW Washington DC

BURGESS, CECIL EDMUND, educator, mathematician; b. Happy, Tex., Jan. 21, 1920; s. John Wesley and Sallie (Crawford) B.; B.S., W. Tex. State U., Canyon, 1941; Ph.D., U. Tex. at Austin, 1951; m. Charlotte June Stevenson, Feb. 20, 1948; children—Grant Lewis, Carol Jean. Tchr., Sudan (Tex.) pub. schs., 1941; instr. math. U. Tex., 1941-42, 46-51; with Naval Ordnance Lab., 1942-43; mem. faculty U. Utah, 1951—, prof. math., 1961—, chmn. dept., 1967—; vis. lectr. U. Wis., 1956-57; vis. mem. Inst. Advanced Study, 1962-63. Mem. Commn. Undergrad. Program in Math., 1965-67. Served to lt. (j.g.) USNR, 1943- 46. Mem. Am. Math. Soc., Math. Assn. Am., Nat. Council Tchrs. Math. Research in topology, structure of continua, surfaces in Euclidean space. Home: 2236 Logan Av Salt Lake City UT 84108

BURGESS, CHARLES HARRY, mining co. exec.; b. Sheridan, Wyo., Apr. 3, 1910; s. James Henry and Mary Helen (Helvey) B.; A.B., Harvard, 1931, A.M., 1933, Ph.D., 1936; m. Linda Cannon, May 24, 1934 (div. 1954); children—Walter Pierce, Heather, James Helvey, Pamela, Martha; m. 2d, Elisabeth Blessing Halliday, July 1, 1961; stepchildren—Donald A. Halliday, Jr., Barry Halliday. Instr. geology Harvard, 1934-36; geologist Anaconda Copper Mining Co., 1936-38; mine leasee and cons., 1938-41; analyst Adminstrn. Export Control, Bd. Econ. Warfare, also dep. chief aluminum and magnesium sect. OPA, 1941- 42; chief wire, rod and bar sect., aluminum and magnesium div. WPB, 1942- 44; geologist Hoover, Curtice and Ruby, N.Y.C., 1944-46, M.A. Hanna Co., 1946-47; dep. dir., then dir. strategic materials div. ECA, 1948-50; treas. United Electric Coal Co., Chgo., 1950-52; dist. geologist Bear Creek Mining Co., Mpls., 1952-56, pres., dir. N.Y.C. and Salt Lake City, 1956-60, now dir.; v.p. exploration Kennecott Copper Corp., 1960—; pres., dir. B.C. Molybdenum Ltd., 1963-66, now dir.; pres., dir. Kennecott Exploration, Inc., Kennecott Panama, Inc., Kennecott Costa Rica, S.A., P.T. Kennecott Indonesia; chmn. bd. Kennecott Explorations (Australia) Pty. Ltd.; v.p., dir. Kennecott Coal Co.; dir. Kennco (Stikine) Mining Ltd., Stikine Copper Ltd., Kennarctic 42- (Can.), Ltd., Kennco Explorations (Western), Ltd., N.C. Phosphate Corp., Bear Creek Mining Co., Flambeau Mining Corp., Kennecott Explns. (S.W. Africa) (Pty.) Ltd., Bear Tooth Mining Co., Great Lakes Exploration, Inc., Kennecott Italia, S.P.A. Mem. vis. com., dept. geol. scis. Bd. Overseers, Harvard, 1963-68, 70-71. Mem. Am. Inst. Mining a Engrs., Am. Geol. Inst. (pres. 1970), Mining and Metall. Soc., Soc. Econ. Geologists, Harvard Grad. Soc. for Advanced Study and Research, Phi Beta Kappa. Club: Harvard of New York City. Home: 127 Guinea Rd Cos Cob CT 06807 Office: 161 E 42d St New York City NY 10017

BURGESS, CONSTANCE HOEY, orgn. exec.; b. Boston, Oct. 12, 1906; d. Henry L. and Helen (Quinlan) Hoey; m. Nelson A. Burgess, Oct. 10, 1935; children—Robert McDonald, Constance (Mrs. Noel Coletti), Jane (Mrs. Louis Flanagan), Holly Richards. Exec. sec. Alliance Unitarian Women, 1952-63; exec. dir. Unitarian Universalist Women's Fedn., 1963—. Legislative chmn. Mass. League Women Voters, 1952-54; pres. Council Nat. Orgn. for Adult Edn., 1962- -; bd. dirs. Adult Edn. Assn., Coalition Adult Edn. Orgns. Club: Boston Women's City. Home: 10 Emerson Pl Boston MA 02114 Office: 25 Beacon St Boston MA 02108

BURGESS, GEORGE VAN TRUMP, ret. cons. engr.; b. Pitts., Mar. 13, 1903; s. George Heckman and Harriet (Van Trump) B.; B.S., Yale, 1925; E.D. (hon.), Case Inst. Tech., 1950; m. Helen G. Steers, June 6, 1930; children—Claire Louise (Mrs. Burt W. Phillips), George Van Trump. Field clk. Eire R.R., Wanaque, N.J., 1925-26; resident engr. G., M. & N. R.R., Jackson, Miss., 1926-27; field engr., structural designer Dwight P. Robinson & Co. at Am. Rolling Mill Co., Middletown, O., 1927-29; constrn. mgr. F.H. McGraw & Co., N.Y.C., 1929-31; accoustical cons. engr. Elec. Research Products, Inc., N.Y.C., 1931-34, v.p., 1934-38, comml. relations mgr., 1938-41; gen. mgr. Gen. Service Studios, Long Island City, N.Y., sr. staff engr. Coverdale & Colpitts, N.Y.C., 1941-42, partner, 1943-69. Mem. Am. Inst. Cons. Engrs., Am. Soc. C.E., Engring. Inst. Can., Am. Soc. Appraisers, Yale Engring. Assn. Home: Pilgrim Rd Rye NY 10530

BURGESS, GEORGE W., b. East Orange, N.J.; grad. Mass. Inst. Tech. With Kroger Co., Cin.; v.p. Dole Corp., Hawaii; v.p. mfg., v.p. marketing Fibreboard Corp., 1958-64, pres., dir., 1964—. Office: 55 Francisco St San Francisco CA 94133*

BURGESS, HAROLD DEMPSTER, lawyer; b. Dundee, Ill., July 10, 1895; s. John W. and Sadie E. (Dempster) B.; ed. pub. schs., Beatrice, Neb.; student U. Colo., 1913- 14; student U. Neb. 1914-17, A.B. in absentia, 1920; student U. Chgo., 1920-21; m. Mary Ellen Evans, Sept. 16, 1964. Admitted to Ill. bar, 1921, since practiced in Chgo.; mem. firm Price, Cushman, Keck & Mahin, 1934—. Mem. Am., 7th Circuit, Ill., Chgo. bar assns., Legal Club Chgo., The Law Club. Republican. Episcopalian. Clubs: Mid-Day (Chgo.), Edgewood Valley Country (LaGrange). Home: 644 S County Line Rd Hinsdale IL 60521 Office: 134 S LaSalle St Chicago IL 60603

BURGESS, ISABEL ANDREWS, govt. ofcl.; b. Cleve.; d. William Hayward and Alice (Ball) Andrews; student Mills. Coll., 1930-31, Western Res. U., 1931-32; m. Richard Burgess, June 15, 1939 (div. Nov. 1967); children—Richard Ball, Susan Berry (Mrs. Allen Cordsen), Thomas Hayward. Mem. Ariz. Ho. of Reps., 1952-53, 56-57, 60-65; mem. Ariz. Senate, Phoenix, 1966-69; mem. Nat. Transp. Safety Bd., Washington, 1969—; dir. Ball Co., Chgo. Pres. Heard Mus. Guild, 1959-60; chmn. Senate Hwys. and Transp. Com. First vice chmn. Ariz. Republican Com., 1965-67. Sec. exec. com. Heard Mus. Mem. Council State Govts. (exec. bd. Western conf. 1966-69). Clubs: Capitol Hill, Aero of Washington, 1925 F Street, Federal Aviation (Washington). Home: 2510 Virginia Av NW Washington DC 20037 Office: 800 Independence Av SW Washington DC 20591

BURGESS, JAMES E., journalist; b. La Crosse, Wis., Apr. 5, 1936; s. William T. and Margaret (Forseth) B.; B.S. in Journalism, U. Wis., 1958; m. Catherine E. Qualey, Dec. 20, 1958; children—Karen E., J. Peter, Sydney A., R. Curtis. Bus. mgr. Daily Cardinal, U. Wis., 1957-58; with Mpls. Star Tribune, 1958; reporter Wis. State Jour., 1962-63; intern Davenport (Ia.) Times- Democrat, 1964; prodn. and bus. mgr. Missoula (Mont.) Missoulian, 1964- 67; pub. Helena (Mont.) Ind. Record, 1968—; asst. pub. LaCrosse (Wis.) Tribune, 1970—. Served with USAF, 1958-62. Mem. Mont. Press Assn. (bd. dirs.), Beta Theta Pi, Iron Cross of U. Wis. Presbyn. Home: 4681 Norseman Dr LaCrosse WI 54602 Office: 435 S 4th St LaCrosse WI 54602

BURGESS, JOHN HERBERT, medical educator; b. Montreal, Que., Can., May 24, 1933; s. John Frederick and Willa Reta (McGinness) B.; B.Sc., McGill U., 1954, M.D., C.M., 1958; m. Andrea Clouston Rutherford, May 30, 1958; children—Willa, Cynthia, Lynn, John. Med. resident Montreal (Can.) Gen. Hosp., 1958-60, 62-64; Nuffield research fellow U. Birmingham, Eng., 1960-62; McLaughlin research fellow Cardiovascular Inst., San Francisco, 1964-66; asst. prof. medicine McGill U., 1966-69, asso. prof., 1969—. Examiner in internal medicine Royal Coll. Physicians and Surgeons Can., 1969—. Med. Research Council Can. scholar, 1966-71. Fellow Am. Heart Assn.; mem. Med. Research Soc. Gt. Britain, Am. Physiol. Soc., Canadian Soc. Clin. Investigation, Canadian Cardiovascular Soc., N.Y. Acad. Sci., Alpha Omega Alpha. Home: 639 Murray Hill Montreal 217 Quebec Canada Office: Montreal General Hospital Montreal 109 Quebec Canada

BURGESS, JOHN LAWIE, journalist; b. Carlisle, Eng., Nov. 17, 1912; s. Robert Nelson and Jean Hope (Lawie) B.; student Trinity Coll., Glenalmond, Scotland, 1926-31; m. Alice Elizabeth Gillieron, Mar. 31, 1948; childrenAnne, Robin, Charles. With Cumberland Newspapers Ltd., pub. 1 daily and 4 weekly papers, 1934-, mng. dir., editor-in-chief, 1945-; chmn. Reuters Ltd., 1959-68, Border T.V. Ltd., 1961—. Bd. dirs. Press Assn., 1950-57, chmn., 1955. Justice of peace, dep. lt. County Cumberland. Served with British Army, 1939-45. Decorated Order British Empire, Territorial decoration. Mem. Inst. Journalists. Address: The Old Hall Rockcliffe Carlisle England

BURGESS, JOHN MELVILLE, bishop; b. Grand Rapids, Mich., Mar. 11, 1909; s. Theodore Thomas and Ethel Inez (Beverly) B.; A.B., U. Mich., 1930, M.A., 1931, L.H.D., 1962; B.D., Episcopal Theol. Sch., 1934; LL.D., St. Augustine's Coll., 1963; m. Esther J. Taylor, Aug. 2, 1945; children—Julia Beverly, Margaret Olivia. Ordained to ministry Episcopal Ch., 1934; vicar in Mich. and Ohio, 1934-46; Episcopal chaplain Howard U., 1946-56; canon Washington Cathedral, 1951-56; archdeacon Boston, supt. Episcopal City Mission, 1956-62; suffragan bishop Mass., 1962-69; bishop coadjutor Episcopal Diocese Mass., 1969-70; diocesan bishop Episcopal Diocese Mass., 1970—. Bd. dirs. Ch. Pension Fund Episcopal Ch., Nat. Exec. Council Episcopal Ch. Mem. gen. bd. Greater Boston YMCA, Boston Com. Fgn. Relations; mem. Mass. adv. com. U.S. Commn. Civil Rights. Trustee St. Augustine's Coll., Raleigh, N.C. Home: 46 Berwick Rd Newton Center MA 02159 Office: 1 Joy St Boston MA 02108

BURGESS, LLOYD ALBERT, constrn. co. exec.; b. Culver, Ore., Oct. 4, 1917; s. Estell Elmer and Arrista (Ditterline) B.; B.S. in Civil Engring., Ore. State U., 1939; m. Wanda Marie Gregory, Dec. 18, 1955; children—Gregory Scott, Elizabeth Anne, Jeffrey Lloyd; 1 son by previous marriage, Jason M. Engr., C.E., Portland, Ore., 1939-40, 41; engr. Douglas Aircraft Co., 1940-41, Tidewater Asso. Oil Co., 1941-42; pres. Burgess Constrn. Co., Fairbanks, Alaska, 1946-69, now chmn.; pres. Spruce Equipment, Inc., Fairbanks, 1955- 64, Grove Inc., Fairbanks, 1955-64, Alaska Freight Lines, 1959-60, Burgess Internat. Inc., Seattle; dir. Concrete Products Alaska, Alaska Title & Guarantee

Co., Alaska Interstate Co., Houston, Seattle N.W. Securities, Oceanic Industries, Seattle, Holosonics, Richland, Wash., Energy Co. Alaska, Dallas, Coral Constrn. Co., Ltd., Suva, Fiji. Chmn. Alaska Rep. Finance Com., 1958- 62; del. Rep. Nat. Conv., 1960, 64, 68; mem. nat. platform com., 1968; mem. Nat. Rep. Com. from Alaska, 1964-69. Served to lt. comdr. USNR, 1942-46; PTO. Mem. Asso. Gen. Contractors (pres. Alaska 1960), Am. Legion, Fairbanks C. of C. Elk. Clubs: Mercer Island Country; Fairbanks Petroleum; Seattle Golf and Country, Harbor, Washington Athletic (Seattle). Home: 5911 77th Av SE Mercer Island WA 98040 Office: 4706 Seattle 1st Nat Bank Bldg Seattle WA 98104

BURGESS, NEIL, elec. engr.; b. Melrose, Mass., Aug. 2, 1918; s. Neil and Lucia (Payne) B.; B.S. in Mech. Engring., U. Rochester, 1939; B.S. in Elec. Engring., M.S., Mass. Inst. Tech., 1941; grad. Advanced Mgmt. Program, Harvard, 1952; m. Evelyn Ruth Lent, Sept. 18, 1942; children—Nancy, Susan, Mark Neil, Cynthia Payne, Wendy. With Gen. Electric Co., 1939—, beginning as design engr., successively turbojet engine project engr., mgr. devel. operation, project mgr. turbojet engine, 1953-57, mgr. engine projects, 1939-58, mgr. comml. engine operations, Cin., 1958-62, mgr. Western region def. programs operation, 1962-68, mgr. airline relations, aircraft engine group, 1968—. Recipient Collier Trophy award for devel. turbojet engine, 1959. Fellow Royal Aero. Soc.; asso. fellow Inst. Aero. Scis. (v.p. 1958); mem. Soc. Automotive Engrs., Theta Delta Chi. Club: Bel Air (Los Angeles). Home: 1645 N Amalfi Dr Pacific Palisades CA 90272 Office: 6151 W Century Blvd Los Angeles CA 90045

BURGESS, ROBERT MILLER, educator; b. Mt. Crawford, Va., Sept. 4, 1906; s. John William and Ida Luella (Rogers) B.; B.A., Bridgewater Coll., 1928; M.A., U.Va., 1936; Ph.D., U. Cal. at Los Angeles, 1951; postgrad. U. Paris, 1934-35, U. So. Cal., 1937-38, U. Cal. at Los Angeles, 1940-42, 46-47, U. Mexico, summer 1946. Asst. prin. Central High Sch., Low Moor, Va., 1929-32, 35- 36; instr. French, Black-Foxe Mil. Inst., Los Angeles, 1936-40; teaching asst. dept. French, U. Cal. at Los Angeles, 1940-42, 46-47; asst. prof., asso. prof. Mont. State U., 1947-55, prof., 1955—, chmn. dept. fgn. langs., 1952-63. Dir. Nat. Def. Edn. Act fgn. lang. insts. Mont. State U., summers 1960, 61, 62; pres. Pacific N.W. Conf. Fgn. Langs., 1956, 64; mem. teaching staff Am. Heritage Assn. Study Abroad Program, Paris, summer 1969. Served from pvt. to 1st lt. AUS, 1942-46. Decorated Chevalier des Palmes Academiques, France, 1958. Mem. Am. Assn. U. Profs., Modern Lang. Assn., Internat., Am. comparative lit. assn., Am. Assn. Tchrs. French, Renaissance Soc. Am., Assoc. des Membres de l'Ordre des Palmes Academiques. Author: Platonism of Desportes, 1954. Address: Dept Fgn Langs U Mont Missoula MT 59801

BURGESS, ROGER, ch. exec.; b. Sioux City, Ia., Oct. 1927; s. Frederick Earl and Mable (Irwin) B.; B.A., Morningside Coll., Sioux City, 1950, LL.D., 1965; spl. student Center Alcohol Studies, Yale, 1955; grad. student Am. U. Grad. Sch. Journalism, 1966; m. Dorah Jean Salyer, 1953; three boys, one girl. Dir. Morningside Coll. Press Bur., also corr. Sioux City papers, 1948- 50; mem. staff Nat. Conf. Methodist Youth, Nashville, also editor youth publns. Power and Concern, 1950-51; projects sec. Nat. Conf. Meth. Youth, 1951-53; editor publns., dir. communications Meth. Gen. Bd. Temperance, 1953-56, asso gen. sec., 1956-60; dir. communications Meth. Gen. Bd. Christian Social Concern, also editor news mag. Concern, 1960- 61, asso. gen. sec. with responsibility div. alcohol problems and gen. welfare, 1961-65; exec. v.p. charge creative planning in advt., graphic arts and audio visual Design Center, Inc., 1965-67; exec. dir. Joint Action in Community Service, 1967-68; gen. sec. bd. health and welfare ministeries United Meth. Ch., 1968—. Mem. gen. bd. Nat. Council Chs.; bd. dirs. Joint Action in Community Service; mem. council secs. United Meth. Ch.; mem. Nat. Inter-faith Com. Health and Welfare, Bd. dirs. Scarritt Coll. Served U.S. Navy, 1945-46, USNR, 1946-48. Contbr. profl. jours. Address: 1200 Davis St Evanston IL 60201

BURGESS, WARREN RANDOLPH, ex-govt. ofcl. b. Newport, R.I., May 7, 1889; s. Isaac Bronson and Ellen (Wilbur) B.; A.B., Brown U., 1912, LL.D., 1937, U. Rochester, 1948, Bowdoin Coll., 1959, U. Cal., 1962; Ph.D., Columbia, 1920; m. May Ayres, May 17, 1917 (dec. July, 1953); m. 2d, Helen Hamilton Woods, Mar. 5, 1955; children—Leonard Randolph, Julian Ayres. With Fed. Res. Bank, N.Y.C., 1920-38, dep. gov., 1930-36, v.p., 1936-38; vice chmn. Nat. City Bank of N.Y. 1938-48, chmn. exec. com., 1948-52; chmn. bd. City Bank Farmers Trust Co.; dir. Discount Corp., Internat. Banking Corp., U.P.R.R. Royal-Liverpool Group Ins. Cos. in U.S.; dep. to Sec. Treasury, 1953-54, undersec. of Treasury, 1955-57; U.S. permanent rep. on NATO, 1957-61; Regent prof. U. Cal. at Berkeley, 1962. Served as maj., asst. acting chief of statistics br. Gen. Staff World War I. Fellow Brown U. Trustee Robert Coll. Tchrs. Coll., (Columbia). Chmn., N.Y. State War Finance Com., 1943-44. Pres., Per Jacobsson Found. Fellow Am. Statis. Assn. (pres. 1937), Acad. Polit. Sci. (trustee, pres. 1939), Am. Hist. Assn., N.Y. State Bankers Assn. (pres. 1940-41, Res. City Bankers Assn. (pres. 1952), Am. Bankers Assn. (chmn. econ. policy Commn., 1940-44, pres., 1944-45, chmn. com. public debt policy, 1946- 47); mem. Internat. C. of C. (chmn. monetary com., 1946-47), Atlantic Treaty Assn. (chmn. 1961-63, vice chmn. 1963—), Atlantic Council U.S. (chmn. 1971), Am. Econ. Assn., Am. Philos. Soc., Fgn. Policy Assn. (dir.), Delta Upsilon, Phi Beta Kappa. Clubs: Metropolitan (Washington); Century Assn., University, River, Chevy Chase, Cosmos. Author: Trends of School Costs, 1920; The Reserve Banks and the Money Market, 1927, rev. edits. 1936, 46. Editor: Interpretations of Federal Reserve Policy (by Benjamin Strong), 1930; (with James R. Huntley) Europe and America—The Next Ten Years. Contbr. articles to profl. jours. Home: Queenstown MD Office: Atlantic Council US 1616 H St N W Washington DC

BURGESS, WILLIAM HENRY, financier; b. Mpls., June 30, 1917; s. Gerald Henry and Louise (Bailey) B.; B.B.A., U. Minn., 1939; M.B.A., Harvard, 1941; m. Clara Ethel Woodward, June 21, 1941; children—Sarah Louise, Margaret Warren. Indsl. engr. R.R. Donnelly & Sons Co., 1941-42; mgmt. engr. Hollister & Evans, Los Angeles, 1946; pres. Electronic Splty. Co., Los Angeles, 1949-66, chmn. bd., 1949-69; entrepreneur, 1969—; pres., chmn. William H. Burgess Found., 1954—. Vice chmn. commerce and industry United Crusade, 1968-70. Mem. adv. bd. Pasadena YWCA; bd. dirs. Jr. Achievement So. Cal., 1965—; founding mem. Los Angeles Music Center, 1964; v.p., bd. dirs. Cal. Inst. Tech. Assos., 1964—; board overseers, vis. com. Harvard, 1964-69; bd. dirs. Huntington Meml. Hosp. Tumor Clinic, 1958-60; trustee Pasadena Arts Mus., 1956—; mem. pres.'s council Cal. Inst. Tech., 1968—; bd. govs. Otis Art Inst., 1965—; bd. dirs. Inst. Internat. Edn., 1970—, L.S.B. Leakey Found., 1969—; founder L.S.B. Leakey Fellows, 1969; trustee San Gabriel Valley Found. Boy Scouts Am., 1968—; nat. adv. bd. Am. Security Council, 1971—. To lt. USNR, 1941-45. Recipient Bus. Achievement award Harvard Bus. Sch. Club So. Cal., 1963; Citation for Distinguised Service, D.A.V., 1963; Outstanding Achievement award U. Minn., 1964. Mem. Nat. Inst. Social Scis., Chief Execs. Forum (dir. 1969—), Young President's Orgn. (nat. dir. 1958-67, internat. pres. 1965), Pasadena Art Mus. (life mem.; dir.), Harvard Bus. Sch. Club So. Cal. (pres., dir. 1955-56), Newcomen Soc., Internat. Marketing Inst. (adv. council 1959-), Los Angeles C. of C., World Affairs Council Los Angeles (v.p. and dir. 1962—, treas. 1964- -), Tennis Patrons Assn. So. Cal. (bd. govs. 1966), Pasadena Foothill Tennis Patrons Assn. (hon. bd. mem.), Phi Delta Theta Alumni Assn., Phi Delta Theta. Republican. Episcopalian. Clubs: Verdugo (Glendale, Cal.); Valley Hunt, Annandale Golf Flintridge Riding (Pasadena); Gardiner Tennis (Carmel Valley); Los Angeles Tennis, Harvard, California, Lincoln, West Hills Hunt (Los Angeles); Harvard, River (N.Y.C.); Palm Springs Racquet, Palm Springs Tennis; Eldorado Golf (Palm Desert, Cal.); Dana Strand Beach and Tennis (Dana Point, Cal.); Lake Arrowhead Yacht. Home: 945 Hillcrest Pl Pasadena CA 91106 also 550 Palisades Dr Palm Springs CA 92262 Office: 222 E Glenarm St Pasadena CA 91106

BURGESS, WILLIAM THOMAS, newspaper publisher; b. La Crosse, Wis., Mar. 14, 1907; s. Frank Henry and May (Thomas) B.; B.A., U. Wis., 1929; m. Margaret Solveig Forseth, Nov. 21, 1930; children—Stephen, James, Thomas. Advt. salesman La Crosse Tribune, 1929-36, advt. mgr., 1936-37, bus. mgr., 1937-39, publisher, 1939—; sec. Lee Enterprises, Lee Found; dir. Lee Enterprises, Inc., Davenport, Ia., Mem. Am. Newspaper Pubs. Assn., La Crosse Indsl. Assn. (pres.). Republican. Conglist. Club: La Crosse. Home: Rural Rt 1 Dakota, MN 55925. Office: 4th and Cass Sts La Crosse WI 54601

BURGIN, CHARLES DAVID, journalist; b. Somerset, Ky., Feb. 12, 1939; s. Lester E. and Lillian (Mounce) B.; B.A. in Engliish, Miami U., Oxford, O., 1961; m. Diane Josephy, Dec. 14, 1968. Reporter, N.Y. Herald Tribune, 1964-66; news editor, Washington corr. Newspaper Enterprise Assn., 1966-67; sports editor Washington daily News, 1967-69; exec. sports edititor San Francisco Examiner, 1969—. Served with AUS, 1961-64. Mem. Beta Theta Pi. Home: 2052 Green St San Francisco CA 94123 Office: 110 5th St San Francisco CA 94133

BURGIN, RICHARD, orch. condr.; b. Warsaw, Poland, Oct. 11, 1892; s. Maurice and Rachel (Krisow) B.; grad. Petrograd Conservatory Music, 1912; D. Mus., Hartt Coll. Music, New Eng. Conservatory, 1962; m. Ruth Posselt July 3, 1940; children—Diana, Richard. Child prodigy on violin; debut Dec. 7, 1903, as soloist with Warsaw Philharmonic Orch.; concertmaster Helsingfors Symphony, Finland, Fitelberg's Orchestra, Pavovsk, Russia, 1915; founded string orch. and toured Scandinavia, 1916-18; became concertmaster Boston Symphony under Pierre Monteux, later under Koussevitsky and Muench, 1920; concurrently taught at N.E. Conservatory; faculty Boston U.; asso. condr. Boston Symphony Orch.; violinist, tchr., guest condr. Boston U. Symphony Orch., music dir. Congress of Strings, 1967; distinguished prof. violin Fla. State U., Tallahassee; mem. Florestan Quartet. Decorated chevalier French Legion of Honor. Mem. Am. Acad. Arts and Scis., Sinfonia, Phi Gamma Lambda. Home: 1118 Lothian Dr Tallahassee FL 32303.

BURGISON, RAYMOND MERRITT, educator; b. Balt., Aug. 17, 1917; B.S., Loyola Coll., 1941; M.S. (Ohio Chem. Co. fellow), U. Md., 1948, Ph.D. in Chemistry (Lilly fellow), 1950. Chemist, Continental Oil Co., 1941-42, Air Reduction Co., 1942-45, U.S. Indsl. Chem. Co., 1945-47; pharmacologist U. Md., 1947-50, asst. prof. pharmacology, 1950-56, asso. prof., 1956-63, prof., 1963—, also head dept. pharmacology and cell biology. Chmn. chem. panel Nat. Insts. Mental Health, 1962—. Mem. Am. Chem. Soc., Am. Soc. Pharmacology and Exptl. Therapeutics. Office: Grad Sch U Md College Park MD 20742*

BURGOON, CARROLL FOSTER, Jr., physician; b. Harrisburg, Pa., Feb. 21, 1916; s. Carroll Foster and Helen (Watson) B.; A.B. in German, Franklin and Marshall Coll., 1939; M.D., Temple U., 1943; m. V. Jane Smiley, June 19, 1947; children—Carroll Foster, Helen, Janet, Anne, Thomas, Peter, Michael, Susan, Elizabeth. Intern Phila. Gen. Hosp., 1943-44, U.S. Naval Hosp., Portsmouth, Va., 1944-45; assigned U.S. Naval Hosp., Phila., 1945-46; fellow dermatology U. Pa. Hosp., 1946-49, Skin and Cancer Hosp., Phila., 1947-48; mem. research staff Children's Hosp., Phila., 1948-52; mem. faculty Hahnemann Med. Sch., Phila., 1950-58, prof. dermatology, 1953- 58, chmn. dept., 1955-58; chief dermatology Phila. Gen. Hosp., 1954-66; cons. staff Sacred Heart, Montgomery hosps., Norristown, Pa., 1949—; dir. Skin and Cancer Hosp. of Temple U. Med. Sch., 1958-66, chmn. dept. dermatology, 1961-66, prof. dermatology Health Scis. Center, 1967—; cons. U.S. Army Hosp., Valley Forge, Pa., 1950-59, Norristown State Hosp., 1950-55, Phila. VA Hosp., 1950-58, Camden (N.J.) Municipal Hosp. Served with USNR, 1944-46. Diplomate Am. Bd. Dermatology and Syphilology. Fellow Am. Dermatol. Assn., A.C.P.; mem. Soc. Investigative Dermatology, Am. Acad. Dermatology and Syphilology, A.M.A., Pa. Med. Soc., Phila. Dermatol. Soc. Home: Fox Hollow Farms Yellow Springs Rd Chester Springs, PA 19425. Office: 3322 N Broad St Philadelphia PA 19140 also 1539 DeKalb St Norristown PA 19401

BURGOON, NORMAN AARON, Jr., surety bond and ins. co. exec.; b. Balt., Oct. 27, 1916; s. Norman Aaron and Nellie (Ricker) B.; student Balt. City Coll., 1931-34; LL.B., U. Balt., 1939; m. Doris Hunter, June 30, 1939; children—Norman Richard, Harvey Ronald, Alan Charles, Michele Doris. With Fidelity & Deposit Co. Md., 1935—, exec. v.p., 1966—, also dir. Admitted to Md. bar, 1940. Past v.p., dir. Bur. Contract Information, Inc. Pres., dir. Commerce and Industry Combined Health Appeal, Balt., 1967—; mem. finance com. Presbyn. Hosp., Balt., 1955—; exec. com. Presbyn. Synod Chesapeake, 1960—. Bd. dirs. Greater Balt. Med. Center, 1966—; trustee Presbyn. Assn., 1965—, U. Balt., 1971—. Served with AUS, World War II. Mem. Am. Ins. Assn. (exec. com.), Am. Mgmt. Assn., Surety Assn. Am. (past chmn. contract bond adv. com.), Newcomen Soc. N. Am., Md. Hist. Soc., Casualty and Surety Club, Tail of the Fox, Soc. War 1812. Presbyn. (ruling elder). Clubs: Center (Balt.); Towson Golf & Country. Home: 304 Wynell Ct Timonium MD 21093 Office: Fidelity Bldg Baltimore MD 21201

BURGREEN, DAVID, educator; b. N.Y.C., Aug. 1, 1917; s. Max and Minnie (Dresner) B.; B.Civil Engring., Coll. City N.Y., 1943; M.Aero. Engring., Bklyn. Poly. Inst., 1947, Ph.D., 1950; m. Lillian Mandel, Apr. 6, 1941; children—Vicki Joan (Mrs. Alex Grunski), Bruce Lawrence, Rosalind Susan, William Scott. Adv. engr. atomic power div. Westinghouse Electric Corp., 1950-51; engring. specialist Asso. Nucleonics Co., 1951-56; cons. engr. United Nuclear Corp., 1956-65; prof. mech. engring. Bklyn. Poly. Inst. 1966—. Served to lt. (j.g.) USNR, 1943-47. Mem. Am. Soc. M.E., Am. Soc. C.E., Am. Nuclear Soc., Am. Inst. Aero. and Astronautics, Sigma Xi, Tau Beta Pi. Author papers in field. Home: 80-60 190th St Jamaica, NY 11423. Office: 333 Jay St Brooklyn NY 11201

BURGSTAHLER, ALBERT WILLIAM, educator; b. Grand Rapids, Mich., July 10, 1928; s. Albert Ernest and Constance (Foster) B.; B.S. in Chemistry magna cum laude, U. Notre Dame, 1949; A.M. in Organic Chemistry, Harvard, 1950, Ph.D., 1953; m. Patricia Lois Boker, Aug. 12, 1957; children—Judith Marie, Albert Paul, Janet Lynn, Jennifer Ann, David Frederick. Eli Lilly, NRC post-doctoral fellow Birkbeck Coll., U. London, Eng., 1952-53; instr. U. Notre Dame, 1953-54; project asso. U. Wis.-Madison, 1955-56; mem. faculty U. Kan., Lawrence, 1956—, prof. chemistry, 1965—; cons. Parke-Davis Research Labs., 1960-67. Pres. PTA Council, Lawrence, 1965-66. Alfred P. Sloan research fellow, 1961-64; recipient Notre Dame Centennial Sci. award, 1965. Fellow Chem. Soc. London; mem. Am. Chem. Soc. (past chmn. U. Kan sect.), Internat. Soc. Fluoride Research (pres. 1970-71), Internat. Soc. Research Civilization Diseases (sci. council), Kan. Acad. Sci. Contbr. profl. jours. Home: 1620 Massachusetts St Lawrence KS 66044

BURGUM, KATHERINE KILBOURNE, mem. Republican Nat. Com.; b. Minneapolis, Kan., Feb. 26, 1915; d. Burton K. and Daisy (Conwell) Kilbourne; B.S., N.D. State U., Fargo, 1939; M.A., Columbia Tchrs. Coll., 1941; m. Joseph B. Burgum, Apr. 8, 1944 (dec. Jan. 1971); children—Bradley J., Barbara K., Douglas J. Tchr. art and home econs. Sayville (N.Y.) Jr. and Sr. High Sch., 1939-41; asst. prof. home econs., also research asso. air cargo studies, Sch. Bus. Admintrn., Wayne State U., 1941-47. Farm mgr., dir. Farmers Elevator Co., Arthur, N.D. Pres. 11th Dist. Cass County Rep. Women's Club, 1961-62; exec. bd. Cass County Rep. Com., 1961-64; Rep. precinct com., Arthur, N.D., 1965—; del. Rep. Nat. Conv., 1968; mem. Rep. Nat. Com. for N.D., 1968—. Pres. N.D. Hosp. Hosp. Auxs. Assn., 1965-66, 66-67; mem. Arthur Sch. Bd., 1968-69, 71—; mem. Nat. Motor Vehicle Safety Council, 1971; del. from N.D., McCalls mag. Congress Better Living, 1958. Trustee N.D. State U. Recipient Aviation Writers prize for contbn. to comml. aviation, 1949; Alumni Achievement award N.D. State U., 1971. Author: (with others) Markets for Airborne Seafood, 1948. Address: Box 57 Arthur ND 58006

BURHOE, RALPH WENDELL, educator; b. Somerville, Mass., June 21, 1911; s. Winslow Page and Mary Trenaman (Stumbles) B.; student Harvard, 1928-32, Andover Newton Theol. Sch., 1934-36; m. Frances Bickford, Aug. 4, 1931 (dec. Aug. 1967); children—Winslow, Laura, Thomas Allen, Diana May; m. 2d, Calla Crawford Butler, Apr. 6, 1969. Observer, research asst. Blue Hill Meteorol. Obs., Harvard, 1936-47; asst. sec. Am. Meteorol. Soc., Milton, Mass., 1936-47, treas., 1942-47; exec. officer Am. Acad. Arts and Sciences, Boston, 1947-64; prof., chmn. theology, scis. Meadville Theol. Sch., Chgo., 1964- -, dir. Center for Advanced Study in Theology and Scis. Co-founder, hon. pres. Inst. Religion in an Age of Sci. Fellow World, Am. acads. arts aand scis., A.A.A.S. (council); mem. Société Européenne de Culture, Acad. Religion and Mental Health, Am. Theol. Assn., Fedn. Am. Scientists, Religious Research Assn., Soc. Gen. Systems. Research, Soc. Sci. Study Religion, World Future Soc. Author-editor: (with Hudson Hoagland) Evolution and Man's Progress, 1962; Science and Human Values in the Twenty-first Century, 1971. Editor: Zygon, Jour. Religion and Sci., 1965—. Home: 5711 Woodlawn Av Chicago IL 60637. Office: 5700 S Woodlawn Av Chicago IL 60637

BURHOP, JOHN WALTER, banker; b. Detroit, Oct. 13, 1923; s. Walter George and Viola (Bruderick) B.; B.A., Wayne State U., 1949, LL.B., 1956; postgrad. Stonier Grad. Sch. Banking, Rutgers U., 1967; m. Marilyn Morden, Aug. 26, 1949. Asst. examiner Fed. Res. Bank, Chgo., 1949-51; operations officer Detroit Bank & Trust Co., 1951-60; controller Bank of Hawaii, Honolulu, 1960-63, v.p., 1964-69; v.p., controller First Nat. State Bank of N.J., Newark, 1969-70, exec. v.p., 1971—; treas. 1st Nat. State Bancorp., 1971—; auditor City Bank & Trust Co., Jackson, Mich., 1963-64; tchr. econs., accounting, bank mgmt. Am. Inst. Banking, 1957-70. Served with USMCR, 1942-46. Mem. Financial Execs. Inst., Mich. Bar Assn. Home: 50 Thackeray Dr Short Hills NJ 07078 Office: 550 Broad St Newark NJ 07101

BURK, DEAN, biochemist; b. Oakland, Cal., Mar. 21, 1904; s. Frederic and Caroline (Frear) B.; B.S., U. Cal., 1923, Ph.D., 1927; fellow NRC and Internat. Edn. Bd., 1927-29 at U. London (Univ. Coll.), Kaiser Wilhelm Inst. for Biology, Harvard; m. Mildred Chaundy; children—Diana (Mrs. Richard A. Barker), Wendy, Frederic Chaundy. Asso. phys. chemist Fixed Nitrogen Research Lab., Dept. Agr., Washington, 1929, chemist, 1937-39; sr. chemist Nat. Cancer Inst., NIH, Bethesda, Md., 1939-48, prin. chemist, 1948-51, head chemist, 1951-58, chief chemist, 1958—; asso. prof. biochemistry Cornell U. Med. Coll., 1939-41; research master grad. faculty George Washington U., 1947—. Guest research worker U.S.S.R. Acad. Scis. (Biochem. Inst.), Moscow, 1935. Recipient Domagk prize for cancer research, 1965; decorated knight comdr. Med. Order Bethlehem. Fellow A.A.A.S. (organizer, chmn. research confs. on cancer, 1942-45); mem. Am. Chem. Soc. (Hillebrand award 1952), Am. Soc. Biol. Chemists, Am. Assn. Cancer Research, Am. Soc. Plant Physiologists, Soc. Exptl. Biology and Medicine (chmn. 1949-50, sec.-treas. 1948-49), N.Y., Washington acads. sci., Soc. Gen. Physiology, L.I. Biol. Assn., Harvey Soc., Chem. Soc. Washington, Max Planck Assn. Goettingen, Inst. for Cell Physiology Berlin, Royal Soc. Medicine London, Nat. Trust Gt. Britain, Dolmetsch Found. Haslemere (fgn.), Gamma Alpha, Sigma Xi. Club: Cosmos (Washington). Author: Cancer, 1945; Approaches to Tumor Chemotherapy, 1947; Cell Chemistry, 1953. Asso. editor: Record Chem. Progress, 1943—; Proc. Soc. Exptl. Biology and Medicine, 1948-53, Enzymologia since 1937. Contbr. sci. articles. Home: 4719-44 St N W Washington DC 20016 Office: Nat Cancer Institute Nat Institutes of Health Bethesda MD 20014

BURK, RICHARD DALE, physician; b. Denver, Oct. 15, 1922; s. George John and Marybelle (Smith) B.; B.S., Regis Coll., 1943; M.D., Creighton U., 1951; M.S., Ohio State U., 1955; m. Mary Imogene Sullivan, Jan. 6, 1944; children—Richard, Daniel, Kathy, Kevin. Intern St. Joseph Creighton Meml. Hosp., Omaha, 1951-52; Ohio State U. Hosp., 1952-55; asso. prof., dir. Rehabilitation Center Ohio State U., 1958-65; prof., chmn. dept. dean Sch. Allied Health Professions, U. Tex. Med. Sch., Dallas, 1966-70; asso. dir. dept. phys. medicine and rehab. St. Elizabeths Med. Center, Dayton, O. 1971—. Mem. com. tng. VA, Washington; mem. Joint Commn. Accreditation, Chgo.; mem. Gov.'s Commn. Blind, 1959-65. Served with USNR, 1944-46. Named Ohio Physician of Yr., 1963, Tex. Physician of Yr., 1966. Mem. Am., Tex., Ohio med. assns., Am. Acad. Phys. Medicine and Rehab., Am. Cong. Rehab. Medicine, Nat. Rehab. Assn. (pres. 1970-71), Nat. Assn. Rehab. Facilities (pres. 1961-65). Home: 5327 Salem Bend Dr Dayton OH 45426 Office: 601 Miami Blvd W Dayton OH 45408

BURK, WILLIAM EMMETT, Jr., architect; b. Louisville, Apr. 9, 1909; s. William Emmett and Mable (Martin) B.; B.F.A., U. So. Cal., 1931; m. Suzanne Sweet, Oct. 31, 1933; children—William Emmett III, Charles S. Profl. sculptor, Los Angeles, 1928-33; practice architecture, Albuquerque, 1933—; head dept. architecture U. N.M., 1935-42; pres. Asso. Research Design, Inc., 1942-55; dir. Security Fed. Savs. & Loan Assn. Cons. Rand Corp., Santa Monica, Cal., Miter, Boston, Joint Air Def. Bd., Colorado Springs. Recipient OSRD citation, 1946. Mem. A.I.A. (pres. N.M. chpt. 1948-50), Kappa Sigma, Delta Delta Delta. Elk. Home: 611 Loma Linda Pl SE Albuquerque NM 87108 Office: 512 Yale Blvd SE Albuquerque NM 87106

BURKE, ADRIAN P., judge; b.N.Y.C., Oct. 2, 1904; s. Thomas F. and Rose Mary (Daw) B.; A.B., Holy Cross Coll., 1927; LL.B., Fordham U., 1930; m. Edith Martin, Dec. 28, 1934; children—Adrian P., Edith Martin, Francis. High sch. tchr.; v.p. James R. Murphy, real estate; admitted to N.Y. bar; corp. counsel City N.Y., 1954; asso. judge Ct. of Appeals, N.Y., 1955—. Del. Constitutional Conv., 1938.

Founder, past pres. Youth Counsel Bur., N.Y.C.; founder, past sec. Youth House, N.Y.C.; founder, past pres. Children's Center Neglected Children, N.Y.C. Clubs: University (N.Y.C.); Fort Orange (Albany). Address: 60 E 42d St New York City NY 10017

BURKE, ARLEIGH ALBERT, ret. naval officer, corp. exec.; b. Boulder, Colo., Oct. 19, 1901; s. Oscar A. and Claire (Mokler) B.; B.S., U.S. Naval Acad., 1923; M.S., U. Mich., 1932, LL.D.; D.Sc. (hon.), U. Notre Dame, U. Colo.; LL.D., Tufts Coll., Loras Coll.; D.End., Pa. Mil. Coll.; H.H.D., U. So. Ill.; m. Roberta Gorsuch, June 7, 1923. Commd. ensign USN, 1923, advanced through grades to adm., 1955; comdr. Destroyer Squadron 23, chief staff Task Force 58, 1942-45; chief staff Atlantic Fleet, 1945-47; comdr. Cruiser Div. 5, Korea, 1950-52; mem. mil. armistice negotiating group, 1951; dir. strategic plans Navy Dept., 1952-54; comdr. Cruiser Div. SIX, 1954-55; comdr. Destroyer Force, U.S. Atlantic Fleet, 1955; adm. and chief U.S. Naval Operations, 1955-61; ret. 1961; dir., mem. exec. com. Texaco, Inc., 1961—, Freeport Sulphur Co.; dir. Thiokol Chem. Corp., First Nat. Bank of Washington, DuKane Corp., Financial Gen. Corp., Foster Wheeler Corp. Bd. dirs. Freedoms Found., Marineland of Pacific, Center for Strategic Studies of Georgetown U.; mem. exec. bd. Nat. Capital Area Council Boy Scouts Am. Decorated Navy Cross, Legion of Merit (two gold stars and oak leaf cluster), Purple Heart, other U.S. and fgn. decorations. Mem. Am. Chem. Soc., Am. Legion, Am. Ordnance Assn., I.R.E., Am. Soc. Naval Engrs., Mil. Order World Wars, Navy League (mem. nat. adv. council), Naval Acad. Alumni Assn., Fleet Res. Assn., U. Mich. Alumni Assn., Nat. Geog. Soc., Newcomen Soc. N. Am., Naval Hist. Found., N.Y. State Soc. Cincinnati (hon.), Pilgrims U.S., Iota Alpha, others. Clubs: Metropolitan (Washington); Army-Navy, International, Chevy Chase, Lotos, Salmagundi, Alfalfa, Brook, Inner Wheel, Circus Saints and Sinners; Bohemian (San Francisco). Home: 8624 Fenway Dr Bethesda MD 20034 Office: 1800 K St NW Washington DC 20006

BURKE, ART, journalist; b. New Orleans, July 30, 1914; s. Arthur I. and Sophia (Meyer) B.; student Loyola U., New Orleans, 1938; m. Enola Celeste Schulz, Jan. 3, 1942; children-Arleen Enola (Mrs. Joseph Nicosia), Barbara Kay (Mrs. Carl Bartling), Donald A., Arthur I. With Times- Picayune, New Orleans, 1934—, gen. sports reporter, 1936-48, columnist, 1948-64, exec. sports editor, 1964—; editor La. Legionnaire Am. Legion monthly publ., 1948—; dir. Dixie Brewing Co. Served to lt. comdr. USNR, 1940-46; PTO. Mem. Am. Legion (post and dist. comdr.), V.F.W. (co- founder sports com., Greater New Orleans Hall of Fame). Lutheran. Home: 10113 Gail Ct New Orleans LA 70123 Office: 3800 Howard Av New Orleans LA 70140

BURKE, AUBREY FRANCIS, corp. exec.; b. Apr. 21, 1904; m. Rosalind Laura Norman, 1936. Dep. mng. dir. vice chmn. Hawker Siddeley Group Ltd.; dep. chmn., Hawker Siddeley Dynamics Ltd., dep chmn., mgr. dir. Holdings Ltd. Hawker Siddeley Diesels Ltd.; dep. chmn. Hawker Siddeley Electric Ltd.; chmn. Mirrlees Nat. Ltd., Petters Ltd., Hawker Siddeley Bldg. Supplies Pty. Ltd., Gloster Saro Ltd., Thomas Green & Son Ltd., Hands Trailers Ltd., Saro Products Ltd., Blackstone & Co. Ltd., Hawker Siddeley Brush Pty. Ltd., Kelvin Constrn. Ltd.; dir Hawker Siddeley Aviation Ltd., Hawker Siddeley Internat. Ltd., Hawker Siddeley Brush Lt., Hawker Siddeley Internat. N.Z. Ltd. Hawker Siddeley Internat. (Pty.) Ltd., Hawker Siddeley Australia Pty. Ltd., Hawker de Havilland Australia Pty. Ltd., Harrison Lister Engring. Ltd., Racair Ltd. Pres. Soc. British Aircraft Constructors, Ltd., 1958-60. High Sheriff of Hertfordshire, 1966-67. Home: Rent St Barns Bovingdon Herts England also Ramster Chiddingfold Surrey, England.

BURKE, BERNARD FLOOD, educator, physicist; b. Boston, June 7, 1928; s. Vincent Paul and Clare (Brine) B.; S.B., Mass. Inst. Tech., 1950, Ph.D., 1953; m. Jane Chapin Pann, May 30, 1953; children—Geoffrey Damian, Elizabeth Chapin, Mark Vincent, Matthew Brine. Staff mem. terrestrial magnetism Carnegie Instn. of Washington, 1953-65, chmn. radio astronomy sect., 1962-65; prof. physics Mass. Inst. Tech., 1965—; cons. Nat. Sci. Found., NASA. Recipient Helen Warner prize, Am. Astron. Soc., 1963. Fellow A.A.A.S.; mem. Nat. Acad. Scis., Am. Acad. Arts and Scis., Am. Phys. Soc., Am., Royal astron. socs., Internat. Astron. Union, Internat. Sci. Radio Union. Research on microwave spectroscopy, radio astronomy, galactic structure, antenna design. Home: 10 Bloomfield St Lexington MA 02173 Office: Mass Inst Tech Cambridge MA 02139

BURKE, BROTHER DANIEL, pres. LaSalle Coll. Address: LaSalle Coll Olney Av and 20th St Philadelphia PA 19141*

BURKE, COLEMAN, lawyer; b. Summit, N.J., Feb. 1, 1914; s. Daniel and Kate (Bundy) B.; grad. Pingry Sch., 1930; A.B., Hamilton Coll., 1934; J.D., Harvard, 1938: LL.D. Rikkyo U., Tokyo, Japan, 1958; m. Mary Poston, Nov. 20, 1937; children—Daniel II, Coleman P., Mary C. Admitted to N.Y. bar, 1938, N.J. bar, 1943; asso. atty. Burke & Burke, N.Y.C., 1937-42, partner, 1942—; partner Burke & Schmid and predecessors, Summit, N.J., 1943—. Dir. Champion Products, Inc., LFE Corp., Wiltek, Inc., Summit & Elizabeth Trust Co., other corps. Chmn. bd. Hamilton Coll., Humane Soc. U.S.; chmn. exec. com. Am. Bible Soc. Mem. Am., N.Y. State, N.J. bar assns., Assn. Bar City N.Y., Phi Beta Kappa, Chi Psi. Methodist (trustee). Clubs: Harvard, Down Town Assn. (N.Y.C.); Short Hills, Baltusrol Golf, Cotton Bay. Author: Voting Trust Currently Observed, 1940. Home: 45 Stewart Rd Short Hills NJ 07078 Office: 1 Wall St New York City NY 10005 also 382 Springfield Av Summit NJ 07901

BURKE, DANIEL BARNETT, communications corp. exec.; b. Albany, N.Y., Feb. 4, 1929; s. J. Frank and Mary (Barnett) B.; A.B., U. Vt., 1950; M.B.A., Harvard, 1955; m. Harriet Shore, Aug. 31, 1957; children—Steve, James, Sarah, William. Various positions product mgmt. and devel. Jell-O div. Gen. Foods Corp., 1955-61; gen. mgr. WTEN-TV, Albany, 1961-64, corporate v.p., 1962; gen. mgr. WJR AM/FM, Detroit, 1964-69, corporate exec. v.p., dir. 1967; pres. pub. div. Capital Cities Broadcasting Corp., N.Y.C., 1969—; dir. Palm Beach Co., First Independence Nat. Bank Detroit. Pres. United Cerebral Palsy Assn., Detroit, 1968-69. Chmn. adv. bd. dirs. Med. Mission Sisters, Phila. Served to 1st lt., inf., AUS, 1951-53; Korea. Mem. Phi Delta Theta. Office: 24 E 51st St New York City NY 10022

BURKE, DENNIS MAURICE, coll. ofcl.; b. Casco, Wis., May 27, 1905; s. Patrick F. and Catherine (Smithwick) B.; B.A., St. Norbert Coll., 1926; S.T.D., Gregorian U., Rome (Italy), 1930; J.C.D., Angelic Inst., Rome, 1932. Ordained priest Roman Catholic Ch., 1929; prof. philosophy St. Norbert Coll., 1932-49, chmn. dept. philosophy, 1935-46, v.p., 1934-47, pres., 1955-68, chancellor, 1968—; prior St. Norbert Abbey, 1934-47; prosynodal judge Green Bay Diocesan Matrimonial Ct., 1933—. Mem. Cath. Philos. Assn., Canon Law Soc. Am. K.C. (4). Club: Green Bay Kiwanis. Address: St Norbert Coll De Pere WI 54115

BURKE, EDWARD NOLAN, pub. relations; b. Orange, N.J., Sept. 5, 1918; s. John I. and Marie (Burke) B.; A.B., Columbia, 1940; student Harvard Bus. Sch., 1943-44; m. Marjorie Madden, Nov. 9, 1941; children—Elizabeth, David. Exec. trainee R.H. Macy & Co., N.Y.C., 1940-41; with advt. dept. Procter & Gamble Co., 1941-43; with Newark News, 1946-71, bus. and financial editor, 1957- 69, mem. editorial bd., 1969-71; pub. information officer 1st Nat. State Bank N.J., Newark, 1971—. Served with USNR, 1943-46; PTO. Mem. Phi Beta Kappa. Club: Bond of N.J. Home: 205 Sterling Dr Orange NJ 07050 Office: 550 Broad St Newark NJ 07102

BURKE, ELLEN COOLIDGE, ret. librarian; b. Alexandria, Va., May 10, 1901; d. Henry Randolph and Rosella (Trist) Burke; B.A., Catholic U. Am., 1938, M.A., 1943. With Alexandria Library, 1939—, successively catalogue, reference, 1st asst. library dir., 1948-69. Mem. Va. Library Assn., Va. Council Human Relations, Common Cause, League Women Voters, Historic Alexandria Found. (charter). Roman Catholic. Club: Zonta. Home: Regency Apts St Matthews Sq Virginia Beach VA 23451

BURKE, FRANK WELSH, mayor; b. Louisville, June 1, 1920; s. Joseph M. and Ann (Welsh) B.; student U. So. Cal., 1938-39; Ph.B., Xavier U., 1942; LL.B., U. Louisville, 1948; m. Evalyne Hackett, Apr. 6, 1943; children—Lynn (Mrs. Dennis Clare), JoAnn (Mrs. George Schuhmann), Lucy, Frank Welsh. Admitted to Ky. bar, 1948, since practiced in Louisville; asst. city atty., Louisville, 1950-51; dir. pub. safety, Louisville, 1952; exec. asst. to mayor of Louisville, 1952-53; mem. Ky. Ho. of Reps., 1957; mem. U.S. Ho. of Reps. from Ky., 1958-62; mayor of Louisville, 1969—. Del Democratic Nat. Conv., 1968. Served to 1st lt. AUS, 1942-45. Mem. Ky., Louisville bar assns., Am. Legion, V.F.W., Phi Alpha Delta, Alpha Sigma Nu, Phi Kappa Psi. Catholic. K.C. Home: 1234 Eastern Pky Louisville KY 40204 Office: City Hall Louisville KY 40202

BURKE, FREDERIC GERARD, physician, educator; b. England, Feb. 19, 1917; s. Patrick John and Frances (Smitton) B.; naturalized U.S. citizen by derivation; B.S., Seton Hall U., 1938; M.D., Georgetown U., 1942; m. Ruth Elizabeth Derouin, Dec. 27, 1945; children—Frederic Gerard, Mary Elizabeth, Patrick, Frances, John, Barbara, Frank, Thaddeus. Intern Georgetown U. Hosp., 1942-43; resident, fellow pediatrics Childrens Hosp., Washington, 1943-45, dir. pediatric edn., 1945-49; asst. prof. pediatrics George Washington U., 1944-49; asst. prof. pediatrics Georgetown U., 1945-50, prof. pediatrics, 1950—, chmn. dept., 1950-63; dir. Children's Convalescent Hosp., Washington, 1950—; cons. to surgeon gen. U.S., NIH. Co- founder Retarded Children's Clinic, Georgetown U., 1955. Diplomate Am. Bd. Pediatrics. Mem. A.M.A., D.C. Med. Soc., So. Soc. Pediatric Research, Am. Acad. Pediatrics, Am. Assn. Clin. Research, Alpha Omega Alpha. Mem. editorial bd. D.C. Med. Annals, Clin. Proc. Children's Hosp. Home: 3307 Woodbine St Chevy Chase MD 20015 Office: 3740 Military Rd NW Washington DC 20015

BURKE, FRED GEORGE, state ofcl.; b. Collins, N.Y., Jan. 1, 1926; s. Fred F. and Sophie (Blesy) B.; B.A., Williams Coll., 1953; M.A., Princeton, 1955, Ph.D., 1958; postgrad. Oxford U., 1955-56; m. Daphne Elaine Ruttenbur, Sept. 17, 1949; children—Rebecca Lynel, Frederick Donald, Daniel George, Adam Terry. Prof., dir. Arneson Inst. Politics, Ohio Wesleyan U., Del. 1957-60; prof. polit. sci., dir. East African Studies Program Syracuse (N.Y.) U., 1960-68; dean internat. studies State U. N.Y., Buffalo; commr. edn. State R.I., Providence, 1971—. Mem. Del. City Council, 1958-60. Chmn. Ohio Citizenship Clearing House. Served with USAAF, World War II; USAF, Korean War. Recipient Social Sci. Research Council Kimborough-Owen award, 1958; Woodrow Wilson fellow, 1953- 54. Mem. Am. Polit. Sci. Assn., African Studies Assn., Am. Soc. Pub. Adminstrn. (chmn. CAG). Author: Africa's Quest For Order, 1964; Local Government and Politics in Uganda, 1965; The Transformation of East Africa, 1966; Pre-Planning in Tanganyika, 1966. Home: 32 Seaview Av Cranston RI 02905 Office: 199 Promenade St Providence RI

BURKE, HAROLD P., U.S. dist. judge; b. Rochester, N.Y., June 6, 1895; s. Peter and Jennie (Noonan) B.; LL.B., U. Notre Dame, 1916; m. Margaret M. McKay, June 30, 1927. Admitted to N.Y. bar, 1920, and practiced in Rochester; 2d dep. atty. gen. for N.Y., 1931-34; corp. counsel for Rochester, 1934-37; U.S. dist. judge, Rochester, 1937—. Democrat. K.C. Home: 30 Lake View Park Rochester NY 14613 Office: Federal Bldg Rochester NY 14613

BURKE, HYLE GILMORE, lawyer, communications exec.; Bancroft, Neb., Aug. 29, 1907; s. Allen Gilmore and Emily Margaret (McManus) B.; A.B., U. Neb., 1930, LL.B. cum laude, 1932; m. Mardele Rucker, Jan. 11, 1933; childrenAlan Rucker, Robert Gilmore. Admitted to Neb. bar, 1932, Ind. bar, 1952; pvt. practice law Moodie & Burke, West Point, Neb., 1932-37; county atty. Cuming County, Neb., 1935-37; asst. trust officer Continental Nat. Bank of Lincoln, 1937; atty. Northwestern Bell Telephone Co., Omaha, 1937-52; gen. atty. Ind. Bell Telephone Co., Indpls., 1952-53, gen. counsel, 1954-, v.p., gen. counsel, 1956-. Pres. Family Service Assn., 1943; trustee Bishop Clarkson Meml. Hosp., (both Omaha), 1946-51. Mem. Am., Neb., Ind. bar assns., Am. Judicature Soc., Newcomen Soc. N.A., Fgn. Policy Assn. Omaha (sec. 1941-48), Order of Coif, Phi Delta Phi, Sigma Phi Epsilon. Republican. Episcopalian. Mason. Clubs: Omaha (dir., sec. 1950-52); Columbia, Woodstock (Indpls.). Home: 538 W 91st St Indianapolis IN 46260 Office: 240 N Meridian St Indianapolis IN 46204

BURKE, J. HERBERT, congressman; b. Chgo., Jan. 14, 1913; s. Joseph Patrick and Catherine (Lobert) B.; student Northwestern U., 1934-35; A.A., Central YMCA Coll., 1936; J.D., Kent Coll. Law, 1940; L.H.D. (hon.), Drake Coll., 1967, Ft. Lauderdale U., 1970; LL.D., Chgo. Coll. Law, 1969; m. Evelyn Krumtinger, Sept. 4, 1946; children—Michele Kathleen, Kelly Ann. Admitted to Ill. bar, 1940, Fla. bar, 1949, U.S. Supreme Ct., 1949; practiced in Chgo., 1940-49, Hollywood, Fla., 1949—; asso. firm Pam, Hurd & Reichmann, 1940-49; sr. partner Abrams, Anton, Robbins, Resnick & Burke; mem. 90th-92d Congresses 10th Dist. Fla., mem. Com. on Fgn. Affairs, Subcoms. on European Affairs, Asian and Pacific Affairs, Fgn. Econ. Policy. Chmn. March Dimes S. Broward County, 1955; chmn. Broward County Heart Fund, 1956, 58; mem. adv. bd. Small Bus. Adminstrn., 1956-60; adviser Nat. Rivers and Harbors Congress, 1958. Mem. Broward County Commn., 1952-66, chmn., 1956-58, dean, 1958-64; Rep. state committeeman, 1954-58. Served to capt. AUS, 1942-45; ETO. Decorated Purple Heart, Bronze Star medal; recipient Outstanding Service medal Heart Assn., 1957, Good Govt. award Hollywood Jr. C. of C., 1963; Hollywood Civitan Outstanding Citizenship award, 1964; Distinguished Service award Ams. Constnl. Action, 1967-70; Watchdog Treasury award Nat. Assn. Businessmen, 1967-70; Service to Israel award, 1969; citation for meritorious Service Nat. Assn. Ret. Civil Employees, 1971; meritorious citation AMVETS, 1969. Mem. Fla., Broward County, Hollywood bar assns., Nat. Assn. Army Judge Advocates, Am. Legion (past post comdr.), 40 and 8, V.F.W., D.A.V., AMVETS (life), Hollywood C. of C., Phi Delta Phi. Roman Catholic. Eagle (past state dir.), Elk, Moose, Kiwanian. Home: 1218 Hollywood Blvd Hollywood FL 33020 Office: Longworth Bldg U S Ho of Reps Washington DC 20515

BURKE, JAMES A., congressman; b. Boston, Mar. 30, 1910; student Lincoln Prep. Sch., Suffolk U.; m. Aileen McDonald. Former registrar vital statistics, Boston. Served as spl. agt. in Counter Intelligence, World War II. Mem. Mass. Gen. Ct., 10 years; asst. majority leader Mass. Ho. of Reps., 4 years; mem. 86th-87th Congresses, 13th Mass. Dist., 88th-92d Congresses, 11th Dist. Mass. Home: Milton MA 02186 Office: House Office Bldg Washington DC 20515

BURKE, JAMES BUNDY, lawyer; b. Bklyn., Nov. 25, 1904; s. Daniel and Kate Hull (Bundy) B.; student Summit Acad., 1916-21; A.B., Hamilton Coll., 1925; LL.B., Harvard, 1928; m. Margaret Clark Sessions, Oct. 18, 1930 (dec. Dec. 1968); children—Gilman S., Kate S.; m. 2d, Muriel K. Atkinson, Aug. 1, 1970. Admitted to N.Y. bar, 1928; mem. firm Burke & Burke, N.Y.C., 1929—; dir. R.T. French Co., Simmons Co., Summit & Elizabeth Trust Co., China Safe Deposit Co., Greatermans Buying & Shipping, Chinese Am. Bank. Formerly pres., bd. dirs. Family Welfare Soc., YMCA, Summit, N.J.; trustee Drew U. Mem. Am., N.Y. State bar assns., Assn. Bar City of N.Y., Phi Beta Kappa, Chi Psi. Methodist. Clubs: Downtown Assn., Harvard (N.Y.C.). Home: 6 Llewellyn Rd Summit NJ 07901 Office: 1 Wall St New York City NY 10005

BURKE, JAMES EDWARD, bus. exec.; b. Rutland, Vt., Feb. 28, 1925; s. James Francis and Mary (Barnett) B.; B.S. in Econs., Holy Cross Coll., 1947; M.B.A., Harvard, 1949; m. Alice Eubank, Apr. 27, 1957; children—Mary Clotilde, James Charles. Salesman, Procter & Gamble, 1949, asst. brand mgr., 1949-52, brand mgr., 1952; product dir. Johnson & Johnson, 1953- 54, dir. new products, 1954-57, dir. advt. and merchandising, 1957-58, v.p. advt. and merchandising, 1958-62, gen. mgr. Robert Wood Johnson Co. div., 1962-64, exec. v.p. marketing, 1964-65, gen. mgr. domestic operating div., 1965-66, pres. Domestic Operating Co., 1966-70, chmn. bd., 1970—, chmn. bd. Personal Products Co., 1970—; dir., vice chmn. exec. com. Johnson & Johnson. Home: 158 Springdale Rd Princeton NJ 08530 Office: 500 George St New Brunswick NJ 08901

BURKE, JAMES GIBBONS, lawyer; b. New Orleans, Dec. 21, 1902; s. Patrick Edward and Catherine (Gibbons) B.; A.B., Georgetown U., 1924; LL.B., Harvard, 1927; m. Mary Shea, June 2, 1930; children—Deirdre (Mrs. Michel O. Provosty), James Gibbons, Peter Gibbons, Sheela (Mrs. David D. Plater), Sean Gibbons. Admitted to La. bar, 1928, since practiced in New Orleans; partner firm Burke & Ballard; Equity prof. Loyola U., New Orleans, 1930-33. Vice pres. Paramount Gulf Theatres, Inc.; adviser to bd. Motion Picture Advt. Corp. Sec., Variety Children's Home. Bd. dirs. New Orleans chpt. A.R.C., 1930-35, Richards Found., Weiss Found., George Found., Information Council Americas, Home for Incurables. Recipient Merrick medal Georgetown Coll., also Hamilton medal. Mem. Am., La., New Orleans bar assns., Assn. Bar City N.Y., Am. Judicature Soc. (life). Democrat. Roman Catholic. Clubs: Boston, Pickwick (pres. 1943), Harvard, Georgetown, Variety (counsel tent 45), Plimsoll (New Orleans); Knickerbocker (N.Y.C.); Lancers (Dallas). Home: 452 Audubon St New Orleans LA 70118 Office: Ten Ten Common St New Orleans LA 70112

BURKE, JAMES VINCENT, Jr., lawyer; b. Pitts., Dec. 28, 1911; s. James Vincent and Alice (Hesson) B.; B.A. cum laude, Notre Dame U., 1933; LL.B., U. Pitts., 1936; m. Mary E. Brown, Jan. 26, 1952. Admitted to Pa. bar, 1937; asso. with firm Campbell, Thomas & Burke and predecessors, Pitts., 1937-42, 46-59, 61—, partner, 1946-59, 61—; gen. counsel Dept. of Def., 1959- 61. Dir. Tyson Metal Products, Inc., Allegheny Installations, Inc. Pitts. Metal Polishing Co., Inc., Tafco, Inc., La Shall Realty Co., Inc.; pres., dir. Allegheny Indsl. Park Corp.; sec., dir. ATV, Inc., Three Rivers Enterprises, Inc. Bd. dirs. St. Francis Gen. Hosp. Served to lt. USNR, 1942-46; ETO. Mem. Am. (ho. of dels. 1952- 60, 62-71), Pa., Fed., Allegheny County (pres. 1958) bar assns., Am. Law Inst., Fellows Am. Bar Found. Clubs: Duquesne, University, Notre Dame (Man of Year award 1960) (Pitts.). Home: 127 Spring House Lane Pittsburgh PA 15238 Office: Peoples Bank Bldg Pittsburgh PA 15222

BURKE, JOHN B., lawyer; b. McGregor, Ia., Apr. 21, 1901; s. James J. and Mildred (Goedert) B.; LL.B., William Mitchell Coll. Law, 1922; m. Margaret Barrett, June 17, 1925 (dec. Aug. 1970); children—Mary C. (Mrs. John Stryker), Patricia J. (Mrs. Warren Kump), John B., Margaret A. (Sister Joanne Charlotte, VHM), Geraldine H. (Mrs. Howard Boyer). Admitted to Minn. bar, 1922; title atty. Fed. Land Bank, St. Paul, 1922-24; chief counsel Minn. Fed. Savs. & Loan Assn., 1924—; partner firm Burke & Scott, and predecessors, St. Paul, 1924—. Treas. Minn. Tb and Health Assn., 1945. Trustee William Mitchell Coll. Law; bd. dirs. Minn. State Bar Found. Fellow Am. Bar Found.; mem. Am. (ho. of dels., chmn. credentials and admissions com.), Minn. (past pres., bd. govs.), Ramsey County bar assns., Am. Judicature Soc. (dir.), Sierra Club. Roman Catholic. K.C. Home: 1371 Goodrich Av St Paul MN 55105 Office: 355 Minnesota St St Paul MN 55101

BURKE, JOHN DOUGHERTY, advt. exec.; b.Bklyn., Apr. 15, 1917; s. John F. and Agnes (Dougherty) B.; B.A. cum laude, Prinnceton, 1938; m. Elizabeth Ann Hourigan, May 14, 1949; children-John Dougherty, Christopher, Brian, Andrew, Elizabeth. Copy chief, v.p. Erwin & Wasey, N.Y.C., 1946-56; sr. v.p., head creative dept., dir. Compton Advt., Inc. N.Y.C., 1956—. Promotion chmn. Community Chest, Greenwich, Conn., 1967-69. Served from ensign to lt., USNR, 1942-45. Club: Riverside Yacht. Home: 92 Meadow Rd Riverside CT 06878 Office: 625 Madison Av New York NY 10022

BURKE, JOHN EMMETT, librarian; b. Chgo., Aug. 22, 1908; s. James Joseph and Susan Marie (Haffey) B.; A.B., DePaul U., 1930, B.S., 1931, A.M., 1936; B.S. in L.S., U. Chgo., 1947; Ed.D., U. Denver, 1957; m. Lois Evelyn Perkins, Mar. 11, 1950; children—James Joseph, Daniel Redmond, Suzanne Maureen, Sean Patrick. Asst. prin., tchr. English, Evanston, Ill., 1930-36; dean men, asst. librarian St. Mary's Coll., Winona, Minn., 1936-40; asst. librarian Christian Bros. Coll., St. Louis, 1943-49; head librarian, asst. prof. library sci. George Peabody Coll., 1949-53; dir. library service, prof. library sci. E. Tex. State Coll., Commerce, 1953-68, prof. library sci., 1968—. Group leader Jr. Coll. Terminal Edn. Workshop, 1941; profl. asst. survey Clear Creek (Tex.) pub. schs., 1953; coordinator Internat. Tchr. Edn. Program, 1956; cons., library planner U. Dallas, 1961. Mem. Am. (chmn. nominating com. library edn. div. 1958, state legislative chmn. 1962), Cath. (chmn. secondary sch. sect. 1949), Southwestern, Tex. library assns., Lang. Tchrs. Assn. (pres. 1945-47). Assn. Coll. and Research Libraries (chmn. membership 1949-52), Am. Assn. Coll. Tchr. Edn., N.E.A., Spl. Libraries Assn., Phi Delta Kappa. Author: The School Librarian at Work, 1954; Guideposts to Improved Library Service, 1958; Planning the Modern Functional College Library, 1961; Specifications Covering Furniture and Equipment for the Library, 1963; The Rising Tide-More Research Libraries, 1966; also articles. Contbr. encys., profl. jours. Home: 1201 Earl St Commerce TX 75428

BURKE, JOHN J., co. dir.; b. Danville, Kan., Jan. 21, 1923; s. John Harrison and Mary (Oliver) B.; B.S., Cal. Inst. Tech., 1946, M.S., 1948; m. Joyce L. Simmons, Dec. 4, 1954; children—Cheryl Lynn, Robert Lawrence, Merriann Lorraine, Philip Francis. Research engr. Hughes Aircraft Co., Los Angeles, 1946-48; div. mgr. jet propulsion lab. Cal. Inst. Tech., Pasadena, Cal., 1948-56, now mem. adv. com.; sr. v.p. Lear Siegler, Inc., Los Angeles, 1956- 65; pres., dir. Howmet Corp., N.Y.C., 1965-69, chmn., 1969-70, now dir.; pres., dir.

Automation Industries, Inc., Los Angeles; dir. Howmedica Corp., Reuben H. Donnelly Co. (all N.Y.C.), Sergent Industries, Computer Equipment Corp., Systems Devel. Corp. (all Los Angeles), Collins Radio Co., Dallas; mem. adv. committee Chase Manhattan Bank, N.Y.C., Jet Propulsion Lab, Pasadena, Cal.; past cons. to adminstr. NASA. Served with USNR, 1942-46. Mem. Am. Rocket Soc., I.E.E.E., Am. Ordanance Assn. (dir.), Sigma Xi, Tau Beta Pi. Participated as engr. mgr. devel. U.S. ballistic missile Corporal and 1st U.S. satellite Explorer. Home: 1690 Alta Mura Pacific Palisades CA 90272

BURKE, JOHN P., banker. Sr. v.p., controller Waterbury Savs. Bank (Conn.). Office: 60 N Main St Waterbury CT 06720*

BURKE, JOHN RICHARD, fgn. service officer; b. Madison, Wis., Dec. 7, 1924; s. Patrick J. and Katherine M. (Boyle) B.; A.B., U. Wis., 1948, M.A., 1950. Teaching fellow U. Wis., 1954-55; spl. asst. to dir. Wis. Hist. Soc., 1954-55; joined U.S. Fgn. Service, 1956; various assignments, 1957-68; dir. Office Viet Nam Affairs, State Dept., 1968-69; assigned Nat. War Coll., 1969-70; dep. chief mission, Port-au-Prince, Haiti, 1970—. Served to lt. comdr. USNR, 1943-46, 50-53. Recipient Superior Honor award State Dept., 1966. Mem. Chi. Phi. Address: Am embassy Port-au-Prince Haiti

BURKE, JOHN STEPHEN, Jr., merchant; b. N.Y.C., Mar. 3, 1923; s. John Stephen and Helen (Churchill) B.; ed. Canterbury Sch. and Yale; m. Stan O'Connell, Apr. 26, 1947; children—Mary Kathryn, Anne Bridget, Mary Stan, John Stephen III, Margaret Helen. With B. Altman & Co., N.Y.C., 1946—, pres., 1954—, chmn. bd., 1969—; dir. Frederick Atkins, Inc. Bd. dirs. Better Bus. Bur. Met. N.Y., Fifth Av. Assn., N.Y. Conv. and Visitors Bur., Met. N.Y. Retail Mchts. Assn., Ireland-U.S. Council Commerce and Industry. Pres., trustee Altman Found.; trustee Canterbury Sch., Catholic Charities Archdiocese N.Y., Manhattanville Coll., Alfred E. Smith Found. Decorated Knight of Malta. Mem. Soc. Friendly Sons St. Patrick N.Y.C. (pres.). Clubs: Union League (N.Y.C.); Misquamicut (R.I.). Home: 1185 Park Av New York City NY 10028 Office: 361 Fifth Av New York City NY 10016

BURKE, JOHN T., educator; b. Escanaba, Mich., Nov. 23, 1924; s. John Thomas and Sophronia (Hickey) B.; B.S. in Econs., Carroll Coll., Waukesha, Wis., 1949; M.A., Mich. State U., 1950, Ph.D., 1958; m. Jean Marion Salter, Aug. 25, 1947; children—John T., Susan J. Instr. accounting Mich. State U., 1950-56; asst. prof. Wis. State U., Whitewater, 1956-57; asst. prof. asso. prof. Syracuse U., 1957-62, acting chmn., chmn. dept., 1961-62; prof. accounting, head dept. Western Mich. U., 1962—. Served with AUS, 1943-46. C.P.A., Wis. Mem. Am. Accounting Assn., Nat. Accounting Assn., Am. Inst. C.P.A.'s, Am. Inst. C.P.A.'s, Beta Gamma Sigma, Beta Alpha Psi, Alpha Kappa Psi. Home: 1321 Edington St Kalamazoo MI 49002

BURKE, JOSEPH ALOYSIUS, coll. dean; b. Phila., June 23, 1918; s. Michael Joseph and Mary (Killen) B.; A.B., St. Joseph's Coll., Phila., 1940; M.S., Fordham U., 1956, Ph.D., 1959. Ordained priest Roman Catholic Ch., 1951; instr. St. Joseph's Coll., Phila., 1945-48, acad. dean, 1970—; biology tchr. Gonzaga High Sch., Washington, 1953-54; asst. prof. biology Loyola Coll., Balt., 1958-63, asso. prof., 1963-64; dean Wheeling (W.Va.) Coll., 1964-70. Trustee Wheeling Coll., Georgetown U. Fellow A.A.A.S. Office: St Joseph's Coll Philadelphia PA 19131

BURKE, KENNETH, (Duva), author; b. Pittsburgh, Pa., May 5, 1897; s. James Leslie and Lillyan May (Duva) B.; ed. Ohio State U., Columbia; D.Litt. (hon.), Bennington Coll. 1966, Rutgers U., 1968, Dartmouth, 1970; L.H.D. (hon.), Fairfield U., 1970; m. Lily Mary Batterham, May 19, 1919 (div.); children—Jeanne Elspeth, Eleanor Duva, Frances Batterham; m. 2d, Elizabeth Batterham, Dec. 18, 1933; children—James Anthony, Kenneth Michael. Research work, Laura Spelman Rockefeller Memorial, 1926-27; music critic, The Dial, 1927-29; editorial work Bureau Social Hygiene, 1928-29; vis. prof. English, U. Chicago, 1949-50. Writer of stories, Translations, critical articles, book reviews; music critic of The Nation, 1934-36; lectures on practice and theory of lit. criticism, New Sch. for Social Research, 1937; lectures on psychology of lit. form and on Samuel Taylor Coleridge, U. of Chicago, 1938; course in theory and practice, lit. criticism Bennington Coll., 1943-61; lit. critic Drew U., 1962, 64; modern lit. critic Pa. State U., 1963; Regents prof. U. Cal. at Santa Barbara, 1964-65; prof. Central Washington State Coll. 1966; lit. critic, Fannie Hürst vis. prof. Washington U., 1970-71. fellow Center for Advanced Study Behavioral Scis., 1957- 58. Winner Dial award $2,000 for dist. service to Am. Letters 1928; Guggenheim Memorial fellowship, $2,000, 1935; Am. Acad. Arts and Letters and Nat. Inst. Arts and Letters grant, $1000 1946; Rockefeller Found, grant for $10,000, 1966; Creative Arts award Brandeis U., 1967; Poet of Yr. award N.J. Assn. Tchrs. English, 1968; award $7,000 Nat. Endowment for Arts, 1969; Horace Gregory award New Sch. Social Research, 1970. Mem. Am. Acad. Arts and Letters, Am. Acad. Arts and Scis. Club: Century. Author: The White Oxen and Other Stories, 1924; Counter-Statement, 1931, rev. edit. 1953, 1968; (novel) Towards a Better Life; a Series of Declaration on Epistle, 1932, rev. edition, 1966; Permanence and Change Anatomy of Purpose, 1935, rev. edit. 1954; Attitudes Toward History (Vol. I. Acceptance and Rejection; The Curve of History; Vol.II, Analysis of Symbolic Structure), 1937, rev. 1 vol. edit., 1959; Philosophy of Literary FormStudies in Symbolic Action, 1941, abridged edit., 1957, revised unabridged edit. 1967; A Grammar of Motives, 1945, new edit., 1969; A Rhetoric of Motives, 1950, new edit., 1969; Book of Moments, Poems, 1915-54, 1955; The Rhetoric of Religion, 1961; Perspectives by Incongruity, Terms for Order, 1964; Language as Symbolic Action, 1966; Collected Poems, 1915-1967, 1968; (short stories) The Complete White Oxen, 1968. Translator several books. Contbr. to leading mags. Club: Century. Home: RD 2 Andover NJ 07821

BURKE, KENNETH KARL, publisher; b. Rochester, N.Y., July 19, 1910; s. John Alexander and Cora (Keeler) B.; grad. Mt. Hermon Prep. Sch., 1929; B.A., Colgate U., 1933; m. Mildred Fischer, Apr. 20, 1940 (dec. Aug. 1968); 1 dau., Susan Fischer (Mrs. Clemow); m. 2d, Evelyn Gallager Stewart, Nov. 1969. Advt. depts. Rochester and Albany newspapers, 1933-40; bus. mgr. Saratogian, Saratoga Springs, N.Y., 1940-50; gen. mgr. Danville (Ill.) Comml. News, 1951-55; gen. mgr., v.p. Niagara Falls (N.Y.) Gazette, 1955-60; pub. Hartford Times, 1960-67; now pub. Portsmouth (N.H.) Herald. Trustee Nat. Mus. Racing, Saratoga Springs. Served to lt. (s.g.) USNR, 1942-45. Mem. Alpha Tau Omega. Home: 546 Washington Rd Rye NH 03870 Office: 82 Congress St Portsmouth NH 03801

BURKE, LLOYD HUDSON, judge; b. Oakland, Cal., Apr. 1, 1916; s. James H. and Edna L. (Taylor) B.; A.B., St. Mary's Coll., 1937; LL.B., U. Cal., 1940; m. Virginia Joan Kerchum, Apr. 27, 1941; children—Brian Hudson, Bruce Thomas. Dep. dist. atty. Alameda County, Cal., 1940-53, sr. criminal trial dep., 1950-53; U.S. atty., 1953-58; U.S. dist. judge Northern Dis. Cal. 1958—. Served with U. S. Army, 1942-46. Mem. Native Sons Golden West, Phi Delta Phi. Elk. Club: Press and Union League (San Francisco). Home: 250 La Salle Av Piedmont CA 94610 Office: US Court House 450 Golden Gate Av San Francisco CA 94102

BURKE, LOUIS HARRY, state justice; b. Montebello, Cal., Jan. 4, 1905; s. Joseph and Lucie (Dion) B.; Ph.B., Loyola U., Los Angeles, 1926, LL.B., 1926, LL.D. (hon.), 1964; m. Ruth Ann Horsfall, July 1, 1933; children—Michael, Kathleen (Mrs. Donald Peters), Sheila (Mrs. Matt Moore), Mary Eileen (Mrs. Lawrence Coulombe), Patrick. Admitted to Cal. bar, 1927; gen. practice law, Los Angeles, 1927-51; city atty., Montebello, 1928-47; gen. counsel League Cal. Cities, 1932-46; judge Los Angeles County Superior Ct., 1951-61, presiding judge, 1958-61; presiding judge div. 4, 2d Appellate Dist., Cal. Dist. Ct. Appeal, 1961-64; asso. justice Cal. Supreme Ct., 1964—. Mem. Joint Com. for Effective Adminstrn. of Justice, 1962-65; faculty mem. Nat. Coll. State Trial Judges, Boulder, Colo., 1964, Seminar for Intermediate Appellate Ct. Judges, N.Y. U. Sch. Law, 1965. Bd. regents Immaculate Heart Coll., Los Angeles, 1958—; mem. president's council Loyola U., Los Angeles, 1959—. Served to maj. AUS, 1943-46. Recipient Town Hall award for service to So. Cal. community, 1960. Mem. Am. Judicature Soc. (v.p. 1963-66), Am. Bar Assn. (mem. bd. appellate judges conf. 1963—, chmn. com. continuing edn. to judiciary 1966—), Order of Coif, Alpha Sigma Nu, Delta Theta Phi. Roman Catholic. Club: Commonwealth (San Francisco). Author: With This Ring, 1958. Home: 66 Cleary Ct San Francisco CA 94109 Office: 350 McAllister St San Francisco CA 94102

BURKE, MICHAEL, broadcasting co. exec.; b. Enfield, Conn., June 8, 1918; s. Patrick and Mary (Fleming) B.; B.S., U. Pa., 1939; m. Faith Long, June 10, 1939 (div. Dec. 1945); 1 dau., Patricia; m. 2d, Timothy Campbell, Nov. 17, 1946; children—Michele, Doreen, Peter. Spl. adviser to U.S. high commnr. for Germany, 1951-54; v.p., gen. mgr. Ringling Bros. Barnum & Bailey Circus, 1954-56; program exec. CBS TV Network, 1956-57; program dir. CBS TV Network, Europe, 1957-58; mng. dir., pres. CBS Europe, Zurich, Switzerland, 1958-62, CBS Ltd., London, Eng., 1958-62; mng. dir. CBS Prodns. Ltd., London, 1958-62; v.p. CBS, Inc., N.Y.C., 1962—; chmn., pres. N.Y. Yankees, Inc., 1966—. Vice pres., bd. dirs. Reperatory Theatre of Lincoln Center, N.Y.C. Served to lt. (j.g.) USNR, 1942-45. Decorated Navy Cross, Silver Star; Medaille de la Resistance (France). Clubs: Garrick, Special Forces (London). Home: 17 E 89th St New York City NY 10028 Office: Yankee Stadium Bronx NY 10458 also CBS 51 W 52d St New York City NY 10019

BURKE, MOTHER MARGARET, coll. pres.; b. Morris, Minn.; grad. Duchesne Coll., Omaha; M.A. in Philosophy, Ph.D. in Psychology, Loyola U., Chgo.; grad. student St. Louis U., Cath. U. Am. Mem. faculty Barat Coll., Lake Forest, Ill., 1941—, formerly chmn. dept. psychology, now pres. Mem. Chgo. Archdiocesan Commn. on Ecumenism. Trustee Lincoln Acad. Mem. Am. Philos. Assn., Am. Psychol. Assn. Address: Barat Coll Lake Forest IL 60045

BURKE, RAY ALBERT, oil co. exec.; b. Elgin, Tex., Dec. 5, 1921; s. Wade Hampton and Lula Belle (Rhodes) B.; B.S. in Geology, U. Tex., 1947; grad. Advanced Mgmt. Program, Harvard, 1960; m. Jimmye Winkler, Apr. 24, 1945; children—Rodney Ray, Robert Winkler, Glenn Rhodes. Geologist, Stanolind Oil & Gas Co., 1947-51; with Union Oil Co. Cal., 1951-, dir. exploration, 1961-62, v.p., 1962-66, sr. v.p., dir., mem. exec. committee, 1966—, head internat. div., 1966—. Served to lt. (s.g.), A.C., USNR, 1942-45. Decorated Air medal with 5 oak leaf clusters, D.F.C. Mem. Am. Assn. Petroleum Geologists, Houston, New Orleans, Corpus Christie (Tex.) geol. socs. Home: 830 Singingwood Dr Arcadia CA 91006 Office: 461 S Boylston St Los Angeles CA 90017

BURKE, RICHARD S., mfg. co. exec.; b. Chgo., May 11, 1908; s. Samuel T. and Mabelle (Signor) B.; A.B., Dartmouth, 1929; m. Mary Cadley, Sept. 16, 1939; children—Helen (Mrs. Aldo Rostagno), Mary, Martha. Various merchandising positions Sears, Roebuck & Co., 1929-41, asst. merchandising v.p., 1941- 44, mgr. mdse. devel. design and testing lab., 1946-56, operating asst. to pres., 1956-60; staff purchasing div. U.S. Navy Aviation Supply Dept., 1944-46; pres. Roper Corp., Kankakee, Ill., 1960-64, chmn., 1964-68, chmn. exec. com., dir., 1968—. Home: 14 Marquette Lane Route 5 Kankakee IL 60901 Office: Roper Corp Kankakee IL 60901

BURKE, RITA MARGARET, educator, orgn. ofcl.; b. Carbondale, Pa., Jan. 13, 1917; d. Luke A. and Margaret V. (Golden) Farrell; B.S., Maywood Coll., Scranton, Pa., 1963, M.S. in L.S., 1964; m. Thomas Joseph Burke, Dec. 28, 1942; 1 son, Tommy (dec.). Tchr., Eldred (N.Y.) Central Sch., 1962; librarian, tchr. history nursing and communication skills St. Joseph's Hosp. Sch. Nursing, Carbondale, 1964—. Mem. Nat. Council Cath. Women, 1957—, nat. vice chmn. com. coop. with Cath. Charities, 1965-67, nat. dir. Province Phila., 1968—, nat. pres., 1970—; treas. Carbondale Cath. Social Services, 1968—; pres. Scranton Diocesan Council Cath. Women, 1959-63; cons.-observer to exec. bd. Pa. Ch. Women United, 1968—. Pres., Muscular Dystrophy Assn. Northeastern Pa., 1959-63; chmn. Upper Lackawanna United Fund campaign, 1958-59. Bd. dirs. Lackkawanna County Crippled Children's Soc. Recipient Benjamin Rush award Muscular Dystrophy Assn. Am., 1957. Home: 32 Spring St Carbondale PA 18407

BURKE, ROBERT E., corp. sec.; b. Dexter, Ind., Sept. 7, 1900; s. William and Mary L. (George) B.; A.B., Ind. State U., 1924; postgrad. DePaul U., 1925; LL.B., Chgo.-Kent Coll. Law, 1928; m. Rose McHale, Feb. 1938; children—Barbara (Mrs. John Dunn), Rosemary, Robert, Janet, Nancy. Admitted to Ill. bar, 1928; pvt. practice law, Chgo., 1928-67; sec. Standard Kollsman Industries, Inc., 1965—. Mem. Am., Ill., Chgo. bar assns., Delta Theta Phi. Republican. Roman Catholic. Home: 1330 Castle St Park Ridge IL 60068 Office: 2085 N Hawthorne Av Melrose Park IL 60160

BURKE, ROBERT EUGENE, educator, historian; b. Chico, Cal., July 22, 1921; s. Ralph Ambrose and Frieda (Rupp) B.; A.B., Chico State Coll., 1946; M.A., U. Cal. at Berkeley, 1947, Ph.D., 1950; m. Helen Blom, Oct. 31, 1952; 1 dau., Elizabeth Anne. Dir. Bancroft Library research project, Eng., 1950-51; head manuscript div. Bancroft Library, U. Cal. at Berkeley, 1951-56; asst. prof. history U. Hawaii, 1956-57; faculty U. Wash., Seattle, 1957—, prof. history, 1965—, chmn. dept., 1962-67; vis. prof. Columbia, summer 1960, Stanford, summer 1968, U. Wyo., 1969, U. Ore., summer 1971, Yugoslav-Am. Seminar, Novi Sad, summer 1965. Served with AUS, 1942-45; PTO. Mem. Am., So. hist. assns., Orgn. Am. Historians (exec. bd. 1967-70), Agrl. History Soc. (exec. bd. 1968-71), Western history Assn. Author: Olson's New Deal for California, 1953; (with J.D. Hicks and G.E. Mowry) The American Nation, 5th edit., 1971, The Federal Union, 5th edit., 1970, A History of American Democracy, 4th edit., 1970. Mng. editor Pacific N.W. Quar., 1959—; gen. editor Americana Library Series. Home: 7336 19th Av NE Seattle WA 98115

BURKE, ROBERT GRANVILLE, lawyer; b. Buffalo, Dec. 24, 1905; s. Michael J. and Kathryn (Daly) B.; grad. St. Joseph's Collegiate Inst., 1922; B.S., Canisus Coll., 1926; LL.B., Georgetown U., 1929; m. Lora Meadows, Sept. 12, 1934; children—Robert Granville (dec.), John Michael. Admitted to D.C. bar, 1929, N.Y. bar, 1931; pvt. law practice, 1929-35; spl. tax counsel City N.Y., 1935-39, dir. emergency revenue div., 1939-43; mem. McGoldrick, Winn, Dannett & Burke, 1947-52; mem. Chapman & Burke, 1952—. Dir. gen. counsel Nat. Strategy Information Center, Inc. Served as counsel Nat. Strategy Information Center, Inc. Served as capt., active duty USNR, 1943-47, comdg. officer Naval Res. Law Co. 3-3, 1948—; rear adm. N.Y. Naval Militia, comdg. officer, 1963-70. Mem. N.Y. County Lawyers Assn., Res. Officers Assn. U.S. (nat. pres. 1952-53), Mil. Order Fgn. Wars (comdr. gen. 1967-69), Naval Res. Assn. (nat. v.p. 1970—), Guild Cath. Lawyers (pres. 1949-51), Navy League (nat. dir. 1962-64), Army and Air N.G. and Naval Militia Assn. State N.Y. (Pres. 1957-58), Soc. Wars, Mil. Order World Wars, N.Y. Soc. Mil. and Naval Officers World Wars (pres. 1967-68), Am. Legion, Am., N.Y. State bar assns., Judge Advs. Assn. (pres. 1955-56, 59-60), Naval Order U.S. (comdr. N.Y. commandry 1965-67, comdr.-gen. 1969—), Friendly Sons St. Patrick. Clubs: Patrick. Clubs: Athletic (life mem.), Army-Navy (pres. 1963-64, 68-69) (N.Y.C.); Army and Navy (Washington). Contbr. legal jours. Home: 3 Peter Cooper Rd New York City NY 10010 Office: 420 Lexington Av New York City NY 10017

BURKE, RUDOLPH CARL, clergyman; born McPherson, Kan., June 1, 1907; s. August and Anna (Petterson) B.; B.A., Bethany Coll., 1930; B.D., Augustana Theol. Sem., Rock Island, Ill., 1933; m. Nellie E. Berg, Sept. 2, 1931; children—Dorothy (Mrs. David Freedland), Alan, Ronald. Ordained to ministry Lutheran Ch., 1933; pastor in Forest Lake, Minn., 1934-39, Los Angeles, 1939-46, Mpls., 1946-51; asso. dir. Bd. World Missions, Augustana Luth. Ch., 1951-61, exec. dir., 1961-63, mem. Bd. Youth Activities, 1943-46, pres. Cal. conf., 1944-46; sec. for Africa, Bd. World Missions, Luth. Church in Am., 1963-65; pastor Am. congregation, Luth. Ch. Am., Stockholm, Sweden, 1965-71. Mem. div. fgn. missions, commn. missionary edn. Nat. Council Chs. of Christ; commn. world mission Luth. World Fedn.; com. Latin Am., also dep. world missions coop. dept. Luth. world fedn. affairs Nat. Luth. Council. Address: 4744 12th Av S Minneapolis MN 55407

BURKE, THOMAS A., lawyer, former senator; b. Cleve., Oct. 30, 1898; s. Thomas A. and Lillian (McNeil) B.; A.B. cum laude, Holy Cross Coll., 1920, LL.D. (honorary), 1954; LL.B., Western Res. U., 1923; m. Josephine Lyon, June 25, 1924; children—Jo Ann, Barbara. Admitted to Ohio bar, 1923; asst. pros. atty., Cuyahoga County, O., 1930-36; spl. counsel to atty. gen. of Ohio, 1937; mem. firm McConnell, Blackmore, Cory & Burke, Cleve., 1937-41; dir. law, City of Cleve., 1941-44; mayor of Cleve., 1945-53; U.S. senator from Ohio, 1953-54; now partner firm Burke, Haber & Berick, Cleve. Mem. Phi Alpha Delta. K.C. Clubs: Shaker Heights (O.) Country; Cleveland (O.) Athletic. Address: Central National Bank Bldg E 9th and Superior Av NE Cleveland OH 44114

BURKE, THOMAS JOHN M., clergyman, univ. dean; b. Boston, Nov. 19, 1920; s. Thomas J. and Agnes (Cahill) B.; A.B., Boston Coll., 1944, M.A., 1945; licentiate in theology Weston Coll., 1952; certificate dramatics Fordham U., 1946; Ph.D., N.Y. U., 1962. Joined Soc. of Jesus, 1938, ordained priest Roman Cath. Ch., 1951; religion editor America, 1953-54; dir., asso. editor Jesuit Missions, N.Y.C., 1954-63; dir. pub. relations Fairfield (Conn.) U., 1963-66, dean grad. sch. corporate and polit. communication, 1964—, dir., founder Center for Advancement Human Communication, 1964—. Coordinator, author TV series Face of the World, 1958-59. Mem. Pub. Relations Soc. Am., Cath. Inst. Press, Cath. Press Assn., Am. Soc. Pub. Adminstrn., Nat. Soc. Study Communications, N.Y. Soc. Gen. Semantics, Am. Acad. Polit. and Social Scis., Mgmt. Council Southwestern Conn. Editor, contbr.: Beyond All Horizons, 1957; Sinews of Love, 1961; Mary and Modern Man, 1954. Address: Fairfield U Fairfield CT 06430

BURKE, VINCENT JOHN, journalist; b. Chgo., June 17, 1919; s. Victor and Marie (Larke) B.; B.A. in History, U. Chgo., 1941; m. Velma Lois Whitgrove, Dec. 5, 1942; children—Douglas, Barbara, Judith, Patricia. With U.P.I., 1940-42, 46- 63, assigned Washington, 1947-63; mem. staff Los Angeles Times, 1964—, Moscow (USSR) bur., 1965-66, reporter, Washington, 1967—. Home: 3336 Quesada St N W Washington DC 20015. Office: 1700 Pennsylvania Av NW Washington DC 20006

BURKE, WALTER JAMES, trade union exec.; b. Antioch, Ill., Sept. 14, 1911; s. Anthony Frederick and Margaret Luella (Burke) B.; ed. pub. schs., Ill.; m. Aletha Phyllis Luff, Aug. 12, 1939; children—Phillip, Charles, Mary Ellen (Mrs. Patrick McGrath), Barbara, Kevin. Asst. instr. printing Waukegan (Ill.) Township High Sch., 1930-32; insp. metal finishing div. San, Refrigerator, Fond du Lac, Wis., 1932-37; organizer, 1st pres. local union 1935, Amalgamated Assn. Iron, Steel and Tin Workers N. Am., 1937; mem. staff Steel Workers Organizing Com., 1937-39; sec.-treas. Wis. Indsl. Union Council, CIO, 1939-41; labor mem. tripartite disputes panel WLB, Chgo., 1941-43; mem. United Steelworkers Am., 1937—, dir. dist. 32, Milw. area, 1948-65, internat. sec.-treas., 1965—; rep. com. polit. edn. AFL-CIO, 1965—; v.p. indsl. union dept. AFL-CIO, 1965—. Mem. Gov. Wis. Blue Ribbon Tax Study Com., 1959-63; vice chmn. Com. of 25, Wis., 1963-65; mem. Milw. Expressway Commn., 1964-65; mem. Gov. Wis. Coordinating com. Higher Edn., 1963-65; Fed. Adv. Council Employment Security, 1966—; mem. industry-labor team auspices State Dept. to conduct seminars on Utilization Human Resources, India, 1961; rep. Am. Trade Unions at 75th anniv. conv. German Metalworkers Fedn., Frankfurt, 1966; mem. President's Nat. Labor-Mgmt. Panel, 1967—, sec. Labor's Nat. Adv. Com. Safety and Health, adv. council Social Security Dept. Health, Edn., Welfare. Mem. Milw. council exec. com. Boy Scouts Am., 1964-65, rep. Nat. council, 1964-65. Bd. dirs. Pitts. Symphony Soc., 1967—; pres. Insts. Achievement Human Potential; trustee Nat. Safety Council of Am. Mem. Nat. Council Catholic Men, Am. Amateur Radio Relay League. Democrat. Home: 642 Maryland Av Pittsburgh PA 15219 Office: Commonwealth Bldg Pittsburgh PA 15222

BURKE, WILLIAM ALDEN, army officer; b. Muskogee, Okla., Feb. 8, 1921; s. Marion and Inza Lee (Younger) B.; grad. Okla. Mil. Acad., 1942; B.A., George Washington U., 1964; advanced mgmt. program Harvard, 1965; m. Martha Jane Horton, Nov. 19, 1945; children—William Steven, Michael Mario. Commd. 2d lt. U.S. Army, 1942, advanced through grades to maj. gen., 1970—; with 803d Tank Destroyer Bn., ETO, 1942-45; exec. officer Office Res. Components, Dept. of Army, also Office Joint Chiefs Staff, Washington, 1963-66; chief army sect. Joint U.S. Military, 1966-68; asst. div. comdr. 1st Armored Div., Ft. Hood, Tex., 1968-69; dep. chief of staff III Marine Amphibious Force, U.S. Mil. Assistance Command, Vietnam, 1969; comdg. gen. 1st Brigade, 5th Inf. Div., Vietnam, 1969-70, 4th Inf. Div., Vietnam, 1970; dir. Systems Directorate, Office Asst. Chief of Staff for Force Devel., Dept. of Army, Washington, 1971—. Decorated D.S.M., Silver Star with 2 oak leaf clusters, Legion of Merit with oak leaf cluster, D.F.C., Bronze Star with oak leaf cluster, Meritorious Service medal, Air medal, Army Commendation medal, Purple Heart. Home: 1600 Stonebridge Rd Alexandria VA 22304 Office: Office Asst Chief Staff Dept Army Washington DC 20310

BURKE, WILLIAM EDWARD, ret. electronics exec.; b. Portland, Ore., July 22, 1906; s. Edward and Marie (Mueller) B.; B.S., Ore. State Coll., 1928; m. Margaret A. Holmes, Sept. 3, 1932; children—Robert H., Cara E. Mem. tech. staff Bell Telephone Labs., 1928-32; comml.

engr. Consol. Edison Co., 1932-36; mfg. engr. Western Electric Co., N.Y.C., 1936-47, supt. mfg. engring. Kearny Works, 1947-52, asst. works mgr. Point Breeze Works, 1952-54, comptroller mfg. div., 1954-56, v.p. def. projects div., 1956-61, v.p. mfg., div. for transmission equipment, 1961-69, v.p. mfg. div. for electronic components and gen. communications equipment, 1969-71. Mem. Am. Ordnance Assn., Armed Forces Communications and Electronics Assn., Montclair Soc. Engrs., Tau Beta Pi, Eta Kappa Nu, Phi Kappa Phi. Clubs: Glen Ridge (N.J.) Country; Lords Valley (Pa.) Country. Home: 11 Bellegrove Dr Upper Montclair NJ 07043 also Hemlock Farms Lords Valley PA

BURKE, WILLIAM JAMES, chemist, educator; b. Lowellville, O., May 24, 1912; s. Sylvester L. and M. Catherine (Saltzman) B.; A.B., Ohio U., Athens, 1934; Ph.D., Ohio State U., 1937; m. Katherine M. King, June 21, 1940; children—Mary Katherine (Mrs. Frank Noyes), Susan E., Thomas W.J., D. Kevin. Research chemist central chem. dept. E.I. duPont de Nemours & Co., Henry Clay, Del., 1937-46; asso. prof. Ohio U., Athens, 1946- 47; asso. prof. U. Utah, 1947-50, dept. head, 1949-62, prof., 1950-62; v.p., prof. chemistry Ariz. State U., Tempe, 1962—, dean Grad. Coll., 1963—; cons. U.S. Army, 1956-62, Monsanto Co., 1961-70. Mem. ICA team to survey higher edn. in Ethiopia U.S. State Dept., 1959-60; pres. Western Assn. Grad. Schs; mem. exec. com. Nat. Assn. State Univs. and Land Grant Colls. Past pres., dir. Catholic Charities Salt Lake City. Fellow A.A.A.S.; mem. Am. Chem. Soc. (vis. asso. com. on profl. tng. 1953—, councilor for Central Ariz. sect. 1967-70), Ariz. Acad. Sci., Midwest Conf. on Grad. Study and Research (past chmn.), Phi Beta Kappa, Sigma Xi, Phi Lambda Upsilon, Gamma Alpha, Phi Kappa Phi. Contbr. articles profl. jours. Patentee in field. Home: 501 Bishop Dr Tempe AZ 85281

BURKE, WILLIAM MILLER, educator; A.B., Duke, 1934, A.M., 1937; Ph.D., U. Pa., 1949. Dean freshman year studies and prof. English, U. Notre Dame, now asst. provost. Address: Provost Office U Notre Dame Notre Dame IN 46556

BURKET, HARRIET, (Mrs. Francis B. Taussig), mag. editor; b. Findlay, O.; d. John Franklin and Betty (Hoege) Burket; A.B., Vassar Coll., 1931; m. Maurice C. Reinecke, Sept. 24, 1935 (div. Apr. 1952); 1 dau., Rosalind; m. 2d, Francis Brewster Taussig, Oct. 8, 1960 (dec. May 1970). Asso. editor Arts and Decoration, 1933-35, Creative Design, 1935- 37; asso. editor House and Garden, 1937-44, home furnishings mdse. editor, 1952-55, exec. editor, 1955-58, editor-in-chief, 1958—; partner Editors Inc.; interior design editor Woman's Home Companion, 1944-52. Mem. Internat. Fashion Group (bd. govs. 1953-55, v.p. 1958-59), Home Fashions League, Am. Inst. Decorators, Internat. Platform Assn. Clubs: Field (Sarasota, Fla.); Decorators, Cosmopolitan, Vassar, Harvard. Editor: House & Garden's Complete Guide to Interior Decorating, 7th edit., 1970; House & Garden's Complete Guide to Creative Entertaining, 1971. Home: 14 Sutton Pl S New York City NY 10022 Office: 420 Lexington Av New York City NY 10017

BURKET, LESTER W., educator, dentist, physician; b. Bozeman, Mont., Feb. 18, 1907; s. William Barnard and Mary (Roe) B.; A.B., U. Pa., 1929, D.D.S., 1932; M.D., Yale, 1936; Hon. Prof., Nat. U., Bogota, Columbia; Sc.D. (hon.), U. of Anitoquia, Madellin, Colombia, 1950, Temple U., 1956, U. Athens, 1969; m. Grace Travers, May 5, 1934. Sterling fellow, Grad. sch. of medicine Yale, 1936-37; mem. faculty U. Pa., prof. oral medicine, dental sch. (also dean) and grad. sch. medicine, dir. postgrad. courses, dental sch.; chief oral medicine Phila. Gen. Hosp.; cons. to Army, Navy and V.A. dental services, to Council on Dental Edn., 1969. Mem. Spl. Med. Adv. Group to Chief VA, 1969. Organizer Ivory Cross Expdn. to Holland, 1946. Mem. Am. Dental Assn., Nat. Assn. for Dental Research, Sigma Xi. Author: Oral Medicine. Mem. bd. editors Jour. Oral Medicine, Jour. of Oral Pathology, Jour. of Oral Surgery. Home: 105 Landover Rd Bryn Mawr PA 19010 Office: 4001 Spruce St Philadelphia PA 19104

BURKETT, HOWARD BENTON, educator; b. Putnam County, Ind., Feb. 26, 1916; s. Zefa Benton and Jennie (Hills) B.; A.B., DePauw U., 1938; Ph.D., U. Wis., 1942; m. Lucile Eloise Nichols, Aug. 4, 1936; children—Nancee Lou (Mrs. Alfred A. Dickson), Harvey Benton, David Howard, Richard Allen. Research chemist Eli Lilly and Co., 1942-45; mem. faculty DePauw U., 1945—, prof. chemistry, 1954—, head dept., 1967—; research asso. U. Wash., 1953-54, 62-63; vis. lectr. Ind. U., summer 1965; vis. prof. Stanford, summer 1966; cons. to industry, 1945-52; sr. engring. asso. Naka works Hitachi Co., Katsuta, Japan, 1970-71. Mem. Am. Chem. Soc., Am. Assn. U. Profs., Sigma Xi, Phi Lambda Upsilon. Mem. Christian Ch. Mason. Home: 700 Shadowlawn Greencastle IN 46135

BURKETT, LOWELL ABNER, vocational educator; b. Palestine, Ill., May 4, 1912; s. Fred Harlin and Alta M. (Richards) B.; student Blackburn Coll., 1930-31, Eastern Ill. U., 1931-32; B.S., U. Ill., 1946, M.S., 1952; m. Mary E. Cawood, Apr. 16, 1938; children—Rebecca Marilyn (Mrs. James Stillwell), Cynthia Sue (Mrs. Samuel Bowlin), Andrew Cawood. Tchr. in Ill., 1932-49; dir. vocational edn., Robinson, Ill., 1946-49; supr. trade and indsl. edn. in Ill., 1949-55; asst. exec. sec. Am. Vocational Assn., 1955-66, exec. dir., 1966—. Mem. Am. Soc. Tng. and Devel., Am. Assn. Sch. Adminstrs., Am. Vocational Assn., Phi Delta Kappa, Iota Lamba Sigma. Home: 6312 Anneliese Dr Falls Church VA 22044 Office: 1510 H St NW Washington DC 20005

BURKHALTER, DAVID ALEXANDER, city mgr.; b. McKenzie, Tenn., May 14, 1912; s. David A. and Mamie (Mays) B.; A.B., Bethel Coll., 1934; m. Nell Sparks, Aug. 25, 1938; 1 dau., Diane (Mrs. Edward Michael Hill). High sch. adminstr., Mo. and Tenn., 1934-40; mem. staff reservoir properties dept. TVA, 1940-52; city mgr., Elizabethton, Tenn., 1952-56, Johnson City, Tenn., 1956-66, Springfield, Mo., 1966-71, Charlotte, N.C., 1971—. Mem. Mo. Law Enforcement Assistance Council. Bd. dirs. Nat. Center Vol. Action. Served to lt. USNR, 1943-46. Mem. Internat. City Mgmt. Assn. (pres. 1969-70). Office: City Hall Charlotte NC 28202

BURKHALTER, GEORGE LEWIS, mfg. exec.; b. Metter, Ga., Sept. 23, 1922; s. George Lewis and Henrietta (Pierce) B.; LL.B., Mercer U., 1948, A.B., 1949; m. Helen Wood, Aug. 9, 1944 (dec.); 1 dau., Sandra. Admitted to Ga. bar, 1949; pvt. practice law, Macon, 1949-50; spl. agt. FBI, Phila., N.Y.C., 1950-52; with Bibb Mfg. Co., Macon, 1952—, asst. credit mgr., 1952-56, asst. sec., credit mgr., 1956-62, credit mgr., sec., 1962—; v.p., sec. Star Chems., Inc., Macon, Ga. Served to 1st lt. USAAF, 1942-45; ETO. Decorated D.F.C., Air medal with three oak leaf clusters. Mem. Ga. Assn. Credit Mgmt. (dir., pres.). Mason (33, Shriner), Moose, Elk. Home: 5320 Rivoli Dr Macon GA 31204 Office: PO Box 4207 Macon GA 31208

BURKHALTER, N. LAURENCE, educator, musician; b. Landour, India, June 30, 1920 (parents Am. citizens); s. Noah L. and Adah (Good) B.; B.Mus., Bluffton Coll., 1947; M.Mus., Northwestern U., 1949; Ph.D., Ohio State U., 1962; m. Holly A. Mosiman, Aug. 14, 1943; children—Kathlynn, Karol Jean, Paul Gareth, Holly Joanne, Ruth Eileen. Mem. faculty Bluffton Coll., 1949-55, Ohio State U., 1955-66; prof. music, head dept. Ia. State U., 1966—, condr. symphony orch., 1966—; prin. violist Columbus Symphony, 1955-66; violist Hughes Quartet, Ohio State U., 1955-56. Mem. Music Educators Nat. Conf., Phi Delta Kappa, Pi Kappa Lambda, Phi Mu Alpha. Presbyn. Home: 228 N Riverside Dr Ames IA 50010

BURKHALTER, WILLIAM MAYS, govt. ofcl.; b. McKenzie, Tenn., Nov. 21, 1914; s. David Alexander and Mamie (Mays) B.; student Bethel Coll., 1932-35, B.S., U. Tenn., 1936, LL.B., 1939; m. Thelma Kanatzar, Dec. 30, 1944; children—Susan Marguerite, Mary Scott (Mrs. John Allen Loveless), David Alexander, Sara Louise. Admitted to Tenn. Louise. Admitted to Tenn. bar, 1939, D.C. bar, 1953; atty. TVA, 1939-42; asso. firm Brown & Lund, Washington, 1946-61; atty. Office Emergency Planning, 1961-62; mem. Renegotiation Bd., 1962-69, asst. gen. counsel, 1969—. Ann. corporate mem. Children's Hosp. D.C. mem. Children's Hosp. D.C. Served to lt. (s.g.) USNR, World War II; lt. comdr. Res. ret. Mem. Am., Fed. bar assns. Presbyn. (past deacon, elder, trustee, chmn. bldg. com.). Clubs: Nat. Lawyers (Washington); Kenwood Golf and Country (Bethesda, Md.). Home: 5817 Madawaska Rd Washington DC 20016 Office: 1910 K St NW Washington DC 20446

BURKHARDT, ERDMAN WALTER, architect; b. Leipzig, Germany, Jan. 23, 1894; s. Ernest Wilhelm and Emma (Heilmann) Burckhardt; B.S., Wash. State U., 1917; M.S., Columbia, 1923; m. Varian Carpenter, Feb. 14, 1924; children—Ellwood Walter, Beverley Ann (Mrs. Albert Thomas, Jr.), Erdman Carlyle. Engaged in naval constrn., 1917-19; designer N.Y.C. archtl. offices, 1919-20, 23-26; head design Architect's Office, Fla. Bd. Instns. Higher Learning, 1926-29; head prof. design, chmn. design, chmn. terminal problems, acting head dept. architecture Auburn U., 1929-64, emeritus, 1964—; dist. officer for Ala., Historic Am. Bldgs. Survey, 1933-37; planning cons., Auburn, 1930—; restoration cons. Ala. Div. Parks and Historic Sites, 1970—. Del. State Dept. and A.I.A. XIV Internat. Congress Architects, Paris, 1937; mem. Nat. Trust Historic Preservation, 1940—. Mem. Auburn Planning Bd., 1936-59. Medalist, Beaux Arts Inst. Design; recipient 1st medal, XV Paris prize, 1922. Fellow A.I.A. (pres. Ala. 1940-41); mem. Ala. Bd. Registration Architects, Scarab, Phi Kappa Phi (pres. Auburn U. 1947-49). Presbyn. (past deacon). Mason, Rotarian. Author articles. Home: 337 Payne St Auburn AL 36820

BURKHARDT, FREDERICK H., educator; b. Bklyn., Sept. 13, 1912; s. Louis and Marie (Neumaier) B.; A.B., Columbia U., 1933, Ph.D., 1940; B.Litt., Oxford U., 1935; fellow to Oriel Coll., Oxford, 1933-35; LL.D., U. Mich., 1968; m. Margret Mary Ross, Jan. 9, 1936; children—Jane, Ross, Susan. Instr. and asst. prof. in philosophy U. Wis., 1937-43; research analyst in Central European Affairs, OSS, 1943-45; acting chief, Div. Research for Europe, State Dept., 1945-46, asso. prof. philosophy U. Wis., 1946-47; pres. Bennington Coll., 1947-57; pres. Am. Council of Learned Socs., 1957—. Dep. dir. Office Pub. Affairs, Office of U.S. High Commr. for Germany, 1950-51; mem. U.S. Nat. Commn. for UNESCO, 1959-64; mem. panel on ednl. research and devel. Office Sci. and Tech., Exec. Office of Pres., 1962-68. Vice chmn. Nat. Adv. Commn. on Libraries, 1967; chmn. Nat. Commn. on Libraries and Information Sci., 1971—; Trustee Center for Applied Linguistics, N.Y. Pub. Library, Bennington Coll., Harcourt Found. Mem. Bd. Higher Edn., City of N.Y., 1966—, chmn., 1969—. Served with USNR, 1944-46. Mem. Council Fgn. Relations, Am. Acad. Arts and Scis., Am. Philos. Assn., Am. Antiquarian Soc., Am. Assn. U. Profs., Phi Beta Kappa. Clubs: Century (N.Y.C.); Cosmos (Washington). Translator and editor: God, Some Conversations on Spinoza's System, by J.G. Herder, 1940. Editor: The Cleavage in our Culture, 1952. Office: Am Council Learned Socs 345 E 46th St New York City NY 10017

BURKHARDT, HANS GUSTAV, artist; b. Basel, Switzerland, Dec. 20, 1904; s. Gustav and Anna (Schmidt) B.; came to U.S., 1924, naturalized, 1930; student Cooper Union, 1924-25, Grand Central Sch. Art, N.Y.C., 1928-29; pvt. student with Gorky, 1930-37; m. Louise Thile, Mar. 25, 1929 (div. 1938); 1 dau., Elsa (Mrs. Kenneth Brown); m. 2d, Thordis Olga Westhassel, June 18, 1955. One-man exhbns. include Los Angeles County Mus., Ore. State U., Museo de Bellas Artex, Gualalajara, Mexico, Occidental Coll., Inst. de Allende, San Miguel de Allende, Mexico, Mt. St. Mary Coll., Palos Verdes Community Art Assn., Pasadena Art Mus., Valley Jr. Coll., Van Nuys, Santa Monica Pub. Library, Glendale Pub. Library, Whittier Art Assn., U. So. Cal., Santa Barbara Mus. Art, Palace Legion of Honor, Los Angeles Municipal Art Gallery, La Jolla Art Center, Pierce Coll., Los Angeles, Freie Schule, Basel, Switzerland, San Fernando Valley State Coll., Bay City Jewish Community Center, Laguna Beach Art Assn., San Diego Art Inst. (forty year retrospective), ACA-American Masters Gallery, Los Angeles, Cal., San Diego Fine Arts Gallery; represented in Mus. Modern Art Stockholm, Los County Art Mus., Pasadena Art Mus., Santa Barbara Mus. Art, Long Beach Art Mus., La Jolla Art Mus., San Diego Fine Art Center, Jocelyn Art Center, Lincoln, Neb., Kunstmuseum, Basel, Switzerland; exhibited numerous group shows; asst. prof. art Long Beach State U., 1959; prof. art U. So. Cal., 1959-60; parttime instr. U. Cal. at Los Angeles, Chouinard Art Inst., 1962—; artist, asst. prof. art San Fernando Valley State Coll. Cal. Recipient purchase prize in oil Los Angeles County Mus., 1946, cash awards, 1954, 57; award Terry Art Inst., Miami, Fla., 1951; purchase prize Santa Barbara Mus. Art, 1957; award Cal. Watercolor Soc., 1961; purchase oil Los Angeles All-City Show, 1958, 61, purchase watercolor, 1961. (Cal.) Mus., Long Beach Mus., Pasadena Art Mus., Los Angeles County Mus., Santa Barbara Mus. Art, La Jolla Art Center, Emily and Joe Lowe Mem. Mus. Modern Art N.Y.C., Am. Fedn. Art, Santa Barbara Mus. Assn., Los Angeles Art Assn., Cal. Watercolor Soc., Los Angeles Mus. Art (graphic arts council), Santa Barbara Art Mus., UN Orgn., Internat. Platform Assn. Kappa Pi. Address: 1914 Jewett Dr Los Angeles CA 90046

BURKHARDT, RICHARD WELLINGTON, univ. ofcl.; b. Newton, Mass., May 18, 1918; s. Edgar and Ruth (Wellington) B.; A.B., Knox Coll., 1939; A.M., Harvard, 1940, A.M.T., 1942, Ed.D., 1950; m. Dorothy Josephine Johnson, June 18, 1941; children—Jon Edgar, Richard W., Claire Elizabeth. Tchr. Lenox (Mass.) Sch., 1941, Tulsa Central High Sch., 1941-44, Syracuse U., 1945- 52; dean Ball State U., Muncie, Ind., 1952-62, now v.p. instructional affairs and dean faculties, v.p. Coop. Ednl. Research Lab., 1966. Mem. Ind. Commn. on Aged and Aging, 1958-66, Ind. Scholarship Commn., 1965-70; nursing rev. com. U.S. Dept. Health, Edn. and Welfare, 1966-71; mem. Gov.'s Commn. on Med. Edn., 1969. Vice pres. bd. dirs. Muncie YMCA, 1959-65; bd. dirs. United Fund Delaware County, 1968-71; evaluation bd. Nat. Commn. on Accreditation Tchr. Edn., 1971. Mem. No. Central Assn. Acad. Deans (pres. 1965), North Central Assn. (commn. on research and service, chmn., 1966-68, dir. 1964—), Ind. Congress Parents and Tchrs. (exec. bd. 1963-66), Phi Beta Kappa, Phi Delta Kappa, Phi Gamma Delta. Episcopalian (vestryman, mem. Indpls. Diocesan Council 1965- 66). Rotarian (pres. 1957-58). Author: (with Ann McGuinness) Elementary Social Studies Series, 1954; (with Lawhead and Bell) Introduction to College. Contbr. articles to profl. jours. Home: 6 Woodridge Dr Muncie IN 47304

BURKHARDT, ROBERT JAMES, state ofcl.; b. Chgo., June 10, 1916; s. Ernest R. and Dale (Messinger) B.; student Purdue U.; m. Lucille Frances Hogan, Dec. 29, 1936; children—Constance R., Robert James, Ross M., and Valerie L. (Mrs. Philip Rulon Tamis). Engaged as regional organizer 1948 presdl. campaign, N.Y. State; pres. N.Y. State Young Democrats, 1949-50; dir. speakers bur. Dem. Nat. Com., 1951-53; exec. sec. to Gov. Meyner, N.J., 1953-57; exec. dir. N.J. Dem. Com., 1957-60, Nat. Voters Registration Com., 1960, Inaugural Com., 1960-61; asst. postmaster gen. U.S., 1961- 62; sec. state State of N.J., 1962-70; exec. dir. Dem. State Com. N.J. to direct re-election campaign Gov. Hughes, 1964—, state chmn. com., 1965-69. Mason, Elk. Home and office: 130 W State St Trenton NJ 08608

BURKHART, CHARLES BARCLAY, advt. exec.; b. Atchison, Kan., May 18, 1914; s. Charles Bert and Claudene (Barclay) B.; grad. Ft. Scott Jr. Coll., 1932; m. Elinor Karr, Apr. 19, 1936; children—Sherry (Mrs. Peter C. John), Janette (Mrs. W. Scott Miller). Pres. Stalcup, Inc., Kansas City, Mo., 1945-54, Cream City Outdoor Advt. Co., Milw., 1954-58, Naegele Outdoor Advt. Co., Milw., 1958-62, Outdoor Advt. Assn. Am., Chgo., 1962-64; pres. Burkhart Advt., Inc., South Bend, Ind., 1964—; dir. Signacast Corp., Milw. Mem. advt. adv. com. Dept. Commerce; dir. Am. Fedn. Advt., Advt. Council Am., Traffic Audit Bur. N.Y., Nat. Sign Assn. Mem. at large nat. council Boy Scouts Am. Chmn. founding bd. govs. Inst. Outdoor Advt.; bd. dirs., exec. com. Central Outdoor Markets. Mem. Young Pres. Orgn. Clubs: Indiana, South Bend (Ind.) Country; Wisconsin (Milw.); Chicago Athletic Assn. Home: 55721 Country Club Rd South Bend IN 46615 Office: 1247 Mishawaka Av South Bend IN 46615

BURKHART, G.A., banker. Sr. exec. v.p. Barclays Bank of Cal., San Francisco. Office: 111 Pine St San Francisco CA 94111*

BURKHEAD, LLOYD RUSSEL, food and mfg. co. exec.; b. Oakdale, Neb., Nov. 4, 1908; s. George L. and Viola (Bailey) B.; attended U. Cal.; m. Margaret Snowden, July 16, 1933; children—Helen Pauline (Mrs. Robert L. Stanley), Robert Eugene. Accountant, Libby McNeil and Libby, 1935-41; with Stokely-Van Camp, Inc., 1941—, asst. treas., controller, 1960—. Dist. chmn. Boy Scouts Am., 1957-59. Mem. Financial Execs. Inst., Newcomen Soc. N.Am. Mason (Shriner). Home: 9001 N Braeside Dr Indianapolis IN 46260 Office: 941 N Meridian St Indianapolis IN 46206

BURKHEAD, MARGARET BRISTOW, ret. library dir.; b. St. Louis, Nov. 5, 1905; d. Harry L. and Mary V. (Safford) Bristow; student Harris Tchrs. Coll., St. Louis, Mt. Holyoke Coll., Ill. U. Library Sch.; grad. Strassburger Conservatory Music; m. Lingurn S. Burkhead, June 24, 1925. Exec. sec. legal firm Thompson, Mitchell, Thompson & Young, St. Louis, 1930-37; tchr. Miss Hickey's Sch. for Secs., St. Louis, 1937-39; pvt. tutor, Little Rock, 1939-42; exec. sec. Little Rock Pub. Library, 1942-56, adminstr., 1956-57, dir., 1957-70. Mem. Ark. Library Assn., Nat. Soc. Arts and Letters, D.A.R. (regent Little Rock chpt.), P.E.O. (past pres.), Order of Bookfellows (past pres.). Home: Bookfellows (past pres.). Home: Little Rock AR 72207

BURKHOLDER, DONALD LYMAN, educator, mathematician; b. Octavia, Neb., Jan. 19, 1927; s. Elmer and Susie (Rothrock) B.; B.A., Earlham Coll., 1950; M.S., U. Wis., 1953; Ph.D., U. N.C., 1955; m. Jean Annette Fox, June 17, 1950; children—Kathleen, Peter, William. Asst. prof. U. Ill. at Urbana, 1955-60, asso. prof., 1960-64, prof. math., 1964—. Fellow Inst. Math. Statistics; mem. Am. Math. Soc., Inst. Math. Statistics. Editor Annals Math. Statistics, 1964-67. Contbr. research articles in probability theory and allied subjects to Am., European math. jours. Home: 506 W Oregon St Urbana IL 61801

BURKHOLDER, HENRY CLAY, lawyer; b. West Earl Twp., Pa., Jan. 7, 1898; s. Amos E. and Clara E. (Bolster) B.; A.B., Franklin and Marshall Coll., 1918; m. Catharine H. Falck, June 12, 1936; children—J. Nicholas, H. Clay, Peter F. Admitted to Pa. bar, 1925, since practiced in Lancaster; solicitor City Sch. Dist., 1927-29; mem. sch. bd. City of Lancaster, 1933-37; judge Orphans' Ct. of Lancaster County, 1937; mem. zoning bd. appeals, 1949-55; judge Ct. of Common Pleas of Lancaster County, 1955; solicitor of City of Lancaster, 1958-59; mem. Lancaster City Charter Commn., Lancaster City Parking Authority. Treas. Denver and Ephrata Tel. and Tel. Co. Pres. Lancaster YMCA, 1950-56, YMCA of Pa., 1956-59; trustee Meadville Theol. Sch., Chgo., 1951-56, 59-65, chmn., 1954-56. Del. Pennsylvania Constitutional conv., 1967-68. Mem. Am., Pa. Lancaster (pres. 1954-55), Fed. bar assns., Am. Judicature Soc., Am. Unitarian Assn. (moderator 1956-58), Cliosophic Soc. (v.p.1958-59), Lancaster C. of C. (pres. 1966, dir. 1964-67), Phi Alpha Delta, Phi Kappa Tau. Mason. Elk. Clubs: Hamilton, Torch. Home: 504 State St Lancaster PA 17603 Office: 121 E King St Lancaster PA 17602

BURKHOLDER, PAUL RUFUS, educator, microbiologist; b. Orrstown, Pa., Feb. 1, 1903; s. William Rankin William Rankin and Mary Ellen (Schubert) B.; A.B., Dickinson Coll., 1924; Ph.D., Cornell U., 1929; NRC fellow in botany, Harvard, 1932- 33, Columbia, 1933-34; M.A. (hon.), Yale, 1944; Sc.D. (hon.), Dickinson Coll., 1949; m. Lillian Miller, Feb. 4, 1930; children—Franz M., Peter M., Karl M. Instr. botany Cornell U., 1924-28; biol. curator Buffalo Mus. Sci., 1929-32; asst. prof. Conn. Coll., 1934-37, asso. prof., 1937-38; asso. prof. U. Mo., 1938-40; asso. prof. Yale, 1940-43, Eaton prof. botany, 1944-53; chmn. dept. plant sci., 1950- 53; head dept. bacteriology U. Ga., 1953-56; dir. research Bklyn. Botanic Garden, 1956-61; chmn. marine biology programs Lamont Geol. Obs. Columbia, 1961-69; vis. prof. microbiology U.P.R., Mayaguez, 1969—. Mem. A.A.A.S., Nat. Acad. Sci., Bot. Soc. Am. (sec. 1940-45), Am. Soc. Naturalists (pres. 1948), Am. Soc. Microbiologists, Soc. Protozool., Soc. Gen. Microbiol., Torrey Bot. Club, Sigma Xi. Contbr. papers in field. Office: Lab Marine Biology U P R LaParguera PR 00708

BURKLE, HOWARD RUSSELL, educator; b. Monticello, Ark., July 15, 1925; s. Howard Russell and Crystal (Kizer) B.; B.A., Central Mo. State Coll., 1945; B.D., Yale, 1948, S.T.M., 1949, Ph.D., 1954; m. Wanda Jeanne Mayo, June 18, 1948; children—Michael Mayo, Heidi, Amy. Asst. prof. religion Colo. Coll., 1951-54, Dickinson Coll., 1954-58; mem. faculty Grinnell (Ia.) Coll., 1958—, prof. philosophy, 1966—; vis. prof. (Lilly Found.) Christian ethics Internat. Christian U., Tokyo, Japan, 1961-62. Served with USNR, 1943-46. Lilly Found. fellow Christianity and politics, 1959; Ford Found. fellow U. Wis., 1965. Mem. Am. Philos. Assn., Soc. Phenomenology and Existential Philosophy. Mem. United Ch. Christ. Author: The Non-Existence of Existence of God. Home: 1326 Broad St Grinnell IA 50112

BURKLEY, GEORGE GREGORY, ret. physician, naval officer; b. Pitts., Aug. 29, 1902; s. Frank George and George and Anna (O'Donnell) B.; B.S., U. Pitts., 1926, M.D., 1928, D.Sc., 1963; postgrad. U. Minn., 1929-32; m. Isabel Winburn, Nov. 30, 1933; children—Isabel B. (Mrs. Michael Starling), Nancy A. (Mrs. Leo Denlea), George W., Richard M. Intern St. Francis Hosp., Pitts., 1928-29; resident fellow internal medicine Mayo Clinic, 1929-32; fellow cardiology U. Pitts., 1933-34, asst. prof. medicine, 1934-41; practic medicine, specializing internal medicine and cardiology, Pitts., 1934-41; commd. lt. comdr. M.C., USN, 1941, advanced through grades to vice adm., 1964; served in S. Pacific, 1942- 44, chief medicine naval hosps., Charleston, S.C., Memphis, Newport, R.I., Portsmouth, Va., 1946-57, comdg. officer Naval Dispensary, Washington, 1959-61; physician to Pres. John F. Kennedy, 1961-63, to Pres. Lyndon B. Johnson, 1963-69. Mem. vis. com. Sch. Medicine, U. Pitts. Diplomate Nat. Bd. Med. Exam. Fellow A.C.P.; mem. A.M.A., Pitts. Acad. Medicine, Alpha Omega Alpha, Phi Sigma. Home: Grand View Farm RD 2 Box 27 Blairsville PA 15717

BURKS, ARTHUR WALTER, educator; b. Duluth, Minn., Oct. 13, 1915; s. Walter Demoree and Cora Belle (Voyles) B.; A.B. (Rector scholar), DePauw U., 1936; A.M., U. Mich., 1937, Ph.D. (Univ. fellow, Rackham predoctoral and postdoctoral fellow), 1941; m. Alice Grace Rowe, Feb. 27, 1943; children—Edward A., Nancy, Douglas. Teaching and research, a prin. designer ENIAC, Moore Sch. Engring., U. Pa., 1941-36; cons. Inst. Advanced Study Digital Computer, 1946-48; cons. digital computers Burroughs Corp., 1948-54; cons. Oak Ridge Computer, Argonne Nat. Lab., 1950-51; asst. prof. philosophy U. Mich., 1946-48, asso. prof., 1948-54, prof., 1954—, chmn. dept. communication scis., 1967-71; research asso. U. Chgo., 1950-51, Harvard, 1955; vis. prof. applied math. U. Ill., 1960; vis. prof. Indian Inst. Tech., Kanpur, India, 1965-66. John Simon Guggenheim Meml. fellow, 1953-54; recipient (with others) Louis E. Levy medal Franklin Inst., Phila., 1956; fellow Center for Advanced Study in Behavioral Scis., 1971-72. Fellow Am. Council Learned Socs.; mem. Assn. Symbolic Logic (council, exec. com.), Am. Philos. Assn. (program, exec. com., v.p. 1971-72), Assn. Computing Machines, Philosophy Sci. Assn. (gov.), Charles Peirce Soc. (pres. 1954-55), Sigma Xi, Phi Beta Kappa, Phi Eta Sigma, Delta Sigma Rho, Phi Kappa Phi, Eta Kappa Nu. Contbr. numerous articles in field. Editor: Collected Papers of Charles Sanders Peirce (vols. 7, 8, 1958); John von Neumann's Theory of Self-Reproducing Automata; Essays on Cellular Automata. Editor Philosophy of Science Synthese. Home: 1413 Morton Av Ann Arbor MI 48104

BURKS, CRAIGHILL STONER, sch. adminstr.; b. Berryville, Va., Sept. 3, 1921; s. Harry Hunter and Elizabeth Price (Butler) B.; B.S., Hampden-Sydney Coll., 1941; postgrad. U. Va., 1941-42, 46; M.A., George Washington U., 1952; Andelot fellow Am. Studies U. Del., 1964-66; m. Mary Joyce Rowland, June 21, 1952; children—Clary, Rebekah, Timothy. Tchr., Fairfax County, Va., 1942-43, 46-49. asst. high sch. prin., 1949-51, supr. secondary schs., 1951-55, dir. secondary edn., 1966-67; prin. McLean (Va.) High Sch., 1955-64; headmaster The Masters Sch., Dobbs Ferry, N.Y., 1967-71; dean faculty Everglades Sch., Miami, Fla., 1971—. Bd. govs. St. Margaret's Sch., Tappahannock, Va. Served with M.C., AUS, 1943-46; CBI. John Hay fellow Williams Coll., summer 1960. Episcopalian (vestryman). Contbr. articles on parasitology, edn., Am. studies to profl. jours.

BURLAGE, HENRY MATTHEW, educator, pharmacist; b. Rensselaer, Ind., May 23, 1897; s. Max and Mary Anne (Linzbach) B.; A.B., Ind. U., 1919; A.M., Harvard, 1921; Ph.G., B.S., Purdue, 1924, D.Sc., 1961; Ph.D., U. Wash., 1929; m. Alleda Virginia Robb, Dec. 29, 1925; 1 son, Robb Kendrick. Austin teaching fellow Harvard, 1919-20; instr. pharmacy and pharm. chemistry Purdue, 1921-24, asso. prof., 1929-31; instr. pharmacy U. Wash., 1924-27; asso. prof. drug analysis and insp. Ore. State Bd. Pharmacy, 1927-29; prof. pharmacy U. N.C., 1931-47; prof. pharmacy and pharm. chemistry U. Tex., 1947—, dean, 1947-62. Registered pharmacist in Tex. Fellow Am. Coll. Apothecaries, A.A.A.S.; mem. Am. (council 1961-64, hon. pres. 1966-67), Tex. (treas. 1966-68) pharm. assns., Am. Chem. Soc., Am. Assn. Colls. Pharm. (mem. exec. com. 1959-60, pres. 1960-61), Phi Beta Kappa, Sigma Xi, Phi Kappa Phi, Rho Chi, Kappa Psi, Alpha Chi Sigma, Phi Lambda Upsilon. Mason (K.T.). Author: Study Guide to Essential Literature of Pharmacy, rev. 1969; (with M.L. Jacobs) Index to the Plants of North Carolina with Reputed Medicinal Uses, 1959; Index to the Plants of Texas with Reputed Medicinal and Poisonous Properties, 1968; also other lab. manuals. Editor: Orientation to Pharmacy, 1959; Physical and Technical Pharmacy, 1963; Experiments in Physical and Technical Pharmacy, 1968. Home: 702 E 43d St Austin TX 78751

BURLESON, ELIZABETH (Mrs. Gamewell David Burleson), author; b. Kerrville, Tex., Nov. 2, 1912; d. Edward Elijah and Mary (Sproul) Morriss; student U. Tex., 1932-33, San Antonio Coll., summer 1936, Trinity U., nights 1949-50; m. Gamewell David Burleson, May 17, 1951. Tchr. pub. schs. rural Tex., 1932-36; with USAF, 1941-53, edn. specialist, 1952-53. Recipient Cokesbury award Tex. Inst. Letters, 1965, Gold Spur award Western Writers Am., 1968. Baptist. Club: Cactus Study (Junction). Author: A Man of the Family, 1965; Middl'un, 1968; Eine Ranch in Texas (German trans. A Man of the Family), 1970. Home: Junction TX 76849

BURLESON, IRA LEE, ins. co. exec.; b. Athens, Ala., June 6, 1920; s. Luther A. and Marie (Witt) B.; B.S., Florence (Ala.) State Coll., 1940; student U. Ala., 1941; LL.B., U. Va., 1948; m. Anna Kate Givens, Sept. 7, 1948. Admitted to Ala. bar, 1948; with firm Spain, Gillon, Grooms & Young, Birmingham, 1948-50; with Liberty Nat. Life Ins. Co., Birmingham, 1950-, v.p., sec., gen. counsel, 1967—, also sec. to bd. dir., dir.; sec. dir. Brown Service Funderal Homes Co., Inc., 1960—; mem. adv. bd. Service Ins. Co. Ala., 1960—; Chmn. joint com. on state taxation of ins. cos. Am. Life Conv. Life Ins. Assn. Am. Trustee, Birmingham-So. Coll. Served to comdr. USNR, 1942-46; PTO. Mem. Am., (vice chmn. com. life ins. law), Ala. bar assns., Am. Life Conv. (v.p. Ala.), Assn. Life Ins. Counsel, Am. Soc. Corp. Sec., Ala. Life Ins. Cos. (dir.). Methodist (chmn. ofcl. bd. 1964-66). Contbr. legal periodicals. Home: 3924 Forest Av Birmingham AL 35213 Office: 301 S 20th St Birmingham AL 35202

BURLESON, OMAR, congressman; b. Anson, Tex., Mar. 19, 1906; s. Joseph and Bettie (Couch) B.; student Abilene (Tex.) Christian Coll., 1924-26, Hardin-Simmons U., 1926-27, Cumberland U., 1927-29; Ruth DeWeese, Apr. 21, 1929. County atty., Jones County, Tex., 1931-35, county judge, 1935-41; spl. agent, F.B.I., 1940-41; sec. Congressman Sam Russell, 1941-42; gen. counsel Nat. Capitol Housing Authority, Washington, Jan.-Dec. 1942; mem. of 80th-92d Congresses from 17th Tex. Dist. Served to lt. comdr. comdr. USNR, 1942-46; PTO. Pres. Tex. Welfare Assn., 1936-38; pres. County Judges and Commrs. Assn. of Tex. Mem. Lions Internat.; dist. gov. Lions Clubs, 1937-38. Democrat. Mem. Ch. of Christ. Mason. Home: Anson TX 79501 also 2801 New Mexico Av N W Washington DC 20007 Office: House Office Bldg Washington DC 20515

BURLEW, JOHN SWALM, scientist; b. Washington, Sept. 10, 1910; s. Ebert Keiser and Marion Kate (Swalm) B.; A.B., Bucknell U., 1930, Sc.D., 1955; Ph.D. in Chemistry, Johns Hopkins, 1934; Sc.D., Drexel Inst. Tech., 1956; m. Grace Anne Schaum, June 16, 1934; children—David Schaum, Thomas Ebert. Sterling Fellow in chemistry, Yale, 1934-36; phys. chemist Geophys. Lab., Carnegie Instn. of Washington, 1936-43, 47-52; tech. aide NDRC, 1943-47; tech. dir. Cambridge Corp., 1952-54; asst. dir. Franklin Inst., 1954-55, dir., 1955-56, exec. v.p., 1956-59; dir. research Carrier Corp., 1960-66; dir. Conn. Research Commn., 1966-71; pres. New Directions Inc., Glastonbury, Ct., 1971—. Decorated Presdl. Medal for Merit, 1948. Fellow A.A.A.S.; mem. Am. Chem. Soc., Am. Nuclear Soc., Am. Geophys. Union, Phi Beta Kappa, Sigma Xi. Club: Cosmos (Washington). Editor: Algal Culture from Laboratory to Pilot Plant, 1953. Home: 93 Russet Rd Glastonbury CT 06033 Office: PO Box 418 Glastonbury CT 06033

BURLEY, GEORGE FRANKLIN, corp. exec.; b. Harris, Ia., Jan. 13, 1908; s. Adelbert Willis and Agnes (Campbell) Burley; student Ia. State Tchrs. Coll., 1926; m. Alice Emma Haapanen, July 9, 1932; children—Marian Alice (Mrs. John McMillan Adams), George Franklin, Kathleen Anne (Mrs. Don Patrick Kelly); m. 2d, Corinne Mabel Beeler, Nov. 17, 1962. Asst. dir. purchase Budd Co., Detroit, 1945-48; dir. transp. and supply Lustron Corp., Columbus, O., 1948-50; purchasing mgr. Hotpoint, Inc., Chgo., 1950-52; dir. purchases Motor Products Corp., Detroit, 1952-56, Warwick Mfg. Corp., Chgo., 1956-58; v.p. marketing and procurement Crane Co., 1958-59, v.p. trade relations, 1959-62, gen. mgr. plumbing heating air conditioning group, 1960-61; v.p., gen. mgr. Whitinsville (Mass.) div. Whitin Machine Works, 1962-64; gen. purchasing agt. E.W. Bliss Co., Canton, O., 1964-67; pres. Burley Volkswagen Inc., 1966- -. Mem. Ill. C. of C., Chgo. Assn. Commerce and Industry, Am. Ordnance Assn., Nat. Assn. Purchasing Agts., N.A.M., Nat., Akron, Ohio automobile dealers assns., Am. Mgmt. Assn. Mason. Club: Detroit Yacht. HOme: 2121 Amarillo Dr N W Canton OH 44720 Office: 3100 Manchester Rd Akron OH 44319

BURLEY, ORIN EVERETT, educator; b. West Union, O., Dec. 23, 1905; s. John Frederick and Jennie (Hayslip) B.; B.S., Okla. A. & M. Coll., 1928; M.A., Ohio State U., 1930, Ph. D., 1937; m. Shirley Smith, Apr. 14, 1946; children—Don Orin David Everett. Asst. prof. Ala. Poly Inst. Auburn, 1928-30, Ohio State U., 1930-39, asso. prof., 1939-44; economist Fed. Res. Bank of Cleveland, 1944-45; prof. U. Pa., 1945-, now chmn. dept. marketing and foreign commerce. Dir. Statis. sect. Nat. Wholesale Druggists Assn. since 1947, operating cost study Nat. Assn. Retail Druggists 1949—. Mem. Am. Econ. Assn., Am. Marketing Assn. (editorial bd. 1950—). Author: The Consumers' Cooperative as a Distributive Agency, 1939; An Introduction to Business Management (with H. H. Maynard and W. C. Weidler), 1941: Drug Store Operating Costs and Profits (with A. B. Fisher and R. Cox), 1956; also spl. study pamphlets and articles. Home: 33 Roselawn Av Lansdowne PA 19050

BURLIN, ROBERT BRADFORD, educator; b. Cleve. Oct. 7, 1928; s. Leslie Robert and Helen (Svoboda) B.; B.A., Yale, 1950, M.A., 1952, Ph.D., 1956; m. Katrin Ristkok, June 27, 1970. Instr., Yale, 1955-59; asst. prof., asso. prof., prof. Bryn Mawr (Pa.) Coll., 1960—, chmn. dept. English, 1968—. Mem. Modern Lang. Assn., Mediaeval Acad. Am. Author: The Old English Advent, 1968. Home: 140 Morris Av Bryn Mawr PA 19010

BURLINGAME, MARK VELZY, natural gas cons.; b. Fond du Lac, Wis., Aug. 5, 1902; s. Mark V. and Elizabeth (Snyder) B.; B.S., Mich. State U. 1926, D.Sc., 1966; m. Gladys Litfin, Aug. 2, 1929; children—Joanne Elizabeth (Mrs. Charles A. Bryan III), Robert Everitt. Reconnaissance engr. Lago Petroleum Co., Maracaibo, Venezuela, 1926-27; field supt. Continental Oil & Gas Co., Muskegon, Mich., 1928-29; chief insp. Continental Constrn. Co. (now Natural Gas Pipeline Co. Am.), 1930-48, v.p., 1948-57, exec. v.p., 1957-66, sr. v.p., 1966-67; pres. TARGET (industry fuel cell research group), 1966-69. Trustee New Coll., Sarasota, Fla. Recipient Distinguished Alumni award Mich. State U., 1961. Registered profl. engr., Ill. Mem. Am. Inst. Profl. Geologists, Am. Assn. Petroleum Geologists, Am. Gas Assn. (award merit operating sect.), Am. Petroleum Inst. Ind. Nat., So. gas assns., Soc. Am. Mil. Engr. Clubs: Bradenton (Fla.) Country; Yacht; Sarasota University. Address: 6008 Shore Acres Dr NW Bradenton FL 33505

BURLINGHAM, CHARLES, lawyer; b. N.Y.C., June 8, 1884; s. Charles C. and Louisa (Lawrence) B.; A.B., Harvard, 1906, LL.B., 1908; m. Cora Weir, Apr. 2, 1929; 1 son, Charles. Admitted to N.Y. bar, 1908, since practiced in N.Y.C.; partner firm Burlingham, Underwood, Wright, White & Lord, and predecessors, 1912—. Trustee Community Service Soc. N.Y.C., 1936-67, sec., 1942-67. Mem. N.Y. State Bar Assn., Assn. Bar City N.Y.; Maritime Law Assn. U.S. Democrat. Episcopalian (past vestry). Home: 1220 Park Av New York City NY 10028 Office: 25 Broadway New York City NY 10004

BURLISON, BILL D., congressman; b. Wardell, Mo., Mar. 15, 1933; s. John I. and Lilly (Marler) B.; LL.B., U. Mo., 1956; m. Barbara Ann Humphreys, Feb. 1, 1955; children—James David, Laura Ann, Andrew Jefferson. Admitted to Mo. bar, 1956, also U.S. Supreme Ct.; practice in Cape Girardeau, 1959-68; pros. atty. Cape Girardeau County, Mo., 1963-68; asst. atty. gen. Mo., 1960-62; mem. 91st and 92nd Congress 10th Dist. Mo. Past pres. Cape Girardeau County Sch. Bd. Served with USMCR, 1956-59. Mem. Am., Mo. (vice chmn. com. criminal law 1966), Cape Girardeau County bar assn., Mo. Pros. Attys. Assn. (pres. 1967). Democrat. Office: Longworth House Office Bldg Washington DC 20515

BURMA, JOHN HARMON, sociologist; b. Dallas, Tex., Apr. 2, 1913; s. John Harmon and Manetta (Knock) B.; A.B., Trinity U., Waxahachie, Tex., 1933; A.M., U. Tex., 1938; Ph.D., U. Neb., 1941; m. Hughlette Beasley, June 3, 1937; 1 dau., Susan Bea; m. 2d, Dorothy Ann Pulley, Feb. 14, 1953. Tchr., adminstr. and coach in Tex. pub. schs., 1933-39; teaching fellow U. Neb., 1939-41; chmn. dept. sociology Grinnell (Ia.) Coll., 1941-45, 47-68, prof. sociology, 1968-70, marshall, 1947-52, chmn. social studies div., 1949-50, 60-62; prof. sociology Cal. State Poly. Coll., Pomona, 1970—; tchr. div., 1949-50, 60-62; prof. sociology Cal. State Poly. Coll., Pomona, 1970—., tchr. (summers) U. Tex., 1936, 37, 45. Pomona Coll., 1946-47, N.M. Highlands U., 1948, 49, 56-58, U. Redlands, 1951. U. Minn. 1952, Whittier Coll., 1959, 64, U. Nev., 1962, U. So. Cal., 1966. Mem. Am., Midwest (exec. com; pres. 1954-55) sociol. socs. Conglist. Author: Spanish-Speaking Groups in the United States; Mexican Americans in the United States; also articles and monographs in scholarly and popular periodicals. Co-author: Workbook in United States; also articles and monographs in scholarly and popular periodicals. Co-author: Workbook in Introductory Sociology, Migratory Agricultural Workers in the United States; Life in Society. Editor MidWest Sociologist, 1948-52. Home: 114 Monterrey Dr Claremont CA 91711

BURMAN, BEN LUCIEN, writer; b. Covington, Ky., Dec. 12, 1895; s. Sam and Minna B.; A.B., Harvard, 1920; m. Alice Caddy, Sept. 19, 1927. Began as reporter Boston Herald, 1920; asst. city editor Cin. Times Star, 1921; spl. writer N.Y. Sunday World, 1922; staff contbr. N.E.A. (Scripps Howard Newspapers), 1927; wrote literary revs. for The Nation and other publs.; regular contbr. Readers Digest; contbr. Saturday Rev. regular contbr. Readers Digest; contbr. Saturday Rev. Served as mem. 2d Div., A.E.F., severely wounded at Soissons, France, July 1918. Bd. dirs. Authors' League of America, P.E.N. Author: Steamboat Round the Bend, 1933 (filmed starring Will Rogers); Blow for a Landing, 1938 (awarded Southern Authors prize for most distinguished book); Rooster Crows for Day, 1945 (Thomas Jefferson Meml. prize); Everywhere I Roam, 1949; Children of Noah, 1951; High Water at Catfish Bend, 1952; The Four Lives of Mundy Tolliver, 1953; Seven Stars for Catfish Bend, 1956; It's a Big Country, 1956; The Street of The Laughing Camel, 1959; The Owl Hoots Twice at Catfish Bend; It's a Big Continent, 1962; The Generals Wear Cork Hats, 1963, The Sign of the Praying Tiger, 1966; Blow A Wild Bugle for Catfish Bend, 1967. Was the first writer to reach Free French in Africa after French collapse; war corr. attached Free French and British 8th Army, 1941. Decorated French Legion of Honor, 1946; recipient Gold medal for distinguished services to Am. lit. Dutch Treat Club. Address: care Taplinger Pub Co 29 E 10th St New York City NY 10003

BURMAN, MARSHALL LYLE, lawyer; b. Chgo., July 22, 1929; s. Henry L. and Florence (Rosin) B.; B.S., Northwestern U., 1951; LL.B., Yale, 1954; m. Marian Sondheimer, June 28, 1953 (div. July 1966); children—Julie Anne, Jamie Alison. Admitted to Ill. bar, 1954; practice in Chgo., 1957—; asso. firm Arvey, Hodges & Mantynband, 1957-60, mem., 1961—. Dir. Belscot Retailers, Inc., Heitman Mortgage Investors, Fabric Mart Draperies, Inc., Calandra Photo, Inc., TCT, Inc., DoRay Lamp Co. Mem. financial investment adv. panel Railpax. Pres. Young Mens Jewish Council, 1965; chmn. bus. assistance program New Ill. Com., 1965-66. Served with AUS, 1954-56. Recipient medallion Boys Clubs Am., 1966. Mem. Ill., Chgo. bar assns., Phi Alpha Delta, Phi Epsilon Pi (pres. 1950). Clubs: Standard, Yale (Chgo.); Green Acres Country (Northbrook, Ill.) Home: 260 E Chestnut St Chicago IL 60611 Office: 1 N LaSalle St Chicago IL 60602

BURMEISTER, CLIFTON ALVIN, educator; b. Mason City, Ia., Mar. 11, 1913; s. Alfred Edmund and Amelia Molly (Zittzke) B.; B.A., (scholarship 1930-34), Carleton Coll., 1933, postgrad., 1933-35; Mus.M., Northwestern U., 1941; Ph.D. (fellow 1949-50), U. Kan., 1953; m. Mildred Lorraine Landsberg, June 7, 1937; children—Judith Ann, Robert Allen. Teaching asst. Carleton Coll., 1933- 35; tchr. music pub. schs., Woodward, Ia., 1935-37, Clarion, Ia., 1937- 40; teaching asst. Northwestern U. Sch. Music, 1940-41; tchr. music pub. schs., Lorain, O., 1941-43; dir. band and music edn. Central Mo. State Coll., Warrensburg, 1946-52; dir. music Dist. 65 schs., Evanston, Ill., 1952-60; mem. faculty Northwestern U., 1952—, prof. music, 1959—, John W. Beattie prof., 1962—, chmn. dept., 1952—. Mem. Ill. Com. Prepare Curriculum Guide Music Ill. Secondary Schs., 1963-64; adviser ednl. policies commn. N.E.A., 1964-68; chmn. music com. 1st Methodist Ch., Evanston, 1963-65; bass trombonist Evanston Symphony, 1961-65. Served to 1st lt. USAAF, 1943-46. Recipient Steinway award for contbns. to music edn., 1969. Mem. Music Educators Nat. Conf. (pres. N. central div. 1960-62, past. nat. counselor student mem. chpts., also exec. com. of bd. dirs., nat. chmn. commn. music higher edn.), Pi Kappa Lambda, Phi Mu Alpha, Phi Delta Kappa. Author: (with Hazel B. Morgan) Music Research Handbook, 1962. Cons. Birchard Music Series, 1962. Mem. prodn. staff, contbr. Basic Concepts in Music Education, 1958; editorial bd. Music Educators Jour., 1964-68. Home: 1601 Riverwoods Rd Lake Forest IL 60045

BURMESTER, HARRY FREDERICK, former banker; b. San Francisco, May 17, 1903; s. Henry D. and Erna (Hesse) B.; student Coll. of Pacific, U. Cal.; LL.D., Baldwin-Wallace Coll.; D.Sc., Fenn Coll.; D.C.S., Cleve. State U.; m. Edna Jensen, Aug. 17, 1924; 1 dau., Maren (Mrs. R.B. Houghton). Vice pres. Union Commerce Bank, Cleve., 1938-43, sr. v.p., 1943-56, pres., 1956-68, dir., chmn. exec. com., 1968-69; dir. Samuel Moore & Co., Steel Improvement & Forge Co. Chmn., chief exec. officer Cleve.-Cuyahoga County Port Authority. Bd. dirs. Fenn Ednl. Found. Mason (33, Shriner, K.T., Jester). Clubs: Pepper Pike Country, Union (Cleve.); Shaker Heights Country, 50. Home: 13415 Shaker Blvd Cleveland OH 44120 Office: Union Commerce Bldg 917 Euclid Av Cleveland OH 44115

BURN, HARRY THOMAS, lawyer, banker, orgn. ofcl.; b. Niota, Tenn., Nov. 12, 1895; s. James LaFayette and Febb King (Ensminger) B.; studied law with lawyers, 1919- 23; m. Ellen Folsom Cottrell, Feb. 14, 1937; 1 son, Harry Thomas. Admitted to Tenn. Bar, 1923; practice in Rockwood, 1923-27, Sweetwater, 1927-50; pres., chmn. 1st Nat. Bank & Trust Co., Rockwood, 1950—; sr. v.p. Belted Galloway Soc., Inc., 1967—. Mem. S.A.R., 1931, treas. gen., 1962-64, pres. gen., 1964-65, Minute Man award, 1962. Mem. Tenn. Ho. of Reps. from McMinn County, 1919-23, Tenn. Senate from 7th Dist., 1949-53; mem. Tenn. Planning Commn., 1952—; del. Tenn. Constl. Conv., 1953, 59, 65, 71. Mem. Am., Tenn. bar assns. Republican. Presbyn. Clubs: Burns (Atlanta); Civitan (pres. Rockwood 1960-61). Home: RFD 1 Niota TN 37826

BURNAM, PAUL WAYNE, educator, accountant; b. Abilene, Tex., Jan. 2, 1913; s. Joseph Edward Joseph Edward and Opha Carrie (Jobe) B.; B.A. in Math. and Accounting, Hardin-Simmons U., 1934; M.B.A., U. Tex., 1939; Ph.D., U. Ala., 1959; postgrad. La. State U., 1946; m. Anita Maxie Kellow, June 8, 1941; children—Roy Edward and Ray Thomas (twins). Grad. asst. U. Tex., 1934-35; head dept. math. Conroe (Tex.) High Sch., 1935-41; mem. faculty U. Southwestern La., 1942—, prof. accounting, 1950—, head dept., 1952—; auditor, adviser U. Southwestern La. Found., 1960—; real estate broker in La., 1966- -. Vis. prof. McNeese State Coll., Lake Charles, 1969. Chmn. bd. trustees Kellow's Tech. Coll., Houston, 1961-. Served with AUS, 1942- 45. C.P.A., La. Mem. Am. Inst. C.P.A.'s, Am. Accounting Assn., Soc. La. C.P.A.'s (exec. bd. 1961), Beta Gamma Sigma, Beta Alpha Psi, Phi Kappa Phi, Phi Eta Sigma, Theta Xi. Baptist. Contbr. profl. jours. Home: 188 Ronald Blvd Lafayette LA 70501

BURNES, JAMES ALTON, educator; b. Boston, Jan. 2, 1921; s. Charles D. and Dora (Appel) B.; B.S. in Econs., Wharton Sch. U. Pa., 1942; LL.B., Harvard, 1944; LL.M., Boston U., 1949; D.Phil., Magdalen Coll., Oxford U., 1958; m. Olga E. Pillau, Aug. 9, 1950; 1 dau., Bettina Danielle. Asso. prof. law U. Miami, 1948-51, prof. 1951-62, also dean Law Sch., 1957-61; now prof. law U. Fla., Gainesville. Mem. Mass. Bar Assn., Fla. Bar. Home: 2732 SW 4th Pl Gainesville FL 32601

BURNET, ARTHUR LINING, Jr., textile co. exec.; b. Camden, S.C., July 29, 1908; s. Arthur L. and Annie Lee (Alexander) B.; A.B., Mercer U., 1930; m. Martha Jones McCowen, June 30, 1931; children—Arthur Lining III, Martha Ann, Duncan M., J. Alexander. Trainee, B.F. Goodrich Co., 1929-33; plant supt. Riegel Textiles Co., 1932-40, Deering Milliken Co., 1940-42; with Burlington Industries, 1942—, v.p., 1963—. Bd. dirs. Greensboro Community Council. Presbyn. (elder). Home: 1004 Cornwallis Dr Greensboro NC 27405 Greensboro NC 27405 Office: 301 N Eugene St Greensboro NC 27401

BURNET, FRANK MACFARLANE, med. scientist; b. Traralgon, Victoria, Australia, Sept. 3, 1899; s. Frank and Hadassah (Mackay) B.; M.D., Melbourne U., 1923, LL.D., 1962; Ph.D., London U., 1927, D.Sc., 1960; Sc.D., Cambridge (Eng.) U.; D.Sc., U. Western Australia U., New Zealand, 1957, Harvard, 1960, Sydney (Australia) U., 1961; m. Edith Linda Druce, July 10, 1928; children—Elizabeth (Mrs. P.M. Dexter), Ian, Deborah (Mrs. John Giddy). Asst. dir. Walter and Eliza Hall Inst. Med. Research, 1928-31, 34-43, dir., 1944-65; prof. exptl. medicine U. Melbourne, 1944-65. Flexner lectr. Vanderbilt U., 1958. Chmn., Commonwealth Found., London, 1966-69. Recipient Royal medal, Copley medal Royal Soc. London, Lasker award Am. Pub. Health Assn., 1952; Nobel prize for medicine, 1960. Fgn. asso. Nat. Acad. Sci., U.S.A., 1954. Mem. Australian Acad. Sci. (pres. 1965- 69), Royal Australian Coll. Physicians, N.Y. Acad. Sci., Royal Soc. Medicine. Author: Virus as Organism, 1945; Natural History of Infectious Disease (rev. edit.), 1953; Principles of Animal Virology, 1955; Clonal Selection Theory, 1959; Integrity of Body, 1962; (with

I.R. MacKay) Autoimmune Diseases, 1963; Changing Patterns (autobiography), 1968; Cellular Immunology, 1969; Immunological Surveillance, 1970; Dominant Mammal, 1970; Genes, Dreams and Realities, 1971. Home: 13 Edward St Kew Melbourne 3101 Australia Office: Dept Microbiology U Melbourne Parkville Australia 3052

BURNET, GEORGE, Jr., educator; b. Ft. Dodge, Ia., Jan. 30, 1924; s. George and Myrtle Violet (Hutchinson) B.; B.S. in Chem. Engring., Ia. State U., 1948, M.S., 1949, Ph.D., 1951; m. Betty Arlene Riggs, Oct. 8, 1944; children—Kathryn Ann, Betty Jo, Dolores Unalee, Joan Marie, Elaine Kaye, George VI. Mem. faculty Ia. State U., 1949-51, 56—, prof. chem. engring., 1958—, head dept., 1961—; process design engr. Comml. Solvents Corp., 1952-56; successively engr., sr. engr., div. chief Ames Lab., AEC, 1956—; Phillips lectr. Okla. State U., 1970. Dir. for planning Ia. State U. Civil Def. Orgn., 1961-69; AID cons. in higher edn. to India, 1967. Trustee Ia. State U. Alumni Achievement Fund; adv. com. Ia. State U. Center Agrl. Econ. Devel. Recipient Distinguished Faculty citation Ia. State U., 1969; Ia. Citizen Chem. Engr. award, 1970. Registered profl. engr., Ia. Mem. Am. Inst. Chem. Engrs. (chmn. Terre Haute sect. 1956, chmn. Ia. sect. 1967, nat. rep. to Engrs.' Council for Profl. Devel., 1969—, chmn. nat. com. on chem. engring. tech. 1969-70; Ia. Citizen Chem. Engr. award 1970), Am. Soc. Engring. Edn. (chmn. chem. engring. div. 1964), Am. Chem. Soc. (chmn. div. fertilizer and soil chemistry 1969), Sigma Xi, Tau Beta Pi, Phi Lambda Upsilon, Phi Kappa Phi, Alpha Chi Sigma, Tau Kappa Epsilon, Omega Chi Epsilon (nat. pres. 1970). Methodist (chmn. ofcl. bd.). Author articles, patentee in field. Home: 2060 Cessna St Ames IA 50010

BURNETT, ALLISON LEE, educator, biologist; b. St. Francis, Me., Mar. 3, 1932; s. Ray Lawrence and Julie (Kelley) B.; A.B. cum laude, Bates Coll., 1953; M.S., Cornell U., 1956, Ph.D., 1958; m. Marie Grace Miranti, June 12, 1955; children—Gene Paul, Allison James, Carla Marie. Instr. Cornell U., 1958-59; NSF fellow U. Brussels, 1959-60; asst. prof. U. Va., 1960-61; instr. embryology Wood Hole Inst., 1962-66; asso. prof. biology Case Western Res. U., 1961-66, prof., 1967-69; prof. biology Northwestern U., 1969—. Cons. for NASA project for N.Am. Airlines, 1964-65; exec. dir. Project Survival, Northwestern U., 1970. Recipient career development award NIH, 1964. Mem. A.A.A.S., Am. Soc. Zoologists, Am. Soc. Naturalists, Soc. Developmental Biology, Am. Soc. Anatomists, Marine Biol. Assn., N.Y. Acad. Sci., Sigma Xi. Author: Animal Adaptation, 1964. Contbr. articles profl. jours. Poet with 30 published poems. Home: 207 Lake St Evanston IL 60201

BURNETT, CAREY CORLEY, civil engr.; b. Montgomery, Ala., Nov. 28, 1915; s. James Leonard and Louise (Davie) B.; student U. Fla., 1934-35; B.S., U. Ga., 1938; postgrad. Ala. Poly. Inst., 1939-40; m. Mary Elizabeth Parker, July 5, 1946; children—Mary Kay, Carey Parker. City engr., Newnan, Ga., 1940-42; city engr. and asst. city mgr., Thomasville, Ga., 1946-47; city engr. and acting city mgr., Valdosta, Ga., 1947-51; chief design engr. J.E. Greiner Co., Balt. on USMC Supply Center Constrn. project, Albany, Ga., 1951-54; city mgr., Albany, Ga., 1954-61, Columbia, S.C., 1961-70; v.p. Wilbur Smith & Assos., cons. engrs. and planners, Columbia, 1970—. Mem. Albany-Dougherty County Bd. Health, 1954-61, City-County Airport Com. Albany, 1954-61; mem. adv. com. Richland (S.C.) Tech. Edn. Center, 1966—, also Greater Columbia Indsl. Devel. Com., Central City Devel. Com.; mem. navagational study com. Nat. Rivers and Harbors Congress; chmn. Elec. Exam. Bd. Albany, 1954-61; chmn. original plumbing code com. So. Bldg. Code Congress, 1956-61. Bd. dirs. Columbia United Community Services, 1963-64, chmn. pub. employees div. for Lexington-Richland counties, 1964. Served with USAAF, 1942-45. Recipient certificate of merit for leadership Am. City mag., 1964-68. Registered profl. engr., Fla., Ga., S.C. Mem. Nat. Soc. Profl. Engrs., S.C. Soc. Engrs. (regional dir. 1969—), Nat. Soc., San. Engrs., Am. Pub. Works Assn., Am. Water Works Assn., Inst. Municipal Engrs., Ga. (pres. 1958-59), S.C. (sec., pres. 1968-70), Internat. (regional v.p. 1968-70) city mgrs. assns. Presbyn. Contbr. articles to profl. jours. Home: 3333 Devereaux Rd Columbia SC 29205 Office: 4500 Jackson Blvd Columbia SC 29203

BURNETT, CARLOS EARLE, mfg. co. exec.; b. Dallas, Apr. 8, 1909; s. John Earle and Cecil (Rush) B.; B.S. in Elec. Engring., S. Meth. U., 1931; B.S. in Elec. Engring., Mass. Inst. Tech., 1932, M.S., 1933; grad. Inst. for Mgmt. Northwestern U., 1955; m. Charlotte Reinhard, Feb. 3, 1939; children—Rush Darress, Charlotte Randall, Bonnie Elizabeth. With tube div. RCA, 1933—, mgr. indsl. tube products dept., 1957-60, div. v.p. dept., 1960-63, div. v.p., gen. mgr., indsl. tube and semicondr. div., 1963-67, solid state and receiving tube div., 1967-69, solid state div., 1969-70, indsl. tube div., 1970—. Mem. Assn. U.S. Army, So. Meth. U., Mass. Inst. Tech., Northwestern U. alumni assns. Contbr. articles to profl. jours. Patentee in field. Home: 263 Brook Farms Rd Lancaster PA 17601 Office: Box 1140 Lancaster PA 17604

BURNETT, CAROL, comedienne, singer; b. San Antonio, Apr. 26, 1935; d. Jody and Louise (Creighton) Burnett; student U. Cal. at Los Angeles, 1952-54; m. 2d, Joseph Hamilton; 3 daus. Introduced comedy song, I Made a Fool of Myself Over John Foster Dulles, 1957; Broadway debut in Once Upon a Mattress, 1959; regular performer Garry Moore TV show, 1959-62; starred in musical comedy, Fade Out-Fade In; TV shows include Julie and Carol at Carnegie Hall; Carol Plus Two-with Lucille Ball and Zero Mostel; Carol Burnett TV show. Recipient 1st outstanding comedienne award Am. Guild Variety Artists, 1959, 1st Emmy for outstanding performance in variety or mus. program or series A.F.T.R.A., 1962, Peabody award, 1963. Address: care Goodman 667 Madison Av New York City NY 10021

BURNETT, CLINTON BROWN, indsl., bldg. mfg. co. cons.; b. Waukegan, Ill., July 29, 1908; s. Henry Clinton and Bessie (Brown) B.; B.S., Washington U. St. Louis, 1930; postgrad. Chgo. Kent Coll. Law, 1930-31; m. Margaret Warner, Dec. 6, 1930; 1 dau., Polly Ann (Mrs. Gerald Dirvin). With Johns-Manville, 1931-70, cost reduction mgr. Waukegan plant, operating mgr. Kan. Ordnance Plant, prodn. mgr. Bldg. Products div., dir. engring. Johns-Manville Corp., asst. gen. mgr., then gen. mgr. Celite div., gen. mgr. packings and friction materials div., 1931-57, exec. v.p., dir. corp., 1957-59, pres., chief operating officer, 1959-60, pres., chief exec. officer, dir., 1960-70, chmn. bd., 1970, ret., 1970, cons., 1970—. Mem. Tau Kappa Epsilon, Alpha Kappa Psi. Club: Ridgewood Country (Danbury, Conn.). Home: Candlewood Isle New Fairfield CT 06430 also 425 W Stevens Rd Palm Springs CA 92262

BURNETT, CORDAS CHRIS, coll. pres., assn. exec.; b. Mounds, Ill., Feb. 6, 1917; s. Christopher prof., Columbus and Lucy Virginia (Cline) B.; student Central Bible Inst., Springfield, Mo., 1934-35, U. Notre Dame, 1942-44; B.A. cum laude, DePaul U., 1948; student Washington U., St. Louis, 1949-50; D.D. (hon.), Southeastern Bible Coll., Birmingham, Ala., 1958; m. Dorothy Charlene Talley, June 3, 1937; children—Barbara Celeste, Marilyn Kay. Ordained to ministry Assemblies of God, 1937; minister in S. Bend, Ind., 1940-45, Chgo., 1945-48, Cin., 1952-54; instr. history and philosophy Central Bible Inst., 1948-52, v.p. inst., 1954-58; mem. bd. edn. Assemblies of God, 1958— sec. dept. edn., 1958-59; sec. Nat. Assn. Evangs., 1956—, mem. bd. adminstrn., 1953—, treas. commn. on higher edn., 1964—; pres. Bethany Bible Coll., Santa Cruz, Cal., 1959—. Mem. exec. com. Accrediting Assn. Biblle Colls., 1959-64; treas. N. Am. Assn. Bible Insts. and Bible Colls., 1956—. Pres. Scotts Valley County Water Dist., 1962—. Bd. dirs. Berean Sch. Bible, Springfield, 1958-59, Evangel Coll., Springfield, 1958-59. Home: 505 Tabor Dr Santa Cruz CA 95060

BURNETT, COY, business exec.; b. McCook, Neb., Dec. 15, 1888; s. William David and Mary (Smith) B.; student, McCook High School; Neb. State U.; m. Mildred Kingsburg, Aug. 22, 1915. Admitted to bar, Supreme Court, Neb., Dec. 15, 1909; practiced law, Lincoln, Neb., Dec. 1909-Feb. 1911, Portland, Ore., 1911-1920; helped found Monolith Portland Cement Co., Los Angeles, 1920, pres., chmn.; pres., dir. Monolith Portland Midwest Co., Laramie Valley Ry. Co., Monolith Portland Cement Co.; founder Mel Dar Corp., 1950, now chairman bd. Former dir. All-Year Club of Southern Calif.; former mem. exec. com. Calif. Tax Payers' Assn. Mem. Portland Cement Assn. Republican. Episcopalian. Mason (K.T., 32). Mem. St. John's Episcopal Ch. (vestryman). Home: 104 S Fremont Pl Los Angeles CA 90005 Office: 643 S Olive St Los Angeles CA 90014

BURNETT, EARLE MOODY, realtor; b. Marion, Ky., June 4, 1900; s. Granville Moody and Millie Eleanor (Sullivan) B.; student Neb. Wesleyan Acad., 1916-18; m. Eugenia Frost, June 7, 1921; children—Eugenia Nelle (Mrs. Howard Edgar Hall), Earle M (Tad), Muriel Cassandra (Mrs. Robert Eugene Miller). Asst. editor The Neb. Printer, 1918-19; editor Midwest Printer & Publisher, Lincoln, Neb., 1920; mgr. Globe Printing Co., Quincy, Ill., 1921; salesman, mgr. printing dept. of office equipment and supply co., 1922-23; salesman, city sales mgr. Heat Equipment Corp., 1923-24; salesman, asst. mgr. real estate dept. Woods Bros. Corp., 1926-31; agt. Sun Life Assurance Co. Can., 1932-41; sales mgr. Sweeney Constrn. Co., 1942-51; pres. Lincoln Town Teller, Inc., shopping paper, 1951-53; past dist. mgr. Woodmen Accident & Life Co.; founder, also cons. pub. relations and sales Earle Burnett Co., real estate and ins., Lincoln, 1954. Founder Nat. Salemen's Week, 1950, Am. Heartland Devel. Month, 1950, Nat. Automobile Month, 1952. Mem. Neb. Real Estate Assn. (co-chmn. indsl. devel. com. 1950-51), Nat. Assn. Real Estate Bds., Lincoln Bd. Realtors, Internat. Platform Assn. Democrat. Methodist. Author: Clicking with the ClassifiedsClassified Dynamics, 1948; Device for Decision, 1951; Operation Opportunity, 1955; Rank of a Region, 1956. Compiler: Multifax Master Real Estate Listing Form C, 1943; Slapstick Stopper of Accidents on the Streets and Highways, 1965; Small Busines—My Foot! 1965. Office: Anderson Bldg PO Box 80035 Lincoln NB 68501

BURNETT, GRAYDON EARL, cons. engr.; b. Madison, S.D., Sept. 15, 1908; s. Frank Leslie and Mary Eva (Marquart) B.; student Dakota State Coll., 1926-28; B.S., U. Utah, 1930; m. Jane Lucille Donohue, Dec. 3, 1958; children—Barbara (Mrs. Herbert Marsolek), William, Kathleen, Graydon. Engr. U.S. Bur. Reclamation, Denver, 1936-62, chief research scientist, 1962-70; cons. engr., Denver, 1971—. Served to capt. AUS, 1942-45; ETO. Decorated Bronze Star; recipient distinguished service award Dept. Interior, 1968. Mem. Am. Concrete Inst. (dir., pres. 1968), Nat. Assn. Corrosion Engrs., Am. Water Works Assn. Research and publs. on concrete and protective coatings. Home: 11537 W 26th Pl Lakewood CO 80215

BURNETT, HALLIE SOUTHGATE (Mrs. Whit Burnett), author, editor; b. St. Louis; d. John McKnight and Elizabeth (Baker) Southgate; m. 2d, Whit Burnett, 1942; children—John Southgate, Whitney Ann Beekman. Co-editor Story mag., Story Press, N.Y.C., 1942-70. Asso. prof. lit. Sarah Lawrence Coll., 1960-64; tchr. short story writing N.Y.C. Writers Conf., Wagner Coll., S.I., N.Y., summers 1955-60, Hunter Coll., 1959-61; sr. fiction editor Prentice-Hall, Inc., 1958-60. Mem. Authors League, Woman Pays Club, P.E.N. (bd. dirs.), Jr. League N.Y.C. Club: Overseas Press (N.Y.C.). Author: (short stories, novellas) The Boarders in the Rue Madame, 1966; (novels) A Woman in Possession, 1951, This Heart, This Hunter, 1953, The Brain Pickers, 1957, Watch on the Wall, 1965; Daughter-in-Law's Cookbook, 1969; also short stories, articles in mags., anthologies. Editor: (with Whit Burnett) The Fiction of the Forties, 1949; Story No. 1, 2, 3, 4, 1951-54; Best College Writing, 1962; Prize College Stories, 1963; The Stone Soldier, 1964; The Modern Short Story in the Making, 1964; Story Jubilee, 1965; Story: The Yearbook of Discovery, 1968-70; (with Eleanor Gilchrist) Welcome to Life, 1947. Episcopalian. Address: 174 Huckleberry Hill Rd Wilton CT 06897

BURNETT, HAMILTON SANDS, former justice; b. Jefferson City, Tenn., Aug. 20, 1895; s. J.M. and Caroline (Sands) B.; A.B., Carson-Newman Coll., 1916; LL.B., U. Va., 1920, LL.D. (hon.), 1948; m. Mary Griffin, Oct. 10, 1923 (dec. Nov. 1952); children—Jamie Knox, Adeline Sands, Hamilton Sands; m. 2d, Marjie Reaman, Dec. 1953 (dec. July 1964). Admitted to Tenn. bar, 1920, practiced in Knoxville, 1920-34; mem. Poore, Testerman & Burnett; circuit judge, Knoxville, 1932-42; judge Ct. Appeals, Tenn., 1942-47; asso. justice Supreme Ct. Tenn., Nashville, 1947, justice, 1947-63, chief justice, 1963-70, ret., 1970. Pres., Empty Stocking Fund, Knoxville, 1943—; mem. YMCA. Trustee Carson-Newman Coll. (chmn.). Mem. Am., Tenn. bar assns., Am. Judicature Soc., Knoxville C. of C., Order of Coif, Phi Delta Phi. Democrat. Baptist. Mason (33, Shriner), Kiwanian. Home: 3478 Kingston Park Dr Knoxville TN 37919

BURNETT, JAY A., accountant; b. Seattle, Oct. 2, 1936; s. Fred and Elizabeth (Smith) B.; B.A. in Bus. Adminstrn., U. Wash., 1959; m. Jeanne D. Earnheart, Oct. 8, 1955; children—Brian, Keven. With Ernst & Ernst, C.P.A.'s, 1959-69, as mgr.; accounts mgr. Brit. Petroleum Alaska, Inc., 1969—. C.P.A., Wash., Alaska. Mem. Am. Inst. C.P.A.'s, Petroleum Accountants Soc. (Alaska chpt.). Republican. Methodist. Home: 2610 Teleguana Dr Anchorage AK Office: PO Box 4-CCC Anchorage AK 99503

BURNETT, JOE RAY, educator; b. Welch, W.Va., May 7, 1928; s. James B. and Vada Christine (Watson) B.; B.A. in Philosophy, U. Tenn., 1951, M.A., 1952; Ph.D. in Philosophy of Edn., N.Y.U., 1958; m. Jacquetta Hill, Jan. 2, 1953. Tchr. English, Columbia Grammar Sch., N.Y.C., 1954-55; asst. instr. philosophy and sociology N.Y.C. Community Coll., 1955-56; asst. prof. philosophy edn. Kansas City U., 1956-57; instr., then asst. prof. philosophy of edn. N.Y.U., 1957-59; mem. faculty U. Ill. at Urbana, 1959—, prof. philosophy of edn., 1966—; vis. asso. prof. ad honorem U. P.R., fall 1965; vis. lectr. U. B.C., summers 1969, 70. Fellow Am. Philos. Assns., Am. Ednl. Research Assn.; mem. John Dewey Soc. (pres. 1966-68), Philosophy of Edn. Soc. (pres. 1968-69), Midwest Philosophy of Edn. Soc. (pres. 1963-64). Co-author: Democracy and Excellence in American Secondary Education, 1964. Bd. editors Coop. Research on Dewey Publns., So. Ill. U., 1961—; editorial bd. Studies in Philosophy and Education, 1962—; asso. editor Educational Theory, 1962-65, 1970—, editor elect, 1971. Home: 1210 W John St Champaign IL 61820 Office: Coll of Edn Univ Ill Urbana IL 61801

BURNETT, JOHN GRANT, lawyer, bus. exec.; b. Milw., Dec. 29, 1923; A.B., Princeton, 1947, postgrad. N.Y. U., 1947; LL.B., Yale, 1950; m. Jane Holmer; children—David Mitchell, John, Barbara, Anthony, Mark. Admitted to D.C. Bar, 1951; law clk. to justice William O. Douglas, U.S. Supreme Ct., 1950-51; atty. TCA, 1952-54; gen. counsel Inst. Inter-Am. Affairs, 1954; asso. gen. counsel ICA, 1955-58, gen. counsel, 1958-60; gen. counsel Devel. Loan Fund, 1958; exec. v.p., gen. counsel Devel. and Resources Corp., N.Y.C., 1960—, also dir. urban devel., 1960—. Mem. Bar Assn. City N.Y., Am. Soc. Internat. Law, Internat. Law Assn., Yale Law Assn., Council Fgn. Relations, Nat. Planning Assn. Home: 54 W 13th St New York City NY 10061 Office: 1 Whitehall St New York City NY 10002

BURNETT, JOHN GRANT, lawyer, bus. exec.; b. Milw., Dec. 29, 1923; A.B., Princeton, 1947, postgrad. N.Y. U., 1947; LL.B., Yale, 1950; m. Jane Holmer; childrenDavid Mitchell, John, Barbara, Anthony, Mark. Admitted D.C. Bar, 1951; law clerk to Justice William O. Douglas, U.S. Supreme Court, 1950-51; attorney TCA, 1952-54; gen. counsel Inst. Inter-Am. Affairs, 1954; asso. gen. counsel ICA, 1955-58, gen. counsel, 1958-60; gen. counsel Devel. Loan Fund, 1958; exec. v.p., gen.counsel Development and Resources Corp., 1960—, also dir. urban development, 1960—. Mem. Bar Assn. City of New York, American Soc. Internat. Law, Internat. Law Assn., Yale Law Assn., Council Fgn. Relations, Nat. Planning Assn. Home: 57 W 13th St New York City, NY 10061 Office: 1 Whitehall St New York City NY 10002

BURNETT, LAWRENCE FREDERICK, obstetrician, gynecologist; b. Newark, Sept. 5, 1915; s. Nicholas J. and Madeline (Schultze) B.; B.S. cum laude, U. Notre Dame, 1937; M.D., Jefferson Med. Coll., 1941; m. Ann Jane McNally Olini, Oct. 19, 1946; children—Lawrence Frederick II, Alyson, Gregory, Candace. Intern Newark City Hosp., 1941-42; pvt. practice, Newark, 1946-47, 50—; resident Margaret Hague Maternity Hosp., Jersey City, also Jersey City Med. Center, 1947-50; postgrad. Seton Hall U. Med. Sch., 1951; attending obstetrician and gynecologist Presbyn. Hosp., 1957—, chmn. dept. obstetrics, 1963—; attending obstetrician and gynecologist St. Michael's Hosp., 1958-70, cons., 1970—; dir. dept. obstetrics and gynecology Presbyn. unit United Hosps. of Newark, 1967- -, asso. chief staff of hosps., 1968—. Served to capt., M.C., AUS, 1942-46; ETO. Decorated Bronze Star. Diplomate Am. Bd. Obstetricians and Gynecologists. Fellow A.C.S., Am. Coll. Obstetricians and Gynecologists; mem. Am., World med. assns., N.J., Essex County, Pan Am. med. socs., Acad. Medicine N.J., N.J. Soc. Obstetricians and Gynecologists. Spl. research use intravenous pitocin. Home: 370 Roseville Av Newark NJ 07107 Office: 386 Roseville Av Newark NJ 07107

BURNETT, LEWIE WOODROW, psychology, edn. dir.; b. Seligman, Mo., Aug. 16, 1914; s. James Wesley and Susan Victoria (Collier) B.; B.Ed., Central Wash. Coll., 1937; Ed.D., Stanford, 1948; postgrad. U. Cal., 1938-39, U. Wash., 1940; m. Charlotte Virginia Adams, Feb. 16, 1943; children—Richard, Keith, Susan, Nancy. Classroom tchr. Seattle pub. schs., 1935-46; elementary prin. Ravenswood Schs., East Palo Alto, Cal., 1946-47; dir. student teaching Central Wash. Coll., 1948-50; asso. prof. edn. George Washington U., 1950-53; dir. curriculum and personnel Monroe (Mich.) pub. schs., 1953-55; dean Coll. Edn., U. Toledo, 1955-57; dir. tchr. edn., head div. edn. Fresno State Coll., 1957-61; asst. supt. schs. Laura Lee Great Neck, L.I., N.Y., 1961-62; prof. edn. Cal. State Coll., Hayward, Cal., 1962-63; chmn. dept. sch. adminstrn. and supervision Cal. State Coll., Hayward, 1963-64, Instr. prof., head div. edn., 1964-70, dean. Sch. Edn., 1970—; vis. summer instr. Angeles, 1942-48, U. Mich., 1952, U. Toledo, 1960; Fulbright prof. U. Amsterdam, 1967-68. Dir. Greater Toledo Manpower Project, 1955-56; dir. Operation Fair Chance, 1965-67. Mem. Assn. Supervision and Coll., U. London, 1956-57. Fellow A.A.A.S.; mem. Am. Chem. Soc., Curriculum Devel., Nat. Dept. Elementary Sch. Prins., Cal. Council on Tchr. Edn., Cal. Tchrs. Assn., N.E.A., Phi Delta Kappa, Kappa Delta Pi, Phi Kappa Phi. Presbyn. Home: 3180 Cromwell Pl Hayward CA 94542

BURNETT, R. WILL, educator; b. Runnels, Ia., Sept. 9, 1912; s. Milo and Adeline (Tidball) B.; A.B., U. Kan., 1934; M.A., Columbia, 1939, Ph.D., 1940; m. Bernice Ester Dawson, Dec. 21, 1932; children—Michael Joseph, Robin Dawson. Sci. tchr. Osawatomie (Kan.) High Sch., 1934-35; head sci. dept. Concordia (Kan.) High Sch., 1935-38; research asso. instr. Tchrs. Coll., Columbia, 1939-41; asst. prof. edn. Stanford, 1941-46; prof. biol. sci. and edn., chmn. div. natural sci. San Francisco Coll., 1946-47; prof. sci. edn. U. Ill., 1947—, chmn. dept. secondary edn., 1947—. Smith-Mundt prof. sci. edn. Am. U., Beirut, Lebanon, 1958-60; cons. sci. teaching to East Africa, Ford Found., 1960, 62; cons. sci. edn. U.S. AID project in India, 1964-65. Dep. dir. Army Specialized Tng. Program exams. project, 1943, dep. regional dir. Army and Navy Qualifying exams. project for civilians, 1943; head tng. specialist in sci. edn. War Dept., 1943; cons. Armed Forces Inst. Examining Staff, 1943-45. Cons. Soil Conservation Service, 1944-47, Tchr. Coll., Columbia, 1948; chief cons. in sci. aeros. project for elementary schs. with CAA, 1944. Fellow A.A.A.S. (mem. coop. com. on teaching sci., math.; mem. Nat. Com. on Sci. Teaching (dir. research for sub-com. on teacher edn. 1939-41), N.E.A., Am. Council Sci. Tchrs. (chmn. resolutions com.; mem. yearbook com., 1943), Assn. for Edn. Sci. Tchrs. (pres. 1963-64), Nat. Sci. Teachers Assn. (exec. com., 1943; mem. pub. relations com. 1944), Nat. Assn. Research in Sci. Teaching. Democrat. Author: Atomic Energy—Double Edged Word of Science, 1948; Life Through the Ages, 1947; Teaching Science in the Elementary School, 1953; Teaching Science in the Secondary School, 1957; (with others) Photography, 1956, Weather, 1957, Zoology, 1958, Life Goes On, 1958, Electricity and Magnetism, 1958; (with Atkin) Air, Wind and Weather, 1958, Plants, 1959, Animals, 1959; (with others) Life: Its Forms and Changes, 1968; Matter: Its Forms and Changes, 1968; Energy: Its Forms and Changes, 1968. Dept. editor, mem. editorial bd. Sci. Edn., 1944-50. Office: coll Edn U Ill Urbana IL 61801 ☆

BURNETT, ROBERT A., publisher; b. Joplin, Mo., June 4, 1927; s. Lee Worth and Gladys (Plummer) B.; A.B., U. Mo., 1948; m. Gloria M. Cowden, Dec. 25, 1948; children—Robert A., Stephen, Gregory, Douglas, David, Penelope. Salesman, Cowden Motor Co., Guthrie Center, Ia., then Equitable Life Assurance Soc., Joplin, Mo.; now exec. v.p. operations Meredith Corp. Bd. dirs. Discover Am. Travel Orgns., Consumer Research Inst., Advt. Research Found. Served with AUS, 1945-46. Mem. Mag. Pubs. Assn. (dir.), Phi Delta Theta. Conglist. Home: 5231 Waterbury Dr Des Moines IA 50312 Office: 1716 Locust St Des Moines IA 50303

BURNETT, THEODORE SWARTS, ret. life ins. exec.; b. Wichita, Kan., Nov. 8, 1904; s. William Ward and Adeline (Swarts) B.; A.B., U. Kan., 1928; m. Mary Engel, Nov. 29, 1930; children—Theodore Swarts, William, Molly. Joined Pacific Mut. Life Ins. Co., Los Angeles, 1928, v.p. mortgage loan and real estate dept., 1946- 52, financial v.p., 1952-55, exec. v.p., 1955-56, pres., 1956-63, vice chmn. bd., 1963-64, chmn., 1964-69; hon. dir. United Cal. Bank. Mayor, mem. City Council. Bd. dirs., chmn. investment com. Childrens Hosp. Los Angeles; dir., past pres. Cal. Taxpayers' Assn.; vice chmn. bd. trustees, finance and investment Claremont Men's Coll.; trustee Kan. U. Endowment Assn. Recipient distinguished service award U. Kan., 1960. Mem. Inst. Life Ins. (past dir.), So. Cal. Mortgage Bankers Assn. (past pres., past dir.), Cal. C. of C. (dir., chmn. statewide com. on ins. and employee cash fringe benefit programs), Life Assos. Cal. Inst. Tech., Life Ins. Assn. Am. (past chmn., com. on govt. relations and joint com. on urban problems), Assn. Cal. Life Ins. Cos. (dir., past pres.), So. Cal. Visitors Council (past pres., dir., mem. mgmt. com.), Phi Gamma Delta. Clubs: California (Los Angeles); Annandale Golf (Pasadena, Cal.). Home: 1555 Wilson Av San Marino CA 91108

BURNETT, WHIT, editor, writer; b. Salt Lake City, Utah, Aug. 14, 1899; s. Benjamin James and Anna Marian (Christensen) B.; student U. of So. Cal. 1918; U. Utah, 1920, U. Cal. 1921; m. Martha Foley, 1930 (div.); 1 son, David; m. 2d, Hallie Southgate Abbett, 1942; children—John, Whitney Ann Beekman. Reporter, Salt Lake newspapers, 1916; reporter on Evening Express, Los Angeles, 1918; editor Asso. Press, Los Angeles, 1919-20, San Francisco, 1921, asst. city editor, N.Y. 1926-27; city editor, N.Y. Herald, Paris edition, 1927- 28; organizer Balkan news service for N.Y. Sun Fgn. Service and Consol. Press, Vienna, Austria, 1929-31; founder, with Martha Foley, of magazine, Story, Vienna, 1931, transferred magazine to New York, 1933; with J. B. Lippincott Co. 1939-49, E. P. Dutton, other cos. 1949—; instr. advanced short story, Columbia U., 1936-43. Queens Coll., 1940, Hunter Coll., 1957-58; editor Hawthorn Books, N.Y.C., 1958- 61; editor (with Hallie Burnett) Story Mag., Story Press, 1942-65; mem. editorial bd. Story (acquired by Scholastic Mags., Inc.), 1966, dir. Story's Coll. Creative Awards Contest, 1966-71. Charter Member Anglo- Am. Press Assn. Vienna, Overseas Press Club, N.Y., gov., 1963-67, 71; chmn. nat. awards com. 1966-67, 69, 70, sec. of P.E.N., Am. Center, 1944-46. Editor (with Martha Foley): A Story Anthology, 1933, Story in America, 1934; The Flying Yorkshireman, novellas, 1937. Editor: This Is My Best, anthology of 93 of America's greatest living authors, 1942; Two Bottles of Relish, a book of strange stories, 1942; The Seas of God, great stories of the human spirit, 1944; Time To Be Young, 1945; The Story Pocket Book, 1945; American Writers Today (with C.E. Slatkin), 1947; Story: The Fiction of the Forties, and Sextet (with Hallie Burnett), 1949, 51; The World's Best, 1950; Story, No. 1, 2, 3, 4 (with Hallie Burnett) 1951-54; editor and collaborator on This Is My Best, radio series, 1944-45. Author: The Maker of Signs (short stories), 1934, The Literary Life and the Hell With It (essays), 1939; Immortal Bachelor, The Love Story of Robert Burns (with John Pen), 1942; contbr. articles and stories to mags. Editor: This is My Best Humor, 1955; The Spirit of Adventure, 1956; Animal Spirits, 1956; This is My Philosophy, 1957; The Spirit of Man, 1958; Firsts of the Famous, 1962; (with Hallie Burnett); Best College Writing, 1962, Prize College Stories, 1963, The Stone Soldier, 1964, The Modern Short Story in the Making, 1964, Story Jubilee, 1965; Story: The Yearbook of Discovery, 1968, 69, 70, 71, That's What Happened to Me, 1969; This Is My Best, 1970; Black Hands on a White Face, 1971. Home: 174 Huckleberry Hill Rd Wilton CT 06897 Office: Scholastic Mags Inc 53 W 43d St New York City NY 10036

BURNETT, WILLIAM CLYDE, Jr., journalist; b. East Point, Ga., May 22, 1928; s. William Clyde and Grace (Childers) B.; B.F.A., U. Ga., 1951; m. Elizabeth Jean Puckett, Aug. 16, 1957; children—Karen Susan, Kenneth William. Display advt. mgr. Sears Roebuck & Co., Sarasota, Fla., 1953-56; mem. retail advt. dept. Sarasota Herald Tribune, 1956-61, fine arts editor, spl. assignment writer conservation, 1961-69; art and music editor, art critic Atlanta Jour., 1969—; free-lance writer, photographer, artist. Served with Hosp. Corps, USNR, 1946-48. Recipient Gov.'s award for conservation writing, Fla. Wildlife Fedn. and Sears Found., 1963. Mem. Outdoor Writers Assn. Am. (asso.). Home: 812 S Candler St Decatur GA 30030 Office: 10 Forsyth St Atlanta GA 30303

BURNETT, WILLIAM RILEY, author; b. Springfield, O., Nov. 25, 1899; s. Theodore Addison and Emily Updike Colwell (Morgan) B.; student Ohio State U., 1919- 20; m. 2d, Whitney Forbes Johnstone: children—William Riley III, James Addison. Statistician, State of Ohio, 1921-27; writer, 1928—. Recipient O. Henry Meml. award for best short story, 1930. Mem. P.E.N. (Internat.; Acad. Motion Picture Arts and Scis. Democrat. Episcopalian. Club: Players (N.Y.). . Author: Little Caesar, 1929; Iron Man, 1930; Saint Johnson, 1930; The Silver Eagle, 1931; The Giant Swing, 1932; Dark Hazard, 1933; Goodbye to the Past, 1934; The Goodhues of Sinking Creek, 1934; King Cole, 1936; The Dark Command, 1938; High Sierra, 1940; The Quick Brown Fox, 1942; Nobody Lives Forever, 1944; Tomorrow's Another Day, 1945; Romelle, 1946; The Asphalt Jungle, 1949; Little Men, Big World, 1951; Vianty Row, 1952; Adobe Walls, 1953; Captain Lightfoot, 1954; Pale Moon, 1956; Underdog, 1957; Bitter Ground, 1958; Mi Amigo, 1959; The Goldseekers, 1962; The Widow Barony, 1963; also fiction Harpers, Esquire, others; story The Ivory Tower, in The Best Short Stories of 1946; has received 3 book club selections; Little Caesar (Lit. Guild); Iron Man, Dark Hazard (Book of the Month), Little Caesar, and The Asphalt Jungle translated into 12 languages; The Great Escape (Screen Writers award for best drama 1963); The Roar of the Crowd, 1964; Coal Man, 1968. Author many screen plays, including Wake Island, 1942. Address: HN Swanson Inc 8523 Sunset Blvd West Hollywood CA 90069

BURNETT, WINSTON A., constrn. co. exec.; b. N.Y.C.; ed. Manhattan Tech. Inst., Columbia, Coll. City N.Y.; m. Jean Burnett; children—Spencer Anthony, Pamela Alicia. Chmn. bd., chief exec. officer Burnett Internat. Devel. Corp. and subsidiaries Winston A. Burnett Internat., Ltd., Nassau, Bahamas, Burnett Internat., Nigeria, Burnett Constrn. Ltd., Rivers State; founder Winston A. Burnett Constrn. Co. and subsidiaries; involved in 32 urban renewal projects, also devel. and constrn., Nigeria, Bahamas, Lybia, Egypt. Served with AUS, 1943-46. Decorated 4 Bronze Stars, Silver Star; recipient Horatio Alger award, Internat. Constrn. Bldg Orgn. Business Achievement, JFK Meml. award; others. Address: 15 Columbus Circle New York City NY 10023

BURNETTE, WELLS DEWEY, pub. relations co. exec.; b. San Antonio, Sept. 14, 1915; s. LaSalle Dewey and Margaret (Seits) B.; A.B., U. Chgo., 1937; postgrad. John Marshall Law Sch., 1942-43; m. Cora A. Clauson, Sept. 9, 1939; children—Mark Clauson, James Dewey (dec.), Linnéa Margaret. Own bus., Pueblo, Colo., 1933-35; editor U. Chgo. mag., 1935-36; asst. bus. mgr. Pitts. Sun-Telegraph, 1937; social sci. editor Wonderland of Knowledge Ency., Chgo. 1938; asst. sales promotion mgr. Scott, Foresman & Co., Chgo., 1938-43; asso. dir. Midwest area Nat. Conf. Christians and Jews, Chgo., 1946-49; v.p. Roosevelt U., Chgo., 1950-60; exec. v.p. Charles R. Feldstein & Co., Inc., pub. relations, Chgo., 1960-61; pres. Wells Burnette Assos., Inc., pub. relations and fund raising consultants for ednl. and welfare orgns., Chgo., 1961—; dir. Library of Living Philosophers, Inc. Vice Chmn. Budget rev. com. Chgo. Community Fund, 1960. Served as personnel classification specialist USNR, 1943-46. Mem. Am. Civil Liberties Union, Chgo. Urban League, U.S. Assn. UN (dir. Ill. chpt.), Assn. for Family Living, Kappa Sigma. Unitarian (former ch. chmn.). Editor: Story of the Rights of Man, 1942. Author ednl. monographs, articles. Home: 513 Edens Lane Northfield IL 60093 Office: 176 W Adams St Chicago IL 60603

BURNEY, CECIL EDWARD, lawyer; b. Riesel, Tex., Oct. 6, 1914; s. Frank Edward and Allye Stacie (Goodman) B.; A.B., U. Tex., 1936, LL.B., 1937; m. Kara Hunsucker, Jan. 15, 1949; children—Cecil Edward, Kara Lisa, Frank Burleson. Admitted to Tex. bar, 1938, since practiced Corpus Christi; partner Wood, Burney, Nesbitt & Ryan and predecessor firms, 1941—; pres. Merc. Nat. Bank, 1955-56; dir. Parkdale State Bank, Nat. Bank of Commerce of Brownsville, Merc. Nat. Bank, Kingsville, Stonewall Bank, Corpus Christi, 1st Nat. Bank, Ingleside; sec. Corpus Christi Broadcasting Co. K-SIX T.V. Inc. Spl. asst. atty. gen. Tex., 1956; mem. exec. bd. Gulf Coast council Boy Scouts Am.; chmn. Gov.'s Traffic Safety Com., 1956; past chmn. Corpus Christi Housing Authority, Nueces County Red Cross; past pres. Jr. C. of C. Served to lt. comdr. USNR, 1942-45. Fellow Am. Bar Found.; mem. State Bar Tex. (pres. 1951-52), Am. Bar Assn. (bd. govs. 1965-68), Am. Judicature Soc. (pres. 1960-62), Nat. Legal Aid Assn. (dir.), Nat. Conf. Bar Pres. (chmn. 1955-56), Tex. Hist. Found. (pres. 1970—), Southwestern Legal Found. (adv. com.). Presbyn. Rotarian. Clubs: Town, Petroleum (Corpus Christi). Home: 4895 Ocean Dr Corpus Christi TX 78412 Office: Petroleum Tower Corpus Christi TX 78401

BURNEY, LEROY E., physician; b. Burney, Ind., Dec. 13, 1906; B.S., Ind. U., 1928, M.D., 1930; M.P.H., Johns Hopkins, 1932; D.Sc., Jefferson Med. Coll., 1957, DePauw U., 1958, Ind. U., 1959, Woman's Med. Coll. Pa., 1960; LL.D., Seton Hall U., 1957; m. Mildred Hewins, Feb. 20, 1932; children—Robert, Kay Susanne. Entered USPHS, 1932, surgeon gen., 1956-61; cons. WHO, Geneva, Switzerland, 1961; v.p. for health scis. Temple U., Phila., 1961-71; pres. Milbank Meml. Fund, 1971—. Home: 901 Rock Creek Rd Bryn Mawr PA 19101 Office: 40 Wall St New York City NY 10005

BURNEY, VIRGIL DAN, mfg. co. exec.; b. Ft. Worth, May 12, 1927; s. William Homer and Grace (Carter) B.; student Tex. Christian U., 1944-45, 47-49; LL.B., So. Meth. U., 1953; m. Diane Owen King, July 14, 1962; children—Kendall King, King Carter. Admitted to Tex. bar, 1953, N.Y. bar, 1958, U.S. Supreme Ct. bar, 1967; asst. supr. joint agreements Atlantic Refining Co., Dallas, 1953-57; asso. firm White & Case, N.Y.C., 1957-62; with Ling-Temco-Vought, Inc., Dallas, 1962—, gen. counsel, 1966—, sec., 1966-69, v.p., 1967-70, sr. v.p., 1970—. Served with USNR, 1945-46, 50-51. Mem. Am., N.Y. State, Tex., Dallas bar assns., Am. Soc. Corp. Secs. (pres. Dallas region 1969-70), Phi Alpha Delta. Home: 4405 Highland Dr Dallas TX 75205 Office: 1600 Pacific Av Dallas TX 75201

BURNHAM, ALAN, architect; b. Englewood, N.J., Feb. 10, 1913; s. Enoch Lewis and Cora (Sellers) B.; student Avon (Conn.) Old Farms, 1929-30, Fountain Valley Sch. of Colo., Colorado Springs, 1930-32; B.S., Harvard, 1936; B.Arch., Columbia, 1940; m. Frances Hotchkiss Berking, Mar. 22, 1947; children—Roderick Hotchkiss, Cora Lewis. With Bur. Yards and Docks USN (camouflage), Washington, 1941-43; overseas duty USN, Trinidad, B.W.I., 1944-46; with Alex D. Crosett & Assos., architects, N.Y.C., 1946, Walter Dorwin Teague, indsl. designer, N.Y.C., 1946-47, Frederick L. Ackerman and Harold R. Sleeper, architects, N.Y.C., 1947-48, Trio Industries, Inc., N.Y.C., 1948-49, Lorimer Rich & Robbins Conn, architects, N.Y.C., 1949-50, office of Henry S. Churchill, N.Y.C., 1950-52, indsl. div., Ebasco Service, Inc., 1952-60, Burns & Roe, Inc., 1960-62, Shanley & Sturges, 1962-65; exec. dir. Landmarks Preservation Commn., 1965—; lectr. New Sch., 1965—. Fellow A.I.A.; mem. Nat. Council Archtl. Registration Bds., Soc. Archtl. Historians, Nat. Trust, L.I., N.Y. hist. socs., Municipal Art Soc. (dir.) Clubs: Harvard (N.Y.C.); Century Assn. Contbr. to jours. and mags. Edited Richard Morris Hunt Family Papers, 1939, New York Landmarks, 1963. Home: 65 Fairfield Rd Greenwich CT 06830

BURNHAM, CHARLES WILSON, educator; b. Detroit, Apr. 6, 1933; s. Charles Hubbard and Anne (Wilson) B.; S.B., Mass. Inst. Tech., 1954, Ph.D., 1961; A.M., Harvard, 1966; m. Mary Sue Morgan, June 21, 1958; children—Jeffrey Wentworth, David Wilson. Postdoctoral fellow Geophys. Lab. Carnegie Instn., Washington, 1961-63, staff scientist, 1963-66; asso. prof. mineralogy Harvard, 1966-69, prof., 1969—. Served as 1st lt. USAF, 1955-57. Fellow Mineral. Soc. Am.; mem. Am. Crystallographic Assn., A.A.A.S., Mineral. Soc. (London), Am. Geophys. Union, Geochem. Soc., Sigma Xi, Phi Gamma Delta. Episcopalian. Club: Appalachian Mountain (Boston). Home: 6 Captain Browns Lane Acton MA 01720 Office: 20 Oxford St Cambridge MA 02138

BURNHAM, DAVID BRIGHT, journalist; b. Boston, Jan. 24, 1933; s. Addison Center and Dorothy (Moore) B.; B.A., Harvard, 1955; m. Sophy Taylee Deub, Mar. 12, 1960; children—Sarah Taylee, Molly Bright. Reporter, U.P.I., Washington, 1959- 61, reporter Newsweek mag., Washington, 1961-63; writer CBS, N.Y.C., 1963-65; asst. dir. President's Commn. Law Enforcement and Adminstrn. of Justice, 1965-67; reporter N.Y. Times, N.Y.C., 1967—. Recipient George K. Polk award, L.I. U., 1968, Silurians award, 1968, N.Y. Newspaper Guild award, 1968. Clubs: Spee, Hasty Pudding (Cambridge, Mass.). Home: 9 Pierrepont St Brooklyn NY 11201 Office: The New York Times 229 W 43d St New York City NY 10036

BURNHAM, DONALD CLEMENS, mfg. co. exec.; b. Athol, Mass., Jan. 28, 1915; s. Charles Richardson and Freda (Clemens) B.; B.S. in Mech. Engring., Purdue U., 1936, D.Engring. (hon.), 1959; D.Eng., Ind. Inst. Tech., 1952, 1963, Drexel Inst. Tech., 1964, Poly. Inst. of Bklyn., 1967; m. Virginia Gobble, May 29, 1937; children—David Charles, Joan (Mrs. Fred Koloc), John Carl, William Lawrence, Mary Barbara. With Gen. Motors Corp., 1936-54, asst. chief engr. Oldsmobile div., 1953-54; with Westinghouse Electric Corp., 1954—, group v.p., 1962-63, pres., chief exec. officer, 1963-68, chmn., chief exec. officer, 1969—, also dir.; dir. Mellon Nat. Bank & Trust Co.; mem. internat. adv. council Chase Manhattan Bank N.Y. Mem. Bus. Council, Nat. Indsl. Pollution Control Council; exec. com. Allegheny Conf. on Community Devel. Life trustee Carnegie-Mellon U.; trustee Com. for Econ. Devel., Carnegie Inst.; bd. dirs. Am. Wind Symphony Orch., Purdue Research Found., United Fund Allegheny County. Served to maj. AUS, World War II. Recipient Outstanding Achievement in Mgmt. award Am. Inst. Indsl. Engrs., 1964. Mem. Am. Soc. M.E., (Richards Meml. award 1958), Soc. Automotive Engrs. I.E.E.E., Nat. Acad. Engring., Am. Mgmt. Assn., Tau Beta Pi, Pi Tau Sigma, Alpha Pi Mu. Clubs: Duquesne, Chartiers Country (Pitts.); Sky (N.Y.C.); Rolling Rock (Ligonier, Pa.); Laurel Valley Golf (Latrobe, Pa.). Home: 615 Osage Rd Pittsburgh PA 15243 Office: Westinghouse Bldg Gateway Center Pittsburgh PA 15222

BURNHAM, FORBES LINDEN SAMPSON, prime minister Guyana; b. Kitty Village, Guyana, Feb. 20, 1923; s. James Ethelbert and Rachel A. (Sampson) B.; student Queen's Coll., B.A. (hon.), LL.B. (hon.), London U.; m. Sheila Bernice Lataste, 1951; children—Roxanne, Annabelle, Francesco; m. 2d, Viola Harper, 1967. Called to bar, 1948; engaged in local politics, 1949; mem. Guyana Legislature; leader opposition, 1961-64; minister edn., 1953; councillor, 1952; mayor Georgetown, 1959-64; prime minister Guyana, 1966—. Pres., W. Indian Students Union, then Kitty Brotherhood, 1947-48, Guyana Bar Assn., 1959, Brit. Guiana Labour Union, 1953-54, 63-65; co-founder People's Progressive Party, People's Nat. Congress; former minister edn. Clubs: Demerara Cricket, Maltenoes Sports, Georgetown Cricket, Non Pareil. B.G.C.C. (Guyana). Home: The Residence Botanic Gardens Vlissengen Rd Georgetown Guyana WI Office: Pub Bldgs Georgetown Demerara Guyana WI

BURNHAM, HARRY G., Jr., newspaper editor; b. Hibbing, Minn., July 30, 1914; s. Harry G. and Harriet M. (Belding) B.; B.A. in Journalism, U. S.D., 1947; m. Juanita M. Schoene, Feb. 14, 1946; children—Barbara, Harry G. III, Ellen, Thomas. City editor Watertown (S.D.) Pub. Opinion, 1948; news editor Salt Lake Telegram, 1948-52; asst. mng. editor Duluth News-Tribune, 1952- 59; mng. editor St. Paul Pioneer Press, 1959-62, St. Paul Dispatch, 1962-. Mem. Internat. Press Inst., Am. Press Inst., A.P. Mng. Editors Assn. Home: 8867 Hallmark Av S Cottage Grove MN 55016 Office: 55 E 4th St St Paul MN 55109

BURNHAM, JAMES, author; b. Chgo., Nov. 22, 1905; s. Claude George and Mary May (Gillis) B.; B.A., Princeton, 1927; B.A., Oxford (Eng.) U., 1929, M.A., 1932; m. Marcia Lightner. Mar. 31, 1934; children—Marcia, James Bernard, John Lightner. Prof. dept. philosophy Washington Sq. Coll., N.Y. U., N.Y. U., 1929-53. Editor: The Symposium (with Philip E. Wheelwright), 1930-33; What Europe Thinks of America, 1953. Author: (with Philip E. Wheelwright) Introduction to Philosophical Analysis, 1931; The Managerial Revolution, 1941; The Machiavellians, 1943; The Struggle for the World, 1947; The Case for De Gaulle (with André Malraux); The Coming Defeat of Communism, 1950; Containment or Liberation?, 1953; The Web of Subversion, 1954; Congress and the American Tradition, 1959; Suicide of the West, 1964; The War We Are In, 1967. Mem. editorial bd. Nat. Rev., 1955—. Home: Kent CT 06757

BURNHAM, JOSEPH ANDREW, retail co. exec.; b. Berryville, Ark., Mar. 11, 1920; s. Joseph Andrew and Tommie (Wade) B.; B.S., U. Ark., 1941; postgrad. Inst. for Mgmt., Northwestern U., 1955; m. Ruth Merrifield Drover, Sept. 26, 1943; children—Bruce, Stephen, Philip, Gregory, Ann. With Marshall Field & Co., various positions, 1948—, exec. v.p., gen. mgr. Chgo. stores, 1970-71, exec. v.p. operations, 1971—, also dir. Vice chmn. bd. dirs. Chgo. Health Research Found.; trustee Community Hosp., Geneva, Ill. Served to lt. USNR, 1942-46. Mem. Econ. Club Chgo. Republican. Conglist. (trustee). Clubs: Chicago, Chicago Athletic. Home: 433 Main St Batavia IL 60510 Office: 111 N State St Chicago IL 60690

BURNHAM, WILBUR HERBERT, artist, designer stained glass murals; b. Boston, Feb. 4, 1887; s. Wilbur Leroy and Mary (Oxley) B.; student Mass. Sch. Art, 1904-08; also France, Eng., Italy and Spain; m. Etta Mae Miller, June 22, 1912; 1 son, Wilbur Herbert. Began as designer stained glass, 1906; designer Harry E. Goodhue, Boston, 1906-16, Horace J. Phipps Co., Boston, 1916-18; mem. firm Ball & Burnham, 1918-20, Phipps, Ball & Burnham, 1920-22; in bus. alone, 1922—. Stained glass represented in Cathedral of St. John the Divine, Washington Cathedral, Ch. St. Vincent DePaul, Los Angeles, many others. Fellow Royal Soc. Arts; mem. Mediaeval Acad. Am. Am. Fedn. Arts. Stained Glass Assn. Am. (pres. 1939-41), Boston Soc. Arts and Crafts (master craftsman), Mass. Sch. Art Alumni, Copley Soc. (pres. 1951-53). Recipient Gold medal Boston Tercentenary Art Exhbn., 1930; diplome de Medaille d'Argent, Paris Expn., 1937; Craftsmanship medal A.I.A., 1947. Republican. Episcopalian. Writer, lectr. on stained glass. Home: 14 Overlook Rd Wakefield MA 01880 Office: 458 Main St Wakefield MA 01880

BURNIGHT, ROBERT GALEN, educator; b. Lancaster, Pa., Aug. 6, 1918; s. Franklin Gilpin and Edith (Lawrence) B.; A.B., Franklin and Marshall Coll., 1940; M.A., U. Pa., 1947, Ph.D., 1952; m. Catherine Alice Glazier, May 25, 1963. Instr. sociology U. Pa., 1947-49; asst. prof., then prof. rural sociology U. Conn., 1949-61; adj. prof. sociology Brown U., 1961-62, prof. sociology, 1962—. Adviser, Center Population and Social Research, U. Med. Scis., Bangkok, Thailand, 1967-68; mem. adv. com. epidemiology and biometry Nat. Inst. Gen. Med. Scis., 1962-67; mem. developmental behavioral scis. study sect. NIH, 1968—. Bd. dirs. World Affairs Council R.I. Served with AUS, 1941-45. Guggenheim fellow, Mexico, 1959. Mem. Population Assn. Am. (dir.), Am. Sociol. Assn., Am. Statis. Assn., Internat. Union Sci. Study Population, Gerontological Soc. Contbr. articles, monographs to profl. lit. Home: 160 Brown St Providence RI 02906

BURNIM, KALMAN AARON, educator; b. Malden, Mass., Mar. 7, 1928; s. Jack K. and Sadie (Levy) B.; B.A., Tufts Coll., 1950; M.A., Ind. U., 1951; Ph.D., Yale, 1958; m. Verna Ruth Lesser, Sept. 12, 1948; children—Ira, Judith, Susan. Vice pres. New Eng. Adding Machine Co., 1951-55; asst. prof. Valparaiso U., 1958-59, U. Pitts., 1959-60; mem. faculty Tufts U., 1960—, prof. drama, 1965—, mng. dir. Tufts Univ. Theatre, 1961-65, exec. dir., 1966—, chmn. dept. drama and speech, 1966—. Served with AUS, 1946-47. Folger Library fellow, 1957, 69; Guggenheim fellow, 1964-65; Sterling fellow, 1957-58. Mem. Am. Ednl. Theatre Assn., Am. Soc. Theater Research (exec. com. 1960-69, program chmn. 1963-65), Modern Lang. Assn., Brit. Soc. Theatre Research, Phi Beta Kappa. Author: David Garrick Director, 1961; (with William Appleton) The Prompter, 1966; also articles. Asso. editor Ednl. Theatre Jour., 1968-70. Home: 22 Cranmore Lane Melrose MA 02176 Office: Tufts Univ Theatre Medford MA 02155

BURNOR, ROMAN G., lawyer, business exec.; b. Toledo, Feb. 16, 1916; s. Roman G. and Victoria (Farber) B.; A.B., U. Detroit, 1937; J.D., U. Mich., 1940; m. Marjorie Ann Nyquist, May 12, 1945; children—David Jonathon, Richard Neal, Douglas Kent. Admitted to Ohio bar, 1941, gen. practice law, 1941-47, corporate law, 1947—; asso. Wm. A. Finn, Toledo, 1941-42, Williams Eversman & Morgan, 1942-47; law dept. N.Y., C. & St.L. R.R., Cleve., 1947-50; sec., counsel Indsl. Rayon Corp., 1950-61; asst. sec., counsel Harshaw Chem. Co., 1962-64, sec., gen. counsel, 1964—, v.p., 1965—; corporate sec. Kewanee Oil Co., 1967—; dept. counsel Gen. Electric Co., 1969—; instr. U. Toledo, 1946, Cleve.-Marshall Law Sch., 1947-50. Mem. Am., Ohio, Cleve. bar assns., Assn. Bar City N.Y., Ohio, Cleve. chambers commerce, Am. Soc. Corporate Secs. Clubs: Mid Day, Clevelander, Paly House, Centerbury Country. Home: 3193 Somerset Rd Shaker Heights OH 44122 Office: Nela Park Cleveland OH 44112

BURNS, ALAN LINCOLN, mfg. co. exec.; b. Saco, Me., May 16, 1925; s. Alan Lincoln and Mildred (Emmitt) B.; B.A., Amherst Coll., 1949; M.B.A., Harvard Bus. Sch., 1949- 51; m. Cary Sutherland Sturges, June 17, 1950; children—Gordon, Sarah, Martha, Duncan. Various personnel and mfg. positions Westvaco Corp., N.Y.C., 1951-67; pres. U.S. Envelope Co., Springfield, Mass., 1967—, also dir. Served to 2d lt. AUS, 1943-46. Mem. Delta Kappa Epsilon. Clubs: Union League (N.Y.C.); Manursing Island (Rye, N.Y.). Episcopalian. Home: Manursing Island Rye NY 10580 Office: PO Box 3300 Springfield MA 01101

BURNS, ARTHUR EDWARD, economist, educator; b. Oakland, Cal., Sept. 3, 1908; s. William Thomas and Anne (Bruns) B.; A.B., U. Cal., 1931, M.A., 1934; Ph.D., George Washington U., 1935; m. Marcella Eugenic Wyss, Oct. 30, 1933; 1 son, Robert Lee. Instr., George Washington U., 1934-35, asst. prof., 1935-37, asso. prof., 1937-40, adj. prof., 1940-45, prof. econs., 1945—, acting dean Sch. Govt., 1946-49, dean, 1949-57, dean, chmn. grad. council, 1957—, dean Grad. Sch. Arts and Scis., 1967—. Vis. prof. econs. U. Cal., summer 1949, Getulio Vargus Found., nat. faculty econ. scis. U. Brazil, Rio de Janeiro, 1952. Economist, Fed. Emergency Relief Adminstrn., 1934-35; economist, asst. dir. research W.P.A., 1935-40, adviser, 1941- 42; spl. cons., O.P.A., 1942-43; dep. dir. Office of Materials and Facilities, War Food Adminstrn., 1943-45; cons. White House Office, 1957-60, Renegotiation Bd., 1961—, U.S.-P.R. Status

Commn., 1965-66; vis. lecturer at Indsl. Coll. Armed Forces, 1950—; pub. mem. Fgn. Service Selection Bd., Dept. State, 1951; cons. Fgn. Operations Adminstrn., ICA, 1953-57, Operations Research Office, 1951-60, Italian Govt., Rome, 1955. Fellow A.A.A.S.; mem. Am. Econ. Assn. Artus, Delta Phi Epsilon (nat. pres. 1948-50). Clubs: Cosmos. Author: (with Neal and Watson), Modern Economics, 1948, rev. edit. 1953; (with D.S. Watson), Government Spending and Economic Expansion, 1940; (with E.A. Williams), Federal Work, Security, and Relief Programs, 1941. Contbr. articles and revs. to profl. jours., govt. publs. Home: 4000 Massachusetts Av Washington DC 20016 Office: George Washington U Washington DC 20006

BURNS, ARTHUR F., economist, educator; b. Stanislau, Austria, Apr. 27, 1904; s. Nathan and Sarah (Juran) B.; A.B., Columbia, 1925, A.M., 1925, Ph.D., 1934, LL.D., 1970; LL.D., Lehigh U., 1952, Brown U., 1956, Dartmouth, 1956, Oberlin Coll., 1956, Wesleyan U., 1958, Swarthmore Coll., 1958, L.I. U., 1960, U. Chgo., 1960, Rikkyo U., Tokyo, 1965, Fordham U., 1969, N.Y. U., 1970, U. Cal., 1970; D.Sc., U. Pa., 1958, U. Rochester, 1963; L.H.D., Rutgers U., 1955; D.Econ., Chung-ang U., Korea, 1970; D.Phil., Hebrew U., Israel, 1970; L.H.D., Pepperdine Coll., 1970; m. Helen Bernstein, Jan. 25, 1930; children—David, Joseph. Instr. econs. Rutgers U., 1927-30, asst. prof., 1930-33, asso. prof., 1933-43, prof., 1943-44; asst. statistics Columbia, 1926, Gilder fellow, 1926-27, vis. prof., 1941-44, prof., 1944-59, John Bates Clark prof., 1959—; research asso. Nat. Bur. Econ. Research, 1930-31, mem. research staff, 1933—, dir. research 1945-53, pres., 1957-67, chmn., 1967-68, hon. chmn., 1968—. Millar lectr. Fordham U., 1957; Murray lectr. State U. Ia., 1964; Fairless lectr. Carnegie Inst. Tech., 1965; Moskowitz lectr. N.Y. U., 1967; vis. prof. econs. Stanford, spring 1968; cousellor Pres. U.S., 1969-70; chmn. bd. govs. Fed. Res. System, Washington, 1970—; trustee 20th Century Fund. Chief statistician Ry. Emergency Bd., 1941; cons. various govtl. agys. and depts.; chmn. Pres.'s Council Econ. Advisers, 1953- 56, Adv. Bd. on Econ. Growth and Stability, 1953-56, Cabinet Com. on Small Bus., 1956; mem. Pres.'s Adv. Com. on Labor-Mgmt. Policy, 1961-66, Gov.'s Com. on Minimum Wage, 1964; mem. research adv. bd. Rutgers U., 1947-61; adv. bd. Indsl. Coll. Armed Forces, 1958-64; bd. mgrs. Swarthmore Coll., 1959-62; mem. U.S. Adv. Council on Social Security Financing, 1957-58, N.Y. Temp. State Commn. on Econ. Expansion, 1959-60. Recipient Alexander Hamilton medal Columbia, 1969; Distinguished Pub. Service award Tax Found., 1969; Mugungwha decoration (Korea), 1970. Fellow Am. Statis. Assn., Econometric Soc., Am. Acad. Arts and Scis.; mem. Pilgrims Soc., Am. Philos. Soc., Council Fgn. Relations, Am. Econ. Assn. (pres. 1959, distinguished fellow), Acad. Polit. Sci. (pres. 1962-68), Institut de Sci. Economique Appliquee (corr.), Phi Beta Kappa. Clubs: Cosmos (Washington); Men's Faculty of Columbia Century Assn. (N.Y.C.). Author: Production Trends in the U.S. Since 1870, 1934; Economic Research and the Keynesian Thinking of Our Times, 1946; Frontiers of Economic Knowledge, 1954; Prosperity Without Inflation, 1957; The Management of Prosperity, 1966; The Business Cycle in a Changing World, 1969; (with W.C. Mitchell) Measuring Business Cycles, 1946; (with P.A. Samuelson) Full Employment, Guideposts and Economic Stability, 1967; (with Jacob Javits, Charles Hitch) The Defense Sector and the American Economy, 1968. Home: Watergate East 2510 Virginia Av NW Washington DC 20037 Office: Fed Res Washington DC 20551

BURNS, CHARLES FOWLER WILLIAMS, investment dealer; b. Vancouver, B.C., Can., Sept. 27, 1907; s. Herbert Deschamps and Marguerite (Williams) B.; student U. Toronto, 1926-28; m. Janet Mary Wilson, Feb. 23, 1934; children—Joan Harrison (Mrs. John Addison), Janet (Mrs. James Day), Herbert Michael. Floor mem. Campbell, Stratton & Co., Toronto, Ont., Can., 1929-31; investment dealer R.A. Daly & Co., Toronto, 1931-32; chmn. bd. Burns Bros. & Co. Ltd., 1932—, Burns Bros. & Denton Ltd., Toronto, 1932—, Burns Bros. & Denton, Inc., N.Y.C., 1952—, Crown Life Ins. Co., Toronto, 1959—; dir. Canadian Breweries Ltd., Denison Mines Ltd., Rothmans of Pall Mall Can., Algoma Central Ry., Argonaut Football Club, Mogal of Ireland Ltd., Lake Ont. Cement Ltd., Can. Permanent Trust Co., Royal Winter Fair, Maple Leaf Gardens Ltd., Jockey Club Ltd., Gen. Accident Assurance Co. Can., Scottish Canadian Assurance Corp., Telegram Pub. Co. Ltd. Bd. dirs. Toronto Redevel. Adv. Council; vice chmn. bd. trustees Sunnybrook Hosp. Hon. Chmn. Bd. United Community Life: life gov. Trinity Coll. Sch., Port Hope, Ont. Served to wing comdr. RCAF, 1941- 45. Mem. Zeta Psi. Mem. Anglican Ch. Mem. Liberal Party. Mason. Clubs: Toronto, York, Hunt (Toronto); Halifax (N.S.); University. Rolling Rock National Steeplechase and Hunt Association Canada (hon. pres.). Home: Kingfield Farms King Ontario Canada Office: PO Box 39 Toronto 1 Ontario Canada also 140 Broadway New York City NY 10005

BURNS, CRANFORD HERMAN, former supt. schs.; b. Cullman, Ala., July 1, 1907; s. John Henry and Lexer and Lexer (Grant) B.; B.S., U. Ala., 1936, M.A., 1941; Ed.D., Columbia, 1948; m. Dorothy Rienstadier, Aug. 27, 1936; children—Caroline, Jimmy. Tchr., Cullman County (Ala.) schs., 1930-31, attendance worker, 1933-36; prin. Cold Springs Jr. High Sch., Bremen, Ala., 1931-33, Cold Springs High Sch., 1936-44; prin. Scottsborough High Sch., Jackson County, Ala., 1944-45; dir. guidance services U. Ala., 1945-46, 47-48; asst. supt. charge curriculum Mobile County Schs., 1948-52, supt. schs., 1952-70. Home: 2500 Oakview Dr Mobile AL 36606

BURNS, DANIEL MATTHEW, advt. exec.; b. Bklyn., Aug. 1, 1918; s. Isaac M. and Mary (Hodell) B.; B.A., St. Francis Coll., Bklyn., 1940; postgrad. Fordham U., 1940-41; m. Adele Valerie Casey, July 28, 1945; children—Daniel Matthew, Eugene, Clare, Margaret, Christopher, Adele, Theresa, Stephen, Barbara. Vice pres., editor Bottling Industry, Gussow Publs., 1946-53; with William Esty Co., Inc., N.Y.C., 1953—, sr. v.p., 1968—, dir. merchandising, 1965—. Mem. council regents St. Francis Coll., 1965—. Served to 1st lt., inf. AUS, 1942-46; ETO. Mem. St. Francis Coll. Alumni Assn. (pres. 1958). Republican. Roman Catholic. Author: The Gray Bonnets: Combat History of the 121st Infantry, 1946. Home: 212 Stewart Av Garden City NY 11530 Office: 100 E 42d St New York City NY 10017

BURNS, DAN WILLIAM, mfg. co. exec.; b. Auburn, Cal., Sept. 10, 1925; s. William and Edith Lynn (Johnston) B. Dir. materials Menasco Mfg. Co., 1951-56; v.p., gen. mgr. Hufford Corp., 1956-58; pres. Hufford div. Siegler Corp., 1958-61; v.p. Siegler Corp., 1961-62, Lear Siegler, Inc., 1962-64; pres., dir. Electrade Corp., Culver City, Cal., 1964, Arnonx Corp., Culver City, 1964; now pres., chief exec. officer, dir. Sargent Industries; dir. Republic Corp. Served to capt. AUS, 1941-47. Club: Bel Air Country (Los Angeles). Home: 10851 Chelon Rd Bel Air Los Angeles CA 90024

BURNS, DAVID MITCHELL, govt. ofcl.; b. Pineville, Ky., Dec. 1, 1928; s. Judge Mitchell and Mary Louise (Cooke) B.; A.B., Princeton, 1953; student Sch. Advanced Internat. Studies, John Hopkins, 1957, 60, Howard U., 1957, 60, Fgn. Service Inst., Tangier, Morocco, 1967-69; m. Sandra Lynn Dunlop, June 8, 1955; children—David A.D., Patrick C.C. Advt. trainee Gen. Electric Co., 1953; instr. English, U. Kan., 1954-55; asst. cultural affairs officer Am. embassy, Damascus, Syria, 1955-56, Beirut, Lebanon, 1956; dir. Iran-Am. Soc., Isfahan, 1957; information officer Am. consulate general, Salisbury, Fedn. Rhodesia and Nyasaland, 1957-59; pub. affairs officer Am. embassy, Bamako, Mali, 1960-62, cultural affairs officer, Tunis, Tunisia, 1962-63; cultural policy officer Africa, USIA, Agy., 1963-67; pub. affairs officer Am. interests sect. embassy of Switzerland, Algiers, Algeria, 1969—. Served with USAAF, 1946-49. Fulbright grant l'Universite de Lille, Salzburg Seminar in Am. Studies, 1953-54. Contbr. articles lit. and profl. jours. Home: 1618 Highland Dr Augusta KS 67010 Office: US Information Agency 1776 Pennsylvania Av NW Washington DC 20520

BURNS, DEAN CARL, surgeon; b. Petoskey, Mich., Dec. 19, 1896; s. Dean Samuel and Emma Caroline (Bohm) B.; Sc.B., U. Chgo., 1919; M.D., Rush Med. Coll. (now dept. U. of Chgo.), 1922; postgrad. Harvard, 1930, Columbia, 1932; m. Marcella Ann Whalen, Oct. 29, 1930; children—Ann Emma (Mrs. John Behan), Mary Juanita (Mrs. William E. McKee II), Dean Daniel. Asst. in dept. materia medica Rush Med. Coll. 1919-21; lectr. chemistry and toxicology Presbyn. Hosp. Tng. Sch., Chgo., 1921; mem. resident staff St. Luke's Hosp., Chgo., 1921-23, chief of resident staff, 1923; practiced in Petoskey, 1923—; attending surgeon, v.p. Petoskey Hosp., 1923—; med. dir., chief of staff Little Traverse Hosp., Petoskey, 1939-60, mem. active staff, 1939—; founder, dir. Burns Clinics (now Burns Clinic Med. Center); 1938—; surgeon for P.M. and Pa. rys.; mem. archtl. commn. for constrn. No. Mich. State Sanatorium. Mem. State Cancer Control Com., 1946—, Mich. Coordinating Council for Pub. Higher Edn., 1962—. Pres. bd. trustees North Central Mich. Coll., 1958—; trustee Mich. YMCA, 1970—; pres. Mich. Assn. Community-Jr. Coll. Governing Bds. Recipient Outstanding Community Service award Jr. C. of C., 1963. Served in Med. R.C., 1918-19, World War. Fellow A.C.S. (Mich. regional com. on fractures and other traumas, councilor Mich. chpt.), Royal Soc. Health (Gt. Britain); mem. A.M.A., A.A.A.S., N.Y. Acad. Scis., Am. Cancer Soc. (state exec. com., trustee Mich. div.), Internat. Coll. Surgeons, Mich. Med. Soc., No. Mich. Med. Soc., Internat. Platform Assn., Tau Kappa Epsilon, Phi Beta Pi. Republican. Episcopalian. Mason. Clubs: Petoskey, Petoskey Country; University (Chgo.); Walloon Lake Country. Contbr. articles to med. jours. Home: Indian Garden Rd Petoskey MI 49770 Office: Burns Clinic Petoskey MI 49770

BURNS, DONALD BRUCE, detective agy. exec.; b. Ossining, N.Y., July 16, 1921; s. William Sherman and Dorothy (Abell) B.; student Union Coll., Schenectady, 1940- 42; children—Donald Bruce, Patricia Anne, Sharon Lynne, Diana Sue. With William J. Burns Internat. Detective Agy., Inc., 1942—, v.p., 1955-64, pres., 1964-70, chmn. bd., chief exec. officer, 1970—. Served as pilot USAAF, 1942-46, USAF, 1951-52. Mem. Am. Legion (past post comdr.), Quiet Birdmen, Phi Delta Gamma (pres. Chi Assn. 1962). Elk. Clubs: Winged Foot Country (Mamaroneck, N.Y.); Sleepy Hollow Country (Scarborough, N.Y.); Desert Forest Golf (Carefree, Ariz.); Key Biscayne Yacht (Fla.); Shattemuc Yacht (Ossining, N.Y.). Home: 161 Orchard Rd Briarcliff Manor NY 10510 Office: 320 Old Briarcliff Rd Briarcliff Manor NY 10510

BURNS, DONALD SNOW, banker; b. Cambridge, Mass., July 31, 1925; s. Jules and Ruth (Snow) B.; grad. Phillips Acad., Andover, Mass., 1943; student Williams Coll., 1943- 44; grad. Am. Inst. Banking, 1947; m. Lucy Keating, July 15, 1947; children—Julie, Patty, Laurie, Wendy, Lonnie, Robin. Sales supr. O'Rourke Baking Co., Buffalo, 1947-49; gen. mgr., then v.p. Glaco Co. So. Cal., 1949-51; with Ekco Products Co. and subsidiaries, 1951-63, pres. subsidiary McClintock Mfg. Co., 1958-60, v.p. builders and indsl. div., 1959-66, dir parent co., 1963-66; pres. Don Burns, Inc. Volkswagen, 1966—; pres. Oceanaire Leasing, Inc., 1968—; chmn. bd. Newport Nat. Bank, Newport Beach, Cal., 1963—; dir. Dura Fiber Co. Inc., Sentinel Equities Corp.; officer, dir. Lifeguard Ins. Co. Mem. Cal. State Coll. Found. Adv. Com., 1964—. Chmn. bd. trustees Orme Sch., Mayer, Ariz. Mem. Am. Soc. Bakery Engrs., U.S. Navy League, Am. Ordnance Assn., Airplane Owners and Pilots Assn. Clubs: Jonathan (Los Angeles); Balboa Bay, Newport Harbor Yacht, Irvine Coast Racquet (Newport Beach); Porsche Owners; Sports Cars of America. Home: 4621 Brighton Rd Corona del Mar CA 92625 Office: 13731 Harbor Blvd Garden Grove CA 92640

BURNS, EDWARD DERMOTT, lawyer;b. Marlboro, Mass., Nov. 17, 1905; s. Edward P. and Mary A. (McDermott) B.; A.B., Manhattan Coll., 1927; LL.B., Fordham U., 1930; m. Anne Loretta Gallagher, July 30, 1934; children—Edward Dermott, Patrick O., Cornelia A., John R. Admitted to N.Y. bar, 1930; with firm Burns, Kennedy, Schilling & O'Shea and predecessors, N.Y.C., 1927—. Sec., dir. Pitman Pub. Corp., N.Y.C.; dir. Hamilton Adams Imports, Ltd. Asst. to chmn. N.Y. State Democratic Law Com., 1935-57. Mem. Am., N.Y. State bar assns., N.Y. County Lawyers Assn., Nat. Assn. R.R. Trial Counsel. Democrat. Roman Catholic. Contbr. articles to profl. jours. Office: 598 Madison Av New York City NY 10022

BURNS, EDWARD MCNALL, ret. educator, author: b. Burgettstown, Pa., Feb. 18, 1897; s. James McNall James McNall and Lucy (Gilliland) B.; student Washington and Jefferson Coll., 1917- 18; A.B., U. Pitts., 1925, A.M., 1927, Ph.D., 1935, LL.D., 1962; student U. Chgo., 1926-29; m. Marie K. Bentz, June 29, 1936; 1 dau., Eleanor W. Asst. in polit. sci. U. Pitts., 1925-27; instr. history and polit. sci. Rutgers, 1928-31, asst. prof. history, 1931-41, asso. prof., 1941-47, prof. history 1947-51, prof. polit. sci., 1951-62, emeritus, 1962—, chmn. dept. history and polit. sci. 1950-51, chmn. dept. polit. sci., 1951-62, sec. faculty Coll. Arts and Scis., 1943- 62; lectr. Vanderbilt U., summer 1963, U. Cal. at Santa Barbara, 1964-65; lectr. South Orange-Maplewood (N.J.) Adult Sch., 1935-40; 1935-40; Fulbright prof. U. Berlin, 1959-60; James Taylor lectr. S.W. Tex. State Coll., 1966. Recipient Distinguished Research award Rutgers Research Council, 1957. Mem. Am. Hist. Assn., Am. Polit. Sci. Assn., Am. Assn. U. Profs., Phi Beta Kappa, Tau Kappa Alpha, Phi Alpha Theta. Author: James Madison, Philosopher of the Constitution, 1938; Western Civilizations, Their History and Their Culture, 1941; David Starr Jordan: Prophet of Freedom, 1953; The American Idea of Mission, 1957; Ideas in Conflict, 1960; The Counter Reformation, 1964; (with Phillip L. Ralph) World Civilizations, 1955. Home: 4346 Via Presada Hope Ranch Park Santa Barbara CA 93105

BURNS, EEDSON LOUIS MILLARD, ret. govt. ofcl.; b. Westmount, Que., Can., June 17, 1897; s. George Eedson and Louise (Wills) B.; student Lower Can. Coll., Montreal, Royal Mil. Coll., Kingston, 1914-15; grad. Staff Coll., Quetta, India, 1929; m. Eleanor Phelan, Dec. 3, 1927; 1 dau., Mary Eleanor. Served with 17th Hussars, 1913; commd. Royal Canadian Engrs., 1915; advanced through grades to lt. gen.; assigned 4th Div. Signal Co., 1916-18; staff capt. 12th Canadian Inf. Brigade, 1919; instr. mil. engring. Royal Mil. Coll., 1926- 28; assigned gen. staff geog. sec. Nat. Def. Hdqrs., Ottawa, Can., 1930; col. gen. staff Canadian Mil. Hdgrs., London, 1940; brig. gen. staff, 1st Canadian Corps, 1941; assigned 4th Canadian Armored Brigade, 2d Canadian Div., 1941-44; comdr. 5th Canadian Armored Div., Italy 1944, 1st Canadian Corps, 1944; gen. officer charge Canadian sect., hdqrs. 21st Army Group, Northwest Europe, 1945; dir.-gen. rehab. Canadian Dept. Vets. Affairs, Ottawa, 1945, asst. dep. minister vets. affairs, 1946-50, dep. minister, 1950; alternate del. Can., 4th session UN Gen. Assembly, N.Y.C., 1949; chief staff UN Truce Supervision Orgn., Palestine, 1954; comdr. UN Emergency Force, Cairo, 1956-59; adviser on disarmament to Canadian Govt., 1960-68. Canadian rep. at Disarmament Confs., Geneva, Switzerland, 1960, 62-68. Decorated Mil. Cross, Order Brit. Empire, Distinguished Service Order (Britain); companion Order of Can. Mem. Canadian Inst. Survey (pres. 1936-37), NRC, UN Assn. in Can. (nat. pres. 1952-53). Mem. Anglican Ch. Author: Man Power in Canadian Army, 1939-45; Between Arab and Israeli; Megamurder; General Mud; also articles Am., Brit., Canadian periodicals. Home: 6 Park Rd Ottawa Ontario Canada

BURNS, EVELINE MABEL, economist; b. London, Eng., Mar. 16, 1900; d. Frederick Haig and Eveline Maud (Falkner) Richardson; B.Sc. in Econs., London Sch. Econs., U. London, 1920, Ph.D., 1926; L.H.D., Western Coll., 1962, Adelphi, 1968, Columbia U., 1969; LL.D., Western Res. U., 1963; m. Arthur Robert Burns, Apr. 8, 1922. Came to U.S., 1926, naturalized, 1937. Adminstrv. asst. Ministry of Labour, 1917-21; asst. lectr., London Sch. Econs., 1921-26, asst. editor Economics, 1923-26; Laura Spelman Rockefeller fellow traveling in U.S., 1926-28; lectr., grad. dept. econs. Columbia, 1928-42; sr. staff mem. com. on social security Social Sci. Research Council, 1937-39, chief econ. security and health sect. Nat. Resources Planning Bd., 1939-43; cons. on social security Nat. Planning Assn., 1943-45; prof. social work N.Y. Sch. Social Work, Columbia, 1946-67, prof. emeritus, 1967—; prof. social work N.Y. U. Grad. Sch. Social Work, 1968-70; Robb vis. prof. Barnard Coll., 1970-71. Cons. N.Y. State Dept. Labor, U.S. Treasury Dept., Com. on Econ. Security, Fed. Res. Bd. and Social Security Bd.; mem. Fed. Adv. Council on Employment Security; mem. consultants on social security Sec. Health, Edn. and Welfare, 1953; mem. Nat. Adv. Com. on Area Redevel., 1961-65, Nat. Adv. Com. on Econ. Devel., 1965-69, N.Y.C. Mayor's Commn. on Health Services, 1966-67. Active YMCA (mem. social welfare com. nat. bd. 1933-39). Recipient Adam Smith medal for outstanding econ. research, 1926; Florina Lasker award, 1960; Blanche Ittelson award, 1968. Guggenheim fellow, 1954-55; hon. fellow London Sch. Econs., 1964. Mem. Consumers League N.Y. (pres. 1934-35, 48-51, vp. 1935-40), Am. Assn. Social Security (v.p. 1935-43), Am. Pub. Welfare Assn. (v.p. 1969-70), Am. Assn. U. Women (nat. social studies com., Woman of Achievement award 1968), Nat. Conf. Social Welfare (sec. 1950-51, v.p. 1955-56, pres. 1957-58), Am. Econ. Assn. (exec. com. 1945-48, v.p. 1953-54). Club: Women's City (N.Y.C.). Author: Wages and the State, 1926; (with Arthur Robert Burns) The Economic World, 1927; Toward Social Security, 1936; British Unemployment Programs, 1920-38, 1941; The American Social Security System, 1949; Social Security and Public Policy, 1956. Editor: Security Work and Relief Policies, 1943; Children's Allowances and the Economic Welfare of Children, 1968. Contbr. to encys., year books. Home: Box 986 Christiansted St Croix VI 00820

BURNS, FINDLEY, Jr., U.S. ambassador; b. Balt., May 4, 1917; s. Findley and Susan Waters (Penniman) B.; A.B., Princeton, 1939; m. Martha A. Lobeck, Oct. 31, 1953. Fgn. service officer, 1942—; 3d sec., vice consul, Madrid, Spain, 1942-44, Brussels, Belgium, 1944-45; assigned Dept. of State, Washington, 1945-47, 49-51, 56-58; 2d sec., vice consul, Warsaw, 1947- 49; consul, Martinique, 1950; 2d sec., consul, Vienna, Austria, 1951-53; fgn. service inspector, 1953-56; chief polit. sect., dep. asst. chief U.S. Mission, Berlin, Germany, 1958-60; spl. asst. to dep. undersec. of state for adminstrn., 1960-61; student Nat. War Coll., 1961-62; counselor for adminstrn. Am. Embassy, London, Eng., 1962-66; U.S. ambassador to Jordan, 1966-68; dep. asst. sec. for mgmt. Bur. Interam. Affairs, Dept. State, Washington, 1968-70; U.S. ambassador to Ecuador, 1970—. Mem. Inst. for Strategic Studies, London. Episcopalian. Home: 4101 Cathedral Av NW Washington DC 20016 Office: Am Embassy Quito Ecuador

BURNS, FLOYD WILLIAM, lawyer; b. Martinsville, Ind., Oct. 29, 1910; s. Sherman and Catherine Catherine (Owens) B.; LL.B., Ind. U., 1932; postgrad. Mich. U. Law Sch., 1937; m. Madge Mae Fesler, Aug. 26, 1932; children—Sandra K. (Mrs. Gene L. Fisher), Stephen F. Admitted to Ind. bar, 1932, since practiced in Indpls.; mem. firm Cadick, Burns, Duck & Neighbours. Fellow Am. Coll. Trial Lawyers, Am. Bar Found.; mem. Am., Ind. (pres. 1968), Indpls. (pres. 1951) bar assns. Home: 5151 Brendonshire Ct Indianapolis IN 46226 Office: Union Fed Bldg Indianapolis IN 46204

BURNS, FRITZ BERNARD, real estate developer; b. Mpls., Oct. 9, 1899; s. Patrick Henry and Marie Elise (Schreyer) B.; student U. Minn., 1918, U. Pa., Wharton Sch. Finance, 1919-20; LL.D., Loyola U., Los Angeles, 1963; m. Lucille Robison, June 10, 1924; 1 son, F. Patrick; m. 2d, Gladys Carson Scheller, Nov. 6, 1940. Successivley salesman, sales mgr., exec. v.p., pres. Dickinson & Gillespie Corp., 1916-32; partner Robert S. Burns in Del Rey Drilling Co., 1932-36; gen. partner Marlow-Burns Devel. Co., 1937-44, also Pasadena-Hastings Shopping Center; partner Munro-Burns Constrn. Co., 1968—, S. Pasadena Shopping Center; partner Henry J. Kaiser in bldg. communities, 1944-54; with Kaiser- Burns Devel. Co., builder Hawaiian village, Waikiki, 1954-60; chmn., chief exec. officer Fritz B. Burns & Assos., Los Angeles, 1960—, Santa Clara Indsl. Park, Airport-Marina Hotel, Fritz B. Burns & Son, Lincoln- Manchester Properties, Inc.; pres. Burns- Wilshire Corp., Panorama City Shopping Center, Playa del Rey Devel. Corp., Hilton-Burns Hotels Co., Inc., Hawaii; owner San Fernando Indsl. Park, Fritz Burns Reindeer Ranch; vice chmn. bd., dir. Hilton Hotels Corp.; dir. Dominguez Water Corp. Chmn. bd. trustees Burns Found. Served as 2d lt., inf., U.S. Army, 1918-19. Decorated knight sovereign Order of Malta; grand knight Knightly Order of St. Brigitte; recipient Builder of Yr. award Los Angeles Bldg. Contractors Assn., 1952, Man of Achievement award Los Angeles C. of C., 1955. Mem. Nat. Assn. Home Builders (pres. 1943), Home Builders Assn. Los Angeles (pres. 1942), Zeta Psi. Clubs: California (Los Angeles); Pacific (Honolulu). Home: 365 S Hudson Av Los Angeles CA 90020 Office: 4950 Wilshire Blvd Los Angeles CA 90010 also 4423 Kahala Av Honolulu HI 96815

BURNS, GEORGE, comedian; b. N.Y.C., Jan. 20, 1896; student pub. schs., N.Y.C.; m. Gracie Allen, Jan. 7, 1926 (dec.); adopted children—Sandra Jean, Ronald John. Began as dancer, vaudeville performer; formed team with Gracie Allen, 1923, team toured U.S. and Europe, making radio debut with B.B.C.; team began own radio show, 1932; screen debut, 1932, pictures include, The Big Broadcast (1932, 36, 37), International House, Love in Bloom, Two Girls and a Sailor; began own TV show, Oct. 1950; appeared TV show Wendy and Me, 1964-65. Home: Beverly Hills CA 90201

BURNS, GEORGE WASHINGTON, educator; b. Cin., Nov. 20, 1913; s. George Washington and Caroline (Little) B.; A.B., U. Cin., 1937; Ph.D., U. Minn., 1941; m. Hermine McDonald, June 15, 1942; children—George McDonald, Barbara Lynette, Theodore Scott. Teaching fellow botany U. Minn., 1937-41, instr., 1945- 46, faculty summer sessions, 1948-49; asst. prof. botany Ohio Wesleyan U., 1946-50, asso. prof., 1950-54, prof. botany, chmn. dept., 1954—, acting v.p., dean, 1957-59, acting pres., 1958-59, v.p., dean, 1959-61; vis. prof. Kerala U., India, 1964, U. Bombay (India), 1965, 66. Cons. State Dept. Edn. Mission to India, AID, summers 1964-67. Head insts. sect. NSF, 1961-62. Served as lt. USNR, 1942-45. Fellow A.A.A.S., Ohio Acad. Sci. (v.p. 1956-57, sec. 1957-63, pres. 1969-70); mem. Am. Genetic Assn., Am. Soc. Human Genetics, Bot. Soc.

Am., Arctic Inst. in N.Am. Sigma Xi. Methodist. Author: The Science of Genetics, 1969, 72; also articles in tech. jours. Home: 354 Troy Rd Delaware OH 43015 also Box 743 Eastham MA 02642

BURNS, HOBERT WARREN, coll. ofcl.; b. Los Angeles, Oct. 13, 1925; s. Hobert Washington and Ruth (Price) B.; A.A., Menlo (Cal.) Coll., 1948; A.B., Stanford, 1950, A.M., 1951, Ed.D. (trustees scholar, grantee Arthur A. Newhouse Found.), 1957; m. Patricia Rowe, 1954; children—Carol Lynne, Janifer Marie, Charles Rowe. Tchr., La Tuna Camp High Sch., Los Angeles, summer 1951, Muir Jr. High Sch., Burbank, Cal., 1951-53, Wilbur Jr. High Sch., Palo Alto, Cal., 1953-54, Jordan Jr. High Sch., Palo Alto, 1954-56; instr. Stanford, 1956-57; asst. prof. Rutgers U., 1957-60; asso. prof. Syracuse U., 1960-63, J. Richard Street lectr., 1963; prof. edn., dean Hofstra U. Sch. Edn., 1963-66; prof. edn., v.p. acad. affairs San Jose (Cal.) State Coll., 1966—, acting pres., 1969-70. Fulbright prof. U. de Chile, 1959; vis. prof. U. Hawaii, summer 1962, U. So. Cal., summer 1963, U. Cal. at Los Angeles, summer 1966. Field adviser UNESCO, 1959-60; cons. Conf. Bd. Asso. Research Councils, 1960, Council Higher Edn. in Am. Republics, 1960; adviser com. internat. relations in edn. Am. Assn. Colls. Tchr. Edn., 1961-62, mem. com. internat. relations, 1970—; adviser Fulbright tchr. exchanges Inst. Internat. Edn., 1961; adviser univ. relations and tng. Peace Corps, 1962; cons. higher edn. in Bolivia, AID, 1963; team mem. study tour higher edn. in Israel for State Dept., Israel Ministry Edn. and Culture, also Am. Assn. Colls. Tchr. Edn., 1965. Vice chmn. bd. trustees N. Shore Jr. Sci. Mus., 1964-66; trustee Citizens Exchange Corps.; bd. advisers Human Resources Sch. for Handicapped, 1965-67. Mem. Am. Assn. U. Profs. (editor bull. Rutgers U. 1958-59, mem. exec. bd. Rutgers U. chpt. 1959-60), Am. Philos. Assn., Comparative Edn. Soc., John Dewey Soc., Middle Atlantic States Philosophy Edn. Soc., Nat. Soc. Study Edn., Philosophy Edn. Soc. (sec.-treas., exec. bd. 1958-59), Phi Delta Kappa (cons. com. internat. edn. 1962). Author: The Critical Incident Technique as an Instrument of Educational Research: A Philosophic Analysis, 1957; The Great Debate: Our Schools in Crisis, 1959; (with C. J. Brauner) Essays in the Philosophy of Education, 1961; (with C.J. Brauner) Philosophy of Education: Essays and Commentaries, 1962, Problems in Education and Philosophy, 1965. Acad. editor Prentice-Hall Paperbacks in Founds. of Edn. Contbr. articles to profl. jours., chpts. in books. Home: 1527 Waverley Palo Alta CA 94301 Office: Adminstrn Bldg San Jose State College San Jose CA

BURNS, JAMES MACGREGOR, polit. scientist; b. Melrose, Mass. Aug. 3, 1918; s. Robert Arthur and Mildred Curry (Bunce) B.; B.A., Williams Coll., 1939; postgrad. Nat. Inst. Pub. Affairs, 1939-40; M.A., Ph.D., Harvard, 1947; postgrad. London Sch. Econs., 1949; m. Janet Rose Dismorr Thompson, May 23, 1942; children—David MacGregor, Timothy Stewart, Deborah Edwards, Margaret Rebecca Antonia; m. 2d, Joan Simpson Meyers, Sept. 7, 1969. Exec. sec. non ferrous metals commn. NWLB, 1942-43; faculty polit. sci. Williams Coll., Williamstown, Mass., 1941—, prof., 1953—. Mem. staff Hoover Commn., 1948; faculty Salzburg Seminar in Am. Studies, 1954, 61. Mem. Mass. delegation Democratic Conv., 1952, 56, 60, 64; Berkshire County delegation Mass. state conv., 1954; Dem. candidate for Congress, 1st Dist. Mass., 1958. Trustee Stockbridge Sch., Woodrow Wilson Internat. Center for Scholars. Served with AUS, 1943-45, combat historian Guam, Saipan, Okinawa. Recipient Tamiment Inst. award for best biography, 1956; Woodrow Wilson prize, 1957; Pulitzer prize in history, 1971; Nat. Book award, 1971; Francis Parkman prize, 1971. Mem. Am., New Eng. (pres. 1960-61) polit. sci. assns., Am. Hist. Assn., Am. Philos. Soc., Am. Civil Liberties Union, Am. Legion, Phi Beta Kappa, Delta Sigma Rho. Author: Guam: Operations of the 77th Infantry Div. 1944; Okinawa: The Last Battle (with others), 1947; Congress on Trial, 1949; Government by the People (with Jack W. Peltason), 1951; Roosevelt: The Lion and the Fox, 1956; John Kennedy: A Political Profile, 1960; The Deadlock of Democracy: Four Party Politics in America, 1963; Presidential Government: The Crucible of Leadership, 1966; Roosevelt: The Soldier of Freedom, 1970. Contbr. to periodicals. Home: High Mowing Bee Hill Williamstown MA 01267

BURNS, JAMES PATRICK, Sr., lawyer; b. Nickerson, Kan., June 13, 1896; s. John Edward and Dora May (Harden) B.; student Mont. State Coll., 1913-17; LL.B., George Washington U., 1924; m. Ada Lee Hall, Aug. 22, 1921 children—James Patrick, Wendell E.; m. 2d, Esther Green, 1957. Admitted to D.C. bar, 1923; sr. partner Burns, Doane, Benedict & Irons, (now Burns, Doane, Sweeker & Mathis), Washington, 1936—. Advt. com. sec. Commerce, 1955—. Served with USN, 1917-19; AEF. Mem. Am. Patent Law Assn. (pres. 1955-56), Am. (ho. of dels. 1957), D.C. bar assns., Delta Theta Phi. Mason. Home: 640 Park Av N Winter Park FL 37289 Office: 815 Connecticut Ave NW Washington DC 20006

BURNS, JAMES WILLIAM, ins. co. exec.; b. Winnipeg, Man., Can., Dec. 27, 1929; s. Charles William and Helen Gladys (Mackay) B.; B.Comm., U. Man., 1951; M.B.A., Harvard, 1953; m. Barbara Mary Copeland, Aug. 12, 1953; children—James F.C., Martha J., Alan W. With Great-West Life Assurance Co., 1953—, asst. in agy. dept., Winnipeg, 1953-55, supr. Chgo. br., 1955-57, mgr. field tng., Winnipeg, 1957-61, supt. agys., 1961-68, regional dir. Marketing, 1968-69, dir. U.S. marketing, 1969-70, exec. v.p., 1970, pres., dir., 1971—. Bd. dirs. Man. Mus. Man and Nature. Mem. U. Man. Alumni Assn. (pres. 1962-63). Clubs: Winter, St. Charles Country, Manitoba (Winnipeg); Albany (Toronto). Home: 116 Ash St Winnipeg 9 Manitoba Canada Office: 60 Osborne St N Winnipeg 1 Manitoba Canada

BURNS, JOHN ANTHONY, gov. Hawaii; b. Ft. Assinneboine, Mont., Mar. 30, 1909; s. Harry Jacob and Anne Florida (Scally) B.; student U. Hawaii, LL.D., (hon.), 1964; LL.D., St. Benedicts Colls., 1964, Gonzaga U., 1965; L.H.D., Chaminade Coll., 1963; m. Beatrice Majors Van Vleet, June 8, 1931; children—John Anthony, Mary Elizabeth, James Seishiro. Mem. Honolulu Police Dept., 1934-45, chief espionage bur., 1941-43; retail store operator, 1945-53; pres., mgr. Burns & Co., Ltd., real estate, 1946-62; Hawaii del. to Congress, 1956-59; gov. Hawaii, 1962—. Adminstr., Oahu Civil Def. Agy., 1951-55; presdl. rep. to South Pacific Conf., 1962; presdl. rep., spl. ambassador, head U.S. delegation to inauguration Korean pres., 1963; presdl. rep., spl. ambassador Independence of Botswana, 1966; presdl. rep., head U.S. delegation coronation King of Tonga, 1967. Organizer, Democratic party Hawaii; chmn. County Dem. Com., 1948-52, Central Com., 1952-56; del. Dem. Nat. Conv., 1952, 56, 60, 64. Named Outstanding Cath. Layman, 1959. Mem. Nat. Soc. Crippled Children and Adults (1st pres. Hawaii chpt.), 442d Vets., Honolulu C. of C. (hon.). Clubs: Waialae Country, Mid-Pacific Country, Aloha Civitan (hon.). Lion. Home: Washington Pl Honolulu HI Office: Governor's Office Honolulu HI 96813

BURNS, JOHN BRENDAN, communications cons.; b. Chgo; Apr. 20, 1918; s. John A. and Mary (Tighe) B.; student Northwestern U., De Paul U., John Marshall Law Sch.; m. Margaret Trude, Aug. 28, 1947. Librarian pub. schs., Chgo., 1939-40; newscaster, sportscaster radio sta. WTMA, Charleston, S.C., 1944-45; mem. sales staff radio sta. KROC, Rochester, Minn., 1949-50, radio sta. WGN, Chgo., 1950-52, ABC Radio Network central div., 1952-53; Midwest mgr. ABC Films, Inc., 1953-55, dir. nat. sales, 1955-59; dir. nat. sales MGM-TV, 1959-60, gen. sales mgr., 1960; v.p. Metro-Goldwyn-Mayer, Inc., 1960-70; communications cons., N.Y.C., 1970—. Mem. Acad. TV Arts and Scis., Internat. Radio and TV Soc. Elk. Clubs: Friars (N.Y.C.); Shawnee (Pa.) Country. Home: 50 Sutton Pl S New York City NY 10022 Office: 765 Fifth Av New York City NY 10022

BURNS, JOHN HOWARD, ambassador; b. Pauls Valley, Okla., Dec. 12, 1913; s. Arthur Parsons and Susan Elizabeth (Matthews) B.; student Denison U., 1931-32; A.B., U. Okla., 1935. Sec. to mem. U.S. Congress, 1939-41; fgn. service officer, 1941; vice consul, Ciudad Juarez, Mexico, 1941-43, Belem, Para, Brazil, 1943-44; 3d sec., later 2d sec. Am. embassy, Rio de Janeiro, Brazil, 1944-47; assigned Dept. of State, 1948-49; 1st sec. Am. embassy, Port-au-Prince, Haiti, 1949-51; fgn. service insp., 1952; Nat. War Coll., 1954; consul gen., Frankfurt-am-Main, Germany, 1955-57; assigned to Dept. State, 1957; 1st sec. Am. embassy, Bonn, Germany, until 1961; U.S. ambassador to Central African Republic, 1961-63; spl. asst. for internat. affairs to supreme allied comdr. Europe, SHAPE, 1963; U.S. ambassador to Tanzania, 1965—; dir. gen. Fgn. Service, 1969—. Clubs: Brook (N.Y.); Metropolitan, University, Federal City (Washington). Home: Pauls Valley OK 73075

BURNS, JOHN JOSEPH, research dir.; b. Flushing, N.Y., Oct. 8, 1920; s. Thomas F. and Katherine (Kane) B.; B.S., Queens Coll., 1942; M.A., Columbia, 1948, Ph.D., 1950. With lab. chem. pharmacology Nat. Heart Inst., 1950-60, dep. chief lab., 1957-60; head sec. clin. pharmacology, also adj. asst. prof. biochemistry N.Y.U. research service, Goldwater Meml. Hosp., Welfare Is., N.Y., 1950-57; dir. research pharmacodynamics div. Wellcome Research Labs., Burroughs Wellcome & Co. (U.S.A.) Inc., Tuckahoe, N.Y., 1960-66; v.p. for research Hoffman-LaRoche Inc., Nutley, N.J., 1967—. vis. prof. pharmacology Albert Einstein Coll. Medicine, 1960-68, Cornell U. Medical Coll. 1969—; sr. cons. pharmacology-toxicology programs NIH. Chmn. com. problems drug safety Drug Research Bd. Served with AUS, 1944-46. Fellow Am. Inst. Chemists; mem. Inst. Medicine, Nat. Acad. Scis., N.Y. Acad. Scis. (v.p.), Am. Soc. Pharmacology and Exptl. Therapeutics (pres.), Am. Soc. Biol. Chemists, Am. Inst. Nutrition, Am. Coll. Neuropsychopharmacology. Author articles metabolism drugs, vitamins and carbohydrates. Home: 500 E 77th St New York City NY 10021 Office: Hoffman-LaRoche Inc Nutley NJ 07110

BURNS, JOHN TOLMAN, mfg. exec.; b. Montgomery, Ala., May 16, 1922; s. Loren J. and Harriett (McFerran) B.; B.S., U. Louisville, 1943; m. Patricia Jacques, Sept. 25, 1954; children—Scott, Kent. Asst. hydraulic group engr. Douglas Aircraft Co., 1946-56; dist. sales mgr. aerospace div. Vickers, Inc., Torrance, Cal., 1956-58, gen. sales mgr., 1958-61, marketing mgr., 1961- 62, gen. mgr. European div. internat. div., 1962-64, v.p., gen. mgr., 1964-68; pres. Vickers div. Sperry Rand Corp., Troy, Mich., 1968—. Served to lt. (j.g.) USNG, 1944-46. Home: 4423 Ardmore Dr Bloomfield Hills MI 48013 Office: PO Box 302 Troy MI 48084

BURNS, JOSEPH BERNARD, mfg. co. exec.; b. Waterbury, Conn., July 22, 1915; s. Bernard John and Mary E. (Carroll) B.; B.A., U. Conn., 1936, LL.B., 1942; m. Dorothy E. Fitzpatrick, Nov. 30, 1939; children—Diane (Mrs. George D. Royster, Jr.), Sheila Jo (Mrs. Joel B. Rockwell). Admitted to Conn. bar, 1942; counsel Mfrs. Assn. Conn., 1943; prof. U. Conn. Coll. Law, 1942-68; with Fuller Brush Co., East Hartford, Conn., 1945—, v.p., 1964-68, pres., 1968- -; dir. Hartford Electric Light Co., United Bank & Trust Co., Hartford, Mohawk Brush Co., Albany, N.Y. Civilian aide to sec. army, 1968—. Pres. U. Conn. Found., 1965—, Central Conn. Communities Cultural and Civic Corp., 1967—. Mem. Am., Conn. bar assns. Republican. Roman Catholic. Clubs: Hartford, Hartford City; Avon (Conn.) Golf. Home: 112 Cliffmore Rd West Hartford CT 66107 Office: 88 Long Hill St East Hartford CT 06108

BURNS, KENNETH JONES, Jr., lawyer; b. Cleve., Oct. 3, 1926; s. Kenneth Jones and Isabel (Nanson) B.; B.S., Northwestern U., 1948, J.D., 1951; m. Edith Louise Mitten, June 23, 1949; children—Deborah, Kenneth Jones III, Sarah, Elizabeth, Nancy, Andrew. Admitted to Ill. bar, 1951; asso. Jenner & Block, Chgo., 1951-60, partner, 1961—; sec., dir. Enginuity, Inc. Legal counsel Chgo. Jr. Assn. Commerce and Industry, 1955-58; lectr. Northwestern U. Sch. Law, 1955; pres. Wilmette Civic Improvement Assn., 1958-62; v.p., dir. Citizens of Greater Chgo., 1961-64. Served with USNR, 1945-46, 51-52. Recipient Key award Chgo. Jr. Assn. Commerce, 1956. Mem. Am. (chmn. jr. bar conf. 1961-62, ho. of dels. 1962-64, 71—, asst. sec. 1967-71, sec. 1971—), Ill., Chgo. (bd. mgrs.) bar assns., Am. Judicature Soc., Chgo. Barrister Inn (pres. 1966-67), Order of Coif, Sigma Chi, Phi Delta Phi. Clubs: Skokie (Ill.) Country; Legal, Law (Chgo.). Home: 1511 Highland Av Wilmette IL 60091 Office: 135 S LaSalle St Chicago IL 60603

BURNS, LAWRENCE, lawyer; b. Corning, O., May 3, 1910; s. Lawrence and Anna (Amberge) B.; student Aquinas Coll., Columbus, O., 1928; J.D., Ohio State U., 1933; m. Elinor Bresnahan, Oct. 8, 1935; children—Lawrence (dec.), David William. Admitted to Ohio bar, 1933; practice of law, Coshocten, 1933—; atty. Coshocton Nat. Bank, Pa. R.R., Ohio Power Co. Bd. dirs. Nat. Bank of Dover (O.), Novelty Advt. Co., Buckeye Fabric Finishing Co., Auto Supply Co., Muskingum Valley Lumber Co., Coshocton. City solicitor, Coshocton, 1942-44; chmn. Republican County Exec. Com., 1943-62. Trustee Ohio Legal Center, Columbus. Served to lt. (s.g.) USNR, 1942-46. Mem. Am., Ohio (pres.), Coshocton County bar assns., Am. Judicature Soc., Ohio State U. Alumni Assn., C. of C., Internat. Assn. Ins. Counsels, Am. Coll. Probate Counsel. Rotarian. Home: Kensington Rd Coshocton OH Office: Coshocton Nat Bank Bldg Coshocton OH 43812

BURNS, MARVIN GERALD, lawyer; b. Los Angeles, July 3, 1930; s. Milton and Belle (Cytron) B.; B.A., U. Ariz., 1951; J.D., Harvard, 1954; m. Barbara Irene Fisher, Aug. 23, 1953; children—Scott Douglas, Jody Lynn, Bradley Frederick. Admitted to Cal. bar, 1955; partner firm Fulop, Rolston, Burns & McKittrick Beverly Hills, 1956—. Served with AUS, 1955-56. Club: Calabasas Park (Cal.) Tennis. Home: 5401 Aldea Av Encino CA 91316 Office: 9601 Wilshire Blvd Beverly Hills CA 90210

BURNS, MURRAY EDWIN, ret. constrn. co. exec.; b. Spokane, Wash., Nov. 29, 1898; s. Cyrus R. and Cyrus R. and Marietta (Tilsley) B.; grad. high sch.; m. Betty Bonnell, Apr. 23, 1921; children—Murray W., Robert N., Bartlett J., Bonny Jean (Mrs. Donald J. Baranco), Mary Ellen (Mrs. Leon W. Nowierski), Betty (Mrs. Charles Holt), Nancy Ann (Mrs. Dan Davis). Successively rodman, levelman, transitman Ore. Hwy. Dept., 1920-22; resident engr. Ida. Hwy. Dept., 1922-23; asst. engr. S.P. Co., 1923-30; constrn. supt. Morrison-Knudsen Co., Inc., 1930-32, dist. mgr., 1932-43, v.p., dir., 1946-69. Mem. lay bd. St. Alphonsus Hosp., Boise. Served with USMC, 1918-19; as col. C.E., AUS, 1943-46. Decorated Bronze Star, Legion of Merit. Mem. Asso. Gen. Contractors (pres. Ida. 1958). Republican. Episcopalian. Mason. Home: Sgay Ranch Route 2 Boise ID 83702

BURNS, NORMAN, econ., edn. cons.; b. Versailles, O., Nov. 14, 1905; s. Marley A. and Mabel (Bigler) B.; B.A., Wittenberg U., 1927, LL.D., 1962; M.A., Yale, 1929; postgrad. U. Montpellier, France, 1932-33; m. Constance Albrech, July 8, 1935. Asst. prof. econs. Am. U. of Beirut, 1929-32; lectr. Middle East econ. problems Sch. Advanced Internat. Studies, Johns Hopkins, 1951-53; tariff economist U.S. Tariff Commn., Washington, 1934- 41; adviser internat. trade policy U.S. Dept. State, 1944-49, prin. economist Middle East affairs, 1949-51, dir. Fgn. Service Inst., also dep. examiner Bd. Examiners for Fgn. Service, 1951- 53, chief econ. adviser to UN Relief and Works Agency, Beirut, 1953-56, dep. regional dir. for Near East, South Asia and Africa, ICA, Dept. of State, 1956-59; dir. U.S. Operations Mission to Jordan, 1959-61; pres. Am. U. of Beirut (Lebanon), 1961-65. Bd. govs. Middle East Inst., Washington, 1967—; bd. dirs., v.p. Am. Near East Refugee Aid Inc., 1968- 1968- . Mem. Am. Fgn. Service Assn. Clubs: Dacor, Cosmos (Washington). Home: 3813 N 37th St Arlington, VA 22207

BURNS, NORMAN, educator; b. Syracuse, N.Y., Apr. 4, 1907; s. Arthur P. and Ivy (Van Norman) B.; B.S., U. Buffalo, 1929; M.B.A., Northwestern U., 1933; Ph.D., U. Chgo., 1945; LL.D., U. Ark., 1956; D.Litt., U. Cin., 1970; m. Imogene Stark, m. Imogene Stark, June 26, 1935; 1 dau., Imogene Ruth. Asst. prof. edn. U. Chgo., 1945-48, asso. prof. edn., 1948-53. prof. edn., 1953—; dir. Survey State- Controlled Higher Edn. in Ark., 1949-50; participant numerous ednl. surveys higher edn., 1940—; dir. leadership tng. project under auspices North Central Assn. Colls. and Secondary Schs., financed by Carnegie Corp., 1957—; sec. commn. on colls. and univs. North Central Assn., 1946—, exec. exec. sec. and editor publs., 1960—; exec. dir. Fedn. Regional Accrediting Commns. Higher Edn.; ednl. cons. groups and colls., also govts. Pakistan and Iraq. Mem. N.E.A., Assn. Higher Edn., Am. Assn. U. Profs. Author: (with R.J. Kibbee) State Controlled Higher Education in Arkansas, 1951, also numerous articles. Editor: The Administration of Higher Institutions under Changing Conditions, 1947; (with C.O. Houle) The Community Responsibilities of Institutions of Higher Learning, 1948. Mem. yearbook com., contbg. author Public Junior College, 57th yearbook of Nat. Soc. Study Edn., 1956. Frequent keynote speaker. Home: 10 Crest Dr Dune Acres Chesterton IN 46304

BURNS, PAUL YODER, univ. adminstr.; b. Tulsa, July 4, 1920; s. Paul Patchin and Mary Emily (Knowles) B.; B.S., U. Tulsa, 1941; student N.Y. U., 1942; M.F., Yale, 1946, Ph.D., 1949; m. Kathleen Iola Chase, Dec. 4, 1942; children—Virginia Kathleen, Margaret Evelyn, Nancy Chase. Asst. prof. forestry U. Mo., 1948-53, asso. prof., 1953-55; dir. Sch. Forestry, prof. forestry La. State U., 1955—. Mem. La. Forestry Commn.; dir. La. Forest Festival Assn.; chmn. forestry com. So. Regional Edn. Bd. Served from cadet to capt. USAAF, 1942-45; weather officer. Mem. La. Forestry Assn. (dir.), Council Forest Sch. Execs., Forest Farmers Assn. (mem. So. Weed Conf.), Univ. Christian Council Assn. (dir.), Am. Assn. U. Profs., Weed Soc. Am., Soc. Am. Foresters, Am. Forestry Assn., Forest Products Research Soc., Sigma Xi, Alpha Zeta, Xi Sigma Pi, Phi Kappa Phi. Presbyn. (elder). Editor: Forest Management in Plan and Practice, 1956; Southern Forest Soils, 1959. Author sci. papers, bulls. Home: 2137 Cedardale St Baton Rouge LA 70808

BURNS, RALPH ARTHUR, educator; b. Vinalhaven, Me., Apr. 5, 1897; s. Willie Horace and Carrie (Hopkins) B.; A.B., Bates Coll., 1920; Ed.M., Harvard, 1926; A.M. (hon.), Dartmouth, 1934; LL.D., Farleigh Dickinson Coll., 1954; Ed.D., Northeastern U., 1968; L.H.D., Emerson Coll., 1968; Ed.D., Northeastern U., 1969; Ped.D., Franklin Pierce Coll., 1971; m. Ethel Emroye Magwood, July 7, 1920; children—Robert Edwin, Elizabeth, William Arthur. Supervising prin. pub. schs., Cornish, Rockport, Me., 1920-24; prin. Am. Sch. Found., Mexico City, 1924-25; instr. Carleton Coll., 1926- 27; faculty Dartmouth, 1927—, prof. edn., chmn. dept., 1934-63, emeritus, 1963—. Dir. evaluation program Commn. on Instns. Higher Edn., New Eng. Assn. Colls. and Secondary Schs., Boston, 1964—; chief cultural affairs br. Edn. and Cultural Relations Div., Office Mil. Govt. U.S., Bad Nauheim, Germany, 1948-49. Chief exchanges div. Office U.S. High Commr. Germany, 1949-52; Am. specialist Dept. State to Nat. U. Asuncion, Paraguay, 1959-60. Served as lt. col. USAF, 1942-45. Recipient Gold medal Paraguay, 1959; Bundesverdienst-kreuz, Germany, 1960; named hon. prof. Nat. U. Asuncion, 1960. Mem. Am. Legion, N.E.A., Soc. Mayflower Descs., Descs. Colonial Clergy Soc., Hanover Hist. Soc., S.A.R., Internat. Platform Assn., Dragon, Phi Beta Kappa, Phi Delta Kappa, Sigma Phi Epsilon. Mem. Ch. of Christ. Home: 4 Hovey Lane Hanover NH 03755

BURNS, RAYMOND JOSEPH, detective agy. exec.; b. Columbus, O., Mar. 25, 1886; s. William J. and Annie M. (Ressler) B.; student Ohio State U., 1905-06; m. Gladys Sykes, Apr. 9, 1907; 1 son, William J. With William J. Burns Internat. Detective Agy., Inc., 1909—, pres., 1948-55, chmn. bd. 1954-64, chmn. exec. com., 1964-70, also dir. Mem. Ohio Soc. N.Y., Delta Chi. Clubs: Union League, N.Y. Athletic, Sky, Cloud (dir. N.Y.C.); Sleepy Hollow Country (Scarborough, N.Y.); Lyford Cay (Nassau, B.W.I.). Home: 30 E 65th St New York City NY 10021 Office: 320 Old Briarcliff Rd Briarcliff Manor NY 10510

BURNS, ROBERT EDWARD, editor, publisher; b. Chgo., May 14, 1919; s. William Joseph and Sara (Foy) B.; student De Paul U., 1937-39; Ph.B., Loyola U., Chgo., 1941; m. Brenda Coleman, May 15, 1948; children—Maddy F., Martin J. Pub. relations dir. Cath. Youth Orgn., Chgo., 1943-45, 47-49; exec. dir. No. Ind. region Nat. Conf. Christians and Jews, 1946; exec. editor U.S. Cath. mag., gen. mgr. Claretian Publs., Chgo., 1949—. Trustee Rosary Coll.; bd. dirs. Thomas More Assn. Home: 616 High Rd Glen Ellyn IL 60137 Office: 221 W Madison St Chicago IL 60606

BURNS, ROBERT HENRY, hotel exec.; b. Orange, N.J., July 5, 1929; s. Robert Henry and Lillian (Giessen) B.; B.A., Mich. State U., 1958; postgrad. U. Mich., 1959. Exec. positions Sheraton Corp. Am., Honolulu, 1958-62; gen. mgr. Colony Surf Hotel, Honolulu, 1962-63; gen. mgr. Kahala Hilton Hotel, Honolulu, 1963—; vis. lectr. U. Hawaii, 1962—, also chmn. bus. adv. coml.; East-West Center cons.-Far East; adviser Sch. Hotel, Restaurant and Inst. Mgmt. Mich. State U.; U.S. State Dept. sponsored seminars Far East (Bangkok, Thailand, Manila, Philippines, Seoul, Korea); vis. lectr. Peace Corps Tng. Camp, Molokai, 1966. Treasurer, Hawaii Nani-Loa Committee. Served to capt., arty., with U.S. Army, 1953-56. Recipient Dist. Service award Coll. Bus. U. Hawaii, 1966. Mem. Hawaii Hotel Assn. (pres. 1968). Address: 5000 Kahala Av Honolulu, HI 96815

BURNS, ROBERT KENNETH, coll. dean; b. Alberta, Can., Jan. 6, 1909; s. Ira A. and Benedicta (Sawby) B.; A.B., U. Wash., 1933; student London Sch. Econs., 1934-35; Ph.D., U. Chgo., 1940; m. Ara Lee Malach, 1945; children—Malcom, Alan, Lawton. Came to U.S., 1915, naturalized, 1916. Researcher Social Sci. Research Council, 1932, Twentieth Century Fund, 1939; mem. Round-the- World Debater's Tour, U.S. Office Edn., 1933-34; organizer Sci. Research Asso. (with Lyle M. Spencer), 1937; staff sch. bus. and social scis., div. U. Chgo., 1940—, exec. officer indsl. relations center, 1946—, prof. bus. social sci., 1948-68, now prof. bus. Admin. former asso. dean school of business. Pres., Veritas Co., 1960—; dir. Am. Photocopy Equipment Co., Exchange Nat. Bank, Chgo., Paddock Corp. Pres. Allied Education Council. Principal mediation officer with the Nat. War Labor bd., 1942, regional dir. 6th dist., 1942-43, chmn., 1943-45, now mem. staff. Elected one of 10 outstanding young men U.S. Jr. C. of C., 1942. Mem. Am. Econ. Assn., Royal Econ. Soc., Sigma Phi Epsilon. Presbyn. Author: Collective Bargaining in the Daily Newspaper Industry, 1941; The Employment Opportunities of Today, 1941; Uncle Sam's Fighting Men, 1942; Youth Goes to War, 1943; White Collar Unionism, 1954. Home: 5533 S Woodlawn Av Chicago IL 60637

BURNS, ROBERT KYLE, former embryologist, anatomist; b. Hillsboro, W.Va., July 26, 1896; s. William McLauren and Sarah Elizabeth (White) B.; student U. Va., summer 1915; A.B., Bridgewater Coll., 1916; Sc.D., 1953; Ph.D., Yale, 1924; m. Emily Lucile Moore, June 21, 1924; children—Robert Kyle, William Moore, John McLauren. Instr. biology Bridgewater Coll., 1916-17; fellow in zoölogy Yale, 1920-24; instr. zoölogy U. Cin., 1924-25, asst. prof. 1925-28; asst. prof. anatomy U. Rochester, 1928-30, asso. prof., 1930-40; staff mem. Carnegie Instn. Washington, Balt., 1940-62; interim prof. zoology Bridgewater (Va.) Coll., 1962-67. Lectr. zoology U. Cal., Santa Barbara, 1965; staff, biol. sta. U. Va., 1940-46; hon. prof. zoology Johns Hopkins, 1945—; vis. prof. U. Fla., 1955; exchange prof. Sorbonne, U. Paris, 1955-56; adj. prof. zoology U. Fla., Tampa. Served as pvt. USMC, 1918-19. Mem. A.A.A.S., Nat. Acad. Scis., Internat. Inst. Embryology, Am. Soc. Zoology, Am. Assn. Anatomists, Am. Soc. Naturalists, Soc. for Growth and Devel., Sigma Xi, Gamma Alpha. Contbr. articles to sci. jours., various books. Home: 303 N 2d St Bridgewater VA 22812

BURNS, ROBERT M., automotive exec.; b. Spurgeon, Ind., Nov. 8, 1915; s. Reece A. and Clara (Scales) B.; A.B., Ind. U., 1937; m. Mary E. Jackson, May 12, 1938; children—Sandra Sue (Mrs. Robert J. Kessler), Betsy Ann (Mrs. Lee Clark), Richard Reece. Prodn. mgr. P.R. Mallory, Inc., N. Tareytown, N.Y., 1945-55; v.p. Mallory Plastic div., Chgo., 1955-57; exec. v.p. Victor Mfg. & Gasket Co., Chgo., 1957-66; gen. mgr. Victor div. Dana Corp., Chgo., 1966-69; pres., dir. Holley, Inc. Carburetor, subsidiary of Colt Industries, Warren, Mich., 1969—; dir. Bowling Green Mfg. Co. (Ky.), Paris Mfg. Co. (Tenn.), Mickey Thompson Enterprises, Inc., Warren. Mem. sch. bd., Croton, N.Y., 1954-55. Bd. dirs. Elmhurst (Ill.) YMCA, 1966-69. Mem. Soc. Automotive Engrs. Clubs: Detroit Athletic; Oakland Hills Country (Birmingham). Home: 2061 Avon Lane Birmingham MI 48009 Office: 11955 E Nine Mile Rd Warren MI 48090

BURNS, ROBERT OBED, engr., physicist; b. Emporia, Kan., Jan. 16, 1910; s. Elmer Emmett and Catherine (Crocker) B.; B.S., Knox Coll., 1931; M.S., U. Ill., 1933, Ph.D., 1937; m. Margaret Holte, Sept. 7, 1937. Physicist, Celotex Corp., 1937-42, asst. dir. research engring., 1942-43; physicist U. Cal. div. war research, San Diego, 1943, engring. mgr., 1943-45, asst. dir. 1945; head devel. dept. Navy Electronics Lab., San Diego, 1946-49, head systems dept., 1949-52; chief scientist Electronics Warfare Center, Ft. Monmouth, N.J., 1952-54, Army Electronic Proving Ground, Ft. Huachuca, Ariz., 1954-56; devel. coordinator USN, 1956-59, dir. devel. planning, 1959-62, dir. tech. analysis and adv. group, 1962—. Mem. I.E.E.E., Accoustical Soc. Am., A.A.A.S., Operations Research Soc. Am., Am. Soc. for Pub. Adminstrn., Phi Beta Kappa, Sigma Xi, Phi Sigma Kappa, Phi Kappa Phi, Mason. Home: 5007 Dodson Dr Annandale VA 22003 Office: Office Chief of Naval Operations Washington DC 20350

BURNS, ROBERT WHITEHALL, clergyman; b. Merchantville, N.J., Jan. 20, 1904; s. Walter S. and Emily (Elms) B.; student Drake U., 1921-24, D.D., 1963; B.A., Washington U., 1927; B.D., Eden Theol. Sem., 1930; D.D., Oglethorpe U., 1936; D.S.T., Milligan Coll., 1967; m. Agnes Neff, June 25, 1927; children—Robert Whitehall, Frank Neff, Virginia (Mrs. C.R. Anderson), J. Bricker. Ordained to ministry Christian Ch., 1924; pastor Chesterfield Christian Ch., Des Moines, 1923- 24, Webster Groves (Mo.) Christian Ch., 1924-28; First Christian Ch., Maryville, Mo., 1928-30, Peachtree Christian Ch., Atlanta, 1930—. Pres., Internat. Youth Conv. Christian Chs., 1928-30, Internat. Conv. Christian Chs. U.S. and Can., 1962-63, Child's Service Assn., 1934-38; mem. bd. Christian Chs. of Ga.; dir. Christian Coll. of Ga.; exec. trustee Atlanta Child's Home; pres., sr. counselor Christian Ch. Counseling, Inc., 1967—. Clubs: Campbell (Chgo.); Authors (London); Atlanta Athletic, Piedmont Driving (Atlanta). Author: The Christian Life, 1930; The Art of Staying Happily Married, 1963. Home: 1730 Barnesdale Way Atlanta GA 30309 Office: 1580 Peachtree St Atlanta GA 30309

BURNS, ROBERT WIYGUL, air force officer; b. Nettleton, Miss., Dec. 8, 1916; s. Eliam Baxter and Virginia Mary (Wiygul) B.; B.S., U. So. Miss., 1938; grad. USAAF Advanced Flying Sch., 1939, Armed Forces Staff Coll., 1949, Nat. War Coll., 1958; M.A., George Washington U., 1966; m. Ruth Josephine Blackburn, Oct. 23, 1945; children—Robert Andrew, Susan Jane, Mary Rebecca. Commd. 2d lt. USAAF, 1939, advanced through grades to maj. gen. USAF, 1965; dep comdr., then comdr. 351st Bomb Group, Eng., World War II; chief Mil. Assistance Adv. Group, Pakistan, 1965-67; comdr. 19th Air Force Tactical Air Command, 1967-68, 4th Air Force Aerospace Def. Command, 1968—. Mem. exec. council San Francisco area Boy Scouts Am., 1968—. Bd. dirs. San Francisco Bay Area USO. Decorated Silver Star, Legion of Merit with one oak leaf cluster, D.F.C. with one oak leaf cluster, Air medal with four oak leaf clusters, Army Commendation medal; Croix de Guerre with palm. Mem. Air Force Assn. Methodist. Mason (Shriner), Rotarian. Home: 2440 Pretty Bayou Panama City FL 32401 Office: PO Box 1997 Panama City FL 32401

BURNS, ROY RASBURY, petroleum co. exec.; b. Florence, Ala., July 1, 1905; s. Lytle and Ida (Rankin) B.; B.S. in Chem. Engring., Auburn U., 1927; m. Elizabeth Brittain, Oct. 2, 1930; children—Elizabeth Mayfield (Mrs. Ed R. Davies), Robert Brittain, Cecelia Vance. With Tennessee Corp., 1927-71. mgr. copper div., 1954-61, corp. v.p., dir., mem. research com., 1962-63, pres., 1963-71. pres. Capital Fertilizer Co., 1964-71, New Haven Copper Co., 1964-71; group v.p. chems. and metals div. Cities Service Co., 1971—. Dir. Cities Service Co. Dir. So. States Indsl. Council. Vice pres. Tenn. area council Boy Scouts Am., 1950. Mem. Am. Inst. Mining and Metall. Engrs., Am. Chem. Soc., Am. Inst. Chemists, Am. Ordnance Assn., Mining and Metall. Soc. Am. Conglist. Kiwanian. Clubs: Mining, Lawyers (N.Y.C.); Morris County Golf, Atlanta Athletic. Home: Nottingham Rd Short Hills NJ 07078

BURNS, STEPHEN JOSEPH, corp. lawyer; b. Bklyn., Nov. 7, 1929; s. John Aleysius and Florence (Doyle) B.; B.S., Fordham Coll., 1951, LL.B., 1956; m. Helen Carter McGrover, Aug. 11, 1956; children—Mary Jo, Stephen Joseph, Ellen. Admitted to N.Y. bar, 1957, Ohio bar, 1966; gen. counsel Underwood Corp., N.Y.C., 1960-61; asst. sec., counsel Worthington Corp., 1962—; sec. subsidiary Alco Products, Inc., 1965-66; sec., gen. counsel Reliance Electric Co., Cleve., 1966—. Served as 1st lt. USMCR, 1951-53. Mem. Am. Bar Assn., Assn. Bar City N.Y. Democrat. Roman Catholic. Home: 21316 Fairmount Blvd Shaker Heights OH 44118 Office: 24701 Euclid Av Cleveland OH 44177

BURNS, THAGRUS ASHER, life ins. co. exec.; b. Columbia City, Ind., Feb. 19, 1917; s. Harlow A. and Hazlette (Wise) B.; A.B., Wabash Coll., 1939; m. Dorothy Kimble, May 1, 1942; children—Steven L., Gerald A. With Lincoln Nat. Life Ins. Co., Ft. Wayne, Ind., 1939—, treas., 1967—; treas. Lincoln Nat. Life Co., 1967—, Lincoln Nat. Corp., 1968—. Treas., dir. Lincoln Nat. Life Found. Served to lt. USNR, 1942- 45. Mem. Financial Execs. Inst., Phi Beta Kappa. Inventor automatic feeder for typewriter and inserting machine. Home: 8710 Maraville Dr Fort Wayne IN 46805 Office: 1301 S Harrison St Fort Wayne IN 46801

BURNS, THOMAS DAVID, lawyer; b. Andover, Mass., Apr. 4, 1921; s. Joseph Lawrence and Catherine (Horne) B.; grad. Phillips Andover Acad., 1938; student Brown U., 1938-41; LL.B., Boston U., 1943; m. Sylvia Lansing, Sept. 14, 1946; children-Wendy (Mrs. Christopher L. Tilghman), Lansing, Diane, Lisa. Admitted to Mass. bar, 1944, since practiced in Boston; asso. Friedman, Atherton, King & Turner, 1946-50, partner, 1950-60; sr. partner Burns & Levinson, 1960—; sponsor, lectr. New Eng. Law Innst. Chmn. Planning Bd. Appeal, Andover, 1955-57. Chmn. Republican Andover Finance Com., 1950- 51; mem. Rep. Town Com., 1953-57. Trustee, clk. mem. exec. com. Pike Sch., Andover; mem. alumni council Phillips Andover Acad., Boston U. Law Sch. Served to lt. USNR, 1942-46; ETO, PTO. Fellow Am. Coll. Trial Lawyers (bd. regents, 1970—, past state chmn.); mem. Found. Am. Coll. Trail Lawyers (dir. 1969—), Internat. Assn. Ins. Counsel, Def. Research Inst. (past state chmn.), Am., Boston (mem. exec. council) bar assns., Delta Kappa Epsilon. Clubs: Union (Boston), North Andover Country. Author: Cross Examination, 1963; Medical Advocacy, 1961. Home: 675 Great Pond Rd North Andover MA 01845 Office: 77 Franklin St Boston MA 02110

BURNS, VINCENT GODFREY, poet, lectr., writer; b. Bklyn., Oct. 17, 1893; s. James H. and Katherine (Rossberg) B.; B.S., Pa. State Coll., 1916 (John W. White prize fellowship); A.M., Harvard, 1917; B.D., Union Theol. Sem., 1922; postgrad. Columbia, 1922-24; m. Edna Rodenberger, June 15, 1924; 1 dau., Barbara; m. 2d, Katherine Howard, Aug. 21, 1945; 2 sons, Vincent Howard, Victor David. Ordained to ministry Congl. Ch., 1920; successively pastor of City Park Chapel (Presbyn.) Bklyn. South Congl. Ch., Pittsfield, Mass., Central Christian Ch., N.Y.C., until 1929, pastor Union Ch. (Community), Palisade, N.J., 1929-36; leader Log Cabin Shrine, 1936—; pastor Community Ch., Washington, 1953—; spl. lectr. U. Kan., 1952-53, U. Wis., 1953-54; radio artist (as Bobby Burns, poet of the air), recitalist (chiefly poetry) and lecturer. Served to lt. U.S. Army, 1918; grad. Saumur F.A. Sch.; served on staff of Gen. Foote, 193d F.A. Brigade. Chmn. bd. Ft. Lee Pub. Library, N.J. Recipient Gold medal Freedoms Found., 1958; named poet laureate of Md., 1962; founder Poet Laureate's Com. of 100. Mem. Internat. Platform Assn. (poet laureate), Composers, Authors and Artists Am. (pres. chpt.), Vets. World War I, Md. Poetry Soc. (pres. 1964), Am. Legion, Alpha Zeta, Delta Sigma Rho, Phi Kappa Phi. Mason, Odd Fellow, Jr. O.U.A.M. Founder Nat. Poetry Clubs, Santa Barbara Theatre Guild. Club: Rockland County Golf (Nyack, N.Y.). Author: The Master's Message for the New Day, 1926; (with brother Robert Burns), I am a Fugitive from a Georgia Chain Gang, 1932; I'm in Love with Life, 1933; Female Convict, 1934; Heavenly Vision, 1939; Out of These Chains, 1942; I Am My Brother's Keeper (play) 1942; Heart on Fire, 1943; also author (brochures) Fosdick and the Fundamentalists, Health Is Life; Redwood and Other Poems, 1952; World on Fire (play), 1952; poem A Nation Prayed (awarded Freedoms Found. Gold Medal), 1953; America, I Love You, 1957; Vagabond's Luck, 1958; Flame Against The Night (poems), 1960; Poetry for Young Americans 1962; Maryland's Revolutionary Hero, story of Col. Tench Tilghman, 1963; Memories and Melodies of Maryland, 1964; Still Life (poems), 1969; Red Fuse on a World Bomb, 1969; The Sunny Side of Life (poems), 1970. Editor: The Red Harvest (verse), 1930, Youth Dreams (mag.); The Rainbow (poetry mag.); An American Poet Speaks, 1965; Four Tests of a Loyal American, 1966; The Man Who Broke a Thousand Chains, 1968; Songs of the Free State Bards, 1968; Ballads of the Free State Bard, 1968; asso. editor, Poetry Caravan. Contbr. to mags. Public address Four Fundamentals of American Idealism (Freedoms Found. top honors, George Washington Gold Medal, 1955). Home: Epping Forest Annapolis MD 21401

BURNS, WARD, textile co. exec.; b. New Bedford, Mass., May 31, 1928; s. Frederick Lloyd and Pauline (Ward) B.; grad. St. Paul's Sch., Garden City, N.Y., 1946; B.A., Amherst Coll., 1950; M.B.A., Harvard, 1952; spl. student N.Y.U., 1955-57; m. Cynthia A. Butterworth, Dec. 19, 1964; children—Helen Abby, David Ward. Mgr. Price Waterhouse & Co., C.P.A.'s, N.Y.C., 1954-62; asso. Laurence S. and David Rockefeller, Brussels, Belgium, 1962-65; with J.P. Stevens & Co., Inc., N.Y.C., 1965—, comptroller, 1969—; dir. J.P. Stevens & Co. (U.K.), Ltd., SOVCOR, BARA (both Paris), ELRON, Tel Aviv, Israel; cons. ARS, Milan, Italy, HVL, Brussels, ARCO, Florence and Milan, 1963-65. Treas., dir. Internat. Sch. Brussels, 1963-65; pres. bd. dirs. Internat. Sch. Brussels Found., N.Y.C., 1965—. Served as capt. USAF, 1952-53. C.P.A., N.Y. Mem. Am. Inst. C.P.A.'s, N.Y. State Soc. C.P.A.'s, Financial Execs. Inst., St. Andrews Soc., Phi Alpha Psi, Phi Kappa Psi. Club: University (N.Y.C.). Mem. editorial adv. bd. Jour. Accountancy, 1969—. Home: Angus Lane Greenwich CT 06830 Office: 1185 Av of Americas New York City NY 10036

BURNS, WARREN W., hosp. supt., psychiatrist; b. Manchester, N.H., Aug. 21, 1912; s. Harrison M. and Winnifred (Whitcomb) B.; B.S., U. N.H., 1933; M.D., C.M., McGill U., 1939; m. Mary H. Griggs, Dec. 15, 1939; children—Allan, Carol (Mrs. Bruce McDermott), Alison (Mrs. Warner Seeger), David, Diane (Mrs. Richard Marcott), Dorothy, Victoria. Intern, Lynn (Mass.) Hosp., 1940-41; psychiat. resident Norwich (Conn.) Hosp., 1953-56; pvt. practice, Monroe, N.H., 1941-45, Manhattan, Kan., 1945-53; psychiatrist Norwich Hosp., 1953-66; supt. N.H. Hosp., Concord, 1966-69; dep. supt. Laconia (N.H.) State Sch. and Tng. Center, 1969—. Fellow Am. Psychiat. Assn.; mem. New Eng. Soc. Psychiatry (pres. 1965), Hartford Psychiat. Assn. (pres. 1960). Address: Laconia State Sch and Tng Center Laconia NH 03246

BURNS, WILLIAM A., museum adminstr., author; b. N.Y.C., Oct. 7, 1909; s. William A. and Florence (Willis) B.; B.A., Manhattan Coll., 1934; M.A., Columbia, 1937, Ed.D., 1949; m. Adelaide Jordan, Oct. 7, 1955; Field dir. Occupational Adjustment Study, 1939-40; with Am. Mus. Natural History, N.Y.C., 1940-62, asso. curator dept. edn., asst. chmn. dept., 1945-51, asst. to dir., membership sec., editor popular publs., 1951-62; dir. Witte Meml. Mus., San Antonio, 1962-70; exec. dir., sec. bd. dirs. San Diego Natural History Mus., 1970—. Mem. adv. bd. Florence (S.C.) Mus., Gay Head Mus., Fairfield County (Conn.) Mus. Art, Sci. and Industry, Nimitz Mus.; mem. cultural adv. com. Hemis Fair '68; mem. Inter-Am. Ednl. Commn., Latin Am.. Studies Conf. Mem. environmental ednl. adv. com. U.S. Dept. Health, Edn. and Welfare; mem. Creative Ednl. Resources Com. Exec.. Council, City of San Diego; mem. inter-museums council Balboa Parks Museums. Bd. dirs. San Antonio A.R.C., Children's Symphony Music Fair, Craft Guild, Weavers' Guild; trustee San Antonio Art League. Served to 1st lt. AUS, 1943-46. Mem. Mexican- Am. Art Council, San Antonio Little Theater, Am. Assn. Museums (council), Assn. Sci. Mus. Dirs. (pres.), Internat. Council Museums, Tex. Mus. Conf., Tex. Art Mus. Conf., Tex., Bexar County (survey commn.) hist. socs., Trinity U. Library Council, Sci. Dirs. Assn., San Antonio Conservation Soc., San Antonio Art Guild, Rocks and Minerals Soc., Nat. Speleological Soc., Chamber Music Soc., Kappa Delta Pi, Gamma Theta Upsilon. Rotarian. Clubs: Jazz Society, Torch, Alamo, Press, Argyle, Shell, Manuscript; University. Author: A World Full of Homes; Horses and Their Ancestors; Man and His Tools; Exploring for Fun; Your Future in Museums. Editor: Natural History of the Southwest; Witte Mus. Quar., 1963-70. Co-editor: Illustrated World Geography. Home: 5030 Merrimac Ct San Diego CA 92117 Office: San Diego Natural History Mus PO Box 1390 San Diego CA 92112

BURNS, WILLIAM ALBERT, mfg. exec.; b. Chgo., Dec. 14, 1911; s. William Albert and Helen Mary (Maurice) B.; Ph.B., U. Chgo., 1936; M.B.A., U. Cal., Berkeley, 1969; m. Florence Gerwig, Feb. 27, 1937; children—William Albert, Robert Gerwig, Bonnie Louise. Cons. A.T. Kearney Co., 1935-40; v.p., gen. mgr. James H. Rhodes & Co., 1940-45, Wesco Foods Co. (subsidiary of Kroger Co.), 1945-50; v.p., sales mgr. Trailmobile Co., Cin., 1950-66; pres. Trailmobile, Inc., Cin., 1952-64; dir. Martin Marietta Corp., Nuclear Chgo. Corp.; lectr. Grad. Sch. Bus. Adminstrn., U. Cal., Berkeley, 1965—. Home: 40 N Hill Ct Oakland CA 94618

BURNS, WILLIAM GRADY, lawyer; b. Ashdown, Ark., Apr. 16, 1907; s. William Franklin and Ida (Graham) B.; Ph.B., U. Chgo., 1929, J.D., 1931; m. Margaret McDonald, Nov. 28, 1934; children—Margaret Ann, Susan, Catherine, Graham William, David John. Admitted to Ill. bar, 1931, since practiced in Chgo.; mem. firm Bell, Boyd, Lloyd, Haddad & Burns and predecessors, 1943—. Mem. Joseph Sears Bd. Edn., Kenilworth, 1956-62, pres. bd., 1960; trustee Village of Kenilworth, 1965-69; chmn., vice chmn. rev. coms. Community Fund Chgo., 1965-70; mem. citizens bd. and nat. devel. council U. Chgo.; mem. nat. panel Am. Arbitration Assn., 1965—. Mem. Am., Ill., Chgo. bar assns., Law Club Chgo., Legal Club Chgo., U. Chgo. Law Sch. Alumni Assn. (pres., dir.), Phi Beta Kappa, Order of Coif, Delta Tau Delta, Phi Delta Phi. Republican. Baptist. Clubs: University (Chicago), Economic, Commercial, Attic (dir.) (Chgo.), Kenilworth (pres. 1965-66), Westmoreland Country (Wilmette, Ill.). Home: 320 Cumberland Av Kenilworth IL 60043 Office: 135 LaSalle St Chicago IL 60603

BURNS, WILLIAM OLIVER, ins. co. exec.; b. Monticello, Ill., June 24, 1930; s. Guy O. and Nellie (McWhorter) B.; B.S., U. Ill., 1954; m. Marilyn Cannon, Aug. 10, 1962; children—Lindsay Clodfelter, Michael Clodfelter. With State Farm Life Ins. Co., Bloomington, Ill., 1959—, controller, 1961-64, v.p., controller, 1964-67, v.p., 1967—. Mem. adv. bd. St. Josephs Hosp. Served with AUS, 1951-53. Fellow Soc. Acturaries, Life Office Mgmt. Inst.; mem. Am. Coll. Life Underwriters, Financial Execs. Inst. Home: 302 Granada Rd Bloomington IL 61701 Office: 112 E Washington St Bloomington IL 61701

BURNS, WILLIAM S., business exec.; b. Lebanon, Va., Aug. 30, 1917; s. Clarence Clifton and Nora (Shuler) B.; A.B., Washington and Lee U., 1938, LL.B., 1940; m. Mary Ann Swanger, Feb. 3, 1944; children—William Shuler, Suzanne Swanger. Vice pres. John H. Swanger, Inc., Lancaster, Pa., 1945-61; gen. mgr., pres. Houdaille-Duval-Wright Co. div. Houdaille Industries, Inc., Jacksonville, Fla., 1961—, v.p. Houdaille Industries, Inc., Buffalo, 1965—. Served to comdr. USNR, 1940-45. Decorated Navy Cross, D.F.C., Air medal with 6 oak leaf clusters. Mem. Soc. Mil. Engrs. Rotarian. Home: 4816 Yacht Club Rd Jacksonville FL 32201 Office: 1000 Riverside Av Jacksonville FL 3220189

BURNS, WILLIAM SHERMAN, ret. detective agy. exec.; b. Columbus, O., Feb. 10, 1891; s. William J. and Annie M. (Ressler) B.; A.B., Stanford, 1914; m. Dorothy Abell, Sept. 6, 1916; children—Donald Bruce, Ashley John (dec.), William Sherman (dec.). With Burns Internat. Security Services, Inc., 1915—, pres., 1955-64, chmn. exec. com., 1964-71, also dir., now ret.; cons., 1971—. Served to capt. U.S. Army, 1917-18; AEF in France and Germany. Mem. Am. Legion. Elk. Clubs: Sky (N.Y.C.); Sleepy Hollow Country (Scarborough). Home: Meade Creek Ranch Route 1 Sheridan WY Office: 320 Old Briarcliff Rd Briarcliff Manor NY 10510

BURNSHAW, STANLEY, writer; b. N.Y.C., June 20, 1906; s. Ludwig Behr and Sophia (Kievmann) B.; B.A., U. Pitts., 1925; M.A., Cornell U., 1933; m. Lydia Powsner; children—Sandra Bonnie, Valerie, Amy. Advt. bus., Pitts., N.Y.C., 1925-27, 28-32; drama critic, co-editor New Masses, N.Y.C., 1933-36; v.p. The Cordon Co., Inc., pubs., N.Y.C., 1936-39; pres., gen. mgr. Dryden Press, Inc., N.Y.C., 1939-58; v.p. Holt, Rinehart & Winston, Inc., N.Y.C., 1958-65, adviser to pres., 1965-67. Mem. organizing group, then lectr., dir. studies in World lit. Grad. Inst. of Book Publishing, N.Y. U., 1958-62. Bd. judges Nat. Book Award, 1967, 72; awards adv. com. Nat. Book Com., 1967—. Mem. organizing bd. editors, then cons. editor Adult Leadership (mag. supported by Fund for Adult Edn., Ford Found.), 1953-55. Recipient award for lit. Nat. Inst. Arts and Letters, 1971. Mem. Am. Inst. Graphic Arts (dir. 1960-61), Coll. Pubs. Group. Author: The Wheel Age, 1928; André Spire and His Poetry, 1933; The Iron Land, 1936; The Bridge, 1945; The Revolt of the Cats in Paradise, 1945; The Sunless Sea, 1949; Early and Late Testament, 1952; Caged in an Animal's Mind, 1963; The Seamless Web, 1970. Editor: Two New Yorkers, 1934; The Poem Itself, 1960; Varieties of Literary Experience, 1962; The Modern Hebrew Poem Itself, 1965; Poetry Folio (mag.), 1926-28. Contbg. editor Modern Quar., 1932-33, Theatre Workshop, 1935-38. Contbr. Columbia U. Dictionary Modern European Literature, 1947, Dictionary World Literature, L'Approdo Letteraria (Italy), Delphica Tetradia (Greece), Nouvelle Revue Francaise; N.Y. Times Book Rev., Poetry, Atlantic Monthly, Sewanee Rev., Sat. Rev. Home: RFD Vineyard Haven MA 02568

BURNSIDE, FRANK BOYLE, mcht.; b. Hazleton, Pa., Feb. 23, 1914; s. Malcolm and Helen L. (Deremer) B.; B.A., Haverford Coll., 1935; m. Peggy R. Davis, Dec. 30, 1937; children—Diane, Patricia, Priscilla, Frank Boyle. Vice pres., gen. mgr. Fowler, Dick & Walker, Wilkes-Barre, Pa., now pres., dir.; dir. Glen Alden Corp., Miners Nat. Bank of Wilkes-Barre. Trustee Wyoming Sem., Wilks Coll. Served with Supply Corps, USNR, 1943-45. Mem. Nat. Retail Dry Goods Assn. (dir.), Pa. Retailers Assn. (dir.). Presbyn. (trustee). Mason (Shriner). Clubs: Westmoreland, Wyoming Valley Country (Wilkes-Barre); University (N.Y.C.). Home: Box 23 Harveys Lake PA 18618 Office: 15-25 S Main St Wilkes-Barre PA 18701

BURNSIDE, MAURICE GWINN, former congressman, tobacco co. exec.; b. nr. Columbia, S.C., Aug. 23, 1902; s. James Walter and Olivia America (McCants) B.; student The Citadel, 1919-22; student law Furman U., B.S., 1926; A.M., U. Tex., 1928; Ph.D., Duke, 1938; m. Evelyn Jackson Pell, May 29, 1937; 1 dau., Marilyn B. Weaver. Instr., Greenville (S.C.) High Sch., 1931-32; purchaser for Duke Library, 1933-35; grad. research in office gov. S.C., 1935-36; instr. Auburn U., 1936-37; faculty polit. sci. Marshall U., 1937-48, head dept., 1941-45; mem. 81st, 82d, 84th Congresses, 4th W.Va. Dist.; br. chief Nat. Security Agy., Washington, 1952; mfrs. rep., 1953; legislative rep. N.E.A., 1958-60; asst. to Sec. Def., Ho. of Reps., 1961-68; pres. Tri- State Tobacco Warehouse Co., 1956-70. Lectr. polit. sci. Wilson Tech. Coll., 1970-71. Head citizen's recreation program, Huntington, 1943-45; mem. Parole and Probation Exam. Bd. W.Va., 1939- 41, head workers edn., 1943-45; bd. mem. Community

Welfare Council of Cabell County, 1945-48, regional co-ordinator Inter-Am. Affairs, W.Va., eastern and so. Ohio, eastern Ky., cultural and bus. relations; mem. E. Carolina council Boy Scouts Am., 1969—, Wilson County Council on Alcoholism, 1969—. Del., mem. platform com. Democratic Nat. Conv., 1960. Mem. W.Va. Soc. (pres.), Am. Pub. Adminstrn. Assn., Internat. Relations Am. (a founder), Am. Assn. U. Profs., Am., So. polit. sci. assns., Lambda Chi Alpha, Pi Gamma Mu. Democrat. Presbyn. (elder). Moose, Rotarian. Author: Pardon, Parole, and Indeterminate Sentence with Special Reference to South Carolina, 1938; (with Conley Dillon) Government of West Virginia, 1949. Compiler: (with others) Union Check List of Newspapers in the United States and Canada, 1937. Home: 2009 Hermitage Rd Wilson NC 27893

BURNSIDE, PHILLIPS BROOKS, educator; b. Columbus, O., July 20, 1927; s. Lewis Brooks and Mary (Gilbert) B.; Ph.D., Ohio State U., 1958; m. Christel Amalie Rossmann, July 3, 1954; children—Thomas Brooks, Paul Theodore, John Douglas. Instr., Ohio State U., 1957-59, research asso. Research Found., 1958-62, project supr., 1961; asst. prof. Ohio Wesleyan U., Delaware, 1959-63, asso. prof., 1963-69, prof. physics, 1969—. Served with AUS, 1945-48. Mem. Optical Soc. Am., Am. Assn. Physics Tchrs., A.A.A.S., Sigma Xi. Presbyn. Contbr. articles profl. jours. Home: 136 W Lincoln Av Delaware OH 43015

BURNSTAN, ROWLAND, business exec.; b. Scranton, Pa., Nov. 9, 1901; s. Arthur H. and Lucie (Rowland) B.; B.S., Lafayette Coll., 1925, A.M., 1926, LL.D., 1961; Ph.D. (traveling fellow Western Europe), Columbia, 1929; postgrad. Heidelberg U., Germany, 1930-31; Sc.D., Chgo., 1938; m. Naomi Sloan, Oct. 19, 1929; children—Rowland, Alex Sloan. Comml. work, S.Am., 1926-27; research economist N.Y. State Tax Commn., 1927-28; research in comml. geography, Tunis and Algeria, N. Africa, 1929-30; economist N.Y. State Commn. for Revision Tax Law, 1930; lectr. econs., Heidelberg, Germany, 1930-31; economist U.S. Dept. Commerce, asso. editor Survey of Current Bus., 1931-32; dir. marketing research Armour & Co., Chgo., 1932- 33; mem. J.O. McKinsey & Co., Chgo., 1933-35; bus. mgr. Chgo. Times, 1935-37; lectr. econs. U. Chgo., 1933-37; prof. econs. Carleton Coll., Northfield, Minn., 1937, chmn. dept., 1941; dir. aero. div. Mpls.-Honeywell Co., 1941-43; pres. Lawrence Aero. Corp. 1943-50; dir. Sch. Aero. Electronics, U. Minn., 1941-43; pres. Indian Motorcycle Co., 1944-45; dir. European operations Pepsi-Cola Corp., mng. dir., Pepsi-Cola de France, 1950-54; pres., dir. Borg-Warner Internat. Corp., 1954-61; asst. sec. commerce Dept. Commerce, 1961-62; pres. Indsl. Relations Counselors, Inc., 1962-64; chmn. Export Procurement Corp., 1969—; chmn. York Shipley, Ltd. (Eng.), Euromat A.G. (Switzerland); dir. Borg & Beck do Brasil (Brazil), B.W.I. Panama (Panama), Borg-Warner A.G. (Switzerland), Freymon (Spain), Matfroid S.A., Fiby S.A., (France), Torque, Wobron (all Argentina), Yorkaire Py. (Australia), Skofel Italiana, S.R.L. (Italy), Henninger Internat. (Germany), First Fed. Savs. & Loan Assn. (Chgo.), Colonial Trust Co. (N.Y.C.), Federated Purchaser Corp., Intelectron Corp. Treas., World Fedn. for Mental Health, 1965-70; mem. adv. com. Minn. Inst. Govtl. Research; rep. N.Y. State at Nat. Tax Assn., 1929; mem. League of Nations Commn. to Study Orgn. of Peace. Trustee Chgo. Med. Sch., Meadville Theol. Sem., U. Chgo.; bd. dirs. Unitarian Service Com., Nat. Tb Assn. Decorated chevalier Legion d'Honneur (France); commendador del Orden Merito Civil (Spain); recipient Man of Year award in internat. relations, Chgo., 1961. Fellow Royal Econ. Soc.; mem. Am. Econ. Assn., Acad. Polit. Sci., A.A.A.S., Inst. Aero. Sci. (asso.); mem. Nat. Aero. Assn., Am. Mgmt. Assn. (v.p., dir., council, steering com.), N.Y. Acad. Medicine, Royal Aero. Soc. Eng., Nat. Fgn. Trade Council, Phi Gamma Delta. Unitarian. Mason. Clubs: University, Congressional Country (Washington); University (N.Y.C.); Nassau (Princeton, N.J.). Author books on taxation, other econ. subjects (pub. English, German); articles on aeros., fgn. bus. Home: 44 Winfield Rd Princeton NJ 08540 Office: 101 Park Av New York City NY 10017

BURNUM, JAMES HOWARD, banker; b. Trussville, Ala., Jan. 15, 1905; s. Henry Clay and Dora (Elgin) B.; grad. Rutgers U. Grad. Sch. Banking, 1946; m. Martha Isobel Presley, Aug. 5, 1926; children—Sara Elizabeth, Martha Jane (Mrs. Marion Duncan). With First Nat. Bank, Birmingham, Ala., 1923—, v.p., 1946—, also cashier. Active local A.R.C., Community Chest. Clubs: Country of Birmingham, Club, Executive, Metropolitan Dinner, Exchange (Birmingham). Home: 905 Conroy Rd Birmingham AL 35222 Office: 17 N 20th Birmingham AL 35203

BUROW, RICHARD E., mfg. co. exec.; b. Houston, Minn., July 25, 1923; s. Norman E. and Elsie (House) B.; B.S. in chemistry, Beloit (Wis.) Coll., 1947; m. Ena McLaughlin, Jan. 11, 1957; children—Michael, Scott, Lynn, Lisa. Chem. engr. Pa. Salt Mfg. Co., 1947-48; underwriter Mass. Mut. Life Ins. Co., 1948-49; with Kroehler Mfg. Co., 1940—, exec. v.p., 1967-68, pres., 1968—, also dir.; dir. Murphy-Miller, Inc., Bank of Naperville. Chmn. Home Furnishings Council, Inc.; bd. dirs. Brand Name Found. Industry chmn. Nat. Bible Week. Trustee Beloit Coll. Served with AUS, World War II. Recipient Innovator award, 1969. Mem. Nat. Assn. Furniture Mfrs. (past pres.), So. Furniture Mfrs. Assn., Beta Theta Pi. Home: 1021 Lexington St Wheaton IL 60187 Office: 222 5th Av Naperville IL 60540

BURPEE, DAVID, seedsman; b. Phila., Apr. 5, 1893; s. Washington Atlee and Blanche (Simons) B.; student Cornell U., 1913; D.Sc. (hon.), Bucknell U., 1959; m. Lois Torrance, July 18, 1938; children—Jonathan, Blanche Elizabeth (Mrs. Michael R. Dohan). Asst. to father in seed bus., Phila., 1914; chief exec. officer W. Atlee Burpee Co., 1915-70, now dir. Hon. dir. Del. Valley Coll. Sci. and Agr., Doylestown, Pa., Bucknell U.; bd. dirs. N.Y., Welcome House; dir. emeritus Abington Meml. Hosp. Recipient gold seal Nat. Council State Garden Clubs. 1964; Am. Home Achievement medal, 1964. Mem. Am. Seed Trade Assn. (dir., past pres.), Soc. War 1812, Canadian Soc. Phila. (hon. life pres.), English-Speaking Union, Pa. Soc. N.Y. (v.p.), Pa. S.R., Am. Hort. Council (citation 1958), Royal Hort. Soc., Nat. Sweet Pea Soc. Gt. Britain (Henry Eckford Meml. medal 1964), Scottish Nat. Sweet Pea Soc., Société Nationale d'Horticulture de France, Newcomen Soc. N.A., Phila. Soc. Promoting Agr. (Agrl. award 1950) Men's Garden Clubs Am., Quaker City Farmers Club, Delta Mu Delta (hon.), Alpha Zeta (hon.), Delta Upsilon. Republican. Clubs: Union League (v.p. 1933-35), Poor Richard, Penn (dir.), Racquet, Germantown Cricket (Phila.); Hillsboro (Fla.). Plant breeder; created, introduced new hybrid flowers, vegetables. Home: Fordhook Farm Doylestown PA 18901

BURR, ARTHUR ALBERT, coll. dean; b. Manor, Sask., Can., Aug. 23, 1913; s. Charles A. and Mary (Hay) B.; B.S., U. Sask., 1938, M.S., 1940; Ph.D., Pa. State U., 1943; m. Leslie Dickin, July 1, 1941; children—Janet Leslie, Leonard Charles. Came to U.S., 1940, naturalized, 1950. Teaching asst. U. Sask. 1938-40, Pa. State U., 1940-43; research physicist Armstrong Cork Co., 1943-46; faculty Rensselaer Polytech. Inst., 1946-, prof., asso. head dept. metall. engring., 1953-55, prof., head dept., 1955-61, acting dean Sch. Engring, 1961-62, dean, 1962—. Me. Soc. Metals (award outstanding ability tchr. metallurgy, 1952; chmn. Eastern N.Y. chpt. 1958), Soc. Nondestructive Testing (chmn. Mohawk Hudson chapter 1949), Am. Phys. Soc., Am. Soc. Mining, Metall. and Petroleum Engrs. (chmn. Hudson Mohawk chpt. 1959), Am. Soc. Engring. Edn., Sigma Xi, Sigma Pi Sigma, Phi Lambda Upsilon. Presbyn. (elder). Presbyn. (elder). Home: 983 Spring Av Troy NY 12180

BURR, ARTHUR HOUGHTON, educator; b. Worcester, Mass., May 27, 1908; s. Thomas Shepard and Ethel Mae (Houghton) B.; B.S., Worcester Poly. Inst., 1929; M.S., U. Pitts., 1931; Ph.D., U. Mich., 1947; m. Phyllis Carter, Oct. 6, 1932; children—Arthur Houghton, Merrill (dau.), Thomas Shepard. Research engr. Westinghouse Electric Corp., East Pittsburgh, 1929-33; instr. Rice U., Houston, 1933-41; asst. prof. U. Mo., 1941-44; asst. dir. aerial measurements lab. Northwestern U., 1944-47; prof. and head dept. machine design Cornell U., 1947-68, Sibley prof. mech. engring., 1953—, cons. aero. lab., 1951-53; prof. Instituto Tecnologico de Aeronautica, Brazil, 1953-54; vis. prof. Pontificia Universidade Católica de Rio de Janeiro, 1966; Ford Found. vis. prof. Universidad de los Andes, Bogota, Colombia, 1968, 69; vis. prof. Indian Inst. Sci., Bangalore, also NSF-U.S. AID Summer Insts., India, 1970. Fellow Am. Soc. M.E. (chmn. N.Y. So. Tier sect. 1956-57); mem. Am. Soc. Engring. Edn., Sigma Xi, Tau Beta Pi, Pi Tau Sigma, Lambda Chi Alpha. Contbr. papers in engring. jours. Address: 308 Upson Hall Cornell U Ithaca NY 14850

BURR, DONALD DAVID, corp. exec.; b. N.Y.C., Apr. 20, 1923; m. Jeanne Parry, May 22, 1948; children—Cynthia Parry, Cory Howell. Account exec. Bache & Co., 1946-47; gen. mgr. LaPlaya Products, Inc., 1948-52; gen. sales mgr. Hazel Bishop, Inc., 1952-54, v.p. marketing, 1954, pres., 1955-57, also dir.; pres. Parry Labs., Inc., 1957-61, also dir.; v.p., dir. Am. Motor Scooter Corp., 1960-61, dir. Tracey Enterprises, Inc., 1960-61; v.p. Rayette, Inc., 1961-63, exec. v.p., 1963-64; v.p. Parfum Lorle, Inc., 1961-64, Odell Co., Inc., 1962-64; v.p. Yardley of London, Inc., 1964-66, exec. v.p., 1966-68, pres., 1968-69, also dir.; chmn., pres. Burr Corp., 1970—; chmn. Am. Pharm. Co., Inc., Devon Products Co., Inc., Trylon Products Co. Inc., 1970—. Served with USNR, 1942- 44, as lt. (j.g.) USCGR, 1944-46. Clubs: New York Athletic; Devon Yacht (Amagansett, L.I.); Maidstone (East Hampton, L.I., N.Y.). Home: 430 E 56th St New York City NY 10021 Office: 1290 Av Americas New York City NY 10000

BURR, EDWARD BENJAMIN, investment co. exec.; b. Worcester, Mass., Dec. 19, 1923; s. Guy Weatherbee and Bertha Mary (Clark) B.; A.B. cum laude, Bowdoin Coll., 1945; M.B.A., Wharton Sch. U. Pa., 1948; C.L.U., 1951; m. Mary Elizabeth Hayes, Sept. 2, 1944; children—Susan Jean, Nancy Carol. Ednl. dir. Inst. Life Ins., N.Y.C., 1948-54; dir. pub. information Nat. Assn. Investment Cos., 1954-55, exec. dir., 1955-58; bd. govs., 1958-61; exec. v.p., dir. One William St. Fund, Inc., N.Y.C., 1958-62; pres., dir. William St. Sales, Inc., N.Y.C., 1958-62; dir. One William Dept. Lehman Bros., 1960-62; chmn. bd. Hugh W. Long & Co., 1962—; vice chmn. Fundamental Investors, Inc., Diversified Investment Fund, Inc., Diversified Growth Stock Fund, Inc., Westminster Fund, Inc., 1964—; pres. Anchor Corp., Inc., 1964—; chmn. Anchor Life Ins. Co., Los Angeles. Bd. overseers Bowdoin Coll. Served with Inf. AUS, 1943-46. Decorated Silver Star medal, Bronze Star medal (2). Mem. Am. Soc. C.L.U.'s, Kappa Sigma. Clubs: Wall Street (N.Y.C.). Home: 8 Coach Lane Westport CT Office: Westminster at Parker Elizabeth NJ 07208

BURR, EUGENE, TV exec., producer; b. N.Y.C., July 27, 1910; s. Eugene Paul and Alvine (Fredericks) B.; B.A., Columbia, 1930; m. Marian Alden, Apr. 13, 1938. Company mgr. Charles Frohman, 1930-32; editor, drama critic Billboard, 1932-42; night editor N.Y. Jour. Am., 1942-44; gen. mgr. for Billy Rose, 1944-45; play editor Warner Bros., 1945-48; author theatre column Playbill mag., 1948-58; head TV-radio programming Dancer, Fitzgerald and Sample, N.Y.C., 1953-54; TV supr. Young & Rubicam, N.Y.C., 1954-56; producer CBS, 1957-60; v.p. program devel. NBC, 1960- 61; pres., producer Eugene Burr Prodns., Inc., 1961—; editor, producer TV programs Ford TV Theatre, 1951-52, Ellery Queen, 1952-53, The Web, 1952-54, Date with Life, 1954-55, The Verdict is Yours, 1957-60, DuPont Play of Week, 1961, My Five Daughters, 1962, The Troubled Years, 1963, The Young Marrieds, 1964, Day in Court, 1964. Contbr. Ency. Brit. Yearbook, 1940-66. Home: 12821 Mulholland Dr Beverly Hills CA 90210 Office: 1041 N Formosa St Los Angeles CA 90046

BURR, FRANCIS HARDON, lawyer; b. Nahant, Mass., July 21, 1914; s. I Tucker and Evelyn (Thayer) B.; A.B. cum laude, Harvard, 1935, LL.B., 1938; m. Nancy Blagden, Mar. 24, 1951. Admitted to Mass. bar, 1938; asso. firm Ropes & Gray, 1938-45, partner firm, Boston, 1947—; dir. New Eng. Electric System, Fiduciary Trust Co. N.Y., Am. Airlines, Inc., State St. Investment Corp., Am. Employers Ins. Co., Employers Fire Ins. Co., Fed. St. Fund, Inc., Equitable Life Assurance Soc. U.S., First Nat. Stores, Inc., Second Fed. Street Fund, Thorndike, Doran, Paine & Lewis, Inc.; corporator Provident Instn. for Savs.; mem. trust bd. First Nat. Bank Boston; trustee Union Warren Savs. Bank, Employers' Group Assos. Fellow Harvard Coll., 1954—; trustee Humane Soc. Commonwealth of Mass., Mass. Taxpayers Found., Indsl. Sch. for Crippled Children, Mass. Gen. Hosp., Radcliffe Coll., Noble and Greenough Sch.; bd. mgrs. Adams House; bd. dirs. Boston Legal Aid Soc. Fellow Am. Acad. Arts and Scis.; mem. Am. Law Inst., Am., Boston bar assns. Clubs: Somerset (Mass.); Myopia Hunt (Hamilton, Mass.); Links (N.Y.). Home: South Hamilton MA 01982 Office: 225 Franklin St Boston MA 12110

BURR, HELEN GUNDERSON, (Mrs. Horace Burr), educator; b. Iowa City, Dec. 30, 1918; d. George Byron and Grace (Farrell) Gunderson; B.A., Stanford, 1937; M.A., U. So. Cal., 1940; Ph.D., Columbia, 1949; post-doctoral study U. So. Cal., summer 1950, U. Mich., summer 1952; m. Horace Burr, July 24, 1954; 1 son, David Stanford. Speech pathologist, N.Y.C. and Los Angeles, 1944-50; asst. prof., dir. speech clinic State U. N.Y., 1950-53; asst. prof. U. Va., Charlottesville, 1953-60, asso. prof. speech pathology and audiology, 1961-66, prof., 1966—, dir. Speech and Hearing Center, 1961—, chmn. dept. speech pathology and audiology, 1962—. Bd. dirs. Va. Hearing and Speech Found.; professional adv. bd. Va. Soc. for Crippled Children and Adults; mem. coordinating com. on crippled children's services Va. Council on Health and Med. Care. Fellow Am. Speech and Hearing Assn., N.Y. Acad. Scis., Speech and Hearing Assn. Va. (pres. 1960); mem. Am. Assn. U. Women, English Speaking Union, Albemarle Hist. Assn., Albemarle Art Assn., A.A.A.S., Am. Assn. U. Profs., Linguistic Soc. Am., Speech Assn. Am., Internat. Soc. for Gen. Semantics, Delta Delta Delta, Pi Lambda Theta, Kappa Delta Pi, Delta Kappa Gamma. Editor: SHAV Jour., 1961—, The Aphasic Adult, 1965. Home: Carrsgrove Stribling Av Charlottesville VA 22903

BURR, HENRY I., book mfg. co. exec.; b. N.Y.C., Mar. 24, 1928; s. Emanuel and Geraldine (Satenstein) B.; B.S., Yale, 1948; m. Suzanne C. Conhaim, Nov. 5, 1950; children—John, Aimee. Exec. v.p., sec., dir. Am. Book-Stratford Press, Inc., N.Y.C. Bd. dirs., v.p. Book Mfrs. Inst.; bd. dirs. Manhattan League Hebrew Kindergarten and Infants Home. Clubs: Friars, Yale (N.Y.C.); Fenway Golf (White Plains, N.Y.). Author: Observations on Trade Book Sales, 1949. Home: 6 Stonewall Lane Mamaroneck NY 10543 Office: 75 Varick St New York City NY 10013

BURR, JOHN GREEN, educator; b. Ft. Sill, Okla., Mar. 12, 1918; s. John Green and Ruth Guyer (Oeschlin) B.; B.S., Mass. Inst. Tech., 1940, M.S., 1940; Ph.D., Northwestern U., 1948; m. Irma Therese Garrigan, June 12, 1943; children—John G., Sara Margaret (Mrs. Michael Sheehan), Kathleen Burr (Mrs. James Oliver), Maryellen, Elizabeth, Mark C., Matthew E. Asst. prof. Miami U., Oxford, O., 1947-48; sr. scientist Oak Ridge Nat. Lab., 1948-57; sr. scientist N.Am. Rockwell Corp., Los Angeles, 1957-69; prof. chemistry and radiology U. Okla., 1969—. Served with USNR, 1945-46. Guggenheim fellow, 1964; USPHS sr. fellow, 1953-54; Eastman fellow Northwestern U., 1946-47. Fellow Am. Inst. Chemistry; mem. Am. Chem. Soc., A.A.A.S., Radiation Research Soc., Biophys. Soc., Okla. Acad. Sci. Democrat. Roman Catholic. K.C. Club: Cosmos (Washington). Contbr. articles profl. jours. Home: 1101 Woodland Dr Norman OK 73069

BURR, JOHN ROY, educator; b. Oshkosh, Wis., July 18, 1933; s. Lester John and Dorothy Ann (Hoffman) B.; B.A., U. Wis., 1955; M.A. (Univ. grantee), Columbia, 1956, Ph.D., 1959; m. Marjorie Jean Bakirakis, July 4, 1963; children—Michael John, Christopher Scott. Adj. faculty Franklin and Marshall Coll., 1959-61; asst. prof. philosophy Hood Coll., 1961-64; faculty dept. philosophy Wis. State U., Oshkosh, 1964—, asso. prof., 1966-68, prof., 1968—, chmn. dept., 1966—, chmn. humanities div., 1966—. Pres., Oshkosh Community Players, 1968-69, bd. dirs., 1966-69. Ford Found. grantee, 1963-64; Wis. State U. Regents Research grantee, 1971-72. Mem. Am. Philos. Assn., Metaphys. Soc. Am., Assn. Asian Studies, Am. Assn. U. Profs., Wis. Acad. Arts, Scis. and Letters, Aurelian Soc. Mason. Club: Candlelight (Oshkosh). Contbr. articles to profl. jours. Home: 2114 Doemel St Oshkosh WI 54901

BURR, LEONARD WAYNE, naval officer; b. Lebam, Wash., Mar. 5, 1913; s. Byron Orestes and Margaret May (Brumfield) B.; B.C.S., Benjamin Franklin U., Washington, 1950; grad. Naval Sch. Hosp. Adminstrn., 1951, Army Mgmt. Sch., 1964; m. Kathryn Geraldine McCann, July 18, 1943; children—Wayne, Michael. Enlisted as seaman U.S. Navy, 1931, advanced through grades to capt., 1966; assignments afloat and ashore in med. adminstrv. dept., 1931-; now adminstrv. officer USN Hosp., San Diego. Address: USN Hosp San Diego CA 92134

BURR, RAYMOND, actor; b. New Westminster, B.C., Can., May 21, 1917; student Stanford, U. Cal., Columbia, U. Chungking. Appeared on stage numerous countries, in Night Must Fall, Mandarin, Crazy with the Heat, Duke in Darkness; dir. Pasadena Community Playhouse, 1943; formerly radio actor; star Perry Mason Show, TV series (recipient Emmy award as best actor), 1961, 62, now star Ironside TV series; appeared numerous motion pictures, latest being They Were So Young, You're Never Too Young, A Man Alone, Count Three and Pray, Please Murder Me, Godzilla King of the Monsters, Great Day in the Morning, Secret of Treasure Mountain, Cry in the Night, Criss Cross, others. Office: care Lester Salkow 8780 Sunset Blvd Los Angeles CA 90069

BURR, ROBERT NATHAN, educator; b. Rochester, N.Y., Oct. 15, 1916; s. John Edwin and Ethel J. (Bills) B.; A.B., U. Rochester, 1939; Ph.D. (Social Sci. Research Council pre-doctoral field fellow 1942, Penfield Travelling scholar 1942- 43, Social Sci. Research Council demobilization award 1947-48), U. Pa., 1948; m. Virginia Ward, June 10, 1940 (div. 1949); children—Tracy E., Robert F.; m. 2d, Elizabeth Evarts, Apr. 30, 1952. Asst. to prodn. engr. Gen. Ry. Signal Co., 1943-45; gen. mgr., treas. Idylbrook Farms, also treas., dir. Country Gentleman Corp. and Turpin Corp., 1945-46; instr. history Rutgers U., 1946-48; mem. faculty U. Cal. at Los Angeles, 1948-, prof. history, 1963-, Mem. for U.S., Commn. on History of Pan Am. Inst. Geography and History, 1957-64, vice chmn. U.S. delegation 7th gen. assembly, Buenos Aires, 1961; chmn. U.S. delegation 4th consultation Commn. History, Cuenca, Ecuador, 1959; mem. joint com. Latin Am. studies Social Sci. Research Council-Am. Council Learned Socs., 1959-60, chmn., 1960-67; mem. Latin Am. nat. selection com. Fgn. Area Tng. Fellowship Program, 1961-64; staff asso. Brookings Instn., 1962-67. Recipient Bolton prize, 1966. Doherty Found. Travelling fellow, 1951-52; Eisenhower Exchange fellow, 1957; Rockefeller fellow, 1961-62, Mem. Am. Hist. Assn., Conf. Latin Am. Hist. (chmn. gen. com. 1965), Pacific Coast Council Latin Am. Studies (gov. bd. 1955-58). Author: The Stillborn Panama Congress; Power Politics in Chilean-Columbia Relations during the War of the Pacific, 1962; By Reason or Force, 1965; Our Troubled Hemisphere, 1967. Co-editor; Documents on Inter-American Cooperation, 2 vols., 1955. Home: 10856 Wellworth Av Los Angeles CA 90024

BURRELL, BERKELEY GRAHAM, trade assn. exec., dry cleaning exec.; b. Washington, June 12, 1919; s. Hayward G. and Fannie (Miles) B.; student Howard U., 1941-43; m. A. Parthenia Robinson, June 10, 1951; 1 son, Berkeley. Owner Burrell's Superb Cleaners, Washington, 1946—; pres. Mcht. Prince Corp., Burrell Assos.; chmn. bd. dirs. Nat. Bus. Corp.; partner Graham Assos.; dir. Indsl. Bank of Washington, Tradewinds Corp.; adjunct prof. Howard U., Morgan State Coll.; vis. scholar Fisk U.; guest lectr. Vanderbilt U., Am. U. Pres. Nat. Bus. League, Washington, 1962—. Mem. bldg. research adv. bd. Nat. Acad. Scis.; dir. YMCA, D.C. Soc. Crippled Children, Housing Devel. Corp. Vice chmn. Pres.'s Adv. Council Minority Enterprises; dir. Interracial Council Bus. Opportunity. Trustee Robert Russa Moton Found., LeMoyne- Owen Coll. (Memphis); pres. Booker T. Washington Found.; dir. Doctors, Rogers Meml. hosps. Served with AUS, World War II. Mem. Met. Washington Bd. Trade (dir.). Author: (with John Seder) Getting It Together: Black Businessmen in America, 1971. Home: 1346 Jackson St NE Washington DC 20017 Office: 4324 Georgia Av NW Washington DC 20011

BURRELL, DONALD SAMUEL, mcht.; b. Lebanon, N.J., Feb. 18, 1931; s. Lloyd Wilbur and Elizabeth Catherine (Mahoney) B.; B.S., Drexel U., 1954; M.B.A., U. Pa., 1958; m. Grace Palmer, Apr. 19, 1958; 1 dau., Jean Elizabeth. Sr. auditor Union Camp Corp., N.Y.C., 1963-68, Johnson & Johnson, New Brunswick, N.J., 1958-63; treas. Moore-Handly, Inc., Pelham, Ala., 1968—. Served with Finance Corps, AUS, 1954-56. Home: 3716 Briar Oak Circle Birmingham AL 35223 Office: Moore-Handly Inc Pelham AL 35202

BURRELL, KENNETH EARL, guitarist; b. Detroit, July 31, 1931; s. William Henry and Elizabeth (Day) B.; Mus.B., Wayne State U., 1955. Guitarist, Oscar Peterson Trio, 1955-57, Benny Goodman Orch., 1957-59, Jimmy Smith Trio, 1959; formed Kenny Burrell Trio, 1960, Kenny Burrell Quartet, 1963. Recipient Internat. Jazz Critics awards, 1957, 60. Mem. Phi Mu Alpha.

BURRELL, LOOMIS, mfr.; b. Little Falls, N.Y., July 31, 1872; s. David Hamlin and Louisa (Loomis) B.; B.S., Pa. Mil. Coll., 1892, D.Sc., 1961; Ph.B., Yale, 1894; m. Lois Watson Wing, June 20, 1912; children—Lilian Wing (Mrs. Edwin M. Fisher), Elizabeth Loomis (Mrs. William Slater Barkentin, Jr.), Jean (Mrs. G. Dickinson). Various positions with D. H. Burrell & Co., manufacturers of dairy machinery equipment and supplies, 1895-1919, D.H. Burrell & Co., Inc., 1919-28; chmn. bd. Cherry- Burrell Corp. 1928-54; pres. Herkimer Co. Trust Co. 1941-48, chmn. bd. 1948-63; v.p., dir. Reed Tissues Corp., 1929-61, Mohawk Valley Paper Co., Burrows Paper

Corp., mgr. N.Y. Tng. Sch. for Girls, 1908-09; Cons. U.S. Pub. Health Service, 1932-37. Del. to World's Diary Congress. Berlin, 1937. Dir. Auburn Theol. Sem., 1908-55, Little Falls Pub. Library, 1910-57. Recipient award for services to dairy industry from Cornell Dairy Sci. Assn., 1952. Mem. Sci. Research Soc. Am., Inst. Food Tech., Am. Dairy Sci. Assn. Republican. Presbyn. Clubs: Mohawk Valley Country (Little Falls); Yale (N.Y.C.); University (Winter Park, Fla.), Home: 676 E Main St Little Falls, NY . 13365. Office: Burrell Bldg Little Falls NY 13365

BURRELL, SIDNEY ALEXANDER, educator; b. Choteau, Mont., Feb. 24, 1917; s. Sidney Harris and Frances (Timmis) B.; student DePauw U., 1934-35; A.B., U. Chgo., 1938; Ph.D., Columbia, 1953; m. Ann Theresa Gibbons, Sept. 2, 1945; children—John A., Sidney Antony, Andrew J. Mem. faculty seamanship and navigation U.S. Naval Acad., 1945-46; instr. history Columbia, 1948-50, Barnard Coll., 1950-52; mem. research staff Center Research on World Polit. Instns., Princeton, 1952-53; mem. faculty Barnard Coll., 1953-66; prof., chmn. dept. history Boston, U., 1966—. Served with USNR, 1942-46; PTO. Guggenheim fellow, 1961-62. Mem. Am., New Eng. (exec. com.) hist. assns., Am. Soc. Ch. History, Acad. Polit. Sci., Conf. Brit. Studies, Colonial Soc. Mass., Econ. History Soc. (Great Britain), Author: (with others) Political Community in the North Atlantic Area, 1957. Editor: Amiable Renegate: Memoirs of Capt. Peter Drake, 1671-1753, 1960. Editor, compiler: Role Religion in Modern European History, 1964. Contbr. to Some Modern Historians of Britain, 1951, The Protestant Ethic and Modernization (S.N. Eisenstadt, ed.), 1968. Contbr. articles profl. jours. Home: 43 Walker Lane Needham MA 02192 Office: Boston Univ Boston MA 02215

BURRESS, JAMES RUSSELL, Jr., govt. ofcl.; b. Hampton, Va., Aug. 22, 1913; s. James Russell and Marian (East) B.; B.S., N.C. A. and T. State U., 1937; M.S., Columbia, 1941; m. Ruth R. Nicholson, July 17, 1942; children—Melvin L., Cynthia K., Margaret J. Vocational rehab. adviser specialist Office Vocational Rehab., U.S. Dept. Health, Edn. and Welfare, Washington, 1951-59, asso. regional rep. Vocational Rehab. Adminstrn., Region VIII, Denver, 1959-67, regional commr. Social and Rehab. Service, 1967—. Mem. bd. Metro-Denver Fair Housing Center, Inc., ., 1966-70; chmn. adv. com. Com. Civil Rights and Minority Employment, 1965-71; mem. Denver Fed. Exec. Bd., 1967-71. Recipient Spl. Service award, 1966, Superior Service award, 1969, Distinguished Service award, 1970 (all Dept. Health, Edn. and Welfare), Man of Year award Omega Psi Phi, 1969. Mem. Nat. Assn. Social Workers, Nat. Rehab. Assn. (pres. 1971-72), Nat. Rehab. Counseling Assn., Am. Pub. Welfare Assn., Nat. Conf. for Social Welfare, Nat. Assn. Hearing and Speech Agys. (nat. bd.). Delivered first Louis P. Ortale Meml. lecture on placement services 1970 Ann. Conf. Nat. Rehab. Assn., San Diego. Home: 3290 Leyden St Denver CO 80207 Office: Fed Bldg 19th and Stout Sts Denver CO 80202

BURRESS, RICHARD THOMAS, lawyer, govt. ofcl.; b. Omaha, Dec. 22, 1922; s. Burrell Jackson and Lea (Dickinson) B.; A.B., Omaha U., 1943; J.D., U. Ia. 1948; LL.M., N.Y. U., 1953; m. Jan Eaton, June 16, 195l; children—Bonny, Lee. Admitted to Ia. bar, 1948, Cal. bar, 1959, D.C. bar, 1965, also U.S. Supreme Ct.; spl. agt. FBI, Richmond, Va., N.Y.C., Honolulu, 1948-53; dep. asst. gen. counsel NLRB, Washington, 1953-58; corp. atty, Lockheed Aircraft Corp., Sunnyvale and Burbank, Cal., 1958-61; practice law, Palo Alto, Cal., 1963-64; dir. govt. relations Cal. C. of C., 1964; with firm Veder, Price, Kauffman, Kamholz & McGuiness, Washington, 1964-65; minority counsel edn. and labor com. U.S. Ho. of Reps., 1961-63; staff dir. Republican policy com., counsel Rep. conf. of Ho. of Reps., also minority sqt.-at-arms, 1965-69; dep. asst. to pres. Nixon, 1969-70; chmn. Renegotiation Bd., 1970—. Served with USMCR, 1943-46. Mem. Am., Cal. bar assns., Soc. Former FBI Agts. Republican. Home: 5521 Mohican Rd Washington DC 20016 Office: 1910 K St NW Washington DC 20006

BURRILL, DAN YOUNGS, educator; b. Chgo., May 9, 1907; s. James Alfred and Bertha (Youngs) B.; A.B., U. Mich., 1929, LL.B., 1931; D.D.S., Northwestern U., 1939, M.S., 1942; m. Marie Wecker, June 9, 1931; 1 dau., Elizabeth Ann (Mrs. Guy Mullenbach). Admitted to Ill. bar, 1932; practice in Chgo., 1932-36; practice dentistry, specializing in orthodontia, Chgo., 1939-44; instr., asst. prof. oral pathology Northwestern U. Dental Sch., Chgo., 1942-46. prof. oral diagnosis, dept. head, 1957—; prof. oral medicine, dept. head U. Louisville Sch. Dentistry, 1946-57. Diplomate Am. Bd. Oral Medicine. Fellow A.A.A.S.; mem. Am., Ill. dental assns., Chgo. Dental Soc., Am. Coll. Dentists, Am. Acad. Oral Pathology, Internat. Assn. for Dental Research (past pres.), Sigma Xi, Omega Kappa Upsilon, Phi Kappa Phi. Contbr. articles profl. jours. Home: 1320 Maple Av Wilmette IL 60091 Office: 311 E Chicago Av Chicago IL 60611

BURRILL, FLOYD IRVIN, agrl. coop. exec.; b. Harrington, Wash., Feb. 3, 1916; s. Thomas O. and Maude G. (Graff) B.; student Coll. Puget Sound, 1934-36; B.S. in Bus. Adminstrn., U. So. Cal., 1938; m. Maxine P. Florence, Sept. 4, 1938; children—Judith Ann (Mrs. Jerry J. Mabey), Richard L. With Sunkist Growers, Inc., Los Angeles, 1938—, controller, 1963-64, sec., 1964—, sec. retirement bd., sec. investment bd., 1964—. Mem. Orange Adminstrv. Com., 1950-52, Naval Orange Adminstrv. Com., 1953—, Valencia Orange Adminstrv. Com., 1954—, Lemon Adminstrv. Com., 1958—, chmn. Joint exec. coms. Naval Orange, Valencia Orange, Lemon adminstrv. coms., 1963—; bd. dirs. Cal.-Ariz. Citrus League, 1964-65, sec. treas., 1964-; mem. So. Cal. Research Council, 1954-57, Town Hall, Los Angeles, 1959-64,, U.S. Nat. Fruit Export Council, 1962—. Scoutmaster, dist. Explorer adviser local Boy Scouts Am., 1949-59. Served to lt. USNR, 1943-46. Mem. Am. Mgmt. Assn. (pres. student chpt. 1938), Los Angeles C. of C., Am. Soc. Corporate Secs., Alpha Phi Omega. Methodist. Home: 555 Camino Verde South Pasadena CA 91030 Office: 14130 Riverside Dr Sherman Oaks CA 91403

BURRILL, GERALD FRANCIS, clergyman; b. Bangor, Me., June 8, 1906; s. William George and Clara Mary (McCafferty) B.; A.B., U. of Me., 1929, D.H.L., 1953; S.T.B., Gen. Theol. Sem., 1932, S.T.D., 1951; D.D. (honorary), U. of South, 1951; D.D., Seabury-Western Seminary, 1954; D.D., Nashota Sem., 1970; m. Elna Jean Thompson, July 3, 1933; children—William George, James Thompson. Ordained to ministry Episcopal Ch., 1933, served as priest in charge All Saints' Ch., Mariner's Harbor, S.I., N.Y., 1932-35; rector St. Paul's Ch., Morrisania, N.Y.C., 1935-44; asso. sec. Forward in Service, 1944-45, exec. sec., 1945-46; mem. Bd. Religious Edn., N.Y.C., 1939, pres. bd., 1941-44; rector Christ Ch., Williamsport, Pa., 1946-50; Suffragan Bishop of Diocese of Dallas, 1950-54; bishop of Chgo., 1954-71; ret., 1971. Pres. N.Y. Churchmen's Clericus, 1943; chmn. Commn. Christian Edn. 2d Providence, 1944. Home: 5563 Shadow Lawn Dr Sarasota FL 33581

BURRILL, MEREDITH FREDERIC, geographer; b. Houlton, Me., Dec. 23 1902; s. Fred Wilson and Carrie Louise (Odiorne) B.; A.B., Bates Coll., 1925, D.Sc., 1960; M.A., Clark U., 1926, Ph.D., 1930; m. Sarah Bannister, May 30, 1927; children—Robert Meredith, Elizabeth Ellen (Mrs. David Henry Allard). Instr. geography schs. and colls., 1926-30; asst. prof. geography Okla. A. and M. Coll., 1930-31, asso. prof., 1931-37, prof., 1937-40; research adviser McGill U., 1931; unit head and acting regional chief Land Use Planning Sect., Region 8, Resettlement Adminstrn., 1935-37; econ. geographer Gen. Land Office, Dept. of Interior, 1940-42, chief Div. of Research and Analysis, 1942-43; dir. U.S. Bd. on Geog. Names, Dept. Interior, 1943-48, exec. sec., 1948—, dir. Office of Geography, 1948-68; geographer Directorate of Mapping, Charting and Geodesy, Dept. Def., 1968—. Chmn. com. on social geography NRC, 1948-51, vice chmn. adv. com. to geog. br., Office Naval Research, 1949-52. Del. internat. geog. congresses, 1949, 52, 60, 64, 68; chmn. UN Group of Experts on Geog. Names, 1960, 66, 67; pres. UN Conf. on Standardization Geographic Names, 1967. Trustee Bates Coll., 1966-71. Decorated Order of Alfonso X, El Sabio; recipient So. Regional Grant-in-Aid, Social Sci. Research Council, 1932; Distinguished Service medal, 1968; Antarctic medal. Fellow Royal Geog. Soc., Am. Geog. Soc.; corr. mem. Geog. Soc. Lima; mem. Assn. Am. Geographers (pres. 1966), Am. Name Soc. (pres. 1955), Am. Dialect Soc., A.A.A.S., Am. Geophys. Union, Phi Beta Kappa, Pi Gamma Mu. Clubs: Cosmos, Explorers (N.Y.): Trojan Sierra (hon. mem.). Author: A Socio- Economic Atlas of Okla., 1936; Water for Industry, 1956. Home: 5503 Grove St Chevy Chase MD 20015 Office: Bd Geog Names Dept Interior Washington DC 20240

BURRIS, B. CULLEN, psychiatrist; b. Miss., 1924; M.D., U. Tenn., 1946; married; 2 children. Intern Wesley Meml. Hosp., Chgo., 194647, resident internal medicine, 1949, resident neuropsychiatry, 1949-50, mem. staff, 1953-58; resident Johns Hopkins Hosp., 1950; fellow psychiatry Northwestern U. Med. Sch., 1952-53, clin. instr. psychiatry, 1953-58, asso. prof. psychiatry, 1967—; also mem. staff Evanston (Ill.) Hosp. Assn.; mem. attending staff W. Allis Meml. Hosp., Milw., 1961-66; med. dir. Milw. Sanitaarium Found., Wauwatosa, Wis., 1961-67; now mem. attending staff Passavant Meml. Hosp., Chgo.; asso. prof. psychiatry Marquette U. Med. Sch., 1958- 67. Served with M.C., USNR, 1950-52. Address: 707 N Fairbanks Ct Chicago IL 60611

BURRIS, CONRAD TIMOTHY, educator; b. Edmonton, Can., May 17, 1924; s. James Edward and Mary Elizabeth (Salzl) B.; B.Chem. Engring., U. Alta., 1946, M.Chem. Engring., 1948; Ph.D., Cath. U. Am., 1955. Came to U.S., 1950, naturalized, 1956. Asst. prof. Manhattan Coll., Bronx, N.Y., 1958-61, asso. prof., 1961-63, prof., 1963—, head dept. chem. engring., 1961-71, dean engring., 1971—. Dir. Particulate Solid Research, Inc. Mem. Am. Inst. Chem. Engrs., Am. Chem. Soc., Sigma Xi. Address: Manhattan Coll Bronx NY 10471

BURRIS, JOSEPH JENNINGS, lawyer; b. Aberdeen S.D., Dec. 29, 1913; s. Joseph Henry and Lura Stella (Jennings) B.; A.B., Stanford, 1936, J.D., 1940; children—Joseph Steven, Susan Dirksen. Admitted to Cal. bar, 1942; practice in Los Angeles, 1946—; mem. firm Burris, Lagerlof, Swift & Senecal, 1953—. Chmn. disciplinary com. 3, dist. 7 State Bar Cal. Dir. Stauffer Chem. Co., Thistle Inn Club, Raffles, Inc. Chmn., Stanford Athletic Bd., 1961-65; asst. sec. Orthopaedic Hosp., Los Angeles, Orthopaedic Found., Los Angeles Orthopaedic Med. Center, Crippled Children's Hosp.; treas. John and Beverly Stauffer Found.; sec. Louis McDonald Pollution Abatement Found. Mem. bd. World Trade Libraries, San Francisco; bd. overseers Hoover Instn. of Stanford U.; mem. exec. com. bd. trustees Republican Assos. Served to lt. comdr. USNR, World War II. Mem. Am., Cal., Los Angeles bar assns., Phi Delta Theta, Stanford Alumni Assn. (pres. 1952-53), Stanford Law Soc. So. Cal. (pres. 1957), Stanford Assos. (bd. govs. 1954-60), Pasadena-Foothill Tennis Patrons Assn. (bd. govs.). Clubs: Annandale Golf (Pasadena); Los Angeles, Stanford (pres 1948-50) (Los Angeles); Buck (bd. dirs. 1955, chmn. 1955-57) (Stanford); Bohemian (San Francisco). Home: 827 W Inverness Dr Flintridge Pasadena CA 91103 Office: 500 S Virgil Av Los Angeles CA 90020

BURRIS, ROBERT HARZA, biochemist, educator; b. Brookings, S.D., Apr. 13, 1914; s. Edward T. and Mable C. (Harza) B.; B.S., S.D. State Coll., 1936, D.Sc., 1966; M.S., U. Wis., 1938, Ph.D., 1940; m. Katherine Irene Brusse, Sept. 12, 1945; children—Jean Carol, John Edward, Ellen Louise. NRC fellow Columbia, 1940-41; faculty U. Wis., Madison, 1941- -, prof., 1951- -, chmn. biochemistry Coll. Agr., 1958-70. Guggenheim fellow Cambridge U., 1954. Mem. Am. Chem. Soc., Am. Soc. Biol. Chemistry, Am. (Stephen Hales award 1968, pres. 1960), Scandinavian socs. plant physiology, Biochem. Soc., A.A.A.S., Soc. Gen. Physiology, Am. Soc. for Microbiology, Nat. Acad. Scis. Home: 1015 University Bay Dr Madison WI 53705

BURRISS, STANLEY WILLIAM, aircraft mfg. co. exec.; b. Bklyn., July 15, 1910; s. Charles Scott and Elwine (Dreyer) B.; B.S., Newark Coll. Engring., 1938, D. Eng., 1964; postgrad. nuclear physics Los Alamos Lab., 1948-49, radar and electronics Bowdoin Coll., Mass. Inst. Tech., 1943, math. and electronics City Coll. N.Y., 1942; m. Maria Sartori, Oct. 25, 1958; 1 son, Richard S. with Los Alamos Sci. Lab., 1946-53, chief of staff to test dir. Operation Greenhouse, 1950-51, comdr. sci. task group Operation Ivy, 1952; project analyst Oriole project Patrick AFB, Glenn L. Martin Co., 1953-54, dir. Polaris missile system, 1956-61; v.p., gen. mgr. Missile Systems div. Lockheed Missiles & Space Co., Sunnyvale, Cal., 1961-69 pres., 1969—; v.p. Lockheed Aircraft Corp., 1961-69, group v.p., 1969—. Served to lt. comdr. USNR, 1943-46. Recipient Certificate of Appreciation sec. Army, 1953, Meritorious Pub. Service award U.S. Navy, 1961, Edward F. Weston Distinguished Alumnus award Newark Coll. Engring., 1962. Fellow Am. Inst. Aero. and Astronautics, Royal Aero. Soc.; mem. Nat. Acad. Engring., Am. Ordnance Assn., Navy League. Home: 98 Catalpa Dr Atherton CA 94025 Office: Box 504 Sunnyvale CA 94088

BURROUGHS, EDMUND, lawyer; b. Amherst, Mass., Feb. 16, 1890; s. George Stockton and Emma (Plumley) B.; A.B., Oberlin Coll., 1911; LL.B., Harvard, 1914; m. Esther Anne Swinehart, Sept. 24, 1921; children—Anne Caroline (Mrs. Halbert Frank), Elizabeth Frances (Mrs. Paul Addison Frank, Jr.). Admitted to Ohio bar, 1914; asso. firm M.B. & H.H. Johnson, Cleve., 1914-16; mem. firm Buckingham, Doolittle & Burroughs, Akron, O., 1943—. Instr., Akron Night Law Sch., evening session Akron U.; dir. Burkhardt Consol. Co., Gilbert Lumber Co., Inc., Met. Investment Co., Skillwood Products, Inc., Spiral Brushes, Inc. Served as 2d lt. U.S. Army, 1918-19; AEF in France. Mem. Am., Ohio Akron (pres. 1933-34) bar assns., Am. Judicature Soc., Akron C. of C. (1st v.p. 1950-51). Conglist. (chmn. trustees 1938). Rotarian. Club: City (pres. 1956 Akron). Home: 1206 Sunset View Dr Akron OH 44303 Office: Akron Center Bldg 1 Cascade Plaza Akron OH 44308

BURROUGHS, HENRY DASHIELL, photographer; b. Washington, Aug. 1, 1918; s. Henry D. and Clara (Mattes) B.; m. Elizabeth Anderson, Jan. 18, 1940; 1 dau., Patricia Ellen; m. 2d, Anne Simpson Moore, June 13, 1964; stepchildren—Lyford M. Moore III, Patricia Ann Moore; m. 3d, Margaret Mary Wohlgemuth, Oct. 2, 1971. Staff photographer Washington Post, 1938- 44; staff photographer A.P., 1944—, assigned Paris, France, 1945, Berlin, Germany, 1945-49, Washington, 1949—. Pres. U.S. Berlin Press Club, 1947. Recipient A.P. Mng. Editors 1st annual award for photog. performance, 1964; work represented in Pictures of Year Traveling Exhibit, 1964. Mem. White House News Photographers Assn. (pres. 1956, sec. 1954-55). Clubs: Nat. Press (Washington); Overseas Press (N.Y.C.). Home: Rt 1 Box 65 West River MD 20881 Office: 1300 Connecticut Av NW Washington DC 20006

BURROUGHS, JAMES R., banker; b. Flint, Mich., 1909. Chmn., chief exec. officer Citizens Comml. & Savs. Bank, Flint; v.p., dir. Flint Mortgage Co., Gauranty Title & Mortgage Co. Elk. Home: 3302 Westwood Pky Flint MI 48503 Office: 328 S Saginaw St Flint MI 48502*

BURROUGHS, NELSON MARIGOLD, clergyman; b. Bridgeport, Conn., July 12, 1899; s. Robert Nelson and Lillie Mae (Dunworth) B.; B.A., Wesleyan U., 1922; S.T.B., Berkeley Div. Sch., 1925, S.T.D., 1950; D.D., Wesleyan U., 1942, Kenyon Coll., 1949; m. Ann Bywater Cluett, Dec. 28, 1938; children—Anita Cluett, Margaret Gorham, Robert Nelson, Timothy Rockwell. Ordained to ministry P.E. Ch., deacon, 1925, priest, 1925; curate St. Paul's Ch., Syracuse, N.Y., 1925-27; rector St. Mark's Ch., Syracuse, 1927-30, St. John's Ch., Troy, N.Y., 1930-39, Christ Ch., Cin., 1939-49; bishop coadjutor Ohio, 1949-52, bishop, 1952-68; pres. Fifth Province of P.E. Ch., 1957-63, mem. nat. council, 1963- 68, vice chmn. Ho. of Bishops, 1958-68. Mem. council Diocese of Albany, N.Y., 1935-39, chmn. dept. religious edn., 1934-38; organizer, chaplain Silver Bay Conf. Young People, 1934-38; chaplain Troy Police Dept., 1933-39, Troy Citizen's Corp., 1936-39; lectr. religion Russell Sage Coll. Dept. Gen. Convs., 1937, 40, 43, 46, 49; mem. Bishop Chpt. Diocese So. O., 1943-49, standing com., 1944-48, sec., 1945-48. Trustee Ch. Pension Fund, N.Y. 1945—; dir. Cin. A.R.C. 1948-49; trustee Children's Home, Western Res. U., Kenyon Coll., Cin. Council Chs., also chmn. Comity Com.; pres. Troy Good Will Industries. Mem. Troy Ministerial Assn. (pres. 1936), Newcomen Soc., Phi Sigma Kappa. Clubs: Cleveland, Union, Kirtland Hills; Rotary (Troy past pres.) (Cleve.); University, Cincinnati Country (Cincinnati). Home: 3490 Holly Lane Chatham MA 02633

BURROUGHS, RAYMON, coll. dean; b. Union, Miss., Oct. 11, 1913; s. H.J. and Ethel (Arnold) B.; B.A., Bethel Coll., McKenzie, Tenn., 1939, D.D., 1959; M.A., Western Ky. State Coll., Bowling Green, 1946; B.D., Vanderbilt U., 1942; m. Elizabeth Rives, Apr. 30, 1934; 1 dau., Judith Ray. Ordained to ministry Presbyn. Ch., 1934; mem. faculty Bethel Coll., 1945-, acad. dean, 1947- -. Moderator Cumberland Presbyn. Ch., 1967—. Active local Boy Scouts Am. Mem. Reelfoot Regional Library Bd. Mem. McKenzie C. of C. Rotarian. Home: 219 Magnolia St Mckenzie TN 38201

BURROUGHS, ROBERT PHILLIPS, pioneer designer of pension plans; b. Manchester, N.H., Jan. 13, 1900 s. Sherman Everett and Helen Sophie (Phillips) B.; A.B., Dartmouth, 1921; M.C.S., Amos Tuck Sch. Bus. Adminstrn. and Finance, 1922; m. Dorothy Hall Wellman, Apr. 20, 1927; children—James Wellman, Helen Burroughs Stern, Harriet Burroughs McGraw; m. 2d, Martha Cluverius Parsons, June 19, 1965. Exec. in shoe mfg., 1922-27; entered ins. bus., 1927; pension plan engr., 1930-66; designed and installed pension systems and other employee benefit plans for many leading corps. throughout eastern half of U.S.; v.p. Marsh & McLennan, Inc., 1966—; dir. N.H. Ins. Co., Manchester Corp., Loon Mountain Recreation Corp., Hitchener Co. Spl. U.S. ambassador to Cameroun, 1959, Liberia, 1960. Mem. Republican Nat. Com., 1932-44, mem. exec. com., 1936-40, 1940-44, del. at large Rep. Nat. Conv., 1936, 44, 52, 56, spl. adviser to Gen. Eisenhower during campaign for presidency, 1952, 56; cons. to study Fed. Social Security Act, 1953. Bd. dirs. N.E. Council, 1942-43, Boys Club Am., Child and Family Services of N.H.; chmn. N.H. March of Dimes, 1953-55. Served to 1st lt., AS, U.S. Army, 1918-19. Decorated cross Order Vasco Nuneẑ de Balboa (Panama); recipient Ben Thompson citation U. N.H. Mem. Dartmouth Coll. Alumni Assn. (pres. 1950- 51), Soc. Protection N.H. Forests (sec.), N.H. Soc. S.A.R., Soc. Colonial Wars, Def. Orientation Conf. Assn. (dir.), Am. Forestry Assn. (dir.), Newcomen Soc. Eng., Am. Legion, Sphinx Sr. Soc. Kappa Kappa Kappa. Episcopalian (trustee P.E. Ch. N.H.). Mason. Clubs: Union League (N.Y.); Union, St. Botolph (Boston); Appalachian Mountain: Country, Rotary (Manchester); Metropolitan (Washington); Cotton Bay (Eleuthera). Home: 1280 Union St Manchester NJ 03105 Office: 1015 Elm St Manchester NJ 03105

BURROUGHS, SHERMAN EVERETT, Jr., ret. mfg. co. exec.; b. Manchester, N.H., Feb. 22, 1903; s. Sherman Everett and Helen Sophie (Phillips) B.; B.S., U.S. Naval Acad., 1924; grad. U.S. Navy Postgrad. Sch., 1933, Nat. War Coll., 1951; m. Katherine Earle, Apr. 6, 1929; children—Katherine (Mrs. James A. Sontheimer), Julia Phillips (Mrs. James E. DeBettencourt). Commd. ensign U.S. Navy, 1924, advanced through grades to capt., 1943; designated naval aviator, 1926; staff Adm. Halsey, 1940-42; comdr. Saratoga Air Group, 1942-43, Naval Ordnance Test Sta., China Lake, Cal., 1944-45; chief of staff COMCARDIV 5, 1947-48; assigned Bur. Ordnance, 1949-50; comdg. officer Naval Air Sta., Quonset Point, R.I., 1952-54; ret. as rear adm., 1954-59; v.p. Gen. Precision-Librascope div., 1960—, spl. rep. in Washington. Decorated Silver Star (2), Legion of Merit, D.F.C. Asso. fellow Am. Inst. Aeros. and Astronautics; mem. Naval Order U.S. (comdr. S.W. commandery 1961), Navy League. Episcopalian (vestryman). Clubs: N.Y. Yacht; Army-Navy (Washington); Army-Navy Country (Arlington, Va.). Home: 810 Glorietta Blvd Coronado CA 92118

BURROUGHS, WILLIAM SEWARD, writer; b. St. Louis, Feb. 5, 1914; s. Perry Mortimer and Laura (Lee) B.; A.B., Harvard, 1936; grad. studies ethnology and archeology; med. student U. Vienna; m. Jean Vollmer, 1945; 1 son, William Seward. Formerly newspaper reporter, pvt. detective, exterminator; now full-time writer. Served with AUS, World War II. Author: Junkie: Confessions of an Unredeemed Drug Addict, 1953; Naked Lunch, 1959; The Exterminator, 1960; Minutes to Go, 1961; The Soft Machine, 1961; The Ticket That Exploded, 1962; Dead Fingers Talk, 1963; (with Allen Ginsburg) The Yage Letters, 1963; Nova Express, 1964. Address: care Calder and Boyars 18 Brewer St London W1 England*

BURROW, WILLIAM FITE, lawyer; b. Milan, Tenn., July 2, 1907; s. Richmond Jarrell and Nancy (Jackson) B.; A.B., Vanderbilt U., 1929; LL.B., Yale, 1931; postgrad. Harvard, 1931-32, Cambridge U., Eng., 1932; m. Josephine Worsham, Oct. 12, 1938 (div. Feb. 1967); children—William Fite, Nancy Marian, Bruce Raguet, Christopher Randolph; m. 2d, Marjorie Hanley, Mar. 7, 1968. Admitted to Tex. bar, 1932, since practiced Dallas; asso. Turner, Rodgers & Winn, 1932-37; sr. partner Worsham, Burrow & Worsham, 1938-47; partner Leake, Henry, Golden & Burrow, 1948-58; sr. partner Leake, Henry, Golden, Burrow & Potts, 1959-66, Golden, Burrow, Potts & Beckman, 1967—. Pres. Big D Theatre Co.; past pres. Dallas Oil Syndicate. Dean Jefferson U. Law Sch., 1935-36. Tex. rep. Brit. Govt.'s Civilian Tech. Corp., 1941. Democratic candidate for Congress, 1946; founder 1st Eisenhower Rep. Club in U.S., 1951. Mem. grad. bd. Yale Law Sch., 1955-60; alumni bd. Vanderbilt U., 1959-63; bd. dirs. Yale Law School Fund; trustee St. Mark's Sch. of Tex., 1958-65. Served from capt. to lt. col. 8th Inf. Div., AUS, World War II; col. Res. Decorated Legion of Merit, Bronze Star medal with cluster; Croix de Guerre with palm (Belgium), Medaille Liberté (France). Mem. Am. Arbitration Assn. (nat. panel arbitrators), Am., Tex. (chmn. pub. utilities com.), Dallas (v.p., chmn. grievance com.) bar assns., Jr. Bar Assn. Dallas (pres.), S.A.R., Dallas Interacial Com., S.C.V., Anglo-Texas Soc. (chmn.), Yale Law Sch. Assn. (exec. com. 1958-65), Alpha Tau Omega, Phi Delta Phi. Republican. Episcopalian (vestryman; chmn. dept. social relations Diocese of Dallas). Clubs: Yale (past pres. Dallas); Vanderbilt (past pres.), Idlewild, Northwood Country, Variety (Dallas). Asso. editor Tex. Bar Jour., 1939-42. Contbr. articles law jours. Home: 10122 Gaywood Rd Dallas TX 75229 Office: Republic Nat Bank Tower Dallas TX 75201

BURROWS, ABE, playwright, dir.; b. N.Y.C., Dec. 18, 1910; s. Louis and Julia (Salzberg) B.; student Coll. City N.Y., 1928-29, Sch. of Finance, N.Y.U., 1929, 30, 31; m. Carin Smith Kinzel, Oct. 2, 1950; children—James Edward, Laurie Ellen (Mrs. Peter Grad). Writer of This is New York, for CBS, 1938-39, Texaco Star Theatre, CBS, 1939, Rudy Vallee-John Barrymore program, NBC, 1940, Duffy's Tavern, CBS and NBC, 1941- 45; writer-producer Paramount Pictures, 1946; writer Joan Davis program, CBS, and Ford Program, 1946; writer and star Abe Burrows Show, CBS, 1946-47; made personal appearances in theatres and night clubs, 1947-48; writer-performer-producer, CBS, 1949; writer and star of Breakfast with Burrows, CBS, 1949, Abe Burrows Almanac, CBS-TV, 1950; also in This is Show Business, CBS-TV and We Take Your Word, CBS Radio and TV, 1950; co-author, musical comedy Guys and Dolls, 1950; dir. musical Two on the Aisle, 1951; co-author, dir. musical Three Wishes for Jamie, 1952; author, dir. musical Can-Can, 1953, First Impressions, 1959; dir. play Reclining Figure, 1954, Golden Fleecing, 1959; author, dir. play, Say, Darling, 1958; co-author, dir. How To Succeed in Business without Really Trying, 1961; dir. musical What Makes Sammy Run?, 1964; author, dir. Am. version Cactus Flower, 1965; dir. Broadway play Forty Carats, 1968; Broadway musical Happy Hunting; co-author, dir. Broadway play Four on a Garden, 1971. Recipient Radio Critics award for best comedy show, 1947, N.Y. Drama Critics Award as co-author Guys & Dolls, 1951, as co-author How To Succeed in Business without Really Trying, 1961; Pulitzer prize as co-author How To Succeed in Business without Really Trying, 1961, Tony award as co-author and dir. How to Succeed in Business without Really Trying, 1961. Mem. Dramatists Guild (v.p. 1964), A.S.C.A.P., A.F.T.R.A., Writers Guild Am. West, Musicians Union, Am. Guild Variety Artists. Composer, lyricist and performer Decca Record Album, Columbia Record album, Abe Burrows Sings?, 1950. Author song: The Girl with the Three Blue Eyes, 1944; Abe Burrow's Song Book, 1955; Solid Gold Cadillac (screenplay), 1956; co-author Silk Stockings (Broadway musical comedy). Office: William Morris Agency 1350 6th Av New York City NY 10009

BURROWS, ALBERT COLLINS, former naval officer, lectr. and bus. edn. cons.; b. Shawnee, Okla., Sept. 23, 1905; s. Arthur George and Alice (Guinn) B.; B.S., U.S. Naval Acad., 1928, student Postgrad. Sch., 1935-36; postgrad. Georgetown U. Law Sch., 1940-42; m. Gloria Knight Mangum, Apr. 5, 1952. Commd. ensign USN, 1928, advanced through grades to rear adm., 1958; comdg. officer submarines, 1937-39, exec. officer, destroyer, 1939- 40; comdr. submarines U.S.S. Swordfish and Whale, 1942-44, submarine divisions 12 and 13, Submarine Force Atlantic, 1944-45; comdg. officer U.S.S. Shenandoah, 1945-46; pub. information officer for comdt. 13th Naval Dist., 1946-48; comdg. officer U.S.S. Tappahannock, 1948-50; staff Office Chief of Naval Operations, div. undersea warfare, Washington, 1950-53; comdr. Destroyer Squadron 9, 1953-55; dep. chief staff to comdr. in chief Alaskan Command, 1955-56; comdr. Naval Tng. Center, Gt. Lakes, Ill., 1956-58. Pres., Council Profit Sharing Industries, Chgo., 1958-61, Profit Sharing Research Found., 1958-61. Decorated Navy Cross, Silver Star with 2 gold stars. Named hon. col. Ky., Okla.; Ark. traveler; adm. Neb. Navy, Tex. Navy; chief Tribe of Sycamores; chief Sagamore of the Wabash, Ind.; hon. citizen, states of Tenn., Ohio, Colo., city of New Orleans. Mem. U.S. Naval Acad. Alumni Assn., Navy League U.S. (bd. advisers Chgo. council), Naval Order U.S., Mil. Order World Wars (comdr. Chgo. chpt. 1960-62, chmn. dept. Ill. 1962- 63, Ill. Mfrs. Assn. (vice chmn. nat. security com. 1964—). Clubs: Army- Navy (Washington). Home: 222 Center St Lake Bluff IL 60040

BURROWS, BENJAMIN, educator, physician; b. N.Y.C., Dec. 16, 1927; s. Samuel and Theresa Helen (Handelsman) B.; M.D., Johns Hopkins, 1949; m. Nancy Kreiter, June 14, 1949; children—Jan C., Susan K., Lynn A., Steven M. Intern, Johns Hopkins Hosp., 1949-50; resident King County Hosp., Seattle, 1950-51, U. Chgo., 1953-55; instr. to asso. prof. medicine U. Chgo., 1955-68; prof. internal medicine, head sect. pulmonary diseases U. Ariz. Coll. Medicine, Tucson, 1968—. Cons. Tucson VA Hosp.; dir. Chronic Pulmonary Disease Program for Ariz., USPHS Specialized Center for Research Tng. Program in Pulmonary Diseases. Bd. dirs. Ariz. Tb and Respiratory Disease Assn., Tb and Respiratory Disease Assn. Pima County. Served to capt. USAF, 1951-53. Research grantee USPHS, 1958—. Fellow Am. Coll. Chest Physicians (regent 1969—), A.C.P.; mem. Am. (counsilor), Ariz. (pres.) thoracic socs., Am. Soc. Clin. Investigation, Central Soc. Clin. Research, Am. Physiol. Soc. Mem. editorial bd.: Am. Rev. Respiratory Disease, 1967-71. Contbr. articles to profl. jours., chpts. to books. Home: 350 Sierra Vista Dr Tucson AZ 85719

BURROWS, CHARLES ROBERT, govt. ofcl.; b. Detroit, Feb. 25, 1910; s. John Robert and Martha (Schultz) B.; A.B., Otterbein Coll., 1931; Ph.D., 1964; M.S., N.Y. U., 1932; postgrad. law sch. George Washington U., 1934-35, Nat. War Coll., 1952-53; m. Lucy Mullin, June 12, 1940; children—James Christian, Joan Davidson. Adminstrn. asst. Dept. Agr., 1936-39; apptd. fgn. service officer Dept. State, 1939, vice consul, Havana, 1939, 3d sec., vice consul, La Paz, 1940-43; 2d sec. Buenos Aires, 1943-47, 1st sec., consul, chargé d'affaires Cuidad Trujillo, 1947-49; 1st sec., polit. counselor Mexico City, 1949-51; dir. Middle Am. affairs Dept. State, 1953-54; counselor, dep. chief mission Am. embassy, Manila, 1954, minister-counselor, 1955, Caracas, Venezuela, 1956-60; ambassador to Honduras, 1960-65; dir. C. Am. affairs State Dept., 1965-69; pvt. cons. Latin Am. relations Standard Fruit & S.S. Co.; dir. Found. Coop. Housing. Address: 2519 Massachusetts Av NW Washington DC 20008

BURROWS, DONALD ALBERT, museum dir., educator; b. Chgo., June 26, 1937; s. Charles Frederick and Bertha (Olesen) B.; student So. Ill. U., 1955-56; B.F.A., Art Inst., U. Chgo., 1961, M.F.A., 1963; m. Philomena Durkin, Mar. 3, 1962; children—Jennifer Maria, Charles Frederick. Instr., Sch. Art Inst. Chgo., 1961-64; mus. dir. Mobile (Ala.) Art Gallery, 1964-66; mus. dir. Ft. Worth Art Center Mus., 1966-67, Detroit Art Sch. of Soc. Arts and Crafts, 1967-68; asst. prof. humanities Loop Coll., Chgo. City Coll. Mem. Mobile and Birmingham Festival Arts Adv. Com., 1964-65; mem. adv. council Tex. Fine Arts Commn., 1966-67; pvt. collections Chgo. Ryerson Fgn. Traveling fellow, Chicago, 1961. Mem. Alumni Assn. Art. Inst. Chgo. Am. Assn. Museums, Am. Fedn. Arts Mus. audiovisual applications group, Sigma Tau Gamma. Home: 4839 Imperial Dr Richton Park IL 60471 Office: 64 E Lake St Chicago IL 60601

BURROWS, FRANK FERGUSON, bldg. contractor; b. Salt Lake City, July 21, 1901; s. Frank Edmond and Elsie (Lang) B.; student U. Utah, 1918-20; B.S. in Civil Engring., U. Cal. at Berkeley, 1922; A.B., San Francisco Law Sch., 1937; m. Alice Elizabeth Small, June 30, 1927; children—Frank Robert, Nancy Alice, William Douglas. Asst. hydraulic engr. State of Cal., 1922-24; sec., dir. G.W. Williams Co., 1926—; sec., dir. Am. Homes Co., 1926—, Am. Homes Devel. Co., 1943—; v.p., dir., gen. mgr. Williams & Burrows, Inc., now pres. Mayor, City of Burlingame, 1943-44, councilman, 1940-44. Chmn. Cal. Council Home Builders, 1947; pres. Peninsula Gen. Contractors Assn., 1946-47. Mem. Asso. Gen. Contractors (nat. dir., pres. central chpt. 1953, nat. pres. 1962), Newcomen Soc., Cons. Constructors Am. Mason (Shriner). Clubs: Engineers (San Francisco); Menlo Country; Commonwealth. Home: 120 Fallenleaf Dr Hillsborough CA 94010 Office: 500 Harbor Blvd Belmont CA 94002

BURROWS, LESLIE RAYMOND, univ. dean; b. La Junta, Colo., Nov. 1, 1929; s. Berwyn G. and Leo A. (Willis) B.; student La Junta Jr. Coll., 1947-48; B.A., U. Colo., 1953; D.D.S., U. Kansas City, 1957; Ph.D., U. Rochester, 1962; m. Bertha Jean Pabst, Sept. 2, 1951; children—Eric, Amy, Julie, David. Asst. sec. Council on Dental Research, Am. Dental Assn., 1962-66; cons. Dental Sch. adv. com. U. Colo., Denver, 1966-67, dean Sch. Dentistry, 1967—. Chmn. VA instl. research programs evaluation com., 1968-70; mem. dental program-projects com. Nat. Insts. Dental Research, 1968-70. Served with Colo. N.G., 1948-51; with USAF, 1951-52. Recipient Pattison award for dental research U. Kansas City Dental Sch., 1957, certificate of merit Am. Acad. Dental Medicine, 1960. Mem. Am. Assn. for Accreditation Lab. Animal Care (chmn. bd. trustees), Internat. Assn. for Dental Research, Am. Dental Assn., A.A.A.S., Am., Internat. colls. dentists, Sigma Xi. Home: 1968 Ivy St Denver CO 80220

BURROWS, RICHARD ALAN, ins. co. exec.; b. Detroit, Feb. 5, 1928; s. Sumner Kelsey and Adeline (Oselett) B.; A.B., Albion (Mich.) Coll., 1951; A.M., Yale, 1952; m. Marguerite E. Milici, Sept. 1, 1962; children—Sumner S., Melanie L., Rachel K., Pamela M. Asst. mathematician Equitable Life Assurance Soc., 1961-64; actuary Fidelity Mut. Life Ins. Co., 1966-70; v.p., actuary Asso. Hosp. Service N.Y., N.Y.C., 1971—. Served with AUS, 1946-48. Fellow Soc. Actuaries; mem. Am. Acad. Actuaries, Soc. Indsl. and Applied Math, Phi Beta Kappa, Kappa Mu Epsilon. Home: 979 Post Rd Scarsdale NY 10583 Office: Associated Hospital Service of NY 80 Lexington Av New York City NY 10016

BURROWS SELIG SAUL industrialist; b. N.Y.C., June 1, 1913; s. Louis A. and Julia (Salzberg) B.; student Fordham U., 1930-33. N.Y.U. Law Sch., 1933-36; m. Gladys Spatt, Sept. 18, 1938; childrenKenneth David, Jonathan Lowell, Patricia. Pres., Central Coat Apron & Linen Service, Inc., N.Y.C., 1959—, Bur-Sam Communications Corp., 1965—, Central Industries, Inc., Jersey City, Realty Enterprises of N.J., Inc., Real Estate Indsls., N.Y.C.; partner Burmel Enterprises Co., Spatt Textile & Trading Co., Jersey City. Mem. Presdl. Ann. Assay Commn., 1963. Pres. Burrows Found., Inc.; bd. dirs. N.Y. Worlds Fair 1964 Corp., 1959-; dir. Friends Whitney Mus. Am. Art; trustee L.I. Jewish Hosp., New Hyde Park, N.Y., North Shore Hosp., Manhasset, N.Y.; mem. Pres. council Hofstra U., vice chmn. Fedn. Jewish Charities, L.I.; L.I. exec. com. United Jewish Appeal; exec. adv. council United Cerebral Palsy of N.Y.C.; chmn. Arts Council of Great Neck, N.Y.; mem. adv. bd. Skowhegan Sch. Painting and Sculpture; trustee L.I. Theatre Soc. Clubs: Lotos, Fresh Meadows Country, Country, Dutch Treat (N.Y.C.); Palm Beach (Fla.) Country. Home: Serena Horseshow Rd Mill Neck NY 11020 also 6 W 56th St NYC NY 10019 also 100 Sunrise Av Palm Beach FL 33480 Office: 514 W 49th St New York City NY 10019

BURROWS, VERNON WILSON, coll. dean; b. Claremore, Okla., Oct. 30, 1909; s. Charles C. and Laura (Julian) B.; B.S., East Central State Coll., 1929; M.S., Okla. State U., 1942, D.Ed., 1958; m. Mary Helen Chew, June 10, 1939; children—Linda Kay (Mrs. James R. Priest), Barbara H., Philip V. Prin. Pernell (Okla.) High Sch., 1929-30, prin. Weleetka (O.) High Sch., 1930-39, prin. Beggs (Okla.) High Sch., 1939-41, prin. Stigler (Okla.) High Sch., 1941-42; chmn. math. dept. Jr. Coll., El Reno, Okla., 1945-47; mem. faculty Northeastern State Coll., 1947—, dean Grad. Sch., 1963—. Mem. Okla., Nat edn. assns., Assn. Higher Edn., Nat. Council Tchrs. Math., Kappa Mu Epsilon. Mem. Christian Ch. (trustee 1960—). Home: 1200 N Grand St Tahlequah OK 74464

BURROWS, WILLIAM, bacteriologist, educator; b. New Haven, Mar. 6, 1908; s. William and Winifred Elizabeth (Johnson) B.; B.S., Purdue U., 1928; M.S., U. Ill., 1930; Ph.D., U. Chgo., 1932; m. Margaret Pound, June 24, 1931; 1 dau., Mary. Gen. Edn. Bd. fellow, 1935-37; research asst. U. Chgo., 1932-35; asst. prof., 1937-42, asso. prof., 1942-47, prof. microbiology, 1947-; responsible investigator Office Sci. Research and Devel., 1942-46, 58—, U.S. Army Research and Devel. Command, 1963—, USPHS, 1946-49, 53—, biol. div. chem. corps U.S. Army, 1950-; cons. Argonne Nat. Lab.; mem. WHO, expert adv. Panel Cholera. Recipient Ricketts prize, 1932. Fellow A.A.A.S., Am. Acad. Microbiology, Inst. Medicine Chgo.; mem. Chgo. Hist. Soc., Am. Soc. Microbiologists, Am. Assn. Immunologists, Am. Pub. Health Assn., Soc. Exptl. Biology and Medicine, Soc. Ill. Microbiologists (pres. 1949), Sigma Xi, Gamma Alpha, Sigma Alpha Epsilon. Republican. Episcopalian. Clubs: Quadrange, Literary (Chgo.). Author: Textbook of Microbiology, 1968; research papers med. jours. Mem. editorial bd. Am. Med. Dictionary. Home: 5550 Dorchester Av Chicago IL 60637

BURROWS, WILLIAM FREDERICK, diesel engine mgr.; b. Gates Wills, O., Apr. 27, 1915; s. George Frederick and Amy Clair (Neff) B.; B.S. in Mech. Engring., Cornell U., 1939. Engring. devel., then asst. chief engr. Aircooled Motors Corp., Syracuse, N.Y., 1939-49; engr. White Motor Co., Cleve., 1950- 55, gen. mgr. White Diesel Engine div., Springfield, O., 1955-58, v.p., gen. mgr., Cleve., 1958-65; pres. White Superior div., 1965-68; dir. Quick Mfg., Inc., Lagonda Nat. Bank, Springfield. Active Jr. Achievement. Mem. Am. Soc. M.E., Soc. Automotive Engrs., Soc. Exptl. Stress Analysis, C. of C. Home: 1420 Garfield Av Springfield OH 45504 Office: 1401 Sheridan Av Springfield OH 45505

BURRUS, GEORGE BERNARD, retail drug exec.; b. Woodland Mills, Tenn., Apr. 14, 1906; s. George Brasfield and Mosell (Davis) B.; grad. Max-Morris Sch. Pharmacy, 1925; m. Beulah Jefferson Ross, Jan. 19, 1929; children—Margaret Louise (Mrs. John Drerup), Patricia Swan (Mrs. Rudolf A. Ruda). Soda dispenser Peoples Drug Stores, 1923-24, sales clk., 1924- 26, pharmacist, 1926, mgr., 1927, asst. advt. mgr., 1927-28, asst. dist. mgr., 1928-34, advt. mgr., 1934-40, v.p. charge store operations, 1940- 49, dir., 1945—, exec. v.p. 1949-50, pres., 1950-70, chmn. bd., 1958—; dir. Am. Security & Trust Co., Acacia Mut. Life Ins. Co. Dir. Fed. City Council, Washington, Interracial Council for Bus. Opportunity, Washington. Bd. dirs. United Givers Fund, Am. Found. Pharm. Edn. (treas. 1966-69), Children's Hosp. Mem. Nat. Assn. Chain Drug Stores (dir., pres. 1955-57), Washington Bd. Trade (dir. 1959-63), D.C. Pharm. Assn., Asso. Chain Drug Stores (dir. 1960-68, pres. 1964-66), Newcomen Soc., Soc. Friendly Sons St. Patrick (dir., past pres. Washington). Episcopalian. Mason. Clubs: Advertising (pres. 1940-41), Columbia Country, Metropolitan, Circus Saints and Sinners, Burning Tree (Washington). Home: 4100 52d St NW Washington DC 20016 Office: 60 Florida Av NE Washington DC 20002

BURSIEK, RALPH CARL, univ. ofcl.; b. Rockford, Ill., Nov. 25, 1906; s. William and Emma (Bucks) B.; Comm. Eng., U. Cin., 1931, A.M., 1932, postgrad. econs., 1932-34; student Sch. Banking U. Wis., 1948-50; LL.D., Xavier U., m. Marjorie DeCamp, October 23, 1927; children—Carolyn Patricia (Mrs. Bergen Merrill), Ralph David. Taft teaching fellow U. Cin., 1932-34, instr. coll. bus. adminstrn., 1934-39, asst. prof., dir. Student Union, 1939-42, asso. prof., asst. dean, 1946-51, prof. econs., dean univ. adminstrn., 1951—, exec. v.p., 1967—; research asst. Fed. Emergency Relief Adminstrn., 1934. Pres., Mid-Am. Conf., 1949-50, Mo. Valley Conf., 1959-60. Sec. bd. dirs., exec. sec. U. Cin. Research Found., 1951-59; trustee Lichter Found., Hosp. Care Corp., U. Cin. Endowment Fund Assn. Served as maj. Med. Adminstrn. Corps, AUS, 1942- 46; ETO. Mem. Am. Econ. Assn., Am. Finance Assn., Soc. for Advancement Mgmt. (dir. Cin.), Ohio Soc. N.Y., Newcomen Soc. Eng., Engring. Soc. Cin., Am. Acad. Polit. and Social Sci., Beta Gamma Sigma (past. sec.-treas., editor 1950-51), Omicron Delta Kappa, Alpha Kappa Psi, Scabbard and Blade. Rotarian. Clubs: University, Queen City, Kenwood Country. Home: 2930 Scioto St Cincinnati, OH 45219.

BURSK, EDWARD COLLINS, editor; b. Lancaster, Pa., Apr. 16, 1907; s. John Howard and Sarah Katharine (Mull) B.; student Mercerburg Acad., 1923-24; A.B., Amherst Coll., 1928; A.M., Harvard, 1929; m. Catherine Hertzler Irwin, June 26, 1930; children—Edward Collins, John Howard, Christopher Irwin. Instr. Greek and Latin, Dartmouth, 1931-33; pres. J.H. Bursk Co., 1933-41; instr. Greek, econs. Franklin and Marshall Coll., 1941-42; instr. bus. adminstrn. Harvard, 1942, asst. prof., 1943, asso. prof., 1946-51, prof., 1953-67, mng. editor Harvard Bus. Rev., 1943-47, editor, 1947—. Chmn., Internat. Mgmt. & Marketing Group, Inc.; pres. Intermark, Inc.; dir. Newsome & Co., Inc., Gum Products, Inc., N.Am. Investment Fund N.V., N.Am. Bank Stock Fund N.V., Rumford Ins. Co., Underwriters Investment Corp., Conf. Service Corp., Interliving Corp., Hamilton Internat. Corp. Named to Distbn. Hall of Fame, 1962. Mem. Internat. Marketing Research and Planning Dirs. (council), Internat. Marketing Inst. (ednl. dir.), Am. Marketing Assn. (v.p. marketing mgmt. 1962-63), Kappa Theta, Phi Beta Kappa, Delta Tau Delta. Unitarian. Author: Text and Cases in Marketing: A Scientific Approach, 1962; Cases in Marketing Management, 1965. Co-author: Advanced Cases in Marketing Management, 1968. Editor: Thinking Ahead for Business, 1952; Getting Things Done in Business, 1953; How to Increase Executive Effectiveness, 1953; The Management Team, 1954; Human Relations for Management, 1956; Business and Religion, 1959; Planning the Future Strategy of Your Business, 1956. Co-editor: The World of Business, 1962; New Decision-Making Making Tools for Managers, 1963; Modern Marketing Strategy, 1964; Salesmanship and Sales Force Management, 1971. Home: Beach Island Cohasset MA 02025 Office: Soldiers Field Boston MA 02163

BURSON, HAROLD, pub. relations exec.; b. Memphis, Feb. 15, 1921; s. Maurice and Esther (Bach) B.; B.A., U. Miss., 1940; m. Bette Ann Foster, Oct. 30, 1947; children—Scott, Mark. Corr., reporter Memphis Comml. Appeal, 1938- 40; dir. Ole Miss News Bur., Oxford, Miss., 1939-40; dir. pub. relations H.K. Ferguson Co., N.Y.C., 1941-43; chmn. Burson-Marsteller, N.Y.C., 1953—; dir., mem. exec. com. Marsteller, Inc., N.Y.C.; pres., dir. Burson-Marsteller (Can.), Ltd., Toronto, 1958—, Marsteller Internat. S.A., Geneva, Switzerland, 1961—; dir. Marsteller (Belgium) S.A., Brussels, Marsteller-Bruder Internat. GmbH. Stuttgart, Germany, Burson-Marsteller Ltd. (London). Bd. dirs., exec. com., v.p. pub. information Nat. Safety Council; trustee Hackley Sch., Tarrytown, N.Y. Served with AUS, World War II. Mem. Pub. Relations Soc. Am., Internat. Advt. Assn., Internat. Pub. Relations Assn., N.Y. Soc. Security Analysts, Indsl. Publicity Assn., Am. Philatelic Soc., Blue Key, Omicron Delta Kappa. Clubs: Overseas Press, Marco Polo, Fifth Avenue (N.Y.C.); Mid-America (Chgo.); International (Washington). Home: 260 Beverly Rd Scarsdale NY 10583 Office: 866 3d Av New York City NY 10022

BURSON, PHYLLIS S., librarian; b. Seattle, Mar. 31, 1914, d. Harry E. and Theodosia (Porter) Sheidler; B.A., U. Wash., 1938, B.A. in Librarianship, 1939; student U. Ida. Coll. Law, 1939-45; children—Theo Lynne, Marilyn Kay. Asstships, univ. libraries, 1934-40; head librarian U. Ida. Coll. Law, Moscow, 1940-45; asst. librarian Del Mar. Coll., Corpus Christi, Tex., 1951-53; asst. librarian La Retama Pub. Library, Corpus Christi, 1953- 56, head librarian, 1956-66, dir., 1966—; cons. in field. Sec., treas. Nueces County Hist. Survey Com., 1962—; mem. library services and facilities com. Coastal Bend Regional Planning Commn., 1968—. Bd. dirs. Paisano Girl Scout Council, 1964-66, personnel chmn., 1968-70. Named Corpus Christi Woman of Year, 1963. Mem. A.L.A., Tex. (past div. chmn., exec. bd. mem.-at-large; librarian of year 1966, legislative chmn. 1967-69, pres. 1970-71), Southwestern (mem. council, exec. com. Southwestern library collaborative effort 1971—) library assns., Am. Assn. U. Women. Episcopalian. Home: 3102 Santa Fe Corpus Christi TX 78404 Office: 505 N Mesquite St Corpus Christi TX 78401

BURSTONE, CHARLES JUSTIN, educator; b. Kansas City, Mo., Apr. 4, 1928; s. Lester and Rose (Farb) B.; M.S., Ind. U., 1955; D.D.S., Washington U., St Louis, 1950. Faculty Ind. U. Sch. Dentistry, Indpls., 1955-70, prof. orthodontics, 1966-70, chmn. dept., 1959-70; prof., head dept. orthodontics Sch. Dental Medicine U. Conn., 1970—. Served to capt. USAF, 1951-53. Diplomate Am. Bd. Orthodontics. Mem. Am. Assn. Orthodontists, Am. Dental Assn., Angle Soc., Ind. (pres. 1967-68) Great Lakes Socs. orthodontists (pres. 1967-68), Omicron Kappa Upsilon (pres. 1969-70). Author articles on mechanics, physics, growth amd devel., soft tissue analysis. Home: 8 Gloucester Lane West Hartford CT 06107

BURT, ALVIN VICTOR, Jr., newspaperman; b. Carlton, Ga., Sept. 11, 1927; s. Alvin Victor and Mabel Sorrow) B.; B.A., in Edn., U. Fla., 1949; m. Gloria White. With U.P., 1949-50, Atlanta Jour., 1950-51, Jacksonville (Fla.) Jour., 1951-55; with Miami (Fla.) Herald, 1955-66, Latin Am. editor, 1962-66, assigned Washington, 1962; editor Hartwell (Ga.) Sun, 1966-67; editorial writer for Miami Herald, 1967—. Recipient Ernie Pyle award for newspaper writing, 1961; State award A.P. for feature writing, 1964; citation Fla. Legislature, 1965; Scripps-Howard award for best interviews in nation, 1966. Mem. Sigma Delta Chi. Co- author; Papa Doc, 1969. Home: 10701 SW 69th Av Miami FL 33156 Office: Miami Herald Miami FL 33101

BURT, CLEON LEROY, diversified co. exec., lawyer; b. Central Cove, Ida., May 23, 1923; s. Charles Andrew and Grace (Godfrey) B.; student U. Ida., 1940-43, Midwestern U., 1946-47; J.D., St. Louis U., 1950; m. M. Imogene Troop, Dec. 23, 1949; children—Karen, Glenna. Admitted to Mo. bar, 1950; practiced in St. Louis, 1950-51; asst. sec., asst. gen. counsel Mississippi River Corp., St. Louis, 1952-60, gen. counsel, 1960-69, v.p. sec., sec.,, 1969—. Mem. adv. council St. Louis U. Law Sch., 1955-60. Dist. capt. sustaining membership St. Louis Girl Scouts Council, 1969-71. Served with USAAF, 1944-46. Mem. Am., Mo., St. Louis, St. Louis County, Fed. Power bar assns., Alpha Sigma Nu, Phi Alpha Delta, Tau Kappa Epsilon. Home: 605 N Woods Mill Rd St Louis MO 63017 Office: Mississippi River Corp 9900 Clayton Rd St Louis MO 63124

BURT, GEORGE DOLE WADLEY, newspaperman; b. Bolingbroke, Ga., Oct. 1, 1909; s. William Giroud and Sarah Lois (Wadley) B.; ed. Woodbury Forest, Va., and Lanier High Sch., Macon, Ga.; student Ga. Sch. Tech., 1926-27; m. Gwyneth Margaret Miller. Reporter, Macon Telegraph, 1928-36; writer and editor Asso. Press, 1936-38; editor Macon (Ga.) Evening News and exec. editor Macon Telegraph, 1938-40; staff Courier-Jour. and Louisville Times, 1940—, chief editorial writer, 1948-56; editorial page editor Louisville Times, 1956—. Capt. U.S. Army, World War II, asst. intelligence officer, Bermuda Base Command, a.d.c. to comdg. gen. Harbor Defs., Portland, Me. Army Civil Communications Intelligence Sch., Stanford U.; instr. press censorship Civil Censorship Group, Camp Stoneman, Cal. Mem. Am. Soc. Newspaper Editors, Nat. Conf. Editorial Writers, Inter-Am. Press Assn. Democrat. Home: Prospect KY 40222 Office: Louisville Times Louisville KY 40202

BURT, JOHN HARRIS, bishop; b. Marquette, Mich., Apr. 11, 1918; s. Bates G. and Emily May (Bailey) B.; B.A., Amherst Coll. 1940, D.D. (hon.), 1960; B.A., Va. Theol. Sem., 1943, D.D., 1967; D.D., Youngstown U., 1958, Kenyon Coll., 1967; m. Martha M. Miller, Feb. 16, 1946; children—Susan, Emily, Sarah, Mary. Boys worker Christodora House, N.Y.C., 1940-41; ordained to ministry Episcopal Ch., 1943; canon Christ Ch. Cathedral, rector St. Paul's Ch., St. Louis, 1943-44; chaplain to Episcopal students U. Mich., 1946-50; rector St. John's Ch., Youngstown, O., 1950-57, All Saints Ch., Pasadena, Cal., 1957-67; bishop coadjutor Ohio, 1967-68; Episcopal bishop of Ohio, 1968—. Pres. So. Cal. Council Chs., 1962-65; mem. bd. Ch. Soc. Coll. Work, 1964—, chmn. joint commn. deployment Episcopal Ch., 1967—. Pres. Youngstown Coordinating Council, 1954-56, Pasadena Community Council, 1964-66. Trustee Pomona Coll., 66, Va. Theol. Sem., 1967—, Colgate-Rochester Div. Sch., 1968—, Kenyon Coll., 1967—; bd. dirs. United Way Los Angeles, 1964-67, Cleve. Urban Coalition, 1968-70, Inst. Am. Democracy, 1967—; gen. bd. Nat. Council Chs., 1970—. Served as chaplain USNR, 1943-46. Recipient Arvona Lynch Human Relations award Youngstown, 1956; Rissica Human Relations award Jewish War Vets., 1966; Pasadena Community Relations award, 1967. Mem. Phi Gamma Delta. Co-author: World Religions and World Peace, 1969. Home: 18200 Shelburne Rd Shaker Heights OH 44118 Office: 2230 Euclid Av Cleveland OH 44115

BURT, MILLARD PAYLOR, coll. ofcl.; b. Fuquay, N.C., Feb. 27, 1917; s. Raymond A. and Ella (Stanfield) B.; A.B., Atlantic Christian Coll.; 1934-38; M.A., U. N.C., 1948, Ph.D., 1952; m. Beulah Aycock, June 29, 1940; children—Charles Aycock, Carolyn Aycock, Dir. band Raleigh (N.C.) Pub. Schs., 1938-40, 46- 52; chmn. dept. edn. Atlantic Christian Coll., 1952-55, dean of coll., 1958-63; dean Meth. Coll., Fayettville, N.C., dir. Ft. Bragg br. N.C. State U., Raleigh, 1965—; asst. dir. prisons N.C. Prison Dept., 1955-58. Mem. N.C. N.G., 1932—. Served with AUS, 1940-46. Mem. Nat., N.C. edn. assns., N.C. Bandmasters Assn. (past pres., exec. sec.), Shrine Bandmasters Assn. N.A. (past pres.), Phi Delta Kappa. Mason (Shriner, dir. band), Elk. Club: Sertoma (pres. Wilson, gov. E. N.C. dist.). Home: 258 Prince Charles Rd Fayetteville NC 28301

BURT, RICHARD LAFAYETTE, educator, physician; b. Springfield, Mass., Dec. 7, 1915; s. Lafayette and Theresa (Maines) B.; B.S., Springfield Coll., 1938; Sc.M., Brown U., 1940, Ph.D., 1942; M.D., Harvard, 1946; m. Regina Meed, June 27, 1942; children—Jonathan M., Duncan T., Deborha D., Priscilla M. Research fellow Harvard, 1942-43; intern U.S. Navy Hosp., Chelsea, Mass., 1946- 47; asst. resident obstetrics and gynecologyy N.C. Baptist Hosp., 1949- 52, chief resident, 1952-53; mem. faculty Bowman Gray Sch. Medicine, 1949—, prof. obstetrics and gynecology, 1958—, chmn. dept., 1966—; cons. NIH, 1964-68; research prof. USPHS, 1960-64. Served to lt. (j.g.) USNR, 1946-49. Mem. Am. Gynecol. Soc., Soc. Gynecol. Investigation, Ednocrine Soc., St. Atlantic Assn. Obstetricians and Gynecologists, Am. Diabetes Assn., A.M.A., N.C. Soc. Obstetricians and Gynecologists, Sigma Xi, Alpha Omega Alpha. Author papers in field. Mem. editorial bd. Obstetrics and Gynecology, 1966—. Home: 2801 Robin Hood Rd Winston-Salem NC 27106

BURT, RUSSELL JEFFORDS, lawyer; b. Charleston, W.Va., Jan. 2, 1886; s. Benjamin R. and Lillian Allen (Jeffords) B.; B.A., m. Hilda J. Corwin, June 23, 1913 (dec. Dec. 1926); children—John C., Ben R.; m. 2d, Adelaide Wise, Jan. 27, 1928; 1 son, Richard J. Admitted to Ohio bar, 1910; with firm Goulder, Day, White, Garry & Duncan, Cleve., 1910-12; practice in Canton, O., 1912—; partner firm Amerman, Burt & Jones, 1957—. Tchr. corp. law William McKinley Law Sch., Canton, 1928-32; dir. Peoples-Mchts. Trust Co., Canton, 1958-66. Fellow Am. Coll. Trial Lawyers; hon. mem. Ohio Bar Assn.; mem. Delta Upsilon. Republican. Home: 1601 Logan Av NW Canton OH 44703 Office: Peoples Bank Bldg Canton OH 44702

BURT, WAYNE VINCENT, oceanographer, educator; b. South Shore, S.D., May 10, 1917; s. John David and Mary Pearle (McDuffee) B.; B.S. in Math, Pacific Coll., 1939; M.S., U. Cal. at Los Angeles, 1948, Ph.D. in Phys. Oceanography, 1952; D.Sc. (hon.), George Fox Coll., Newberg, Ore., 1963; m. Grace Louise DuBois, Jan. 15, 1941; children—John Alan, Christine Louise, Laurence W., Darcy Jean. Instr., Ore. high schs., 1939-42; material engr. Kaiser Co., Inc., Wash. State, 1942; instr. math. U. Ore., 1946; asst. Scripps Instn., 1946-48, asso. oceanographer, 1948-49; asst. prof. oceanography, research oceanographer Chesapeake Bay Inst., Johns Hopkins, 1949-53, asst. dir., 1953; research oceanographer dept. oceanography U. Wash., 1953-54; asso. prof. oceanography Ore. State U., Corvallis, 1954-59, prof., chmn. dept., 1959-67, asso. dean research, 1967—; dir. marine sci. center, 1964—. Mem. sci. expdns. to Eastern tropical Pacific Ocean, Scripps Instns. Oceanography, 1955, 58; rep. XIV Limnology Congress, Vienna, Austria, 1959; rep. to UN Research Vessel Forum, Tokyo, Japan, 1961; rep. UNESCO Inter-govtl. Oceanographic Commn., Paris, 1965. Served to lt. USNR, 1942-46; comdr. Res. Recipient Alumni Distinguished Prof. award Ore. State U., 1968, Centennial award, 1968; Gov.'s Scientist award Ore. Mus. Sci. and Industry, 1969; Man of Year award Willamette Valley Research Council, 1971. Mem. Meteorol. Soc. (council 1969), Am. Geophys. Union (pres. oceanography sect. 1964), Am. Soc. Limnology and Oceanography (pres. Pacific sect. 1958, editorial bd. 1963-64), Ore. Acad. Sci., Ore. Marine Biol. Soc. Contbr. articles to profl. jours. Home: 1615 Hillcrest Dr Corvallis OR 97330

BURT, WILLIAM HENRY, ret. zoologist, mammalogist; b. Haddam, Kan., Jan. 22, 1903; s. Frank P. and Hattie (Carlson) B.; A.B., U. Kan., 1926, A.M., 1927; Ph.D., U. Cal., 1930; m. Leona S. Galutia, Sept. 15, 1928. Teaching fellow in zoology U. Kan., 1926-27, U. Cal., 1927-28, in paleontology, 1928-29; research fellow Cal. Inst. Tech., 1930-35; instr. in zoology U. Mich., 1935-41, prof., 1949-69, asst. curator mammals Mus. Zoology, 1935-38, curator, 1938-69, emeritus prof., curator, 1969—. NRC, 1963—. Mem. Am. Soc. Mammalogists (corr. sec. 1935-38, dir., v.p. 1951-53, pres. 1953-55), hon. mem. Izaak Walton League of Am. (pres. Mich. div., 1949), Soc. Systematic Zoology (council 1957-60). Wilson, Cooper ornithol. socs., Phi Beta Kappa, Sigma Xi, Phi Sigma. Author: The Mammals of Michigan, 1946, rev., 1948; A Field Guide to the Mammals, 1951, rev. edit., 1964; Mammals of the Great Lakes Area, 1957. Editor: Journal of Mammalogy 1947-52. Contbr. articles to scientific publs. Home: 2995 Glenwood Dr Boulder CO 80301

BURTENSHAW, CLAUDE JUNIOR, univ. adminstr.; b. Bonneville County, Ida., Feb. 24, 1918; s. W.F. and Olive (Humphrey) B.; A.A., Ricks Coll., 1941; B.S., U. Utah, 1947, M.S., 1948, Ph.D., 1955; m. Frances Davis, May 27, 1942; children—Claudene, Bonita, Bruce, Rick, LuAnn, Julene Gina Kay, Francene. Elementary sch. tchr. Bonneville County Sch., 1941; tchr. Ricks Coll., Reburg, Ida., 1947-59, pub. relations dir., 1951-59; ins., implement, investment businesses, 1950-59; pres. Coll. Eastern Utah, 1959-62; v.p. Utah State U., Logan, 1962—, prof. polit. sci., 1965—, program dir. Peace Corps, 1963—. Mem. Ida. Democratic Central Com., 1948-50; mem. Ida. Ho. of Reps., 1952, Senate, 1958—; mem. Reorgn. Study Com. Ida. Govt., 1953-54; Dem. chmn. Madison County, Ida., 1954; nominee U.S. Senate, 1950. Served with USAAF, 1942-45. 15th Dist. Fed. Res. Seminar fellow, 1955. Recipient Distinguished Service award Jr. C. of C., 1952. Mem. Western States Polit. Sci. Assn., N.W. Sci. Assn. (editorial staff 1955- -). Mem. Ch. of Jesus Christ of Latter-day Saints (past missionary). Rotarian, Toastmaster (pres.). Home: 1439 E 8th N Logan UT 84321

BURTIN, WILL, designer; b. Cologne, Germany, Jan. 27, 1908; s. August and Gertrude (Sieger) B.; student Kolner Werkschulen, 1927-30; m. Hilda Munk, Apr. 12, 1932 (dec. Oct. 1960); 1 dau., Carol; m. 2d, Cipe Pineles Golden, Jan. 28, 1961; 1 stepson, Tom. Came to U.S., 1938, naturalized, 1943. Designer exhbns. and graphic projects, Germany, 1930-38; free-lance designer, N.Y.C., 1938-43; tchr. exptl. design Pratt Inst., Bklyn., 1939- 43; art dir. Fortune mag., 1945-49; designer for industry and govt., N.Y.C., 1949—; design dir., cons. Upjohn Co., Kalamazoo, 1950-70. Program chmn. Internat. Design Conf., Aspen, Colo., 1954-56, Vision 65, World Communication Congress; speaker numerous design confs. in U.S. and fgn. countries, 1948; pres. Internat. Congress Communication Arts and Scis.; v.p. Internat. Com. Graphic Design Assn., London. Served with USAAF, 1943-44; with OSS, 1944-45. Recipient numerous medals and awards from N.Y. Art Dirs. Club, Detroit Art Dirs. Club, Am. Inst. Graphic Arts. Mem. Am. Inst. Graphic Arts (past dir.), Alliance Graphique Internationale (pres. Am. Sect.), Soc. Typographers and Artists (hon.), N.Y. Art Dirs., Am. Society Information Sci. Club: New York Type Dirs. Club. Designer The Cell, The Brain, Chromosone, Def. of Life exhbns. for Upjohn Co., 1958-69, also Atom in Action for Union Carbide Corp., 1960. Home: Filors Lane Stony Point NY 10980 Office: 132 E 58th St NY 10022

BURTIS, THEODORE ALFRED, chem. engr.; b. Jamaica, N.Y., May 17, 1922; s. Theodore Alfred and Florence Angela (Whalen) B.; B.Sc., Carnegie Inst. Tech., 1942; M.Sc., Tex. A. and M. Coll., 1946; m. Billie Joyce King, June 2, 1945; children—Barbara, Theodore, Pamela. Research engr. Magnolia Petroleum Co., 1943-45; sales engr. Owens-Corning Fiberglas Corp., 1946-47; with Houdry Process Corp., Phila., 1947—, pres., 1956-62, also chmn.; dir. comml. devel. Sun Oil Co., 1967-68, adminstrv. dir. research and engring., 1969-70, v.p. research and devel., 1970—; chmn. Catalytic Constrn. Co.; pres. Houdry Process & Chem. Co.; v.p., dir. Air Products & Chems. Inc., 1962-67. Trustee Carnegie Mellon Inst. Fellow Am. Inst. Chem. Engrs. (pres. 1967); mem. Am. Chem. Soc., Coordinating Research Council (dir.), Kappa Sigma, Tau Beta Pi. Clubs: Union League (Phila.); Chemists (N.Y.C.); Springhaven (Wallingford, Pa.). Home: 109 Sycamore Lane Wallingford PA 19086 Office: 1608 Walnut St Philadelphia PA 19103

BURTNER, CHARLES ALLEN, assn. exec.; b. White Post, Va., Mar. 18, 1929; s. William Dorsey and Golda Virginia (Dearmont) B.; diploma Randolph-Macon Acad., 1947; B.A., Randolph-Macon Coll.; m. Janet Ellen Flora, Dec. 12, 1959; children—Tamsey Leigh, Sydney Ann. Reporter, advt. salesman South Boston News & Halifax County Record-Advertiser, South Boston, Va., 1952-54; sports editor, spl. assignment reporter Waynesboro (Va.) News-Va., 1954-57; exec. sec. Bedford (Va.) County C. of C., 1957-60; dir. pub. relations Charlotte (N.C.) C. of C., 1960-62; dir. New River Indsl. Commn., 1962-66; v.p., sec. Lynchburg (Va.) C. of C., 1966-68; exec. mgr. Greater Richmond (Va.) C. of C., 1968—. Bd. dirs. Better Bus. Bur. Richmond, 1968—. Mem. Va. Assn. C. of C. Execs. (pres. 1968-70), Va. C. of C. (indsl. com. 1966—), Pi Delta Epsilon. Club: Downtown (Richmond). Home: 10505 Covent Rd Richmond VA 23233 Office: 616 E Franklin St Richmond VA 23219

BURTNER, DALE CHARLES, educator; b. Portland, Ore., Oct. 20, 1926; s. William Reed and Eleanor (Cooper) B.; B.A., Reed Coll., 1948; M.A., U. Wash., 1951, Ph.D., 1954; m. Leona May Wright, Dec. 16, 1950; children—Don Reed, Ann. Research chemist Shell Devel. Co., 1954-58; faculty Fresno (Cal.) State Coll., 1958—, prof. chemistry, 1967—, chmn. dept., 1965—, dean arts and scis., 1966-69. Mem. Am. Chem. Soc., Assn. Cal. State Coll. Profs. (v.p. 1965-66, pres. 1970-71), United Profs. Cal. (state v.p. 1970-71), Sigma Xi (asso.), Phi Lambda Upsilon. Home: 5648 N Safford St Fresno CA 93705

BURTNESS, HAROLD WILLIAM, r.r. exec.; b. Chgo., Nov. 16, 1897; s. Theodore and Marie (Rone) B.; student Met. Bus. Coll., 1915-16, LaSalle Extension U., 1920-21; m. Grace M. Reinholtzen, Aug. 16, 1924; children—Roger William, James Harold. Clk., C., B.&O. R.R., 1914; clk., stenographer, sec. to mgr. Star Union Line, later gen. freight agt., traffic mgr. Pa. R.R., 1915-22; sec. to pres., chmn. bd. C.G.W. R.R. Co., 1922-33; sec. to chmn. Western Assn. Ry. Execs., 1925-30; asst. to pres., sec. C.G.W. R.R. Co., 1933-41, in charge transp. div. operating dept.; v.p., dir. 6 subsidiary cos. C.G.W. R.R., pres. Gt. Western Coal Co., 1934—; v.p. C.G.W. R.R., 1941-46, pres., dir., chmn. exec. com., 1946-48; chmn. bd. Luth. Mut. Life Ins. Co., 1965—; dir. Kansas City Terminal Ry. Co., St. Paul Union Depot Co., Minn. Transfer Ry. Co. Mem. 1st Div. Nat. R.R. Adjustment Bd., 1949—. Pres., Bethesda Home for Aged. Pres. bd. trustees Luth. Deaconess Home and Hosp. Mem. Am. Assn. R.R. Supts. Republican. Lutheran. Clubs: Union League, Chicago. Home: 1225 N Euclid Av Oak Park IL 60302 Office: 433 W Van Buren St Chicago IL 60607

BURTNESS, PAUL SIDNEY, coll. dean; b. Chgo., June 30, 1923; s. Sidney Thorander and Anna Margaret (Johnsen) B.; student U. Chattanooga, 1941-43; A.M., U. Chgo., 1947, Ph.D., 1953; m. Jean Winifred Bordwell, Dec. 26, 1945; children—Karen Lynn, Neil Jeffrey. Instr. English lang. and lit. U. Kan. City, 1949-53; mem. faculty Northern Ill. U., 1953—, prof. English, 1962—, dean Coll. Liberal Arts and Scis., 1969—; cons. communications Coronet Instructional Films; cons. exec. communications Motorola Corp. Chmn. citizens adv. com. Sycamore Bd. Edn., 1961-62; mem. faculty adv. com. Ill. Bd. Higher Edn., 1963-65. Served with USNR, 1943-46. Intern in Acad. Adminstrn., Ellis L. Phillips Found., Stanford 1965, U. Mich., 1966. Mem. Modern Lang. Assn., Nat. Council Tchrs. English, Conf. Coll. Composition and Communication, Am. Assn. Higher Edn., Council Colls. Arts and Scis., Lyric Opera Assn., Art Inst. Chgo. Co-author: Effective English for Business Communication, 1970. Co-editor: The Strategy of Prose—Structure, Purpose, Style, 1970. Home: 395 Parkside Dr Sycamore IL 60178 Office: Watson Hall East No Ill Univ De Kalb IL 60115

BURTON, A. PAUL, publisher; b. Camden, N.J., June 10, 1909; s. Paul and Beatrice (Eadson) B.; B.Sc., Rutgers U., 1932; grad. Advanced Mgmt. Program, Harvard, 1951; m. Mildred S. Leonard, Feb. 1, 1936 (dec. 1967); 1 son, A. Paul; m. Agnes S. Donahue, June 1968. Dist. mgr. Curtis Pub. Co., 1932-40; with W.B. Saunders Co., Phila., 1940—, v.p. sales, 1950-56, exec. v.p., 1956—, also dir.; dir. Rutgers U. Pres, W.B. Saunders Co., Ltd., London, Eng. Mem. cons. panel internat. uses of textbooks State Dept., 1963—. Mem. bd. edn., Pitman, N.J., 1938-41, pres., 1940-41; mem. Pitman Borough Council, 1948-50. Trustee Rutgers-The State U. N.J., 1963—; vice chmn. bd. trustees Gloucester County Coll. Served to lt. USNR, 1943-46; PTO. Mem. Med. Exhibitors Assn. (dir. 1948-50, pres. 1950-52), Assn. Am. Med. Schs. World Med. Assn., Mil. Order World Wars. Methodist. (ofcl. bd.). Mason. Clubs: Union League, Downtown (Phila.); Seaview Country (Absecon, N.J.). Home: 11201 3d Av Stone Harbor NJ 08247

BURTON, ALEXANDER TENNILLE, aero. exec.; b. Montgomery, Ala., Apr. 21, 1909; s. Warren Beal and Eloise (Tennille) B.; B.S., Ala. Poly. Inst., 1932; grad. Advanced Flying Sch., Kelly Field, Tex., 1934; m. Louise Nicholson Jones, Aug. 5, 1942; children—Cameron (Mrs. Riddell), Barbara. Commd. 2d lt. USAC Res., 1934, 1st lt., 1937; served as airplane pilot 9th Bombardment Sqdn., 7th Bombardment Group, 1934-36, then resigned; civilian engr. AC Procurement Insp. Div., Wright Field, Dayton, O., 1936; trans. AC Procurement Office, Boeing Airplane Co., Seattle, 1936-37; with N.Am. Rockwell Corp., Los Angeles, 1937—, v.p. 1950—. Mem. Am. Inst. Aeros. and Astronautics, Soc. Automotive Engrs., Air Force Assn., Assn. U.S. Army, Navy League, Kappa Sigma. Clubs: Army and Navy, National Press, National Aviation, Burning Tree, Metropolitan (Washington); Los Angeles Country; Eau Gallie Yacht; Royal Oaks Country. Home: 253 Bimini Rd Cocoa Beach FL 32931 Office: 1355 N Atlantic Av Cocoa Beach FL 32931

BURTON, BERNARD HOWARD, financial exec.; b. Berlin, Germany, Apr. 7, 1924; s. Sherman and Ray (Backer) B.; B.S., Rutgers U., 1951; M.B.A., N.Y. U., 1954; m. Helga Rosemarie Riemer, June 5, 1949; children—Vivian Jane, Monica Lynn, Michelle Annette. Came to U.S., 1945, naturalized, 1946. Sr. accountant Peat, Marwick, Mitchell & Co., N.Y.C., 1951-57; controller internat. div. div. Olin Mathieson Chem. Corp., 1957-62; treas. Minerals & Chems. Philipp Corp., N.Y.C., 1962-67; v.p. Engelhard Minerals & Chems. Corp., 1967—. Mem. Financial Execs. Inst., Am. Inst. C.P.A.'s, N.Y. State Soc. C.P.A.'s, Am. Accounting Assn., Inst. on U.S. Taxation Fgn. Income, Inc. Home: 142 Monterey Dr Manhasset Hills NY 11040 Office: 299 Park Av New York City 10017

BURTON, C. GRANT, coll. dean; b. Ogden, Utah, July 14, 1916; s. C.W. and Mary May (Faddis) B.; A.A., Weber Coll., 1936; B.A., U. Utah, 1938, M.A., 1940; postgrad. U. Cal., 1940-41; Ph.D., U. So Cal., 1954; m. Beulah Larsen, Nov. 28, 1947; children—Mary Ilene, Kathryn Joyce, Steven Grant, Richard Thomas. Tchr., Lewis High Sch., Ogden, 1938-40; tchr. English, U. Utah, 1945-46; tchr. English, speech Long Beach City Coll., 1946-51, 53-54; exec. dean San Jose (Cal.) State Coll., 1954—. Mem. adv. bd. San Jose Hosp. Nursing Sch.; mem. San Jose Citizens Community Improvement Com. Served from pvt. to lt. col. AUS, 1941-45, USAF, 1951-53; col. Res. Decorated Bronze Star medal; Croix de Guerre with vermilion star. Mem. Phi Rho Pi, Kappa Delta Pi. Rotarian. Contbr. articles to mil. publs. Home: 1848 Marlyn Way San Jose CA 95125

BURTON, CHARLES, lawyer; b. Bayonne, N.J., Aug. 23, 1932; s. Leon and Mildred (Sapon) B.; A.B. cum laude, Rutgers U., 1954; LL.B., Columbia, 1957; LL.M., N.Y. U., 1961; m. Ann Marilyn Labiner, Aug. 16, 1959; children—Peter W., Jonathan H. Admitted to N.Y. bar, 1957; asso. firm Finley & Lans, N.Y.C., 1959-61; asso. firm Battle, Fowler, Stokes & Kheel, N.Y.C., 1961-66, mem. firm, 1966—. Lectr. estate and gift taxation Am. Inst. Banking, 1961-63; dir. Beck/Arnley Corp., Melville, N.Y., Winston Devel. Corp., Atlanta, Winston Securities Corp., N.Y.C. Mem. Assn. Bar City N.Y. Home: 286 Rockingstone Av Larchmont NY 10538 Office: 280 Park Av New York City NY 10017

BURTON, CHARLES WESLEY, Jr., ret. mfg. exec.; b. Balt., Nov. 26, 1897; s. Charles W. and Eurith Ann Hargest (Leach) B.; grad. Balt. City Coll.; A.B., St. Johns' Coll., Annapolis, Md., 1918; C.P.A., Pace Inst., 1923; m. Mildred M. Meyer, July 12, 1922; children—Charles L., Mildred (Mrs. Lee S. Pyles), William Kenneth, Phyllis (Mrs. Fielding Watson). C.P.A., Haskins & Sells, 1922-29; accountant Anchor Post Products, Balt., 1929-37, treas., 1938-45, v.p., 1945-50, exec. v.p., 1950-56, pres., 1956-59, chmn. bd., pres., 1959-70, now dir.; dir. Sunshine Mining Co., Heritage Savs. & Loan Assn., Indsl. Corp. Baltimore City; adv. bd. Liberty Mut. Ins. Co. Served as 2d lt., inf., U.S. Army, World War I. Mem. Balt. Assn. Commerce, Md. Assn. C.P.A.'s, Financial Execs. Inst., N.A.M., Kappa Alpha. Clubs: Enterprise, Sherwood Forest, Baltimore Country, Kiwanis. Home: 3115 Juneau Pl Baltimore MD 21214 Office: 6500 Eastern Av Baltimore MD 21224

BURTON, COURTNEY, mining and shipping co. exec.; b. Cleve., Oct. 29, 1912; s. Courtney and Sarita (Oglebay) B.; student Mich. Coll. Mining and Tech., 1933-34, B.S., 1956; m. Marguerite Rankin, Sept. 7, 1933; children—Sarita Ann (Mrs. John Limbocker Jr.), Marguerite Rankin (Mrs. George M. Humphrey II). Dir. E.W. Oglebay Co., Cleve., 1934-57, pres., 1947-57; v.p. Ferro Engring. Co., Cleve., 1950-57; pres. Fortuna Lake Mining Co., Cleve., 1950-57; treas., dir. Columbia Transp. Co., Cleve., 1950-57; v.p. Montreal Mining Co., Cleve., 1950-57; pres. North Shore Land Co., Cleve., 1950-57; v.p., dir. Brule Smokeless Coal Co., Cleve., 1950-57; chmn. bd., chmn. exec. com. Oglebay Norton Co., Cleve., 1957—; dir. Nat. Bank W.Va., 1951-59, Central Nat. Bank Cleve., 1941-42, Cleve. Trust Co., 1950—. Dir. Ohio Civilian Def. and Rationing, 1941-42; exec. asst. Office Coordinator Inter-Am. Affairs, 1942-44, Mayor, Village of Gates Mills, O., 1948-61; mem. Cleve. Met. Park Bd. Chmn. Ohio Republican Finance Com., 1954-61, Rep. Nat. Finance Com., 1961-64. Trustee, founder, mem. adminstrv. bd. Nat. Recreation and Park Assn.; bd. dirs. Nat. Park Found.; trustee Bethany Coll., Univ. Hosp., Cleve., Oglebay Inst., Wheeling, W.Va.; pres. America's Future Trees Found. Served to lt., USNR, 1944-46. Mem. Am. Iron and Steel Inst., Nat. Coal Assn., Cleve. Zool. Soc. (pres. 1968—). Episcopalian. Clubs: Chagrin Valley Hunt (master of hounds 1946-54) (Gates Mills); Tavern, Union (Cleve.); Rolling Rock (Ligonier, Pa.); Lake Placid (N.Y.); Fort Henry (Wheeling, W.Va.); Kirtland, (Willoughby, O.); Capitol Hill (Washington). Office: Hanna Bldg Cleveland OH 44115

BURTON, DAVID LEE, detective agy. exec.; b. Kansas City, Mo., July 20, 1930; s. Aaron F. and Stella Mae (Henson) B.; A.A., Kansas City Jr. Coll., 1950; B.S., U. Kan., 1952, M.S., 1954; m. Mary Jean Dillon, June 2, 1951; children—Laura Michele, Melinda Leigh. Spl. agt. FBI, 1954-59; asst. to gen. mgr. Lawn-Boy, Lamar, Mo., 1959-60; asst. dir. security T.W.A., 1960-61; asst. v.p. personnel, mgr. security Western Auto Supply Co., Kansas City, Mo., 1961-66; mgr. security Western Electric Co., 1966-70; exec. v.p., dir. Burns Internat. Security Services, Inc., Briarcliff Manor, N.Y., 1970—. Dir. Westchester County Assn., 1970-71. Campaign chmn. Johnson County (Kan.) Republican Party, 1964. Served with CIC, AUS, 1952-54. Mem. Soc.

Former Spl. Agts. FBI (chmn. N.Y. 1970-71), Internat. Assn. Chiefs Police, Am. Soc. Indsl. Security. Presbyn. Home: 42 Whitlaw Lane Chappaqua NY 10514 Office: 320 Old Briarcliff Rd Briarcliff Manor NY 10566

BURTON, DWIGHT LOWELL, educator; b. Carson Lake, Minn., Aug. 9, 1922; s. Benjamin Otis and Beryl (Green) B.; B.S., U. Minn., 1943, M.A., 1947, Ph.D., 1951; m. Claudia Holland, Feb. 15, 1968; children—Barbara Kay, Christine Beryle. High sch. tchr. English, Superior, Wis., 1946-47; tchr. English, head dept. U. Minn. High Sch., 1947-52; prof. English edn. Fla. State U., 1952-60, now head dept. Served from pvt. to capt. AUS, 1943-46. Decorated Bronze Star; Croix de Guerre (France). Mem. Nat. Conf. on Research in English, Conf. on English Edn. (past chmn.), Nat. Council Tchrs. English (2d v.p. 1966), Phi Delta Kappa, Sigma Tau Delta. Author: Literature Study in the High Schools, 1958, rev. edit., 70; co-author Teaching English in Today's High Schools, 1965, rev. edit., 1970. Editor: English Jour., 1955-64. Home: 423 Vinnedge Ride Tallahassee FL 32303

BURTON, EDWIN, (Weisman), physician; b. McKinney, Tex., July 19, 1899; s. Edwin Lee, Jr. and Elizabeth (Duer) B.; student U. Tex., 1916-17, Sch. Medicine, 1920- 22; B.A., Rice Inst., 1920; M.D., U. Pa., 1924; m. Mary Elizabeth Dalgety-Kerr, Aug. 4, 1928. Interne Hosp. of U. Pa., 1924-26; house surgeon N.Y. Eye and Ear Infirmary, N.Y.C., 1927-29; instr. ophthalmology, dept. medicine U. Va. 1930-33, asst. prof., 1933-35, asso. prof., 1935-38, prof. ophthalmology, 1938-70, prof. emeritus, 1970—, chmn. dept., 1938-65; practice medicine specializing in ophthalmology, Charlottesville, Va., 1930—. Fellow A.C.S.; mem. Am. Ophthalmol. Soc., Am. Acad. Ophthalmology and Otolaryngology, A.M.A., Va. Soc. Ophthalmology and Otolaryngology (sec. 1935, v.p. 1936, pres. 1937), Alpha Mu Pi Omega, Alpha Omega Alpha. Democrat. Episcopalian. Author article, Progressive Myopia-A Possible Etiologic Factor (Transactions of Am. Ophthalmol. Soc., 1942); contbr. chpt. to Lawyers Med. Cyclopedia, Vol. VI, 1962. Home: 1841 Wayside Pl Charlottesville VA 22903 Office: 1400 Jefferson Park Av Charlottesville VA 22903

BURTON, GARY, vibraharpist; b. Anderson, Ind., Jan. 23, 1943; student piano and composition in high sch. and coll.; self-taught on vibraharps; m. Donna Hanley, May 29, 1969. Debut, Nashville, 1960; own group, S. Am., 1962; with George Shearing, 1963, Stan Getz, 1964-66; composer, arranger album Out of the Woods, 1964; recording artist for RCA Records, Atlantic Records; films include The Hanged Man; Get Yourself a College Girl. Home: PO Box 98 Little Neck NY 11363 Office: care Festival Prodns 33 Riverside Dr New York City NY 10023

BURTON, GEORGE ALLAN, merchant; b. Toronto, Ont., Can., Jan. 20 1915; s. Charles Luther and Ella (Leary) B.; student U. Toronto, 1933; m. Audrey Caro Syer, May 12, 1938; children—Audrey Gail (Mrs. Dr. John Michael Kendall), James Allan, Lynn Dell, Janice Caro. With Robert Simpson Co., Ltd., Toronto, 1935-54, gen. mgr., 1951-54; dir. Simpsons, Ltd., Toronto, 1954—, v.p., mng. dir., 1958-64, now pres., chmn.; dir. Simpson-Sears, Ltd., Simpsons Acceptance Co., Ltd., Royal Bank Can., St. Lawrence Cement Co., Pres. Bd. Trade Met. Toronto, 1962-63. Chmn. United Appeal Met. Toronto, 1961; pres. Toronto Indsl. Commn., 1967—; founding chmn. Toronto Indsl. Commn., 1960—; founding chmn. Toronto Redevelopment Adv. Council, 1960- 62, mem. exec. bd., 1962—. Trustee Hosp. For Sick Children. Served to maj. Gov. Gen.'s Horse Guards, 1940-45, lt. col., 1965. Decorated Dist. Service Order (Italy); Knight St. Lazarus Jerusalem, Officer St. John Jerusalem. Mem. Psi Upsilon, Mason. Home: Limestone Hall Farm Rural Rt 2 Milton Ontario Canada Office: 176 Yonge St Toronto 1 Ontario Canada

BURTON, GLENN WILLARD, geneticist; b. Clatonia, Neb., May 5, 1910; s. Joseph Fearn and Nellie (Rittenburg) B.; B.Sc., U. Neb., 1932, D.Sc. (hon.), 1962; M.Sc., Rutgers U., 1933, Ph.D., 1936, D.Sc. (hon.), 1955; m. Helen Maurine Jeffryes, Dec. 16, 1934; children—Elizabeth Ann (Mrs. John Edward Fowler), Robert Glenn, Thomas Jeffryes, Joseph William, Richard Bennett, With U.S. Dept. Agr. and U. Ga. at Tifton Expt. Sta., 1936-, prin. geneticist, 1952-, chmn. div. agronomy, 1950-64; Univ. Found. prof. U. Ga., 1957. Mem. Tift County Bd. Edn., 1953-58. Recipient 1st ann. agrl. award So. Seedsmen Assn., 1950, Sears-Roebuck research award, 1953, 60, Superior Service award Dept. Agr., 1955, 1st Ford Almanac Crops and Soils Research award, 1962; named Man of Year in So. Agr., Progressive Farmer, 1954; numerous other awards and citations. Fellow Am. Soc. Agronomy (Stevenson award 1949, John Scott award 1957; v.p. 1961, pres. 1962); mem. Am. Genetic Assn., Am. Soc. Range Mgmt., Genetics Soc. Am., Sigma Xi, Alpha Zeta, Gamma Sigma Delta. Home: 421 W 10th St Tifton GA 31794

BURTON, HAROLD BERNARD, author, editor; b. Mpls., Apr. 15, 1908; s. Barney and Josephine (Deutsch) B.; student U. Wis., 1927; m. Henrietta Kimberly Ward, Sept. 24, 1948; children—Mary Ward and Frederick Barney (twins). Editorial writer N.Y. Daily News, 1934-41; chief editorial writer Newsday, Garden City, N.Y., 1958-68, book editor, 1968—. Writer amendment to N.Y. State Constn. permitting devel. skiing in Adirondack Forest Preserve, 1939; chmn. Gov.'s Com. on Skiing in N.Y. State, 1938-41, 55-57; commr. Adirondack Mountain Authority, 1957-68. Served to capt., inf., AUS, 1942- 45. Mentioned in dispatches Household Cav. Regt. (Brit.) Italy, 1944. Republican. Episcopalian. Clubs: American Alpine (N.Y.C.); Adirondack Mountain (Gabriels, N.Y.). Author: The City Strikes Back, 1957. Contbr. articles popular mags. Home: Mt Porter Rd Keen Valley NY 12943 Office: Newsday Inc 550 Stewart Av Garden City NY 11530

BURTON, HARRY JAMES, engring. and constrn. co. exec.; b. Glasgow, Mont., Aug. 22, 1910; s. Harry and Ruth (Soule) B.; B.A., Carleton Coll., 1931; M.A., Columbia 1936; C.P.A., Cal., 1949; m. Kathryn Koons, Jan. 27, 1951. Tchr., Brainerd (Minn.) High Sch. and Jr. Coll., 1931-40; asst. prof. accounting Lehigh U., 1946-56; sr. v.p., treas. Ralph M. Parsons Co., Los Angeles, 1956—. Served to capt. AUS, 1940-45; ETO. Decorated Bronze Star. Mem. Am. Inst. C.P.A.'s, Cal. Soc. C.P.A.'s. Phi Beta Kappa. Episcopalian. Mason (Shriner). Club: California. Home: 179 S Hudson Av Los Angeles CA 90004 Office: 617 W 7th St Los Angeles CA 90017

BURTON, JAMES BONDURANT, ins. co. exec.; b. Sharon, Tenn., Sept. 23, 1910; s. James William and Fannie (Bondurant) B.; student Freed-Hardeman Coll., 1927-29; B.A., Vanderbilt U., 1931; m. Virginia Lynn Lamm, Nov. 10, 1945; children—James William, Mary Virginia, Frances Elizabeth, Walter Lamm. Treas., Life & Casualty Ins. Co. Tenn., Nashville, 1931—; treas. WLAC- Radio and Nashville Mag., Inc. Councilman, Boy Scouts Am., Bd. dirs. Freed-Hardeman Coll., Fanning Orphan Sch. Fund, Nashville chpt. A.R.C. Served with USAAF, 1942-46. Mem. Mortgage Bankers Assn., Nashville C. of C., Delta Tau Delta. Mem. Ch. of Christ. Clubs: Nashville City, Seven Hills. Home: 934 Battery Lane Nashville TN 37720 Office: Life and Casualty Tower Nashville TN 37219

BURTON, JOE WRIGHT, editor, clergyman; b. Miles, Tex., Sept. 7, 1907; s. William Thomas and Martha Ellen (Davison) B.; A.B., Hardin-Simmons U., 1929, D.D., 1946; Th.M., Southwestern Bapt. Theol. Sem., Ft. Worth, 1932; postgrad. U. Mo. Sch. Journalism, summer 1940; m. Lula Grace Williams, Sept. 9, 1931; children—Mary Lu (Mrs. H. David Smith), John Williams, Robert Henry. Ordained to ministry Bapt. Ch., 1928; pastor Thornberry Ch., nr. Wichita Falls, Tex., 1933, Big Lake, 1934-35; sec. edn. So. Bapt. Conv. Home Mission Bd., Atlanta 1936-45, sec. So. Bapt. Conv., 1947-65, sec. family life dept. Bapt. Sunday Sch. Bd., Nashville, 1946-66, also editor Home Life, 1947—. Preacher home revivals, evangelistic meetings throughout South; condr. Clin. Study Sch. Pastoral Care, Winston-Salem, 1968, Inst. Advanced Pastoral Studies, Detroit, 1970, family study tours, No. Europe, 1952, Near East, 1955, Israel 1969, Europe, 1971. Recipient citation from Lambda Lambda Lambda for distinctive service in religious journalism, 1947. Author: Missionary Illustrations, 1938; Epochs of Home Missions, 1945; Prince of the Pulpit, 1946; The Church and Family Life, 1948; Tomorrow you Marry, 1950; Family Life—A Bible View, 1964. Editor 42 vols. pub. by Home Mission Bd., 1936-45; Altar fires for Family Worship, 1954; So. Bapt. Family Life quar., 1954-60; Light From Above, 1968. Home: 6222 Vosswood Dr Nashville TN 37205 Office: 127 9th Av N Nashville TN 37203

BURTON, JOHN EDWARD, univ. adminstr.; b. North Bloomfield O., Mar. 2, 1908; s. Josh Henry and Lena Endora (Hyde) B.; B.A., Hiram Coll., 1928; M.B.A., Northwestern U., 1929, postgrad. study, 1929-31; m. Dorothy Jean Coleman, Feb. 8, 1930; children—Coleman Henry, Thomas Richard. Research asso. Inst. Econ. Research, Inc., 1929-33, exec. sec. 1933-35; research sec. Committee on Taxation, President's Conference on Home Bldg. and Home Ownership, 1931; dir. research Mortgage Commn. of State of N.Y., 1935-38; dir. own research group, 1938-42; lectr. Northwestern U., 1931-33, N.Y.U., 1937- 38, 1941; dir. of budget N.Y. State 1943-50, and chmn. of Post-War Pub. Works Planning Commn., 1943-47; v.p. business, Cornell U., 1950—. Chmn. N.Y. State Power Authority, 1950-54, trustee, 1950-58; mem. State Vets. Commn., 1944-50. Gov.'s Com. on State Edn. Program, 1945-50, Gov.'s Com. on StateLocal Fiscal Relations, 1945, State Commn. on Municipal Revenue, 1945. Tax Com. Council State Govts., 1945-46. State U. Commn. 1946-48, Grants-in-Aid Com. Council of State Govts., 1947-48; chmn. Governor's Thru-way Com., 1950; FederalState Relationships Com. of Commn. on Orgn. Exec. Br. Fed. Govt., 194748. Fed. Commn. Intergovernmental Relations, 1950-55, trustee bd. govs. Council of State Govts., 1954—; mem. Fed. Adv. Commn. Intergovernmental Relations, 1959-62; chmn. N.Y. Gov's Com. on Power Resources, 1959; mem. Fed. Adv. Com. on Pub. Assistance, 1959; dir. research N.Y. Joint Legislative Com. Sch. Financing, 1960-63; mem. N. Y. State Citizens Com. on Welfare Costs, 1968; mem. N.Y. State Commn. on Expenditure Review, 1970—. Mem. Nat. Assn. State Budget Officers (pres. 1946), Am. Soc. Pub. Author research monographs and reports on pub. adminstrn. Home: 44 Uptown Village Ithaca NY 14850

BURTON, JOHN FLACK, plastic surgeon; b. Wicklyffee, Ky., July 10, 1897; s. Leslie D. and Martha (Flack) B.; A.B., Okla. U., 1918; B.S., 1921; M.D., Columbia, 1923; m. Naomi McCasland, May 5, 1925; children—John Flack (dec.), James Leslie; m. 2d, Barbara Jean Cook Iselin, June 21, 1962. Intern 1st surg. div. Bellevue Hosp., N.Y.C., 1923-24; gen. practice in Tex., 1924-29; mem. faculty Okla. U. Med. Sch., 1931—, clin. prof. surgery 1940—; founder, 1st chief dept. plastic surgery Okla. U. Med. Center, 1932, now med. dir. plastic surgery sect.; cons. Will Rogers VA Hosp., bur. family service of Dept. Health, Edn. and Welfare; attending surgeon Okla. U., St. Anthonys, Mercy, Baptist, Presbyn., Mid-West City hosps.; surg. cons. Okla. Dept. Pub. Welfare. Founder mem., v.p. Okla. Blue Shield Plan; pres. Okla. U. Sooner Scholarship Trust Plan. Bd. dirs. Okla. Soc. Crippled Children, 1958; adv. bd. Goodwill Industries Oklahoma City, 1958-59. Diplomate Am. Bd. Plastic Surgery. Fellow A.C.S.; mem. A.M.A. (ho. dels. 1949-56, council med. service 1956- 63, chmn. 1962-63, chmn. com. indigent care 1956-62, Okla. Med. Assn. (past pres.). Republican. Conglist. Rotarian. Clubs: Doctors Dinner, Mens Dinner, Beacon, Touchdown (Oklahoma City). Author sci. papers. Home: 801 NW 7th St Oklahoma City OK 73106 Office: 807 NW 7th St Oklahoma City OK 73106

BURTON, JOHN FLETCHER, pub. utility exec.; b. Portsmouth, Va., Sept. 19, 1906; s. Perry G. and Mary (Hamilton) B.; student pub. schs.; m. Virginia Elizabeth Holmes, Jan. 4, 1930; 1 dau., Betty Lou (Mrs. J. Lawrence Sherrin). Accountant, spl. analyst Va. Electric & Power Co., Portsmouth, Norfolk, Richmond, Va., 1925-36; asst. treas. Stone & Webster Service Corp., N.Y.C., 1936-48, Tampa Electric Co. (Fla.), 1938-48, Okla. Natural Gas Co., Tulsa, 1941-48; v.p., treas. Colonial Utilities Corp. and subsidaries, N.Y.C., 1945-48; asst. treas. Savannah Electric & Power Co. (Ga.), 1945-48; treas. Jamaica Pub. Service, Ltd. and subsidiaries, Kingston, Jamaica, B.W.I., 1946-48, West Gas Improvement Co. Am., Inc., N.Y.C., 1946-48; v.p., treas. Transcontinental Gas Pipe Line Corp., Houston, financial v.p., 1955-69, sr. v.p., 1969—, also dir. Mem. Am., So. gas assns., Ind. Natural Gas Assn., U.S., Houston chambers commerce, Tex., Mid-Continent oil and gas assns., Am. Mgmt. Assn. Clubs: India House (N.Y.C.); Houston, Petroleum, Houston Country, University (Houston). Home: 9 Pine Hill Lane Houston TX 77019 Office: 3100 Travis St Houston TX 77006

BURTON, JOSEPH ASHBY, chemist; b. Onley, Va., Aug. 22, 1914; s. Vernon Swanger and Loleta (Boggs) B.; B.S., Washington and Lee U., 1934; Ph.D. in Chemistry, Johns Hopkins, 1938; m. Denison Laws, Aug. 29, 1936; children—Delano (Mrs. Leroy M. May), W. Butler, John D. Mem. tech. staff Bell Telephone Labs., Murray Hill, N.J., 1938—, head semicondr. physics research dept., 1954-58, dir. chem. physics research, 1958-71, dir. phys. research, 1971—. Mem. NRC. Mem. Am. Phys. Soc. (treas., exec. com. 1969—), Am. Inst. Physics (governing bd. 1969—), Am. Chem. Soc. Home: 22 Linden Lane Chatham NJ 07928 Office: Mountain Av Murray Hill NJ 07974

BURTON, LAURENCE J., govt. ofcl.; b. Ogden, Utah, Oct. 30, 1926; s. Laurence S. and Marguerite (Roghaar) B.; B.S., U. Utah, 1951; M.S., Utah State U., 1956; grad. student Georgetown U., George Washington U.; m. Janice Shupe, Sept. 16, 1947; children—Carol, Susan, Sally Laurence S. Legislative asst. to Congressman Dixon, 1957-58; asst. prof. polit. sci. Weber Coll., Ogden, 1958-60; adminstrv. asst. to Gov. Clyde of Utah, 1960-62; mem. 88th-91st Congresses from Utah; dir. Office Congl. Relations, Dept. Transp., Washington, 1971—. Editor Juco Rev., mag. Nat. Jr. Coll. Assn., 1951- 61; regional and state dir. Am. Coll. Pub. Relations Assn., 1954-55. Mem. Pub. Lands Law Rev. Commn. Bd. dirs. Coll-Community Theatre, Ogden, Weber Coll. Alumni. Served with Air Corps, USNR, World War II. Republican. Mem. Ch. Jesus Christ of Latter-Day Saints. Club: Ogden Quarterback, Ogden Kiwanis. Home: 9354 Reid Circle Captain's Cove Ft Washington MD 20022 Office: Dept Transp 400 7th St SW Washington DC 20590

BURTON, LEONARD PATTILLO, educator; b. Jasper, Ala., June 8, 1918; s. James Robert and Fannie (Pattillo) B.; student Ga. Inst. Tech., 1935-36; A.B., U. Ala., 1939, M.A., 1940; student Lehigh U., 1940-41, U. Chgo., 1948-49; Ph.D., U. N.C., 1951; m. Evalyne Rankin Hiller, Apr. 4, 1942; children—Evelyn Pattillo (Mrs. David G. Whitman), Dorothy Jean, James Robert. Instr. U. Ala., 1946-48; instr. U. Cal. at Davis, 1951-52, asst. prof., 1952-54; asst. prof. math. Auburn U., 1954-56, asso. prof., 1956-60, prof., 1960—, head prof., 1965—. Dir. Burton Mfg. Co. Inc., Jasper, Ala. Bd. dirs. Presbyn. Community Ministry, Inc., Auburn. Served with AUS, 1941-45. Decorated Bronze Star medal. Mem. Ala. Acad. Sci., Am. Math. Soc., Math. Assn. Am., Phi Beta Kappa, Sigma Xi (pres. Auburn chpt. 1962), Phi Delta Theta. Presbyn. (elder 1959—). Kiwanian (dir. 1958-59). Club: Saugahatchee Country (Auburn). Home: 755 Moores Mill Rd Auburn AL 36830

BURTON, MALCOLM KING, clergyman, author; b. Mpls., Mar. 28, 1905; s. Charles Emerson and Cora (King) B.; student Phillips Acad., Andover, Mass., 1919-23; B.A., Carleton Coll., 1927; postgrad. Chgo. Theol. Sem., 1927-29; m. Carol Berkemeier, Feb. 24, 1930. Ordained to ministry Congl. Ch., 1928; pastor in Massena, N.Y., 1929-33, Pelham, N.Y., 1933-38, New London, Conn., 1938-52, 1st Congl. Ch., Pontiac, Mich., 1952-71. Exec. vice chmn. dir. Com. Continuation Congl. Christian Chs. in U.S., 1954—; chaplain Police Protective Assn., Massena, 1930-33; moderator Nat. Assn. Congl. Christian Chs., 1968-69. Served as chaplain AUS, 1945. Recipient citation Nat. Assn. Congl. Christian Chs., 1964. Mem. Delta Sigma Rho. Club: Pontiac Exchange. Author: Destiny for Congregationalism, 1953; Constitution for Congregationalism, 1954; How Church Union Came, 1966; also numerous pamphlets, articles. Home: 1159 River Rd Agawam MA 01001

BURTON, MILTON, chemist; b. Stapleton, N.Y., Mar. 4, 1902; B.S. in Chem. Engring., N.Y. U., 1922, M.S., 1923, Ph.D., 1925; m. Frances Louise Paperno, May 19, 1934 (dec. 1944); 1 son, James; m. 2d, Sarah Holt Foust, May 18, 1946; 1 son, Thomas. Teaching fellow N.Y. U., 1922-24, U. fellow, 1924-25; various indsl. positions, 1925-35; with N.Y. U., 1935-36, 38-42, U. Cal., 1937-38; chief radiation chem. sect., atomic energy project Metall. Lab., U. Chgo., 1942-45, Clinton Labs., Oak Ridge, 1945-46; mem. Radiol. Safety Sect., and cons. Office Q.M. Gen., Operation Crossroads, Bikini, 1946; prof. chemistry U. Notre Dame (Ind.), 1945-71, emeritus, 1971—, dir. Radiation Lab., 1945-71. Fulbright lectr., guest prof., Guggenheim fellow, Göttingen, 1955-56. Recipient AEC citation and gold medal, 1971. Fellow Am. Inst. Chemists (sec.-treas. N.Y. chpt. 1941-42); mem. Radiation Research Soc. (councillor-at-large 1956-57, pres. 1958-59), Société de Chimie Physique France, Am. Chem. Soc. (treas. St. Joseph sect. 1946-47, chmn. 1958-59, chmn. div. phys. and inorganic chemistry 1950-51, S.C. Lind award Knoxville-Oak Ridge sect. 1969), A.A.A.S., Ind. Acad. Sci. (W.A. Noyes award 1952), Faraday Soc. U.K., Fedn. Am. Scientists (councillor-at-large 1957- 59), Am. Assn. U. Profs., Sigma Xi (pres. Notre Dame club 1948-49), Phi Lambda Upsilon. Clubs: University (Notre Dame); Cosmos (Washington); Quadrangle (Chgo.); N.Y. U. Chemistry Alumni. Author: (with G.K. Rollefson) Photochemistry and the Mechanism of Chemical Reactions, 1939. Co-editor: Comparative Effects of Radiation; Advances in Radiation Chemistry (series). Mem. editorial bd. Jour. Phys. Chemistry, 1949-54; asso. editor Jour. Chem. Physics, 1965-67. Contbr. articles to profl. jours. Home: 15631 Embers Dr Mishawaka IN 46544 Office: Radiation Lab U Notre Dame Notre Dame IN 46556

BURTON, OSMOND ALEXANDER, Jr., lawyer; b. Tucson, Feb. 20, 1934; s. Osmond Alexander and Mattie Lee (Handley) B.; LL.B., U. Ariz., 1960; m. Virginia Lee Richards, Apr. 20, 1957; children—Lee Walker, Susan Rachelle, Bethanne. Admitted to Ariz. bar, 1960; city atty., Scottsdale, Ariz., 1961-65; asso. firm Bellamak, Zepp & Mitchell, Scottsdale, 1965-67; partner firm Burton & Weeks, Scottsdale, 1967-70; pvt. practice law, Scottsdale, 1970—. Sec.-treas., dir. Waste Control of Ariz. Vice pres., dir. Scottsdale Indsl. Devel. Corp.; v.p. Ecumenical Counselling Service, 1970—; mem. Scottsdale Bd. Edn., 1969—; acting city mgr., Scottsdale, 1964; chmn. bd. dirs. Scottsdale-Temple br. YMCA, 1967-69. Mem. State Bar Ariz., Maricopa County Bar Assn., Am. Arbitration Assn., Scottsdale Charros. Home: 2323 N 80th Pl Scottsdale AZ 85257 Office: 7020 3d Av Scottsdale AZ 85251

BURTON, PHILIP WARD, advt. exec., educator; b. Chgo., May 23, 1910; s. Carl Marshall and Gladys (Mann) B.; A.B. summa cum laude, Stanford, 1944, A.M., 1945; m. Ellen Schell Garber, Dec. 21, 1941; children—Elisabeth, Philip Ward and Bruce Garber (twins). With advt. dept. Colgate-Palmolive Co., 1929-31; sales promotion adminstr. Bird & Son, Inc., 1932-34; mgr. med. promotion Bell & Howell Co., 1935-37; copy editor Procter & Gamble Co., 1938- 41; asst. prof. Syracuse U. Sch. Journalism, 1945-46, prof., head advt. dept., 1949-55, chmn. advt. dept., 1956-; asso. prof. journalism and bus. adminstrn. State U. Ia., 1946, prof., head dept., 1947-49; creative dir. Bruce B. Brewer Advt. Agy., Mpls., 1955-57; dir. marketing and research Barlow Advt. Agy., 1956—; copy chief T.A. Best Co.; dir. Auburn Pub. Co. Book rev. editor Auburn Citizen-Advertiser; editor Internat. Corr. Schs., also editor- cons. internat. textbook div. Named Advt. Educator in U.S., 1961. Fellow Am. Acad. Advt. (regional dean); mem. Advt. Fedn. Am. (dir. 1953-57), Nat. Indsl. Advertisers Assn., Alpha Delta Sigma (nat. pres. 1953-57, chmn. nat. council 1957-59; recipient citation for contbns. to frat.), Sigma Delta Chi, Delta Upsilon. Author: Advertising Copywriting, 1949, rev. edit., 1962; Retail Advertising for Small Stores, 1951; Putting Advertising to Work, 1953; Principles of Advertising, 1955; Making Media Work, 1958; Which Ad Pulled Best, 1969; Advertising Fundamentals, 1970; also articles in mags. Home: 108 E Genesee St Skaneateles NY 13152 Office: Sch Journalism Syracuse U Syracuse NY 10310

BURTON, PHILLIP, congressman; b. Cin., June 1, 1926; A.B. in Polit. Sci., U. So. Cal., 1947; LL.B., Golden Gate Law Sch., 1952; m. Sala Galant; 1 dau., Joy. Admitted to Cal. bar, 1952, U.S. Supreme Ct. bar, 1956; practice law, San Francisco; mem. Cal. Assembly, 1956-64, chmn. com. social welfare; mem. 88th-92d congresses 5th dist. Cal. mem. interior and insular affairs coms., edn. and labor com. U.S. del. Atlantic Treaty Assn. Conf., Paris, France, 1959. Past nat. officer Young Democrats; a founder Cal. Dem. Council; sec.-treas. 88th Congress Dem. Club. Served with AUS, World War II, Korea. Mem. Blue Key. Home: 450 Golden Gate Av San Francisco CA Office: House Office Bldg Washington DC 20525

BURTON, RALPH ASHBY, educator; b. Shreveport, La., Oct. 31, 1925; s. Cleveland Cunningham and Sadie (King) B.; B.S., U. Ark., 1947; M.S., U. Tex. at Austin, 1951, Ph.D., 1952; m. Nancy Gaines, Aug. 4, 1948; 1 son, Ralph Gaines. Asst. prof. Mass. Inst. Tech., 1952-54; asso. prof. U. Mo. at Columbia, 1954-58; sect. mgr., staff scientist Southwest Research Inst., San Antonio, 1958-67; liaison scientist U.S. Office Naval Research, London, Eng., 1967-69; prof., chmn. mech. engring. and astronautical scis. Northwestern U., 1969—. Mem. Am. Soc. M.E., Am. Inst. Astronautics and Aero., Am. Soc. Engring. Edn., Am. Assn. U. Profs., Am. Soc. Lubrication Engrs., Sigma Xi, Alpha Chi Sigma, Sigma Tau Delta, Pi Kappa Alpha. Author: Vibration Impact, 1958, 1968. Editor: Bearings and Seal Design in Nuclear Power Machinery, 1967. Home: 619 Library Pl Evanston IL 60201

BURTON, RALPH JOSEPH, internat. devel. cons.; b. Syracuse, N.Y., Nov. 7, 1911; s. Louis and Sarah Burton; A.B., Syracuse U., 1932; Ph.D., U. Chgo., 1939; m. Elaine Becker, June 24, 1934 (div. Nov. 1961); children—Sharone L., Brenda R., Rhoda S.; m. 2d, Helena Felton, May 1962. With Chgo. City Govt., 1935- 40, adminstrv. asst. to corp. counsel, 1938-40; with U.S. Bur. Budget, 1940-56, asst. chief govt. orgn. br., 1947-52, asst. chief internat. div., 1952-56; mem. U.S. Fgn. Service, 1956-68; spl. asst. to asst. sec. state for adminstrn., 1956-58; spl. detail to Pres.'s Adv. Com. on Govt. Orgn. 1957, to Pres.'s Com. to Study U.S. Mil. Assitance Program, 1959; dep. prin. officer U.S. consulate gen., Sao Paulo, Brazil, 1958-61; officer charge Brazilian affairs Dept. State and Alliance for Progress, 1962-65; dir. AID Mission to Nicaragua, 1965-68; gen. adv. loan adminstrn. Inter Am. Devel. Bank 1968-71. Cons. to com. pub. adminstrn. Social Sci. Research Council, 1941; cons. gov. P.R., 1948; lectr. polit. sci. Syracuse U., George Washington U., Am. U.; 1940-50; cons. Pub. Adminstrn. Mission to Colombia, 1950-51; mem. U.S. delegation Internat. Inst. Adminstrv. Sci., Florence, Italy, 1950; U.S. delegation to NATO, Lisbon, Portugal, 1952; cons. gov. P.R., 1954. Mem. Am. Fgn. Service Assn., Am. Acad. Polit. and Social Scis. Author: (with Edward B. Strait) The Central Machinery of Government: Its Role and Functioning, 1951. Home: 4410 Exeter Dr Sarasota FL 33577

BURTON, RICHARD, (Richard Jenkins), actor; b. Pontrhydfen, South Wales, Nov. 10, 1925; ed. Exeter and Oxford; m. Sybil Williams (div. 1963); 2 children; m. 2d, Elizabeth Taylor, Mar. 15, 1964. lst stage appearance in Druid's Rest, Royal Court Theatre, Liverpool, Eng., 1943, later on London stage; Brit. debut in film, Last Days of Dolwyn, 1948; on London stage in The Lady's Not for Burning, A Phoenix Too Frequent; N.Y. stage debut, Phoenix Too Frequent, 1950, later appeared Legend for Lovers, 1951; on Broadway in Time Remembered, then musical Camelot; title role in Hamlet, Old Vic Company, Edinburgh Festival, 1953, continued 1953-54 season with Old Vic Company, later appeared in King John, Twelfth Night, The Tempest, Othello, Henry V; Hollywood film debut in My Cousin Rachel, 1954; other films include The Robe, Prince of Players, Alexander the Great, Rains of Ranchipur, The Bramble Bush, The Longest Day, Cleopatra, Look Back in Anger, Becket, Night of the Iguana, The Sandpiper, The Spy Who Came in from the Cold, Who's Afraid of Virginia Woolf, The Taming of the Shrew, Doctor Faustus, The Comedians, Candy, Where Eagles Dare, Boom, Staircase, Anne of the Thousand Days, Raid on Rommel, Villain, Under Milk Wood, Hammersmith is Out, Tito, The Assassination of Trotsky; TV role in Wuthering Heights, 1958. Served with RAF, 1944-47. Author: A Christmas Story, 1964; Meeting Mrs. Jenkins, 1965. Office: care John Springer Assos Inc 667 Madison Av New York City NY 10021

BURTON, ROBERT COOPER, mfg. co. exec.; b. Memphis, Aug. 17, 1909; s. Madison Theodore and Lula (Cooper) B.; B.S. in Chem. Engring., U. Tenn., 1930; D.Sc. (hon.), Emory and Henry Coll., 1965; m. Anna Beatrice Johnson, Oct. 5, 1959. With Tenn. Eastman Co., Kingsport, 1930—, sr. v.p., 1969—; vice chmn. bd. Eastman Chem. Products, Inc., 1969—, Tex. Eastman Co., 1969—; v.p. Carolina Eastman Co., 1966—; pres. Holston Def. Corp., 1966—; dir. First Nat. Bank Sullivan County. Chmn. exec. com. Emory and Henry Coll., 1968—; mem. devel. council U. Tenn., 1969—. Bd. dirs. Kingsport Community Chest, Holston Valley Community Hosp.; joint bd. trustees Emory and Henry, Hiwassee, and Tenn. Wesleyan colls. Mem. Am. Chem. Soc., Am. Inst. Chem. Engrs., Am. Ordnance Assn., Tau Beta Pi, Alpha Chi Sigma. Republican. Methodist. Club: Ridgefields Country (Kingsport). Home: 3600 Orebank Rd Kingsport TN 37664 Office: Eastman Rd Kingsport TN 37662

BURTON, ROBERT JAY, music licensing orgn. exec.; b. N.Y.C., Sept. 21, 1914; B.S., Columbia, 1935, LL.B., 1937; m. Linda Patterman; children—Theodore D., Cathy Lizbeth, William Michael. Admitted to N.Y. bar, 1937; head legal staff Broadcast Music, Inc., N.Y.C., 1941—, sec., v.p. domestic performing rights adminstrn., 1956-63, exec. v.p., 1963-64, pres., 1964—, also dir.; lectr. N.Y.U., Coll. City N.Y., Columbia Sch. Law, Yale Law Sch., U. Cal. at Los Angeles, others. Past acting city judge, New Rochelle, N.Y. Former mem. New Rochelle Bd. Edn. Mem. Patent, Trademark and Copyright Found., George Washington U. Mem. Urban League Westchester County (dir., mem. adv. com.), Copyright Soc. U.S. (past trustee), Am. Bar Assn. (past chmn. copyright office affairs com.), Fed. Bar Assn. N.Y., N.J. and Conn. (chmn. radio and TV com.), Radio and TV Execs. Soc. (pres. N.Y.C. 1955-57, chmn. Am. soc. broadcast arts com.), Assn. Bar City N.Y., N.Y. State Bar Assn., Am. Judicature Soc., Am. Patent Law Assn. (chmn. copyright com.). Mason, Elk. Clubs: Broadcasters (bd. govs.), Broadcast Pioneers (pres.), Columbia U. Home: 75 Crawford Terrace New Rochelle, NY Office: Broadcast Music Inc 589 Fifth Av New York City NY 10017

BURTON, ROBERT ROBINSON, advt. exec.; b. Joplin, Mo., May 9, 1912; s. Perlee Ellis and Cordelia (Gamble) B.; B.S., Washington U., 1933; m. Mary Frances O'Neil, Nov. 16, 1911; children—Robert Robinson, Lynn Obear, John Gamble. Account exec. Gardner Advt. Co., St. Louis, 1933-41; sales rep. MacFadden Publs., Chgo., 1941-42; v.p., account supr. Young & Rubicam, Chgo., 1946-53, Needham, Louis & Brorby, Chgo., 1953-57; v.p., mgr. Chgo. office Kenyon & Eckhardt, 1957-59, sr. v.p., account mgmt., dir., N.Y.C., 1957-62, exec. v.p., mgr. Chgo. office Campbell-Mithun, Inc., 1962-69, chmn. bd., 1969—, pres., 1970—. Bd. dirs. Nat. Safety Council, 1962-66, Goodwill Industries, Chgo., 1970—. Served from capt. to lt. col. AUS, 1942-46. Mem. Am. Assn. Advt. Agys. (bd. govs. central region 1962-63), Phi Delta Theta. Clubs: Exmoor Country (Highland Park, Ill.); Tavern, (Chgo.); John's Island (Vero Beach, Fla.); Caledonian Curling (Hastings on Hudson, N.Y.). Home: 666 Rosemary Rd Lake Forest IL 60045 Office: Campbell Mithun Inc 111 E Wacker Dr Chicago IL 60601

BURTON, ROD BAXTER, advt. exec.; b. Detroit, Dec. 2, 1926; s. Riley League and Ola (Braswell) B.; B.A. in Journalism, Mich. State U., 1949; m. Patricia Stricklen, Aug. 16, 1958; 1 son, Barry R. With Latimer & Bayle, Detroit, Mem. Nat. Assn. State Budget Officers (pres. 1946). photgrapher, corr. A.P., 1949; with Maxon Inc., advt., 1949-64; pres. Burton Schigian Advt. Agy., Detroit, 1966—; former chmn. bd. Burton Schigian Can. Ltd.; dir. Sav-AOFund. Inc., B.L.K. Distbg. Co. Mem. Detroit council Boy Scouts Am.; chmn. Detroit United Found.; adviser to New Detroit, Inc. Served with USAAF, 1944-47. Mem. Adcrafter, Lambda Chi Alpha. Home: 1163 Buckingham Rd Grosse Point MI 48230 Office: Penebscot Bldg Detroit MI 48226

BURTON, WILFORD MOYLE, lawyer; b. Salt Lake City, Feb. 5, 1910; s. Theodore Taylor and Florence (Moyle) B.; A.B., U. Utah, 1931, LL.B., 1933; m. Dorothy Boud, June 28, 1934; children—Dorothy Ann, Wilford Boud, Margaret Jane. Admitted to Utah bar, 1934; mem. Armstrong & Burton, 1934-39; judge of City Ct., Salt Lake City, 1939-44; mem. McKay, Burton, McMillan & Richards, 1948- 58, McKay and Burton, attys., Salt Lake City, 1958-. Pres., Indsl. Uranium Co., Indsl. Western Inc. Mem. Salt Lake City, Utah (exec. sec.) restaurants assns., Am., Utah, Salt Lake City bar assns., Sigma Chi. Mem. Church of Jesus Christ of Latter Day Saints (pres. Eastern Atlantic states mission, regional rep. quorum of 12). Clubs: Salt Lake Country, Exchange, Booneville Knife and Fork; Timpanogas. Home: 668 17th Av Salt Lake City UT 84103 Office: Kennecott Bldg Salt Lake City UT 84111

BURTON, WILLIAM LESTER, educator; B. Moundsville, W.Va., Sept. 20, 1928; s. William Lester and Harriet (Hicks) B.; B.A., Bethany Coll., 1949; M.S., U. Wis., 1952, Ph.D., 1958; m. Ruthann Buzzard, Aug. 24, 1958; children—James Stewart, Carol Louise. Instr. Craig County (Va.) High Sch., 1949-50; from asst. prof. to prof. Western Ill. U., 1957-68, chmn. dept. history, 1969—. Research asso. Ill. Civil War Centennial Commn.; history textbook cons.; curriculum cons. sch. dists. Mem. Am. Hist. Assn., Orgn. Am. Historians, Danforth Assos., Am. Assn. Univ. Profs. (state v.p., chpt. pres.). Author: A Descriptive Bibliography of Civil War Manuscripts in Illinois, 1966; A Manual for History Teachers, 1967; Illinois: a Student's History of the Prairie State, 1969. Editorial bd. Jour. Developing Areas, 1968—. Contbr. articles profl. jours. Home: 817 Orchard Dr Macomb IL 61455

BURTON, WILLIAM SMITH, lawyer; b. Salt Lake City, Oct. 10, 1915; s. Harold Hitz and Selma Florence (Smith) B.; B.S., Bowdoin Coll., 1937; LL.B., Harvard, 1940; m. Nancy Lea Conners, Sept. 9, 1939 (div.); children—Susan Smith (Mrs. Bruce J. Shapiro), Betsey Lea (Mrs. George C. Wick, Jr.), Dianne Conners (Mrs. George S. Sherwin); m. 2d, Anne R. Hillman, Dec. 18, 1965. Admitted to Ohio bar; asso. Garfield, Baldwin, Jamison, Hope & Ulrich, 1940-51; partner Arter, Hadden, Wykoff & Van Duzer, Cleve., 1951- 70, Arter & Hadden, 1970—. Mem. Bd. Edn. Shaker Heights, O., 1956-63, pres., 1961-63; pres. Neighborhood Settlement Assn., 1954; mem. Cuyahoga County Charter Commn., 1959, chmn. Cleve. Unreached Youth Project, 1954-58. Rep., 99th and 100th Gen. Assemblies Ohio. Served from ensign to lt. USNR, 1942-46. Decorated Purple Heart. Fellow Am. Bar Found.; mem. Am. (chmn. standing com. aero. law 1954-58, 63-64), Ohio, Cuyahoga County, Cleve. bar assns., Am. Acad. Polit. and Social Sci., Phi Beta Kappa, Delta Kappa Epsilon. Unitarian. Clubs: City (pres. 1958), Cleveland Skating. Home: 2761 N Park Blvd Cleveland Heights OH 44118 Office: Union Commerce Bldg Cleveland OH 44115

BURTS, CHARLES WATSON, univ. adminstr.; b. Anderson, S.C., Aug. 28, 1907; s. Charles Elford and Sadie Amanda (Watson) B.; A.B., Furman U., 1929; B.D., Yale, 1932, Ph.D., 1939; spl. student Columbia, 1935; m. Ruth Littlejohn, June 12, 1933; 1 son, Watson Lee. Dir. Camp Ridgecrest for Boys, Ridgecrest, N.C., 1930-38; successively instr. psychology, asst. prof., asso. prof., prof., asst. dean, Furman U., Greenville, S.C., 1933- 42, 1945-46, dean grad. studies, 1958-63, chmn. dept. psychology, 1963—; dean Meredith Coll., Raleigh, N.C., 1946-48; pres. Shorter Coll., Rome, Ga., 1948-53. Vis. scholar U. Chgo., summer 1941, Columbia, 1953, 59, U. Mich., 1965, Stanford, 1968; mem. S.C. Bd. Exams. in Psychology, 1968—. Dir. Community College, 1957-59. Served from lt. (j.g.) to lt. comdr. personnel and research, USNR, 1942-45. Mem. So. Soc. for Philosophy and Psychology, Am., S.C. psychol. assns., Tau Kappa Alpha, Sigma Alpha Epsilon. Democrat. Baptist. Rotarian. Author: (with Allen Post) Background Factors Important in the Selection of Officers of the Line for Sea Duty (restricted publ. of Bur. of Naval Personnel), 1945. Home: Altamont Rd Paris Mt Greenville SC 29609

BURTS, THERON EUGENE, lawyer; b. Dublin, Ga., July 2, 1919; s. Theron E. and Agnes (Harper) B.; B.S. in Chem. Engring., U. Ala., 1946, LL.B., 1949, J.D., 1969; m. Elizabeth Sigler, Mar. 11, 1948; 1 dau., Ann Elizabeth. Admitted to Ala. bar, 1949; asso. law office Thomas E. Scofield, Kansas City, Mo., 1949- 50, 50-70; gen. practice law, Florence, Ala., 1950—; patent counsel to corps. and govt. agys., NASA. Dir. Financial Adjustment Bur., Inc., Highway Grassing Co., Inc., Masonry Services, Inc. Mem. speakers bur. United Fund, 1960; chmn. dist. leadership tng. Boy Scouts Am., 1957; mem. Shoals Labor Mgmt. Com., 1965- -, Lauderdale Indsl. Expansion Com., 1970—; chmn. Florence City Planning Com., 1960. Chmn. Lauderdale Republican Exec. Com., 1966. Bd. dirs. Muscle Shoals Concert Assn., Inc. Served with U.S. Army, 1937-38, N.G., 1938-40, M.I., AUS, 1943-46; ETO. Mem. Am., Ala., Lauderdale County (pres. 1964) bar assns., Am. Patent Law Assn., Sigma Pi Alpha, Sigma Pi. Episcopalian (vestryman, lay reader). Contbr. articles on history of World War II, Army Hist. Div.; lectr. on mil. history. Home: 2119 Chickasaw Dr Florence AL 35630 Office: Greater Alabama Bldg Florence AL 35630

BURTT, EVERETT JOHNSON, Jr., economist, educator; b. Jackson, Mich., Aug. 6, 1914; s. Everett Johnson and Eva Mildred (Meisenhelter) B.; A.B., Berea Coll., 1935; M.A., Duke, 1937, Ph.D., 1950; m. Cynthia Webb, June 15, 1940; children—Michael Coburn, Judith. Instr. econs. U. Me., 1939-41; instr. Denver U., 1941- 42; labor market analyst War Manpower Commn., 1942-43; employment analyst U.S. Bur. Labor Statistics, Boston, 1946-47; asst. prof. Boston U., 1947-52, asso. prof., 1952-57, prof. econs., 1957—, chmn. dept. Coll. Liberal Arts and Grad. Sch., 1952-68, chmn. all-univ. dept., 1956-68. Mem. Am. Econ. Assn., Indsl. Relations Research Assn. (pres. Boston 1966-67), Am. Assn. U. Profs. Author: Labor Markets, Unions and Government Policies, 1963; Plant Relocation and the Core City Worker, 1967. Contbr. profl. periodicals, reports. Home: 399 Clapboardtree St Westwood MA 02090 Office: 725 Commonwealth Av Boston MA 02215

BURWELL, JAMES ROBERT, educator; b. Anderson, Ind., Mar. 28, 1929; s. James M. and Alice Lucile (Merrick) B.; B.S., Ind. U., 1952, M.S., 1954, Ph.D., 1957; m. Joyce Elaine Wilson, Feb. 4, 1951; children—Anthony Duane, David Carl, Donald Eric. Grad. asst. Ind. U., 1952-54, research asst., 1954-57, postdoctoral research asso., 1957-59; asst. prof. U. Okla., 1959-63, asso. prof., 1963-68, prof., 1968—, chmn. dept. physics, 1963-64, asst. dean Coll. Arts and Scis., 1966-69, asso. dean, 1969—; physicist Lawrence Radiation Lab., U. Cal. at Berkeley, 1963. Mem. Am. Phys. Soc., Am. Assn. Physics Tchrs., Sigma Xi. Home: 1512 Ann Arbor Dr Norman OK 73069

BURWELL, MELVIN BLAINE, glass co. exec.; b. Toledo, Oct. 10, 1907; s. Arthur N. and Harriet (Blaine) B.; m. Edna C. Ehrenfried, July 5, 1941 (dec. 1966); children— Melvin Blaine, James Carroll, Patrice Blaine; m. 2d, Williamene N. Marshall, Mar. 9, 1970. With Libbey-Owens-Ford Glass Co., 1931—, gen. dir. employee relations, 1961—, v.p. employee relations, 1963—. Mem. Toledo Labor-Mgmt.-Citizens Com. Trustee Toledo Hosp. Mem. U.S. C. of C., Am. Mgmt. Assn., N.A.M. Home: 5005 W Central Av Toledo OH 43615 Office: 811 Madison Av Toledo OH 43624

BURWELL, ROBERT LEMMON, Jr., chemist; b. Balt., May 6, 1912; s. Robert Lemmon and Anne Hume (Lewis) B.; A.B., St. John's Coll., Annapolis, Md., 1932; Ph.D. (Procter fellow), Princeton, 1936; m. Elise Frank, Dec. 23, 1939; children—Mary Elise, Augusta Somervell. Instr. chemistry Trinity Coll., 1936-39; instr. Northwestern U., 1939-45, asst. prof., 1946, asso. prof., 1946- 52, prof., 1952—, chmn. dept. chemistry, 1952-57; dir. Internat. Congress on Catalysis, 1956-65; chmn. Gordon Research Conf. on Catalysis, 1957; com. phys. chemistry Nat. Acad. Sci.-NRC, 1962-64; sec. Council Internat. Congress Catalysis, 1968—. Served as lt. USNR, 1942- 45. Fellow Chem. Soc. (London); mem. Am. Chem. Soc. (chmn. div. phys. chemistry 1958-59, mem. council policy com. 1969—), Catalysis Soc. (dir.), Internat. Union Pure and Applied Chemistry (titular mem. colloid and surface chemistry commn. 1969—), Faraday Soc., Sigma Xi. Research in heterogeneous catalysis and surface chemistry. Home: 2759 Girard Av Evanston IL 60201

BURWELL, STEVE L., banker; b. Lexington, Miss., 1910. Sr. v.p. Deposit Guaranty Nat. Bank, Jackson, Miss.; pres., dir. Credit Life Agy., Inc.; partner Burwell Bros. Home: 3640 Crane Blvd Jackson MS 39216 Office: 200 E Capitol St Jackson MS 39205*

BURY, POL, sculptor; b. Haine-St-Pierre, Belgium, Apr. 26, 1922; s. Jules and Augusta (Modave) B.; student Athene Dulentre La Louviere, 1934, Acad. des Beaux Arts, Mons, 1938; m. Claudine Strebbelle, July 18, 1951; 1 dau., Michele; m. 2d, Velma Horne, Nov. 3, 1968. Kinetic sculpture, 1953—; one man shows, Los Angeles, 1965, U. Cal. at Berkeley, 1970, Walker Art Center, Minn., 1970-71, U. La., Chgo. Fine Arts Club, Houston Mus., Guggenheim Mus., N.Y.C., 1970-71; exhbns. at Lefebre Gallery, N.Y.C., Iris Clert La Hume Gallery, Paris, France, Kasmin Gallery, London, Eng., 1964, Venice Biennale, 1964, Gallerie Maeght, Paris, 1968, 1969; Kinetic Fountain, U. Ia. Mus., 1969; represented in permanent collections Mus. Modern Art, Guggenheim Mus., Allbright Knox Gallery, Ridgfield Mus., Amsterdam, Krefeld Mus., Brussels, Tate Gallery, London. Guest prof. U. Cal., Berkeley, 1970. Home: 236 Blvd Raspail Paris 14e France

BURZLE, JOHN ANTHONY, educator; b. Munich, Germany, May 20, 1908; s. Anton and Barbara (Schmelz) B.; Diplome de langue et literature, U. Dijon (France), 1927; Ph.D., U. Munich, 1932; m. Muriel M. Wittman, Oct. 3, 1935. Came to Can., 1935, U.S., 1945, naturalized, 1952. Instr., U. Munich, 1930-35; asst. prof. German, U. Man. (Can.), 1935; mem. faculty U. Kan., 1945—, prof. German, 1950—, chmn. dept., 1947-67, asso. dean Coll. Liberal Arts and Scis., 1967—, dir. Orientation Center for Scholars, 1951—; vis. prof. Stanford, 1963; cons. Inst. Internat. Edn., Inter Nationes, Bonn. Mem. adv. bd. Austro-Am. Bd. Edn.; cons. Goethe Inst., Munich. Decorated Grand Order Merit (Fed. German Govt.), Alexander von Humboldt medal. Mem. Kan. Modern Lang. Assn. (pres. 1962-64), Assn. Tchrs. German (pres. Kan. chpt. 1961-62), Am. Assn. U. Profs., Modern Lang. Assn., Kan. Hist. Soc. Author books and articles on German lang., German-Am. lit. Home: 1321 Strong Av Lawrence KN 66044

BUSBEE, CYRIL B., ednl. adminstr.; b. Wagener, S.C., Dec. 17, 1908; s. William J. and Minnie (Toole) B.; B.S., U. S.C., 1928, M.A., 1938, LL.D., 1969; postgrad Coll. William and Mary, 1941, Columbia, 1955; LL.D., Wofford Coll., 1970; m. Thelma Ecord, July 20, 1929; children—Carolyn (Mrs. Robert Carpenter), Cyril B. Supt., Windsor Sch., Aiken County, S.C., 1930-35, Baron DeKalb Sch., Kershaw County, S.C. 1935-43, Brookland-Cayce (S.C.) Schs., 1943-67; supt. edn. S.C., Columbia, 1967—. Dir. Citizens and So. Nat. Bank, Columbia, S.C. Mem. steering com. Edn. Commn. of States; mem. exec. com. Regional Edn. Lab. of Carolinas and Va. Served with USNR, 1943-46. Mem. Nat. Council Chief State Sch. Officers (chmn. policy com.), S.C. Edn. Assn. (pres. 1965-66), W. Columbia-Cayce C. of C. (pres. 1962). Democrat. Methodist (ofcl. bd., trustee). Lion (pres. Cayce-W. Columbia 1959), Kiwanian (pres. Camden 1940). Home: 900 N Av Cayce, SC 29033 Office: Rutledge Bldg Columbia SC 29201

BUSBY, ELDEN B., ednl. adminstr.; b. Venus, Tex., Nov. 3, 1907; s. Horace W. and Viola May (Wise) B.; B.A., Abilene Christian Coll., 1930; M.A., Tex. Christian U., 1931; Ed.D., Stanford, 1948; m. Ruby Tunstill, Aug. 20, 1929. Tchr., Ft. Worth Pub. Schs., 1931-33, vice prin., 1935-37, prin., 1937-46, asst. supt. gen. adminstrn., 1946-61, dep. supt., 1961-63, supt. schs., 1963- 67; exec. dir. Edn. Service Center, Region XI, 1934-35, 67—. Personnel dir. W. C. Stripling Co. Mem. Ft. Worth Library Bd., 1957-63. Bd. dirs. Southwestern Expn. and Fat Stock Show. Recipient award of appreciation for developing excellence in edn. Ft. Worth Classroom Tchrs. Assn., 1964. Mem. N.E.A., Am., Tex. assns. sch. adminstrs., Nat. Sch. Pub. Relations Assn. (past v.p. Tex chpt.), Tex. Tchrs. Assn., Ft. Worth Classroom Tchrs. Assn., Ft. Worth C. of C., Am. Assn. Sch. Adminstrs., Nat. (life), Tex. congresses parents and tchrs., Phi Delta Kappa, Iota Lambda Sigma. Clubs: Knife and Fork, Kiwanis (pres. 1950) (Ft. Worth). Home: 3551 Westcliff Rd S Fort Worth, TX 76109. Office: 2821 Cullen St Fort Worth TX 76107

BUSBY, JACK KEMP, utilities exec.; b. Chgo., June 16, 1917; s. Leonard Asbury and Esther (Boardman) B.; B.A., Princeton, 1938; LL.B., Yale, 1941; m. Elise Sophie Hohle, Oct. 4, 1947 (dec. 1966); children—Leonard Asbury, Louise Wheeler; m. 2d, Mary Rose McWilliams, May 10, 1969. Admitted to N.Y. bar, 1941; asso. Simpson, Thacher & Bartlett, N.Y.C., 1941- 51; gen. counsel Pa. Power & Light Co., Allentown, 1951-54, v.p., gen. counsel, 1954-56, exec. v.p., dir., 1956—, pres., 1957- -, chief exec. officer, 1964—; dir. Cryotherm, Inc., Air Products & Chems., Inc., Lehigh Portland Cement Co., Allentown. Met. chmn. Nat. Alliance Businessmen. Adv. regional com. Boy Scouts Am.; chmn. Pa. Planning Bd. Trustee Found. for Ind. Colls., Sacred Heart Hosp., Cedar Crest Coll.; bd. dirs. United Fund Lehigh County, Geisinger Med. Center. Served with USNR, 1942-46. Mem. Am. Bar Assn. Clubs: Saucon Valley Country; Lehigh Country. Home: RFD 1 Zionsville PA 18092 Office: 901 Hamilton St Allentown PA 18101

BUSCAGLIA, CHRIS JOSEPH, mental health center adminstr.; b. Milw., July 12, 1907; s. Lucian and Rose (Costa) B.; B.S., Marquette U., 1931, M.D., 1933; postgrad. neuropathology and neuroanatomy U. Mich., 1939-40, 45-46; children—Lou, Chris Joseph, Mary. Intern St. Mary's Hosp., Milw., 1932- 33; res. officer Civilian Conservation Corps, 1934-36; resident Ypsilanti State Hosp., 1937-40, psychiat. tng., 1940; asst. supt. Huntington (W.Va.) State Hosp., 1948-49; pvt. practice, Wauwatosa, Wis., 1950-58; med. dir. Milwaukee County Mental Health Center (North), 1958- 71; cons. staff Elmbrook Meml. Hosp., Brookfield, 1971—; cons. Mental Health Center (South), 1971—; asst. prof. Marquette U. Med. Sch., 1958—; cons. psychiatrist St. Joseph Hosp., Milw.; mem. hon. staff St. Michael Hosp., Milw. Served with M.C., AUS, 1941-45. Mem. Am., Wis. psychiat. assns., A.M.A., Milw. Neuro-psychiat. Soc. (past pres.), Milw. Urban League, Phi Beta Pi. K.C. Address: 5310 S Magellan New Berlin WI 53151

BUSCH, ALFRED EUGENE, mfg. co. exec.; b. Riga, Latvia, Aug. 14, 1914; s. Eugene and Ottilie (Keuffel) B.; B.S., Mass. Inst. Tech., 1937; m. Elinor Thomsen, June 1940 (dec. June 1962); children—Madelaine Jean (Mrs. John Lansing Zabriskie, Jr.), Elizabeth Thomsen (Mrs. John B. Crosby, Jr.), Carolyn Keuffel; m. 2d, Maria de Sellern, Oct. 26, 1963. Naturalized Am. citizen, 1938. Salesman, N.Y. Dept., 1938-43; mfg. Kneffel & Esser Co., Hoboken, N.J., 1943-45, asst. treas., 1945-48, financial v.p., 1948-55, v.p., treas., 1955-61, pres., 1961-70, chmn., 1970—; dir. First Jersey Nat. Bank, Leslie Co., Columbia Mut. Life Ins. Co.; vice chmn., dir. N.J. Mfrs. Ins. Co.; vice chmn., trustee N.J. Mfrs. Assn.; vice chmn. N.J. Internat. Trading Corp.; mem. adv. bd. Arkwright-Boston Ins. Mem. Newcomen Soc. Clubs: Deke, Baltusrol Golf, Short Hills. Home: 91 Western Dr Short Hills NJ 07078 Office: 20 Whippany Rd Morristown NJ 07960

BUSCH, ALFRED H., corp. exec.; b. Chgo., 1919; ed. U. Wis., 1942; LL.B., De Paul U., 1947. Vice pres., sec., treas. Stewart-Warner Corp. Office: 1826 Diversey Pkwy Chicago IL 60614

BUSCH, ARTHUR WINSTON, educator, cons. engr.; b. Houston, Oct. 9, 1926; s. Arthur Clarence and Vere (Hillsman) B.; B.S. in C.E., Tex. Tech. Coll., 1950; S.M. in San. Engring., Mass. Inst. Tech., 1952; m. Elray Carter, Sept. 5, 1948; children—Randolph, Juliet. Asst. to dir. research and devel. Infilco, Tucson, 1952-55; mem. faculty Rice U., 1955—, prof. environmental engring., 1964—, chmn. dept., 1967-70; cons. in field, 1955—. Cons. to Water Quality Office, Environmental Protection Agy. Mem. Pres.'s Air Quality Adv. Bd. Served with AUS, 1944-46. Co-recipient Harrison Prescott Eddy medal Water Pollution Control Fedn., 1961. Mem. Am. Chem. Soc. (certificate of merit 1952), Am. Water Works Assn., Water Pollution Control Fedn., Am. Inst. Chem. Engrs. (nat. dir. environmental div. 1970-71), Am. Geophys. Union, A.A.A.S., Sigma Xi, Tau Beta Pi. Club: Cosmos (Washington). Author book, also papers in field. Home: 5239 Braes Valley Houston TX 77035

BUSCH, AUGUST A., Jr., brewing exec.; b. St. Louis, Mo., Mar. 28, 1899; s. August A. and Alice (Zisemann) B.; ed. Smith Acad.; m. Gertrude Buholzer, Mar. 22, 1952. With Mfrs. Ry. Co., Lafayette South Side Bank & Trust Co.; gen. supt. Anheuser-Busch, Inc., 1924-26, 6th v.p., gen. mgr., 1926-31, 2d v.p., gen. mgr., 1931-34, 1st v.p., gen. mgr., 1934-41, pres., 1946—, also chmn. bd.; dir., pres. August Busch & Co., Mass., Mo., So. Syrup & Brokerage Co.; pres. St. Louis Cardinals; dir., v.p. Mfrs. Ry. Co.; dir., 1st v.p. Adolphus Busch Estate, Inc.; v.p. St. Louis Refrigerator Car Co.; dir. St. Louis Union Trust Co., Huttig Sash & Door Co., Gen. Am. Life Ins. Co., U.S. Brewers Found., 1st Nat. Bank; v.p., dir. August A. Busch & Co., Inc., Tex.; pres., dir. St. Louis Nat. Baseball Club. Mem. brewing industry adv. com. WPB, 1942; chmn. bd. Civic Progress, Inc., St. Louis U. Devel. Fund drive; mem. bd. St. Louis Symphony Orch., St. Louis Municipal Opera, Civic Center Redevel. Corp.; chmn. St. Louis Bi-centennial Celebration Com. Served to col. Ordnance Dept., AUS, 1942-45. Clubs: Missouri Athletic, Racquet, Old Warson, Log Cabin, Bridlespur Hunt (St. Louis); Rolling Rock (Ligonier, Pa.). Home: Grant's Farm 10501 Gravois Av St Louis MO 63123 Office: 721 Pestalozzi St St Louis MO 63118

BUSCH, AUGUST ADOLPHUS, III, brewery exec.; b. St. Louis, June 16, 1937; s. August Anheuser and Elizabeth (O'Fallon) B.; student U. Ariz., 1957-59, Siebel Inst. Tech., 1960-61; m. Susan Marie Hornibrook, Aug. 17, 1963; children—August Adolphus IV, Susan Marie II. With Anheuser-Busch, Inc., St. Louis, 1958—, sales mgr., 1962-64, v.p. marketing operations, 1964-65, v.p., gen. mgr., 1965—, also dir.; dir. St. Louis Nat. Baseball Club, Comml. Bank St. Louis County, 1st Nat. Bank of St. Louis. Active Muscular Dystrophy campaign; bd. govs. Cardinal Glennon Hosp.; mem. adv. bd. Wharton Sch. U. Pa., Coll. William and Mary Sch. Bus. Adminstrn.; mem. pres.'s council St. Louis U.; bd. dirs. St. Louis Municipal Opera, St. Louis Research Council, United Fund Greater St. Louis, Boy Scouts Am., St. Louis Symphony. Mem. St. Louis Jr. C. of C. Clubs: St. Louis, Racquet (St. Louis). Home: 00 Fordyce Lane St Louis MO 63124 Office: 721 Pestalozzi St St Louis MO 63118

BUSCH, BENJAMIN, lawyer; b. N.Y.C., June 12, 1912; s. S. Henry and Dorothy (Busch) B.; student City Coll. N.Y., 1928-30; LL.B., St. Lawrence U., 1933; m. Phyllis Toby Schnell, Nov. 8, 1935; children—Frederick Matthew, Eric Edwin. Admitted to N.Y. bar, 1934; partner firm Katz & Somerich, 1946—. Explorer, adviser Boy Scouts Am. Served with AUS, 1944-45. Decorated Bronze Star medal, Purple Heart. Mem. Am. (div. vice chmn. sect. internat. and comparative law, div. comparative law), N.Y.C., N.Y. State bar assns., Am. Judicature Soc., Am. Fgn. Law Assn. (pres. 1969-70), Consular Law Soc. (bd. dirs.), Am. Soc. Internat. Law. Author: (with Otto C. Sommerich) Foreign Law-A Guide to Pleading and Proof, 1959; also articles. Office: 120 Broadway New York City NY 10005

BUSCH, DARYLE HADLEY, educator, chemist; b. Carterville, Ill., Mar. 30, 1928; s. Dwight H. and Ione (Bauman) B.; B.A., So. Ill. U., 1951; M.S., U. Ill., 1952, Ph.D. (Bersworth fellow), 1954; m. Geraldine Barnes, Mar. 11, 1951; children—Derek H., Michael C., Steven J., Cheryl Ann, Kristina Marie. Mem. faculty Ohio State U., Columbus, 1954—, prof. chemistry, 1963—, head div. inorganic chemistry, 1959-66; cons. E.I. duPont, 1956—, NIH, 1961-65, NSF, 1965—, Beaunit Fibers, 1966—; cons. editor Allyn & Bacon; plenary lectr. 10th Internat. Conf. Coordination Chemistry, St. Moritz, Switzerland, 1966. Served with AUS, 1946-48. Unrestricted grantee Research Corp., 1960-63; recipient Am. Chem. Soc. award inorganic chemistry, 1963. Mem. Am. Chem. Soc., A.A.A.S., Sigma Xi, Pi Mu Epsilon, Phi Lambda Upsilon, Sigma Pi Sigma. Editorial bd. Chem. Revs., 1967-70, Internat. Letters, Inorganic and Nuclear Chemistry, 1965—, Am. Chem. Soc. Monographs, 1964—. Contbr. numerous articles to profl. jours. Studies in transition metal chemistry, application of phys. measurements to study of their compounds, nature of interactions between metal ions and groups bound to them, function of metal ions in the control of chem. reactions. Home: 1930 Cambridge Blvd Columbus OH 43212

BUSCH, HARRIS, educator; b. Chgo., May 23, 1923; s. Maurice Ralph and Rose Lillian (Feigenholtz) B.; B.S., U. Ill., 1944, M.D. with honors, 1946; M.S., U. Wis., 1950, Ph.D., 1952; m. Rose Klora, June 16, 1945; children—Daniel Avery, Laura Anne (Mrs. Mitchell Smolkin), Gerald Irwin, Fredric Neal. Intern, Cook County Hosp., Chgo., 1946-47; asst. surgeon, sr. asst. surgeon USPHS, 1947-49; postdoctoral fellow Nat. Cancer Inst., 1950-52; asst. prof. biochemistry, internal medicine Yale, 1952-55; asso. prof., prof. pharmacology U. Ill., 1955-60; prof. biochemistry, chmn. dept. Baylor U. Coll. Medicine, 1960-62, prof. pharmacology, chmn. dept., 1960—, also dir. Cancer Research Center. Vis. prof. U. Chgo., 1968, 71, Northwestern U., 1968, Ga. Med. Coll., 1971; cons. lectr. U. Tenn., U. Tex., San Antonio, 1971; cons. VA, Meth. hosps. (both Houston); mem. cons. bd. Eli Lilly Co. Mem. personnel panel Am. Cancer Soc.; cancer chemotherapy study sect. USPHS. Baldwin scholar oncology Yale Sch. Medicine, 1952-55; scholar cancer research Am. Cancer Soc., 1955. Mem. Am. Soc. Biol. Chemists, Am. Assn. for Cancer Research, Am. Chem. Soc., Soc. pharmacology and Exptl. Therapeutics, Soc. Exptl. Biology and Medicine, Sigma Xi, Alpha Omega Alpha. Author: Chemistry of Pancreatic Diseases, 1959; An Introduction to the Biochemistry of the Cancer Cell, 1962; Histones and Other Nuclear Proteins, 1965. Co-author: Chemotherapy, 1966; The Nucleolus, 1970. Editor: Frontiers in Medical Biochemistry, 1962; The Nucleus of the Cancer Cell, 1963; Jour. Phys. Chemistry and Physics; Methods in Cancer Research; Molecular Pharmacology; asso. editor Cancer Research; Methods in Cancer Research, vol. I, 1966, vols. II, III, 1967, vol. IV, 1968; vol. V, 1970, vol. VI, 1971. Home: 4966 Dumfries Dr Houston TX 77035

BUSCH, JOSEPH PETER, county dist. atty.; b. Chgo., Feb. 12, 1926; s. Joseph Peter and Clara Henrietta (Schukenecht) B.; B.S., U. Tex., 1947, J.D., Loyola U., Chgo., 1951; m. Jennie Frances Roasio, Feb. 22, 1947; children—Joseph, Steven, David. Admitted to Cal. bar, 1952; mem. dist. attys. office Los Angeles County 1952-65, chief trial dep., 1965-68, dir. bur. spl. operations, 1968, asst. dist. atty., 1969, chief dep. dist. atty., 1970, dist. atty., 1970—. Served with USNR, 1944-46. Mem. Nat. Dist. Attys. Assn., Dist. Attys. and County Counsels Assn. Cal. Home: 1619 Chetney Dr W Convina CA 91790 Office: Hall Justice Los Angeles CA 90012

BUSCH, NIVEN, author; b. N.Y.C., Apr. 26, 1903; s. Birton Niven and Christine (Fairchild) B.; grad. Princeton, 1926; m. Teresa Wright, May 12, 1942 (div. 1952); m. 2d, Carmencita Baker, Mar. 14, 1956 (div. Sept. 1969); children—Peter, Briton, Terence, Mary Kelly, Joseph, Nicholas and Eliza (twins). Asso. editor Time mag., 1927, 31; asso. editor, contbr. New Yorker mag., 1927, 31; motion picture writer, 1931-40, with Warner Brothers, 20th Century, Goldwyn, Paramount, Universal studios. Regents' prof. English, fine arts U. Cal., Irvine, 1970, 71. Nominated for Acad. Motion Picture Arts and Scis. award for best original screen play, In Old Chicago, 1937. Mem. Acad. Motion Picture Arts and Scis., Authors Guild, Writers Guild Am. Author: Twenty-One Americans (originally pub. New Yorker mag.), 1930; (novels) The Carrington Incident, 1941, Duel in the Sun, 1944, They Dream of Home, 1944, Day of the Conquerors, 1946, The Furies, 1948, The Hate Merchant, 1953, The Actor, 1955, California Street, 1958; The San Franciscans, 1961, The Gentleman from California, 1965; (original screen-plays): Pursued, 1946; The Capture, 1946; Distant Drums, 1951; Man from the Alamo, 1952; The Moonlighter, 1953; The Treasure of Pancho Villa, 1955; Galveston, 1956; California Street, 1959; The San Franciscans, 1961; The Gentleman From California, 1965. Clubs: Press, Union League (San Francisco), Lakeside (Los Angeles). Home: 3139 Jackson St San Francisco CA 94115

BUSCH, NOEL FAIRCHILD, author, editor; b. N.Y.C., Dec. 27, 1906; s. Briton Niven and Christine (Fairchild) B.; student St. Bernard's Sch., 1917-21, St. George's Sch., 1921-25; student Princeton, 1925-27; m. Mary Smart, June 5, 1950; children—Mary Fairchild, Beatrix. Asso. editor Time mag., 1927-38; sportswriter N.Y. Daily News, 1928-31; sr. editor Life mag., 1938- 42, war corr., 1942-45, sr. writer, 1945-52; rep. The Asia Found., Tokyo, 1952-54, Bangkok, 1954-58, spl. asst. to the pres., 1958-59; staff writer Reader's Digest, 1959—. Mem. Am. Hist. Soc. Clubs: PEN, Princeton, Century Assn., Racquet and Tennis (N.Y.C.); Millbrook Golf and Tennis. Author: My Unconsidered Judgment, 1944; What Manner of Man, a biography of Franklin Delano Roosevelt, 1944; Lost Continent, 1945; Fallen Sun, a Report on Japan, 1948; Briton Hadden, a biography of the co-founder of Time, 1949; Adlai E. Stevenson of Ill., a biography, 1952; Thailand: An Introduction to Modern Siam, 1958; Two Minutes to Noon, The Story of the Great Tokyo Earthquake, 1962; T.R.: The Story of Theodore Roosevelt, 1963; The Emperor's Sword, 1969. Contbr. New Yorker, Atlantic Monthly, Sat. Eve. Post. Horizon, other mags. Home: South Rd Millbrook NY 12545

BUSCHE, EUGENE MARVIN, ins. co. exec.; b. Decatur, Ind., July 2, 1926; s. Louis Martin and Ruby (Smith) B.; B.B.A., Ind. U., 1950; m. Barbara Ann Sherow, Aug. 1, 1954; children—David Alan, Sara Lynn. Agt. Am. United Life Ins. Co., Lafayette, Ind., 1950-55; asst. gen. agt. State Mut. Life Assurance Co., Indpls., 1955-56; field supr. Indpls. Life Ins. Co., 1956-63, ednl. dir. 1963-70, adminstrv. v.p., dir., 1970—, prin., dir. LINSCO Corp., Washington. Asst. scoutmaster Kikthawenund council Boy Scouts Am., 1970-71. Served with USNR, 1944-46. C.L.U. Mem. Indpls. Soc. C.L.U.'s (past pres.), Delta Tau Delta (pres. Delta Tau Delta Bldg. Corp. 1965-67, past pres. Alumni chpt. Methodist (chmn. council ministeries 1969-71). Rotarian Club: Toastmasters. Home: 1320 Lawrence Rd Carmel IN 46032 Office: 2960 N Meridian St Indianapolis IN 46208

BUSCHMAN, ARTHUR WILLIAM, Jr., govt. ofcl., indsl. economist; b. Phillipsburg, N.J., Apr. 26, 1917; s. Arthur William and Nina Kellum (Segraves) B.; student Northwestern U., 1935-37, Rider Coll., 1937-38; A.B., George Washington U., 1941, postgrad., 1941-42; m. Eleanor Virginia Kennedy, June 21, 1945; 1 dau., Michal Mary. With N.Y. Life Ins. Co., 1936, 38, ICC, 1941; spl. asst. to dir. regional officers Bur. Labor Statistics, 1941-43, dep. chief aircraft sect., 1943-45, spl. studies 1946-48; spl. studies potential mfg. capacity multi-product producers Munitions Bd., Dept. Def., 1948-49, orgn. indsl. preparedness measures, 1949, spl. studies for chmn. on guided missiles, 1950, adviser to chief Office Prodn. Planning, 1950, chief officer components, 1951, staff dir. indsl. readiness and econ. analysis div. Dept. Def., dir. indsl. mgmt., 1964—, chmn. industry adv. com. for integrated logistic support, 1968—. Founder mem. Republican Club D.C. Served with USAAF, 1946-47. Mem. Am. Legion, Soc. for Preservation and Encouragement Barber Shop Quartet Singing in Am., Delta Phi Epsilon. Episcopalian. Elk. Clubs: Capitol Hill, Tuesday Musical, Washington Golf and Country, National Aviation. Contbr. articles to profl. jours., govt. reports. Home: 6311 Beachway Dr Lake Barcroft Estates Falls Church VA Office: Asst Sec Def Dept of Defense Washington DC 20301

BUSCHMAN, HOWARD CHARLES, Jr., mfg. co. exec.; b. N.Y.C., Sept. 2, 1917; s. Howard Charles and Lillian L. (Ruopp) B.; A.B., Williams Coll., 1939; LL.B., Albany Law Sch., 1949; m. Elizabeth L. Heisler, Dec. 13, 1941; children—Howard Charles III, Charles G. H., Henrietta E. Admitted to N.Y. bar, 1949; law clk. to justice U.S. Supreme Ct., 1949-50; law asso. firm Milbank, Tweed, Hope & Hadley, N.Y.C., 1950-52; with Abex Corp. (name formerly Am. Brake Shoe Co.), N.Y.C., 1952—, gen. counsel, 1958—, sec., 1960—; v.p., dir. Superston Corp., N.Y.C., 1960-62. Bd. dirs. Family Consultation Service Eastchester, N.Y. Served to capt. AUS, 1941-46. Mem. Am. Bar Assn., Bar Assn. City N.Y., Phi Beta Kappa, Delta Phi, Episcopalian. Club: Williams (N.Y.C.). Office: 530 Fifth Av New York City NY 10036

BUSCHMAN, LEONARD VICTOR, clergyman; b. McGirks, Mo., Sept. 15, 1893; s. Kasten D. and Lydia (Mellies) B.; B.A., Westminster Coll., Fulton, Mo., 1915, D.D., 1928; M.A., Princeton, 1918; postgrad. Princeton Theol. Sem., 1918; m. Lillian Martin, Oct. 16, 1918. Ordained to ministry Presbyn. Ch., 1918; pastor First Presbyn. Ch., Woodbridge, N.J., 1918-25, Tyler Pl. Presbyn. Ch., St. Louis, 1925-29, Central Presbyn. Ch., Buffalo, 1929-41, Central Presbyn. Ch., Summit, N.J., 1941-58, pastor emeritus, 1958-; asso. minister First Congl. Ch., Sarasota, 1961-63. Mem. Bd. Christian Edn. U.P. Ch. U.S.A.; regional rep. Presbyn. Found. Mem. Beta Theta Pi. Republican. Mason, Rotarian. Club: Ivy League (pres. Sarasota). Home: 1523 Flower Dr Sarasota FL 33779

BUSCHMANN, CHARLES SEVERIN, lawyer; b. Indpls., June 19, 1896; s. Charles Louis and Laura Blanche (Miller) B.; A.B., Ind. U., 1917; postgrad. Sorbonne, Paris, 1919; LL.B., Yale, 1921, LL.M., 1931; m., Dorothy Ford, Aug. 24, 1918; children—Charles Severin, Jr., Joan F. (Mrs. Charles Hicks), George Harry; m. 2d, Betty Jeanne Davis, June 19, 1941. Admitted to Ind. bar, 1921, since practiced in Indpls.; partner firm Buschmann, Carr & Schabel; former instr. Ind. Law Sch. Pres. Sheffield Hotel, Indpls., Fairfield Apts., Ft. Wayne, Ind. Served with U.S. Army, 1917- 19; disch. as capt. Inf.; mem. O.R.C., 1919-48; disch. as col. Inf., 1948; with AUS 1942-45; served at SHAEF, G/1 Div., 1944-45. Decorated Croix de Guerre avec Etoile de Vermeil. Mem. Am., Ind., Indpls. bar assns., Phi Delta Phi, Phi Kappa Psi, Sigma Delta Psi. Clubs: Columbia, Athletic, Athenaeum, Woodstock, Players (Indianapolis). Contbr. articles to Ind. Law Jour. Home: 4750 North Meridian St Indianapolis IN 46208 Office: Fidelity Bldg Indianapolis IN 46204

BUSCHMEYER, FRED SHERMAN, clergyman; b. Carpinteria, Cal., Oct. 22, 1899; s. August H. and Rachel (Sherman) B.; B.R.E., Boston U., 1925, S.T.B., 1927; Litt.D., U. N.H., 1937; D.D., Pacific Sch. Religion, 1951; LL.D., Ursinus Coll., Collegeville, Pa., 1957; m. Myrna Dresser Elbert, Dec. 27, 1922; children—Myrna Helen (Mrs. Nielson Marshall), Fred S., Barabara (Mrs. William Funcke). Ordained to ministry Methodist Episcopal Ch., 1926; transferred to Congl. Christian chs., 1934; asso. minister Leyden Congl. Ch., Brookline, Mass., 1924-27; minister Durham (N.H.) Community Ch., 1927-36, First Congl. Ch., Manchester, N.H., 1936-39, Mt. Pleasant Congl. Ch., Washington, 1939-48; asso. minister, dir. dept. ministry Gen. Council Congl. Christian Chs., N.Y.C. 1948-57. Chmn. Congl. European Relief Study Tour, 1947; del. First Assembly of World Council of Chs., Amsterdam, 1948; mem. Gen. Commn. on Chaplains, 1939—; mem. life and work div. Nat. Council of Churches of Christ in Am., 1949-53, chmn. dept. ministry, 1952-56, asst. gen. sec. of council and dir. Washington Office, 1957-61; sec. United Ch. of Christ, N.Y.C., 1961-67; minister Pitt St. Congl. Ch., Sydney, Australia, 1967- 69; dir. personal relations and admissions Pilgrim Place, Claremont, Cal., 1970—. Mem. armed services com. Nat. YMCA, 1961-67. Bd., govs., chmn. com. on field operations U.S.O., 1961-67. Home: Melvin Village NH 03850 Office: 660 Priscilla Way Claremont CA 91711

BUSE, HENRY WILLIAM, Jr., marine corps officer; b. Ridley Park, Pa., Apr. 10, 1912; s. Henry William and Estelle (Tichenor) B.; student Severn Sch., 1929-30; B.S., U.S. Naval Acad., 1934; grad. Armed Forces Staff Coll., 1949; m. Dorothy Virginia Snow, June 27, 1936; children—Barbara (Mrs. Roger C. Johnson), Henry William III. Commd. 2d lt. USMC, 1934, advanced through grades to lt. gen., 1964; assigned to various divs., Guadacanal, 1942-43, Cape Gloucester, 1943-44, Japan, 1946-47; asst. chief staff G-4 supply, Pacific area, 1947-49; comdg. officer 2d div. Sixth Marines, 1950-51; chief of staff 1st div., Korea, 1952-53, Marine Corps Recruit Depot, Parris Island, S.C., 1953-56; chief of staff Fleet Marine Force, Pacific 1956-57, Atlantic, 1957-58; liaison officer to vice chief naval operations, 1958-61; asst. chief of staff G-3 Hdqrs., 1961-62; comdr. 3d div., Okinawa, 1962-63; dep. chief of staff, plans and programs Hdqrs. Offce Comdt., Washington, 1963-67, chief of staff, 1967-68; comdg. gen. Fleet Marine Force, 1968—. Mem. exec. com., bd. govs. U.S. Olympic Com. Decorated D.S.M., Silver Star, Legion of Merit with combat V, Bronze Star medal with combat V and gold star, Legion of Merit; Netherlands Order of Orange Nassau with swords; Korean Ulchi medal with silver star; Order Nat. Security Merit, 2d class Republic Korea; Medal Cloud and Banner with Grand Cordon, Govt. Republic China. Mem. U.S. Naval Inst., Marine Corps Assn. Mason (32). Home: 35 Makalapa Dr Honolulu HI 96818 Office: Hdqrs Fleet Marine Force Pacific FPO San Francisco CA 96610

BUSH, BEVERLY, assn. exec., artist; b. Kelso, Washington; d. Edward Lawrence and Gunild Hedvig (Hansen) Stover; B.A., U. Wash.; student Art Student's League, Nat. Acad. Design; m. William Bush, Jan. 8, 1944. Nat. exhbns. include Audubon Artists, N.A.D., Nat. Assn. Women Painters, USA 59; rep. pvt. colls. with Artists Equity Assn., Inc., 1956—, exec. sec., 1958—. Zeta Phi Eta. Home: 3521 E Spruce St Seattle WA 98104 Office: 229 Broadway E Seattle WA 98102

BUSH, BURL HEBER, coll. dean; b. New Castle, Pa., Dec. 3, 1906; s. Frank Layton and Flora Belle (Ricker) B.; B.S., U.S. Naval Acad., 1929; M.S., State U. Ia., 1931; grad. Advanced Mgmt. Program Harvard, 1947; m. Eloise Walker, Aug. 11, 1932; children—Signy Eloise (Mrs. J.T. Brown), Susan Gertrude (Mrs. P.M. Moriarty), Henry Veblen. Commd. ensign USN, 1929, advanced through grades to comdr., 1962; with power br. Office Naval Research, 1953-56; indsl. officer Naval Engring. Expt. Sta., 1947- 51, Navy Electronics Lab., 1960-62; design supt. San Francisco Naval Shipyard, 1956-60, Long Beach (Cal.) Naval Shipyard, 1951-52; ret., 1962; mem. engring. faculty Fenn Coll., Cleve. State U., 1931-41, dean engring., 1962—. Registered profl. engr., Ohio. Mem. Am. Soc. Engring Edn., Am. Soc. M.E., Cleve. Engring. Soc. Presbyn. Home: 2640 Berkshire Rd Cleveland OH 44106

BUSH, CHARLES KETTRON, Jr., psychiatrist, state ofcl.; b. Owensboro, Ky., June 29, 1907; s. Charles Kettron and Lillie (White) B.; M.D., U. Louisville, 1929; m. Edna Mae Redmon, June 18, 1936 (div. Mar. 1946); children—Barbara Ellen, Charles Kettron, Nina Ruth; m. 2d, Nancy Mae DeGrafft, June 15, 1946; 1 son, James Maxwell. Gen. practice medicine, Irvington, Ky., 1929-32, Louisville, 1932-42; resident in psychiatry Elgin (Ill.) State Hosp., 1946-49; supt. Dixon (Ill.) State Hosp., 1949-54; dir. archtl. study project Am. Psychiat. Assn., 1954-56, chief insp., central inspection bd., 1956-60; dep. supt. Del. State Hosps., Newcastle, 1961, supt., 1961- 64; commr. mental health Del., 1964; asst. dir. mental health div. Ga. Dept. Pub. Health, Atlanta, 1964—; clin. asst. prof. psychiatry Emory U. Med. Sch., 1965—. Cons. VA Hosp., Wilmington, Del., 1962-64. Served from lt. to capt. AUS, 1942-46; ETO. Diplomate Am. Bd. Psychiatry and Neurology; fellow Am., So. psychiat. assns., Am. Pub. Health Assn.; mem. A.M.A., Med. Assn. Ga., Fulton County Med. Soc., Ga. Psychiat. Assn., Am., Ga. pub. health assns., Am. Assn. on Mental Deficiency, Soc. Philatelic Ams., Phi Chi. Rotarian (pres. Dixon club 1954), Mason; mem. Order Eastern Star. Home: 4425 Harris Trail NW Atlanta GA 30327 Office: 47 Trinity St SW Atlanta GA 30303

BUSH, CHILTON ROWLETTE, media research cons.; b. Pleasureville, Ky., July 13, 1896; s. Charles and Pearl (Ireland) B.; B.A., U. Wis., 1925, M.A., 1927, Ph.D., 1935; Litt.D., Georgetown (Ky.) Coll., 1940; m. Myrtle Stocking, June 15, 1929; 1 son, John. Engaged in newspaper work, 1917-23, mem. faculty Sch. Journalism, U. Wis., 1925-34; prof., exec. head dept. communication and journalism Stanford U., 1934-61; vis. asso. prof. U. Minn., summer 1929; vis. prof. U. Ore., 1962; dir. news research center Am. Newspaper Pubs. Assn., 1964—; tech. cons. in measurement pub. opinion, media and employee attitudes. Recipient Sidney S. Goldish award, 1969; Paul J. Deutschmann award, 1969. Mem. Am. Assn. Schs. and Depts. of Journalism (chmn. council on research, 1939-42, pres. 1942-44), Am. Statis. Assn., Am. Soc. Newspaper Editors (distinguished service mem.), Am. Market Assn., Am. Assn. Pub. Opinion Research, Pi Kappa Alpha, Sigma Delta Chi (Nat. v.p., 1939-41, Distinguished Teaching award 1969), Alpha Delta Sigma, Kappa Tau Alpha. Clubs: Press (San Francisco); Faculty (Stanford U.). Author books latest being: News Research for Better Newspapers, Vol. I, 1966, Vol. II, 1967, Vol. III, 1968, Vol. IV, 1969, Vol. V, 1971; Free Press-Free Trial: Some Dimensions of the Problem, 1970. Contbr. to profl. jours. Address: 669 Cabrillo Stanford CA 94305

BUSH, D., mfg. co. exec. Controller, Am. Hoechst Corp., Somerville, N.J. Office: Am Hoechst Corp PO Box 2500 Somerville NJ 08876*

BUSH, DONALD LEE, vet. med. exec.; b. Augusta, Me., Mar. 10, 1920; s. Peter, Jr. and Winnifred G. (Harrington) B.; D.V.M., Mich. State U., 1944, M.S. in Pathogenic Parasitology and Bacteriology, 1948; m. Phyllis J. Elworthy, Sept. 6, 1944; children—Donald Lee, Deborah Leah, Johanna Karen, Jane Frederica. U.S. Govt. veterinarian, 1944-45; pvt. practice, 1945-46; research parasitologist Park, Davis & Co., 1946-48; civilian veterinary cons. for U.S. Army in Japan, 1948-51, I.I.A.A. in Uruguay, 1952; joined U.S. fgn. service as vet. parasitologist, 1952; dep. chief agrl. and natural resources mission, dir. Haitian-Am. Agrl. Coop. Program, Haiti, 1952-57; chief agr. and natural resources, food and agr. officer, also vet. adviser ICA, Havana, Cuba, 1957-59; U.S. Operation Mission veterinary adviser, co-dir. Imperial Vet. Services, Ethiopia, 1959-61; coordinator labs., dept. vet. medicine Chas. Pfizer & Co., Inc., 1962-63, head clin. research and drug devel., 1963-65; mgr. animal health research Olin Mathieson Internat., N.Y.C., 1965-66; dir. research E.R. Squibb & Sons, Inc., Squibb Internat. subsidiary Olin Mathieson Chem. Co., 1966-67, vet. med. dir., 1967-68; mgr. fgn. operations animal health Rohm and Hass Co., 1969—. Consultant S. Am. govts., 1951-61. Served as maj. Vet. Corps, U.S. Army Res. to 1962. Recipient letters of commendation from Japanese Govt., SCAP, 8th Army, Cuban Nat. Agronomists Assn. and Coll.; Letter of Appreciation, Japan; Govt. Certificate of Meritorious Service. Mem. Am., Mich., Me. vet. med. assns., Indsl. Veterinarians Assn., Am. Assn. Avian Pathologists, Mich. State U. Alumni Assn., Alpha Psi. Office: Inddependence Mall W Philadelphia PA 19105

BUSH, DOROTHY VREDENBURGH, sec. Dem. Nat. Com.; b. Baldwyn, Miss., Dec. 8, 1916; d. Will Lee and Lany (Holland) McElroy; student George Washington U., summer 1935; B.S., Miss. State Coll. for Women, 1937; m. Peter Vredenburgh, 3d, Dec. 27, 1940 (dec.); stepson, Peter (dec.); m. 2d, John W. Bush, Jan. 13, 1962. Sec. to dir. ins. bus., Tenn. Coal, Iron & R.R. Co., subsidiary U.S. Steel, Birmingham, Ala., 1937-40. Nat. committeewoman Ala. Young Democrats, 1941-50; asst. sec. conv. Young Dems. Am., 1941, v.p., 1943-48; co- chmn. Jackson Day dinners of Ala., 1944; sec. Dem. Nat. Com., 1944— (1st woman to hold this position), acting pres. Young Dems. Am., 1944; sec. Dem. Nat. Convs., 1944—. Life mem. Ark. Traveler, Beta Sigma Phi. Baptist. Clubs: Maskers (Miss. State Coll. for Women), Jane Jefferson (life), National Fedn. Business and Profl. Women's. Home: 4201 Cathedral Av NW Washington DC 20016 Office: Democratic Nat Com Washington DC 20037

BUSH, GEORGE HERBERT WALKER, diplomat; b. Milton, Mass., June 12, 1924; s. Prescott Sheldon and Dorothy (Walker) B.; grad. Phillips Acad., Andover, Mass., 1942; B.A. in Econs., Yale, 1948; m. Barbara Pierce, Jan. 6, 1945; children—George W., John E., Neil M., Marvin P., Dorothy W. Co- founder, dir. Zapata Petroleum Corp., 1953-59; pres. Zapata Off Shore Co., Houston, 1956-64, chmn. bd., 1964-66; mem. 90th- 91st congresses, 7th Dist. Tex., mem. Ways and Means com.; U.S. ambassador to UN, 1970—. Tex. chmn. Heart Fund. Chmn. Republican Party Harris County, Tex., 1963-64; del. Rep. Nat. Conv., 1964, 68; Rep. candidate U.S. senator from Tex., 1964, 70; Served to lt. (j.g.), pilot, USNR, World War II. Decorated D.F.C., Air medals (3). Home: Waldorf Towers 50th St and Park Av New York City NY 10022 Office: 799 UN Plaza New York City NY 10017

BUSH, GEORGE MONROE, army officer; b. Ft. Sheridan, Ill., July 9, 1923; s. James Emerson and Nellie (Chappelle) B.; B.S., U.S. Mil. Acad., 1945; M.S., Harvard, 1953; student Command and Gen. Staff Coll., 1957, Nat. War Coll., 1963; m. Theo Dell Gerstenberger, Oct. 19, 1947; children—James Emerson, Carol Ann. Commd. 2d lt., U.S. Army, 1945, advanced through grades to maj. gen., 1971—, engr. group comdr., Vietnam, 1966-67; mil asst. to undersec. army, 1967-69; dep. comdr. Tank Automotive Command, comdg. gen., U.S. Army Mobility Equipment Command, 1969-71, asst. dep. chief of staff for logistics, programs and budget, Dept. of Army, Washington, 1971—; mem. bd. policy council Fed. Exec. Bd., 1970—. Decorated Silver Star, Bronze Star, Legion of Merit, Air medal. Mem. St. Louis Soc. West Point (pres. 1970-71), Assn. U.S. Army, Soc. Am. Mil. Engrs., Am. Ordnance Assn., Mecom Mgmt. Assn. Home: 3656 Military Rd Arlington VA 22207 Office: Dept Army Pentagon Washington DC 20310

BUSH, GERALD WILLIAM, mgmt. cons.; b. San Francisco, Mar. 20, 1937; s. Bernard Joseph and Anne Josephine (Kelly) B.; B.S., U. Santa Clara, 1958; M.A., Claremont Grad. Sch., 1959; postgrad. U. Cal. at Berkeley, 1959-61; Ph.D., No. Ill. U., 1969; m. Jean Pond Wentworth, June 15, 1960; children—Michael Joseph, Patrick Kevin, Mark William, Robert Timothy. Adminstrv. asst. Cal. C. of C., 1958-59; instr., then research asso. U. Cal., Berkeley, 1959-61; staff mem. Com. Fgn. Affairs Personnel, Washington, 1961-62; asst. dir. tng. in Far East, Peace Corps, 1962-64, spl. asst. to dir., exec. sec., 1964-65; mem. dept. polit. sci., dir. Peace Corps programs No. Ill. U., DeKalb, 1965-67; spl. asst. to sec. U.S. Dept. Labor, 1967-68, asst. v.p., 1968; sr. staff Arthur D. Little, Inc. Mem. Am. Polit. Sci. Assn., Am. Soc. Pub. Adminstrn., Comparative Adminstrn. Group, Alpha Phi Omega, Phi Sigma Alpha. Author: Recent Trends in Government Finances, 1961; Inter- university Case Study: A Business Office for the West, 1965; The Peace Corps a study in Open Organization, 1965. Home: 333 Main Concord MA 01742

BUSH, HENRY TATNALL, Jr., mfg. co. exec.; b. Wilmington, Del., Feb. 9, 1911; s. Henry Tatnall and Lydia (Moore) B.; B.A., Williams Coll., 1932; postgrad. Yale, 1932- 33; m. Anne Douglas McCoy, Feb. 7, 1941; children—Anne Douglas (Mrs. J. Glenn Little 2d), Henry Tatnall 3d. With E.I. duPont De Nemours & Co., Inc., 1933—, sec. company, dir. sec.'s dept., 1966—; v.p., dir. Union Library Catalog Pa., 1961—. Trustee Wilmington Med. Center. Served to lt. comdr. USNR, 1942-45. Mem. Soc. Colonial Wars, Williams Alumni Assn. (exec. com. 1968—), Am. Soc. Corporate Secs. (dir. 1968-71). Clubs: Wilmington, Wilmington Country. Home: 913 Blackshire Rd Wilmington DE 19805 Office: Du Pont Bldg Wilmington DE 19898

BUSH, IAN ELCOCK, research exec.; b. Bristol, Eng., May 25, 1928; s. Gilbert B. and Jean (Elcock) B.; B.A., U. Cambridge (Eng.), 1949, Ph.D., 1952, M.B., B.Chir., 1957; m. Alison Pickard, Aug. 26, 1951 (div. 1966); children—Charles Fabian, Philippa, Caroline; m. 2d, Joan Morthland, Sept. 16, 1967; children—Andrew, Georgia. Came to U.S., 1964. Med. Research Council scholar Cambridge Nat. Inst. Med. Research, London, 1949-52; Commonwealth fellow U. Utah at Mass. Gen. Hosp., Boston, 1952-53; research asso. St. Mary's Hosp., Boston, 1952-53; research asso. St. Mary's Hosp. Med. Sch., London, 1953-56; grad. asst. U. Oxford (Eng.), 1956-60; prof., chmn. dept. physiology U. Birmingham (Eng.), 1960-64; sr. scientist Worcester Found. Exptl. Biology, 1964-67; prof., chmn. dept. physiology Med. Coll. Va., 1967-70; v.p. research and devel. Cybertek Inc., 1970—; prof. physiology N.Y. U. Med. Sch., part-time ,1970—; cons. in field, 1949—. Past mem. panels NSF, Am. Cancer Soc., Med. Research Council Eng. Fellow Am. Acad. Arts and Scis.; mem. Physiol. socs. Am., Eng., endocrine socs. Am., Eng., A.A.A.S., N.Y. Acad. Scis., The Players. Author: Chromatography of Steroids, 1961; also papers. Home: 8 Seawanhaka Pl Oyster Bay NY 11771

BUSH, IRVING M., urol. surgeon; b. N.Y.C., Jan. 19, 1934; s. Arthur M. and Mirra (Guttman) B.; B.A., N.Y. U., 1954; M.D., Chgo. Med. Sch., 1958; m. Ronnie Beth Schwartz, June 23, 1958; children—Alan Michael, Steven Douglas. Rotating intern, asst. resident surgery, resident urology Beth Israel Hosp., N.Y.C., 1959-63, asst. adj. urology, 1963-66; fellow Sican Kettering Inst., 1963-65, asst. clinician, 1965-66; clin. research trainee Meml. Hosp., N.Y.C., 1963-65, clin. asst. surgeon, 1965-66; clin. asst. surgeon James Ewing Hosp., N.Y.C., 1965-66; attending urologist, chmn. dept. Cook County Hosp., Chgo., 1966—; prof., chmn. dept., urology Cook County Grad. Sch. Medicine, 1966—; prin. investigator urology, med. sci. group Hektoen Inst. Med. Research, 1966—; asst. prof. urology Northwestern U. Med. Sch., 1966-68; clin. prof., chief div. urology Chgo. Med. Sch., 1968—; attending urologist, chmn. div. Mt. Sinai Hosp., Chgo., 1968—; cons. Oak Forest Hosp., 1968. Valentine fellow N.Y. Acad. Medicine, 1964; Mosley scholar, 1958. Recipient Valuable Service citation Chgo. Med. Sch., 1958. Mem. Am. Urol. Assn. (1st prize 1964, grand prize 1965, 1st prize lab. research 1968, Wirt R. Dankin hist. award 1968, 69, 1st prize lab. research 1970), A.M.A. (John B. Morrisey award 1965, Hektoen medal for research 1970), Ill. Med. Soc., Chgo., N. Central urol. socs., James Ewing Soc., A.C.S., Am. Med. Writers Assn., Am. Soc. Nephrology, Soc. U. Urologists, Assn. Acad. Surgery, Am. Assn. History Medicine. Editor-in-chief Chgo. Med. Sch. Quar., 1958; cons. editor urology Jour. Student A.M.A., 1966; urology editor Geriatrics Digest, 1968. Home: 908 Euclid St Oak Park IL 60302 Office: 1825 Harrison St Chicago IL 60612

BUSH, JIM, business exec. Comptroller, Gem Internat. Inc., Kansas City, Mo. Office: 6000 Manchester Trafficway Terrace Kansas City MO 64141*

BUSH, JOHN NASH DOUGLAS, educator; b. Morrisburg, Ont., Mar. 21, 1896; s. Dexter C. and Mary E. (Nash) B.; B.A., U. Toronto, 1920, M.A., 1921; Ph.D., Harvard, 1923; Sheldon traveling fellow, Harvard, in Eng. 1923-24; Guggenheim Meml. fellow, Eng., 1934-35; Litt.D., Tufts U., 1952; Princeton, 1958, U. Toronto, 1958, Oberlin Coll., 1959, Harvard, 1959, Swarthmore, 1960; Boston Coll., 1965, State U. Mich., 1968, Merrimack Coll. 1969; L.H.D., So. Ill. U., 1962, Marlboro Coll, 1966; m. Hazel Cleaver, Sept. 3, 1927; 1 son, Geoffrey Douglas. Instr. and tutor in English, Harvard, 1924-27; asst. prof. U. Minn., 1927-28, asso. prof., 1928-31, prof., 1931-36; asso. prof. English, Harvard U. 1936-37, prof. 1937-66, Gurney prof. 1957-66. Recipient award Am. Council Learned Soc. 1957. Corr. fellow Brit. Acad.; mem. Modern Humanities Research Assn. (pres. 1955), Am. Philos. Soc. Phi Beta Kappa. Author: Mythology and the Renaissance Tradition in English Poetry, 1932, rev. 1963; Mythology and the Romantic Tradition in English Poetry, 1937; The Renaissance and English Humanism, 1939; Paradise Lost in Our Time, 1945; English Literature in the Earlier Seventeenth Century (Oxford History Eng. Lit.), 1945, rev. edit., 1962; Science and English Poetry, 1950; Classical Influences in Renaissance Literature, 1952; English Poetry, the Main currents from Chaucer to the Present, 1952; John Milton, 1964; Prefaces to Renaissance Literature, 1965; John Keats, 1966; Engaged and Disengaged, 1966; Pagan Myth and Christian Tradition, 1968; Mathew Arnold 1971. Editor: Portable Milton, 1949; Tennyson Selections, 1951; Keats Selections, 1959; (with A. Harbage) Shakespeare's Sonnets, 1961; Complete Poetical Works of John Milton, 1965; Variorum Commentary on Milton, Vol. 1, Latin and Greek Poems, 1970, Vol. 2, Minor English Poems (with A.S.P. Woodhouse and E. Weismiller), 1971. Home: 3 Clement Circle Cambridge MA 02138 (summer) Norwich VT 05055

BUSH, JOHN WILLIAM, govt. ofcl.; b. Columbus, O., Sept. 17, 1909; s. William Hayden and Esther (Brushart) B.; B.S. in Bus. Adminstrn., Va. Polytech. Inst., 1931; m. Mary Elizabeth Van Doren, June 4, 1932 (dec. 1958); children—Jan Hayden (Mrs. Richard L. Jennings), Emily Ann (Mrs. Thomas P. Bennett); m. 2d, Dorothy Vredenburgh, Jan. 13, 1962. With Standard Oil Co. La., 1932-37, T.K. Brushart Oil Co., Portsmouth, O., 1937-49; pres. Ohio System, Inc., 1946—; dir. purchasing Ohio, 1949-57, dir. commerce, 1959-61; commr. ICC, 1961—. Chmn. bd. Old Judge Foods Corp., St. Louis, 1957-59; dir. R.C. Williams & Co., Inc., N.Y.C. Mem. U.S. nat. comm. Pan Am. Ry. Congress Assn. Councilman, Portsmouth, 1941- 44; Democratic nominee for Congress, 1944. Pres. Nat. Assn. State Purchasing Ofcls., 1954. Home: 4201 Cathedral Av NW Washington DC 20016 Office: Interstate Commerce Bldg Washington DC 20423

BUSH, LAURENS EARLE, ret. educator; b. Martins, S.C., Mar. 24, 1900; s. Laurens Ashley and Mary Elizabeth (Oswald) B.; B.S., The Citadel, 1919; S.M., U. N.C., 1926; student U. Chgo., 1929; Ph.D., Ohio State U., 1931; m. Winnie Davis Kearse, June 23, 1920; children—Patricia Earle (Mrs. Jerome Long), Edward Ashley. Instr. U. N.C., 1926-30, Ohio State U., 1931-33; prof., chmn. dept. math. Coll. St. Thomas St. Paul, 1933-53; prof. math. Kent State U. 1953-70, prof. emeritus, 1970—, head dept. math 1953-64; vis. prof. North Tex. State Coll., Summers 1938- 41. Dir. William Lowell Putnam math. competition for Math. Assn. Am., 1948-65. Mem. Math. Assn. Am. (bd. govs. 1947-49, past chmn. Minn. sect., chmn. Ohio sect. 1958-59, Sigma Xi, Pi Mu Epsilon (mem. nat. council 1966—). Bd. editors Nat. Math. mag., 1935-45. Contbr. articles profl. jours. Home: 408 Burr Oak Dr Kent OH 44240

BUSH, MILLARD MUNDELL, lawyer; b. Jackson, Miss., Feb. 21, 1928; s. Millard Mundell and Clara Baur (Johnston) B.; B.A., U. Miss., 1950; LL.B., 1951; LL.M., George Washington U., 1957; m. Peggy Ann Bennett, Nov. 23, 1951; children—Pamela Gay, Millard Mundell III. Spl. agt. FBI, 1951-55; admitted to Miss. bar, 1951, U.S. Supreme Ct. bar, 1957; asst. U.S. atty. So. Dist. Miss., 1957-59; practice law, Jackson, 1959—, mem. firm Binder & Bush, 1959—. Vice chmn. exec. com. Miss. Agrl. and Indsl. Bd., 1964, now exec. dir.; mem. Miss. Marketing Council, 1964- -, Miss. Research and Devel. Council, 1964—. Served to 1st lt. USAF, 1955-57. Mem. Am., Hinds County bar assns., Miss. State Bar, Phi Delta Theta, Phi Delta Phi. Methodist. Mason, Kiwanian. Home: 2539 Eastover Jackson MS Office: 511 E Pearl St Jackson MS 29201

BUSH, OLIVER FRANKLIN, anesthesiologist; b. Birmingham, Ala., Jan. 5, 1919; s. Oliver Franklin and Mary Ethel (Martin) B.; M.D., Emory U., 1942; m. Madelaine Gerhart, Sept. 9, 1945; children—Michael G., Robert L., John C., Joseph O., James F., Mary Madelaine. Intern Met. Hosp., N.Y.C., 1942-43; gen. practice Medicine, Menard, Tex., 1946-49; resident anesthesiology Charity Hosp., New Orleans, 1949-51; pvt. practice anesthesiology, Dallas, 1951—; dir. dept. anesthesiology St. Paul Hosp., Dallas, 1951—. Served as flight surgeon USAAF, 1943-46; PTO. Mem. Am. Soc. Anesthesiologists (pres. 1963- 64), Am. Tex. med. assns., Kappa Alpha, Alpha Kappa Kappa. Home: Route 1 Lewisville TX 75067 Office: St Paul Hosp Dallas TX 75235

BUSH, PETER BIRDSALL, newspaper exec.; b. Milw., Oct. 1, 1924; s. Fred Randall and Marie (Donner) B.; grad. Advanced Mgmt. Program, Harvard, 1960; S.M., Syracuse U., 1958; m. Mary Ann Kumler, May 5, 1945; children—Carol Lynnlee, Marc Randall. Advt. dir. Norfolk (Va.)-Portsmouth Newspapers, Inc., 1960-64; v.p., gen. mgr. Greensboro (N.C.) Daily News and Rec., now pres.; dir. Landmark Communications, Inc. Served as aviator USNR, World War II. Mem. Newspaper Advt. Execs., Assn. (v.p. Va. 1964), Am. Newspaper Pubs. Assn., Greensboro C. of C., Greensboro Better Bus. Bur., So. Newspaper Pubs. Assn., Greensboro Mchts. Assn., Sales and Marketing Execs. Norfolk-Portsmouth (pres. 1964-65). Rotarian. Club: Starmount Forest County. Author: Newspaper Advertising Ethics, 1964; Newspaper Advertising Effectiveness Studies, 1963. Home: Office: 200 N Davie St Greensboro ND 27401

BUSH, ROBERT BENJAMIN, mfg. co. exec.; b. Attica, Ind., Jan. 15, 1928; s. Robert Lincoln and Virginia (Leath) B.; B.S. in Elec. Engring., Purdue U., 1949; J.D., Ind. U., 1956; m. Patricia Ann Gosnell, Jan. 6, 1951; children—Robert Benjamin II, Anne Elizabeth. Admitted to Ind. bar, 1956; engr. Naval Ordnance Plant, Indpls., 1950; with Bur. Naval Ordnance, 1951-53; gen. counsel Cummins Engine Co., Inc., 1956—; dir. Transinterbank, Geneva, Cummins Internat. Finance Corp. Pres. Columbus Redevel. Commn., 1965—. Commr. to 182d. Gen. Assembly U.P. Ch., 1970; elder 1st Presbyn. Ch., Columbus. Served to lt. (j.g.) USNR, 1951-53. Mem. Am., Ind. (bd. dirs., chmn. corp. law sect.) bar assns., Phi Delta Phi (pres. Foster Inn 1955). Author articles. Home: 210 Newsom Av Columbus IN 47201 Office: 432 Washington St Columbus IN 47201

BUSH, VANNEVAR, ret. adminstr., elec. engr.; b. Everett, Mass., Mar. 11, 1890; s. Richard Perry and Emma Linwood (Paine) B.; B.S., M.S., Tufts Coll., 1913, hon. Sc.D., 1932; Eng.D., Mass. Inst. Tech., Harvard, 1916; hon. degrees from twenty univs. and colls., 1939—; latest Sc.D., Boston U. 1959; m. Phoebe Davis, Sept. 5, 1916; children—Richard Davis, John Hathaway. With test dept. Gen. Electric Co., 1913; with inspection dept. U.S. Navy, 1914; instr. math. Tufts Coll., 1914-15, asst. prof. elec. engring., 1916-17; research on submarine detection, with spl. bd. on submarine devices, U.S. Navy, 1917-18; asso. prof. elec. power transmission Mass. Inst. Tech., 1919-23, prof., 1923-32; v.p. and dean engring., 1932-38; pres. Carnegie Instn. of Washington, 1939-55, trustee, 1958—. Trustee Carnegie Corp. of N.Y., 1939-55, now trustee emeritus. Mem. adv. com. Nat. Security Resources Bd. Trustee Tufts Coll., Johns Hopkins, 1943-55; life mem. Mass. Inst. Tech. Corp., hon. chmn. corp., 1959—; chmn. bd. Graphic Arts Research Found.; trustee Putnam Funds; regent Smithsonian Instn., 1943-55. Recipient some twenty prizes, awards and medals, 1928, including Founders' medal Nat. Acad. Engring., 1966, Atomic Pioneer award U.S. Govt., 1970; decorated knight comdr. Order Brit. Empire. Mem. numerous adv. coms. and bds., govtl. orgns., research projects including chmn. Nat. Def. Res. Commn., World War II. Fellow or mem., sometime honoree several scientific and profl. socs. Clubs: St. Botolph (Boston). Author: (with W.H. Timbie) Principles of Electrical Engineering, 1922; Operational Circuit Analysis, 1929, Endless Horizons, 1946; Modern Arms and Free Men (book), 1949; Science is Not Enough, 1967; Pieces of the Action, 1970. Was the builder of differential analyzer (machine for solving differential equations). Contributor numerous articles to American Institute Elec. Engring. and other scientific publs. Address: Mass Inst Technology Cambridge MA 02139 ☆

BUSH, WILBUR KIRKTON, railroad ofcl.; b. Chgo., May 30, 1911; s. Edward H. and Isabelle (Kirkton) B.; student U. Munich, Bonn U., 1932-33; B.S. (Austin scholar 1929-34), Northwestern U., 1934, M.B.A., 1937; grad. advanced mgmt. program Harvard Grad. Sch. Bus., 1966; m. Loretta Bell, Apr. 19, 1941; children—Thomas Hale, Meredith Nancy. Railroad assessor Ill., 1938-40; gen. tax agt. C.B. & Q. R.R., 1941, 45-58, dir. land and tax dept., 1958-61, treas., 1961-62, sec., treas., 1962-64, v.p., 1964-70; sec., treas. Ft. Worth & Denver R.R., 1961-64, v.p., 1964-70; v.p. Colo. & So. Ry., 1964-70; v.p. exec. dept. Burlington No., Inc., St. Paul, 1970—; chmn. board Burlington Truck Lines, 1964-66, now dir.; dir. Trailer Train Co. St. Paul Union Depot. Pres. Civic Fedn. Chgo., 1957-59; dir., 1957-70. Served to capt. Transp. Corps, AUS, 1942-45. Mem. Western Assn. Ry. Tax Commrs. (pres. 1951), Taxpayers Fedn. Ill. (exec. com. 1952). Club: Minnesota; University; White Bear Yacht. Home: 400 Summit St Paul MN 55102 Office: 176 E 5th St St Paul MN 55101

BUSH, WILLIAM GEORGE, mfg. co. exec.; b. Independence, Kan., Sept. 14, 1923; s. William Edward and Flava Inez (Griggs) B.; B.B.A., North Tex. State U., 1950; m. Miriam Hooks Ditto, Oct. 2, 1948; children—William Ward, Robert Earl, Benton Edward. With Mobil Oil Co., 1950-53; with Williamson-Dickie Mfg. Co., Ft. Worth, 1953—, sec., treas., dir., 1960—; sec., treas., dir. Work Clothes Rental Service Co. Served with AUS, 1942-46. Methodist. Club: Glen Garden Country (Ft. Worth). Home: 8109 Meadowbrook Dr Fort Worth TX 76112 Office: 509 W Vickery St Fort Worth TX 76101

BUSH, WILLIAM LAWRENCE, forest products corp. exec.; b. San Francisco, Nov. 9, 1914; s. William L. and Helen F. (Killian) B.; B.S., U. Cal. at Berkeley, 1934; postgrad. U. So. Cal., Stanford; m. Margaret Jane Pierson, Apr. 18, 1942; children—William Lawrence III, Barbara Jane. Chief clk. traffic dept. Port Stockton, Cal., 1934-36; exec. sec., research dir. Contra Costa (Cal.) County Devel. Assn., 1936-39; asst. to traffic mgr. Standard Oil Co. Cal., 1939-61; dir. transp. Weyerhaeuser Co., Tacoma, 1961—; pres. Columbia & Cowlitz Ry., Chehalis Western Ry. Mem. Comprehensive Planning Com. Tacoma; pres. Tacoma Art Mus. Served with Ordnance dept. AUS, 1943-45. Mem. Assn. ICC Practitioners (pres. 1964- 65), Nat. Indsl. Traffic League, Am. Soc. Traffic and Transp. (founder mem.), Delta Sigma Pi, Lambda Chi Alpha. Clubs: Tacoma, Tacoma Country and Golf Contbr. articles to profl. jours. Home: 110 Country Club Dr Tacoma WA 98498 Office: Tacoma Bldg Tacoma WA 98401

BUSH, WILLIAM McDONALD, ret. bus. exec.; b. Kirriemuir, Scotland, Oct. 10, 1903; s. Allan B. and Elizabeth (McDonald) B.; student U. Hawaii; grad. Advanced Mgmt. Program, Harvard, 1944; m. Mary E. Lindsay, June 7, 1933; children—Sheila L. (Mrs. Rober Myhre), Kathleen M. (Mrs. Robert A. Jones), Alan M. With Castle & Cooke, Inc., Honolulu, 1926-68, asst. treas., 1935-44, treas., 1944-58, v.p., 1955-61 exec. v.p., 1961-68, dir. Ewa Sugar Co., Inc., Kohala Sugar Co., Waialua Sugar Co., Inc., First Ins. Co. Hawaii, Ltd., Castle & Cooke, Inc. Mem. Hawaiian Bot. Soc. Hawaiian Acad. Sci. Club: Pacific. Home: 999 Wilder Av Honolulu HI 96822 Office: Castle & Cooke Inc PO Box 2990 Honolulu HI 96802

BUSHACHER, H.W., railroad exec.; b. Topeka, Sept. 16, 1917; s. Oscar Louis and Mary (Ward) B.; student Washburn U., 1935-39, Am. U., 1947, Northwestern U., 1966-67; m. Barbara Jean Miller, Dec. 25, 1940; children—Marcia L., Robert Ward. With Bank of Am., San Diego, 1940-41; with Rio Grande R.R., Denver, 1941—, asst. comptroller, 1954-59, mgr. revenue for Denver, 1959-60, dir. data processing, 1960-62, comptroller, 1965—, v.p. finance, 1969—; dir. Tensleep Petroleum Corp., Rio Grande Land Co., Leavell Devel. Co. Bd. dirs. Denver City Employees Pension Fund, Denver Met. YMCA. Served to capt., inf. AUS, 1942-46. Decorated Silver Star, Purple Heart with oak leaf cluster. Mem. Financial Execs. Inst., Accounting div. Assn. Am. Railroads, Denver Presidents' Round Table. Republican. Mem. Christian Ch. (elder, trustee). Clubs: Denver, Kiwanis (pres.). Home: 2905 S Clayton St Denver CO 80210 Office: Rio Grande Railroad 1531 Stout St Denver CO 80202

BUSH-BROWN, ALBERT, univ. adminstr.; b. West Hartford, Conn., Jan. 2, 1926; s. James and Louise (Carter) Bush-B.; A.B., Princeton, 1947, M.F.A., 1949, Ph.D., 1958; LL.D., Emerson Coll., 1965; H.H.D., Providence Coll., 1966; m. Frances Wesselhoeft, Aug. 28, 1948; children—David, Frances, Lesley, Martha. Instr. art, archaeology Princeton, 1949-50; jr. fellow Soc. Fellows, Harvard, 1950-53; Lowell lectr. Boston, 1952; asst. prof. art and architecture Western Res. U., Cleve., 1953-54; asst. prof. architecture Mass. Inst. Tech., 1954-58, asso. prof., 1958-62, exec. officer dept., 1958-61; prof. extension courses Harvard, 1956-61; pres. R.I. Sch. Design, Providence, 1962-68, chmn. Research and Design Center, Inc.,

1964-67; dir. council urban and regional studies State U. N.Y., Buffalo, 1968-71, vis. prof., 1968-69, v.p., 1969-71; chancellor L.I. U., 1971—; faculty asso. Joint Center Urban Studies, Mass. Inst. Tech.-Harvard, 1968-69. Mem. Providence City Plan Commn., 1962-67, Robie House Com., Chgo., 1962—; nat. adv. com. Archives Am. Art, 1962—; spl. adviser to sec. Dept. Housing and Urban Devel. 1968-69; nat. adv. council Urban Am., Inc. adviser U.S. Dept. State 1960, OES, 1969, U. Ill., Chgo., 1968-69, U. Mass., 1970—; mem. White House Nat. Council on Arts. 1965-70. Woodrow Wilson fellow Princeton, 1947-48; Howard Found. fellow Brown U., 1959-60; fellow Inst. Politics, J.F. Kennedy Sch. Govt., Harvard, 1968-69. Mem. Coll. Art Assn. (dir.), A.I.A. (hon.). Club: Century Assn. Author: Louis Sullivan, 1960; (with J.E. Burchard) The Architecture of America: A Social Interpretation, 1961; Books, Bass, Barnstable, 1967; also numerous articles. Contbr. Encys., Jours. Home: Piping Rock Rd Locust Valley NY 11560

BUSHBY, WILKIE, former lawyer; b. Shoreham, Vt., Sept. 11, 1897; s. James Cloud and Jessie M. (Wilkie) B.; A.B., Yale, 1918; LL.B., Harvard, 1921; m. Laura Cheney, July 5, 1924; children—James Cheney, Anne Kimberly (Mrs. Wm. J. Roome, 2d). Admitted to N.Y. bar, 1921, D.C. bar, 1947; mem. Dewey, Ballantine, Bushby, Palmer & Wood, and predecessor firms, N.Y.C., 1921-70, mem. firm, 1928-70. Nat. chmn. Harward Law Sch. Fund, 1950- 52, nat. pres. Law Sch. Assn., 1957-59, vis. com. Law Sch., 1949-56; mem. Yale Alumni Bd. Mem. Conn. finance com. Republican party; chmn. Greenwich finance com., 1947-52; presdl. elector from Conn., 1948. Served to capt. F.A., U.S. Army, 1918. Mem. Am., N.Y. State, N.Y.C., N.Y. County bar assns., Am. Law Inst., Am. Judicature Soc., Harvard Law Sch. Assn. N.Y.C. (past pres.), Phi Beta Kappa, Delta Kappa Epsilon, Elihu. Clubs: Round Hill (Greenwich, Conn.); Racquet and Tennis, Anglers, Down Town, Yale, Wall (N.Y.C.); Amabelish Fish and Game (P.Q.); Ekwanok Country (Manchester, Vt.); Stratton Mountain Country (Vt.). Home: Deer Park Greenwich CT 06830 Office: 140 Broadway New York City NY 10005 Died Apr. 4, 1970

BUSHEL, ARTHUR, educator; b. Bklyn., Mar. 18, 1921; s. Harry and Bertha (Levine) B.; A.B., Bklyn. Coll., 1940; D.D.S., Columbia U., 1943, M.P.H., 1947; m. Marian Rubin, Apr. 11, 1948; children—Glenn E., Faith E., Betsy L. Asst. dir. dentistry N.Y. State Dept. Health, 1947-55; dir. dentistry N.Y.C. Dept. Health, 1955-62, asst. commnr., 1962-66, 1st dep. commnr., 1966-69, acting commnr., 1966; prof., chmn. pub. health adminstrn. Johns Hopkins, 1969—; cons. USPHS; lectr. U. Md. Coll. Dentistry. Served with AUS, 1944-46. Diplomate Am. Bd. Dental Pub. Health (pres. 1963-64); mem. Am. Pub. Health Assn., Am. Coll. Dentists, Pub. Health Assn. N.Y.C. (pres. 1966-67), Sigma Xi. Home: 1 Velvet Ridge Dr Owings Mills MD 21117 Office: 615 N Wolfe St Baltimore MD 21205

BUSHELL, W.J., business exec.; b. Eng., 1913. Chmn., Courtaulds N.Am., Inc., Mobile, Ala.; dir. Courtaulds, Ltd. Office: PO Box 2648 Mobile AL 36601*

BUSHER, GEORGE DEWEY, real estate exec.; b. Bronx, N.Y., Oct. 10, 1898; s. Eugene J. and Anna (Crantz) B.; B.S., Dartmouth, 1922; LL.B., Fordham U., 1926; m. Josephine Lane, Jan. 18, 1929; children—Joan E. (Mrs. Wallace M. Kain), Eugene L. Admitted to N.Y. bar, 1927; v.p., dir. Eugene J. Busher Co., Inc., N.Y.C., 1922—; dir., mem. adv. bd. Mfrs. Hanover Trust Co.; trustee Bronx Savs. Bank. Mem. adv. bd. Bronx Community Coll. Hon. trustee Fordham U. Mem. Am. Bar Assn., Bronx Real Estate Bd. (dir., past pres.), Bronx Bd. Trade (dir., past pres.). Clubs: Winged Foot Golf (Mamaroneck, N.Y.); Union League, Dartmouth (N.Y.C.); Rhode Island Country. Home: 22 Cassilis Av Bronxville NY 10708 Office: 141 Parkway Rd Bronxville NY 10708

BUSHEY, JOSEPH HOBART, educator; b. Balt., Dec. 19, 1903; s. Arthur Clifton and Alberta (King) B.; B.S., Johns Hopkins, 1924; Ph.D., U. Mich., 1930; m. Jewell Constance Hughes, June 25, 1935. Instr. mathematics Hollins Coll., 1924-26, U. Mich., 1926-30; prof. mathematics Hunter Coll. of City U. N.Y., 1930—. Mem. N.Y.C. Tchrs. Retirement Bd., 1953—; pension cons. City U. N.Y. Mem. Am. Math. Soc., Inst. Math. Statistics. Contbr. articles profl. jours. Home: 200 E 66th St New York City NY 10021

BUSHKIN, JOSEPH, pianist; b. N.Y.C., Nov. 7, 1916. Played with Louis Prima, Bunny Berigan, Joe Marsala, Muggsy Spalner; recordings with Eddie Condon, Sharkey, Bonano, Lee Wiley; with Tommy Dorsey, 1940; trumpet player Army Band, 1942; asst. to David Rose, Winged Victory Air Force Show; with Benny Goodman, 1946; free-lance, TV shows, 1947; actor Broadway play Rat Race, 1949; own quartet, Embers, N.Y.C., 1951; with Louis Armstrong, 1953; singer radio, TV; songwriter Oh Look at Me Now and many more. Address: 435 E 52d St New York City NY 10022

BUSHMILLER, ERNIE, cartoonist; b. N.Y.C., Aug. 23, 1905; s. Ernest George and Elizabeth (Hall) B.; student N.A.D.; m. Abby Bohnet, July 9, 1930. Former comedy writer for Harold Lloyd, comedian, Hollywood, Cal.; former cartoonist N.Y. World, N.Y. Graphic; with United Features Syndicate, 1931—; creator cartoon Fritzi Ritz, also comedy strip Nancy (syndicated to Am. newspapers, trans. and pub. in fgn. newspapers); Fritzi Ritz and Nancy comic books pub. monthly. Mem. adv. bd. Salvation Army. Mem. Soc. Illustrators, Nat. Cartoonists Soc. Clubs: Dutch Treat, Artists and Writers; Banshees. Home: 552 Haviland Rd Stamford CT 06903 Office: United Features Syndicate 220 E 42d St New York City NY 10017

BUSHNELL, ASA SMITH, ret. athletic adminstr.; b. Springfield, O., Feb. 2, 1900; s. John Ludlow and Jessie Manton (Harwood) B.; grad. The Hill Sch., 1917; B.S., Princeton, 1921; student law sch., Columbia, 1922; LL.D., Syracuse U. 1955, Hobart and William Smith Colls., 1965; P.D., St. John's U., 1961; m. Thelma Lucille Clark, Feb 11, 1924; children—Asa S., Barbara C. (Mrs. John C. Leonard). Teller Morris Plan Bank, Springfield, 1922-23, dir., 1924-25; treas., office mgr. Direct Products Co., 1924- 25; editor Lagonda Pub. Co., 1924, Princeton (U.) Alumni Weekly, 1925- 30; founder Princeton Athletic News, 1932, editor, 1932-37; grad. mgr. athletics Princeton, 1927-37, acting dir. athletics, 1942-44; commr. Eastern Coll. Athletic Conf., 1938-70, cons. 1970-71. Apprentice seaman USNR, 1918. Dir. sports sect. Office Coordinator Inter-Am. Affairs, 1941-42; mem. Nat. Com. on Phys. Fitness, 1942-44; asst. to dir. schs. and tng. br. OSS, 1944; spl. cons. athletic br. Spl. Services Div., U.S. Army, 1944-45. Originator Princeton Invitiation Track Meet, 1934, dir., 1934-38. Sports adv. com. N.Y. World Fair, 1939. Sec. Nat. Football Found. and Hall Fame, Inc., 1948-51, 70—; dir., 1952—. Recipient Olympic Torch, U.S. Olympic Com., 1966; Austrian Olympic medal, Austria, 1966; Distinguished Service award from Princeton Class of 1921, 1955; Sportsmanship Brotherhood award, 1954; Touchdown Club award, 1957; meritorious service award N.Y. Track Writers Assn., 1958; named to Helms Athletic Found. Rowing Hall Fame, 1958; James Lynah Meml. award Eastern Collegiate Athletic Conf., 1959; distinguished service award Del. Chpt. Valley Football Found., 1967; Madison Square Garden Hall of Fame, 1967; James Corbett Meml. award Nat. Assn. Coll. Dirs, Athletics, 1969; Helms Athletic Found. Commrs. and Athletic Dirs. Hall Fame, 1970. Mem. Amateur Athletic Union of U.S. (gov.), Nat. Coll. Athletic Assn. (exec. com. 1943-44, 1947-51; dir. TV program 1952-70, cons. 1970—). Collegiate Commrs. Assn. (pres. 1947-52), S.R., U.S. Olympic Com. (asst. treas. 1936-37, mem. exec. com. 1937-45, sec. 1945-65, dir. 1965-70), Order Founders and Patriots Am. Episcopalian (vestryman). Club: University Cottage (gov.). Editor: 1948 and 1952 U.S. Olympic Book. Co-contbr. sects. on football in Ency. Brit. and Collier's Ency. Home: 71 Palmer Sq Princeton NJ 08540

BUSHNELL, CLARENCE W., hosp. adminstr. Adminstr., Bridgeport Hosp. Office: 267 Grant St Bridgeport CT 06602*

BUSHONG, JAMES WILLIAM, educator; b. Portland, Ore., Mar. 28, 1911; s. James Alvin and Nora (Barrett) B.; B.S., Pacific U., 1934; M.Ed., U. Ore., 1941, Ed.D., 1953; Edn. fellow Harvard, 1950-51; Ph.D. (hon.), Pacific U., 1970; m. Victoria Helen Seymour, July 29, 1934; children—Joyce (Mrs. James Ellis), Janice (Mrs. Richard Siemon), Helen Elizabeth, Linda (Mrs. W. James LeDuc). Tchr., coach Elgin (Ore.) High Sch., 1934- 36; supt. Imbler (Ore.) schs., 1936-39, Nyssa (Ore.) Union High Sch., 1939-40; prin. Bend (Ore.) Jr.-Sr. High Sch., 1940-42, supt. schs., 1946- 49; supt. Grosse Pointe (Mich.) schs., 1951-62; pres. Kamehameha Schs., Honolulu, 1962—; vis. prof. ednl. adminstrn. U. Wis., 1954, 58, Central Mich. U., 1955, Western Mich. U., 1960. Dir. First Ins. Co. Hawaii, Ltd. Pres. Ore. City Sch. Supts. Assn., 1949-50, Wayne County (Mich.) Supts. Assn., 1957-58; trustee Ore. Edn. Assn., 1948-50; mem. Legislative Interim Com. Study Post High Sch. Edn. Ore., 1949-50, Survey Team Studying Adminstrv. Orgn., Buffalo schs., 1950; mem. dean adv. com. Sch. Edn., Mich. State U., 1960-61; mem. pres.'s adv. com. Eastern Mich. U., 1956; adv. com. Mid-West Airborne Ednl. TV Project, 1959; bd. dirs. Met. Detroit Bur. Coop. Sch. Studies, 1957-60, chmn. exec. bd., 1961; v.p. Mich. Assn. Sch. Adminstrs., 1961-62, chmn. com. preparation sch. adminstrs., 1959-60, com. coll. relations, 1960-61; del. Am. Assn. Sch. Adminstrs. to Am. Council Edn., 1956, 60, to nat. meeting profs. ednl. adminstrs., 1953. Mem. army adv. com. U.S. Army Hawaii. Bd. dirs. Wayne County Tb and Health Soc., 1960-61, v.p., 1961; bd. dirs. Hawaii div. Am. Cancer Soc., state crusade chmn., 1969-71. Served to lt. comdr. USNR, World War II. Mem. Am. Assn. Sch. Adminstrs., Nat. (nat. adv. com. tech. devel. project 1960), Hawaii edn. assns., Nat. Assn. Ind. Schs., Navy League, Hawaii C. of C. (dir.). Conglist. Mason, Rotarian. Clubs: Oahu Country (dir.), Pacific. Contbr. profl. jours. Address: The Kamehameha Schs Honolulu HI 96817

BUSHOVEN, CORNELIUS JOHN, trust co. exec.; b. Propsect Park, N.J., July 4, 1932; s. Jacob and Jennie (Tanis) B.; B.B.A., Pace Coll., 1953; M.B.A., Rutgers U., 1960; m. Ann M. Sybesma, June 4, 1952; children—Cynthia, A., Roy D., Glenn E., Douglas J., Kenneth J. Tax accountant Star Expansion Indsl. Corp., Mountainville, N.Y., 1958-60; dir. adminstrn. Curtiss Wright Corp., Wood Ridge, N.J., 1960- 70; comptroller L.I. Trust Co., Garden City, N.Y., 1970—; instr. Sch. Bus., Fairleigh Dickinson U., Rutherford, N.J., 1965—. Served with AUS, 1953-55. C.P.A., N.J. Mem. Nat. Assn. Accountants (pres. West Bergen chpt. 1969-70), Am. Inst. C.P.A.'s, N.J. Soc. C.P.A.'s, Eastern Christian Sch. Assn. (chmn. finance com. 1969—, bd. dirs. 1969—), Pace Coll. Alumni Assn. (bd. dirs.). Home: 450 Glendale Rd Wyckoff NJ 07481 Office: 1401 Franklin Av Garden City NY 11530

BUSIA, KOFI ABREFA, prime minister of Ghana, sociologist; b. Wenchi, Ghana, July 11, 1913; student Wesley Coll., Kumasi, Ghana, 1931-32, Achimota Coll., 1935-36; B.A. with honors in history, London (Eng.) U., 1941; B.A. with honors in politics, philosophy, econs., Oxford U., 1943, M.A., 1946, D.Phil. in Social Anthropology, 1947; m. Naa Morkor, Aug. 14, 1950; children—Kofi, Abena, Yaw, Akosua. Mem. faculty Wesley Coll., Kumasi, Ghana, 1933-34, Achimota Coll., Accra, Ghana, 1936-39; adminstrv. officer Gold Coast Govt., 1942-49; research lectr. Univ. Coll., Accra, 1949-51, sr. researcher, 1954-55, prof. sociology, 1954-59; prof. sociology Inst. Social Studies, The Hague, Netherlands, 1959-62; prof. sociology and culture of Africa, U. Leiden (Netherlands), 1960-62; dir. studies World Council Chs., Birmingham, Eng., 1962-64; prof. sociology, sr. asso. mem. St. Antony's Coll. U. Oxford, 1964—; mem. Parliament, prime minister Republic of Ghana, 1969—; vis. prof. Northwestern U., 1954, Nuffield Coll., Oxford U., 1955, Agrl. U. Wageningen (Netherlands), 1956, El Colegie de Mexico, 1962, others. Mem. Internat. Social Sci. Council UNESCO, Paris, 1955-64. Chmn. nat. adv. com. Nat. Liberation Council, 1967; chmn. Centre for Civic Edn., 1967. Mem. Ghana Parliament, 1951-59, leader parliamentary opposition, 1956-59. Mem. Internat. Sociol. Assn. (exec. com. 1953-59). Author: A Social Survey of Sekondi-Takoradi, 1950; The Position of the Chief in the Modern Political System of Ashanti, 1951; The Influence of Colonialism and Racial Conflicts in the Development and Maintenance of Free Societies, 1955; The Challenge of Africa, 1962; Purposeful Education for Africa, 1964; Urban Churches in Britain, 1966; Africa in Search of Democracy, 1967. Home: Wenchi BA Region Ghana Office: The Castle Accra Ghana

BUSICK, CHARLES J., copper co. exec.; b. Bklyn., Feb. 16, 1912; s. Charles J. and Edna (Frisbie) B.; B.S., N.Y. U., 1937; m. Olga E. Smith, Oct. 20, 1934. Vice pres. Anaconda Co., N.Y.C.; v.p. dir. Jamaica Alumina Security Co., Chile Copper Co.; controller Golden Reward Mining Co., dir. Andes Copper Mining Co., Chile Exploration Co., Gen. Astrometals. Corp., Mines Investment Co., Farms Jamaica Ltd. Served to lt. USNR, 1944-46. Mem. Am. Inst. C.P.A.'s, Tax Execs. Inst., Am. Inst. Mining Engrs. Home: 82 Tahlulah Lane West Islip NY 11795 Office: 25 Broadway New York City NY 10004

BUSIGNIES, HENRI GASTON, electronic-communications engr.; b. Sceaux, France, Dec. 29, 1905; s. Henri and Juliette (Benoit) B.; degree in elec. engring., Paris, 1926; D.Sc. Newark Coll. Engring., 1958; D.Engring., Poly. Inst. Bklyn., 1970; m. Cecile Phaeton, July 15, 1931; 1 dau., Monique (Mrs. Henri Charles Honeck). Came to U.S., 1940, naturalized, 1953. Research, devel. engr. Les Laboratoires, Le Materiel Telephonique, Paris labs. Internat. Tel.& Tel. Corp., 1928-35, dept. head, 1935-38, head project on direction finders, radar, instrument landing, receivers, antennas, 1938-41; lab. head Fed. Telecommunication Labs. Internat. Tel.&Tel. Corp., Nutley, N.J., 1941-46, dir., 1946-48, tech. dir., 1948-54, exec. v.p., 1954-56, pres. 1956—, pres. I.T.&T. labs. div., 1958—, v.p., 1960-65, gen. tech. dir. corp., 1960—, sr. v.p., chief scientist; dir. Internat. Standard Electric Corp.; Am. Optical Corp. Recipient Lakhovsky award Radio Club of France, 1926; certificate commendation for outstanding service USN, 1947; Presdl. certificate of Merit, 1948; Pioneer award air navigation I.R.E., 1959; Indsl. Research Inst. medal, 1971. Fellow I.E.E.E. (David Sarnoff award 1964, Internat. Communications award 1970); mem. French Engrs. in U.S., Soc. French Civil Engrs., French Soc. Advancement Scis. Nat. Acad. Engring. Roman Catholic. Club: Alliance Francaise. Contbr. articles to profl. publs. Patentee in field; inventor MTI Radar. Home: 71 Melrose Pl Montclair NJ 07042 Office: 320 Park Av New York City NY 10022

BUSKIN, MARTIN, journalist; b. Bklyn., July 9, 1930; s. Harry and Frances (Drimmer) B.; A.B., N.Y.U., 1951; m. Saundra Rosman, June 3, 1956; children—Linda, Randi. Reporter, Newsday, Garden City, N.Y., 1953-55, copy editor, 1955-59, feature editor, 1959-61, edn. editor, 1962—. Cons. U.S. Office Edn. Served with U.S. Army, 1951-53. Recipient 1st prize for outstanding coverage local edn. issues Edn. Writers Assn., 1964, 65, 1st prize for outstanding columns on brotherhood Nat. Conf. Christians and Jews, 1966. Mem. Edn. Writers Assn. (pres.), Nat. Council for Advancement Edn. Writing (vice chmn.). Author: (with Howard Hagler) Great Moments in Sports, 1968. Contbr. to Naked Came The Stranger, 1969. Contbr. articles profl. jours. Home: 40 Raybor Rd Commack NY 11725 Office: 550 Stewart Av Garden City NY 11530

BUSS, CLAUDE ALBERT, educator; b. Sunbury, Pa., Nov. 29, 1903; s. W. Claude and Clara (Fetter) B.; A.B., Washington Missionary Coll., Takoma Park, D.C., 1922; M.A., Susquehanna U., 1924; Ph.D., U. Pa.; LL.D., U. So. Cal., 1945; student Ecole Libre des Science Politiques, Paris, 1927-28; Fulbright scholar U. Philippines, 1957, 1959; m. Evelyn Lukens, Jan. 20, 1928; one dau. Lynne. Carnegie teaching fellow in internat. law, Europe, 1927-28; attaché for language study U.S. Legation in China, U.S. Dept. State, 1929-31; U.S. vice consul, Nanking, China, 1931-34; prof. internat. relations U. So. Cal. 1934-41; prof. history Stanford, 1946-69, prof. emeritus, 1969; prof. Inst. Fgn. Studies, Monterey Cal, 1968—; prof. San Jose State Coll. Exec. asst. U.S. High Commr. to Philippine Islands, 1941-44; chief San Francisco office, O.W.I., 1944-46; exec. cons. petroleum div. U.S. Strategic Bombing Survey, Japan, 1945-46; cons. Civil Information and Edn. Sect., Gen. Hdqrs., Tokyo, 1948. U.S. del. 10th Internat. Conf., Inst. Pacific Relations, 1947, also 12th Conf., 1954; mem. Seminar on U.S. Fgn. Policy, Brookings Instn., Lake Forest (Ill.) Coll., 1949; dir. studies Nat. War Coll., Washington, 1949, mem. civilian faculty, 1963-64; adviser Bur. E. Asia and Pacific Affairs U.S. Dept. State, 1967-68. Author: War and Diplomacy in Eastern Asia, 1941; The Far East, 1955; South-east Asia and World Today, 1958; Arc of Crisis, 1961; People's Republic of China, 1962; Asia in the Modern World, 1964; Contemporary Southeast Asia, 1970; also articles in various mags. Home: 1234 Pitman Av Palo Alto Ca 94301

BUSS, DWIGHT B., lawyer; b. Cleve., Apr. 3, 1908; A.B., Yale, 1929, LL.B., 1932. Admitted to Ohio bar, 1932, since practiced in Cleve.; now mem. firm Baker, Hostetler & Patterson. Fellow Am. Coll. Trial Lawyers; mem. Am., Ohio, Cleve. (pres. 1967) bar assns. Home: Cedar Rd Cleveland OH 44124 Office: Union Commerce Bldg Cleveland OH 44115*

BUSSARD, CLARENCE LEASE, farm supply co. exec.; b. Frederick, Md., Feb. 9, 1911; s. Clarence A. and Katharine Elizabeth (Lease) B.; B.S., U. Md., 1932; B.E., Western Md. Coll., 1934; m. Frances Lovina Thomas, June 22, 1935; 1 dau., Jeanne Frances (dec.). Coach, organizer comml. dept. Clearspring (Md.) High Sch., 1934-35; opened fertilizer dept. father's bus. Farmers Supply Co., 1935, added feeds, seeds and insecticides, 1940, built feed processing and plant as Farmers Feed & Supply Co., 1951- -, since owner; owner-mgr., operator dairy farm, Frederick County, 1935-51; pres., owner Three Springs Fisheries, Lilypons, Md. Pres., Frederick County Civil War Centennial, 1961-64; pres. Francis Scott Key Meml. Found.; exec. v.p. Antietam-South Mountain Civil War Centennial, 1962—; treas., charter pres. Central Md. council. Girl Scouts U.S.A. Bd. dirs. Frederick Optimist Boys Found., Big Bros. Balt., Md. Civil War Commn. Centennial, Frederick County Assn. for Retarded Children, Frederick County Hist. Soc.; active YMCA, Community Chest. Trustee Western Md. Coll. Mem. Mil. Manpower Commn., 2d Corps Area, World War II, 1st lt. Army Res. Mem. Western Md. Alumni Assn. (Alumni award 1957, pres.), S.A.R., Gamma Beta Chi. Lutheran. Elk. Clubs: Optimist of Honolulu; Los Angeles Breakfast. Home: Route 9 Box 109 Frederick MD 21701 Office: E All Saint St Box 310 Frederick MD 21701

BUSSARD, PAUL, clergyman, editor; b. Essex, Ia., Nov. 22, 1904; s. William and Catherine (Howard) R.; A.B., St. Thomas Coll., St. Paul, 1922; S.T.B., St. Paul Sem., 1928; Ph.D., Cath. U. Am., 1937; postgrad. German Univs., 1934; LL.D. (hon.), U. Notre Dame, 1949. Asso. editor Worship (formerly Orate Fratres), 1931—; pub. Cath. Digest, 1936—, editor fgn. edits., French, Dutch, Irish, 1945—, German, 1947. Dir. Mag. Pubs. Assn. Author: If I Be Lifted Up, 1936; The Living Source, 1936; Staircase to a Star, 1938; The Sacrifice, 1939; The Vernacular Missal in Religious Education, 1937; The Meaning of the Mass (with Dr. Kirsch), 1942. Mem. Cath. Press Assn. U.S. (sec. 1943-45, pres., 1948-50). Home: 911 24th NE Minneapolis MN

BUSSE, EWALD WILLIAM, psychiatrist; b. St. Louis, Aug. 18, 1917; s. Frederick Ewald and Emily Louise (Stroh) B.; A.B., Westminster Coll., 1938; M.D., Washington U., St. Louis, 1942; D.Sc., Westminster Coll., 1960; m. Ortrude Helen Schnaedelbach, July 18, 1941; children—Ortrude Susan, Barbara Ann, Ewald Richard, Deborah Emily. Intern, St. Louis City Hosp., 1942-43; resident in psychiatry Colo. Psychopathic Hosp., U. Colo. Med. Center, 1946-48; instr. U. Colo., 1946-47, asst. prof., 1947-49, asso. prof., 1949-50, prof., head psychosomatic medicine, 1949-53; prof. Duke U. Sch. Medicine, Durham, N.C., 1953-66, J.P. Gibbons prof. psychiatry, 1966—, chmn. dept. psychiatry, 1953—, dir. Center for Study of Aging and Human Devel., 1957-70. Cons. psychiatry VA, AUS, USAF, USPHS; mem. profl. adv. council Nat. Assn. Mental Health, 1967-71; mem. Nat. Adv. Child Health and Human Devel. Council, 1967-71. Served as maj. AUS, 1943-46, chief electroencephalography, asst. chief neuropsychiat. service. Diplomate Am. Bd. Psychiatry and Neurology (dir., sec.-treas. 1959-69). Fellow A.C.P., Am. Psychiat. Assn. (v.p. 1966-67, pres.-elect 1970-71). Gerontological Soc. (council pres. 1967-68); mem. So., World Psychiat. Assns., N.C. Neuropsychiat. Assn., Am. Geriatrics Soc., Am. Psychosomatic Soc., Am. Orthopsychiat. Assn., Eastern, Central electroencephalographic socs., A.M.A., So. Electroencephalographic Assn., Am. Psychopath. Assn., Sigma Xi, Phi Delta Theta, Phi Beta Pi, Omicron Delta Kappa. Mason, Rotarian. Contbr. sci. articles to profl. publs. Home: 1132 Woodburn Rd Durham NC 27706

BUSSE, FREDERICK EUGENE, lawyer; b. St. Louis, June 18, 1910; s. F. Ewald and Emily L. (Stroh) B.; student Westminster Coll., 1926-28; LL.B., St. Louis U., 1931; postgrad. Northwestern U. Law Sch., 1932; m. Muriel A. Reineke, June 15, 1935; 1 son, Frederick C. Admitted to Mo. bar, 1931, since practiced in St. Louis; asso. Abbott, Fautleroy, Cullen & Edwards, 1931-35; with Wesley Nail, 1936; with Thomas, Busse, Cullen, Clooney, Weil & King and predecessors, 1937—, mng. partner, 1952—; price atty. OPA, Dallas 1941- 44, chief price atty., Washington, 1943, territorial atty., Terr. of Hawaii, 1944-45. Chmn. St. Louis Bd. Childrens Services, 1950-56; chmn. Mo. Hills Correctional Instn. for Boys, 1953-54; mem. Charter Bd. Freeholders, St. Louis, 1955-56; mem. Bd. Edn., St. Louis, 1961—, v.p., 1965, pres., 1966-67. Gen. counsel bd. dirs. Gen. Protestant Childrens Home; bd. dirs. North Side br. YMCA, Good Samaritan Home for Aged; trustee Deaconess Hosp. Mem. Am., Mo., St. Louis bar assns., Delta Theta Pi, Kappa Alpha. Mem. Reformed Ch. (past pres. ch. council). Mason. Home: 1740 Grape Av St Louis MO 63147 Office: 418 Olive St St Louis MO 63147

BUSSEWITZ, DONALD B., financial exec.; b. Milton, Wis., July 22, 1920; s. Raymond H. and Lillian (Baker) B.; Ph. B., Milton (Wis.) Coll., 1942; m. Bette Kumlien, Dec. 9, 1943; children—Bruce D., Kay S. With Air Reduction Co., Inc., 1946—, controller, 1969—. Chmn. budget and admission com. United Givers, Madison, Wis., 1962. Served with AUS, 1943-46. Mem. Financial Execs. Inst. (pres. Madison, 1961). Nat. Assn. Accountants. Club: Whippoorwill (treas. 1969-70) (Armouk, N.Y.). Home: 56 Brandon Dr Mount Kisco NY 10549 Office: 150 E 42d St New York City NY 10017

BUSSEY, THOMAS PATRICK, state justice; b. Parksville, S.C., May 7, 1905; s. John Morgan and Lillie Mobley (Conner) B.; LL.B., U. S.C., 1927; m. Louise McKelvey Florence, Dec. 6, 1931; 1 dau., Patricia (Mrs. B. Wheeler); stepson, Quinton Florence Jr. Admitted to S.C. bar, 1926; practiced in Charleston until 1958; judge 9th Jud. Circuit S.C., 1958-61; asso. justice Supreme Ct. S.C., 1961—. Mem. Am. Bar Assn. Episcopalian. Mason. Home: 8 Broughton Rd The Crescent Charleston SC 29407 Office: Charleston County Ct House PO Box 326 Charleston SC 29401

BUSSING, WILFRID CHARLES, ret. pub. co. exec.; b. Evansville, Ind., Nov. 8, 1889; s. Bernard J. and Alice (Doyle) B.; grad. high sch., Evansville, Ind.; m. Katherine Kittinger, Jan. 25, 1915 (dec. 1927); children—Marilyn, Wilfrid, Charles; m. 2d, Lois MacCammon, Mar. 26, 1929. Advt. mgr. Terre Haute (Ind.) Post, 1909; pub. Evansville (Ind.) Rev. 1912; bus. mgr. Evansville Press Co., 1916-26, became pres., 1936; advt. dir. Rocky Mountain News, Denver, 1926-29; gen. mgr. Indpls. Radio Sta. WKBF, 1929-31; advt. dir. Balt. Post, 1931-34; bus. mgr. Evansville Press, 1934-39; pres. Evansville Printing Corp., 1939-65, pubs. Evansville Courier, Evansville Press, Sunday Courier and Press, Bussing Investment Corp., 6th and Lincoln Corp., Mich. and Main Corp.; v.p., sec. Lois Anne Investments Inc. Trustee, exec. com. U. Evansville; past pres. bd. overseers St. Meinrad Coll.; bd. dirs. Evansville Indsl. Found. Chmn. adv. bd. Little Sisters of the Poor. Mem. C. of C. Roman Catholic. Knight of Malta. Clubs: Evansville Country, Evansville Petroleum; University of Notre Dame. Home: 52 S Oriole Evansville IN 47715 Office: 3 Brentwood Evansville IN 47715

BUSSMANN, CHARLES HAINES, publisher; b. Pitts., Mar. 9, 1924; s. Amos George and Ann (Haines) B.; student Colgate U., 1946. With Pit & Quarry Publs., Inc., 1946-63, v.p., 1957-63, dir., 1960-63; pres., dir. Compass Publs., Inc., Arlington, Va., 1963-. Served with USAAF, 1942-43. Mem. Indsl. Marketers Cleve. (past bd. dirs.), Nat. Bus. Publs. Inc. (past chmn. sales com.), Marine Tech. Soc., Am. Oceanographic Orgn., Advt. Club Cleve., T.F. Club Cleve. (past pres.), Theta Chi. Office: 1111 N 19th St Arlington VA 22209

BUSSOTTI, SYLVANO, composer, painter; b. Florence, Italy, Oct. 1, 1931; s. Gino and Inez (Zancanaro) B.; ed. Conservatorio Musicale L. Cherubini, Florence, in Paris, 1956-58, Feriaukursen Für Neuen Musik, Darmstadt 1958-59. Asso. Teatro di Marionette, Florence, 1948-49, Recontres Internationales de Jennesse, Aix-en-Provence, 1955-56; concerts in cities including Darmstadt, Cologne, Vienna, N.Y.C., Los Angeles, Madrid, Paris, Rome, Venice, Stockholm, Brussels, Warsaw, Munich, Bremen, Duesseldorf, Florence, Berlin, Amsterdam. Tokyo, Milan, Copenhagen, Toronto, 1958-64; came to U.S. under auspices Rockefeller Found., Center Creative and Performing Arts, 1965, concert Carnegie Hall, 1965; wrote opera La Pasion Selon Sade, performed Palermo Festival, 1965, Theatre Odeon, Paris, 1966; wrote Solo, performed TV, Stockholm, 1967, Rara (chamber music), London, 1967; also actor in theater and exptl. films, painter, writer and critic. Works include: Five Piano Pieces for David Tudor; Torso; Pour Clavier; Memoria; Fragmentations; All'Italia. Contbr. articles to various publs. Home: 9 via Del Portico d'Ottavia Rome Italy

BUSTAMANTE, MIGUEL E., pub. health adminstr.; b. Oaxaca, Mexico, May 2, 1898; s. Manuel and Luz (Vasconcelos) B.; student Inst. Sci. and Art, Oaxaca, 1914-19; M.D., Nat. U. Mexico, 1925; D.P.H., Johns Hopkins, 1928; m. Alice Mary Connolly, Oct. 6, 1928; children—Nancy Jane, Mary Elizabeth, Charles Joseph. Intern, Gen. Hosp., Mexico City, 1924-25; fellow Rockefeller Found., 1926-28; chief health unit Veracruz, 1930; asst. chief Fed. Health Service Republic Mexico, 1931, chief, 1932-35; prof. Med. Sch. Nat. U. Mexico, 1931—, dir. dept. med. sociology and preventive medicine, 1956-58; chief Mexican States welfare services, 1938; sci. investigator Inst. de Salubridad Enfermedades Tropicales, 1939; dir. Inst. Pub. Health and Tropical Diseases, 1942-43, 46-47; sec.-gen. Pan-Am. San. Bur., Washington, 1947-56; gen. dir. health services secretaria de Salubridad y Asistencia, Mexico, 1958-59, undersec. health, 1959-64; sec. gen. Nat. Health Council, 1965—. Health del. in Ixtlahuaca, 1935; mem. Mexican Nat. Commns. drafting san code, 1934, 68—, pub. health laws for coordination fed., state, and municipal services; mem. study groups for nat. health program, 1934-35, 45-46; mem. spl. Yellow Fever Studies, 1942-43, Spotted Fever Commn. 1943-47, spl. lectr. tropical med., U.S. univs., 1942-43; hon. prof. faculty medicine, Halti, 1943; chmn. UNICEF exec. bd., 1962-69; mem. expert com. WHO, 1958—. Decorated: Dr. Eduardo Liceaga medal for spl. pub. health service, Mexico, 1946; Finlay Order, Cuba. Hon. mem. Soc. Parasitology and Tropical Medicine Caracas, Am. Acad. Tropical Medicine; mem. Am. Pub. Health Assn., Soc. Mexicana de Pediatria, Soc. Medica Veracruzana, Am. Soc. Tropical Medicine Soc. Mexicana de Hist. Natural, Acad. Nacional de Medicine de Mexico. Author med. reports. Contbr. articles to profl. jours. Home: Viena 22 Coyoacán Mexico City 21 Mexico Office: Consejo de Salubridad General Secratariade Salubridad y Asistencia Lieja y Paseo de la Reforma Mexico ☆

BUSTAMANTE Y RIVERO, JOSE LUIS, ret. judge Internat. Ct. Justice; b. Arequipa, Peru, Jan. 15, 1894; s. Manuel Bustamente y Barreda and Vitoria Rivero de Bustamante; D.Law, U. San Agustin, Arequipa, 1918, D.Polit.Scis., 1929; D.Philosophy and Letters, U. San Antonio Abad, Cuzco, 1918; m. Maria Jesús Rivera de Bustamante, Dec. 16, 1923; children—Beatriz (Mrs. St. Ricardo Bouroncle), Jose Luis. Practice of law in Arequipa, 1918-34; Lima, 1956-60; substitute judge, substitute atty. Ct. Arequipa, 1925-33; prof. Faculty Letters, U. Arequipa, 1921, prof. civil law, 1930-34; spl. envoy and M.P. to Bolivia, 1934-38, to Uruguay, 1939-42; spl. ambassador to Bolivia, 1942- 45, to Paraguay, 1939; minister justice and instrn., 1930-31; pres. Peruvian delegation to Congreso de Jurisconsultos, Montevideo, 1939-40; constl. pres. Peru, 1945-48; dean Coll. Lawyers of Lima, 1960; judge Internat. Court of Justice, The Hague, Netherlands, from 1960, pres., from 1967, now ret. Delegate, Colegio de Abogados de Lima to V and XI confs. Inter-americanas de Abogados, Rio de Janeiro and Miami, Fla., 1943, 59; mem. Peru, 1960. Hon. mem. Interam. Bar Assn.; mem. Sociedad Peruana de Derecho Internat., Instituto Hispano-Luso-Americano de Derecho Internat. (founder), Asociación Francisco de Vitoria de Derecho Internacional de Madrid; mem. Academia Nacional de Derecho y Ciencias Politicas (Peru), Academia Peruana de la Lengua. Author: La ONU en el Palacio de Chaillot, 1952; Panamericanismo e Ibero-americanismo, 1953; La subestimación del Derecho en el mundo moderno, 1954; Las clases sociales en el Peru, 1959. Home: PO Box 2161 Lima Peru Office: Avenida Miro Quesada 58 S Isidro Lima Peru

BUSTEED, ROBERT CHARLES, educator; b. Milan, Ind., Sept. 4, 1907; s. Robert and Emma (Elble) B.; student Hanover Coll., 1925-27; A.B., Ind. U. 1930, M.A., 1932, Ph.D., 1936; m. Ada Flora Kohlerman, June 6, 1931; children—Philip Gene, Robert Louis, Richard Charles, Wallace Bruce. Grad. asst. botany dept. and U., 1930-33, tutor, 1934-35, instr., 1935-36; prof., head dept. biology Appalachian State Tchrs. Coll., 1937-45; prof. botany, chmn. sci. div. U. Ga., Savannah div., 1946-48; prof., head dept. biology, chmn. sci. div., grad. council West Tex. State Coll., 1948-. Faculty sponsor West Tex. State chpt. Tex. Collegiate Acad. Sci. Mem. adminstrv. council Kilgore Research Center, 1967-, Dir. Am. Brittany Spaniel Club, 1946. Dist. commr. Boy Scouts Am., Boone, N.C., 1944-46. Mem. Texas Coll. Tchrs. Assn., Tex. Panhandle Sci. Council (dir. 1959, pres. 1967- 68), Ind. Acad. Sci., Sigma Xi, Theta Kappa Nu, Alpha Phi Omega (sponsor), Beta Beta Beta (sponsor). Lutheran. Mason, Lion (pres. Boone). Home: Box 195 Sta 1 Canyon TX 79015

BUSWELL, ARTHUR STEPHEN, univ. adminstr.; b. Pocantico Hills, N.Y., Apr. 11, 1922; s. Fred Lacy and Lena Mary (Webster) B.; B.S., U. Me., 1949, M.S., 1950; Ph.D., U. Wis., 1959; m. Frances Jean Allen, June 21, 1947; children—Marjorie Lena, Arthur Stephen III, Gregg Allen. Mem. faculty U. Alaska, 1951—, Asso dir. Coop. Extension Service, head dept. agr., 1954-61, dean div. statewide services, dir. Coop Extension Service, 1961-68, now v.p. pub. service, dir. coop. extension service. Vice chmn. Alaska Ednl. Broadcasting Commn.; chmn ESEA Title III State Adv. Council; mem. State Arts Council, Northwest Manpower Devel. Adv. Commn. Fellow A.A.A.S.; mem. Adult Edn. Assn. (mem. del. assembly), N.W. Adult Edn. Assn. (dir.), Am. Assn. U. profs. (past pres. U. Alaska), Western Interstate Commn. Higher Edn. (Alaska devel. program com.), Delta Tau Delta. Presbyn. (elder). Mason, Lion (pres. College club). Home: 1033 Pedro St Fairbanks AK 99701

BUSWELL, CHARLES ALBERT, bishop; b. Homestead, Okla., Oct. 15, 1913; s. Charles J.D. and Bridget M. (Doherty) B.; student St. Benedict's Coll., Atchison, Kan., 1931-33, St. Louis Prep. Sem., 1933-35, Kenrick Sem., St. Louis, 1935-36; Ph.B., Am. Coll. of Louvain U. (Belgium), 1939. Ordained priest Roman Catholic Ch., 1939; asst. pastor, Tonkawa, Okla., 1939-42; asst. pastor Our Lady of Perpetual Help Cathedral, Oklahoma City, 1942-47, vice chancellor, 1942- 45, diocesan master ceremonies, 1945-59; founding adminstr. Christ the King Parish, Oklahoma City, 1947-59; papal chamberlain, 1949, domestic prelate, 1955; bishop Diocese of Pueblo, 1959-. Bd. dirs. Nat. Liturgical Conf., 1960-68. Mem. Louvain U. Am. Alumni Assn. (pres. 1961- 62). Home: 325 W 15th St Pueblo CO 81003 Office: 1426 Grand Av Pueblo CO 81003

BUTCHER, DEVEREUX, assn. exec.; b. Radnor, Pa., Sept. 24, 1906; s. Henry Clay and Constance (Devereux) B.; grad. St. George's Sch.,; student Pa. Acad. Fine Arts, 1926-28; m. Mary Frances Taft, Dec. 13, 1935; 1 son, Russell Devereux. Free lance writer, photographer, 1936-39; editorial asst. Am. Forests mag. Am. Forestry Assn., 1940-41; exec. sec. Nat. Parks Assn. 1942-50, field rep., 1950-57, editor Nat. Parks Mag., 1942-57; editor, pub. Nat. Wildlands News, 1959-62; dir. Hawk Mountain Sanctuary Assn., 1963—, John Burroughs Meml. Assn., 1965—. Mem. adv. com. on conservation Sec. Interior, 1952-53. Mem. Wilderness Soc., Defenders Wildlife (sec. 1947-59), Nat. Parks Assn. Author: Exploring Our National Parks and Monuments, 1947; Exploring the National Parks of Canada, 1951; Seeing America's Wildlife in Our National Refuges, 1955; Exploring Our National Wildlife Refuges, 1963; Our National Parks in Color, 1964. Home: Wessex House 505 E Lancaster Av St Davids PA 19087

BUTCHER, ERNEST DELL, transp. co. exec.; b. Ernest Dell and Katherine (Brown) B.; B.S. in Chem. Engring., Rice U., 1934; m. Rosadel Block, Dec. 22, 1934; children—John Erwin, Allen Dell. Technologist, Shell Oil Co., 1934-41; with Tex. Gas Transmission Corp., and predecessors, 1941—, v.p., 1968- , also dir.; dir. Harrisburg Bank, Houston, Clear Lake Savs. & Loan Assn., Houston, First Participating Fund, Inc. Bd. govs. Rice U. Mem. Am. Bur. Shipping. Methodist. Clubs: Petroleum, Houston Country (Houston). Home: 5623 Shady River Houston TX 77027 Office: 2919 Allen Pky Houston TX 77019

BUTCHER, FANNY, (Mrs. Richard Drummond Bokum), lit. critic; b. Fredonia, Kan. Feb. 13, 1888; d. L. Oliver and Hattie May (Young) Butcher; prep. edn. Lewis Inst., Chgo., A.B., U. Chgo., 1910; m. Richard Drummond Bokum, Feb. 13, 1935. With Chgo. Tribune, 1912-63, as soc. editor, asst. woman's editor, spl. corr., lit. editor also writer Lit. Spotlight. Past sec. to first little theatre movement in Am. Former owner Fanny Butcher-Books (bookshop). Recipient Friends of Lit. award, 1952; Constance Lindsay Skinner award, 1955; Communicator of Yr. award U. Chgo., 1964; citation Alliance of Bus. and Profl. Women, 1964. Mem. Soc. Midland Authors, Adult Edn. Council (dir.), Modern Poetry Assn. (dir.), Internat. P.E.N. Club (past pres. Chgo. chpt.) Friends of Am. Writers (hon.), Officer d'Academie of France, Friends of Chgo. Pub. Library (chmn. bd.). Clubs: Friday, Fortnightly, Arts, Scribblers, Chicago Women's Press (hon.), Kappa Phi Delta. Chicago Press. Author: Many Lives-One Love (autobiography), 1972. Contbr. revs. to Chgo. Tribune, 1963—. Home: 1209 Astor St Chicago IL 60610

BUTCHER, HOWARD, III, investment broker; b. Ardmore, Pa., Jan. 28, 1902; s. Howard and Margaret (Keen) B.; A.B., U. Pa., 1923; m. Elizabeth Crosswell McBee, Jan. 8, 1936; children—Howard, McBee, Jonathan. Partner, Butcher & Sherrerd, Phila.; pres., dir. 1500 Walnut Corp., Internat. Light & Power Co., Ltd., Toronto; v.p., dir. Juniper Securities Corp.; dir. Bankers Securities Corp., Honokaa Sugar Co., Phila. Bourse; chmn., dir. Yellow Cab Co. Phila. Life trustee, mem. investment, exec. coms. J. Pa.; trustee Phila. Art Mus.; bd. dirs. Hillsboro Assos. Mem. Zeta Psi. Clubs: Merion Cricket, Racquet; Pacific (Honolulu). Home: Villanova PA 19085 Office: 1500 Walnut St Philadelphia PA 19102

BUTCHER, REGINALD WILLIAM, educator; b. Bay Shore, L.I., N.Y., May 4, 1930; s. Reginald William and Elizabeth (Porper) B.; B.S., U.S. Naval Acad., 1953; student U. Va., 1956-57; Ph.D., Western Res. U., 1963; m. Joan Weiterer, June 6, 1953; children—David, Elizabeth, Jane. Instr. physiology Vanderbilt U., 1963-66, asst. prof., 1966-68, asso. prof., 1968-69; prof., chmn. dept. biochemistry U. Mass., 1969—; sr. scientist The Worcester Found. for Exptl. Biology, Shrewsbury, Mass. Served with USAF, 1953-56. Mem. Am. Physiol. Soc., Am. Soc. Biol. Chemistry. Research molecular level actions of hormones, with emphasis on the role of cyclic AMP in control of cellular activities. Home: 62 Newton St Northboro MA 01532 Office: 419 Belmont St Worcester MA 01604

BUTCHER, WILLARD CARLISLE, banker; b. Bronxville, N.Y., Oct. 25, 1926; s. Willard F. and Helen (Calhoun) B.; student Middlebury Coll., 1945; B.A., Brown U., 1947; m. Sarah Catherine Payne, Oct. 8, 1949 (dec. Jan. 1955); children—Sarah Carlisle, Helen Catherine, m. 2d, Elizabeth Allen, Jan. 28, 1956; children—Barbara Downs, John Carlisle. With Chase Nat. Bank (now Chase Manhattan Bank), N.Y.C., 1947—, asst. treas. Grand Central br., 1953-56, asst. v.p., 1956-58, v.p. 1958-61, sr. v.p., 1961-69, exec. v.p. 1969—; dir. Nederlandsche Credietbank N.V., Amsterdam, Netherlands, Chase Internat. Investment Corp., N.Y.C. Treas., trustee Mus. Modern Art N.Y.C. Served with USNR, 1944-45. Mem. Phi Beta Kappa, Sigma Nu, Conglist. Clubs: Union League, Economic (N.Y.C.); Silver Spring Country (Ridgefield, Conn.); Winged Foot Golf (Mamaroneck, N.Y.). Home: 24 Topfield Rd Wilton CT 06897 Office: 1 Chase Manhattan Plaza New York City NY 10015

BUTCHER, WILLIAM LEWIS, banker; b. Newark, Aug. 31, 1907; s. William Lewis and Mae (Lewis) B.; A.B., Williams Coll., 1928; grad. Rutgers Sch. Banking, 1939; m. Aimee Tweedy, May 24, 1929 (dec. 1967); children—Gayle (Mrs. Foster Nichols), Lynne (Mrs. Merrell Mays Clark), Tweedy (Mrs. Derek Lee Tattersall); m. 2d, Kathleen R. Cox, Jan. 20, 1968; children—Abigail, Thomas, Coletta Cox. Exec. sec. Zeta Psi Frats; N.Y.C., 1929-35; v.p. Central Trust Co., Cin., 1935-46; exec. v.p. County Trust Co., White Plains, N.Y., 1946-57, pres., 1957-60, chmn. bd., 1960—; dir. Dictaphone Corp. Faculty, Rutgers Sch. Banking, 1949-58. Mem. N.Y. State Met. Transp. Authority. Trustee Pace Coll.; bd. dirs. White Plains Hosp., N.Y. Sch. for Deaf, Burke Found. (White Plains), Westchester County Assn., Westchester Med. Center Found. Mem. Zeta Psi. Episcopalian. Mason. Clubs: Scarsdale (N.Y.) Golf; Shenorock (Rye, N.Y.); University, Williams (N.Y.C.); Club at Point O'Woods (N.Y.). Home: 223 Saxon Woods Rd White Plains NY 10605 Office: 235 Main St White Plains NY 10601

BUTCHER, WILLIAM WILLIAMS KEEN, investment banker; b. Ardmore, Pa., Jan. 17, 1916; s. Howard, Jr. and Margaret (Keen) B.; grad. Hill Sch., 1934; A.B. with honors, Williams Coll., 1938; m. Madeleine Kilrert, July 13, 1963; 1 son, William K.; children by previous marriage—Somer K., Noel; stepchildren—Garrett D. Pagon, Madeleine K. Pagon, Marshall W. Pagon, Nicholas A. Pagon, Alexandra B. Pagon. With Butcher & Sherrerd, Phila., 1938—, gen. partner, 1950—; dir. Yellow Cab Co. Phila. Mem. finance com. Inglis House; financial adviser Widows and Single Women's Soc.; mem. Com. of Seventy. Trustee Agnes Irwin Sch.; bd. mgrs. Hosp. U. Pa. Served to maj. AUS, 1941-46. Mem. Zeta Psi. Clubs: Union League, Racquet (Phila.). Home: 8811 Towanda St Philadelphia, PA 19118. Office: 1500 Walnut St Philadelphia PA 19102

BUTENANDT, ADOLF, biochemist, assn. exec.; b. Bremerhaven-Lehe, Germany, Mar. 24, 1903; s. Otto Louis Max and Wilhelmine (Thomfohrde) B.; ed. Oberrealschule, Bremerhaven-Lehe, U. Marburg (Germany); Ph.D., U. Goettingen, 1927; Ph.D. (hon.), U. Graz; M.D. honoris causa, U. Tübingen, Dr. rer. nat. (hon.); D.V.M., U. Munich, D.Sc. (honoris causa), U. Leeds, Cambridge, St. Louis U.; M.D. (hon.), U. Thessaloniki, Vienna, Bucharest, Med. and Pharm. Inst. (Med. Acad.); Dr. rer. nat. h.c. U. Madrid: Dr. Ing. e.h., Berlin; M.D. honoris causa, Med. Pharm. Inst., Bucharest; m. Erika von Ziegner, Feb. 28, 1931; children—Ina, Otfrid, Heide, Eckart, Anke, Imme, Maike. Privatdozent in biochemistry U. Goettingen, 1931-33; prof. organic chemistry Technische Hochschule, Danzig, 1933-36; dir. Kaiser-Wilhelm Inst. for Biochemistry, Berlin, also hon. prof. U. Berlin, 1936-45; dir. Max-Planck Inst. for Biochemistry, Tübingen, also prof. physiol. chemistry U. Tübingen, 1945-56; dir. Max-Planck Inst. for Biochemistry, Munich, also prof. physiol. chemistry U. Munich, 1956—; pres. Max-Planck Soc., 1960—. Recipient Nobel prize for chemistry, 1939. Mem. N.Y. Acad. Scis., Bavarian Acad. Sci. Goettingen Acad. Sci., other sci. socs. Address: 8 München 60 Morsopstrasse 5 Germany

BUTENHOFF, ROBERT LOWELL, nuclear scientist; b. Markesan, Wis., Apr. 25, 1921; s. Leo Eric and Ella Emma (Menke) B.; B.S. in Chemistry, North Central Coll., Ill., 1943; m. Evelyn A. Hoover, June 2, 1944; children—Judith Ann, John Lowell, and Roger William. Research asso. Oak Ridge Nat. Lab., 1943-48; chief radiation instruments br. AEC, 1948-57; program dir. Office Sci. Information, NSF, 1957; sci. coordinator Office U.S. Commnr. Gen., Brussels Worlds Fair, 1958; mgr. nuclear measurements dept. Lockheed Nuclear Products, Lockheed Aircraft Corp., Atlanta, 1959-61; dep. chief chemistry br. U.S. Army Sci. Liaison and Adv. Group, Washington, 1961- 67; program mgr. radiation analysis and control staff, div. isotopes devel. U.S. AEC, Washington, 1967—. Tenor soloist various chs., 1945—. Mem. Am. Phys. Soc., I.E.E.E., Health Physics Soc. Methodist lay leader 1968—. Home: 11511 Hitching Post Lane Rockville, MD 20852. Office: US AEC Washington DC 20545

BUTHOD, ARTHUR PAUL, chem. engr. educator, b. Tulsa, May 5, 1917; s. Charles Paul and Buelah Ellen (Butler) B.; B.S., U. Tulsa, 1939, M.S., 1943; m. Mary R. Dougherty, June 4, 1943; children—Mary, Ellen, Ruth, Alice, Patrick (dec.) Lynn, Paula, William Anthony. Chem. engr. pilot plant Pure Oil Co. Chgo., 1939-41; faculty chem. engring. U. Tulsa, 1942—, successively instr., asst. prof., asso. prof., 1942-50, prof., 1950—, also head computer dept., 1964-70. Cons. on heat transfer Western Supply Co. Tulsa, 1946-58; Indusl. Fabricating Co., Tulsa, 1968—; pilot plant work Blaw Knox Co., Refinery Engring. Co., Nat. Carbon Co., George Armistead Co., 1952—. Mem. Am. Inst. Chem. Engrs. Am. Chem. Soc., Am. Gas Assn., Assn. for Computing Machinery. Author: Class Outline for LP-Gas Training Course, 1946 Contbr. articles to profl. publs. Home: 5894 S Kingston St Tulsa OK 74135

BUTLAND, RALPH ALBERT, assn. exec.; b. Lawrence, Mass., July 12, 1895; s. Francis Augustus and Maude (Hanford) B.; student Lawrence Indsl. Sch., 1909-12. Lowell Textile Inst., 1913-16; m. Julia Anna Zigray, Oct. 3, 1923. Apprentice, Am. Woolen Co., 1920; Cons. engr. various chem., dyestuff, textile and related firms, 1920-36; civilian Q.M.C., U.S. Army, 1936-46, insp. to prin. textile technologist, OQMG, Washington, World War II; spl. asst. to chmn. J.P. Stevens & Co., Inc., N.Y.C., 1946-56; John P. Maguire & Co., Inc., N.Y.C., 1956-60; ret., 1960; ret., 1960; pres. Am. Tariff League, N.Y.C. 1958—; dir. Multifuser Associates; dir. Textile Export Assn. U. S., 1954- -. Pres. Northcastle Bus. Property Owners Assn., Inc., Armonk, N.Y., 1957—. Chmn. bd. trustees Trade Relations Council U.S., Inc., 1959-60, now v.p. Served to sgt. 1st Mass., F.A., U.S. Army, Mexican Border Service, 1916, 101st F.A., Med. Detachment; AEF in France, 1917-19. Recipient meritorious civilian citation Q.M. Gen., 1944. Club: Arkwright (N.Y.C.). Holder patents on blood tranfusion and x-ray apparatus, insulation testing apparatus for textiles used by Army for cold climate clothing, other testing apparatus. Home: 1000 15th St N St Petersburg FL 33704

BUTLER, ALGERNON LEE, U.S. judge; b. Clinton, N.C., Aug. 2, 1905; s. George Edwin and Eva Boykin (Lee) B.; student Trinity Coll., U.N.C. (asso. editor Law Rev. 1927-28); m. Josephine Lydia Broadwell, June 5, 1935; children—Eva Josephine (Mrs. Louis B. Daniel, Jr.), Algernon Lee, George Edwin. Admitted to N.C. bar, 1928; gen. practice, Clinton, 1928-59; county atty. Sampson County, 1938-51; U.S. dist. judge Eastern Dist. N.C., 1959- -. Mem. N.C. Gen. Assembly, Sampson County, 1931; organizer, 1st chmn. Young Republican Clubs N.C., 1932-34; del. Rep. Nat. Conv., 1936, 40, 48; mem. Rep. Exec. Com. N.C., 1942-59, asst. chmn., 1946-50. Mem. Am., N.C., Sixth Dist. (pres. 1953), Sampson County (pres. 1958) bar assns., Sigma Nu. Episcopalian (vestry). Rotarian (pres. Clinton 1935). Home: 403 Butler Dr Clinton NC 28328 Office: Post Office Bldg Clinton NC 28328

BUTLER, ALLAN CHURCHILL, banker; b. Cambridge, Mass., Apr. 26, 1926; s. Allan Macy and Mabel (Churchill) B.; B.S., Harvard, 1946; M.A., Johns Hopkins, 1949; m. Shirley Lewis Oakes, Apr. 8, 1961; children—Ellen Pardee, Allan Shaw, Robert Agassiz. Publisher, Valley News, Lebanon, N.H., 1952-57; European rep. 1st Nat. Bank Boston, 1958-59; financial v.p. Fairbanks, Morse & Co., Chgo., 1959-60; chmn. bd. Butlers Bank Ltd., Nassau, Bahamas, 1962—; dir. Security Capitol Corp. Ltd., Toronto, Ont., Can. Hon. Netherlands consul, Nassau, 1968—. Mem. Bahamas Hist. Soc. (treas. 1968—). Home: Jacaranda House Nassau Bahamas Office: Box 981 Nassau Bahamas

BUTLER, ALLAN MACY, physician; b. Yonkers, N.Y., Apr. 3, 1894; s. George P. and Ellen (Mudge) B.; student Hill Sch., Potstown, Pa., 1908-12; Litt.B., Princeton, 1916; M.D., Harvard, 1926; m. Mabel H. Churchill, June 1921; children—Margaret B., Allan C., Beverly A. With Cunard S.S. Co., N.Y.C. 1919-21; research asst. Rockefeller Inst., 1926-28; tutor prof. pediatrics, biochem. scis., Harvard, 1928-30, staff, dept. pediatrics Harvard, 1930-42, prof. of Pediatrics, Harvard, chief children's med. service Mass. Gen. Hosp., Boston, 1942- 60, prof. emeritus 1960—; dir. med. clinics, chief pediatric service Met. Hosp. Clinics, Detroit, 1960-62. Spl. Cons. Cal. Dept. Pub. Health, 1962-63; lectr. Stanford Med. Sch., 1963-66; cons. AID, 1964-65; med. cons. Head Start, Office Econ. Opportunity, 1965-69, Chgo. Bd. Edn., 1969-71, dir. med. edn. St. Lukes Hosp., San Francisco, 1965-66; fellow Center for Study Democratic Instns. Santa Barbara, 1966-67. Team dir. Nat. Nutrition Survey N.Y.C., 1969. med. officer Civil Def., New Eng. area, 1941-42; Am. Acad. Pediatrics coordinator Head Start, region I 1970—. Mem. Soc. for Pediatric Research, Am. Soc. Clin. Investigation, Am. Acad. Arts and Scis., Assn. Am. Physicians, Am. Pediatric Soc. (pres. 1955, Howland award 1969), Am. Acad. Pediatrics, Com. Physicians for Improvement Med. Care (sec., treas.), Physicians Forum (chmn. 1960), Nat. Council Infant and Child Care (pres. 1958). Asso. editor New Eng. Jour. Medicine, 1936-38, Jour. Clin. Investigation. 1940-46. Contbr. articles on biol. chemistry, nutrition, metabolic disease, clin. medicine, med. econs. to profl. jours. Home: Tashmoo Farm Vineyard Haven MA

BUTLER, BROADUS NATHANIEL, univ. pres.; b. Mobile, May 28, 1920; s. John Nathaniel and Mary Lillian B.; B.A., Talladega (Ala.) Coll. 1941; M.A., U. Mich., 1947, Ph.D., 1952; m. Lillian P. Rutherford, Dec. 27, 1947; children—Bruce N., Janet Cecile. Instr. philosophy St. Augustine's Coll., Raleigh, N.C., 1953; dean guidance, asst. prof. humanities Talledega Coll., 195865; grad. officer coll. liberal arts Wayne State U., 195864; acad. adviser, asst. to dean, 195865; asst. to U.S. commr. edn., 196465; spl. asst. to asso. commr. for higher edn., 196566; dean coll. arts and scis. Tex. So. U., 1969; pres. Dillard U., New Orleans, 1969—. Dir. Fed. Reserve Bank of Atlanta, New Orleans. Asso. dir. Project PRESCAD, 1966-68. Bd. dirs. Assn. Study Negro Life and History, Burton Mercy Hosp., Flint-Goodridge Hosp., Met. Hosp. Detroit, Nat. Merit Scholarship Corp.; trustee Lane Coll. Served with USAAF, 194245. Named Citizen of Year, Mich. Chronicle, 1962; recipient Social Action award Phi Beta Sigma, 1961, Pan-Africa Student Union Service award, 1963; decorated Grand Comdr. Order Star of Africa (Liberia). Mem. N.A.A.C.P. (life), Am. Assn. U. Profs., Coll. English Assn., Mich. Coll. Personnel Assn., Hist. Soc. Mich. Am. Acad. Polit. and Social Sci., Am. Pub. Health Assn., Omega Psi Phi. Episcopalian. Author: Heritage in Black, 1965; The Negro Self- Image, 1965. Address: Dillard U 2601 Gentilly Blvd New Orleans LA 70122

BUTLER, CHARLES, indsl. designer; b. Perth Amboy, N.J., Aug. 10, 1914; s. Wilfred and Letitia (Powell) B.; B.A., Pa. Coll. Art, 1936; postgrad. in Architecture, U. Pa., 1939; m. Irene Reynolds, June 30, 1939 (div., Sept. 1954); children—Wendy, Malcolm; m. 2d Leta Counihan, Oct. 1, 1955; 1 dau., Tracy. Civilian adviser U.S. Navy Bur. Spl. Devices, Ridgefield Mfg. Corp. (N.J.), 1940-44; transp. designer Raymond Loewy Assos., N.Y.C., 1945- 50; pres. Charles Butler Assos., N.Y.C., 1950—, London, Eng., 1958—; mng. dir. Charles Butler Assos. Design for Industry, Ltd., London, 1959- -. Recipient Design awards mil., comml. aircrafts interiors, 1960. Mem. Design Inst., Royal Aero. Soc., Royal Aero. Club. Clubs: Greenwich Country; Union League (N.Y.C.). Designer interiors for transport. Concorde SST mil., comml. aircraft. Home: 23 Copper Beech Rd Greenwich CT 06830 Office: 230 Park Av New York City NY 10017

BUTLER, CHARLES FREDERICK, govt. ofcl.; b. Quincy, Mass., July 10, 1933; s. Percy and Ethel Garrett (Sutermeister) B.; A.A., Boston U., 1957, A.B., 1959; J.D. with honors, George Washington U., 1964; m. Alice Ryan, June 21, 1959; children— Charles Frederick, Colin, Christopher, Alison. Admitted to Mass. bar, 1965; air transp. examiner CAB, 1959-63; adminstrv. asst. to Congressman Hastings Keith, Mass., 1959-65; Washington rep. for internat. proceedings Eastern Airlines, 1965-69; cons. to Spl. Asst. to Pres., Harry Flemming, 1969; U.S. rep. Internat. Civil Aviation Orgn., Montreal, 1969—; lectr. unlawful seizure of aircraft McGill Inst. Air and Space Law. Served with AUS, 1963-65. Recipient award of merit, C.A.B., 1961. Mem. Nat. Lawyers Club, Nat. Aviation Club, Phi Delta Phi. Republican. Club: Capitol Hill (Washington). Author symposium report, article. Home: 1323 Redpath Crescent Montreal 109 Quebec Canada Office: Internat Aviation Bldg Montreal 101 Quebec Canada

BUTLER, CHARLES HARVEY, former ins. co. exec.; b. Camden, N.J., Nov. 19, 1903; s. Leslie Richard and Martha D. (VanLeir) B.; student Pierce Bus. Sch., Phila., 1922-23; m. Anna Williams Smith, June 13, 1928; 1 son, Leslie Richard II. With Penn Mut. Life Ins. Co., Phila., 1922-68, asst. to treas., 1948-55, asst. treas., 1955-65, treas., 1965-68. Pres., Pitman (N.J.) Borough Council, 1946-50; chmn. Pitman Youth Counseling Com., 1950-62; sec. Pitman Bd. Edn., 1953-58; mem. exec. com. Gloucester County March Dimes, 1960-67, sec., 1967-68; mem. Pitman Zoning Bd., Adjustment, 1965—, chmn. 1966. Kiwanian. Home: 108 Pitman Av Pitman NJ 08071 Office: 530 Walnut St Philadelphia PA 19105

BUTLER, CHARLES RANDOLPH, lawyer; b. N.Y.C., Jan. 18, 1906; s. Frank A. and Maude (Williamson) B.; A.B., Colgate U., 1927; LL.B., Fordham U., 1931; m. Venetia Neville Bacon, Feb. 25, 1936; children—Venetia Neville (Mrs. John H. Friend), Charles Randolph. Admitted to N.Y. bar, 1932, Ala. bar, 1951; practice in N.Y.C., 1932-51, Mobile, 1951—; mem. firm Perkins & Butler, 1932-51; mem. firm Hamilton, Butler, Riddick & Latour, 1951—. Dir. Mobile Fed. Savs. & Loan Assn. Mem. Ala. Republican Exec. Com., 1958-66; vice chmn. Mobile County Rep. Exec. Com., 1954-66. Pres. emeritus Am. Camellia Soc. Served with USAAF, 1942-45. Recipient Maroon citation Colgate U., 1969. Mem. Beta Theta Pi, Phi Delta Phi. Episcopalian. Clubs: Athelstan, Bienville, Mobile Country (Mobile). Home: 2401 Venetia Rd Mobile AL 36605 Office: P O Box 1743 Mobile AL 36601

BUTLER, CHAUNCEY W., Jr., banker; b. Memphis, June 28, 1909; s. Chauncey W. and Katherine (Dillard) B.; student U. of South, 1931; m. Ann Butler (dec.); 1 son, Chauncery W.; m. 2d, Kathryn Brown, July 10, 1953. With First Nat. Bank Memphis, 1930-42; with Union Planters Nat. Bank, Memphis, 1947—, sr. v.p., 1947-69, now exec. v.p. Served with USMCR, 1942-45. Home: 4217 Gwynne Rd Memphis TN 38117 Office: Union Planters Nat Bank 67 Main Av Memphia TN 38103

BUTLER, COULA P., (Mrs. Leon L. Butler), lawyer; b. Chgo., May 18, 1911; d. Stelios and Mary (Markas) Psaras; student Crane Jr. Coll., 1928, Northwestern U., 1929-32; J.D., John Marshall Law Sch., Chgo., 1936; m. Leon L. Butler, Feb. 6, 1942; children—Sandra Lee, Carla Penelope. Admitted to Ill. bar, 1936; since practiced in Chgo.; partner Endler, Harris & Butler, 1946—. Parents assn. fund chmn. Knox Coll., Galesburg, Ill., 1970-71. Republican candidate for judge ct. Chgo., 1950-52. sec. trustee Edward T. Lee Found., 1944—; trustee John Marshall Law Sch. Mem. Nat. Assn. Women Lawyers (corr. sec. 1964-65), Chgo. Bar Assn. Women's Bar Assn. Ill. (pres. 1948-49), Hon. Order John Marshall, Kappa Beta Pi. Clubs: Central Business and Professional Womens, Republican Business Women's (pres. 1963-64). Home: 224 N Elmwood Av Oak Park IL 61611 Office: 33 LaSalle St Chicago IL 60602

BUTLER, EDWARD FRANCIS, lawyer; b. N.Y.C., Mar. 10, 1909; s. William and Katherine (Mahan) B.; B.S., U.S. Naval Acad., 1929; LL.B., Harvard, 1933; m. Maybelle McManus, June 23, 1934; childrenMichael, Katherine (Mrs. Claiborne H. Johnson, Jr.), Norah, Martha. Admitted to N.Y. bar, 1934, since practiced in N.Y.C.; partner firm Conboy, Hewitt, O'Brien & Boardman, 1946-; spl asst. to atty. gen. Dept. Justice, 1942. Mem. N.Y.C. Commn. Health Services, 1959-61. Trustee St. John's Hosp., Cath. Med. Center Bklyn. Served to comdr. USNR, 1942-46. Mem. Assn. Bar City N.Y., Am., N.Y. bar assns., Nat. Assn. R.R. Trial Counsel, Knights of Malta. Roman Cath. Clubs: Down Town Assn., Downtown Athletic, Harvard (N.Y.C.): Westchester Country (Rye; N.Y.). Home: 40 Fifth Av New York City, NY 10011. Office: 20 Exchange Pl New York City NY 10005

BUTLER, ELMER GRIMSHAW, biologist; b. Parish, N.Y., Feb. 13, 1900: s. Frank Alexander and Elizabeth Jane (Grimshaw) B.; A.B., Syracuse U., 1921; A.M., Princeton, 1925, Ph.D., 1926; Sc. D., Syracuse U., 1941; m. Eleanor Brill, June 30, 1927. Instr. Zoölogy U. Vt., 1921-23; fellow biology Princeton, U. 1923-26, instr. biology, 1926-28, asst. prof. 1928-31. asso. prof., 1931-37, Class of 1877 prof. zoölogy 1937- 60, Henry Fairfield Osborn prof. biology, 1960-, chmn. dept. biology, 1933-48. Mem. vis. com. for biol. scis. Johns Hopkins; chmn. cell biology study sect. NIH, 1959—. Trustee Asso. Univs., Inc. (Brookhaven Nat. Lab.). John Simon Guggenheim fellow, 1950. Fellow Internat. Inst. Embryology, A.A.A.S., N.Y. Acad. Sci.; Mem. Am. Soc. Zoölgists (pres. 1956-57), Am. Soc. Naturalists, Am. Assn. Anatomists, Soc. for Exptl. Biology and Medicine, Am. Inst. Biol. Scis. (chmn. 1949.) Soc. for Growth and Devel. (pres. 1951-52), Am. Soc. for Cell Biology, Marine Biol. Lab. Woods Hole (trustee), Bermuda Biol. Sta., Am. Philos. Soc., Mt. Desert Island Biol. Lab., Internat. Soc. Cell Biology, Phi Beta Kappa, Sigma Xi. Phi Kappa Psi. Presbyn. Club: Nassau (Princeton). Asso. editor Jour. Morphology, 1941-43, mng. editor, 1946-54; mem. editorial bd. Jour. Exptl. Zoölogy, Am. Zoölogist, Biol. Bull. 1955-58; cons. editor Developmental Biology. Contbr. articles to profl. jours. Home: 19 Lake Lane Princeton NJ 08540

BUTLER, EUGENE, editor, pub.; b. Starkville, Miss., June 11, 1894; s. Tait and Dell (Bell) B.; B.S., Miss. Agrl. and Mech. Coll. (now Miss. State U.), 1913; B.S., Cornell U., 1915; M.S., Ia. State U., 1917; m. Mary Britt Burns, June 11, 1921; children—Eugene Britt, Mary Jean. With Progressive Farmer, 1917—, editor Tex. edit., mgr. Dallas office, pres., 1953-68, chmn. bd. dirs., 1964—, editor-in- chief. Mem. agrl. adv. com. State Fair Tex.; agrl. information specialist M.S.A. trip to Europe 1952; mem. Nat. Cotton Adv. Com.; 1962 -66; Nat. Cotton Council Boll Weevil Eradication Com. Mem. group educators and journalists selected by Carnegie Endowment for Internat. Peace to make goodwill trip to S.Am., 1941. Bd. dirs. Miss. State U. Devel. Found. Recipient Hoblitzelle award for advancement Tex. rural life, 1953; award for outstanding contbn. to Tex. agr. Tex. Cottonseed Crushers Assn., 1957; award for profl. writers Am. Seed Trade Assn., 1961; Tex. Fedn. Co-ops. Agrl. Press award 1962; Distinguished Service award Nat. Future Farmers Am., 1968. Mem. Tex. Agrl. Workers Assn. (pres. 1940-41), Dallas Agrl. Club (pres. 1935), Tex. Forestry Assn., Phi Kappa Phi, Alpha Zeta, Sigma Delta Chi. Clubs: Dallas Hardware and Implement, Dallas Athletic; Tenglewood-on-Lake. Democrat. Home: 5514 Ursula Dallas TX 75229 Office: 3612 Noble Dallas TX 75204

BUTLER, FREDERICK GEORGE, drug co. exec.; b. Greenwich, Conn., Mar. 25, 1919; s. Harold Nassau and Rosa (Rhinhart) B.; A.B., Middlebury (Vt.) Coll., 1941; M.B.A., Columbia, 1947; m. Sarah Lou Allred, Sept. 23, 1945; children—Pamela Sue, Frederick Houston. With Price Waterhouse & Co., C.P.A.'s, 1941-42, 47-49; with McKesson & Robbins, Inc., N.Y.C., 1949-63, asst. comptroller, 1952-61, comptroller, 1961-63; comptroller Bristol-Myers Co., N.Y.C., 1963-66, v.p., controller, 1966-69, v.p. operations, 1970—. Active Little League Baseball. Village mayor Briarcliff Manor, N.Y., 1968—. Served to comdr. USNR, 1942-46, 51-52. C.P.A., N.Y. Mem. Am. Inst. C.P.A.'s, N.Y. State Soc. C.P.A.'s, Financial Execs. Inst., Chi Psi. Congligst. Clubs: Scarsdale (N.Y.) Golf; Boardroom (N.Y.C.). Home: 77 Dalmeny Rd Briarcliff Manor NY 10510 Office: 345 Park Av New York City NY 10022

BUTLER, GEORGE A., lawyer; b. Emmett County, Ia., Dec. 20, 1899; s. Allen R. and Josephine (Grettenburg) B.; LL.B., Nat. U., 1925; m. Anne Garrett, Nov. 19, 1924; children—George A., Ida (Mrs. Grainger), Anne (Mrs. Cater, Jr.). Sr. partner firm Butler, Binion, Rice, Cook & Knapp. Pres., Houston Corp.; chmn. bd. Bank of Tex., Post Oak Bank, Houston; dir. Gulf Resources and Chem. Corp., Houston Post Co., Am. Gen. Ins. Co., Md. Casualty Co. Past chmn. Community Chest; first pres. and campaign mgr. of United War Chest of Tex.; past pres. Houston Y.M.C.A.; Chmn. exec. com. Tex. Democratic Com., 1943-44. Trustee S.W. Legal Found. U. Houston Law Found., Grand Central Art Galleries, N.Y.C., George Washington U.; bd. dirs. Tex. Law Enforcement Found., Tex. Dept. Welfare. Member Am., Tex., Houston bar assns., Washington-on-Brazos State Park Assn. (pres.), Spl. Com. on Hist. Preservation (speaker), Delta Tau Delta. Democrat. Episcopalian. Mason (Shriner, 32). Clubs: Bayou, Houston Country. Home: 3416 Chevy Chase Dr Houston TX 77019 Office: Esperson Bldg Houston TX 77027

BUTLER, GEORGE ALFRED, hosp. dir.; b. San Francisco, Sept. 13, 1911; s. Alfred John and Virginia (Davis) B.; B.A., Coll. of Pacific, 1936, M.A., 1943; M.D., U. Cal., 1947; m. Margaret Lawry Moore, Aug. 1, 1942; children—Alan Moore, Ann Virginia. Intern San Francisco County Hosp. 1947-48; grad. tng. psychiatry Met. State Hosp., 1957-60; dir. health Santa Ana (Cal.) Schs., 1948-57; asso. supt., med. dir. Sonoma State Hosp., Eldridge, Cal., 1963-69, supt., med. dir., 1969—. Served with AUS, 1943-46, 51-53. Fellow Am. Assn. Mental Deficiency; mem. A.M.A., Am. Psychiat. Assn. Home: 505 Jackson Dr Santa Rosa CA 95405 Office: Sonoma State Hospital Eldridge CA 95431

BUTLER, GEORGE ANDREWS, banker; b. Westmont, N.J., Apr. 14, 1928; s. John T. and Kathryn B.; B.S. In Econs., U. Pa., 1950; m. Barbara J. Thomas, June 17, 1950; children—Lynn B., William E. Thomas S., Pamela S. With First Pa. Banking and trust Co., 1950—. exec. v.p., 1968—; dir. V.I. Nat. Bank. Mem. adv. bd. Salvation Army. Trustee Presbytery Phila., Phila. Presbyn. Found. Served with AUS. 1946-47. Home: 1824 Ludwell Dr Maple Glen PA 19002 Office: 555 East City Line Bala Cynwyd PA 19004

BUTLER, GEORGE HARRISON, lawyer; b. Jackson, Miss., Mar. 9, 1917; s. George H. and Mamie (Gardner) B.; B.A., U. Miss., 1938, LL.B. with distinction, 1940; m. Jean Word Baker, Aug. 25, 1951. Admitted to Miss. bar, 1940, since practiced in Jackson; partner firm Butler, Snow, O'Mara, Stevens and Cannada, 1954—. Served to capt. AUS, 1941-45. Mem. Am., Miss., Hinds County bar assns., Jackson C. of C., Omicron Delta Kappa, Phi Delta Phi, Sigma Chi. Methodist. Home: 4005 Old Canton Lane Jackson MS 39206 Office: Petroleum Bldg Jackson MS 39205

BUTLER, GEORGE PAUL, author, editor, b. Chester, Pa., Oct. 23, 1900; s. William Austin and Katherine Maud (Anthony) B.; A.B., Lawrence Coll., 1923; Ph.D., Milton U., 1929; A.M., U. So. Cal.; 1932; postgrad. Drew U. Theol. Sem., Columbia; LL.D., Atlanta Law Sch., 1971; m. Erica Helene Bracher; children—George Paul II, Eric and Paula Renate (twins), Jolyan Anthony. Ordained to ministry Meth. Ch., 1923; pastor, Wis., N.J., staff N.Y. Times, 1924-27; head English dept., West Side YMCA, N.Y.C., 1924-27; head dept. history, Silver Bay Sch., 1928-29; prof. history, lectr. Southwestern U., Los Angeles, 1929-38; English faculty Los Angeles Jr. Coll., 1932-38; head dept. English lit. Chapman Coll., Los Angeles, 1936-38; editor, mgr. books, chs., Schs., religious and book editor N.Y. Mirror, 1938-63. Research in lit., rare books, history Bibliotheque Nationale de Paris, Shakespeare Library, Stratford-on-Avon, Library Brit. Mus., U. Strassbourg, U. Heidelberg, U. Geneva, League of Nations, Vatican libraries, Bodleian Library, U. Oxford (Eng.); lectr. books, life today. Recipient Freedoms Found. citation, 1956; certificate Nat. Conf. Christians and Jews, 1956; USAF citation, 1956. Mem. Author's Club N.Y. Author, editor: Best Sermons, vols. I-XII, 1943- 71 (1st world wide anthologies contemporary preaching, selected from 55 countries); Butler's South America, 1960; Butler's Mexico, 1960; Butler's Caribbean, 1960; Great Catholic Sermons, 1964-71; Butler's Europe, and the Mediterranean; 1971; Butler's Hawaii, The Pacific, The Orient and Round The World, 1971. Contbr. numerous articles to profl. jours., book revs. Address: 114 SW 57th Terrace Cape Coral FL 33904

BUTLER, HAROLD, restaurant exec.; b. Montreal, Que., Can., July 6, 1921 (parents Am. citizens); s. Joseph S. and Celia (Shapiro) B.; ed. pub. schs.; m. Jean Parker, Apr. 16, 1963; children (by previous marriage)—Steven A., Gail (Mrs. Neil Kirkwood), Cathy, Cheryl. Owner, Ridge Lumber Co., Rochester, N.Y., 1945-50; dir. Denny's Restaurants, Inc., 1955—. Active Harold Butler Leukemia Research Fund, City of Hope, 1963—. Recipient Indsl. Acheivement award City of Hope, 1963. Address: 14256 E Firestone Blvd La Mirada CA 90638

BUTLER, HARRY ALLISON, univ. librarian; b. Dallas, Apr. 25, 1931; s. Woodda Byron and Mabel (Walton) B.; B.A., Abilene Christian Coll., 1951; M.A. Pepperdine Coll., 1952; Ph.D., Vanderbilt U., 1959; M.S., U. So. Cal., 1962; m. Mary Jane Reagen, Aug. 27, 1956; children—Daniel, Mary, Melanie. Instr., David Lipscomb Coll., Nashville, 1955-58; instr., chaplain Whittier (Cal.) Coll., 1960-61; reference librarian Pepperdine Coll., Los Angeles, 1961-62, asst. librarian, 1962-63, librarian, 1963-66; asso. prof. Fla. State U., 1966-67; librarian Iliff Sch. Theology, Denver, 1967-70; asso. librarian U. Mo., Columbia, 1970—. Vis. lectr. U. So. Cal., 1965, U. Denver, 1967. Mem. A.L.A., Am. Acad. Religion. Mem. Ch. of Christ. Home: 305 Rockingham Dr Columbia MO 65201

BUTLER, J.A., bag mfg. co. exec. Sec., Chase Bag Co. Office: 2 Greenwich Plaza Greenwich CT 06830*

BUTLER, JACK, physician, govt. ofcl.; b. Lubbock, Tex., Sept. 21, 1931; s. Edmond L. and Ella May (Burney) B.; B.A., Tex. Technol. Coll., 1951; M.D., U. Tex., Galveston, 1955; M.P.H., U. Pitts., 1965; m. Marjorie Lee Fillman, June 20, 1954; children—Steven Craig, Cynthia Kay. Intern, Good Samaritan Hosp., Phoenix, 1955-56; resident Allegheny County Health Dept., 1963-64; practice medicine, Waco, Tex., 1958-62; med. officer div. med. care adminstrn. Health, Edn. and Welfare Dept. USPHS, Rockville, Md., 1965-66, chief profl. services Fed. Health Programs Service, 1966-68, dep. dir., 1968-69, acting dir., 1969-70, dir., 1970—. Mem. Alpha Omega Alpha. Methodist. Home: 4008 Simms Dr Kensington MD 20795 Office: 5600 Fisher's Lane Rockville MD 20795

BUTLER, JACK GRIFFITH, banker; b. Paducah, Ky., Aug. 5, 1906; s. Joseph Columbus and Tommie Jefferson (Young) B.; m. Estelle White, June 29, 1929; children—Jack Griffith, Suzanne (Mrs. Jackson D. Waterbury II). Chmn. Bd. dir. Bank of St. Louis, Gen. Bancshares Corp., St. Louis; chmn. exec. com. Jefferson Gravis Bank; chmn. bd. Northwestern Bank & Trust Co., St. Louis, Comml. and Indsl. Bank of Memphis; dir. Bader Bank, Comml. Bank of St. Louis County (all St. Louis), Lindbergh Bank, Hazelwood, Mo., Ill. State Bank, Quincy. Home: 900 S Hanley Rd Clayton MO 63105 Office: 720 Olive St St Louis MO 63101

BUTLER, JACK LAWRENCE, newspaper editor; b. Seymour, Tex., Oct. 21, 1917; s. Wash Cain and Margaret (Lawrence) Gravois; B. Journalism, U. Tex., 1939; m. Mary Lou Ford, Oct. 26, 1940; children—Lawrence Ford, Helen (Mrs. David Hays). Mng. editor Tyler (Tex.) Morning Telegraph, 1940, Gladewater (Tex.) Times Tribune, 1941; news editor Austin (Tex.) Tribune, 1942; mem. staff Ft. Worth Star-Telegram, 1943—, asst. mng. editor, 1958-63, editor, 1963—. mem. adv. com. dept. communications Tex. Tech. U.; mem. adv. council U. Tex. at Arlington. Bd. dirs. Tex. Christian U. Research Found. Mem. Am. Soc. Newspaper Editors, A.P. Mng. Editors Assn., Sigma Delta Chi. Home: 1613 Scenery Hill Rd Fort Worth TX 76103 Office: 400 W 7th St Fort Worth TX 76102

BUTLER, JAMES H., educator; b. Cathlament, Wash., Dec. 16, 1908; s. Don Carlos and Maude (Kimball) B.; A.B., Western Wash. Coll. Edn., 1937; A.M., U. So. Cal., 1939, Ph.D., 1948; m. E. Willena Barnhart, June 5, 1937. Tchr. pub. schs., Kelso, Wash., 1934-38, Tulare (Cal.) Union High Sch., 1939-40; asst. prof. speech West Tex. State Coll., Canyon, 1940-42, 43-44; asst. prof. speech San Jose (Cal.) State Coll., 1945-46; asst. prof. drama U. So. Cal., Los Angeles, 1946-57, prof. drama. 1957—, head dept. drama, 1953-70, Demille prof. drama, 1953—. Served as pvt. U.S. Army, 1942-43. Mem. Am. Ednl. Theater Assn. (pres. 1968), Nat. Coll. Players (past pres.), Western Speech Assn., Am. Legion, Blue Key, Phi Beta Kappa, Phi Kappa Phi, Phi Delta Kappa. Editorial adviser theater and motion picture sects. Ency. Brit. Author numerous filmstrips on history of theater; contbr. articles to theater jours. Home: 5030 W Slauson Los Angeles CA 90056

BUTLER, JAMES THOMAS, broadcasting exec.; b. Peoria, Ill., May 30, 1921; s. Thomas A. and Estelle (Maloney) B.; grad. Bradley U., 1942; m. Jean Claire Eliel; children—Nancy (Mrs. Chester Davis Rudolf III), James T., Jeffrey, Cynthia. Exec. v.p. Hearst Radio, Inc., Milw., 1966—; v.p. WISN div. Hearst Corp., Milw., 1959—; gen. mgr.

Sta. WISN-TV, Milw., 1965—, v.p., 1959—. Served with AUS, 1942-46. Mem. Broadcast Pioneers, Nat. Broadcasters Club, Milw. Assn. of Commerce. Clubs: North Hills Country, Milwaukee Athletic (Milw.). Home: 12855 Lee Ct Elm Grove WI 53122 Office: 759 N 19th St Milwaukee WI 53233

BUTLER, J. DONALD, educator; b. Ewing, Neb., Apr. 8, 1908; s. James A. and Ora (Comstock) B.; A.B., U. Neb., 1929; M.R.E., N.Y. Theol. Sem., 1933; Ph.D., N.Y. U., 1937; m. Linda Marie Bradway, Aug. 18, 1933; children—James Bradway, Peter C., Mark H. Ordained to ministry Presbyn. Ch., 1933; asst. minister Second United Presbyn. Ch., Jersey City, N.J., 1933-39; instr. edn. N.Y. U., 1939-42; prof. history and philosophy of edn. Princeton Theol. Sem. (N.J.), 1944-58; prof. Christian edn. Austin (Tex.) Theol. Sem., 1958-61; James Wallace prof. religion Macalester Coll., St. Paul, Minn., 1961—. Pres. Council Community Services, Princeton, 1955-60; mem. Planning Bd., Princeton, 1947-52; mem. Bd. Edn., Princeton, 1952-58. Fellow Philosophy of Edn. Soc.; mem. Am. Philos. Assn. Author: Religious Education, 1962; Four Philosophies and Their Practice in Education and Religion, 3d ed., 1968; also contbr. jours. Home: 1630 Edgcumbe Rd St Paul MN 55116 Office: Macalester Coll St Paul MN 55101

BUTLER, JEFFREY ERNEST, educator, historian; b. Cradock, S. Africa, Sept. 27, 1922; s. Ernest Collett and Allison (Stringer) B.; B.A., Rhodes U., S. Africa, 1947; M.A., Oxford (Eng.) U., 1956, D.Phil., 1963; m. Valerie Joy de la Harpe, Nov. 29, 1947; children—Katherine, Peter, Jonathan. Came to U.S., 1957, naturalized, 1966. Tchr., Kingswood Coll., S. Africa, 1947-50; tutor Delegacy of Extra Mural Studies, Oxford U., 1953-57; research asso. African studies program Boston U., 1957-64; vis. asso. prof. history U. Cal. at Los Angeles, 1964; faculty Wesleyan U., Middletown, Conn., 1964—, prof. history, 1967—. Served with S.African Army, World War II. Fellow African Studies Assn.; mem. Am. Hist. Assn. Author: The Liberal Party and the Jameson Raid, 1968. Home: 296 Pine St Middletown, CT 06457.

BUTLER, JEREMY EDWARD, lawyer; b. Grand Forks, N.D., Apr. 9, 1930; s. Edward William and Gwenyth (Goar) B.; grad. Phillips Exeter Acad., 1948; B.A., Yale, 1952, LL.B., 1959; M.A., Coluumbia, 1956; m. Penelope Wells, Nov. 29, 1952; children—Jeremy Gaylord, Reid William, Lydia Gwenyth Katharine, Starin Wells. Admitted to Ariz. bar, 1960, since practiced in Phoenix; law clk. to Chief Justice Fred C. Struckmeyer, Jr., 1959-60; mem. firm Lewis & Roca, 1960—, partner, 1965—. Mem. dist. governing bd. Maricopa County Jr. Coll. Served with USNR, 1952-56. Mem. Am., Ariz., Maricopa County bar assns. Author: (with Fred C. Struckmeyer, Jr.) Water, a Review of Rights in Arizona, 1960. Home: 6534 N 13th St Phoenix AZ 85014 Office: 144 W Adams St Phoenix AZ 85003

BUTLER, JOHN, choreographer, dancer; b. Memphis, Sept. 29, 1920; s. Kent and Minnie (Nielson) B.; student Miss. State Coll., 1937-38, Martha Graham Sch., 1940-41, Am. Sch. Ballet, 1940-41. Concert dancer Martha Graham Co., N.Y.C., 1945, 47-48; danced leading role in musicals Oklahoma, N.Y.C., 1946, Inside U.S.A., N.Y.C., 1948-49, also motion picture Words and Music; dancer, choreographer CBS-TV, 1948-49, NBC-TV, 1950-51; choreographer Broadway prodn. The Consul, 1950, St. Louis Municipal Opera, summer 1950; Choreographer N.Y.C. Center Opera Co., Ice Capades, 1952; choreographer; dir. John Butler Dance Theatre, ANTA Theatre, and others; leading dancer Rogers and Hammerstein Festival, St. Louis, 1950; creator numerous ballets; choreographic dir. 1958 Spoleta Festival, Italy; choreographer numerous TV shows; including: Rogers and Hammerstein. Spectacular, Omnibus, Studio One, Steve Allen, Herb Shriner, Chevy Show, and others; choreographer play A Family Affair. Address 1125 6th Av New York City NY 10036

BUTLER, JOHN M., educator, psychologist; b. Hector, Minn., May 12, 1917; s. John P. and Myrtle (Schroeder) B.; B.S., U. Minn., 1939, Ph.D., 1949; m. Helen Machat, July 12, 1956; children—James T., Steven. Mem. faculty U. Chgo., 1947—, prof. psychology, 1960—; cons. Nat. Inst. Mental Health, VA. Served USAAF, 1942-43, AUS, 1943-45. Mem. Am. Psychol. Assn., Soc. Multivariar Exptl. Psychologists, A.A.A.S., Sigma Xi. Home: 2243 Braeborn Av Flossmoor IL 60422 Office: Dept Psychology Univ Chicago Chicago IL 60637

BUTLER, JOHN P., banker; b. Mt. Calm, Tex., Dec. 19, 1901; s. H.R. and Sophronia Jane (Findley) B.; ed. pub. schs.; m. Alva Wallace, June 30, 1926; 1 dau., Alva Jane (Mrs. H.B. Arnold, Jr.). Formerly with First State Bank, Mt. Calm, then bookkeeper First Nat. Bank, Waco, Tex.; asst. cashier First Nat. Bank, Littlefield, Tex., until 1927; with First Nat. Bank, Midland, Tex., 1927—, chmn. bd., 1962—; also dir.; dir. Tex. Electric Service Co., Mem. Midland C. of C. (past pres.). Lion. Home: 1701 W Illinois St Midland TX 79701 Office: First Nat Bank Midland TX 79701

BUTLER, JOHN VERNON, clergyman; b. Worcester, Mass., Apr. 29, 1906; s. John Vernon and Ruth Ethel (Nelson) B.; B.A., Amherst Coll., 1927, D.D., 1952; S.T.B., Gen. Theol. Sem., 1932, S.T.D., 1952; D.D., Ripon Coll., 1946, Brown U., 1960, Trinity Coll., 1968; S.T.D., Hobart, 1968; m. Mary Eleanor McKee, Sept. 13, 1930 (dec. 1966); children—Janet M. (Mrs. William P. Haugaard), Mary Vernon (Mrs. Donald R. Nickerson); m. 2d, Ruth Dear Towner, June 14, 1969. Ordained deacon Episcopal Ch., 1930, priest, 1931; curate, Springfield, Mass., 1930-31, N.Y.C., 1931-33; rector, Springfield, 1933-42, Providence, 1942-48, Princeton, N.J., 1948-60; dean Cathedral Ch. St. John the Divine, N.Y.C., 1960-66, now hon. canon; rector Trinity Church, N.Y.C., 1966—. Am. canon Cathedral and Diocese of Aberdeen and Orkney, 1952—; dep. Gen. Conv. Episcopal Ch., 1946, 49, 55, 58, 64, 67, 70; mem. Nat. Council Episcopal Ch., 1952-58; mem. delegation Ch. of S. India, 1956; gen. bd. Nat. Council Chs. Christ, 1953-65; exam. chaplain N.Y., 1961—; chaplain N.Y. Altar Guild; past standing com., exec. council Diocese of N.Y.; vice chmn. Joint Commn. Ecumenical Relations. Bd. dirs. Bible and Common Prayer Book Soc., Episcopal Peace Fellowship, Leake and Watts Children's Home, trustee Cathedral St. John; sec. Josiah Macy Jr. Found.; v.p. Manhattanville Community Centers; trustee Ch. Pension Fund, St. Hilda's and St. Hughe's Sch., Sailors' Snug Harbor; chmn. bd., pres. Trinity Ch. Assn.; trustee General Theol. Sem., 1945—, chmn. standing com., 1951—. Mem. Pilgrims, St. George's Soc., Soc. for Promoting Religion and Learning (v.p.), N.Y. C. of C., Chi Phi. Clubs: British Luncheon, Columbia Men's Faculty (N.Y.C.); Union; Down Town Assn.; Athenaeum (London); University. Author: (with W. Norman Pittenger) What is the Priesthood?, 1952. Address: 74 Trinity Pl New York City NY 10006 also 89 Highland Av Montclair NJ

BUTLER, JULIAN DAVID, lawyer; b. Cullman, Ala., Sept. 24, 1939; s. Julian P. and Dorothy (Gold) B.; B.S., U. Ala., 1961, J.D., 1963; m. Margaret Rose Miller, Nov. 28, 1964; 1 son, David Miller. Adminstrv. asst. U.S. Senator Lister Hill, Washington, 1962-63; adminstrv. asst. Congressman Carl Elliott, Jasper, Ala., 1964; law clk. Seybourn H. Lynne, chief judge U.S. Dist. Ct., Birmingham, 1965; admitted to Ala. bar, 1963; practice in Huntsville, 1966—; mem. firm Bell, Richardson, Cleary, McLain & Tucker, 1966—; instr. bus. law U. Ala., 1967—. Sec., Young Democrats Ala., 1962—; regional dir. Young Dem. Clubs of Am., 1966-68. Bd. dirs. Legal Aid Soc. Madison County, Youth Franchise Coalition; trustee U. Christian Student Center. Served to 1st lt. U. S. Army, 1964-65. Named Outstanding Young Dem. of Ala., 1962. Mem. Am., Ala. bar assns., Ala. Def. Lawyers Assn., Omicron Delta Kappa, Kappa Alpha, Phi Alpha Delta, Mem. Ch. of Christ. Home: 702 Cleermont Dr S E Huntsville AL 35801 Office: 408 Franklin St S E Huntsville AL 35801

BUTLER, LEE DAVID, business exec.; b. Dunmore, Pa., Feb. 6, 1897; s. James Samuel and Ethel Blanch (Frey) B.; A.B., Princeton, 1922, M.A., 1924; m. Margaret Burchard Fine, June 20, 1930; children—Lee David, Margo (Mrs. Eugene Lorig), Adele (Mrs. Hugh McLennan). Pres., treas. Lee D. Butler, Inc., Washington, 1930—; owner-mgr. Kinloch Farm, 1941—; dir., mem. exec. com. Potomac Electric Power Co. dir. Woodward & Lathrop, also chmn. exec. com. First v.p., dir. Nat. Symphony Orch.; pres. United Community Services, Washington, 1950-52; chmn. blood donor service D.C. chpt. A.R.C., World War II, chmn. war fund campaign Washington area, 1945; member Essex County (Va.) Planning Commn. Mem. bd. Emergency Hosp. Washington; bd. dirs. Atlantic Rural Expn., 1951—; alumni trustee Princeton, 1952-56. Mem. Va. Angus Assn. (pres. 1962), Phi Beta Kappa. Episcopalian. Clubs: Princeton (pres. 1942-45), Metropolitan (Washington); Chevy Chase (Md.). Home: Kinlock Farm Supply PO VA 22559 Office: 1121 21st St Washington DC 20036

BUTLER, LEWIS CLARK, univ. dean; b. Hornell, N.Y., July 11, 1923; s. H. McKey and Evelyn (Clark) B.; B.A. cum laude, Alfred (N.Y.) U., 1944; M.S., Rutgers U., 1948; Ph.D., U. Ill., 1957; m. Margaret M. Kelley, June 19, 1948; children—Lewis Clark, Andrew McKey, Charles Kelley, Elizabeth Lee. Research asst. Rutgers U., 1946-47; instr. math. Alfred U., 1947-49, prof. math., dean Grad. Sch., 1963—; teaching asst. U. Ill., 1949-54; instr., then asst. prof. math. Pa. State U., 1954-57; asst. prof., then asso. prof. math. State U. N.Y. Coll. Ceramics at Alfred, 1957-60. Dir. Inst. Central de Matematicas, U. Concepcion (Chile), 1960-63; cons. in field, 1964—. Served with AUS, 1944-46; ETO. Decorated Bronze Star. Mem. Am. Math. Soc., Delta Sigma Phi, Phi Kappa Phi. Mason. Home: 8 Terrace St Alfred NY 14802

BUTLER, MARY JOSETTA, SISTER, see Josetta, Sister Mary.

BUTLER, MERTON DAVID, poultry industry exec., assn. ofcl; b. Ray, N.D., Jan. 31, 1910; s. George Rufus and Olive Margaret (Tomson) B.; student Santa Ana (Cal.) Coll., 1930; m. Tessie Helen Childers, June 17, 1937, 1 dau. Nancy Jane. Partner, Childers Hatchery, Santa Ana, 1946—, Childers Cheraw Turkey Hatchery (Colo.), 1957-62; pres. Colo. Turkey Breeders, Inc., Cheraw, 1951-67, Childers B-K Turkey Hatchery, Lakeview, Cal., 1962—, Roasters, Inc. 1965—. Sec., Antelope Valley Turkey Growers Assn., Lancaster, Cal., 1963-64, Valley Turkey Growers Assn., Lancaster, 1963-64, v.p. 1962, dir. 1961-64; pres. Western Poultry Congress, 1955, parliamentarian, 1962—, dir., 1947-62; Cal. del. Nat. Turkey Fedn., 1948; mem. Cal. Poultry Improvement Adv. Bd., 1955-70, sec., 1963; mem. Cal. Egg Promotional Adv. Bd., 1962-66. Mem. Am. Poultry and Hatchery Fedn. (Cal. del., dir., 1955-62, exec. bd. 1962-67, pres. 1963, sec.-treas. 1966, chmn. finance com. 1968). Wine and Food Soc. Orange County. Mason (Shriner). Clubs: Newport Harbor Yacht, El Bandito Shrine. Home: 1922 Omega Dr Santa Ana CA 92705 Office: 618 N Baker St PO Box 1793 Santa Ana CA 92702

BUTLER, MICHAEL, producer; b. Chgo., Nov. 26, 1926; s. Paul Butler. Former v.p. Butler Co.; former exec. v.p., dir. Butler Engring. & Constrn., Butler Overseas; prin. Michael Butler Assos.; chmn. Natoma Prodns., Inc., Talisman Co.; dir. Butler Paper Co., Internat. Sports Core; land devels. Oak Brook, Sugarbush, Talisman; coal washeries in India, Dugda I, producer (play) Hair, (motion picture) You Are What You Eat; chancellor Lincoln Acad.; chmn. Orgn. Econ. Devel.; dir., commr. Chgo. Regional Port Dist.; spl. adviser on Indian and Middle East affairs to Senator John F. Kennedy. Decorated Order of Lincoln, Order Sword and Cutlass, Soc. Colonial Wars. Mem. Oceanographic Inst., Chgo. Hist. Soc., English Speaking Union, Chgo. Natural History Mus., U.S. Polo Assn. (gov.). Clubs: Racquet, Arts (Chgo.); Oak Brook Hounds, Oak Brook Polo (gov.); Racquet and Tennis, Explorers, Knickerbocker (N.Y.C.); Talisman Corinthian Yacht (vice commodore Port Antonio). Address: Natoma Oak Brook IL 60521

BUTLER, MRS. EDWARD H., newspaper exec.; b. Atlanta, d. Augustus Marcellus and Jennie (Maddux) Robinson; student Gunston Hall and France; m. Edward Hubert Butler, Feb. 2, 1909; 1 dau., Kate Robinson (Mrs. James Haslam Righter). Dir. Buffalo Evening News, Inc., 1951—, pres., 1956—; v.p. WBEN, Inc., 1956-67 pres., 1967—. Hon. mem. council U. Buffalo; mem. corp. Am. Hosp. Paris (France); mem. Buffalo Fine Arts Acad. Mem. Frontier of Republican Women Buffalo. Mem. Colonial Dames Am. Presbyn. Clubs: Buffalo Country, Garret, Saturn; Adirondack League (Old Forge, N.Y.). Home: 672 Delaware Av Buffalo NY 14209 Office: Buffalo Evening News Buffalo NY 14240

BUTLER, OGBOURNE DUKE, Jr., educator; b. Orange, Tex., Sept. 29, 1918; s. Ogbourne Duke and Vivian (Jarvis) B.; B.S., Tex. A. and M. U., 1939, M.S., 1947; Ph.D., Mich. State U., 1953; m. Jane Gray, Jan. 16, 1943; children—Jan, James Gray, Ogbourne Duke III. Grad. asst. Mich. State U., 1951-53; faculty Tex. A. and M. U., College Station; 1953—. prof., head dept. animal sci., 1956—. Cons. Wortham Research Found., 1961—. Served to maj. AUS, 1941-45; col. Res. Recipient award outstanding service beef cattle industry Tex. and Southwestern Cattle Raisers Assn., 1963; named Man of Year in So. Agr., Progressive Farmer mag., 1965. Mem. Am. Soc. Animal Sci v.p., Am. Meat Sci. Assn., Sigma Xi, Phi Kappa Phi. Methodist (steward). Home: 700 Thomas St College Station, TX 77840.

BUTLER, PAUL, bus. exec.; b. Chgo., June 23, 1892; s. Frank O. and Fannie (Bremaker) B.; grad. U. Ill., 1916. Pres., Butler Co., Chgo.; chmn. bd. J.W. Butler Paper Co.; pres., gen. mgr. Butler Paper Cos., Kansas City, Detroit, Los Angeles, New Orleans, Mpls., Phoenix, Denver, Southwestern Paper Cos., Dallas, Ft. Worth, Houston, Pacific Coast Paper Co., San Francisco, Standard Paper Co., Milw., Butler Paper Co., Inc., Ft. Wayne, Ind.; chmn. bd. Butler Aviation Co. bases at Midway, O'Hare, Meigs (Chgo.), Alexander Field (Wisconsin Rapids), Logan Internat. (Boston), Palm Beach (Fla.) Internat., Washington Nat., LaGuardia (N.Y.C.); Helicopter Air Lift (Chgo.), San Francisco Internat. Airport, Palm Springs (Cal.) Airport; pres., gen. mgr. Mid-States Paper Co., Terre Haute, Ind., Sun Ranch, Cameron, Mont. Served as lt. AS, U.S. Army. Mem. Soc. Colonial Wars, Chgo. Hist. Soc., Art Inst., Chgo. Natural History Mus. Clubs: Oak Brook (Ill.) Polo (pres. 1924-30); Army and Navy (v.p., acting pres. 1924-26); York Golf (pres. 1926-35); Racquet Attic, Union League, Chicago Golf; India House, Meadow Brook (N.Y.C.); Everglades, Seminole (Palm Beach, Fla.). Home: Oak Brook IL 60521 Office: 1000 Oak Brook Rd Oak Brook IL 60521 also 100 Wisconsin River Dr Port Edwards WI 54469

BUTLER, PHILIP LIVINGSTON, banker; b. N.Y.C., 1909; grad. U. Ala., 1931. Sr. v.p. LaSalle Nat. Bank, Chgo. Home: 914 Juniper Rd Glenview IL 60025 Office: 135 S LaSalle St Chicago IL 60690*

BUTLER, PIERCE, lawyer; b. Ancon, C.Z., May 24, 1918; s. Pierce and Hilda (Vallandigham) B.; A.B., Harvard, 1939; LL.B., U. Minn., 1947; m. Janine de Coster, Admitted to Minn. bar, 1947, since practiced in St. Paul; partner firm Doherty, Rumble & Butler, 1953—. Served to capt. C.E., AUS, 1942-45; PTO. Mem. Am., Minn. bar assns. Club: Minneapolis. Home: 737 Blue Gentian Saint Paul MN 55118 Office: First Nat Bank Bldg Saint Paul MN 55101

BUTLER, REGINALD COTTERELL, sculptor; b. Hertfordshire, Eng., Apr. 28, 1913; s. Frederick William and Edith (Barltrop) B.; ed. privately, Eng.; Gregory fellow sculpture, Leeds U., 1950-53. Lectr., Archtl. Assn. Sch., 1937-39; tech. editor, Archtl. Press, 1946-51; 1st one man show, London, 1949; retrospective exhbn. J. B. Speed Art Mus. Louisville, 1963; exhibited in Hanover Galery, London, Pierre Matisse Gallery, N.Y.C. Grand prize winner Unknown Polit. Prisoner Internat. Sculpture Competition, 1953. Asso. Acad. Royale des Scis., des Lettres et des Beaux-Arts de Belgique, 1965. Author: Creative Development, 1962. Address: Ahs Berkhamsted Pl Berkhamsted Hertfordshire England

BUTLER, RICHARD AUSTEN, (Lord Butler), ednl. amdinstr.; b. Attock Serai, India (now Pakistan), Dec. 9, 1902; s. Montagu Sherard Dawes and Ann Gertrude (Smith) B.; student Marlborough; M.A., Pembroke Coll., Cambridge; LL.D., Cambridge, 1952, Nottingham, 1953, Bristol, 1954, Sheffield, 1955, St. Andrews U., Glasgow, Reading, 1959; D.H.L., Oxford, 1952; m. Sydney Elizabeth Courtauld, Apr. 20, 1926 (dec.); children—Richard Clive, Adam Courtauld, Samuel James, Sarah Teresa Mary; m. 2d, Mollie Montgomerie Courtauld, 1959. Fellow Corpus Christi Coll., Cambridge, 1925-29; mem. Parliament, Saffron- Walden, 1929-65; parliamentary under-sec. State for India, 1932-37; sec. Ministry of Labour, 1937-38; under-sec. of state for Fgn. Affairs, 1938- 41; pres. Bd. Edn., 1941-45, minister of labor, 1945; chmn. Nat. Union of Conservative and Unionist Assns., 1945-51; chancellor of the Exchequer, 1951-55; Lord Privy Seal, 1956-59; also leader House of Commons, 1956-62, home sec., 1957-62, chmn. Conservative Party, 1959-62; first sec. of state, 1962-63, sec. of state for fgn. affairs, 1963-65. High steward Cambridge U., chancellor Sheffield U., 1959—; now master of Trinity College, Cambridge U. Mem. Indian Franchise Com., 1931; mem. Privy Council com. for Reform of Channel Islands Govt., 1946. Privy councillor, 1945. Decorated Companion of Honour, 1954; hon. fellow Corpus Christi Coll. of Cambridge, 1952. President of Union Soc., 1924, Modern Lang. Assn., 1946, Nat. Assn. for Mental Health, 1946, Royal Soc. Lit., 1951, Brit. and Fgn. Schs. Socs., 1945; chmn. council Royal India Soc., Anglo Netherlands Soc., 1946. Clubs: Athenaeum, Carlton, Farmers, Beefsteak, Grillions (London). Address: Master's Lodge Trinity Coll Cambridge, England.

BUTLER, RICHARD COLBURN, banker, lawyer; b. Little Rock, Jan. 1, 1910; s. R. Colburn and Edna (Clok) B.; student Little Rock Jr. Coll., 1929; A.B., U. Ark., 1931; m. Gertrude Remmel, Mar. 7, 1936; 1 son, Richard Colburn III. Admitted to Ark. bar, 1933, U.S. Supreme Ct. bar; gen. practice law, Little Rock, 1933-63; partner firm House, Holmes, Butler & Jewell, 1941-63; pres., chmn. bd. Comml. Nat. Bank Little Rock, 1963—; pres., dir. Ark. Nat. Stockyards Co., 1958—; dir. Peoples Savs. & Loan Assn. Little Rock, Rock Island R.R., Ark. Power & Light Co., Coca Cola Bottling Co. Ark., Interstate Hwy. Sign Co., Comml. Nat. Mortgage Co., Indsl. Devel. Co. of Little Rock. Pres. bd. trustees Little Rock U., 1961-63; bd. dirs. Little Rock Boys Club, pres., 1960; nat. asso. for Ark., Boys Clubs America, 1964—; trustee Hendrix Coll., Conway, Ark. Served to maj. USAAF, 1942-46; CBI. Decorated Bronze Star. Mem. Am. Judicature Soc., Am., Ark. bar assns., Am. Iris Soc. (life, regional v.p. 1960-61), Bookfellows (pres. 1961), Little Rock C. of C. (pres. 1952). Methodist (chmn. bd. trustees). Clubs: Little Rock Country, Little Rock, XV, Top of Rock (pres. 1961). Home: 36 River Ridge Rd Little Rock AR 72207 Office: 200 Main St Little Rock AR 72203

BUTLER, ROBERT CHARLES, chewing gum co. exec.; b. Bloomington, Ill., Nov. 4, 1904; s. George Walker and Josie (O'Brien) B.; student U. Chgo., Northwestern U.; m. Louise D'Andrea, Dec. 25, 1931; children—Mary (Mrs. Robert C. Hastings, Jr.), Carolyn (Mrs. Robert F. Mensik). Joined Wrigley Orgn., Chgo., 1921—, sales office mgr., 1938-47, asst. gen. office mgr., 1947-51, gen. office mgr., 1951-53, v.p., 1953-61, v.p., treas., 1961—, also dir.; v.p. Wrigley S.A. France; sr. v.p., treas. Wm. Wrigley Jr. Co., 1970—; pres., dir. Zeno Equipment Co.; treas. Northwestern Chem. Co., dir. Wrigley Philippines, Inc., Wrigley Co. (N.Z.), Aukland, Amurol Bldg. Corp., Wrigley Espana, S.A., Wrigley Co. (Hong Kong) Ltd., Wrigley Kabushiki Kaisha, Japan, Wrigley Co. (East Africa) Ltd., Amurol Products Co. Asst. treas. Wrigley Fund. Mem. Japan Am. Soc. of Chgo. Clubs: Chicago Athletic Assn., Economic (Chgo.). Home: 1325 N State Pkwy Chicago IL 60610 Office: 410 N Michigan Av Chicago IL 60611

BUTLER, ROBERT CLIFTON, chem. co. exec.; b. Newark, Aug. 29, 1930; s. Thomas C. and Helen V. (Woods) B.; B.S.C., U. Notre Dame, 1952; M.B.A., Wharton Sch. U. Pa., 1956; m. Eileen Hudson, Apr. 14, 1956; children—Christopher R., John H., Thomas C. Dir. planning Gen. Telephone & Electronics Internat., 1965-66; 66; v.p., treas. Isotopes Inc., 1966-67; v.p., controller Inmont Corp., 1967—. Served with AUS, 1954-55. Home: 30 Fellscrest Rd Essex Fells NJ 07021 Office: 1133 Av Americas New York City NY 10036

BUTLER, ROBERT ERNEST, coll. ofcl.; b. W. Hartford, Conn., Apr. 13, 1922; s. Ernest Lee and Grace (Jacobs) B.; B.A., Wesleyan U., Middletown, Conn., 1943, M.A., 1946; Ph.D., Rutgers U., 1950; m. Doris Cook Douglas, June 14, 1945; children—Douglas Robert, Donald Lee. Instr. English, U. Conn., 1946-48, Rutgers U., 1950-51, head English dept. Hun Sch., 1951-52; from instr. to asst. prof. Douglass Coll., 1952-60; master English, Choate Sch., 1960-62, head English dept., 1962-64; headmaster St. Johnsbury (Vt.) Acad., 1964-65, Tilton (N.H.) Sch., 1965-69; dir. devel. Gettysburg (Pa.) Coll., 1969—. Served to 2d lt. USAAF, 1943-45. Mem. Cum Laude Soc., Sigma Chi. Republican. Methodist. Address: RD 6 Box 365 Gettysburg PA 17325

BUTLER, ROY FRANCIS, educator; b. Atlanta, May 4, 1914; s. Roy Edward and Mae (Kenner) B.; A.B. (Chattanooga Times scholar), U. Chattanooga, 1935; M.A. (Latin scholar), U. Tenn., 1938; Ph.D. (Univ. scholar), Ohio State U., 1942; m. Barbara Goehring Scott, Nov. 17, 1943; children—Roy Francis John Scott. Instr. U. Tenn., 1946, Ohio State U., 1946-47; asst. prof. U. Tenn., 1947, 48, Baylor U., 1947-49; faculty Baylor U., Waco, Tex., 1947—, prof. classics, 1952—, chmn. dept. classics, 1958—. Served with USAAF, 1942-45, Mem. Am. Philol. Assn., Linguistic Soc. Am., Am. Oriental Soc., Renaissance Soc. Am., Classical Assn. Middle West and S. A.A.A.S., Mensa, Phi Kappa Phi, Blue Key. Author: Vocabulary Building Through Etymology, 1948; Handbook of Medical Terminology, 1957. Editorial cons. Dorland's Illustrated Medical Dictionary, 1965. Home: 2613 Starr Dr Waco, TX 76710.

BUTLER, T. J., bldg. materials mfr.; b. Austin, Tex., May 25, 1884; s. Michael and Mary J. Butler; student jr. coll.; m. Hazel O. Butler, Feb. 14, 1924; children—T.J., Martin, Mary Jo (Mrs. W. Douglas Cooper). Pres., dir. Elgin-Butler Brick Co., Austin, Teci Prodn. Co. Mem. Structural Clay Products Inst. Washington (dir.), Clay Products Assn. S.W. (pres., dir.). Roman Catholic. K.C. Clubs: Austin, Austin Country. Home: 1801 Lavaca Austin TX 78701 Office: 4000 East Av Austin TX 78751

BUTLER, THOMAS CLIFTON, chain food store exec.; b. Granville, N.Y., Nov. 14, 1900; s. Thomas A. and Agnes T. (Matthews) B.; studen Green Mt. Coll., 1917; LL.D., St. Joseph's Coll., Phila., 1965; m. Helen V. Woods, Oct. 15, 1927; children—Robert C., Norman W. With Grand Union Co., 1918- -, sec.-treas., 1946-58, v.p., treas., 1958-60, pres., 1960-66, chief exec. officer, chmn., 1966-68, chmn. bd., 1968—; dir. Eastern Shopping Centers, Inc. First Nat. Bank Passaic County, N.J.; bd. mgrs. Bloomfield Savs. Bank (N.J.). Dir. finance World Food Congress, Washington, 1963; dir. 5th Internat. Food Congress and Exhbn.; N.Y.C., 1962. Mem. N.J. Ednl. Facilities Authority, Citizens Com. Higher Edn. (N.J.); regional exec. com. Boy Scouts Am. Mem. borough council Gen. Ridge, N.J., 1948-54, mayor, 1954-58. Trustee Nat. Conf. Christians and Jews, chmn. exec. com. N.J. region; trustee N.J. Citizens Transp. Council, Acad. Food Marketing, St. Joseph's Coll.; chmn. bd. trustees Marymount coll.; v.p. trustee Hosp. Service Plan (Blue Cross) N.J.; Recipient Nat. Brotherhood award Nat. Conference Christians and Jews, 1960; Meier Merchandising award Advt. Club N.Y., 1964; Human Relations award Am. Jewish Com., 1965; Freedoms Found. George Washington medal, 1967. Mem. Nat. Assn. Food Chains (sec., dir. exec. com.). U.S. (dir. chmn. pvt. pension plan com.), N.J. (pres.), Bergen County (v.p., dir.) chambers commerce, Retail Mchts. Assn. (dir.), better bus. burs. Met. N.Y. (dir.), Bergen County (dir.), N.J. Clubs: Mercier (pres.), Serra (Montclair, N.J.); Glen Ridge Country. Home: 565 Ridgewood Av Glen Ridge, NJ Office: 100 Broadway East Paterson NJ 07407

BUTLER, WENDELL PACE, state ofcl.; b. Sulphur Well, Ky., Dec. 18, 1912; s. Henry and Pearl (Pace) B.; A.B., Western Ky. State Coll., 1936; M.A., U. Ky., 1950, postgrad. 1951; m. Edna Ford, Jan. 15, 1947; children—Rendell and Kendell (twins), Wendell Ford. Tchr. pub. schs., Metcalfe County, Ky., 1931-36, supt. schs., 1938-42; supt. pub. instrn., Ky. Dept. Edn., 1952-63; commr. agr. Commonwealth of Ky., 1964-68, supt. pub. instruction, 1968—. Pres., mgr. Sch. Service Co., Frankfort, Ky., 1956-60. Mem. state senate Ky., 1947-51, mem. com. on edn., 1950. Served with USNR, World War II. Mem. Nat. Ky. edn. assns., Farm. Bur., Am. Legion, Vets. Fgn. Wars, Phi Delta Kappa, Kappa Delta Pi. Methodist. Mason. Home: 121 Crittendon Rd Frankfort KY 40601 Office: State Dept Edn Frankfort KY 40601

BUTLER, WILLIAM ROBERT, univ. ofcl.; b. Robinson, Ill., May 10, 1926; s. George Edward and Blondell Etelka (Smith) B.; B.S. in Edn., Ohio U., 1950, M.A., 1951; Ed.D., U. Kan., 1956; m. Virginia Lou Ault, Aug. 18, 1951; children—Michael Allan, Barbara Lou, Jennifer Ann, Rebecca Joan. Teaching fellow human relations U. Kan., 1951- 52, research asst., 1952-54, asst. dean men, fgn. student adviser, 1953- 57; research psychologist USAF, Topeka, Kan., summer 1953; dean men, asst. prof. student affairs U. Wis., 1957-59; asst. prof. human relations Ohio U., Athens, 1959-62, dean of men, 1959-62, dean students, 1962-65; v.p. student affairs, prof. edn. U. Miami, 1965—. Cons. North Central Assn. Colls. and Secondary Schs., 1958-65, So. Assn. Colls. and Secondary Schs., 1966—; research cons., Am. Bar Assn., 1963-65; pres. House Corp. Sigma Chi, Athens, 1959-65. Mem. Fla. Gov.'s Commn. Scholarships and Loans, 1965—. Served with USNR, 1944-46. Recipient Distinguished Alumni award Ohio U., 1970. Mem. Nat. Vocation Guidance Assn., Am. Psychol. Assn., Am. Coll. Personnel Assn. (pres. 1971-72), Ohio U. Alumni Assn. (dir., treas. 1962), Sigma Chi, Omicron Delta Kappa, Phi Delta Kappa, Alpha Phi Omega, Phi Mu Alpha. Presbyn. Rotarian. Address: U Miami Coral Gables FL 33124

BUTOR, MICHEL M., lectr., writer; b. Mons en Baroeul, France, Sept. 14, 1926; s. Emile and Anne (Brajeux) B.; Licence and D.E.S. philosophie, Sorbonne, Paris, France, 1949; m. Marie-Josephe Mas, Aug. 1958; children—Cecile, Agnes, Irene, Mathilde. Vis. prof. Bryn Mawr Coll., Middlebury Coll., 1960, State U. N.Y. in Buffalo, 1962, Northwestern U., 1965, U. N.M., Albuquerque 1969-70. Author: Passage de Milan, 1954; L'Emploi du Temps, 1956; La Modification, 1957; Le Genie du Lieu, 1958; Degres, 1960; Repertoire, 1960; Histoire Extraordinaire, 1961; Mobile, 1962; Reseau Aerien, 1962; Description de San Marco, 1963; Repertoire II, 1964; Illustrations, 1964; 6,810,000 Litres D'eau Par Seconde, 1965; Portrait de l'Artiste en jeune Singe, 1967; Repertoire III, 1968; Essais sur les Essais, 1968; Illustrations II, 1969; Les Mots dans la Peinture, 1969; La Rose des Ventes 1970; Dialogue avec 33 Variations de Ludwig van Beethoven sur une valse de Diabelli, 1971. Address: le Valfleuri A Alleé Pasteur 06-St Laurent du Var France

BUTT, HUGH ROLAND, physician; educator; b. Belhaven, N.C., Jan. 8, 1910; s. Harry Frederick and Maybelle (Jarvis) B.; student Va. Poly. Inst., 1927-29; M.D., U. Va., 1933; post grad. Mayo Found. U. Minn., 1937; m. Mary Dempwolf, Apr. 8, 1939; children—Selby, Lucy, Charles, Frances. Intern St. Luke's Hosp., Bethlehem, Pa., 1933-34; fellow medicine Mayo Found., 1934-37, 1st asst., 1937-38, instr., 1938-43, asst. prof., 1943-47, asso. prof., 1947- 52, prof., 1952—; cons. physician Mayo Clinic, St. Mary's Hosp., 1938- -. Chmn. sci. counselors Nat. Cancer Inst., 1961-62; mem. Nat. Adv. Cancer Council, 1966—. Served as lt. comdr. M.C., USNR, 1942- 46. Recipient John Horsley Meml. prize U. Va., 1938. Diplomate Am. Bd. Internal Medicine (mem. bd., subsplty. gastroenterology). Fellow A.C.P., Royal Coll. Physicians; mem. Am. Soc. Clin. Investigation, Am. Gastroent. Assn. Central Soc. Clin. Research, Assn. Am. Physicians, A.M.A. Episcopalian. Author: (with Snell), Vitamin K, 1941. Author papers, monographs. Home: 1014 7th St SW Rochester MN 55901

BUTT, JIMMY LEE, orgn. exec.; b. Tippo, Miss., Oct. 13, 1921; s. H.W. and Jimmie O. (Davis) B.; B.S., Auburn U., 1943, M.S., 1949; m. Jane F. Williams, June 23, 1943; children—Janie Lake, Melanie Maryanne, Jimmy Lee. Grad. asst. agrl. engring. dept. Auburn U., 1947-48, asst. 1948-50, asso. agrl. engr., 1950-56; exec. sec. Am. Soc. Agrl. Engrs., 1956—. Served as capt. F.A., AUS, 1943-46. Registered profl. engr., Ala. Fellow A.A.A.S., Am. Soc. Agrl. Engrs. mem. Sci. Research Soc. Am., Nat. Soc. Profl. Engrs., Sigma Xi, Tau Beta Pi, Phi Kappa Phi, Gamma Sigma Delta, Alpha Zeta, Omicron Delta Kappa. Lion. Club: Economic. Home: 1860 Smyers Dr Benton Harbor MI 49022 Office: 2950 Niles Rd St Joseph MI 49085

BUTT, WILLIAM RALPH, hosp. adminstr.; b. Bay Roberts, Nfld., Can., Aug. 10, 1914; s. Charles C. and Winifred E. (Parsons) B.; student Columbia; m. Marjorie B. Beard, Aug. 31, 1940; children—John Charles, Sharon Lee. Mgr. post Hudson's Bay Co., 1941; bus. mgr. Saginaw (Mich.) Osteo. Hosp., 1946-47, adminstr., 1947—; trustee Mich. Blue Cross. Bd. dirs. Saginaw United Fund, 1960-62, mem. bd. central health council, campaign orgn., 1964—; bd. dirs. Saginaw Big Bros.; trustee Jr. Achievement. Fellow Am. Coll. Osteo. Hosp. Adminstrs.; mem. Am. (pres. 1965), Mich. (sec. 1951, pres. 1953) osteo. hosp. assns. Conglist. (pres. joint bd. 1951). Mason, Elk. Clubs: Saginaw Country, Optimists Internat. Home: 4703 Ironwood Dr Saginaw MI 48603 Office: 515 N Michigan Av Saginaw MI 48602

BUTTEL, ROBERT WILLIAM, educator; b. Bklyn., June 10, 1923; s. Louis and Helen (Reese) B.; A.B., Williams Coll., 1947; M.A., Columbia, 1949, Ph.D., 1961. Instr. English, Williams Coll., 1949-51; lectr., instr. English, Columbia, 1951-59; instr. English, U. Cin., 1959-62; from asst. prof. to asso. prof. English, Temple U., 1962-64, prof., 1967—, chmn. dept., 1968-71. Served to 1st lt. USAAF, 1942-45. Mem. Modern Lang. Assn., Nat. Council Tchrs. of English, Coll. Conf. Composition and Communication (exec. com. 1967-70). Author: Wallace Stevens: the Making of Harmonium, 1967. Home: 309 Maple Av Wyncote PA 19095 Office: English Dept Temple Univ Philadelphia PA 19122

BUTTENHEIM, DONALD VOORHEES, publishing co. exec.; b. Hastings-on-Hudson, N.Y., July 23, 1915; s. Edgar J. and Marion R. (Voorhees) B.; B.A., Williams Coll., 1937; m. Kathleen H. Coursen, May 20, 1939; children—Richard M., Peter V., Deborah (Mrs. J. David Brumell), Judith C., Nancy C. With Buttenheim Pub. Corp., Pittsfield, Mass. 1937—. pres., 1957-68, chmn. bd., 1968—. Dir., Am. Bus. Press, pres., 1969. Mem. Bd. Edn. Bedford Central Sch. Dist. No. 2, 1952-58, pres., 1953-55, 57-58. Vice pres. bd. trustees Emma Willard Sch., trustee Taft Sch. 1950-60. Mem. Constrn. Industry Mfrs. Assn. (pres. 1960, dir.), Am. Road Builders Assn. (dir.). Episcopalian. Home: Hickory Lane Mt Kisco NY 10549 Office: Berkshire Common Pittsfield MA

BUTTENHEIM, EDGAR MARION, publishing co. exec.; b. Yonkers, N.Y., Dec. 23, 1922; s. Edgar J. and Marian R. (Voorhees) B.; grad. cum laude Taft Sch., Watertown, Conn., 1940; A.B. magna cum laude, Princeton, 1943; M.B.A., N.Y. U., 1955; m. Mary Elizabeth Robertson, Aug. 22, 1947; children—Margaret Collier, Anne Robertson, Elizabeth Gay, Martha Bradford. Instr., Hotchkiss Sch., Lakeville, Conn., 1946-47; with Buttenheim Pub. Corp., Pittsfield, Mass., 1947—, exec. v.p., 1963-68, pres., 1969—; dir. Newark Brush Co., Kenilworth, N.J., Berkshire Bank & Trust Co., Pittsfield. Mem. Westchester County Republican Com., 1957-61. Served to 1st lt. F.A. AUS, 1943-46, 51-52. Decorated Bronze Star. Mem. UN Assn., Phi Beta Kappa. Home: 65 Crofut St Pittsfield MA 01201 Office: Berkshire Common Pittsfield MA 01201

BUTTENWIESER, BENJAMIN JOSEPH, banker; b. N.Y.C., Oct. 22, 1900; s. Joseph L. and Caroline (Weil) B.; ed. student Columbia; m. Helen Lehman, Oct. 3, 1929; children—Lawrence Benjamin, Carol (dec.), Peter Lehman, Paul Arthur. Ltd. partner Kuhn, Loeb & Co.; dir. Title Guarantee Co., N.Y.C., Chock Full O' Nuts, Tishman Realty & Constrn. Co., Revlon, Inc. Past U.S. asst. high commr. Germany. Trustee Fedn. Jewish Philanthropic Socs., Columbia, Fisk U., Nashville, N.Y. Philharmonic of C. (exec. com.). Symphony Soc., Lenox Hill Hosp., Parkinson's Disease Found. Mem. N.Y. C. of C. (exec. com.). Clubs: Midday, Century Country (N.Y.C.). Home: 450 E 52nd St New York City NY 10022 Office: 40 Wall St New York City NY 10005

BUTTERBRODT, JOHN ERVIN, dairy co. exec.; b. Beaver Dam, Wis., Feb. 14, 1929; s. Ervin E. and Josephine M. (O'Mare) B.; U. Agriculture short course, 1946-47; m. June Rose Bohalter, Sept. 27, 1952; children—Claire, Daniel, Larry. Vice-pres. Pure Milk Assn., 1967-69; pres. Asso. Milk Producers, Inc., Chgo., 1969—; pres. State Brand Creameries, Madison, Wis., 1970—; dir. Town Mut. Ins. Co. Pres. Sch. Bd. 1968. Recipient Am. Farmer degree Future Farmers of Am., 1949; Outstanding Wis. Farmer award, 1965. Home: Route 1 Burnett WI 53922 Office: 1707 S Park Madison WI 53713

BUTTERFIELD, ALEXANDER PORTER, former air force officer, govt. ofcl.; b. Pensacola, Fla., Apr. 6, 1926; s. Horace Bushnell and Susan A. (Alexander) B.; B.S., U. Md., 1956; M.S., George Washington U., 1967; m. Charlotte Mary Maguire, Sept. 9, 1949; children—Leslie Carter (dec.), Alexander Porter, Susan Carter, Elisabeth Gordon. Commd. 2d lt. USAF, 1949, advanced through grades to col., 1966; fighter pilot, mem. Skyblazers, U.S. jet aerobatic team, Europe, 1949-53; aide to comdr. 4th Allied Tactical Air Force NATO, 1954- 55; operations officer interceptor squadron, 1955-56; instr. USAF 1957-59; sr. aide to comdr.-in-chief U.S. Pacific Air Forces, 1959-62; comdr. fighter squadron, S.E. Asia, 1962-64; policy planner USAF hdqrs., 1964-65; mil. asst. to spl. asst. sec. def., 1965-66; student Nat. War Coll., 1966-67; sr. U.S. mil. rep., comdr.-in-chief Pacific rep., Australia, 1967-69; ret., 1969; dep. asst. to Pres. Richard M. Nixon, 1969—; sec. to Cabinet, 1969—. Mem. Nat. Armed Forces mus. adv. bd. Smithsonian Instn., 1970—. Decorated Legion of Merit, D.F.C., Bronze Star medal, Air medal, with 3 oak leaf clusters. Mem. Acad. Polit. Sci., Sigma Nu. Republican. Contbr. articles to profl. jours. Home: 7416 Admiral Dr Alexandria VA 22307 Office: The White House Washington DC 20500

BUTTERFIELD, CHARLES WILLIAM, composer, musician; b. Middletown, O.; student Transylvania Coll., Lexington, Ky.; m. Dotty Smith; children—Debby and Judy (twins). With Bob Crosby Orchestra, 1937, later Artie Shaw; with Benny Goodman, 1940- 41; recordings with Gramercy Five; organized Billy Butterfield and His Orchestra, toured U.S.; recordings R.C.A.-Victor, also Capitol, Decca, Essex, Westminster; now recording exclusively for RCA-Victor; appearances include, indsl. shows, social functions, colls. Served with U.S. Army.

BUTTERFIELD, CLAIR JOSEPH, educator; b. Waterloo, Ia., June 12, 1900; s. Almon Frank and Josephine (Gibbons) B.; student Grinnell Coll., 1923-24; A.B., U. Ia., 1926, A.M., 1936, Ph.D., 1945; m. Ione Genevieve Waldron, Jan. 14, 1927; children—Thomas Dean, Larry Duane. High sch. tchr., prin., supt. schs., Upper Mich., 1926-32; elementary prin., Iowa City, 1933-43; dir. elementary edn., Davenport, Ia., 1943-46; prof. edn. Edinboro (Pa.) State Tchrs. Coll., 1946-51, head dept. edn., 1959-66, acting pres., 1966; prof. edn. Alliance Coll., Cambridge Springs, 1966-68 Vis. summer lectr. Augustana Coll., 1946;, U. Ia., 1947, 49, U. Collo., 1948; dir. servicio cooperativo Inter-Americano de Educacion, ICA, Honduras, 1951-57, Nicaragua, 1957-59. Served with USN, 1918-19. Mem. N.E.A., Phi Delta Kappa. Home: 217 Ash St Edinboro PA 16412

BUTTERFIELD, HARRY DURHAM, banker; b. Pembroke, Bermuda, Sept. 1, 1898; s. Harry Durham and Anna (Darrell) B.; student McGill U. (Can.), 1915; B.A., Oxford U. (Eng.), 1922; m. Florence Heywood, Sept. 17, 1925; children—H. Chester, Richard D., Nathanial. Called to bar Middle Temple, Sandon, 1922; with Bank of Butterfield, Hamilton, Bermuda, 1923—, now chmn. bd.; dir. Bermuda Electric Light Co., Bermuda Telephone Co., Bermuda Fire & Marine Ins. Co., numerous others. Mem. Colonial Parliament, 1937-56, mem. exec. council, 1947-56, mem. legislative council, 1956-68. Decorated count Brit. Empire. Mem. India Ho. N.Y., Alpha Delta Phi. Mason. Clubs: Atlantic Phoenix; Royal Bermuda Yacht; Royal Hamilton Digby; Royal Thames Yacht; Canadian of N.Y. Office: Butterfield Bank Hamilton Bermuda*

BUTTERFIELD, HARVEY DEAN, bishop; b. North Troy, Vt., Mar. 13, 1908; s. Hugh Harvey and Evangeline Gladys (Barrows) B.; B.A., Vt., 1931, D.D., 1962; S.T.B., Gen. Theol. Sem., N.Y.C., 1934, S.T.D., 1961; m. Carolyb Zeruah Whitney, Aug. 7, 1934; children—Harvey Whitney, Deborah Ann. Ordained to ministry Episcopal Ch., 1934, consecrated bishop, 1961; vicar St. Mary's Chapel, Carle Pl., N.Y., 1934-35; curate Ch. of Good Shepherd, Rosemont, Pa., 1935-36; rector Christ Ch., Media, Pa., 1936- 41, St. Luke's Ch., Phila., 1941-43, Trinity Ch., Rutland, Vt., 1943-56; dir. religious edn. Diocese Vt., 1958-61; 6th bishop Diocese Vt., Burlington, 1961- -. Dep. to gen. convs. P.E. Ch., 1943, 46, 49, 55, 58; chmn. dept. Christian edn. Province New Eng., 1957-60. Chaplain, Vt. N.G., 1947-61; served to maj., chaplain, inf. AUS, 1950-52. Home: Rock Point Burlington VT 05401

BUTTERFIELD, LYMAN HENRY, historian; b. Lyndonville, N.Y., Aug. 8, 1909; s. Roy Lyman and Ethel (Place) B.; A.B., Harvard, 1930, A.M., 1934; Litt.D., Franklin and Marshall Coll., 1952, Bucknell U., 1953; D.Hum., Washington Coll., 1963; m. Elizabeth Anne Eaton, June 15, 1935; children—Fox, Hester Lee. Instr., tutor English, Harvard, 1930-37; asst., asso. prof. English, Franklin and Marshall Coll., 1937-46; asst., asso. editor Papers of Thomas Jefferson, Princeton, 1946-51; dir. Inst. Early Am. History and Culture, Williamsburg, Va., 1951-54; editor-in-chief Adams Papers, sponsored by Mass. Hist. Soc. and pub. by Harvard U. Press, 1954—. Bd. editors Quar., lectr. history Coll. of William and Mary, 1951-54; lectr. on history Harvard, 1955-64; cons. editor history Harvard U. Press, 1965—. Dir. Council on Library Resources, Inc., Harry S. Truman Library Inst. John Simon Guggeheim fellow, 1958-59. Fellow Am. Acad. Arts and Scis., Soc. Am. Archivists; mem. Am., N.Y. State hist. assns., N.Y., Mass., Pa., Va. hist. socs., Orgn. Am. Historians, Nat. Parks Assn. (life), Am. Civil Liberties Union, Am. Philos. Soc., Am. Antiquarian Soc., Colonial Soc. Mass., Phi Beta Kappa. Clubs: Century (N.Y.C.); St. Botolph, Odd Volumes (Boston). Author: John Witherspoon Comes to America, 1953. Editor: Anticipation (Richard Tickell), 1941; Letters of Benjamin Rush, 1951; (with others) Papers of Thomas Jefferson, vols. 1-5, 1950-52. Editorial bd. New Eng. quar. Home: 5 Berkeley Pl Cambridge MA 02138 Office: 1154 Boylston St Boston MA 02215

BUTTERFIELD, PAUL, singer; b. Chgo., 1941. Singer, harmonica player; performed at Blue Flame, 1015 clubs, Big John's (all Chgo.), also on TV programs; recorded The Paul Butterfield Blues Band with Elektra. Address: 4800 Chicago Beach Chicago, IL 60614.*

BUTTERFIELD, PHILIP H., ret. banker; b. Antrim, N.H., May 8, 1899; s. Charles F. and Annie (Goodwin) B.; student Grad. Sch. Banking, Rutgers U., 1939; m. Nettie M. Jewell, Oct. 6, 1923; children—Philip H., John J, Hugh G. Messenger, First Nat. Bank, Concord, N.H., 1919; with Concord Nat. Bank, and predecessors, 1919—, now chmn. bd. dirs.; dir. Concord Savs. Bank, Concord Investment Co., Former trustee New Eng. Coll. Mem. Am. Legion, Concord C. of C. Republican. Rotarian. Home: 56 A Beacon St Concord NH 03301

BUTTERFIELD, RICHARD DAVID, architect; b. Dover, N.H., Apr. 26, 1909; s. Ernest Warren and Edith (Thompson) B.; A.B., Dartmouth, 1930; B.F.A., Yale, 1934; m. Genevieve Benezet, Sept. 25, 1934; children—Ann (Mrs. Moffat), Joan (Mrs. Roger P. Whitcomb). With archtl. office J. Fredrick Larson, Hanover, N.H., 1930-32, 37-39, Ernest Sibley, Litchfield, Conn., 1935-37; propr. Richard D. Butterfield, architect, Hanover, 1939-42, Perkinsville, Vt., 1942-49; partner Nichols & Butterfield, architects, West Hartford, Conn., 1949-61; prin. Butterfield & Assos., Farmington, Conn., 1961—. Mem. adv. com. sch. constrn. economy service Conn. Dept. Edn., 1959—; chmn. Farmington Historic Dist. Commn., 1965—. Recipient award of merit A.I.A.-Am. Assn. Sch. Adminstrs., 1952; hon. mention citation Sch. Exec. competition better sch. design, 1954; award citation Progressive Architecture mag., 1954. Fellow A.I.A. (pres. Conn. 1958-60). Rotarian. Prin. works include East Hartford (Conn.) High Sch., 1952-54, F.U. Conard High Sch., West Hartford, 1956-58, Torrington (Conn.) High Sch., 1961-62, Windham High Sch., Willimantic Conn., 1966-67; master plan and bldgs. new campus Quinnipiac Coll., Hamden, Conn., 1963—. Home: 199 Garden St Farmington CT 06032 Office: 1 Professional Park Farmington CT 06032

BUTTERFIELD, SAMUEL HALE, govt. ofcl.; b. Moscow, Ida., Nov. 8, 1924; s. Rolston Samuel and Leone (Hamilton) B.; student U. Ida., 1942-43, 46-47; B.S. in Fgn. Service, Georgetown U., 1949, M.A. in Am. History, 1953; m. Lois Herrington, Feb. 10, 1948; children—Charles Oliver, Stephen Crandall, Susan Hale. Retail salesman, 1949-50; labor economist Dept. Labor, 1950-53; examiner, fiscal economist, internat. div. Bur. Budget, 1953-58; with AID, and predecessors 1958-68, dir. office East and So. Africa, 1960- 62, dep. dir. mission to Tanganyika, 1962-64, Sudan, 1964-65; dir. mission to Tanzania, 1966-68, mem. sr. seminar in fgn. policy Dept. State, 1968-69, asso. asst. adminstr. for tech. assistance AID, 1969—. Served with USAAF, 1943-46. Mem. Am. Acad. Social and Polit. Sci., Beta Theta Pi. Address: 4016 Rickover Rd Silver Spring MD 20902

BUTTERFIELD, VICTOR LLOYD, educator; b. Kingston, R.I., Feb. 7, 1904; s. Kenyon Leach and Harriet (Millard) B.; grad. Deerfield Acad., 1923; B.A., Cornell U., 1927, M.A., 1928; Ph.D., Harvard, 1936, LL.D., 1961; M.A. (hon.), Wesleyan U., 1942, L.H.D., 1967; LL.D. (hon.), Brown U., 1943, Amherst Coll., 1944, Williams Coll., 1944, Lawrence Coll., 1947, Columbia, 1954, Tulane U., 1957, Mount Allison (Can.), 1958, Dartmouth, 1967; Litt. D., Bowdoin Coll., 1955; L.H.D., Trinity Coll., 1946, U. Hartford, 1959, Boston Coll., 1965; D.Sc., Union U., 1961; m. Katherina Geyer, June 10, 1928; children—Margot (Mrs. Robert Siekman), Daniel Kenyon. Tchr. English, Deerfield Acad., 1928-29, Riverdale Sch., N.Y.C., 1929-31; instr. philosophy Lawrence Coll., 1934-35; dir. admissions Wesleyan U., Middletown, Conn., 1935-41, dean freshmen, 1938-41, asso. dean, 1941-42, acting pres., 1942-43, pres., 1943-67, pres., emeritus, 1967—. Chmn., Conn. Commn. Selection for Rhodes Scholarships, 1946-49; chmn. com. faculty fellowships Fund for Advancement of Edn., Ford Found., 1951-54, study assignment ednl. situation in Near East, 1952-53; mem. coll. grants adv. com. Ford Found., 1955; mem. New Eng. Bd. Higher Edn., 1955-61; mem. vis. com. Harvard Divinity Sch., 1956-61, Philosophy Dept., Harvard, 1962-65; v.p. New Eng. Colls. Fund, Inc., 1958-60; cons. Ford Found. Humanities and Arts Program, 1960; mem. com. plans and objectives for higher edn. Am. Council of Edn., 1962-65; mem. adv. council Danforth Grad. Fellowship Program, 1963-65; mem. Nat. Com. on Accrediting Adv. Commn. to Study Influence on Higher Edn., 1963; mem. commn. coll. and soc. Assn. Am. Colls., 1966-69, mem. com. on liberal learning, 1966-69, chmn. spl. com. liberal studies, 1965—; chmn. bd. selection E. Harris Harbison Award for Gifted Teaching, Danforth Fond., 1967-69; cons. liberal studies Ford Found., 1969—; mem. council Coll. Arts and Scis., Cornell U., 1958—; cons. Acad. for Ednl. Devel., 1969-70; pres. Nat. Council on Religion in Higher Edn., 1949-56, fellow, 1927-61. Alumni trustee Cornell U., 1946-51; trustee Edward W. Hazen Found., 1947-67; bd. regents U. Hartford, 1959-63; trustee Deerfield Acad., 1956—, Wilbraham Acad., 1957-65, New Coll., 1965—. Carnegie Corp. grantee, 1939, 52. Fellow Soc. for Religion in Higher Edn. (bd. dirs. 1962—); mem. Am. Acad. Arts and

Scis., Phi Beta Kappa, Beta Theta Pi. Clubs: University, Century Association. Author: The Life of the Teacher, 1954; The Faith of a Liberal College, 1955; Counter Attack in Liberal Learning, 1966; numerous essays. Home: 1193 Randolph Rd Middletown CT 06457

BUTTERFIELD, WILLIAM HENRY, corr. cons., author; b. Norfolk, Neb., July 5, 1910; s. George and Alice M. (Doe) B.; student Phillips Exeter Acad., Exeter, N.H., U. Berlin, summer 1932; A.B., U. Neb., 1933; A.M. (Phi Gamma Delta fellow), U. Okla., 1935; postgrad. U. Pa. 1933, U. Neb., 1934, Columbia, summer 1936, Harvard, summer 1939; m. Virginia Shire, June 11, 1936 (div.); 1 son, William Henry; m. 2d, Betty Jennings Doak, Jan. 9, 1965. Acting instr. bus. communication U. Okla; 1935-36, instr., 1936-37, asst. prof., 1937-38, asso. prof. chmn. dept., 1939-42, asst. dean admission, 1942-43, prof., chmn. dept., 1944-46; ednl. dir. Nat. Retail Credit Assn., 1946-48; v.p. De Pauw U., 1948; exec. dir. U. Ill. Found., 1948-58; v.p. devel. Tex. Technol. Coll., 1959-64; so. rep. Prentice-Hall, Inc., 1938-39. Vis. asso. prof. bus. writing U. Tex., summer 1941. Mem. Am. Bus. Writing Assn. (pres. 1943-45), Phi Beta Kappa Assos., Phi Beta Kappa, Phi Gamma Delta, Sigma Delta Chi, Delta Sigma Pi. Rotarian. Author numerous books including; The Business Letter in Modern Form, 1938, enlarged edit., 1941; Goodwill Letters That Build Business, 1940; Successful Collection Letters, 1941; Twelve Ways to Write Better Letters, 1943; How to Use Letters in College Public Relations, 1944; Effective Personal Letters, 1945, rev. edit., 1951; How to Write Good Credit Letters, 1947; Tested Credit and Collection Letters, 1950; Letters That Build Bank Business, 1953; Common Sense in Letter Writing, 1958, enlarged edit., 1963. Editor: Better Letters Service of Nat. Retail Credit Assn., 1946-48. Contbr. articles to trade publs. Contbr. numerous letter-writing clinics for bus., profl. groups. Address: PO Box 666 Idyllwild CA 92349

BUTTERS, JOHN KEITH, educator, economist; b. Oak Park, Ill., Aug. 28, 1915; s. Thomas M. and Anna L. (Milan) B.; A.B., U. Chgo., 1937; A.M., Harvard, 1939, Ph.D., 1941; m. Helena Renaud, Dec. 25, 1942; children—Elizabeth A., Gerald R., Nancy L. Instr. econs. Harvard, 1941-43, faculty Grad. Sch. Bus. Adminstrn., 1943—, prof. bus. adminstrn., 1954—, Ford Found. fellow Inst. Basic Math., 1959-60. Cons. Treasury Dept., 1942-53, OPA, 1942-43, also various bus. firms; spl. adviser to dir. OSRD, 1945; trustee Home Savs. Bank, Boston. Mem. Nat. Tax Assn., Am. Econ. Assn., Am. Finance Assn., Phi Beta Kappa. Conglist. Author: (with John Lintner) Effect of Federal Taxes on Growling Enterprises, 1945; (with others) Problems of Accelerating Aircraft Production during World War II, 1947; (with D.T. Smith) Taxable and Business Income, 1949; Effects of Taxation on Inventory Accounting and Policies, 1949; (with J. Lintner, W.L. Cary) Effects of Taxation on Corporate Mergers, 1951; (with L.E. Thompson, L.L. Bollinger) Effects of Taxation on Investments by Individuals, 1953; Case Problems in Finance, 1969. Editor: Nat. Tax Jour., 1951-57; (with Arthur Smithies) Readings in Fiscal Policy, 1955. Home: 1445 Massachusetts Av Lexington MA 02173 Office: Baker Library Soldiers Field Sta Boston MA 02163

BUTTERWORTH, JAMES DONALD, educator; b. Columbus, O., Feb. 9, 1919; s. Alfred Harold and Helen Kathryn (Kinney) B.; B.S., Miami U. (O.), 1940; M.B.A., Northwestern U., 1941, Ph.D. in Marketing, 1950; m. Jayne Marie Bubridge, Nov. 14, 1941; 1 son, Timothy. Lectr. marketing Northwestern U., 1946-49; asst. prof. marketing Ind. U., 1949-55; asso. prof. marketing U. Fla., Gainesville, 1944-58, prof., head dept., 1958—. Marketing analyst Small Bus. Adminstrn., Richmond, Va., 1959; mem. U.S. Regional Export Expansion Council, 1971—. Served with USAAF, 1941-42, to 1st lt. AUS, 1942-46. Decorated Medalla de Guerra (Brazil), 1944. Mem. Am. Marketing Assn., So. Econs. Assn., Beta Theta Pi, Beta Gamma Sigma, Delta Sigma Pi, Pi Sigma Epsilon. Presbyn. (deacon). Rotarian. Author: (with Barker, Anderson) Principles of Retailing, 1956. Home: 2136 NW 28th St Gainesville FL 32601

BUTTERWORTH, JULIAN SCOTT, physician; b. Iowa City, Sept. 24, 1910; s. Julian Edward and Veta (Scott) B.; A.B., Cornell U., 1932, M.S. in Chemistry, 1933, M.D., 1937; Med.Sci.D., Columbia, 1942; m. Marjorie Moore, June 6, 1942; children—Barbara, David Scott. Intern, resident N.Y. Post Grad. Hosp., 1937-39, Mellville fellow cardiology, 1939-41; pvt. practice, N.Y.C., 1941—; asso. prof. medicine N.Y. U. Sch. Medicine, 1949—; mem. staff Bellevue, Univ. hosps. Served to maj. USAAF, 1942-45. Diplomate Am. Bd. Internal Medicine (cardiovascular diseases). Fellow A.C.P.; mem. Am. Heart Assn. (award of merit 1959, Gold Heart award 1965, pres. 1961-62), 62), A.M.A. (Frank Billings Gold medal 1953), Sigma Xi. Author: Cardiac Auscultation, 1960. Office: 104 E 40th St New York City NY 10016

BUTTERWORTH, OLIVER, educator, author; b. Hartford, Conn., May 23, 1915; s. Paul McMillan and Clarabel (Smith) B.; grad. Kent Sch., 1933; B.A., Dartmouth, 1937; M.A., Bread Loaf Sch. English, 1947; m. Miriam Ford Brooks, June 30, 1940; children—Michael, Timothy, Dan Kate. Tchr. Latin and English, Kent Sch., 1937-48; tchr. English, Hartford Coll. Women, 1948—, asso. prof., 1959- -. Trustee Mark Twain Meml. Commn., Hartford. Author: The Enormous Egg, 1956; The Trouble with Jenny's Ear (Herald Tribune Spring Festival of Books award), 1960. Home: Sunset Farm West Hartford CT 06107 Office: Hartford Coll 1265 Asylum Av Hartford CT 06105

BUTTFIELD, HENRY ADAMS, packaging co. exec.; b. Plainfield, N.J., Jan. 15, 1929; s. Gibson and Anita (Adams) B.; grad. Taft Sch., Watertown, Conn., 1946; B.A., Yale, 1950; M.B.A., N.Y. U., 1957; m. Margaret L. Gee, Mar. 21, 1952; children—William H., James G., Brewster G. Financial analyst Royal Ins. Co.. 1953-58; with Diamond Nat. Corp., N.Y.C., 1958—, asst. sec., 1960, sec., 1960-62, 67—, v.p. finance, 1962—. Served to 1st lt., inf. AUS, 1951-53. Home: 118 Av of Two Rivers Rumson NJ 07760 Office: 733 3d Av New York City NY 10017

BUTTLE, EDGAR ALLYN, lawyer; b. N.Y.C., May 7, 1903; s. Norman Alexander and Ella Tice (Collins) B.; A.B., Columbia, 1928; J.D., N.Y.U., 1931, J.S.D., 1935; postgrad. Princeton, 1945; m. Erika Lucille Heydolph, Aug. 9, 1931, dau., Dagmar Jo Ann. Admitted to N.Y. bar, 1933, D.C. bar, 1948; spl. asst. atty. gen. N.Y. State, 1933; law asso. George Gordon Battle, 1936- 49; N.Y. regional counsel War Assets Adminstrn., 1946-48; spl. asst. to atty. gen. of U.S., 1950-52; counsel in admiralty matters Caddy & Shephard, attys., N.Y.C., 1960-70; hearing examiner FTC, 1959—; chmn. bd. dirs. Buttle-Baker Chemical Corp., 1953-58; mem. adv. com. on vets. re-employment Dept. Labor; referee Appeals Council Social Security Adminstrn.; pres. Fed. Trial Examiners Conf. 1961-62. Served as comdr. USNR, 1942-45, navy liaison officer, Selective Service Hdqrs., N.J. and Del., 1943-45. Recipient Army Commendation Ribbon. Mem. S.A.R., Fed. Trial Examiners Conf. (vice pres. 1960-61), Am. Irish Hist. Soc., Assn. Bar City N.Y., Am., Fed. (exec. council, 1947-48, chmn. adminstrv. law com. 1965-66) bar assns., Am. Legion, V.F.W., Mil. Order of World Wars, Delta Sigma Phi, Phi Delta Phi. Episcopalian. Clubs: University, Church (N.Y.C.); Nat. Lawyers (Washington). Author: The Perplexities of Trade Regulation, 1956; The Search for Administrative Justice, published 1958; A Guide to the Law and Legal Literature of Peru (in collaboration with Library of Congress), 1947; Trial Problems in Antitrust Legislation), 1953; also articles law jours. Home: 5400 Pooks Hill Rd Bethesda, MD 20014. Office: Fed Trade Commn Washington DC 20580

BUTTLER, JOHN HOWLAND, lawyer; b. Bridgeport, Conn., Aug. 4, 1923; s. Frank D. and Ruth (Curtis) B.; A.B., Darmouth, 1947; LL.B., Columbia, 1950; m. Ann Elizabeth Stover, Aug. 18, 1947; children—Suzanne, John, Dana, Elizabeth, Barbara. Admitted to D.C. bar, 1950, Ore. bar, 1951, also U.S. Supreme Ct.; practice in Portland, Ore., 1951—; partner firm Cake, Jaureguy, Hardy, Buttler & McEwen, 1956—. Mem. Ore. Bd. Bar Examiners, 1966-68. Mem. Ore. exec. bd. Am. Civil Liberties Union, 1957-62; chmn. Ore. Bd. Parole and Probation, 1965. Bd. dirs. Portland Children's Center, 1965—; trustee John Wesley Housing Corp., 1968—, pres., 1970. Served to lt. (j.g.), USNR, 1943-46. Decorated Air medal (2). Mem. Ore.,, Multnomah County bar assns. Democrat. Clubs: City (bd. govs. 1970- -), Multnomah Athletic. Home: 3131 NW Skyline Blvd Portland OR 97229 Office: 1408 Standard Plaza Portland OR 97204

BUTTLES, BRUCE, investment analyst; b. Vienna Twp., Mich., Aug. 26, 1906; s. Cephas and Lillian (Voelker) B.; A.B., U. Cal., 1930; B.S. in Printing, Carnegie Inst. Tech., M.S. in Journalism, Columbia, 1936; m. Virginia Lee Gilmer, Oct. 14, 1949; children—Suzanne L., John S. Staff corr. Christian Sci. Monitor, 1930-38; staff reporter, asst. city editor Pitts. Post-Gazette, 1939-40; asso. prof. graphic arts, head dept. printing Carnegie Inst. Tech., 1947; chief information control br. U.S. Mil. Govt., Berlin, 1948; with Allied Control Comm., Vienna, 1949; asst. officer-in-charge German and Austrian pub. affairs Dept. State, 1949-51; 1st sec. Am. embassy, Belgrade, 1951-53; chief linotype publs., asst. to pres. Mergenthaler Linotype Co., 1953-56; chief div. pub. services Dept. State, 1956-58; consul, Calcutta, India, 1958-63; 1st sec. Central Treaty Orgn., Ankara, Turkey, 1963-66; v.p. George A. Rogers & Co., N.Y.C., 1967—; dir. Timetable & Folder Distbrs., Inc., N.Y.C. Served to col. USAAF, 1940-47; asst. mil. attache Am. embassy, Moscow, 1946-47. Decorated Legion of Merit, Bronze Star. Mem. Am. Soc. Internat. Law, Asiatic Soc., Sigma Chi. Clubs: Army-Navy Country (Arlington, Va.); Royal Calcutta Golf, Swimming, Bengal, Calcutta (Calcutta, India); Oriental (London, Eng.); Sea Bright Lawn Tennis and Cricket (Rumson, N.J.). Author: America's New Army, 1942. Home: 66 Ward Av Rumson NJ 07760 Office: 15 Exchange Pl Jersey City NJ 07302

BUTTNER, CARL A., business exec. Controller, Guedron Industries, Inc., Southfield, Mich. Office: 17600 W Eight Mile Rd Southfield MI 48075*

BUTTON, DANIEL EVAN, assn. exec., b. Dunkirk, N.Y., Nov. 1, 1917; s. Roy and Alice (Root) B.; A.B., U. Del., 1938; M.S., Columbia, 1939. Reporter, News-Jour. Papers, Wilmington, A.P., N.Y.C., 1939-46; dir. pub. relations U. Del. 1947-51; asst. to pres. State U. N.Y., 1952-58; asso. gen. sec. Renesselaer Poly. Inst., 1959; editor editorial page Times-Union, Albany, N.Y., 1959-60, exec. editor, 1960-66; mem. 90th to 91st Congresses, 29th Dist. N.Y.; exec. dir. Arthritis Found., N.Y.C., 1971—. Co-producer, co-moderator TV series Speak for Yourself, 1963-66. Republican. Author: Lindsay: A Man for Tomorrow, 1965. Home: 1 Lincoln Plaza New York City NY 10023 Office: 1212 Av Americas New York City NY 10036

BUTTON, HENRY WARREN, educator; b. Phila., Pa., Sept. 6, 1922; s. Henry Warren and Luella (Barber) B.; A.B., Washington U., 1946, M.A., 1950, Ph.D., 1961; m. Lee Parrish, Dec. 24, 1943; children—Judith Lee, (Mrs. Jerome A. Challman), Nancy Graham, Robert Warren, Rachael Sue. Tchr., St. Louis pub. schs., 1954-58; lectr. St. Louis U., 1957-58, Washington U., St. Louis, 1958-61; with State U. N.Y. at Buffalo, 1961—, chmn. dept. Social Founds. Edn., 1968—. Editor Urban Edn., 1965—. Home: 36 Highgate Av Buffalo NY 14214

BUTTON, JACK BLAIR, fgn. service officer; b. Lebanon, Kan., Feb. 12, 1926; s. Elgin R. and Mabel (Van Tries) B.; A.B., U. Kan., 1947, M.A., 1948; postgrad. Yale, 1957-58; m. Jean Stodard, Dec. 20, 1947; children—Alexander, Van Tries, Margaret, Jonathan. Instr. polit. sci. U. Kan., 1947-48; intern Nat. Inst. Pub. Affairs, 1948-49; joined U.S. Fgn. Service, 1949, assigned Baghdad, Iraq, 1949-51, Berlin, Germany, 1951-56, Tel Aviv, Israel, 1960- 63; assigned State Dept., 1956-60, 63-67, asst. chief foodstuffs div., 1964-67; assigned Nat. War Coll., 1967-69, faculty, 1968-69; adviser U.S. delegation UN Gen. Assembly, 1969; econ. counselor AID liaison officer Am. embassy, Tel Aviv, 1970—. Home: 44 Hakidma Herzliya-Pituach Israel Office: c/o Dept State Washington DC 20521

BUTTON, JAMES WILSON, dept. store exec.; b. Chgo., Apr. 17, 1917; s. Bland Ballard and Aleene (Wilson) B.; B.A., U. Chgo., 1939; m. Lurena Lejuene Stubbs, July 3, 1940; children—James Wilson, Douglas S., Katherine T. With Sears, Roebuck & Co. and affiliates, 1939—, asst. v.p., gen. mgr., N.Y.C., 1959-62, pres., dir. Simpsons-Sears Ltd., Toronto, Ont., Can., 1962-66; v.p. merchandising Sears, Roetuck & Co., 1966-68, sr. v.p. merchandising, 1968—, also dir.; dir. Simpsons-Sears Ltd., Gen. Telephone & Electronics Co., Allstate Ins. Co., Harris Bank. Mem. Nat. Bus. Council for Consumer Affairs, U.S. Dept. Commerce; mem. Navy Resale System Adv. Com. Trustee U. Chgo., mem. council Grad. Sch. Bus.; trustee La Rabida Children's Hosp. and Research Center; bd. dirs. Sears-Roebuck Found., Nat. Better Bus. Bur., N. Shore Country Day Sch., Joint Council on Econ. Edn. Served to lt. (j.g.) USNR, 1944-46. Named Marketing Man of Year, Chgo. chpt. Am. marketing Assn., 1971, recipient Charles Coolidge Parlin award Phila. chpt., 1971. Mem. Psi Upsilon. Clubs: Indian Hill; Shoreacres; Chicago, Commercial, Mid-Am., Arts (Chgo.); York (Toronto). Home: 85 Indian Hill Rd Winnetka IL 60093 Office: Sears Roebuck & Co 925 S Homan Av Chicago IL 60607

BUTTON, ROBERT YOUNG, former state ofcl.; b. Culpeper, Va., Nov. 2, 1899; s. John Young and Margaret Agnes (Duncan) B.; LL.B., U. Va., 1922; m. Kathleen Mary Antoinette Cheape, Aug. 20, 1931; children—Kathleen Margaret (Mrs. L.H. Ginn), Robert Young. Admitted to Va. bar, 1922; practice in Culpeper, 1922-61; atty. gen. Va., 1962-70. Dir. Mut. Fire Ins. Co. Loudoun, Mchts. Grocery Co. Culpeper, 2d Nat. Bank Culpeper, Central Hardware Co. Mem. Va. Commns. on Pub. Edn., 1954, 59, Potomac River Commn., 1958, Va. Bd. Edn., 1945-60, Va. Parole Bd., 1942-45. Mem. Va. Senate, 1946-61. Trustee Jamestown Corp. Fellow Am. Coll. Trial Lawyers, Am. Judicature Soc., Va. State Bar (council 1950-56), Am., Va., Richmond City bar assns. Democrat. Baptist. Mason, Rotarian. Clubs: Culpeper Country; Commonwealth (Richmond). Home: 139 W Davis St Culpeper VA 22701

BUTTONS, RED, actor; b. N.Y.C., Feb. 5, 1919; s. Michael and Sophie (Baker) B.; student pub. schs.; m. Helayne McNorton Dec. 8, 1949 (div. Jan. 1963); m. 2d, Alicia Pratt, Jan. 27, 1964. Burlesque comedian Minsky, 1938-41; appeared in Broadway plays, Admiral Had a Wife, 1941, Vicki, 1942, Wine, Women and Song, 1942, Winged Victory, 1943, Barefoot Boy with Cheek, 1947, Hold It, 1948, also vaudeville theatres, cafes throughout U.S.; TV actor Red Buttons Show, 1952-55; motion pictures include Winged Victory, 1944, Sayonara, 1957, Imitation General, 1958; The Big Circus, 1959; Hatari, The Longest Day, One-Two-Three, 1961, Gay Paree, Five Weeks in a Balloon, 1962, A Ticklish Affair, 1963, Your Cheatin' Heart, 1964, From the Beach, 1964, Harlow, They Shoot Horses Don't They. Recipient Michael award for best comedian Acad. Radio TV Arts and Scis., 1953; Fgn. Press Golden Glove award for best supporting actor (Sayonara), 1957, Oscar award, 1957. Served USAAF, World War II. Club: Friars of N.Y. (sec.). Address: Robert Raison Agy 9000 Sunset Blvd Los Angeles CA 90069

BUTTREY, THEODORE VERN, Jr., educator; b. Havre, Mont., Dec. 29, 1929; s. Theodore Vern and Ruth (Scoutt) B.; grad. Phillips Exeter Acad., 1946; B.A., Princeton, 1950, Ph.D., 1953; m. Marisa Macina, Sept. 9,, 1953 (div.); children—Stephanie, James, Claude, Samuel; m. 2d, Ann Johnston, July 26, 1967. Instr., Yale, 1954-58, asst. prof., 1958-64, Morse fellow, 1960-61; asso. prof. Greek and Latin, U. Mich., Ann Arbor, 1964-68, prof., chmn. dept. Classical studies, 1968—, dir. Kelsey Mus. Ancient and Medieval Archeology, 1969—. Chmn. adv. council Am. Acad. at Rome, 1970. Recipient Henry Russel award for teaching and research U. Mich., 1967. Fulbright fellow U. Rome (Italy), 1953-54. Mem. Am. (life, gov. 1963—), Azteca (hon.) numis. socs., Am. Philol. Assn., Archeol. Inst. Am.; mem. Sociét é Française de Numismatique. Contbr. articles on ancient and modern numismatics to profl. jours. Home: 1256 Ferdon Rd Ann Arbor MI 48104

BUTTRICK, GEORGE ARTHUR, clergyman, educator; b. Seaham Harbour, Northumberland, Eng., Mar. 23, 1892; s. Tom and Jessie (Lambert) B.; grad. Lancaster Ind. Theol. Coll., Manchester, 1915, Victoria U. (honors in philosophy), 1915; D.D., Hamilton Coll., 1927, Middlebury Coll., 1930, Princeton, 1940, Harvard, 1960, Grinnell Coll., 1963; Bucknell U., 1965; S.T.D., Yale, 1932, Miami U., 1934; LL.D., Bethany Coll., 1940, Davidson Coll., 1970; Litt.D., Albright Coll., 1940; D.S.T., Columbia, 1944; L.H.D., Wooster Coll., 1967; m. Agnes Gardner, June 27, 1916; children—John Arthur, George Robert, David Gardner. Ordained minister Congl. Ch. 1915; pastor 1st Union Congl. Ch., Quincy, Ill., 1915-18, 1st Congl. Ch., Rutland, Vt., 1919-21, 1st Presbyn Ch., Buffalo, 1921-27, Madison Av. Presbyn. Ch., N.Y.C., 1927-54; preacher to univ., Plummer prof. Christian morals Harvard, 1954-60, emeritus; Harry Emerson Fosdick vis. prof. Union Theol. Sem., N.Y.C., 1960-61; prof. preaching Garrett Theol. Sem., Northwestern U., 1961-70; vis. prof. Vanderbilt U. Div. Sch., 1970—. Joseph Cook lectr. various fgn. countries, 1951-52; William Belden Noble lectr. Harvard, 1962; vis. prof. Chgo. Theol. Sem., 1962, Union Theol. Sem., Richmond, Va. 1963, Agnes Scott Coll., 1965; vis. lectr. Scripps Coll., So. Cal. Sch. Theology, 1966, Davidson Coll., 1970. Past pres. Fed. Council Chs. Christ in Am. Recipient Gutenberg award Chgo. Bible Soc., 1966. Mem. Am. Acad. Arts and Scis. Author: The Parables, 1925; Jesus Came Preaching, 2d edit., 1970; Prayer, 1942; Christ and Men's Dilemma, 1946; So We Believe, So We Pray, 1951; Faith and Education, 1952; Sermons Preached in a University Church, 1959; Biblical Thought and the Secular University, 1960; Christ and History, 1963; God, Pain and Evil, 1966; The Beautitudes, 1968; The Power of Prayer Today 1970. Gen. editor: The Interpreter's Bible, 12 vols., 1952. Editor: The Interpreter's Dictionary (4 vols.), 1959. Home: 5967 Post Rd Nashville TN 37205 ☆

BUTTRICK, JOHN ARTHUR, educator, economist; b. Rutland, Vt., Sept. 12, 1919; s. George Arthur and Agnes (Gardner) B.; B.S., Haverford Coll., 1941; M.A., Yale, 1947, Ph.D., 1950; m. Ann Tatlow, July 24, 1958; children—Peter M., Hilary J., Michael S. Asst. prof. econs. Northwestern U., 1949-53; faculty U. Minn., Mpls., 1953—, prof. econs., 1958—, chmn. dept., 1960-63, dir. grad. studies, 1967-69. Vis. prof. U. Cal. at Berkeley, 1957- 59, U. Tokyo, 1963-64, U. de los Andes, Colombia, 1964-65, York U. (Can.) , 1970-71; summer vis. prof. Vanderbilt U., Stanford, Harvard, Singapore; vis. lectr. Govt. Pakistan, 1961. Mem. Mpls. Com. for Responsible Govt., Minn. Council Econ. Edn. Fellow Fund for Advancement Edn., 1952-53; Ford Found. fellow, 1959-60; Fulbright fellow, Japan, Singapore, 1963-64. Mem. Am. Econ. Assn., Econometric Soc., Am. Civil Liberties Union, Nat. Com. for Sane Nuclear Policy, Congress Racial Equality, Minn. Resist (chmn.). Co- author: Economic Development, 1954, Spanish edit., 1958; Theories of Economic Growth, 1960, Spanish edit., 1964; Consumer, Producer and Social Choice, 1968. Office: Dept Econs U Minn Minneapolis MN 55414

BUTTRILL, SIDNEY EUGENE, pub. co. exec.; b. Krum, Tex., Mar. 2, 1920; s. William John Burl and Stella (Sanderford) B.; B.S., N. Tex. State U., 1940; B.S. in Mech. Engring., U. Tex., 1946-48; m. Elinor Frances Brous, June 15, 1941; children—Sidney Eugene, Joe Brous, John Charles, Betsy Ruth. With Houston Post Co., 1950-61, v.p., 1958-61, also dir.; v.p. N.Y. Herald Tribune, Inc., 1961-63; dir. prodn. Gannett Co., Inc. Rochester N.Y., 1963—, asst. sec., 1967—; v.p., dir. Empire Newspaper Supply Corp., 1970—; dir. Charlevoix Paper Co., Ltd., Served to lt. USNR, 1943-46. Registered profl. engr., Tex. Mem. Am. Soc. M.E. Methodist: Home: 103 Danbury Circle S Rochester NY 14618 Office: 55 Exchange St Rochester NY 14614

BUTTS, HUGH FLORENZ, psychiatrist; b. N.Y.C., Dec. 2, 1926; s. Lucius C. and Edith (Higgins) B; B.S., City Coll. N.Y., 1949; M.D., Meharry Med. Coll., 1953; ceritifate psychoanalytic medicine, Columbia Psychoanalytic Clinic Tng. and Research, 1962; m. June Dobbs, June 11, 1953 (div. Jan. 1971); children-Lucia Irene, Florence Dobbs, Eric Hugh. Intern Morisania City Hosp., Bronx, N.Y., 1953, 55; resident Bronx VA Hosp., 1956-58; psychiatric cons. Neuropsychiatric Center N.Y., 1957, Jewish Bd. Guardians, N.Y.C., 1962; pvt. psychiatric practice, N.Y.C., 1959—, psychoanalytic practice, 1962—; staff psychiatrist Hillcrest Center Children, Bedford Hills, N.Y., 1959-61; clin. dir. Wiltwyck Sch. Boys, N.Y.C., 1961-63; asst. attending psychiatrist Gracie Sq. Hosp., N.Y.C., 1961—, Montefiore Hosp., Bronx, N.Y., 1961-65, Mt. Morris Park Hosp., N.Y.C., 1961-65, Beth Israeel Hosp., N.Y.C., 1962-63, Vanderbilt Clinic of Presbyn. Hosp., N.Y.C., 1963-65, St. Luke's Hosp., N.Y.C., 1968—; asst. attending psychiatrist adolescent service N.Y. Psychiat. Inst., 1962—, asso. attending, 1969; chief in-patient psychiat. service Harlem Hosp. Center, 1962-69, asso. dir. psychiatry, 1965-69, asst. vis. psychiatrist, 1962-69; cons. N.Y. State Dept. Vocational Rehab., 1963—; mem. faculty Coll. Coll. Phys. and Surg., 1962—, asso. psychiatry, 1966- 69, asst. clin. prof. psychiatry, 1969—. Served with USAAF, 1945. Diplomate Am. Bd. Psychiatry and Neurology. Mem. Am., Nat. med. assns., N.Y. County Med. Assn., Am. Psychiat. Assn., Am. Psychoanalytic Assn., Assn. Psychoanalytic Medicine (council 1968—, chmn. com. social issues and community psychiatry 1969—), Am. Orthopsychiat. Assn. (bd. dirs. 1970-73), Alumni Assn. Psychoanalytic Clinic for Tng. and Research (pres. 1968-70). Author numerous articles in field. Home: 63 W 92d St New York NY 10025 Office: 16 E 79th St New York NY 10021

BUTTS, R. FREEMAN, educator; b. Springfield, Ill., May 14, 1910; s. R.F. and Cornelia Ann (Paddock) B.; A.B., U. Wis., 1931, A.M., 1932, Ph.D., 1935; m. Florence Randolph, May 30, 1936; children—Stephen, Anne (Mrs. Griffiths). Faculty, Tchrs. Coll. Columbia, 1938—, exec. officer div. founds. of edn., 1946-56, dir. div., 1956-60, prof. edn., 1947—, head dept. social and philos. found., 1948-58, William F. Russell prof., found. of edn., 1958—, dir. internat. studies, 1961-64, asso. dean for internat. studies, 1964—, dir. Inst. Internat. Studies, 1965—. Vis. prof. edn. U. Wis., 1949; cons. Dict. Am. Biography, Am. Council Learned Socs., U.S. Dept. Health, Edn.

and Welfare, 1967—; sr. specialist in residence East-West Center, U. Hawaii, 1965. Chief, Tchrs. Coll. Ednl. Mission to India, 1959; mem. advanced placement com. Coll. Entrance Exam. Bd., 1963-64; exec. com. bd. govs. Center Research and Edn. in Am. Liberties; vis. com. UN Internat. Sch., 1966-68. Fulbright Research scholar on Edn. in Australia, 1954; Carnegie Travel grantees Africa and Asia, 1961-62; 6th John Dewey Soc. lectr., 1963. Mem. Am. Hist. Assn., Am. Ednl. Research Assn., Am. Ednl. Services Assn. (pres. 1968-69), Am. Assn. U. Profs., N.E.A. (chmn. com. internat. relations 1965-67). Assn. for Higher Edn., John Dewey Soc., Philos. Edn. Soc., Nat. Soc. Coll. Tchrs. Edn. (pres. 1953), Nat. Soc. for Study Edn., History Edn. Soc. (dir.), Internat. Council Edn. Teaching, African Studies Assn., Soc. Internat. Devel., Am. Acad. Polit. and Social Sci., Am. Soc. for Pub. Adminstrn., Comparative and Internat. Edn. Soc. (pres. 1964-65), Kappa Delta Pi (laureate chpt.). Author: The College Charts Its Course, 1939; A Cultural History of Education, 1947; The American Tradition in Religion and Education, 1950; co-author: History of Education in American Culture, 1953; Assumptions Underlying Australian Education, 1955; A Cultural History of Western Education, 1955; American Education in International Development, 1963. Chmn. editorial bd. World Year Book of Edn. Home: 1 Conifer Lane Ho-Ho-Kus NJ 07423 also 89 West Wharf Rd Madison CT

BUTTS, WILLIAM ELLENBERGER, mfg. exec.; b. Buffalo, Mar. 31, 1906; s. Charles G. and Augusta (Ellenberger) B.; student mech. engring. Cornell U., 1923-26; m. Marie Hagener, May 5, 1933; children—William W., Judith L. Plant mgr. Gen. Metals Corp., subsidiary Transamerica Corp., San Francisco, 1928-36, v.p., 1936-50, pres., 1950-64, chmn., 1964—, v.p. parent co., 1964- -; chmn. bd. dirs. DeLaval Turbine Inc., 1964—. Mem. Diesel Engine Mfrs. Assn. (dir.), Nat. Security Ind. Assn., Am. Ordnance Assn. Clubs: Family (San Francisco); California (Los Angeles). Home: 246 Seaview Av Piedmont CA 94611 Office: Transamerica Bldg 701 Montgomery St San Francisco CA 94111

BUTZ, EARL LAUER, univ. dean; b. Albion, Ind., July 3, 1909; s. Herman Lee and Ada Tillie (Lower) B.; B.S.A., Purdue, 1932, Ph.D., 1937; postgrad. U. Chgo., summer 1936; m. Mary Emma Powell, Dec. 22, 1937; children—William Powell, Thomas Earl. Farmer, Noble County, Ind., 1933; grad. research asst. agrl. econs. Purdue U., Lafayette, Ind., 1934-35, instr. agrl. econs., 1937-39, asst. prof., 1939-43, asso. prof., 1943-46, prof., head agrl. econs. dept., 1946-54, dean agr., 1957-67, dean continuing edn., v.p. Research Found., 1968—. Research economist Fed. Land Bank, Louisville, 1935-36, Brookings Inst., 1944, 51; research staff Nat. Bur. Econ. Research, 1944-45, lectr. Sch. Banking, U. Wis., 1946-65, Rutgers U., 1950-58; asst. sec. Dept. Agr., 1954-57, dir. CCC. Dir. Standard Life Ins. Co. Ind., Stokely-Van Camp Co., Indpls., Ralston Purina Co., St. Louis, Internat. Minerals & Chem. Corp., Chgo. Chmn. U.S. delegation FAO, Rome, 1955, 57; mem. White House Task Force Fgn. Econ. Devel., 1969-70. Bd. dirs. Farm Found., Chgo., 1960-70, Found. Am. Agr., Washington; trustee Nutrition Found., N.Y.C. Mem. Am. Farm Econ. Assn. (v.p. 1948, sec. treas. 1953-54), Am. Soc. Farm Mgrs. and Rural Appraisers, Ind. Acad. Social Sci. (v.p. 1948), Canadian Am. Com., Internat. Conf. Agrl. Economists, Sigma Xi, Alpha Gamma Rho (nat. pres. 1948-50), Sigma Delta Chi, Tau Kappa Alpha, Alpha Zeta, Scabbard and Blade, Skull and Crescent. Kiwanian. Author: The Production Credit System for Farmers, 1944; various bulls. Home: 312 Jefferson Dr West Lafayette IN 47906 Office: Purdue University Lafayette IN 47907

BUTZ, OTTO WILLIAM, educator; b. Floesti, Roumania, May 2, 1923; s. Otto E. and Charlotte (Engelmann) B.; B.A., Victoria Coll., U. Toronto, 1947; Ph.D., Princeton, 1953; m. Velia DeAngelis, Sept. 13, 1961. Came to U.S., 1949, naturalized, 1959. Asst. prof. polit. sci. Swarthmore Coll., 1954-55; asst. prof. politics Princeton U., 1955-60; asso. editor Random House, N.Y.C., 1960-61; prof. social sci. San Francisco State Coll., 1961-67; academic v.p. Sacramento State Coll., 1967-69, acting pres., 1969-70; pres. Golden Gate Coll., 1970—. Recipient Cal. State Colls. Outstanding Tchr. award, 1966. Mem. Am. Polit. Sci. Assn. Author: German Political Theory, 1955; The Unsilent Generation, 1958; Of Man and Politics, 1960; To Make a Difference—A Student Look at America, 1967. Home: Wolfback Ridge Sausalito CA 94965 Office: 536 Mission St San Francisco CA 94105

BUTZ, WILLIAM BRINTON, banker; b. Alburtis, Pa., Mar. 6, 1902; s. William Brinton and Mary Alice (Ettinger) B.; B.A., Yale, 1926, LL.B., 1928. Admitted to Pa. bar, 1929; Fed. Cts.; dir. Lehigh Valley Trust Co., 1946-68, gen. counsel, 1946-70, pres., 1963-68; vice-chmn. bd. dirs. Indsl. Valley Bank & Trust Co., Allentown, Pa., 1968—; sr. atty. Bd. Econ. Warfare, 1940-42; U.S. asst. to atty. gen., 1943-46; mem. Com. on World Trade, 1946; mem. State Dept. Mission, Tokyo, 1946. Pres. Allentown Art Mus.; trustee N.Y. Infirmary, Trexler Found. Mem. Am., Pa., Lehigh County bar assns., Delta Theta Phi. Clubs: Livingston, Lehigh Valley, Lehigh Country (Allentown), Saucon Valley Country (Bethlehem, Pa.), Seaview Country (Absecon, N.J.), Metropolitan Opera, Metropolitan (both N.Y.C.). Home: 1411 Hamilton St Allentown PA 18102 Office: 634 Hamilton St Allentown PA 18101

BUTZER, KARL WILHELM, educator; b. Mülheim-Ruhr, Germany, Aug. 19, 1934; s. Paul A. and Wilhelmine (Hansen) B.; B.Sc. honours Math., McGill U., 1954, M.Sc., 1955; D.Sc., U. Bonn (Germany), 1957; m. Elisabeth Schlösser, May 12, 1959. Asst. prof., then asso. prof. geography U. Wis., 1959-66; prof. anthropology and geography U. Chgo., 1966—. Author: Environment and Archeology, 1964; revised, 1971; Desert and River in Nubia, 1968; History of an Ethiopian Delta, 1971. Home: Flossmoor IL 60422 Office: Univ Chicago Chicago IL 60637

BUTZNER, JOHN DECKER, Jr., circuit judge; b. Scranton, Pa., Oct. 2, 1917; s. John Decker and Bess Mary (Robison) B.; B.A., U. Scranton, 1939; LL.B., U. Va., 1941; m. Viola Eleanor Peterson, May 25, 1946; 1 son, John Decker III. Admitted to Va. bar, 1941; practice in Fredericksburg, 1941-58; judge 15th and 39th Jud. Circuit of Va., 1958-62; U.S. judge Eastern Dist. Va., 1962-67; U.S. circuit judge 4th circuit Ct. Appeals, Richmond, Va., 1967—. Served with USAAF, 1942-45. Home: 5507 Dorchester Rd Richmond VA 23225 Office: P O Box 2188 Richmond VA 23217

BUXTON, CHARLES INGRAHAM II, ins. co. exec.; b. Owatonna, Minn., Dec. 17, 1924; s. John Anthony and Vera Helen (Moore) B.; student Carleton Coll., 1942- 43; B.S. with distinction, U.S. Naval Acad., 1946; postgrad. Wharton Sch. Finance and Commerce U. Pa., 1949-50; m. Norma Pat Lee, Oct. 21, 1950; children—Cynthia Lee, John Anthony II, Sarah, Patricia, Elizabeth. In home office dept. Federated Mut. Implement & Hardware Ins. Co., 1950- 51, office, personnel mgr. Central div., 1953-55, mgr. Minn. div., 1956, v.p., asst. to pres., 1957, pres., dir., 1957—; pres., dir. Federated Life Ins. Co., 1958—, chmn. bd., 1966—; dir. Am. Mut. Ins. Alliance, Security Bank & Trust Co., Owatonna; mem. bd. govs. Mut. Loss Research Bur.; dir., v.p. Minn. Ins. Information Service. Trustee, sec. bd. trustees Asso. Chs. Owatonna. Served as ensign USNR, 1946-49, to lt. 1951-53. Mem. Am. Legion. Mason, Rotarian. Club: Owatonna Country. Home: 1143 Austin Rd Owatonna MN 55060 Office: Federated Mut Implement & Hardware Ins Co 129 E Broadway Owatonna MN 55060

BUXTON, CHARLES ROBERTS, newspaper editor, pub.; b. Corvallis, Ore., Mar. 20, 1913; s. Harry E. and Lucille (Roberts) B.; B.A., Ore. State U., 1935; m. Janet Millard, Sept. 12, 1937; children—Cynda (Mrs. Philip C. Wilcox, Jr.), Charles Roberts, Richard M., Janet Anne. Reporter, The Oregonian, Portland, Ore., 1935-37, sports news editor, 1937, pix editor, 1938, asst. news editor, 1939-40, night city editor, 1946; asst. bus. mgr. Denver Post, 1946-50, advt. dir., 1950-51, bus. mgr., 1951-65, gen. mgr., 1965-70, v.p., 1970, editor, pub., 1971—; dir. Denver Post, Inc., Sunday Met. Newspaper Group. Bd. dirs. Salvation Army, Frederick G. Bonfils Found., Helen G. Bonfils Found.; trustee Denver Post Employees Stock Trust. Served from 1st lt. to lt. col., inf., AUS, 1940-45. Decorated Silver Star medal with oak leaf cluster, Bronze Star medal. Mem. Am. Newspaper Pubs. Assn., Grav. Tech. Assn. (past dir.), Grav. Research Inst. (past dir.), Inst. Newspaper Operation (past dir.), Denver Press Club, Denver C. of C. (dir.), Am. Legion, V.F.W., Sigma Delta Chi, Phi Kappa Phi. Presbyn. (past trustee). Kiwanian. Clubs: Cherry Hills Country (Englewood, Colo.); Denver, Denver Athletic, Denver Country. Home: 5215 Sky Trail Littleton CO 80123 Office: 650 15th St Denver CO 80202

BUXTON, CHESTER L., coll. pres.; b. Salineville, O., July 22, 1903; s. James and Eleanor (Madison) B.; student Mt. Union Coll., 1922-23, Western Res. U., 1936-37; B.S., Case Inst. Tech. 1930, M.S., 1933; D.Sc. (hon.), Clarkson Coll., 1954; m. Mildred D. Zimmer, June 27, 1927; 1 son, Lorn Alan. With Nat. Carbon Co., 1925-27; rural sch. tchr., Ohio, 1923- 25; tchr., Cleve., 1930-31, 36; instr. Case Inst. Tech., 1931- 32; instr. math. Clarkson Coll., Potsdam, N.Y., 1937-42, asst. prof., 1942-43, asso. prof. physics, 1943-46, prof. of physics, 1946, dir. Clarkson, 1946-48; pres. Paul Smith's (N.Y.) Coll., 1948—. Pres., Paul Smith's Electric Light & Power Co., 1963-66; adv. bd. Marine Midland Trust. Mem. Am. Phys. Soc., Math. Assn. Am., Phi Kappa Tau. Methodist. Mason, Rotarian, Elk. Club: Lake Placid. Address: Paul Smith's Coll Paul Smiths NY 12970

BUXTON, CLAUDE ELMO, educator; b. Cromwell, Ia., Nov. 15, 1912; s. Montrose and Caroline Mae (Goldner) B.; A.B., Neb. Wesleyan U., 1933; A.M. U. Ore., 1935; Ph.D., U. Ia., 1937; m. Virginia Carr, Sept. 12, 1938; children—Katherine Cox, Elizabeth Bennett, James Laurence, Andrew Prior. Research asso. Swarthmore Coll., 1938-39; instr. Northwestern U., 1939- 42, asso. prof., 1946-49; instr. U. Ia., 1937-38, asst. prof., 1942- 46; prof. psychology Yale, 1949—, chmn. dept., 1951-66, dir. div. social scis., 1961-63. Chmn., Conn. Bd. Examiners of Psychologists, 1957-59. Mem. Am. Psychol. Assn. (pres. div. for teaching psychology 1950-51), Soc. Exptl. Psychologists, Psychonomic Soc., Am. Assn. U. Profs., Mid-western (sec.-treas. 1946-49, pres. 1949-50), Eastern psychol. assns., Conn. Psychol. Soc. (pres. 1954-55), Sigma Xi. Home: 21 Cooper Rd North Haven CT 06473 Office: Inst Human Relations 333 Cedar St New Haven CT 06510

BUZARD, RALPH MURRAY, mfg. exec.; b. Greenwich, O., Aug. 17, 1904; s. Charles and Martha (Murray) B.; B.A., Ashland Coll., 1927; m. Marian McHose, July 30, 1929. With Internat. Harvester Co., 1922—, regional mgr. Western region, 1943- 46, asst. sales mgr. Motor Truck div., 1946-54, sales mgr., 1954-57, gen. mgr., v.p., 1957, now exec. v.p., dir.; ret. Home: 66 Balmoral Northfield IL 60093 Office: 180 N Michigan Av Chicago IL 60601

BUZBEE, JOHN PAUL, lawyer; b. Allen, Okla., Sept. 17, 1936; s. Glenwood and June (Coburn) B.; B.A., Okla. Bapt. U., 1959; LL.B., U. Okla., 1960; m. Marilyn Dorff, Nov. 25, 1959; children—John Paul, Nancy Elizabeth. Admitted to Okla. bar, 1960, since practiced in Anadarko; asst. county atty. Caddo County, 1960-61; pvt. practice, 1960-61; atty. solicitors office U.S. Dept. Interior, 1961-63; partner Wilhite & Buzbee, 1963-71; municipal judge, Anadarko, 1965-66; asst. dist. atty., Anadarko, 1966-70. Sec.-treas., dir. Washita Devel. Co.; dir. Indian City U.S.A., A Corp., Chmn. Caddo County Red Cross drive, 1961; mem. Anadarko Municipal Airport Bd., 1967- 71. Caddo County chmn. Jed Johnson Congl. Campaign, 1964-66. Trustee Anadarko Municipal Hosp. Bd., Anadarko Campfire Council. Recipient Outstanding Service award Okla. Bar Assn., 1966; named Outstanding Young Man, Anadarko Jr. C. of C., 1967. Mem. Am., Okla., Caddo County (v.p.) bar assns., Anadarko C. of C. (dir.). Presbyn. (elder). Rotarian, Odd Fellow. Clubs: Caddo County U. Okla. Alumni (pres.), Caddo Golf and Country (past dir.). Home: 705 W Colorado St Anadarko OK 73005 Office: 111 NW 2d St Anadarko OK 73005

BUZICK, WILLIAM ALONSON, Jr., diversified co. exec.; b. Sylvan Grove, Kan., Nov. 4, 1920; s. William Alonson and Mildred (Hickman) B.; A.B., Kan. U., 1942; LL.B., Washburn U., 1950; m. Mary Lee Emerson, Nov. 18, 1954; children—William Alonson III, Bonnie Lee. Vice pres., dir. Sylvan State Bank, Sylvan Grove, 1946-48; 1st sec. Alcoholic Beverage Bd. Kan., 1948-50; admitted to Kan. bar, 1950; pres. Shasta Water Co., San Francisco, 1950-60; pres. Shasta div. Consol. Foods Corp., Chgo., 1960- 66; exec. v.p. Consol. Foods Corp., 1966-68, pres., 1968-69, chmn. bd., chief exec. officer, 1969—, also dir., mem. exec. com., mem. finance com.; dir. Am. Nat. Bank. Young Republican nat. committeeman for Kan., 1949. Bd. dirs. A.R.C. Served to lt. U.S. Navy, 1942-46. Mem. Am., Kan. bar assns. Mem. Washburn Law Rev. Bd., 1949. Home: 50 Woodley Rd Winnetka IL 60093 Office: 135 S La Salle Chicago IL 60603

BUZZELL, ROBERT DOW, educator; b. Lincoln, Neb., Apr. 18, 1933; s. Dow Alan and Grace (Blomquist) B.; A.B., George Washington U., 1953; M.S., U. Ill., 1954; Ph.D., Ohio State U., 1957; m. Edith F. Moser, June 5, 1953; children—Susan, Robert Dow, Barbara, William. Faculty, Ohio State U., 1957-61; faculty Harvard Grad. Sch., Bus. Adminstrn., 1961—, prof., 1967—. Vis. prof. Inst. European d'Adminstrn. des Affaires. 1967; exec. dir. Marketing Sci. Inst., 1968—; dir. Mgmt. Horizons, Inc.; cons. in field, 1960—. Mem. Wellesley (Mass.) Republican Town Com. Mem. Am. Marketing Assn., Phi Beta Kappa. Conglist. Author or co-author: Wholesaling, 1959; Mathematical Models and Marketing Management, 1964; Marketing: An Introductory Analysis, 1964, rev., 1972; Marketing Research, 1969. Home: 15 Swarthmore Rd Wellesley MA 02181 Office: Harvard Bus Sch Boston MA 02163

BYARS, WALTER RYLAND, Jr., lawyer; b. Birmingham, Ala., Oct. 5, 1928; s. Walter Ryland and Essie (Hooper) B.; B.S., U. Ala., 1948, LL.B., 1952, J.D., 1969; m. Mildred Lucile Rhodes, Dec. 22, 1950; children—Debra Leigh, Walter Ryland III, Rebecca Lynn, John Baxter. Admitted to Ala. bar, 1952, also U.S. Supreme Ct., U.S. Circuit Ct. of Appeals, 5th Circuit, U.S. Dist. Cts. No., Middle and So. dists. Ala.; practiced in Troy, 1953-57, Birmingham, 1959- 68, Montgomery, 1968—; pvt. practice, 1953-57; atty. legal dept. So. Bell. Tel. & Tel. Co., Atlanta, 1957-59, Ala. atty.; Birmingham, 1959- 60, gen. atty., Birmingham, 1960-68; partner Steiner, Crum & Baker, 1968- -. Mgmt. rep. Ala. Unemployment Bd. Appeals, 1962-63; vice chmn. Ala. chpt. Americans for Constl. Action, 1966—, Montgomery Dist. chmn., 1968- -. Republican committeeman Montgomery County, 1970. Served to lt. (j.g.) USNR, 1952-53. Fellow Internat. Soc. Barristers; mem. Am. (past mem. exec. council, com. chmn.), Ala. (past pres. Young Lawyers, sect. chmn., past com. chmn.), Pike County (past pres.), Birmingham (past com. chmn.), Montgomery County (past com. chmn.) bar assns., Fed. Jud. Conf., Sigma Chi, Phi Alpha Delta. Methodist. Mason (Shriner). Bd. editors: Ala. Law Review, 1951-52. Home: 1616 S Hull St Montgomery AL 36104 Office: First Nat Bank Bldg P O Box 668 Montgomery AL 36101

BYCK, MARY HELEN, mem. Democratic Nat. Com., b. Louisville, June 28, 1907; d. Cyrus Lincoln and Alice Belle (Goldsmith) Adler; A.B. Vassar Coll., 1928; L.H.D., Catherine Spalding Coll., Louisville, 1961; m. Dann C. Byck, June 27, 1931 (dec. 1960); children—Lucy (Mrs. Jack Shapero), Betty (Mrs. Stephen N. Goodman), Dann C. Pres., Bych Bros. & Co., 1942-45, 60- 64, chmn. bd., chief exec. officer, 1964—; pres., chmn. operating com. Consol. Foods Corp. Mem. Ky. Democratic Central Com., 1964—; Dem. mem. Conv. Center Bd., 1962—; mem. Dem. Nat. Com. for Ky., 1964—; chmn. primary and gubernatorial race Jefferson County, spring and fall, 1963, senate and presdl. race, 1964, woman's chmn. campaigns spring and fall, 1965; mem. Ky. Woman's Adv. Com., gubernatorial race, 1963; mem. adv. com. City/County Dem. Com., 1962—. Mem. exec. com. Louisville Central Area, 1962—, Gov. Ky. Commn. Human Rights, 1959—; Coordinating Com. Jefferson County and Louisville Schs., 1944—; pres. Louisville Orch., 1949-56, life mem., 1956—; bd. overseers U. Louisville, 1960—; bd. counselors Catherine Spalding Coll., 1961—; exec. bd. com. Louisville Fund, 1956—; disbursing com. Louisville Found., 1959—. Recipient Citizen Laureate award Younger Woman's Club Louisville, 1963; Blanche C. Ottenbeimer award Jewish Community Center, 1964. Home: 332 Penruth Av Louisville KY 40207 Office: 532 S 4th St Louisville KY 40202

BYDALEK, THOMAS JOSEPH, educator; b. Grand Rapids, Mich., Apr. 22, 1935; s. Henry and Anna (Fron) B.; B.S., Aquinas Coll., 1957; Ph.D. in Analytical Chemistry, Purdue U., 1961; m. Marilyn Frances Schubert, Aug. 24, 1957; children—Thomas Michael, Ann Marie, Elizabeth Ann. Instr., U. Wis., Madison, 1961, asst. prof., 1962-65; asst. prof. U. Minn., Duluth, 1965-66, asso. prof., 1966-69, prof. chemistry, 1969—. Research grantee NSF, 1963-65, 67—. Mem. Am. Chem. Soc., Sigma Xi. Contbr. articles to profl. jours.

BYE, RICHARD EARLE, publisher; b. Worcester, Mass., Mar. 12, 1920; s. Terschak F. and Odele B. (Johnson) B.; B.S cum laude, Bowdoin Coll., 1942; m. Delia F. Grubb, Feb. 15, 1947; children—Juliana, Jonathan, Matthew, Amelia. With Ronald Press Co., N.Y.C., Alonzo J. Harriman, arch.-engr.; sales rep. Pub.'s Weekly, 1947-50, advt. mgr., 1950—, dir., 1955—, v.p., 1963—; v.p., pub. R.R. Bowker Co., N.Y.C., 1963-69; pres. LJ Cards, Inc., 1965-68; sr. v.p., pub. R.R. Bowker Co. (Xerox), 1969—. Commnr. shade trees Clarkstown, N.Y.; pres. Friends of New City (N.Y.) Library. Democratic committeeman Rockland County, N.Y. Served to lt. USNR, 1942-46; PTO. Mem. Am. Bach Soc. (pres. 1963), Pubs. Adclub (past pres.). Theta Delta Chi. Club: Players (N.Y.C.). Home: 220 Piermont Av South Nyack NY 10960 Office: 1180 Av of Americas New York City NY 10036

BYERLY, PERRY, educator, seismologist; b. Clarinda, Ia., May 28, 1897; B.A., M.A., Ph.D., U. Cal., 1920-21, postgrad., 1921-24; LL.D., U. Cal. at Berkeley, 1966; children— Perry Edward, David Donald; m. 2d, Lillian Lizee, 1941. Instr. physics U. Nev., 1924-25; successively instr., asst. prof., asso. prof., prof. seismology U. Cal., 1925-64, chmn. dept. geol. scis., 1949-54, now dir. emeritus seismographic stas., prof. emeritus. Guggenheim fellow, 1929, 52; Smith-Mundt Act lectr. Nat. U. Mexico, 1954; Condon lectr. U. Ore.; Sr. Fulbright scholar U. Cambridge (Eng.), 1960-61. Fellow Royal Astron. Soc., Geol. Soc. Am., Am. Geophys. Union, Internat. Assn. Seismology and Physics of Interior of Earth (pres. 1960-63); mem. Am. Acad. Arts and Scis., NRC, Wash., Nat. (chmn. sect. geophysics 1957-60, chmn. panel seismology and gravity Internat. Geophys. Year 1956-58) acads. scis., Earthquake Engring. Research Inst., Seismol. Soc. Am. (hon.). Author: Seismology, 1942. Contbr. articles profl. jours. Home: 5340 Broadway Terrace Oakland CA 94618 Office: Earth Scis Bldg U Cal Berkeley CA 94720

BYERLY, RUSSELL WAYNE, wholesale grocer; b. Velva, N.D., July 30, 1901; s. William Edward and Edna (Bowning) B.; student U. Minn., 1916-19; m. Mildred Boyd, 1925; 1 son, Russell William; m. 2d, Margaret Mae Thompson, July 18, 1935; 1 son, Donald Duane. Partner, Ford Agy., Velva, to 1929; farm loan dept. Bank of N.D., Bismarck, 1929-32; with Super Value Stores, Inc. (formerly Winston & Newell), 1932—, bookkeeper, mgr., Aberdeen, S.D., Minot, N.D., Des Moines, exec. v.p., Mpls., 1932-58, pres., 1958-64, chief exec., 1960-64, chmn. bd., 1964—,also dir.; past v.p., dir. Dahl Food Enterprises, Dahl's Food Mart, Fluer Foods, Waveland Food Center (all Des Moines); dir. S.M. Flickenger Co., Buffalo; v.p., dir. Byerly Devel. Corp., Byerly Foods Golden Valley, Byerly Foods St. Paul, Byerly Liquors (all mpls.). Mason (Shriner), Odd Fellow. Clubs: University, Minneapolis. Home: Longboat Key Towers 601 Longboat Club Rd Sarasota FL 33577 Office: 5725 Duluth St Minneapolis MN 55422

BYERLY, THEODORE CARROLL, govt. ofcl.; b. Melbourne, Ia., May 3, 1902; s. William Henry and Lulu May (Crook) B.; A.B., U. Ia., 1923, M.S., 1925, Ph.D., 1926; m. Helen Frances Freeman, May 31, 1929 (dec.); children—Carroll (Mrs. N. Holcomb), David, Nora (Mrs. T.D. Bolita); m. 2d, Imogene J. McCarthy, Aug. 7, 1967. Instr. zoology U. Mich., 1926-28, Hunter Coll., 1928-29, Peabody Coll., summers 1927- 28; physiologist div. animal husbandry Bur. Animal Industry, Dept. Agr., 1929—, sr. poultry husbandman charge poultry husbandry investigation, 1941—, chief animal husbandry div., 1947—, asst. dir. livestock research Agrl. Research Service, 1955-57, dep. adminstr., 1957-62, adminstr. coop. state exptl. sta. service, 1962-63, adminstr. Coop. State Research Service, 1963-69, now asst. dir. sci. and edn. Dept. Agr.; prof. Md. U., 1937-41. Chmn. div. biology and agr. NCR, 1963-65; mem. U.S. Nat. Commn. for UNESCO, 1954-60; chmn. U.S. delegation Internat. Conf. Rational Use Biosphere, 1968. Fellow A.A.A.S., Poultry Sci. Assn. (Borden award 1943, pres. 1960-61), Am. Soc. Animal Sci.; mem. Am. Inst. Biol. Scis., Am. Soc. Zoologists, Soc. Exptl. Biology and Medicine, Soc. Growth and Devel., Acad. Medicine D.C. Club: Cosmos (Washington). Home: 6-J Ridge Rd Greenbelt MD Office: U S Dept Agr Washington DC 20250

BYERRUM, RICHARD UGLOW, coll. dean; b. Aurora, Ill., Sept. 22, 1920; s. Earl Edward and Florence (Uglow) B.; A.B., Wabash Coll., 1942, D.Sc. (hon.), 1967; Ph.D., U. Ill., 1947; m. Claire Somers, Apr. 3, 1945; children—Elizabeth, Robert, Mary, Carey. Teaching asst. U. Ill., 1942-44; research asso. U.S. Chem. Corps, toxicity dept. U. Chgo., 1944-47; faculty Mich. State U., East Lansing, 1947—, prof. biochemistry, 1957—, acting dir. Inst. Biology and Medicine, 1961-62, dean Coll. Natural Sci., 1962- -. Mem. Project Hope, 1961—. Trustee Mich. Health Council, 1961—, pres., 1966. Travel grantee Internat. Congress Biochemistry, Vienna 1958, Montreal, 1959. Mem. Am. Chem. Soc. (lectr. vis. scientist program, awards com., visitor for com. profl. tng.), N. Central Assn. Colls. and Secondary Schs., A.A.A.S., Am. Soc. Plant Physiologists, Am. Soc. Biol. Chemists, Soc. Exptl. Biology and Medicine, Mich. Acad. Arts, Sci. and Letters, Phi Beta Kappa (pres. local chpt. 1962), Sigma Xi (awards com., Jr. Research award Mich. State U. chpt. 1958), Phi Kappa Phi (pres. 1968-69), Phi Lambda Upsilon, Alpha Chi Sigma, Beta Theta Phi. Author: (with others) Experimental Biochemistry, 1956. Editorial bd. Phytochemistry, 1961—. Contbr. numerous articles to profl. jours. Patentee cancer tumor inhibiting material. Home: 602 Wildwood Dr East Lansing MI 48823

BYERS, BUCKLEY MORRIS, business exec.; b. Pitts., Jan. 7, 1917; s. John Frederic and Caroline Mitchell (Morris) B.; student St. Paul's Sch., Concord, N.H., 1932-36; A.B., Yale, 1940; m. Rosamond Farrell Murray, Nov. 19, 1940; children—Buckley Morris, Joseph Murray, Christopher Farrell. Salesman, A. M. Byers Co., Pitts., 1940-42, asst. mgr., Washington, 1942, N.Y.C., 1945-51, mgr. export dept., 1946-51, asst. mgr. steel sales, 1951-53, gen. mgr. wrought iron sales, 1953-54, v.p. charge sales, 1954-57, pres., 1957-62, dir., 1948-70; v.p., spl. asst. to pres. Blaw-Knox Co., Pitts., 1962-64; pres., dir. Secretarial Services, Washington, 1965—; also bus. cons. Trustee Sewickley Valley Hosp., Sewickley, Pa. Served from ensign to lt., USN Intelligence, 1942-45, overseas 4 major invasions in ETO, PTO. Recipient Presl. citation and Individual commendation. Mem. Nat. Steeplechase and Hunt Assn. Clubs: Washington, F Street, Capitol Hill, Carlton, Internat., Metropolitan (Washington); Rolling Rock, Duquesne, Allegheny County (Pitts.). Fence, Book and Snake (Yale); Racquet and Tennis (N.Y.C.). Home: 5208 Upton Terrace Washington DC 20016 Office: 35 Wisconsin Circle N W Washington DC 20015

BYERS, CHARLES FRANCIS, educator, writer; b. Johnstown, Pa., Nov. 18, 1902; s. Charles Alexander and Texas Rachel (Blauch); student Marine Biol. Lab., Woods Hole, Mass., 1922; A.B., U. Mich., 1925, M.S., 1926, Ph.D., 1929; postgrad. Cornell U., 1926-27; m. Jeannette M. Radin, Dec. 19, 1935; 1 dau., Sarah Frances. Faculty, U. Fla. 1927-59, head prof. biol. scis., acting dean grad. sch. 1951-52, asst. dean Coll. Arts and Scis., 1953-59, asso. prof. biology U. Ida., 1959-60; chmn. div. natural scis., prof. biology Elmira (N.Y.) Coll., 1960, dean faculty, 1963-68, acting pres., 1964, curriculum cons., 1968-70; prof. biology Ripon (Wis.) Coll., 1968-69; vis. prof. biology Rollins Coll., Winter Park, Fla., 1969—. Fulbright lectr. India, 1957. Mem. A.A.A.S., Ida. Acad. Sci., Entomol. Soc. Am., Am. Assn. U. Profs., Fla. Acad. Sci., Sigma Xi, Gamma Alpha, Delta Sigma Phi, Phi Sigma. Elk. Author: (with Rogers, Hubbell) Man and the Biological World, 1953; numerous other books, papers on N.A. dragonflies, gen. edn. in relation to biology. Home: 937 Lakeview Dr Winter Park FL 32789

BYERS, DONALD N., lawyer; b. Montreal, Que., Can., Dec. 11, 1912; B.A., McGill U., 1933; L.L.L., U. Montreal, 1936. Admitted to Que. bar, 1936; now partner firm Byers, McDougall, Casgrain & Stewart, Montreal. Pres., Montreal Bd. of Trade, 1962-63. Mem. Canadian, Que. bar assns., Canadian (chmn. exec. council 1969- 70) Que. (pres. 1970-71) chambers commerce. Office: 800 Victoria Sq Montreal 115 Quebec Canada*

BYERS, EDNA HANLEY, ret. librarian; b. Trenton, O., Mar. 30, 1900; d. James H. and Ida. K. (Augspurger) Hanley; A.B., Bluffton Coll., 1923; A.B. in L.S., U. Mich., 1927, A.M. in L.S. (Carnegie fellow 1934), 1934; m. Noah E. Byers, Dec. 16, 1950 (dec. June 1962). Librarian Bluffton (O.) Coll., 1927-32, Agnes Scott Coll., 1932-69; cons. library bldg. plans Bennett Coll., 1937-38, Rockford Coll., 1939-40. Conn. Coll., 1940-41, Columbia Theol. Sem., 1951-52; reference asst. N.Y.C. Pub. Library, summers 1943, 44, 45; cons. book collection Tex. Wesleyan Coll., 1946-47; lectr. U. Mich. Library Sch., summers, 1952-55, 57. Chmn. Univ. Center Ga. Library Commn., 1955-58. Mem. A.L.A. (bldg. com. 1937-45), Assn. Coll. and Reference Libraries (bldg. com. 1955-59), Ga. Library Assn., Beta Phi Mu. Republican. Mennonite. Author: College and University Library Buildings, 1939. Compiler: Robert Frost at Agnes Scoll, a bibliography, 1963. Home: 226 E Hancock St Decatur GA 30030

BYERS, HORACE ROBERT, educator, meteorologist; b. Seattle, Mar. 12, 1906; s. Charles Hopkins and Harriet (Ensminger) B.; A.B., U. Cal., 1929; S.M., Mass. Inst. Tech., 1932, Sc.D., 1935; m. Frances Isabel Clark, Oct. 6, 1927; 1 dau., Henrietta Louise (Mrs. T.W. Billhorn). With Scripps Instn. Oceanography, 1932-33; instr. meteorology Transcontinental & Western Air Inc., Kansas City, Mo., 1932-34; meteorologist U.S. Weather Bur., Washington, 1935-40; asso. prof. meteorology U. Chgo., 1940-44, prof. 1944-65, chmn. dept. meterology, 1948-60; Distinguished prof. meteorology Tex. A. and M. U., College Station, 1965—, dean Coll. Geoscis., 1965-68, acad. v.p., 1968-71; dir. Thunderstorm Project, 1945-49; cons. U.S. Weather Bur., 1954-62, Dir. Gulf Univs. Research Corp., 1965-71, chmn. bd., 1967-69. Mem. subcom. meteorol. problems NACA 1948-59. Trustee U. Corp. for Atmospheric Research, 1960—, chmn. bd. trustees, 1962-64. Recipient Robert M. Losey award Inst. Aero. Scis., 1941; award of merit Chgo. Tech. Socs. Council 1959. Fellow Am. Geophys. Union, Am. Meteorol. Soc. (pres. 1952-53, Charles F. Brooks award 1960); mem. A.A.A.S., Am. Geog. Soc., Nat. Acad. Sci., Internat. Assn. Meteorology, Internat. Geophys. Union (pres. 1960-63), Sigma Xi. Clubs: Warwick (Houston); Briarcrest Country (Bryan); Cosmos (Washington). Author: Synoptic and Aeronautical Meteorology, 1937; General Meteorology, 2d edit., 1959; (with R.R. Braham, Jr.) The Thunderstorm, 1950; Elements of Cloud Physics, 1965. Contbr. articles to profl. jours. Home: 305 Brookside Dr Bryan TX 77801 Office: Tex A and M U College Station TX 77843

BYERS, JAMES, banker; b. San Francisco, Apr. 25, 1906; s. William J. and Grace (Kamp) B.; student San Jose State Coll., 1927; grad. Pacific N.W. Banking Sch., U. Wash., 1957; m. Ruth M. Sherburne, Nov. 17, 1940; 1 son, William S. Auditor, insp. Bank of Am., 1927-41; from asst. cashier to v.p. Nat. Bank Wash., Tacoma, 1941-57; pres. Bank of Ida., Boise, 1957-61, First Nat. Bank Ariz., 1961-65; exec. v.p. Western Bancorp., Los Angeles, 1965-67; chmn. exec. com., dir. Walker Bank & Trust Co., Salt Lake City, 1967—, Chmn., Tacoma Bank Mgmt. Commn., 1956; dir. Pacific Banking Sch., 1962-65. Chmn., Pierce County (Wash.) Tax Payers Assn., 1957, chmn. Wash. Gov.'s Com. Employment Handicapped, 1959; mem. Wash. Gov.'s Mil. Adv. Council, 1958-60, Phoenix Com. Handicapped, 1961-65, Ariz. Town Hall, 1963, hosp. budget com. United Crusade, Los Angeles, 1965-67. Served with USAAF, 1942-45. Mem. Nat. Arbitration Assn., Wash. (pres. 1957), Ida. (exec. council 1957-61), Ariz. (v.p., exec. council 1961-65), City bankers assn., Nat. Assn. Bank Auditors and Controllers (pres. Puget Sound chpt.), Tax Execs. Inst. (treas. Boise). Home: 2337 E 13th South Salt Lake City UT 84108 Office: 175 S Main St Salt Lake City UT 84110

BYERS, NINA, educator, physicist; b. Los Angeles, Jan. 19, 1930; d. Irving M. and Eva (Gertzoff) Byers; B.A., U. Cal. at Berkeley, 1950; M.S., U. Chgo., 1953, Ph.D., 1956. Research fellow U. Birmingham (Eng.), 1956-58; research asso., asst. prof. Stanford, 1958-61; mem. faculty U. Cal. at Los Angeles, 1961—, prof. physics, 1967—; vis. fellow Inst. Advanced Studies, Princeton, 1964-65; fellow Somerville Coll., faculty lectr. Oxford (Eng.) U., 1967-68; Janet Watson vis. fellow Somerville Coll., 1968-71. Guggenheim fellow, 1964-65. Research theory high energy physics and superconductivity. Office: Dept Physics U Cal Los Angeles CA 90024

BYERS-BROWN, WILLIAM, educator; b. Glasgow, Scotland, Nov. 6, 1929; s. William and Jean (Thomson) Byers-B.; B.S., U. Manchester (Eng.), 1950, M.S., 1953, D.Sc., 1967; m. Pauline E. Knight, July 29, 1955; children—Lesley Helen, Jennifer Ann, David Byers; m. 2d, D. Betty Fitch, Jan. 11, 1964; m. 3d, Karen A. Arneson, Nov. 25, 1970. Lectr. theoretical chemistry U. Manchester, 1955-60, prof. theoretical chemistry, 1967—; lectr. theoretical chemistry U. Edinburgh (Scotland), 1960-62; prof. theoretical chemistry U. Wis. Theoretical Chem. Inst., Madison, 1962-67. Served with RAF, 1953-55. Mem. Faraday Soc., Chem. Soc. (London), Am. Inst. Physics, Sigma Xi, Alpha Chi Sigma. Contbr. articles to profl. jours. Home: 207 Rusholme Gardens Manchester M14 5 LS England

BYINGTON, HOMER MORRISON, Jr., fgn. service officer, ex-ambassador; b. Naples, Italy, May 31, 1908, of Am. parents; s. Homer Morrison and Jeannette Lindsley (Gregory) B.; student Phillips Acad., Andover, Mass., 1923-26; A.B., Yale, 1930; m. Jane Craven McHarg, Sept. 31, 1932; 1 son, Homer Morrison. Apptd. fgn. service officer and sec. in Diplomatic Service, 1930; assigned Dept. State, Washington, 1930-32; press officer U.S. del. to UN Conf. on Internat Orgn., San Francisco, 1945; lst sec. Am. embassy, Rome, 1945-47; dep. U.S. polit adv. to Supreme Allied Comdr., Allied Force H.Q., MTO 1945-46; counselor Am. embassy, Rome, 1947, with rank minister plenipotentiary, 1948; dir. Office Western European Affairs, Dept. State, 1950; counselor Am. embassy, Madrid, Spain, with rank minister plenipotentiary, 1954-57; ambassador to Malaya, 1957-61; spl. asst. to dep. undersec. of state for adminstrn. Dept. State, 1961-62; Am. consul gen., Naples, Italy, 1962—. U.S. rep. 14th session Econ. Commn. for Asia and Far East, 1958. Decorated Medal of Freedom, 1946. Clubs: Metropolitan, Chevy Chase. Office: Am Consulate Gen Naples Italy ☆

BYKOVSKY, VALERIY FEDOROVICH, cosmonaut; b. Pavlovo-Posad, USSR, 1934; grad. Kacha Mil. Aviation Acad., 1955; m. With Soviet Army, 1952—; student pilot, 1952; pilot in fighter regiment, 1955—; jet pilot, 1956—; pilot class II, 1959—; former instr. parachute tng. sch.; space pilot, 1960—; stand- in for Maj. Adriam Nikolaev's space flight, 1962; made 81 orbits, 119 hours in space vehicle Vostok 5, June 1963. Mem. All-Union Konsomol, 1952-63; mem. Communist Party, 1963—. Hon. master of sport USSR; decorated Order Red Star, Order Lenin, Hero Soviet Union. Address: Arbatskaya Pl Ministerstvo Oborony SSSR Moscow USSR

BYLER, JOHN GRAY, found. exec.; b. Sedalia, Mo., Dec. 23, 1900; s. James William and Bertha (Gray) B.; B.S. in Comml. Engring., Carnegie Inst. Tech., 1922; m. Marion Lowerre, Feb. 8, 1930 (dec. 1967); m. 2d, Mary M. Murphy, Sept. 8, 1968. Instr., Wharton Sch., U. Pa., 1922-23; with Life Ins. Sales Research Bur., 1923-24; with W.T. Grant Co., 1924-55, v.p., treas., 1930-55; dir., 1930—; treas. Grant Found., Inc., 1955-70; chmn. Am. Retail Fedn., 1952-53; dir. Nat. Consumer- Retailer Council, 1948-52; pres. Inst. Distbn., 1946-50. Mem. Nat. Republican Club. Mem. Tau Beta Pi, Delta Upsilon. Republican. Episcopalian. Clubs: Union League (N.Y.C.); Country of N.C. (Pinehurst); Ekawnok County (Manchester, Vt.); Larchmont (N.Y.) University; Nat. Press, Capitol Hill (Washington). Home: Pinehurst NC 28374 also South Londonderry VT 05155 Office: 130 E 59th St New York City NY 10022

BYLINSKY, GENE MICHAEL, mag. editor; b. Belgrade, Yugoslavia, Dec. 30, 1930; s. Michael Ivan and Dora (Shadan) B.; B.A. in Journalism, La. State U., 1955; m. Gwen Gallegos, Aug. 14, 1955; children—Tanya, Gregory. Staff reporter Wall St. Jour., Dallas, 1957-59, San Francisco, 1959-61, N.Y.C., 1961; sci. writer Nat. Observer, Washington, 1961-62; sci. writer Newhouse Newspapers, Washington, 1962-66; asso. editor Fortune Mag., N.Y.C., 1966—. Served with AUS, 1956. Recipient 21st Ann. Albert Lasker Med. Journalism award, 1970, Deadline award Sigma Delta Chi, 1970, hon. mention Nat. Soc. Med. Research, 1970, spl. commendation A.M.A., 1967, 68. Mem. Nat. Assn. Sci. Writers. Mem. Russian Orthodox Ch. Home: 32 Chapel Lane Riverside CT 06878 Office: Time and Life Bldg Rockefeller Center New York City NY 10020

BYNUM, WILLIAM, corp. exec.; b. Oneonta, Ala., Sept. 1, 1902; s. Dalton Perry and Lena (Hendricks) B., A.B., U. Ala., 1924, D.Sc., 1957; E.E., Auburn U., 1930; LL.D., Syracuse U., 1966; m. Margaret Garrett, Nov. 18, 1935; children—William, Robert Fluornoy. Athletic dir., football coach Troy (N.Y.) U., 1925-27; with Carrier Corp., Syracuse, 1930—, exec. v.p., 1951-56, pres., 1956-65, chief exec. officer, 1963-68, chmn. bd., 1965-68, also dir.; dir. Marine Midland Grace Trust Co. N.Y., Otis Elevator Co., Grouse Hinds Co., Marine Midland Trust Central N.Y. Mem. N.A.M. (dir.), Nat. Indsl. Conf. Bd., Eta Kappa Nu, Tau Beta Pi, Phi Kappa Phi. Episcopalian. Clubs: Century; Onondaga Golf and Country; University, Sky (N.Y.C.). Home: Hunt Lane Fayetteville NY 13066 Office: Carrier Corp Carrier Pkwy Syracuse NY 13202

BYRAM, E. T., physicist; b. Toledo, Sept. 29, 1914; s. Charles E. and Eva (Taylor) B.; B.Engring., U. Toledo, 1940. Head rocket astronomy sect., upper air physics br., atmospheric and astrophysics div. Naval Research Lab., 1948—. Spl. research x-ray astronomy. Served with AUS, 1943-45. Home: 3713 Elmwood Dr Alexandria VA 22303 Office: Naval Research Lab Hulbert Center Space Research Washington DC 20390

BYRAM, HAROLD MOORE, retired educator; b. Waverly, Ia., Mar. 26, 1902; s. Arthur Ray and Jennie Evelyn (Moore) B.; B.S., Ia. State Coll., 1924, M.S., 1928; Ph.D., Columbia, 1933; m. Edythe Lenore Tegland, Dec. 28, 1926; children—Marilyn, Barbara. High sch. tchr. vocational agr., Northfield, Minn., 1924-26, Kelley, Ia.; instr. vocational edn. Ia. State Coll., 1926-30; grad. asst. higher edn. Tchrs. Coll., Columbia, 1930-31; asst. prof. vocational edn. Ia. State Coll., 1932-36; asso. prof. edn. Mich. State U., East Lansing, 1936-44, prof. edn., chmn. staff in agrl. edn. Coll. Edn., 1944-72. Mem. Am., Mich. vocational assns., Mich. Assn. Tchrs. Vocational Agr., Am. Assn. Tchr. Edn. in Agr. (Distinguished Service award 1966), Mich. Occupational Edn. Assn., Phi Delta Kappa, Kappa Delta Pi, Alpha Zeta, Phi Mu Alpha Sinfonia, Pi Kappa Phi. Club: Lansing Orpheus (pres. 1947-48). Author: Guidance in Agricultural Education, 1966; (with Ralph C. Wenrich) Vocational Education and Practical Arts in the Community Sch., 1956. Author or co-author numerous bulls. Editor: Agr. Edn. mag., 1939-42. Contbr. articles to ednl. jours. Home: 13859 Tan Tara Dr Sun City AZ 85351

BYRCZEK, JAN, married; 1 dau., Balbina. Formerly bass player with K. Komeda, A. Kurylewicz, J. Wroblewski and Z. Namyslowski groups; pres. Polish Jazz Soc., 1964—. Gen. sec. organizing com. Internat. Festival Jazz Jamboree; v.p. European Jazz Fedn. Mgr. promotor vocal group NOVI. Mem. Assn. Polish Music Artists. Editor-in-chief Jazz Forum, Polish Music Forum. Contbr. articles to music mags. Address: Warszawa 1 PO Box 282 ul Rutkowskiego 20 Poland*

BYRD, CECIL KASH, univ. librarian; b. Winchester, Ky., Oct. 23, 1913; s. George Madison and Eliza Jane (Marrow) B.; A.B., Anderson Coll., 1937; A.M., Ind. U., 1938, Ph.D., 1942; m. Esther Irene Sample, Feb. 25, 1938; children—Jean Scott, Clare Ann, Charles Thomas. Tutor history Ind. U., 1939-41, curator rare books, 1942-46, asst. dir. libraries, 1946-48, asso. dir. libraries, 1948—. univ. librarian, 1964—. Library adviser Indonesian Nat. Inst. Adminstrn., Djakarta, 1961-62. Served to lt. USNR, 1943-45. Fellow Carnegie Project in Advanced Library Adminstrn., Rutgers U., 1958. Mem. Am., Ind. library assns., Civil War Round Table, Bibliog. Soc. Am., Caxton, Grolier clubs. Author: (with H.H. Peckham) A Bibliography of Indiana Imprints, 1955; Illinois Imprints, 1966; (with C. Walter Stone, David Kaser) Librarianship in Eight Asian Countries, 1969; Books in Singapore, 1970; Early Printing in the Straits Settlements, 1970. Joint editor Ind. U. Bookmen, 1946-54; editor 1964—; joint editor Ind. U. Library Publs., 1946—. Contbr. articles to profl. jours. Home: 410 Park Ridge Rd Bloomington IN 47401

BYRD, CHARLES LEE, musician; b. Suffolk, Va., Sept. 16, 1925; s. Newman H. and Mary (Holland) B.; student Va. Poly. Inst., 1942-43, Hartnett Sch. Music, N.Y.C., 1946; m. Virginia Marie Darpino, Apr. 23, 1950; children—Jeffrey C., Carol Marie. Jazz guitarist, 1936—, classical guitarist, 1948—; performed with Sol Yaged, Joe Marsala, Alvy West, Freddie Slack; student composition with Thomas Simmons, classical guitar with Sophocles Papas and Andres Segovia; rec. artist Savoy, Offbeat, Riverside, Verve and Columbia records; played at Showboat Lounge, Washington, 1957- 67, Byrd's Nest, Silver Spring, Md., 1967—; numerous TV appearances, 1958—, also jazz festivals; tours of Eng., Saudi Arabia, S. and Central Am., Far East, Africa (State Dept. Cultural Exchange 1969); leader Charlie Byrd Quintet, 1967—; tchr. Am. U., 1963- -. Bd. dirs. Big Bros. Am. Served with AUS World War II. Named Guitarist of Year, Playboy mag., 1964-67; recipient Internat. Critics Poll award Downbeat mag., 1963. Composer original compositions, 1950—. Address: 6435 Barnaby St NW Washington DC 20015

BYRD, CONLEY F., judge; b. Poughkeepsie, Ark., Jan. 14, 1925; s. Robert Lee and Artie (Barnes) B.; LL.M., U. Ark., 1950; m. Frances Hardin, Sept. 4, 1949; children—Conley, Susan, J. Paul. Asst. atty. Ark. Dept. Revenue, 1952; reporter Supreme Ct., 1954-60; law clk., judge U.S. Dist. Ct., 1963-65; formerly practice law, asso. William R. Butler and Omar Greene, Little Rock; now asso. justice Supreme Ct., Little Rock. Served with USNR. Home: PO Box 61 Redfield AR 72132 Office: Justice Bldg Little Rock AR 72201

BYRD, DANIEL MADISON, Jr., mfg. co. exec.; b. Madison, Ga., Nov. 16, 1914; s. Daniel Madison and Nannaline (King) B.; B.Ph., Emory U., 1936; M.A., George Washington U., 1937, J.D., 1939; m. Mary Jeanne McKay, Nov. 29, 1939; children—Daniel Madison II, Jeanne McKay (Mrs. Patterson W. Brown), Mitchell King, Edward Llewellyn. Admitted to D.C. bar, 1939, Tenn. bar, 1945, Ga. bar, 1950, S.C. bar, 1967; atty. NLRB, 1939-45; gen. practice law, Chattanooga, 1946-47; gen. atty. So. Bell Tel. & Tel. Co., 1947-67; v.p., gen. counsel, sec. Springs Mills, Inc., Ft. Mill. S.C., 1967—. Mem. Am. (chmn. adminstrv. law sect. 1969, past sec., mem. council), S.C. bar assns., State Bar Ga. (past chmn. adminstrv. law sect.), Corp. Counsels Assn. (past mem. exec. com., ofcl. bd.), U.S. C. of C., Am. Soc. Corporate Secs., Chi Phi. Methodist (past mem. ofcl. bd.). Clubs: Commerce, Ansley Golf (Atlanta); Palmetto. Home: 200 Fairway Dr Fort Mill SC 29715 Office: Springs Mills Inc Fort Mill SC 29715

BYRD, DAVID HAROLD, diversified industry exec.; b. Detroit, Tex., April 24, 1900; s. Edward and Mollie (Easley) B.; student Trinity U., 1917-18, U. of Tex., 1919-21; D.Sc., Coll. Osteo. Medicine and Surgery, Des Moines, 1962; m. Martha Caruth, June 8, 1935; children—David Harold, Caruth Clark. Geologist; oil and gas producer; chmn. bd. Space Corp., Anchor Motel Corp., Newport Dunes, Inc., Meat Producers, Inc.; pres. Dallas Trust Co., Byrd Farms, Inc., Byrd Cattle Co., Byrd & Cheshier Grain & Supply Co.; dir. emeritus Ling-Tempo-Vought; dir. Home Theaters, Inc., Antarctic Assos., Inc. Chmn. emeritus Civil Air Patrol; hon. life mem. Air Cadet League Can. Adv. council S. W. Center Advanced Studies. Mem. Cotton Bowl Athletic Assn. (dir.), Am. Assn. Petroleum Geologists, Ind. Petroleum Assn. Tex. (pres.). Democrat. Presbyn. Mason (32, Shriner), Elk. Clubs: Dallas Athletic, Petroleum, Brook Hollow Golf, Calyx, Terpsichorean, Dallas, City, Preston Trails Golf (Dallas); Petroleum (Houston); Wings (N.Y.C.); Koon Kreek (Athens, Tex.). Home: 6909 Vassar Dr Dallas TX 75205 Office: Tower Petroleum Bldg Dallas TX 75201 ☆

BYRD, DAVID LAMAR, dentist, educator; b. Houston, June 3, 1922; s. William Leslie and Gabie O. (Cissell) B.; D.D.S., U. Tex., 1946; M.S.D. in Oral Surgery, Northwestern U., 1949; m. Carobeth Weeber, Feb. 1, 1947; 1 dau., Sharon Ann. Intern, Jackson Meml. Hosp., Miami, Fla., 1949-50; resident oral surgery Charity Hosp., New Orleans, 1950-51; prof., chmn. dept. oral surgery and anesthesiology Baylor U., Dallas, 1951—, dir. grad. tng. in oral surgery, 1951—; clin. asst. prof. oral surgery Southwestern Med. Sch. U. Tex.; cons. oral surgery VA Hosp., Bonham, Tex., 1952—, Terrell State Hosp., 1956—, U.S. Army, Ft. Hood, Tex.; dir. oral surgery tng. program, chief dept. dentistry Baylor U. Med. Center; attending staff St. Pauls, Presbyn., Parkland Meml. hosps. Mem. com. grad. dental edn. Am. Cancer Soc., 1955—, bd. dirs. Tex. div.; sr. cons. U.S. 4th Army, Bd. dirs. Dallas chpt. Med. Benevolence Found., Hemophiliac Found. Served as lt. USNR, 1946-48. Recipient Distinguished Tchr. award Acad. Gen. Practice of Dentistry, 1971. Diplomate Am. Bd. Oral Surgery. Fellow Am. Coll. Dentists; mem. Internat., Am., S.W. socs. oral surgeons, Am., Tex. dental assns., Omicron Kappa Upsilon. Editor: Current Therapy in Dentistry, 1st, 2d, 3d, vols. Contbr. articles to profl. jours. Home: 7222 Wild Valley Dr Dallas TX 75231

BYRD, DONALD, musician, educator; b. Detroit, Dec. 9, 1932; s. Elijah Thomas and Cornelia (Taylir) B.; Mus.B., Manhattan Sch. Music, 1962, M.Music Edn., 1963; postgrad., Fountaibleau, France, 1963, Columbia Tchrs. Coll., 1967-68, Howard U. Law Sch., 1969-71. Music tchr. Music and Arts High Sch., N.Y.C., 1962-63, Pub. Sch. 55, N.Y.C., 1967-68, Alexander Berger Intermediate Sch., Bronx, N.Y., 1963-64; band conductor Rutgers U., 1967-68; music conductor Bklyn. Coll., 1968; asso. prof., dir. Inst. Jazz Studies, Howard U., 1968—; pres., founder Jaguar Ednl. Corp.; numerous part-time positions with music clinics; soloist, writer for TV and musical groups, also orchestras; guest conductor Detroit Symphony, summer 1967; TV show Donald Byrd Music Series, N.Y.C., 1969-70; master ceremonies, moderator 1st ann. festival of Left Bank Jazz Soc., Smithsonian Instn., 1970; recording artist for Transition, Columbia records, 1954-58. Cons., mem. adv. bd. Psi Systems, N.Y.C., 1971—. Served with band USAF, 1951-53. Named Best Trumpeter, Down Beat mag., 1967, Trumpeter, Playbook mag. poll, 1957, Best Soloist, Japanese Jazz poll, 1957, Best Trumpeter, Record World mag., 1968-69; recipient Ann. Achievement award Phila. Jazz Club, 1970; Legion of Honor, Chapel of Four Chaplains, Phila. Mem. Black Composers Soc., Harlem Jazz Center, Am. Fedn. Musicians, Congress African Peoples, Inst. Black Am. Music, Inst. of Black World (asso.), Black Acad. Arts and Letters, Kappa Alpha Psi, Phi Mu Alpha. Recording artist for Blue Note Records: Fancy Free, 1969; New Perspective, 1964; Electric Byrd, 1970. Composer score French film Port Oceans, 1958; background music film Montgomery to Memphis, 1970. Home: 490 M St SW Washington DC 20024

BYRD, ELON EUGENE, biologist; b. Richton, Miss., June 9, 1905; s. Henry Webster and Eleanor Elizabeth (Hinton) B.; B.S., Miss. A. and M. Coll., 1929; M.S., Miss. State Coll., 1931; Ph.D., Tulane U.

1934; m. Margaret Elizabeth Powell, Sept. 3, 1938. Instr., Miss. State Coll., 1929-32; faculty U. Ga., Athens, 1934—, prof. zoology-parasitology, 1945—. Spl. cons. filarial studies USPHS, 1951-62; cons. parasitology Southeastern Coop. Wildlife Disease Study, 1968—. Trustee, exec. com. Highlands Biol. Lab., 1950—, Highland (N.C.) Biol. Sta., 1957—. Served to lt. Med. Service Corps. USNR, 1942-45. Decorated B.S.M. Recipient Michael award for research in parasitology, 1948. Fellow A.A.A.S.; mem. Am. Micros. Soc., Am. (editorial bd. 1949-55, mem. council 1952-55), Southeastern (pres. 1970) socs. parasitologists, Am. Soc. Tropical Medicine, Assn. Southeastern Biologists (sec.-treas. 1947-49, pres. 1950), Tenn. Acad. Sci., Am. Soc. Systematic Zoologists. Club: Men's Garden (organizer, pres. Athens). Asso. editor: Am. Midland Naturalist, 1960-66. Contbr. articles to profl. jours. Home: 580 Milledge Circle Athens GA 30601

BYRD, HARRY FLOOD, U.S. senator, newspaper exec.; b. Winchester, Va., Dec. 20, 1914; s. Harry Flood and Anne Douglas (Beverley) B.; student Va. Mil. Inst., 1931-33, U. Va., 1933-35; hon. degrees of LL.D., L.H.D., D. Internat. Service; m. Gretchen B. Thomson, Aug. 9, 1941; children—Harry, Thomas Thomson, Beverley (Mrs. George P. Greenhalgh III). Editor, Winchester Evening Star 1935—; pub. Harrisonburg (Va.) Daily News-Record, 1937—; Pres., dir. Rockingham Pub. Co., 1946; dir. A.P., 1950-66, v.p., mem. exec. com.; mem. Va. Senate, 1947-65 (author state automatic tax reduction law); mem. U.S. Senate from Va., 1965—. Mem. Va. Democratic Central Com., 1940-66. Served to lt. comdr. USNR, 1942-46. Recipient Honor medal Freedoms Found. Mem. V.F.W., Am. Legion. Rotarian. Clubs: National Press, Army-Navy. Home: 411 Tennyson Av Winchester VA 22601 Office: Senate Office Bldg Washington DC 20510

BYRD, HUBERT L., former corp. exec.; b. S.C., Jan. 4, 1906; s. John Lee and Cora Elizabeth (Ulmer) B.; B.S., Clemson A. and M. Coll., 1926; m. Mary Elizabeth Palmer, Apr. 9, 1934; 1 dau., Mary Ann. Various engring. positions Gen. Electric Co., Schenectady, 1926-46; with Food Machinery & Chem. Corp. (now FMC Corp.), San Jose, Cal., 1946-71, exec. v.p., 1960-71, exec. com., 1965-71, also dir. Mem. Farm Equipment Inst. (past chmn.), I.E.E.E. Home: 25640 Moody Rd Los Altos Hills CA 94022

BYRD, HY, former bus. exec.; b. Elgin, Tex., Oct. 8, 1900; s. Walter Collin and Alice (Hartsfield) B.; m. Gertrude Fitzgerald, June 29, 1932; children—Robert H., James H., Sally, Susan. Pres., dir. Gulf Interstate Co.; dir. Pearsall Chem. Co.; ret. Clubs: Racquet and Tennis (N.Y.C.); Jefferson Islands (Washington); River Oaks Country (Houston). Home: 5131 Bayou Timber Houston TX 77027

BYRD, ISAAC BURLIN, fishery biologist, fisheries adminstr.; b. Canoe, Ala., Mar. 14, 1925; s. Isaac Britt and Mary Adline (Wright) B.; B.S., Auburn U., 1948, M.S., 1950; m. Marjorie Fé Elmore, Sept. 24, 1949; children—Cathy Ann, Teresa Carol, Gary Curtis. Grad. asst. Auburn U., 1949-50; chief fisheries sect. Ala. Dept. Conservation, 1951-65; fed. aid coordinator fisheries research and devel. Bur. Comml. Fisheries, Dept. Interior, 1965—; initiated 1st fisheries mgmt. and fisheries research program in Ala. Served with USAAF, 1943-46. Recipient Gov. Ala. award outstanding tech. accomplishments conservation, 1964. Mem. Am. Fisheries Soc. (pres. So. div. 1958, pres. 1965-66, asso. editor trans. 1955- 58), A.A.A.S., Gulf and Caribbean Fisheries Inst., Phi Kappa Phi, Omicron Delta Kappa, Gamma Sigma Delta, Alpha Zeta, Alpha Gamma Rho. Baptist (Sunday sch. tchr.). Contbr. articles sci. jours. Office: Fed Office Bldg 144 1st Av S St Petersburg FL 33701

BYRD, JOHN BAXTER, govt. ofcl.; b. Lexington, Miss., Feb. 26, 1916; s. John B., Sr., and Mary Hunter (Wilkes) B.; ed. pub. schs., U. Tenn. extension; m. Nellie Brooks Shute, Aug. 12, 1938; 1 dau., Phyllis. Co. comdr. CCC, 1941-42; adminstrv. officer Air Tech. Service, 1942-46; with VA, 1946—, dir. adminstrv. services VA Area Med. Office, Atlanta, 1964-65, dir. VA Hosp., Kerrville, Tex., 1965-68, dir. VA Center, Jackson, Miss., 1968—. Mem. adminstrs. forum U.S. Civil Service Commn., Jackson-Vicksburg Hosp. Council; mem. gov.'s adv. commn. Miss. Council on Aging; mem. Comprehensive State Health Planning Council, Miss. Regional Med. Adv. Group; mem. bd. UA; mem. finance com. Jackson United Givers campaign, 1970-71. Served with AUS, World War II. Mem. Fed. Execs. Assn., Am. Coll. Hosp. Adminstrs. Mason. Home: 6143 Waverly Dr Jackson MS 39206 Office: 1500 Woodrow Wilson St Jackson MS 39216

BYRD, MANFORD, Jr., schs. adminstr.; b. Brewton, Ala., May 29, 1928; s. Manford and Evelyn (Turk) B.; B.A., Central Coll., Ia., 1949, H.H.D., 1969; M.A. in Ednl. Psychology, Atlanta U., 1954; postgrad. De Paul U., U. Chgo.; m. Cheribelle Warfield, Mar. 31, 1956; children—Carl, Bradley, Donald. Tchr., Quincy, Ill., 1949-54; with Chgo. Pub. Schs., 1954—, asst. gen. supt. schs., 1967-68, dept. supt. schs., 1968—. Moderator, Met. Assn. United Ch. Christ, 1967, vice moderator Gen. Synod, 1971. Trustee Central Coll., Pella, Ia.; bd. dirs. Chgo. State Coll. Found. Recipient Distinguished Service award Central Coll., 1964. Mem. Am. Assn. Sch. Adminstrs., Phi Delta Kappa. Toastmaster (dist. ednl. chmn. Chgo. 1961). Home: 9515 S Parnell Av Chicago IL 60628 Office: 228 N LaSalle St Chicago IL 60601

BYRD, MILTON BRUCE, coll. pres.; b. Boston, Jan. 19, 1922; s. Max Joseph and Rebecca (Malkiel) B.; A.B. cum laude, Boston U., 1948, M.A., 1949; Ph.D., U. Wis., 1953; postgrad. (fellow) U. Mich., 1961-62; m. Susanne J. Schwerin, Aug. 30, 1953; children—Deborah, Leslie, David. Teaching asst. English, U. Wis., 1949-53; instr., asst. prof. English, Ind. U., 1953-58; asst. prof., asso. prof. humanities So. Ill. U., 1958-62, head div. humanities, 1958-60, supr. acad. advisement, 1959-60, asso. dean, 1960- 62; v.p. acad. affairs No. Mich. U., 1962-66; pres. Chgo. State Coll., 1966—. Bd. dirs Chgo. Council for Urban Edn., Union for Experimenting Colls. and Univs. Served with USAAF, 1943-46. Mem. Modern Lang. Assn., Nat. Council Tchrs. English, Am. Studies Assn., Am. Assn. U. Profs., Assn. for Higher Edn., N.E.A., Mich. Edn. Assn., Phi Beta Kappa. Author: (with Arnold L. Goldsmith) Publication Guide for Literary and Linquistic Scholars, 1958; contbr. to profl. jours. Home: 824 Bonnie Brae River Forest, IL 60305. Office: Chgo State Coll Chicago IL 60621

BYRD, OLIVER ERASMUS, educator, physician; b. Little Rock, Feb. 25, 1906; s. Erasmus A. and Clara Isabel (Alsbury) B.; A.B., Stanford, 1929, A.M., 1932, Ed.D., 1940; M.D., U. Cal., 1947; m. Jennnie C. Sonnichsen, Dec. 21, 1930; children—Beverly Joan, Thomas Russell. Tchr. English, Harvard Mil. Sch., Los Angeles, 1930-31; health educator, athletic coach San Mateo Jr. Coll., 1932-37; faculty, Stanford, 1937—, prof. health edn., 1947—, chmn. dept. health edn., 1947—. Pres., Med. Readings, Inc., 1969. Recipient Internat. certificate Merit for distinguished service to health edn., 1968; Hall of Fame, Nat. Jr. Coll. Athletic Assn. Fellow Am. Sch. Health Assn. (Distinguished Service award 1966), Am. Pub. Health Assn., Am. Acad. Phys. Edn., A.A.A.S. Athletic Assn. Author: Health Yearbooks (15 vols.) 1943-57; Workbook for Health, 1948; Health Attitude Scale, 1949; Patients Self-History Form, 1948; Textbook of College Hygiene, 1957; School Health Scourcebook, 1955; Nutrition Sourcebook, 1955; Family Life Sourcebook, 1956; New Road to Health Series, 1960; Health, 1961; School Health Administration, 1964; Laidlaw Health Series, 1966; Health, 1966. Home: 1533 Madrono Av Palo Alto CA 94306 Office: Sch Edn Stanford U Stanford CA 94305

BYRD, ROBERT CARLYLE, U.S. senator; b. North Wilkesboro, N.C., Jan. 15, 1918; s. Cornelius Sale and Ada (Kirby) B.; student Beckley Coll., Concord Coll., Morris Harvey Coll., 1950-51, Marshall Coll., 1951-52; J.D., Am. U., 1963; m. Erma Ora James, May 29, 1937; children—Mona Carole, Marjorie Ellen. Elected mem. W. Va. Ho. of Dels., 1946-50, Senate, 1950-52. Mem. 83d-85th Congresses, 6th Dist., W. Va.; U.S. senator from W. Va., 1959- -. Democrat. Baptist. Home: Sophia WV 25921 Office: Senate Office Bldg Washington DC 20510

BYRD, WILLIAM ROWLAND, Jr., banker; b. Sanford, Va., Jan. 19, 1918; s. William Rowland and Laura (Witham) B.; student U. Pa., 1950; m. Audrey Grace Kilmon, July 25, 1938; children—William Rowland III, Elizabeth Lee. With Phila. Nat. Bank, 1935—, asst. v.p., 1956-59, v.p., 1959-66, sr. v.p., 1966-70, exec. v.p., 1970—. Past vice-chmn., trustee United Fund Norristown; bd. dirs. Eastern Bapt. Coll. Served with USNR, World War II; ETO. Mem. Phila. Bank Officers Club, Am. Inst. Banking U. Pa. Evening Sch. Alumni Soc., Phila. Clearing House Assn. (bd. dirs., bank operations com.), Bank Adminstrn. Inst. (operations com. chmn.), Pa. (bank operations com.), Am. (bank mgmt. com.) bankers assns. Rotarian (past dir.). Clubs: Union League (Phila.); Plymouth Country (Norristown). Home: Valley View Apts King of Prussia PA 19406 Office: Broad and Chestnut Sts Philadelphia PA 19101

BYRNE, BRENDAN, pub. affairs cons.; b. N.Y.C., Dec. 28, 1908; s. Thomas J. and Clara (Janson) B.; A.B. magna cum laude, Fordham U., 1930, M.A., 1936; m. Rena H. Faecher, July 1, 1937; children—Mary P., Michael K., Judith A. Chmn. social studies dept. John Adams High Sch., N.Y.C., 1931-42; editor Facts mag., Read mag., New Books Digest, 1946; research dir., copywriter Grady Advt. Agy., 1947; dir. programs Am. Heritage Found., 1947-50, asso. dir., 1956, exec. dir., 1956, exec. dir., 1957-65; pub. affairs cons. Fed. Electric Corp., 1965—; trustee Hill Savs. Bank, 1969—. Pub. relations dir. Nat. Citizens Commn. for Better Schs., 1950; v.p. Valley Forge Found., 1951-52; exec. v.p. Goldby & Byrne. Inc., philanthropic cons., N.Y.C., 1954-55; pub. affairs cons. Mem. Pres.'s Commn. on Registration and Voter Participation, 1962-65, vice chmn. N.Y. Commn. on Hist. Observances, 1960-63; dir. Nat. Conf. on Citizenship, 1962—; dir. nationwide campaign Contribute to Your Polit. Party, 1958-65, nonpartisan program to modernize archaic election laws, 1957-65 Register, Inform Yourself and Vote Program, 1957-65; mem. N.Y.C. Bd. Edn. 1961-64; mem. N.Y.C. Nat. Shrines Com., 1969—. Served from lt. (j.g.) to lt. comdr. USNR, 1942-45. Decorated Sec. of Navy Letter of Commendation; recipient Freedoms Found. George Washington honor medal for pub. speaking, 1963; S.A.R. Gold Good Citizenship medal, 1948. Mem. Pub. Relations Soc. Am., N.Y. Hist. Soc., Am. Polit. Sci. Assn., Authors League Am., Authors Guild, Am. Mgmt. Assn., Am. Acad. Polit. Scis., Nat. Municipal League, Adult Edn. Assn., Advt. Club N.Y.C., Fordham U. Alumni Assn., Am. Polit. Sci. Assn. Club: Naval Reserve Officers (N.Y.C.). Author: Guide to the Study of History, 1936; American Heritage Manual, 1950; Alert America Public Relations Guide, 1951; Three Weeks to a Better Memory, 1951; Let's Modernize Our Horse-and-Buggy Election Laws, 1961; How to Help or Hurt Your Country, 1963. Contbr. articles to profl. jours. Home: 85-19 118th St Kew Gardens NY 11415 Office: 621 Industrial Av Paramus NJ 07652

BYRNE, CHARLES RAYMOND, editor, pub.; b. Bklyn., Mar. 17, 1916; s. Charles Ambrose and Rose Cecilia (Garrity) B.; A.B., Fordham U., 1938, student Law Sch., 1938-40; postgrad. Columbia, 1948-50, N.Y.U., 1950-52; m. Dorothy Grace Smith, June 30, 1941; children—Anthony Richard, Adrian Michael, Nicholas Charles, Alison Andrea. With N.Y. Post, 1938-40; v.p., editor-in-chief Avon Pub. Co., 1946-54; pres., editor-in-chief Berkley Pub. Corp., 1954- 60; editor-in-chief Avon Brooks, pub. by Hearst Corp., 1960-61; pub. editor-in-chief paperback book div. Macfadden Publs., Inc., 1961-66, v.p. book div., 1965-66; mgr. subsidiary and fgn. rights, editor Meredith Press div. Meredith Pub. Company, 1966—; dir. gen. trade book pub. Consumer Book div. Meredith Corp.; dir. Carroland Realty Corp. Rep. of Macfadden Publs. to Am. Book Pubs. Council. Served to capt., arty., AUS, 1940-45. Clubs: New York Athletic; Racquet (Yonkers, N.Y.), Home: 2728 Henry Hudson Pkwy Riverdale New York City NY 10463 Office: Meredith Corp 750 3d Av New York City NY 10017

BYRNE, CORNELIUS JAMES, former dept. store exec.; b. Kansas City, Mo., July 18, 1907; s. Frank P. and Agnes (Smith) B.; B.S., U. Ill., 1929. With Mandel Bros., Chgo., 1929- 43, mdse. mgr., 1934-39, 41-43; with Famous-Barr, St. Louis, 1939-41; with Frederick & Nelson, Seattle, 1946-70. v.p., gen. mgr., 1954-61, pres., gen. mgr., 1962-70; v.p. Marshall Field & Co., Chgo.; dir. News Pub. Co. Trustee Central Assn.; v.p., trustee Greater Seattle; bd. dirs. Seattle chpt. A.R.C.; trustee World Trade Center; bd. govs. Am. Nat. Red Cross, 1963-66; bd. regents Seattle U. Served with USNR, 1943-46. Mem. Nat. Retail Mchts. Assn. (dir., v.p.), Seattle Municipal League. Clubs: Wash. Athletic, Rainier, Harbor, Golf (Seattle). Home: 2611 42d Av W Seattle WA 98199

BYRNE, JAMES A., congressman; b. Phila., June 22, 1906; s. James P. and Catherine C. (Foody) B.; student St. Joseph's Coll.; m. M. Virginia Mullen, June 7, 1939. Local registrar Bur. Vital Statistics, Phila. County; del. Democratic Nat. Conv., Phila., 1936; mem. Dem. County Com., Phila.; chief dep. U.S. marshal Eastern Div. Pa., also chief U.S. marshal; funeral dir., 1937-50; sr. disbursing officer Pa. State Treasury; mem. Pa. State Legislature, 1950-52. mem. commn. on Independence Hall Mall; mem. 83d-92d U.S. Congresses, 3d Pa. Dist. Mem. Nat., Pa. State, Phila. funeral dirs. assns. Home: 239 E Girard Av Philadelphia PA 19125 Office: House Office Bldg Washington DC 20525

BYRNE, JAMES JOSEPH, archbishop; b. St. Paul, July 28, 1908; s. Philip J. and Mary (McMonigal) B.; student Nazareth Hall Prep. Sem., 1924-27, St. Paul Sem., 1927-33; S.T.B., Cath. U. Am., 1933; summer student U. Minn., 1933; S.T.D., U. Louvain (Belgium), 1937; LL.D., Portland (Ore.) U., 1960. Ordained priest Roman Cath. Ch., 1933; prof. theology and philosophy St. Thomas Coll., St. Paul, 1937-45; part time prof. theology St. Catharine Coll., St. Paul, 1941-47; prof. theology St. Paul Sem., 1945-47; aux. bishop of St. Paul, 1947-56; bishop of Boise, Ida., 1956-62; archbishop of Dubuque (Ia.), 1962—. Home: 1105 Locust St Dubuque IA 52001 Office: 11th and Bluff Sts Dubuque IA 52001

BYRNE, JOHN JOSEPH, Jr., ins. co. exec. b. Passaic, N.Y., July 11, 1932; s. John Joseph and Winifred (Mohr) B.; B.S., Rutgers U., 1954; postgrad. Harvard Law Sch., 1957; M.S., U. Mich., 1959; m. Dorothy M. Cain, July 22, 1958; children-John Joseph III, Mark James, Patrick Michael. With Lincoln Nat. Life Ins. Co., Ft. Wayne, Ind., 1959-63; exec. v.p. Mass. Life Ins. Co., Boston, Mass., 1963-67; sr. v.p. The Travelers Ins. Co., Hartford, Ct., 1967—. Mem. Museum of Fine Arts, Boston; active United Fund Boston, Hartford. Served to capt. USAF, 1954-57. Mem. Soc. Actuaries, Cap and Skull, Zeta Psi. Republican. Roman Catholic. Home: 6 Cedar Hill Rd W Simsbury CT 06092 Office: 1 Tower Sq Hartford CT 06115

BYRNE, JOHN VINCENT, educator; b. Hempstead, N.Y., May 9, 1928; s. Frank E. and Kathleen (Barry) B.; A.B., Hamilton Coll., 1951; M.A., Columbia, 1953; Ph.D., U. So. Cal., 1957; m. Shirley O'Connor, Nov. 26, 1954; children—Donna, Lisa, Karen, Steven. Research geologist Humble Oil & Refinery Co., Houston, 1957-60; asso. prof. Ore. State U., Corvallis, 1960-66, prof. oceanography, 1966—, chmn. dept., 1968—. Program dir. oceanography NSF, 1966-67. Recipient Carter teaching award, 1964. Fellow Geol. Soc. Am.; mem. Am. Assn. Petroleum Geologists, A.A.A.S., Am. Geophys. Union, Sigma Xi, Chi Psi. Research oceanography, marine geology. Home: 1501 N 12th St Corvallis OR 97330

BYRNE, LEO CHRISTOPHER, bishop; b. St. Louis, Mar. 19, 1908; s. Patrick and Eleanor (Sale) B.; grad. Kenrick Theol. Sem., Webster Groves, Mo., 1933; M.A., St. Louis U., 1942, M.S., 1946, D.D. (hon.), 1954. Ordained priest, Roman Cath. Ch., 1933; exec. sec. Cath. Charities of St. Louis, 1944-50; nat. moderator Lay Women's Retreat Movement, 1950-53; auxiliary bishop of St. Louis, 1954-60; co-adjutor bishop, Diocese of Wichita, Kan., 1960-63, apostolic adminstr., 1963-67; coadjutor archbishop St. Paul and Minn., 1967—. Episcopal moderator Nat. Laywomen's Retreat Movement. Address: 226 Summit Av St Paul MN 55102

BYRNE, MARGERY ELEANOR LITTLE (Mrs. Thomas E. Byrne), banker; b. N.Y.C., Feb. 28, 1918; d. George Packer and Dorothy (Beard) Little; grad. Elmira Bus. Inst., 1938; m. Thomas E. Byrne, Nov. 8, 1953; 1 dau., Melody Anne. With Marine Midland Bank So. (formerly Elmira Bank & Trust Co.), Elmira, N.Y., 1938-41, 46—, sec., 1962—; with Citizens Bank & Trust Co., White Plains, N.Y., 1941-43, Netherlands Information Bur., N.Y.C., 1943-45, George P. Little Co., Cleve., 1945- 46. Pres. Elmira Little Theatre, 1951. Mem. Nat. Secs. Assn. (chpt. pres. 1967; named Sec. of Year 1966), Beta Sigma Phi. Presbyn. (trustee). Home: 1448 W Water St Elmira NY 14905 Office: 150 Lake St Elmira NY 14902

BYRNE, THOMAS RICHARD, mayor; b. St. Paul, Mar. 9, 1924; s. Philip Joseph and Mary (McMonigal) B.; B.A. cum laude, Coll. St. Thomas, 1947; M.A., U. Minn., 1960; m. Mary Therese Barrett, June 9, 1945; children—Mary Ellen, Patrick, Timothy, Joseph, Thomas. Instr. Latin, St. Thomas Acad., 1947-53; instr., student counselor St. Paul pub. schs., 1953-66; mayor, St. Paul, 1966—; vice chmn. Minn. Municipal Commn., 1966-67; mem. exec. com. Nat. League Cities, 1967. Mem. St. Paul Council on Human Relations; pres., dir. Little League Baseball, 1962-66. Treas. Minn. Democratic Farmer- Labor Legislative Dist., 1963; chmn. Lyndon B. Johnson-Hubert H. Humphrey Presdl. Campaign, Minn. 4th Congl. Dist., 1964. Served to 1st lt. USAAF, 1943-45. Decorated Air medal with two clusters. Mem. Nat. Congress Parents and Tchrs., Am. Legion, V.F.W., (past post comdr.). K.C. (4). Home: 2170 Wellesley Av St. Paul, MN 55105. Office: City Hall and Courthouse St Paul MN 55102

BYRNE, WILLIAM MATTHEW, judge; b. Bakersfield, Cal., July 10, 1896; s. John Joseph and Mary Ellen (Mills) B.; LL.B., Loyola U. of Los Angeles, 1929; m. Julia Ann Lamb, June 2, 1925; children—Margaret Moira, William Matthew. Admitted to Cal. bar, 1929; mem. Cal. State Legislature, 1925-31, speaker pro tempore State Assembly, 1927-31; judge Los Angeles Municipal Ct., 1943- 48, Superior Ct. of Cal., 1948-50, U.S. dist. judge since 1950. Mem. Los Angeles Bar Assn., Phi Alpha Delta, Alpha Sigma Nu. Home: 520 N Cherokee Los Angeles CA 90004 Office: Federal Bldg Los Angeles CA 90012

BYRNES, ALLEN WILLIAM, psychiatrist; b. Lake Park, Ia., Mar. 20, 1910; s. Roscoe Conklin and Anna (Leese) B.; B.S., M.D., State U. Ia., 1934; m. Elizabeth Earley, Dec. 25, 1934; children—Eva Ann (Mrs. James Elmer), Barbara Jean (Mrs. Paul Reddington). Intern, Ia. Meth. Hosp., Des Moines, 1934-35; pvt. practice medicine, Traer, Ia. 1936-37; physician Civilian Conservation Corps, Ia., 1938-40; physician VA Hosp., Ft. Custer, Mich., 1940-42, chief continued treatment service, 1946-49; chief neuropsychiat. sect. VA Hosp., Dayton, O., 1949-52, chief phys. medicine and rehab. service VA Hosp., Downey, Ill., 1952-54, VA Hosp., Danville, Ill., 1954-58; chief staff VA Hosp., St. Cloud, Minn., 1958-61; dir. VA Hosp., Knoxville, Ia., 1961-63, VA Hosp., Battle Creek, Mich., 1963-67. Served with M.C., AUS, 1942-46; ETO, Africa. Decorated Bronze Star. Diplomate Am. Bd. Psychiatry and Neurology. Mem. Am. Psychiat. Assn., Acad. Religion and Mental Health, Law-Sci. Found. (founding mem.), Am. Acad. Forensic Scis., Am. Legion, V.F.W., D.A.V. Mason. Address: 13833 Kaanapail Dr Sun City AZ 85351

BYRNES, ARTHUR F., govt. ofcl.; b. N.Y.C., June 28, 1917; s. Arthur I. and Barbara (Young) B.; B.S., Manhattan Coll., 1940; student Springfield (Mass.) Coll., 1942; Ph.D., N.Y. U., 1951; m. Anne Louise Schug, Dec. 24, 1941; children—Arthur Everett, Sue Anne, John Mitchell, Timothy Francis. Asst. prof. orgn., adminstrn. and mgmt. Springfield Coll., 1940-42; supt. schs., Monroe, Ind., 1945-49; dir. communications Eastern Ill. State U., Charleston, 1949-53; dir. research, 1953-55; ICA cons. Ministry Edn., Govt. Brazil, 1955-57; div. chief AID, 1957-62, dep. dir. mission, N.E. Brazil, 1962-63, dir. mission, 1963-64, asst. dir., Rio de Janeiro, Brazil, 1964; dep. dir. U.S., also attaché, econ. and social devel. Am. embassy, Quito, Ecuador, 1965-66; with U.S. Army War Coll., Carlisle, Pa., 1966-67; dir. internat. and regional programs AID, 1967-70, asst. dir. office internat. tng., Washington, 1970—. Mem. Brazilian-U.S. Exchange Commn., 1957—; acad. affairs com. Escola Americana, Rio de Janeiro, 1960—. Served to capt. USAAF, 1942-45. Decorated Cruziero do Sul (Brazil), 1960. Mem. Am. C. of C., Am. Soc., Am. Assn. U. Profs., Fgn. Service Assn. Soc. Internat. Devel., Phi Delta Kappa. Home: 116 88th St Brooklyn NY 11209 Office: AID U S Dept State Washington DC 20523

BYRNES, CLIFFORD HAMILTON, lawyer; b. Mpls., Sept. 8, 1893; s. Timothy Edward and Clara M. (Goodrich) B.; grad. Phillips Exeter Acad., 1911; B.A., Yale, 1915; LL.B., Harvard, 1919; m. Blanche Edith Trainor, Aug. 1, 1925. Admitted to Mass. bar, 1920; spl. asst. U.S. atty. gen., Washington, 1922-26, 27-31; asst. U.S. atty., Boston, 1926-27; partner firm Hale, Sanderson, Byrnes & Morton, Boston, 1927—. Served to 2d lt., inf. U.S. Army, 1917-19. Mem. Alpha Delta Phi. Republican. Unitarian. Mason. Clubs: Cohasset; Laurel Brook; Union (Boston); Yale (N.Y.C., Boston). Home: 152 Summer St Hingham MA 02043 Office: 10 Post Office Sq Boston MA 02109

BYRNES, EDWARD T., educator; B.A., Seton Hall U.; M.A., Ph.D., N.Y. U. Asso. prof. English, chmn. Dept. English, Seton Hall U., South Orange, N.J. Office: Seton Hall U South Orange NJ 07079•

BYRNES, FRANK ALBERT, lawyer, former ins. co. exec.; b. Bklyn., Feb. 17, 1905; s. Edward Joseph and Mary Patricia (Brennan) B.; A.B., N.Y. U., 1925; LL.B., Fordham U., 1931; m. Mary Elizabeth Finan, Nov. 26, 1938; 1 dau., Elizabeth Anne (Mrs. William Anthony Watt). Admitted to N.Y. bar; mem. legal staff N.Y. Life Ins. Co., 1934-70, counsel, 1951-54, asst. gen. counsel, 1954-57, asso. gen.

counsel, 1957-65, v.p., gen. counsel, 1965-70. Fellow Am. Bar Found.; mem. Am., N.Y. bar assns., Assn. Bar City N.Y., Am. Land Title Assn., N.Y. State Title Assn., N.Y. Law Inst., Assn. Life Ins. Counsel, Am. Judicature Soc., L.I. Hist. Soc. Home: 43 Ridge Rd New Rochelle NY 10804

BYRNES, GEORGE BARTHOLOMEW, pension-ins. cons.; b. Kansas City, Mo., Oct. 19, 1911; s. James C. and Hannah (Haffey) B.; student Rockhurst Coll., Kansas City, 1929-31; grad. U. N.M., 1935; m. Grace E. Mehren, Apr. 11, 1942; children—Marygrace, Patrick, Robert, Brian, Kathleen. Rep., Equitable Life Assurance Soc., Albuquerque, 1935-42, dist. mgr., Phoenix, 1942-45, Pasadena, Cal., 1945-54; gen. agt. New Eng. Mut. Life Ins. Co., N.Y.C., 1954-60; cons. pension and profit-sharing planning, bus. and personal estate plans, Los Angeles, 1960—. Pres., Pasadena Tb Assn., 1954, Nat. Epilepsy League, 1960. Mem. bd. fellows U. Santa Clara (Cal.). Named Honor agt. Equitable Life Assurance Soc., 1949. Mem. C.L.U.'s Assn. Los Angeles (v.p. 1952-53, nat. bd. 1958-60), Life Ins. and Trust Council Los Angeles (sec.-treas. 1951-52, v.p. 1952-53, pres. 1953-54), Million Dollar Round Table (chmn. exec. com.), Pasadena C. of C. (mem. bd. 1950, 53, sec.-treas. 1952, 2d v.p. 1953, 1st v.p. 1954), Tournament of Roses Assn., Phi Kappa Phi, Sigma Chi. Clubs: University (Pasadena, Cal.); Palos Verdes Golf (Palos Verdes Estates, Cal.); California (Los Angeles); Los Angeles Country. Home: 2017 Paseo del Sol Palos Verdes Estates CA 90274 Office: Union Bank Tower Torrance CA 90503

BYRNES, JAMES BERNARD, museum dir.; b. N.Y.C., Feb. 19, 1917; s. Patrick J.A. and Janet E. (Geiger) B.; student N.A.D., 1936-38, Am. Artist Sch., 1938- 40, Art Students League, 1940-42, U. Perugia (Italy), 1951, Istituto Meschini, Rome, 1952; m. Barbara A. Cecil, June 10, 1946; 1 son, Ronald L. Art tchr. mus. activity program N.Y.C. Bd. Edn., 1936-40; indsl. designer Michael Saphier Assos., N.Y.C., 1940-42; docent Los Angeles County Mus., 1946-47, asso. curator modern contemporary art, 1947-48, curator, asst. to dir., 1948-53; dir. Colorado Springs Fine Arts Center, 1954-55; asso. dir. N.C. Mus. Art, 1956-58, acting dir., 1958-59, dir., 1959-60; dir. Isaac Delgado Mus. Art, New Orleans, 1962—. Vis. lectr. U. Fla., 1961, Newcomb Coll., Tulane U., 1963; art cons. Mem. Western (sec.-treas. 1955), S.E. (council) assns. art mus. dirs., Am. Soc. Aesthetics, Am. Assn. Museums, Art Mus. Dirs. Assn., Am. Fedn. Arts, Am. Inst. Design (hon.). Author: Masterpieces of Art, W.R. Valentiner Memorial, 1959; Tobacco and Smoking in Art, 1960; Fates de la Palette, 1963; Edgar Degas, His Family and Friends in New Orleans, 1965; Odyssey of an Art Collector, 1966; Art of Ancient and Modern Latin America, 1968; also numerous mus. catalogs. Home: 1243 Bourbon St New Orleans LA 70116 Office: Isaac Delgado Mus Art City Park New Orleans LA 70119

BYRNES, JAMES FRANCIS, former U.S. sec. state, gov. S.C.; b. S.C.; s. James Francis and Elizabeth E. Byrnes; student pub. schs.; m. Maude Busch, May 2, 1906. Admitted to bar, 1903; editor Jour. and Rev. Aiken, 1903- 07; ofcl. ct. reporter 2d Circuit, S.C., 1900-08; solicitor 2d Circuit, S.C., 1908-10; mem. 62d to 68th Congresses (1911-25), 2d S.C. Dist.; practiced law, Spartanburg, 1925-31; elected U.S. senator, 1931-43; apptd. justice U.S. Supreme Ct., June 1941, resigned from U.S. Supreme Ct. Oct. 1942 to accept appointment as dir. econ. stblzn., 1942-43, dir. war mblzn., 1943-45; sec. state, 1945-47; gov. S.C., 1951-55. Democrat. Author: Speaking Frankly; All in One Lifetime. Home: Heathwood Circle Columbia SC

BYRNES, JOHN W., congressman; b. Green Bay, Wis., June 12, 1913; s. Charles W. and Harriet (Schumacher) B.; A.B., U. Wis., 1936; LL.B., 1938; m. Barbara Preston, 1947; children—John, Michael, Bonnie, Charles, Barbara, Elizabeth. Admitted to Wis. bar, 1939; mem. Wis. senate, 1941- 45; mem. 79th-92d Congresses, 8th Wis. Dist. Mem. Wis. Bar Assn. Elk. Republican. Office: 101 N Jefferson St Green Bay WI 54301

BYRNES, ROBERT FRANCIS, educator; b. Waterville, N.Y., Dec. 30, 1917; s. Michael Joseph and Pauline (Albecker) B.; B.A., Amherst Coll., 1939; M.A., Harvard, 1940, Ph.D., 1947; sr. fellow Columbia, 1948-50; LL.D., Coe Coll., 1964; D.H.L., Amherst Coll., 1964; D.Litt., St. Mary's College, 1967; married Eleanor Frances Jewell, June 6, 1942; children—Shaun, Sheila, Sally, Susan, Robin, Charles, James. With Fgn. Econ. Adminstrn., 1943-44; instr. Swarthmore Coll., 1945-46, vis. lectr., 1946-48; asst. to asso. prof. Rutgers U., 1946-53; faculty Inst. Advanced Study, 1950; staff Office Nat. Estimates, CIA, 1951-54; dir. Mid-European Studies Center, N.Y.C., 1954-56; prof. history Ind. U., 1956—, chmn. dept., 1958-65, dir. Russian and East European Inst., Ind. U., 1959-62, director International Affairs Center, 1965-67, Distinguished professor of history, 1967—; chairman Conf. on Slavic and East European Affairs, 1959. Civilian service M.I., AUS, 1944-45. Guggenheim fellow, 1953; Am. Council Learned Socs. fellow, 1962-63. Member American Historical Association (mem. exec. council 1963-67), Am. Cath. Hist. Assn. (pres. 1961), Phi Beta Kappa. Author: Anti-semitism in Modern France; The Prologue to the Dreyfus Affair, 1950; Bibliography of American Publications on East Central Europe, 1945-57, 1959; The Non-Western Areas in Undergraduate Education in Indiana, 1959; (with others) The College and World Affairs, 1964; Pobedonoster: His Life and Thought, 1967; The United States and Eastern Europe, 1967. Editor: East- Central Europe under the Communists, 7 vols., 1956-57. Contbr. articles profl. jours. Home: 402 Reisner Dr Bloomington IN 47401

BYRNSIDE, JOHN HILL, utility co. exec.; b. Madison, W.Va., Jan. 20, 1908; s. Marshall A. and Mary (Hill) B.; LL.B., W.Va. U. 1933; m. Mary Gray Silver, Aug. 21, 1933 (dec. Oct. 1970); children—Anne (Mrs. Robert B. Davis), Jane (Mrs. Richard A. Kuehn), John Hill. Admitted to W.Va. bar, 1933; practiced in Madison, 1933-35; atty. Hope Natural Gas Co., Charleston, Clarksburg, W.Va., 1936- 54, asst. sec., 1955-58, sec., gen. counsel, dir., 1959-65; sec. Consol. Gas Supply Corp., Clarksburg, 1965—; asst. sec. River Gas Co., Clarksburg, 1955-58, sec., gen. counsel, dir., 1959—. Mem. exec. com. Harrison County United Fund, pres., 1971. Mem. Am., W.Va., Harrison County bar assns., Am. Judicature Soc., W.Va., Clarksburg chambers commerce, Phi Alpha Delta, Sigma Nu. Republican. Presbyn. Club: Clarksburg Country. Home: 517 Stanley Av Clarksburg WV Office: 445 W Main St Clarksburg WV 26301

BYROADE, HENRY ALFRED, U.S. ambassador; b. Allen County, Ind., July 24, 1913; s. Ernest C. and Carrie B.; B.S., U.S. Mil. Acad., 1937; M.S. in Engring., Cornell U., 1941; m. Jitka Donda Henson, Feb. 1962; 1 dau., Linda; children by previous marriage—Gene, Alan, John. Commd. 2d lt. U.S. Army, 1937, advanced through grades to brig. gen. (temp.), 1946; served in CBI, 1937-44; dep. chief, acting chief Asiatic Theater sect. Operations div. Office Chief of Staff, Washington, 1944-45; mil. attache Gen. Marshall, China, 1945-46; activated cessation of hostilities, exec. Hdqrs., Peiping, China, Peiping Hdqrs. Group, service as dir. operations, exec., comdg. gen. Hdqrs. Group. Jan. 1946; student Armed Forces Staff Coll.; chief internat. affairs sect. Gen. Staff U.S. Army; on loan to Dept. State, 1949-52, dep. dir. bur. German affairs, 1949, dir., 1949-62; resigned, 1952; asst. sec. state Nr. Eastern, S. Asian, African affairs, 1952-55; U.S. Ambassador to Egypt, 1955-56, Union South Africa, 1956-59, Afghanistan, 1959- 62; sr. adviser Arms Control and Disarmament Agy., Washington, 1962; U.S. ambassador Burma, 1963-68, Philippines, 1969- -. Decorated D.S.M., Legion of Merit with 2 oak leaf clusters, Air medal; Spl. Breast Order of Yun Hua (3d and 4th class, China). Address: Dept of State Washington DC 20521

BYROD, FRED JACOB, sports editor; b. Sunbury, Pa., Jan. 5, 1911; s. Fred Jacob and Edna (Farra) B.; B.S., Temple U., 1933; m. Doris M. Fish, Nov. 3, 1942; children—Fred Jacob 3d, Robert W. Sports staff Phila. Inquirer, 1933—, asst. sports editor, 1952-58, sports editor, 1958—. Served to capt. USAAF, 1942-45. Mem. Vets. Fgn. Wars, Phila. Sports Writers Assn. (pres. 1950-51), Sigma Delta Chi. Home: 1422 Wynnewood Rd Ardmore PA 19003 Office: 400 N Broad St Philadelphia PA 19130

BYROM, FLETCHER LAUMAN, chem. mfg. co. exec.; b. Cleve., July 13, 1918; s. Fletcher L. and Elizabeth M.A. (Collins) B.; B.S. in Metallurgy, Pa. State U., 1940; m. Marie M. McIntyre, Feb. 17, 1945; children—Fletcher Lauman, Carol A., Susan J. Sales engr. Am. Steel & Wire Co., Cleve., 1940-42; procurement and adminstrv. coordination Naval Ordnance Lab., also Bur. Ordnance and Research Planning Bd., Navy Dept., 1942-47; asst. to gen. mgr. Tar Products div. Koppers Co., Inc., Pitts., 1947-54, asst. v.p., mgr. operations Tar Products div., 1954-55, v.p., asst. mgr. gen. Tar Products div., 1955-58, v.p., gen. mgr., 1958-60, pres., chief administrative officer, dir., 1960-67, chief exec. officer, 1968—, chmn., 1970—; dir. Mellon Nat. Bank and Trust Co., Am. Smelting and Refining Co., Blue Cross Western Pa., Bell Telephone Co. Pa., Northwestern Mut. Life Ins. Co., Phillips Electronics and Pharm. Industries Corp. Mem. adv. com. on bus. programs Brookings Instn. Bd. dirs. Hosp. Planning Assn. Allegheny County, Regional Indsl. Devel. Corp., Pitts. Regional Planning Assn., Allegheny Conf. on Community Devel. (v.p.); v.p. bd. trustees Presbyn.-Univ. Hosp.; chmn. bd. trustees Kiskiminetas Springs Sch.; trustee Council Ams., Allegheny Coll., Pa. State U. Recipient Distinguished Civilian Service award U.S. Navy Dept. Mem. Am. Coke and Coal Chems. Inst., Am. Wood Preservers Assn., Eastern States Blast Furnace and Coke Assn., Engrs. Soc. Western Pa., Am. Iron and Steel Inst., Pitts. C. of C., Com. Econ. Devel. (bd mem.), Mfg. Chemists Assn. (dir.), Fgn. Policy Assn. (dir.), The Conf. Bd. (sr. execs. adv. council), Phi Kappa Psi. Presbyn. Clubs: Duquesne, Fox Chapel Golf (Pitts.); Rolling Rock (Ligonier, Pa.); Laurel Valley Golf (N.Y.C.); Links (Beach Haven, N.J.); Little Egg Harbor Yacht. Home: 1420 Centre Av Pittsburgh PA 15219 Office: Koppers Bldg Pittsburgh PA 15219

BYRON, GOODLOE EDGAR, congressman; b. Williamsport, Md., June 22, 1929; s. William D. and Katharine (Edgar) B.; B.A., U. Va., 1951; J.D., George Washington U., 1953; m. Beverly Barton Butcher, Dec. 20, 1952; children—Goodloe Edgar, Barton Kimball, Mary McComas. Admitted to Md. and D.C. bars, 1953; law clk. to Judge Andrew Hood, D.C. Municipal Ct. Appeals, 1954; practice law, Frederick, Md., 1958—; county atty., 1959-62; mem. Md. Ho. of Dels., 1963-66, Md. Senate, 1967-70; mem. 92d Congress 6th Dist. Md., 1970—. Legal adviser Frederick County San. Commn., 1960-66, Frederick County Planning Commn., 1960-63; chmn. Md. Planning and Zoning Law Study Commn., 1967-70. Pres. Young Democratic Clubs Md., 1961-62, chmn. Western Md. caucus, 1963-66. Mem. Md. Hist Trust, 1963—, Appalachian Trail Nat. Adv. Council, 1969—; bd. visitors Md. Sch. for Deaf, 1964—. Served from 1st lt. to capt., AUS, 1955-58. Mem. Frederick Soc. soc. (pres. 1962), Am., Md., Frederick County bar assns. Episcopalian. Mason (Shriner), Elk, Eagle, Red Man, Optimist. Club: Lewistown Ruritan. Home: 306 Grove Blvd Frederick MD 21701 Office: Law Bldg W Church St Frederick MD 21701

BYRON, JAMES GERALD, corp. exec.; b. St. Louis, Apr. 17, 1906; s. Michael G. and Agnes K. (Howard) B.; A.B., U. Detroit, 1927, LL.B., 1929; m. Vivian Tinkham, Apr. 24, 1935; children—Michael Gerald, James Woodford, Susan Catherine. Admitted to Mich. bar, 1929; partner Byron & Dorn, 1929-34; asst. account exec. Campbell-Ewald Co., 1934-36; territorial mgr. Detroit Gen. Motors Corp., Phila., 1936-42; dir. indsl. relations Bendix Aviation Corp., 1942-50; v.p. personnel, dir. Curtiss-Wright Corp., Wood-Ridge, N.J., 1950-57, exec. v.p., dir., 1957-70; also chmn., pres. Canadian Curtis Wright Ltd. Bd. dirs. Passaic Gen. Hosp. Mem. Air Force Assn., Am. Ordnance Assn., Gamma Eta Gamma. Clubs: Pennington (bd. govs.) (Passaic, N.J.); Economic, Wings (N.Y.C.). Home: Holly Rd Amberley Annapolis MD 21401 Office: Curtiss-Wright Corp Wood-Ridge NJ 07075

BYRON, JOHN P., lawyer; b. Waseca, Minn., Mar. 4, 1930; student Coll. St. Thomas; B.S.L., U. Minn., 1950, LL.B., 1952. Admitted to Minn. bar, 1952, U.S. Supreme Ct. bar, 1955; now mem. firm Fredrickson, Byron, Colburn Ltd., Mpls. Fellow Am. Coll. Probate Counsel; mem. Am., Minn. (chmn. probate ct. com. 1969—), Hennepin County bar assns., Phi Delta Phi. Mem. editorial bd. Minn. Law Rev., 1951-52. Office: Northwestern Bank Bldg Minneapolis MN 55402*

BYRUM, WOODROW ROBERT, coll. dean; b. Phoebus, Va., Jan. 24, 1914; s. Robert Lafayette and Mattie Alice (Clark) B.; student William and Mary Coll., 1933-34; B.S. in Pharmacy, Med. Coll. Va., 1937; Ph.D. (Am. Found. Pharm. Edn. fellow), Ohio State U., 1947; m. Mary Ceceila Byrum Collier, Apr. 11, 1939; children—Linda Susan, Nancy Lou, Beverly Ann. Asst. prof. Ohio State U., 1947-48; asso. prof. U. Ariz., 1948-50; prof., head dept. pharmacology U. Ga., 1950-52; dean Sch. Pharmacy Samford U., Birmingham, Ala., 1952—. Mem. Am. Assn. Colls. Pharmacy, Am., Ala. pharm. assns., Am. Assn. U. Profs., Sigma Xi, Kappa Psi, Omicron Delta Kappa, Rho Chi. Rotarian. Home: 2204 Lester Lane Birmingham AL 35226

BYSE, CLARK MILTON, educator, lawyer; b. Oshkosh, Wis., Aug. 23, 1912; s. Charles Henry and Jennett (Carew) B.; B.E., State Tchrs. Coll. Oshkosh, 1935; LL.B., U. Wis., 1938; LL.M., Columbia, 1939, J.S.D., 1952; M.A. (hon.), Harvard, 1958; m. Merwin Helen Scott, Dec. 19, 1939; children—James Clark, Barbara Helen. Admitted to Wis. bar, 1938, Pa. bar, 1953; with firm Thompson, Gruenwald & Frye, Oshkosh, 1938; instr. law U. Ia., 1939-40, asst. prof., 1940-41; staff office gen. counsel SEC, 1941, legal asst. commrs., 1941-42, staff office solicitor, 1945-46; office gen. counsel Bd. Econ. Warfare, 1942, spl. rep. bd. Econ. Warfare and Def. Supplies Corp., Colombia, S.Am., 1942-43; counsel office war areas trade Dept. Commerce, 1946; asst. prof. law U. Pa., 1946-47, asso. prof., 1947-48, prof., 1948-58; prof. law Harvard, 1958-70, Bussey prof., 1970—. Vis. prof. law Stanford, summer 1947, U. Wis., 1955, Harvard, 1957-58, U. Tex. 1962, U. Minn., 1969-70; Salzburg Seminar in Am. Studies, 1958, 65. Mem. Mass. adv. com. U.S. Com. Civil Rights, 1962—. Served with USNR, 1943-45. Mem. Adminstrv. Conf. U.S., Am. Civil Liberties Union (Mass. dir.), Am. Assn. U. Profs. (counsel 1962-64, pres. 1966-68), Phi Beta Sigma, Phi Kappa Delta, Kappa Delta Pi, Pi Gamma Mu, Order of Coif. Roman Catholic. Author: Administrative Law Cases and Comments (with W. Gellhorn), 1970; (with Louis Joughn) Tenure in American Higher Education, 1959. Editorial bd. law book dept. Little, Brown & Co., 1956—, James Madison Constl. Law Inst., 1968—. Contbr. articles to Ency. Brit., legal publs. Home: Leverett House Towers Cambridge MA 02138 Office: Langdell Hall Harvard Cambridge MA 02138

BYTHELL, R. K., advt. exec.; b. Cochrane, O., Sept. 23, 1912; s. John Ruben and Anne (Simcock) B.; B.A., U. Western Ont., 1936; m. Helen Louise Babe, Sept. 21, 1940; children—David, Sara. Business editor Maclean Publns., 1936-39; copywriter London Life, 1946-47; marketing mgr. Salada Tea Co., 1947-55; with McCann Erickson Advt. Can. Ltd., 1955—, sr. v.p., 1963—. Served to lt. comdr. Royal Canadian Navy, 1941-45. Home: 31 Baby Point Crescent Toronto Ontario Canada Office: 151 Bloor St W Toronto Ontario Canada

BYWATERS, JERRY, artist, educator; b. Paris, Tex., 1906; s. Porter A. and Hattie (Williamson) B.; B.A., So. Meth. U., 1927; student Art Students League, N.Y.C., 1927; studied in Mexico. Europe; m. Mary McLarry, Nov. 3, 1930; children—Jerry, Dick. Prof. art So. Meth. U., 1936—, head art department, 1965-67; director Pollock Galleries, 1965-71; director of Dallas Museum of Fine Arts, 1943-64; works exhibited Met. Mus., San Francisco Mus., others; painter, printmaker, lectr. art, 1930—; art critic Dallas News, 1933-39; art editor Southwest Review, Dallas, 1950- 60. Home: 3625 Amherst Dallas TX 75225 Office: Southern Methodist U Dallas TX 75222

BZOCH, KENNETH RUDOLPH, educator; b. Chgo., Nov. 6, 1927; s. Rudolph and Mildred (Novoteny) B.; B.A., DePaul U., 1951; M.A., Northwestern U., 1952, Ph.D., 1956; m. Lorraine Marie Caoli, Oct. 29, 1950; children—Kathleen Marie, Kevin Jude, Instr., Northwestern U., 1951, asst. prof., dir. Cleft Palate Inst., 1957-59; asst. prof. Loyola U., Chgo., 1953-57; asso. prof. U. Fla., Gainesville, 1960-64, prof., chmn. dept. communicative disorders, 1964—; cons. U.S. Dept. Health, Edn. and Welfare, Nat. Inst. Dental Research, 1967-70, Div. Hosp. and Med. Facilities, 1964, VA Hosp., Gainesville, 1968-70. Served with USMCR, 1947. Fellow Am. Speech and Hearing Assn. (asso editor); mem. Fla. Speech and Hearing Assn. (pres.), Am. (sec.-treas.), Fla. (pres.) cleft palate assns. Author: Receptive-Expressive Emergent Language Scale and Manual, 1971. Co-editor: Cleft Lip and Palate, 1971. Contbr. articles profl. jours. Home: 640 NW 57th St Gainesville FL 32601

BZOCH, RONALD CHARLES, educator, mathematician; b. Chgo., Mar. 16, 1930; s. Rudolph and Mildred (Novotny) B.; B.A., DePaul U., 1953, M.S., 1954; Ph.D., Ill. Inst. Tech., 1957; m. Ann Cathrine Grill, Feb. 3, 1951; children—Mary Anne, James Joseph. Asst. prof. U. Minn., 1957-60, U. Utah, 1960-61; asso. prof. La. State U., 1961-66; prof. math., chmn. dept. U. N.D., 1966. Mem. cons. bur. Com. Undergrad. Program Math., 1966—; mem. com. examiners algebra-trigonometry, coll. level. exam. program Ednl. Testing Service, 1967-68. Recipient Outstanding Tchr. award U. N.D., 1969. Mem. Am. Math. Soc., Math. Assn. Am. (high sch. and coll. lectr. 1962—), Am. Assn. U. Profs. Roman Cath. Research on Stieltje's integration theory. Home: 914 Boyd Dr Grand Forks ND 58201

CABALLE, MONTSERRAT, soprano; m. Bernabé Martí; 1 son, Bernabé. N.Y.C. debut in Donizetti's Lucrezia Borgia, with Am. Opera Soc., 1965; also appeared with La Scala, Milan, Vienna Staatsoper, Glydebourne Festival, Met. Opera, Covent Garden, Rome Opera, Chgo. Lyric Opera; recitals and orchestral concerts in every maj. concert hall, Europe, N.Am. Address: care Columbia Artists Mgmt Inc 165 W 57th St New York City NY 10019*

CABANA, GEORGES, archbishop; b. Granby, Can., Oct. 23, 1894; s. Joseph and Marie V. (Desgrés) C.; student St. Charles Coll., Sherbrooke, 1908-10, St. Hyacinthe Sem., 1910-14; B.A., Laval U., 1914; B. Canon Law, Sem. of Theology, Montreal, 1917; D.C.L. Bishop's U.; Doct. Un., U. Sherbrooke. Ordained to priesthood Catholic Ch., 1918; prof. St. Hyacinthe Sem., 1918-21, St. Augustine's Sem., Toronto, 1921-31; prof., asst. St. Hyacinthe and Sorel, 1931-34; chaplain St. Charles Hosp., 1935; spiritual dir. St. Hyacinthe Sem. of Theology, 1936-41; consecrated archbishop-coadjutor of St. Boniface, Manitoba, 1941-52; archbishop of Sherbrooke, P.Q., 1952-68; titular See, archbishop of Succuba, 1968—; chancellor Sherbrooke U., 1954-68. Address: 104 E Sherbrooke Montreal 129 Quebec Canada

CABANISS, JAMES ALLEN, educator; b. Tuscumbia Ala., Dec. 8, 1911; s. Lem and Frances (Allen) C.; B.A. with honors, Southwestern at Memphis, 1932; M.Div., Louisville Presbyn. Theol. Sem., 1935; Ph.D., U. Chgo., 1939. Ordained to ministry Presbyn. Ch., 1935; pastor, Hazlehurst, Miss., 1935-37, Columbia, 1939- 43; prof. history U. Miss., 1946-68, research prof. history, 1968—, chmn. dept., 1961-64. Mem. Inst. Advanced Study, 1952- 53; stated clk. Presbyn. Synod Miss., 1960-64. Served from 1st lt. to maj. USAAF, 1943-46. Decorated Order Palmes Academiques. Fellow Royal Hist. Soc.; mem. Medieval Acad. Am., Am. Soc. Ch. History, Studiorum Novi Testamenti Societas, geneal. socs., Phi Beta Kappa, Omicron Delta Kappa. Mason (grand master Miss. 1962). Author: Life and Thought of a Country Preacher, 1942; History of the University of Mississippi, 1949, (2d edit. rev. titled The University of Mississippi: Its First Hundred Years 1971); Agobard of Lyons: Churchman and Critic, 1953; Amalarius of Metz, 1954; (with G.E. McCracken) Early Medieval Theology, 1957; Son of Charlemagne, 2d edit., 1965; Charlemagne's Cousins, 1967; Liturgy and Literature, 1970. Home: Box 253 University MS 38677

CABELL, CHARLES PEARRE, business cons.; b. Dallas, Oct. 11, 1903; B.S., U.S. Mil. Acad. 1925; grad. Air Corps Primary Flying Sch., 1931, Advanced Flying Sch., observation course, 1931, Command and Gen. Staff Sch., 1940; Army and Navy Staff Coll., 1943; m. Jacklyn DeHymel, 1934; children—Charles, Catharine, Ben. Commd. 2d lt., F.A., A.U.S., 1952, advanced to gen., U.S.A.F., 1958; served successively as asst. chief operations sect., tng. and operations div., as chief, photo unit, chief, tech. coordination br., Office of Chief of Air Corps, Washington, 1941-42; mem. advisory council Hdqrs. Army Air Forces, Washington, 1942-43; assigned 8th Air Force, ETO, Oct. 1943, comdr. combat Wing Dec. 1943; dir. plans, U.S. Strategic Air Forces, Apr.-July 1944; mil. air adviser to U.S. rep. on European Adv. Commn., London, May-July 1944; dir. operations and intelligence, Mediterranean Allied Air Forces, July 1944-May 1945; chief strategy and policy div. of air plans, Hdqrs. A.A.F., Washington, 1945; dep. and U.S. air rep. on mil. staff com. of UN, N.Y.C., 1946-47; dir. intelligence, Hdqrs., USAF, Washington, 1948; dir. Joint Staff, Joint Chiefs of Staff, 1951; dept. dir. Central Intelligence, 1953-62; now business cons. Awarded D.S.M., Legion of Merit, Air medal with oak-leaf cluster, D.F.C., Bronze Star; Distinguished Intelligence medal; Hon. comdr. Brit. Empire; Officer French Legion of Honor, Croix de Guerre; mem. Order of St. Laurice and Lazarus of Italy. Died May 25, 1971. Address: 2506 Ft Scott Dr Arlington VA 22202

CABELL, EARLE, congressman; b. nr. Dallas, Oct. 27, 1906; s. Ben E. and Sadie (Pearre) C.; student Tex. A. and M. Coll., 1952-26, So. Meth U., 1926; m. Elizabeth Holder, Feb. 22, 1932; children—Elizabeth Lee (Mrs. Pulley), Earle. Salesman, Morning Glory Creameries, Houston, 1926-28; plant supt. Mistletoe Creameries, Amarillo, Tex., 1928-30; owner Cabell's Dairy, Pine Bluff, Ark., 1930-32; with Cabell's Inc., 1932— successively sec.-treas., exec. v.p., 1932-52, pres., 1952—, chmn. bd., 1961-64; chmn. bd. Cabell's Dairies, Dallas; dir., exec. com. Grand Av. State Bank, 1945-65; mayor City of Dallas, 1961-64; mem. 89th-92d congresses 5th Dist. Tex. Pres. Dallas Crime Commn., 1954-56; mem. Gov.'s Econ. Adv. Commn., 1954- 56; adv. bd. Tex. Indsl. Commn.; active Boy Scouts Am.; sec., mem. exec. com. Tex. Law Enforcement Found.

Bd. dirs., Jr. Achievement. Served from capt. to lt. col., Tex. State Guard, 1941-46. Mem. Southwestern Law Enforcement Inst. (exec. com.), East Tex., Dallas chambers commerce, Dallas Sales Execs. Club (past pres.), Dairy Products Inst. Tex. (past pres.), Tex. Mfrs. Assn. (past pres.), Dallas Salemanship Club, Dallas Sales Execs. Clubs: Dallas Country, Dallas Athletic (past dir.), McKinney Lake (past pres.), City. Home: 3701 Turtle Creek Blvd Dallas TX 75219 Office: 1114 Commerce St Dallas TX 75201 also House Office Bldg Washington DC 20515

CABELL, RICHARD AYLETT, corp. exec.; b. Big Stone Gap. Va., Aug. 4, 1912; s. Mayo and Clara (Cabell) C.; B.A., U. Va., 1935, LL.B., 1939; m. Cyane Mason, May 11, 1940; children—Frances Mason, Richard Aylett, John Norton, Nicholas, Admitted to N.Y. bar, 1939; with firm Sullivan & Cromwell, N.Y.C., 1939- 44; with Internat. Nickel Co., Inc., N.Y.C., 1944—, asst. v.p., 1952- 58, v.p., 1958-64, exec. v.p. 1964-71, v.p., sec., 1971—, also dir.; with Internat. Nickel Co. of Can., Ltd., N.Y.C., 1945—, asst. v.p., 1958-60, v.p., 1960-67, exec. v.p., 1967-71, v.p., sec., 1971—; dir. Toronto- Dominion Bank Trust Co.; chmn. bd. Asso. Hosp. Service N.Y. Mem. Raven Soc., Order Coif, Phi Beta Kappa, Delta Psi, Phi Delta Phi. Clubs: Knickerbocker, One New York Plaza, Broad Street, Nat. Arts (N.Y.C.); Waccabuc Country. Home: Post Office Rd Waccabuc NY 10597 Office: 1 New York Plaza New York City NY 10004

CABELL, ROBERT GAMBLE, Jr., lawyer; b. Richmond, Va., Feb. 12, 1932; s. Robert Gamble and Jeanne (Witt) C.; B.A., U. Va., 1954, LL.B., 1957; m. Julia Carrington Riggs, June 6, 1950; children—Robert Gamble III, Julia Carrington, Temple Witt, Anne Norrison; m. 2d Shelley Louise Wessel, Apr. 2, 1959; children—Lynn Trude, Virginia Miller. Admitted to Va. bar, 1957; practice in Phila., 1957, Richmond, 1958—; mem. firm Pepper, Bodine, Frick, Scheetz & Hamilton, 1957, Williams, Mullen, Pollard & Rodgers, 1958-60, William, Cabell, Geisler & Glascock, 1960-65, White, Roberts, Cabell & Paris 1965—. Mem. Henrico County Democratic Com., 1962-65. Vice pres., bd. dirs. Richmond Tennis Patrons Assn.; bd. dirs. Va. Tennis Assn. Mem. Am., Va., Richmond bar assns., Phi Delta Phi, Delta Kappa Epsilon. Club: Country of Virginia, Author: (with others) The Virginia Lawyer, 1966. Home: Route 1 Box 178 Doswell VA 23047 Office: 721 E Main St Richmond VA 23219

CABELL, WILLIAM DANIEL, lawyer; b. Big Stone Gap, Va., Sept. 1, 1908; s. Mayo and Clara (Cabell) C.; grad. Va. Episcopal Sch., 1922-26; B.A., U. Va., 1939; m. Ellen Elspeth Rolston, Dec. 27, 1941; children—Kathleen Rolston (Mrs. Robert A. Hildreth), Willliam Daniel. Admitted to N.Y. bar, 1936, Va. bar, 1942, also U.S. Supreme Ct.; practice in N.Y.C., 1932-42, 46—, in Richmond, Va., 1942-45; partner firm McKenzie, Cabell, Martin & Greene, 1967—. A founder United Fund No. Westchester, N.Y., 1958, bd. dirs., sec., 1959- 61; chmn. Chappaqua Community United Fund campaign, 1961, Chappaqua Adv. Council United Fund, 1962; mem. men's com. N.Y.C. campaign United Negro Coll. Fund, 1950-60; mem. interacial conf. Nat. Council Chs., Richmond, 1944-45; mem. com. Washington Iriving council Boy Scouts Am., 1959-60. Mem. 5th Dist. Republican Com., New Castle, Westchester County, 1956-62; editor Voters Voice, 1952-53. Served as lt. (j.g.) USNR, 1942. Mem. Am., Va., Westchester County bar assns., Assn. Bar City N.Y., Delta Psi. Clubs: Town (Chappaqua); Waccabuc Country (Westchester County); St. Anthony, Knickerbocker (N.Y.C.). Home: 255 Quaker St Chappaqua NY 10514 Office: 555 Madison Av New York City NY 10022

CABLE, DONALD AUBREY, lawyer; b. Chgo., Aug. 7, 1927; s. Forbes and Clara (Henderson) C.; B.A., Lake Forest Coll., 1949; J.D., George Washington U., 1957; m. Joan B. Swanton, June 27, 1953; children—Bruce Cameron, Neil Alexader, Alison Clare. Staff auditor Main & Co., Washington, 1954-57; admitted to Wash. bar, 1957; agt. IRS, Seattle, Wash., 1957-58; mem. firm Short, Cressman & Cable and predecessor firms, Seattle, 1958—, partner, 1962—. Served with USNr, 1945-46, 52-54. Mem. Jr. C. of C. (past nat. bd. dirs.). Rotarian. Home: 6227 83d Av SE Mercer Island WA 98040 Office: 3000 Seattle-First Nat Bank Bldg 1001 4th Av Seattle WA 98104

CABLE, JOHN ARTHUR, ceramic tile mfr.; b. Canton, O., Aug. 15, 1912; s. Davis A. and Gail (Watson) O.; B.S. in Indsl. Engring., Lehigh U., 1947; m. Janet Vandervort, Sept. 9, 1950; childrenJennifer Alison, Philip Eric. With U.S. Ceramic Tile Co., Canton, 1947-, pres., 1955-66, chmn. bd., 1966- -. Served as 1st lt. Chem. Corps, AUS, 1943-46. Mem. Am. Ceramic Soc., Ohio Profl. Engrs. Home: 3435 Guilford Rd N W Canton OH 44718 Office: 1375 Raff Rd S W Canton OH 44710

CABLE RAYMOND MILLARD, univ. prof. and zoologist; b. Campton, Ky., Apr. 11, 1909; s. Casper and Rosa May (Smith) C.; A.B., Berea (Ky.) Coll., 1929, Sc.D., 1955; Sc.M., N.Y. U., 1939, Ph.D., 1933; Mary Caswell Tupper, Dec. 26, 1936; children—Margaret Treadway William Heyburn, June Perry, Daniel Hobbs. Grad. asst. N.Y.U., 1931- 33; asso. prof. biology Berea Coll., 1933-35; asst. in parasitology U. Chgo., summer 1934; ass. prasst. prof. zoology Purdue U., 1935-38, asso. prof. 1939-47, prof., 1948—; summer research, Marine Biol. Lab., Wood Hole, Mass., 1931-33, 1935-42; Guggenheim fellow U. P.R., 1951-52; research supported by NSF at Craibisch Marine-Biologisch Inst., Curacao, N.A., U. Coll. of W.I. Jamaica, 1961. Fellow A.A.A.S., Ind. Acad. of Sci., N.Y. Acad. Sci; mem. Helminthological Soc. Washington, Am. Soc. Zoologists, American Soc. Parasitologists (past pres.), Am. Soc. Naturalists, American Micros. Society, Sigma Xi. Republican. Presbyn. Author: An Illustrated Laboratory Manual of Parasitology, 1941, 58; also research papers on animal parasities. Mem. editorial bd. Jour. of Parasitology. Home: 820 Carrolton Blvd West Lafayette, IN 47906. Office: Dept Biol Scis Purdue U Lafayette IN 47907

CABOT, CHARLES CODMAN, lawyer; b. Brookline, Mass., Nov. 22, 1900; s. Henry Broomfield and Anne Macmaster (Codman) C.; A.B., Harvard, 1922, LL.B., 1925; m. Ellen P. White, July 1, 1929; children—Charles Codman, Walter M. Admitted to Mass. bar; practice in various Boston offices; partner Ropes, Gray, Best, Coolidge and Rugg, 1933-43; asso. justice Mass. Superior Ct., 1943-47; partner firm Herrick, Smith, Donald, Farley and Ketchum. Sec. U.S. Strategic Bombing Survey, 1945. Chmn. Greater Boston United War Fund campaign, 1943; moderator, former chmn., Bd. of Selectmen, Dover, Mass.; chmn. bd. dirs. Mass. Bay Transp. Authority, 1966-69. Trustee New Eng. Center Hosp. Milton Acad.; overseer Harvard Coll. 1944-50. Served as pvt. USMC, World War I. Mem. Mass., Boston bar assns. Participates in various charitable, civic and polit. enterprises. Home: Dedham St Dover MA 02030 Office: 294 Washington St Boston MA 02108

CABOT, HAROLD, bus. exec.; b. Waltham, Mass., Nov. 28, 1899; s. Chilton and Louise (Richardson) C.; student Harvard, 1922; m. Adeline Eveleth, May 14, 1924; children—Lucia Lee, Harold, Daniel Breck. Advt. work various agys. and corps., 1922-29; established Harold Cabot & Co., advt. agy., Boston, 1930, now chmn.; dir. Union Mut. Life Ins. Co. Trustee, past pres. bd. Concord Acad.; past pres. and trustee Emerson Hosp., Concord, Mass. Mem. Am. Assn. Advt. Agys. (sec.-treas.), Boston C. of C. Clubs: Union: Downtown; Country (Concord, Mass.). Home: Ripley Hill Rd Concord MA 01742 Office: 136 Federal St Boston MA 02110

CABOT, HENRY B., univ. trustee; b. Boston, Dec. 7, 1894; s. Henry B. and Anne M. (Codman) C.; A.B., Harvard, 1917, LL.B., 1922; L.H.D. Tufts U.; m. Olivia Ames, June 18, 1927; 1 son, Henry B. Jr. Practicing lawyer, Boston, 1922-30; research asso., Harvard Law Sch., 1930-38, trustee since 1938. Dir. Samuel Cabot, Inc. Mem. bd. overseers Harvard, 1954-60; trustee emeritus Boston Symphony Orch. Author: (with S.B. Warner) Judges and Law Reform, 1937. Home: Dover MA 02030 Office: 225 Franklin St Boston MA 02110

CABOT, JOHN GODFREY LOWELL, chem. co. exec.; b. Rio de Janeiro, Brazil, Aug. 8, 1934 (parents Am. citizens); s. John Moors and Elizabeth (lewis) C.; grad. Groton Sch., 1952; A.B., Harvard, 1956, M.B.A., 1960; m. Carroll Lloyd Trimble, July 9, 1960; children—John Ridgeway, Andrew Lowell. Instrumentation engr. Martin Co., Balt., 1956-57; with Cabot Corp. and subsidiaries, Boston, 1960—, mgr. financial planning, 1962-64, asst. mgr. machinery div., 1964-65, dir. planning, 1965-67 gen. mgr. Cabot Utilities, Inc. Div., 1967—, also dir. parent co., mgr. European operations. Vice pres. Boston Opera Group. Mem. Pan Am. Soc. New Eng. (gov.) Clubs: Metropolitan (Washington) ; Somerset (Boston); Essex County (Manchester, Mass). Home: 146 Mt Vernon St Boston MA 02108 Office: 125 High St Boston MA 02110

CABOT, JOHN M., former U.S. ambassador; b. Cambridge, Mass., Dec. 11, 1901; s. Godfrey Lowell and Maria (Buckminster) Moors C.; A.B. magna cum laude, Harvard, 1923; B.Litt., Brasenose Coll., Oxford, Eng., 1925; LL.D., Tufts U., 1956; D.Fgn. Service (hon.), Suffolk U., 1966; m. Elizabeth Lewis, Apr. 2, 1932; children—Majorie Moors (Mrs. Antonio Enriquez-Savignac), John G.L., Lewis Pickering, Elizabeth Tracy (Mrs. Bogislav von Wentzel). U.S. fgn. service officer, 1926—; vice consul, Callao-Lima, Peru, 1927-28; 3d sec., Dominican Republic, 1929-31, Mexico, 1931-32; 3d sec. and 2d sec., Rio de Janeiro, Brazil, 1932-35; 2d sec., The Hague, Netherlands, 1935-38; sec., Stockholm, Sweden, 1938-39, Guatemala, 1939- 41; assigned Dept. of State; Asst. chief div. Am. Republics, 1942; chief div. Caribbean and Central Am. affairs, 1944; counselor of embassy, Buenos Aires, Argentina, 1945-46, Belgrade, Yugoslavia, 1947; apptd. career minister, 1948; consul gen., Shanghai, China, 1948-49; minister to Finland, 1950-52; ambassador to Pakistan, 1952-53; asst. sec. of state for Inter-Am. affairs, 1953; U.S. A.E. and P. to Sweden, 1954-57; ambassador Colombia, 1957-59, Brazil, 1959-61, Poland, 1962-65; dep. comdt. Nat. War Coll., 1965-66; lectr. Fletcher Sch. Law and Diplomacy, Tufts U., 1967-68; tech. officer U.S. delegations to Dumbarton Oaks, Mexico City and San Francisco Confs. Del. Conf. Am. States, Caracas, Venezuela, 1954. Decorated Grand Cross Order of So. Cross (Brazil). Mem. Am. Acad. Arts and Scis. Clubs: Metropolitan, Chevy Chase, University (Washington); Brook (N.Y.C.); Somerset (Boston). Author: The Racial Conflict in Transylvania, 1926; Toward Our Common American Destiny, 1955. Home: 1610 28th St NW Washington DC 20007

CABOT, LOUIS WELLINGTON, chem. mfr.; b. Boston, Aug. 3, 1921; s. Thomas Dudley and Virginia (Wellington) C.; A.B., Harvard, 1943, M.B.A., 1948; LL.D. (hon.), Norwich U., 1961; m. Mary Louise Bass, Nov. 24, 1945; children—James Bass, Anne Louise, Godfrey Lowell II, Amanda Chilton, Helen. With Cabot Corp., 1948—, dir., financial v.p., 1953-60, pres., 1960-69, chmn. bd., 1969—; dir. Owens-Corning Fiberglas Corp., R.R. Donnelley & Sons Co., Chgo., New Eng. Tel. & Tel. Co., Fed. Res. Bank Boston, U.S. rep. 15th Plenary Session UN Econ. Commn. for Europe, 1960; mem. steering com. bus. ethics adv. council Dept. Commerce, 1961-63; New Eng. chmn., dir. Nat. Alliance Businessmen. Pres. Beverly Hosp., 1958-61; chmn. Harvard Coll. Fund Council, 1963-65; mem. corp. Mass. Inst. Tech., 1963-68, Boston Hosp. Women; trustee Carnegie Corp. N.Y., Northeastern U., Norwich U., Brookings Instn., Boston Mus. of Sci.; bd. overseers Harvard U., Boys Clubs Boston, Inc.; dir. Mass. Bay United Fund. Served to lt. USNR, 1943-46. Recipient Bus. Statesman award Harvard Bus. Sch. Assn., Boston, 1966. Fellow Am. Acad. Arts and Scis.; mem. Bus. Council, Conf. Bd., Com. Corporate Support Am. Univs., Bus. Com. for the Arts, Council Fgn. Relations, Phi Beta Kappa, Sigma Xi. Clubs: Harvard (N.Y.C.); Somerset (Boston); Metropolitan (Washington); Kandahar Ski; Myopia Hunt. Home: 97 Larch Row Wenham MA 01984 Office: 125 High St Boston MA 02110

CABOT, PAUL CODMAN, banker; Brookline, Mass., Oct. 21, 1898; s. Henry Bromfield and Anne MacMaster (Codman) C.; A.B., Harvard, 1921, M.B.A., with distinction, 1923, LL.D., 1966; LL.D., Yale, 1965; m. Virginia C. Converse, Sept. 20, 1924; children—Virginia C. (Mrs. John M. Wood, Jr.), Elizabeth M. (Mrs. Henry W. Minot, Jr.), Paul Codman, Edmund C., Frederick C. With First Nat. Bank, Boston, 1923-24; treas. State St. Investment Corp., 1924-34, pres., 1934-58, chmn. bd. dirs., 1958—; partner State St. Research & Mgmt. Co., 1928—; dir. J. P. Morgan & Co., Continental Can Co., Ford Motor Co., Inc., Nat. Dairy Products Corp., The B.F. Goodrich Co., M.A. Hanna Co. Mem. bus. adv. council Dept. of Commerce. Treas. Harvard U., 1948-65. Served as 2d lt. F.A., U.S. Army, 1917-18; as nat. dir. salvage div. WPB, 1941-42. Mem. Eastern Gas and Fuel Assn. (trustee, mem. exec. com.). Clubs: Harvard, Union (Boston); Links (N.Y.C.); Dedham Country and Polo; Porcellian; Somerset. Home: 653 Chestnut St Needham MA 02192 Office: Franklin St Boston MA 02110

CABOT, TED, U.S. dist. judge; b. Hobe Sound, Fla., Feb. 5, 1917; s. Frederick Mortimer and Sallie Belle (Crenshaw) C.; LL.B., U. Miami (Fla.), 1953; m. Louise Morris Cook, June 28, 1947; children—Nathalie Ann, Bruce, Sallie, Louise, Mary Beth. Engaged in accounting, Ft. Lauderdale, Fla., 1936-44; clk. circuit ct. Broward County, Fla., 1945-53; admitted to Fla. bar, 1953; pvt. practice, Ft. Lauderdale, 1953-59; mem. Fla. Senate from Borward County, 1954-58; circuit judge Broward County, 1959-66; U.S. dist. judge So. Dist. Fla., 1966—. Democrat. Presbyn. (trustee). Home: 3333 Riverland Rd Fort Lauderdale FL 33312 Office: 300 NE 1st Av Miami FL 33101

CABOT, THOMAS DUDLEY, corp. exec.; b. Cambridge, Mass., May 1, 1897; s. Godfrey Lowell and Maria Buckminster (Moors) C.; A.B., Harvard, 1919; L.H.D., Tufts U., 1951, Boston U., 1961; LL.D., Northeastern U., 1952, Morris Harvey Coll., 1953, Harvard, 1970; m. Virginia Wellington, May 15, 1920; children—Louis Wellington, Thomas Dudley, Robert Moors, Linda, Edmund Billings. Former pres. United Fruit Co., Boston; pres. Godfrey L. Cabot, Inc. (name changed to Cabot Corp., 1960), chmn. bd., 1960-68, hon. chmn. bd., 1968- -; former dir. John Hancock Mut. Life Ins. Co., First Nat. Bank of Boston, Am. Mut. Liability Ins. Co.; trustee Boston Five Cents Savs. Bank; adv. bd. Colonial Growth Shares, Inc. Chmn. Mass. Aero Commn., 1944-45; dir. office Internat. Security Affairs, Dept. of State, 1951, cons. Spl. Mission to Egypt, 1953. Bd. overseers Harvard, 1953-59, 62-68; trustee Radcliffe Coll., Escuela Agricola Panamericana; mem. corp. Mass. Inst. Tech.; trustee Com. Econ. Devel., Children's Med. Center; dir. Affiliated Hosp. Center, Inc. Served as 2d lt., A.S., U.S. Army, flying instr., 1917-18. Decorated chevalier Legion of Honor (France); commendatore Al Merito della Republica Italiana. Fellow A.A.A.S.; mem. Council Fgn. Relations, Internat. C. of C. (trustee U.S. council). Republican. Unitarian. Author: Quick Water and Smooth. Home: 31 Farm Rd Weston MA 02193 Office: 125 High St Boston MA 02110

CABOT, THOMAS DUDLEY, Jr., chem. co. exec.; b. Boston, Oct. 15, 1922; s. Thomas Dudley and Virginia (Wellington) C.; A.B., Harvard, 1944; m. Anne Flint, May 13, 1950; children—Thomas Dudley III, Moors, Cecily; m. 2d, Mary McGrath, Nov. 7, 1963; childrenRobert M., Laura, James W. Engaged as a scientist, Bikini Bomb Test, 1946; tech. exec. Am. Research and Devel. Corp., Boston, 1947- 52; officer small cos., Boston, 1953-57; treas. Cabot-France S.A., Paris, 1957-58; v.p., then pres. Tex. Butadiene & Chem. Internat., Ltd., Switzerland, 1959-62; pres. Tex. Butadiene & Chem. Corp., N.Y.C., 1962-63; v.p. corp. devel. Cabot Corp., N.Y.C. and Boston, 1963—. Served with USNR, World War II. Home: 10 Copper Beech Rd Greenwich CT 06830 Office: 522 Fifth Av New York City NY 10017 also 125 High St Boston MA 02110

CACCIA, LORD HAROLD ANTHONY, Brit. diplomat; b. India, Dec. 21, 1905; s. Anthony and Fanny Theodora (Birch) C.; student Eton, Trinity Coll., Oxford, Eng.; Laming Travelling fellow Queen's Coll., Oxford, 1928; m. Anne Catherine Barstow, Oct. 4, 1932; childrenDavid, Clarissa, Antonia. Entered Her Majesty's Fgn. Service, 1929—, assigned Peking, China, 1932. Fgn. Office, 1935; asst. pvt. sec. to Sec. of State, 1936; assigned Athens, Greece, 1939; with resident minister, North Africa, 1943. Allied Control Commn. in Italy, 1943-44; then polit. adviser to Gen. Officer Comdg. Officer Comdg.-in Chief Land Forces, Greece, 1944; asst. under- sec. state, 1946, dep. under-sec. state, 1949; Brit. high commr., Austria, 1950-54, Brit. ambassador, 1951-54; dep. under-sec. state Fgn. Office, 1954-56; permanent under-sec. State, 1962-65; A.E. and P. to U.S., 1956-61; provost Eton Coll., Windsor, Eng., 1965—. Chmn. Standard Telephones & Cables, Ltd.; dir. Prudential Assurance, Ltd., Nat. Westminister Bank, Ltd., Fgn. and Colonial Investment Trust, Orion Bank, Ltd. Decorated knight grand cross Most Distinguished Order of St. Michael and St. George; knight grand cross Royal Victorian Order; grand cross of Order St. John Jerusalem; created Baron of Abernant, 1965. Lord prior Order of St. John, 1969. Home: Abernant Builth-Wells Wales also 1 Chester Pl Regents Park London England Office: Provost's Lodge Eton College Windsor England

CACKLER, HAROLD WAYNE, clergyman; b. Lucas County, Ia., Sept. 30, 1912; s. Jacob Clark and Catharine Ann (Thomas) C.; ed. pub. schs., Ia.; m. Arline Fae Fowler, Apr. 18, 1941; 1 son; John Wayne. With J.D. Trelkeld & Son, Ins., Chariton, Ia., 1931-34, Ford Motor Co., Des Moines, 1934-43, Gibbs-Cook Tractor and Equipment Co., Des Moines, 1942-47; mem. Reorganized Ch. of Jesus Christ of Latter Day Saints, part-time minister, 1932-47; bishop, 1947—; asst. to presiding bishop internat. hdqrs., Independence, Mo., 1947-48; bishop for Independence area, 1948-66; counselor to presiding bishop, also mem. internat. orgn. of ch., 1966—. Vice pres. Central Devel. Assn.; dir. Bellevista Devel. Assn. Past pres. Community Welfare League Indepencence, bd. dirs.; bd. dirs. Jackson County (Mo.) United Fund Council. Rotarian. Home: 117 S Union St Independence MO 64050 Office: The Auditorium Independence MO 64501

CACOYANNIS, MICHAEL, stage and film dir.; b. Cyprus, June 11, 1922; s. Panayotis and Angeliki (Efthyvoulos) C.; Barrister-at-Law, Gray's Inn, London, Eng., 1942; student Central Sch. Dramatic Art, London, 1942-43, Old Vic Sch., London, 1945-46. Appeared on London stage in Salome, 1946, Caligula, 1949, others; author, dir. films Winfall in Athens, 1953, Stella, 1955, A Girl in Black, 1956, A Matter of Dignity, 1958, Our Last Spring, 1960, The Wastrel, 1961, Electra, 1962, Zorba the Greek, 1964, The Day the Fish Came Out, 1966-67, The Trojan Women, 1970-71; dir. stage prodns., Athens, Greece, 1954-62, The Trojan Women, N.Y.C., 1963-65, Mourning Becomes Electra, 1967, Iphigenia in Aulis, N.Y.C., 1967-68, Romeo and Juliet, Paris, France, 1968. Recipient Cannes Jury award for Electra, 1962, also 24 other internat. awards for film; 3 Acad. awards for Zorba the Greek, 1965; Drama Critics Spl. award, also Lola D'Annunzio Meml. award for Trojan Women, 1964; decorated Order Gold Phoenix (Greece). Address: 96 Blvd Montparnasee Paris France

CADBURY, HENRY JOEL, educator; b. Phila., Pa., Dec. 1, 1883; s. Joel and Anna Kaighn (Lowry) C.; A.B., Haverford Coll., 1903, Litt.D., 1933; A.M., Harvard, 1904, Ph.D., 1914; D.D., U. Glasgow, 1937; LL.D., Whittier Coll., 1951, Swarthmore Coll., 1954; L.H.D., Howard U., 1959, Earlham Coll., 1967; m. Lydia Caroline Brown, June 17, 1916; children—Elizabeth (Mrs. John K. Musgrave, Jr.), Christopher Joel, Warder Henry, Winifred (Mrs. Martin M. Beer). Asso. with Haverford Coll. 1910-19, Harvard, 1919-26, Bryn Mawr Coll. 1926-34; Hollis prof. divinity Harvard, also Dexter lectr. Bib. lit., 1934-54, now emeritus; lectr. Pendle Hill, Wallingford, Pa., 1954—, Haverford Coll., 1954- 63; adj. prof. Temple U., 1962-66; sec. Am. Schs. Oriential Research, 1934-54; dir. Andover-Harvard Theol. Library, 1938-54; Lowell lectr., Boston, 1935, 53, Carew lectr. Hartford Sem., 1935; Shaffer lectr. Yale Div. Sch., 1946; Samuel A. Crozer lectr. Crozer Sem., 1953; Edward Cadbury lectr. U. Birmingham, 1956; Swarthmore lectr. at London Yearly Meeting, 1957. Chmn. bd. dirs. Bryn Mawr Coll., 1956-68. Mem. Am. Friends Service Com. (chmn. 1928-34, 1944-60; hon. chmn. 1960- -, engaged child-feeding in Germany, summer 1920; commissioner to England, winter 1941); mem. Am. Standard Bible Com., 1930—. Fellow Am. Acad. Arts and Scis.; hon. mem. Oxford Soc. Hist. Theology; mem. Am. Oriental Soc. Soc. Bib. Lit. (sec. 1916-33, pres. 1936; del. Am. Council Learned Socs., 1929-50), Am. Antiquarian Soc., Am. Philos. Soc., Studiorum Novi Testamenti Societas (pres. 1958- 59), Phi Beta Kappa. Mem. Soc. of Friends. Author books including: The Making of Luke-Acts, 1927; George Fox's Book of Miracles, 1948; Letters to William Dewsbury, 1948; The Book of Acts in History, 1955; also articles on history of Quakerism, Bibl. subjects. Editor Annual of Am. Schs. of Oriental Research, 1927-32. Home: 774 Millbrook Lane Haverford PA 19041 ☆

CADBURY, WILLIAM EDWARD, Jr., educator; b. Phila., Apr. 19, 1909; s. William Edward and Mary Yarnall (Brown) C.; S.B., Haverford Coll., 1931, A.M., 1932; Ph.D., U. Pa., 1940; m. Charlotte May, June 12, 1933; children—William Edward, III, Sarah T. (Mrs. Donald G. Giddings). Member of faculty of Haverford College, 1932—, successively instr. chemistry, asst. and asso. prof., prof., 1954—, dean, 1951-66, dir. post-baccalaureate fellowship program, 1966—; acting asso. prof. U. N.C. 1943-44. Exec. dir. Nat. Med. Med. Fellowships, Inc., N.Y.C., 1969—. Mem. com. charge Westtown Sch., 1942-68. Mem. A.A.A.S., Am. Conf. Acad. Deans (chmn. 1962-63), Phi Beta Kappa. Mem. Soc. of Friends. Author: (with A.E. Severinghaus and H.J. Carman) Preparation for Medical Education in the Liberal Arts College, 1953, Preparation for Medical Education: A Restudy, 1961. Asso. editor Jour. Chem. Edn., 1950-55. Home: 404 Riverside Dr New York City NY 10025

CADDELL, JOHN A., lawyer; b. Tuscumbia, Ala., Apr. 23, 1910; s. Thomas Arthur and Florence Lee (Huff) C.; A.B., U. Ala., 1931, LL.B., 1933; m. Lucy Bowen Harris, Sept. 1, 1935; children—Thomas A., Lucinda Lee, Henry Harris and John A. (twins). Admitted to Ala. bar, 1933, since practiced in Decatur. Sec., dir. Southeastern Metals Co., Inc., Birmingham, 1946-68; dir. First Nat. Bank Decatur. City atty., Decatur, 1936-59; counsel com. Ho. Reps. U.S. investigating campaign expenditures, 1944; bd. commrs. Ala. State Bar, 1939-54, Jud. Council Ala., 1946-58; mem. bd. Bar Examiners Ala., 1949, 50. Trustee U. Ala. Fellow Am. Coll. probate counsel, Am. Coll. Trial

Lawyers; mem. Am., Ala. (pres. 1951-52), Morgan County bar assns., U. Ala. Alumni Assn. (pres. 1953), Decatur C. of C. (pres. 1943- 44), Pi Kappa Alpha, Omicron Delta Kappa, Phi Delta Phi. Democrate (mem. Ala. exec. com. 1938-50). Presbyn. (elder). Clubs: Athletic, U. Alabama; Decatur Kiwanis (pres. 1939). Home: 2200 Country Club Rd SE Decatur AL 35601 Office: 230 E Moulton St Decatur AL 35601

CADDOO, WILLIAM HENRY, retired carton co. exec.; b. Yonker, N.Y., July 18, 1908; s. William A. and Nettie Cole (Jones) C.; B.S., Colby Coll., 1932; grad. Advanced Mgmt. Program, Harvard, 1957; m. Barbara Louise King, Dec. 11, 1948. From chemist to v.p. boxboard div. Robert Gair, Inc., 1937-56; company merged with Continental Can Co., Inc., 1956, v.p., gen. mgr. boxboard and folding carton div., 1958-60, gen. mgr. mfg. boxboard until 1970, retired, 1970. Club: Wee Burn Country. Home: Forest Hill Rd Darien CT 06820

CADDY, E. REID, hosp. exec.; b. Canonsburg, Pa., Dec. 6, 1914; s. Charles Edward and Mary (Reid) C.; A.B., Miami U., Oxford, O.; B.S. in Hotel Adminstrn., Cornell U.; M.P.H. in Hosp. Adminstrn., U. Pitts.; m. Margaret M. Montgomery, June 29, 1936. Dir. Ch. Charity Found. and St. John's Episcopal Hosp., Bklyn., 1947-51; dir. sec. Westmoreland Hosp. Assn., Greensburg, Pa., 1951-68; exec. v.p. Monsour Hosp., Jeanette, Pa., 1968- -; cons. Monsour Med. Found., 1968—; dir. hosp. div. W.L. Canong Cons. Co., Pitts., 1959-70; pres. E. Reid Caddy Cons. Group, Greensburg. Pres. Westmoreland Health and Welfare Assn., 1964- 67; exec. com. Regional Med. Program Adv. Group, 1968—; mem. Westmoreland Comprehensive Health Planning Council; bd. dirs. Md. and Western Pa. Blue Cross, Southwestern Heart Assn. Fellow Am. Pub. Health Assn., Am. Coll. Hosp. Adminstrs., Royal Soc. Health, Am. Acad. Sci. Episcopalian (vestry). Home: 213 Blackridge Dr Greensburg PA 15601 Office: 70 Lincoln Way E Jeannette PA 15644

CADDY, EDMUND HARRINGTON HOMER, Jr., architect; b. N.Y.C., Apr. 17, 1928; s. Edmund Harrington Homer and Glenna Corinne (Garratt) C.; B.A., Princeton, 1952, M.F.A. (grad. sch. fellow), 1955; m. Mary Audrey Ortiz, Dec. 22, 1951; children—Edmund Harrington Homer III, Mary Elizabeth. With firm Louis E. Jallade, architect, N.Y.C., 1949; Eggers & Higgins, architects, N.Y.C., 1953; dir. design Dalton-Dalton Assos., architects and engineers, Cleve., 1955-60; asso. mem. firm Raymond & Rado, architects, N.Y.C., 1960-68; gen. parnter Raymond & Rado and Partners, architects, N.Y.C., 1968—; maj. works include Suburban Hosp., Cleve., 1957; J.M. Smucker Co., Salinas, Cal., 1957; Brookpark (O.) City Hall, 1959; Cleve. Transit System addition, 1959; adminstrn. bldg. Metropolitan Water Treatment System, Saigon, 1960; Franklin D. Roosevelt High Sch., N.Y.C., 1963; Crown Heights Intermediate Sch., N.Y.C., 1966; J.C. Penney dept. stores in Kansas City, Mo., 1968, Greensburg, Pa., 1969, Ft. Wayne, Ind., 1969, and Mpls., 1970; engring. complex Stony Brook Campus, State U. N.Y., 1970. Mem. adv. com. arts, John F. Kennedy Center Performing Arts, 1963—. Mem. Richard Nixon Assos., 1968—. Bd. Trustees Montclair (N.J.) Community Hosp. Served with USMC, 1946-48, USMCR, 52-53. Mem. A.I.A., Architects Soc. Ohio, N.Y. State Architects Assn., USMCR Officers Assn. Clubs: Tower (Princeton); Raquet and Tennis (N.Y.C.); Montclair Golf. Home: 2 Wendover Rd Montclair NJ 07042 Office: 299 Park Av New York City NY 10017

CADE, ARTHUR JOSEPH, ins. co. exec.; b. Oak Park, Ill., Apr. 3, 1917; s. Joseph P. and Clara D. (Reisch) C.; A.B., Yale, 1939; m. Patricia Pfau, Apr. 17, 1942; children—Scott R., Melissa R., Phillip R.; m. 2d, Ione Rogers, Dec. 8, 1962. Agt. Equitable Life Assurance Soc. U.S., 1939-40; field rep. Old Republic Life Ins. Co., Chgo., 1940-42, 45-47, v.p., 1947- 53, exec. v.p., 1953-59, Old Republic Ins. Co., Greensburg, Pa., 1955- 60; pres., dir. Security Funding Corp., Chgo., 1960-; v.p., dir. So. Provident Life Ins. Co.; dir. Tilden Life Ins. Co., Genesee Valley Life Ins. Co. (all Phoenix), 1st Provident Co., Sanford, N.C. Chmn. bd. Consumer Credit Ins. Assn. Served as lt. comdr., USNR, 1942-45. Mem. U.S., Ill. chambers commerce, Yale Alumni Assn. Home: 9S174 Drew Av Hinsdale, IL 60521. Office: 310 Oak Brook Exec Plaza Oak Brook IL 60521

CADES, JULIUS RUSSELL, lawyer; b. Phila., Oct. 30, 1904; s. Isaac and Ida Frieda (Russell) C.; A.B., U. Pa., 1925, LL.B. cum laude, 1928, LL.M. (Gowan research fellow corp. law), 1930; m. Charlotte Leah McLean, Nov. 28, 1938; 1 son, Russell McLean. Admitted to Pa. bar, 1928, Hawaii bar, 1930; practice in Honolulu, 1929—; partner firm Cades, Schutte, Fleming & Wright, and predecessor, 1934—. Chem. com. to promote uniformity of legislation of U.S. for Hawaii, 1949-60, mem., 1962-66; mem. Jud. Council State Hawaii, 1966—. Dir. Universal Motor Co. Ltd., Advertisers Pub. Co., Ltd., Kekaha Sugar Co., Ltd., Lihue Plantation Co., Ltd., Puna Sugar Co., Ltd., Pacific Devel. Co., Ltd., Hawaiian Life Ins. Co. Ltd., Pacific Concrete & Rock Co., Ltd., Oahu Sugar Co., Ltd., Pioneer Mill Co. Ltd. Chmn. bd. commnrs. Hawaii Bd. Pub. Instrn., 1945; counsel, violin and viola player Honolulu Symphony Orch., 1935—. Chmn. bd. regents U. Hawaii, 1941-43: trustee, dir. Honolulu Acad. Arts, 1950-51, Watumull Found., 1955—; treas., dir. Honolulu Art Soc., 1936-50. Fellow Am. Bar Found.; mem. Am. Bar Assn. (del. Hawaii 1950-53), Bar Assn. Hawaii (pres. 1946-48), Am. Law Inst., Order of Coif. Writer on taxation, gen. semantics, law. Home: 2186A Round Top Dr Honolulu HI 96822 Office: First Hawaiian Bank Bldg Honolulu HI 96813

CADES, MILTON, lawyer; b. Phila., Mar. 14, 1903; B.S., U. Pa., 1924, LL.M., 1937; LL.B., Temple U., 1932. Admitted to Pa. bar, 1932, Hawaii bar, 1937; now mem. firm Cades, Schutte, Fleming & Wright, Honolulu. Mem. Am. Bar Assn., Bar Assn. Hawaii. Office: Cades Schutte Fleming & Wright 1st Hawaiian Nat Bank Bldg Honolulu HI 96808*

CADGE, WILLIAM FLEMING, art dir.; b. Phila., May 5, 1924; s. Arthur and Janet (Fleming) C.; student Phila. Mus. Sch. Art, 1945-49; m. Anne Marie English, Feb. 5, 1949; children—Stephen Anthony, Jeffrey John, Catherine Anne. Free lance designer, Phila., 1949-50; asst. art dir. Eve. Bull., Phila., 1950-52, Woman's Home Companion, 1952-56; art dir. Doyle, Dane & Bernbach, advt., N.Y.C., 1956-57; asso. art dir. McCall's mag., 1959-61; art dir. Redbook mag., 1961—; photog. covers nat. and European mags., also fashion, reportage and illustration. Served with RAF, 1941-43, with USAAF, 1943- 45. Recipient 2 gold medals, 8 award distinctive merit Art Director's Club N.Y.; 1 gold medal, 1 award distinctive merit Art Director's Club Phila.; 1 award excellence Art Director's Club N.J., also N.J. 2 awards of excellence.; 1 award outstanding achievement for 1966, Soc. Illustrators; 5 awards excellence Type Director's Club N.Y.; 1 award excellence for 3 consecutive issues of Redbook in 1966, 1969, Soc. Publn. Designers, also 1 award excellence best typography in 1966, and award distinctive merit for 3 consecutive issues Redbook, 1970; awards excellence CA Mag. Show, 1967, 68, Soc. Publication Designers, 1968, Soc. Illustrators, 1968. Mem. Soc. Illustrators, Art Director's Club N.Y. (exec. bd. 1966-68). Home: 33 Colonial Av Dobbs Ferry NY 10522 Office: Redbook Magazine 230 Park Av New York City NY 10017

CADIEUX, LEO, Canadian govt. ofcl.; b. St. Jerome, Que., Can., May 28, 1908; s. Joseph E. and Rosa (Paquette) C.; ed. Comml. Coll. St. Jerome, Sem. Ste. Thérèse de Blainville; m. Monique Plante, Aug. 1, 1962; 1 son, Fabrice. Engaged in pub. relations work with the Canadian Army, 1941- 44; war corr. La Ore Presse, Montreal, Que., 1944; engaged in journalism; dir. L'Avenir du Nord, La Revue Moderne; prothonotary Superio Ct., Terrebonne Dist.; mayor St. Antoine des Laurentides, 1948; mem. Ho. of Commons, 1962—, apptd. asso. minister nat. def., 1965; ambassador of Can. in France, 1970—. Mem. Liberal party. Roman Catholic. Home: 135 rue du Fauborg St Honoré Paris 8e France Office: 35 avenue Montaigne Paris 8e France

CADIEUX, MARCEL, ambassador; b. Montreal, Que., Can., June 17, 1915; s. Romeo and Bertha (Patenaude) C.; B.A., Andre Grasset Coll. (Can.), 1936; Licentiate Laws, U. Montreal, 1939; postgrad. McGill U., 1939-40; LL.D. univs. Montreal, 1964, Poitiers, 1966, Ottawa, 1968; m. Anita Comtois, Jan. 21, 1956; children—Francois, Rene. Called to Canadian bar, 1939, named Queen's counsel, 1962; with Canadian Dept. External Affairs, Ottawa, Ont., 1941- 56, London, Eng., 1944-45. Brussels, Belgium, 1945-47, Paris, France, 1951-54, Hanoi, Vietnam, 1954-55; asst. under-sec. state for external affairs, legal adviser, Ottawa, 1956-60. dep. under-sec., legal adviser, 1960-64, under-sec., 1964-70; Canadian ambassador to U.S., Washington, 1970—; prof. pub. internat. law Faculty of Law, U. Ottawa, 1956-63. Mem. UN Internat. Law Commn., 1962-67. Bd. govs. Nat. Film Bd. Can., 1962-70. Decorated Order of Companion of Can.; recipient Vanier gold medal Inst. Pub. Adminstrn. Can., 1969, Outstanding Achievement award of Pub. Service, 1969. Mem. Royal Soc. Roman Catholic. Clubs: Metropolitan, Chevy Chase (Washington); Rideau (Ottawa). Author: Le Ministere des Affaires Exterieures, 1949; Premieres Armes, 1950; Embruns, 1951; Le Diplomate Canadien, 1961; also articles. Home: 2825 Rock Creek Dr NW Washington DC 20008 Office: 1746 Massachusetts Av NW Washington DC 20036

CADIGAN, GEORGE LESLIE, bishop; b. Mt. Vernon, N.Y., Apr. 12, 1910; s. Edward J. and Christina (Lindblom) C.; B.A., Amherst Coll., 1933, also D.D.; student Episcopal Theol. Sch., 1935, Jesus Coll., Cambridge U., 1936; D.D., Hobart Coll., U. of the South; m. Jane Jones, Aug. 15, 1944; children—Peter, David, Rufus, Christine. Ordained deacon P.E. Ch., 1935, priest, 1936; rector St. Paul's Ch., Brunswick, Me., 1936-41, Grace Ch., Salem, Mass., 1941-47, St. Paul's Ch., Rochester, N.Y., 1947-59; bishop Diocese of Mo., 1959—. Trustee U. of South. Home: 11 Litzinger Lane St Louis MO 63124 Office: 1210 Locust St St Louis MO 63103

CADIGAN, ROBERT JAMES, journalist, b. Mt. Vernon, N.Y., Jan. 22, 1912; s. Edward J. and Christina (Lindblom) C.; A.B., Swarthmore Coll., 1934; M.A., U. Chgo., 1942; Litt.D., Waynesburg Coll., 1950; H.L.D., U. Dubuque, 1956; LL.D., Carroll Coll., 1958; m. Rosemary Cowden, June 24, 1936; childrenKevin Robert, Rosemary. Tchr. Amherst (Mass.) High Sch., 1935; chmn. English dept. Friends' Central Sch., Phila., 1935-44; free-lance mag. writer, 1944-45; asso. editor Holiday Mag., 1945-47; gen. mgr. Presbyn. Life Mag., 1947—, editor, 1954—; pres. Asso. Ch. Press, 1955-57. Served AUS, 1945. Mem. Phi Delta Kappa. Presbyn. Editor: (with H.H. Giles), Playwrights Present, 1942; September to June, 1942. Contbr. to popular mags. and tech. jours. Home: Swarthmore PA 19081 Office: Witherspoon Bldg Philadelphia PA 19107

CADLE, DON DUANE, banker; b. Omaha, June 25, 1929; s. Paul Hicks and Ella Mae (Reed) C.; B.A., Yale, 1950; Ph.D., Oxford U. (Eng.), 1953; m. Ingeborg Plelenz, June 30, 1956; 1 dau., Caron Patricia. Budget examiner Bur. of Budget, Washington, 1956-61; dir. Resources programming div. Dep. Dir. Adminstrn. NASA, Washington, 1961-63; mgr., dir. Amann & Sons, Boennigheim, Germany, 1964-67; dir. investment promotion div. AID, Washington, 1967-68; dep. dir. Office Fgn. Direct Investments Commerce Dept., Washington, 1968-69; dir. plans analysis and coordination div. Chase Manhattan Bank N.A., N.Y.C., 1969, sr. v.p., 1971—, dir. financial controls group, 1970—; treas., chief financial officer Chase Manhattan Corp., N.Y.C., 1970—. Active youth groups, 1959—. Served with AUS, 1954-56. Rhodes scholar, 1950-53; recipient citation NASA, 1963, AID, 1968, Commerce Dept. gold medal, 1969. Mem. N.Y. Clearing House, Bank Adminstrn. Inst. Phi Beta Kappa. Democrat. Presbyn. Club: Yale (N.Y.C.). Home: 237 Wendover Dr Princeton NJ 08540 Office: 1 Chase Manhattan Plaza New York City NY 10015

CADMAN, BAILEY M., architect; b. Bklyn., July 14, 1924; s. Samuel and Miriam (Remer) C.; student Coll. City N.Y., 1941-43, U. Cin., 1944, Bklyn. Coll., 1946, Inst. Constrn. and Design, 1947; B.Arch., Rensselaer Poly. Inst., 1950; m. Joyce Beryl Plotkin, May 26, 1948; children—Lesley Ann, Bruce Michael, Douglas Jed, Glenn R. Draftsman, Hurwit-Kraus, architects, 1946, H. Silverman, architect, 1947-48; chief draftsman F. Morgan, architect, 1950-51; fellow, instr. Rensselaer Poly. Inst., Troy, N.Y., 1950-51, 52-53; mem. design faculty, prin. architect Group Practice, 1953, Morrow & Cadman, Albany, N.Y., 1954, B. M. Cadman, architect, Troy, 1955-56, B. M. Cadman Assos., 1958, Cadman, Klinger & Droste, Troy, 1959-62, Cadman & Droste, 1962-71; pres. Cadman & Droste P.C., 1971—; cons. Troy Planning Commn., 1959—; adviser Troy Citizens Com. for Redevel., 1960—. Mem. Troy Mayor's Adv. Com., 1959-60. Served to capt., inf., AUS, 1943-36; to capt., C.E., 1952-53. Decorated Bronze Star. Registered architect, N.Y., Vt. Fellow A.I.A. (pres. East N.Y. chpt. 1956-57, design award 1961); mem. N.Y. State Assn. Architects (dir. 1958-59), Troy C. of C. (dir.), Rensselaer Poly. Inst. Alumni Assn. (pres. Capital dist. 1954-56); charter mem. Assn. of the Professions. Mem. B'nai B'rith (pres. Troy). Club: Shaker Ridge Country, Troy. Prin. works include: Weinstock House, Troy, 1956, master plan for Troy, 1959-61, Averill Park Meth. Ch., Troy, 1960, Cobleskill Library and Classroom Bldg., 1961, South End Bowling Lanes, Albany, 1960, Kennedy Towers, Troy, 1965, Saratoga County Courthouse Complex, 1966, Farm and Horticultural Complex, Cobleskill, 1965, Adminstrn. Bldg., Cobleskill, 1966, H. V. C.C. Library, 1969, Dormitory Group, Cobleskill, 1971, Rehab. Center, Hudson River State Hosp., 1971. Home: Oxford Rd Troy NY 12180 Office: 405 Broadway Troy NY 12180

CADMUS, PAUL, painter, etcher; b. N.Y.C., Dec. 17, 1904; s. Egbert and Maria (Latasa) C.; student Nat. Acad. Design, N.Y. City, 1919-26, Art Students League of N.Y., 1926-27. Advertising work, 1928-31; lived and painted in Europe, 1931-33; first one-man show, N.Y.C., 1937. Represented in Met. Museum of Art, Whitney Museum Am. Art, Library of Congress, Chgo. Art Inst., Baltimore Museum, New York Pub. Library, Seattle Museum, Milw. Mus., Sara Roby Found., Smithsonian Inst.; works include "The Fleet's in", "Greenwich Village Cafeteria," "Coney Island," 1934, "Gilding the Acrobats," 1935; "Sailors and Floosies," 1938; Hinky Dinky Parley Voo, 1939; The Seven Deadly Sins, 1945-49; Bar Italia, 1952-55; pub. Paul Cadmus/Prints and Drawings, 1922-67. Recipient Nat. Inst. Arts and Letters grant, 1961, purchase award Norfolk Mus. Arts and Scis., 1964. Mem. Soc. Am. Graphic Artists. Home: 128 Remsen St Brooklyn NY 11201

CADOFF, IRVING BERNARD, educator; b. N.Y.C., Aug. 7, 1927; s. Max and Rose (Stutman) C.; B.M.E., Coll. City. N.Y., 1947; M.M.E., N.Y.U., 1948, D.Eng. Sci., 1953; m. Harriet Rudes, June 5, 1949; children—Susan, Evan. Instr., N.Y.U., 1949-53, asst. prof., 1953-57, asso. prof., 1957-65, prof., 1965-68, prof., chmn. dept. metallurgy and materials sci. Sch. Engring. and Sci., 1968—; guest prof. U. Vienna (Austria), fall 1970. Cons. N.Am. Aviation Co., Western Electric Co., U.S. Magnet and Alloy Corp., Frankford Arsenal; dir. Laser Scis. Inc. Mem. Am. Ins. M.E., Am. Phys. Soc., Am. Soc. Metals, Sigma Xi, Pi Tau Sigma, Alpha Sigma Mu. Contbr. articles profl. jours. Research thermoelectric materials, epitaxiel thin films, fracture of solids. Home: 39 Lark Av White Plains NY 10607 Office: New York U Bronx NY 10453

CADWELL, SIDNEY MARSH, chem. engr.; b. Bozeman, Mont., Mar. 5, 1893; s. Edward Payson and Laura (Marsh) C.; B.S., U. Chgo., 1914, Ph.D. magna cum laude, 1917; m. Elizabeth Hazelton Nicol, July 12, 1919 (dec. Sept. 1962); children—Loraine Hazelton (Mrs. Lewis A. Dibble, Jr.), Elizabeth Ellen (Mrs. William O. Dance); m. 2d, Agnes Brandon Brossy, Feb. 8, 1964. Research asst. U. Chgo., 1914-17; asso. mem. Sprague Inst., 1916; research chemimst Fed. Dyestuff & Chem. Corp., 1917-18; research chemist U.S. Rubber Co., 1919-30, asst. dir. gen. labs., 1930, dir. tire devel., 1930-45, asst. gen. mgr. tire div., 1945-46, dir. research and devel., 1946-58; prof., dept. chem. engring. Coll. Engring., Wayne State U., 1958-66, dir. Inst. Applied Chemistry and Physics, 1964- 66. Mem. sch. bd., Leonia, N.J., 1924-30. Served from 2d lt. to capt., C.W.S., U.S. Army, 1918. Recipient Charles Goodyear gold medal for outstanding accomplishment in rubber, div. rubber chemistry Am. Chem. Soc., 1956, Thomas Midgley award Detroit sect., 1966. Mem. Am. Chem. Soc. (chmn. div. rubber chemistry, also Detroit sect. 1935), Am. Inst. Chem. Engrs., Am. Inst. Chemists (hon.), Sigma Xi. Presbyn. (elder 1940- 46). Clubs: Country, Torch (Detroit). Contbr. articles learned jours. Patentee processes for prodn. rubber products. Home: 436 Washington Rd Grosse Pointe MI 48236

CADY, EDWIN HARRISON, educator; b. Old Tappan, N.J., Nov. 9, 1917; s. Edwin Laird and Ethel Sprague (Harrison) C.; A.B., Ohio Wesleyan U., 1939, Litt.D., 1964; M.A., U. Cin., 1940; Ph.D., U. Wis., 1943; Litt.D., Oklahoma City U., 1967; m. Norma Woodard Aug. 31, 1939; children—Frances (Mrs. Edward Hitchcock), Elizabeth (Mrs. Larry Saler). Instr. English, U. Wis., 1945, Ohio State U., 1946; from asst. prof. to prof. Syracuse U., 1946-59; Rudy prof. English, Ind. U., 1959—, cons. to pres. athletics and library affairs, 1963—; vis. prof. Am. lit., Uppsala and Stockholm, Sweden, 1951-52. Mem. exec. com. Center Am. Editions, 1964-68; mem. U.S. Nat. Commn. for UNESCO, 1969—. Served with Am. Field Service, Italy, 1943-44, with USNR, 1945. Guggenheim fellow, 1953-54. Mem. Am. Studies Assn., Modern Lang. Assn., Nat. Council Tchrs. English, Guild Scholars, Phi Beta Kappa, Omicron Delta Kappa, Phi Gamma Delta. Episcopalian. Author: The Gentleman in America, 1949; The Road to Realism; The Early Years, 1837-1885, of William Dean Howells, 1956; The Realist at War: The Mature Years, 1885-1920, of William Dean Howells, 1958; Stephen Crane, 1962; John Woolman: The Mind of the Quaker Saint; The Light of Common Day, 1971. Editor: (with H.H. Clark) Whittier on Writers and Writing, 1950; Literature of the Early Republic, rev. edit., 1969; (with L. Ahnebrink) An Anthology of American Literature, 1953; (with L.G. Wells) Stephen Crane's Love Letters to Nellie Crouse, 1954; (with F.J. Hoffman and R.H. Pearce) The Growth of American Literature, 1956; W.D. Howells, The Rise of Silas Lapham, 1957; Corwin K. Linson, My Stephen Crane, 1958; (with D.L. Frazier) The War of the Critics Over William Dean Howells, 1962; W.D. Howells, The Shadow of a Dream and An Imperative Duty, 1962; William Cooper Howells, Recollections of Life in Ohio, 1963; The American Poets, 1800-1900, 1966; (with D.F. Hiatt) W. D. Howells, Literary Friends and Acquaintances, 1968; Nathaniel Hawthorne, The Scarlet Letter, 1969. Gen. editor A Selected Edition of W.D. Howells, 1966-68. Home: Box 204 RFD 12 Bloomington IN 47401

CADY, ERNEST ALBERT, newspaper editor; b. Newark, O., Oct. 25, 1899; s. Charles Adelbert and Bird Lenore (Bollwine) C.; student Ohio State U., 1920-22; m. Frances D. Fairchild, June 11, 1923; childrenCharles Sherman, Jocelyn Sue (Mrs. Richard Ritter), Judith Ann (Mrs. Raymond Duda), Jerilou. Mem. staff Columbus (O.) Dispatch, 1922-, editorial writer, asst. editor of editorial page, 1936-65, lit. editor, columnist, 1948-. Mem. book awards com. Ohioana Library Assn., 1950-, chmn., 1965-66. Co- incorporator, trustee Ohio Childrens' Soc., pvt. adoption agy., 1953-. Mem. Sigma Delta Chi (organizing pres. Central Ohio profl. chpt. 1950). Republican. Methodist. Clubs: Press, Gridiron, Columbus Dispatch Country (Columbus). Author: We Adopted Three, 1952; (with Frances Cady) How to Adopt a Child, 1956; also articles. Home: 693 Yaronia Dr Columbus, OH 43214. Office: Columbus Dispatch 34 S 3d St Columbus OH 43216

CADY, GEORGE HAMILTON, educator, chemist; b. Lawrence, Kan., Jan. 10, 1906; s. Hamilton P. and Stella (Gallup) C.; A.B., U. Kan., 1927, A.M., 1928; Ph.D., U. Cal., 1930; m. Alpha Anna Marsh, June 2, 1929; children—Howard H., Carl M. Asst. prof. U. S.D., 1930-31; instr. Mass. Inst. Tech., 1931-34; research chemist U.S. Rubber Co., 1934-35, Pitts. Plate Glass Co., Columbia Chem. div., 1935-38; with U. Wash., 1938—, asst. prof., asso. prof., 1938-47, prof., 1947-, chmn. chemistry dept., 1961-65; with Manhattan project Columbia, 1942-43; G.N. Lewis Meml. lectr. U. Cal., 1967. Recipient U.S. Navy citation for Meritorious Pub. Service, 1970. Mem. Am. Chem. Soc. (award for Distinguished Service to Inorganic Chemistry 1966, chmn. Puget Sound sect. 1955; chmn. div. inorganic chemistry 1963), A.A.A.S., Deutsche Akademie der Naturforscher Leopoldina, Phi Beta Kappa, Sigma Xi, Alpha Chi Sigma, Phi Lambda Upsilon. Conglist. Home: 10625 Culpeper Ct NW Seattle WA 98177

CADY, HAYDEN HOWARD, airline exec.; b. Green Bay, Wis., Sept. 18, 1908; s. Lewis Denton and Elizabeth (Mannebach) C.; student U. Wis., 1933; m. Audrey E. Meyer, Dec. 27, 1932; children—Lewis C., Steven H. With Continental Air Lines, Inc., 1945—, v.p., treas., 1958—. Home: 7727 Beland Av Los Angeles CA 90045 Office: Continental Air Lines Inc Los Angeles Internat Airport Los Angeles CA 90009

CADY, HOWARD STEVENSON, editor; b. Middlebury, Vt., July 28, 1914; s. Frank William and Marian (Kingsbury) C.; A.B., Middlebury Coll., 1936; m. Marjory Arnold, Dec. 31 1938; children—Peter, Janet (Mrs. Janet McCoy), Susan (Mrs. Timothy Y. Hayward), Anne, and Ellen. Employed in the editorial dept. of The Macmillan Co., N.Y.C., 1937-41; mng. editor Stephen Daye Press, Brattleboro, Vt., 1941-42; editor Doubleday & Co., Inc., N.Y.C., San Francisco, 1942-52; editor-in-chief Little Brown & Co., Inc., Boston, 1952-54, Henry Holt & Co., N.Y.C., 1954-57; editor-in-chief, v.p., dir. G. P. Putnam's Sons, 1957-62; gen. mgr., editor-in-chief gen. book div. Holt, Rinehart & Winston, Inc., 1962-64; exec. editor David McKay Co., Inc., 1964-68; sr. editor Wm. Morrow & Co., Inc., 1968—. Lectr. editing and publishing Sch. Gen. Studies, Columbia, 1958-60. Served with OSS, 1943-45. Served with AUS, 1945-46. Mem. Delta Upsilon. Democrat. Conglist. Club: Century Assn. Home: 10 Prospect Av Darien CT 06820 Office: 105 Madison Av New York City NY 10016

CADY, JOHN F., educator; b. Boonville, Ind., July 14, 1901; s. J. Frank and Katie (Johnson) C.; A.B., DePauw U., 1923; A.M., U. Cin., 1924; Ph.D., U. Pa., 1929, L.H.D., Franklin Coll., 1962; m. Vivian C. Thomas, June 8, 1935; children—John T., Susan G., George F. Instr. history U. Me., 1925-26, U. Pa., 1926-27; asso. prof. history Marshall Coll., 1929-30; prof. history and polit. sci. Franklin Coll., 1930-35; lectr. history Judson Coll., U. Rangoon (Burma), 1935-38; dean, prof. history Franklin Coll., 1938-43; research analyst OSS, 1943-45; officer State Dept., Washington, 1945-49, as chief S. Asian sect., div. research Near East and Africa; fgn. service res., assigned to Consul Gen., Rangoon, 1945-46; prof. history Ohio U., 1949-71, past chmn. history dept., emeritus distinguished prof. history, 1971—; vis. prof. history Cornell U., 1952; Guggenheim Found. fellow and Fulbright research scholar U. Rangoon, 1955-56; Guggenheim Found. fellow, London, 1961; Rockefeller Found. grant lectr. history Thamassat U. Bangkok, Thailand, 1967-68. Recipient Ohioana Library award for best book in non-fiction category, 1956; Distinguished Professorship award Ohio U., 1959. Mem. Am. Hist. Assn., Phi Beta Kappa. Author books including: Burma's Pre-War Govt. and Problem of Law and Order, 1948; The Roots of French Imperialism in Eastern Asia, 1954 (Carnegie award, Am. Hist. Assn.); A History of Modern Burma, 1958; South East Asia; Its Historical Development, 1964; Italian translation, 1965); Thailand, Burma, Cambodia, Laos, 1966; book chpt., also articles hist. jours. Home: 45 Maplewood Dr Athens OH 45701 ☆

CADY, JOHN LODGE, publishing co. exec.; b. Boston, July 17, 1922; s. Joseph Patrick and Mildred (Lodge) C.; A.B., Harvard, 1943, J.D., 1948; LL.M., N.Y. U., 1956; m. Margaret Ann Foley, Aug. 8, 1944; 1 son, Robert Lodge. Admitted to N.Y. bar, 1951; atty. firm Chadbourne, Hunt, Jaeckel & Brown, N.Y.C., 1948-52, RCA, 1952-57; tax dir. McGraw-Hill, Inc., 1957-63, v.p. taxes, 1963—; dir. McGraw-Hill Internat., Inc., McGraw-Hill Publs. Overseas Corp., Opec, Inc., Data News, Inc. Sec. adv. bd. Tax Mgmt., Inc., 1959—. Pres. Bronxville P.T.A., 1967-68. Bd. dirs. Donald C. McGraw Found. Served to 1st lt. AUS, 1943-45. Mem. Tax Execs. Inst. (chmn. publs. com. 1965-70), Am., N.Y. State bar assns., Bar Assn. City N.Y., Commerce and Industry Assn. N.Y.C. (tax coms.), N.A.M., Am. Bus. Press. Clubs: Harvard (N.Y.C.); Bronxville Field. Contbr. articles profl. jours. Home: 46 Summit Av Bronxville NY 10708 Office: 330 W 42d St New York City NY 10036

CAEN, HERB, newspaper columnist, author; b. Sacramento, Cal., Apr. 3, 1916; s. Lucien and Augusta (Gross) C.; student Sacramento Jr. Coll., 1934; m. Sally Gilbert, Feb. 15, 1952 (div. 1959); 1 step dau., Deborah; m. 2d, Maria Theresa Shaw, Mar. 9, 1963; one son, Christopher. Engaged as daily newspaper columnist with the San Francisco (Cal.) Chronicle, 1938-50, 1958-; columnist, San Francisco Examiner, 1950-58. Author: The San Francisco Book, 1948; Baghdad-by-the-Bay, 1949; Baghdad 1951, 1950; Don't Call It Frisco, 1953; Caen's Guide to San Francisco, 1957; Only in San Francisco, 1960; (with Dong Kinghman) City on Golden Hills, 1968. Enlisted as private U.S. Army Air Force, 1942; disch. capt., 1945. Decorated by French Govt. in Paris with Medaille de la Liberation, 1949. Democrat. Club: Cal. Tennis. Home: 2459 Pacific Av San Francisco, CA 94115. Office: San Francisco Chronicle San Francisco CA 94103

CAESAR, ANDREW LEE, former mfg. co. exec.; b. Clifton, N.J., Aug. 16, 1927; s. Frank and Sophie (Podgurski) C.; B.S. in Engring., Columbia, 1950; M.B.A, Harvard, 1952; m. Betty Jane Bradshaw, Mar. 6, 1954; children—Holly Logan, Tracey Lee, Andrew Lee, Cameron Logan. With IBM Corp., 1957—, became controller IBM World Trade Corp. Served with AUS, World War II. Mem. Tau Beta Pi. Home: 11 Harscrabble Circle Armonk NY 10504

CAESAR, HENRY A., II, factors exec.; b. N.Y.C., Oct. 20, 1914; s. Harry I. and Doris (Porter) C.; A.B., Princeton, 1937; LL.B., Yale, 1940; m. Allison Garver, Mar. 15, 1941; childrenSanderson, Porter Dean, Austin Brewster, John Garver. Attorney Dwight, Harris Koegel & Caskey, N.Y.C., 1940-41; partner H. A. Caesar & Co., N.Y.C., 1946-69, pres., dir. H.A. Caesar & Co., Inc., 1969—. Trustee, former chmn. bd. trustees N.Y. Inst. Credit; trustee, v.p. New Canaan Nature Center. Engine capt. Old Faithful Hose Co. 1, New Canaan, Conn. Served as lt. USNR, World War II. Mem. N.Y. Credit and Financial Mgmt. Assn. Clubs: Union League, Racquet and Tennis (N.Y.C.); New Canaan Country. Home: 50 Hemlock Hill New Canaan CT 06840 Office: 360 Lexington Av New York City NY 10017

CAESAR, IRVING, author and composer; b. N.Y.C.; s. Morris and Sofia (Selinger) C.; student N.Y.C. pub. schs., Chappaqua Mountain Inst., City Coll. of N.Y.; unmarried. Sec. and corr. Ford Peace Ship; then with Ford Motor Co.; now writer of songs and Broadway and Hollywood musicals. Dir. A.S.C.A.P., Songwriters Protective Assn. Composer: Sing A Song of Safety; Sing a Song of Friendship; Songs of Health; Tea for two; The Pledge of Allegiance (in song). Author: Peace by Wireless; Plan to Eliminate the Surprise Attack. Home: Park Sheraton Hotel New York City NY 10016 Office: 1619 Broadway New York City NY 10019

CAESAR, MARION FRANCES, naval officer; b. Lawrence, Mass., June 27, 1913; d. Julius Joseph and Anne (Maguire) Caeser; diploma Addison-Gilbert Hosp. Sch. Nursing, Gloucester, Mass., 1935; certificate Boston Lying-in Hosp., 1937; B.S., Boston U., 1954, M.S., 1961. Commd. ensign, Nurse Corps, U.S. Navy, 1943, advanced through grades to comdr., 1961; assigned naval hosp. at Chelsea, Mass., 1943-44, Key West, Fla., 1944-45, Seattle, 1945, Portsmouth, N.H., 1946-48, San Diego, 1954-58; with hosp. ship U.S.S. Samariton, 1945-46; assigned Bur. Medicine and Surgery, 1949-52; former chief nursing service U.S. Naval Hosp., Nat. Naval Med. Center, Bethesda, Md. Chmn. Nursing Br. Neonatal Soc., San Diego, 1956-58. Mem. Grad. Nurses Assn. D.C. (chmn. nursing service br. 1962-64), Am., D.C. (pres. 1965—) nurses assns., Nat. League Nursing, Assn. Adult Edn., Sigma Theta. Club: Bull Run Hunt (Manassas, Va.). Home: 270 Salem Rd Dracut MA 01826

CAESAR, SID, actor, comedian; b. Yonkers, N.Y., Sept. 8, 1922; s. Max and Ida (Raphael) C.; grad. Yonkers High Sch., 1939; studied saxophone and clarinet, N.Y.C.; m. Florence Levy, June 17, 1943; children—Michele, Richard, Karen. Played in small bands, later orchestras of Charlie Spivak, Shep Fields and Claude Thornhill; following World War II, toured leading theatres and night clubs as comedian; appeared in Tars and Spars Revue also film version; in film Guilt of Janet Ames; in Broadway musical prodn. of Make Mine Manhattan, 1948; on television as the star of Admiral Broadway Revue, 1948, Your Show of Shows, 1950-54; star of own show, Caesar's Hour, 1954-57; star and producer Sid Caesar Invites You, 1958, also As Caesar Sees It, 1962- 63; TV guest appearances include Jackie Gleason Show, Carol Burnett Show, Robert Morse Show, star of Broadway musical Little Me, 1962-63; in film It's a Mad, Mad, Mad, Mad World, 1963. Recipient Look magazine award as best comedian on television, 1951, 56; Emmy award, best comedian, 1956; Sylvania award best comedy-variety show of 1958; named to U.S. Hall of Fame, 1967. Clubs: Old Falls Rod and Gun (Fallsburgh, N.Y.). Office: 59 E 54th St New York City NY 10022

CAETANO, MARCELO, premier of Portugal. Address: Presidencia do Conselho Palacio de S Bento Lisbon Portugal*

CAFFERTY, NEIL GEORGE, univ. adminstr.; b. Elroy, Wis., Aug. 5, 1900; s. Michael Patrick and Catherine Amelia (Garrigan) C.; B.S. in Elec. Engring., U. Wis., 1923; m. Margaret Teresa Boyle, Aug. 30, 1930; children—Mary Kathryn (Mrs. Ronald Kelly), Margaret Ellen (Mrs. Michael Dean). Engr., Ill. Power & Light Corp., 1923-26; mem. staff U. Wis. at Madison, 1926—, bus. mgr., 1957-62, v.p. bus. affairs, 1962-65, v.p. bus. and finance, trust officer, 1965—; pres. Wis. U. Bldg. Corp., 1965—. Treas., dir. Starks Farms. Mem. Wis. Personnel Adv. Com., 1957-61, Madison Bd. Rev., 1959-61; co-chmn. Wis. Employees U.S. Bond Sales, 1964- 65. Bd. dirs. Univ. Catholic Center, 1965—. C.P.A., Wis. Mem. Nat. Assn. Coll. and U. Bus. Officers, Beta Alpha Psi, Phi Kappa Phi (hon.). Roman Catholic. Club: University (bd. dirs. 1962-65) (Madison). Home: 5906 Cable Av Madison WI 53705 Office: U Wis 1220 Linden Dr Madison WI 53706

CAFFERY, JEFFERSON, retired diplomat; b. Lafayette, La., Dec. 1, 1886; s. Charles Duval and Mary Catherine (Parkerson) C.; B.A., Tulane U., 1906, LL.D., 1968; LL.D., Cath. U. Am., 1941, U. Lyon (France), 1947, Seattle U., 1955, U. Southwestern La., 1971; J.S.D., Holy Cross Coll., Ph.D. (hon.), U. Brazil, 1943; m. Gertrude McCarthy, Nov. 20, 1937. Admitted to La. Bar, 1909; sec. U.S. legation, Caracas, Venezuela, 1911-13, followed by various fgn. service appointments (including Paris, 1917-19), 1913-19; assigned Dept. State for U.S. visits King of Belgian and Prince of Wales, 1919; various assignments abroad, 1919-24; E.E. and M.P. to Salvador, 1926-28, to Columbia, 1928; spl. presdl. rep. with rank of ambassador, at inauguration Pres. Herrera of Columbia, 1930; spl. rep. Dept. State, Salvador, 1931-32; apptd. asst. sec. state, mem. personnel bd. Fgn. Service, personal presdl. rep. to Cuba, with rank of ambassador, 1933; A.E. and P. to Cuba, 1934-37; ambassador to Brazil, 1937; U.S. rep. with rank of ambassador to de facto French authority, 1944; ambassador to France, 1944-49, to Egypt, 1949-55; ret., 1955. Personal rep. of Pres. Eisenhower for inauguration Pakistan Republic and 1st Pakistan pres., Karachi; rep. U.S. Senate spl. com. to study fgn. aid programs in France, Italy, Spain, Portugal, U.K., 1956; U.S. rep. numerous confs., delegations; signer for U.S. internat. agreements, treaties. Recipient Cath. Action medal, 1944, State Dept. Distinguished Service award, 1950, Laetare medal, 1954, Bellarmine Coll. medal., Pres.'s medal Canisius Coll.; named hon. papal chamberlain (Pius XII, John XXIII, Paul VI); decorated grand cross Legion of Honor (France); Roman Cath. Grand Cross Pius IX; Order of Cordon of Egypt 1st class; grand cross of Carlos Cespedes Order Prder of Boyaca (Colombia); Order of Simon Bolivar (Venezuela); honored with establishment Jefferson Caffery Chair polit. sci. S. Western La. U., also Jefferson Caffery La. Room; numerous fgn. honors. Mem. Am. Fgn. Service Assn., S.A.R. Roman Catholic. Knight of Malta. Clubs: Metropolitan (Washington); Jockey (Paris); Boston (New Orleans). Address: care of Fendrich Industries Inc 1PO Box 3645 Evansville IN 47701 ☆

CAFFERY, PATRICK THOMSON, congressman; b. Franklin, La., July 6, 1932; s. Ralph Earl and Letitia (Decuir) C.; B.A., U. Southwestern La., 1955; J.D., La. State U., 1956; m. Anne Bercegeay, Jan. 30, 1954; childrenPatrick Thomson, Kevin, Michael St. M. Partner firm Helen, Simon & Caffery, 1957, Caffery, Duhe & Davis, 1965-69; asst. dist. atty. 16th Jud. Dist. La., 1958-62; mem. La. Ho. of Reps., 1964-68; mem. 91st and 92d Congresses 3d Dist. La. Past Past pres Iberia Parish United Givers Fund; mem. exec. bd. Evangeline area council Boy Scouts Am., past dist. commr. Bd. dirs. Iberia Crippled Children's Assn. Rotarian (past pres.). Asso., mng. editor La. Law Rev., 1955-56. Home: 116 Hacker St New Iberia, LA 70560. Office: Cannon House Office Bldg Washington DC 20515

CAFFEY, GUY HAMILTON, Jr., banker; b. Montgomery, Ala., Feb. 16, 1926; s. Guy Hamilton and Mamie Susan (Barber) C.; B.S., Samford U., 1951; grad. Stonier Sch. Banking, 1963; m. Marjorie Sue Courtney, Dec. 26, 1948; children—Guy Hamilton III, William Courtney, Mamie Susan. With Birmingham Trust Nat. Bank (Ala.), 1951—, pres., dir., 1969—; instr. Am. Inst. Banking, 1961-64; lectr. Banking Sch. South, 1965-67. Chmn. Jefferson County (Ala.) Heart Fund, 1964; chmn. outlying div. United Appeal, 1965, chmn. met. div., 1968. Chmn. Vestavia Hills Sch. Bd. Mem. met. bd. Birmingham YMCA; pres. Warrior Tomigbee Devel. Assn. Served with USAAF, 1944-46. Named Outstanding Young Banker of Year, Ala. Bankers Assn., 1961; recipient Distinguished Alumni award Samford U., 1967. Mem. Am. Bankers Assn. (installment credit com.). Clubs: Relay House, The Club, Country Vestavia Country, Mountain Brook (Birmingham). Home: 1245 Graylynn Dr Birmingham AL 35216 Office: 112-118 N 20th St Birmingham AL 35202

CAFFREY, ANDREW AUGUSTINE, U.S. judge; b. Lawrence, Mass., Oct. 2, 1920; s. Augustine J. and Monica A. (Regan) C.; A.B. cum laude, Holy Cross Coll., 1941; LL.B. cum laude, Boston Coll., 1948; LL.M., Harvard, 1948; m. Evelyn F. White, June 26, 1946; children—Augustine J., Andrew A., James E., Mary L., Francis J., Joseph H. Admitted to Mass. bar, 1948, U.S. Supreme Ct. bar, 1958; asso. prof. law Boston Coll. Law Sch., 1948-55; asst. U.S. atty., chief civil div., Dist. Mass., 1955-59, 1st asst. U.S. atty. Dist. Mass., 1959-60, U.S. dist. judge, 1960—. Served with AUS, World War II; ETO. Mem. Am., Fed., Boston bar assns., Am. Law Inst., Harvard Law Sch. Assn. Mass., Alpha Sigma Nu, Delta Epsilon Sigma. Club: Merrimack Valley, Holy Cross Alumni (past pres., dir.).‡

CAFKY, WILLIAM BRADFORD, assn. exec.; b. Wetherford, Okla., June 5, 1908; s. Otis Homer and Ella (Wright) C.; LL.B., Southeastern U., Washington, 1940, postgrad., 1941, 42; m. Elma Pinney, Dec. 31, 1933; 1 dau., Floann (Mrs. Gerald Lee Kamens). Cashier, 1st State Bank, Forgan, Okla., 1928-32; dir. research Conn. C. of C., Hartford, 1945-51, exec. v.p., 1951—; job counselor. Mem. Open Hearth Assn., 1955—. Recipient plaque for Outstanding Leadership as Pres., Council State Chambers Commerce, 1963-65. Mem. Am., Fed. bar assns., Nat. Lawyers Club Washington, Am. C. of C. Execs., Council State Chambers Commerce (past pres.), Sigma Delta Kappa. Universalist. Home: 23 Linwold Dr West Hartford CT 06107 Office: 410 Asylum St Hartford CT 06103

CAGE, JOHN, composer; b. Los Angeles, Sept. 5, 1912; s. John Milton and Lucretia (Harvey) C.; student Pomona Coll., 1928-30; studied with Richard Buhlig, Adolph Weiss, Henry Cowell, Arnold Schoenberg; m. Xenia Kashevaroff, June 7, 1935 (div.). Faculty Cornish Sch., Seattle, Wash., 1936-38, Sch. Design, Chgo., 1941-42; tchr. composition New Sch. for Social Research, N.Y.C., 1955-60; musical dir. Merce Cunningham and Dance Co., N.Y.C., 1944-66; fellow Center Advanced Studies, Wesleyan U., Middletown, Conn., 1960-61; composer-in residence U. Cin., 1967; research prof. and asso. Center Advanced Studies, U. Ill., Urbana, 1967-69. Dir. concert percussion music sponsored by Mus. Modern Art and League Composers, 1943; commd. by Ballet Soc. to write The Seasons, 1947, by Donaueschinger Musiktage to write work for two prepared pianos 34'46, 766 or Two Pianists, 1954; by the Montreal Festivals Soc. to write work for full orch. Atlas Eclipticalis, 1961; recorded Fontana Mix on magnetic tape for Studio di Fonologia, Milan, Italy, 1958; organized group of musicians and engrs. for making music directly on magnetic tape, 1951; produced (with Lejaren Hiller) HPSCHD for seven harpsichords and 52 computer generated tapes, 1967-69. Mem. bd., past pres. Cunningham Dance Found.; mem. Found. for Contemporary Performance Arts. Guggenheim fellow, 1949; award for extending boundries mus. art Nat. Acad. Arts and Letters, 1949; recipient first prize Woodstock Art Film Festival for score of Works of Calder, 1951, ann. award from the People to People Com. on Fungi, 1964; Thorne Music Fund grantee, 1967-69. Mem. A.S.C.A.P., N.Y. Mycol. Soc. (a founder); also The Nat. Inst. Arts and Letters. Author: (with Kathleen O'Donnell Hoover) The Life and Works of Virgil Thomson, 1958; Silence, 1961; A Year from Monday, 1967; (with Alison Knowles) Notations, 1969. Address: 107 Bank St New York City NY 10014

CAGIE, MALCOLM WINFIELD, naval officer, author; b. Grand Junction, Colo., Sept. 6, 1918; s. Victor Malcolm and Anna Leila (Cross) C.; B.S., U.S. Naval Acad., 1941; grad. Nat. War Coll., 1958; m. Virginia Lee Power, Aug. 20, 1941; children—Patrick, Mary Winfield, Jane Forrest. Commd. ensign U.S. Navy, 1941, advanced through grades to rear adm.; Served in World War II, Korea and Vietnam. Decorated Navy Cross, Legion of Merit, D.F.C., Air medal. Presbyn. (elder 1965-68). Author: Sen War in Korea; Battle Report; Naval Aviation Guide; Pilot's Meteorology; The New World of Flying Ships. Home: 412 Wolfe St Alexandria VA Office: Comdr Carrier Div 1 FPO San Francisco CA 96602

CAGLAYANGIL, IHSAN SABRI, minister fgn. affairs Turkey; b. Istanbul, Turkey, 1908; s. Sabri and Belkis Caglayangil; grad. faculty law, U. Istanbul, 1931; m. Fürüzende Caglayangil, Apr. 16, 1933; 1 dau., Fatos (Mrs. Mansur Shokrai). Formerly security service in various Turkish cities; gen. dir. Turkish Security Service; gov. Yozgat, Antalya, Canakkale, Sivas, Bursa; senator of Bursa; minister of labour; now minister fgn. affairs. Served as 2d lt. Turkish Army, 1933-34. Recipient decorations and medals from numerous countries. Mem. Turkish Edn. Found., Touring and Tourism Assn. Turkey. Author: Police Psychology; The Science of Arcive. Home: Hariciye Köshü Cankaya Ankara, Turkey Office: Ministery of Foreign Affairs Ankara Turkey

CAGLE, FREDRIC WILLIAM, Jr., educator; b. Metropolis, Ill., Dec. 17, 1924; s. Fredric William and Hattimay (Stalcup) C.; B.S., U. Ill., 1944, M.S., 1945, Ph.D., 1946. Mem. Sch. Math. Inst. for Advanced Study, Princeton, N.J., 1947-48; fellow in chemistry U. Utah, 1948-49, research asst. prof., 1949-53, asst. prof., 1953-54, asso. prof., 1954-60, prof., 1960—; cons. Pacific Northwest Pipeline Corp., 1958-61, Dow Chem. Co., 1963-67. Mem. Am. Chem. Soc., Am. Crystallographic Assn., Sigma Xi, Phi Kappa Phi, Sigma Pi Sigma. Club: University Club of Salt Lake City. Research X-ray crystallography and crystal structure; chemical thermodynamics. Home: 352 University St Salt Lake City UT 84102

CAGNEY, JAMES, actor; b. N.Y.C., July 17, 1904; ed. grammer sch.; left high school to go to work; m. Frances Vernon, 1922. Began in vaudeville, 1924; worked in motion pictures, 1931—; pres. Cagney-Montgomery Productions, Los Angeles; has appeared in many pictures among which were "Public Enemy," "Ceiling Zero," "Great Guy," "Something to Sing About," "Boy Meets Girl" "Angels with Dirty Faces," "Each Dawn I Die," "Roaring Twenties," "The Fighting 69th," "The Strawberry Blond," "The Bride Comes C.O.D.," "Captains of the Clouds", Yankee Doodle Dandy, What Price Glory?, A Lion is in the Streets, Run for Cover, Love Me or Leave Me, Mr. Roberts, 1, 2, 3. Given "Best Male Actor of 1942" award from Critics Circle for his acting in "Yankee Doodle Dandy", Vice pres. Cagney Productions, 1942—. Films they have since released through United Artists are "Johnny Come Lately," "Blood on the Sun," and Saroyan's "The time of Your Life," "Never Steal Anything Small", "Shake Hands With The Devil", and "The Gallant Heart", Heart." Address: MGM Studios Culver City CA 90230

CAGWIN, LELAND GEORGE, army officer; b. Norwich, N.Y., July 12, 1915; s. Fred L. and Elizabeth (House) C.; student Mass. Inst. Tech., 1935; B.S., U.S. Mil. Acad., 1940; grad. Inf. Sch., 1945, Command and Gen. Staff Coll., 1947, Armed Forces Staff Coll., 1952, Nat. War Coll., 1957; m. Jacquiline Elizabeth Smith, May 11, 1941; children—Timothy Douglas, Thomas Leland, Rondelle Ellen. Commd. 2d lt. U.S. Army, 1940; advanced through grades to maj. gen. 1966; assigned 25th Inf. Div., PTO, 1941-45, Army Gen. Staff, 1947-51; comdr. 27th Inf. Regt., Korea, 1952-53; sr. U.S. adviser 3d Turkish Brigade, 1953; dir. airborne tng. U.S. Army Inf. Sch., 1953-56; spl. asst. to chief of staff SHAPE, 1957-60; comdr. 325th Airborne Inf. Regt., 82d Airborne Div., 1961-62; mem. group to establish U.S. Strike Command, 1962-63; chief U.S. Mil. Assistance Adv. Group, Ethiopia, 1963- 65; comdg. gen. U.S. Army Combat Devel. Experimentation Command, 1965- 66, U.S. Army Test and Evaluation Command, 1966-68; comdg. gen. 2d Inf. Div., 1968-69; dir. operations U.S. European Command, 1969—. Decorated D.S.C., D.S.M. with oak leaf cluster, Silver Star, Legion of Merit with 2 oak leaf clusters, Bronze Star medal, Army Commendation medal, Combat Inf. badge with star, Master Parachutist badge. Mem. Assn. Grads. U.S. Mil. Acad., Legion of Honor, Nat. Rifle Assn., 25th Inf. Div. Assn. (pres. 1947, v.p. 1966), Monterey (Cal.) History and Art Assn. Methodist. Club: Army-Navy (Washington). Home: P O Box 4642 Stewart Pl Carmel CA 93921 Office: Div J-3 Operations Hdqrs US EUCOM APO New York City NY 09128

CAHAL, MAC FULLERTON, lawyer, orgn. exec.; b. Kiowa, Kan., Mar. 28, 1907; s. Frank Bastian and Carrie (Fullerton) C.; A.B., U. Kan., 1931; postgrad. Northwestern U., 1937; J.D., De Paul U., 1942; m. Wilma Marshall, June 1, 1935; children—Carolyn, William Marshall. Newspaper reporter, feature writer Wichita (Kan.) Beacon, 1928; pub. relations dept. Grigsby-Grunow, Kansas City, 1929; 1st exec. sec. Sedgwick Co. (Kan.) Med. Soc., 1931-37; exec. dir. Am. Coll. Radiology, Chgo., 1937-48, admitted to Ill. bar, 1942; exec. v.p. Southwestern Med. Found., Dallas, Tex., 1934-44; exec. dir., gen. counsel Am. Acad. Gen. Practice (pub. Am. Family Physician), Kansas City 1948—; lectr. legal, social medicine U. Kan. Cons. Med. Task Force of Hoover Commn. for Orgn. Exec. Br. Govt., 1953-55; founder Med. Soc. Execs. Assn., pres., 1947-48. Fellow A.M.A.; mem. Am., Mo., Chgo. bar assns., Pub. Relations Soc. N.Am., U.S. C. of C. (bd. regents Inst. for Assn. Mgmt., mem. tax council), Am. Soc. Assn. Execs. (dir.), Chartered Assn. Execs. (trustee), C. of C. Episcopalian. Rotarian. Clubs: Indian Hills County (Kansas City); Carriage; Wine and Food; Lawyers (Washington); Kansas City; Bohemian (San Francisco); Mission Valley Hunt; Saddle and Sirloin; University (Chgo.). Author monographs on legal, social and econ. aspects of medicine. Contbr. articles to med., legal publs. Home: 6610 Indian Lane Shawnee Mission KS 66208 Office: Volker Blvd at Brookside Kansas City MO 64112

CAHALANE, VICTOR H., mammalogist; pres., dir. Defenders of Wildlife; mem. Sierra Club. Author: Mammals of North America; (with others) Alive in the Wild. Editor: Audubon Game Animals. Office: Defenders of Wildlife 2000 N St NW Washington DC 20036*

CAHAN, WILLIAM GEORGE, physician; b. N.Y.C., Aug. 2, 1914; s. Samuel George and Flora (Gomperts) C.; B.S., Harvard, 1935; M.D., Columbia, 1939; m. Mary Arnold Sykes, Dec. 26, 1952; children—Christopher, Anthony. Surg. pathology Presbyn. Hosp.,

N.Y.C., 1939; intern, house surgeon Hosp. Joint Diseases, N.Y.C., 1940-41; fellow cancer surgery Meml. Hosp., N.Y.C., 1942-48; thoracic cons. Strang Clinic, 1949-53, attending surg. staff thoracic service, 1949-; asst. attending surgeon Manhattan Eye, Ear and Throat Hosp., 1950-58, cons. gen. surgeon, 1964—; asso. vis. surgeon James Ewing Hosp., N.Y.C. 1959-68; cons. tumor service Newark Beth Israel Hosp., 1968; instr. surgery Cornell U. Med. Coll., 1950-56, mem. faculty, 1956—, clin. asso. prof. surgery, 1966—; asst. clinician Sloan-Kettering Inst., 1953-68; vis. scholar Univ. Center in Va., Richmond, 1967. Pres. Treadwell Farm Hist. Dist., N.Y.C., 1966-69; mem. overseers vis. com. music Harvard, 1968-69. Served to maj., M.C., USAAF, 1943-46. Diplomate Am. Bd. Surgery. Fellow A.C.S.; mem. Am. Assn. Thoracic Surgery, Am. Cancer Soc., Am. Coll. Chest Physicians, A.M.A., Am. Radium Soc., Internat. Congress Smoking and Health (adv. bd.), N.Y. Cancer Soc. (sec. 1955-58), N.Y. County, N.Y. State med. socs., N.Y. Surg. Soc., N.Y. Soc. Thoracic Surgeons, Royal Soc. Medicine (affiliate), Soc. Cryobiology, Soc. Thoracic Surgeons. Author: (with Hans von Leden) Cryogenics in Surgery, 1971. Author numerous articles in field. Editorial bd. Jour. Cryosurgery. Home: 209 E 62d St New York City NY 10021 Office: 444 E 68th St New York City NY 10021

CAHANEY, GEORGE ROGER, movie exec.; b. Dennison, O., Aug. 22, 1919; s. James Michael and Cora Regina (Riffle) C.; B.A. cum laude, Notre Dame U., 1949; m. Myra Faye Long, June 24, 1950; children—Matthew Leslie, Timothy Hugh, Mark Liam, Dara Ann, Nan Marie. Began career as an advt. and sales promotion specialist Gen. Electric Co., 1949-51; asso. account exec. Fuller & Ross, Cleve., 1951-53; exec. sec. Cath. Press Assn. of U.S., Inc., 1953-58; gen. promotion mgr. Sterling Movies USA, 1958-61, v.p., 1961-63, exec. v.p. 1963-68; became pres. Sterling Movies, Inc.; sr. v.p., dir. Sterling Communications. Mem. Farmingdale (N.Y.) Sch. Bd., dist. 22, 1962-65, pres., 1964-65. Mem. bd. dirs. Pro Arte Symphony Orch., L.I. Mem. pub. relations adv. com. Hofstra U. Served as sgt. maj. 9th Air Force, USAAF, 1942-45. Decorated Bronze Star Medal. Home: 25 Rogers Dr Cold Spring Harbor NY 11724 Office: 375 Park Av New York City NY 10022

CAHILL, ARTHUR RIPLEY, financial exec.; b. Springfield, Mo., July 7, 1907; s. Frederic Arthur and Louise (Ripley) C.; Ph.B., U. Chgo., 1931; m. Jeannette Smith, Sept. 15, 1934; children—Douglas, Steven, Susan. With loan and discount dept. Harris Trust & Savs. Bank, Chgo., 1931-34; asst. to gen. auditor Fed. Res. Bank, 1934-41; asst. treas. Montgomery Ward & Co., 1941-42, treas., 1948-49, v.p., treas., 1949-52; asst. treas. Internat. Minerals & Chem. Corp., Chgo., 1953, v.p., treas., 1954-56, v.p. finance, 1956-60, dir., 1957-61; v.p. finance Brunswick Corp., 1960—, also dir.; dir. Oak Park Trust & Sav. Bank, Bradshaw-Praeger Co. Clubs: Economics, Commonwealth, University, Executives (Chgo.); Oak Park (Ill.) Country. Home: 737 Keystone Av River Forest IL 60305 Office: 69 W Washington St Chicago IL 60602

CAHILL, CHARLES LESLIE, univ. adminstr.; b. El Reno, Okla., Feb. 23, 1933; s. Leslie T. and Charlene (McCluskey) C.; A.B., Okla. Bapt. U., 1955; M.S., U. Okla., 1957, Ph.D., 1961; m. Dorotha Cleek, Feb. 14, 1954; children—Steven Charles, Terri Ann, Susan Beth. Clin. chemist Med. Arts Labs., Oklahoma City, 1960-61; asst. prof. chemistry Oklahoma City U., 1961-63, asso. prof., chmn. dept., 1963-67, asso. dean Coll. Arts and Scis., 1967-70, prof. chemistry, asso. dean, dir. research, 1970-71; vice-chancellor acad. affairs U. N.C., Wilmington, 1961—. Cons. McBride Bone and Joint Found., Bio-Analytic Lab., Bio-Tech. Lab. Mem. Okla. Gov.'s Commn. Sci. and Industry, 1965; chmn. Okla. Commn. Air Quality Control, 1970, Commn. Water Quality Control Oklahoma City, 1969-71; mem. Okla. Sci. and Arts Found., 1970. NASA grantee, 1962-68; NIH grantee, 1961-71; NSF grantee, 1967. Mem. Am. Chem. Soc., A.A.A.S., N.Y. Acad. Sci., Endocrine Soc., Sigma Xi. Contbr. articles to profl. jours. Home: 2216 Parham St Wilmington NC 28401

CAHILL, FRED VIRGIL, educator; b. Davton, Wash., Feb. 13, 1916; s. Fred Virgil and Grace Violet (Crossler) C.; B.A., U. Neb., 1937, M.A., 1938; Ph.D., Yale, 1941; m. Nan Walker Hardin, Mar. 25, 1952. Instr. govt. U. Ore., 1941-42, asst. prof., 1946-47; asst. prof. govt. Yale, 1947-51, prof. govt. U. Mass., 1953-55, dean arts and scis., 1955-60; dean gen. studies N.C. State Coll., 1960-63, dean of liberal arts, 1963-71, prof. politics, 1971—. Served to lt. col. AUS, 1942-46, 51-53. Mem. Am., So. polit. sci. assns., Phi Beta Kappa, Phi Kappa Phi. Democrat. Conglist. Author: Judicial Legislation, 1952; (with R.J. Steamer) The Constitution, Cases and Comment, 1960. Home: 4801 Yadkin Dr Raleigh NC 27609

CAHILL, HARRY HOLMES, ret. newspaper exec.; b. London, Ont., Can., Apr. 7, 1901; s. Thomas Joseph and Hanna Anita (Lewis) C.; m. Alice E. Mehan, Sept. 11, 1926; children—John L., Margaret Ann (Mrs. John Kay Martin, Jr.). Came to U.S., 1923, naturalized, 1932. Circulation mgr. Vancover (B.C.) World, 1921-23, Fresno (Cal.) Morning Republican, 1923-26; asst. circulation mgr. Seattle Times, 1926-28, circulation mgr., 1928-38, bus. mgr., 1938-41, gen. mgr., 1942-70, v.p., dir.; former dir. Metro Sunday Newspapers, Inc. Past dir. Am. Newspaper Pubs. Assn. Past mem. Seattle C. of C. (v.p. 1962-63, exec. com., trustee). Clubs: Rotary (pres. 1960-61), Washington Athletic; Broadmoor Golf, Seattle Golf. Home: 4939 NE Laurelcrest Lane Seattle WA 98105

CAHILL, JAMES FRANCIS, educator; b. Ft. Bragg, Cal., Aug. 13, 1926; s. James Francis and Mae (Bond) C.; B.A., U. Cal. at Berkeley, 1950; M.A., U. Mich., 1952, Ph.D., 1958; m. Dorothy Dunlap, July 15, 1951; childrenNicholas, Sarah. Became curator Chinese art Freer Gallery Art, Smithsonian Instn., Washington, 1957; now prof. art, curator Oriental art U. Cal. at Berkeley; became adj. prof. art Am. U., Washington, 1958; guest dir., adviser Asia House, N.Y.C., 1962-. Served to 1st lt. AUS, 1945-48. Mem. Assn. Asian Studies, Coll. Art Assn. Author: Chinese Painting, 1960. Home: 2422 Hillside Av Berkeley, CA 94704.

CAHILL, JOSEPH T., univ. pres.; b. Phila.; student Mary Immaculate Sem.; LL.D., Niagara U., 1967; Litt.D., China Acad., 1969; LL.D., Nat. Chengchi U., Taipei, Taiwan, 1971. Ordained priest Roman Catholic Ch., 1946; mem. faculty St. Joseph's Coll., until 1953, pres., 1962-65; prof. history Niagara U., Niagara Falls, N.Y., 1953, dir. dramatics, 1953-56, dir. athletics, 1956-58, dean Grad. Sch. and Sch. Edn., 1958- 59, acad. v.p., dean Coll. Arts and Scis., 1959-62, pres., 1964-65; pres. St. John's U., Jamaica, N.Y., 1965—. Address: St John's U Jamaica NY 11432

CAHILL, LAURENCE JAMES, Jr., educator, physicist; b. Frankfort, Me., Sept. 21, 1924; s. Laurence J. and Wilma (Lord) C.; student U. Me., 1942-43; B.S., U. Chgo., 1950; B.S., U.S. Mil. Acad., 1946; M.S., U. Ia., 1956, Ph.D., 1959; m. Alice Adeline Krieger, Sept. 10, 1949; children—Laurence James III, Thomas G., Daniel A. Staff, U. Ia., 1954-59, research asso., 1959; mem. faculty U. N.H., 1959-68, prof. physics, 1965-60, dir. Space Scis. Center, 1966-68; prof. physics, dir. Space Sci. Center, U. Minn., Mpls., 1968—; chief physics NASA Hdqrs., Washington, 1962-63, cons., 1962—; vis. prof. U. Cal. at San Diego, 1965-66; cons. NSF, 1965—. Recipient NASA award for sustained superior performance, 1963. Fellow Am. Geophys. Union; mem. Am. Phys. Soc., A.A.A.S., Sigma Xi. Research and publs. on measurement by rocket-borne magnetometer of elec. currents in ionosphere, measurement boundary between earth's magnetic field and interplanetary medium, ring current of charged particles encircling earth and causing magnetic storms. Home: Box 294 Afton MN 55001 Office: U Minn Dept Physics Minneapolis MN 55455

CAHILL, LAWRENCE PATRICK, former coll. pres.; b. Middletown, O., Jan. 20, 1922; s. Jones Martin and Florence Elizabeth (Smith) C.; student John Carroll U., 1942, M.A., 1956; student St. Mary Sem., Cleve., 1947, Cath. U. Am., summers, 1956, 57, Western Res. U., 1956-60. Ordained priest Roman Cath. Ch., 1947; named very reverend monsignor, 1960, right reverend monsignor, 1962; asst. pastor in Barberton, O., 1947-53, Cleve., 1954; prof. history Borromeo Sem., Wickliffe, O., 1954-60, vice rector, 1958- 60; pres. St. John Coll., Cleve., 1960-71. Mem. Cleve. Diocesan Bd. Edn., 1960; pres. Cleve. Council Information Communism, 1961-62; mem. Cleve. Community Relations Bd. Chmn. Ohio Found. Ind. Colls., 1968-70; mem. Am. Assn. Colls. Tchr. Edn. study tour Israel, 1965. Mem. Nat. Cath. Ednl. Assn., Am. Cath. Hist. Assn., N.E.A., Am. Hist. Assn., Phi Alpha Theta. Club: Cleve. Athletic. Home: 28700 Euclid Av Wickliffe OH 44092

CAHILL, WILLIAM THOMAS, gov. N.J.; b. Phila., June 25, 1912; s. William P. and Rose (Golden) C.; A.B., St. Joseph's Coll., 1933; LL.B., Rutgers South Jersey Law Sch., 1937; m. Elizabeth M. Myrtetus, Feb. 1, 1941; children—Kathleen, Mary, William Thomas, Regina, John Patrick, Patricia, Eileen, Theresa. Tchr., Camden City Sch. System, 1933-37; spl. agt. FBI, Washington, Little Rock, Ark., also St. Louis; admitted to N.J. bar, 1939, practiced in Camden; former mem. firm Cahill & Wilinski; city pros., Camden, 1941; 1st asst. county pros., Camden County, 1948-51; spl. dept. atty. gen., 1951; assemblyman from Camden County, N.J. Legislature, 1951- 53; member 86th to 91st Congresses, First Congressional District of New Jersey; gov. N.J., 1970—. Member American, N.J., Camden County bar assns., Former Spl. Agts. of FBI, Nat. Assn. Claimants' Compensation Attys., Internat. Acad. Trial Lawyers. Republican. Home: Morven Princeton NJ 08540 Office: State House Trenton NJ 08625

CAHN, JOHN WERNER, educator, metallurgist; b. Germany, Jan. 9, 1928; s. Felix H. and Lucie (Schwarz) C.; came to U.S., 1939, naturalized, 1945; B.S., U. Mich., 1949; Ph.D., U. Cal. at Berkeley, 1953; m. Anne Hessing, Aug. 20, 1950; children—Martin Charles, Andrew David, Lorie Selma. Instr., U. Chgo., 1952-54; with research lab. Gen. Electric Co., 1954-64; prof. metallurgy Mass. Inst. Tech., 1964—; vis. prof. Israeli Inst. Tech., Haifa, 1971-72; cons. in field, 1963—. Chmn. Gordon conf. Phys. Metallurgy, 1964. Guggenheim fellow, 1960. Mem. Am. Inst. Metall. Engrs., A.A.A.S. Home: 5 Field Rd Lexington MA 02173 Office: Mass Inst Tech Cambridge MA 02139

CAHN, ROBERT, govt. ofcl.; b. Seattle, Mar. 9, 1917; s. Adolph and Edna (May) Cahen; B.A., U. Wash., 1939; LL.D. (hon.), Allegheny Coll., 1970; m. Patricia Lovelady, Dec. 8, 1951, Reporter, Seattle Star, 1939-41, Pasadena (Cal.) Star-News, 1946-48; corr. Life mag., 1948-51; corr., sr. editor Collier's mag., 1951-56; free-lance mag. writer, 1957-61; Midwest bur. chief Sat. Eve. Post, 1962; White House reporter USIA, 1963-64; staff corr. Christian Sci. Monitor, 1965- 69; mem. President's Council Environmental Quality, 1970—. Served with AUS, 1942-46; ETO. Decorated Bronze Star; recipient Conservation Service award Dept. Interior, 1968; Pulitzer prize in journalism for nat. reporting, 1969. Mem. Sigma Delta Chi. Christian Scientist. Author: (with Perle Mesta) Perle, My Story, 1960. Home: 3416 O St NW Washington DC 20007 Office: 722 Jackson Pl Washington DC 20006

CAHN, SAMMY, lyric songwriter; b. N.Y.C., June 18, 1913; s. Abraham and Alice (Reiss) Cohen; student pub. schs., N.Y.C.; m. Gloria Delson, Sept. 5, 1945 (div. May 1964); children—Steven, Laurie. Violinist since boyhood; organizer of a band with Saul Chaplin; songwriter, 1935—, for motion pictures, 1940—. Writer for stage show High Button Shoes; songs written include: Rhythm in my Nursery Rhymes, Bei Mir Bist Du Schoen, Until the Real Thing Comes Along, Please be Kind, I've Heard that Song Before, I'll Walk Alone, Shoe Shine Boy, Victory Polka, Let it Snow, Let it Snow, Let it Snow, It's Magic, Teach me Tonight, The Tender Trap, Love and Marriage (TV Emmy award; Christopher award), Be My Love, Because You're Mine, Three Coins in the Fountain (Acad. award), All the Way (Acad. award 1957), High Hopes (Acad. award 1959), Second Time Around, Call Me Irresponsible (Acad. award 1963). Office: care Edward Traubner and Co 1901 Av of the Stars Los Angeles CA 90067

CAILLOUET, LOUIS ABEL, bishop; b. Thibodaux, La., Aug. 2, 1900; s. Louis Philip and Marie Adele (Lagarde) C.; M.A., St. Mary's Sem., Balt., 1921; student U. of Propaganada Fide, Rome, 1921-25; S.T.L. Ordained to priesthood Roman Catholic Ch., 1925, consecrated bishop, 1947; aux. bishop Archdiocese of New Orleans. Home: 1342 Moss St New Orleans LA 70119

CAIN, C.R., rubber co. exec. Controller, Cooper Tire and Rubber Co., Findlay, O. Office: Lima and Western Avs Findlay OH 45840*

CAIN, EDMUND JOSEPH, coll. dean; b. Chico, Cal., Mar. 18, 1918; s. Edmund Joseph and Myrtle Ellen (Perdue) C.; B.S., Columbia, 1946, M.A., 1947, Ed.D., 1950; m. Virginia Hartigan, Dec. 3, 1944; children—Edmund Joseph III, Mary Ellen, James Michael. Tchr., Horace Mann-Lincoln Sch., N.Y.C., 1946-47; research asst. Columbia, 1947-48; asso. prof. edn. Danbury (Conn.) State Coll., 1948-55; vis. prof. edn. San Francisco State Coll., 1951, San Diego State Coll., summer 1952, U.N.M., summers 1953, 54, 58; dir. student teaching programs and grad. and postgrad. program tchr. edn. U. Del., 1955-64; dean Coll. Edn., U. Nev., 1964—, also chmn. tchr. edn. bd. and mem. human rights bd. Expert in edn. UNESCO, Chile, 1961- 62; cons. Inst. Internat. Edn., 1962-63; rep. Study Higher Edn. in Yugoslavia, 1967; chmn. subcom. Gov. Nev. Com. Edn.; chmn. and vice chmn. bd. dirs. Far West Lab. Ednl. Research and Devel., 1968-71; co-chmn. Bishop Nev. Ednl. Bd. Served to capt. AUS, 1941-46. Mem. N.E.A., Am. Assn. Colls. Tchr. Edn. (state rep.), Nat. Soc. Study Edn., Phi Delta Kappa (Edn. Leadership award 1971), Kappa Delta Phi. Rotarian. Contbg. author: Applied Principles of Education Sociology, 1954. Contbr. profl. jours. Home: 3710 Clover Way Reno NV 89502

CAIN, FREDRICK LORIMER, fgn. service cons.; b. Haverhill, Mass., May 10, 1915; s. Frederick J. and Mary Ann (Lorimer) C.; student Worcester Acad., 1935-36; B.S., Syracuse U., 1940, postgrad. Naval Air Acad., Pensacola, 1942, Harvard, 1958, 65; m. Lorraine Leyfield, May 8, 1943; children—Michael Layfield, Diana, Frederick Lorimer. Account exec. Batten, Barton, Durstine & Osborn, N.Y.C., 1950-58; marketing and new product devel. cons., N.Y.C., 1958-63; marketing cons., U.S. AID, Turkey, 1963-64, indsl. devel. cons., Brazil, 1965-68; founder pres. Lorimer Internat., 1968—. UN expert, Malaysia, 1970-71. Served with USNR, 1942-45. Mem. Am. Mgmt. Assn., Am. Marketing Assn., Acad. Polit. Sci., Soc. for Internat. Devel. Episcopalian. Home: 3606 Mockingbird Dr Vero Beach FL 32960 Office: 501 Date Palm Rd Vero Beach FL 32960

CAIN, GEORGE HARVEY, lawyer, bus. exec.; b. Washington, Aug. 3, 1920; s. J. Harvey and Madeleine (McGettigan) C.; B.S., Georgetown U., 1942; LL.B., Harvard, 1948; m. Patricia J. Campbell, Apr. 23, 1946; children—George Harvey, James C., John P., Paul J. Admitted to N.Y. bar, 1949, since practiced in N.Y.C.; sec., gen. counsel Nat. Carloading Corp., 1949-54; mem. firm Spence & Hotchkiss, 1954-55; gen. atty., asst. sec. Cerro Corp., 1955- 68, sec., gen. atty., 1968—; sec. Cerro Sales Corp., 1955—; dir., sec. Leadership Housing Systems, Inc.; dir., gen. counsel Atlantic Cement Co., Inc.; dir. Cerro Exploration Co., Inc., Cerro Gas & Oil Corp. Served to 1st lt. USAAF, 1942-46; to capt. USAF, 1951-52. Mem. Am., N.Y. State, N.Y.C. bar assns., Am. Soc. Corporate Secs., Georgetown U. Alumni Assn. (mem. Alumni senate). Home: 4 Sachem Rd Greenwich CT 06830 Office: 300 Park Av New York City NY 10022

CAIN, GEORGE R., pharm. exec.; b. Noblesville, Ind., Sept. 9, 1910; s. Rolly Morton and Dersie Alberta (Myers) C.; A.B., Williams Coll., 1933; m. Jane Gent, Oct. 20, 1934; childrenDenis G., Tyler R., Michael G. Group dept. rep. Equitable Life Assurance Soc. of U.S., 1933-37; gen. ins. broker W.A. Alexander & Co., Chicago, 1937-40; in sales dept. Abbott Labs., North Chicago, 1940-47, dir. and adminstrv. asst. to pres., 1947-50, dir. since 1947, exec. v.p., chmn. exec. com., 1950-58, pres., 1958-67, chmn. bd., 1962-; dir. Abbott Universal, Ltd., Ill. Bell Telephone Co., Internat. Harvester Co., Continental Ill. Nat. Bank & Trust Co. Chgo., Skil Corp., Standard Oil Co. (Ind.), Conill Corp. Trustee Northwestern U.; hon. dir. Evanston Hosp.; dir. Pharm. Mfrs. Assn. Mem. Northwestern U. Assos., Phi Gamma Delta. Republican. Episcopalian. Mason. Clubs: Commonwealth, Mid- America, Chicago, Commercial (Chgo.); Glen View (Golf, Ill.); Old Elm (Ft. Sheridan, Ill.); Shoreacres (Lake Bluff, Ill.). Home: 691 Sheridan Rd Winnetka IL 60093 Office: Abbott Labs Abbott Park North Chicago IL 60064

CAIN, GERALD IRWIN, architect; b. Champaign, Ill., Nov. 28, 1923; s. Curtis Irwin and Lila Catherine (Cain) C.; B.S. in Archtl. Engring., U. Ill. 1946; m. Jeanne H. Smith, Dec. 26, 1954 (div. Mar. 1971); children—Jeffrey Winston, Alora Jean, Michael Curtis. Pvt. practive, 1952-54; partner Starkweather & Cain architects, Tucson, Cain, Nelson & Wares, architects, Tucson, 1960-70, Cain, Nelson, Wares, Cook & Assos., Inc., Tuscon, 1970—; prin. works include Ariz. Western Coll., 1st. Nat. Bank, Tucson Community Center, U.S. Govt. Fed. Bldg., U. Ariz. Math bldg. Mem. City Tucson Archtl. Approval Bd., 1967. Recipient Architecture West mag. award 1965; Rocky Mt. Region awards, A.I.A., 1963-66; Ariz. Masonry Guild award, 1968. Mem. Tucson Execs. Assn. (pres. 1967-68), A.I.A. Democrat. Club: Mt. Oyster (Tucson). Home: Ranch House Lodge 4531 Caminito de la Puerta Tucson AZ 85718 Office: 405 W Franklin St Tucson AZ 85705

CAIN, GORDON ARBUTHNOT, chem. co. exec.; b. Baton Rouge, May 31, 1912; s. Gordon Dunn and Ola (Arbuthnot) C.; B.S., La. State U., 1933; grad. Advanced Mgmt. Program, Harvard, 1959; m. Lucia La Madrid, January 28, 1956 (decased September 1968). Engineer with the La. Power and Light Co., 1933-35, Freeport Sulphur Co., 1935-41, 46-49, Merck & Co., 1941-42; v.p. Standard Perlite Co., Pasadena, Cal., 1949-50; self employed cons., N.Y.C. 1950-51; engr. F.M.C. Corp., 1951-55; v.p. Petro-Tex. Chem. Corp., Houston, 1955-64; v.p., gen. mgr. petrochem. dept. Continental Oil Co., 1964-. Served to lt. col. AUS, 1942-46. Decorated Bronze Star (2), Purple Heart. Mem. Am. Inst. Chem. Engrs. Clubs: Houston, River Oaks Country (Houston); University (Washington); Union League (N.Y.C.). Home: 25 Sutton Pl S New York City, NY 10022. Office: 9 Rockefeller Plaza New York City NY 10020

CAIN, HARVEY SWENNES, retired pipeline co. exec. b. Lake Forest, Ill., June 15, 1908; s. James Joseph and Lisa Julia (Swennes) C.; B.A. in Bus. Adminstrn., Lake Forest (Ill.) Coll.; m. Ruth A. Dunning, June 15, 1929 (dec. 1959) children—Harvey Dunning, Ruth Weldon (Mrs. Richard Burkholder), Lenora Mary (Mrs. Michael Hoffman); m. 2d, Jean Celia Wyse, Aug. 20, 1960; 1 stepchild, Susan Dedrick. With Natural Gas Pipeline Co. Am., 1931-71, asst. comptroller, 1960-61, treas., 1961-69, asst. v.p., asst. treas., 1969-71 retired, 1971. Mem. Ind. Natural Gas Assn. Am. (treas. 1965—), Am. Gas Assn., Chgo. Assn. Commerce and Industry, Ill. C. of C. Home: 295 Grace St Elmhurst IL 60126

CAIN, HOWARD BRUCE, architect; b. Lakewood, O., Dec. 30, 1918; s. Oscar Clyde and Meta Matilda (Gusse) C.; B.S., Western Res. U., 1942; postgrad. Princeton, 1942-43; m. Helen Lynch Shaner, Mar. 21, 1942; children—Margaret (Mrs. C. Lamb), Christopher, Catherine (Mrs. R. Rybak), Walker Scott, Bruce, Elizabeth, Carolyn. With spl. devices div. Naval Research, 1946-48, Outcalt & Guenther, 1948-50, Richard Hawley Cutting & Assos., 1950-52; pvt. archtl. practice, Cleve., 1952—; mem. faculty architecture Kent State U., 1970-71. Mem. Ohio Bd. Examiners Architects, 1969-74; mem. Archtl. Bd. Gates Mills, 1968-71, Archtl. bd. Beachwood, 1958—. Mem. Architects Soc. Ohio (pres. 1962), A.I.A. (pres. Cleve. 1968-69), Growth Assn. Cleve. Clubs: City of Cleveland (dir. 1963-65); Cleveland-West Rotary (pres.). Home: County Line Rd Gates Mills OH 44040 Office: Park Bldg Cleveland OH 44114

CAIN, J. B., savs. and loan assn. exec. Exec. v.p., mgr. Uptown Fed. Savs. and Loan Assn. Office: 4545 Broadway Chicago IL 60640*

CAIN, JAMES CLARENCE, physician; b. Kosse, Tex., Mar. 19, 1913; s. Thomas Marshall and Aileen (Jackson) C.; B.A., U. Tex., 1933, M.D., 1937; M.A., U. Minn., 1948; m. Ida May Wirtz, June 6, 1938; childrenStephaine Cannon (Mrs. Karl H. Van D'Elden), Mary Lucinda (Mrs. William Carleton Moore), Katherine May (Mrs. Jerry Wayne Snider), James Alvin. Intern Protestant Episcopal Hosp., Phila., 1937-39; instr. pathology U. Tex. Med. Sch., 1939-40; fellow Mayo Found., 1940-41, 46-48; cons. medicine Mayo Clinic, Rochester, Minn., 1948, head of sect., 1966—; prof. medicine U. Minn.; personal physician to Pres. Johnson, 1946—. Mem. nat. adv. heart council NIH; v.p. Minn. Bd. Med. Examiners; chmn. nat. adv. commn. for selection drs., dentists and allied med. personnel SSS; mem. Nat. Adv. Commn. on Med. Manpower; cons. to surgeon gen. Dept. Army. Chmn. Johnson for Pres. vols., Minn., 1964. Diplomate Pan Am. Med. Assn. Mem. Soc. Med. Cons. Armed Forces, A.A.A.S., A.M.A. (vice chmn. council on nat. security, recipient Billings gold medal award 1963), So. Minn. Med. Assn. A.C.P. (life mem., gov. for Minn.), Am. Gastroenterol. Assn., Assn. Study Liver Diseases, Am. Fedn. Clin. Research, Mayo Clinic Alumni Assn., Am. Radio Relay League, Amateur Radio Emergency Corps, Sigma Xi, Delta Kappa Epsilon, Alpha Kappa, Alpha Epsilon Delta. Baptist. Contbr. articles profl. jours., chpts. books. Home: Cain's Mesa Rochester MN 55901 Office: Mayo Clinic Rochester MN 55901

CAIN, JAMES MALLAHAN, newspaper man; b. Annapolis, Md., July 1, 1892; s. James William and Rose Cecilia (Mallahan) C.; A.B., Washington Coll., Chestertown, Md., 1910, A.M., 1917; m. Florence Macbeth, 1947. Mem. staff of the Baltimore (Md.) Am., 1917-18, Baltimore Sun, 1918-23; prof. journalism, St. John's Coll., Annapolis, Md., 1923-24; editorial writer New York World, 1924- 31; magazine, syndicate, and moving picture work since 1931. Served as pvt. 1st class, Hdqr. Troop, 79th Div., A.E.F., 1918-19; editor-in- chief,

Lorraine Cross, official newspaper 79th Division, 1919. Democrat. Author: Our Government (sketches), 1930; novels, The Postman Always Rings Twice, 1934, (play, 1936); Double Indemnity, 1936; Serenade, 1937; Career in C Major, 1938; The Embezzler, 1940; Mildred Piece, 1941; Love's Lovely Counterfeit, 1942; Three of a Kind, 1943; Past All Dishonor, 1946; The Butterfly, 1947; Sinful Woman, 1947; The Moth, 1948; Jealous Woman, 1950; Galatea, 1953; The Root of His Evil, 1954; Mignon, 1962; The Magician's Wife, 1965. Address: 6707 44th Av Unversity Park Hyattsville MD 20782

CAIN, JAMES RICHARD, mfg. co. exec.; b. Centralia, Ill., Feb. 11, 1929; s. Paul M. and Bernice (Wilson) C.; B.S. in Accountancy, U. Ill., 1951; m. Marilyn J. Stanford, Feb. 5, 1950; childrenRichard S., Jeffrey A., David G., Lise A., Harold S. Pub. accountant Murphey Nash & Jones, Decatur, Ill., 1952- 54; controller, asst. sec.-treas. Norge div. Borg-Warner Corp., 1954-68; controller Fedders Corp., Edison, N.J. 1968-70; dir. accounting York div. Borg-Warner Corp., York, Pa., 1970—. Mem. Nat. Assn. Accountants. Home: 2171 Blenheim Ct York PA 17403 Office: York div Borg-Warner Corp Grantley Rd York PA 17405

CAIN, JOSEPH ALEXANDER, artist, educator; b. Henderson, Tenn., May 27, 1920; s. Thomas Watson and Rose Anna (Wimberly) C.; B.F.A., U. Cal. at Berkeley, 1947, M.F.A., 1948; m. Mable Louise Barton, Aug. 21, 1945; 1 dau., Jonizo. Exhibited one man shows including Centennial Mus., Corpus Christi, Tex., 1950, Richmond Art Center, 1951, Tex. Coll. Arts and Industries, 1952, Little Theatre, Corpus Christi, 1956, Victoria, Tex., 1957. Southwestern U., Georgetown, Tex., 1961, Incarnate Word Coll. San Antonio, 1961, Legoa Duncan Gallery, N.Y.C., 1963, U. Ore., 1964, Williamantic (Conn.) State Coll., 1965, Laguna Gloria Austin, Fine Arts Library, Jersey City, 1968, others; exhibited group shows Grand Central Galleries, Petite Gallerie, N.Y.C., Los Angeles County Mus., other museums, galleries U.S., Mexico, France; tchr. art Corpus Christi High Sch., 1948-50, W.B. Ray High Sch., 1950—, Corpus Christi Fine Arts Colony Workshops, Cain Studio, Corpus Christi; asso. prof. art Delmar Coll., Corpus Christi; with art editor, critic Corpus Christi Caller-Times, 1955—; rep. permanent collections including Collection Contemporary Tex. Art, Michael M. Engel, M. Grubacher, Inc., also Seton Hall U., Del Mar Coll., Goliard Library Rosenberg Gallery, Beaumont Mus., others; exhbn. casein paintings on nat. tour Old Bergen Art Guild, 1964-66, acrylic paintings on tour Old Bergen Art Guild, 1967—; executed mosaic murals Spohn Hosp., Buccaneer Bowl, 1961. Mem. Corpus Christi Municipal Art Commn., 1968-72. Served to capt. USMCR, 1942-46, 50-52; col. Res. Recipient Gold medal Seton Hall U., 1958; Sarah Goode award, 1963; Phila. Water Color Club prize Pa. Acad. Fine Arts, 1965; Purchase award Cal. show Nat. Watercolor Soc., 1969; numerous other awards nat., regional, local exhbns. Fellow Royal Soc. Arts (London); mem. S. Tex. Art League (pres. 1970-71), Tex. Watercolor Soc. (regional dir. 1958—, 3d v.p. 1964- 66), Tex. Fine Arts Assn. (regional dir. 1957—), Sarasota, Miss. art assns., Cal., Ala. watercolor socs., Western Artists Assn., N.E.A., Nat. Platform Assn., Corpus Christi Art Found., Tex. Classroom Tchrs. Assn., Nat. Soc. Painters in Casein (Grumbacher 1st award 1965), Nat. Artists and Art Patrons Soc. Contbr. articles to various publs. Home: 402 Troy Dr Corpus Christi TX 78412

CAIN, ROBERT EDGAR, petroleum co. exec.; b. Toledo, Mar. 7, 1925; s. C. Edgar and Lumina (St. Pierre) C.; A.B., Miami (O.) U., 1948; m. Jean Turman, Sept. 11, 1948; children—Barbara Joan, Julie Marie. Geologist, Magnolia Petroleum Co., 1948-53; div. geologist Tex. Eastern Transmission Corp., 1953-60; chief geologist Ramada Oil Co., 1960-61; with Southland Royalty Co., Ft. Worth, 1961—, exec. v.p., 1964-66, pres., dir., 1966—; dir. Gateway National Bank, Fort Worth, Texas. Bd. dirs. Tarrant County Assn. Mental Health. Served with USMCR, World War II. Decorated Purple Heart. Mem. Am. Assn. Petroleum Geologist, Am. Petroleum Inst., Mid-Continent Oil and Gas Assn., Ind. Petroleum Assn. Am., Am. Inst. Profl. Geologists, Ft. Worth Petroleum Club, Sigma Chi fraternity. Clubs: Ft. Worth, River Crest Country (Ft. Worth). Home: 324 N Bailey St Fort Worth TX 76107 Office: First Nat Bldg Fort Worth TX 76102

CAIN, STITH M., librarian; b. Nashville, Sept. 25, 1911; s. Henry B. and Ellie F. (Ford) C.; A.B., Vanderbilt U., 1934; M.A., U. Va., 1936; B.S. in L.S., Peabody Coll., 1938; Ed.M., 1945; m. Mary Elizabeth Woodcock, Aug. 27, 1949; children—Edit Malone, Irene Woodcock. Dir. sch. libraries, Haines City, Fla., 1938-40; asst. librarian State Tchrs. Coll., Morehead, Ky., 1940- 42; staff Vanderbilt Med. Sch. Library, 1944-45; head librarian N.M. State Tchrs. Coll., 1945, Union Coll., 1946-47, Central Coll., Fayette, Mo., 1947-53; librarian Ill. Wesleyan U., Bloomington, 1953-57, Wis. State U., Whitewater, 1957—. Mem. adv. council pub. schools, Bloomington; mem. Wis. consulting com. to Fed. Historic Sites Preservation Act of 1966, 1969; mem. Gov.'s Commn. Edn. for Wis., 1969, Wis. Historic Site Commn. Served as sgt., AUS, 1942-44. Mem. A.L.A., Tennessee, Kentucky, Missouri (chmn. coll. and univ. sect. 1949-50, bus. mgr. Quar.), N.M. (v.p. 1946), Ill., Wis. (chmn. coll. and univ. sect. 1967-68), McLean County (pres. 1955-56) library assns., Am. Assn. U. Profs., Wis. Edn. Assn., Assn. Coll. and Reference Librarians, Tenn., Boonslick hist. socs., Civil War Round Table, Phi Delta Kappa, Pi Gamma Mu Phi Kappa Phi. Democrat. Methodist. Mason (Shriner), Rotarian, Kiwanian (pres. Whitewater 1965). Contbr. articles edn. publs. Home: 775 W Main St Whitewater WI 53190

CAIN, VICTOR M., tool mfg. exec.; b. Nokomis, Ill., Sept. 25, 1904; s. Daniel B. and Elsie M. (Manning) C.; student U. Ill., 1927; m. Eula Spelman, June 12, 1927; 1 dau., Barbara (Mrs. Lynn A. Ameche). With Snap-On Tools Corp., Kenosha, Wis., 1929—, successively accountant, asst. treas., controller, 1929-57, v.p., controller, dir., 1957-59, pres., dir., 1959- 66, chmn. bd., 1966—; dir. Snap-on Tools of Can., Ltd., Weidenhoff Corp., Nat. Blvd. Bank of Chgo., Nat. Standard Co., Niles, Mich., Employers Muts. Ins. of Wausau. Trustee Wis. Council of Safety. Mem. Kenosha C. of C. (past pres.), Kenosha Mfrs. Assn. (pres.). Home: 523 78th St Kenosha WI 53140 Office: 8028 28th Av Kenosha WI 53140

CAIN, WALKER O., architect; b. Cleve., Apr. 14, 1915; s. Oscar Clyde and Meta Mathilde (Gusse) C.; Diploma in Arch., Ecole de Beaux Arts Americaine, Fontainbleau, France, 1937; B.Arch., Western Res. U., 1938; M.F.A., Princeton, 1940; fellow Am. Acad. Rome, 1947-48; m. Abby Jane Huston, June 1941 (div.); children—Susan Berry, Tamma Huston. With firm McKim, Meade & White, architects, N.Y.C., 1940-51, asso., 1951-61; partner Steinmann, Cain & White, architects, N.Y.C., 1961-65, Steinmann & Cain, architects, N.Y.C., 1965-67, Walker O. Cain & Assos., 1967—; prin. works include Gould Acad., Campus Plan Dormitories, Bethel, Me., Me. State Cultural Bldg., Schenectady Mus., dormitories U. Conn.; Jafet Library, Engring. Sch., Hosp. addition, faculty apts., American Univ., Beirut, Lebanon; Ballou Hall, Tufts College; campus plan dormitories, Liberial Arts Center, Science Center, Union College, Schenectady; Museum History and Tech. at Smithsonian Institution; library, field house, Jadwin Gymnasium, Computer Center, Princeton Univ.; library, Bowdoin Coll.; St. Vartan Cathedral and cultural center Armenian Ch. Am., N.Y.C.; Casco Bank & Trust Co. office bldg., Portland, Me.; additions to New Eng. Center Hosp., Boston; illustrator archtl. mags. and books. Mem. Manhattan Boro President Community Planning Bd., 1965-67; dir. Park Assn. N.Y.C., 1962-65, chmn. City Parks Week, 1962-63; mem. Taconic State Park Commn., 1966—, Nat. Capitol Com., 1969-70, East Hudson Pkwy. Authority, 1966—. Trustee American Acad. Rome, 1952—; hon. chmn. bd. trustees Garrison's Landing Assn. Museum Transp.; mem. vis. com. visual arts Western Res. U., 1963-66. Served to lt. USNR, 1943-46. Recipient Prix de Rome, 1940. Fellow A.I.A. (chmn. urban design com. N.Y. chpt. 1963-65)); mem. N.A.D (asso.), Am. Arbitration Assn., Soc. Archtl. Historians, Nat. Inst. Archtl. Edn. Clubs: Century assn. (N.Y.C.). Home: 400 E 52d St New York City NY 10022 Office: 101 Park Av New York City NY 10017

CAIN, WOFFORD, gas exec.; b. Athens, Tex., Oct. 19, 1891; s. Smith M. and Mattie (Wofford) C.; B.S., Tex. A. and M. Coll., 1913; m. Effie Marie Arrington, Nov. 11, 1941. Asst. supt. Italy Com; pres. various subsidiaries; chmn. Aztec Oil & Gas Co., Ennis, Tex., 1923-28; v.p. So. Union Gas Co., Dallas, 1928-43, pres., 1943-60, chmn.; also chmn. and pres. various subsidiaries; chmn. Aztec Oil & Gas Co., Dallas, So. Union Prodn. Co.; dir. Mercantile Nat. Bank. Dir., past pres. Dallas Heart Assn. Home: 4408 St Johns Dr Dallas TX 75205 Office: First Nat Bank Bldg Dallas TX 75202

CAINE, LOUIS VERNON, coll. pres.; b. Wall Lake, Ia., Sept. 30, 1904; s. Philip and Lucetta (Smith) C.; B.A., Jamestown Coll., 1927, LL.D., 1951; M.A., U. Minn., 1934; postgrad. U. Wis., Columbia, N.Y.U.; m. Elizabeth Holland, June 29, 1932; childrenClifford, Alan, Stanley. Prin. Bryant (S.D.) High Sch., 1927-29; supt. schs., Hayti, S.D., 1929-34, DeSmet, 1934-42; successively pub. relations dir., coordinator AAF coll. tng., asst. prof. physics, asst. to pres., v.p., acting pres. Jamestown Coll., 1942- 50; v.p. Macalester Coll., 1950-56; pres. Ill. Coll., 1956-. Mem. exec. com. Fedn. Ill. Independent Colls. and Univs.; pres. Congl. Christian Coll. Council; exec. sec. com. on arrangements 165th Gen. Assembly, Presbyn. Ch. U.S.A. Active Boy Scouts of America; trustee Lincoln Academy of Illinois. Presbyn. (chmn. gen. council Synod Ill., elder). Rotarian. Home: 310 Lockwood Pl Jacksonville IL 62650

CAINE, MARTIN GEORGE, plastics co. exec.; b. Worcester, Mass., Feb. 1, 1916; s. Myer and Rose (Glesen) C.; B.S., Worcester Poly. Inst., 1937; M.S., Bklyn. Poly. Inst., 1941; m. Ada Fay Curley, June 22, 1947; children—Jonathan L., Robin M. Chief chemist Siemon Co., Bridgeport, Conn., 1937-41; with Monsanto Chem. Co., 1941-42, 46-67, mgr. comml. devel., 1961-67; chief exec. officer Tenneco Plastics div. Tenneco Chems. Inc., Piscataway, N.J., 1967—; dir. Tenneco Chems., Inc. Served with USNR, 1942-46: ETO. Mem. Am. Chem. Soc., Soc. Plastics Engrs., Am. Soc. Naval Engrs., Res. Officer Assn., Soc. Commd. Officers, Alpha Epsilon Pi. Developer PVC plasticized drybiends, 1949. Home: 25 Bonnyview Dr Livingston NJ 07039 Office: PO Box 2 Piscataway NJ 08854

CAINE, MICHAEL, actor; b. Eng., 1933; m. Patricia Haines (div.); 1 dau. Actor with Theatre Workshop and Royal Ct. Theatre, London; understudied Peter O'Toole in The Long and the Short and the The Tall; film appearances include How to Murder a Rich Uncle, Zulu, The Ipcress File, Alfie, Gambit , Funeral in Berlin, Hurry Sundown, Billion Dollar Brain, Deadfall, The Magus, Play Dirty, Italian Job, The Battle of Britain, Too Late the Hero. Served with Royal British Fuisiliers, 1953; Korea. Address: care CMA 600 Madison Av New York City NY 10022 also care Harry Saltzman 1 Tilney St London England*

CAINE, WALTER EUGENE, utility exec.; b. Buffalo, Apr. 4, 1908; s. Howard Ellsworth and Dora (Squier) C.; B.B.A., U. Buffalo, 1930; M.B.A., Northwestern U., 1931; m. Jeanette Wenborne, Dec. 22, 1932; children—Stephen Howard, Edward Arthur, Martin Squier. Sr. rate analyst Pub. Service Commn. of Wis., Madison, 1932-38; asst. chief rate div. Rural Electrification Adminstrn., Washington, 1936; asst. chief div. rates and research Fed. Power Commn., Washington, 1938-44; asso. dir. Survey Electric Industry, Twentieth Century Fund, N.Y.C., 1940; dir. bur. statistics, sec. accounting sect. Am. Gas. Assn., N.Y.C., 1944-48; dir. gas planning div. Petroleum Adminstrn. for Def., Dept. Interior, Washington, 1951-52; sec., treas. Texas Eastern Transmission Corp., Shreveport, La., 1948-50, v.p., treas., 1950-53, v.p. gas sales and marketing, Houston, N.Y.C., 1953-67, v.p. corporate services div., 1967—; instr. U.S. Dept. Agr. Grad. Sch., Washington, 1943-44. Mem. gas industry adv. council Dept. Interior, 1954-57, mil. petroleum adv. bd., 1957-62. Mem. future requirements com. Denver Research Inst., U. Denver, 1961—, vice chmn., 1970—. Mem. Am. Gas Assn., Am. Ordnance Assn. (mem. nat. council 1960-61), U.S. C. of C. (com. on econ. policy 1963-66, task force on financing state, local govt. 1966-67), N.Y. Soc. Security Analysts, N.Y. Soc. Gas Lighting, Newcomen Soc. N.Am., Am. Econ. Assn., Nat. Planning Assn. (nat. council 1969—). Clubs: Cosmos (Washington); Sky, Economic (N.Y.C.); Seaview Country (Absecon, N.J.); Bald Peak Colony (Melvin Village, N.H.); Shreveport, Shreveport Country; Houston, Lakeside Country (Houston). Author: (with A.R. Burns) Electric Power and Government Policy, 1948; Gas Facts, 1948. Home: 426 Westminster Dr Houston TX 77024 Office: Box 2521 Houston TX 77001

CAIRNCROSS, ALEXANDER KIRKLAND, economist; b. Lesmahagow, Scotland, Feb. 11, 1911; s. Alexander Kirkland and Elizabeth Andrew (Wishart) C.; grad. Hamilton Acad., 1928; M.A., U. Glasgow, 1933; Ph.D., Cambridge U., 1936; LL.D., Mt. Allison U., 1962; LL.D., Glasgow Univ., 1966, Exeter U., 1969; D.Litt., Reading U., 1968, Heriot Watt U., 1969; D.Sc., University Coll., Swansea, 1971; m. Mary Frances Glynn, May 29, 1943; children—Frances Anne, Philip Wishart, Alexander Messent, David John, Elizabeth Mary. Lectr., U. Glasgow, 1935-39, prof. applied econs., dir. dept. social and econ. research, 1951-61; econ. adviser to Her Majesty's Govt., 1961-64; head of Her Majesty's Govt. Econ. Service, 1964-69; master St. Peters Coll., Oxford, Eng., 1969—; War Cabinet offices, Bd. Trade, Ministry Aircraft Prodn., 1939-45, econ. adviser Bd. Trade, 1946-49; head econ. adv. panel, Berlin, 1945-46; staff London Economist, 1946; econ. adviser OEEC, 1949-50; dir. Econ. Devel. Inst., Washington, 1955-56. Trustee Urwick Orr and Partners; extraordinary dir. Scottish Amicable Life Assurance Soc. Bd. govs. London Sch. Econs. Decorated comdr. Order St. Michael and St. George, 1950, Knight comdr., 1966. Fellow Brit. Acad.; mem. Royal (v.p.), Scottish (pres.) econ. socs., Nat. Inst. Econ. and Social Research of London (bd. govs.). Author: Introduction to Economics, 1944; Home and Foreign Investment, 1870-1913, 1953; Monetary Policy in a Mixed Economy, 1960; Factors in Economic Development, 1962; Essays in Economic Management, 1971. Editor: The Scottish Economy, 1954, Scottish Jour. Polit. Economy, 1954-61; The Managed Economy, 1970; Planning and Economic Management, 1970, Britain's Economic Prospects Reconsidered, 1971. Home: Master's Lodgings St Peter's Coll Oxford England

CAIRNES, JOSEPH FRANCIS, bldg. constrn. exec.; b. Somerville, Mass., May 26, 1907; s. Edward and Bridget (Shiel) C.; student State Steam Engring. Sch., Boston, 1926, Lowell Inst., Cambridge, Mass., 1937-38; m. Helen Mary Tobin, Sept. 21, 1940; children—Joseph Francis, Edward, Mary Gilberta, Thomas, Anne Clare, Ellen Bernadette. Regional engr. Fed. Works Agy., N.Y., Pa., Conn., Mass., N.H., Vt., Maine, R.I., 1940-44; commr. pub. works Commonwealth of Mass., 1945-46; exec. v.p. Boston Braves, 1952; exec. v.p. Milwaukee Braves, 1953-56, pres., 1958-61, vice chmn. bd., 1961-63; pres. Perini Westward Developers, Inc., 1958-62, vice chmn. bd. dirs. 1961-63; v.p., dir. Perini Corp., 1960—. Mem. adv. council Mass. Bldg. Congress, 1970—. Mem. president's adv. council Marquette U. Mem. Nat. Soc. Profl. Engrs., Asso. Gen. Contractors Mass. (pres. 1967-68, dir. 1966—). K.C. (4). Clubs: Charles River Country; Engineers (Boston); Sailfish of Fla.; Wamsutta (New Bedford, Mass.). Home; 175 Richardson Dr Needham MA 02192 Office: 73 Mt Wayte Av Framingham MA 01701

CAIRNS, EARLE EDWIN, clergyman, educator; b. Woodworth, Man., Can., May 26, 1910; s. Frederick and Amelia (Gompf) C.; A.B., Municipal U. Omaha, 1938; Th.B., Presbyn. Theol. Sem., 1938; M.A., U. Neb., 1939, Ph.D., 1942; m. Helen Frances Purdie, Aug. 29, 1938 (dec. Apr. 1967); 1 son, Bruce Earle; Earle; m. 2d, Jo Ann Patricia Jordan, June 11, 1968. Came to U.S., 1935; naturalized, 1954. Ordained to ministry Presbyn Ch., 1938; prof. N.T., Presbyn. Theol. Sem., Omaha, 1941-43; prof. history Wheaton (Ill.) Coll., 1943-, chmn. history and polit. sci. dept., 1948-, div. chmn., 1969—. Named Tchr. of Year, Wheaton Coll., 1962. Mem. Am. Hist. Assn., Am. Soc. Ch. History. Author: Christianity Through the Centuries, 1954, Japanese edit., 1957, Italian edit., 1970; Saints and Society, 1960; Christianity in the United States, 1964. Contbr. chpt. to Contemporary Evangelical Thought. Home: 515 E Prairie Av Wheaton, IL 60187.

CAIRNS, GORDON MANN, educator; b. Bklyn., July 14, 1911; s. John A. and Mary Harriet (Mann) C.; B.S., Cornell, 1936, M.S., 1938, Ph.D., 1940; m. Ruth Marion Sharp, July 1, 1938; children—John, Barbara. Asso. prof., head dept. animal husbandry U. Me., 1939-40, prof., head dept., 1940-45; prof. dairy husbandry, head dept. U. Md., 1945-51, dean of agr., 1950—. Dir. Balt. br. Fed. Res. Bank, Richmond, 1957-62. Fellow A.A.A.S.; mem. Sigma Xi, Alpha Zeta, Phi Kappa Phi. Presbyn. Rotarian. Home: 8528 Pineway Dr Laurel MD 20810 Office: Coll of Agr U Md College Park MD 20740

CAIRNS, HUNTINGTON, lawyer, author; b. Balt., Sept. 1, 1904; s. James Duncanson and Helen Huntington (Heath) C.; grad. Balt. City Coll., 1922; LL.B., U. Md., 1925; LL.D., N.Y. U., St. Andrews U., Johns Hopkins, U. Md.; L.H.D., Tulane U., Kenyon Coll.; m. Florence F. Butler, May 29, 1929. Admitted to Md. bar, 1926, D.C. bar, 1943; asso. Piper, Carey & Hall, 1926-37, partner 1933-37; spl. legal adviser U.S. Treasury Dept., 1934-37, 43-65. Lectr. taxation U. Md. Law Sch., 1935-37; chmn. radio program Invitation to Learning, 1940-41; asst. gen. counsel U.S. Treasury, 1937-43; mem. com. on practice Treas. Dept., 1944-52. Sec., mem. Am. Commn. for Protection and Salvage of Artistic and Historic Monuments, War Areas, 1943-46; sec., treas., gen. counsel Nat. Gallery Art, 1943-65; James Schouler lectr. polit. sci. Johns Hopkins, 1947, lectr. criticism, 1949-59; mem. Md. Tax Revision Commn., 1938-41. Trustee Bollingen Found., Textile Mus.; mem. Dumbarton Oaks adminstrv. com. Harvard; bd. dirs. Jr. Hist. of Ideas; mem.-at-large Am. Council Learned Socs. Benjamin N. Cardozo lectr., 1962; John Randolph Tucker lectr., 1970. Recipient Civic medallion for most significant contbn. to progress of Balt. in field professions and sci., 1935, Rockefeller Pub. Service award. Mem. Am. (council sect. legal edn. and admissions to bar), D.C., Md. bar assns., Am. Law Inst., Am. Philos. Assn., Am. Soc. for Aesthetics, Phi Beta Kappa. Clubs: Hamilton Street, 1925 F Street, Md., Cosmos, Wranglers. Author: Law and the Social Sciences, 1935; The Theory of Legal Science, 1941; Invitation to Learning (with Allen Tate and Mark Van Doren), 1941; (with John Walker), Masterpieces of Painting from the National Gallery of Art, 1944; The Limits of Art, 1948; Legal Philosophy from Plato to Hegel, 1949; (with John Walker) A Pageant of Painting; The Two-Story World; Selected Writings of James K. Feibleman; Law and its Premises, 1962. Editor: Tax Laws of Maryland, 1937; Malinowski, A Scientific Theory of Culture, 1944; Saintsbury, French Literature and Its Masters, 1945; Lectures in Criticism, 1949; (with John Walker) Great Paintings from the National Gallery of Art, 1952; (with Edith Hamilton) The Collected Dialogues of Plato, 1961; (with John Walker) Treasures from the National Gallery of Art, 1962; H.L. Mencken; The American Scene, A Reader, 1965. Contbr. to various mags., symposia, Dictionary Am. Biography. Home: 2219 California NW Washington DC 20008

CAIRNS, ROBERT WILLIAM, govt. ofcl.; b. Oberlin, O., Dec. 23, 1909; s. William D. and Iva (Crofoot) C.; student U. Cal. at Berkeley, 1926-27; A.B., Oberlin Coll., 1930; Ph.D., Johns Hopkins, 1932; D.Sc., U. Del., 1969; m. Katherine Kuhn, Oct. 22, 1932; children—Lindsey Ann, Michael John, Robert Christopher, Stephen William Waldo. Research chemist Firestone Tire & Rubber Co., Akron, O., summers 1930-33; fellow Bartol Research Found., Swarthmore, Pa., 1933-34; research chemist explosives research div. research center Hercules, Inc., 1934-40, asst. to dir. research, 1940-41, dir. research center, 1941-45; dir. devel. dept. Radford Ordnance Works, Va., 1942-43, asst. dir. research, 1945- 55, dir. research, 1955-66, dir., 1960-71; v.p. research Hercules, Inc., 1966-71; dep. asst. sec. sci. and tech. Dept. Commerce, 1971—. Vice chmn. research and devel. bd. Dept. Def., Washington, 1953, spl. asst. to sec. def., 1953-54, dep. asst. sec. def. for research and devel., 1953- 54; spl. asst. to asst. sec. def., 1955-56, cons. Office Asst. Sec. Def., 1956-69, mem. def. sci. bd., 1956-62, 65-69, chmn. panel gen. sci., 1957-61; cons. Nat. Def. Research Com., 1943-46; panel chmn. com. on ordnance Research Devel. Bd., 1947-48; mem. sci. adv. bd. Naval Ordnance Test Sta., 1949-53; trustee Gordon Rsearch Confs., 1958-61, chmn., 1960-61. Dir. Family Service, Inc., Wilmington; v.p. Travelers Aid Soc., Wilmington, 1946-54. Mem. math and physical scis. com. NSF, 1958-60; chmn. res. com., bd. trustees U. Del. Research Found.; chmn. com. on sci. and tech. communication Nat. Acad. Sci. NRC, 1965-70; mem. res. adv. bd. AID, Dept. State; cons. to Arms Control and Disarmament Agy.; sci. adviser to Gov. Del., 1969-71; chmn. Gov.'s Council Sci. and Tech., 1969-71; mem. macromolecular div., pres. applied chemistry div. Internat. Union Pure and Applied Chemistry, 1968—. Pres., U. Del. Research Found., 1966- 70. Recipient Perkin medal Soc. Chem. Industry, 1969. Fellow A.A.A.S., N.Y. Acad. Scis.; mem. Am. Chem. Soc. (dir. 1961—, chmn. finance com. 1964-67, pres. 1968, chmn. com. on corp. assos., chmn. Del sect. 1944-45, councilor 1948-49), Nat. Planning Assn. (com. overseas devel.), Engrs. Joint Council (dir. 1967-69), Am. Phys. Soc., Indsl. Research Inst. (pres. 1959-60), Soc. Chem. Industry (chmn. American sect. 1961-62), Nat. Acad. Engring. (mem. exec. com. 1969—), Dirs. of Ind. Research, Nat. Sec. Indsl. Assn., Am. Inst. Chem. Engring., Am. Ordnance Assn., Phi Beta Kappa, Sigma Xi, Phi Lambda Upsilon. Episcopalian. Home: 900 Burnt Mill Rd Wilmington DE 19807 Office: Dept Commerce Washington DC 20230

CAIRNS, STEWART SCOTT, educator; b. Franklin, N.H., May 8, 1904; s. James George and Laure (Dorion) C.; A.B. magna cum laude, Harvard, 1926, A. M., 1927, Ph.D., 1931; m. Kathleen Hand, June 20, 1928; childrenJames Donald, Charles Edward. Part-time instr. Harvard, 1927-28, traveling fellow, 1928-29; instr. Yale, 1929-31; instr. Lehigh U., 1931-33, asst. prof., 1933-38; mem. Inst. for Advanced Study, 1936-37, 59-60, 62-63; assistant professor Queens College, Flushing, Long Island, N.Y., 1938-46; prof., chmn. dept. Syracuse U., 1946-48; head dept. mathematics U. Ill., 1948- 58, prof., 1948-; Fulbright lectr. U. Strasbourg, France, 1954-55; vis. fellow U. Cambridge, 1964, U. Warwick, 1966. Cons. USAAF, 1944-46, Dept.

Def., Rand Corp. Fellow A.A.A.S.; mem. Math. Assn. Am., Am. Math. Soc., Phi Beta Kappa, Sigma Xi, Pi Mu Epsilon. Author: Introductory Topology, 1961; also articles in field; co-author: Critical Point Theory in Global Analysis and Differential Topology, 1969. Home: 607 W Michigan Av Urbana IL 61801

CAIRNS, THEODORE LESUEUR, chemist; b. Edmonton, Can., July 20, 1914; s. Albert Williams and Theodora (MacNaughton) C.; came to U.S., 1937, naturalized, 1945; B.S., U. Alta., 1936, LL.D., 1970; Ph.D., U. Ill., 1939; m. Margaret Jean McDonald, Aug. 17, 1940; children—John Albert, Margaret Eleanor (Mrs. James R. Latimore), Elizabeth Theodora, James Richard. Instr. organic chemistry U. Rochester, 1939-41; research chemist central research dept. E.I. duPont de Nemours & Co., Wilmington, Del., 1941-45, research supr., 1945-51, lab. dir., 1951-63, dir. basic scis., 1963-66, dir. research, 1966-67, asst. dir. central research dept., 1967-71, dir., 1971—. Mem. adv. bd. Organic Syntheses, 1958—; mem. President's Sci. Adv. Com., 1970-73. Recipient award for creative work in synthetic organic chemistry Am. Chem. Soc., 1968. Mem. Nat. Acad. Scis., Am. Chem. Soc. (chmn. organic div. 1964-65), A.A.A.S., Sigma Xi, Phi Lambda Upsilon, Alpha Chi Sigma, Phi Lambda Upsilon (hon.). Editorial bd. Organic Reactions, 1959—, Jour. Organic Chemistry, 1965-69. Home: Hillside Rd Greenville Wilmington DE 19807 Office: Central Research Dept DuPont Wilmington DE 19898

CAIRNS, THOMAS WILLIAM, educator; b. Hutchinson, Kan., Nov. 13, 1931; s. Edmund Alexander and Gladys Lorene (Upstone) C.; B.S. in Physics, Okla. State U., 1953, M.S. in Math., 1955, Ph.D., 1960; m. Sharon Louise Kellet, May 26, 1959; children—Janet Lorraine, Michael Scot. Asst. prof. math. U. Tulsa, 1959-65, asso. prof., 1965-69, head of dept., 1967—, prof., 1969—. Cons. to Def. Dept., Cities Service Oil Co., Amoco Research Co., Hillcrest Med. Center. Mem. Gov.'s Com. on Computing in Edn., 1968-70. Served to 1st lt. AUS, 1954-56. Mem. Am. Math. Soc., Math. Assn. Am. (pres. Okla.-Ark. sect. 1971—), Soc. Indsl. and Applied Math. Assn. Computing Machinery. Author: (with N.A. Rutledge) Mathematics for Business Analysis, 1963; research in computer sci. and biomath. Home: 1357 S 101 E Av Tulsa OK 74128

CAIRO, WILLIAM PASQUALE, mfg. co. exec.; b. Phila., Dec. 10, 1905; s. Frank and Chiara G. (Nicoletti) C.; A.B. with honors, U. Pa., 1929; LL.B., Harvard, 1932; m. Marion M. Middleton, July 21, 1934; children—Barbara Ann, Jeanne C. (Mrs. Hugh C. Sutherland). Admitted to Pa. bar, 1932; practice in Phila., 1932-42; with Electric Storage Battery Co., 1942—, asst. sec., 1957-59, sec., 1959-71, v.p., gen. counsel, 1971—; dir. Bd. City Trusts Phila. Mem. exec. bd. Com. of Seventy, Phila. Mem. Am., Phila. bar assns., Phi Beta Kappa. Episcopalian (vestryman). Clubs: Cricket, Union League (Phila.). Home: 509 E Gorgas Lane Philadelphia PA 19119 Office: 5 Penn Center Plaza Philadelphia PA 19102

CAKE, RALPH HARLAN, savs. and loan assn. exec.; b. Portland, Ore., June 26, 1891; s. William M. and Lulu (Riley) C.; A.B., U. Ore., 1913; LL.D., Harvard, 1916; m. Katherine Myers, Apr. 6, 1963; children by previous marriageMartha, Ralph Harlan. With Equitable Savs & Loan Assn., Portland, 1922-, v.p., 1933-38, pres., 1938-64, chmn. bd., 1964-68, chmn. finance com., 1968—, also dir.; dir. Ore. Portland Cement Co., Hayden Island, Inc., Gerber Legendary Blades, KATU, Portland, Ore., Panama Canal Co. Pres. Portland Rose Festival Assn., 1938, Multonomah Civic Stadium Assn., 1936. Mem. Republican Nat. Com. for Ore., 1940-52. Mem. U.S. Savs. and Loan League (pres. 1942-43), U. Ore. Alumni Assn. (pres. 1937-38), Phi Delta Gamma (trustee 1964-66, pres. 1952-53, pres. ednl. found. 1970—). Clubs: Waverly Country, Multonomah Athletic, Arlington, University (Portland); University (N.Y.C.); Capitol Hill (Washington). Home: 321 NW Royal Blvd Portland, OR 97210. Office: 1300 SW 6th Av Portland OR 97201

CALABI, EUGENIO, educator, mathematician; b. Milan, Italy, May 11, 1923; s. Giuseppe and Maria (Bassani) C.; B.s. in Chem. Engring., Mass. Inst. Tech., 1946; M.A., U. Ill., 1947; Ph.D., Princeton, 1950; m. Giuliana Calabi, Sept. 3, 1952; children—Nora J., Joseph A. Asst. prof. La. State U., 1951-55; from asst. prof. to prof. U. Minn., 1955-64; prof. math. U. Pa., 1964—, Thomas A. Scott prof. math., 1967—. Served with AUS, 1943-46. Mem. Am. Math. Soc. Home: 516 Sabine Circle Wynnewood PA 19096 Office: U Pa Philadelphia PA 19104

CALABRESI, GUIDO, legal educator; b. Milan, Italy, Oct. 18, 1932; s. Masimo E. and Bianca (Finzi-Contini) C.; came to U.S., 1939, naturalized, 1948; B.S. in Analytical Econs., Yale, 1953, LL.B., 1958, M.A. (hon.), 1962; B.A. in Politics, Philosophy and Econs., Magdalen Coll., Oxford (Eng.) U., 1955. M.A., 1959; m. Anne Gordon Audubon Tyler, May 20, 1961; childrenBianca Contini, Anne Gordon Audubon, Massimo Franklin Tyler. Admitted to Conn. bar, 1958; law clk. to Supreme Ct. Justice Hugo L. Black, 1958-59; mem. faculty Yale, 1959—, prof. law, 1962—, John Thomas Smith prof. law, 1970, fellow Timothy Dwight Coll., 1960—. Dir. Crosby Co., Mpls., First New Haven Nat. Bank, Concord Computing Corp. Mem. bd. ednl., Woodbridge, Conn., 1967-69; mem. Woodbridge Democratic Town Com., 1968—. Bd. dirs. Dixwell Community House, St. Thomas More Chapel (Yale); trustee Carolyn Found., Mpls. Rhodes scholar, 1953. Named One of Outstanding Young Men in Am., U.S. Jr. C. of C., 1962. Mem. Conn. Bar Assn., Phi Beta Kappa. Roman Cath. Home: Amity Rd Woodbridge, CT 06525. Office: 127 Wall St New Haven CT 06520

CALABRESI, PAUL, educator, physician; b. Milan, Italy, Apr. 5, 1930; s. Massimo E. and Bianca (Contini) C.; A.B., Yale, 1951, M.D., 1955; m. Celia Treadway Gow, Apr. 3, 1954; children—Steven Gow, Janice Louise, Peter Arthur. Intern. then asst. resident Harvard med. service Boston City Hosp., 1955- 59; project asso. medicine U. Wis. Med. Sch., 1956-58; field investigator Nat. Cancer Inst., 1956-60; from research fellow to asso. prof. medicine and pharmacology Yale Sch. Medicine, 1959-68; head div. clin. pharmacology and chemotherapy, dir. Clin. Pharmacology Research Center, Yale-New Haven Med. Center, 1965-67; prof. med. sci. Brown U., 1968—. Chmn. dept. medicine, also physician-in-chief Roger Williams Gen. Hosp., Providence, 1968—; vis. scientist U. Lausanne (Switzerland) 1966-67. Mem. cancer chemotherapy collabortive program rev. com. NIH, 1965-66, pharmacology-toxicology rev. com., 1967—; mem. clin. pharmacology tng. program com. VA, 1969—; policy and planning com., drug research bd. Nat. Acad. Scis.-NRC, 1969—. Mem. Corp. R.I. Philharmonic, Providence Child Guidance Clinic; Pres. Woodbrige (Conn.) PTA, 1965-66. Served with USPHS, 1955-60. Burroughs Wellcome scholar clin. pharmacology, 1964-68; Eleanor Roosevelt Internat. Cancer fellow Am. Cancer Soc., 1966-67. Diplomate Am. Bd. Internal Medicine. Fellow A.C.P.; mem. Am. Soc. Clin. Investigation (sec.-treas. 1971—), Am. Assn. Cancer Research, Am. Cancer Soc., Am. Soc. Hematology, Am. Fedn. Clin. Research (councillor Eastern sec. 1962-65), Am. Soc. Clin. Oncology (pres. 1969- 70), Am. Soc. Pharmacology and Exptl. Therapeutics (exec. council div. clin. pharmacology 1965-68), Sigma Xi. Club: Sachem's Head Yacht (Guilford, Conn.). Author articles, revs., chpt. in books. Home: 27 Glen Av Barrington RI 02806 Office: 825 Chalkstone Av Providence RI 02908

CALALANG, ALFONSO, banker; b. Paniqui, Tarlac, Aug. 1, 1899; s. Casimiro and Romasa (Tolentino) C.; B.Sc. with honors, U. Philippines, 1922; M.S. in Bus., Columbia, 1927; D.Sc. in Bus., Nat. U. Manila, 1967, Far Eastern U., 1968; m. Virginia Tiongson, June 20, 1926; children—Augusto, Araceli (Mrs. Rodolfo R. Mondonedo), Benjamin, Conrado. Income tax examiner Bur. Internal Revenue, 1921-29; bank examiner Bur. Banking, 1929-36; v.p. Finance Mining Investment Corp., 1936-38; v.p. Philippine Bank Commerce, 1938-47, mem. Central Bank Council, 1947-48; dep. gov. Central Bank Philippines, 1949-51; pres. Security Bank & Trust Co., 1951-63; chmn. finance com. Trans-Philippines Investment Corp. and subsidiaries, 1963-66; chmn., pres. Filipinas Bank & Trust Co., 1964-66; chmn. Nat. Econ. Council, Republic of Philippines, 1966-67; gov. Central Bank Philippines, 1968-70; chmn. Filipinas Orient Airways, 1966, Guacods, Inc., 1966, Philippine Overseas Telecommunications, 1966; dir. Internat. Harvester Macleod Co., Internat. Chems. Corp. Chmn. Pres. Garcia's Spl. Bankers Mission to Japan, 1956. Chmn., pres. U. Philippines Endowment Found., Dilimon, Quezon City, 1963—. Named Banker of Year, 1951, Econ. Leader of Year, 1958, Finance Leader of Year, 1961; decorated Order Brilliant Star (Nationalist China). Mem. Bankers Assn. Philippines (pres. 1954-60), Beta Gamma Sigma. Office: Central Bank Philippines Aduana St Intramuros Manila Philippines*

CALAMARAS, LOUIS BASIL, assn. exec.; b. Peabody, Mass., Jan. 6, 1908; s. Basil James and Margo (Papalexaton) C.; prep. L'école-Metax a, Athens, Greece; pre-law Columbia, 1931; LL.D., Georgetown U., 1934; postgrad. student law and commerce Northwestern U.; m. Pauline Spirrison, May 2, 1937; children—Margo, Basil, Georgia. Dept. commr. Ind. Securities Commn., 1935-37; supr. Ill. Labor Dept., 1937-40; counsellor Labor Indsl. Relations, 1940-44; exec. sec. Nat. Electronic Distbrs. Assn., 1944-51, exec. v.p., 1951—; mng. dir. Midwest Elec. Distbrs. Assn.; dir. Montclare Theatre Corp., Elm Theatre Corp.; trustee, Nat. Assn. Wholesalers; mgmt. cons. Lawn and Garden Assn., Suburban Restaurant Assn. Mem. Wholesalers Adv. Com. to Sec. of Commerce; chmn. Radio-TV Industry FTC Trade Practice Conf.; mem. Electronic Coordinating Com. Chmn. Park-Recreation Bd., Planning Commn., Zoning Bd., Village of Lincolnwood. Mem. Chgo. Exchange, Electric Assn., Am. Acad. Polit. Sci., Phi Delta Theta. Rotarian, Mason, K.P. Clubs: Variety, Tam O'Shanter Country, Lake Shore Athletic (Chgo.); Ridgemore Country (v.p., dir.), Columbia University; Lake Michigan (sec.), Electric Golf. Editor, pub. Nat. Electronic Distbrs. Assn. Jour. Contbr. jours. Home: 6712 N Leroy St Lincolnwood IL 60645 Office: 600 W Jackson Blvd Chicago IL 60606

CALAME, ALEXANDRE EMILE, educator; b. Lausanne, Switzerland, Apr. 9, 1913; s. Jules and Edwige (Mittel) C.; student univs. Lausanne, Fribourg and Paris, 1934-40; Docteur es Lettres, Sorbonne, Paris, 1960; m. Jeanne Burollet, Mar. 27, 1947; children—Isabelle, Beatrice, Mireille, Marianne. Came to U.S., 1960. Lectr. of French in Hungary, 1942-44; asst. prof., Saabrüecker Germany, 1948-56; asso. prof. U. Algiers (Algeria), 1956-60; prof. French, U. Cal. at Berkeley, 1960, chmn. dept., 1963-68. Author books and articles on French classicism. Home: 1837 Sonoma Av Berkeley CA 94707

CALAME, DON L., educator; b. Fort Scott, Kan., Dec. 22, 1914; s. Arthur B. and Lula N. (Barnett) C.; B.S., S.W. Mo. State Coll., Springfield, 1947; M.A., Northwestern U., 1949, Ph.D., 1956; m. Penelope F. Alexander, Oct. 25, 1936; children—Ross Edwin, Donna Lou, Betty June (Mrs. Stephen E. Staten). Tchr. pub. schs., S.W. Mo., 1935-44, Aurora, Ill., 1946-48; tchr. bus. dept. S.W. Mo. State Coll., 1948-53; dir. Methodist Men, 1953-62; exec. dir. dept. united ch. mem. Nat. Council Chs., 1962-67; prof., head dept. bus. S.W. Mo. State Coll., Springfield, 1967—. Bd. dirs. Religion In Am. Life, 1962—, Am. Leprosy Mission, 1962—. Served to 1st lt. AUS, 1944-46. Mem. Am. Assn. U. Profs., Pi Omega Pi, Delta Pi Epsilon. Methodist. Kiwanian. Home: 2661 S Belview Av Springfield MO 65804

CALAME, GERALD PAUL, educator, physicist; b. Lelocle, Switzerland, Nov. 27, 1930; s. Paul Arnold and Jessie (Beesley) C.; came to U.S., 1935, naturalized, 1953; B.A., Coll. Wooster, 1953; M.A., Harvard, 1955, Ph.D., 1960; m. Jocelyn Florence Sullivan, July 26, 1958; 1 son, Jeffrey Paul. Physicist, Knolls Atomic Power Lab., 1959-61; asst. prof. Rensselaer Poly. Inst., 1961-63, asso. prof., 1963-66; asso. prof. physics U.S. Naval Acad., 1966-69, prof., 1969—. Mem. Am. Phys. Soc., Am. Nuclear Soc., Am. Assn. Physics Tchrs., A.A.A.S., Am. Assn. U. Profs., Sigma Xi. Research on neutron transport theory. Home: 695 Americana Dr Annapolis MD 21403

CALANDRA, JOSEPH CARL, educator, physician; b. Chgo., Mar. 17, 1917; s. Domenic W. and Angela (Palma) C.; B.S., Lewis Inst., 1938; Ph.D., Northwestern U., 1942, M.D., 1950; m. Patricia Mader, Sept. 9, 1944; children—Carolyn P., Susan J., Joseph D., David B. Intern Henrotin Hosp., Chgo., 1950-51; asst. prof. biochemistry Northwestern U., Chgo., 1942-50, asso. prof., 1950-53, prof., 1954—, prof. pathology Dental and Med. Sch., 1955—. Pres. Indsl. Bio-Test Labs., Northbrook, Ill., 1952—; dir. Nalco Chem. Co., Chgo. Bd. dirs. Cancer Prevention Center, Chgo. Diplomate Am. Bd. Clin. Chemists. Fellow Soc. Clin. Pharmacology and Chemotherapy; mem. A.M.A., A.A.A.S., Am. Chem. Soc., Am. Indsl. Hygiene Assn., Am., European socs. toxicology, Sigma Xi, Phi Lambda Upsilon, Omicron Kappa Upsilon. Roman Catholic. Contbr. articles profl. jours. Home: 4630 Elm Terrace Skokie IL 60076 Office: 1810 Frontage Rd Northbrook IL 60062

CALAPAI, LETTERIO, artist; b. Boston, s. Biagio and Emanuela (Planeta) C.; grad. Mass. Sch. Art, Boston Sch. Fine Arts and Crafts, Art Students League N.Y.C. One-man shows in N.Y.C., Nat. Gallery of Art, Smithsonian Instn., Washington, D.C., Paris and London; rep. in permanent collections of Metropolitan Museum of Art, The Boston Museum of Fine Arts, Chgo. Art Inst., The Fogg Museum, Brooklyn Museum, Albright Art Gallery, Library of Congress, N.Y. Pub. Library, Boston Pub. Library, Free Library Phila., Rose Mus., Brandeis U., The Biblioteque Nationale, Paris, Princeton U. Library, The Houghton Library (Harvard), Va. Mus. Fine Arts, Nat. Mus. of Bezalel, National Mus. Jerusalem, Israel, Tokyo Mus., Japan, Gorakhpur U. Mus. Art, India, Kunsthaus, Zurich, Switzerland, Rosenwald Collection; illustrator (with wood engravings) How God Fix Jonah; The Mohawk; One Hundred Years Ago; head graphics Albright Art Sch., Buffalo, 1949-54; became asso. Contemporaries Graphic Art Center, 1956; faculty mem. New Sch. Social Research, N.Y.C., 1957-61; founder, dir. Intaglio Workshop, N.Y.C., 1960- 65; lectr. dept. art edn. N.Y.U., 1962-65; asso. professor Brandeis Univ., 1964-65; vis. asso. prof. Kendall Coll., Evanston, Ill., 1965-69; lectr. dept. art and architecture U. Ill., Chgo. Circle, 1966. Mem. adv. panel Ill. Arts Council, 1971—. Recipient prize award America In the War Exhibition, 1943; work chosen for Fifty Best Prints of the Year, 1944; Albert H. Wiggins purchase prize First Boston Printmakers Exhbn., 1948; John Taylor Arms prize Soc. Am. Graphic Artists, 1954; Library of Congress purchase prize, 1950, 51, 54; William J. Keller prize Western N.Y. Exhbn., 1954; Tiffany Found. grant in graphic arts, 1959; Audubon Artists medal for creative graphics, 1967. Mem. Soc. Am. Graphic Artists (hon. mem. council), Print Council Am., Am. Fedn. Arts, Cal. Soc. Etchers, Boston Printmakers. Home: 1458 Wilmette Av Wilmette IL 60091 Office: The Workshop Gallery 344 Tudor Ct Glencoe IL 60022

CALAWAY, MARTIN CURTIS, lawyer; b. Fresno, Cal., Nov. 16, 1925; s. Allison A. and Geneva (Gean) C.; student U. So. Cal., 1947-50; B.S., U. Cal., Los Angeles, 1952, LL.B., 1955; m. Beverly Ann Eiffler, Feb. 3, 1948; children-Kathleen Ann, Bradely Brian. Admitted to Cal. bar, 1956 since practiced in Beverly Hills; law clk. Erb, French, Picone & Griffin, 1953-56, asso., 1956-58, jr. partner, 1958-60; sr. partner Erb, Picone & Calaway, 1960- 66; partner Law Offices of Martin C. Calaway, 1966—. Dir. Advanced Found. Engring., Inc., Twining Labs. of So. Cal., Inc., Robert Morris & Assos., Inc. Mem. Mayor's Civil Adv. Com., Los Angeles, 1965—. Bd. dirs. W.A.I.F., Served with USMCR, 1943-46. Decorated Air medal. Mem. Am. Trial Lawyers Assn., Am. Bd. Trial Advs., Am. Judicature Soc., Internat. Acad. Law and Sci., Am. Bar Assn., Am. Arbitration Assn., Thailians, Phi Delta Phi. Home: 3911 Mandeville Canyon Los Angeles CA 90049 Office: 9454 Wilshire Blvd Beverly Hills CA 90212

CALBERT, HAROLD EDWARD, educator; b. Edinburg, Ind., Mar. 20, 1918; s. James Irmer and Ethel Ethel Margaret (Feight) C.; A.B., Allegheny Coll., 1939; M.S., U. Wis., 1947, Ph.D., 1948; m. Mary Jane Fargo, Sept. 5, 1942; children—Mary Bonita, Barbara Jane, Brad Wallace. Mem. faculty U. Wis., 1948—, prof. food sci. and industries, chmn. dept., 1961—. Served to lt. col. AUS, 1942-45. Fellow A.A.A.S.; mem. Inst. Food Tech., Am. Dairy Sci. Assn., Internat. Assn. Dairy and Food Technologists, Sigma Xi, Phi Sigma, Gamma Alpha, Alpha Zeta. Lutheran (trustee). Kiwanian (pres.). Home: 5514 Barton Rd Madison WI 53711

CALCAGNO, LAWRENCE, painter; b. San Francisco, Mar. 23, 1913; s. Vincent and Anna (de Rosa) C.; student Cal. Sch. Fine Arts, San Francisco, 1947-50. Asst. prof. art U. Ala., 1955-56, Albright Art Sch of U. Buffalo, 1956-58; vis. artist in residence U. Ill., 1958-59; partime tchr. N.Y.U., 1960; Andrew Mellon prof. Painting Carnegie Inst. Tech., 1965-68; vis. artist in residence Honolulu Acad. Arts, 1968-69; one man shows LaBaudt Gallery, San Francisco, 1948, 54, Galleria Numero, Florence, Italy, 1951, 52, Galeria Clan, Madrid, 1955, Studio Paul Fachetti, Paris, France, 1955, Martha Jackson Gallery, N.Y.C., 1955, 58, 60, 62, U. Ala., 1956, Albright Art Gallery, 1956, Inst. de Atre Contemporaneo, Lima, Peru, 1957, U. Ill., 1959, Fairweather-Hardin Gallery, Chgo., 1959, Phila. Art Alliance, 1960, New Arts Gallery, Houston, 1960, Ciudad Universitaria, Mexico City, 1961, McRoberts & Tunnard, London, Eng., 1961, Carnegie Inst. Tech., 1965, Houston Mus. Fine Arts, 1965; retrospective Westmoreland County Mus., Greensburg, Pa., 1967, Honolulu Acad. Arts, 1968-69, Franklin Siden Gallery, Detroit, 1965, 67, 69; represented in permanent collections Honolulu Acad. Arts, Santa Barbara Mus., Boston Mus. Fine Arts, Rochester Memorial Gallery, Houston Museum of Fine Arts, also Carnegie Inst., Albright-Knox Gallery, Whitney Mus., U. Neb., Inst. Contempory Art, Lima, San Francisco Mus. Art, Walker Art Center, Walter P. Chrysler Mus., U. Ill., Mus. Modern Art, N.Y.U., Cal. Palace of Legion of Honor, Phoenix Art. Mus., U. Ala., Dayton Art, Mus., Chase Manhattan Bank, Smithsonian Instn., Balt. Mus. also numerous pvt. collections. Residence fellowships Yaddo Corp., 1965, Ford Found. Humanities Program, 1965, Macdowell Colony, 1967-68. Recipient 2d Drawing prize Nat. Army Arts Contest, Nat. Gallery Art, 1945. Address: 215 The Bowery New York City NY 10002

CALCIA, LILLIAN ACTON, retired educator; b. Paterson, N.J., Mar. 28, 1907; d. James and Isabel (Barrie) Acton; student Montclair State Normal Sch., 1923-25; B.S., Columbia, 1931, M.A., 1936; D.Ed., N.Y.U., 1941; m. Peter Calcia, Aug. 9, 1939. Tchr., Passaic (N.J.) schs., 1925-28; tchr. Paterson schs., 1928-35; tchr. Newark State Tchrs. Coll., 1935-55; chmn. fine arts dept., prof. Montclair State Coll., Upper Montclair, N.J., 1955-69, prof. emeritus, 1969—. Lillian A. Calcia Visual Arts Center dedicated at Montclair State Coll., 1969. Mem. N.E.A., N.J. Edn. Assn., Assn. Suprs. and Curriculum Dirs., Eastern Arts Assn., Nat., N.J. (past pres.) art edn. assns. Home: 301 Rea Av Extension Hawthorne NJ 07506

CALDECOTT, RICHARD STANLEY, educator; b. Vancouver, B.C., Can., Apr. 15, 1924; s. Godfrey and Ethyl (Snellgrove) C.; came to U.S., 1946, naturalized, 1954; B.S.A., U. B.C., 1946; M.S., Wash. State Coll., 1948, Ph.D., 1951; m. Lucille Peggy Ingalls, Aug. 16, 1947; children—Richard Robert, Ann Elizabeth, Lisa Barbara. Research fellow Am. Cancer Soc., 1949-51; asst. prof. U. Neb., 1951-53; asso. radiobiologist Brookhaven Nat. Lab., 1953-54; geneticist Dept. Agr., 1954-60, 63-65, AEC, 1960-63; prof. genetics, dean Coll. Biol. Scis., U. Minn., 1965—. Del. UN Atoms for Peace Conf., 1955; mem. subcom. radiation biology Nat. Acad. Sci.-NRC, 1965—. Bd. trustees Argonne Univs. Univs. Assn., 1970—; v.p. Fresh Water Biol. Research Found., 1969—; bd. trustees Minn. Project Planned Parenthood. Fellow A.A.A.S.; mem. Radiation Research Soc., Genetics Soc. Am., Am. Inst. Biol. Scis. (chmn. edn. com. 1970—), Sigma Xi. Club: Cosmos (Washington). Editor: Radio-isotopes in the Biosphere, 1960. Asso. editor Radiation Research, 1963-66. Home: 1837 Ryan St Paul MN 55113

CALDER, ALEXANDER, sculptor; b. Phila., July 22, 1898; s. Alexander Stirling and Nanette (Lederer) C.; M.E., Stevens Inst. Tech., 1919; m. Louisa James, Jan. 17, 1931; children—Sandra. Mary. Devised Wire Sculpture, Paris, 1927, Stabiles, 1931, Mobiles,1932, Constellations, 1943, gongs, towers, 1951; numerous one-man exhbns.; represented in many collections. Awarded 1st prize for non-Italian sculptor Biennale di Venezia, 1952; 1st prize sculpture Internat. Exhbn. Contemporary Painting and Sculpture, Pitts., 1958. Mem. Nat. Inst. Arts and Letters (recipient Gold Medal award 1971). Address: Painter Hill Rd RFD Roxbury CT 06783

CALDER, ALEXANDER, Jr., business exec.; b. Bklyn., July 14, 1916; s. Alexander and Adelaide Fancher (Gunnison) C.; A.B., Dartmouth, 1938; M.B.A., Harvard, 1940; m. Rebecca Jane Holmes, Aug. 17, 1940; children—Christie Holmes (Mrs. Richard E. Salomon), Alexander III. Began with Union Camp Corp., N.Y.C., 1940, sales trainee, 1940-41, asst. to dir. indsl. relations, 1941-42, 46, asst. to v.p. charge sales, 1947-49, v.p., 1949-52, exec. v.p., gen. mgr., 1952-56, pres., dir., chief exec. officer, 1956—; dir. Bank of N.Y. Co., Inc., Seaboard Coast Line Industries, Inc. Intelligence analyst Bd. Econ. Warfare, 1942-43; trustee Tax Found., Inst. Paper Chemistry; bd. dirs. Am. Arbitration Assn.; exec. com. Am. Paper Inst., Fourdrinier Kraft Bd. Inst. Bd. overseers Amos Tuck Sch. Bus. Adminstrn., Dartmouth. Served as lt. (j.g.) USNR, 1943-46. Mem. Am. Paper and Pulp Assn., Phi Kappa Psi. Clubs: Montclair (N.J.) Golf; Augusta (Ga.) Nat.; Pine Valley (N.J.) Golf; Madison (Conn.) Beach; Oglethorpe (Savannah, Ga.); University (N.Y.C.). Home: 18 Heller Dr Upper Montclair NJ 07043 Office: 1600 Valley Rd Wayne NJ 07470

CALDER, ROBERT GEORGE, Jr., food co. exec.; b. Honolulu, Hawaii, June 11, 1916; s. Robert George and Maude (Martin) C.; grad. Deerfield Acad., 1933; B.A., Amherst Coll., 1937; LL.B., Yale, 1940; student U. Heidelberg (Germany), 1936; m. Erin E. Mason, May 1, 1946; children—John K., Stephen M., Erin E. Admitted to

N.Y. bar, 1940; law sec. N.Y. Ct. Appeals, 1941; gen. practice, N.Y.C., 1946-51; gen. counsel Chesapeake Industries, Inc., 1951-58; v.p., dir. Portsmouth Gas Co., 1956-58; gen. counsel Campbell Soup Co., 1959—, sec., 1965—. Mem. Phila. Crime Com. Served with USCGR, 1942-46. Mem. Am., N.Y. State bar assns., Am. Soc. Corporate Secs., St Andrews Soc. Phila., Psi Upsilon. Clubs: Mid Ocean (Bermuda); Merion Golf; Yale (N.Y.C.). Home: 800 Amies Lane Bryn Mawr PA 19010 Office: Campbell Pl Camden NJ 08101

CALDERA, RAFAEL, pres. of Venezuela; b. San Felipe, Venezuela, Jan. 24, 1916; s. Rafael Caldera; m. Alicia Pietri Montemayor, Aug. 6, 1941; children—Mireya, Rafael Tomas, Juan Jose, Alicia Elena, Cecilia, Andres Caldera Pietri. File clk. U. Central de Venezuela, 1931-32; asst. mgr. Nat. Labor Office, 1936-39; corr. ILO, 1937-38; co-dir. law sch. mag. for Distrito Fed., 1941; mem. editing commn. complete works Andres Bello, 1948, then dir., 1949; prof. sociology U. Central de Venezuela, 1943—, prof. labor legislation, 1945—; prof. sociology U. Catolica Andres Bello, 1953—, prof. Labor legislation, 1956—; dir. Venezuelan Inst. Social Legislation, 1958-66; sec.-gen. Patrido Nacional, 1941-45; rep. Nat. Congress for State of Yaracuy, 1941-44; atty. gen. Venezuela, 1946; adviser polit. orientation COPEI, 1946-48; rep. Distrito Fed. Nat. Constituent Assembly, 1946-47; presdl. candidate, 1947; sec. gen. COPEI Party, 1948—; mem. spl. editing commn. Electoral Senate, 1949-50: dep. to Constituent Assembly, 1952—; presdl. candidate, 1958, 63; pres. Chamber Reps. Nat. Congress, 1959-61; pres. Christian Democratic Orgn. Latin Am., 1964—, also mem. World Com. Christian Democracy; pres. Republic of Venezuela, 1968—, Hon. prof. U. Mayor de San Marcos, 1951, U. de Los Andes, 1958, U. del Zulia, 1958, U. Catolica de Quito, 1960, U. Notre Dame, 1964; recipient ann. award Inter-Am. Cath. Coop. Program, 1965; decorated Order Andres Bello 1st class, Order Jose Matias Gonzales 1st class, Order El Sol de Peru 1st class, grand Cordon Order Liberator, grand cross de Duarte Sanchez y Mella, Order Au Merite 1st class (France), grand cross de San Gregorio Magno, Orden al Merito (Italy). Mem. Venezuelan Acad. Lang. (Andres Bello award 1935), Venezuelan Assn. Sociology (pres. 1958—), Venezuelan Acad. Polit. and Social Sci., Mexican Acad. Labor Law, Inst. Labor Law U. San Fe (Argentina), Inst. Labor U. Sao Paulo (Brazil), Internat. Social Legislation Soc., Internat. Inst. Sociology, Latin Am. Sociol. Assn. (founding mem., v.p.), Venezuelan (founder 1958, pres. 1958-67), Am. social. assns., Rural Social. Assn., Cath. Economy Assn., Am. Acad. Polit. and Social Sci. Author: Andres Bello; Derecho del Trabajo; El Bloque Latinoamericano; Moldes para la Fragua; Democracia Cristiana y Desarrollo; Idea de una Sociologia; Sociologia Juridaca; also numerous articles. Address: Office of the President Caracas Venezuela

CALDERINI, CHARLES JOHN, lawyer; b. Chgo., Aug., 14, 1905; s. Dominic and Catherine (Becker) C.; LL.B., DePaul U., 1926; student U. Mich., 1927-28; m. Eleanor Sieren, Oct. 31, 1931; children—Charles, Marilyn; m. 2d Dorothy Lee, Aug. 9, 1960. Admitted to Ill. bar, 1928; asso. Winston, Strawn & Shaw, Chgo., 1928-41, partner, 1942-52; partner Winston, Strawn, Smith & Patterson, 1952—; dir. The Hubinger Co., Drake Hotel, Stewart-Warner Corp., Scot Lad Foods, Inc., Rockwell-Barnes Co., Elk Grove Village, Ill. Hon. patron Chgo. Museum of Natural History, Shedd Aquarium. Mem. Am., Ill., Chgo. bar assns., Law Club of Chgo., Phi Alpha Delta. Republican. Clubs: Mid-Day, Chicago (Chgo.); Tavern (Chgo.); Galena Golf; Dubuque (Ia.) Golf and Country. Home: 1212 N Lake Shore Dr Chicago IL 60610 Office: 38 S Dearborn St Chicago IL 60603

CALDER-MARSHALL, ANNA LUCIA, actress; b. Kensington Garden Sq., London, Jan. 11, 1947; d. Arthur and Phyllis (Sales) Calder-M.; Ellen Perry Scholarship, London, 1965-67. Appeared on TV, 1967; mem. Birmingham Repertory, 1967; appeared Edinburgh Festival, 1968, 69; film Pussy Cat, Pussy Cat I Love You, 1969; played in Edinburgh as Ophelia; as Hedvig in Wild Duck; as Beatrie in The Changling; as Sonya in Uncle Vanya, in West End London Film Wuthering Heights; Cathy for A.I.P. Mem. Ch. of Eng. Address: care Larry Dazell 35 Curzon St London SW 1 England

CALDERON, ANTONIO, Mexican economist; b. Parras, Coahwila, Mexico, Oct. 12, 1930; s. Antonio and Aurora (Martinez) C.; degree econs., U. Nacional Autonoma de Mexico, 1952; student Am. U., 1955; m. Margarita Madrigal, Mar. 1, 1958; 1 dau., Claudia Guadalupe. With Centrl Bank Mexico, 1952-56, 58-65, head Latin Am. dept., 1960-65; head customs tariff dept. Ministry Finance, 1956-59; dep. dir. gen. Nat. Fgn. Trade Bank, Mexico City, 1965—; prof. econs. Escuela Superior de Econ., Nat. Poly. Inst., Escuela Nat. de Economia; prof. fgn. trade of bus. adminstra. Sch. Escuela de Aminstrn. de Empresas dela U. Iberoamericana; tech. dir. Nat. Fgn. Trade Inst., Mexican rep. Latin Am. Free Trade, Montevideo, Uruguay, 1962-63. Dir. Transp. Maritime Mexicaba, S.A., Almancenes Nacionales de Desposito, S.A., Credito Central Mexicano, S.A. Mem. Am. Statis. Assn. Colegio de Economistas de Mexico, Sociedad Mexicana de Economia. Author: De la Alalc al Mercado Comun Latinoamericana; others. Home: 220 Picacho Mexico City 20 DF Mexico Office: 80 Au Cuavhtemoc Mexico City DF Mexico

CALDERON, RODRIGO, hotel exec.; b. Madrid, Spain, Mar. 3, 1920; s. Antonio and Mercedes (Domenchina) C.; Bachelor degree, Instituto Cardenal Cisneros, Madrid, 1935; student math. U. Madrid, 1935-36; Accountant degree, Bankers Sch., Mexico City, 1943; m. Maria E. Lopez Figueroa, Nov. 28, 1946. Came to U.S., 1960. Exec., Hotel Reforma, Mexico City, 1945-47; engaged as pub. accountant, Mexico City, 1947-60; mem. bd. dirs. several banking cos., Mexico City, 1950-60; exec. Nacional Hotelera, Mexico City, 1960; became v.p. Balsa Hotels Corp., N.Y.C., 1960. Home: 45 E 72d St New York City NY 10021

CALDERONE, FRANK ANTHONY, physician; b. N.Y.C., 1901; M.D., N.Y.U., 1924; M.P.H., Johns Hopkins, 1937. Med. dir. health service UN, 1951-54; pres. Occupational Health Inst., N.Y.C., 1955-57; exec. dir. N.Y.C., Cancer Com., 1949; dir. hdqrs. office WHO, 1946-49; dep. commnr. health, N.Y.C., 1944-46; sec. dept. health, Hempstead, L.I., N.Y., 1942-44, dist. health officer, 1938-42, now Cons. pub. and indsl. health; dir. Reproductive Biology Research Found. 1967—; instr. pharmacology and physiology N.Y.U. Sch. Medicine; cons. War Dept., World War II. Recipient Meritorious Service citation. Diplomate Am. Bd. Preventive Medicine. Fellow Am. Pub. Health Assn.; mem. Am., World. Internat. med. assns., Royal Soc. Medicine, Alpha Omega Alpha. Address: 120 Mineola Blvd Mineola NY 11501*

CALDERONE, MARY STEICHEN, (Mrs. Frank A. Calderone), physician; b. N.Y.C., July 1, 1904; d. Edward J. and Clara (Smith) Steichen; B.A., Vassar Coll., 1925; M.D., U. Rochester, 1939; M.P.H., Columbia, 1942; D.Med. Sci. (hon.), Women's Med. Coll., 1967; L.H.D. (hon.), Newark State Coll., 1971; Sc.D. (hon.), Adolphi U., 1971; m. Frank A. Calderone, Nov. 1941; children—Linda Martin (Mrs. Stuart Hodes), Francesca S. (Mrs. J. Thomas Stuart II), Maria S. Intern, Bellevue Hosp., N.Y.C., 1939-40; med. dir. Planned Parenthood-World Population, 1953-64; co-founder, dir. Sex Information Edn. Council U.S., N.Y.C., 1964—. Lectr. sex edn.; 33d Lower lectr. Acad. Medicine and Cleve. Clinic, 1970. Recipient 4th Ann. award for distinguished service to humanity Women's Aux. Albert Einstein Med. Center, Phila., 1966; Woman of Consience award Nat. Council Women, 1968; citation Merrill-Palmer Inst. Human Devel. and Family Life, Detroit, 1969; Woman of Achievement award Greater N.Y. chpt. women's div. Albert Einstein Coll. Medicine, Yeshiva U., 1969; Haven Emerson award N.Y.C. Pub. Health Assn., 1970. Fellow Am. Pub. Health Assn; mem. Am. Assn. Marriage Counselors (affiliate), Am. Assn. World Health (dir.). Mem. Soc. of Friends. Author: Release From Sexual Tensions, 1960. Editor: Abortion in U.S., 1958; Manual of Contraceptive Practice, rev. edit., 1970. Contbr. articles profl. jours., mags. Home: 55 Hoagland Lane Glen Head NY 11545 Office: SIECUS 1855 Broadway New York City NY 10023

CALDERWOOD, STANFORD MATSON, mgmt. cons.; b. Scottsbluff, Neb., Nov. 6, 1920; s. Herbert Merle and Hazel Emjore (Matson) C.; B.A., U. Colo., 1942; m. Norma Jean Smith, Mar. 17, 1942. Reporter-photographer Manchester (N.H.) Union-Leader, 1946-48; staff corr. U.P.I., 1948-51, bus. rep., 1951-52; pub. relations writer Eastern Gas & Fuel Assos., Boston, 1952-53; with Polaroid Corp., Cambridge, Mass., 1953-70, v.p. advt., 1960-62, v.p. sales and advt., 1962-66, v.p. marketing 1966-69, exec. v.p., 1969-70; pres., dir. Polaroid of Japan, 1962-70, Polaroid Overseas, 1962-70, Polaroid Can., 1962-70, Polaroid France, 1965-70; pres. Polaroid GmbH, 1965-70, Polaroid (Italia) S.p.A., 1965-70; gen. mgr. dir. Polaroid (Nederlands), N.V., 1962-70; gen. mgr. Polaroid (Internat.) N.V., 1965-70; pres. WGBH Ednl. Found., Boston, 1970-71; cons. Corp. Pub. Broadcasting, 1971—, Endowment Mgmt. & Research Corp., Boston, 1971—; dir. Omega Fund, Tahoma Devel., Inc. Bd. dirs. Internat. Student Assn., 1965-69, MacDowell Colony; bd. overseers Old Sturbridge (Mass.) Village; trustee Radcliffe Coll., Boston Inst. Contemporary Art; corporator Boston Museum Sci.; vis. com. Harvard. Served to lt. USNR, 1942-46. Mem. Pi Gamma Mu. Club: St. Botolph (Boston). Home: 136 Fletcher Rd Belmont MA 02178 Office: 77 Franklin Av Boston MA 02110

CALDWELL, ALEX CRAIG, govt. ofcl.; b. Ennis, Tex., Aug. 12, 1915; s. Robert Lee and Emily Idell (Haynes) C.; student Washington U., St. Louis, also U. Tex. Various accounting and financial positions in pvt. industry, N.Y.C., 1945-50; with Commodity Exchange Authority, Dept. Agr., 1950-, adminstr., 1960—. Served with AUS, 1941-45. Recipient Dept. Agr. Distinguished Service award, 1970. Home: 3200 Holly St Alexandria VA 22305 Office: Dept of Agriculture Washington DC 20250

CALDWELL, CARLYLE G., corp. exec.; b. 1914; D. Chemistry, Ia. State Coll., 1939. With Nat. Starch and Chem. Corp., 1940—, pres., 1969—, also dir. Address: Nat Starch and Chem Corp 750 3d Av New York City NY 10017*

CALDWELL, ERSKINE, author; b. White Oak, Ga., Dec. 17, 1903; s. Ira Sylvester and Caroline Preston (Bell) C.; student Erskine Coll., S.C., 1920, 21, U. Va., 1922, 25, 26, U. Pa., 1924; m. Helen Lannigan, Mar. 3, 1925; children—Erskine Preston, Dabney Withers, Janet; m. 2d, Margaret Bourke-White, Feb. 27, 1939; m. 3d, June Johnson, Dec. 21, 1942; 1 son, Jay Erskine; m. 4th, Virginia Moffett Fletcher, Jan. 1, 1957. Newspaper writer, 1925; cotton picker, stage hand, profl. football player, book reviewer, lectr., editor; motion picture screen writer, Hollywood, Cal., 1933-34, 42-43; corr., Mexico, Spain, Czechoslovakia, 1938-39, China, Mongolia, Turkestan, 1940; editor Am. Folkways, 1940-55; war corr. Life mag., PM, CBS, Russia, 1941. Recipient Yale Rev. $1,000 award for fiction, 1933. Mem. Authors League Am., Nat. Inst. Arts and Letters, Internat. P.E.N., Euphemian Lit. Soc., Raven Soc. Clubs: Overseas Press (N.Y.C.); Phoenix Press; San Francisco Press. Author: The Bastard, 1929; Poor Fool, 1930; American Earth, 1931; Tobacco Road, 1932; God's Little Acre, 1933; We Are The Living, 1933; Journeyman, 1935; Kneel to the Rising Sun, 1935; Some American People, 1935; (with Margaret Bourke-White), You Have Seen Their Faces, 1937; Southways, 1938; (with Margaret Bourke- White) North of the Danube, 1939; Trouble in July, 1940; Jackpot, 1940; Say! Is This the U.S.A.? (with Margaret Bourke-White), 1941; All-Out on the Road to Smolensk, 1942; Moscow Under Fire, 1942; All Night Long, 1942; Georgia Boy, 1943; Stories, 1944; Tragic Ground, 1944; A House in the Uplands, 1946; The Sure Hand of God, 1947; This Very Earth, 1948; Place Called Estherville, 1949; Episode in Palmetto, 1950; Call It Experience, 1951; The Courting of Susie Brown, 1952; A Lamp for Nightfall, 1952; The Complete Stories of Erskine Caldwell, 1953; Love and Money, 1954; Gretta, 1955; Erskine Caldwell's Gulf Coast Stories, 1956; Certain Women, 1957; Molly Cottontail, 1958; The Sacrilege of Alan Kent, 1958; Claudelle Inglish, 1959; When You Think of Me, 1959; Jenny by Nature, 1961; Close to Home, 1962; The Last Night of Summer, 1963; (with Virginia M. Caldwell), Around About America, 1964; In Search of Bisco, 1965; The Deer at Our House, 1966; In The Shadow of The Steeple, 1966; Writing in America, 1966; Miss Mamma Aimee, 1967; Deep South, 1968; Summertime Island, 1968; The Weather Shelter, 1969; The Earnshaw Neighborhood, 1971. Contbr. to mags. Home: PO Box 820 Dunedin FL 33528 Office: care McIntosh & Otis Inc 18 E 41st St New York City NY 10017

CALDWELL, FRANK HILL, clergyman, educator; b. Corinth, Miss., Jan. 26, 1902; s. Rufus Lusk and Frances (Hill) C.; student U.S. Mil. Acad., 1919-20, U. Miss., 1920- 22; B.D., Louisville Presbyn. Sem., 1925 (Humphrey fellowship); A.B., Centre Coll., Danville, Ky., 1926, D.D., 1936, LL.D., 1947; Ph.D., Edinburgh (Scotland) U., 1934; D.D., Maryville (Tenn.) Coll., 1953; Litt.D., Southwestern Coll., 1964; LL.D., Davidson (N.C.) Coll., 1965; m. Fannie Wells, Sept. 14, 1926; children—Frances Patricia (Mrs. Frank S. McKnight), Ann Starling, John Beale Howard. Ordained to ministry Presbyn. Ch., 1925; pastor in Bradfordsville, Ky., 1925-26; acting prof. Bible, Centre Coll., 1927-28; pastor J. J. White Meml. Ch., McComb, Miss., 1928-30; prof. homiletics, Louisville Presbyn. Sem., 1930-64, pres., 1936-64; exec. dir. Presbyn. Found. U.S., Inc., Charlotte, N.C., 1964-71. Chmn. adv. council Christian edn. Presbyn. Ch. U.S., 1944, vice chmn. council theol. edn., 1954-56; chmn. council Christian edn. Presbyn. Ch. U.S., 1944, vice chmn. council theol. edn., 1954-56; chmn. council Christian relations Gen. Assembly Presbyn. Ch., 1959-60, mem. joint com. worship, 1958-70, moderator 106th Gen. Assembly. Montreat, N.C., 1966; rep. 18th Gen Council, World Presbyn. Alliance, Sao Paulo, Brazil, 1959; del. 3d Assembly, World Council Chs., New Delhi, 1961. Bd. corporators Presbyn. Ministers Fund; bd. visitors Davidson Coll. Mem. Presbyn. Ednl. Assn. South (pres. 1952). Am. Assn. Homiletics Profs. (pres. 1942-43), Omicron Delta Kappa. Clubs: Rotary, City (Charlotte). Author: Preaching Angles, 1954. Asso. editor, contbr. The Church Faces the Isms, 1958. Home: 1117 Lingamore Pl Charlotte NC 28203

CALDWELL, GAYLON LORAY, univ. adminstr.; b. Hyrum, Utah, Sept. 11, 1920; s. Morris Snow and Marie (Christensen) C.; B.S., Utah State U., 1947; M.A., U. Neb., 1948; Ph.D., Stanford U., 1952; student Yale U., 1957-58; m. Victoria Mae Bigler, Aug. 1, 1947; children—Thomas Snow, Camden Stanford, Melissa Marie, Kimerly Edith. Asst. prof. polit. sci. Brigham Young U., 1951-53, asso. prof., 1953-60, instr. Trinity Coll., 1956-58, 59; dir. Am. Cultural Center, Guatemala City, 1960-62, Lima, Peru, 1962-63; U.S. cultural attache, Lima, 1963-65, Mexico City, 1968-70; provost Elbert Covell Coll., U. Pacific, 1970—. Served with USAF, 1942-45. Lilly fellow, 1958. Mem. Am. Polit. Sci. Assn., Am. Assn. U. Profs., Sigma Alpha Epsilon, Pi Sigma Alpha. Author: American Government Today, 1963. Translator: El Gobierno Estadounidense Actual, Teoria y Practica, 1971. Home: 2904 Bonnie Lane Stockton CA 95204

CALDWELL, HARRY BURKHEAD, agrl. ins. co. exec.; b. Woodsfield, O., Nov. 23, 1908; s. Oliver F. and Elizabeth (Burkhead) C.; Dr. Humanities, N.C. State Coll., 1962; m. Margaret Virginia Hood, Apr. 3, 1930; children—Harry Burkhead, Robert Hood. Dir. orgn. and edn. N.C. State Grange, 1929-37, master, 1937, 47- 61; sec.-treas. N.C. Grange Mut. Ins. Co., 1935—; chmn. exec. com. Nat. Grange, 1951-67, chmn. fgn. relations com., 1939, agrl. com., 1938, 42, 47, legislative com., 1943, co-op. com., 1945, transp. com., 1948; del. Internat. Fedn. Agrl. Producers, Rome, 1953, Lafayette, Ind., 1957, Dublin, Ireland, 1963. Mem. interim agrl. adv. com. U.S. Dept. Agr., 1953; chmn. Nat. Agrl. Adv. Commn., 1961-65. Mem. N.C. Adv. Budget Commn., 1949-53, planning bd., 1942-43; exec. dir. Farm Labor Commn., N.C., 1943; mem. N.C. Tax study Commn., 1965-66, 67-68, Food and Fiber Commn., 1966-67, Commn. Study Revenue Structure of State. Exec. sec. N.C. Good Health Assn., 1946-47; mem. United Forces for Edn., 1947-61; pub. dir. Blue Cross Hosp. Savs. Assn., 1948-62. Recipient Distinguished Service award Faculty of U. N.C. Sch. Medicine, 1957. Mem. Am. Agrl. Assn. (chmn. cotton adv. com.), Nat. Planning Assn. (trustee 1944-45), N.C. Farmers Coop. Council of N.C. (exec. v.p.), N.C. Milk Producers Fedn. (dir.), Farmers Coop. Exchange (dir.), Tobacco Assos., Inc., Gamma Sigma Delta (hon.), Alpha Zeta (hon.). Baptist (v.p. gen. bd. 1951). Home: 1000 Sunset Dr Greensboro NC 27401 Office: 437 W Friendly Av Greensboro NC 27401

CALDWELL, IRENE CATHERINE SMITH, educator, clergywoman; b. Sublette, Kan., Aug. 29, 1908; s. O. Herbert and Eva L. (Henage) Smith; B.A., Northwestern State Coll., Okla., 1930; M.A., U. Okla., 1936; B.Th., Anderson (Ind.) Coll., 1938; M.A., Oberlin Sch. Theology, 1945; Ph.D., U. Soc. Cal., 1959; m. Mack M. Caldwell, Dec. 16, 1944. Prof. Warner Meml. U., Eastland, Tex., 1930-32; tchr. Cherokee (Okla.) High Sch., 1932-38; exec. sec. nat. bd. Christian edn. Ch. of God, 1939-45; chmn. dept. Christian edn. Warner Pacific Coll., Portland, Ore., 1945-66, Anderson (Ind.) Coll. Sch. Theology, 1966—. Del. World Council Christian Edn. Assembly, Toronto, 1950, Lima, Peru, 1971. Bd. dirs. Community Action Council Madison County, Ind., 1967—. Grantee World Council Chs., U. West Indies, 1968. Mem. Religious Edn. Assn. Author: Solving Church School Problems, 1945; Our Concern Is Children, 1948; Teaching That Makes a Difference, 1950; Adults Learn and Like It, 1955; Responsible Adults in the Church School Program, 1961; Basics for Communication in the Church, 1971. Home: 1704 Hill Ct Anderson IN 46012

CALDWELL, J. PHILO, retired constrn. co. exec.; b. Winnsboro, S.C., 1904. Past sr. v.p. J. A. Jones Constn. Co., now dir. emeritus. Home: 2085 Hopedale Av Charlotte NC 28207 Office: 521 E Morehead St Charlotte NC 28202

CALDWELL, JANET TAYLOR, (Mrs. Marcus Reback), author; b. Preswich, Manchester, Eng., Sept. 7, 1900; d. Arthur F. and Anna (Marks) Caldwell; A.B., U. Buffalo, 1931; Litt.D., D'Youville Coll., Bufallo, 1964; L.H.D., Niagara U., 1971; m. William Fairfax Combs, May 27, 1919 (div. 1931); 1 dau., Mary Margaret (Mrs. Gerald Fried); m. 2d, Marcus Reback, May 12, 1931; 1 dau., Judith Ann (Mrs. Theodore Roosevelt Goodman). Began as stenographer, court reporter; court reporter Workmen's Compensation Div., N.Y. State Dept. Labor, Buffalo, 1923-24; sec. Bd. Spl. Inquiry, U.S. Immigration and Naturalization Service, Dept. Justice, Buffalo, 1924-31. Served as yeomanette, USNR, 1918-19. Recipient nat. award D.A.R. 1956; McElligott medal Marquette U., 1964. Fellow Internat. Inst. Arts and Letters; mem. Am. Legion, St. Francis Guild, Nazareth Guild, Legion of Mary. Republican. Roman Catholic. Club: Women's Nat. Rep. Author: Dynasty of Death, 1938; latest include: Melissa, 1948; Let Love Come Last, 1949; The Balance Wheel, 1951; The Devil's Advocate, 1952; Never Victorious, Never Defeated (Grand Prix, Prix Chatrain, Paris), 1956; Tender Victory, 1956; The Sound of Thunder, 1957; Dear and Glorious Physician, 1959; The Listener, 1960; A Prologue to Love, 1961; Grandmother and The Priests, 1963; A Pillar of Iron, 1965; No One Hears But Him, 1966; Dialogues with the Devil, 1967; Testimony of Two Men, 1968; Great Lion of God, 1970; Captains and Kings, 1972. Contbr. nat. mags. Home: 34 Audley End Eggertsville NY 14226

CALDWELL, JOHN MARS, educator, ret. army officer; b. Augusta, Ga., Nov. 29, 1904; s. John Mars and Mary Ethel (Bennett) C.; B.S., U. Ga., 1925, M.D., 1928; M.S., U. Minn., 1932; m. Dorothy Driskell, Oct. 8, 1932; children—Caroline, John Mars III. Intern Duval County Hosp., Jacksonville, Fla., 1928-29; fellow medicine Mayo Clinic, 1929-32, Med. Field Service Sch., 1934, St. Elizabeth's Hosp., Washington, 1940; commd. 1st lt. U.S. Army, 1932, advanced through grades to col., 1944; assigned Ft. Snelling, Minn., Carlisle, Pa., Ft. Howard, Md., Gorgas and Corozal hosps., Canal Zone; staff Walter Reed Gen. Hosp., Washington; comdr. 54th Gen. Hosp., 1943; assigned New Guinea, Hollandia, Bantagas, P.I., Tokyo, Japan, 1944-46; chief neuropsychiatry cons. div. Office Surg. Gen., U.S. Army, 1946-52; chief dept. neuropsychiatry Walter Reed Hosp., 1952-53, Letterman Army Hosp., 1953-55; ret., 1955; prof. psychiatry, chmn. dept. Med. Coll. Ga., 1955-57; chmn. dept. psychiatry U. Miami, 1957-70, prof. emeritus, 1970—; cons. psychiatry VA, Social Security Adminstrn., Dept. Def., Fed. Aviation Adminstrn. Decorated Bronze Star. Diplomate Am. Bd. Psychiatry and Neurology. Fellow A.C.P., Am. Psychiat. Assn.; mem. So. Psychiat. Soc., A.M.A., Am. Psychoanalytic Assn., Am. Acad. Neurology, Florida Psychoanalytic Society, Fla. Psychiat. Soc., Society Residents and Ex-Residents Mayo Found., Med. Soc. St. Elizabeth's Hosp., Am., S. Fla. orchid socs., Alpha Omega Alpha, Delta Tau Delta, Alpha Kappa Kappa. Presbyn. Contbr. articles profl. pubs. Home: 4421 Santa Maria Coral Gables FL 33146 Office: The Institute Jackson Meml Hosp Miami FL 33136

CALDWELL, JOHN TYLER, univ. chancellor; b. Yazoo City, Miss., Dec. 19, 1911; s. Joseph Redford and Lilley (Tyler) C.; B.S., Miss. State Coll., 1932; A.M., Duke, 1936, LL.D., 1965; Ph.D. Princeton, 1939; student U. Wis., summer 1938; student Naval Sch. Military Government, Columbia, 1943, M.A., 1945; LL.D., Coll. Ozarks, 1955, Wake Forest Coll., 1960, U. Md., 1970; m. Catherine Wadsworth Zeek, May 16, 1947 (dec. Feb. 1961); children—Alice Beaulieu, Andrew Morton, Charles Franklin, Helen Tyler; m. 2d, Carol Schroeder Erskine, June 29, 1963; children—Carol Case Erskine (Mrs. Lawrence Wurn), Melanie Ann Erskine (Mrs. M.F. Johnston). Tchr. social scis. and band dir. Holmes Junior Coll., Goodman, Miss., 1932-36; jr. economist U.S. Resettlement Adminstrn., State Coll., Miss., and Little Rock, 1936-37; asst. economist, land use planning, Bur. Agrl. Economics, U.S. Dept. Agr., Vicksburg, Miss., summer, 1939; instr. polit. science Vanderbilt U., 1939-42, asst. prof., 1942-46 (leave of absence 1942-46), asso. prof. 1946-47; pres. Alabama Coll., Montevallo, Ala. 1947-52; pres. U. Ark., Fayetteville, 1952-59; chancellor N.C. State U., Raleigh, 1959—; ednl. cons. Ford Found. in Pakistan, 1954. Ofcl. mem. for Ala. So. Regional Edn. Bd., 1948-52; mem. Com. Aid-U. Relations, 1965-69; bd. trustees Ednl. Testing Service, 1957-60, 65-69, 70—, chmn. bd., 1966-67, 68-69; past mem. com. Advancement Sch. Adminstrn.; past mem. Nat. Commn. on Accrediting; chmn. commn. on internat. edn. Am. Council on Edn., 1967-69; mem. U.S. National Commission UNESCO, 1968-69; bd. dirs. Overseas Devel. Council, 1969—; pres. Nat. Assn. State Univs. and Land-Grant Colls., 1962, chmn. internat. affairs con., 1966-69. Bd. visitors Air U., Maxwell AFB, 1970—. Served from ensign to lt. comdr. USN, 1942-45. Recipient Bronze Star; Julis Rosenwald fellow Princeton, 1937-39. Mem. Am., So. polit. sci. assns., Am. Soc. Pub. Adminstrn., N.E.A., Phi Kappa Phi, Blue Key, Pi Kappa Alpha. Dem. Christian Scientist. Rotarian. Home: 1903 Hillsborough Raleigh NC 27607

CALDWELL, LAFAYETTE HARDWICK, stove co. exec.; b. Chattanooga, Aug. 14, 1897; C.; student U. Va., 1915- 17. With Modern Maid, Inc. (formerly known as Tenn. Stove Works), Chattanooga, 1917—, became pres., 1927, now chmn. bd.; dir. mem. exec. com. Dixie Mercerizing Co.; dir. Am. Nat. Bank & Trust Co., Chattanooga, Krystal Co. Mayor, Lookout Mountain, Tenn., 1943-51. Pres. Hardwick Caldwell Found. Served as aviator U.S. Navy, 1918. Home: 523 Fleetwood Dr Lookout Mountain TN 37350 Office: Modern Maid Inc Chattanooga TN 37402

CALDWELL, MILLARD F., Jr., judge; b. Knoxville, Tenn., Feb. 6, 1897; s. Millard Fillmore and Martha Jane (Clapp) C.; student Carson and Newman Coll., 1913-14, U. of Miss., 1917-18, U. Va., 1919-22; LL.D., Rollins Coll., U. Fla., Fla. So. U., Fla. State U.; m. Mary Rebecca Harwood, Feb. 14, 1925; children—Millard Fillmore III (dec.), Sally. Perkins McCord, Susan B. Admitted to Tenn. bar 1922, Fla. bar, 1925; served as pros. atty. and county atty., Santa Rosa County, Fla., and city atty., Milton; elected to Fla. State Legislature, 1928 and 1930; mem. 73d to 76th Congresses (1933-41), 3d Fla. Dist.; voluntarily retired from Congress to resume practice of law at Milton and Tallahassee, Fla.; elected gov. of Florida for term 1945-49; Fed. Civil Def. administrator 1950-52; justice Florida Supreme Court 1962—, chief justice, 1967—. Del. Interparliamentary Union. Chmn. Nat. Govs. Conf., 1946-47; pres. Council of State Govts., 1946-48; chmn. bd. of control So. Regional Edn., 1947-50; chmn. Fla. Commn. Constl. Govt., 1957-66. Served as pvt. and 2d lt., F.A., U.S. Army, World War I. Mem. Am. Judicature Soc., Newcomen Soc., Huguenot Soc., S.A.R., Alpha Kappa Psi, Blue Key, Kappa Sigma, Phi Alpha Delta. Democrat. Home: Harwood Plantation Old Bainbridge Rd Tallahassee FL 32301 Office: Supreme Court Bldg Tallahassee FL 32302

CALDWELL, NATHAN GREEN, reporter; b. St. Charles, Mo., July 16, 1912; s. Albert Green and Sara (Jetton) C.; student Southwestern Coll., 1933, Cumberland U., 1934; Nieman fellow Harvard, 1940; m. Camilla Frances Jonston, Nov. 16, 1936; 1 son, John Sam. Polit. writer Nashville Tennessean, 1934-56, econs. and regional resource devel. reporter, 1956—. Co-recipient Pulitzer prize for nat. affairs reporting, 1961. Rosenwald fellow, 1947. Author: The Cotton Picker Moves People, 1947; The Strange Romance of John L. Lewis and Cyrus Eaton, 1961. Home: 1216 Eastdale Av Nashville TN 37216 Office: 1100 Broad St Nashville TN 37203

CALDWELL, OLIVER JOHNSON, educator, former govt. ofcl.; b. Foochow, China, Nov. 16, 1904 (parents U.S. citizens); s. Harry Russell and Mary Belle (Cope) C.; student U. Wash., 1922-23; A.B., Oberlin Coll., 1926, M.A., 1927; student music, aesthetics, 1927-29; student Army Civil Affairs Tng. Sch., U. Chgo., 1943; L.H.D., Baldwin-Wallace Coll.; LL.D., Ithaca U., Albright Coll.; m. Eda Joslin Holcombe, June 29, 1935; children—Eda Joslyn (Mrs. Edmund Becker), Gail Edna (Mrs. Warren Robinson). Head social scis. Harvey Sch., Hawthorne, N.Y., 1929-35; asso. prof. English, U. Amoy, China, 1935-36; prof. English, U. Nanking, China, 1936-37, acting head dept. fgn. langs., 1937-38 (assisted univ. move through gorges Yangtze River to Chengtu after Japanese attack); pub. relations officer Asso. Bds. Christian Colls. in China, 1938-43; chief student br., fed. programs br., div. exchange of persons Dept. State, 1947-51; chief program devel. staff ednl. exchange service U.S. Internat. Information Adminstrn., 1951-52; asst. commr. internat. edn., dir. div. internat. edn. U.S. Office Edn., later acting asso. commr., 1952- 64; vis. prof. comparative edn. U. Md., 1964-65; dean internat. services So. Ill. U., Carbondale, 1965-69, prof. higher edn., 1969—. Mem. sch. bd., Falls Church, 1952-56. Served to maj. AUS, 1943-45. Mem. Am. Soc. Cybernetics, Am. Peace Soc., Phi Delta Kappa. Methodist. Rotarian. Collaborator: The Asian Legacy and American Life; The Task of the Universities in a Changing World. Contbr. articles profl., popular jours. Home: RFD 1 Cobden IL 62929 Office: Internat Program Devel So Ill U Carbondale IL 62901

CALDWELL, PHILIP, machinery mfg. co. exec.; b. Bourneville, O., Jan. 27, 1920; s. Robert Clyde and Wilhelmina (Hemphill) C.; B.A. in Econs., Muskingum Coll., 1940; M.B.A. in Indsl. Mgmt., Harvard, 1940; m. Betsey Chinn Clark, Oct. 27, 1945; children—Lawrence Clark, Lucy Hemphill, Désirée Branch. With Navy Dept., 1946-53, dep. dir. procurement policy div., 1948-53; with Ford Motor Co., 1953—, v.p., gen. mgr. truck operations, 1968-70; v.p., 1970—; pres., dir. Philco-Ford Corp., Phila., 1970—. Mem. bus. adv. council Kent State U. Bus. Adminstrn., 1968—. Trustee United Fund Phila. Area; bd. dirs. World Affairs Council Phila; trustee Muskingum Coll. Served to lt. USNR, 1942-46. Recipient Meritorious Civilian Service award U.S. Navy, 1953; 1st William A. Jump Meml. award, 1950. Mem. Soc. Automotive Engrs., Engring. Soc. Detroit, Automobile Mfrs. Assn. (mem. motor truck mfrs. com. 1964-70), U.S. C. of C. (mem. transp. com. 1968-70). Clubs: Detroit Athletic; Sunday Breakfast (Phila.); Pennsylvania Society (N.Y.C.). Home: 1221 Ridgewood Rd Bryn Mawr PA 19130 Office: Philco-Ford Corp Tioga and C Sts Philadelphia PA 19134

CALDWELL, RALPH MERRILL, cons. cereal breeding; b. Brookings, S.D., June 27, 1903; s. Peter and Margaret (Christie) C.; B.S., S.D. State U., 1925; M.S., U. Wis., 1927, Ph.D., 1929; m. Margaret Dunlap, Sept. 12, 1931; 1 dau., Janet Harriet (Mrs. Ralph W. Storts). Asst. botany U. Wis., 1925-28; state leader in barberry cradication in Wis., U.S. Dept. Agr., 1928-30; agent plant pathology U.S. Dept. Agr., Purdue U., 1930-31, asso. pathologist, 1931-37, chief, dept. botany and plant pathology Purdue U. Agrl. Expt. Sta., 1937-50, head dept. agrl. botany Purdue U., 1943-50, head dept. botany and plant pathology, 1950-54, prof. plant pathology, 1937-71, cons. cereal breeding, 1971—. Fellow A.A.A.S., Am. Soc. Agronomy, Am. Phytopath. Soc. (treas.; bus. mgr. Phytopathology, 1944-46, nat. councilor-at-large 1964-66); mem. Indiana Acad. Sci., Sigma Xi, Gamma Alpha, Phi Sigma, Alpha Zeta. Clubs: Rotary International, University (Lafayette); Torch. Editor: Phytopathology, 1954-57. Contbr. sci. papers profl. jours. Breeder disease and insect resistant wheat and oats and barley varieties. Home: 628 Terry Lane West Lafayette IN 47906

CALDWELL, ROBERT CRAIG, univ. dean; b. Detroit, Nov. 20, 1927; s. Robert and Elise (Bass) C.; student Anderson Coll. Medicine, Scotland, 1945-47; L.D.S., U. Glasgow, 1950, H.D.D., 1951; M.S., U. Rochester, 1957; D.M.D., U. Ala., 1957, Ph.D., 1964; F.D.S., Royal Coll. Phys. and Surg., Glasgow, 1970; m. Marjorie Eleanor Hane, June 19, 1954; children—Robert Wallace, Lisa Marie, Jeffrey Bowman. Mem. faculty U. Ala. Sch. Dentistry, 1957-70, prof. dentistry, 1964-70, chmn. dept. oral biology, 1964-67, asso. dean, dir. Inst. Dental Research, 1967-70; prof., dean Sch. Dentistry, U. Cal. at Los Angeles, 1970—; cons. VA Hosp., Los Angeles. Mem. Nat. Inst. Dental Reseach Dental Research Insts. and spl. programs adv. com. Served as flight lt. RAF, 1951-53. Fulbright fellow, 1953; sr. research fellow NIH, 1959-61, recipient Research Career Devel. award, 1961-63. Mem. A.A.A.S., Am. Chem. Soc., Am. Dental Assn. (chmn. research sect.), Fedn. Dentaire Internat., Internat. Assn. Dental Research, Am. Soc. Dentistry Children, Sigma Xi, Omicron Kappa Upsilon. Mem. editorial adv. bd. Jour. Dental Research. Address: Sch Dentistry Univ Cal Los Angeles CA 90024

CALDWELL, ROBERT GRAHAM, educator; b. Phila.; s. Robert Graham and Rebecca Jane (Stuart) C.; B.S. in Econs. cum laude, U. Pa., 1928, M.A. in Sociology, 1934, Ph.D., 1939; LL.B., Jackson Sch. Law, 1947; m. La Merle Sutton, Aug. 22, 1935. Employee, Bell Telephone Co., Pa., 1928-36; on sociology dept. U. of Pa., 1936-38, U. of Del., 1938-43; with Fed. Security Agy., 1943- 45; prof. sociology Coll. of William and Mary, 1945-48; prof. sociology and research cons. State U. of Ia., 1948—; cons., research analyst Ia.'s correctional instns. law and behavioral sci. Sr. fellow, U. Chgo., 1959. Mem. Am. Correctional Assn., Am. Acad. Polit. and Social Sci., Internat., Am. socs. criminology, Nat. Council Crime and Delinquency, Del. Hist. Soc., Am., Midwest sociol. socs., N.Y. Acad. Scis., Va. Social Service Assn., Va. Bar Assn., Alpha Delta Kappa, Pi Gamma Mu. Mason (Shriner). Author: The New Castle County Workhouse, 1940; The Penitentiary Movement in Delaware, 1946; Red Hannah, Delaware's Whipping Post, 1947; Criminology (textbook), 1956, rev., 1965; (with James Block) Juvenile Delinquency (textbook), 1971. Contbr. profl. jours. Specialist in criminology. Home: 325 Beldon Av Iowa City IA 52240

CALDWELL, ROBERT TATE, lawyer; b. Taylor County, Ky., May 7, 1882; s. James Thomas and Annie (Read) C.; B.S., Centre Coll., Danville, Ky., 1903; student Centre Coll. Law Sch., 1906-08; m. Virginia B. Hoge, Dec. 27, 1916 (dec. 1962); m. 2d, Ruth Turner, 1963. Admitted to Ky. bar, 1908; instr. and coach Selma Mil. Inst., 1908-10; practiced in Louisville, 1910-14; asst. atty. gen. for Ky., 1914-16; chmn. Ky. Workmen's Compensation Bd. (author of Ky. Workmen's Compensation Act), 1916-18; pvt. practice, Ashland, Ky., 1919—; mem. firm Caldwell & Hughes. Enlisted Field Arty., 1918; commd. capt., Nov. 1918. Adviser U.S. delegation Internat. Labor Conf., 1935; mem. Nat. Conf. of Commrs. Uniform State Laws (1944-50). Trustee Pikeville Coll. Mem. regional adv. conf. NLRB.; mem. Ky. All Industries Wage Bd., Ky. Adv. Com. on Nuclear Energy. Mem. Am., Ky. (pres. 1934, 35), Boyd County bar assns., Order of Coif, Kappa Alpha (So.). Democrat. Presbyn. Address: 1920 Lexington Av Ashland KY 41101

CALDWELL, SAMUEL WELCH, army officer; b. Brighton, Ala., Jan. 14, 1916; s. Samuel Welch and Anna Dean (Sawyer) C.; A.B., U. Ala., 1936; M.D., N.Y.U., 1940; M.P.H., Harvard, 1959; m. LeVerle Kelley, June 3, 1948; 1 son, Samuel Edwin. Intern Hillman Hosp., Birmingham, Ala., 1940-42; practice medicine, specializing in surgery, Huntsville, Ala., 1946-50; commd. 1st lt. U.S. Army, 1942, advanced through grades to col., 1959; group surgeon 1169th C.E. Group, Ft. Campbell, Ky., 1950-51; div. surgeon 24th Inf. Div. FECOM, 1951; instr. Med. Field Service Sch., Ft. Sam Houston, Tex., 1952- 53, chief field med. service br., 1953, asst. chief dept. mil. sci., 1953; chief med. sect. TUSAG, JAMMAT, Turkey, 1955-58; chief preventive medicine div. U.S. Army Garrson, Ft. Bragg, N.C., 1959-60; chief preventive medicine div. Hdqrs. Third U.S. Army, Ft. McPherson, Ga., 1960-63; preventive medicine officer Hdqrs. USARPAC, Ft. Shafter, Hawaii, 1963-65; comdg. officer U.S. Army Hosp., Ft. Ord, Cal., 1966-68; dep. comdr. 9th Hosp. Center, Landstuhl, Germany, 1968-69; comdr. Landstuhl Army Med. Center, also 2d Gen. Hosp., Landstuhl, Germany, 1969-71; command surgeon STRICOM, 1971—; asst. prof. dept. preventive medicine Loma Linda U., 1968. Decorated Legion of Merit, Bronze Star medal with oak leaf cluster, Combat Med. badge. Diplomate Nat. Bd. Med. Examiners. Mem. A.M.A., Ala. Med. Assn., Madison County Med. Soc., Phi Chi, Kappa Sigma, Gamma Sigma Epsilon. Home: 1628 Sunnybrook Lane Clearwater FL 33516 Office: Command Surgeon STRICOM MacDill AFB Tampa FL 33608

CALDWELL, SARAH, opera producer, condr.; b. Maryville, Mo.; student violin New Eng. Conservatory. Mem. faculty Tanglewood (Mass.) Sch. Music; created dept. of music theater at Boston U. and conducted Am. premiere of Hindemith's Mathis der Maler; founder, artist dir. Opera Co. of Boston which has produced 45 operas including Schoenberg's Moses and Aaron, 1966, Stravinsky's Rakes Progress, 1967; presenting Falstaff, Tosca and Berg's Lulu in San Francisco, Chgo., Dallas and N.Y.C. Address: 46 Fenway Boston MA 02215*

CALDWELL, SHIRLING SAM, state ofcl.; b. East Point, Ga., Jan. 22, 1929; s. Paul Favor and Minnie (Baker) C.; student N. Ga. Coll., 1948-50; A.B., U. Ga., 1952; m. Jeanette Josephine Nemie, July 16, 1952; children—Josette Tina, Valerie Jean, Rachael Angela, Patrick Shirling Victor. Pub. relations pvt. industry and govt., 1956-62; personnel dir. GA. Hwy. Dept., Atlanta, 1962-66; commr. labor Ga., Atlanta, 1966—. Mem. exec. com. Ga. Democratic Party. Bd. dirs. Model Cities Project Atlanta, People to People. Served with USMCR, 1946-48; with AUS, 1952-54. Mem. Farm Bur., V.F.W., Am. Legion, Woodmen of World, Sigma Delta Chi. Baptist. Elk. Home: 2703 Hawaii Ct Decatur GA 30033 Office: State Labor Bldg Atlanta GA 30334

CALDWELL, THEODORE JOSEPH SHAUT, banker; b. Huntington, W.Va., Sept. 10, 1920; s. Foree Dabney and Edna (Shaut) C.; grad. Phillips Exeter Acad., 1939; A.B., Princeton, 1943; postgrad. Sch. Banking, Rutgers U., 1955; m. Elizabeth Guthrie Williamson, Jan. 18, 1950; children—Margaret Lynn, Barbara O'Bannon, Elizabeth Dabney, Theodore Joseph Shaut. With Allied Chem. & Dye Corp., South Point, O., 1943-44; with First Huntington Nat. Bank, 1947—, v.p., 1959-68, cashier, 1963-68, chmn. bd., 1968—; pres., dir. J.L. Caldwell Co., Wayne County Land & Mineral Co.; treas., dir. Dingess Rum Coal Co., Ben Williamson & Co., Williamson Realty Co.; v.p., dir. Big Sandy Coal Co., Eagle Coal Co., C.L. Ritter Lumber Co.; pres., dir. Realty Co.; dir. Chesapeake & Potomac Telephone Co. W.Va., Warfork Land Co., Central Realty Co., Frederick Hotel. Treas. Downtown Improvement Group, 1964-66; pres. Huntington Indsl. Corp., 1969-70; exec. com. Tri-State Area council Boy Scouts Am., 1966—. Treas., trustee United Community Service; trustee Huntington Galleries; bd. dirs. Cammack's Children Center. Served with USNR, 1944-46. Mem. Greater Huntington Area C. of C., Am. Legion (vice comdr. post 1946), W.Va. Bankers Assn. (pres. trust div. 1959-60). Episcopalian (vestryman 1963-69, trustee 1965—), Elk. Clubs: City (pres. 1955-56), Gypsy, Guyan Golf and Country, Square Dance (Huntington); Kreeneland (life) (Lexington, Ky.). Home: 2101 Cherry Av Huntington WV 25701 Office: PO Box 179 Huntington WV 25701

CALDWELL, THOMAS ALLISON, Jr., lawyer; b. Chattanooga, Sept. 4, 1924; s. Thomas Allison and Mamie (Hartwig) C.; B.S cum laude, Harvard, 1944, LL.B., 1949; m. Anne Gunter, Feb. 14, 1954; children—Thomas Allison III, Joanne G., Grant H., Craig J. With ECA, 1949-53, asst. controller, 1949-53, atty., 1952-53; admitted to Tenn. bar, 1949; asso. firm Witt, Gaither, Abernathy & Finlay, Chattanooga, 1953-58; partner firm Witt Gaitherm Abernathy, Caldwell & Wilson, Chattanooga, 1958-64, Stophel, Caldwell & Heggie, Chattanooga, 1964—. Bd. dirs. Orange Grove Center for Retarded, Inc., Chattanooga (pres. 1955-56), United Fund Greater Chattanooga, Ga.-Tenn. Regional Health Commn., and others. Served as ensign USNR, 1944-46; PTO. Recipient Distinguished Service award Jr. C. of C. as outstanding young man yr. Chattanooga, 1958. Home: Box 400 Wilson Rd Route 1 Signal Mountain TN 37377 Office: 450 Maclellan Bldg Broad St Chattanooga TN 37402

CALDWELL, WARREN W., educator; b. Davenport, Ia., Dec. 28, 1925; B.A., Stanford, 1948, M.A., 1949; Ph.D., Wash. U. at Seattle, 1956; married; one child. Curator anthropology and history Seattle Mus. History and Industry, 1941-52; asst. curator anthropology State Mus. Wash., Seattle, 1953-54; archaeologist Mo. Basin project Smithsonian Instn., 1956-63, chief, 1963-65, dir. River Basin Survey, 1965—; from asst. prof. anthropology to prof., chmn. dept. anthropology U. Neb., Lincoln, 1960—. Fellow A.A.A.S., Am. Soc. Archaeology, Am. Anthropology Assn. Contbr. articles to profl. publs. Office: Dept Anthropology U Neb Lincoln NB 68508*

CALDWELL, WILLIAM MACKAY, III, furniture co. exec.; b. Los Angeles, Apr. 6, 1922; s. William Mackay II and Edith Ann (Richards) C.; B.S., U. So. Cal., 1943; M.B.A., Harvard, 1948; m. Mary Louise Edwards, Jan. 16, 1946; children—William Mackay IV, Craig Edwards, Candace Louise. Sec.-treas., dir. Drewry Photocolor Corp., 1957-60, Adcolor Photo Corp., 1957-60; treas., dir. Drewry Bennetts Corp., 1959-60; v.p., chief financial officer Am. Cement Corp., 1960-67, sr. v.p. corp., pres. cement and concrete group, 1967-69; pres., chief exec. officer Van Vorst Co., 1969—; chmn., chief exec. officer Van Vorst Co., Washington, 1969—; chmn. bd. Hawaiian Cement Corp., 1967-69; pres. dir. Am. Cement Internat. Corp., 1967-69. Bd. dirs. Am. Cement Found., 1966-68. Served to lt., USNR, 1943-46. Mem. Newcomen Soc., Commerce Assos. (dir.), Friends Huntingdon Library, Kappa Alpha (pres. U. So. Cal. Cal. 1943- 44), Alpha Delta Sigma, Alpha Pi Omega. Presbyn. Clubs: Harvard Business Sch. of So. Cal. (dir. 1960-63); Toastmasters (pres. San Marino 1956- 57); Los Angeles, Metropolitan Dinner, Town Hall, California, Los Angeles Country (Los Angeles); Trojan; Annadale Golf. Home: 1880 Lombardy Rd San Marino CA 91108 Office: 1000 S St Andrews Pl Los Angeles CA

CALDWELL, WILLIAM VIRGIL, educator, mathematician; b. Boyd, Tex., Sept. 3, 1917; s. Joseph Floyd and Fanny (Long) C.; B.A., Tex. Christian U., 1951; M.A., U. Mich., 1955, Ph.D., 1959; m. Beatrice Marjorie Thompson, June 14, 1953; children—Deborah Ellen, Thomas Jefferson. Asst. prof. U. Del., 1959-61, Flint Coll., U. Mich., 1961-66, prof. math. U. Mich., Flint, 1968—, chmn. dept., 1966—. Served with USNR, 1937-45. Mem. Am. Civil Liberties Union, Am. Math. Soc., Math. Assn. Am., Am. Assn. Univ. Profs., Sigma Xi. Research in the theory of light interior functions. Home: 2119 E 2d St Flint MI 48503 Office: 1321 E Court St Flint MI 48503

CALDWELL, ZOE, actress; b. Australia, Sept. 14, 1933. Appeared in The Madwoman of Chaillot, Goodman Theater, Chgo., 1964, in repertory Stratford-on-Avon, 2 seasons, in The Way of the World and The Caucasian Chalk Circle, Mpls., in Slapstick Tragedy (Tony award for best supporting actress), N.Y.C., 1966; appeared in Antony and Cleopatra, Richard III and The Merry Wives of Windsor at Stratford (Ont.) Shakespeare Festival, 1967, The Prime of Miss Jean Brodie (Tony award for best supporting actress 1968).*

CALE, EDGAR BARCLAY, ednl. adminstr.; b. Uniontown, Pa., Aug. 31, 1910; s. Charles H. and Myrtle (Barclay) C.; student U. Pitts., 1928-30; B.A., U. Pa., 1932, M.A., 1934, Ph.D., 1940; m. Lynetta Gerhardt, June 20, 1932; children—Audrey Arlene, Barbara Jeanne (Mrs. Jack S. Overton), Edgar Barclay, Patricia Anne (Mrs. Gerald Beaver). Mem. faculty polit. sci. U. Pa., 1937-53; exec. sec. Phila. Charter Commn., 1949-51; chief edn. div. U.S. mission to Thailand, 1953-56; prof. polit. sci. U. Buffalo, 1956-61, dir. devel., 1956-58, vice chancellor planning and devel., 1958-61; vice chancellor devel., also prof. higher edn. U. Pitts., 1961-66; pres. Univ. and Coll. Assos., Washington, 1966-68; dean Motorola Exec. Inst., Vail, Ariz., 1968—; ednl. cons. Motorola, Inc. Asst. dir. U. Pa. Bi-Centennial, 1939-40; acad. dir. U.S. Naval Flight Prep. Sch., 1943-44, Refresher Sch. V-7 Officers Candidates, 1944-45; moderator, dir. U. Pa. Forum of Air, 1944-53. Mem. sch. bd., Upper Darby, Pa., 1948- 53. Bd. dirs. Pitts. History and Landmarks Found., Consultants Overseas Relations, Park Sch., Buffalo. Rockefeller social sci. fellow, 1941-42; Penfield traveling scholar diplomacy, 1942-43. Mem. Am. Coll. Pub. Relations Assn., Am. Polit. Sci. Assn., Am. Arbitration Assn. Presbyn. Club: University (Pitts.). Home: 3545 E 3d St Tucson AZ 85716 Office: Motorola Exec Inst Oracle AZ 85623

CALEF, WESLEY CARR, geographer, educator; b. Alma Center, Wis., June 22, 1914; s. Ellis Neil and Hazel (Carr) C.; B.A., U. Wis., 1936; M.S., U. Cal. at Los Angeles, 1944; Ph.D., U. Chgo., 1948; m. Beulah Waller, Apr. 13, 1941. Mem. faculty U. Chgo., 1947-69, prof. geography, 1959-69, chmn. dept., 1961-67; 1961-67; mem. faculty Ill. State U., 1970—. Mem. Assn. Am. Geographers. Author: Private Grazing and Public Land, 1960. Home: 810 Manchester Rd Normal IL 61761

CALEY, EARLE RADCLIFFE, educator, chemist; b. Cleve., May 14, 1900; s. John Radcliffe and Minnie (Mitchell) C.; student Case Inst. Applied Science, 1918-20; B.Sc., Baldwin-Wallace College, Berea, Ohio, 1923, Doctor of Sci. (hon.), 1967; M.S., Ohio State U., 1925, Ph.D., 1928; m. Grace Fowles Cochran, Dec. 24, 1925; childrenGrace Virginia (Mrs. Walter F. Feist), Robert Cochran, Paul Cochran. Instr., then asst. prof. Princeton, 1928-42; chemist Agora Excavation staff, Athens, Greece, 1937; chief chemist Wallace Labs., New Brunswick, N.J., 1942-46; mem. faculty Ohio State U., 1946-, prof. chemistry, 1957-, vice chmn. dept., 1949-60. Recipient Lewis prize Am. Philos. Soc., 1940, Research prize Ohio Jour. Sci., 1952, citation Am. Classical League, 1954. Fellow A.A.A.S., Internat. Inst. Conservation Historic and Artistic Works, Ohio Acad. Sci., Am., Royal numismatic socs.; mem. Am. Chem. Soc. (Dexter award 1966), Archeol. Inst. Am. (pres. Columbus 1959), History Sci. Soc. Presbyn. (elder). Author: Analytical Factors and Their Logarithms, 1932; The Composition of Ancient Greek Bronze Coins, 1939; Composition of Parthian Coins, 1954; (with J.F.C. Richards) Theophrastus on Stones, 1956; Orichaleum and Related Ancient Alloys, 1964; Analysis of Ancient Metals, 1964; Metrological Tables, 1965; also articles. Home: 87 Erie Rd Columbus, OH 43214.

CALFEE, JOHN BEVERLY, lawyer; b. Cleve., May 2, 1913; s. Robert M. and Alwine (Haas) C.; grad. Hotchkiss Sch., 1931; B.A., Yale, 1935; LL.B., Western Res. U., 1938; m. Nancy Leighton, Feb. 8, 1944; children—John Beverly, David L., Peter H., Mark E. Admitted to Ohio bar, 1938, since practiced in Cleve.; partner firm Calfee, Halter, Calfee, Griswold & Sommer. Dir. Ajax Mfg. Co., Curtis-Noll Corp.; dir., gen. counsel Lamson & Sessions Co. Dir. civil def., Cleve., 1951. Served to maj. U.S. Army, 1942-46. Mem. Am., Ohio, Cleve. bar assns. Presbyn. Mason (Shriner), Rotarian. Clubs:

University (N.Y.C.); Chevy Chase (Washington); Mayfield, Union, Pepper Pike (Cleve.). Home: 4892 Clubside Dr Lyndhurst OH 44124 Office: Central Nat Bank Bldg Cleveland OH 44114

CALFEE, WILLIAM NOWARD, sculptor, painter; b. Washington, Feb. 7, 1909; s. Lee Price and Carrie L. (Whitehead) C.; studied sculpture Beaux Arts, Paris, also Cranbrook Acad., Mich.; m. Gertrude H. Dunn, 1951; children—Adriana, Richard, Judy, Helme, William, Alan Edward. Instr. spl. skills div. Resettlement Adminstrn., Cumberland Homesteads, Tenn., 1935; executed murals, sculptures, fine arts sect. procurement div. U.S. Treasury Dept., 1936-41; psychotherapy worker St. Elizabeth's Hosp., Washington, 1942-43; works exhibited most museums; one-man show painting Wehye Gallery, N.Y.C., sculpture Graham Gallery, Balt. Mus., Corcoran Gallery, Philbrook Art Mus., Tulsa; rep. in Root Collection, Phillips Gallery, Corcoran Gallery. Tchr. mural technique Centre d'Art, Port au Prince, Haiti, 1949; guest asso. prof. painting U. Cal. at Berkeley, 1951; chmn. dept. painting and sculpture Am. U., Washington until 1954, now artist in residence; initiated Watkins Meml. Collection, Watkins Gallery; executed altar, font, candle sticks St. Augustine's Chapel, Washington, District Columbia, 1968. Home: 4817 Potomac Av NW Washington DC 20007

CALHOON, JESSE MAYO, labor union ofcl.; b. Belhaven, N.C., Apr. 4, 1923; s. Ephraim Franklin and Nancy (Mayo) C.; grad. U.S. Merchant Marine Officer Candidate Sch., 1942-43; m. Jean Nolan, Jan. 9, 1965; children-Richard Earl, Tamara Kay, Ronald Lee, Curtis Sean. Service with U.S. Merchant Marine, 1940-55; pres. Marine Engrs. Beneficial Assn., AFL-CIO, 1955—, also chmn. trustee pension and welfare fund; mem. gen. bd., also maritime com. AFLCIIO. Home: 2 Madison Pl Jericho NY 11753 Office: 17 Battery Pl New York NY 10004

CALHOON, RICHARD PERCIVAL, educator; b. Sewickley, Pa., Feb. 3, 1909; s. George Percival and Elizabeth Cavett (Sigman) C.; A.B., U. Pitts., 1930, A.M., 1932; m. Frances Clark Abercrombie, July 2, 1940; children—Kathryn, Susan, Carol, Bruce. Instr., U. Pitts., 1930-34; labor adminstr. NRA, 1934-35; referee under Davis-Bacon Act, 1936; asst. to factory mgr. Ansco Corp., Binghamton, N.Y., 1936-37; pub. relations and tng. dir. U.S. Rubber Co., Naugatuck, Conn., 1937-41; personnel dir. Kendall Mills, Charlotte, N.C. 1941-46; prof. personnel adminstrn. U. N.C., 1946—; cons. in personnel adminstrn. Arbiter Am. Arbitration Assn., Fed. Conciliation and Mediation Service, N.C. Dept. Labor. Mem. Indsl. Relations Research Assn., S.E. Personnel Conf. (bd.), Acad. Mgmt., Am. Assn. U. Profs., Eugene Field Soc. (hon.), Delta Sigma Pi (hon.), Beta Gamma Sigma (hon. pres.). Democrat. Author: Moving Ahead on Your Job, 1946; Problems in Personal Administration, 1949, (with C. A. Kirkpatrick) Influencing Employee Behavior, 1956; (with E. W. Noland and A. M. Whitehill) Cases on Human Relations in Management, 1958; Managing Personnel, 1963; Cases in Personnel Management and Supervision, 1966; Personnel Management and Supervision, 1967; also research publs., articles. Home: 104 Pine Lane Chapel Hill NC 27514

CALHOUN, ALEXANDER DEWEY, cons.; b. Phila., May 9, 1898; s. Robert and Mary (Thomas) C.; student U. Pa., 1917-18; m. Minna Schick, Apr. 4, 1923; children—Alexander Dewey, Thomas B. With First Nat. City Bank N.Y. 1919-63, v.p., 1951-60, sr. v.p., 1960-63; cons. Nat. Econ. Council, Republic of Philippines, 1964, AID, Dept. State, 1964-66, Nat. Bank Detroit, 1964-68, Wells Fargo Bank, San Francisco, 1966-67, Western Am. Bank (Europe), Ltd., 1967, Security Pacific Nat. Bank, 1967—. Mem. Shanghai Municipal Council, 1936-37; adv. com. Govt. of India Investment Centre. Pres. China Inst. Am., 1958-64, 66-67; chmn. exec. com. Am.-Philippine Sci. Found., 1960-66; bd. dirs. Internat. Schs. Found., 1960-64. Served with U.S. Army, 1918. Decorated Order of Sikatuna (Republic P.I.). Mem. Asia Soc. (trustee), Far East Am. Council Commerce and Industry (dir. 1958-63), Philippine Am. C. of C. (pres. 1961-63), Am. Arbitration Assn. (nat. panel arbitrators), Council on Fgn. Relations. Presbyn. (trustee, elder). Clubs: Metropolitan, India House (N.Y.C.); University, Manila Polo (past pres.), Manila Golf, Army and Navy, Manila, Casino Espanol (Manila); Baguio (P.I.) Country; Royal Bombay (India) Yacht. Home: 200 E 66th St New York City NY 10021

CALHOUN, BYRON CLARENCE, textile co. exec.; b. Greensboro, N.C., Aug. 29, 1916; s. Henry Willis and Arena (Henderson) C.; ed. pub. schs. With Cone Mills Corp., 1942—, sec., 1961—. Home: 1520 Countryside Dr Greensboro NC 27405 Office: Cone Mills Corp 4th and Maple Sts Greensboro NC 27405

CALHOUN, DANIEL FAIRCHILD, educator; b. Fairfield, Conn., June 21, 1929; s. Philo Clarke and Doris Antoinette (Wheeler) C.; grad. Phillips Exter Acad., 1946; B.A., Williams Coll., 1950; M.A., U. Chgo., 1951, Ph.D., 1959; m. Janet Montgomery McGovern, July 12, 1952; children—Carol Victoria, Philo Clark, Virginia Stuart Blair. Instr., Coll. Wooster (O.), 1956—, instr. history, 1956-60, asst. prof., 1960-63, asso. prof., 1963-66, prof., 1966—, chmn. dept. history, 1971—. Dir. Steels and Basks, Ltd., Leicester, Eng. Mem. Am. Hist. Assn., Ohio Acad. History, Phi Beta Kappa. Democrat. Episcopalian. Home: 1150 N Bever St Wooster OH 44691

CALHOUN, DONALD EUGENE, Jr., lawyer; b. Columbus, O., May 15, 1926; s. Donald E. and Esther (Cope) C.; student John Carroll U., 1945, U. Mich., 1946; B.A. in Polit. Sci., Ohio State U., 1949, J.D., 1951; m. Shirley Claggett, Aug. 28, 1948; children-Catherine C., Donald Eugene III, Elizabeth C. Admitted to Ohio bar, 1951, since practiced in Columbus; partner Folkerth, Calhoun, Webster, Maurer & O'Brien, 1968—. Gen. counsel Ohio Conf. United Ch. of Christ, 1964—. Chmn., City-wide Citizens Com. for Neighborhood Seminars on Sch. Program and Finance, 1963. Mem. Columbus Bd. Edn., 1963—, pres., 1966-70. Republican 21st Ward committeeman, 1962—. Served with USNR, 1944-46. Mem. Am. (Nat. Conf. Bar Presidents), Ohio, Columbus (pres. 1967-68) bar assns., Am. Arbitration Assn., Columbus Jr. C. of C. (life). Conglist. Mason. Home: 216 W Beechwold Blvd Columbus OH 43214 Office: 230 E Town St Columbus OH 43215

CALHOUN, EDWARD H., exec. v.p. Cunningham and Walsh, Inc. Address: 260 Madison Av New York City NY 10016*

CALHOUN, F. PHINIZY, Jr., med. educator; b. Atlanta, 1910; M.D., Johns Hopkins, 1936; Diploma in Ophthalmology, Oxford U. (Eng.), 1943. Intern Johns Hopkins, 1936-37; resident in internal medicine Mass. Gen. Hosp., Boston, 1937-38; resident in ophthalmology Presbyn. Hosp. and Columbia U., 1939-42; prof., chmn. dept. ophthalmology Emory U. Sch. Medicine, also dir. Montgomery Lab. of Ocular Pathology. Served from capt. to maj. MC., AUS, 1942-44. Diplomate Am. Bd. Ophthalmology. Office: Dept Ophthalmology Emory U Med Sch Atlanta GA*

CALHOUN, HARLAN MAYBERRY, state justice; b. Franklin, W.Va., Oct. 25, 1903; s. Harrison Mayberry and Virginia (Mullenax) C.; student Potomac State Coll., 1921-23; LL.B., U. W.Va., 1926; m. Alberta Dorsey, Nov. 16, 1929 (dec. Oct. 1, 1953); children—Ann Fredlock (Mrs. G. Thomas Williams), Joseph Harlan; m. 2d, Florene S. Baker, Sept. 4, 1954. Admitted to W.Va. bar, 1926; pros. atty., Hardy County, W.Va., 1933-36; judge 22d Jud. Circuit W.Va., 1937-58, W.Va. Supreme Ct. Appeals, 1958—. Chmn. W.Va. Jud. Council. Mem. Am., W.Va., South Branch Valley bar assns., W.Va. State Bar, W.Va. Jud. Assn. (past pres.), Am. Judicature Soc., Mountain Soc., Kappa Sigma, Phi Delta Phi. Democrat. Methodist. Mason. Home: 1549 Virginia St Charleston WV 25311 Office: State Capitol Charleston WV 25305

CALHOUN, HAROLD, architect; b. Mineral Springs, Ark., Oct. 11, 1906; s. Albert Sidney and Willie (Reeder) C.; B.A., Rice U., 1932; m. Annie Louise Robertson, Dec. 3, 1932; 1 dau., Nancy Ann. Freelance delineatro and archtl. draftsman, 1925-29; organized firm Wirtz & Calhoun, architects, 1932; with Robert & Co., architects and engrs. on design of Corpus Christi Naval Air Center, Corpus Christi, Tex., 1940-43; vis. critic, grad. students archtl. dept., Rice U., 1846; with Wirtz, Calhoun, Tungate & Jackson, Houston, 1947-66, Calhoun, Tungate & Jackson, Houston, 1966-. Recipient first hon. mention House Beautiful competition, 1946; 3d prize Georgia Builds competition, 1947; certificate of award Houston chpt. A.I.A., 1947, hon. mention, 1953; award of merit Tex. Soc. Architects, 1954, architecture of merit award, 1960. Served to lt. (s.g.) USNR, 1943-46. Fellow Am. Inst. Architects; mem. Texas Society of Architects (past president), Houston Engineering and Scientific Soc., La Sociedad de Arquitectos Mexicanos (hon.). Baptist (deacon). Mason, Lion. Club: Champions Golf. Home: 1 Concord Circle Houston TX 77024 Office: 2506 Richton St Houston TX 77006

CALHOUN, JOHN ARCHIBALD, U.S. ambassador; b. Berkeley, Cal., Oct. 29, 1918; s. George Miller and Ellinor McKay (Miller) C.; B.A., U. Cal., 1939; M.A., Harvard, 1940. Vice consul, Tijuana, Mexico, 1941-42; 3d sec., vice consul, Tehran, Iran, 1942-44; fgn. service officer, consul, Berlin, Germany, 1946-49; dep. dir. Office German Polit. Affairs, Dept. State, Washington, 1950; 1st sec. Am. embassy and consul, Seoul, Korea, 1953-55; adviser U.S. delegation Geneva Conf. on Korea and Indo-China, 1954; assigned Air War Coll., Maxwell AFB, 1955-56; 1st sec. Am. embassy, Paris (U.S. delegation to NATO), 1956-57; dep. dir., then dir. Exec. Secretariat, Dept. State, 1957-60; counselor Am. embassy, Athens, Greece, 1960-61; ambassador to Republic of Chad, 1961-63; American minister to Berlin, Germany, 1963-67; minister counselor polit. affairs Saigon, Vietnam, 1967-68; ambassador to Republic of Tunisia, 1969—. Served as ensign, Supply Corps, USNR, overseas duty, 1944-46. Mem. Am. Fgn. Service Assn., Delta Tau Delta. Clubs: Federal City, University (Washington). Address: Foreign Service Mail Room Dept of State Washington DC 20521

CALHOUN, JOHN C., Jr., coll. adminstr.; dean; b. Betula, Pa., Mar. 21, 1917; s. John C. and Martha (Rowe) C.; B.S. in Petroleum and Natural Gas Engring., Pa. State U., 1937, M.S., 1941, Ph.D., 1946; m. Ruth Elizabeth Huston, June 10, 1941; children—John, Emily, Mary Beth, Ruth Ellen. Research asst., instr. Pa. State U., 1937-46, prof. petroleum and natural gas engring., head dept., 1950-55; asso. prof., then prof., then chmn. Sch. Petroleum Engring. U. Okla., 1946-50, 50, chmn. Sch. Petroleum Engring., 1948-50; dir. Am. Petroleum Inst. dean Sch. Engring., A. and M. Coll. Tex., 1955-57; dir. Tex. Engring. Expt. Sta., Tex. Enging. Extension Service, 1955-57, v.p. engring., Tex. A. and M. Coll. system, 1957-59. vice chancellor for engring., 1959-60, for devel., 1960-63, v.p. programs, 1967-71; asst., also sci. adviser to sec. of Interior, Washington, 1963-65; distinguished prof. petroleum engring., Tex. A. and M. U., 1965—, distinguished dir. office sea grant programs, 1968—; dean geoscis., 1969-71, v.p. acad. affairs, 1971—. Acting dir. Office Water Resources Research, 1964; cons. petroleum engr., research cons.; mem. Fed. Council for Sci. and Tech., 1963-65; chmn. com. on oceanography Nat. Acad. Scis., 1967-70, chmn. ocean sci. affairs bd., 1970—; mem. Environmental Pollution Panel, Pres.' Sci. Adv. Com., 1964-66; chmn. com. on marine resources program devel. Dept. Interior, 1966, chmn. spl. study group on sonic boom in relation to man, 1967-68, chmn. marine affairs action group, 1970; mem. Presdl. Task Force on Oceanography, 1969; chmn. Pres.' Santa Barbara Oil Spill Panel and Panel on Union Oil Lease, 1969; Vice chmn. Engring. Coll. Research Council, 1959-62. Chmn. Coll. Station United Fund, 1961. Trustee U. Corp. for Atmospheric Research, 1959—, chmn. bd., 1968-71; trustee Tex. A. and M. Research Found.; bd. dirs. EDUCOM, 1966- 69; exec. dir., pres. Gulf Univs. Research Corp., 1966-69. Mem. A.A.A.S., Am. Inst. Mining, Metall. and Petroluem Engrs., Am. Soc. Oceanography, Sigma Xi, Tau Beta Pi, Sigma Gamma Epsilon, Phi Kappa Phi, Tau Kappa Epsilon. Presbyn. Club: Cosmos. Author: Fundamentals of Reservoir Engineering, 1953. Contbr. profl. jours. Home: 1106 Ashburn St College Station TX 77840

CALHOUN, JOSEPH DUKES, lawyer; b. Norwood, Pa., June 25, 1907; s. Joseph Hoe and Mary Agnes (Dukes) C.; B.A. with honors, Swarthmore Coll., 1929; B.L., U. Pa., 1932; m. Mary Hooton Roberts, Sept. 28, 1939. Admitted to Pa. bar, U.S. Supreme Ct. bar; practice law, Media, Pa.; asst. dist. atty., Delaware County, 1940-43. Chmn. Delaware County council Econ. Stblzn. Agy., 1950-51. Mem. Am. Bar Assn. (sec. 1957-63, life mem. Fellows, Housing Authority, Delaware County Welfare Council, 1946-50; asso. gen. council Econ. Stblzn. Agy., 1950-51. Mem. Am. Bar Assn. (sec. 1957-63, mem. Fellows, life mem. ho. of dels), Jr. Bar (nat. chmn. 1942-48), Delaware County Bar Assn. (pres. 1963). Home: 210 Mohawk Av Norwood PA 19074 Office: 218 W Front St Media PA 19063

CALHOUN, LAWTON MILLER, sugar co. exec.; b. Macon, Ga., June 28, 1910; s. Patrick Noble and Katharine (Miller) C.; A.B., Washington and Lee U., 1937; m. Mary Anne Train, Feb. 25, 1941; children—Lawton Miller (dec.), Mrs. Mary Anne Farmer, Mrs. Lilla Comer Olmstead, Katharine. With Savannah Sugar Refining Corp. (Ga.) (now Savannah Food & Industries, Inc.), 1940—, successively asst. sales mgr., sales mgr., sec., v.p., 1940-60, exec. v.p., pres., 1961-71, pres., chmn. bd., 1971—, also dir.; chmn. bd., dir. Stevens Shipping Co., Savannah; pres. Atlantic Towing Co., Savannah; dir. Liberty Nat. Bank & Trust Co., chmn. exec. com. 1959-68; dir. Trust Co. of Ga. Assos., Atlanta, U.S. Sugar Corp., Clewiston, Fla. Bd. dirs. Savannah United Community Services, pres. 1964-65; bd. dirs. Savannah Port Authority, chmn., 1970-71; trustee Candler Gen. Hosp., St. Joseph's Hosp. Served to lt. comdr. USNR, 1942-46. Mem. Savannah C. of C. (pres. 1959-60, dir.), Sugar Assn. N.Y. (dir., chmn. 1967-69), U.S. Cane Sugar Refiners Assn. (dir., policy com.), Kappa Alpha. Democrat. Presbyn. Clubs: Savannah Golf, Savannah Yacht and Country, Oglethorpe (pres. 1953-54), Chatham (Savannah). Home: 504 E St Julian St Savannah GA 31401 Office: Savannah Bank and Trust Co Bldg PO Box 339 Savannah GA 31402

CALHOUN, PATRICK NOBLE, Jr., banker; b. Atlanta, Sept. 2, 1911; s. Patrick Noble and Katherine Hurt (Miller) C.; B.S. in Civil Engring., Clemson U., 1932; student Grad. Sch. Banking, Rutgers U., 1947-49; m. Mary Gertrude Pitts, June 17, 1950; children—Constance DeG., Mary M., Parick N., Margaret P., Alexander M., Emily P. With the Guaranty Trust Co. N.Y. 1932-42; from asst. treas. to v.p. Bank of Manhattan Co., 1946-55; v.p. Chase Manhattan Bank, 1955; exec. v.p. Guilford Nat. Bank, Greensboro, N.C., 1955-57, pres., 1958-60; exec. v.p. N.C. Nat. Bank, Charlotte, 1960—; dir. Hermitage Cotton Mills, Hermitage Hosp. Products, Hermitage MIlls, Inc. Mem. Charlotte City Council, 1971—. Bd. dirs. United Community Services, pres., 1969; life trustee Clemson U.; mem. bd. Clemson Univ. Found. Served to maj. USAAF, 1942-46. Mem. Alumni Assn. Clemson U. (pres. 1960), Charlotte C. of C. (pres. 1967), N.C. Bankers Assn., Assn. Res. City Bankers. Clubs: Charlotte City; Quail Hollow Country. Home: 737 Edgehill Rd S Charlotte NC 28207 Office: NC Nat Bank Box 120 Charlotte NC 28202

CALHOUN, ROBERT B., paper co. exec.; b. Montreal, Can., 1906; B.A., McGill U., 1930; B.C.L., 1933; m. Margaret Mackay, June 29, 1940; children—Heather, Douglas, Bruce. Practicing lawyer, Montreal, Que., Can., 1934-36; estates officer Capital Trust Corp., Ottawa, 1936-38; sec.-treas. J.W. Kilgour & Bros., Ltd., Beauharnois, Que., 1938-56; sec. Consolidated-Bathurst, Ltd., 1956—, Anticosti Shipping Co., Consol.-Bathurst Packaging Ltd., Consol.-Bathurst Newsprint Ltd., Gillies Gillies Bros. & Co., Ltd. Commr. West Island Sch. Commn., 1959-69. Home: 168 Juniper St Beaconsfield Quebec Canada Office: 800 Dorchester Blvd W Montreal Quebec Canada

CALHOUN, RORY, (Francis Timothy Durgin), actor; b. Los Angeles, Aug. 8, 1922; m. Lita Baron, 1948; 2 children. First appeared in motion picture Something for the Boys, 1944, numerous others, latest being Nob Hill, Rogue River, 1950, The Great John L., I'd Climb the Highest Mountain, 1951, With a Song in My Heart, 1952, How to Marry a Millionaire, 1955, The Spoilers, 1956, Apache Territory, 1958; Raw Edge, Flight to Hong Kong, Young Fury, Colossos of Rhodes; TV Series The Texan, 1958. Home: 939 N Beverly Dr Beverly Hills CA 90210*

CALHOUN, WALTER BOWMAN, ednl. adminstr.; b. Mt. Olive, Miss., May 19, 1917; s. William Sidney and Fannie (Holloway) C.; B.S., Miss. State U., 1938; M.B.A., La. State U., 1939; m. Eva Burnell Linton, Sept. 23, 1946; children—Eva Suzanne, Mai Fran. Mem. staff La. State U. and A. and M. Coll., 1940—, comptroller, 1958-62, v.p. charge finance, 1962—. Treas. La. State U. Found. Mem. exec. bd. Istrouma Area council Boy Scouts Am. Served as aviator USNR, 1942-45; lt. comdr. Res. ret. Mem. Am. Legion, Phi Kappa Phi, Beta Gamma Sigma, Beta Alpha Psi, Omicron Delta Kappa. Methodist. Home: 1348 Meadow Lee Dr Baton Rouge LA 70808

CALHOUN, WILLIAM ADLEY, lawyer; b. nr. Stewbenville, O., Jan. 20, 1915; s. William H. and Sarah (Billett) C.; student Kent State U., 1932; LL.B., Ohio State U., 1939; m. Pearl M. Beach, June 30, 1939; children—James A., Florence Ann. Admitted to Ohio bar, 1939; practice in Columbus, 1939-42, Mansfield, 1946—; spl. agt. FBI, 1942-46. Dir. Gorman-Rupp Co., Richland Trust Co., Mid-Ohio Banc-Shares, Inc., Servisteel Corp. Chef Systems, Inc., Car-Burger, Inc., De-Kal, Inc., Campus Foods, Inc., Ky. Enterprises, Inc. Chmn. Richland County Democratic Exec. Com., 1950-56. Pres. United Community Services; pres., trustee Mansfield U. Found.; trustee Mansfield Cancer Found. Mem. Am., Ohio, Richland County bar assns. Methodist. Mason (Shriner). Home: 1872 Autumn Dr Mansfield OH 44907 Office: 70 Park Av W Mansfield OH 44902

CALIFANO, JOSEPH ANTHONY, Jr., lawyer; b. Bklyn., May 15, 1931; s. Joseph Anthony and Katherine (Gill) C.; A.B., Holy Cross Coll., 1952; LL.B., Harvard, 1955; m. Gertrude Zawacki, July 4, 1955; children—Mark Gerard, Joseph Anthony II, Claudia Frances. Admitted to N.Y. State bar, 1955; with firm firm Dewey, Ballatine, Bushby, Palmer & Wood, N.Y.C., 1958-61; spl. asst. to gen. counsel Dept. Def., 1961-62; spl. asst. to sec. army, 1962-63; gen. counsel Dept. Army, 1963-64; spl. asst. to sec. and dep. sec. def., 1964- 65; spl. asst. to Pres., 1965-69; mem. firm Arnold & Porter, Washington, 1969-71; partner firm Williams, Connolly & Califano, Washington, 1971—. Gen. counsel Democratic Nat. Com., 1970—. Served to lt. USNR, 1955-58. Recipient Distinguished Civilian Service award Dept. of Army, 1964; Man of Year award Justinian Soc. Lawyers, 1966; One of Ten Outstanding Young Men of Year, 1966; Distinguished Service medal Dept. Def., 1967. Mem. Am., Fed. bar assns., Am. Judicature Soc. Democrat. Author: The Student Revolution: A Global Confrontation, 1969. Home: 3551 Springland Lane NW Washington DC 20008 Office: 1229 19th St NW Washington DC 20036

CALIRI, JOSEPH LOUIS, lawyer, corp. exec.; b. Rochester, N.Y., Mar. 16, 1916; s. Salvatore and Maria Teresa (Bottazzi) C.; A.B., U. Rochester, 1938; LL.B., Cornell, 1941; m. Dorothy Ann McGrath, Aug. 19, 1944; children—Robert Redmond, Barbara Jane. Admitted to N.Y. bar, 1941; law dept. Nat. Dairy Products Corp. (name changed Kraftco Corp.), N.Y.C., 1941-51, asst. sec., 1951-52, sec., 1952—, v.p., 1971—. Past pres., Bd. Edn. Union Free Sch. Dist.. 9, West Islip, N.Y. Mem. A.I.M., Am. Judicature Soc., Am. Soc. Corporate Secs., Am., N.Y. bar assns., Cornell Law Assn., Phi Beta Kappa, Alpha Phi Delta. Republican. Roman Catholic. Clubs: Southward-Ho Country (Brightwaters, N.Y.); Magoun Landing Yacht (West Islip); South Bay Cruising (Babylon, N.Y.); Cornell (N.Y.C.). Home: 24 Davison Lane W West Islip NY 11795 Office: 260 Madison Av New York City NY 10016

CALISHER, HORTENSE, (Mrs. Curtis Harneck), author; b. N.Y.C., Dec. 20, 1911; d. Joseph Henry and Hedvig (Lichtstern) Calisher; A.B., Barnard Coll., 1932; children by former marriage—Bennet Hughes, Peter Heffelfinger; m. 2d, Curtis Harnack, Mar. 23, 1959. Adj. prof. English, Barnard Coll., N.Y.C., 1956- 57; vis. lectr. State U. Ia., 1957, 59-60, Sarah Lawrence Coll., Bronxville, N.Y., 1962; adj. prof. Columbia, N.Y.C., 1968- ; vis. prof. lit. State U. N.Y. at Purchase, 1971-72. Guggenheim fellow, 1952, 55; Dept. of State Am. Specialist's grantee to S.E. Asia, 1958; recipient Nat. Council of Arts and Letters award. Author: In the Absence of Angels (short stories), 1951; False Entry, 1961; Tale for the Mirror (short stories), 1962; Textures of Life, 1963; Extreme Magic (novella and short stories), 1964; Journal from Ellipsia, 1965, The Railway Police and The Last Trolley Ride (novellas), 1966; The New Yorkers, 1969; Queenie (novel), 1971. Contbr. short stories, articles, revs. to New Yorker, Harper's, Harper's Bazaar, Mademoiselle, Reporter, N.Y. Times, Am. Scholar, anthologies, others. Office: care Candida Donadio-Robert Lantz 111 W 57th St New York City NY 10019

CALISTI, LOUIS J. P., univ. pres.; b. Trenton, N.J., Dec. 16, 1925; s. Philip Calisti; student Rutgers U., 1943-45; D.D.S. with honors, U. Pa., 1949; M.P.H., Harvard, 1960, grad. Advanced Mgmt. Program, 1971; m. Kathryn McEwen, Feb. 14; children—Scott Philip, Bruce McEwen, Robyn Lou. Pvt. practice dentistry, 1949-50, 52-56; instr. oral diagnosis U. Pa., 1956; dental dir. Brookline (Mass.) Health Dept., 1957- 61; mem. faculty Tufts U. Sch. Dental Medicine, 1957-71, asso. prof., chmn. dept. social dentistry, 1961-63, dean 1963-71, prof. social dentistry, 1967; pres. U. Me., Portland and Gorham, 1971—. Mem. Nat. Bd. Dental Hygiene Examiners. Mem. dean's com. VA Hosp., Boston; mem. study sect. continuing edn. NIH; mem. Bd. Health, Westwood, Mass., 1970; del., panelist White House Conf. Children and Youth, 1970; cons. to USPHS Hosp., Boston. Served to capt., Dental Corps, USAF, 1950-52. Fellow Am. Pub. Health Assn., Am. Assn. Dental Schs. (dean's council); mem. Am. Dental Assn., Mass. Dental Soc., Omicron Kappa Upsilon. Author articles in field. Home: E Grand Av Old Orchard Beach ME 04064 Office: College Av Gorham ME 04038

CALKINS, CARROLL CECIL, former mag. editor; b. Springfield, Ore., Oct. 7, 1918; s. Herman Cecil and Gladys (Riggs) C.; B.A., U. Ore., 1946; m. Ruth Geneva Monroe, Sept. 27, 1947; children—Christopher Carroll, Robin Ruth, Melissa Howard. Comml. photographer Dotson Photo, Engene, Ore., 1947-49; self employed comml. photographer, Eugene, 1949-53; N.W. editor Sunset mag., 1953-56, asso. editor, 1956-57; asso. editor House Beautiful mag., 1957- 67, former editor-in-chief, House Garden mag. Founding pres. Common Interest Group, Norwalk, Conn., 1963-67. Bd. govs. Norwalk Symphony Orch. Served to maj. USAAF, 1941-45. Decorated D.F.C., Air medal with 5 oak leaf clusters. Mem. Am. Soc. Mag. Editors, Alpha Delta Sigma. Home: 23 Saw Mill Rd Norwalk CT 06851

CALKINS, CHARLES RICHARD, research dir.; b. Racine, Wis., May 30, 1921; s. Bert L. and Bonieviere (Clark) C.; B.A., Lawrence Coll., 1942; M.S., Inst. Paper Chemistry, 1947, Ph.D., 1949; m. Julia Elizabeth Spencer, Feb. 25, 1944; childrenSarah E., Susan D., Julia B. With Riegel Paper Corp., 1949-, corp. dir. research and devel., 1957-65, v.p., dir. research and devel., 1965-68, vice pres. planning and corporate devel., 1968—. Served to lt. (j.g.) USNR, 1943-46. Decorated Purple Heart. Mem. Am. Chem. Soc., T.A.P.P.I. (chmn. Del. Valley sect. 1954-55, nat. bd. dirs. 1965-), Packaging Inst., British Paper and Board Makers Assn., A.A.A.S., Phi Beta Kappa, Phi Delta Theta, Inst. Paper Tech. Alumni Assn. (past pres.). Club: Chemists (N.Y.C.). Home: RD 1 Kintnersville, PA 18190. Office: Riegel Paper Corp 260 Madison Av New York City NY 10016 10016

CALKINS, EVAN, physician, educator; b. Newton, Mass., July 15, 1920; s. Grosvenor and Patty (Phillips) C.; grad. Milton Acad., 1939; A.B., Harvard, 1942, M.D., 1945; m. Virginia McC. Brady, Sept. 9, 1946; children-Sarah Whiton, Stephen, Lucy McCormick, Joan Grosvenor, Benjamin, Hugh, Ellen Rowntree, Geoffrey, Timothy. Intern, asst. resident medicine Johns Hopkins, 1946-47, 48-50; practice medicine, specializing in internal medicine, Boston, 1951-61, Buffalo, 1961—; Nat. Research fellow med. scis. Harvard, 1950-52, instr., asst. prof. medicine, 1952-61; staff mem. Mass. Gen. Hosp., 1952-61; prof. medicine State U. N.Y., Buffalo, 1961—, chmn. dept., 1965—; head dept. medicine Buffalo Gen. Hosp., 1961-68; dir. medicine E.J. Meyer Meml. Hosp., 1968—; cons. Nat. Inst. Arthritis and Metabolic Diseases Tng. Grants Com., 1958-62, Program Project Com., 1964-68; cons. Nat. Insts. Spl. Study Sect. for Health Manpower, 1969—. Served to capt., M.C., AUS, 1943-45, 46-48. Mem. A.M.A., Am. Soc. Internal Medicine, Am. Soc. for Exptl. Pathology, Gerontol. Assn., Am. Rheumatism Assn. (pres., past chmn. Med. Council), A.C.P., Am. Clin. and Climatological Assn., Am. Soc. Clin. Investigation,, Assn. Am. Physicians, Assn. Profs. Medicine (sec.- treas.). Home: 40 Windover Hamburg NY 14075 Office: 462 Grider St Buffalo NY 14215

CALKINS, FRANCIS JOSEPH, educator; b. Chgo., Oct. 15, 1910; s. Frank M. and Anna (Masilko) C.; A.B., Loyola U., Chgo., 1932, A.M., 1933; Ph.D., Northwestern U., 1947; m. Rose Marie Schreiber, June 24, 1944; children—Edward J., Richard F., Anne R., Timothy J. Statistician, asst. supr. WPA, Chgo., 1933-38; analyst Standard & Poor's Corp., N.Y.C., 1938-39; asst. prof. econs., finance U. Notre Dame, 1939-45; prof. finance Marquette U., 1945-65, chmn., 1949-61; prof., chmn. banking, finance Western Res. U., 1965-67; prof. banking, finance Case Western Res. U., Cleve., 1967-69; prof. finance Cleve. State U., 1969—. Trustee, cons. credit Counseling Service Greater Cleve., 1969—. Mem. Am. Finance Assn., Am. Econ. Assn., Cleve. Soc. Security Analysts, Chartered Financial Analysts, Blue Key, Alpha Kappa Psi, Pi Gamma Mu, Beta Gamma Sigma. Author: Case and Problems in Investments, 1955; (with Dowrie and Fuller) Investments, 1961. Home: 16064 Brewster Rd East Cleveland OH 44112

CALKINS, GARY NATHAN, lawyer; b. N.Y.C., Mar. 1, 1911; s. Gary Nathan and Helen R. (Williston) C.; student Ecole Internationale, Geneva, Switzerland, 1926-27, Storm King Sch., 1927-29; A.B., Columbia, 1933; LL.B., Harvard, 1936; m. Susannah Eby, Nov. 19, 1949; children-Helen, Margaret, Sarah, Abigail. Admitted to N.Y. bar, 1936, D.C. bar, 1955; asso. Beekman & Bogue, N.Y.C., 1936-41; staff CAB, 1941-56, chief internat. and rules div., 1947-56; partner Galland, Kharasch & Calkins, Washington, 1956-62; partner Galland, Kharasch, Calkins & Lippmann, 1962-69, Galland Kharasch, Calkins & Brown, 1970—. Mem. U.S. del. legal com. internat. Civil Aviation Orgn., 1947-55, delegation chmn. 1st, 3d, 5th, 9th and 10th meetings; chmn. U.S. delegation internat. Diplomatic Conf. for Revision of Warsaw Conv., The Hague, 1955; chmn. legal div. U.S. Air Coordinating Com., 1955-56. Served as lt. USNR, 1943-45. Mem. Am., D.C. bar assns., Am. Judicature Soc., Soc. Quiet Birdmen, Psi Upsilon. Asso. editor United States and Canadian Aviation Reports, 1956; asso. editor Jour. Air Law and Commerce, 1956-58, editor-in-chief, 1958-63. Contbr. articles profl. jours. Home: 6504 Dearborn Dr Falls Church VA 22044 Office: 1054 31st St NW Canal Sq Washington DC 20007; also 40 Wall St New York NY 10022

CALKINS, HOWARD W., advt., pub. relations; b. Cortland, N.Y., May 30, 1902; s. Chauncey E. and Minnie L (Lang) C.; B.S., U. Pa., 1924; m. Mary Ellen McGovern, Aug. 21, 1932; children—Carole E., Howard W. Reporter, financial writer, N.Y. News, bur. assn. pub. Wall Street News, 1924-35; financial writer N.Y. Times, 1935-45; became v.p., dir., dir. publicity dept., Albert Frank- Guenther Law, Inc., 1945, chmn. bd., 1951-70, pres., 1958-60. Served with USNR, 1942-45; disch., lt. comdr. Home: 81 Cayuga Rd Yonkers NY 10710 Office: 61 Broadway New York City NY 10006

CALKINS, HUGH, lawyer; b. Newton, Mass., Feb. 20, 1924; s. Grosvenor and Patty (Phillips) C.; student Phillips Exeter Acad., 1938-41; A.B., Harvard, 1945, LL.B., 1949; m. Ann Burnett Clark, June 14, 1953; children—Peter Burnet, Andrew Whiton, Margaret Phillips, Elizabeth Walker. Admitted to Ohio bar, 1961; since practiced in Cleve.; asso. firm Jones, Day, Cockley & Reavis, mem. firm, 1968—; dir. Browne & Sharpe Mfg. Co., Premier Indsl. Corp. Pres. Cleve. Commn. Higher Edn., 1971—; mem. Council on Fgn. Relations, Manpower Planning and Devel. Commn. of Cleve. Welfare Fedn., Businessmen's Interracial Com.; dir. Cleve. Small Bus. Opportunity and Devel. Corp., Cleve. City Club; trustee Greater Cleve. Neighborhood Centers Assn.; mem. Cleve. Bd. Edn., 1965—. Mem. Am., Cleve., Ohio bar assns., Am. Law Inst. Home: 2477 Guilford Rd Cleveland Heights OH 44118 Office: Union Commerce Bldg Cleveland OH 44115

CALKINS, JOHN UBERTO, Jr., lawyer; b. San Francisco, Apr. 26, 1889; s. John Uberto and Harriet Louise (Bates) C.; B.L., U. Cal., 1911, J.D., 1913; m. Deborah Dyer, Dec. 21, 1916; children—Deborah Hathaway, John Uberto III; m. 2d, Lucille Dougherty, Feb. 25, 1933; 1 dau., Sally Jane. Admitted to Cal. bar, 1913; asst. city atty., Oakland, 1916-17; asst. dist. atty., Alameda County, 1919-22; pvt. practice, 1922—; atty. for regents U. Cal., 1923-55; lectr. U. Cal. Sch. Jurisprudence, 1914-40; law prof. Hastings Coll. Law, U. Cal., 1956-59. Mem. Cal. Crime Commn., 1924-25; mem. Crime Problem Adv. Com. Cal., 1931-32. Trustee Cal. Coll. Arts and Crafts, 1947-57, mem. adv. bd., 1957—. Served as 1st U.S. Army, 1918-19; AEF in France, 1918-19 served to lt. gen. AUS, 1941-46. participated in campaigns, Bismarck Archipelago, New Britain, New Guinea, LEyte, Luzon; with Army of Occupation, Japan; brig. gen., asst. div. comdr. 52d Div., N.G., 1946-48, maj. gen., comdg. 49th Div., 1948-49. Decorated D.S.M., Legion of Merit, Bronze Star with cluster, Combat Inf. badge; Medal of Merit with cluster (Cal.). Mem. Am., Cal. bar assns., Ry. and Locomotive Hist. Soc., Am. Judicature Soc., Legion, Am. Arbitration Assn. (arbitrator), Order of Coif, Phi Delta Phi, Phi Kappa Sigma. Democrat. Rotarian, Elk. Clubs: Marine Memorial (San Francisco); Faculty (Univ. Cal.); City (Berkeley). Asso. editor Cal. Law Rev., 1914-40 (co-founder, 1st student editor); chmn. editorial com. Cal. Bar Jour. Home: 1445 Stockton St St Helena CA 94574 Office: American Trust Co Bldg Berkeley 4 CA

CALKINS, KINGSLEY MARK, artist, educator; b. South Lyon, Mich., May 13, 1917; s. Russell E. and Sadie (Hodgeman) C.; B.S., Eastern Mich. U., 1948; M.A. (State Coll. scholar), U. Mich., 1949; postgrad. Detroit Soc. Arts and Crafts, 1951- 53. Haystack Sch., summer 1964; m. Anna Josephine Woods, June 1, 1944; children—Mark, Peter, Amy. Instr., Eastern Mich. U., Ypsilanti, 1950-54, asst. prof., 1954-58, dept. head, 1959—; exhibited group shows South Bend (Ind.) Mus., 1958, 59, Audubon Artists Ann., 1956; one man shows Forsythe, Gilman, Chgo., 1965, Detroit Artists Market, 1966; perm. colls. at South Bend Mus., Mich. Consol. Gas Co., Ind. Mus. Natural History, Ford Motor Co.; executed mural Mayflower Hotel, Plymouth, Mich.; juror Wis. State Fair Art Exhbn., 1957. Chmn. sub. com. Improvement of Ypsilanti, 1967—. Served with AUS, 1941-45; ETO. Recipient numerous painting awards, 1949—. Mem. Mich. Art Edn. Assn. (past treas.), Mich. Water Color Soc. (chmn., past exhbn. chmn.). Home: 1327 Collegewood Ypsilanti MI 48197 Office: 118 Sill Hall Ypsilanti MI 48197

CALKINS, ROBERT DE BLOIS, economist; b. Lebanon, Conn., Jan. 19, 1903; s. Robert D. and Ethel Mae (Chambers) C.; B.S., Coll. William and Mary, 1925, LL.D., 1942; M.A., Stanford, 1929, Ph.D., 1933; LL.D., Emory U., 1954, Lehigh U., 1955, U. Pitts. 1958, Tulane U., 1959, Brown U., 1960, U. Cal., George Washington U., 1962; L.H.D., Southwestern U., 1962; m. Mary Gertrude Gilmer, 1929; children—Elizabeth Dixon, Robert Gilmer. Mem. staff Food Research Institute, Stanford, 1925-27, 30-32; univ. fellow, 1928- 29, teaching asst., instr., 1929-30; lectr. econs. U. Cal., 1932, asst. prof., 1933-36, asso. prof., 1936-40, prof., 1940- 41, chmn. dept., 1935-40, dean Coll. Commerce, 1937-41; prof. business econ., dean Sch. Bus., Columbia, 1941-47; v.p., dir. Gen. Edn. Bd., 1947-52; pres. Brookings Instn., Washington, 1952-67, dir., 1952—; vice chancellor social scis., prof. econs. U. of Cal. at Santa Cruz, 1967-70; vis. fellow New Eng. Center Continuing Edn., Durham, N.H., fall 1970. Vice chmn. San Francisco Regional Labor Bd., 1934, pub. rep., 1935; arbitrator labor disputes, 1935-46; temporary rep. on staff N.R.A. and AAA, 1933-35; mem. Ry. Labor Panel 1943-45; dir. N.Y. Fed. Res. Bank, 1943-49; mediator War Labor Bd., 1942-45. Vice pres. San Francisco chpt. Am. Statis. Assn., 1933-34; v.p. Pacific Coast Econ. Assn., 1938, pres. 1941; chmn. Pacific Coast regional com. Social Sci. Research Council, 1939-41; cons. U.S. Bur. Reclamation, 1939-40, Nat. Resources Planning Bd., 1940-42, OPA, 1942, War Dept., 1942, res. advisory bd. Com. Econ. Devel. 1942-52, 55-59; dir. Washington Center Met. Studies, 1959-67, chmn., 1959-61; dir. Washington Inst. Fgn. Affairs, 1962-67, Ednl. Radio and TV Center, 1953-59, Salzburg Seminar Am. Studies, 1963—, Nat. Inst. Pub. Affairs, 1965-67, Consortium of Univs. Washington, 1966-67. Mem. Phi Beta Kappa, Sigma Alpha Epsilon. Clubs: University (N.Y.C.); Cosmos (Washington). Home: 5225 Connecticut Av Washington DC 20015 Office: 1775 Massachusetts Av Washington DC 20036

CALL, CHARLES WARREN, Jr., food co. exec.; b. Hackensack, N.J., Sept. 25, 1925; s. Charles Warren and Ruth (Adelsperger) C.; A.B., Harvard, 1949; LL.B., Northeastern U., 1954; m. Eloise Faxon, June 16, 1953; 1 son, Charles Bradford. Pres., dir. Noma Corp., N.Y.C., 1963-66; pres., chief exec. officer Ward Foods, Inc., 1966—. Mem. nat. adv. com. N.Y.C. Hall of Sci.; mem. Northeastern U. Corp.; trustee Worcester Acad. Served with inf. AUS, 1943-46. Mem. Am. Bakers Assn. (gov.). Home: 52 Springbrook Rd Morristown NJ 07960 Office: 2 Pennsylvania Plaza New York City NY 10001

CALL, DAVID LINCOLN, educator; b. Batavia, N.Y., Feb. 12, 1932; s. Robert V. and Lucille (Hale) C.; B.S., Cornell U., 1954, M.S., 1957, Ph.D., 1960; m. Mary Gentry, July 3, 1954; children—Laura Ellen, David Stokes, Barbara Ruth, Carolyn Mary. Grad. asst., instr. Cornell U., 1956-60, H. E. Babcock prof. food econs., 1962—, dir. Cornell Agribusiness Execs. program, 1964-68; asst. prof. Mich. State U., 1960-62; vis. prof. Mass. Inst. Tech., 1968-69. Dir. Agribus Council Inc.; staff economist Nat. Commn. Food Marketing, 1965-66; mem. food and nutrition bd. Nat. Acad. Sci.-NRC; cons. food and agrl. bus., trade orgns. Served with U.S. Army, 1954-56. Mem. Am. Farm Econ. Assn. (chmn. audit com. 1964, 65), Am. Econ. Assn., Am. Assn. U. Profs., Alpha Gamma Rho, Phi Kappa Phi, Ho-Nun-De-Kah. Club: Adirondack League. Author: Private Label Products in Food Retailing (monograph). Author numerous sci. papers, articles. Home: 108 Comstock Rd Ithaca, NY 14850.

CALL, REX VANCE, educator; b. El Paso, Tex., Sept. 2, 1912; s. Willard Everett and Estella (Walker) C.; B.A., U. Wash., 1949, M.B.A., 1950; Ph.D., Ohio State U., 1955; m. Arta Louise Shippee, Sept. 14, 1940; childrenDavid Clayton, Christine Louise. Instr. Ohio State U., 1950-52; asst., then asso. prof. U. Omaha, 1952-55; mem. faculty U. Ariz., 1955-, prof. bus. adminstrn., pharmacy adminstrn., 1955-, head dept. marketing, 1959-; Ford Found. vis. prof. U. Rangoon (Burma), 1958-59, Harvard Bus. Sch., 1961, U. Cal. at Berkeley, summer 1960; Fulbright lectr. Am. U., Beirut, Lebanon, 1963-64; vis. professor Monterrey (Mexico) Inst. Tech., 1968- 69. Bd. dirs. Arizona Children's Home. Mem. American Marketing Assn., Am. Assn. U. Profs., Am. Assn. Tchrs. Pharmacy Adminstrn., Sales and Marketing Execs. Club, Delta Sigma Pi, Alpha Delta Sigma, Beta Gamma Sigma. Mem. Ch. of Jesus Christ of Latter-Day Saints (high council Tucson stake). Kiwanian. Home: 712 S Magnolia Blvd Tucson AZ 85711

CALLAGAN, DWIGHT A., naval med. officer; b. Sheridan, Ill., Sept. 26, 1917; s. Ralph J. and Amine (Hapeman) C.; B.S. in Medicine, U. Ill., 1942, M.D., 1942; m. Anne King, Sept. 26, 1943; children—Sharon Anne, Dwight Allen, Brian King, Wayne Reed. Commd. lt. (j.g.) U.S. Navy, 1942, advanced through grades to capt., 1957; intern U.S. Naval Hosp., Mare Island, 1943; resident in gen. surgery U.S. Naval Hosp., Nat. Naval Med. Center, Bethesda, Md., 1945-46, resident in obstetrics and gynecology, 1945-50, chief obstetrics and gynecology service, 1962-65; chief obstet. and gynecol. service U.S. Naval Hosp., Camp LeJeune, N.C., 1950-51, Guantanamo Bay, Cuba, 1951-53, Bremerton, Wash., 1953-55, Portsmouth, Va., 1955-62; exec. officer, chief profl. services U.S. Naval Hosp., Great Lakes, Ill., 1966-67; comdg. officers U.S. Naval Hosp., Subic Bay, 1968-69; with Naval Dispensary, Treasure Island, Cal., 1969—; asst. clin. prof. obstetrics and gynecology George Washington U. Med. Sch., 1962-65. Decorated Bronze Star medal with combat V. Diplomate Am. Bd. Obstetrics and Gynecology. Mem. A.M.A., Am. Coll. Obstetricians and Gynecologists, Alpha Omega Pi, Phi Rho Sigma. Contbr. numerous articles on electrocardiographic diagnosis of multiple pregnancies. Inventor ultrasonic doppler fetal heart detection instrument. Home: Quarters 326A YBI San Francisco CA 94130 Office: Naval Dispensary Treasure Island San Francisco CA 94130

CALLAGHAN, B., journalist. Book editor Toronto Telegram. Office: 440 Front St W Toronto Ontario Canada*

CALLAGHAN, JAMES, Brit. govt. ofcl.; b. Portsmouth, Eng., Mar. 27, 1912; s. James and Charlotte G. (Cundy) C.; student elementary sch., Portsmouth; m. Audrey Elizabeth Moulton, 1938; children—Margaret Ann (Mrs. Peter Jay), Julia Elizabeth (Mrs. Ian Hubbard), Michael James. Tax officer Inland Revenue Dept., 1929-36, br. asst. sec., Inland Revenue Staff Fedn., 1936-47; parliamentary pvt. sec. to under-sec. state for dominion affairs, 1945; chmn. Labour Party's Def. and Services Com., 1945-47; mem. parliamentary delegation to West Africa, 1947, substitute rep. Consultative Assembly Council Europe, 1949, rep. 2d session, 1950, Strasbourg, 1954; parliamentary and sec. to Ministry Transport, 1947-50; parliamentary and financial sec. to Admiralty, 1950-51; attended 6th Unofficial Commonwealth Relations Conf. Royal Inst. Internat. Affairs, New Zealand, 1959; mem. parliamentary delegation, Zanzibar, Mauritius, Madagascar, 1961; attended Conf. African Socialism, Senegal, 1962-63; mem. nat. exec. com. Labour Party, 1957-67, treas., 1967-, chief spokesman on treasury affairs, 1961-64; chancellor of exchequer, 1964-67, privy councillor, 1964; Labour M.P. for Cardiff South-East, 1945—; home sec. Brit. Cabinet, 1967—. Served to lt. Royal Navy, 1942-45. Hon. life fellow Nuffield Coll. Oxford U. Pres., U.K. Pilot's Assn. Address: House of Commons London S W 1 England

CALLAGHAN, MORLEY EDWARD, author; b. Toronto, Ont., Can., Sept. 22, 1903; s. Thomas and Mary (Dewan) C.; student St. Michael's Coll., U. Toronto, 1925; LL.B., Osgoode Hall, 1928; LL.D. (hon.), U. Western Ont., 1965; m. Loretto Dee, Apr. 16, 1929; children—Michael, Barry. Author: Strange Fugitive, 1928; A Native Argosy, 1929; It's Never Over, 1930; Broken Journey, 1932; Sick is my Beloved, 1934; They Shall Inherit The Earth, 1935; Now That April's Here, 1936; More Joy in Heaven, 1937; The Loved and the Lost, 1957; The Many Colored Coat, 1960; A Passion in Rome, 1961; That Summer in Paris, 1963; Luke Baldwin's Vow, 1948; Morley Callaghan's Stories, 1958. Stories and articles have been widely translated. Recipient Gov. Gen. Can. medal, 1952, medal of merit City Toronto, 1962, gold medal Royal Soc. Can., 1958. Address: 20 Dale Av Toronto Ontario Canada

CALLAGHAN, WILLIAM JEROME, educator; b. Cleve., Mar. 28, 1912; s. James C. and Elsie J. (Hanley) C.; A.B., Harvard, 1937, A.M., 1947; Ph.D., Columbia, 1958; m. Mary E. Sacco, May 31, 1942; childrenVirginia M., James E. Instr. philosophy Queens Coll., 1947-49; mem. faculty Mich. State U., E. Lansing, 1949-, prof. philosophy, chmn. dept., 1961-; Fulbright research scholar, Bologna, Italy, 1964-65. Mem. Am. Philos. Assn., Philosophy Sci. Assn., Am. Assn. U. Profs. Home: 835 Collingwood Dr East Lansing MI 48823

CALLAHAM, JOHN ROBERT, publishing exec., chem. engr., editor; b. Townville, S.C., June 5, 1911; s. William C. and Stella Mae (Moore) C.; B.S., U. S.C., 1933; grad. study Columbia, 1937; m. Ludmilla G. Thoro, May 16, 1937; children—Michael Lee, Donn Robert, Neil Gregory, Patricia Elizabeth. Chemist, S.C. Land Uses Survey, Clemson Coll., 1934-35; plant chemist Gen. Chem. Co., Marcus Hook, Pa., 1935-37, chemist, N.Y.C. and El Segundo, Cal., 1937-41; asst. editor Chem. and Metall. Engring., McGraw-Hill Pub. Co. N.Y.C., 1941-45, Pacific Coast editor Chem. Engring., San Francisco, 1945-49, exec. editor, N.Y.C., 1949-50, chief editor, 1950-59; v.p. editorial McGraw-Hill Publs. div. McGraw-Hill, Inc., 1959—. Chmn. bus. publ. com. Pres.'s Com. for Employment Handicapped, 1963— (Distinguished Service award 1966). Mem. N.A.M., Am. Inst. Chem. Engrs., Western Chmn. Market Research Soc. (pres. 1948), Jr. Chem. Engrs. Greater N.Y. (pres. 1944), Soc. Chem. Industry (exec. com), Am. Chem. Soc., T.A.P.P.I., Tau Beta Pi. Contbr. Chem. Engring., 1941—. Home: Glen Ridge NJ 07028 Office: 330 W 42d St New York City NY 10036

CALLAHAM, THOMAS HUNTER, govt. ofcl.; b. Lynchburg, Va., Nov. 29, 1915; s. Charles Edwin and Celina (Rector) C.; B.S., Va. Poly. Inst., 1937; m. Patricia Mae Murphy, Oct. 16, 1953; children—Sandra Colleen (Mrs. Bill C. Herrmann), Thomas Hunter, Kathleen Louise, Michael Merriman. Started career as an accountant with the Standard Oil Co. of N.J., also Godfrey L. Cabot, Inc., Charleston, W.Va., 1937-40; budget officer Office U.S. High Commr. for Germany, 1949-53; budget and programs officer MSA, FOA, ICA, 1953-56; bus. specialist, chief fiscal mgmt., asst. dir. mgmt., dir. Ft. Worth regional office Pub. Housing Adminstrn., 1956-66, asst. regional adminstrn., Housing Assistance Office, Region V, 1966-70; asst. regional adminstr. Housing Mgmt. and Community Services, 1970—. Served with AUS, 1940-49; col. Res. ret. Mem. Nat. Assn. Housing and Redevel. Ofcls. (exec. com. 1968-69), Internat. Platform Assn. Democrat. Catholic. Elk. Home: 5305 Garrick Av Fort Worth TX 76133 Office: 819 Taylor St Fort Worth TX 76102

CALLAHAN, ALSTON, physician; b. Vicksburg, Miss., Mar. 16, 1911; s. Neil and Effie (Alston) C.; A.B., Miss. Coll., 1929; M.D., Tulane, 1933, M.S. in Opthalmology, 1936; m. Eivor Holst, Feb. 23, 1941; children—Kristina Alice, Patrick Alston, Michael Alston, Timothy Alston, Karin Eivor, Kevin (dec.). Intern, Charity Hosp., New Orleans, 1933-35, resident ophthalmology, 1936- 37; mem. staffs Eye Found Hosp. (co-founder), Carraway Meth., Univ. hosps.; pres., Eye Found., Inc., Birmingham. Pres. Horizon, Inc., Vertex, Inc., Gemini, Inc., Callahan Properties, Inc., Aesculapius Pub. Co. Served from 1st lt. to capt., M.C., AUS, 1943-46, eye sect. Northington Gen. Hosp., Tuscaloosa, Ala., 1944-46; disch. Fellow A.C.S.; mem. A.M.A., Am. Acad. Ophthalmology and Otolaryngology, So. Med. Assn., Alpha Omega Alpha, Sigma Alpha Epsilon, Nu Sigma Nu. Clubs: Mountain Brook; Relay House; Explorers; Club. Author: Surgery of the Eye, Injuries, 1950; Surgery of the Eye, Diseases, 1956; Reconstructive Surgery of the Eyelids and Ocular Adnexa, 1966; (with John C. Mustardé, Lester T. Jones) Opthalmic Plastic Surgery Up-to-Date. Contbr. articles profl. jours. Dir. med. motion pictures eye surgery. Home: 2175 Crest Rd Birmingham AL 35209 Office: 903 S 21st St Birmingham AL 35205

CALLAHAN, CARROLL BERNARD, lawyer; b. Montello, Wis., June 14, 1908; s. John and Rose (Reardon) C.; LL.B., U. Wis., 1931; m. Phyllis Luchsinger, Sept. 27, 1939; 1 son, Timothy Sean. Admitted to Wis. bar, 1931, since practiced in Columbus. Pres. First Nat. Bank, Columbus, 1960-; v.p. Columbus Fed. Savs. & Loan Assn., 1939-; sec., dir. Fall River Canning Co. (Wis.), 1939-; dir. Rio-Fall River Union Bank, Fall River. Served to 1st lt. AUS, 1943-46. Fellow Am. Coll. Trial Lawyers; mem. State Bar Wis. (pres. 1960-61), Am. Bar Assn., Am. Legion, Phi Alpha Delta. K.C. (4). Home: 856 S Charles St Columbus WI 53925 Office: Law Bldg 159 S Ludington St Columbus WI 53925

CALLAHAN, DANIEL JOHN, inst. dir.; b. Washington, July 19, 1930; s. Vincent Francis and Anita (Hawkins) C.; B.A., Yale, 1952; M.A., Georgetown U., 1957; Ph.D., Harvard, 1965; m. Sidney Cornelia de Shazo, June 5, 1954; children—Mark Sidney, Stephen

Daniel, John Vincent, Thomas Hawkins, Peter Thorn, Sarah Elisabeth, David Lee. Exec. editor The Commonweal, N.Y.C., 1961-68; vis. asst. prof. religion Temple U., 1964; vis. asst. prof. religious studies Brown U., 1965; vis. prof. theology Marymount Coll., 1966; vis. prof. U. Pa., 1970; dir. Inst. Soc. Ethics and the Life Scis., 1969—. Served with CIC, AUS, 1952-55. Author: The Mind of the Catholic Layman, 1963; Honesty in the Church, 1965; The New Church, 1966; Abortion: Law, Choice and Morality, 1970; also essays, articles. Co-editor: Christianity Divided: Protestant and Roman Catholic Theological Issues, 1961. Editor: Federal Aid and Catholic Schools, 1964; Secular City Debate, 1966; The Catholic Case for Contraception, 1969; The American Population Debate, 1971. Home: 84 Summit Dr Hastings-on-Hudson NY 10706 Office: 623 Warburton Av Hastings-on-Hudson NY 10706

CALLAHAN, DANIEL JOSEPH, III, banker; b. Washington, May 7, 1932; s. Daniel Joseph and Anne Bailey (Scott) C.; B.A., Williams Coll., 1954; m. Colleen Adrienne Mount, May 5, 1956; children—Daniel Joseph IV, Carey Scott, Caren Anne, Carolyn Patricia, Colleen Gerry. Trainee, Riggs Nat. Bank, Washington, 1956-58; v.p. Chase Manhattan Bank, N.Y.C., 1958-69; exec. v.p. Hambro Am. Bank and Trust Co., N.Y.C., 1969—, also dir.; dir. People's Am. Bank, Atlanta, Govt. Employees Life Ins. Co. N.Y., Hambro Am. Corp. Trustee Am. Sch., London, 1965-69; bd. dirs. Am. Sch. in London Found., Inc., 1969. Served to capt. USAF, 1954-56. Mem. Delta Kappa Epsilon. Republican. Roman Catholic. Clubs: American (London); Metropolitan (Washington); Chevy Chase (Md.); Morris County Golf (Convent, N.J.). Home: Old Chester Rd Gladstone NJ 07934 Office: 25 Broad St New York City NY 10004

CALLAHAN, GEORGE HAROLD, ins. co. exec.; b. Glen Ridge, N.J., July 13, 1920; s. George Leo and Katherine (Higgins) C.; B.S., Seton Hall Coll., 1942; LL.B., Harvard, 1948; m. Regina Ann Heslin, Feb. 17, 1943; children—G. Kevin, Jeanne C. (Mrs. Robert D. Sarg), Virginia, Barbara, John. Admitted to N.J. bar, 1948; asso. Riker, Emery & Danzig, Newark, 1948-56; partner Lowenstein, Del Tufo, Callahan & Kean, Newark, 1957-58; partner Consodine, Callahan & Farley, Newark, 1958-60; asso. counsel, sec., v.p., now sr. v.p., gen. counsel, sec. Colonial Life Ins. Co. Am., East Orange, N.J., 1960—; atty. Borough of Glen Ridge, 1956—. Mem. Character and Fitness Com. and Com. Unauthorized Practice Law N.J. Chmn. East Orange Juvenile Conf. Com., 1970—. Served to lt. USNR, World War II. Decorated Silver Star with oak leaf cluster. Mem. Am., N.J., Essex County bar assns., Assn. Life Ins. Counsel. Home: 104 Forest Av Glen Ridge NJ 07028 Office: 111 Prospect St East Orange NJ

CALLAHAN, KENNETH, artist; b. Spokane, Wash., Oct. 30, 1906; s. John Lafayette and Martha Anna (Cross) C.; student U. Wash., 1922-25; spl. study in Mexico, 1931, Paris, France, London, Eng. and Florence, Italy, 1936; m. Margaret Macauley Bundy, Oct. 11, 1930 (dec. 1961); 1 son, Brian Tobey; m. 2d, Beth Inge Gotfredsen, 1964. Asst. dir. Seattle Art Mus., 1931-35, curator, 1935-53; Guggenheim fellow creative painting, 1954-55; art writer Seattle Times, 1932-53; art mag. free lance writer since 1932. One man show Am.-Brit. Art Center, N.Y.C., 1946; exhibited Whitney Mus. Contemporary Am. Painting, Carnegie Inst. Painting in U.S., 1946, Pepsi Cola painted of the yr.; exhibited France, Eng., Germany, Italy, Denmark, Formosa, Japan, Australia, New Zealand, P.I., 1957; work in permanent collections Met. Mus. Art, Mus. Modern Art, Bklyn., Phila. and Springfield art museums, Whitney Mus. Art, Pa. Acad. Art, others. Author articles profl. mags. Home: 1216 1st Av W Seattle WA 98101 ; also Long Beach, WA 98631. Office: 1055 Madison Av New York City NY 10028

CALLAHAN, NICHOLAS PETER, govt. ofcl.; b. Washington, Dec. 26, 1913; s. Stephen Benjamin and Helen R. (Hancock) C.; B.C.S., Benjamin Franklin U., Washington, 1937; m. Lillian Christine Pepper, Jan. 2, 1936; childrenNicholas Peter, Patricia (Mrs. Joseph F. Lamb), Michael Stephen. With FBI, 1935-, designated insp., 1948, asst. dir. charge adminstrv. div., 1959-. Home: 5611 Chesterbrook Rd Washington, DC 20016. Office: Fed Bureau Investigation 9th and Pennsylvania Av NW Washington DC 20535.

CALLAHAN, NORTH, author, educator; b. nr. Sweetwater, Tenn., Aug. 7, 1908; s. Robert B. and Naomi (North) C.; student pub., pvt. schs., Tenn., 1914-26; A.B., U. Chattanooga, 1930, L.H.D., 1964; grad. student U. Tenn., 1930-32; M.A., Columbia, 1950; Ph.D., N.Y.U., 1955 (class rep.); m. Jennie Waugh, Sept. 27, 1939; children—Mary Alice, North. Educator, 1930-34; ednl. pub. relations counselor TVA-Civilian Conservation Corps. 1934-37; reporter, columnist, spl. writer Chattanooga Times, Chattanooga News, Knoxville Jour., Tyler (Tex.) Courier-Times, Morning Telegraph; N.Y.C. corr. Dallas News, 1939-44; writer syndicated column, So This is New York, 1943-68; pub. relations cons. various firms and orgns., N.Y.C., 1945-55; Penfield fellow N.Y.U., 1954-55; prof. Am. hist., head soc. sci. dept. Finch Coll., N.Y.C., 1956- 57; asso. prof. N.Y.U., 1957-62, prof. history, 1962—. Served from 1st lt. to lt. col. AUS 1940-46; supr. Army radio show, Voice of Army. Recipient N.Y.U. Founders Day Honors award, 1956. American Revolution Round Table plaque, Henry Knox, 1958; vis. scholar Huntington Library, 1960. Fellow Am. Studies Assn.; mem. Am., So. hist. assns., Am. Acad. Polit. and Social Sci., So. Soc. (historian), Civil War Round Table N.Y. (pres. 1954-55), Tenn. Soc. N.Y. (historian), Confr. Brit. Studies, Tenn. Hist. Soc., Am. Revolution Round Table (chmn.), Delta Sigma Pi, Kappa Tau Alpha, Theta Alpha Phi, Delta Theta Phi, Sigma Delta Chi. Clubs: Columbia (N.Y.C.); Lookout Mountain (Tenn.); Fairyland (Chattanooga). Author: The Army, 1941; The Armed Forces as a Career, 1947; Smoky Mountain Country, 1952; Henry Knox: General Washington's General, 1958; Daniel Morgan, Ranger of the Revolution, 1961; Royal Raiders: the Tories of the American Revolution, published in 1963, Flight from the Republic (Vol. II), pub. 1967; Carl Sandburg, a Biography, 1970. Editor Army Life mag., 1943-46, Europe's View of America, 1954; contbg. editor So. Observer mag. Composer (with Norman Cloutier) Voice of the Army, adptd. by War Dept. as ofcl. song Army Recruiting Service. Home: 110 Bleeker St New York City NY 10012

CALLAHAN, THOMAS THEODORE, pub. relations exec.; b. Chgo., Aug. 2, 1919; s. Daniel Joseph and Rose Catherine (Long) C.; B.Edn., Western Ill. State U., 1942; m. Dorothy Jane Hrack, June 5, 1943; children—Kathleen Joy, Thomas Daniel. Reporter, Macomb (Ill.) Daily Jour., 1940-42; editorial asst. TAXES, the tax mag., 1946-47; staff corr. Wall St. Jour., 1947-49; mgr. community and press relations Quaker Oats Co., 1950-54; asso. editor Commerce mag., 1955-59; editor Finance mag., 1959-66; v.p. Finance Pub. Corp., 1964-68; asso. pub. relations dept. Swift & Co., 1966-69, asst. mgr. pub. relations dept., 1969, mgr. pub. relations dept., 1970—. Served to capt. USAAF, 1942-46; ETO. Mem. Headline Club Chgo., Execs. Club Chgo., Chgo. Press Club, Sigma Delta Chi. Home: 6932 W 29th St Berwyn IL 60402 Office: 115 W Jackson Blvd Chicago IL 60604

CALLAHAN, WILLIAM FRANCIS, Jr., pub. co. exec.; b. Medford, Mass., Apr. 23, 1915; s. William Francis and Florence E. (Bailey) C.; LL.B., Suffolk U., Boston, 1938; m. Ruth S. MacDonald, Aug. 31, 1940; children—William Francis III, Richard Paul. New Eng. sales supr. Curtis Pub. Co., 1938-42; New Eng. sales supr. Dell Pub. Co., Inc., 1942-46, Eastern regional sales mgr., 1946-53; sales mgr. Dell Books, 1953-55, asst. v.p., 1955-57, v.p. charge Dell Books, 1957; v.p. Dell Distbg., Inc., also Dell Internat. Inc., 1957-60; former exec. v.p., chief operating officer, dir. Dell Pub. Co., Inc., Dell Distbg., Inc., Dell Internat., Inc.; vice chmn. bd. Nobel & Noble Publs., Inc.; dir. Mayflower Books Ltd., London, The Dial Press, Inc., Montville Warehousing Co., Inc., Pine Brook, N.J. Mem. Am. Book Pubs. Council, Mag. Pubs. Assn. (dir.), Bur. Ind. Pubs. and Distbrs. Clubs: Greenwich (Conn.) Country; Westchester Country (Rye, N.Y.); Lyford Cay (B.W.I.); Oyster Harbors, Wianno Yacht (Osterville, Mass.). Home: 16 Sutton Pl New York City NY 10022

CALLAN, JOHN HENRY, univ. dean; b. Lambertville, N.J., Nov. 2, 1920; s. Harry Joseph and Emma (Weiss) C.; B.S., Trenton State Coll., 1943; M.A., Columbia, 1949, Ed.D., 1953; m. Nancy Clare Burkle, July 12, 1952; children—John Robert, Jane Marie, Daniel Edward. Adminstrv. asst., div. higher edn. N.J. Dept. Edn., 1946-49; asso. prof. bus., chmn. div. bus. West Liberty State Coll., 1950-54; dir. tchr. edn. Ferris State Coll., 1954- 57; dean Seton Hall U. Sch. Edn., 1957—. Mem. pres.'s adv. council Caldwell Coll. Mem. bd. edn., Lambertville, N.J., 1948-49; mem. bd. Edn., Archdiocese of Newark. Served from pvt. to 1st lt., USMCR, 1943-46; maj. Res. Mem. Nat. Cath. Edn. Assn., Am. Assn. Higher Edn., Am. Assn. Sch. Adminstrs., Nat., N.J. edn. assns., N.J. Council Edn., Internat. Council Edn. Teaching, Nat. Soc. Study Edn., Kappa Delta Pi, Pi, Phi Delta Kappa, Delta Pi Epsilon, Democrat. Roman Catholic. Kiwanian. Author: Community Resources Handbook in Business Education, 1954. Contbr. chpt. to Am. Bus. Edn. Yearbook, 1961; also articles profl. jours. Home: 26 Sherwood Av Madison NJ 07940 Office: South Orange NJ 07079

CALLAS, MARIA, singer; b. N.Y.C., Dec. 2, 1923; d. George and Evangelia (Demitriadu) Callas; ed. pub. schs., N.Y.C., and Conservatoire d'Athene et Nat. Singer (dramatic soprano) in operas at La Scala, Milan, Italy, Metropolitan, N.Y.C., Covent Garden, London, State Opera House of Vienna, Opera House of Paris; appeared in operas at Lyric Theatre, Chgo., 1954 and 1955. Made hon. citizen, Mexico, also Dallas; recipient numerous medals. Address: 36 Av George Mandel Paris, France.

CALLAWAY, BEN ANDERSON, journalist; b. Oakland, Cal., Mar. 16, 1927; s. Owen M. and Aulis (Anderson) C.; student Stanford, 1946-47; B.A., Denison U., 1950; m. Patricia Hurd, Apr. 7, 1951; children-Randall Owen, Karen Anne. Sports writer, wildlife editor Denver Post, 1950-57; with Phila. Daily News, 1957—, sports editor, outdoor columnist, 1961—; free-lance magazine writer-photographer. Sports chmn. Phila. United Fund, 1966—; active local Boy Scouts Am. Served with USNR, 1945-46. Recipient Old Salt award N.J. Resort Assn., 1967; Henshall award Am. Fishing Tackle Mfrs. Assn., 1964. Mem. Phila. Sports Writers Assn. (pres. 1968-70), Denver Sports Writers and Broadcasters Assn. (pres. 1957), Outdoor Writers Am., Pa. Outdoor Writers, Baseball Writers Am., Blue Key, Beta Theta Pi, Pi Delta Epsilon, Omicron Delta Kappa. Home: 420 Kingston Dr Cherry Hill NJ 08034 Office: 400 N Broad St Philadelphia Pa 19101

CALLAWAY, CARL BYRON, lawyer; b. Corsicana, Tex., Oct. 7, 1895; s. LeRoy Rowland and Ida (McConnico) C.; LL.B., U. Tex., 1920; m. Katherine McLaurin, Apr. 23, 1929; 1 dau. Katherine McLaurin. Admitted to Tex. bar, 1920; former mem. Callaway & Reed now Callaway, Reed, Kidwell & Brooks, now in pvt. practice, became v.p., gen. counsel Transcontinental Bus. System, Inc., Dallas, 1948; dir. Empire State Bank. Served as 1st lt. 90th Div., U.S. Army, World War I. Mem. Am., Tex. State, Dallas (pres. 1928) bar assns., Phi Kappa Psi, Delta Sigma Rho. Mason. Clubs: Country, City Brookhollow Country, Idlewild (Dallas). Home: 4315 Lorraine St Dallas TX 75205 Office: Continental Bldg Dallas TX 75201

CALLAWAY, DAVID HENRY, Jr., investment banker; b. N.Y.C., July 3, 1912; s. David Henry and Mary (Sampson) C.; A.B., Amos Tuck Sch., Dartmouth, 1934; m. Virginia A. Devoe, June 5, 1937; children—Nancy A. (Mrs. James C. Tompkins), Patricia J. With Halsey Stuart & Co., Inc., 1934-36; with First Mich. Corp., N.Y.C., 1936—, sr. v.p., 1956-62, pres., 1963-70, chmn. bd., chief exec. officer, 1970—, also dir. Pres., Municipal Forum N.Y., 1959-60; asso. mem. Am. Stock Exchange. Clubs: Bond, Municipal Bond, Stock Exchange, Luncheon (N.Y.C.); Detroit; Wee Burn Country (Darien). Home: 17 Holly Lane Darien CT 06820 Office: 2 Wall St New York City NY 10005 also Buhl Bldg Detroit MI 48226

CALLAWAY, ELY REEVES, Jr., textile exec.; b. LaGrange, Ga., June 3, 1919; s. Ely Reeves and Loula (Walker) C.; A.B., Emory U., 1940; D. Textiles, Phila. Coll. Textiles and Sci., 1968; m. Jeanne Delaplaine Wiler, Oct. 7, 1942 (div. Jan. 1960); children—Ely Reeves III, Louise Wiler, Nicholas Delaplaine; m. 2d, Jane Dudley Atkins, Dec. 28, 1961. Sales exec. Deering, Milliken & Co., 1946-54; v.p., dir. Amerotron Corp. div. Textron, Inc., 1955-56; joined Burlington Industries, Inc., 1956, successively pres. various divs., then v.p. of corp., 1960, exec. v.p., 1961, pres., 1968—, also dir., mem. exec. com., mgmt. com. Bd. dirs., chmn. corp. giving United Negro Coll. Fund, 1970-71; bd. Greater N.Y. council Boy Scouts America; board visitors Emory U.; trustee Hampshire Coll., Amherst, Mass., Menninger Found., Topeka, Kan. Served from 2d lt. to maj., Q.M.C., AUS, 1940-45; purchasing and contracting officer cotton clothing Phila. Q.M. Depot. Recipient Golden Fleece award Nat. Assn. Wool Mfrs., 1965; Brotherhood award Nat. Conf. Christians and Jews, 1966; Good Scout award Greater N.Y. councils Boy Scouts Am., 1966. Mem. Kappa Alpha, Omricon Delta Kappa. Clubs: University, Blind Brook (N.Y.); Wee Burn Country (Darien, Conn.); Eldorado Country (Palm Desert, Cal.); Pine Valley (N.J.) Golf. Home: 55 Talmadge Hill Rd New Canaan CT 06840 Office: Burlington Industries Inc 1345 Av of Americas New York City NY 10019

CALLAWAY, FULLER EARLE, Jr., mfr.; b. LaGrange, Ga., Jan. 1, 1907; s. Fuller Earle and Ida Jane (Cason) C.; student Ga. Inst. Tech., Eastman Bus. Sch. N.Y.; LL.D., LaGrange Coll., 1971; m. Alice Hinman Hand, Aug. 6, 1939; children—Fuller Earle III, Ida Cason (Mrs. Charles D. Hudson). Treas., Valley West Mills, 1927; treas., gen. mgr. Truline, Inc., 1928; dir. Callaway Mills, 1932-46, pres., treas., 1935-36, pres., 1936-45, ret., 1945- 59, chmn. bd., chief exec. officer Callaway Mills Co., 1959-61, pres., chief exec. officer, 1961-65, chmn., chief exec. officer, 1965- 68, chmn. Callaway Mills, Inc., 1961-68, pres., 1962-65; chmn. Internat. Leasing Corp., 1961-65, pres., 1962-65; pres. Internat. Products & Services, Inc., 1965-70, chmn., 1970—; propr. Hills & Dales, dir. Habersham Mills. Trustee Callaway Found., Fuller E. Callaway Found., Ga. Tech. Research Inst., Ga. Tech. Found., Habersham Mills Found.; chmn., trustee Callaway Ednl. Assn.; past dir. West Ga. council Boy Scouts Am. Commd. capt. Ga. State Guard, 1942, comdg. Troop County Co., lt. col., comdg. 3d Bn., 1943; transferred to D.O.L., 1944; a.d.c., staff gov. Ga., 1943-71. Recipient Silver Beaver award Boy Scouts Am., 1939. Fellow Textile Inst. (Eng); mem. Ga. Textile Mfrs. Assn. (treas., v.p., pres. 1938-39, dir.), Am. Textile Mfrs. Inst. (chmn. 1945, v.p., dir., chmn. 1947-48), Phi Delta Theta. Democrat. Baptist. Mason, Rotarian. Clubs: Southern Society (N.Y.C.); Field, Long Boat Key Golf, Capital City, Highland Country, Piedmont Driving; Big Eddy. Home: 1200 Vernon Rd LaGrange GA 30240 Office: 200 Ferrell Dr LaGrange GA 30240

CALLAWAY, HOWARD HOLLIS, corp. exec., former congressman; b. LaGrange, Ga., Apr. 2, 1927; s. Cason Jewell and Virginia (Hand) C.; grad. Episcopal High Sch., Alexandria, Va., 1939-44; student Ga. Inst. Tech., 1944-45; B.S., U.S. Mil. Acad., 1949; m. Elizabeth Walton, June 11, 1949; childrenElizabeth Walton, Howard Hollis, Edward Cason, Virginia Hand, Ralph Walton. Chmn. bd. dirs. Gardens Services, Inc., Pine Mountain, Ga.; Ga.; mem. 89th Congress, 3d, Dist. Ga. Mem. Nat. 4-H Service Com., 1957—; pres. Ida Cason Callaway Found., Pine Mountain. Former mem. bd. regents U. System Ga.; chmn. bd. trustees Freedoms Found. at Valley Forge; trustee Nat. Recreation Assn. Republican candidate for gov. Ga., 1966. Served to 1st lt., inf. AUS, 1949-52 . Mem. Mem. Young Presidents Orgn. (past pres.), Phi Delta Theta. Episcopalian . Clubs: Clubs: Capital City, Piedmont Driving (Atlanta); 29 (N.Y.C.). Home: Pine Mountain GA 31822 Office: Callaway Gardens Pine Mountain GA 31822

CALLAWAY, JAMES THORPE, advt. exec.; b. St. Louis, Dec. 10, 1937; s. Willaim F. and Rosemary (Thorpe) C.; B.Journalism, U. Mo., 1959, M.A., 1961; m. Elizabeth Ann Neal, Sept. 10, 1960; children—David Arthur, John Patrick. Account exec. Benton & Bowles, Inc., N.Y.C., 1961-64; mgmt. supr. Papert Koenig Lois Inc., N.Y.C., 1965-67; prin., exec. v.p., treas. Lois Holland Callaway Inc., N.Y.C., 1967—. Served to 2d lt. AUS, 1960. Mem. Sigma Nu. Democrat. Roman Cath. Home: 605 Park Av New York City NY 10021 Office: 745 Fifth Av New York City NY 10022

CALLAWAY, JASPER LAMAR, physician; b. Cooper, Ala., Apr. 5, 1911; s. Lucien Adkin and Dora Belle (Robinson) C.; B.S., U. Ala., 1935; M.D., Duke, 1932; m. Catherine Dater Van Blarcom, Oct. 11, 1941; children—Frederick, Catharine, Elizabeth. Intern, Duke Hosp., Durham, N.C., 1933-35, dermatologist, chief dermatology service, 1937—, prof. medicine, specializing dermatology, 1937—, James B. Duke prof. dermatology, 1967—; cons. USPHS, VA, secretary of war; national consultant dermatology surgeon gen. USAF; mem. spl. med. adv. group to VA, Washington. Diplomate Am. Bd. Dermatology and Syphilogy (president 1958-59). Fellow A.C.P.; mem. National Adv. Serology Council, American Academy Dermatology (pres. 1971, dir.), So. Med. Assn. (past chmn. dermatology and syphilology), Southeastern Dermatology Assn. (pres. 1950), Am. Medical Assn. (chairman sect. dermatology 1962-63), N.C. Med. Soc. (chmn. sect. dermatology 1968), Am. Derm. Assn. (secretary 1953, president 1958-59), Society of Investigative Dermatology (president 1956), Baltimore-Washington Dermatol. Society, Sigma Xi, Theta Kappa Psi, Delta Sigma Phi, Alpha Omega Alpha. Co-author: Manual of Clinical Mycology, 1971; Dermatology for Students, 1961. Editorial bd. Archives of Dermatology and Syphilology, Medicine, Jour. Investigative Dermatology. Home: 828 Anderson St Durham NC 27706

CALLAWAY, JOSEPH, educator; b. Hackensack, N.J., July 1, 1931; s. Joseph and Sybil Leigh (Mock) C.; B.S., William and Mary Coll., 1951; M.A., Princeton, 1953, Ph.D., 1956; m. Mary Louise Eldred Morrison, July 30, 1949; children—Joseph A., Paul E., Jessie S. Asst. prof. U. Miami (Fla.), 1954-60, asso. prof., 1960-64; prof. U. Cal. at Riverside, 1964-67; prof. physics La. State U., Baton Rouge, 1967—, chmn. physics dept., 1970—; cons. Philco-Ford Corp., 1961-67. Fellow Am. Phys. Soc.; mem. Phi Beta Kappa. Author: Energy Band Theory, 1964; also articles. Home: 16250 Phillip Hickey Baton Rouge LA 70808

CALLAWAY, LLEWELLYN LINK, Jr., former mag. pub.; b. Virginia City, Mont., Sept. 12, 1907; s. Llewellyn Link and Ellen N. (Badger) C.; A.B., Dartmouth, 1930; M.B.A., Harvard, 1932; m. Helene Anderson, Oct. 10, 1936; children—Peter Anderson, Elizabeth Woodson. With Conde Nast Publs., 1932-37; with Time Inc., 1937- 63, advt. dir. Fortune, 1954-59, advt. dir. Sports Illus., 1959-63; former pub. Newsweek mag.; mem. bd. dirs. Washington Post Co. Acting adminstr. forest products div. WPB, 1945; mem. bd. dirs. Near East Found. Pres. Citizens Planning Assn., Westport, Conn., 1961, Westport Commuters Assn., 1959. Mem. Westport Republican Town Com., 1962—. Trustee, Mt. Holyoke Coll. Served with USNR, 1943-45. Mem. Mil. Order World Wars, Harvard Bus. Sch. Assn. (pres. 1968-69), Casque and Gauntlet, Psi Upsilon. Conglist. Clubs: Harvard, University (N.Y.C.). Home: 923 Fifth Av New York City NY 10021

CALLAWAY, PAUL SMITH, organist; b. Atlanta, Ill., Aug. 16, 1909; s. Ralph Vernon and Mattie (Cubbage) C.; student Westminster Coll., Fulton, Mo., 1927-29, Mus.D. (hon.), 1959; Mus.D. (hon.), Washington Coll., Chestertown, Md., 1967. Organist, choirmaster St. Thomas Chapel, N.Y., 1930-35, St. Mark's Ch., Grand Rapids, Mich., 1935-39, Washington Cathedral, 1939—; cond. Cathedral Choral Soc., Washington, 1942—; mem. faculty Peabody Conservatory, Balt., 1953-57, Coll. Ch. Musicians, Washington, 1962-69. Berkshire Music Center, Tanglewood, Mass., 1965-67, Blossom Music Center, 1968; condr. Opera Soc. Washington, 1956—, Lake George Opera Festival, 1967—. Served AUS, 1942-46. Fellow Am. Guild Organists; mem. Lit. Soc. Wash. Episcopalian. Clubs: Cosmos, City Tavern Assn. (Washington); St. Wilfred (N.Y.C.). Composer: An Hymne of Heavenley Love, 1935; The Office of the Holy Communion, 1945; Hark! The Glad Sound!, 1946; O Saving Victim, 1947. Home: 2230 Decatur Pl NW Washington DC 20008 Office: Washington Cathedral Mount St Alban Washington DC 20016

CALLAWAY, SAMUEL RODGER, banker; b. N.Y.C., Apr. 25, 1914; s. Trowbridge and Elsie (McIntosh) C.; grad. St. Paul's Sch., 1932; A.B., Harvard, 1936; m. Dorothy Harding, Apr. 24, 1937; children—Joan (Mrs. Charles W. Pratt), Samuel Rodger, Dorothy (Mrs. Michael Belknap). With Morgan Guaranty Trust Co., N.Y.C., 1936—, exec. v.p., 1968—. Pres. St. Timothy's Sch., 1960-65, East Woods Sch., 1952-56; treas. United Hosp. Fund N.Y. Trustee N.Y. Pub. Library, St. Paul's Sch.; treas., trustee Julliard Mus. Found. Served with USN, 1945. Clubs: Piping Rock (Locust Valley, N.Y.): Huntington (N.Y.) Country: Shinnecock Hills Golf (South Hampton, N.Y.); Cold Spring Harbor Beach. Home: White Hill Rd Cold Spring Harbor NY 11724 Office: 23 Wall St New York City NY 10015

CALLAWAY, TROWBRIDGE, Jr., retired sugar co. exec.; b. N.Y.C., Feb. 25, 1912; s. Trowbridge and Elsie McI. (Kellogg) C.; student Gunnery Sch., Washington, Conn., 1929-32; diploma Harvard, 1932-33; m. Ruth E. Tooker, June 25, 1935 (div.); m. 2d, Diana Stokes, Sept. 21, 1957; children—Trowbridge III, Norman Tooker, Tyler. Gen. brokerage and investment tng. George H. Farrington & Co., Farrington & Coleman & Co., N.Y.C., 1934-36; with research dept. Clark Dodge & Co., 1936-42; mem. investment adv. dept. Brown Bros. Harriman & Co. 1942-52; dir. N.Am. Sugar Industries, Inc. (formerly Cuban American Sugar Co.), 1944-71, sec., 1952-64, treas., 1952-70, v.p., 1964-70, past mem. exec. com.; cons. in field. Club: Harvard (N.Y.C.). Address: Quogo Neck Lane Quogue NY 11959

CALLAWAY, WILLIAM HOWARD, govt. ofcl.; b. Washington, Ga., Jan. 23, 1914; s. Abner M. and Katie Lou (Echols) C.; grad. Young Harris Coll., 1933; night studies Southeastern U., Am. U., Washington; B.S., American University, 1956; married to Catherine Sibley, December 4, 1938; children—Janis Carole, William Howard.

Various positions with business firms, Washington, 1933; tchr. John Mason Sch., Mystic, Conn., 1933-34; desk clk. Washington Pub. Library, 1934-35; graphotype operator Treasury Dept., V.A., 1935; with Rural Electrification Adminstrn. since 1935, field auditor, 1937-41, field rep. and regional head applications and loans div., 1941-52, area dir. S.E. area, 1952-53, became regional dir., so. region, 1953, spl. asst. program operations, 1954-61, area dir. N.E. area electric program, 1961-. Served from pvt. to 1st lt. U.S. Army, 1943-45. Baptist. Home: 5722 Arlington Blvd Arlington, VA 22204. Office: care Rural Electrification Administration Washington DC 20250

CALLEN, EARL ROBERT, educator, physicist; b. Phila., Aug. 28, 1925; s. Abraham and Mildred (Goldfarb) C.; A.B., U. Pa., 1948, M.A., 1951; Ph.D., Mass. Inst. Tech., 1954; m. Anita Blatt, Dec. 16, 1949; children—Liza, Melany, Jane, Jody. Physicist, Nat. Security Agy., 1955-59; physicist U.S. Naval Ordnance Labs., Silver Spring, Md., 1959-68; research prof. Catholic U., 1961-67; prof. physics Am. U., 1968—. Fellow Am. Phys. Soc., Washington Philos. Soc. Contbr. chpt. to Reinhold Ency. of Physics, 1966. Research on temperature dependence of magnetic anisotropy and magnetostriction; statis. mechanics of ferro and antiferromagnetism; metal semiconductor transitions. Home: 9110 LeVelle Ct Chevy Chase MD 20015 Office: Am U Dept Physics Washington DC 20016

CALLEN, HERBERT BERNARD, educator; b. Phila., July 1, 1919; s. Abraham and Mildred (Goldfarb) C.; B.S. in Edn., Temple U., 1941, M.A., 1942; Ph.D., Mass. Inst. Tech., 1948; m. Sara Smith, Jan. 21, 1945; children—Jill, Jed. With Manhattan Project, N.Y.C., 1944-45; with Guided Missile Project, Princeton, 1945; mem. faculty physics dept. U. Pa., Phila., 1948—, prof., 1956—; cons. Sperry Rand Univac, 1950—. Mem. adv. com. physics NSF, 1966-69; chmn., 1969; mem. adv. com. Nat. Magnet Lab., 1965-68, chmn., 1968. Vice chmn. Am. Profs. for Peace in Middle East, 1970—. Bd. dirs. Jewish Community Relations Council Phila. Fellow Am. Phys. Soc. (council, officer div. solid state physics). Author: Thermodynamics, 1960; also articles. Home: 2136 St James Pl Philadelphia PA 19103

CALLENDER, JOHN HANCOCK, architect; b. Kansas City, Mo., Jan. 18, 1908; s. Alonzo Lee and Lola (Hancock) C.; B.A., Yale, 1928, student Sch. Architecture, 1928-30; B.Arch., N.Y.U., 1939; m. Mary Carnwath, Aug. 5, 1933; 1 dau., Janet. Research methods and materials low-cost housing John B. Pierce Found., N.Y.C., 1931-43; pvt. practice architecture, specializing in residences, 1945—; faculty Columbia, 1953-54, Princeton, 1954-57, Pratt Inst., 1954—, asso. prof., 1958-63, prof., 1963—; cons. architect for Nat. Housing Agency, Staff Army Engrs., Manhattan project, Columbia, 1943-45. Vis. prof. Cheng Kung U., Taiwan, China, 1967-68. Author: Before You Buy a House, 1953; (with others) Curtain Walls of Stainless Steel, 1955. Editor-in-chief: Time-Saver Standards, a Handbook of Architectural Design, 1966. Contbr. popular mags., profl. publs. Home: 182 Emerson Pl Brooklyn NY 11205 Office: 170 Fifth Av New York City NY 10010

CALLERY, FRANCIS ANTHONY, investments; b. Pitts., Aug. 14, 1898; s. James Dawson and Marcella (Howley) C.; prep. edn., Newman Sch., Hackensack, N.J., 1912- 16; war diploma, Princeton, 1920; m. Virginia R. Annan, Dec. 6, 1924; children—Roberdeau (Mrs. Arthur B. DuBois), Joanne Dawson (Mrs. T. P. Heffelfiner II), James; m. 2d, Holly Simonds. Various positions Marland Oil Co., Ponca City, Okla., 1919-21, Ladenburg, Thalmann & Co., N.Y.C., 1921-23, 25-32, Guinness, Mahon & Co., London, Eng., 1923-24, Mellon Nat. Bank, Pitts., 1924-25; partner Emanuel & Co., N.Y.C., 1932-41; v.p., dir. Consol. Vultee Aircraft Corp., San Diego, 1942-46; partner Lehman Bros., Investment bankers, 1946-58, oil producer, Houston, 1944—. Clubs: University, Seawanhaka Corinthian Yacht, Quiet Birdmen, Brook, Union, Sky (N.Y.C.); Bayou, Ramada (Houston). Home: 133 E 64th St New York City NY 10021 Office: 375 Park Av New York City NY 10022 also First City Nat Bank Bldg Houston TX 77002

CALLERY, MARY, sculptor; b. N.Y.C., June 19, 1903; d. James Dawson and Julia (Welch) Callery; student Art Students League, 1924-28; m. Frederic R. Coudert, Jr., June 23, 1923; 1 dau., Caroline (Mrs. Simon Boosey) (dec.); m. 2d, Carlo Frua de Angeli, May 7, 1934. One-man shows art Curt Valentin Gallery, 1944, 47, 50, 52, 55, Arts Club, Chgo., 1945, Galerie Mai. Paris, 1949, Margaret Brown Gallery, 1951, Galerie Cahiers d'Art, Paris, 1954, B.C. Holland Gallery, Chicago, Illinois, 1968, Daniel Morris Gallery, Detroit, Michigan, 1968, 69; also exhbn. Knoedler & Co., 1957, 61, 62-64; commns. include Laughlin Children's Center, Sewickley, Pa., Internat. Exposition, Brussels, 1958; public commns. include 3 hanging birds, also portrait heads, Pitts.; grille in pub. sch., N.Y.C.; relief Bklyn. Ct. House; sculpture arch Lincoln Center Opera; work rep. Mus. Modern Art, Mus. Fine Arts Toledo, Mus. Fine Arts Cin., Mus. Fine Arts San Francisco, Addison Gallery, Andover, Atheneum, Hartford, Mus. Fine Arts, Richmond, Va., also numerous pvt. collections. Address: 168 E 68th St New York City NY 10021

CALLIARI, DAVID FRANCIS, mfr.; b. Pitts., Feb. 15, 1925; s. Frank and Emma (Maccani) C.; B.S. cum laude, Rider Coll., 1949; m. Ida Zafarana, Aug. 28, 1948; children—Anne, David. Accountant Kearney Trecker Corp., Plainfield, N.J., 1950; sr. auditor Haskins & Sells, N.Y.C., 1951-54; treas. Permacel div. Johnson & Johnson, New Brunswick, N.J., 1954-68; v.p. finance, treas., dir. Raybestos-Manhattan, Inc., Bridgeport, Conn., 1968—. Mem. Middlesex Bd. Edn., 1960-66, pres., 1963. Bd. dirs. Parents and Friends of Mentally Retarded, Bridgeport, 1969—, Raritan Valley chpt. Nat. Assn. Retarded Children, 1965-68. Served with USNR, 1943-46. Club: Rotary (Bridgeport). Home: 5380 Congress St Fairfield CT 06430 Office: PO Box 9140 205 Middle St Bridgeport CT 06603

CALLICUTT, LAURIE TIMMONS, educator; b. Athens, Tex., Oct. 2, 1907; s. Sidney Archer and Harrie (Watts) C.; A.B., Southwest State Coll., San Marcos, 1928; M.A., U. Tex., Austin, 1934, Ph.D., 1942; m. Dorothy Gretta Hinds, June 22, 1938; children—Anne Kathryn, Richard Lawrence. Tchr. pub. schs., McAllen, Tex., 1927-35, Salinas, P.R., 1935-36; instr. U. P.R., 1936-40; faculty U. Houston, 1946—, prof., 1949—, chmn. dept. psychology, 1950-68; cons., adv. bd. Women's Inst. of Houston. Mem. com. So. Regional Edn. Bd., Atlanta. Mem. Mil. Order World Wars (past comdr. Houston), Mental Health Assn., Houston and Harris County (past pres.), Am. Southwestern, Tex. psychol. assns., Tex. Assn. Mental Health. Episcopalian. Contbr. articles profl. publs. Home: 8903 S Rice Av Houston TX 77035

CALLIHAN, E. L., educator; b. Lockhart, Tex., Dec. 6, 1903; s. Jefferson Davis and Elizabeth (Horner) C.; B.J., U. of Tex., 1929; M.S.J., Northwestern U., 1939; m. Lillian Edwards, Nov. 28, 1928. Free lance writer, editor and reporter Tex. newspapers, 1923-30; sports editor. Sherman (Tex.) Daily Democrat, 1930-32; publicity writer, Austin Coll., 1931-32; publicity dir., instr. journalism, Ft. Worth (Tex.) Pub. Schs., 1933-40; prof. journalism, Drake U., 1940-45; prof. journalism, univ. news bur. dir., Baylor U., 1945-46; chmn. dept. journalism, So. Methodist U., 1946—. Mem. Assn. for Edn. in Journalism, Southwestern Journalism Congress, Am. Soc. Journalism Sch. Aminstrs., Sigma Delta Chi, Key Club, Kappa Tau Alpha (nat. pres). Author: Grammar for Journalists, 1957, rev. edit., 1969. Co-author: Exercises and Tests for Journalists, 1970; Instructor's Manual of Corrected Exercises, 1970. Editor: Drake Creative Awards anthologies, 1940-45. Contbr. publs. in field. Home: Rancho Poquito Rt 2 Mesquite TX 75149 Office: Southern Methodist U Dallas TX 75222

CALLIS, ROBERT, educator; b. Grand Tower, Ill., June 1, 1920; s. Marion J. and Edith (Todd) C.; B.Ed., So. Ill. U., 1942; M.A., U. Minn., 1946, Ph.D., 1948; m. Thelma Lewis, Oct. 23, 1942; children—Ronald W., Steven M. Mem. faculty U. Mo., 1948—, prof. edn., 1955—, dean extra divisional adminstrn., 1964-69. Served with USNR, 1942-46. Fellow Am. Psychol. Assn.; mem. Am. Coll. Personnel Assn. (pres. 1959-60), Am. Personnel and Guidance Assn. Author: A Casebook of Counseling, 1955; Minnesota Teacher Attitude Inventory, 1951; Missouri College English Test, 1965; Stanford Achievement Test, High School Level, 1966. Editor Jour. Coll. Student personne, 1964-70. Home: 1548 Towne Dr Columbia MO 65201

CALLIS, THEODORE EDWIN, advt. exec.; b. Kokomo, Ind., Aug. 27, 1908; s. Theodore Orner and Genevieve (Baker) C.; A.B., DePauw U., 1930; m. Kathryn Homan, July 9, 1932 (dec. Jan. 1955); children—Theodore H., William J., Deborah J., Mary K.; m. 2d, Virginia Rae Gould, May 10, 1956. With The Wall Street Jour., N.Y.C., 1930-62, advt. mgr., 1945-48, advt. dir. 1948-62; mem. exec. com., gen. sales mgr. Dow Jones & Co., Inc., N.Y.C., 1962-65, v.p., 1965-69, cons., 1969—; treas. dir. Dow Jones-Irwin, 1966-69, dir., 1969-71. Mem. Phi Gamma Delta, Alpha Delta Sigma. Club: Manhasset Bay Yacht. Home: 123 Manhasset Woods Rd Manhasset NY 11030 Office: 30 Broad St New York City NY 10004

CALLISEN, STERLING ADOLPH, educator; b. N.Y.C., Mar. 30, 1899; s. Adolph W. and Dora (Sterling) C.; A.B., Princeton, 1920; M.A., Harvard, 1934, Ph.D., 1936; m. Sara T. Limerick, Dec. 26, 1938; childrenJosephine S., Mary T. Staff, N.Y. Aquarium, 1920-22; instr. prep. sch., 1922-25, 1927-32; hunter, Kenya, 1925-27; asst. fine arts Harvard, 1934-36; asst. prof. Rochester U., 1936-41; asso. dean Wesleyan U., 1945-49; dean edn. Met. Mus., 1949-59; pres. Parsons Sch. Design, 1959-64, pres. emeritus, 1964- ; prof. art history Pace Coll., 1964-. Trustee Scarsdale Adult School, Met. Ednl. TV Assn., Westchester Orch. Soc., Scarsdale Pub. Library; chmn. Dance in Edn. Fund. Served USN, World War I, chief evaluation officer, OSS, World War II., Mem. Sch. Art League (pres.), Coll. Art Assn., Scarsdale Art Assn., Am. Archtl. Historians, Mus. Assn. Clubs: Scarsdale Golf; Century Assn. (N.Y.C.); Cosmos (Washington); Manursing Island (Rye, N.Y.). Home: 10 Ridgecrest W Scarsdale, NY 10583. Office: 41 Park Row New York City NY 10038

CALLISON, CHARLES HUGH, conservation orgn. exec.; b. Lousana, Alta., Can., Nov. 6, 1913; s. Guy A. and Dorinda (Stuart) C; came to U.S., 1918, naturalized, 1937; B. Journalism, U. Mo., 1937; m. Amelia D. Ferguson, June 7, 1951; children—Charles Stuart, Joyce Marie (Mrs. Robert Melville), Karen Sue, Bettye Ruth (Mrs. Dennis Bradford). Editor, Garnett (Kan.) Rev., 1937-38, Boonville (Mo.) Advertiser, 1938-41; editor, information div. chief Mo. Conservation Commn., 1941-46; exec. sec. Conservation Fedn. Mo., 1947-51; asst. conservation dir., then conservation dir. Nat. Wildlife Fedn., 1951-60; asst. to pres. Nat. Audubon Soc., 1960-66, exec. v.p., 1967—. Chmn. Nat. Resources Council Am., 1957-59; mem. organizing and exec. coms. 5th World Forestry Congress, 1960; chmn. legislative com. Internat. Assn. Game, Fish and Conservation Commrs., 1955-59; mem. Fed. Water Pollution Control Adv. Bd., 1961-64; mem. of Pres.-Elect's Task Force on Resources and Environment, 1968; mem. N.Y. State Environmental Bd., 1970—. Village trustee, 1969-71. Mem. Canadian Audubon Soc. (bd. dirs. 1967-69), Wildlife Soc., Sierra Club, Wilderness Soc., Am. Ornithologists Union, Wilson Ornithol. Soc., Sigma Delta Chi, Kappa Tau Alpha. Democrat. Mem. Reformed Ch. Am. Club: Nat. Press (Washington). Author: Man and Wildlife in Missouri, 1952. Editor: America's Natural Resources, rev. edit., 1967. Home: 43 S Calumet Av Hastings-on-Hudson NY 10706 Office: 950 3d Av New York City NY 10022

CALLISON, MASTON KENNERLY, coll. dean, physician; b. Knoxville, Tenn., Jan. 14, 1917; s. John Clairborne and Eunice (Ogle) C.; B.S., U. Tenn., 1937, M.D., 1939; certificate U. Pa. Grad. Sch. Medicine; m. Harriett Meier, Jan. 15, 1943; children—Susan, John, Bettye Jeanne. Intern, Knoxville Gen. Hosp.; asst. resident John Gaston Hosp., Memphis, 1942-43, resident, 1943-44; instr. to asso. prof. dept. medicine U. Tenn., 1947-58, dean Coll. Medicine, prof. medicine, 1958-70, clin. prof. medicine, 1970—. Bd. dirs. Soc. Crippled Children and Adults. Mem. Mayor's Commn. on Drug Abuse. Served from lt. to capt., AUS, 1944-47. Fellow A.C.P.; mem. Assn. Am. Med. Colls., A.M.A., Tenn. State (Distinguished Service award 1970), Shelby County, Memphis med. socs., Am. Heart Assn., Am. Rheumatism Assn., Sigma Xi, Alpha Omega Alpha, Kappa Sigma, Phi Chi. Home: 4206 Longleaf Dr Memphis TN 38117

CALLMER, JAMES PETER, architect; b. Aurora, Ill., May 6, 1919; s. Carl L. and Anna (Hegg) C.; B.S. in Architecture, U. Ill., 1942; m. Sally-Lee Maxwell Young, Mar. 21, 1944; children—Melinda-Lee, Sally Susanne, Shelley Ann. Architect with Justement, Elam, Callmer & Kidd, Washington, 1956-66, Justement & Callmer, Washington, 1966-68, Callmer & Milstead, Washington, 1968—; prin. works include Nat. Guard Meml. Bldg., Washington, Sibley Meml. Hosp., Washington, Pan Am. Health Orgn., Washington, master plan for Judiciary Sq., Washington. Bd. govs. Washington Bldg. Congress, 1968-71; mem. Bd. Examiners and Registrars Architects Washington, 1970—; chmn. design and decoration com. 1969 Inaugural Com. Mem. panel arbitrators Am. Arbitration Assn.; past pres. Western Bethesda Community Planning Assn. Served to lt. comdr. USNR, 1942-46. Mem. A.I.A. (pres. Washington Met. chpt. 1968), Alpha Chi Rho (v.p. Phi Kappa chpt. 1941). Clubs: Cosmos (Washington); Columbia Country (Bethesda). Home: 5625 Huntington Pky Bethesda MD 20014 Office: 2011 K St NW Washington DC 20006

CALLOWAY, AUGUSTUS JAMES, Jr. utilities exec.; b. Texarkana, Tex., June 24, 1908; s. Augustus James and Alice Ann (Hawkins) C.; A.B., U. Mich., 1936; postgrad. Washington and Jefferson U., 1943-44; m. Mary Frances Billups, May 31, 1937; children—Augustus James III, Brian Joseph. Letter carrier Fed. Govt., 1936-37; investigator Welfare Dept., Detroit, 1938-40; comml. rep. Mich. Bell Tel. Co., Detroit, 1940-43, 46-50, mgr. pub. office, 1950-55, 57-61, staff rep. comml. personnel, 1955-57, mgr. bus. office, 1961-62, mgr. pub. relations, 1962-63, asst. mgr. customer relations, 1963-64, mgr. customer relations, 1964-67, dir. community affairs, 1967—. Mem. Trade Union Leadership Council, 1962—. Bd. dirs. San Antoine YMCA, 1958-59, chmn. com. mgmt., 1958-60; chmn. Ambassador Bridge dist. Boy Scouts Am., 1961-63; mem. exec. com. Family Services Met. Detroit, 1964—; pres. Mich. United Fund, 1965—; mem. Detroit Community Council, 1951-52, pres., 1953-55, mem. exec. com., 1954-56; mem. Detroit Council Polit. Edn., 1965—. Trustee Mich Coll. Osteo. Medicine, Burton Mercy Hosp.; bd. dirs. Delta Sigma Theta Home for Girls; chmn. bd. govs. Wayne State U. Served with USAAF, 1943-45. Mem. Inst. Black Elected Ofcls., Booker T. Washington Bus. Assn (pres. 1957-58), Alpha Phi Alpha. Democrat. Optimist. Home: 4075 W Outer Dr Detroit MI 48221 Office: Mich Bell Tel Co 1365 Cass Av Detroit MI 48226

CALLOWAY, CABELL CAB, singer, bandleader; b. Rochester, N.Y., Dec. 24, 1907. Leader, Alabamians, Chgo., 1928, N.Y.C., 1929; leader Missourians, 1929, Cab Calloway Band, 1930—; recorded Minnie the Moocher, 1931; appeared motion picture Singing Kid, Big Broadcast of 1933, Stormy Weather, Sensations of 1945; toured U.S., Europe with Porgy and Bess, 1952-54, also appeared in Hello Dolly with Pearl Bailey; appeared night clubs with quartet, 1954—. Address: 1619 Broadway New York City NY 10019*

CALLOWAY, EARL, tenor, choral dir., music columnist; b. Birmingham, Ala.; s. James and Mary Magdalene (Williams) C.; student Oakwood Coll., 1946-47; Mus. B. in Voice, Chgo. Mus. Coll.; student Roosevelt U. Appeared recitals, oratorio, guest appearances, prin. Am. cities; soloist, Japan, Korea, 1952-53; music critic Chgo. Courier, 1960—; fine arts editor Asso. Negro Press, 1960—; music editor Chgo. Defender, 1964—; fine arts editor Negro Press Internat., 1964—. Tchr., Reed Elementary Sch., Chgo.; founder, dir. Philharmonic Youth Choir, Shiloh Oratorio Soc.; syndicated columnist; dir. radio program Artists' Circle, radio sta. WXFM, Chgo., 1966-67. Founder, dir. Shiloh Pathfinder Youth Club, Chgo., 1954-57. Served with AUS, 1951-53. Mem. Oakwood Coll. Nat. Alumni Assn. (pres. Chgo. chpt. 1958-63, 64—, also regional v.p.), Chgo. Jr. C. of C. (chmn. religion in Am. life program 1960-62), Phi Mu Alpha. Mem. Seventh Day Adventist Ch. (chmn. music dept.). Club: R. Nathaniel Dett Music. Home: 6527 S Green St Chicago IL 60621 Office: Chgo Daily Defender 2400 S Michigan Av Chicago IL 606166

CALLOWAY, JEAN MITCHENER, educator, mathematician; b. Indianola, Miss., Dec. 18, 1923; s. James Earl and Mittie Lou (Mitchener) C.; B.A. with high honors, Millsaps Coll., 1944; A.M., U. Pa., 1949, Ph.D., 1952; m. Anne Marie Whitney, June 21, 1952; children—Nancy Lou, Catherine Anne. With Millsaps Coll., 1944, McCallie Sch., Chattanooga, 1944-47, U. Pa., 1947-52; from asst. prof. to asso. prof., acting chmn. dept. Carleton Coll., 1952-60; Olney prof. math., chmn. dept. Kalamazoo Coll., 1960—. Mem. sch. math. study group Inst. Advanced Study, 1959; math. workshop Ednl. Services, Inc., Mombasa, Kenya, 1965. Mem. Am. Math. Soc., Math. Assn. Am. (chmn. Mich. sect. 1963-64), Am. Assn. U. Profs. (pres. Kalamazoo Coll. chpt. 1964-65), Sigma Xi. Author: Fundamentals of Modern Mathematics, 1964. Home: 1341 Bunker Hill Dr Kalamazoo MI 49009

CALMAN, ROBERT FREDERICK, diversified industry exec.; b. Mineola, N.Y., May 14, 1932; s. William Arthur and Ida (Alberswerth) C.; B.A., Yale, 1954; M.S., Mass. Inst. Tech., 1967; m. Susan Jean Raphael, June 20, 1959; children—Andrew Frederick, Camille, Matthew Alexander. With Chase Manhattan Bank, N.Y.C., 1954-61, asst. treas., 1961; with Mobil Oil Corp., N.Y.C., 1961-70, treas. N.Am. div., 1964-68, treas. Internat. div., 1968-69; v.p. finance, treas. Internat. Utilities Corp., Phila., 1970—; lectr. N.Y.U., 1968-69. Trustee Portledge Sch., Locust Valley, N.Y.; bd. govs. Soc. Alfred P. Sloan Fellows, Mass. Inst. Tech. Served to 1st lt., arty., U.S. Army, 1955-57. Recipient E.P. Brooks prize Mass. Inst. Tech., 1967. Mem. Am. Petroleum Inst. (chmn. financial research com.), Phi Beta Kappa. Republican. Presbyn. Author: Linear Programming and Cash Management/ Cash Alpha, 1968. Home: 212 Avon Rd Haverford PA 19041 Office: 1500 Walnut St Philadelphia PA 19102

CALMER, NED, author, journalist; b. Chgo., July 16, 1907; s. Henry Edgar and May (Regan) C.; student U. Va., 1930; m. Priscilla A. Hatch, Mar. 1929; 1 dau., Alden; m. 2d, Carol Church, Aug. 1957; 1 son, Regan. Reporter, fgn. corr. Chgo. Tribune and N.Y. Herald-Tribune, 1927-34; fgn. news editor in N.Y. for Agence Havas, France, 1934-40; news editor, broadcaster C.B.S., 1940-67; war corr. with U.S. armed forces, Eng., France, Belgium, Germany, Holland, Italy, 1944-45; Mediterranean corr., 1951-53. Clubs: Players; Rockaway Hunting. Author: Beyond the Street, 1934; When Night Descends, 1936; The Strange Land, 1950; All the Summer Days, 1961; The Anchorman, 1970. Home and office: 125 Ocean Av Lawrence NY 11559

CALS, JOSEPH MARIA LAURENS THEO, minister of state of The Netherlands; b. Roermond, Netherlands, July 18, 1914; s. Jacques and Elise (Smeets) C.; LL.D., U. Nijmegen, 1940; m. Geertruide Catrien van der Heijden, May 7, 1941; children—Gidi, Noud, Maria, Jos, Marga. Engaged as lawyer, also tchr. economy and policy, 1940; chmn. Netherlands Counsel for Mining Industry, 1948-50; mem. Parliament, 1948-50, 63-65; sec. of state for edn., arts and scis., 1950-52; minister edn., arts and scis., 1952-63; prime minister, 1965- 66; minister of state, 1966—. Decorated grand cross Order Oranje-Nassau, numerous others. Address: van Ouwenlaan 4 The Hague Netherlands

CALVER, JAMES LEWIS, geologist; b. Pontiac, Mich., June 15, 1913; s. William and Emma Catherine (Stever) C.; A.B., U. Mich., 1936, M.S., 1938, Ph.D., 1941; m. Lela M. Mynatt, Apr. 11, 1945 (dec. Oct. 1969); children—James Stevan, Lewis Edward; m. 2d, Evelyn Slaven Eddy, June 13, 1970. Instr. geology U. Wichita, 1940-41; asst. prof. U. Mo., 1941-42; geologist TVA, 1942-47, Fla. Geol. Survey, 1947-57; commr. mineral resources, also state geologist, Va., 1957—. Mem. adv. com. on geology Commonwealth of Va. Fellow Geol. Soc. Am.; mem. Geol. Soc. Washington, Am. Am. Inst. Mining Engrs., Am. Assn. Petroleum Geologists, Assn. Am. State Geologists, Am. Mineral. Soc., Am. Ceramic Soc., Am. Water Works Assn., Appalachian Geol. Soc., Va. Acad. Sci., Am. Geophys. Union, Am. Mining Congress, Am. Inst. Profl. Geologists, Sigma Xi. Author numerous articles in field. field. Home: 1614 Oxford Rd Charlottesville VA 22903 Office: PO Box 3667 Charlottesville VA 22903

CALVERT, JACK GEORGE, educator; b. Inglewood, Cal., May 9, 1923; s. John George and Emma (Eschstruth) C.; B.S. in Chemistry, U. Cal. at Los Angeles, 1944, Ph.D., 1949; m. Doris Arlene Breimon, Nov. 8, 1946; children—Richard John, Mark Steven. Mem. faculty Ohio State U., 1950—, prof. chemistry, 1960—, chmn. dept., 1964-68; spl. research photochemistry, reaction kinetics, environmental chemistry, mechanisms free radical reactions. Cons. air pollution tng. com. USPHS, 1964-66; mem. Nat. Air Pollution Control Manpower Devel. Com., 1966-69, chmn. 1968-69; mem. air pollution control research grants com. Environmental Protection Agy., 1970—, chmn., 1971—; chmn. air pollution com. Conservaion Found., 1968- 70; bd. dirs. Gordon Research Confs., 1969—. Served to ensign USNR, 1944 -46. Named Honor Prof. of Year, Coll. Arts and Scis., Ohio State U., 1957, recipient Alumni award distinguished teaching, 1961. Fellow Nat. Research Council Can., 1949. Fellow Ohio Acad. Sci., Am. Inst. Chemists; mem. Am. Chem. Soc., Am. Assn. U. Profs., Air Pollution Control Assn., Phi Beta Kappa, Sigma Xi, Pi Mu Epsilon, Phi Lambda Upsilon, Alpha Chi Sigma. Author: (with J. N. Pitts, Jr.) Photochemistry, 1966; also articles. Home: 2535 McVey Blvd W Worthington OH 43085 Office: 140 W 18th Av Columbus OH 43210

CALVERT, JAMES FRANCIS, naval officer; b. Cleve., Sept. 8, 1920; s. Charles Spence and Grace (Gholson) C.; student Oberlin Coll., 1937-39, D. Sc. (hon.), 1960; B.S., in Elec. Engring., 1937-39; D.Sc. (hon.), 1960; B.S. in Elec. Engring., U.S. Naval Acad., 1942; m. Nancy Ridgeway King, Aug. 9, 1942 (dec. Dec. 1965); children—James, Margaret, Charles; m. 2d, Margaretta Harrison Battle, Apr. 8, 1968. Commnd. ensign U.S. Navy, 1942, advanced through grades to vice-adm., 1970; served in submarines, PTO, World War II; comdr. diesel submarine U.S.S. Trigger, 1952-55, nuclear power submarine U.S.S. Skate, 1956-59; U.S.S. Skate engaged in polar operations, 1958, 59, 1st submarine to break through ice and surface in Arctic Ocean, 1958, 1st ship to surface in Arctic Ocean, 1958, 1st ship to surface at North Pole, 1959; dir. politico-mil. policy Navy Dept., 1965-67; comdr. Cruiser-Destroyer Flotilla Eight, 1967-68; supt. U.S. Naval Acad., Annapolis, Md., 1968—. Decorated Silver Star (2), Legion of Merit (4), Bronze Star (2), Navy Commendation ribbon, Dept. Def. Commendation medal; French Govt. Merite Maritime. Mem. U.S. Naval Inst. (v.p.). Author: Surface at the Pole, 1960; A Promise to Your Country, 1961; The Naval Profession, 1965. Home: Supt's House US Naval Acad Annapolis MD 21402 Office: Supt US Naval Acad Annapolis MD 21402

CALVERT, JAMES HENRY, bus. exec., rancher; b. Widnes, Eng., Oct. 22, 1898; s. Albert Ellis and Annie (Spencer) C.; student Wade Deacon Sch., Widnes; m. Carolyn Rice, Sept. 29, 1923; childrenJames Spencer, David Rice, Jonathan, Richard. Mdse. mgr. C.F. Hovey Co., Boston, 1925-29; mdse. mgr. Jordan Marsh Company, 1930-32; chmn. Joske Bros. Co., dept. store, San Antonio, Tex., 1932-. Trustee San Antonio Med. Found., Meth. Hosp., Southwest Research Found. Trinity U. Methodist. Home: 326 Park Dr San Antonio TX 78212 Office: 100-20 Alamo Plaza San Antonio TX 78205

CALVERT, ROBERT S., state ofcl.; b. Tex., Apr. 27, 1892; s. Cleon H. and Sallie (Neff) C.; student Howard Payne Coll., 1909; m. Josie Moody, Mar. 24, 1920; 1 dau., Josephine (Mrs. Leonard Baker). Asst. cashier 1st Nat. Bank Sweetwater (Tex.), 1917-30; statistician for state comptroller Tex., Austin, 1930-44, chief clk., 1944-49; state comptroller Tex., Austin, 1949—. Bd. dirs. Fedn. Tax Adminstrs. Served with U.S. Army, World War I. Named Man of Year, Howard Payne Coll., 1957. Mem. Am. Legion, V.F.W., S.A.R., Sons Confederacy, Nat. Assn. State Auditors, Comptrollers and Treasurers, Nat. Tax Assn., Austin C. of C. Mem. Christian Ch. Mason, Lion. Home: 2115 Enfield Rd Austin TX 78703 Office: State Capitol Austin TX 78711

CALVERT, ROBERT WILBURN, judge; b. nr. Pulaski, Tenn., Feb. 22, 1905; s. Porter and Maud (Richardson) C.; LL.B., U. Tex., 1931; m. Frances Freeland, June 6, 1933 (div. 1958); children—Carolyn, James Porter; m. 2d, Corinne Lundgren, Jan. 26, 1962. Admitted to Tex. bar, 1931, practiced Hillsboro, Tex., 1931-50 with Morrow & Calvert, 1934-50; dist. atty. Hill County, Tex., 1943- 47; asso. justice Supreme Ct. of Tex., 1950-61, chief justice, 1961—. Mem. Tex. Ho. of Reps., 1933-39, speaker, 1937-39. Chmn. Dem. State Exec. Com., 1946-48. Home: 1411 W 29th St Austin TX 78703 Office: Supreme Court Austin TX 78711

CALVET, PIERRE LOUIS, banker; b. Troyes, France, June 27, 1910; s. Louis and Marthe (Bauer) C.; student Faculte de Droit, Paris, 1927-30, Ecole des Sciences Politiques, Paris, 1927-33; m. Luce Petitjean, Oct. 12, 1933; children—Bernard, Arlette. Insp. finances French Treasury, 1933; financial counselor French Embassy, London, Eng., 1945-47; vice chmn. European Payments Union, 1950-58; dep. gov. Bank of France, Paris, 1952—; v.p. Banque Nationale de Paris. Bd. dirs. French Nat. Museums, 1945—. Decorated comdr. Legion of Honor. Home: 33/35 rue de Valois Paris France Office: 16 Blvd des Italiens Paris France

CALVIN, LYLE DAVID, statistician, educator; b. Dannebrog, Neb., Apr. 12, 1923; s. David A. and Muriel (Harvey) C.; grad. Parsons (Kan.) Jr. Coll., 1943; B.S. in Meteorology, U. Chgo., 1948; B.S., N.C. State Coll., 1947, Ph.D., 1953; m. Shirley Jeanne Schmidt, Apr. 19, 1952; children—James Arthur, Ronald David, Janet Lee. Biometrician, G.D. Searle & Co., Chgo., 1950-52; asst. statistician N.C. State Coll. at Raleigh, 1952-53; statistician Agrl. Expt. Sta., asso. prof. Ore. State U., 1953-57, prof. 1957—, chmn. dept. statistics, 1962—; vis. prof. U. Edinburgh, 1967. Served from pvt. to 1st lt. USAAF, 1943-46. Fellow A.A.A.S. Am. Statis. Assn.; mem. Inst. Math. Statis., Biometric Soc. (pres WNAR 1964-65), Royal Statis. Soc., Sigma Xi. Home: 3463 Crest Dr Corvallis OR 97330

CALVIN, MELVIN, chemist, educator; b. St. Paul, Apr. 8, 1911; s. Elias and Rose I. (Hervitz) C.; B.S., Mich. Coll. Mining and Tech., 1931, D.Sc., 1955; Ph.D., U. Minn., 1935, D.Sc., 1969; hon research fellow U. Manchester (Eng.), 1935- 37; Guggenheim fellow, 1944; D.Sc., Nottingham U., 1958, Oxford (Eng.) U., 1959, Northwestern U., 1961, Wayne State U., 1962, Gustavus Adolphus Coll., 1963, Polytech. Inst. Bklyn., 1962, Notre Dame, 1965, U. Gent (Belgium), 1970, Whittier Coll.; m. Marie G. Jemtegaard, 1942; children—Elin, Karole, Noel. With U. Cal., at Berkeley, 1937—, successively instr. chemistry, asst. prof., prof., dir. Lab. Chem. Biodynamics, 1963—, asso. dir. Lawrence Radiation Lab., 1967—. Peter Reilly lectr. U. Notre Dame, 1949, Harvey lectr. N.Y. Acad. Med., 1951, Harrison Howe lectr. Rochester sect. Am. Chem. Soc., 1954, Falk-Plaut lectr. Columbia U., 1954, Edgar Fahs Smith Meml. lectr. U. Pa. and Phila. sect. Am. Chem. Soc., 1955, Donegani Found. lectr. Italian Nat. Acad. Sci., 1955, Max Tishler lectr. Harvard, 1956, Karl Folkers lectr. U. Wis., 1956; London lectr., 1961; Eastman prof. Oxford (Eng.) U., 1967-68. Recipient prize Sugar Research Found., 1950, Flintoff medal prize Brit. Chem. Soc., 1953, Stephen Hales Award Am. Soc. Plant Physiologists, 1956, Chem. Soc. Nichols medal N.Y. sect. Am. Chem. Soc., 1958; Nobel prize in chemistry, 1961; Davy medal Royal Soc. 1964. Mem. Britain's Royal Soc. London (fgn. mem.), Am. Chem. Soc. (Richards medal N.E. sect. 1956, award for nuclear applications in chemistry; pres. 1971), Am. Acad. Arts and Scis., Nat. Acad. Scis., Royal Dutch Acad. Scis., Am. Philos. Soc., Sigma Xi, Tau Beta Pi, Phi Lambda Upsilon. Author: The Theory of Organic Chemistry (with G. E. K. Branch), 1940; Isotopic Carbon (with others), 1949; Chemistry of Metal Chelate Compounds (with Martell), 1952; Path of Carbon in Photosynthesis (with Bassham), 1957; Chemical Evolution, 1961; (with Bassham) Photosynthesis of Carbon Compounds, 1962; Chemical Evolution, 1969. Contbr. chem., sci. jours. Home: 2683 Buena Vista Berkeley CA 94708

CALVINO, ITALO, writer; b. Oct. 15, 1923. Editorial staff Giulio Einaudi Editore. Author: Il Sentiero dei Nidi di Ragno, 1947; Ultimo viene il Corvo, 1949; Il Visconte dimezzato, 1951; L'Entrata in Guerra. 1954; Fiabe Italiane, 1956; Il Barone Ramante, 1957; I Racconti, 1958; Il Cavaliere Inesistente, 1959; La Giornata di uno Scrutatore, 1963; Le Cosmicomiches, 1966; Ti con zero (short stories), 1967. Address: care Giulio Einaudi Editore Via Umberto Biancamano 1 Turin Italy

CAMACHO, ALVRO MANUEL, educator, physician; b. Trinidad, W.I., Mar. 1, 1927; s. Lewis F. and Hilda (Periera) C.; came to U.S. 1946, naturalized, 1965; M.D. Creighton U., 1953; m. Phyllis Jean Stanislav, June 16, 1956; children—Lisa Marie, Laura Jean, Christopher Lewis, Lydia Patrice. Intern Charity Hosp., New Orleans, 1953-54; postgrad. tng. pediatrics U. Tex. Med. Br. Hosps., Galveston, 1955-58; postgrad. tng. pediatric endocrinology Children's Hosp., Ohio State U., 1958-60, Johns Hopkins Hosp., 1960-61; instr. pediatrics Johns Hopkins Hosp., 1961-63; clin. dir. pediatrics Detroit Receiving Hosp., asst. prof. pediatrics Wayne State U. Sch. Medicine, 1963-64; mem. faculty U. Tenn. Coll. Medicine, 1965—, asso. prof. pediatrics, head sec. pediatric endocrinology, 1965—. Recipient Lederle Med. Faculty award, 1966. Mem. Am. Soc. Pediatric Research, Endocrine Soc., Am. Fedn. Clin. Research, So. Soc. Pediatric Research. Author articles in field. Home: 495 N McLean Blvd Memphis TN 38112

CAMACHO, CARLOS GARCIA, gov. of Guam; b. Agana, Guam, Nov. 16, 1924; s. Felix M. and Antonia C. (Garcia) C.; student Aquinas Coll., 1947-50; D.D.S., Marquette U., 1952; m. Lourdes Duenas Perez, May 15, 1955; children—Carlos Anthony, Felix James, Thomas John, Mary Margaret, Ricardo Jose, Francis Gerard, Victor Charles. Mem. dental staff Guam Meml. Hosp., 1952-53, Cath. Med. Center, 1953-56, 58-69; gov. of Guam, 1969—. Senator 8th Guam Legislature, 1964-66. Served as capt., Dental Corps, U.S. Army, 1956-58. Republican. Roman Catholic. K.C. (4). Address: Government House Agana Guam 96910

CAMACHO GUIZADO, EDUARDO, author, educator; Licenciado en Filosofia y Letras, U. Andres, Bogota, Columbia; Dr. en Filosofia y Letras, U. Madrid, 1962. Now prof. State U. N.Y., Albany; vis. prof. Middlebury Coll. Spanish Sch., 1967, 68, 69, 70, 71. Author: Estudios de literatura colombiana, Siglos XVI y XVII, 1965; La poesia de Jose Asuncion Silva, 1967; La elegá funeral en la poesia espaola, 1969. Address: Dept Romance Langs State U New York Albany NY 12203

CAMBEILH, EUGENE GERALD, cement co. exec.; b. Galveston, Tex., Dec. 28, 1919; s. Michel J. and Mary (Byrne) C.; student Soule Bus. Coll., New Orleans, 1937-38, Internat. Accountants Soc., 1946-47; m. Casilda Margaret Hufft, Dec. 21, 1942; children—Eugene Gerald, Sandra Mary, Barry Edward, Joyce Casilda. With Lone Star Cement Corp., N.Y.C., 1938—, asst. treas., 1960- 65, comptroller, 1965—. Served to capt. AUS, 1941-45; PTO. Mem. Financial Execs. Inst. Roman Catholic. Home: 9 Cedar Ct Closter, NJ 07624. Office: 100 Park Av New York City NY 10017

CAMBEL, ALI BULENT, engr., univ. ofcl.; b. Merano, Italy, Apr. 9, 1923; s. H. Cemil and Remziye (Hakki) C.; B.S., Robert Coll., Istanbul, Turkey, 1942; postgrad. U. Istanbul, 1942-43, Mass. Inst. Tech., 1943-45; M.S., Cal. Inst. Tech., 1946; Ph.D., U. Ia., 1950; m. Marion dePaar, Dec. 20, 1946; children—Metin, Emel, Leyla, Sarah. Came to U.S., 1943, naturalized, 1951. Instr., State U. Ia., 1947-50, asst. prof., 1950-53; asso. prof. mech. engring. Northwestern U., 1953-56. prof. mech. engring., 1956-61, Walter P. Murphy distinguished prof., 1961-68, dir. gas. dynamics lab., 1953-68, chmn. dept. mech. engring. and astrophys. scis., 1957-68; dir. research and engring. support div. Inst. Def. Analyses, 1966-67, v.p. for research, 1967-68; dean Coll. Engring., Wayne State U., Detroit, 1968-70, exec. v.p. for acad. affairs, 1970—. Tech. cons. govt. agys., various firms; staff dir. Pres.'s Interdeptl. Energy Study; engring. scis. adv. com. USAF Office Sci. Research, 1961-63; mem. Commn. Engring. Edn., 1966—; mem. Army Sci. Adv. Panel, 1966—; nat. lectr. Sigma Xi, 1961-62. Bd. dirs. YMCA. Washburn scholar, 1938; recipient leadership award YMCA, 1953; J. Edward Pendray award Am. Inst. Aeros. and Astronautics, 1959; Curtiss McGraw award Am. Soc. Engring. Edn., 1960, George Westinghouse award, 1966. Fellow Am. Inst. Aeros. and Astronautics (nat. dir.); mem. Am. Soc. Engring. Edn. Mem. Soc. of Friends. Author: Plasma Physics and Magnetofluidmechanics, 1963; co-author Gas Dynamics, 1958; Real Gases, 1963; Plasma Physics, 1965. Editor: The Dynamics of Conducting Gases, 1960; asso. editor Am. Inst. Aeros. and Astronautics jours., Jet Propulsion, 1955-60; editor Transport Properties in Gases, 1958; co-editor Magnetohydrodynamics, 1962. Author numerous papers in field. Home: 1929 Pembridge Pl Detroit MI 48207

CAMBERE, ARA ANGELE, investment banker; b. N.Y.C., Nov. 7, 1911; s. Haroutioun A. and Leontine (Canzuch) C.; B.S. in Econs., Wharton Sch. of U. Pa., 1933; m. Marion S. Quinn, Jan. 31, 1942 (dec. Mar. 1968); children—Yvonne (Mrs. Alan Mellinggaard), Mary-Frances (Mrs. G. Peter Mymbach), Peter, Kathleen, John, Richard; m. 2d, Francesca P. Cuzzi, 1971. Mem. promotion dept. N.Y. Sun. 1933-35; mem. buying dept. Hayden, Stone & Co., 1936-49; v.p., dir. Mfrs. Capital Corp., N.Y.C., 1949-51; pres., dir. Berry Motors, Inc., Corinth, Miss., 1951; v.p., dir. Oliver Steel & Iron Coop. Pitts., 1951-55; asst. to pres. Stewart-Warner Corp., Chgo., 1955-60; partner Hayden, Stone & Co., 1960-62; exec. v.p., dir. Hayden, Stone, Inc., N.Y.C., 1962-65, pres., dir., mem. exec. com., 1965- 68, vice chmn., dir., mem. exec. com., 1968-70; chmn. bd. Haywood Mgmt. Corp., 1969-71; v.p. Hornblower & Weeks-Hemphill, Noyes, 1971—. Former mem. Midwest Stock Exchange, Chgo. Bd. Trade. Republican. Roman Cath. Clubs: Duquesne (Pitts.); Chicago, Bond (Chgo.); Harbor View, Bond, Veterans 7th Regiment (N.Y.C.); Stanwich (Greenwich, Conn.). Home: 348 Highbrook Av Pelham NY 10803 Office: 8 Hanover St New York City NY 10004

CAMBIO, FRANK CAESAR, lawyer; b. Providence, Aug. 14, 1895; s. Camillo Guiseppe and Maria Sophia (Mercurio) C.; A.B., Brown U., 1917; student Harvard Law Sch., 1918-20; m. Adelina Benevenga, June 11, 1923; children—Maria Alberta, Frank Caesar. Admitted to R.I. bar, 1922, since practiced in Providence; asst. atty. gen., 1938-40. Chmn. R.I. Bd. Bar Examiners, 1964—; chmn. R.I. Bd. Tax Equalization; mem. bd. tax assessment review City Providence. Mem. commn. on reapportionment Ho. of Reps. Candidate atty. gen. for R.I., 1954. Dir. United Fund, Inc., Fed. Hill House. Mem. Am., R.I. (pres. 1957-58) bar assns., Aurora Civil Assn. Club: Republican of R.I. (v.p.). Home: 19 Havenswood Av Providence RI 02908 Office: 58 Weybosset St Providence RI 20903

CAMBRE, ROLAND JOSEPH, educator; b. LaPlace, La., Aug. 14, 1901; s. Charles Francis and Ernestine (Vicknair) C.; B.S., U. Southwestern La., 1926; postgrad. La. State U., Va. Poly. Inst., U. Wis.; M.Sc., La. State U., 1952; m. Bernice Babin, Aug. 26, 1929; children—Thomas K. (dec.), Louis Charles. Sales engr. Wagner Electric Corp., 1926-30; power sales engr. Asso. Gas & Electric Co., 1930-39; supt. bldgs. and grounds U. Southwestern La., 1939-41, asst., then asso. prof. mech. engring., 1941-56, prof., head gen. engring., 1956-68. Mem. Am. Soc. Engring. Edn., La. Engring. Soc., La. Tchrs. Assn., Nat. Football Hall Fame Assn. (charter mem.), Am. La., Southwest La. (pres. 1967, 68) camellia socs., Am. Petroleum Inst., So. Intercollegiate Athletic Assn. (sec.- treas.) (Lafayette). Clubs: Acadian Hills Country; S (life) (U. Southwestern La.). Home: 902 Myrtle Pl Lafayette LA 70501

CAMBRIDGE, GODFREY, comedian; b. N.Y.C., Feb. 26, 1933; s. Alexander and Sarah Cambridge; grad. Hofstra Coll.; student Coll. city N.Y.; student dramatic coaches; m. Barbara Anne Teer, 1962 (div.) First profl. appearance in off- Broadway prodn. Take a Giant Step. 1956; Broadway appearances include Nature's Way, Detective Story, Lost in the Stars, The Blacks, Purlie Victorious, The Living Promise, A Funny Thing Happened on the Way to the Forum, How to be a Jewish Mother; film appearances include The Last Angry Man, Gone Are The Days!, Purlie Victorious, The Troublemaker, The President's Analyst, The Busy Body, The Biggest Bundle of Them All, Bye Bye Braveman, Cotton Comes to Harlem; numerous TV appearances including Jack Paar show; recording artist for Epic Records; nightclub and coll. campus appearances. Recipient Obie award, 1961. Author: Put Downs and Put-Outs, 1967; also articles. Address: care United Artists 729 7th Av New York City NY 10019*

CAMDEN, CHARLES CARROLL, educator; b. Parkersburg, W. Va., Mar. 24, 1903; s. Charles Carroll Carroll and Sarah Edna (Timmons) C.; A.B., Centre Coll. Ky., 1925; postgrad. Harvard, 1926-27; Ph.D., U. Ia., 1930; m. Louise Smith, Sept. 1, 1925; children—Charles Carroll III, Barbara Brooke (Mrs. John H. Burns). Instr. English, U. Ia., 1928-30; faculty Rice U., Houston, 1930—, prof. English, 1950—, chmn. dept., 1957-63. Lectr. on Shakespeare, U. P.R., 1964; vis. lectr. U. Tex., 1946-47; vis. prof. So. Methodist U., summer 1959, U. Wis., 1965-66, U. Cal. at Santa Barbara, summer 1970; 1970; del. Internat. Shakespeare Conf., Stratford, Eng., 1955, 64; research fellow Folger Library, 1954, 62, English Speaking Union, 1955. Mem. Modern Lang. Ass. Am., South Central Modern Lang. Assn., Shakespeare Assn. Am., Malone Soc., Renaissance Soc. Am. (del. 1961—), South Central Renaissance Conf. (pres. (pres. 1959-60), Am. Hist. Assn., Houston Philos. Soc. (pres. 1943-44). Author: Elizabethan Almanacs and Prognostications, 1931; Elizabethan Woman, 1952; co-author Essays in Honor of Hardin Craig, 1941, Essays in Honor of Baldwin Maxwell, 1962, Shakespeare 400, 1964; Studies in Honor of DeWitt T. Starnes, 1967. Editor: Restoration and Eighteenth- Century Essays in Honor of A.D. McKillop, 1963; Critical and Historical Essays, 1964; mem. editorial bd. English Lit. Renaissance; founding editor Studies in English Lit., 1960—. Contbr. articles to profl. jours. Home: 5309 Brae Burn Dr Bellaire, TX 77401. Office: Rice U Houston TX 77001

CAMERINI, UGO, educator; b. Milan, Italy, Mar. 27, 1925; s. Oscar and Livia (Dalseno) C.; B. Sc. in Physics, U. Sao Paulo (Brazil), also B.Sc. in Math.; hon. prof., U. Mayor de San Andres (Brazil); m. Ingrid Clareus, Nov. 1, 1948; children—Michael O.R., U. Roberto L., David P.J. Came to U.S., 1957. Tech. asst. expert UNESCO, Brazil, 1951-57; mem. faculty U. Wis., 1957—, now prof. physics. Hon. prof. U. Mayor de San Andres (Bolivia). Home: 3925 Plymouth Circle Madison WI 53705

CAMERON, ALISTER, educator; b. Glasgow, Scotland, Feb. 20, 1904; s. Alexander Forrester and Marion Cooper (Stark) C.; A.B., Union Coll., 1926; M.A., Princeton, 1927; postgrad., U. Edinburgh, 1930-31; Ph.D., (univ. fellow), Columbia, 1938; m. Elizabeth Ridley Moore, May 26, 1934; 1 dau., Elizabeth (Mrs. Michael Ward). Instr. classics St. John's Coll., Annapolis, Md., 1927-28; instr. classics Union Coll., 1928-30; asst. to asso. prof. Greek, Bryn Mawr Coll., 1935-46; prof. classics U. Cin., 1946—, fellow Grad. Sch., 1970—. Served with OSS, 1944-45. Club: Literary (Cin.). Author: Thr Pythagorean Background of the Theory of Recollection, 1938; The Identity of Oedipus The King, 1968. Home: 240 Loraine Av Cincinnati OH 45220

CAMERON, ALLEN, corp. exec. b. New Rockford, N.D., Mar. 29, 1911; s. John Steward and Edith Leslie (Allen) G.; m. Ruth Isabel Trankler, Mar. 15, 1944; children—Mrs. Suzanne Cameron Black, Laurie Ellen. Successively asst. port capt., v.p., gen. mgr. Pacific Tankers, Inc., San Francisco, 1944-49; v.p. Joshua Hendy Corp., 1949; exec. v.p., dir. Transworld Carriers, Inc.; asst. to exec. v.p. and treas. Nat. Bulk Carriers, Inc., 1959-60; v.p. 1960-67; pres. Rogers, Slade & Hill, Inc., 1968—. Seaman USN, 1930-34; U.S. Mcht. Marine, 1934-44, advancing from able seaman to master. Mem. N.E. Coast Inst. Engrs. and Shipbuilders, Soc. Naval Architects and Marine Engrs., Council Am. Master Mariners, Soc. Maritime Arbitrators, Marine Tech. Soc., Newcomen Soc., Propeller Club. Clubs: Greenwich Country; Bohemian; Circum- navigators, Union League. Home: Buckfield Lane Greenwich CT 06830 Office: 30 E 42d St New York City NY 10017

CAMERON, BARNEY GEORGE, newspaper exec.; b. Spokane, Wash., Jan. 3, 1911; s. Gilbert L. and Minnie (Bond) C.; student Willamette U., 1929-30, U. Ore. extension, 1934; m. Betty Hayford Fosdick, July 24, 1932; children—Ann, Joan. Circulation exec., Salem, Ore., also Los Angeles Examiner, 1930-34; circulation mgr. Portland (Ore.) News-Telegram, 1939-42; Seattle Star, 1942-46. Pitts. Post-Gazette, 1946-51; circulation dir. N.Y. Herald Tribune, 1951-56, v.p., bus. mgr., dir. 1956-61: v.p., bus. mgr. Pitts. Press, 1961-65, v.p. bus mgr., 1965—. also dir. First v.p. St. Francis Hosp.; bd. dirs. Pitts. Opera, Inc., Boy Scouts Am., Jr. Achievement S.W. Pa., Pitts. Regional Planning Assn., Pitts. Conv. and Visitors Bur., Better Bus. Bur., Pa. Newspapers Pubs. Assn., C. of C. Greater Pitts., Met. Sunday Newspapers; trustee Community Services of Pa. Mem. Newcomen Soc. North Am., St. Andrews Soc. State N.Y. , Golden Triangle Assn. (v.p., dir.), Amen Corner, Pa. Soc. Mason (Shriner), Rotarian. Clubs: New York Athletic Assn. (N.Y.C.): Pittsburg Press, Duquesne (dir.), Allegheny (dir.), Pittsburgh Advertising, Chartiers Country, Variety (former asst. chief barker), (Pitts.); Overseas Press of Am. Home: 682 Osage Rd Pittsburgh PA 15243 Office: Pittsburgh Press Pittsburgh PA 15230

CAMERON, CHARLES CLIFFORD, banker; b. Meridian, Miss., Jan. 4, 1920; s. Daniel Baker and Bertha (Morris) C.; B.S., La. State U., 1941; m. Yvonne Smith, June 4, 1942; children—Sheryl, Randolph Morris, Cynthia and Cathy (twins). Engr. Engr. Standard Oil Co. N.J., 1945-49; with Cameron-Brown Co., Raleigh, N.C., 1949—, pres., 1951-66, chmn. bd., 1966—; pres., chmn. bd., chief exec. officer First Union Nat. Bank of N.C., 1966—; dir. Charlotte br. Fed. Res. Bank of Richmond. Mem. Gov.'s Council for Econ. Devel.; treas. Bus. Devel. Corp. N.C.; mem. Army Adv. Com. N.C. Pres. United Fund Raleigh, Bd. dirs. Raleigh YMCA, Carolinas United Community Service; trustee U. N.C.; v.p. Chapel Hill; chmn. bd. trustees Meredith Coll. Served to col. AUS, 1941-45; ETO. Decorated Bronze Star. Named Boss of Year, Raleigh Jr. C. of C., 1964. Mem. Assn. of Reserve City Bankers, Newcomen Soc. N.Am. Nat. Assn. Real Estate Bds. (v.p. 1961), Raleigh Bd. Realtors (past pres.), N.C. Assn. Realtors (past pres.; Realtor of year award 1959), Am. (pres. 1964: Distinguished Service award 1961), Carolinas (pres. 1955) mortgage bankers assns., Am. Inst. Real Estate Appraisers, U. S. C. of C., Scabbard and Blade, Alpha Chi Sigma, Phi Lambda Upsilon, Theta Xi (pres. 1941), Baptist (deacon). Clubs: Carolina Country (Raleigh); Country of N.C. (Pinehurst); Charlotte (N.C.) City, Charlotte Country, Quail Hollow Country, Home: 3915 Foxcroft Rd Charlotte NC 28211 Office: First Union Nat Bank Charlotte NC 28202

CAMERON, CHARLES FRANKLIN elec. engr.; b. Enid, Okla., Jan. 22, 1898; s. William J. and Carrie (Nelson) C.; diploma Northwestern (Okla.) State Coll., 1919; student U. Okla., 1920-21; B.S., Okla. A. and M. Coll., 1923, E.E., 1936; M.S.E., Purdue U., 1939; postgrad. summers, Ia. State Coll., 1927, 29, 30, Colo. Agrl. Coll., 1928; m. Helen Fash, June 28, 1920 (dec. 1950); children—Jean (Mrs. Milton L. Levy), Joanna (Mrs. W. Philip Pipkin, II); m. 2d, Eleanor Drummond Hanna, 1951. Instr. electronics high sch., Rock Springs, Wyo., 1923-28, dir. indsl. edn., 1928-41; dir. war tng. trade sch., 1941; asst. prof. elec. engring. Okla. State U., 1941-44, asso.

prof., 1944-47, prof. elec. engring. specializing in power machinery, 1947-51, research prof. elec. engring. 1951-63, prof. emeritus, 1963—, acting head Sch. Elec. Engring., 1959- 61; cons. engr.; cons. electric projects; researcher electromagnetic relays; vis. prof. elec. engring. Assiut (Egypt) U. Vice pres. Internat. Conf. Electromagnetic Relays, 1963, chmn. com., 1965. Mem. I.E.E.E., Am. Soc. Engring. Edn., Nat., Okla. socs. profl. engrs., Acacia, Sigma Xi, Eta Kappa Nu, Sigma Tau. Republican. Mason (K.T.). Author engring. dept. sta. bulls., publs. on electro- mech. relays. Research prediction performance of induction motors, both poly-phase and single-phase. Home: PO Box 601 Stillwater OK 74074

CAMERON, CHARLES METZ, Jr., educator; b. Morristown, Tenn., Dec. 20, 1923; s. Charles Metz and Mildred (Brown) C.; student U. Tenn., 1942, N.C. State Coll., 1943, U. Ky., 1944, U. Miss., 1945; M.D., Vanderbilt U., 1948; M.P.H., U. N.C., 1955; m. Vera L. Cheek, Nov. 25, 1948; children—Charles Metz III, Cheryl Lynn, David Alan. Rotating intern U.S. Marine Hosp. System, 1949; dist. health officer Tenn. Dept. Pub. Health, 1949-52; physician USPHS, 1951-53; chief communicable disease control sect., accident prevention sect. N.C. Rd. Health, 1953-55; asso. prof., prof. U. N.C. Sch. Pub. Health, 1955-68, acting chmn. dept., 1960-61; dir. N.C. Office Comprehensive Health Planning, 1967-68; prof., chmn. dept. health adminstrn. U. Okla. Med. Center Grad. Sch. Health, Oklahoma City, 1968—, also dir. Mid-Continent Comprehensive Health Planning Ednl. Center and Health Resources Information Center. Served with AUS, 1943-45. Mem. Delta Omega (nat. pres. 1962). Contbr. papers to profl. lit. Home: 3132 Goshen Dr Oklahoma City OK 73120

CAMERON, CHARLES SHERWOOD, orgn. exec., physician; b. Phila., June 22, 1900; s. Charles Sherwood and Ella (Baker) C.; A.B., U. Pa., 1931; M.D., Hahnemann Med. Coll., Sc.D. (hon.), 1955. Intern Phila. Gen. Hosp., 1935-37, surg. resident, 1937-38; postgrad. cancer surgery N.Y. Meml. Hosp. (Rockefeller fellowship), 1938-42; pres. Hahnemann Med. Coll. and Hosp.; v.p. Phila. Bd. Health. Mem. Nat. Bd. Med. Examiners. Trustee Eastern Pa. Psychiat. Inst. Served with USN, 1942-46; chief tumor service Bklyn. Naval Hosp., 1945-46; disch. comdr. M.C. Fellow Coll. of Physicians of Phila., A.C.S., mem. Am. Cancer Soc. (v.p., med. and sci. dir. 1946-56, bd. dir. Phila. div.), Phila. Health and Welfare Council (mem. health div.), A.M.A., Am., World Med. Assn., N.Y. Med. Soc., Coll. Physicians Phila. Author: The Truth about Cancer. Adv. editor Geriatrics, Excerpta Medica. Clubs: Union League (Phila.); Penn. Home: 6473 Drexel Rd Philadelphia PA 19151

CAMERON, COLIN CAMPBELL, pineapple co. and land devel. exec.; b. Paia, Maui, Hawaii, Feb. 2, 1927; s. J. Walter and Frances (Baldwin) C.; A.B., Harvard, 1950, M.B.A., 1953; m. Margaret Hartley, Aug. 25, 1951; children—Douglas, Richard, Margaret, Frances. Spray operations supr. Maui Pineapple Co., Ltd., 1953-57, cannery operations supt., 1957-59, v.p., operations mgr., 1959-62, exec. v.p., 1962-67; engaged in land devel., 1967—; pres. Maui Land and Pineapple Co., Inc., 1969—, Honolua Plantation Land Co., Inc., 1970—; sec., dir. Haleakala Ranch Co., Ltd., Haleakala Dairy, Inc.; dir. Bishop Trust Co., Ltd., Hawaiian Electric Co., Inc., Maui Savs. & Loan Assn., Maui Electric Co., Ltd., Maui Pub. Co. Chmn. Maui County Com. Republican Party, 1957-62. Chmn. bd. trustees Mauna Olu Coll.; v.p., bd. dirs. Lahaina Restoration Found. Served with USNR. 1945-46. Unitarian. Clubs: Pacific; Maui Country. Home: Spreckelsville HI 96779 Office: Box 187 Kahului HI 96732

CAMERON, DALE CORBIN, physician, orgn. exec.; b. Hendley, Neb., July 10, 1912; s. Joseph R. and Veda L. (Corbin) C.; A.B., U. Neb., 1933, M.D., 1936; M.P.H., Johns Hopkins, 1951; m. Irma C. Lippold, June 10, 1936; children—Robert W., Marsha K. Intern USPHS Hosp., San Francisco, 1936-37; resident psychiatry U. Colo., 1939-40, USPHS Hosp., Ft. Worth, 1940-43; commissioned officer USPHS, 1936, asst. surgeon gen., 1962, clin. dir. USPHS Hosp., Ft. Worth, 1940-41, exec. officer, 1941-43; asst. chief Nat. Inst. Mental Health, 1945-50; dir. med. services Minn. Dept. Welfare, 1954-60; clin. prof. psychiatry and neurology U. Minn. Med. Sch., 1954-60; asst. supt. St. Elizabeths Hosp., Washington, 1960-62, supt., 1962-67; clin. prof. psychiatry George Washington U. Med. Sch., 1960—; chief drug dependence unit WHO, 1967—. Chmn. com. drug addiction and narcotics Nat. Acad. Scis.- NRC, 1961-65, chmn. com. problems drug dependence, 1965-67; chmn. mental health project grants rev. com. Nat. Inst. Mental Health, 1957-60. Diplomate Am. Bd. Psychiatry and Neurology. Fellow Am. Psychiat. Assn. (treas. 1963-68, mem. budget com. 1962-67); mem. A.M.A. (chmn. com. alcoholism and addiction 1963-67), Minn. (pres. 1958-59), Washington (council 1961-64, chmn. liaison with standing com. jud. conf. D.C. 196-67) psychiat. socs., Nat. Assn. Mental Health, Central, Minn. neuropsychiat. assns., Am. Pub. Health Assn., D.C. Med. Soc. (com. mental health 1961-67). Author articles in field. Address: Av Appia 1211 Geneva Switzerland

CAMERON, DONALD ANGUS, book pub., editor; b. Indpls., Dec. 25, 1908; s. Joseph A. and Minnie I. (Groeschel) C.; A.B., DePauw U., 1930; m. Sheila K. Smith, Apr. 30, 1936; childrenKevin A., Catherine P. Sales promotion mgr. Hurty-Peck Co., Indpls., 1931-34; sales promotion mgr. Bobbs-Merrill Co., Indpls., 1934-38, editor, N.Y.C., 1938; editor Little Brown & Co., N.Y.C., 1938- 43, editor-in-chief, Boston, 1943-51, sec. of corp., 1944-46. v.p., 1946-51, dir., 1944-51; pres. Cameron and Kahn, pubs. and Cameron Assos., Assos., N.Y.C., 1954-59, Liberty Book Club, N.Y.C., 1954-59; editor Alfred A. Knopf, Inc. (now part of Random House), N.Y.C., 1959-67, sr. editor, v.p., 1967—. State chmn., nat. treas. Progressive Party of Mass., 1948. Mem. Phi Delta Theta. Home: 358 Westport Rd Wilton CT 06897 Office: 201 E 50th St New York City NY 10022

CAMERON, EMMET GEORGE, electronics co. exec.; b. San Francisco, Nov. 29, 1911; s. Francis John and Elizabeth (Murphy) C.; B.S. in Elec. Engring., U. Cal. at Berkeley, 1935; m. Juliet Schellenbach, Oct. 28, 1939; children—Donald William, Carol, Barbara. Became exec. v.p. Varian Assos., Palo Alto, Cal., 1957, now dir., v.p. corporate devel. Past. dir. Western Electronic Show and Conv. Sr. mem. I.E.E.E. (chmn. conf. bd.); mem. Western Electronic Mfrs. Assn. (pres., bd. dirs.), Palo Alto C. of C. (pres., bd. dirs.), Phi Beta Kappa, Sigma Xi, Tau Beta Pi, Eta Kappa Nu. Clubs: Sharon Heights Country; Palo Alto. Home: 76 James Av Atherton CA 94025 Office: 611 Hansen Way Palo Alto CA 94304

CAMERON, EUGENE NATHAN, educator; b. Atlanta, Aug. 10, 1910; s. Nathan Massey and Jessie Roberta (Bennett) C.; B.S. N.Y. U., 1932; M.S., Columbia, 1934, Ph.D., 1939; m. Adrienne M. Macksoud, Aug. 5, 1939; children—Beatrice A., James N., Donald E. Lectr., then instr. geology Columbia, 1937-42; asso. geologist U.S. Geol. Survey, 1942-44. geologist, 1944-46, commodity geologist indsl. minerals, 1946-57, sr. geologist, 1946-51; asso. prof. geology U. Wis., 1947-50, prof., 1950—, chmn. dept., 1955-60, Van Hise Distinguished prof., 1970—; cons. geologist, 1951—. Chmn. panel raw materials of beryllium Materials Adv. Bd., 1957- 58, vice-chmn. panel raw materials of chromium, 1958-59; cons. NASA, 1965—; U.S.A. del. Internat. Commn. on Ore Microscopy, 1964-68. Fellow Geol. Soc. Am., Geol. Assn. Can., Soc. Econ. Geologists (v.p. 1969, sec. research found. 1966—), Mineral. Soc. Am. (council 1965-68); mem. Am. Inst. Mining, Metall. and Petroleum Engrs., Geol. Soc. S. Africa, Am. Bus. Club (pres. 1953-54). Author: Ore Microscopy, 1961. Contbr. articles profl. jours. Home: 4414 Rolla Lane Madison WI 53711

CAMERON, FRANCIS, retired mining geologist; b. Washington, Mar. 14, 1902; s. Frank K. and Katherine (Boyle) C.; A.B., Leland Stanford U., 1924; D. Engring. (hon.), U. Mo., 1961; m. Louise Lang, Mar. 5, 1932; children—Frank K., William L. Asst. foreman, engr. Chief Consol. Mining Co., Eureka, Utah, 1924-25; asst. geologist Internat. Smelting Co., Salt Lake City, 1926-28; geologist Anaconda Copper Mining Co., N.Y.C., various U.S., fgn. cities, 1928-45; adviser Metals Res. Co., Washington, 1942- 45; asst. to exec. v.p. St. Joe Minerals Corp., N.Y.C., 1945-46, v.p., 1946-60, pres., 1960-67, chmn. 1967-71; retired, 1971; pres. Bonne Terre Framing & Cattle Co., 1960-67; v.p., dir. Meramec Mining Co.; chmn., dir. St. Joseph Internat. Explorations, Ltd.; pres., dir. St. Joseph Explorations Ltd.; dir. Companie Minerales Santander, Inc., P. & L.E. R.R., Jododex Australia Pty. Ltd., Mine La Motte Corp. Fellow Geol. Soc. Am.; mem. Am. Inst. Mining and Metall. Engrs., Mining and Metall. Soc. Am., Canadian Inst. Mining and Metallurgy, Soc. Econ. Geologists. Clubs: Sharon (Conn.) Country; University, Mining (N.Y.C.); Cosmos (Washington). Home: Lakeville CT 06039 Office 250 Park Av New York City NY 10017

CAMERON, FRANK B., corp. exec.; b. Greenville, S.C., 1924; ed. Clemson A. and M. Coll., 1949. Formerly with Fiber Industries, Inc.; v.p. Interchem. Corp. Address: PO Box 10038 Charlotte NC 28201*

CAMERON, GEORGE GLENN, educator; b. Washington, Pa., July 30, 1905; s. William Byers and Elizabeth (Smith) C.; student Washington and Jefferson Coll., 1923-25; A.B., Muskingum Coll., New Concord, O., 1927, Litt. D., 1952; A.M., U. Chgo., 1930, Ph.D., 1932; m. Frances Thomas, June 25, 1932 (dec. Aug. 1955); children—Thomas W., Douglas R.; m. 2d, Margaret F. Bell, Aug. 18, 1956; children—Elizabeth B., Mary M. Traveling fellow Oriental Institute, U. Chgo., 1930-32, instr. Oriental langs., asst. prof. of ancient Oriental hist., 1933-45, asso. prof., 1945-48; prof. of Near Eastern cultures, dept. Near Eastern langs. and lits. U. Mich., 1948—. chmn. dept., 1948-69; annual prof., Baghdad Sch. of Am. Schs. of Oriental Research, organizer expdn. to Bisitun inscription of Darius, 1948-49; dir. U. of Mich. expdn. to the Near East, 1951; Haskell lectr. Oberlin College, 1954; Fulbright research scholar U. Göttingen, Germany, 1956-57. Decorated Order of Homayoun 2d class (Iran), 1949. Mem. Am. Oriental Soc. (pres. Midwest br. 1952-53), Am. Hist. Assn., Archaeol. Inst. America. Author: History of Early Iran, 1936, also French trans.; Persepolis Treasury Tablets, 1948. Editor of posthumous work of Edward Chiera, They Wrote on Clay, 1938, trans. into French, German, Danish, Dutch; Am. Jour. of Semitic Langs. and Lits., 1940-41, Jour. of Near Eastern Studies, 1940-48. Home: 1515 Ottawa Dr Ann Arbor MI 48105

CAMERON, GORDON BRENT, restaurant exec.; b. Hardy, Neb., Aug. 6, 1933; s. H. Milo and Gladys M. (Loetterle) C.; B.A., Ore. State U., 1955; m. Marcellene Ruth Hauge, Aug. 27, 1960; children—Jacqueline Rene, Scott Charles. With A & W Root Beer Co., Santa Monica, Cal., 1959-61; exec. v.p. McDonalds Corp., Los Angeles, Atlanta, Chgo., 1961—. Served as capt. USMCR, 1955-59. Office: McDonald's Plaza Oakbrook IL 60521

CAMERON, J. ELLIOT, univ. dean; b. Panguitch, Utah, Feb. 9, 1923; s. B.A. and Leonia (Sargent) C.; B.S., M.A., Brigham Young U., 1946-49; Ed. D., 1966; m. Maxine Petty, Dec. 23, 1942; children—Bruce, Kim, Kerry Lynn, Preston. Former high sch. prin., supt. schs. Duchesne, Sevier, Utah, later pres. Snow Coll., Ephraim, Utah, then dean students Utah State U.; now dean students, prof. edn. Brigham Young U., Provo, Utah. Served with AUS, World War II. Mem. N.E.A., Nat. Assn. Student Personnel Adminstrs., Am. Assn. Sch. Adminstrs., Phi Delta. Kappa. Mem. Ch. of Jesus Christ of Latter-day Saints. Home: 2802 N 700 East Provo. UT 84601.

CAMERON, J. WALTER, fruit canner; b. Canton, Mass., June 6, 1896; s. Colin Campbell and Mary E. (Pond) C.; student pub. schs., Brookline, Mass.; m. Frances H. Baldwin, July 17, 1924; children—Colin Campbell, Mary Ethel. With Street & Smith Pub. Co., Boston 1920-21, Hearst's Internat. mag., Boston, 1921- 23; Advertisers Pub. Co., Honolulu, T.H., 1923-24; foreman Haleakala Ranch, Maui, T.H., 1924-26; mgr. Haleakala Pineapple Co., 1926-33; chmn. dir. Maui Pineapple Co. Ltd., 1933—; pres., dir. Haleakala Ranch Co., Ltd., Maui Electric Co., Ltd., Maui Pub. Co., Ltd., H.P. Baldwin Ltd.; dir. Bank of Hawaii, Hawaiian Telephone Co., Sheraton Corp. Hawaii, Hawaiian Airlines Ltd. Served from 2d lt. to capt. U.S. Army, 1917-19. Mem. Hawaiian Sugar Planters Assn. (exec. com.). Clubs: Maui Country; Pacific (Honolulu); Pacific Union (San Francisco). Address: Kahului Maui HI 96732

CAMERON, JAMES, advt. agy. exec. Sr. v.p., mgmt. supr. Young & Rubicam, N.Y.C. Office: 285 Madison Av New York City NY 10017*

CAMERON, JAMES M., pipe line co. exec. Vice pres., gen. counsel Trans-Can. Pipe Lines, Ltd. Office: 150 Edlinton Av E Toronto 12 Ontario Canada*

CAMERON, JOHN LANSING, govt. ofcl.; b. Sanford, N.C., Sept. 14, 1916; s. William John and Lena (Rosser) C.; A.B., Elon Coll., 1937; M.A., U. N.C., 1947, D.Ed., 1965; m. Beulah Arena Bradley, Sept. 7, 1940; children—William John, Elizabeth Ann (Mrs. Irvin A. Pearce), David Bradley. Dir. school planning N.C. Dept. Pub. Instrn., 1949-59; with U.S. Office of Edn., Washington, 1959—, dir. facilities devel. staff, acting dir. ednl. tech., 1971—. Chmn. U.S. delegation to Internat. Edn. Bldg. Conf., London, 1962, U.S. delegation to Latin Am. Ednl. Bldg. Conf., Mexico City, 1966. Served to lt. comdr. USNR, 1942-46. Recipient Superior Service award Dept. Health, Welfare and Edn., 1966. Mem. Am. Nat. Standards Inst., Illuminating Engring. Soc., A.I.A. (hon.), Am. Assn. Sch. Adminstrs., Council Ednl. Facility Planners (pres. 1966-67), Soc. Coll. and Univ. Planners, Phi Delta Kappa. Methodist (trustee). Mem. adv. bd. Am. Sch. and Univ., 1968—; cons. school planning of Nation's Schools, 1964—. Home: 3030 Sleepy Hollow Rd Falls Church VA 22042 Office: US Office Edn 7th and D Sts NW Washington DC 20202

CAMERON, JOHN LAWSON, ins. exec.; b. Bklyn., Feb. 20, 1902; s. William F. and Jessie R. (Wyatt) C.; A.B., Williams Coll., 1922; m. Eleanor V. A. Moak, Aug. 20, 1932. With Guardian Life Ins. Co. Am., 1930-, v.p., 1943-57, pres., 1957-64, chmn. bd., 1964—, hon. chmn. bd., also dir., 1943—. Past pres. bd. reps. Stamford. Fellow Soc. Actuaries; mem. Phi Beta Kappa. Home: 5179 Hidden Harbor Rd Sarasota, FL 33581. Office: 201 Park Av S New York City NY 10017

CAMERON, MERIBETH ELLIOTT, retired coll. prof. and adminstr.; b. Ingersoll, Ont., Can., May 22, 1905; d. John Shaw and Margaret Alberta (Elliott) Cameron; brought to U.S., 1906, naturalized 1936; A.B. with great distinction, Stanford, 1925, A.M., 1926, Ph.D., 1928; A.M., Radcliffe Coll., 1927; L.H.D., Wheaton Coll., 1958; Litt.D., Oberlin Coll., 1961; D.Lit., U. Western Australia, 1962; LL.D., Mt. Holyoke Coll., 1970. Instr. history Reed Coll., 1928-34, Flora Stone Mather Coll., Case-Western Res. U., 1934-37, asst. prof., 1937-41; prof. history, dean Milw.- Downer Coll., 1941-48; vis. prof. Far Eastern history Claremont Grad. Sch., summers 1944, 45, Stanford, 1945-46; acad. dean, prof. history Mt. Holyoke Coll., 1948-70, acting pres., 1954, 66, 60-69, emeritus, 1970—. Mem. Mass. adv. com. U.S. Commn. Civil Rights, 1958-61. Trustee Westover Sch. Research grantee for study in China by Am. Council of Learned Soc., 1936-37. Mem. Am. Hist. Assn., Assn. Asian Studies, Am. Assn. U. Profs., Am. Assn. U. Women (chmn. com. internat. relations 1953-59), Nat. Assn. Women Deans and Counsellors, Internat. Fedn. U. Women (council 1953-56, pres. 1959-62), Phi Beta Kappa. Author: Reform Movement in China, 1898-1912-1931, reprints published 1963, 69; The United States and Eastern Asia, A Study Guide, 1950; China, Japan and the United States, A Study Guide, 1956; China in Revolution, A Study Guide, 1959. Co-author: China, Japan and the Powers, 1952, rev. edition, 1960. Book rev. editor Far Eastern Quar., 1942-51, Jour. Nat. Assn. Deans of Women, 1947- 58. Contbr. articles on Chinese and Japanese history profl. jours. Home: 30 Ashford Lane South Hadley MA 01075

CAMERON, NORMAN ALEXANDER, psychopathologist, educator; b. Longueuil, Que., Can., Apr. 24, 1896; came to U.S., 1907, naturalized, 1937; A.B. U. Mich., 1923, Ph.D., 1927; postgrad. U. Wis. Med. Sch., 1929-31; M.D., Johns Hopkins, 1933; M.A. (hon.), Yale, 1953; m. Eugenia Sue Cass, Nov. 22, 1922. Asst. in psychology U. Mich., 1923-24; instr., asst. prof. U. Wis., 1924-30; asst., instr., asso. in psychiatry Johns Hopkins Med. Sch., 1933-38; house officer, asst. resident, sr. resident psychiatrist Johns Hopkins Hosp., 1933-37, diagnostic clinic psychiatrist, 1937-38; asso. prof. psychology Cornell U. Med. Coll., 1938-39; attending psychiatrist N.Y. Hosp., 1938- 39; prof. psychology U. Wis., 1939-47, prof. psychology and psychiatry, 1947-53; prof. psychiatry Yale Sch. Medicine, 1953—, asso. psychiatrist Yale Psychiat. Inst., 1953—. Mem. Conf. on Psychiat. Edn., 1950-52; spl. commn. on psychodynamics, 1951-52; mem. mental health panel Pres.'s Commn. on Health of Nation, 1952-53. Recipient Fromm-Reichmann award for research in schizophrenia Am. Acad. of Psychoanalysis, 1969. Fellow Am. Psychoanalytic Assn., Am. Psychol. Assn. (life, award for distinguished contbns. in clin. psychology 1964), Am. Psychiat. Assn. (life); mem. Internat. Psychoanalytic Assn., Western New Eng. Psychoanalytic Soc., Western New Eng. Psychoanalytic Inst. (lectr.), Group for Advancement Psychiatry, Sigma Xi, Phi Beta Kappa, Phi Sigma, Gamma Alpha, Nu Sigma Nu. Club: University (New Haven). Author: Cerebral Destruction in Its Relation to Maze Learning, 1928; Reasoning, Regression and Communication in Schizophrenics, 1938; Psychology of Behavior Disorders, 1947; co-author; Personality and the Behavior Disorders, 1944; Language and Thought in Schizophrenia, 1944; Mental Disorders in Late Maturity, 1945; Behavior Pathology, 1951; co-author, asso. editor American Handbook of Psychiatry, 2 vols. 1959; Personality Development and Psychopathology, 1963. Address: 36 Foote Hill Rd Northford CT 06472

CAMERON, PAUL A., mfg. co. exec.; b. 1921; married. With Purolator, Inc., 1964—, now pres., also dir. Address: 970 Brunswick Av Rahway NJ 07065

CAMERON, RICHARD RAY, psychiatrist; b. Wheeling, W.V., Sept. 17, 1910; s. Albert Ernest and Zoe Shockley (Barker) C.; B.A., W.Va. U., 1932; M.D., Jefferson Med. Coll., 1936; m. Ellen Irene Jones, Mar. 2, 1935; children—Richard Douglas, Bonnie Jean (Mrs. Gary Dukes), Bruce Robin. Heather Anne, Scott Kenneth. Rotating intern George F. Geisinger Meml. Hosp., Danville, Pa., 1936-37; instr. pathology U. Ark. Sch. Medicine, 1937-38; commd. 1st lt., M.C., U.S. Army, 1938, advanced through grades to col., 1954; assigned Philippines, 1945-46; resident psychiatry Fitzsimons Army Hosp., 1948-51, chief dept., 1951-52; asst. chief psychiat. cons. div. Office Surgeon Gen., U.S. Army, 1952-53; sr. resident neurology Walter Reed Army Hosp., 1953-54; chief psychiatry and neurology service Ft. Dix, N.J., 1954-55: chief psychiat. service Brooke Army Hosp., Ft. Sam Houston, Tex., 1955-56, chief dept. neuropsychiatry, 1956-58; ret., 1958; clin. dir. Mental Health Inst., Independence, Ia., 1958-59; pvt. practice psychiatry and neurology, Cedar Rapids, Ia., 1959-60; dir. psychiat. services for correctional and juvenile instns. Ia. Dept. Mental Health, 1960-61, also supt. Security Mental Hosp., Anamosa, Ia.; cons. Mich. Dept. Mental Health, 1961-62; med. supt. Newberry (Mich.) State Hosp., 1962-65; dir. Shiawasse County (Mich.) Mental Health Center, 1965-68; clin. dir. edn., tng. and research San Antonio (Tex.) State Hosp., 1968—; professorial lectr. neuroanatomy George Washington Sch. Medicine, 1952- 53, 53-54; asso. clin. prof. psychiatry U. Tex. Med. Sch. at San Antonio, Antonio, 1970—; dir. dept. neuropsychiatry, lectr. Army Med. Service Sch., Brooke Army Med. Center, 1956-58. Diplomate Am. Bd. Psychiatry and Neurology. Fellow Am. Psychiat. Assn.; mem. A.M.A., Tex. Med. Assn., Phi Beta Kappa, Delta Phi Alpha, Alpha Kappa Kappa, Kappa Beta Phi. Contbr. profl. jours. Address: 8930 Callaghan Rd San Antonio TX 78230 Office: San Antonio State Hosp PO Box 23310 San Antonio TX 78223

CAMERON, ROBERT HORTON, mathematician; b. Bklyn., May 17, 1908; s. Henry Horton and Florence (Brown) C.; A.B., Cornell U., 1929, M.A., 1930, Ph.D., 1932; m. Ethel Cartmell, June 27, 1931; children—Alice (Mrs. Richard Bostrom), Jean (Mrs . Darrel Hiel). Instr., Cornell U., 1929-33; Nat. Research fellow Brown U., Princeton U. and Inst. for Advanced Study (Princeton, N.J.), 1933-35; instr. Mass. Inst. Tech., 1935-37, asst. prof. math., 1937-43, asso. prof., 1943- 45; prof. math. U. Minn., 1945—, also chmn. math. dept., 1957-63; vis. mathematician Inst. of Numerical Analysis, Nat. Bur. of Standards, U. Cal. at Los Angeles, summer 1948. Mem. applied math. group OSRD, N.Y.U., 1944-45, Inst. for Advanced Study, 1953-54. Recipient Chauvneet prize Math. Assn. Am., 1944. Mem. Math. Assn. Am., Am. Math. Soc., A.A.A.S., Am. Assn. U. Profs., Sigma Xi. Baptist. Contbr. articles on math. research to profl. jours. Home: 3519 Stinson Blvd Minneapolis MN 55418

CAMERON, RONALD G., financial co. exec.; b. Los Angeles, Dec. 30, 1941; grad. cum laude, U. Redlands, 1963; m. Shirley A. Shears, May 10, 1968; 1 son, Mark Daniel. Vice pres. Corporate Securities, Inc., 1964-67; founder Independent Securities Corp., Pasadena, Cal., 1967, pres., dir., 1967—. Author: Technical Analysis of Stock Trends, 1963. Home: 140 W Orange Grove St Arcadia CA 91006 Office: 201 S Lake Av Pasadena CA 91101

CAMERON, RONDO, economist, educator; b. Linden, Tex., Feb. 20, 1925; s. Burr S. and Annie May (Dalrymple) C.; A.B., Yale, 1948, A.M., 1949; Ph.D., U. Chgo., 1952; m. Claydean Zumbrunnen, July 26, 1946; children—Alan, Cindia. Instr., Yale, 1951-52; asst. prof. U. Wis. at Madison, 1952-56, asso. prof., 1957-61, prof. econs. and history, dir. grad. program econ. history, 1961-69; William Rand Kenan Univ. prof. Emory U., 1969—; vis. prof. U. Chgo., 1956-57; spl. field rep. Rockefeller Found., S.A., 1965- 67. Chmn. Council Research Econ. History, 1967-69. Fulbright scholar, France, 1950-51; Guggenheim fellow, Europe, 1954-55, 70-71; fellow Center Advanced Study Behavioral Scis., 1958-59; Fulbright prof. U. Glasgow, 1962-63. Mem. Am. Econ. Assn., Am., Econ. hist. assns. Author: France and the Economic Development of Europe, rev. edit., 1966 (trans. French and Spanish 1971); Banking in the Early Stages of Industrialization,

1967; The European World, 2d edit., 1970. Editor: Essays in French Economic History, 1970; Civilization Since Waterloo, 1971; Banking and Economic Development, 1972. Am. rev. editor of Econ. History Rev., 1960-65; rev. editor Jour. Econ. History, 1968-69. Contbr. articles profl. jours. Home: 860 Castle Falls Dr NE Atlanta GA 30329

CAMERON, THOMAS BROWN, educator, chemist; b. Newburgh, N.Y., Mar. 22, 1916; s. T. Brown and Rose Ethel (Taylor) C.; B.S. in Chemistry, Rensselaer Poly. Inst., 1937, M.S., 1938, Ph.D. in Inorganic Chemistry, 1942; m. Virginia Leggett, June 24, 1944; children—Ann Leggett, Beth Leggett, John Taylor. Mem. faculty Rensselaer Poly. Inst., 1941-36, instr. chemistry 1942-46; mem. faculty U. Cin., 1946—, prof. chemistry, 1956—, dir. undergrad. studies in chemistry, 1959-62, chmn. dept., 1962-66. Asso. chemist Argonne Nat. Lab., 1948-49. Area radiol. officer Ohio Civil Def. Orgn., 1950-56: faculty chmn. com. coll. work P.E. Diocese So. Ohio, 1954-59. Recipient of Clin. Chemist award, 1966. Mem. Am. Chem. Soc. (chmn. Cin. Sect. 1956-57, nat. councillor 1951-53, 61—), A.A.A.S., Ohio Acad. Sci., Am. Assn. U. Profs., Sigma Xi, Phi Lambda Upsilon (nat. pres. 1960- 63). Home: 5747 Davey Av Cincinnati OH 45224

CAMERON, THOMAS WILLIAM LANE, investment co. exec.; b. Newton, Mass., Feb. 19, 1927; s. Percy G. and Mary W. D. (Mitchell) C.; A.B. cum laude, Harvard, 1948, M.B.A., 1951; m. Carol Louise Soliday, June 17, 1950; childrenHelen Delone, Thomas Mitchell. With sales dept. Procter & Gamble, Boston, 1951-53; with Hopper, Soliday, Brooke, Sheridan, Inc., Phila., 1953—, partner, 1961- -, pres., 1966—. Chmn. Phila.-Balt.-Washington Stock Exchange, 1970- -. bd. govs., 1963—. Bd. dirs. Paoli Meml. Hosp. Served with USNR, 1944-46. Mem. Pa. Economy League (chmn. finance com.). Clubs: Waynesborough Country (pres. 1965-67) (Paoli, Pa.); Harvard (pres. 1965-66, Harvard Bus. Sch. (pres. 1962-64) (Phila.). Home: 15 Horseshoe Lane Paoli PA 19301 Office: 1420 Walnut St Philadelphia PA 19102

CAMERON, WILLIAM KIMMEL, govt. ofcl.; b. Toledo, Dec. 22, 1922; s. Donald E.A. and Edith E. (Kimmel) C.; student Miami U., Oxford, O.. 1941-43; B.A., J.D., George Washington U., 1950; m. Kathleen Norris Depue, June 3, 1950; children—Susan Ruxton, Amy Barton, Deborah Ames, William Kimmel, Christine Ayres. Admitted to D.C. bar, 1950; atty., adviser Gen. Services Adminstrn., Washington, 1950-55, asst. regional counsel region 3, 1955-63, dir. utilization and disposal services region 3, 1963-65; asst. commr. property disposition FHA, Dept. Housing and Urban Devel., Washington, 1965, now dir. property disposition div. Renewal and Housing Mgmt. Served with USAAF, 1943-46. Recipient Spl. Service award for performance as atty. adviser Office of Regional Counsel, Gen. Services Adminstrn., 1957, Outstanding Rating Superior Performance, 1962, Meritorious Service award, 1965; FHA Commendation award for performance, 1968. Mem. Fed. Bar. Assn., Phi Delta Phi (exchequer 1948- 49), Phi Delta Theta. Episcopalian. Mason. Home: 7405 Shenandoah Av Annandale VA 22003 Office: 451 7th St SW Washington DC 20410

CAMICIA, NICHOLAS THOMAS, holding co. exec.; b. Welch, W.Va., Apr. 23, 1916; s. Anthony and Antonia (Santini) C.; B.S. in Mining Engring., Va. Poly. Inst., 1938; m. Virginia Brown, May 11, 1941; children—Karen, Thomas (dec.). Mining engr. Pond Creek Pocahontas Co., 1938-41; supt. Island Creek Coal Co., Holden, W.Va., 1949-49, div. mgr., 1949-53, gen. mgr., 1953-57, v.p., gen. mgr. 1957-63, exec. v.p., 1963-64, dir., 1964; exec. v.p. Freeman Coal Mining Corp., 1965-68, pres. 1968-69; pres. United Electric Coal Cos., 1968-69; president, dir. Pittston Co., 1969—, chief exec. officer, 1970—; dir. Brink's, Inc. Served from 2d lt. to maj., AUS, 1941-45. Decorated Bronze Star; Order Orange-Nassau with swords (Netherlands). Mem. Am. Mining Congress (bd. dirs.), Nat. Coal Assn. (bd. dirs.), Bituminous Coal Operators Assn. (bd. dirs.), Nat. Mgmt. Assn., W.Va. Coal Mining Inst. (past pres.), Am. Mgmt. Assn., Nat. Mine Rescue Assn. (past pres.), Am. Inst. Mining, Metall., and Petroleum Engrs., Va. C. of C., Rocky Mountain Coal Mining Inst. Clubs: Pelham Country; Sky; Chicago Athletic. Home: 85 Country Club Lane Pelham Manor NY 10803

CAMINOS, HORACIO, educator, architect; b. Buenos Aires, Argentina, Apr. 5, 1914; s. Carlos N. and Maria E. (Crottogini) C.; arquitecto, U. Buenos Aires, 1939: m. Elena Ines Chapman, Sept. 13, 1943; children—Carlos H., José, Miguel, Maria I.. Maria P., Ana M. Came to U.S., 1952, naturalized, 1965. Prof. architecture and town planning U. Tucuman (Argentina), 1946-50; chief architect Univ. City, Tucuman, 1948-50; prof. architecture Archtl. Assn., London, Eng., 1951-52, U. N.C., 1952-61, Harvard, fall 1962, Mass. Inst. Tech., 1962—; prin. works include univ. campus plans and bldgs. U. Buenos Aires, 1961-67, U. Los Andes-Merida (Venezuela), 1963- 67, campus plan U. Carabobo, Valencia, Venezuela. Author: (with John Turner and John Steffran) Urban Dwelling Environments. Spl. research and design two types of membrane structures, also low cost housing and urban settlements in developing countries. Home: 83 Fairmont Av Newton MA 02158 Office: Mass Inst Tech Cambridge MA 02139

CAMINOS, RICARDO AUGUSTO, educator, Egyptologist; b. Buenos Aires, Argentina, July 11, 1915; s. Carlos Norberto and Maria (Crottogini) C.; M.A., U. Buenos Aires, 1938; Ph.D., U. Chgo., 1947; D.Phil., U. Oxford, 1952. Research asst. Oriental Inst., U. Chgo., 1943-44; Rockefeller fellow U. Chgo. and Oxford, 1944-46; Oriental Inst. research fellow U. Chgo., 1946-47, epigraphist, expdn. at Luxor, Upper Egypt, 1947-50; asst. prof. Egyptology Brown U., 1952-57, asso. prof., 1957-64, prof., 1964—, chmn. dept., 1971—; field dir. Egypt Exploration Soc. and Brown U. expdn. to Gebel es-Silsilah, Upper Egypt, 1955-59, Semna, Sudanese Nubia, 1962-63, Kumma, Sudanese Nubia, 1963-65. Guggenheim Meml. Found. fellow in Europe and Egypt, 1958-59; vis. prof. Egyptology, U. Buenos Aires, 1960. Mem. Oxford Soc., Egypt Exploration Soc., Deutches Archaologisches Institut (corr. mem.). Author: Late-Egyptian Miscellanies, 1954; Literary Fragments in the Hieratic Script, 1956; The Chronicle of Prince Osorkon, 1958; Gebel es-Silsilah, Vol. I, 1963; Shrines and Rock-Inscriptions of Ibrim, 1968; The New-Kingdom Temples of Buhen, Vols. I and II, 1972; also articles in field. Office: Brown U Providence RI 02912

CAMM, FRANK AMBLER, army officer; b. Ft. Knox, Ky., Mar. 13, 1922; s. Frank and Felicia (Taylor) C.; B.S., U.S. Mil. Acad., 1943; M.S., Harvard, 1951; M.A., George Washington U., 1964; grad. advanced mgmt. program Harvard, 1966; m. Arlene Margaret Brinkman, June 21, 1947; children—Frank Ambler, Arlene Hartley. Commd. 2d lt. U.S. Army, 1943, advanced through grades to maj. gen., 1972; mem. army staff Pentagon, Washington, 1957-60, 68-69, Office Sec. Def., 1963-67; comdg. officer Engr. Group, Germany, 1961-62; planner 7th Army, Germany, 1962-63; assigned Mil. Assistance Command, J-33, Saigon, Vietnam, 1967-68; S. Pacific div. engr., San Francisco, 1969—. Chmn. Cal. Debris Commn., 1969—, Pacific S.W. Interagy. Com., 1969—; mem. Cal. Fed. Interagy. Group, 1969—, Coastal Engring. Research Bd., 1970—, Bd. Engrs. Rivers and Harbors, 1971—. Pres. local P.T.A., 1955; active Boy Scouts Am., 1958-60, 62, 64. Decorated Legion of Merit with oak leaf cluster, Meritorious Service medal, Bronze Star with V and 3 oak leaf clusters; recipient award for scholarship in soil mechanics Harvard Grad. Sch. Engring., 1951. Registered profl. engr., D.C. Mem. Assn. U.S. Army, Soc. Am. Mil. Engrs., Am. Soc. C.E., Episcopalian. Clubs: Commonwealth of Cal., Sierra (San Francisco); Army-Navy Country (Arlington, Va.). Home: 342 Arguello Blvd Presidio of San Francisco CA 94129 Office: 630 Sansome St San Francisco CA 94111

CAMMACK, CECIL CAGLE, oil co. exec.; b. Matador, Tex., Mar. 24, 1908; s.William Richard and Jennie E. (Cagle) C.; B.A., Simmons U., Abilene, Tex., 1931; LL.B. with highest honors, U. Tex., 1936; m. Ruth Estelle Reed, Mar. 24, 1933; children—Virginia (Mrs. Donald L. Cotten), Cecil Cagle. Tchr., band dir. Saunderson (Tex.) pub. schs., 1931-34; admitted to Tex. bar, 1936, Okla. bar, 1956; pvt. practice, Ft. Worth, 1936-37, Dallas, 1937-38; asst. atty. gen. Tex., 1939-43; with Cities Service Oil Co., 1943—, gen. counsel, dir., 1965—; dir. Cities Service Pipeline Co. Bd. dirs. Children's Med. Center. Mem. Am., Tex., Okla., Tulsa County, Washington County, Fed. Power bar assns., Ind. Natural Gas Assn. Mid-Continent Oil and Gas Assn., Am. Petroleum Inst., Assn. Oil Pipe Lines, Order of Coif. Democrat. Baptist. Clubs: Austin (Tex.); Petroleum (Ft. Worth); Hillcrest Country (Bartlesville, Okla.): Tulsa, Southern Hills Country (Tulsa). Home: 2946 E 57th St Tulsa OK 74105 Office: PO Box 300 Oil Center Bldg Tulsa OK 74012

CAMMANN, FRED G., advt. agy. exec. Sr. v.p. TV comml. prodn. Compton Advt., Inc., N.Y.C. Office: 625 Madison Av New York City NY 10022*

CAMMAROSANO, JOSEPH RAPHAEL, economist, educator; b. Mt. Vernon, N.Y., Mar. 12, 1923; s. Louis Raphael and Mary Nancy (Sansone) C.; student Stanford, 1943-44; B.S. cum laude, Fordham U., 1947, Ph.D., 1956; M.A., N.Y.U., 1949; m. Rosalie Nancy Esposito, Nov. 22, 1952; children—Louis, Nancy, Joseph. Inspector, U.S. Bur. Customs, 1948-50; asst. prof. Iona Coll., 1950-55; asst. prof. Fordham U., Bronx, N.Y., 1956-60, asso. prof., 1962-67, dir. Inst. Urban Studies, 1964—, prof. econs., 1967—, chmn. dept. econs., 1969, exec. v.p., 1969—; fiscal economist U.S. Bur. of Budget, Washington, 1961-62. Fiscal cons. N.Y. State Temp. Commn. on Constl. Conv., 1957-58, N.Y. State Spl. Legislative Com. on Revision and Simplification of the Constn., 1958-60, N.Y. State Tax Structure Study Com., 1962—, N.Y. State Temp. Commn. on the Constn., 1966-67; econ. cons. N.Y. Bell Telephone Co., 1960; cons. N.Y.C. Econ. Devel. Adminstrn., 1969; vice chmn. Regional Manpower Adv. Com. to Sec. Labor, 1970—. Trustee Fordham Rd. Devel. Corp., Cathedral Coll., Douglaston, N.Y. Served with AUS, 1943-46; ETO. Mem. Am. Econ. Assn., Phi Delta Kappa. Author: Highway Finance in New York State, 1958; A Profile of the Bronx Economy, 1967; A Plan for the Redevelopment of the Brooklyn Navy Yard, 1968; The Long Range Forecasting of Telephone Demand, 1960. Home: 76 N Fulton Av Mount Vernon NY 10550

CAMP, CARLTON LEWIS, architect, state ofcl.; b. Stockton, Cal., June 11, 1914; s. Clarence Edson and Alice (Kibbee) C.; grad. Los Angeles Art Center Sch., 1935; student U. So. Cal. Extension, 1937, 42, 45, Los Angeles City Coll., 1938-39, U. Cal. at Los Angeles, 1946-48; m. Pearl E. Gutterman, Mar. 16, 1940 (div. Apr. 1958); children—Walter Dean, Carol Ann. Archtl. designer Luminous Structures, Inc., Los Angeles, 1935-39, Fed. Home Service Bur., 1940, H. W. Sampson, 1941-42, David C. Jones Steel Co., 1942-44; architect Pub. Works, City of Los Angeles, 1944-49; supervising architect Cal., Los Angeles, 1949-60, prin. architect, Sacramento, 1960—. Leader, Boy Scouts Am., Los Angeles, 1950-55. Mem. A.I.A., Cal. State Employees Assn., Cal. State Mgmt. Club. Democrat. Presbyn. Clubs: California Men's, Sierra. Archtl. works include comml., religious, state colls., instns., office bldgs. Home: 956 4th Av Sacramento CA 95818 Office: 1500 5th St Sacramento CA 95814

CAMP, DAVID BENNETT, educator; b. Alberta, Va., Jan. 30, 1910; s. David Oscar and Eva Sylvester (Bennett) C.; B.S., Coll. William and Mary, 1941; Ph.D., U. Rochester, 1950; m. Eunice Moore Richardson, Feb. 7. 1948; childrenDavid Paul, Thomas Adams. Instr. chemistry Coll. William and Mary-Va. Poly. Inst., 1942-46; asso. prof. phys. sci. U. Ida., 1949-50; asso. prof. chemistry Oglethorpe U., 1950-52, U. S.D., 1952-54; mem. faculty U. of South, 1954—, prof. cehmistry, chmn. dept., 1956—. Mem. Am. Chem Soc., Tenn. Acad. Sci., Phi Beta Kappa, Sigma Xi. Address: Dept Chemistry Univ of South Sewanee TN 37375

CAMP, EARL D., educator: b. Magazine, Ark., June 12, 1918; s. Chester Clyde and Minnie Mae (Chappell) C.; B.S., Tex. Tech. Coll., 1941; M.S., U. N.M., 1943; Ph.D., State U. Ia., 1952; m. Hattie Charlotte Ballow, July 17, 1948; 1 son. William Earl. Mem. war research staff Columbia, 1943-44; mem. faculty Tex. Tech. Coll., 1945—, prof. biology, head dept., 1959—. Mem. evaluation panels NSF. Fellow A.A.A.S., (exec. com., chmn. and sec. bot. sect. Southwestern and Rocky Mountain div.. pres. 1965-66); mem. Am. Inst. Biol. Socs., Sigma Xi, Sigma Chi. Baptist. Co-author tech. papers. Home: 3704 46th St Lubbock TX 79414

CAMP, EHNEY ADDISON, Jr., ins. exec.; s. Wheeler and Pearl (Hendrick) C.; grad. U. Ala., 1928; m. Mildred Tillman, February 25, 1933; children—Patricia (Mrs. Faulkner), Mary Eugenia (Mrs. Boulware), Ehney Addison, III. With Ward, Sterne & Co., investment bankers, Birmingham, Ala., 1928, Bankers Mortgage Bond Co., Birmingham, 1929-32; mgr. mortgage loan dept. Liberty Nat. Life Ins. Co., Birmingham, 1932-34, asst. treas., 1934-35, treas., 1935-43, dir., 1940—, v.p., treas., 1943-60, exec. v.p., 1960—, treas., 1960-64; former pres. First Nat. Bank of Columbiana, Ala.; dir. Brown Service Funeral Homes Co., Am. Cast Iron Pipe Co. Mem. adv. com. Fed. Housing Commr. Washington; mem. nat. com. Vol. Home Mortgage Credit Program; mem. vol. credit restraint com. life ins. firms apptd by Fed. Res. Bd., 1951-52; mem. Adv. Com. Fed. Housing Policies. Co-chmn. Community Chest, Jefferson County; pres. Anti-Tb Assn. Trustee, mem. statewide adv. com. med. sch., mem. alumni council U. Ala.; past trustee and pres. Jefferson County Tb Sanitorium. Mem. Am. Life Conv. (past chmn. financial sect.), Life Ins. Assn. Am. (joint com. on securities and valuation of assets, chmn. com. housing and mortgage lending), Mortgage Bankers Assn. Am. (bd. govs.), U. Ala. Alumni Assn. (past pres.), Birmingham Mortgage Bankers Assn. (past pres.), Phi Beta Kappa, Beta Gamma Sigma, Sigma Nu, Omicron Delta Kappa. Methodist (past chmn. bd. stewards, now chmn. bd. trustees). Clubs: Kiwanis (past pres.), Mountain Brook, Country, The Club, Birmingham Country (Birmingham); Indian Hills (Tuscaloosa); Relay House. Home: 3232 E Briarcliff Rd Birmingham AL 35223

CAMP, HUGH DOUGLAS, paper products mfg. exec.; b. Franklin, Va., Apr. 4, 1903; s. James James Leonidas and Caroline Fountain (Savage) C.; student Wake Forest Coll., U. Va., Phila. Textile Sch.; m. Ada Norris Coleman, 1927; 1 dau., Caroline (Mrs. Frank Robertson Motley). Vice pres. Roanoke Mills Co., Roanoke Rapids, N.C., 1926-37; v.p. Camp Mfg. Co., 1937-54, exec. v.p., 1954-56, pres., Franklin, Va., 1956—; exec. v.p. Union Bag-Camp Paper Corp., N.Y.C. 1956-60, chmn. bd., 1960—, also dir.; dir. First Merchants Bank of Richmond, Vaughan & Co. Bank, Franklin, Va. Bd. dirs. Camp Found. Mem. Newcomen Soc. N.A. Clubs: Canadian, New York Yacht, Commonwealth, Merchants, Union League, Rotary (N.Y.C.). Home: 25 Sutton Pl New York City NY 10022 Office: 233 Broadway New York City NY 10007

CAMP, JAMES LEONIDAS, Jr., business exec.; b. Franklin, Va., June 7, 1895; s. James Leonidas and Carrie Fountain (Savage) C.: A.B., Wake Forest Coll., 1914; student Columbia. 1914-15; D.Sc. (hon.), U. Richmond, 1958; m. Mary Clav, May 21, 1918; 1 son, James Leonidas, III. Began as lumber plant worker, 1915-19; with Camp Mfg. Co., Franklin, 1919-56, successively salesman, v.p., head sales, 1919-26, pres., dir., 1926-56, chmn. bd., dir., 1956; chmn. exec. com. Union Camp Corp., 1956-69; dir. Va. Nat. Bank; trustee Am. Forest Products Industries, Inc. Pres. J.L. Camp Found., Inc.; trustee U. Va. Grad. Sch. Bus. Adminstrn., Va. Found. Ind. Colls., Nat. Fund for Med. Edn., Bapt. Orphanage, Salem, Va., U. Richmond. Served with USN, 1918. Mem. Am. Paper and Pulp Assn. (exec. com.), Nat. Assn. Mfrs. (past bd. dirs.), Nat. Lumber Mfrs. Assn. (bd. dirs.), Va. Mus. Fine Arts, Newcomen Soc. N.A., English-Speaking Union, Phi Kappa Sigma. Democrat. Baptist. Clubs: Princess Anne Country (Virginia Beach); Country, Commonwealth, Virginia (Richmond); Union League, Merchants (N.Y.C.); Farmington Country (Charlottesville, Va.). Home: Wyndie Crest Franklin VA 23851 Office: Union Camp Corp Franklin VA 23851

CAMP, JOHN N., Happy, congressman; b. Enid, Okla., May 11, 1908; s. John Rowland and Minnie Catherine (Newbold) C.; ed. Phillips U., Enid; m. Vera Juanita Overman, Nov. 26, 1930; children—Patricia (Mrs. Roy G. Rainey), Kay (Mrs. Dan Dillingham), John N. III, Steven Richard. Mem. Okla. Legislature; chmn. Okla. Bd. Pub. Affairs; mem. 91st and 92d Congress 6th Dist. Okla. Pres. Great Salt Plains council Boy Scouts Am.; Legislative supt. Okla. Girls State; area dir. Okla. Northwest. Bd. dirs. Miss Okla. Pageant; mem. grad. sem. council Phillips U.; mem. gov. com. Christian Ch. Found. Recipient Silver Beaver award Boy Scouts Am.; Master Farmers certificate Future Farmers Am. Hon. mem. 4-H Clubs Okla.; mem. Okla. C. of C. (bd. dirs.), Hist. Soc. Disciples of Christ (Charter). Republican. Mem. Christian Ch. (elder). Mason (32, Shriner, Jester). Office: House Office Bldg Washington DC 20005

CAMP, KATHERINE MERRILL LINDSLEY, peace orgn. exec.; b. Mt. Kisco, N.Y., July 10, 1918; d. Horace Nelson and Louise Elizabeth (Keyes) Lindsley; B.A. in Psychology and Edn., Swathmore Coll., 1940-42; cryptographer War Dept., 1942-43 children—David Lindsley, Nelson Evans, Anthony Merrill. Tchr., Buxton Sch., Short Hills, N.J., founder, dir. Fairmount Kindergarten, Haverton, Pa., 1948-51; pres. U.S. sect. Womens Internat. League Peace and Freedom, 1966—, cons. internat. exec. com., 1965-67. Pres. P.T.A., Plymouth Meeting Friends Sch., 1958-59; founder, pres. Citizens Bi-Racial Study Group, Norristown, Pa., 1962-64. Recipient Bersh Community Brotherhood award, 1965. Mem. Soc. of friends. Home: 200 Hughes Rd King of Prussia PA 19406 Office: 1 N 13th St Philadelphia PA 19103

CAMP, PAUL RICE, educator; b. Middletown, Conn., Dec. 29, 1919; s. Burton H. and Rachel (Rice) C.; B.A., Wesleyan U., 1941; M.A., Harvard, 1946; Ph.D., Pa. State U., 1951; m. Polly A. Newton, June 28, 1958; children—Elizabeth, Susan, Jennifer. Engr., Naval Research Lab., Washington, 1941-44; instr. physics Wesleyan U., 1947-48; physicist RCA Research Lab., Princeton, N.J., 1951-53; Ford fellow Reed Coll., 1953-54; asst. prof. physics Poly. Inst. Bklyn., 1954-57, asso. prof., 1957-61; chief materials research br. U.S.A. Cold Regions Research and Engring. Lab., 1961-63, physicist at large, 1963-65; staff mem., Commn. on Coll. Physics, U. Mich., 1965-67; head dept. physics U. Me., Orono, 1967—. Served with USNR, 1944-45. Mem. Am. Phys. Soc., Am. Assn. Physics Tchrs., A.A.A.S., Sigma Xi, Sigma Pi Sigma. Home: 38 N Main Orono ME 04473

CAMP, THOMAS JAMES, Jr., army officer; b. Des Moines, Ia., Mar. 10, 1918; s. Thomas James and Mary (Mattis) C.; B.A., Yale U., 1940; M.A., U. Va., 1951; student Naval War Coll., 1962; m. Margaret Gibson Forsythe, Feb. 16, 1946; children—Thomas James III, Lawrence F., John L., David C. Commd. 2d lt. U.S. Army, 1941, advanced through grades to brig. gen., 1966—; comdg. officer 3d Inf. Div., 1963-64; asst. div. comdr. 7th Inf. div., Korea, 1967; dir. orgn. and tng. Dept. Army, 1968; asst. div. comdr. 25th Inf. Div., Vietnam, 1969-70; asst. chief staff Hdqrs. MACV, Saigon, 1970—. Decorated D.S.M., D.F.C., Legion of Merit. Home: 3505 Springland Lane NW Washington DC 20008 Office: Hdqrs MACV APO San Francisco CA 96222

CAMP, THOMAS RINGGOLD, hydraulic and san. engr.; b. San Antonio, Nov. 5, 1895; s. Harmon Clark and Mildred Stella (Dashiell) C.; B.S., Tex. A. and M. Coll., 1916; M.S., Mass. Inst. Tech., 1925; D.Sc. (hon.), Clarkson Coll., 1970; m. Margaret Alice Evans, June 15, 1925; children—Frances, John, Emilie (Mrs. R. F. Stouffer). Practicing engr., Tex., N.C., N.Y., N.J., 1916-29; hydraulic and san. engr., 1921—; asso. prof. san. engring., Mass. Inst. Tech., 1929-44; cons. engr., 1944—; founded Camp Dresser & McKee, Boston, 1947. Mem. adv. com. revision USPHS Drinking Water Standards, 1962. Served with U.S. Army, 1917-19. Recipient san sect. prize Boston Soc. C.E., 1941, hydraulic sect. prize, 1944, Desmond FitzGerald medal, 1949, Clemens Herschel award, 1970; Karl Emil Hilgard prize Am. Soc. C.E., 1941, J.C. Stevens hydraulic prize, 1945, J. James R. Croes medal, 1947, Samuel Arnold Greeley award, 1969; Dexter Brackett meml. medal N.E. Water Works Assn., 1943, 56; Fuller award Am. Water Works Assn., 1955; Rudolph Hering medal Am. Soc. C.E., 1956; New Eng. award Engring. Socs. New Eng., 1963; Distinguished Service award Nat. Clay Pipe Inst., 1966. Diplomate Am. Acad. Environmental Engrs., 1955. Fellow Am. Pub. Health Assn.; mem. Am. Soc. C.E. (Friedman award 1964; hon. mem.), Boston Soc. C.E. (pres. 1950; hon.), N.E. (pres. 1950; hon.), Am. water works assns., N.E. Sewage Works Assn. (pres. 1947), Environmental Engring. Intersoc. Bd. (founder, chmn. 1956-62), Am. Inst. Cons. Engrs., Water Pollution Control Fedn. (hon. mem.; fedn. established Thomas R. Camp medal 1964), Sigma Xi, Tau Beta Pi. Author: Water and Its Impurities, 1963 . Contbr. profl., tech. articles to profl. jours. Patentee in field. Office: 1 Center Plaza Boston MA 02108

CAMP, TRUMAN WILDES, educator; b. Newington, Conn., Dec. 6, 1904; s. Norman P. and Bertha (Wildes) C.; B.A., Yale, 1926, Ph.D., 1935; postgrad. U. Tex., 1928-31; m. Virginia I. Chapman, Aug. 1, 1940; 1 son, Roger C. Master, Collegiate Sch., New Haven, 1926-28; instr. English, U. Tex., 1928-31, 33-34, Conn. Coll. Commerce, 1934-35; instr. English, Tex. Technol. Coll.. 1935- 42, prof., 1950—, head dept., 1946-62. President Friends of Lubbock Pub. Library, 1960-61. Served to capt. USAAF, 1942-46. Mem. Nat. Council Tchrs. English, Tex. Conf. Coll. Tchrs. English (sec., treas. 1956-61, pres. 1963-64), South Central Modern Lang. Assn., Coll. English Assn., Modern Lang. Assn. Clubs: After Dinner Forum, Questers (Lubbock). Home: 2611 25th St Lubbock TX 79410

CAMP, WESLEY DOUGLASS, educator; b. Bedford Hills, N.Y., Jan. 2, 1915; s. Douglass Fletcher and Edna Mary (Westcott) C.; grad. Pennington (N.J.) Sch., 1932; A.B., Columbia, 1936, A.M., 1940, Ph.D., 1957; diplome d'etudes francaises, U. Lille (France), 1937; m. Kathleen Virginia Bamman, Dec. 22, 1936; children—Mary Virginia,

Wesley Douglass. Asst. d'anglais Lycee Faidherbe, Lille, 1936-37; mem. faculty Monmouth (N.J.) Coll., 1941-60, prof., chmn. social sci. dept., 1946-60; research Bibliotheque Nationale, Paris, France, 1960-61; asso. prof. history Carnegie Inst. Tech., 1961-62; prof. history, chmn. dept. history and govt. Adelphi U., 1962-65, chmn. history dept., 1965—; guest lectr. Hofstra U., Hempstead, N.Y., 1968-69. Trustee Elberon (N.J.) Meml. Ch. Mem. Am. Hist. Assn., Societe d'Histoire Moderne, Population Assn. Am., Am. Assn. U. Profs. Author: Marriage and the Family in France: An Essay in the History of Population, 1961; also revs. Home: 481 Dogwood Av West Hempstead NY 11552 Office: Adelphi U Garden City NY 11530

CAMP, WILLIAM BACON, govt. ofcl.; b. Greenville, Tex., Nov. 25, 1913; s. William Hille and Marguerite (Bacon) C.; student Tex. Mil. Coll., 1932, Baylor U., 1933; m. Lida Eileen Conner, Nov. 23, 1947. With U.S. Office Comptroller, 1937—, comptroller of currency, 1967—; mem. faculty Stonier Sch. Banking, Rutgers U., 1962—. Mem. Christian Ch. (chmn. trustees, elder). Rotarian. Home: 1397 Canterbury Way Rockville MD 20854 Office: Main Treasury Bldg Washington DC 20220

CAMP, WILLIAM PERRINE, psychiatrist; b. Bridgeport, Conn., Apr. 8, 1917; s. William E. and Helen M. (Olp) C.; A.B., Swarthmore Coll., 1940; postgrad. Rutgers U., 1945- 46; M.D., U. Pa., 1950; grad. Phila. Psychoanalytic Inst., 1960; m. Katherine M. Lindsley, June 11, 1941; children—David L., Nelson E., Anthony M. Intern Bryn Mawr (Pa.) Hosp., 1950-51; resident psychiatry Norristown (Pa.) State Hosp., 1951-54, mem. staff, 1954-59, supt., 1959- 63; commr. mental health Pa. Dept. Pub. Welfare, Harrisburg, 1963-67; dir. clin. services Pathway Sch., 1967-68; supt., psychiatrist-in-chief Friends Hosp., Phila., 1968—; clin. prof. psychiatry Hahnemann Med. Coll. Bd. dirs. Foulkeways at Gwynedd, Mental Health Assn. Southeastern Pa. (pres.), Pa. Mental Health Inc., Noyes Research Found. Served to capt. AUS, 1942-45; ETO. Decorated Bronze Star. Diplomate Am. Bd. Psychiatry and Neurology. Fellow Am. Psychiat. Assn., Pa., Phila. (pres. 1971) psychiat. socs., Phila. Psychoanalytic Soc.; mem. A.M.A. Mem. Soc. of Friends. Author: (with others) Psychiatric Nursing, 1964. Home: 200 Hughes Rd King of Prussia PA 19406 Office: Friends Hosp Roosevelt Blvd and Adams Av Philadelphia PA 19124

CAMP, WOFFORD BENJAMIN, farmer; b. Gaffney, S.C., Mar. 14, 1894; s. John Clayton and Mary Jane (Atkins) C.; B.S. Clemson Agrl. Coll., 1916; Dr. Agrl. Industries (hon.), 1951; grad. student U. Cal.; LL.D., Limestone Coll. 1955, Whittier Coll., 1958; m. Georgia Anna App, December, 14, 1921 (dec.); children—Wofford Benjamin, Donald Max; m. 2d, Louise Phifer Wise, Jan. 18, 1956. Charge coop. testing field crops U.S.D.A., S.C. 1916-17; founder cotton, San Joaquin Valley, Cal., 1917; agronomist charge cotton breeding and growing expts., San Joaquin Valley, others, 1917—; established, charge U.S. Expt. Sta., Shafter, Cal., 1922-28; agr. appraiser Bank of Am. Nat. Trust & Savs. Assn., 1929; mgr. Cal. Lands, Inc., Bank Am. subsidiary, 1929-33; head agrl. economist, asst. dir. cotton div. and So. region A.A.A., Washington, 1933-36; pres., owner Georgianna Farms, Inc., 1937-45; pres. W.B. Camp & Sons, Inc., 1946—; co-owner Calolina Farms and Calolina Cotton Ginning Co.; author Cal. One-variety Cotton law; founder Cal. Cotton Planting Seed Distbrs.; co-founder Cal. Cotton Coop. Assn.; founder Camp Irrigation Fund, S.C., and first to urge large scale conservation of water for irrigation in entire rainfall belt. Mem. com. on conservation and devel. soil and water resources U.S. Dept. Agr.; bd. dirs. Nat. Indsl. Conf. Bd. Founder W.B. Camp Found. (scholarship); bd. dirs. Nat. Rivers and Harbors Congress, co-chmn. com. conversions and uses saline water; trustee Bur. Water Resources, Clemson Alumni Found., Whittier Coll., Freedom's Found., Valley Forge; bd. govs. Agrl. Hall of Fame and Nat. Center, also chmn. nat. devel. com.; mem. pres.'s bd. Pepperdine Coll.; mem. adv. bd. Sch. Bus., Am. Univ. Mem. Kern County Potato Seed Assn. (founder, pres.), Nat. Potato Council (co-founder, v.p.), Asso. Farmers Cal. (past pres.), Kern County Mus. Assn., Am. Cancer Soc. (Cal. dir.), Crippled Children Soc. Cal., U.S. (v.p., treas., dir., chmn. agrl. com.) Chambers Commerce, Farm Bur., Phi Kappa Phi, Blue Key. Baptist. Mason, Rotarian. Club: Commonwealth (San Francisco). Author several agrl. bulls. Contbr. articles mags., newspapers. Home: 701 Oleander Av Bakersfield CA 93304 Office: PO Box 2028 Bakersfield CA 93303

CAMPA, ARTHUR LEON, educator; b. Guaymas, Mexico, Feb. 20, 1905 (parents U.S. citizens); s. Daniel and Delfina (Lopez) C.; A.B., U. of N.M. (Cutting research fellow, 1929), 1930, A.M., 1930; Ph.D., Columbia, 1940; was married to Lucille Cushing April 23, 1943; children—Mary Del (Mrs. Larry Price), Arthur L., Danielle Lucille, Celia, David. Chmn. dept. modern langs., Albuquerque High Sch., 1928; instr., French and Spanish, U. of N.M., 1929, asst. prof. modern langs., 1932-34, asso. prof., 1937-42, prof. modern langs., 1942-46; chmn. div. langs. and lit., U. of Denver, 1946; Guggenheim fellow for 1952; cultural attache Am. Embassy, Lima, Peru, 1955-57. Dir. Fiestas, U.S. Coronado Exposition Commn. 1940. Served as capt., Air Corps., Combat Intelligence, AUS, 1942. Awarded Bronze star, Mediterranean Theatre and 10 campaign stars, 1945. Mem. Am. Dialect Soc., Am. Assn. Tchrs. of Spanish and Portuguese, Am. Folklore Soc. (councillor), Folklore Soc. Brazil, Venezuela, Argentina, etc., Folklore Soc. Ams., Nat. Folk Festival Assn. (pres.), Folklore Soc. Mexico, Rocky Mountain Modern Lang. Assn., Colo. Authors League, Colo. Folklore Soc. (pres. 1950), The Westerners, Denver Corral, Roundup Foreman. Author: Spanish Folk Poetry in New Mexico, 1946; Acquiring Spanish, 1944; Mastering Spanish, 1945; Spanish Commercial Correspondence (with Bedichek), 1945; Treasure of the Sangre de Cristos; also bulls. on Spanish folklore. Home: 2031 S Madison St Denver CO 80210 Office: Univ Denver Denver CO 80210

CAMPAIGNE, CURTIS, UN ofcl.; born Mendham, N.J., July 6, 1912; s. Curtis and Edna Amory Amory (Foote) C.; grad. Montclair Acad., 1930; A.B. cum laude, Williams Coll., 1934; LL.B., Yale, 1938; m. Alice Marie Livesey, Oct. 1, 1938; children—Custis, Anthony Livesey, Jonathan Foote, Cathryn Marie. Admitted to N.Y. bar, 1939; joined Internat. Paper Co., 1942, asso. counsel, 1942-53; exec. dir. World Vets. Fund, U.S., 1953-54; sec.-gen. World Vets. Fedn., 1954-61, hon. v.p. 1961—; dir. U.S. AID Mission to Cambodia, 1962-63, dir. U.S. AID Mission to Guinea, 1964-67; spl. asst., human rights div. UN, 1967-68; UN ofcl. resident in Liberia, 1968- -. Nat. chmn. Am. Vets. Com., 1952-53. Served as cpl. USMC, 1944-45. Decorated Order of Merit (Italy); Order of Red Banner (Yugoslavia). Mem. N.Y.C. Bar Assn. Club: University. Home: 71 Plymouth St Montclair NJ 07042

CAMPAIGNE, ERNEST EDWIN, educator, chemist; b. Chgo., Feb. 13, 1914; s. John Herbert and Nellie (Daufel) C.; B.S., Northwestern U., 1936, M.S., 1938, Ph.D. in Biochemistry, 1941; m. Jean Hill White, Jan. 1, 1941; children—David Alan, Claudia Jean (Mrs. Ronald L. Buskirk), Barbara Naomi. Instr., Bowdoin Coll., 1940-41; research asso. Northwestern U., 1941-42; asso. biochemist M.D. Anderson Hosp. for Cancer Research, Galveston, Tex., 1942-43; faculty dept. chemistry Ind. U., Bloomington, 1943—, prof. chemistry, 1953—; vis. prof. U. Cal. at Los Angeles, 1954-55; cons. NIH, 1960-64, 66—; indsl. chem. cons., 1952—. Fellow N.Y. Acad. Scis., Ind. Acad. Sci.; mem. Am. Chem. Soc., Chem. Soc. (London), A.A.A.S. Author: (with J. C. Muhler and C. H. Rohrer) Introduction to Chemistry, 1960; Elementary Organic Chemistry, 1962. Research and publs. on synthesis of drugs, antihistamines, anticonvulsant drugs for treatment of epilepsy, molecular dimensions of drugs to interpret their optimum dimensions and nature of receptor sites. Home: 1240 E Wylie St Bloomington IN 47401

CAMPAIGNE, JAMESON GILBERT, columnist, writer; b. Bklyn., Jan. 16, 1914; s. Curtis and Edna Amory (Foote) C.; A.B., Williams Coll., 1936; m. Edith Louise Baker, Jan. 15, 1938; children—Jameson, Markham Baker, Jeffrey, Catherine. Sales work Yarkley & Co., Ltd., 1936-40; radio writer Compton Advt., Inc., N.Y.C., 1940-43; chief editorial writer Indpls. Star, 1946-51, editor editorial page, 1952-60, editor, 1960-69, editorial writer, columnist, 1969—; v.p. Audio Visual Services, Inc., Indpls.; dir. Calumet Publ. Co., Chgo. Served with USMCR, 1943-46. Recipient Lincoln Nat. Life Found. award for best editorial on Lincoln (2); Freedoms Found. medal, 1951, 53, award, 1952, 57; Ind. U. Writers Conf. award, 1960. Mem. Mont Pelerin Soc. Author: American Might and Soviet Myth, 1960; Check-off, 1961. Home: 746 Broadway Sonoma CA 95476 Office: 307 N Pennsylvania St Indianapolis IN 46204

CAMPANA, RICHARD JOHN, educator, botanist; b. Everett, Mass., Dec. 5, 1918; s. Joseph and Sarah Agnes (Shea) C.; B.S. in Forestry, U. Ida., 1943; M.F., Yale, 1947, Ph.D., 1952; m. Jean M. MacKenzie, July 2, 1945; children—Jane Helen, Mark Robert. Instr. forestry Pa. State U., 1947; asst. prof. botany N.C. State Coll., 1947-49; asst. plant pathologist, div. forestry pathologist Dept. Agr., 1949-52; asst. asso. plant pathologist Ill. Natural History Survey, 1952-56, 56-58; prof. botany U. Me., 1958—, head dept. botany and plant pathology, 1958-68; vis. prof. N.Y. State Coll. Forestry, Syracuse U., 1967; guest botanist Brookhaven Lab., 1967—. Adv. council Trees mag.; exam. mem. Me. Arborist Bd. Mem. Orono (Me.) Planning Bd., 1970—. Served with AUS, 1943-46. Decorated Bronze Star; recipient Bartlett research fellowship grant Yale. Mem. Am. Phytopath. Soc. (chmn. teaching com. 1965-67, editor jour. 1970—), Bot. Soc. Am., Mycol. Soc. Am., Internat. Shade Tree Conf. (pres. 1966-67, gov., pres. New Eng. chpt. 1965-67), Orono Conservation Com. (chmn. 1970—), Air Pollution Control Assn., A.A.A.S., Am. Inst. Biol. Scis., Me. Biol. Assn., Nature Conservancy Soc., Internat. Soc. Plant Pathology, Josselyn Bot. Soc., Me. Natural Resources Council, No. New Eng. Acad. Sci., Am. Assn. U. Profs., Sigma Xi, Phi Kappa Phi, Xi Sigma Pi. Author research and ednl. articles on tree diseases. Home: 25 Sunrise Terrace Orono ME 04473

CAMPANELLA, ROY, former profl. baseball player; b. Homestead, Pa., Nov. 19, 1921; s. John Campanella; m. Ruthe Willis, Jan. 3, 1939; five children. Mem. Negro profl. baseball teams prior to 1946; mem. Bklyn. Dodgers farms teams, 1946-48; catcher for Bklyn. Dodgers Profl. Baseball Team, 1949- 58; now propr. Roy Campanella, Inc., N.Y.C. Named Most Valuable Player in Nat. League three times; named to Baseball Hall of Fame, 1969; set maj. league records for catcher with home runs and runs batted in, 1953. Home: 114-1 179th St St Albans NY*

CAMPBELL, ALAN KEITH, univ. dean; b. Elgin, Neb., May 31, 1923; s.Charles E. and Anna (Schneckloth) C.; A.B., Whitman Coll., 1947; M.P. (Volker fellow), Wayne State U., 1949; Ph.D. (Sheldon Traveling fellow), Harvard, 1952; m. Linna Jane Owen, Mar. 9, 1945; children—Kimberly Ann, Charles Duncan. Asst. dir. Harvard Summer Sch., 1950-54, instr., 1952-54, vis. lectr., 1957; prof., chmn. polit. sci. dept. Hofstra Coll., Hempstead, N.Y., 1954-60; dep. comptroller adminstrn. State N.Y., Albany, 1960-61; vis. prof. Columbia, 1961-62; prof. polit. sci., dir. met. studies program Maxwell Grad. Sch., Syracuse (N.Y.) U., 1961-68, dean Maxwell Sch. Citizenship and Pub. Affairs, 1969—; mem. staff N.Y. Commn. on Govtl. Operations, N.Y.C., 1959; mem. faculty Salzburg (Austria) Seminar Am. Studies, 1965. Mem. com. instrn. and evaluation Am. Council Edn., 1957-68; mem. adv. com. improvement mgmt. in govt. Com. Econ. Devel., 1965-68; mem. com. urban econs. Resources For Future, 1965-68; mem. adv. com. to sec. Dept. Housing and Urban Devel., 1967-68; mem. Gov.'s Council Econ. Advisers, 1969—. Chmn. adv. platform com. N.Y. State Democratic Party, 1962; co-chmn. platform, resolutions sub-com. N.Y. State Dem. Com., 1964; co-chmn. Citizens for Johnson, Humphrey and Kennedy, Syracuse Met. Area, 1964; mem. Temp. N.Y. State Commn. on Revision and Simplification of Constn., 1965-66; del.-at-large N.Y. State Constl. Conv. 1967, chmn. com. on local govt. and home rule, 1967. Mem. exec. bd. Inter-Univ. Case Program. Served to ensign, CIC, USNR, 1943- 46. Recipient Alumnus of Merit award Whitman Coll., 1970. Mem. Am. Polit. Sci. Assn., Am. Soc. Pub. Adminstrn., Nat. Acad. Pub. Adminstrn., Council of Nat. Municipal Leagues, Phi Beta Kappa. Author (with Seymour Sacks) Metropolitan America: Governmental Systems and Fiscal Patterns, 1967. Editor: (with Edwin Bock) Case Studies in American Government, 1962. The States and the Urban Crisis, 1969; (with John Callahan) Redirecting State Educational Aid, 1969; Reshaping Government in Metropolitan Areas, Project Dir., Com. for Econ. Devel., 1970; (with others) Pattern of Allocation of Federal Aid to Education, 1970. contbr. articles profl. jours. Home: Ten Eyck Av RD 1 Cazenovia NY 13035

CAMPBELL, ALBERT ANGUS, social psychologist, educator; b. Leiters, Ind., Aug. 10, 1910; s. Albert Alexis and Orpha (Brumbaugh) C.; B.A., U. Ore. 1931, M.A., 1932; Ph.D., Stanford, 1936; Dr. Letters, Strathclyde, 1970; m. Jean Winter, June 29, 1940; children—Bruce, Joan, Carol. Instr. dept. psychology Northwestern U., Evanston, Ill., 1936-39, research fellow Social Sci. Research Council, 1939- 40, asst. prof. psychology, 1940-42; asst. head, div. program surveys U.S. Dept. Agr., 1942-46; asso. prof. psychology and sociology U. Mich, Ann Arbor, 1946-49, prof. 1949—, asst. dir. Survey Research Center, 1946-48, dir., 1948-70, asso. dir. Inst. Social Research, 1948-70, dir., 1970—. Fulbright research fellow, Norway, 1958-59. Fellow Am. Acad. Arts and Letters; mem. Am. Psychol. Assn., Am. Sociol. Assn., Soc. Psychol. Study Social Issues, Am. Assn. U. Profs. Home: 1009 Berkshire Rd Ann Arbor MI 48104

CAMPBELL, ALEXANDER, editor, author; b. Edinburgh, Scotland, Oct. 19, 1912; s. Alexander Maclean and Elizabeth (Morgan) C.; M.A. with first honours in Econs., Edinburgh U., 1934; m. Jane Young Lowe Shand, June 8, 1937; children—Morgan Brand, Kenneth Maclean, Lesley Ann. Came to U.S. 1961. Editorial writer Scotsman Edinburgh, 1935-37, East London (South Africa) Daily Dispatch, 1937-42; asst. to editor The Star, Johannesburg, South Africa, 1942-50; bur. chief for Time-Life, Johannesburg, 1950-54, New Delhi, India, 1954-56, Tokyo, Japan, 1956-60, Middle East, 1960-61; Washington corr. The Economist, London, Eng., 1961-63; mng. editor New Republic, 1964-71 mem. editoral bd. Toronto (Ont., Can.) Daily Star, 1971—. Recipient award outstanding accomplishment fgn. corr. Sigma Delta Chi, 1954. Mem. Overseas Writers. Author: The Heart of Africa, 1954; The Heart of India (Overseas Press Club Am. award, 1959), 1958; The Heart of Japan, 1961; Unbind Your Sons, 1970; The Trouble With Americans, 1971. Home: 11 Crescent Pl Toronto 13 Ontario Canada Office: Toronto Daily Star 80 King St W Toronto 1 Ontario Canada

CAMPBELL, ALEXANDER BRADSHAW, premier of P.E.I.; b. Summerside, P.E.I., Can., Dec. 1, 1933; s. Thane Alexander and Cecilia (Bradshaw) C.; B.A., Dalhousie U., 1958, LL.B., 1959; LL.D. (hon.), McGill U., 1967; m. Marilyn Gilmore, Aug. 19, 1961; childrenBlair Alexander, Heather Kathryn, Graham Melville. Called to Prince Edward Island bar, 1959, created Queen's counsel, 1966; practice in Summerside, 1959-66; mem. P.E.I. Legislature, 1965, premier, 1966—, atty.-gen., 1966-69, minister of devel., 1969—; mem. Privy Council Can., 1967—. Past sec. Summerside Bd. Trade. Leader, Prince Edward Island Liberal Party, 1965—. Mem. United Ch. Can. (elder). (elder). Home: 215 Maple Av Summerside Prince Edward Island Canada Office: Provincial Adminstrv Bldg Charlottetown Prince Edward Island Canada

CAMPBELL, ALISTAIR MATHESON, ins. co. exec.; b. Argyllshire, Scotland, July 3, 1905; s. Peter and Catherine (MacRae) C.; student Inverness Royal Acad., 1917-23; M.A., U. Aberdeen, 1927; m. Barbara Hampson Alexander, Apr. 2, 1948; children—Michael Alexander, Catherine, Barbara, Jill. Joined Sun Life Assurance Co. of Can., Montreal, Que., 1928, chief clk., 1930-34, asst. actuary, 1934-40, asso. actuary, 1940-46, asst. gen. mgr., actuary, 1947, v.p., actuary, 1950, v.p. and chief actuary, 1954, exec. v.p., dir. 1956-62, pres., 1962-70, chmn., 1970—; chmn., dir. Sun Life Assurance Co. Can. (U.K.) Ltd., Sun Life Assurance Co. Can. (U.S.); dir., chmn. exec. com. Canadian Enterprise Devel. Corp. Ltd.; dir., mem. exec. com. Asbestos Corp. Ltd., Canadian Pacific Investments Ltd., Royal Trust Co., Steel Co. Can.; dir. Canadian Industries, Ltd., Royal Trust Mortgage Co., Digital Equipment Can., Ltd., Am. Research & Devel. Corp., Boston. Past provincial v.p. (Que.) Am. Life Conv., 1962-63, mem. exec. com. 1965. Bd. dirs. Can. Safety Council; divisional trustee, mem. bd. Quebec div. Canadian Red Cross Soc. Served with Royal Canadian Arty., 1940-45. Fellow Inst. Actuaries, Soc. Actuaries (past gov.); mem. Canadian Life Ins. Assn. (pres. 1957-58), Canadian Assn. Actuaries (pres. 1947-48), Life Ins. Assn. Am. (dir.). Home: 3660 The Boulevard Westmount Quebec Canada Office: Sun Life Bldg Dominion Sq Montreal 110 Quebec Canada

CAMPBELL, ANNE, (Mrs. George W. Stark), writer; b. Lynn, Mich., June 19, 1888; d. High J. and Mina (Atkinson) Campbell; ed. high sch.; hon. LL.D., Wayne U., 1949; m. George W. Stark, Aug. 28, 1915 (dec.); children—George Winter, Alison Jean (Mrs. Allan F. Wilson), Richard Campbell. Writer of verse for Asso. Newspapers of N. Y. for 46 years; Author: Companionship and Other Poems; Back Home (collection of farm verse); The Heart of Home; Jesus and His Twelve Apostles; Four Songs from the Lord's Prayer; Songs from the Beatitudes (with Ward-Stephens); The House That Love Built; Two Heads Are Better. Named Mich. Mother, Goodwill Woman of the Year. Home: 2067 W Boston Blvd Detroit MI 48206 Office: Detroit News Detroit MI 48226

CAMPBELL, ARTHUR BERL, banker; b. Tulsa, Jan. 28, 1914; s. George Albert and Edna (Summers) C.; B.S., U. Utah, 1950; grad. mgmt. and indsl. engring. Rensselaer Poly. Inst., 1952; m. Thelma Jean Chanfield, Apr. 10, 1935; 1 son, Robert Arthur. Enlisted U.S. Navy, 1931, advanced through grades to comdr., 1959; ret., 1959; with First Nat. Bank Ariz., Phoenix, 1959—, v.p., cashier, 1967—. Bd. dirs. Family Service Phoenix, 1961-67, pres., 1966; bd. dirs. Phoenix United Fund. Mem. Phoenix C. of C., Central Phoenix Devel. Assn., Navy League U.S. (pres. Ariz. 1966, nat. dir. 1966). Founder monthly econ. bull. profile of Ariz., 1963. Office: 411 N Central Av Phoenix AZ 85002

CAMPBELL, ASHLEY SAWYER, educator; b. Montclair, N.J., Dec. 24, 1918; s. George Ashley and Caroline Gillis (Sawyer) C.; A.B. Harvard, 1940, S.M., 1947, D.Sc.,1949; m. Mary Letitia Fishler, July 18, 1942; childrenAshley Sawyer, Christopher Stuart, Martha Overton, Gordon Hovey, Philip LaRoche, Benjamin Hill. Mech. engr. Wright Aero. Corp., 1940-45; asst. prof. Harvard Harvard , 1949-50; dean coll. tech. U. Me., 1950-57; dean coll. engring., Tufts U., 1957-68; prof. mech. engring. U. Me., 1968-. Mem. Am. Soc. Engring. Edn., Combustion Inst., Am. Soc. M.E., Sigma Xi, Tau Beta Pi. Episcopalian. Home: 16 Spencer St Orono ME 04473

CAMPBELL, BEN SINGLETON, bus. exec.; b. Houston, July 8, 1918; s. Ben Singleton and Lucille (Towles) C.; B.A., Rice U., 1936; m. Dorothy Darby, June 17, 1939; children—Ben Singleton, III, Laura Elaine, Dorothy Ann. With Houston Oilfield Material Co., 1938-41. Hughes Tool Co., Houston 1941-42, 46; banking mgr. Tenneco, Inc., (formerly Tenn. Gas), Houston, 1947-52, asst. treas., 1953-66, treas. 1966—; officer KCL Corp., Tenneco West Inc. Served with AUS, 1942-46. Decorated Bronze Star. Baptist. (deacon). Home: 7522 Middlewood Houston TX 77042 Office: PO Box 511 Houston TX 77001

CAMPBELL, BYRON ADAMS, educator; b. Portland, Ore., Jan. 16, 1927; s. Robert Henry and Estelle (Grettie) C.; B.S. magna cum laude, U. Wash., 1950; M.S., Yale, 1951; Ph.D., 1954; m. Enid Margaret Hobart, June 19, 1954; children—Andrea Adams, Ian Hobart, NSF postdoctoral fellow Harvard, 1954-56; mem. faculty dept. psychology Princeton 1956—, asso. prof., 1963-68, prof., 1968-71, Eugene Higgins prof., 1971—. Served with USNR, 1945-46. Fellow Am. Psychol Assn., A.A.A.S.; mem. Eastern Psychol Assn. (bd. dirs.), Psychonomic Soc., Soc. Neuroscience, N.Y. Acad. Scis., Sigma Xi, Phi Beta Kappa. Editor: (with Russell M. Church) Punishment and Aversive Behavior, 1969. Home: 111 Maclean Circle Princeton NJ 08540

CAMPBELL, C. WILLIAM, lawyer; b. Plumer, Pa., Nov. 3, 1891; s. George M. and Ella (Emery) (Emery) C.; A.B., Grove City Coll., 1911, LL.D., 1955; student U. Philippines, 1912- 13; LL.B., U. Pitts., 1916; m. Edith Scharpf, June 20, 1918; 1 dau., Virginia. Admitted to Pa. bar, 1916, since practiced in Pitts.; partner firm Campbell, Thomas & Burke (now Tucker, Burke, Campbell & Arensberg), 1924—. Dir. emeritus N.Am. Rockwell Corp.; mgmt. com. Coraopolis office Union Nat. Bank of Pitts. Home: King Edward Apts Pittsburgh PA 15213 Office: Peoples Bank Bldg Pittsburgh PA 15222

CAMPBELL, CATHERINE HARTSHORN (Mrs. Crawford Campbell), civic worker; b. N.Y.C., July 23, 1916; d. Stewart Henry and Jennette (Vorce) Hartshorn; student U. Chgo., 1947-48; m. Crawford Campbell, July 22, 1939; children—Jennette, James, Joanna, Cowles. Artist, Whitman Pubs., N.Y.C., 1938-40; exhibited one-man show Inst. History and Art, Albany, N.Y.; group shows Amateur Art Show, Cooperstown, N.Y., 1950, N.Y. Art Assn., 1951, Studio Guild of N.Y., 1954, others. Sec., Planned Parenthood Fedn. Am., 1958-64; mem. exec. com. Pintard fellows N.Y. Hist. Soc. Bd. dirs., Albany Planned Parenthood Assn.; chmn. womens council, v.p. Albany Inst. History and Art. Mem. Colonial Dames Am. Episcopalian. Club: Cosmopolitan (N.Y.C.). Speaker on population problems, sex edn. Home: 33 Old Niskayuna Rd Loudonville NY 12211

CAMPBELL, CECIL RAYMOND, former retail drug co. exec.; b. Gilman, Ill., Aug. 17, 1907; s. Jason R. and Gertrude (Baker) C.; student U. Wis., 1926-30; M.B.A., U. Chgo., 1945; m. Jean C. Bartholomy, Apr. 27, 1935; children—Robert S., Charles R., James C. Asst. buyer Mandel Bros. Dept. Store, Chgo., 1930-31; partner

Anderson & Campbell Real Estate, Chgo., 1932-33; with Walgreen Co., Chgo., 1934-70, v.p., treas., dir. until 1970; dir. Mickelberry's Food Products Co. Mem., past pres. U. Chgo. Exec. Program; exec. com. U. Chgo. Grad. Sch. Bus. Mem. Ill. C. of C. (past dir.), Urban Land Inst., Beta Gamma Sigma. Clubs: Executives, Economist (Chgo.); North Shore Country (Glenview); Chicago Curling (past pres.) (Northbrook, Ill.). Home: 1005 Barton Ct Glenview IL 60025 Office: 4300 Peterson Av Chicago IL 60646

CAMPBELL, CHARLES BRYAN, constrn. co. exec.; b. Burley, Ida., Mar. 9, 1922; s. James R. and Jane (Kelly) C.; B.S., U. Ida., 1949; m. Jo Anne Voiten, Apr. 12, 1952; children—Bryan Joe, Douglas James. Pub. accountant Wells, Baxter & Miller, Boise, Ida., 1949-51; with Morrison-Knudsen Co., Inc., Boise, 1951—, asst. controller taxes, 1961-65, asst. controller, 1965-69, controller, 1969—. Mem. Boise City Park Bd., 1966—. Employer trustee Ida. Am. Gen. Contractors-Teamsters Health and Welfare Fund, 1968—, Ida. Am. Gen. Contractors-Operating Engrs. Health and Welfare, Pension and Apprenticeship Funds, 1968—. Served with AUS, 1942-46. Mem. Am. Inst. C.P.A.'s, Ida. Soc. C.P.A.'s, Financial Execs. Inst. Home: 6008 Lubkin St Boise ID 83704 Office: 400 Broadway Boise ID 83707

CAMPBELL CHARLES DUNCAN, educator; b. Ann Arbor, Mich., Nov. 12, 1905; s. Edward DeMille and Jennie Maria (Ives) C.; student U. Ariz., 1925-27; B.S., U. Mich., 1930, M.S., 1931; Ph.D., Stanford, 1934; m. Dorothy Jones, Apr. 4, 1938. Faculty, Wash. State U., Pullman, 1934-42, 45-71, asso. prof., 1946-50, prof., 1950-71; chmn. dept. geology, 1950-61; geologist U.S. Geol. Survey, 1942-45. Fellow Geol. Soc. Am. (emeritus), Mineral. Soc. Am.; mem. Nat. Assn. Geology Tchrs. (pres. 1960-61), Geochem. Soc. Contbr. articles on petrology, rock magnetism to profl. jours. Home: 2103 Orchard Dr Pullman WA 99163

CAMPBELL, CHARLES KING, corp. exec.; b. Westerly, R.I., Dec. 22, 1911; s. Clifford W. and Effie (King) C.; student Choate Sch., 1928-30; Ph.B., Brown U., 1934; m. Phyllis Lord, Mar. 17, 1939; childrenSally Lord, Judith King, Charles King. Vice pres., dir. IBM World Trade Corp., N.Y.C., 1952-; dir. Am. Brazilian Assn., Inc. Mem. bus. adv. council U. Mass. Mem. Pan Am. Soc., U.S. Inter-Am. Council, Council for Latin Am. (trustee), Am. Soc. Friendship with Switzerland (bd. dirs.), Argentine-Am. (bd. dirs.), Netherlands (bd. dirs.), German Am. (pres.) chambers commerce, Peruvian Am. Assn. (pres.), Sales and Marketing Execs. Internat. (sec.-treas.), Newcomen Soc. Clubs: Brown, University, Wee Burn Country. Home: Ridge Acres Darien CT 06820 Office: 821 United Nations Plaza New York City NY 10017

CAMPBELL, CLARENCE SUTHERLAND, sports assn. exec.; b. Fleming, Sask., Can., July 9, 1905; s. George A. and Annie M. (Haw) C.; B.A., LL.B. (Rhodes scholar), U. Alberta, 1926; M.A., Oxford U., 1928, B.C.L., 1929; m. Phyllis L. King, Nov. 17, 1955. Queen's Counsel, Alta.; barrister, Edmonton, Alta., 1929-40; pres. Nat. Hockey League, Montreal, Can., 1946—. Pres. Lakeshore Gen. Hosp. Found. Served to lt. col., Canadian Army, 1940- 46. Decorated Order Brit. Empire. Mem. Law Soc. Alberta. Home: 3465 Redpath St Montreal Quebec Canada Office: Sun Life Bldg Montreal Quebec Canada

CAMPBELL, CLIFFORD BLAINE, railway ofcl.; b. Cin., Mar. 24, 1908; s. Allen Baline and Anna Blanche (Orr) C.; B.S., U. Ill., 1931; grad. Advanced Mgmt. Program, Harvard, 1953; m. M. Jeanne Maher, Dec. 22, 1946; children—Allen Barry, John T., Susan C. Gibbs, Cynthia Ann, Douglas Lee, Elizabeth Jeanne. Mem. corp. buying dept. Halsey, Stuart & Co., Inc., Chgo., 1931-45, v.p. corp. buying dept., 1945-48; asst. to v.p finance N.Y.C. & St. L. R.R. Co., 1948-52, asst. v.p. finance, treas., 1954-60, v.p. finance and accounting, 1960-64; v.p. N & W. Ry. Co., 1964—; dir. Detroit & Toledo Shore Line R.R. Co., Nickel Plate Devel. Co., Inc., Nickel Plate Improvement Co., Nickel Plate Properties Co., Cleve. Union Terminals Co.; dir. v.p. Wheeling & Lake Erie Ry. Co.; dir., mem. finance com. Trailer Train Co.; v.p. Toledo Terminal R. R. Co. Mem. Assn. Am. R.R.'s, Delta Phi. Clubs: Cleveland Athletic, Mayfield Country (Cleve.); Harvard; Roanoke Country, Hidden Valley Country (Roanoke). Home: 3136 Somerset St SW Roanoke VA 24014

CAMPBELL, COLIN, clergyman; b. Antigonish, N.S., Can., June 12, 1931; s. Peter Smyth and Ida (Tompkins) C.; B.A., St. Mary's U., Halifax, N.S., 1952; B.Th., Holy Heart Sem., 1956; M.A., U. Montreal, 1964. Ordained priest Roman Cath. Ch., 1956; asst. various parishes, 1956-64; dir. social services Archdiocese of Halifax, 1964-69, vicar gen., 1969—, also pastor St. Thomas Acquinas Ch.; lectr. social work Dalhousie U. Pres. N.S. Family and Child Welfare Assn., 1967-69; chmn. Halifax Housing Authority, 1969—. Vice chancellor St. Mary's U., 1969—. Mem. Profl. Assn. Social Workers N.S. Address: 1725 Oxford St Halifax Nova Scotia Canada

CAMPBELL, COLIN DEARBORN, educator, economist; b. Cooperstown, N.Y., Feb. 10, 1917; s. James Samuel and Marion (Jennings) C.; B.A., Harvard, 1938; M.A., U. Ia., 1941; Ph.D., U. Chgo., 1950; M.A., Dartmouth, 1965; m. Rosemary Garst, June 18, 1949; children—William Garst, Janet Adele. Instr. Rensselaer Poly. Inst., 1946-47; asst. prof. Drake U., 1949-51; economist CIA, 1952-54, Fed. Res. System, 1954-56; mem. faculty Dartmouth, 1956—, prof. econs., 1964-, chmn. dept., 1965-66. Dir. Dartmouth Nat. Bank, 1961-. Mem. U.S. Tax Adv. Group to Republic Korea, 1959-60. Served to capt., Ordnance Corps, AUS, 1941-46, 51-53. Mem. Am. Econ. Assn. Contbr. profl. jours. Home: 9 N Park St Hanover, NH 03755.

CAMPBELL, COLIN GOETZE, univ. pres.; b. N.Y.C., Nov. 3, 1935; s. Joseph and Majorie (Goetze) C.; A.B., Cornell U., 1957; J.D., Columbia, 1960; m. Nancy Nash, June 20, 1959; children—Elizabeth, Jennefer, Colin. Admitted to Conn. bar, 1961; atty. Cummings & Lockwood, Stamford, Conn., 1960-62; asst. to pres. Am. Stock Exchange, N.Y.C., 1962-63, sec., 1963-64, v.p., 1964-67; adminstrv. v.p. Wesleyan U., Middletown, Conn., 1967-69, exec. v.p., 1969-70, pres., 1970—. Dir. Middletown Savs. Bank, Hill Devel. Corp. Pres., Middlesex County Legal Assistance Assn., Inc., 1968—; mem. Cornell U. Council, 1966—. Mem. Psi Upsilon, Phi Delta Phi. Episcopalian. Home: 269 High St Middletown CT 06457

CAMPBELL, DAN HAMPTON, scientist, educator; b. Freemont, O., Jan. 18, 1907; s. Ralph and Edna Catherine (Moses) C.; A.B., Wabash Coll., 1930, Sc.D., 1960; M.S., Washington U., 1932; Ph.D., U. Chgo., 1935; m. Margaret Kathryn Dorr, May 12, 1930; 1 son, John Hampton. Instr. comparative anatomy and embryology, Washington U. 1930-33; research fellow, U. Chgo., 1933-37, instr. bacteriology and immunology, 1937-39, asst. prof. immunology, 1940-42; asst. prof. immunochemistry Calif. Inst. Tech., 1942-45, asso. prof., 1945-50, prof. immunochemistry 1950—. Fellow Rockefeller Found. Ednl. Bd. 1940-41; mem. research adv. bd., City of Hope Medical Center, 1952-60, Nat. Nephrosis Found., 1954-58, Los Angeles Children's Hosp., 1955-57, mem. Com. Advanced Advanced Sci. Training, 1957—, served as responsible investigator of plasma substitute program for Com. of Med. Research, World War II; cons. for Manhattan project and Atomic Energy Commn., 1943-45, 1948-49; responsible responsible investigator for U.S. Pub. Health Research program on chemistry of blood and plasma substitute and for Office of Naval Research program for immunochemical research of Arctic animals, 1948—; cons. NIH on immunochem. problems, 1957—; chmn. com. standardization allergen Nat. Inst. Allergy and Infectious Diseases, 1959-; sci. adv. council St. Jude Hosp.; sci. adv. bd. Hastings Found., chmn. bd. for research and devel., bd. dirs. Internat. Chemical and Nuclear Corp., 1962—. Fellow N.Y. Acad. Sci., Am. Acad. Allergy (hon.; distinguished service award), Internat. Soc. Hematology, A.A.A.S.; member Am. Assn. Immunologists (council midwinter conf.), Editorial Coll. Physiol. Chemistry and Physics, Am. Chem. Soc., Soc. Exptl. Biology and Medicine, Arctic Inst. N.A., Sigma Xi, Phi Chi, Tau Kappa Epsilon. Author: Principles of Immunology, 1957; co-author Methods in Immunology, 1963, 1970; Adv. editor Jour. Infectious Diseases, 1941-38; asso. editor Jour. of Immunology, 1953-58, mem. editorial bd., 1960; chmn. editorial bd. Immunochemistry, 1964—. Contbr. chpt. profl. publs. and articles. Home: 11 54 Mount Lowe Dr Altadena CA 91001 Office: Div Chemistry and Chem Engring Cal Inst Tech Pasadena CA 91104 ☆

CAMPBELL, DEAN STERLING, chain store co. exec.; b. Wichita, Kan., July 20, 1913; s. William A. and Z. Myrtle (Rice) C.; m. Wandalee Parsons, May 3, 1936; children—Donald S., Robert D. Asst. treas., v.p. J. J. Newberry Co., N.Y.C., 1960-63, financial v.p., 1963-66, exec. v.p., 1966-69, pres., 1969-70, now dir. Office: 245 Fifth Av New York City NY 10016

CAMPBELL, DONALD ALFRED, govt. ofcl.; b. St. Louis, Mar, 31, 1928; s. Clarence Alfred and Dorothy Ethyl (Eggeman) C.; student Mercer U., 1945, Ga. Inst. Tech., 1945-46; J.D., George Washington U., 1949; m. Mary Kathryn McKay, June 17, 1951; children—Cynthia Kathleen, Jean Elizabeth. Admitted to U.S. Dist. Ct. D.C. bar, 1949, U.S. Ct. Appeals D.C. bar, 1951, U.S. Supreme Ct. bar, 1955; atty. Office Gen. Counsel, Dept. Agr., Washington, 1949-62, asst. to asst. gen. counsel, 1959-62, dir. packers and stockyards div. Consumer and Marketing Service, 1962-67, adminstr. Packers and Stockyards Adminstrn., 1967-71, judicial officer, 1971—. Served with USNR, World War II; lt. comdr. Res. ret. Mem. Am., Fed. bar assns., Order of Coif. Presbyn. (deacon, elder). Contbr. articles to legal jours. Home: 4207 Wynnwood Dr Annandale VA 22003 Office: Dept of Agriculture Washington DC 20250

CAMPBELL, DONALD BROUGHTON, hotel exec.; b. St. Louis, Jan. 3, 1929; s. William Roland and Isabelle (Jackson) C.; B.S., Okla. State U., 1951; m. Dorothy Blanche Reed, Nov. 2, 1956; children—David Reed, Dawn Elisabeth, Daniel McMullen, Douglas Jackson. Associated with Hotel Peabody, Memphis, 1956-63, mgr., 1961-63; with Standard Oil Co. (Ohio), 1963-, gen. mgr., v.p. Hospitality Motor Inns, Inc. subsidiary. Served to 2d lt. AUS, 1952-54. Mem. Cleve. C. of C., Lambda Chi Alpha. Mason (Shriner, Jester). Home: 14214 Shaker Blvd Shaker Heights OH 44120 Office: Midland Bldg Cleveland OH 44115

CAMPBELL, DONALD G., broadcasting co. exec. Chmn., Maclean-Hunter, Ltd. Office: 481 University Av Toronto 2 Ontario Canada*

CAMPBELL, DONALD GUY, journalist, author; b. Brownsburg, Ind., June 27, 1922; s. George Guy and Ella (Menefee) C.; A.B. in Journalism, Ind. U., 1948; m. Jean Farson, Oct. 15, 1949; children—Scott Guy, Jennifer Lee. Reporter, feature writer St. Petersburg (Fla.) Time, 1948-49; writer Nat. Safety Council, 1949-52; reporter Indpls. Star, 1952-54, bus. and financial editor, 1954-65; exec. bus. and financial editor Ariz. Republic, Phoenix, 1965—; chief researcher, writer Dow Theory Trader, 1956—; contbr. N.Am. Newspaper Alliance, 1967—; columnist real estate Register and Tribune Syndicate, 1968—; hon lectr. Am. Inst. Fgn. Trade, 1966—. Served with AUS, 1942-45; ETO. Mem. Soc. Am. Bus. Writers (sec.), Author's Guild, Sigma Delta Chi, Phi Gamma Delta. Clubs: Ariz. Country, University, Press (Phoenix). Author: Let's Take Stock, 1959; What Does Daddy Do All Day, 1962; Understanding Stocks, 1965 (Kiplinger Book Club best seller 1965); The Handbook of Real Estate Investment, 1968. Home: 5601 E Montecito Av Phoenix AZ 85018 Office: 120 Van Buren St Phoenix AZ 85001

CAMPBELL, DONALD HILL, corp. exec.; b. New Orleans, Mar. 8, 1927; s. Philip and Marjorie (Hill) C.; B.A., Rice U., 1951; m. Patty June McMillian, Aug. 1, 1948; children—Kathy Jo, Marjorie Kaye, Sally Eileen. With Tenneco Inc., 1951- -, controller, 1968—. Served with AUS, 1943-46. Mem. Financial Execs. Inst., Am. Petroleum Inst., Rice U. Assn. Home: 12467 Kimerley Lane Houston TX 77024 Office: PO Box 2511 Houston TX 77001

CAMPBELL, DONALD ROBERT, educator, historian; b. Glenwood Springs, Colo., Apr. 16, 1905; s. John Henry and Margaret (McDonald) C.; A.B., U. Cal. at Berkeley, 1941, M.A., 1947, Ph.D., 1950; student Oriental langs., U. Mich., 1943-44; m. Lois Agnes Nagle, June 4, 1943. Mem. faculty Eastern Wash. Coll. at Cheney, 1949-52; mem. faculty U. San Francisco, 1952—, prof. history, 1964—, chmn. dept., 1957-68. Served with AUS, 1942-46; PTO. Mem. Am. Hist. Assn., Am. Assn. U. Profs., Soc. Asian Art, DeYoung Museum Soc., Phi Beta Kappa. Club: Commonwealth (San Francisco). Author: articles, book revs. Home: 1891 17th Av San Francisco CA 94122

CAMPBELL, DONALD THOMAS, educator, psychologist; b. Grass Lake, Mich., Nov. 20, 1916; s. Arthur Lawrence and Hazel (Crafts) C.; A.B., U. Cal. at Berkeley, 1939, Ph.D., 1947; m. Lola Sheaff, June 6, 1942; children—Thomas Sheaff, Martin Crafts. Asst. prof. psychology Ohio State U., 1947-50, U. Chgo., 1950- 53; mem. faculty Northwestern U., Evanston, Ill., 1953—, prof. psychology, 1958—. Fellow Center Advanced Study Behavioral Scis., Stanford, Cal., 1965-66; Fulbright lectr., vis. prof. social psychology Oxford U., 1968-69. Served to lt. USNR, 1943-46. Mem. Am. (pres. div. personality and social psychology 1968-69, recipient Distinguished Sci. Contbn. award 1970), Midwestern (pres. 1966- 67) psychol. assns. Co-author: Experimental and Quasi-Experimental Designs for Research, 1966; Unobtrusive Measures: Nonreactive Research in the Social Sciences, 1966; The Influence of Culture on Visual Perception, 1966; also numerous articles. Home: 2024 Orrington Av Evanston IL 60201

CAMPBELL, DOUGLAS, asso. artistic dir. Tyrone Guthrie Theatre, Mpls. until 1965, dir., 1965—.*

CAMPBELL, DOUGLASS, consultant; b. N.Y.C., Aug. 31, 1919; s. William Lyman and Helene (Underwood) C.; A.B., Yale, 1941; m. Marion Danielson Strachan, Jan. 13, 1962; stepchildren—Richard and Stephen Strachan. With N.Y. Central System, 1939-67, timekeeper, traveling car agt., asst. train master, train master, asst. supt. asst. to freight traffic mgr., asst. to pres., supt. exec. rep., 1939-58, v.p. N.Y.C. R.R. and subsidiaries, 1958-67, also in charge pub. relations and advt. dept., 1960-67, also dir. affiliates and subsidiaries; chmn. pres. Bowater Paper Co., Inc., 1967-68; pres. Argyle Research Corp. consultants, N.Y.C., 1968—. Served as maj. AUS, 1942-46. Episcopalian. Clubs: Down Town Assn., Yale (N.Y.C.); University, Chagrin Valley Hunt (Cleve.); Mill Reef (Antigua, B.W.I.); Buffalo, Saturn (Buffalo); River (N.Y.C.); Chicago. Racquet (Chgo.). Home: 765 Park Av New York City NY 10021 Office: 345 Park Av New York City NY 10022

CAMPBELL, EDMUND DOUGLAS, lawyer; b. Lexington, Va., Mar. 12, 1899; s. Henry Donald and Martha (Miller) C.; A.B., Washington and Lee U., 1918, LL.B., 1922; M.A., Harvard, 1920; m. Esther Butterworth, June 9, 1925 (dec. July 1934); childrenEdmund D., Virginia (Mrs. Evertt W. Holt); m. 2d, Elizabeth Pfohl, June 16, 1936; childrenH. Donald, Benjamin P. Admitted to D.C. bar, 1924, Va. bar, 1924; practice in Washington and Arlington, Va., 1924-; mem. firm Douglas, Obear & Campbell, Washington, 1929-. Dir. Fairfax County Nat. Bank (Va.). Pres. Arlington Council Chs., 1949, Arlington Community Chest, 1951, Bd. dirs. Washington Council Chs., 1967—; mem. D.C. Police Complaint Rev. Bd., 1966-69; mem. Arlington County Bd. Suprs., 1941-47; chmn. Arlington Pub. Utilities Commn. 1935. chmn. Arlington Civil Service Commn., 1964-67; Democratic candidate for Congress, 1952. Trustee Mary Baldwin Coll., chmn., 1945-62. Served as pvt. U.S. Army, 1918. Recipient Algernon Sydney Sullivan award Mary Baldwin College, 1949. Member American (ho. dels. 1964-70), Va., D.C. (Distinguished Lawyers award, 1965; pres. 1961-62), Internat. bar assns., Phi Beta Kappa, Omicron Delta Kappa, Phi Delta Phi, Alpha Tau Omega. Episcopalian. Clubs: Metropolitan, Barristers, Lawyers (Washington). Home: Home: 2912 N Glebe Rd Arlington VA 22207 Office: 1425 H St Washington DC 20005

CAMPBELL , EDWARD FAY, Jr., educator, clergyman; b. New Haven, Jan. 5, 1932; s. Edward Fay and Edith Louise (May) C.; grad. Haverford Sch. Boys, 1949; B.A., Yale, 1953; B.D., McCormick Theol. Sem., 1956; Ph.D., Johns Hopkins, 1959; m. Phyllis Kletzien, Sept. 4, 1954; children—Thomas Edward, Sarah Ives. Ordained to ministry Presbyn. Ch., 1956; asst. pastor 1st Presbyn. Ch., Balt., 1956-58; instr. O.T., archaeology McCormick Theol. Sem. Chgo., 1958-59, asst. prof., 1959-62, asso. prof., 1962-66, prof. O.T., 1966—; acting dir. Am. Sch. Oriental Research, Jerusalem, 1964-65, annual prof., 1965; staff mem. Drew-McCormick Archeol. Expdn. to Shechem, 1957, 60, 62, 64, asst. dir., 1960-62, treas., 1960—, asso. dir., 1964, archaeol. dir. expdn., 1966, 68; instr. Bib. Hebrew, Harvard, summer 1961; with Presbytery of Chgo., 1956—. Pres. W.F. Albright Inst. Archaeol. Research. Mem. Am. Schs. Oriental Research (1st v.p. 1967- 70), Am. Oriental Soc., Aurelian Soc., Am. Civil Liberties Union. Author: The Chronology of the Amarna Letters, 1964. Editor: The Bibl. Archaeologist (guar.); (with David N. Freedman) The Biblical Archaeologist Reader, 2, 1964, 3, 1970. Contbr. to Schechem, 1965, The Bible and the Ancient Near East, 1961. Home: 841 Chalmers Pl Chicago IL 60614

CAMPBELL, EDWARD GRANT, mfg. co. exec.; b. Dayton, Ky., May 17, 1920; s. Albert John and Selma B. (Carmichael) C.; B.A., U. Denver, 1947; m. Evelyn J. Keating, Dec. 20, 1942; children—Gail (Mrs. Douglas F. Valentine), Teri L., Guy T. Printer, Schraffenbergers, Cin., 1938-41; sr. auditor, M. Earl Tedtman, C.P.A., Cin., 1941-43; prodn. supt., corp. controller Gates Rubber Co., Denver 1946-47; v.p., gen. mgr. Lear jet Stereo, Inc., pres. Ansco Inc., 1968—; v.p. Gates Learjet Corp. Past pres. Gates Credit Union; past supervisory auditor Mile High United Fund. Served with USMCR, 1943-46. Mem. Nat. Assn. Accountants (past pres. Denver, past nat. bd. dirs.), Financial Execs. Inst., Stuart Cameron McCloud Soc. Author articles in field. Office: 6868 S Plumer St Tucson AZ 85706

CAMPBELL, EDWIN DENTON, ednl. inst. exec.; b. Boston, June 25, 1927; s. William Edwin and Mildred (Altmiller) C.; grad. Bentley Coll., Boston, 1948, grad. Advanced Mgmt. Program, Harvard, 1965; m. Adele Distelhurst, Dec. 28, 1957; children—Geraldine, Linda, David. Mgr., Arthur Andersen & Co., C.P.A.'s, Boston, 1948-53; v.p. Lab. for Electronics, Inc., Boston, 1953-62, also dir.; exec. v.p. Itek Corp., Lexington, Mass., 1962-70, now dir.; pres. Edn. Devel. Center, Newton, Mass., 1971—; dir. Leesona Corp., Keystone Apollo Fund, OSTI. Faculty, Bentley Coll., Boston, 1956-58, trustee, 1963—. Vice pres. Mass. Assn. Mental Health, 1965-68, now dir.; mem. Mass Commn. Vocational Rehab., 1966-68. Mem. finance com. Town of Carlisle, Mass., 1965-68. Trustee, Boston Urban Found., 1969—, Fenn Sch., 1970—. Served with USMCR, 1943-45. C.P.A., Mass. Mem. A.I.M. (pres. 1967—, dir.). Home: River Rd Carlisle MA 01741 Office: 55 Chapel St Newton MA 02160

CAMPBELL, ERNEST QUEENER, educator; b. Stephens, Ga., Sept. 15, 1926; s. George McLaughlin and Margaret (Queener) C.; B.A., Furman U., 1945; M.A., U. Pa., 1946; Ph.D., Vanderbilt U., 1956; m. Berdelle Taylor, Aug. 28, 1949; children—John McLaughlin, Ernest Paul, Alison Leigh, Scott Wallace. Instr. sociology Coll. of Wooster (O.) 1951-54; asst. prof. Fla. State U., 1956-57; postdoctoral research tng. fellow Social Sci. Research Council, Lab. Social Relations, Harvard, 1957-58; asst. prof., then asso. prof. U. N.C., 1958-63, research prof. Inst. Research Social Sci., 1958-63; prof. sociology, chmn. dept. sociology and anthropology Vanderbilt U., Nashville, 1963—. Vis. prof., chmn. dept. sociology U. East Africa, Nairobi, Kenya, 1968-69. Co-dir. Equal Ednl. Opportunities Survey, U.S. Office Edn., 1965-66. Mem. rev. panel sociology and social psychology NSF, 1966-68; Am. Social. Assn. rep. NRC-Nat. Acad. Scis., 1971-73. Mem. Am. Sociol. Assn., So. Sociol. Soc. (pres. 1967-68), Sociol. Research Assn. Democrat. Methodist. Co-author: Christians in Racial Crisis, 1959. Editor: Racial Tensions and National Identity, 1971; asso. editor Social Forces, 1958-63, Sociol. Inquiry, 1964-70, Am. Sociol. Rev., 1971-73; mem. editorial bd. Sociometry, 1966-71; adv. editor in sociology Houghton-Mifflin Co., 1966-; mem. editorial adv. bd. So. Edn. Report, 1966-68. Home: 4407 Howell Pl Nashville TN 37205

CAMPBELL, EUGENE EDWARD, educator; b. Tooele, Utah, Apr. 26, 1915; s. Edward and Betsy Ann (Bowen) C.; A.A., Snow Jr. Coll., 1935; B.A., U. Utah, 1939, M.A., 1940; Ph.D., U. So. Cal., 1952; m. Beth Larsen, Aug. 11, 1939; childrenBruce L., Mary Ann, Jean, Sharon, Edward L. Tchr., prin. high sch.-sem. Mormon Church Ednl. System, 1940-44; dir. Latter Day Saints Inst. Religion, Ida. State Coll., 1946-49; asso. dir. Latter Day Saints Inst. Religion, Utah State U., 1950-56; prof. history Brigham Young U., 1956-, chmn. dept., 1960-67, dir. travel tours to Europe; vis. prof. history Church Coll. Hawaii, 1967-68. High priest Ch. Jesus Christ of Latter Day Saints. Served to capt., Chaplains Corps, AUS, 1944-46. Mem. Utah Hist. Soc., Mormon History Assn. (pres. 1966), Danforth Assos., Phi Beta Kappa, Phi Kappa Phi, Phi Alpha Theta, Phi Delta Kappa (pres.). Co-author: (coll. text) The United States: An Interpretative History, 1964. Contbr. articles on Mormon and Western history. Address: 1305 E Briar Av Provo UT 84601

CAMPBELL, EUGENE PAUL, physician, fgn. service officer; b. St. Paul, July 22, 1907; s. Eugene Paul and Fan (Berry); C.; B.A. in Zoology, U. Cal. at Los Angeles, 1929; M.D., Johns Hopkins, 1933; M.P.H., Pa. Sch. Pub. Health, 1942; m. Dr. Reba Lowe, Oct. 3, 1936; 1 dau., Marilyn Joyce. Asst. physiology Johns Hopkins Sch. Medicine, 1933; intern, asst. resident medicine Balt. City Hosp., 1933-35; ward officer Communicable Disease Hosp., Walter Reed Hosp., 1935-39; asst. prof. epidemiology U. Pa. Sch. Pub. Health, 1939-42; chief coop. health program, Guatemala, 1942; field dir. Central Am. Coop. Health Programs, 1943-45; chief coop. health program, Brazil, 1945-55; dep. chief pub. health div. ICA, 1955-57, chief pub. health div., 1957-59, dir. Office Pub. Health, 1959-62; chief pub. health div. AID, New Delhi, India; attache health Am. embassy, India; now chief pub. health div. AID. Mem. U.S. delegation WHO Gen. Assembly, 1957, 58, 60. Bd. dirs. Am. Sch., 1952-55, Strangers Hosp., 1953-55 (both Rio de Janeiro). Decorated grand ofcl. Order Med. Merit, Brazil, 1955; recipient Meritorious Service citation U.S. Govt., 1956, Merit citation Nat. Civil Service League, 1958. Fellow Am. Pub. Health Assn. (life), A.C.P., Royal Acad. Tropical Medicine and Hygiene; mem. Royal Soc. Health, Tropical Medicine Assn., Med. Soc. D.C., Brazilian Soc. Hygiene, Indian Assn. Advancement Med. Edn., Am. Orchid Soc. Office: AID State Dept Washington DC 20523

CAMPBELL, GEORGE STUART, educator; b. Sauquoit, N.Y., Nov. 29, 1926; s. Ralph Douglass and Grace Adaline (Dennis) C.; B.S., Rensselaer Polytech. Inst., 1947, B. Aero. Engring., 1949; M.S., Cal. Inst. Tech., 1951, Ph.D. (Douglas Aircraft, Howard Hughes fellows), 1956; m. Roy Evelyn Stallings, Sept. 21, 1951; children—John Stuart, Robert Douglas. Aero. research scientist NACA, Hampton, Va., 1947-53; research engr. Hughes Aircraft Co., El Segundo, Cal., 1954-59, sr. staff engr., 1959-62, sr. scientist, 1962-63; prof., head, aerospace engring. dept. U. Conn., Storrs, 1963—. Served with USNR, 1944-46. Asso. fellow Am. Inst. Aeros. and Astronautics, Canadian Aeros. and Space Inst.; mem. Am. Phys. Soc., Combustion Inst. Contbr. articles to tech. jours. Home: 30 Hillyndale Rd Storrs CT 06268

CAMPBELL, GEORGE WILBUR, univ. dean; b. Dadeville, Ala., Oct. 10, 1915; s. George H. and Felicia (Gresham) C.; A.B., U. Ala., 1936, M.A., 1937; student U. Ill., summers 1939-41; Ed.D., Columbia, 1957; m. Florinne Clarke, Oct. 7, 1944; children—Karen, Breckinridge. Asst. dir. engring. sci. and mgmt. war tng. program U. Ala., Birmingham, 1941-44, mem. faculty, 1946—, dir. Birmingham Center, 1958-66, asso. dean extension div., 1958-66, dean Coll. Gen. Studies, 1966—. Served with AUS, 1944-46. Home: 253 Big Springs Dr Birmingham AL 35216

CAMPBELL, GERARD JOHN, clergyman, educator; b. St. Marys, Pa., Aug. 26, 1919; s. Nicholas J. and Clare (Zimmerman) C., A.B., Loyola U., Chgo., 1943, Licentiate in Philosophy, 1945; S.T.L., Woodstock (N.Y.) Coll., 1952; postgrad. Fordham U., 1953-54; Ph.D., Princeton, 1957, postdoctoral fellow, 1963, LL.D., 1965; Ed.D. (hon.), St. Vincent Coll. Joined Soc. of Jesus, 1939, ordained priest Roman Catholic Ch., 1951; prof. history and polit. sci. St. Joseph's Coll., Phila., 1945-48; prof. history Loyola Coll., Balt., 1957-62; exec. v.p. Georgetown U., Washington, 1963-64; pres., 1964-69; asst. for higher edn. Md. Province, Soc. of Jesus, Balt., 1969—. Trustee Woodstock Coll., Marquette U. Mem. Am. Hist. Assn., Mediaeval Acad. Am. Address: 5704 Roland Av Baltimore MD 21210

CAMPBELL, GLEN, entertainer; b. Delight, Ark., Apr. 22, 1936; s. Wesley and Carrie (Stone) C.; ed. pub. schs., Ark. and N.M.; m. Billie Jean Nunley, Sept. 20, 1959; children—Debby, Kelli, Travis, Kane. Appearances include N.M.-Bick Bills (uncle), 1953, Hollywood Champs, 1960, 63-64 Shindig, 1964; studio musician 1962-66; host summer Smothers Brothers Show, 1968; film appearance in True Grit, 1968, Norwood, 1969; host Glen Campbell Good Time Hour, 1969—. Named Best Country Entertainment, 1968, Best Country Vocalist, 1968; recipient 4 Grammy awards, 5 Country Assn. awards; named Best Male Vocalist, 1967. Author: (song) Less of Me. Address: PO Box 69500 Hollywood CA 90069

CAMPBELL, GRAHAM RUTHERFORD, advt. exec.; b. Winnipeg, Man., Can., June 6, 1929; s. Alan Charles and Christina (Wright) C.; B.Commerce, U. Man., 1950; m. Nora Kathleen Bowman, Oct. 27, 1952; children—Timothy, Sandra, Linda, Heather, Jill. Asst. dept. mgr. Hudson's Bay Co., Winnipeg, 1950-53; brand mgr. Procter & Gamble, Toronto, Ont., 1953-57; product mgr. Nestle Can., Ltd., Toronto, 1957-58; with Foote, Cone & Belding, Toronto, 1958—, pres. gen. mgr., 1969—; dir. Bryn Enterprises, Ltd. Chmn. advt. div. Canadian Cancer Soc. campaign, 1970. Mem. Advt. and Sales Club Toronto (dir.), Zeta Psi. Home: 11 Tetbury Crescent Don Mills Ontario Canada Office: 10 St Mary St Toronto 5 Ontario Canada

CAMPBELL, HARRY MODEAN, educator; b. Terrell, Tex., Nov. 18, 1908; s. Harry Leroy and Nora Emily (McNutt) C.; B.A., So. Meth. U., 1926, M.A., 1935; Ph.D., Vanderbilt U., 1942; m. Meredith Eleanor Keller, Jan. 20, 1940; 1 dau., Alice Nora. Prof. English, Okla. State U., 1960-67, chmn. dept., 1960-67, part-time teaching and research, 1967—. Fulbright lectr. in Italy, 1955-57. Ford Found fellow Harvard, 1952-53. Mem. Modern Lang. Assn. (chmn. comparative lit. group 1957), Am. Studies Assn. (regional pres. 1960), Coll. English Assn. (nat. dir. 1967-69), Nat. Council Teachers English. Presbyn. (elder). Co-author: Faulkner, 1951; Elizabeth Madox Roberts, 1956. Mem. editorial bd. Midcontinent Am. Studies Jour., 1960-64. Contbr. numerous articles to profl. jours. Home: 126 S Duck St Stillwater OK 74074

CAMPBELL, HENRY CUMMINGS, librarian; b. Vancouver, B.C., Can., Apr. 22, 1919; s. Henry and Margaret (Cummings) C.; B.A., U. B.C., 1940; B.L.S., U. Toronto, 1941; M.A., Columbia, 1949; m. Sylvia Woodsworth, Sept. 13, 1943; children—Shiela (Mrs. David Macrae), Bonnie, Robin. Librarian, film producer Nat. Film Bd. Can., Ottawa, 1941-46; with Secretariat UN, N.Y., 1946-48; with UNESCO, Paris, 1949-56; chief librarian Toronto (Can.) Pub. Library, 1956—. Lectr., U. Toronto Sch. Library Sci., 1970-71, cons. on information systems and library services Canadian Govt., Social Sci. Research Council Can., UNESCO. Mem. Internat. Assn. Met. City Libraries (pres. 1971—), Canadian Library Assn., Ont. Continuing Edn. Assn. (pres. 1966), Toronto Hist. Assn. (dir. 1958—). Author: How To Find Out About Canada, 1967; Canadian Libraries, 1970; Early Days on the Great Lakes, 1971. Home: 373 Glengrove Toronto Ontario Canada Office: 40 St Clair Av E Toronto Ontario Canada

CAMPBELL, HERBERT PETERKIN, business exec.; b. Ravenswood, W.Va., Nov. 11, 1898; s. Charles Mitchell and Eugenia C. (Fairfax) C.; student Marshall Coll., 1916-17; m. Mary Louise Dyer, June 10, 1920; children—John William, Robert Lee. Salesman wholesale dry goods, 1919-26; sec. Guthrie-Morris-Campbell Co., 1926-41, pres., 1941—. Trustee, mem. exec. com. Morris Harvey Coll. Served with 38th, 78th Inf. Divs., U.S. Army, 1917-19. Mem. Nat. Assn. Textile and Apparel Wholesalers, Nat. Assn. Wholesalers, U.S. (past nat. councilor), Charleston (past pres.), W.Va. (past pres.) chambers commerce. Methodist. Mason (Shriner), Rotarian. Home: 1 Morris St Charleston WV 25301 Office: 816 Virginia St E Charleston WV 25301

CAMPBELL, HOWARD ERNEST, educator, mathematician; b. Detroit, Sept. 20, 1925; s. Howard E. and Marie (Brown) C.; student Stevens Inst. Tech., 1943-44; B.S. in Elec. Engring., U. Wis., 1946, M.S. in Math., 1947, Ph.D. in Math., 1949; m. Ruth Mary Noland, June 27, 1950; children—Tanaquil Ruth, Howard Blaine, Thane George, Lowell Lete. Grad. asst. U. Wis., 1946-49; instr. U. Pa., 1949-51; asst. prof. Emory U., 1951-56; asst. prof., then asso. prof. Mich. State U., 1956-63; prof. math., chmn. dept. U. Ida., 1963—; spl. research associative and non-associative algebras. Chmn. com. gen. exams. math. Coll. Entrance Exam. Bd.; chmn. com. examiners for math. test of gen. examinations of coll. level examination program Coll. Entrance Exam. Bd. and Ednl. Testing Service. Served with USNR, 1943-46. Mem. Math. Assn. Am. (cons. bur. of com. undergrad. program math. 1963-65), Am. Math. Soc., Sigma Xi (treas. Emory U. chpt. 1953-55), Pi Mu Epsilon. Author: The Structure of Arithmetic, 1971. Home: 205 S Garfield St Moscow ID 83843

CAMPBELL, HUGH M., accountant; b. Detroit, 1916; ed. Yale, 1936. Partner Price, Waterhouse & Co., C.P.A.'s, Chgo. Home: 23 Indian Hill Rd Winnetka IL 60093 Office: Price Waterhouse & Co 130 E Randolph St Chicago IL 60601

CAMPBELL, HUGH STEWART, ins. co. exec.; b. Hartford, Conn., Oct. 29, 1910; s. Frederick Stewart and Anna (Dow) C.; B.A., Trinity Coll., 1932; LL.B., Hartford Law Coll., 1937; m. Sally Tuttle Moore, Aug. 8, 1936; children—Peter Dow II, Pamela Sanford. Admitted to Conn. bar, 1937; with Phoenix Mut. Life Ins. Co., Hartford, 1933—, asst. counsel, 1946, counsel, 1948, sec., counsel, 1951, v.p., counsel, 1958-68, sr. v.p., gen. counsel, 1968—. Former chmn. Wethersfield Library Bd.; mem. Wethersfield Library Survey Com., Town Hall-Library Bldg. Com. Bd. dirs. Hartford County Legal Aid Soc., Inc.; corporator Inst. of Living; bd. dirs. Hartford Pub. Library; alumni trustee Trinity Coll. Served to lt. USNR, 1943-46. Mem. Am., Conn., Hartford County bar assns., Am. Judicature Soc., Assn. Life Ins. Counsel, Am. Life Conv. (chmn. legal section 1964), Conn., Wethersfield hist. socs., Trinity Coll. Alumni Assn. (Alumni medal, 1958; past pres.), Wadsworth Atheneum (trustee ; past pres. bd. trustees), Antiquarian and Landmark Soc., Mark Twain Meml., Phi Beta Kappa, Alpha Chi Rho. Republican. Clubs: University (Hartford); Dauntless; Essex. Contbr. articles to profl. jours. Home: 161 Garden St Wethersfield CT 06109 Office: 1 American Row Hartford CT 06115

CAMPBELL, IAN, geologist; b. Bismarck, N.D., Oct. 17, 1899; s. Dugald and Agnes (Gilkison) C.; A.B., U. Ore., 1922, A.M., 1924; Ph.D., Harvard, 1931; Univ. fellow, Northwestern U., 1923-24; m. Catherine Robbins Chase, Sept. 16, 1930; 1 son, Dugald Robbins. Asst. prof. geology, La. State U., 1925-28; instr. mineralogy and petrography Harvard, 1928-31; mem. faculty Cal. Inst. Tech., Pasadena 1931—, prof. petrology, 1946-59, exec. officer div. geol. scis., 1952-59, research asso. in geology, 1959-70, prof. emeritus, 1970—; state geologist, chief Cal. Div. Mines and Geology, 1959-69; dir. Cal. Dept. Conservation, 1966-67; adv. council U. Cal. Inst. Marine Resources, 1962-68; commr. Am. Commn. on Stratigraphic Nomenclature, 1962- 68; sec. Cal. Geothermal Resources Bd., 1967-69; research asso. geology Carnegie Instn. of Wash., 1932-38; mem. div. war research U. Cal., 1944-46; vis. com. geol. scis. Harvard Bd. Overseers, 1970—. Cons. geologist, 1926-59, 70—. Served with U. S. Army, 1917-19; AEF. Del. of 3 sci. socs. to 18th Internat. Geol. Congress, Gt. Britain, 1948; del. to 23d Internat. Geol. Congress, Prague, 1968. Recipient Scholarship Found. award, Am. Fedn. Mineral Socs., 1969. Mem. Am. Assn. Petroleum Geologists, Assn. Am. State Geologists (editor 1960-63, pres. 1965-66), Am. Assn. U. Profs. (nat. council 1957-60), Am. Inst. Mining and Metall. Engrs. (exec. com. San Francisco sect. 1961-70, chmn. 1967, Hardinge award 1962), Mineral. Soc. Am. (pres. 1962). Am. Geol. Inst. (pres. 1961, dir. 1955-64), Cal. Acad. Scis. (trustee 1960—, research asso. geology 1969, sec. 1970-71, pres. 1971—), Geol. Soc. Am. (councillor 1951-55, asso. editor 1963-67, pres. 1968), Le Conte Geol. Soc. (pres. 1963-64), Soc. Econ. Geol., A.A.A.S. (pres. Pacific div. 1957-58), Branner Geol. Soc. (pres. 1938), Am. Geophys. Union, Assn. of Engring. Geologists, Geochem. Soc., Nat. Assn. Geology Tchrs., Internat. Union Geol. Scis. (U.S. com. 1961-65), Soc. Mining Engrs. (western vice- chmn. 1966-69), Am. Inst. Prof. Geologists (Ben H. Parker Meml. medal 1970), Laymen's League, Cal. Bd. Registration for Geologists, 91st Division Assn., Phi Beta Kappa, Sigma Xi, Gamma Alpha, Unitarian. Clubs: Athenaeum, Commonwealth, Engineers (San Francisco). Mason. Asso. editor Am. Mineralogist, 1954-57. Contbr. articles to geol. jours. Home: 1333 Jones St San Francisco CA 94109 Office: Cal Acad Scis Golden Gate Park San Francisco CA 94118

CAMPBELL, IAN CADOGAN, mining co. exec.; b. Kingston, Ont., Can., July 3, 1917; s. Percy Cadogan and Evelyn (Rogers) C.; B.A., Queen's U., 1940; m. Elizabeth McNeill, Aug. 3, 1940; children—Peter, Douglas, Elspeth, Robert. With Asbestos Corp. Ltd., Thetford Mines, Que., Can., 1946—, asst. sec., 1948-54, asst. sec.-treas., 1954-58, sec.-asst. treas., 1958—, sec.-treas., 1958-64, v.p., sec.-treas., 1964—; sec. Minorex Ltd., Hudson Strait Asbestos, Gen. Minerals Beneficiation Ltd. Mem. Montreal Port Authority, 1971—. Served with Canadian Army, 1940-45. Home: 1142 Coleraine Av Thetford Mines Quebec Canada Office: PO Box 9 Thetford Mines Quebec Canada

CAMPBELL, IRVING HAYNER, investment banker; b. Toronto, Can., June 14, 1914; s. Frank O. and Helen (Hayner) C.; ed. N. Toronto Collegiate Sch.; m. Lillian Jeannette Greenwood, June 15, 1940; childrenJudith Annette, Carolyn Jeannette. With Bell, Gouinlock & Co., Ltd., Toronto, 1934-, dir., 1949-, v.p., 1957-; pres., dir. Bell, Gouinlock & Co., Inc., N.Y.C., 1957-. Served with Royal Canadian Navy Vol. Res., World War II. Mem. Investment Bankers Assn. Am. (bd. govs. 1961). Clubs: Toronto, Hunt (Toronto); Hartford (Conn.); Glen Major (Ont.) Angling. Home: 200 Dawlish Av Toronto Ontario Canada Office: 44 King St Toronto Ontario Canada

CAMPBELL, J. FRANK, coll. dean; b. Big Rapids, Mich., Mar. 11, 1912; s. Earl R. and Adeline (Davenport) C.; student Eastern Mich. U., 1932-35; B.A., Central Mich. U., 1938; M.A., U. Mich., 1940, Ed.D., 1951; m. Dorothy A. Stackable, Jan. 2, 1943; 1 son, Terence W. Social studies tchr., athletic coach, also Boy Scout dir. Davison (Mich.) pub. schs., 1938-39; history tchr., homeroom counselor Monroe (Mich.) High Sch., 1939-40; counselor Detroit Counseling Center, 1940-42; personnel counselor Westinghouse Electric Corp., Chgo., 1944-45; dir. psychol. counseling and rehab. program VA, Detroit, 1945-50; vis. instr. Eastern Mich. U., 1950-51; mem. faculty Wayne State U., 1951—, prof. ednl. psychology, asso. dean Coll. Edn., 1965—; cons. Mich. Soc. Mental Health, 1958—. Served with USNR, 1942- 44; PTO. Recipient Faculty Service award Wayne State U., 1966. Mem. Am. Psychol. Assn., Am. Assn. Curriculum and Devel., Nat. Mental Health Assn., Phi Delta Kappa, Delta Pi Epsilon (hon.). Author: Effective Supervisor-Employee Relations, 1963. Home: 9246 Penrod St Detroit MI 48228

CAMPBELL, JACK M., ex-gov. N.M.; b. Hutchinson, Kan., Sept. 10, 1916; s. John M. and Blanche E. (Chain) C.; A.B. magna cum laude, Washburn Coll., 1938, LL.B., 1940; m. Ruthanne DeBus, Nov. 17, 1945; children—Patty, Mike, Kathy, Terry. Admitted to N.M. bar, 1944; practiced in Albuquerque, 1940; agt. FBI, 1941; exec. sec. N.M. Oil and Gas Assn., partner firm Campbell & Russell, Roswell, 1953-63; gov. N.M., 1963-66; counsel firm Olmsted & Cohen, 1970—; dir. Inst. for Sociol Research and Devel., U. N.M., 1969—. Mem. atomic safety and licensing bd. AEC, 1967—; pres. Fedn. Rocky Mountain States, 1969—; chmn. Inst. State Program for 70's, U. N.C., 1967-69. Mem. N.M. Ho. of Reps., 1955-62, speaker, 1961-62; mem. N.M. Bd. Finance, 1955-59, N.M. Legislative Council, 1962. Chmn. Interstate Oil Compact Commn., 1963-64. Served to 1st lt. USMCR, World War II. Democrat. Roman Catholic. Home: 1431 Seville Santa Fe NM 87501

CAMPBELL, JACKSON JUSTICE, educator, Medievalist; b. Nowata, Okla., Jan. 9, 1920; s. Thomas Bernard and Isis (Justice) C.; B.A., Yale, 1941, Ph.D., 1950; M.A., U. Pa., 1946; m. Margarita Monal, Apr. 24, 1943; children—Catherine, Thomas, Robert. Tchr., Ruston Acad., Havana, Cuba, 1941-42; instr. English lit. Yale, 1948-51; asst. prof. English, U. Ill., Urbana, 1951- 54, prof., 1964—; asst. prof., asso. prof. Princeton, 1954-64; Fulbright lectr. U. Havana, 1952; Annan preceptorship for research in Eng., 1956-57; asso. Recording for the Blind Assn., Princeton, N.J., 1957-64. Served to capt. USAAF, 1942-45. Mem. Medieval Acad. Am., Linguistic Soc. Am., Modern Lang. Assn. Author: The Advent Lyrics of the Exeter Book, 1959; Shakespeare's Troilus and Cressida, 1956; Poems in Old English, 1962. Contbr. articles profl. jours. Office: English Bldg U Ill Urbana IL 61801

CAMPBELL, JAMES ALEXANDER, accountant; b. Bklyn., Jan. 6, 1911; s. Philip S. and Gladys (Tapscott) C.; A.B., Harvard, 1932, M.B.A., 1934; m. Dorothy Claire Ray, Mar. 26, 1938; children—Priscilla A., Robert A. With Arthur Andersen & Co., C.P.A.'s, 1934—, partner, 1948—, charge Los Angeles office, 1951-66. Mem. C.P.A. qualifications com., dept. consumer affairs Cal. Bd. Accountancy, 1966—. Mem. Jr. Achievement Los Angeles County, 1954—; sect. chmn. Los Angeles County Heart Assn. fund drive, 1966; sustaining mem. Los Angeles YMCA, 1953—; sustaining mem. Coro Found., 1964—; mem. audit com. Episcopal Diocese Los Angeles, 1965-66. Mem. Republican Assos., 1957—, United Rep. Fund Los Angeles, 1959—. Bd. dirs. So. Cal. Industry Edn. Council 1965—; sustaining mem. C.P.A., Cal., other states. Mem. Am. Inst. C.P.A.'s, Cal., Ill., N.Y. socs. C.P.A.'s Am. Accounting Assn., Canadian Soc. Los Angeles. Clubs: Town Hall, California, Harvard Business School, University, Los Angeles (Los Angeles). Contbr. articles to profl. jours. Home: 665 Santa Anita Av San Marino CA 91108 Office: 1920 W 3d St Los Angeles CA 90017

CAMPBELL, JAMES ALLAN, physician, educator; b. Moweaqua, Ill., Nov. 29, 1917; s. Frank Arthur and Gertrude Mary (Dowling) C.; A.B., Knox Coll., Galesburg, Ill., 1939, D. Sc., (hon.), 1965; student U. Chgo., 1939-41; M.D., Harvard, 1943; L.H.D. (hon.), Lake Forest (Ill.) Coll., 1968; m. Elda Schaffer Crichton, Sept. 23, 1944; children—James Allan, Bruce Crichton, Douglas Karr. Asst. resident Billings Hosp., Chgo., 1941-42; asst. pathology Sch. Medicine, U. Chgo., 1941-42; intern Boston City Hosp., 1943-44, asst. resident, 1944-45, resident 1945-46; teaching fellow medicine Harvard Med. Sch., 1944-45, asst. medicine Thorndike Meml. Lab., 1945-46; Harvey Cushing fellow Johns Hopkins Hosp., also Med. Sch., 1947-48; prof. medicine U. Ill., 1951-71; attending physician Albany Hosp., 1951- 53; dean, prof. medicine Albany Med. Coll., 1951-53; asst. attending physician Presbyn. Hosp., Chgo., 1948-51, asso. attending physician, 1951, chmn. dept. medicine, 1953, now pres. Rush-Presbyn.-St. Luke's Med. Center, Chgo., also trustee; prof. medicine Rush Med. Coll., Chgo., 1971—. Planning dir. edn. in health fields Ill. Bd. Higher Edn., 1964-68. Alumni council Harvard Med. Sch.; trustee Knox Coll. Served as capt., M.C., U.S. Army, 1946-47, clin. research sect., exec. officer med. div. Army Chem. Center, Edgewood Arsenal, Md. Diplomate Am. Bd. Internal Medicine. Fellow A.C.P.; mem. Central Soc. Clin. Research, Central Soc. Clin. Investigation, N.Y. Acad. Sci., A.M.A., Alpha Omega Alpha (nat. sec.). Contbr. articles profl. jours. Home: 1530 N State Pkwy Chicago IL 60611 Office: 1753 W Congress St Chicago IL 60612

CAMPBELL, JAMES ARTHUR, profl. baseball exec.; b. Huron, O., Feb. 5, 1924; s. Arthur A. and Vanessa (Hart) C.; B.S., Ohio State U., 1949; m. Helene G. Mulligan, Jan. 16, 1954 (div. July 1969). Bus. mgr. Thomasville (Ga.) Baseball Club, 1950, Toledo Baseball Club, 1951, Buffalo Baseball Club, 1952; bus. mgr. Detroit Minor League System, 1953, asst. farm dir. Detroit Baseball Club, 1954- 56, v.p., farm dir., 1957-61, v.p., gen. mgr., 1962-65, exec. v.p., gen. mgr., 1965—. Served with AC, USNR, 1943-46. Named Maj. League Exec. of Year, 1968. Mem. Ohio State U. Varsity O Assn., Assn., Delta Upsilon. Presbyn. Clubs: Detroit Athletic, Detroit Press. Home: 1511 1st St Detroit MI 48216 Office: Tiger Stadium 2121 Trumbull St Detroit MI 48226

CAMPBELL, JAMES ARTHUR, educator; b. Elyria, O., Oct 1, 1916; s. James Allen and Helen (Metcalf) C.; A.B., Oberlin Coll., 1938; M.Sc., Purdue U., 1939; Ph.D., U. Cal. at Berkeley, 1942; m. Dorothy Carnell, Nov. 12, 1938; children—Kathleen Annette (Mrs. Gerald Bruce Fischer), Christine (Mrs. Ronald Edmundson). Instr., U. Cal. at Berkeley, 1942-45; prof. Oberlin Coll., 1945-56; program dir. NSF, 1956-57; prof. chemistry Harvey Mudd Coll., Claremont, Cal., 1957—, dir. chem. edn. material study, 1960-63. Sci. adviser UNESCO, Asia, 1969-70; adviser Ford, Sloan, Danforth founds., Research Corp. Recipient James Flack Norris award N.E. sect. Am. Chem. Soc., 1963; Mfg. Chemists award, 1963; So. Cal. Industry award, 1965; Fund for Advancement Edn. fellow Cambridge U., 1952-53; Guggenheim fellow Kyoto U., also Cambridge U., 1963-64; Nat. Sci. Faculty fellow Harvard, 1970- 71. Mem. A.A.A.S., Am. Assn. U. Profs., Am. Chem. Soc., Conglist. Author: (with L.E. Steiner) General Chemistry, 1955; Why Do Chemical Reactions Occur? 1965; Chemical Systems, 1970; Teacher's Guide to Chemical Systems, 1970; also articles, motion pictures. Home: 754 W 10th Claremont CA 91711

CAMPBELL, JAMES CARL, mdse. exec.; b. Paxton, Ill., Aug. 15, 1906; s. J. Pam and Mary (Kenard) C.; B.S., Knox Coll., 1928; M.A. (hon.), 1956; m. Mildred Kirkpatrick, June 13, 1928; children—Sue (Mrs. James E. Charlesworth II), James Carl. Dept. mgr. Marshall Field & Co., 1945-49; with Carson Pirie Scott & Co., Chgo., v.p., gen. mdse. mgr., 1964-67, former exec. v.p., gen. mgr.; dir. Nat. Retail Mchts. Assn. N.Y.C., Millinery Inst. N.Y.C.; lectr. Northwestern U., 1951-56. Active various community fund dirs.; bd. dirs. Boy Scouts Am., Chgo., 1962—. Mem. Newcomen Soc., Tau Kappa Epsilon. Presbyn. (ch. trustee). Clubs: University, North Shore Country Executives (Chgo.); Cornell (N.Y.). Home: 3027 Indianwood Rd Wilmette IL 60091

CAMPBELL, JAMES DOW, educator; b. Nashville, Oct. 26, 1907; s. James Dow and Nannie (Pegram) C.; B.A., Vanderbilt U., 1934; Ph.D., U. Ill., 1946; m. Priscilla Humphreys, June 30, 1949. Mem. faculty Rensselaer Poly. Inst., 1938-68, 68—; prof. Tenn. Technol. U. at Cookeville, 1968. Mem. Am. Math. Soc. Home: Box 44 RD 5 Troy NY 12180

CAMPBELL, JAMES HOBART, pub. utility exec.; b. Jackson, Mich., Oct. 18, 1910; s. Birum Gould and Helen May (Chapel) C.; B.S. in M.E., Purdue U., 1933, D. Engring. (hon.), 1964; student Mass. Inst. Tech. (Alfred P. Sloan fellow), 1939-40; m. Jane Hewett, June 11, 1936; children—Bruce Hobart, James Birum, Scott Richard. Power engr. Consumers Power Co., Lansing, Mich., 1933-39, Ohio Edison Co., Youngstown, 1940-42; asst. to div. mgr. Consumers Power Co., Grand Rapids, Mich., 1946-47, div. mgr., 1947-49, asst. to pres., 1949-50, v.p., Jackson, Mich., 1950-56, sr. v.p., 1956-60, pres., chief operating officer, 1960—, also dir.; dir., v.p. mem. exec. com. Power Reactor Devel. Co.; dir. Nat. Bank Jackson, Tecumseh Products Co. (Mich.), Hayes-Albion Corp. Vice pres., dir. Atomic Indsl. Forum; chmn. Nat. Assn. Electric Cos., 1962-63. Served to lt. col., Fifth Army, AUS, 1942-46; ETO. Mem. Newcomen Soc., Beta Theta Pi. Clubs: Town, Country, Rotary (Jackson); Metropolitan (Washington). Student history of Am. Revolution. Home: 3515 Stonewall Rd Jackson MI 49203 Office: 212 W Michigan Av Jackson MI 49201

CAMPBELL, JAMES PHILANDER, Jr., govt. ofcl.; b. Athens, Ga., Apr. 9, 1917; s. James Philander and Lorraine (Proctor) C.; student George Washington U., 1934; student agr., Denmark, 1938-39; B.S.A., U. Ga., 1940; m. Elizabeth Anne McCreery, Mar. 20, 1943; children—Elizabeth Ann (Mrs. Phil Prichard), Vivian Lorraine, James Philander III, John Alan, Jennifer Claire, Janice. Mem. Ga. Ho. of Reps. from Oconee County, 1949-54; commnr. agr. Ga., 1955-69; under sec. Dept. Agr., 1969—. Mem. nat. adv. com. to sec. agr. for hog cholera eradication, 1962-69, nat. adv. com. sec. agr. wholesome meat and food inspection, 1967-69. Mem. Stone Mountain Meml. Assn., 1958-69, sec.- treas., 1960-64, chmn. bd., 1964-68. Trustee U. Ga. Found., 1957—. Served to 1st lt. USAAF, 1942-45. Mem. Am. Legion, U. Ga. Alumni Soc. (pres. 1956), Farm Bur., Phi Kappa Phi. Republican. Baptist. Rotarian. Clubs: Athens (Ga.) Country; Atlanta Athletic, Atlanta Commerce. Home: 8822 Fircrest Pl Alexandria VA 22308 Office: Dept of Agriculture 14th and Independence Av Washington DC 20250

CAMPBELL, JAMES WINCHESTER, former found. exec.; b. Ayshire, Scotland, May 1, 1903; s. Andrew and Agnes McGill (Ferguson) C.; ed. in Scotland, 1925-28; extension student Columbia Sch. Bus. Adminstrn.; m. Kathleen M. Woods, Aug. 11, 1928; 1 son, James Winchester. Came to U.S., 1923, naturalized, 1944. Engaged as pub. accountant, 1925-33; with Carnegie Corp., N.Y.C., 1933-69, treas., 1961-69; treas. Carnegie Found. Advancement Teaching, 1961-69; past dir. Home Trust Co., Hoboken, N.J. Bd. dirs. Norwalk chpt. A.R.C., 1953-54. Club: 60 East (N.Y.C.). Home: 38 Sandra Circle Westfield NJ 07090 also Miller Rd Pennsburg Rd PA 18073

CAMPBELL, JOHN ALEXANDER, medical educator; b. Cin., June 29, 1914; s. Archibald and Elizabeth M. (Harris) C.; B.S., U. Cin., 1935, M.D., 1937; m. Willie Dickins, July 9, 1938; children—Nancy, Duncan, Jamie. Intern Detroit Receiving Hosp., 1937-38; postgrad. tng. radiology Henry Ford Hosp., Detroit, 1938- 41; asst. radiologist St. Joseph Hosp., Ann Arbor, Mich., 1941; instr. radiology USPHS, 1942-45; mem. faculty radiology Ind. U. Med. Center, 1941—, prof., 1956—, chmn. dept., 1957—; dir. acad. radiol. services Univ., Marion County Gen., Indpls. VA hosps., Ind. U. Student Health Service; chief radiology Marion County Gen. Hosp., 1969, Martin L. King Jr. Gen. Hosp., Los Angeles; chmn. dept. radiology Charles R. Drew Postgrad. Med. Sch., Los Angeles; cons. radiology USAF, 1968—; cons. radiation adv. control commn. Ind. Bd. Health; radiol. cons. Ind. Civil Def. Bd. Mem. com. radiology Nat. Acad. Scis.-NRC. Mem. Marion County Civil Def. Bd. Dir. Indpls. Council World Affairs, Doctors Dixieland Band, Indpls. Civic Theatre; mgr. Pony League Baseball; mem. Indpls. Mayor's Citizens Adv. Com., 1965-. Diplomate Am. Bd. Radiology in radiology and nuclear medicine. Fellow Am. Coll. Radiology (councilor, mem. com. on edn.); mem. Am. Roentgen Ray Soc., Radiol. Soc. N. Am. (1st v.p.), Council Acad. Socs., Assn. Am. Med. Colls. (mem. council of acad. socs.), Assn. U. Radiologists (pres. 1964-65), A.M.A., Ind. Roentgen. Soc., Ind., Marion County med. socs., Alpha Omega Alpha, Delta Tau Delta, Nu Sigma Nu. Author civil def. bull. Home: 5201 Grandview Dr Indianapolis IN 47208 Office: 1100 W Michigan St Indianapolis IN

CAMPBELL, JOHN ANDREW, mining co. exec.; b. Toronto, Ont., Can., Nov. 5, 1929; s. Andrew and Alice (Sharpe) C.; B.A., U. Toronto, 1953, LL.B., 1957; m. Gwenith Muriel Yeates, Dec. 23, 1955; children—John Malcolm, Timothy Andrew. Called to Law Soc. Upper Can., 1957—; with firm Hogg, Colbert & Campbell, Sarina, Ont., Can., 1958, firm Smith Rae Greer, Toronto, 1958-69; partner firm Seed, Greer, Long, Campbell & Howard, Toronto, 1969—. Gen. counsel, sec. Steep Rock Iron Mines Ltd., Atikokan, Ont., Can., 1969—. Named Queen's Counsel, 1970. Mem. Canadian Bar Assn., Lawyers Club, Med.-Legal Soc., Donalda Club. Home: 34 Parmbelle Crescent Toronto Ontario Canada Office: 220 Bay St Toronto Ontario Canada

CAMPBELL, JOHN COERT, author, polit. scientist; b. N.Y.C., Oct. 8, 1911; s. Allan Reuben and Gertrude Helen (DuBois) C.; A.B., Harvard, 1933, M.A., 1936, Ph.D., 1940; m. Mary Elizabeth Hillis, Aug. 1, 1936; childrenAllan Reuben II, Alexander Bruce. Instr. polit. sci. U. Louisville, 1940-41; specialist Eastern Europe, State Dept., 1942-46; sec. U.S. delegation, polit. adviser Council Fgn. Ministers, also Paris (France) Peace Conf., 1946; polit. adviser U.S. delegation Danube Conf., 1948; officer charge Balkan affairs, mem. policy planning staff State Dept., 1949-55; dir. polit. studies, sr. research fellow Council Fgn. Relations, 1955-; cons. and adv. State Dept., 1963—, mem. policy planning council, 1967-68. Gov., v.p. Middle East Inst.; mem. joint com. Slavic studies Am. Council Learned Soc. Fellow Middle East Studies Assn.; mem. Council Fgn. Relations, Am. Hist. Assn., Am. Assn. Advancement Slavic Studies. Author: The United States in World Affairs, 3 vols., 1947-49; Defense of the Middle East; Problems of American Policy, rev. edit., 1960; American Policy Toward Communist Eastern Europe; The Choices Ahead, 1965; Tito's Separate Road; America and Yugoslavia in World Politics, 1967. Mem. editorial bd. Slavic Rev. Home: 399 Bedford Rd Chappaqua, NY 10514. Office: 58 E 68th St New York City NY 10021

CAMPBELL, JOHN G., banker; b. 1923; married. With Crocker-Citizens Nat. Bank, 1940—, v.p. comml. loans, 1962-68, regional v.p., 1968-69, sr. v.p., regional mgr., Oakland, Cal., 1969—. Office: 393 13th St Oakland CA 94604*

CAMPBELL, JOHN LLOYD, oral surgeon, educator, b. Leavenworth, Kan., Jan. 29, 1914; s. Lloyd Gully and Lorena Mary (Starry) C.; student DePauw U., 1932-33; D.D.S., Ind. U., 1939; M.S., U. Md., 1953; m. Ruth Elizabeth Lee, June 15, 1939; children—Margaret Lee (Mrs. John Cremer), Sally Ann (Mrs. Darrel Hicks); m. 2d, Eleanor Lois Ingebretsen, Oct. 4, 1947; children—Catherine Louise, John Lloyd Campbell. Intern, Columbia Presbyn. Med. Center, 1939-40; commd. 1st lt., Dental Corps, U.S. Army, 1940, advanced through grades to lt. col., 1951; ret. 1960; prof. oral surgery, chmn. dept. W.Va. U. Sch. Dentistry, Med. Center, Morgantown, 1960—, also chief hosp. dental service; oral surgery cons. VA Hosp., Clarksburg, W.Va., Ireland Gen. Hosp., Ft. Knox, Ky. Bd. dirs. W.Va. chpt. Nat. Hemophilia Found. Friendship Manor, A.R.C., state Am. Cancer Soc. Diplomate Am. Bd. Oral Surgeons. Fellow Internat. Coll. Dentists, A.A.A.S., Am. Coll. Dentists; mem. Internat. Assn. Oral Surgeons, Assn. Internat. Dental Research, Assn. Mil. Surgeons, Royal Soc. Health, Am. Assn. Hosp. Chiefs, Am., W.Va. dental assns., Monongahela Valley Dental Soc., Fedn. Dentaire Internat., Pan Am. Med. Assn., Am., Middle Atlantic, W.Va. Southeastern socs. oral surgeons, Morgantown C. of C., Am. Legion, V.F.W., Omicron Kappa Upsilon, Delta Upsilon, Alpha Phi Omega, Delta Sigma Delta. Presbyn. (trustee). Mason (Shriner), Kiwanian, Elk. Home: 601 Valley View St Morgantown WV 26505

CAMPBELL, JOHN MORGAN, engr.; b. Virden, Ill., Mar. 24, 1922; s. John M. and Ione Marie (Whittler) C.; B.S. in Chem. Engring., Ia. State U., 1943; M.S., U. Okla., 1948, Ph.D., 1951; m. Gwendolyn Thompson, Aug. 27, 1945; childrenJohn Morgan, Robert, Charles. Devel. engr. and supr. E. I. duPont de Nemours & Co., Inc., 1943-46; spl. instr. chem. engring. U. Okla., 1946-50; tech. adviser to v.p. Black Sivalls and Bryson, Oklahoma City, 1951-54; mem. faculty U. Okla. Sch. Petroleum Engring., 1954-69, chmn. dept., 1956-63, Erle P. Halliburton prof., 1963-69, dir. 1969; Petroleum Research Center, 1964—; pres. John M. Campbell & Co., engring. counselors, mgmt. cons., 1954—. Mem. Am. Inst. M.E. (exec. com. council edn. 1963-), Soc. Petroleum Engrs., Am. Arbtration Assn. (arbitration panel), Internat. Petroleum Inst. (pres. 1968—), Sigma Alpha Epsilon, Phi Lambda Upsilon, Pi Epsilon Tau. Lion. Presbyn. (trustee). Author: Oil Property Evaluation, 1959; Gas Conditioning and Processing, 1970; Effective Technical Communications, 1969; The Professional - From Puberty to Semlity, 1970; Decision Methods For Petroleum Investments, 1969; also articles, chpts. in books. Home: 234 Foreman Av Norman, OK 73069.

CAMPBELL, JOHN PALMER, lawyer; b. Utica, N.Y., Sept. 1, 1923; s. Samuel R. and Sophia (Doolittle) C.; grad. Middlesex Sch., 1942; A.B. Harvard, 1947; LL.B., Columbia, 1949; m. Eleanor M. Seggerman, Aug. 27, 1949; children—Samuel R., Frederick B., Louisa D., Mary Camilla. Admitted to N.Y. bar, 1950; mem. firm Reynolds, Richards & McCutcheon, N.Y.C., 1950-51; with J.P. Morgan & Co., Inc., 1951-52; asst. counsel com. to investigate crime in interstate commerce U.S. Senate, 1951; mem. firm Curtis, Mallet-Prevost, Colt & Mosle, .N.Y.C., 1953-59, partner, 1959—; dir. pvt. corps.; conservator, trustee Continental Vending Machine Corp., 1963-64. Mem. Nassau County (N.Y.) Republican Com., 1954-57. Trustee, Middlesex Sch., Concord, Mass., 1952-55, 57—, Clarkson Coll. Tech., Potsdam, N.Y., 1969—, Mus. Am. Indian, 1964—. Served to capt. USAAF, 1942- 45. Decorated Air medal. Home: 76 Shore Rd Cold Spring Harbor NY 11724 Office: 100 Wall St New York City NY 10005

CAMPBELL, JOSEPH, former comptroller gen. U.S.; b. N.Y.C., Mar. 25, 1900; s. Thomas and Anne (Conneil) C.; A.B., Columbia, 1924, LL.D.; LL.D., Colgate U.; children by previous marriage—Frederick, Douglas, Robert, Alan, Colin; m. 2d, Dorothy Bostwick; stepchildren—Mrs. John V.B. Dean, Mrs. Henry A. Rudkin, Jr., W.T. Sampson Smith, Jr. With Lingley Baird & Dixon, accountants, 1924-27; asst. comptroller Valspar Corp., 1927-29, comptroller, 1929-32; partner R.T. Lingley & Co., accountants, 1932-33, Joseph Campbell & Co., accountants, 1933-41; asst. treas. Columbia, 1941-48, treas., v.p. 1949-55; comptroller gen. U.S., 1954-65. Trustee emeritus Trinity Coll., Conn. Mem. AEC, 1953-54. Mem. Am. Inst. Accountants, Alpha Delta Phi. Republican. Episcopalian. Clubs: Union League, Madison Square Garden (N.Y.C.); Seawanhaka Corinthian Yacht (L.I.); Chevy Chase. Home: 3111 Woodland Dr NW Washington DC 20008 also Cooperstown NY 13326

CAMPBELL, JOSEPH, educator, author; b. N.Y.C., Mar. 26, 1904; s. Charles William and Josephine (Lynch) C.; grad. Canterbury Sch., 1921; student Dartmouth, 1921-22; A.B., Columbia, 1925, M.A., 1927; postgrad. U. Paris, 1927-28, U. Munich, 1928-29; m. Jean Erdman, May 5, 1938. Tchr., Canterbury Sch., 1932-33; mem. faculty lit. dept., Sarah Lawrence Coll., Bronxville, N.Y., 1934—; lectr. Fgn. Service Inst., Dept. State, Washington, 1956—, Columbia, 1959. Pres. Creative Film Found., 1954-63; trustee Bollingen Found., 1960-69. Mem. Soc. for Arts, Religion and Contemporary Culture (bd. dirs.). Author: (with Jeff King, Maud Oakes) Where the Two Came to Their Father, A Navaho War Ceremonial, 1943; Grimm's Fairy Tales; Folkloristic Commentary, 1944; (with Henry Morton Robinson) A Skeleton Key to Finnegans Wake, 1944; The Hero with a Thousand Faces, 1949; The Masks of God, Vol. I, Primitive Mythology, 1959, Vol. II, Oriental Mythology, 1962, Vol. III, Occidental Mythology, 1964, Vol. IV, Creative Mythology, 1967; The Flight of the Wild Gander, 1969. Editor: The Viking Portable Arabian Nights, 1952; Papers from the Eranos Yearbooks (vols. 1 to 6), 1954, 55, 57, 61, 64, 68; Myths, Dreams and Religion, 1970; Viking Portable Jung, 1971; (with Heinrich Zimmer) Myths and Symbols in Indian Art and Civilzation, 1946, The King and the Corpse, 1948, Philosophies of India, 1951, The Art of Indian Asia, 1955. Contbr. articles to profl. pubis. Home: 136 Waverly Pl New York City NY 10014 Office: Sarah Lawrence College Bronxville NY 10708

CAMPBELL, JOSEPH BRADBURN, state senator; b. Denver, Mar. 21, 1908; s. Joseph D. and Naomi (Bradburn) C.; student Colby Coll.; LL.B., Georgetown U., 1931, LL.M., 1932; m. Dorothy Murphy, June 8, 1934; children—Susan (Mrs. Law), Sheila (Mrs. Rhoades), Martha (Mrs. Murphy). Admitted to Me. bar, 1932; solicitor City of Hallowell, Me., 1938-47, judge Municipal Ct., 1949-53; atty. Kennebec County, Me., 1953-54; past acting city mgr. Augusta, Me.; mem. Me. Ho. of Reps., 1949-51; mem. Me. Senate, 1963—, pres., 1967—; sec. Depositors Corp., Augusta. Served from 1st lt. to maj., USAAF, 1942-45; ETO, NATOUSA; col. in Res., 1961—. Mem. Am. Coll. Trial Lawyers, Am. Judicature Soc., Am., Me., Kennebec County bar assns., Am. Legion, Zeta Psi. Roman Catholic. Home: 76 Willow St Augusta ME 04330 Office: 286 Water St Augusta ME 04330

CAMPBELL, JOSEPH RICHARDSON, banker; b. Monaca, Pa., July 13, 1909; s. Robert C. and Grace (Ellis) C.; B.S. in Econs., Wharton Sch., U. Pa., 1931; M.B.A., Temple U., 1954; m. Gertrude V. Nash, Feb. 12, 1934; children—Joseph Richardson III, Mary Elizabeth (Mrs. Olen D. Thornton), Robert C. III. With Fed. Res. Bank Phila., 1931—, sr. v.p. charge bank exam., 1969—; past instr. Bank-Examiner Inter-Agy. Sch., Washington, Temple U. Mem. Nat. Rifle Assn., Newcomen Soc., Theta Xi. Episcopalian. Club: Bank Officers (Phila.). Home: 5023 Bond Av Drexel Hill PA 19026 Office: 925 Chestnut St Philadelphia PA 19101

CAMPBELL, KENNETH, cons. engr.; b. San Francisco, June 1, 1899; s. William Wallace and Elizabeth Ballard (Thompson) C.; grad. Hotchkiss Sch., Lakeville, Conn., 1917; A.B., Harvard, 1921, S.B., 1923; D.Sc. (hon.), Bard Coll., 1952; m. Margaret Bruce Macon, Nov. 8, 1930; children—Janet Bruce, Elizabeth Wallace, Margaret Macon, Martha Madison. Mem. staff Lick Obs. solar eclipse expdn., Kiev, USSR, 1915, eclipse party, Freyburg, Me., 1932; with various operating depts. Bethlehem Steel Co., 1923-26, foreman blast furnace dept., 1926- 28; indsl. engr. Sanderson & Porter, 1928-33; aircraft power plant research, devel. engring. Wright Aero. div. Curtiss-Wright Corp., 1933-64, dir. research, 1950-51, tech. dir., 1951-55, gen. mgr. research div. Curtiss-Wright Corp., 1966-60, chief scientist- propulsion, 1960-64; cons. Thiokol Chem. Corp., Dover, N.J., 1964—, also Inst. for Def. Analyses, Gregory Assos. Chmn. subcom. compressors and turbines NACA, 1940-45, subcoms. heat exchangers, 1945-47 combustion, 1948-49, compressors and turbines, 1950-51; vice chmn. vis. com. for engring. scis. Harvard, 1955—; mem. bd. cons. Nuclear Energy Power Plant for Aircraft, 1949-51; mem. tech. mission to Germany, USN, 1945; mem. panel on engines Air Tech. Intelligence Center, USAAF, 1951—. Served as ambulance driver A.R.C., Capo Sile, Italy, 1918; 2d lt. RAF, 1918-19. Decorated Croce di Guerra (Italy); Wright Bros. medal. Soc. Automotive Engrs., 1944, Charles Matthews Manley medal, 1945. Fellow Inst. Aero. Sci.; mem. Soc. Automotive Engrs., Harvard Engring. Soc., Sigma Xi. Episcopalian. Contbr. articles profl. publs. Home: 144 S Maple Av Ridgewood NJ 07450

CAMPBELL, KENNETH NIELSEN, chemist, educator; b. Hillsdale, Mich., May 31, 1905; s. Royal Burke and Vivian Winifred (Nielsen) C.; student Kalamazoo Coll., 1924-26; B.S., U. Chgo., 1928, Ph.D., 1932; m. Barbara Harriet Knapp, June 17, 1933. Post-doctoral research asst. organic chemistry Pa. State Coll., 1933-35, U. Ill. at Urbana, 1935-36; instr. organic chemistry, U. Notre Dame, South Bend, Ind., 1936-38, asst. and asso. prof., 1938-46, prof., 1946-54; dir. medicinal chemistry Mead Johnson Research Labs., Evansville, Ind., 1954—; cons. USPHS, 1949-52; vis. lectr. pharm. scis. U. Tex. at Austin, 1958. Chmn. 2d Nat. Medicinal Chemistry Symposium, 1950. Dir. projects on anti-malarials for Com. on Med. Research, World War II, on explosives for Nat. Def. Research Com. Recipient citation of merit Ind. Tech. Coll., 1958, alumni science award University Notre Dame, 1965. Fellow A.A.A.S., Brit. Chem. Soc., Am. Inst. Chemists; mem. Research Soc. Am., Am. Chem. Soc., (chmn. local sect. 1944-45, councilor 1946-48, chmn. meml. div. 1949-50; councilor local sect. 1955- 57), Ind. Acad. Sci. (chmn. chemistry sect. 1942-43), Ind. Chem. Soc. (director), N.Y. Acad. of Sci., Sigma Xi. Research on chemotherapy of cancer with NIH; on aliphatic hydrocarbons for Office of Naval Research; on other problems in organic and medicinal chemistry. Contbr. numerous papers in sci. jours. Patents on heterocyclic compounds, antimalarials, synthetic drugs. Home: 8216 Petersburg Rd Evansville, IN 47711. Office: Mead Johnson Research Center Evansville IN 47721

CAMPBELL, L. MERLE, retired banker; b. Emlenton, Pa., Sept. 17, 1886; s. Joseph A. and Lucy A. (Bell) C.; student Pa. State Normal Sch.; m. Ada McFeeters, Mar. 20, 1908; children—Geraldine (Mrs. Charles A. Perry), Gretchen (Mrs. William H. Liddle). Chmn. emeritus N.W. Pa. Bank & Trust Co., Oil City; dir. McCoy Natural Gas Co., Oil City Scarcroft Securities, Ltd., Toronto, Monongahela Connecting R.R., Aliquippa & So. R.R. Co., Cuyahoga Valley Ry. Co., Peoples Bldg. & Loan, Oil City. Past sec. banking Commonwealth Pa. Mason (32, Shriner). Clubs: Wanango Country, Oil City. Home: Plincak Dr Oil City PA 16301 Office: 13 E 1st St Oil City PA 16301

CAMPBELL, LAURENCE RANDOLPH, educator; b. Batavia, Ia., Mar. 11, 1903; s. Frank Thomas and Flora May (Harris) C.; A.B., San Jose State Coll., 1926; M.S., Northwestern, 1931, Ph.D., 1939; grad. study, summers, Stanford, U. Wash., U. Colo.; m. Katheryn Belle Gourley, June 9, 1942; childrenMalcolm Randolph, Douglas Gourley, Laurence Barrett. Tchr. S. San Francisco Jr.-Sr. High Sch., 1926-28, Menlo (Cal.) Sr. High Sch. and Jr. Coll., 1928-33, Marysville U. High Sch. and Yuba Co. Jr. Coll., 1933-36; asst. Northwestern U., 1936- 39; editorial asst. The Rotarian, 1938-39; asst. Prof. U. Ill., 1939-41, U. Cal., 1942-43; asso. editor Drug Progress, 1942; news editor San Francisco edition Wall St. Jour., 1943-44; asso. prof. Temple U., 1944-45; prof., acting dean sch. journalism Syracuse (N.Y.) U., 1945-46, prof., 1946-47, U. Ore., 1947-50; prof., dean sch. journalism Fla. State U., 1950-59, prof. edn., 1960-61, head dept. ednl. founds. School Edn., 1961-63, prof. English edn., 1963; lectr. Am. journalism, Jordan, Egypt, and Syria, 1956 (under auspices Dept. of State Internat. Edn. Exchange Service). Mem. Assn. Edn. Journalism (Carl Towley award service to journalism, 1967), Sigma Delta Chi, Phi Delta Kappa, Kappa Tau Tau Alpha. Republican. Presbyn. Author: Exploring Journalism. 1949 (with R.E. Wolseley), rev., 1957; News Beat, 1949 (with John Paul Jones); Newsmen at Work, 1949 (with R. E. Wolseley); Guide to Radio-TV Writing, 1950 (with Henry Heath, Raymond Johnson); How to Report and Write the News, 1961 (with R. E. Wolseley). Editor: Careers in Journalism 1950, rev., 1955; Social Basis for Education in Florida 1962. Book editor of Sch. Press Rev.; asso. editor Quill and Scroll; dir. Quill and Scroll Studies, 1965-. Home: 2103 E Randolph Circle Tallahassee FL 32303

CAMPBELL, LEONARD MARTIN, lawyer; b. Denver, Apr. 12, 1918; s. Bernard Francis and May (Moran) C.; A.B., U. Colo., 1941, LL.B., 1943; m. Dot J. Baker, Sept. 23, 1944; children— Brian T., Teri Pat, Thomas P. Admitted to Colo. bar, 1943, since practiced in Denver; mem. firm Gorsuch, Kirgis, Campbell, Walker & Grover, 1946; cons. pub. utility matters City and County Denver, also Colo. Municipal League, 1953—; city atty., Denver, 1951-53. Mem. Denver Charter Com., 1947; mgr. Safety and Excise for Denver, 1947-48; chmn. Denver Com. Human Relations, 1954; mem. Denver Planning Bd., 1950-51; mem. Bd. Water Commrs. Denver, 1965-70, pres., 1968-69. Chmn. U. Colo. Law Alumni Devel. Fund, 1962. Served with USAAF, 1943-46. Mem. Am., Colo. (chmn. legislative com. 1961), Denver (pres. 1969) bar assns., Am. Coll. Trial Lawyers, Cath. Lawyers Guild Denver (pres. 1962), Nat. Inst. Municipal Law Officers (v.p. 1952). Democrat. Roman Catholic. K.C. Clubs: Denver Athletic (sec. 1960-61, pres. 1962), Cherry Hills Country (Denver). Home: 3447 S Birch St Denver CO 80222 Office: Security Life Bldg Denver CO 80202

CAMPBELL, LINZY LEON, microbiologist, educator; b. Panhandle, Tex., Feb. 10, 1927; s. Linzy Leon and Eula Irene (McSpadden) C.; B.A. in Bacteriology and Chemistry, U. Tex., 1949, M.A., 1950, Ph.D., 1952; m. Alice P. Dauksa, Feb. 7, 1953. Research scientist U. Tex., 1947-51; predoctoral research fellow NIH, 1951-52; postdoctoral research fellow Nat. Microbiol. Inst., U. Cal. at Berkeley, 1952-54; asst. prof., asso. prof. Wash. State U., 1954-59; asso. prof. Western Res. U. Sch. Medicine, 1959-62; sr. research fellow USPHS, 1959-62; prof. microbiology U. Ill., Urbana, 1962—, head dept., 1963-71, dir. Sch. Life Scis., 1971—. Fellow Am. Acad. Microbiology; mem. Am. Soc. Microbiology (chmn. publ. bd. 1965—, councilor at large 1962-64), Soc. Gen. Microbiology, Am. Soc. Biol. Chemists, A.A.A.S., Am. Chem. Soc. Served with USNR, 1944-46. Mem. editorial bd. Jour. Bacteriology, 1961-65, editor, 1964-65, editor-in-chief, 1965—. Contbr. articles to profl. jours. Office: Dept Microbiology U Ill Urbana IL 61801

CAMPBELL, LORAINE LEESON, (Mrs. Walter E. Campbell), assn. exec.; b. Newton Center, Mass., May 12, 1905; d. Robert Ainsworth and Mildred Carruth (Dix) L.; A.B. with honors, Vassar Coll., 1928; m. Walter Edward Campbell, Apr. 7, 1934; children—Leeson, Dix, Charles Lanning. Asso. birth control movement, Mass., 1934—, U.S., 1941—; clinic chmn. Brookline and Boston, Mass., 1936-37; dir. Birth Control League of Mass. (became Mass. Mothers' Health Council, later Planned Parenthood League Mass.), 1936—, pres., 1940-43, 1945-49, v.p., 1943- 45, 1949-56; dir. Planned Parenthood Fedn. Am., 1941-62, 63-69, pres., 1956-59. Bd. overseers Shady Hill Sch., Cambridge, Mass., 1944-47; bd. dirs. Asso. Alumnae, Vassar Coll., 1949-52. Mem. League Women Voters (dir. 1942-45), Civil Liberties Union Mass. (dir. 1949-52, exec. com. 1950-52), Phi Beta Kappa. Unitarian. Home: 11 Lowell St Cambridge MA 02138

CAMPBELL, MARION (Mrs. Douglass Campbell), publisher; b. Ipswich, Mass., July 14, 1921; d. Richard Ely and Barbara (Deering) Danielson; B.A. Vassar Coll., 1943; m. Malcolm Strachan, 1949 (dec.); children—Richard, Stephen Malcolm; m. 2d, Douglass Campbell, Jan. 1962. Editorial asso. Atlantic Monthly, 1943, 45-50, dir., 1953- -; pres. Atlantic Monthly Co., 1957—; mem. editorial dept. Washington Post, 1944. Staff aide casework Am. Red Cross, 1944-46. Office: 8 Arlington St Boston MA 02116

CAMPBELL, MILDRED L., educator; b. Sheffield, Tenn., May 31, 1897; d. John Martin and Rosannah (Medsger) Campbell; A.B., Maryville (Tenn.) Coll., 1920, Litt.D., 1961; A.M., Columbia, 1923; Ph.D., Yale, 1932; A.M., Oxford (Eng.) U., 1951; LL.D., Rockford Coll., 1955. History tchr. Central High Sch., Chattanooga, 1920-22; instr., later asst. prof. history, Rockford (Ill.) Coll., 1923-29; mem. faculty Vassar Coll., Poughkeepsie, N.Y., 1932—, prof. history, 1941-62, now prof. emeritus. Guggenheim fellow, 1951-52; Fulbright fellow, Oxford, Eng., 1951-52. Mem. Ford Found. Com. for Selection of Teaching Fellows, 1951, Fulbright Nat. Selection Com., 1953-56. Mem. council Williamsburg Inst. Early Am. History and Culture, Williamsburg, Va. Trustee, Dowling Coll., 1968-71. Recipient Ann. award Am. Assn. U. Women, 1964. Fellow Royal Hist. Soc. London; mem. Am. Hist. Assn. (council 1958-62), Econ. Hist. Assn. (trustee 1964-68). Author: The English Yeoman Under Elizabeth and the Early Stuarts, 1942; contbg. author Seventeenth Century America, 1959; Conflict in Stuart England, 1960. Editor: More's Utopia (Classics Club edit.), 1947; mem. editorial bd. Jour. Modern History, 1942-45, Am. Hist. Rev., 1957-62, Jour. Econ. History, 1959-65. Contbr. to hist. jours. Home: 162 College Av Poughkeepsie NY 12603

CAMPBELL, NORMAN LLOYD, life ins. co. exec.; b. Toronto, Ont., Can., Oct. 22, 1912; s. John Norman and Blanche (LeHuquet) C.; B.A., U. Toronto, 1935; m. Mary Simmons, July 8, 1967; children by previous marriage—Judith Marilyn, Carla Call, William Call. Came to U.S., 1949, naturalized, 1959. With Mfrs. Life Ins. Co., Toronto, 1935-41; life sec. Royal Ins. Co., 1947- 49; asst. actuary Tchrs. Ins. & Annuity Assn., 1949-52, Coll. Retirement Equities Fund, 1949-52; with Nat. Life Ins. Co., Montpelier, Vt., 1952—, asst. actuary, 1952-55, asso. actuary, 1955-60, actuary, 1960-65, v.p., actuary, 1965-69, sr. v.p. plans and operations, 1969—; pres., dir. Sentinel Income Fund, Inc., 1968—, Sentinel Growth Fund, Inc., 1968—, Adminstrv. Services, Inc., 1969—, Sentinel Trustees Fund, Inc., 1970—; dir. Equity Services, Inc., Nat. Life Investment Mgmt. Co., Inc. Served with RCAF, 1942-45. Fellow Soc. Actuaries; mem. Canadian Assn. Actuaries, Am. Acad. Actuaries. Clubs: Woodway Country (Darien, Conn.); Burlington Country. Home: 1411 Spear St Burlington VT 05401 Office: Nat Life Ins Co Montpelier VT 05602

CAMPBELL, ORVIN WATSON, univ. ofcl.; b. Lodi, Cal., May 4, 1906; s. Gordon Jerome and Rose Elizabeth (Watson) C.; A.B., Stanford, 1929; postgrad. U. Cal., 1932-35; m. Evelyn Louise Pimentel, Feb. 22, 1935; children—Beverly Ann (Mrs. Richard Tremper), John Richard. Pub. adminstrn. service, 1937-40; cons. pub. adminstrn. fed. and state govts., 1940-43; city mgr., San Jose Cal., 1946-50, San Diego, 1950-57; county mgr. Dade County (Miami), Fla., 1957-61; vice- chancellor for bus. and finance U. Cal. at Berkeley, 1961—. Past pres. League Cal. Cities. Trustee Eno Found.; dir. Univ. Corp. for Atmospheric Research. Served with AUS, 1943-46; ETO. Mem. Am. Soc. Pub. Adminstrn., Internat. City Mgrs. Assn., Berkeley C. of C. (v.p.). Home: 10 Cascade Lane Orinda CA 94563 Office: Sproul Hall U of Cal Berkeley CA 94720

CAMPBELL, OTIS W., telephone co. exec. Pres., Gen. Telephone Co. Ky. Office: 2001 Harrodsburg Rd Lexington KY 40503*

CAMPBELL, PATRICK, business exec.; b. Manchester, Eng., Dec. 24, 1909; s. John and Dorothy (Philips) C.; student Blundells Sch., Tiverton, Eng., 1922-26; B.Sc., London U., 1931. Trainee, salesman Horlicks, Ltd., 1928-35, mgr. Far East, 1939-41, mng. dir., 1954—; mng. dir. Horlicks Proprietary, Ltd., Australia, 1935-38; exec. v.p. Horlicks Corp., Racine, Wis., 1951-53, pres., 1953-54, dir., 1953-69. Served as squadron leader RAF, 1942-46. Fellow Royal Inst. Chemistry. Home: 6 Burlington Lane London W4 England Office: Horlicks Ltd Slough Buckinghamshire England

CAMPBELL, PATTON, costume designer; debut as Broadway designer for 27 Wagons Full of Cotton; other Broadway shows include The Glass Menagerie, A Hole in the Head, Fallen Angels, All American; costume designer Man of La Mancha; formerly with N.Y. City Opera, Santa Fe, Central City operas; former tchr. stage design Barnard Coll.; now mem. faculty N.Y.U.

CAMPBELL, RALPH NORTON, educator; b. Minotola, N.J., Mar. 7, 1910; s. Edward Baylell and Rebecca White (Paris) C.; A.B., Rutgers U., 1931; M.B.A., Harvard, 1947; m. Mary Elizabeth Garland, Aug. 22, 1936 (dec.); childrenPeter Norton, Patricia Audrey; m. 2d, Marian McCauley, Apr. 1, 1966; stepchildrenPhillip McCauley IV, Nancy McCauley, Patricia McCauley. Reporter New Brunswick (N.J.) Daily Home News, 1931-32; grad. asst. polit. sci. Rutgers U., 1932-33, asst. dir. alumni and pub. relations, 1934-37, dir. personnel and placement, 1937-40; salesman Conn. Mut. Life Ins. Co., 1940; prof. indsl. and labor relations N.Y. State Sch. of Indsl. and Labor Relations, Cornell U., Ithaca, N.Y., 1948—, dir. extension 1948-56 1948-56 , 60-63, dir. summers, 1956-58; prof. edn. Cornell U., 1956— chmn. dept. human resources, adminstrn., 1960. Pres. Nat. Inst. Labor Edn.; mem. nat. com. on study grants in adult edn. Fund for Adult Edn., 1952- 54; roster of arbitrators Fed. Mediation and Conciliation Service, 1953—; impartial chmn. N.Y. State Adv. Council on Farm Minimum Wages, 1969—. Trustee, sec. Nat. Center for Arts at Ithaca, co-founder and 1st exec. dir. Ithaca Festival. Served from 1st lt. to col. AUS, 1946. Decorated Bronze Star medal, French Croix de Guerre. Pres. N.J. Jr. C. of C., 1940; nat. panel labor arbitrators Am. Arbitration Assn. Mem. field service com., N.Y. State Citizens Council, 1949-52. Mem. Indsl. Relations Research Assn., Acad. Mgmt., Phi Beta Kappa, Tau Kappa Alpha. Theta Chi. Mem. editorial bd. Indsl. and Labor Relations Rev., 1952-55. Home: 101 The Parkway Ithaca NY 14850

CAMPBELL, RAYMOND ROOSEVELT, lawyer; b. Shepherd, Mich., Oct. 24, 1904; s. David W. and Emma (Ingleson) C.; student Kalamazoo Coll., 1922-24; A.B., Western Mich. U., 1926; postgrad. U. Wis., 1932-33; J.D., U. Mich., 1942; m. Violet Evelyn McBrian, June 13, 1936; 1 son, Briar Raymond. Head social studies Lansing, Mich., 1929-38; asst. atty. TVA, 1942-43; admitted to Mich. bar, 1942; asso. atty. Fed. Power Commn., 1943-45; atty. Chrysler Corp., Detroit, 1945-48; spl. asst. prosecuting atty., Lansing, Mich., 1948-52; partner Foster, Campbell, Lindemer & McGurrin, Lansing, 1952—; city atty., E. Lansing, 1955-67. Dir. East Lansing State Bank, 1954—. Chmn. Lansing Library Com., 1958-60. Mem. Am., Ingham County (past pres.) bar assns., State Bar Mich., Am. Judicature Soc., Lansing C. of C. (past chmn. exec. com.). Presbyn. Mason, Kiwanian (pres. 1965). Clubs: City, Country (Lansing). Home: 124 Oxford Rd East Lansing MI 48823 also 5330 Calle del Norte Phoenix AZ 85018 Office: Am Bank & Trust Co Lansing MI 48933

CAMPBELL, RICHARD CUNNINGHAM, ret. ins. exec.; b. Lynn, Mass., Feb. 5, 1904; s. Frederick Joseph and Harriet (Cunningham) C.; student Middlebury (Vt.) Coll., 1923-25; B.S., Columbia, 1927; M.B.A., N.Y.U., 1936; m. Doris Isabell Byers, Apr. 11, 1933; children—Richard Cunningham II, William B. Asst. mgr. econ. research dept. Gen. Motors Acceptance Corp., N.Y.C., 1927-29; asst. mgr. market and research dept. Johns Manville Corp., N.Y.C., 1929-30; v.p. Continental Bank & Trust Co., N.Y.C., 1930-49; v.p., treas. SAFECO Ins. Co. Group, Seattle, 1949-67; dir. UDPA, Inc., Seattle. Mem. investment com. Episcopal Diocese Olymphia, Wash., 1956-67. Adv. Children's Home Soc. Wash., 1955-67. Mem. Bldg. Owners and Mgrs. Assn. Seattle (trustee, pres. 1936-37), N.Y. Soc. Security Analysts. Kappa Delta Rho, Alpha Kappa Psi. Conglist. Kiwanian. Club: University (Seattle). Home: 4516 48th Av NE Seattle WA 98105

CAMPBELL, RICHARD RICE, newspaperman; b. Athens County, O., Mar. 25, 1923; s. Arthur Donald and Marguerite (Rice) C.; A.B. summa cum laude, Ohio U., 1947; m. Margaret Jandes, Feb. 9, 1946; children—Christopher, Constant. With Cleve. Press, 1947—, asst. city editor, 1959-62, chief editorial writer, 1962-66, asso. editor, 1966-68, mng. editor, 1968—. Served with AUS, 1943-46. Recipient Alumni award outstanding achievement journalism Ohio U., 1962. Mem. Am. Soc. Newspaper Editors, Cleve. C. of C., Cleve Ad Club, Phi Beta Kappa, Sigma Delta Chi, Sigma Chi. Methodist. Clubs: Rotary, City, Mid-Day (Cleve.). Home: 20219 Mercedes Dr Rocky River OH 44116 Office: Cleveland Press 901 Lakeside Av Cleveland OH 44114

CAMPBELL, ROALD FAY, educator; b. Ogden, Utah, Dec. 4, 1905; s. U. Fay and Pearl (Wilson) C.; student Ida. State Coll., 1923-25; A.B., Brigham Young U., 1930, M.A., 1933; Ed.D., Stanford, 1942; m. Della Jones, 1931; children—Patricia, Bruce, Judith, Adele. Supt. schs., Preston, Ida., 1933-42; prof. edn. U. Utah, 1942-51, Ohio State U., Columbus 1952-57, Fawcett prof. ednl. adminstrn., 1970—; faculty U. Chgo., 1957-70, Reavis prof. edn. adminstrn., 1961-70, dean Grad. Sch. Edn., 1964-70. Cons. sch. systems, state depts. edn., profl. orgns., univs. U.S., Can., Pakistan. Mem. Nat. Acad. Edn., Am. Assn. Sch. Adminstrs., Nat. Conf. Profs. Ednl. Adminstrn., Am. Ednl. Research Assn. (pres. 1969), Phi Delta Kappa. Author: (with J.T. Wahquist) Administration of Public Education, 1952; (with J.A. Ramseyer) Dynamics of School Community Relationships, 1955; (with R. T. Gregg) Administrative Behavior in Education, 1957; (with J.E. Corbally, J.A. Ramseyer) Introduction to Educational Administration, 1958; (with J.M. Lipham) Administrative Theory as a Guide to Action, 1960; (with R. A. Bunnell) Nationalizing Influences on Secondary Education, 1963; (with L.L. Cunningham and R.F. McPhee) The Organization and Control of American Schools, 1965; (with J.W. Getzels and J. M. Lipham) Educational Administration as a Social Process, 1968. Editor Ednl. Adminstrn. Quar., 1964-67. Contbr. articles to profl. jours. Home: 3852 Mountview Rd Columbus OH 43220

CAMPBELL, ROBERT, educator, economist; b. San Mateo, Cal., Apr. 4, 1921; s. Harry Archibald and Aradath (Post) C.; A.B., U. Cal. at Berkeley, 1947, Ph.D., 1953; B.S., U.S. Mcht. Marine Acad., 1950; m. Beth Mildred Neighbor, Oct. 9, 1943; children—Byd Robert, Geoffrey Howard. Asst. prof. econs. U. Ill., 1949-52; asst. prof., asso. prof., prof. econs. U. Ore., Eugene, 1952—, head dept., 1963-71; Fulbright exchange lectr., Ireland, 1961-62. Mem. Ore. Legislative Interim Com. on Jud. Adminstrn., 1957- 59; chmn. Eugene Municipal Commn. on Human Rights, 1966-67. Mem. Am., Western (past mem. exec. com.) econ. assns., Am. Assn. U. Profs., A.A.A.S. Author: (with others) Libraries of the Pacific Northwest, 1960; (with others) The Social Sciences View School Administration, 1965. Home: 3575 Glen Oak Dr Eugene OR 97405

CAMPBELL, ROBERT CRAIG, food co. exec.; b. E. Providence, R.I., Feb. 13, 1917; s. Robert Newton and Vivian Z. (Savini) C.; grad. Bryant & Stratton Bus. Coll., Boston, 1938; m. Margaret R. Fry, Jan. 17, 1941; children—Robert Craig II, Colin, Bruce, Scott, Glenn, Dorothy. With Lever Bros. Co., 1936-53, nat. accounts sales mgr., mem. marketing staff Benton & Bowles Advt., 1954-55; v.p., gen. mgr. foods div. Mead Johnson Co., 1955-59; propr. Product Acceptance & Research, Inc., Evansville, Ind., 1959-62; v.p., dir. world marketing operations Internat. Packers, Ltd., Chgo., 1962-69; pres., chief exec. officer Welch Foods, Inc., Westfield, N.Y., 1969—. Club: Union League (Chgo.). Address: Welch Foods Inc Westfield NY 14787

CAMPBELL, ROBERT DALE, educator; b. Omaha, Neb., Dec. 2, 1914; s. Robert Ward and Emma Mary Augusta (Klempnauer) C.; B.A., U. Colo., 1938, M.A., 1940; Ph.D., Clark U., 1949; m. Anna Elizabeth Abel, Sept. 4, 1941; 1 son, Robert William Duncan; m. 2d, Marian MacAnelly Tucker, Dec. 30, 1962; stepchildren—Ken D., Margaret M., Diane C. Tucker. prof. geography, chmn. dept. George Washington U., 1947-66; Fulbright lectr. Alexandria (Egypt) U., 1952-53, U. Peshawer (Pakistan), 1957-58; prin. investigator George Washington U.- C.E., U.S. Army, Hist. Records Project, 1953-57, Q.M.C. Intelligence Research Project, 1958-60, Outdoor Recreation Resources Rev. Commn., Shoreline and Beach Recreation Resources Study, 1960, Urban Planning Data Systems Project, Md. Nat. Capital Park and Planning Commission, 1961—; pres. AREA, Inc., research, Arlington, Va.; v.p. Matrix Corp., Arlington, 1966-70; prof. geography U. N.M., 1970—; lectr. Conf. Am. Studies, Oxford (Eng.) U., 1955; chmn. theory group Army Logistics Research Project, 1955-56; cons. Office Q.M. Gen., 1947-49, George Washington U.-Office Naval Research Logistics Research Project, 1949—, Spl. Operations Research Office of Am. U., 1959—, Arctic Inst., 1960—; regional planning cons. Ford Found. Adv. Planning Group, Calcutta Met. Planning Orgn., Calcutta, 1964-65. Served with USNR, 1943-46. Mem. Am. Assn. Geographers (pres. Middle Atlantic div. 1948), Am. Assn. U. Profs., Regional Sci. Assn., Phi Beta Kappa, Sigma Xi, Pi Gamma Mu, Kappa Delta Pi. Author: Pakistan, Emerging Democracy, 1963; A Question of Place (with Fisher and Miller), 1967; also articles, papers. Office: Dept Geography U NM Albuquerque NM 87106

CAMPBELL, ROBERT ERLE, bus. exec.; b. Storm Lake, Ia., Mar. 13, 1888; s. John and Minna (Bentley) C.; B.S., U. of Neb., 1910; m. Dorothy Tibbets Miller, June 27, 1912; childrenRobert E., John M., Dorothy M. (Mrs. L.E. Hurtz, Jr.). Asst. to gen. mgr. sales Nat. Electric Lamp Div. of Gen. Electric Co., Cleve., 1910-15; sec., gen. mgr., Miller & Paine, Lincoln, Neb., 1915-38, now chmn. bd.; chmn. bd. First Trust Co., Lincoln, (merged with Nat. Bank Commerce, Lincoln), 1956- 61, past dir.; dir. Omaha br. Fed. Res. Bank, Kansas City, 1934-41, Security Mut. Life Ins. Co., Lincoln Devel. Co. Chmn. bd. commrs. Housing Authority, Lincoln, 1946-52; exec. com. Neb. Resources Found., 1947—; pres. Lincoln Community Chest, 1931. Mem. Lincoln City Council, 1937-41; mayor, Lincoln, 1940-41. Pres. U. Neb. Found.; trustee Cooper Found., Midwest Research Found. Mem. U.S. (bd. dirs. 1937-40), Lincoln (pres. 1929), chambers commerce, Neb. Reclamation Assn., Nat. Retail Dry Goods Assn., Nat. Better Bus. Bur., U. Neb. Alumni Assn. (pres. 1925), Newcomen Soc. Eng., Alpha Tau Omega, Beta Gamma Sigma, Alpha Kappa Psi. Republican. Presbyn. Mason. Clubs: Country, University. Home: 2600 Woodscrest Av Lincoln NB 68502 Office: 1227-49 O St Lincoln NB 68508

CAMPBELL, ROBERT FARISS, lawyer; b. Cleburne, Tex., June 25, 1890; s. Clark Calhoun and Annie Juriah (Fariss) C.; student U. Tex., 1914; m. Genevieve Atkinson Carver, Mar 12, 1918 (dec.); 1 son, Robert Fariss. Admitted to Tex. bar, 1914, since practiced Houston, mem. Andrews, Kurth, Campbell & Jones, attys. Served as 1st lt. 61st F.A., U.S. Army, 1917-19. Mem. Am., Houston bar assns., Phi Delta Theta, Phi Delta Phi. Democrat. Episcopalian. Mason. Clubs: River Oaks Country, Petroleum (Houston). Home: 2701 Westheimer Rd Houston, TX 77006. Office: Humble Bldg Houston TX 77002

CAMPBELL, ROBERT FRANCIS, educator; b. Cleve., Sept. 22, 1917; s. Oscar James and Emily Lyon (Fuller) C.; A.B., Yale, 1939; A.M., Columbia, 1940, Ph.D., 1947; m. Hope Lenore Leiken, Oct. 3, 1941 (div. 1946); m. 2d, Emma-Elizabeth Thomson Little, May 30, 1949 (div. 1967); children—Charles Fuller, Susan Frances; m. 3d, Minette Anderson, July 28, 1967. Jr. communications analyst Office Facts and Figures, Washington, 1942; economist OPA, 1942-45, historian, 1945-46; asso. in Am. history George Washington U., 1943-46; asst. prof. Am. history Clark U., Worcester, Mass., 1946-50, asso. prof., 1950-57, prof., 1960—, dir. U. Inst. of Liberal Studies for Execs., 1956-57, dean of coll., 1960-69, asst. to pres., 1969-70; ednl. dir. Nat. Coal Assn., Washington, 1957-59; staff asso. Center Study Liberal Edn. for Adults, Chgo., 1959-60. Pres., Worcester Citizens Plan E Assn., 1955-57, Worcester Charter Com., 1962. Chmn. Worcester Vols. for Stevenson, 1952. Mem. Am. Hist. Assn., Orgn. Am. Historians. Democrat. Unitarian. Author: The History of Basic Metals Price Control in World War II, 1947; also articles in profl. jours., encys. Home: 103 King Philip Rd Worcester MA 01606

CAMPBELL, ROBERT GORDON, educator, aero. scientist; b. Richland Center, Wis., June 1, 1915; s. Doan A. and Cora (Kohout) C.; B.Aero. Engring., Rensselaer Poly. Inst., 1939, Ph.D., 1956; M.S., Case Inst. Tech., 1942; m. Hilda Ruth Barnhouse, Dec. 25, 1941; children—Robert Scott, Marcia Burton. Research asst. Case Inst. Tech., 1939-41; sr. aerodynamicist B.F. Goodrich Co., 1941-44; sect. head icing research NACA, Cleve., 1944-47; mem. faculty Rennsselaer Poly. Inst., 1947-55; prof. aero. scis. Rensselaer-Hartford Grad. Center, 1955—; cons. fluid dynamics, 1956—. Mem. ethics com. Engring. Council for Profl. Devel., 1965-70. Vice chmn. Manchester (Conn.) Town Bldg. Commn., 1958-62. Registered profl. engr., Ohio. Mem. Am. Inst. Aero. and Astronautics, Am. Soc. Engring. Edn., A.A.A.S., N.Y. Acad. Scis., Sigma Xi, Tau Beta Pi. Republican. Methodist. Club: Westerly (R.I.) Yacht. Spl. research spherical blast phenomena; conceived and used first conical shock tube, dynamics of real gases. Home: 94 Ferguson Rd Manchester CT 06040 also 53 Lawton Av Misquamicut RI 02891 Office: Windsor St Hartford CT 06120

CAMPBELL, ROBERT JAMES, mfg. co. exec.; b. Watertown, N.Y., Dec. 23, 1929; s. Robert Everett and Etta (Jessmore) C.; student U. So. Miss., 1949-52, Tex. Christian U., 1957-58; m. Carole Ann Kenesky, July 8, 1966; children—Robert James, Stephen Phillip. Sr. field engr. Reeves Instrument Co., 1952-56; from dist. mgr. to pres. Link group Gen. Precision Co., 1956-68; pres. Friden div. Singer Co., San Leandro, Cal., 1968-71; chmn. bd. Magna Tek Systems, Inc., Hayward, Cal., 1971—; dir. Duplican, Inc.; mgmt. and investment cons., 1971—. Bd. dirs. Bay Area Mgmt. Council, 1969—; past chmn. tng. adv. subcom. Nat. Security Indsl. Assn. Served with USAF, 1948-52. Club: Lomas Santa Fe Country (Cal.). Address: 2562 Calle de Oro La Jolla CA 92037

CAMPBELL, ROBERT WELLINGTON, educator, economist; b. Wichita, Kan., Feb. 4, 1926; s. Robert Wellington and Kathleen (Payton) C.; A.B., U. Kan., 1948, M.A., 1950; M.A., Harvard, 1952, Ph.D., 1956; m. Laura Mason, June 7, 1950; children—Sarah Kathleen, Andrew Robert, Polly Louise, Benjamin Charles, Emily Jane, Alice Laura. Instr., then asso. prof. U. So. Cal., 1956-60; prof. econs. Ind. U., 1961-. Mem. Am. Econ. Assn., Am. Assn. Advancement Slavic Studies. Author: Soviet Economic Power, 1960; Accounting in Soviet Planning and Management, 1963; Economics of Soviet Oil and Gas, 1968. Home: 919 E Hunter St Bloomington IN 47401

CAMPBELL, ROLAND A., air force officer; b. Persia, Ia., Sept. 20, 1917; s. Charles E. and Anna (Schnecloth) C.; student Spokane Jr. Coll., 1937, Eastern Wash. Coll., 1938; grad. Air Command and Staff Coll., 1949, Air War Coll., 1957; m. Elizabeth J. Cady, July 26, 1941; children—Caly Anne (Mrs. Joseph D. Welch Jr.), Gregory Scott. Commd. 2d lt. USAAF, 1940, advanced through grades to maj. gen. USAF, 1971—; dir. materiel SAC, 1969-70, Pacific Air Forces, 1971—; chief staff Pacific Air Forces, 1970-71; comdr. 21st Air Force, 1971—. Decorated Legion of Merit with 2 oak leaf clusters, D.F.C., Bronze Star, Air medal with 4 oak leaf clusters, D.S.M. Home: 3704 Circle Dr McGuire AFB NJ 08641 Office: Hdqrs Pacific Air Forces APO San Francisco CA 96553

CAMPBELL, ROLLA DACRES, lawyer; b. Huntington, W.Va., Jan. 5, 1895; s. Charles William and Jennie Elena (Ratiff) C.; B.A., Harvard, 1917, LL.B., cum laude, 1920; m. Ruth Cammack, Jan. 1, 1918; children—Rolla Dacres, William C. Practiced law, 1920—; sr. partner firm Woods, Bagley, Emerson, McNeert, Hernden, and predecessors 1935—; pres., dir. Dingess-Rum Coal Co., Huntington; pres., dir. C.W. Campbell Co.; v.p. dir. Caldwell-Campbell Co.; dir. D-R Stores, Inc.; gen. and cons. counsel Island Creek Coal Co., and affiliated cos., 1935-60; pres., dir. Nat. Council Coal Lessors, Inc., Washington, 1951-71; mem. vice chmn., chmn. Property Owner's Com., 1935-63; mem. Cabell County Bd. Edn., 1933-35; past dir. Huntington Community Chest; former dir. and pres. Family Welfare Soc.; former dir. State Assn. YMCA's; former mem. Cabell-Huntington Bd Health. Mem. Am. (chmn. natural resources sect., past chmn. mineral law sect.), W. Va. (former mem. exec. com.), Cabell County bar assns., Ohio Valley Improvement Assn. (past trustee, chmn. adv. council), Nat. Waterways Conf. (former dir.), Nat. Coal Assn. (former mem. transp. com.), W.Va. (past dir.), Huntington (pres. 1931-32) chambers commerce. Episcopalian. Clubs: D.U., Inst. of 1770, Speakers, Varsity (Harvard Coll.); Gypsy, Guyan Golf and Country, City (Huntington); Everglades (Palm Beach, Fla.). Mem. editorial bd. Harvard Law Rev. (vol. 33), 1919-20. Home: 1030 Ritter Park Huntington WV 25701 also 369 S Lake Dr Palm Beach FL 33480 also (summer) 419 E Washington St Lewisburg WV 24901 Office: First Huntington Nat Bank Bldg Huntington WV 25701

CAMPBELL, RUSSELL RAYMOND, comml. finance co. exec.; b. Trafalgar, Ind., Nov. 13, 1907; s. James William and Maxia (Phillips) C.; A.B., Franklin (Ind.) Coll., 1929, LL.D., 1963; grad. bus. tng. course, Gen. Electric Co., 1933; m. Lynne Fountaine, June 26, 1930; children—Virginia (Mrs. William Furst), Barbara (Mrs. James McDermid), Julie (Mrs. William Esrey). With Gen. Electric Co., 1929-55, Midwest regional mgr. Gen. Electric Credit Co., 1941-55; v.p. charge Chgo. operations James Talcott, Inc., 1955-60, central regional mgr., 1960—, sr. v.p., 1962-65, exec. v.p., 1964—, also dir., mem. operations council com.; dir. several financial cos. in U.S. Bd. dirs. Nat. Comml. Financial Conf., 1958—, v.p., 1960—. Mem. Newcomen Soc. North Am., Blue Key, Kappa Delta Pi, Theta Alpha Phi, Pi Kappa Delta, Kappa Delta Rho. Roman Catholic. Clubs:

Executives, University (Chgo.); Sunset Ridge (Winnetka, Ill.); Kenilworth (Ill.). Home: 2939 Indian Wood Rd Wilmette IL 60091 Office: 209 S LaSalle St Chicago IL 60604

CAMPBELL, STANLEY HOWARD, univ. adminstr.; b. Front Royal, Va., June 16, 1906; s. Charles P. and Mary (Reller) C.; B.A. in Bus. Adminstrn., Pa. State U., 1932; m. Louise Will, Nov. 11, 1932; childrenThomas W., Richard W. Mem. staff Pa. State U., 1932-69, dir. housing food service, 1960-61, v.p. business, 1962-69, ret., 1969. Mem. Nat. U. Extension Assn. (bd. dirs. 1955-58), Eastern (mem. exec. com.), Nat. assns. coll. and univ. bus. officers, Acacia. Mason, Elk. Address: 2800 Gulf Shore Blvd N Naples FL 33940

CAMPBELL, STEPHEN JAMES, fgn. service officer; b. Pitts., Aug. 26, 1916; s. Daniel and Margaret Frances (Yinger) C.; student Pa. State Coll., 1934-37; m. Elisabeth Barbier, Nov. 9, 1945 (dec. Apr. 1968); children—Stephen Sean, Patrick. Newspaper reporter, 1937-41; with ECA, Paris, 1949-51; joined U.S. Fgn. Service, 1952; information officer, press attache embassy, Paris, 1952- 54; 2d sec. embassy, Tehran, Iran, 1954-56; assigned Bur. Near East- South Asian Affairs, State Dept., 1957-60; consul, prin. officer consulate, Aden, Arabia, 1960-62; with Office UN Polit. Affairs, Dept. State, Washington, 1962-67; consul gen., Jerusalem, 1967—. Served with USAAF, 1942-48. Decorated D.F.C., Air medal with 4 oak leaf clusters. Home: 612 23d St NW Washington DC 20037 Office: American Consulate Gen 118 Agron Rd Jerusalem Israel

CAMPBELL, THOMAS CORWITH, Jr., educator; b. Enfield, Va., Mar. 19, 1920; s. Thomas Corwith and Pearl (Gravatt) C.; A.B., Lynchburg Coll., 1942; M.A., U. Pitts., 1947, Ph.D., 1948; student U. Wis., summer 1947; m. Burdine Gordon, Apr. 17, 1943; children—Thomas Corwith III, Maxwell Gordon. Mem. faculty W.Va. U., 1948- -, asst. to asso. prof., 1948-58, asst. dean Coll. Commerce, 1955-64, prof., 1958—, dean Coll. Commerce, 1964-68; adviser to Ministry of Econ. Planning and Devel. Govt. of Kenya, 1968-70. Chmn. Gov's. Council Econ. Advisers, 1963-65; mem. Charleston Regional Export Expansion Council, 1964—. Served to lt. USNR, 1942-46. Mem. Am. Econ. Assn., Am. Assn. U. Profs., Soc. Cincinnati, Beta Gamma Sigma. Mem. Christian Ch. Contbr. articles profl. jours. Home: 1445 Woodland Dr Morgantown WV 26505

CAMPBELL, THOMAS NOLAN, educator; b. Munday, Tex., July 3, 1908; s. Finis Oscoe and Minnie Bell (Nelson) C.; student McMurry Coll., 1925-27; B.A., U. Tex., 1930, M.A., 1936; M.A., Harvard, 1940, Ph.D., 1947; m. Lorene Merle Gregg, June 26, 1940; 1 dau., Tommy Jo. Faculty U. Tex., Austin, 1938—, prof. anthropology, 1953-, chmn. dept., 1947-62, dir. research in anthropology, 1947-62; editor American Antiquity, 1962-66; dir. Texas Archeol. Salvage Project, 1958-62. Served to capt. USAAF, 1942-45. Fellow Am. Anthrop. Assn., Soc. Am. Archeology, A.A.A.S., N.Y. Acad. Scis., Sociedad Mexicana de Antropologia. Author articles in field. Editor Tex. Jour. of Sci., 1953-56. Home: 2209 Quarry Rd Austin, TX 78703.

CAMPBELL, THOMAS PATTERSON, retired metall. engr.; b. Denver, July 27, 1896; s. Richard Crawford and Margaret Montjoy (Patterson) C.; grad. Phillips Exeter Acad., 1914; B.S., Dartmouth, 1918; B.S., Mass. Inst. Tech., 1921; Sc.D., Colo. Sch. Mines, 1924; m. Miriam Margaret Savage, Apr. 23, 1918 (dec. Dec. 1968); children—Richard Crawford III, Thomas Patterson (dec. 1922), Donald Carr. Metallurgist, Consol. Mining and Smelting Co. of Can., 1924-25; asso. prof. metallurgy Colo. Sch. Mines, 1927-38; pres. Campbell Investment Co., 1930-50; pres. Creede Mills, Inc.; pres. Wright Engring. Supply Co., 1942-44; v.p., dir. Patterson Bldg. Co., 1945-50, Albany Hotel Co., 1950-55; dir. Met. TV Co., 1952—. Pres. Denver Air Show, Inc., 1940- 41; dir. Denver C. of C., 1938-41. Mgr. improvements and parks (dep. mayor), City and County of Denver, 1947-55; mem. Bd. of Water Commrs., City and County of Denver, 1957-63, pres., 1958-61; dir. Metro-Denver Sewage Disposal Dist., 1964-66. Trustee Denver Art Mus.; pres. Child Research Council Denver; alumni councillor Dartmouth, 1943-46 (pres. 1946). Served as 2d lt., res. mil. aviator, Air Service, U.S. Army, 1917-19. Fellow A.A.A.S.; mem. Electrochem. Soc. Am., Am. Chem. Soc., Am. Inst. Mining and Metall. Engrs., Colo. Mining Assn. (dir.), Psi Upsilon, Sigma Gamma Epsilon. Republican. Episcopalian. Clubs: Denver Country, Denver Club, Denver Athletic, Cactus (past pres.), Mile High Club (past v.p.) (Denver); Grand Lake Yacht (past commodore); 1,000,000 Mile Club. Contbr. tech. articles jours. Home; 90 Corona St Denver CO 80218

CAMPBELL, THOMAS ROBERTSON, steamship co. exec.; b. Peebles, Scotland, Nov. 11, 1912; s. John and Catherine (Robertson) C.; m. Esther McKim Brackbill, Aug. 13, 1939; 1 son, J. Cameron. Came to U.S., 1926, naturalized, 1936. With U.S. Lines Co., 1937—, asst. sec., 1956-60, sec., 1960—; sec. U.S. Lines, Inc., 1966—; sec., dir. U.S. Lines Operations, Inc., 1961—, Roosevelt Steamship Co., Inc., 1961—, One Broadway Corp., 1958—, U.S. Lines Co (Can.) Ltd., 1957—, Balt. Mail Steamship Co., 1961, USL Leasing corp., 1966—, Walter Kidde Leasing of Me., Inc., 1969—; sec., adminstr. U.S. Lines Retirement Fund, 1959—. Mem. Am. Soc. Corporate Secs. Presbyn. Club: Downtown Athletic (N.Y.C.). Office: 1 Broadway New York City NY 10004

CAMPBELL, WALTER EDWARD, architect; b. Chgo., Nov. 11, 1901; s. James Edward and Mineva Alice (Smith) C.; student U. Ill., 1921-23; B.S., Mass. Inst. Tech., 1925, M.Arch., 1926; m. Loraine Leeson, Apr. 7, 1934; childrenLeeson, Dix McDill, Charles Lanning. Designer, Maginnis & Walsh, 1926-29; partner Hogg & Campbell, 1929-45, Campbell & Aldrich, Boston, 1945-64; partner Campbell, Adrich & Nulty, 1964-70, cons., 1970—; architectural work include Simmons Coll. Library, Am. embassy, Taiwan (asso. architect), Dartmouth Coll. bldgs., Tufts U. Library, N.E. Pavilion N.Y. World's Fair, Data Processing Center Bldg., 1st Nat. Bank, Boston; Inner Belt Hwy. design Boston Fenway; new main office bldg. 1st Nat. Bank Boston; library for Episcopal Theol. Sch., Cambridge, Mass.; water colors exhibited Irving Casson Galleries, Children's Mus., Boston. Mem. Cambridge Historic Dists. Commn.; chmn. bd. survey on youth activities and community services, Boston. Corp. mem. Simmons Coll.; v.p. Robert Gould Shaw Settlement House. Permanent mem. Rotch Traveling Fellowship in Architecture,1955-65, sec., mem. bd. trustees, 1965—. Served with AUS, 1942- 45. Fellow A.I.A. (chmn. nat. com. on research 1954-60; jury of fellows); mem. Nat. Acad. Scis. (bldg. research adv. bd.). Boston Soc. Architects (v.p.), Mass. Assn. Architects (v.p.). Clubs: Cosmos (Washington); St. Botolph (pres.) (Boston). Home: 11 Lowell St Cambridge MA 02138 Office: 100 Boylston St Boston MA 02116

CAMPBELL, WESLEY GLENN, economist, educator; b. Komoka, Ont., Can., Apr. 29, 1924; s. Alfred E and Delia (O'Brien) C.; B.A., U. Western Ont., 1944; M.A., Harvard, 1946, Ph.D., 1948; m. Rita Ricardo, Sept. 15, 1946; children—Barbara, Diane, Nancy. Teaching fellow econs. Harvard, 1946-48, instr. 1948-51; research economist U.S. C. of C., 1951-54; dir. research Am. Enterprise Assn., 1954-60; dir. Hoover Instn. War, Revolution and Peace, Stanford, 1960—. Mem. com. welfare Commn. Co-dir. project on Am. competitive enterprise, fgn. econ. devel. and aid program, spl. com. to study fgn. aid program U.S. Senate, 1956-57; mem. Pres.'s Commn. on White House Fellows, 1969—; Chmn. bd. trustees Inst. Social Sci. Research, 1962—; regent U. Cal., 1968—; bd. dirs. Belgian Am. Ednl. Found.; trustee Herbert Hoover Birthplace Found. Fellow Royal Econ. Soc.; mem. Am. Econ. Assn., Phila. Soc. (pres. 1965-67), Mont Pelerin Soc. Clubs: Bohemian, Commonwealth (Cal.). Co-author: The American Competitive Enterprise Economy, 1952. Editor, prin. author: The Economics of Mobilization and War, 1952. Contbr. articles to profl. jours. Home: 26915 Alejandro Dr Los Altos Hills CA 94022 Office: Hoover Instn Stanford Stanford CA 94305

CAMPBELL, WILBURN CAMROCK, bishop; b. Waynesville, N.C., Nov. 9, 1910; s. Wilburn Camrock and Stella (Brown) C. (stepfather Arthur M. Waldron); A.B. cum laude, Amherst Coll., 1932, D.D. (hon.), 1957; B.D. cum laude, Bexley Hall Theol. Sem., 1935; S.T.D. (hon.), Gen. Theol. Sem. (student 1934-35), 1951; D.D. (hon.), Kenyon Coll., 1950; LL.D., Morris Harvey Coll., Charleston, W.Va., 1951; L.H.D., Concord Coll., Athens, W.Va., 1968; m. Janet Louise Jobson, June 17, 1935; children—Jane Jobson, Arthur Waldron. Ordained to ministry Episcopal Ch., 1935; curate St. Stephen's Ch., Port Washington, N.Y., 1935-36; rector St. Luke's Ch., Sea Cliff, N.Y., 1936-39, All Saints' Ch., Bklyn., 1939-42, Ch. of Ascension, Pitts., 1946- 50; dir. Presiding Bishop's Com. for Layman's Work, N.Y.C., 1942-46; bishop coadjutor Episcopal Diocese W.Va., Charleston, 1950-55, bishop, 1955—; chaplain Episcopal students U. Pitts., 1942-46; instr. religion Penn Coll. Women, 1944-46, acting chaplain, 1945-46; priest-in- charge St. Thomas Chapel, Amagansett, N.Y., summers 1941-46; founder Ascension Acad., Pitts., 1947. Mem. Civic Center Bd., Charleston, 1957—; chmn., pres. Buckskin council Boy Scouts Am., 1965-68, exec. bd. region IV, 1968—. Trustee Va. Theol. Sem., Episcopal High Sch., Alexandria Va.; pres. W.Va. Council Chs., 1954-56; pres. bd. dirs. Reynolds Meml. Hosp., Glen Dale, W.Va. Served as chaplain, U.S. Army Res., 1937-39; 106th Inf., N.Y. N.G. (Bklyn.), 1939-40. Recipient Silver Beaver award, Silver Antelope award Boy Scouts Am. Mem. Delta Upsilon. Author: The Episcopal Church-Some Interesting Facts, 1945. Editor: Sermons for Lay Readers (originator 1942), 1942-46; Guide for Lay Readers, 1942; Pastoral Staff, 1969. Contbr. ch. publs. Address: 1608 Virginia St E Charleston WV 25311

CAMPBELL, WILFRED ESSELMONT, educator, research chemist; b. Durhan, So. Africa, June 28, 1903; s. Walter D. and Charlotte (Mauger) C.; B.Sc., U. Witwatersrand (S. Africa), 1923, D.Sc., 1948; tchrs. certificate, Johannesburg (S. Africa) U., 1923; A.M., Columbia, 1930; m. Mary Eliza Maxted, Sept. 28, 1928; children— Keith Stuart, Alan Maxted, Bruce Davidson. Came to U.S., 1926, naturalized, 1939. Analytical chemist New Transvaal Chem. So., Delmore S. Africa, 1918-20; tchr. chemistry and physics Forest High Sch., Johannesburg, 1924-26; mem. tech. staff Bell Telephone Lab., Murray Hill, N.J., 1926-54; dir. materials research Clevite Corp., 1954-56; cons. chemist, Cleve., 1956-63; prof. materials engring. Rensselaer Poly. Inst., 1963—. Mem. United World Federalists, 1946—, chmn. Summit (N.J.) chpt. 1950-54, Cleve. chpt., 1957-59. Fellow Am. Soc. M.E. (chmn. lubrication div. 1962-64); mem. Am. Soc. Lubricating Engrs. (pres. 1954), Am. Chem. Soc. Author articles in field. ‡

CAMPBELL, WILLARD DONALD, lawyer; b. New Philadelphia, O., June 6, 1901; s. Dr. Howard N. and Eloise (Gray) C.; A.B., Muskingum Coll., 1922; student U. Pitts. 1922-23, Cornell, 1924; LL.B., Yale U. (fellowship), 1925; m. Rosanna L. Vance, November 25, 1936 (dec. Dec. 1965); childrenRosanna Vance (Mrs. Michael Guy), and Willard Donald. Admitted to Ohio bar, 1925; Florida bar, 1926; acting city solicitor, Cambridge, O., 1928-30; pros. atty., 1930-34 senator, representing 17th, 18th 19th, 28th dists., Southeastern O. 1935-37; chief enforcement counsel O.P.A., Columbus, 1941-46; dir. Bur. Code Revision Ohio, 1946- 53; private law practice, Columbus, 1953-63; chmn. bd. rev. Ohio Bur. Unemployment Compensation, 1963-; sr. partner Campbell, Potts, Alban & Watson; spl. asst. atty. gen. Ohio, 1957-58; chmn. Ohio Bd. Rev., Bureau Unemployment Compensation. Chmn. Columbus Park Commn., 1963-71. Named Fraternalist of Year, Ohio Council Fraternal and Service Orgns., 1962. Mem. Am. Judicature Soc., Am., Ohio, Florida, Columbus, Guernsey County bar assns., Cambridge C. of C. (past bd. dir., v.p.) Phi Delta Theta, Delta Theta Phi, Tau Kappa Alpha (hon.). Presbyn. Elk, Mason (32, Shriner), Moose (state pres. 1939-40, supreme councilman 1946-51, supreme prelate 1951, supreme gov. 1953). Clubs: Scioto Country, Torch, Athletic of Columbus; Agonis; Ohio Commodores. Author: Ohio Revised Code, 1953; Accumulated Index Attorney General Opinions, 1959. Home: 3249 Tremont Rd Columbus, OH 43221. Office: Bd Rev Bureau of Employment Services 145 S Front St Columbus OH 43215

CAMPBELL, WILLIAM ALEXANDER, music educator; b. Dayton, Pa., Feb. 2, 1913; s. James M. and Margaret E. (Ross) C.; B.Mus., Eastman Sch. Music, 1935, postgrad., 1950-51; M.A., N.Y.U., 1940; postgrad. Syracuse U., 1939-40; m. Alice Louise Williams, July 6, 1942; childrenMichal A., Deborah A. Supr. music, pub. schs., Oneida, N.Y., 1935-41; organist, choir dir. First Presbyn. Ch., 1937-41; tchr. music East High Sch., Auburn, N.Y., 1941-42; dir. instrumental music, theory tchr. St. Lawrence U., 1946-47; dir. bands, prof. music Cornell U., 1947-66, chmn. dept. music, 1963-66; prof., chmn. music Ore. State U., Corvallis, 1966-. Cons. pub. schs., Binghamton, N.Y., 1958; guest condr., adjudicator at county, state music festivals. Served with AUS, 1942-46. Mem. Ore. State Music Assn., Coll. Band Dirs. Nat. Assn., Music Educators Nat. Conf., Phi Mu Alpha, Kappa Kappa Psi. Home: 1470 N 13th St Corvallis OR 97330

CAMPBELL, WILLIAM BEVERLY, air force officer; b. Carrollton, Ga., May 21, 1916; s. William Scott and Eva Lee (Thomasson) C.; B.S., U.S. Mil. Acad., 1940; grad. Indsl. Coll. Armed Forces, 1956; m. Blanche Evans, June 19, 1940; childrenWilliam Beverly, James, Robert. Commd. 2d lt. USAF, 1940, advanced through grades to maj. gen., 1964; served as air insp. Hq. 55th Bomb Wing, 15th Air Force, Italy, 1944-45; comdr. SAC Zebra, Europe, 1952-53; insp. gen. Hdqrs 7th Air Div., Eng., 1954-55; comdr. 816th Air Div. SAC, Altus Air Force Base, Okla., 1961-64, 4th Strategic Aerospace Div., Grand Forks Air Force Base, N.D., 1964-65; dep. insp. gen. OTIG, USAF, Norton Air Force Base, Cal., 1965-68, dir. manpower and orgn. Hdqrs. USAF, 1968, asst. dep. chief staff, programs and resources, 1968- 70; chief Army and Air Force Exchange Service, Dallas, 1970—. Decorated Distinguished Service Medal, Legion of Merit, Decorated D.F.C. with oak leaf cluster, Air medal with 3 oak leaf clusters, Purple Heart (U.S.), Croix de Guerre with palm (France). Home: 4157 Allencrest Lane Dallas TX 75234 Quarters 27 Bolling AFB Washington DC 20332 Office: Hdqrs Army and Air Force Exchange Service 3911 Walton Walker Blvd Dallas TX 75236

CAMPBELL, WILLIAM BLOUNT, former advt. exec.; b. Wilmington, N.C., May 31, 1918; s. William B. and Jeannette M. (Robbins) C.; A.B., U. N.C., 1939, student Law Sch., 1939-41; m. Gertrude L. Rittenhouse, Sept. 10, 1948. Asst. to div. sales mgr. L. Sonneborn Sons, N.Y.C., 1946-47; mdse. dept. asst., sr. mdsg. exec. Young & Rubicam, Inc., 1947-50; partner syndicated advt. agy. Stanley Musselman, Inc., 1950-51; asst. nat. advt. mgr. Borden Co., 1951-54, nat. advt. mgr., 1954-57, mgr. gen. advt. dept., 1957, dir. advt. and promotion, 1958-59; dir. advt. and promotion Borden Milk & Ice Cream Co., N.Y.C., 1961-64; sr. v.p. account service, mem. exec. com Weightman, Inc., Phila., 1965-67, exec. v.p., 1967-70. Mem. Phi Delta Theta. Episcopalian. Home: 247 Church Rd Devon PA 19333 Office: 1700 Market St Philadelphia PA 19103

CAMPBELL, WILLIAM CLARKE, lawyer; b. Haileybury, Ont., Can., Dec. 3, 1918; s. Reuben Yacht and Maude (Moses) C.; B.A., Victoria Coll., U. Toronto (Ont. Can.); m. Kathleen Joan Jenkins, July 3, 1943; children—Kathleen (Mrs. David Thomas), William Clarke, Bryan James. Admitted to Ont. bar, 1943; partner Day, Wilson, Campbell, and predecessors, Toronto, 1946—. Pres., dir. Consolidated Canadian Faraday Ltd., Toronto, 1969—. Served with Royal Canadian Navy, 1943-45. Mem. Bailli Delegue, Confrerie de la Chaine des Rotisseurs, Engrs. Club (Toronto), Royal Canadian Mil. Inst. Club: Eglinton Hunt (Toronto). Home: 95 Dunvegan Rd Toronto Ontario Canada Office: 250 University Av Toronto 110 Ontario Canada

CAMPBELL, WILLIAM DURANT, assn. exec.; b. Flint, Mich., Mar. 18, 1907; s. Edwin Rutheven and Margery (Durrant) C.; A.B., Princeton, 1929; m. Beatruce Hawn, Aug. 16, 1940; 1 dau., Margot. Field asso. dept. mammals Am. Mus. Natural History, N.Y.C., 1935-41; collector, leader African expdns. for museums, Okapi, Black Rhino, Sudan Desert, Upper Nile River groups. Former chmn. Region 6 (N.C., S.C., Ga., Fla.) Boy Scouts Am., mem. nat. exec. bd., 1950-65, 69—, former v.p., internat. commr., hon. v.p. world com., 1969—. Pres. Woodland Found. Served as maj., F.A., AUS, 1941-45. Decorated comdr. Star of Africa (Liberia), comdr. Order of Merit (Dahomey), comdr. Order of Merit (Gabon), comdr. Nat. Order Merit (Cameroons). Fellow Royal Geog. Soc.; mem. St. Andrews Soc., Nat. Audubon Soc. (dir. 1963-67). Episcopalian (warden). Clubs: Union, Explorers, Racquet and Tennis, Links, The River, N.Y. Yacht (N.Y.C.); Royal Aero, Royal Thames Yacht (London); Travellers (Paris, France); Piping Rock. Home: 1 Beekman Pl New York City NY 10022

CAMPBELL, WILLIAM EDWARD, state hosp. sch. supt.; b. Kansas City, Kan., June 30, 1927; s. William Warren and Mary (Bickerman) C.; student U. Neb., 1944-45, U. Mich., 1945, Drake U., 1948; B.A., U. Ia., 1949, M.A., 1950; m. Joan Josselyn Larimer, July 26, 1952; children—William Gregory, Stephen James, Douglas Edward. Psychologist, Dept. Pub. Instrn., State of Ia., 1951-52; hosp. adminstr. Mental Health Inst., Cherokee, Ia., 1952-68; dir. planning and research Dept. Social Services, State of Ia., 1968-69; supt. Glenwood (Ia.) State Hosp. Sch., 1969—. Bd. dirs. Polk County Mental Health, United Cerebral Palsy. Served with AUS, 1944-46. Decorated Army Commendation medal. Mem. Assn. Med. Adminstrs., Assn. Mental Health Adminstrs. (nat. com. chmn. 1970), Ia. Hosp. Assn., Health Planning Council of Midlands, Am. Assn. on Mental Deficiency, Nat. Rehab. Assn., Assn. for Retarded Children, Mental Health Assn., Phi Beta Kappa. Address: Glenwood State Hosp Sch Glenwood IA 51534

CAMPBELL, WILLIAM J., judge; b. Chgo., Mar. 19, 1905; s. John and Christina (Larsen) C.; J.D., Loyola U., 1926, LL.M., 1928, LL.D. 1955; m. Marie Agnes Cloherty, 1937; children—Marie Agnes (Mrs. Howard G. Krane), Karen Christina (Mrs. James T. Reid), Heather Therese (Mrs. Patrick Henry), Patti Ann (Mrs. Peter V. Fazio, Jr.), Roxane (Mrs. Wesley Sedlacek), William J., Christian Larsen, Thomas John. Admitted to Ill. bar, 1927; gen. practice, Chgo., 1927-40; Ill. adminstr. Nat. Youth Adminstrn., 1935-39; U.S. dist atty. No. Dist. Ill., 1938-40; judge U.S. Dist. Ct., 1940—, chief judge No. Dist. Ill., 1959-70. Mem. nat. exec. bd. Boy Scouts Am., 1934—, mem. regional exec. com., 1937—, mem. exec. bd., Chgo. council, 1930—. Chmn. bd. trustees Barat Coll., Lake Forest, Ill.; mem. citizens bd. U. Chgo., Loyola U., Chgo.; bd. dirs. Catholic Charities Chgo. Clubs: Ill. Athletic, Saddle and Cycle, Union League, Standard, Mid-America (Chgo.). Home: 199 E Lake Shore Dr Chicago IL 60611 Office: US Ct House Chicago IL 60604

CAMPBELL, WILLIAM STEEN, mag. publisher; b. New Cumberland, W.Va., June 27, 1919; s. Robert N. and Ethel (Steen) C.; grad. Steubenville (O.) Bus. Coll., 1938; m. Rosemary J. Bingham, Apr. 21, 1945; children—Diana J., Sarah A., Paul C., John W. Cost accountant Hancock Mfg. Co., New Cumberland, 1938-39; cashier, statistician Weirton Steel Co. (W.Va.), 1939-42; tavel exec. Am. Express Co., N.Y.C., 1946-47; adminstr., account exec. Good Housekeeping mag., 1947-55; pub. Cosmopolitan mag., 1955-57; asst. dir. circulation Hearst Mags., N.Y.C., 1957-61, v.p., dir. circulation, 1962-67, v.p. mags., 1967—; gen. mgr. Motor Boating mag., 1961-62; with Periodical Pubs. Service Bur., Inc., Sandeasky, O., 1964—, v.p., chief exec. officer, pres., 1971—; dir. Nat. Mag. Co., Ltd., Randolph Jamaica Ltd. Chmn. Central Registry-PDS Bd., Mag. Pubs. Assn. Trustee Hearst Employees Retirement Plan. Served to lt. col. USAF, 1942-46; ETO. Mason. Home: 33 Shore Dr Plandome NY 11030 Office: 959 8th Av New York City NY 10019

CAMPBELL, WILLIS L., ins. exec.; b. Spokane, Wash., Feb. 17, 1898; s. John P. and Elizabeth (McEachran) C.; B.B.A., U. Wash., 1922; m. Catherine Thompson, Sept. 24, 1924; children—James R., Thomas J. Partner, Dean Witter & Co., mems. N.Y. Stock Exchange, 1926-42; v.p., treas. Gen. Ins. Co. of Am., 1st Nat. Ins. Co. of Am., Gen. Am. Corp., Seattle, 1946-52, pres., dir., 1952-66, chmn., dir., 1966—; chmn., dir. SAFECO Ins. Group, until 1970; trustee Wash. Mut. Savs. Bank. Trustee Seattle Art Mus., Seattle Found. Served as lt. col., Gen. Staff Corps, AUS, 1942-46. Mem. Greater Seattle, Inc., Seattle C. of C. Episcopalian. Clubs: University, Seattle Golf, Seattle Tennis; Seven Lakes Country (Palm Springs, Cal.). Home: 1834 Parkside Dr E Seattle WA 98102 Office: 4347 Brooklyn Av NE Seattle WA 98105

CAMPER, HARRY GREEN, Jr., lawyer; b. Kansas City, Mo., Jan. 22, 1924; s. Harry Green and Lena (Harrell) C.; grad. Ky. Mil. Inst., 1942; student U. Richmond, 1942-43, 49, Centre Coll., 1947; LL.B. cum laude, Washington and Lee U., 1952; m. Mary Elizabeth Bankhead, Apr. 1, 1945; children—Mary Ann, Linda Kay, Harry Green III. Admitted to W.Va. bar, 1952, Va. bar, 1951, also U.S. Supreme Ct.; pvt. practice, Welch, W.Va., 1952—; pros. atty., McDowell County, W.Va., 1958-61; U.S. atty. So. Dist. W.Va., Charleston, 1961-64; partner firm of Bailey, Worrell, Camper & Viers, Welch, Pineville, W.Va., 1964—. Vice pres. So. Ins. Agy., Welch. Chmn. fund drive McDowell County chpt. A.R.C., 1948; county chmn. Heart Fund drive, 1953. Sec. McDowell County Democratic Exec. Com., 1959. Served to capt. AUS, 1943-46. Decorated Bronze Star; recipient award W.Va. Jr. C. of C., 1956. Mem. W.Va. Jr. C. of C. (internat. dir. 1956, pres. 1957), Am., W.Va. bar assns., W.Va., Bar, Va. state bars, Am. Legion, 40 and 8, Phi Delta Phi. Mason (Shriner), Elk, Lion. Home: Southwood Addition Welch WV 24801 Office: 1st Nat Bank Bldg Welch WV 24801

CAMPIOLI, MARIO ETTORE, architect; b. Parma, Italy, Sept. 3, 1910; s. Marcello and Genevieve (Pesci) C.; student Columbia Sch. Architecture, 1930; B.Arch., N.Y.U., 1937; m. Margaret Giordano, May 28, 1933; children—Genevieve (Mrs. Irwin W. Kemp), Elizabeth (Mrs. J.R. Lovewell), Margaret (Mrs. Wesley W. Dement), Carl Michael. Asso., Dwight James Baum, architect, N.Y.C., 1928- 39; prodn. mgr. Eggers & Higgins, architects, N.Y.C., 1940-49; dir.

architecture Colonial Williamsburg, Inc., 1949-57; asso. Alfred Easton Poor, architect, N.Y.C., 1957-59; asst. architect of U.S. Capitol, 1959- -. Mem. bd. archtl. cons. Old Georgetown Act, Washington Commn. Fine Arts, 1965-71; bd. cons. U.S. Capitol Hist. Soc., 1966—; mem. Fairfax County History Commn., 1971—. Recipient Water Color award, Morse prize N.Y.U., 1931; medal in design Soc. Beaux Arts Architects, 1935. Mem. A.I.A., Soc. Archtl. Historians, Producers' Council (hon.). Home: 1136 Basil Rd McLean VA 22101 Office: U S Capitol Washington DC 20515

CAMPION, DONALD RICHARD, editor, publisher; b. Bklyn., Aug. 29, 1921; s. Richard Michael and and Josephine (Gayne) C.; A.B., St. Louis U., 1945, Ph.L., 1946, M.A., 1949; S.T.L., Woodstock (Md.) Coll., 1953; Ph.D., U. Pa., 1960. Joined Soc. of Jesus, 1939, ordained priest Roman Cath. Ch., 1952; tchr. Xavier High Sch., N.Y.C., 1946-47; instr. LeMoyne Coll., Syracuse, N.Y., 1947-49; asso. editor America, 1947-65, editor-in-chief, 1968—; nat. dir. self-evaluation Soc. of Jesus, 1965-68; editor Cath. Mind, 1968—; lectr. Woodstock Coll., Inst. Religious and Social Studies, Union Theol. Sem., Fordham U. Mem. adv. bd. Vera Found., 1962-64; trustee, sec. bd. Fordham U., 1966—; trustee Woodstock Coll., 1968—, Holy Cross Coll., 1969—. Mem. Am., Am. Cath. sociol. assns., Religious Edn. Assn. (bd. dirs. 1964—), Council Religion and Internat. Affairs (bd. dirs. 1970—). Contbr. numerous books. Address: 106 W 56th St New York City NY 10019

CAMPION, ROBERT THOMAS, mfg. co. exec.; b. Mpls., June 23, 1921; s. Leo P. and Naomi (Revord) C.; student Loyola U., Chgo., 1939-41, 46-48; m. Wilhelmina Knapp, June 8, 1946; 1 son, Michael. With Alexander Grant & Co., Chgo., 1946-57, partner, 1954-57; with Lear Siegler, Inc., Santa Monica, Cal., 1957—, pres. chief exec. officer, dir., 1971—. Served with AUS, 1942-46. C.P.A., Ill. Mem. Am. Inst. C.P.A.'s, Ill. Soc. C.P.A.'s. Republican. Clubs: Union League (Chgo.); Bel Air (Cal.) Country; Metropolitan (N.Y.C.). Home: 4188 High Valley Rd Encino CA 91316 Office: 3171 S Bundy Dr Santa Monica CA 90406

CAMPO, ALFRED FELICE, oil co. exec.; b. Castel di Lucio, Italy, Jan. 22, 1905; s. Placido and Matilde (lo Forti) C.; LL.D., Royal U., Palermo and Catania; m. Thelma Bradburn, June 18, 1926; 1 dau., Giovanna (Mrs. Ross Reade). Gen. sales mgr. McColl-Frontenac Oil Co., Ltd., 1927-53; pres., dir. Canadian Petrofina, Ltd., from 1953, now chmn. bd., chief exec. officer; dir. Calvan Consol. Oil & Gas Co., Ltd., Western Leaseholds, Ltd., Am. Petrofina, Inc. Life gov. Montreal Gen. Hosp. Clubs: Manitoba (Winnipeg); Montreal, Forest and Stream, Mt. Royal (Montreal); Mt. Bruno Golf. Home: 3468 Drummond St Montreal Quebec Canada Office: 505 Dorchester St W Montreal 1 Quebec Canada

CAMPOLI, ALFREDO, violinist; b. Rome, Italy, Oct. 20, 1906; s. Romeo and Elvira (Celi) C.; m. Joy Burbridge, May 9, 1942. Appeared in series Internat. Celebrity subscription concerts, 1921; regular broadcaster BBC, 1921—; first world concert tour, 1950; Am. debut Carnegie Hall, N.Y.C., 1953; tour of Russia as soloist with London Philharmonic Orch., 1956; tour in Australia, New Zealand, India, Malaya, Hong Kong, Japan, South Africa, S. Am., Can., Europe; recording artist for London, Decca, H.M.V. records. Recipient Gold medal for performance of Mendelssohn Concerto at London Mus. Festival, 1919. Home: 50 Eversley Park Rd Winchmore Hill London N 21 England

CAMPOLI, COSMO PIETRO, sculptor; b. South Bend, Ind., Mar. 21, 1922; s. Paoulo and Lena (Focosi) C.; diploma Art Inst. Chgo., 1950, student L'Ecole de la Grand Chaumiere, Paris, France, 1950-51; m. Kathryn Marie Carolye, May 20, 1950; children—Anna Pietra, Paoulo Uccello. Rep. permanent collections Mus. Modern Art, Richmond (Va.) Art Mus., So. Ill. U. Carbondale, Unitarian Ch., Chgo., Willowbrook High Sch., Villa Park, Ill., Exchange Nat. Bank, Chgo., also pvt. collections; one-man show at Marjorie Dell Gallery, Chgo., 1968, Whitney Mus. Am. Art. N.Y.C., 1969, Mus. Contemporary Art, Chgo., 1969, 71; asso. prof. Inst. Design of Ill. Inst. Tech., 1952—, Contemporary Art Workshop, Chgo., 1956—, vis. prof. Midway Studios of U. Chgo., summers 1964-69; pres. Fine Arts Faculty Gallery, Chgo., 1966; sculpture include Birth of Death, 1951, Birth, 1958, Jonah and the Whale, 1952, David and Goliath, 1954, Prodigal Son, 1958, Madonna and Child, 1962, Great Peace Symbol, 1962, Bird Birth, 1966. Great Peace Symbol erected permanently in Chgo. Pub. Park at 54th and Kimbark Sts., 1970. Recipient Bronze medal, green ribbon, 25,000 pesetas for showing of An Expression of the Automobile Obsession at II Bienal Internat. Del Deporte en las Bellas Artes, Madrid, Barcelona, Spain, 1969. Anna Louise Raymond traveling fellow Art Inst. Chgo., 1950; grantee Ford Found., 1959. Served with AUS, 1943-46. Address: 5307 S University St Chicago IL 60615

CAMPORA, GUISEPPE, tenor; b. Tortona, Italy, Sept. 30, 1924; s. Luigi and Santina (Orso) C.; ed. Liceo and Conservatorio, Genova, Italy; m. Franca Nespoli, Sept. 29, 1956; 1 dau., Daniela Victoria. Debut, La Scala, Milan, 1950; N.Y.C. debut, 1954; has appeared at La Scala, Teatro Dell'Opera (Rome), San Carlo (Naples), Maggio Musicale Fiorentino (Florence), Liceo (Barcelona), Belles Artes (Mexico), Caracas (Venezuela), Colon (Buenos Aires), Met. Opera (N.Y.C.), San Francisco, New Orleans and Miami operas, State Theatre of Bucharest (Roumania), O'Keefe Center, Toronto, Can.; TV appearance on Voice of Firestone, CBC-TV (Can.) network in Rigoletto; rec. artist for Decca records. Home: Via Leopardi 7 Milan Italy

CAMPOS, SALOS, OCTAVIANO, Mexican govt. ofcl.; b. Mar. 22, 1916; ed. Escuela Nacional de Economia, U. Nacional Autonoma de Mexico, also U. Chgo. Formerly mgr. Bank of Mexico; exec. sec. Mexican Com. Latin Am. Free Trade Area: dir. Sch. Econs; Nat. U. Mexico; dir.-gen. Polit., Econ. and Social Studies of Partido Revolucionario Institucional; coordinator gen. planning Partido Revolucionario Institucional; dir.-gen. commerce, sec. industry and commerce; later sec. finance and public credit; formerly chief dept. econ. studies Bank of Mexico; economist UN Com. Latin Am., Internat. Monetary Fund; vis. prof. U. Mexico; sec.-gen. Tchrs.' Union Mexico. 1938-40: pres. Colegio de Economistas de Mexico, 1956-58; mem. exec. council Internat. Soc. Econometrics, 1961-63; sec. industry and commerce, 1964—. Author articles in field. Address: Secretaria de Industria y Comercio Mexico DF Mexico*

CAMRAS, MARVIN, engr., inventor; b. Chgo., Jan. 1, 1916; s. Samuel and Ida (Horwich) C.; B.S., Armour Inst., Tech., 1940; M.S., Ill. Inst. Tech., 1942, LL.D., 1968; m. Isabelle Pollack, 1951; children—Robert, Carl, Ruth, Michael, Louis. Mem. staff Armour Research Found., Chgo., 1940—, asst. physicist, 1940-45, asso. physicist, 1945-46, physicist, 1946-49, sr. physicist, 1949-58, sr. engr., 1958-65, sci. adviser, 1965- 69, sr. sci. adviser, 1969—. Chmn. S-4 com. Am. Nat. Standards Inst., 1966, mem., 1966—. Recipient Distinguished Service award Ill. Inst. Tech. Alumni Assn., 1948; Achievement award for outstanding contbn. motion picture photography U.S. Camera mag., 1949; John Scott medal, 1955; Ind. Tech. Coll. citation, 1958; Achievement award I.R.E., 1958; Indsl. Research Mag. Product award, 1966; John S. Potts Meml. award Audio Engring. Soc., 1969. Profl. engr., Ill. Fellow I.E.E.E. (sec.-treas. 1951-53; Consumer Electonics award 1964; nat. chmn. profl. group on audio 1953-54 of I.R.E.), Acoustical Soc. Am., (patent rev. bd.), A.A.A.S., Soc. Motion Picture and Television Engrs.; mem. Physics Club Chgo. (dir. 1969—), Radio Engrs. Club Chgo., Chgo. Acoustic and Audio Group (dir. 1967-68), Sigma Xi (chpt. pres. 1959-60), Audio Engring. Soc. (hon., gov. 1970—), Tau Beta Pi, Eta Kappa Nu. Editor: Inst. of Radio Engrs. Transactions on Audio, 1958-63. Patentee in field, devels. in wire and tape recorders and stereo sound reproduction, motion picture sound, video recorders. Home: 560 Lincoln Av Glencoe IL 60022 Office: Technology Center Chicago IL 60616

CAMU, PIERRE, govt. ofcl.; b. Montreal, Que., Can., Mar. 19, 1923; s. Pierre and Jeanne (Duval) C.; B.A., U. Montreal, 1944, M.A., 1947, Ph.D., 1951; postgrad. Johns Hopkins, 1947-49; m. Marie Trudeau, Nov. 4, 1950; children—Suzanne, Marie-Helene, Pierre. With Dept. Mines and Tech. Surveys, Ottawa, Ont., Can., 1949-56; dir. Research Centre Sch. Commerce Laval U., Quebec, Que., 1956-60; v.p. St. Lawrence Seaway Authority, Ottawa, 1960-65, pres., 1965—; adminstr. Canadian Marine Transp. Adminstrn., Ministry Transport, 1970—; pres. Seaway Internat. Bridge Co. Dir. Tech. Service Council. Pres., St. Louis Marie de Monfort Hosp. Fellow Royal Soc. Can., Royal Soc. Arts (life); mem. Royal Canadian Geog. Soc. (pres.) Author: (with Weeks and Sametz) Economic Geography of Canada, 1964. Home: 358 Somerset St E Ottawa 4 Ontario Canada Office: Place de Ville 330 Sparks St Ottawa Ontario Canada

CAMUS, JACQUES PIERRE, hotel exec.; b. Brussels, Belgium, July 5, 1931; s. Paul Joseph and Berthe (Bellevaux) C.; coll. degree, Inst. St. Marie, Brusels, 1948; degree with highest honors, Hotel Sch., Namur, Belgium, 1951. Came to U.S., 1959, naturalized, 1966. Receptionist, cashier, auditor Hotel Metropole, Brussels, 1952-57; asst. to mgr. Hotel Amico, Brussels, 1957-59; asst. mgr. Hotel Delmonico, N.Y.C., 1959-61; exec. asst. mgr. Hotel Summit, N.Y.C, 1961-64; gen. mgr. Drake Hotel, N.Y.C., 1964-69; mng. dir. Regency Hotel, N.Y.C., 1969—; French tchr. Union Carbide Co., 1962-64. Served with Belgian Army, 1950- 52. Mem. Hotel Execs. Club, Hotel Sales Assn. Home: 160 E 55th St New York City, NY 10022. Office: 540 Park Ave New York City NY 10021

CANADA, ROBERT OWEN, Jr., retired naval med. officer; b. Grottoes, Va., July 16, 1913; s. Robert Owen and Mary Patterson (Crawford) C.; grad. Augusta Mil. Acad., Ft. Defiance, Va., 1931, M.D., U. Va., 1937; m. Julia Dent Salter, July 16, 1938; 1 son, Robert Owen III. Intern U. Va. Hosp., 1937-38; commd. lt. (j.g.) U.S. Navy, 1938, advanced through grades to rear adm., 1964; med. officer oiler U.S.S. Salinas, 1940-41; sr. med. officer U.S.S. Pasadena, 1944-45; then shore assignments naval hosps. Charleston, S.C., Oakland, Cal., Portsmouth, Va., Sampson, N.Y., Fitzsimons Gen. Hosp., Denver; comdg. officer U.S. Naval Hosp., Jacksonville, Fla., 1961-62, Bethesda, Md., 1962-65; dep. surg. gen., asst. chief Bur. Medicine and Surgery, Navy Dept., 1965-68; comdg. officer Nat. Naval Medical Center, Bethesda, 1968-69; ret., 1969; mem. staff Greenbrier Clinic, White Sulphur Springs, W. Va., 1969—. Decorated Legion of Merit. Diplomate Am. Bd. Internal Medicine. Fellow A.C.P. (gov. for Navy), Am. Coll. Chest Physicians; mem. Am. Clin. and Climatol. Assn., Am. Thoracic Soc., A.M.A. Home: 209 Dwyer Lane Lewisburg WV 24901 Office: Greenbrier Coll White Sulphur Springs WV 24986

CANADAY, JOHN E., writer, art critic; b. Ft. Scott, Kan., Feb. 1, 1907; s. Franklin and Agnes F. (Musson) C.; B.A., U. Tex., 1929; M.A., Yale, 1933; m. Katherine S. Hoover, Sept. 19, 1935; children—Rudd Hoover, John Harrington. Tchr. art history, dept. architecture U. Va., 1938-50; head sch. art Newcomb Coll., Tulane U., 1950-52; chief div. edn. Phila. Mus. Art, 1953-59; art critic N.Y. Times, 1959—. Served with USMCR, 1944-45. Author: The Metropolitan Seminars in Art (24 portfolios); Mainstreams of Modern Art, 1959; Embattled Critic, 1962; Culture Gulch: Notes on Art and Its Public in the 1960's, 1969; Keys to Art; Lives of the Painters, 4 vols.; also 7 mystery novels underpseudonym Matthew Head.

CANADAY, WARD MURPHEY, advt., housing financing, automobile mfg. co. exec.; b. New Castle, Ind., Dec. 12, 1885; s. Miles Murphey and Sarah Helena (Smith) C.; student U. Colo., 1903-05; A.B., Harvard, 1907; LL.D., Toledo U., 1945; Hum.D., Wooster (O.) Coll., 1967; m. Mariam Louise Coffin, June 15, 1912; 1 dau., Doreen Damaris (Mrs. Lyman Spitzer, Jr.). Advt. mgr. Hoosier Kitchen Cabinet Co., New Castle, 1907-16; pioneered time payment plan, 1907; advt. mgr. to dir. Willys-Overland Co., Toledo, 1916-21, chmn. bd. Willys-Overland Motors, Inc. (now Overland Investment Corp.), 1936-46, chmn. finance com., 1946-53, chmn. bd., 1949—, pres., 1950-63; dir. State St. Research & Mgmt. Co., Boston. Asst. in orgn. 1st automobile credit co., 1917; organizer U.S. Advt. Corp., Toledo, 1921, pres., 1921—; organizer Dealers' Finance Co. (automobile), 1925, later merging with Comml. Credit Co., Balt., dir., until 1961; apptd. chmn. orgn. rep. group Toledo bank depositors during crisis 1933; promoted passage Nat. Housing Act, 1933; asst. adminstr., dir. pub. relations FHA, 1933, 35. Mem. War Industries Bd., Non-War Constrn. Div., World War I; dir. devel. and prodn. of mil. vehicle later trademarked Jeep, World War II; U.S. co- chmn. Caribbean Commn., 1948-52; mem. bd. Nat. Indsl. Cont. Bd. Bd. dirs. Toledo Area Med. Coll. and Found., Fund for Peaceful Atomic Devel.; chmn. bd. trustee Toledo U. Endowment Found.; trustee Toledo Mus. Art, Archaeol. Inst. Am.; hon. trustee Green Mountain Horse Assn.; chmn. bd. trustees Am. Sch. Classical Studies, Greece; pres. Friends of Toledo U. Library. Decorated comdr. Order of Orange Nassau; Grand Cross Order of Phoenix (Greece); named hon. citizen City of Athens (Greece); recipient Eloy Alfaro medal, Cross Eloy Alfaro. Mem. Am. Ordnance Assn. (dir.). Unitarian. Clubs: Toledo Toledo Country, Inverness Country, Harvard (Toledo); Harvard (Vt.); Bohemian (San Francisco); Harvard, Recess. Economic, Brook, Explorers (N.Y.C.); 1925 F Street, Metropolitan, Nat. Press (Washington); Lake Placid (N.Y.); Detroit Athletic; Tennis, Country (St. Croix, V.I.); Lakota, Country (Woodstock, Vt.). Home: Inlands 4455 Brookside Rd Ottawa Hills OH 75875 Office: Security Bldg Toledo OH 46304

CANAGA, BRUCE LIVINGSTON, Jr., ret. naval officer, physician; b. Honolulu, Apr. 25, 1915; s. Bruce Livingston and Margaret (Edwards) C.; student U. Cal. at Berkeley, 1937; B.S. in Med. Sci., M.D., Washington U., St. Louis; m. Ruth Belding, Dec. 24, 1940; 1 son, Bruce Livingston III. Commd. lt (j.g.) U.S. Navy, 1941, advanced through grades to capt., 1956; intern U.S. Naval Hosp., San Diego, 1941- 42; resident internal medicine U.S. Naval Hosp., Phila., 1948-49, 50-51; assigned in U.S.S. California, also Naval Hosp., Guam, World War II; assigned Naval Hosp., Phila., then fellow internal medicine Northwestern U. Sch. Medicine, 1949; embassy physician Am. embassy, Moscow, USSR, 1951-53; sr. med. officer Philippine Islands, 1957-59, Da Nang, Vietnam, 1965-66, U.S. Naval Acad., 1966-68, ret., 1968; med. dir. Portsmouth (Va.) Gen. Hospital, 1968—. Decorated Legion of Merit. Diplomate Am. Bd. Internal Medicine. Fellow A.C.P.; mem. A.M.A. (chmn. sect. mil. medicine 1964), Am. Coll. Chest Physicians (gov. 1964—). Home: 3205 High Point Dr Portsmouth VA 23703 Office: Portsmouth Gen Hosp Portsmouth VA 23704

CANAN, ROBERT HARVEY, aerospace co. exec.; b. Findlay, O., Dec. 1, 1911; s. James Harvey and Carrie (DeVoe) C.; A.B., U. Cal. at Los Angeles, 1933, LL.B.; J.D., U. Cal. at Berkeley, 1936; m. Molly Brown, Aug. 10, 1935; children—Michael J., Patrick H. Joyce. Admitted to Cal. bar, 1936; atty. with U.S. Govt., 1936-42; regional atty. Fed. Security Agy., San Francisco, 1942-43; with Lockheed Aircraft Corp., 1943—, asst. chief consel, 1961-68, sec., 1968- -; sec. lockheed Aircraft Corp. Can. Ltd. Mem. Cal. Gov.'s Com. Employment and Retirement Problems; active Crescent Bay area Boy Scouts Am. Bd. dirs. Pacific Palisades Civic League, 1963-66; sec. Lockhead Leadership Fund, 1962—. Mem. Am., Los Angeles County, Burbank bar assns., Cal. State Bar. Home: 1314 Goucher St Pacific Palisades CA 90272 Office: 2555 N Hollywood Way Burbank CA 91503

CANARY, SUMNER, lawyer; b. Bowling Green, O., Jan. 7, 1905; s. Spencer A. and Lucy (Chaney) C.; Ph.B., Denison U., 1924; J.D., Case Western Res. U., 1927; Althea L. Gilbert, May 29, 1930; 1 son, Richard L. Admitted to Ohio Bar, 1927, since practiced in Cleve.; U.S. atty. for No. Dist. Ohio, 1954-59; judge Ct. Appeals Ohio, 8th Jud. Dist. 1967-68. Trustee Cleve. Marshall Law Sch., 1954-70, Denison U., 1958—, Fairview Park Hosp., 1959- -. Mem. Am., Fed., Ohio, Cleve. bar assns., Fla. Bar, Am., Coll. Trial Lawyers. Home: 12520 Edgewater Dr Cleveland OH 44107 Office: Union Commerce Bldg Cleveland OH 44115

CANAVAN, JOHN JOSEPH, coll. dean; b. Ridgefield Park, N.J., Aug. 18, 1921; s. Frederick Louis and Esther (Buckley) C.; A.B., Loyola U., Chgo., 1944, M.A., 1946; Ph.L., W. Baden (Ind.) Coll., 1945; S.T.L., Woodstock Coll., 1952; Ph.D., Cornell U., 1956. Joined Soc. of Jesus, 1938, ordained priest Roman Cath. Ch., 1951; tchr. Latin and English, Bklyn. Prep. Sch., 1945-47, Loyola Sch., N.Y.C., 1947-48; prof. Classical langs. Canisius Coll., Buffalo, 1956-65, dean Coll. Arts and Scis., 1965—. Address: Canisius Coll Buffalo NY 14208

CANAVAN, WILLIAM JOHN, mfg. co. exec.; b. N.Y.C., 1923; grad. Stevens Inst. Tech., 1944. With Union Carbide Corp., N.Y.C., 1944-70, successively sales engr. Plastics div., div. mgr. Wire and Cable div., mgr. new product devel. plastics, 1944-66, v.p., 1966, exec. v.p. Plastics div., 1966-67, pres. Fibers and Fabric div., 1967-70, also pres. subsidiary Englander Co.; v.p. chem. group, gen. mgr. plastic operations Olin Corp., Stamford, Conn., 1970-71, corporate v.p., gen. mgr. plastics operations, 1971—; also pres. Stanwood Industries. Home: RFD 3 Meadow Lane Huntington NY 11743 Office: 120 Long Ridge Rd Stamford CT 06905*

CANBY, HENRY MATHEWS, lawyer; b. Wilmington, Del., Nov. 25, 1910; s. Henry Mathews and Marjorie Tatnall (Bush) C.; grad. Phillips Exeter Acad., 1928; B.A., Princeton, 1932; LL.B., U. Pa., 1935; m. Elizabeth Gawthrop, Nov. 4, 1938; childrenElizabeth F. (Mrs. Thomas L. Pulling), Marjorie B. (Mrs. Hubert E. Pipin), Sheila R. Admitted to Del. bar, 1935, since practiced in Wilmington; partner firm Richards, Layton & Finger, 1951-, Group Hosp. Service, Inc., 1958-. Mem. Del. Legislature from New Castle County, 1939-40; dep. atty. gen. Del., 1940-42. Trustee United Found. Served to maj. USAAF, 1942-46. Mem. Del. Bar Assn. (pres. 1963-65), Am. Law Inst. Home: West Farm Greenville, DE 19807. Office: DuPont Bldg Wilmington DE 1981

CANCELL, BENTON RUSSELL, paper co. exec.; b. N.Y.C., Nov. 11, 1909; s. Henry and Ann (Russell) C.; B.S.F., U. Mich., 1938, M.S., 1938; m. Theodora Shipley, Feb. 5, 1939; children—June Catherine, Jean Margaret. With Powell River Co., Ltd., 1945, v.p., 1948; v.p. St. Regis Paper Co., Deferiet, N.Y., 1948- 57, exec. v.p., 1957-62; v.p. Rhinelander Paper Co. (Wis.), 1950-54, pres., 1955-62; pres., chief exec. officer Potlatch Forests, Inc., San Francisco, 1962-71; cons., dir., 1971—; dir. First Security Corp., Salt Lake City, Bank of Cal., Clorox Co., Oakland, Cal. N.A. Wartime dir. forest products bur. WPB. Mem. Inst. Paper chemistry (trustee), Am. Forest Inst. (pres.), Nat. Paperboard Assn. (pres.). Clubs: Chicago; Fifth Avenue (N.Y.C.); Bankers of San Francisco. Home: 2200 Pacific Av San Francisco CA 94115 Office: Bank of Am Center San Francisco CA 94104

CANCELLARE, FRANK EDWARD, news photographer; b. Bklyn., July 4, 1912; s. Charles and Rose (Marinella) C.; ed. pub. schs., Bklyn.; m. Rose A. Koprivic, June 26, 1956. Photo printer, photographer Acme Newspictures, N.Y.C., 1928-39; newsphotographer Acme News, Washington, 1938-57, U.P.I., 1957-. Chmn. standing com. U.S. Senate Press Gallery, 1962. Served as war corr., CBI, World War II. Recipient Headliners award, 1954, Mo. Sch. Journalism award, 1947. Mem. White House Photographers Assn. (Pres. 1960; Grand Prize photo contest 1949). Home: 109 S Utah St Arlington, VA 22204. Office: 1013 13th St NW Washington DC 20005

CANCELLIERE, MARION A., banker; b. Pitts., 1911; ed. Brown U., 1932. Chmn., dir. Western Pa. Nat. Bank, Pitts., sec., treas., dir. Daily News Pub. Co.; chmn., pres., dir. WPNB Corp.; dir. Pitts. Indsl. Chem. Corp., Allied Bank Internat. Bd. dirs. Action Housing, Symphony Soc. Mem. Pa. Bankers Assn. (1st v.p.), Am. Ordnance Assn. (dir. Pitts. chpt.). Club: University. Home: Windsor Rd Fox Chapel Pittsburgh PA 15215 Office: Western Pa Nat Bank 5th Av and Smithfield St Pittsburgh PA 15222

CANCIO, HIRAM RAFAEL, U.S. judge, educator; b. San Sebastian, P.R., Aug. 26, 1920; s. Miguel Cancio-Cores and Camelia Vilella-Malaret; B.A., U. P. R., 1942; LL.B., 1948; m. Carlota Alfaro Bou, Aug. 11, 1951; childrenCamelia, Hiram Fafael, Rosa Matilde. Psycometrist, VA, 1946-48; trial examiner P.R. Labor Relations Bd., San Juan, 1948, asst. chmn. head legal div., 1949- 52; chmn. wages and hours coms. under Fair Labor Standards Act, Dept. Labor, 1952-58; dir. Labor Relations Inst., U. P.R., San Juan, 1952-55, dean adminstrn., 1955-58, prof. labor relations and labor law, 1952-; atty. gen. Commonwealth P.R., 1959; now chief judge U.S. Dist. Ct., San Juan. Served with AUS, 1944-46. Recipient Merit award P.R. Bar Assn., 1960. Mem. Am. Judicature Soc., P.R. Bar Assn., Am. Soc. Pub. Adminstrn., Pub. Personnel Assn., Phi Sigma Alpha. Roman Catholic. Author: Labor Management Arbitration in Puerto Rich, 1954; Workers Education in Labor Relations Institutes, 1954. Home: 566 Ramon Gandia St San Juan PR 00918 Office: U S Court House San Juan PR 00901

CANDAU, MARCOLINO GOMES, health orgn. exec., physician; b. Rio de Janeiro, May 30, 1911; s. Julio and Augusta (Gomes) C.; M.D., M.P.H., Sch. Medicine, State Rio de Janeiro, 1933, postgrad. U. Brazil, 1937, Johns Hopkins, 1940-41; LL.D., U. Mich., 1961, Johns Hopkins, 1962, U. Edinburgh (Scotland), 1963, Queen's U., Belfast, 1965, Gt. Britain, Seoul (Korea) U., 1965, Royal U. Malta, 1970; M.D. (hon.), U. Geneva (Switzerland), 1963; Sc.D., Bates Coll., 1963; Doctor (hon.), U. Brazil, 1963, U. Sao Paulo (Brazil), 1965. U. Bordeaux (France), 1967, Charles U., Prague, 1967, Institute Medicine and Pharmacy, Bucharest, Romania, U. Abidjan (Ivory Coast), 1970; m. Ena de Carvalno, May 16, 1936; children— Marcos de Carvalho, Nelson de Carvalho. Charge various health services State Rio de Janeiro 1934-38; participated in mosquito eradication campaign waged by N.E. Malaria Service, 1939; chief health services

State Rio de Janeiro, 1941-42, asst. chief med. services, 1943; asst. supt., later supt. Co-op. Health Services, Brazilian Govt., 1944-50; asst. prof. hygiene Sch. Medicine, State Rio de Janeiro, 1938-50; dir. Div. Orgn. Health Services, WHO, Geneva, Switzerland, 1950, asst. dir.-gen. dept. adv. services, 1951; asst. dir. Pan Am. San. Bur., Washington, 1952-53, also dep. dir. Regional Office for Ams., WHO; dir-gen. WHO 1953—. Recipient Bronfman prize Am. Pub. Health Assn., 1961, Eduardo Liceaga medal Govt. of Mexico, 1963, Mary Kingsley medal Liverpool Sch. Tropical Medicine, 1966, Moinho Santista prize Sao Paulo, 1967; Sesquicentennial award U. Mich., 1967; Centennial award Mass. Dept. Health, 1969; Jo. Baptistae Morgagni Internat. prize Assn. Artistico Letteraria Internat., Florence, Italy, 1970. Hon. fellow Am. Coll. Dentists, Argentina Med. Assn. (fgn.), Am. Pub. Health Assn., Royal Soc. Promotion Health (gold medal 1966), Nat. Acad. Med. (Peru), Peruvian Pub. Health Assn., Royal Acad. Med. (Ireland), Royal Soc. Med. (London); fellow Royal Coll. Physicians (London); mem. Geneva Med. Soc. (hon.), Am. Hosp. Assn. (hon.), Am. Veneral Disease Assn. (hon.), Brazilian Soc. Hygiene, Soc. Medicine and Surgery (Rio de Janeiro), Royal Soc. Tropical Medicine and Hygiene (Gt. Britain), Inter-Am. Assn. San. Engring. (hon.), Canadian Pub. Health Assn. (hon.), Bolivian Pub. Health Soc. (hon.), Nat. Acad. Medicine Brazil (hon.), Panamanian Pub. Health Assn. (hon.), numerous other hon. memberships. Author sci. papers in field. Home: 14 av Dumas Geneva Switzerland Office: WHO Avenue Appia Geneva Switzerland

CANDEE, MARK CHUNN, lawyer, food co. exec.; b. New Haven, Oct. 22, 1903; s. Judge Nehemiah and Annie (Chunn) C.; Ph.B., Yale, 1925, LL.B., 1927, J.D., 1971; m. Kathleen O'Donnell, Feb. 15, 1933; 1 son, Mark Chunn. Admitted to Conn. bar, 1927, N.Y. bar, 1928, U.S. Supreme Ct. bar, 1951; asst. counsel Gen. Foods Corp., 1942-50; gen. counsel, Clinton Foods Corp., N.Y.C., 1950—, v.p. 1952—; pres. Am. Partition Co. div. Standard Brands, Inc.; pres. Traver Partition Corp., Chgo.; dir. Minute Maid Corp. Mem. Am. Bar Assn., Assn. Bar City N.Y. Episcopalian. Home: Pentreath Belle Haven Greenwich CT 06830 Office: 625 Madison AV New York City NY 10022

CANDELA, FELIX, architect; b. Madrid, Spain, Jan. 27, 1910; s. Felix Candela Magro and Julia Outerino Echeverria; Architect, Escuela Superior de Arquitectura de Madrid, 1935; D.F.A. (hon.), U. N.M., 1965; Dr. en Ingenieria, U. Santa Maria, Caracas, Venezuela; m. Eladia Martin, May 3, 1940 (dec. Sept. 1963); children—Antonia, Manolita, Teresa and Pilar (twins); m. 2d, Dorothy Davies, Oct. 20, 1967. Came to Mexico, 1939, naturalized, 1941; came to U.S., 1971. Practice of architecture in Mexico City, also Acapulco; builder reinforced concrete shells, 1951—, important works include Church La Virgen Milagrosa, Mexico City, Sports Palace for Olympics, Mexico City, 1968; pres. Cubiertas Ala S.A., 1950—; prof. structures Escuela Nacional de Arquitectura, Universidad Nacional Autonoma de Mexico, 1953-71, also chmn. dept.; Charles Eliot Norton prof. poetry Harvard, 1963-62; Jefferson Meml. prof. U. Va., 1966; Andrew D. White prof.-at-large Cornell U., 1969-74; hon. prof. Escuela Tecnica Superior de Arquitectura de Madrid, 1969; prof. architecture U. Ill. at Chgo. Circle, 1971—; lectr. in field. Served as capt., C.E., Republican Army, Spanish Civil War. Recipient Gold medal Instn. Structl. Engrs., London, 1961; Auguste Parret prize Internat. Union Architects, 1961. Mem. Am. Concrete Inst. (Alfred E. Lindau award 1965), Sociedad y Colegio de Arquitectos Mexicanos (Plomada de Oro 1963), Am. Concrete Inst., Internat. Assn. Bridge and Structural Engring.; hon. mem. Internat. Assn. of Shell Structures, Venezolana de Arquitectos, Sociedad de Arquitectos Colombianos, Institut Technique du Batiment of Des Travaus Publics, A.I.A., Royal Inst. Brit. Architects, Ch. Archtl. Guild Am., Asociacion Costarricense de Arquitectos, Colegio de Arquitectos del Peru, Sociedad Bolivariana de Arquitectos. Contbr. articles profl. jours. Home: 2440 Lakeview Av Chicago IL 60614

CANDELL, VICTOR, artist; b. Budapest, Hungary, May 11, 1903; s. Adolph and Esther (Fuchs) C.; m. Clara Steiner, 1927. Came to U.S., 1922, naturalized, 1927. Profl. artist, 1924—; exhibited French galleries, 1928-31; mem. Whitney Art Project, 1934; mem. fine arts sect., art project WPA, 1936; exhibited Met. Mus. Art, Art Inst. Chgo., Albany Art Inst., U. Ill., Audubon Painters Soc., Whitney Mus. Art; executed mural for govt. of Iraq bldg., N.Y. Worlds Fair, 1939; rep. pvt. collections and collections of U.S. Govt., Met. Mus. Art, Corcoran Gallery Art, Washington, Newark Art Mus., U. Neb. Galleries, Montclair Mus. Art, Inst. Art and Letters, Whitney Mus. Am. Art, Carnegie Inst., Munson-Williams-Proctor Inst. (Utica, N.Y.), Brandeis U., Krannert Mus., Urbana, Ill., Tex. U. Mus., Austin, Notre Dame (Ind.) U. Coll.; lectr. tchr., art, 1941—; mem. faculty Bklyn. Mus. Sch. Art, 1946-54, Cooper Union, 1954-68; asst. prof. art N.Y.U., 1969—; tchr. Silvermine Coll. Art, 1961—; vis. instr. Ohio U., 1951, Cranbrook Acad., 1958; guest critic Columbia Sch. Painting, 1952, 54; co- founder, dir. Provincetown (Mass.) Workshop, 1959—. Recipient award Mus. Modern art exhbn., 1940, 2 awards U.S. Treasury, 1942, 1st prize drawing 30th Annual, Bklyn. Soc. Arts, 1st prize painting 34th Ann., 1950, Artists prize in painting 10th Ann., Audubon Artists, 1952, Emily Lowe prize, 1956, Lamont award for painting, 1961; Silver Mine Guild painting prize New Eng. Ann., 1968. Mem. Artists Equity Assn. (dir.), Allied Mems. Edward McDowell Assn., Provincetown Art Assn. (trustee), Audubon Artists (dir.). Home: 22 E 10th St New York City NY 10003

CANDIB, MURRAY A., dept. store exec.; b. Chelsea, Mass., 1915; ed. Boston U.; m. Sylvia Candib; children—Mark, Wendy, Nancy. Pres., dir. King's Dept. Stores, Inc., Newton, Mass. Fellow Brandeis U., 1966. Recipient Nat. Award for community service Jewish Theol. Sem. Am., 1965. Mason (Shriner). Home: 172 Shaker Rd Longmeadow MA 01106 Office: 150 California St Newton MA 02158 also 505 8th Av New York City NY 10018

CANDILIS, GEORGES, architect; b. Bakou, USSR, Apr. 11, 1913; s. Panayotis and Vera (Skanavi) C.; grad. Athens Poly. Sch., 1936; m. Christiane Richard, July 21, 1959; children by previous marriage—Drina, Taki, Alexis. With LeCorbusier, 1946-54; dir. agy. for housing in N. Africa, 1954-56; with S. Woods and A. Josic in housing firm, 1956-63; pvt. archtl. practice, Paris, 1963—; architect new town Toulouse- Mirail; works include U. Berlin, multiple housing Languedoc Roussillon Coast; pres. Agy. for Devel. of Languedoc-Roussillon Coast; prof. Ecole des Beaux-Arts. Served as lt. Greek Army, 1940-42. Decorated Greek War Cross. Hon. fellow A.I.A. Author: Candilis-Josic-Woods, 1964. Home: 17/3 Campagne Premiere St Paris XIVe France Office: 18 Dauphine St Paris VIe France

CANDIOTTY, MAX, retail co. exec.; b. N.Y.C., May 10, 1923; s. Isaac and Dora (Amira) C.; A.A., U. Cal., Los Angeles, 1943; B.S., U. So. Cal., 1946, J.D., 1951; m. Lillian Steinkeler, Sept. 5, 1948; children-Doreen, Edward, Mark. Pub. accountant Candiotty & Beck, Los Angeles, 1948—; admitted to Cal. bar, 1951; practice in Los Angeles, 1951-66, Beverly Hills, 1966—; co- founder, sec.-treas. Daylin, Inc., 1960-68, pres., 1968—; sr. partner Adam Assos., 1965; dir. Am. Med. Enterprises; mem. Beverly Hills adv. bd. Union Bank. Mem. Citizens Efficiency Economy Com. Los Angeles County, 1965-69; co-founder Fund for Job Corps Grads., 1965-70; mem. Beverly Hills Mall Com., 1969-70. Bd. dirs. Jewish Fedn. Council, Am. Friends of Hebrew U.; mem. exec. com. Israel Bonds. Served with AUS, 1943-45. Recipient Israel Freedom medal, 1968, Bd. Suprs. commendation County of Los Angeles, 1968, Man of Year award Sephardic Jewish Community, 1964. Mem. Soc. Attys. and C.P.A.'s, Sephardic Jewish Community and Brotherhood (pres. Los Angeles). Home: 632 N Arden Dr Beverly Hills CA 90210 Office: 9606 Santa Monica Blvd Beverly Hills CA 90210

CANDLAND, DOUGLAS KEITH, educator; b. Long Beach, Cal., July 9, 1934; s. Horace George and Erma Louise (Downing) C.; B.A., Pomona Coll., 1956; Ph.D., Princeton, 1959; m. Mary Homrighausen, June 18, 1959; children—Kevin, Christopher, Ian. Postdoctoral research fellow U. Va., 1959-60; asst. prof. Bucknell U., 1960-64, asso. prof., 1964-67, prof., 1967—, dir. grad. sch., 1962-64, chmn. subdept. animal behavior, 1969—, chmn. dept. psychology, 1970—. Postdoctoral research fellow Delta Regional Primate Center, Tulane U., 1967-68, anthropology dept. Pa. State U., 1968-69; cons. Princeton, Susquehanna U., NSF, Am. Council Grad. Schs. Democratic committemen Union County, Pa., 1968—. Recipient research awards NSF, 1966—, NIH, 1960—, Office Edn., 1963-65. Mem. Pa. (sec., pres. acad. div.), Am., Eastern psychol. assns., Animal Behavior Soc., Soc. Mammalogists, Internat. Soc. Primatologists, Phi Beta Kappa. Author: Exploring Behavior, 1960; Psychology, the Experimental Approach, 1968; Emotion: Bodily Change, 1962, rev., 1972. Contbr.: Sensory Deprivation, 1960; Conformity and Deviation, 1962; Experimental Investigations of Emotional Behavior, 1969; Ontogeny of Vertebrate Behavior, 1971. Editor: Experimental Psychology, 1968—; The Primates, 1970—. Home: 125 Stein Lane Lewisburg PA 17837

CANDLER, ASA WARREN, lawyer; b. Atlanta, Aug. 30, 1914; s. Asa W. and Hattie Lee (West) C.; A.B., U. Ga., 1936; LL.B., Emory U., 1938; m. Elaine M. Davidson, Oct. 21, 1939; children—Gail Mary, Asa Warren III, David McDowell. Admitted to Ga. bar, 1938, since practiced in Atlanta; mem. firm Chandler, Cox & Andrews, 1946—; spl. agt. FBI, 1939-40; spl. asst. atty. gen., Ga., 1940. Sec. Pershing Point Pharmacy, Inc., Removable Outdoor Carpets, Inc., Marler Oil Co.; dir. Palmer, Inc. Served to col. USAAF, 1941-45; brig. gen. Res. ret. Decorated Legion of Merit. Mem. Am., Ga., Atlanta (past pres.) bar assns., Am. Legion. Clubs: Touchdown (past pres.), Peachtree Racket (past pres.), Atlanta Athletic (bd. dirs.), Lawyers (past pres.) (Atlanta). Home: 2479 Peachtree Rd NE Atlanta GA 30303 Office: Atlanta Gas Light Tower Bldg Atlanta GA 30303

CANDLER, JOHN SLAUGHTER II, lawyer, novelty co. exec.; b. Atlanta, Nov. 30, 1908; s. Asa Warren and Harriet Lee (West) C.; A.B. magna cum laude, U. Ga., 1929; J.D., Emory U., 1931; m. Dorothy Bruce Warthen, June 13, 1933; children-Dorothy Warthen (Mrs. Joseph W. Hamilton, Jr.), John Slaughter. Admitted to Ga. bar, 1931, since practiced in Atlanta; partner Candler, Cox & Andrews and predecessor firms, 1931—; pres., chmn. bd., dir. So. Toy & Novelty Co., 1940—; v.p., gen. counsel, dir. Palmer, Inc., 1939—; dep. asst. atty. gen., Ga., 1951-68; gen. counsel, sec., dir. D.M. Weatherly Co., Weatherly Corp. Dir. Peachtree Realty & Ins. Co., Propane Gas Service, Inc., P.D. Christian Co., Sungas, Inc., Leon Propane, Inc., Equipment Sales Co., Inc. Pres. Atlanta Estate Planning Council, 1963-64. Trustee Ga. Student Ednl. Fund; pres. Kappa Alpha Scholarship Fund; exec. com. U.S.O. Council Greater Atlanta; chmn. bd. trustees Northside Atlanta Kiwanis Found. Served from capt. to col., AUS, 1941-46. Decorated Army Commendation Ribbon. Fellow Am. Coll. Probate Law (bd. regents 1968—), Internat. Acad. Law and Sci.; mem. Am., Atlanta bar assns., State Bar Ga. (chmn. sect. fiduciary law 1964-65), Lawyers Club Atlanta, Tax Inst. Am. (adv. council 1969-71), Am. Legion (post comdr. 1949-50), Res. Officers Assn. (state pres. 1949, nat. exec. com. 1947), Am. Judicature Soc., Internat. Platform Assn., Mil. Order World Wars, English Speaking Union, Phi Beta Kappa, Phi Kappa Phi, Phi Delta Phi, Kappa Alpha, Sigma Delta Chi. Episcopalian. Mason, Kiwanian. Home: 413 Manor Ridge Dr NW Altanta GA 30305 Office: Atlanta Gas Light Tower Atlanta GA 30303

CANDLER, SAMUEL CHARLES, merchant; born Oxford, Ga., Dec. 9, 1895; s. Warren Akin and Sarah Antoinette (Curtright) C.; A.B., Emory U., 1916; m. Mary Frances Godfrey, Nov. 29, 1917; childrenCaroline (Mrs. Lowry W. Hunt), Frances (Mrs. Frances C. Shumway). Pres., Godfrey's Warehouse, Madison, Ga., 1937-70, ret. chmn. bd. Mem. Southeastern Jurisdictional Conf., 1948, 52, member comm. on chaplains, 1948-64. Trustee emeritus Emory University, Atlanta, Georgia; ret. trustee Wesleyan Christian Advocate, Salem Camp Ground. Served as capt., inf., U.S. Army, World War I. Mem. Am. Legion, Kappa Alpha. Mason. Clubs: Atlanta Athletic. Home: 102 Eatonton Rd Madison GA 30650 Office: 315 W Jefferson St Madison GA 30650

CANDLER, WILLIAM LOVE, life ins. co. exec.; b. Dallas, Apr. 29, 1908; s. Daniel Beville and and Dora (Candler) C.; B.B.A., U. Tex., 1929; m. Felicia Holloway, Feb. 27, 1935; children Nan (Mrs. Charles C. Freed, Jr.), William Love, George Holloway. With Southland Life Ins. Co., Dallas, 1929-, sr. v.p., 1967- -, dir. Served with AUS, 1944-46. Mem. Life Office Mgmt. Assn., Inst. Home Office Underwriters, Dallas Mgmt. Assn., Kappa Alpha. Methodist. Clubs: Dallas Country, Chaparral (Dallas). Home: 10232 Daria Dr Dallas, TX 75229. Office: P O Box 2220 Dallas TX 75221

CANDY, WALTER WEAVER, Jr., business exec.; b. St. Louis, Dec. 11, 1905; s. Walter Weaver and Rose (Dehlendorf) C.; grad. Lawrenceville Sch., 1924; B.S., Princeton, 1928; m. Kate Irene Winnett, June 19, 1929; children—Walter Weaver, Glenn Winnett, Peter William. vice pres. Busy Bee Candy Co., St. Louis, 1928-35; with Bullock's, Inc., Los Angeles, successively as v.p., mem. bd. dirs., chmn.; past v.p., dir. Federated Dept. Stores; now dir. Security Pacific Nat. Bank, Pacific Indemnity Co., Chubb Corp., Am. Airlines, Inc. Served with USNR, 1942-46. Decorated Bronze Star. Republican. Presbyn. Clubs: Country (dir.), California, The Beach. Home: 875 Comstock St Los Angeles CA 90024

CANE, MELVILLE HENRY, lawyer, poet; b. Plattsburg, N.Y., Apr. 15, 1879; s. Henry William and Sophia (Goodman) C.; A.B., Columbia, 1900, LL.B., 1903; m. Florence Naumburg, Dec. 23, 1909; children—Katherine (Mrs. Paul Marcus), Mary (Mrs. Arthur Robinson). Admitted to N.Y. bar, 1903; mem. firm Ernst, Lowenstein & Cane, and successors, N.Y.C., 1905—, now Ernst, Cane, Berner & Gitlin; specializes in copyright law, allied fields. Awarded medal for conspicuous alumni service Columbia, 1933; Columbia U. Medal for excellence in law, poetry, 1948. Mem. Assn. Bar of N.Y.C., Poetry Soc. Am. (Gold medal 1971). Club: Columbia University. Author poetry including: A Wider Arc, 1947; Making a Poem (prose). 1953; and Pastures New, 1956; Bullet-Hunting 1960; To Build A Fire, 1964; So That It Flower, 1966; All and Sundry (autobiography), 1968; Eloquent April, 1971. Co-editor: The Man from Main Street, 1953; The Golden Year, 1960. Contbr. articles, fiction and verse to leading mags. Home: 400 E 57th St New York City NY 10022 Office: 5 W 45th St New York City NY 10036

CANELLAKIS, EVANGELO STAMATIOS, educator, biochemist; b. Tientsin, China, June 20, 1922; s. Stamatios Charitos and Demeter (Rappas) C.; B.Sc., U. Athens (Greece), 1947; Ph.D., U. Cal. at Berkeley, 1951; m. Zoe Katherine Nakos, Aug. 28, 1948; children—Thomas Nakos, Arthur John. Came to U.S., 1947, naturalized, 1953. Postdoctoral fellow U. Wis. at Madison, 1951-54; postdoctoral fellow Yale, 1954-55, mem. faculty, 1955—, prof. pharmacology, 1963—. Served with Greek Underground Forces, 1941-44, with Greek Nat. Guerilla Forces, 1944-45. Recipient Career Research award USPHS, 1963—. Mem. Am. Soc. Biol. Chemists, Am. Cancer Soc., Biochem. Soc. (London, Eng.), Greek Chem. Soc., Sigma Xi. Editor Biochemica Biophysica Acta, 1969—. Spl. research biosynthesis nucleic acids, intermediary metabolism. Home: 206 Livingston St New Haven CT 06511.

CANEVER, VICTOR WILLIAM, automobile exec.; b. Detroit, Dec. 22, 1914; s. John and Elsie Emma (Berry) C.; A.B., U. Mich., 1939; m. Betty Marie Rohrer, Sept. 28, 1940; children—Constance Ann, Susan Mary, Jane Ellen, John Howard, Richard Stephan. Sales rep. Underwood Corp., 1939-42; Salvage engr. Murray Corp. Am., 1942-45; sales promotion mgr. GMC Truck & Coach div. Gen. Motors Corp., 1945-52; successively sales promotion writer, sales promotion mgr., asst. accountant exec., account exec. and v.p., account supr., mgmt. supr. and sr. v.p. D.P. Brother & Co. Detroit, 1952-69; owner, pres. Vic Canever Chevrolet, Inc., Fenton, Mich., 1969—. Mem. Fenton Area C. of C. (dir.). Kiwanian. Clubs: Flint Golf; Spring Meadows Country. Home: 1320 Fairfax Av Birmingham MI 48009

CANFIELD, CASS, publishing co. exec.; b. N.Y.C., Apr. 26, 1897; s. August Cass and Josephine (Houghteling) C.; student Groton Sch., 1909-15; A.B., Harvard, 1919; postgrad. Oxford U. (Eng.), 1919-20; m. Katharine Emmet, May 24, 1922; children—Cass, Michael Temple; m. 2d, Jane White Fuller, May 27, 1938. With Harris. Forbes & Co., 1921-22, N.Y. Evening Post, 1922- 23, Fgn. Affairs, 1923-24; mgr. London (Eng.) office Harper & Bros., 1924-27; with Harper & Bros., N.Y.C., 1927-62, pres., 1931-45, chmn. bd., 1945-55, chmn. exec. com. and editorial bd., 1955-62; chmn. exec. com., and Harper editorial bd. Harper & Row, N.Y.C., 1962-67; vice chmn. Harper's Mag., Inc. Chmn. exec. com. Planned Parenthood Fedn. Am.- World Population Emergency Campaign, 1962-67; chmn. governing body Internat. Planned Parenthood Fedn., 1963-69. Trustee, Woodrow Wilson Fellowship Found., Farfield Found. Mem. N.Y. State Council on Arts, 1960-64. Mem. Bd. Econ. Warfare, Washington, 1942-43; spl. adviser to Am. ambassador, London, in charge Econ. Warfare Div.; dir. O.W.I., France, 1945. Served as 2d lt., World War I. Recipient Albert Lasker award. Pres. Nat. Assn. Book Pubs., 1932-34. Mem. Am. Assn. UN (dir.), Phi Beta Kappa (hon.). Clubs: Century Assn., River. Author: The Publishing Experience, 1969; Up and Down and Around, 1971. Home: Mount Kisco NY 10549 Office: 49 E 33d St New York City NY 10016

CANFIELD, DELOS LINCOLN, educator; b. Cleve., Dec. 13, 1903; s. Delos Wilford and Mary Miriam (Thompson) C.; A.B., U. Tex., 1926. M.A., 1927, Ph.D., 1934; m. Mary Elizabeth Walker, Aug. 24, 1928 (dec. June 1970); children—Lewis Randall, Cynthia, Janet Elizabeth; m. 2d, Muriel Nixon Rising, Aug. 2, 1971. Instr. Spanish, U. Rochester, 1927-31, asst. prof., 1934-42, asso. prof., 1942-46, prof. Spanish, 1952-70, prof. emeritus, 1970, chmn. dept. langs. and linguistics, 1962-67; instr. Spanish, Columbia, 1932-34; prof. modern langs., head dept. Fla. State U., 1946-52; prof. Spanish, So. Ill. U., Carbondale, 1970—. Vis. prof. U. Guatemala, summer 1949; condr. tours to Mexico, summers 1926-41; research cons. U. Sal Salvador, 1952; Fulbright lectr. Spanish linguistics, Instituto Caro y Cuervo, Bogota, Colombia, 1960; prof. linguistics NDEA Summer Insts., 1961-69; cons. nat. NDEA panel, 1964; producer, voice for the radio series Spanish Today, Empire State Sch. of Air, 1958-62; TV series Spanish Today, also Our Spoken Lang., 1954, 58. Inter-Am. consul U.S. Office Edn., summer 1945; cons. U.S. Dept. State in Mexico, 1945- 46; chmn. immigration com. Rochester C. of C.; chmn. curriculum com. Fla. State U., 1948-49. Mem. Nat. Fulbright Selection Com., Latin Am., 1965-66. Mem. Modern Lang. Assn., Am. Assn. Tchrs. Spanish and Portuguese (pres. 1945, pres. Upper N.Y. chpt. 1939, Fla. chpt. 1948- 49), Fla. Edn. Assn., Am. Assn. U. Profs., Hispanic Soc. Am., Sigma Delta Pi, Phi Sigma Iota. Republican. Presbyn. Clubs: Kiwanis, Circulo Hispano, Cosmopolitan (Rochester). Author: Spanish Literature in Mexican Languages as a Source for the Study of Spanish Pronunciation, 1934; La Pronunciación del Espaol en America, 1962; East Meets West, South of the Border, 1968; also articles on regional pronunciation of Spanish, Co-author: El espaol a través de sus escritores, 1968. Asso. editor Hispania; contbg. editor Handbook of Latin Am. Studies, 1964—. Home: 1609 Taylor Dr Carbondale IL 62901

CANFIELD, EARLE LLOYD, univ. dean; b. Des Moines, Oct. 24, 1918; s. Lloyd Angle and Margaret Melissa (Earle) C.; B.A., Drake U., 1940; M.A., Northwestern U., 1944; Ph.D., Ia. State U., 1950; m. Betty Alice Fosher, Jan. 30, 1947; children—Irving Nelson. Ward Evan. Marcia Elice. Math. and sci. tchr. Moorhead (Ia.) High Sch., 1940-42; math. and sci. tchr., prin. Winterset (Ia.) High Sch., 1942-46; faculty dept. math. Drake U., Des Moines, 1946—. prof., 1958—, grad. dean. 1957—. Edn. research adviser Colo. State U., summers 1952-57. Bd. coll. visitors Ia. Synod (Presbyn. Colls.). 1964, chmn. 1967—; chmn. Ia. Coop. Study Post High Sch. Edn., Grad. Instrn. and Research Com., 1965-66; mem. com. on instnl. membership Council Grad. Schs. in U.S., 1971-72. Fellow Ia. Acad. Sci. (chmn. program com. for long range planning 1967-68); mem. Math. Assn. Am. (sec. Ia. 1956-67), A.A.A.S., Am. Ednl. Research Assn., Phi Beta Kappa, Phi Delta Kappa, Pi Mu Epsilon. Presbyn. (elder). Mason. Home: 3820 SW 31st St Des Moines IA 50321

CANFIELD, EDWARD FRANCIS, business exec.; b. Phila., Apr. 7, 1922; s. Frank James and Eunice C. (Sullivan) C.; B.A. magna cum laude, St. Joseph's Coll., 1943; LL.B., U. Pa., 1949; m. Janet Powell Trotter, Jan. 12, 1952; children—Andrew Trotter, Janet Powell. Admitted to Pa. bar, 1949; practice in Phila., 1949-51; with RCA, 1953-60, marketing mgr. def. electronics products, 1957-60; with Philco Corp., 1960-69, corp. dir. marketing, 1961-63, v.p. govt. planning and marketing 1964-66, v.p. electronic group marketing, 1966-69; pres. Leisure Time Industries, Inc., 1969—; dir. Woodlawn Nat. Bank, Alexandria, Va. Served as officer USNR, 1942-46, 51-43. Mem. Phila. Bar Assn., I.E.E.E., Am. Ordnance Assn., Armed Forces Communications and Electronics Assn., Alpha Sigma Nu. Roman Catholic. Clubs: Congressional Country (Bethesda. Md.); Internat. (Washington). Home: 9600 Weathered Oak Ct Bethesda MD 20034 Office: 923 15th St NW Washington DC 20008

CANFIELD, FAYETTE CURTIS, educator; b. Bridgeport, Conn., July 29, 1903; s. Andrew A. and Elizabeth M.C.V. (O'Connor) C.; A.B., Amherst Coll., 1925, L.H.D., 1955; M.A. (hon.), Yale, 1954; LL.D., Emerson Coll., 1956; m. Katharine Fitz Randolph Newbold, May 21, 1927; 1 dau., Sylvia Huntington (Mrs. Peter H. Winn), Instr. dramatics Amherst Coll., 1927, prof., 1938, Stanley King prof. dramatic arts, 1952-54, dir. Kirby Meml. Theatre, 1938-54; prof. drama Yale, 1954-68, chmn. dept. 1954-55, dir. U. Theatre, 1954-65, 1st dean Drama Sch., 1955-65, fellow Saybrook Coll. (Yale); Univ. prof. theatre arts U. Pitts., 1968—. Trustee, Am. Shakespeare Festival Theatre and Acad., 1963-68; mem. exec. com. Shakespeare Anniversary. Served as lt. comdr. USNR, World War II. Mem. Nat. Theatre Conf. (trustee 1958-62, pres. 1964). Club: Century Assn.

Author: The Seed and the Sowers, 1955, Plays of the Irish Renaissance, 1929; Plays of Changing Ireland, 1936; The Craft of Play Directing, 1963. Home: 3955 Bigelow Blvd Pittsburgh PA 15213

CANFIELD, FRANCIS XAVIER, clergyman, educator; b. Detroit, Dec. 3, 1920; s. Edward and Adelle (Berg) C.; B.A., Sacred Heart Sem., Detroit, 1941; M.A., Catholic U., 1945; A.M. in L.S., U. Mich., 1950; Ph.D., U. Ottawa, 1951; spl. courses Notre Dame U., Wayne U., U. Detroit. Ordained priest Roman Cath. Ch., 1945, named domestic prelate, 1963; with English dept. Sacred Heart Sem., Detroit, Mich., 1946—, librarian, 1948-63, rector-president, 1963-70; pastor St. Paul's Parish, Grosse Pointe Farms, Mich., 1971—. Instr. library sci. Immaculate Heart Coll., Los Angeles, summers 1955-61. Chaplain, Detroit Police Dept., 1965—. Mem. Cath. Library Assn. (chmn. Mich. unit 1950-52, 54-56, exec. council 1957-63, pres. 1961-63), Council Nat. Library Assns. (vice chmn. 1962-63). Club: First Saturday (spiritual dir. 1952-60). Editor; Philosophy and the Modern Mind, 1961; Literature and the Modern Mind, 1963; Political Science and the Modern Mind, 1963. Author articles, book revs. Home: 157 Lake Shore Grosse Pointe Farms MI 48236

CANFIELD, FRANK BALLEW, Jr., educator; b. Searcy, Ark., Dec. 6, 1936; s. Frank Ballew and Velma Leone (Shute) C.; B.S. in Chem. Engring., U. Ark., 1958; Ph.D., Rice U., 1962; m. Betty Ann Fortner, Sept. 7, 1956; children—Philip Alan, Mark Fortner. Asst. prof. chem. engring. U. Okla., 1962-65, asso. prof., 1965-69, prof., 1969—, dir. Sch. Chem. Engring. and Materials Sci., 1966-70; acad. visitor Imperial Coll. Sci. and Tech., London, 1969-70. Chmn. bd. ChemShare Corp., 1969—, also dir. Bd. dirs. U. Okla. Research Inst., 1966-70, mem. exec. com., 1966-68. Mem. Am. Inst. Chem. Engrs., Am. Chem. Soc., Am. Soc. Engring. Edn. Contbr. articles profl. jours. Home: 1720 Homeland St Norman OK 73069

CANFIELD, FREDERICK WEBER, business exec.; b. Cambridge, Mass., Feb. 1, 1930; s. Haskins Bishop and Anne (Waterman) C.; A.B., Williams Coll., 1952; postgrad. Boston U. Sch. Law, 1952; M.B.A., Harvard, 1958; m. Janet Billings Littlefield, Sept. 6, 1952; children—Scott Weber, Leigh Pierce, Clarke Bishop, Amanda Billings. Asst. treas., dir. planning East Tenn. Natural Gas Co., 1958-60; treas. Dysatech Corp., Cambridge, 1960-62, Littlefield Lumber Co., Cambridge, 1962-65, Mississippi River Transmission Corp., St. Louis, 1965-67; asst. to exec. v.p. Ralston Purina Co., St. Louis, 1967- 69; pres., treas., dir. Servicetime Corp. and all operating subsidiaries, 1969—; dir. West-Time, Inc., Rock Island, Ill. Served to lt. USNR, 1953-56. Mem. Harvard Bus. Sch. Assn. St. Louis (dir.), St. Louis Soc. Security Analysts Mo. Amateur Ice Hockey Assn. (sec.), Ducks Unlimited, Kappa Alpha. Republican. Conglist. Clubs: St. Louis, Harvard, Arena (St. Louis); Williams (N.Y.C.). Home: 412 Somerset Av Webster Groves MO 63119 Office: 7700 Clayton Rd St Louis MO 63117

CANFIELD, THOMAS HARRISON, educator; b. Butte, Mont., Jan. 19, 1916; s. Robert W. and Florence (Hiatt) C.; B.Arch., Ohio State U., 1939; A.F.D., Ithaca Coll., 1970; m. Dorothy Fogle, May 6, 1942; children—Anne (Mrs. Zoltan Soos), Thomas H. Mem. faculty Coll. Architecture, Art and Planning, Cornell U., 1946—, prof., 1951—, chmn. dept. archtl. tech., 1960—; archtl. practice, 1947-58; design cons., 1959—; architect with Harvard-Cornell Archeol. Exploration Sardis, 1958-59. Mem. Ithaca Planning Bd., 1959-61. Served as lt. USNR, 1945. Recipient Sch. medal A.I.A., 1939; Alpha Rho Chi medal, 1939. Home: 128 Eddy St Ithaca NY 14850

CANFIELD, WILLIAM NEWTON, editorial cartoonist; b. Orange, N.J., Oct. 8, 1920; s. Walter L. and Mildred (Apgar) C.; student Am. Sch. Design, N.Y.C., 1940-41; m. Dorothy J. Levins. Feb. 23, 1946. children—Craig R., Susan A. Cartoonist, Morning Telegraph and Racing Form, N.Y.C., 1941-46; with Newark News, 1946—, sports cartoonist, 1946-60, editorial cartoonist, 1960—. Served with USNR, World War II. Home: 143 Wayside Rd New Shrewsbury NJ 07701 Office: 215 Market St Newark NJ 07102

CANFIELD, WRIGHT, electric utility co. exec.; b. Yale, Okla., Apr. 11, 1907; s. George Washington and Roxie (Wright) C.; B.S. in Elec. Engring., Okla. State U., 1929; m. Edith Adair, Aug. 16, 1941. With Pub. Service Co. Okla., Tulsa, 1930—, v.p., 1949-67, pres., 1967—, also dir.; dir. Tulsa Fed. Savs. & Loan Assn. Vice chmn. Tulsa area A.R.C., 1961-62; chmn. Tulsa Area Safety Council, 1960. Trustee Tulsa Psychiatric Found., 1966—, Frances E. Willard Girls Home, Tulsa, 1959—, Oklahoma City U., 1961—, U. Tulsa, 1970—. Registered profl. engr., Okla. Fellow I.E.E.E.; member Nat., Okla. (pres. Tulsa 1952) assns. profl. engrs., Tulsa C. of C., Tulsa Engrs. Club (v.p. 1951-52). Methodist (steward). Kiwanian (pres. Tulsa 1962). Office: 600 S Main St Tulsa OK 74102

CANGELOSI, VINCENT EMANUEL, educator; b. Baton Rouge, Feb. 5, 1928; s. Philip Vincent and Angelina Elizabeth (Roccaforte) C.; B.S., La. State U., 1954, M.B.A., 1956; Ph.D. in Econs., U. Ark., 1961; postdoctorate Carnegie-Mellon U., 1964; m. Mary Jean Johnson, Feb. 23, 1952; children—Philip William, Phyllis Ann, Angyln Marie, Mary Jean, Joan. Instr., then asst. prof. U. Ark., 1956-59; instr. La. State U., 1959-60; asso. prof. U. Ark., 1960-65; asso. prof. U. Tex., 1965-67; prof. La. State U., Baton Rouge, 1967-70, prof., chmn. dept. quantitative methods, 1970—. Chmn. bd. vis. Postal Service Inst.; spl. cons. Postmaster Gen., 1968. Chmn. parish council Catholic Student Center, La. State U., 1969-70. Served with AUS, 1950-52. Recipient First Annual Distinguish Service award Am. Inst. Decision Scis., 1970. Mem. Am. Inst. Decision Scis. (v.p.), Southwestern Social Sci. Assn., Acad. Mgmt., Beta Gamma Sigma, Pi Gamma Mu, Pi Tau Pi, Alpha Kappa Psi. Editor: Mathematics and Quantitative Methods Series, 1967; Compound Statements and Mathematical Logic, 1967. Editorial bd. Decision Sci. and Social Sci. Quar. Contbr. World Book Encyclopedia. Home: 1370 Ashland Dr Baton Rouge LA 70806

CANHAM, ERWIN DAIN, newspaper editor, radio and TV commentator; b. Auburn, Me., Feb. 13, 1904; s. Vincent Walter and Elizabeth May (Gowell) C.; B.A., Bates Coll., 1925, Litt. D., 1946; B.A., M.A. (Rhodes scholar), Oxford U. (Eng.); recipient numerous honorary degrees, including L.H.D., Boston U., 1948, Yale, 1949; LL.D., Principia Coll., 1951, Tufts U., 1958, Temple U. 1959; Litt.D., Brigham Young U., 1962; LL.D., Lafayette Coll., Bowdoin Coll., 1967; m. Thelma Whitman Hart, May 10, 1930 (dec.); children—Carolyn (Mrs. R. Shale Paul), Elizabeth (Mrs. Lyle Davis); m. 2d, Patience M. Daltry. Reporter, Christian Sci. Monitor, 1925, covered annual sessions of League of Nat. Assn., 1926, 27, 28. Chief corr. Christian Sci. Monitor at Lon. Naval Conf., 1930; corr. Geneva, Switzerland, 1930-32; head of Wash. Bur., Christian Sci. Monitor, 1932-39 gen. news editor, 1939-41, mng. editor, 1941-44, editor, 1945-64, editor in chief, 1964—; nation wide polit. surveys and covered trips of Am. Presidents; attended inauguration Philippine Commonwealth Govt. and wrote on Far East, 1935; dep. chmn. U.S. delegation U.N. Conf. on Freedom of Information, 1948; U.S. alternate del. U.N. Gen. Assembly, 1949; mem. U.S. Commn. for Information, U.S. Nat. Commn. for UNESCO, 1948-51; mem. Pres.'s Commn. on Campus Unrest, 1970. dir. John Hancock Mut. Life Ins. Co., Keystone Custodian Funds, Inc.; chmn. Fed. Reserve Bank of Boston, 1962-67. Bd. dirs. Nat. Safety Council, v.p. religious leaders, 1964-68; dir. Resources for Future. Trustee, Boston Pub. Library (pres. 1968—), Robert A. Taft Inst. of Govt., 20th Century Fund, Bates Coll., Simnons Coll., Wellesley Coll.; mem. corp. Northeastern U. Radio commentator, 1938-39, 45—. Decorated hon. comdr. Order Brit. Empire; officer French Legion Honor; Order of George I (Greece); grand distinguished service cross Order of Merit (German Federal Republic); Grand Silver Badge of Honor (Austria); recipient John Peter Zenger award U. Ariz., 1970. Fellow Am. Acad. Arts and Scis.; mem. U.S. C. of C. (chmn. bd. 1960, dir.), Am. Soc. Newspaper Editors (pres. 1948-49), Assn. Am. Rhodes Scholars, Phi Beta Kappa, Delta Sigma Rho. Christian Scientist. Mason (33). Clubs: Gridiron, Nat. Press, Overseas Writers (Washington pres. 1938- 40); Tavern; Harvard (Boston); Saturday. Author: (with others) Awakening: The World at Mid-Century, 1951; New Frontiers for Freedom, 1954; Committment to Freedom, 1958; (with DeWitt John) The Christian Science Way of Life, with A Christian Scientist's Life, 1962. Editor: Man's Great Future, 1959. Home: 6 Acorn St Boston MA 02108 Office: 1 Norway St Boston MA 02115

CANHAM, ROBERT ALLEN, assn. exec.; b. Virden, Ill., Jan. 3, 1921; s. Howard Ambrose and Rhoda Ann (Haneline) C.; B.S. in Civil Engring., Purdue U., 1942, M.S. (Nat. Polio Found. fellow), 1947; m. Margie Lu Bruton, Dec. 21, 1951; children—Patricia Ann, Robert Allen, Jane Claire. Civil engr. M.W. Kellogg Co., 1942-47; san. engr. Nat. Canners Assn., 1947-57; asso. editor Water Pollution Control Fedn., Washington, 1957-64, asst. sec., editor, 1964-69, exec. sec., 1969—. Adj. prof. san. engring. Howard U., Washington, 1967—; cons. USPHS, 1962-65, Food canning industry, 1957—. Pres., P.T.A., 1966; treas. Fairfax County Council P.T.A.'s, 1970—; citizen adviser Fairfax County Sch. Bd., 1968—. Served from ensign to lt. (j.g.), USNR, 1944-46. Registered profl. engr., Del., Ind. Diplomate Am. Acad. Environmental Engrs. Mem. Water Pollution Control Fedn., Am. Soc. C.E., Am. Water Works Assn., Va. Water Pollution Control Assn., Inter-Am. Assn, San. Engrs., Am. Acad. Environmental Engrs., Sigma Nu. Methodist. Editor, Jour. Water Pollution Control Fedn., 1957-69. Contbr. articles profl. jours. Home: 3612 Bent Branch Ct Falls Church VA 22041 Office: 3900 Wisconsin Av NW Washington DC 20016

CANIFF, MILTON ARTHUR, cartoonist; b. Hillsboro, O., Feb. 28, 1907; s. John William and Elizabeth (Burton) C.; A.B., Ohio State U., 1930; LL.D., Atlanta Law Sch.; A.F.D. (hon.), Rollins Coll.; m. Esther Parsons, Aug. 23, 1930. Began as cartoonist, summer 1921; successively on Dayton (O.) Journal-Herald, Miami (Fla.) Daily News, Columbus, (O.) Dispatch, A.P. Feature Service, N.Y.C., Chgo. Tribune-N.Y. News Syndicate, N.Y.C., 1934-46; now with Publishers-Hall Syndicate div. Field Enterprises, Inc.; creator of Male Call and of Steve Canyon. Awarded Scroll of Merit, Dayton Art Inst.; War Dept. citation for Male Call; Billy DeBeck Meml. award (now Reuben award), 1947; Distinguished Service award Sigma Delta Chi, 1950; Freedoms Found. award, 1950; certificate of merit, 1953; Medal of Merit award Air Force Assn., 1952, Arts and Letters award, 1953; U.S. Treas. citation, 1953; Ohioana Career medal, 1954; USAF exceptional service award, 1957; Ohio gov.'s award, 1957; Silver Beaver award Boy Scouts Am., 1960; Silver medallion N.Y. World's Fair, 1964; Goodwill Industries award, 1965; N.Y. Philanthropic League award, 1965; Aerospace Edn. Council award, 1966; named Man of Yr., USAF Assn., 1966; YMCA Service-to-Youth award, 1966; Freedoms Found. Nat. Service medal, 1967, Freedoms Found. George Washington Honor medal, 1969; Distinguished Eagle award Boy Scouts Am., 1969. Mem. Newspaper Comics Council, Soc. Illustrators, Nat. Cartoonists Soc. (pres. 1948- 49, now hon. chmn.; recipient Golden Scroll 1964), Air Force Assn., Arnold Air Soc. (hon. nat. comdr.), Exec. Order Ohio Commodores (charter), Sigma Chi, Sigma Delta Chi. Clubs: Players, Overseas Press, Dutch Treat (N.Y.C.); Nat. Press, Nat. Aviation (Washington); Office: King Features 235 E 45th St New York City NY 10017

CANIVET, LOUIS, archbishop; b. Verneuil-Sur-Seine, France, Mar. 30, 1916; ed. Coll. Poissy (Yvehnes), Evreux (Eure). Employed in bank, 1933-34; elementary sch. tchr.; prof. coll.; now prof. French Mfg. Tng. Technic Sch., Lorraine, France; pvt. gen. Lahn Cath. Ch., France, Orthodix Ch. of Nigeria, also United Chs. of Congo. Recipient numerous awards. Mem. Internat. Research Inst., Societe des Gems de Lettres de france. Author books and essays. Address: 33 Allee de la Liberation 57 Thionville France

CANIZA, GILBERTO, Paraguayan diplomat; b. Asuncion, Paraguay, Sept. 1, 1940; s. Carlos Antonio and Francisca (Sanchiz) C.; lawyer degree, Sch. Law Nat. U. Asuncion, 1967; m. Craciela Martinez-Varela, Feb. 3, 1968; 1 dau., Claudia Carolina. Officer, Dept. Stats. Ministry Treasury, Asuncion, 1962-64, Ministry Fgn. Office, 1964-67; vice dir. treaties div. Ministry Fgn. Office, 1967-69, dir. treatives div., 1969-70; counselor, Washington, 1970—. Roman Catholic. Home: 501 Slaters Lane Alexandria VA 22314 Office: 2400 Massachusetts Av Washington DC 20008

CANJAR, LAWRENCE NICHOLAS, coll. dean; b. Pitts., Mar. 5, 1923; s. Michael and Catherine (Kosturic) C.; B.S., Carnegie Inst. Tech., 1947, M.S., 1948, D.Sc., 1951; m. Patricia McWade, Aug. 4, 1951; 1 son, Robert Michael. Mem. faculty Carnegie Inst. Tech., 1951-65, asso. prof. chem. engring., 1954-59, prof. chem. engring., 1959-65, asso. dean Coll. Engring. and Sci., 1962-65; dean Coll. Engring., U. Detroit, 1965—; prin. cons., research chem. engr. Research Project 44, Am. Petroleum Inst., 1952—; partner Asso. Chem. Engrs., 1955-61; cons. L'Air Liquide, Montreal, Que., 1951-59. Served with C.E., AUS, 1942-45. Recipient Teaching award Carnegie Inst. Tech., 1954; Pro Eclesia et Pontifice award Pope Paul, 1964. Mem. Am. Inst. Chem. Engrs., Am. Chem. Soc., Am. Soc. Engring. Edn. (Western Electric teaching award 1968), Am. Soc. M.E. Home: 18011 Hamilton Rd Detroit MI 48203

CANMANN, DAVID LEO, mfg. co. exec.; b. Chgo., Feb. 1, 1915; s. Harry L. and Lillian P. (Porges) C.; B.A., Carleton Coll., 1936; LL.B., U. Mich., 1939; m. Fern H. Admitted to Ill. bar, 1939; practice in Chgo., 1939-42; v.p., treas. Ekco Products Co., Chgo., 1941-50, sr. v.p., 1950-61, exec. v.p., treas., 1961-66, also dir.; exec. v.p., treas. and dir. of Unarco Industries, Inc., Chgo., 1966; now asst. to pres. Ekco Housewares Co.; dir. Chgo. Guarantee Survey Co., S.P.R. & P. Corp. Bd. dirs. Canmann Found. Served with USNR, 1944-46. Mem. Ill., Chgo. bar assns. Home: 188 Lakewood Pl Highland Park IL 60035 Office: 9234 W Belmont Av Franklin Park IL 60131

CANN, WILLIAM HOPSON, aviation co. exec.; b. Newark, June 17, 1916; s. Howard W. and Ruth (Hopson) C.; A.B. magna cum laude, Harvard, 1937; LL.B., 1940; m. Mildred E. Allen, Mar. 7, 1942; children—William Hopson, Sharon Lee, John Allen, Lawrence Edward. Admitted to N.Y. State bar, 1941, Cal. bar, 1947; asso. firm Chadbourne, Parke, Whiteside & Wolfe, and predecessors, N.Y.C., 1940-53; asst. to pres. N.Am. Rockwell Corp., 1953-60, v.p., sec., 1960—. Mem. adv. bd. Family Service of Los Angeles. Served to 1st lt. USAAF, 1942-45. Mem. Am. Soc. Corporate Secs., Phi Beta Kappa, Episcopalian. Club: Harvard of Southern Cal. (Los Angeles). Home: 835 Toulon Dr Pacific Palisades CA 90272 Office: North Am Rockwell Corp 1700 E Imperial Hwy El Segundo CA 90245

CANNEGIETER, CORNELIS ANTONIUS, educator; b. Grootebroek, Holland, June 25, 1913; s. Henrik Gerrit and Maria (Kuipers) C.; B.Ec., Amsterdam U., 1934; Drs.Ec., Netherlands Sch. Commerce, 1937; Dr.Ec., Netherlands Sch. Econs., 1959; postgrad. Institut du Pantheon (Paris), 1937-38; m. Ingrid Petronella Cornelia Den Toom, Nov. 10, 1950; children—Arthur Marinus, Hendrik Willem Adriaan, Fenny Maria. Came to U.S., 1966. Adviser The Hague, 1938-39; tchr. econs. and polit. sci. Zutphen High Sch., 1939-41; economist Dutch Govt., 1941-49; budget controller Indonesian Govt., Djakarta, 1949-50; economist Central Planning Bur., The Hague, 1950-59; prof. econ. research, adviser Econ. Research Centre of U. Nuevo Leon, Mexico, 1960-62; sr. research fellow, sr. lectr. U. Western Australia, 1962-67; prof. econs. Am. U. in Cairo, 1967-69; Andrew Wells Robertson prof. econs. Allegheny Coll., 1969—. Vis. financial controller Dutch New Guinea, 1954-57; tchr. accountancy High Sch. of Hollandia, New Guinea, 1955-57; vis. prof. econs. U. Tex., 1966; prof. econs. Egyptian U. of Cairo, also Ein Shams U., Cairo, 1968-69; coordinator Soc. Internat. Devel. group, Cairo, 1968-69. Mem. Am. Econ. Assn., Soc. Internat. Devel., Am. Assn. Univ. Profs., Nat. Social Sci. Honor Soc. Author: The Economic Prospects of Dutch New Guinea, 1959. Research on how to feed future population, human aspects of econ. development, econ. consequences of Ord River scheme in Western Australia. Home: RD 1 Conneaut Lake PA 16316 Office: Allegheny Coll Meadville PA 16335

CANNELL, CHARLES FREDERICK, educator, psychologist; b. Antrim, N.H., Sept. 10, 1913; s. William J.B. and Hattie (Morse) C.; A.B., U. N.H., 1936; M.A., Ohio State U., 1940, Ph.D., 1952; m. Martha Phyllis Osgood, Aug. 23, 1937; children—John Charles, Edward Lincoln. Head field sect., div. program surveys Bur. Agrl. Econs., Dept. Agr., 1942-46; mem. faculty U. Mich., 1954—, prof. psychology in journalism, 1962—, mem. staff Inst. Social Research, Survey Research Center, 1946—, program dir., 1963—; cons. research methods USPHS, 1955—. Fellow Am. Psychol. Assn.; mem. Soc. Psychol. Study Social Issues, Am. Assn. Pub. Opinion Research. Author: (with R. L. Kahn) The Dynamics of Interviewing, 1957; also articles. Home: 13 Heatheridge St Ann Arbor, MI 48104.

CANNELL, PETER BEST, investment banker; b. Glen Ridge, N.J., May 8, 1926; s. John and Hildegarde (Best) C.; B.A., Princeton, 1949; m. Ann Eberstadt, June 10, 1950; children—William, Peter F., Cynthia, Michael, James. With ECA, Paris, 1949-50; advt. copywriter Batten, Barton, Durstine & Osborn, Inc., 1951-54; with Merrill, Lynch, Pierce, Fenner & Smith, brokerage, 1954-55; with F. Eberstadt & Co., investment bankers, 1955-69, partner, 1959-69; with Chemical Fund, Inc., 1955-64, exec. v.p., 1959-62, pres., dir. 1962-64; chmn. Cannell, Breed & Musser, 1969-70; with Werthelm & Co., Co., investment bankers, 1970—. Member N.Y. Soc. Security Analysts. Clubs: Madison Square Garden, River, Princeton, Recess (N.Y.C.); University Cottage (Princeton, N.J.). Home: 164 E 72d St New York City NY 10021 Office: 65 Broadway New York City NY 10006

CANNELLA, JOHN MATTHEW, U.S. judge; b. N.Y.C., Feb. 8, 1908; s. Joseph and Laura (Gullo) C.; B.S., Fordham U., 1930, LL.B., 1933; m. Ida Rutnik, Dec. 26, 1938; children—Lauretta (Mrs. Robert Stublick), Christine (Mrs. John J. Phelan 3d), John Matthew. Admitted to N.Y. bar, 1934; gen. practice, N.Y.C., 1934-40; asst. U.S. atty., 1940-42; commnr. Water Supply Gas and Electricity, N.Y.C., 1946-48, Dept. Licenses, 1948-49; mem. Ct. Spl. Sessions, N.Y.C., 1949-59; mem. Ct. Gen. Sessions, N.Y.C., 1957-58, City Ct., N.Y.C., 1959-61; mem. Criminal Ct., N.Y.C., 1963; U.S. judge So. Dist. N.Y., 1963—. Served with USCGR, 1942-45. Mem. Assn. Bar City N.Y., Cath. Lawyers Guild, Fed. bar Assn., Columbia Lawyers Assn. Home: 3 Consulate Dr Tuckahoe NY 10707 Office: US Dist Courthouse Foley Sq New York City NY 10007

CANNEY, DONALD JAMES, mayor; b. Iowa City, Ia., Oct. 8, 1930; s. John J. and Alice E. (Mickle) C.; student Ia. State Coll., 1954-57; B.S., State U. Ia., 1959; m. Gloria F. Oberer, Aug. 20, 1955; children—Kevin, Timothy, Michael. With engring. dept. City of Riverside (Cal.), 1954; spl. projects engr. City of Cedar Rapids (Ia.), 1954-62, commr. pub. improvements, 1966-69, mayor, 1969—. Mem. adv. com. Functional Rd. Classification of Ia., 1970—; mem. legislative com. Ia. League Municipalities, 1971—. Co-chmn. Iowans Care Orgn., 1971. Served with USMC, Korean Conflict. Mem. adv. council Coll. of Engring. of Ia. State Coll., 1968—. Mem. Ia. Hwy. Research Bd. (past chmn.), Cedar Rapids Engrs. Club, Cedar Rapids C. of C., Nat. Assn. County Engrs., Nat. Soc. Profl. Engrs., Phi Eta Sigma. Home: 436 Fleetwood Rd SW Cedar Rapids IA 52404 Office: City Hall Cedar Rapids IA 52401

CANNING, LEONARD, newspaper editor. Asst. mng. editor Mpls. Star. Office: 5th and Portland Sts Minneapolis MN 55415*

CANNING, RICHARD FRANCIS, lawyer; b. Providence, Apr. 29, 1912; s. Joseph P. and Mary V. (Lovett) C.; A.B., Brown, 1932; LL.B. cum laude. Harvard, 1935; m. Ann M. Loughery, Apr. 10, 1937; 1 dau., Judith A. (Mrs. Lovett). Admitted to R.I. bar, 1935, since practiced in Providence; partner firm Letts & Quinn, 1937—; city solicitor, Cranston, 1945-54, Pres. Am. Hockey League, 1957-61, bd. govs., 1954-57, 62-66; dir. R.I. Auditorium, Inc., Moore Fabrics, Inc. Mem. Am., R.I. bar assns., Phi Gamma Delta. Club: Wannamoisett Country. Home: 82 Woodstock Lane Cranston RI 02910 Office: Hospital Trust Bldg Providence RI 02903

CANNON, ABRAM H., educator, radiologist; b. Salt Lake City, Nov. 30, 1915; s. Calude Qualye and Emily (Barnes) C.; B.A., U. Utah, 1938; M.D., Northwestern U., 1941; m. Aino Sylvia Marsell, Mar. 30, 1942; children—James Qualye, Margaret, Carol. Asso. radiologist Chgo. Wesley Meml. Hosp., 1949-50, chmn. dept., 1950—; mem. faculty Northwestern U. Med. Sch., 1949—, now asso. prof. radiology; spl. research retrograde brachial augiographic roentgen studies. Served to maj. USAAF, 1942-46. Mem. Am. Roentgen Ray Soc., Radiol. Soc. North Am., Am. Coll. Radiology, A.M.A. Home: 194 Michael John Dr Park Ridge IL 60068 Office: 250 E Superior St Chicago IL 60611

CANNON, ALLEN EUDELLE, music educator; b. Crystal Falls, Mich., June 24, 1920; s. Lester H. and Lena (Tobin) C.; B.S., Mus. B., U. Ill., 1941, Mus.M., 1942; Mus.D., Chgo. Mus. Coll., 1954; m. Marilyn C. Levy, June 22, 1945; children—David Stuart, Michael Richard. With Rome Opera Co. Orch., 1944-45; head violin dept. Bradley U., Peoria, Ill., 1945-54, head music dept., 1957—; concertmaster Peoria Symphony, 1947—, also soloist; faculty TV course WMBD-TV, 1959; former mgr., bassoonist Peoria Municipal Band; counselor B'nai B'rith Hillel Found., Bradley U. Campus, 1957-62; charter mem. Central Ill. Youth Symphony Bd.; mus. adviser, dir. Peoria Civic Ballet Co. Served with USAAF, World War II. Decorated Presidential citations, Mem. Am. String Tchrs. Assn., Nat. Assn. Sch. Music, Music Tchrs. Nat. Conf., Am. Fedn. Musicians, Alpha Epsilon Pi, Pi Kappa Lambda, Phi Mu Alpha, Phi Kappa Phi (sec. 1963-67). Jewish religion (mem. synagogue bd.). Mem. B'nai B'rith. Home: 2721 W Parkridge Dr Peoria IL 61604

CANNON, BRADFORD, surgeon; b. Cambridge, Mass., Dec. 2, 1907; s. Walter Bradford and Cornelia (James) C.; B.S., Harvard, 1929, M.D., 1933; m. Ellen DeNormandie, June 25, 1938; children—Walter Bradford, Philip Yardley, Robert Laurent, Sarah, Woodward, Intern, asst. resident, resident surgery Barnes Hosp., St. Louis, 1933-37, fellow plastic surgery, 1938- 39; asst. surgery Washington U., St. Louis, 1934-39; vis. surgeon, chief plastic surgery Mass. Gen. Hosp., Boston, 1941—; clin. asso. surgery Harvard, 1941-68, asso. clin. prof. surgery, 1968—; cons. VA, AEC; sr. cons. surgeon Crippled Children's Program, Mass. Served from lt. to lt. col., M.C., AUS, 1943-47; asst. chief, then chief plastic surgery Valley Forge Gen. Hosp., Phoenixville, Pa. Decorated Legion of Merit. Diplomate Am. Bd. Surgery, Am. Bd. Plastic Surgery (sec.-treas. 1950-55). Fellow A.C.S.; mem. A.M.A., Am. Surg. Assn., Soc. U. Surgeons, Am. Assn. Plastic Surgeons (pres. 1957-58), Harvard Med. Sch. Alumni Assn. (v.p. 1968-71), Am. Soc. Plastic and Reconstructive Surgery (v.p. 1959-60), New Eng. Surg. Soc., Soc. Plastic and Reconstructive Surgery (pres. 1962-63), Am. Soc. Surgery the Hand, Mass. Med. Soc., Scoiete Internationale Chirurgie, Soc. Mayflower Descs., Sigma Xi. Unitarian. Club: Harvard Aesculapian (Boston). Mem. editorial bd. Jour. Plastic & Reconstructive Surgery, 1958-63, co-editor, 1966—. Author articles, papers on plastic and reconstructive surgery. Home: Weston Rd Lincoln MA 01773 Office: 275 Charles St Boston MA 02114

CANNON, BROWN W., food co. exec.; b. Denver, June 16, 1916; s. Hugh Brown and Margaret (Reynolds) C.; A.B., Stanford U., 1938; M.B.A., Harvard, 1940; m. Charla Gates Apr. 9, 1941; children—Brown W., Charles, Reynolds. With Beatrice Foods Co., Denver, 1940—, v.p. and dist. mgr., 1948—, also dir.; dir. United Bank of Denver, United Bank of Colo., Pub. Service Co. of Colo., Van Schaack & Co. Commr. Colo. Commn. Higher Edn. Trustee Nat. Jewish Hosp. and Research Center. Served as lt., USNR, 1942- 45. Mem. Mountain States Employers Council (dir.), Zeta Psi. Rotarian. Home: 575 S Elizabeth St Denver CO 80209 Office: 2401 E 2d Av Denver CO 80206

CANNON, CARROLL CONWAY, lawyer; b. St. Louis, July 22, 1909; s. Thomas D. and Marguerite (Carroll) C.; student Washington U., St. Louis, 1926-28; LL.B., City Coll. Law, 1933; m. Helen Harrelson, Nov. 2, 1940; children—Carroll C., Cathlyn II, Helen M. Abstractor, Title Ins. Corp., St. Louis, 1928-33; admitted to Mo. bar, 1932, Ark. bar, 1946; atty. Fed. Land Bank, St. Louis, 1933-38; practice in St. Louis, 1938-41; spl. agt. FBI, 1942-46; practice in Forrest City, Ark., 1946—. Owner St. Francis County Abstract Co. Pres. St. Louis Jr. C. of C., 1942; dir., mem. exec. com. Forrest City C. of C., 1947-51. Mem. Am., Ark., St. Francis County (pres. 1963) bar assns., Ark Land Title Assn. (pres. 1951-52), Lion (pres. Forrest City 1955). Home: 2917 E Broadway Forrest City AR 72335 Office: 108 S Izard St Forrest City AR 72335

CANNON, EDMUND RASHA, Jr., lawyer; b. Mobile, Ala., Dec. 17, 1926; s. Edmund Rasha and Kate (Davis) C.;; A.B., U. Ala., 1949, LL.B., 1952. Admitted to Ala. bar, 1952 since practiced in Mobile, asso. Joseph C. Sullivan, Esq., 1952-55; asso. Hand, Arendall, Bedsole, Greaves & Johnston, 1956—, partner, 1958—. Bus. mgr. Ala. Law Review, 1951-52. Served with AUS, 1945-46. Mem. Am., Ala., Mobile (treas., 1962) bar assns., Am. Legion, V.F.W., Phi Delta Theta, Phi Delta Phi (magister de Graffenried Inn, 1951). Democrat. Presbyn. Clubs: Bienville, Athelstan, Alba Fishing and Hunting, Mobile. Home: 2200 N Levert Dr Mobile AL 36607 Office: 1st Nat Bank Bldg 30th Floor Mobile AL 36602

CANNON, EDWARD WHITNEY, mathematician; b. Sussex County, Del., June 20, 1907; s. John Robert and Josephine (Whitney) C.; B.S., U. Del., 1928, M.S., 1931, D.Sc., 1966; Ph.D., Johns Hopkins, 1935; m. Irene Ellen McDermott, Aug. 3, 1943; children—John E., E. Raymond. Elec. engr. Gen. Electric Co., 1928-29; tchr. elec. engring. U. Del., 1929-31, tchr. applied math., 1935-42; asst. chief applied math. div. Nat. Bur. Standards, Washington, 1947-53, chief applied mathematics div., 1955—; prin. investigator Logistics Research Project, George Washington U., 1953-55. Served from lt. to comdr., USNR, 1942-46. Fellow A.A.A.S.; mem. Washington Acad. Sci., Philos. Soc., Soc. for Indsl. and Applied Math., Am. Math. Soc., Sigma Xi. Home: 5 Vassar Circle Glen Echo MD 20768 Office: National Bureau of Standards Washington DC 20234

CANNON, FRANCIS ALLISON, bus. exec.; b. Plainfield, N.J., Sept. 23, 1903; s. Arthur A. and Henrietta M. (Blatz) C.; student N.Y.U.; m. Barbara Dunn, May 16, 1930; childrenWilliam Dunn, Peter Byam. Asso. First Boston Corp. (and predecessor firms), 1921—, asst. mgr., 1931-32, mgr., 1932-35, asst. v.p., 1935-40, v.p., 1940-46, dir., 1946—, mem. exec. com. 1950—, adminstrv. v.p., ret.; mgr. Savs. Bank of Central Jersey, Chmn. bd. Plainfield chpt. A.R.C. Jury commr. Plainfield chpt. A.R.C.; bd. dirs. United Community Service Plainfield. Mem. Investment Bankers Assn. Am. (chmn. N.Y. group). Clubs: Plainfield Country; Bond (N.Y.C.); Board Street; Stock Exchange, Bay Head Yacht. Home: 981 Fox Hill Lane Plainfield NJ 07060 Office: 15 Broad St New York City NY 10005

CANNON, GARNETT EDWARD, ins. co. exec.; b. Toronto, Ont., Can., July 30, 1906; s. Alfred Edwin and Emma (Hughes) C.; B.A., U. Toronto, 1928; m. Gyla C. Kemmer, Sept. 12, 1931; children—Anne (Mrs. Lester H. Jochum), Nancy (Mrs. Stanley A. Goodell). Came to U.S., 1928, naturalized, 1936. Clk. Excelsior Life, 1928; mgr. actuarial dept. Standard Ins. Co., 1928-32; asst. acturary, asst. actuary and asst. sec., v.p., actuary, exec. v.p., 1932-57, pres., 1957—; pres. Standard Mgmt. Inc.; dir. Pacific Northwest Bell Telephone Co. Hon. v.p. Portland Area council Boy Scouts Am., mem. regional exec. com.; mem. regional adv. com. U.S. Forest Service; adv. council Pacific Crest Nat. & Scenic Trail. Bd. overseers Whitman Coll. Fellow Soc. Actuaries; mem. Portland C. of C. (dir., past pres.), Fedn. Western Outdoor Clubs (past pres.), Internat. Congress Actuaries, Am. Arbitration Assn. (Portland adv. council), Keep Ore. Green Assn. (past pres.). Rotarian. Clubs: Trails, Aero, City, Arlington (past pres.). Home: 4470 SW Greenleaf Dr Portland OR 97221 Office: PO Box 711 Portland OR 97207

CANNON, GEORGIUS YOUNG, architect; b. Salt Lake City, Mar. 6, 1892; s. George Quayle and Caroline (Young) C.; student U. Utah, 1909-11; B.Arch., Mass. Inst. Tech., 1918; m. Phyllis Winder, Dec. 1, 1921, (dec. June 1953); 1 dau., Dorothy (Mrs. Allen Paul Webb). Office mgr. Wallace Neff, Pasadena, Cal., 1925-30; pvt. practice architecture, Pasadena, Cal., 1935-41; with Los Angeles shipyards, San Pedro, Cal., 1941-43; draughtsman 20th Century Fox Studio, Hollywood, Cal., 1943-45, MGM Studio, Hollywood, 1945-46; pvt. practice architecture, Pasadena, Cal., 1946-53, Salt Lake City, 1953—. Served to 2d lt. U.S. Army, 1918. Fellow A.I.A. (pres. Utah chpt. 1957-58), Utah Heritage Found. Home: 105 E South Temple Salt Lake City UT 84101 Office: 19 W South Temple Salt Lake City UT 84101

CANNON, HENRY CECIL, Jr., architect; b. Fitzgerald, Ga., Dec. 1, 1935; s. Henry Cecil and Corinne (Ellis) C.; student Ga. Inst. Tech., 1954-55; Asso. Sci. in Bldg. Constrn., So. Tech. Inst., 1959; m. Beth Kirkley McRee, Mar. 21, 1964; 1 son, Thomas Elliot. Mem. staff Veran O. Blackburn, Architect, 1960-62; asso. firm Zeb V. Lackey & Assos., Architects, Valdosta, Ga., 1963—. Served with AUS, 1956-57. Registered profl. architect, Ga. Mem. A.I.A. (past sec. S.W. Ga. chpt.; alternate dir. Ga. assn.), Tau Alpha Pi. Prin. work Ben Hill-Irwin Vocational Tech. Sch., Fitzgerald, Ga., 1970. Home: 1807 Canterbury Dr Valdosta GA 31601 Office: PO Box 431 Valdosta GA 31601

CANNON, HERBERT SETH, corp. exec.; b. Bklyn., Dec. 3, 1931; s. Joseph and Gertrude (Kimmel) C.; B.A., Washington and Jefferson Coll., 1953; student Cornell U. Law Sch., 1953-54; LL.B., Fordham U., 1960; m. Edith Marks, June 20, 1954; children—Naomi Sue, Nina Louise. Salesman, Manhattan Scalloping & Embroidery Co., N.Y.C., 1956-57; stock broker Hirsch & Co., N.Y.C., 1957- 61, Wineman, Weiss & Co., N.Y.C., 1961-62; pres. Weis, Voisin, Cannon, Inc., N.Y.C., 1963-70; chmn. bd. Elgin Nat. Industries, Inc., N.Y.C., 1967-70; chmn. bd., pres. Cannon, Jerold & Co., Inc., 1970—; chmn. bd. Cannon Industries, Inc., 1970—, dir. Elgin Nat. Industries, Inc., Electro- Catheter Corp., Generics Corp. Am., Nation-Wide Check Corp., Product Applications, Inc., Solvent Chem. Co., Inc., Data Information Services Inc. Trustee Washington and Jefferson Coll. Served with AUS, 1954-56. Mem. Young Pres. Orgn. Home: 140 Tekening Dr Tenafly NJ 07670 Office: 77 Water St New York City NY 10005

CANNON, HOWARD HENRY, lawyer; b. Lyons Falls, N.Y., June 26, 1903; s. George C. and Joanna (Cassidy) C.; A.B., Hamilton Coll., 1923; LL.B., Harvard, 1927; m. Marion E. Schermerhorn, Aug. 31, 1929; children—Mary Ellen (Mrs. N. Austin Weston), Elizabeth A. (Mrs. Frank E. Gump). Admitted to N.Y. bar, 1927, since practiced in Syracuse; asso. Bond, Schoeneck & King, 1927-45, partner, 1945—. Sec., dir. A.E. Nettleton Co., Coyne Indsl. Laundry, Inc.; chmn. bd. Cogar Corp.; dir., mem. exec. com. Lincoln Nat. Bank & Trust Co.; dir. Lincoln First Banks, Inc., Unity Mut. Life Ins. Co. Mem. vis. com. Harvard Law Sch., 1961-67; chmn. com. Harvard Law Sch. Fund, Harvard Law Sch. Sesquicentennial Fund Upstate N.Y., 1966-70. Bd. dirs. Blue Shield of Central N.Y., Inc.; bd. dirs., chmn. N.Y. Higher Edn. Assistance Corp.; trustee Ct. of Appeals Library; treas., bd. dirs. J. Stanley Coyne Found.; pres., trustee Cogar Found., Inc.; bd. dirs. Community Found. Syracuse and Onondaga County. Recipient Man of Year award for community service Greater Syracuse C. of C., 1966. Fellow Am. Bar Found.; mem. Am., N.Y. State (past sect. chmn., mem. exec. com.), Onondaga County bar assns., Am. Judicature Soc., Greater Syracuse C. of C. (past pres.), Harvard Law Sch. Assn. Upstate N.Y. (past pres.). Democrat. Roman Catholic. Clubs: University, Onondaga Golf and Country, Century (Syracuse). Home: 106 Bradford Lane Syracuse NY 13224 Office: State Tower Bldg Syracuse NY 13202

CANNON, HOWARD WALTER, U.S. senator; b. St. George, Utah, 1912; s. Walter and Leah (Sullivan) C.; B.E., Ariz. State Tchrs. Coll., 1933; LL.B., U. Ariz., 1937; LL.D., Ariz. State Coll., 1962; m. Dorothy Pace, Dec. 21, 1945; children—Nancy Lee, Alan Howard. Admitted to Ariz. bar, 1937, Utah bar, 1938, Nev. bar, 1946; reference atty. Utah Senate, 1939; county atty., Washington County, Utah, 1940-41; mem. firm Hawkins & Cannon; city atty., Las Vegas, Nev., 1949-58; U.S. senator from Nev., 1959—. Mem. Nev. Bd. Bar Examiners, 1950-55. Past chmn. Clark County Democratic Central Com. Served with USAF, 1941-46; maj. gen. AF Res. Mem. Ariz., Clark County, Nev., Utah bar assns., Air Force Assn., Nat. Space Club, Res. Officers Assn., V.F.W., D.A.V., C. of C. (pres. 1955), Am. Legion. Club: Lions (pres. 1956-57, past dist. gov., internat. counsellor). Home: 5312 Portsmouth Rd Spring Hill, MD 20016. Office: Senate Office Bldg Washington DC 20510

CANNON, JACK A., surgeon; b. Salina, Kan., July 17, 1919; s. Charles Heaton and Bess May (Beadle) C.; B.A., U. Cal. at Los Angeles, 1940; M.D., Harvard, 1943; m. Helen Stacia Sineszko, Feb. 15, 1949; children—Susan Gail, Patricia Bess, Jack Charles, Michael Gerald, Deborah Christine. From intern to asst. resident surgery Mass. Gen. Hosp., Boston, 1944-46; admitting room physician, then surg. resident Los Angeles County Gen. Hosp., 1948-49, sr. surg. resident, 1949-50; instr. surgery U. So. Cal. Med. Sch., 1919- 50; mem. faculty U. Cal. at Los Angeles Med. Center, 1950—, prof. surgery, 1963—, also mem. staff Center for Health Scis.; head physician surgery Harbor Gen. Hosp., Torrance, Cal., 1951-52; staff surgeon Wadsworth VA Hosp., 1950-51, 52-60; mem. staff St. John's, Santa Monica hosps. (both Santa Monica). Grantee USPHS, 1954—. Served to capt., M.C., AUS, 1946-47; with M.C., USAF, 1953. Diplomate Nat. Bd. Med. Examiners, Am. Bd. Surgery. Fellow A.C.S.; mem. Am., Cal., Los Angeles County (bd. dirs. Bay dist.) med. assns., Am. Surg. Assn., Soc. Univ. Surgeons, Soc. Vascular Surgery, Internat, Cardiovascular Soc., Pan-Pacific, Pacific Coast, Western surg. assns., Bay (bd. dirs. past pres.), Los Angeles surg. socs., Soc. Grad. Surgeons Los Angeles County Gen. Hosp., Alpha Omega Alpha. Spl. research homotransplantability of tissues by host alteration, studies in reconstructive arterial surgery. Home: 121 Udine Way Los Angeles CA 90024

CANNON, JIMMY, columnist; b. N.Y.C., Apr. 10, 1909; s. Thomas J. and Loretta (Monahan) C. Reporter, N.Y. Daily News, 1927-1930, N.Y. World-Telegram, 1930-34; feature writer, Internat. News Service, 1935-36; sports writer, N.Y. Jour. Am., 1936-39; columnist (specializing in sports, also covering other important nat. events), N.Y. Post, 1946, also war corr. in Korea; now columnist N.Y. Jour. Am. Served with AUS, 1941-45; 3d Army corr. for Stars and Stripes in 4 campaigns. Recipient Dutton award 3 times. Author: The Sergeant Says, 1942; Nobody Asked Me, 1950; Who Struck John?. Home: Edison Hotel New York City NY 10036 Office: 75 West St New York City NY 10006

CANNON, JOSEPH HARRIS, textile co. exec.; b. York County, S.C., Sept. 19, 1916; s. Roscoe S. and Lida (Adams) C.; B.S., Clemson Coll., 1937; m. Frances E. Cash, Dec. 21, 1938; children—Alice A., Joseph B. With Cannon Mills Co., Kannapolis, N.C., 1944—, beginning as personnel employee, successively personnel dir., 1944-53, v.p., dir., 1953—, sec., 1964—. Home: 201 Cannon Blvd Kannapolis NC 28081 Office: Cannon Mills Co Kannapolis NC 28081

CANNON, LEGRAND, Jr., author; b. New Haven, Conn., Dec. 1, 1899; s. LeGrand and Florence (Pond) C.; Ph.B., Yale U., 1920; M.B.A., Harvard U., 1922; m. Jeannette Peabody, Dec. 30, 1922; children—Jeannette, LeGrand, 3d, Winthrop, Margaret. Author: A Mighty Fortress, 1937; The Kents, 1938; Look to the Mountain, 1942; Come Home at Even, 1951. Home: 56 Laurel Rd New Haven CT 06511

CANNON, MARY ALICE, educator; b. Milw., Oct. 19, 1918; d. Raymond J. and Alice (Carry) Cannon; Ph.B., Marquette U., 1940, M.A., 1941; Ed.D., U. Colo., 1961. Tchr., Mil. County Sch. System, 1941-42; civilian instr. USAAF, Truax Field, Madison, Wis., 1943-44; case worker A.R.C., 1944-45; asst. dean of women Marquette U., 1945-58, dean of women, 1958-70, asst. prof. edn. Grad. Sch., 1970—. Mem. Milw. County Civil Service Commn., 1960—. Mem. Nat., Wis. assns. women deans, Am. Assn. U. Women, Am. Personnel and Guidance Assn. Home: 731 Glenview Milwaukee WI 53213

CANNON, MELVIN CROXALL, chemist, educator; b. Salt Lake City, July 25, 1913; s. Tracy Young and Lettie (Taylor) C.; B.S., U. Utah, 1933, M.S., 1938; Ph.D., Boston U., 1941; postdoctoral student, U. Pitts., Cornell U.; m. Anne Holland, Aug. 26, 1937; children—Bonnie Gay, Melvin Croxall, Marcia Anne, Kenneth Holland. Research fellow Merck & Co., 1941; indsl. fellow Mellon Inst. Indsl. Research, 1941-44; dir. research Sapphire products div. Elgin Nat. Watch Co., 1944-46; asst. prof. chemistry U. Denver, 1946-47; mem. faculty Utah State U., 1947—, prof. chemistry, 1951—, chmn. dept., 1955-68. Cons. sci. teaching program A.A.A.S., 1957. Bishop, Ch. of Jesus Christ of Latter-day Saints, 1959-63. Mem. Am. Chem. Soc. (chmn. Salt Lake City 1952), Utah Acad. Arts, Scis. and Letters. Home: 748 E Center St Logan, UT 84321.

CANNON, NORMAN LAWRENCE, publishing co. exec.; b. Kansas City, Kan., Oct. 9, 1936; s. William Lawrence and Norma (Purvis) C.; B.A. in Econs. cum laude, Harvard, 1959, M.B.A., 1961; m. Alyce Diane Blanton, Sept. 26, 1964; 1 dau., Charlotte Walker. With Johns-Manville Co., 1961-63, W.Va. Pulp & Paper Co., 1963-64; from project dir.. to asst. to pres. Air Reduction, Inc., 1964-69; with Harper & Row Publishers, N.Y.C., 1969—, treas., 1970—. Republican. Episcopalian. Home: 19 W Brookside Dr Larchmont NY 10538 Office: 49 E 33d St New York City NY 10016

CANNON, NORMAN S., educator; b. Bountiful, Utah, Oct. 16, 1916; s. George M. and Ellen Christina (Steffensen) C.; B.S., U. Utah, 1938; M.S., Columbia, 1939, Ph.D., 1957; m. Virginia Bateman, Mar. 4, 1944; children—Norman Scott, Bradford Allen, Jeffrey David, Kyle Robert. Accounting labs. asst. U. Utah, 1937-38; accountant E.B. Packard Co., N.Y.C., 1938-40; instr. Coll. City N.Y., 1940-52; prof. accounting Utah State U., Logan, 1947—, now also head dept.; instr. Columbia, 1956-57; practice pub. accounting, 1947—. Treas. Utah State U. Credit Union, 1958-63. Served with USAAF, 1942-45. C.P.A., Utah. Mem. Am. Accounting Assn., Am. Inst. C.P.A.'s, Utah Assn. C.P.A.'s, Phi Kappa Phi, Alpha Kappa Psi. Home: 354 Lauralin Dr Logan UT 84321

CANNON, ORSON SLIVER, educator, plant pathologist; b. Salt Lake City, Nov. 21, 1908; s. Quayle and Eugenia (Silver) C.; B.S Utah State U., 1935, M.S., 1937; Ph.D., Cornell U., 1943; m. Dorothy Knowlton, May 29, 1934; children—Lawrence O., Rozanne (Mrs. N. Kent Hogan), James W., Kathleen, Kristine. Extention plant pathologist Pa. State Coll., 1942-43; dept. head crops research lab. H. J. Heinz Co., Bowling Green, O., 1943-48; plant pathologist Agrl. Research Service, Dept. Agr., Logan, Utah, 1948-57; prof., head dept. botany and plant pathology Utah State U., 1957—; spl. research fungicides to control tomato diseases, wilt resistant tomato varieties, mosaic resistant cucumber varieties. Mem. Am. Phytopathol. Soc., Am. Genetic Assn., Sigma Xi. Mem. Ch. of Jesus Christ of Latter Day Saints (bishop). Home: 1407 E 17th N Logan UT 84321

CANNON, ROBERT HAMILTON, Jr., govt. ofcl.; b. Cleve., Oct. 6, 1923; s. Robert Hamilton and Catherine (Putnam) C.; B.S., U. Rochester, 1944; Sc.D. (du Pont fellow 1947-48), Mass. Inst. Tech., 1950; m. Dorothea Alta Collins, Jan. 4, 1945; children—Philip Gregory, Douglas Charles, Beverly Jo, Frederick Scott. David John, Joseph Collins, James Robert. Research engr. Baker Mfg. Co., Evansville, Wis., 1946-50; instr. Mass. Inst. Tech., 1949-50; research engr. Bandix Aviation Research Labs., Detroit, 1950-51; with Autonetics div. N.Am. Aviation Inc., Downey, Cal., 1951-57, research specialist, systems, engr. inertial naviation instruments and systems, 1954-57; vis. asst. prof. U. Cal. at Los Angeles, 1955-57; asso. prof. mech. engring. Mass. Inst. Tech., 1957-59; mem. faculty Stanford, 1959-70, prof. aero. and astronautics, 1962-70, dir. Guidance and Control Lab., 1960-69, vice chmn. dept. aeros. and astronautics, 1968; chief scientist USAF, 1966- 68; asst. sec. transp., Washington, 1970—; cons. to industry, 1957-66. Del. Am. Inst. Aero. and Astronautics to Am. Automatic Control. Council, 1964-; chmn. research adv. subcom. guidance, control and navigation NASA, 1967-70, chmn. electronics research center adv. group, 1968-69. Served to lt. (j.g.) USNR, 1944-46. Fellow Am. Inst. Aero. and Astronautics (chmn. tech. com. guidance and control 1964-66, dir., 1968—). Sigma Xi, Theta Chi (local pres. 1943-44). Presbyn. Author: Dynamics of Physical Systems, 1967; also articles. Participated devel. hydrofoil boats, automatic flight control, inertial guidance instruments and systems, space vehicle control, drag free satellite, gyro test of gen. relativity. Home: 9221 Laurel Oak Dr Bethesda MD 20034 Office: Dept of Transportation Washington DC 20590

CANNON, ROBERT JAMES, co. dir.; b. Los Angeles, Dec. 6, 1913; s. James H. and Vinna (Hale) C.; student Los Angeles Jr. Coll., 1932-33; m. Elizabeth H. Bennett, Aug. 21, 1937; children—Jeffrey Douglas, Janis Bundschu. With Cannon Electric Co., Los Angeles, 1933-64, successively shopworker, foreman, salesman-engr., plant mgr., gen. mgr., 1941-50, pres., 1950-64, dir., 1930—64; owner Four 'C' Enterprises, Los Angeles, Cal.; dir. Western Gear Corp., Transcon Lines, Warwick Electronic, Chgo. Pacific United Services Corp., Security Pacific Nat. Bank; past dir., past chmn. Los Angeles br. Fed. Res. Bank San Francisco. Trustee Occidental Coll.; pres. James H. Cannon Found.; pres. Jr. Achievement Los Angeles County, 1954-55. Mem. Mchts. and Mfrs. Assn. (pres. 1957-58, dir.). Clubs: Rotary (pres. 1948-49), California, Los Angeles Country, Eldorado Country, Electrical Manufacturers, Beach. Home: 10375 Wilshire Blvd Los Angeles CA 90024 Office: 10889 Wilshire Blvd Los Angeles CA 90024

CANNON, ROWLAND MORRELL, sugar co. exec.; b. Logan, Utah, June 2, 1914; s. Clawson Young and Winnifred (Morrell) C.; B.S., Ia. State U., 1936; m. Elithe Fillmore, July 16, 1940; children—Rowland Morrell, Douglas Fillmore, Maurine. With Utah-Ida. Sugar Co., 1936—, v.p., prodn. mgr., 1964-67, exec. v.p., 1967-69, pres., also chief exec. officer, 1969—, also dir., mem. exec. com.; mem. Salt Lake adv. bd. First Security Bank of Utah; dir. 1st Security Corp. Mem. water pollution adv. council Ida. Bd. Health, 1962-64. Mem. Am. Soc. Sugar Beet Technologists (past dir.), U.S. Beet Sugar Assn. (trustee), Sigma Chi. Mem. Ch. of Jesus Christ of Latter-day Saints. Rotarian, Elk. Club: Alta (Salt Lake City). Home: 3424 Loren Von Ciole Salt Lake City UT 84117 Office: Beneficial Life Bldg Salt Lake City UT 84110

CANNON, RUSSELL CARROLL, educator; b. McNab, Ark., Dec. 11, 1916; s. William Manton and Eva (Raley) C.; B.A., Harding Coll., 1939; M.A., Pepperdine Coll., 1948; M.A., N.Y.U., 1952, Ed.D., 1953; m. Nona Hanes, June 1, 1939; adopted children—Lynona Marie, Lisa Carol. Ordained to ministry Ch. of Christ, 1938, Disciples of Christ, 1963; minister, 1939-47; v.p. Ibaraki Christian Coll., Japan, 1949-51; prof. religious edn. Harding Coll., 1953-54; prof. religious edn., dean students Pepperdine Coll., 1954-58; dean students Cal. Western Campus, U.S. Internat. U., 1958-60, asso. prof. edn., 1958—, dean Coll. Arts and Scis., 1960-64, acad. v.p., 1964-67, provost, 1967-70. Pres. United Cerebral Palsy Found., San Diego County. Mem. N.E.A., Am. Personnel and Guidance Assn., Nat. Vocational Guidance Assn., Religious Edn. Assn., Kappa Delta Pi. Home: 870 Moana Dr San Diego CA 92106

CANNON, WILLIAM BERNARD, ednl. adminstr.; b. Cascade, Ia., Nov. 10, 1920; s. Charles Bernard and Irma (White) C.; Ph.B., U. Chgo., 1947; M.A., 1949; m. Jeanne Adair Ketchum, Aug. 16, 1944; children—Julia, Dominic, William, Robert. Budget examiner Bur. Budget, 1951-54, 59-62; asst. v.p. U. Chgo., 1954-59, v.p. programs and projects, 1968—; asst. chief, office legislative reference for health, edn. and welfare programs Bur. Budget, 1962-65, chief edn., manpower and sci. div., 1965-67; dep. chmn., Nat. Endowment for the Arts, 1968. Served with AUS, 1943-46. Mem. Phi Beta Kappa. Home: 5545 University Av Chicago, IL 60637.

CANNON, WILLIAM RAGSDALE, bishop; b. Chattanooga, Apr. 5, 1916; s. William Ragsdale and Emma (McAfee) C.; A.B., U. Ga., 1937; B.D. summa cum laude, Yale, 1940, Ph.D., 1942; D.D., Asbury Coll., 1950; LL.D., Temple U., 1955 Ordained to ministry Methodist Ch., 1940; pastor Allen Meml. Methodist Ch., Oxford, Ga., 1942-43; prof. ch. history and hist. theology Candler Sch. Theol., Emory U., 1943-68, dean sch. theology, 1953-68; bishop Raleigh area United Meth. Ch., 1968—; lectr. Fondren Found., Southern Meth. U., 1948; vis. prof. Garrett Bib. Inst., summer 1949, Richmond Coll., U. London, 1930. Mem. comm. on ritual and worship Meth. Ch.; chmn. bd. ministerial tng. N. Ga. Conf., Meth. Ch.; del. to gen. and jurisdictional confs. Meth. Ch., 1948, 52, 56, 60, 64, also mem. commn. on worship, commn. ecumenical affairs; del. Ecumenical Conf. Methodism, Oxford, Eng., 1951, World Meth. Conf., Lake Junalaska, N.C., 1956; fraternal del. from World Meth. Council to World Conf. on Faith and Order, Lund, Sweden, 1952; accredited visitor World Council Chs., Evanston, Ill., 1954; Meth. ch. del. 3d assembly World Council of Chs., New Delhi, 1961; del. World Meth. Conf., Oslo, Norway, 1961; Meth. Ch. del. Conf. on Faith and Order, Montreal Can., 1963; mem. exec. com. World Methodist Council; ofcl. protestant observer from council to II Vatican Council of Roman Catholic Church. Trustee La Grange (Ga.) Coll., Asbury Coll.; chmn. trustees Protestant Radio and TV Center. Mem. Oxford Inst. Wesleyan Studies, Phi Beta Kappa, Phi Beta Kappa Assos. (exec. com.), Theta Phi, Phi Kappa Phi. Methodist. Author: A Faith for These Times, 1944; The Christian Church, 1945; The Theology of John Wesley, 1946; Accomplishments to Wesley's Death in Methodism (edited by W. K. Anderson), 1947; Our Protestant Faith, 1949; The Redeemer, 1931; History of Christianity in the Middle Ages, 1960; journeys after St. Paul, 1963. Editor: Selections from Augustine, Table Talk (Martin Luther), 1950. Address: 1307 Glenwood Av Raleigh NC 27605

CANO ABASCAL, JUAN JOSE, consul gen. of Spain in New Orleans. Address: Internat Trade Mart New Orleans LA 70130*

CANOYER, HELEN GERTRUDE, univ. dean; b. Melrose, Minn.; d. John Newton and Myrtle Ellen (Nickey) Canoyer; A.B., U. Minn., 1925, M.A., 1930, Ph.D., 1940. Asst. prof. marketing and econs. U. Minn. 1941-44; economist, distbn. div. Bur. Fgn. and Domestic Commerce, Dept. Commerce, Washington, 1944-45; asst. chief, div. research and statistics Office Allen Property Custodian, Washington, 1945-46; asso. prof. marketing and econs. U. Minn., 1944-50, prof., 1950-53; dean N.Y. State Coll. Home Econs., 1953-68; dean Sch. Home Econs., U. Mass. at Amherst, 1968—. Mem. adv. com. Nat. Study Home Econs. in State Univs. and Land-Grant Colls.; mem. Gov.'s Com. on Consumer Information and Services; mem. cons. team to U. Philippines, 1967. Dir. Grand Union Co. Mem. Women's council N.Y. State Dept. Commerce, Women's com. N.Y. State Expn.; chmn. President's Consumer Adv. Council, 1962-63; mem. Consumer Adv. Council and Presidents' Com. on Consumer interests, 1963-64. Mem. N.E.A., Am. Assn. U. Profs., Am. Econs. Assn., Am. Marketing Assn. (dir.), Am. Home Econs. Assn., N.Y. State Home Demonstration Agts. (hon.), Internat. Fedn. Home Econs., Delta Sigma Rho, Omicron Nu, Epsilon Sigma Phi, Alpha Lambda Delta, Phi Kappa Phi. Author: Selecting a Store Location; (with R.S. Vail) Social Aspects of Consumption in the Depression; (with R. S. Vaile) Economics of Income and Consumption; (with R. S. Vaile) Income and Consumption Mem. U.S. team educators workshops problems African Women and Girls, 1961. Home: 15 Hickory Lane Amherst MA 01002

CANT, GILBERT, writer; b. London, Eng., Sept. 16, 1909; ed. Leeds (Eng.) Boys Modern Sch.; m. Barbara Nickelhoff, Sept. 20, 1930 (div.); children—Geoffrey David, John Gilbert Hubbard; m. 2d, Ruth Abramson, Dec. 18, 1966. Came to U.S., 1930, naturalized, 1940. Reporter, Yorkshire Post, Leeds, 1927-28, No. Whig, Belfast, No. Ireland, 1929; asst. editor Royal Gazette and Colonist Daily, Bermuda, 1929-30; N.Y. corr. for Brit. newspapers, 1930-37; feature writer N.Y. Post, 1937-42, war editor, 1942- 44; contbg. editor Time mag., 1944-52, asso. editor, 1952—. Recipient Russell L. Cecil award Arthritis and Rheumatism Found., 1957, 1966; Albert Lasker Med. Journalism award, 1961, 1965. Mem. Am. Ornithologists Union. Clubs: Orienta Yacht (Mamaroneck); Coral Reef Yacht (Miami, Fla.). Author: The War at Sea, 1942; America's Navy in World War II, 1943; The Great Pacific Victory, 1946; also articles, pamphlets. Editor: This Is the Navy, 1944. Office: Time Inc Rockefeller Center New York City NY 10020

CANTAROW, ABRAHAM, biochemist, educator; b. Hartford, Conn., Jan. 27, 1901; s. Joseph and Helen (Karp) C.; student Tufts Coll., 1917-20; M.D., Jefferson Med. Coll., 1924, D.Sc. (hon.), 1968; m. Elizabeth Stern, Aug. 1, 1932; 1 dau., Ellen. Intern Jefferson Med. Coll. Hosp., 1924-27, resident instr., asst. prof., asso. prof. medicine Jefferson Med. Coll., 1927-45, prof. biochemistry, head dept., 1945-66, prof. biochemistry emeritus, 1966—; biochemist Jefferson Med. Coll. Hosp., 1932-45, asst. physician, 1936-45; research planning officer Nat. Cancer Inst., Bethesda, Md., 1966—; cons. in biochemistry Bur. Medicine and Surgery, U.S. Navy, 1947—. Mem. study sect. NIH, 1960-64. Recipient Silver medal U. Helsinki, 1963, Sci. award Phi Lambda Kappa, 1963. Mem. Am. Assn. Cancer Research (dir., pres. 1969), Am. Physiol. Soc., Am. Soc. Pharmacology Exptl. Therapeutics, Endocrine Soc., A.A.A.S., Soc. Exptl. Biology and Medicine, Phila. Biochemists Club, Sigma Xi, Alpha Omega Alpha. Author: Textbook of biochemistry, 1954; Clinical Biochemistry, 1932; Clinical Endocrinology, 1954; Calcium Metabolism, 1932; Lead Poisoning, 1940. Mem. editorial bd. Metabolism. Home: 2939 Van Ness St NW Washington DC 20008 Office: Nat Cancer Institute Bethesda MD 20014

CANTELLA, VINCENT MICHELE, stock broker; b. Boston, Oct. 27, 1917; s. Michele and Josephine (Sapienza) C.; B.S., Boston U., 1939; m. Josephine R. Castanien, Nov. 19, 1944; children—Betsy Ann, David V., Steven M. Mng. partner Cantella & Co., Boston, 1963—. Mem. Boston Stock Exchange, 1953—, bd. govs., mem. exec. com., 1963—; mem. Midwest Stock Exchange, 1965—, Pacific Coast Stock Exchange, 1965—, N.Y. Stock Exchange, 1969—. Served to maj. USMCR, World War II. Mem. Boston Financial Research Assn. Clubs: Lewis Bay Yacht (Cape Cod, Mass.); Winchester (Mass.) Yacht. Home: 53 Swain Rd Winchester MA 01890 Office: 53 State St Boston MA 02109

CANTER, FLOYD MARTIN, glass co. exec.; b. nr. Hartford City, Ind., Dec. 18, 1908; s. Edward J. and Della (Martin) C.; student Ind. Bus. Coll., 1927, Internat. Accountants Soc., 1932; m. Marianna McGarrell, July 19, 1936; 1 son, Stephen E. Supr. accounting Chevrolet div. Gen. Motors Corp., 1935-45; with Am. Coating Mills Co., 1945-53, v.p., asst. treas., dir., 1952-53; v.p., dir. R.L. Snideman & Co., Chgo., 1953-54; with Owens-Ill., Inc., 1947—, comptroller, 1957-61, v.p. corp. planning, 1961-64, v.p. new products and marketing devel., 1964-66, exec. v.p. comml. and tech. adminstrn., 1966—, dir. 1970—. Mem. Financial Execs. Inst., Tech. Soc. Toledo, Toledo C. of C. Clubs: Toledo, Inverness (Toledo); Economic (Detroit). Home: 3252 Corey Rd Toledo OH 43615 Office: Owens-Ill Glass Co PO Box 1035 Toledo OH 43651

CANTER, JACOB, former govt. ofcl.; b. Newton, Mass., July 13, 1911; s. Max and Sophia (Helfman) C.; B.A., Harvard, 1932, M.A., 1933, Ph.D., 1940; m. Alva I. Leo, May 29, 1947; 1 dau., Emily A. Instr., Harvard, 1936-37, 38-39, 39- 40, Sheldon travelling fellow, Europe, 1937-38; instr. U.S. Naval Acad., 1941-42, asst. prof., 1946; pub. affairs officer Am. embassy, Managua, 1946-47; cultural attache Am. embassy, Bogota, Colombia, 1947-49; cultural attache, pub. affairs officer Am. embassy, Havana, Cuba, 1950-54; cultural affairs adviser USIA, 1954-57; cultural attache Am. embassy, Mexico, 1957-58, Madrid, Spain, 1958-62; dir. Inter- Am. programs Bur. Ednl. and Cultural Affairs, Dept. State, 1962-66, dep. asst. sec. of state ednl. and cultural affairs, 1966-69, acting asst. sec., 1969. U.S. mem. exec. com. Inter-Am. Cultural Council, Orgn. Am. States, 1968-69: E.R. Murrow fellow, vis. prof. pub. diplomacy Fletcher Sch. Law and Diplomacy, Tufts U., 1969-71; research asso. in edn. Harvard, 1970-71. Served from lt. (j.g.) to lt. comdr., USNR, 1942- 45. Editor: Cuentos Norteamericanos, 1956. Home: 5209 38th St NW Washington DC 20015

CANTER, MILTON ERNEST, lawyer, corp. exec.; b. Poughkeepsie, N.Y., Nov. 21, 1908; s. Jacob and Jennie (Abrams) C.; B.A., Union Coll., Schenectady, 1929; LL.B., St. Lawrence U., 1932, J.D., 1967. Reporter, Bklyn. Eagle, 1930-31; editor-in-chief, founder Bklyn. Law Rev., 1932; editor-in-chief Justinian, legal newspaper, 1931-33; admitted to N.Y. bar, 1935, D.C. bar, 1947; pub. relations counsel N.Y.C. Housing Authority, 1934; asst. counsel Joint Legislative Com. Investigate Pub. Utilities State N.Y., 1934-36; gen. practice, N.Y.C., 1935-37; assn. counsel N.Y. State Pub. Service Commn., 1937-39; spl. prosecutor to investigate N.Y. State Ins. Fund, 1939-40; referee N.Y. State Tax Commn., 1941; dir. priorities div. War Assets Adminstrn., 1945- 46, chief small bus. div., 1946; sr. mem. firm Canter, McLaughlin & Urow, Washington, 1947—, Dir. Washington-Balt. Helicopter Airways Service, B. Manischewitz Co. and affiliated cos., 1960—; chmn. bd. Am. Rail & Steel Co., 1948-68; pres. Potomac Investment Corp. Mem. U.S. Expn. of Sci. and Industry; sec. Mayor N.Y.C. Com. Real Property Inventory, 1934; mem. com. investigate 3d degree methods N.Y. Criminal Bar, 1934; Mem. N.Y. State Democratic Pub. Relations Bur., 1929-30; vice chmn. finance com. Dem. Nat. Com., 1946- 47; mem. Nat. Dem. Club. Nat. affiliate. Nat. bd. dirs. Boys' Clubs Am.; bd. dirs., trustee Freedoms Found. at Valley Forge; mem. adv. council George Washington U., 1969—. Served to capt. USAAF, 1942-45. Mem. Am., N.Y. State, D.C. bar assns., Washington Bd. Trade, Am. Legion (comdr. Nat. Def. Post 1966), Tau Kappa Alpha. Clubs: Army and Navy, Federal City (Washington). Author: Rates and Ratemaking for Public Utilities, 1937; Weather Flying, 1943. Home: 4201 Cathedral Av NW Washington DC 20016 also Doncaster MD 21914 Office: 1025 15th St NW Washington DC 20005

CANTER, STANLEY D., advt. exec.; b. N.Y.C., Dec. 10, 1923; s. Frank and Rose (Posner) Kanter; B.S., City Coll. N.Y., 1944; M.A., Columbia, 1947; m. Shirley Zolov, June 19, 1948; children—Leonard A., Robert G. Econ. analysist Economteric Inst., N.Y.C., 1944-45; dir. marketing research McCann-Erickson, 1947-57; sr. v.p., dir. Ogilvy & Mather, 1957—. Served with USAAF, 1945-46. Mem. A.A.A.S., Inst. Math. Statistics, Am. Statis. Assn., Am. Marketing Assn., Market Research Council, Copy Research Council. Home: 3905 Franklin Av Seaford NY 11783 Office: 2 E 48th St New York City NY 10017

CANTERBURY, WILLIAM MONTE, scientist; b. Muskogee, Okla., Jan. 14, 1910; s. Walter Milton and Zona (Gatewood) C.; student U. Okla., 1928-29; B.S., U.S. Mil. Acad., 1934; student AC Primary and Advanced Flying Schs., 1934-35, AC Electronics Sch., 1938-39, Mass. Inst. Tech. Radar Sch., 1941; m. Mary Ellen Looney, July 24, 1934; children—Ellen Blair, William Monte. Commd. 2d lt. USAF, 1934, advanced through grades to maj. gen., 1957; asst. dir. AC, chief radar br. Hdqrs. AAF. Washington, 1943; comdr. 346th Bomb Group, Dalhart, Tex., 1944; asst. dep. chief staff operations 2d Air Force, Colorado Springs, Colo., 1945, 8th Air Force, Okinawa, 1945, asst. dep. chief staff Air Staff, Research and Devel. Armed Service Spl. Weapons Projects, Sandia Base, N.M., 1947; dir. devel. Air Research and Devel. Command, Balt., 1950; dep. asst. Atomic Energy, dep. chief staff operations hdqrs. USAF, Washington, 1951; comdr. 1009th Spl. Weapons Squadron, Washington, 1952; comdr. Air Force Spl. Weapons Center, Kirtland AFB, N.M., 1954-59; dep. chief staff, research, engring. ARDC, Andrews AFB, 1959-60; comdr. Air Force Missle Devel. Center, Holloman AFB, N.M., 1960-61; sr. staff scientist Lockheed Missiles & Space Co., 1961-66;; cons., 1966—. Decorated officer Order Brit. Empire; outstanding unit award USAF; Legion of Merit. Mem. Phi Kappa Psi. Episcopalian. Address: 5821 Box Canyon Rd La Jolla, CA 92037.

CANTEY, EMORY AMBLER, lawyer; b. Ft. Worth, Apr. 25, 1917; s. Samuel Benton and Grace (Ambler) C.; student Washington and Lee U.; LL.B., U. Tex., 1939; m. Joyce Oatherine Ernst, July 14, 1962; children—Sandra Aileen (Mrs. Peter Wolf), Emory Ambler. Admitted to Tex. bar, 1939, since practiced in Ft. Worth; partner firm Cantey, Hanger, Gooch, Cravens & Munn, and predecessors, 1946—. Dir., mem. exec. com. First Nat. Bank Ft. Worth; dir., sec., gen. counsel Components, Inc., Graham Magnetics, Inc., Shenandoah Oil Corp. Trustee Fuller Found., William P. Smallwood Found. Served with USMCR, 1943-46. Mem. Kappa Sigma Mason. Clubs: Ft. Worth, Shady Oaks Country (Ft. Worth); La Concha Beach (Acapulco, Mexico); Squadron A (N.Y.C.). Home: 4840 Crestline Rd Fort Worth TX 76107 Office: First Nat Bank Bldg Fort Worth TX 76102

CANTEY, JAMES WILLIS, banker; b. Columbia, S.C., Mar. 3, 1917; s. J.M. and Elizabeth (Childs) C.; B.A., U.S.C., 1938; m. Nancy Moorer, Apr. 19, 1941; children—James Willis, Joseph Moorer, John Childs. With Columbia Outdoor Advt., Inc. 1945-58, pres., 1947-58, also dir.; with Citizens & So. Nat. Bank S.C., Charleston, 1958—, pres., 1960—, also dir.; pres. dir. State Investment Co., Inc., Columbia, 1950—; dir. Liberty Life Ins. Co., State- Record Newspaper, Charlotte br. Fed. Res. Bank. Chmn. S.C. Ports Authority, 1956-64. Served with inf. AUS, World War II. Decorated Silver Star (3), Bronze Star (4), Legion of Merit, Purple Heart; Croix de Guerre (France). Mem. S. C. Bankers Assn. (pres. 1966- -), Sigma Alpha Epsilon. Episcopalian. Kiwanian. Home: 1400 Westminster Dr Columbia SC 27925 Office: PO Box 727 Columbia SC 29202

CANTIN, J. MAURICE, lawyer; b. Que., Can., Mar. 25, 1929; B.A., St. Jean Eudes, 1949; LL.B., Laval U., 1953. Admitted to Que. bar, 1953. Partner firm Gagnon, de Billy, Cantin & Dionne. Mem. Canadian, Que. (mem. council 1966-68) bar assns. Office: 100 d'Youville Quebec 4 Quebec Canada*

CANTINFLAS, MARIO MARENO REYES, actor; b. Mexico City, Mexico, Aug. 12, 1917; m. Valentina Zubaroff, 1937. Dancer, traveling tent show; created tramp character Latin-Am. variety stage; first feature film Ahi Esta del Detalle, also Ni Sangre Ni Arena, 1941; first appeared to U.S. audiences as bicycle rider in film Around the World in 80 Days, 1956; prod., partner Pasa Films; imitates style of famous matadors in mock bullfights Plaza de Toros, 4 times ann.; appeared in Pepe, Sube y Baja. Address: Av Insurgentes Sur #377 Mexico DF Mexico

CANTLAY, GEORGE GORDON, army officer; b. Honolulu, Aug. 2, 1920; s. George Gordon and Helen (Reid) C.; student U. Hawaii, 1938-39; B.S., U.S. Mil. Acad., 1943; grad. Armor Sch., 1952, Command and Gen. Staff Coll., 1955, Army War Coll., 1962; M.A., George Washington U., 1963; m. Wilhelmina Shannon Davison, Apr. 27, 1946; children—George Gordon III, Donald Davison, Carolyn Reid. Commd. 2d lt. U.S. Army, 1943, advanced through grades to brig. gen., 1969; instr. armor tactics, chief doctrine sect. Combat Devels. Group, Command and Staff Dept., Armor Sch., 1952-54; instr., asst. prof. dept. mil. art and engring. U.S. Mil. Acad., 1955-58; comdr. 2d Medium Tank Bn., 1st Cav., 3d Armored Div., Europe, 1958-60; assigned gen. staff Hdqrs. U.S. Army Europe, 1960-61; faculty Army War Coll., 1962-65; brigade comdr. 2d Inf. Div., Korea, 1965-66; chief congl. activities div. Office Chief of Staff of Army, 1966-68; asst. div. comdr. 1st Inf. Div., Vietnam, 1968-69; dep. comdg. gen. Delta Mil. Assistance Command, Vietnam, 1969-70; comdg. gen. U.S. Army Tng. Center, Armor, 1970; dep. comdg. gen. U.S. Army Armor Center and Fort Knox, Ky., 1970—. Decorated D.S.M., Silver Star medal, Legion of Merit with oak leaf cluster, Bronze Star with V device and oak leaf cluster, Army Commendation medal with oak leaf cluster, Purple Heart; RVN Army Distinguished Service Order 1st Class, RVN Gallantry Cross with palm, RVN Armed Forces Honor medal 1st Class. Mem. Armor Assn., Assn. U.S. Army, Assn. Grads. U.S. Mil. Acad. Episcopalian. Clubs: Army and Navy, Army Navy Country (Washington). Home: 1401 Fifth Av Fort Knox KY 40121 Office: Hdqrs US Army Armor Center Fort Knox KY 40121

CANTLON, JOHN EDWARD, ednl. adminstr.; b. Sparks, Nev., Oct. 6, 1921; s. John Edward and Anna (Riddle) C.; B.S., U. Nev., 1947; Ph.D., Rutgers U., 1950; m. Carolyne Irene Riley, Aug. 20, 1944; children—John Edward (dec.), William Howard, Carolyne Ann, Robert Dean. Asst. prof. George Washington U., 1950-52, asso. prof., 1952-53; sr. ecologist Boston U., 1953-54; asso. prof. Mich. State U. at East Lansing, 1954-58, prof. botany and plant pathology, 1958, provost, 1969—. Program dir. environmental biology NSF, Washington, 1965-66, adv. com. div. environmental sci., 1966-69, adv. com. instl. devel. program, 1970—; adv. com. health physics Oak Ridge Nat. Lab., 1966-69, mem. adv. council, 1970—; mem. nat. research council, exec. com., div. biology and agr. U.S. Nat. Acad. Sci., 1969—. Served with USNR, 1942-45. Recipient Distinguished Faculty award Mich. State U., 1964. Mem. Ecol. Soc. Am. (sec. 1958-61, v.p. 1965-66, pres. 1968-69), A.A.A.S. (exec. com. 1970—), Am. Inst. Biol. Scientists (gov. bd. 1962-65). Contbr. articles profl. jours. Home: 1795 Bramble St East Lansing MI 48823

CANTOR, B. GERALD, bus. exec.; b. N.Y.C., Dec. 17, 1916; s. Julius and Rose (Delson) C.; student N.Y. U., 1935-37; m. Leona Witzel, Mar. 10, 1940; 1 son, Jay S. Chmn., pres. Cantor, Fitzgerald & Co., investment bankers, Beverly Hills, Cal. Home: 9475 Sunset Blvd Beverly Hills CA 90210 Office: 232 N Canon Dr Beverly Hills CA 90210'

CANTOR, DAVID GEOFFREY, educator; b. London Eng., Apr. 12, 1935; s. Joseph and Sally (Heller) C.; came to U.S., 1940, derivative citizen; B.S., Cal. Inst. Tech., 1956; Ph.D., U. Cal. at Los Angeles, 1960; m. Hariet Lebedinsky, Dec. 21, 1958; children—Judith, Michael. Instr. Princeton, 1960-62; asst. prof. U. Wash., 1962-64; mem. faculty U. Cal. at Los Angeles, 1964—, prof. math., 1969—; cons. to govt. and industry. Sloan fellow, 1968-70. Sr. mem. I.E.E.E.; mem. Am. Math. Soc., Math. Assn. Am. Author: (with others) A Fortran Program for Elastic Scattering Analyses with the Nuclear Optical Model, 1958; also research papers. Office: Dept Math Univ Cal Los Angeles CA 90024

CANTOR, NORMAN FRANK, educator, historian; b. Winnipeg, Can., Nov. 19, 1929; s. Max W. and Elizabeth (Niznick) C.; came to U.S., 1951, naturalized, 1968; B.A. with honors (Gold medalist), U. Man. (Can.), 1951; M.A., Princeton, 1953, Ph.D. (Jacobus fellow 1953-54), 1957; Rhodes scholar, Oxford U., 1954- 55; m. Mindy Mozart, Aug. 25, 1937; children—Howard, Judy. Instr., then asst. prof. history Princeton, 1955-60; asso. prof., then prof. Columbia, 1960-66; prof. history Brandeis U., 1966-70, Leff prof history, 1968-70; Distinguished prof. history, chmn. dept. history State U. N.Y. at Binghamton, 1970—; cons. in field, 1953—. Can. Council fellow, 1960; Am. Council Learned Socs. fellow, 1960. Mem. Am. Hist. Assn., Medieval Assn. Am., Conf. Brit. Studies. Republican. Jewish religion. Author: Medieval History: The Life and Death of a Civilization, 2d edit., 1969; The English: A History of Politics and Society to 1760, 1968; How to Study History, 1967; Western Civilization, 1969. Home: 41 E Hamton Rd Binghamton NY 13903

CANTOR, SAMUEL CHARLES, lawyer; b. Phila., Mar. 11, 1919; s. Joseph and Miriam (Ginzberg) C.; B.S.S., Coll. City N.Y., 1940; LL.B., Columbia, 1943; m. Dorothy Van Brink, Apr. 9, 1943; childrenJudith Ann, Barbara Ann. Admitted to N.Y. bar, 1943; asst. dist. atty. N.Y.C., 1943-48; legislative counsel N.Y. State Senate, counsel N.Y.C. Affairs Com. on State Senate, 1949-59; mem. firm Newcomb, Woolsey & Cantor, Newcomb & Cantor, N.Y.C., 1951-59; 1st dep. supt. ins. State of N.Y., 1959-64, acting supt. ins., 1963-64; 2d v.p., gen. solicitor Mut. Life Ins. Co. N.Y., 1964-66, v.p., gen. counsel, 1967—. Mem. spl. com. on ins. holding cos. N.Y. Supt. Ins., 1967. Fellow Am. Bar Found.; mem. Ins. Fedn. N.Y. (v.p. 1967-68), Am., N.Y. State bar assns., Am. Life Conv. (pres. N.Y. State 1965—), Assn. Life Ins. Counsel, Am. Judicature Soc. Mason. Club: Fairview Country (Greenwich, Conn.). Home: Audubon Lane Greenwich CT 06830 Office: 1740 Broadway New York City NY 10019

CANTOR, SOL WILLIAM, dept. store exec.; b. N.Y.C., Jan. 6, 1911; s. Abraham and Pearl (Rosencupf) C.; student St. John's Law Sch., 1931; m. Hermina Rosenberg, Dec. 15, 1940; children—Ellen T., Robert I. With Interstate Stores, Inc., N.Y., 1933—, pres., 1952-68, chmn. bd., 1968—, dir., 1948—; dir. Beneficial Standard Life Ins. Co. Exec. com. United Cerebral Palsy; trustee, founder Albert Einstein Coll. Medicine. Club: Glen Oaks (Great Neck, N.Y.). Home: 200 Central Park S New York City NY 10011 Office: 111 8th Av New York City NY 10011

CANTRELL, CLYDE HULL, librarian; b. Caroleen, N.C., Sept. 23, 1906; s. James Volney and Sarah Nancy Florence (Hull) C.; A.B., U. N.C., 1933, A.M., 1936, A.B. in L.S., 1937; postgrad. W.Va. U., 1941-42; Ph.D., U. Ill. 1960; m. Ethel Marie Williams, June 5, 1940; 1 dau., Nancy Elizabeth (Mrs. William Kent Kennedy). Engaged as bookkeeper Charlotte (N.C.) News, 1926-29; asst. circulation dept. U. N.C. Library, 1930-32, supr. 1933-37; periodicals librarian N.C. State U., 1937-39, circulation librarian, 1939-41; head circulation div. W.

Va. U. Library, 1941-42, asst. librarian, 1942- 43; asso. prof. Spanish and dir. library, Birmingham So. Coll., 1943-44; dir. libraries Auburn (Ala.) U., 1944-59, dir. libraries. prof., 1959—. Mem. A.L.A., Ala. Acad. Sci. (archivist 1954—), Ala. Writers Conclave, So. Hist. Assn., Southeastern Library Assn. Am. Assn. U. Profs., Council for Basic Edn., Ala. Hist. Assn., Ala. Library Assn. (v.p., 1945-46, pres. 46-47), Soc. Am. Archivists, South Atlantic Modern Lang. Assn., Instituto Internacional de la Literature Iberoamericana, Assn. Coll. and Research Libraries, Modern Lang. Assn., Phi Beta Kappa, Mu Beta Psi, Phi Sigma Iota, Beta Phi Mu. Episcopalian. Author: Graduate Degrees Awarded and Titles of Theses, 1894-1940, 1941; (with Walton R. Patrick) Southern Literary Culture: A Bibliography of Masters' and Doctors' Theses, 1955. Editor: A History of the Alabama Academy of Science, 1963. Contbr. to lit. and profl. jours. Home: 175 Woodfield Dr Auburn AL 36830

CANTRELL, JOHN HOWARD, lawyer, business exec.; b. Dardanelle, Ark., July 17, 1898; s. John Marion and Martha Jane (Bearden) C.; A.B., U. Okla., 1921, LL.B., 1924; m. Lucille Josephine Farish, June 6, 1925; 1 son, John Edward. Admitted to Okla. bar, 1924; with firm Cantrell, Douglas, Thompson & Wilson, Oklahoma City, 1960—; v.p., gen. counsel C.R. Anthony Co., Oklahoma City 1954-60. Mem. Oklahoma City Charter Revision Com., 1954. Served with USMC, 1918-19; AEF. Fellow Am. Bar Found. (Okla. chmn. 1970-71); mem. Am. (state del. 1942- 46), Okla. (pres. 1941-42), Oklahoma County (pres. 1938), Tulsa County (pres. 1931) bar assns., Am. Coll. Trial Lawyers (Okla. chmn. 1970-71), Oklahoma City C. of C. (chmn. govtl. relations div. 1954), Am. Legion, Order of Coif, Phi Delta Phi, Sigma Alpha Epsilon. Methodist. Rotarian. Clubs: Mens Dinner, Beacon. Home: 2607 Warwick Dr Oklahoma City OK 73116 Office: 1st Nat Bldg Oklahoma City OK 73102

CANTRELL, ROY HERBERT, coll. pres.; b. Kansas City, Mo., Nov. 4, 1904; s. Herbert H. and Mable (Munch) C.; student Pasadena Coll., 1921-22; Asbury Coll., 1922-25; A.B., U. Ky., 1925-26; student Biblical Sem., 1926-27; A.M., N.Y.U., 1928; B.D., Asbury Sem., 1927; D.D., Northwest Nazarene Coll., 1944; D.R.E., Southwestern Baptist Sem., 1955; m. Evelyn Mikkelson, June 19, 1929. Ordained to ministry Ch. of Nazarene, 1927; prof. Eastern Nazarene Coll., Wollaston, Mass., 1927-29, dean of men, 1928-29; pastor Ch. of the Nazarene, Syracuse, N.Y., 1929-34, Binghamton, N.Y., 1934-39; dist. supt. Ch. of Nazarene, Ont. Dist., Toronto, 1939-42, Minn. Dist., St. Paul, 1941-46, Kan. Dist., Wichita, 1946-47; pres. Bethany-Peniel Coll., Bethany, Okla., 1947—. Mem. gen. bd. and mem. dept. edn. ch. schs. Ch. of Nazarene. Dir. Community Nat. Bank; trustee Okla. County Utility Service Authority. Trustee Eastern Nazarene Coll., 1930-41, Northwestern Nazarene Coll., 1942-46, Sem. of Kansas City, Mo., 1944-47, Bethany Hosp. Kiwanian. Co-author: Exploring Christian Faith. Home: 4300 N College Av Bethany OK 73008

CANTRICK, ROBERT BIRDSALL, educator; b. Monroe, Mich., Dec. 8, 1917; s. George T. and Laura (Birdsall) C.; A.B. cum laude, U. Rochester, 1938, M.A., 1946; Ph.D., U. Ia., 1959; student Harvard, 1941, Julliard Sch. Music, 1946, Berkshire Music Center, 1950, U. Mich., 1951, Oberlin Coll., 1951-52; m. Margaret A. Gesell, July 16, 1943; children—Robert A., Joel, Anthony, Timothy, Susan, Catherine. Reporter, Monroe Eve. News, 1938-40; mem. conducting staff Juilliard Summer Sch., 1946; asst. prof. music Furman U., 1946-51; founder-conductor Greenville (S.C.) Symphony Orch., 1948-51; apprentice condr. to George Szell with Cleve. Orch., 1951-52; asst. prof. music Carnegie Inst. Tech., 1952-55, Cornell Coll., Mt. Vernon, Ia., 1955-59; head div. fine arts Jacksonville (Ala.) State Coll., 1959-64; arts commentator radio sta. WHMA, Anniston, Ala., 1961-62; dean Sch. Fine Arts, Wis. State U. at Stevens Point, 1964-67; dir. arts and humanities State U. N.Y. Coll. at Buffalo, 1967-69, prof. music, 1969—. Served with AUS, 1943-45. Recipient grant-in-aid for musical composition Carnegie Found., 1948, 49; fellowship for conducting and composition Ford Found., 1951-52; award for composition Birmingham (Ala.) Festival Arts, 1960. Mem. Music Educators Nat. Conf., Am. Music Center, Music Tchrs. Nat. Assn., Southeastern Composers League, Soc. Aesthetics and Art Criticism, Wis. Acad. Scis., Arts and Letters, Phi Beta Kappa, Delta Upsilon. Rotarian. Contbr. profl. publs. Home: 159 Bidwell Pkwy Buffalo NY 14222

CANTWELL, CONAN, lawyer; b. Corsicana, Tex., July 2, 1907; s. James William and Ada (Westmoreland) C.; A.B., U. Kan., 1928, LL.B., 1930; m. Pauline Bramlette, July 28, 1937; children—Carolyn, Conan, Nancy Lawrence. Admitted to Tex. bar 1930; practice in Dallas, 1936—; mem. firm Jackson, Walker, Winstead Cantwell & Miler; spl. dist. judge, 1934. Past chmn. grievance com. Fifth Congl. Dist of Tex. Trustee St. Mark's Sch. of Tex. Served to lt. USNR, World War II. Mem. Am., Tex., Dallas (pres. 1958) bar assns., Am. Judicature Sec., Tex. Surveyors Assn., Phi Delta Phi, Beta Theta Pi. Clubs: Dallas, Brookhollow Golf, (Dallas). Author publs. in field. Home: 3700 Alice Circle Dallas TX 75205 Office: 1st Nat Bank Bldg Dallas TX 75202

CANTWELL, JAMES FRANCIS, former state ofcl.; b. Trenton, N.J., June 24, 1908; s. James Francis and Mary J. (Sebring) C.; Architecture, U. Pa., 1932; m. Blanche Elizabeth Minnick, Oct. 11, 1944; children—James Francis, Betsy Jane. Maj. gen. N.J. Dept. of Def., 1946-54, chief of staff, adj. gen., 1954-70. Served to lt. col. AUS, 1941-45. Mem. Adj. Gen. Assn. of U.S. (pres. 1960-63), N.G. Assn. of U.S. (pres. 1963—), Engrs. Club. Lion, Elk. Home: 622 Latona Av Trenton NJ 08618

CANTWELL, JOHN WALSH, advt. exec.; b. Fall River, Mass., July 16, 1922; s. William J. and Esther (Walsh) C.; B.S., in Econs., Holy Cross Coll., 1944; M.A., Georgetown U., 1945; postgrad. Columbia, 1949-50; m. Barbara Kirwin, Mar. 4, 1944; children—Sharon, Peter, Paul, Asst. sales mgr. Internat. Milling Co., 1947-48; v.p. mgmt. supr. Compton Advt., N.Y.C., 1948-60; sr. v.p. mgmt. supr. Sullivan, Stauffer Colwell & Bayles, N.Y.C., 1960- 65; pres., chief exec. officer Pritchard, Wood, advt., N.Y.C., 1965-68; pres. Carlin Hall, Inc., N.Y.C., 1965—; pres., chief exec. officer Parkson Advt. Agy., Inc., 1968-69; sr. v.p. J. B. Williams Co., Inc., 1968—; pres. Jack Cantwell, Inc., 1970—. Home: 45 Sherwood Rd Tenafly NJ 07670 Office: 420 Lexington Av New York City NY 10017

CANTWELL, KENNETH ROBERT, dentist, educator; b. Smithfield, Utah, Feb. 22, 1916; s. William Haemer and Eliza Jane (Mourtisen) C.; B.S., Utah State U., 1938; D.M.D., North Pacific Coll. of Ore., 1943; m. Margaret Sue Jarrell, Sept. 1, 1945; 1 son, Gary Kenneth. Instr. U. Ore. Dental Sch., 1946-47, asst. prof., head dept. operative dentistry, 1947-49, asso. prof., head dept., 1949-31, prof., head dept., 1949-51, prof., head dept., 1951—. Served as capt. Dental Corps, AUS, 1944-46. Fellow Am. Coll. Dentists, Acad. Gen. Dentistry; mem. Am. Dental Assn., Am. Acad. Gold Foil Operators. Home: 1613 SW Westwood Ct Portland OR 97201

CANTWELL, RAYMOND JOSEPH, accountant; b. Yonkers, N.Y., July 14, 1916; s. Joseph P. and Margaret (Lynch) C.; B.B.A., Manhattan Coll., 1938; M.S., Columbia Grad. Sch. Bus., 1941; m. Dorothy Quill, Apr. 12, 1947; children—Joseph, Patrick Kathleen. Jr. accountant, Westchester County, N.Y., 1938-41; accountant Price Adjustment Bd., 1941-46; with Babcock & Wilcox Co., N.Y.C., 1946—, comptroller, 1957-63, v.p. comptroller, 1963-65, v.p. finance, 1965—, dir., 1966—; dir. Bailey Meter Co., Cleve., Diamond Power Supply Corp., Lancaster, O., A.M. Lockett & Co., Ltd., New Orleans, Standard Refractories, Ltd., Burlington, Ont. Mem. Financial Execs. Inst., Nat. Assn. Accountants, Machinery and Allied Products Inst. (accounting council). Home: 5 Cotswold Way Scarsdale NY 10583 Office: Babcock & Wilcox Co 161 E 42d St New York City NY 10017

CANTWELL, ROBERT EMMETT, author; b. Little Falls (now Vader), Wash., Jan. 31, 1908; s. Charles James and Nina Adelia (Hanson) C.; student U. Wash., 1924-25; m. Mary Elizabeth Chambers; children—Joan McNiece (Mrs. George Stolz), Betsy Ann (Mrs. Walter Pusey III), Mary Elizabeth (Mrs. Lars-Erik Nelson). Plywood factory veneer clipper operator, Hoquiam, Wash., 1925-29; contbr. to publs., 1929-35; editorial staff Time, 1935-36, Fortune, 1937; asso. editor Time, 1938-45; lit. editor Newsweek, 1949-54; editorial cons. Sports Illustrated, N.Y.C., 1956-61, sr. editor, 1961—. Mem. Battery A. 248th Coast Arty., Washington N.C., 1925-26. Mem. N.Y. Hist. Soc., N.Y. Geneal. and Biog. Soc., Sigma Delta Chi. Author: Laugh and Lie Down, 1931; The Land of Plenty, 1934; Nathaniel Hawthorne: The American Years, 1948; American Men of Letters, 1956; Alexander Wilson, Naturalist and Pioneer, 1961; The Real McCoy: the Life and Times of Norman Selby, 1971. Home: 520 West 114th Street New York City NY 10025 Office: Sports Illustrated Time and Life Bldg Rockefeller Center New York City NY 10020

CANTWELL, WILLIAM PATTERSON, lawyer; b. Saranac Lake, N.Y., Dec. 2, 1921; s. Francis Barry and Genevieve (Godfrey) C.; B.A. with highest honors, Williams Coll., 1942; J.D., Yale, 1948; m. Hendrika Antonia Restebreurtje, June 19, 1947; children—Peter F., Rebecca D., Christopher A. Admitted to N.Y. bar, 1948, Colo. bar, 1953; asso. firm Moot, Sprague, Marcy & Gulick, Buffalo, 1948-52; with Holland & Hart, Denver, 1953-64, mem. firm, 1955-64; mem. firm Dawson, Nagel, Sherman & Howard, 1964—. Vis. lectr. law U. Denver, 1956- 60, 64-65, U. Colo., 1962; lectr. various continuing legal edn. insts. and legal meetings; mem. Estate Planning Council, Denver. Adminstr. Waterman Fund, 1963-65. Mem. Am. Coll. Probate Counsel (sec. 1971-72), Am. (mem. ho. of dels. 1964-66, chmn. real property probate and trust law sec. 1971-72), Colo. (pres. 1970-71, gov. 1959-65, chmn. taxation law sect. 1959-60, probate and trust law sect. 1960-61), Denver (pres. 1962-63, award of merit 1969) bar assns., Greater Denver Tax Counsel Assn. (pres. 1957-58), Order of Coif. Clubs: 26 Club, Denver Country, Rotary (Denver). Contbr. articles to profl. jours.; lectr. profl. orgns. Home: 375 Lafayette St Denver CO 80218 Office: 1st Nat Bank Bldg Denver CO 80202

CANTY, DONALD JAMES, writer, editor; b. Oakland, Cal., Feb. 8, 1929; s. Harry Vincent and Mabel (Turner) C.; Ph.B., U. Santa Clara (Cal.), 1950; M.S. in Journalism, Northwestern U., 1951; m. Joan McGowan, Feb. 23, 1952; children—Kevin, Dennis, Mary, Hilary, Susan, Brendan. Editor, Lake County Bee, Lakeport, Cal., 1952-53; asso. editor Daily Pacific Builder, San Francisco, 1954-56; exec. asst. Cal. council A.I.A., 1956-59; editor in chief Western Architec and Engr. 1959-61; pub. information dir. A.I.A., Washington, 1962; sr. editor Archtl. Forum, 1962-64, mng. editor, 1965-66; dir. Urban Information Center, editor in chief City mag., Urban Am., Inc., Washington, 1967—. Commnr., Englewood (N.J.) Housing Authority, 1966; chmn. Cath. Council Interracial Justice No. N.J., 1963-65. Recipient Jesse H. Neal award Asso. Bus. Publs., 1963. Home: 3315 Highland Pl NW Washington DC 20008. Office: 1717 Massachusetts Av NW Washington DC 20036

CANUP, WILLIAM CALEB, govt. ofcl.; b. N.Y.C., Oct. 19, 1921; s. Martin Luther and Inez (Bollinger) C.; B.A. in History with high distinction, Wayne State U., 1943; M.A. in Anthropology, Harvard, 1947; m. Mireille Anne Rousselet, Dec. 2, 1950; children—James William, Eric Anthony. Joined U.S. Fgn. Service, 1947; vice consul, econ. officer, Marseille, France, 1947-49; visa officer displaced persons program, Stuttgart and Frankfurt, Germany, 1949-50; 2d sec. econ. affairs, Luxembourg, 1950-52; vice consul, econ. and comml. officer, Casablanca, Morocco, 1952-55; engaged in African research and polit. affairs State Dept., 1955-59; consul, prin. officer, Elisabethville, Republic Congo, 1959-61; 2d sec., later 1st sec., polit.-mil. affairs sect. Am. embassy, Paris, France, 1962-64; dep. dir. pvt. office sec.-gen. NATO, Paris, 1965; Congolese affairs, State Dept., 1965-66: dep. exec. dir. Nat. Mil. Information Disclosure Policy Com., Washington, 1966-67; mem. mgmt. staff State Dept., 1967-68; internat. transp. adviser Transp. Dept., 1969; dir. city bus pilot demonstration project Met. Washington Council of Govts., 1969—. Served as navigator USAAF, 1943-45; prisoner of war in Germany. Home: 7204 Ridgewood Av Chevy Chase MD 20015 Office: Met Washington Council of Govts Washington DC 20036

CANZONA, EDMUND JOHN, lawyer; b. Red Bank, N.J., Jan. 27, 1904; s. Michael and Luisa (Juliano) C.; student Dickinson Coll., 1923-25; B.S., Lafayette Coll., 1927; LL.B., Georgetown U., 1930; m. Helen A. MacFadden, Apr. 6, 1939. Admitted to N.J. bar, 1931, since practiced in Red Bank; mem. firm Parsons, Canzona, Blair & Warren, and predecessors, 1942—. Mem. Red Bank Bd. Edn., 1940-70, pres., 1950-70. Mem. Am., N.J., Monmouth County (pres. 1960, chmn. ethics com. 1964-65) bar assns. Republican. Roman Catholic. Rotarian. Clubs: Navesink Country (Middletown, N.J.); Red Bank Root Beer and Checker. Home: 63 Fisher Pl Red Bank NJ 07701 Office: 18 Wallace St Red Bank NJ 07701

CAPALBO, CARMEN CHARLES, director, producer; b. Harrisburg, Pa., Nov. 1, 1925; s. Joseph and Concetta (Riggio) C.; student Yale Sch. Drama, 194546; m. Patricia McBride, July 9, 1950 (div. June 1961); children—Carla, Marc. Dir., co- producer Juno and the Paycock, Shadow and Substance, Dear Brutus, Awake and Sing, The Threepenny Opera, The Potting Shed, A Moon for the Misbegotten, The Cave Dwellers, the Rise and Fall of the City of Mahagonny, 1970. dir. A Connecticut Yankee, The Good Soldier Schweik, Seidman and Son, The Strangers, The Sign in Sidney Brustein's Window, Enter Solly Gold, also TV prodn. The Power and the Glory; story editor Studio One, 1951-52; prodn. mgr. Emlyn Williams as Charles Dickens. 1952-53; Jean-Louis Barrault-Madeleine Renaud Co., 1952; dir., producer, writer 200 radio plays. Served with AUS, 194445. Decorated Bronze Star, Purple Heart; recipient Tony award, 1956, Obie award, 1956. Mem. League N.Y. Theatres, Screen Dirs. Guild, Soc. Stage Dirs. and Choreographers, Dramatists Guild, League OffBroadway Theatres (co-founder 1958, exec. bd. 1958-60). Address: 21 E 11th St New York City NY 10003

CAPARN, RHYS, (Mrs. Herbert Johannes Steel), sculptor; b. Onteora Park, N.Y., July 28, 1909; d. Harold Rhys and Clara (Jones) Caparn; student Brearly Sch., N.Y.C., 1918-27, Bryn Mawr Coll., 1927-29, Ecole Artistique des Animaux, Paris, 1929-30, Archipenko Sch. Art, 1931-33; m. Herbert Johannes Steel. Sept. 9, 1935. Instr. sculpture, Dalton Sch., 1946-53, 60—. One man show at Riverside Mus., 1961, Delphic Studios, N.Y.C., 1933-35; exhibited in group shows at Archtl. League, N.Y.C., 1941, Whitney Annuals, 1941, 53, 54, 56, 60, N.Y. Zool. Park, 1942, Wildenstein & Co., 1944, 47, Dartmouth Coll., 1949, 55, John Heller Gallery, 1953, Art Colony Gallery, Cleve., 1953, Meltzer Gallery, N.Y.C., 1956, 59, 60, La Boetie Gallery, N.Y.C., 1970; represented in permanent collections City Art Mus., St. Louis (Morton May collection), Colorado Springs Fine Arts Center, Dartmouth, Fogg Mus., Whitney Mus. Am. Art, Concoran Gallery Art, Barnard Coll. Library, Bryn Mawr Coll., Mus. City of N.Y.; also represented in exhbn. 8 Am. Painters and Sculptors, touring Asia and Europe under auspices Dept. State, 1957. Recipient 2d prize for Am. sculpture Met. Mus. Art, 1951; medal of honor, Nat. Assn. Women Artists, 1960, 61. One of 11 Am. sculptors representing U.S. in competition Unknown Political Prisoner, Tate Gallery, London, 1953, Fellow internat. Inst. Arts and Letters; mem. Fedn. Modern Painter and Sculptors (pres. 1944-45, 61-63), Sculptors Guild, Am. Abstract Artists. Office: Taunton Hill Rd Route 1 Newtown CT 06470

CAPE, DONALD PAUL MONTAGU STEWART, Brit. diplomat; b. Kildare, Ireland, Jan. 6, 1923; s. John Scarvell and Olivia (Lyons) C.; B.A. with honors, Oxford U., 1946; m. Cathune Agnes Johnston, July 14, 1948; children—Andrew, John, Francis, Nicholas, Katherine. With Brit. Fgn. Service, 1946—; 1st sec., Holy See, Rome, 1962-67; head information adminstrn. dept. Fgn. Office, London, 1967-70; counsellor Brit. embassy, Washington, 1970—. Home: 5212 Portsmouth Rd Washington DC 20016 Office: British Embassy 3100 Massachusetts Av Washington DC 20008

CAPEHART, HOMER EARL, Jr., lawyer; b. Green Bay, Wis., Oct. 29, 1922; s. Homer Earl and Irma (Mueller) C.; A.B., DePauw U., 1945; LL.B., Harvard, 1948; m. Harriet Jane Holmes, June 17, 1950; children—Craig Earl, Caroline Mary. Admitted to Ind. bar, 1948, since practiced in Indpls.; partner firm Krieg, DeVault, Alexander & Capehart, 1952—. Dir. Secured Ins. Co., Indpls., 1950-62; sec., dir. Packard Mfg. Corp., 1949-65. Mem. Ind. Bd. Bar Examiners, 1963-67. Mem. Ind. Flood Control and Water Resources Commn., 1953-60. Bd. dirs. Indpls. Symphony Orch., 1958-63. Mem. Am., Ind., Indpls. bar assns., S.A.R. (pres. Ind. 1960), Ind. Hist. Soc., Ind. Soc. Pioneers, Phi Beta Kappa, Beta Theta Pi. Republican. Mason (32). Clubs: Literary, Exchange (pres. 1969, nat. dist. dir. 1970-71), Columbia, Woodstock, Contemporary (Indpls.). Home: 445 Pine Dr Indianapolis IN 46260 Office: 1 Indiana Sq Indianapolis IN 46204

CAPEHART, W. J., banker; b. Roxobel, N.C., 1897; m. Velma S. Caperhart; children—Mrs. William T. Bland, Jr., Charles R. Mem. adv. bd. First Nat. Bank at Orlando; chmn. emeritus South Orlando Nat. Bank; adv. mem. Central Brevard Nat. Bank, Cocoa, Fla. Mayor, City of Bay Lake; mem. bd. advisers Reedy Creek Improvement Dist. (Walt Disney World). Mem. adv. bd. Salvation Army. Mem. Greater Orlando C. of C. Club: University (Orlando). Home: 1354 Spring Lake Dr Orlando FL 32804

CAPEK, MILIC, educator, author: b. Trebechovice, Bohemia, Jan. 26, 1909; s. Josef and Elisabeth (Sebesta) C.; Ph.D., U. Prague, 1935; m. Stephanie Rezabek, June 24, 1947; 1 dau., Stella Milica. Came to U.S., 1941, naturalized, 1954. Instr. U. Ia., 1943-44, U. Neb., 1944-46; lectr. physics U. Olmutz (Czechoslovakia), 1946-47; asst. prof. to prof. philosophy Carleton Coll., 1948-62; prof. philosophy Boston U., 1962—. Distinguished vis. prof. U. Cal. at Davis, 1968-69. Mem. adv. bd. Masaryk Inst. of N.Y. Recipient Ford Found. grant, 1953-54. Mem. Am. Philos. Assn., Philos. Assn., Metaphys. Soc. Am. Author: The Philosophical Impact of Contemporary Physics, 2d edit., 1969. Mem. editorial bd. of Philos. Forum, 1967—, Process Studies, 1970—. Contbr. articles U.S. and fgn. profl. jours. Home: 143 Hobart St Hingham MA 02043 Office: 232 Bay State Rd Boston MA 02215

CAPEL, CHARLES EDWARD, educator, mathematician; b. Troy, N.Y., Dec. 26, 1922; s. Charles Edward and Frances (Albert) C.; A.B., N.Y. State Coll. Tchrs., Albany, 1947; M.A., U. Rochester, 1950; Ph.D., Tulane U., 1953; m. June Arlene Semple, Sept. 22, 1945; children—Janice Roberta, Gail Ann. Instr., Geneseo (N.Y.) State Tchrs. Coll., 1947-49; asst. prof. U. Miami (Fla.), 1953-58; mathematician Westinghouse Electric Corp., 1958-60; prof. math. Miami U., Oxford, O., 1960—, chmn. dept. math., 1960-63. Served with AUS, 1943-45. Mem. Am. Math. Soc., Math. Assn. Am., Am. Assn. U. Profs., Sigma Xi, Pi Mu Epsilon. Author math. articles, co-author textbook. Home: 5 Patrick Dr Oxford, OH 45056.

CAPELLE, HENRY THEODORE, natural gas co. exec.; b. Loyal, Wis., Sept. 10, 1917; s. Henry Edward and Emma Elizabeth (Helmke) C.; student Wis. State U., 1939-42; B.S. in Mining Engring., Mo. Sch. Mines, 1947; m. Marion Hulda Reineking, Dec. 25, 1942; children—Stephen Henry, Kathryn Jean, Helen Christine. With Shell Oil Co., 1947-69, engring. geologist, mgr., Wichita, Kan., Wichita Falls, Tex., Ardmore, Okla., Midland, Tex., Houston, 1947-66, regional mgr. Tex. and N.M. charge gas dept. and prodn., Houston, 1967-69, v.p. gen. mgr. Blue Dolphin Pipeline Co. div. Shell, Houston, 1966-69; sr. v.p. charge gas div. Coastal States Gas Producing Co., Corpus Christi, Tex., 1969-71, pres. subsidiaries Lovaca Gathering, S. Tex. Natural Gas Gathering, Tex. Southeastern Gas, 1971—, mem. exec. com., dir. parent co., 1971—; guest lectr. Shell Mgmt. Sch., Galveston, Tex., 1963-66. Chmn., regional forum on offshore gas handling, Natural Gas Processing Assn., 1966-67. Mem. long range planning com. City of Houston, 1966-67. Served to capt. USAF, 1942-46; PTO. Mem. Nat. Alliance of Bus. Men (jobs. mgr. Houston 1967-68), Am. Petroleum Inst. (v.p. electric logging div. 1952). Presbyn. (ruling elder 1962-64). Home: 5130 Cape Ann Corpus Christi TX 78412 Office: PO Drawer 521 Corpus Christi TX 78403

CAPENER, HAROLD R., educator. Prof. rural sociology Cornell U., Ithaca, N.Y. Address: 523 The Parkway Ithaca NY 14850*

CAPERS, CHARLOTTE, state ofcl.; b. Columbia, Tenn.; d. Walter B. and Louise (Woldridge) Capers; student Millsaps Coll., 1930-32, U. Colo., 1932; B.A., U. Miss., 1934. With Miss. Dept. Archives and History, 1938—, successively sec., research and editorial asst., asst. dir., 1938-55, dir., 1955-69, dir. spl. projects, 1969—; asst. editor Jour. Miss. History, 1942-43, asso. editor, 1943-55, State Times, 1955, Dixie Roto Mag., 1957; book revs. N.Y. Times Book Rev., various hist. jours. Chmn. Miss. Hist. Commn. Fellow Soc. Am. Archivists; mem. Jr. League Jackson, Miss. State Hist. Soc. (sec.-treas.), Am., So. hist. assns., Am. Assn. Museums. Episcopalian. Editor: (with William D. McCain) Papers of the Washington County Historical Society, 1954; editorial dir. Mississippi in the Confederacy, 1961; mem. adv. editorial bd. Jefferson Davis Papers, Rice U.; publs. com. Mississippi as a Province, Territory and State (J.F.H. Claiborne), 1964; contbg. editor The Delta Rev., 1966-70. Home: 1622 Poplar Blvd Jackson MS 39202 Office: Box 571 Jackson MS 39205

CAPERS, FRANCIS LEGRAND, drug co. exec.; b. Pueblo, Colo., May 31, 1914; s. Francis L. and Ethel (Davis) C.; A.B., Stanford, 1935; M.B.A., Harvard, 1937; m. Caretta Miles, Aug. 31, 1935; children—Francis LeGrand IV, Anne Elizabeth (Mrs. Donald Freiday), Catharine May (Mrs. Stephen Fairfield). With Arthur Andersen & Co., Chgo., 1937; trainee, accountant, buyer, sales mgr., div. mgr., v.p. and nat. sales mgr. McKesson & Robbins, Inc., 1938-60; v.p. planning and devel. Norcliff Labs., 1961-67; pres. McKesson & Robbins Drug Co., N.Y.C., 1967—; exec. v.p., dir. Foremost-McKesson, Inc. Served with USNR, 1943-45. Mem. Nat. Wholesale Druggists Assn. (pres. 1970-71), Sigma Nu. Clubs: New

York Yacht; Cruising of America; Riverside Yacht. Home: Twin Lakes Lane Riverside, CT 06878. Office: 155 E 44th St New York City NY 10017

CAPERS, GERALD MORTIMER, Jr., educator; b. New Orleans, May 30, 1909; s. Gerald Mortimer and Vivia (Deane) C.; B.A., Southwestern Coll., 1930; Ph.D., Yale, 1936; m. Roberta Alford, Dec. 27, 1962. Tchr. math. Fairview Jr. High Sch., Memphis, 1930-32; instr. history Yale, 1936-40; faculty mem. Tulane U., 1940—, chmn. history dept. Sophie Newcomb Coll., 1941—, prof. history, 1948—. Served from 2d lt. to capt., USAAF, 1942-45. Recipient Engleston prize Yale, 1936; Guggenheim fellow, 1959-60. Fellow Am. Council Learned Socs.; mem. Am., So., hist. assns., Orgn. Am. Historians, Phi Beta Kappa, Omicron Delta Kappa. Author: Biography of a Rivertown, 1939; Stephen A. Douglas, Defender of the Union, 1959; John C. Calhoun, Opportunist, 1960; Occupied City, New Orleans Under the Federals, 1862-1865, 1965; also articles in hist. jours., Ency. Americana, Ency. Brit. Home: 244 Vinet St New Orleans LA 70121

CAPLAN, FRED HARRY, state justice; b. Clarksburg, W.Va., Dec. 3, 1914; s. Henry A. and Hannah (Siegelman) C.; A.B., W.Va. U., 1939; LL.B., U. Richmond, 1941, LL.D., 1971; m. Miriam Kessler, Nov. 12, 1941; 1 dau., Betty Lee. Admitted to W.Va. bar, 1941; practiced in Clarksburg, 1946-53; asst. atty. gen. W.Va., 1953- 61; chmn. Pub. Service Commn. W.Va., 1961-62; judge Supreme Ct. Appeals W. Va., 1962—, pres. Supreme Ct. Appeals W.Va., 1966, 71. Mem. W.Va. Legislature from Harrison County, 1949-53. Served with AUS, 1941-46; PTO. Mem. Am., W.Va., Harrison County bar assns., W.Va. State Bar, W.Va. Jud. Assn. Democrat. Jewish religion. Mem. B'nai B'rith. Home: 4218 Noyes Av SE Charleston WV 25304 Office: WVa Supreme Court Appeals Charleston WV 25305

CAPLAN, GERALD, psychiatrist, educator; b. Liverpoool, Eng., Mar. 6, 1917; s. David and Sophia (Zassman) C.; B.S.C., U. Manchester, Eng., 1937, M.B., Ch.B., 1940, M.D., 1945; D.P.M., Royal Coll. Physicians and Surgeons, London, 1942; m. Ann Siebenberg, Mar. 29, 1942; 1 dau., Ruth. Came to U.S., 1952, naturalized, 1958. Asst. med. officer Birmingham Mental Hosp., 1940-43; dep. med. supt. Swansea Mental Hosp., 1943-45; psychiatrist Tavistock Clinic Adult Dept., Eng., 1945-48; adviser in psychiatry Ministry Health, Israel, 1948-49; psychiat. dir. Lasker Mental Hygiene and Child Guidance Center of Hadassah, Jerusalem, 1949-52; asso. prof. mental health, head community mental health program Harvard Sch. Pub. Health, 1954-64, dir. lab. of community psychiatry dept. psychiatry Harvard Med. Sch., 1964—, clin. prof. psychiatry, 1964-70, prof. psychiatry, 1970—; chmn. Mass. Adv. Council on Mental Health and Retardation, 1968—. Sr. psychiat. cons. U.S. Peace Corps, 1961, Office Econ. Opportunity, 1967. Trustee, Law and Soc. Assn. Fellow Am. Pub. Health Assn., Am. Psychiat. Assn., Am. Orthopsychiatric Assn., Am. Coll. Psychiatrists; mem. Internat. Assn. for Child Psychiatry and Allied Professions (hon. pres.), Royal Soc. Medicine, Royal Medico-Psychol. Assn., Delta Omega. Author: An Approach to Community Mental Health, 1961; Principles of Preventive Psychiatry, 1964; Adolescence: Psychosocial Perspectives, 1969; (with Ruth B. Caplan) Psychiatry and the Community in Nineteenth Century America, 1969; Theory and Practice of Mental Heath Consultation, 1970. Editor: Emotional Problems of Early Childhood, 1955; Prevention of Mental Disorders in Children: Initial Explorations, 1961. Home: 93 Fresh Pond Pkwy Cambridge MA 02138 Office: 58 Fenwood Rd Boston MA 02115

CAPLAN, HARRY, univ. prof.; b. Hoag's Corners, N.Y., Jan. 7, 1896; s. Jacob and Sarah (Tolehin) C.; A.B., Cornell U., 1916, A.M., 1917, Ph.D., 1921; Litt.D., Wesleyan U., 1967. Grad. scholar in archeology and comparative philology, Cornell U., 1916-17, grad. fellow in Latin and Greek, 1917-18; instr. pub. speaking, Cornell U., 1919-23, in classics, 1924-25, asst. prof. classics, 1925-30, prof. classics, 1930-67, chmn. dept., 1929- 46, Goldwin Smith prof. classical langs. and lit. 1941-67, emeritus, 1967—. Vis. prof., summers, U. Wis., 1925, U. Mich., 1932, Northwestern U., 1938, Stanford, 1942, 48, U. Chgo., 1945, Columbia, 1946; fellow Center for Advanced Studies, Wesleyan U., 1962-63, 64; Andrew Mellon vis. prof. U. Pitts., 1967-68; Walker Ames vis. prof. U. Wash., 1968; Ziskind vis. prof. Brandeis U., 1968-69; vis. prof. U. Minn., 1969, Stanford, 1969, U. Ill., 1970-71; asst. editor Quar. Jour. Speech, 1923; joint editor Cornell Studies in Classical Philology. Served with U.S. Army during World War, 1918-19. Fellow Mediaeval Acad. Am.; mem. Am. Philol. Assn. (pres. 1955), Speech Assn. Am., Renaissance Soc. of Am., Modern Lang. Assn. Am., Linguistic Soc. Am., Am. Assn. U. Profs., Classical Assn. of Eng. and Wales, Phi Beta Kappa, Phi Eta Sigma, Delta Sigma Rho, Phi Delta Kappa, Phi Kappa Phi. Fellow John Simon Guggenheim Meml. Found., 1928-29 (studying medieval rhetoric in libraries of Europe), also 1956. Jewish religion. Author and editor: Gianfrancesco Pico della Mirandola On the Imagination, 1930; Mediaeval Artes Praedicandi, 1934; Medieval Arts praedicandi—A supplementary Hand-List, 1936; Rhetorica ad Herennium, 1954; (with H. H. King) Pulpit Eloquence-English, 1955; Pulpit Eloquence-German, 1956; Of Eloquence (edited by Anne King and Helen North), 1970. Contbr. articles and revs. in fields of classical and medieval lit. Home: East Greenbush NY 12061 Office: 121 Goldwin Smith Hall Ithaca NY 14850

CAPLAN, HOWARD, lawyer; b. Balt., Aug. 16, 1904; s. Henry A. and Hannah (Seigeltman) C.; LL.B., W.Va. U., 1928. Admitted to W.Va. bar, 1928, since practiced in Clarksburg; mem. Caplan and Caplan; dist. counsel, asst. state counsel and state counsel Home Owners Loan Corp., W.Va. agy., 1933- 38; city atty. Clarksburg, 1938-39; asst. U.S. atty., 1939-42, 46- 51; U.S. atty. No. Dist. W.Va., 1951-54; mem. Stotler, McReynolds & Caplan, 1954-60, McReynolds & Caplan, 1960—. Pres. Harrison County Soc. for Crippled Children, 1960, now mem. bd. dirs. Served with AUS, 1942-46. Fellow Am. Coll. Trial Lawyers; mem. Am., W.Va., Harrison County (pres. 1958) bar assns., W.Va. State Bar (bd. govs. 1960-64, pres. 1965), Am. Legion, Pi Lambda Phi. Elk; mem. B'nai B'rith; Kiwanian. Home: 225 N Chestnut St Clarksburg WV 26301 Office: Goff Bldg Clarksburg WV 26301

CAPLAN, LOUIS, lawyer; b. Sept. 15, 1886; s. David and Rachel C.; LL.B., U. Pitts., 1912, LL.D., 1966. Admitted to Pa. bar, 1912, since practiced in Pitts.; mem. firm Sachs & Caplan, 1919-45. Dir. May, Stern & Co., Comml. Bank & Trust Co., (Pitts.), Ruben Furniture Co., McKeesport, Pa. Bd. dirs. Chatham Center, Action Housing Pitts.; pres., bd. dirs. Louis J. and Mary E. Horowitz Found.; bd. govs. (hon.) Hebrew Union Coll.-Jewish Inst. Religion, Cin.; trustee Pitts. United Jewish Fedn., Assn. Improvement poor, Leon Falk Family Trust, Lehman- Epstine Trust, Halpern Found. Past pres., hon. pres. J.M. Gusky Hebrew Orphanage and Home of Western Pa.; past nat. v.p., chmn. exec. bd. Am. Jewish Com., pres., 1961-62, hon. pres., 1962—. Served as 1st lt., Q.M.C., U.S. Army, 1918-19; alien enemy hearing officer, World War II. Recipient award Nat. Conf. Christians and Jews, 1953; Louis Caplan Human Relations award given annually by Pitts. chpt. Am. Jewish Com.; Louis Caplan lectures in law established in his honor U. Pitts. Law Sch.; Louis Caplan vis. lectureship Jewish law founded in his honor Hebrew Union Coll.-Jewish Inst. Religion; named Man of Year, Jewish War Vets. Post 49, Pitts., 1961. Mem. Am., Pa., Allegheny County (pres. 1954) bar assns., 3d Circuit Fed. Jud. Conf., Am. Law Inst. Home: 3955 Bigelow Blvd Pittsburgh PA 15213 Office: Grant Bldg Pittsburgh PA 15219

CAPLENOR, DONALD, univ. dean, botanist; b. Smith County, Tenn., Feb. 10, 1922; s. John W. and Daisy (Purnell) C.; student Cumberland U., 1943-44; B.S. in Biology, George Peabody Coll. Tchrs., 1948, M.A., 1949; Ph.D., Vanderbilt U., 1954; summer student U. Chgo., 1959-60, Cal. Inst. Tech., 1961; m. Sue Cooksey, June 9, 1946; children—Deborah Kay (Mrs. Lanny D. Glick), Terry Michael, Donna Sue. Instr. biology George Peabody Coll. Tchrs., 1949-51, Vanderbilt U., 1951-53; asso. prof. biology, chmn. dept. Ga. Tchrs. Coll., 1953-55; asso. prof. George Peabody Tchrs. Coll., 1955-57, prof., chmn. div. sci. and math., 1963- 66; prof. biology, chmn. dept. Millsaps Coll., 1957-63; dean Coll. Arts and Sci., prof. biology Tenn. Tech. U., 1966-70; dean faculty, prof. biology U. Ala., Huntsville, 1970—; biologist USPHS, summer 1957. NSF sci. faculty fellow, summers 1959-61. Mem. Tenn. Acad. Scis. (sec. 1955- 57, editor jour. 1965-70), Ecol. Soc. Am., Bot. Soc. Am., Assn. Southeastern Biologists, Sigma Xi, Beta Beta Beta, Alpha Epsilon Delta, Omicron Delta Kappa. Contbr. profl. jours. Home: 9107 Camille Dr SE Huntsville AL 35802

CAPLES, JAMES STEPHEN, architect; b. Ft. Leavenworth, Kan., July 12, 1911; s. William Goff and Alice Keller (Thomas) C.; A.R., Vienna Technicale Sch., 1935; B.F.A., Yale, 1938; postgrad. Armed Forces Staff Coll., 1948; diploma Indsl. Coll. Armed Forces, 1957; m. Barbara Gunning Barrett, June 29, 1940; children—Cynthia Barrett, Sara Elizabeth. Archtl. desinger J.H. Lapish/Roberts & Schaeffer, Washington, 1938-41; commd. 2d lt. USAF, 1940, advanced through grades to 1st lt., 1941, capt., 1942, maj., 1942, lt. col., 1943, col., 1951; co. officer 121st Engr. Regt., 1941; staff officer Engring. Hdqrs., Washington, 1942; dep. engr. for air 14th Brit. Army/RAF, Burma, 1942-45; engr. Caribbean Air Command, Panama, 1946-48; engr. Eastern Air Def. Force, Newburgh, N.Y., 1951-53; engr. 5th Air Force, Korea, 1953; dep. engr. Air Def. Command, Colorado Springs, Colo., 1954-56; regional civil engr. Missouri River Region, Omaha, 1957-60; chief constrn. Allied Air Forces, Central Europe, Fountainebleau, France, 1960-63; chief engring. div. Hdqrs., Washington, 1963-66; ret., 1966; project architect, sr. asso. Perkins & Will Architects, Washington, 1966—. Decorated Legion of Merit (U.S.); Order Brit. Empire; Order of Cloud Banner (China). Mem. A.I.A., Nat. Soc. Profl. Engrs., Iktinos, Beta Theta Pi. Episcopalian. Club: Army-Navy (Washington). Prin. archtl. works include design and constrn. over 100 air bases, constrn. surveillance 1st 9 Atlas ICBM squadrons, 1st TITAN wings, 1st Minuteman wing, 1957-60, internat. constrn. allied missile belt Central Europe, 1960-63; project architect Duke Med. Center, 1966-71. Home: 1111 Roan Lane Alexandria VA 22202 Office: 1828 L St NW Washington DC 20036

CAPLES, JOHN, advt. exec.; b. N.Y.C., May 1, 1900; s. Byron H. and Edith Jessie (Richards C.; student Columbia, 1918-19; B.S., U.S. Naval Acad., 1924; m. Mabel Veronica Watson, June 12, 1931 (dec. 1956). With engring. dept. N.Y. Telephone Co., 1924-25; advt. writer Ruthrauff & Ryan, Inc., 1925- 27; writer, exec. Batten, Barton, Durstine & Osborn, Inc., 1927-41, v.p., 1941—; tchr. advt. Grad. Sch. Bus. Columbia, 1952-53; mem. guiding faculty Famous Writers Sch., Westport, Conn., 1958—. Mem. council of judges Advt. Hall of Fame, 1970. Mem. nat. adv. council Episcopal Ch. Found., 1968; mem. pub. relations com. Nat. Multiple Sclerosis Soc., 1969. Served as seaman USNRF, 1918; from lt. comdr. to comdr., USNR, 1942-45. Recipient Ann. award Nat. Assn. Direct Mail Writers, 1969. Mem. Assn. Direct Mktg. Agys. (adv. council 1971—), Market Research Council N.Y., Copy Research Council N.Y., Jury Ann. Advt. Awards, Naval Acad. Assn., Alpha Delta Sigma. Episcopalian. Club: University of N.Y. Author: Tested Advertising Methods, 1932, rev. 1961; Advertising for Immediate Sales, 1936; Advertising Ideas, 1938; Making Ads Pay, 1957; co-author: Copy Testing, 1939. Author two advertisements included in book The 100 Greatest Advertisements, 1950. Contbr. to The Advertising Handbook, 1950, Saturday Rev., various advt. trade jours. Home: 35 Park Av New York City NY 10016 Office: 383 Madison Av New York City NY 10017

CAPLES, WILLIAM GOFF, coll. pres.; b. Pitts., Oct. 4, 1909; s. William Goff and Alice Keller (Thomas) C.; Ph.B., Kenyon Coll., 1930, LL.D., 1961; J.D., Northwestern U., 1933; LL.D., Loyola U., 1969; m. Julia D. Pringle, Oct. 3, 1936; 1 dau., Pamela Gunning (Mrs. Gilbert V. Wilkes); m. 2d, Jean Coburn Dunbar, Dec. 1, 1945; children—William Goff, Cynthia Keller. Admitted to Ill. bar, 1933, practiced in Chgo., 1933-38; gen. atty. Continental Casualty Co., v.p. Nat. Casualty Co., 1938-42; mgr. indsl. relations Inland Steel Co., 1946-50, v.p., 1953-68; pres., dir. Inland Steel Container Co., 1950-53; pres. Kenyon Coll., Gambler, O., 1968—. Dir. First-Knox Nat. Bank, Mt. Vernon, O. Adv. council Sch. Indsl. and Labor Relations Cornell U., 1960; mem. City Chgo. Bd. Edn., pres. 1961; mem. Nat. Adv. Com. Manpower Devel. and Tng. Act, 1962—; mem. Pres.'s Adv. Com. Labor-Mgmt. Policy; mem. adv. com. civilian personnel mgmt. Dept. Army. Served to lt. col. C.E., AUS, 1942-46 Pres., bd. dirs. United Charities, Chgo.; trustee Kenyon Coll. Mem. Better Govt. Assn., Indsl. Relations Assn. Chgo. (pres. 1951-52), Am. Mgmt. Assn., N.A.M. (v.p. 1954-61), Am. Iron and Steel Inst. (chmn. com. indsl. relations 1960-63, Am. Arbitration Assn. (dir.), Phi Beta Kappa. Clubs: University, Tavern, Commonwealth, Commercial (Chgo.); Union (Cleve.). Address: Gambier OH 43022

CAPLICE, WILLIAM FRANCIS, newspaper co. exec.; b. Chgo., Mar. 24, 1923; s. Michael J. and Irene (Murphy) C.; B.S., DePaul U., 1945, J.D., 1947; m. Jeanne M. McCurdy, Jan. 14, 1950; children—Mary Beth, William, James, Thomas, Daniel, Robert, John, Michael, Timothy. Admitted to Ill. bar, 1948; agt. Internal Revenue Service, Chgo., 1949-52; accountant Arthur Anderson & Co., 1952-55; asst. sec, gen. counsel Am. Linen Supply Co., 1955-59; sec.-asst. treas. Tribune Co., Chgo., 1959—. Commr., Westchester Park Bd., 1970—. Trustee DePaul U. Served with AUS, 1942-44. C.P.A., Ill. Mem. Chgo. Bar Assn., Ill. Soc. C.P.A.'s, Chgo. Tax Club, Financial Execs. Inst. Home: 1509 Hull Av Westchester IL 60153 Office: 435 N Michigan Av Chicago IL 60611

CAPLIN, MORTIMER MAXWELL, lawyer; b. N.Y.C., July 11, 1916; s. Daniel and Lillian (Epstein) C.; B.S., U. Va., 1937, LL.B., 1940; J.S.D., N.Y.U., 1953; LL.D., St. Michael's Coll., 1964; m. Ruth Sacks, Oct. 18, 1942; children—Lee, Mary Ellen, Michael, Jeremy, Catherine. Admitted to bar Va., 1941, N.Y. State bar, 1942, D.C. bar, 1964; law clk. to judge U.S. Ct. Appeals, 1940-41; with firm Paul, Weiss, Rifkind, Wharton & Garrison, N.Y.C., 1941-50; prof. law U. Va., 1950-61; counsel firm Perkins, Battle & Minor, Charlottesville, Va., 1952-61; U.S. commr. internal revenue Treasury Dept., 1961-64; partner firm Caplin and Drysdale, Washington, 1964—. Vis. prof. law U. Va., 1964—. Bd. dirs., chmn. finance com. Prentice-Hall, Inc.; dir. Variable Annuity Life Ins. Co., Peoples Drug Stores, Inc., Standard Prudential Corp., Gulf States Land and Industries, Pueblo Internat., Inc. Bd. dirs., pres. Nat. Civil Service League; bd. dirs. People-to-People Sports Com., Council on Founds., Inc., Airlie Found.; trustee George Washington U.; overseer Coll. of V.I. Served to lt. USNR, 1942-45; ETO. Recipient Army Distinguished Unit award 7th USN Beach Bn., France, D-Day; award coms. taxation Va. Bar Assn. and Va. Soc. C.P.A.'s; Alexander Hamilton award U.S. Dept. Treas.; Learned Hand Human Relations award; Distinguished Service award Tax Execs. Inst., Achievement award Tax Soc. of N.Y. U. Mem. Am., Fed., D.C., N.Y. State, Va. bar assns., Bar Assn. D.C. Am. Law Inst., Nat. Tax Assn., Order of Coif, Raven Soc., Phi Beta Kappa, Omicron Delta Kappa. Author and lectr. tax and corp. matters. Editor-in-chief Va. Law Rev., 1939-40. Home: 4536 29th St NW Washington DC 20008 Office: 1101 17th St NW Washington DC 20036

CAPLOW, THEODORE, educator, sociologist; b. N.Y.C., May 1, 1920; s. Samuel Nathaniel and Florence (Israel) C.; A.B., U. Chgo., 1939; M.A., U. Minn., 1941, Ph.D., 1946; m. Christine Allen. Mem. faculty U. Minn., 1940-60; prof. sociology Columbia, 1961-70; prof., chmn. sociology and anthropology U. Va., Charlottesville, 1970—; vis. prof. U. Bordeaux (France), 1950, U. Aix-Marseille (France), 1951, U. Utrecht (Netherlands), 1954-55, Stanford, 1957, U. Bogota (Colombia), 1962, Sorbonne, Paris, France, 1968-69. Pres. Mendota Research Group Inc., 1957-65. Served with AUS, 1943-45; PTO. Decorated Purple Heart. Clubs: Keswick Hunt (Charlottesville); Tarratine (Dark Harbor, Me.). Author: Sociology of Work, 1954; The Academic Marketplace, 1957; Principles of Organization, 1964; Two Against One, 1968; L'Enquete Sociologique, 1970; Elementary Sociology, 1971. Home: Rivanna Farm Charlottesville VA 22901

CAPOBIANCO, TITO, opera dir.; b. La Plata, Argentina, Aug. 28, 1931; s. Donato and Felicia (Basciano) C.; student Law and Philosophy Sch., Argentina; m. Elena Denda, Dec. 26, 1955; children—Danilo, Renato. Dir. N.Y.C. Opera, Deutch Opern Berlin, Hamburg Opera, San Francisco Opera Co., Teatro Colon, Argentina; artistic dir. Channel 9 Television, Argentina; dir. Mexico Internat. Opera Festival, Nat. Council Arts in Argentina, Kennedy Center, Washington, Chile Opera Season, Acad. Vocal Arts, Phila., dir., founder Am. Opera Center, Juilliard Sch., N.Y.C. Gen. dir. Phila. Mus. Acad. Producer: Julius Caesar, Mephistophele, Manon, Don Rodrigo Bomarzo, Roberto Deverreux, Lucia de Lamermoor, Tales of Hoffman, Love for Three Oranges, Salome, Tannhauser, Meistersingers, Ariodante. Office: care Peter Witt 37 W 57th New York City NY 10019

CAPOGROSSI, GIUSEPPE, painter; b. Rome, Italy, Mar. 7, 1900; s. Gugliemo Capogrossi Guarna and Beatrice Tacchi Venturi; classical diploma, Inst. Massimo, Rome, 1917; M.A. in Jurisprudence, U. Rome, 1921; m. Costanza Mennyey, June 2, 1959; children—Beatrice, Olga, Engaged in painting, 1921—; a founder Roman Sch., 1932, Origine Group, 1950; prin. works in abstractionism, 1949—; pvt. shows include Rome, 1950, 64, 68, 69, Milan, 1951, 68, Venice, 1952, 54, 62-66, Florence, 1952, Paris, 1956, 61, London, 1957, N.Y.C., 1958, Berlin, 1967; Brussels, 1959; Tokyo, 1963, others throughout Europe; Frankfort, N.Y.C., Paris, Berlin, London, Lausanne, Brussels, group shows include N.Y.C., 1954, 55, 57, 58, 60-62, 63, 68; San Francisco, 1954, 59; Sao Paulo, Brazil, 1955, 58; London, 1956, 57, 64; Paris, 1956, 60-62, 63; Los Angeles, 1956; Milan, 1956, 57, 58, 59, 60-62, 63, 65-66, 67, 69-70; numerous others throughout the world. Recipient 1st certificate, Kassel, 1955, 2d certificate, 1959, Prix Einaudialla XXVII biennale di Venezia, 1954, Prix Bari, 1957, le premier prix XXXI biennale di Venezia, 1962, prix d'Honneur alla VIII biennale internazionale di Lubiana. Author: (monographs) Michel Seuphor, 1954; Michel Tapié, 1962; G.C. Argan- Capogrossi, 1968. Home: Viale Marco Polo Rome 80 Italy Office: Via Le Marco Polo 80 00154 Rome Italy

CAPOLINO, JOHN JOSEPH, artist, art dir.; b. Phila., Feb. 22, 1896; s. Francis and Maria (di Nucci) C.; student Pa. Acad. Fine Arts, 1915-20; studied in Eng., France and Italy; m. Gertrude Rowan, June 13, 1928; 1 dau., Ann; m. 2d, Ila Junod, Dec. 26, 1959; children—John Joseph, Maria Francesca. Represented with many murals and pictures in bldgs. and instns. including 1st Regt. Armory, Phila., Truxton Decatur Mus., Washington, Naval War Coll., Newport, R.I., Marine Corps Sch., Quantico, Va., Children's Hosp., Phila., Loyola Coll. at Balt., Farragut Acad., U.S. Banknote Co., State Capitol Del., U. Del., Phila. City Hall, U.S. Senate and House Armed Forces Com. Rooms, Washington, also numerous mil. camps and installations, also U.S. Marine Corps Bldg., Phila.; A.I.A.; Circolo Italiano, Phila.; USMC Hdqrs., Washington; Friends Central Sch., Overbrook, Phila.; Jenks Sch., Chestnut Hill, Pa., Century of Progress, Chgo.; Municipal Ct. Bldg., Phila.; decorations Bur. of Aeros. and Navy Bldg., Washington; USMC Q.M. Depot, San Francisco; portraits for Milton B. Medery, Jr., A.I.A., Judge Thomas D. Finletter, Phila., Nathan Hayward, Franklin Ins. (Phila.); also others of Marine Corps officers, Spring Garden Inst., Phila.; dir. Chestnut Hill (Pa.) Art Center; curator Woodmere Art Gallery, Chestnut Hill; designed New Marine Corps standard. Recipient two traveling scholarships, 1917-18, Toppan prize, 1918, Edward T. Stotesbury prize, 1924 (all Pa. Acad. Fine Arts); gold medal Spring Garden Inst.; gold medal Sesqui-Centennial Expn., Phila., 1926; Best poster award Phila. Printing Industries, Inc.; commd. 1st lt. USMC Res. for marine corps decorations exhibited at Sesqui-Centennial, Phila., also Century of Progress, Chgo. Fellow Pa. Acad. Fine Arts; mem. Phila. Water Color Club, Franklin Inst., Mil. Order World Wars, Marine Corps League. Roman Catholic. Clubs: Philadelphia Cricket, Officers. Home: 8510 Navahoe St Chestnut Hill Philadelphia PA 19118

CAPON, FRANK SAMUEL, retired mfg. co. exec.; b. Romford, Eng., Dec. 15, 1915; s. Frank C. and Lillian (Apps) C.; grad. Royal Liberty Sch., Romford, 1930; m. Marjorie O'Connell, Apr. 27, 1940; children—Gail Frances, Susan Mary. With firm Riddell, Stead, Graham and Hutchison, chartered accountants, Montreal, Can., 1930-38; with Canadian Industries Ltd., 1938-54, treas., 1949-54; sec., treas. Du Pont of Can. Ltd., Montreal, 1954-57, treas., 1957-60, v.p., 1960-69, v.p. corporate planning, 1969-70, dir. Loomis-Sayles Canadian and Internat. Fund Ltd., Dennison Mfg. Co. of Can. Ltd. Chartered accountant Can., 1938. Mem. Financial Execs. Inst. (pres. 1960-61, chmn. bd. 1961-62), Canadian Inst. Chartered Accountants (1st v.p. 1970-71). Home: 2 Westmount Sq Montreal 216 Quebec Canada Office: 630 Dorchester Blvd W Montreal Quebec Canada

CAPONE, ALPHONSE WILLIAM, indsl. exec.; b. Pitts., Oct. 22, 1919; s. Aniello and Mary (Manzione) C.; B.B.A., Duquesne U., 1942; postgrad. Harvard, 1959, Am. U. Sch. Internat. Service, Washington, 1965, Brookings Instn., 1966; m. Eleanor M. Polis, Aug. 16, 1947; 1 dau., Margaret Ellen. With Koppers Co., Inc., Pitts., 1946—, mgr. finance dept. internat. operations, 1964-67, asst. treas., 1958-67, v.p., chief financial officer, treas., 1967—; v.p., dir. Buffalo Gravel Corp., Buffalo Slag Co., Inc., Crestrock N.Y., Inc., Eastern Rock Products, Inc., Erie Sand S.S. Co., Erie Sand & Gravel Co., Gen. Crushed Stone Co., Swanson Lumber Co., Ltd., U.S. Plastic & Chem. Corp.; Dir. L'Industriale Koppers, S.p.A., Internat. Cons. Services, Inc., Koppers Constrn. (Venezuela) S.A., Koppers (Far East), Inc., Koppers Interam. Co., Koppers Internat. (Australia), Ltd., Koppers Internat., C.A., Koppers of Can., Ltd., Koppers, Ltd., Koppers Products, Ltd., Koppers of Turkey, Inc., Koppers de Venezuela, C.A., Mfrs. Leasing Corp. Served to lt. USNR, 1943- 46. Mem. Am., Pa. insts. C.P.A.'s, Financial Execs. Inst., Pitts. C. of C., World Affairs Council Pitts., Duquesne U. Alumni Assn. (pres., gov.), Harvard Advanced Mgmt. Assn., Harvard Bus. Sch. Assn. Pitts., Pa. Soc. Clubs: Duquesne, St.

Clair Country; University, Cornell (N.Y.C.). Home: 1703 Hastings Mill Rd Pittsburgh PA 15241 Office: Koppers Bldg Pittsburgh PA 15219

CAPONIGRI, ALOYSIUS ROBERT, educator; b. Chgo., Nov. 16, 1915; s. Nicholas and Lucia (Sorrocco) C.; A.B., Loyola U., Chgo., 1935, M.A., 1936; student Harvard Grad. Sch., 1937-39; Ph.D., U. Chgo., 1942; m. Winifred Phyllis Franco, Oct. 6, 1946; children—Victoria Marie, Robert John, Lisa Marie, Instr., State U. Ia., 1943-46; mem. faculty U. Notre Dame, 1946—, prof. philosophy, 1956—; lectr. Inst. Luigi Sturzo, Rome, 1961; distinguished vis. prof. Loyola U., Chgo., 1963; vis. lectr. U. Padova, Bologna, spring 1964, 68, 71; vis. lectr. Genoa, Milan, also Luigi Sturzo Inst., Rome, 1964, 65; vis. prof. philosophy U. Madrid (Spain), 1964-65; mem. editorial bd. U. Notre Dame Press, also mem. univ. Grad. Council. Sec.-treas. Assos. Philos. Inquiry; mem. nat. selection bd. Fulbright Program, 1958-60. Fulbright fellow, 1950-51; Rockefeller fellow, 1953; grantee Am. Philos. Soc., 1960, Am. Council Learned Socs., 1963. Mem. Am., Am. Cath. philos. assns., Metaphysics. Soc. Am., Cath. Commn. Cultural and Intellectual Affairs, Instituto Luigi Sturzo Roma (corr.). Author: Time and Idea, 1953; History and liberty, 1955; History of Western Philosophy, 5 vols. 1964-70. Editor: Modern Catholic Thinkers, 1960; Masterpieces of Catholic Literature, 2 vols., 1964; Contemporary Spanish Philosophy, 1967. Translator: Major Trends in Mexican Philosophy, 1966. Home: 317 E Napoleon Blvd South Bend IN 46617

CAPOTE, TRUMAN, author; b. New Orleans, Sept. 30, 1924; s. Joseph G. and Nina (Faulk) C.; ed. Trinity Sch., St. John's Acad. (N.Y.), pub. schs. of Greenwich, Conn. Writer from early years. Mem. Nat. Inst. Arts. and Letters. Recipient O. Henry Meml. award for short story, 1946, 48, 51; creative writing award Nat. Inst. Arts and Letters, 1959. Author: Other Voices. Other Rooms, 1948; Tree of Night (short stories), 1949; Observations, 1949; Local Color, 1950; The Grass Harp, 1953; The Muses Are Heard, 1956; Breakfast at Tiffany's, 1958; Selected Writings, 1963; In Cold Blood (Book-of-Month Club selection), 1965; A Christmas Memory, 1966; (with H. Arlen) House of Flowers, 1968; Thanksgiving Visitor, 1969. Contbr. short stories, non-fiction, nat. mags. Home: Wainscott NY 11975 Office: care Random House 457 Madison Av New York City NY 10022

CAPOUYA, EMILE, author From Rebellion to Responsibility, 1965; contbg. editor Sat. Rev. Address: 380 Madison Av New York City NY 10017.

CAPP, AL, cartoonist, columnist; b. New Haven, Sept. 28, 1909; s. Otto and Matilda (Davidson) C.; student Pa. Acad. Fine Arts, Museum Fine Arts, Boston; m. Catherine Wingate Cameron; children—Julie Ann (Mrs. Julian Cairol), Catherine Jane (Mrs. Michael Pierce), Colin C. Author Comic strip Li'l Abner, also columnist N.Y. Daily News Syndicate; daily syndicated radio-TV commentator. Address: Capp Enterprises 122 Beacon St Boston MA 02116

CAPP, GLENN RICHARD, educator; b. Westminster, Tex., Sept. 21, 1910; s. Cal W. and Margaret Angeline (Middlebrooks) C.; A.B., Okla. Baptist U., 1933, LL.D., 1965; J.D., Baylor U., 1938; A.M., Northwestern U., 1948; m. Thelma Robuck, May 25, 1940; 1 son, Glenn Richard. Dir. forensics Okla. Baptist U., 1933-34; instr. Baylor U., 1934-38, asst. prof., 1938-42, asso. prof., 1942-48, prof., 1948-49, prof. speech, chmn. speech dept., 1949—, now chmn. dept. oral communication. Served to capt. USAAF, 1942-46. Mem. Am. Assn. U. Profs., Speech Communication Assn. Am. (chmn. nat. questions com.), So. Speech Assn. (pres. 1949-50, v.p. 1937-42, 48), Tex. Poetry Assn., Tex. Speech Assn., Am. Forensic League, Eugene Field Soc., Waco Jr. C. of C., Pi Kappa Delta (nat. pres. 1942). Baptist (sch. tchr.). Author: Practical Debating (with Courtney, L. W.), 1949; How To Communicate Orally, rev. edit., 1966; Famous Speeches in American History, 1963; (with Thelma Robuck Capp) Principles of Argumentation, 1965; The Great Society: A Sourcebook of Speeches, 1967; Basic Oral Communication, 1971; Student Guide to Communication, 1971; five handbooks on debating for high sch. students. Home: 3000 Cumberland Av Waco TX 76707

CAPP, MARTIN PHILIP, coll. dean; b. Boulder, Colo., Aug. 5, 1912; s. Martin Philip and Susie Belle (Hannah) C.; B.S. in Archtl. Engring. cum laude, U. Colo., 1935, M.S. in Civil Engring., 1936; m. Beryl Almyra Bentson, June 16, 1937; children—Maryl Susann (Mrs. Jack D. Waggoner), Martin Philip, Jennifer Beryl (Mrs. Philip M. Groves). Chief draftsman Denver Builders, Inc., 1935-38; instr., then asst. prof. civil engring. Colo. Sch. Mines, 1938-46; asso. prof., then prof. head dept. civil engring. U. Denver, 1946-53; faculty San Diego State Coll., 1953—, chmn. div. engring., 1958-61, dean Sch. Engring., 1961—. Field rep. engring. war tng. program U.S. Office Edn., 1944-45; prin. field engr. Bur. Reclamation, Dept. Interior, 1945-46; chief engr., prin. partner Bond Engring. Co., Denver, 1949-53; engring. examiner civil service dept. City of San Diego, 1958-60. Mem. Am. Soc. Engring. Edn. (council 1950-52), Am. Inst. Indsl. Engrs. (Achievement award 1959), Tau Beta Pi, Omicron Delta Kappa; Sigma Tau, Theta Chi, Chi Epsilon. Episcopalian (past vestryman). Rotarian. Clubs: Teknik (Denver); University (San Diego). Home: 4561 Seminole Dr San Diego CA 92115

CAPPIELLO, TONY, advt. exec.; b. Bklyn., Aug. 17, 1932; s. Anthony J. and Sophie (Inserillo) C.; grad. N.Y. Sch. Art and Design, 1950; A.A.S. in Advt. Design, Pratt Inst., 1960; m. Marilyn Rotoli, Feb. 21, 1954; children—Douglas Anthony, Jeanne Marie. With Maxon Inc., 1950-53, St. Georges & Keyes, 1956-58, Popular Sci. Pub. Co., 1958-61, Marsteller Inc., 1961-63; exec. v.p., prin. treas. Ries Cappiello Colwell, N.Y.C., 1963—, also dir.; dir. Ries Cappiello Colwell Profit Sharing Plan, Visual Verbal Inc.; asso. dir., instr. Visual-Verbal Workshop, 1967—. Served with AUS, 1953-55. Recipient awards advt. N.Y. Art Dirs. Club, N.J. Art Dirs. Club, Direct Mail Advt. Assn., Advt. Club N.Y., Andy awards, Comml. Art mag. awards. Mem. Art Dirs. Club N.Y. (co-chmn. awards com. 1968-69), Am. Inst. Graphic Arts, U.S. Power Squadron (South Shore div.). Author articles in field. Home: 2758 Clubhouse Rd Merrick NY 11566 Office: 200 E 42d St New York City NY 10017

CAPPON, ALEXANDER PATTERSON, ret. educator; b. Milw., May 11, 1900; s. John, Jr., and Charlotte Curry (Paterson) C.; student Milw. State Tchrs. Coll., 1919-20, Harvard, 1921, 1929-31; Ph.B., U. Chgo., 1925, M.A., 1926, Ph.D., 1935; m. Dorothy Churchill, Nov. 13, 1922; 1 dau., Frances Burney (Mrs. Hardison J. Geer). Instr. English, U. Tulsa, 1926-27; asso. English lit. U. Wash., 1927-29; lit. editor The New Humanist, 1931-35; instr. English, Mont. State. Coll., 1932-33, asst. prof., 1934-37; instr. Western Ill. State Tchrs. Coll., 1934; asso. editor U. Kansas City Rev., 1937, 42-52, editor in chief, 1938-42, 53-70, asst. prof. English, U. Kansas City, 1937-41, asso. prof., 1941-45, chmn. dept. English, 1941-44, 48-51, prof. English lang. and lit., 1945-63; prof. English lit., editor in chief Univ. Rev., U. Mo. at Kansas City, 1964-70. Mem. Modern Lang. Assn. Am. Assn. U. Profs., Phi Kappa Phi. Contbr. articles profl. pubs. Home: 16 E 52d St Kansas City MO 64112

CAPPON, LESTER JESSE, historian; b. Milw., Sept. 18, 1900; s. Jesse and Mary Elizabeth (Geisinger) C.; student State Tchrs. Coll., Milw., 1918-20; diploma Wis. Conservatory Music, 1920; A.B., U. Wis., 1922, M.A., 1923; M.A., Harvard, 1925, Ph.D., 1928; m. Dorothy Elizabeth Bernet, June 25, 1932; children—Mary Elizabeth (Mrs. William B. Yarbrough) (dec.), Stanley Bernet. Tchr. English, Boy's Tech. High Sch., Milw., 1923-24; research asso. history, inst. for research social sci. U. Va., 1926-27, 1928-30, archivist library, 1930-40, asst. prof. history, 1930-45, cons. archives, 1940-45, hon., 1945—, asso. prof. history, 1945; dir. Va. Hist. Records Survey, 1936-37, Va. World War II History Commn., 1944-45; editor publs. Inst. Early Am. History and Culture, Williamsburg, Va., 1945-55, dir., 1955-69; archivist Colonial Williamsburg, Inc., 1945-52, archival cons., 1952-69; sr. fellow Newberry Library, Chgo., 1969-70; editors-in-chief Atlas of Early American History, Newberry Library, 1970—; lectr. history Coll. William and Mary, 1946-69, emeritus, 1969—; lectr. archives Am. U., 1947-53; dir. Inst. on Hist. and Archival Mgmt., Radcliffe Coll., 1956-60. Mem. community council, Williamsburg, 1951-53; bd. dirs. Univ. Press Va., 1962-66. Fellow Soc. Am. Archivists (sec. 1942-50, v.p. 1955, pres. 1957); mem. Am. Antiquarian Soc., Am., So. (pres. 1949) hist. assns., Am. Assn. State and Local History, Orgn. Am. Historians, Mass., Va., Wis. Albemarle County (editor 1940-45) hist. socs., Colonial Soc. Mass., Nat. Parks Assn., Am. Forestry Assn., Wilderness Soc., Phi Beta Kappa (hon.), Sigma Pi, Phi Mu Alpha-Sinfonia, Sigma Delta Chi. Episcopalian. Democratic. Clubs: Sierra, Caxton. Author: Bibliography of Virginia History Since 1865, 1930; Virginia Newspapers, 1921-1935, A Bibliography, 1936; A Plan for the Collection and Preservation of World War II Records, 1942; Virginia Gazette Index, 1736-80, 1950; others. Editor: William and Mary Quar., 1955-56, 62-63; The Adams-Jefferson Letters, 1959. Contbr. articles to profl. jours. Home: 416 Griffin Av Williamsburg VA 23185 Office: 60 W Walton St Chicago IL 60610

CAPPS, BENJAMIN FRANKLIN, author; b. Dundee, Tex., June 11, 1922; s. Benjamin Franklin and Ruth Kathleen (Rice) C.; student Tex. Tech. Coll., 1938-39; B.A., U. Tex., Austin, 1948, M.A., 1949; m. Millie Marie Thompson, Dec. 12, 1942; children—Benjamin, Franklin, Kathleen Marie, Mark Victor. Surveyor, Civilian Conservation Corps, Grand Junction, Colo., 1939-40; surveyor Corps Engrs., Grand Junction, 1940, Greenville, Tex., 1942; truck driver Atkinson Co., Denison, Tex., 1941; instr. journalism Northeastern State Coll., Tahlequah, Okla., 1949-51; tool and die maker Comml. Engring. Co., other cos., Grand Prairie, Tex., 1951-61; free-lance writer, Grand Prairie, 1961—. Served to 1st lt. USAAF, 1942-45. Mem. Tex. Inst. Letters, Western Writers Am., Phi Beta Kappa. Author: Hanging at Comanche Wells, 1962; Trail to Ogallala, 1964; Sam Chance, 1965; A Woman of the People, 1966; The Brothers of Uterica, 1967; The White Man's Road, 1969. Address: 2529 SE 8th St Grand Prairie TX 75050

CAPPS, ETHAN LEROY, oil co. exec.; b. Sherman, Tex., Dec. 2, 1924; s. Ethan Daniel and Annie Mae (Anderson) C.; B.S., Tex. A. and M. U., 1948; grad. Advanced Mgmt. Program, Harvard, 1965; m. Emily Ann Tyson, Sept. 8, 1951; children—Richard LeRoy, Nancy Elizabeth. With Tenn. Gas Transmission Co., Houston, 1948-59, asst. treas., budget dir., 1960-61; chief accountant Midwestern Gas Transmission Co., Houston, 1959; v.p. Tenneco Corp., Houston, 1961-63; adminstrv. v.p. Tenneco Oil Co., Houston, 1961-63, v.p., controller financial controls dept., chief financial officer charge credit, treasury, accounting and Budget, 1968—. Treas., bd. dirs. Planned Parenthood Houston, 1963-69. Served to 1st lt. AUS, 1944-46. C.P.A., Tex. Mem. Am. Inst. C.P.A.'s, Tex. Soc. C.P.A.'s. Presbyn. Clubs: Petroleum, Racquet (Houston). Home: 6206 Cedar Creek Houston TX 77027 Office: PO Box 2511 1010 Milam St Houston TX 77001

CAPPS, JOHN GRIERSON, Jr., investment banker; b. Gary, Ind., Aug. 20, 1929; s. John Grierson and Ellen (McCurley) C.; B.S., U. Wis., 1952; m. Edith Row, Nov. 3, 1957; childrenPerrie G., Sandra Ellen, Susan Anne. With Paine, Webber, Jackson & Curtis, Chgo., 1955—; gen. partner, 1965-70, v.p., 1970—. Bd. govs. Midwest Stock Exchange, 965-70, chmn. exec. com. bd. govs. 1969; mem. Chgo. Bd. Bd. Trade, Chgo. Merc. Exchange, Midwest Stock Exchange, Mem. Hammond (Ind.) City Plan Comm., 1969-70. Served to lt. (j.g.) USNR, 1952-55 Home: 9235 Greenwood Munster IN 46321 Office: 208 S LaSalle St Chicago IL 60604

CAPPS, RICHARD BROOKS, physician; b. Chgo., Mar. 14, 1906; s. Joseph A. and Christy (Brooks) C.; B.S., Princeton, 1927; M.D., Harvard, 1931; m. Mary F. Grulee, July 8, 1930; 1 son, Richard Brooks. Intern, Mass. Gen. Hosp., Boston, 1931-33; asst. resident Thorndike Meml. Lab., Boston City Hosp., 1933- 35; pvt. practice internal medicine, Chgo., 1936-, asso. prof. medicine Northwestern U., 1953-57; asso. clin. prof. medicine U. Ill., 1957-62, clin. prof., 1962—; sr. attending physician Presbyn.-St. Lukes Hosp., Chgo., pres. staff, 1962-64, 66-67. Dir. Chgo. Blue Cross Plan. Served as lt. col. M.C., AUS, 1942-46. Diplomate Am. Bd. Internal Medicine in cardio-vascular disease. Fellow A.C.P.; mem. Am. Assn. Study Liver Disease (treas. 1954-57, pres. 1959), Soc. Med. Consultants Armed Forces, Am. Assn. Physicians, Am. Soc. Clin. Investigation, Central Soc. Clin. Research, Am. Clin. and Climatical Assn. (mem. council 1948-53, v.p. 1962-63), Constantinian Med. Sco., Chgo. Inst. Medicine (bd. govs. 1950-55, 69—), Chgo. Soc. Internal Med. (pres. 1954), Am., Chgo. (bd. govs. 1952-57) heart assns.; Am. Therapeutic Soc. (mem. council 1962-64), A.M.A., Chgo. Zool. Soc. (gov.), Phi Beta Kappa, Sigma Xi, Alpha Omega Alpha. Clubs: Commonwealth, Economic, University, Central Interurban Clinical (Chgo.); Commercial, Indian Hill, Old Elm. Contbr. articles to profl. jours. Home: 505 N Lake Shore Dr Chicago IL 60611. Office: 1725 W Harrison St Chicago IL 60612

CAPPS, RICHARD HUNTLEY, educator, physicist; b. Wichita, Kan., July 1, 1928; s. Charles M. and Anna (Palmer) C.; B.A., U. Kan., 1950; M.A., U. Wis., 1952, Ph.D., 1955; m. Joan P. Salatino, June 18, 1955. Research asso. U. Cal. at Berkeley, 1955-57; faculty U. Wash., 1957-58; research asso. Cornell U., 1958-60; faculty Northwestern U., Evanston, Ill., 1960-67, prof., 1965-67; prof. physics Purdue U., Lafayette, Ind., 1967—. Cons. Argonne Nat. Lab., 1960—. Mem. Am. Phys. Soc. Contbr. articles profl. jours. Research on theoretical investigation of basic laws of fundamental sub-atomic particles. Home: 135 Indian Rock Dr West Lafayette IN 47906 Office: Purdue U Lafayette IN 47907

CAPPS, WILBUR DEAN, lawyer; b. Roseville, Ill., Apr. 21, 1913; s. Elbert Henry and Anna (Davis) C.; student Western Ill. U., 1934-36; A.B., U. Ill., 1938, J.D., 1940; LL.D., Carthage Coll., 1965; m. Martha Ann Simmons, Mar. 10, 1941. Admitted to Ill. bar, 1940 since practiced in Carthage; mem. firm Johnson & Capps, 1940-42; sr. partner Capps & Ripple, 1964—; city atty., Carthage, 1949-55; spl. asst. atty. gen., 1961-69. Pres. Hancock Savs. & Loan Assn.; sec. Hancock Pellets, Inc.; dir. Attys. Title Guaranty Fund, Inc. Mem. Carthage Sch. Dist. Bd. Edn., 1947-53; Mem. Hancock County Housing Authority, 1946—. Sec. Robert Morris Coll. Ednl. Found.; bd. dirs. Lamoine Valley Assn.; sec., bd. trustees Robert Morris Coll.; trustee Carthage Coll. Served to maj. AUS, 1941-46. Mem. Am., Ill., Hancock County (past pres.) bar assns., Am. Legion, V.F.W., Carthage C. of C. (past pres.). Presbyn. Mason, Kiwanian. Clubs: Keokuk (Ia.) Country; Carthage Golf. Mem. bd. student editors Ill. Bar Jour., 1938-40. Home: 114 Parkway Dr Carthage IL 62321 Office: 55 S Adams St Carthage IL 62321

CAPPUYNS, HENRI FRANS FERDINAND, photog. products co. exec.; b. Lier, Belgium, Apr. 24, 1913; s. Henry and Carolina (van Dingenen) C.; J.D., U. Louvain, 1936; m. Judith Smeets, Sept. 5, 1942; children—Jan, Martina. Practiced law, Brussels, 1936-37; sec. gen. Belgian R.R. cy., 1938-45; sec. gen. Gevaert Photo- Producten N.V. Mortsel, Antwerp, Belgium, 1945-52, gen. mgr., 1952-64, dir., 1956—, mng. dir., 1957—; pres. Agfa-Gevaert N.V. Mortsel-Antwerp, 1964—; pres. Agfa-Gevaert Group, 1971—; dir. Soc. Reunies D'Energie du Bassin de L' Escaut, Royale Belge, Union Chimique Belge. Censor Nat. Bank Belgium. 1962-67, regent, 1967—; bd. dirs. Found. Industry-Univ., 1962—, Nat. Investment Co., 1962-66, Nat. Co. for Credit to Industry, 1964-66. Decorated knight Leopold Order, officer Crown Order, officer Order Orange-Nassau (Netherlands). Mem. Flemish Econ. Assn. (past pres.), Fedn. Belgian Chem. Industry (v.p.), Fedn. Belgian Industries (v.p.), Internat. C. of C. (dir. Belgian com.). Home: 109 Hortsebaan Schoten Antwerp Belgium Office: 27 Septestraat Mortsel Antwerp Belgium

CAPRA, FRANK, producer and director motion pictures; b. Palermo, Italy, May 18, 1897; s. Salvatore Capra; came to U.S. at age of 6; ed. Cal. Inst. Tech.; m. Lucille Warner, 1933; 3 children. Producer motion pictures 1921—; produced, directed: The Strong Man, Submarine, Flight, Dirigible, Bitter Tea of General Yen, American Madness, Platinum Blonde, Lady for a Day, It Happened One Night, Mr. Deeds Goes to Town, Mr. Smith Goes to Washington, Lost Horizon, Broadway Bill, You Can't Take It With You, Meet John Doe, Arsenic and Old Lace, It's a Wonderful Life, State of the Union, Riding High, Here Comes the Groom, Pocketful of Miracles. Served as pvt., advancing to 2d lt., U.S. Army, World War I; commd. maj., U.S. Army, 1942; made series of army orientation films, Why We Fight; disch. with rank of col., 1945. Decorated D.S.M., Legion of Merit; Order British Empire. Recipient 3 Academy awards (Oscars) for best direction of year; twice produced pictures which received Acad. award as best of the year. Bd. dirs. Calif. Inst. Tech. Pres. Acad. of Motion Picture Arts and Sciences, 4 times; pres. Screen Directors Guild, 3 times. Address: Red Mountain Ranch Fallbrook CA 92028

CAPRILES, I. H., banker. Mng. dir. Maduro and Curiel's Bank N.V., Curacao, Netherlands Antilles. Address: De Ruyterplein 2 Curacao Netherlands Antilles*

CAPRON, WILLIAM MOSHER, acad. adminstr.;b. N.Y.C., July 30, 1920; s. Charles Alexander and Margaret Eleanor (Mosher) C.; A.B., Swarthmore Coll., 1942; student Maxwell Sch. Citizenship, Syracuse U., 1942; M.P.A., Harvard, 1947, M.A., 1948; m. Margaret Morgan, June 13, 1942; children—Alexander M., Margaret Wells, Barry Lincoln, Seth Thompson. Fiscal analyst Bur. Budget, 1945-46, asst. dir., 1964-65; research asso. Harvard Econ. Research Project, 1948-49; asst. prof. econs. U. Ill., 1949-51; economist Rand Corp., Santa Monica, Cal., 1951-56, cons., 1956-62; asst. prof. econs. Stanford, 1956-62; sr. staff Council Econ. Advisers, 1962-64; sr. fellow econ. studies div. Brookings Instn., 1966-69; asso. dean John F. Kennedy Sch. Govt., Harvard, 1969—. Served to 1st lt. AUS, 1942-45. Decorated D.C. S. Fellow A.A.A.S.; mem. Am. Econ. Assn., Econometric Soc., Am. Assn. U. Profs., Fedn. Am. Scientists (council). Unitarian. Home: 248 Gray St Arlington MA 02174 Office: Littaur Center Cambridge MA 02138

CAPSHAW, HULTON, former judge; b. Cookeville, Tenn., June 2, 1891; s. Robert Byrd and Alice (Whitson) C.; grad. Peabody Coll., 1911; A.B., U. Tenn., 1913; scholar Columbia, 1914-16, LL.B., 1916. Admitted to N.Y. bar, 1916, bar U.S. Supreme Ct., 1926; with Cravath & Henderson, 1916-18, Olney & Comstock, 1919-21; pvt. practice, 1921-28; mem. Capshaw & Capshaw, 1928-29; judge N.Y. City Magistrates Cts., 1929- 40. Del. Democratic Conv., 1st Jud. Dist., N.Y., 5 times. Served to ensign USNRF, World War I. Mem. N.Y. So. Soc. (sec. 1926-29), Tenn. Soc. in N.Y. (pres. 1935-37), Pilgrims of U.S., S.R., N.Y. Soc. Mil. and Naval Officers World War, Kappa Alpha (pres. nat. conv. Louisville 1929). Episcopalian. Mason. Clubs: University, Kappa Alpha (Southern) (pres. 1926-34), Down Town, Laymen's Cathedral of St. John the Divine (pres. 1935-37). Home: 90 Morningside Dr New York City NY 10027 Office: 36 W 44th St New York City NY 10036

CAPUCINE, GERMAINE LEFEBVRE, actress; b. Toulon, France. Motion pictures include Song Without End, The Lion, North to Alaska, Walk on the Wild Side, The Pink Panther, The Seventh Dawn, What's New, Pussycat, Honey Pot, Fraulein Doktor, The Exquisite Cadaver, Fellini Satyricon, The Red Sun. Address: care Kurt Frings Agy 9025 Wilshire Blvd Beverly Hills CA

CAPURSO, ALEXANDER ALEXIS, educator; b. Gioia del Colle, Italy, May 22, 1910; s. John and Vita Maria (Semeraro) C.; came to U.S., 1913, naturalized, 1938; student Pa. State U., 1930-31, Temple U., 1931-32; B.S., U. Ky., 1933, A.M., 1934, Ph.D., 1938; Mus. D. (hon.), Phila. Mus. Acad., 1957; LL.D., Oklahoma City U., 1968; m. Martha Honerkamp, Aug. 24, 1940; children—John Alexander, Vita Marie. Dir. instrumental music Lab. Sch., U. Ky., 1934-38, exec. dir. music dept., 1940-44, head music dept., 1944-48, distinguished prof. Coll. Art and Scis., 1945; asst. dir. Carnegie Community Music Study Project, Ky., 1938-40; dir. sch. music Syracuse U., 1948-61, gen. chmn. Festival Arts, 1960-61; prof., asso. chmn. creative arts San Francisco State Coll., 1961-63; pres. Stanislaus State Coll., Turlock, Cal., 1963-69; prof. music Cal. Sate Poly. Coll., San Luis Obispo, 1969—; research asso. office chancellor Cal. State Colls., 1962; conductor Syracuse Symphony Orch., 1949-52; vis. prof. music U. Wis., summer 1950, 62, Appalachian State Tchrs. Coll., summer 1958. Chmn. artist-lecture series Cal. State Colls., 1966; mem. research com. Music Research Found., Inc.; guest condr. symphony orchs. U. Kan., Ohio State U., Transylvania Coll., others. Decorated knight officer Order of Merit (Italy); named to Hall of Fame, U. Ky. Alumni, 1966. Mem. Am. Assn. State Colls. and Univs. (com. cultural affairs), Am. Council Edn., Assn. Higher Edn., Am. Assn. Colls. Tchrs. Edn., N.E.A., Am. Assn. Sch. Adminstrs., Am., Cal. psychol. assns., Sigma Xi (asso.), Phi Delta Kappa, Phi Mu Alpha, Theta Beta Phi. Co-author: Music and Your Emotions, 1952. Contbr. chpt. in Curriculum Planning for the Gifted Child; also articles profl. jours. Home: 260 Westmont Av San Luis Obispo CA 93401

CAPUTI, ANTHONY, educator; b. Buffalo, Dec. 22, 1924; s. Anthony and Jessie (Storms) C.; B.A., U. Buffalo, 1949, M.A., 1951; Ph.D., Cornell U., 1956; postgrad. Oxford U., 1954-55; m. Marjein O'Neill, June 19, 1948; children—David, Pauline, Mary, Carol. Mem. faculty Cornell U., Ithaca, N.Y., 1956—, prof. English, 1966—. Served with AUS, 1943-46; ETO. Fulbright fellow, 1964-65, 54-55; Guggenheim fellow, 1964-65. Author: John Marston, Satirist, 1961; Norton Anthology of Modern Drama, 1966; Masterworks of World Drama, 6 vols, 1968. Home: 123 N Quarry St Ithaca NY 14850

CAPWELL, RICHARD LEONARD, univ. dean; b. E. Greenwich, R.I., May 6, 1920; s. Walter Henry and Grace (Knowles) C.; A.B., Brown U., 1942; M.A., Yale, 1946; Ph.D., Duke, 1964; m. Margaret

Ruth Johnston, Dec. 19, 1959; children—Richard Johnston, Alton Robert. Instr., Adm. Billard Acad., New London, Conn., 1942-44; instr. Milton (Mass.) Acad., 1944-45, U. Mo., Columbia, 1946-49, Ohio Wesleyan U., Delaware, 1952-54; asst. prof. E. Carolina U., Greenville, N.C., 1957-64, asso. prof., 1964-66, prof. 17th Century English lit., 1966—, dean Coll. Arts and Scis., 1969—. Mem. Modern Lang. Assn. Am., S. Atlantic Modern Lang. Assn., Southeastern Renaissance Conf., Am. Assn. U. Profs., Phi Beta Kappa, Phi Kappa Phi. Methodist. Club: Greenville Golf and Country. Contbg. editor: Abstracts of English Studies, 1961—. Home: 206 Dalebrook Circle Greenville NC 27834

CARACRISTI, ANN Z., cryptologist; b. Bronxville, N.Y., Feb. 1, 1921; d. Virginius Z. and Jessie (Donald) Caracristi; B.A., Russell Sage Coll., 1942. Cryptologist, Nat. Security Agy. Recipient Fed. Woman's award, 1965. Home: 1222 28th St NW Washington DC 20007 Office: Nat Security Agy Fort Meade MD 20755

CARADON, LORD HUGH MACKINTOSH , retired Brit. diplomat; b. 1907; ed. Leighton Park Sch., Reading, also St. John's Coll., Cambridge. Pres. Cambridge Union, 1929; adminstrv. officer, Palestine Govt., 1929-37; attached to Colonial Office, 1938-39; asst. Brit. resident, Transjordan, 939-42; Brit. mil. adminstr., Cyrenaica, 1943; colonial sec., Cyprus, 1943-45, Jamaica, 1945-47; chief sec., Nigeria, 1947-50; capt.-gen., gov.-in-chief, Jamaica, 1951-57; gov., comdr. in chief, Cyprus, 1957-60; permanent rep. UN Trusteeship Coucil, 1961-62; cons. UN Spl. Fund., 1963-70; minister state for fgn. affairs, permanent rep. UN, 1964-70; mem. UN export group on South Africa, 1964. Author: A Start in Freedom, 1964. Home: Trematon Castle Saltash Cornwall England

CARAM, ANGEL RAMON, Argentinian economist; b. Buenos Aires, Argentina, Apr. 9, 1921; s. Assad Neme and Yamile (Meouchi) C.; Pub. Accountant, U. Buenos Aires, 1942, D. Econs., 1947; m. Yolanda Elies, July 27, 1956. With Central Bank Argentina, 1939-45, Indsl. Bank, 1945-48; pvt. cons., 1948-52; with Argentine Ministry Trade, 1952-57, dep. dir. econ. and financial policy, 1958, dir., 1963, undersec. economy, 1965; financial counsellor Argentine embassy, Washington, 1965; exec. dir. for Argentina, World Bank, 1968-70; financial minister Argentine embassy, Washington, 1970—. Mem. Soc. Internat. Devel., Assn. Economists. Author articles. Home: 1300 Army Navy Dr Arlington VA 22202 Office: 1818 H St NW Washington DC 20443

CARAPETYAN, ARMEN, editor, musicologist, publisher; b. Isfahan, Iran, Oct. 11, 1908; s. Mackertoum and Miriam (Khazarian) C.; diploma, Am. Coll., Teheran, 1927; student in Paris, France, then N.Y.C.; M.A., Harvard, 1940, Ph.D., 1945; m. Harriet Esther Norris, Nov. 4, 1937; children—Francelle, Peter Anthony. Came to U.S., 1928. naturalized, 1942. Founder, 1945, since dir. Am. Inst. Musicology, specializing Medieval and Renaissance music, Cambridge, Mass.; spl. work in fostering research and publs. in field, directing project, also editor and pub. Mem. Am., Internat. musicological socs., Renaissance Soc. Am. Office: PO Box 30665 Dallas TX 75230 also CP 515 San Silvestro Rome Italy

CARAS, ROGER ANDREW, author, motion picture co. exec.; b. Metheun, Mass., May 24, 1928; s. Joseph J. and Bessie (Kasanoff) C.; student Northeastern U., 1948-49, Western Res. U., 1949-50; B.A. in Cinema, U. So. Cal., 1952; m. Jill Langdon Barclay, Sept. 5, 1954; children—Pamela Jill, Barclay Gordon. Asst. to v.p., also nat. dir. mdsg. for U.S. and Can., Columbia Pictures Corp., 1955-65; v.p. Stanley Kubrick's Polaris Prodns., N.Y.C., 1965-68, Hawk Films Ltd., London, Eng., 1965-68; coll. lectr. on wildlife and conservation, 1955-65; sci. editor Armed Forces Radio and TV Service, 1963—; columnist Register & Tribune Syndicate; star CBS radio show Pets and Wildlife. Mem. adv. bd. Zero Population Growth. Chmn. zoo and wildlife com. Morris Animal Found.; bd. dirs. Humane Soc. U.S., Fund for Animals. Fellow Royal Soc. Arts; mem. Authors League, Outdoor Writers Assn., Mensa, Blue Key, Delta Kappa Alpha (past nat. pres.). Author: Antarctica: Land of Frozen Time, 1962; Dangerous to Man, 1964; Wings of Gold, 1965; (pseudonym Roger Sarac) The Throwbacks, 1965; The Custer Wolf, 1966; Mammals of North America, 1966; Last Chance on Earth, 1966; Sarang, 1968; Monarch of Deadman Bay, 1969; Source of the Thunder, 1970; Panther!, 1970; Death as a Way of Life, 1971. Home: 46 Fenmarsh Rd East Hampton NY 11937

CARAVATI, CHARLES M., physician, retired educator; b. Richmond, Va., May 31, 1899; s. Henry L. and Lena (Mahoney) C.; student U. Richmond, 1916-18; M.D., Med. Coll. Va., 1922; m. Virginia Mason, Oct. 19, 1956; 1 son, Charles M. Intern Providence Hosp., Washington, 1922-23, resident, 1923-24; practice medicine, specializing in internal medicine and gastroenterology, Richmond, 1924-66; prof. medicine Med. Coll. Va., Richmond, 1961-70, emeritus prof. medicine, 1970—, asst. dean, dir. continuation edn., 1966-70. Dir. First & Mchts. Nat. Bank, Richmond Fed. Savs. & Loan Assn. Bd. dirs. Adult Devel. Center, St. Joseph's Villa, Med. Coll. Va. Found. Served to col., M.C., AUS, 1942-46. Recipient 1st Ann. award Louise Obici Hosp., Suffolk, Va., 1965; named knight of St. Sylvester. Diplomate in gastroenterology Am. Bd. Internal Medicine. Fellow A.C.P. (v.p., past gov., regent, master); mem. Am. Gastroenterology Soc., Phi Chi. Contbr. numerous articles med. jours. Home: 208 Gun Club Rd Richmond VA 23221

CARAVATT, PAUL JOSEPH, Jr., advt. agy. exec.; b. New Britain, Conn., Dec. 13, 1922; s. Paul Joseph and Bessie (Avery) C.; A.B., Dartmouth, 1945, M.C.S., 1947; m. B. Laura Bennett, June 22, 1946; childrenCynthia Diane, Suzanne Laura. With Nat. Dairy Assn., 1947-49, Young & Rubicam, 1949-50; advt. mgr. Hunting and Fishing mag., 1950-52, Biow Co., 1952-56; v.p. Ogilvy, Benson & Mather, 1956-69; sr. v.p. Foote, Cone & Belding, 1960-64, LaRoche, McCaffrey & McCall, advt. agy., N.Y.C., 1964-66; pres. Carl Ally, Ind., advt. agy., N.Y.C., 1966-67; chmn. bd. Marschalk Co., Inc., N.Y.C., 1967—. Mem. Newcomen Soc., S.A.R., Zeta Psi. Republican. Conglist. Clubs: University, N.Y. Athletic (N.Y.C.); Shore and Country (Norwalk, Conn.). Home: 274 Westport Rd Wilton, CT 06897. Office: Time and Life Bldg 1271 Av of Americas New York City NY 10020

CARAWAY, PAUL WYATT, ret. army officer and lawyer; b. Jonesboro, Ark., Dec. 23, 1905; s. Thaddeus H. and Hattie (Wyatt) C.; B.S., U.S. Mil. Acad., 1929; LL.B., Georgetown U., 1933; diploma Inf. Sch., 1934, Command and Gen. Staff Sch., 1942; student Imperial Def. Coll., London, 1946; m. Indel Roberts Little, June 30, 1934. Commd. 2d lt. Inf., 1929, advanced through grades to lt. gen., 1961; assigned 15th Inf. Regt., Tientsin, China, 1935-37; instr. law U.S. Mil. Acad., 1938-42; staff operations div., strategy sect. War Dept. Gen. Staff, 1942-44; chief plans group, dep. chief staff plans, operations and intelligence China Theater, Chungking, China, 1944-45; comdg. gen. Chungking Liaison Group, 1945-46; faculty Nat. War Coll., Washington, 1947-49; regt. comdr. 351st Inf. Regt., TRUST, Trieste, Free Ty. Trieste, 1949-51; sr. U.S. instr., Army dep. NATO Def. Coll., Paris, France, 1951-53; chief plans div. Dept. Army Gen. Staff, Washington, 1953-55; comdg. gen. 7th Inf. Div., Korea, 1955-56; asst. chief staff J-3, hdqrs. Far East command-UN command, Tokyo, Japan, 1956-57; chief staff hdqrs. U.S. Forces, Japan, 1957-58; mem. joint strategic survey council Office Joint Chiefs of Staff, Washington, 1958-61; high commr. Ryukus Islands, comdg. gen. U. S. Army, Ryukyus Islands and IX Corps, CINCPACREP Ryukyus, 1961-64; mem. firm Reed and Caraway, Heber Springs, Ark., 1965-68; instr. bus. law, business financing Benjamin Franklin U., Washington, 1968—; cons. mil.-polit. affairs. Admitted to Ark. bar, 1933. Decorated D.S.M. with oak leaf cluster, Legion of Merit with oak leaf cluster (U.S.); Order of Pao Ting (China); comdr. Order British Empire; Order of Rising Sun (Japan), 1958. Mem. Assn. Grads. U.S. Mil. Acad., Council Fgn. Relations, Nat. Rifle Assn. (life), Nat. Muzzle Loading Rifle Assn. (life), Co. Mil. Historians, Am. Orchid Soc. Club: Army and Navy (Washington). Home: 9143 Santayana Dr Fairfax, VA 22030. Office: Benjamin Franklin U 16th and L Sts Washington DC 20036

CARBAUGH, GLENN I., vending machine co. exec.; b. Kansas City, Mo., June 22, 1927; s. Glenn Claiborne and Fay (Whitman) C.; A.B., Yale, 1949; J.D., U. Mich., 1952; m. Doreen Ann Collins, June 19, 1952. Asso. firm Lathrop. Righter, Gordon & Parker, Kansas City, Mo., 1952-54; with Vendo Co., Kansas City, Mo., 1954—, sec., gen. counsel, dir., officer charge communications div., 1967—. Past finance chmn. Citizens Assn. Kansas City, Mo. Past committeeman, precinct capt. Johnson County (Kan.) Republican Central Com. Bd. dirs., treas. Children's Cardiac Center, Kansas City, Mo. Served with AUS, 1945-47. Mem. Am., Mo. bar assns., Lawyers Assn. Kansas City, Mo., English Speaking Union, Phi Beta Kappa, Order of Coif, Phi Alpha Delta. Mem. Disciples of Christ Ch. Club: University (Kansas City, Mo.). Home: 2201 Stratford Rd Shawnee Mission KS 66208 Office: 7400 E 12th St Kansas City MO 64126

CARBAUGH, HARRY CLARKE, mem. Republican Nat. Com.; b. Tasso, Tenn., May 11, 1895; s. Harvey Francis and Bertha (Fletcher) C.; student U. Chattanooga, 1914-16; m. Alyce Katherine Huffaker, Dec. 10, 1917; 1 dau., Betty Carolyn (Mrs. Richard Fancher). Partner Carbaugh & Co.,Chattanooga, 1918-20; gen. mgr. Tenn. Egg Co., 1920-, v.p., 1920-27, pres., 1927-63; pres. Scenic City Investment Corp.; dir. Hamilton Nat. Bank, Interstate Life & Accident Ins. Co., Interstate Fire Ins. Co. Chmn. City-Wide Eastern Sunrise Service, 1947-55; exec. com., pres. Community Chest, 1946-47; exec. com. United Fund, 1959-69. Vice chmn. for So. states Nat. Republican Finance Com., 1960-63; mem. Rep. Nat. Com. for Tenn., 1961-; chmn. Tenn. Rep. Finance Com., 1944-62; del. Rep. Nat. Conv., 1948-68. Vice chmn. bd. trustees U. Chattanooga, 1950-69; dir. YMCA. Served from 2d lt. to lst lt. inf. U.S. Army, 1916-19. Mem. U.S. (dir. 1959-65), Chattanooga (pres. 1941, dir. 1940) chambers commerce, Inst. Am. Poultry Industries (dir., exec. com. 1958), Nat. Butter and Egg Assn. (pres. 1947-48), Sigma Chi. Baptist (deacon). Clubs: Rotary (pres. 1943-44), Executive (pres. 1943-44); Fairyland, Mountain City (Chattanooga). Home: 219 W Brow Oval Lookout Mountain TN 37350 Office: Maclellan Bldg Chattanooga TN 37402

CARBERRY, JAMES JOHN, educator; b. Bklyn., Sept. 13, 1925; s. James Thomas and Alice (McConnin) C.; B.S., U. Notre Dame, 1950, M.S., 1951; Dr. Engring., Yale, 1957; m. Judith Ann Bower, Sept. 12, 1959; children—Alison Ann, Maura O'Malley. Process engr. E.I. duPont de Nemours & Co., Gibbstown, N.J., 1951-53, sr. research engr., Wilmington, Del., 1957-61; teaching, research fellow Yale, 1953-57; prof. chem. engring. U. Notre Dame (Ind.), 1961—. NSF fellow Cambridge U. (Eng.), 1965-66; cons. in field. Served with USNR, 1944-46. Recipient Distinguished Lectr. citation U. Mich., 1967, award for advancement pure and applied sci. Yale Engring. Assn., 1968. Allied Chem. & Dye Corp. fellow, 1955-56. Mem. Am. Chem. Soc., Am. Inst. Chem. Engrs., Yale Engring. Assn., Sigma Xi. Roman Catholic. Address: Dept Chem Engring U Notre Dame Notre Dame IN 46556

CARBERRY, JOHN J., cardinal; recipient degrees; D.D., S.T.D., Ph.D., J.C.D., LL.D. Ordained priest Roman Cath. Ch., 1929; apptd. titular bishop of Elis, coadjutor cum lure successions, 1956; consecrated, 1956, succeeded to See, 1957; bishop of Columbus, O. until 1968; archbishop of St. Louis, 1968—; named to Coll. Cardinals, 1960. Pres. Center Applied Research in the Apostolate, 1970—. Home: 4445 Lindell Blvd St Louis MO 63108

CARBERRY, MURIEL R., dean Sch. Nursing, Cornell U. Address: 1320 York Av New York City NY 10021*

CARBERY, JOHN HUGH, Irish diplomat; b. Bandon, Ireland, Jan. 24, 1939; s. Austin Hugh and Josephine (Heffernan) C.; B.A., Univ. Coll. Dublin, 1959, B.C.L., 1962; barrister at law Kings Inn Dublin, 1962; diplome des hautes etudes Europeanes U. Strasbourg, 1960, U. Rome (Italy), 1969; M.A., U. Ga., 1963; m. Marie- Francoise Ponsar, Sept. 3, 1966. Sec. Irish embassy, Holy See, Rome, Italy, 1966-70; 1st sec. Irish embassy, Washington, 1970—. Decorated knight comdr. Order St. Gregory the Great. Mem. Phi Beta Kappa. Club: University (Dublin). Home: 4325 Verplanck Pl Washington DC 20016 Office: 2234 Massachusetts Av NW Washington DC 20008

CARBINE, JOHN DUGAN, lawyer; b. Rutland, Vt., Jan. 5, 1914; s. William Charles and Mary (Dugan) C.; A.B., U. Notre Dame, 1935; LL.B., Harvard, 1938; m. Muriel Brown, Apr. 13, 1940 (dec.); children—Stephen Anthony, Sandra Ann; m. 2d, Renny Weaver Downey, July 3, 1968. Admitted to Mass. bar, 1938, Vt. bar, 1939; partner firm Ryan, Smith & Carbine, Rutland, Vt., 1948—. Pres. Ethan Allen Nat. Bank; dir. Vt. Electric Power Co., Inc. Del. Rep. Nat. Conv., 1952, 64. Fellow Am. Bar Found.; mem. Vt. Bar Assn. (pres.), Am. Bar Assn. (chmn. standing com. commerce 1964-65. bd. govs. 1966—), Am. Judicature Soc. Home: 234 Grove St Rutland VT 05701 Office: 98 Merchants Row Rutland VT 05701

CARBON, MAX WILLIAM, educator; b. Monon, Ind., Jan. 19, 1922; s. Joseph William and Mary Olive (Goble) C.; B.S. in Mech. Engring., Purdue U., 1943, M.S., 1947, Ph.D., 1949; m. Phyllis Camille Myers, Apr. 13, 1944; children—Ronald Allen, Jean Ann, Susan Jane, David William, Janet Elaine. With Hanford works Gen. Electric Co., 1949-55, head heat transfer unit, 1951-55; with research and advanced devel. div. Avco Mfg. Corp., 1955-58, chief thermodynamics sect., 1956-58; prof., chmn. nuclear engring. dept. U. Wis. Coll. Engring., 1958—, group leader Ford Found. program, Singapore, 1967-68. Served to capt. ordnance dept., AUS, 1943- 46. Mem. Am. Nuclear Soc., A.A.A.S., Am. Soc. Engring. Edn., Am. Soc. M.E., Am. Assn. U. Profs., Sigma Xi, Tau Beta Pi. Office: Engring Research Bldg U Wis Madison WI 53706

CARD, ANNON MELTON, oil co. exec.; b. Lufkin, Tex., June 22, 1919; s. Henry Martin and Elizabeth (Durden) C.; B.B.A., U. Tex., 1941; m. Frances Marie Holt, Mar. 3, 1946; children—Michael, Carol (Mrs. George Lord III), Cathy, Richard. With Texaco, Inc., 1947—, asst. to v.p., 1964, asst. to pres., 1964, gen. mgr. sales, 1965, v.p. Texaco Inc. (Sales U.S.), 1966-69, chmn. chief exec. officer Texaco Europe Ltd., 1969, sr. v.p., 1970—. Served with USNR, 1943-47. Office: 135 E 42d St New York City NY 10017

CARDEGNA FELIX F., pres. Woodstock Coll. Address: Woodstock Coll Woodstock MD 21163*

CARDENAS, ROBERT LEON, air force officer; b. Merida, Yucatan, Mexico, Mar. 10, 1920; s. Robert Leon and Maria (Lopez-Alonzo) C.; brought to U.S., 1926, naturalized, 1936; B.S. in Mech. Engring., U. N.M., 1955; grad. Air Command and Gen. Staff Sch., 1949, Air War Coll., 1958; m. Gladys V. Gisewite, May 29, 1948; children—Diana, Richard, Robin, Debra, Michael, Mark, Maria. Joined Cal. Nat. Guard, 1939, commd. 2d lt. USAAF, 1941, advanced through grades to brig. gen., 1968; experimental jet test pilot, 1947-53; chief aircraft and guided missiles program div. Office Dep. Chief Staff for Plans and Programs, 1958-60, chief aerospace vehicles div., 1960-62; chief spl. plans div. U.S. Strike Command, MacDill AFB, Fla., 1962-64; comdr. 18th Tactical Fighter Wing, Okinawa, 1964-66, 835th Air Div., McConnell AFB, Kans., 1966-68, Air Force Spl. Operations Force, Eglin AFB, Fla., 1968-69; vice comdr. 16th Air Force Torrejon AFB, Spain, 1969-70; U.S. dep. chief staff Live Oak, Supreme Hdqrs. Allied Powers in Europe, Belgium, 1970—. Pres. Wichita Fed. Exec. Assn. (Kan.), 1967-68. Decorated Legion Merit with 1 oak leaf cluster, D.F.C., Meritorious Service Medal, Air Medal with 4 oak leaf clusters, Joint Service Commendation medal, Air Force Commendation medal with oak leaf cluster, Purple Heart; Grand Cross Order Aero. Merit, Spain. Mem. Soc. Exptl. Test Pilots, Order Daedalians (named mem.), Phi Kappa Phi, Sigma Tau, Pi Tau Sigma, Sigma Chi. Roman Catholic. Home: 186 Church St Brookville OH 45309 Office: US Dep Chief Staff LIVE OAK-SHAPE APO New York City NY 09055

CARDIN, CHRISTIAN MAURICE, banker; b. Paris, France, Nov. 17, 1908; s. Maurice and Elvira (Klingelhofer) C.; LL.D., U. Paris, 1935; m. Annette Simon, Sept. 8, 1939; children—Catherine (Mrs. Francois Grandchamp des Raux), Dominique. Came to U.S., 1960. Active service Insp. des Finances, 1934- 51; comml. counsellor French embassy, Ottawa, Can., 1947, Buenos Aires, Argentina, 1951; rep. Banque de Paris et des Pays Bas for Western Hemisphere, 1960—; exec. v.p. Paribas Corp., N.Y.C., 1961-66, pres., chief exec. officer, 1966—, chmn. bd., 1971—, chmn. bd. Santa Fe Co., Buenos Aires; dir. Bendix Corp., I.B.E.C. Served from lt. to capt., French Army, 1939-40. Decorated officer Legion of Honor, Croix de Guerre. Home: 1080 Fifth Av New York City NY 10028 also 148 Blvd Malesherbes Paris France Office: 40 Wall St New York City NY 10005

CARDIN, PIERRE, fashion designer; b. Venice, Italy, July 7, 1922 (parents French citizens); ed. St. Etienne, France. Tailor with Manby, men's tailor, Vichy, France, 1939-40; adminstr. with French Red Cross, World War II; designer with Paquin, Paris, 1945-47, House of Dior, Paris, 1947-50; propr. own design house, Paris, 1950—. Address: 118 Rue du Faubourg Saint-Honore Paris 8e France

CARDINALE, CLAUDIA, actress; b. Tunis, Tunisia, 1939; student Centro Sperimentale di Cinemato grafica, Rome, Italy. Motion picture appearances include I soliti ignoti, Girl With a Suitcase, The Pink Panther, Blindfold, The Centurions, Running World. Home: Via Flaminia Rome, Italy. Office: Vides Piazza Pitagora Rome Italy

CARDON, MARRINER PAUL, lawyer; b. Albuquerque, May 17, 1932; s. Louis Sanders and Winnafred (Bellamy) C.; B.A., U. Utah, 1954; LL.B., U. Colo., 1962; m. Ruth Hanks, Aug. 9, 1957; children—Stephan, Laurie, Roslyn, Bradley, Lamont. Admitted to Ariz. bar, 1962; practice in Phoenix, 1963—; law clk., research asst. Ariz. Supreme Ct., 1962; asso. Kramer, Roche, Burch & Streich, 1963-66; partner Kramer, Roche, Burch, Streich & Cracchiolo, 1966-70; partner Streich, Lang, Weeks, Cardon & French, 1970—. Sub- chmn. Phoenix Growth Com., 1969; mem. Phoenix Planning Commn., 1970. Served to lt. (j.g.) USNR, 1954-57. Mem. Am., Ariz., Maricopa County bar assns., Order of Coif, Phi Alpha Delta. Republican. Mem. Ch. of Jesus Christ of Latter-day Saints. Club: Arizona Country Phoenix. Co-author: American Law of Mining, 1962. Editor U. Colo. Law Rev., 1961. Home: 3148 N 53d St Phoenix AZ 85018 Office: First Nat Bldg Phoenix AZ 85004

CARDONA, MANUEL, educator; b. Barcelona, Spain, Sept. 7, 1934; s. Juan and Angela (Castro) C.; B.Sc., U. Barcelona, 1955; Ph.D., U. Madrid, 1958; M.Sc., Harvard U., 1957, Ph.D., 1959; m. Inge Hect, Feb. 11, 1959; children—Michael, Angela, Steven. Came to U.S., 1956, naturalized, 1967. Mem. staff RCA Labs., Zurich, Switzerland, 1959-61, Princeton, N.J., 1961-64; asso. prof. physics Brown U., 1964-66, prof., 1966—; dir. Max Planck Inst. Solid Stae Physics, Stuttgart, Germany, 1971—. Sloan fellow, 1966-68; Guggenheim fellow, 1969-70. Author: Modulation Spectroscopy, 1969. Home: Daumlingway 18 Stuttgart West Germany

CARDONI, HORACE ROBERT, lawyer, precision electronic instrument mfg. co. exec.; b. Jessup, Pa., July 24, 1916; s. Louis and Maria (Saldi) C.; B.A., U. Scranton, 1938; LL.B., U. Pa., 1941; m. Florence D'Arienzo, July 2, 1945; children—Mary Clare, Ann, Louise, Robert L., Joseph J., John J. Admitted to Pa. bar, 1941; pvt. practice, Scranton, 1941-42; area rent atty. Office Housing Expediter, OPA, Scranton, 1946-51; with Daystrom, Inc. (name changed to Weston Instruments, Inc. 1964), Newark, 1953—, sec., 1962—, gen. counsel, 1963—; dir. Weston P.R., Inc., Ponce, Weston Caribe, Inc., Ponce. Treas. cub pack Boy Scouts Am., Mountain Side, N.J., 1964-66, Mountain Side Little League, 1965-66. Dist. committeeman Democratic Party, 1967—. Served with USNR, 1942-45, 51-52. Mem. Nat. Security Indsl. Assn., Am., Pa. bar assns. Home: 326 Short Dr Mountainside NJ 07092 Office: 614 Frelinghuysen Av Newark NJ 07114

CARDOZO, MANOEL, educator; b. Ribeiras, Pico, Azores, Dec. 24. 1911; s. Jose Silveira and Rosalina Soares (de Sousa) C.; came to U.S., 1915, naturalized, 1944; B.A., Stanford, 1931, M.A., 1934, Ph.D., 1939. Teaching asst. U. Cal. at Berkeley, 1935-36; curator Oliveira Lima Library, Catholic U. Am., Washington, 1940—, prof. history, 1954—; head dept., 1961-71, dir. Inst. Ibero-Am. Studies; Smith-Mundt lectr., Portugal, 1958; lectr. in U.S., Brazil, Portugal, Peru, Argentina, Azores; spl. research Brazilian and Portuguese history; asso. sec.-gen. First Internat. Colloquim Luso-Brazilian Studies, Washington 1950. Fellow Inst. de Alta Cultura, Lisbon, Portugal, 1936-38; recipient Rio Branco medal Brazilian Fgn. Office, 1945; decorated chevalier Order So. Cross (Brazil). Social Sci. Research Council grantee; Am. Philos. Soc. grantee; OAS grantee; Instituto de Alta Cultura (Lisbon) grantee. Mem. Am. Cath. (pres. 1962), Am. hist. assns., Sociedade de Geografia (Lisbon), Inst. Historico (Terceira, Azores), Institute Histórico Geográfico (Saõ Paulo and Saõ Luis do Maranhaõ), Inst. do Ceara. Am. Assn. U. Profs., Cath. Commn. Intellectual and Cultural Affairs, Inter-Am. Council (pres. Washington 1964-65), Sociedad Peruana de Historia. Author numerous hist. studies pub. in U.S., Portugal, Spain, Brazil, Venezuela, Mexico, Germany. Contbr. articles to hist. jours., encys. Home: 1004 Sigsbee Pl NE Washington DC 20017

CARDOZO, MICHAEL HART, assn. exec.; b. N.Y.C., Sept 15, 1910; s. Ernest A. and Emily (Wolff) C.; grad. Phillips Acad., Andover, Mass., 1928; A.B., Dartmouth, 1932; LL.B., Yale, 1935; m. Alice Corneille, July 31, 1937; children—Michael Hart V, Julia Aline (Mrs. Charles R. Eisendrath,) Alice Rebecca. Admitted to N.Y. bar, 1936; with firm Parker & Duryee. N.Y.C., 1935-38; mem. temporary nat. econ. com., life ins. investigation SEC, 1938-40; atty. U.S. Dept. Justice, 1940-42; with U.S. Lend-Lease and Fgn. Econ. Adminstrns.,

1942-45, Lend-Lease rep. in Turkey, 1943-44; with Office of Legal Adviser, Dept. State, 1945-52, asst. legal adviser for econ. affairs, 1950-52; from asso. prof. to prof. law Cornell U., Ithaca, N.Y., 1952-63; Fulbright and Guggenheim fellow, Belgium, 1958-59; exec. dir. Assn. Am. Law Schs., 1963—; vis. prof. law Northwestern U., 1961- 62, U. Pa., 1964-65, Howard U., 1965-66, Georgetown U., 1966-67, Salzburg Seminar in Am. Studies, summer, 1968; cons. Dept. State, fgn. relations com. U.S. Senate sumcom. on patents, trade marks and copyrights Ho. of Reps., Naval War Coll., Fellowship review bd. Dept. Health, Edn. and Welfare, Nat. Sci. Found. Named Officer of the Order of Orange, Nassau. The Netherlands. Mem. Am., Fed., N.Y. State bar assns., Am. Law Inst. Author: Diplomats in International Cooperation, 1963; also contbr. articles to jours. Home: 2602 36th st NW Washington DC 20007 Office: One Dupont Circle NW Washington DC 20036

CARDWELL, ALVIN BOYD, physicist; b. Lenoir City, Tenn., Oct. 16, 1902; s. John Wesley and Martha (Duff) C.; B.S., U. Chattanooga, 1925, D.Sc., 1961; M.S., U. Wis., 1927; Ph.D., 1930; m. Edna Evangeline Zirkle, Dec. 27, 1930; children—Edward (dec.), Nancy, Charles Evan. Asst. in physics U. Wis., 1926-29, fellow, 1929-30; asst. prof. Tulane U., 1930-35, asso. prof., 1935-36; prof. Kan. State U., Manhattan, 1936—, head dept., 1937-53, 1957-67, asso. dean sch. arts and scis., 1953-55, dir. Bur. of Gen. Research, 1953-68; research physicist Manhattan Project, 1944-46; asso. editor Trans. Kan. Acad. Sci., 1942—; dir. Asso. Midwest Univs., 1959-66. Recipient distinguished prof. award, 1956; named Kan. Scientist of Yr., Topeka Daily Capital, 1958, Kan. Educator of Yr., 1968. Fellow Am. Phys. Soc., A.A.A.S.; mem. Kan. Acad. Sci., Am. Assn. Physics Tchrs., Sigma Xi, Phi Kappa Phi, Gamma Alpha, Gamma Sigma Delta. Author: Kansas Weather and Climate, 1942. Contbr. articles to prof. jours. Home: 1506 N 10th St Manhattan KS 66502

CARDWELL, GUY ADAMS, educator; b. Savannah, Ga., Nov. 14, 1905; s. Guy Adams and Ethel (Parmele) C.; A.B., U. N.C., 1926, Ph.D., 1936; A.M., Harvard, 1932; m. Margaret Randolph Bullitt, Dec. 21, 1935; children—Evelyn Bullitt, Margaret Randolph, Ethel Parmele, Lucy Adams. Instr., later asst. prof. English, Wake Forest Coll., 1936-38; mem. faculty Tulane U., 1938-45, prof. English, 1943-45; prof. English, head dept. U. Md., 1945-49; prof. English, Washington U., St. Louis, 1949-68, prof. emeritus, 1968—, chmn. dept., 1949-56, 59-63; prof. English, State U. N.Y. at Albany, 1968-71; guest prof. on Fulbright appt. U. Vienna, 1951-52; research fellow Henry E. Huntington Library, 1954-55; vis. prof. U. Buenos Aires, 1957; Fulbright-Smith-Mundt vis. prof. Nat. U. Mexico, 1960-61. Traveling fellow Gen. Edn. Bd., 1930-31; Faculty study fellowship Am. Council Learned Socs., 1951. Mem. Modern Lang. Assn. Am., Phi Beta Kappa. Democrat. Episcopalian. Author: Twins of Genius, 1953; Der amerikanische Roman, 1954; Charleston, S.C., Periodicals, 1960. Editor: The Uncollected Poems of Henry Timrod, 1942; Readings from the Americas, 1947; Discussions of Mark Twain, 1963; Life on the Mississippi (Mark Twain), 1968. Contbr. articles to profl. jours., essays, poems and stories to periodicals and anthologies. Home: PO Box 163 Moose WY 83012

CAREGA, GIORGIO, consul gen. of Italy in Boston. Address: 101 Tremont St Boston MA*

CARELLI, GABOR PAUL, opera singer; b. Budapest, Hungary, Mar. 20, 1915; s. Bela Krausz and Lenke Deutsch; Dr. Law. U. Budapest, 1937; studied singing Liszt-Ferenc Acad., Budapest, 1935-36, with Gigli, Rome, Italy, 1936- 39. Came to U.S., 1939, naturalized, 1949. Made debut in Boheme, Florence, Italy, 1938; opera, concert tours in U.S., 1939—; singer with symphonies, recorded with Toscanini, Antal Dorati for RCA-Victor, also recorded in Hungary; mem. of Met. Opera Assn., 1950—; singer Am. premiere Puccini-Mass, Chgo., 1951; artistic adviser opera and concerts, San Salvador 1951—; singer premiere Requiem-Mass by Verdi, Israel, 1954; regular radio appearances. 1944-51, guest appearances on operatic TV programs; concert opera appearances, Europe, 1958—; prof. voice Manhattan Sch. Music, N.Y.C. Mem. Am. Guild Mus. Artists (dir.). Home: 41 W 86th St New York City NY 10024 Office: Metropolitan Opera Assn New York City NY 10018

CARETTO, ALBERT ALEXANDER, chemist, educator; b. Baldwin, N.Y., May 16, 1928; s. Albert A. and Mary (Magnasco) C.; B.S., Rensselaer Poly. Inst., 1950; Ph.D., U. Rochester, 1954; m. Virginia L. Ahman, Apr. 30, 1960; children—Joseph A., Ann M. Postdoctoral research Brookhaven Nat. Lab., Upton, N.Y., 1954-56, U. Cal. at Berkeley, 1956-57; asst. prof. Carnegie Inst. Tech., Pitts., 1957-58, 59-64, asso. prof. 1964-67; research chemist U. Cal. at Livermore, 1958-59; with CERN, European Lab. for Nuclear Research, Geneva, Switzerland, 1964-65; prof. Carnegie-Mellon U., Pitts., 1967—, chmn. dept. chemistry, 1970—. Treas., trustee Richland Pub. Library Gibsonia, Pa. Mem. Am. Chem. Soc. (membership chmn.), Am. Phys. Soc., A.A.A.S., Sigma Xi, Phi Kappa Phi. Contbr. articles to profl. jours. Home: 1231 Woodhill Dr Gibsonia PA 15044 Office: Dept Chemistry Carnegie-Mellon U Pittsburgh PA 15213

CAREW, HERMAN JOHN, educator; b. N.Y.C., Feb. 12, 1920; s. Herman and Julia (Reynolds) C.; B.S., Pa. State U., 1940; Ph.D., Cornell U., 1947; m. Patricia Shellenberger, Sept. 30, 1944; children—Shelly Ann, William Rolfe, Jacqueline Ray, John Herman. Mem. faculty Cornell U., 1947-55; prof. horticulture Mich. State U., 1955—, chmn. dept., 1962—; OECD sr. vis. scientist, Eng., 1961-62. Mem. joint univ. council U. Nigeria, 1962-65. Served to 1st lt. AUS, 1943-46; CBI. Named Vegetable Man of year, Vegetable Growers Assn. Am., 1961. Fellow A.A.A.S.; mem. Am. Soc. Horticultural Sci. (past pres.), Internat. Soc. for Hort. Sci., Sigma Xi, Phi Kappa Phi, Alpha Zeta, Pi Alpha Xi, Gamma Alpha. Co-author: Vegetable Production and Marketing, 1954. Contbr. articles encys., profl. jours. Asso. editor Am. Vegetable Grower mag., 1953—. Home: 725 Whitehills Dr East Lansing MI 48823

CAREW, ROD, second baseman with Minn. Twins Profl. Baseball Team. Address: care Metropolitan Stadium 8001 Cedar Av Bloomington MN 55420*

CAREWE, SYLVIA, artist, tapestry designer; b. N.Y.C.; d. Lewis and Esther (Oghstal) C.; student Columbia; 1 son. John. One-man shows (tapestries) French & Co., 1960, 62, (tapestries and banners) Community Ch., N.Y.C., 1964-69, Fordham U., 1970, (paintings) A C A Gallery, 1948, 53, 54, 56, 58, 61, Riley Gallery (both N.Y.C.), 1959, Three Arts (Poughkeepsie, N.Y.), 1947, 52, 54, 58, 60, Barnett Aden Gallery (Washington), 1950, Tersa Karlis Gallery, Westport. Conn., 1955, Decatur (Ill.) Art Center, Ball State Tchrs. Coll., Art Assn. Richmond (Ind.), Butler Inst. Am. Art. U. Ind., 1955, Wittenborn's One-Wall Gallery, N.Y.C., 1957, Galerie Katie Granoff, Paris, France, 1957, Butler Inst. Am. Art. tapestries, 1960, U. N.C., 1962, also various colls., univs.; headdresses for Aristophanes The Birds, Cooper Union, 1960; exhbn. pastel paintings for tapestry Donnell Art Library, N.Y.C., 1968; exhibited works in many group shows including Mus. Modern Art, Whitney Mus., Mus. Bruge, Belgium, Standliche Mus., Rotterdam, Boston Mus. Fine Arts, Bklyn. Mus., Phila. Print Club, Smith Mus. Springfield, Mass., Columbia (S.C.) Mus. Art, Ga. Mus. Arte; represented in permanent collections Whitney Mus. Am. Art, Musee de l'Arte Moderne, Finch Coll. Art Mus., Paris, Nat. Mus., Djakarta, Indonesia, Brandeis U., Butler Art Inst., Howard U., Tel Aviv Mus., also pvt. collections; designer mag. covers; appeared in Liberated Laundromat (film), 1971. Recipient ann. award A C A Gallery competition for 1st one-man show, 1947. Mem. Artists Equity, Am. Soc. Contemporary Artists, Archtl. Guild, Am. Watercolor Soc., Phila. Print Club, N.Y. Soc. Women Artists, Nat. Soc. Women Artists, Atelier 17, Friends of Whitney Mus., Mus. Modern Art, Guggenheim Mus., Municipal Art Soc. Club: Women's City. Address: 500 E 83d St New York City NY 10028

CAREY, ARCHIBALD J., Jr., clergyman, judge; b. Chgo., Feb. 29, 1908; s. Bishop Archibald J. and Elizabeth (Davis) C.; student U. Chgo., 1925-27; B.S., Lewis Inst., 1928; B.D., Northwestern U., 1932; LL.B., Chgo. Kent Coll. Law, 1935; D.D., Wilberforce U., 1943; LL.D. (hon.), John Marshall Law Sch., 1954; m. Hazel Harper, Jan. 1, 1931; 1 dau., Carolyn Eloise. Ordained to ministry, A.M.E. Ch., 1930; pastor Woodlawn Ch., Chgo., 1930-49, Quinn Chapel, 1949-67; admitted to Ill. bar., 1936, practiced in Chgo.; mem. Prescott, Taylor, Carey & Cooper; judge Circuit Ct. of Cook County, 1966- -; dir., past pres. Ill. Fed. Savs. & Loan Assn. Elected alderman 3d Ward, Chgo., 1947, 51. Chmn. Pres.'s Com. on Govt. Employment Policy, 1957-61, vice chmn., 1955-57; mem. U.S. delegation 8th Gen. Assembly UN, 1953. Rep. nominee 1st Ill. Dist., U.S. Congress, 1950. Received 1st prize oratorical contest Chgo. Daily News, 1924; Edmund W. Burke law scholarship, 1935. Mem. Alpha Phi Alpha (past pres.). Home: 4934 S Michigan Av Chicago IL 60615 Office: Civic Center Chicago IL 60602

CAREY, BENJAMIN WATSON, physician; b. Pleasant Hill, Ill., Feb. 26, 1907; s. Benjamin Watson and Nellie (Smith) C.; B.S., U. Ill., 1928; M.D., Harvard, 1932; m. Eleanor L. Rose, Mar. 2, 1935; 1 dau., Susan (Mrs. William S Bainbridge). Intern Johns Hopkins Hosp., 1932-33; intern, then resident Children's Hosp., Boston, 1933-35; instr. bacteriology and pediatrics Harvard Med. Sch., 1935-38; asst. prof. pediatrics Wayne U., 1938-41; dir. labs. Pearl River Research Labs., Lederle Labs., Am. Cyanamid Co., 1941-57, med. dir., 1957-68; adminstrv. asst. for med. affairs Pascack Valley Hosp., Westwood, N.J., 1968—. Mem. nat. com. Program Harvard Medicine. Mem. N.Y. Acad. Scis., A.M.A., Am. Acad. Pediatrics. Republican. Author: Chemotherapy in Diseases of Infancy and Childhood, Vol. I, 1942. Home: 142 2d Av Westwood, NJ 07675. Office: Pascack Valley Hosp Westwood NJ 07675

CAREY, CHARLES THOMAS, hotel exec.; b. Omaha, Feb. 27, 1911; s. William Lafayette and Elizabeth Gertrude (Jeffers) C.; grad. Creighton Prep Sch., 1928, Worcester Acad., 1929, Cornell U. Coll. Fine Arts, 1934. Asst. passenger traffic mgr. U.P. R.R., 1938-51; v.p. Allied Properties, San Francisco, 1951-53; gen. mgr. Santa Barbara Biltmore, 1951-53; mgr. William Penn Hotel, 1953-56, gen. mgr. Penn-Sheraton Hotel (formerly William Penn), 1956-61; gen. mgr. Sheraton Fontennelle and Logan Hotels, 1961-63; v.p., gen. mgr. Sheraton-Ritz Hotel, Mpls., 1963-66, St. Regis-Sheraton Hotel, Inc., N.Y.C., 1966—. Served as lt. col. AUS, USAAF, 1942-46. Mem. Newcomen Soc. N. Am., Am. Hotel and Motel Assn., Internat. Hotel Assn., Chi Psi. Knight of Malta, Knight of Holy Sepulchre. Address: St Regis-Sheraton Hotel 2 E 55th St New York NY 10022

CAREY, DAVID MARSDEN, mfg. co. exec.; b. Concord, Mass., 1922; ed. Boston Coll., 1947; m. Eve Casey; children—Norine Patricia, David Marsden, Eva Marie, Peter Doyle, Caroline Mary. Vice pres. finance, treas. Am. Chain & Cable Co., Inc.; dir. Parsons Chain, Ltd., Dominon Chain, Brit. Wire Products, M.H.S., Internat. Home: 7 Leslie Lane Westport CT 06880 also (summer) Brewster MA Office: 230 Park Av New York City NY 10017

CAREY, EDWARD, nat. comdr. Salvation Army; b. Eng., Jan. 13, 1906; s. James Joseph and Jane Leila (Quellin) C.; student Salvation Army Tng. Coll., 1923-24; B.S. in Edn., N.Y. U., 1950; m. Faith Seaver, Sept. 19, 1928; children—Donald E., Constance (Mrs. Bruce Samuel), Florence Jane (Mrs. Marion Kim). Various appointments in field work with Salvation Army, divisional comdr., internat. sec., London, 1963-68, territorial comdr. U.S., 1968-69, nat. comdr. U.S., 1970—. Bd. dirs. Christian Children's Fund, Richmond, Va., Nat. Council Boy Scouts Am.; mem. nat. budget com. U.S.O. Recipient Golden Rule award St. George's Assn. Police Dept. N.Y., 1961, Distinguished Service award N.Y. U., 1969. Mem. Nat. Assn. Social Workers, Acad. Certified Social Workers, Nat. Conf. Social Work, Kappa Delta Pi. Home: 720 West End Av New York City NY 10025 Office: 120-130 W 14th St New York City NY 10011

CAREY, EDWIN WILLIAM mfg. exec.; b. Lima, O., Apr. 1, 1932; B.S., U. San Francisco, 1954; M.S., Stanford University, 1956; m. Rosemarie Lois Brown, May 15, 1955; 1 son, Anthony Robinson. Sales rep. Ames-Brockton Fabricated Products, Akron, O., 1956-58, sales mgr. Coshocton, Ohio, 1959-61, gen. manager plant, 1961-68, v.p. sales, 1968--. Instr. bus. Coshocton Jr. College, 1968-69. Secretary Coshocton YMCA, 1960-61; active Boy Scouts of America. Named Man of Year, Coshocton Junior Chamber of Commerce, 1968. Mem. Coshocton C. of C. (vice president 1967-68, pres. 1969-70), English Speaking Union, Coshocton Sertoma Club, Nat. Assn. Mfrs., Sales Executives Institute, Phi Beta Kappa, Sigma Chi, Phi Mu. Democrat. Mem. Christian Ch. (lay leader). Mason (32, Shriner). Clubs: Coshocton Country, Coshocton City, Running Deer Country. Home: 2d Av Coshocton OH Office: 3d Av Coshocton OH

CAREY, ERNESTINE GILBRETH, (Mrs. Charles E. Carey), author, lectr.; b. N.Y.C., Apr. 5, 1908; d. Frank Bunker and Lillian (Moller) Gilbreth; B.A., Smith Coll., 1929; m. Charles Everett Carey, Sept. 13, 1930; children—Lillian Gilbreth (Mrs. Henry C. Clark III), Charles Everett. Buyer, R. H. Macy & Co., N.Y.C., 1930-44, James McCreery, N.Y.C., 1947-49; lectr., book reviews, syndicated newspaper articles, 1951—. Bd. dirs. Right to Read, Inc., 1968—, co-chmn., 1967; lay adv. com. Manhasset Pub. Library, 1953-59, v.p., 1956-59; trustee Smith Coll., 1967—. Recipient French Internat. humor award for Cheaper by the Dozen, 1950, (with Lillian Mollen Gilbreth) McElligott medallion Assn. Marquette U. Women, 1966. Mem. Am. Assn. U. Women (chmn. edn. com. N. Shore, L.I. br. 1956-57, mem. legislative com. 1956-57), Authors Guild Am. (life mem., mem. guild council 1955-60), P.E.N. Republican. Conglist. Clubs: Smith College (asst. chmn. scholarship com. 1950-59) (L.I.); Smith Coll. (N.Y.); Smith College Phoenix (chmn. scholarship com. 1967), 7 College Conf. Council (Phoenix). Author: Jumping Juniper, 1952; Rings Around Us, 1956; Giddy Moment, 1958; (with Frank B. Gilbreth) Cheaper by the Dozen, 1949; Belles on Their Toes, 1951; also mag. articles and book revs. Home: 6148 E Lincoln Dr Paradise Valley AZ 85253 also Pond Point Westhampton Beach NY 11978

CAREY, FRANCIS E., sci. writer; b. Lowell, Mass., Aug. 1, 1909; s. Francis J. and Theresa (Egan) C.; B.A. cum laude, Coll. Holy Cross, 1930; Nieman fellow, Harvard, 1946-47; m. Anna Gertrude Carney, July 13, 1938; children—Barbara Anne (Mrs. Arthur H. Hayes, Jr.), Eleanor Frances (Mrs. Kurt Kroeger), Susan Mary (Mrs. William B. Bell III). Reporter, Lowell Sun, 1931-38; newsman A.P., Boston, 1938-43, sci. writer, Washington, 1943—. Recipient Westinghouse A.A.A.S. award, 1948, Christopher award, 1952, Am. Heart Assn. award, 1956, Epilepsy Found. award, 1964, Grady award Am. Chem. Soc., 1965, journalism award Am. Soc. Abdom. Surgeons, 1966; Spl. commendation A.M.A. Journalism Competition, 1965, 66, Med. Journalism award, 1970; Atomic Indsl. Forum award, 1968, Am. Assn. Blood Banks award, 1969. Fellow A.A.A.S.; mem. Nat. Assn. Sci. Writers (past sec.-treas.), Washington Acad. Scis. K.C. Home: 12 N Edison St Arlington VA 22203 Office: 1300 Connecticut Av NW Washington DC 20036

CAREY, FRANCIS JAMES, Jr., lawyer; b. Balt., Mar. 24, 1926; s. Francis James and Marjorie (Armstrong) C.; student Princeton, 1943-44; A.B., U. Pa., 1945, J.D., 1949; m. Emily Norris Large, June 8, 1956; children—Francis James III, Elizabeth Page, Augustus, Emily Norris, Frances Whelen. Admitted to Pa. bar, 1950; law sect. to justice Supreme Ct. Pa., 1950-51; with firm Townsend, Elliott & Munson, Phila., 1951—, mem. firm, 1958—; mem. faculty U. Pa., 1946-47. Dir. Western Savs. Bank, Phila. Nat. Sugar Securities Co., Broadsan Corp., Internat. Leasing Corp. Mem. Com. of Seventy, Phila., 1957-58; mem. Lower Gwynedd Twp. Planning Commn., 1962—. sec., 1962-65. Trustee, Germantown Acad., 1961—, pres., 1966—; mgr. Law Alumni Soc. U. Pa., 1962-66. Served to lt. USNR, 1943-45; PTO. Mem. Am., Pa. (chmn. real property, probate and trust sect. 1965-66), Phila. (chmn. com. civil legislation 1962) bar assns. Republican. Episcopalian. Clubs: Philadelphia, Fourth Street (past officer), St. Anthony (past officer) (Phila.); Penllyn (Pa.). Home: Norristown Rd Spring House Philadelphia PA 19477 Office: Western Saving Bank Bldg Philadelphia PA 19107

CAREY, FRANK J., ins. exec.; b. Boston, Feb. 16, 1907; s. Henry M. and Mary T. (Coughlin) C.; student Georgetown U., 1926-28; m. Alice M. Lynch, Oct. 5, 1929; children—Frank J., Marilyn A. Joined Employers' Liability Assurance Corp., Ltd., Am. Employers' Ins. Co., Employers' Fire Ins. Co., Boston, 1928; first dep. mgr. U.S. br. Employers' Liability Assurance Corp., Ltd., 1959—; pres., dir. Hallifax Ins. Co. Mass., 1959—, Am. Employers' Ins. Co., 1959—, Employers' Fire Ins. Co., 1959—; trustee, 1st v.p. Employers' Group Assos. Clubs: Down Town, Algonquin (Boston); Wianno (Osterville, Mass.). Home: 75 Hampshire Rd Wellesley Hills MA 02181 Office: 282 Beacon St Boston MA 02116

CAREY, GERARD V., banker; b. N.Y.C., Nov. 20, 1926; s. George J. and Helen M. (Curley) C.; B.B.A., Adelphi U., 1950; m. Doris L. Walz, May 23, 1953; 1 dau., Diane L. Sr. accountant Price, Waterhouse & Co., N.Y.C., 1953-59; asst. controller Stahl-Meyer Corp. of N.Y., 1959-60; mgr. systems and spl. studies Standard Brands, N.Y.C., 1960-65; v.p. audit, accounting and control functions First Pa. Banking & Trust Co., Phila., 1965-68, sr. v.p., chief financial officer, 1968-70, exec. v.p., 1970—; v.p. First Pa. Corp., 1968—; dir. Asso. Mortgage Companies, Inc., Investors Loan Corp., Indsl. Finance & Thrift Corp., Tinicum Real Estate Holding Corp., Asso. Advisers, Inc., Vestaur Corp. Trustee Magee Meml. Hosp. for Convalescents, Phila. C.P.A., N.Y. Mem. Am. Inst. C.P.A.'s, N.Y. State Soc. C.P.A.'s, Nat. Assn. Accountants, Bank Adminstrn. Inst., Financial Execs. Inst. (bd. dirs. Phila.). Home: 11 N Riding Dr Cherry Hill NJ 08034 Office: 15th and Chestnut Sts Philadelphia PA 19101

CAREY, GUILLERMO, lawyer; b. Chile, Feb. 19, 1912; s. Francisco Carey and Elena Bustamante de Carey; LL.B., U. Santiago, 1934; m. Anita Tagle de Carey, Nov. 23, 1939; children—Guillermo, Jorge, Marianne (Mrs. Michael Patrick Shea), Francisco, Jaime. Came to U.S., 1964. Prof. law U. Santiage Law Sch., 1938-60; admitted to Chile bar, 1934; corp. lawyer, partner Carey and Carey, 1935-64; founder, chief counsel, chmn. bd. Banco Sud Americano, 1944-64; dir., v.p., chief counsel, dir. Anglo Lautaro Nitrate Corp., 1945-64; dir. Nitrate Sales Corp., 1945-64, Compania Sue Americana de Vapores, 1952-64, Compania de Aceros del Pacifico, 1952-64, Embotelladora Andina (Coca Cola), 1944-65, Coia (Grace & Co.), 1958-64, Compania de Sequros La Americana, 1948-64; dir., v.p. Chile Exploration Co., 1964—, Santiago Mining Co., 1964—, Greene Cananea Copper Co., 1964—, Andes del Peru, 1964—; v.p. Anaconda Co., 1966—, sr. v.p. Latin Am. affairs, 1968—, Bd. dirs. Nat. Fqn. Trade Council. Bd. dirs. Leukemia Soc., Americas Found., Inc. Clubs: Recess, Metropolitan (N.Y.C.); Piping Rock (Locust Valley, L.I.); Club de la Union, de Golf, de Polo (Santiago). Author: The Monetary Problems and the Crises, 1934; The Inflaton and the Law, 1960. Home: 535 Park Av New York City NY 10021 Office: 25 Broadway New York City NY 10004

CAREY, HARVEY LOCKE, lawyer; b. Parkin, Ark., Jan. 19, 1915; s. Gregory and Willie Belle (Locke) C.; student U. Ark., 1932-34, La. Poly. Inst., 1934-35; J.D., Tulane U., 1939; postgrad. Dartmouth, 1942, Princeton, 1943; m. Katie Elizabeth Drew, Oct. 15, 1933 (div.); children—Richard Drew, Thomas Gregory, Katie Lucile; m. 2d, Nellie A. Deatherage, Apr. 14, 1956 (dec. Nov. 1967). Admitted to La. bar, 1939; practice in Shreveport, 1940—; as Harvey L. Carey, atty., 1950—; spl. asst. atty. gen. La., 1948; U.S. dist. atty. for Western Dist. of La., 1950-52; spl. counsel Caddo Levee Bd., 1948—; judge ad hoc City Ct., Shreveport, 1968—. Clerk, La. Ho. Reps., 1948-50. Served to lt. comdr. USNR, 1943-46; comdg. officer of U.S.S. LCI(L) 466, 1943-44. Mem. Am., La., Shreveport bar assns., Am. Judicature Soc., Assn. ICC Practitioners, Am. Legion, V.F.W., Disabled Am. Vets., Mil. Order Purple Heart (local comdr. 1949, state comdr. 1950, 56-57, nat. vice comdr. 1962-63), Phi Delta Phi, Sigma Phi Epsilon. Democrat (mem. Caddo Parish exec. com. 1948-50; candidate for U.S. rep. from La. 1948). Methodist. Home: 1901 Centenary Blvd Shreveport LA 71101 Office: Lane Bldg Shreveport LA 71101

CAREY, HIRAM BISSELL, Jr., utility exec.; b. Farmington, Conn., July 30, 1915; s. Hiram Bissell and Mary Elizabeth (Barney) C.; B.A., Yale, 1937, LL.B., 1940; m. Anne Holladay Shafer, Feb. 13, 1943; children—Hiram Bissell III, Mary Holladay, Dallas Shafer, Nancy Sheldon. Admitted to Conn. bar, 1940; with firm Buck & McCook, Hartford, 1940-45, Hoppin, Carey & Powell, Hartford, 1945-51; with Hartford Electric Light Co., 1949-66, gen. counsel, 1951-53, v.p., gen. counsel, 1954-64, sr. v.p., 1964-66; v.p. N.E. Utilities, 1966—; sr. v.p. dir. N.E. Utilities Service Co., 1966—; dir. Conn. Light & Power Co., Hartford Electric Light Co., Holyoke Water Power Co., Western Mass. Electric Co., Millstone Point Co., Farmington Savs. Bank, Hartford Courant, Conn. Internat. Corp., Windsor Locks. Bd. dirs. Hartford Hosp. Mem. Am., Fed. Power, Conn., Hartford County bar assns. Home: Mountain Spring Rd Farmington CT 06032 Office: PO Box 270 Hartford CT 06101

CAREY, HUGH L., congressman; b. Bklyn., Apr. 11, 1919; s. Dennis J. and Margaret (Collins) C.; LL.B., St. John's Coll., 1951; LL.D., St. John's Law School, 1967; m. Helen Owen, Feb. 27, 1947; children—Alexandria, Christopher, Susan, Peter (dec.), Hugh L. (dec.), Michael Donald, Marianne, Nancy, Helen, Bryan, Paul, Kevin and Thomas Carey. Admitted to the N.Y. State bar, 1951, U.S. Supreme Ct., 1963; practiced in Bklyn.; past dir., officer several indsl. firms; mem. 87th Congress 12th Dist. N.Y., 88th-92d Congress 15th dist. N.Y., mem. house edn. and labor com., interior and insular affairs com., elected to com. on ways and and means, 1970. Active local Boys, League Sch., Gallaudet Coll. for Deaf, St. Joseph Coll., Marymount Coll., Nat. Tech. Inst. for the Deaf at Rochester. Mem. bd. visitors U.S. Mcht. Marine Acad. del. Interparliamentary Union Conf., Brussels, Belgium, 1961. Mem. bd. govs. Nat. Democratic Club. Served to maj., inf., AUS, World War II; col. res. Decorated Bronze Star, Combat Inf. award; Croix de Guerre with silver star

(France); named knight Holy Sepulchre of Jerusalem (Pope Pius XII). Mem. V.F.W., Am. Legion, Cath. War Vets., Emerald Assn. (dir.), Phi Delta Phi. Democrat. Catholic. K.C. Club: Cathedral (dir.) (Bklyn.). Home: 61 Prospect Park W Brooklyn NY 11215 Office: House Office Bldg Washington DC 20515

CAREY, J. EDWIN, lawyer; b. N.Y.C., Aug. 29, 1923; s. Edwin J. and Nora L. (Greene) C.; student Manhattan Coll., 1941-43; LL.B., St. John's U., 1951; m. Marian G. Burke, May 23, 1954; children—Brianne, Christopher. Admitted to N.Y. bar, 1951, since practiced in N.Y.C.; sr. partner firm Hill, Rivkins, Warburton, McGowan & Carey, and predecessors, 1961—. Lectr. admiralty law Practicing Law Inst., 1959—. Served with inf. AUS, 1943-46; ETO. Mem. Am., N.Y. State bar assns., Maritime Law Assn. U.S. (chmn. membership com. 1958-60, membership sec. 1960-66, sec. 1966-69, 1st v.p. 1970—, del. internat. confs.), Am. Judicature Soc. (1st v.p. 1970—), Assn. Average Adjusters, Ins. Soc. N.Y., St. Thomas More Soc. (pres. 1948-49), Phi Delta Phi. Clubs: Drug and Chemical (N.Y.C.); North Jersey Country (Wayne, N.J.). Home: 393 Carriage Lane Wyckoff NJ 07481 Office: 96 Fulton St New York City NY 10038

CAREY, JAMES BARRON, labor exec.; b. Phila., Pa., Aug. 12, 1911; s. John and Margaret (Loughery) C.; student Drexel Inst., evenings., 1929-31, Wharton Evening Sch., U. Pa., 1931-32; LL.D., Rollins Coll., 1947; m. Margaret McCormick, Jan. 8, 1938; children—James Barron, Patricia Ann. Elec. worker, radio lab. Phila. Storage Battery Co., 1929-34; nat. pres. Radio and Allied Trades, 1933-40; apptd. gen. organizer for U.S. by A.F. of L., July 1934; nat. sec. Congress Indsl. Orgn., 1938—, sec.-treas., 1942—; gen. pres. United Elec., Radio and Machine Workers Am., 1936-41; pres. Internat. Union Elec., Radio and Machine Workers, AFL-CIO, 1950-65; v.p. AFL-CIO, 1955-65, sec.- treas. Indsl. Union Dept.; apptd. mem. prodn. planning bd. Office Prodn. Mgmt., Washington, 1941; exec. officer Utility Workers Organizing Com.; chmn. Congress Indsl. Orgn. Com. to Abolish Discrimination; del., London, 1945, Paris, 1945. Moscow, 1946, Paris, 1947. Rome, 1948, meetings of World Fedn. Trade Unions; del founding meeting Internat. Confedn. Free Trade Unions, London, 1949; worker del. ILO, Geneva, 1956; mem. presdl. commn. on civil rights, 1946; presdl. non-partisan (Harriman) Commn., 1947; mem. adv. com., ECA, 1948; labor rep. Commn. on Jud. and Congl. Salaries, 1953; mem. labor adv. com. FOA, 1954, Dept. Labor, 1955; mem. Commn. on White House Fellows, 1964-65; dir. labor participation UN Assn. U.S. Mem. fgn. policy and labor policy adv. coms. Dem. Nat. Com., 1958; mem. nat. bd. Ams. for Dem. Action. Recipient award for service to youth Parent Mag. 1940; Quadragesimo Anno award Assn. Catholic Trade Unionists, 1961; James B. Carey Labor Library, Rutgers U., named in his honor, 1962. Mem. Am. Arbitration Assn. (dir.), Workers Def. League (v.p.), League for Indsl. Democracy (nat. council), Nat. Planning Assn. (trustee). Contbr. to labor jours. Home: 8 Hilltop Rd Silver Spring MD 20910 Office: 1126 16th St NW Washington DC 20036

CAREY, JAMES HENRY, banker; b. Elizabeth, N.J., May 22, 1932; s. Charles C. and Adelyne (Bilyeu) C.; B.A. cum laude, Brown U., 1953; postgrad. Sch. Bus. Adminstrn., N.Y. U., 1956-59; m. Nancy Mershon Ferrenz, Aug. 14, 1954; children—Jane Meredith, Christopher James, George Mershon, David James. With Chase Manhattan Bank, N.Y.C., 1955-68, asst. v.p., 1961-63, v.p., 1963-68; exec. v.p. Hambro Am. Bank & Trust Co., N.Y.C., 1968-69, pres., 1969—, dir. 1969—; dir. Hambros Bank Ltd., London, Hambro Internat. N.V., Eurus, Inc., Essex Internat., Inc. Served to lt. (j.g.) USNR, 1953- 55. Mem. India House, Phi Beta Kappa, Delta Tau Delta. Episcopalian. Club: Sleepy Hollow Country. Home: 44 Sleepy Hollow Rd Briarcliff Manor NY 10510 Office: 25 Broad St New York City NY 10004

CAREY, JAMES WILLIAM, cons. civil and elec. engr.; b. Duluth, Minn., Aug. 28, 1892; s. Peter and Marie (Nichols) C.; ed. various schs. in Minn., Ohio, N.Y.; m. Sally B. Lofthus, Dec. 5, 1942. Transitman on railroad constrn. work, Wash., 1908-09; constrn. engr. bldg. railroads, docks, power and sewer systems for Pacific Coast Steamship Co., Pacific Coast Coal Co., Pacific Coast R.R. Co., 1909-15; charge valuation work Pacific Coast R.R. Co. of Wash. and Pacific Coast Ry. Co. of Cal. for ICC, 1915-17; constrn. engr., various positions, 1919-21; constrn. engr., transmission lines Stone & Webster Engring. Corp., 1921-22; chief engr. Wash. Dept. Pub. Works and Wash. Tax Commn., 1922-28; cons. engr., Portland, Ore., and Tacoma, engaged in valuation, reports on water power sites, including present Bonneville power site; outlined present pub. service laws Ore., 1928-33; chief engr. Wash. Dept. Pub. Service, 1933-36; state engr. charge constrn. P.W.A., Wash., 1936- 38; cons. civil and elec. engr., Seattle and Tacoma, 1938-43; mem. firm James W. Carey & Assos. Carey & Kramer, cons. engrs. Mem. U.S.-Alaskan Internat. Hwy. Commn., 1938- 54; mem. Nat. Rivers and Harbors Congress; engaged as cons. engr., rebldg. City of Renton, Wash., as def. matter; now streets, water and sewer system, sewage disposal plant, 1944; designed Des Chutes Basin Project, dam, spillway; Tolt River Dam for Seattle Water Supply; design for USN, largest drydock in world, Bremerton, Wash. with N.Y. firm; co- designer met. sewage project, Seattle; engaged in work with Hydro- Electric Project, Sitka, Alaska; widely known in electric light, power, water, sewerage and sewage disposal, appraisals. Served as officer USNR, 1917-19. Mem. Soc. Am. Mil. Engrs., Wash. Soc. Profl. Engrs. (pres. 1942), Am. Legion, 40 and 8, Seattle Exec. Assn., Seattle C. of C., Am. Water Works Assn., Northwest Sewage Assn., Am. Concrete Inst., Am. Arbitration Assn., Cons. Engrs. Assn., Nat. Rivers and Harbor Congress, Alaska-Yukon Pioneers (past pres.). Mason (K.T.). Clubs: Rainier, Blue Ridge (past pres.), Washington Athletic, Arctic, Engineers (Seattle). Author numerous engring. papers. Home: 10005 Bayard Av NW Blue Ridge Seattle WA 98177 Office: Alaska Trades Bldg Seattle WA 98101

CAREY, JANE PERRY CLARK, polit. scientist; b. Washington; d. John C. and Addie (Burr) Clark, A.B., Vassar Coll.; A.M., Columbia, Ph.D., 1931; m. Andrew Galbraith Carey, Jan. 10, 1942. Research sec. Internat. Migration Service, 1922-28; instr. econs. Mt. Holyoke Coll., 1928-29; cons. Com. on Ellis Island, U.S. Sec. Labor, 1933; staff mem. Pres.'s Com. on Econ. Security, 1934-35; cons. U.S. Social Security Bd., 1935-43; prin. tng. specialist U.S. Civil Service Commn., 1943; mem. various fed., state wage bds., 1934-40; asst. adviser on displaced persons U.S. Dept. State, 1944-46; cons. U.S. State Dept., 1946-47; expert cons. Germany, U.S. Mil. Govt., 1948, cons. Dept. State, 1951, 64-67; chief investigator U.S.A. and Can. refugee survey UN High Commr. for Refugees, 1952; asst. prof. govt. Barnard Coll., Columbia, 1938-53. Research guest Greek Govt., 1965, Sweden, 1968, 70, Turkey, 1969, Iran, 1970; mem. U.S. Fulbright Commn. for Italy, 1953-54. Pres., Consumers League N.Y., 1941-42. Trustee Vassar Coll., 1943-51, Mt. Vernon Jr. Coll. and Sem. for Girls; bd. dirs. Robert Coll., Istanbul, Anatolia Coll., Thessaloniki, Greece, Salzburg Seminar in Am. Studies; past bd. dirs. Am. Women's Vol. Service, Consumers' League N.Y. Recipient Robert Noxon Toppan prize in constl. law Columbia, 1928 (1st time to a woman), research awards Council for Research Social Sci., 1935, 38, 48. Decorated Order Italian Solidarity. Mem. Am. Polit. Sci. Assn., Fgn. Policy Assn. (dir., exec. com.), Am. Acad. Polit. Sci., Am. Soc. Pub. Adminstrn. (internat. com.), Am. Soc. Internat. Law, Internat. Polit. Sci. Assn., Am. Soc. Pub. Adminstrs. Democrat. Methodist. Clubs: Cosmopolitan, Colony (N.Y.C.); Sulgrave (Washington). Author: Deportation of Aliens from United States to Europe, 1931; The Rise of a New Federalism, 1938; The Uprooted People of Europe and European Recovery, 1948; Italy: Change and Progress, 1963; (with A.G. Carey) The Web of Modern Greek Politics, 1968. Contbr. articles to profl. publs. Address: Godfrey Rd Weston CT 06880 also 30 Sutton Pl New York City NY 10022

CAREY, JOHN, lawyer; b. Phila., June 11, 1924; s. Henry Reginald and Margaret Howell (Bacon) C.; grad. Milton Acad., 1942; B.A., Yale, 1947; LL.B., Harvard. 1949; LL.M. in Internat. Law, N.Y.U., 1965; m. Patricia F. Frank, Feb. 24, 1951; children—Henry Frank, John, Douglas, Jennifer Patricia. Admitted to Pa. bar, 1950, N.Y. bar, 1957; practiced in Phila., 1949-55, N.Y.C., 1956—; asst. dist. atty., Phila., 1952-54; cons. spl. com. fed. loyalty-security program Assn. Bar City N.Y., 1955- 56; partner firm Coudert Bros., 1961—. Dir., Walker & Co. Mem. Faculty N.Y. U. Law Sch., 1966—. Mem. city council, Rye, N.Y., 1964-68. Alternate mem. UN Subcommn. on Prevention Discrimination and Protection of Minorities, 1966—; alternate U.S. rep. UN Human Rights Commn., 1968. Trustee, Little Harbor Chapel, Portsmouth, N.H. Mem. Am. Fgn. Law Assn., Am., Internat., N.Y. State, Phila. bar assns., Assn. Bar City N.Y. (rep. at UN), Internat. League for Rights of Man (chmn. bd.), Am. Soc. Internat. Law, Phi Beta Kappa. Rotarian. Author: UN Protection of Civil and Political Rights, 1970. Mem. bd. editors Am. Jour. Internat. Law. Home: 860 Forest Av Rye NY 10580 Office: 200 Park Av New York City NY 10017

CAREY, JOHN LEO, lawyer; b. Morris, Ill., Oct. 1, 1920; s. John Leo and Loretta (Conley) C.; B.S., St. Ambrose Coll., Davenport, Ia., 1941; J.D., Georgetown U., 1947, LL.B., 1949; m. Rhea M. White, July 15, 1950; children—John Leo III, Daniel Hobart, Deborah M. Legislative asst. Sen. Scott W. Lucas, 1945-47; spl. atty. Internal Revenue Service, Washington, 1947- 54; admitted to Ind. bar, 1954, since practiced in South Bend; partner Thornburg, McGill, Deahl, Carey & Murray, 1954—; law prof. taxation Notre Dame Law Sch., 1968—. Trustee LaLumire Prep. Sch., Laporte, Ind. Served with USAAF, World War II; to lt. col. USAF, Korean War. Decorated D.F.C., Air medal. Mem. Am., Ind., South Bend bar assns. Club: South Bend Country (sec.). Home: 1326 Ridgedale Rd South Bend IN 46614 Office: First Bank Bldg South Bend IN 46601

CAREY, JOHN THOMAS, educator; b. Wilmont, Minn., Aug. 23, 1917; s. Thomas Joseph and Elizabeth (Mahon) C.; B.S., Milw. State Tchrs. Coll., 1946, U. Wis., 1947; Ph.D., Ohio State U., 1954; m. Eileen Frances Schumann, Sept. 23, 1947; children—Thomas George, Michael John. Instr. art dept. U. Wis., 1947-48; supr. art Janesville (Wis.) pub. schs., 1948-49; asst. prof. Ill. State Normal U., 1949-51; asst. prof. art dept. Bowling Green (O.) State U., 1954-56; chmn. dept. art No. Ill. U., 1956-62, prof., 1956-66; vis. prof. art history Rollins Coll., Winter Park, Fla. 1966-67; 67; chmn. faculty art U. West Fla., Pensacola, 1967—; vis. prof. World Campus Afloat div. internat. edn. Chapman Coll., Orange, Cal., spring 1969. Served from pvt. to capt., C.E., AUS, 1941-46. Mem. Am. Assn. U. Profs. Southeastern Coll. Art Assn., Fla. Art Edn. Assn. Home: 412 Sunnydale Lane Cantonment FL 32533 Office: U West Fla Pensacola FL 32504

CAREY, LAWRENCE BERNARD, retired banker; b. Bklyn., Feb. 7, 1892; s. Michael F. and Eliza (Byron) C.; student Fordham U., 1915-17, also Columbia and N.Y.U.; m. Agnes Monetti, Sept. 15, 1920 (dec. Nov. 1946); m. 2d, Francesca Ferris, July 31, 1954. With Irving Trust Co., N.Y.C., 1920-35, asst. v.p., 1929-35; pres. First Nat. Bank, Plainfield, N.J., 1936-39, Plainfield Nat. Bank, 1939-45; commr. banking and ins. N.J., 1945-48; exec. v.p. The Trust Co. of N.J., 1948-58, pres., 1958-64, chmn. bd., 1964-70; cons., 1971—. Served with U.S. Navy, World War I. Mem. Fordham Alumni Assn., Club: Plainfield Country (treas. 1941-43). Home: 1110 Martine Av Plainfield NJ 07060 Office: 35 Journal Sq Jersey City NJ 07603

CAREY, LEN, advt. exec.; b. Los Angeles, Apr. 29, 1915; s. Olie Leonard and Edith (Taylor) C.; ed. U. Ariz., 1934; m. Elizabeth Poulson, Oct. 5, 1934; children—Jeffrey Taylor, Christopher Ann; m. 2d, Shirley Welton, June 16, 1948; 1 dau., Leslie Taylor. Owner Len Carey & Assos., Long Beach, Cal., 1936-42; v.p. Batten, Barton, Durstine & Osborn, Inc., N.Y.C., 1946-60, also dir.; exec. v.p. C.J. La Roche & Co., Inc., N.Y.C., 1960—; pres. Len Carey, Inc., 1961-63, Compton-Carey, Inc., 1964-70, Barnes-Carey Advt., Inc., San Diego, 1970—. Served to maj. USMCR, 1942-45. Mem. Am. Assn. Advt. Agys. (gov. N.Y. council 1958-60). Clubs: La Jolla Country; Westminster Kennel, Westchester Kennel (chmn.). Author: Your Doberman Pinscher, 1954; also short stories. All-breed judge Am. Kennel Club. Home: 7320 Encelia Dr La Jolla CA 92037 Office: 1010 2d Av San Diego CA 92001

CAREY, RAYMOND BERNARD, Jr., elec. co. exec.; b. Cambridge, Mass., Nov. 13, 1926; s. Raymond Bernard and Irene (Lawton) C.; B.S., Holy Cross Coll., 1948; M.B.A., Harvard, 1950; m. Dennice Rioux, Aug. 18, 1951; children—Shelia, Lisa, Michael. With Gen. Dynamics Corp., 1951-66, pres., gen. mgr. Electro Dynamic div., 1960-66; v.p., dir. Robert Morse Corp., Montreal, 1966-70; pres. Howe Richardson Scale Co., Clifton, N.J., 1966-68; pres., dir. Am. Dist. Telegraph Co., indsl. and residential protection, N.Y.C., 1970—. Served with USNR, 1944-46. Home: Browndock Rd Locust NJ 07760 Office: 155 6th Av New York City NY 10013

CAREY, ROBERT S., iron ore and shipping co. exec.; b. Cleve., July 27, 1915; s. Charles S. and Martha (Boggis) C.; A.B., Yale, 1937; m. Judith Feather, Mar. 23, 1940; 1 dau., Linda F. (Mrs. D.O. Kyle Felt). With Pickands Mather & Co., Cleve., 1937—, exec. v.p., 1967-69, pres., 1969—, also dir.; dir. William Feather Co., Labrador Steamship Co., Toledo Lakefront Dock Co. Served to lt. (j.g.) USNR, 1943-46. Mem. Lake Carriers Assn. (bd. dirs.), Am. Bur. Shipping, Am. Iron Ore Assn. (bd. dirs.). Clubs: Union, Tavern, Mayfield (Cleve.); Duquesne (Pitts.); Laurel Valley (Ligonier, Pa.). Home: 3076 Fairmount Blvd Cleveland Heights OH 44118 Office: Union Commerce Bldg Cleveland OH 44115

CAREY, ROSS SHUGART, lawyer; b. Cranberry, Pa., Oct. 22, 1907; s. Charles M. and Mary L. (Sayers) C.; A.B., Allegheny Coll., 1929; LL.B., U. Pa., 1940; m. Margaret E. Dougherty, June 27, 1936; children—Kathleen M., Helen S., Alice R. Tchr. high sch., Meadville, Pa., 1930-37; admitted to Pa. bar, 1940; law clk. Pa. Supreme Ct., 1940-43; dep. atty. gen. Commonwealth Pa., 1943-44; asso. firm Cahill, Gordon, Zachry & Reindel, N.Y.C., 1944-48; asst. gen. counsel Libbey-Owens-Ford Co., Toledo, 1948-60, gen. counsel, 1960—, sec., 1954-63, v.p., 1963—, dir., 1971—; dir. Societa Italiano Vetro, Italy. Trustee Allegheny Coll., Toledo Orch. Assn. Mem. Am., Ohio, Toledo bar assns., Order of Coif, Phi Beta Kappa, Alpha Chi Rho. Club: Toledo Iverness. Home: 6234 Valley Park Dr Toledo OH 43623 Office: 811 Madison Av Toledo OH 43603

CAREY, THOMAS LAWRENCE, chem. co. exec.; b. Shullsburg, Wis., Apr. 10, 1917; s. Wilfred W. and Mary (Lewis) C.; B.S. in Mining Engring., Mich. Tech. U., 1941; m. Mable M. Marksbury, Jan. 24, 1945; children—Thomas Lawrence, Carol Jean (Mrs. W. H. Frizell III), Deborah Ann, William, Michael. Mining engr., mine supr. Kennicott Copper Corp., 1941-42; mining engr., staff engr., adminstrv. asst. Potash Co. Am., 1945-56; resident mgr., v.p., dir. asst. sec. Potash Co. Am. Ltd., Sask., Can., 1956-59; dir. exploration and mine devel. mgr. phosphate mining and mfg. operations Armour Agrl. Chem. Co., Atlanta, 1959-66; with Escambia Chem. Corp., Pensacola, Fla., 1966-71, pres., chief exec. officer, dir., 1968-71; v.p. Air Products & Chems., Inc., 1971—. Mem. adv. com. Bapt. Hosp.; charter mem. U. W. Fla. Found. Bd. dirs. United Fund, Jr. Achievement, Pensacola. Served with USAAF, 1942-45. Mem. Fla. C. of C. (dir.), Indsl. Mgmt. Assn. Pensacola (exec. com.), Am. Inst. Mining and Metall. Engrs., Pensacola Sports Assn., Santa Ross County C. of C. and Indsl. Bd. Roman Catholic. Club: Pensacola Country, Scenic Hills Country (Pensacola). Patentee in field. Home: 205 Palmetto Rd Gulf Breeze FL 32561 Office: Box 467 Pensacola FL 32502

CAREY, TOM MAX, oil co. exec.; b. Guthrie, Okla., Sept. 26, 1928; s. Glen T. and Ora Jo (Mitchell) C.; B.S., Okla. State U., 1950; M.B.A., So. Meth. U., 1957; m. E. Joyce Derden, June 18, 1953; children—Ellen, Martha. Accounting mgr. Mobil Oil Co., Dallas, 1954-61; v.p., dir., treas., Koch Industries, Wichita, Kan., 1961—; v.p., dir. Koch Engring. Co.; pres. Matador Cattle Co.; dir. Great No. Oil Co., Matador Chem. Co. Served to 1st lt. USAF, 1952-54. Home: 562 Brookfield St Wichita KS 67206 Office: PO Box 2256 Wichita KS 67220

CAREY, WESLEY GORDON, lawyer; b. nr. Zion, Ill., May 6, 1907; s. Eustace L. and Susan (Watkinson) C.; A.B., Lake Forest U., 1931; J.D., John Marshall Law Sch., Chgo., 1936; m. Ute Lehmann, Oct. 29, 1964; children-Barbara Ann (Mrs. Shane Hunt), Wesley Gordon, Robert, Michele, Sonia. Admitted to Ill. bar, 1935, Fla. bar, 1952; practice in Waukogan, Ill., 1935-52, Miami, Fla., 1953—; sr. partner Carey, Dwyer, Austin, Cole & Selwood. Trustee Lake Forest U. Served from lt. (j.g.) to lt., USNR, 1952-55. Mem. Internat. Assn. Ins. Council, Am., Inter-Am., Fla., Ill., Chgo., Dade County bar assns., Am. Judicature Soc., Am. Soc. Internat. Law, Internat. Soc. Barristers, C. of C. of Ams. Clubs: Coral Reef Yacht Coconut Grove, Fla., Ocean Reef (Key Largo, Fla.); American (Miami). Home: 1270 Mariola Ct Miami FL 33134 Office: Seybold Bldg Miami FL 33132; also Court House Sq Bldg Fort Lauderdale FL 33301

CAREY, WILLIAM DANIEL, mgmt. cons.; b. N.Y.C., Jan. 29, 1916; s. Daniel Joseph and Elizabeth (Galloway) C.; B.A., Columbia, 1940, M.A. (Curtis fellow 1941), 1941; M.P.A. (Littauer fellow 1941-42), Harvard, 1942; m. Mary Margaret Rhodin, May 20, 1944; childrenEric, Teresa, Jane, Julia, Elizabeth. With Bur. of Budget, Exec. Office of President, 1942-69, asst. dir., 1966-69; with Arthur D. Little, Inc., Washington, 1969-; lectr. pub. policy, govt. orgn. Faculty Salzburg Seminar in Am. Studies, 1964. Mem. Commerce Tech. Adv. Bd., human resources bd. Nat. Acad. Scis., com. on pub. engring. policy Nat. Acad. Engring. Bd. dirs. Nat. Capitol Health and Welfare Council; trustee Am. Cancer Soc. Recipient Career Service award Nat. Civil Service League, 1958, Exceptional Service award Bur. of the Budget, 1960, Rockefeller Public Service award, 1964. Mem. Am. Polit. Sci. Assn., Am. Soc. Pub. Adminstrn., A.A.A.S., Nat. Acad. Pub. Adminstrn., Phi Beta Kappa. Catholic. Home: 3724 Northampton St NW Washington DC 20015 Office: 1735 Eye St NW Washington DC 20006

CAREY, WILLIAM DAVID PUTERBAUGH, lawyer; b. Hutchinson, Kan., Sept. 4, 1901; s. Emerson and Anna May (Puterbaugh) C.; A.B., LL.B., Cornell U., 1926; B.A. with 1st class honours (Rhodes scholar 1922), Sch. Jurisprudence, Oxford (Eng.) U., 1925, M.A., 1950; m. Moscelene Cambell, Oct. 1, 1923; children—William David Puterbaugh, Gwendolyn (Mrs. Everett). Admitted to Kan. bar, 1926, U.S. Supreme Ct. bar, 1931; mem. firm Martindell, Carey Hunter & Dunn, Hutchinson, 1926—; dir. Central Fibre Products Co., Quincy, Ill., 1933—, pres., 1954-59; dir. Packaging Corp. Am., Evanston, Ill., 1959—, pres., 1959-62, chmn. bd., chief exec. officer, 1962-66, chmn. exec. com., 1966—; dir. Tenneco Inc., Tenn. River Pulp & Paper Co., Hutchinson Nat. Bank & Trust Co., McAlester Fuel Co., Krause Plow Corp., Kan. Oxygen, Inc. Mem. Kan. Bd. Law Examiners 1953-66. Mem. Kan. Rhodes Scholarship Selection Com., 1928—, sec., 1928- 70. Bd. dirs. Charles E. Carey Found., Burger Sandzen Meml. Found.; trustee Cornell U., 1941, now trustee emeritus; pres. Trans Miss. Golf Assn., 1948, bd. dirs., 1937—. Served to lt. col. USAAF, 1942-46. Decorated Legion of Merit. Mem. Am. Bar Assn. (past ho. of dels.), Am. Legion, 40 and 8, Phi Beta Kappa, Chi Psi. Mason (Shriner), Elk; mem. Order Eastern Star. Clubs: University (N.Y.C.); Chicago, Union League (Chgo.); Kansas City (Mo.); California (Los Angeles). Home: Willowbrook Hutchinson KS 67501 Office: Wolcott Bldg Hutchinson KS 67501

CAREY, WILLIAM NELSON, Jr., assn. exec.; b. Ft. Snelling, Minn., July 11, 1915; s. William Nelson and Mary Helen (Wade) C.; B.Civil Engring., U. Minn., 1937; m. Joan Margaret Lockhart, June 25, 1955; children (by previous marriages)—Joanna (Mrs. L.R. Jenkin), Gail (Mrs. K.R. Clark), Susan (Mrs. Ned Block), Sandra (Mrs. D.K. Smith), William N. III, Catherine (Mrs. J.B. Moody). Civil engr. C.E., Tex., 1938-39; research engr. Carney Cemeent Co., Minn., 1939-41; asst. to dir. Hwy. Research Bd., Nat. Acad. Scis., Washington, 1946-51, project engr. WASHO Road Test, Ida., 1951-54, chief engr. for research AASHO Road Test, Ill., 1955-61, dep. dir., Washington, 1961-66, exec. dir., 1966—. Mem. adv. com. Inst. Transp. and Traffic Engring., U. Cal. at Berkeley. Bd. dirs. Nat. Safety Council. Served to lt. col. AUS, 1941-46. Mem. Am. Soc. C.E., Instrument Soc. Am., Am. Soc. Testing Materials, Sigma Xi. Democrat. Episcopalian. Clubs: Cosmos (Washington); Belle Haven Country (Alexandria, Va.). Inventor (with R.C. Leathers and Henry Huckins) CHLOE Profilometer; developer (with P.E. Irick) psi system of measurement of pavement performance based on concept of serviceability; developer nuclear soil test gages. Editor procs. Hwy. Research Bd., 1946-51; contbr. articles tech. lit. Home: 5063 Macomb St NW Washington DC 20016 Office: 2101 Constitution Av NW Washington DC 20418

CAREY, WILLIAM POLK, investment banker; b. Balt. May 11, 1930; s. Francis J. and Marjorie A. (Armstrong) C.; grad. Pomfret Sch., 1948; student Princeton, 1948-50; B.S. in Econs., Wharton Sch. of U. Pa., 1953. Vice pres., gen. mgr. A. J. Orbach Co., Plainfield, N.J., 1955-58; prin. W. P. Carey & Co., Bloomfield, N.J., 1958-63; pres., dir. Internat. Leasing Corp., N.Y.C., 1959—; prin. Carey Internat., N.Y.C., 1960-64; chmn. bd. Carey Internat. (Australia) Pty. Ltd., 1962—; chmn. exec. com., dir. Hubbard, Westervelt & Mottelay, Inc., N.Y.C., 1964-67; dept. head Loeb, Rhoades & Co., Inc., N.Y.C., 1967—, v.p., 1968—; pres., dir. Seabalt Corp., Balt., 1965—; v.p. Fulton Assos., Inc., 1967—; pres., dir. Aerospace Mortgage Corp., 1967—. Rescent Corp., MGT Corp., Kona Corp., 1968—; limited partner Airloeb Co., 1967—, Reloeb Co., 1968—, Loebox Co., 1968—, Hapaloeb Co., 1968-70; dir. Nat. Sugar Securities Co. Mem. pres.'s council Cal. Inst. Tech.; trustee, treas. Delta Phi Found., 1969—; ex-officio trustee pomfret Sch. Served to 1st lt. USAF, 1953-55. Mem. Fgn. Policy Assn. (nat. council), Pomfret Sch. Alumni Assn. (pres.), Am. Acad. Polit. and Social Sci., Soc. Mayflower Descs., Soc. N.Y. Hosp., Newcomen Soc. N. Am., Delta Phi (v.p., gov.). Republican. Episcopalian. Clubs: Racquet and Tennis, Princeton, Brook, Down Town Assn. (N.Y.C.); St. Elmo (gov.)

(Phila.); Royal Motor Yacht (Sydney, Australia). Home: 145 E 84th St New York City NY 10028 Office: 42 Wall St New York City NY 10005

CARFAGNO, EDWARD CHARLES, art dir.; b. Los Angeles, Nov. 28, 1907; s. Salvatore and France Mary (Sereno) C.; M.Arch., U. So. Cal., 1933; m. Lois Doty, Dec. 14, 1939; childrenEdward Louis, Carol Louis, Linda Louise. Archtl. draftsman, designer Metro-Golwyn-Mayer, 1933-40, head drafting room, 1940-42 art dir., 1942—. As motion picture art dir. won Acad. Award for black and white art direction Bad and the Beautiful, 1953, Julius Caesar, 1954, for color art direction Ben Hur, 1959. Mem. Tau Sigma Delta. Home: 3001 Benedict Canyon Dr Beverly Hills CA 90210 Office: Metro Goldwyn Mayer Studios Culver City CA 90230

CARGILL, HENSON, country and Western singer; b. Oklahoma City; student Colo. State U., 2 years. Appeared in night clubs in Nev., Cal., Mo., N.M., Ariz., Las Vegas; recorded Skip a Rope. Address: Monument Records 530 W Main St Hendersonville TN 37075*

CARGILL, IAN PETER M., internat. bank ofcl.; ed. Oxford U. With Indian Civil Service, 1938-47, British Treasury, London and Washington 1948-52; with Internat. Bank Reconstrn. and Devel., 1952—, asst. dir. dept. operations Far East, 1957-61, dir. South Asia dept., 1968—. Address: 1701 N Kent St Arlington VA 22209

CARGILL, JAMES NELSON, advt. exec.; b. Portsmouth, Va., Oct. 15, 1914; s. Woodson Hughes and Barbara (Revels) C.; B.S. in Arch., Va. Poly. Inst., 1936; m. Frances Virginia McDaniel, Sept. 9, 1939; childrenJames Nelson, Nancy Virginia, Sally (Mrs. Carroll B. Jarvis), Anne Barksdale. Office mgr. Comml. Credit Co., Miami Fla., 1937-41; sales mgr. Richmond Oil Equipment Co. (Va.), 1946-48; exec. v.p. Cabell Eanes, Inc., Richmond, 1948-50; founder Cargill, Wilson & Acree, Inc., Richmond, 1950, pres., 1950-65, chmn. bd., 1965—; mem. Richmond adv. bd. First & Mchts. Nat. Bank. Past bd. dirs. United Givers Fund, Richmond chpt. A.R.C. Served to lt. col. AUS, World War II. Named Advt. Man of Year, Richmond Advt. Club, 1961; decorated Legion of Merit, Bronze Star (U.S.); Croix de Guerre (France and Belgium). Mem. Am. Assn. Advt. Agys. (past nat. bd. dirs., chmn. educator/student relations com. 1964-66), Richmond Sales and Marketing Execs. (past pres.), Richmond C. of C., Richmond Better Bus. Bur., Va. Poly. Inst. Alumni Assn. (bd. dirs.), Omicron Delta Kappa. Kiwanian. Clubs: Commonwealth, Country of Virginia, Rotunda (Richmond). Home: 8917 Tresco Rd Richmond VA 23229 Office: 201 E Cary St Richmond VA 23219

CARGILL, OSCAR, educator, editor; b. Livermore Falls, Me., Mar. 19, 1898; s. Carrol David and Rose (Farrington) C.; B.S., Wesleyan U., 1922; postgrad. Stanford, 1924-25; Ph.D., Columbia U., 1930; D.Litt., N.Y.U., 1967; L.H.D., Ohio U., 1968; m. Gladys Gertrude Lermond, June 14, 1924; children—Elizabeth Anne, Marcia Jean. Instr. English, Mich. State Coll., 1922-23, Marietta Coll., 1923-25, N.Y.U., 1925-27, 1928-30; Cutting traveling fellow Columbia, 1927-28; asst. prof. English, N.Y.U., 1930-36, prof. 1945—, chmn. dept. English, 1949-63, head grad. dept. English, 1956-63; McGuffey vis. prof. English, Ohio U., 1966-67; distinguished lectr. Nat. Council Tchrs. English, 1968—; cons. Internat. Inst. Edn., 1953-63; co-sponsor 1st closed-circuit TV composition expt. Fund for Advancement Edn., 1955-56; dir. Am. Civilization Program, 1948-63; lectr. Pelham Adult Sch., 1939-40; vis. prof. N.J. State Tchrs. Coll., Montclair, 1940-41, U. So. Cal., summer 1957. Am. specialist State Dept., Japan, summer 1962. Bd. dirs. N.Y.U. Press, Inc., 1957. Dir. W.P.A. Index to Am. Periodicals, N.Y. C., 1932-39. Cons. editor, English texts, The Macmillan Co., 1935-63; gen. editor Gotham Library, 1959—; mem. editorial bd. Garrett Press, 1969—. Mem. poetry jury of Nat. Book Award, 1954. Mem. Am. Studies Assn., Modern Lang. Assn. (rep. Copyright Bill 1965—), Nat. Coll. Tchrs. English, Phi Beta Kappa. Author and co-author several books, including the Novels of Henry James, 1961; Toward a Pluralistic Criticism, 1965. Editor: Walt Whitman's The Wound Dresser, 1949; Walt Whitman's Leaves of Grass, 1950; Thoreau's Selected Writings on Nature and Poetry, 1952; (with T.C. Pollock) The Wolfe-Watt, Correspondence, 1953; Henry James' Daisy Miller and Washington Square, 1956; (with J.W. Bennett and V. Hall) Studies in the English Renaissance Drama, 1959; (with N.B. Fagin and W.J. Fisher) O'Neill and His Plays, 1961; The Ambassadors, 1962, Portrait of a Lady, 1963 (Henry James); The Octopus (Frank Norris), 1963. Contributor essays, revs. to mags., article on Am. lit. to Crowell-Collier Ency., Collier's Yearbook, 1960-68. Home: 593 Upper Mountain Av Upper Montclair NJ 07043 Office: NYU Press 62 Fifth Av New York City NY 10011

CARGO, DAVID FRANCIS, lawyer b. Dowagiac, Mich., Jan 13, 1929; s. Francis Clair and Mary E. (Harton) C.; A.B., U. Mich., 1951, M.Pub. Administrn., 1953, LL.B., 1957; m. Ida Jo Anaya, Sept. 22, 1960; children—Veronica Ann, David Joseph, Patrick Michael, Maria Elena Christina. Admitted to Mich., N.M. bars, 1957; practice in Albuquerque, 1957; asst. dist. atty. Albuquerque, 1958-59; mem. N.M. Ho. of Reps., 1962; gov. N.M., 1967-70; practice law, Santa Fe, 1970—. Chmn. N.M. Young Republicans, 1959-61. Served with AUS, 1953-55. Named Man of Year, Albuquerque Jr. C. of C., 1964. Mem. Mich., N.M., Albuquerque bar assns., Issac Walton League (N.M. v.p.).

CARGO, WILLIAM IRA, govt. ofcl.; b. Detroit, Feb. 27, 1917; s. Ira Wiles and Nina (Lathrop) C;. A.B., Albion Coll., 1937, LL.D., 1963; A.M., U. Mich., 1938, Ph.D., 1941; student Russian lang. Naval Tng. Sch., Boulder, Colo., 1944-45; m. Margaret Grace Ludwig, June 21, 1938; children—David Paul, Ruth (Mrs. Robert C. Smith). Instr. polit. sci. U. Mich., 1941-42, Colo. Coll., 1942-43; staff Dept. State, 1943—, Bur. UN Affairs, 1946-53, dep. dir. office dependent area affairs, 1952, assigned Nat. War Coll., 1953-54; adviser U.S. delegations Gen. Assembly, Trusteeship Council Sessions, 1946-53; alternate U.S. rep. UN Com. on Non-self-governing Terrs., 1952; U.S. rep. UN vis. mission, Trust Terrs. Tanganyika, Italian Somaliland, Ruanda-Urundi, 1951; assigned to U.S. Mission to NATO and European regional orgns. in connection with spl. internat. trade problems, Paris, 1954-57; dep. dir. Office of UN Polit. and Security Affairs, Dept. State, 1957-58, dir., 1958-61; dep. U.S. rep. Internat. Atomic Energy Agy., Vienna, Austria, 1961-63; dep. chief of mission, minister-counselor Am. embassy, Karachi and Rawalpindi, Pakistan, 1963-67; dep. U.S. rep. to NATO, minister Brussels, 1967-69; career minister U.S. Fgn. Service, 1969; dir. planning and coordination staff Dept. State, Washington, 1969—. Adviser U.S. delegation UN Gen. Assembly, 1957, Gen. Conf. of Internat. Atomic Energy Agency, Vienna, 1958. alternate U.S. rep. 1961, 62; adviser U.S. delegation Conf. Discontinuance Nuclear Weapons Tests, Geneva, 1959. Served with U.S. Navy, 1944-46. Recipient Meritorious Service award Dept. State 1958. Mem. Phi Beta Kappa. Methodist. Home: 4312 N 39th St Arlington VA 22207 Office: Dept of State Washington DC 20525

CARHART, RAYMOND T., educator, audiologist; b. Mexico City, Mexico, Mar. 28, 1912; s. Raymond Albert and Edith (Noble) C.; A.B., Dak. Wesleyan U., 1932; M.A., Northwestern U., 1934, Ph.D., 1936; m. Mary Ellen Westfall, Aug. 2, 1935; children—Richard Alan, Robert Noble, Raymond Edgar. Instr. speech re-edn. Northwestern U., 1936-40, asst. prof., 1940-43, dir. Edn. Deaf and Hard of Hearing, 1942-55, asso. prof., 1943-47, prof. audiology 1947—, asst. prof. otolarynology, 1948-52, prof. 1952—; instr. 1st Internat. Course in Audiology, Stockholm, 1950; cons. U.S. Army, 1946-52; com. on hearing NRC, 1948-52; cons. com. on conservation of hearing Am. Acad. Opthalmology and Otolaryngology, 1944-65; cons. audiology VA, 1955-61. Mem. nat. adv. council Nat. Inst. Neurol. Diseases and Blindness, NIH, 1965-69; dir. Am. Bd. Examiners in Speech Pathology and Audiology, 1960-61. Served as capt. Med. Adminstrv. Corps, U.S. Army, acoustic physicist, Deshon Gen. Hosp., Pa., 1944-46. Recipient award of merit Am. Acad. Opthalmology and Otolarynology, 1960; Research Career award Nat. Inst. Neurol. Diseases and Blindness, 1963. Fellow Am. Speech and Hearing Assn. (pres. 1957), Am. Acad. Ophthalmology and Otolaryngology (hon.), A.A.A.S., Acoustical Society Am. Otosclerosis Study Group, Am. Triological Soc., Am. Otol. Soc. Author articles in profl. publs. Research on psychophysis of hearing loss, hearing aids, edn. of the acoustically handicaped, training non-med. specialists in audiology. Home: 1310 Sheridan Rd Wilmette IL 60091 Office: Auditory Research Lab Northwestern University Evanston IL 60201

CARIANI, ANTHONY, educator; b. Boston, June 13, 1918; s. Walter and Elena (Govoni) C.; A.B., Boston U., 1953, M.A., 1954, Ph.D., 1958; m. Vanda Bertazzoni, June 18, 1949; children—Peter, Karen. Asst. prof. geology U. Miss., 1956-58, asso. prof., 1958-64; prof. geology Memphis State U., 1964-66, chmn. dept., 1966—. Served with AUS, 1942-45. Fellow Geol. Soc. Am. Home: 722 Eaton St Memphis TN 38117

CARIS, THEODORE, pub. co. exec.; b. Boston, Mar. 20, 1934; s. Nicholas and Dimitra (Hedgianov) C.; B.S., Northeastern U., 1957; m. Chrysoula Kazantzi, Apr. 1, 1962; children—Chris, Theo. Editor, Allyn-Bacon, Boston, 1960-62, Macmillan Co., N.Y.C., 1962-63; v.p. for editorial programs Random House and Knopf, N.Y.C., 1963-70; pres. Xerox Coll. Pub., Lexington, Mass., 1970—. Served to 1st lt. AUS, 1958-60. Mem. Assn. Am. Pubs., Am. Sociol. Assn., Am. Econ. Assn., Am. Anthrop. Assn. Greek Orthodox. Responsible (while at Random House) for publ. of distinguished series of textbooks in sociol., anthrop. and econs. fields, including The Social Bond (Robert Nisbet). Home: 116 Sherburn Circle Weston MA 02193 Office: 191 Spring St Lexington MA 02173

CARITHERS, HUGH ALFRED, physician; b. Winder, Ga., July 21, 1913; s. Hugh A. and Starr (Blasinfame) C.; A.B., Emory U., 1933, M.D., 1937; m. Cornelia Davis Morse, July 27, 1942; children—Susan (Mrs. John F. Callender), Hugh Alfred, Starr (Mrs. Roy W. Waddell). Intern Germantown Dispensary, Phila., 1937-39; resident St. Christophers Hosp. of Phila., 1939-40, Bellevue Hosp., N.Y.C., 1940-41; practice medicine specializing in pediatrics Jacksonville, Fla., 1945—; chief pediatrics Jacksonville Hosps. Edn. Program, 1958-69; chief dept. pediatrics St. Vincent's Hosp., 1952-64, staff pres., 1956-58; clin. asso. prof. pediatrics U. Fla. Coll. Medicine, 1969—. Served with M.C., AUS, 1941-45. Diplomate Am. Bd. Pediatrics. Fellow Am. Pub. Health Assn.; mem. Fla. Pediatric Soc. (pres. 1949-50), Duval Med. Soc. (pres. 1963-64), Phi Delta Theta, Alpha Kappa Kappa. Clubs: Fla. Yacht, Timequana Country (Jacksonville). Editorial bd. Am. Jour. Diseases Children, 1970—. Home: 3010 St Johns Av Jacksonville FL 32205 Office: 1661 Riverside Av Jacksonville FL 32204

CARL, MARION EUGENE, marine corps officer; b. Hubbard, Ore., Nov. 1, 1915; s. Herman Lee and Ellen (Ellingsen) C.; B.S. in Mech. Engring., Ore. State U., 1938; grad. Air War Coll., Maxwell AFB, Ala., 1959; m. Edna Theresa Kirvin, Jan. 8, 1943; children—Lyanne Theresa, Bruce Robert. Commd. 2d lt. U.S. Army Res., 1938, resigned, 1938; joined as Marine aviation cadet. 1938; commd. 2d lt. USMC, 1939, advanced through grades to maj. gen., 1967; test pilot Naval Air Test Center, Patuxent River, Md., 1945-47, 49-52; re-assigned, 1949-53; 1st helicopter pilot USMC, 1945; comdr. 1st jet squadron USMC, 1947-48; 1st Marine to qualify in rocket powered aircraft in USMC, 1953; operations officer Air Sta., Quantico, Va., 1953-54; comdr. photog. squadron, Korea, also exec. officer Aircraft Group 11, Japan, 1954-56; comdg. officer Marine Aircraft Group 33, asst. chief of staff G-3, 1956-58; mem. staff joint chiefs staff, 1959-61; asst. dir. aviation, dir., asst. dep. chief of staff for air USMC hdqrs., 1961-63; chief of staff 1st Marine Brigade, Hawaii, then comdr. brigade, 1963-65; assigned to Okinawa and Vietnam, 1965-66; asst. wing comdr. 1st Marine Aircraft Wing, 1965-66; comdr. air bases East... Area, also comdg. gen. Air Sta., Cherry Point, N.C., 1966-68, comdg. gen. officer 2d Marine Aircraft Wing, Cherry Point, 1968-70, insp. gen. U.S. Marine Corps, 1970—. Decorated Navy cross (2), D.F.C. with 4 gold stars, Legion of Merit (2), Air medal (13), also numerous area ribbons; holder of world speed record. 1947, world altitude record, 1953. Mem. Am. Fighter Aces Assn., Soc. Exptl. Test Pilots, Early and Pioneer Aviators Assn. Home: 18338 Sharon Rd Triangle VA 22172 Office: Inspector Gen Hdqrs US Marine Corps Washington DC 20380

CARL, RALPH FLETCHER, educator; b. Jeromesville O., Nov. 7, 1916; s. Walter H. and Hallie (Fletcher) C.; B.A., Coll. Wooster, 1938; postgrad. U. Paris (France), 1938-39, Ohio State U., 1940-41; M.A., U. Mich., 1949, Ph.D., 1956. Tchr. French and world history Westerville (O.) High Sch., 1941-42; instr. Spanish, Coll. Wooster, 1945-47; prof. Romance langs. DePauw U., 1947-48, 52—, head dept., 1968—; interpreter, escort Dept. State, 1958- 66. Served with AUS, 1942-45. Fulbright scholar, 1951-52. Mem. Am. Assn. U. Profs., Modern Lang. Assn., Am. Assn. Tchrs. French. Democrat. Home: 108 S Arlington St Greencastle IN 46135

CARLANDER, KENNETH DIXON, educator, fishery biologist; b. Gary, Ind., May 25, 1915; s. Lester William and Ruth Emelia (Larson) C.; B.A. cum laude, U. Minn., 1936, M.S., 1938, Ph.D., 1943; m. Harriet Coleman Bell, June 23, 1939. Ornithologist, Panhandle Plains Hist. Soc. Mus., Canyon, Tex., 1933; lab. technician U. Minn., 1936-38; aquatic biologist Minn. Dept. Conservation, 1938-46; asst. prof. Ia. State U., 1946-48, asso. prof., 1948-57, prof., 1957—; leader Ia. Coop. Fishery Research Unit, 1946-66. Exec. bd. 15th Internat. Congress Limnology, 1960-62; editorial referee Fisheries Research Bd. Can., 1957; mem. Ia. Natural Resources Council, 1961, Iowa Water Resources Research Inst., 1964—; mem. panel fishery Experts FAO of UN: Ford Found. assignment, Egypt, 1965-66. Research grantee AEC, NSF. Fellow Am. Inst. Fishery Research Biologist (bd. control 1957-61), A.A.A.S. (council 1963-65); mem. Am. Inst. Biol. Scis., Am. Soc. Ichthyologists and Herpetologists (bd. govs. 1952-56), Am. Soc. Limnology and Oceanography, Wildlife Soc., Am. (pres. 1960-61), Brit. fisheries socs., Biometric Soc., Ecol. Soc. Am., Internat. Assn. Theoretical and Applied Limnology (central com. 1962—), Am. Soc. Naturalists, Nat. Assn. Biology Tchrs., Am. Assn. U. Profs., Izaak Walton League, United World Federalists (chpt. chmn.), Ia. Acad. Sci. (dir. 1959-64, pres. 1968-69), Nature Conservancy, Japanese Soc. Population Ecology, Sigma Xi (chpt. pres. 1963), Phi Kappa Phi, Gamma Sigma Delta. Conglist. Author: Handbook of Freshwater Fishery Biology, 3d edit., 1969. Editorial bd. Progressive Fish Culturist, 1951-52, Jour. Wildlife Mgmt., 1952-53, Am. Fishery Soc. trans., 1956-59, proc. Ia. Acad. Sci., 1957. Home: 2322 Knapp St Ames IA 50010

CARLE, LELAND LESTER, food co. exec.; b. Stuttgart, Ark., Feb. 9, 1929; s. Elmer G. and Mary Margaret (Walters) C.; student Internat. Accountants Soc. Corr. Sch.; m. Helen R. Stavhes, Aug. 14, 1949; children—Leslie, Timothy. Clk., Ark. Rice Growers Coop. Assn. (now Riceland Foods), Stuttgart, 1946-49, asst. office mgr., 1949-59, office mgr., 1959-62, sec., treas., 1962-71, v.p. finance, sec.-treas., 1971—; dir. S.A.R.I. Real Estate Corp. Chmn. Ark. County Heart Fund, 1962, 63. Mem. Nat. Assn. Accountants, Stuttgart C. of C., Nat. Assn. Accountants for Co-ops. Lutheran. Kiwanian. Home: 53 Gran vue Dr Stuttgart AR 72160 Office: PO Box 927 Stuttgart AR 72160

CARLEN, SISTER CLAUDIA, librarian; b. Detroit, July 24, 1906; d. Albert B. and Theresa Mary (Ternes) Carlen; A.B. in L.S., U. Mich., 1928, A.M., 1938. Asst. librarian St. Mary Acad., Monroe, Mich., 1928-29; asst. librarian Marygrove Coll., Detroit, 1929-44, librarian, 1944—; on leave as index editor New Cath. Ency., 1964-67, Catholic Theol. Ency., 1968- ; supr. orgn. and servicing Community Center Libraries staffed by vols. Bd. dirs. Corpus Instrumentorum, Inc. Mem. instructional materials com. Mich. Curriculum Study; cons. McGraw Hill Ency. World Biography, 1968—, World Book Ency. 1969—. Mem. A.L.A. (council 1959-62, 68—), Cath. Library Assn. (chmn. com. membership 1946- 49, chmn. Mich. unit. 1952-54, chmn. coll. and univ. sect. 1954-56, chmn. publs. com. 1961-62, pres. 1965-67), Bibliog. Soc. Am., Nat. Fedn. Cath. Coll. Students (moderator nat. lit. commn.), Spl. Libraries Assn., Mich. Library Assn. (chmn. coll. sect. 1956-57, chmn. recruiting com. 1959-60), Cath. Assn. Internat. Peace, Phi Beta Kappa, Phi Kappa Phi, Beta Phi Mu. Author: Guide to Encyclicals of the Roman Pontiffs, 1939; Guide to the Documents of Pius XII, 1951; Dictionary of Papal Pronouncements, 1958. Editor column At Your Service, Cath. Library World, 1950-52, Reference Book Rev. Sect., 1952-64, 66—; Books for the Home column. monthly news release Nat. Cath. Rural Life Conf., 1952- 61; adv. bd. The Pope Speaks, 1953—; contbr. New Catholic Ency., Cath. Youth Ency., also Catholic Bookmen's Guide, 1961, Dictionary Western Chs., 1969. Address: 8425 W McNichols St Detroit MI 48221

CARLEN, RAYMOND NILS, steel co. exec.; b. Rockford, Ill., May 3, 1919; s. Charles and Hannah (Nystrom) C.; B.S. in Metall. Engring., U. Ill., 1942; M.S. in Bus. Adminstrn., U. Chgo., 1950; m. Jean Lovejoy, June 15, 1946; children—Cynthia Jean, Susan Joy. With Joseph T. Ryerson & Son, Inc., Chgo., 1946—, v.p. Eastern region, 1963-64, exec. v.p., 1964-68, pres., 1968—, also dir.; dir. Inland Steel Co., Am. Nat. Corp., Chgo., Inland-Ryerson Construction Products, Inc., Am. Nat. Bank and Trust of Chgo., Internat. Scientific, Ltd., Barbados, West Indies, Pecker Plada Corp., Ltd., Tel Aviv, Israel, Ryerson (Holland) N.V., Amsterdam, Hinsdale Fed. Savs. & Loan Assn. (Ill.), Riverside Real Estate Investment Trust. Mem. Ill. Emergency Resources Planning Com., 1964—. Chmn. Hinsdale (Ill.) Community Caucus, 1963-64; v.p. Chgo. area council Boy Scouts Am.; active fund raising U. Chgo., Loyola U., Chgo., Passavant Meml. Hosp., Chgo., Met. Crusade of Mercy. Bd. dirs. Hinsdale Community House, 1957-60, Hinsdale P.T.A., 1957-60; mem. adv. council U. Chgo., 1960—, adv. council Coll. Engring., U. Ill., 1952—. Served to maj., C.E., AUS 1942-45; ETO. Mem. Chgo. Assn. Commerce and Industry, Ill. C. of C. Nat. (Leadership award 1961), Ill. mfrs. assns., Exec. Program Club Chgo., Newcomen Soc. N.Am. Clubs: Chicago Golf (pres. 1965, 66, dir. 1960-67) (Wheaton, Ill.); Hinsdale (Ill.) Golf; Chicago, Commerical, Economic (Chgo.). Home: 321 N Adams St Hinsdale IL 60521 Office: P O Box 8000-A Chicago IL 60680

CARLETON, ALSIE HENRY, bishop; b. Oglesby, Tex., June 22, 1910; s. Thomas Jefferson and Ethel (Hudson) C.; B.A., McMurry Coll., 1933, LL.D., 1969; B.D., So. Meth. U., 1935, D.D., 1971; D.D., Tex. Wesleyan U., 1952; m. Artha Blair Crutchfield, Oct., 13, 1936; children—Tom, Jon, Carolyn (Mrs. Michael Stewart). Ordained to ministry Methodist Ch., 1938; pastor in Big Spring, Tex., 1948-52, University Park, Dallas, 1952-61; supt. Dallas N.E. Dist., 1961-64; prof. ch. adminstrn., dir. field edn. and Conf. Courses of Study Sch., Perkins Sch. Theology, So. Meth. U., Dallas, 1964-68; bishop So. Central Jurisdictional Conf., 1968—; assigned N.W. Tex.-N.M. Area, 1968-72. Mem. Gen. Bd. of Laity United Meth. Ch., 1968—; mem. Gen. Bd. Missions, 1968—. Trustee Tex. Mission Home, San Antonio, Meth. Hosp., Lubbock, Tex., Meth. Home, Waco, Tex., Meth. Found., N.M. Meth. Found., Tex. Meth. Edn., Harwood Sch., Albuquerque, McCurdy Sch., Espanola, N.M., McMurry Coll., Tex. Coll., So. Meth. U., Mt. Sequoyah Assembly, Fayetteville, Ark. Mem. Chi Alpha. Mason, Kiwanian. Home: 810 Morningside Pl SE Albuquerque NM 87108 Office: First Nat Bank Bldg East Albuquerque NM 87108

CARLETON, EDWARD HERCULES, physician; b. Ayer, Mass., Oct. 25, 1904; s. Phillips Alexander and Susan Lillian (Smith) C.; M.D., U. Louisville. 1932; m. Pauline Edmonda Bessire, July 7, 1933; children—Sue (Mrs. Karl H. Brenner), Christy (Mrs. M.L. Sass), Edward Hercules. Intern, Louisville Gen. Hosp., 1932-34; gen. practice medicine, Louisville, 1934-35, practice orthopedic surgery, 1935-37; asst. resident physician Wheelwright Coal Mine, Inland Steel Co., Wheelwright, Ky., 1937-40; asst. med. dir. Inland Steel Co., East Chicago, Ind., 1940-44, med. dir. 1944-53, gen. med. dir., 1953-69, in charge of health and indsl. hygiene for entire co. and its subsidiaries. Liaison rep. N.W. Ind. area on Chgo. Med. Civil Def. Com.; mem. tech. com. President's Conf. on Indsl. Safety; mem. adv. com. Research Council for Econ. Security. Mem. vis. com. Harvard Sch. Pub. Health; mem. med. com. and research adv. council Mellon Inst. Indsl. Hygiene Found.; mem. profl. adv. com. Portal House, Chgo. Recipient Meritorious Service award Indsl. Med. Assn., 1952. Diplomate Am. Bd. Preventive Medicine Fellow Central States Soc. Indsl. Medicine and Surgery; mem. Am. Coll. Preventive Medicine, Med. Dirs. Club Chgo., Am. Med. Writers Assn., Am. Foundrymen's Soc., A.M.A.; World (mem. U.S. com.), Ind. Lake County med. assns., Order Ky. Cols., Am. Acad. Polit. and Social Scis., N.A.M. (mem. subcom. on indsl. health industry liaison group), Am. Forestry Assn., Chgo. Assn. Commerce and Industry (mem. cleaner air com.), Am. Assn. Indsl. Physicians and Surgeons (pres. 1950-51). Occupational Health Inst. (trustee), Assn. Am. Phys. and Surgs., Am. Indsl. Hygiene Assn. (dir. Chgo. sect.), Am. Pub. Health Assn., A.A.A.S., Am. Iron and Steel Inst., Nat. Safety Council, NRC, Am. Inst. Biol. Scis., C. of C., Ramazzinian Soc. Republican. Mason. Contbr. articles on indsl. health. Address: 1730 Eucalyptus Dr Solvang CA 93463

CARLETON, GEORGE, Jr., retired metal products mfr.; b. Detroit, Jan. 3, 1905; s. George and Laura (Boyd) C.; A.B., Colgate U., 1927; m. Charlotte Kilbourne, Nov. 25, 1931. Treas., sec. Standard Electric Products, Inc., 1927-28; with Nice Ball Bearing Co. (became div. Channing Corp. 1950, div. SKF Industries, Inc., 1960), Phila., 1929-70, exec. v.p. to 1950, pres., 1950-69, chmn., 1969-70; pres., dir. Channing Corp., N.Y.C., 1954-60; v.p. SKF Industries, Inc. Mem. Anti-Friction Bearing Mfrs. Assn. (chmn.), Beta Theta Pi. Clubs: Cricket, Racquet (Phila.); Delray Beach (Fla.) Yacht; Little (Gulf Stream, Fla.). Home: 2665 Av au Soleil Gulf Stream Delray Beach FL 33444 Office: 2901 Hunting Park Av Philadelphia PA 19140

CARLETON, JIM G., univ. chancellor; b. Stratford, Okla., Aug. 5, 1928; s. Robert Edward and Ethel (Edwards) C.; B.A., Okla. U., 1949; Ph.D., Syracuse U., 1969; m. Frances Bee, June 7, 1952; children—Timothy B., Anelia J., Brenda C. Mem. faculty Syracuse U.,

1952—, dir. financial aids, 1961-63, dean men, 1963-66, dean student services, 1966-69, vice chancellor student affairs, 1969—, instr. pub. affairs, 1956-69, asst. prof.,1969—. Served with AUS, 1954-56. Mem. Nat. Assn. Student Personnel Adminstrs., Am. Acad., Phi Beta Kappa, Phi Eta Sigma, Phi Delta Kappa. Democrat. Methodist. Home: 1633 Westmoreland Av Syracuse NY 13210

CARLETON, JOHN WALKER, ins. co. exec.; b. Alameda, Cal., July 8, 1914; s. Harry M. and Beulah (Potts) C.; A.B., U. Cal. at Berkeley, 1935; m. Phoebe Rawles, Oct. 21, 1939; children—Catherine (Mrs. John Washburn), Elizabeth. With Fireman's Fund Idemnity Co., 1935-39, State Compensation Ins. Fund, San Francisco, 1939-41; with Liberty Mut. Ins. Co., 1941—, v.p., 1955—. Served with USNR, 1944-46. Fellow Casualty Actuarial Soc. Home: 39 Nehoiden Rd Waban MA 02168 Office: 175 Berkeley St Boston MA 02117

CARLETON, R. V., airline exec.; b. Elk City, Okla., Sept. 4, 1905; s. Virgil Francis and Olga M. (Smallwood) C.; student Okla. U., 1927-29; m. Alice Ruth Calmes, July 22, 1928; 1 dau., Rosemary Leigh. With Curtiss-Wright Flying Service, Portland, Me., 1929-31; airline capt. Braniff Airways, 1931-42, chief pilot, 1942-45, dir. flight operations, 1945-52, operations mgr., 1952-54, v.p. operations, 1954-61, became sr. v.p., 1961, exec. v.p., asst. to chmn. bd., 1964-70, dir., 1956-70, also mem. exec. ocm. Pres., Goodwill Industries, Dallas, 1966-67. Bd. dirs. Am. Cancer Soc., Dallas, 1968-71, Blakley-Braniff Found., 1954-64. Mem. Internat. Air Transport Assn. (tech. com. chmn. 1961), Air Transport Assn. Operators Conf. (pres. 1960). Presbyn. Clubs: Northwood Country; Dallas Salesmanship. Home: 4314 Willow Grove Rd Dallas TX 75220 Office: Love Field Dallas TX 75235

CARLETON, ROBERT HOWARD, assn. exec.; b. Dayton, O., Jan. 23, 1909; s. Guy and Lena Maude (Hulse) C.; B.S. in Edn., Ohio State U., 1930; M.A., N.Y.U., 1945; student Mich. State U., 1947-48; m. Dorothy Evelyn Johnson, Aug. 18, 1938; children—Nancy Eleanor (Mrs. Walter Childs), Sally Jean (Mrs. Paolo Barucchieri), Guy Henry. Sci. tchr., Dayton, 1926-28, 30-35, Summit, N.J., 1935-46; instr. N.Y.U., 1938-42; asst. prof. chemistry Newark Coll. Engring., 1946-47; asst. prof. phys. sci. Mich. State U., 1947-48; exec. sec. Nat. Sci. Tchrs. Assn., 1948—. Fellow A.A.A.S.; mem. Phi Beta Kappa. Author or co-author 14 sci. textbooks for jr. and sr. high sch. Home: 2029 Lanier Dr Silver Spring MD 20910 Office: 1201 16th St NW Washington DC 20036

CARLEY, CHARLES TEAM, Jr., ednl. adminstr.; b. Greenville, Miss., Dec. 27, 1932; s. Charles Team and Ruby (McClendon) C.; B.S., Miss. State U., 1955; M.S., Va. Poly. Inst., 1960; Ph.D., N.C. State U., 1965; m. Shirley Holland, May 28, 1955; children—Karen, Mary McClendon, Charles Team III, Holland. Engr., Gen. Elec. Co., 1955; instr. Va. Poly. Inst., 1958-60; asst. prof. Miss. State U., 1960-61; Ford Found. fellow N.C. State U., 1961-64; asso. prof. Miss. State U., 1964-68, prof., 1968—, head mech. engring. dept., 1969—. Pres. Oktibeha County unit Am. Cancer Soc., 1970-72; sec.-treas. Starkville Park and Recreation Commn., 1968-71. Chmn. Municipal Exec. Com. Miss. Republican Party, 1968-72. Served with USNR, 1955-58. Mem. Engrs. Council Miss. (pres. 1970-71), Am. Soc. Mech. Engrs. (v.p. Region XI, 1972—), Sigma Xi, Omicron Delta Kappa, Phi Kappa Phi. Methodist (chmn. N. Miss. Conf. bd. Christian social concerns 1968-72). Home: Rt 3 Box 371A Starkville MS 39759 Office: Drawer ME State College MS 39762

CARLEY, DONALD S., wholesale co. exec.; b. Spokane, Wash., May 25, 1927; s. John Lewis and Freda (Stiles) C.; student U. Ida., 1951, Thunderbird Grad. Sch. Internat. Mgmt., 1955; m. Joan M. Davidson, Sept. 2, 1950; children—David Stiles, Clayton Neal. Auditor United Pacific Ins. Co., 1955-58; credit mgr. Mountain States Wholesale Co., Boise, Ida., 1958-62, v.p., 1962-67, pres., 1967—; dir. Ida. First Nat. Bank, Boise, Saxon Oil Co., Denver, Boise Sales Co., Pioneer Co., Boise, Landa Farms, Inc., Othello, Wash. Bd. dirs. Boise Philharmonic Assn., 1970-71. Served with USNR, 1945-46. Mem. Nat. Am. Wholesale Grocers Assn., Beta Theta Pi. Home: 1513 Claremont Dr Boise ID 83702 Office: 506 S 11th St Boise ID 83707

CARLILE, THOMAS, physician; b. Grand Rapids, Mich., May 6, 1914; s. Thomas Burnham and Margaret (Stephenson) C.; A.B., U. Mich., 1936, M.D., 1939; m. Roberta Ault, Aug. 20, 1937; children—Thomas D., Craig M., Catherine J. Intern, Virginia Mason Hosp., 1939-40, resident internal medicine, 1940-42, resident radiology, 1942-45, chmn. dept., 1945—; clin. asso. prof. radiology U. Wash. Sch. Medicine, 1948-; cons. Mary Swift Tumor Clinic, Butte, Mont. Chief emergency med. service Office Civil Def., Seattle, 1942-45. Bd. dirs., past pres. Virginia Mason Hosp.; sec., dir. Virginia Mason Ednl. Research Found.; hon. life dir. Wash. div. Am. Cancer Soc., also nat. dir., chmn. med. and sci. com., 1939-60, v.p., 1960-61, pres. Am. Cancer Soc., 1961-62; bd. govs. Eleanor Roosevelt Cancer Found.; vice chmn. cancer coordinating com. State of Wash.; adv. com. cancer control br. USPHS, 1963-66; adv. com. Regional Med. Program Alaska and State Wash., 1967, 68; trustee, mem. exec. com. Pacific Sci. Center Found. (pres. 1966-68). Fellow Am. Coll. Radiology; mem. Wash. State Radiol. Soc., Soc. Nuclear Medicine (founders com., 1st pres. 1954), A.M.A., Wash., Alaska (hon.) med. assns., King Co. Med. Soc., Pacific N.W., Wash. radiol. socs., Radiol. Soc. N. Am., Am. Roentgen Ray Soc., Phi Rho Sigma. Republican Episcopalian. Clubs: Heckman, Rainier, Overlake Golf, Seattle Rotary (dir.). Home: 8825 NE 28th St Bellevue WA 98004 Office: 1118 9th St Seattle WA 98101

CARLIN, DONALD WALTER, lawyer; b. Gary, Ind., Aug. 27, 1934; s. Walter Joseph and Mabel (Ebert) C.; B.S. in Engring., U. Notre Dame, 1956; LL.B., U. Mich., 1959; m. Kathleen Susan McCone, Jan. 21, 1961; children-Michael Scott, Karen Mary, Mark Steven. Admitted to Ind. bar, 1959, Ill. bar, 1960; practice in Chgo., 1960—; mem. firm Anderson, Luedeka, Fitch, Even and Tabin, 1965—. Mem. Am., Ind., Chgo. (chmn. parent sub-com., anti-trust com. 1964-70) bar assns., Patent Law Assn. Chgo. (chmn. younger mems. com. 1966). Clubs: Chgo. Athletic Assn., Notre Dame (Chgo.). Home: 2709 Simpson St Evanston IL 60201 Office: 135 S LaSalle St Chiicago IL 60603

CARLIN, EDWARD AUGUSTINE, univ. dean; b. Gardiner, N.Y., Sept. 21, 1916; s. Edward A. and Mary (Mulligan) C.; B.S., N.Y.U., 1946, M.A., 1947, Ph.D., 1950; m. Eleanor Helen Bigos, Feb. 20, 1943; children—Mary Ellen, Edward Augustine. Instr. econs. and govt. Packard Bus. Coll., 1946-47; asst. prof. Mich. State U., 1947-51, asso. prof., 1952-56, asst. dean, prof., 1956, dean Univ. Coll., 1956—; cons. to Coll. Gen. Studies, U. Nigeria, 1961, 62. Served to 1st lt., inf., AUS, 1942-46. Decorated Purple Heart. Mem. Am. Econ. Assn., Assn. Gen. and Liberal Studies (pres. 1963-64), Am. Acad. Polit. and Social Sci., Am. Assn. U. Profs., Pi Gamma Mu. Author numerous articles. Co-editor: Curriculum Building in General Education, 1960. Home: 834 Rosewood East Lansing MI 48823

CARLIN, HERBERT JACOB, educator; b. N.Y.C., May 1, 1917; s. Louis Aaron and Shirley (Salzman) C.; B.S., Columbia, 1938, M.S., 1940; D. Elec.Engring., Bklyn. Poly. Inst., 1947; m. Esther Beth Sherry, Sept. 8, 1940; children—Seth Andrew, Elliot Michael. With Westinghouse Co., 1940-45; mem. faculty Bklyn. Poly Inst., 1945-66, prof. electrophysics, 1955-61, chmn. dept., 1961-66; dir. Sch. Elec. Engring., Cornell U., 1966—, J. Preston Levis prof. engring., 1966—. Mem. radio engring. adv. panel Nat. Bur. Standards. Vis. com. Lehigh U. Recipient award outstanding achievement Air Force Systems Command, 1965; NSF sr. research fellow, 1964-65. Fellow I.E.E.E.; mem. A.A.A.S. Author: (with A. B. Glordano) Network Theory: An Introduction to Reciprocal and Nopreciprocal Circuits, 1964. Patentee relaying, microwave instruments, circuits. Home: 121 Heights Court Ithaca NY 14850

CARLIN, JAMES LAWRENCE, govt. ofcl.; b. N.D., July 26, 1921; s. James Lawrence and Anna (Schwinden) C.; student U. Minn., 1940-41, 47, U. Md., 1952-55; m. Annemarie Aeberhard, Oct. 15, 1957. Supr. distbn. relief supplies UNRRA, Austria, 1946-47; supr. supply distbn. IRO, Austria, 1947-50, chief U.S. Resettlement br., Geneva, Switzerland, 1950-52; chief liaison office Intergovtl. Com. European Migration, Frankfurt, Germany, 1952-53; dep. chief Austrian mission in charge operations, 1954-60, chief mission, 1960-63; UN high commr. for refugees, Hong Kong, 1963; with coordinator refugee program western Europe and Near East, liaison, coordination refugee and migration activities, liaison Internat. Red Cross and League Red Cross socs. State Dept., Geneva, 1963—, active relief man-made natural disasters, 1963—. Served with AUS, USAAF, 1942-46; ETO. Home: 5 Rue des Alpes Geneva Switzerland Office: US Mission 80 Rue de Lausanne Geneva Switzerland

CARLIN, LEO JOSEPH, lawyer; b. Grodno, Russia, Dec. 25, 1895; s. Joseph and Rachel (Cohen) C.; came to U.S., 1901, naturalized, 1906; Ph.B., U. Chgo., 1917, J.D., 1919; LL.D., Chgo. Med. Sch., 1969; m. Celia Cohn. Aug. 15, 1920; children—Florence E. (Mrs. Chester M. Epstein), Jerome Edward. Admitted to Ill. bar, 1919, since practiced in Chgo.; with firm Sonnenschein, Levinson, Carlin, Nath & Rosenthal and predecessors, 1919—, partner, 1926—. Dir. Sun Electric Corp. Hon. life dir. Mt. Sinai Hosp. (pres. 1955-58); trustee Chgo. Med. Sch. (vice chmn. bd.), Francis W. Parker Sch. (all Chgo.), Retina Found., Boston. Mem. citizens bd. U. Chgo., mem. bd. overseers, recipient nat. award for community service Jewish Theol. Sem. Am. Recipient citation for pub. service U. Chgo. Mem. Am., Ill., Chgo. bar assns., U. Chgo. Law Sch. Alumni Assn., Phi Beta Kappa, Order of Coif. Jewish religion (pres. synagogue). Clubs: Bryn Mawr Country (pres. 1941-43); Standard (pres. Chgo. 1952-54). Home: 2920 Commonwealth Av Chicago IL 60657 Office: 69 W Washington St Chicago IL 60602

CARLIN, ROBERT BURNELL, educator; b. St. Paul, Nov. 13, 1916; s. Robert James and Madeleine Eleanor (Howell) C.; B.Ch., U. Minn., 1937, Ph.D., 1941; Lalor post- doctoral fellow, U. Ill., 1941-42; m. Catherine Margaret Patzke, May 28, 1941 (dec. Nov. 1950); m. 2d, Mary Elizabeth Janes, Aug. 16. 1952; children—Barbara Ann, Robert James, Mark Thomas, John Frederick, Richard Howell. Instr. chemistry U. Ill., 1942-43, U. Rochester, 1943-46; asso. prof. chemistry Carnegie Inst. Tech., 1946-52, Becker prof. organic chemistry, 1952—, head dept. chemistry, 1960-67, asso. dean Coll. Engring. and Sci., 1967-71. Wartime research NDRC and Com. Med. Research; mem. com post doctoral fellowships in chemistry and on awards in chemistry under Fulbright Act, Nat. Acad. Scis.-NRC; chmn. Gordon Research Conf. Organic Reactions and Processes, New Hampton, N.H., 1956. Fellow A.A.A.S.; mem. Am. Chem. Soc. (chmn. Pitts. 1960-61), Pitts. Chemists (pres. 1954-55), Sigma Xi, Alpha Chi Sigma, Phi Lambda Upsilon, Gamma Alpha. Author articles research mags. Home: 928 Pennsylvania Av Oakmont PA 15139

CARLIN, THOMAS L., newspaper exec.; b. Bird Is., Minn., Dec. 19, 1921; s. Leo Joseph and Agnes (Hentschell) C.; B.S. in Elec. Engring., U.S. Naval Acad., 1943; m. Dawn Van Eyck, Mar. 31, 1948; children—Thomas, Mark, Paul, Mary, Sara, Andrew. Account exec. Arnold Niemeyer & Assos., 1949-51; sales corr. Am. Hoist & Derrick, 1951-53; advt. rep. St. Paul Dispatch and Pioneer Press, 1953-56, asst. prodn. mgr., 1956-57, asst. to pub., 1957- 58, bus. mgr., 1958-66, gen. mgr., 1966—; dir. Northwest Publns., Inc.; pres. Twin Cities Newspaper Service. Pres. St. Paul Jr. Achievement, 1965; gen. chmn. St. Paul Arts and Sci. Fund drive, 1965. Served to lt. (s.g.) USNR, 1943-47. Decorated Silver Star; recipient Outstanding Community Service award St. Paul Jr. C. of C., 1967. Mem. St. Paul Serra Club (pres. 1967), Navy League. Republican. Roman Cath. Rotarian. Clubs: Minnesota, St. Paul Athletic, North Oaks Golf (St. Paul), Home: 17 Oak Knoll Dr White Bear Lake MN 55110 Office: 55 E 4th St St Paul MN 55101

CARLISLE, JAMES MALLORY, physician; b. Thomasville, Ga., Jan. 20, 1904; s. James Mallory and Annie (Carroll) C.; B.S., U. Ala., 1930; M.D., Temple U., 1932; LL.D., Dublin, 1950; m. Lillian Burt, Aug. 16, 1934; children—James Mallory III, Margaret Anne, Janet Ruth, Lillian Dixie. Resident, chief resident pathology Temple U. Hosp., 1931-34; dir. med. research Merck & Co., Inc., Rahway, N.J., 1934-53; staff anesthetist Temple U., 1934, staff medicine, lectr. indsl. medicine, 1942-52, asst. prof. indsl. medicine, 1951-54; staff Rahway Meml. Hosp., 1936-53, head dept. clin. research, 1945-53; mem. med. staff Bapt. Sacred Heart hosps., Pensacola, Fla., 1955—. Pres., N.J. State Health dept., 1943. Recipient 1st award; certificate of merit for exhibit on cortisone A.M.A., So. Med. Assn., 1950. Diplomate Am. Bd. Preventive Medicine. Fellow A.M.A., Am. Assn. Indsl. Physicians and Surgeons, N.Y. Acad. Medicine, N.Y. Acad. Scis., Am. Pub. Health Assn., Am. Acad. Occupational Medicine, Am. Coll. Chest Physicinas; mem. Escambia County Med. Soc., Fla. Assn. Indsl. Physicians and Surgeons, Assn. Mil. Surgeons U.S., (chmn. med. res. com.), Am. Soc. Anesthetists, Am. Soc. Tropical Medicine and Health, NRC, Am. Trudeau Soc., Am. Acad. Gen. Practice, Babcock Surg. Soc., So. Med. Assn., Alpha Kappa Kappa, Alpha Tau Omega. Mason, Rotarian. Contbr. sects. to med. books, articles to profl. jours. Address: 1125 N Palafox St Pensacola FL 32501

CARLISLE, KITTY, singer, actress; b. New Orleans, Sept. 3, 1915; d. Joseph and Hortense (Holtzman) Conn; studied with Miss McGhees, New Orleans, Chateau Mont Cohoise, Lausanne with Princesse Metcherssy, Paris, also Royal Acad. Dramatic Art, London; m. Moss Hart, Aug. 10, 1946 (dec.); children—Christopher, Catherine. Motion pictures include Murder at the Vanities, She Loves Me Not, Here is My Heart, A Night at the Opera, White Horse Inn, Three Waltzes, The Anniversary Waltz; regular panel mem. TV program To Tell the Truth.‡

CARLITZ, LEONARD, educator; b. Phila., Dec. 26, 1907; s. Michael and Anna (Schneyer) C.; A.B., U. Pa., 1927, M.A., 1928, Ph.D., 1930; m. Clara Skaler, Sept. 1, 1931; children—Michael, Robert. Mem. faculty Duke, 1932—, prof. math., 1944—, James B. Duke prof. math., 1964—. Mem. Am. Math. Soc., Math. Assn. Am. Author numerous research papers. Editor Duke Math. Jour., 1938- -, Fibonacci Quar., 1963—; asso. editor Acta Arithmetica, 1958—, Am. Math. Monthly, 1963—. Home: 2303 Cranford Rd Durham NC 27706

CARLOCK, JOHN K., lawyer; b. Globe, Ariz., Aug. 16, 1912; s. Frank H. and Judith (Kavanaugh) C.; LL.B., U. Ariz., 1941; m. Hallie Leavitt, Dec. 27, 1941. Admitted to Ariz. bar, 1941; atty. Treasury Dept., 1941-42, 45-48, spl. asst. to gen. counsel, 1948-49, asst. gen. counsel, 1949-62, fiscal asst. sec. treasury, 1962—. Served as ensign to lt. USCG, 1942-45. Recipient Tom C. Clark award as outstanding govt. career lawyer, 1962; award Nat. Civil Service League, 1969. Mem. Ariz. Bar Assn., Phi Delta Phi. Home: 2301 E St NW Washington DC 20037 also Vernon AZ 85940 Office: Treasury Dept Washington DC 20220

CARLONI, ANTONIO, Italian diplomat; b. Florence, Italy, June 8, 1907; s. Francesco and Eleanor Graham (Allen) C.; LL.B., U. Florence, 1935; m. Isabella Guadagni, June 16, 1943; children—Francesco, Bernardo, Eleonora. With Italian Diplomatic Service, 1947-; vice consul, Tunis, 1949-52; with Fgn. Office, Rome, 1952-54; consul, Detroit, 1954-57; consul, Brussels, Belgium, 1957-61; counsellor Italian embassy, Tel Aviv, 1961-63; consul gen., Caracas, Venezuela, 1963-67, Phila., 1967—. Home: The Dorchester W Rittenhouse Sq Philadelphia PA 19103 Office: 2128 Locust St Philadelphia PA 19103

CARLOUGH, EDWARD F., labor union ofcl.; b. Bronx, N.Y., Aug. 31 1903; ed. pub. schs.; m. Florence Sweeney. Journeyman sheet metal worker, N.Y.C., 1924-40; pres., bus. mgr. local 28, Sheet Metal Workers Internat. Assn., N.Y.C., 1940- 51, gen. sec.-treas., Washington, 1951-59, gen. pres., 1959—. Office: 1000 Connecticut Av Washington DC 20036

CARLS, JOHN NORMAN, educator, geographer; b. Virginia, Ill., Dec. 22, 1907; s. John Homer and Katherine Barbara (Bins) C.; B.E., Ill. State Normal U., 1932; A.M., Clark U., 1934, Ph.D., 1935; grad. study extension U. Ill., 1940-42; m. Catharine Montague Driver, July 11, 1945; 1 dau., Catherine Trice. Tchr. elementary sch., Bluff Springs, Ill., 1927-29; instr., later asst. prof. Ore. Coll. Edn., 1935-40; head dept. geography Eastern Ill. U., 1940-46; chief operations geography div. Bur. Census, 1946-47; asso. prof. Am. U., Washington, 1949-51, prof. geography, 1951-55; prof. geography, U. Pitts., 1955-61, adj. prof., 1961-64, chmn. dept. 1955- 58; vis. prof. Columbia, 1963-64; prof. geography Shippensburg (Pa.) State Coll., 1964—, chmn. dept. geography, 1966—. Mem. Secretariat, Pan Am. Consultation on Geography, 1952; del. Mid-Century White House Conf. on Children and Youth, 1950. Served as lt. to lt. comdr., U.S.N.R., 1942-45; staff officer Naval Air Tng. Command, 1944-45. Mem. N.E.A., Nat. Council Geographic Edn. (pres. 1956), Nat. Council Social Studies, Assn. Am. Geographers, Assn. Pacific Coast Geographers, Am. Geog. Soc., Pa. Council Geol. Edn. (pres. 1970-71), Gamma Theta Upsilon, Pi Gamma Mu, Theta Alpha Phi. Author: (with Frank E. Sorenson) Neighbors Across the Seas, 1950; (with Frank E. Sorenson and Margery D. Howarth) Neighbors in Latin America, 1951; Our United States in a World of Neighbors, 1958; Knowing Our Neighborsin Canada and Latin America, 1964; Knowing Our Neighborsin the United States, 1965; Knowing Our Neighbors-Around the Earth, 1966; Knowing Our Neighborsin the Eastern Hemisphere, 1968. Office: Shippensburg State Coll Shippensburg PA 17257

CARLSBERG, ARTHUR WALTER, Jr., corporation executive; b. Stockton, Cal., Mar. 16, 1933; s. Arthur Walter and Lillian (Preston) C.; B.A., U. So. Cal., 1953; student Southwestern Law Sch., Founder, Land Investment Research Corp., Sherman Oaks, Cal., 1961; pres. Telezone, Inc., Encino, Cal., 1964-; pres. Carlsberg Financial Corp., Los Angeles, 1966—; a founder Am. Growth Properties Mgmt. Co., Ltd., Nassau, Bahamas, 1969—; v.p. Microwave Communications Ltd., 1965—; also presently pres. 22 corps., dir. 36 corps. Club: Safari (Inglewood, Cal.). Home: 16970 Knollwood Dr Granada Hills CA 99344 Office: 1801 Av of Stars Los Angeles CA 90067

CARLSEN, ALBERT, utilities exec.; b. St. Paul, June 29, 1910; s. Alfred and Marin (Jensen) C.; student U. Ida., 1931-34; m. Frances Elizabeth Nixon, June 19, 1935; children—Richard C., James A., Nancy Ann, Kenneth M. With Ida. Power Co., 1934—, dir., 1964—, pres., 1967-71, chmn., chief exec. officer, 1971—; gen. mgr. Ida. Potato Starch Co., Blackfoot, 1941-56, pres., 1956-66; v.p., dir. Safety Savs. & Loan Assn., Blackfoot, Ida., until 1968; dir. Provident Savs. & Loan, Boise. Chmn. Blackfoot Sch. Bd., 1947-59. Bd. dirs. Rocky Mountain Fedn. States, 1967—. Mem. Ida. C. of C. (dir.), Asso. Industries Ida. (dir., past pres.), Ida. Sch. Trustees Assn. (past pres.). Mason (Shriner), Elk, Rotarian. Home: 4120 Hillcrest Dr Boise ID 83705 Office: PO Box 70 Boise ID 83707

CARLSEN, NORMAN C., machinery mfg. co. exec.; b. Chgo., Jan. 2, 1911; s. I.C. and N. (Nielson) C.; student Central YMCA, La Salle Extension U.; grad. Drake U. Exec. Devel. Program; m. Thelma Berg, Aug. 8, 1936; children—Raymond C., Dennis L. With Chgo. Title & Trust Co., 1930-45; with Maytag Co., Newton, Ia., 1945-, controller, 1960-, v.p., 1963-, dir. Maytag Co. Ltd. Can. Past mem. Newton Planning and Zoning Bd.; past town treas. Lambs Grove, Ia. Mem. Newton C. of C., Financial Execs. Inst. (mem. bd., past pres. Ia. chpt.). Presbyn. (trustee). Kiwanian. (past pres.). Home: 611 S 5th Av W Newton IA 50208 Office: 403 W 4th St N Newton IA 50208

CARLSMITH, CARL WENDELL, lawyer; b. Hilo, Hawaii, Jan. 22, 1904; s. Carl S. and Nelle (Wood) C.; B.A., Stanford, 1926, J.D., 1928; m. Edith Mattson, June 14, 1928; children—Donn Wendell, Carl Duane, Edith Gayle (Mrs. Frank Palmer, Jr.). Admitted to Hawaii bar, 1928, since practiced in Hilo; partner firm Carlsmith & Carlsmith, Hilo, Honolulu, 1932-37, sr. partner, 1937-49; sr. partner Carlsmith, Carlsmith & Cox, Hilo, 1949-59, Carlsmith, Carlsmith, Wichman & Case, Honolulu and Hilo, 1959—. Partner Dillingham Partners' Co.; v.p., dir. Dillingham Investment Corp., Inter-Island Resorts, Ltd., Maui Land & Pineapple Co., Inc. Mem. exec. com. bd. visitors com. Stanford Law Sch., 1962-65. Mem. Stanford Assos., Am., Hawaii bar assns. Clubs: Pacific (Honolulu); Hilo Yacht. Home: 625 Hakaka Pl Honolulu HI 96815 Office: 810 Richards St Honolulu HI 96813

CARLSMITH, MERRILL LAWRENCE, lawyer; b. Hilo, Hawaii, Nov. 2, 1905; s. Carl Schurtz and Nelle (Wood) C.; LL.B., Stanford, 1928, J.D., 1930; m. Maxine Walters, Dec. 17, 1939; children—Marilyn Maxine (Mrs. James Thomas Van Winkle), Curtis Wade, Robert Wood. Admitted to Hawaii bar, 1930; partner Carlsmith, Wichman & Case and predecessor firms, Hilo, also Honolulu, 1930—. Trustee Hilo Boarding Sch.; bd. dirs. Hilo Boys Club. Mem. U.S. Golf Assn. (sr. golf champion 1962, 63, world sr. golf champion 1970). Elk, Rotarian (past pres.). Clubs: Hilo Country (pres. 1946-48). Home: PO Box 686 Hilo HI 96720 Office: 121 Wainnenue St Hilo HI 96720

CARLSON, ALBERT SIGFRID, educator; b. Worcester, Mass., July 4, 1907; s. Albert and Anna (Norling) C.; B.A., Clark U., 1929, M.A., 1931, Ph.D., 1939; m. Mildred Swenson, June 10, 1933; children—Russell Albert, Betty Ann, Warren Herbert. Instr. geography Darmouth, 1929-37, asso. prof., 1937-44, prof., 1944—; pres. Lebanon (N.H.) Coll., eves. 1970-71, dean faculty, 1971-72. Econ. cons. New Eng. region Nat. Resources Planning Bd., 1942-43; exec. sec. Dartmouth-Lake Sunapee Region Assn., 1945—; mem. indsl. devel. com. New Eng. Council. Mem. Assn. Am. Geographers, Nat. Council Geography Tchrs., New Eng. Geog. Conf., Am. Geog. Soc. Editor in chief: Industrial Economic Geography, 1956. Contbr. geog. publs. Home: 7 Conant Rd Hanover NH

CARLSON, ALBIN EDMUND, business exec.; b. Chgo., Nov. 16, 1905; s. Victor and Sophie (Mattson) C.; B.S., Northwestern U., 1928; m. Esther Virginia Stevens, June 20, 1931; children—Stephen Edmund (dec.), Candace. Former vice chmn., dir. Hartford Plaza bank, Chgo.; former pres., dir. Comptometer Corp (now Victor-Comptometer Corp.); former exec. v.p., dir. Continental Telephone Co., Wilmington, Del., Theodore Gary & Co., Gary Service & Investment Co.; pres., dir. Asso. Tel. & Tel. Co.; v.p., dir. Inland Telephone Co., Middle States Utilities, Inc., Automatic Electric (Can.), Ltd., Community Telephone Co., Automatic Electric Sales (Can.), Ltd., Automatic Electric Co., Chgo., Anglo-Canadian Telephone Co., Montreal. Trustee Nat. Coll. Edn., Evanston, Ill., Asso. Colls. Ill.; bd. regents Marymount Coll., Boca Raton, Fla. C.P.A., 1941. Mem. Am. Inst. Accountants, Beta Alpha Psi, Republican. Methodist, Clubs: Chicago, Economic, (Chgo.); Westmoreland Country; Boca Raton Hotel, Boca Tecca Country. Address: 1480 Royal Palm Way Boca Raton FL 33432

CARLSON, ARNOLD WILLIAM, publishing exec.; b. Lake Forest, Ill., Aug. 4, 1906; s. William and Ellen (Petersen) C.; B.S., Lake Forest Coll., 1928, LL.D., 1957; M.B.A., Harvard, 1932; m. Alice Retzlaff, Feb. 9, 1935. Auditor, Lawrence Scudder & Co., 1928-30, Columbia Gas & Electric Co., 1932, Interstate Fuel & Light Co., 1932; asst. treas. Nat. Bancservice Corp., 1932-36; with Time, Inc., N.Y.C., 1936-69, asst. to comptroller, 1936-43, asst. sec., 1943-60, comptroller, 1946-57, v.p., 1957-69, asst. to pres., 1960-69; v.p., dir. Bleakwood Timber Co., San Augustine Timber Co., Newton Timber Co., (all Jasper, Tex.), Venezuela TV, Inc., N.Y.C., Time-Life Broadcast, Inc. (Mich., Denver, N.Y.C.) Eastex, Inc., Evadale, Tex., Time- Life Brasil, Inc., N.Y.C.; dir. Time-Life Internat., Inc., Printing Devels., Inc., Selling Areas-Marketing Inc. (all N.Y.C.), Time Internat. Can., Ltd. (Montreal), Time-Life Internat. de Mexico, S.A. (Mexico City), Jasper Timber Co. (Tex.), David M. Co., Printing Devels. (P.R.), Inc., Research Products, Inc., (all San Juan, P.R.) Nat. trustee Lake Forest Coll.; chmn. nat. finance com. Girl Scouts U.S.A. C.P.A., N.Y., 1937. Mem. Financial Execs. Inst., Harvard Bus. Sch. Assn. (exec. council), New York C. of C. (ednl. com.). Clubs: Harvard (N.Y.C.); Shawnee (Pa.) Country; Buck Hill Falls (Pa.) Country. Home: 11 Riverside Dr New York City NY 10023 also Canadensis PA Office: Time Inc Time & Life Bldg Rockefeller Center New York City NY 10020

CARLSON, BILLE CHANDLER, educator; b. Boston, June 27, 1924; s. John Rudolph and Henrietta C. (Peabody) C.; grad. Phillips Exeter Acad., 1941; A.B. summa cum laude, Harvard, 1947, A.M., 1947; D.Phil. (Rhodes scholar), U. Oxford, 1950; m. Louise Winston, May 30, 1947; children—Marian Bille, John Russell. Instr., research asso. Princeton, 1950-54; mem. faculty Ia. State U., staff mem. Ames Lab. of A.E.C., 1954—, prof. math. and physics, sr. physicist, 1961—; sr. research fellow mathematics Cal. Inst. Tech., 1962-63. Fellow Am. Phys. Soc.; mem. Am. Math. Soc., Soc. Indsl. and Applied Mathematics, Math. Assn., Am. Assn. Univ. Profs., Phi Beta Kappa, Sigma Xi. Served with USNR, 1944-46. Research and publs. on spl. function of math. physics, especially R-fuctions and symmetric elliptic integrals. Home: 430 Westwood Dr Ames IA 50010

CARLSON, BRUCE ROBBINS, electronics co. exec.; b. Chgo., May 4, 1921; s. Earl C. and Elsie (Robbins) C.; B.A., Stanford, 1943; postgrad. Northwestern U., 1946-47; m. Rubydonna Joseph, Feb. 27, 1943; childrenLawrence B., Nancy J., Gregg P., Christine A. Investment analyst Stein, Roe & Farnham, Chgo., 1947-53; statis. asst. to pres. Sprague Electric Co., North Adams, Mass., 1953-60, v.p. corporate planning and systems, 1960-65, treas., 1965-68, sr. v.p. finance, 1968, pres., 1968—, also dir. Inst. bus. statistics Northwestern U., Chgo., 1948-51. Mem. Sch. Com., Williamstown, Mass., 1959-62, Mt. Greylock Regional Dist., 1960-70. Bd. dirs. North Adams YMCA, 1960-66, pres., 1961; bd. dirs. Williamstown Boys' Club, 1957-60. Served to lt. (j.g.) USNR, 1943-45. Mem. Investment Analysts Soc. Chgo., Am. Statis. Assn., Operations Research Soc. Am., Phi Beta Kappa, Theta Xi. Republican. Conglist. Home: 8 Hill Province Rd Williamstown, MA 01267. Office: 87 Marshall St North Adams MA 01247

CARLSON, CLARENCE SELMER, prof. mathematics; b. Dalesburg, S.D., Jan. 6, 1901; s. Erick August and Bertha (Hovde) C.; A.B., St. Olaf Coll., Northfield, Minn., 1926; M.S., State U. of Ia., Iowa City, 1928, postgrad. 1930-31, 1932-33, also 5 summer sessions; m. Lorraine Bauman, July 17, 1931; 1 son, Erik Edvard. Buyer and bookkeeper Carlson's Dept. Store, Beresford, S.D., 1919-22; asst. in instr. St. Olaf Coll., Northfield, Minn., 1925- 26, instr. mathematics, 1928-29, asst. prof., 1929-31, asso. prof., 1931-42, prof. mathematics, 1942—, chmn. department, 1931-68; grad. asst. State U. of Ia., Iowa City, 1926-28. Mem. Math. Assn. of Am., National Council Tchrs. Math., Am. Math. Soc. Lutheran. Home: 1 Walden Pl Northfield MN Office: Saint Olaf College Northfield MN

CARLSON, CURTIS LEROY, trading stamp co. exec.; b. Mpls., July 9, 1914; s. Charles A. and Letha (Peterson) C.; B.A. in Econs., U. Minn., 1937; m. Arleen Martin, June 30, 1938; children—Marilyn (Mrs. Glen Nelson), Barbara (Mrs. Edwin C. Gage III). Salesman, Procter & Gamble Co., Mpls., 1937-39; founder chmn. bd., pres. Gold Bond Stamp Co., Mpls., 1938—; chmn. bd., chief exec. officer Mgmt. Corp., Radisson, 1961—, also Schimmel Hotels Corp.; pres., chmn. bd. Premium Service Corp., Mpls. Indsl. Park, Inc., Premium Corp. Am., Inc.; chmn. bd. Performance Incentives Corp.; pres., dir. Gold Bond Co., Ltd., Toronto, Ont., Can., Naegele Outdoor Advt. Co. of Travel, Inc., Red Scissors, Inc., Commonwealth Premium Co. Ltd. (Can.), N.S. Gold Bond Inc., Western Gold Bond, Ltd.; Mich., Naegele Midwest Outdoor Inc., Custom Travel, Inc., Red Scissors, Inc., Commonwealth Premium Co. Ltd. (Can.), N.S. Gold Bond Ltd., Western Gold Bond, Ltd.; v.p., dir. Lamar Dean Outdoor Advt. Co., Inc., Lamar Dean Outdoor Advt. Co. of N.C., Inc.; dir. Premiums Internat. Ltd., Gold Bond Stamps Co. Ltd. U.K., Gold Bond de Espana S.A., Premiums de Espana S.A., Boers Ver Zendhuis N.B., Melior S.A., Gold Bond Japan Ltd., Canning & Co. Ltd. Marquette Nat. Bank of Mpls., Apache Corp., Bank Shares, Inc., North Star Center, Inc., N.Am. Life & Casualty Co., Minn. Enterprises, Inc., Peters Foods, Inc. Trustee, treas. U. Minn. Found.; bd. dirs. Fairview Hosp., Boys Club Mpls. (also founder), Minn. Orchestral Assn., Mpls. Downtown Council. Minn. Orchestral Assn., Mpls. Downtown Council. Mem. Trading Stamp Inst. Am. (dir., founder, pres. 1959-60), Mpls. C. of C. (dir., v.p. exec. com.), Minn. Alumni Assn. Sigma Phi Epsilon. (nat. trustee). Methodist (mem. financial adv. bd.). Mason (Jester, Shriner). Clubs: Minneapolis, Minneapolis Athletic; Edina (Minn.) Country; Wayzata (Minn.) Country; North Country (Duluth); Minikahda; Ocean Reef Yacht; Palm Bay. Home: 4907 Sunnyside Rd Edina MN 55424 Office: 12715 B State Hwy 55 Minneapolis MN 55427

CARLSON, DEAN BERNARD, ins. co. exec.; b. Mpls., May 3, 1917; s. Per August and Delia (Chellsen) C.; B.B.A., U. Minn., 1947; m. Amy Yeakel, July 2, 1947; children—Christine, William, Sarah. With accounting dept. First Nat. Bank & Trust Co., Mpls., 1935-42; audit firm Touche, Niven, Bailey & Smart, Mpls., 1948; asst. supr. policyholders service N. Am. Life & Casualty Co., Mpls., 1948-50, asst. field auditor, 1950-53, auditor, 1953-57; v.p., sec. treas. Investors Syndicate Life Ins. & Annuity Co., Mpls., 1967—. Mem. Citizens League, 1966—. Mem. bd. mgrs. YMCA, Mpls., 1963-67. Served with USNR, 1942-46; PTO. Fellow Life Mgmt. Inst.; mem. Mpls. C. of C., Soc. Advancement Mgmt. (pres.), Minn Ins. Information Center (bd. dirs.). Home: 12122 Robin Circle Minneapolis MN 55343 Office: Investors Bldg Minneapolis MN 55402

CARLSON, DEVON MCELVIN, univ. dean; b. Topeka, Dec. 1, 1917; s. Gustave Elvin and Gertrude M. (Swanson) C.; B.S. in Architecture (Alice Chittenden prize 1938), U. Kan., 1941; B.S. in Archtl. Engring. with honors, U. Colo., 1947; M.S. in Architecture (scholarship 1948), Columbia, 1949; m. Mary E. Ackley, June 14, 1949; children—Mitchell Lans, Martha Sue, Judith Ann, Peter DeVon. Engaged in archtl. practice, 1941-43; mem. faculty U. Colo., 1943- -, prof., chmn. dept. archtl. engring. and architecture, 1959-62, dean Sch. Architecture, 1962—, mem. steering com. creative arts program, 1959—; lectr. civic and profl. groups. Past mem. Colo. Bd. Examiners Architects, pres., 1964-65; mem. exams. com. Nat. Council Archtl. Registration Bds. Mem. A.I.A. (dir. Colo. 1966-67, pres. 1969), Assn. Collegiate Schs. Architecture (chmn. nat. program com.), Am. Soc. Engring. Edn. (past chmn. Colo.), Boulder C. of C., Rocky Mountain Liturgical Art Assn., Scarab, Tau Beta Pi, Delta Phi Delta, Chi Epsilon, Triangle. Rotarian. Co-author: An Approach to Architectural Design, 1950; Architecture/Colorado, 1966. Contbr. articles profl. jours. Home: 502 Mapleton Avenue Boulder CO 80302

CARLSON, DONALD HERBERT EDWARD, automobile co. exec.; b. Edmonton, Alta., Can., Aug. 25, 1918; s. Theo Gustav and Grace (Ockenden) C.; B.A., U. Alta., 1940; m. Madeline Frances Beetlestone, Mar. 5, 1941; children—Madeline Anne (Mrs. Desmond P. Ellis), Elizabeth Jane (Mrs. Richard B. Davis), Susannah Pamela Grace (Mrs. John D. Wyndham), Anthony Ernest Theo, Gustav Donald Michael. Reporter and editor Toronto Daily Star, Vancouver Sun, Vancouver Province and Vancouver News-Herald, 1942-53; dir. pub. relations James Lovick & Co., Ltd., 1953-55, Crown Zellerbach Can. Ltd., 1955-59; with Ford Motor Co., Can., 1959—, v.p., sec., 1966—. Pres. Oakville Jr. Baseball Assn., 1968-70; chmn. joint steering com. Canadian Univs. Assn., 1966; press dir. World Anglican Congress, 1963, Bd. dirs., pub. relations chmn. Nat. Council YMCA, 1965-67. Mem. Canadian Pub. Relations Soc., Toronto Bd. Trade. Clubs: Nat. Press (Ottawa, Can.); Newsmen's National (Toronto, Can.); Terminal City (Vancouver). Home: 32 Colonial Crescent Oakville Ontario Canada Office: Ford of Canada The Canadian Road Oakville Ontario Canada

CARLSON, EARLAND IRVING, coll. pres.; b. Chgo., Jan. 7, 1925; s. Carl Joseph and Esther Anna (Johanson) C.; student N. Park Coll., Chgo., 1942-43, 46-47; A.B., Wheaton (Ill.) Coll., 1949; M.A., U. Ill., 1950, Ph.D. in History, 1955; m. Ethel Taylor, Oct. 4, 1953; 1 dau., Nancy Lynn. Grad. fellow history U. Ill., 1949-51, 53-54; instr. social sci. N. Park Coll., 1954-55; instr. history, then asst. prof. Colo. Coll., 1955-57; dean coll. N. Park Coll., 1957-62, asso. prof. history, 1960-62; v.p. acad. affairs, prof. history Millikin U., 1962- 67; pres. Westminster Coll., New Wilmington, Pa., 1967—; cons., examiner Commn. Colls. and Univs., N. Central Assn. Colls. and Secondary Schs., 1959—; evaluator Commn. on Instns. Higher Edn., Middle States Assn. Colls. and Secondary Schs., 1968—. Nat. chmn. Christian citizenship commn. Evang. Covenant Ch. Am., 1960-62; mem. citizens cons. com. Decatur Bd. Edn., 1964-67; mem. task force ch. and higher edn. United Presbyn. Ch., 1970—. Served to 1st lt. USAAF and USAF, 1943- 46, 51-53, Mem. Am. Hist. Assn., Orgn. Am. Historians, Am. Assn. U. Profs., Phi Kappa Phi. Presbyn. Rotarian. Club: Duquesne (Pitts.). Contbr. articles profl. jours. Home: 521 New Castle St New Wilmington PA 16142

CARLSON, EDGAR MAGNUS, clergyman, educator; b. Amery, Wis., July 12, 1908; s. David and Hilda (Swanson) C.; A.B., Gustavus Adolphus Coll., St. Peter, Minn., 1930; B.D., Augustana Theol. Sem., Rock Island, Ill., 1933; postgrad. U. Minn., 1934-37; Ph.D., U. Chgo., 1944; m. Ebba Edquist, July 11, 1934; children—David Jon, Joanna Linda, Samuel Edquist. Ordained to ministry Lutheran Ch., 1933; pastor Mount Olivet Luth. Ch., Mpls. 1933-37; prof. Bible and ethics Gustavus Adolphus Coll., 1937-42; asst. prof. ch. history and English Bible, Augustana Theol. Sem., 1942-44; pres. Gustavus Adolphus Coll., 1944-68; exec. dir. Minn. Pvt. Coll. Council, 1968—. Mem. theol. commn. Luth. World Fedn., 1963-70; mem. bd. Found. Reformation Research; mem. planning commn. World Council Chs. Gen. Assembly, 1953; rep. Lutheran World Fedn. Europe, summer 1951. Mem. Am. Ch. History Soc., Royal Order North Star, Pi Gamma Mu, Pi Kappa Delta. Rotarian. Author: The Reinterpretation of Luther, 1948; The Church and the Public Conscience, 1956; The Classic Christian Faith, 1959; Church Sponsored Higher Education in Lutheran Church in America, 1967. Home: 5320 Brookview Av Minneapolis MN Office: 550 Cedar St St Paul MN

CARLSON, EDWARD ELMER, hotel co. exec.; b. Tacoma, June 4, 1911; s. Elmer E. and Lula (Powers) C.; student U. Wash., 1928-32; m. Nell Hinckley Cox, June 26, 1936; children—Edward Eugene, Jane Leslie. Mgr. President Hotel, Mt. Vernon, Wash., 1936-37, Rainier Club, Seattle, 1937-42; with Western Internat. Hotels, Inc., Seattle, 1946—, exec. v.p., 1953-61, pres., 1961-69, chmn., 1969-70, dir., 1953—; pres., chief exec. officer, dir. UAL, Inc., 1970—, United Air Lines, 1970—; dir. 1st Nat. Bank of Chgo., 1st Chgo. Corp., Seattle First Nat. Bank, Safe Co. Pres. Century 21 Exposition, Inc., Seattle, 1957-59, chmn. bd., 1959-61; chmn. Wash. World's Fair Commn., 1955-63; mem. Navy Ship's Store Office adv. com. to undersec. navy, 1965—; hon. chmn. Pacific Sci. Center Found., 1967-68; bd. dirs. Va. Mason Hosp.; trustee Passavant Hosp., Chgo., 1971—, Mus. Sci. and Industry, Chgo., 1971—; mem. adv. bd. U. Wash. Grad. Sch. Bus. Adminstrn. Mem. Am. Soc. Order St. John of Jerusalem. Clubs: Seattle Golf, Seattle Yacht Rainier (Seattle); Economic, Executives (Chgo.); Wings (N.Y.C.); Bohemian (San Francisco). Home: 175 E Delaware St Chicago IL 60611 Office: PO Box 66100 Chicago IL 60666

CARLSON, FRANCIS DEWEY, biophysicist; b. Syracuse, N.Y., June 29, 1921; s. Frank Dewey and Mary Ann (O'Brien) C.; A.B., Johns Hopkins, 1942; student Harvard, 1942-43; Ph.D., U. Pa., 1949; m. Carolyn Stout, July 14, 1950; childrenNils William, Christopher Francis, Peter Kirk. Research asst. acoustic communication devices Electroacoustic Lab., Harvard, 1942-46; research muscle mechanochemistry Johns Hopkins, 1949-62, prof., chmn. dept. biophysics, 1956—. Con. NIH. Trustee Marine Biol. Lab., Woods Hole, Mass. Recipient sr. (postdoctoral fellowship NSF, 1961-62. Mem. Biophys. Soc. (council), Soc. Gen. Physiologists (past pres.), A.A.A.S., Sigma Xi. Editorial bd. Jour. Gen. Physiology. Home: 2302 West Rogers Av Baltimore MD 21209

CARLSON, GUSTAV GUNNAR, educator, anthropologist; b. Gwinn, Mich., Nov. 21, 1909; s. A. Victor and Brita (Mattson) C.; A.B., No. Mich. U., 1932; M.A., U. Mich., 1934, Ph.D., 1940; m. E. Elizabeth Erickson, Nov. 22, 1911; children—Karen Elizabeth (Mrs. John T. Ogden), Eric Gustav. Mem. faculty U. Cin., 1936- 43, 46—, prof. anthropology, 1952—, head dept. anthropology and sociology, 1961-69, chmn. dept. of anthropology, 1969—; chief intelligence OWI, Kunming, China, 1943-46; ethnol. field work among Comanche Indians, Okla., 1933, in Mexico, 1948, 51. Trustee Miami Purchase Assn., Cin., 1964—. Recipient A. B. Cohen award excellence univ. teaching U. Cin., 1962. Fellow Am. Anthrop. Assn.; mem. Phi Beta Kappa, Sigma Xi, Phi Kappa Phi. Editor: Bull. of Central States Anthrop. Soc., 1971—. Home: 6404 Edwood Av Cincinnati OH 45224

CARLSON, HENNING MAURICE, educator, mech. engr.; b. Moline, Ill., Feb. 13, 1916; s. Henning E. and Gerda (Peterson) C.; student Augustana Coll., 1935-37; B.S., U. Minn., 1939, B.S. in Mech. Engring., 1943; M.E., U. Louisville, 1955; m. Phyllis A. Tjernlund, Sept. 18, 1943; children—Diane A., Marcia A., Sharon L., Rebecca J. High sch. tchr., Morris, Minn., 1939-41; teaching asst. mech. engring. dept. U. Minn., 1941-43, instr., 1943-44; research engr. Battelle Meml. Inst., Columbus, O., 1944-49; asst. prof. mech. engring. U. Louisville, 1949-55, asso. prof., 1955-57; prof., chmn. dept. mech. engring. Lafayette Coll., Easton, Pa., 1957—, dir. engring., prof., chmn. dept. mech. engring., 1959-62. Registered profl. engr., Ohio, Pa. Mem. Am. Soc. M.E. (chmn. Anthracite-Lehigh Valley sect. 1965-66, chmn. region III mech. engring. dept. heads 1968-70), Am. Soc. Engring. Edn. (chmn. ethics com. 1966-68, sec. mech. engring. div. 1969-70, vice chmn., program chmn. 1970-71, chmn. 1971-72), Engring. Council for Profl. Devel. (chmn. student devel. com. 1962-66), Pa. Soc. Profl. Engrs. (pres. Lehigh Valley chpt. 1967-68). Office: Dept Mech Engring Lafayette College Easton PA 18042

CARLSON, HOWARD R., banker; b. 1921; grad. Healds Bus. Coll., 1941; student Columbia Exec. Sch. Bus. Adminstrn., 1963; married. With Crocker-Citizens Nat. Bank, 1946—, asst. mgr., Palo Alto, Cal., 1950-55, Stanford Center, 1955-64, applied tech. v.p., dir., 1964-65, v.p., regional mgr. central coast region, 1969-70, sr. v.p., regional mgr., 1970—. Served with USAF, 1941-46. Office: 101 W Santa Clara St San Jose CA 95108*

CARLSON, JAMES GORDON, zoologist; b. Port Allegany, Pa., Jan. 24, 1908; s. James August and Mabel (Johns) C.; A.B. (Univ. scholar, Pa. Senatorial Scholar), U. Pa., 1930, Ph.D., 1935; m. Margaret Elizabeth Shirley, Dec. 24, 1936; children—Shirley Johns, Bette Walker, James Marvin. Asst. in zoology U. Pa., 1929-30; demonstrator in biology Bryn Mawr Coll., 1930-31, instr., 1931-35; instr. zoology U. Ala., 1935-39, asst. prof., 1939-45, asso. prof., 1945-46; sr. biologist, indsl. hygiene research lab., USPHS, Bethesda, Md., 1946-47; spl. cons. in biology, 1943-46, 1947-48, asso. biologist, summer 1943, biologist, summers 1945, 46; prof. zoology U. Tenn., Knoxville, 1947—, chmn. dept. zoology and entomology, 1947-67, dir. Inst. of Radiation Biology, 1955—, distinguished service prof. 1962—. Cons. biology div. Oak Ridge Nat. Lab., 1947—; Rockefeller fellow in natural scis., 1940-41; instr. cytology Mt. Lake Biol. Sta., U. Va., summer 1936; guest investigator, Carnegie Instn. Washington, Cold Spring Harbor, summers, 1937, 38, 40. Mem. N.R.C. com. on fellowships in biology and agriculture, 1950-52. USPHS spl. fellow U. of Heidelberg, 1964-65. Fellow A.A.A.S. (v.p. 1955), Tenn. Acad. Sci. (pres. 1961); mem. Am. Inst. Biol. Scis., Am. Assn. U. Profs., Am. Soc. Naturalists, Assn. Southeastern Biologists, Am. Soc. for Cell Biology, Radiation Research Soc., Phi Beta Kappa, Sigma Xi, Phi Sigma, Phi Kappa Phi, Alpha Epsilon Delta. Presbyn. Contbr. papers on cytology and radiation biology to profl. jours. Home: 2134 Island Home Blvd SE Knoxville TN 37920

CARLSON, JOHN CLAYTON, utilities exec.; b. Soldier, Ia., May 18, 1919; s. John Magnus and Dena Maria (Hansen) C.; B.S. in Commerce, U. Ia., 1940; postgrad. Grinnell Coll., 1943, U. Wis., 1943-44, Sch. Mil. Govt., Rheims, France, 1945, Indsl. Coll. Armed Forces, 1963-64, Ia. State U., 1965; m. Catherine Maurine Hughes, Aug. 12, 1946. Parts and service mgr. Internat. Harvester Co., Omaha, 1940-42; partner Carlson Hardware, Soldier, 1942-46; tng. officer VA, Des Moines, 1946-47; office mgr., asst. mgr. A.Y. McDonald Mfg. Co., Sioux City, Ia., 1947-56; utility accountant Ia. Pub. Service Co., Sioux City, 1956-61, asst. sec., 1961-63, asst. sec., asst. treas., 1963-67, dir. purchases and stores, asst. sec., 1967-70, sec., dir. purchases and stores, 1970—. Mem. adv. bd. on office occupation Sioux City Community Sch. Dist.; mem. exec. com. Briar Cliff Coll. Campaign. Served to 1st lt. AUS, 1943-46; ETO. Decorated U.S. Army Spl. Commendation award, Personal decoration King Haakon VII of Norway. Mem. Edison Electric Inst. (mem. purchasing and stores com. Exec. Planning Group), Am., Midwest gas assns., N.Central Electric Assn., Sioux City C. of C., Am. Legion, Delta Chi. Roman Catholic. K.C. (4), Rotarian, Lion. Clubs: Knife and Fork, Sioux City Country; Blessed Sacrament Mens (Sioux City). Home: 3525 Nebraska St Sioux City IA 51104 Office: Orpheum Electric Bldg Sioux City IA 51101

CARLSON, JOHN ROY, (pseudonym of Avedis Arthur Derounian), writer, lectr.; b. Alexandropolis, Greece, Apr. 9, 1909; s. Boghos and Elizabeth (Aprahamian) D.; brought to U.S., 1921, naturalized, 1926; B.S. in Journalism N.Y.U., 1932; post- grad. Columbia, Reporter, writer and editor, 1928—; asso. with Service Bur. for Intercultural Edn., N.Y.C., which conducted research for series of 26 nation-wide broadcasts, Americans All, Immigrants All, sponsored by U.S. Office Edn., 1938-39; with Friends of Democracy to 1952; pub. Armenian Reporter (quar. polit.- cultural jour.); lectr.; conducted research for Fortune and Life mags. Recipient Jefferson award Council Against Intolerance in Am. Mem. Armenian Ch. St. Gregory the Illuminator, N.Y.C. Mem. Legion of Honor, Order De Molay. Author: Under Cover, 1943; The Plotters, 1946; Cairo to Damascus, 1951. Contbr. articles to mags. Address: care Club Program Service 515 Park Av New York City NY 10022

CARLSON, JOHN SWINK, lawyer, petroleum co. exec.; b. Ft. Collins, Colo., June 16, 1911; s. George A. and Rosa (Alps) C.; A.B., U. Colo., 1932; LL.B., Harvard, 1936; m. Sara A. Mott, June 22, 1940; children—John Swink, Lucie Pamela, Ann Brockenbrough, Virginia Charles, Thomas (dec.). Admitted to Okla. bar, 1937; legal staff Shell Oil Co., 1936-37, Turman Oil Co., 1937-38; legal asso. Yancey & Spillers, Tulsa, 1938-39; legal counselor Chapman, Barnard & McFarlin, oil, cattle and investments, Tulsa, 1939-42; gen. counsel Seismograph Service Corp., Tulsa, 1942-49; practiced in Tulsa, 1949-51; gen. counsel Okla. Natural Gas Co., 1951-61; sr. partner firm Carlson, Lupardus, Matthews, Holliman & Huffman, Tulsa, 1951-61; head legal firm John S. Carlson, Tulsa, 1961—. Sec., gen. counsel, dir. Century Geophys. Corp., 1951-71, sr. v.p., 1957-71, sec. exec. com., 1951, chmn. exec. com., 1965, dir.; gen. counsel Hayward-Wolff Research Corp., 1951; v.p., sec., dir., gen. counsel Exploration Cons., Inc., 1951-60, Canadian Geophys. Measurements, Ltd., 1954-65, Venezuela Geophys. Measurements, S.A., 1957-65; pres., dir., gen. counsel Petroleum Research Corp., 1957-65; chmn. bd., gen. counsel Community Merchandisers, Inc., 1959; pres., dir., gen. counsel Western Petroleum Co., Inc., 1960; v.p., sec., dir., gen. counsel Enterprises & Businesses, Inc., 1960; sec., dir. Western Hemisphere Trade & Credit Corp., 1960, v.p. 1961; sec., dir. Hemisphere Constrn. Co., 1960, v.p., 1961-64; v.p., sec., dir., gen. counsel Jameson Corp., 1961-63; pres., chmn. bd. T'Oil, Inc., 1962—. Pres. Maple Ridge Assn., 1964- 70. Mem. Am., Okla., Okla. Jr. (pres. 1943-44), Tulsa County, Fed. Power bar assns., Am. Judicature Soc., Tulsa C. of C., Am. Soc. Internat. Law, Mid-Continent Oil and Gas Assn., Phi Beta Kappa, Delta Sigma Rho. Clubs: Tulsa, Harvard (pres. 1949-50) (Tulsa). Editor: Compendium of Laws Relating to Problems of Men in the Armed Forces, 1943. Contbr. sect. to report on 34th Nat. Fgn. Trade Council. Home: 1001 East 19th St Tulsa OK 74120 Office: Fourth Nat Bank Bldg Tulsa OK 74199

CARLSON, KAREN LOUISE, univ. dean; b. Milw., Apr. 15, 1906; d. Duane Lloyd and Jennie (Boothroyd) Carlson; A.B., Carroll Coll., 1929; M.A., Northwestern U., 1937, Ph.D., 1948. Sec. to pres. Carroll Coll., 1929-34, registrar, 1934- 44, instr. Latin, 1934-37, asst. prof., 1937-44; counselor Northwestern U., 1944-45; asst. dean women U. Ariz., Tucson, 1945-49, dean women, 1951-71; registrar Woman's Coll of U. N.C. 1949-51. Mem. adv. bd. Guidance Research Group. Mem. Nat., Ariz., So. Ariz. assns. women deans and Counselors, Am. Assn. U. Women, Nat. Council Adminstrv. Women in Edn., Pima County Assn. Mental Health, Mortar Bd., Pi Lambda Theta, Delta Kappa Gamma, Alpha Xi Delta, Alpha Lambda Delta (hon.). Home: 201 N Norton St Tucson AZ 85719

CARLSON, LELAND HENRY, educator; b. Rockford, Ill., Mar. 25, 1908; s. Henry John and Bessie (Nilson) C.; B.A., Beloit Coll., 1931, LL.D., 1956; B.Th., North Park Theol. Sem., 1934; B.D., Chgo. Theol. Sem., 1938; Ph.D., U. Chgo., 1939; m. LaVerne Shirley Larson, June 10, 1933; children—Timothy, Kay (Mrs. John Roberts III). With North Park Coll., 1932-42, dean, 1938-42; with Northwestern U., 1942-54; pres. Rockford Coll., 1954-59; prof. history Claremont Grad. Sch., prof. ch. history Sch. Theology, Claremont (Cal.) Coll., 1959—. Colin Rhys Lovell prof. English history U. So. Cal., 1970-72. Trustee Rockford Coll., 1954-59. Recipient King Gustav V Royal Swedish medal, 1951; Northwestern U. Centennial award, 1951, Folger Shakespeare Library fellow, 1953, 58, 60; Rockefeller fellow, 1962-63. Fellow Royal Hist. Soc. London; mem. Phi Beta Kappa, Sigma Xi, Phi Theta Kappa. Author: A History of North Park College, 1941; An Alaskan Gold Mine, 1951; Cartwrightiana, 1951; The Writings of Robert Harrison and Robert Browne, 1953; The Writings of Henry Barrow, 1587-1590, 1962; The Writings of John Greenwood, 1587-1590, 1962; The Writings of Henry Barrow, 1590- 1591, 1966; The Writings of John Greenwood and Henry Barrow, 1591-1593, 1970. Sect. editor Am. Hist. Rev., 1949—. Office: 1325 North College Av Claremont CA 91711

CARLSON, LENNART H., mining co. exec.; b. Deer River, Minn., Sept. 14, 1921; s. John W. and Alma (Hagbloom) C.; B.B.A. in Accounting, U. Minn. 1947; m. Dora E. Bugliosi, Aug. 23, 1943; children—Alan G., Curtis D. Accountant, M.A. Hanna Co., Hibbing, Minn., 1947-53; chief accountant, adminstrv. mgr. Hanna Nickel Smelting Co., Riddle, Ore., 1954-61; with Hanna Mining Co., Cleve., 1961—, comptroller, 1965—. Served with USAAF, 1943-46. Mem. Nat. Assn. Accountants, Financial Execs. Inst. Republican. Mason. Home: 3570 Eldorado Drive Rocky River OH 44116 Office: 100 Erieview Plaza Cleveland OH 44114

CARLSON, LOREN DANIEL, physiologist, educator; b. Davenport, Ia., May 5, 1915; s. Frank Daniel and Esther (Lind) C.; B.S., St. Ambrose Coll., 1937; Ph.D., U. Ia., 1941; Ph.D. honoris causa, U. Osio (Norway), 1969; m. Marion Dudley Gross, June 7, 1941; children—Eric Daniel, Christopher Dean, Allen David, Katherine Dudley. Research asso. cellular physiology dept. zoology U. Ia., 1941-42; instr. zoology U. Wash., 1945, asst. prof. to prof. physiology and biophysics, 1946-60; prof., chmn. dept. physiology and biophysics U. Ky. Coll. Medicine, 1960-66; chief of scis. basic to medicine U. Cal. at Davis, 1966—. Mem. sci. adv. bd. to USAF, 1957-62. Served to maj. USAAF, 1942-46. Decorated Legion of Merit; recipient USAF Exceptional Civilian Service medal, 1962; John Jeffries award Am. Inst. Aeros. and Astronautics, 1968, Outstanding Achievement award Office Aerospace Research, Dept. Air Force, 1970. Asso. fellow Inst. Aeros. and Astronautics; fellow Aerospace Med. Assn., Am. Acad. Arts and Scis.; mem. Am. Physiol. Soc. (pres. 1968-69), Fedn. Am. Socs. Exptl. Biology (pres. 1969-70), Soc. Exptl. Biology and Medicine, Am. Soc. Zoologists, A.A.A.S., Internationalis Astronautica Academia, Sigma Xi. Contbr. articles to sci. jours. Home: 22 Meadowbrook Dr Davis CA 95616

CARLSON, M. W., rubber mfg. co. exec. Comptroller, Firestone Synthetic Rubber & Latex Co., Akron, O. Office: PO Box 2786 Akron OH 44301*

CARLSON, MARGERY CLAIRE, educator; b. Arthur, Ill., Nov. 21, 1892; d. John Emerich and Nellie Nellie Marie (Johnson) Carlson; B.S., Northwestern U., 1916; M.S., U. Wis., 1920, Ph.D., 1925. Tchr. biology high schs. in Ill., 1916-19; grad. asst. U. Wis., 1919-20, 22-25, 27-28; instr. botany Wellesley Coll., 1920-22; research fellow Boyce Thompson Inst. Plant Research, Yonkers, N.Y., 1925-27; mem. faculty Northwestern U., 1928-, asso. prof. botany, 1954-58, asso. prof. emeritus, 1958-; research asso., collector tropical plants Field Natural History Mus., 1945; dir. Nature Center and Wild Flower Trail, Evanston, Ill., 1958-; sec. Ill. chpt. Nature Conservancy, 1964-; lectr. plants and conservation, 1940-. Mem. Ill. Nature Preserves Commn., 1963-; Gov. Ill. Com. Ill. Beach State Park, 1945-. Chmn. Evanston Victory Garden Com., 1942-50. Bd. dirs. Wild Flower Preservation Soc., 1935-. Fellow A.A.A.S.; mem. Am. Inst. Biol. Scis., Bot. Soc. Am., Ill. Acad. Scis., Garden Club Am. (Eloise Payne Luquer medal 1952, Sarah Gildersleeve Fife award 1954), Garden Club Evanston (hon.), Evanston Bird Club (cons.), Alumni Assn. Northwestern U. (award of merit 1944, hon. life mem. 1953), Sigma Xi, Sigma Delta Epsilon (charter mem.; pres. Lambda chpt. 1933, 35, sec., v.p. grand chpt. 1936-40). Club: Zonta Internat. (pres. Evanston club 1942, hon. pres. 1946). Author monograph. Address: 2308 Hartzell Street Evanston, IL 60201.

CARLSON, MARVIN ALBERT, educator; b. Wichita, Kan., Sept. 15, 1935; s. Roy Edward and Gladys (Nelson) C.; B.S., U. Kan., 1957, M.A., 1959; Ph.D., Cornell U., 1961; m. Patricia Alene McElroy, Aug. 20, 1960; children—Geoffrey, Richard. Instr. speech and drama Cornell U., Ithaca, N.Y., 1961-62, asst. prof., 1962-66, asso. prof. theatre arts, 1966—, chmn. dept., 1966-68; dir. Univ. Theatre, 1963-64, 65-66. Guggenheim fellow, 1968. Mem. Am. Ednl. Theatre Assn., Am. Soc. Theatre Research, Nat. Collegiate Players, Am. Assn. U. Profs., Phi Kappa Phi. Author: Andre Antoine's Memories of the Theatre-Libre, 1964; The Theatre of the French Revolution, 1966. Home: 121 Thurston Av Ithaca NY 14850

CARLSON, MAXWELL, banker; b. Aberdeen, Wash., Nov. 9, 1905; s. Gust A. and Eleanor (Lind) C.; A.B., Dartmouth, 1928; M.C.S., Amos Tuck Sch. Adminstrn. and Finance, 1929; m. Willadee E. Hart, Sept. 15, 1931; children—Deanne, Karen. Dir., Nat. Bank of Commerce of Seattle, 1947—, pres., 1948-71; pres. Internat. Bank of Commerce, 1963-69, dir., 1963—, chmn., 1969—; dir. Marine Bancorp., 1953—, chmn., 1971—; pres. Nat. Bank of Commerce of Seattle (Internat.), 1969-71, dir., 1969—, chmn., 1971—. Pres., Clearing House Assn. of Seattle, 1953- 54, 65-66. Dir. United Good Neighbors, 1952—, campaign dir., 1954, pres., 1963. Mem. Wash. Bankers Assn. (pres. 1956-57). Clubs: Rainier, Harbor (Seattle). Home: 1626 Federal Av E Seattle WA 98102 Office: PO Box 3966 Seattle WA 98124

CARLSON, MICHAEL ERNST, banker, lawyer; b. Chgo., Jan. 30, 1925; s. Carl Ernst and Elizabeth (Huber) C.; student Loras Coll., 1942-43, Willamette U., 1944-45; J.D., Chgo, Kent Coll. Law, 1949; m. Kathleen Marie Green, Aug. 23, 1947; children—Michael, Ralph, Brigid, David, Mary, Charles, Judith, Christopher, Paul, Nora. Admitted to Ill. bar, 1950, N.Y. bar, 1963; atty. Cities Service Oil Co., Chgo. and N.Y.C., 1952-63; with Chase Manhattan Bank N.A., 1963—, v.p., sec., 1968—. Served to lt. USNR, 1943-46, 51-52. Mem. Am., Ill. bar assns. Home: 65 Wildwood Rd New Rochelle NY 10804 Office: 1 Chase Manhattan Plaza New York City NY 10015

CARLSON, NATALIE SAVAGE, author; b. Winchester, Va., Oct. 3, 1906; d. Joseph Hamilton and Natalie Marie (Villeneuve dit Vallar) Savage; student parochial schs., Cal.; m. Daniel Carlson, Dec. 7, 1929; children—Stephanie Natalie (Mrs. Robert David Sullivan), Julie Ann. Newspaper reporter Long Beach (Cal.) Sun, 1926-29. Author: The Talking Cat and Other Stories of French Canada, 1952 (N.Y. Herald Tribune award Children's Spring Book Festival 1952); Alphonse, That Bearded One, 1954 (in N.Y. Herald Tribune award Children's Spring Book Festival 1954); Wings Against the Wind, 1955; Sashes Red and Blue, 1956; Hortense, the Cow for a Queen, 1957; The Happy Orpheline, 1957; The Family Under the Bridge, 1958; A Brother for the Orphelines 1959; Evangeline, Pigeon of Paris, 1960; The Tomahawk Family, 1960; The Song of The Lop-Eared Mule, 1961; A Pet for the Orphelines, 1962; Carnival in Paris, 1962; Jean-Claude's Island, 1963; The Empty Schoolhouse, 1965; Sailor's Choice, 1966; Chalou, 1967; Luigi of the Streets, 1967; Ann Aurelia and Dorothy, 1968; Befana's Gift, 1969; The Half Sisters, 1970; Luvvy and the Girls, 1971. Republican. Roman Catholic. Home: Periwinkle Newport RI

CARLSON, NORMAN ALBERT, govt. ofcl.; b. Sioux City, Ia., Aug. 10, 1933; s. Albert N. and Esther (Hollander) C.; B.A., Gustavus Adolphus Coll., 1955; M.A., State U. Ia., 1957; Nat. Inst. Pub. Affairs fellow, Princeton, 1965-66; m. Patricia Helen Musser, Sept. 8, 1956; children—Lucinda M., Gary N. Parole officer Dept. Justice, U.S. Penitentiary, Leavenworth, Kan., 1957-58, casework supr. Fed. Correctional Inst., Ashland, Ky., 1958-60, asst. supr. Dept. Justice, Washington, 1960-62, project officer, 1962-65, exec. asst. to dir., 1966-70, dir. Fed. Bur. Prisons, 1970—. Mem. Am. Correctional Assn. Home: 8702 Piccadilly Pl Springfield VA 22151 Office: Dept Justice Washington DC 20530

CARLSON, OSCAR NORMAN, educator, metallurgist; b. Mitchell, S.D., Dec. 21, 1920; s. Oscar and Ruth Belle (Gammill) C.; B.A., Yankton Coll., 1943; Ph.D., Ia., State U., 1950; m. Virginia Jyleen Forsberg, July 30, 1946; childrenGregory Norman, Richard Norman, Karen Virginia. Mem. faculty Ia. State U., 1943- , prof., sr. metallurgist Ames Lab., 1960-, chmn. dept. metallurgy, chief metallurgy div. Ames Lab., 1962-66; spl. research nuclear metals and alloys, phase studies binary alloy systems, brittle-ductile behavior metals and alloys; developed process preparing and purifying yttrium, vanadium, zirconium, calcium, hafnium metals. Mem. Am. Soc. Metals (chmn. Des Moines 1957-58), Am. Chem. Soc., Am. Inst. Metall. Engrs., Am. Soc. Engring. Edn., Ia. Acad. Scis., Sigma Xi, Phi Kappa Phi, Phi Lambda Upsilon. Lion. Home: 811 Ridgewood Ames, IA

CARLSON, OSCAR RUDOLF, telephone co. exec.; b. Beverly, Mass., Mar. 27, 1907; s. John A. and Emma (Nicklasson) C.; A.B., Harvard, 1928; m. Gertrude Phelps, Aug. 30, 1940. Econ. statistician New Eng. Tel. & Tel. Co., 1930—, treas., 1967- -. Past mem. Lexington (Mass.) Appropriation Com.; mem. Lexington Town Meeting, 1964—. Mem. Financial Execs. Inst., Newcomen Soc. Club: Treasurers (Boston). Home: 23 Hayes Av Lexington MA 02173 Office: 185 Franklin St Boston MA 02107

CARLSON, PHILIP EBEL, former cement co. exec.; b. Mpls., Mar. 25, 1915; s. John F. and Laura (Ebel) C.; B.Chem. Engring., U. Minn., 1938; m. Louise Richards Burger, May 19, 1942; children—Philip B., John C. With Mpls.-St. Paul San. Dist., 1938- 41, Collins & Aikman, 1945-46; with Lehigh Portland Cement Co., 1946-70, asst. v.p. mfg., 1958-62, v.p. engring., 1962-70. Served to lt. comdr. USNR, 1941-45. Mem. I.E.E.E., Portland Cement Assn., Engrs. Club Lehigh Valley. Club: Livingston (Allentown). Home: RD1 Alburtis PA 18011

CARLSON, RAYMOND, magazine editor; b. Leadville, Colo., Sept. 1, 1906; s. Carl and Hulda (Bengtson) C.; student U. Ariz., 1924-25, 26-27; A.B. in Romance langs., Stanford, 1929; m. Helen Mary Hooker, Oct. 12, 1937. Reporter, editor Ariz. Silver Belt., Miami, Ariz., 1929-35; editor Ariz. Hwys., 1937- -. Served with inf. AUS, World War II; PTO. Decorated Bronze Star. Mem. Hammer and Coffin Soc. (Stanford), Phi Beta Kappa, Phi Delta Theta. Editor: Gallery of Western Paintings, 1951; The Flowering Cactus, 1954. Home: 1123 W Palo Verde Dr Phoenix AZ 85013 Office: 2039 W Lewis Street Phoenix AZ 85008

CARLSON, REYNOLD ERLAND, former U.S. ambassador; b. Chgo., Sept. 7, 1912; s. Amel Reynold and Lillian (Evald) C.; B.S., Northwestern U., 1936, M.A., 1937; Ph.D., Harvard, 1946; m. Patricia Proctor, July 27, 1964; 1 dau., Marie Louise Roehm. Asst. prof. econs. Johns Hopkins, 1940-48; econ. cons. UN, 1946- 47, Econ. Commn. Latin Am., Santiago, Chile, 1948; asso. prof. econs., dir. Inst. Brazilian Studies, Vanderbilt U., 1949-53; economist Joint Brazilian-U.S. Devel. Commn., Inst. Inter-Am. Affairs, Rio de Janeiro, 1951-52; sr. economist Western Hemisphere operations World Bank, 1953- 58; prof. econs., dir. grad. program econ. devel. Vanderbilt U., 1958- 63; cons. Ford Found., 1959-61, rep. in Rio de Janeiro, 1961-65, asso. dir. Latin Am. program, 1965-66; U.S. ambassador to Colombia, 1966-69; Ford Found. rep. in Buenos Aires, 1969—. Served to 2d lt. USAAF, 1942-45. Decorated Cruzeiro de Sul (Brazil). Mem. Am. Econ. Assn., Phi Beta Kappa, Delta Sigma Pi. Clubs: Harvard (N.Y.C.): Yacht (Rio de Janeiro). Home: Ayacucho 2151 Buenos Aires Argentina Office: Ford Found Casilla Correo 4199 Buenos Aires Argentina

CARLSON, ROBERT LEE, educator; b. Gary, Ind., May 22, 1924; s. Herman and Eva (Larson) C.; B.S., Purdue U., 1948, M.S., 1950; Ph.D., Ohio State U., 1962; m. Betty Christine Nelson, Oct. 21, 1950; chilen—David Lee, Richard Ray, Karen Christine, Robert Lee, Carol Lynn. Research engr. Battelle Inst., Columbus, O., 1950-62; research engr. U.S. Steel Research Lab., Monroeville, Pa., 1962-63; research asso., lectr. Stanford, 1963-66; prof. Ga. Inst. Tech., Atlanta, 1966—; invited lectr. Internat. Union Theoretical and Applied Mechanics, 1960; cons. EIMAC div. Varian Assos., USAF Flight Dynamics Lab. Served with AUS, 1943-45. Recipient Charles Dudley medal Am. Soc. Testing Materials, 1959. Mem. Am. Inst. Aeros. and Astronautics, Am. Soc. for Exptl. Stress Analysis (chmn. S.E. chpt. 1968-69), Sigma Xi, Pi Tau Sigma, Tau Beta Pi. Contbr. to Folke Odquist Vol., 1967. Contbr. articles profl. jours. Home: 4738 Cambridge Dr Dunwoody GA 30338 Office: Dept Aerospace Engring Ga Inst Tech Atlanta GA 30332

CARLSON, ROBERT SCOTT, univ. dean; b. Chgo., June 16, 1934; s. Robert F. and Helen (Pierce) C.; S.B., Mass. Inst. Tech., 1956; M.B.A., Stanford U., 1962, Ph.D., 1964; m. Sandra Lynn Stolz, June 21, 1962; children—Cynthia Lynn, Scott Edward. Prodn. engr. E.I. duPont de Nemours & Co., 1956-57; financial analyst Ford Motor Co., 1962, Standard Oil N.J., 1963; instr. Stanford U., 1963-64; asst. prof. Columbia, 1964-66; vis. prof. Robert Coll., Istanbul, Turkey, 1966; asst. prof. Harvard, 1966-69; dean Babcock Grad. Sch. Mgmt. of Wake Forest U., also prof. mgmt., 1969—; dir. 4 corps.; cons. to industry. Active Common Cause, United Fund, Pres. Babcock Grad. Sch. Mgmt. Found., 1970—. Served from ensign to lt. (j.g.), USNR, 1957-70, Named adminstr. of year Wake Forest U., 1970. Billings fellow, 1953; Ford Found. fellow, 1963; M.I.T. Club of Chgo. fellow, 1952. Mem. Am. Econ. Assn., Am. Finance Assn. Contbr. articles profl. jours. Research on measuring investment performance, new teaching-learning systems in mgmt. edn. Home: 2535 Woodberry Dr Winston-Salem NC 27106

CARLSON, SUZANNE OLIVE, architect; b. Bakham, Mass., Aug. 20, 1939; d. Sigfrid and Helga (Larson) Carlson; B.S., R.I. Sch. Design, 1963. Jr. partner Dingnam-Fauteux & Partners, Worcester, Mass., 1969-70; partner firm Richard Lamoureux Asso., Worcester, 1970—; guest lectr. Holy Cross Coll., 1969-70. Mem. Worcester Art Museum, Worcester Craft Center. Recipient European Honors Program grant, Rome, Italy, 1961-62; recipient A.I.A. School medal for excellence, 1963. Mem. Worcester Heritage Soc., A.I.A. (Central Mass. exec. bd. 1969-71, sec.-treas. 1970-71), Mass. Assn. Architects, New Eng. Regional Assn. Architects. Home: Old Turnpike Rd Bakham MA 01068 Office: 14 E Worcester St Worcester MA 01604

CARLSON, WILLIAM DONALD, educator, former dean; b. Sandstone, Minn., Jan. 15, 1914; s. C. Oscar and Jennie A. (Biorklund) C.; B.E. with high honors, St. Cloud State Teachers Coll., 1939; M.A., U. Minn., 1951, Ph.D., 1955; m. Marian A. Finseth, Feb. 15, 1942; children—John W., Marcia A., Audrey J., Meridee J. Tchr. elementary schs., Minn., 1932-36, tchr., prin., secondary schs., 1937-41; with U.S. Bur. Prisons, 1941-42, 46-47; research asst. bur. ednl. research U. Minn., 1947-48, dir. student personnel Coll. Edn. High Sch., 1948-52; dean student affairs U. Nev., Las Vegas, 1952-57, dean so. regional div., 1957-65, prof. edn., 1952—. Mem. adv. council U.S. Civil War Centennial Commn. Member U.S. Regional Export Expansion Council. Served to capt., inf., AUS, 1942-46. Decorated Bronze Star with oak leaf cluster. Mem. Clark County (pres.), Nev. (v.p.) mental health assn, Nev. Psychol. Assn., Am. Personnel and Guidance Assn., Am. Coll. Personnel Assn., Higher Edn. Assn., Phi Delta Kappa, Psi Chi, Kappa Delta Pi, Phi Kappa Phi, Tau Kappa Alpha. Mason (33), Rotarian; mem. Order Eastern Star. Home: 1308 Cashman Dr Las Vegas NV 89102

CARLSON, WILLIAM DWIGHT, univ. pres.; b. Denver, Nov. 5, 1928; D.V.M., Colo. State U., 1952, M.S., 1956; Ph.D. in Radiology, U. Colo., 1958; m. Beverley Ann Bradshaw, 1950; children—Susan Elaine, Earl Dwight. Pres., prof. radiation biology U. Wyo., Laramie, 1968—; affiliate prof. radiology, radiation biology Colo. State U., Fort Collins, 1968—. Dir. Cheyenne Nat. Bank (Wyo.), 1968—, Heath Consol. Industries, Fort Collins, Colo., 1967—. Mem. subcom. Nat. Council on Radiation Protection and Measurements. 1965—; adv. dir. Wyo. Indsl. Devel. Corp., 1967—; commr. Wyo. Western Interstate Commn. Higher Edn., 1968—; bd. commnrs. Nat. Commn. Accrediting, 1969—; mem. president's council and senate Assn. Land Grant Colls. and State Univs., 1968—; exec. com. Assn. Western Univs., 1970—; regional adv. com. Inst. Internat. Edn., 1969—. Mem. exec. com. Longs Peak council Boy Scouts Am., 1966—, v.p. exec. com. region 8, 1970—. Named Outstanding Young Man of Year, Colo. Jr. C. of C., 1960, Top Prof., Colo. State U., 1961, Vet. of Year, Am. Animal Hosp. Assn., 1967. Diplomate Am. Bd. Vet. Radiology (founding mem.). Fellow A.A.A.S.; mem. Laramie C. of C., Am., Wyo. vet. med. assns., Nuclear Medicine Soc. Am. (nat. trustee 1964-68), Wyo. Higher Edn. Council, Radiation Research Soc., Wyo. Med. Soc., Am. Vet. Radiology Soc. (charter, pres. 1965), Am. Inst. Biol. Scis., N.Am. Radiol. Soc. Rotarian. Author: Veterinary Radiology, 2d edit., 1968. Editor: procs. Internat. Symposium on the Effects of Ionizing Radiation of the Reproductive System, 1964. Contbr. articles profl. jours. Home: 1306 Ivinson Av Laramie WY 82070

CARLSON, WILLIAM SAMUEL, univ. pres.; b. Ironwood, Mich., Nov. 18, 1905; s. Samuel and Mary (Lamsted) C.; A.B., U. Mich., 1930, M.S., 1932, Ph.D., 1938, LL.D., 1950; postgrad. U. Copenhagen (Denmark), 1931, Columbia, 1935; LL.D., Dickinson Coll., 1948, U. Del., 1950, Middlebury Coll., 1951; D.Sc., Alfred U., 1953, Bowling Green State U., 1964; L.H.D., U. Cin., 1970; m. Maryjane Rowe, Dec. 17, 1932; 1 dau., Kristin Rowe. Asst. geology U. Mich., 1927; spl. observer U.S. Weather Bur., 1928; field leader U. Mich. Greenland Expdn., 1928-29; tech. adviser on Greenland to Chgo. Tribune, 1929; asst. geology U. Mich., 1929-30, leader 4th expdn. to Greenland, 1930-31; Henry Goddard Leach fellow Am.-Scandinavian Found., 1931- 32; instr. geology U. Mich., 1932-33, grad. fellow, 1933; instr. Ironwood (Mich.) High Sch., 1933-34; prin. Wakefield (Mich.) High Sch., 1934-36, East Lansing (Mich.) High Sch., 1936-37; asst. prof. U. Minn., 1937-39, asso. prof., 1939-41, dir. admissions and records, 1941- 45, dean, prof., 1946; pres. U. Del., 1946-50, U. Vt., 1950-52, State U. N.Y., 1952-58, U. Toledo, 1958—. Dir. Toledo Trust Co., Toledo Edison Co. Mem. Gov. Minn. Adv. Com. Edn., 1941; chmn. Ohio Civil War Centennial Commn., 1959-63, Greater Toledo War Centennial Commn., 1959-63; mem. N.Y. State Citizens Com. for Pub. Schs.; chmn. N.Y. State Com. Fulbright Scholarships, 1952-58; elector Hall of Fame. Bd. visitors Air U., 1949-52; bd. dirs. Toledo Hosp., Inst. Med. Research; adv. bd. St. Vincent Hosp. Special cons. on arctic problems to comdg. gen., USAAF, 1941; commd. maj. USAAF, 1942, advanced through grades to col., 1945; asst. chief, spl. projects br., plans div., Hdqrs. USAAF, 1942-43, exec. Western Hemisphere br., plans div., 1943-44, dir. Arctic, Desert and Tropic br., USAAF Tactical Center, 1944-45; col. Res., 1945—. Decorated Legion of Merit. Mem. Geophys. Union, State Univs. Assn. (sec.-treas.), N.Y. Acad. Scis., Am. Council Edn., Met. Ednl. TV Assn. (past trustee), Minn. Assn. Secondary Sch. Prins. (sec. 1937-41), Ohio Coll. Assn. (pres. 1969), A.A.A.S., Am. Legion, Newcomen Soc., Sigma Xi, Sigma Gamma Epsilon, Phi Delta Kappa, Phi Kappa Phi, Omicron Delta Kappa, Blue Key, Tau Beta Pi, Alpha Kappa Psi, Pi Delta Theta, Beta Gamma Sigma, Phi Eta Sigma, Pershing Rifles. Clubs: Explorers, Century (N.Y.C.); Toledo Country; M (U. of Mich.). Author: Greenland Lies North, 1940; Report of the Northern Division of the Fourth University of Michigan Greenland Expedition, 1941; (with C. W. Boardman) Student Teachers Handbook, 1940; Lifelines Through the Arctic, 1962; The Municipal University, 1962. Editor: Manual for the Supervising Teacher, 1940. Contbr. articles tech. jours. Home: 3425 W Bancroft St Toledo OH 43606

CARLSSON, PERCY ALLAN, educator; b. San Jose, Cal., Feb. 3, 1927; s. Percy Gustav and Esther (Anderson) C.; student U. Tex., 1947, U. Neb., 1947-48; B.A., Wheaton (Ill.) Coll., 1951, M.A., 1956; B.D., Trinity Evang. Div. Sch., 1954; Ph.D., Northwestern U., 1961; m. Marian Inga Carlsson, June 27, 1952. Instr. philosophy Wheaton Coll., 1957-58; instr. philosophy and religion, registrar, dir. admissions Trinity Coll., Chgo., 1958-61; prof. philosophy, registrar, adminstrv. asst. to dean of faculty Va. Mil. Inst., Lexington, 1961—. Bd. dirs. Lexington Research Center. Served with USNR, 1945-46. Mem. Am. Philos. Assn., Soc. for Philosophy of Religion, So. Soc. Philosophy and Psychology, Metaphysical Soc., Soc. for Sci. Study Religion, Va. Humanities Conf., Am. Assn. U. Profs., Am. Assn.

Higher Edn., Am., Va. assns. coll. registrars and admissions officers. Author: Butler's Ethics, 1964. Contbr. articles profl. jours. Home: 110 Rebel Ridge Dr Lexington VA 24450

CARLTON, DOYLE ELAM, lawyer; b. Wauchula, Fla., July 6, 1887; s. Albert and Martha (McEwen) C.; A.B., Stetson U., 1910, also LL.D.; A.B., U. Chgo., 1910, LL.D., 1912; LL.B., Columbia, 1912; LL.D., U. Fla., 1933; L.H.D., Fla. South Coll., 1953, U. Tampa, 1953; m. Nell Ray, Aug. 30, 1912; children—Martha (Mrs. David Ward), Mary (Mrs. W. J. Ott), Doyle Elam. Admitted to Fla. bar, 1912, since practiced in Tampa; partner firm Carlton, Fields, Ward, Emmanuel, Smith & Cutler, 1912—; city atty., Tampa, 1926-28. Mem. Pres. Eisenhower's Commn. Civil Rights, 1957-61, Pres. Kennedy's Nat. Agrl. Adv. Commn., 1961-63; pres. Pan Am. Commn. of Tampa. Mem. Fla. Senate, 1917-19; gov. of Fla., 1929-33. Trustee Stetson U. Named Outstanding Citizen of Tampa, Civitan Club, 1954. Mem. Am., Fla., Tampa, Hillsborough County bar assns., Fla. C. of C. (past pres.), Com. of 100. Baptist. Kiwanian (dist. gov. 1922), Mason (Shriner), Elk, K.P. Home: 2401 Bayshore Harbor House Tampa FL 33609 Office: Exchange Nat Bank Bldg Tampa FL 33601

CARLTON, PAUL KENDALL, air force officer; b. Manchester, N.H., Apr. 14, 1921; s. R.W. and Julia Anne (Jameson) C.; student U. Pitts., 1939-40, Ohio State U., 1940-41, George Washington U., 1961; grad. Nat. War Coll., 1962; m. Helen Sweat, Oct. 4, 1942; children—Paul K., Dorothy E. (Mrs. Peter Alan Sievert). Commd. 2d lt. USAAF, 1942, advanced through grades to lt. gen. USAF, 1969; aricraft comdr. 468th Bomb Group, 58th Bomb Wing, CBI, 1944; dep. comdr. 93d Bomb Wing, Castle AFB, Cal., 1957-59, 4126th Strategic Wing, Bealee AFB, Cal., 1959-61, 379th Bomb Wing, Wurtsmith AFB, Mich, 1962-63, 305th Bomb Wing, Bunker Hill AFB, Ind., 1963-65; chief operations plans div. SAC Hdqrs., Omaha, 1965-67, asst. dept. chief staff operations, 1967-68, dep. chief staff operations, 1969; comdr. 1st Strategic Aerospace Div., Vandenberg AFB, Cal., 1968, 15th Air Force, March AFB, Cal., 1969—. Decorated Silver Star, Legion Merit with oak leaf cluster, D.F.C., Air medal with 5 oak leaf clusters, Army Commendation medal, Purple Heart. Mem. Air Force Assn. Presbyn. Rotarian. Contbr. mil. jours. Home: Quarters 176 March AFB CA 92508 Office: Hdqrs 15th Air Force March AFB CA 92508

CARLTON, STEVE, pitcher with St. Louis Cardinal Profl. Baseball Team. Address: care Busch Meml Stadium Plaza St Louis MO 63102*

CARMACK, GEORGE, newspaper editor; b. Troy, Tenn., Feb. 20, 1907; s. Dan Meacham and Frances (Burnett) C.; student Union U., Jackson, Tenn., 1922-24; A.B., U. Tenn., 1927; m. Bonnie Tom Robinson, Oct. 1943; 1 dau., Judith Anne. Reporter, Knoxville Sentinel, 1926-28, Memphis Evening Appeal, 1928-30; city editor Memphis Press- Scimitar, 1930-35; mng. editor, 1935-37; editor Knoxville News-Sentinel, 1937; editor Houston Press, 1946-64; staff writer Scripps-Howard Newspaper Alliance, 1964-66; editor Albuquerque Tribune, 1966—. Served as pvt. in 6th Cav., 1940; commd., 1942; ETO. PTO. Episcopalian. Home: 1800 San Patricio S W Albuquerque, NM 87104. Office: Albuquerque Tribune Albuquerque NM 87103

CARMACK, MARVIN, educator; b. Dana, Ind., Sept. 1, 1913; s. Robert R. and Elsie (Jackson) C.; B.A. in Chemistry, U. Ill., 1937; M.S. in Chemistry, U. Mich., 1939, Ph.D. in Chemistry, 1940; m. Joan M. Scully, July 9, 1960. Research asso. U. Ill., 1940-41; instr. U. Pa., Phila., 1941-44, asst. prof., 1944-46, asso. prof., 1946-51, prof. chemistry, 1951-53; prof. chemistry Ind. U., Bloomington, 1953—. Responsible investigator Nat. Def. Research Com., 1942-45, Com. Med. Research, 1945-46, office Sci. Research and Devel., 1945-46; cons. Los Alamos Sci. Labs., 1953-55; cons. in chem. industry. Bd. dirs. Boys Club, Bloomington, Ind., 1971—. Guggenheim Found. fellow, 1949-50; Fulbright research fellow, 1960-61. Mem. Am., Swiss chem. socs., Chem. Soc. London, N.Y., Ind. acads. scis., A.A.A.S., Am. Inst. Chemists, Am. Soc. Pharmacognosy, Soc. Econ. Botany, Sigma Xi, Phi Beta Kappa, Phi Lambda Upsilon. Patentee in field. Contbr. articles to scientific jours. Home: Rural Route 12 Box 73 3516 Bradley St Bloomington IN 47401

CARMAN, GLENN ELWIN, educator, entomologist; b. Waterloo, Ia., June 8, 1914; s. Herbert Elwin and Corna Anne (Peck) C.; B.S., Ia. State U., 1936; Ph.D., Cornell U., 1942; m. Sophie Gertrude Quick, Apr. 12, 1941; children—Donna Gail, Gary Bruce. Research fellow Ia. State U., 1936-37, Cornell U., 1937-41, Rohm & Haas Co., 1942-43; mem. faculty U. Cal. at Riverside, 1943—, successively jr. entomologist, asst. entomologist, asso. entomologist, 1943-53, entomologist, 1953—, prof. entomology, 1963—, chmn. dept., 1963-68. Vice chmn., mem. bd. ICCAP, Inc. Bd. dirs., exec. com., chmn. disaster com. Riverside County chpt. A.R.C.; vector control adv. com. Cal. Dept. Health. Mem. Entomol. Soc. Am. (chmn. Pacific br. 1951, mem. governing bd.), A.A.A.S., Am. Chem. Soc., Sigma Xi, Phi Kappa Phi. Home: 5368 Pinehurst Drive Riverside CA 92504

CARMAN, IAN, journalist. Bus. and financial editor Toronto Globe and Mail. Office: 140 King St W Toronto 1 Ontario Canada*

CARMAN, JAMES WALMSLEY FREDERIC, bishop; b. Denver, Sept. 26, 1903; s. Frederic and Rosa (Cook) C.; B.A., Carleton Coll., 1929; B.D., Seabury Div. Sch., Fairbault, Minn., 1930; D.D., Seabury-Western Theol. Sem., Evanston, Ill., 1949; m. Phyllis Churchill, Aug. 13, 1930; children—Catherine (Mrs. Stephen W. Edwards), Charles Churchill. Ordained deacon Episcopal Ch., 1929, priest, 1930; rector St. Luke's Ch., Denver, 1930-34, Ascension Ch., Pueblo, Colo., 1934-44; field officer Nat. Council P.E. Ch., 1944-47, mem. dept. promotion, 1948-53; dean Trinity Cathedral, Phoenix, 1954-56; bishop coadjutor Diocese Ore., 1956-58; diocesan bishop, 1958—. Pres. trustees Good Samaritan Hosp., Corvallis, Ore., Good Samaritan Hosp., Portland, Ore., Rogue Valley Meml. Hosp., Medford, Ore., Ore. Episcopal Schs., Portland; trustee Church Div. Sch. of Pacific, Berkeley, Cal. Home: 51 SW Touchstone Lake Oswego OR 97034 Office: 11800 S W Military Lane Portland OR 97219

CARMAN, JOHN BRAISTED, educator. Prof. comparative religion, acting dir. Center for Study of World Religions Harvard. Office: Dept Religion Harvard U Cambridge MA 02138*

CARMAN, WILLIAM BRAINERD, lawyer; b. Detroit Lakes, Minn., Oct. 5, 1905; s. William B. and Frances P. (Fritzsche) C.; A.B. magna cum laude, Carleton Coll., 1926; LL.B. magna cum laude, Harvard, 1929; m. Dorothy J. Day, Sept. 15, 1930; children—Patricia Jeanne McEldowney, Mary Elisabeth Kneale. Admitted to Cal. bar, 1930; mem. firm O'Melveny & Myers, 1920-40, partner, 1940-70, gen. counsel, 1970—; instr. law Southwestern U., 1936-39. Mem. Carleton Nat. Alumni Assn. (pres. 1964-66), Harvard Legal Aid Soc. (pres. 1928), Carleton Coll. So. Cal. Alumni Assn. (pres. 1947-50), Am., Cal. State (chmn. radio com. 1950-51), Los Angeles bar assns., Cal., S.C. hist. socs., Phi Beta Kappa, Phi Delta Epsilon. Clubs: University, Chancery, Zamorano; El Niguel Country. Mem. editorial bd. Harvard Law Rev., 1928-29. Author numerous legal and hist. articles. Home: 422 S Orange Grove Blvd Pasadena CA also 31671 Crystal Sands Dr. Laguna Niguel CA Office: 611 W 6th St Los Angeles CA 90017

CARMER, CARL, author; b. Cortland, N.Y., Oct. 16, 1893; s. Willis Griswold and Mary (Lamson) C.; Ph.B., Hamilton Coll., Clinton, N.Y., 1914, Ph.M., 1917; M.A., Harvard U., 1915; Litt.D., Elmira Coll., 1937; L.H.D., Hamilton Coll., 1941; Litt.D., Susquehanna University, 1944; LL.D., U. Buffalo, 1962; m. Elizabeth Black, Dec. 24, 1928. Instr. in English, Syracuse U., 1915-16, U. of Rochester, 1916-17; chmn. pub. speaking dept., Hamilton Coll., 1919; asst. prof. English, U. Rochester, 1919-21; asso. prof. U. of Ala., 1921-24, prof., 1924- 27; columnist New Orleans Morning Tribune, 1927; asst. editor Vanity Fair, 1928-29, Theatre Arts Monthly, 1929-33; pres. Boscobel Restoration, Inc. Bd. overseers Coll. of Virgin Islands, 1963. Served as 1st lt. F.A., World War I. Recipient merit award Am. Assn. of State and Local History, patriotic achievement medal Order Founders and Patriots of America. Association, P.E.N., Poetry Society America. Authors Guild of Authors Fellow New York State Hist. Assn. (v.p.); mem. MacDowell Association, P.E.N., Poetry Soc. Am., Authors Guild of Authors League Am. P.E.N, Poetry Soc. Am., Authors Guild of Authors League Am. N.Y. State Folklore Soc. (v.p.). Soc. Am. Historians (bd. dirs.), 56. Mem. Nat. Assn. Student Personnel Adminstrs., Am. Acad., Phi Beta Victorian Soc. in America (bd. dirs.), Hudson River Conservation Soc. (1st v.p.), Phi Beta Kappa, Psi Upsilon. Presbyn. Clubs: Pilgrims, Century. Author: Stars Fell on Alabama, 1933; Listen for a Lonesome Drum, 1936; The Hudson, 1939; Dark Trees to the Wind, 1949; Windfall Fiddle, 1950; The Susquehanna, 1955; The Screaming Ghost, 1956; My Kind of Country, 1966; The Farm Boy and the Angel, 1970. Editor: Rivers of America Series; The Rivers of America Series; The Tavern Lamps Are Burning. Address: Octagon House Irvington-on-Hudson NY ☆

CARMI, EUGENIO, artist; exhibited silk screens Mus. Modern Art, N.Y.C., Kiko Galleries, Houston, also Mexico City and Japan; exhibited Stripsody (interpretation of Cathy Berberian composition) Venice Biennale, 1966. Office: Kiko Galleries 419 Lovett Blvd Houston TX 77006*

CARMICHAEL, ALEXANDER DOUGLAS, educator; b. Sliema, Malta, July 19, 1929; s. Adam and Jane (Hamilton) G.; B.Sc., Plymouth Tech. Coll., London U., 1949; Ph.D., Cambridge U., 1958; m. Rose Margaret Whittaker, Sept. 1, 1951; children—Gillian Ruth, Alison Rose, Peter Stewart. Chief engr. Dracone Developments Ltd., London, Eng., 1960-61; sr. project engr. No. Research and Engring. Corp., Cambridge, Mass, 1961-64; research fellow Imperial Coll. Sci. and Tech., London, 1964-68; tech. adv. English Elec. Co. Ltd., Rugby, 1968-70; prof. power engring. Mass. Inst. Tech., 1970—. Mem. Soc. Naval Architects and Marine Engrs., Whitworth Soc. (London), Sigma Xi. Home: 69 Otis St Newtonville MA 02160 Office: Mass Inst Tech Cambridge MA 02139

CARMICHAEL, ALLAN RUSSELL, banker; b. New Haven, Sept. 5, 1902; s. Alian John and Lisette (Shaw) C.; B.S., Yale, 1924; m. Ruth Hoppen, July 10, 1948; stepchildren—William E. Gwatkin, Richmond N. Gwatkin. Civil engr. Sperry & Treat Co., New Haven, 1924-32, C.W. Blakeslee & Sons, New Haven, 1932-39; with Conn. Savs. Bank, New Haven, 1939—, asst. treas., v.p., 1939-58, exec. v.p., 1958-62, pres., 1962-67, chmn. 1967—, also trustee; dir. New Haven Water Co., First New Haven Nat. Bank; sr. v.p. Savs. Bank Life Ins. Co., 1964-67, dir., 1964-68; dir. C.W. Blakeslea & Sons. Bd. dirs. Quinnipiac council Boy Scouts Am., 1957-67, Taxpayers Research Council; trustee Savs. Banks Life Ins. Fund Conn., 1959-63. Served to lt. comdr. USNR, 1942-46. Mem. Nat. Assn. Savs. Banks (bd. dirs. 1958-62), Savs. Banks Assn. Conn. (pres. 1959-60), New Haven C. of C. Conglist. Mason (32), Rotarian. Home: 42 Deer Run Road Woodbridge CT 06525 Office: 47 Church St New Haven CT 06501

CARMICHAEL, DONALD SCOTT, lawyer, bus. exec.; b. Toledo, February 19, 1912; s. Grey Thornton and Edna Earle (Jaite) C.; A.B., Harvard, 1935, law student, 1935-37; LL.B., U. Mich., 1942; m. Mary Glenn Dickinson, May 28, 1940; children—Mary Brooke, Pamela Hastings. Staff dept. law City of Cleve., 1938-40; admitted to Ohio bar, 1942; chief renegotiation br. Cleve. Ordnance Dist., War Dept., 1942-46; practiced in Cleve., 1946; asst. sec. Diamond Alkali Company, 1946-48, sec., 1948-59, gen. counsel, 1957-59; v.p.-gen. counsel Stouffer Corp., 1959-60, exec. v.p., 1960-64; practiced in Cleve., 1964-70; pres. Food Service div. Pet, Inc., N.Y.C., 1971—; officer, dir., various corps. Mem. Cuyahoga County Charter Commn., 1959—, chmn. Mem. Cleve. Met. Services Commn., 1957-59; President's Task Force on War Against Poverty, 1964. Del., Democratic Nat. Conv., 1960, 64; mem. Cuyahoga County Dem. Exec. Com. Chmn. bd. trustees Cuyahoga County Hosps., 1958-64, Urban League, Karamu House. Mem. Am., Ohio, Cleve. bar assns., Phi Gamma Delta. Clubs: Harvard (pres.), Union, Fifty, Chagrin Valley Hunt (Cleve.); Harvard (N.Y.C.). Editor: F.D.R.; Columnist, 1947. Contbr. to law revs. Home: Hunting Valley Village OH Office: 50 W 23d St New York City NY 10010

CARMICHAEL, DOUGLAS, educator; b. Greenwich, Conn., July 24, 1923; s. George Edgar and Helen Gertrude (Fox) C.; A.B. summa cum laude, Bowdoin Coll., 1947; M.A., Harvard, 1948; Ph.D., Ind. U., 1954; m. Helen Sanborn Edgerly, June 26, 1949; children—Douglas Alasdair, Megan Margaret, Elspeth Edgerly. Tchr. English, Loomis Sch., Windsor, Conn., 1948-49; head, English dept. St. Mark's Sch. Tex., Dallas, 1949-52; instr. philosophy U. Mass., 1954-56; instr. philosophy and acad. counselor Ind. U., S.E. Extension, Jeffersonville, 1956-58; asst. prof. philosophy St. Lawrence U., Canton, N.Y., 1958-63, asso. prof., 1963-65, prof., 1965—, chmn. dept., 1964—. Served with AUS, 1943-46. Mem. Am. Philos. Assn., Am. Metaphys. Soc., Soc. Ancient Greek Philosophy, Phi Beta Kappa, Kappa Sigma. Republican. Trans. Pico della Mirandola (Heptaplus), 1965. Home: 14 Elm St Canton NY 13617

CARMICHAEL, EMMETT BRYAN, biochemist; b. Shelbyville, Mo., Sept. 4, 1895; s. George Frank and Amelia Grant (Tingle) C.; student Central Coll., 1914-16; A.B., U. Colo., 1918; M.S., 1922; Ph.D., U. Cin., 1927; postgrad. summers Northwestern, 1935, Harvard, 1936; m. Lelah Marie Van Hook. Instr. organic chemistry U. Colo., 1919-24; biochemistry U. Cin., 1924-26; asst. prof., head dept. physiol. chemistry U. Ala., 1927, asso. prof., 1928-32, prof., 1932-45; prof. biochemistry Med. Coll. Ala., 1945-66, Sch. Dentistry, 1948-66, asst. dean Med. Coll. Ala., Sch. Dentistry, 1959-66, prof. biochemistry emeritus, asst. dean emeritus, 1966. Chmn., N. Central Ala. Regional Sci. Fair, 1954-57. Trustee Gorgas Scholarship Found., 1952—, chmn., 1957—. Served in Ordnance Dept., U.S. Army, 1918-1919, 2d lt. Res., 1919. Acting sec.- mgr. So. Med. Assn., 1948. Recipient citations Central Coll., 1954, U. Ala., 1966; William Crawford Gorgas award Med. Assn. Ala., 1966. Fellow A.A.A.S. (chmn. acad. conf. 1933), Am. Inst. Chemists (hon., nat. councilor 1952-54, pres. Ala. 1962-63, nat. pres. 1967-69, chmn. bd. 1969-71), Internat. Coll. Anesthetists; mem. A.M.A., Am. Assn. Clin. Chemists (nat. exec. com. 1956-57), Am. Bd. Clin. Chemistry, Am. Chem. Soc. (So. Chemist award Memphis sect. 1965, vice chmn. Ala. sect. 1932-34, chmn. 1934-35), Am. Soc. Biol. Chem., Soc. Exptl. Biology, Med. (past vice chmn. So. sect.), Am. Physiol. Soc., Ala. Acad. Sci. (pres. 1930-31, editor jour. 1942-48), Am. Assn. Hist. Med., Sigma Phi Epsilon (alumni citation 1967, dist. gov. 1942-46), Sigma Xi, Alpha Chi Sigma, Alpha Epsilon Delta (Distinguished Service award 1966, grand pres. 1932-38, So. councilor 1938-40, nat. councilor 1940-51), Gamma Sigma Epsilon, Phi Beta Pi (So. praetor 1934-39, mem. council 1943-67, Man of Year 1954, supreme archon 1950-52). Democrat. Methodist. Mason (32, Shriner), Acacia (Order of Pythagoras 1966). Assembler, editor, bibliographies of faculty mems. U. Ala., 1934, ann. supplements, 1935-40; mem. editorial adv. bd. Scalpel of Alpha Epsilon Delta, 1938-40; editor Phi Beta Pi Quar., 1945-49; editor Ala. Jour. Med. Scis., 1962-66, cons. to editorial bd., 1966—. Contbr. to sci. jours. Home: 3501 Redmont Rd Birmingham AL 35213 Office: 1919 7th Av S Birmingham AL 35233

CARMICHAEL, HOAGLAND HOWARD (Hoagy Carmichael), composer; b. Bloomington, Ind., Nov. 22, 1899; s. Howard Clyde and Lida Mary (Robison) C.; LL.B., U. Ind., 1926; m. Ruth Mary Meinardi, Mar. 14, 1936; children—Hoagy Bix, Randy Bob. Composer, radio artist, recording artist; writer for Broadway shows and moving pictures, TV shows; star of own radio program CBS; also TV show Saturday Night Rev., and Laramie; Played feature roles in films to Have and Have Not, Johnny Angel, Canyon Passage, Best Years of Our Lives, Night Song, Young Man with a Horn, 1950, Belles on Their Toes, 1952, Las Vegas Story, Timberjack. Mem. A.S.C.A.P., Kappa Sigma, Theta Tau Alpha, Theta Nu Epsilon. Republican. Mem. Christian Church. Elk. Club: Belair Country. Compositions include: Stardust, Rockin' Chair, Lazybones, Little Old Lady, Washboard Blues, Skylark, Two Sleepy People, Blue Orchids, Georgia on My Mind, Ole Buttermilk Sky, Lazy River, Hongkong Blues, In the Cool, Cool, Cool of the Evening (Oscar award 1951). Author: The Stardust Road (biographical), 1946; (with Stephen Longstreet) Sometimes I Wonder 1965. †

CARMICHAEL, HOWARD NELSON, shoe mfg. co. exec.; b. Lauderdale, Miss., Sept. 4, 1912; s. William M. and Mary (Williams) C.; student Bowling Green Coll. Commerce, 1932-34; m. Helen Leighton, June 17, 1937; children—Carolyn, Leighton, Linda, Howard. Asst. sec. Genesco, Nashville, 1942-47, asst. v.p., dir., 1947-51, v.p., dir., 1951-67, group v.p., dir., 1967—; dir. Commerce Union Bank, Nashville, Mem. Tenn. Small Bus. Adv. Council. Trustee Scarritt Coll.; hon. mem. nat. council Duke U. Methodist. Club: Hillwood Country (Nashville). Home: Regency Park 690 Timer Lane Nashville TN 37215 Office: 111 7th Av N Nashville TN 37203

CARMICHAEL, HUGH THOMPSON, psychiatrist, psychoanalyst; b. Peterborough, Ont., Can., Feb. 10, 1898; s. Duncan Nevin and Jessie Eliza (Bolster) C.; M.D., C.M., Queen's U., Kingston, Ont., 1923; M.S., U. Minn., 1931; m. Charlotte L. Greenwood, June 27, 1923; children—William Greenwood, Donald Keith, Charlotte Elizabeth; m. 2d, Carolyn G. Ruhland, July 10, 1937; children—Sandra Jennifer, Peter John Hugh. Came to U.S., 1926, naturalized, 1932. Pvt. practice medicine, Omemee, Ont., 1924-26; fellow internal medicine and neurology Mayo Found., Mayo Clinic, 1927-30; sr. fellow neuropsychiatry and instr. neuropathology Albany Med. Coll., 1930-31; asso. neuropsychiatrist, 1930-31; jr. physician to chief psychiatrist research service Worcester (Mass.) State Hosp., Meml. Found. for Neuroendocrine Research, 1931-35; psychiatrist Neuropsychiat. Inst. and Hosp. of Hartford (Conn.) Retreat, 1935; instr. to asst. prof. psychiatry U. Chgo., 1935-43; Rockefeller fellow Inst. Psychoanalysis, Chgo., 1936-40; asso. attending physician Cook County Psychopathic Hosp., 1939-40, 42; asso. prof. psychiatry U. Ill., 1943-47, prof., 1947- 52, clin. prof., 1952-61, prof. psychiatry, 1961-66, prof. emeritus, dept. psychiatry, 1966—; dir. office continuing edn. for psychiatrists Am. Psychiat. Assn., Washington, 1967—; on leave as professorial lectr. psychiatry U. Chgo. Sch. Medicine, 1960, 61; cons. psychiatry Surgeon Gen. U.S. Army, 1960; adv. com. psychiatry and neurology service VA Dept. Medicine and Surgery, 1960-64; asso. dir. psychiat. div. Ill. Neuropsychiat. Inst., 1943-52; attending psychiatrist Research and Edn. Hosps., Chgo., 1943-66; attending psychiatrist Chgo. Meml. Hosp., 1943-51, hon. staff, 1951-54; courtesy staff Inst. Psychiatric and Psychosomatic Research and Tng., Michael Reese Hosp., 1954-67. Mem. Joint Com. on Mental Illness and Health, 1955- 61, trustee, 1955-57; commr. Joint Commn. on Accreditation of Hosps., 1958-67, treas., 1963-67; sr. cons. continuing edn. br. Nat. Inst. of Mental Health, 1966-67; adv. bd. Med. Specialties, Inc., 1958-65, mem. com. on standards, 1962-65, chmn., 1963-65, exec. com., 1963-65; mem. White House Conf. on Aging, 1971. Served with C.E.F., 1917-18. Diplomate Am. Bd. Psychiatry and Neurology (dir. 1957-65, v.p. 1963-64). Fellow Am. Psychiat. Assn. (life; v.p. 1963-64), Am. Orthopsychiat. Assn., Am. Coll. Psychiatrists, Am. Coll. Psychoanalysts, Eastern Psychoanalytic Assn.; mem. A.M.A. (council on mental health 1953- 61), Chgo., D.C. med. socs., A.A.A.S., World Med. Assn., Central Neuropsychiat. Assn., Am. Psychoanalytic Assn. (exec. council 1954- 56), Am. Psychosomatic Soc., Ill. (pres. 1956-57), Washington psychiat. socs., Chgo. Psychoanalytic Soc. (pres. 1952-54), Inst. Medicine Chgo., Chgo. Neurol. Soc. (pres. 1952), World Fedn. Mental Health (asso.), Internat. Psychoanalytic Assn., Alumni Assn. Mayo Found., Group Advancement Psychiatry (exec. com. 1956-58), Am. Assn. U. Profs., Canadian Psychiat. Assn. (corr.), Sigma Xi. Contbr. tech. articles to profl. jours. Home: 3122 Ordway St NW Washington DC 20008 Office: 1700 18th St NW Washington DC 20009

CARMICHAEL, IAN STUART EDWARD, educator, geologist; b. London, Eng., Mar. 29, 1930; s. Edward Arnold and Jeanette (Montgomerie) C.; B.A., Cambridge (Eng.) U., 1954; Ph.D., Imperial Coll. Sci., London U., 1958; m. Dione Gilmore Thatcher, Sept. 12, 1970; children by previous marriage—Deborah, Graham, Alistair. Came to U.S., 1964. Lectr. geology Imperial Coll. Sci. and Tech., 1958-63; NSF sr. fgn. sci. fellow U. Chgo., 1964; mem. faculty U. Cal. at Berkeley, 1964—, prof. geology, 1967—. Home: 784 Cragmont Av Berkeley CA 94708

CARMICHAEL, JAMES H., aircraft exec.; b. Newark, Apr. 2, 1907; s. James H. and Margaret (Miner) C.; ed. Suffield Mil. Acad., Conn.; student Univ. So. Cal.; m. Jessie Northrup. July 4, 1930; children—Joan, Judith. Chief pilot Pa.- Central Airlines, 1936, v.p. charge operations, 1940, exec. v.p., 1945; dir. Capital Airlines-P.C.A., 1941—, pres., 1947-57, chmn. bd. dirs., 1957-58; corporate v.p. Fairchild Engine & Aircraft Corp., 1958-59, pres., 1959-60; now pres. J. H. Carmichael & Assos., Washington; chmn. bd. Airlift Internat., Inc. Head Tech. Indsl. Intelligence Com. to study German comml. and mil. transp. aviation; mem. industry adv. com. NACA. Mem. Fed. City Council, Washington, Nat. Capital Planning Com. Mem. bus. adv. com. Am. U. Recipient Airmail Flyer's Congl. Medal of Honor, 1935, Horatio Alger award, 1958. Mem. Transp. Assn. Am., Air Trans. Assn. Am. (dir.), U.S. C. of C. (v.p.), Soc. Automotive Engrs. Clubs: Wings, Nat. Press, University, Conquistadores del Cielo, Sky. Home: 4101 Cathedral Av N W Washington DC 20016 Office: 1700 K Street NW Washington DC 20006

CARMICHAEL, JAMES VINSON, bus. exec.; b. nr. Smyrna, Ga., Oct. 2, 1910; s. John Vinson and Emma Mae (Nolan) C.; LL.B., Emory U., Ga., 1933; m. Frances Elizabeth McDonald, June 3, 1938; children—Mary Emma, James Vinson, Frances Elizabeth. Admitted to Ga. bar, 1933, practiced in Marietta, 1933-44; elected state legislator, 1936-40; exec. dir. state revenue commn., 1943; mem. commn. to redraft state constrn.; gen. mgr., v.p. Bell Aircraft Corp.,

Marietta, 1944-46; candidate for gov., Ga., 1946; asst. to pres. Scripto, Inc., 1946, pres., 1947-64, chmn. bd. dirs., 1964- 68, hon. chmn. bd., 1968—; v.p., gen. mgr. Ga. div. Lockheed Aircraft Corp., Marietta, 1951-52, dir., 1952—; dir. Trust Co. of Ga., Scripto Pens, Ltd. (London), So. Co., Ga. Internat. Life Ins. Co.; cons. under sec. army on prodn. problems of tank procurement program. Trustee Com. Econ. Devel., Emory U., Interdenominational Theol. Center, Atlanta U. Recipient Order St. John (England); Presidential Citation of Merit; Ga. medal for distinguished pub. service. Mem. Atlanta Arts Alliance (trustee, vice chmn., past pres.), Atlanta Music Festival Assn. (vice chmn., trustee), Atlanta Symphony Guild (past pres.), Bus. Council (grad member), Am. Bar Assn., Atlanta Opera Guild, Emory Nat. Alumni Assn. (past pres.), Blue Ridge Bar (past sec.), Nat. Foundation Pen and Mech. Pencil Mfg. Assn. (past pres.), Alpha Kappa Psi, Sigma Pi, Phi Alpha Delta, Omicron Delta Kappa. Presbyn. Mason, Woodman of World. Clubs: Kiwanis (past dist. gov.), Capital City, Piedmont Driving (Atlanta); Buck's (London, Eng.); Century Assn. (N.Y.C.). Address: 1031 Cherokee Av Marietta GA 30060

CARMICHAEL, JOHN P., retired sports editor; b. Madison, Wis., Oct. 16, 1902; s. George J. and Margaret (Mooney) C.; student Campion Coll., Praire du Chien, Wis., also U. Wis; m. Kay Naughton, Dec. 27, 1956; children (by previous marriage)—John P., Joan Marie. Reporter, Milw. Jour.; reporter, columnist Milw. Leader; sports reporter Chgo. Herald- Examiner; Barber Shop columnist and sports editor Chgo. Daily News until 1971. K.C. Author: Biggest Days in Baseball. Editor (with Marshall B. Cutler) Who's Who in the Major League, 1950. Home: 660 Irving Park Road Chicago IL 60613

CARMICHAEL, KATHERINE KENNEDY, univ. dean; b. Birmingham, Ala., Oct. 1, 1912; d. Daniel Malcolm and Ruby (Kennedy) Carmichael; A.B., Birmingham-So. Coll., 1932; M.A., Vanderbilt U., 1939, Ph.D., 1943. High sch. tchr. nr. Birmingham, 1932- 36; elementary sch. tchr., Birmingham, 1936-38; instr. English, mem. staff of dean of women Tex. State Coll. Women, 1939-40; asst. prof. English, dean of women Western Md. Coll., 1942-44; instr., later chmn. dept. English, Hockaday Sch., Dallas, 1944-46; vis. lectr. English, U. Wis., summer 1946; dean of women, instr. English, U. N.C. 1946—; Fulbright lectr. English, Philippine Normal Coll., Manila, 1951-52; vis. Smith-Mundt prof. U. Saigon (Viet Nam), 1961-62. Bd. visitors Peace Coll., 1968-71. Fellow Vanderbilt U., 1940-41; Delta Kappa Gamma scholar, 1955-56. Mem. Am. Assn. U. Women (Md. bd. dirs. 1941-42, N.C. bd. dirs. 1952-54), D.A.R., N.C. Assn. Women Deans and Counselors (pres. 1963-65), N.C. Lit. and Hist. Soc. (bd. awards 1952-54), Modern Lang Assn., Delta Kappa Gamma (N.C. scholarship chmn. 1952-54, chpt. pres. 1965-67), Chi Delta Phi, Alpha Chi Omega, Mortar Board. Democrat. Presbyn. Clubs: Altrusa Internat., Faculty (U.N.C.) (sec. 1954-55), Author: A Critical Edition of the Early Poems of John Keats, with a Philosophical Supplement, 1943. Home: Graham Ct Apts Chapel Hill NC

CARMICHAEL, LEONARD, assn. exec.; b. Germantown, Phila. Nov. 9, 1898; s. Thomas Harrison and Emily Henrietta (Leonard) C.; grad. Germantown Friends Sch., 1917; B.S. summa cum laude, Tufts Coll., 1921, Sc.D., 1937; Ph.D. (Sheldon traveling fellow), Harvard, 1924, LL.D., 1952; postgrad. U. Berlin, 1924; LL.D., Boston U., 1938, Colgate U., 1938, Northeastern U., 1941, R.I. State Coll., 1942, St. Lawrence U., 1943, Boston Coll., 1951, Amherst Coll., 1954, U. Mass., 1954; Litt.D., Portia, 1939, Clark U., 1953; L.H.D., U. Me., 1949, Sc.D., Brown U., 1952, Lowell Inst. Tech., 1955, George Washington U., 1956, Tulane U., 1958; D.C.L. (hon.), Dickinson Coll., 1955; LL.D., Fairleigh Dickinson U., 1959; D.Sc., Drexel Inst. Tech., 1959; Sc.D., Trinity Coll., 1960, Worcester Polytech. Inst., 1964; m. Pearl Kidston, June 30, 1932; 1 dau., Martha (Mrs. S. Parker Oliphant). Instr. biology, part time, Tufts Coll., 1923-24; instr. psychology Princeton, 1924-26, asst. prof., 1926-27, Langfeld lectr., 1968; asso. prof. psychology Brown U., 1927-28, prof., 1928-36, also dir. psychol. lab., 1927-36, and dir. lab. sensory physiology, 1934-36; chmn. dept. psychology, dean faculty arts and sci. U. Rochester, 1936-38; pres. Tufts Coll. and dir. lab. sensory psychology and physiology, 1938-52; sec. (the 7th) Smithsonian Instn., 1953-64; v.p. research and expln. Nat. Geog. Soc., 1964—; lectr. Harvard, summers 1927-31; vis. prof. exptl. psychology Clark U., 1931-32; vis. prof. psychology Harvard, 1935; vis. prof. Radcliffe Coll., 1935, U. Wash., 1940; lectr. Naval War College to 1952; Arthur D. Little lectr. Mass. Inst. Tech., 1953. Dir. Nat. Roster Sci. and Specialized Personne, 1940-44; mem. sci. com. Nat. Resources Planning Bd., 1941-43; chmn. com. sci. research personnel War Manpower Commn., 1941-43; chmn. anthropology and psychology div. NRC 1941-44; mem. applied psychology panel OSRD, 1942-45; mem. adminstr.'s spl. com. on vocational rehabilitation, edn. and tng. problems, VA, 1945-52; dir. human resources NSRB, 1948; mem. com. on human resources Research & Devel. Bd., 1952-53, mem. Naval Research Adv. Com., 1947-52; mem. Internat. Union Sci. Psychology, 1948; vice- chmn. Harvard Found. Advanced Study and Research, 1951-54, 58-64; mem. com. on research Ednl. Testing Service, 1952-57; mem. NACA, 1952-58, vice. chmn., 1956-58. Chmn. U.S. delegation Internat. Conf., The Hague, signer for U.S., Treaty for Protection Cultural Property in Time of War, 1954. Chmn. selections com. Time Capsule, N.Y. World's Fair; mem. Army Sci. Adv. Panel, 1956-62, cons., 1963—. bd. sci. overseers, trustee Jackson Lab., Bar Harbor, Me., 1952—; chmn. com. N.E. (comprehensive econ. survey of N.E.), 1950-54. Trustee Brookings Instn., to 1969, hon. trustee, 1969—; bd. dirs. Research Corp. (N.Y.); pres. bd. trustees Sci. Service, 1955-67, trustee, 1967—. trustee Tufts U., George Washington U.; bd. fellows (trustee) Brown U.; bd. dirs. White House Hist. Assn.; bd. sci. dirs. Yerkes Labs. Primate Biology, 1942-69, chmn., 1942-60; mem. sci. adv. bd. Tulane Delta Regional Primate Research Center, to 1971. Decorated knight comdr. Order of Alfonso the Wise (Spain); knight comdr. cross with star Order of Merit of Federal Republic of Germany; comdr. Order of Dannebrog (Denmark), commendatore dell' Ordine Al Merito della Republica Italiana (Italy). Fellow Am. Acad. Arts and Scis., A.A.A.S.; mem. Am. Physiol. Soc., Internat. Primatological Soc. (pres. 1964-68), Am. Philos. Soc. (pres. 1970—), Nat. Acad. Sci. (chmn. sect. psychology 1950-53), N.R.C., Soc. Exptl. Psychologists, Soc. Research in Child Devel., Nat. Geog. Soc. (trustee), Am. Psychol. Assn. (pres. 1939-40), Soc. Exptl. Biology and Medicine, Internat. Union Biol. Scis. (pres. sect. exptl. psychology and animal behavior 1961-69), Soc. of Cincinnati, S.A.R., Am. Legion, Newcomen Soc., Lit. Soc., Phi Beta Kappa, Sigma Xi; hon. mem. Ergonomics Research Soc. Eng., Soc. Francaise de Psychologie. Episcopalian. Clubs: St. Botolph, Algonquin (Boston); Century Assn. (N.Y.C.); Alfalfa, Metropolitan, Chevy Chase, Cosmos (Washington). Co-author books, 1925—; part-author Carmichael's Manual of Child Psychology, 3d edit., 1970. Editor, part-author; Manual of Child Psychology, 2d edit., 1954; co- editor: The Selection of Military Manpower, 1952; Basic Psychology, 1957; asso. editor Jour. Genetic Psychology, Genetic Psychology Monographs, Brit. Jour. Ednl. Psychology. Editor Houghton Mifflin Co. series of books on psychology. Contbr. articles to psychol. jours. Home: 4520 Hoban Rd NW Washington DC 20007 Office: Nat Geog Soc 17th and M Sts NW Washington DC 20036 ☆

CARMICHAEL, MARY MULLOY, educator; b. Miles City, Mont., Aug. 6, 1916; d. John William and Laura (Maher) Mulloy; Ph.B., Marquette U., 1939, M.A., 1940; postgrad. Am. U., Washington, 1943-49; m. John Buford Carmichael, (dec. June 1949). Asst. to dean Women Marquette U., 1935-40; dean women Thompson Falls (Mont.) pub. schs., 1940-42; personnel officer War Dept., Washington, 1942-44; chief overseas classification and wage adminstrn. OWI, Washington and London, 1944-45; successively chief salary adminstrn. sect., asst. planning adviser, asst. chief pay leave and retirement br. State Dept., 1945-56; fgn. service officer, 1956-69; 1st sec., consul, Brussels, Belgium, 1959-64; 1st sec., econ. officer Am. embassy, Leopoldville, Congo, 1964-65; econ. officer U.S. delegation OECD, Paris, 1964-65; asst. econ. adviser U.S. delegation NATO, 1965-66, spl. asst. to ambassador, also U.S. rep. to coordinating com. of govt. experts, 1966-69; chmn. internat. bus. adminstrn. and econs. dept. Am. Coll. Switzerland, Leysin, 1969—. Mem. Fgn. Service Assn., Alpha Kappa Delta. Office: Am Coll Switzerland Leysin Switzerland

CARMICHAEL, OLIVER CROMWELL, Jr., business exec.; b. Birmingham, Ala., Mar. 10, 1920; s. Oliver Cromwell and Ruth Mae (Crabtree) C.; A.B., Vanderbilt U., 1940; LL.B., Duke, 1942; M.A., Columbia, 1951, Ph.D., 1953; m. Ernestine Morris, Sept. 28, 1946; children—Carmen Murphy, Oliver Cromwell III, Ernestine Morris, Stanley Clark. Admitted to Tenn. bar, 1942, Ind. bar, 1948; asst. gen. counsel Assos. Corp. N.Am., S. Bend, Ind., 1946-49, chmn. bd., 1960—; chmn. bd. Marshall County Bank & Trust Co., Plymouth, Ind.; dir., mem. exec. com. Gulf & Western Industries, Inc., N.Y.C.; dir. Wheelabrator Corp., W.R. Grace & Co.; chmn. bd. FAS Internat., Inc. Gen. chmn. Com. Higher Edn. No. Ind.; pres. Citizens Nat. Com. Higher Edn. Trustee Vanderbilt U., U. Notre Dame; bd. dirs. United Community Services, S. Bend; chmn. bd. trustees Converse Coll., Spartanburg, S.C.; bd. dirs. Vanderbilt U. Med. Center. Served to lt. USNR, 1942-46. Mem. Phi Beta Kappa, Order of Coif, Omicron Delta Kappa. Republican. Presbyn. Clubs: Ocean (Delray Beach, Fla.); Pickwick (Niles, Mich.); New York Athletic; Country of Florida. Home: South Bend IN 46624 Office: Asso Corp NAM 1700 Mishawaka Av South Bend IN 46624

CARMICHAEL, STOKELY, civil rights worker; b. Port-of-Spain, Trinidad, B.W.I., June 29, 1941; s. Adolphus and Mabel F. Carmichael; came to U.S., 1952; B.A., Howard U., 1964; m. Miriam Makeba, Apr. 1968. Former field sec. Student Non- Violent Coordinating Com. for Ala., later nat. chmn., now field comdr.; organized Lowndes County Freedom Orgn.; continued Meredith March through Miss., 1966; originator term Black Power. Address: Student Non-Violent Coordinating Com 360 Nelson SW Atlanta GA 30313*

CARMICHAEL, WILLIAM DANIEL, found. ofcl.; b. Denver, Sept. 5, 1929; s. Fitzhugh Lee and Anna Devona (Sullivan) C.; A.B., Yale, 1950; M.A., M.P.A., Princeton, 1952, Ph.D., 1959; B.Litt. (Rhodes scholar), Oxford (Eng.) U., 1955; m. Faith Young, June 21, 1958; children—Amy, Philip Fitzhugh. Legislative analyst U.S. Bur. Budget, 1955-56, budget analyst, 1956-57; lectr. econs. and pub. affairs Princeton, 1957-60, asst. prof., 1960-62, dir. undergrad. program Woodrow Wilson Sch. Pub. and Internat. Affairs, 1958-62; prof. econ. policy, dean Grad. Sch. Bus. and Pub. Adminstrn., Cornell U., 1962-68; rep. Ford Found., Brazil, 1968-71, head office for Latin Am. and Caribbean, N.Y.C., 1971—. Mem. Assn. Am. Rhodes Scholars, Am. Econs. Assn., Am. Soc. Pub. Adminstrn., Phi Beta Kappa. Home: Van Hornesville NY 13475 Office: 320 E 43d St New York City NY 10017

CARMIN, ROBERT LEIGHTON, geographer, educator, univ. dean; b. Muncie, Ind., Nov. 28, 1918; s. Zora and Florelda May (Harrison) C.; B.S. in Edn., Ohio U., 1940; M.A., U. Neb., 1942; Ph.D. (Salisbury fellow geography), U. Chgo., 1953; m. Marie Jane Carr, Nov. 2, 1940; children—Thomas Nelson, James Harrison. Instr. geography Mich. State U., 1942-44, asst. prof., 1947-50; cartographer OSS, 1944-45; from asst. prof. to prof. geography U. Ill., 1951-62, dir. Center Latin Am. Studies, 1959-62; head Latin Am. studies sect. U.S. Office Edn., 1962; dean Coll. Scis. and Humanities, prof. geography Ball State U., 1962—. Cons. lang. devel. br. U.S. Office Edn., 1963-64; cons. NSF, 1964-69, internat. programs com. Assn. State Colls. and Univs.; com. geography Nat. Acad. Sci.-NRC, 1961—; sec.-treas. Asso. Univs. for Internat. Edn., Inc., 1968-70, v.p., 1970—; U.S. del. 6th Gen. Assembly Pan Am. Inst. Geography and History, Buenos Aires, Argentina, 1961. Pan Am. World Airways travel fellow, Brazil, 1948; adviser A.I.D., Brazil, 1965; grantee U.S. Office Edn., Brazil, 1948-49, Office Q.M. Gen., Brazil, 1956; Fulbright scholar U. de Cuyo, Mendoza, Argentina, 1958; grantee U. Ill. Research Bd., Brazil, 1961, Am. Assn. Colls. Tchr. Edn., Peru, 1963. Mem. Ill. Acad. Sci. (chmn. membership com. 1955-60, geography sect. 1955-56), Ind. Acad. of Social Scis. dir. 1967-68), Assn. Am. Geographers (past pres. West Lakes div., ofcl. rep. to Internat. Council Edn. for Teaching, Brazil 1963), A.A.A.S., Assn. Latin Am. Studies (past pres.), Nat. Council Geog. Edn., Assn. dos Geografos Brasileiros, Latin Am. Studies Assn., Sigma Xi, Sigma Delta Pi. Rotarian. Author: Anápolis, Brazil: Regional Capital of an Agricultural Frontier, 1953; also articles. Home: 2505 Johnson Road Muncie IN 47304

CARMINES, ALVIN ALLISON, clergyman, composer; b. Hampton, Va., July 25, 1936; s. Alvin Allison and Katherine (Graham) C.; B.A., Swarthmore Coll., 1958; B.D., Union Theol. Sem., 1961, S.T.M., 1963. Ordained to ministry; asso. minister Judson Meml. Ch., N.Y.C., 1961—; tchr. N.Y.U., Earlham (N.Y.) Seminar; now TV dir., also movie columnist Motive mag.; composer: Home Movies, 1964; Gorilla Queen, 1967; In Circles, 1967. Recipient Obie award for best off-Broadway prodn. Home Movies, 1964; Vernon Rice award for composing and performing, In Circles, 1968, Peace, 1968, Promenade, 1969; A.S.C.A.P. award for popular A.S.C.A.P. award for popular music, 1968. Home: 237 Thompson Street New York City, NY 10012. Office: 55 Washington Sq S New York City NY 10012

CARMODY, DAVID WETHERILL, ret. state justice; b. Denver, Apr. 22, 1908; s. Thomas E. and Mary Jane Mary Jane (McBride) C.; A.B., U. Colo., 1931, LL.B., 1933; m. Jessie McGillivray, May 13, 1935; children—Thomas David, Douglas Edward; m. 2d, Hazel Greenbacker, Jan. 11, 1954; m. 3d, Hazelbel H. Via, Jan. 20, 1971. Admitted to N.M. bar, 1933; dist. atty., N.M., 1937-47; judge 1st Jud. Dist., N.M., 1947-59, Supreme Ct. of N.M., 1959, chief justice, 1965-66, justice, 1966-69. Pres. Jud. Council N.M. Judges, 1953, 54, 55; mem., pres. Santa Fe City Council, 1938-42. Mem. Am. (chmn. appellate judges' conf. 1966-67, 68-69), N.M. bar assns., Am. Law Inst., Am. Judicature Soc. (dir. 1965—), Inst. Jud. Adminstrn. Democrat. Episcopalian. Lion. Home: Santa Fe NM 87501 Office: Supreme Ct Bldg Santa Fe, NM 87501.

CARMODY, FRANCIS JAMES, educator; b. San Francisco, Dec. 4, 1907; s. Frank Edward and Mary (Turner) C.; A.B., U. Cal. at Berkeley, 1928, M.A., 1929; Ph.D., Harvard, 1932; m. Carol Hink, May 3, 1934; children—Robert F., Jean (Mrs. Carl Linder). Mem. faculty U. Cal. at Berkeley, 1932—, now prof. French. Author articles mediaeval lit. and sci., Celtic langs., modern French lit. Home: 2535 Buena Vista Way Berkeley CA 94708

CARMODY, JOHN JOSEPH, lawyer; b. Washington, Aug. 28, 1901; s. Cornelius J. and Margaret (Dee) C.; LL.B., Georgetown U., 1924; m. Helen M. Donahoe, Jan. 28, 1930; children—Margaret (Mrs. George T. Marcou), Helen (Mrs. Charles J. Steele), John Joseph, Kathleen (Mrs. L. Maurice Rowe), Kevin. Admitted to D.C. bar, 1924; practiced in Washington, 1924—; sr. partner firm Whiteford, Hart, Carmody & Wilson, 1933—. Dir., Am. Fed. Savs. and Loan Assn. Bd. dirs. Washington Soc. for Blind. Mem. Bar Assn. D.C. (pres. 1944-45), Am. Bar Assn. (mem. ho. of dels. 1945-50, standing com. on fed. judiciary 1948-50), Catholic Youth Orgn., Barristers, John Carroll Soc., Friendly Sons of St. Patrick (pres. 1960-61). K.C. Clubs: University, Columbia Country, Rotary (pres. 1962-63) (Washington); Merrick Boys (pres. 1945-46). Home: 6121 Nevada Av Washington DC 20015 Office: 815 15th St Washington DC 20005

CARNELL, PAUL HERBERT, educator, chemist; b. Oakfield, Wis., May 27, 1917; s. Herbert Clyde and Fannie (Carstens) C.; A.B. with high honors, Albion Coll., 1939; Ph.D. (Wyandotte research fellow), Case. Western Res. U., 1943; postgrad (USPHS fellow), Yale, 1959-60; m. Phyllis Martha Whipple, June 21, 1942; children—Nancy, Michael, Cheryl, Beth, Cara. Research chemist Phillips Petroleum Co., 1943-47; dir. research Leonard Refineries, Inc., Alma, Mich., 1947-48; asst. prof., Marietta Coll., 1948-49; faculty Albion Coll., 1949-66, prof. chemistry, chmn. dept., 1954-66; edn. specialist U.S. Office Edn., Washington, 1966-68, asst. dir. div. coll. support, 1966—. Vis. scientist div. chem. edn. Am. Chem. Soc., 1959-66; inservice inst. dir. NSF, 1961-62, asso. program dir. Acad. Yr. Insts., 1964-65; mem. sci. com. Mich. Dept. Pub. Instrn., 1961-65; vis. scientist Mich. Acad. Sci., Arts and Letters, 1960-66. Grantee Research Corp., 1952, NIH, 1959-66. Mem. Am. Chem. Soc., Mich. Coll. Chemistry Tchrs. Assn. (past pres.), Midwest Assn. Chemistry Tchrs. Liberal Arts Colls. (past mem. exec. com., pres. 1963-64), Yale Chemists Assn., Sigma Xi. Contbr. articles to profl. jours. Patentee petroleum processing and refining. Home: 1209 Highland Dr Silver Spring MD 20910 Office: U S Office Edn Washington DC 20202

CARNER, DONALD CHARLES, hosp. adminstr.; b. Chgo., Sept. 19, 1917; s. Chester E. and Anna (Forester) C.; grad. Morgan Park Jr. Coll., 1937; A.B., U. Chgo., 1939, M.B.A., 1948; m. Hazel Kruse, Sept. 21, 1940; children—Dianne (Mrs. Frank Robert Hodges), Nancy (Mrs. Stephen L. Salzman), Donald C. Admitting officer U. Chgo. Hosps. and Clincis, 1939-41; asst. adminstr. Northwestern Hosp., Mpls., 1947-50; adminstr. Parkview Meml. Hosp., Ft. Wayne, Ind., 1950-55; exec. v.p. Meml. Hosp. and Med. Center, Long Beach, Cal., 1955—; founder, v.p., mem. bd. dirs. Hosp. Research and Devel. Inst., Inc., 1963—; v.p., sec. Hosp. Information Service, 1967-69; hosp. and mgmt. cons., 1955—. Pub., editor Executive Director's Letter, 1963—; editor Hospital Letter, 1963—; partner Long Term Fund Devel. Inst., 1963—. Served to maj. AUS, 1941-46. Rotarian. Contbr. articles profl. jours. ‡

CARNES, DEL, former newspaper drama editor; b. Wichita, Kan., Jan. 4, 1931; s. Merle L. and Lucille (Winniger) C.; student Wichita U., 1949-50, Boston U., 1956; B.A. in Polit. Sci., Denver U., 1960; m. Barbara J. Pitts, June 28, 1958; children—Philip, Gary. Reporter, Wichita Beacon, 1951-54; reporter Denver Post, 1956-61, TV editor, 1961-66, drama editor, 1966, former motion picture, theatrical editor; free-lance writer 1950—. Chmn. Larry Tajiri Meml. Found. Dist. capt. Denver Republican Com., 1960-62. Served with AUS, 1954-56. Recipient Pall Mall Big Story Journalism award, 1954, TV award Am. Legion, 1967. Mem. Writers Guild Am., Am. Newspaper Guild. Republican. Mem. United Ch. of Christ. Club: Denver Press. Home: 10493 Lincoln Ct Denver CO 80233

CARNES, JOHN ROBB, Jr., educator; b. Lima, O., Dec. 7, 1924; s. John Robb and Kathryn (Wyre) C.; B.S., U. Mich., 1948, M.S., 1948, Ph.D., 1957; m. Corinne Ann Stevens, May 21, 1949; children— John Steven, Benjamin Grant. Mathematician, physicist Fairchild Engine & Airplane Corp. (NEPA Project), Oak Ridge, 1948-50; tech. editor, writer Engrng. Research Inst., U. Mich., 1952-56; instr., asst. prof., asso. prof., prof. U. Colo., Boulder, 1956—, asso. dean arts and scis., 1963—. Served with USAAF, 1943-46. Mem. Am. Mountain Plains philos. assns., Sigma Nu. Democrat. Episcopalian. Contbr. articles profl. jours. Home: 5927 S Vale Rd Boulder CO 80303

CARNES, WILLIAM GRAY, landscape architect, educator; b. LaPlata, Mo., Jan. 7, 1907; s. Percy Thomas and Ann Mary (Nichols) C.; B.S. in landscape architecture, U. Cal., 1930; m. Hazel Marian Troutwine, Feb. 2, 1938 (dec. Mar. 1969); 1 dau., Karen Diane. With Nat. Park Service, U.S. Dept. Interior 1930-62, asst. chief landscape architect, 1936-46, chief landscape architect, 1946-55, chief advance planning, 1955-62; prof., chmn. landscape architecture dept. U. Ill., Urbana, 1962-70, emeritus prof., 1970—. Guest lectr. colls. and univs.; mem. Arctic Research Lab., Office Naval Research, 1953. Recipient Meritorious Service award Dept. Interior, 1956, Distinguished Service award, 1962. Fellow Am. Soc. Landscape Architects (chmn. com. on edn.; sec.). Contbr: Accreditation in Higher Education, 1959; Modern Land Policy, 1961. Home: 468-A Paseo Lobo Green Valley AZ 85614 Office: Mumford Hall U Ill Urbana IL 61801

CARNES, WILLIAM HENRY, Jr., physician, educator; b. Ft. Worth, Nov. 2, 1909; s. William Henry and Sarah Paine (Thompson) C.; A.B., Columbia, 1932; M.D., Johns Hopkins, 1936; m. Elizabeth Ann Irwin, June 27, 1950. Intern, then resident pathology Balt. City Hosp., 1936-38; asso. pathology Johns Hopkins, 1938- 39; instr. Pathology Columbia, 1939-41; asst. prof. to prof. pathology Stanford, 1941-56; asst. prof., then asso. prof. pathology Johns Hopkins, 1947-51; prof. pathology, head dept. U. Utah, 1956-68; prof. pathology U. Cal. at Los Angeles, 1968—. Mem. Am. Assn. Pathologists and Bacteriologists, Soc. Exptl. Biology and Medicine, Am. Soc. Exptl. Pathology, Internat. Acad. Pathology, Am. Assn. Cancer Research, Sigma Xi. Office: U Cal Center for Health Scis Los Angeles CA 90024

CARNEY, ART, actor; b. Mt. Vernon, N.Y., Nov. 4, 1918; s. Edward M. and Helen (Farrell) C.; student pub. schs.; m. Jean Myers, Aug. 15, 1940; children—Eileen, Brian, Paul. Mem. Horace Heidt Orchestra, 1936-39; vaudeville and club entertainer, 1939-40; radio performer, 1942-44, 45- 49; TV actor, featured in comedy and dramatic roles with Morey Amsterdam, Henry Morgan, Jackie Gleason. Studio One, Kraft Theater, Omnibus, Climax, Playhouse 90, The Chevy Show, and several others, 1949- -, Rope Dancers, 1957-58, Harvey, 1958; actor in Broadway play Take Her, She's Mine, 1961-62, Odd Couple, 1965, in motion picture The Yellow Rolls Royce, 1964, in stage play Lovers, 1968. Recipient 1959-60 TV Acad. Emmy award for outstanding humor program, 1960; Emmy award for individual achievement, 1968. Mem. Screen Actors Guild, A.F.T.R.A., Actors Equity. Club: Players. Office: 501 Madison Avenue New York City NY 10022

CARNEY, CHARLES J., congressman; b. Youngstown, O., Apr. 17, 1913; s. Michael G. and Florence Grogan (Grimm) C.; student Youngstown State U.; LL.D. (hon.), Central State U., Wilberforce, O., 1959; m. Mary Lucille Manning, Nov. 12, 1938; children—Mary Ellen (Mrs. John Leshinsky), Ann (Mrs. James Murphy). Mem. United Rubber Workers Union, 1934-50, former pres. Local Union 102, pres. Dist. Council No. 1, 1940-43, staff rep., dist. dir., 1942-50; staff rep. United Steelworkers of Am., 1950-68; mem. of Congress from Ohio, 1970—. Active Youngstown Cath. Service League. Mem.

Ohio State Senate, 1950-70, minority leader, 1969-70. Trustee Mahoning County CIO Indsl. Council. Mem. Farm Grange. K.C., Elk, Moose, Eagle. Home: 2405 Volney Rd Youngstown OH Office: Longworth Bldg US House of Representatives Washington DC 20515

CARNEY, CHESNEY M., lawyer, banker; b. Silver Hill, W.Va., Apr. 16, 1901; s. Ellis B. and Julia (Jones) C.; A.B., W.Va. U., 1924, LL.B., 1926; m. Elise Gibson, Sept. 23, 1933. Admitted to W.Va. bar, 1926, since practiced in Clarksburg; partner firm Steptoe & Johnson, Clarksburg, Charleston, W.Va. and Washington, 1930-69. Chmn. bd. dirs., mem. exec. com. Clarksburg Community Bank (W.Va.). Dir., sec. bd. dirs. Monongahela Valley Hosp. Service and Med.-Surg. Service, Clarksburg. Mem. Newcomen Soc. Eng., Order of Coif, Theta Chi, Phi Delta Phi. Republican. Episcopalian. Clubs: Rotary, Jrough (Romney, W.Va.). Home: 150 Carpenter St Clarksburg WV 26301 Office: Union Bank Building Clarksburg WV 26301

CARNEY, DENNIS JOSEPH, steel co. exec.; b. Charleroi, Pa., Mar. 19, 1921; s. Walter Augustus and Ann (Nandor) C.; B.S. in Metallurgy, Pa. State U., 1942; Sc.D., Mass. Inst. Tech., 1949; m. Virginia M. Horvath, June 12, 1943; children—Colleen A., Dennis Joseph, Glenn P., Lynn C., Dianne V. With U.S. Steel Corp., Pitts., 1942—, gen. supt., 1963-65, v.p. long range planning, 1965-68, v.p. applied research, 1968—. Vice pres. Mon-Yough council Boy Scouts Am., 1959—. Served to lt. (j.g.) USNR, 1943-46. Mem. Am., Brit. iron and steel insts., Am. Soc. Metals (Grossman award Pitts. chpt. 1959), Am. Inst. Mining, Metall. and Petroleum Engrs. (McKune award 1951), Am. Iron and Steel Engrs., Sigma Xi, Tau Beta Pi, Sigma Nu. Clubs: South Hills Country, Duquesne (Pitts.). Author: (with others) Gases in Metals, 1956. Home: 4536 Brownsville Rd Pittsburgh PA 15236 Office: 600 Grant St Pittsburgh PA 15230

CARNEY, HARRY HOWELL, musician; b. Boston, Apr. 1, 1910; s. Harry F. and Jennie (King) C.; ed. high sch.; m. Dorothy Streat, Nov. 4. 1929. Player bass saxophone, bass clarinet Duke Ellington's Orch., 1927—. Recipient Numerous musical awards. Home: 450 W 147th St New York City NY 10031 Office: 333 Riverside Dr New York City NY 10025

CARNEY, JOHN HAYES, Jr., inn exec.; b. Memphis, Dec. 10, 1923; s. John Hayes and Eula (White) C.; B.S., U. Tenn., 1949; m. Frances Irene Garrett, June 7, 1947; 1 son, John Garrett. Clk., Richman-Crosby Co., 1949; accountant M. O. Carter Co., 1950-51; controller Continental Mortgage Co., 1951-57; auditor Holiday Inns of Am., Inc., Memphis, 1958-60, asst. controller, 1960-63, asst. treas., 1963-67, controller, 1963-67, treas., 1967—, v.p., 1969—. Served with USAAF, 1942-45. Mem. Financial Execs. Inst., Am. Mgmt. Assn., U.S. Power Squadron, U.S. Coast Guard Aux. (financial officer 1965), Nat. Assn. Accountants, Am. Legion, V.F.W., W.Tenn. Sport Assn., Nat. Rifle Assn. Moose. Clubs: Army-Navy, Mariners. Home: 3349 Lakeview St Memphis TN 38116 Office: 3742 Lamar Av Memphis TN 38118

CARNEY, JOSEPH ROBERT, former paper co. exec.; b. Toledo, Dec. 11, 1922; s. James Theodore and Emma Louise (Maynard) C.; student Yale, 1939-41; m. Barbara Waterman, Apr. 29, 1943; children—Patrick Alan, Timothy James, Kathleen Ann. With Oxford Paper Co., 1946-71, v.p. operations, 1964-67, sr. v.p., dir., 1967-71; Served to maj., F.A., AUS, 1942-46; CBI. Home: 902 Silvermine Road New Canaan CT 06840 Office: 227 Park Av New York City NY 10017

CARNEY, PRICE FELTS, ins. co. exec.; b. Nashville, Apr. 28, 1917; s. Herschel Koster and Ida May (Price) C.; B.A., Vanderbilt U., 1941; m. Lois Jeanne Hudson, Aug. 14, 1954; 1 son, Price Felts. Clk. cashier's office Equitable Life Assurance Soc. U.S., Nashville, 1934-37; clk. Life & Casualty Ins. Co., Nashville, 1937-41, asst. sec., 1946-59, sec., 1959—. Mem. Nashville City Bd. Edn., 1957-62, chmn. vocational and recreation com., 1957-62; mem. Nashville, Motion Picture Bd. Censors, 1953-63. Dir., past v.p. Nashville-Davidson County unit Am. Cancer Soc. Served to maj. AUS, 1941- 45. Decorated Bronze Star. Mem. Nashville C. of C., 80th Div. Vets. Assn., Sigma Nu Alumni Assn. Democrat. Mem. Ch. of Christ. Mason (32). Clubs: City (v.p. 1964, dir.), Nashville Quarterback (dir.), Nashville-Vanderbilt, Green Hills Civitan (past lt. gov. valley dist., past pres.) (Nashville). Home: 733 Richfield Dr Nashville TN 37205 Office: Life and Casualty Tower Nashville TN 37219

CARNEY, ROBERT A., hosp. adminstr. Exec. dir. Jewish Hosp. Cin. Office: 3200 Burnet Av Cincinnati OH 45229*

CARNEY, ROBERT FORREST, lawyer, corp. exec.; b. Chgo., Oct. 22, 1905; s. Joseph Michael and Rose Margaret (McShane) C.; Ph.B., U. Wis., 1927; LL.B., Harvard, 1930; m. Lucille Kelly, May 24, 1946; children (by former marriage)—Michael Kerwin, Robert McShane. Admitted to Wis. bar, 1930, Ill. bar, 1937; sr. partner firm Carney, Crowell & Leibman, Chgo., 1945-51; chmn. bd. Foote, Cone & Belding, Inc., N.Y.C., 1951-66, chmn. finance com., 1966-69, dir., 1970—. chmn. bd. dirs. Southampton (N.Y.) Hosp.; treas. bd. dirs. Finch Coll., N.Y.C. Served with USNR, 1943-45. Decorated chevalier French Legion of Honor. Mem. Chgo. Bar Assn. Clubs: Brook, Racquet and Tennis (N.Y.C.); Nat. Golf Links Am., Shinnecock Hills Golf, Southampton (Southampton, N.Y.); Everglades, Seminole Golf Club (Palm Beach, Fla.). Home: 161 Woodbridge Rd Palm Beach FL

CARNEY, ROBERT GIBSON, educator, dermatologist; b. Ann Arbor, Mich., Apr. 25, 1914; s. Robert John and Frances (Gibson) C.; A.B., U. Mich., 1935, M.D., 1939; m. Dorothy Ann Briscoe, June 18, 1939; children—Robert Gibson, Patricia Lee (Mrs. Hentzel), Kathleen Ann (Mrs. Hill), Margaret Lou. Intern U. Ia. Hosps., 1939-40, resident dermatology, 1940-43; mem. faculty U. Ia. Med. Sch., Iowa City, 1947—, prof. dermatology, chmn. dept. 1961—. Mem. com. revision U.S. Pharmacopcia. Served with USNR, 1943-46. Mem. Am. Dermatol. Assn., Am. Acad. Dermatology, Soc. Investigative Dermatology, A.M.A., Ia. Dermatol. Soc., Phi Beta Kppa, Alpha Omega Alpha. Author: Dermatology for the Student and Physician. Home: 519 W Park Rd Iowa City IA 52240

CARNEY, THOMAS PATRICK, pharm. mfr.; b. DuBois, Pa., May 27, 1915; s. James P. and Margaret (Senard) C.; B.S., U. Notre Dame, 1937, L.L.D., 1969; M.S., Pa. State U., 1939, Ph.D., 1941; postdoctoral student U. Wis., 1943-44; m. Mary Elizabeth McGuire, Oct. 3, 1942; childrenThomas P., Sheila, James K., Janet. Research chemist Reilly Tar & Chem. Corp., Indpls., 1937-39, 1941-43; v.p. research, devel. control Eli Lilly & Co., Indpls., 1944-64, dir.; v.p. research and devel. G.D. Searle & Co., 1964-66, sr. v.p., 1966-70, sr. v.p. research and corporate devel., 1970—. Trustee U. Notre Dame, Barat Coll, Fellow A.A.A.S., Am. Inst. Chemists, N.Y. Acad. Scis.; mem. Chem. Soc. (London), Soc. Chem. Industry (London), Am. Chem. Soc., Swiss Chem. Soc., Sigma Xi, Phi Lambda Upsilon. Author: Laboratory Fractional Distillation, 1949. Home: 277 Bluff's Edge Dr Lake Forest IL 60045 Office: Post Office Box 5110 Chicago, IL 60680.

CARNICERO, JORGE, aviation co. exec.; b. Buenos Aires, Argentina, July 17, 1921; student U. LaPlata (Argentina), 1939-41; Aero. Engr., Rensselaer Poly. Inst., 1945; m. Jacqueline Damman, Feb. 22, 1946; children—Jacqueline Denise, Jorge Jay. Came to U.S., 1942, naturalized, 1950. Chief engr. Dodero Airlines, Argentina, 1945, Flota Aerea Mercante, Argentina, 1945-46; v.p. Air Carrier Service Corp., Washington, 1946, exec. v.p., 1947-55, chmn. bd., dir., 1955—; chmn. bd., dir. Dynalectron Corp., Washington (formerly Cal. Eastern Aviation), Air Carrier Service Corp., Hydrocarbon Research Inc.; pres. dir. Trans-Am. Aero. Corp.; pres. Inter-Financial Corp.; dir. Hydrocarbon Engring. S.A. France, Metrodyn Corp., Dytel Ltd., Bahama Islands, Internat. Fuel Corp., Liberia, Hydrocarbon Realty, Inc., Pan-Am. Hydrocarbon Research, Airtech Service, Inc., Gen. Aircraft Supplies, Inc., Dynair, Inc., Vegas Valley Electric, Inc., Baytel S.A., Argentina, Huyck Corp., Huyck Argentina S.A.I.C., Seeger Electric Co., Airtech Service, Inc., Griffin Constrn. Co. Asso. fellow Royal Aero. Soc.; mem. Am. Inst. Aeros. and Astronautics. Clubs: University, Surf, Nat. Aviation, Indian Creek; Metropolitan (N.Y.C.). Home: 3949 52d St NW Washington DC 20007 Office: 2233 Wisconsin Av Washington DC 20007

CARNOVSKY, MORRIS, actor; b. St. Louis, Sept. 5, 1897; s. Isaac and Jennie (Stillman) C.; A.B., Washington U., St. Louis; m. Phoebe Brand, Sept. 17, 1941; 1 son, Stephen Brand. Acting debut with Henry Jewitt Players, Boston; 1st N.Y. appearance with Provincetown Players in God of Vengence, 1922; mem. Theatre Guild Acting Co., N.Y.C., 1924-30, prodns. include St. Joan, Marco's Millions, Hotel Universe; founding mem. Group Theatre, N.Y.C., 1930-39, prodns. include Men in White, Doctor's Dilemma, Awake and Sing, Golden Boy; on Broadway in An Enemy of the People, Uncle Vanya, Tiger at the Gates, Nude with Violin, A Family Affair, others; actor, tchr. at Am. Shakespeare Festival, Stratford, Conn., 1956-63, with repertory co. in Hamlet, Midsummer Night's Dream; motion pictures include Cyrano de Bergerac, Dead Reckoning, Rhapsody in Blue, Edge of Darkness, Our Vines Have Tender Grapes, Cornered, Deadly is the Female; dir. Volpone, Monday's Heroes, for Actor's Lab. in Cal.; past prof. theatre arts Brandeis U. Address: 309 W 104th Street New York City NY 10025

CARNS, EDWIN HUGH JOHN, ret. army officer; b. N.Y.C., May 22, 1907; s. Hugh John and Mary (Sullivan) C.; B.S., U.S. Mil. Acad., 1929; student Nat. War Coll., 1949-50; m. Jeannette Anne Chamberlain, Dec. 23, 1935; children—Michael, Mary, Hugh John, Jeannette Anne. Commd. 2nd Lt., Cav., U.S. Army, 1929, advanced through grades to maj. gen., 1956; with cav. service, Tex., 1929-33; student, instr. Cavalry Sch., Fort Riley, Kan., 1933-39; cav. instr., West Point, 1939-42; staff duty Hodqrs. Army Ground Forces, Washington, 1942-44; combat comdr., chief staff 20th Armored Div., 1944-46; staff duty Hdqrs. U.S. Forces in Austria, 1946-49; dep. sec., sec. Joint Chiefs of Staff, Washington, 1950-55; asst. div. comdr. 24th Inf. Div., 1955; sr. adviser 1st ROK Army, 1956; comdg. gen. 1st Cav. Div., 1956; staff duty Hdqrs. US Army Pacific, 1957-59; comdg. gen. U.S. Army Corps, 1959-61; Army mem. Joint Strategic Survey Council, Joint Chiefs of Staff, 1961; asst. dep. chief staff for mil. operations Dept. Army, 1961-63; comdg. gen. USATC, Ft. Ord, Cal., 1963-65; ret., 1965; cons. Stanford Research Inst., Menlo Park, Cal., 1965—. Decorated Legion of Merit, D.S.M., Croix de Guerre. Address: 1112 Presidio Road Pebble Beach, CA 93953.

CARO, ANTHONY, sculptor; b. London, Eng., Mar. 8, 1924; s. Alfred and Mary (Haldinstein) C.; M.A., Christ's Coll., Cambridge U., 1943; grad. Royal Acad. Schs., London, 1952; D.Litt., East Anglia U.; m. Sheila Girling, Dec. 17, 1949; children—Timothy Martin, Paul Gideon. Asst. to Henry Moore, 1951-53; one-man shows include Galleria Naviglio, Milan, Italy, 1956, Gimpel Fils Gallery, London, 1957, Whitechapel Art Gallery, London, 1963, Emmerich Gallery, N.Y.C., 1964, 66, 68, 70, Washington Gallery Modern Art, 1965, Kasmin Gallery, London, 1965, 67, Mirvish Gallery, Toronto, 1966, 71, Galerie Bischofberger, Zurich, 1966, Kröller Müller Mus., Holland, 1967, Haywood Gallery, London, 1969, San Paulo Biennale, 1970; part-time teacher sculpture St. Martin's Sch. Art, London 1952-71; tchr. sculpture Bennington Coll., 1963—; exhibited group shows including Documenta III, Kassel, 1964; represented in permanent collections Tate Gallery, Mus. Modern Art, Albright Knox Gallery, Nat. Gallery of Victoria, Melbourne, Australia. Recipient prize 18th Paris Biennele for Young Artists, 1959, Venice Biennele, 1966. Address: 111 Frognal Hampstead London N W 3 England

CARO, JOSEPH HENRY, advt. exec.; b. Poland, Feb. 13, 1901; s. Albert and Ernestine (Rayner) C.; student Northwestern U., DePaul U., Art Inst. Chgo.; m. Theresa DeLott, Jan. 28, 1923; children—Mrs. Stanford J. Reinisch, Howard M. Advt. mgr. Albert Pick & Co., 1922-35; v.p., dir. Earle Ludgin & Co., 1935-51; formerly v.p., treas. Buchen Co. Chgo., N.Y.C., South Orange, N.J., then sr. v.p., treas., exec. v.p., 1963-65; exec. v.p. Buchen Advt., Inc., Chgo., N.Y.C., Denver, 1965-68; adminstrv. officer Bozell & Jacobs, Inc., Chgo., 1968—. Past vice pres. Highland Park Community Concert Assn. Past trustee Highland Park Community Chest; life trustee Highland Park Hosp. Mem. Ill. C. of C. Club: Executives (Chgo.). Home: 1675 Green Bay Rd Highland Park IL 60035 Office: 120 S Riverside Plaza Chicago IL 60606

CAROL, NORMAN, concertmaster; b. Phila., 1928; s. Max. N. Carol; grad. Curtis Inst. Music; studied under Efrem Zimablist; m.; 1 son, 1 dau. Began as recitalist, Boston; N.Y. debut, Town Hall, 1949, debut Phila. Orch., 1954; concertmaster Mpls. Symphony, 1960-66; concertmaster Phila. Orch., 1966—. Prof. music U. Minn. Office: 230 S 15th St Philadelphia PA 19102

CAROLLA, WILLIAM LAURENCE, aviation co. exec.; b. Oneida, N.Y., Dec. 17, 1917; s. James Marten and Antona N. (Fischine) C.; student Niagara U., 1938-39; m. Shirley Andrews, Sept. 25, 1948; 1 son, Laurence W. Div. mgr. Hollinshead Corp., Camden, N.J., 1946-54; v.p., gen. mgr. Air Assos., Inc., Teterboro, N.J., 1954-60; pres. Van Dusen Air, Inc., Minneapolis, 1970—, also dir.; dir. Bellanca Aircraft Corp., Speed-o-Laq Corp. Served with USNR, 1942-46. Clubs: Decathlon Athletic (Mpls.); Edina Country. Home: 5011 Wooddale Lane Edina MN 55424 Office: 2801 E 78th St Minneapolis MN 55420

CARON, LESLIE (Leslie Clare Margaret Caron), film and stage actress; b. Boulogne, France, July 1, 1931; d. Claude and Margaret (Petit) Caron; student Convent of the Assumption, Paris, France; m. George Hormel, May 1953; m. 2d, Peter Reginald Frederick Hall, Aug. 6, 1956; children—Christopher John, Jennifer Caron; m. 3d, Michael Laughlin, Jan. 1, 1969. With Ballet des Champs Elysees, 1947-50, Ballet de Paris, 1954; appeared in motion pictures, including American in Paris, Lili, Glass Slipper, Daddy Long Legs, Gigi, The Doctor's Dilemma, The Man Who Understood Women, Fanny, The L Shaped Room, Father Goose, The Favour, Promise Her Anything, Is Paris Burning, Head of the Family, The Beginners; also appeared in Renoir play Orvet, Paris, 1955; Gigi, London, 1956; Ondine, 1961. Address: 31 Montpelier Sq London SW 7 England

CAROTHERS, BARRETT MANVILLE, former electric utility co. exec.; b. Kirksville, Mo., Apr. 10, 1908; s. Manville and Mabel (Barrett) C.; B.S. in Elec. Engring., U. Ill., 1932; m. Eva Evelyn Atteberry, Feb. 22, 1934; 1 son, James B. With Union Electric Co., 1932-44, 46-71, v.p. operations, St. Louis, 1966-68, exec. v.p. 1968—. Served with USNR, 1944-46. Home: PO Box 212 Warrenton MO 63383

CARPENDER, JAMES WOOD JOHNSON, physician; b. New Brunswick, N.J., Nov. 18, 1911; s. Sydney B. and Louise W. (Johnson) C.; A.B., Yale, 1934; M.D., Columbia, 1938; m. Mary Bliss. June 25, 1935 (div.); 1 dau., Constance; m. 2d, Pauline Toy, Mar. 2, 1946; children—Stephen, Patricia, Anne. Intern Robert Packer Hosp., Sayre, Pa., 1938-39, fellow radiology, 1939-42; instr. radiology U. Chgo., 1947, asst. prof., 1948-51, asso. prof., 1951-55, prof., 1955-66; chief irradiation therapy U. Chgo. Hosps. and Clinics, 1948-66; co-chmn. dept. radiology Robert Packer Hosp., Sayre, 1966—. Served to lt. comdr. MC, USNR, 1942-46. Diplomate Am. Bd. Radiology. Mem. A.M.A., A.A.A.S., Am. Coll. Radiology, Radio. Soc. N.A., Am. Roetgen Ray Soc., Am. Radium Soc. Mason (32, K.T.). Contbr. articles to med. jours. Home: 329 Chemung Street Waverly NY Office: Robert Packer Hosp Sayre PA

CARPENTER, ANN-MARY PASSIER, educator; b. Ambridge, Pa., Jan. 14, 1916; d. Samuel U. and Adele M. (Passier) Carpenter; B.A., Geneva Coll., 1936, D.Sc. (hon.), 1968; M.S., U. Pitts., 1937, Ph.D., 1940; M.D., U. Minn., 1958. Research asst. U. Pitts., 1938-40; instr. Moravian Coll. Women, Bethlehem, Pa., 1941-42; chmn. biology curricula Keystone Coll., Scranton, Pa., 1942-44; research asso. pathology Children's Hosp., lectr. mycology Sch. Medicine, Pitts., 1946-53; instr. Sch. Medicine U. Minn., Mpls., 1954-57, asst. prof., 1957-58, asso. prof., 1959-65, prof. anatomy, 1965—. Mem. A.A.A.S., Am. Diabetes Assn., Histochem. Soc., Am. Assn. Anatomy, Internat. Soc. Mycology. Internat. Soc. Stereology. Author: Color Atlas of Human Histology, 1968. Home: 153 Orlin Av SE Minneapolis MN 55414

CARPENTER, BENJAMIN HOWARD, life ins. exec., cattle rancher; b. Dallas, Mar. 10, 1924; s. John William and Flossie (Gardner) C.; B.B.A., U. Texas, 1948; m. Betty Dupree, June 18, 1948; children—Laura Lucinda, John William III, Elizabeth Carolyn, Barbara Dupree, Ellen Belle Gardner. Chmn. bd., chief exec. officer Southland Life Ins. Co.; pres. The Crockett Co., Beeftex Cattle Co., Nat. Real Estate Devel. Corp., Trinity Valley Cattle Co.; dir. Nat. Finance Credit Corp., Republic Nat. Bank of Dallas, Community Gen. Stores, Inc., Kroger Co. Chmn., Livestock San. Commn. of Texas, 1951-57. Bd. dirs. first pres. Trinity River Authority; chmn. bd. dirs. dir. Trinity Improvement Assn. Served as 1st lt. AUS, 1943-46. Decorated Silver Star. Mem. Tex. Livestock Marketing Assn. (dir.), Tex. Beef Council (dir.), Am. Brahman Breeders Assn. (dir.), Tex. and Southwestern Cattle Raisers Assn. (dir.), Dallas Agrl. Club (dir.), Phi Eta Sigma, Sigma Alpha Epsilon. Home: Box 99 Route 6 Dallas TX 75220 Office: Box 2220 Dallas TX 75221

CARPENTER, CHARLES COLCOCK JONES, educator, physician; b. Savannah, Ga., Jan. 5, 1931; s. Charles Colcock Jones and Alexandra (Morrison) C.; A.B., Princeton, 1952; M.D., Johns Hopkins, 1956; m. Sally R. Fisher, Nov. 29, 1958; children—Charles Morrison, Murray Douglas, Andrew Fisher. Intern, Johns Hopkins Hosp., 1956-57, resident, 1957-59, 61-62; practice medicine, specializing in infectious disease, Balt., 1962—; asst. prof. medicine Johns Hopkins, 1962-67, asso. prof., 1967-69, prof., 1969—; physician-in-chief Balt. City Hosps., 1969—; dir. Cholera Research Program, Johns Hopkins Center Med. Research and Tng., Calcutta, India, 1962-64; chmn. cholera panel U.S.-Japan Coop. Med. Sci. Program, 1965—. Served as sr. asst. surgeon USPHS, 1959-61. Fellow A.C.P.; mem. Am. Soc. Clin. Investigation. Home: 209 Goodwood Gardens Baltimore MD 21210

CARPENTER, CHARLES IRVING, clergyman; b. Wilmington, Del., Jan. 13, 1906; s. Frank Freeman and Anne Virginia (Milligan) C.; A.B., Bucknell U., 1927, D.D. (hon.), 1955; B.D., Drew U., 1931; S.T.D., Boston U., 1950; L.H.D., U. Del. 1956; D.D., Houghton Coll., 1958; m. Miriam Byrd Dryden, Sept. 4, 1928. Ordained to ministry Meth. Ch., 1928, pastor Bethany Meth. Ch., Fort Lee, N.J., 1928-31, Rehoboth Beach, Del. and Federalsburg, Md., 1931-36; commd. chaplain (1st lt.) U.S. Army, 1936; assigned Ft. H.G. Wright, N.Y., 1936-37, Ft. Randolph, C.Z., 1937-39, Langley Field, Va., 1939-42; air chaplain hdqrs. USAAF, 1942-45; staff chaplain Hdqrs. U.S. Strategic Air Force, Europe, 1945-46, Hdqrs. USAF, Washington, 1946-58; designated chief air force chaplain, 1949, and promoted maj. gen.; chmn. Armed Forces Chaplains Bd., 1952-54, 56-57; Protestant cadet chaplain, col., USAF Acad., 1958-60; minister Av. Meth. Ch., Milford, Del., 1960-68. Decorated Legion of Merit with oak leaf cluster, D.S.M.; Belgian Mil. Cross 1st class. Mem. Ocean Grove Camp Meeting Assn. (pres. 1963—). Kappa Delta Rho. Home: PO Box 206 Milford DE 19963 Office: Ocean Grove Camp Meeting Assn Ocean Grove NJ 07756

CARPENTER, CLARENCE RAY, educator; b. Lincoln County, N.C., Nov. 28, 1905; s. C. E. and Gaddie Lee (Harrelson) C.; B.A., Duke, 1928, M.A., 1929; N.R.C. fellow Yale, 1931-33; Ph.D., Stanford, 1932; m. Mariana Evans, July 16, 1932 (dec. July 1963); children—Richard Lee, Lane Evans; m. 2d, Ruth Jones Chamblee, October 8, 1966. Research asst. Yale, 1931-34; fellow, asst. prof. Bard Coll. Columbia, 1934- 38, co-leader Asiatic Primate expdn., Thailand, Sumatra, 1937, comdr. Indian Primate expdn., 1938, asst. prof. Coll. Phys. and Surg., 1938-40; developed Santiago Primate Research Colony, P.R.,1938-40; asso. prof. psychology Pa. State U., 1940-46, prof., 1946-65, research prof. psychology and anthropology, 1965-69, emeritus research prof., 1969—, dir. div. instructional research services, 1954-63; mem. bd. control, New U. Planning Commn. State of Fla., 1960- 62; exec. dir. survey com. Hershey Med. Center, 1963-64; Ford vis. prof. U. N.C., 1964-65; research prof. psychology and anthropology U. Ga., Athens, 1969—. Dir., State Coll. Fed. Savs. and Loan Assn.; v.p., dir. State Coll. Flying Service, 1958-62; cons. long range devel. com. Pa. U., ednl. products project Gen. Electric, RCA, Holt, Rinehart & Winston; prin. planner Nat. Complement Learning Research Center for U.S. Office Edn.; mem. Community Planning Com; mem. appraisal com. pub. sch., TV project Fund for Advancement of Edn., Ford Found., 1957-58; mem. evaluation com. Midwest Airborne Instrnl. TV Project, 1961-65; dir. Center Applied Ednl. Research, Washington, 1960-65; mem. Joint Council Ednl. Telecommunications, pres., 1968-70; mem. team experts on communications and media advisers Indian Govt. on devel. communication system (Ford Found.-Indian Govt.), 1963; mem. planning meeting U.S.-Japan Coop. Program in Sci., 1964; mem. adv. com. U.S. Office of Edn., 1966-68; mem. exec. com. Nat. Commn. Instrnl. Tech., 1968-69; mem. EDUCOM; mem. Ga. Instructional Television Adv. Council; mem. sci. adv. com. Yerkes Regional Primate Research Lab., Emory U., 1967-69, chmn., 1969—; UNESCO lectr., Spain, 1971; NRC lectr., West Coast, 1971. Bd. dirs. Internat. Psychiat. Found., 1971—. Served capt. to maj. USAAF 1943-46, head research sect., dept. psychology and sociology Biarritz Am. Army U., 1945- 46; organized German Youth Re-edn. Program; lt. col. USAF Res. Fellow Animal Behavior Soc., N.Y. Zool. Soc. (research coordinator 1948-50), Nat. Council Religion in Higher Edn.; member A.A.A.S., Am. Soc. Zoologists, Pa. Psychol. Assn., Am. Anthrop. Assn., Nat. Acad. Sci. (del 13th Pacific sci. congress 1966), Am. Assn. U. Profs., Am. Acad. Sci., N.E.A., Internat.

Primatological Soc. (Am. sec. 1964-68), Assn. Higher Edn. (pres. 1965- 66), Phi Beta Kappa, Sigma Xi. Author: Naturalistic Behavior of Nonhuman Primates. Editor: Behaviour, internat. jour.; Telecommunications: Toward a National Policy for Education; Behavioral Regulators of Behavior in Nonhumans; U.S. editor: Jour. Human Evolution; editorial bd. Ednl. Broadcasting Rev., 1967—. Address: 295 Gatewood Circle Athens GA 30601

CARPENTER, CLIFFORD EARL, newspaperman; b. East Syracuse, N.Y., Mar. 15, 1909; s. Edmund B. and Helen (Pehl) C.; student U. Rochester; m. Ethel LeFevre, Oct. 20, 1933; 1 son, Scott E. With Democrat & Chronicle, Rochester, 1933—, police reporter, gen. assignments reporter, yachting columnist, asst. city editor, Sunday editor, copy reader, copy desk chief, acting mng. editor, editorial writer, 1953-57, editor editorial page, 1957-60, editor, 1960-67, editorial columnist, 1967—; reporter Canadaigua Daily Messenger, 1931-33. Pres. Nat. Conf. Editorial Writers, 1963-64, now life mem.; editorial bd. Rochester Gannett Newspapers. Bd. mem. Monroe County Arts Com., Grovetown. Named goodwill ambassador to S.A., Rochester, 1958. Fellow Rochester Mus. Arts and Scis.; mem. U.S. Power Squadron (sr.), Inter-Am. Press Assn. (life), U.S. Coast Guard Aux. Clubs: Rochester, Rochester Yacht. Home: 144 Gibbs St Rochester NY 14605 Office: Democrat and Chronicle Rochester NY

CARPENTER, COY CORNELIUS, medical educator; b. Carpenter, N.C., Apr. 24, 1900; s. Rufus Jackson and Betty (Rogers) C.; B.A., Wake Forest (N.C.) Coll., 1922; M.D., Syracuse U., 1924; m. Dorothy Mitten, Oct. 23, 1926; children—Harry Mitten, Coy Cornelius. Began practice medicine, 1924; instr. pathology, asst. attending pathologist U. Hosp., Syracuse U., 1924-25, resident physician, instr. clin. medicine, 1925-26; pathologist various hosp. in N.C., 1926—; prof. pathology Bowman Gray Sch. Medicine, Wake Forest U., 1926-70, prof. emeritus, 1970—, dean, 1936-60, v.p. med. affairs, 1960-68, v.p. emeritus med. affairs, 1968—; Fulbright lectr. pathology Fouad U. Faculty Medicine and Ibrahim U. Faculty Medicine, Cairo, Egypt, 1953-54. Diplomate Am. Bd. Pathology. Fellow A.M.A.; mem. N.C., Forsyth County med. socs., Assn. Am. Med. Colls., Winston-Salem C. of C., Nu Sigma Nu, Alpha Omega Alpha. Democrat. Baptist. Clubs: Rotary, Old Town. Home: 3154 Bonhurst Dr Winston-Salem NC 27106

CARPENTER, DAVID BAILEY, educator; b. Webster Groves, Mo., June 4, 1915; s. Fred Green and Mildred (Bailey) C.; B.A., Wash. U., 1937, M.A., 1938; M.A., Columbia U., 1944; Ph.D., U. Wash., 1951; m. Yoshi Horikawa, Aug. 6, 1946; children—Mary Yoshiko, Teresa Teiko, Gary Bailey, James Burton. Instr. sociology U. Wash., 1941-42; civilian chief of statistics div. MacArthur HQ, Tokyo, 1946-48; instr. sociology U. Wash., 1948-49; asst. prof. sociology Wash. U., 1949-52, asst. prof., 1952-63, prof., 1963—, dean Grad. Sch. Arts and Scis., 1965-67, Chief Grad. Academic Programs br. U.S. Office Edn., 1967-68. Served with USNR, 1942-46. Mem. Ethical Soc. St. Louis (pres. 1969-71), Phi Beta Kappa. Author: (with Stuart A. Queen) The American City, 1953; (with Stuart A. Queen) St. Louis; The Social Life of a Modern Metropolis, 1954. Home: 715 W Oak Dr Glendale MO 63122 Office: Dept Sociology Wash U St Louis MO 63130

CARPENTER, DELMA RAE, Jr., educator, physicist; b. Salem, Va., Apr. 15, 1928; s. Delma Rae and Gladys (Jamison) C.; B.S., Roanoke Coll., Salem, 1949; M.S., Cornell U., 1951; Ph.D., U. Va., 1957; m. Jane Augusta Grant, Aug. 2, 1952; children—Delma Rae III, Cita Anne, Gordon Grant, Barbara Elizabeth. Instr. physics Va. Mil. Inst., Lexington, 1951-55, asst. prof., 1955-59, asso. prof., 1959-63, prof., 1963—, head dept. physics, 1969—, dep. dir. research Research Labs., 1963-66, dir. research, 1966—, bd. dirs., 1966—; industry control, devel. engr. Gen. Electric Co., summer 1962; cons. Army Research Office; summer research Depts. Army and Commerce, 1953—. Fellow A.A.A.S.; mem. Am. Assn. Physics Tchrs., Va. Acad. Sci. (pres.), Sigma Xi. Rotarian. Home: 401 Overlook Circle Lexington VA 24450

CARPENTER, DONALD DUBOIS, banker; b. Bklyn., Sept. 11, 1910; s. Jacob Greene and Marion (Metcalf) C.; student N.Y.C., 1950; postgrad Stonier Grad. Sch., Rutgers U., 1956- 58, Columbia Grad. Sch., 1966; m. Eleanor Jane Bressan, Dec. 19, 1941; children—Bruce D., Jane M. With Hanover Nat. Bank, N.Y.C., 1928-29, Central Hanover Bank and Trust Co., N.Y.C., 1929-41; with United Nat. Bank of Central Jersey, 1946—, pres., chief exec. officer, 1967—. Bd. dirs. Plainfield Area YMCA, 1962-68. Plainfield Pub. Library, 1956-68, John H. VanWinkle Home, 1960—. Muhlenberg Hosp., 1969—. Served with AUS, 1941-46. Decorated Bronze Star. Presbyn. (past deacon). Home: 5 Knollcroft Rd Basking Ridge NJ 07920 Office: 202 Park Av Plainfield NJ 07061

CARPENTER, EDWARD LESTER, banker; b. Cleve., Sept. 12, 1904; s. Frank B. and Edna (Woods) C.; B.S., Princeton, 1926; grad. Stonier Sch. Banking, Rutgers U.; m. Elizabeth Howland, 1934; children—William H., Frank H., Elizabeth (Mrs. Bruce M. Listerman). With Central Nat. Bank of Cleve., 1928—, sr. v.p., 1958-64, 1st v.p., 1964-67, chmn. chief exec., 1967—, also dir. Hon. trustee U. Sch., Cleve.; trustee John Carroll U.; chmn. bd. advisers Notre Dame Coll., Real Property Inventory of Cleve.; trustee, mem. pres.'s adv. council for devel. Ashland Coll. Mem. Res. City Bankers Assn., Ohio Bankers Assn., Cleve. Soc. Security Analysts, Greater Cleve. Growth Assn. (dir.), Newcomen Soc., Bluecoats. Clubs: Union, Country The 50, Pepper Pike (Cleve.). Home: Topping Lane Hunting Valley Chagrin Falls OH 44022 Office: 800 Superior Av Cleveland OH 44114

CARPENTER, FRANCES, see Huntington, Frances Carpenter.

CARPENTER, FRANCIS WARNER, former govt. ofcl.; b. Decherd, Tenn., July 29, 1907; s. Clyde Millard and Ida Mae (Warner) C.; A.B., Emory U., 1928; m. Dorothy Sweeny, June 1, 1935; children—David, Martha, Elizabeth Ann. Reporter, Atlanta Georgian, 1928-29; editor, corr. A.P., 1929-57; dir. news services U.S. Mission to UN, 1957-66, sr. adviser pub. affairs, 1966-67; pub. affairs officer Vietnam bur. AID, 1967-69; spl. asst. pub. affairs Bur. Internat. Orgn. Affairs, U.S. Dept. State, 1969-70, ret., 1970; cons. Bur. Internat. Orgn. Affairs, State Dept., 1970; spl. sec. for Asia-Pacific affairs Am. Bible Soc., 1971—. Pres. board edn. Harrison, N.Y., 1962-65. Served to capt., AUS, 1943-45. Decorated Bronze Star. Methodist. Author: Men in Glass Houses, 1951. Home: 115 Harrison Av Harrison NY 10528

CARPENTER, FRANK MORTON, zoologist; b. Boston, Sept. 6, 1902; s. Edwin Arthur and Maude Frances (Wall) C.; A.B. magna cum laude, Harvard, 1926, M.S., 1927, D.Sc., 1929; m. Ruth Frances Scace, June 1, 1932; children—Alden Bliss, Ellen Ruth, Cynthia. NRC fellow biol. scis., 1928-31; asso. entomology Harvard, 1931-32; research asso. Carnegie Inst., 1931- 32; asst. curator invertebrate paleontology Harvard, 1932-36; curator fossil insects Mus. of Comparative Zoology, Harvard, 1936—, asst. prof. palentology, 1936-39, asso. prof. entomology, 1939-45, prof. entomology, Agassiz prof. zoölogy, 1945-69, Fisher prof. natural history, 1969—. Fellow Am. Acad. Arts and Scis. (v.p. 1961-63); mem. Phi Beta Kappa, Sigma Xi (nat. pres.). Author tech. articles on insect evolution. Home: 94 Pleasant Street Lexington MA Office: Harvard U Cambridge MA

CARPENTER, GENE BLAKELY, educator; b. Evansville, Ind., Dec. 15, 1922; s. Leland A. and Juanita (Blakely) C.; B.A., U. Louisville, 1944; M.A., Harvard U., 1945, Ph.D., 1947; m. Elizabeth E. Corkum, Apr. 15, 1949; children—Jonathan R., Anne E. NRC fellow Cal. Inst. Tech., 1947-48, research fellow, 1948-49; instr. Brown U., 1949-52, asst. prof., 1952-56, asso. prof., 1956-63, prof., 1963—; Guggenheim fellow U. Leeds (Eng.), 1956-57; vis. prof. U. Groningen, The Netherlands, 1963-64. Mem. Am. Crystallographic Assn., Am. Chem. Soc. Author: Principles of Crystal Structure Determination, 1969. Contbr. articles sci. jours. Home: 6 Wilson Av Rumford RI 02916 Office: Dept Chemistry Brown U Providence RI 02912

CARPENTER, GENE F., banker; b. 1931; B.S., Ind. U., 1957. With Nat. City Bank Cleve., 1957—, asst. cashier, 1961-65, asst. v.p., 1964-67, v.p., 1967-69, v.p., cashier, 1969—. Served with USAF, 1955. Office: PO Box 5756 623 Euclid Av Cleveland OH 44101*

CARPENTER, HELEN MCCRACKEN, educator; b. Norwalk, O., July 31, 1909; d. Irving and Myrtle (McCracken) Carpenter; B.A., Ohio Wesleyan U., 1931; M.A., Columbia, 1934, Ed.D., 1942; student Ohio U., summers 1931, 35, 36. Tchr. high sch., Crestline, O., 1931-33, Norwalk, O., 1934-36, Ohio Wesleyan U., 1936-38, Columbia Tchrs. Coll. 1940-42, Wilson Tchrs. Coll., 1942-43, R.I. State U., 1943-44; with Trenton State Coll., Trenton, N.J., 1944—, chmn. history and govt., dept. social studies, 1947-58, now prof. history; summer tchr. Columbia Tchrs. Coll., Syracuse U., Northwestern U. Dir. Nat. Council for Social Studies, 1951-52, 57-59, 2d v.p., 1954, 1st v.p., 1955, pres., 1956; sec. Commn. Econs. Tchr. Edn., 1952-54; ednl. cons. U.S. Steel Corp., 1954-67, Enrichment Teaching Materials, 1952-71; cons. Inst. Life Ins., 1964-66; edn. cons. social studies curriculum sch. systems, 1964—; field reader U.S. Office Edn., 1965—; cons. Am. Assn. Sch. Librarians, H. H. Wilson Co. Grace Dodge fellow Columbia Tchrs. Coll., 1938-39. Mem. Am., Trenton hist. assns., Am. Assn. U. Profs., Nat., N.J. edn. assns. Assn. Supervision and Curriculum Devel., League Women Voters (dir. N.J. 1951-52), Am. Assn. U. Women, Nat., Middle States, N.J. councils social studies, Phi Beta Kappa, Delta Sigma Rho, Kappa Delta Pi, Pi Lambda Theta, Delta Kappa Gamma. Club: Zonta. Author: Gateways to American History, 1942; Leads to Listening, 1952-71; co-author: Scribner Social Studies Series for Schools, 1948-62. Editor: Skills in Social Studies, 1953; Skill Development in Social Studies, 1963. Contbr. profl. jours. Home: 301 W State Street Trenton NJ 08618

CARPENTER, JAMES D., lawyer; b. Woodbury, N.J., Feb. 10, 1885; s. James D. and Harriet (Fish) C.; grad. Brown Coll. Prep. Sch., 1905; LL.B., U. Pa. 1909; m. Emily M. Atkinson, Oct. 17, 1912 (dec. Jan. 1960); children—Emily A. (Mrs. Lawrence Pratt), William A., Frances H. (Mrs. Albert E. Betteridge, Jr.); m. 2d, Mildred L. Pearson, 1961. Practiced in Newark; sr. mem. firm Carpenter, Bennett & Morrissey; U.S. Commr. Jersey City, 1910-1920; spl. asst. atty. gen. N.J., prosecuting jury fixers and racketeers at Paterson, 1933-34. Mem. N.J. Crime Commn., 1934. Fellow Am. Bar Found. (recipient 50 Year award from fellows 1965); mem. Internat. (patron), Am. (ho. of dels.), Inter-Am., N.J. (pres. 1933-34), Hudson County (pres. 1923), Essex County bar assns., Assn. Bar City N.Y., N.Y. County Lawyers Assn. Democrat. Conglist. Clubs: Lawyers (N.Y.C.); Upper Montclair Country; Essex. Home: 12 S Mountain Av Montclair NJ 07042 Office: 744 Broad St Newark NJ 07114

CARPENTER, JAMES HENRY, mfg. co. exec.; b. Camden, Mo., Sept. 3, 1908; s. John J. and Bernice (Galle) C.; student Kansas City (Mo.) U., 1927-30; m. Ruby Stephens, Aug. 16, 1946; 1 son, James Stephens. With Colgate-Palmolive Co. and affiliates, 1928—, pres. Colgate-Palmolive Internat., 1968—, mem. bd., v.p. parent co., 1970—, also dir. numerous fgn. subsidiaries. Bd. dirs. Nat. Fgn. Trade Council, Philippine Am. C. of C. Civilian interned by Japanese in Manila, Philippines, 1941-45. Clubs: Rosedale Golf (Toronto, Can.); Coral Ridge Country (Ft. Lauderdale, Fla.); American (London); Manila Polo; Canadian (N.Y.C.). Home: 815 Park Av New York City NY 10021 Office: 300 Park Av New York City NY 10022

CARPENTER, JAMES MORTON, educator; b. Glens Falls, N.Y., Dec. 7, 1914; s. William Morton and Beulah (Mason) C.; A.B., Harvard, 1937, Ph.D., 1943; m. Dorothy Neal Sauer, Nov. 4, 1939; children—William Morton, Stephen Sparrell, Elizabeth Ashley, Jane Mason. Instr., then asst. prof. Harvard, 1943-50; mem. faculty Colby Coll., 1950—, prof. art, chmn. dept., 1953—; dir. Colby Coll. Art Mus., 1959-65. Mem. Me. Commn. Arts and Humanities. Trustee Haystack Mountain Sch. Crafts; bd. govs. Skowhegan Sch. Painting and Sculpture. Author: (with others) Maine and Its Role in American Art, 1963. Home: 1 Edgewood St Waterville ME 04901

CARPENTER, JOHN MELVIN, educator; b. Terre Haute, Ind., May 21, 1910; s. John R. and Maude M. (Batchelder) C.; B.A., U. Tex., 1936, M.A., 1940, Ph.D., 1946; m. Mary W. Meadors, July 2, 1946; children—Mary M., Gene B., John H. Research asso. Clayton Found. Research, 1938-45; tutor zoology U. Tex., 1942-45, instr., 1945-46; asst. prof. zoology U. Tenn., 1946-53; prof., head dept. zoology U. Ky., 1953-62, prof., 1953—, chmn., 1963, chmn. biol. sci. div., 1954; dir. NSF Summer Inst. for Secondary Sch. Tchrs., 1961, 62, 63, asso. dir., 1964. Del. Tex. Democratic County Conv., 1944. Mem. Tex. N.G., 1930-36. Grantee Clayton Found. Research, 1944, Tenn. Acad. Sci., 1953, NSF, 1956, 64, U. Ky. Faculty Research Fund, 1953, 58, 65, 66, NIH, 1962, AEC, 1962, 65; asso. Danforth Found. Fellow A.A.A.S.; mem. Ky. Acad. Sci. (asso. editor biology transl., pres., 1966), Found. Preservation Hist. Lexington, Assn. Southeastern Biologists (exec. com. 1962-65, pres. 1968-70), Soc. Study Evolution, Ecol. Soc. Am., Am. Assn. U. Profs. (pres. U. Ky. chpt. 1966), Assn. Higher Edn., Genetics Soc. Am., Am. Inst. Biol. Scis., Am. Soc. Zoologists, Am. Genetic Assn., Sigma Xi, Phi Sigma, Alpha Epsilon Delta. Presbyn. (deacon). Author: (with A. W. Jones) A Students Guide to Slide Making, rev. edit., 1960; (with R. W. Barbour and J. M. Edney) Laboratory Studies in the Principles of Zoology, rev. edit., 1958; also articles. Home: 208 Tahoma Rd Lexington KY 40503

CARPENTER, JOHN WILSON, III ret. air force officer, ednl. adminstr.; b. Starkville, Miss., Aug. 11, 1916; s. John Wilson and Alice Margaret (McBee) C.; student Okla. State U., 1934, Miss. State U., 1935; B.S., U.S. Mil. Acad., 1939; grad. Air Command and Staff Sch., 1947, Air War Coll., 1954; m. Dorothy Bigelow Goding, June 13, 1939; children—Carol Sue (Mrs. James P. Rogers), John Wilson IV, Jean McBee (Mrs. Martin V. Murray). Commd. 2d lt. USAAF, 1939, advanced through grades to lt. gen., USAF, 1965; vice-comdr. 13th Air Force, 1949-54; plans and programming office, dep. for operations and chief of staff Air Research and Devel. Command, 1950; vice-comdr. Arnold Engring. Center, 1954; insp. gen., chief plans and programming, asst. vice comdr. Air Research and Devel. Command, 1955, 57-58; comdr. Flight Test Center, 1959-62; dir. plans hdqrs. USAF, 1962-64, asst. dep. chief of staff for plans and operations. (JCS matters), 1964-65; comdr. Air U., Maxwell AFB, Ala., 1965-68; dep. chief staff, personnel Hdqrs. U.S. Air Force, 1968-69, asst. vice chief staff, 1969-70; supt. Culver (Ind.) Mil. Acad., 1970—. Decorated D.S.M. with oak leaf cluster, also Silver Star with two oak leaf clusters, Legion of Merit with two oak leaf clusters, D.F.C. with two oak leaf clusters, Air Medal with oak leaf cluster, Presdl. Citation (U.S., P.I.). Asso. fellow Am. Inst. Aeros. and Astronautics; mem. Soc. Exptl. Test Pilots (asso.), Order Daedalians, Tau Beta Pi, Sigma Alpha Epsilon. Home: Culver IN 46511 Office: Culver Mil Acad Culver IN 46511

CARPENTER, LESLIE E., newspaper corr.; b. Austin, Tex., Feb. 20, 1922; s. John W. and Edleen (Falwell) C.; B.J., U. Tex., 1943; m. Mary Elizabeth Sutherland, June 17, 1944; children—Scott Sutherland, Christy. Reporter, Austin Am.-Statesman, 1942; Washington corr. Ft. Worth Star- Telegram, Dallas Times Herald, Houston Chronicle, New Orleans States, other newspapers, 1945-51; chief Washington bur. Variety mag., Variety (N.Y.C.), Daily Variety (Hollywood), Ark. Gazette (Little Rock), Springfield (Mass.) Daily News, Beaumont (Tex.) Enterprise and Jour., Abiliene (Tex.) Reporter-News, Lubbock (Tex.) Avalance-Jour., San Antonio Express and Evening News, Corpus Christi (Tex.) Caller-Times, San Angelo (Tex.) Standard-Times, Honolulu Advertiser, Amarillo News-Globe, Austin Am.- Statesman, Waco (Tex.) Tribune-Herald, Wichita Falls (Tex.) Record-News & Times, numerous others, 1951—; columnist Hall Syndicate, 1963—. Served to lt. USNR, 1943-45. Mem. Sigma Delta Chi. Episcopalian. Clubs: Congressional Country, Nat. Press, Internat. (Washington). Home: 4701 Woodway Lane NW Washington DC 20016 Office: National Press Building 14th and F Streets NW Washington DC 20004

CARPENTER, MALCOLM BRECKENRIDGE, educator, neurologist; b. Montrose, Colo., July 7, 1921; s. Grover B. and Haidee (Moritz) C.; A.B., Columbia, 1943; M.D., L.I. Coll. Medicine, 1947; m. Carolyn I. Sloan, July 20, 1949; children—Duncan B., Gregory S., Rustin I. Intern Bellevue Hosp., N.Y.C., 1947-48; resident neurology Neurol. Inst. N.Y., 1950-53; fellow neurology Columbia Coll. Phys. and Surg., 1948-50, mem. faculty, 1953—, prof. anatomy, 1962—; cons. NIH, 1962-66, 1968—; adviser Parkinson Disease Found., 1962—. Served with M.C., USNR, 1950- 52. Markle Sch. med. sci., 1953-58. Diplomate American Bd. Psychiatry and Neurology. Author: (with R.C. Truex) Human Neuroanatomy, 1969; also articles. Editorial bd. Neurology, 1963—, Neurobiology, 1970, Jour. Comparative Neurology, 1971—; asso. editor Am. Jour. Anatomy, 1968—. Home: 185 Delhi Road Scarsdale NY 10583 Office: 630 W 168th Street New York City NY 10032

CARPENTER, MALCOLM SCOTT, astronaut; b. Boulder, Colo., May 1, 1925; s. Marion Scott and Florence Kelso (Noxon) C.; B.S. in Aero. Engring., U. Colo., 1962; m. Rene Louise Price, Sept. 9, 1948; children—Marc Scott, Robyn Jay, Kristen Elaine, Candace Noxon. Commd. ensign U.S. Navy, 1949, advanced through grades to lt. comdr., 1959; assigned various flight tng. schs., 1949-51, Patrol Squadron 6, Barbers Point, Hawaii, 1951, also in Korea, 1951-52; grad. Navy Test Pilot Sch. 1954; assigned electronics test div. Naval Air Test Center, 1954-57, Naval Gen. Line Sch., 1957, Naval Air Intelligence Sch., 1957-58; air intelligence officer U.S.S. Hornet, 1958-59; joined Project Mercury, man-in-space project, NASA, 1959; completed 3 orbit space flight mission in spacecraft Aurora 7, May 1962; mem. U.S. Navy Aquanaut Project, 1965-67; retired from U.S. Navy, 1969; now engaged in pvt. business. Fellow Inst. Environmental Scis. (hon.); mem. Delta Tau Delta. Home: Timbercove Houston TX

CARPENTER, MILTON, church ofcl.; b. St. Louis, Mar. 4, 1905; s. Francis James and Emma Louise (Vedder) C.; night student Washington U., St. Louis, 1923-25, Morse Sch. Expression, St. Louis, 1925-28; m. Jaunet Naomi Parham, Sept. 24, 1942. Engaged in jewelry bus., 1923-31, constrn. bus., 1932-49; comptroller City St. Louis, 1949-57; dir. revenue Mo., 1957-61, treas., 1961—; treas. Lutheran Ch., Mo. Synod, 1963—; v.p. Am. Credit Ins. Co., 1963—, Bobette, Inc., 1964—; dir. Security Mut. Life Ins. Co. Treas. Luth. Laymen's League, 1952. Bd. dirs. St. Louis Symphony Assn., 1951; nat. adv. bd. Valparaiso U., 1953—. Served with AUS, World War II. Recipient award Met. St. Louis Ch. Fedn., 1951, N.W. St. Louis Optimist Club, 1957, Mo. Jewish War Vets., 1961, Am. Legion Mo., 1964; Merit award Pres.'s Com. Employment Handicapped, 1960. Mem. Mo. Assn. Social Welfare (v.p.), Mo. Hist. Soc. (bd. dirs.), Am. Legion, D.A.V. (aide to comdr.), Amvets (past post comdr.), Bach Soc. St. Louis (past pres.). Democrat. Rotarian. Clubs: Missouri Athletic, Optimist (St. Louis). Home: 1640 Grape Avenue St Louis MO 63147 Office: Capitol Building Jefferson City MO 65101

CARPENTER, NOBLE OLDS, banker; b. Cleve., May 8, 1929; s. John W. and Maribel (Olds) C.; A.B. cum laude, Princeton, 1951; m. Ann Lindemann, Oct. 13, 1956; children—John L., Noble Olds, Robert W. Vice pres. Central Nat. Bank, Cleve., 1951-65; pres., chief exec. officer First Nat. Bank, Canton, O., 1965—; treas., dir. Mountain Lake Tree & Land Co., Ltd.; pres., dir. First Canton Corp., 1st Ohio BancCorp.; dir. Carways Corp., Ohio Ferro-Alloys Corp. Dep. sheriff, Stark County. Trustee Stark County Found., United Fund Central Stark County, UMCA Camp Bd., YMCA, Canton Scholarship Found., Canton Country Day Sch. Named outstanding Young Man of Year, Jr. C. of C., 1965. Mem. Canton C. of C., Ohio Bankers Assn. (past sec., treas., mem. exec. com.), Robert Morris Assos., Young Presidents Orgn. Clubs: Country, Union, Swdohaha Field (Cleve.); Canton, Brookside Country, Canton Athletic (Canton). Home: 3441 Croydon Dr NW Canton OH 44718 Office: 101 Central Plaza S Canton OH 44702

CARPENTER, PAUL LEONARD, lawyer; b. Norwalk, O., Jan. 21, 1920; s. Irving and Myrtle (McCracken) C.; A.B., Ohio Wesleyan U., 1941; M.B.A., Harvard, 1943; LL.B., U. Mich., 1948; m. Barbara Jane Chambers, Aug. 28, 1948; chiildren—Susan A., Deborah L., Helen C. Admitted to Ohio bar, 1948; with firm Doyle, Lewis & Warner, Toledo, 1948-55; partner firm Carpenter & Paffenbarger, Norwalk, O., 1955—. Dir. Citizens Nat. Bank, Norwalk. Trustee Norwalk City Hosp. Assn., 1959—, pres., 1966-68. Served to lt. USNR, 1943-46. Recipient joint award Cleve. Toledo chpts. A.I.A., 1969. Mem. Am., Ohio bar assns. Republican. United Methodist. Home: 54 W Main St Norwalk OH 44857 Office: Citizens Nat Bldg Norwalk OH 44857

CARPENTER, PETER C.A., banker; b. Eng., 1911; exec. v.p. J. Henry Schroder Banking Corp., N.Y.C.; sr. v.p., dec., dir. Schroder Trust Co.; dir. Christiania Gen. Ins. Corp., Deltec Internat. Ltd., Deltec Panam., S.A. Mem. Colombian-Am. C. of C. (v.p., dir.). Home: 1 E 62d St New York City NY 10021 Office: 57 Broadway New York City NY 10004*

CARPENTER, PHILIP LEWIS, educator; b. Newtown, Conn., Mar. 17, 1912; s. Warren Lewis and Lucia (Avery) C.; B.S., Middlebury Coll., 1933; Sc.M., Brown U., 1934; Ph.D., U.Wis., 1937; m. Helen Maria Easton, Dec. 24, 1935; 1 son, Robert. Intr. to asst. prof. bacteriology Ia. State U, 1937-42; successively asst. prof., asso. prof., prof. and chmn. dept. bacteriology and biophysics U. R.I., 1942-70, prof. bacteriology, 1970—. Mem. Am. Soc. Microbiology, A.A.A.S., Am. Acad. Microbiology, N.Y. Acad. Scis., Brit. Soc. Immunology, Sigma Xi, Phi Kappa Phi, Kappa Delta Rho. Author: Microbiology, 1961; Immunology and Serology, 1956. Home: 42 College Rd Kingston RI 02881

CARPENTER, PHILIP NATHANIEL, educator; b. Port Royal, Pa., Mar. 6, 1908; s. Frederick Michael and Ellen Stitzel (Lamm) C.; B.S., Grove City (Pa.) Coll., 1930, Sc.D. (hon.), 1966; M.S., U. Wash.,

1932; student Pa. State Coll., 1936, U. Pitts., 1937-39; m. Ethel Orr, Aug. 15, 1931; children—Shirley Elva, Patricia Joyce. Grad. asst., math. dept. U. Wash., 1930-32; prin. of schs., Port Royal, 1932-37; instr. physics and math. Grove City Coll., 1937-40, asst. prof. math., 1940- 42, asso. prof., 1942-45, prof. math., chmn. dept. 1945—; pvt. practice land and mine surveying, 1940—; instr. in E.S.M.D.T. and E.S.M.W.T. courses, Army Air Corps Pre-Flight Sch., Naval Tng. Sch., World War II. Mem. Grove City Bd. Edn., 1946-57; pres. Grove City Joint Consol. Sch. Bd., 1949-54. Registered surveyor, Pa. Mem. Lancaster County Hist. Assn., S.A.R., Math. Assn. Am. (past gov. Allegheny Mountain sect.), Pi Mu Epsilon, Theta Alpha Phi, Kappa Mu Epsilon, Omicron Delta Kappa (past dep. Province I). Republican. United Presbyn. (ruling elder). Mason (32, past master), Rotarian. Home: 214 E Pine St Grove City PA ☆

CARPENTER, RHYS, author, archeologist; b. Cotuit, Mass., Aug. 5, 1889; s. William Henry and Anna Morgan (Douglass) C.; A.B., Columbia, 1908, Ph.D., 1916; B.A., Balliol Coll., (Oxford U., Eng.), 1911, M.A., 1914; Litt.D., Rutgers U., 1941; studied Am. Sch. Classical Studies, Athens, Greece, 1912-13; m. Eleanor Houston Hill, Apr. 23, 1918. Instr. classical archeology, 1913-15, asso., 1915-16, asso. prof., 1916- 18, prof., 1918-55, prof. emeritus, 1955—, Bryn Mawr Coll.; dir. Am. Sch. Classical Studies, Athens, Greece, 1927-32, 46-48, vis. prof., 1956-57; in charge Classical Sch., Am. Acad., Rome, 1939-40; Sather prof. classical lit., U. Cal., 1945. Served as 1st lt. M.I. Staff, A.U.S., 1918-19; attached Am. Commn. to Negotiate Peace, Paris, 1919. Mem. Am. Philos. Soc., Archeol. Inst. Am., Phila. Oriental Club, Am. Philol. Assn., Linguistic Soc. Am., Phi Beta Kappa; hon. mem. Greek Archaeol. Soc., German Archaeol. Inst., Austrian Archeol Inst., Hispanic Soc. Am. Corr. mem. Pontifical Roman. Acad. Archaeology. Author: Folk Tale, Fiction Saga in the Homeric Epics, 1946; others; also profl. articles in jours. Home: Goose Walk RD1 Chester Springs PA 19425

CARPENTER, ROBERT BEACH, advt. exec.; b. Bklyn., Apr. 30, 1930; s. Hiram Beach and Melvina Liana (LaPointe) C.; A.B., U. Mich., 1953, M.B.A., 1956; m. Karin Carlson, (dec. 1963); children—Robert Beach, John Wesley, Kristin Anne, Scott Thomas, Charles Andrew; m. 2d, Sandra Kay Mitchell, July 13, 1963. Asst. dir. research Old Republic Ins. Co., Chgo., 1955-56; research account exec. Campbell Ewald, Detroit, 1956-59; exec. v.p. Fink, Carpenter & Rau, 1960-62; pres. Robert B. Carpenter, Advt., Inc., Detroit, 1963-70; chmn. bd. Specialized Communications, Inc., 1971—. Mem. Detroit Bd. Commerce. Pres. Birmingham (Mich.) Little League, Detroit City Ballet, 1962. Served with USMCR, 1953-54. Mem. Alpha Delta Phi (dir. Penninsular chpt.). Republican. Presbyn. Clubs: University of Michigan (bd. dirs. 1967-68) (Detroit); Oakland Hills Country (Birmingham). Home: 564 Overhill St Birmingham MI 48010 Office: Foxcroft Bldg Birmingham MI 48010

CARPENTER, ROBERT PHILLIPS, steel co. exec.; b. Pueblo, Colo., May 18, 1917; s. Howard B. and Ella (Soddy) C.; grad. Mercersburg Acad., 1936; B.S., Washington Jefferson Coll., 1940; postgrad. Harvard, 1957; m. Helen Mitchell, Aug. 10, 1940; children—Elizabeth Bruce, Jean Frances, Barbara, Constance. With Republic Steel Corp., 1940—, mgr. Buffalo dist., 1957-60, mgr. Cleve. dist., 1960-62, v.p. bar, alloy and pipe operations, Cleve., 1962-66, v.p. bar and alloy operations, 1966-68, v.p. raw materials and steel divs., 1968-70, v.p. environmental control, 1970—. Bd. dirs. local Cancer Soc., A.R.C., YMCA, Boy's Club, Brentwood Hosp. Mem. Masillon C. of C. (dir.), Am. Iron and Steel Inst., Am. Inst. Mining, Metall. and Petroleum Engrs., Beta Theta Pi. Presbyn. (trustee, chmn. investment com.). Home: 19333 Van Aken Blvd Shaker Heights OH 44120 Office: Republic Steel Corp Cleveland OH 44101

CARPENTER, ROBERT R. M., baseball club exec.; b. Chgo., Dec. 12, 1917; grad. high sch., Chgo.; married; children—Robert R. M. III, Mary Kaye. Played football Tower Sch., also Duke; staff pub. relations dept. E. I. DuPont de Nemours & Co.; pres. Phila. Baseball Club, 1943—; owner Wilmington Bombers, Am. Baseball League. Served with AUS, 1944-46. Club: Wilmington Sportsmen's (pres.). Office: Philadelphia Baseball Club Veterans Stadium Philadelphia PA 19148*

CARPENTER, SAMUEL RAYMOND, bank exec.; b. Evanston, Wyo., June 23, 1901; s. Samuel Felix and Hannah (Lake) C.; LL.B., George Washington U., 1932; m. Kathleen Romney, Sept. 12, 1930; children—Craig Romney, Jon Carvel, Kathleen Anne. Sec. to exec. Salt Lake council Boy Scouts Am., 1919-20; missionary Ch. of Jesus Christ of Latter-day Saints (Mormon) to Holland, 1921-23; sec. to purchasing agt. Utah Copper Co., 1923-26; mem. staff Fed. Res. Bd., 1926, asst. sec., 1933-45, sec., 1945-58; pres. central states mission Ch. of Jesus Christ of Latter-day Saints, 1958-61; v.p., personnel dir. First Security System Banks, Salt Lake City, 1961-70, ret., 1970. Mem. Delta Theta Phi. Republican. Mem. Ch. of Jesus Christ of Latter-day Saints. Home: 4065 Evelyn Dr Salt Lake City UT Office: First Security Co 79 S Main St Salt Lake City UT

CARPENTER, SAMUEL THEODORE, educator, cons. engr.; b. Montpelier, O., Sept. 2, 1906; s. Otto A. and Bernice (Brownwell) C.; B.C.E., Ohio State U., 1930, C.E., 1935, M.S., 1939; m. Mary Nofzinger, Mar. 31, 1934; 1 dau., Shirley Marie. Instr. Swarthmore (Pa.) Coll., 1935-39, asst. prof., 1939-42, asso. prof., 1942- 46, prof., chmn. civil engring. dept., 1946-64, chmn. dept. engring.; pvt. cons. engr., 1932—. Council mem. Engring. Coll. Adminstrv. Council; bd. visitors Sch. Engring., U. Pitts. Mem. Swarthmore- Rutledge Union Sch. Bd. Mem., chmn. Swarthmore Planning Commn., 1971—. Named Engr. of Year, Del. County chpt. Pa. Soc. Profl. Engrs., 1967; recipient Centennial Distinguished Alumnus award, Ohio State U., 1970. Registered profl. engr., Ohio, Pa. Mem. Am. Soc. Engring. Edn., Am. Soc. C.E., Soc. for Exptl. Stress Analysis, Sigma Xi, Tau Beta Pi, Sigma Tau, Triangle. Club: Rotary. Author: Structural Frameworks (with C. T. Morris), 1943; Structural Mechanics, 1960. Contbr. articles to engring. jours. Home: 612 Ogden Av Swarthmore PA 19081

CARPENTER, STANLEY SHERMAN, fgn. service officer; b. Boston, Feb. 27, 1917; s. Lloyd and Adeline (Sherman) C.; A.B., Wheaton Coll., 1940; A.M., U. Ill., 1941, Ph.D., 1943; student U. Mich., 1943; m. Alice Luken, June 7, 1941; children—Wendell Sherman, Terry Ann. Fgn. service officer, 1947—; vice- consul Am. consulate, Kobe, Japan, 1948-49; consul, 2d sec. Am. embassy, Tokyo, Japan, 1949-52, 1st sec., 1955-59; consul, 2d sec. Am. embassy, London, Eng., 1953-55; assigned Nat. War Coll., 1959-60; dep. chief personnel operations Dept. State, 1960-62; dep. chief mission Am. embassy, Copenhagen, Denmark, 1962-65; dir. Performance Evaluation Program, Dept. State, 1965-67; civil adminstr. Ryukyn Islands, 1967-69; exec. dir. Bur. European Affairs, Dept. State, 1969—. Served to 1st lt. AUS, 1943-47. Decorated U.S. Army Distinguished Civilian Service award, 1969. Mem. Phi Beta Kappa, Sigma Pi Sigma. Home: 3169 N Pollard St Arlington VA Office: Dept State Washington DC

CARPENTER, THOMAS EARL, publishing co. exec.; b. Nashville, Dec. 1, 1925; s. Charles Hugo and Ethel Powers (Wilson) C.; student Carson Newman Coll., Jefferson City, Tenn., 1944-45, Duke, 1945-46; B.S., George Peabody Coll., 1947, M.A., 1948; m. Mildred Ann Reynolds, Dec. 18, 1946; children—Mary Stephanie, Thomas Earl, Emily Reynolds, Laurale. Tchr. math. Springfield (Tenn.) High Sch., 1948-52; gen. mgr. Reynolds Co., Nashville, 1952-58; with Abingdon Press, Nashville and N.Y.C., 1958-61, 63-70, mgr., 1963-70; v.p. Methodist Pub. House, Nashville, 1970—. Trustee Martin Coll., Pulaski, Tenn. Mem. Protestant Ch.-Owned Pubs. Assn., Religious Pubs. Group, Assn. Am. Meth. Socs., Coop. Publn. Assn. (officer 1970—), Nashville Met. C. of C., Phi Delta Kappa. Meth. (exec. com., chmn. com. membership materials, 1963—; chmn. ofcl. bd. 1963-69). Home: 512 Alta Loma Dr Goodlettsville TN 37072 Office: 201 8th Av S Nashville TN 37203

CARPENTER, THOMAS G., univ. pres.; b. Atlanta, Feb. 27, 1926; s. Walker Glenn and Loretta (Jackson) C.; student Ga. Inst. Tech., 1943-45; B.S., Memphis State U., 1949; M.A., Baylor U., 1950; Ph.D., U. Fla., 1963; m. Oneida P. Carpenter, Oct. 30, 1948; children—Debra, Thomas Glenn. Gen. mgr. Laundry & Cleaning Co., Memphis, 1950-54; instr. econs. U. Fla., Gainesville, 1957-59; asst. dir. housing, 1959-64; bus. mgr. U. W. Fla., 1965, dean adminstrn. affairs, 1965-67, v.p. for adminstrn. affairs, 1967-69; pres. U. N. Fla., Jacksonville, 1969—. Mem. Jacksonville Symphony Assn., Beta Gamma Sigma, Phi Delta Theta. Clubs: University, Deerwood, St. Johns, Ponte Verde. Address: U North Fla Jacksonville FL 33606

CARPENTER, WALTER SAMUEL, Jr., industrialist; b. Wilkesbarre, Pa., Jan. 8, 1888; s. Walter S. and Belle (Morgan) C.; prep. edn., Wyoming Sem., Kingston, Pa., 1902- 06; student Cornell U., 1906-10; m. Mary Wootten, June 3, 1914; children—Walter Samuel III, John W., Edmund N. II. With E.I. du Pont de Nemours & Co., Wilmington, Del., 1909—, v.p., 1919- 40, pres. 1940-48, chmn., 1948-62, now hon. chmn.; dir. Christiana Securities Co. Trustee emeritus Wyoming Sem., Kingston, Pa.; trustee, past pres. U. Del. Methodist. Clubs: Wilmington, Wilmington Country; Fisher's Island (N.Y.); Racquet and Tennis (N.Y.C.). Home: 17th St and Rising Sun Lane Wilmington DE 19807 Office: du Pont Bldg Wilmington DE 19801

CARPENTER, WILLIAM BERNARD, utilities exec.; b. Sallisaw, Okla., June 18, 1918; s. William H. and Gussie (McPeters) C.; B.S., U. Okla., 1949; m. Emma Elizabeth Ambrister, Oct. 10, 1942; children—William Bernard, Pamela E. (Mrs. W.R. Stewart), Deborah K. With Pub. Service Co. of Okla., Tulsa, 1949—, spl. asst. to controller, 1952-60, asst. controller, 1960-65, controller, 1965—. Scoutmaster, asst. area commr. Indian Nations council Boy Scouts Am., 1960-67. Pres. Tulsa Area Christian Church Ministry; bd. dirs. Tulsa Christian Found. Served with USAAF, 1943-45. Mem. Adminstrv. Mgmt. Soc. (pres. Tulsa chpt. 1964-65). Mem. Christian Ch. (past chmn. bd.). Kiwanian (pres. Tulsa 1969-70). Home: 3817 S 90th East Av Tulsa OK 74145 Office: 600 S Main St Tulsa OK 74102

CARPER, WOOD BOWYER, Jr., clergyman, retired educator; b. Iron Gate, Va., June 29, 1909; s. Wood Bowyer and Louise Burks (Cox) C.; A.B., U. of South, 1932; student Va. Episcopal Sem., 1933-35; S.T.B., Episcopal Theol. Sch., 1936; D.D., Seabury-Western Theol. Sem., 1953; m. Eleanor Robson, June 10, 1935; children—Thomas Robson, Nicholas Wood, Timothy Scott. Ordained priest P.E. Ch., 1936, deacon, 1936; curate St. Peter's Ch., Morristown, N.J., 1936-37; rector Trinity Ch., Pawtucket, R.I., 1937-39, Calvary Ch., Fletcher, N.C., 1939-40; chaplain Episcopalian students Princeton, 1940-44; rector Ch. of the Holy Spirit, Lake Forest, Ill., 1946-56; Eugene Augustus Hoffman prof. pastoral theology Gen. Theol. Sem., N.Y.C., 1956-71. Served as lt., Chaplains Corps, USNR, 1944- 46. Mem. Ch. Hist. Soc., Phi Beta Kappa. Home: 300 Ruffner Dr Lewisburg WV 24901

CARPINO, LOUIS A., educator, chemist; b. Des Moines, Dec. 13, 1927; s. Pete and Angela (Ortale) C.; B.S., Ia. State Coll., 1950; M.S., U. Ill., 1951, Ph.D., 1953; m. Barbara Pepe, Aug. 30, 1958; children—Philip, Alexandra, Nicholas, Christine, Elizabeth, Margaret. Mem. faculty U. Mass., Amherst, 1954—, prof. chemistry, 1967—. Mem. Am., German chem. socs., Chem. Soc. London. Research, publs. on devel. new synthetic techniques in field of organic chemistry. Home: 11 Mount Pleasant St Amherst MA 01002

CARR, ALBERT ZOLOTKOFF, writer, former govt. ofcl.; b. Chgo., Jan. 15, 1902; s. Leon and Fannie (Ogus) Z.; B.S., U. Chgo., 1921; A.M., Columbia, 1926; student London Sch. Econs., 1936; m. Anne Kingsbury, Dec. 13, 1943. Editor, Business Tng. Corp., 1927-30; asst. to pres. Tradeways, Inc., 1931-33; author of books and contbr. to Sat. Eve. Post, Harpers mag., Cosmopolitan, Life, This Week, 1931-41; asst. to chmn. WPB, 1942-44; econ. adviser White House staff, 1944-46; cons. Inter-Allied Reparation Agy., Brussels, Belgium, 1946-47, 49; cons. to Pres. Truman, 1948-52; mem. WPB Mission to Eng., 1943, to China, 1944; mem. White House Mission to Pres. of China, 1945, of Inter-Allied Reparations Mission to Germany, 1947. Decorated Order of Victory (Republic of China), 1945. Author: Juggernaut: The Path of Dictatorship, 1939; Men of Power, rev. edit., 1956; American's Last Chance, 1940; Napoleon Speaks, 1941; Truman, Stalin and Peace, 1950; How to Attract Good Luck, 1952; The Black Kitten (1st prize Queen's Awards 1955); The Coming of War, 1960; John D. Rockefeller's Secret Weapon, 1962; The World and William Walker, 1963; A Matter of Life and Death: How Wars Get Started or Are Prevented, 1966; Business As a Game, 1968; (pseudonym A.B. Carbury) The Girl With the Glorious Genes, 1968; Finding Maubee, 1971. Home: Truro Cape Cod MA Office: 290 9th Av New York City NY

CARR, ARCHIE F., biologist; b. Mobile, June 16, 1909; s. Archibald Fairly and Louise Gordon (Deaderick) C.; B.S., U. Fla., 1932, M.S., 1934, Ph.D., 1937; m. Marjorie Harris, Jan. 1, 1937; children—Marjorie, Archie III, Stephen, Thomas, David. Mem. faculty U. Fla., 1937—, now prof. zoology, also curator zool. scis. Fla. State Mursum; prof. biology Escuela Agricola Panamericana, Honduras, 1945-49; research asso. Am. Mus. Natural History, 1951—; tech. dir. Caribbean Conservation Corp., 1961, exec. v.p., tech. dir., 1968—; Am. Philos. Soc. expdn. to Panama, Costa Rica, Trinidad, 1953, NSF expdn. Central Am., 1955, Brazil, French West Africa, Portugal and Azores, 1956, Union of South Africa, Argentina, Chile, 1958, Africa, Madagascar, 1963, Caribbean, yearly 1960—; prin. investigator marine turtle migrations project NSF, 1955—, Office Naval Research, 1961—. Recipient Daniel Giraud Elliott medal Nat. Acad. Sci.; O'Henry award for prize stories of 1956; John Burroughs medal for exemplary nature writing; 1st ann. research award Sigma Xi, U. Fla., Merit award Fla. Audubon Soc., 1961. Mem. Am. Soc. Ichthyologists and Herpetologists, Am. Soc. Naturalists, Fla. Acad. Sci. (1st Ann. Honors medal 1963), East African Wildlife Soc., Internat. Union Conservation Nature (survival service commn.), Phi Beta Kappa, Sigma Xi. Author: Handbook of Turtles, 1952; High Jungles and Low, 1952; The Windward Road, 1955; (with Coleman Goin) Guide to the Reptiles, Amphibians and Freshwater Fishes to Florida, 1956; Guideposts of Animal Navigation, 1962; The Reptiles, 1963; Ulendo, 1964; African Wildlife, 1964; So Excellent a Fishe: A Natural History of Sea Turtles, 1967. Home: Micanopy FL 32667 Office: U Fla Gainesville FL 32601

CARR, ARTHUR JAPHETH, educator; b. Bad Axe, Mich., Apr. 21, 1914; s. Arthur Wellesley and Margaret (McAuslan) C.; A.B., U. Mich., 1935; A.M., Syracuse U., 1937; Ph.D., U. Ill., 1947; m. Penelope Gall, Feb. 1, 1964; children by previous marriage—Jennifer (Mrs. John McGee), Adam Fyfe, Daniel Arthur, Alice (Mrs. Jan A. Van den Broek III). Instr. English, Syracuse U., 1937-40, U. Ill., 1947-49; mem. faculty U. Mich., 1949-67, prof. English, 1961- 67; prof. English, chmn. dept. Williams Coll., Williamstown, Mass., 1967—, Edward Dorr Griffin prof., 1970—; cons. U.S. Office Edn., 1965-69. Ednl. Testing Service, Coll. Entrance Exam. Bd., 1966-71; dir. Nat. Def. Edn. Act Inst. U. Mich., 1965. Served with USNR, 1943-45; PTO. Mem. Modern Lang. Assn., Nat. Council Tchrs. English, Am. Assn. U. Profs., Phi Beta Kappa, Phi Eta Sigma, Phi Kappa Phi. Editor: Victorian Poetry; Clough to Kipling, 1959; co-editor: Norton Anthology of Poetry, 1970. Contbr. articles to profl. jours. Home: Green River Rd Williamstown MA 01267

CARR, BRAXTON BRAGG, assn. exec.; b. Enterprise, Ala., Apr. 1, 1911; s. Richard and Arrie (Culpepper) C.; A.B., Howard Coll., 1932; m. Jordan McMurry, Apr. 4, 1939; children—Braxton Bragg, Rebecca Jordan, Rena Deborah. Reporter, Birmingham (Ala.) News, 1929-32, Birmingham Age Herald, 1932-33; reporter, news editor Birmingham Post, 1933-40; cables editor Pitts. Press, 1941-42; pub. relations staff various trade assns., 1946-51; exec. v.p. Warrior-Tombighee Devel. Assn., Birmingham, 1952-55; with Am. Waterways Operators, Inc., 1956—, pres., 1957—. Served with USNR, 1943-45. Mem. Internat. Assn. Nav. Congresses (mem. U.S. nat. commn.). Home: 11008 Ardwick Dr Rockville MD 20852 Office: 1250 Connecticut Av Washington DC 20036

CARR, CHALMERS RANKIN, orthopedic surgeon; b. Asheville, N.C., Oct. 27, 1907; s. Claude and Annie (Rankin) C.; A.B., Davidson Coll., 1928; postgrad. U. N.C. Med. Sch., 1931-33; M.D., Jefferson Med. Coll., Phila., 1936; m. Willie Alexander, May 8, 1933; children—Chalmers Rankin, William A., Alice Alexander. Intern, Jefferson Med. Coll. Hosp., 1936-38; commd. lt. (j.g.) M.C., USN, 1938, advanced through grades to capt., 1951; fellow orthopedic surgery Lahey Clinic, Boston, 1943, N.C. Orthopedic Hosp., Gastonia, 1947; chief orthopedic surgery U.S. Naval Hosp., Oakland, Cal., 1948-51, U.S. Naval Hosp., Bethesda, Md., 1951-54; separated, 1954; practice in Charlotte, N.C., 1954—; pres. Miller Clinic, Inc., Charlotte, 1954—; chief orthopedic surgery Charlotte Meml. Hosp., 1958-60, 66-69; mem. staff Presbyn., Mercy hosps. Fellow Soc. Internat. de Chirurgerie Orthopedia et Traumautologic; mem. A.C.S. (bd. govs. 1966—), Am. Orthopedic Assn., Am. Acad. Orthopedic Surgeons, A.M.A., Mecklenberg County Med. Soc. (past pres.), Med. Soc. State N.C. (speaker ho. of dels. 1969-70), Assn. Surgeons So. R.R.'s (pres. 1966), Charlotte C. of C., N.C. Orthopaedic Soc. (past pres.), Pi Kappa Phi, Phi Chi. Republican. Presbyn. Clubs: Charlotte Country; Quail Hollow. Contbr. articles to med. jours. Home: 1715 Queens Rd Charlotte NC 28207 Office: 1822 Brunswick Av Charlotte NC 28207

CARR, CHARLES ALBERT, tobacco co. exec.; b. Greenville, N.C., Aug. 23, 1907; s. Charles S. and Pattie (Skinner) C.; B.S. in Commerce, U. N.C., 1929; m. Sarah P. Badham, Oct. 22, 1938; children—Sarah Paxton, Charles Albert, Henrietta Skinner. Supr. purchases E. B. Ficklen Tobacco Co., Greenville, 1929-33, 34-38, also dir.; mgr. Pacific Leaf Tobacco Co., Shanghai, China, 1933-34; supr. purchases Dibrell Bros., Inc., Danville, Va., 1938-42, v.p., 1943-58, pres., 1959-68, chmn. bd., 1968—, also dir.; pres. Am. Interiors, Inc., Danville, 1969—; dir. Am. Nat. Bank, Danville. Bd. dirs., mem. exec. com. Danville Meml. Hosp.; bd. dirs. Danville YMCA; trustee Va. Episcopal Sch., Lynchburg; chmn. bd. trustees St. Paul's Coll., Lawrenceville, Va. Mem. Soc. Cincinnati. Episcopalian (sr. warden). Clubs: Stratton Mountain (Vt.) Country; Farmington Country (Charlottesville, Va.); Danville Golf. Home: PO Box 681 Danville VA 24541 Office: 512 Bridge St Danville VA 24541

CARR, CHARLES FREEMAN, banker, lawyer; b. Cambridge, O., June 11, 1898; s. William T. and Jane (McCulley) C.; A.B., Western Res. U., 1921, LL.B., 1922; m. Alvira Ott, June 30, 1923; 1 dau., Barbara Jane (Mrs. William B. Roe). Admitted to Ohio bar, 1922; practice in Cleve., 1922-57; judge Common Pleas Ct., 1957-59; v.p., trust officer Soc. Nat. Bank, Cleve., 1959; now sr. v.p.; mem. firm Herbert, Laylin, Carr & Graham, 1936-42, Herbert & Carr, 1942-57; spl. counsel to atty. gens. Gilbert Bettman and John W. Bricker; spl. duty supt. under Govs. John W. Bricker, Frank J. Lauche and Thomas J. Herbert. Served with U.S. Army, 1918. Mem. Phi Gamma Delta, Phi Delta Phi. Rotarian. Clubs: Union (Cleve.); Country (Pepper Pike, O.). Home: 3248 Belvoir Blvd Beachwood OH 44122 Office: 127 Public Sq Cleveland OH 44114

CARR, CHARLES HARDY, U.S. judge; b. Coahoma, Miss., Aug. 18, 1903; s. Charles Hardy and MaiBelle (Landers) C.; A.B., Vanderbilt U., 1925; LL.B., Yale, 1926; m. Margaret Applewhite, Aug. 1, 1936; foster sons—Darrell V. Cole, James Applewhite Cole. Admitted to Tenn. bar, 1926, Cal. bar, 1931, U.S. Supreme Ct. bar, 1937; practice law, Memphis, 1926-29, Los Angeles, 1931-33, 40-43, 46-62; asst. U.S. atty. for Los Angeles, 1933- 36; spl. asst. to atty. gen. U.S., 1936-40; U.S. atty. So. Dist. Cal., 1943-46; judge U.S. Dist. Ct., Los Angeles, 1962—. Instr., Southwestern U., Los Angeles, 1930-31. Mem. regional loyalty bd. U.S. Civil Serv. Commn., 1949-52. Mem. Am., N.Y. State, Los Angeles County, Internat. (patron) bar assns., Phi Alpha Delta, Kappa Alpha. Clubs: Bel-Air Country, Bel Air Bay (Pacific Palisades, Cal.); Oahu Country, Outrigger Canoe (Honolulu). Home: 655 Endrino Pl Beverly Hills CA 90210 Office: US Ct House 312 N Spring St Los Angeles CA 90012

CARR, CHARLES JELLEFF, pharmacologist, educator; b. Balt., Mar. 27, 1910; s. Joshua Barney and Pearl (Jelleff) C.; B.S. (Garvan scholar), U. Md., 1933, M.S., 1934, Ph.D. (Emerson fellow), 1937; D.Sc. (hon.), Purdue U., 1964; m. Mary Agnes McGrath, June 14, 1932; children—Daniel Jelleff, Noel Edward, Joseph Barney. Teaching asst. pharmacology Sch. Medicine, U. Md., 1934-35, instr., 1935-37, asst. prof., 1937-39, asso. prof., 1939-50, prof., 1950-55, adj. prof., 1957—; prof., chmn. dept. pharmacology Sch. Pharmacy, Purdue U., 1955-57; chief pharmacology unit Psychopharmacology Service Center, Nat. Inst. Mental Health, Bethesda, Md., 1957-63; chief sci. analysis br., life scis. div. Army Research Office, Office Chief Research and Devel. U.S. Army, Arlington, Va., 1963-67; dir. Life Scis. Research Office, Fedn. Am. Socs. for Exptl. Biology, Bethesda, 1967—; spl. lectr. Georgetown U. Sch. Medicine; instr. physicians course chem. warfare Emergency Med. Service, Balt. Third Civilian Def. Region, 1943. Merit badge councilor for chemistry and pub. health Boy Scouts Am., 1957- -. Recipient U.S. Army Meritorious Civilian award, 1965, 68. Fellow N.Y. Acad. Scis., Am. Coll. Neuropsychopharmacology; mem. Am. Soc. Pharmacology and Exptl. Therapeutics, Am. Chem. Soc. (life), Am. Pharm. Assn., Soc. Exptl. Biology and Medicine, Sigma Xi, Kappa Psi. Author: (with Krantz) Pharmacologic Principles of Medical Practice, 7th edit., 1969; also articles. Home: 6010 River Meadow Dr Ellicott City MD 21043 Office: 9650 Rockville Pike Bethesda MD 20014

CARR, DAVID TURNER, physician; b. Richmond, Va., Mar. 12, 1914; s. John Ernest and Mary Lela (King) C.; student U. Richmond, 1931-33; M.D., Med. Coll. Va., 1937; M.S. in Medicine, Mayo Grad. Sch. Medicine, 1947; m. Rosemary Rudow, June 18, 1948 (div. 1953); 1 dau., Jennifer Anne. Intern, then asst. resident Grady Hosp., Atlanta, 1937-39; resident chest diseases Bellevue Hosp., N.Y.C.,

1940-41; fellow medicine Mayo Clinic, 1943-47, cons. medicine, 1947—; prof. clin. medicine Mayo Grad. Sch. Medicine, 1964—. Mem.-at-large bd. dirs. Nat. Tb and Respiratory Disease Assn., 1959—, v.p., 1971-72. Bd. dirs. Rochester Civic Theatre, 1951-70, pres., 1965-67; bd. dirs. at large Am. Cancer Soc. Fellow A.C.P., A.A.A.S.; mem. Central Soc. Clin. Research, Am. Thoracic Soc. (v.p. 1963-64), Rochester C. of C. (pres. 1959-60); hon. mem. Peruvian Anti-Tb Assn.; affiliate mem. Royal Soc. Medicine (Eng.). Spl. research pulmonary diseases. Home: 1211 8 / St SE Rochester MN 55901 Office: Mayo Clinic Rochester MN 55901

CARR, DONALD, lawyer; b. Leeds, Eng., June 23, 1928; grad. Osgoode Hall. Admitted to Ont. bar, 1951; partner firm Goodman & Carr, Toronto. Mem. Queens Counsel, 1964. Chmn. bd. United Jewish Welfare Fund Toronto; treas. Canadian Jewish Congress. Mem. Canadian Bar Assn. (mem. comml. law sect.), Law Soc. Upper Can., Lawyers Club Toronto (corr. sec. 1965-66), Internat. Council Shopping Centers (mem. law com.) County York Law Assn., Canadian Tax Found. Office: 44 Victoria St Toronto 1 Ontario Canada*

CARR, EARLE WESTCOTT, lawyer, milling co. exec.; b. Solomon, Kan., Feb. 8, 1906; s. Clement V. and Lillian (Fasold) C.; A.B., Earlham Coll., 1927; LL.B., Harvard, 1930; m. Penelope Keifer, Aug. 17, 1933; children—Robert W., David W. Admitted to Mass. bar, 1930, since practiced in Boston; sr. partner firm Gaston, Snow, Motley & Holt, and predecessors, 1955—. Dir. Bay State Milling Co., Winona, Minn., First County Nat. Bank, Brockton, Mass., The Talbots of Hingham, Mass., Howe & Bainbridge, Inc., Boston, Morton C. Tuttle Co., Boston. Moderator, Hingham, 1955-60. Republican. Clubs: Harvard (Boston); Hingham Tennis; Cohasset (Mass.) Tennis. Home: 52 Fearing Rd Hingham MA 02043 Office: Prudential Center Boston MA 02199

CARR, EDWARD HALLETT, historian, author; b. June 28, 1892; ed. Trinity Coll., Cambridge (Eng.) U. Temporary clk. Brit. Fgn. Office, 1916; with Brit. delegation to Peace Conf., 1919; temporary sec. Brit. embassy, Paris, France, 1920-21; assigned Fgn. Office, 1922-25, 29-30; 2d sec. legation, Riga, 1925-29; asst. adviser League of Nations affairs, 1930-33, 1st sec., 1933; resigned from Fgn. Service, 1936; Wilson prof. internat. politics Univ. Coll., Wales, Aberystwyth, 1936- 47; dir. fgn. publicity Ministry Information, 1939-40; asst. editor The Times, 1941-46; tutor politics Balliol Coll., Oxford U., 1935-55; fellow Trinity Coll., Cambridge U., 1955—. Decorated comdr. Order Brit. Empire, 1920. Author: Dostoevsky, 1931; The Romanitc Exiles, 1933; Karl Marx: A Study in Fanaticism, 1934; International Relations Since the Peace Treaty, 1937; Michael Bakunin, 1937; The Twenty Years Crisis, 1919- 1939, 1939; Britain: A Study in Foreign Policy from Versailles to the Outbreak of the War, 1939; Conditions of Peace, 1942; Nationalism and After, 1945; The Soviet Impact on the Western World, 3946; Studies in Revolution, 1950; A History of Soviet Russia, vol. I, 1950, vol. II, 1952, vol. III, 1953 (all under title The Bolshevik Revolution, 1917- 1923), vol. IV, 1954 (The Interregnum, 1923-1924), vol. V, 1958, vol. VI, 1959 (Socialism in One Century, 1924-1926), vol. VII (2 parts), 1964, vol. VIII (Foundations of a Planned Economy) 2 parts, 1969; German-Soviet Relations Between the Two World Wars, 1919-1939, 1951; The New Society, 1951; What is History?, 1961. Clubs: Oxford and Cambridge. Address: Trinity Coll Cambridge England

CARR, FRANCIS THOMAS, lawyer; b. Mahanoy City, Pa., Dec. 9, 1923; s. James Francies and Anne (Durkin) C.; B.S. in Chem. Engring., Lehigh U., 1944; LL.B., U. Va., 1948; m. Cora Virginia Gay, Aug. 12, 1950; children- Gay Margaret, David Francis. Admitted to N.Y. bar, 1949; asso. firm Kenyon & Kenyon, N.Y.C., 1948-56, mem. firm, 1956—; sr. partner Kenyon & Kenyon, Reilly, Carr & Chapin, N.Y.C., 1969—. Bd. dirs. Stewart House, N.Y.C., 1964-68. Served with USNR, 1944-46; PTO. Mem. Am. Bar Assn., N.Y. Patent Law Assn., N.Y. County Lawyers Assn., Internat. Patent and Trademark Assn., Lawyers' Club, Order of Coif, Phi Delta Theta, Delta Theta Phi. Republican. Episcopalian. Club: New Seabury Country (Mass.). Home: 70 E 10th St New York NY 10003 also 80 Waterway New Seabury MA Office: 59 Maiden Lane New York NY 10038

CARR, FRANK CHARLES, ins. co. exec.; b. Chgo., Mar. 4, 1913; s. Harry Landis and Mabel (Teed) C.; student pub. schs.; m. Elizabeth Frye, Feb. 10, 1940; children—Stephanie, Frank, Victoria. With First Nat. Bank, Palm Beach, Fla., 1935-36; with John Nuveen & Co., Chgo., 1936-69, retiring as chmn. bd.; pres. Am. Municipal Bond Assurance Co., Milw., 1971—; dir. Ontario Motor Speedway, Inc. (Cal.). Mem. Municipal Forums N.Y. and Washington. Clubs: Milw. Athletic; Municipal Bond, Union League, Executives (Chgo.); Bankers (N.Y.C.). Home: 3357 N Lake Dr Milwaukee WI 53211 Office: 600 Marine Plaza Milwaukee WI 53201

CARR, FRANKLIN DAVID, hosp. adminstr.; b. Kansas City, Mo., Dec. 10, 1912; s. David F. and Ruth (Stewart) C.; B.S. in Physiology, U. Chgo., 1935; m. Annetta Lang Purvis, June 28, 1956. Tech. sales corr. E.I. duPont de Nemours & Co., Chgo., 1936-42; hosp. adminstr. Door County Meml. Hosp., Sturgeon Bay, Wis., 1946-48, Waukesha (Wis.) Meml. Hosp., 1948-54, Detroit Meml. Hosp., 1954; now adminstr. Detroit-Macomb Hosps. Assn.; dir. Mich. Med. Service, 1958-64; mem. exec. com., dir. Greater Detroit Area Hosp. Council, 1958-64; chmn. research com. Mich. Hosp. Service, 1959-61; dir., mem. exec. com. Hosp. Research and Ednl. Res. Mich., Inc., 1965-68. Served to maj. USMCR, 1942-46. Fellow Am. Coll. Hosp. Adminstrs.; mem. Am. (chmn. purchasing, simplification, standardization com. 1965-68), Mich. (trustee, mem. exec. com. 1961-65) hosp. assns. Clubs: Econ., Detroit Golf (Detroit). Home: 339 Grosse Pointe Blvd Grosse Pointe Farms, MI Office: 1420 St Antoine St Detroit MI 48226

CARR, GILBERT RANDLE, railroad ofcl.; b. Rockford, Ill., Jan. 4, 1928; s. Audra Clifford and Marjorie (Lantz) C.; B.S. in Accounting and Mgmt., U. Ill., 1950; m. Marion Minnie Heinemann, Mar. 28, 1953; children—John W., J. Michael. With Arthur Andersen & Co., C.P.A.'s, Chgo., 1950-57; with C.& N. W. Ry., 1957—, comptroller, 1967—. Served with AUS, 1946-47. Lutheran. Home: 8467 W Sunnyside Av Chicago IL 60656. Office: 400 W Madison Av Chicago IL 60606

CARR, HAROLD NOFLET, airlines exec.; b. Kansas City, Kan., Mar. 14, 1921; s. Noflet B. and Mildred (Addison) C.; B.S., Tex. A. and M. U., 1943; postgrad. Am. U., 1945-46; m. Mary Elizabeth Smith, Aug. 5, 1944; children—Steven Addison, Hal Douglas, James Taylor, Scott Noflet. Asst. dir. route devel. Trans World Airlines, Inc., 1943-47; exec. v.p. Wis. Central Airlines, Inc., 1947-52; mem. McKinsey & Co., 1952-54; now chmn. bd., chief exec. officer North Central Airlines, Inc., Mpls.; professorial lectr. mgmt. engring. Am. U., 1952-62; pres. T.L.&C. Co.; dir. April Corp., First Internat. Corp., GCO, Inc., Temp Con, Inc. Mem. bd. nominations Nat. Aviation Hall of Fame. Councilor Tex. A. and M. Research Found.; bd. dirs. Met. Area Safety Council Minn. Mem. Nat. Aero. Assn., World Bus. Council, Am. Assn. Airport Execs., A.I.M. (pres.'s council), Smithsonian Assos., Minn. Execs. Orgn., Nat. Def. Transp. Assn., Pine Beach Peninsula Assn., Young Presidents' Orgn., Am. Econ. Assn., Mpls., St. Paul chambers commerce, Tex. A. and M. Former Students Assn., Air Transport Assn. Am. (dir.), Assn. Local Transport Airlines (dir.). Episcopalian. Clubs: Midway Civic (St. Paul); Nat. Aviation, Aero (Washington); Minneapolis; Racquet (Miami); Gull Lake Yacht (Brainerd, Minn.); Southdale Racquets; Stearman Alumnus; Briarcrest Country (Bryan). Home: 3505 Parkway Terrace Bryan TX 77801 Office: 7500 Northliner Dr Minneapolis MN 55450

CARR, HOWARD EARL, educator, physicist; b. Headland, Ala., Sept. 16, 1915; s. Samuel Tilden and Annie Bell (Freeman) C.; B.S., Auburn U., 1936; M.A., U. Va., 1939, Ph.D., 1941; m. Carolyn Taylor, June 25, 1939; children—Howard Earl, Carolyn Ann. Research asst. U.Va., 1939-41; asso. prof. physics U. S.C., 1941-43; physicist for Ford, Bacon & Davis, Oak Ridge diffusion plant, 1944; asst. prof. physics U.S. Naval Acad., 1946-48; asso. prof. physics Auburn U., 1948-53, prof., head dept., 1953—; researcher Oak Ridge Nat. Lab., 1950, cons., 1951-55; cons. USAF, 1957-61, U. S. Army, 1966-68; spl. research separation isotopes, negative ion studies, ion optics, Mossbauer effect. Regional coordinator Ala. Sci. Fair. Served with USNR, 1944-46. Fellow Am. Phys. Soc. (sec. S.E. sect. 1956-67, pres. 1968), A.A.A.S.; mem. Ala. Acad. Sci. (pres. 1957), Am. Inst. Physics (counselor Ala. 1962-69), Am. Assn. Physics Tchrs., Ala. Edn. Assn., Sigma Xi, Phi Kappa Phi, Sigma Pi Sigma, Raven Soc., Blue Key. Methodist. Kiwanian. Home: 342 Payne St Auburn AL

CARR, HUBERT FRANKLIN, steamship co. exec.; b. Pitts., Nov. 20, 1920; s. Peter J. and Grace (Franklin) C.; student N.Y.U., 1942-48; LL.B., Bklyn. Law Sch., 1952; m. Pierina Paccioretti, June 7, 1947; children—John P., Peter J. Admitted to N.Y. bar, 1953; clk. Mason Dixon Lines, Newark, 1938-39, L.C. Smith Typewriter Co., 1939-41; with Moore-McCormack Lines, Inc., N.Y.C., 1941—, sec., 1960—, v.p. claims and ins., 1971—; dir. Container Terminals N.Y., Portsmouth Terminals. Bd. dirs. A.V. Moore Found., E.J. McCormack Found., St. Joseph Regional High Sch., Montvale, N.J. Mem. N.Y. County Lawyers Assn., N.Y. State Bar Assn., Maritime Law Assn., Am. Soc. Corporate Secs. Home: 51 Woodland Dr Woodcliff Lake NJ 07675 Office: 2 Broadway Av New York City NY 10004

CARR, ISAAC NEWTON, coll. dean emeritus; b. Gatlinburg, Tenn., Feb. 29, 1892; s. Marion and Rosan (McCarter) C.; A.B., Carson-Newman Coll., 1916, LL.B., 1941; postgrad. U. Poitiers (France), 1919; A.M., U. N.C., 1925; postgrad. (Angier Duke fellow) Duke, 1927-29; m. Lena Bird, June 26, 1920 (dec. Apr. 1962); children—James Clyde, Wilbur Lloyd, Glenn Frank, Marion Turley; m. 2d, Freda West Blanc, July 6, 1963. Supt. schs., Willacoochee, Ga., 1916-17; prin. Church Hill (Tenn.) High Sch., 1919-20, Yancey Collegiate Inst., Burnsville, N.C., 1920-23; dean, prof. polit. sci. and history Mars Hill (N.C.) Coll., 1923-42; instr. Wake Forest-Meredith Coll., summer sessions, 1934-41; prof. history and polit. sci. Carson-Newman Coll., 1945—, chmn. history and polit. sci. dept., 1968—; acad. dean, 1947-57, emeritus, 1957—; vis. prof. history and polit. sci. Grand Canyon Coll., Phoenix, 1959-61, Beimont Coll., 1965-67. Chmn. Madison County (N.C.) Welfare Bd., 1937-42; mem. N.C. Gov.'s Interracial Commn., 1927-42. Bd. dirs. Cherokee-Douglas Tb Assn., Carson-Newman Alumni Assn. Served to lt. col. U.S. Army, 1917-19, 42-45. Recipient certificate award U.S. Army, 1945; resolution of appreciation Carson-Newman Coll. faculty, 1948. Mem. Am., Miss. Valley, East Tenn., Tenn., So. hist. assns., Am. Assn. U. Profs., Civitan, Southeastern Athletic Assn. of Jr. Colls. (pres., 1930-31), S.A.R. Democrat. Baptist. Mason. Club: Schoolmaster's (pres. Asheville, N.C.). Author: History of Carson-Newman College, 1962. Contbr. numerous articles to newspapers and mags., 1925—. Home: 710 S Russell Av Jefferson City TN 37760

CARR, JAMES KENNEDY, city ofcl.; b. Redding, Cal., Jan. 15, 1914; s. Francis and Mary (Kennedy) C.; B.S. in Civil Engring., U. Santa Clara (Cal.), 1934; D.Eng. (hon.), 1968; m. Katherine Kergan, Oct. 14, 1939; children—Mary, Ann (Mrs. Gene Dahlosto), Susan (Mrs. Michael Taylor), Margaret (Mrs. Dino Boito). Engr. with WPA, geol. surveyor Dept. Interior, Shasta County (Cal.) Surveyor's Office, city engr.'s office, Redding, 1934-36; with Bur. Reclamation, Dept. Interior, 1936-51, planning, constrn. and operations dir. Shasta Dam, 1936-40, Keswick Dam, 1945-51, Orland Project, 1945-51, dir. studies Trinity and Feather River projects, 1946-51, dist. mgr. all activities in Cal. north of Sacramento, 1946-51; engring. cons. com. interior and insular affairs U.S. Ho. of Reps., 1951-53; asst. gen. mgr. Sacramento Municipal Utility Dist., 1953-61; under sec. Dept. Interior, Washington, 1961-64; gen. mgr. pub. utilities City-County of San Francisco, 1964-70; dir. San Francisco Internat. Airport, 1970—. Chmn. Cal. Water Commn., 1959-61. Bd. regents U. Santa Clara, 1959-65. Registered profl. engr., Cal., D.C. Fellow Am. Soc. C.E. (Civil Govt. award 1964); mem. Sacramento C. of C., Airport Operators Internat. (2d v.p. 1970). Rotarian, K.C. Club: Serra (San Francisco). Home: 1420 Marlborough Rd Hillsborough CA 94010 Office: San Francisco Internat Airport San Francisco CA 94128

CARR, JAY PHILLIP, newspaper critic; b. N.Y.C., Aug. 19, 1936; s. Andrew Joseph and Florence (Glassman) C.; B.S., City Coll. N.Y., 1958; m. Nancy Lou Hutchison, Oct. 27, 1962; children—Diane Elizabeth, Richard Joseph, Julia Veronica. Reporter, Jersey City Jour., 1957; editorial asst., amusement dept. staff writer N.Y. Post, 1957-64; drama and music critic Detroit News, 1964—. Served with AUS, 1960-62. Office: Detroit News Bldg Detroit MI 48231

CARR, JESSE LAWRENCE, pathologist; b. Pembina, N.D., Oct. 8, 1901; s. Harry C. and Ethel (Purdy) C.; B.S., U. Cal., 1923; M.D., Harvard, 1927; m. Louise Barrows, Aug. 28, 1930 (dec. 1951); m. 2d, Elsie Marclay, Apr. 7, 1957. Intern surg. staff L.I. Coll. Hosp., Bklyn., 1928; ambulance surgeon, N.Y.C., 1928; asst. resident surgery U. Cal. Hosp., 1929, asst. resident pathology, 1929-30, asst. vis. pathologist, 1930-32; instr. pathology and legal medicine, 1944-50, clin. prof. pathology, 1950—, prof. legal medicine, 1949—, also chmn. dept.; lectr. dept. criminology U. Cal.; vis. pathologist San Francisco City and County Hosp., 1930-32, vis. pathologist, chief staff, 1932—; vis. pathologist Laguna Home, 1930-32; pathologist, dir. labs. Franklin Hosp., San Francisco, 1937-63, Shriner's Hosp., 1939-65, Garden Hosp., 1946-63, Chinese Hosp., 1947-69; vis. prof. pathology U. Indonesia, 1955-56. Decorated Kings Naval Medal (Sweden). Mem. A.M.A., Am. Soc. Clin. Pathologists, Am. Soc. Exptl. Pathology, Am. Assn. Pathologists and Bacteriologists, A.A.A.S., Cal. Heart Assn., Soc. Exptl. Biology and Medicine, San Francisco County Med. Soc., San Francisco County Pathol. Soc., Harvard Med. Alumni Assn., Cal. Delta Chi Alumni Assn., Nu Sigma Nu Alumni Assn. Clubs: Aesculapias (Boston); St. Francis Yacht (San Francisco); Cruising Club Am. Contbr. profl. publs. Home: 337 Margarita Dr San Rafael, CA Office: San Francisco Hosp San Francisco CA 94110

CARR, JOE CORDELL, sec. state Tenn.; b. Cookeville, Tenn., June 20, 1907; s. Sidney Forrest and Laura (Burton) C.; student pub. schs., Nashville; m. Mary Oliver Hart, Sept. 12, 1934; children—Carolyn (Mrs. George N. Welch III), Joe Cordell. Bill clk. Tenn. Ho. of Reps., 1929-33, asst. chief clk., 1933-37, reading clk., 1937-39, chief clk., 1939-41, 53-55; sec. state State of Tenn., Nashville, 1941-45, 47-49, 57—. Pres. Tenn. Bapt. Brotherhood. Organizer, sec. Young Democratic Clubs Tenn., 1933, pres., 1934; sec. Young Dem. Clubs Am., 1937, pres., 1941. Trustee Belmont Coll. Served with AUS, 1944-45. Mem. Am. Legion, 40 and 8, Soc. Amateur Chefs. Baptist (deacon). Mason (33, Shriner, Jester). Clubs: Cumberland, Richland Country, Exchange (pres. 1954), Elks. Home: 3508 Hampton Av Nashville TN 37215 Office: State Capitol Nashville TN 37215

CARR, JOHN ARTHUR, clergyman, publisher; b. Oneonta, N.Y., Sept. 18, 1911; s. John and Mary (Rudden) C.; student Niagara U., 1930-33; S.T.B., St. Paul's Coll., Washington, 1940; M.A., Cath. U., 1943. Joined Paulist Fathers, 1933, ordained priest Roman Cath. Ch., 1940; dir. vocations Paulist Fathers, 1946-49; dir. edn. Paulists Houses Study, 1949-52; prof. philosophy St. Paul's Coll., 1944-52, prof. theology, 1952-57; exec. pub. Paulist Press, Paramus, N.J., 1957-70, Newman Press, Paramus, N.J., 1962-70, also mags. Catholic World, The Ecumenist; exec. dir. Newman Book Stores, Balt. and Washington, 1962-70, Cath. Library Service, Glen Rock, 1962-70; exec. dir. Am. Library and Ednl. Service, Glen Rock, 1963-70, dir., 1970—; dir. Paulist/Newman Press, 1970—. Vicar gen. Paulist Fathers, 1964—; v.p. Paulist Soc., 1946—. Chmn. Eckenrode Found., Westminster. Mem. American Mgmt. Assn., Cath. Ednl. Assn., Cath. Press Assn., Book Pubs. Council, Nat. Conf. Christians and Jews. Home: 86 Dromore Rd Scarsdale, NY 10583.

CARR, JOHN DICKSON, (pseudonyms, Carr Dickson, Carter Dickson), author; b. Uniontown, Pa., 1906; ed. Hill Sch., Haverford Coll.; m. Clarice Cleaves, 1931; 3 children. Writer of mystery fiction, 1930—; lived in Eng., 1931-48; worked with Adrian Conan Doyle on life of Sir Arthur Conan Doyle, 2 yrs.; now a leading authority on Sir Arthur Conan Doyle. Worker with BBC, Eng., World War II. Mem. Baker Street Irregulars. Clubs: Savage, Garrick (London). Author numerous books; latest publs.: Life of Sir Arthur Conan Doyle, 1949; Bride of Newgate, 1950; Devil in Velvet, 1951; Behind the Crimson Blind, 1952; Poison in Jest, 1952; Waxworks Murder, 1952; Nine Wrong Answers, 1952; Eight of Swords, 1953; Cavalier's Cup, 1952; Third Bullet, 1954; Captain Cut-Throat, 1955; The Dead Man's Knock, 1958; Fire Burn; Fear is the Same; Patrick Butler for the Defense; Scandal at High Chimneys; The Arabian Nights Murder; The Burning Court; In Spite of Thunder, 1960; Most Secret, 1964; Blind Barber; Case of the Constant Suicides; Corpse in the Waxworks; Dark of the Moon, 1967; House of Satan's Elbow, 1967; Castle Skull, 1968; Pappa La-Ba, 1968; Crooked Hinge; Death Watch; Emperor's Snuff Box; Four False Weapons; Ghosts' High Noon; Hag's Nook; It Walks By Night ; Lost Gallows; Mad Hatter Mystery; Men Who Explained Myster-ies; The Problem of Green Capsules; To Wake the Dead. Home: Mamaroneck NY 10543*

CARR, JOHN FISHER, mfg. co. exec., lawyer; b. Boston, Aug. 4, 1921; s. Arthur Wyman and Elsie (Laughney) C.; B.A., Williams Coll., 1946; LL.B., Harvard, 1948; m. Ruth J. Huffman, Aug. 16, 1952; children—Douglas, Jeffrey, Elizabeth. Admitted to N.Y. bar, 1949; atty. firm Sage, Gray, Todd & Sims, N.Y.C., 1948-50; asst. counsel Office Gen. Counsel, Dept. Navy, 1950-52; contract negotiator Mpls. Honeywell Regulator Co., 1953-55; with Grumman Corp., Bethpage, N.Y., 1955—, gen. counsel, 1960—, sec., 1966-70, v.p., 1970—; sec. Grumman Allied Industries, Inc., 1964-68. Pres. bd. edn., Cold Spring Harbor, N.Y., 1963-66. Served to lt. (s.g.) USNR, 1942- 45. Mem. Am. Bar Assn. Clubs: Huntington Country (sec.); Lloyd Neck Bath (Lloyd Harbor, N.Y.). Home: 24 Wawapek Rd Cold Spring Harbor, NY 11724. Office: Grumman Corp Bethpage NY 11714

CARR, MILTON L., fgn. service office; b. New Tazewell, Tenn., Feb. 15, 1917; s. Charles Ross and Mona Sue (Stanifer) C.; student U. Tenn.; corr. student U. Chgo.; spl. studies U. P.R., San Marcos U.; m. Laura Myrtle McWhorter Dec. 12, 1936; children—Susan Michael (Mrs. Charles K. House), Barbara Jane (Mrs. Richard W. Peterson), Catherine Anne, Millicent Emilie, Laura Sally. Theatre mgr., Knoxville, Tenn., 1938- 39, Miami, Fla., 1940; with U.P.I., and predecessor, 1941-62, internat. mgr. for Mexico, C.A., Panama and Cuba, 1957-60, bus. rep., Atlanta, 1960-62; dir. Peace Corps in Ecuador, 1962-63, in Venezuela, 1963-64, in Colombia, 1965-66; spl. asst. to regional dir. program devel. and operations for Latin Am., 1966; adviser govt. Thailand, AID, Dept. State, 1967-71; dep. multi-sector officer AID, Bangkok, Thailand, 1971—. Mem. Am. Fgn. Service Assn., Sigma Delta Chi. Episcopalian. Home: 20/29 Krungsri Nai Rd Muang Surin Thailand Office: US AID Am Embassy APO San Francisco CA 96346

CARR, OSCAR CLARK, Jr., cotton producer; b. Memphis, Aug. 4, 1923; s. Oscar Clark and Blanche (Busby) C.; student Cornell U., 1941-42; B.S. with distinction, U.S. Naval Acad., 1945; m. Billie Fisher, June 21, 1950; children—Oscar Clark, Blanche Busby, Palmer Scott, John T. Fisher, Elane Tucker. Pres. Carr Planting Co., cotton producer, Clarksdale Miss., 1948—; organized First Nat. Bank Clarksdale, 1964, chmn. bd., 1964-70; chmn. bd. Samuelson Cigar Co., 1964-68; pres. Holiday Inn of Clarksdale, 1957-71; mem. exec. com. Planters Oil Mill, N. Delta Congress. Pres. Planters Club Coahoma County. 1953: bd. dirs. Cotton Council Internat., 1965-68; king Memphis Cotton Carnival, 1956; pres. Delta Council 1961. Pres. Episcopalian Laymen of Miss; 1963; del. Episcopalian Gen. Conv., 1967, 1969, 70; mem. standing com. Episcopal Diocese Miss., 1967-71; participant Am. Assembly, 1969; mem. Presiding Bishop's Renewal Commn., 1965-66; mem. Joint Commn. on Ch. in Human Affairs; v.p. exec. council Episcopal Ch. for Devel., 1971—. Del. Democratic Nat. Conv., 1968; chmn. Mississippians for Robert Kennedy, 1968. Trustee St. George's Episcopal Day Sch., 1958-64. Hutchinson's Sch., All Saint's Sch., Okolona Coll., 1962-67; mem. president's council Southwestern U. Served to lt. (j.g.) USNR, 1945-47. Mem. Nat. Cotton Council, Newcomen Soc., Psi Upsilon. Home: Route 2 Box 156 Clarksdale MS 38614 Office: Route 2 Box 161 Clarksdale MS 38614 also 815 2d Av New York City NY 10017

CARR, ROBERT KENNETH, educator; b. Cleve., Feb. 15, 1908; s. Clifford A. and Sue (Stewart) C.; A.B., Dartmouth, 1929, A.M., Harvard, 1930, Ph.D., 1935; LL.D., Dartmouth, Concord, Ohio Wesleyan U., 1960, U. Pitts., 1962, Ripon College, 1967, Denison U., 1970; m. Olive Grabill, Aug. 25, 1933; children—Norman Stewart, Elliott Grabill, Robert Clifford. Mem. dept. govt., also dir. bur. municipal research U. Okla., 1931- 37; mem. dept. govt. Dartmouth, 1937-59; Parker prof. of law and polit. sci. 1948-59, dir. Great Issues course, 1955-57; Guggenheim fellow, 1954-55; pres. of Oberlin (O.) Coll., 1960-70; research scholar Am. Council Edn., 1970—. Cons. U.S. Civil Rights Commn., 1959; mem. adv. com. higher edn. Dept. Health, Edn. and Welfare, 1967-68; exec. sec. Pres.'s Com. on Civil Rights, 1947. Chmn. Hanover Democratic Com., 1940-44; mem. Hanover Sch. Bd., 1943-52. Exec. com., trustee Carnegie Found. Advancement Teaching, 1964-70; trustee Am. Council Edn., 1964-67; mem. vis. com. dept. govt. Harvard, 1965-70; acad. adv. bd. U.S. Naval Acad., 1969-71. Mem. Am. Polit. Sci. Assn. (council 1949-51), Am. Assn. U. Profs. (council 1952-53, 2d v.p. 1956-58, gen. sec. 1957-58, chmn. acad. freedom and tenure com. 1958-60), Am. Acad. Arts and Scis., New Eng. Polit. Sci. Assn. (pres. 1955-56), Phi Beta Kappa. Clubs: Century (N.Y.C.); Cosmos (Washington). Author: The Supreme Court and Judicial Review, 1942; Federal Protection of Civil Rights, 1947; American Democracy in Theory and Practice (with others), rev. edit., 1971; The Unamerican Activities Committee, 1952. Home: 2450 Virginia Av NW Washington DC 20037 Office: 1 Dupont Circle Washington DC 20036 ☆

CARR, RUSSELL EVAN, educator, mathematician; b. Evanston, Ill., Jan. 31, 1919; s. Arthur Blaine and Josie K. (Cross) C.; B.A., Simpson Coll., 1940; M.S., Ia. State U., 1942, Ph.D., 1946; m. Zoe F. Zondervan, June 1, 1940; children—Cathi (Mrs. Cathi Hankinson), Jonna (Mrs. Ira Zipperer), Bruce, David. Instr. math. Ia. State U., 1946-47; asst. prof. Mich. State U., 1947-51; research engr. N. Am. Aviation Corp., 1951-52; research specialist Jet Propulsion Lab., Cal. Inst. Tech., 1952-61; prof. geophysics Geophys. Inst., U. Alaska, 1961-64, prof. math. 1964-67; prof. math. U. Wyo., 1967—. Served with USNR, 1942-44. Mem. Am. Math. Soc., Math. Assn. Am., Soc. Indsl. and Applied Math., Sigma Xi. Club: Sierra (San Francisco). Address: Dept Mathematics U Wyo Laramie WY 82070

CARR, WAGGONER, lawyer; b. Fairlie, Tex., Oct. 1, 1918; s. Vincent and Ruth (Warlick) C.; B.A., Tex. Tech. Coll., 1940; LL.B., U. Tex., 1947; LL.D., McMurry College, Abilene, Tex., 1968; m. Ernestine Story, Dec. 21, 1941; 1 son, David William. Admitted to Tex. bar, 1946; asst. dist. atty. 72d Jud. Dist. of Tex., 1947; atty. Lubbock County, 1948-50; partner Key, Carr, Carr & Clark, Lubbock, 1951-62; atty. gen. Tex., 1963-67; partner Key, Carr, Carr & Clark, Austin, 1967-69, Carr, Osorio, Palmer, Dickson, Long & Coleman, 1969—. Mem. Tex. Ho. Reps., 1951-61, speaker, 1957-61. Served with USAAF, 1942- 45. Recipient Nat. medal Tex. Heritage Found., 1957; Distinguished Service award Vocational Agr. Tchrs. Assn. Tex., 1956; named Outstanding Atty. Gen. in Nation, Nat. Assn. Attys. Gen., 1966. Mem. Tex., Travis County bar assns., Am. Legion, Delta Theta Phi. Mason. Home: 6903 Mesa Dr Austin TX 78731 Office: Capital Nat Bank Bldg Austin TX 78701

CARR, WILLARD HERBERT, business exec.; b. N.Y.C., Sept. 28, 1904; s. Herbert Joseph and Florence Nightingale (Rosenbaum) C.; A.B., Yale, 1925; m. Adrienne Huyler Tinnerello, July 3, 1969; stepson, Joseph G. Tinnerello; 1 dau. by previous marriage, Susan (Mrs. Paul Hirschman). Served to comdr. USNR, 1941-45. Decorated Mexican Order of Aztec Eagle. Fellow Photog. Soc. Am.; mem. Royal Photog. Soc. Eng. (London), Profl. Photographers Am., Profl. Photographers Soc. N.Y., Profl. Photographers Assn. New Eng., Mil. Order World Wars (life), U.S. Naval Commandery. Republican. Conglist. Clubs: India House, Yale (N.Y.C.); U. Mexico, Mexico City Country, Bankers of Mexico; Washington (Conn.) Golf; Army-Navy (Washington). Home: Route 47 Washington CT 06793 Office: 667 Madison Av New York City NY 10021

CARR, WILLIAM BOUVARD, publisher's rep.; b. Houston, May 3, 1905; s. Walter William and Hettie Ebenezer (Minter) C.; A.B., U. Tex., 1926; student Harvard, 1926-27; m. Bess Nance, June 28, 1938 (div. June 1958); foster children—Howard Clark, Beverly Ann; 1 dau., Susan Nance (Mrs. Dudley Alan Voorhees); m. 2d, Estelle Lane, Dec. 8, 1958. Instr. English, athletic coach Austin Mil. Sch., 1923-24; salesman Crowell Pub. Co., 1927-29, Spur Pub. Co., 1929; asst. sec. Central Hanover Bank & Trust Co., N.Y.C., 1929-33; with Time mag., 1934-50; v.p., dir. McCall Corp., advt. dir. McCall's mag., 1950-58; v.p. N. W. Ayer & Sons, Inc., 1958-59; pres. Million Market Newspapers, Inc., 1959-60; partner Byron & Carr, Inc., N.Y.C., 1961; exec. v.p. Drew and Carr, Inc., Chgo., 1961-63; Midwest sales mgr. Newsweek, Inc., 1963-68; owner William B. Carr Co., Ft. Lauderdale, 1968- -. Nat. chmn. wastepaper salvage div. Periodical Pubs. Nat. Com., 1944- 45. Bd. dirs. Harris Sch., Chgo. Mem. Chgo. Fedn. Advt. Clubs (pres. 1941-42), Delat Theta Phi. Methodist. Club: Coral Ridge (Ft. Lauderdale). Address: 2500 NE 48th Lane Fort Lauderdale FL 33308

CARR, WILLIAM EMSLEY, news orgn. exec.; b. London, Eng., May 30, 1912; s. Emsley and Jenny (Carr) C.; B.A., Trinity Coll., Cambridge (Eng.) U., 1935; m. Jean Mary Forsyth, Sept. 22, 1938; children—William, Sarah. With News of World Orgn. Ltd., 1945—, pres., 1969—, chmn., 1952-69. Served to maj. Brit. Army, 1939-45. Created knight bachelor. Clubs: Walton Health Golf (Surrey); Buck's, Hamilton, Crockford's, Lucifer Golfing Soc. (London); Royal and Ancient Golf (St. Andrews, Scotland); Royal Liverpool (Eng.) Golf; Oxford and Cambridge Golfing Soc. Home: Cliveden House Cliveden Pl London SW 1 England

CARR, WILLIAM HERBERT, business exec.; b. Matagorda, Tex., May 11, 1905; s. Charles M. and Ida May (Day) C.; A.B., Stanford, 1928, M.B.A., 1930; m. Winifred Barton Nichols, Sept. 4, 1928; children—Barbara (Mrs. Acevedo), Eleanor (Mrs. Murray Korngold), Shirley Louise (Mrs. Gerald M. Patterson), William Lee, Dorothy (Mrs. Troy Parker), Walter, Catherine (Mrs. Ronald Guest). Auditor Bancraft-Whitney Co., 1930-33; gen. auditor, asst. sec. Yosemite Park & Curry Co., 1933-41; dir. Yosemite Credit Union, 1937-41, v.p., 1937-38, pres., 1938-41; cons. prof. accounting, grad. sch. bus. Stanford, 1937-64; asst. comptroller Cal. Packing Corp. (co. name changed to Del Monte Corp.), 1941-42, comptroller, asst. treas., 1942-46, treas., 1946-65, finance com., 1946-70, v.p., dir., 1948-71, mgmt. com., 1948, v.p. finance, 1955-65, exec. v.p. finance, 1965- 70, chmn. finance com. 1963-70, v.p. Del Monte Sales Co., 1970—; dir. Crocker- Citizens Nat. Bank, Crocker Citizens Internat. Corp., Crocker Nat. Corp., Yosemite Park & Curry Co., Mem. Canners Exchange Subscribers Adv. Com. Chmn. Stanford Bus. Sch. Trust; trustee, chmn. bd. dirs., Freedoms Found. at Valley Forge; bd. dirs. Children's Health. Council of Mid-Peninsula. Mem. Financial Execs. Inst. (nat. dir. 1946-51, pres. 1949, 50, chmn. bd. dirs. 1950- 51, nat. dir. at large 1951-53), Nat. Assn. Accountants, Beta Alpha Psi. Mason, Rotarian. Clubs: Olympic, Menlo Country, Bohemian. Home: 400 Selby Lane Atherton CA 94025 Office: 215 Fremont St San Francisco CA 94119

CARR, WILLIAM NED, educator; b. Thayer, Mo., June 5, 1936; s. Earl S. and Jessie A. (Rice) C.; B.S. in Elec. Engring., M.S., Carnegie Mellon U., 1959, Ph.D., 1962; M.S. in Engring. Adminstrn., So. Meth. U., 1966; m. Sandra M. Savinelli, June 8, 1963; 1 child, Darian. Mem. tech. staff Tex. Instruments, Inc., Dallas, 1962-66; dir., prof. Electronic Scis. Center, So. Meth. U., 1966-71; clin. asso. prof. radiology Baylor Coll. Medicine, Houston, 1968—; chmn. bd. Zentron, Inc., 1968—, Carr Forest Products, Inc., Mountain View, Mo., 1967—. Mem. Soc. Nuclear Medicine, I.E.E.E., Am. Soc. Engring. Edn. Democrat. Unitarian. Contbr. articles to profl. jours. Home: 13709 Peyton St Dallas TX 75240

CARRACIO, GEORGE VICTOR, accountant; b. Chgo., Oct. 15, 1917; s. Anthony and Marie (Eulo) C.; B.S., U. Ill., 1938; grad. Advanced Mgmt. Program, Harvard, 1956; m. Lee Kravek, May 13, 1942; 1 son, George Victor. With Arthur Young & Co., C.P.A.'s, Chgo., 1938-42, 45—, now gen partner. Asst. treas. Pub. Bldg. Commn. Chgo.; adv. com. to atty. gen Ill. Mem. dean's adv. com. Coll. Commerce, U. Ill., also adv. com. Coll. Bus. Adminstrn.; mem. bd. trustees, vice chmn. bd. trustees Ill. Inst. Tech.; exec. com. Ill. Inst. Tech. Reseach Inst.; mem. Citizens Com. U. Chgo.; gov. Community Meml. Gen. Hosp., La Grange, Ill. Served to maj. AUS, 1942-45; ETO. Decorated Bronze Star. C.P.A., Ill., Mich., Ia. Mem. Am. Inst. C.P.A.'s, Ill. Soc. C.P.A.'s, Alumni Assn. Coll. Commerce and Bus. Adminstrn. U. Ill., president's clubs U. Ill., Ill. Inst. Tech. Clubs: Harvard Business Sch., Illini, Chicago, Econ., Mid-America, Mid-Day (Chgo.); Edgewood Valley Country (La Grange); Grandfather Country (Linnville, N.C.). Home: 635 Courtland Circle Western Spring IL 60558 Office: 111 W Monroe St Chicago IL 60603

CARRARA, ARTHUR ALFONSO, architect, designer, graphic designer; b. Chgo., Apr. 8, 1914; s. Cesare and Georgia (Marcucci) C.; B.A. in Arch., U. Ill., 1937; apprenticeship John S. VanBergen, Prairie Sch. Architect, Highland Park, Ill., 1938; m. Charlotte A. Bartels, Sept. 23, 1944. Pvt. practice architecture, Chgo., 1946—; tchr., lectr. various archtl. schs. and museums; mem. editorial staff Inland Architect, 1964-67; one-man archtl. shows include Milw. Art Center, 1960, Walker Art Center, Mpls., 1962, Albright-Knox Art Mus., 1965, Munson-Williams-Proctor Mus. Art, Utica, N.Y., 1965; introduction hydraulic/moving parts to architecture, Cafe Borranical, Melbourne, Australia, 1944; architect master plan, Manila, P.I., 1944, Cebu, P.I., 1945; 1st magnetic sculpture exhbn. Renaissance Soc., U. Chgo., 1947; design 1st magnetic lamp, 1946; designer, inventor magnet master playtool, 1947, inflata lamp, 1954, transfer print, 1957; one man show prints Gilman Gallery, 1963; introduction paper flexagon Chgo. Art Inst., 1957, prin. magnetic and electro-magnetic into modern architecture, 1960; designer sky-spider duct column Graphic Controls Bldg., 1962, 1st large scale one piece fibre-glass skylite into modern architecture, 1963; introduced air supported forms into architecture, 1964; pioneer large scale fibreglass archtl. mech. forms; designed 1st stapled plywood furniture, 1st paper-core house with paper-core furniture; collector, curator Prairie Sch. Architects work. Mem. Nat. Council Architects Registration Bd. Served to maj. AUS, 1942-45. Mem. A.I.A., Alpha Rho Chi. Contbr. articles profl. jours. Address: 715 W Briar Pl Chicago IL 60657 also Townline Rd Whitewater WI 53190

CARRAWAY, GERTRUDE SPRAGUE, orgn exec., journalist, editor; b. New Bern, N.C., Aug. 6, 1896; d. John Robert Bennett and Louise (Elgie) Carraway; A.B., Woman's Coll., U. N.C., 1915; grad. work Columbia; LL.D., Northland Coll., Ashland, Wis., 1955; L.H.D., Lincoln Meml. U., Harrogate, Tenn., 1957, Woman's Coll., Univ. of N.C., 1961. Tchr. high schs. of N.C., 1915-20; newspaper work, New Bern, 1922-37; editor Smithfield (N.C.) Observer, 1920-22; city editor New Bern (N.C.) Sun Jour., 1929-37; free lance journalist, 1937—; editor D.A.R. mag., Washington, 1950-53; editor and pub. Coastal Topics, summer mag., New Bern, 1949-51; dir. Tryon Palace Restoration, New Bern, 1956-71. Sec. Tryon's Place Commn., N.C., 1945-56; mem. exec. com. N.C. Dept. Archives and History, also other statewide commns.; regional chmn. women's div. War Finance Com., 1943-44; N.C. vice chmn. women's sect. U.S. Savs. Bonds programs, 1944-45; served as publicity dir. bond drives and A.R.C. campaigns in Craven County, N.C., World War II. Trustee U. N.C., 1947-55; bd. dirs. Good Shepherd Hosp. for Negroes, New Bern, 1952-53; bd. dirs. pub. libraries many years. Recipient 12 awards from Treasury Dept., A.R.C., Elks, D.A.R. and other orgns. for World War II work; named North Carolinian of 1962, The State mag. Mem. D.A.R. (state regent 1946-49, v.p. gen. 1949-52, pres. gen. 1963-56, hon. pres. gen. for life 1953—, pres. Nat. Officers Club 1966-68), Daughters Am. Colonists, Daus. Colonial Wars, Soc. Colonial Dames, Am. Pen Women, N.C. Lit. and Hist. Assn. (pres. 1966-67). Episcopalian. Club: Woman's Garden. Home: 207 Broad St New Bern NC

CARRE, JEFFREY JAMES, educator; B.A., Bowdoin Coll., 1940; Ph.D., Columbia, 1950; M.A. (hon.), Amherst Coll., 1964. Chmn. Dept. Fine Arts, Amherst Coll. Office: Dept Fine Arts Amherst Coll Amherst MA 01002*

CARREIRO, JOSEPH ALVAREZ, educator, indsl. designer; b. Cambridge, Mass., Mar. 13, 1920; s. Camillo A. and Maria (Borges) C.; B.S., Mass. Coll. Art, 1950; postgrad. Cranbrook Acad., 1947-48, Harvard, 1951-53; m. Dorothy Rita Bellefleur, Nov. 22, 1947; children—Joel, Christine, Donald, Anthony, Suzanne, Michele, Amanda. Instr. dept. housing and design Cornell U., Ithaca, N.Y., 1950-54, prof., chmn. dept., 1965—; dir. indsl. design dept. Phila. Coll. Art, 1954-60, dir. indsl., interior and dimensional design depts., 1960-63, dean faculty, 1963-65; pres. Carreiro Design Asso., Carreiro Indsl. Designers. Mem. planning com. Design in Govt. Conf., Dept. Agr., Washington, 1964; mem. planning com. Role of Crafts in Edn. Conf., Dept. Health, Edn. and Welfare, Washington, 1964-65; chmn. Fulbright Com. design div. Inst. Internat. Edn., 1963-65. Recipient Nat. Design Div. award Am. Ceramic Soc., 1964. Mem. Indsl. Design Edn. Assn. (past pres.), Indsl. Designers Soc. Am. (bd. govs.), Am. Assn. Housing Educators (v.p., chmn. edn. com). Coll. Art Assn., N.E.A. Project dir., research publn. The New Building Block: A Report on the Factory-Produced Dwelling Module. Home: 152 Oakwood Lane Ithaca, NY 14850.

CARRERA, JOSEPH ANTHONY, banker; b. Santa Clara, Cal., Jan. 20, 1916; s. Joseph William and Gertrude (Gilardin) C.; m. Virginia Smith, Aug. 19, 1945; 1 dau., Virginia Jane. With Bank of Am. NT & SA, 1937—, v.p. charge br. and internat. operations, 1958-64, sr. v.p. internat. banking, 1963-71, sr. v.p., dir. personnel; dir. Bank of Am. (Internat.), Bamerical Financial Corp. Mem. Am. Inst. Banking. Home: 13641 Ronnie Way Saratoga CA Office: 555 California St San Francisco CA

CARRET, PHILIP LORD, business exec.; b. Lynn, Mass., Nov. 29, 1896; s. James R. and Hannah (Todd) C.; A.B., Harvard, 1917; student Harvard Grad. Sch. Bus. Adminstrn., 1916-17; m. Elisabeth Osgood, Sept. 4, 1922; children—Gerard, Donald, Diane. Chmn. bd. Pioneer Fund, Inc.; pres. Carret & Co., Inc.; director of other corporations. Trustee Scarsdale Bd. Edn., 1941-46. Mem. N.Y. Security Dealers Assn. (dir.), Nat. Assn. Securities Dealers (past member board governors), American Legion. Republican. Conglist. Rotarian. Clubs: Bankers of America, Harvard (New York); Scarsdale (N.Y.) Golf. Author: Buying a Bond, 1924; The Art of Speculation, 1926. Contbr. mag. articles to Barron's and other publications. Home: 28 Circle Rd Scarsdale NY 10583 Office: 22 E 40th St New York City NY 10016

CARRETTA, ALBERT ALOYSIUS, educator, lawyer; b. N.Y.C., Dec. 23, 1907; s. Vincent and Concetta (De Florio) C.; B.S., Coll. City of N.Y., 1930; J.D., Georgetown U., 1940; postgrad. N.Y. U.; m. Gertrude Elizabeth Lynch, Nov. 29, 1934; children—Albert Aloysius, John Vincent, William Joseph. Instr. econs., finance Coll. City N.Y. Sch. Bus. and Civic Adminstrn., 1930-34; financial analyst, atty. SEC, Washington, 1934-42; instr. finance Columbus U., Washington, 1935-36; admitted to D.C. bar, 1940, Va., 1941; bus. specialist OPA, Washington, 1942-44; lectr. corp. law, corp. finance, unfair trade practices, fed. antitrust legislation Cath. U. Am., Wash., 1942-54; instr. finance U. Cal., 1945; vice chief, bd. mem. services and sales renegotiation sect. Navy Dept., Washington, 1946-47; lectr. accounting dept., sch. fgn. service Georgetown U., 1946-52; pvt. practice law, Washington, also Arlington, Va., 1947-52; mem. FTC, 1952-54; pvt. practice law, Washington, 1954—. Pres., Cath. Charities No. Va., 1955-57, U.S.N., 1944-45. Decorated knight Order of the Star of Italian Solidarity. Mem. Am., D.C., Fed., Va. bar assns., Am. Arbitration Assn. (nat. panel). K.C. Home: 1823 N Glebe Rd Arlington VA 22207 Office: 1815 H St NW Washington DC 20006

CARRICK, ROBERT BRUCE, librarian; b. Winnipeg, Man., Can., Feb. 10, 1907; s. Andrew Alexander and Annie (Petrie) C.; B.A., U. B.C., 1929; B.L.S., McGill U., 1936; m. Barbara Mary Brockley, Dec. 14, 1940; children—Jennifer (Mrs. John Dicken), Sandra Maureen. Came to U.S., 1949, naturalized, 1954. Regional librarian Fraser Valley Regional Library, Abbotsford, B.C., Can., 1940- 45; city librarian Brandon War Meml. Pub. Library, Man., 1946-48; county librarian Whitman County Library, Colfax, Wash., 1949-50, Spokane County Library, 1950-60; city librarian Spokane Pub. Library, 1961—. Mem. Wash. (pres. 1958-59), Pacific N.W. library assns., Photog. Soc. Am., Delta Upsilon. Democrat. Presbyn. Home: W 1309 19th Av Spokane WA 99203 Office: W 906 Main Av Spokane WA 99201

CARRICO, HARRY LEE, state justice; b. Va., Sept. 4, 1916; s. William Temple and Nellie Nadalia (Willett) C.; jr. certificate George Washington U., 1938, J.D., 1942; m. Betty Lou Peck, May 18, 1940; 1 dau., Lucretia Ann. Admitted to Va. bar, 1941; with firm Rust & Rust, Fairfax, 1941-43; trial justice Fairfax County, Va., 1943-51; pvt. practice, Fairfax, 1951-56; judge 16th Jud. Circuit Va., 1956-61; justice Supreme Ct. Appeals Va., 1961—. Served to ensign USNR, 1945-46. Mem. Phi Delta Phi. Episcopalian. Home: 9303 Cragmont Dr Richmond VA 23229 Office: Courthouse Fairfax VA 22030 also Supreme Ct Bldg Richmond VA 23219

CARRICO, JAMES LEON, educator; b. Sanger, Tex., Nov. 22, 1906; s. James Edward and Mary G. (Champion) C.; B.A., N. Tex. State U., 1927, B.S., 1929; M.A., U. Tex., 1931; Ph.D., Cal. Inst. Tech., 1935; m. Mary Lou Jones, July 9, 1933; children—Charles James, William Raymond, Mary Elizabeth. Tchr. high sch., Elizabeth, La., 1927, McLean, Tex., 1928; tutor chemistry dept. U. Tex., 1929, 30; asso. prof. chemistry North Tex. State U., Denton, 1931, mem. staff chemistry dept., 1938—, chmn. dept., 1942-69; Henry Lawes teaching fellow Cal. Inst. Tech., 1932-35; prof. chemistry and physics Lamar Coll., Beaumont, Tex., 1936; chemist Texas Co., 1937, photochemistry of hydrocarbons, 1938-71. Del. Tex. Democratic Conv., 1939. Exec. bd. Longhorn council Boy Scouts Am., 1950—. Recipient award of merit A.R.C. Fellow Tex. Acad. Sci.; mem. Am. Chem. Soc., Sigma Xi, Kappa Delta Pi, Alpha Chi Sigma, Phi Lambda Upsilon. Presbyn. Club: Kiwanis. Home: 1819 Mistywood Lane Denton TX

CARRIER, GEORGE FRANCIS, engr.; b. Millinocket, Me., May 4, 1918; s. Charles Mosher and Mary (Marco) C.; M.E., Cornell, 1939, Ph.D., 1944; m. Mary Casey, June 30, 1946; children—Kenneth, Robert, Mark. Research asso. Harvard, 1944-46. Gordon MacKay prof. mech. engring., 1952—; asst. prof. Brown U., 1946- 47, asso. prof., 1947-48, prof., 1948-52; asso. mng. editor Quar. Applied Mathematics since 1952. Mem. com. on atmospheric scis. Nat. Acad. Scis. Fellow Am. Acad. Scis.; mem. Am. Soc. M.E., Sigma Xi, Phi Kappa Phi. Author: (with M. Krook and C.E. Pearson) Functions of a Complex Variable: Theory and Technique, 1966; (with C. Pearson) Ordinary Differential Equations, 1968. Editor: The Foundations of High Speed Aerodynamics, 1951. Asso. editor Jour. Fluid Mechanics. Contbr. articles tech. jours. Home: Rice Spring Lane Wayland MA 01778 Office: Harvard U Cambridge MA 02138

CARRIER, LORAN FRANCIS, composer, educator; b. Scobey, Mont., May 27, 1936; s. Aime Joseph and Alma (Parent) C.; student Assumption Abbey Jr. Coll., 1954-56, Queen of Apostles Coll., 1956-58, Boston Coll., summer 1957, Boston U., summer 1959; Mus. B., Catholic U., 1966, Mus. M., 1967; Mus. M., Washington Mus. Inst., 1967; Dr. Mus. Arts, Md. U., 1970; m. Marjorie B. Arvidson, July 13, 1961; children—Mark F., Genine M., Jeffrey L. Tchr. philosophy and contemporary humanities Good Counsel High Sch., Wheaton, Md., 1969—; founder Fresh Music Group, 1967. Nat. Def. Edn. Act fellow, 1967-68. Composer: Opera Game 1; Brass Quartet 1 and 2; Christmas is Y-Come; also electronic music compositions. Home: 440 Ridge Rd Greenbelt MD 20770 Office: 11601 Georgia Av Wheaton MD 20902

CARRIER, RONALD EDWIN, coll. pres.; b. Bluff City, Tenn., Aug. 18, 1932; s. James Murphy and Melissa (Miller) C.; B.S., E. Tenn. State U., 1955; M.S., U. Ill., 1957, Ph.D., 1960; m. Edith Marie Johnson, Sept. 7, 1955; children—Michael Lavon, Linda Lois, Jennine Maria. Asso. prof. econs. U. Miss., 1960-63; dir. Bur. Bus. and Econ. Research, Memphis State U., 1963-66, provost, prof. econs., 1966-69, v.p. for acad. affairs, 1969-71; pres. Madison Coll., Harrisonburg, Va., 1971—. Dir. Leader Fed. Savs. & Loan Assn., Memphis, Rockingham Nat. Bank, Harrisonburg; cons. Harland Bartholomew & Assos. Internat., Inc. St. Louis. Mem. Southeastern Regional Manpower Adv. Com. Trustee, Madison Coll. Found. Earheart fellow, 1958-60. Recipient Ben Franklin award Memphis Printing Industry, 1966; Faculty award E. Tenn. State U., 1955; Distinguished Service award Jr. C. of C., 1965. Mem. Am. Econs. Assn., Regional Sci. Assn., Am. Mgmt. Assn., So. Econ. Assn., Va. Edn. Assn., Omicron Delta Kappa, Omicron Delta Gamma, Sigma Phi Epsilon. Rotarian. Methodist. Author books and articles on econs. and indsl. location. Home: Hillcrest Madison Coll Harrisonburg VA 22801

CARRIER, WARREN PENDLETON, coll. dean; b. Cheviot, O., July 3, 1918; s. Burly Warren and Prudence (Alfrey) C.; student Wabash Coll., 1937-40; A.B., Miami U., Oxford O., 1942; M.A., Harvard, 1948; Ph.D., Occidental Coll., 1962; m. Marjorie Jane Regan, Apr. 3, 1947; 1 son, Gregory Paul. Asst. prof. English, State U. Ia., 1949-52; asso. prof. Bard Coll., 1953-57; mem. lit. faculty Bennington, 1955-58; vis. prof. Sweet Briar (Va.) Coll., 1958- 60; prof. Deep Springs (Cal.) Coll., 1960-62, Portland (Ore.) State Coll., 1962-64; prof., chmn. English dept. U. Mont., Missoula, 1964-68; asso. dean. prof. English and comparative lit., chmn. comparative lit. Livingston Coll., Rutgers U., 1968-69; dean Coll. Arts and Letters, San Diego State Coll. 1969—. Vol., Am. Field Service attached to Brit. Army, India-Burma, 1944-45. Mem. Modern Lang. Assn., Phi Beta Kappa. Author: The Hunt, 1952; Bay of the Damned, 1957; Toward Montebello, 1966. Founder: Quar. Rev. of Lit. Asso. editor: Western Rev., 1949-51. Cons. editor N.W. Rev., 1964-. Co-editor: Reading Modern Poetry, 1955. Contbr. numerous articles, poems, revs. to lit. mags. Home: 5908 La Jolla Corona Dr La Jolla, CA 92037. Office: College of Arts and Letters San Diego State College, San Diego, CA 92115.

CARRIERE, CHARLES MONTBRUN, business exec.; b. New Orleans, July 2, 1908; s. Victor Montbrun and Eveline (D'Aquin) C.; student Loyola U. of South, 1929-33; m. Mary Augusta Barnett, Jan. 13, 1934; children—Mary Evelyn (Mrs. Gerard E. Ruch), Elizabeth Rosemary, Jean Louise, Charles Montbrun, Victor Montbrun, Janet Ann, Carolyn Judith. Clk., So. Clk. Oil Co., 1925-34, now v.p., treas.; prof. accounting Loyola U. of South, 1933-40; accountant So. Shell Fish Co., 1934-39, office mgr., 1934-44, asst. sec., 1939-44, v.p., dir., 1944-48, now exec. v.p., treas., dir.; treas., asst. sec. Wesson Oil & Snowdrift Co., Inc., 1948-56, v.p., treas., 1956- 60; v.p., Hunt Foods & Industries, Inc., 1960—; v.p., treas. S. Tex. Cotton Oil Co. Mem. Pres.'s Food Com., World War II; mem. adv. council Loyola U. Coll. Bus. Adminstrn., New Orleans, chmn., 1969. C.P.A., La. Mem. La. Soc. C.P.A.'s, Am. Inst. Accountants, C. of C., Financial Execs. Inst. (pres. New Orleans control 1956-57), Budget Execs. Inst. (pres. New Orleans chpt. 1962-63), Holy Name Soc., Cath. Evidence Guild. K.C. Home: 6655 Vicksburg St New Orleans LA 70124 Office: 401 Veterans Memorial Hwy Metairie LA also PO Box 24219 New Orleans LA 70124

CARRIGER, JOHN SHIELDS, lawyer; b. Morristown, Tenn., Aug. 7, 1902; s. John Stonewall and Elizabeth (Gammon) C.; A.B., U. Tenn., 1925, LL.B., 1927; m. Helen Fletcher, June 25, 1935; children—John Fletcher, William Converse, Martha (Mrs. Gordon P. O'Neill). Admitted to Tenn. bar, 1927; partner Strang, Fletcher, Carriger, Walker & Hodge, Chattanooga, 1933—. Dir. Chattanooga Gas Co.; sec., dir. Tenn. Paper Mills. Mem. Am., Tenn., Chattanooga (pres. 1954-55, bd. govs. 1955-56) bar assns., World Peace Through Law Center, U. Tenn. Alumni Assn. (past pres. Hamilton County), U. Tenn. Coll. Law Alumni (pres. 1949-50), Order of Coif, Phi Delta Phi, Phi Kappa Phi, Alpha Tau Omega. Methodist (chmn. ofcl. bd. local ch. 1959-60). Kiwanian. Clubs: Executives (pres. 1946-47), Mountain City, Fairyland, Metropolitan Dinner (Chattanooga). Home: 1009 E Brow Rd Lookout Mountain TN 37350 Office: Maclellan Bldg Chattanooga TN 37402

CARRILLO, MANUEL, amateur photographer; b. Mexico City, Mexico, Jan. 17, 1906; s. Lauro and Guadalupe (Palacios) C.; m. Consuelo Cadena, Feb. 19, 1951; 1 son by previous marriage, Manuel. Gen. agt. I.C. R.R. in Mexico city; amateur photographer; seventy exhibits in U.S., Europe, Central and South Am. under titles Mi Pueblo and The Inseparables. Recipient 1st prize black and white photography Sat. Rev., 1967. Mem. Liga Defensora de los Animales S.A., Soc. Protectora de los Animales South Am., Traffic Club Mexico City. Lion. Address: Bolivar No 21 Mexico City, Mexico

CARRINGTON, ALEXANDER BERKELEY, Jr., former tobacco mcht., banker; b. Danville, Va., Jan. 26, 1895; s. Alexander Berkeley and Mary Miller (Taylor) C.; A.B., Hampden-Sydney Coll., 1915, LL.D., 1942; A.M., U. Va., 1917; m. Ruth Simpson, Oct. 30, 1920. With Dibrell Bros., Inc., Danville, since 1919, pres., 1936-51, chmn. bd. dirs., 1951-69; chmn. bd. Am. Nat. Bank & Trust Co., 1949-69; dir. Dan River Mills. Trustee Hampden- Sydney Coll., Stratford Coll., Meml. Hosp., Danville. Served as capt. C.A.C., with AEF, 1917-19. Home: Forest Hills Danville VA 24541 Office: Dibrell Bros Inc Danville VA 24541

CARRINGTON, GORDON GREGORY, Jr., oil co. exec.; b. Gilmer, Tex., May 12, 1930; s. Gordon Gregory and Mae (Taylor) C.; B.B.A., Baylor U.; m. Patricia Ann Baldridge, Feb. 28, 1951; children—Richard Carl, Alicia Arlene. Staff accountant F.W. LaFrentz & Co., Dallas, 1954; accountant Creole Petroleum Corp., Caracas, Venezuela, 1955-64; asst. treas. Creole Caracas, 1965-68, treas., 1969, comptroller, 1969—. Bd. dirs. Escuela Campo Alegre, Caracas, 1967-68. Served to 2d lt. USAF, 1952-53. C.P.A., Tex. Mem. Tex. Soc. C.P.A.'s. Baptist. Home: Quinta Gloria Calle Oriente Prados Del Este Caracas Venezuela Office: Apartado 889 Caracas Venezuela

CARRINGTON, MALCOLM, Jr., utility exec.; b. Chgo., Apr. 28, 1916; s. Malcolm and Irene (Ashford) C.; grad. Manlius (N.Y.) Sch., 1935; B.S. in Bus. Adminstrn., Lehigh U., 1939; m. Barbara Anne Klipstein, Aug. 28, 1947; children—Anne Seddon, Hollyce Ashford, Malcolm III, Steven Wallace, David Christie. With Pub. Service Electric & Gas Co., Newark, 1939—, sec., 1963—. Dir. Am. Competitive Enterprise System. Bd. dirs. YMCA and YWCA of Newark and vicinity, United Community Fund Essex and W. Hudson; trustee Garden State Ballet, Lehigh U. Served to maj. AUS, 1942-46; PTO. Mem. Greater Newark C. of C., Nat. Lehigh Alumni Assn. (pres. 1967-68, dir. 1965—), Am. Soc. Corporate Secs. (dir. 1970—), Kappa Alpha, Omicron Delta Kappa, Alpha Kappa Psi. Mem. Covenant Ch. Am. Rotarian (dir., pres. 1971-72 Newark). Clubs: N.J. Automobile (dir.); Down Town (Newark); Lehigh No. N.J. (dir.). Home: 50 Billingsley Dr Livingston NJ 07039 Office: 80 Park Pl Newark NJ 07101

CARRINGTON, PAUL, lawyer; b. Mexico, Mo., Sept. 23, 1894; s. William Thomas and Mary (Holloway) C.; A.B., U. Mo., 1914; LL.B., Harvard, 1917; m. Francis DeWitt, Nov. 5, 1921; children—Frances (Lee), Paul DeWitt. Admitted to Tex. bar, 1919, since practiced civil law, Dallas; mem. Carrington, Coleman, Sloman, Johnson & Blumenthal. Chmn., N. Tex. Com. on Econ. Devel., 1943-46, Allen Enemy Hearing Bd. for N. Tex., 1942-45; pres. Greater Dallas Planning Council, 1948-53; chmn. bd. Dallas Council on World Affairs, 1953-54; v.p. Dallas Boy Scouts Am., nat. councilor, 1945-63; pres. Dallas YMCA, 1946-49. Trustee S.W. Legal Found.; bd. dirs. Am. Bar Endowment. Served as 2d lt., instr. primary flying U.S. Army, 1918- 19. Fellow Am. Bar Found. (chmn. 1965-66); mem. E. Tex. (pres. 1950-51), Dallas (pres. 1940-42, chmn. legislative com. 1943-70) chambers commerce, Tex. Assn. Commerce (pres. 1946-49), Am. (ho. dels. 1958—, chmn. com. on lawyer referral 1959-63), Dallas (pres. 1939-40) bar assns., State Bar Tex. (pres. 1960-61 1st chmn. sect. corp. banking, bus. law 1954), Am. Soc. Internat. Law (exec. council 1961-67), Am. Arbitration Assn. (dir. 1935—), World Peace Through Law Center (chmn. corporate law commn. 1963—), Am. Law Inst., Am. Judicature Soc., Harvard Law Sch. Assn. (pres. 1959-61, nat. council 1953—), S.A.R. Democrat. Mem. Christian Ch. (elder). Mason (32). Clubs: Dallas Country, Petroleum (Dallas); Harvard (N.Y.C.); Metropolitan (Washington); Austin. Author: (with William A. Sutherland) Articles of Partnership for Law Firms, 1962. Home: 6315 Lupton Dallas, TX 75225. Office: 1 Main Pl Dallas TX 75250

CARRION, RAFAEL, Jr., banker; b. Santurce, P.R., Aug. 27, 1914; s. Rafael and Ernestina (Ruiz) C.; student Wharton Coll., 1931; m. Nellie Rexach, Aug. 19, 1935; children—Nellie, Eileen, Marilyn, Rafael, Richard, Janet. With Banco Popular de Puerto Rico, San Juan, 1932—, exec. v.p., dir., 1952, now pres., chmn.; dir. P.R. Telephone Co., Banco de Cooperativas de P.R. Bd. dirs. A.R.C., YMCA, Presbyn. Hosp.; trustee Com. for Econ. Devel. Mem. Bankers Assn. Fgn. Trade (dir.), Am. Bankers Assn. (v.p. for P.R.). Roman Catholic. Elk. Clubs: Swimming and Tennis of the Caribe Hilton (dir.), Casa de Espana (San Juan); Berwind Country (Rio Piedras, P.R.); Casino de Puerto Rico, Nautico (Santurce, P.R.); Dorado Beach. Home: N Loiza St Santurce PR 00908 Office: Banco Popular Center Hato Rey PR 00901

CARRIUOLO, CHRISTOPHER WILFRED, liquor co. exec.; b. Brockton, Mass., Oct. 12, 1920; s. Joseph W. and Emily (LaRocca) C.; B.S. in Bus. Adminstrn., Boston U., 1942; grad. Advanced Mgmt. Program, Harvard, 1944; m. Florence M. Picanzi, Oct. 12, 1947; children—Carol Lynne, Peter Michael. With Reynolds Corp., 1945-48; with Four Roses div. House of Seagram, 1948-59, nat. sales promotion mgr., 1959; with Heublein, Inc., 1959—, sr. v.p., 1964—, dir., 1965—, gen. mgr. wine and spirits div., 1968—; pres. Beaulieu Vineyard, 1969—, Smirnoff Beverage & Import Co., 1970—; v.p., dir. Vinifere Devel. Corp., 1970—; dir. Don Q Imports, J.M. de Fonseca, Internacional-Vinhos, Lda., Hartford Fed. Savs. & Loan Assn. Mem. exec., finance and budget coms., bd. dirs. Distilled Spirits Inst. Trustee Syracuse U. Grad. Sch. Bus.; chmn. parents com., mem. devel. com. Wheelock Coll.; bd. dirs. Hartford Symphony Soc., Conn. Opera Assn. Mem. Am. Marketing Assn., Sales Execs. Club N.Y., Sales Promotion Execs. Assn., Sales and Marketing Club Hartford, Sales and Execs. Internat., Boston U., Harvard alumni assns., Nat. Assn. Alcholic Beverage Importers (bd. dirs.), Newcomen Soc. Clubs: City (Hartford); Golf (Avon); Wampanoag Country. Home: 77 Stony Corners Avon CT 06001 Office: 330 New Park Av Hartford CT 06101

CARROL, LOUIS, dept. store exec.; b. Toronto, Ont., Can., Apr. 1, 1913; m. Lillian Neibart, Feb. 22, 1939; children—Phyllis (Mrs. Alan Zeitlin), Richard. With L. Bamberger & Co., Newark, 1933-50; furniture buyer May Co., Los Angeles, 1953-55; with Rich's, Inc., Atlanta, 1951-52, 57—, now exec. v.p., also dir., mem. exec. com. Mem. Atlanta C. of C. Clubs: Standard, Commerce (Atlanta). Home: 2841 Ridgewood Rd NW Atlanta GA 30307 Office: Broad St Atlanta GA 30303

CARROLL, BARBARA, pianist; b. Worcester, Mass., Jan. 25, 1925; d. David L. and Lillian (Lavine) Coppersmith; grad. New Eng. Conservatory Music, 1941; m. Joseph Shulman, Sept. 20, 1954 (dec. Aug. 1957); m. 2d, Bert Block, Oct. 7, 1960; 1 dau., Suzanne Elizabeth. Jazz pianist, leader Barbara Carroll Trio, 1951—; frequent nightclub appearances throughout U.S., 1947—; appeared on TV in Today Show, Tonight Show, others; on Broadway in Me and Juliet, 1953; concerts for univs. in U.S., 1957—; recording artist for RCA Victor, Verve, Kapp, Warner Bros. records. Mem. A.S.C.A.P., Actor's Equity. Composer: Barbara's Carol, 1952; Fancypants, 1956; Today, 1958. Address: 450 E 63d St New York City, NY 10022.

CARROLL, CLIFFORD ANDREW, coll. ofcl., clergyman; b. Duluth, Minn., Apr. 23, 1906; s. Andrew P. and Nellie (Beladeau) C.; student Gonzaga U., 1927-28, A.B., 1933, A.M., 1934; student Santa Clara U., 1932; S.T.L., Alma (Cal.) Coll., 1942; Ph.D., St. Louis U., 1946. Entered Soc. of Jesus, 1928; ordained priest Roman Cath. Ch., 1941; instr. Seattle Coll., 1935-38, vis. prof., summer 1942; dean Gonzaga U. Sch. Econs. and Bus., Spokane, Wash., 1945- 53, regent, 1953-63, dir. libraries, prof., 1963—. Mem. Indsl. Relations Inst.; chmn. Pacific N.W. Cath. Regional Library Conf., 1961-63; Wash. State adv. council to libraries, 1971—. Mem. Am. Arbitration Assn. (nat. panel), Am., Cath. econ. assns., Royal Econ. Soc. Address: Gonzaga Univ Spokane WA 99202

CARROLL, COLEMAN FRANCIS, bishop; b. Pitts., Feb. 9, 1905; s. William J. and B. Margaret (Hogan) C.; B.A., Duquesne U., 1926; L.S.T., St. Vincent's Sem., Latrobe, Pa., 1930; J.C.D., Cath. U. Am., 1942. Ordained priest Roman Cath. Ch., 1930; asst. pastor various chs., 1930- 49; pastor St. Maurice Parish, Pitts., 1949-51, Sacred Heart Ch., East End, Pitts., 1951-58; 1st Bishop, Miami, Fla., 1958—; domestic prelate, rt. rev. msgr., 1952; aux. bishop Pitts., 1953-58; became bishop Miami, 1958, now archbishop Miami. Address: 1633 Northview Dr Sunset Island Miami Beach FL 33140

CARROLL, DAVID SHIELDS, physician; b. Morristown, Tenn., Jan. 3, 1917; s. Charles Thomas and Zoe Marvin (Wells) C.; B.S., U. Tenn., 1938, M.D. 1940; m. Mary Kathryn McGuire, Nov. 9, 1941 (dec. May 1960); children—Kathryn (Mrs. Hal W. Canary), Elizabeth Jane, David Shields; m. 2d, Peggy Land Leppert, Nov. 10, 1961. Intern John Gaston Hosp., Memphis, 1940-41; resident radiology U. Tenn. Hosp., 1946-47; chmn. dept. radiology City of Memphis Hosps., 1947-64; prof., chmn. dept. radiology U. Tenn. Coll. Medicine, 1957-64, clin. prof., 1964—; staff radiologist Meth. Hosp.; cons. Oak Ridge Inst. Nuclear Studies, 1952-62, Le Bonheur Children's Hosp., 1965—, Kennedy VA Hosp., 1959—, Meth. Hosp., 1962—, St. Jude Children's Hosp., 1963—. Pres. bd. dirs. Les Passees Treatment Center, 1960-61; pres. Memphis and Shelby County unit Am. Cancer Soc., 1963, bd. dirs. Tenn. div., 1960—; bd. dirs. West Tenn. Cancer Clinic, 1954—. Served to maj., M.C., AUS, 1941-46; ETO. Diplomate Am. Bd. Radiology. Fellow Am. Coll. Radiology (chmn. bd. chancellors 1963, pres. 1964); mem. Radiol. Soc. N.Am. (v.p. 1956, chmn. bd. 1971), Am., So. med. assns., Tenn. Radiol. Soc. (pres. 1958), Memphis and Shelby County Med. Soc., Am. Radium Soc. Episcopalian. Rotarian. Clubs: University, Chickasaw Country. Conbtr. articles to med. jours. Home: 350 Sweetbriar Rd Memphis TN 38138 Office: 1265 Union Av Memphis TN 38104

CARROLL, DIAHANN, actress, singer; b. N.Y.C., July 17, 1935; d. John and Mabel (Faulk) Johnson; student N.Y. U., 1 yr.; m. Monte Kay (div.); 1 dau., Suzanne. Began career as model; actress motion pictures, including: Carmen Jones, Porgy and Bess, Goodbye Again, Paris Blues; on Broadway in House of Flowers, No Strings; TV series Julia. Address: care Merrick Shefrin Co 18 E 48th St New York City NY 10017

CARROLL, DONALD KINGERY, judge; b. Hartington, Neb., Apr. 16, 1909; s. Charles Eden and Blanche Elsie (Kingery) C.; A.B., Harvard, 1930; postgrad. U. Miami, 1931-33; J.D., U. Fla., 1935. Asst. to editor Nat. mag., Boston, 1930- 31; admitted to Fla. bar, 1935, since practiced in Jacksonville, mem. Milam, McIvanine, Carroll & Wattles, 1938-57; asst. atty. gen. of Fla., 1941; judge Ct. of Appeal First Dist., Fla., 1957—, chief judge, 1961-63. Dir. Greater Jacksonville Crime Commn., 1952—; exec. com. Fla. Citizenship Clearing House, 1954-56, pres., 1957-63; pres. of the Civic Round Table, 1950-51. Served as capt. Judge Adv. Gen. Dept., AUS, 1942-46. Mem. Am. Judicature Soc. (bd. dirs., mem. exec. com. 1956), Am. (exec. council jr. bar conf. 1941-43, ho. of dels. 1952—), Fla., Jacksonville (treas. 1938-40, sec. 1946-48, pres. 1949) bar assns., Fla. Bar (pres. 1955-56), Nat. Conf. Bar Pres. (exec. council 1955-56), Am. Legion (state comdr. 1950-51), Vets. Fgn. Wars, Mil. Order World Wars, Judge Advs. Assn., Jr. C. of C. (pres. 1942), Phi Kappa Phi, Phi Delta Phi, Blue Key. Democrat. Meth. Mason (32, Shriner), Elk. Club: Torch (Jacksonville). Editor: Handbook for Judges, 1961. Home: 420 E Park Av Tallahassee FL Office: Supreme Ct Bldg PO Box 87 Tallahassee FL

CARROLL, EDWIN WINFORD, architect; b. Elizabeth, La., Mar. 6, 1912; s. Rupert A. and Maude Marie (Ping) C.; B.Arch., U. Tex., 1936; m. Alyce Moter Outlaw, Mar. 27, 1937. Designer, draftsman Trost & Trost, architects, El Paso, Tex., 1936-41; architect, supt. bldgs. El Paso Pub. Schs., 1941-45; partner Carroll, Daeuble Du Sang & Rand, El Paso, 1945—; prin works include Mesita Elementary Sch., Eastwood High Sch., El Paso Natural Gas Co. Office Bldg., El Paso Pub. Library, Ft. Bliss Arty. and Guided Missile Center, Providence Meml. Hosp., First Presbyn. Ch., El Paso Mus. Art, Chelmont Shopping Center, El Paso Nat. Bank Bldg., Sun Bowl Stadium, El Paso, Liberal Arts bldg., library and dormitory complex U. Tex. at El Paso, El Paso Civic Center, Hotel Dieu Sch. Nursing, Tex hdqrs. bldg. Mountain Bell Co., also others in Big Spring, Tex., Mexico; cons. architect met. water treatment plant, Salt Lake City. Chmn. Tex. Bd. Archtl. Exam., 1953; vice chmn. internat. border devel. commn. A.I.A. and Sociedad de Arquitectos Mexicanos, 1960-63; mem. El Paso Bldg. Code Bd., 1951—, chmn., 1953; pres. Am. delegation XI Congress of Fedn. Pan- Am. Architects, 1965. Mem. exec. bd. Yucca council Boy Scouts Am.; Pres. Tex. Archtl. Found., 1958-59; mem. devel. bd. Tex. Christian U.; mem. Tex. Western Coll. Mission 173. Fellow A.I.A. (chmn. nat. border com. 1964-66); mem. Tex. Soc. Architects (pres. 1954), Soc. de Arguitectos Mexicanos (hon.). U. Tex. Ex-Students Assn. Mem. Christian Ch. (elder, past pres. congregation). Clubs: El Paso Country (pres. bd. govs. 1957), Coronado Country (pres. 1967, 68). Home: 901 Cherry Hills Lane El Paso TX 79912 Office: 250 N Mesa St El Paso TX 79902

CARROLL, ELISABETH, ballerina; b. Paris, Jan. 19, 1937; d. Jean and Suzanne (Beneyton) Pfister; ed. Ecole Elementaire de Filles, 1942-47, Coll. de Jeunes Filles, 1948-51; m. Felix Smith, July 18, 1957; 1 dau., Ariane Smith. Soloist, Monte Carlo Opera Ballet, Monte Carlo, 1952-54; 1st soloist Am. Ballet Theatre, 1954-61; prin. dancer Robert Joffrey Co., 1961-63, Harkness Ballet, 1964—. Recipient hon. award Dance Masters Am., 1969. Address: RD 2 Box 296 Stockton NJ 08559

CARROLL, FRANCIS BRIAN, physician; b. Whitinsville, Mass., Aug. 19, 1902; s. John F. and Ellen (McGuiness) C.; D.M.D. cum laude, Tufts U., 1924; M.D., U. Rochester, 1935; M.P.H., Harvard, 1939; m. Helen M. Collins, June 27, 1936; childrenBrian Cushing, Joan (Mrs. Lyman Matthew Beggs III), John Brian. Intern Highland Hosp., Rochester, N.Y., 1935-36; field dir. W. K. Kellogg Found., Battle Creek, Mich., 1936-38; dist. health officer Mass. Dept. Pub. Health, 1938-41, also mem. Pub. Health Council, Hosp. Adv. Council; asst. br. med. dir. VA, Boston, 1946-47, br. med. dir., 1947-49 area med. dir. New Eng. States, N.Y. State, 1949-63; hosp. dir. VA Hosp., Boston, 1963—; vis. lectr. Harvard, Mass. Inst. Tech., Boston U. Mem. Fed. Exec. Bd. Boston; VA Liaison rep. to Office Civil Defense, Office Emergency Planning, 1954—; mem. civil defense disaster com. Mass. Hosp. Council, 1962—. Served to lt. col., M.C., AUS, 1941-46. Decorated Legion of Merit; recipient Meritorious Service award Adminstr. Vets Affairs, 1965. Diplomate Am. Bd. Preventive Medicine and Pub. Health. Fellow A.C.P., Am. Coll. Preventive Medicine, Am. Pub. Health Assn.; mem. Am., Mass. hosp. assns., Assn. Mil. Surgeons, New Eng. Med. Assembly, Mass. Med. Soc., Mass. Pub. Health Assn., Louis Pasteur Club, Robt. R. Andrews Soc., Psi Omega, Omicron Kappa Upsilon. Home: 55 Wilde Rd Waban, MA 02168. Office: VA Hosp 150 S Huntington Av Boston MA 02130

CARROLL, GLADYS HASTY, author; b. Rochester, N.H., June 26, 1904; d. Warren Verdi and Emma Frances (Dow) Hasty; A.B., Batas Coll., Lewiston, Me., 1925, Litt.D., 1945; A.M. (hon.), U. N.H., 1934; Litt.D., U. Me., 1939; m. Herbert A. Carroll, June 23, 1925; children—Warren, Sarah (Mrs. Hazen L. Watson). Author juvenile books, novels, and non-fiction, including: As the Earth Turns, 1933; A Few Foolish Ones, 1935; Neighbor to the Sky, 1937; Head of the Line, 1942; While The Angels Sing, 1947; West of the Hill, 1949; Christmas Without Johnny, 1950; Dunnybrook, 1952; One White Star, 1954; Sing Out the Glory, 1957; Come With Me Home, 1960; Only Fifty Years Ago, 1962; To Remember Forever, 1963; The Road Grows Strange, 1965; The Light Here Kindled, 1967; Christmas Through the Years, 1968; Man on the Mountain, 1969; also short stories. Mem. Phi Beta Kappa. Contbr. to mags.; stories appearing as screenplays on TV. Home: South Berwick ME 03908 ☆

CARROLL, GORDON, author, editor; b. Balt., Apr. 29, 1903; s. Charles Gordon and Elizabeth (Swann) C.; grad. Balt. Poly. Inst., 1920; student U. Md., 1921-23; m. Phyllis Oliver Fechtig, Sept. 6, 1926; children—Gordon, Robert McHenry. Reporter, editor various met. newspapers, 1924-34; mng. editor Am. Mercury, 1934-38; sr. editor Reader's Digest, 1938-41; editor publs. Office Civilian Def., 1942; editor Time, Inc., 1943-45; exec. editor Coronet, 1945-48, editor in chief, 1948-52, pub., 1952-55; now internat. dir. Famous Writers School, Westport, Conn. Editor: Saturday Evening Post Reader of Civil War Stories; The Desolate South; Writing, Revising and Editing; Famous Writers Annual. Home: Aspetuck Corners Weston, CT 06880.

CARROLL, GRAYSON, physician, surgeon; b. Dallas, Tex., Feb. 10, 1895; s. Washington Irving and Lettie Catherine (Mosher) C.; student Austin Coll., 1913-14; student Univ. of Tex. at Austin 1914-15; M.D., Univ. of Tex. at Galveston, 1919; m. Thelma Hayman, November 20, 1924; children—Gaye (Mrs. Shelton Voges), Elizabeth (Mrs. Robert Hensley). Intern Bellevue Hosp., N.Y.C., 1919-21; urologist U.S. VA Hosp., Jefferson Barracks, Mo., 1921-24; asst. urologist Baylor Univ. Med. Sch., Dallas, 1924-26; asso. with Bransford Lewis, urologist, St. Louis, 1926-41; asst. prof. urology St. Louis U., 1945-50, asso. prof., 1950-58, prof., 1959—; cons. urology St. Louis City Hosp.; urologist St. John's Hosp., 1933—, asso. chief of staff, 1952—, chief urol. staff, 1959—; cons. urologist Jewish Hosp. Diplomate Am. Bd. Urology (past pres.). Mem. A.M.A. (chmn. sect. urology 1947), A.C.S., Am. Urol. Assn. (pres. 1962-63; past pres. S. Central Sect.), So. Med. Assn. (past chmn. urol. sect.), Delta Tau Delta Presbyn. Club: Bellerive Country. Home: 710 S Hanley Rd Clayton, MO 63105. Office: 316 Beaumont Blvd St Louis MO 63108

CARROLL, HELENA, actress, producer; b. Glasgow, Scotland; d. Paul Vincent and Helena (Reilly) Carroll; student Webber-Douglas Sch. Drama, London, 1949-49. Theatrical appearances include A Babble of Green Field, 1949; repertory in Worthing, Eng., Croyden, Eng., Southport, Eng; appeared in London in Riders to the Sea. 1949, The Monkey Puzzle, 1950, The Common Property, 1951; tour U.S. with Dublin Players, 1951-53; N.Y.C. debut in The Wise Have Not Spoken. 1954; tour in The Seven Year Itch, 1956; Broadway debut in Separate Tables, 1956; a founder. Irish Players, 1957; other appearances include A Touch of the Poet; Shadow and Substance; Happy as Larry; Little Moon of Albion, 1960; The Hostage (tour), 1961; Sharon's Grave, 1961; Oliver, 1963; film appearance in Midnight Episode narrator travel film; The Spell of Ireland, 1953; numerous TV appearances. Mem. Artists Equity Assn., A.F.T.R.A., Screen Artists Guild. Address: 325 W 45th St New York City NY 10036*

CARROLL, HOLBERT NICHOLSON, educator; b. Charleroi, Pa., June 30, 1921; s. James Russell and Mary Leola (McDonough) C.; A.B., U. Pitts., 1943, M.A., 1947; postgrad. Yale, 1943-44; Ph.D., Harvard, 1953. Faculty, U. Pitts., 1946-48, 50—, prof. polit. sci., 1960—, chmn. dept., 1960-68; teaching fellow Harvard, 1949-50. Cons. Brookings Instn., 1959. Served with AUS, 1943-46; CBI. Mem. Am. Polit. Sci. Assn., Am. Acad. Polit. and Social Sci., Phi Beta Kappa, Omicron Delta Kappa, Delta Sigma Rho, Pi Sigma Alpha. Author: The House of Representatives and Foreign Affairs, 1958, rev. edit., 1966; contbr. chpt. to The Congress and America's Future, 1965. Office: Dept Polit Sci U Pitts Pittsburgh PA 15213

CARROLL, JAMES MATTHEW, utility exec.; b. Springfield, Mass., Dec. 9, 1908; s. Alfred Joseph and Margaret E. (Cruse) C.; A.B. magna cum laude, Holy Cross Coll., 1931; LL.B., Yale, 1934; m. Ruth Madelyn Crowe, Feb. 14, 1942; children—James Matthew, Deborah V., Kathleen M., Nancy C. Admitted to Mass. bar, 1934; asst. city solicitor Springfield, 1938-39, city solicitor, 1940-43; spl. counsel SEC, Phila., 1944-46; spl. asst. to U.S. atty., Los Angeles, 1945; commnr. Mass. Dept. Pub. Utilities, 1949-51; counsel, sec. Am. Bosch Arma Corp., 1951-55; asst. gen. counsel Boston Edison Co., 1956-63, v.p., gen. counsel, 1963—, also dir. Incorporator, Cath. Scholarships for Negroes, 1946. Mem. Am., Mass., Hampden County, Boston bar Boston bar assns. Democrat. Roman Catholic. Clubs: Algonquin (Boston); Wellesley. Home: 44 Skyline Dr Wellesley Hills, MA 02181. Office: 800 Boylston St Boston MA 02199

CARROLL, JEFFERSON ROY, Jr., architect; b. Phila., Sept. 25, 1904; s. J. Roy and Mary (Greenaway) C.; B.Arch., U. Pa., 1926, M.Arch. (fellow), 1928; m. Doris Hansen Packard, Dec. 15th, 1945; children—Spencer Packard (Mrs. Charles K. Fassett), Mary Margaret

(Mrs. Robert Rigby Morrison), Patricia Carroll. Partner firm Carroll, Grisdale & Van Alen, architects, 1946—. Asst. prof., exec. chmn. design staff U. Pa., 1945; vis. lectr. architecture Pa. State U., 1953-54; archtl. cons. Dept. Army, 1964—; mem. archtl. rev. bd. Dept. Navy, 1965—. Chmn., Delaware County Adv. Com. on archtl. rev. bd. Dept. Navy, 1965—. Chmn., Delaware County Adv. Com. on Housing and Planning, 1947-52; pres. Citizens Council Housing and Planning of Delaware County, 1953-56; Mem. Swarthmore Borough Council, 1955-60. Asso. trustee, chmn. fine arts bd. U. Pa.; adv. bd. Temple U. Sch. Architecture. Recipient award Sch. Architecture. Recipient award Appammattox Monument competition, 1932. Registered architect, Pa., N.J., Md., N.Y., Wash., Va., Tenn., D.C., R.I. Fellow A.I.A. (Phila. pres. 1951-52, gold medal Phila. chap. 1963, regional dir. 1956, nat. sec. 1959-62, 1st v.p. 1962-63, pres. 1963-64, pres. A.I.A. Found. 1964-68, Phila. architects charitable trust 1968—, chancellor Coll. of Fellows), Royal Soc. Arts (London, Eng.), Philippine Inst. Architects (hon.), Royal Archtl. Inst. Can. (hon.); mem. Colegio de Arquitectos de Mexico (hon.), Pa. Soc. Architects (gold medal 1963, pres. 1945-46), Phila. Housing Assn. (dir.), Phila. Art Alliance, Franklin Inst. Phila., Archtl. League N.Y., Phila. Numis. and Antiquarian Soc. Phila., Pa. Acad. Fine Arts, Gen. Alumni Soc. U. Pa. (pres. 1944-45, Alumni award of merit 1948), Sigma Xi, Tau Sigma Delta. Presbyterian (pres. bd. trustees 1952, elder, mem. session 1965-68). Clubs: Union League (Phila.); Cosmos (Washington); Carpenters Company Phila. (mgmt. com.); Century Assn. (N.Y.C.). Contbr. articles to profl. publs. Bldgs. designed by firm include: Youth Study Center, Phila. Internat. Airport Terminal, Student Union Bldg. at La Salle Coll., Law Sch. Bldg. U. Pa. (all Phila.); FAA Office Bldg., The Mall, NASA Bldg. (both Washington). Home: 501 Riverview Rd Swarthmore PA 19081 Office: 6 Penn Center Plaza Philadelphia PA 19103

CARROLL, JOHN BISSELL, psychologist; b. Hartford, Conn., June 5, 1916; s. William James and Helen M. (Bissell) C.; B.A., Wesleyan U., 1937; Ph.D., U. Minn., 1941; A.M., Harvard, 1953; m. Mary Elizabeth Searle, Sept. 6, 1941; 1 dau., Melissa (Mrs. F. Stuart Chapin III). Instr., Mt. Holyoke Coll., 1940-42, Ind. U., 1942-43; lectr. U. Chgo., 1943-44; research psychologist Dept. Army, 1946-49; asst. prof. Harvard Grad. Sch. Edn., 1949-53, asso. prof., 1953-57, prof. edn., 1957-62, prof. ednl. psychology, 1962-67; sr. research psychologist Ednl. Testing Service, Princeton, New Jersey, 1967—. Mem. com. aptitude examiners Coll. Entrance Exam. Bd., 1952-65, commn. tests, 1967-70; adv. com. on new ednl. media U.S. Office Edn., 1961-64. Served to lt. (j.g.) USNR, 1944-46. Recipient E.L. Thorndike award for distinguished service to ednl. psychology, 1970. Fellow Am. Psychol. Assn.; mem. Psychometric Soc. (pres. 1960- 61), Linguistic Soc. Am., Nat. Acad. Edn. Author: The Study of Language, 1953; Modern Language Aptitude Test, 1958; Language and Thought, 1964. Editor: Language, Thought and Reality, 1956. Home: 33 Eglantine Av Pennington NJ 08534 Office: Ednl Testing Service Princeton NJ 08540

CARROLL, JOHN EDWARD, indsl. exec.; b. Hibbing, Minn., 1912; student U. Minn. Pres., dir. Am. Hoist & Derrick Co., St. Paul; dir. Smith Industries Internat., Inc., Old Fort Industries, Inc., Am. Nat. Bank & Trust Co., First Midwest Capital Corp., Eastern Ry. Supplies, Inc. Bd. dirs. St. Joseph's Hosp., St. John's U. Home: 772 Linwood Av St Paul MN 55105 Office: 63 S Robert St St Paul MN 55107*

CARROLL, JOHN WALLACE, journalist; b. Milw., Dec. 15, 1906; s. John Francis and Josephine (Meyer) C.; B.Litt., Marquette U., 1928; LL.D. (hon.), Duke, 1968; m. Margaret Sawyer, May 25, 1938; children—Margaret, John, Rosamond, Patricia. With U.P.I., 1928-1941, London, 1929-31, Paris, 1931-34, Geneva, 1934-38, corr. Spanish Civil War, 1938, diplomatic corr., London, 1938, mgr. bur., London, 1939; covered Eng.'s first 2 yrs. of war, Russian front, 1941; dir. London office OWI, 1942-44, dep. dir. Overseas br. (for Europe), 1944-45; exec. news editor Winston-Salem (N.C.) Jour. & Sentinel, 1949-55, editor, pub. 1963—; Washington news editor N.Y. Times, 1955-63. Cons. Dept. State, Dept. Army, Psychol. Strategy Bd., 1947-52, Mass. Inst. Tech., 1952-54, U. N.C. 1952-54; lectr. Nat. War Coll., Air War U., other service instns. Adv. com. Pulitzer Prizes, 1969—. Trustee N.C. Sch. Arts. Winner Nat. Headliners Club award for outstanding dispatches on war in Russia, 1942. Author: We're in This With Russia, 1942; Persuade or Perish, 1948. Home: 852 Wellington Rd Winston-Salem NC 27102 Office: Jour & Sentinel Winston-Salem NC 27102

CARROLL, JOSEPH FRANCIS, assn. exec., former air force officer; b. Chgo., Mar. 19, 1910; s. James Michael and Sara (Kane) C.; A.B., St. Mary's, Mundelein, Ill., 1933; J.D. (Chief Justice White scholar), Loyola U., Chgo., 1940; m. Mary Ann Morrissey, Aug. 21, 1937; children—Joseph Francis, James Michael, Brian Patrick, Dennis Thomas, Kevin Martin. Admitted to Ill. bar, 1940. Spl. agt. various field offices FBI, 1940-44, chief gen. criminal sect., Washington, asst. div. chief, gen. investigations div., 1944-45; dir. compliance enforcement div. Surplus Property Adminstrn., War Assests Adminstrn., 1945-47, insp. in charge fraud and accounting matters, FBI, 1947; commd. col. USAF, brig. gen., 1948; now maj. gen.; dir. Office Spl. Investigations, Insp. Gen. USAF, 1948-50; dep. insp. gen. for security, 1950-58; dep. comdr. USAFE, (REAR), 1958-60; lt. gen. Insp. Gen. USAF, 1960-61; dir. Def. Intelligence Agy., Washington, 1961-68; ret., 1968; exec. dir. Nat. Council Cath. Men., Washington, 1968—. Decorated Legion of Merit, D.S.M. Mem. Ill. Bar Assn. Roman Catholic. Home: 7306 Rippon Rd Alexandria VA Office: 1312 Massachusetts Av NW Washington DC 20005 Office: Def Intelligence Agy Pentagon Washington DC 20301

CARROLL, LEO G., actor; b. Weedon, Eng., 1892; m. Nancy De Silva, 1927; 1 son, William First appeared in English prodn. Liberty Hall, 1908; Broadway appearances: The Vortex, 1925, Green Bay Tree, 1935, Two Bouquets, 1938, You Never Can Tell, 1948; Someone Waiting, 1956; role in Angel Street, 1941-44, Late George Apley, 1945-46; motion pictures include Wuthering Heights, 1939, Waterloo Bridge, Rebecca, 1940, Spellbound, House on 92d Street, 1945, Paradine Case, 1948, The Swan, 1956; also The Barretts of Wimpole Street, Forever Amber, Father of the Bride, Strangers on a Train, Snows of Kilmanjaro, We're No Angels, North by Northwest, Desert Fox, Bad and the Beautiful, Young Bess, The Parent Trap, others; played role of Cosmo Topper Television series, 1953; co-star Going My Way TV series, The Man from U.N.C.L.E., 1964-67. Office: care Players Club 16 Gramercy Park S New York City NY 10003

CARROLL, LOREN, fgn. service officer; b. Scanlon, Minn., Mar. 5, 1904; s. John and Mary (Noonan) C.; m. Sheila M. Baker, May 9, 1949; children—Alexander, Nicholas. Various positions newspapers 1924-33; corr. Internat. News Service, Europe, 1933; city editor N.Y. Herald Tribune, European edit., 1934-37; fgn. editor, Newsweek, N.Y., 1940; chief OWI Psychol. Warfare Operations, Western Europe, hdqrs. London, 1942-43; press attache, Am. Diplomatic Mission Algiers, Am. embassy, Paris, 1944; chief Paris bur. Newsweek, 1945-51; pub. affairs officer attached to NATO, Paris, France, 1952-56; U.S. consul- gen., Que., 1956-60, Palermo, Sicily, Italy, 1960-64; editor Fgn. Service Jour., Washington, 1964—. Author: Wild Onion, 1930; Conversation Please, 1939. Home: 105 Grafton St Chevy Chase MD 20015 Office: Fgn Service Jour 815 17th St Washington DC 20009

CARROLL, LOUIS FRANCIS, lawyer; b. Davenport, Ia., May 31, 1905; s. Edward John and Lydia (Keller) C.; B.A., U. Ia., 1927; J.D., State U. Ia., 1929; m. Lina Katherine Sidney, July 18, 1930; children—Michael Edward, Sidney Ann (Mrs. David Peter Knapp), Mary Lydia, Terence John, Timothy Thomas. Admitted to N.Y. bar, 1930, since practiced in N.Y.C.; partner firm Willkie, Farr & Gallagher, N.Y.C., and predecessors, 1941—. Mem. Am., N.Y. State bar assns., Assn. Bar City N.Y., N.Y. County Lawyers Assn., Am. Judicature Soc., Order of Coif, Phi Beta Kappa, Delta Sigma Rho, Delta Upsilon. Republican. Roman Catholic. Clubs: Board Room, Wall Street (N.Y.C.); St. Andrews Golf (Hastings-on-Hudson, N.Y.); Larchmont Yacht. Home: 11 Locust Av Larchmont NY 10538 Office: 1 Chase Manhattan Plaza New York City NY 10005

CARROLL, LUKE PAUL, newspaper editor; b. N.Y.C., Oct. 18, 1915; s. Michael J. and Delia (Farley) C.; m. Christine Francis Murphy, June 1, 1941; children—Christine N. (Mrs. Vincent Avell), Judith E. (Mrs. William Stull), Paul F., Deborah D. (Mrs. William Brinkmann), Susan E. (Mrs. Charles Hardy), Geoffrey M., Frances Joanne, Geraldine F. Reporter, N.Y.C. News Assn., 1936-40; reporter N.Y. Herald Tribune, 1940-44, Chgo. corr., 1944-49, asst. to editor, 1949-52, news and fgn. editor, 1952-54, city editor, news editor, nat. editor, fgn. editor, 1954-58, asst. exec. editor, 1958- 60; mng. editor Chgo.'s American, 1960-70; editor Chgo. Today, 1970-71, exec. v.p., gen. mgr., 1971—; Am.; dir. Hygrade Food Products Corp. Mem. Archdiocesan Commn. on Human Relations and Ecumenism. Bd. dirs. Chgo. Am. Charities, Mid-Am. chpt. A.R.C.; trustee Barrington Hills Countryside Fire Protection Dist. Mem. Am. Soc. Newspaper Editors, Am. Newspaper Pubs. Assn. Clubs: Tavern, Chicago Press: Barrington Hills Country. Home: Bateman Rd Barrington IL 60010 Office: 445 N Michigan Av Chicago IL 60611

CARROLL, MARK SULLIVAN, publisher; b. Boston, Apr. 25, 1924; s. Francis M. and Barbara (Blum) C.; A.B., Harvard, 1950; m. Jane Hartenstein, Apr. 25, 1953; children—Alison, Jeremy, John. Corr., reporter Boston Post, 1948-50; news editor radio sta. WORL, Boston, 1950- 51; promotion mgr. Yale U. Press, 1951-56; asst. to dir. Harvard U. Press, 1956-59, asso, dir., 1959-67, dir. Harvard U. Press, 1968—; cons. Pahlavi U., Shiraz, Iran, 1966. Vice pres. Am. Inst. Graphic Arts, 1962-64; mem. exec. com. Assn. Am. Univ. Presses, 1963-64. bd. dirs., 1970—; bd. dirs., sec. Assn. Am. Pubs., 1970—; mem. publs. com. Unitarian Universalist Assn., 1962-65. Served with AUS, 1943-47; ETO. Decorated Purple Heart. Ford Found. grantee, Turkey, 1966. Mem. Am. Book Pubs. Council (dir. 1969-70). Democrat. Unitarian. Home: 29 Oakland St Lexington MA 02173 Office: 79 Garden St Cambridge MA 02138

CARROLL, MARSHALL ELLIOTT, architect; b. Durham, N.C., May 14, 1923; s. Dudley Dewitt and Eleanore (Elliott) C.; A.B., Harvard, 1943; student Grad. Sch. Design, 1947-51; m. Dorothy Jane Grune, Mar. 28, 1953; children—Jane Dudley, Marshall Elliott, Frederick Grune. Asso. G. Milton Small & Assos., architects and engrs., Raleigh, N.C., 1957-60; various positions to dep. exec. v.p. A.I.A., Washington, 1960-71; parnter Vincent G. Kling & Partners, architects, planners and engrs., Phila., 1971—. Pres. N.C. Symphony Soc., 1955-60. Served to capt. USNR, 1944-46, 51-53. Fellow A.I.A.; mem. Harvard Grad. Sch. Design Assn. (v.p.), U.S. Naval Inst. Democrat. Episcopalian. Club: Cosmos (Washington). Project dir.; Urban Design, the Architecture of Towns and Cities, 1965; Architectural Graphic Standards, 6th edit., 1970. Home: 460 Foxchase Lane Media PA 19063 Office: 1401 Arch St Philadelphia PA 19102

CARROLL, SISTER MARY THOMAS AQUINAS, religious ofcl., educator; b. Pitts., Mar. 24, 1913; d. Edward Joseph and Estelle (Bonner) Carroll; B.A., U. Pitts., 1934, L.H.D. 1964; M.A., U. Toronto, 1939; Ph.D., Cath. U. Am., 1946. Joined Soc. of Sisters of Mercy, 1935; faculty Mt. Mercy Coll., Pitts., 1939-66, prof. history, 1949-63, dean, 1952-63, pres., 1963-66; lectr. Cath. U. Am., 1947-51, Marquette U., 1959-61, 63. Mem. nat. exec. com. Sister Formation Conf., 1960—, nat. chmn., 1969-71; mother gen. Congregation Pitts. Sisters of Mercy, 1964—. Am. del. Internat. Union Superiors Gen., Rome, 1967, 70, mem. council, 1970-73. Trustee Mt. Mercy Coll., Mercy Hosp., Pitts., Holy Cross Hosp., Ft. Lauderdale. Mem. Leadership Conf. Women Religious (pres. 1971-72, exec. com.). Author: The Venerable Bede: His Spiritual Teaching, 1946. Contbr. articles to profl. jours. Address: 3333 5th Av Pittsburgh PA 15213

CARROLL, MATTHEW EUGENE, mfg. co. exec.; b. Chillicothe, Ill., Nov. 8, 1916; s. Henry C. and Anne (O'Bryne) C.; grad. Spalding Inst., Ill., 1936; m. Ellen Estep, June 1, 1940; children—Janet (Mrs. Dennis Geraghty), Patricia E. (Mrs. Luis Garcia), Susan (Mrs. Thomas Tremba), Thomas, Molly. Vice pres. marketing Mpls.-Moline Co., 1959-61; pres. dir. Clinton Engines Co., 1961-63; chmn., dir. Amalgamated Metal Industries, 1963—; pres., dir. Sterling Precision Corp., 1965—; dir. Resource Exploration Corp., Larson Industries. Served with USNR, 1945-46. Home: 8 Westhill Circle Stamford CT 06902 Office: 1 Rockefeller Center New York City NY 10020

CARROLL, MITCHELL BENEDICT, lawyer; b. Richmond Va., July 2, 1898; s. Mitchell and Caroline Moncure (Benedict) C.; B.A., Johns Hopkins, 1920; postgrad. U. Grenoble, Ecole Libre des Sciences Politiques, U. Madrid, U. Geneva, Academie de Droit Internat., The Hague; Licencie en Droit, Université de Paris, 1922; J.D., U. Bonn, Germany, 1923; J.D., George Washington U., 1927; m. Catharine Breen, May 20, 1931. Admitted to D.C. bar, 1926, N.Y. bar, 1933; chief sect. European law and taxes U.S. Dept. Commerce, 1924-29; mem. Conf. Tech. Experts on Double Taxation, London,1927, Conf. Govtl. Experts on Double Taxation, Geneva, 1928, Law Commn. Fed. Aeronautique Internationale, 1929-31; spl. atty. internat. tax matters U.S. Treasury Dept., 1930-31; mem. Am. Commn. to negotiate double taxation treaty with France, 1930; dir. survey tax systems in 35 countries Fiscal Com. League Nations, 1931-33, Am. mem. Fiscal Com., 1934- 1946, chmn., 1938-39, acting pres. meeting Mexico City, June 1940, regional fiscal conf. Mexico City, 1943; chmn. com. Problems of Fgn. Investments League of Nations, 1944-45; cons. State Dept. U.S., 1942; pres. Internat. Fiscal Assn. (cons. fiscal commn. UN 1948-55); congresses The Hague 1939, 47, Rome 1948, 56, Monte Carlo 1950, Zurich 1951, Brussels 1952, Paris (medal) 1953, Cologne 1954, Amsterdam, 1955, Vienna, 1957, Knokke, Belgium, 1958, Madrid, 1959, Basle, Switzerland, 1960, Jerusalem, Israel, 1961, Athens, Greece (awarded medal of honor), 1962, Paris, 1963, Hamburg, 1964, London, 1965, Lisbon, 1966, Stockholm, 1967, Rotterdam, 1969, Brussels, 1970. Decorated officer Order of Leopold 1, 1952. Mem. Inst. Finances Publiques, Am. (past chmn. double taxation com., chmn. sect. internat. and comparative law 1943-45), N.Y. State bar assns., Council on Fgn. Relations, Am. Fgn. Law Assn., Am. Soc. Internat. Law, Am. Br. Internat. Law Assn. (del. conf. 1948), Academie Diplomatique Internat., Inter-Am. Bar Assn. (del. numerous confs.), Bar Assn. City N.Y., Chevalier du Tastevin de Bourgogne (France). Clubs: Metropolitan (N.Y.C., Washington); Pilgrims. Author books on taxation, contbr. articles on internat. tax law to law publs. Home: 180 E 79th St New York City NY 10021 Office Coudert Bros 200 Park Av New York City NY 10017

CARROLL, MOLLIE RAY, educator; b. Des Moines; d. Alonzo Neighton and Rachel Pauline (Gullette) Carroll; Ph.B., M.A., Ph.D., U. Chgo. Asso. prof., prof., chmn. dept. econs. and sociology Goucher Coll., 1921-30; asso. prof. social economy U. Chgo., exec. head resident U. Chgo. Settlement, 1930-35; councilor on labor studies Div. Rev., NRA, 1935; research dir. Workers Edn. Bur., 1936-37; indsl. economist Div. Labor Standards, U. S. Dept. Labor, 1937-42; tng. specialist in Social Security, 1942-55. John Simon Guggenheim Found. fellow, 1927-28. Trustee Am. Found. for Homeopathy. Author: Labor and Politics; Unemployment Insurance in Germany; Our Wants and How They are Satisfied; Unemployment Insurance in Austria; American Workers' Education (with Spencer Miller Jr.); What Is Collective Bargaining? Contbr. to Trade Unionism in the U.S., also to labor, social service and econ. jours. Home: 10507 Cedar Av Fairfax, VA 22030

CARROLL, PAUL BERTRAND, paper co. exec.; b. Springfield, Mass., Oct. 11, 1909; s. Michael J. and Mary (Noone) C.; A.B., Fordham U., 1929, LL.B., 1932; m. Ann Joyce Cramer, Oct. 28, 1939; children—Peter, Ann (Mrs. William J. Nealon), Jane, Paula, Elizabeth. Admitted to N.Y. bar, 1933; asso. firm Lorenz & Lorenz, N.Y.C., 1934-37; full time mem. faculty Fordham U. Law Sch., 1937-42, part time, 1942-47; with Internat. Paper Co., 1942—, gen. solicitor, 1961-65, gen. counsel, sec., 1965-70, v.p., sec., gen. counsel, 1970—; pres. Internat. Records Corp.; sec. Ariz. Chem. Corp., Internat.-Stanley Corp.; dir. Red River Paper Mill, Inc. Bd. dirs., sec. Speech Rehab. Inst. Mem. Am., N.Y. State bar assns., Assn. Gen. Counsel, Am. Soc. Corp. Secs., New Eng. Soc. in N.Y. Roman Catholic. Clubs: Union League (N.Y.C.); Larchmont Yacht. Home: 7 Lyons Pl Larchmont NY 10538 Office: 220 E 42d St New York City NY 10017

CARROLL, PHIL, cons. indsl. engr.; b. Bucyrus, O., June 20, 1895; s. Phil and Martha Ada (Couts) C.; B.S. in Elec. Engring., U. Mich., 1918, M.E., 1940; m. Margaret Birdsell, Mar. 20, 1920; children—Margaret Birdsell (Mrs. L. Terry Finch), Jeane Durrell (Mrs. Thomas G. Custin), Phil III, Patricia Anne (Mrs. Martin H. Buchler, III). Engaged in r.r. work, track constrn., automatic signals, summers 1911-17; with Westinghouse, East Pittsburgh, 1919, timestudy Krantz Mfg. Co. (Westinghouse), Bklyn., 1921-22, Westinghouse, Mansfield, O., 1922-23; with Hydraulic Pressed Steel Co., Cleve., 1923-24; a founder Dyer Engrs., Inc., Cleve., 1924, engr., chief engr., v.p. in charge operations, 1924-40; own bus. specializing in timestudy, wage incentive, cost control, 1940—. Lectr., Newark Newark Coll. Engring., Stevens Inst. Tech., univs. Pa., Mich., Wis., Conn., N.Y. Chmn., Maplewood (N.J.) Planning Bd., 1965-69; mem. indsl. engring. adv. com. U. Mich. Served with Signal Corps, adv. com. U. Mich. Served with Signal Corps, U.S. Army, 1918. Awarded Gilbreth medal in 1950, Indsl. Incentive award, 1953, Distinguished Alumnus, U. Mich., 1953. Fellow Am. Soc. M.E. (Gantt medal bd. 1949-53, chmn. mgmt. div. 1954, chmn. gen. engring. dept., mem. bd. tech. 1962-63), Internat. Acad. Mgmt. (Frank and Lillian Gilbreth award 1970), Am. Inst. Indsl. Engrs. (regional v.p. 1956), Gilbreth award 1970), Am. Inst. Indsl. Engrs. (regional v.p. 1956), Soc. for Advancement Mgmt. (Distinguished Service award N.J. chpt. 1958, nat. sec. 1947, nat. treas. 1948-49, nat. sec. 1947, nat. treas. 1948-49. v.p. membership 1955-57, 1st v.p. 1957, pres. 1958, chmn. bd. 1959; mem. Wallace Clark Bd. Award 1960-66, chmn. 1962); mem. N.J. Tech. Socs. Council (pres. 1951), U.S. Adv. Group on European Productivity, Am. Mgmt. Assn., Nat. Soc. Profl. Engrs., Acad. Mgmt. Republican. Methodist (ofcl. bd.). Mason. Author: Timestudy for Cost Control, 1938; Timestudy Fundamentals for Foremen, 1944; Discussion Leaders Manual, 1948; How to Chart Data, 1950; rev., 1960; How to Control Production Costs, 1952; How Foremen Can Control Costs, 1955; Better Wage Incentives, 1957; Cost Control Through Electronic Data Processing, 1958; Profit Control, 1962; Overhead Cost Control, 1964; Practical Production and Inventory Control, 1966. Contbr.: Foremen's Handbook, 1943, 66; Industrial Engineering Handbook, 1956; profl. jours., encys. in field. Editorial bd. Advanced Mgmt. and Supervision. Address: 6 Crestwood Dr Maplewood NJ 07040

CARROLL, RICHARD C., ednl. adminstr.; b. Burlington, Vt., Mar. 16, 1909; s. Carl H. and Lena Nina (Cushman) C.; grad. Phillips Andover Acad., 1928; A.B., Yale, 1932, M.A., 1940; m. Esther Helen Peck, Aug. 2, 1935; children—Richard C., Nana. Asst. dean Yale, 1939-43, dean army students, 1943-48, asso. dean, 1948-49, dean students, 1949-51, dean of undergraduate affairs, 1957-68, asso. sec. of the univ., 1968—. Fellow Timothy Dwight Coll. Trustee Hopkins Grammar Sch., pres. bd., 1961—; bd. dir. Prospect Hill Sch., 1957-59, Conn. Radio Found., Inc. Mem. Zeta Psi. Home: 165 Huntington St New Haven CT

CARROLL, ROBERT LLOYD, educator; b. Rapid City, S.D., Mar. 22, 1931; s. Foster George and Jeannette A. (Kooima) C.; B.A., U. Cin., 1953, M.A., 1955; Ph.D., U. Mich., 1960; m. Wanda Kennedy, July 24, 1953; children—Steve, Beth, Scott. Teaching fellow U. Mich., 1956-58, instr., 1958-60, 60-63; asst. prof. sociology Cornell U., 1963-66; asso. prof. U. Cin., 1966-68, asst. v.p. research, dir. Inst. Social, Behavioral and Bus. Studies, 1968, prof., head dept. sociology, 1969—. Cons. in field; lectr. Wittenberg U., Bucknell U., Harvard, 1971. Chmn. com. long range research and planning Community Chest, Cin., 1971—. Mem. Am., Rural sociol. socs., Population Assn. Am. Home: 3560 Interwood St Cincinnati OH 45220

CARROLL, ROBERT WAYNE, educator; b. Chgo., May 10, 1930; s. Walter Scott and Dorothy (Le Monnier) C.; B.S., U. Wis., 1952; Ph.D., U. Md., 1959; m. Berenice Jacobs, Sept. 7, 1957; 1 son, David Leon. Aero. research scientist NASA, Cleve., 1952-54; NSF postdoctoral fellow, 1959-60; asst. prof. Rutgers U., 1960-63, asso. prof., 1963-64; asso. prof. U. Ill., Urbana, 1964-67, prof. math., 1967—. Served with U.S. Army, 1954-57. Mem. Am., French math. socs. Author: Abstract Methods in Partial Differential Equations, 1969. Asso. editor: Jour. Applicable Analysis, 1970—. Home: 2010 Silver Ct E Urbana IL 61801

CARROLL, ROBERT WILLIAM, r.r. exec.; b. Ossining, N.Y., May 29, 1923; s. John Francis and Catherine Veronica (Coyne) C.; student Sch. Commerce, N.Y.U., 1952-56, Mgmt. Inst., 1957; m. Mary Bernardine Dugan, June 1, 1946; children—Kevin, Dennis, Terrence, Maura, Monica. With N.Y. Central R.R. 1942-68, sec., 1959-68; sr. asst. sec. Penn Central Transp. Co., 1968-70, sec., 1971—, also sec. 110 subsidiaries. Served with USCGR, 1942-46. Mem. Am. Soc. Corporate Secs., V.F.W., Soc. Friendly Sons St. Patrick. K.C. (4). Club: Overbrook Golf (Bryn Mawr, Pa.). Home: 9 Ridgewood Rd Radnor PA 19087 Office: Transportation Center 6 Penn Center Plaza Philadelphia PA 19103

CARROLL, THOMAS SYLVESTER, business exec.; b. N.Y.C., Oct. 1, 1919; s. Thomas Jeremiah and Johanna (Mulvihill) C.; A.B. cum laude, Catawba Coll., 1941; postgrad. Mass. Inst. Tech., 1941-42; M.B.A. with distinction, Harvard, 1947; m. Sidney Burke, Sept. 27, 1947; children—Jeffrey Burke, Thomas Jeremiah, James Francis,

Matthew, Charles Laurence. Brand man Procter and Gamble Co., 1947-53; product dir. Gen. Foods Corp., 1953-55; marketing mgr. Colgate-Palmolive Co., 1955-57; v.p. George Fry & Assos., 1957-58; gen. mgr. marketing services Lever Bros. Co., 1958- 59, marketing v.p., 1959-63, merchandising v.p., 1963-64, dir., 1963—, exec. v.p., 1964-67, pres., chief exec., 1967—; dir. Interpace Corp. Police commr. City of New Canaan, Conn., 1963-67; mem. Greater N.Y. com. United Negro Coll. Fund; chmn. comml. div. United Fund Greater N.Y.; adv. bd. Better Bus. Bur. Harlem; mem. N.Y. Share in Freedom Com. Bd. dirs. Whitby Sch., Greenwich, Conn., 1962-66, Inst. for Applied Behavioral Sci., 1970-71; trustee Catawba Coll., 1967; bd. dirs. Fifth Av. Assn. Served from cadet to lt. col., USAAF, 1941-46. Mem. Grocery Mfrs. Assn. (dir.), Harvard Bus. Sch. Assn. (exec. council), Nat. Inst. Social Scis. Clubs: Country of New Canaan, New Canaan Winter, New Canaan Field; Racquet and Tennis, Economic (dir.) (N.Y.C). Home: Oenoke Ridge New Canaan CT 06840 Office: 390 Park Av New York City NY 10022

CARROLL, VINCENT P., surgeon; b. Kirksville, Mo., Mar. 14, 1904; s. Edward and Mary (Winter) C.; B.S., Mo. State College; M.D., D.Sc., Cal. Coll. Medicine at Los Angeles; m. Ann Claire Zachow, 1928; children—Patricia (Mrs. John H. Farnworth), Mary (Mrs. Thomas Mahoney), Vincent Patrick. Intern Laughlin Hosp., Kirksville, Mo., 1929- 30; resident surg. tng. Los Angeles Co. Hosp., 1932-34; practice gen. surgery So. Cal., 1937—; mem. surg. staff Santa Ana Community Hosp., 1934—; chief staff South Coast Community Hosp., Laguna Beach. Chmn. adv. com. Regional Med. Program, U. Cal. at Irvine. Mem. adv. bd. Security Pacific Nat. Bank, Laguna Beach; dir. Laguna Fed. Savs. and Loan. Chmn. Orange County Inter-Agy. Council on Smoking and Health. Mem. World, Am. (del.), Cal. (del.) Orange County med. assns., Cal. (mem. bd.), Orange County, (past pres.) Tb and health assns., Am. Med. Writers Assn., Laguna C. of C., Sigma Tau Gamma. Roman Catholic. Elk. Clubs: Jonathan (Los Angeles); Santa Ana Country; Irvine Country (Corono-Del Mar); Rotary of Laguna Beach (pres. 1933-34). Contbr. articles to profl. jours. Home: 1920 Glenneyre St Laguna Beach CA 92651 Office: 265 Laguna Av Laguna Beach CA 92651

CARROLL, WALLACE EDWARD, corp. exec.; b. Taunton, Mass., Nov. 4, 1907; s. Patrick J. and Katherine (Feely) C.; Ph.B., Boston Coll., 1928, LL.D., 1957; postgrad. Mass. Inst. Tech., 1929, Harvard Bus. Sch., N.Y.U., 1933, Northwestern U. 1936; m. Lelia Holden, Nov. 7, 1936; childrenWallace E., Denis H., Barry J., Lelia K.H. Various positions, 1924-29; with N.Y. Telephone Co., 1930-33, Reed & Barton, 1933-34, Fed. Products, 1934-40; chmn., dir. Wacker Sales, 1940—, Size Control Co., 1941—, Walsh Press & Die Co., 1945-, Am. Gage & Machine Co., 1948-, Simpson Electric Co., 1950—, Standard Transformer Co., 1956—: chmn. bd. Katy Industries, Inc. 1970—, Hawthorne Bank Wheaton, Dei-Con Co., Australia; vice chmn., dir. Ludlow Typograph Co.; vice chmn. M.-K.-T. R.R.; pres. Affiliated Screw Products Co., 1951-; treas., dir. Midwest Gage Lab., G.M. Diehl Machine Co., Bativa Body Co., Champion Pneumatic Machinery Co., 1957—; dir. Binks Mfg. Co., Burgmaster Corp., Chgo. Helicopter Corp., Merc. Nat. Bank, First Drovers Corp., Consol. Packaging, Firth Sterling, Inc., Mich. Av. Financial Group, Inc., Matsuoka-Binks Kiki Kabushiki Kaisha, Ruttonsha-Simpson Private Ltd., Ga, Internat. Corp., Warwick Mfg. Co., Brit. Labour Pump Co., Ordnance Engring, Assos. Dir, metal-working equipment div. BDSA, Dept. Commerce, Washington, 1957; with U.S. Trade Mission to India, 1958-59, UAR, 1960, Ireland and Portugal, 1966. Chmn. fed. agencies Community Fund drive, 1959. Bd. dirs. Catholic Charities, 1962. Chgo. Boys Club; bd. regents Boston Coll; trustee Christine and Alfred Sonntag Found. Cancer Research. DePaul U. Served as cadet with Air Corps, U.S. Army, 1929; with N.Y.N.G., 1930-33. Mem. Tool and Die Inst. (pres. 1952-53), U.S. C. of C., Nat. Machine Tool Builders Assn. (pres. 1962-63). Roman Catholic. Clubs: Chicago Athletic, Chicago, Massachusetts Institute Technology, Harvard, Harvard Business, Boston College, New York University (Chgo.); Burning Tree (Bethesda, Md.); Exmoor Country (Highland Park, Ill.); Everglades, Bath and Tennis (Palm Beach, Fla.); Nat. Aviation; The Hundred (dir.); Edgartown Yacht; Metropolitan (Washington). Home: 900 N Waukegan Rd Lake Forest, IL Office: 853 Dundee Av Elgin IL 60120

CARROLL, WALTER WILLIAM, surgeon; b. Chgo., June 25, 1915; s. Emmett P. and Claudia Mary (Flynn) C.; B.S. magna cum laude, Loyola U., 1936; M.S., Northwestern U., 1944, M.D., 1941; m. Jean Lawler Gayton, June 13, 1942; children—Michael, Christopher. Intern, Passavant Meml. Hosp., 1940-41, surg. resident, 1941- 42, surg. fellow, 1942-44; surg. asso. Cook County Hosp., 1944-46; surg. attending staff Passavant Meml. Hosp., 1945, VA Research Hosp., 1954; active tchr. Northwestern U. Med. Sch., now prof. surgery, dir. tumor clinic. Asso. dir. for edn. and research Joint Commn. on Accreditation of Hosps., 1968—. Diplomate Am. Bd. Surgery. Fellow A.C.S.; mem. Am. Pub. Health Assn., Am. Radium Soc., Ill., Chgo. med. socs., A.M.A., Pan-Pacific, Chgo., Central, Western (past pres.), Pan- Am. surg. assns., Soc. Surgery Alimentary Tract (founder mem.), Internat. Surg. Soc. (sec.), Halsted Soc., Geriatric Soc., U.S. Pub. Health Assn., Sigma Xi. K.C., Elk. Clubs: South Shore Country, Saddle and Cycle. Cons. editor: Surgery, Gynecology and Obstetrics. Contbr. articles to profl. jours. Home: 230 E Delaware Pl Chicago IL 60611 Office: 700 N Michigan Av Chicago IL 60611

CARRON, MALCOLM, univ. pres., clergyman; b. Detroit, May 15, 1917; s. Harold Gregory and Florence Irene (McLeod) C.; A.B., U. Detroit, 1939; Ph.L., W. Baden Coll., Ind., 1945, S.T.B., 1952; M.A., Loyola U., Chgo., 1949; Ph.D., U. Mich., 1956. Joined Soc. of Jesus, 1939, ordained priest Roman Cath. Ch., 1951; instr. English St. Ignatius High Sch., Cleve., 1945-48; faculty U. Detroit, 1956—, asso. prof. edn., dean Coll. Arts and Scis., 1960-63, acad. v.p., dean, 1963-66, pres., 1966—. Bd. dirs. New Detroit, Detroit Urban League, Detroit Ednl. TV Found., Met. Fund, Round Table Catholics, Jews and Protestants. Mem. Greater Detroit C. of C. (bd. dirs.), Philosophy Edn. Soc., Jesuit Edn. Assn., Assn. Higher Edn., Blue Key, Alpha Sigma Nu, Phi Delta Kappa, Phi Kappa Phi. Clubs: University, Economic (bd. dirs.) (Detroit). Author: The Contract Colleges of Cornell UniversityA Cooperative Educational Enterprise, 1958; Readings in the Philosophy of Education, 1964. Address: U Detroit Detroit MI 48221

CARROW, BURTON STIMSON, educator; b. Phila., Feb. 12, 1925; s. Harold Jones and Anita (Jones) C.; B.S., Temple U., 1949; postgrad. N.Y.U., 1949-51. Research, U. Basle, 1951-52. Marburg U., 1951-52. Brussels Conservatory, 1951-52; mem. faculty Rutgers U., 1949-51; prof. Temple U., 1952—; minister music 1st Unitarian Ch., Phila., 1957-69. Mem. fine arts adv. com. State of Pa., 1966—. Pres. Delaware Valley Philharmonic Orch. Assn. Served with AUS, 1943-46. Recipient Distinguished Teaching award Lindbach Found., 1964, Distinguished Alumni award Temple U., 1970. Mem. Am. Musicol. Soc., Am. Assn. U. Profs., Music Educators Nat. Conf., Unitarian-Universalist Assn. Contbr. articles profl. jours. Home: 423 S Jessup St Philadelphia PA 19147

CARROW, MILTON MICHAEL, lawyer; b. N.Y.C., Sept. 13, 1912; s. Samuel and Ethel (Berlin) C.; A.B., Syracuse U., 1933, postgrad., 1933-34; LL.B., Harvard, 1937; m. Betsey Wood Hall, Nov. 2, 1940 (div. 1968); children-David M., Thomas E., Deborah, James H., Emily W.; m. 2d, Eve Wagner Cooper, Feb. 28, 1969. Admitted to N.Y. bar, 1938; asso. Legal Aid Soc., Rochester, N.Y., 1937-38: asso. Lincoln Epworth & Nathan Sweedler, 1938-42, Emil Schlesinger, 1946-48; pvt. law practice, 1948-53; partner firm Lavine & Carrow, N.Y.C., 1953-59, Landis, Carrow, Benson & Tucker N.Y.C., 1959- 70, Carrow, Bernson, Hoeniger, Freitag & Abbey, 1970—; adj. asst. prof. N.Y.U. Law Sch., 1964—; mem.faculy appellate judges seminar Inst. Jud. Adminstrn., 1969, 70, cons. Nat. Adv. Com. Civil Disorde rs, 1967—. Vice Chmn. Weston (Conn.) Charter Commn., 1965-66; chmn. citizens adv. com. Weston Bd. Edn., 1965-66; counsel UN We Believe, 1962—. Served wwith AUS, 1943-46. Mem. Am. Arbitration Assn. (panel arbitrators), Assn. Bar City N.Y. (Chmn. com. adminstrv. law 1964-67), Am. Bar Assn (chmn. elect sect. adminstrv. law 1970-71). Author: Background of Administrative Law, 1948; The Licensing Power in New York City, 1968; also articles. Home: 32 W 88th St New York NY 10024 Office: 1 E 33th St New York NY 10017

CARRUTH, CHARLES WELDON, newspaper editor; b. Haleyville, Ala., Feb. 6, 1921; s. Charles and Getha Gale (Morgan) C.; student in journalism Emory U., 1939-42; A.B., M.A. in Theatre Arts, Pasadena Coll. Theatre, 1948; student Glastonbury Monastery, Hingham, Mass. and St. Bernard Abbey, Cullman, Ala., 1959-61. Radio producer and dir., 1948-55; pub. relations, prodn. mgr. conv. and conf. programs Pub. Relations Soc. Am., Direct Mail Advt. Assn., other profl. orgns., 1955-59; with Catholic News, Roman Catholic Archdiocese N.Y., N.Y.C., 1961-69, asst. editor, 1961-64, asso. editor, 1964-66, editor, 1966-69; exec. editor Med. Counterpoint, monthly med. jour., 1969 -70, Twin Circle, nat. Catholic weekly newspaper, 1970-71; v.p., exec. editor U.S. Press Assn., 1971—. Mem. Gov. N.Y. Com. Employment Minority Groups in News Media, 1968—. Served with USAAF, 1942-45. Mem. Pi Kappa Alpha. Contbr. to periodicals, yearbooks. Address: 421 E 64th St New York City NY 10021

CARRUTH, CLARENCE URI, Jr., lawyer; b. Buffalo, Nov. 15, 1901; s. Clarence Uri and Elizabeth (Hutt) C.; student Hamilton Coll., 1918-19; A.B. Columbia, 1922, A.M., 1925, J.D. 1925; m. Nancy Stikeleather Wall, Oct. 14, 1939; 1 son, Clarence Uri III. Admitted to N.Y. bar 1926, since practiced in N.Y.C.; asso.; Curtis, Mallet-Prevost, Colt & Mosle, 1926-45, sr. partner, 1945—. Dir. Natural Resources Fund, Inc., Natural Resources of Can. Fund, Inc.; mem. temporary N.Y. State Commn. Use TV for Ednl. Purposes, 1952-53. Nat. chmn. Trinity Coll. Parents Fund, 1961-62; bd. dirs. Trinity Coll. Parents Assn., 1960—; chmn. vis. com. dept. religion Trinity Coll., 1964—. Bd. dirs. Highand Christian Mission Found. Mem. Am. Bar Assn., Assn. Bar City N.Y., N.Y. Law Inst., Phi Beta Kappa, Chi Psi. Republican. Presbyn. (deacon, trustee, elder). Mason. Clubs: Wall Street (N.Y.C.) Westchester Hills Golf (White Plains, N.Y.), Home: 32 Kingston Rd Scarsdale NY 10583 Office: 100 Wall St New York City NY 10005

CARRUTH, GORTON VEEDER, editor; b. Woodbury, Conn., Apr. 9, 1925; s. Gorton Veeder and Margery Tracy Barrow (Dibb) C.; Ph.B., U. Chgo., 1948; B.A., Columbia, 1950, M.A., 1954; m. Gisele Leliet, Dec. 28, 1955; children—Gorton Veeder III, Hayden III, Christopher Leliet. Editor ref. books Thomas Y. Crowell Co., N.Y.C., 1954-63; exec. editor McGraw-Hill Book Co., N.Y.C., 1963-68; editor-in-chief Funk & Wagnalls, N.Y.C., 1968-71. Mem. Linnaean Soc., Lab. Ornithology Cornell U. (hon.), Phi Beta Kappa. Author: Encyclopedia of American Facts and Dates, rev. ed., 1970. Home: Box 168 Pleasantville NY 10570

CARRUTH, HAYDEN, poet; b. Waterbury, Conn., Aug. 3, 1921; s. Gorton Veeder and Margery Tracy Barrow (Dibb) C.; A.B., U. N.C., 1943; M.A., U. Chgo., 1948; m. Sara Anderson, Mar. 14, 1943; 1 dau., Martha Hamilton; m. 2d. Eleanore Ray, Nov. 29, 1952; m. 3d, Rose Marie Dorn Oct. 28, 1961; 1 son, David Barrow II. Editor-in-chief Poetry mag., 1949-50; asso. editor U. Chgo. Press, 1950-51; project adminstr. Intercultural Publs. Inc., N.Y.C., 1952-53. Recipient Vachel Lindsay prize, 1954, Bess Hokin prize, 1956, Levinson prize, 1958, Annual Poetry award Brandeis U., 1959. Harriet Monroe Poetry prize U. Chgo., 1960; Helen Bullis prize U. Seattle, 1962; Carl Sandburg prize, 1963; Emily Clark Balch prize, 1964. Fellow Bollingen Found., N.Y.C., 1962, John Simon Meml. Guggenheim Found., 1965; $10,000 grantee Nat. Found. on Arts and Humanities, 1967; Morton Zabel prize, 1968. Author: The Crow and the Heart, 1959; Journey to a Known Place, 1961; Norfolk Poems, 1962; Appendix A, 1963; North Winter, 1964; Nothing for Tigers, 1965; Contra Mortem, 1967; After the Stranger, 1965; For You, 1970; The Clay Hill Anthology, 1970; The Voice That is Great Within Us; 1970; The Bird/ Poem Book, 1970. Home: Johnson VT 05656

CARRUTH, IRBY BREWSTER, supt. schs.; b. Comanche, Tex., July 6, 1900; s. Robert Edwin and Cora (Brewster) C.; B.A., West Tex. State Coll., Canyon, 1927; M.A., U. Chgo., 1931; LL.D., Tex. Christian U., 1957; postgrad. Stanford, U. Tex.; m. Tip Bradford, Aug. 25, 1924; children—Robert Bruce, Stanley Bradford. Successively classroom tchr., prin., supt. schs., Canyon, Tex., 1927-38; supt. schs., Ronham, Tex., 1938-44, Waco, Tex., 1944-50, Austin, Tex., 1950-71. Adv. council Nat. Def. Counseling and Guidance Commn.; bd. mgrs. Tex. P.T.A.; mem. Joint Council on Econ. Edn.; mem. aerospace adv. council Air Force Assn.; mem. Tex. Com. of Ten. Bd. dirs. Nat. council Boy Scouts Am., Tex. Safety Assn. Mem. Am. (exec. com. 1943-48, v.p., 1960, pres., 1962-63), Tex. (past pres.), N.W. Tex. (chmn.) assns. sch. adminstrs., N.E.A. (life), Tex. tchrs. assn., Austin C. of C., Phi Delta Kappa. Rotarian. Home: 5 Niles Rd Austin TX 78703

CARRUTH, LAURENCE ADAMS, educator, entomologist; b. Mansfield, Mass., June 11, 1907; s. Charles Mason and Sarah Millicent (Cole) C.; B.S., Mass. Agrl. Coll., 1929; M.S., S.D. State Coll., 1931; Ph.D., Cornell U., 1935; m. Wynne Eleanor Caird, June 26, 1937; children—James Charles, Susan Wynne (Mrs. J.J. Ellington). Entomologist, N.D. Agr. Expt. Sta., summers 1931-33, N.Y. State Agr. Expt. Sta. (Cornell U.), 1935-49; prof. entomology, entomologist Agr. Expt. Sta., U. Ariz., 1949—, head dept., 1949-67, head dept. emeritus, 1967—. Fellow A.A.A.S.; mem. Entomol. Soc. Am., Sigma Xi, Gamma Sigma Delta. Presbyn. Home: 2904 E Kleindale Rd Tucson, AZ 85716

CARRUTH, PHILIP WILKINSON, mathematician, educator; b. Cleve., July 19, 1914; s. Harold Massey and Bertha (Wilkinson) C.; A.B., Hamilton Coll., 1936; M.A., Syracuse U., 1937; Ph.D., U. Ill., 1941; m. Mary Notestein, July 11, 1942; children—William W., Frank W. Instr. math U. Ill., 1945-47; asst. prof., asso. prof. Swarthmore Coll., 1947-66; prof. math. Middlebury (Vt.) Coll., 1966—. Served with AUS, 1941-45. Mem. Am. Math. Soc., Math. Assn. Am., Sigma Xi. Home: 1 Adirondack View Middlebury, VT 05753

CARRUTHERS, PETER AMBLER, physicist, educator; b. Lafayette, Ind., Oct. 7, 1935; s. Maurice Earl and Nila (Ambler) C.; B.S., Carnegie Inst. Tech., 1957, M.S., 1957; Ph.D., Cornell U., 1960; m. Jean Ann Breitenbecher, Feb. 26, 1955; children—Peter, Debra, Kathryn; m. 2d, Lucy J. Marston, July 10, 1969. Asst. prof. Cornell U., 1961-63, asso. prof., 1963-67, prof. physics, atomic and solid state physics, nuclear studies, 1967—; vis. asso. prof. Cal. Inst. Tech., 1965, vis. prof., 1969-70. Alfred P. Sloan Research fellow, 1963-65; NSF sr. postdoctoral fellow U. Rome, 1967-68. Mem. Am., Italian phys. socs. Author: (with R. Brout) Lectures on the Many-Electron Problem, 1963; Introduction to Unitary Symmetry, 1966. Address: 115 W Upland Rd Ithaca NY 14850

CARRY, CHAMP, former mfg. co. exec.; b. Lockport, Ill., May 31, 1896; s. Joseph Carles and Arabella C. (Dill) C.; M.E., Cornell U., 1918; m. Marion Osborne, Oct. 14, 1922; children—Marion (Mrs. Jerome Rich), June (Mrs. Irving Seaman, Jr.). Began in shops of Haskell & Barker Car Co., mfrs. freight cars, 1919; with Pullman Car & Mfg. Corp., 1922-32; v.p., 1929-32; v.p. Pullman Co., 1932-41, exec. v.p., 1941-46; pres. Pullman- Standard Car Mfg. Co., 1946-50; pres., Pullman, Inc., 1950-61, chmn. bd., 1961-66, hon. chmn. bd. irs., 1966-70, also dir. Lt. 18th F.A., 3d Div. U.S. Army, World War I. Decorated D.S.C. Clubs: Chicago, Chicago Commonwealth, Onwentsia, Commercial, Old Elm, Shoreacres, Links (New York). Home: 155 E Onwentsia Rd Lake Forest IL 60045

CARRY, JAMES M., former bus. exec.; b. Chgo., Jan. 2, 1908; s. Joseph Charles and Arabella C. (Dill) C.; A.B., Cornell U., 1930; m. Mary Trigg Waller, Oct. 4, 1930; children—William C., Trigg W.; m. 2d, Margaret Swing Thomas, Apr. 5, 1952; m. 3d, Gladys R. Pope, Dec. 23, 1969. Stenographer pres.'s office Pullman Co., Chgo., 1930-32, chief clk. sec.'s office, 1932-33, asst. sec., 1933-36, asst. to v.p., exec. v.p.'s office, 1936-42, asst. v.p., 1942-44, v.p. operating dept., 1944-47, became asst. to pres. Pullman, Inc., 1951; asst. to pres. M.W. Kellogg Co., N.Y.C., subsidiary Pullman Inc., 1954-70, v.p., 1958-70, ret., 1970; cons. Belmas Industries, Houston, 1970—; dir. Kellogg Internat. Corp., Canadian Kellogg Co., Soc. Kellogg, Compania Kellogg Espanola; v.p. Carl Byoir & Assos., N.Y.C., 1948-51. Mem. Kappa Alpha. Clubs: Chicago; University, Cornell (N.Y.C.). Home: 11402 Shadow Way Houston TX Office: Fannin Bank Bldg Holcombe and Main Sts Houston TX 77725

CARRYER, HADDON MCCUTCHEN, physician; b. Unionville, Mo., Aug. 25, 1914; s. Carl Haddon and Margaret Dill (McCutchen) C.; B.A., Drake U., 1935; M.B., M.D., Northwestern U., 1939, M.S. in Physiology, 1939; Ph.D. in Medicine, U. Minn., 1948; m. Mabel Jane Jones, Feb. 15, 1941; children—Haddon Carl, Peter Ward, Diane Elizabeth. Intern, Evanston (Ill.) Hosp., 1938-40; fellow Mayo Grad. Sch. Medicine, 1940-43; mem. staff sect. medicine Mayo Clinic, 1943—, head a clin. sect. internal medicine and allergy, 1959- 70; faculty Mayo Grad. Sch. Medicine, U. Minn., 1946—, asso. prof. medicine, 1962—. Spl. research allergy, exec. health care. Mem. med. adv. com. Minn. Dept. Pub. Welfare, 1952—. Recipient Alumni Achievement award Drake U., 1963. Diplomate Am. Bd. Internal Medicine. Fellow Am. Acad. Allergy, A.C.P.; mem. Am., Minn. (speaker ho. dels. 1957-63, pres. 1962, alternate del. ho. dels. A.M.A. 1965—) med. assns., Zumbro Valley Med. Soc., Sigma Xi, Alpha Tau Omega, Nu Sigma Nu. Republican. Episcopalian. Contbr. numerous articles to profl. jours. Home: 25 Skyline Dr Sunny Slopes Rochester MN 55901 Office: 200 1st St SW Rochester MN 55901

CARSON, ALBERT BEN, educator; b. Sedalia, Mo., Aug. 10, 1913; s. Albert Edwin and Alice Ben (McGee) C.; A.B., Colo. Coll., 1935; M.B.A., Northwestern U., 1937; Ph.D., U. Neb., 1943; m. Ruth Bradley, Dec. 24, 1937; children—Mary Beth, Nancy Jean. Instr. accounting Morningside Coll., 1937-38, U. Neb., 1938-43; accountant Kaiser Co., Inc., 1943-45; asst. prof. accounting U. Utah, 1945-47; accountant Beesley, Wood and Co., C.P.A.'s, Salt Lake City, 1946-47; faculty U. Cal. at Los Angeles, 1947—, prof. accounting, 1958—, vice chmn. dept. bus. adminstrn., 1957-65, acting asso. dean Sch. Bus. Adminstrn., 1958-59. Fulbright lectr., Australia, summer 1962; vis. prof. Ariz. State U., 1965-66, Australian Nat. U., Canberra, 1968. Mem. Educator-Cons. Com. to Comptroller Gen. U.S., 1959-64. C.P.A., Utah. Mem. Am. Accounting Assn. (dir. research 1959, pres. 1961), Am. Inst. C.P.A.'s, Beta Theta Pi, Alpha Kappa Psi. Author: (with A.E. Carlson, C. Boling) College Accounting, 8th edit., 1967; The Public Accounting Profession in California, 1956. Contbr. articles to profl. jours., to Accountants' Cost Handbook, 2d edit., 1960; also Ency. Brit. Home: 1407 Allenford Av Los Angeles, CA 90049

CARSON, ALLAN GRANT, lawyer; b. Salem, Ore., Sept. 7, 1897; s. John A. and Helen (Fraser) C.; student U. Ore., 1919-20; J.D., Willamette U., 1922; LL.B., LaSalle Extension U., 1935; m. Merle Hamilton, Nov. 4, 1922; children—Allan H., Marian Andree (Mrs. Donald A. Fager). Admitted to Ore. bar, 1922, U.S. Dist. Ct., 1924, U.S. Supreme Ct., 1927; gen. prqctice law, 1922-42, 46—; dep. dist. atty., Marion County, Ore., 1922-27; spl. legal counsel Gov. Ore., 1927, 29. Mem. Ore. Ho. of Reps., 1940-42, Senate, 1942-46, 46-50. Mem. bd. control Salem Gen. Hosp., 1933-57, Salem Boxing Commn., 1946—; chmn. Ore. Law Improvement Com., 1963—. Served with inf. Mexican Border Expdn., 1916; to 1st lt., inf. AEF, U.S. Army, World War I; to lt. col. USAAF, World War II; CBI. Decorated Air medal. Mem. Willamette U. Coll. Law Alumni Assn. (pres. 1947-49), Am., Ore. (pres. 1937-38), Marion County (pres. 1951) bar assns., V.F.W. (post comdr. 1923), Am. Legion (post comdr. 1933), Mil. Order World Wars, Retreads, Kappa Sigma, Delta Theta Phi. Republican. Episcopalian. Mason. Home: 2185 Church St S E Salem OR 97302 Office: Pioneer Trust Bldg Salem OR 97303

CARSON, CALE WELLMAN, banker; b. Ashland, Kan., Nov. 19, 1891; s. Cale Wellman and Mattie (Congelton) C.; A.B., U. Kan., 1915; m. Alice Coors, Nov. 29, 1922 (dec.); children—Kathryn, Cale Wellman; m. 2d, Ruth Eaves, June 6, 1959. Cashier, First Nat. Bank, Spearman, Tex., 1919-25; v.p. First Nat. Bank, Amarillo, Tex., 1925-29; liquidating agt. Nat. Bank of Commerce, 1931; dep. land bank commr., Washington, 1933; pres. First Nat. Bank, Albuquerque, 1933-61, chmn bd., 1961-69; past dir. Denver br. Fed. Res. Bank Kansas City. State chmn. War Finance Com., World War II; former mem. State Bd. Finance. Trustee emeritus Lovelace Found. for Med. Edn. and Research, S.W. Research Inst., San Antonio; bd. dirs. Presbyn. Hosp. Center. Served as maj., inf. U.S. Army, AEF, 1917-18. Mem. N.M. (past pres.), Am. bankers assns., N.A.M., Albuquerque C. of C. Rotarian. Clubs: Country, Petroleum (Albuquerque). Home: 716 Morningside Dr NE Albuquerque NM 87110 Office: First Nat Bank Albuquerque NM 87108

CARSON, CHARLES AVERETTE, III, lawyer; b. Idaho Springs, Colo., Oct. 28, 1921; s. Charles Averette, Jr., and Carrie (Burger) C.; J.D., U. Ariz., 1947; m. Phyllis Peterson, Apr. 19, 1947; children—Kristin, Abigail, Charles Averette IV. Admitted to Ariz. bar, 1947; mem. firm Carson, Messinger, Elliott, Laughlin & Ragan (formerly Cunningham, Carson & Messinger), Phoenix, 1947—. Dir. Kitchell Corp. Trustee Orme Sch., Mayer, Ariz.; pres. bd, trustees St. Luke's Hosp., Phoenix. Served as tech. sgt., inf. Med. Dept., AUS, 1943-46. Mem. Ariz. (gov. 1955-59, pres. 1958-59), Maricopa County (dir. 1950-55, pres. 1954), Am. (gov. 1969-72), Ariz. (del. 1960—) bar. assns., Am. Judicature Soc. (dir.), Am. Coll. State Trial Judges (dir.), S.A.R., Phoenix C. of C., Phoenix Thunderbirds Order of Coif, Phi Kappa Phi, Phi Delta Phi. Democrat. Episcopalian (chancellor diocese Ariz. 1965-70). Clubs: Arizona, Kiva, Phoenix Country (Phoenix). Home: 53 N Country Club Dr Phoenix AZ 85014 Office: United Bank Bldg 3550 N Central Av Phoenix AZ 85012

CARSON, CHARLES CLIFTON, fgn. service officer; b. Conehatta, Miss., Mar. 18, 1918; s. Clarence Clifton and Nan (Williams) C.; student Bowling Green (Ky.) Bus. U., 1936-38; m. Corinth Winston Eckman, Apr. 2, 1947; children—Charles Clifton II, James Howard Winston, Peter Jonathan, Thomas Williams. Joined U.S. Fgn. Service, 1940; assigned Am. embassy, Montevideo, 1940-41, Asunción, 1941-43, Lima, 1943-44, Vancouver, 1946-50, Lisbon, 1950-52, Brisbane, 1952-53, Saigon, 1953-55, Prto Alegre, 1955-58, Rio de Janeiro, 1962-65, Matamoros, 1965-68; assigned State Dept., 1958-62; consul gen., Seville, 1968—. Served with USMC, 1938-40, 44-46. Club: Pineda de Golf (Seville). Home: Route 1 Conehatta MS 39057 Office: State Dept Washington DC 20520

CARSON, CHARLES WILLIAM, banker; b. Bethany, N.Y., Dec. 23, 1897; s. Theodore W. and Eunice E. (Blood) C.; student U. Rochester, 1920-22; m. Dorothy B. Knight, Sept. 16, 1924; children—Charles William, Mary H. Sec., YMCA, Batavia, Buffalo and Rochester, N.Y., 1915-35; treas. Colgate-Rochester Div. Sch., 1935- 43; exec. v.p. Community Savs. Bank of Rochester, 1944-45, pres., 1946- 64, chmn. bd., 1965-68, adv. council, 1968—; dir. M.S.B. Fund. Bd. dirs. Highland Hosp.; bd. dirs., past pres. YMCA, Rochester; bd. dirs., treas. Planned Parenthood League; trustee Colgate-Rochester Div. Sch., Rochester Center for Govtl. and Community Research. Mem. Savs. Bank Assn. N.Y. State (past pres.), Nat. Assn. Mut. Savs. Banks (past chmn. com. edn. and mgmt. devel.), Rochester C. of C. (past pres.), Rochester Assn. UN (chmn. bd.). Presbyn. Clubs: City (past pres.), University, Country (Rochester); Princeton of N.Y. Home: 2505 East Av Rochester NY 14610 Office: 235 Main St E Rochester NY 14604

CARSON, CYRIL FREDERICK HARSHAW, lawyer; b. Toronto, Ont., Can., May 18, 1900; s. David John and Erminie (Harshaw) C.; grad. Osgoode Hall Law Sch., 1921; LL.D. (hon.), Queen's U., 1957; m. Dorothy Rogers, Oct. 15, 1927 (dec. 1964); children—Valerie Anne (Mrs. Robert Kilpatrick), John Cyril; m. 2d, Jocelyn Jackson, June 28, 1966. Called to Ont. bar, 1921, created King's Counsel, 1936; mem. firm Tilley, Carson and Findlay, and predecessor firms, Toronto; gen. counsel Bank of N.S.; dir. Falconbridge Nickel Mines, Ltd., Hiram Walker-Gooderham & Worts, Ltd., Can. Permanent Trust Co., Mfrs.' Life Ins. Co., Canadian Pacific Ry. Co. Mem. Law Soc. Upper Can. (bencher for life, treas. 1950-58), Canadian Bar Assn. (hon. treas. 1944-48). Clubs: Toronto, Lawyers (pres. 1932). York (Toronto). Home: 89 Ardwold Gate Toronto Ontario Canada Office: 44 King St W Toronto Ontario Canada

CARSON, DAVID BYERS, cons.; b. Pitts., Sept. 1, 1890; s. Theodore Freulingheuysen and Louise (Ochsenhirt) C.; C.E., Ohio State U., 1913; m. Rose Steinfeld, Nov. 29, 1917; children—Susan Marion, David Byers III, Robert Sterling; m. 2d, Helen Foster, Oct. 20, 1945. Rodman, later draftsman, asst. to valuation engr. Toledo & Ohio Central Ry., Columbus, O., 1913-15; insp., later clk., sales agt. Carbon Steel Co., Pitts., 1915-17, dist. sales mgr., 1919-20; dist. sales mgr. Tacony Steel Co., Cleve., 1921-23; asst. sales mgr., later sales mgr., mgr. research and devel. dept. Central Alloy Steel Corp., Massillon, O., 1923-29; v.p., treas. Asso. Alloy Steel Corp., Cleve., 1930-32; v.p. Pitts. Steel Co., 1935-44; v.p. sales, exec. v.p., dir. Sharon steel Corp., 1932-59, now cons. Dir. iron and steel div. NPA, Washington, 1950, mem. Moblzn. Controls Task Force. Served as 1st lt. AUS, 1917-19. Mem. Army Ordnance Assn., Nat. Sales Execs., A.I.M., Am. Iron and Steel Inst., (dir.), Am. Soc. Metals, Delta Upsilon. Republican. Presbyn. Clubs: Duquesne (Pitts.); Cleveland Athletic; Youngstown, Youngstown Country (Youngstown, O.); Coral Ridge Country (Ft. Lauderdale, Fla.); Sharon Country (Pa.). Home: 330 SE 7th Av Delray Beach FL 33444

CARSON, EDWARD MANSFIELD, banker; b. Tucson, Nov. 6, 1929; s. Ernest Lee and Earline (Masfield) C.; B.S. in Bus. Adminstrn., Ariz. State U., 1951; grad. Stonier Sch. Banking, Rutgers U., 1963; m. Nadine Ann Severns, Dec. 13, 1952; children—Dawn Marie, Tod Edward. With First Nat. Bank Ariz., Phoenix, 1951—. Exec. v.p., dir. banking, 1969—. Chmn. Ariz. State U. Library Assos.; mem. men's art council Phoenix Art Mus.; adviser exec. devel. Ariz. State U. also chmn. award com., chmn. alumni fund.; chmn. fund com. Ariz. chpt. A.R.C., also chmn. members com.; v.p. Jane Wayland Child Center, also treas., chmn. pesonnel com. Treas., v.p., bd. dirs. Phoenix Symphony Assn.; bd. dirs. Ariz. State U., Sun Angel Found. Named 1 of 3 Outstandinng Young Men, Ariz., 1960. Mem. Ariz. Acad. (bd. dirs.), Ariz. State Alumni Assn. (past pres.), Ariz. State U. Law Soc., Nat. Assn. Bank Auditors and Comptrollers (past pres.), Robert Morris Assos. (chmn. new mem. com. Ariz. chpt.), Ariz. Council Econ. Edn. (hon. dir.), Ariz. Bankers Assn., Alpha Tau Omega (pres. Ariz. 1956). Clubs: de Concho; Paradise Valley; Kiva; University; Phoenix Executive (bd. dirs., treas.). Home: 233 E Glenn Dr Phoenix AZ 85020 Office: 411 N Central Av Phoenix AZ 85004

CARSON, GEORGE BARR, Jr., educator, historian; b. Ancon, C.Z., Oct. 16, 1915; s. George Barr and Edna (Hess) C.; B.A., Coll. Wooster, 1935; M.A., U. Chgo., 1940, Ph.D., 1942; m. Dorothy Alberta Klemer, Sept. 5, 1936; children—Michael Frederic, Donald Richard, Jane Isabelle. Instr., Monticello Coll., 1942- 45; asst. prof. U. Ky., 1945-47; prof. history, chmn. div. social sci. N.Y. State Tchrs. Coll., New Paltz, 1947-49; asst. prof. U. Chgo., 1949- 56, also editor Jour. Modern History; sr. fellow Russian Inst., Columbia, 1951-52; dir. service center for tchrs. history Am. Hist. Assn., also editor publ. series, 1956-61; prof. history, chmn. dept. Ore. State U., 1961—; vis. prof. U. Colo., summer 1955, George Washington U., spring 1958, 61. Mem. Am. Hist. Assn., Am. Assn. Advancement Slavic Studies (chmn. Far Western Slavic cong. 1966-67), Am. Assn. U. Profs. Author: (with Louise F. Brown) Men and Centuries of European Civilization, 1948; Electoral Practices in the USSR, 1955; (with T. Walter Wallbank and Alastair M. Taylor) Civilization Past and Present. Vol. II, 1969; also numerous articles. Editor: Latvia: An Area Study, 2 vols., 1956. Adv. bd. Hist. Abstracts, 1953-60; exec. bd. Social Edn., 1960-61. Home: 1399 N 14th St Corvallis OR 97330

CARSON, GORDON BLOOM, engr., univ. exec.; b. High Bridge, N.J., Aug. 1, 1911; s. Whitfield R. and Emily (Bloom) C.; B.S. in Mech. Engring., Case Inst. Tech., 1931, D.Eng., 1957; M.S., Yale, 1932, M.E., 1938; m. Beth Lacy, June 19, 1937; children—Richard Whitfield, Emily Elizabeth (Mrs. Lee A. Duffus), Alice Lacy (Mrs. William P. Allman), Jean Helen (Mrs. Michael J. Gable). With Western Electric Co., 1930; instr. mech. engring. Case Inst. Tech., 1932-37, asst. prof., 1937- 40, asso. prof. indsl. engring. charge indsl. div., 1940-44; with Am. Shipbldg. Co., 1936; patent litigation, 1937; research engr., dir. research Cleve. Automatic Machine Co., 1939-44; asst. to gen. mgr. Selby Shoe Co., 1944, mgr. engring., 1945-49, sec. of corp., 1949-53; sec., dir. Pyrrole Products Co., 1948-53; dean engring. Ohio State U., Columbus, 1953- 58, v.p. bus. and finance, treas., 1958-71; dir. Engring. Exptl. Sta., 1953-58; exec. v.p. Albion (Mich.) Coll., 1971—. Dir., Indsl. Nucleonics. Trustee White Cross Hosp. Assn., 1960-71 Engring. Service Index; bd. dirs. Knowledge Communication Fund, 1966—; dir. Goodwill Industries, 1959-67, 1st v.p., 1963-64; dir. Orton Found. 1953-58; v.p. Ohio State U. Research Found., 1958-71; v.p., chmn. adv. council Center for Automation and Soc., U. Ga. Chmn. tool and die com. 5th Regional War Labor Bd., 1943-45; chmn. Ohio State adv. com. for sci., tech. and specialized personnel SSS. Fellow Am. Soc. M.E., A.A.A.S.; mem. Columbus Soc. Financial Analysts (pres. 1964-65), Financial Analysts Fedn. (dir. 1964- 65), C. of C. (dir., treas. 1952-53), Am. Ordnance Assn., Am. Inst. Indsl. Engrs. (pres. 1957-58), Am. Soc. Engring. Edn., Asso. U. for Research in Astronomy (dir.), Midwestern Univs. Research Assn. (dir. 1958-71), U.S. Naval Inst. Sigma Xi, Tau Beta Pi, Zeta Psi, Phi Eta Sigma, Alpha Pi Mu, Romophos, Sphinx. Mason (32). Editor: The Production Handbook, 1958, cons. editor, 1971—. Author of tech. papers engring. subjects. Home: 810 Michigan Av Albion MI 49224

CARSON, HAMPTON LAWRENCE, geneticist, educator; b. Phila., Nov. 5, 1914; s. Joseph and Edith (Bruen) C.; A.B., Pa., 1936, Ph.D., 1943; m. Meredith Shelton, Aug. 14, 1937; children—Joseph II, Edward Bruen. Instr., U. Pa., 1938-42; mem. faculty Washington U., St. Louis, 1943-70, prof. biology 1956-70; prof. genetics U. Hawaii, 1970—; vis. prof. biology U. Sao Paulo (Brazil), 1951. Fulbright Research scholar zoology dept. U. Melbourne (Australia), 1961. Mem. Genetics Soc., Soc. for Study Evolution, (pres. 1971), Am. Soc. Naturalists (v.p.), Soc. Zool. Population Genetics, A.A.A.S., Phi Beta Kappa, Sigma Xi. Author: Heredity and Human Life, 1963. Contbr. articles profl. jours. Address: Univ Hawaii Honolulu HI

CARSON, JAMES, fgn. service officer; b. Hermiston, Ore., July 8, 1926; s. C.L. and Nell Amy (Chamberlain) C.; student Ore. State Coll., 1946-48, Portland State Coll., 1949-50; B.S., U. Ore., 1951, M.A., 1953; m. Virginia Shelton, Sept. 2, 1949; childrenWendy Elaine, Thomas Leonard, Nancy Elizabeth. Joined U.S. Fgn. Service, 1955; vice consul, Frankfurt-am-Main, Germany, 1955-57; fgn. affairs officer, Exec. Secretariat, State Dept., 1957 ˙ 60; 2d sec. embassy, Abidjan, Ivory Coast, 1961; 1st sec. embassy, Cotonou, Dahomey, 1961-63, counselor of embassy, 1964; fgn. affairs officer U.S. Mission, Berlin, Germany, 1964-67, Canadian Nat. Def. Coll., Kingston, Ont., 1967-68, Dept. of State, Washington, 1968-. Served with USNR, 1942-45. Mem. Am. Fgn. Service Assn., Theta Chi, Sigma Delta Chi. Home: 6915 Southridge Dr McLean, VA Office: Executive Secretariat Dept of State Washington DC 20500

CARSON, JOHNNY, TV entertainer; b. Corning, Ia., Oct. 23, 1925; s. Homer and Ruth (Hook) C.; B.A., U. Neb., 1949; m. Jody Wolcott, 1948 (div. 1963); children—Chris, Ricky, Cory; m. 2d, Joanne Copeland, Aug. 1963. Announcer, radio Sta. KFAB, Lincoln, Neb., 1948, later at Sta. WOW, WOW- TV, Omaha; became announcer Sta. KNXT, Los Angeles, 1950, started TV show Carson's Cellar, 1951; next became writer for Red Skelton; emcee TV quiz show Earn Your Vacation, 1954; star The Johnny Carson Show, CBS, 1955; emcee quiz show Who Do You Trust, ABC-TV, 5 years; other TV appearances include To Tell The Truth, Password, Garry Moore Show, What's My Line?, Playhouse 90, U.S. Steel Hour; host Tonight show, NBC- TV, 1962—. Author: Happiness Is a Dry Martini, 1965. Club: Friars (knight). Address: care NBC 30 Rockefeller Plaza New York City NY 10020

CARSON, RALPH, advt. exec.; b. Milw., May 12, 1914; s. Israel and Ester (Carson) Feingold; B.S., Boston U., 1937; postgrad. U. Wis., 1939, U. Minn., 1939; m. Maida Berger, Oct. 27, 1943; children—Cary Martin, Janis. Partner, Coll. Boys Butter & Egg Co., 1931; announcer, writer, actor sta. WIXAL, WNAX, Boston, 1933-37; salesman John Irving Shoe Co., 1933- 37; tchr. Peabody Playhouse, 1936-37; newswriter NBC, N.Y.C., 1937-38; announcer, writer sta. WRJN, Racine, Wis., 1939; with Packard-Bell Advt., Los Angeles, 1945; advt. mgr. Carson-Roberts Advt., Los Angeles, 1946—; now chmn. bd., chief exec. officer Carson-Roberts, Inc. Seminar tchr. U. Cal. at Los Angeles, Conf. Center, Arrowhead. Vice pres. Bel Air Democratic Club, 1960. Served with USNR, 1941-45. Home: 2461 Roscomare Rd Los Angeles CA 90024 Office: 8322 Beverly Blvd Los Angeles CA 90048

CARSON, RALPH MOORE, lawyer; b. Indpls., Aug. 22, 1896; s. Oliver Howard and Mary (Dowdigan) C.; A.B., U. Mich., 1917, J.D., 1923, LL.D., 1959; B.A. (Rhodes scholar), Oxford U., 1922; m. Cécile Bellé, Oct. 14, 1928; 1 son, Jean- Philippe. Admitted to N.Y. bar, 1926; with Davis Polk & Wardwell, and predecessor law firms, N.Y.C., 1923—, partner firm, 1935—. Served with USNRF, 1918. Mem. Oxford Union Soc. (pres. 1922), Am., N.Y. County bar assns., Bar Assn. City N.Y., Phi Beta Kappa, Delta Sigma Rho. Clubs: Downtown Assn., Century Assn. (N.Y.C.); Univ. of Mich. Lawyers. Editor: Jurisprudence in Action, 1953. Contbr. articles to legal periodicals. Home: Quaker Hill Pawling NY 12564 Office: 1 Chase Manhattan Plaza New York City NY 10005

CARSON, RICHARD BROWN, steel co. exec.; b. Scotland, Nov. 28, 1910; s. Richard Brown and Jessie (Leitch) C.; m. Cecily Grace Webb, Dec. 17, 1948. Exec. v.p., dir. Ont. Steel Products Co., Ltd., Toronto; dir. Tycos Tool & Dye Co. Ltd., Worcester Moulded Plastics Co. Mem. Bd. of Trade of Met. Toronto. Mem. Canadian C. of C. Clubs: Mississaugua Golf and Country; Essex Golf and Country (Windsor, Ont.); Ontario; Empire; Canadian. Home: 1276 Clarkson Rd N Clarkson Ontario Canada Office: 7 E King St Toronto 1 Ontario Canada*

CARSON, ROBERT, author; b. Clayton, Wash., Oct. 6, 1909; s. Franklin Pierce and Blanche Ethel (McClaren) C.; student Am. Inst. Banking; m. Mary Jane Irving, Feb. 11, 1938. Various positions, 1928-35; scenarist, novelist, mag. writer, 1935-42, writer 1945—; producer CBS-TV, 1954-55; motion pictures written include Men with Wings, Light That Failed, Bundle of Joy, Action of the Tiger, sound version Beau Geste, Western Union, Desperados; movies from serials, short stories include Across the Pacific, Perilous Holiday, You Gotta Stay Happy, Reformer and the Redhead. Served as lt. col. USAAF, 1942-45. Received Acad. award for motion picture A Star is Born, 1937. Mem. Writers Guild Am., Screen Writers' Guild (exec. bd. 1951-53). Author: The Revels are Ended, 1936; Stranger in our Midst, 1947; Magic Lantern (Book-of-the-Month Club selection), 1952; Quality of Mercy, 1954; Love Affair, 1958; My Hero, 1961; An End to Comedy, 1963; The Outsiders, 1966; The December Syndrome, 1969; The Golden Years, 1970. Contbr. fiction to nat. mags. Works transl. Danish, Italian, German, Dutch, Norwegian, Swedish. Home: 10565 Fontenelle Way Los Angeles CA 90024

CARSON, ROBERT GORDON, Jr., univ. dean; b. Seneca, S.C., Mar. 29, 1918; s. Robert Gordon and Sue Ellen (Hunter) C.; B.S., Clemson U., 1939; M.S., Ga. Inst. Tech., 1950; Ph.D., U. Mich., 1953; m. Mary Elizabeth White, Aug. 17, 1941; children—Robert Gordon III, Mary Elizabeth, Virginia Sue. Jr. engr. Callaway Mills, LaGrange, Ga., 1939-42; plant mgr. Carwood Mfg. Co., Cornelia, Ga., 1946-47; asst. prof. to asso. prof. Sch. of Textiles of Clemson U., 1947-55; prof., head indsl. engring. dept. N.C. State U., 1955-57, asso. dean engring., 1957—. Sr. asso. Bruce Payne & Assos., 1953-55; arbitrator Fed. Mediation and Conciliation Service, Am. Arbitration Assn., N.C. Dept. Labor; chmn. steering com. Kabul-Afghan Am. Program, 1970-73. Served from 2d lt. to capt. inf., AUS, 1942-46; CBI. Recipient distinguished service award Am. Inst. Indsl. Engrs., 1967, Region III award of excellence, 1970; named Tar Heel of the week Raleigh News and Observer, 1970. Mem. Am. Soc. Engring. Edn. (gen. council 1960-62), Am. Inst. Indsl. Engrs. (regional v.p. 1964-65), Alpha Pi Mu (nat. pres. 1960-62). Contbr. articles profl. jours. Home: 1202 Brooks Av Raleigh NC 27607

CARSON, SAMUEL GOODMAN, banker; b. Glens Falls, N.Y., Oct. 6, 1913; s. Russell M.L. and Mary (Goodman) C.; B.A. magna cum laude, Dartmouth, 1934; m. Alice Williams, Oct. 14, 1939; children—Russell L., Frances Elizabeth (Mrs. Thomas E. Brady, Jr.), Mary Goodman (Mrs. John A. Fedderke), Kathryn Williams, Samuel Goodman. With Aetna Life Ins. Co., 1934-68; dir. Toledo Trust Co. 1967—, exec. v.p., 1968, pres., 1969—; dir. Kiemle-Hankins Co., Nat. Family Opinion, Inc., Lamson Bros. Co., Toledo Edison Co., Bostwick-Brawn Co., Toledo Discount Co. Mem. Ottawa Hills Bd. Edn., 1954-64; pres. United Appeal Greater Toledo Area, 1969, campaign chmn., 1964. Bd. dirs., trustee Toledo chpt. A.R.C., 1950—, chmn., 1959- 61; trustee Toledo Hosp., 1960—, v.p., 1963-65, pres., 1966-69; bd. dirs. Community Chest Greater Toledo, 1962-65, pres., 1965; pres. Boys' Club Toledo, 1961-64, trustee, 1957—; sec.-treas. Toledo Mus. Art 1969. trustee, 1967—. Recipient Service to Mankind award Sertoma Club Toledo, 1965, Man and Boy award Boys' Clubs Am., 1966, Pacemaker of Yr. award U. Toledo Coll. Bus. Adminstrn. Alumni Assn., 1969. Mem. Toledo Area C. of C. (trustee 1961-62), Phi Beta Kappa, Phi Gamma Delta. Republican. Conglist. Clubs: Toledo Country, Toledo, Belmont Country (Perrysburg, O.). Home: 3404 Chestnut Hill Rd Toledo OH 43606 Office: 245 Summit St Toledo OH 43603

CARSON, SAMUEL OLIVER, lawyer; b. Kissimmee, Fla., Aug. 3, 1912; s. Marion Bryan and Ruby (Oliver) C.; B.S. in Bus. Adminstrn., U. Fla., 1937, LL.B. with highest honors, 1940; m. Helen Watson, Aug. 4, 1937; children—Samuel Oliver, James Monroe, Thomas Lane. Admitted to Fla. bar, 1940; research asst. Fla. Supreme Ct., 1940-41; asst. states atty. Fla., 1945-51; practiced in Miami, Fla., 1941—; partner firm Walton, Lantaff, Schroeder, Carson & Wahl, 1944—. Served with USNR, 1943-45. Mem. Am., Fla., Dade County bar assns., Blue Key, Phi Delta Phi, Phi Kappa Phi. Baptist (chmn. bd. deacons, chmn. finance com., supt. Sunday sch.). Home: 2269 SW 23d St Miami, FL 33145 Office: Alfred I DuPont Bldg Miami FL 33131

CARSTENSEN, HANS LOUIS, Jr., advt. exec.; b. Cambridge, Mass., Sept. 18, 1916; s. Hans Louis and Elizabeth (Butcher) C.; B.S., Harvard, 1938, M.B.A., 1940; m. Judson Scribner, Feb. 20, 1943 (dec.); m. 2d Jane Burnham Van Pelt Toland, Aug. 25, 1967; children—Judson (Mrs. Thomas M. Niver), Hans Louis III, Carolie S., Julia R. Toland, Jane B. Toland, Alexander B. Toland, Mariana G. Toland. Salesman Scott Paper Co., Chgo., 1940-41, dist. sales mgr., Balt., 1945-47, market research, Chester, Pa.,1947-48; staff marketing dept. N.W. Ayer, Phila., 1948-55, v.p., mgr. marketing, 1955-61, v.p., mgr. account service, 1961-66, sr. v.p., dir. media, 1966—. Bd. dirs. Children's Aid Soc. Pa. Served to lt. comdr. USNR, 1941-45. Republican. Episcopalian. Clubs: Harvard (N.Y.C. and Phila.); Gulph Mills Golf; Corinthian Yacht (Phila.). Home: 334 Aubrey Rd Wynnewood PA 19096 Office: West Washington Sq Philadelphia PA 19106

CARSTENSEN, VERNON, historian, educator; b. Cherokee County, Ia., Dec. 28, 1907; s. Frederick Herman and Amelia (Kruse) C.; B.A., Ia. State Tchrs. Coll., 1928; M.A., State U. Ia., 1932. Ph.D., 1936; m. Mary Buffum Hill, May 30, 1936; children—Peter Christian, Frederick Vernon. High sch. tchr., Minn. and Ia., 1928-31; tchr. history Central Wash. Coll. Edn., 1935-42; historian War Dept., 1942-45; research asso. U. Wis., 1945-48, asst. prof., 1948-50, asso. prof., 1950-54, prof., 1954-64, asso. dean Grad. Sch., 1960-64; prof. history U. Wash., Seattle, 1964—. Vis. prof. U. Wash., 1941, U. Ore., summer session 1954. U. Cal. at Berkeley, 1958; vis. prof. under Smith-Mundt grant, U. Stockholm, 1956-57. Fellow Wis. Hist. Soc.; mem. Agrl. History Soc. (pres. 1958-59), Am. Hist. Assn., Orgn. Am. Historians, A.A.A.S., Western, Wash., Ore. hist. socs., Am. Assn. U. Profs. Author: (with Merle Curti) The University of Wisconsin; A History, 2 vols., 1949. Editor; Letters of George Gibbs, 1954; Farms or Forests, 1958; The Public Lands, 1962; Agrl. History, 1953-57, Pacific N.W. Quar., 1965-66; bd. editors Jour. Am. History, 1963-66, Agrl. History, 1965—. Home: 4815 Purdue Av NE Seattle, WA 98105

CARSWELL, ARCHIBALD A., corp. exec.; b. 1908; B.S. in Civil Engring., Northeastern U., 1925; m. Project mgr. Turner Constrn. Co., 1925-40; with contractors Pacific Naval Air Base, 1940-43; project mgr. Rone Anderson Co., Ridge, 1943-46; with Dillingham Corp., 1946—, sr. v.p. 1961—, also dir.; dir. subsidiaries. Home: 2980 Makalei Pl Honolulu HI 96815 Office: PO Box 3468 Honolulu HI 96801

CARSWELL, GEORGE HARROLD, lawyer; b. Irwinton, Ga., Dec. 22, 1919; s. George Henry and Esther Claire (Wood) C.; A.B., Duke, 1941; postgrad. U. Ga. Law Sch., 1941-42, U.S. Naval Acad., 1945; LL.B., Mercer U., 1948; m. Virginia Simmons, Sept. 5, 1944; children—Virginia Ramsay, Sarah Nan, George Harrold, Scott Simmons. Editor weekly newspaper Irwinton Bull., 1940-41, 45-48; admitted to Ga. bar, 1948, practiced in Macon, Irwinton and Gordon, 1948; with Ausley Collins & Truett, Tallahassee, 1948-51, partner firm Carswell, Cotton & Shivers, 1951-53; U.S. atty. No. Dist. Fla., 1953-58; chief judge U.S. Dist. Ct., No. Dist. Fla., 1958-69; judge U.S. Ct. Appeals for 5th circuit, 1969-70; practiced in Tallahassee, 1970—. Served as lt. USNR, 1941-45. Mem. Am., Ga., Fla. bar assns., Am. Judicature Soc., Phi Alpha Delta, Sigma Nu. Episcopalian. Club: National Exchange. Home: 833 Lake Ridge Dr Tallahassee FL 32301

CARSWELL, ROBERT, lawyer; b. Bklyn., Nov. 25, 1928; s. William Brown and Charlotte Edna (Riegger) C.; A.B. magna cum laude, Harvard, 1949, LL.B. cum laude, 1952; m. Mary Kileen Wilde, Dec. 28, 1957; children—Kate, William. Admitted to N.Y. bar, 1952, Cal. bar, 1954; with firm Shearman & Sterling, N.Y.C., 1955-62, partner, 1965—; spl. asst. to sec. treasury, 1962-65. Dir. Aiken Industries, Inc., Chgo. Musical Instrument Co., Graniteville Co. Sec. Caledonian Hosp., N.Y.C., 1959—. Served to lt. (j.g.) USNR, 1952-55. Mem. Am. Bar Assn., Bar Assn. City N.Y., Japan Soc., St. Andrews Soc. N.Y., Phi Beta Kappa. Club: Harvard (N.Y.C.). Home: 7 W 81st St New York City NY 10024 Office: 53 Wall St New York City NY 10005

CARTA, ALVARO LUIS, sugar co. exec.; b. Santa Isabel de ls Lajas, Las Villas, Cuba, Mar. 7, 1927; s. Manuel and Clara (Ramos) C.; came to U.S., 1959, naturalized, 1965; grad. Valley Forge Nil. Acad. 1946; m. Vivian Maria Latour, Jan. 19, 1958; children—Vivian Maria, Maria Teresa, Alina Maria. Officer, dir. Okeelanta Sugar Refinery, Inc., 196064; with S. P.R. Sugar Co., 1965-70, pres., dir. 1968-70; v.p., dir. Scott-Mattson Farms, Inc., 1967-70; v.p. Gulf & Western Industries, Inc., 1969—; pres., dir. Gulf Western Americas, 1968—; pres. dir. S.P.R. Sugar Corp., 1968-70, Central Romana By-Products, Inc., 1968—, Abaco Farms Ltd., 1968—, Corporacion Financiera Asociada, S.A., 1969—; pres. Gulf & Western Food Products. Co., 1970—; dir. Fla. Molasses Exchange Inc. Hon. consul from Dominican Republic, 1969—. Mem. Fla. Thoroughboro Breeders Assn. Roman Catholic. Clubs: Miami (Fla.); Jockey (N.Y.C.); Vero Beach Country; Riomar Bay Yacht (Vero Beach, Fla.). Home: 255 Live Oak Rd Vero Beach FL 32960 Office: PO Box 3448 Vero Beach FL 32960

CARTELYON, WILLIAM T., ednl. adminstr. Dean Grad Sch. Depauw U., Chgo. Office: Grad Sch Depauw U Chicago IL 60611*

CARTER, ALAN, fgn. service officer; b. Rochester, N.Y., Apr. 16, 1923; s. Daniel Benjamin and Sonya (Gordon) C.; student George Washington U., 1940-41; B.A., U. Mich., 1946; m. Marjorie Leo Lawyer, Sept. 27, 1953; 1 dau., Pamela Dale. Radio announcer, Rochester, Albany, N.Y., 1946-49; program dir. radio sta. WNYC, N.Y.C., 1949-51; staff producer radio sta. WNBC, N.Y.C., 1951-53; campaign dir. San Antonio Council Ednl. TV, 1953- 55; joined U.S. Fgn. Service, 1955; radio officer USIS, Karachi, Pakistan, 1956-58; information officer, press attache USIS, New Delhi, India, 1958- 62; spl. asst. to dep. dir. USIA, Washington, 1962-63, dir. TV service, 1963-65, asst. dir. Nr. East, 1965-70; minister-counsellor for pub. affairs Am. embassy, Tokyo, Japan, 1970—. Recipient Meritorious Service award USIA, 1963. Mem. Sigma Alpha Mu. Home: 6242 29th St NW Washington DC 20015 Office: USIA 1776 Pennsylvania Av NW Washington DC 20006

CARTER, ALAN, musician; b. Greenwich, Conn., July 29, 1904; s. Herbert Swift and Mabel (Pettit) C.; student Taft Sch., Watertown, Conn., 1920-22, Mannes Music Sch., N.Y.C., 1922-23, Conservatory of Music, Cologne, Germany, 1923-24; Mus. D. (hon.), U. of Vt., 1955; m. Marianne Townsend, May 18, 1926; children—Joan Pettit, Alan Peter; m. 2d, Barbara Kent, July 7, 1934; children—Timothy, Eric, Kent, Thayer. Musician since 1923; founder and condr. Vt. State Symphony Orch.; mem. musical faculty, Middlebury Coll., 1939-69, chmn. music dept., 1955-69; music dir. of the Vt. Symphony Orch. Assn., Inc.; dir. Bennington Composers' Conf. and Chamber Music Center, 1946—. Trustee Vt. Council on the Arts. Capt. U.S. Army, music officers Hdqrs. 4th Service Comd., Atlanta, 1942-44; Hdqrs. 1st Service Comd., Boston, 1943-44. Recipient Alice M. Ditson condr.'s award Columbia U., 1968. Contbr. articles on music and music edn. Home: 36 Seminary St Middlebury VT 05753

CARTER, ALBERT EDWIN, writer-photographer, former fgn. service officer; b. Big Stone Gap, Va., Nov. 4, 1909; s. Joel Miles and Mary (Cass) C.; student U. Chattanooga, 1929-33, U. Mich., 1939; m. Dorothy Eastmary Sharp, Apr. 19, 1946; children—Robert Sharp, Janet Eastmary, Deborah Cass, Alice Priscilla. Cartoonist, reporter, feature writer Chattanooga News, 1929-36; fgn. affairs editor, columnist Chattanooga Times, 1936-40; asso. editor Norfolk (Va.) Pilot, 1941- 42; sr. bus. analyst Bd. Econ. Warfare, 1942-43; chief Latin Am. sect., div. internat. information Dept. State, 1944-45; cultural attache, pub. affairs officer Am. embassy, San Jose, Costa Rica, 1945-48; pub. affairs officer, Montevideo, 1948-50; 1st sec., consul, Panama, 1950-51; chief pub. affairs policy staff Berlin Element, High Commr. Germany, 1951-52; pub. affairs officer, Bremen, 1952-54; chief Latin Am. div. Office Policy and Programs, USIA, 1954-56, policy adviser for Latin Am., 1956; 1st sec., Asuncion, 1957-58, counselor of embassy, dep. chief mission, 1958-61; with Bur. Intelligence and Research, State Dept., 1961-65, mem. Bd. Examiners, 1965-68; chief pub. relations office S.W. regional office Office Econ. Opportunity, 1968-69; writer, photographer, 1969—. Rosenwald fellow for study travel Latin Am. countries, 1939-41. Mem. Am. Fgn. Service Assn., Internat. Exec. Service Corps. Author: The Battle of South America, 1941. Address: 208 Gannet Cove Austin TX 78746

CARTER, ALEXANDER, bishop; b. Montreal, Que., Can., Apr. 16, 1909; s. Thomas and Mary (Kerr) C.; M.Th., M.C.L., LL.D., Montreal Coll. 1930; ed. Sem. Philosophy and Grand Sem. Montreal, 1936; M.Th., M.C.L., Canadian Coll., Rome, 1939; LL.D., (hon.) Laurentian U., Sudbury, Ont., 1962. Ordained priest Roman Cath. Ch., 1936; bishop of Sault Ste. Marie, 1957—. Chancellor U. Sudbury, 1962—. Pres. Canadian Cath. Conf., 1967-69. Mem. Vanier Inst. Address: 480 McIntyre St W North Bay Ontario Canada

CARTER, AMON, Jr., publisher; b. Ft. Worth, Dec. 23, 1919; s. Amon G. and Nenetta (Burton) C.; B.B.A., U. Tex., 1941. With Carter Pubs., Fort Worth, 1936—, pres., 1952—; dir. Gt. So. Corp., Am. Airlines, Inc. Served as capt. AUS, 1941-45; prisoner of war, Germany, 1943-45. Decorated Purple Heart, Bronze Star. Mem. Kappa Sigma. Club: Exchange. Home: 29 Valley Ridge Rd Fort Worth TX 76107 Office: 400 W 7th St Fort Worth TX 76102

CARTER, ANN, journalist; b. N.Y.C., Feb. 8, 1943; d. Sam F. and Jane (Downs) Carter; student Coll. du Leman, Geneva, Switzerland, 1960-61, W.Va. U., 1961-62; B.S. in Journalism, U. Fla., 1965; postgrad. Ga. State Coll., 1966-67, Sch. Art Inst. Chgo., 1969-71. With Office Press Information, European Common Market, summer 1963, Daytona Beach (Fla.) News-Jour., summer 1964; gen. assignment and arts editor Atlanta Jour., 1965-69; contbg. editor Architecture Midwest monthly mag., 1970. An organizer Atlanta chpt. Expts. in Art and Tech., 1969. Mem. Theta Sigma Phi (v.p. 1964-65), Zeta Phi Eta (sec. 1965). Democrat. Mem. Christian Sci. Ch. Home: 3631 N Broadway Chicago IL 60613

CARTER, BENJAMIN CHADWICK, business exec.; b. Rainier, Ore., Jan. 14, 1907; s. Frank Fair and Mary Ruth (Chadwick) C.; student Menlo (Cal.) Sch., 1920-24; A.B., Stanford, 1929; m. Thelma Grothe, June 30, 1934; children—Nancy Jean, Dennis Benjamin, Linda Ann, Sharon Ruth. With Price- Waterhouse & Co., 1929-34; with Food Machinery Corp., San Jose, Cal., 1934—, Food Machinery & Chem. Corp. (co. name changed to FMC Corp.), 1934—, asst. controller, 1934-41, controller, 1941-52, dir., 1946—, v.p., 1946-52, exec. v.p., 1952-60, exec. v.p. finance, 1960-66, vice chmn. bd. dirs., 1966-71, chmn. bd. dirs., 1971—; dir. Bank of Cal., W.P. R.R. Co., Ketchikan Pulp Co., Petro-Tex Chem. Corp., Avicon, Inc. Mem. city council, San Jose, 1944-48. Trustee Menlo Sch. and Coll., 1949—, chmn. bd. trustees, 1968-70. C.P.A., Cal. Mem. Machinery and Allied Products Inst. (exec. com.). Clubs: Sainte Claire, San Jose Country; Pacific Union (San Francisco); Pinnacle (N.Y.C.). Home: 15600 Alum Rock Av San Jose CA 95127 Office: 1105 Coleman Av San Jose CA 95110

CARTER, BENNETT LESTER BENNY, musician, bandleader; b. N.Y.C., Aug. 8, 1907; student theology Wilberforce U. Early career as alto saxophonist, clarinetist, trumpeter; with Duke Ellington, Charlie Johnson, Fletcher Henderson, Chick Webb, McKinney's Cotton Pickers, Willie Bryant; with Willie Lewis band, Paris, France, 1935; studio band arranger Henry Hall's BBC Studio, Eng., 1936; leader own band, 1938-41, leader sextet, 1941; arranger, writer sound-track music for movies including Five Pennies, Flower Drum Song, Gene Krupa Story, Snows of Kilimanjaro, others; appeared motion picture Snows of Kilimanjaro, 1952; rec. star, then free-lance artist, swing arranger; mus. dir., arranger for various singers, background music TV shows. Recipient silver award Esquire, 1943, gold award, 1946. Address: 2325 Kimridge Rd Beverly Hills CA

CARTER, BOYD GEORGE, educator, author; b. Duffield, Va., May 8, 1908; s. James David and Viola (Fraley) C.; student Coll. William and Mary, 1925-26, A.B., 1929; student U. Toulouse (France), 1926-27; A.M., U. Ill., 1933, Ph.D., 1937; postgrad. U. Ia., 1942; m. Mary Eileen Barry, June 16, 1965. With A.P., summer 1929; tchr. Beaver High Sch., Bluefield, W.Va., 1929- 31; grad. asst. U. Ill., 1931-37; instr. U. Ida., 1937; asst. prof. U. Wyo., 1938; prof., chmn. dept. modern langs. Coe Coll., Cedar Rapids, Ia., 1939-45; prof. U. Neb., 1945-59, chmn. dept. Romance langs., 1950- 56; prof. So. Ill. U., 1959-67, U. Mo., Columbia, 1967—. Lectr., Mexico City, 1962, Managua, Nicaragua, 1967. Mem. adv. com. project Mass. Council Pub. Schs., 1959—. Decorated palmes academiques (France), 1956. Mem. Modern Lang. Assn. Am. Assn. Tchrs. French (pres. West Central chpt. 1948-50), Am. Assn. Tchrs. Spanish and Portuguese, Latin Am. Studies Assn., 82d Airborne Div. Assn. (hon.), Phi Beta Kappa, Phi Kappa Phi, Omicron Delta Kappa, Phi Sigma Iota, Phi Kappa Tau. Author: (with C.G. Rowe) A French Review Grammar, 1948; Manuel Gutiérrez Nájera; estudio y escritos inéditos, 1956; Las revistas literarias de Hispanoamerica, 1959; En torno a Gutiérrez Nájera, 1960; (with Joan L. Carter) Manuel Gutiérrez Nájera; florilegio crítico- conmemorativo, 1966; La Revista de Américá de Rubén Darío y Ricardo Jaimes Freyre, 1967; Historia de la literatura hispanoamericana a través de sus revistas, 1968. Editor: (Ross S. Carter) Those Devils in Baggy Pants, 1951; (D.E. Allison) German Review Grammar, 1965. Adv. editor Prairie Schooner, 1949-59. Contbr. articles, stories, poetry to periodicals. Home: 1108 W Stewart Rd Columbia MO 65201

CARTER, BYRUM EARL, univ. chancellor; b. Shawnee, Okla., Mar. 3, 1922; s. Byrum Earl and Myrtle (Madison) C.; A.B., U. Okla., 1943; Ph.D., U. Wis., 1951; m. Beth Peter, May 14, 1944; children—Terry Elizabeth (Mrs. Robert Hedrick), Keith M. Wage rate analyst, 1944; mem. faculty Ind. U., Bloomington, 1947—, prof. govt., 1961—, dean Coll. Arts and Scis., 1966-69, chancellor Bloomington campus, 1969—. Served with USMCR, 1943. Recipient Frederic Bachman Lieber award distinguished teaching Ind. U., 1957. Mem. Am. Polit. Sci. Assn, (exec. com. 1962-64), Midwest Conf. Polit. Scientists. Author: The Office of Prime Minister, 1956. Home: 1900 Ruby Lane Bloomington IN 47401

CARTER, C. I., feed co. exec.; b. Weogufka, Ala., Aug. 7, 1919; s. Claude I. and Irona (Strickland) C.; B.S. in Agrl. Sci., Auburn U., 1941; m. Ruth Laubenthal, Oct. 2, 1943; children—Constance, Michael, Ann, Theresa. With Con Agra, 1941—, exec. v.p., gen. mgr. feed div., 1964—. Mem. Am. Feed Mfrs. Inst. (past chmn. bd.). Lion (past pres. Decatur, Ala.). Home: 1705 N 102d St Omaha NB 68114 Office: 500 Kiewit Plaza Omaha NB 68131

CARTER, CHARLES, journalist. Edn. editor Denver Post. Office: 650 15th St Denver CO 80202*

CARTER, CHARLES EDWARD, educator, pharmacologist; b. Boise, Ida., Aug. 25, 1919; s. Charles Ernest and Ethel (Rude) C.; B.A., Reed Coll., 1941; M.D., Cornell U., 1944; m. Polly Byers Whitrow, Sept. 7, 1945; children—Diana, Geoffery. With Nat. Cancer Inst., 1945-47; biology div. Oak Ridge Nat. Lab., 1947-50; dept. medicine Western Res. U. Sch. Medicine, 1950-53; dept. pharmacology Yale Sch. Medicine, 1953-64; prof., dir. dept. pharmacology Case Western Res. U. Sch. Medicine, Cleve., 1964—. Mem. Bd. Edn. Town of Orange, Conn. Mem. Am. Biol. Chemists. Home: 31500 Jackson Rd Moreland Hills OH 44221 Office: Case Western Res U Sch Medicine Cleveland OH 44106

CARTER, CHARLES VAL, savs. and loan assn. exec.; b. Reno, Nev., Feb. 14, 1907; s. Charles R. and Jessie G. (Carter) C.; B.A., U. Nev., 1928. With Union Fed. Savs. & Loan Assn., Reno, 1939—, sec.-treas., dir., 1939—, chmn. bd., 1970—; dir. Fed. Home Loan Bank San Francisco. Bd. dirs. Nev. Humane Soc.; trustee YMCA. Served with USNR. Mem. U.S. Savs. and Loan League (dir., mem. legislative and nominating coms.), Reno C. of C. (dir.). Baptist (dir.). Mason (Shriner), Odd Fellow, Kiwanian (past pres.). Home: 1445 California Av Reno NV 89502 Office: 195 S Sierra St Reno NV 89505

CARTER, CHESTER CHARLES, corp. exec.; b. Emporia, Kan., Feb. 14, 1921; s. Chester Charles and Mary Lenore (Johnson) C.; A.B., U. So. Cal., 1949, M.A., 1952; LL.B., Loyola U., Los Angeles, 1958; m. Claudia June Bernard, Mar. 9, 1956; children—Chester Charles, Marise Sue, Carol Jill. Asst. dir. Los Angeles Bur. Charities, 1955-56; probation officer Los Angeles County Ct., 1956- 60; juvenile referee Los Angeles County Superior Ct., 1960-62; dir. Peace Corps, Africa, 1962-63; dep. asst. sec. state Dept. State, Washington, 1963-64, dep. chief protocol, 1964-68; exec. Seagram Overseas Sales Co., N.Y.C., 1968—. Mem. Pres.'s Com. on UN, 1964—. Served to 2d lt. AUS, 1942-46; to 1st lt., 1950-52. Mem. Fgn. Service Assn., Skull and Dagger, Blue Key, Kappa Alpha Psi. Home: 140 West End Av New York City NY 10023 Office: 375 Park Av New York City NY 10022

CARTER, CLARENCE HOLBROOK, artist; b. Portsmouth, O., Mar. 26, 1904; s. Clarence William and Hettie May (Holbrook) C.; student Cleve. Sch. Art, 1923-27; studied abroad under H. Hoffman, Capri, Italy, summer 1927; m. Mary B. Griswold, May 4, 1929; children—John Holbrook, Peter Griswold, Clarence Blakesley. Represented in permanent collections Met. Mus., Mus. Modern Art, Whitney Mus. Am. Art (all N.Y.C.), Bklyn. Mus., Cleve. Mus. Art, Toledo Mus. Art, Arnot Art Mus., Elmira, N.Y., Meml. Art Gallery, Rochester, N.Y., Montclair (N.J.) Art Mus., N.J. State Mus., Trenton Fogg Art Mus. Harvard, Corcoran Gallery Art, Washington, Butler Inst. Am. Art, Youngstown, O., Oberlin Coll., Coll. Wooster (O.), Sheldon Swope Art Gallery, Terre Haute, Ind., Nelson Gallery Art, Kansas City, Mo., U. Neb., U. Tex. at Austin, Pasadena (Cal.) Art Mus., Mus. Boymans-Van Beuningen, Rotterdam, Netherlands, Victoria and Albert Mus., London, Eng.; executed murals for sect. of painting and Sculpture, Treasury Dept., Portsmouth, O. and Ravenna, O. Post offices; murals for Cleve. Pub. Auditorium; represented by Gimpel and Weitzenhoffer Gallery Ltd., N.Y.C., Henri Gallery, Washington. Awarded 13 first prizes, numerous (2d and 3d prizes in ann. exhbns. by Cleve. artists and craftsmen (Cleve. Mus. Art); Pitts. Asso. Artists, 1st prize oils, 1943, 1st prize water color, 1944, Popular prize, "Painting in the United States," Carnegie Inst. 1943, First popularity prize, 1936, 1st prize for oils, 1940, 2d prize for oils, 1943, Butler Art Inst., Youngstown, O. Instr. Cleve. Mus. Art, 1930-37; asst. prof. painting and design Carnegie Inst. Tech., Pitts., 1938-44; guest instr. painting Cleve. Inst. Art, summer 1948, Mpls. Sch. Art., fall 1949, Lehigh U., 1954, Ohio U., 1955; Atlanta Art Inst., 1957; guest artist U. Ia., Spring 1970; artist-in-residence Lafayette Coll., 1961-69, cons., 1970-71; retrospective one-man shows in largest cities represented in exhibit 200 Years of Am. Painting, Tate Gallery, London, 1946; European tour of Modern Am. Art, 1955-56. S.A., gathering material for series of paintings for Alcoa S.S. Co. Gen. supt. Fed. Art Project, Cleve, Dist., 1937-38. Mem. N.A.D., Conglist. Home: Box 311 Route 1 Milford NJ 08848

CARTER, COLLINS L., mfg. Co. exec.; b. Jackson, Mich., Jan. 30, 1906; s. Philander Lothrop and Nelle (Collins) C.; M.E., Cornell U., 1929; D. in Bus. Adminstrn., (hon.), Albion Coll., 1967; m. Mary Bursley, 1938; children—Deborah, Virginia, Mary Victoria, Philander Lothrop III. With Albion Malicable Iron Co., Jackson, 1929-67, pres., 1938-67; pres. Hayes-Albion Corp. (merger Albion Malleable Iron Co., and Hayes Industries), 1967—, also dir.; dir. City Bank and Trust Co., Jackson. Cons. Small Bus. Adminstrn., 1955-60. Exc. mem. Lando' Lakes council Boy Scouts Am.; chmn. fund raising campaign Sheldon Meml. Hosp., Albion, Mich.; v.p. Albion Housing Commn., 1950-58; pres. Albion Community Concert Assn., 1957-59; mem. New Jackson Com., 1968—. Mem. Mich. Republican Finance Com., 1956-61. Bd. dirs. Culver Ednl. Fund.; trustee Starr Commonwealth for Boys, Albion. Served to maj. AUS, 1941-44. Recipient Silver Beaver award Boy Scouts Am., 1961; McCrea medal Malleable Founders' Soc. Mem. Albion Mfrs. Assn. (pres. 1947), Am. Ordnance Assn. dir. Mich. dhpt. 1967—, Am. Legion. Episcopalian (past sr. warden). Rotarian clubs: Duck Lake Golf (Albion); Country of Jackson, Town (Jackson); Detroit Athletic; Clubs: Town (Ann Arbor, Mich.); Union League (Chgo.). Home: 1715 Probert Rd Jackson MI 49203 Office: 437 Fern Av Jackson MI 49202

CARTER, CREED FULTON, Jr., former merchandising exec., horse farm owner; b. Roxie, Va., May 26, 1909; s. Creed Fulton and Caroline Kyle (Fulton) C.; student McGuire U. Sch., 1927-29, Emory and Henry Coll., 1929-30; m. Mary Virginia Monteiro, June 8, 1929; 1 dau., Evelyn Nan (Mrs. Robert A. Sadler III). Mgr., McCrory Stores, N.J., Conn., Va., 1939-46, dist. mgr., Carolinas, Pa., Tex., 1947-59, gen. supt. McCrorоy-McLellan Stores, N.Y.C., 1960, v.p., 1960-64, v.p., east central regional mgr., 1964-67, v.p. co., 1968-69, ret., 1970; v.p. new stores planning and devel. McCrory, McLellan-Green Stores, 1960-63; treas., chief exec. officer Car-Nan-Sa Farms, Inc., Allentown, Pa.; partner Nanco Corp., 1969—; dir. Blacks Poultry, Supreme Products Co.; dealer horses, Hereford cattle. Bd. dirs., regent , chmn., pres. Swain Sch., Allentown., mem., bd. dirs. Allentown Symphony Assn. Mem. adv. bd. on retailing Leigh County Community Coll. Named to Wisdom Hall of Fame recipient Wisdom award of Honor., 1970; col. W.Va. Centennial, 1965. Mem. Am. Mgmt. Assn., Nat. Steeplechase and Hunt Assn., Northeast Pa. Horse Assn., Pa. Horse Breeders Assn., Pa. Soc., 100,000 Pennsylvanians, Allentown Art Mus., Pa. Chain Store Council, Pa. Retailers Assn., Penn-Jersey Horse Show Assn. (chmn. show com.), Allenton Art Mus., Allentown Civic Little Theatre, Internat. Platform Assn. Methodist (trustee, regent, mem. ofcl. bd.). Rotarian, Mason (32); mem. Order Eastern Star. Clubs: Lehigh Country, Lehigh Valley; Three Oaks Riding and Hunt (dir., pres.); Orange County Hunt; United Hunt and Racing; Ridglea Country. Home: Car-Nan-Sa Farms Allentown PA 18105 Office: 471 S Cedarbrook Rd Allentown PA 18103

CARTER, DAN T., educator; b. Florence, S.C., June 17, 1940; s. Dewey L. and Lalla (Lawhon) C.; B.A., U. S.C., 1962; M.A., U. Wis., 1964; Ph.D., U. N.C., 1967; m. Jane Winkler, Aug. 29, 1964; children—Alicia Lee, David Charles. Asst. prof. U. Md., 1967-69, asso. prof., 1970-71, prof., 1971—; vis. asso. prof. U. Wis., 1969-70. Woodrow Wilson fellow 1962-63; recipient Bancroft prize, 1969, Anisfield-Wolfe award, 1969, Jules Landry prize, 1970, Lillian Smith award, 1969. Mem. Orgn. Am. Historians, So. Hist. Assn., Soc. Am. Historians. Presbyterian. Author: Scottsboro: A Tragedy of the American South, 1969; A Reasonable Doubt, 1968. Home: 4217 Woodberry St University Park MD 20782 Office: Hist Dept U Md College Park MD 20740

CARTER, DEANE MILTON, educator; b. Sharon Springs, Kan., Oct. 2, 1926; s. Edward Lee and Doris Mabel (Smith) C.; B.S., U. Colo., 1950, M.S., 1956; Ph.D., U. Ia., 1965. Instr. pub. high schs., Lamar and Denver, Colo., Los Alamos, 1950-56; instr. bus. dept. Pueblo (Colo.) Jr. Coll., 1956-58; asso. prof. bus. data processing Colo. State U., Ft. Collins, 1958-62, chmn. adminstrv. services dept. Coll. Bus., 1962—; ednl. cons. Data Processing Mgmt. Assn., Park Ridge, Ill., 1968-70, Infatron Systems, Inc., Ft. Collins, 1969-70; data processing cons. Colo. Vocational Edn. Dept., Denver, 1960- 66, U.S. Office Edn., Washington, 1962-65, U.S. Bur. Reclamation, Denver, 1966, Am. Software Corp., Ft. Collins, 1967-69, Boise Cascade Corp. (Ida.), 1967-70, Cities Service Oil Corp., Tulsa, 1970; editorial cons. McGraw-Hill Book Co., N.Y.C., 1965-70, Wadsworth Pub. Co., Belmont, Cal., 1965-70; v.p. Profl. Cons., Inc., Ft. Collins. Chmn. adv. com. Computer Information Systems, Pub. Schs., Ft. Collins, 1967-70, mem. adv. com. City Govt., 1970. Served with USNR, 1944-46. Recipient Nat. award of merit Biennial Conclave, Acacia Fraternity, 1968. Mem. Data Processing Mgmt. Assn. (past internat. dir.), Admnstrv. Mgmt. Soc. (past systems and planning dir.), Am. Mgmt. Assn., Internat. Bus. Assn., Nat., Mountain-Plains, Colo. bus. edn. assns., Am. Assn. Coll. Tchrs. Edn., Nat. Assn. Bus. Tchrs. Edn., Am. Assn. U. Profs., Soc. for Automation in Bus., Am. Vocational Edn. Assn., Acacia, Beta Gamma Sigma, Delta Pi Epsilon, Omicron Delta Kappa, Pi Gamma Mu. Republican. Methodist. Mason. Contbr. articles profl. jours. Home: 136 Yale Av Fort Collins CO 80521

CARTER, DONALD PATTON, advt. exec.; b. Richmond, Mo., July 30, 1927; s. R.D. and Lillian (Patton) C.; student U. Louisville, 1945-46; B.S., U. Mo., 1948; M.B.A., Wharton Sch. U. Pa., 1950; m. Susan Virginia Wurst, Apr. 22, 1950; children—Jeffrey, Stephen, Carol. With Continental Color Press, Inc., Kansas City, Mo., 1950-52; pres. Nasco, Inc., Kansas City, Kan., 1953- 54; v.p., then pres. Biddle Co., Bloomington, Ill., 1955-68; pres. chief operating officer Post-Keyes-Gardner Inc., Chgo., 1968—, also dir. Tchr. econs., bus. adminstrn. Kansas City (Mo.) Jr. Coll., 1950-52. Active local fund raising campaigns. Served with USNR, 1945-47. Named Young Man of Year, Jr. C. of C., 1951. Mem. Phi Kappa Psi. Presbyn. Clubs: Lake Shore (Chgo.); Knollwood Country. Home: 120 W Westminster Lake Forest IL 60045 Office: 875 N Michigan Av Chicago IL 60611

CARTER, DON EARL, newspaper editor; b. Plains, Ga., June 22, 1917; s. William Alton and Annie Laurie (Gay) C.; student Ga. Southwestern Coll., 1934-36; A.B., U. Ga., 1938; m. Carolyn McKenzie, Oct. 3, 1942. Reporter, Atlanta Jour., 1938-39, farm editor, 1940-41, municipal govt. reporter, asst. city editor, 1946-50, city editor 1951-59; editor Baxley (Ga.) News-Banner, 1939-40; exec. dir. Newspaper Fund, Wall Street Jour., 1959-61; founding mng. editor Nat. Observer, 1961-67; exec. editor The Record, Hackensack, N.J., 1967-71, Morning Call, Paterson, N.J., 1967-69; v.p. Bergen Evening Record Corp., 1968-71; exec. editor Macon (Ga.) Telegraph and Macon News, 1971—. Tchr. journalism eve. div. Ga. State Coll., 1950-59; lectr. Am. Press Inst., Columbia, 1953—. Pulitzer award juror, 1968-70. Bd. dirs. Newspaper Fund; adv. council journalism St. Bonaventure U., N.Y.U.; trustee Ramapo Coll. of N.J., 1969-71. Served to capt. AUS, 1941-45. Decorated Bronze Star; recipient citation service to journalism Theta Sigma Phi, 1961, U. Neb. Sch. Journalism, 1962. Mem. A.P. Mng. Editors Assn. (pres. 1971), Am. Soc. Newspaper Editors, Am. Newspaper Pubs. Assn., Phi Beta Kappa, Sigma Delta Chi (pres. Atlanta 1957-59, nat. dir. 1958- 59, 66-67, 69-71), Omicron Delta Kappa, Phi Kappa Phi, Phi Delta Epsilon, Kappa Tau Alpha. Clubs: Nat. Press (Washington); Idle Hour Country (Macon); Atlanta Athletic. Home: PO Box 684 244 DeSoto St Sea Island GA 31561 Office: 120 Broadway Macon GA 31208

CARTER, EDGAR BROCK, research cons.; b. Elkinsville, Ind., Apr. 22, 1886; s. Tobe Wilford and Nannie Elizabeth (Brock) C.; A.B., U. Ind., 1911; m. Susie Field Huffines, June 4, 1914 (dec. 1918); 1 son, John Robert; m. 2d, Ruth Ann Cheney, June 17, 1922; 1 dau., Carol Ruth (Mrs. H. Dale Clark). Analytical, cons. chemist Landon C. Moore, Dallas, 1911-15; dir. biol. lab. Swan-Myers Co., Indpls., 1915-20, dir. sci. work, 1920-31; with Abbott Labs., North Chicago, 1931—, bd. dirs., 1935-52, asso. dir. research 1942-46, exec. dir. research, asst. sec., 1946-52, now cons. Chmn. sub-com. sterile products, mem. exec. com. U.S. Pharmacopoeia Revision Com., 1950-60; pres. Highland Park (Ill.) Social Service Com., 1938-40. Fellow Am. Pub. Health Assn., A.A.A.S., Am. Inst. Chemists, Royal Soc. Health; mem. Am. Chem. Soc., Am. Pharm. Assn., Am. Soc. for

Microbiology, Sigma Xi, Alpha Chi Sigma. Presbyn. (elder). Mason (32), Kiwanian. Club: Chemists. Author chpt. in Drug. Research and Development, 1948. Home: 140 E Ridge Village Dr Miami FL 33157

CARTER, EDWARD FRANCIS, former judge; b. Middlebranch, Neb., Mar. 11, 1897; s. Edward Charles and Allie Margaret (Waring) C.; LL.B., U. Neb., 1919; m. Vera Marie Hofrichter, June 2, 1920; children—Dolores Jean, Lyle Allen, Edward Francis, Robert Le Roy, Barbara Jean. Admitted to Neb. bar, 1919; practiced in Bayard until 1927; judge 17th Jud. Dist., Neb., 1927-35; asso. justice Neb. Supreme Ct., 1935-71; dir. Neb. Criminal Code Revision, 1971—. Judge, 5th Mil. Tribunal, Nurnberg, Germany, to try maj. German war criminals, 1947-48. Past pres. Cornhusker Council Boy Scouts Am. Served with U.S. Army, World War. Mem. Am., Neb., Western Neb., Lancaster County, Scotts Bluff bar assns., Am. Interprofl. Inst. (past nat. pres.), Am. Legion, Cornhusker Boys' State (pres.), Order of Coif, Phi Alpha Delta. Republican. Conglist. Mason (33). K.P. Club: Hiram. Home: 1615 Skyline Dr Lincoln NB 68506 Office: Anderson Bldg Lincoln NB 68508

CARTER, EDWARD JENNINGS, educator; b. Mars Hill, N.C., Aug. 25, 1906; s. Horace Judson and Sophronia Ann (Sams) C.; A.B., Lenoir Rhyne Coll., 1926; M.A., U. N.C., 1938, Ph.D., 1942; m. Charlotte Annette Booth, Aug. 6, 1930; 1 son, David Edward. Tchr., adminstr. N.C. pub. schs., 1922-23, 26-42; dir. tng. program overseas personnel UNRRA, 1944-45; supr. pub. instrn. Ala. Dept. Edn., 1945-46; chmn. dept. edn. Murray (Ky.) State Coll., 1946-50; chmn. dept. edn. East Carolina Coll., Greenville, N.C., 1950—, dir. field services, 1951- 57, dir. edn. dept., 1957-61, dir. grad. studies div., 1961—, prof. Sch. Edn., 1963—. Served with A.R.C., 1942-44. Mem. Am. Assn. Sch. Adminstrs., Nat., N.C. edn. assns., Ala. Acad. Sci., Ky. Hist. Assn., Kappa Delta Pi, Phi Delta Kappa. Methodist. (steward). Kiwanian. Home: 1207 E Rock Spring Dr Greenville NC 27834

CARTER, EDWARD WILLIAM, mcht.; A.B., U. Cal. at Los Angeles, 1932; M.B.A. cum laude, Harvard, 1937; LL.D., Occidental Coll., 1962; m. 2d, Hannah Locke Caldwell, 1963; children—William Dailey, Mrs. Ann Carter Huneke. Pres., dir. Broadway-Hale Stores, Inc., Los Angeles; dir. Am. Tel & Tel. Co., Del Monte Corp., Western Bancorp., Pacific Mut. Life Ins. Co., So. Cal. Edison Co., United Cal. Bank. Mem. Nat. Commn. on Productivity, Nat. Indsl. Conf. Bd. Bd. dirs. Council for Financial Aid to Edn., San Francisco Opera Assn., So. Cal. Symphony, Hollywood Bowl Assn., James Irvine Found., Stanford Research Inst.; trustee Brookings Instn., Com. Econ. Devel., Los Angeles County Mus. Art, Occidental Coll., Santa Anita Found.; mem. overseers vis. com. Harvard Grad. Sch. Bus.; vis. com. U. Cal. at Los Angeles regent U. Cal.; adv. com. Stanford Bus. Sch. Clubs: California, Los Angleles Country (Los Angeles); Pacific Union, Bohemian, Burlingame Country (San Francisco). Home: 626 Siena Way Los Angeles CA 90014 Office: 600 S Spring St Los Angeles CA 90014

CARTER, ELLIOTT COOK, Jr., composer; b. N.Y.C., Dec. 11, 1908; s. Elliott Cook and Florence (Chambers) C.; A.B., Harvard, 1930, A.M., 1932. hon. degree, 1970; Mus. D. (hon.), New Eng. Conservatory Music, 1961, Swarthmore Coll., 1956, Princeton, 1967; hon. degrees Boston U., Yale, Oberlin Coll., 1970; m. Helen Frost-Jones, July 6, 1939; 1 son, David Carter. Tutor, chmn. music St. John's Coll., Annapolis, Md., 1939-41, tchr. Greek and math.; tchr. music theory and composition Peabody Conservatory, Balt., 1946-48; tchr. in Am. studies Salburg Seminars, Austria, 1958; asso. music Columbia, 1948-50; mus. dir. Ballet Caravan, 1937-39; cons. O.W.I., 1942-44; critic League of Composers Quar. Modern Music, 1937- 42; prof. musical composition Yale U., 1960—; lectr. Princeton music seminar, 1959-60; composer in residence City of West Berlin, 1964. Commd. by N.Y., Zagreb philharmonic orchs. Trustee Am. Acad. in Rome. Guggenheim fellow, 1945-46, 50-5l. Awarded choral prize for To Music, WPA music div., 1938; Am. Composers Alliance prize for Quartet for Four Saxophones, 1943; League of Composers commn. for symphony, 1952; First prize in internat. music competition for composers, Leige, Belgium, 1953; Ford Found. award for piano concerto, 1959; Pulitzer prize for music, 1960; Music Critics Circle N.Y. award, 1962, Creative Arts award Brandeis U., 1965; Premio delle Muse, City of Florence, Italy 1969. Mem. League Composers (dir. 1939-52), Internat. Soc. Contemporary Music (dir. 1946-52, pres. U.S. sect. 1952). Nat. Inst. Arts and Letters (Gold medal for music 1971), Am. Acad. Arts and Letters, Am. Composers Alliance (dir. 1939-52, treas. 1949-50). Composer: Tarantella, 1937; Ballet Pocahontas (Ballet Caravan commn. 1939, Julliard Publ. award for suite 1941), 1938; Incidental Music for the Merchant of Venice, 1938; The Defense of Corinth, 1941; First Symphony, 1942-43; The Harmony of Morning, 1945; Piano Sonata, 1945; Holiday Overture (Ind. Music Pubs. prize 1945), 1945; ballet The Minotaur (Ballet Soc. commn.), 1946-47; Woodwind Quintet, 1947; Sonata for Cello and Piano, 1948; Emblems for men's chorus and piano, 1948; Eight Etudes and a Fantasy for Woodwind Quartet, 1949; String Quartet, 1950-1951; Sonata for Flute, Oboe, 'Cello, Harpsichord (Naumburg award 1956), 1952; Variations for Orch. (Louisville commn.), 1955; Double Concerto (From Foun. commn.), 1956; Concerto for Orch. (N.Y. Philharmonic Soc. commn.), 1969. Home: 31 W 12th St New York City NY 10011

CARTER, EMMETT FINLEY, research exec., engr.; b. Elgin, Tex., July 1, 1901; s. Alfred Hinds and Lutie (Stevens) C.; B.S. cum laude, Rice Inst., 1922; m. Charlotte Reid, May 16, 1925; children—Everett Carter, Caryl Ruth (Mrs. Peter Mezey). Radio transmitter, receiver, and TV devel. Gen. Electric Co., Schenectady, 1922-29; dir. radio engring. div. United Research Corp. (subsidiary of Warner Pictures), N.Y.C., 1929-32; cons. engr. Sylvania Electric Products Inc., N.Y.C., 1932, radio div. engr., 1932-38, asst. chief engr., 1938-41, dir. indsl. relations, 1941-45, v.p. in charge engring., 1946- 53, v.p. and tech. dir., 1953-54; mgr. research operations Stanford Research Inst., 1954-56, dir., 1956-65, mem. exec. com., pres., 1959-63, sr. mgmt. counselor, 1963-65; dir. Itek Corp., URS Systems Corp., Eitel-McCullough, Inc. Mem. research and devel. adv. council Chief Signal Officer, 1954-62; mem. Gov's Bus. Adv. Council, 1961-65. Pres. bd. trustees Silver Bay Assn., 1950-54; trustee, v.p. World Affairs Council No. Cal.; bd. dirs. Oscar Project; mem. fund council Rice U., 1971—. Recipient Founders award I.E.E.E., 1969. Registered profl. engr., Cal., N.Y. Fellow I.E.E.E. (dir. at large and del. 1961-63); mem. Nat. Soc. Profl. Engrs., A.A.A.S., Research Soc. Am., Am. Ordnance Assn. (dir. 1957-63, past pres. and dir. San Francisco post, regional v.p. 1963—), Tau Beta Pi. Clubs: University (N.Y.); University (Palo Alto); Commonwealth Cal.; Stanford Faculty. Patentee in field. Home: 137 Ash Lane Portola Valley CA 94025 Office: Portola Valley CA 94025

CARTER, EVERETT, educator; b. N.Y.C., Apr. 28, 1919; s. Ben and Myra (Rosenberg) C.; B.A., U. Cal. at Los Angeles, 1939, M.A., 1943; Ph.D., 1947; m. Cecile Doudna, June 29, 1940; children—Dale Everett, Timothy Howard. Writer, So. Cal. Gas Co., 1939-42, Universal Pictures, 1942-46; instr., then asst. prof. English, Claremont Men's Coll., 1946-49; asst. prof. English, U. Cal. at Berkeley, 1949-57, spl. asst. to pres., 1963-64; univ. dean research, 1964-66; vis. lectr. Harvard, 1957-58; faculty U. Cal. at Davis, 1958-63, prof. English, 1966—; dir. Center for Studies, U. Cal. at Bordeaux (France), 1970—. Fulbright lectr. U. Copenhagen (Denmark), 1954- 55, 61-62; participant Salzburg Seminar Am. Studies, 1953; Fulbright lectr. Nice Seminar Am. Studies, 1958, 62, Seminar Am. Studies, Hyderabad, India, 1964; Fulbright prof. U. Strasbourg, 1966-67. Guggenheim fellow, 1952-53, 61-62. Recipient Commonwealth gold medal non-fiction 1955. Mem. A.S.C.A.P., Modern Lang. Assn. Author: Howells and the Age of Realism, 1954. Contbr. articles to profl. jours. Home: 734 Hawthorn Lane Davis CA 95616

CARTER, EVERITT A., electronics co. exec.; b. Phila., May 9, 1919; s. Robert A. and Florence Emma (Everett) C.; B.S., Mech. Engring., Duke, 1940; m. Mary M. Cragoe, Oct. 9, 1943; children—Nickola Mary, Robert Edward, Timothy John, Susan Catherine. Engring. and sales positions Wright Aeros. div. Curtiss-Wright Corp., 1940-46, dir. sales west coast, 1952-55; dir. sales and service Hughes Aircraft Co., 1946-49; v.p. Faber Labs., N.Y.C., 1949-52; gen. mgr. Curtiss-Wright Can., Ltd., 1955-56; v.p., gen. mgr. Canadian Curtiss-Wright, Ltd., 1957-59; chmn. bd., chief exec. officer Oak Electro/Netics Corp., Crystal Lake, Ill., 1959—; dir. Home State Bank Crystal Lake, United Card Co.; Palatine, Ill. Mem. No. Ill. U. Forum for Pres.'s Council. Bd. dirs. Crystal Lake Hosp. Assn. Mem. Soc. Automotive Engrs., Canadian Aero. Inst., World Trade Council, Chgo. Assn. Commerce and Industry, Midwest-Japan Assn., Newcomen Soc., Phi Kappa Psi, Delta Epsilon Sigma. Republican. Clubs: Inverness Country; Crystal Lake Country; Economic, Chicago, University (Chgo.); Canadian; Barrington (Ill.) Tennis, West Side Tennis (Forest Hills, N.Y.); Balboa Bay (Newport Beach, Cal.). Home: 1175 Blackburn Inverness Countryside Palatine IL 62451 Office: Oak Electro/Netics Corp Crystal Lake IL 60014

CARTER, FOREST CHARLES, coll. dean; b. Indpls., Mar. 12, 1922; s. Forest C. and Myra (Fortney) C.; student Butler U., 1939-41; B.B.A., U. Mich., 1946, M.B.A., 1947; D.B.A., Ind. U., 1962; m. Marilyn Eunice Meyers, Aug. 22, 1945; children—Cecelia Ann, Karen Louise. Accountant Cinder Block and Material Co., Indpls., 1940-41; asst. prof. U. Tenn., 1947-54; teaching asso. Ind. U., 1954-56; prof., head dept., asso. dean Colo. State U., 1956-67; dean bus. adminstr. Clarion State Coll. (Pa.), 1967—; asst. dir. edn. Am. Inst. C.P.A.'s, 1959-60. Served with USNR, 1941-45. Mem. Am. Accounting Assn., Am. Inst. C.P.A.'s, Nat. Assn. Accountants (dir. 1948-49, 69-71), Colo., Pa. socs. C.P.A.'s, Beta Gamma Sigma, Phi Kappa Phi. Author: (with Vrendenburg and Patty) A Historical, Economic and Statistical Study of the Electrical Sign Industry. Home: RD 1 Shippenville PA 16254 Office: Clarion State College Clarion PA 16214

CARTER, FRANCIS BAYARD, obstetrician, gynecologist; b. Wilmington, Del., Jan. 20, 1899; s. George and Ann Bowen (Foard) C.; A.B., U. Del., 1920, D.Sc.; B.A. (Rhodes scholar), Oxford U., 1923; M.A. 1932; M.D., Johns Hopkins, 1925; m. Harriet Cook Roberts, June 21, 1930; 1 stepdau., Anne Hamilton Roberts. Intern obstetrics and gynecology New Haven Hosp., Yale Sch. Medicine, 1925-26, asst. resident 1926-27, resident, 1927-28, asst. resident medicine, 1928-29; asso. prof. obstetrics and gynecology U. Va., 1929-31; prof. obstetrics and gynecology, Duke Sch. Medicine, 1931—. Examiner, Am. Bd. Obstetrics and Gynecology (pres. 1955). Served as 2d lt. inf. U.S. Army, (pres. 1955). Served as 2d lt. inf. U.S. Army, World War. Fellow Royal Coll. Obstetricians and Gynecologists (Eng.); mem. Am. Acad. Obstetricians and Gynecologists (pres. 1954), A.M.A., So. Med. Soc., Am. Assn. Obstetricians and Gynecologists (pres. 1956), Am. Gynecol. Soc. (pres. 1966), N.C., So. Atlantic, Canadian, Va. obstet. and gynecol. socs., Am. Com. Assn. for Maternal Welfare, Soc. Pelvic Surgeons (pres. 1965), Sigma Phi Epsilon, Alpha Omega Alpha. Democrat. Episcopalian. Mason. Clubs: Cosmos (Washington); River (Jacksonville, Fla.); Keswick Country (Va.); Vincents, Gridiron, Annandale (Oxford, Eng.); Pithotomy (Balt.); Octopus; To Bac, Hope Valley Country (Durham, N.C.), Contbr. to med. jours. Home: 5 Sylvan Rd Durham NC 27701 Office: Hilton Inn 2424 Erwin Rd Durham NC 27705

CARTER, FREDERICK ELBE, mfg. co. exec.; b. Rockford, Ill., May 18, 1909; s. John Munday and Effie (Green) C.; student U. Ill., 1925-28; m. Violette Elaine Stakemiller, June 26, 1946; children—Frederick E., Sharon Kay. Cost accountant Woodward Governor Co., 1940-42, supr. cost and payroll dept., 1942-64, asst. treas., 1964-65, treas., mgr. accounting, 1965-68, corporate sec., 1968—. Bd. dirs., v.p. Rockford Library Bd. Mem. U.S., Ill., Rockford chambers commerce, Nat. Assn. Accountants, Ill. Mfrs. Assn., Accounting Council of Machinery and Allied Products. Republican. Mem. Evang. Free Ch. Home: 4042 Alpine Ct Rockford IL 61107 Office: 5001 N 2d St Rockford IL 61111

CARTER, GARNETT ALONZO, banker; b. Chattanooga, Dec. 2, 1909; s. Frank A. and Minerva (DeMars) C.; grad. Am. Inst. Banking, 1934, Grad. Sch. Credit and Financial Mgmt., Dartmouth, 1952; m. Margaret Virginia Simms, Nov. 16, 1929; 1 dau., Barbara Virginia. Became asso. with Fulton Nat. Bank, Atlanta, 1927; asst. cashier, then br. mgr., asst. v.p., 1944, v.p.; pres. Peoples Am. Bank of Atlanta, 1966-67; v.p. Gen. Acceptance Corp., 1968—. Past pres., dir., Atlanta Better Bus. Bur.; dir. Internat. Better Bus. Burs., Inc. Mem. Adv. Council of Naval Affairs. Regent, Grad. Sch. Banking, Rutgers U.; bd. dirs. Atlanta Childs Home. Recipient Certificate of Merit and Treasury medal, 1945. Mem. Am. Inst. Banking (nat. pres. 1947-48, past pres. Atlanta chpt., mem. nat. exec. council, 1939-42, past chmn. ednl. adv. com.), Exec. Assn. (past pres.), Druid Hills Civic Assn. (past pres.), Am., Ga. (past chmn. ednl. extension com.) bankers assns., U.S., Atlanta C of C., Ga. State Coll. Found. Execs. Assn. (pres.). Episcopalian. Clubs: Commerce, Kiwanis (dir.). Brookhaven Country, Capital City. Home: 45 S 4th St Allentown PA 18101 Office: 1105 Hamilton St Allentown PA 18101

CARTER, GEORGE EDWARD, ret. newspaper exec.; b. Kenton, O., Aug. 24, 1910; s. Lloyd Denver and Sarah Lucretia (Quayle) C.; A.B. Western Res. U., 1932, A.M., 1933, student law sch., 1933-34; m. Harriette Withington, Aug. 19, 1944; children—William, Cornelia, Sarah (Mrs. Charles L. West). Employed with Scipps-Howard newspapers since 1934, sales rep. Times Press, Akron, O., 1934-37; as sales rep., gen. office, Chgo., 1937-45; pres. and bus. mgr. Ft. Worth Press, 1945-52; bus. mgr. Cleve. Press and News, 1952-70; asst. v.p. E.W. Scipps Co. Mem. Am. Newspaper Pubs. Assn., Phi Gamma Delta. Clubs: Mid-day City, Cleveland Skating, Union, Chagrin Valley Hunt. Home: Berkshise Rd Gates Mills OH 44040

CARTER, GEORGE FRANCIS, geographer; b. San Diego, Apr. 6, 1912; s. Thomas Fontaine and Catherine Harriet Anne (Brennan) C.; student San Diego State Coll., 1930- 31; A.B., U. Cal., 1934, Ph.D., 1942; m. Alberta Ruth Richter, Jan. 1, 1939; children—George, Robert, Anne. Curator anthropology San Diego Mus. of Man, 1934-38; asst. instr. Geography San Diego State Coll., 1937-38, instr., 1940-41; teaching asst. U. Cal., 1938-40, 41-42; research analyst, OSS, Washington, 1942-43; mem. dept. geography, Johns Hopkins, 1943-67, prof. 1948-67, chmn. 1944-58; Distinguished prof. geography Tex. A. and M. U., College Station, 1967—. Field work, San Nicolas Island, 1930, Mohave and Colo. deserts, 1930-38, coastal San Diego County, summers, 1947-48, 50, 53, 54; study Southwestern Indian agr., summer 1940-41; Pleistocene man, So. Cal., 1947—; Chesapeake Bay region, 1951-52, Sierra Nevada moraines, 1956—, Brazos Valley archeology, 1968-69, pre-Columbran chicken, 1970-71. Fellow Am. Geog. Soc. 1944, A.A.A.S., 1951. John Simon Guggenheim fellow, 1953-54, Instituto Interamericano, 1958. Mem. John Henry Cardinal Newman Hon. Soc., Assn. Am. Geographers, Soc. Am. Archeology. Roman Catholic. Clubs: Bucks Harbor Yacht, Iron Bridge Hunt. Author: Plant Geography and Culture History in the American Southwest, 1945; Pleistocene Man at San Diego, 1957; Man and the Land, 1964. Home: Route 3 Box 224A Bryan TX 77801 Office: Tex A and M U College Station TX 77840

CARTER, GERALD EMMETT, bishop; b. Montreal, Can., Mar. 1, 1912; s. Thomas Joseph and Mary (Kelty) C.; B. Th., Grand Sem. Montreal, 1936; B.A., U. Montreal, 1933, M.A. 1940, Ph.D., 1947, L.Th., 1950, D.H.L., Duquesne U., 1962; LL.D., U. Western Ont., 1966. Ordained priest Roman Cath. Ch., 1937; prin., prof. St. Joseph Tchrs. Coll., Que., 1939-61; chaplain Newman Club, NcGill U., 1941-56; charter mem., 1st pres. Thomas More Inst. Adult Edn., Montreal, 1945-61; mem. Montreal Cath. Sch. Commn., 1948-61; hon. canon Cathedral Basilica Montreal, 1952-61; aux. bishop London and titular bishop Altiburo 1961-62; bishop of London, Ont., 1964—. Chmn. Episcopal Commn. Liturgy Can., 1966; mem. Consilium of Liturgy, Rome, 1965. Author: The Catholic Public Schools of Quebec, 1957; Psychology and the Cross, 1959; The Modern Challenge to Religious Education, 1961. Office: 1070 Waterloo St London Ontario Canada

CARTER, GRANVILLE WELLINGTON, sculptor: b. Augusta, Me., Nov. 18, 1920; s. Brooks Eaton and Araletta Tarr (Payne) C.; student Coburn Classical Inst., 1938-39, Portland Sch. Fine and Applied Art, 1944-45, N.Y. Sch. Indsl. Art, 1945-49, N.A.D., 1945-48. Grand Chaumiere de Paris, 1954, Scuolo del Circolare Internazionale di Roma, 1955; m. Senta Jacobshagen, Oct. 15, 1955; children—Juliana S., Richard S. Exhibited in U.S., Paris, Rome, Hofstra Coll., Washington Cathedral, also collections; important works include Bullfighter Fountain Group, Neptune Fountain Urns, Gilded Terra Cotta Capitols, Toro Malo Bronze Relief, limestone St. Augustine of Canterbury, heroic size limestone Archangels Michael and Gabriel, Jane Addams portrait bust for Hall of Fame for Gt. Ams., also medals for Hall of Fame for Great Ams., at N.Y U., Nat. Commemorative Soc., Ofcl. Sesquicentennial medal for State Me. Bd. dirs. Am. Artist Socs. Recipient First prize N.A.D. Art Sch., 1946; Louis Comfort Tiffany fellow, 1954, 55; Lindsey Morris Meml. prize Nat. Sculpture Soc., 1966. N.A.D. Fellow Nat. Sculpture Soc., Am. Artists Profl. League. Address: 625 Portland Av Baldwin NY 11510

CARTER, GWENDOLEN MARGARET, educator, author; b. Hamilton, Ont., Can., July 17, 1906; d. Charles and Nora (Ambrose) Carter; B.A., U. Toronto, 1929; B.A., Oxford (Eng.) U., 1931, M.A., 1936; M.A., Radcliffe Coll., 193, Ph.D., 1938; D.H.L., Wheaton Coll., 1962, Russell Sage Coll., 1963; LL.D., Western Coll. for Women, 1964; LL.D., Goucher Coll., 1964, Carleton U., 1965, Boston U., 1966, McMaster U., 1966, Toronto U., 1970. Came to U.S., 1935; naturalized, 1948. Instr. McMaster U., Hamilton, 1932-35, Wellesley Coll., 1938-41, Tufts U., 1942-43; asst. prof. Smith Coll., 1943-47, asso. prof., 1947-52, prof. govt., 1952-64, Sophia Smith prof., 1961-64; Melville J. Herskovits prof. African affairs, dir. program of African studies. prof. polit. sci. Northwestern U., Evanston, Ill., 1964—. Mem. grant-in-aid com. Social Sci. Research Council, 1957; selection com. Ford Found. Tng. Program Africa, 1959-60; mem. adv. council for Africa, State Dept., 1962-67. Bd. trustees African-Am. Inst.; Mem. bd. U. of North Africa Assn. Recipient George V medal pub. service, 1935; Achievement award Am. Assn. U. Women, 1962; Distinguished Tchrs., 1962. Fellow Am. Acad. Arts and Scis.; mem. Am. (council 1954-56, v.p. 1963-64), New Eng. (pres. 1959-60). Internat. polit. sci. assns., Canadian Hist. and Polit. Sci. Assns., Internat. Inst. Pacific Relations, African Studies Assn. (council 1956-58, pres. 1958-63, chmn. com. and linguistics 1959-64), Am. Assn. U. Women, Internat. Union for Conservation Nature (N.Am. com. on edn. 1968), African-Am. Inst. (dir. 1964—), Chgo. Council Fgn. Relations (dir. 1967—). Author: British Commonwealth and International Security, 1947; (with John Herz) Major Foreign Powers, 1949, 52, 57, 62, 67, 71; The Politics of Inequality, 1958; Independence for Africa, 1960; (with John Herz) Government and Politics in the Twentieth Century, 1961, rev., 1966; The Government of United Kingdom, 1964, rev., 1968; The Government of Soviet Union, 1964, rev., 1968; (with Thomas Karis and Newell Stultz) South Africa's Transkei: The Politics of Domestic Colonialism, 1967; The Government of France, 1968. Editor: (with W.O. Brown) Transition in Africa; Problems of Political Adaptation, 1959; African One-Party States, 1962; Five African States; Responses to Diversity, 1963; Politics in Europe, 1965; Politics in Africa, 1966; National Unity and Regionalism, 1966; Africa in the Modern World series. Home: 222 Lake St Evanston IL 60201

CARTER, HAROLD FREEMAN, stockbroker; b. Port Monmouth, N.J., Oct. 16, 1906; s. James G. and Lillian M. (Thorne) C.; A.B., Swarthmore Coll., 1930; m. Ruth B. Cleaver, July 4, 1933; children—Jean, Ann. Analyst Halsey Stuart & Co., 1931-35, analyst Hornblower & Weeks, 1935-38, sales mgr., 1938-50, partner Hornblower & Weeks-Hemphill Noyes, 1950—. Mem. Phila. Securities Assn. Presbyn. (trustee). Clubs: Union League (Phila.); Bond. Home: 329 Owen Av Lansdowne PA 19050 Office: 120 Wall St New York City NY 10005

CARTER, HARRY TYSON, lawyer; b. Norristown, Pa., Apr. 17, 1924; s. John S. and Katharine M. (Tyson) C.; grad. Haverford Sch., 1941; A.B., Dartmouth, 1944; LL.B., Harvard, 1949; m. Elizabeth A. Edge, Aug. 25, 1956; children—Harry Tyson, Elizabeth Hamlin, Robert Edge. Admitted to D.C. bar, 1949; legal asst. to chmn. minority policy com. U.S. Senate, 1949-50; atty. ECA and successors, 1950-53; legal counsel Sen. Smith of N.J., 1953-55; spl. asst. to asst. sec. def. for internat. security affairs, 1955-56; asst. to Pres.'s spl. rep. for Hungarian Refugee Relief, also to chmn. Pres.'s Com. for Hungarian Refugee Relief, 1956-57; dep. gen. counsel USIA, 1957-58; gen. counsel, congrl. liaison, 1959-60; resident partner Shanley & Fisher, and predecessor law firms, Washington, 1960—. Pub. mem. 24th Fgn. Service Officer Selection Bd., 1970. Served with USMCR, 1942-46. Mem. Phi Beta Kappa, Zeta Psi. Republican. Episcopalian. Clubs: Chevy Chase, Metropolitan (Washington). Home: 5211 Norway Dr Chevy Chase MD 20015 Office: 1815 H St NW Washington DC 20006

CARTER, HARVEY LEWIS, educator; b. Forest, Ind., Dec. 2, 1904; s. Harry Holmes and Martha Frances (Wyatt) C.; A.B., Wabash Coll., 1927; A.M., U. Wis., 1928, Ph.D., 1938; m. Ruth Thornton, June 20, 1929; children—Harvey Thornton, Cherry (Mrs. John J. Kinney). Faculty Ursinus Coll., Collegeville, Pa., 1928-45, prof. history and pub. speaking, 1941-45; prof. history Colo. Coll., Colorado Springs, 1945—, chmn. dept., 1955-60, John and Harriet Parker Campbell prof. Am. history, 1956—; curator Archer B. Hulbert Meml. Collection Western Americana, Colorado Coll., 1960—; summer vis. prof. U. Denver, 1945, Western State Coll. Colo., 1954, 62. Mem. Rocky Mountain Social Sci. Assn. (pres. 1950-51), Am. Assn. U. Profs. (nat. council 1956-59), Am. Civil Liberties Union, Am., Western, and Miss. Valley hist. assns., Tau Kappa Alpha, Pi Gamma Mu. Democrat. Club: Winter Night (Colorado Springs). Author: Zebulon Montgomery Pike: Pathfinder and Patriot, 1956; The Far

West in American History, 1960; 'Dear Old Kit'; The Historical Christopher Carson, 1968; articles. Editor: The Pikes Peak Region; A Sesquicentennial History, 1956. Contbr. Dictionary Am. History, Ency. Britannica, Mountain Men and the Fur Trade of the Far West. Home: 4 Cragmor Village Colorado Springs CO 80907

CARTER, HENRY ZAC, shipyards exec.; b. Troy, Ala., Mar. 4, 1907; s. Cada Sanders and Lucy L. (Kelly) C.; B.S., U. Ala., 1931; LL.B., Georgetown U., 1939; m. Myrtle E. Mooneyham, June 1, 1932; children—Henrietta Sue (Mrs. Jack C. Watson), Henry Zac, Stephanie Ellen. Gen. auditor U.S. Maritime Commn., 1940-47; with Avondale Shipyards, Inc., New Orleans, 1947—, pres. 1965—, also dir.; dir. La. and So. Life Ins. Co., Whitney Nat. Bank, So. Ry. Active local Girl Scouts, United Fund. Named Maritime Man of Year in La., 1962; recipient New Orleans Press Club award, 1964; named Man of Year in La., Sales Execs. C. of C., 1966. Mem. New Orleans C. of C. (1st v.p. 1967). Clubs: Propeller, Internat. House (New Orleans). Home: 28 Audubon Pl New Orleans LA 70118 Office: PO Box 50280 New Orleans LA 70150

CARTER, HERBERT EDMUND, ednl. adminstr.; b. Mooresville, Ind., Sept. 25, 1910; s. George Benjamin and Edna (Pidgeon) C.; A.B., DePauw U., 1930, Sc. D., 1952; A.M., U. Ill., 1931, Ph.D., 1934; m. Elizabeth Winifred DeWees, Aug. 30, 1933, children—Anne Winsett, Jean Elizabeth. Instr. chemistry U. Ill., 1933-35, asso., 1935-37, asst. prof. 1937-43, asso. prof. 1943-45, prof., 1945-71, acting dean grad. coll., 1963-64, head dept. chemistry and chem. engring., 1954-67, now vice chancellor for acad. affairs, 1967-71, coordinator interdisciplinary programs U. Ariz., Tucson, 1971—. Mem. Pres.'s Com. on the Nat. Medal of Sci., 1963-66; mem. nat. sci. bd. NSF, 1963—, chmn., 1970-72. Awarded Rector Scholarship, Rector Fellowship, DePauw U., Eli Lilly & Co. Annual award ($1,000 and bronze medal to biochemist under 35 years of age showing promise in research), 1943; Am. Oil Chemist's Soc. award in lipid chemistry, 1966. Mem. exec. com. div. chemistry and chem. tech., NRC, 1949-55, 57-68. Mem. Am. Chem. Soc. (dir., asso. editor Bio-Chemistry 1961—; recipient William H. Nichols medal N.Y. sect., also Spencer award Kansas City sect. 1969), Am. Inst. Nutrition (sec. 1945-47), Am. Soc. Biol. Chemists (editorial bd. 1951-60, editorial com. 1963-66, pres. 1956-57), Nat. Acad. Scis. (chmn. section biochemistry 1963-66, mem. council 1966-69), Blue Key, Phi Beta Kappa, Sigma Xi, Phi Eta Sigma, Lambda Chi Alpha, Gamma Alpha, Alpha Chi Sigma. Democrat. Presbyn. Mem. editorial bd. Bio Chem. Preparations, editor-in-chief, Vol. I. Contbr. to tech. publs. Home: Cerrada de Promesa Tucson AZ 85718

CARTER, HODDING, publisher, author; b. Hammond, La., Feb. 3, 1907; s. William Hodding and Irma (Dutatre) C.; B.A., Bowdoin Coll., 1927; postgrad. journalism Columbia, 1927-28, Tulane U., 1928-29, (Nieman fellow) Harvard, 1939; M.A. (hon.) Harvard, 1947; Litt.D. (hon.), Bowdoin Coll., 1947; L.H.D. (hon.), Washington U., 1945, P.E. Theol. Sem., 1965; H.H.D., Coe Coll.; LL.D., Allegheny Coll., 1960; m. Betty Werlein, Oct. 14, 1931; children—William Hodding III, Philip Dutartre. Teaching fellow Tulane U., 1928-29; reporter New Orleans Item-Tribune, 1929; night bur. mgr. U.P.I., New Orleans, 1930; mgr. A.P. Bur., Jackson, Miss., 1931-32; started Daily Courier, Hammond, La., editor, pub., 1932-36; started Delta Star, Greenville, Miss., editor, pub., 1936-38; editor, pub. Delta Democrat-Times, Greenville, Miss., 1939—; newspaper editor PM, 1939. Civilian aide sec. army, 1952-60; writer in residence Tulane U., 1962-70. Bd. overseers Bowdoin Coll.; mem. Nat. Citizens Council for Better Schs.; bd. visitors Tulane U., 1953-69; mem. Pulitzer Prize Adv. Bd., 1951-61. Joined N.G., 1938; pub. Dixie, 31st div. paper, Camp Blanding, Fla., 1940; Army Bur. Pub. Relations, Washington, 1940-41; editor Stars and Stripes, Yank, Middle East edits., Cairo, Egypt; ret. as maj., 1945. Recipient War Dept. citation, 1946; Pulitzer prize, 1946; So. Lit. award, 1945; William A. White Found. nat. citation of journalistic merit, 1961; Bowdoin Prize, 1963; First Fed. Found. award for outstanding Mississippians, 1968; Journalism Alumni award Columbia, 1971. Guggenheim fellow, 1945; fellow Sigma Delta Chi, 1954. Mem. Am. Soc. Newspaper Editors. Author: (with Ernest Dupuy) Civilian Defense of the United States, 1941; Where Main Street Meets the River, 1953; Robert E. Lee and The Road of Honor, 1954; Marquis de Lafayette, Bright Sword for Freedom, The Angry Scar, So Great A Good; Doomed Road of Empire, 1962; First Person Rural, 1963; The Ballad of Catfood Grimes and Other Verse, 1964; So the Heffners Left McComb, 1965; The Commandos of World War II, 1966; Their Words Were Bullets, 1970; Man and the River: The Mississippi, 1970. Contbr. to mags. Home: Feliciana Farm Greenville MS 38701 Office: Delta Democrat-Times Greenville MS 38701

CARTER, HOMER MUNROE, Sr., co. exec.; b. Van Zant County, Tex., Dec. 16, 1901; s. Jessee O. and Mary E. (Barber) C.; B.S., Ga. Sch. Tech., 1923; m. Mary Jane McGinnis, June 30, 1925; 1 son, Homer Munroe. Joined Pepperell Mfg. Co., 1925, gen. mgr. Ala. div., 1931-59, exec. v.p., 1959-61, pres., 1961-66, dir., 1952-65; pres., West Point-Pepperell, Inc., 1965-68, vice chmn., 1968-69, dir., 1965-70; dir. Farmers Nat. Bank, Opelika, Ala. Mem. Phi Delta Theta, Phi Kappa Phi. Methodist. Clubs: Union League (N.Y.C.); Captial City (Atlanta). Home: 2637 Peachtree Rd NE Atlanta GA 30305

CARTER, JAMES BUTLER, ins. co. exec.; b. Queenstown, Md. Oct. 16, 1916; grad. Goldey Beacom Bus. Coll. With tabulating dept. Standard Accident Ins. Co., 1936, br. office auditor, 1938-41, systems analyst, 1946-51, mgr. field coordination, 1951-56, asst. br. mgr., 1956-59; br. mgr. Standard Accident & Reliance, 1959-67; asst. v.p., controller, 1967-68; v.p., controller Reliance Ins. Co., Phila., 1968—; v.p., gen. mgr. Cananwill, Inc.; dir. Planet Ins. Co. Served with AUS, 1941-46. Home: 709 Mancill Rd Wayne PA Office: 4 Penn Center Plaza Philadelphia PA 19103

CARTER, JAMES EARL, Jr., gov. Ga.; b. Plains, Ga., Oct. 1, 1924; s. James Earl and Lillian (Gordy) C.; student Ga. Southwestern U., 1941-42, Ga. Inst. Tech., 1942-43; B.S., U.S. Naval Acad., 1947; postgrad. Union Coll., 1952; m. Rosalynn Smith, July 7, 1946; children—John William, James Earl III, Donnel Jeffrey, Amy Lynn. Commd. ensign USN, 1947, advanced through grades to lt., 1950; ret., 1953; farmer, warehouseman, 1953—; mem. Ga. Senate, 1962-66; gov. Ga., 1971—. Democrat. Lion. Home: 1 Woodland Dr Plains GA 31780 Office: State Capitol Atlanta GA 30334

CARTER, JAMES JOHNSTON, lawyer; b. Samson, Ala., Apr. 13, 1913; s. Castilla L. and Mary Ann (Smith) C.; LL.B., Jones Law Sch., 1934; postgrad. U. Mich., 1940, U. Va., 1941; m. Eva Jane Edwards, Sept. 6, 1947; children—Harold M., David E. (step sons), James M., Kathy Jane. Admitted to Ala. bar, 1934; mem. firm Carter & Park, Montgomery, 1934-35; atty. Montgomery County Probate Ct., 1935-38; law clk., sec. U.S. circuit judge, Montgomery, Ala., also New Orleans, 1938-47; mem. Hill, Hill, Stovall, Carter & Franco, Montgomery, 1947—; spl. judge 15th Jud. Circuit Ala., 1949, 51, 55, 60; spl. asst. atty. gen. Ala., 1969-70. Prof. constl. law Jones Law Sch., 1936—, pres., 1964- -. Served to 1st lt. AUS, 1943-46. Recipient Distinguished Service award U.S. Jr. C. of C., 1937. Mem. Am., Tenn. (hon.), Montgomery County (pres. 1957) bar assns., Ala. State Bar (pres. 1962-63), Jud. Conf. Ala., Jud. Conf. 5th Circuit, Jr. C. of C. (past pres.), Am. Judicature Soc., Am. Law Inst. (council mem.), Fedn. Ins. Counsel, Sigma Delta Kappa. Presbyn. (elder). Clubs: Country, Beauvoir, Civitan. Home: 2602 Wildwood Dr Montgomery AL 36111 Office: Hill Bldg PO Box 116 Montgomery AL 36101

CARTER, JAMES MARSHALL, judge; b. Santa Barbara, Cal., Mar. 11, 1904; s. James Madison and Belle A. (Hicks) C.; A.B., Pomona Coll., 1924; student Harvard Law Sch., 1924-25; J.D., U. So. Calif., 1927; LL.D. (hon.), U. San Diego, 1962; m. Dorothy Freeland, 1927; one dau., Joan F.; m. 2d, Ruth Doty, Sept. 17, 1938; m. 3d, Bina Cheney, Dec. 30, 1953. Admitted to Cal. bar, 1928, and practiced in Los Angeles, 1928-40; dir. State Dept. Motor Vehicles for Cal., 1940-43; chief asst. U.S. atty. So. Dist. Cal., 1943-46, U.S. atty., 1946-49; U. S. dist. judge, 1949-67; judge ninth circuit U.S. Ct. of Appeals, 1967—. chmn. of the Cal. State Hwy. Traffic Adv. Com. to War Dept., 1941-42; mem. Commn. on Interstate Cooperation, State of Cal., 1941-42, of Interstate Commn. on Crime, 1941-42, mem. gov.'s council, 1940-42. Mem. various committees Jud. Conf. of U.S.; mem. adv. council judges Nat. Council Crime and Delinquency. Member Am. Bar Assn., Inst. Jud. Adminstrn., Order of Coif, Phi Kappa Phi, Sigma Tau, Phi Alpha Delta. Ephebian Soc. Democrat. Eagle, Elk. Office: Charter Oil Bldg San Diego CA 92101

CARTER, JAMES R., corp. exec.; b. Newton, Mass., July 14, 1907; s. Hubert Lazell and Edith Harriet (Adams) C.; grad. Worcester Acad., 1925; student Harvard, 1925-29, Harvard Bus. Sch. 1932-33; m. Placidia White, Apr. 2, 1954. With Townsend, Anthony & Tyson, stockbrokers, 1930-32, Am. Pulp & Paper Assn., 1933-34; with Nashua Corp. (N.H.), 1934—, now chmn., dir.; dir., chmn. bd. Nashua Can., Ltd., Copycat Ltd. (Eng.); vice chmn., dir. Copygraph G.m.b.H. (Germany); dir. N.E. Electric System, State Street Bank and Trust Co., Boston, State Street Boston Financial Corp.; mem. policyholders adv. com. New Eng. Mut. Life Ins. Co. Trustee New Eng. Colls. Fund. Mem. paper adv. com. Lowell Technol. Inst. Pres., dir. N.H. Charitable Fund. Served as lt. col. USAAF, 1942-46. Mem. Am. Mgmt. Assn., Sons Colonial Wars, Newcomen Soc. Clubs: Leash, Brook (N.Y.C.); Union (Boston). Home: Powersbridge Peterborough NH 03458 Office: 44 Franklin St Nashua NH 03060

CARTER, JAY BOYD, govt. ofcl.; b. Turlock, Cal., Apr. 12, 1925; s. Arthur Wesley and Gail Bernice (Jaderberg) C.; student U. So. Cal., 1943-44, B.S. in Elec. Engring., 1946, B.S. in Civil Engring., 1951; student U. N.M., 1944-46; m. Mary Louise Cross, Apr. 12, 1946; children—Jay Boyd, Kathleen Susan (Mrs. Harold E. Melle, Jr.), Brian Douglas, Annette Marie, Daniel Edward, Mary Beth, Jeannette Marie, Lawrence Scott. Engr., City of Los Angeles Dept. Water and Power, 1946-51; engr., supt. various cons. engring. and constrn. firms, 1951-55; with State Dept., ICA, then AID, power engr., Thailand, 1955-58, gen. engr., Taiwan, 1958-63, power engr., India, 1963-66, gen. engr., Washington, 1966-68, dep. chief engr., Brazil, 1968—. Served with USNR, 1943-46. Mem. I.E.E.E. Home: Estrada da Gavéa 722 Rio de Janeiro Brazil Office: U S AID Rio de Janeiro Enro APO New York City NY 09676

CARTER, SIR JOHN, diplomat of Guyana; b. Guyana, Jan. 27, 1919; s. Kemp Ridley and Gertrude (Humphry) C.; B.A., U. London (Eng.), 1940, LL.B., 1942; barrister-at- law, Middle Temple, 1942; m. Sara Lou Harris, July 25, 1949; children—John, Brian. Admitted to Supreme Ct. Guyana, 1945; Queen's counsel, 1962; practice in Guyana until 1966; Guyana ambassador to U.S., 1966-70; Guyana high commr. to U.K., 1970—; ambassador to Yugoslavia, Fed. Republic Germany, France, Netherlands, U.S.S.R.; high commr. to India. Mem. Guyana Legislature, 1948-53, 61-64; chmn. Ruling People's Nat. Congress, Guyana, 1960. Pro-chancellor U. Guyana, 1963-66. Created knight, 1966. Home: 44 Lowndes Sq London SW1 England

CARTER, JOHN, jazz musician, composer. Address: 9312 Denker Av Los Angeles CA 90047*

CARTER, JOHN, bibliographer; b. Eton, Eng., May 10, 1905; s. Thomas Buchanan and Margaret Teresa (Stone) C.; student Eton Coll., King's Coll., Cambridge; m. Ernestine Marie Fantl, Dec. 26, 1936. European rep. rare book dept. Scribners, N.Y.C., 1927-39, mng. dir. Charles Scribner's Sons, Ltd., London, 1946-52; staff Ministry Information, 1939-43; with Brit. Information Services, N.Y.C., 1944-45; counsellor embassy, personal asst. to Brit. ambassador in Washington, 1953-55; asso. for Am. operations Sotheby & Co., auctioneers, London; bibliog. cons., 1956—; dir. Parke- Bernet Galleries, Inc., N.Y.C. Decorated comdr. Order Brit. Empire, 1956; named Hon. Ky. col., Sandars reader bibliography U. Cambridge, 1947. Mem. Arts Council Gt. Britain (exec. com. 1951-53), Bibliog. Soc. (pres. 1968-69). Clubs: Garrick, Double Crown, Eton Ramblers, Beefsteak (London); Grolier; Rowfant. Author: ABC for Book Collectors, 1952, 4th edit., 1966; Taste and Technique in Book Collecting, 1948, enlarged, 1970; (with Graham Pollard) An Enquiry into the Nature of Certain 19th Century Pamphlets, 1934, Books and Book Collectors, 1957. Editor: Selected Prose of A.E. Housman, 1961: (with Percy H. Muir) Printing and the Mind of Man, 1967. Home: 113 Dovehouse St Chelsea London SW 3 England

CARTER, JOHN COLES, steel co. exec.; b. Eolia, Mo., Jan. 21, 1920; s. Charles William and Ollie (Brown) C.; A.B., Lake Forest (Ill.) Coll., 1943; LL.B., Chgo.- Kent Coll. Law, 1950; m. Dorothy Mary Strong, Jan. 29, 1944; children—Carolyn L., Charles W. Pub. accountant Price Waterhouse & Co., Chgo., 1946-47, Paul Pettingill Co., Waukegan, Ill., 1950-51; instr. Lake Forest Coll., 1947-50; with Inland Steel Co., Chgo., 1951—, sec., 1962—; instr. John Marshall Sch. Law, 1964—. Commr., past pres. Lake Bluff (Ill.) Park Dist. Past pres. Lake Bluff Village Library; bd. dirs. Tb Inst. Chgo. and Cook County. Served to lt. (j.g.) USNR, 1943-46; PTO. Decorated Presdl. Commendation Medal. Mem. Am., Chgo. bar assns., Am. Soc. Corporate Secs. (pres. 1964-65, mem. nat. board dirs. 1966—), Lake Forest Alumni Assn. (past pres. exec. bd.), Scholarships and Guidance Assn. (bd. dirs.), Chgo. Assn. Commerce and Industry, World Peace Through Law Assn., Am. Iron and Steel Inst., Am. Assn. U. Profs. Clubs: Legal, Law, Economic, Literary, University (Chgo.) . Home: 246 Ravine Forest Dr Lake Bluff, IL 60044 Office: Inland Steel Co 30 W Monroe St Chicago IL 60603

CARTER, JOHN DEWEESE, state judge; b. Denton, Md., June 2, 1904; s. John Tilghman and Elizabeth (DeWeese) C.; J.D., Washington and Lee U., 1927. Admitted to Md. bar, 1927; practice in Caroline County, 1928-49; asso. Judge 2d Jud. Circuit Md., 1949-57, chief judge, 1957-71, asso. judge Ct. Spl. Appeals of Md., 1971—. Mem. standing com. on rules of practice and procedure Md. Ct. of Appeals, 1967-71; chmn. Circuit Adminstrv. Judges of Md., 1969-71, Md. Commn. on Jud. Disabilities, 1971—; mem. numerous study commns. apptd. by gov. Chmn. arbitration com. McCready Meml. Hosp., Crisfield, 1966-67; co-sponsor, pres. Caroline County Pub. Library, 1962-63. Chmn. Md. Democratic Central Com. for Caroline County, 1942-46. Trustee Meml. Hosp. Easton, 1952-58, Peninsula Annual Conf. Methodist Ch., 1954-63; Md. gen. chmn. Wesley Coll. Devel. Com., 1962; trustee, mem. exec. com. Wesley Coll., 1963—. Served to maj. AUS, World War II; PTO. Fellow Am. Bar Found. (state chmn.); mem. Md. Bar Found. (dir., 1st pres. 1966-71), Am. (standing com. on Am. citizenship, acting chmn. 1966; ho. of dels. 1964-66), Md. (pres. 1964-65), bar assns., Am. Law Inst., Nat. Conf. State Trial Judges (Md. del. 1966-69), Am. Judicature Soc. (dir. 1968—), Order of Coif (hon.), Phi Kappa Sigma, Phi Delta Phi, Omicron Delta Kappa. Methodist (trustee). Mason, Rotarian (hon. mem.). Clubs: Chesapeake Bay Yacht (Easton, Md.); Maryland, Center (Balt.); Caroline Country (1st pres. County); (Caroline County); Rehoboth Beach (Del.) Country. Editor: Tax Laws of Maryland; trustee Md. Law Rev., 1964-65. Contbr. articles to profl. jours. Home: 201 Carter Av Denton MD 21629 Office: 304 Market St Denton MD 21629

CARTER, JOHN MACK, mag. editor; b. Murray, Ky., Feb. 28, 1928; s. William Z. and Martha (Stevenson) C.; student Murray State Coll., 1944-46, LL.D., 1971; B.J., U. Mo., 1948, M.A., 1949; m. Sharlyn Emily Reaves, Aug. 30, 1948; children—Jonna Lyn, John Mack II. Reporter, Murray Ledger & Times, 1945; asst. editor Better Homes & Gardens mag., 1949-51; mng. editor Household mag., Topeka, 1953-57, editor, 1957-58; exec. editor Together, 1958-59; editor Am. Home, 1959-61; exec. editor McCall's, 1961, editor, 1962-65; v.p., dir. McCall Corp., N.Y.C., 1962-65; editor-in-chief of Ladies Home Jour., 1965—, pub., 1967—; pres. Downe Pub. Co. Served as lt. (j.g.) USNR, 1951-53. Recipient Walter Williams award for writing, 1949. Mem. Sigma Delta Chi. Home: 20 Ridge Rd Bronxville NY 10708 Office: 641 Lexington Av New York City NY 10022

CARTER, JOHN PACKARD, govt. ofcl.; b. Smithville, Tex., Sept. 26, 1928; s. Clifton and Zetta (Crawford) C.; student N. Tex. State Coll.; m. Louis Byrum, June 16, 1953; children—Charlene, James David, Clifton Floyd. Mem. research dept. Dow Chem. Co., Freeport, Tex., 1955-61; with P.O. Dept., 1962-67, former dir. Office Regional Adminstrn., Office Postmaster Gen.; now exec. dir. Nat. Assn. Postmasters U.S. Served with USAF, 1950-53. Democrat. Mason (Shriner). Home: 7221 Churchill Rd McLean VA 22101 Office: 348 Pennsylvania Bldg Pennsylvania Av NW Washington DC 20004

CARTER, JOHN ROBERT, physician; b. Buffalo, Apr. 21, 1917; s. John Harvey and Gertrude Ann (Buckpitt) C.; B.S., Hamilton Coll., 1939; M.D., U. Rochester, 1943; m. Adelaide Briggs, May 8, 1943; children—Marilyn Anne, Jeanne Catherine. Intern State U. Ia., 1943-44, resident, 1944-48, asst. dept. pathology, 1944, from instr. to asso. prof., 1944-55, prof., 1955-59; prof., chmn. dept. pathology and oncology U. Kan. Med. Center, 1960-66; prof. pathology, dir. Inst. Pathology, chmn. dept. pathology Case Western Res. U., Cleve., 1966—; cons. VA Hosp., U.S. Army Hosp., U.S. Penitentiary, Watkins Meml. Hosp. Chmn. pathology study sect. NIH; mem. pathology tng. grant com. Nat. Inst. Gen. Med. Scis.; mem. pathology adv. council Central VA Office; mem. sci. adv. bd. Armed Forces Inst. Pathology Bd. dirs. Univs. Asso. Research and Edn. Pathology. Served to lt. USNR, 1946-48. Diplomate Nat. Bd. Med. Examiners. Mem. A.M.A., A.A.A.S., Cleve. Acad. Medicine, Path. Soc. Gt. Britain and Ireland, Am. Assn. Pathologists and Bacteriologists (past pres.), Internat. Acad. Pathology, Am. Soc. Clin. Pathology, Am. Soc. Exptl. Pathology, Coll. Am. Pathologists, Soc. Exptl. Biology, Am. Assn. U. Profs., Central Soc. Clin. Research, Phi Beta Kappa, Sigma Xi. Alpha Omega Alpha. Mem. editorial bd. Am. Jour. Pathology. Home: 36570 Ridge Rd Willoughby OH 44094 Office: Inst Pathology Case Western Res U Cleveland OH 44106

CARTER, JOHN S., banker; b. Martins Ferry, O., July 15, 1907; s. Hervey F. and Pearl C. C. Carter; B.S., Washington and Jefferson Coll., 1929; LL.B., Cornell, 1933; m. Mary Jane Dalton, Jan. 5, 1932; children—John S., Nancy Lyn, Jeffrey W. Joined RCA, Camden, N.J., 1935, formerly finance RCA Victor div., then v.p. finance adminstrn. RCA; now chmn. South Jersey Nat. Bank. Bank. Home: 219 E Main St Moorestown NJ 08057 Office: S Jersey Nat Bank Broadway Cooper and 6th Sts Camden NJ 08103

CARTER, JOHN STEWART, author Full Fathom Five (novel).*

CARTER, JOSEPH L., A.R.C. ofcl.; b. Altoona, Pa., May 5, 1908; s. Joseph W. and Eva (Evans) C.; B.A., Am. U., 1932; m. Dorothy Mathews, Jan. 7, 1933; children—Joseph L., Richard M. Asst. dir., br. mgr. Boys Club, Washington, 1929-32; dir. transient bur. Pa. Emergency Relief Bd., 1932- 33, relief adminstr. Blair County, 1933-35; dir. boys dept. Neighborhood Settlement House, Washington, 1935-37; mng. dir. Boys Club-Big Bro. Orgn., Scranton, Pa., 1937-42; disaster field rep. A.R.C., 1942-43, dir. disaster service Eastern area, 1943-45, asst. mgr. Eastern area, 1945- 49, dep. mgr. Eastern area, 1949-56, mgr. Eastern area, 1956-59, exec. officer Greater N.Y., 1959—. Mem. Am. Mgmt. Assn. Methodist (steward). Rotarian. Club: University (N.Y.C.). Home: 67-00 192d St Flushing NY 11365 Office: 150 Amsterdam Av New York City NY 10023

CARTER, LAMORE JOSEPH, educator; b. Carthage, Tex., Apr. 18, 1925; s. Peter and Nancy (Fite) C.; student Wiley Coll., 1946-47; A.B., Fisk U., 1950; M.S., U. Wis., 1952; Ph.D., State U. Ia., 1958; postgrad. U. Chgo., summer 1954, U. Tex., summer 1966, Columbia, summer 1967, Emory U., summer 1970; m. Lena Mae Jones, Aug. 18, 1957; children—Greta Lisa, Kris-Lana. Tchr., Union High Sch., Gallatin, Tenn., 1950-51; instr. Grambling (La.) Coll., 1952-54, asst. prof., 1954-56, asso. prof. edn. and psychology, dir. spl. edn. center, 1961-66, adminstr. Instl. Research, 1966-68; postdoctoral research fellow So. Assn. Colls. and Schs., 1967-70; dean of faculties Tex. So. U., Houston, 1970—; research asst. State U. Ia., 1956-58; distinguished prof. psychology Morehouse Coll., spring 1970; licensed to practice psychology Grambling, La., 1965—. Dir. Grambling Motel Internat. Cons. Social Security Adminstrn. Bd. Hearings and Appeals, 1965—, bur. edn. handicapped U.S. Office Edn., 1967. Served with AUS, 1943-46. Decorated Bronze Star Mem. Am. Assn. U. Profs. (chpt. pres. 1960-63), Am., Southwestern, La. psychol. assns., Nat. Council Univ. Research Adminstrs., Assn. for Instl. Research, Am. Ednl. Research Assn., Assn. for Higher Edn., Nat. Soc. for Study Edn., Am. Assn. on Mental Deficiency, La. Assn. Mental Health, N.E.A., Phi Beta Sigma, Phi Delta Kappa. Democrat. Methodist. Mason (32). Contbr. articles profl. jours., monographs, books. Home: 110 Richmond Dr Grambling LA 71245 Office: Tex So U Houston TX 77004

CARTER, LAUNOR FRANKLIN, sci. adminstr.; b. Friday Harbor, Wash., Jan. 23, 1914; s. Alvia F. and Hazel Agnes (Shull) C.; B.S., U. Wash., 1936, M.S., 1939; Ph.D., Princeton, 1941; certicicate Exec. Tng. Program U. Cal. at Los Angeles, 1961; m. Mary Ann Wickersham, Feb. 14,1941; 1 son, James Franklin. Chief examiner Wash. State Dept. Social Security Merit System Office, 1937-38; personnel technician Social Security Bd., Washington, 1940-41, Adj. Gen. Office, Dept. Army, 1941-42; research psychologists Aero-Med. Lab., Wright Field, O., 1946; asst., then asso. prof. psychology U. Rochester, 1946-52; dir. research Human Research Unit 2, Continental Army Command, Ft. Ord, Cal., 1952-55; v.p., dir. research System Devel. Corp., Santa Monica, Cal., 1955-62, v.p., mgr. pub. systems div., 1963- -; chief scientist USAF, 1962-63. Mem. USAF Sci. Adv. Bd., 1955- 68; adv. com. dept. psychology Princeton, 1962-68; mem. Nat. Adv. Commn. Libraries, 1966-68; mem. sci. information council NSF, 1965-69; mem. computer sci. and engring. bd. Nat. Acad. Sci. Served with USAAF, 1942-46. Benjamin Franklin fellow Royal Soc. Arts. Fellow A.A.A.S.; mem. Am. (rec. sec., dir. 1955-61, chmn. program com. 1953, chmn. ad hoc conv. com. 1954), Western psychol. assns., Soc. for Psychol. Study Social Issues, Am.

Fedn. Scientists, Assn. for Computing Machinery. Clubs: Princeton (N.Y.C.); Riviera Country; Cosmos (Washington). Cons. editor Psychol. Bull., 1955-60, Jour. Abnormal and Social Psychology, 1955-68; asso. editor Sociometry, 1955-64. Contbr. numerous articles to profl. jours. Home: 249 Mantua Rd Pacific Palisades CA 90272 Office: 2500 Colorado Av Santa Monica CA 90404

CARTER, LESTER CLYDE, food co. exec.; b. Warren, Ark., June 10, 1909; s. T.A. and Mary Elizabeth (Moseley) C.; B.S. in Agronomy, U. Ark., 1931; LL.D., 1969; postgrad. U. Wis., 1941; m. Vera Barton, Nov. 18, 1933; children—Shirley (Mrs. F.M. Henderson), Jerry (Mrs. Norton A. Pope), Mary (Mrs. Homer Dale Keeton). Tech. asst. Rice br. Expt. Sta., U. Ark., 1931-34; county agt. Montgomery County, Ark., 1934-35, Howard County, Ark., 1935-36; asst. state 4-H Club agt. U. Ark. Agrl. Extension Service, 1936-37, supr. univ. Rice br. Expt. Sta., 1937-44; gen. mgr. Ark. Rice Growers Coop. Assn. (now Riceland Foods), Stuttgart, 1944—, exec. v.p., 1961—, gen. mgr. affiliated coops., 1962—; exec. v.p. Ark. Grain Corp. (now Riceland Foods), Stuttgart, 1958—; mem. midwest adv. bd. Awkright-Boston Ins. Co., 1970—; dir. Ark. Power & Light Co., Union Nat. Bank, Little Rock. Past chmn. Fed. Farm Credit Bd.; dir. Am. Inst. Coop., Nat. Fedn. Grain Coops.; mem. liaison com. Rice Millers Assn.; chmn. Rice Council, Houston; past pres., dir. Rice Council for Market Devel. Bd. dirs. Stuttgart Meml. Hosp. Named Man of Year in Agr., Progressive Farmer, 1965; Man of Year, Stuttgart C. of C., 1960; Distinguished Alumni citation U. Ark., 1960, Trustee Emeritus award, 1963. Mem. Am. Farm Bur. Fedn. Baptist (deacon). Rotarian. Home: 39 Circle Lane Stuttgart AR 72160 Office: PO Box 927 Stuttgart AR 72160

CARTER, LYNDALL FREDERIC, mfg. co. exec.; b. Needham, Mass., 1902; s. Horace Albert and Bertha Louise (Manson) C.; grad. Williams Coll., 1924, Harvard Bus. Sch., 1926; m. Margaret Walker, June 29, 1925 (dec. May 1962); m. 2d, Ruth Plummer Reynolds, Sept. 21, 1963; children—Dana Pierce, Mary Lee. With William Carter Co., Needham, Mass., 1926—, pres., 1959-69, chmn., 1969—, also dir.; dir. Needham Nat. Bank. Trustee Modern Sch. Fashion Design. Home: 40 Black Oak Rd Weston MA 02193 Office: 963 Highland Av Needham Heights MA 02194

CARTER, MARSHALL SYLVESTER, found. exec., former army officer; b. Ft. Monroe, Va., Sept. 16, 1909; s. Clifton Carroll and Mai (Coleman) C.; B.S., U.S. Mil. Acad., 1931; M.S., Mass. Inst. Tech., 1936; grad. Nat. War Coll., 1950; m. Préct Nicholas; children—Josephine Stoney, Marshall Nichols, Mary Coleman. Commd. 2d lt. U.S. Army, 1931; advanced through grades to lt. gen., 1962; plans and operations div. War Dept. Gen. Staff, 1942-45; dep. and asst. chief of staff G-5, Hdqrs., China Theater, 1945-46; spl. rep. in Washington for Gen. Marshall (China Mission), 1946-47; spl. asst. Sec. State, 1947-49; minister Am. embassy, London, Eng., 1949; comdg. 138th AAA Group and AA officer Air Defs. Central Japan, 1950; dir. exec. office Sec. Def., 1950-52; dep. comdg. gen. U.S. Army, Alaska, asst. div. comdr. 71st Inf. Div., 1952-55, comdg. gen. 5th AA Regional Command, Ft. Sheridan, 1955-56; chief of staff N. Am. Air Def. Command, 1956-59; chief of staff U.S. 8th Army, Korea, 1959-60; comdg. gen. Army Air Def. Center, Ft. Bliss, Tex., 1961-62; dep. dir. CIA, Washington, 1962-65; dir. Nat. Security Agy. 1965-69 (now cons.); ret., 1969; pres. George C. Marshall Research Found., Lexington, Va., 1969—. Vice pres. Cheyenne Mt. Zool. Soc. Bd. dirs. Am.-Korean Found., N.Y.C. Decorated D.S.M., with two oak leaf clusters, Legion of Merit and oak-leaf cluster, Bronze Star (U.S.); spl. Breast Order of Yun Hui with Rosette (China), 1945 and Oak-Leaf Cluster, 1947; comdr. Order of Orange Nassau with swords (Netherlands); Order of Service Merit (Republic Korea). Clubs: Boone and Crockett (N.Y.C.); Broadmoor Golf, Cheyenne Mountain, Garden of Gods, Kissing Camels Golf (all Colorado Springs); Army-Navy Country (Arlington, Va.). Home: 2520 Hill Circle Colorado Springs CO 80904 Office: George C Marshall Research Found Lexington VA 24450 ☆

CARTER, MATTHEW GAMALIEL, mayor, chem. co. exec.; b. Danville, Va., Oct. 16, 1913; s. Clarence and Henrietta (Curley) C.; B.A., Va. Union U., 1939, B.D., 1942, D.D. (hon.), 1960; postgrad. Columbia, Union Theol. Sem.; LL.D. (hon.) Bloomfield (N.J.) Coll., 1969; m. Frances A. Hill, Dec. 10, 1944; children—Bettye Frances, Nanette Carolyn. Ordained to ministry Bapt. Ch., 1939; minister in Petersburg, Va., , 1940; exec. dir. Leigh St. YMCA, Richmond, Va., 1940-48; asso. exec. dir. S.W. area council Nat. council YMCA, 1948-51, exec. dir. Spring St. br. YMCA, Columbus, O., 1951- 58; asst. dir. Assn. Press, pub. dept. nat. council YMCA, 1958-69; dir. community affairs Hoffmann-LaRoche, Inc., Nutley, N.J., 1969—. dir. First Fed. Savs. & Loan Assn., Montclair, N.J. Bd. commnrs. Montclair, 1964-68; mayor Montclair, 1968—. Mem. exec. bd. N.J. Conf. Mayors; mem. N.J. Civil Rights Commn.; mem. commuter adv. com. N.J. Dept. Transp. Recipient N.J. Fedn. Negro Women's Club award for being 1st Negro elected mayor maj. N.J. city, 1968; achievement award Phi Delta Kappa, 1968; award outstanding leadership in govt. Montclair chpt. Nat. Council Negro Women, 1965; Man of Year award Phila. YMCA Y's Men's Club, 1962; Distinguished Service award Bankers Nat. Life Ins. Co., 1969; Achievement award North N.J. Alumni chpt. United Negro Coll. Fund, 1964- -. Republican. Home: 215 Orange Rd Montclair, NJ 07042 Office: Hoffmann-LaRoche Inc Nutley NJ 07110

CARTER, MOTHER MAYBELLE, folk singer; appearance at Newport (R.I.) Folk Festival, 1965; rec. artist for Smash records.*

CARTER, OLIVER, lawyer; b. Memphis, June 6, 1907; s. Oliver and Kate (Clift) C.; LL.B., Wilmington Law Sch., 1931; student Wake Forest College, 1931; m. Annie Lois Barden, June 24, 1930; 1 dau., Barbara Ann (Mrs. Joseph Richard McKeever); m. 2d, Mary Virginia Fisher, Nov. 27, 1946; children—Mary Virginia, James Oliver. Admitted to N.C. bar, 1931, U.S. Dist. Ct. Eastern Dist. N.C., 1932, U.S. Supreme Ct., 1945, U.S. Ct. Appeals, 1948, U.S. Ct. Claims, U.S. Tax Ct., F.C.C., 1953; practice of law, Elizabethtown, N.C., 1932-34; elected judge Bladen Co. Ct., N.C., 1934- 40; asst. U.S. Atty. Eastern Dist. N.C., 1941-43; enforcement trial atty., gen. counsel's office CAB, Washington, 1946- 48, acting chief enforcement and litigation sect., 1948, chief office of enforcement, 1948-53; practice of law, Wilmington, N.C., 1953- -. Dist. commr. Cape Fear area Boy Scouts of Am., 1938; v.p. Community Council, 1956. Mem. state farm debt adjustment com., N.C., 1939. Served as enlisted man USAF, 1943-44; capt. Judge Adv. Gen. Corps, U.S. Army, 1944-46. Mem. N.C. (mem. bd. govs. 1966-69), Ninth Jud. Dist. (pres. 1940) bar assns. Episcopalian. Mason. Clubs: Rotary (pres. Elizabethtown 1937), Optimist (lt. gov. 18th Dist. 1955-56). Home: 122 Pine Cone Rd Wilmington NC 28401 Office: Carolina Power & Light Bldg Wilmington NC 28401

CARTER, OLIVER JESSE, judge; b. San Francisco, Apr. 7, 1911; s. Jesse W. and Tiny E. (Gish) C.; student Stanford, 1928-32; LL.B., U. Cal., 1935; m. Hildur Emlyn Westlind, Oct. 11, 1941, (dec. Dec. 1969); 1 dau., Karin Westlind; m. 2d, Mary D. Wallace, Apr. 18, 1970. Admitted to Cal. bar, 1936; asso. Carter, Barrett, Finley & Carlton, 1936-38; asst. dist. atty. Shasta County, 1938-39; partner Carter, Barrett & Carlton, Redding Cal., 1940-41, pvt. practice, 1941-50; mem. Cal. Senate, 5th Senatorial Dist., 1941-49; U.S. dist. judge No. Dist. Cal., 1950—. Sec., Shasta County Democratic Central Com., 1941-48; vice chmn. Cal. State Central Com. for 2d Congl. Dist., 1948; chmn. Dem. State Central Com. Cal., 1948-51. Mem. Hastings Coll. Law Alumni Assn. U. Cal. Presbyn. Elk. Home: 3446 Broderick St San Francisco CA 94123 Office: 450 Golden Gate Av San Francisco CA 94102

CARTER, PAUL DOUGLAS, univ. adminstr.; b. Palmyra, N.Y., Mar. 10, 1934; s. Charles Wesley and Harriett (Miner) C.; A.B., Hamilton Coll., 1956; B.A., M.A. (Rhodes scholar), Oxford (Eng.) U., 1958; m. Elizabeth Heard Baker, June 18, 1960; children—Michael Scott, Catherine Elizabeth, Stephen Christopher. Mem. staff office dean of students U. Minn., 1960-62; asst. provost Columbia, 1962-65, asso. provost, 1965-67, vice provost, 1967-69, provost, 1969; v.p., provost Hamilton Coll., Clinton, N.Y., 1969-71; exec. v.p. for adminstrn. Columbia, 1971—. Mem. Phi Beta Kappa, Alpha Delta Phi. Home: 24 Palmer Ct Ridgewood NJ 07450

CARTER, RICHARD, author; b. N.Y.C., Jan. 24, 1918; s. Samuel J. and Alice (Kulka) C.; B.A., Coll. City N.Y., 1938; m. Gladys Chasins, Oct. 20, 1945; children—Nancy Jane (Mrs. Scott FitzGibbon), John Andrew. Music editor Billboard mag., 1940-46; staff organizer N.Y. Newspaper Guild, 1946-47; writer N.Y. Daily Mirror, 1947-49, N.Y. Daily Compass, 1949-52; author, contbr. mags., 1952—. Served with USAAF, 1942-45; PTO. Recipient George Polk Meml. award, 1952. Mem. Authors Guild, Nat. Assn. Sci. Writers, N.A.A.C.P. Author: The Man Who Rocked the Boat, 1956; The Doctor Business, 1958; The Gentle Legions, 1961; Your Food and Your Health, 1964; Breakthrough: The Saga of Jonas Salk, 1966; Superswine, 1967; (with Curt Flood) The Way It Is, 1971; (under pseudonym Tom Ainslie) The Compleat Horseplayer, 1966, Ainslie's Jockey Book, 1967, Ainslie's Complete Guide to Thoroughbred Racing, 1968; The Handicapper's Handbook, 1969, Theory and Practice of Handicapping, 1969, Ainsile's Complete Guide to Harness Racing, 1970. Address: 165 Pinesbridge Rd Ossining NY 10562

CARTER, ROBERT ELDRED, med. educator, adminstr.; b. Mpls., July 14, 1923; s. Cuthbert Smith and Margaret (Foque) C.; B.S., U. Minn., 1945, M.D., 1946; m. Lota Ahrens, June 22, 1946; children—Jonathan, Ann, David. Intern Cleve. City Hosp., 1947-48; pediatrics resident U. Chgo. Clinics, 1954-56; teaching asst. U. Minn., 1947; staff mem. Los Alamos Sci. Lab., U. Cal. at Los Alamos, N.M., 1948-51; instr., then asst. prof. pediatrics U. Chgo., 1957-59; from asst. prof. to prof. pediatrics U. Ia. Sch. Medicine, 1959-67, asso. dean, 1966-67; prof. pediatrics, dean Med. Sch., U. Miss., also dir. U. Miss. Med. Center 1967—; attending physician Univ. Hosp., Jackson. Mem. regional health advt. com. USPHS, 1951-53. Recipient Markle scholarship in med. scis., 1957-62. Fellow Am. Acad. Pediatrics; mem. Am. Cancer Soc. (bd. dirs. Miss.), Soc. Pediatric Research, Midwest Soc. Pediatric Research, Sigma Xi, Alpha Omega Alpha. Author articles in field. Home: 4626 Hickory Ridge Dr Jackson MS 39211

CARTER, RONALD, musician; b. Royal Oak Twp., Mich., May 4, 1937; s. Lutheran Morris and Willie (Howard) C.; Mus.M., Eastman Sch. Music, 1959; Mus.M., Manhattan Sch. Music; m. Janet Clarice Hosbrouck, June 7, 1958; children—Ronald Carter, Myles. First Negro in Rochester (N.Y.) Philharmonic, 1958-59; 1st bassist Eastman Philharmonia, 1959, Manhattan Symphony Orch., 1960- 61; faculty Nat. State Bank Camp; tchr. U. Buffalo, 1968; tch. jazz, ensemble, guidance counselor Washington U., St. Louis, 1969; tchr. jazz history Manhattan Sch. Music, N.Y.C.; rec. artist for Embryo records; leader group performing in colls., night clubs. Named Outstanding Cellist in Mich., Sch. System Mich., 1951, Internat. Jazz Bassist of Year, Internat. Jazz Critics-Downbeat mag., 1965, Jazz Bassist of Decade in Detroit, Detroit Free Press, 1966; winner Japan All Star Jazz Poll on bass, 1969-70. Mem. Jazz Musicians Assn. (adv. bd.). Author 3 tech. books on jazz and classical bass. Home: 156-20 Riverside Dr W New York City, NY 10032 Office: care Ronald Carter Music Co Box 316 New York City NY 10032

CARTER, SAMUEL E., bishop; b. St. Andrew, Jamaica, July 31, 1919; s. Wilfred George and Marie (Williams) C.; M.A., Boston Coll., 1950; S.T.L., Weston Coll., 1955; M. Social Work, Boston Coll., 1958; LL.D., Holy Cross Coll., 1970. Ordained priest, Roman Catholic Ch., 1954; pres. St. George's Coll., 1964-66, Bishop, Jamaica, 1966; pres. Antilles Episcopal Conf., 1969; apptd. Second Synod of Bishops, Rome, 1969; archbishop of Jamaica, 1970. Mem. Churches Adv. Bur.,1967—; chmn. Commn. on Liturgy Antilles Episcopal Conf., 1967; chmn. Organizing Com. Caribbean Christian Conf., 1970—. Pres. Save the Children Fund, 1967; mem. exec. com. Jamaica Mental Health Assn., 1961-63; chmn. Schools' Labour Relations Council, 1965-66. Decorated Comdr. Order of Distinction, 1970. Address: 21 Hopefield Av Kingston 6 Jamaica

CARTER, SIDNEY, physician; b. Boston, Dec. 8, 1912; s. Jack and Rose (Laurence) C.; A.B., Dartmouth, 1934; M.D., Boston U., 1938; m. Elizabeth M. Crosby, Mar. 24, 1945; children—Jeffrey, Jonathan, Jeremy. Intern St. Mary's Hosp., Waterbury, Conn., 1938-39; resident psychiatry Waterboro (Mass.) State Hosp., 1939-40; resident neurology Boston City Hosp., 1940-42; adj. attending neurologist Montefiore Hosp., N.Y.C., 1946-48; mem. staff Columbia-Presbyn. Med. Center, N.Y.C., 1948—, attending neurologist, 1952—, chief div. pediatric neurology, 1952—; Dwight D. Eisenhower prof. neurology Columbia Coll. Phys. & Surg., 1962—. Served with AUS, 1943-46. Mem. Am. Acad. Neurology (pres.), A.M.A., Assn. Research Nervous and Mental Disease, Am. Epilepsy Soc., N.Y. Neurol. Soc., N.Y. Acad. Scis. Author articles in field. Home: 53 Rockland Av Yonkers NY 10705 Office: 710 W 168th St New York City NY 10032

CARTER, THERESA HOWARD, (Mrs. Edward C. Carter, II), archaeologist; b. Millbrook, N.Y., May 15, 1929; d. Clarence K. and Ann (Warren) Howard; A.B., Syracuse U., 1950; M.A., U. Pa., 1954; Ph.D. in Classical and Near Eastern Archaeology, Bryn Mawr Coll, 1962; m. Edward C. Carter II, Mar. 24, 1951; 1 dau., Laura Coffin. With reprodns. dept. Univ. Mus., Phila., 1950-52, student asst. ethnology dept. 1953-55, research asst. Mediterranean sect., 1960-62, research asso., 1962-64, dir. Iraq excavations, sect. Bibl. archaeology, 1964—, teaching asst. Bryn Mawr. Coll., 1961-62, deptl. asst., 1962-63; ann. prof. Am. Sch. Oriental Research, Baghdad, 1965-66; vis. lectr. dept. Near Eastern studies Johns Hopkins, Balt., 1969-71, asst. prof., 1971—; Middle East Studies Assn. fellow. Mem. staff U. Pa. Gordion Expdn., Polati, Turkey 1955, 57; dir. U. Pa., Phoenician excavations, Lepcis Magna. Homs. Libya, 1960, 61; dir. Cyrenaican Coastal Survey, U. Pa., 1962; participated Bryn Mawr Coll. excavations Kara Tash, Elmali, Turkey, 1963; co-dir. Tell al-Rimah Expdn., No. Iraq, 1964-66; collaborator for Univ. Mus. with Soprentendenza alle Antichitá di Napoli at Pithecusa, Lacco Ameno. Ischia, 1965; field dir. Sybaris project of Univ. Pa. in Calabria, Italy, 1968. Bd. dirs. Theatre of Living Arts, Phila., 1964-67, chmn. Women's com., 1964-65. Mem. Archaeol. Inst. Am., Am. Oriental Soc. Contbr. articles to profl. jours. Home: 2620 Quebec St N W Washington DC 20008 Office: Dept Near Eastern Studies Johns Hopkins Baltimore MD 21218

CARTER, THOMAS SMITH, Jr., r.r. exec.; b. Dallas, June 6 1921; s. Thomas S. and Mattie L. (Dowell) C.; B.S. in Civil Engring., So. Meth. U., 1944; m. Janet R. Hostetter, July 3, 1946; children—Janet Diane, Susan Jean, Charles T., Carol. With M.-K.-T. R.R., 1941-44, 46-66, asst. engr., St. Louis, asst. dist. engr., Franklin, Mo., dist. engr., Parsons Kan., asst. chief engr., St. Louis, chief engr., St. Louis, Dallas, 1946-61, v.p. operations, Dallas, 1961-66; v.p. KCS Ry. Co., L&A Ry. Co. Served with C.E., AUS, 1944-46. Registered profl. engr., Mo., Kan., Okla., Tex., La., Ark. Fellow Am. Soc. C.E.; mem. Am. Ry. Engring. Assn., Nat. Soc. Profl. Engrs., Shreveport C. of C., Alpha Tau Omega, Chi Epsilon. Presbyn. Home: 8614 W Wilderness Way Shreveport, LA 71106. Office: 4601 Blanchard Rd Shreveport LA 71101

CARTER, TIM LEE congressman; b. Tompkinsville, Ky., Sept 2, 1910; s. James Clark and Idru (Tucker) C.; A.B., Western Ky. U.; M.D., U. Tenn., 1937; m. Kathleen Bradshaw, Nov. 15, 1931; 1 son, Billy Starr. Pub. sch. tchr., 1927-32; intern U.S. Marine Hosp., Chgo. Maternity Center; practice medicine, Tompkinsville, 1939-42, 46-65; mem. 89th-92d congresses 5th Dist. Ky. Engaged in farming, Tompkinsville; owner T.L. Carter Devel. Co.; chief staff Monroe County Meml. Hosp. Chmn. Monroe County Bd. Edn.; mem. President's Commn. on Marihuana and Drug Abuse. Chmn. Monroe County Republican Exec. Com. Served to capt. M.C., AUS, 1942- 46. Decorated Bronze Star; recipient Tom Wallace award for conservation. Mem. Am., Ky. med. assns., Am., Ky. acads. gen. practice, Alpha Omega Alpha. Baptist Mason (32, Shriner). Home: 701 N Main St Tompkinsville KY 42167 Office: House Office Bldg Washington DC 20515

CARTER, VICTOR M. bank exec.; b. Rostov, Russia, Aug 21 1910; s. Mark and Fanya (Rudnick) C.; m. Adrea Zucker, July 15, 1928; 1 dau., Fawn. Dir., United Cal. Bank, Benefical Standard Corp. Past pres. United Way, City of Hope; chmn. bd. govs. Tel Aviv U. Bd. dirs. Fedn. Jewish Welfare Orgns. Mason; mem. B'Nai B'rith. Home: 10375 Wilshire Blvd Los Angeles CA 90024 Office: 1900 Av of Stars Los Angeles CA 90067

CARTER, VINCENT, lawyer; b. St. Clair, Pa., Nov. 6, 1891; s. William J. and Julia Anna (Clarke) C.; ed. Cath. U., Washington, Fordham U.; m. Helen Carlson, July 2, 1921 (dec.), 1 son, James Vincent (dec.); m. 2d, Mary Crowley, Aug. 13, 1929; children—Helen, Jerome, Roch. Admitted to Wyo. bar, 1919, began practice at Casper; dept. atty. gen. Wyo. 1919-23; state auditor, Wyo., 1923-29; state purchasing agt., 1923-29; former pres. Golconda Oil Co. Mem. 71st to 73d Congresses, 1929-35, Wyo. Republican nominee for U.S. Senate, 1934. Capt. cav. Wyo. N.G. 1919-21. Mem. Bd. Charities and Reform, Wyo., 1923-29. Served as lt. USMC, World War I. Mem. Am. Legion, Pi Gamma Mu. Elk. Home: 1331 Park Av SW Albuquerque NM 87102

CARTER, WALTER COLQUITT, lawyer; b. Atlanta, June 12, 1904; s. Walter Colquitt and Nannie Sue (Hill) C.; A.B., U. Ga., 1924; LL.B., Harvard. 1927. m. Marion Cobb Bryan, June 4, 1930; children—Florence Bryan, Nancy Hill. Admitted to Ga. Bar, 1927, since practiced in Atlanta; mem. Bryan, Carter, Ansley & Smith. Dir. Jefferson Standard Life Ins. Co., DeKalb County Fed. Savs. & Loan Assn. Mem. Commn. on Uniform State Laws, 1940-50; Bd. dirs. Family Welfare Soc. Fulton and DeKalb Counties, 1940-48, Atlanta Tb Assn. (pres. 1948- 49), Atlanta Legal Aid Soc. (pres. 1945-47). Mem. Am. (life ins. law com. 1941-52, legal aid com. 1941-42), Ga. (v.p. 1936), Atlanta bar assns., Am. Law Inst., Am. Judicature Soc., Phi Beta Kappa, Phi Kappa Phi, Chi Phi (nat. v.p. 1941-42). Democrat. Episcopalian. Lion. Clubs: Lawyers (pres. 1943-44), Harvard (pres. 1945-47), Piedmont Driving (Atlanta); Capital City. Contr. to law jours. Home: 52 W Wesley Rd Atlanta GA 30305 Office: First Nat. Bank Bldg Atlanta GA 30303

CARTER, WARREN RAY, diversified co. exec.; b. Ashtabula, O., Apr. 18, 1922; s. Laddie F. and Mary Elizabeth (Braké) C.; B.B.A., Western Res. U., 1950; m. Ruth Lillian Danes, Apr. 10, 1943; children—Gary, Jane. Supr. Thompson Products, Cleve., 1942; with Gen. Motors Corp., Detroit, 1950-53, asst. supr., 1953; plant supt. Borg Warner Corp., Decatur, Ill., 1953-58, works mgr., 1958-60; with Sealed Power Co., Muskegon, Mich., 1960-70, v.p., 1961-69, group v.p., 1970; sr. v.p. Weatherhead Co., Cleve., 1970-71, exec. v.p., 1971—; pres., 1971—, also dir.; dir. East Shore Chem. Co., Muskegon, Mich. Pres., founder, Jr. Achievement Muskegon, 1963-70. Served to 1st. lt. USAAF, 1943-46. Recipient Law Day award Mich. Young Lawyers Group, 1966. Mem. Soc. Automotive Engrs. Mason (Shriner). Clubs: Tangelwood Country, Clevelander, Mid-Day (Cleve.). Office: Home: 30700 Shaker Blvd Pepper Pike OH 44124

CARTER, WENDELL EUGENE, ret. air force officer; b. Lincoln, Neb. Nov. 19, 1915; s. Joseph Albert and Amanda (Higginbotham) C.; B.S. in Bus. Adminstrn., Wichita State U., 1938; M.B.A., Harvard, 1947; m. Helen Rebecca Inness, Aug. 14, 1940; children—Sandra Leigh, David Inness, Karen Lou. Commd. 2d lt. U.S. Army Res., 1939, entered active duty as 2d lt., 1940, advanced through grades to maj. gen. USAF, 1966, assigned Wright Field, 1940-46; with budget directorate Hdqrs. USAF, 1947-49; asst. to comptroller USAF 1949-51; chief adminstrv. mgmt. Air Material Command, 1951-52, chief accounting 1952-55; assigned Air War Coll., 1956; comptroller Alaska Air Command, 1956-59; dep. comptroller Mil. Air Transp. Service, 1959-60, comptroller, 1960-63; dept. dir. budget Hdqrs. USAF, 1963-64; comptroller Air Force Systems Command, Andrews AFB, 1964-67; dept. asst. sec. of def. (information), 1967-69. Decorated D.S.M., Legion of Merit with three oak leaf clusters, Air Force Commendation medal, Army Commendation medal with 1 oak leaf cluster; named Man. of Distinction, Am. Mgmt. Assn., 1966. Mem. Am. Soc. Mil. Comptrollers (nat. pres.), Armed Forces Mgmt. Assn. (dir.). Home: 3200 Candlelight Dr NE Albuquerque NM 87111

CARTER, WILBUR LEE, Jr., ins. co. exec.; b. Greensboro, N.C., Jan. 23, 1922; s. Wilbur Lee and Marie (Cranford) C.; B.S., Davidson Coll., 1943; m. Martha Virginia Sauvain, Dec. 16, 1943; children—Judith Marie, Carolyn S. (Mrs. David E. Yawars), Wilbur Lee III. Exec. v.p. So. Life Ins. Co., Greensboro, 1946-64, pres., 1964—, also dir.; dir. Jefferson Standard Life Ins. Co., Jefferson-Pilot Corp., N.C. Nat. Bank; mem. Greensboro Investors, Inc. Mem. exec. com. Life Insurers Conf. Bd. dirs. United Fund Greensboro, Greensboro Sports Council, Greensboro Jr. Achievement, Excellence Fund; trustee Wesley Long Community Hosp., L. Richardson Hosp. Served to capt. inf., AUS, World War II; ETO. Decorated Purple Heart. C.L.U. Mem. Life Underwriters Assn. (dir.). Presbyn. (elder). Clubs: Sedgefield Hunt (master foxhounds); Greensboro Country (bd. dirs.); Country of N.C. (Pinehurst). Home: 1012 Country Club Dr Greensboro NC 27408 Office: 330 S Greene St Greensboro NC 27402

CARTER, WILLIAM DANIEL, life ins. co. exec.; b. Reading, Mass., Sept. 16, 1911; s. Frank Clifford and Mary (Daniel) C.; B.A., Amherst Coll., 1933; m. Elizabeth Cooke Alling, May 7, 1938; children—Nancy Chute, Elizabeth C. (Mrs. Michael S. Welch). Clk., Prudential Life Ins. Co. Am., Newark, 1934-40; with Conn. Mut. Life Ins. Co, Hartford, 1940—, sec., 1958-70, 2d v.p., 1970—. Group chmn. Hartford Commmity Chest, 1959. Mem. Conn. Ho. of Reps.

from North Brantford, Conn., 1963, 65. Chmn., Bd. Finance North Branford, 1965- -. Fellow Life Office Mgmt. Assn.; mem. Alpha Delta Phi. Republican. Home: Middletown Av Northford CT 06471 Office: 140 Garden St Hartford CT 06105

CARTER, WILLIAM GILBERT, lawyer; b. Chgo., Jan 15, 1927; s. William Curtis and Maye (Corbin) C.; B.A., Yale, 1948; LL.B., Columbia, 1952; m. Mary Carlyle Fitzgerald, Aug. 20 1955; children—Elizabeth, Sarah,Zoë. Admitted to N.Y. bar 1953; asso. firm Hughes, Hubbard, Blair & Reed, N.Y.C., 1952-53, Lewis and MacDonald, 1953-54; asso. Coudert Bros., Paris office, 1954-60, partner, 1961-62; spl. asst. to dept. adminstr. AID, 1962; spl. asst. internat. space communications to asst. sec. state econ. affairs, 1962-64, chief of private investment div., 1964-65; asso. asst. adminstr. for private enterprise, AID, State Dept. Washington, 1965-67, asso. asst. adminstr., officer pvt. resources, 1967-68, dep. asst. adminstr., 1968-70; cons. Overseas Pvt. Investment Corp., agy. of U.S. govt., 1970-71; partner law firm Nicholson & Carter, Washington, 1971—. Trustee Am. Overseas Meml. Day Assos., Inc., 1959-62, Am. Sch. Paris, 1960-62, Am. Library Paris, 1959-62, Am. Coll. Paris, 1961—. Vol. Am. Field Service, 1945. Recipient Superior Honor award Dept. State, 1964. Mem. Assn. Bar City N.Y., Am. Soc. Internat. Law, Am. Fgn. Law Assn., Internat. Bar Assn. (patron), Chi Psi, Phi Delta Phi. Clubs: Yale (N.Y.C.); Travellers (Paris); Boodles (London); National Lawyers (Washington) Home: 3450 Ordway St NW Washington DC 20016 Office: 21 Dupont Circle NW Washington DC 20036

CARTER, WILLIAM HARRISON, educator; b. Gloucester City, N.J., Apr. 20, 1905; s. William Harrison and Olive Edna (Taylor) C.; A.B., Amherst Coll., 1926; M.A. Harvard, 1930, Ph.D., 1932; m. Joan L. Cooke, Aug 22, 1931; 1 dau., Alice E. Instr. econs. Amherst Coll., 1927-28, Brown U., 1930-31; instr. to prof. U. Conn., Storrs, 1931-66, prof., 1942-66, head dept. econs., 1945-54, dean Coll. Liberal Arts and Scis., 1954-66, dean emeritus, 1966—, coordinator of nat. def. tng., 1954-66. Price economist OPA, Conn., 1943-44; chmn. Conn. Minimum Wage Bd., 1951-52. Mem. Am. Econ. Assn., Phi Beta Kappa. Conglist. Mason. Author: Economic Geography, 1939; Economic Theory, 1948; Economic Analysis, 1952; Intermediate Economic Analysis, 1961. Home: 21 Hillside Circle Storrs CT 06268

CARTER, WILLIAM HOYT, Jr., educator; b. Ferrisburg, Vt. Aug. 14, 1914, s. William Hoyt and Angeline (Wilcox) C.; A.B., Middlebury Coll., 1936; postgrad. U. Heidelberg, 1936-37; A.M. Harvard, 1938, Ph.D., 1951; m. Lorna Adele Little, Apr. 4, 1941 (div.); m. 2d, Harriet Rhodes Meigs, July 19, 1969; stepchildren—Joe V., Rebecca W., Stephen R., Sarah P., Thomas M. Instr. English, Conn. Coll. for Women, 1940-42, Mass. Inst. Tech., 1942-43, Yale, spring 1949; faculty Clark U., Worcester, Mass., 1949—, prof. English, 1967—, chmn. dept., 1966—. Mem. Am. Assn. U. Profs., Coll. English Assn., Nat. Assn. Tchrs. English, Phi Beta Kappa. Home: 88 Sagamore Rd Worcester MA 01609 Office: English House Clark U Worcester MA 01610

CARTER, WILLIAM LEE, univ. pres.; b. Flora, Ill., Jan 19 1925; s. Emerson Lee and Zola (King) C.; student Kenyon Coll., 1943-44; B.S., Eastern Ill. U., 1948; M.A., Ohio State U., 1949, Ph.D., 1952; m. Phyllis Lee Cisne, Oct. 28, 1944; children—Kanda Sue, William Brand. Tchr., Ashmore (Ill.) High Sch., 1947 - 48; research asst. Ohio State U., 1948-50; instr. Western High Sch., Macomb, Ill., 1950-52; prof. Coll. of Guam, Agana, 1952-54; prof. edn. U. Cin., 1954-67, asst. dean faculties, 1963-64, asso. dean faculties, officer acad. planning, 1964-66, dean Coll. Edn. and Home Econs., 1966- 67; pres Wis. State U., Whitewater, Wis., 1967—. Cons. Hamilton County Schs., Cin., 1957-63. Hon. life mem. Ohio Congress P.T.A. Served with USAAF, 1943-46. Mem. Math. Assn. Am., Am. Assn. Sch. Adminstrs., Phi Sigma Epsilon, Phi Delta Kappa, Kappa Delta Pi, Kappa Mu Epsilon, Iota Lambda Sigma (hon. life), Phi Kappa Phi. Mason (Shriner), Kiwanian. Author: Learning to Teach in the Elementary School, 1959; Learning to Teach in the Secondary School, 1962. Home: 724 W Main St Whitewater WI 53190

CARTER, WILLIAM RADCLIFFE, lawyer; b. Newark, Jan. 6, 1917; s. Clyde and Ruth (Radcliffe) C.; A.B., Dartmouth, 1939; LL.B., Harvard, 1942; m. Ethel Ann Grow, Oct. 10, 1942; children—Virginia Ann, Ellen Ruth, William Radcliffe, Robert Clyde. Admitted to N.Y. State bar, since practiced in N.Y.C.; asso. atty. firm Chadbourne, Hunt, Jaeckel & Brown, 1945-56; partner firm Brown, Wood, Fuller, Caldwell & Ivey, 1956—. Dir. Checker Motors Corp. 1965—. Active local fund-raising campaigns. Served to Capt. USNR, 1942- 45. Mem. and past pres. Peter Tare, orgn. former MT Navy boat officers. Presbyn. (trustee). Clubs: Fairmount Country (Chatham Twp., N.J.) (bd. dirs.), Dartmouth Essex and Morris counties, N.J. (bd. dirs.). Home: 333 Woodland Rd Madison NJ 07040 Office: 70 Pine St New York City NY 10005

CARTER, WILLIAM THOMAS, III, investment co. exec.; b. Houston, June 6, 1913; s. William Thomas and Lillie (Neuhaus) C.; student Lawrenceville Sch.; B.S., Yale 1935; m. Patricia Barrett, Mar. 7, 1939; children—William Thomas IV, Patricia B., Robert B. With Carter Investment Co., 1935—, pres., 1957—; with Commerce Fund, Inc., 1949—, pres., 1957-60, now dir.; dir. Gibraltar Savs. Assn. Mem. Chi Phi. Clubs: Houston Country, Eagle Lake Rod and Gun (Houston). Office: 1616 W Loop So Houston TX 77027

CARTER, WILLIAM WALTON, physicist; b. Pensacola, Fla. Nov. 7, 1921; s. Eugene Hudson and Nannie (Ledyard) C.; B.S., Carnegie Inst. Tech., 1943; M.S., Cal. Inst. Tech., 1948, Ph.D., 1949; m. Elizabeth Jean Dedick, June 11, 1945; children—Carolyn A., Susan J., Judith J., Paul W. Atomic, thermonuclear Weapon research and devel., group leader applied physics group, weapons div. Los Alamos (N.M.) Sci. Lab., 1949-59, also mem. joint working com. Los Alamos Sci. Lab. and Sandia Corp.; chief scientist Army Missile Command, Redstone Arsenal, 1959-67; asst. dir. nuclear programs, def. research and engring. Office Sec. Def., Washington, 1967-71, asso. dir. Harry Diamond Labs., 1971—. Chmn. steering com. Huntsville Research Inst. Served to lt. USNR, 1944-46. Asso. fellow Am. Inst. Aeros. and Astronautics; mem. Am. Phys. Soc., Assn. U.S. Army, Am. Inst. Physics, Am. Nuclear Soc. Home: 1124 Ormond Ct McLean VA 22101 Office: Harry Diamond Labs Washington DC 20438

CARTER, WILLIS MERLE, educator; b. Paris, Ky., Nov. 28, 1916; s. Wallace Franklin and Lucy Cora (Young) C.; B.S. in Mech. Engring., U. Ky., 1934-38, M.S., 1944-46; Ph.D., U. Mich., 1953; m. Mildred K. Brown, Apr. 18, 1940; children—David Brown, Linde Merle. Engine designer Mawen Motor Corp., Lexington, Ky., 1938-43; project engr. Wenner-Gren Aero. Lab., U. Ky., Lexington, 1944-46, prof. machine design, 1946-60, head dept. mech. engring., 1960- 65, prof. mech. engring., 1960—. Mem. Am. Soc. M.E., Am. Soc. Engring. Edn., Ky. Soc. Profl. Engrs. Baptist. Lion. Home: 729 Malabu Dr Lexington KY 40502

CARTHY, MARGARET, educator; b. N.Y.C., Oct. 15, 1911; d. Patrick and Ellen (Hosburg) Carthy; A.B., Coll. of New Rochelle, 1933; postgrad. Columbia, 1934- 36; M.A., Catholic U. Am., 1948, Ph.D., 1957. Asst. to bus. mgr. Tchrs. Coll., Columbia, 1933-37; asst. registrar Coll. of New Rochelle, 1941- 49, dean, 1950-57, pres, 1957-61; staff editor New Cath. Ency., 1962-66; editor Corpus Instrumentorum, Inc., 1966-67; asso. prof., asst. dir. gen. edn. program U. Md., College Park, 1968—; lectr. Cath. U. Am., 1963-66. Mem. Am. Cath. Hist. Assn., Nat. Assn. Fgn. Student Advisers, Am. Assn. U. Women. Home: 1404 Hampshire West Ct Silver Spring MD 20903 Office: Skinner Bldg U Md College Park MD 20742

CARTIER-BRESSON, HENRI, photographer; b. France, Aug. 22, 1908; m. Ratna Mohini, 1937. Asso., Magnum Photos, Paris, also N.Y.C., 1947—; creater documentary films, TV films, filmstrips; photographs exhibited Madrid, 1933, Palacio de Bellas Artes, Mexico, 1934, Mus. Modern Art, N.Y.C., 1946, 68, Musee du Louvre, Paris, France, 1956, Tokyo, 1965, Victoria and Albert Mus., London, 1969, Grand Palais, Paris, 1970. Recipient award for story death of Gandhi, U.S. Camera, 1948, for best photographic reporting from abroad Overseas Press Club Am., 1949, for most contbn. progress of mag. photography Am. Soc. Mag. Photograph, 1953; internat. understanding through photography award Photography Soc. of Am., 1958; Overseas Press Club awards for Russia, 1954, for Red China 1960, and for Cuba, 1964. Author: The Decisive Moment (also French editor), 1952; Moscow, 1955; From One China to the Other (text Han Suyin), 1956; Photographs by Cartier-Bresson (text Lincoln Kirstein, Beaumont Newhall), 1963; The World of HCB, 1968; Man and Machine, 1969; Vive la France (text Francois Nourrissier), 1970. Office: 125 rue de Faubourg Saint-Honore Paris 8e France Office: care Mrs Helen Wright 135 E 74th St New York City NY 10021

CARTLIDGE, ALVA RAY, clergyman; b. Shelburn, Ind., Sept. 26, 1906; s. Frank and Winifred (Jacobs) C.; A.B., U. Cin., 1929; B.D., Lane Sem. Cin., 1932; D.D., Milliken U., 1947; m. Mary Ann Caldwell, Feb. 15, 1928; children—David R., Mary Ann. Ordained to ministry Presbyn. Ch. 1932; pastor, Wilmington, O., 1932-34, Cin., 1934-39, Champaign, Ill., 1939- 54, Ch. of Covenant, Erie, Pa., 1954—. Mem. bd. nat. missions United Presbyn. Ch., 1956-68; mem. Exec. and Field Service Commn., 1960-68, Council on Evangelism, 1960-68; moderator Synod of Ill., 1949, Synod of Pa., 1969-71. Trustee McCormick Theol. Sem., Grove City (Pa..) Coll., Lane Sem. Endowment. Mem. Pi Kappa Alpha. Mason. Home: 5598 West Wind Lane Fort Myers FL 33901

CARTMELL, PETER, banker; b. Clydebank, Scotland, Apr. 30, 1921; s. George Jack and Kate Banks (Griffin) C.; came to U.S., 1924, naturalized, 1942; B.S. in Bus. Administn., Rutgers U., 1943; m. Constance Wingerter, May 26, 1945; children—Virginia, Peter B., Jennifer B., Elizabeth B., George D. With Fidelity Union Trust Co., Newark, 1946—, v.p., 1958-62, sr. v.p., 1962-64, exec. v.p., 1964-69, pres., 1969—, dir., 1966; pres., dir. Fidelity Union Bancorp., dir. Bro-Dart Industries, Firemen's Ins. Co. of Newark (N.J.), Foster Wheeler Corp. Mayor, Borough Rumson N.J., 1958-61. Trustee Rutgers U. Served to 1st lt. AUS, 1943-46. Mem. Phi Beta Kappa. Episcopalian. Home: 11 Holly Tree Lane Rumson NJ 07760 Office: 765 Broad St Newark NJ 07101

CARTMELL, VINTON AIKINS, pulp and paper co. exec.; b. Glen Ridge, N.J., Oct. 11, 1925; s. Nathaniel Madison and Madeline (Aikins) C.; grad. Phillips Acad., 1944; B.S., Yale, 1949; m. Jane Ann Thomson, Feb. 16, 1957; children—Jennifer Anne, Geoffrey Wayne Thomson, Matthew Frederick Lindsay, Barbara Jane. With Chase Manhattan Bank, 1949-55; with Westvaco Corp., 1955—, treas., 1968—. Served with inf. AUS, 1944-46, 50-52. Decorated Bronze Star. Mem. Chi Phi Clubs: Yale, Board Room (N.Y.C.). Home: 21 Prospect Av Darien CT 06820 Office: 299 Park Av New York City NY 10017

CARTMILL, GEORGE EDWIN, Jr., hosp. adminstr.; b. Plover, Wis., Dec. 26, 1918; s. George Edwin and Elsie Evelyn (Dobbie) C.; B.S., Central State Tchrs. Coll., Stevens Point, Wis., 1938; M.S. Columbia, 1947; m. Helen Marie Heimburg, Feb. 20, 1948; children—George Thomas, William Charles, Sara Jane. High sch. tchr., Wis., 1938-41; asst. dir. Harper Hosp., Detroit, 1947-50, asso. dir., treas., 1950-52, dir., 1952—, pres., 1966—, also trustee, 1966—. Mem. adv. com. hosps. div. W. K. Kellogg Found., 1956-61; pres. Greater Detroit Area Hosp. Council, 1952; trustee Mich. Hosp. Service (Blue Cross), 1952—, vice chmn. bd., 1962—; v.p. Tri-State Hosp. Assembly, 1958-59; com. adminstrn. Wayne State U. Coll. Medicine, 1953-57; trustee v.p. Community Health, Inc., 1968; mem. Pres.'s Nat. Adv. Com. Health Facilities, 1968; mem. Task Force on Medicaid and Related Problems, Dept. Health, Edn. and Welfare, 1970. Asso. mem. corp. Merrill-Palmer Inst. Served with AUS, 1941-45. Recipient Award of Merit, Tri-State Hosp. Assembly, 1965; Meritorious Service award Mich. Hosp. Assn., 1966. Fellow Am. Coll. Hosp. Adminstrs. (regent 1970-72); mem. Am. Dietetics Assn. (hon., adv. bd. 1963-69), Am. (chmn. council adminstrv. practice 1959-62, trustee 1962-68, pres. 1966), Mich. (pres. 1958, trustee 1952-60) hosp. assns., Nat., Mich. leagues nursing, Assn. Am. Med. Colls. (exec. council 1970-72, chmn. council of teaching hosps. 1971- 72). Presbyn. Rotarian. Clubs: Detroit, Detroit Athletic, Country of Detroit. Home: 333 Touraine Rd Grosse Pointe Farms MI 48236 Office: 3825 Brush St Detroit MI 48201

CARTON, J. GERALD, lawyer; b. Asbury Park, N.J., May 9, 1906; B.S., Brown U., 1929; LL.B., Harvard, 1932. Admitted to N.J. bar, 1932; now mem. firm Carton, Nary, Witt & Arvanitis, Asbury Park. Mem. Am., N.J. State, Monmouth County bar assns. Office: 601 Grand Av Asbury Park NJ 07712*

CARTON, JAMES D., Jr., lawyer; b. Asbury Park, N.J., May 22, 1903; LL.B., Columbia, 1928. Admitted to N.J. bar, 1928; now mem. firm Carton, Nary, Witt & Arvanitis, Asbury Park. Mem. N.J. State, Monmouth County bar assns. Office: 601 Grand Av Asbury Park NJ 07712*

CARTON, JOHN VICTOR, lawyer; b. Asbury Park, N.J., Feb. 7, 1900; s. James D. and Mary M. (Ludlow) C.; A.B., Georgetown U., 1922; LL.B., Columbia, 1925; m. Joan E. McGregor, June 20, 1939; children—Malcolm V., Gail T., Joan E., Kerry, Michael. Admitted to N.J. bar, 1926, since practiced in Asbury Park; mem. firm Durand, Ivins & Carton, 1935-63, Carton, Nary, Witt & Arvanitis, 1964—. Dir. counsel Keystone Savs. & Loan Assn., Asbury Park. Asst. pros. atty. of the Pleas, Monmouth County, N.J., 1930-35; county pros. atty. Monmouth County, 1945-55. Bd. dirs. Jersey Shore Med. Center, Neptune. Fellow Am. Bar Found.; mem. N.J. Bar Assn., Am. Coll. Trial Lawyers. Clubs: Deal (N.J.) Golf and Country, Pinhurst (N.C.) Country. Home: Riverfront Neptune City NJ 07753 Office: PO Box 1229 Asbury Park NJ 07712

CARTON LAURENCE ALFRED lawyer; b. Chgo., Oct. 11, 1918; s. Alfred Thomas and Mildred (Wells) C.; grad. Hotchkiss Sch., Lakeville, Conn., 1936; A.B., Princeton, 1940; J.D., U. Chgo., 1947; m. Ann Fontaine Schmidt, July 2, 1949; childrenKatherine Lynch, Ellen, John Laurence, Mary, Evelyn. Admitted to Ill. bar, 1947, since practiced with Gardner, Carton, Douglas, Chilgren & Waud, Chgo., mem. firm, 1952—. Trustee Morton Arboretum, Ferry Hall, John G. Shedd Aquarium, James C. King Old Men's Home, Chgo., Sunday Evening Club. Served as lt. comdr. USNR, 1942-46. Mem. Am., Ill., Chgo. bar assns., Chgo. Zool. Soc., Art Inst. Chgo. (gov.), Orchestral Assn. Clubs: Chicago, University, Onwentsia. Home: 285 W Laurel Av Lake Forest IL 60045 Office: 1 First National Plaza Chicago IL 60670

CARTON, MYER FRED, bus. exec.; b. N.Y.C., Mar. 18, 1898; s. Saul and Ethel (Freeman) C.; B.S. in Ch.E., Poly. Inst. Bklyn., 1919; m. Harriet Ethyl Sims, Feb. 24, 1921; 1 son, Alan Robert. Pres., Heller- Deltah Co., 1921-23, sales mgr., 1926-35; exec. v.p., dir. Longiness-Wittnauer Watch Co., 1935-45; chmn. bd., treas., chief exec. officer, 1945—. Served with Engrs. Res. Corps., U.S. Army, World War I. Mem. Poly. Alumni Assn., Phi Delta Pi, Tau Beta Pi. Clubs: 24K; Marmaroneck Beach Yacht. Office: 580 Fifth Av New York City NY 10020

CARTTER, ALLAN MURRAY, educator; b. Westfield, N.J., June 17, 1922; s. Allan Murray and Bertha Louise (Baker) C.; A.B., Colgate U., 1946; A.M. Yale, 1949, Ph.D., 1952; m. Marietta S. Macklin, June 26, 1943. Instr. econs. Colgate, 1946-48; from asst. prof. to asso. prof. econs. Duke, 1952-57, prof., dean Grad. Sch., 1959-62; v.p. Am. Council on Edn., 1963-66; chancellor N.Y. U., 1966—; program asso. Ford Found., 1957-59. Mem. Inter-Univ. Com. Econ. Devel. of South, 1960- 64; dir. Commn. Plans and Objectives for Higher Edn., 1963-66; com. grad. sch. Yale, 1966-70; mem. Pres.'s Econ. Survey Team, Indonesia, 1961-62; mem. task group on manpower Pres.'s Sci. Adv. Com., 1963-64, mem. Commn. on Human Resources, 1963-70, N.Y. Gov.'s Council Econ. Advisers, 1968—. Bd. dirs. Tchrs. Ins. Annuity Assn., Theol. Fund. Served with AUS, 1942-45. Mem. Am. Econ. Assn., Royal Econ. Soc. Clubs: Cosmos (Washington); Century (N.Y.C.). Author: Redistribution of Income in Postwar Britain, 1955; Theory of Wages and Employment, 1959; An Assessment of Quality in Graduate Education, 1966. Co-author: Economic Survey of Indonesia, 1962; Labor Economics, 1967. Editor: American Universities and Colleges, 1964: Home: 34 W 11th St New York City NY 10011

CARTUN, WALTER PAUL, mfg. co. exec.; b. Cleveland Heights, O., Jan. 15, 1916; s. Paul O. and Gertrude (Bauer) C.; B. Sc., Ohio State U., 1937; M.B.A., Harvard, 1939; m. Lavette S. Watterson, Jan. 17, 1941; children—David, William (dec.), Richard. With Gen. Electric Co., 1936-62; v.p. Westinghouse Air Brake Co., 1962-69; pres. Railroad, Friction Products Corp., 1966-69; exec. v.p. Emhart Corp., 1969—. Vice pres. Pitts. C. of C., 1966-69 Vice pres. Jr. Achievement Southwest Pa., 1963-69. Trustee Indsl. Health Found., Pitts. Served to lt. USNR, 1941-45. Decorated Commendation ribbon. Mem. Soc. Advancement Mgmt. (Profl. Mgr. citation 1965; regional v.p. 1970—), Inst. Mgmt. Scis. Home: 75 Reverknolls Avon CT 06001 Office: 950 Cottage Grove Rd Bloomfield CT 06002

CARTWRIGHT, DAVID PHILIP, ins. co. exec.; b. Pasadena, Cal., Feb. 10, 1918; s. Paul W. and Mabel (Stone) C.; B.B.A. with distinction, U. Minn., 1939; m. Carol Hemberson, Aug. 24, 1940; children—Dian (Mrs. James W. Gardner), David W. Accountant, mgr. payroll div., mgr. policy issues div. underwriting asst., asst. underwriting officer, underwriting officer, 2d v.p. Minn. Mut. Life Ins. Co., St. Paul, 1960-63, v.p., 1963-66, sr. v.p., 1966—; dir. Financial Life Ins. Co. of N.Y. Instr. U. Minn., 1946-47. Mem. exec. bd. Indian Head council Boy Scouts Am. Village trustee, Falcon Heights, Minn., 1954- 56; chmn. Falcon Heights Planning Commn., 1957-61. Bd. dirs., sec. Jr. Achievement of St. Paul; bd. dirs. Family Service of St. Paul. Mem. Home Office Life Underwriters Assn. (past pres., dir.), Life Ins. Assn. Am., Inst. Home Office Underwriters, Life Office Mgmt. Assn., Delta Upsilon, Beta Alpha Psi, Beta Gamma Sigma. Republican. Conglist. Mason. Clubs: St. Paul Athletic (v.p.) Rotary (past pres.), Minnesota, Midland Hills Country. Home: 3030 Little Bay Rd St Paul MN 55113 Office: 345 Cedar St St Paul MN 55103

CARTWRIGHT, DORWIN PHILIP, social psychologist; b. Des Moines, Mar. 3 1915; s. Lin Dorwin and Inez (Scott) C.; A.B. Swarthmore (Pa.) Coll., 1937; M.A. Harvard, 1938, Ph.D., 1940; m. Barbara Elizabeth Weiss, Aug. 9 1938; children— Patricia Alice, Susan Carol, Peter Scott. Research fellow U. Ia., 1940- 42; research dir. div. program surveys, bur. agrl. econs. U.S. Dept. Agr. 1942-45; asst. prof. Mass. Inst. Tech., 1945-47, asso. prof. dir. Research Group Center Group Dynamics, 1947-48; asso. prof. psychology U. Mich., 1948-50, prof. psychology 1950—, dir. Research Center Group Dynamics, 1947-58, research coordinator, 1959—. Mem. policy com. Nat. Tng. Lab. Group Devel., 1948-59; fellow Center Advanced Study in Behavioral Scis., Stanford, Cal., 1960-61; mem. behavioral scis. study sect. NIH, 1964-67, chmn. social sci. research rev. com. Nat. Institute Mental Health, 1968-69. Bd. dirs. Social Scis. Research Council. Mem. Soc. Psychol. Study Social Issues (pres. 1952- 53), Am. Psychol. Assn. (chmn. bd. sci. affairs 1958- 59), Am. Sociol. Assn., Phi Beta Kappa, Sigma Xi. Mem. Soc. of Friends. Author: (with Alvin Zander) Group Dynamics: Research and Theory, 1953; (with Frank Harary and Robert Z. Norman) Structural Models, 1965. Editor: Field Theory in Social Science (by Kurt Lewin), 1951; Studies in Social Power, 1959; editor Human Relations 1947—: co-editor Public Opinion and Propaganda, 1954. Home: 2030 Dhu Varren Rd Ann Arbor MI 48105

CARTWRIGHT, EDWIN ORVILLE, investment co. broker; b. Jonesboro, Ark., Sept. 18, 1901; s. Eugene Orville and Lulu Bell (Barnett) C.; student pub. schs.; m. Frances Lucille Crunk, Mar. 27, 1920; children—Edwin Orville, William Eugene. Editorial dept. Dallas Morning News, 1921-22; securities dept. M.H. Thomas & Co., Dallas, 1922-27; account exec. E.A. Pierce & Co., Dallas, 1927-28; mgr. Fenner & Beane, Dallas, 1929-40; partner Merrill, Lynch, Pierce, Fenner & Beane, Dallas 1929-40, Merrill Lynch, Pierce, Fenner & Smith, Inc., 1949- 59, v.p., dir., 1959-62, sr. v.p., dir., 1962-66; pres. Cartwright Co., Investments, 1940-48, Willis Electronic Corp.; owner Cartwright Oil Co., dir. Midwest Video Corp., Home Theatres, Inc. Chmn., Dallas Pub. Transit Bd.; Bd. dirs. Dallas County United Fund; chmn. emeritus area Ednl. TV Found. past pres., bd. dirs. Richman Freeman Meml. Clinic for Children; bd. dirs., v.p. Children's Med. Center; bd. dirs. Dallas Citizens Council, Central Bus. Dist. Assn; trustee DeGolyer Found., Tex. Research Found., E.O. Cartwright Found.; bd. dirs. So. Meth. U. Grad Assos., Southwestern Bus. Found. Mem. Dallas C. of C. (pres. 1966-67, dir.), Investment Bankers Assn. Am., Nat. Security Traders Assn., Assn. Stock Exchange Firms, Dallas Hist. Soc., Dallas Symphony Soc., Dallas Council World Affairs (past pres.). Mem. Christian Ch. Mason (33, Shriner), Rotarian. Clubs: Dallas Athletic, Dallas Petroleum, D.A.C. Country, Imperial, Brook Hollow Golf. Home: 6146 Yorkshire Dr Dallas TX 75230 Office: 1st Nat Bank Bldg Dallas TX 75202

CARTWRIGHT, GEORGE EASTMAN, med. educator; b. Lancaster, Wis., Dec. 1, 1917; s. Walter Clark and Vera (Eastman) C.; B.A., U. Wis., 1939; M.D., Johns Hopkins, 1943; m. Helene Cleare, Sept. 1, 1948; children—Jane Ann, Margaret Ann, Christine Ann, Candace Helene, Peter Edmund. Intern, Johns Hopkins, 1943-44, resident, 1944-45; practice medicine, specializing in internal medicine, Salt Lake City, 1947—; prof., head dept. medicine U. Utah Coll. Medicine, 1967—. Served to capt., M.C., AUS, 1945-47. Author: Diagnostic Laboratory Hematology, 1968. Home: 2870 Floribunda Dr Salt Lake City UT 84117

CARTWRIGHT, JAMES GLENN, utilities exec.; b. Hinton, Okla., Oct. 26, 1915; s. Oscar Glenn and Ella (Shawler) C.; B.S., Okla. State U., 1937; postgrad. Ga. Inst. Tech., 1964; m. Thelma Rosa Smith, Dec. 4, 1938; children—Clifford Glenn, Randall Joe. With Okla. Gas & Electric Co., Oklahoma City, 1937- -, asst. treas., 1962-65, asst. treas., asst. controller, 1965-69, controller, 1969—. Served to ensign USNR, 1942-45. Mem. Inst. Internal Auditors, Nat. Assn. Accountants (pres.), Edison Electric Inst., Missouri Valley Electric Assn., Kappa Tau Pi, Pi Gamma Mu, Phi Kappa Phi, Beta Alpha Psi. Baptist. Home: 3732 N W 69th Terrace Oklahoma City OK 73116 Office: 321 N Harvey Av Oklahoma City OK 73101

CARTWRIGHT, JOHN PHILIP, mfg. co. exec.; b. Ellwood City, Pa., June 7, 1926; s. Paul Joseph and Agnes (Johnson) C.; student Dartmouth, 1944-45; B.S. in Mech. Engring., U.S. Naval Acad., 1949; m. Dawn Denise Powell, Jan. 5, 1950; children —Caren Dawn, John Philip, Susan Crystal. With Joy Mfg. Co., 1950-61, v.p., 1958-61; operating v.p. Dresser Industries, Dallas, 1961-64; pres. Clark Bros. Co. subsidiary, 1963-64; exec. v.p. Studebaker Corp., 1964- 65; chmn. bd. Jet Air Products Co., Dallas, 1966—. Served to ensign USN, 1944-50. Mem. U.S. Naval Acad. Alumni Assn., Pa. Soc. Republican. Presbyn. Clubs: Duquesne (Pitts.); Petroleum, Brook Hollow Golf (Dallas). Home: 5131 DeLoache Av Dallas TX 75220 Office: 125 Majesty Dr Dallas TX 75201

CARTWRIGHT, OSCAR LING, museum curator; b. Sharpsville, Pa., Apr. 12, 1900; s. William Robert and Lydia Blanche (McDowell) C.; B.S. Allegheny Coll., 1923; M.Sc., Ohio State U., 1925; m. Sara Marie Richbourg, Dec. 18, 1928. Research entomologist S.C. Agr. Expt. Sta., 1925-45, 47; sanitarian USPHS, 1945- 46; asso. curator div. insects U.S. Nat. Mus., Smithsonian Instn., 1948- 63, curator coleoptera, dept. entomology, 1963-70, entomologist emeritus, 1970—. Spl. taxonomic research in Scarabaeidae; field studies, Tex., Costa Rica, 1951, Ariz., 1956, El Salvador, 1958, Fla., 1959, Andros, Bahamas, 1966. Recipient Smithsonian Service award, 1954. NSF grantee, 1963. Fellow Entomol. Soc. Am.; mem. Entomol. Soc. Washington, Assn. Tropical Biology, Biol. Soc. Washington, Soc. Systematic Zoology, A.A.A.S., Sigma Xi, Alpha Chi Rho, Phi Beta Phi, Gamma Alpha. Club: Cosmos (Washington). Contbr. numerous reports, articles to profl. lit. Home: 2110 Greenwich St Falls Church VA 22043 Office: Dept Entomology US Nat Mus Washington DC 20560

CARTWRIGHT, STEPHANIE DOROTHEA COY, textile designer; b. N.Y.C., Feb. 18, 1914; d. James Joseph and Esther (McGrann) Coy; William K. Vanderbilt scholar to study in France and Italy, 1931; student Paris br. Parsons Sch. Design, N.Y. Sch. Fine and Applied Art, 1932, also Columbia; m. Arnold Zavell, Feb. 15, 1946; children—Margot, Arnold. Designer window and interior displays Bonwit Teller; designer, stylist Susquehanna Silk Mills; with Fabrics by Cartwrights, div. Roth Fabrics; v.p. Coutoure Fabrics, Ltd., 1945-54, pres., 1954—, also dir.; v.p., dir. Pavillon Fabrics Corp., Fabric Mart Corp.; lectr. textile design Parsons Sch. Design, Fashion Group of Am. Career Course. Mem. N.Y. fund-raising coms. N.Y. Infirmary, Comeback, Inc., Kidney Disease Found.; vice chmn. adv. council LaGuardia House Nursery; vol. painting class Yorkville Youth Council. Bd. overseers Parsons Sch. Design; bd. govs. Boys and Girls Service League. Recipient Cover Design award Art et Industrie, 1932; gold medal Cal. Fair Textile Expn., 1953-55. Mem. Council Fashion Designers Am. (charter), Parsons Alumni Assn. (council, pres. 1959), Republican Women in Industry and Professions (past pres. N.Y. chpt.), Women's Nat. Fashion Group Am. (legislative com., past chmn. membership com. N.Y.), Nat. Council Women, Internat. Platform Assn., N.Y. Advt. Club. Club: York. Contbr. chpt. to Your Future in Fashion Design, 1966. Home: 912 Fifth Av New York City NY 10021 Office: 1040 6th Av New York City NY 10018

CARTWRIGHT, WALTER JOSEPH, educator; b. Carona, Kan., Apr. 26, 1922; s. James William and Agnes (Whitehead) C.; student Texarkana Coll., 1939-41; A.B., So. Meth. U., 1943, M.Th., 1946; M.A., U. Tex., 1960, Ph.D., 1964; m. Elizabeth Daniel Atkins, June 6, 1948; children—Joseph Daniel, Deborah. Ordained to ministry Meth. Ch., 1944; pastor, McLeod-Lodi, Tex., 1944-45, Douglassville, Tex., 1945-47, Mount Pleasant West-Side, Tex., 1948, Johnson City, Tex., 1948-49, Hebbrenville, Tex., 1949-52, Weimar, Tex., 1952-55, Goldthwaite, Tex., 1955-58, Bastrop, Tex., 1958-62; asst. prof. Tex. Tech. U., Lubbock, 1962-65, asso. prof., 1965-68, prof., chmn. dept. sociology and anthropology, 1968—. Cons. Tex. Commn. on Alcoholism, 1965-67; mem. projects bd. Internat. Center Arid and Semi-Arid Land Studies, 1968—, Lubbock Met. Council Govts. Com. Crime Prevention, 1966-70, Tech. Adv. Com. Canyon Lakes Project, Lubbock, 1970-71, manpower com. Lubbock County Community Action Agy. Office Equal Opportunity, 1967-70. Bd. dirs. Golden Age Home, Lockhart, Tex., Coordinating Bd. Tex. Coll. and Univ. System. Mem. Am., So., Southwestern Sociol. systems, Law and Soc. Assn., Rocky Mountain, Southwestern social sci. assns., Am. Assn. U. Profs. Author: (with Mhyra S. Minnis) Sociological Perspectives, 1968. Contbr. articles to profl. jours. Home: 5417 8th Pl Lubbock TX 79416 Office: P O Box 4509 Lubbock TX 79409

CARTWRIGHT, WILLIAM HOLMAN, educator; b. Pine Island, Minn., Sept. 12, 1915; s. William Holman and Ada Caroline (Frisbie) C.; B.S., U. Minn., 1937, M.A., 1942, Ph.D., 1950; m. Elaine Mary McGladrey, Sept. 3, 1934; children—John Morris, Mary Elaine, Margaret Ann. Dairy farmer, 1934-36; tchr. pub. sch., Mabel, Minn., 1937-40, Rochester, Minn., 1940-43; tchr. Univ. High Sch., Mpls., 1943-45; instr. U. Minn., 1943-45, Macalester Coll., 1944; historian Mil. Dist., Washington, 1945-46; asst. prof. edn. Boston U., 1946-50, asso. prof., 1950-51; prof. edn. Duke, 1951—, chmn. dept. edn., 1951-65, 67-70. Vis. prof. summers U. Cal., 1950, U. Colo., 1957; curriculum cons.; staff Study of Edn. Am. Tchrs., 1961-63. Recipient Army Commendation Ribbon for hist. writing, 1946; Outstanding Achievement award U. Minn., 1959. Mem. Nat. Council Social Studies (pres. 1957), So. Council on Tchr. Edn. (pres. 1959), Am. Hist. Assn., N.E.A., Am. Assn. U. Profs., N.E. History Tchrs. Assn. (pres. 1949-50), N.C. Council Social Studies, N.C. Edn. Assn., Phi Delta Kappa, Phi Alpha Theta, Pi Gamma Mu, Kappa Delta Pi. Unitarian. Author: A History of Newburg Township and the Village of Mabel, 1943; The Military District of Washington during the War Years, 1946; (with Arthur C. Bining) The Teaching of History in the United States, 1950; (with Miriam E. Mason) Trailblazers of American History, 1961, rev. 1966; (with Oscar O. Winther) The Story of Our Heritage, 1962, last rev. edit., 1970; (with Edgar B. Wesley) Teaching Social Studies in Elementary Schools, 1968; also chpts. in yearbooks The National Council Social Studies; numerous articles, revs. ednl., hist. publs. Editor: (with Richard L. Watson) Interpeting and Teaching American History, 1961. Home: 3610 Britt St Durham NC 22705

CARTY, JOHN N., elevator co. exec.; b. Phila., Nov. 10, 1920; s. Harry A. and K. Ethel (Adelhelm) C.; B.S., Drexel Inst. Tech., 1942; m. Ann Marie Kenney, Nov. 29, 1947; children—James D., Janice A., Carol M. Asst. treas., treas. Continental Can Co., N.Y.C., 1946-65; treas. Eastern Airlines, N.Y.C., 1965-67; treas. Otis Elevator Co., N.Y.C., 1967—. Served to 1st lt., C.E., AUS, 1943-46; ETO. Club: Treasurers, Union League (N.Y.C.); Patterson (Westport). Home: 146 Bayberry Lane Westport, CT 06880. Office: 260 11th Av New York City NY 10001

CARTY, JOHN VICTOR, utility exec.; b. N.Y.C., Apr. 12, 1904; m. Edna M. Lynch, 1928 (dec.); m. 2d, Ruth E. Riddle, 1960. With Ohio Water Service Co., 1935—, v.p., sec., 1945-52, exec. v.p., 1952-63, pres., treas., 1963-69, chmn. bd., 1969—, also dir. Mem. Am. Water Works Assn., C. of C. Kiwanian. Club: Youngstown. Home: 131 Diana Dr Poland OH 44514 Office: 235 State St Struthers OH 44471

CARTY, ROLAND KENNETH, corp. exec.; b. Midland, Ont., Can., Jan. 5, 1919; s. Roland Dennis and Kenina (Morrison) C.; B.Com., Queen's U., 1941; m. Catherine Elizabeth Matheson, Sept. 26, 1942; children—Roland Kenneth, Donald John, Robert Matheson, William George, Douglas Alan, Carolyn Elizabeth. With Canadian Gen. Electric Co., 1941-42, 46-48, 52-55, dist. mgr., Toronto, Ont., 1952-55; sec.-treas. Canadian Allis Chalmers, Montreal, Que., 1949-51; with Canron, Ltd., Montreal, 1955—, v.p. finance, 1962-65, exec. v.p. finance, 1965—. Bd. dirs. Que. div. Canadian Nat. Inst. Blind. Served to flight lt. RCAF, 1942-45. Mem. United Ch. Can. Clubs: Canadian, University St. Jame's (Montreal). Home: 220 Surrey Dr Mount Royal 304 Quebec Canada Office: 1120 Place Ville Marie Montreal Quebec Canada

CARTY, WALTER VINCENT, pub. relations exec.; b. Boston, Jan. 22, 1927; s. John and Mary Ellen (Moran) C.; B.S., Boston Coll., 1951; postgrad. Harvard, 1952; m. Sally Clarke, Sept. 14, 1957; children—Mary Ellen, Elizabeth Seton, Jennifer Jane, Michael Clarke, Thomas More. Corr., Boston Herald-Traveler, 1948-50; columnist, editor Boston Pilot, 1950-52; reporter-writer Time-Life Publs., N.Y.C., 1952-54; asso. editor Curtis Publs., N.Y.C., 1954; with John Moynahan & Co., Inc., N.Y.C., 1955—, now pres.; lectr. A.M.A., N.Y.U. Capt., United Fund of Larchmont, 1967-70. Bd. dirs. Mens Club, St. Augustines, Larchmont, 1963-66. Served with USNR, 1944-46. Mem. Pub. Relations Soc. Am. (program chmn. N.Y. chpt. 1962, 64, 68, program chmn. nat. conf. Atlanta 1970, dir. N.Y. chpt. 1969, pres. 1971-72. Contbr. articles profl. jours. Home: 6 Soundview Dr Larchmont NY 10538 Office: 155 E 44th St New York City NY 10017

CARUCCI, SAMUEL ANTHONY, lawyer; b. Bronx, N.Y., Dec. 16, 1935; s. Anthony and Rose (Russo) C.; B.S., N.Y.U., 1956; LL.B., St. John's U., 1959; m. Joan Elizabeth Kelly, Aug. 18, 1962; children—Patricia, Caroline, Samuel. Admitted to N.Y. bar, 1960; asst. legal counsel, asst. sec. Royal McBee Corp., 1963-65; counsel office communications equipment group Litton Industries, N.Y.C., 1968—; counsel Litton Industries Credit Corp., 1965—. Served with AUS, 1959-60. Mem. Am. Bar Assn., N.Y. State Bar Assn., Bar Assn. City N.Y., Assn. Comml. Finance Attys., Phi Lambda Phi, Delta Theta Phi. Roman Catholic. Home: 21 Herkimer Av Jericho NY 11753 Office: 850 3d Av New York City NY 10022

CARUS, HERMAN DIETRICH, business exec.; b. LaSalle, Ill., Feb. 26, 1899; s. Paul and Marie (Hegeler) C.; student Haverford (Pa.) Coll., 1917-18, Mass. Inst. Tech., 1918; Ph.B., U. Chgo., 1921; student Sch. Mines, Freiberg, Germany, 1922- 23; m. Emily Roxana Chadbourne, 1940; 1 son, Frederick Leonard. Research chemist Carus Chem. Co., 1923-24, v.p., dir., 1924-67; mineral exploration M & H Zinc Co., Joplin, Mo., 1925-28; research dept. Matthiessen & Hegeler Zinc Co., LaSalle, 1928-30, chief research, 1930-33, plant supt., 1934-40, v.p., treas., dir., 1940-49, pres., 1949-64, chmn. bd., chief exec. officer, 1964-70, also dir.; pres., dir. LaSalle & Bureau County R.R. Co., 1937-67, Carusbrooke Farms, Inc., 1958—; chmn. bd. Apollo Metals, Chgo., Mowes Seed Co., Granville, Ill.; dir. Willroy Mines Ltd. Mem. Internat. Lead and Zinc Research Orgn. (past dir.) Am. Inst. Mining, Metall. and Petroleum Engrs., Am. Soc. Metals, Am. Iran and Steel Inst., Ill. Mfrs. Assn. (dir. 1958), Zinc Inst. (v.p.), Ill. Valley Indsl. Assn. Clubs: Union League, Cliff Dwellers (Chgo.); Deer Park Fishing, Deer Park Golf (La Salle); St. Joseph River Yacht. Home: 2209 Elmwood Rd Peru IL 61354 Office: care M & H Zinc Co Box 463 LaSalle IL 61301

CARUSI, EUGENE CASSIN, lawyer; b. Washington, June 3, 1905; s. Charles Francis and Marie (Cassin) C.; B.S., U.S. Naval Acad., 1928; LL.B., Nat. U., 1934, LL.D., 1954; m. Cecil Perry, Mar. 1, 1933. Admitted to D.C. bar, 1935; asst. U.S. atty., Washington, 1935-38; practice law, Washington, 1938-41, 46—. Mem. adv. com. USCG Acad., New London, 1951, chmn. com., 1955; trustee George Washington U., 1954—. Served from ensign to lt. (j.g.) USN, 1928-31; comdr. USNR, 1941-46, comdg. officer 6th Beach Bn., Normandy Beach, June 1944. Decorated Silver Star, Purple Heart, Croix de Guerre, others. Mem. D.C. Bar Assn. (dir. 1961-63). Home: 4800 Dexter St NW Washington DC 20007 Office: 1629 K St NW Washington, DC 20006.

CARUSO, MARIANO, tenor; appearances with Met. Opera and Chgo. Lyric Opera. Address: care Metropolitan Opera 147 W 39th St New York City NY 10018 *

CARUTH, WILLIAM WALTER, Jr., investment co. exec.; b. Dallas, Feb. 11, 1912; s. William Walter and Earle (Clark) C.; B.S., So. Meth. U., 1933; M.B.A., Harvard, 1935; m. Mabel Morrow Peters, Jan. 2, 1936; children—William Walter III, George Peters, John Clark, Robert Morrow. Pres. Caruth Bldg. Service, 1936—, Caruth Corp., 1947—, Kaywood Corp., 1942-65, Climax Timber Co., 1943-70, Park Cities Corp., 1951—, Hillside Corp., 1953—, Central Control Co., 1959—, Central Land Co., 1959—, Saber Ranch Co., 1959-66, Lande Co., 1960-71, Caruth Properties, Inc., 1958—, Dolphin Houseboats Inc. (Fla.), Dolphin Properties, Inc., St. Petersburg; dir. Tex. Industries, Brookhollow Properties, Southwestern Financial Co. Past mem. exec. bd. Urban Land Inst.; pres. Caruth Found.; bds. dirs. Wadley Research Inst. Molecular Medicine, Caruth Meml. Rehab. Center; trustee Hillcrest Found. Mem. Phi Delta Thera, Phi Delta Sigma, Alpha Kappa Psi. Cycen Fjodr. Presbyn. (deacon). Clubs: Dallas, Dallas Country; St. Petersburg Yacht. Home: 7411 Greenbrier Dr Dallas TX 75225 Office: 5803 Greenville Av Dallas TX 75206

CARUTHERS, OSGOOD, journalist; b. Raton, N.M., Jan. 2, 1915; s. John L. and Mary (Osgood) C.; student Bucknell U., 1931; m. Rosemarie Falcone, Dec. 8, 1945. Reporter, Denver Post, 1935-40; corr. Middle East, Balkans, London, then fgn. news desk editor A.P., 1945-55; corr. Middle East and USSR, N.Y. Times, 1955-61; pres. dir., spokesman for sec. gen. UN, 1961-65; corr., Germany, East Europe, Los Angeles Times, 1965—. Served to capt. USAAF, 1941-45; PTO. Decorated Air medal with oak leaf cluster. Mem. Kappa Sigma. Club: Overseas (v.p. 1965) (N.Y.C.). Home: Europastrasse 10 Bad Godesberg West Germany Office: Heussalle 18 Bonn West Germany

CARUTHERS, REXFORD HENRY, lawyer; b. Louisville, July 28, 1923; s. Alberdina (Vieweg) C.; B.S. in Pub. Adminstrn., Washington U., St. Louis, 1947, LL.B., 1949; m. Megan Ruth O'Connor, July 28, 1963; children—Rexford Henry, Regan O'Conner. Admitted to Mo. bar, 1949, since practiced in St. Louis; mem. firm Guilford, Caruthers, Symington, Montrey & Petzall; now mem. firm Lashy, Caruthers, Rava, Hyndman & Rutherford. Faculty, Wash. U. Law Sch., 1952—. Pres., Legal Aid Soc. St. Louis and St. Louis County, 1965-66; bd. govs. Mo. bar, 1966—. Served to capt., inf. AUS, 1942-46. Recipient Trial Lawyer's award Mo. Bar Found., 1956. Mem. Bar Assn. St. Louis (pres. 1964-65), Am., Mo. bar assns., Am. Law Inst., Order of Coif. Democrat. Home: 230 S Brentwood Blvd St Louis MO 63105 Office: 818 Olive St St Louis MO 63101

CARUTHERS, ROBERT MACK, educator, petroleum engr.; b. Shreveport, La., Jan. 19, 1938; s. John DeWitt and Veva (Ozley) C.; B.S. in Liberal Arts, La. Tech. U., 1960, B.S. in Petroleum Engring., 1961; Ph.D., U. Tex., 1965; m. Valleau Renee Resweber, June 25, 1960; children—Carol Renee, Aimee Katharine, Shelton DeWitt. Reservoir engr. Humble Oil & Refining Co., Dallas, 1965, New Orleans, 1965-67; head, dept. petroleum engring. La. Tech. U., Ruston, 1967—. Chmn. Lincoln Parish chpt. A.R.C., 1968-70. Bd. dirs., treas. Wesley Found.; v.p. La. Tech. Alumni Found. Registered profl. engr., La. Mem. Am. Inst. M.E. (edn. and accrediation com. of Soc. of Petroleum Engrs. sect.), Am. Soc. Engring. Edn., La. Engring. Soc. Home: 430 Forest Circle Ruston LA 71270

CARVEL, ELBERT NOSTRAND, ex.-gov. Del., fertilizer co. exec.; b. Shelter Island Heights, N.Y., Feb. 9, 1910;; s. Arnold Wrightson and Elizabeth (Nostrand) C.; engring. course, Balt. Poly. Inst., 1924-28; LL.B., U. Balt., 1931; m. Ann Hall Valliant, Dec. 17, 1932; children—Elizabeth Nostrand (Mrs. Charles L. Palmer), Edwin Valliant, Ann Hall, Barbara Jean. Sales engr. Consol. Gas and Electric Power and Light Co., Balt., 1931-36; gen. mgr. and dir. Valliant Fertilizer Co., Laurel, Del., 1936-45, pres. 1945—; dir. Milford Fertilizer Co., Del., 1937—, v.p., 1941-59, chmn. bd., 1959—; chmn. Fischer Enterprises, 1969—; v.p. Laurel Grain Co.; dir. Peoples Bank and Trust Co. Lt. gov. Del., 1945-49, gov., 1949-53, 61-65; Vice pres. Del. Safety Council; exec. bd. Delmarva council Boy Scouts Am.; mem. Del. Bicentennial Commn., 1968—; pres. Del. Bd. Pardons, 1945-49. Chmn. Del. Democratic Com., 1946-47, 54 -56; del. Dem. Nat. Conv., 1948, 52, 56, 60, 64; jointly nominated Adlai Stevaison Dem. candidate for pres. nat. conv., 1952; chmn. Del. Dem. Renewal Commn., 1970; Dem. candidate U.S. Senate, Del., 1958, 64; chmn. Del. Const. Revision Commn.; mem. Dem. League, Wilmington, Del. Trustee U. Del., U. Balt.; chmn. March of Dimes of Del., 1951- 62. Mem. exec. com. Govs.' Conf., 1950-51, 62-63. Decorated comdr. Order Orange Nassau (Netherlands); recipient Good Govt. award Com. of 39, Wilmington, Good Citizenship medal Nat. Soc. S.A.R., 1967, Vrooman award Prisoners Aid Soc. Del., 1965, Silver Beaver award Boy Scouts Am., 1970. Mem. Lewes, Milford hist. socs., Wilmington Savs. Fund Soc. Am. Contract Bridge League, Del. Hist. Soc., Sussex County Laymen's League, Am. Soc. Agronomy, Del. Ducks Unlimited, Swedish Colonial Soc. Del., Sigma Delta Kappa, Alpha Zeta. Episcopalian (del. gen. conv. 1946, 52). Mason (33, Shriner), Lion. Clubs: Church, Seaford Golf and Country, Tail Cedars of Lebanon, Sussex County Whist, Antique Automobile of America, Del. Motor, Queen Anne Golf. Address: Box 111 Laurel DE 11956

CARVER, DALE RINGWALT, educator; b. Oakely, Kan., Sept. 21, 1923; s. Harleigh Dean and Ruth Dorcas (Ringwalt) C.; B.S. in Civil Engring., Kan. State Coll., 1946, M.S. in Applied Mechanics, 1949; Ph.D., U. Ill., 1952; m. Irva Miller Smith, June 28, 1947; children—Carol Lee, Nancy Lynn, Barbara Anne, Susan Dale, David Ringwalt. Instr. applied mechanics Kan. State Coll., 1946-50, asso. prof., 1952-54; instr. theoretical and applied mechanics U. Ill., 1950-52; prof., head dept. engring. sci La. State U., 1954—; structural research engr. Convair, Ft. Worth, summer 1956; research participant Oak Ridge Inst. Nuclear Studies, 1959, 60. Pres. Stress Analysis, Inc., Baton Rouge. Served from pvt. to 1st lt., inf., AUS, 1943-46. Decorated Silver Star. Mem. Am. Soc. M.E., Am. Soc. Engring. Edn., Sigma Xi, Phi Kappa Phi, Tau Betta Pi. Author papers on theoretical mechanics. Research dynamic loading of structures and thick shells. Reviewer Applied Mechanics Revs. Home: 1645 Ingleside Dr Baton Rouge LA 70808

CARVER, EUGENE PENDLETON, Jr., lawyer; b. Arlington, Mass., Nov. 9, 1891; s. Eugene P. and Clare (Porter) C.; A.B., Harvard, 1913, LL.B., 1916; student U. London (Eng.), 1919; m. Dorothy Bell, Sept. 20, 1917. Admitted to Mass. bar. 1916, since practiced in Boston. Selectmen, Town of Brookline, Mass., 1942-60. Served as sgt. Mexican Border, 1916, as 1st lt. U.S. Army, 1917-18. Mem. V.F.W. (past comdr.-in-chief), S.A.R. (past nat. pres. gen.). Soc. War 1812 (past nat. pres. gen.), D.A.V., Mass. Soc. Mayflower Descendants. Mason (Shriner), Elk (past exalted ruler, dist. dept.). Home: 15 Buckminster Rd Brookline MA 02146 Office: 84 State St Boston MA 02109

CARVER, FREDERICK LEWIS, lawyer; b. Bklyn., Dec. 31, 1896; s. John and Gertrude (Goeltz) C.; LL.B., N.Y.U., 1918; m. Carol Kane, Aug. 22, 1922; children—Frederick Carrol, Robert Quentin. Admitted to N.Y. bar, 1919, since practiced in N.Y.C.; with firm Sage, Gray, Todd & Sims, and predecessor, 1911-69, sr. partner now ret. Served with U.S. Army, World War I. Mem. Assn. Bar City N.Y., N.Y., Bklyn. bar assns., Am. Legion. K.C. Home: 1047 E 3d St Brooklyn NY 11230 Office: 40 Wall St New York City NY 10005

CARVER, GEORGE ALLEN, ret. army officer; b. Rome, Ga., Feb. 27, 1909; s. William and Rose Ella (Kelley) C.; B.S., U.S. Mil. Acad., 1933; grad. F.A. Schs., 1938, 40, 43, Command and Gen. Staff Coll., 1948, Armed Forces Staff Coll., 1951, Army War Coll., 1956; m. Barbara Ellen Bristol, Mar. 3, 1937; children—Barbara Bristol (Mrs. William H. Schneider), George Allen. Commd. 2d lt., F.A., U.S. Army, 1933, advanced through grades to maj. gen., 1962; comdr. 155 MM Howitzer Battalion, 42d Inf. Div., ETO, World War II; assigned staff U.S. Forces in Austria, Vienna, 1946-47; instr. Command and Gen. Staff Coll., 1948-50; comdr. 18th F.A. Group in Europe, 1953-54, 2d Guided Missile Group, 1956-57, U.S. Army Tng. Center, Air Def., Ft. Bliss Tex., 1957-59; comdg. gen. 1st Guided Missile Brigade, Ft. Bliss, 1959-60, 7th Inf. Div., Arty, Korea, 1960-61; chief arty. officers div. Dept. Army, 1961-62; comdg. gen. IV U.S. Army Corps., Miss., Ala., and Fla., 1962-65; comdg. gen. U.S. Army Alaska, 1965-66; dir. Army Emergency Relief, Dept. Army, Washington, 1966—. Decorated Legion of Merit, D.S.M., Bronze Star with oak leaf cluster, various service and area ribbons. Recipient D.S.M., service medal State of Ala. Mem. Assn. Grads. U.S. Mil. Acad., Assn. U.S. Army, Am. Ordnance Assn., Res. Officers Assn. (Distinguished Service citation), Am. Legion. Protestant Episcopalian. Mason. Home: 3333 N Albermarie St Arlington VA 22207 Office: Army Emergency Relief Dept Army Washington DC 20315

CARVER, JOHN ALFRED, Jr., govt. ofcl.; b. Preston, Ida., Apr. 24, 1918; s. John Alfred and La Verne (Olson) C.; A.B., Brigham Young U., 1939; LL.B., Georgetown U., 1947; m. Ruth Patricia O'Connor, June 7, 1942; children—John Alfred III, Craig, Candace Elaine. With various depts. U.S. Govt., 1940-47; admitted to Ida. and D.C. bars, 1946; asst. atty. gen. Ida., 1947-48; practice law, Boise, Ida., 1948-56; adminstrv. asst. to U.S. Senator Church, 1957- 61; asst. sec. interior pub. land mgmt., 1961-64, under sec. interior, 1964-66; commr. FPC, 1966—. Served with USAAF, 1943- 46. Mem. Am., Fed., Ida. bar assns. Home: 4421 25th St N Arlington VA 22207 Office: GAO Bldg 441 G St NW Washington DC 20426

CARVER, NORMAN F., Jr., architect, photographer; grad. Yale; m. Joan Willson; children—Norman III, Cristina. Practice architecture, Kalamazoo; vis. lectr., critic Carnegie Inst. Tech., Mich. State U., Yale, Mass. Inst. Tech.; exhibited photography U.S. and abroad; photographs pub. in Apertrure, House Beautiful, Horizon, others. Recipient Fulbright awards to Japan, 1953- 54, 64; silver medal Archtl. League 1962; award Archtl. Record, 1960, 61, 62. Author: Form and Space of Japanese Architecture (photographs of Japan), 1955; Silent Cities, Mexico and the Maya, (photog. study ancient Mayan and Mexican architecture), 1966. Address: 3201 Lorraine Kalamazoo MI 49001

CARVER, THOMAS RIPLEY, physicist, educator; b. Rochester, N.Y., Mar. 6, 1929; s. Emmett Kirkendall and Ruth (Ripley) C.; A.B., Harvard, 1950; Ph.D., U. Ill., 1954; M.A., Oxford (Eng.) U., 1964; m. Eleanore Bie Benson, Feb. 5, 1951;; children—Davis Benson, Alison. Instr., U. Ill., 1954; faculty Princeton, (N.J.), 1954—, prof., physics, 1967—. Cons. to industry, 1954—. Sloan fellow, 1956-58; Guggenheim fellow, 1964-65. Fellow Am. Phys. Soc.; mem. Am. Assn. Physics Tchrs., Sigma Xi (local sec. 1966-68). Research on dynamic nuclear polarization, gas cell atomic clocks, spin transmission resonance, magnetic resonance, optical pumping, solid state physics. Home: 374 Cherry Hill Rd Princeton NJ 08540

CARY, CHARLES, lawyer; b. Buffalo, Oct. 24, 1916; s. George and Allithea (Birge) C.; B.S., Harvard, 1939; LL.D., U. Va., 1942; m. Rhoda G. Coogan, Feb. 1, 1947; children—Charles C., George G., Trumbull, Thomas C. Admitted to N.Y. bar, 1947, since practiced in Buffalo. First v.p. Buffalo and Erie County Planning Assn., 1955. Dir., mem. art com. Albright-Knox Art Gallery; dir., v.p. Buffalo Hist. Soc., 1949-67; mem. overseers com. to visit dept. fine arts Harvard, 1967-69. Served to lt. comdr. USNR, World War II. Mem. Harvard Alumni Assn. (nat. regional dir. 1966-69), Newcomen Soc., Phi Delta Phi. Episcopalian. (vestryman). Clubs: Harvard (pres. 1956), Saturn (Buffalo,); Fly (Cambridge, Mass.); River (N.Y.C.); Ft. Erie Jockey (bd. dirs.). Home: Sweet Rd East Aurora NY 14052 Office: Marine Trust Bldg Buffalo NY 14203

CARY, CHARLES OSWALD, govt. ofcl.; b. Boston, July 10, 1917; s. Charles P. and Adeline J. (Oswald) C.; student Northeastern U., 1937-39, Mass. Inst. Tech., 1941- 42; m. Jean M. Cochran, May 8, 1948; children—Peter Cochran, Jean Scott, Anne, Charles, Elizabeth. With comml. airlines, 1936-44; exec. asst. to chmn. CAB, 1944-46; spl. asst. to asst. sec. navy for air, 1946-48; mem. Civil Transp. Aircraft Evaluation and Devel. Bd., 1948-49; exec. sec. Air Coordinating Com., 1949-54; gen. sec. Air Transp. Moblzn. Survey, Nat. Security Resources Bd., 1950-51; dep. adminstr. Def. Air Transp. Adminstrn., 1951-54; dir. marketing electronics div. Curtiss-Wright Corp., 1954-63; v.p. Hazeltine Corp., 1963-65; asst. adminstr. dept. transp. FAA, 1965—. Mem. U.S. delegation 1st assembly Provisional Internat. Civil Aviation Orgn., 1946, mem. U.S. delegations assemblies, 1947, 51, 53, 70; cons. to adminstr. FAA, 1963. Asso. fellow Am. Inst. Aeros. and Astronautics; mem. Acad. Polit. Sci. Clubs: Wings (N.Y.C.); University, Congressional, National Aviation (Washington). Home: 7703 Arrowwood Ct Bethesda MD 20034 Office: 800 Independence Av SW Washington DC 20590

CARY, FRANK TAYLOR, bus. machines co. exec.; b. Gooding, Ida., Dec. 14, 1920; s. Frank Taylor and Ida C.; B.S., U. Cal. at Los Angeles, 1943; M.B.A., Stanford, 1948; m. Anne Curtis, 1943; children—Marshall, Bryan, Steven, Laura. With IBM, 1948—. dist. mgr., San Francisco, 1957-61, pres. Service Bur. Corp., N.Y.C., 1959-61, asst. dir. corporate staff, 1961-62, v.p. data processing div., White Plains, N.Y., 1962-64, pres., 1964—. v.p., group exec., 1966-, now sr. v.p., Armonk, N.Y. Served with AUS, 1944- 46. Home: 6 Haskell Lane Darien CT 06820 Office: IBM Corp Armonk NY 10504

CARY, FRENCH STROTHER, Jr., advt. exec.; b. El Paso, Tex., Mar. 18, 1912; s. French Strother and Edith (Jones) C.; Ph.B., U. Chgo, 1934; m. Barbara Fortune, Nov. 26, 1936; children—Eliza (Mrs. Peter Hatton), French Strother III. With Erwin, Wasy, Ltd., 1934-35; with Leo Burnett Co., Chgo, 1935—, successively office boy, copywriter, account exec. 1935-52, adminstrv. v.p., 1952-58, dir., 1955—, vice chmn. exec. com., 1956-70, exec. v.p., 1970—, also treas. dir. Leo Burnett Internat. Ltd., London, Eng., Richard Heath, Ltd., London, Leo Burnett Co. of Canada, Ltd. Jackson-Wain Pty., Sydney, Australia. Past dir. Off The Street Club for Boys; life trustee, past vice chmn., mem. exec. com. Ravinia Festival Assn.; mem. alumni council Sch. Bus. Adminstrn., mem. citizens com. U. Chgo., trustee, bd. dirs., v.p. U. Chgo. Cancer Research Found. Served to lt. comdr. 7th Amphibious Force, USNR, World War II. Mem. Chicago Art Inst. (life), Am. Assn. Advt. Agys. (dir., gov.), Internat. Advt. Assn., Brit. Am. C. of C., Am. C. of C. in France, Chgo. Hist. Soc. (life), Chgo. Orch. Assn. (governing mem.), Chgo. Zool. Soc., Pi Alpha Mu, Alpha Delta Phi. Episcopalian. Clubs: University, Mid-America, Arts, Executives (Chgo.); Bird Key Yacht, Field (Sarasota, Fla.). Home: 1153 Pine St Winnetka IL 60093 also Sarasota FL 33577 Office: Prudential Plaza Chicago IL 60601

CARY, HENRY HOWARD, mfg. co. exec.; b. Los Angeles, May 3, 1908; s. Henry Gardner and Bessie Howard (Brown) C.; B.S., Cal. Inst. Tech., 1930; m. Barbara Ward, July 22, 1933. Sec.-treas. H.G. Cary Corp., Los Angeles, 1930-32: v.p., gen. mgr. Allied Pipe Corp., Los Angeles, 1932-35; engr. instruments devel. Nat. Tech. Lab., div. Beckman Instruments, 1935-37; v.p. charge devel. Beckman Instruments, 1937-46; pres. Cary Instruments (formerly Applied Physics Corp.), Monrovia, Cal., 1946-68, chmn. bd., 1968-70; v.p. Research Instruments Corp., Pasadena, Cal., 1949- 62; dir. Varian Assos., 1961—. Mem. Tau Beta Pi. Clubs: Altadena (Cal.) Town and Country; Balboa Bay (Cal.); Jamaica Tennis (Carona Del Mar, Cal.); Jonathan, Electronic (Los Angeles). Office: 2724 S Peck Rd Monrovia CA 91016

CARY, JOHN BURROUGHS, mil. analyst; b. Emporia, Kan., Nov. 11, 1911; s. Harvey M. and Cora (Webster) C.; B.S., U.S. Mil. Acad., 1934; grad. Nat. War Coll., 1950; m. Theresa Russo, Sept. 22, 1951. Comm. 2d lt. U.S. Army, 1934. advanced through grades to maj. gen., USAF, 1956; served with 7th, 5th. 13th Bomb Groups, Hawaii and U.S., 1935-41; assigned Hdqrs. 3d Air Force, 1942-43, War Dept., 1943, Southeast Asia Command, 1943-44; dep. chief strategy and policy group, gen. staff. War Dept. 1944-46; asst. chief staff for plans Air Def. Command, 1946-47; assigned directorate of plans Hdqrs. USAF, 1947-49; dir. plans 8th Air Force, 1950; chief plans div. USAF, Europe, 1951-52; dir. operations SHAPE, 1952-54; comdr. 35th Air Div. (Def.) Air Def. Command, 1954-56; dir. plans Hdqrs. USAF, 1956- 58; dep. chief staff plans and operations, Hdqrs. PACAF, 1958-61; analyst Inst. for Def. Analyses, Washington, 1961-; cons. to dir. U.S. Arms Control & Disarmament Agy., 1961-63; cons. Dept. Def., 1962. Decorated D.S.M., Legion of Merit, Commendation Ribbon, Mem. Washington Inst. for Fgn. Affairs, Inst. for Strategic Studies (London), Council on Fgn. Relations. Clubs: Army and Navy Country (Arlington, Va.) Army- Navy (Washington). Office: Inst Defense Analyses 400 Army-Navy Dr Arlington, VA 22202.

CARY, JOHN H., educator, historian; b. Eau Claire, Wis., May 4, 1926; s. John Bernard and Mary Ann (Beschta) C.; B.S., U. Wis., 1950; M.A., Pa. State U., 1951; Ph.D. (Univ. fellow 1952-53, Babcock fellow 1954-55), U. Ill., 1959; m. Kathryn Marie Ditter, June 9, 1956; children—Sean Bernard, Paul Alexander, Kenneth George, Carolyn Ann. Instr., DePaul U., 1955-57; asst. prof. Mich. State U., 1958-63; head dept. history Lehigh U., 1963- 66, prof. history, 1965-67; prof., chmn. dept history Cleve. State U., 1967—; cons. Nat. Park Service. 1964-65. Served with USAAF, 1944-46. Mem. Am. Hist. Assn., Ohio Hist. Soc., Conf. of British Studies, Orgn. Am. Historians, Conf. Early Am. History. Author: Joseph Warren: Physician, Politician, Patriot, 1961. Home: 3368 Blanche Av Cleveland Heights, OH 44118. Office: Dept of History Cleve State U Cleveland OH 44115

CARY, VERONICA FRANCES, librarian; b. N.Y.C., Feb. 8, 1911; d. James J. and Wanda (Plawska) Cary; :A.B., Douglas Coll., 1933; B.S. in L.S., Columbia, 1945. Gen. asst. Trenton (N.J.) Free Library, 1935-46, chief circulation, 1946-56, dir., 1961—; field cons. N.J. State Library, 1956-61. Bd. dirs. Trenton YMCA, 1964—. Mem. Am., N.J. (pres. 1965-66) library assns., Am. Assn. U. Women (pres. Trenton 1944-46). Club: Zonta. Home: 230 Garfield Av Trenton, NJ 08629. Office: 120 Academy St Trenton NJ 08608

CARY, WILLIAM LUCIUS, lawyer, educator; b. Columbus, O., Nov. 27, 1910; s. William Lincoln and Ellen (Taugher) C.; A.B., Yale, 1931, LL.B., 1934; M.B.A., Harvard, 1938; LL.D., Amherst, 1965; m. Katherine L.F. Cooper, 1954; children—Linn F.C., Katherine F.C. Admitted to Ohio bar, 1934, also Mass., D.C., N.Y., Ill. bars; atty. Squire, Sanders & Dempsey, Cleve., 1934-36, SEC, Washington, 1938-40; spl. asst. to atty. gen. tax div. Dept. Justice, Washington, 1940-42; counsel Office Coordinator of Inter-Am. Affairs, Brazil, 1942; lectr. finance, law Harvard Grad. Sch. Bus. Adminstrn., 1946-47; prof. law Northwestern U. Sch. Law, 1947-55; prof. law Columbia, 1955—, Dwight prof. law, 1964—. Vis. prof. U. Cal. at Berkeley, summer 1950, Stanford, summer 1954, Yale, 1957-58; dir. Newark (O.) Telephone Co.; counsel Patterson, Belknap & Webb. Chmn., SEC, 1961-64. Served as maj. USMCR; with OSS, Rumania and Yugoslavia, 1944-45; dep. dept. counsellor for procurement, Dept. Army, 1951. Trustee Robert Coll., Istanbul, Turkey. Mem. Am., N.Y. bar assns., Am. Law Inst., Am. Acad. Arts and Scis., Phi Beta Kappa. Presbyn. Clubs: Century (N.Y.); Metropolitan (Washington). Co-author: Effects of Taxation on Corporate Mergers, 1951; The Law and the Lore of Endowment Funds, 1969. Author: Politics and the Regulatory Agencies, 1967; Cases and Materials on Corporations, 1958, 69. Office: Columbia U Sch Law New York City NY 10027

CASADESUS, GABY l'HOTE, pianist; b. Marseilles, France, Aug. 1901; m. Robert Casadesus, July 16, 1921; children—Jean, Guy, Therese (Mrs. David Rawson). Tchr., Am. Conservatory Fontainebleau, 1936-48; numerous dual piano performances with husband in concert and recs.; appeared with husband in his concerto for 2 pianos, N.Y. Philharmonic, 1950, also in concertos with husband and son; broadcast performances Telephone Hour. Mem. jury Internat. Competition. Recipient 1st prize Paris Conservatory, Pages prize. Home: 54 rue Vaneau Paris 7e France

CASADESUS, ROBERT, concert pianist, composer; b. Paris, France, Apr. 7, 1899; studied harmony and piano, Paris Conservatory; m. Gaby Lhote; children—John, Guy, Therese. Soloist with orchestras and recitalist throughout Europe and North Africa, Mexico, S.Am., Palestine, Japan, and in about 1000 concerts, throughout U.S. First concert in U.S. with N.Y. Philharmonic Symphony Orch., Arturo Toscanini, conductor, 1935; gen. dir. Am. Conservatory of Fountainebleau, France, 1948—. Awarded first prize, piano, Paris Conservatory, 1913, first prize, harmony, 1919; Diémer prize, 1921; comdr. of Legion of Honor (France); comdr. Order Orange-Nassau (Netherlands); gold medal World's Fair, Paris, 1937; Brahms medal, Hamburg, Germany, 1958. Composer numerous concertos, quartettes, trios, sonatas and pieces for piano; 7 symphonies; 4 orchestra suites. Home: 2565 Wayland Rd Berwyn PA 19312

CASAGRANDE, ARTHUR, educator; b. Haidenschaft, Austria, Aug. 28, 1902; s. Angelo and Anna (Nussbaum) C.; Ing. (civil engr.), Tech. Univ. Vienna, 1924, Dr. techn., 1933, Dr.h.c., 1965; S.M. (hon.), Harvard, 1942; Dr. (hon.), Nat. U. Mexico, 1952; m. Erna M. Maas, Nov. 9, 1940; children—Vivien Alice, Sandra Maas. Came to U.S., 1926, naturalized, 1931. Asst. hydraulics Tech. U., Vienna, 1924-26; research asst. U.S. Bur. Pub. Rds., Mass. Inst. Tech., 1926-32; lectr. Harvard, 1932-34, asst. prof., 1934-40, asso. prof., 1940-46, prof. soil mechanics and found. engring., 1946—; cons. numerous fed., state, municipal and pvt. engring. orgns. on found. and earth dams in U.S., Can., Latin Am., Europe, Near and Far Eastern Countries; cons. U.S. C.E., 1936—, Panama Canal, 1940—. Organizer 1st Internat. Conf. Soil Mechanics and Found. Engring., Cambridge, June 1936. Recipient Desmond Fitzgerald medal Boston Soc. Civil Engr., 1936, Clemens Herschel prize, 1932, 51, structural sect. prize, 1947; Arthur M. Wellington prize Am. Soc. C.E., 1950, research prize, 1959, Karl Terzaghi award 1963; Distinguished Civilian Service medal from sec. army, 1967. Fellow Geol. Soc. of Am.; mem. A.A.A.S., Am. Acad. Arts and Scis., Am. (hon.), Boston (pres. 1957-58; hon.), socs. civil engrs., Am. Soc. Engring. Edn., Hwy. Research Bd., Am. Geophys. Union, Mexican Soil Mechanics Soc. (hon.), Soil Mechanics Soc. Venezuela (hon.), Harvard Engring. Soc., Internat. Soc. Soil Mechanics and Found. Engring. (pres. 1961-65), Nat. Acad. Engring., Sigma Xi. Home: 16 Rockmont Rd Belmont MA 02178 Office: Pierce Hall Harvard U Cambridge MA 02138

CASAGRANDE, JOSEPH BARTHOLOMEW, educator; b. Cin., Feb. 14, 1915; s. Louis Bartholomew and Alma (Hausske) C.; B.A., U. Wis., 1938, Wis. scholar, 1938-39; Ph.D. (Univ. fellow 1940-41), Columbia, 1951; m. Mary Deveney, Aug. 15, 1945 (dec. July 1967); children—Louis Bartholomew, Mary Leonora, Laurie Jean, Katherine Alma; m. 2d, Mabel Stevenson Navarro, Sept. 23, 1969. Instr. anthropology Queens Coll., summer 1949, U. Rochester, 1949-50; adj. asso. prof. Am. U., 1953-56; lectr. Fgn. Service Inst., 1956; prof. anthropology U. Ill., Urbana, 1960—, head dept. anthropology, 1960-67, dir. Center Internat. Comparative Studies, 1968—. Exec. sec. 29th Internat. Congress Americanists, N.Y.C., 1949; field trips to Comanche, Okla., 1940, Ojibwa, Wis., 1941, Navaho, Ariz., 1956, Ecuador, 1962, 63, 64, 65, 66-67, 68, 69, 70; staff mem. Social Science Research Council, 1950-60, dir., 1961-63; mem. adv. panel in anthropology NSF, 1962-64, adv. com. for social scis., 1966; mem. behavioral scis. study section NIH, 1965-69; mem.-at-large div. behavioral scis. Nat. Acad. Scis.-NRC, 1969—. Served to 1st lt. AUS, 1942-46. Recipient Demblzn. award Social Sci. Research Council, 1946-47, 48-49; Guggenheim fellow, 1966-67; NSF research grantee, 1966-67, 70-71. Fellow Am. Anthrop. Assn. (exec. bd. 1961-63), Royal Anthrop. Soc. Great Britain and Ireland; mem. Am. Ethnol. Soc. (past pres.), Soc. Applied Anthropology (regional v.p. 1960-61), Anthrop. Soc. Wash. (sec. 1953-56), Linguistic Soc. Am., Phi Beta Kappa. Author: Comanche Linguistic Acculturation, 1955; also numerous articles. Editor: In the Company of Man; Twenty Portraits by Anthropologists, 1960. Home: 302 W Florida Av Urbana IL 61801

CASAGRANDE, LEO, educator, found. engr.; b. Haidenschaft, Austria, Sept. 17, 1903; s. Angelo and Anna (Nussbaum) C.; Dipl. Ing. (Civil Engring.); Tech. U. of Vienna, 1928, Dr. Ing., 1933; m. Carla Maria Busch May 6, 1939; children— Christian E., Dirk R., Raif R., Imogen R., Carl N. Design engr., Augburg, Germany, 1928-30; research asst. soil mechanics Mas. Inst. Tech., 1930-32; asst. to Prof. Karl Terzaghi, Tech. U., Vienna, Austria, 1932-33; charge orgn. soil mechanics inst. Tech. U., Berlin, Germany, 1933-34; charge soil mechanics and found. div. Office Inspector Gen. for German Hwys., 1934-41; cons. engr. Germany, 1941-44; lectr. applied soil mechanics Tech. U., Braunschweig, Germany, 1940-45; chief engr. Orgn. Todt, Berlin, 1944-45; dir. Hwy. Div., Luebeck, Germany, 1945-46; research engr. bldg. research sta., Brit. Dept. Sci. and Insl. Research, Watford, Hertfordshire, Eng., 1946-50; cons. engr. founds. and earthworks, 1950—; research fellow Harvard, 1953- 57, vis. prof. practice of found. engring., 1957-58, prof. practice foundation engring., 1959—. Named honorary prof. Tech. U., Braunschweig, Germany, 1940; recipient structural section prize Boston Soc. C.E., 1952, 66-67; citations for contbns. Am. Soc. C.E., 1966. Mem. Am., Boston socs. civil engrs., Mass. Soc. Profl. Engrs., Sigma Xi. Home: 24 Arlington St Winchester MA 01890 Office: Pierce Hall Cambridge MA 02138

CASALS, JORDI, physician; b. Viladrau, Girona, Spain, May 15, 1911; s. Martin and Margarida (Ariet) C.; Bachiller en Ciencias, Instituto Nacional, Barcelona, Spain, 1928; Licenciado en Medicina y Cirurgia con Grado, U. Barcelona, 1934; m. Ellen Evelyn Brock, Dec. 6, 1941; 1 dau., Christina. Came to U.S., 1936, naturalized, 1946. Intern Med. Sch. Hosp., Barcelona, 1934-36; research asso. Cornell U. Med. Coll., N.Y.C., 1936- 38; asso. Rockefeller Inst. Med. Research, N.Y.C., 1938-52; mem. staff The Rockefeller Found., N.Y.C., 1952—; prof. epidemiology Yale, 1964—. Served with Spanish Army, 1933. Recipient Kimble Methodology award Am. Pub. Health Assn., 1969. Fellow Am. Soc. Tropical Medicine and Hygiene (Taylor award 1968); mem. Soc. Exptl. Biology and Medicine, Harvey Soc., A.A.A.S., N.Y. Acad. Medicine, N.Y. Acad. Scis. Contbr. articles profl. jours. Home: 25 Claremont Av New York City NY 10027 Office: 60 College St New Haven CT 06510

CASALS, PABLO, (Pau Carlos Salvador Defillo de), cellist, composer, condr.; b. Vendrell, Spain, Dec. 29, 1876; s. Carlos Casals and Pilar Defillo; studied music under father; later studied in Barcelona and Madrid; hon. degrees, U. Edinburgh, 1934, U. Barcelona, 1939, U. Montpellier, 1946; m. Susan Metcalfe, 1914; m. 2d, Marta Montanez, Aug. 1957. Made profl. debut Crystal Palace, London, and with Lamoureux Orch. Paris, 1898; concert tour, U.S., 1901, N.Y. debut, 1904, last N.Y. recital, 1928; founder, condr. Orquesta Pau Casals, Barcelona, 1920-36; founder Workers Concert Soc., Barcelona, 1923; soloist Brit. Broadcasting Orch., 1945; guest condr. orchs. in capital cities throughout world; last pub. profl. appearance U. Montpellier, 1947; mus. dir. Prades Festival (12 concerts) celebrating Bach bicentenary, June 1950; instr. various colls., univs. Compositions include: oratorios, symphonies, several masses, choral works, string quartets. Made numerous recs. Columbia. Decorated grand officer Legion of Honor (France); Grand Cross Republic of Spain, Rep. of Austria, Grand Cross Isabella the Cath.; hon. citizen many cities. Recipient Beethoven gold medal, 1912, gold medal Worshipful Co. of Musicians (London), 1937; Freedom awards, 1968. Fellow Royal Coll. Music (Eng.); hon. mem. Spanish Acad., Acad. Scis. et Lettres of Montpellier, Royal Philharmonic Soc., Friends of Music Soc. (Vienna). Address: Route de Ria Prades Pyrenees Orientales France

CASARELLA, EDMOND, artist, educator; b. Newark, Sept. 3, 1920; s. Antonio and Natalina (Feliciani) C.; student Cooper Union, 1942; m. Mary Peters, July 21, 1946; 1 dau., Demetra. Group exhbns. include Mus. Modern Art, Whitney Mus., Bklyn. Mus., Jewish Mus., N.Y.C., Trenton (N.J.) Mus., Newark Mus., Montclair (N.J.) Mus., Phila. Mus.; tchr. Yale, 1964-65, Columbia Tchrs. Coll., 1964-65, 66-67, N.Y. U., 1964-65, Hunter Coll., 1964-65; Pratt Inst., 1964-65, Pratt Graphic Center, 1965, Rutgers U., 1964-65, Manhattanville Coll. Sacred Heart, 1965-66; instr. graphics and sculpture Cooper Union, 1965-68, instr. sculpture, 1965-70; instr. graphics and sculpture Finch Coll., 1969; tchr. graphics Art Students League, Tchrs. Coll., Columbia. Mem. adv. bd. Cooper Union, 1959-60. Fulbright grantee, Italy, 1951-52; Guggenheim fellow, 1959; recipient Nat. Print Council award, 1959, Tiffany award in graphics, 1966. Mem. Sculptors Guild. Home: 83 E Linden Av Englewood NY 07631 Office: 52 E 78th St New York City NY 10021

CASASSA, CHARLES STEPHEN, clergyman, educator; b. San Francisco, Sept. 23, 1910; s. Charles S. and Margaret (Power) C.; student U. of Santa Clara, 1930-32; B.S., Gonzaga U., Spokane, 1934, M.A., 1935; S.T.L., Alma (Cal.) Coll., 1939; Ph.D., U. Toronto, 1946. Joined Soc. of Jesus; ordained priest Roman Catholic Ch., 1938; instr. Loyola U., Los Angeles, 1939-41, pres. coll., 1949-69, chancellor, 1969—; asst. prof. philosophy U. Santa Clara, 1946-48, dean coll. arts, 1948-49. Past pres. Ind. Colls. So. Cal., Cal. Coordinating Council Higher Edn. Bd. dirs. Southwest Regional Lab. Research and Devel., Los Angeles Coalition. Recipient Distinguished Citizenship citation Los Angeles County Conf. on Community Relations, 1954; Judge Harry Holzer Meml. award Los Angeles Jewish Community Council, 1955; Outstanding Service award So. Cal. div. Nat. Conf. Christians and Jews, 1958; Ann. Human Relations award Los Angeles chpt. Am. Jewish Com., 1967; Centennial Alumni citation Loyola U., Chgo., 1970 Mem. Los Angeles World Affairs Council (dir.), Assn. Ind. Cal. Colls. and Univs. (exec. com.), Western Coll. Assn. (past pres.). K.C. Rotarian. Club: California. Home: Xavier Hall Loyola U Los Angeles CA 90045

CASAZZA, ALFRED JOHN, banker; b. N.Y.C., Apr. 5, 1899; s. Pasquale John and Catherine (Casazza) C.; B.S., N.Y.U., 1922; M.A., Columbia, 1923; m. Elsie Volpe, Aug. 24, 1923; children—Alfred M., Catherine A. (Mrs. John J. Dillon). Asst. economist Irving Trust Co., N.Y.C., 1924- 31; statistician Dun & Bradstreet's, 1932-33; v.p. Savs. Banks Trust Co., N.Y.C., 1933-64, exec. v.p., 1957-64; investment cons. Eastman Dillon, Union Securities & Co., 1964-66, Hornblower & Weeks-Hemphill, Noyes, 1966-. Mem. Am. Acad. Polit. Sci. Clubs: Garden City Golf, Garden City Country, Wall Street (N.Y.C.); Bankers (Bklyn.). Home: 114 Jackson St Garden City NY 11530 Office: 8 Hanover St New York City NY 10004

CASBERG, MELVIN AUGUSTUS, med. educator; born Poona, India, July 10, 1909 (parents Am. citizens); s. Samuel D. and Jessie (Lively) C.; A.B., Greenville Coll., 1930, D.Sc. (hon.), 1958; M.D., St. Louis U., 1936; m. Olive Van Valin, June 1, 1932; children—Sylvia Mae, Melvin A., Ronald Van. Came to U.S., 1926. Resident in surgery, St. Louis City Hosp., 1937-40; commd. missionary by Free Meth. Ch., 1940, and served as med. missionary as surgeon-in-chief Umri Mission Hosp., Berar, India, 1941-42; chief of staff and surgery, Harriman Jones Hosp., Long beach, Cal., 1946-48; surg. cons. Surgeon Gen. Army, Washington, 1949; dean and asso. prof. surgery, St. Louis U. Sch. of Medicine, 1949-52; chmn. Armed Forces Med. Policy Bd., Office Sec. Def., 1952-53; asst. sec. def. for health and medicine, 1953-54; cons. to sec. def., 1954-58; mem. faculty U. Tex., 1958-59; dir. and prin. Christian Med. Coll., Ludhiana, Punjab, India, 1960-62; adviser U.S. Delegation, 5th World Health Assembly, Geneva, Switzerland, 1952; mem. med. adv. council, MEDICO, Internat. Rescue Com.; chmn. hosp. bd. St. Louis U. Hosp., 1949-52, dir. univ. staff St. Louis City Hosp., 1949-52; v.p. for med. affairs U. Tex.; practice medicine specializing in surgery, Long Beach, 1962—.

Vice pres. Thomas A. Dooley Found.; v.p. and mem. bd. dir. AMDOC, 1966. Govt. Nat. A.R.C., 1953. Served to lt. col., M.C., U.S. Army, 1942-46; in N. Africa, C.-B.-I. (Sta. surgeon, Chungking) and Am. theaters. Decorated Gold Medal of Honor, French Mil. Med. Service. Awarded Certificate of Appreciation, Dept. of Def., 1954. Diplomate Am. Bd. Surgery. Fellow A.C.S., Am. Assn. Surgery Trauma; mem. A.M.A., Soc. Med. Cons. Armed Forces, Assn. Surgs. in India, Nat. Soc. Med. Research (dir., 1950-56), Los Angeles, Long Beach (Cal.) surg. socs., Western Surg. Assn., Los Angeles Acad. Medicine (mem. bd. govs. 1968—), Sigma Xi, Alpha Epsilon Delta, Alpha Omega Alpha. Presbyn. Contbr. nat. sci. and ednl. jours. Home: 1641 Greenbrier Rd Long Beach, CA 90815. Office: 211 Cherry Av Long Beach CA 90802

CASBY, LORRAINE CLARICE, educator; b. St. Paul, May 19, 1925; d. Joseph James and Clara (Croft) Casby; B.S., Winona (Minn.) State Tchrs. Coll., 1945; M.A., U. Neb., 1947, Ph.D. (Regents fellow), 1950; postgrad. U. Minn., U. Chgo., U. London (Eng.), Sorbonne, Paris, U. Heidelberg (Germany). Grad. asst. U. Neb., 1946-49, asst. instr., 1949-50; asst. prof. history York (Neb.) Coll., 1950—; research adviser CRAGLOG, Germany, 1951-52; tour guide, Europe, 1953; asso. prof. history and econs. Poly. Inst., P.R., 1954-56; faculty Inter Am. U. P.R., 1957-65, acad. dean, 1958-60, dean univ., 1960-65; asso. prof. Internat. Inst. Ams., dean univ. World U., Hato Rey, P.R., 1965—. 1st v.p. World U. Inc.; vice chmn. Internat. Ednl. Services, Inc. Fulbright lectr., India, 1961. Mem. Am. Hist. Soc., Am. Assn. Polit. Sci., Quill and Scroll. Mem. E.U.B. Ch. Contbr. articles to profl. jours. Home: El Centro 1401 Hato Rey PR 00918

CASCIERI, ARCANGELO, sculptor, educator; b. Civitaquana, Italy, Feb. 22, 1902; s. Corrado and Marie (Trabucco) C.; came to U.S., 1908, naturalized, 1934; student Sch. Arch., Boston Archtl. Center, 1922-26, Boston U., 1932-36; m. Eda Di Biccari, Sept. 19, 1943. Sculptor, asst. dir. sculpture and wood carving W. F. Ross Studio, Cambridge, Mass., 1923-41; sculptor, asst. dir. Schwab Assos. Studio, Arlington, Mass., 1941-46, sculptor, dir., 1946-52; tchr. pvt. classes, Boston, 1932-37, Craft Center Sch., Boston, 1939- 40; tchr. design New London (Conn.) Jr. Coll., 1941-43; tchr. design Boston Archtl. Center, 1936—, head Sch. Archt., 1938—, also mem. bd. dirs.; partner with Adio Di Biccari in studio for sculpture and decorations, Boston and Arlington, Mass., 1952—; prin. sculptural works include statues in parts of Cathedral St. John the Divine, N.Y.C., Washington Cathedral, Cathedral St. John Evangelist, Seattle, Cathedral Most Holy Redeemer, Cornerbrook, Newfoundland, Cathedral Mary Our Queen, Balt., Riverside Baptist Ch., N.Y.C., East Liberty Presbyn. Ch., Pitts., St. George's Sch. Chapel, Newport, R.I., Boston U. Chapel, St. Ignatius Ch., Chestnut Hill, Mass., Shrine Immaculate Conception, Washington; also works at Boston Coll., Holy Cross Coll., Buffalo Courier Express Bldg., Parlin Jr. High Sch., Everett, Mass., Lexington (Mass.) Jr. High Sch.; Am. War Meml. World War I at Belleau Woods, France, World war II at Margraten, Holland; exterior Meml. Auditorium, Lynn, Mass.; exterior Boys' Stadium, Franklin Field, Dorchester, Mass.; sculpture on fountain Parkman Plaza, Boston; sculpture Backus Estate, Pointe Rose, Mich. Recipient Gold medal citation Nat. Sculpture Soc., 1961; 750th Anniversary citation Boston Archtl. Center, 1964. Fellow A.I.A. (chmn. com. collaborative arts); mem. Dante Alighieri Soc. (hon.), Boston Soc. Architects, Mass. Assn. Architects, New Eng. Sculptors Assn. Catholic. Author articles. Home: 500 Concord Av Lexington MA 02173 Office: 1167 Massachusetts Av Arlington MA 02174 also 27 Tavern Rd Boston MA 02154

CASCINO, ANTHONY ELMO, marketing exec.; b. Chgo., Dec. 15, 1916; s. George E. and Theresa (Cunto) C.; B.S., Ill. Inst. Tech., 1939; M.S., Northwestern U., 1940; m. Lorayne Allergretti Nov. 30, 1946; children—Anthony Elmo, Leonora Marie, Katherine Rose, Christopher Jude. Faculty econs. and statistics Northwestern U., 1940-43; head econs. dept. Ripon Coll., 1943; br. economist, durable goods OPA, Washington, 1944-46; dir. market research, dir. marketing Bendix Home Appliances, 1946-53; dir. marketing Avco Corp., 1953-56; v.p. marketing Internat. Minerals & Chem. Corp., Skokie, Ill., 1956- 63, v.p. agrl. products marketing group, 1963-66, group v.p. for agr., 1966-69, exec. v.p., 1969—. Contbr. articles to trade jours. Home: 439 Grove St Glencoe IL 60022 Office: Old Orchard Rd Skokie IL 60076

CASE, BENTON JANNEY, retail bookstore exec.; b. Mpls., Mar. 13, 1903; s. Charles M. And Helen Mary (Janney) C.; grad. Shattuck Sch., 1921; student Princeton, 1922-24; m. Olive McKnight Crosby, Sept. 11, 1929; children—Olive Crosby (Mrs. Edward C. Brown, Jr.), Benton Janney, Charles W., Carolyn H. (Mrs. E. Cole Graham, Jr.). With Janney, Semple, Hill & Co., Mpls., 1924-61, dir. charge sales, operations and labor relations, 1939—, sec. 1943-48, v.p., 1948-52, pres., 1952-58, chmn. bd., chief exec. officer, 1958-61; pres., treas., dir. Book Case, Inc., 1963—; dir. Kellogg Commn. Co. of Mpls., Northwestern Nat. Bank Mpls., Northwestern Nat. Life Ins. Co., N.W. Bancorp., Crosby Co., trustee Farmers & Mechanics Savs. Bank. Asso. treas., mem. exec. com. Lakewood Cemetery of Mpls. Trustee Mpls. Art Inst., Mpls. Found.; bd. dir., vice chmn. Hennepin County chpt. A.R.C., 1942-46. Democrat. Episcopalian (past mem. exec. com.). Clubs: Minneapolis; Woodhill Country; Racquet, Chicago (Chgo.); Princeton; Century (N.Y.); Minnesota (St. Paul); Kitchi Gammi (Duluth); Wayzata (Minn.) Country. Home: Box 128 Wayzata MN 55391 Office: First Nat Bank 127 S 7th St Minneapolis MN 55402

CASE, CHARLES CARROLL, army officer; b. Raquette Lake, N.Y., Mar. 20, 1914; s. Charles Carroll and Alberta (Williams) C.; B.A., W.Va. U., 1936; postgrad. Command and Gen. Staff Coll., 1952, Army War Coll., 1957; M.A., Am. U., 1960; postgrad. Harvard, 1962; m. Mary Frances Young, Jan. 29, 1938; children—Judith (Mrs. James H. Falkenrath), Charles Carroll III. Commd. 2d lt. U.S. Army, 1936, advanced through grades to maj. gen., 1967; support comdr., chief of staff 3d Div., 1954-56; dir. Office Sec. Def., Washington, 1957-61; comdr. Def. Logistics Service Center, Battle Creek, Mich., 1962-64; q.m. U.S. Army, Europe, 1964-65; chief U.S. Army Supply and Maintenance Agy., Europe, 1965-67; dep. comdg. gen. COMZ, 1965-67; comdg. gen. U.S. Army Mobility Equipment Command, St. Louis, 1967-69; comdr. Def. Fuel Supply Center, Alexandria, Va., 1969—. Leader, tng. dir. Boy Scouts Am., 1957-64. Decorated Legion of Merit with four oak clusters, Bronze Star medal, Army Commendation medal. Mem. Def. Supply Assn. (pres. Washington chpt.). Contbr. articles profl. jours. Home: 1628 N Harrison St Arlington VA 22205 Office: Def Fuel Supply Center Cameron Sta Alexandria VA 22314

CASE, CLIFFORD PHILIP, U.S. senator; b. Franklin Park, N.J., Apr. 16, 1904; s. Clifford Philip and Jeannette (Benedict) C.; A.B., Rutgers U., 1925, LL.D., 1955; LL.B., Columbia, 1928; LL.D., Middlebury Coll., 1956, Rollins Coll., 1957, Rider Coll., 1959, Bloomfield (N.J.) Coll., 1962, Columbia, 1967, Princeton, 1967, Upsala Coll., 1969; m. Ruth M. Smith, July 13, 1928; children—Mary Jane (Mrs. William M. Weaver), Ann (Mrs. John C. Holt), Clifford Phillip III. Asso., Simpson Thacher & Bartlett, N.Y.C., 1928-39, mem. firm, 1939-53. Mem. Rahway (N.J.) Common Council, 1938-42; mem. N.J. House of Assembly, 1943, 44; mem. 79th-83rd U.S. Congresses, from 6th N.J. Dist. resigned 1953; U.S. senator from N.J., 1955—. Pres., Fund for Republic, 1953-54. Trustee Rutgers U., 1945-59, N.J. Com. to Preserve Democratic Process; hon. trustee N.J. Hist. Soc.; mem. adv. council Woodrow Wilson Sch., Princeton; mem. adv. bd. N.J. chpt. Arthritis and Rheumatism Found.; bd. dirs. N.J. Soc. Crippled Children and Adults, Columbia Jour. Law and Social Problems; trustee Roper Pub. Opinion Research Center at Williams Coll., Williamstown, Mass. Mem. Columbia Law Sch. Alumni Assn. (dir.), Assn. Bar City N.Y., Am., N.Y. State, N.Y. County bar assns., Council Fgn. Relations, Phi Beta Kappa, Delta Upsilon, Phi Delta Phi fraternities. Republican. Presbyn. Elk. Clubs: Century Assn. (N.Y.C.); Essex (Newark); Federal City (Washington). Home: Rahway NJ 07065 Office: Senate Office Bldg Washington DC 20510

CASE, DANIEL HIBBARD, lawyer; b. Lihue, Kauai Hawaii, Feb. 25, 1925; s. A. Hebard and Elizabeth (McConnell) C.; student Williams Coll., 1942-44; B.A., U. Denver, 1948, LL.B., 1952; m. Carol Mary Holmes, Aug. 14, 1954; children—Carin Holmes, Daniel Hibbard III, Stephen McConnell, Jeffrey Holmes. Admitted to Hawaii bar, 1953, since practiced in Honolulu; mem. firm Bortz, Case, Stack, Kay, Cronin & Claus and predecessor firms, 1958—; lectr. bus. law U. Hawaii, 1953-54. Pres. Hawaii div. Am. Cancer Soc.; trustee Punahou Sch. Served to lt. (j.g.) USNR, 1943-47. Mem. Am., Hawaii bar assns. Home: 2040 Ahualani Pl Honolulu HI 96822 Office: First Hawaiian Bank Honolulu HI 96822

CASE, EUGENE LAWRENCE, advt. exec.; b. Knoxville, Tenn., Dec. 6, 1937; s. Harry Lawrence and Elinor Alice (Irish) C.; student Cornell U., 1955-59; m. Mary Jane Austin, Apr. 30, 1959 (div. Mar. 1969); children—Christopher Lawrence, Alison Austin, Timothy Punch. Copywriter, J. Walter Thompson, 1961-62, Foote, Cove & Belding, 1963; asst. copy supr. Doyle, Dane, Bernbach, N.Y.C., 1964; partner, creative dir. Jack Tinker & Partners, N.Y.C., 1966-69; partner, founder Case and Krone, Inc., N.Y.C., 1969—. Recipient numerous awards for copywriting from advt. clubs. Mem. Advt. Club N.Y. (dir.). Home: 25 Bethune St New York City NY 10014 Office: 4 W 58th St New York City NY 10019

CASE, EVERETT NEEDHAM, educator; b. North Plainfield, N.J., Apr. 9, 1901; s. James Herbert and Alice (Needham) C.; B.A., Princeton, 1922, LL.D., 1947; B.A., Cambridge U., Eng., 1924, M.A., 1938; postgrad. Harvard, 1924-27; LL.D., Syracuse U., 1942, Temple U., 1943, St. Lawrence U., 1945, U. Rochester, 1948, Colby Coll., 1953, N.Y. U., 1962, Clark U., 1967; L.H.D., Hamilton Coll., Union Coll., 1943, Colgate U., 1957, U. Akron, 1962; D.C.L., Bucknell U., 1947; m. Josephine Young, June 27, 1931; children—Josephine Edmonds, James Herbert III, Samuel, John Philip. Asst. history Harvard, 1926-27; asst. to Owen D. Young, 1927-33; asst. sec. Gen. Electric Co., 1929-33; exec. sec. Central Banking and Industrial Com., Washington, D.C., 1932-33; investigation, study monetary policies and problems, also problems of N.Y. dairy farmer, 1933-41; asst. dean Harvard Grad. Sch. Bus. Adminstrn., 1939-42; pres. Colgate U., 1942-62, pres. emeritus, 1962—; pres. Alfred P. Sloan Found., N.Y.C., 1962-68, adv. trustee, 1968—. Dir. Fed. Res. Bank N.Y., 1961-68, chmn., 1966-68; cons. on Far Eastern Affairs to sec. state, 1949; alumni trustee Princeton, 1957-61; trustee Meml. Sloan-Kettering Inst. Cancer Center, 1963-68, Sloan-Kettering Inst. Cancer Research, 1966-68; trustee Milbrook Sch., 1944—, pres., 1960-68; bd. dirs. Nat. Ednl. TV, 1958—, chmn., 1963-69; hon. trustee Com. Econ. Devel.; trustee Ednl. Broadcasting Corp., 1964-68; chmn. Am. Council Edn., 1951-52; overseers com. to visit Harvard Coll., 1951-61; mem. adv. com. Lindsay A. and Olive B. O'Connor Found., Hobart, N.Y. Mem. Acad. Polit. Sci., Council Fgn. Relations. Democrat. Baptist. Clubs: Economic, Century, University (N.Y.C.). Contbr. articles to profl. jours. Home: Van Hornesville Herkimer County NY 13475

CASE, GEORGE S., Jr., former mfg. exec.; b. Lakewood, O., Dec. 4, 1907; s. George Sessions and Amey (Hall) C. A.B., Dartmouth, 1929, M.C.S., Amos Tuck Sch. Bus. Adminstrn., 1930; m. Katherine Taylor, June 12, 1931; children—Lucien Hall, Lynn Taylor, Joan. Pres., dir. The Lamson & Sessions Co., Cleve., 1939-50, pres., 1950-68, chmn. bd., 1968-70, now dir.; dir. Union Commerce Bank. Dir. Cleve. Bur. Govtl. Research Inst.; past treas., dir. Asso. Industries; past pres. Hardware Mfrs. Assn.; past chmn. Fasteners Research Council, Indsl. Fasteners Inst. Hon. mem. Community Chest; adv. bd. mem., past treas. Citizens League; trustee, life dir., past treas. YMCA; past pres., trustee Jones Home. Served to lt., USNR, 1945-46. Mem. Phi Kappa Psi. Clubs: Union, Pepper Pike Country, Kirtland Country. Home: Hackney Rd Dalsy Hill Hunting Valley OH 44022 Office: 5000 Tiedeman Rd Cleveland OH 44144

CASE, HADLEY, bus. exec.; b. N.Y.C., Mar. 28, 1909; s. Walter Summerhayes and Mary Soule (Hadley) C.; student Kent (Conn.) Sch., 1924-29, Antioch Coll., 1929-33; m. Julie Marguerite Ill, June 8, 1935; children—Mary, C. Durham, Julie Anne, Rosalie C. Clark, Deborah Joan. Geol. field work, Australia, 1933-34, Tex., 1935-36; geol. dept. Case, Pomeroy & Co., Inc., 1936-39, v.p., 1939-41, pres., dir., 1941—; pres., dir. Essex Royalty Corp., Felmont Oil Corp.; dir. N.W. Airlines, Inc., N.Y. Air Brake Co., Copper Range Co., Nashua Corp., Numac Oil & Gas Ltd. Trustee, Kent Sch. Mem. Am. Inst. Mining and Metall. Engrs., Am. petroleum Inst., Ind. Petroleum Assn. Am. (dir.). Episcopalian. Home: Mead's Point Greenwich CT 06830 Office: 6 E 43d St New York City NY 10017

CASE, HAROLD CLAUDE, clergyman, coll. pres.; b. Cottonwood Falls, Kan., May 20, 1902; s. Harry Claude and Rose (Kiger) C.; B.A., Baker U., 1923, D.D. (hon.), 1934; D. D. (hon.), Pacific Sch. Religion, 1951; S.T.B., Boston U., 1927; grad. study Harvard, 1923-24, Garrett Theol. Sem., 1927- 33; Litt.D., Huston-Tillotson Coll., 1944; Sc.D., R.I. Coll. Pharmacy and Allied Scis., 1953; LL.D., W. Va. Wesleyan Coll., 1954, Northeastern U., 1954, Tufts U., 1955, Temple U., Brandeis U., Pratt Inst., 1961, Pasadena Coll., 1964; L.H.D., Whittier Coll., 1970; Ed.D., Franklin Pierce Coll., 1966; m. Phyllis Elizabeth Kirk, June 27, 1927; children—Harold Robert, Phyllis Rosanna (Mrs. Victor Kazanjian), David (dec.). Ordained to ministry Meth. Ch.; instr. Southwestern Coll., 1927-28; pastor North Shore Ch., Glencoe, Ill., 1928- 33, First Meth. Ch., Topeka, 1933-38, Elm Park Ch., Scranton, Pa., 1938- 45, First Meth. Ch., Pasadena, Cal., 1945-51; pres. Boston U., 1951-67, pres. emeritus, 1967—. Dir. Sterling Drug Inc.; dirs. adv. bd. State Street Bank & Trust Co. Trustee N.E. Deaconess Hosp.; chmn. bd. Council on Religion and Internat. Affairs. Hon. dir. Alexander Graham Bell Assn. for Deaf, Inc. Mem. Am. Acad. Arts and Scis., Phi Beta Kappa, Delta Tau Delta, Pi Kappa Delta, Beta Gamma Sigma, Pi Gamma Mu. Mason (33). Author: A Year of Special Parties, 1927; The Prophet Jeremiah, 1953. Home: 2 Lane Rd Annisquam MA 01930

CASE, JOHN CROWTHER, former oil co. exec.; b. Rochester, N.Y., Jan 29, 1892; s. Howard Brown and Elizabeth (Crowther) C.; student Marlborough Coll, Eng., 1906-10, Institut Minerva, Zurich, Switzerland, 1911-12; m. Anne Taylor, Nov. 28, 1916; children—John H., Honor E. (Mrs. John P. Runyon). Joined Vacuum Oil Co., 1912, asst. to mgr. producing dept., N.Y., 1920-25, mgr. producing operations Europe, 1925-37; mgr. producing dept. Socony-Vacuum Oil Co., Inc., 1937, dir. 1943, v.p. dir. charge producing, 1946-57; ret., 1957; dir. Columbian Petroleum Co., Arabian Am. Oil Co. Chmn. bd. trustees Am. U. Beirut, 1955-64; bd. dirs. Near East Coll. Assn. Mem. Morris Twp. Sch. Bd., 1928-50. Served as 1st lt., inf. 78th Div., U.S. Army, World War I, 1918-19. Mem. Am. Geog. Soc., Pilgrims, Council Fgn. Relations, Arctic Inst. N.Am. (chmn. bd. govs. 1955). Clubs: Alpine (London); American Alpine (past pres.), Adirondack Mountain Reserve-Ausable, Century Association (N.Y.C.); Alpine of Canada (Banff); Swiss Alpine, Akademischer Alpen (Zürich). Home: 306 Mt Kemble Av Morristown NJ 07960

CASE, JOSEPHINE YOUNG, (Mrs. Everett Case), author; b. Lexington, Mass., Feb. 16, 1907; d. Owen D. and Josephine (Edmonds) Young; B.A., Bryn Mawr Coll., 1928; M.A., Radcliffe Coll., 1934; Litt.D., Elmira Coll., 1946, Skidmore Coll., 1957, St. Lawrence U., 1959; L.H.D., Colgate U., 1962; m. Everett Case, June 27, 1931; children—Josephine, James Herbert III, Samuel, John Philip. Dir. RCA, 1961—. Mem. gen. adv. com. Fgn. Assistance Programs, 1965-69. Mem. nat. bd. dirs. Girl Scouts Am., 1947-48; bd. dirs. Bryn Mawr Coll., 1935-55; trustee Skidmore Coll., 1938, chmn. bd. trustees, 1960-71; trustee Am. Assembly, 1966—, Colgate U., 1969—; bd. dirs. Overseas Devel. Council, 1969—, Fund Advancement Edn., 1965-67, Nat. Merit Scholarship Corp., 1969—. Democrat. Universalist. Club: Colony (N.Y.C.). Author: At Midnight on the 31st of March, 1938; Written in Sand, 1945; Freedom's Farm, 1946; This Very Tree, 1969. Contbr. chpt. to anthology America Remembers. 1956. Home: Van Hornesville Herkimer County NY 13475

CASE, KEITH EDMOND, educator; b. Creston, Ia., May 11, 1911; s. Roy C. and Eula (Freeman) C.; A.M., Colo. State Coll. Edn., 1935; Ph.D., U. Denver, 1948; m. Leah Young, Nov. 2, 1934; children—Leah Ann Keith, Elizabeth Larie, Kenneth. Dir. forensics Colo. State Coll. Edn., Greeley, 1934-35; chmn. dept. speech and English, Garden City (Kan.) Jr. Coll., 1935-41; chmn. dept. speech, dean men Augustana Coll., Sioux Falls, S.D., 1941-44; coordinator basic communication program U. Denver, 1948-63, chmn. dept. basic communication, 1948-63, chmn. communication div., 1951-63, prof. speech and communications, 1961—; cons. in communication to bus., industry, edn., religious groups, govt. agys. Served to lt. USNR, 1944-46. Mem. Internat. Soc. Gen. Semantics, Speach Assn. Am., Nat. Soc. Study Communication, Pi Kappa Delta, Alpha Psi Omega, Phi Sigma Pi, Kappa Delta Pi. Lutheran. Author: Basic Debate, 1935; Speech Improvement Guide, 1953; Mastering Reading Skills, 1954; Developing Modern Reading Techniques, 1956; Mastering Speech Skills, 1956; Mastering Vocabulary Skills, 1957; Mature Reading and Thinking, 1960; Communicating Effectively Through Speech, 1964. Home: 4990 Larkspur St Bowmar Littleton CO 80120

CASE, KENNETH MYRON, educator; b. N.Y.C., Sept. 23, 1923; s. Louis Francis and Alma (Bierman) C.; B.S. summa cum laude, Harvard, 1944, M.S., 1946, Ph.D., 1948; m. Patia Marian Carpenter, Aug. 19, 1951; children—F. Scott, Laurie, Hope. Scientist Los Alamos (N.M.) Lab., 1944-45; mem. Inst. for Advance Study., Princeton, N.J., 1948-50, 56-57; prof. physics U. Mich., 1950-69, Rockefeller U., N.Y.C., 1969—; cons. Inst. for Def. Analyses. Recipient Certificate of Merit, Am. Nuclear Soc. Fellow Am. Phys. Soc. Contbr. articles to profl. jours. Home: 54 Hardy Dr Princeton NJ 08540 Office: The Rockefeller U New York City NY 10021

CASE, LELAND DAVIDSON, editor; b. Wesley, Ia., May 8, 1900; s. Herbert Llewelyn and Mary Ellen (Grannis) C.; student Dakota Wesleyan U., S.D., 1918-20, Litt.D., 1941; B.A., Macalester Coll., 1922; postgrad. U. Minn.; M.A., Northwestern U., 1926, U. Chgo., 1929; Litt.D., Morningside Coll., 1957, Simpson Coll., 1962; LL.D., McKendree Coll., 1963; m. Josephine Altman, July 28, 1931. City editor Lead (S. D.) Call, 1923-25; staff Paris edit. N.Y. Herald-Tribune, 1926- 27; instr. Medill Sch. Journalism, Northwestern U., 1925-26, asst. prof., 1927-28; co-pub. Evening Star, Hot Springs, S.D., 1928-34; editor Rotarian mag., 1930-50; field editor, 1952; founder-editor Together mag., 1956-63; dir. Pacific Center Western Hist. Studies, U. Pacific, 1965-67, editor Pacific Historia, 1965-68. Co- founder Friends of Middle Border, 1939, Westerners, 1944, pres. Westerners Internat., 1969—. Asso. cons. U.S. Dept. of State at UN Conf., San Francisco, 1945. Recipient of Alumni merit awards Macalester Coll., 1949, Northwestern U., 1951, Dakota Wesleyan U., 1962; St. George's award, 1963; citation Southwestern Coll., 1964. Mem. Soc. Midland Author, Western Hist. Assn. (hon. life), Bibliog. Soc. Am., Sigma Tau Delta, Pi Kappa Delta, Delta Sigma Rho, Sigma Delta Chi, Acacia. Republican. Methodist. Mason, Rotarian. Author: (with George C. Bastian) Editing the Day's News, 1932; (with G.C. Bastian, R.E. Wolsely) Around the Copydesk, 1933; Guidebook to the Black Hills and the Badlands, 1949; contbg. author The Black Hills, 1952, Editor: (series) A World to Live In, 1942; Peace Is a Process, 1944; Peace Requires Action, 1946; (with Edith Grannis) New Hampshire to Minnesota, 1962; Reader's Choice Tresury, 1964. Home: Route 8 Box 397 Tucson AZ 85710

CASE, LYNN MARSHALL, educator; b. Verona, N.Y., Dec. 18, 1903; s. Joseph Arthur and Bertha (Page) C.; A.B., Hamilton Coll., 1925; M.A. (Harrison fellow), U. Pa., 1929, Ph.D., 1931; D.H.C., U. Besancon (France); m. Doris Fellows, May 24, 1930; children—Beverly (Mrs. Rorer), Ronald M. Instr. Rice Inst., 1930-37; asst. prof., then asso. prof. La State U., 1937-46; asso. prof., then prof. and chmn. history dept. U. Pa., 1946—. Served from 1st lt. to maj., AUS, 1942-46. Decorated Legion of Merit, Bronze Star; recipient Beveridge Fund award, 1934, Social Sci. Research Council award, 1933, 48, Am. Philos. Soc. award, 1956. Mem. Am. (chmn. war documents com. 1956-57), So. (mem. council 1943-45) hist. assns., socs. French (pres. 1955- 56), Italian hist. studies, Emerson Lit. Soc., Phi Beta Kappa, Phi Alpha Theta. Democrat. Presbyn. Mason. Author books including: Franco-Italian Relations 1860-65; French Opinion on U.S. and Mexico; French Opinion on War and Diplomacy, 1954; Guide to Diplomatic Archives, 1959; The Bourbon Restoration, 1967; United States and France in the Civil War, 1969. Home: 37 Rodmor Rd Havertown PA 19083 Office: U Pa Philadelphia PA 19104

CASE, MANNING EUGENE, Jr., corp. exec.; b. Sioux City, Ia., Mar. 1916; s. Manning Eugene and Loretta (Seims) C.; A.B., Western Res. U., 1938, J.D., 1941; m. Ernestine Bryan, July 26, 1941; children—Douglas Manning, Randall Bryan. Admitted to Ohio Bar, 1941; asst. counsel B.F. Goodrich Co., Akron, 1941-52; sec., treas., gen counsel, dir. Perfection Industries, 1952-55; sec. Hupp Corp., 1955-57; v.p. service and finance M & M's Candies div. Mars Inc., 1957-60; asst. treas. Standard Brands Inc., N.Y.C., 1961-62, treas. 1962-68, v.p., treas., 1968—. Active in local Boy Scouts Am. Served from pvt. to maj. Judge Adv. Gen. Corps., AUS, 1942-46. Mem. Am. Soc. Corporate Secs., Am., Cleve. bar assns., Phi Beta Kappa, Delta Sigma Rho, Omicron Delta Kappa, Beta Theta Pi, Phi Delta Phi. Home: 25 Lake End Pl Mountain Lakes NJ 07046 Office: 625 Madison Av New York City NY 10022

CASE, RICHARD WERBER, lawyer; b. Washington, Mar. 21, 1918; s. Ralph Hoyt and Erwin (Werber) C.; A.B., U. Md., 1941, LL.B., 1942; m. Elizabeth J. Carson, Sept. 30, 1943. Admitted to Md. bar, 1942, since practiced in Balt.; partner firm Smith, Somerville & Case, and predecessors, 1955—. Dir. T. Rowe Price Growth stock Fund, Inc.; sec., dir. Balt. Ice Sports, Inc.; dir. Charles Center—Inner Harbor Mgmt., Inc., Security Savs. & Loan. Spl. tax counsel County Commrs.

of Baltimore County, 1951; chmn. Baltimore County Tax Survey Commn., 1958-59; mem. Md. Bd. Edn., 1949-52; chmn. Md. Tax Survey Commn., 1949-51; asst. atty. gen. Md., 1947-49; chmn. com. rev. financing Md. Health Activities, 1954-55; mem. com. med. care Md. Planning Commn., 1956-63; chmn. Md. Savs. and Loan Study Commn., 1960-61; mem. Constl. Conv. Commn., chmn. com. state finance and taxation, 1965-67, conv. del., 1967. Trustee Peabody Inst. Balt., Md. Sch. Blind; bd. regents U. Md., 1960—, vice chmn., 1970—. Mem. Am., Md., Balt. bar assns., Am. Law Inst., Order of Coif. Presbyn. Clubs: Maryland, Hamilton Street, Center (Balt.). Contbr. report, articles to profl. jours. Home: Belfast Rd Sparks MD 21152 Office: 1 Charles Center Baltimore MD 21201

CASE, ROBERT OLIVER, lawyer, instrument co. exec.; b. Detroit, Jan. 26, 1922; s. Arthur B. and Elsie (Watts) C.; A.B., Brown U., 1946; LL.B., Columbia 1949; m. Marian Margaret Burke, Nov. 28, 1953; children—Robert A., Leila A., John G., Mary D., Pamela J., Maureen M., Jennifer S. Admitted to Ill. bar, 1949; with Office Gen. Counsel. Navy Dept., 1949-51; atty. Motorola, Inc., Chgo., 1951-54; with firm Ungaro, Sherwood & Groebe, Chgo., 1955-60; partner firm Walsh, Case & Coale, Chgo., 1960—; sec. Cenco Instruments Corp., Chgo., 1961—, gen. counsel, 1965—; sec., dir., gen. counsel Hach Chem. Co.; sec., dir. Cenco Hosp. and Convalescent Home Corp. Trustee Leo T. Norville Found. Home: 1429 Wincanton St Deerfield IL 60015 Office: 104 S Michigan Av Chicago IL 60603

CASE, WELDON WOOD, utility holding co. exec.; b. Cleve., Feb. 22, 1921; s. Harry N. and Alice (Wood) C.; student Western Reserve Acad., 1933-35; student Case Inst. Tech., 1938-40, Ohio Wesleyan U., 1940-41; m. Beatrice K. Kuhn, Jan. 3, 1942; children—Thomas W., William R. With Western Reserve Tel. Co., Hudson, O., 1934-56, gen. mgr., 1946-55, pres., 1955-56; gen. mgr. Elyria Tel. Co., 1956-57, pres., 1957-60; pres., chief exec. officer, dir. Mid-Continent Tel. Corp., Hudson, O., 1960—; dir. Elyria Savs. & Trust Nat. Bank, First Nat. Bank of Akron, Hydrometals Inc., Dallas, Fostoria Corp.; chmn. dirs. Universal Finance Co., Cleve., Bd. dirs. U.S. Ind. Tel. Assn. Trustee Ohio No. U.; mem. adv. bd. Coll. Bus., U. Akron. Served with AUS, 1942-46. Mason. Home: 260 Aurora St Hudson OH 44236 Office: 100 Executive Pkwy Hudson OH 44236

CASE, WILLIBY EUGENE, Jr., lawyer; b. Kansas City, Mo. Dec. 21, 1928; s. Williby Eugene and Ruth (Gwinn) C.; student Stanford, 1946-48; LL.B., U. Ariz., 1952; m. Shirley Stipek, June 7, 1951; children—Susan Elizabeth, Anne Tonia, Margaret Ann, Williby Eugene III. Admitted to Ariz. bar, 1952; atty. Ariz. Code Commn., 1952-53; asso. firm Cox & Cox, Phoenix, 1953-56; pvt. practice, Phoenix, 1956-58; practice in Yuma, 1958-70; partner firm Benton & Case, 1960-70; judge Ct. of Appeals, Ariz., 1970—. Pres. Yuma P.T.A., 1961-62. Precinct and state committeeman Republican, Party, 1958-67; treas. Yuma County Rep. Central Com., 1962. Mem. Yuma County Bar Assn. (pres. 1959-61), State Bar Ariz. (bd. govs. 1962-68, pres. 1966-67), U. Ariz. Alumni Assn. (pres. Yuma 1964-65), Sigma Nu, Phi Delta Phi. Republican. Episcopalian. Elk, Rotarian. Club: Yuma Golf and Country (pres. 1967-68). Home: Route 3 Box 20 Yuma AZ 85364 Office: State Capitol Bldg Phoenix AZ 85007

CASEI, NEDDA, mezzo-soprano; b. Balt., Sept. 9, 1934; d. Howard Thomas and Lyda Marie (Graupman) Casey; grad. high sch., Scarsdale, N.Y., 1950; studied voice with William P. Herman, N.Y.C., 1950-58, Vittorio Piccinini, Milan, Italy, 1959—; also student piano, langs., ballet. Operatic debut Theatre Royal de la Monnaie, Brussels, Belgium, 1960; operatic performances at Basel (Switzerland) Stadttheater, Gran Liceo, Barcelona, Spain, Teatro Carlo Fenice, Genova, Italy, Pitts. Opera, Teatro San Carlo, Naples, Italy, Chgo. Lyric, Vancouver (Can.) Opera, Cape Town Opera, Brno, Bratislava, Kosice and Prague operas, Miami, Houston, San Diego, Hartford, Phila., Toledo, Dayton, Memphis, Los Angeles operas, Met. Opera, N.Y.C.; performances in various mus. festivals and tours, also symphonic concerts, orotorios in Europe, South Africa and U.S., performed in radio and TV in Holland, Brussels, Leipzig, U.S.; performed at White House, Washington, 1967; made various recs. Recipient New Orleans Opera award, 1959, Rockefeller Found. award, 1962, 64. Mem. Actor's Equity, Am. Guild Mus. Artists. Home: 15 W 72d St New York City NY 10023 Office: Met Opera New York City NY 10023 also Hurok Concerts 1370 Av Americas New York City NY 10019

CASELEY, DONALD JOSEPH, physician; b. Sullivan, Ill., Jan. 24, 1912; s. Aubrey L. and Mabelle (Francis) C.; A.B., DePauw U., 1933; M.D., Ind. U., 1937; m. Elizabeth Gorrell, Sept. 8, 1936; children—Jane, David. Practice orthopedic surgery, Indpls., 1942-43, 46; med. dir. Ind. U. Med. Center, 1947-51, Commn. on Financing of Hosp. Care, 1952-53, St. Luke's Hosp., Chgo., 1953-54; med. dir. U. Ill. Research and Ednl. Hosps., also asso. dean U. Ill. Coll. Medicine, Chgo., 1954-69, vice chancellor U. Ill. Med. Center. Commr. Joint Commn. on Accreditation of Hosps.; mem. Fed. Hosp. Council, 1969-72. Mem. bd. trustees Ill. Hosp. Served to maj., M.C., AUS, 1943-46. Diplomate Am. Bd. Orthopedic Surgery. Fellow Royal Soc. Health; mem. A.M.A., Am. Acad. Orthopedic Surgery, Am., Ill. (pres. 1964-65, trustee) hosp. assns., Am. Pub. Health Assn., Assn. Am. Med. Colls. (chmn. teaching hosp. sect. 1960-61), Inst. Medicine Chgo. (gov. 1965-69), Delta Upsilon, Nu Sigma Nu. Home: 5742 S Monroe St Hinsdale IL 60521

CASELLA, P. J., corp. exec.; b. Italy, Oct. 10, 1913; s. Frank and Felice Casella; student U. Pa.; m. Palmina Fiorella, Apr. 11, 1943; 1 son, Mark. Trainee Montgomery Ward & Co., Inc., Binghamton, N.Y., other cities, 1933-34, asst. mgr., Gloversville, N.Y., 1935, gen. store operations mgr., Freeport, L. I., 1935-36, gen. store mgr., Lancaster, Pa., Portsmouth, N.H., Brockton, Mass., Uniontown, Pa., Balt., 1936-42, gen. mgr. Detroit, 1946-48, Albany, N.Y., 1948-54; gen. mgr. distbn. RCA Victor Co., Ltd., Montreal, Can., 1954, v.p. distbn., 1954-55, v.p. consumer products, 1955, pres., chief exec. officer, 1956-60, chmn. exec. com., dir., 1960-61, mng. dir. RCA Italiana, Rome, Italy, 1956; exec. v.p. charge consumer products RCA, N.Y.C., 1958-61; chmn. bd. RCA Sales Corp., Camden, N.J., 1959-61; pres., chief exec. officer Endicott Johnson Corp., 1961-64; pres., chief exec. Elgin Nat. Watch Corp., 1964- 65; exec. v.p., dir., mem. exec. com. BVD Corp., N.Y.C., 1965-68; exec. v.p. Perini Corp., 1969—; pres. Properties Corp. Am., 1971—; v.p., dir. Timely Clothes, Inc.; dir. Marine Midland Trust Co. So. N.Y. Mem. United Shareholders Adv. Com. Bd. dirs. Binghamton Boys Club; trustee N.Y. State Hosp. Rev. and Planning Council. Served to lt. comdr. USNR, 1942-45; comdg. officer Officer Naval Res. Unit, Schenectady-Troy-Albany, N.Y. area, 1949-52. Mem. Am. Civic Assn. (adv. council), Nat. Planning Assn. (nat. council). Roman Catholic. Club: Binghamton City. Home: 56 Larchmont Rd Binghamton NY 13903 also 14 Temple Framingham MA 01701 Office: Mt Wayte Av Framingham MA 01701 also Binghamton NY 13903

CASERIO, MARTIN JOSEPH, automobile mfg. co. exec.; b. Laurium, Mich., July 18, 1916; s. Joseph and Mary (Michela) C.; B.S., Mich. Tech. U., 1936, D.Sc. in Engring. (hon.), 1961; m. Josephine Spolarich, Oct. 7, 1944; children—Richard, Kathleen, Joseph, Patricia. With AC Spark Plug div. Gen. Motors Corp., 1937-58, gen. mgr., 1964-66, gen. mgr. Delco Radio Div., 1958-64, v.p. parent corp., 1964—, gen. mgr. GMC Truck and Coach div., 1966—. Served to 1st lt. C.E., AUS, World War II. Recipient Silver Knight award Nat. Mgmt. Assn., 1963. Fellow Am. Soc. Metals (chmn. Saginaw Valley chpt. 1956); mem. Inst. Aero. Scis., Am. Ordnance Assn., Am. Rocket Soc., Navy League, Air Force Assn., Soc. Automotive Engrs. (chmn. Mid-Mich. sect. 1955), Flint Automobile Club, Flint Indsl. Execs. Club, Tau Beta Pi, Phi Kappa Phi. K.C. Home: 246 Barden Rd Bloomfield Hills MI 48013 Office: GMC Truck and Coach Div Gen Motors Corp 660 S Blvd E Pontiac MI 48503

CASESA, PHILIP ROBERT, physician, hosp. adminstr.; b. Argrigento, Sicily, Italy, June 6, 1909; s. Gerlando and Marie (Florio) C.; came to U.S., 1910, naturalized, 1920; student L.I.U., 1927-29, Tufts Coll., 1929-30; M.D., Boston U., 1934; m. Rose Giammalvo, Dec. 11, 1938; children—Marie, James. Rotating intern St. Elizabeth's Hosp., Boston, 1934-35; gen. practice medicine, Bklyn., 1935-42; med. officer VA Facility, Waco, Tex., 1942-44, VA Hosp., Columbia, S.C., 1944; med. officer, chief outpatient services VA Hosp., Bronx, N.Y., 1946-47; asst. chief med. officer, chief med. officer VA Outpatient Clinic, VA Regional Office, Bklyn., 1947-56; mgr. VA Outpatient Clinic, Bklyn, 1956-60; dir. VA Hosp., Bklyn. 1960—; chief med. con. bur. disability determinations N.Y. State Dept. Social Services; adj. prof. biology, cons. in med. tech. C.W. Post Coll., Greenvale, N.Y. Mem. subcomm. gen. community relations Fed. Exec. Bd., 1965; pres. Better Bklyn. Com., Bklyn. Hall of Fame. Served to maj., M.C., AUS, 1944-46. Recipient award for dedicated med. service to vets. Italian Hist. Soc. Am., 1961. Fellow Am. Coll. Chest Physicians, Am. Coll. Hosp. Adminstrs.; mem. A.M.A., N.Y. State, Kings County (hosp. and profl. relations com.) med. socs., Am., N.Y. State, Bklyn. socs. internal medicine, Am. Legion. Address: VA Hospital 800 Poly Pl Brooklyn NY 11209

CASEY, ALBERT VINCENT, newspaper exec.; b. Boston, Feb. 28, 1920; s. John Joseph and Norine (Doyle) C.; A.B., Harvard, 1943, M.B.A., 1948; m. Eleanor Anne Welch, Aug. 25, 1945; children—Peter Andrew, Judith Anne. With S.P. Ry., 1948- 61, asst. v.p., asst. treas., San Francisco, 1959-61; v.p., treas. Ry. Express Agy., N.Y.C., 1961-63; v.p. finance Times-Mirror Co., Los Angeles, 1963-64, exec. v.p., 1964-66, dir. 1965—, pres., 1966; dir. Bank of Cal., Pacific Ins. Co. Pres. Performing Arts Council Los Angeles. Served to 1st lt. AUS, 1942-46, Clubs: Sky (N.Y.C.); California; Annandale. Home: 2195 Orlando Dr San Marino CA 91108 Office: Times Mirror Sq Los Angeles CA 90012

CASEY, CLAUDE C., Jr., headmaster; b. Anniston, Ala., Apr. 25, 1923; s. Claude C. and Eula (McKee) C.; B.S., U. Chattanooga, 1948; D.V.M., Auburn U., 1955; M.S., Hofstra U., 1962, certificate advanced study, 1964; m. Dorothy Mahr, June 6, 1954. Veterinarian, Crawford Dog and Cat Hosp., Garden City, N.Y., 1955-56; tchr., head sci. dept., registrar, asst. to headmaster St. Paul's Sch., Garden City, 1956-65, headmaster, 1965—. Mem. N.Y. State adv. com. Middle States Assn. Served with AUS, World War II; ETO Mem. Nat. Assn. Ind. Schs., N.Y. State Secondary Sch. Adminstrs. Assn., Headmasters Assn., Middle states Assn. Secondary Schs. and Colls., Newcomen Soc. N.Am., Theta Chi, Alpha Psi, Beta Beta Beta, Alpha Zeta. Address: St Paul's Sch 295 Stewart St Garden City NY 11534

CASEY, EDWARD PAUL, mfg. co. exec.; b. Boston, Feb. 23, 1930; s. Edward J. and Virginia (Paul) C.; A.B., Yale, 1952; M.B.A., Harvard, 1955; m. Patricia Pinkham, June 23, 1950; children—Patricia Estes, Lucile Tyler, Jennifer Paul, Sheila Pinkham, Virginia Louise. With Davidson Rubber Co., Dover, N.H., 1950—, pres., 1965—, dir., 1950—; pres. McCord Corp., Detroit, 1965—, also dir.; dir. Mfrs. Nat. Bank Detroit. Trustee Miss Hall's Sch., Pittsfield, Mass. Mem. Engring. Soc. Detroit (dir.), Soc. Automotive Engrs., Young Pres.'s Orgn. Clubs: Detroit, Detroit Athletic, Recess, Harvard Business School (bd. dirs.) (Detroit); Grosse Pointe; Country Club of Detroit (Grosse Pointe Farms, Mich.); Eastern Yacht (Marblehead, Mass.): Wig and Pen (London, Eng.). Home: 4 Rathbone Pl Grosse Pointe MI 48230 Office: McCord Corp 2850 W Grand Blvd Detroit MI 48202

CASEY, EUGENE BERNARD, former exec. asst. to Pres. U.S.; b. Washington, June 13, 1904; s. Michael B. and Rose (O'Neill) C.; student Pa. State Coll., 1922-24, Georgetown U., 1924-26; m. Helen Stokes, Aug. 29, 1924; children—Virginia, Nancy, Betsy, Eugene, Douglas, Margaret; m. 2d, Betty Brown, Feb. 8, 1955. Sole propr. Casey Enring Co. san., heating, ventilating and elec. engring., designing and constrn., also constrn. housing for personal investment, 1931—; owner, operator cattle and grain farms, Montgomery County, Md., Wis., Va., Minn., S.D.; dep. gov. FCA, 1940-41; exec. asst. to Pres. U.S., 1941-53; dir. Internat. Bank, Nat. Mortgage & Investment Corp. of Washington, Canadian Dredge & Drydock Corp., Financial Gen. Corp., Atlas Gen. Corp., Bowie Race Course, Atlantic City Racing Assn. Navy mem. Army and Navy Munitions Bd. Trustee Patrick Henry Meml. Assn. Past pres. Young Men's Democratic Club. Served with USNR, 1944-45; P.T.O. Mem. Am. Soc. M.E., Am. Soc. Heating and Ventilating Engrs., Am. Soc. Mil. Engrs. Nat. Com. for Agr. (sec.- treas.), Am. Farm Bur. (dir.), Nat. Grange, Newcomen Soc., Am. Legion, U.S. Naval Res. Officers Assn., Navy League, Horsemen's Benevolent and Protective Assn., Delta Upsilon, Lambda Sigma. Democrat. Roman Catholic. Rotarian. Clubs: National Press, Young Men's Democratic (pres.); Winchester (Va.) Golf and Country; Washingtonian Country. Home: Springsbury Farms Berryville VA and Gaitherburg MD 20760 Office: 1 W Deer Park Dr Gaitherburg MD 20760

CASEY, GENEVIEVE MARY, librarian; b. Mpls., July 13, 1916; d. Eugene James and Cecelia (Malerich) Casey; B.S., Coll. St. Catherine, St. Paul, 1937; M.A., U. Mich., 1956. Mem. staff Detroit Pub. Library, 1937-46, 48-61, chief extension dept., 1948-61; librarian U.S. Army Libraries, ETO, 1946-47, Mich. State Library, Lansing, 1961-67; asso. prof. library scis. Wayne State U., 1967—; book reviewer for Mich. Catholic, Sign, Library Jour. Mem. Am. (pres. Assn. Hosp. and Instn. Libraries 1961-62); pres. library edn. div. 1970-72) Mich., Catholic library assns. Address: 574 Goldengate W Detroit MI 48203

CASEY, J. JOSEPH, corp. exec.; b. Boston, July 12, 1921; s. William and Katherine (Wollins) C.; B.S. in Fgn. Service, Georgetown U., 1942; postgrad. N.Y. U. Law Sch., 1947-49; m. Lynn Fallon, June 26, 1948; children—Robin Ann, J. Todd, Reid M. Vice pres., treas. William Casey & Sons, Inc., L.I., 1946-56; asst. treas. Raymond Internat., Inc., N.Y.C., 1957-60, controller, 1961-67; v.p., controller Dillingham Corp., Honolulu, 1967—; exec. v.p. Dillingham Corp. Australia, Ltd. Served to lt. USNR, 1942-46. Mem. Financial Execs. Inst. (chmn. internat. operations com. 1966-67). Home: 134 Niuiki Circle Honolulu HI 96821 Office: 1441 Kapiolani Blvd Honolulu HI 96814

CASEY, JAMES J., lawyer; b. San Francisco, Feb. 2, 1915; s. James M. and Anne (Hodnett) C.; A.B., Columbia, 1937, LL.B., 1940; m. Ann Gambrill, Sept. 27, 1947; children—Anne H., Edith B., Richard G. Admitted to N.Y. bar, 1941, since practiced in N..C.; partner firm Casey, Lane & Mittendorf, and predecessors, 1952—. Dir. Englehard Minerals & Chem. Corp., Inc., Internat. Fund, Inc., Mem. Peapack-Gladstone Zoning Bd., 1956—; mem. adminstrv. tribunal UN, 1960-63. Trustee, pres. of the Upper Raritan Watershed Assn.; bd. of visitors Columbia Law Sch., 1962—; mem. council Columbia Coll., 1963-66. Served to lt. comdr. USNR, 1941-45, Mem. Am., Inter Am., N.Y. State bar assns., Assn. Bar City N.Y., Am. Fgn. Law Assn. Home: Peapackc NJ 07977 Office: 26 Broadway New York City NY 10004

CASEY, JAMES VINCENT, bishop; b Osage, Ia., Sept. 22, 1914; s. James G. and Nina (Nims) C.; A.B., Loras Coll, 1936, LL.D., 1959; student Gregorian U., Rome, Italy, 1936-40; J.C.D., Cath. U. Am., 1949. Ordained priest Roman Cath. Ch., 1939; asst. pastor St. John's Parish, Independence, Ia., 1940-44; sec. Archbishop Leo Binz, Dubuque, 1946-49; bishop of Lincoln, 1957-67; archbishop of Denver, 1967—. Served to lt. (s.g.), Chaplains Corps, USNR, 1944-46. Home: 480 S Marion Pky Denver CO 80209 Office: 938 Bannock St Denver CO 80204

CASEY, JOHN JOSEPH, airlines exec.; b. Boston, Oct. 3, 1918; s. John Joseph and Norine (Doyle) C.; S.B., Mass. Inst. Tech., 1940, postgrad., 1940; postgrad. Cornell U., 1942; m. Mary June Reipe, Apr. 21, 1945; children—John Joseph, David Vaughan, Janet Marjorie, Mary June. Stress engr. Curtiss-Wright Corp., Buffalo, 1940-42; mgr. air cargo engring. Am. Airlines, St. Joseph, Mo., 1946-47, service engr., N.Y.C., 1947-49, asst. v.p. maintenance, Tulsa, 1950-56; v.p. R. Dixon Speas Assos., Manhasset, N.Y., aviation cons., 1956-62; sr. v.p. operations, dir. Seaboard World Airlines, N.Y.C., 1962-68; exec. v.p., dir. Braniff Internat., Dallas, 1968—. Nassau County commr. Boy Scouts Am., 1967-68, mem. exec. bd.; v.p. Circle 10 council, 1969—. Served with USAAF, 1942-46; comdg. officer 320th Squadron, 509th Composite Bomb Group, 1945-46. Mem. Am. Inst. Aeros. and Astronautics, Soc. Automotive Engrs., Mass. Inst. Tech. Alumni Assn. (bd. govs., v.p. N.Y.C. 1959), Air Force Assos. Club: Wings (N.Y.C.); Manhasset Bay Yacht (Port Washington, N.Y.); Braniff Internat. Council. Home: 6837 Meadowcreek Dr Dallas TX 75241 Office: Braniff Internat Exchange Park Dallas TX 75235

CASEY, JOSEPH J., lawyer; b. Albany, N.Y., July 18, 1904; s. James J. and Josephine M. (Wallace) C.; student Christian Bros. Acad., Albany, 1918-22; LL.B., Union U., Schenectady, 1925; LL.D., St. Bernadine of Siena Coll., 1965; m. Julia A. Leddy, June 12, 1929; 1 dau., Mary Faith. Admitted to N.Y. bar, 1926, since practiced in Albany; mem. firm Casey, Yanas and Mitchell; asst. dist. atty. Albany County, 1932-35; asst. corp. counsel, City of Albany, 1935-36, corp. counsel, 1936- 40; v.p. and trustee City & Co. Savs. Bank, 1949—. Bd. trustees St. Agnes Cemetery, Cath. Charities Diocese Albany; v.p. Albany Community Chest, 1950. Pres. Fedn. Bar Assns. Third Jud. Dist. State N.Y., 1950-51. Mem. Am., N.Y. State bar assns., Sons St. Patrick. Roman Catholic. Elk, K.C. Clubs: Fort Orange, Albany Country. Home: 225 Euclid Av Albany NY Office: 100 State St Albany NY

CASEY, LAWRENCE B., bishop; b. Rochester, N.Y., Sept. 6, 1905; s. Joseph L. and Agnes M.(Switzer) C.; student St. Andrew's Minor Sem., Rochester, 1919-24, St. Bernard's Theol. Sem., Rochester, 1924-30. Ordained as priest Roman Cath. Ch., 1930; vice chancellor Diocese of Rochester, 1932-46; pastor Holy Cross Ch., Rochester, 1946-52; rector Sacred Heart Cathedral, Rochester, 1952; titular bishop of Cea and aux. to bishop of Rochester, 1953-66; bishop, Paterson, N.J., 1966—. Home: 178 Derrom Av Paterson NJ 07504 Office: 24 De Grasse St Paterson NJ 07505

CASEY, MAURICE FRANCIS, air force officer; b. Chgo., June 3, 1920; s. Maurice Francis and Marie (Rowan) C.; student U. Chgo., 1939-40, U. Miami, 1948-50, Nat. War Coll., 1962; m. Dora Belle Neubert, Oct. 12, 1946; children—Faith Maureen, Shirley Marie, M.F. Timothy, Georgeanne, Michael Joseph. Commd. 2d lt. USAAF, 1943, advanced through grades to maj. gen. USAF, 1970; leader heavy bomber air armada 8th Air Force, World War II; troop wing comdr. Far East, 1952-54; chief air traffic control USAF, also mem. tech. div. U.S. Air Coordinating Com., 1954-55; mil. adviser Royal Danish Air Force, also chief air force MAAG, 1958-61; dep. dir. air force information, 1955-58, 62-65; comdr. 60th Mil. Airlift Wing, Travis AFB, 1965-68; dir. transp. Hdqrs. USAF, 1968—. Schedule airline insp. CAA, 1947-50. Vice pres. McLean (Va.) Civic Assn., 1961-65; pres. St. John's Men's Council, 1962-65. Decorated Legion of Merit (4), Bronze star, D.F.C. (3), Air medal (5); Croix de Guerre (France): D.F.C. (U.K.); Commendation of Honor (Greece). Mem. S.E. Air Res. Assn. (v.p. 1950), Nat. Def. Transp. Assn. (pres.), Quiet Birdmen. Aviation Space Writers Assn. Lion. Home: 7017 Union Mill Rd Clifton VA 22024 Office: Headquarters USAF Washington DC 20333

CASEY, MORGAN A., retail chain store co. exec.; b. Moravia, N.Y., July 17, 1901; s. Herbert M. and Naomi R. (Decker) C.; B.A., Yale, 1923; m. Irene S. Searles, Mar. 15, 1930; 1 son. Pub. accountant until 1935; with Merc. Stores Co., Inc., N.Y.C., 1936—, now v.p., dir. Active civic affairs, Pelham, N.Y. C.P.A., N.Y. State. Mem. Pelham Manor Assn. (pres.). Presbyn. (trustee). Clubs: Pelham Country, Pelham Men's; Union League (N.Y.C.); Skytop (Pa.). Home: 1028 Esplanade Pelham Manor NY 10803 Office: 128 W 31st St New York City NY 10001

CASEY, RALPH EDWARD, lawyer; b. Boston, May 25, 1911; A.B., Harvard, 1932, LL.B., 1935; LL.M., Georgetown U., 1941. Admitted to Mass. bar, 1935; pvt. practice law, Boston, 1935-39; with Gen. Accounting Office, Washington, 1939-55, asso. gen. counsel charge contracts, litigation and maritime activities, 1948-55; counsel Hardy Com. on U.S. Govt. Operations, 1950-52; chief counsel Mcht. Marine and Fisheries Com., 1955-56; pres. Am. Mcht. Marine Inst., Inc., 1956-68; exec. v.p. Am. Inst. Mcht. Shipping, 1969-70; spl. counsel Mcht. Marine and Fisheries Com., 1970-71, chief counsel, 1971—. Vice pres. Internat. Shipping Fedn., London, Eng., 1965-68; vice chmn. bd., chmn. exec. com. Nat. Com. Internat. Trade Documentation, 1967-70. Address: Longworth House Office Bldg Washington DC 20515

CASEY, LORD RICHARD GARDINER, former gov.-gen. Australia; b. Brisbane, Queensland, Australia, Aug. 29, 1890; s. Richard Gardiner and Evelyn Jane (Harris) C.; student Melbourne U., 1908-09; B.A., Trinity Coll., Cambridge, Eng., 1913; LL.D., Bates Coll. (Me.), 1941, Birmingham U. (Eng.), 1943, Mich. State U., 1958, Monash U., Victoria, Australia, 1966, U. Tasmania, 1966, U. Papua, New Guinea, 1967, Australian Nat. U., 1969; D.Sc., U. New South Wales, 1966, U Sydney (Australia), 1968; D.Engs., Newcastle U., 1967; m. Ethel Marian Sumner Ryan, June 24, 1926; children—Jane Alice Camilla (Mrs. Murray Wynne Macgowan), Richard Charles Donn. Liaison officer Australian Govt. and Fgn. Office, London, 1924-31; mem. Australian Ho. of Reps. for Corio, 1931-40, for Latrobe, 1949-60; asst. fed. treas., 1933-35; fed. treas., 1935-39; rep. Australia at London Conf. on Conduct of War, 1939; minister for supply and devel., 1939-40; minster to U.S.A., 1940-42; minister state resident in Middle East, mem. War Cabinet U.K., 1942-43; gov. Bengal, 1944-46; fed. pres. Liberal Party Australia, 1947-49; minister for works and housing, 1949-51, for supply and devel., 1949-50, for nat. devel., 1950-51; minister charge Commonwealth Sci. and Indsl. Research Orgn., 1950-60, part-time mem. exec., 1960-65; minister external affairs, 1951-60; gov. gen. Commonwealth Australia, Canberra, 1965-69. Served to maj. Gen. Staff, 1914-18. Created life peer, 1961, knight Noble Order Garter, 1969. Hon. fellow Australian Inst. Mgmt., Royal Australian Coll. Surgeons, Royal Australian Chem. Inst., Royal Australian Inst. Architects, Royal Melbourne Inst. Tech.; hon. mem. Instn. Engrs. Australia, Australian Planning Inst. Author: An Australian in India, 1947; Double or Quit, 1948; Friends and Neighbours, 1954; Personal Experience 1939-46, 1962; The Future of the Commonwealth, 1963; Australian Father and Son, 1965. Home: Edrington Berwick 3806 Victoria Australia

CASEY, ROBERT RANDOLPH, congressman; b. Joplin, Mo., July 27, 1915; s. Samuel R. and Mabel (Caywood) C.; student U. Houston, also South Tex. Sch. Law, 1934-40; m. Hazel M. Brann, Aug. 13, 1935; children—Hazel M., Robert R., Catherine, Bonnie, Mike, Shawn, Bridget, Eileen, Tim, Kevin. Admitted to Tex. bar, 1940; practice in Alvin, Tex., 1941-43, Houston, 1943—; asst. dist. atty. Harris County, 1943-47; mem. Tex. Legislature, 1949-50; judge Harris County 1951-58; mem. of the 86th, 88th-92d congresses, 22d District Tex. Democrat. Clubs: Internat., Houston, Yacht (Houston). Home: 2256 Dryden St Houston TX also 5406 Albia Rd NW Washington DC 20016 Office: Rayburn Bldg Washington DC 20515

CASEY, SAMUEL ALEXANDER, lawyer, paper mfr.; b. Perola, Ill., Sept. 10, 1914; s. Richard C. and Chloris (Thomason) C.; A.B., Bradley U., 1936; J.D., U. Ill., 1939; m. Ardean Alexander, Nov. 7, 1942; children—John A., Suzanne E., Page E. Admitted to Ill. bar, 1939, Wis. bar, 1946; practice law, 1939—; asso. Champan & Cutler, Chgo., 1939-42; exec. v.p., treas. Nekoosa- Edwards Paper Co., Port Edwards, Wis., 1946-61, pres., dir., 1962-70, dir., 1962—; pres., dir. Gt. No. Nekoosa Corp., Stamford, Conn., 1971—; dir. Employers Ins. of Wausau, Wis., Gt. No. Paper Co., Marshall & Ilsley Bank, Milw. Trustee Lawrence U., Appleton, Wis., Bradley U., Peoria, Ill. Home: 9 Whaling Rd Darien CT 06820 Office: 75 Prospect St Stamford CT 06901

CASEY, SAMUEL BROWN, Jr., equipment mfg. co. exec.; b. Pitts., Oct. 14, 1927; s. Samuel Brown and Constance (Connelly) C.; B.A., Pa. State U., 1950; m. Margaret Fox, Sept. 9, 1950; children—Samuel Brown III, Ann, Meg. Product mgr. Swindell-Dressler Co., 1950-60; pres. John F. Casey Co., 1960-69, chmn. bd., 1969; pres., chief exec. officer Pullman, Inc., Chgo., 1970—; dir. Amerace-Esna Corp., Joseph Dixon Crucible Co., John F. Casey Co., Ry. Maintenance Co., Nat. Union Ins. Cos. Pres. Pitts. Hosp., 1963-70; vice chmn. bd. Pitts. Stadium Authority, 1964—. Bd. dirs. Carnegie Inst. Served with USAF, 1945-46. Home: 1500 Lake Shore Dr Chicago IL 60610 Office: 200 S Michigan Av Chicago IL 60604

CASEY, THOMAS F., mfg. exec.; b. Rye, N.Y.; 1908; grad. N.Y. U., 1929. Pres., chmn., dir. Tampax, Inc., N.Y.C.; dir. Canadian Tampax Corp., Ltd., Brampton, Ont.; dir. Tampax Ltd., Tampax France S.A.R.L., Tampax Italiana s.p.a., Tampax (Continental) Ltd., Tampax Scandinavia A/B, Tampax (Nederland) N.V. Home: 189 Rockcrest Rd Manhasset NY 11030 Office: 161 E 42d St New York City NY 10017

CASEY, WILLIAM JOSEPH, govt. ofcl.; b. N.Y.C., Mar. 13, 1913; s. William J. and Blanche (La Vigne) C.; B.S., Fordham U., 1934; LL.B., St. John's Law Sch., 1937; m. Sophia Kurz, Feb. 22, 1941; 1 dau., Bernadette. Admitted to N.Y. bar, 1938; chmn. bd. editors Research Inst. Am., 1938-49, Inst. Bus. Planning, 1953-70; partner firm Hall, Casey, Dukle and Hurley, N.Y.C., 1957-71; chmn. SEC, 1971—. Mem. Gen. Advisory Com. Arms Control, 1969-71; mem. Presdl. Task Force Internat. Devel., 1969-70; pres., chmn. L.I. Assn., 1968-71; pres. Internat. Rescue Com., 1970-71. Trustee Fordham U., 1966-71. Served to lt. USNR, 1942-45; ETO. Decorated Bronze Star. Clubs: University (Washington): Sky (N.Y.C.). Author: Lawyers Desk Book, 1965; Tax Sheltered Investments, 1952; Forms of Business Agreements, 1966; Accounting Desk Book, 1967; others. Home: Glenwood Rd Roslyn Harbor NY 11576 Office: 500 N Capitol St Washington DC 20549

CASEY, WILLIAM VAN ETTEN, educator, clergyman; b. Boston, Jan. 7, 1914; s. Thomas Francis and Mary Agnes (Van Etten) C.; A.B., Boston Coll., 1938, M.A., 1940; Ph.L., Weston Coll., 1939, S.T.L., 1945. Joined Soc. of Jesus, 1932; Jesuit novitiate and juniorate, Lenox, Mass., 1932-36; ordained priest Roman Cath. Ch., 1944; instr. English, Holy Cross Coll., 1940-41; instr. theology Boston Coll., 1946-48, chmn. dept., 1948-57, asso. prof. theology, 1948-60, dean Coll. Arts and Scis., 1956-60, also trustee, acad. v.p., 1958-60; prof. theology Coll. of Holy Cross, 1960—; Bibl. archaeology, Jerusalem, 1962-63. Dir. Am. Sch. Oriental Research in Jerusalem, 1967-68. Mem. Soc. Bibl. Lit., Catholic Bibl. Assn. Cath. Theol. Soc., Religious Edn. Assn. Editor: Berrigans, 1971; Holy Cross Quar., 1969—; Cath. editorial adviser Oxford U. Press. Address: Coll of the Holy Cross Worcester MA 01610

CASGRAIN, PHILIPPE, lawyer; b. Rimouski, Que., Can., Apr. 17, 1927; B.A., Laval U., 1948, LL.L., 1952. Admitted to Que. bar, 1952; partner firm Byers, McDougall, Casgrain & Stewart, Montreal. Mem. Montreal (mem. council 1959-60), Que. (mem. gen. council 1968-69), Canadian bar assns. Office: 800 Victoria Sq Montreal 115 Quebec Canada*

CASH, CLAYBOURNE ALLISON, corp. exec.; b. McLean, Tex., Oct. 31, 1914; s. Claybourne Jeremiah and Lavada (Phillips) C.; student Tex. Technol. Coll., 1933-35; m. Juanita Ball, Sept. 13, 1936; 1 dau., Elaine (Mrs. C. D. Culver). With Shamrock Oil & Gas Corp., Amarillo, Tex., 1935-67, beginning as clk., successively chief clk., treating foreman, refinery foreman, chief engr., asst. to v.p. charge operations, v.p., asst. to pres., 1955- 57, exec. v.p., dir., 1957-60, pres., 1960-67; exec. v.p., dir. Diamond Shamrock Corp., 1967, pres., 1967-69, chmn. bd., 1969-71, vice chmn., 1971, pres., 1971—; pres. Diamond Oil & Gas Co. unit, 1967—; dir. First Nat. Bank Amarillo, Terra Chems. Internat., Mc. Bd. dirs. Tex. Research League. Mem. Am. Petroleum Inst. (dir.), Mid-Continent Oil and Gas Assn., Nat. Gas Porcessors Assn. (chmn. gas supply com.), Newcomen Soc., Am. Chem. Soc., (dir.), Panhandle Producers and Royalty Owners Assn. Methodist. Mason. Clubs: Amarillo (pres. 1961), Amarillo Country; Dallas Petroleum; Petroleum (Houston); Union (Cleve.). Home: La Tour Apt 2028 Austin St Amarillo TX 79109 Office: Box 631 Amarillo TX 79105 also: Chmn Commerce Bldg Cleveland OH 44115

CASH, FRANK ERRETTE, Jr., fgn. service officer; b. Oriskany, Va., Mar. 7, 1921; s. Frank Errette and Libbie (Adamson) C.; B.S., Birmingham-So. Coll., 1941, U.S. Mil. Acad., 1944; postgrad. Harvard, 1951-52; m. Naomi Duncan, Dec. 3, 1947; childrenHal Duncan, Susan Hamilton. Commd. 2d lt. U.S. Army, 1944, advanced through grades to capt., 1948; served in ETO, World War II, resigned, 1948; joined U.S. Fgn. Service, 1948; assigned Am. consulate gen., Stuttgart, Germany, 1948-51; polit. officer Am. embassy, Bonn, Germany, 1952-55; consul, polit. officer Am. embassy, Manila, Philippines, 1955-57; head dept. univ. tng. and area studies Fgn. Service Inst., State Dept., 1958-60; officer charge German polit. participant also dep. dir. Berlin task force State Dept., 1960-63. Participant sr. seminar in fgn. affairs Fgn. Service Inst., 1963-64, counselor for mut. security affairs Am. embassy, Ankara, Turkey, 1964-68; country dir. for Turkey, State Dept., 1968-71; Am. minister, dep. chief mission Am. embassy, Bonn, 1971—. Home: 44 Turmstrasse Bonn West Germany Office: Am Embassy APO New York City NY 09080

CASH, JAMES BARRETT, Jr., assn. ofcl.; b. Hazen, Ark., Nov. 8, 1921; s. James Barrett and Annie Laurie (Graves) C.; A.A., George Washington U., 1948, B.A., 1951; certificate emergency mgmt. of nat. economy, Indsl. Coll. Armed Forces, 1956; m. Teresa O'Connor, Dec. 27, 1968. Adminstrv. positions FHA, 1939-53; policy and procedures officer Civil Service Commn., 1953-55; profl. staff mem. com. banking and currency U.S. Senate, 1955-61; dep. commnr. FHA, 1961-62; with AID, Caracas, Venezuela, 1962-64, dir. Latin Am. guaranties, 1964; profl. staff mem. Select Com. on Small Bus., U.S. Senate, 1964-65; legislative asst. Senator J.W. Fulbright, 1965-70; fed. legislative rep. Am. Bankers Assn., 1970—. Served with USAAF, World War II. Mem. Sigma Alpha Epsilon. Home: 7522 Allman Dr Annandale VA 22003 Office: 1120 Connecticut Av NW Washington DC 20036

CASH, JAMES ROBERT, retired physician; b. Chattanooga, May 2, 893; s. James Albion and Elizabeth (Cheney) C.; A.B., U. Va., 1914, A.M., 1915; M.D., Johns Hopkins, 1919; m. Mary Frazier Meade, Sept. 5, 1943. Instr. Johns Hopkins Med. Sch., 1919, asst. prof. pathology, 1922; asso. prof. pathology Peiping (China) Union Med. Coll., 1924-28, prof., 1928; prof. pathology U. Va., 1931-58, 60-63, formerly Walter Reed prof.; vis. prof. Basic Med. Sci. Inst., Karachi, Pakistan, under Internat. Coop. Adminstrn., 1958-60. Mem. Am. Soc. Exptl. Pathology. Specialist in diseases of vascular system; interested in cancer control in Va. Home: Box 265 Crozet VA 22932

CASH, JOHNNY, entertainer; b. Kingsland, Ark., Feb. 26, 1932; s. Ray and Carrie (Rivers) C.; m. June Carter, Mar. 1, 1968; 1 son, John Carter; children by previous marriage—Rosanne, Kathleen, Cindy, Tara. Profl. composer, also recording artist; TV performer the Johnny Cash Show, 1969-71; pres. House of Cash, Inc., Johnny Cash, Inc., Luther Corp., Song of Cash, Inc.; v.p. Family of Man Music, Inc. Mem. adv. com. Peace Corps, Country Music Assn., John Edwards Meml. Found. Served with USAF. Mem. Internat. Platform Assn. Composer: I Walk the Line; Folsom Prison Blues; At Folsom Prison; Man in Black; Don't Take Your Guns to Town; documentary recording: The Holy Land; The True West; composer movie sound tracks: I Walk the Line; Little Fauss and Big Halsy; Subject documentary films: Trail of Tears; Johnny Cash, the Man, His World, His Music; actor movie: A Gunfight; TV documentary film: Johnny Cash at San Quentin. Address: Caudill Dr Hendersonville TN 37075

CASH, PAUL THALBERT, physician; b. Lenox, Ia., July 11, 1911; s. William Henry and Helen (Phalen) C.; student Creston Jr. Coll., 1929-31; M.D., U. Ia., 1935; m. Reva Lamb, Aug. 16, 1958; 1 step-son, Peter Goodwin. Intern, St. Vincents Hosp., Portland, Ore., 1935-36; resident psychiatry Clarkson Meml. Hosp., Omaha, 1936-37, Albany (N.Y.) Hosp., 1937-38; vol. asst. internal medicine U. Ia. Hosps., Iowa City, 1938; resident neurology Neurol. Inst. N.Y., 1939; practice medicine specializing in psychiatry, neurology, Omaha, 1940-48, Des Moines, 1948—; instr. neurology, psychiatry U. Neb. Coll. Medicine, 1946-48; chief service neurology and psychiatry Ia. Meth. Hosp., 1953—; mem. staff Ia. Luth., Mercy, Broadlawsn Gen. hosps.; cons. VA Hosp. Bd. dirs. YMCA Boys Home. Served to maj. M.C., AUS, 1942-46. Diplomate Am. Bd. Psychiatry and Neurology. Fellow Am. Psychiat. Assn., A.M.A.; mem. Central, Ia. neuropsychiat. assns., Am. Acad. Neurology, Assn. for Research in Nervous and Mental Diseases, Am. Electroencephalographic Soc. Contbr. articles to profl. jours. Home: 3422 Wakonda Ct Des Moines IA 50321 Office: 1405 Woodland St Des Moines IA 50309

CASH, WILLIAM BRADBURY, bus. cons.; b. Portland, Ore., Mar. 28, 1915; s. John P. and Irene (Bradbury) C.; B.A. in English, Dartmouth, 1937; grad. Advanced Mgmt. Course, Harvard, 1953; m. Nancy Kirkpatrick, June 14, 1941; childrenPenelope, Nancy, Louise. With Gen. Mills, Inc., 1937-63, dir. marketing, 1960-63, v.p., 1960-63; exec. v.p., gen. mgr. operations United Biscuit Co. Am. (became Keebler Co. 1966), 1963-67; pres., chief exec. officer Hanes Corp., Winston-Salem, N.C., 1967-70; now bus. cons.; dir. Rapistan, Inc., Grand Rapids, Mich., Bemis Co., Inc., Mpls. Chmn. Winston-Salem Housing Inc. Served to lt. comdr. USNR, 1940-45. Mem. A.I.M., Winston-Salem C. of C., Psi Upsilon. Republican. Episcopalian. Clubs: Minneapolis, Wayzata Country (Mpls.); Skokie Country (Glencoe, Ill.); Rotary, Old Town (Winston-Salem). Home: 2848 Bartram Rd Winston-Salem, NC 27106.

CASHIN, BONNIE, designer; b. Oakland, Cal., 1915. Designer, ballet co.; costume designer Roxy Theatre, N.Y.C., 1934-37; sportswear designer Adler & Adler, N.Y.C., 1937-43; fashion designer Twentieth Century Fox Studios, Cal., 1943-49, Adler & Adler, 1949-52; own bus. Bonnie Cashin Designs, Inc., N.Y.C., 1952—. Invited by Indian govt. to assist in revitalization program for handloom industry, 1956. Recipient Nieman Marcus award, N.Y.C. Fashion Critics Winnie, Sports Illustrated award, Knitwear Industry award, Phila. Mus. Coll. of Art citation, Woolknit Assn. award, 1961, N.Y. Fashion Critics award, 1961; named Woman of Year, Lighthouse for Blind, 1961. Home: 32 E 64th St New York City NY 10021 Office: 866 University Pl New York City NY

CASHIN, FRANK M., mfg. co. exec.; b. Duluth, Minn., 1908. Past exec. v.p., dir. Kaiser Aluminum & Chem. Corp. Home: 11 Sotelo Av Piedmont CA 94611

CASHIN, JAMES A., educator; b. Augusta, Ga., May 24, 1911; s. James A. and Mary (Hennessey) C.; B.S., U. Ga., 1932; M.B.A., N.Y. U., 1940; m. Dorothy B. Hamburg, Aug. 29, 1941; childrenJames A., Gary Charles. Accountant, Clearwater Mfg. Co. (S.C.), 1934-36; indsl. engr. Nitekraft Corp., Orange, N.J., 1936-39, prodn. mgr., 1939-41; chief accountant Bristol- Myers Co., N.Y.C., 1941-44, gen. auditor, 1944-50; chief internal auditor St. Regis Paper Co., N.Y.C., 1950-63; faculty N.Y. U., 1954-59; asst. adj. prof. City Coll. N.Y., 1959-64; prof. accounting, chmn. dept. accounting Hofstra U., 1963—. Chmn. coll. proficiency exam. com. in accounting N.Y. State Dept. Edn., 1966. Mem. Am. Accounting Assn., Am. Inst. C.P.A.'s, Am. Assn. U. Profs., Financial Execs. Inst., Inst. Internal Auditors, U. Ga. Alumni Soc. (pres. Met. N.Y. 1962). Publs.: Textbooks, including: Interne Revison, 1962; Auditing, 1963; Careers and Opportunities in Accounting, 1965: Management Controls, 1966; Impact of Medicare on Hospital Costs, 1970; Handbook for Auditors, 1971; also articles in field. Home: 28 Egypt Lane Lettingtown NY 11560 Office: Hofstra U 1000 Fulton Av Hempstead NY 11550

CASHIN, RICHARD MARSHALL, govt. ofcl.; b. Boston, Apr. 3, 1924; s. William David and Anna Genevieve (Keefe) C.; A.B., Harvard, 1946; A.M. Boston U., 1949; grad. Sch. Advanced Internat. Studies, Johns Hopkins, 1959; m. Mary Catherine Walsh, Nov. 25, 1950; children—Anne Jordan, Richard Marshall, Jane Kevill, Stephen Douglas. Mgmt. staff Dept. State, 1949-52; staff U.S. Escapee Program, 1952-56; with ICA, 1956—; program officer USOM to Libya, 1956-59, Ethiopia, 1959-62; dir. Office Central African Affairs, AID, Washington, 1962-66; assigned Sr. Seminar Fgn. Policy, Fgn. Service Inst., Washington, 1966-67; dep. dir. AID mission to Ghana, 1967-68, dir., 1968-70; dir. AID mission to Indonesia, Djakarta, 1970—. Home: Cotuit MA 02635 Office: Am embassy/AID APO San Francisco CA 96356

CASHMAN, JOHN W., govt. ofcl.; b. St. Joseph, Mo., Apr. 26, 1923; s. John Amos and Marguerite (Helphingstine) C.; student U. Rochester, 1940-43, U. Kan., summer 1942; S.B., U. Chgo., 1944, M.D., 1946; M.P.H., Johns Hopkins, 1964; m. Helen Feckanin, Oct. 29, 1948; children—John W., Thomas D. Pvt. practice internal medicine, Kansas City, Mo., 1954-58; career officer USPHS, 1947-54, 58-71; asst. surgeon gen., dir. community-health service, 1968-71; now dir. health State Ohio, Columbus. Served with AUS, 1943-46. Recipient Meritorious Service medal USPHS, 1967; Sec.'s Spl. citation, 1971. Fellow Am. Publ Health Assn. Mem. Ch. of Nazarene (trustee). Home: 1355 Brookwood Pl Columbus OH 43209 Office: 450 E Town St Columbus OH 43215

CASHMAN, ROBERT J., physicist, educator; b. Wilmington, O., Sept. 27, 1906; s. John and Corina (Smithson) C.; A.B., Bethany Coll., 1928, D.Sc., 1953; A.M., Northwestern U., 1930, Ph.D., 1935; student U. Mich., 1931; m. Agnes Jones, June 8, 1940; children—Linda Lloyd, John Elliott. With Northwestern U., 1930—, successively instr. physics, asst. prof., asso. prof., 1937-47, prof. physics, 1947—; govt. research, 1941—. Fellow Am. Phys. Soc., Am. Optical Soc.; mem. Am. Assn. U. Profs., Sigma Xi, Kappa Alpha. Mason. Contbr. articles sci., profl. jours., books. Patentee photoconductive cells, photoemissive cells, sound reprodn. and camera tubes. Home: 830 Indian Rd Glenview IL 60025 Office: Northwestern U Evanston IL 60201

CASHORE, EDWARD DODD, advt. exec.; b. Detroit, June 25, 1918; s. Clarence Edward and Lillian (Dodd) C.; A.B., Princeton, 1940; m. Beryl Kingery, Sept. 25, 1952; children—Patricia L., Peter D. Copywriter, McCann-Erickson, Cleve., 1940, v.p. N.Y.C. 1954-58; advt. dir. Sears Roebuck & Co., Fla. and Ga., 1947-49; pres. Cashore & Co.; Atlanta; v.p. Marschalk Co., N.Y.C., 1958- 67; exec. v.p. Bishopric, Lieberman, Harrison and Fielden (formerly Bishopric Green Fielden), Miami, Fla., 1967, pres., 1968—; dir. W. Kepner Assos., Gerry Dunlop Assos., Ltd., Kingston, Jamaica. Bd. dirs. Tb Assn., 200 Club Miami. Served with RAF, USAF, 1942-46. Fellow Internat. Oceanographic Found.; mem. Am. Marketing Assn. Clubs: Princeton, University (N.Y.C.); Seminole (Fla.); River (Fla.); Kings Bay Yacht and Country (Fla.); Coral Reef Yacht (Miami, Fla.). Office: 3361 SW 3d Av Miami FL 33145

CASIDA, JOHN EDWARD, educator; b. Phoenix, Dec. 22, 1929; s. Lester Earl and Ruth (Barnes) C.; B.S., U. Wis., 1951, M.S., 1952, Ph.D., 1954; m. Katherine Faustine Monson, June 16, 1956; children—Mark Earl, Eric Gerhard. Research asst. U. Wis., 1951-53, mem. faculty, 1954-63, prof. entomology, 1959-63; prof. entomology, insect toxigologist U. Cal. at Berkeley, 1964—. Served with USAF, 1953. Recipient medal 7th Internat. Congress Plant Protection, Paris, 1970: Haight traveling fellow, 1958-59; Guggenheim fellow, 1970-71. Mem. Am. Chem. Soc. (Internat. award research pesticide chemistry 1970), Entomol. Soc. Am. Author research publs. Home: 1570 La Vereda Rd Berkeley CA 94708

CASIDA, LESTER EARL, educator, reproductive physiologist, b. Chula, Mo., Apr. 9, 1904; s. Edward Ellsworth and Minnie (Molloy) C.; B.S. in Edn., N.E. Mo. State Tchrs. Coll., 1926; A.M., U. Mo., 1927, Ph.D., 1932; m. Ruth Barnes, Aug. 2, 1927; children—Lester Earl, John Edward, Betty Ruth (Mrs. Robert Allen Damerau). Tchr. rural sch., Grandy County, Mo., 1922-24; acting prof. biol. sci. Ariz. State Tchrs. Coll., 1929-30; acting prof. agr. Ark. State Tchrs. Coll., 1930-31; NRC fellow U. Wis., 1932-34, mem. faculty, 1934—, prof. genetics, 1946—; cons. NIH, 1962; cons. reproductive physiology Ford Found., India, 1964. Recipient Am. Dairy Sci. Assn. Borden award, 1954, Am. Soc. Animal Sci. Morrison award, 1959, Animal Physiology and Endocrinology Research award Am. Soc. Animal Sci., 1965, Master and Pioneer medal 5th Internat. Congress Animal Reproduction, 1964, Order Cavalier Ufficiale, Republic of Italy, 1966; cited for merit U. Mo. Alumni, 1965. Mem. Endocrine Soc., Soc. Exptl. Biology and Medicine, Am. Soc. Animal Sci., Am. Dairy Sci. Assn., Soc. for Study Fertility, Am. Inst. Biol. Scis., Sigma Xi. Research and numerous publs. on causes of infertility in female mammal, synchronization of estrus in groups of females, physiology of corpus luteum, formation and regression changes in reproductive organs of postpartum female. Home: 4229 Mandan Ct Madison WI 53711

CASKEL, CHRISTOPH, musician, educator; b. Greifswald, Pomerania, Jan. 12, 1932; grad. Französisches Gymnasium, Berlin, Germany; student percussion at Staatliche Hochschule für Musik, Cologne, 1949-54, later student musicology at U. Cologne. Tchr. percussion Internat. Vacation Courses for New Music, Darmstadt, Germany, 1950; percussion concertizer throughout Western world, U.S., 1964; recording artist works of Karlheinz Stockhausen, also Mauricio Kagel for Times Records.*

CASKEY, JOHN LANGDON, educator, archaeologist; b. Boston, Dec. 7, 1908; s. Lacey Davis and Elsie Langdon (Stern) C.; grad. Choate Sch., 1927; B.A., Yale, 1931; Ph.D., U. Cin., 1939; m. 2d, Miriam Ervin, 1967. Mem. staff excavations at Troy, U. Cin., 1932-38, univ. instr. classics, 1939-42, asst. prof., 1946-48, prof. classical archaeology, head dept. classics, 1959—, fellow Grad. Sch., 1961—, chmn. faculty com. Louise Semple Classics Fund, 1961—, field dir. univ. excavations in Ceos, 1960-; asst. dir. Am. Sch. Classical Studies, Athens, 1948-49, dir., 1949-59, field dir. excavations at Heraion of Argos, 1949, Lerna, 1952-58, Eutresis, 1958. Mem. Cin. com. Am. Farm. Sch. of Thessaloniki; vice chmn. mng. com. Am. Sch. Classical Studies at Athens. Served to lt. col. AUS, 1942-46. Decorated Legion of Merit; named comdr. Royal. Order Phoenix (Greece), hon. citizen Athens (Greece). Hon. fellow Archæol. Soc. Athens; mem. Alumni Assn. Am. Sch. Classical Studies at Athens (pres. 1959-62), Archaeol. Inst. Am., Am. Philol. Assn., Vergilian Soc., Am. Philos. Soc., Classical Assn. Can., Soc. Promotion Hellenic Studies, German Aracheol. Inst., Phi Beta Kappa. Contbr. articles to profl. jours., reports in field. Co-author, co-editor: Troy, 1950—. Address: Dept Classics U Cin Cincinnati, OH 45221.

CASLER, HARRY SPROULL, fgn. service officer; b. N.Y.C., Nov. 2, 1908; s. Howard Welford and Pauline Tuthill (Sproull) C.; B.A., Dartmouth, 1931; m. Rosemary Marrow, Jan. 17, 1946; children—Christopher Graham, Alexander Wood, Sarah Ten Eyck, Laurance DeWitt. News reporter, photo editor N.Y. Herald Tribune, 1933-41; with Coordinator Inter-Am. Affairs, 1941-42; information specialist State Dept., 1946-52; information officer, Amsterdam, The Hague, 1952-54; with USIA, 1953; pub. affairs officer, 1st sec., Panama, 1954-57; pub. affairs officer, Caracas, 1957-58; policy officer Voice Am., 1958-61; pub. affairs officer, Kuala Lumpur, 1961-65; pub. affairs counselor Am. embassy, Saigon, Vietnam, 1965-67; with USIA, Washington, 1967—. Served to capt. USAAF, 1942-45. Decorated Air medal (2). Recipient Meritorious Service award USIA, 1959, Vietnam Service medal 1967. Fellow Inst. Pub. Relations Malaysia; mem. Beta Theta Pi, Sphinx. Clubs: Metropolitan (Washington); Baquio (Philippines Country; Bandon Golf (Ireland). Home: Church Hill House Enniskeane County Cork Ireland

CASNER, ANDREW JAMES, educator; b. Chgo., Feb. 7, 1907; s. Andrew James and Margaret Jane (Connell) C.; A.B., U. Ill., 1930, LL.B., 1929; J.S.D., Columbia, 1941; A.M. (hon.), Harvard, 1942, LL.D., 1969; S.J.D. (hon.), Suffolk U., 1970; m. Margaret Snell, June 12, 1936; children—Andrew James, Truman Snell. Admitted to Ill. bar, 1929, Md. bar, 1934, Mass. bar, 1940; instr. law U. Ill., 1929-30, prof. law, 1936-38; prof. law U. Md., 1930-35; prof. law Harvard, 1938—, asso. dean sch., 1961, acting dean, 1967-68; asso. Ropes, Gray, Best, Coolidge & Rugg, Boston, 1945-48. Trustee Old Colony Trust Co.; chmn. law editorial bd. Little, Brown & Co. Served to col. USAAF, 1942-45; E.T.O. Decorated Legion of Merit, Bronze star. Mem. Am., Boston bar assns., Am. Law Inst., Order of Coif, Sigma Chi, Phi Delta Phi, Delta Sigma Rho. Republican. Episcopalian. Author: (with W.B. Leach), Cases and Text on Property, 1950, 2d edit., 1969; Estate Planning, 1953, 3d edition, 2 vols., 1961, supplement, 1971. Editor-in-chief Am. Law of Property, 1951, 66. Adviser, reporter Restatement of Property. Contbr. to legal periodicals. Home: 1572 Massachusetts Av Cambridge MA 02138

CASON, ALBERT, bus. and financial editor Nashville Tennessean. Address: 1100 Broadway Nashville TN 37203*

CASON, CHARLES MONROE, physicist; b. Chattanooga, July 24, 1933; s. Charles Monroe and Cleo (Stargel) C.; B.S., U. Ala., 1954, M.S., 1958; m. Mary Nell Knight, Nov. 14, 1959; children—Tara Nanette, Wendy Karen, Lea Valerie. Atomic and molecular physics Phys. Sci. Lab. U.S. Army Missile Command, Redstone Arsenal, 1957—; dir. Cason, Inc., Expon, Inc. Past trustee Arts Council. Served with USAF, 1955-57, Asso. fellow Am. Inst. Aero. and Astronautics; mem. Am. Phys. Soc., Assn. U.S. Army, Tenn., Ala. archaeol. socs. Methodist. Elk. Clubs: Whitesburg Boat and Yacht; Mason-Dixon Toastmasters (past pres.); Civic Opera Soc. Contbr. articles on plasma physics, aerodynamics, electron beams. Patentee wind tunnels, electronic circuits, laser devices. Home: 1207 Toney Dr S E Huntsville, AL 35802. Office: Phys Sci Lab Redstone Arsenal AL 35809

CASON, JAMES, Jr., educator; b. Murfreesboro, Tenn., Aug. 30, 1912; s. James and Madeliene (Park) C.; A.B., Vanderbilt U., 1934; M.S., U. Cal. at Berkeley, 1935; Ph.D., Yale, 1938; m. Rebecca Marsden, Dec. 28, 1935; children—Roger, Marsden Starbuck. Research asst. Harvard, 1938-40; instr. chemistry DePauw U., 1940-41; instr., then asst. prof. chemistry Vanderbilt U., 1941-45; faculty U. Cal. at Berkeley, 1945—, prof. chemistry, 1952—, asso. dean grad. div., 1970—. Mem. Am. (exec. com. organic div. 1953-55) Swiss chem. socs., N.Y. Acad. Sci., A.A.A.S., Cal. Assn. Chemistry Tchrs., Phi Beta Kappa, Sigma Xi. Author: (with H. Rapoport) Laboratory Text in Organic Chemistry, 1950, latest edit., 1970; Essential Principles of Organic Chemistry, 1956; Basic Experimental Organic Chemistry, 1962; Principles of Modern Organic Chemistry, 1966. Mem. editorial bd. Jour. Organic Chemistry, 1952-56, Organic Syntheses, 1951-59. Contbr. articles to profl. jours. Home: 486 Michigan Av Berkeley CA 94707

CASO Y ANDRADE, ALFONSO, scientist; b. Mexico City, Feb. 1, 1896; s. Antonio and Maria (Andrade) C.; U. Mexico, 1929; dr. h.c. U. Nat. Mexico, U. Mérida, U. Morelia, U. N.M., U. Cal. at Los Angeles; m. Maria Lombardo, Aug. 21, 1922; children—Beatriz (Mrs. Carlos Solorzano), Andrés, Aleiandro Eugenia; m. 2d, Aida Lombardo. Prof. faculty philosophy and letters, 1918-40, Escuela de Layes, 1919-20; dir. Escuela Nacional Preparatoria, 1928; head dept. archeology Museo Nacional, 1930-33, dir., 1933-34; dir. explorations, Monte Albán, Oaxaca, 1931-44; dir. higher learning and sci. investigation, 1944; rector U. Nacional Mexico, 1944-45; sec. nat. properties and adminstrv. inspection, 1946-48; dir. Inst. Nacional Indigenista, Revista Estudios Antropologicos. Recipient 1st medal Viking Fund for Archaeology, 1952. Fellow Royal Anthrop. Inst. Gt. Britain and Ireland (hon.); mem. Nat. Acad. Scis. Antonio Alzate (Pres.), Nat. Coll., Soc. Geography and Statistics, N.Y. Washington acads. scis., Archaeol. Inst. Am. (hon.), Am. Philos. Soc., Soc. Am. Paris (hon.) Brit. Acad. (hon.), Am. Anthrop. Assn., Soc. Geography and History Guatemala, Am. Assn. Tchrs. Spanish, Deutsche Gesellschaft für Volkerkunde. Author numerous books including Urnas de Oaxaca, 1950; The People of the Sun, 1952; Codex Bodley, 1950; Codex Selden, 1964. Dir., founder of the Boletin Bibliog. de Antropologia Am. Home: Av Central 234 Tlacopac Sn Angel Mexico 20 DF Office: Instituto Nacional Indigenista Av Revolucion 1279 Mexico City 20 Mexico

CASPARI, ERNEST WOLFGANG, educator; b. Berlin, Germany, Oct. 24, 1909; s. Wilhelm and Gertrud (Gerschel) C.; Ph.D., U. Göttingen (Germany), 1933; M.A. (hon.), Wesleyan U., Middletown, Conn., 1950; m. Hermine B. Abraham, Aug. 16, 1938. Asst. zoology U. Göttingen, 1933-35; asst. microbiology U. Istanbul (Turkey), 1935-38; fellow, asst. prof. Lafayette Coll., Easton, Pa., 1938-44; asst. prof. zoology U. Rochester, 1944-46; asso. prof. biology Wesleyan U., 1946-47, prof. biology, 1949-60, also Daniel Ayres prof. biology; research asso. dept. genetics Carnegie Instn. Washington, 1947-49; prof. biology U. Rochester (N.Y.), 1960—, chmn. dept. biology, 1960-65. Chmn. program com., mem. gen. organizing com. of 10th Internat. Congress Genetics, Montreal, Can., 1958. Fellow Center Advanced Studies Behavorial Scis., 1956-57, 65-66. Fellow A.A.A.S. (chmn. sect. zool. sci. 1962); mem. Am. Acad. Arts and Scis., Genetics Soc. Am. (pres. 1966), Am. Soc. Zoologists, Soc. Study Devel. and Growth, Soc. Study Evolution, Am. Soc. Naturalists (v.p. 1961), Phi Beta Kappa, Sigma Xi. Editor: Advances in Genetics; Genetics, 1968-72. Contbr. articles profl. jours. Home: 80 Penarrow Rd Rochester NY 14618

CASPARI, MAX EDWARD, physicist, educator; b. Frankfurt/Main, Germany, Mar. 17, 1923; s. Wilhelm Louis and Gertrud (Gerschel) C.; student London (Eng.) U., 1941- 45; A.B., Conn. Wesleyan U., 1948; Ph.D., Mass. Inst. Tech., 1954; m. Sarah Bockoven, Dec. 28, 1951; children—Rachel Elizabeth, Matthew Ernst, Alexander Paul. Came to U.S., 1947, naturalized, 1952. Research asst. Lab. for Insulation Research, Mass. Inst. Tech., 1948-54; from instr. to prof. physics U. Pa., Phila., 1954—, prof., 1964—, chmn. dept. physics, 1968—. Cons. Frankford Arsenal, Phila., 1961—. Fellow Am. Phys. Soc.; mem. Am. Assn. U. Profs., Sigma Xi. Home: 1520 Spruce St Philadelphia PA 19102

CASPARY, SISTER ANITA, educator, adminstr.; b. Herrick, S.D., Nov. 4, 1915; d. Jacob A. and Marie (Bruch) Caspary; B.A., Immaculate Heart Coll., 1937; M.A., U. So. Cal., 1943; Ph.D., Stanford, 1948. High sch. tchr., 1939-42; mem. faculty Immaculate Heart Coll., Los Angeles, 1948-58, chmn. dept. English, 1950-57, dean Grad. Sch., 1950-57, pres. of coll., 1957-63; mother-gen. Sisters of Immaculate Heart, 1963-69; pres. Immaculate Heart Community, 1969—. Merrill fellow Harvard Div. Sch., 1971. Mem. Modern Lang. Assn., Assn. Am. Colls., Nat. Council Tchrs. English, Kappa Gamma Pi. Contbr. articles profl. jours. Address: 5515 Franklin Av Los Angeles CA 90028

CASPARY, VERA, writer; b. Chgo.; d. Paul and Julia (Cohen) Caspary; student Chgo. pub. schs.; m. Isadore Goldsmith, Oct. 5, 1949 (dec.). Author: The White Girl, 1929; Thicker than Water, 1932; Laura, 1942; Bedelia, 1944; Stranger than Truth, 1946; The Weeping and the Laughter, 1950; Thelma, 1957; The Husband, 1957; Evvie, 1950; A Chosen Sparrow, 1964; The Man Who Loved His Wife, 1966; The Rosecrest Cell, 1967; plays include: (with Winifred Lenihan) Blind Mice, 1930, (with George Sklar) Laura, 1946, Wedding in Paris (in London), 1954; original screen stories and adaptations: Night of June 13, 1932; Easy Living, 1936; Bedelia, 1946; Letter to Three Wives, 1949; Three Husbands, 1951; Les Girls, 1958, others. Mem. Authors Guild, Dramatists Guild, Writers Guild West, P.E.N. Home: 55 E 9th St New York City, NY 10003.

CASPER, JOSEPH JOHN, govt. ofcl.; b. Burnside, Minn., June 14, 1918; s. Joseph A. and Elizabeth (Nilan) C.; B.S., Hamline U., 1940; postgrad. U. Minn., 1940; m. June E. Gustafson, Apr. 14, 1941; children—Mary Elizabeth, J. Michael. With FBI, 1941—, insp. charge inspections, 1962-63, asst. dir. charge tng., 1963—. Batchelder Meml. scholar, 1938-40. Mem. Internat. Assn. Chief Police (exec. com. 1963—). Elk. Home: 604 Kenbrook Dr Silver Spring MD 20902 Office: Fed Bureau Investigation Washington DC 20535

CASPER, LEONARD RALPH, educator; b. Fond du Lac, Wis., July 6, 1923; s. Louis and Caroline (Eder) C.; B.A., U. Wis., 1948, M.A., 1949, Ph.D., 1953; m. Linda Velasquez-Ty, June 2, 1956; children—Gretchen Gabrielle, Kristina Elise. Grad. asst. U. Wis., 1949-51; instr. Cornell U., 1952-53; asst. prof. U. Philippines, 1953-56, Fulbright lectr., 1962-63; mem. faculty Boston Coll., 1956—, prof. contemporary Am. lit., 1963—; dir. creative writing U. R.I., summer 1958. Served with F.A., AUS, 1943-46. Stanford creative writing fellow, 1951-52; Bread Loaf creative writing scholar, 1961; research grantee Am. Council Learned Socs.-Social Sci. Research Council, 1965; grantee Asia Soc., 1965; research travel grantee Am. Philos. Soc., 1968-69. Mem. Nat. Cath. Playwrights Circle, Am. Assn. U. Profs., Asia Soc. Author: Robert Penn Warren: The Dark and Bloody Ground, 1960; The Wayward Horizon: Essays on Modern Philippine Literature, 1961; The Wounded Diamond: Studies in Modern Philippine Literature, 1964; New Writing from the Philippines: A Critique and Anthology, 1966. Editor: Six Filipino Poets, 1955; (with T. A. Gullason) The World of Short Fiction: An International Collection, 1962; Modern Philippine Short Stories, 1962. Contbg. editor Panorama (Manila), 1954-61; Drama Critique, 1959-62; Solidarity (Manila), 1966—; Literature East and West, 1969—. Home: 54 Simpson Dr Saxonville MA 01701 Office: Boston Coll Chestnut Hill MA 02167

CASPER, THOMAS PATRICK, supt. schs.; b. Louisville, Feb. 7, 1931; s. Burke and Sara (Husson) C.; B.Phil., Gregorian U., Rome, 1953, Licentiate Sacred Theology, 1957; Ph.D. in Edn., St. Louis U., 1963. Ordained priest Roman Cath. Ch., 1956; asst. supt. schs. Cath. Archdiocese Lousville, 1957-67, supt. schs., 1967—; asst. pastor in Louisville, 1962-63, Clayton, Mo., 1959- 62; mem. faculty Catharine Spalding Coll., Louisville, 1964-66. Bd. dirs. Louisville Health and Welfare Council, Louisville Regional Re-Edn. Center, State Adv. Council-Title III, Louisville Youth Opportunity Center; trustee Louisville Free Pub. Library, 1971—. Mem. Nat. Cath. Edn. Assn., Louisville C. of C. Home: 443 S 5th St Louisville KY 40202 Office: 435 S 5th St Louisville KY 40202

CASPER, WILLIE RAGAN, utilities exec.; b. Raymond, Miss., Nov. 1, 1912; s. Henry A. and Fannie (Summers) C.; grad. high sch.; m. Agnes Claudine Tohill, Nov. 18, 1935; children—Willie Ragan, Robert B. Bookkeeper Miss. Power & Light Co., Jackson, 1930-46, head accountant, 1946-52, asst. treas., 1952-68, treas., 1968—. Scoutmaster Boy Scouts Am., Jackson, 1942-48, mem. troop com., 1954-61; active Boys Baseball Programs, 1955-63. Mem. Nat. Assn. Accountants, Jackson C. of C. Methodist (steward 1944-54, 56-66). Club: Exchange (Jackson). Home: 126 Pimlico Pl Jackson MS 39211 Office: Miss Power & Light Co PO Box 1640 Jackson MS 39205

CASPERSEN, OLAUS WESTBY, corp. ofcl.; b. Risor, Norway, June 15, 1896; s. John A. and Augusta (Bertelsen) C.; grad. Pace Inst., N.Y.C., 1923; m. Freda R., Mar. 3, 1928; children—John W., Finn. With Beneficial Corp., 1920—, successively auditor, v.p., pres., 1944-62, chmn. bd. 1956-62, chmn. emeritus, 1962—; dir. emeritus Bankers Nat. Life Ins. Co.; dir. Peoples Bank and Trust Co. Pres., dir. Beneficial Found., Wilmington; trustee S. Sarasota County Meml. Hosp., Venice, Fla.; emeritus bd. corporators Peddie Sch., Hightstown, N.J. Mason. Home: 613 Granada Av Venice FL 33595

CASPERSSON, TORBJORN OSKAR, scientist; b. Motala, Sweden, Oct. 15, 1910; s. Oskar Fredrik and Eva (Kalen) C.; M.D., Stockholm U., 1936; m. Siv. Gunnarson, 1937; children—Gunnel, Kestin, Lena. Dir. Med. Nobel Inst. for Med. Cell Research and Wallenberg Lab. for Exptl. Cell Research, Stockholm; prof. med. cell research and genetics, 1944—. Mem. natural sci. research council of Sweden, 1946-51, research council Swedish Cancer Soc., 1951-57, Swedish UNESCO Council, 1946—; cons. for UNESCO in Latin Am., 1950. Mem. council Swedish Inst. for Internat. Cultural Relations; mem. bd. Swedish-Am. Found.; mem. UN Radiation Com. Hon. lectureships various U.S. and European univs. Mem. Royal Swedish Acad. Sci., Royal Soc. Sci., Belgian, Brazilian acads. sci. Home: Banérgatan 51 Stockholm, Sweden. Office: Karolinska Institut 10401 Stockholm 60 Sweden

CASS, MILLARD, govt. ofcl. b. Norfolk, Va., Nov. 8, 1916; s. Sigismund and Ridia (Schreier) C.; B.S., U. Va., 1938, LL.B., 1940; m. Ruth Claire Marx, July 19, 1943; children—Sandra (Mrs. Jeffrey A Burt), Ronald, Pamela. Admitted to Va. bar, 1939; pvt. practice law, Portsmouth, Va., 1940-41; atty. SEC, 1941; atty. NLRB, 1941-46, legal asst. to gen. counsel, 1945-46; asst. to Asst. Sec. Labor, 1946-47, Under Sec. Labor, 1947-50; spl. asst. to Sec. Labor, 1950-55, dep. under-sec. labor, 1955-71, moblzn. planning coordinator, 1962-71, liaison officer with State govs., 1969-71; adminstrv. dir. Constrn. Industry Stblzn. Com., 1971—. Exec. officer Manpower Adminstrn., 1963-64; mem. or chmn. numerous departmental coms., internat. delegations; guest speaker U. Va. Law Sch. Pres., Montgomery County Council P.T.A.'s, 1962-64; bd. mgrs. Bd. Parents and Tchrs., 1962-64. Recipient Arthur S. Flemming award for outstanding young men in fed. govt., 1955; Rockefeller Pub. service award, 1966; Dept. Labor Distinguished Service award, 1960, Distinguished Career Service award, 1971; Hornbook award Montgomery County (Md.) Edn. Assn., 1968; Career Service award Nat. Civil Service League, 1969. Mem. Am., Va. bar assns., Raven Soc. Univ. Va., Order of Coif, Phi Beta Kappa, Omicron Delta Kappa. Jewish religion (pres. congregation 1970—). Contbr. articles to legal jours., govt. and other publs. Home: 2103 Plyers Mill Rd Silver Spring MD 20902 Office: Dept Labor Washington DC 20210

CASS, THOMAS FRANCIS, Jr., mfg. exec.; b. Somerville, Mass., Mar. 15, 1912; s. Thomas Francis and Dorothea (Gillet) C.; student Dartmouth, 1934, Wharton Sch. Finance U. Pa., 1936; m. Ruth Wilson, February 10, 1940; children—Linda W. (Mrs. Gordon Humphreys Smith), Deborah G. (Mrs. William Wallace Thornton, Jr.), Victoria J., Laura G. Sales rep. Diamond Match Co., N.Y.C., 1932-36; sales promotion dept. Robert Gair Co., N.Y.C., 1937-38; with Container Corp. Am., 1939—, sales research rep., research project mgr., Chgo., sales mgr., Phila., sales mgr., Los Angeles, gen. mgr., dist. mgr. So. Cal., div. mgr. Pacific Coast Carton and Mill div., v.p. Cal. Container Corp. div., sr. v.p. Cal. Container Corp., 1955-57, v.p., 1957-61, exec. v.p., 1961—, also dir. parent co.; dir. Marcur, Inc., Interstate United Corp., Pioneer Trust & Savs. Bank. Cons. Office Q.M. Gen., 1939-45. Mem. council on med. and biol. research U. Chgo. Bd. dirs. Jr. Achievement. Mem. Marketing Sci. Inst., Folding Paper Box Assn. Am. (former chmn. bd. trustees, dir., mem. exec. com.), Nat. Paperboard Assn., Q.M.'s Assn., Inst. Food Technologists, T.A.P.P.I., Ill. C. of C., Fiber Box Assn. (former mem. exec. com.). Clubs: California (Los Angeles); Mid-America, Chicago (Chgo.); Glen View Golf (Golf, Ill.). Home: 1151 Seneca Rd Wilmette IL 60091 Office: 1 1st National Pl Chicago IL 60670

CASSADY, EDWIN LEONALD, utility exec.; b. Lebanon, Ind., July 13, 1908; s. Albert Alexander and Laura Sylvia (Quick) C.; grad. South Bend Coll. Commerce, 1928, Internat. Accountants Soc., 1933; (student Butler U., 1933-37,) U. Mich., 1956; m. Bernice May Travis, June 26, 1929; children—Dr. Richard L., Dr. James E. With Indpls. Power & Light Co., 1929—, v.p., treas., 1957-70, exec. v.p., 1970-71, pres., 1971—, dir., 1967—; dir. Ind. Ins. Co. and subsidiaries, Consol. Ins. Co., Consol. Nat. Life Ins. Co., Cooling-Grumme-Mumford, Inc., INCO Finance, Inc., Peoples Bank & Trust Co., Mem. Adminstrv. Budget Com. of Mayor's Citizens' Adv. Com., 1962—, chmn., 1965-66; bd. dirs. Central Ind. council Boy Scouts Am., v.p., 1969-70; treas. Ind. Taxpayers Assn., 1966—; trustee Indpls. YWCA; bd. dirs. 500 Festival Assos., 1971—. Mem. Indpls. C. of C., Ind. Elec. Assn. (v.p. 1970-71, dir.), Nat. Assn. Accountants (pres. Indpls. chpt. 1947-48), Financial Execs. Inst. (pres. Indpls. chpt. 1966-67; nat. dir. 1967-71, v.p. North Central area 1970-71; adv. council 1971-74), Edison Elec. Inst. (chmn. exec. com. accounting div.), Butler U. Alumni Assn., Newcomen Soc. N.A., Stuart Cameron McLeod Soc. Methodist. Mason (Shriner). Clubs: Columbia (dir. 1964-70, pres. 1966-67), Indianapolis Athletic, Highland Golf and Country, Kiwanis (Indpls.); Lambs (N.Y.C.). Home: 4821 N Meridian St Indianapolis IN 46208 Office: 25 Monument Circle PO Box 1595 Indianapolis IN 46206

CASSADY, RALPH, Jr., educator; b. Vallejo, Cal., Dec. 30, 1900; s. Ralph L. and Caroline (Luchsinger) C.; B.S., U. Cal. at Berkeley, 1924, M.S., 1927, Ph.D., 1930; m. Dorothea Jatho, Aug. 13, 1927; children—Ralph III, John Michael, Peter William, Patricia Anne. Teaching fellow econs. U. Cal. at Berkeley, 1926-27; instr. econs. Princeton, 1927-28; engaged in study prodn. costs Paramount Pictures, 1928-29; asst. prof. marketing U. Minn., 1930-36; successively asst. prof., asso. prof., prof. emeritus U. Cal. at Los Angeles, 1936—, dir. bur. bus. and econ. research, 1949-68; vis. prof. U. Western Australia, 1963. Mem. price policies com. Social Sci. Research Council, 1942-51, Hall of Fame in distbn. Boston conf. on distbn., 1954; del. Internat. Econ. Assn. Fisheries Roundtable, Rome, Italy, 1956; cons. study world tuna markets for FAO, Japan, summer 1961, mem. panel experts on fisheries devel., 1962—; cons. traditional market study, Oaxaca, Mex., 1965—. Vice pres., dir. Friends of Soochow U., Taiwan, 1963—. Recipient Am. Marketing Assn. Nat. award, 1952. Mem. Am. Econ. Assn., Am. Anthrop. Assn. Author: (with H.J. Ostlund) The Retail Distribution Structure of the Small City; (with W.C. Waite) The Consumer and the Economic Order; (with Wylie L. Jones) The Changing Competitive Structure in the Wholesale Grocery Trade; The Nature of Competition in Gasoline Distribution at the Retail Level; Price Making and Price Behavior In The Petroleum Industry; Competition and Price Making in Food Retailing; Price Warfare in Business Competition; (with Ralph Cassady III) The Private Antitrust Suit in American Business Competition; Auctions and Auctioneering; Negotiated Pricing in Primitive, Peasant and Modern Societies, 1972. Mem. editorial bd. Jour. of Marketing, 1940, 1944-46, mng. editor, 1946-48, editor-in-chief, 1949-51. Contbr. articles bus. and econ. jours. Home: 1732 Midvale Av Los Angeles CA 90024

CASSADY, THOMAS GENTZ, mfg. co. exec.; b. Owen County, Ind., Jan. 5, 1896; s. Otto Ezra and Edith (Gantz) C.; student U. Chgo., 1914-16; m. Elizabeth Harrison, Sept. 1, 1923. Mgr. Mpls. office George H. Burr & Co., 1921-26; partner McGowen, Cassady & White, Chgo., Mpls., Detroit, 1926-41; partner Farwell Chapman & Co., Chgo., 1946-53; v.p., chmn. bd., chmn. exec. com. Chamberlain Mfg. Corp., Elmhurst, Ill., 1953—. Mng. trustee Thomas G. Cassady Found. Served with French Air Force, 1916-18; from lt. comdr. to capt., USNR, 1941-45. Decorated D.S.C. with bronze oak leaf, Legion of Merit; Croix de Guerre with 3 palms and gold star, Comdr. Legion d'Honneur (France); Belgian Mil. medal. Republican. Club: Onwentsia (Lake Forest). Home: 950 E Maplewood Rd Lake Forest IL 60045 Office: 845 Larch Av Elmhurst IL 60126

CASSAT, DAVID BERRYHILL, corp. exec., religious assn. ofcl.; b. Vail, Ia., Jan. 25, 1894; s. David Williams and Lillian (Berryhill) C.; A.B., Parsons Coll., 1916, LL.D., 1955; m. Ruth Boleyn Lyon, Apr. 20, 1922; children—George Lyon, Jean Boleyn (Mrs. Earl S. Christman, Jr.). With Interstate Finance Corp., Dubuque, Ia., 1925-67, pres., 1935-61, chmn., 1961-67; chmn. bd., dir. Sunrise Golf Devel. Corp., Ft. Lauderdale, Fla., Pub. Utilities Corp., Uniflow Gas Corp. (both Sunrise Golf Village, Fla.). Past pres., dir. Presbyn. Life, Inc., Phila.; dir. Am. Trust & Savs. Bank, Dubuque; hon. dir. Am. Finance System, Inc., Wilmington, Del. Mem. City Council Sunrise Golf Village, 1961-67. Voting del. World Council Chs., Evanston Assembly, 1954; treas., mem. exec. com., mem. gen. bd., 1957-69, mem. finance and bus. com., investment com., donor support com. Nat. Council Chs. U.S.A.; mem. planning and function com. Ia. Council Chs., 1968—. Past pres. Dubuque Community Chest; chmn. Ia. Study Com. on Higher Edn., 1957-61; mem. Ia. Coordinating Council on Edn. Beyond High Sch., 1967—. Life bd. dirs. U. Dubuque. Served as 2d lt., inf. U.S. Army, World War I. Mem. Am. Finance Conf. (pres. 1936-37, past chmn. exec., pub. relations coms.), Am. Indsl. Bankers Assn. (life hon. dir., life hon. mem. exec. com), Nat. Council Presbyn. Men (pres. 1954-55). Presbyn. (mem. bd. missions 1947-53). Rotarian (past pres. Dubuque). Home: 890 Mt Carmel Rd Dubuque IA 52001 Office: Am Trust Bldg PO Box 390 Dubuque IA 52001

CASSATA, JOHN J., Cath. bishop Diocese Ft. Worth. Address: 1206 Throckmorton St Fort Worth TX 76102*

CASSAVETES, JOHN, actor; b. N.Y.C., Dec. 9, 1929; ed. Mohawk Coll., Colgate U., N.Y. Acad. Dramatic Arts; m. Gena Rowlands, Mar. 19, 1954. Actor in stock co.; asst. stage mgr. Broadway play Fifth Season; TV credits include: Omnibus, Elgin Playhouse; films include: Taxi, Might Holds Terror, Crime in the Streets, Edge of the City, Fever, The Dirty Dozen, Rosemary's Baby; dir. films including: Shadows, 1960, Too Late Blues, A Child is Waiting, Faces. Address: Care Dir Pub Relations United Artists 729 7th Av New York City NY 10017

CASSEL, JOHN WALTER, singing actor; b. Council Bluffs, Ia., May 15, 1910; s. Thaddeus William and Grace Hester (Cederburg) C.; student Creighton U., 1929-31; m. Nadine Blackburn, June 9, 1930; children—John Walter, William Earl, Catherine Jean, Mary Martha; m. 2d, Gail Manners, 1953; 1 son, Diedrick S. Singer, NBC, N.Y.C., 1934-38; appeared Broadway shows, Great Lady, Stars in Your Eyes, 1939, All in Fun; mus. comedy revivals throughout U.S., Met. Opera Co., 1943-45; traveling concert singer, U.S., 1941—; with N.Y.C. Center Opera Co., 1947—; leading baritone Italian and German rings

Met. Opera, 1956—; opera singer in P.R., Havana, Barcelona, Mexico City; now performing with Deutscher Oper am Rhein, Düsseldorf, Germany, Wiener Staatsoper, Vienna, Austria, Met. Opera Co., N.Y.C. Opera Co.; star Great Waltz, London, Eng., 1971-72. Served as warrant officer 168th Inf., Ia. N.G.; with Council Bluffs band. Mem. Am. Guild Mus. Artists (1st v.p.), Equity, A.F.T.R.A. Office: Sardos Artists Mgmt Inc 180 West End Av New York City NY 10023

CASSEL, WALTER, see Cassel, John Walter. Cassell, Frank Hyde, educator; b. Chgo., Oct. 12, 1916; s. Frank V. Seymour and Alicia (Robinson) C.; A.B., Wabash Coll., 1939; postgrad. U. Chgo., 1946-47; m. Marguerite Ellen Fletcher, Mar. 24, 1940; children—Frank Allan, Thomas W., Christopher B. Exec. with Inland Steel Co., Chgo., 1948-68; on leave as dir. U.S. Employment Service, Washington, 1966-68; prof. indsl. relations Grad. Sch. Mgmt., Northwestern U., 1968—; vis. prof. Inst. Am. Studies, Salzburg, Austria, 1957; cons. to govt. and industry in fields manpower, indsl. relations and mgmt. Chmn. Gov. Ill. Com. Unemployment, 1961-63. Mem. bd. Chgo. Urban League, Community Renewal Soc. Recipient Distinguished Service award U.S. Dept. Labor, 1968. Mem. Indsl. Relations Assn. Chgo. (pres. 1957-58), Indsl. Relations Research Assn., Am. Econ. Assn. Clubs: University, Internat. (Washington); University (Chgo.). Author: The Employment Service: An Organization in Change, 1968; (with Welser and Ginsberg) National Manpower Politics, 1969. Home: 128 Church Rd Winnetka 60093 Office: Deering Library Northwestern U Evanston IL 60601

CASSELL, JOHN WILLIAM, Jr., coll. adminstr.; b. Takoma Park, Md., Mar. 3, 1929; s. John William and Jessie (Swart) C.; B.A., Columbia Union Coll., 1950; M.Ed., U. Md., 1955; Ph.D. Mich. State U., 1961; m. Charlotte Louise Carper, Aug. 13, 1950; children—Janet Louise, John William III. Supervising tchr. Columbia Union Coll., 1950-52; acad. prin. Andrews U., 1955-59, dean students, 1960-63; academic dean So. Missionary Coll., 1963-67; acad. dean Pacific Union Coll., 1967—. Served with AUS, 1952-54. Mem. Am. Assn. Higher Edn., Phi Delta Kappa. Home: 175 Edgewood Pl Angwin CA 94508

CASSELL, MARTIN LEROY, r.r. ofcl., lawyer; b. Vincennes, Ind., Oct. 3, 1910, s. Martin L. and Alice (Shively) C.; A.B., U. Ill., 1933; LL.B., 1935; m. Claudia E. Stone, June 26, 1937; children—Martin Leroy III, Clyde Thomas. Admitted to Ill. bar, 1935, U.S. Supreme Ct. bar, 1941; asso. firm Hamilton, Black & Klatt, Peoria, 1935-40; with C., R.I. & P. Ry., 1940—, gen. solicitor, 1957—. Mem. Barrington (Ill.) High Sch. Bd., 1957-69, pres., 1958-63, 68-69; exec. com. Tri-County div. Ill. Assn. Sch. Bds., 1960-69, chmn., 1961-63, dir. assn., 1960-69, pres., 1965-67. Bd. dirs., v.p. Contemporary Concerts Inc. Mem. Assn. ICC Practitioners (pres. 1962-63), Am., Ill., Chgo. bar assns., Traffic Club Chgo., Beta Theta Pi. Club: Union League (Chicago) Home: RR2 Box 331 Sutton Rd Barrington IL 60010 Office: 139 W Van Buren St Chicago IL 60605

CASSELL, RAY E., ins. co. exec.; b. Baker, Minn., May, 29 1915, s. William H. and Pauline (Dieken) C.; B.S. U. Ia., 1936; m. Margaret H. Farquhar, Oct. 28, 1940; 1 dau., Melissa R. With Bankers Life Ins. Co., Des Moines, 1936—, asst. v.p., 1955-56, sec., 1956-65, v.p., sec., 1965-70, sr. v.p., sec., 1970—. Chmn., United Campaign Greater Des Moines, 1964; pres. United Community Services, 1966; mem. joint com. Life Ins. Industry on Careers for Coll. Grads. Served to capt., inf. AUS, 1942-46, 50-52. Fellow Life Office Mgmt. Inst.; mem. Am. Mgmt. Assn., Life Office Mgmt. Assn. (dir.). Mem. United Ch. of Christ (trustee ch.). Club: Des Moines Golf and Country. Home: 6755 Washington St Des Moines IA 50322 Office: 711 High St Des Moines IA 50307

CASSELLA, WILLIAM NATHAN, Jr., orgn. exec.; b. Alton, Ill., July 14, 1920; s. William Nathan and Martha (Stanly) C.; A.B., U. Ill., 1942; M.S., Syracuse U., 1943; A.M., Harvard, 1951, Ph.D., 1953; m. Margaret Powers Crowley, June 22, 1946; children—John Woodson, Stephen Rowan, Mark Crowley, William Kent. Research asst. Pub. Adminstrn. Clearing House, Washington, 1946; instr., then asst. prof. polit. sci. U. Mo., 1948-54; with Nat. Municipal League, 1953—. exec. dir., 1969—; research asso. Govt. Affairs Found., 1954-57; vis. asso. prof. pub. adminstrn. Columbia, 1957; sr. research asso. Met. Region Program, 1957-61. Mem. adv. com. state and local govt. statistics Bur. Census, 1962-65, chmn., 1963-65; mem. area devel. adv. bd. Com. Econ. Devel., 1964-66; cons. Adv. Commn. Intergovtl. Relations, 1967—. Mem. Greenburgh (N.Y.) Bd. Edn., 1961-64; mem. Westchester County Planning Bd., 1962—, vice chmn., 1967—. Served to lt. USNR, 1943-44. Mem. Am. Polit. Sci. Assn., Am. Soc. Pub. Adminstrn., Govtl. Research Assn., Internat. City Mgmt. Assn., Regional Plan Assn. N.Y., Phi Beta Kappa, Alpha Kappa Lambda, Delta Sigma Pi, Omicron Delta Kappa. Episcopalian. Club: Harvard (N.Y.C.). Author: Constitutional Aspects of Metropolitan Government, 1961; also articles. Contbg. editor Nat. Civic Rev., 1954—, chmn. editorial bd., 1969—. Home: 100 Buena Vista Dr Dobbs Ferry NY 10522 Office: 47 E 68th St New York City NY 10021

CASSELMAN, WILLIAM E. II, govt. ofcl.; b. Washington, Pa., July 8, 1941; s. William E. and Lucy (Bibbs) C.; B.A., Claremont Men's Coll., 1963; postgrad. Universidad de Madrid, 1963-64; J.D., George Washington U., 1968; m. Caroline Murfitt, Dec. 16, 1967; 1 dau., Katharine Carr. Legislative asst. hon. Robert McClory, U.S. Ho. of Reps., 1965-68; staff asst. Office of Pres., 1969; dep. spl. asst. to Pres. Nixon, 1969—. Mem. Nixon staff, Republican nat. conv., 1968; Nixon-Agnew advanceman, Presdl. campaign, 1968; mem. staff transition office of the Pres.-elect, 1968-69. Mem. Va. State Bar, Am., Fed. bar assns., Delta Theta Phi, Theta Chi. Republican. Clubs: Old Town Bath and Racquet (Alexandria, Va.); George Washington U. Washington. Address: The White House Washington DC 20500

CASSELS, DONALD ERNEST, physician, educator; b. Ellendale, N.D., Sept. 8, 1906; s. Ernest E. and Louise (Chambers) C.; B.A., U. N.D., 1932, B.S., 1934; M.D., Harvard, 1936; m. Isabella C.M. Collins, Oct. 8, 1938. Intern pediatrics U. Chgo., 1937-38, resident, 1938-40, asst. prof., 1940-48, asso. prof., 1948-54, prof., 1954—, also dir. pediatric cardiology Wyler Children's Hosp. Served to maj., M.C., AUS, 1943-46; ETO. Decorated Bronze Star medal. Mem. A.M.A., Am. Pediatric Soc., Am. Acad. Pediatrics, Am. Coll. Cardiology (gov. for Ill.), Soc. Pediatric Research, Midwest Soc. Pediatric Research, Am. Heart Assn., Am. Coll. Chest Physicians (chmn. com. cardiology in children). Author, editor books on cardiology Contbr. articles profl. jours. Home: 5617 Dorchester Av Chicago, IL 60637.

CASSELS, LOUIS WELBORN, newspaperman; b. Ellenton, S.C., Jan. 14, 1922, s. Horace Michael Jr. and Molly (Welborn) C.; A.B., Duke, 1942; m. Charlotte Norling, July 10, 1943; 1 son, Michael. Corr., U.P.I., N.Y.C., 1946, mem. staff Washington bur., 1947—, asst. news editor, 1951-56, feature editor, religious news columnist, 1956-64, Washington news analyst, religion editor, 1964-68, sr. editor, nat. news commentator, religion columnist, 1968—. Recipient Christopher award, 1956; Front Page award best U.S. domestic reporting, 1967; Supple ward best religion writing, 1968. Mem. Phi Beta Kappa, Alpha Tau Omega. Episcopalian. Club: Nat. Press. Contbr. articles popular mags., 1948—. Author: Christian Primer, 1964; What's the Difference?, 1965; Your Bible, 1967; The Real Jesus, 1968; The Reality of God, 1971; Haricuts and Holiness, 1972. Syndicated columnist. Home: Coon Tail Lagoon Box 1117 Aiken SC 29801 Office: Nat Press Bldg Washington DC 20004

CASSERLY, JOHN JOSEPH, govt. ofcl.; b. Chgo., Jan. 4, 1927; s. William J. and Hannah (Kane) C.; B.A., St. Mary of Lake, Mundelein, Ill., 1949, Marquette U., 1951; m. Joy Ruth Price, Sept. 17, 1955; children—Kevin, Terence, Jeffrey, Lawrence. Reporter, Milw. Sentinel, 1951; bur. reporter Internat. News Service, 1952, assigned Tokyo bur., 1952, war corr., Korea, 1952-54, assigned Paris bur., 1954, N.Y.C., 1954-56, bur. mgr., Rome, Italy, 1957-58; with CBS News, 1956; Rome bur. chief Hearst Headline service, 1958-61; chief Rome bur. ABC News, 1961-64, assigned Washington bur., 1964-69; part-time fgn. reporting; overseas pub. information mgr. Ford Motor Co., Dearborn, Mich., 1968-70; dir. pub. affairs pub. information Bur. Census, U.S. Dept. Commerce, Suitland, Md., 1970—. Named hon. capt. South Korean Army, 1952-53, hon. cpl. USMC, South Vietnam, 1966. Mem. Sigma Delta Chi. Roman Catholic. Clubs: Press (Milw., Tokyo, Seoul); Rome Foreign Press, American of Rome. Contbr. articles to Cath. lit. mags. Home: 3239 Rittenhouse St NW Washington DC 20015 Office: Bur Census Suitland MD 20233

CASSIBRY FRED JAMES U.S. judge; b. DLo. Miss., Sept. 26, 1918, s. Reginald E. and Lelia (Garner) C.; B.A., Tulane U., 1941, LL.B., 1943; m. Lorraine E. Patterson, Dec. 21, 1940; 1 dau., Elizabeth. Admitted to La. bar, 1944; practice law, New Orleans, 1947-60; mem. firms Cassibry & Zengel, 1946-47, Dymond & Cassibry, 1950-55, Cassibry, Jackson & Hess, 1955-60; judge Civil Dist. Ct., Parish of Orleans, 1960-66; judge U.S. Dist. Ct., Eastern Dist. La., 1966—. Mem. com. on jud. ethics La. Supreme Ct., 1965-66. Mem. city council New Orleans, 1954-60; mem. bd. commrs. New Orleans City Park, 1962-68. Del. Democratic Nat. Conv., 1956. Served from ensign to lt. (j.g.), USNR, 1944-46. Mem. Am. Judicature Soc., Am., Fed., La., New Orleans bar assns., La. Dist. Judges Judges Assn. (pres. 1965), Am. Legion, Tulane U. Alumni Assn. (exec. com. 1962- 65) Home: 6196 Chatham Dr New Orleans, LA 70122. Office: US Dist Ct 400 Royal St New Orleans LA 70130

CASSIDAY, BENJAMIN BUCKLES, Jr., air force officer; b. Honolulu, July 25, 1922; s. Bemjamin Buckles and Harriet (Lucas) C.; B.S., U.S. Mil. Acad., 1943; grad. Nat. War Coll., 1962; m. Barbara C. Dennison, May 14, 1949; children—Benjamin Buckles III, Carol Mary. Commd. 2d. lt. USAAF, 1943, advanced through grades to brig. gen. USAF, 1967; fighter pilot, squadron comdr. 79th Fighter Group, 1943-45; group operations officer, comdr. 81st Fighter Group, 1949-54; dep. comdt. USAF Acad., 1955-59; sec. air staff Hdqrs. USAF, 1963-66; comdr. 36th Fighter Wing, 1966-67; chief air force sect. Joint Mil. Mission to Turkey, 1967-69; commdt. Air Force R.O.T.C., 1969—. Decorated Silver Star, D.F.C., Legion of Merit with 2 oak leaf clusters, Soldier's medal with oak leaf cluster, Air medal with 8 oak leaf clusters; Distinguished Flying Cross (Great Britain). Mem. Air Force Assn., Order of Daedalians. Clubs: Outrigger Canoe (Honolulu); Culver (Ind.) Legion. Home: Box 38 Kahuku HI 96731

CASSIDY, ADRIAN CLYDE, telephone co. exec.; b. Polar, Wis., Jan. 27, 1916, s. William Thomas and Ethel (Jenkins) C.; B.A., U. Wis., 1939, LL.B., 1942; m. Elizabeth Bevans, Mar. 24, 1945; children—David Bevans, Leigh Sheridan, Lynne Porter, Laurie Bevans. Admitted to Wis. bar, 1945, N.Y. bar, 1947, Minn. bar, 1951, N.J. bar, 1962; atty. N.Y. Telephone Co., 1946-50, Am. Tel.& Tel. Co., 1950, 56-51; Minn. atty. Northwestern Bell Telephone Co., 1950-56; gen. atty. N.J. Bell Telephone Co., 1961-63, v.p., 1963-66; v.p. Pacific Tel.&Tel. Co., San Francisco, 1966—. Served to lt. USCGR, 1942-46. Mem. Am. Bar Assn., Am. Judicature Soc., Order of Coif. Clubs: Stock Exchange, World Trade (San Francisco); Canoe Brook Country (Summit, N.J.); Menlo Country (Woodside, Cal.). Exec. editor Wis. Law Rev., 1941-42. Home: 71 Selby Lane Atherton CA 94025 Office: 140 New Montgomery St San Francisco CA 94105

CASSIDY, CLAUDIA, newspaper critic-at-large; b. Shawneetown, Ill.; d. George Peter and Olive (Grattan) Cassidy; A.B., U. Ill.; m. William John Crawford, June 15, 1929. Music, drama critic Chgo. Jour. of Commerce, 1925- 41, Chgo. Sun, 1941-42; music, drama critic Chgo. Tribune, 1942- 65, critic-at-large, 1966—; weekly program Critic's Choice, WFMT, Chgo. Cons. Goodman Theater of Art Inst., Chgo. Home: 33 E Bellevue Pl Chicago IL 60611 Office: Chgo Tribune Tribune Tower Chicago IL 60611

CASSIDY, FREDERIC GOMES educator; b. Kingston, Jamaica, West Indies, Oct. 10, 1907, s. Walter C. and Camilla (Gomes-Casseres) C.; B.A., Oberlin Coll., 1930, M.A., 1932; Ph.D., U. Mich. 1938; m. Hèléne Lucile Monod, Dec. 26, 1931; children—Frederic Monod, Victor Monod, Claire Monod, Michael Monod. Faculty, Oberlin Coll., 1930-31, U. Strasbourg (France), 1935-36, U. Mich., 1936-39; faculty U. Wis., Madison, 1939—, prof. English, 1949—. Vis. prof. Columbia, summer 1956, Stanford, 1963-64; editorial cons. Funk & Wagnalls Co., 1964—. Recipient Silver Musgrave medal Inst. Jamaica, 1961. Fulbright research fellow, 1951-52, 58-59; grantee U.S. Office Edn., 1965-70, Nat. Endowment for Humanities, 1970—. Mem. Am. Dialect Soc. (past pres.). Author: Place Names of Dane County, Wisconsin, 1947; A Method for Collecting Dialect, 1953; Jamaica Talk, 1961; Dictionary of Jamaican English, 1967. Home: Route 1 Waunakee WI 53597

CASSIDY, HAROLD GOMES, educator; b. Havana, Cuba, Oct. 17, 1906; s. Walter Clarence and Camilla (Gomes) C.; student U. Akron, 1923; A.B., Oberlin Coll., 1930, A.M., 1932; Ph.D., Yale, 1939; m. Kathryn Myra Childs, May 19, 1934. Naturalized U.S. citizen. With B.F. Goodrich Tire & Rubber Co., 1924-28; research fellow Oberlin Coll., 1932-33; research chemist William S. Merrell Co., Cin., 1933-36; instr. Oberlin Coll., 1936-37; mem. faculty Yale, 1938—, prof. chemistry, 1958—; sr. fellow in sci. Center Advanced Studies, Conn. Wesleyan U. 1965-66. Cons. Q.M.C., 1954-61; acad. mem.-at-large Gordon Research Council, 1957- 63; del. Conn. Tech. Council, 1945-59; seminar leader Danforth Workship Liberal Arts Edn., 1962, 63, 64, 65; Nat. Sigma Xi lectr., 1960, 63, 65; Ayd lectr., 1962; Korzybski Meml. lectr., 1962; lectr. Assn. Am. Colls. Arts Program, 1968, 71; 1st Lewis lecture St. Joseph's Coll., Hartford, 1969; chmn. Gordon conf. separation and purification 1956; cons. to Coop. Program for Improvement Sci. Edn. in India, 1970; mem. Nat. Humanities Faculty, 1971, 72. Research chemist OSRD and Manhattan Engring Project, 1942-45. Past trustee Choate Sch. Recipient Third John Prymak service award Conn. Sci. Tchr. Assn., 1968. Fellow A.A.A.S. (life mem.); mem. Am. Chem. Soc. (regional lectr. 1952, 56, 59), Conn. Acad. Arts and Scis., Fedn. Am. Socs. Exptl. Biology, Conn. Sci. Tchrs. Assn., Sigma Xi (chmn. com. on grants-in-aid of research). Author: (with J. English) Principles of Organic Chemistry, 1949; Adsorption and Chromatography, 1951; (with J. English) Laboratory Book, 1951; Fundamentals of Chromatography, 1957; The Sciences and the Arts, 1962; (with K.A. Kun) Oxidation-Reduction Polymers, 1965; Knowledge, Experience and Action: An Essay on Education, 1969; Science Restated: Physics and Chemistry for the Non-Scientist, 1970; also numerous articles. Asso. editor Am. Jour. Sci., 1948-67; adv. bd. Analytical Chemistry, 1957-60. Home: 163 East Rock Rd New Haven CT 06511

CASSIDY, HELEN ELIZABETH, social worker, educator; b. New Orleans; d. James Joseph and Lawrentia (Burke) Cassidy; B.A. magna cum laude, Ursuline Coll., Loyola, 1937; M.S.W., Tulane U., 1939; postgrad. Washington U., 1941. U. Cal. at Berkeley, 1969-70. Med. social worker, social service dept. Charity Hosp., New Orleans, 1939-43; social worker, field dir. hosp. service A.R.C., Atlanta, 1943-48; med. social cons. La. Bd. Health, New Orleans, 1948-50; asst. prof. social casework Tulane U., New Orleans, 1950-62, asso. prof., 1962-64, prof., 1964-, coordinator field instrn., 1959-; Fulbright fellow U.K., 1957-58; social casework teaching expert for Spain, UN Tech. Assistance Program, 1961-62. Bd. dirs. La. Conf. Social Welfare, La. Heart Assn., New Orleans Speech and Hearing Center; bd. dirs., profl. adv. com. Social Welfare Planning Council. Recipient Distinguished Service award La. Heart Assn., 1958. Mem. Nat. Assn. Social Workers (pres., past dir.), Council Social Work Edn., Internat. Conf. Social Workers. Author: (with Kindelsperger and Cassidy) Social Work Training Centers; Tentative CAnadian Dredge and Drydock Corp., Financial Gen. Corp., Concepts of Mental Retardation in Medical Care Program for Children, 1957; Modes of Professional Education: The Place of Field Learning in the Social Work Curriculum, 1969. Home: 1526 2d St New Orleans, LA 70130.

CASSIDY, JAMES JOSEPH, pub. relations counsel; b. Norwood, O., Dec. 31, 1916; s. Martin D. and Helen (Johnston) C.; student U. Cin., 1934-38; m. Rita Hackett, Oct. 18, 1941; children—Claudia, James. Dir. spl. events, internat. broadcasts Crosley Broadcasting Corp., 1939-44, war corr., 1944-45, dir. pub. relations, 1946-50; war corr. NBC, 1944-45; account exec. Hill & Knowlton, Inc., N.Y.C., 1950-53, vice president, 1953-61, sr. v.p., 1961- 66, executive vice president, 1966—, also dir. Recipient Variety award, 1944; citation for reporting in combat areas Sec. War, 1945. Mem. Pub. Relations Soc. Am. (pres. N.Y. chpt.), Aviation Writers Assn., Ohio Soc., Council of Profit Sharing Industries (chmn. bd.), Navy League, Air Force Assn. Clubs: Wings, Nat. Press, Metropolitan, Overseas Press. Home: 1261 Madison Av New York City, NY 10028. Office: 150 E 42d St New York City NY 10017

CASSIDY, JOHN EDWARD A., lawyer; b. Ottawa Ill., Jan. 31, 1896; s. Andrew Douglas and Margaret Lucile (Fox) C.; LL.B., U. Notre Dame, 1917; m. Susan Marie Casey, Aug. 11, 1923 (dec.); children—John Edward, James A. (dec.), Susanne Isabella, Colleen Margaret, Marilyn Frances, Thomas Vincent, Owen David, Douglas Joseph and Diane Marie (twins). Admitted to Ill. bar, 1917; gen. practice law, 1921—; mem. firm Cassidy, Cassidy, Quinn & Lindholm; atty. gen. Ill., 1938-41; dir. Peoria-Jour. Star, Inc., Sheridan Bank. Commr., Ill. State Welfare Dept.; Ill. gov. Notre Dame Found.; mem. citizens com. U. Ill.; mem. law council U. Notre Dame. Del., Democratic nat. convs., 1932-36, 40, 56. Mem. Ill. Conf. Repealing 18th Amendment, 1933. Served as lt., inf. 101st Machine Gun Bn., AEF, World War I. Decorated Purple Heart. Mem. Am. (com. coordination law enforcement agys. criminal law sect.), Ill. (bd. govs.), Peoria (pres.) bar assns., Am. Coll. Trial Lawyers, Peoria Assn. Commerce (dir., pres.), U. Notre Dame Alumni Assn., Am. Legion, Ill. C. of C. (nat. councillor, dir.). Roman Catholic. K.C. Clubs: Creve Coeur, Peoria Country; Union League (Chgo.). Home: 6526 St Marys Rd Peoria IL 61614 Office: Jefferson Bldg Peoria IL 61602

CASSIDY, SISTER MARY BRIGH, hosp. adminstr.; b. Eyota, Minn., Feb. 19, 1906; d. Timothy M. and Brigid (Moroney) Cassidy; diploma St. Mary's Sch. Nursing, Rochester, Minn., 1928; B.S. in Nursing Edn., Coll. St. Teresa, Winona, Minn., 1940; M.S., Cath. U., 1942; M.B.A., U. Chgo., 1949. Mem. staff St. Mary's Hosp., Rochester, Minn., 1934—, asst. adminstr., 1949, adminstr., 1949—; instr. lectr. Coll. St. Teresa, 1945—, mem. bd. dirs., 1955—. Recipient Teresa Avilla award, 1965. Mem. Sister 3d Order Regular of St. Francis, 1938-. Fellow Am. Coll. Hosp. Adminstrs.; mem. Am., Cath. (mem. bd. 1956-59, pres. 1967-68), Minn. (pres. 1968-69, mem. bd. 1962-70) hosp. assns., Rochester C. of C. Address: 1216 2d St SW Rochester, MN 55901.

CASSIDY, PATRICK FRANCIS, army officer; b. Pendleton, Ore., Mar. 22, 1915; s. Patrick and Mary Ann (Balcom) C.; student Ore. State Coll., 1933-34; B.S., U. Ore., 1937; postgrad. Command and Gen. Staff Coll., 1945, Army War Coll., 1954, U. Pitts., 1960. Army Mgmt. Sch., 1963; m. Helen Gwendolyn Piggott, Nov. 29, 1940; children—Mary Helen (Mrs. Gabriel R. Robertson), Colleen Gwendolyn (Mrs. Emmette Y. Burton III), Patrick Thomas, Judith Ann, Sean Douglas, Dierdre Kathleen. Commd. 2d lt. U.S. Army, 1937, advanced through grades to lt. gen., 1969; battalion regtl. exec. 101st Airbone Div., World War II; regtl. comdr., chief staff 11th Airborne Div., 1954- 56; chief schs. div. Hdqrs. Continental Army Command, Ft. Monroe, Va., 1959-60, exec. dep. chief staff for operations, plans and tng., 1960-61; sr. adviser V Corps 1st Republic Korea Army, U.S. Army ADGRU, Korea, 1961; adviser to chief staff Detachment L, KMAG, 1962; asst. div. comdr. 101st Airborne Div., Ft. Campbell, Ky., 1962-64; chief staff VII Corps, U.S. Army, Europe, 1964-66; comdg. gen. 8th Inf. Div., 1966-68; dep. chief Office Personnel Operations, Washington, 1968, chief, 1968-69; comdg. gen. I Corps (Group), Korea, 1969-70; dep. comdg. gen. 8th Army, 1970-71; comdg. gen. 5th Army, 1971—. Commr. North Atlantic council Boy scouts Am., 1966-67. Decrated D.S.C., D.S.M., Silver Star, Bronze Star with oak leaf cluster, Purple Heart, Combat Inf. badge, Commendation medal with oak leaf cluster, Legion of Merit; French Croix de Guerre; Belgium Croix de Guerre, Belgium Fourragere; Dutch Orange Lanyard; Luxembourg Medaille Militaire; Spl. Papal award (The Vatican). Mem. Scabbard and Blade. K.C. Address: Comdg General 5th US Army Fort Sam Houston San Antonio TX 78234

CASSIDY, RICHARD THOMAS, army officer; b. Camp Keathley, Philippines, Aug. 16, 1916; s. William Henry and Lillie Christiana (Bergstresser) C.; B.S., U.S. Mil. Acad., 1940; postgrad. Command and Gen. Staff Coll., 1945, U.S. Army War Coll., 1958; m. Annette Nine, June 12, 1940; 1 dau., Camille Gay. Commd. 2d. lt. U.S. Army, 1940, advanced through grades to lt. gen., 1971; dep. chief staff Army Air Def. Command, 1956-57; Army attache to Iraq, 1959-61; comdg. gen. 4th Region, Air Def. Command, 1963-66; comdg. gen. Arty. Brigade, U.S. Army Europe, 1963-66; dir. Air. Def., Pentagon, 1966-68; comdg. gen. Air Def. Center, comdt. Air Def. Sch., Ft. Bliss, Tex., 1968-71; comdg. gen. Army Air Def. Command, Colorado Springs, Colo., 1971—. Decorated Legion of Merit, Bronze Star medal, Army Commendation medal with 2 oak leaf clusters. Home: 820 Vista Grande Colorado Springs CO 80906 Office: Office Comdg Gen Hdqrs US Army Air Command Colorado Springs CO 80912

CASSIDY, WALTER FRANCIS, mathematician, educator; b. N.Y.C., July 1, 1912; s. Francis J. and Mary Ann (Dolan) C.; B.S., Coll. City N.Y., 1932; M.A., Columbia, 1934; Ph D., Fordham U., 1940; m. Theresa A. Trainor, July 1, 1940; children— Walter Trainor, Carol Ann. Faculty, St. John's U., Jamaica, N.Y., 1941—, prof. math., 1951—, chmn. dept., 1961-69. Project dir. Coll. Math. for Disadvantaged, 1969—. Chmn., Cath. Youth Orgns. St. Mary's Parish, Manhasset, N.Y., 1960—. Mem. Math. Assn. Am. (chmn. math. sect. 1965-67), N.Y. Acad. Scis. (math. sect.), Phi Beta Kappa. Co- author: Business Mathematics, 1952; An Introduction to College

Mathematics, 1955; College Mathematics, 1958. Author: History of Insurance (3 vols.) also Am. hist. plays. Home: 70 Strathmore Rd Manhasset NY 11030 Office: Jamaica NY 11432

CASSIDY, WILLIAM FREDERICK, ret. army officer; b. Nome, Alaska, Aug. 28, 1908; s. William and Lillie (Bergstresser) C.; B.S., U.S. Mil. Acad., 1931; M.S., State U. Ia., 1934; grad. Engr. Sch., 1936, Nat. War Coll, 1954; m. Helen Robison, Aug. 15, 1939; children—Anne, Mary. Commd. 2d lt., C.E. U.S. Army, 1931, advanced through grades to lt. gen. 1965; various troop, civil assignments C.E., to 1942; comdr. engr. troops specializing constrn. airfield, ETO, 1942- 44; with war plans div., later operations and tng. div. Office Chief Engrs., 1944-47; asst. div. engr. Lower Mississippi Valley div. C.E., 1947-50; supply officer engr. sect. Hdqrs. Japan Logistical Com., 1950- 52; exec. officer engring. sect. Gen. Hdqrs., AFFE, 1952-53; dep. div. engr. South Pacific Div. C.E., 1954-55, div. engr., 1955-58; sr. logistics adviser Republic Korea Army, 1958-59; dir. civil works Office Chief Engrs., 1959-62, dep. chief engrs., 1962-63; comdg. gen. U.S. Army Engr. Center, also comdt. U.S. Army Engring. Sch., Ft. Belvoir, Va., 1963-65; chief of engrs. U.S. Army, Washington, 1965-69; retired, 1969; recalled to active duty, 1969; chmn. Bd. Engrs. for Rivers and Harbors, 1969-70; retired, 1970. Decorated D.S.M., Legion of Merit with cluster, Bronze Star; Presdl. citation (Republic of Korea). Fellow Am. Soc. C.E.; mem.. Soc. Am. Mil. Engrs., Permanent Internat. Assn. Navigation Congresses, U.S. Com. Large Dams, Nat. Soc. Profl. Engrs., Nat. Acad. Engring., Tau Beta Pi. Contbr. articles profl. jours. Home: 1848 Rivershore Dr Indialantic FL 32901

CASSILL, RONALD VERLIN, author; b. Cedar Falls, Ia., May 17, 1919; s. Howard E. and Mary (Glosser) C.; B.A., U. Ia., 1939, M.A., 1947; m. Karilyn Kay Adams, Nov. 23, 1956; children—Orin, Erica, Jesse. Tchr., Writers Workshop, U. Ia., 1948-52, 60-66; asst. prof. Brown U., 1966—; reviewer for N.Y. Times, Book Week, Chgo. Sun Times. Served to 1st lt. AUS, 1942-46. Mem. Phi Beta Kappa. Methodist. Author: Eagle on the Coin, 1950; Clem Anderson, 1961; Pretty Leslie, 1963; The President, 1964; The Father, 1965; The Happy Marriage, 1966; La Vie Passionnee of Rodney Buckthorne, 1968; In An Iron Time, 1969; Doctor Cobb's Game, 1970; also short stories. Home: 31 Cabot St Providence RI 02906

CASSILLY, PHILIP JACQUEMN, former govt. ofcl.; b. Louisville, Dec. 23, 1904; s. Louis Vincent and Lillie (Jones) C.; student Notre Dame U., 1922-23; m. Ruth Fisher Erickson, May 8, 1943. With Ford Motor Co., Louisville, 1925-26; engr. dam and levee constrn. U.S. C.E., lower Ohio and Miss. Rivers, 1926-29; constrn. maintenance engr. United Fruit Co., Jamaica, B.W.I., 1930-34; state dir. employment WPA, Phoenix, 1935-42; labor relations rep. Consol.-Vultee Aircraft Co., Tucson, 1942-43; personnel officer War Relocation Auth., Poston, Ariz., 1943-46; adminstrv. officer Southwestern Power Adminstrn., Tulsa, 1946-70, asst. adminstr. for adminstrv. operations, 1967-70. Recipient honor award meritorious service sec. of interior, 1970. Home: 3111 E 26th Pl Tulsa OK 74114

CASSIN, RENE, jurist, human rights advocate; b. Bayonne, France, Oct. 5, 1887; s. Henri and Gabrielle (Dreyfus) C.; M.A. (Licenci es lettres); Dr. Juridical, Econ. and Polit. Scis., law schs., Aix (France) and Paris (France); hon. doctorates univs. Oxford (Eng.), Mainz (Germany), London (Eng.), Jerusalem (Israel), Brandeis U., m. Simone Yzombard, Mar. 29, 1917. Prof. law univs. Lille (France), 1920, Paris, 1929-60; prof. Nat. Sch. Colonial Studies, 1935- 40; faculty Acad. Internat. Law, The Hague, Netherlands, U. Inst. Advanced Studies in Internat. Affairs, Geneva, Switzerland; pres. Nat. Sch. Pub. Adminstrn. 1945-60. French del. League of Nations, 1924- 38, UN, 1946-58; French founding mem. UNESCO, 1944, del., 1945-52; past pres. UN Human Rights Commn., chief recorder Universal Declaration of Human Rights, 1947-48; judge, past pres. European Ct. Human Rights, 1959—, pres., 1965-68; permanent sec. Def. Council under DeGaulle, 1940-41; nat. commr. justice and edn. French Govt. in Exile, 1941-43; mem. Interallied Commn. of Inquiry on War Crimes, 1943-45; mem. consulative assembly Algiers, pres. juridical com.; v.p. Council of State, 1944-60, subsequently hon. pres., also founder jour. Researches and Documents, 1947; pres. High Ct. of Arbitration, 1945-46; mem. Constl. Council, 1960-71; founder Internat. Inst. Human Rights, Strasbourg, 1968. Served during World War I, World War II. Decorated grand cross Legion of Honor, Companion of the Liberation, Mil. medal, Croix de Guerre, Resistance Rosette (France). Recipient Nobel Peace prize, 1968, UN Human Rights prize, 1968, Bernard Cogan prize. Mem. Institut de France (pres. Acad. Moral and Polit. Sci. 1962—), Soc. Comparative Legislation (hon. pres.), Assn. Devel. World Law (hon. pres.) Friends of U. Paris (pres.), Inst. Internat. Relations (pres.) Alliance Israélite e Universelle (pres.). Author: L'Exception d'inexécution dans les Contrats. les Droits de l'Etat dans les Successions en Suisse, 1914; Le Domicile dans le Conflit des Lois, 1930; La Déclaration, Universelle et la Mise en Oeuvre des Droits de l'Homme, 1951; Livre Jubilaire du Conseil d'Etat, 1952. Home: 36 Quai de Bethune Paris 4-c France

CASSINI, OLEG LOLEWSKI, designer, mfr.; b. Paris, France, Apr. 11 1913; s. Alexander C. and Marguerite (Cassini) Loiewski; grad. Academia Belle Arti, Florence, Italy, 1934; student Sch. Polit. Sci., Florence, 1932-34; m. Gene E. Tierney, June 1, 1941 (div. Feb. 1952); children—Daria, Christina. Free lance designer, Paris, 1935; designer-owner dress studio, Rome, Italy, 1935-36; designer for Jo Copeland, 1936-38, James Rotherberg, Inc., 1938-39; owner studio, N.Y.C., 1939-40; designer Paramount Pictures Inc., 1940-41, 20th Century Fox, 1941-42; head wardrobe dept. Eagle-Lion Studios, 1946-47; owner firm Cassini-Dardick, 1947-50, Oleg Cassini, Inc., N.Y.C., 1950—; designer mus. comedy As the Girls Go, other Broadway plays. Served as 1st lt., cav. AUS 1942-46. Winner five first prizes Mostra Della Moda, Turin, Italy, 1934. Clubs: Tennis, Lawn Tennis (Florence, Italy); Parioli (Rome); Town and Tennis (N.Y.C.). Home: 135 E 19th St New York City NY 10003 Office: 445 Park Av New York City NY 10022

CASSIRER, HENRY REINHARD, ednl. broadcaster; b. Berlin, Germany, Sept. 2, 1911; s. Kurt H. and Eva (Solmitz) C.; student Odenwaldschule, univs. Frankfurt and Cologne (Germany), 1931-33; B.A. with honors, London (Eng.) U., 1936, Ph.D. in Modern History, 1940; m. Marta Reyto, Mar. 13, 1941; 1 dau., Vivian. Naturalized Am. citizen. Announcer, translator BBC, 1938-40; fgn. news editor, asst. dir. short wave listening sta. CBS, N.Y.C., 1940-44; news editor CBS-TV, 1944-49; free-lance TV and film writer, 1949-52; head radio and TV sect. UNESCO, Paris, France, 1952-66, chief ednl. use mass media, 1965-71, dir. use mass media in out-of-sch. edn., 1971—; producer, dir. art films, 1947—. Lectr. broadcasting New Sch. Social Research, N.Y. U., 1947-52; vis. prof. telecommunications U. So. Cal., 1964; expert adviser govts. India, 1957, Pakistan, 1960, Israel 1961, Venezuela, 1962, Senegal, 1963-70, Brazil, 1967-68, Mali, 1968, Algeria, 1969, Singapore, Alaska, 1970; cons. Mass. Inst. Tech., 1971; organizer internat. confs. broadcasting; charge pilot projects ednl. tech. Author: Television, a World Survey, 1953; Television Teaching Today, 1960; also articles. Producer films: Men of Our Age, the Sculpture of Jo Davidson, 1947; BUMA, African Aculpture Speaks, 1952. Home: 1 rue Alphonse Daudet Paris 14e France Office: Place de Fontenoy Paris 17e France

CASSO, HENRY, educator; A.B., Brown U., 1938, A.M., 1946; D.M.L., Middlebury Coll., 1960. Prof. Italian, asso. dean for acad. programs U. R.I., Kingston. Office: Dept Classics U RI Kingston RI 02881*

CASSON, HUGH MAXWELL, architect; b. London, Eng., May 23, 1910; s. Randal and Mary (Man) C.; ed. Eastbourne Coll., St. John's Coll. of Cambridge U.; Craven scholar, Brit. Sch. at Athens, 1933; m. Margaret MacDonald Troup, Nov. 19, 1938; children—Carola (Mrs. Adam Ritchie), Nicola (Mrs. Ian Hessenberg), Dinah (Mrs. Nicholas Wood). Pvt. archtl. practice, London, Eng., 1937—; dir. architecture Festival of Britain, 1948-51; prof. interior design Royal Coll. Art; mem. Royal Fine Art Commn. Chmn. bd. trustees Arthur Koestler Award; gov. Dorset House Sch. Occupational Therapy. Served with Air Ministry, 1939-45. Fellow Royal Inst. Brit. Architects, Soc. Indsl. Artists and Designers, A.I.A.; mem. Royal Acad., Royal Designers for Industry, Royal Danish Acad. Author: New Sights of London, 1937; Bombed Churches, 1946; Homes by the Million, 1947; Houses—Permanence and Prefabrication, 1947; Victorian Architecture, 1948; Inscape, 1968; also articles. Home: 35 Victoria Rd London W8 England Office: 35 Thurloe Pl London SW7 England

CASTAGNA, EDWIN, librarian; b. Petaluma, Cal., May 1, 1909; s. Frank and Eugenie (Burgle) C.; grad. Santa Rosa Jr. Coll., 1930; A.B., U. Cal., 1935, certificate in librarianship, 1936; m. Rachel Davida Dent, May 3, 1943. With Alameda County Library, 1937; chief librarian Ukiah (Cal.) Pub. Library, 1937-40; dir. Washoe County Library, Reno, 1941-49; chief librarian Glendale (Cal.) Pub. Library, 1949-50; city librarian Long Beach (Cal.) Pub. Library, 1950-60; dir. Enoch Pratt Free Library, Balt., 1960—; vis. lectr. Sch. Library Sci., U. So. Cal., 1958-60; vis. prof. Sch. Library Service, U. Cal. at Los Angeles, summer 1963; cons. on pub. library bldg. and adminstrv. problems to various pub. libraries. Mem. adv. council U. Cal. Sch. Librarianship, 1954-60, U. So. Cal. Sch. Library Sci. 1953-59. Served to capt. AUS, World War II; co-comdr. 771st Tank Bn., Rhineland, Ardennes and Central Europe campaigns. Decorated Bronze Star, Purple Heart. Mem. Am. (council 1946-47, 63—, v.p. 1963-64, pres. 1964-65), Cal. (chmn. jr. mems. round table 1940, pres. 1954), Nev. (pres. 1946-47) library assns., Am. Assn. UN (pres. Long Beach chpt. 1955-57), UN Assn. Md., Md. Library Assn., Balt. Bibliophiles, Internat. Assn. Met. City Libraries (v.p. 1968—), Union de Bibliofilos Taurinos. Democrat. Clubs: 14 West Hamilton Street, Zamorano, Rotary (Balt.). Author: History of the 771 Tank Batallion, 1946; Long Warm Friendship: H.L. Mencken and the Enoch Pratt Free Library, 1966. Co-editor: The Library Reaches Out, 1965. Contbr. library jours. Office: 400 Cathedral St Baltimore MD 21201

CASTAGNETTA, GRACE SHARP, pianist; b. N.Y.C., June 10, 1912; d. Francis and Grace (Sharp) Castagnetta; student Rutherford (N.J.) High Sch.; piano pupil N. Elsenheimer, N.Y.C., student Hochschule fur Musik, Cologne, Germany, 1928-31. First appeared in pub. at age of four; after study in Germany, appeared in prin. German cities; has played with N.Y. Philharmonic Symphony, Nat. Symphony (Washington), symphonies of Portland, Ore., Bridgeport, Conn., and with Fed. and N.Y.C. symphonies, Columbia and Mut. Broadcasting symphonies; made Scandanavian tour, 1938; radio artist; began improvising at piano recitals in 1941, in Town Hall, 1942, 1956; trans-continental tour, 1956-57. Records for Esoteric. Has 3 vols. of recorded music and miscellaneous records. Adviser to faculty of music sch. Lighthouse for Blind, N.Y.C. Mem. Am. Musicol. Soc. Presbyn. Author: (with Hendrick W. Van Loon), The Songs We Sing, 1936; The Christmas Carols, 1937; Folk Songs of Many Lands, 1938; The Last of the Troubadours, 1939; Songs America Sings, 1940; Life and Times of Bach, 1940; Good Tidings, 1941; More Christmas Carols, 1942; Glad Tidings, 1958; Holiday Harmonics, 1959; Concerto series on radio for Treasury Dept., Jan.-Apr. 1943. Made concert transcription of Gershwin Concerto in F for solo piano, 1946; soloist Music For An Hour, MBS, 1945; Annual N.Y. City recital, 1945-46; made coast to coast concert tour, also appeared in solo recitals and with leading orchs., 1946-47; Am. Canadian concert tour, 1948-49, 58-59; appearing Piano Playhouse, ABC coast-to-coast program, 1949; Carnegie Hall recital, 1949; coast-to-coast tour, 1950; extensive Am. concert tour Town Hall Recital, 1954-55; appearing on radio and TV in N.Y.C.; soloist with symphony orchs. throughout the U.S. Appeared in concerts at camps, canteens and hosps. for armed forces, during World War II; now instr. advanced piano Trenton State Coll. Author: Robin Hood Ballads, 1947; Sonata and 4 preludes; Goods Tidings enlarged to pantomime of nativity story, pub., 1960. Recorded improvisations on Christmas carols on Siena pianoforte, 1962. Home: 383 Union Av Wood Ridge, NJ 07075.

CASTANEDA, HECTOR-NERI, philosopher, educator; b. Zacapa, Guatemala, Dec. 13, 1924; s. Ezequiel V. and Sara (Calderón) C.; came to U.S., 1956, naturalized, 1963; B.A., U. Minn., 1950, M.A., 1952, Ph.D., 1954; Brit. Council fellow, Wadham Coll., Oxford, 1955-56; m. Miriam Mendez, Dec. 24, 1946; children—Xmucane (Mrs. Gerald Wiebeck), Kicab, Hector Neri, Omar Sigfrido, Quetzil. Instr., U. Minn., 1953-54; vis. asst. prof. Duke, 1956-57; asst. prof. Wayne State U., 1957-61, asso. prof., 1961-64, prof., 1964-69, acting chmn. philosophy dept., 1965-66, summer 1968, vis. prof. philosophyy, 1970; prof. Ind. U., Bloomington, 1969—; prof. U. San Carlos, Guatemala, 1954-55; vis. lectr. U. Tex., Austin, 1962-63, vis. prof., 1966; vis. prof. U. Cin., 1970. Recipient First award in humanities Wayne State Recognition Fund, 1961. Guggenheim fellow, 1967- 68. Mem. Aristotelian Soc., Am. Philos. Assn., Assn. Symbolic Logic. Author: La Dialéctica de la Conciencia de Sí Mismo, 1960. Editor: (with G. Nakhnikian) Morality and the Language of Conduct, 1963; Intentionality, Minds and Perception, 1967. Founding editor: Nos, 1965- -. Mem. editorial bd. Crítica, 1966—. Contbr. articles profl. jours. Home: 2244 Martha St Bloomington IN 47401

CASTANO, GIOVANNI, artist; b. Gasperina, Calabria, Italy, Oct. 2, 1896; s. Joseph and Maria Therese (Procopio) C.; brought to U.S., 1904; art edn. under Philip L. Hale, Leslie P. Thompson, Huger Elliott, F.M. Lamb, Henry James and at Museum of Fine Arts, Boston, 1916-21; m. Josephine Caruso, Feb. 6, 1926; children—John Elvira (Mrs. Carlo Palmerio), Marie (Mrs. John Robert Lothrop). Works are represented in Pub. Library, Brockton, Mass., Springfield (Mass.) Art Assn. Painter stage settings Boston Opera House; scenic artist and designer Cin. Grand Opera, 1922-27; executed murals First Baptist Ch., Covington, Ky., Mercy Acad., Cin., Met. Theatre, Boston, 1927; painter all stage scenery for Town Hall, Peterborough, N.H., 1936; decorated St. Peter's Church, Boston, 1936; also recently painted individual portraits. Decorated cavaliere Ordine al Merito Della Repubblica Italiana. Recieved hon. mention Pa. Acad. Fine Arts, 1918, Springfield Art Club, 1926. Mem. Accademia Tiberina (Rome, Italy). Republican. Roman Catholic. Clubs: Art (Boston, Cin., Brockton). Home: 245 Hunnewell St Needham MA 02192 Studio: 91 Newbury St Boston MA 02116

CASTEEL, JOHN LAURENCE, educator, clergyman; b. Randolph, Neb., Dec. 17, 1903; s. William Edgar and Geneva Ann (Bell) C.; A.B. with highest distinction, Neb. Wesleyan U., 1927, LL.D., 1947; A.M., Northwestern U., 1929, Ph.D., 1943; m. Audeline Boughn, June 8, 1929, children—Margaret Bell (Mrs. Gilbert Bloom), John Alden. Instr. Northwestern U., 1928-30; acting prof. Neb. Wesleyan U., 1930-31; asst. prof., dir. speech div. U. Ore., 1931-38, asso. prof., 1938-42; ordained to ministry Congl. Christian Ch., 1942; minister in residence Church-in-the-Gardens, Forest Hills, L.I., N.Y., 1944-46; minister 1st Congl. Ch., Sharon, Conn., 1948-51; dir. dept. speech Union Theol. Sem., 1942-43, asso. prof., 1942-51, dir. summer courses, 1946-47, 50-51, prof. pastoral theology, dir. dept. field work, 1956-64; prof. speech Colgate Rochester Div. Sch., 1951-54, Corneilius Woelfkin prof. preaching, 1954-56; gen. sec. for leadership devel. Council for Lay Life and Work, United Ch. of Christ, 1964-68; prof. practical theology, coordinator community edn. and service Hartford (Conn.) Sem. Found., 1969-71; lectr. U. Sch., U. Rochester, 1952-56. Mem. of adv. council Nat. Student YMCA, 1945-51. Mem. Phi Kappa Phi, Pi Gamma Mu, Delta Sigma Rho, Pi Kappa Delta. Author: Rediscovering Prayer, 1955; Pilgrimage in Prayer, 1956; (with others) Spiritual Renewal Through Personal Groups, 1957; Promise of Prayer, 1957; Renewal in Retreats; (with others) The Creative Role of Interpersonal Groups In The Church Today, 1968. Contbr. articles religious periodicals. Address: 2008 Cambridge Dr Muncie IN 47304

CASTEEL, RUSSELL RONAINE, consultant; b. Princeton, Mo., June 1, 1902; s. Edmund Ronaine and Maud L. (Girdner) C.; A.B., U. Mo., 1924, J.D., 1927. Admitted to Mo. bar, 1926, Ill. bar, 1937; practice of law, St. Louis, 1928-29; counsel Stifel Nicolaus & Co., investment bankers, 1929-36; with Olin Industries, Inc., East Alton, 1936-67, sec., counsel dir., then v.p. Olin Mathieson Chem. Corp., now cons. to corp.; v.p., dir. Ill. State Bank, East Alton. Dir., v.p. Jr. Achievement Miss. Valley. Mem. Asso. Employers Ill. (dir.), Alton Dist. Mfg. Assn. (dir.), Ill. Taxpayers Fedn. (exec. com.), Am. Ordnance Assn. (life), Mo., Ill. bar assns., Phi Beta Kappa, Pi Kappa Alpha, Phi Delta Phi. Republican. Mason, Elk. Club: Racquet (St. Louis). Home: East Alton IL 62024

CASTEL, JACK, newspaperman; b. Huntington, Ark., Dec. 29, 1912; s. James P. Castel and Stella (Singleton) C.; student Tex. Western Coll., 1934; m. Alice Jenner McCue, Aug. 13, 1949; children—David Alan, James William, Anthony Jenner. Reporter, The Times, El Paso, Tex., 1933-36; news editor Rocky Mountain News, Denver, 1936-51; mem. staff San Francisco News, 1951-65; chief editorial writer San Francisco Examiner, 1965-. Served with AUS, 1945-46. Recipient awards Denver Press Club, 1950, Cal. Newspaper Pubs. Assn., 1959. Episcopalian. Home: 172 Merced Av San Francisco CA 94127 Office: 110 5th St San Francisco CA 94119

CASTELL, ALBUREY, educator, philosopher; b. Toronto, Can., Jan. 20, 1904; s. William Edward and Adelaide (Maines) C.; B.A., M.A., U. Toronto; Ph.D., U. Chgo.; m. Lillian Munich, July 20, 1939; m. 2d, Lillibel Woll, Aug. 3, 1948. Vis. lectr. dept. philosophy Columbia, 1940-41; asst. prof. philosophy U. Minn., 1935-43, asso. prof., 1943-45, prof., 1945-49; chmn. dept. philosophy U. Ore. 1949-64; Compton prof. philosophy, chmn. philosophy Coll. of Wooster (O.), 1964—. Curriculum study Portland High Sch., spring 1959; vis. prof. U. Wash., 1947, Yale, 1957-58; Machette lectr. Purdue, 1948, Knoles lectr. Coll. of Pacific, 1953, Southwick lectr. Columbia, spring 1963. Author books including: Science as a Goad to Philosophy, 1953; An Elementary Ethics, 1954; Introduction to Modern Philosophy, rev. 2d edit., 1963. Editor several vols.; also editor Selections from T.H. Huxley, 1948; Essays in Pragmatism, by W. James, 1948; The Age of Reason, part I, by Tom Paine, 1948; Nature, by J.S. Mill, 1950; The Self in Philosophy. Home: 942 Quinby St Wooster OH 43085

CASTELL, WILLIAM RENTOUL, librarian; b. Toronto, Ont., Can., Nov. 6, 1908; s. William Edward and Adelaide (Manes) C.; B.A., U. Toronto, 1932; B.Sc., U. Minn., 1935; M.L.S., U. Mich., 1936; m. Mildred Ruth Joyce, Sept. 4, 1937; children—David McFall, Barbara (Mrs. Douglas Ladell). Chief librarian Ft. William (Can.) Pub. Library, 1937-45; dir. Calgary (Can.) Pub. Library, 1945—. Mem. Canadian (pres. 1965-66), Alta. library assns. Home: 2010 Ulster Rd Calgary Alberta Canada Office: 616 Macloud Trail S E Calgary 21 Alberta Canada

CASTELLAN, GILBERT WILLIAM, educator; b. Denver, Nov. 21, 1924; s. John and Eleanor (Pavella) C.; B.S. summa cum laude, Regis Coll., 1945, Sc.D., 1967; Ph.D., Cath. U. Am., 1949; m. Joan Margaret McDonald, Sept. 8, 1956; children—Stephen Joseph, William Andrew, David Matthew, Susan Marie. Instr. chemistry Cath. U. Am., Washington, 1950-54, asst. prof., 1954-58 asso. prof., 1958-64, asst. head dept., 1963-65, prof. chemistry, 1964-69; prof. chemistry, asso. dean phys. scis. and engring. U. Md. Grad. Sch., College Park, 1969—. Cons. electrochemistry br. U.S. Naval Research Lab., 1956-63, Melpar, Inc., Falls Church, Va., 1963-67. Bd. dirs. The Campus Sch., Washington, 1969-70, treas., 1969-70. AEC fellow phys. scis. U. Ill., 1949-50; NSF fellow Max Planck Institut für Physikalische Chemie, Göttingen, Germany, 1962-63. Mem. Am. Chem. Soc., Am. Phys. Soc., A.A.A.S., Albertus Magnus Guild, Electrochem. Soc. (pres. sect. 1964-65), Sigma Xi. Author: Physical Chemistry, 1964, 2d edit., 1971. Home: 3116 Cheverly Av Cheverly MD 20785 Office: U Md Grad Sch College Park MD 20742

CASTELLAN, NORMAN JOHN, educator, engr.; b. Everett, Wash., Jan. 11, 1912; s. John and Eleanor (Pavella) C.; B.S. with spl. honors in Civil Engring., U. Colo., 1933, M.S., 1934; m. Mary Victoria Biebl, May 12, 1933 (dec. May 1968); children—Joanne (Mrs. Howard Chapin Shaw, Jr.), Norman John, Adrienne Marie (Mrs. Gary Leonard LeBlanc). Instr. civil engring. U. Colo., 1934; sr. levelman U.S. Bur. Pub. Rds., Denver, 1935; jr. engr. U.S. Bur. Reclamation, Denver, 1936; instr., asst. prof. Colo. Sch. Mines, 1936-41; asst. to dist. mgr. WPB, Denver, 1941-45, dep. regional dir., 1945; Colo. dist. mgr. Civilian Prodn. Adminstrn., Kansas City, Mo., 1946, regional dir., 1947; cons. civil engring., Denver, 1947-55; asso. prof. charge civil engring. Sacramento State Coll., 1955-59, prof., head dept., 1959-62, chmn. div. engring., 1962-67, prof. civil engring., 1967-68, prof., chmn. dept. civil engring., 1969—. Registered profl. engr., land surveyor, Colo., Cal. Fellow Am. Soc. C.E.; mem. Am. Soc. Engring. Edn., Engring. Council Sacramento Valley (gov. 1963-68, chmn. 1964), Tau Beta Pi, Sigma Tau, Chi Epsilon. Club: Del Paso Country (Sacramento). Home: 824 Commons Dr Sacramento CA 95825

CASTELLO, ALFONSO, bank exec. Statutory auditor Banco Nacional De Mexico, S.A. Office: Avenida Isabel La Catolica 44 Mexico City 1 Mexico*

CASTELLON, FEDERICO, artist; b. Almeria, Spain, Sept. 14, 1914; s. Raimundo and Josefa (Martinez) C.; came to U.S., 1921, naturalized, 1943; ed. pub. schs.; m. Hildegarde Field, Oct. 21, 1940; 1 son, Paul Andrew. Instr. painting Columbia Tchrs. Coll., 1948-61, Pratt Inst., 1951-61, 64—, Queens Coll., 1964, New Sch. Social Research, Art Students League; exhibited one-man shows includiding Albany Mus. History and Art, 1951, Assn. Am. Artists, 1952, 66, Bucknell U., 1953, Mercersberg Gallery, 1953, Phila. Print Club, 1964, Dintewfass Gallery, N.Y.C., 1964, U. Me., 1966, Brandeis U., 1966, also numerous S.Am. galleries; exhibited Galerie Frapier, Paris, France, 1965, Los Angeles Civic Mus., Slater Meml. Mus., 1968; rep. in permanent collections Bklyn., Whitney, Phila. museums, Mus. Modern Art, N.Y. Pub. Library, Pa. Acad. Fine Arts, Chgo. Art Inst., Library Congress, Princeton and Yale; rep. U.S. on cultural exchange 8 countries S.Am., 1956; feature spreads in Life mag. History of Law,

1951, Sumerian Civilization, 1957, also advt., mag. and book illustration. Guggenheim fellow, 1941, 50; grantee Nat. Inst. Arts and Letters, 1950; fellow Spanish Republic, 1934. Recipient Logan prize Chgo. Art Inst., 1939; Eyre medal Pa. Acad. Fine Arts, 1940; 1st prize Library Congress, 1947; Collins prize Phila. Print Club, 1964; Am. Artists group prize, 1964; 1st prize Art Center Madison, Wis. Served with OSS and C.E., AUS, 1943-45. Mem. Soc. Am. Graphic Arts (v.p., Turner prize 1967), Nat. Acad. Arts (membership com.), Nat. Inst. Arts and Letters. Club: Century. Pub. portfolios: Etchings for Asso. Am. Artists, 1967, on Poe's Masque of Red Death, 1968; Images No. 1, 1968; Images No. 2, 1968. Address: 432 W 22d St New York City NY 10011

CASTELLUCCI, JOHN WESLEY, med. care orgn. exec.; b. Boston, Oct. 8, 1906; s. Vincent A. and Sofia (Bruno) C.; student Wayyne U., 1929, Detroit Coll. Law, 1934; m. Faustine Pugliano, Aug. 19, 1933. Asst. dir. Mich. Med. Service, 1943-55; cons. Blue Shield Med. Care Plans, 1947-51; pres. successor Nat. Assn. Blue Shield Plans, 1955—; pres. Blue Shield Found. on Health Care, 1968- -; sec. Med. Indemnity Am., Inc. 1954—. Cons. to Am. Dental Assn. Council on Dental Health. Bd. dirs. Internat. Fedn. Voluntary Health Service Funds, 1968—, v.p., 1970—. Served with AUS, World War II. Decorated knight Order Merit (Italy). Hon. fellow Soc. Med. Care Plan Adminstrs.; mem. Am. Soc. Assn. Execs., Am. Pub. Health Assn., A.I.M., U.S. C. of C. (ins. com. 1962-68). Mem. editorial adv. council Pension and Welfare News, 1964-66. Home: 222 E Chestnut St Chicago IL 60611 Office: 211 E Chicago Av Chicago IL 60611

CASTER, GEORGE BROWN, savs. and loan assn. exec.; b. Leon, Ia., Sept. 21, 1894; s. Joseph A. and Olive (Brown) C.; A.B., U. Cal., 1916; LL.B., Columbia, 1920; m. Bernice A. Browning, Mar. 3, 1948. First v.p., founding dir. Coral Gables Fed. Savs. & Loan Assn. (Fla.), 1934, pres., 1938-66, chmn. bd., 1966—; real estate broker, 1926—; ins. agt., 1930—; pres., dir. Caster Ins. Agy., Inc., 1956—. Served to 1st lt. U.S. Army, World War I; AEF in France. Mem. U.S., Fla. (past pres.) savs. and loans leagues, Greater Miami Ins. Bd. (past v.p., mem. exec. com.), Coral Gables Bd. Realtors (past pres.), Coral Gables C. of C. (past v.p., dir.), Sigma Chi (past pres. Miami alumni chpt.). Rotarian (charter, past pres. Coral Gables), Elk (charter trustee, hon. mem.). Clubs: Century (past pres.), Riviera Country (Coral Gables). Home: 1254 Coral Way Coral Gables FL 33134 Office: 2501 Ponce de Leon Blvd Coral Gables FL 33134

CASTETTER, ROBERT KARL, univ. dean; b. Martinsville, Ind., Aug. 18, 1920; s. Roy Emit and Margaret Henrietta (Tate) C.; B.A. magna cum laude, Washington and Jefferson Coll., 1941, LL.D., 1971; LL.B., Salmon P. Chase Coll. Law, Cin., 1952, J.D., 1962; LL.M., Ind. U., 1954; m. Marjorie Catherine Bruce, Nov. 22, 1947; children—Bruce Robert, Deborah Lynn, Roy Robert, Victoria Leigh. Contract negotiator Cin. ordnance dist. War Dept., 1941-42; gen. mgr. Advance Advertisers Co., Cin., 1946-52; prof. bus. law, head dept. San Diego State Coll., 1954-60; dean Law Sch., Cal. Western U., San Diego, 1960—. Estate planning cons. local banks, 1957-60; founder, organizer Pacific S.W. chpt. Nat. Bus. Law Assn., 1962. Mem. Consumer Protection Com. for Atty. Gen. Cal., 1971—. Bd. dirs. San Diego chpt. A.R.C., 1963—; exec. com., trustee San Diego Legal Aid Soc., 1962-65; incorporating dir. Fed. Defenders, Inc.; bd. dirs. Crofton House. Served with AUS, 1942-46. Mem. Am. Bus. Law Assn., Am. Arbitration Assn. (nat. panel), Phi Delta Phi. Contbr. Ency. Brit., 1963. Home: 9508 Blair Dr La Mesa CA 92041 Office: 3902 Lamaland Dr San Diego CA 92106

CASTIGLIONE, SALVATORE JOSEPH, educator; b. New Haven, Sept. 10, 1910; s. Joseph Frances (DeCarlo) C.; B.A., Yale, 1932, Ph.D., 1939; postgrad. (Exchange fellow) U. Florence (Italy), 1934-35; m. Pierina Borrani, June 29, 1938; 1 dau., Vanna (Mrs. Salvatore Francia). Asst. prof. Yale, 1947-50; mem. Italian faculty ASTP, Rutgers U., 1943- 44; faculty Georgetown U., 1951-66, prof. Italian, 1960-66; Jean Thomson Fulton prof. Italian, Middlebury (Vt.) Coll., 1966—, faculty Italian Summer Sch., 1937-39, 46, dir., 1948—, a founder Grad. Sch. Italian in Italy, dir. studies, 1960-61, 69-70. Examiner in Italian, Coll. Entrance Exam. Bd., 1959-65. Decorated cavaliere ufficiale Ordine al merito delia Repubblica Italiana. Fulbright scholar, Italy, 1950-51. Mem. Modern Lang. Assn., Am. Assn. Tchrs. Italian (pres. 1956), Dante Soc. Translator: Politics and Morals (Benedetto Croce), 1945. Contbr. articles to profl. jours. Home: Route 2 Middlebury VT 05753

CASTIGLIONI, NICCOLO, composer Gymel, for flute and piano. Address: care Time Records Inc Director Recording Personnel 2 W 45th St New York City NY 10036*

CASTILLO, DEL REY, (Antonio Canovas Dal), fasion designer; b. Madrid, Spain, Dec. 13, 1908; s. Jesus Canovas del Castillo and Elvira (del Rey) del Castillo; student Colegio del Pilar, Madrid, U. Madrid, El Sacro Monte, Granada, Spain. Designer dresses, hats, jewelry French countries, including Paquin's, Puguet, also for motion pictures, 1936-44; designer collections custom and ready-made clothes Elizabeth Arden Salon, 1945-50; created theatrical, ballet designs Ballet Russe de Monte Carlo N.Y.C. Center, 1947, also Broadway plays, including Play's the Thing, 1948, My Name is Aquilon, 1949, Medea, 1949, Ring Around the Moon, 1950, Tower Beyond Tragedy, 1950, also Met. Opera Ballets, La Contessa, 1961; with La Maison Jeanne Lanvin, Paris, 1950-63; owner, mgr. La Masion Castillo, Paris 1964—. Home: 25 bis rue de Constantine Paris 7e France Office: La Maison Castillo 95 rue du Faubourg-St Honore Paris 8e France

CASTILLO-VALDES, RAFAEL EDUARDO, diplomat of Guatomala, civil engr.; b. Cunen, Quiche, Guatemala, Jan. 15, 1928; s. Manuel Trinidad and Carmen I. (Valdes) Castillo; B.C.E., Brigham Young U., 1957; C.E., Universidad de San Carlos, Guatemala, 1958; m. Janice Gordon, Apr. 2, 1958; children—Leonel Eduardo, Rafael Eduardo, Manuel Eduardo, Ramon Francisco, June Marie, Ana Patricia, Margaret. Officer Guatemalan Army, aide to pres. Juan Jose Arvalo, 1948-57; civil engr. charge bridges and road constrn. Guatemalan Govt., 1957-59, charge constrn. thermo-elec. plants Empresa Electrica de Guatemala, 1959-61; engr. charge design and constrn. elec. plants, Scotland and Guatemala, 1962-66; mem. Congreso de la Republica de Guatemala, 1966-70; ambassador of Guatemala to UN, 1970—. Mem. Colegio de Ingenieros de Guatemala. Mem. Partido Institucional Democratico (dir.). Club: Reforma Lyons (Guatemala). Home: 45 Sprain Valley Rd Scarsdale NY 10583 Office: 405 Lexington Av New York City NY 10017

CASTLE, ALFRED L., lawyer; b. Honolulu, Mar. 18, 1884; A.B., Harvard, 1906, LL.B., 1908. Admitted to Hawaii bar, 1908; now mem. firm Anthony & Waddoups, Honolulu. Mem. Territorial Ho. of Reps., 1911-13. Trustee Punahou Sch., 1925-45. Mem. Am. Bar Assn., Bar Assn. Hawaii. Office: 333 Queen St Honolulu HI 96813*

CASTLE, EDWARD SEARS, biologist; b. Cambridge, Mass., Dec. 25, 1903; s. William Ernest and Clara (Bosworth) C.; A.B., Harvard, 1925, A.M., 1927, Ph.D., 1929; m. Natalie Watson Berle, June 12, 1930; children—Peter Watson, Philip Sears. Instr. Harvard, 1930-31, asst. prof., 1931-40, asso. prof., 1940- 54, became prof. physiology, 1954, now prof. emeritus, dir. biology labs., 1940-45. Fellow Fund for Advancement Edn., 1953-54. Mem. Am. Physiol. Soc., Am. Assn. Plant Physiologists, Bot. Soc. Am., Soc. Gen. Physiologists, Soc. Growth and Devel., Am. Acad. Arts and Scis. Contbr. tech. papers to profl. lit. Home: 42 Walker St Cambridge MA 02138

CASTLE, EMERY NEAL, educator; b. nr. Greenwood County, Kan., Apr. 13, 1923; s. Sidney James and Josie May (Tucker) C.; B.S., Kan. State U., 1948, M.S., 1950; Ph.D., Ia. State U., 1952; postgrad. N.C. State Coll., 1956; m. Merab Eunice Weber, Jan. 20, 1946; 1 dau., Cheryl Diana. Asst. prof. Kan. State U., 1948-52; agrl. economist Fed. Res. Bank of Kansas City, 1952-54; from asst. prof. to prof. dept. agrl. econs. Ore. State U., Corvallis, 1954-65, dean faculty, 1965-66, prof., head dept. agrl. econs., 1966—, Alumni Distinguished prof., 1970; dir. Water Resources Research Inst.; vis. prof. Purdue U., 1962; cons. to Depts. Agrl., Interior and Def. Dir. 1st Fed. Savs. and Loan, Corvallis. Mem. Water Resources Bd. Ore., 1964—, chmn., 1968-69. Served with USAAF, 1943-45. Decorated Air medal. Mem. Am. Agrl. Econs. Assn. (pres.-elect 1971), Univ. Council on Water Resources (vice-chmn. exec. bd. 1967-70). Author: Farm Business Management, 2d edit., 1971; Water Resources Development, 1964. Contbr. articles profl. jours. Home: 3259 Lincoln Av NW Corvallis OR 97330

CASTLE, GORDON BENJAMIN, educator; b. Portland, Ind., Aug. 10, 1906; s. Arthur D. and May (Brake) C.; A.B., Wabash Coll., 1928; A.M., U. Cal., 1930, Ph.D., 1934; m. Berta Boyd, May 17, 1931; children—Lynn, Margit. Biologist termite investigations com. U. Cal., 1928-31, teaching fellow, 1931-34; instr. U. Mont., 1934-36, asst. prof., 1936-38, asso. prof., 1938-39, prof. 1939-62, chmn. dept. zoology, 1938-48, dir. biol. sta., 1938-62, sr. acad. dean, dean Coll. Arts and Scis., 1949-52, dean Grad. Sch., 1952-57, acting pres., 1958-59; prof. zoology Ariz. State U., Tempe, 1962—, chmn. dept., 1962-64, v.p., 1964-67. Mem. exec. bd. Campfire Girls, 1945-49. Mem. A.A.A.S., Am. Ecol. Soc., Am. Soc. of Zoologists, Ariz. Acad. Scis., Am. Assn. U. Profs. Democrat. Office: Life Sci Center Ariz State U Tempe AZ 85281

CASTLE, HERBERT, corp. exec.; b. Chgo., June 30, 1903; s. John William and Isabelle (Drynan) c.; student pub. schs. and Lewis Inst., Chgo.; m. Esther A. Hutton, June 4, 1937; 1 dau., Linda Letitia. With Meyercord Co., Chgo., 1928— sales mgr., 1937-40, exec. v.p., dir., 1940-64, sr. v.p., 1964- -. Clubs: Oak Park, Oak Park Country, Chicago Athletic Assn. (Chgo.). Home: 525 Edgewood Pl River Forest IL 60305 Office: 365 E North Av Carol Stream IL 60187

CASTLE, JEROME, cement corp. exec.; b. 1935; grad. N.Y. U. Sch. Commerce; married. Pres. Jerome Castle Corp., 1957—; with Hertz, Warner & Co.; security dealers and underwriters, 1965-67; chmn. bd., pres., chief exec officer Penn-Dixie Cement Corp., 1967—; chmn. bd., dir. Continental Steel Corp., 1969—, Castle Chem. Corp., 1968—, Castle Capital Corp., 1967—. Address: 1345 Av Americas New York City NY 10019*

CASTLE, LATHAM, U.S. judge; b. Sandwich, Ill., Feb. 27, 1900; s. John B. and Mollie (Latham) C.; LL.B., Northwestern U., 1924; m. Georgiana Whitcomb, May 1, 1931; 1 son, John W. Admitted to Ill. bar, 1925; city atty., Sandwich, 1925-28; state's atty. DeKalb County, Ill., 1928-40; corp. counsel, Sycamore, Ill., 1933-35; asst. atty. gen. Ill., 1940-42, atty. gen., 1953-59; judge U.S. Ct. Appeals, 7th Circuit, Chgo., 1959—; county judge, DeKalb County, 1942. Served with U.S. Army, 1918. Mem. Am., Ill., DeKalb County bar assns., Phi Kappa Psi, Phi Delta Phi. Republican. Conglist. Club: University (Chgo.). Home: 518 E 6th St Sandwich IL Office: 1212 Lake Shore Dr Chicago IL 60610 also US Ct Appeals 219 S Dearborn Chicago IL 60604

CASTLE, MARIAN JOHNSON, writer; b. Kendall, Ill.; d. Oliver C. and Anna Mary (French) Johnson; student Carroll Coll., 1915, Millikin U., 1916; Ph.B., U. Chgo., 1920; Litt.D., Carroll Coll., 1950; m. Edward Carrick Castle, May 24, 1924. Publicity work for concert and lectr. tours, summers 1918, 19; gen. sec. YWCA, Albuquerque, 1921-22. Recipient Alumni Merit award Millikin U. Mem. Colo. Authors League, Claremont Penwomen, Zeta Tau Alpha. Presbyn. Club: Denver Woman's Press. Author: Deborah (novel), 1946 (serialized Woman's Home Companion, Fiction Book Club choice, reprinted in 7 fgn. countries); The Golden Fury, 1949 (selection 5 book clubs including Book League Am., Dollar Book Club, alternate selection Lit. Guild); Roxana, 1955; Silver Answer, 1960 (made into Talking Books for Blind, 1961). Contbr. to Harper's Mag., Reader's Digest, Good Housekeeping, others. Home: 933 W Bonita Av Claremont CA 91711

CASTLE, RAYMOND NIELSON, chemist, educator; b. Boise, Ida., June 24, 1916; s. Ray Newell and Lula (Nielson) C.; student Boise Jr. Coll., 1934-35; B.S., Ida. State U., 1939; M.A., U. Colo., 1941, Ph.D., 1944; m. Ada Necia Van Orden, June 16, 1937; children—Raymond Norman, Dean Lowell, David Elliott, George Leonard, Elizabeth Anne, Edith Eilene, Christian Daniel, Lyle William. Instr. chemistry U. Ida., 1942-43, U. Colo., 1943-44; research chemist Battelle Meml. Inst., Columbus, O., 1944-46; faculty U. N.M., 1946-70, prof. chemistry, 1956-70, chmn. dept., 1963-70; prof. chemistry Brigham Young U., Provo, Utah, 1970—. Research fellow U. Va., 1952-53. Fellow Chem. Soc. London (Eng.); mem. Am. Chem. Soc., Sigma Xi. Mem. Ch. of Jesus Christ of Latter-day Saints (bishop 1957-61). Contbr. research articles to profl. jours. Editor: Jour. Heterocyclic Chemistry, 1964—. Home: 1175 Mountain Ridge Rd Provo UT 84601

CASTLE, ROBERT WOODS, advt. exec.; b. Oak Park, Ill., June 28, 1925; s. Lester Davis and Dorothy (Woods) C.; B.A., Dartmouth, 1949, M.C.S., Amos Tuck Sch., 1950; m. Mary Wallace Leachman, June 23, 1951; children—Grant B., Steven W., Leslie L. Asst. to dir. market research J. Walter Thompson Co., N.Y.C., 1950-52, account exec., 1952-57; account exec. Ted Bates & Co., N.Y.C., 1957-59, v.p., 1959-61, sr. v.p., 1961—, account group head, 1961-70, bd. dirs., 1969—. chmn. exec. com., mgmt. rep. N.Y. div., 1970—. Served to 2d lt. USAAF, 1943- 45. Republican. Conglist. Clubs: Wee Burn Country (Darien); Northport Point Country (Mich.). Home: 175 Brookside Rd Darien CT 06820 Office: 666 Fifth Av New York City NY 10019

CASTLE, WILLIAM, motion picture dir.; b. N.Y.C., Apr. 24, 1914; m. Ellen Castle; children—Georgeiana, Terry. Former actor, asst. dir. N.Y. stage; dialogue dir. Columbia Pictures; producer Universal Pictures, 1964-65, Paramount Pictures, 1966; motion pictures include Chance of a Lifetime, When Strangers Marry, Mark of the Whistler, Voice of the Whistler, The Crime Doctor's Warning, Texas, Brooklyn and Heaven, Johnny Stool Pigeon, Undertoe, The Fat Man, Hollywood Story, Cave of Outlaws, It's a Small World (also screen play), Fort Ti, Serpent of the Nile, Drums of Tahiti, Battle of Rogue River, Iron Glove, Saracen Blade, Charge of the Lancers, Masterson of Kansas, The American, New Orleans Uncensored, Gun That Won the West, Duel on the Mississippi, Houston Story, Uranium Room, The American; producer, dir. Macabre, House on Haunted Hill, Tingler, 13 Ghosts, Homicidal, The Old Dark House, 13 Frightened Girls, Straight- Jacket, The Night Walker, I Saw What You Did, Let's Kill Uncle, The Spirit is Willing, Busy Body, Project X; producer Rosemary's Baby, Riot; producer, dir. TV show Men of Annapolis. Address: care Paramount Pictures Corp 5451 Marathon St Hollywood CA 90038

CASTLE, WILLIAM BOSWORTH, physician, educator; b. Cambridge, Mass., Oct. 21, 1897; s. William Ernest and Clara Sears (Bosworth) C.; grad. Browne and Nichols Sch., Cambridge, 1914; student Harvard, 1914-17, M.D., 1921, D.Sc., 1964; M.S., Yale, 1933; M.D., U. Utrecht (Netherlands) 1936; D.Sc., U. Chgo., 1952; LL.D., Jefferson Med. Coll., Phila., 1964: D.Sc., U. Pa., 1966, Marquette U., 1969; D.H.L., Boston Coll., 1966; m. Louise Muller, July 1, 1933; children—William Rogers, Anne Louise. Intern, Mass. Gen. Hosp., Boston, 1921-23; asst. medicine Harvard Med. Sch., 1925-27, alumni asst., 1927-28, asst., 1928-29, instr. to asso. prof., 1929-37, prof., 1937-57, George Richards Minot prof. medicine, 1957-63, Francis Weld Peabody faculty prof. medicine, 1963-68, emeritus, 1968—; Distinguished physician VA, 1968—; asso. physician Thorndike Meml. Lab., Boston City Hosp., 1929-48, dir., 1948-63, jr. vis. physician, 1933-48, asst. vis. physician, 1948-55, vis. physician, 1956-63, dir. II and IV Med. Services, 1940-63, cons. physician, 1963—; dir. Rockefeller Found. Commn. for Study Anemia, P.R., 1931-32; sr. cons. hematology Lemuel Shattuck Hosp., 1955—; cons. medicine Beth Israel Hosp., 1956—. Recipient William Procter Jr. Internat. award for distinguished service in scis. Phila. Coll. Pharmacy and Sci., 1935; Walter Reed medal Am. Soc. Tropical Medicine, 1939; Mead Johnson & Co. award for research on vitamin B complex, 1950; Gordon Wilson medal Am. Clin. and Climatol. Assn., 1961; John M. Russell award Markel Scholars, 1964; ann. hon. lecture award Albany Med. Coll., 1964; Distinguished Lecture award Coll. Medicine U. Ky., 1965; Oscar B. Hunter Meml. award Am. Therapeutic Soc., 1965; Joseph Goldberger award A.M.A. and Nutrition Found., 1966; Ann. Am. Coll. Nutrition award for distinguished service in field nutrition and metabolism, 1970. Master A.C.P. (John Phillips prize 1932); fellow Am. Acad. Arts and Scis.; hon. fellow Royal Coll. Physicians London, Royal Coll. Physicians and Surgeons, Royal Australasian Coll. Physicians, Royal Coll. Physicians Edinburgh; mem. Am. Acad. Tropical Medicine, A.A.A.S., A.M.A., Am. Philos. Soc., Am. Soc. Clin. Investigation (pres. 1940-41, emeritus 1943—), Am. Soc. Exptl. Pathology, Am. Soc. Tropical Medicine and Hygiene, Am. Fedn. Clin. Research, Assn. Am. Physicians (George W. Kober medal 1962, pres. 1959-60, emeritus 1960—), Boston Soc. Biologists, Mass. Med. Soc., Nat. Acad. Scis.; corr. mem. Société Internationale Europeene Hematologie, l'Academie royale de Medecine de Belgique, Brit. Med. Assn., Royal Soc. Medicine London; Phi Beta Kappa, Alpha Omega Alpha. Home: 22 Irving St Brookline MA 02146 Office: VA Hosp West Roxbury MA 02132

CASTLE, WILLIAM EUGENE, coll. dean; b. Thomas, S.D., Sept. 5, 1929; s. Eugene Albert and Kathryn (Barkley) C.; B.S., No. State Tchrs. Coll., 1951; M.A., U. Ia., 1958; Ph.D., Stanford, 1963; m. Diane Lee Sklar, Aug. 8, 1963. Tchr., Faulkton (S.D) High Sch., 1951; instr. St. Cloud (Minn.) Tchrs. Coll., 1958-60; instr. Central Wash. Tchrs. Coll., Ellensburg, 1961; asst. prof. U. Va., 1963-65; asso. sec. for research and sci. affairs Am. Speech and Hearing Assn., Washington 1965-68; dean Nat. Tech. Inst. for Deaf, Rochester (N.Y.) Inst. Tech., 1968—. Served with USAF, 1952-56. Mem. Am. Speech and Hearing Assn., Speech Communication Assn., Acoustical Soc. Am., Conf. Execs. for Am. Schs. for Deaf, Conv. Am. Instrs. of Deaf. Author: The Effect of Narrow Band Filtering on the Perception of Certain English Vowels, 1964. Home: 59 Pineview Dr Penfield NY 14526 Office: 1 Lomb Memorial Dr Rochester NY 14623

CASTLEBERRY, DONALD MONTGOMERY, educator; b. Hollis, Okla., Dec. 2, 1914; s. Elisha Marvin and Mamie (Bryant) C.; B.A., Central State Coll., 1935; M.A., U. Okla., 1936; Ph.D., U. Minn., 1943; m. Arline Alrick, Dec. 25, 1941; children—Karen, Marvin. Instr. social sci. U. Minn. High Sch., 1937-42; head social sci. dept. Gen. Coll., U. Minn., 1942-44; asst. dir. Civilian Relief Operations, A.R.C., Russia, 1944-45, dir., Poland, 1945-46; asst. prof. polit. sci. U. Tex., 1947-48; prof. polit. sci., chmn. social sci. div. San Francisco State Coll., 1948-58; vis. prof. polit. sci. Am. U., Beirut, Lebanon, 1959-60; prof. polit. sci. San Francisco State Coll., 1948—, dean ednl. services, 1963-64, dean grad. div., since 1967—; vis. prof. polit. sci. U. Uppsala, Sweden, 1965-66; vis. prof. U. Cal., Los Angeles, summer 1952. Mem. Air War Coll. Seminar, 1958. Trustee Coro Found., 1955-60. Mem. Am. Polit. Sci. Assn., Am. Assn. U. Profs., Assn. Cal. State Coll. Profs., No. Cal. Polit. Sci. Assn. (pres. 1952), Sigma Nu, Kappa Delta Pi, Pi Kappa Delta. Home: 3004 Canyon Rd Burlingame CA 94010 Office: San Francisco State Coll San Francisco CA 94132

CASTLEBERRY, VIVIAN LOU ANDERSON, (Mrs. Curtis Wales Castleberry), newspaper editor; b. Lindale, Tex., Apr. 8, 1922; d. William Clarence and Jessie Lee (Henderson) Anderson; B.S., So. Meth. U., 1944; m. Curtis Wales Castleberry, May 4, 1946; children—Carol Janet (Mrs. Michael Lynn Tate), Chanda Elaine, Keeta Shawn, Kimberley Diana, Catherine Ann. Editorial asst. Petroleum Engr. Pub. Co., 1944-45; editorial asst. Cousins Pub. Co., 1945-46; womens editor Tex. A. and M. Bn., 1948-51; home editor Dallas Times Herald, 1954-56, womens editor, 1957—. Cons. Mgmt. Seminar for Women Execs., 1963—. Mem. women's group Dallas Council World Affairs, 1964—, Dallas Internat. Cultural and Social Circle, 1965—. Recipient awards for womens news reporting U.P.I., 1963, 65; Outstanding Woman award So. Meth. U., 1970; Headliners Club award, 1970; Southwestern Journalism Forum award, 1971. Home: 11311 Buchanan St Dallas TX 75228 Office: 1101 Pacific Av Dallas TX 75202

CASTLEMAN, BENJAMIN, physician; b. Everett, Mass., May 17, 1906; s. Samuel and Rose (Michaelson) C.; B.A., Harvard, 1927; M.D., Yale, 1931; M.D. (hon.), U. Göteborg (Sweden), 1966; m. Anna Alice Segal, Dec. 22, 1935; children—Ruth (Mrs. Emery E. Griffin, Jr.), Jean (Mrs. Lewis Chase), Paul Arnold. House officer pathology Mass. Gen. Hosp., 1931-32, resident pathologist, 1932-35, mem. staff, 1935—, chief dept. pathology, 1953—, editor case records, 1951—; faculty Harvard Med. Sch., 1935—, prof. pathology, 1962—. Cons. pathologist Emerson (Mass.), Worcester (Mass.) Meml. hosps., Mass. Eye and Ear Infirmary, Mass. Soldiers Home; vis. prof. All India Inst. Med. Scis., New Delhi, 1961- 62, Scandinavian univs., 1964. Mem. part III com. Nat. Bd. Med. Examiners, 1964—; chmn. allocations com. Mass Heart Assn., 1962-65; mem. expert com. med. edn. WHO, 1958-62, cons. cancer unit, 1963. Mem. Am., Mass. med. assns., Am. Acad. Arts and Scis., Am. Assn. Pathologists and Bacteriologists, Internat. Acad. Pathology (pres. 1962-63), Am. Soc. Exptl. Pathology, New Eng. Soc. Pathologists, New Eng. Cancer Soc. Home: 335 Marsh St Belmont MA 02178 Office: Dept Pathology Mass Gen Hosp Boston MA 02114

CASTLEMAN, EDWARD, govt. ofcl.; b. Washington, Aug. 22, 1917; s. Alfred and Rebecca (Shusterman) C.; A.B., George Washington U., 1941; m. Mildred Ruth Weiss, Oct. 1, 1944; children—Lynn (Mrs. Robert Seaward), Craig Alfred. Asst. mgr. furniture store, Washington, 1935-42; comml. specialist Fgn. Funds Control, U.S. Treasury Dept., Washington, 1943-45; with U.S. Dept. Interior, Washington, 1949-53; with U.S. State Dept., 1945-49, asst. chief West Coast div., acting dep. regional dir., asst. chief Program Office, Latin Am. Bur., AID, 1953-59, dir. AID mission to Surinam, 1959-63, dep. dir. AID mission to Ecuador, 1963-64, asst. dir. for program Office Internat. Tng., AID, 1965-69, asst. dep. dir. CORDS/Devel., Vietnam, 1970—. Home: Bethesda MD Office: MACV/CORDS Region I APO San Francisco CA 96349

CASTLEMAN, LOUIS SAMUEL, educator; b. St. Johnsbury, Vt., Nov. 24, 1918; s. Max and Fannie (Svetkey) C.; B.S., Mass. Inst. Tech., 1939, D.Sc., 1950; m. Mildred Blanche Rubin, Jan. 25, 1948; children—Michael Z., David A., Steven J., Daniel J. Plant metallurgist Sunbeam Electric Mfg. Co., Evansville, Ind., 1939-41; sr. scientist, supr., acting sect. mgr. Westinghouse Atomic Power Div., Pitts., 1950-54; metall. specialist Gen. Telephone & Electronics Labs., Inc., Bayside, N.Y., 1954-64; prof. phys. metallurgy Poly. Inst. Bklyn., 1964—. Cons. phys. metallurgy. Served with AUS, 1941-46. Mem. Am. Soc. Metals (chpt. chmn. 1963-64), Am. Inst. Mining, Metall. and Petroleum Engrs., Am. Phys. Soc., A.A.A.S., Metal Sci. Club N.Y. (treas. 1970-72). Sigma Xi. Democrat. Jewish religion. Home: 15 Oak St Lynbrook NY 11563 Office: 333 Jay St Brooklyn NY 11201

CASTLEMAN, SAMUEL TORBITT, banker; b. Louisville, Jan. 24, 1922; s. Samuel T. and Margaret (Weissinger) C.; A.B., Yale U., 1943; postgrad. U. Louisville, Jefferson Sch. Law, Stonier Sch. Banking, Rutgers U.; m. Sally Bent Sweetser, July 1, 1949; children—Sally Boone, Samuel Torbitt, Eugenia Bent, Peter Muir. Internat. economist ECA, Washington, 1948-49; spl. asst. to chief ECA Mission to Germany, 1949-50; dep. chief finance div. Office U.S. High Commr. for Germany, Frankfurt, 1950-51; dir. Gen. Joint Export and Import Agy., Germany, 1951-52; with Wachovia Bank & Trust Co., Winston Salem, N.C., 1952-68, asst. v.p., 1953-55, v.p., 1955-58, sr. v.p., 1958-68; sr. v.p. Am. Security & Trust Co., Washington, 1968-71; exec. v.p. Deltec Banking Corp. Ltd., Nassau, Bahamas; dir. Gen. Tel. Co. of S.E. Trustee, treas. Washington Hosp. Center; bd. dirs. Madeira Sch., Greenway, Va., Carolinas United Community Services, N.C. Sch. Arts. Served to lt. AUS, 1943-45. Decorated Purple Heart medal with oak leaf clusters, Silver Star. Mem. N.C. Triangle Yale Alumni Assn., Newcomen Soc. North Am. Democrat. Presbyn. Clubs: F Street (Washington); Old Town. Office: Deltec Banking Corp Ltd Nassau Bahamas

CASTLES, JAMES B., corp. exec.; b. Missoula, Mont., 1915; ed. U. Mont., 1938. Sec., gen. counsel, dir. Tektronix, Inc.; pres., dir. Pacific N.W. Aviation Corp., Melridge Aviation Co., Melridge, Inc. Sec., dir. Millicent Found., Skyline Found.; bd. dirs. Lincoln Meml. Park, Ore. Regional Med. Program; trustee U. Mont. Found. Mem. Multnomah Kennel Club (dir.). Home: 1390 S W Orinda Way Portland OR 97225 Office: 14150 S W Karl Braun Dr Tektronix Industrial Park Beaverton OR 97005

CASTLES, WESLEY, judge; b. Superior, Mont., Sept. 26, 1918; s. William and Catherine L. (Irwin) C.; B.S. in Forestry with honors, Mont. State U., 1939, LL.B., 1949; m. Ruth Blake, 1939; children—Susan Lynn (Mrs. Michael G. Billings), Judith Kay (Mrs. Richard Golberg), Deborah Jane. Forester, 1935-40; border patrol insp., 1940-43; forest ranger, 1946; instr. forestry Mont. State U., 1947-49; admitted to Mont. bar, 1949; pvt. practice law, 1949-50; county atty. Missoula County, 1951- 52; chmn. Mont. Unemployment Compensation Commn., 1953-54; exec. sec. Gov. Aronson, 1955-56; asso. justice Mont. Supreme Ct., Helena, 1957—. Criminal investigator U.S. Army, 1943-45. Named Outstanding Young Man of Mont., Jr. C. of C., 1951. Home: York Route Helena MT 59601 Office: State Capitol Helena MT 59601

CASTLETON, KENNETH BITNER, ednl. adminstr., surgeon; b. Salt Lake City, July 29, 1903; s. Wallace C. and Alice (Bitner) C.; A.B. in Chemistry, U. Utah, 1923, student Sch. Medicine, 1923-25; M.D. with honors, U. Pa., 1927; Ph.D. in Surgery, U. Minn., 1933; children—Elizabeth Ann (Mrs. Boyd A. Blackner), Barbara (Mrs. Dean H. Weaver), Kenneth Bitner, Jane (Mrs. Michale J. Cleary); m. 2d, Heloise Snow Armstrong, Feb. 20, 1964. Practice of medicine, specializing in surgery, Salt Lake City, 1933-62; asso. clin. prof. surgery Coll. Medicine, U. Utah, 1942-62, prof. surgery, dean, 1962-68, v.p. med. affairs, 1968—; mem. med. adv. bd. Sears Roebuck Found., 1962-66; past pres. med. bd., pres. staff Holy Cross Hosp. Dir. First Fed. Savs. & Loan Assn. Chmn. med. sect. U. Utah Med. Center fund campaign. Bd. dirs. Museum Natural History, Community Services Council. Diplomate Am. Bd. Surgery. Mem. A.C.S. (bd. govs. 1960-63), A.M.A. (ho. dels. 1958-60), Utah Med. Assn. (pres. 1952-53; Distinguished Service award), Salt Lake County Med. Soc. (pres. 1949-50), Salt Lake Surg. Soc., Southwestern, Western surg. assns., Sigma Xi, Phi Beta Pi, Alpha Omega Alpha, Beta Theta Pi. Clubs: Alta (bd. dirs.), Salt Lake Country (pres. 1969-70, past dir.), Rotary (pres. 1962-63, past dir.) (Salt Lake City). Contbr. numerous articles on surgery to profl. jours. Home: 1235 E 2d South Salt Lake City UT 84102

CASTONGUAY, AMIL HAROLD, banker; b. Enfield, Conn., June 10, 1905; s. Edward E. and Florence I. (McNamara) C.; LL.B., Boston U., 1933; m. Frances W. Williams, Nov. 10, 1929. Admitted to Mass. bar, 1934, since practiced in Barnstable City; town counsel, Yarmouth, Mass., 1940-60, chmn. planning bd., 1940-45; clk. 1st Dist. Ct., Barnstable County, Mass., 1945; spl. hearing officer Dept. Justice, 1966-68; pres. Hyannis Coop. Bank (Mass.), 1956-70; dir. Cape Cod Bank and Trust Co., Hyannis, Am. Metallic Corp. Mem. Barnstable County Bar Assn. (pres. 1968-69). Author: Two Men on a Mill, 1962. Home: Windswept South Sea Av West Yarmouth MA 02673 Office: 776 Main St Hyannis MA 02601

CASTONQUAY, THOMAS TELLSPHORE, chem. engr.; b. Lead, S.D., Nov. 20, 1909; s. Anselm and Mary (McNally) C.; B.S., U. of Detroit, 1931; student Northwestern U., 1939; Ph.D., Ia. State Coll.; m. Florence Virginia Barr; children—Thomas William, Mary Alexina, John Joseph, Margaret Ann, Jo Ann. Head gen. chemistry dept. U. Detroit, 1931-33; chem. dir. Ames Reliable Products Co., 1933-36; instr. chem. engring. and chemistry Ia. State Coll., 1936-41; successively asst. prof., asso. prof., head chem. engring. dept. U. of Kan., 1941-46; prof. and head chem. engring. dept. U. N.M., 1946—; cons. engr. 1936—; summer cons. Naval Ordnance Testing Labs., China Lake, Cal., 1957—. Mem. Am. Chem. Soc., Am. Inst. Chem. Engrs., Am. Soc. Engring. Edn., Nat. N.M. socs. profl. engrs., Sigma Xi, Phi Lambda Upsilon, Alpha Chi Sigma, Phi Kappa, Blue Key, Sigma Tau. Roman Catholic. Contbr. tech. articles sci. publs. Address: 923 Vassar Dr NE Albuquerque NM 87106

CASTREN, MAUNO JALMAR, Finnish diplomat; b. Rovaniemi, Finland, July 23, 1931; s. Toivo Ilmari and Ester Elina (Soininen) C.; M. in Social Sci., U. Helsinki, 1957; m. Asta Hannele von Hertzen, Mar. 16, 1963; children—Sari Hannele, Tomi Antero. Info. sec., Huhtamaki-Yhtyma Oy, Helsinki, 1957-59; acting sec. gen. Finnish Nat. Com. for UNESCO, Helsinki, 1959-61; attache, Budapest, Hungary, 1963-65; 2d sec., Algiers, Algeria, 1965-67; assigned to Helsinki, 1967-70; 1st sec., Washington, 1970—. Home: 6134 Farver Rd McLean VA 22101 Office: 1900 24th St NW Washington DC 20008

CASTRO, JOAO AUGUSTO DE ARAUJO, diplomat of Brazil; b. Rio de Janeiro, Brazil, Aug. 27, 1919; s. Raimumdo A. and Carmen (Viveiros) C.; grad. Law Sch., Rio de Janiero, 1940; m. Myriam Sanit Brisson, July 1, 1943; children—Luiz Augusto, Carmen, Silvia. Consul, Miami, 1943-44; dep. consul, N.Y.C., 1947-48; sec.-gen. Ministry Fgn. Affairs, 1963; minister external affairs, 1963- 64; head polit. dept. Ministry Fgn. Affairs, 1957-58; sec.-gen. internat. orgns. U.F.A., 1961-62; ambassador to Athens, 1964-65, to Lima, Peru, 1966, 68, to UN, 1968-71, to U.S., 1971—. Decorated grand crosses from Mexico, Bolivia, Peru, Greece and Yugoslavia. Address: 3000 Massachusetts Av NW Washington DC 20008

CASTRO, RAUL HECTOR, lawyer, former ambassador; b. Cananea, Mexico, June 12, 1916; s. Francisco D. and Rosario (Acosta) C.; came to U.S., 1926, naturalized, 1939; B.A., Ariz. State Coll., 1939; LL.B., U. Ariz., 1949; LL.D., No. Ariz. U., 1966; m. Patricia M. Norris, Nov. 13, 1954; children—Mary Pat, Beth. Fgn. service clk. Dept. State, Agua Prieta, Mexico, 1941-46; instr. Spanish, U. Ariz., 1946-49; admitted to Ariz. bar, 1949; practice in Tucson, 1949-51; dep. county atty., Pima County, Ariz., 1951-54, county atty., 1954-58; judge Superior Ct., Tucson, 1958-64, Juvenile Ct., Tucson, 1961-64; U.S. ambassador to El Salvador, San Salvador, 1964-68, to Bolivia, La Paz, 1968-69; practice internat. law, Tucson, 1969—. Operator, Castro Pony Farm, 1954-64. Pres., Pima County Tb and Health Assn., Tucson Youth Bd., Ariz. Horseman's Assn. Bd. dirs. Tucson chpt. A.R.C., Tucson council Boy Scouts Am., Tucson YMCA, Nat. Council Christians and Jews, YWCA Camp Bd. Mem. Ariz. N.G., 1935-39. Recipient Outstanding Naturalized Citizen award Pima County Bar Assn., 1964, Outstanding Am. Citizen award D.A.R., 1964; Pub. Service award U. Ariz., 1966. Mem. Am. Fgn. Service Assn., Am. Judicature Soc., Inter-Am., Ariz., Pima County (Outstanding Naturalized Citizen award 1964) bar assns., Nat. Assn. Trial judges, Nat. Council Juvenile Ct. Judges, Phi Alpha Delta. Democrat. Roman Catholic. Rotarian. Home: 3701 E River Rd Tucson AZ Office: Lawyers Title Bldg 199 N Stone Av Tucson AZ

CASTRO, RUZ FIDEL, prime minister Cuba; b. Mayari, Oriente Province, Cuba, Aug. 13, 1927; s. Angel Castro and Lina Ruz; bachelor degree, Colegio Belélen, Havana, Cuba, 1945; law degree, doctorate U. Havana, 1950; m. Mirta Diaz Balart, Oct. 12, 1948 (div. 1955); 1 son, Fidel. Practiced law, 1950-52. Took part in revolutionary movement expdn. against govt. Dominican Rep., 1947; leader armed forces attacking Batista govt. in Cuba, 1953-58; unsuccessfully attacked Moncada Barracks, Santiago de Cuba, July 1953; captured, imprisoned, 1953-55; in exile, Mexico, N.Y., 1955-56; returned to Cuba, 1956 and led armed attacks against Batista govt., using Oriente Province as hdqrs. for armed forces; forces entered Havana, Jan. 1, 1959; designated Manuel Urrutia provisional pres., named by Pres. Urrutia comdr.-in-chief Cuban armed forces, Jan. 22, 1959; became prime minister, Feb. 1959. Chmn., Agrarian Reform Inst., 1965. Recipient Lenin Peace prize, 1961; named Hero of Soviet Union, 1963. Roman Catholic. Author: Ten Years of Revolution, 1964; History Will Absolve Me, 1968. Address: Havana Cuba*

CASTRO RUZ, RAUL, Cuban govt. ofcl.; ed. Jesuit schs. Sentenced with brother Fidel Castro to 15 years imprisonment for insurrection, 1953; amnestied, 1954; assisted brother's movement in Mexico, later in Cuba after 1956; chief Armed Forces, 1959; head Ministery Revolutionary Armed Forces, 1960—; now also vice prime minister Cuba. Address: Office Vice Prime Minister Havana Cuba*

CASTROVIEJO, RAMON, ophthalmologist; b. Logrono, Spain, Aug. 24, 1904; s. Ramon and Maria Ana (Briones) C.; B.A. and B.S., Inst. Arts and Scis. of Logrono, U. Zargoza, Spain, 1919; M.D., U. Madrid, 1927; hon. Dr., U. San Marcos de Lima, Peru, 1940, U. Santo Domingo, 1945, U. Salamanca (Spain), 1965, U. Granada (Spain), 1966, U. Santa Maria (Brazil), 1969; m. Cynthia Warren Smith, Jan. 30, 1946; children—Cynthia, Ramon. Came to U.S., 1928, naturalized, 1936. Asst. ophthalmology Red Cross Hosp., Madrid, 1927; attending ophthalmologist Chgo. Eye, Ear, Nose and Throat Hosp., 1928- 30; spl. fellow researcch and lab. work Mayo Clinic, 1930-31; with Columbia Presbyn. Med. Center, N.Y.C., 1931-52; now prof. clin. ophthalmology N.Y.U. Post Grad. Med. Sch.; chief emeritus ophthalmology St. Vincent's Hosp. and Med. Center, N.Y.C.; clin. prof. dept. ophthalmology Mt. Sinai Med. Sch.; attending ophthalmic surgeon Mt. Sinai Hosp., N.Y.C.; attending ophthalmology N.Y.U. Med. Center; vis. surgeon eye service Bellevue Hosp., N.Y.C.; hon. dir. of the dept. of spl. corneal surgery, N.Y. Eye & Ear Infirmary; cons. ophthalmologist Lincoln Hosp., St. Clare's Hosp. Med. adviser ophthalmology, bur. hearings and appeals Social Security Adminstn. Decorated grand cross Order Isabel La Catolica, Alfonso El Sabio, Sanidad Civil, Merito Militar con Distintive Blanco (Spain); Nunez de Balboa (Panama); Sol (Peru); gold medal Soc. of Journalists, Oviedo (Spain). Fellow Am. Acad. Ophthalmology and Otolaryngology; mem. A.M.A., N.Y. County Med. Soc., N.Y. State Med. Soc., N.Y. Acad. Medicine, Am., N.Y. ophthal. socs., Am. Soc. Plastic and Reconstructive Surgery, Am. Biol. Assn., Assn. Research Ophthalmology, Assn. Advancement Med. Instrumentation, Biol. Photog. Assn., Royal Med. Soc. (Gt. Britain), Spanish-Am. Med. Assn., Sociedad Medica Hispano-Americana of U.S., Société Francaise d'Ophthalmolgie (France), Sociedad Oftalmologica Espanola (Spain); also hon. mem. ophthelmic socs. in India, Colombia, Brazil, Argentina, Chile, Peru, Panama, Costa Rica, Mexico, Cuba, Greece, Egypt, Australian Coll. Ophthalmologists, Oxford Ophthal. Congress (Eng.). Clubs: New York Athletic; Sewanhaka Corinthian Yacht; Oyster Bay; Piping Rock (Locust Valley, N.Y.). Author: Atlas of Keratectomy and Keratoplasty, 1966. Contbr. over 250 articles Am. Jour. Ophthalmology, other med. jours. Address: 9 E 91st St New York City NY 10028

CATALANO, EDUARDO FERNANDO, architect; b. Buenos Aires, Argentina, Dec. 1, 1917; s. Fernando Catalano; grad. architect U. Buenos Aires, 1940; M.Arch., U. Pa., 1944, Harvard, 1945; m. Gloria Lauersdorf, Dec. 26, 1947; children—Alejandria, Adrian. Acting head dept. architecture N.C. State Coll., Raleigh, 1951-56; prof. architecture Mass. Inst. Tech., 1956—. Designer (with Atilio Gallo, Engr.) hyperbolic paraboloid house, Raleigh, N.C., 1954; Mass. Inst. Tech. Student Center, Social Sci. and Mgmt. Research Center, East Gate Married Student Housing: (with Horacio Caminos) New Campus, U. Buenos Aires, Sch. Sci.; (with Pietro Belluschi) Juilliard Sch. Music, Lincoln Center for Performing Arts and Urban Complex, Civic Center Springfield, Mass.; Govtl. Center Greensboro, N.C., Boston Br. Pub. Library, U.S. embassy Buenos Aires, Argentina. Recipient (with Horacio Caminos) several archtl. awards in U.S. and Argentina. Address: 5 Channing Circle Cambridge MA 02138

CATALANO DI MELILLI, ANTONIO, Italian diplomat; b. Catania, Italy, Jan. 4, 1941; s. Felice and Rosana (Muscatello) Catalano di M.; LL.D., U. Rome, 1964; m. Angela Rosa, May 6, 1970. With Italian Diplomatic Service, 1965—; assigned ministry Fgn. Affairs, 1967-68; 2d sec. Italian embassy, Washington, 1968-70, 1st sec., 1970—. Dep. internat. commr. Italian Catholic Scout Assn., 1966-69. Served as 2d lt. Italian Air Force, 1966-67. Roman Catholic. Home: 1626 32d St NW Washington DC 20007 Office: 1601 Fuller St NW Washington DC 20009

CATALDO, BERNARD FRANCIS, educator, lawyer; b. Phila., Jan. 5, 1907; s. Michael Angelo and Giuseppina (Polcari) C.; A.B. summa cum laude with first honors, U. Pa., 1929, LL.B. summa cum laude with first honors (Gowen law fellow), 1933, LL.M., 1936; Penfield law fellow Harvard, 1933-34; m. Sylvia La Monaca, Jan. 1, 1936; 1 dau., Marlene Annette. Admitted to Pa. bar, 1935; spl. atty. antitrust div. Dept. of Justice, 1935-36; tchr. Wharton sch. U. Pa., Phila., 1936—, prof., 1947—, chmn. dept. bus. law, 1947-61, chmn. dean's adv. com. faculty personel, 1961-65; chief price atty. Phila. regional office OPA, 1943-45; arbitrator Am. Arbitration Assn., 1946-47; cons. Am. Coll. Life Underwriters, Am. Inst. Property and Casualty Underwriters. Member Am. Assn. U. Profs., Order of Coif, Phi Beta Kappa, Beta Gamma Sigma, Eta Sigma Phi. Co-author: Introduction to Law and The Legal Process, 1965; Introductory Cases on Law and the Legal Process, 1967. Contbr. legal jours. Home: 2532 Hillcrest Rd Drexel Hill PA 19026 Office: 3620 Locust St Philadelphia PA 19104

CATANIA, ANTHONY CHARLES, educator; b. N.Y.C., June 22, 1936; s. Charles John and Elizabeth (Lattarulo) C.; B.A., Columbia, 1957, M.A., 1958; Ph.D. (NSF fellow), Harvard, 1961; m. Constance J. Britt, Feb. 10, 1962; children-William John, Kenneth Charles. Postdoctoral research fellow Harvard, 1961-62; sr. pharmacologist Smith, Kline & French Labs., Phial., 1962-64; asst. prof. N.Y. U., 1964-66, asso. prof., 1966-69, prof., chmn. dept. psychology, 1969—. Fellow A.A.A.S., Am. Psychol. Assn.; mem. N.Y. Acad. Sci., Phi Beta Kappa. Editor: Contemporary Research in Operant Behavior, 1968. Editor Jour. Exptl. Analysis Behavior, 1966-69, rev. editor, 1969—. Contbr. articles profl. jours. Home: 19 Center St Cresskill NJ 07626 Office: Dept Psychology Univ Coll Arts and Sci NY U New York City NY 10453

CATE, JAMES LEA, retired educator; b. Little Rock, Nov. 16, 1899; s. Clifford Julian and Nathalie Virginia (O'Hair) C.; B.A., U. Tex., M.A., 1925; student Washington U., 1920-21, U. Ghent and Brussels, 1929-30; Ph.D., U. Chgo., 1935; m. Frances Elizabeth Cohn, Mar. 4, 1927; children—Mary Allison (Mrs. James Hartman), James Lea. Instr. Lockhart (Tex.) High Sch., 1923- 24, Shreiner Inst., Kerrville, Tex., 1925-28; instr. U. Chgo., 1930-36, asst. prof., 1936-40, asso. prof., 1940-48, prof. Medieval history, 1948-65, emeritus, 1968—; con. U.S. Office Edn.; mem. hist. adv. com. AEC, NASA. Served with SATC, 1918; from 1st lt. to maj., USAAF, 1942-46; spl. cons. USAF, 1946-47. Decorated Legion of Merit; recipient Ernest E. Quantrell teaching award U. Chgo.; Arts and Letters award Air Force Assn. Mem. Am. Hist. Assn., Medieval Acad. Am., Air Force Assn. Club: Quadrangle (Chgo.). Co-editor, contbr.; Medieval and Historical Essays in Honor of James Westfall Thompson, 1938; The Army Air Forces in World War II (7 vols.), 1948-58; also articles medieval history. Home; 5545 Woodlawn Av Chicago IL 60637

CATE, WIRT ARMISTEAD, author; b. Hopkinsville, Ky., Nov. 16, 1900; s. James Henry and Mary Lou (Armistead) C.; A.B., Emory U., 1923, A.M. (fellow), 1925; postgrad. (Edward Austin fellow), Harvard, 1926-27, 28-29. Instr., Baylor Sch., Chattanooga, 1923-24, Ga. Sch. Tech., 1925-26, 27-28, asst. prof., 1928-29; lectr. English, Emory U., summers 1926, 28; Julius Rosenwald fellow Am. history, 1937-38; fellow Colonial Williamsburg, Inc. 1940-43; now engaged in biog., hist. research, writing. Mem. Modern Lang. Assn. Am., So. Hist. Assn., Phi Beta Kappa, Sigma Upsilon, Sigma Chi. Democrat. Methodist. Author: Lucius Q.C. Lomar, Secession and Reunion, 1935; History of Richmond, 1959. Editor: Two Soldiers, The Campaign Diaries of Thomas J. Key, C.S.A. and Robert J. Campbell, U.S.A., 1938. Contbr. to hist., philol. and coll. jours., newspapers. Home: 507 N 14th St Nashville TN 37206

CATER, DOUGLASS, educator, writer, editor; b. Montgomery Ala., Aug. 24, 1923; s. Silas D. and Nancy (Chestnutt) C.; grad. Philip Exeter Acad., 1942; A.B., Harvard, 1947, M.A., 1948; m. Libby Anderson, Dec. 20, 1950; children—Silas Douglass III, Rebecca S., Libby M., Benjamin W. Washington editor Reporter mag., 1950-63, nat. affairs editor, 1963-64; spl. asst. to Pres. Johnson, 1964-68; spl. asst. to sec. army, 1951; cons. to dir. Mut. Security Agy., 1952; Ferris vis. prof. pub. affairs Princeton, 1959; vis. prof. pub. affairs Wesleyan U., Middletown, Conn., 1963; Regent prof. U. Cal. at San Francisco, 1971-72; sr. adviser Acad. Ednl. Devel. Adviser on domestic matters Hubert Humphrey Presdl. Campaign, fall 1968. Served with the OSS, World War II. Guggenheim fellow, 1955; Eisenhower exchange fellow, 1957; recipient George Polk Meml. award, 1961; N.Y. Newspaper Guild Page One award, 1961. Mem. Sigma Delta Chi. Presbyn. Clubs: Nat. Press, Overseas Writers (Washington). Author: (with Marquis Childs) Ethics In a Business Society, 1953; The Fourth Branch of Government, 1959; Power in Washington, 1964; Dana: The Irrelevent Man, 1970. Home: 2418 Pacific Av San Francisco CA 94115

CATER, HAROLD DEAN, educator; b. Syracuse, N.Y., Aug. 5, 1908; s. Franklin Ernest and Georgia Anna (McMullin) C.; A.B., Syracuse U., 1933; Ph.D., Columbia, 1946; m. Virginia Hale, July 30, 1936; children—Elizabeth Anne, Harold Dean. Instr. history Clayton High Sch., 1934-36, Mamaroneck Sr. High Sch., 1936-46; hist. div. War Dept. Spl. Staff, 1946-48; dir. Minn. Hist. Soc. 1948-55; dir. Sleepy Hollow Restorations. Inc., Tarrytown, 1955-61; cons. on arts U.S. Office Edn., Washington, 1961-62; dir. admissions and financial aid, prof. Am. history, cons. on arts C.W. Post Coll. of L.I. U., 1963-68; sr. fellow Mackinac Coll., 1968-70; prof., chmn. history and polit. sci. Hillsdale (Mich.) Coll., 1970—. Vis. prof. Ft. Lewis Coll., Durango, Colo., 1969. Mem. Soc. Archtl. Historians, Am. Hist. Assn., Nat. Trust for Hist. Preservation (charter), Am. Mus. Assn., Am. Acad. Polit. and Social Sci. Orgn. Am. Historians, Am. Polit. Sci. Assn., Nat. Assn. State and Local History. Author: Modern Study Guide for American History, 1942; Henry Adams and His Friends, 1947, 68; Washington Irving and Sunnyside, 1957. Home: 31 W Hallett St Hillsdale MI 49242

CATER, JOHN THOMAS, banker; b. Temple, Tex., July 12, 1935; s. B.J. and Guyrene (Thomas) C.; B.B.A., U. Tex., 1958, B.A. in Govt., 1959, LL.B., 1959; m. Margot Kyle Steenland, Feb. 1, 1969. Mem. mgmt. trainee program Tex. Commerce Bank, Houston, 1960, personal trust adminstrn., 1960-67, corporate trust asst. mgr., 1967, nat. div., 1967-68, mgr. adminstrv. services, 1968-69, mgr. data services and bank operations, 1969-70, head operations dept., 1970—. Treas. Republican Party, Harris County, Tex., 1961-65. Bd. dirs. Cerebral Palsy Treatment Center, Harris County, Houston Literacy Council, United Fund, Houston Banks Urban Affairs Com., Inst. Internat. Edn., Tex. Bill of Rights Found. Served with AUS, 1959. Mem. Houston C. of C. (dir.), English-Speaking Union (dir.), Alpha Tau Omega, Phi Alpha Delta. Home: 209 Caruthers Lane Houston TX 77024 Office: P O Box 2558 Houston TX 77001

CATER, WAYLAND HOYT, editor-publisher; b. Alvord, Tex., Oct. 20, 1902; s. Lafayette Walker and Fanny Bell (Cunningham) C.; ed. pub. schs.; m. Ruth Louise Mills, Apr. 12, 1929; children—Michael Wayland and David Anthony (twins). With advt. sales dept. Pasadena (Cal.) Star News, 1940-46; advt. dir. Alhambra (Cal.) Post Adv., 1946-50, Glendale (Cal.) News- Press, 1950-56; pub., editor Burbank (Cal.) Daily Rev., 1956-62, Elgin (Ill.) Daily Courier News, 1962—; v.p., dir. Copley Press, Inc., 1962- -. Mem. exec. com. Elgin Indsl. Devel. Commn. Bd. dirs. Elgin Community Assn. Mem. Am. Assn. Advt. Execs., Am. Soc. Newspaper Editors, Am. Newspaper Pubs. Assn. Republican. Home: 1396 Wing St Elgin IL 60121 Office: 300 Lake St Elgin IL 60120

CATES, JOHN MARTIN, Jr., found. ofcl.; b. Denver, Jan. 20, 1912; s. John Martin and Mary Arden (Randall) C.; grad. Phillips Andover Acad., 1932; B.A., Yale, 1936, J.D., 1939; m. Mary Perkins Raymond, July 4, 1942; 1 son, John Martin III. Admitted to Cal. bar, 1940, D.C. bar, 1946; with McCutchen, Olney, Mannon & Greene, San

Francisco, 1939-41; labor relations San Francisco Warehousemen's Assn., 1941-42; with U.S. Maritime Commn. and War Shipping Adminstrn., Washington, 1942-47; fgn. affairs specialist U.S. Dept. State, 1947-53, legal adviser Am. Embassy, Bonn, 1953-55; legal advisor, 1st sec. Am. Embassy, Mexico, 1955-57; chief polit. officer Am. Embassy, Venezuela, 1957-61; alt. U.S. rep. Council O.A.S., Washington, 1961-63; counsellor U.S. Mission to UN, 1963-70, U.S. Mission to Geneva, 1970-71; pres. Center for Inter-Am. Relations, 1971—; adj. prof. Fairleigh Dickinson U., 1965-68. Committeeman Boy Scouts Am., N.Y.C., 1963-69; mem. Am. Church Council, Bad Godesburg, Germany, 1953-55. Mem. Yale U. Council, 1968—. Recipient superior honor award Dept. of State, 1967. Mem. Council Fgn. Relations, Inter-Am., Cal. bar assns., Bolivian Soc., Cercle de la Presse et Amitie Etrangere (Geneva), Am. Polit. Sci. Assn., S.R., Soc. Colonial Wars (exec. com.), St. Nicholas Soc. (exec. com. 1969). Mason. Clubs: Union, Yale (N.Y.C.), Metropolitan (Washington). Contbr. articles profl. jours. Office: 680 Park Av New York City NY 10021

CATES, LINDLEY ADDISON, Jr., educator; b. Chgo., Nov. 20, 1932; s. Lindley Addison and Alice Lucille (Jewett) C.; B.S., U. Minn., 1954; M.S., U. Colo., 1958, Ph.D., 1961; m. Ruth Elizabeth Gammell, June 16, 1957; children—Catherine Sue, Douglas Addison. Instr. pharmacy Sch. Pharmacy, U. Colo., 1958-61; asst. prof. Coll. Pharmacy, U. Houston, 1961-64, asso. prof., 1964-68, prof., 1968—; vis. prof. Baylor Sch. Medicine, 1970. Served to capt. USAF, 1954-56. NIH research grantees, 1962-65; Robert A. Welch Found. grantee, 1969. Fellow Am. Found. for Pharm. Edn.; mem. Acad. Pharm. Scis., Am. Pharm. Assn., Am. Chem. Soc., Tex. Pharm. Assn., Am. Assn. Colls. Pharmacy Conf. Tchrs., Sigma Xi, Rho Chi, Phi Lambda Upsilon. Methodist. Mason. Contbr. articles profl. jours. Home: 5118 Sleepy Creek Houston TX 77017

CATES, MACFARLANE LAFFERTY, Jr., textile co. exec.; b. Spartanburg, S.C., Nov. 9, 1927; s. MacFarlane Lafferty and Mary (DuPre) C.; A.B., Princeton, 1949; M.B.A., Harvard, 1952; m. Marguerite McGee, Aug. 12, 1949; children—Marguerite DuPre, Elisabeth Quarles, Kathleen MacFarlane, Mary Lafferty. Exec. v.p. Arkwright Mills, Spartanburg, 1954-64, pres., treas., 1964-; dir. Sea Pak Corp.; mem. gen. bd., adv. bd. Citizens & So. Nat. Bank S.C.; dir. adv. bd. Liberty Mut. Ins. Co., Mem. Wofford assos. Wofford Coll.; v.p. United Fund, 1964, pres., 1965. Bd. dirs. Spartanburg Devel. Assn. Mem. Spartanburg C. of C. (dir.), Am. Textile Mfrs. Inst. (pub. relations com.), S.C. Textile Mfrs. Assn. (mem. bd.), Inst. Textile Tech. (mem. bd.), Trout Unlimited S.C. (v.p.) Clubs: Brook; Princeton (N.Y.C.); Biltmore Forest, Piedmont, Spartanburg Country. Home: 1325 Pinecrest Rd Spartanburg SC 29302 Office: PO Box 5628 Spartanburg SC 29301

CATES, WALTER THRUSTON, comml. orgn. exec.; b. Burlington, N.C., Apr. 28, 1913; s. Claud Holt and Ella Lee (Cheek) C.; student U. N.C., 1931-32, Southeastern Inst. for C. of C. Execs., 1942-47; m. Martha Fonville, June 12, 1932; children—George E., Jeanie (Mrs. Rodney O. Siggelkow). Sales mgr. Alamance Motors, Burlington, 1932-41; mgr. Burlington C. of C., 1941-44; Macon (Ga.) C. of C., 1945-52; exec. v.p. Ga. C. of C., Atlanta, 1952—; pres. Empress Hosiery Corp., Atlanta, 1943—; instr., pres., dean of faculty S.E. Inst. Comml. Orgns. Execs., U. N.C., 1951-59. Mem. Regional Export Expansion Council, Gov.'s European Trade Mission, 1962. Mem. Selective Service Bd., 1941-45, adv. bd. Salvation Army, 1961—. Mem. Am. C. of C. Execs. State Economy Study Comm., Sigma Phi Epsilon. Baptist. Elk, Mason, Kiwanian. Home: 97 E Park Lane NE Atlanta GA 30309 Office: Commerce Bldg Atlanta GA 30303

CATHARINE, SISTER MARIE, hosp. exec.; b. S.I., N.Y., Aug. 11, 1904; d. Thomas Joseph and Catharine (McBreen) Blaine; B.A., Coll. Mt. St. Vincent-on-Hudson, 1934; M.S. in Social Work, Cath. U. Am., 1936. Joined Sisters of Charity, 1926; tchr. elementary and secondary schs., 1924-39; dir. boarding dept. N.Y. Foundling Hosp., N.Y.C., 1939-56, asst. adminstr., 1956-57, adminstr., treas., 1957-67; adminstrv. cons. dept. child care Cath. Charities, Archdiocese of N.Y., 1967—. Bd. mgrs. St. Agatha Home for Children. Mem. Acad. Certified Social Workers. Home: 50 E 84th St New York City NY 10028 Office: 122 E 22d St New York City NY 10010

CATHCART, ARTHUR JAMES, lawyer, corp. exec.; b. Palo Alto, Cal., June 22, 1911; s. Arthur Martin and Edna (Wallace) C.; A.B., Stanford U., 1931, LL.B., 1935; m. Martelle Leeper, Jan. 4, 1934; children—Daniel H., David A., Patrick A., Robert J. Admitted to Cal. bar, 1935; gen. practice law, Los Angeles, 1935-42; successively regional rationing atty., regional enforcement exec., regional atty. O.P.A., San Francisco, 1942-45; regional counsel War Assets Adminstrn., San Francisco, 1946-47; gen. practice law, Palo Alto, 1947-59, Hill, Farrer & Burrill, Los Angeles, 1959-67; sec., gen. counsel Baker Oil Tools, Inc., Los Angeles, 1959—; mem. faculty real estate law U. Cal. Extension Div., 1955-59. Mem. Palo Alto City Council, 1949-52. Mem. Am., Cal., Los Angeles County bar assns., Am. Soc. Corporate Secs., Am. Soc. Ins. Mgmt., Theta Delta Chi. Republican. Conglist. Home: 4725 Lincolnshire Av Buena Park CA 90620 Office: PO Box 2274 Terminal Annex Los Angeles CA 90040

CATHCART, HAROLD ROBERT, hosp. adminstr.; b. Odebolt, Ia., Mar. 9, 1924; s. Catham S. and Martha M. (Wells) C.; student Drake U., 1941-43; B.A., State U. Ia., 1947; D.H.A., U. Toronto (Can.), 1948; m. Tressa Bolt, July 20, 1951; 1 dau., Tressa Ann. Fellow W.K. Kellogg Found., 1948-49; mem. staff Pa. Hosp., Phila., 1949—, v.p., 1960-70, pres., 1970—. Mem. nat. adv. allied health professions council USPHS. Served with AUS, 1943-46. Mem. Am. Hosp. Assn. (chmn. council of nursing 1967-68, council on manpower and edn. 1969-71, trustee), Am. Coll. Hosp. Adminstrs., Hosp. Assn. Pa. (pres. 1967-68), Del. Valley Hosp. Council. Address: Pennsylvania Hosp Philadelphia PA 19107

CATHCART, JAMES ARMSTRONG, Jr., ins. exec.; b. Columbia, S.C., Sept. 13, 1909; s. James Armstrong and Ann (Sloan) C.; student U. S.C., 1926-30; LL.B., N.Y. Law Sch., 1936; m. Mary Freeda DePass, June 30, 1932 (dec.); children—James, Charles; m. 2d, Anna A. LeBlanc, Apr. 25, 1946; children—George, John, Sanders, William. With Cathcart Gen. Agy., S.C., 1928-30; admitted to N.Y. bar, 1936; with Gen. Reins. Corp., 1930- 42, 1950—, v.p., 1950-52, pres., 1952—, also dir., named chmn., chief exec. office, 1960; v.p. Peerless Casualty Co., 1942-50; chmn. bd., dir. Herbert Clough, Inc., North Star Reins. Corp.; chmn. Reins Underwriting Services Ltd., London; mem. Midtown adv. bd. Chem. Bank N.Y.; dir. Swedish Atlas Reins. Co., Ltd. Stockholm, Inter Reins. Corp., Zurich, Reins. Co. of Australia, Ltd., Sydney; trustee U.S. Trust Co. Mem. Bd. Zoning Appeals Village of Tuxedo Park, N.Y. Trustee Episcopal High Sch., Alexandria, Va. Mem. N.Y. Bar, Phi Delta Phi, Sigma Nu. Episcopalian. Clubs: Tuxedo (gov.); Downtown Assn., Brook. Home: Tuxedo Park NY 10987 Office: 400 Park Av New York City NY 10022

CATHCART, ROBERT SAMUEL, lawyer; b. Palo Alto, Cal., Mar. 29, 1909; s. Arthur Martin and Edna (Wallace) C.; A.B., Stanford, 1930, LL.B., 1934; m. Barbara East, Feb. 28, 1959. Admitted to Cal. bar, 1934, since practiced in San Francisco; partner firm Bledsoe, Smith., Cathcart, Johnson and Rogers, 1950—. Dir. Alhambra Nat. Water Co., Hong Kong and Eastern Shipping Co., Eastern Mining & Metals Co., Geary Market Investment Co., Redwood-Cal. Ltd. Gen. counsel, gov. San Francisco Heart Assn., 1950—. Served to lt. comdr. USNR, 1942-46. Mem. Am. Bar Assn., State Bar Cal., Am. Judicature Soc., Theta Delta Chi. Republican. Club: Commonwealth (San Francisco). Home: 2423 Leavenworth St San Francisco CA 94133 Office: 650 California St San Francisco CA 94108

CATHCART, ROBERT STEPHEN, educator; b. Los Angeles, Jan. 30, 1923; s. Stephen Joseph and Martha (Morley) C.; A.B., U. Redlands, 1944, M.A., 1947; Ph.D., Northwestern U., 1953; m. Dolores June Hawley, July 1, 1944; children—Linda L., Stephen P. Teaching fellow U. Redlands, 1946-47; instr. Purdue U., 1947-49; teaching fellow Northwestern U., 1949-51; instr. U. Md., 1953-55; prof. rhetorical theory Cal. State Coll. at Los Angeles, 1955-68; chmn. dept. communication Queens Coll., 1968—; cons. USN Officer Tng. Corps, U.S. Army Ordinance Center, Carnation Co. Mem. Pres.'s Adv. Commn. of Scholars, 1967. Served to lt. USNR, 1943-46, 51-53. Sr. visitor in philosophy Oxford U., 1966. Author: (with M. Laser and F. Marcus) Ideas and Issues, 1963; (with J. Dahl and M. Laser) Student, School and Society, 1964; Post Communication, 1966; (with L. Samovar) Small Group Communication, 1970. Home: 1 Oakpoint Dr N Bayville NY 11709 Office: Queens Coll Flushing NY 11367

CATHCART, SILAS STRAW, tool co. exec.; b. Evanston, Ill., May 6, 1926; s. James A. and Margaret (Strawn) C.; student U. Notre Dame, 1944-46; A.B., Princeton, 1948; m. Corlene A. Hobbs, Feb. 3, 1951; children—Strawn, James A., Daniel and David (twins), Corlene. With Ill. Tool Works Inc., Chgo., 1948—, v.p., 1954-62, exec. v.p., 1962-64, pres., 1964—, also dir.; dir. A.B. Dick Co., Jewel Cos., No. Trust Co., Am. Hosp. Supply Corp., Quaker Oats Co. Mem. exec. bd. Chgo. council Boy Scouts Am., 1957—. Bd. dirs. Chgo. YMCA, Lake Forest (Ill.) Hosp., Passavant Hosp., Chgo. Served as ensign USNR, 1944-46. Clubs: Onwentsia (Lake Forest); Chicago (mem. bd.), Old Elm, Commercial, Chicago Commonwealth, Economic (Chgo.) Home: 701 N Mayflower Rd Lake Forest IL 60045 Office: 8501 W Higgins Av Chicago IL 60631

CATHERMAN, BYRON KING, savs. and loan assn. exec.; b. Mifflinburg, Pa., Sept. 26, 1920; s. Milton Carol and Hattie (Dersham) C.; student Pa. State U., 1938-39, Central Pa. Bus. Coll., 1941, U. Ga. Exec. Devel. Sch., 1962-63; m. Margaret Katherine Kerns, July 19, 1944; children—Diane Kay, Jay King. With Commonwealth Pa., 1940, Pa. R.R., 1941; treas. Harris Bldg. & Loan Assn., Harrisburg, 1942—, sec., 1956—, mgr., 1963, pres., 1964—. Mem. Pa. Savs. Assn. Bd., 1965—; treas. Pa. Housing Agy., 1970; mem. Harrisburg Polyclinic Hosp. Council; pres. Harrisburg area YMCA, 1968—; treas. Dauphin County Tb Assn., 1966—. Mem. Am. Savs. and Loan Inst. and Controllers, Pa. Savs. and Loan League (pres. 1971), Harrisburg C. of C. (dir. 1970). Mason, Lion (named Lion of Year Harrisburg 1959-60). Home: 2323 Hoffer St Harrisburg PA 17103 Office: 205 Pine St Harrisburg PA 17105

CATHERWOOD, CUMMINS, financier, philanthropist; b. Haverford, Pa., Jan. 30, 1910; s. Daniel B.C. and Jessica (Davis) C.; prep. edn. St. Georges Sch., Newport, R.I.; student U. Pa., 1931-33; L.H.D., Pa. Mil. Coll.; m. Ellengowen Hood, Feb. 3, 1942; children—Virginia Tucker, Cummins. Asso. various banking firms in Phila.; partner Roberts, Fleitas & Catherwood, Ins.; dir. Fidelity-Phila. Trust Co., 1933-39; co-owner Evening Pub. Ledger, Phila.; v.p., purchasing agt. Fox Munitions Corp., 1940-52; ltd. partner Jenks, Kirkland & Grubbs, Phila., now Hallowell, Sulzberger, Jenks, Kirkland & Co., Phila., Oil & Gas Co., Madison, 1946-57; dir. Bryn Mawr Trust Co.; pres., dir. Mineral Prodn. Corp., Bryn Mawr; chmn. Madeira Oil Corp., Bryn Mawr; dir. Mid-Am. Minerals, Inc., Oklahoma City; dir., mem. exec. com. Vision, Inc. Trustee Catherwood Estates; pres. Catherwood Found.; trustee exec. com. Pa. Mill. Coll.; bd. govs. Phila. Mus. Art. Served to capt. USAAF, 1962-45. Mem. Res. Officers Assn., Am. Ordnance Assn. Home: 622 Rose Lane Bryn Mawr PA 19010 Office: 850 Lancaster Av Bryn Mawr PA 19010

CATHERWOOD, MARTIN PAUL, cons.; b. Battle Ground, Ind., Jan. 28, 1904; s. B.F. and Elsie (Martin) C.; B.S.A., U. Ill., 1926, M.S.A., 1927; Ph.D., Cornell U., 1930; m. Louise Millhouse, June 28, 1930; children—Mary Louise, Kate Millhouse (Mrs. Gustave Fackelman). Asst. prof. bus. mgmt. Cornell U., 1930-36, prof. bus. mgmt., 1936-39, prof. pub. adminstrn., 1939-47, dean N.Y. State Sch. Indsl. and Labor Relations, Cornell, 1947-58; indsl. commr., N.Y., 1959-70. Commr. commerce, N.Y. 1941- 47; chmn. bd. inquiry Longshore Industry Work Stoppage Port of N.Y., 1951-52; spl. cons. N.Y. State Senate Com. on Affairs N.Y.C. investigating labor mgmt., N.Y.C. Transit Authority, 1957-58; chmn. Minimum Wage Bd., P.R., 1955; mem. Presdl. Emergency Bds., 1954- 55. Mem. Indsl. Relations Research Assn., Am. Soc. for Pub. Adminstrn., Nat. Acad. Arbitrators, Phi Kappa Phi, Sigma Xi. Clubs: Cornell (N.Y.C.); Fort Orange (Albany, N.Y.). Home: 304 Highgate Rd Ithaca NY 14850

CATHEY, CORNELIUS OLIVER, univ. dean; b. Davidson, N.C., Apr. 15, 1908; s. Albert Marcellus and Nancy (McAuley) C.; A.B., Davidson Coll., 1928, M.A., 1929; Ph.D., U. N.C., 1948; m. Beulah M. Proctor, June 15, 1929; Tchr. Am. history in jr. colls., 1929-36; camp comdr. Civilian Conservation Corps., 1936-39; mem. faculty U. N.C., 1947—, prof. history, 1957—, chmn. univ. scholarship com., 1956-63, campus coordinator Peace Corps, 1968—, dean student affairs, 1963—; prof. history Rutherford Coll., 1929-33, Brevard Coll., 1933-36; vis. prof. Columbia, 1950-51. Served to col. AUS, 1940-46. Mem. Agrl. History Soc. (exec. com. 1962-63, chmn. book award com. 1963-64), Am., So., Miss. Valley, N.C. hist. assns. Methodist. Author: Agricultural Developments in North Carolina 1783- 1860, 1956; also articles. Editor: A Woman Rice Planter, 1961. Home: 302 Country Club Rd Chapel Hill, NC 27514.

CATHEY, OLIVER EDWARD, elevator co. exec.; b. Arkabutla, Miss., July 30, 1906; s. Thomas Jackson and Donzella (Gillespie) C.; B.S., U. Miss., 1927; m. Frances Charlotte Heck, Sept. 18, 1937; children—Charlotte May (Mrs. Eugene Michell Holder II), Oliver Edward. Accountant, Harter B. Hull Co., Memphis, 1927-30; sec.-treas. Rotary Lift Co., Memphis, 1930-55; sec. Dover Corp., Horn Lake, Miss., 1955-68, N.Y.C., 1969—; sec.-treas., dir. Turnbull Elevator Co., Erie, Pa., Hunter-Hayes Elevator Co., Dallas, Dover Elevator Co., Memphis, Burlington Elevators, Inc., Hoboken, N.J. Trustee Oliver E. Cathey Found. Mem. Nat. Assn. Accountants (past chpt. pres.), Pi Kappa Phi. Republican. Mason, Kiwanian. Club: University (Memphis). Home: 694 Holly St Memphis TN 38112 Office: 277 Park Av New York City NY 10017

CATHLES, LAWRENCE MACLAGAN, Jr., ins. co. exec.; b. Dallas, Sept. 18, 1913; s. Lawrence MacLagan and Esther (Bain) C.; grad. St. Paul's Sch., 1931; A.B., Princeton, 1935; m. Frances Elizabeth Williams, Sept. 21, 1940; children—Lawrence MacLagan III, Frances B. With Aetna Life & Casualty, Hartford, Conn., 1935—, asst. sec. group div., 1949-51, sec., 1952-54, asst. v.p., 1955-56, v.p., 1956-69, sr. v.p., 1969—. Served to lt. comdr. USNR, 1942-46. Home: 61 High Ridge Rd West Simsbury CT 06092 Office: 151 Farmington Av Hartford CT 06115

CATLEDGE, TURNER, ret. newspaperman, author; b. Ackerman, Miss., Mar. 17, 1901; s. Lee Johnson and Willie Anna (Turner) C.; grad. Phila. (Miss.) High Sch.; B.Sc., Miss. State Coll., 1922; Litt.D., Washington and Lee U.; D.H.L., Southwestern at Memphis; LL.D., U. Ky., Tulane U.; m. 2d, Abby Izard, 1958; children (by previous marriage)—Mildred Lee, Ellen Douglas. All-around man on Neshoba (Miss.) Democrat, 1921; resident editor Tunica (Miss.) Times, 1922-23; mng. editor Tupelo (Miss.) Jour., 1923; reporter Memphis Comml. Appeal, 1923- 27, Balt. Sun, 1927-29; mem. city staff N.Y. Times, N.Y.C., 1929, corr. Washington bur., 1930-36, chief Washington news corr., 1936-41, nat. corr., 1943-44, mng. editor, 1951- 64, exec. editor, 1964-68, v.p., 1968-70, also dir.; chief corr. Chgo. Sun, 1941-42, editor in chief, 1942-43. Mem. Pulitzer Prizes Adv. Com. Mem. A.P. Mng. Editors Assn., Am. Press Inst. (adv. bd.), Am. Soc. Newspaper Editors (dir., pres. 1961), Sigma Delta Chi. Clubs: National Press, Gridiron, Overseas Writers, Metropolitan (Washington); Dutch Treat, Overseas Press, Century, Players, Silurians, Creek (N.Y.C.); Boston , New Orleans Country, Internat. House (New Orleans). Author: (with Joseph W. Alsop, Jr.) The 168 Days, 1937; My Life and Times, 1971. Contbr. articles to mag. Home: 2316 Prytania St New Orleans LA 70130 Office: 229 W 43d St New York City NY 10036

CATLETT, GEORGE ROUDEBUSH, accountant; b. Fairmount, Ill., Aug. 14, 1917; s. Shirley Tilton and Effie (Wehrman) C.; B.S., U. Ill., 1939, M.S., 1940; m. Martha Jane Beamsley, May 27, 1944; children—Stanley, Steven, Lawrence, David. With Arthur Andersen & Co., C.P.A.'s, Chgo., 1940—, partner, 1952—; cons. to govt. Pres. bd. dirs. U. Ill. Athletic Assn., 1964-65. Served to maj. AUS, 1942-46. C.P.A., Ill., other states. Mem. Am. Inst. C.P.A.'s (council 1964-70), Ill. Soc. C.P.A.'s (pres. 1966-67), Am. Accounting Assn., Nat. Assn. Accountants, U. Ill. Alumni Assn. (bd. dirs. 1959-65), Beta Theta Pi, Beta Gamma Sigma. Methodist. Clubs: University, Mid-Day (Chgo.); Westmoreland Country (Wilmette, Ill.). Contbr. profl. jours. Home: 615 Earlston Rd Kenilworth IL 60043 Office: 69 W Washington St Chicago IL 60602

CATLETT, LEON BIDEZ, lawyer; b. Dardanelle, Ark., Mar. 26, 1909; s. Samuel Graham and Alix (Bidez) C.; LL.B., U. Ark., 1932; m. Sally Cooper, Mar. 12, 1936. Admitted to Ark. bar, 1932; practice in Little Rock, 1933—; partner firm Catlett & Henderson, 1944—. Sec. Ark. Democratic Com., 1959-63, chmn., 1963-68. Vice chmn. trusteees U. Ark., 1960-70. Served with AUS, 1944-45. Mem. Am. Coll. Trial Lawyers, Am., Fed., Ark., Pulaski County bar assns., Am. Judicature Soc., Am. Coll. Probate Counsel, Am. Legion, Phi Alpha Delta, Kappa Alpha. Presbyn. (elder). Mason (Shriner). Clubs: Little Rock Country, Little Rock, Capitol, North Hills Country (Little Rock). Home: 324 Midland Av Little Rock AR 72203 Office: 727 Pyramid Life Bldg Little Rock AR 72201

CATLIN, GEORGE EDWARD GORDON, philosopher, educator; b. Liverpool, Eng., July 29, 1896; s. George E. and Edith K. (Orton) C.; B.A. summa cum laude (triple prizeman), Oxford U., 1920, M.A., 1924; Ph.D., Cornell U., 1924; m. Vera Brittain, July 24, 1925; children—John, Shirley. Prof. politics Cornell U., 1924-35; asso. with Harold Laswell of Yale in devel. of quantitative polit. sci., 1935-56; Bronman prof. polit. sci., chmn. dept. McGill U., 1956-60, now emeritus; Goethe Centenary lectr. Heidelberg U., 1949; Kierkegaard Commemoration lectr. Copenhagen U., 1949; Weil Lectr. U. N.C., 1957; Tagore Centenary lectr. London Royal Soc. Arts; found. lectr. Calcutta, Peking univs., 1948; lectr. Yale, 1937, U. Cal. at Berkeley, 1953; Walker-Ames lectr. U. Wash., 1963. Spl. adviser late Wendell Willkie, 1940. Arthur Greenwood, dep. leader Brit. Labour Party, 1930-41; pioneer (with Walter Lippmann) proposal for Atlantic community, 1941; draftsman declaration in support Indian independence, 1943. Twice nominated to exec. com. Brit. Labour Party. Decorated comdr. grand cross Order of Merit (Germany). Fellow Royal Soc. Lit.; mem. Fabian Soc. (exec. com.), Am. and Brit. Commonwealth Assn. (co-founder), World Acad. Arts and Scis. (v.p.), Instituto Estudios Politicos (Spain) (hon.), Anglo-German Assn. (v.p.), Popular Television Assn. U.K. (v.p.), Inst. Strategic Studies, Internat., Am., Brit., Canadian polit. sci. assns., Am., Brit. sociol assns., Union Mondiale des Europeens (nat. pres., internat. v.p.). Author: Science and Methods of Politics, 1926 (Spanish translation); Principles of Politics, 1930; History of the Political Philosophers, 1939; One Anglo-American Nation, 1941; (with Vera Brittain) Above All Nations, 1947 (German translation); On Political Goals, 1957; The Atlantic Community, 1959; Systematic Politics, 1962 (Japanese translation); Applications, 1963; The Grandeur of England and the Atlantic Community, 1966 (U.S. title: The Stronger Community;) The Atlantic Commonwealth, 1969. Co-editor (with H.G. Wells, Arnold Bennett, others) The Realist, 1929-30. Home: 4 Whitehall Ct London, S.W. 1, England. also Kingsgate Castle Kent England

CATLIN, KARL AYDELOTTE, physician; b. Cherokee, Okla., Mar. 16, 1910; s. Karl Tracey and Olive Fereba (Aydelotte) C.; B.A., U. Wichita, 1932; M.D., U. Kan., 1939; m. Eunice Fern Gooch, Apr. 1941; children—Sharon Fern, Linda Louise, Karl Eugene. Rotating intern Bethany Hosp., Kansas City, Kan., 1939-40; mem. resident staff Topeka State Hosp., 1940-48; asst. supt. Mental Health Inst., Clarinda, Ia., 1948-55, supt., 1955-67; med. dir. S.W. Ia. Mental Health Center, Atlantic, 1968—; cons. psychiatry Cass County Meml. Hosp., Atlantic. Member bd. Community Fund Clarinda, 1960-67. Served to capt., M.C., AUS, 1942-46. Recipient Achievement award Mental Hosp. Inst., Salt Lake City, 1960. Fellow Am. Psychiat. Assn.; mem. Ia. Psychiat. Soc., Ia., Page County (past pres.), Cass County med. socs. Home: 501 E 14th St Atlantic IA 50022 Office: 1408 E 10th St Atlantic IA 50022

CATLIN, SARA HUNTINGTON, social worker, coll. trustee; b. West Hartford, Conn., July 29, 1912; d. Robert W. and Constance (Willard) Huntington; B.A., Vassar Coll., 1934; grad. Columbia Sch. Social Work, 1936; m. Martin H. Johnson, June 17, 1937 (dec. Aug. 1944); 1 dau., Kate; m. 2d, Herbert P. Catlin, June 10, 1946; children—Mark, Faith, George. Caseworker, Family Service Soc., Hartford, Conn., 1936-37; case supr. A.R.C., Hartford, 1946-47. Active Troy YWCA, 1st v.p. 1956-59, pres., 1961-65; mem. nat. bd. YWCA, 1964—, sec., 1967-70, 1st v.p., 1970—; mem. Capitol Dist. Regional Planning Commn., 1969—; 1st v.p. Family and Children's Services, Troy, N.Y., 1955-59; mem. Human Rights Commn., Troy, Head Start Adv. Bd., Troy. Bd. dirs., exec. com. United Community Services, Mohawk-Hudson Area, 1966—, v.p., 1970—; trustee Vassar Coll. Mem. Vassar Coll. Alumni Assn. (pres. 1960-63), Troy Council P.T.A. (pres. 1959-61). Episcopalian. Home: 212 Pinewoods Av Troy NY 12180

CATLING, PATRICK SKENE, author; b. London, Eng., Feb. 14, 1925; s. Arthur Skene and Sheila (Houlihan) C., student Univ. Coll. Sch., London, also Oberlin Coll., 1942, 46; m. Diane Wheeler-Nicholson, Feb. 5, 1964; children—Charlotte, Desmond. Naturalized U.S. citizen, 1956. Mem. editorial staff Balt. Sun. 194758, Manchester (Eng.) Guardian, 1958-60, Punch mag., London, 1960-61, Newsweek mag., 1963-64; free-lance writer, 1964—. Served with RCAF, 1942-45. Club: Savage (London). Author: The Chocolate Touch, 1952; Better Than Working, 1958; The Right End of the Strick, 1960; Tourist Attraction, 1962; The Experiment, 1967, the

Exterminator, 1969; Freddy Hill, 1969; the Catalogue, 1970. Home: Mary's Acre Broad Campden Gloucestershire England Office: care Collins-Knowlton-Wing 60 E 56th St New York City NY 10022

CATON, CHARLES EDWIN, educator; b. Evanston, Ill., Mar. 21, 1928; s. Harold Dana and Irma (Fruit) C.; A.B., Oberlin Coll., 1950; student Northwestern U., 1949, 53; M.A., U. Mich., 1951, Ph.D., 1956; student Oxford (Eng.) U., 1956- 57; m. Elizabeth Robin McReynolds, Feb. 5, 1955; children—Marcia E., Laura J., John H., George H. Instr. philosophy U. Mich., 1957-58; faculty U. Ill., Urbana, 1958—, prof. philosophy, 1968—. Vis. asso. prof. Purdue U., 1968; vis. prof. U. Western Ont., 1969-70. Mem. Am. Philos. Assn., Linguistic Soc. Am. Editor: Philosophy and Ordinary Language, 1963. Address: Dept Philosophy Univ Ill Urbana IL 61801

CATON, THOMAS GEORGE, journalist; b. Lakin, Kan., Feb. 15, 1913; s. Thomas Stephen and Isabel (Garrettson) C.; A.A., Los Angeles Jr. Coll., 1932; m. Ruby Lee Corbin, Sept. 11, 1948; 1 son, Thomas Stephen. Mng. editor Los Angeles News Jour., 1933-35; staff reporter Los Angeles Times, 1935-46; staff writer Portland (Ore.) Oregonian, 1947-48; staff writer to asst. city editor Los Angeles Evening Herald-Express, exec. city editor to successor paper, Los Angeles Herald-Examiner, 1965—; v.p. Los Angeles News-Jour. Pub. Co., 1934-35; advisor dept. journalism Los Angeles City Coll., 1960-64. Participant Operation Deep Freeze, 1960. Mem. Los Angeles County Juvenile Ct. Citizens Adv. Com., 1937-41. Mem. Antarctica Polar Soc., Sigma Delta Chi, Kappa Tau Alpha. Home: 5252 Stardust Rd LaCanada CA 91011 Office: 1111 S Broadway Los Angeles CA 90054

CATOZELLA, VINCENT ALBERT, financial cons.; b. N.Y.C., July 21, 1907; s. Joseph and Anna (Roberto) C.; student Colgate U., 1926-27, N.Y. U., 1928, Am. Inst. Banking, 1929-30; m. Frances Grove, Aug. 6, 1951; 1 dau. Katherine Douglas. Asst. br. mgr. First Nat. Bank Yonkers, 1930-33; dir. research Merrill Lynch, Pierce, Fenner & Beane, 1934-42; underwriting mgr. Reynolds & Co., 1942-49; pres., chmn. bd., dir. O'Sullivan Rubber Corp., Winchester, Va., 1949-56; dir., pres. Blue Ridge Gas Co., Harrisonburg, Va., 1957-59, Cato- Lyst Research Co., Inc., N.Y.C. Served to maj. AUS, 1943-46. Clubs: Colgate U. (Westchester, N.Y.); Pelham (N.Y.) Country; Congressional Country (Washington); Winchester (Va.) Golf. Contbr. articles on taxes, finance, econs. to various jours. Home: 18 Bolton Gardens Bronxville NY 10708 Office: 200 Park Av New York City NY 10017

CATROW, DAVID JOHNSON, Jr., transp. co. exec.; b. Dayton, O., Mar. 26, 1926; s. David Johnson and Dorothy (Lambert) C.; B.A., Mich. State U., 1951; m. Patricia Sullivan, Nov. 29, 1948; children—Nancy, David Johnson III, Mary Ellen, Sally, Peggy, Daniel. With Ernst & Ernst, C.P.A.'s, 1953-63; asst. sec.-treas. Am. Metal Products Co., 1963-66; group financial officer, asst. sec. Lear Siegler, Inc., 1966-67, div. controller, 1967-69; controller Leaseway Transp. Corp., Cleve., 1969—. Served with USAAF, 1946, AUS, 1952-53. C.P.A., Mich. Mem. Nat. Assn. Accountants (pres. Port Huron, Mich. chpt. 1962). Home: 7223 Saybrook Dr Hudson OH 44236 Office: 21111 Chagrin Blvd Cleveland OH 44122

CATTANI, RICHARD JOHN, writer; b. Detroit, June 17, 1936; s. Primo and Emma (Reis) C.; A.B., Harvard, 1958, M.A. in Teaching, 1959; m. Jacqueline Patricia Hunter, Jan. 23, 1960; children—Jeremy Peter, Ruth Joia, Gabriel Paul. Tchr., Medford (Mass.) pub. schs., 1960-62; pvt. study, Florence, Italy, 1963; financial and bus. pub. relations counselor, exec. v.p. and gen. mgr. Financial Pub. Relations Inc., also Frank Hedge, Inc., Detroit, 1964-66, 67-68; writer cultural affairs, editorial page writer Christian Science Monitor, Boston, 1966-67, 68—. Dir., sec. Harvard Club Eastern Mich., 1967. Home: 400 Wellesley Av Wellesley Hills MA 02181 Office: 1 Norway St Boston MA 02115

CATTELL, EVERETT LEWIS, coll. pres.; b. Kensington, O., Sept. 16, 1905; s. Herman Clifford and Gertrude (Hole) C.; A.B., Marion (Ind.) Coll., 1927; M.A., Ohio State U., 1930; D.D., Asbury Sem., Wilmore, Ky., 1963; m. Catherine DeVol, Aug. 31, 1927; children—David, Barbara (Mrs. John Brantingham), Mary (Mrs. Frederick Boots). Ordained to ministry Friends Ch., 1928; pastor Friends chs. in Columbus, O., Springfield O., and Cleve., 1927-36; missionary to India, 1936-57; supt. Am. Friends India Mission, 1937-57; chmn., exec. sec. Evang. Fellowship India, 1951-57; exec. bd. Nat. Christian Council India, 1951-57; gen. supt. Ohio Yearly Meeting Friends Ch., 1957-60; pres. Malone Coll., Canton, O., 1960—. Pres. World Evang. Fellowship, 1962-68; mem. corp. Inter-Varsity Christian Fellowship, 1961-65. Chmn. bd. govs. Union Bibl. Sem., Yeotmal, India, 1953-55. Mem. Nat. Assn. Evangelicals (bd. adminstrn.). Author: Hinduism in Religions in a Changing World, 1959; An Appraisal of the Wesleyan and Keswick Positions in Insights Into Holiness, 1962; The Spirit of Holiness, 1963. Rotarian. Home: 1735 Vassar Av Canton OH 44703

CATTELL, RAYMOND B., educator; b. Staffordshire, Eng., 1905; s. Alfred Ernest and Mary (Field) C.; B.S., M.A., Ph.D., D.S., King's Coll., U. London; m. Monica Rogers, Dec. 1, 1930; 1 son, Hereward Seagrieve; m. 2d, Alberta Karen Schuettler, Apr. 2, 1946; children—Mary, Heather, Roderic, Elaine. Lectr., U. Exeter, 1927-32; dir. City of Leicester Child Guidance Clinic, 1932-37; G. Stanley Hall prof. genetic psychology, 1938-41; lectr. psychology Harvard, 1941—; research prof. psychology U. Ill., Urbana, 1945—. Civilian cons. personnel research Adj. Gen's Office, War Dept. personnel research Adj. Gen.'s Office, War Dept. Darwin Research fellow, 1935. Recipient Wenner-Gren Prize Essay on Research, Research, 1953; Wisdom award of Honor, 1970. Fellow Brit. Psychol. Soc.; mem. Am. Psychol. Assn., Eugenics Soc., Human Genetics Soc., Psychonomic Soc., Soc. Multivariate Exptl. Psychology, Sigma Xi. Author books including: Psychology, Sigma Xi. Author books including: Personality, A Systematic Study, 1950; Factor Analysis, 1952; Personality and Motivation, Structure and Measurement, 1957; The Meaning and Measurement of Neuroticism and Anxiety, 1961; The Scientific Analysis of Personality, 1965; Handbook of Multivariate Experimental Psychology, 1966; Objective Personality Tests, 1967; Prediction Achievement and creativity, 1968; Abilities, their structure and Growth, 1970; Handbook of Modern Personality Theory, 1971. Contbr. articles, research Achievement and Creativity, 1968; Abilities, their Structure and Growth, 1970; Handbook of Modern Personality Theory, 1971. Contbr. articles, research reports to profl. jours. Office: Psychology Dept U Ill Urbana IL 61801

CATTERSON, WALTER PAUL, mfg. co. exec.; b. Bklyn., Dec. 14, 1919; s. Walter A. and Helen (Jacbara) C.; B.B.A., St. John's U., 1951; M.B.A., N.Y.U., 1954; m. Geraldine M. Stauss, Sept. 4, 1943; children—Robert Paul, Christine Ann. With Miller, Donaldson & Co., C.P.A.'s, N.Y.C., 1947-51; audit supr. Air Reduction Co., 1951-55; with Babcock & Wilcox Co., N.Y.C., 1955—, asst. treas., 1962, treas., 1962—. Served to capt. AUS, 1942- 46. C.P.A., N.Y. Mem. Am. Inst. C.P.A.'s, Am. Mgmt. Assn., Financial Execs . Inst., Assn. Ex-Mems. Squadron A. Club: Cornell (N.Y.C.). Home: 57 Sylvan Rd N Westport CT 06880 Office: 161 E 42d St New York City NY 10017

CATTIER, JEAN, banker; b. Brussels, Belgium, Dec. 15, 1901; s. Felicien and Corinne (Pollard) C.; student Brussels U., 1918-21; m. Carlota Zimmerman, Mar. 6, 1943 (dec. 1961); children—Marie, Suzanne, John; m. 2d, Marianne Vowels, Sept. 13, 1962; children—Alan Richard, Henri Robert. Came to U.S., 1926, naturalized, 1942. Partner, White Weld & Co., investment bankers, N.Y.C., 1930—; chmn. bd. European-Am. Banking Corp., European-Am. Bank & Trust Co. Finance adviser U.S. High Commn., 1950-51, econs. adviser, 1950-51; chief ECA Mission to Germany, 1950-51. Clubs: Stock Exchange Lunch, Links (N.Y.C.); Creek (Locust Valley, N.Y.). Home: Locust Valley NY 11560 Office: 20 Broad St New York City NY 10005

CATTO, HENRY EDWARD, U.S. ambassador; b. Dallas, Dec. 6, 1930; s. Henry Edward and Maurine (Halsell) C.; student Tex. Mil. Inst.; B.A., Williams Coll., 1952; m. Jessica Oveta Hobby, Feb. 15, 1958; children—Heather, John, William, Elizabeth. Partner ins. brokerage firm Catto & Catto, San Antonio, 1952-69; ambassador, dep. U.S. rep. to OAS, 1969—. Mem. Inter-Am. Com. on Edn., 1969-70; mem. permanent exec. com. of Inter-Am. Council on Edn., Sci., and Culture, 1969—; dir. Galveston County Pub. Co., Inc. (Tex.), 1963-67, Houston Post Co., KPRC-TV, KPRC Radio, 1963-69. Mem. Tex. Adv. Com. to U.S. Civil Rights Commn., 1965-69; commr. San Antonio Housing Authority, 1968-69; pres. United Fund San Antonio and Bexar County, 1969. Adv. trustee Southwest Found. for Research and Edn.; bd. dirs. Catto Found., v.p., 1970; adv. council Robert A. Taft Inst. Govt. Mem. Internat. Soc. for Gen. Semantics. Clubs: 1925 F St (Washington); Argyle, Country (San Antonio). Home: 7400 Glenbrook Rd Bethesda MD 20014 Office: Dept State Washington DC 20520

CATTO, ISABEL GORDON, orgn. exec.; b. N.Y.C., Sept. 2, 1912 (parents Brit. citizens); d. Baron and Gladys (Gordon) Catto; ed. sch. in Eng., Paris. With Personal Service League, Women's Vol. Services, head Service Welfare Dept., 1941-43; dep. dir YWCA War Services, Middle East, 1943-46, dir. services Germany, Belgium, France, 1946—; participant YWCA Study Conf., Columbia, 1948; staff hdqrs. YWCA of Gt. Britain, 1951, pres., 1966—; pres. Nat. Hostels Com., 1951; mem. exec. com. World YWCA, 1951, pres., 1955-63; YWCA rep. UN Status of Women Commn., UNESCO. Dir. Yule Catto & Co., S&A Ltd., London, Eng., 1962. Decorated Order Brit. Empire. Club: Oriental (London). Home: 61 Cadogan Gdn London SW 3 England

CATTON, BRUCE, writer, editor; b. Petoskey, Mich., Oct. 9, 1899; s. George R. and Adella M. (Patten) C.; student Oberlin Coll.; hon. Litt.D., Md., Wesleyan, Dickinson colls., 1955, Oberlin, Lincoln colls., 1956, Harvard, Syracuse, Northwestern, Olivet univs., 1957, Ill., Western Mich. colls., 1958; LL.D. (hon.), Knox Coll., 1958; D.L.C. (hon.), Union Coll., 1956; m. Hazel H. Cherry, Aug. 16, 1925; 1 son, William Bruce. Reporter, Cleve. News, Boston Am., later with Cleve. Plain Dealer; became spl. writer, Washington corr. for Newspaper Enterprise Assn., Washington; asso. dir. information WPB, 1942, dir. 1943; dir. information Dept. commerce, 1945-46; spl. asst. Sec. Commerce, 1948. Recipient Pulitzer Prize for hist. work, 1954; Nat. Book award, 1954; non-fiction award for The Coming Fury, Ohioana Library Assn., 1962. Mem. Am. Acad. Arts and Letters. Presbyn. Author: The War Lords of Washington, 1948; Mr. Lincoln's Army, 1951; Glory Road, 1952; A Stillness at Appomatox, 1953; U.S. Grant and the American Military Tradition, 1954; Banners at Shenandoah, 1955; This Hallowed Ground, 1956; America Goes to War, 1958; Grant Moves South, 1960; The Coming Fury, 1961; (with William Catton) Two Roads to Sumter, 1963; Terrible Swift Sword, 1963; Never Call Retreat, 1965; Grant Takes Command, 1969. Editor: Am. Heritage Mag., 1954-59, sr. editor, 1959—. Office: 551 Fifth Av New York City NY 10017

CATTON, JACK JOSEPH, air force officer; b. Berkeley, Cal., Feb. 5, 1920; s. Thomas R. and Jane H. (Sharp) C.; student Loyola U., Los Angeles, 1939-40; grad. Air Force Manpower Mgmt. Tng. Program, 1952; m. Elizabeth Nelson, Jan. 14, 1942; children—Jo Elizabeth (Mrs. Thomas W. Williams), Cheryl Lee (Mrs. Francis E. King), John Joseph. Joined USAAF, 1940, grad. Pilot Sch., 1941, commd. 2d lt., 1941, advanced through grades to gen., USAF, 1969; various assignments, U.S. and Guam, 1941-46; aircraft comdr. Task Group 1.5, Kwajalein, 1946; assigned 393d Bomb Squadron, Roswell, N.M., 1946; comdr. 65th Bomb Squadron, 444th Bomb Group, Davis-Monthan Field, Ariz., 1946-47, Task Unit 741, Project Sandstone, also asst. chief staff Air Task Group 7, Kwajalein, 1947-48; assigned Hdqrs. 43 Bomb Wing, Davis- Monthan AFB, 1948; chief policy br., also chief program br., directorate of plans Hdqrs. SAC, Andrews AFB, Md., 1948, chief plans requirements br., programs sect., directorate of plans Hdqrs. SAC, Offutt AFB, Neb., 1948-50; dir. operations and tng. 22d Bomb Wing, March AFB, Cal., 1950-51; dir. operations 12th Air Div., March AFB, 1951-52; dep. to CINCSAC, SAC Xray, FEAF, Japan, 1951-52; successively dep. comdr. 92d Bomb Wing, comdr. 814th AB Group, comdr. 92d Bomb Wing, Fairchild AFB, Wash., 1952-55; comdr. 43 Bomb Wing, Davis-Monthan AFB, 1955-56; chief requirements div., directorate of operations Hdqrs. SAC, Offutt AFB, 1956-58; chief staff 8th Air Force, Westover AFB, Mass., 1958-59; comdr. 817th Air Div., Pease AFB, N.H., 1959-61, 822d Air Div., Turner AFB, Ga., 1961-62, 823d Air Div., Homestead AFB, Fla., 1962-63, 821st Strategic Aerospace Div., Ellsworth AFB, S.D., 1963-64; dir. operational requirements DCS/P&R. Hdqrs. USAF, 1964-65, dir. operational requirements and devel. plans, DSC/R&D, 1965-66, dir. aerospace programs DSC/P&R, 1966-67, dep. chief staff programs and resources, 1967-68; comdr. 15th Air Force, March AFB, Cal., 1968-69; comdr. Mil. Airlift Command, Scott AFB, 1969- -. Decorated D.S.M., Legion Merit with oak leaf cluster, D.F.C. with oak leaf cluster, Air medal with 3 oak leaf clusters, Purple Heart. Home: Quarters 200 9th St Scott AFB IL 62225 Office: Scott AFB IL 62225

CATTON, WILLIAM BRUCE, historian, educator; b. Cleve., Mar. 21, 1926; s. Bruce and Hazel (Cherry) C.; A.B., U. Md., 1951, M.A., 1952; Ph.D., Northwestern U., 1959; m. Mina Kathryn Sweeney, Dec. 23, 1957; children—David Bruce, Kathryn Cherry. Teaching asst. Northwestern U., 1953-54; instr. U. Md., 1955-58; instr. Princeton, 1958-61, asst. prof., 1961-64; asso. prof. history Middlebury Coll., 1964-68, prof., 1968—, Charles A. Dana prof. history, chmn. div. social scis., 1969—. Served with AUS, 1945-46. Mem. Am., Miss. Valley hist. assns., Phi Alpha Theta. Author: (with Bruce Catton) Two Roads to Sumter, 1963; (with Arthur S. Link) American Epoch, 1963. Home: RD 2 Middlebury VT 05753

CAUBLE, FLORENCE HORKAN, mem. Republican Nat. Com.; b. Moultrie, Ga., July 4, 1929; d. George Arthur and Martha (Olliff) Horkan; A.B., Wesleyan Coll., Macon, Ga., 1950; m. John A. Cauble, Oct. 14, 1950; children—Sally, Susan, David. Tchr., Dekalb County, Ga., 1950-51. Pres. Cherokee Fedn. Republican Women, 1960-64; vice chmn. Rep. Party Cherokee County, 1962-64; treas. Ga. Fedn. Rep. Women, 1965-68; women's activities dir. Congl. campaign, 1964; mem. Rep. Nat. Com. for Ga., 1968—; mem. Ga. Rep. Com., 1966-67, 68—, mem. exec. com., 1968—. Named Outstanding Rep. Woman in Ga., 1966. Methodist. Home: Route 6 Box 51 Sunset Dr Canton, GA 30114.

CAUBLE, GORDON B., army officer; b. Birmingham, Ala., Feb. 15, 1917; s. David Z. and Jessie (Cheek) C.; B.S., Ga. Inst. Tech., 1940; postgrad. Signal Corps Sch., 1942, Command and Gen. Staff Coll., Ft. Leavenworth, 1943; M.B.A., Harvard, 1948; postgrad. Logistics Mgmt. Center, Ft. Lee, 1957, Nat. War Coll., 1963; m. Vernette A. Cedarleaf, Jan. 27, 1945; children—Thomas G., Nancy, Kenneth D., Kathleen. Commd. 2d lt. U.S. Army, 1940, advanced through grades to brig. gen., 1967; chief plans br. Office Chief Signal Officer, 1944-45; chief statis. br. Office Dept. Chief of Staff Logistics, Dept. Army, 1948-52; chief signal adviser Japan Self Def. Force, 1952-53; chief requirements br. Office Chief Signal Office, 1955-59; comdr. 4th Signal Group and 1st Signal Brigade, U.S. Army, Europe, 1959-62; exec. J-6, Joint Chiefs of Staff, 1963-66; dep. comdr. 1st Signal Brigade, Vietnam, 1966; dep. asst. chief of staff, J-6 MACV, 1967; dep. comdr. USASTRATCOM, Ft. Huachuca, Ariz., 1967-69; dep. dir. J-6, Joint Chiefs of Staff, Washington, 1969—. Pres. Pinehurst Citizens Assn., Fairfax County, Va., 1950-51, Heidelberg (Germany) Protestant Men of the Chapel, 1962. Decorated Legion of Merit with 3 oak leaf clusters, Bronze Star, Joint Services Commendation medal with oak leaf cluster, Purple Heart. Mem. Assn. U.S. Army, Armed Forces Communications-Electronics Assn., Ga. Inst. Tech. Alumni Assn., Kappa Sigma, Tau Beta Pi. Methodist (ofcl. bd.). Club: Harvard Bus. Sch. of D.C. Home: 6713 Lainey Ct Annandale VA 22003 Office: J-6 Joint Staff Joint Chiefs of Staff Washington DC 20301

CAUDILL, HARRY MONROE, lawyer, author; b. Whitesburg, Ky., May 3, 1922; s. Cro Carr and Martha (Blair) C.; LL.B., U. Ky., 1948; m. Anne R. Frye, Dec. 16, 1946; children—James Kenneth, Diana Ellen, Harry Frye. Admitted to Ky. bar, 1948, since practiced in Whitesburg. Mem. Ky. Ho. of Reps., 1954-60, chmn. spl. legislative com. on edn., 1960. Mem. Gov.'s Commn. on Edn., 1960, Nat. Com. for Support Pub. Scis., Letcher County Com. Econ. Opportunity; bd. suprs. Letcher County Soil Conservation Dist. Served with AUS, 1942-44; MTO. Recipient Distinguished Alumni medallion U. Ky., 1965; Friends of Am. Writers award, 1964. Mem. Am. Bar Assn., Am. Legion, V.F.W., Council So. Mountains, Ky. Hist. Soc., Phi Delta Phi. Author: Night Comes to the Cumberlands, 1963; also articles on problems of Appalachian mountain area. Address: Box 72 Whitesburg KY 41258

CAUDILL, REBECCA, (Mrs. James Ayars), author; b. Poor Fork, Ky., Feb. 2, 1899; d. George Washington and Susan (Smith) Caudill; A.B., Wesleyan Coll., Macon, Ga., 1920; M.A., Vanderbilt U., 1922; m. James Sterling Ayars, Sept. 8, 1931; children— James Sterling (dec.), Rebecca Jean. Tchr., Collegio Bennett, Rio de Janeiro, 1922-24. Alumnae trustee Wesleyan Coll., 1949-52; trustee Pine Mountain Settlement School, 1967—. Recipient Nancy Bloch Meml. award Intercultural Library, Downtown Community Sch., N.Y.C., 1956. Mem. Delta Kappa Gamma, Theta Sigma Phi. Author: Barrie and Daughter, 1943; Happy Little Family, 1947; Tree of Freedom, 1949; Schoolhouse in the Woods, 1949; Up and Down the River, 1951; Saturday Cousins, 1953; House of the Fifers, 1954; Susan Cornish, 1955; Schoolroom in the Parlor, 1959; Time for Lissa, 1959; Higgins and the Great Big Scare, 1960; The Best Loved Doll, 1962, The Far Off Land, 1964 (Friends Am. Writers juvenile award 1965); A Pocketful of Cricket, 1964; A Certain Small Shepherd, 1965 (Soc. Midland Authors juvenile award 1966); Did You Carry the Flag Today, Charley?, 1966; My Appalachia, 1966; (with James Ayars) Contrary Jenkins, 1969; Come Along, 1969. Address: 510 W Iowa St Urbana IL 61801

CAUDILL, ROBERT PAUL, clergyman; b. Dockery, N.C., July 8, 1904; s. Calvin Millard and Lousina Sernetta Elizabeth (Myers) C.; grad. Mars Hill (N.C.) Coll., 1927; B.A. cum laude, Wake Forest (N.C.) Coll., 1929; Th.M., So. Bapt. Theol. Sem., Louisville, 1934, Ph.D., 1942; D.D., Miss. Coll., 1950; m. Ethel Fern Alderton, Mar. 23, 1929; children—Netta Sue, Robert Paul, Mary Jane (dec.), David Alderton, Mary Fern. Ordained to ministry Bapt. Ch., 1925; pastor rural and village chs., N.C. and Ky., 1927-35, First Bapt. Ch., Carrollton, Ky., 1935-37, First Bapt. Ch., Augusta. Ga., 1937-44. First Bapt. Ch., Memphis, 1944—; Trustee Laubach Lit., Inc. Mem. com. world peace So. Baptist Conv., 1959-65; chmn. relief com. Baptist World Alliance, 1947-60, mem. exec. com., 1950-60; mem. Baptist World Missions Commn., 1957-60; pres. Tenn. Baptist Conv., 1957-58, mem. exec. com., 1970; pres. Am. Bapt. Relief, 1947-60, trustee relief and annuity bd., 1956-59; chmn. distbn. com. Bapt. World Missions Trust Fund; chmn. finance com. So. Bapt. Conv., 1944-52. Founding, pres. Judeo- Christian League for Decency, 1961; dir. Am. Relief for Korea, 1952-54; mem. Nat. Council U.S. Com. for Refugees, 1960; had made many mission journeys in various parts of world. Pres. bd. trustees, chmn. exec. com. Found. for World Literacy; dir. United Tenn. League, Inc., 1946—, Tenn. Bapt. Press, 1957-60; trustee Mercer Univ., 1940-44, Union U., 1945-58, 65-68, Bapt. Meml. Hosp., 1947-58, 60-66, 70—; bd. dirs. United Tenn. League, Inc. 1946—; Commd. hon. chaplain USN Chaplain Corps, 1969. Mem. of the Internat. Platform Assn., Pi Kappa Delta. Rotarian. Clubs: Cross Cut; Executives (Memphis). Author: Broadman Comments (annual edit.), 1949-54; A Minister Looks at His World. Contbr. religious jours. and pamphlets. Toured occupied zones in Germany, Austria, Italy, 1947, in interest of relief program; toured Europe 1948, 1949, 52. Home: 223 Kenilworth St Memphis TN 38112 Office: First Baptist Ch Poplar and Parkway Sts Memphis TN 38112

CAUDILL, WILLIAM WAYNE, architect, educator; b. Hobart, Okla., May 25, 1914; s. Walter H. and Josephine (Moores) C.; B.A., Okla. State U., 1937; M.Arch., Mass. Inst. Tech., 1939; LL.D., Eastern Mich. U., 1957; m. Edith Roselle Woodman, Feb. 5, 1940; children—Susan Kent, William Wayne. Founder firm Caudill, Rowlett & Scott, architects, Houston, 1946; founder architecture div. Tex. Engring. Expt. Sta. Tex. A. and M. Coll, 1948, prof., 1950-61; Wm. Watkin prof. architecture, dir. Rice U. Sch. Architecture, 1961-71. Vis. lectr. Princeton, Harvard, Cornell U., N.C. State Coll., Washington U. Served with C.E., AUS, also USNR, 1942-46. Fellow A.I.A. (chmn. nat. sch. com.). Methodist. Author: Space for Teaching; Building for Learning; So You Want to Build a School; Toward Better School Design; Architecture By Team. Home: 10923 Kirwick Dr Houston TX 77024 Office 1111 West Loop South Houston TX 77027

CAUDLE, JONES RICHARD, Jr., oil co. exec.; b. Foraker, Okla., Nov. 1, 1911; s. Jones Richard and Maude Ethel (Rodgers) C.; student Tulsa U., 1932, Okla. U., 1934, Tulsa Law Sch., 1937; m. Mary Ann Brownlee, June 11, 1943; children—Mary Ann, Jones Richard III. Sales mgr. N.M.Asphalt & Refining Co., 1946-52, Delta Refining Co., 1952-54; v.p. Eastern States Chem. Corp., 1954-57; sr. v.p. Eastern States Petroleum & Chem. Co., 1957-59; v.p. Signal Oil and Gas Co., 1959—, dir., 1968-69; pres. Apex Investment, Inc., Apex Oil Co., Apex Oil Co. of La., Major Industries, Inc. Democratic candidate for state rep. N.M., 1951. Served to capt. USAAF, World War II. Decorated Bronze Star. Mem. Am. Petroleum Inst., Petroleum Industry 25 Year Club, Delta Theta Phi. Presbyn. (elder, deacon). Club: Houston. Home: 11325 Somerland Way Houston TX 77024 Office: 2722 Broad St Houston TX 77017

CAUGHEY, JOHN WALTON, historian; b. Wichita, Kan., July 3, 1902; s. Rudolph Weyerhaeuser and Emily (Walton) C.; B.A., U. of Tex., 1923; M.A., U. of Cal., 1926, Ph.D., 1928; m. LaRee Pfeiffer, Sept. 25, 1928; children—Nancy LaRee, Susan Ariel. Instr. Schreiner

Inst., Kerrville, Tex., 1923-25, San Bernardino (Cal.) Jr. Coll., 1929-30; instr. history, U. of Cal. at Los Angeles, 1930-32, asst. prof., 1932-39, asso. prof., 1936-46, prof., 1946-70, chmn. dept., 1945-47; asso. editor, Pacific Hist. Rev., 1937- 46, mng. editor, 1947-68; gen. editor Chronicles of California, 1946-52; cons. Cal. State Lands Commn. 1949-65. Tech. dir. Paramount Pictures, Cal., 1945-46. Vis. prof. U. Wis., 1957. Regional editor Am. Heritage, 1954-58; lit. editor Frontier, 1956-67. Fellow Native Sons of Golden West, 1928-29, Rockefeller Found. Fellow, 1950-53, Benjamin D. Shreve Fellow, Princeton U., 1955-56; Am. Council Learned Socs. Scholar, 1951-52. Mem. Cal. Landmarks Approval com., 1944-50; council Am. Hist. Research Center, 1950-67. Mem. Am. Assn. U. Profs. (v.p. 1957-58), Am. Hist. Assn. (mem. council 1961-64, pres. Pacific coast br. 1958), Orgn. Am. Historians (pres. 1964-65). Clubs: Zamorano, E Clampus Vitus. Author: History of the Pacific Coast, 1933; Bernardo de Gálvez in Louisiana, 1934, McGillivray of the Creeks, 1938; California, 1940, 53, 70; Hubert Howe Bancroft, 1946; Gold is the Cornerstone, 1948; America Since 1763; A Survey, 1955; In Clear and Present Danger, 1958; Their Majesties the Mob, 1960; (with LaRee Caughey) California's Own History, 1963; (with LaRee Caughey, Katherine Peter) Windows on the Pacific, 1963; (with Ernest R. May) A History of the United States, 1964; (with John Hope Franklin and Ernest R. May) Land of the Free, 1965; School Segregation on our Doorstep; the Los Angeles Story, 1966; The Pueblo Water Right of Los Angeles, 1969; The American West: Frontier and Region, 1969; articles, books revs. Editor: The Emigrant's Guide to California (by J.E. Ware, 1849), 1932; The Los Angeles Star (by W.A. Rice), 1947; Robert Owen, Social Idealist (by Rowland Hill Harvey), 1949; Rushing for Gold, 1949; Seeing the Elephant; Letters of R.R. Taylor, Fortyniner, 1951; The Indians of Southern California in 1852, 1952; Six Months in the Gold Mines (by E. Gould Buffum), 1958; (with LaRee Caughey) California Heritage, 1962, 71. Home: 1897 Mango Way Los Angeles CA 90048 ☆

CAUGHEY, KENNETH WILSON, banker; b. Boulder, Colo., Apr. 8, 1925; s. Clarence H. and Bertha (Hensley) C.; student Miami U., Oxford, O., 1942-43, U. Ariz., 1950-51; LL.B., U. Colo., 1955; m. Judith Stearns, Sept. 4, 1953; children—Peter S., Bruce H., David P. With Colo. Nat. Bank of Denver, 1955—, v.p., trust officer, 1962-69, sr. v.p., trust officer, 1969—, dir., 1969—. Past pres. Denver Estate Planning Council. Treas. Colo. Bar Found., Colo. Hist. Found.; mem. legislative com. Colo. Tb. and Respiratory Disease Assn.; bd. dirs. Craig Rehab. Hosp.; mem. exec. bd. Boy Scouts Am. Served to lt. USMCR, 1943-47. Mem. Am., Colo., Denver bar assns., Colo. Bankers Assn. Rotarian. Clubs: Law (past pres.), University (Denver). Home: 1741 S Newport Way Denver CO 80222 Office: 17th and Champa Sts Denver CO 80202

CAUGHEY, THOMAS KIRK, educator; b. Rutherglen, Scotland, Oct. 22, 1927; s. Robert and Barbara (Frater) C.; B.S. in Mech. Engring., U. Glasgow, 1946, B.S. in Elec. Engring., 1947; M.Mech. Engring., Cornell U., 1952; Ph.D. in Engring. Sci., Cal. Inst. Tech., 1954; m. Jane Suzanne Turner, Dec. 22, 1952; children—Penelope (Mrs. Donia M. LaFave), William Jeffery, Catherine Ball, Christine Anne. Came to U.S., 1951. Research engr. James Howden & Co., Glasgow, 1948-51, cons. engr., 1954-55; mem. faculty Cal. Inst. Tech., 1955—, prof. applied mechanics, 1962—; cons. Tetratech, Jet Propulsion Lab. Bd. dirs. San Gabriel Valley Camp Fire Girls. Mem. Am. Geophys. Soc., A.A.A.S., Am. Assn. U. Profs., Soc. Indsl. and Applied Math., Sigma Xi. Presbyn. (elder). Author papers in field. Home: 2960 San Pasqual Pasadena CA 91107

CAUGHRAN, ROY WILLARD, educator; b. Port Arthur, Tex., Dec. 14, 1917; s. William Isaac and Pearl (Cunningham) C.; A.B., Drury Coll., Springfield, Mo., 1939; M.A., Ball State U., 1949; Ph.D., Northwestern U., 1956; m. Verl Eloise Richman, Oct. 18, 1941; 1 dau., Carol Louise. Tchr., adminstr., Daleville and New Castle, Ind., 1946-51; sch. adminstr., Park Forest, Ill., 1953-54; instr. edn. Northwestern U., 1954-56; mem. faculty Kent (O.) State U., 1956—, chmn. dept. elementary edn., 1961-69; speaker, cons. in field, 1956—. Served with USAAF, 1941- 46, USAF, 1951-53. Mem. Am. Assn. Colls. Tchrs. Edn., Assn. Supervision and Curriculum Devel., Assn. Higher Edn., Am. Assn. Sch. Adminstrs., Nat. Council Profs. Ednl. Adminstr., Nat., Ohio edn. assns., Phi Delta Kappa, Sigma Tau Delta. Home: 514 Valley View Kent, OH 44240.

CAULEY, DOROTHY MARY, steel co. exec.; b. Hamilton, Ont., Can.; d. John Thomas and Dorothy (Forster) Cauley; Student Hamilton Collegiate Inst., Can. Bus. Coll. Sec. to mgr. U.S. Steel Export Corp., Toronto, Ont., Can.; sec. to purchasing agt. Nat. Steel Car Corp. Ltd., Hamilton, Ont., Can., sec. to sales mgr. Dominion Foundries & Steel Ltd., Hamilton, Ont., Can., then mgr. order dept., asst. sect., 1957-68, sec., 1968—. Pres. Hamilton United Appeal, 1968-69; v.p. Mt. St. Joseph Centre, 1970-71; sec. bd. Catholic Children's Aid Soc., 1957-70; mem. operating com. Hamilton Theatre Auditorium, 1971—; mem. Hamilton Art Gallery, 1965—. Bd. dirs. St. Joseph's Hosp. Sch. Nursing. Mem. Hamilton C. of C., Chartered Inst. Secs., Am. Soc. Corp. Secs. Club: Hamilton Golf and Country. Home: 3306 Lakeshore Rd Burlington Ontario Canada Office: 1330 Burlington St Hamilton Ontario Canada

CAULEY, JOHN ROWAN, newspaper corr.; b. Rushville, Ind., Apr. 25, 1908; s. Thomas S. and Mary Ann (Kelly) C.; student Rockhurst Coll., Kansas City, Mo., 1926-28, D.Humane Letters (hon.); L.H.D.; B.J., U. Mo., 1932. Pub. weekly newspaper The Summit News, Kansas City, Mo., 1933-36; mem. staff Kansas City (Mo.) Star, 1936—, news editor, 1954, fgn. affairs editor Washington bur., 1957-64, chief bur., 1964—. Recipient Pro-Meritis award Rockhurst Coll., 1960. Mem. A.P. Mng. Editors Assn. (Bd. dirs. 1953-54). White House Cors. Assn., John Carroll Soc. (gov.), Sigma Delta Chi. Roman Catholic (usher). Clubs: Kansas City Press (pres. 1950), Nat. Press (bd. govs), Federal City, Internat., Gridiron (Washington). Home: 1727 Massachusetts Av NW Washington DC 20006 Office: 1750 Pennsylvania Av NW Washington DC 20006

CAULFIELD, GEORGE F., pub. relations exec.; b. San Francisco, May 31, 1924; s. John Francis and Luise (Peters) C.; B.A., Stanford, 1948; m. Ellen Rescigno, July 14, 1959; children—Tracy, Kevin. Reporter, San Francisco Examiner, 1948-51; pub. relations mgr. Shell Oil Co., various locations, 1951-61; dir. pub. relations Foremost Dairies, San Francisco, 1961-67; dir. corp. communications URS Systems Corp., San Mateo, Cal., 1967-69; mgr. regional office Carl Byoir & Asso., Los Angeles, 1969—. Served with USNR, 1942-46. Mem. Pub. Relations Soc. U.S. (nat. assembly). Home: 10520 Strathmore Dr Los Angeles CA 90024 Office: 900 Wilshire Blvd Los Angeles CA 90017

CAUSEY, BEVERLEY D., Jr., educator; B.A., William Colls., M.A., Harvard, 1934, Ph.D., 1942. Formerly provost, dean faculty, pres. Hobart and William Smith Colls., now exec. v.p. Address: care Hobart and William Smith Coll Geneva NY 11456*

CAUSEY, EDWARD LIVINGSTON, Jr., constrn. co. exec.; b. Coalgate, Okla., Jan. 22, 1908; s. Edward Livingston and Mary (Benham) C.; student Tex. A. and M. Coll., 1925-27; m. Helen Louise Crowley, Feb. 14, 1931; 1 dau., Catherine (Mrs. Dyas Power Boothe, Jr.). With Rock Island Lines, 1924-36; chief engr. Conchas Dam and Friant Dam, Bent Bros. & Griffith, 1936-42; project mgr. P.N.A.B., Samoa, 1942; project mgr. Davis Dam, Utah Constrn., 1943-44; asst. project mgr. Caracas Aqueduct Project, Groves-Drake, 1945-46; project mgr. Aprao Harbor Breakwater, Guam, J.H. Pomeroy Co., 1947; operations supt. AMAG, Greece, Atkinson-Drake- Park, 1948; plant design chief iron ore operations Utah Constrn., San Francisco, 1949-53; v.p., mgr. heavy and indsl. constrn. Marwell Constrn. Co., Vancouver, B.C., Can., 1953-60; v.p., project mgr. Taconite Processing facilities for Res. Mining Co., Silver Bay, Minn., Hunkin-Conkey Constrn. Co., 1960-63; exec. v.p. charge all operations Hunkin-Conkey Constrn. Co., Cleve., 1963—. Mem. U.S. Com. on Large Dams. Mem. Moles, Beavers, Cleve. Engring. Soc. Clubs: Shaker Heights Country; Hermit, Cleveland Athletic (Cleve.); Silver Bay Country; Green Valley Country (Ariz.). Home: 24609 Hazelmere Rd Beachwood OH 44122 Office: 1919 E 13th St Cleveland OH 44114

CAUSEY, ROBERT L., educator; B.S., Western Ky. State Coll.; M.S., U. Ky.; Ph.D., Stanford. Mem. faculty U. Louisville, prof., head dept. engring. math. Office: Grad Sch Dept Engring Math U Louisville Louisville KY 40208

CAUTHEN, BAKER JAMES, clergyman; b. Huntsville, Tex., Dec. 20, 1909; s. James S. and Maude Maude (Baker) C.; A.B., Stephen F. Austin College at Nacogdoches, Tex., 1929; M.A., Baylor U., 1930, D.D., 1945; Th.M., Southwestern Bapt. Theol. Sem., 1933, Th.D., 1936; m. Eloise Glass, May 20, 1934; children—Carolyn, Ralph. Ordained to ministry, Bapt. Ch., 1927; pastor Polytechnic Bapt. Ch., Fort Worth, 1933-39; prof. missions Southwestern Bapt. Theol. Sem., Fort Worth, 1935-39; missionary Fgn. Mission Bd., So. Bapt. Conv., 1939-45, sec. for the Orient, 1945-53, exec. sec., 1953—. Home: 3904 W Weyburn Rd Richmond VA 23235

CAUTHEN, IRBY BRUCE, Jr., univ. dean; b. Rock Hill, S.C., Aug. 24, 1919; s. Irby Bruce and Ruth (Kimbrell) C.; B.A., Furman U., 1940; M.A., U. Va., 1942, Ph.D., 1951; m. Elizabeth Bagby Greear, Aug. 28, 1954; children—Irby Bruce III, James Noah Greear. Asst. prof. English, Hollins Coll., 1951-54; faculty U.Va., Charlottesville, 1954—, prof. English, 1964—, asso. dean, 1958-62, dean coll., 1962—. Chmn., Va. Conf. Summer Session Deans, 1967-68; chmn. regional selection com. Woodrow Wilson Fellowship Found., 1962—. Served with AUS, 1942-46; MTO. Decorated Bronze Star. Mem. Bibliog. Soc. U. Va. (v.p. 1961—), Modern Lang. Assn., Shakespeare Assn., Am. Assn. U. Profs., Phi Beta Kappa (pres. Va. 1969—), Omicron Delta Kappa. Democrat. Presbyn. Clubs: Colonnade, Boar's Head (Charlottesville). Editor: Gorboduc, 1970. Contbg. editor: The Dramatic Works in the Beaumont and Fletcher Canon, 1966. Contbr. articles to profl. jours. Home: 1824 Winston Rd Charlottesville VA 22903

CAUTHEN, JAMES LOUIS, banker; b. Abilene, Tex., Nov. 25, 1911; s. James K. and Lucretia (McCollum) C.; B.A., So. Methodist U., 1967; m. Earla F. Baker, Jan. 25, 1933; children—James Louis, Don Baker. With Fed. Res. Bank Dallas, 1930- -, sr. v..p., controller, 1969—; tchr. banking fundamentals Am. Inst. Banking, 1950-53. Sec. Tex. Lions Eye Bank, 1966-67. Mem. bd. devel. So. Methodist U., 1960-70. Served with Tex. N.G., 1929-31. Mem. Lasso (Tex.) C. of C. (vice chmn. 1960). Methodist (vice chmn. trustees 1955-70). Lion (pres. Dallas 1966-67). Author articles in field. Home: 3240 Daniels Av Dallas TX 75205 Office: 400 S Akard St Dallas TX 75222

CAVA, JAMES M., auditor, Auditor Green Point Savs. Bank, Bkln. Office: 807 Manhattan Av Brooklyn NY 11222*

CAVA, MICHAEL PATRICK, educator, chemist; b. Bklyn., Feb. 13, 1926; s. Michael R. and Catherine (Lombardo) C.; B.S., Harvard, 1946; M.S., U. Mich., 1948, Ph.D., 1951; m. Esther Laden, June 11, 1951; 1 son, John M. Postdoctoral fellow Harvard, 1951-53; from asst. prof. to prof. Ohio State U., 1953-65; prof. Wayne State U., Detroit, 1965-69; prof. chemistry U. Pa., 1969—. Cons., Smith, Kline and French, Phila., 1965—; mem. study sect. NIH, 1966-70. Alfred P. Sloan Found. fellow. Mem. Am. Chem. Soc., Am. Soc. Pharmacognosy. Author: (with M.J. Mitchell) Cyclobutadiene and Related Compounds, 1967; also numerous articles. Reserch on chemistry of 4-membered ring organic compounds; isolation and chemistry of alkaloids of tropical plants. Home: 443 N Highland Av Merion PA 19066 Office: U Pa Dept Chemistry Philadelphia PA 19104

CAVAGLIERI, GIORGIO, architect; b. Venice, Italy, Aug. 1, 1911; s. Gino and Margherita (Maroni) C.; D. Archtl. Engring., Sup. Sch. Engring., Milan, Italy, 1932; student spl. city planning, Sup. Sch. Architecture, Rome, 1934; m. Norma Sanford Jan. 31, 1942. Came to U.S., 1939. naturalized, 1943. Propr. own firm, N.Y.C., 1946—; prin. works in Milan, prior to World War II; apprenticeship N.Y. office R. Candela Balt. offices J.O. Chertkof. also Benjamin Franklin, architect, prior to World War II; propr. own firm, N.Y.C., 1946—; prin. works include Fenton Hall reconstrn. Fredonia (N.Y.) Coll., Astor Library restoration and conversion to N.Y. Pub. Theatre, N.Y. Shakespeare Festival, Jefferson Market Courthouse restoration and conversion to N.Y. Pub. Library, Riverdale, N.Y., Pub. Sch. 32, Staten Is., Kip's Bay br. library; adj. prof. Sch. Architecture, Pratt Inst. Trustee Nat. Inst. Archtl. Edn., chmn. trustees, 1957-60. Served with C.E., AUS, 1943-45, Decorated Bronze Star; recipient Honor award A.I.A., 1968, House Improvement award, 1961; Bard award, spl. citation City Club N.Y., 1968, Illuminated scroll Municipal Art Soc. N.Y., 1966; Clients award N.Y. State Assn. Architects, 1964; Gold medal honor architecture Archtl. League N.Y., 1956; winner 1st prize nat. competition auditorium, Rome, 1935, 3d prize competition city hosp., Cuneo, Italy. 1938, hon. mention Armed Forces bldgs. Rome World's Fair, 1938, 3d prize N.Y.C. Bd. Edn. archtl. competition for modernization Bronx Jr. High Sch., 1967. Fellow A.I.A. (pres. N.Y. chpt. 1970-71); mem. Municipal Art Soc. N.Y. (pres. 1963-65), Archtl. League N.Y. (v.p. 1961-63), Am. Inst. Internat. Designers, N.Y. Council Arts and Govt. Democrat. Home: 75 Central Park West New York City NY 10023 Office: 250 W 57th St New York City NY 10019

CAVALIEREI, LIEBE FRANK, phys. chemist, educator; b. Phila., Aug. 26, 1919; s. Frank and Filomena (Bonacurso) C.; B.S., U. Pa., 1943, M.S., 1944, Ph.D., 1945; m. Doris Koch, Nov. 17, 1945; children—Ralph, Claudia, Frances. Mem. Sloan- Kettering Inst., 1960—; prof. biochemistry Sloan-Kettering div. Grad. Sch. Med. Scis., Cornell U. Med. Coll., 1960—. Mem. Am. Chem. Soc., A.A.A.S., Harvey Soc., Fedn. Am. Socs. Exptl. Biology, Biophys. Soc., Sigma Xi. Home: 255-02 Iowa Rd Great Neck NY 11020 Office: 410 E 68th St New York City NY 10021

CAVALLARO, CARMEN, musician; b. N.Y.C.; ed. high sch. Began career as pianist, early childhood, later appeared with Rudy Vallee orch.; records Decca Rec. Co., album Dancing in the Dark; other recs. include Chopin's Polonaise, adaptations of Rachmaninoff (Full Moon and Empty Arms), Debussy (My Reverie), Tschaikovsky (Tonight We Love); appeared several movies, sound track for Eddie Duchin Story; featured radio and TV Programs; arrangements popular and semi-classical music. Albums: Getting Sentimental Over You, All the Things You Are, I'll See You in My Dreams, Strauss Waltzes and Serenade, Hits from Hollywood, 1962, Swingin' Easy, 1962, Waltzing in the Dark, 1963. Home: 528 N Rodeo Dr Beverly Hills CA 90212*

CAVALLO, DIANA, author; b. Phila., Nov. 3, 1931; d. Genuino and Josephine (Petrarca) Cavallo; B.A., U. Pa., 1953; M.A., Sarah Lawrence Coll., 1965; m. Henry Weiberg, June 5, 1954. Lectr., USIS, 1961-63; tchr. lit. U. Pisa (Italy), 1961-63, Drexel Inst. Tech., 1964; lectr. lit. Queens Coll., Flushing, N.Y., 1966—. Sec.-treas. Mt. Desert Music Festival, 1965. MacDowell Colony fellow, 1960, 67; Fulbright Teaching fellow, 1961-63. Mem. Authors League, Phi Beta Kappa. Author: (novel) A Bridge of Leaves, 1961; (short stories) Certain Fathoms in the Earth, 1964; New York, Its Co-Existing Past and Present, 1969. Home: 75 Montgomery St New York City NY 10002 Office: Queens Coll Flushing NY 11367

CAVALLON, GLORGIO, artist; b. Italy, Mar. 3, 1904; s. Augusto and Agnese (Scarsi) C.; came to U.S., 1920, naturalized, 1929; student Nat. Acad. Design, 1926-30; pupil of Charles Hawthorne, Hans Hofmann; m. Linda Lindberg, Mar. 25, 1954. One man exhbns. include Bottege D'Art, Vicenza, Italy, 1932, Egan Gallery, N.Y.C., 1946-48, 51, 54, Stable Gallery, N.Y.C., 1957-59, Kootz Gallery, N.Y.C., 1961, 63, 65, A.M. Sachs Gallery, N.Y.C., 1969, 71; rep. permanent collections Museum of Modern Art, N.Y.C., U. N.C. at Greensboro, Whitney Mus., Albright Art Gallery, Guggenheim Mus., Union Carbide Corp., Continental Grain Corp., Tishman Collection, Michener Collection U. Tex. at Austin, Chase Manhattan Bank, Singer Mfg. Co., Geigy Chem. Corp., N.Y.U., Univ. Art Mus., Berkeley, Cal., Marine Midland Trust Co., Buffalo, Avco Delta Corp., Cleve., Am. Republic Ins. Co., Des Moines, Rose Mus. of Brandeis U. Artist in residence U. N.C., Greensboro, 1964; vis. critic art Yale, 1967, painting workshop Columbia, summer 1969. Guggenheim fellow, 1966-67; recipient award in painting Nat. Inst. Arts and Letters, 1970. Address: 178 E 95th St New York City NY 10028

CAVANAGH, C.J., assn. exec.; b. Santa Margarita, Cal., Dec. 11, 1908; s. William E. and Josephine (Asberry) C.; ed. Cal. Poly. Sch., U. Cal. at Davis, U. Hawaii; m. Georgia Durden, June 19, 1937; 1 dau., Louise. Tchr. high sch., Honolulu, 1934-37; acting mgr., investigator Nat. Ins. Reference Agy., 1937-40; with Liberty House, Honolulu, 1940-62, asst. gen. supt. 1951-53, gen. supt., 1954-62; exec. v.p. Hawaii C. of C., 1963—. Pres., Honolulu Retail Bd., 1963; mem. Regional Export Expansion Council, U.S. Army Adv. Com. Mem. exec. bd. Honolulu council Boy Scouts Am. Served with U.S. Army, 1930-37; to lt. col. AUS, 1941-45. Mem. Friendly Sons St. Patrick. Mem. Union Ch. Rotarian. Clubs: Pacific, Oahu Country. Home: 6657 Hawaii Kai Dr Honolulu HI 96817 Office: 735 Bishop St Dillingham Bldg Honolulu HI 96813

CAVANAGH, DANIEL JOSEPH, livestock operator; b. St. Charles, Mo., Mar. 20, 1883; s. Daniel and Ann (Martin) C.; B.S. in civil engring., U. Mo., 1905; m. Pearl Langford, Oct. 15, 1915; children—Margaret Ann (Mrs. P.S. Twombly), Barbara Jane (Mrs. G.M. Hoyt). Civil engr. Brenneke & Fay, St. Louis, 1905-07; bridge designer Mo. Valley Bridge & Iron Co., Leavenworth, Kan., 1907-09; bridge contractor Midland Bridge Co., Kansas City, Mo., 1909-21; gen. contractor, Twin Falls, Ida., 1921-46; livestock operator, Twin Falls, Ida., 1934—; pres. Cavanagh Ranch Co., Inc. Mem. Ida. Ho. of Reps., 1933-39, State Planning Bd. Ida., 1935- 37; chmn. Ida. adv. bd. dist. 2 Bur. Land Mgmt., Dept. Interior 1935-53, Idaho rep. nat. adv. council, 1952; adv. bd. Minidoka Nat. Forest, 1935-62; mem. Ida. adv. bd. Bur. Land Mgmt., 1937- 53; mem. Ida. Hosp. Bd., 1946-56; mem. bd. OPA, 1942-46. Democratic precinct committeeman, 1930-60, state committeeman, 1932-56; county chmn. Twin Falls County, 1930-38; Ida. Dem. state chmn., 1946-48; nat. Dem. committeeman Ida. 1948-52; del. Dem. Nat. Conv. 1940, 44, 48, 52, 56; Democratic presdl. elector for Ida., 1960, 64. Mem. Assn. Gen. Contractors Am. Roman Catholic. Elk (life). Clubs: University (life, Salt Lake City); Arid (Boise, Ida.). Home: 127 8th Av N Twin Falls ID 83301 Office: Profl Bldg PO Box 584 Twin Falls ID 83301

CAVANAGH, DENIS, educator; M.B., Ch.B. Former prof. gynecology and obstetrics, chmn. dept. St. Louis Sch. Medicine; now prof., chmn. dept. obstetrics and gynecology U. Tasmania (Australia). Address: care Dept Gynecology and Obstetrics U Tasmania Hobart Tasmania Australia*

CAVANAGH, EDWARD FRANCIS, corp. exec.; b. N.Y.C., Aug. 18, 1908; s. Edward Francis and Mae (Masterson) C.; B.A., Georgetown U., 1929; postgrad. Harvard, 1930-31; LL.B., St. Lawrence U., 1933; m. Nancy Miller, Mar. 26, 1940; children—Edward Francis III, Nannette Christine, Roderick Anthony, Mae A. Admitted to N.Y. bar, 1933, U.S. Supreme Ct., 1938; practice in N.Y.C., 1933-; counsel Curtiss-Wright Corp., N.Y.C., Woodbridge, N.J., 1945-47; dep. commr. N.Y.C. Dept. Marine and Aviation, 1947-49, commr., 1950-54, dep. commr., acting commr. Dept. Hosps., 1949-50, commr. Fire Dept., 1954-62; dep. mayor N.Y.C., 1962-65; v.p., dir. Baker Industries, Inc., 1966—, Wells Fargo Armored Transport Corp., Plant Protection Corp. N.J., Wells Fargo Armored Service Corp., Tenn., Wells Fargo Armored Service Corp. Miss., Wells Fargo Armored Service Corp. Del.; v.p. Wells Fargo Armored Service Corp. Mass., Pacific Plant Protection, Shane & Assos.; dir. Wells Fargo Armored Service of Florida, Coin Auditing Systems, Inc., James Cavanagh Corp., investments, N.Y.C. Mem. Gov.'s Emergency Adv. Com.; chmn. Mayor's Chaplaincy Bd., Mayor's Com. on Harlem Affairs; mem. Mayor's Task Force on Markets; chmn. Interagy. Relocation Coordinating Com.; mem. exec. com. World's Fair, 1964-65; treas., Mercy Hosp., Hempstead, L.I., N.Y., 1950-56; chmn. bd. layman's adv. com. Bellevue Hosp., N.Y.C.; exec. com. Post Coll., L.I. U. Vice pres., dir. Thannawaga Democratic Orgn., N.Y.C.; chmn. N.Y. County Dem. Com. Bd. dirs. Neighborhood House, Glen Cove, L.I., Library Presdl. Papers; trustee L.I. U. Served to lt. col. USAAF, 1942- 45. Decorated Legion of Merit (U.S.); knight grand cross Order Holy Sepulchre of Jerusalem (Papal); Order St. George (Greece); Order Rebuen Dario (Nicaragua); cavaliere ufficiale Order of Merit (Italy); chevalier Order of Crown (Belgium); Ecomeinda of Order of Isabella Catolica (Spain); Medal of Merit (Iran). Recipient William Randolph Hearst gold medal award Downtown Lower Manhattan Assn., 1954; Cath. War Vet award; Achievement award Interfaith Movement, 1964; Anti-Defamation League award, 1965. Mem. Assn. Bar City N.Y., Nat. Fire Protection Assn., Am. Legion (Distinguished Service award N.Y. dept. 1955), Phi Delta Phi. Roman Catholic. Clubs: Racquet and Tennis, Lotos, Whitehall (N.Y.C.); Piping Rock, Beaver Dam Winter Sports (Locust Valley, N.Y.); Harvard of N.Y. Home: 205 E 63d St New York City NY 10021 also Naghward Glen Cove NY 11542 Office 345 Park Av New York City NY 10022

CAVANAGH, HARRY JOSEPH, lawyer; b. Chgo., July 9, 1923; s. John Albert and Mary (Foster) C.; LL.B., U. Ariz., 1950; m. Stella Dominguez, Mar. 20, 1943; children—Kathleen (Mrs. James Barrow), Dianne (Mrs. Charles Albert), Harry Joseph, Patricia, Michael, William, Jamie. Admitted to Ariz. bar, 1950, since practiced in Phoenix; partner firm O'Connor, Cavanagh, Anderson, Westover, Killingsworth & Beshears, 1965—. Exec. v.p. Lawrence & Stegall Ranches, Inc., 1963-64; dir. J.F. Helmold & Bros., Chgo., Ariz. Title & Trust Co., Boys Clubs of Phoenix, Internat. Leisure Hosts, Ltd.

Pres. Am. Bd. Trial Advocates. Served to capt. USAAF, 1943-46. Decorated Silver Star, D.F.C. Mem. Nat. Assn. Ins. Counsel, Internat., Am., Maricopa County (bd. dirs.) bar assns., State Bar Ariz., Am. Judicature Soc., Phoenix Assn. Def. Counsel, Am. Arbitration Assn., Phoenix C. of C., Phi Delta Phi. Home: 7550 Silvercrest Way Paradise Valley AZ 85051 Office: 3003 N Central Av Phoenix AZ 85012

CAVANAGH, JEROME PATRICK, lawyer; b. Detroit, June 16, 1928; s. Sylvester J. and Irene (Timmins) (Timmins) C.; Ph.B., U. Detroit, 1950, J.D., 1954; div.; children—Mark, Patrick, David, Mary Therese, Christopher, Philip, Jerome C., Elizabeth Angela. Admitted to Mich. bar, 1954; practiced in Detroit, 1954-62; mem. firm Cavanagh & Toohey; mayor of Detroit, 1962-70; adj. prof. Inst. Pub. Policy Studies, U. Mich.; pres. Urban Synergistics, Inc. pres. Urban Synergistics, Inc. Past pres. U.S. Conf. Mayors; past pres. Nat. League Cities. Mem. Am., Detroit bar assns., State Bar Mich. Office: First National Bldg Detroit MI 48226

CAVANAGH, JOHN EDWARD, lawyer; b. Winnipeg, Man., Can., Nov. 15, 1918; s. John and Mary Ann (McGarty) C.; came to U.S., 1920, naturalized, 1942; A.B., U. Ore., 1942; J.D., George Washington U., 1949, LL.M., 1952; m. Mary Adele Brophy, May 9, 1953; children—John E., Clare Adele, Cathleen Rose, Sally Ann. Admitted to D.C. bar, 1949, Cal. bar, 1957; grad. asst. social sci. U. Ore., 1941-42; hwy. economist U.S. Bur. Pub. Rds., 1946-49; chief congl. investigations br. Q.M.C., counsel to dep. quartermaster gen. for operations Dept. Army, 1950-56; asst. counsel Lockheed Aircraft Corp., 1956-58; asst. counsel Lockheed Missiles & Space Co., 1958-62, counsel, 1962-68; chief counsel, asst. sec. Lockheed Aircraft Corp., Burbank, Cal., 1968-71, v.p., gen. counsel, 1971—; lectr. U. Santa Clara Law Sch., 1960-68; mem. adv. bd. fed. contracts report Bur. Nat. Affairs, 1968—. Pres. Santa Clara County Taxpayers Assn., 1964-67. Served to maj. AUS, 1942-46; CBI. Mem. Am., Fed. bar assns., Nat. Contract Mgmt. Assn., Order of Coif, Delta Theta Phi. Home: 17341 Gresham St Northridge CA 91324 Office: PO Box 551 Burbank CA 91503

CAVANAUGH, C. EDWARD, bank exec. Auditor, Bank of Commerce, N.Y.C. Office: 56 E 42d St Manhattan NY 10017*

CAVANAUGH, DANIEL PATRICK, lawyer; b. Chgo., Jan. 17, 1903; s. Daniel D. and Josephine (Snowden) C.; studied law with practicing atty.; m. Anna C. Cain, Oct. 1, 1928; children—Marie A. (Mrs. David A. Frink), Patricia A. (Mrs. Thomas C. Boss). Admitted to Conn. bar, 1928; with Aetna Life & Casualty Co., 1923-68, v.p., 1964-68, gen. counsel, 1959-68; pvt. practice law, West Hartford, 1968—. Chmn. bd. finance South Windsor, Conn., 1942, chmn. bd. edn., 1962, town counsel, 1954, mem. town council, 1965-66, town counsel, 1967—. Club: Wampanoog Country (West Hartford, Conn.). Home: 840 Main St South Windsor, CT 06074. Office 968 Farmington Av West Hartford CT 06007

CAVANAUGH, FRANCIS P., educator; b. Owosso, Mich., Apr. 11, 1900; s. Michael and Mary (Keegan) C.; A.B., U. Notre Dame, 1923; Ph.D., Cath. U., Washington, 1928; hon fellowship, U. Minn., 1932-33. Tchr. sociology, U. Notre Dame, 1928-32; head dept. sociology, St. Thomas Coll., St. Paul, 1932-33, Portland (Ore.) U., 1933-34; prof. sociology, U. Notre Dame, 1934-43, acting pres., summer 1945, dean Coll. Arts and Letters, 1943, now prof. sociology, asst. superior of univ., staff chaplain, counsellor lay employees. Mem. Am. Sociol. Soc., Nat. Conf. Cath. Charities. Author: Immigration Restriction on Work Today, 1927; Notes on the Family, 1936. Cons. editor Scott Foresman Co. Contbr. articles to social and religious jours. Address: Notre Dame Univ Notre Dame IN 46556

CAVANAUGH, KENNETH CLINTON, govt. ofcl.; b. Fremont, Mich., Apr. 30, 1916; s. Frank S. and Buryll L. (Preston) C.; B.S., Mich. State U., 1939; m. Emagene Rolyne Hendershot, July 9, 1942; children—Patricia Ann (Mrs. Dwain Arnett), James Lee, John Thomas. County rehab. supr. Farm Security Adminstrn., Dept. Agr., 1939- 43; housing mgmt. officer Fed. Pub. Housing Authority, 1946-47; community mgr. Pub. Housing Adminstrn., Willow Run, Mich., 1947-49, field rep., 1949-54, asst. regional dir., Washington, 1954-61, dir. regional office P.R. and Virgin Islands, 1962-63, dir. fiscal mgmt. br., 1963-66; dir. gen. mgmt. br. Housing Assistance Adminstrn., Dept. Housing and Urban Devel., Washington, 1966-68, dep. dir. tenant services div., 1968-70, asst. to asst. sec. of dept., 1970-71, dir. Office of Housing Programs Mgmt., 1971—; dir. elderly housing loan program Housing and Home Finance Agy., 1961-62. Dir. WCC Land Corp. Served with USNR, 1943- 45. Mem. Nat. Assn. Housing and Redevel. Ofcls. Club: Westwood Country (pres., gov.). Home: 911 Fairway Dr NE Vienna VA 22180 Office: Dept Housing and Urban Devel 7th and D SW Washington DC 20410

CAVANAUGH, ROBERT WILLIAM, internat. banker; b. Oil City, Pa., Jan. 27, 1914; s. Daniel Joseph and Clara Belle (Straub) C.; B.C.S. cum laude, U. Notre Dame, 1936; m. Ruth Virginia Paul, July 24, 1943; 1 son, Robert William. Chief field audit div. Fed. Deposit Ins. Corp., 1936-42; asst. exec. officer Office Alien Property Custodian, 1942-44; chief lend-lease fiscal operations Fgn. Econ. Adminstrn., 1944-45, Dept. State, 1945-46, Treasury Dept., 1946- 47; chief finance div. Internat. Bank Reconstrn. and Devel. 1947-59, treas., 1959-68, also treas. Internat. Finance Corp., Internat Devel. Assn.; chmn., chief exec. officer Chase Manhattan Trust Corp., Ltd., Nassau, Bahamas, 1969—. Treas. Eugene and Agnes E. Meyer Found., 1959-68. Decorated officer Order Leopold II (Belgium), 1947. Club: Notre Dame Alumni (chmn. bd. 1940) (Washington). Home: Sulgrave Manor PO Box 4903 Nassau, Bahamas. Office: PO Box 1543 Nassau Bahamas

CAVANAUGH, WARD ARTHUR, publishing co. exec.; b. Saratoga Springs, N.Y. Mar. 22, 1930; s. Jesse M. and Helen (Gray) C.; B.Mgmt. Engring., Rensselaer Poly. Inst., 1952; M.B.A., Wharton Sch., U. Pa., 1959; m. Elizabeth Louise Whalen, Sept. 21, 1957; children—Mark, Louise, Duncan. Staff indsl. engr. ALCOA, 1954-57; financial analyst Tex. Instruments, Inc., 1959-61; v.p. Schroder Rockefeller Co., Inc., 1961-67; v.p. finance Am. Greetings Corp., 1967- -. Served with AUS, 1952-54. Recipient N.Y. State Regents Vets. scholarship, 1957. Mem. Financial Execs. Inst. Clubs: Downtown Athletic (N.Y.C.); Wharton Graduate, Midday (Cleve.). Home: 7502 Samuel Lord Dr Chagrin Falls OH 44022 Office: 1500 American Rd Cleveland OH 44102

CAVE, ALFRED ALEXANDER, coll. dean; b. Albuquerque, N.M., Feb. 8, 1935; s. Robert L. and Jane (Harscher) C.; B.A., Linfield Coll., 1957; M.A., U. Fla., 1959, Ph.D., 1961; m. Harriett Bennett, Feb. 3, 1960; children—Ruth, Laurence, Elizabeth, Rachel. Instr. U. Fla., 1959-61, Coll. City N.Y., 1961-62; asst. prof. U. Utah, 1962-66, asso. prof., 1966-68, prof. history, 1968—, honors dir., 1965-67, asso. dean Coll. Letters and Sci., 1967-68, dean for humanities, 1968-70, dean Coll. Humanities, 1970—. Mem. Phi Beta Kappa. Democrat. Baptist. Club: Hidden Valley Country (Salt Lake City). Author: Jacksonian Democracy and the Historians, 1964; American Civilization: a Documentary History, 1966; An American Conservative in the Age of Jackson, 1969. Office: Univ Utah Salt Lake City UT 84112

CAVE, EDWIN FRENCH, orthopedic surgeon; b. Mexico, Mo., Sept. 30, 1896; s. Edwin S. and Margaret (French) C.; A.B., U. Mo., 1920; M.D., Harvard, 1924; m. Louise Fessenden, Dec. 9, 1933 (dec. 1966); children—Sally, Patricia (Mrs. Bullis); m. 2d, Joan Tozzer Lincoln, Sept. 26, 1970. Intern gen. surgery Mass. Gen. Hosp., Boston, 1924- 26, intern orthopedic surgery, 1926-28, vis. staff orthopedic surgery, 1928—, chief fracture clinic, 1947-57, cons. vis orthopedic surgeon, 1957-69, bd. consultation, 1969—; intern orthopedic surgery Children's Hosp., Boston, 1926-28; asst. clin. prof. orthopedic surgery Harvard, 1953-57; cons. orthopedic surgeon Faulkner Hosp., Boston, Mt. Auburn Hosp., Cambridge, Groton Community Hosp., Meml. Hosp., North Conway, N.H., Mass. Eye and Ear Infirmary, Boston, New Eng. Peabody Home for Crippled Children, Newton, Mass. (trustee); cons. orthopedics Surgeon Gen., U.S. Army; area cons. orthopedic surgery VA, New Eng. Served from maj. to col. M.C., AUS, 1942-46. Diplomate Am. Bd. Orthopedic Surgery (pres. 1958). Mem. Mass., Boylston med. socs., Am. (pres. 1961), Tex. (hon.), Australian (corr.) orthopaedic assns., Am. Acad. Orthopedic Surgeons, A.C.S. (2d v.p. 1958-59), Am. Assn. for Surgery of Trauma (bd. mgrs., pres. 1966-67), Aesculapian Club, Internat. Soc. Orthopedic Surgery and Traumatology, Boston, New Eng. surg. socs., A.M.A., Houston (hon.), Interurban orthopedic clubs. Clubs: Somerset, Harvard; Country (Brookline). Editor: Fractures and Other Injuries, 1958. Contbr. articles on injuries of knee, wrist, healing of fractures to profl. jours. Home: 340 Hammond St Chestnut Hill MA 02167 Office: 275 Charles St Boston MA 02114

CAVE, JOHN BARNHARDT, textile co. exec.; b. Salisbury, N.C., Aug. 9, 1919; s. J. Russell and Sarah E. (Barnhardt) C.; B.S., The Citadel, 1950; M.B.A., Harvard, 1955; m. Deborah Rugg, Nov. 12, 1955; children—Cynthia Barnhardt, Charles Russell, Elizabeth Rugg. With Burlington Industries, Inc., 1955—, treas., 1962-69, v.p., 1965, financial v.p., dir., 1969—; dir. INA Life Ins. Co. N.Y.; textile adv. bd. Chem. Bank N.Y. Trust Co. Mem. tech. consultants Bus. Council. Trustee Overlook Hosp., Summit, N.J., Com. for Econ. Devel. Club: University (N.Y.C.). Home: 113 Whittredge Rd Summit NJ 07901 Office: 1345 Av of Americas New York City NY 10019

CAVE, NILE EDWIN, bakery co. exec.; b. Redfield, Ia., Oct. 3, 1910; s. Glen and Cecil (Spillers) C.; B.A., Coe Coll., 1932; grad. Advanced Mgmt. Program Harvard, 1954; m. Mary Kathryn Holmes, July 1, 1938; 1 son, Terry. With Nat. Biscuit Co., N.Y.C., 1932—, v.p., 1957-62, sr. v.p., dir., 1962—, apptd. to exec. dept. Served with USNR, 1941-43. Home: 1011 Minisink Way Westfield NJ 07090 Office: 425 Park Av New York City NY 10022

CAVELL, STANLEY LOUIS, educator; b. Atlanta, Sept., 1926; s. Irving H. and Fannie (Segal) Goldstein; A.B., U. Cal. at Berkeley, 1947; postgrad. U. Cal. at Los Angeles, 1948-51; Ph.D., Harvard, 1961; m. Marcia Schmid, July 1955 Schmid, July 1955 (div. Jan. 1963); 1 dau., Rachel Lee; m. 2d, Cathleen Cohen, June 1967. Jr. fellow Soc. of Fellows, Harvard, 1953-56; asst. prof. philosophy U. Cal. at Berkeley, 1956-62; fellow Inst. Advanced Studies, Princeton, 1962-63; Walter M. Cabot prof. aesthetics and gen. theory of value Harvard, Cambridge, Mass., 1963—. Author: Must We Mean What We Say?, 1969; also , 1969; also articles. Home: Adams House Harvard U Cambridge, MA 02138.

CAVEN, HUBBARD SCOTT, sulphur co. exec.; b. Marshall, Tex., May 1, 1903; s. Thomas S. and Virginia (Conway) C.; LL.B., U. Tex., 1927; m. Mary I. Riddle, Jan. 2, 1935; children—Hubbard Scott II, Mary Gay. Admitted to Tex. bar, 1927; with firm Paddock, Massingill & Belew, Ft. Worth, 1927-29; partner firm Caven & Caven, Marshall, 1930-35, Abney & Caven, 1935-47; with Tex. Gulf Sulphur Co., Houston, 1947—, mgr. pub. relations, 1956-59, v.p., 1959-69, head Houston office, 1965-69, cons., 1969—. Mem. Tex. Ho. of Reps., 1931-34. Mem. Am., Tex. Houston bar assns., E. Tex., Houston chambers commerce, Tex. Research League (dir.), Tex. Mid-Continent Oil and Gas Assn. (dir.), Alpha Tau Omega. Clubs: Petroleum, River Oaks (Houston); Sky (N.Y.C.). Home: 2806 Scenic Dr Austin TX 78746 Office: 811 Rusk Av Houston TX 77002

CAVENAUGH, GEORGE KENNETH, ins. co. dir.; b. Benson, N.C., Jan. 13, 1905; s. George W. and Eunice (Betts) C.; A.B., U. N.C., 1928; m. Mary Anderson Oliver, Feb. 9, 1951; children—Adlai S., Sara A. (Mrs. W. Louis Bissette, Jr.). With Jefferson Standard Life Ins. Co., 1928-70, asst. mgr. mortgage loan dept., 1932-46, mgr., 1946-47, mgr. securities dept., 1947-51, v.p., treas., 1951-56, financial v.p., 1956-62, sr. v.p. financial operations, 1962-70, dir., 1959—; dir. Jefferson Pilot Corp., 1968—, v.p., treas., 1969-70. Former mem. bd. regents Life Officers Investment Seminar. Served to lt. col. Ordnance Corps, AUS, 1942-46. Mem. Phi Beta Kappa, Chi Psi. Presbyn. Clubs: Greensboro (N.C.) Country, Home: 2026 St Andrews Rd Greensboro NC 27405 Office: Jefferson Bldg Greensboro NC 27401

CAVENY, ELMER LEONARD, physician; b. Kings Mountain, N.C., May 26, 1907; s. Lebanus High and Lydia (Sarratt) C.; M.D., Emory U., 1930; m. Dorothy Franklin, June 4, 1930; 1 son, Leonard Hugh. Commd. lt. (j.g.) M.C. USN, 1930, advanced through grades to capt., 1945; specialist psychiatry, 1938—; postgrad. tng. psychiatry, Pa. Hosp. and Inst., Phila. Naval Hosp., 1938-41; head psychiatry br. Naval Sch. Aviation Medicine, 1944-47; psychoanalytic tng. Phila. Inst., 1947-52; chief neuropsychiat. center Naval Hosp., Phila., 1948-51; asst. prof. psychiatry Woman's Med. Coll., Phila., 1948- 51; head neuropsychiat. service Naval Med. Center, Bethesda, Md., 1951- 53; head neuropsychiatry br. Bur. Medicine and Surgery, Navy Dept., 1953- 54; clin. prof. psychiatry Georgetown U., 1953-54; prof. psychiatry U. Ala. Med. Coll., 1955—, chmn. dept., 1955-59. Diplomate Am. Bd. Psychiatry, Am. Bd. Preventive Medicine. Fellow Am. Psychiat. Assn., A.C.P.; mem. A.M.A., Group for Advancement Psychiatry, Am. Psychoanalytic Assn., Assn. So. Psychiat. Prof. (pres. 1958-59). Contbr. profl. articles. Address: 3516 Robin Dr Mountain Brook Birmingham AL 35223

CAVERLY, GARDNER A., found. exec.; b. Tuftonboro, N.H., Aug. 2, 1910; s. Arthur L. and Emma (Lamprey) C.; B.S., Northeastern U., 1934; postgrad. Harvard, 1938; m. 2d, Virginia Smith, Aug. 14, 1952; children—Martha, Jon Christian, Jefferson Smith, Nathaniel Eaton; children (by former marriage)—James R., Douglas G. With Bond & Goodwin Inc., Boston, 1935-38; pres. Sargent-Roundy Corp., Randolph, Vt., 1939-45; with Tucker Anthony & Co., N.Y.C., 1941-44; reorgn. mgr. Rutland R.R., 1949-50, trustee, dir., 1950-57, sr. v.p., 1951-54, pres., 1954-57; exec. v.p. New Eng. Council, Boston, 1957-66; pres. Crotched Mountain Found., Greenfield, N.H., 1967—. Chmn. N.H. Comprehensive Health Planning Council, 1968-71. Mem. corp. Northeastern U. Club: Harvard (Boston). Home: Bible Hill Rd Bennington NH 03442 also Crotched Mountain Found Greenfield NH 03047

CAVERLY, ROBERT JAMES, corp. exec.; b. Mpls., Sept. 28, 1918; s. Raymond Nathaniel and Rene Marie (Stacy) C.; B.B.A., Lehigh U., 1941; M.B.A. Harvard, 1943; m. Jane Srill, Sept. 13, 1945; children—Robert James, Lynn Patricia, Kathleen Ann. Supt. dist. research Gen. Foods Corp., 1946-47; asst. to v.p. Hilton Hotels, 1947-52; treas. Hilton Hotels Internat., 1949-52, v.p., 1952-61, exec. v.p., 1961-64; gen. mgr. Caribe Hilton Hotel, 1952-54; asst. v.p. Hilton Hotels Corp., 1954-56, v.p., 1956-60, exec. v.p., dir., 1961-67; chmn. bd., chief exec. officer Sky Chefs, Inc. subsidiary Am. Airlines, N.Y.C., 1967-; dir. Foodco, Inc. Served as maj., exec. officer with Air Transport Command, AUS, 1943-45. Mem. Am. Hotel Assn., Cath. Hosp. Assn. Am. (bd. cons.), Delta Upsilon, Pi Delta Epsilon. Clubs: Baltusrol Golf (Short Hills, N.J.); Berwind Country (Pio Piedras, P.R.); Marco Polo (gov.), Harvard (N.Y.C.); Caesarea Golf (Israel). Home: 12 E 86th St New York City NY 10028 Office: 605 3d Av New York City NY 10016

CAVERS, DAVID FARQUHAR, educator; b. Buffalo, Sept. 3, 1902; s. William Watt and Elizabeth Mitchell (Farquhar) C.; B.S., U. Pa., 1923; LL.B., Harvard, 1926; J.S.D., Suffolk U., 1957; LL.D., Chuo U., Tokyo, Japan, 1964; m. Leile Yeaman, Sept. 8, 1931; 1 son, David Farquhar. Admitted to N.Y. bar, 1928, Mass. bar, 1958; with a N.Y. City law firm, 1926-29; instr. Harvard, 1929-30; asst. prof. W.Va. U. Coll. of Law, 1930-31; asst. prof. Duke U. Sch. of Law, 1931-32, prof. law, 1932-45; prof. Harvard Law Sch. 1945—, Fessenden prof. law, 1952-69, emeritus, 1969—, asso. dean 1951-58; pres. Walter E. Meyer Research Inst. Law, 1958-69; pres. Council Law-Related Studies, 1969 —; vice-chmn. bd. trustees Center for Law and Social Policy, 1970—; fellow Center for Advanced Study in the Behavioral Scis., 1958-59; vis. prof. law Yale U. Sch. of Law, 1936- 37, U. Chgo. Law School, 1940-41; lectr. Hague Acad. Internat. Law, 1970; editor Law and Contemporary Problems, 1933-45; asst. gen. counsel OPA, Washington, 1943-45, asso. gen. counsel, 1945-46; legal adviser U.S. Dept. Agr. in drafting food and drug bills, 1933-34; spl. asst. to U.S. Atty. Gen., 1938. Mem. research adv. bd., Com. for Econ. Devel., 1943-51; mem. Commn. for Revision N.C. Law of Estates, 1935-36; exec. com. Assn. Am. Law Schs., 1967-68. Mem. Am. Acad. of Arts and Scis., Phi Beta Kappa, Delta Upsilon, Beta Gamma Sigma. Clubs: Century (N.Y.C.). Author: (with J.R. Nelson) Electric Power Regulation in Latin America, 1959; The Choice-of-Law Process, 1965. Contbr. articles to jours. Home: 21 Buckingham St Cambridge MA 02138

CAVERT, HENRY MEAD, educator; b. Mpls., Mar. 30, 1922; s. William Lane and Mary (Mead) C.; B.S. in Agrl. Biochemistry, U. Minn., 1942, M.D., 1951, Ph.D. in Physiology, 1952; m. June Lorraine Sederstrom, Jan. 27, 1946; children—John Mead, Harlan McCrea, Winston Peter. Postdoctoral research fellow Am. Heart. Assn., 1951-54; faculty U. Minn. Med. Sch., 1953- -; prof. physiology, 1967—, asso. dean, 1964—. Vis. prof. Nat. Heart Inst.; spl. research fellow biochemistry U. Edinburgh (Scotland), 1961- 62; established investigator Am. Heart Assn., 1954-57; mem. program project com. B, Nat. Heart Inst., 1966-69; cons. Nat. Heart and Lung Inst., 1969—. Mem. bd. parish edn. Am. Luth. Ch., 1958—; mem. met. bd. Mpls. YMCA, 1968-70; bd. mgmt. U. Minn. YMCA, 1955—, chmn., 1968-69. Trustee Minn. Med. Found., 1958—, chmn. scholarship and loan com., 1960-68. Served to capt. USAAF, 1943-46; CBI. Mem. Assn. Am. Med. Colls. (chmn. com. student aspects internat. med. edn. 1967-68, mem. steering com. group on student affairs 1967-68, mem. com. internat. relations med. edn. 1968—), Am. Physiol. Soc., A.M.A., Sigma Xi, Phi Lambda Upsilon, Alpha Omega Alpha, Gamma Sigma Delta. Author: (with A.J. Carlson and V. Johnson) Machinery of the Body, 5th edit., 1961; also numerous articles. Home: 3328 48th Av S Minneapolis MN 55406

CAVERT, SAMUEL MCCREA, clergyman, ch. exec.; b. Charlton, N.Y., Sept. 9, 1888; s. Walter I. and Elizabeth (Brann) C.; B.A., Union Coll., 1910, D.D., 1935; M.A., Columbia, 1914; B.D., Union Theol. Sem., 1915; D.D., Lawrence Coll., 1928; LL.D., Ohio Wesleyan U., 1942; D.D., Yale, 1948, Princeton, 1951, Kalamazoo Coll., 1956; Th.D., U. Göttingen, 1948; L.H.D., Am. U., 1951; Litt.D., Park Coll., 1952; m. Ruth Miller, Nov. 14, 1918 (dec. Feb. 1920); 1 dau., Mary Ruth (Mrs. Harold A. Ramsey); m. 2d, Ruth Twila Lytton, June 28, 1927. Sec., student YMCA, 1910-12, also instr. Greek, Union Coll.; ordained Presbyn. ministry, 1915; asst. systematic theology Union Theol. Sem., 1915-16; fellow Union Theol. sem., Orient, 1916-17; asst. sec. Gen. War-Time Commn. Chs., 1917-18; 1st lt., chaplain U.S. Army, 1918-19; sec. Com. on War and Religious Outlook, 1919-20; asso. sec. Fed. Council Chs. Christ in Am., 1920, gen. sec., 1921-50; gen. sec. Nat. Council Chs. Christ in U.S.A. 1951-54; exec. sec. World Council Chs., 1954-57; William Henry Hoover lectr. Christian Unity, 1958; del. World Conf. of Chs., Jerusalem, 1928, Oxford, Edinburgh, 1937, Utrecht, 1938, Lund, 1952, New Delhi, 1961, Geneva, 1966, Uppsala, 1968. Chmn., Com. on Arrangements for First Assembly of World Council, Amsterdam, Holland, 1948; Protestant liaison ofcl. between German chs. and Am. Mil. Govt. authorities, U.S. Zone Occupation, 1946. Vice chmn. bd. dirs. Union Theol. Sem., 1948-66; trustee Union Coll., hon. chancellor, 1945. Mem. Pres. Roosevelt's Adv. Com. for Polit. Refugees; chmn. com. on ch. center UN, 1963-65; trustee Christian Century Found.; exec. dir. Interch. Center, N.Y.C., 1963-64. Member Phi Beta Kappa, Kappa Alpha. Democrat. Clubs: Century (N.Y.C.); Siwanoy Country (Bronxville, New York). Author: Securing Christian Leaders for Tomorrow, 1926; The Adventure of the Church, 1927; On the Road to Christian Unity, 1961; The American Churches in the Ecumenical Movement: 1900-1968, 1968; Church Cooperation and Unity in America, 1970; (part author or editor) The Church and Industrial Reconstruction, 1920; Christian Unity: Its Principles and Possibilities, 1921; The Teaching Work of the Church, 1923; (with Henry P. Van Dusen) The Church Through Half a Century, 1936. Chmn. adv. bd. Religious Book Club, 1958-68; editorial bd. Religion in Life (quar.); sr. editor Pulpit Digest, 1958-68. Home: 161 Boulder Trail Bronxville NY 10708

CAVERT, WATLER DUDLEY, clergyman; b. Charlton, N.Y., Jan. 18, 1891; s. Walter I. and Elizabeth (Brann) C.; grad. Charlton Acad., 1907; A.B., Union Coll., Schenectady, 1911, D.D., 1931; B.D., Union Theol. Sem., N.Y.C., 1915; m. Harriet Harrer, July 17, 1916; children—Elizabeth Harrer (Mrs. Howard C. Adams), Harriet Morrison (Mrs. Clyde H. McDaniel, Jr.). Ordained ministry Presbyn. Ch., 1915; asst. pastor 1st Congl. Ch., Willimantic, Conn. 1915-16; pastor Stamford, N.Y., 1916-20, North Presbyn. Ch., Elmira, N.Y., 1921-24, Grace Presbyn. Church, Oswego, N.Y., 1925-36, The Presbyn. Ch. (union of Grace and First churches), Oswego, N.Y., 1936-39; supt. of Christian edn. for Synod of N.Y. 1939- 57; vis. prof. of Christian edn., McCormick Theol. Sem., 1957-58, St. Paul's United Theol. Coll., Kenya, 1969; pastor, North Church, Syracuse, 1959-66; dir. pub. relations Charlton Sch., N.Y., 1967—. Moderator Synod N.Y., 1956-57; vice moderator U.P. Gen. Assembly, 1961-62; pres. Syracuse Area Council of Chs., 1961-62. Chaplain, 1st lt. AUS, 1918; chaplain, capt., 390 Inf., O.R.C., resigned. Bd. dirs., N.Y. State Council of Chs. and Religious Edn.; bd. dirs. Charlton Sch., N.Y. del. Presbyn. Gen. Assembly, 1929, 1935; internat. exchange preacher Eng., summer 1934. Mem. Phi Beta Kappa. Republican. Author: Story Sermons from Literature and Art, 1939; Remember Now, 1944; With Jesus on the Scout Trail, 1951; Ours in the Faith, 1960; Prayers for Youth, 1962; Prayers for Scouts, 1964 ; In the Days of Thy Youth, 1971. Contbr. articles to religious mags. Home: 846 Maryland Av Syracuse NY 13210

CAVES, RICHARD EARL, educator, economist; b. Akron, O., Nov. 1, 1931; s. Earl Leroy and Verna Louise (Jobes) C.; A.B., Oberlin Coll., 1953; M.A., Harvard, 1956, Ph.D. (Wells prize 1958), 1958. Asst. prof., asso. prof. econs. U. Cal. at Berkeley, 1957-62; prof. econs. Harvard, 1962—, chmn. dept. econs., 1966-69. Cons. Council Econ.

Advisers, 1961; dep. to spl. asst. to Pres. U.S. for fgn. trade policy, 1961; cons. Treasury Dept., 1961-62, Bur. Budget, 1963-64; mem. White House Task Force on Fgn. Econ. Policy. Recipient Henderson prize Harvard Law Sch., 1967. Ford Found. fellow, 1959-60. Fellow Am. Acad. Arts and Scis.; mem. Am. Econ. Assn. Author: (with R.H. Holton) The Canadian Economy: Prospect and Retrospect, 1959; Trade and Economic Structure, 1960; Air Transport and Its Regulators, 1962; American Industry: Structure, Conduct, Performance, 1964; (with J.S. Bain, J. Margolis) Northern California's Water Industry, 1966; (with others) Britain's Economic Prospects, 1968; (with G.L. Reuber) Capital Transfers and Economic Policy: Canada, 1951-62, 1971; (with R.W. Jones) International Economics, 1972. Contbr. numerous articles to profl. jours. Home: 38 Fernald Dr Cambridge MA 02138

CAVETT, DICK, entertainer; b. Gibbon, Neb., 1937; grad. Yale; m. Carrie Nye. Formerly author comedy lines for TV, then night club performer; host TV show This Morning, until 1969, The Dick Carvett Show, 1969—. Address: care ABC-TV 1330 Av Americas New York City NY 10019*

CAVIER, WILFRED FRANKLYN, electronics co. exec.; b. Sacramento, Cal., May 9, 1911; s. Adolph Gustave and Grace (Dolan) C.; A.B., U. Cal. at Berkeley, 1933; m. Mary Louise Oliver Morgan, Jan. 18, 1941; stepchildren—Edward Charles, Paul Joseph. Accountant, Nat. Ice & Cold Storage Co., San Francisco, 1937-42; with Hewlett-Packard Co., Palo Alto, Cal., 1942—, v.p. finance, 1954-63, v.p., sec., 1963—, also dir., mem. exec. com.; dir., sec.-treas. Palo Alto Engring. Co., 1951-60. Mem. Santa Clara County Mgmt. Study Com., 1964—. Mem. United Republican Finance Com., 1955-66. Bd. dirs. Family Service Assn. Palo Alto, 1955-58, Santa Clara County Taxpayers Assn., 1965—; bd. dirs. Western Electronics Ednl. Fund, 1962-64, chmn., 1964; bd. dirs. Palo Alto YMCA, 1954-56, treas., 1955-56. Mem. Am. Soc. Corporate Secs., Palo Alto C. of C. (bd. dirs. 1955-58), Tau Kappa Epsilon. Club: Menlo Country (Woodside, Cal.). Home: 240 Golden Oak Dr Portola Valley CA 94025 Office: 1501 Page Mill Rd Palo Alto CA 94304

CAVNESS, JACK CHARLEBOIS, lawyer; b. Los Angeles, July 30, 1920; s. Henry Cleburne and Blanche (Charlebois) C.; LL.B., U. Ariz., 1943; m. Lucy Kathryn Cannon, Sept. 22, 1943; children-Marc C., Clay C., Cleve, Kathleen (Mrs. Timothy Jsmes Hughes), Gregory G., John, Laura. Admitted to Ariz. bar, 1944; practiced in Phoenix, 1946—; asso. Cavness, DeRose & Senner, 1962—; spl. asst. atty. gen. Ariz., 1952. Served with USNR, 1943-46. Mem. Am., Ariz., Maricopa County (past dir.) bar assns., Am. Trial Lawyers Assn., Nat. Assn. Def. Lawyers in Criminal Cases. Home: 2627 N 20th Av Phoenix AZ 85009 Office: Luhrs Bldg Phoenix AZ 85003

CAWLEY, EDWARD PHILIP, physician, educator; b. Jackson, Mich., Sept. 1, 1912; s. Michael and Gertrude (Klein) C.; A.B., U. Mich., 1936, M.D., 1940; m. Virginia Anne Cohen, June 17, 1939; children—Janet Anne, Philip Edward. Intern Mercy Hosp., Jackson, 1940-42; teaching fellow, instr. dermatology and syphilology Med. Sch., U. Mich., 1945-48, asst. prof., 1948-51; prof., chmn. dept. dermatology and syphilology Sch. Medicine, U. Va., Charlottesville, 1951—; practice medicine specializing in dermatology and syphilology, Charlottesville, 1951—; investigative and research work in skin diseases, fungus diseases, cancer of skin and dermatopathology. Served from 1st lt. to maj., M.C., AUS, 1942-45. Decorated Bronze Star. Diplomate American Bd. Dermatology (pres., dir.). Fellow A.C.P.; mem. Assn. Profs. Dermatology (pres.), Am. Dermatol. Assn. (dir.), A.M.A., Va., Albemarle County med. socs., Am. Acad. Dermatology (pres.), Soc. for Investigative Dermatology, Chgo. Dermatology Soc., Balt.-Washington, Southeastern dermatol. socs., So. Med. Assn., Sigma Xi, Alpha Omega Alpha. Roman Catholic. Club: Farmington Country (Charlottesville). Contbr. articles to med. jours. Home: Rugby Circle Charlottesville VA 22903 Office: U of Va Hosp Charlottesville VA 22904

CAWLEY, FRANCIS RIGGS, assn. exec.; b. Ottumwa, Ia., May 13, 1911; s. Lawrence Edmund and Mabel Lee (Riggs) C.; Ph.B. in B.A. magna cum laude, U. Notre Dame, 1933; J.D., Georgetown U., 1937; budget adminstrn., Am. U., 1936; m. Ruth Katheryn Nelson, Oct. 12, 1940; children—Mary Helen, Thomas Michael, Marjorie Anne. Admitted to D.C., Supreme Ct. bars; clk. NRA, 1933-36; chief budget, purchase and travel sect. Rural Electrification Adminstrn., 1936-37, budget officer, 1938- 39; budget officer U.S. Housing Authority, 1939-40; chief budget and planning br. OPM, 1941; budget officer, chief mgmt. services br. WPB, 1942, budget officer, dir. div. budget adminstrn., 1943-45; budget officer, dir. office of budget and mgmt. Dept. Commerce, 1945-52; v.p. Mag. Pubs. Assn., 1952-63; exec. dir. Lithographers and Printers Nat. Assn., 1963-64, Label Mfrs. Assn., Inc., 1964—. Washington cons. Agrl. Pubs. Assn.; acting budget officer ECA, 1948; former mem. faculty Syracuse, Georgetown, Fla. State univs. Recipient Outstanding Service award Fed. Govt., Am. Assn. for Pub. Information Edn. Research award. Fellow Soc. for Advancement Mgmt.; mem. Phi Alpha Delta. Democrat. Roman Catholic. Home: 2830 Brook Dr Falls Church VA 22042 Office: Wilson Plaza Bldg 2425 Wilson Blvd Arlington VA 22201

CAWLEY, ROBERT RALSTON, educator, author; b. Canasaraga, N.Y., July 18, 1893; s. Frank Edward and Sarah Haseltine (Brown) C.; A.B., Harvard, 1914, A.M. (honors), 1915, Ph.D., 1921; postgrad. (Harvard traveling fellow) univs. of London, Berlin, Paris, 1921-22; m. Elizabeth Hoon, Sept. 18, 1937; 1 dau., Margaret Elizabeth. Tchr. French, German, Spanish, Thacher Sch., Ojai, Calif., 1915-18; instr. French, German, Spanish, Mass. Inst. Tech., 1919-20; instr. English, Princeton, 1922-25, asst. prof. 1925-27, asso. prof. 1927-44, prof., 1944; acting chmn. dept., 1948-49, 1951-52. Distinguished prof. City U. N.Y., 1963. Pres., London Scholars' Group of Am. U. Union. Served as 2d lt. Q.M. Res. Corps. AUS, 1918. Mem. Modern Lang. Assn. Am. (chmn. English sect. I, chmn. adv. bd. 1947, chmn. Milton group 1948, adv. bd. 1949-51), Am. Assn. U. Profs., Alpha Phi Sigma (Harvard). Presbyn. (elder). Club: Princeton (Phila.). Editor: Truth of Our Times (Henry Peacham), 1942. Author: The Voyagers and Elizabethan Drama, 1938; Unpathed Waters; Studies in the Influence of the Voyagers on Elizabethan Literature, 1940; Milton's Literary Craftsmanship, 1941; Milton and the Literature of Travel, 1951; A Brief History of the First Presbyterian Church of Princeton, 1954; (with George Yost, Jr.) Studies in Sir Thomas Browne, 1965; (with Arthur Link), The First Presbyterian Church of Princeton: Two Centuries of History, 1967; Henry Peacham: His Contribution to English Poetry, 1971. Contbr. articles to Am., fgn. jours. Home: 228 The Western Way Princeton NJ 08540 ☆

CAWS, PETER JAMES, educator; b. Southall, Eng., May 25, 1931; s. Geoffrey Tulloh and Olive (Budden) C.; B.S., U. London, 1952; M.A., Yale, 1954, Ph.D., 1956; m. Mary Ann Rorison, June 2, 1956; children—Hilary, Matthew. Came to U.S., 1953. Instr. natural sci. Mich. State U., 1956-57; asst. prof. philosophy U. Kan., 1957-60, asso. prof., 1960-62, chmn. dept., 1961-62, Rose Morgan vis. prof., 1963; exec. asso. Carnegie Corp. N.Y., 1962-65, cons., 1965-67; prof. philosophy Hunter Coll., N.Y.C., 1965—, chmn. dept., 1965-67; exec. officer Ph.D. program in philosophy City U. N.Y., 1967-70; tchr. New Sch. Social Research, 1965-67; cons. Random House, 1966—; mem. adv. bd. Learning Corp. of Am., 1968—. Mem. Council Philos. Studies, 1965—; bd. dirs. Coordinating Council of Lit. Mags., 1969-70; mem. Scientists Inst. for Pub. Information, 1967—, treas., 1969—. Mem. NRC, 1967-70. Fellow A.A.A.S. (v.p. 1967); mem. Am. Philos. Assn., Philosophy of Sci. Assn. (del.), Soc. For Gen. Systems Research (pres. 1966-67), Mind Assn., Assn. for Symbolic Logic. Clubs: Elizabethan, Yale. Author: The Philosophy of Science, Systematic Account, 1965; Science and the Theory of Value, 1967. Home: 140 E 81st St New York City NY 10028

CAWTHON, WILLIAM CONNELL, former utility exec.; b. Roxton, Tex., Sept. 1, 1922; s. William Arthur and Lura (Denton) C.; B.Mech. Engring., Cornell U., 1944; M.S. in Mech. Engring., U. Tex., 1947; M.Automotive Engring., Chrysler Inst., 1949; m. Flora Keith Campbell, May 31, 1947; children—William Connell, Clark Campbell, Flora Keith. With Chrysler Corp., 1947-62, dir. purchasing, 1959-62; v.p. mfg. Am. Radiator & Standard San. Corp., N.Y.C., 1962-66; dir. world-wide indsl. engring. and mfg. Internat. Tel. & Tel. Corp., N.Y.C., 1966-68, v.p., 1967-68; exec. v.p. Weatherhead Co., Cleve., 1968-70. Served to lt. comdr. USNR, World War II, 1951-53; PTO. Recipient Distinguished Engring. Grad. award U. Tex., 1961. Mem. Am. Ordnance Assn., Phi Kappa Sigma, Kappa Kappa Psi, Phi Theta Kappa. Mem. Ch. of Christ. Club: Cornell of N.Y. (N.Y.C.). Home: 2156 Aurora Rd Hudson OH 44236 300 E 131st St Cleveland OH 44108

CAWTHORNE, DELMAS RICHARD, former bank exec.; b. Glamorgan, Va., Feb. 25, 1907; s. Richard I. and L. Evelyn (Allen) C.; A.B., Georgetown Coll., 1929; M.A., Ohio State U., 1931, Ph.D., 1940; m. Marie H. Gorman, Sept. 24, 1929. Faculty, Miami U., Oxford, O., 1930-42, 46-50, 63-67, prof. econs., 1935-42, 46-50, dean Sch. Bus. Adminstrn., 1963-67; v.p., sr. economist Fed. Res. Bank, Kansas City, 1950-51, 52-63, 67-70; dir. First Citizens Bank, Oxford, Cin. br. Fed. Res. Bank Cleve. Mem. adv. com. Butler County Com. Indsl. Devel., 1963-67. Served to lt. col. USAAF, 1942-46, USAF, 1951-52. Mem. Am. Econ. Assn., Am. Finance Assn., Beta Gamma Sigma, Delta Sigma Pi. Co-author: Money and Banking, 2d edit., 1949; Essays on Commercial Banking, 1963. Home: 11097 Frontier Dr Sun City AZ 85351

CAYCE, ELDRED A., bus. exec.; b. Nashville, July 30, 1900; s. Matthew C. and Susan Thomas (Smith) C.; LL.B., U. Mo. at Kansas City, 1935; m. Amanda Thomasson, Dec. 26, 1923; children—Amanda Ruth (Mrs. Mansel W. Lane), Martha Susan (Mrs. Winfred L. Golden). Admitted to Mo. bar, 1936; pres. A. & E. Co., investments, St. Louis; dir. Ralston Purina Co., St. Louis, Vocational Counseling and Rehab. Service, Inc., St. Louis. Mem. St. Louis Mchts. Exchange (past pres.). Bd. dirs., v.p. Bethesda Dilworth Home, Bethesda Townhouse, Bethesda Gen. Hosp.; regional chmn. Abilene Christian Coll. Design for Devel. Program, Abilene, Tex.; pres., bd. dirs. Wallace Found., Little Rock. Mem. Mo. Bar Assn., Tenn. Soc. St. Louis (past pres.). Mem. Ch. of Christ. Clubs: University, Old Warson Country. Home: 43 Middlesex Dr Brentwood MO 63144 Office: 5100 Oakland Av St Louis MO 63110

CAYCE, KENNETH ODIN, Jr., retail hardware co. exec.; b. Hopkinsville, Ky., Oct. 7, 1920; s. Kenneth Odin and Katherine Rabold (Quarles) C.; student Emory Coll., 1939; A.B., Vanderbilt U., 1942; m. Dorothy E. Kunsman, Nov. 7, 1945; children—Kenneth Odin III, Mary Caroline. With Cayce-Yost Co., Inc., Hopkinsville, 1946—, pres., gen. mgr., 1963—; dir. Cotter & Co., Chgo., First-City Bank & Trust Co., Hopkinsville. Pres. Ky. Retail Hardware Assn., 1951-52, Nat. Retail Hardware Assn., 1963-64, Hopkinsville-Christian County C. of C., 1952; mem. Ky. Econ. Adv. Commn., 1964. Served to lt. (s.g.) USNR, 1942-46. Mem. Ky. Retail Fedn. (v.p. 1967—). Home: Circle Dr Hopkinsville KY 42240 Office: 1000 S Main St Hopkinsville KY 42240

CAYNE, BERNARD STANLEY, editor; b. N.Y.C., Nov. 8, 1924; student Cornell U., 1940-42; B.S., Moravian Coll., 1945; postgrad. U. Pa., 1945-46, (research fellow) Harvard, 1953-55; M.A., Columbia, 1947; m. Helen M. Burgard, Apr. 11, 1953; children—Claudia Elizabeth, Douglas Andrew. Head sci. dept. Adelphi Acad., 1946-47; instr. Bklyn. Coll., 1947-49; tchr. N.Y.C. pub. schs., 1948-49; head sci. sect. test devel. dept. Ednl. Testing Service, Princeton, N.J., 1949-53; dir. research Boston U. Coll. Basic Studies, 1953-54; sr. sci. editor Ginn & Co., Boston, 1955-61; v.p. Crowell-Collier Ednl. Corp., N.Y.C., 1961-68, exec. editor Collier's Ency., 1963-68, Collier's Ency. Yearbook, 1963-68, editor-in-chief Merit Students Ency., 1961-69, asst. editorial dir. corp., 1963-68; mng. editor, sch. div. Macmillan Co., 1968-69; editor-in-chief Ecny. Americana, N.Y.C., 1969—. A.A.A.S.; mem. Am Ednl. Research Assn., Phi Delta Kappa. Chmn. bd. editors Harvard Edn. Rev., 1954. Home: 134 Douglas Rd Chappaqua NY 10514 Office: 575 Lexington Av New York City NY 10022

CAZENAVE, RENE, newspaper editor; b. San Francisco, Dec. 25, 1906; s. Louis and Celine (Marion) C.; ed. pub. schs., San Francisco; m. Evelyn Varni, Apr. 5, 1930; children—Rene, Denise (Mrs. Walter Baccala). With San Francisco News Call Bull., and predecessor, 1924—, news editor, 1946-54, asst. mng. editor, 1954-62, mng. editor, 1962-65; mng. editor San Francisco Examiner, 1965—, Pulitzer Prize Awards juror, 1969-70. Chmn. San Mateo County Democratic Com., 1945. Bd. dirs. Hanna Boys Center, Sonoma, Cal. Mem. Assn. Catholic Newsmen (past pres.), A.P. News Execs. Council (past chmn.), Sigma Delta Chi (bd. dirs. N. Cal. chpt.). Elk. Club: Press (pres.) (San Francisco). Home: 1918 White Oak Way San Carlos CA 94070 Office: 110 5th St San Francisco CA 94119

CEAUSESCU, NICOLAE, Rumanian politician; b. Scornicesti-olt, Jan. 26, 1918; state diploma econs. Acad. Econ. Studies, Bucharest; m. Elena Ceausescu; children—Valentin, Elena, Nicolae. Participant working revolutionary movement, 1932-; mem. Union Communist Youth, 1933— (sec. 1944-45), Romanian Communist party, 1933—; alternate mem. central Com. Romanian Communist party, 1945-48, mem. 1948, sec., 1954-55. 1st sec., 1965, sec.- gen., 1965—, mem. polit. bur., 1955; mem. exec. com., standing pres., 1965—; dep. minister agr., 1948-50, armed forces, 1950-54; pres. Council of State Socialist Republic of Rumania, 1967—, Nat. Council of Front Socialist Unity, 1968—. Named Hero of Socialist Labour, 1964; Hero Socialist Republic Romania, 1971. Address: Central Com of Rumanian Communist Party Bucharest Rumania

CECCHETTI, GIOVANNI, author, educator; b. Pescia, Italy, July 12, 1922; s. Agostino and Adorna (Fattorini) C.; Liceo Machiavelli, U. Lucca, 1939-40; Liceo Michelangiolo, Universita de Firenze, Florence, Italy, 1939-41, Maturita classica, 1941-46, Lit.D., 1947; m. Ruth Elizabeth Schwabacher, Dec. 27, 1953; children-Stephen G., Margaret F. Came to U.S., 1948, naturalized, 1954. Lectr. to asst. prof. U. Cal. at Berkeley, 1948-57; asso. prof., prof. Tulane U., 1957-65; prof. Stanford, 1965-69, charge Italian program, 1965-69; prof., chmn. dept. Italian, U Cal. at Los Angeles, 1969—; cons. U. Colo., U. Ia., 1957. Served with Italian Liberation Army, 1943-45. Decorated Star of Solidarity Italian Govt., Knight Republic of Italy. Mem. Modern Lang. Assn. Am., Am. Assn. Tchrs. Italian, Dante Soc. Am., Leonardo Da Vinci Soc., Il Cenacolo. Author: La poesia del Pascoli, 1954; The She-Wolf and other stories, 1958; Leopardi e Verga, 1962; Diario nomade, 1967; Il Verga maggiore, 1968. contbr. essays and poems to European and Am. jours. Home: 1191 Lachman Lane Pacific Palisades CA 90272 Office: Dept Italian U Cal Los Angeles CA 90024

CECERE, ADA RASARIO, artist; b. N.Y.C., Feb. 24, 1895; d. Stanislaus and Rosa (Lupi) Rasario; student N.A.D., Art Students League, Beaux Arts Inst., N.Y.; m. Gaetano Cecere, Jan. 8, 1924. Portrait and mural painter; tchr.; designer 24 foot sand carved glass decoration for S.S. Pres. Jackson, U.S. Line. Recipient Margaret Fuller prize, oils Nat. Assn. Women Artists, 1946; J. Droege prize, water color, 1948; Newcastle prize, 1960; S. Karasick, oils, 1951; Champman prize, lithograph, 1952; Am. Color Works award Am. Artists Profl. League, 1952; Solo Exhbn. award, Pen and Brush Club, 1951, 62, 1st prize water color, 1952; Knickerbocker Artists oil prize, 1957; M. Tucker prize Nat. Assn. Women Artists, 1958, Lewellyn prize, oil, 1961, Anonymous prize, water color, 1968; E. Reilly Meml. prize Allied Artists America, 1958, M. Cantarella prize, 1967; award for oil Fairleigh-Dickinson U., 1963. Mem. Knickerbocker Artists, Nat. Assn. Women Artists (medal honor 1955, Elizabeth Morse Genius prize 1967, Mabel Hudson Meml. prize 1964), Am. Watercolor Soc., Audubon Artists, Allied Artists of Am., Archtl. League of N.Y., Pen and Brush (Stauffer Meml. prize 1967). Home: 240 Waverly Pl New York City NY 10014 Studio: 41 Union Sq New York City NY 10003

CECERE, GAETANO, sculptor; b. N.Y.C., Nov. 26, 1894; s. Ralph and Catherine (La Rocca) C.; student N.A.D. and Beaux Arts Inst. of Design, N.Y. City; fellow Am. Acad. in Rome, 1920-23; m. Ada Rasario, 1924. Dir. sculpture dept., Beaux Arts Inst. Design; mem. faculty Mary Washington Coll., Fredericksburg, Va., faculty School of Fine Arts, Nat. Acad.; one man show Mary Washington Coll., 1963. Served in AEF, 1916-18. Prin. works include medals, war memls., pediment groups, portrait monuments, etc. Recipient numerous awards including $1,000 Lincoln Meml. prize, Milw., 1933; Am. Acad. in Rome Collaborative medal; hon. mention Art Inst. Chgo., 1927; Medal of Honor, Knickerbcker Artists; Sculpture Award, Allied Artists Am., Audubon Artists, Inc., Frost Sculpture Prize. Audubon Artists, 1957; sculpture prize Knickerbocker Artists, 1963; award in sculpture Nat. Arts Club, 1968; sculpture award Audubon Artists, 1969; Therese Richard meml. award Allied Artists Am., 1970. National Academician; mem. Nat. Sculpture Soc., N.Y. Archtl. League. Home: 240 Waverly Pl New York City NY 10014 Studio: 41 Union Sq New York City NY 10003 ☆

CECIL, EDWARD CHRISTIAN DAVID GASCOYNE, author; b. London, Eng., Apr. 9, 1902; s. 4th Marquess of Salisbury and Lady Alice (Gore) Gascoyne-Cecil; grad. Christ Church, Oxford U.; Litt. D., University of Leeds, 1950, University of London, 1957, University Glasgow, 1962; LL.D., University Liverpool, 1951, U. St. Andrews, 1951; m. Rachel MacCarthy, 1932; children—Jonathan, Hugh, Laura. Fellow, Wadham Coll., Oxford U., 1924-30; fellow New Coll., Oxford U., 1939—, Goldsmiths prof. English lit., 1948—; Rede lectr. Cambridge U., 1955. Trustee Nat. Portrait Gallery, 1937-51. Recipient Hawthornden prize, 1930, James Tait Black prize, 1930, medal Royal Soc. Lit., 1930; created Companion of Honour, 1949. Mem. Poetry Soc. (pres. 1947-48). Author: The Stricken Deer, 1929; Sir Walter Scott, 1933; Early Victorian Novelists, 1934; Jane Austen, 1935; The Young Melbourne, 1939; Hardy, The Novelist, 1943; Two Quiet Lives, 1948; Poets and Story-Tellers, 1949; Lord M., 1954; The Fine Art of Reading, 1957; Max, 1964; Asking Price, 1966; Child Divided, 1966; Brothers in Law; Portrait of a Judge. Address: 7 Linton Rd Oxford England also Red Lion House Cranborne Wimborne Dorset England

CECIL, JOHN LAMONT, business exec., lawyer; b. Fredricktown, Ky., May 15, 1909; s. Robert Logan and Dorthea Bovard (Griffith) C.; student St. Charles Jr. Coll., 1930, Cath. U. Am., 1930; LL.B., Georgetown U., 1935, LL.M., 1937; m. Helen Madigan Breen, Sept. 21, 1954; children—Patricia M., Elaina M. (Mrs. John W. Coyne), Anita J. (Mrs. William D. O'Donovan), Barbara L., John Lamont. Controller, Hamilton Hotel, Washington, 1934-35; admitted to D.C. bar, 1935, Md. bar, 1962; supr. property mgmt. office of counsel F.H. Smith Bondholders Protective Com., Washington, 1935-36; asst. counsel Fed. Deposit Ins. Corp., Washington, 1936-42, counsel, 1946-53, asst. gen. counsel, 1953-62; v.p., sec. Western Bancorp., Los Angeles, 1962-64, exec. v.p., sec., 1964—; v.p., asst. sec. United Cal. Bank Internat.; mem. staff Alien Property Custodian, Washington, 1941-42. Served to comdr. USNR, 1942-46; capt. Res. Recipient John Carroll Alumni award Georgetown U., 1969. Mem. D.C., Fed. bar assns., Navy League, Am. Soc. Corporate Secs., Gamma Eta Gamma. Roman Catholic. K.C. (4). Clubs: Congressional Country, Army and Navy (Washington); Los Angeles Athletic, Stock Exchange, Newman (pres. Los Angeles 1969), Jonathan (Los Angeles). Home: 435 S Lorraine Blvd Los Angeles CA 90005 Office: 600 S Spring St Los Angeles CA 90054

CECIL, LESTER LEFEVRE, judge; b. Miami County, O., Nov. 21, 1893; s. Harry E. and Edna (Furrow) C.; LL.B., U. Mich., 1917; LL.D., Ohio No. U., 1956; m. Celia Carroll, Oct. 18, 1921; children—Nancy (Mrs. Albert Albrecht), Thomas, Martha (Mrs. William Stauffer), David. Admitted to Ohio bar, 1917; atty. E.H. and W.B. Turner, 1917-21; city pros. atty., Dayton, 1922-25, judge Municipal Ct., 1926-29, Common Pleas Ct., Montgomery County, O., 1929-53; U.S. Dist. Ct., So. Dist. Ohio, 1953- 59; judge U.S. Ct. Appeals 6th Circuit, Dayton, 1959-62, chief judge, 1962-63, sr. judge, 1965—. Served with U.S. Army, 1918. Mem. Am., Ohio, Dayton bar assns. Republican. Methodist. Mason (33). Home: 531 Belmont Park N Dayton OH 45405 Office: Fed Bldg Dayton OH 45402

CECIL LORD EDWARD CHRISTIAN DAVID GASCOYNE. see Cecil Edward Christian David Gascoyne

CEDARBAUM, BERNARD, lawyer; b. New Haven, Sept. 1, 1928; s. William and Elsie (Schuster) C.; A.B., Yale, 1950, LL.M., 1956; LL.B., Harvard, 1953; m. Miriam Rachel Goldman, Aug. 25, 1957; children—Daniel Goldman, Jonathan Goldman. Admitted to Conn. bar, 1953, N.Y. bar, 1960; practice in Washington, 1956-59, N.Y.C., 1959—; atty. Dept. Justice, 1956-59; asso. Carter, Ledyard & Milburn, 1959-65, mem. firm, 1965—. Served with AUS, 1953-55. Mem. Am., N.Y. State bar assns., Assn. Bar City N.Y. Club: Town (Scarsdale). Home: 125 Brewster Rd Scarsdale NY 10583 Office: 2 Wall St New York City NY 10005

CEDARQUIST, WAYLAND BERGER, lawyer; b. Denver, Sept. 22 1916; s. Berger E. and Ruth M. C.; B.A. summa cum laude, U. Ill., 1938; LL.B., Harvard, 1941; m. Lois K. O'Brien, Apr. 24, 1943; children—Christin A., Karen A., Katherine. Admitted to Ill. bar, 1941, also U.S. Supreme Ct. bar; practice in Chgo., 1941—; partner firm Boodell, Sears, Foster, Sugrue & Crowley, 1956—. Mem. Ill. Com. for Constl. Revision, 1947-63; gen. counsel Com. Modern Cts. in Ill., 1962-63. Mem. Lake Forest High Sch. Bd., 1961-65. Mem. Am. (chmn. standing com. unauthorized practice law 1963—), Ill., Chgo. bar assns., Phi Beta Kappa. Episcopalian (vestry). Contbr. articles to law revs. Editor Unauthorized Practice News, 1958—. Home: 135 S Maywood Rd Lake Forest IL 60045 Office: 33 N LaSalle St Chicago IL 60602

CEDERBERG, ELFORD ALFRED, congressman; b. Bay City, Mich., Mar. 6, 1918; s. Alvin and Helen (Olson) C.; student Bay City Jr. Coll., 1935-37; children—Tommy, Marilyn. Mgr., Nelson Mfg. Co., Bay City, Mich., 1946-52; mem. 83d-92d Congresses, 10th Mich. Dist., mem. appropriations com. Mayor, Bay City, 1949-53. Served as maj., inf. AUS,, 1941-45. Decorated Bronze Star medal. Mem. Am. Legion, V.F.W. Republican. Mem. Evang. Ch. Mason (33), Elk, Odd Fellow, Lion. Home: 1915 Marsac St Bay City MI 48706 Office: House Office Bldg Washington DC 20515

CEDERQUIST, DENA CAROLINE, educator; b. Madrid, Ia., Aug. 29, 1910; d. Clarence John and Clara (Bork) Cederquist; B.S., Ia. State Coll., 1931, M.S., 1935; Ph.D., U. Wis., 1945. Asst. Dietitian Monmouth Meml. Hosp., Long Branch, N.J., 1932- 33; instr. Kan. State Coll., Manhattan, 1937-41, U. Wis., 1941-42; with Mich. State U., 1944—, asst. prof., asso. prof., 1944-56, prof., head dept. foods and nutrition, 1956—. Mem. Am. Dietetic Assn., Am. Chem. Soc., Am. Home Econ. Assn., Sigma Xi, Omicron Nu, Phi Kappa Phi, Sigma Delta Epsilon. Home: 545 University Dr East Lansing MI 48823

CEDRONE, LOUIS ROBERT, Jr., journalist; b. Balt., June 25, 1923; s. Louis and Lucia (Mazzola) C.; B.S., U. Md., 1951; m. Nancy Nelson, Sept. 11, 1954; children—Linda, David. With Balt. Eve. Sun, 1951—, drama-TV-film critic, 1963—; corr. Variety, 1957—. Swimming instr. A.R.C., 1961—. Served with inf. AUS, 1943-45. Decorated Purple Heart with oak leaf cluster, Bronze Star. Mem. Sigma Nu, Omicron Delta Kappa, Pi Delta Epsilon. Home: 9 Muirfield Ct Lutherville, MD 21093. Office: Balt Eve Sun Calvert and Centre St Baltimore MD 21203

CEFOLA, MICHAEL, educator, chemist; b. Barile, Italy, Oct. 22, 1908; s. Arcangelo and Vincenza (Labella) C.; came to U.S., 1919, naturalized, 1924; B.S., Coll. City N.Y., 1933; Ph.D., N.Y.U., 1941; m. Alice Elizabeth Robertiello, Aug. 14, 1948; 1 son, Michael A. Research asso. U. Chgo. Manhattan Project, 1942-44, Mass. Inst. Tech. Radiation Lab., 1944-45; microchemist Socony Vacuum Oil Co., N.Y.C., 1945-47; nuclear chemist G.E. Knolls Atomic Power Lab., Schenectady, N.Y., 1947-50; prof. chemistry Fordham U., 1950—. Fellow N.Y. Acad. Scis.; mem. Am. Chem. Soc., Am. Microchem. Soc. (hon. past chmn.), New Eng. Assn. Chemistry Tchrs., Sigma Xi, Phi Lambda Upsilon. With Dr. G.T. Seaborg first isolated plutonium at U. Chgo.; patentee on purification of plutonium. Contbr. articles profl. jours. Home: 179 Bell Rd Scarsdale NY 10583 Office: Fordham Univ New York City NY 10458

CEHANOVSKY, GEORGE, baritone; b. St. Petersburg, Russia, Apr. 14, 1892; s. Vincent P. and Sophie (Burago) C.; student St. Petersburg Naval Acad., 1912-16; pupil of Sophie Cehanovska at St. Petersburg Conservatory, 1918-22; m. Elisabeth Rethberg Saettler, June 23, 1956. Came to U.S., 1922, naturalized, 1929. Mem. De Feo Opera Co., Balt., 1923-24, San Carlo Opera Co., N.Y.C., other cities, 1924-25, Met. Opera Co., 1926—, San Francisco Opera Co., 1936-56; recording artist for RCA Victor, Columbia records. Served to lt. Russian Navy, 1912-17. Home: Route 1 Box 92 Yorktown Heights NY 10598

CEITHAML, JOSEPH JAMES, educator; b. Chgo., May 23, 1916; s. Joseph F. and Bessie (Nolc) C.; B.S., U. Chgo., 1937, Ph.D. 1941; m. Ann J. Bednarik, May 9, 1942; children—Lenore Ann, Eric Lee. Prof. biochemistry, dean students biol. scis. U. Chgo., 1942-48, 49—; Gosney fellow biology Cal. Inst. Tech., 1948. Research malaria project OSRD, World War II. Mem. A.A.A.S., Am. Soc. Biol. Chemists, Assn. Am. Med. Colls. (nat. chmn. group student affairs 1966-69). Home: 2337 W 108th Pl Chicago IL 60643

CELEBREZZE, ANTHONY J., judge; b. Anzi, Italy, Sept. 4, 1910; s. Rocco and Dorothy (Marcoguiseppe) C.; student John Carroll U.; LL.B., Ohio No. U., 1936; D.D., Wilberforce U., 1955; LL.D., Fenn Coll., 1962, Boston Coll., 1963, La Salle Coll., 1963, Ohio No. U., 1963; Pd.D., R.I. Coll., 1964; Dr. Humane Letters, Miami U., 1965; m. Anne Marco, May 7, 1938; children—Anthony J., Jean Ann, Susan Marie. Admitted to O. bar, 1938, engaged in practice of law. Senator, Ohio State Legislature, 1952- 53; mayor of Cleve., 1953-62; sec. Dept. Health, Edn. and Welfare, 1962- 65; mem. 6th Circuit Court of Appeals, 1965—. Mem. President's Adv. Commn. on Intergovtl. Relations, 1959—. Served as seaman USN, World War II. Brotherhood award Nat. Conf. Christians and Jews, 1955, Nat. Human relations award, 1962; Order of Merit of the Republic of Italy, 1955; citation United Negro Coll. Fund, 1956; Nat. Fiorello LaGuardia award, 1961, Nat. Catholic Resettlement Council award, 1962, Pub. Service award YMCA, 1962, Gulick award Camp Fire Girls, Inc., 1962, Peter Canisius medal Canisius Coll., 1963, gold medallion City of Rome, 1963; Eleanor Roosevelt Humanities award, 1965. Mem. Am. Municipal Assn. (pres. 1958-59, distinguished service award 1960), Order of Merit. Home: 17825 Lake Rd Lakewood OH 44107 Office: Fed Bldg Cleveland OH 44114

CELIANO, ALFRED VINCENT, educator; b. Orange, N.J., Aug. 8, 1928; s. Alfred John and Theresa (DeSesa) C.; A.B., Seton Hall U., 1949; S.T.L., Catholic U. Am., 1953; M.S., Fordham U., 1957, Ph.D., 1959. Ordained priest Roman Cath. Ch., 1953; instr. Seton Hall U., South Orange, N.J., 1953-54, asst. prof., 1959-62, asso. prof., 1962-67, prof. chemistry, 1967—; hon. research fellow Univ. Coll., London, 1970—. Vice pres. Tamara Enterprises; sec. DeSesa Engring. Co. Fellow A.A.A.S.; mem. Am. Chem. Soc. (councillor N.J. sect. 1966—, chmn. phys. chemistry topical group N.J. sect. 1969- 70), N.Y. Acad. Scis., Am. Assn. U. Profs., Sigma Xi, Phi Lambda Upsilon. Address: Seton Hall U South Orange NJ 07079

CELLA, FRANCIS RAYMOND, economist; b. Harrison, N.J., July 16, 1909; s. Frank L. and Kathryn (Hanlon) C.; A.B., Wesleyan Coll., 1933; A.M., U. Ky., 1937; m. Mildred Russell, Dec. 11, 1944; 1 son, Charles Ronald. Statistician Ky. Agrl. Expt. Sta., 1935-37; research dir. Ky. Unemployment Compensation Commn., 1937-42; dir. bur. bus. research, prof. econs. U. Okla., 1946-68; dir. research Bus. Research, Inc., 1968—, prof. bus. statistics, 1946—, economist Washita Valley Improvement Assn., 1953-56; cons. USAF, 1954-56; mgmt. research cons. Okla. Restaurant Assn., 1966—. Faculty Co-ordinator Com. for Econ. Devel., 1951-57; mem. Gov.'s Council Coal Industry, 1964—; mem. Gov's Gen. Adv. Com., 1964-66; pres. Assn. Univ. Burs. Bus. and Econ. Research, 1962-64. Served as capt. USAAF, 1942-46, lt. col. USAF Res. ret. Mem. Am. Statis. Assn., Operations Research Soc. Am., Inst. for Mgmt. Scis., Econometric Soc., S.W. Social Sci. Assn., S.W. Shippers Assn., Beta Gamma Sigma. Episcopalian. Author brochures, articles. Editor: Okla. Bus. Bull., 1946-68. Home: 719 Hoover St Norman, OK 73069.

CELLARIUS, CHARLES FREDERICK, former architect; b. Dayton, O., July 28, 1891; s. Herman Frederick and Sallie Ellen (Kinder) C.; B.A., Yale, 1913; B.S. in Arch., Mass. Inst. Tech., 1916; L.H.D., Miami U., 1959; m. Madolin Serodino, July 1, 1922 (dec. 1931); m. 2d, Mary Donovan Curtis, Feb. 4, 1950 (dec. 1963). Began practice as architect, Cin., 1921; partner Cellarius & Hilmer. Supervising architect model town Mariemont, O.; cons. architect or architect Miami U., Berea Coll., Coll. of Wooster, W.Va. U., Western Coll. for Women; architect numerous chs., comml. bldgs. including Union Central Life Ins. Bldg., Cin. Served as 2d lt. inf. U.S. Army, 1918-19. Fellow A.I.A.; mem. Ch. Archtl. Guild Am., Phi Beta Kappa, Beta Theta Pi. Methodist. Mason (K.T., Shriner). Clubs: Torch, Literary, University (Cin.); Yale, Technical. Home: 3522 Principio Av Cincinnati OH 45226

CELLER, EMANUEL, congressman; b. Bklyn., May 6, 1888; s. Henry H. and Josephine (Müller) C.; A.B., Columbia, 1910, L.L.B., 1912; LL.D., Yeshiva U., 1971; m. Stella B. Baar, June 30, 1914; children—Jane B. (Mrs. Sydney B. Wertheimer), Judith C. (dec.). Practiced in N.Y.C., 1912—; mem. Weisman, Celler, Allan, Spett & Seinberg; organizer Bklyn. Nat. Bank; dir. Fischbach & Moore, Inc., Oppenheimer Fund; mem. 68th 91st Congresses, 10th N.Y. dist., author: Fed. Register Act, Fgn. Trade Zone Act, India Immigration and Naturalization Act, Celler-Kefauver Anit-Merger Act, Celler Civil Rights Acts of 1957, 60, others. Mem. com. platforms and resolutions Democratic Nat. Conv. 1944, 48, 52, 56, 60; del. N.Y. State Dem. convs. Hon. bd. dirs. Jewish Family Welfare Soc.; bd. dirs. Brookdale Hosp., Bklyn.; Mogen David; trustee Oscar Strauss Meml. Fund, Jewish Nat. Found. Chmn., Am. Red Mogen David; mem. Am. Jewish Com., Am. Jewish Congress; pres. Am. Shield of Israel. Recipient award and medallion of chevalier, commendature Order Merit Republic of Italy. Mem. Am. (state com. sect. jud. adminstrn.), County, Bklyn. bar assns., Columbia Alumni Assn. (N.Y.C.). K.P.; mem. B'nai B'rith. Club: Unity (Bklyn). Author: (autobiography) You Never Leave Brooklyn. Home: 9 Prospect Park West Brooklyn NY 11215 Office: 1501 Broadway New York City NY 10036

CELLI, VITTORIO, educator, physicist; b. Parma, Italy, Aug. 13, 1936; s. Franco and Carolina (Bertazzoli) C.; Dr. Physics, U. Pavia, Italy, 1959; m. Eija Iris Urpalainen, July 6, 1963; 1 son, Carlo. Came to U.S., 1966. Research asso. U. Ill., Urbana, 1959-61, asst. prof., 1961-62; asst. research physicist U. Cal. of San Diego, La Jolla, 1962-64; lectr. U. Bologna, Italy, 1964-66; asso. prof. U. Va., Charlottesville, 1966-69, prof. physics, 1969—. Mem. Am., Italian phys. socs. Home: 210 Magnolia Dr Charlottesville VA 22901

CELLISE, SISTER MARY YVONNE, hosp. exec.; b. Bay City, Mich., Aug. 21, 1934; d. Levi Joseph and Regina (Savage) Gellise; B.S. in Accounting, U. Detroit, 1960; M.Hosp. Adminstrn., St. Louis U., 1965. Jr. accountant Tripp & Laine, C.P.A.'s, Bay City, Mich., 1952-55; joined Sister of Mercy, 1955; bus. gr. Mercy Med. Center, Dubuque, Ia., 1960-63; adminstrv. resident Providence Hosp., Seattle, 1964-65; adminstr. Villa Elizabeth, Grand Rapids, Mich., 1965-67; asso. adminstr. St. Joseph Mercy Hosp., Clinton, Ia., 1967-68; adminstr. St. Joseph Mercy Hosp., Ann Arbor, Mich., 1968—; lectr. hosp. adminstrn. Sch. Pub. Health, U. Mich., 1969—. Pres. bd. trustees St. Joseph Mercy Hosp. of Detroit. Named Boss of Year, Arbor Charter chpt. Am. Bus. Women's Assn., 1969. Mem. Hosp. Financial Mgmt. Assn., Am. Coll. Hosp. Adminstrs. Address: 326 N Ingalls Ann Arbor MI 48104

CENTER, ALLEN HARRY, mfg. co. exec.; b. Quincy, Ill., Oct. 17, 1912; s. Charles Dewey and Louise (Pecinovsky) C.; B.A., Knox Coll., 1933; m. Nancy Creighton Stirton, Apr. 23, 1948; children—Douglas Allen, Dean Montgomery, Laurie Ellen. With editorial dept. N.Y. Times, 1933-36; asst. advt. mgr. Am. Chicle Co., 1936-46; dir. pub. relations Parker Pen Co., 1946-52; with Motorola, Inc., Franklin Park, Ill., 1952-59, v.p. pub. relations, 1961—; v.p. pub. relations Leo Burnett Co., 1959-60. Served with USAAF, 1943-46. Mem. Pub. Relations Soc. Am. (dir., past pres. Chgo.). Clubs: Overseas Press (N.Y.C.); Press, University (Chgo.); Glen View (Ill.) Country. Author: (with Scott Cutlip) Effective Public Relations, 4th edit., 1970; Public Relations Ideas in Action, 1957. Home: 600 Sheridan Rd Winnetka IL 60093 Office: 9401 W Grand Av Franklin Park IL 60131

CENTER, CHARLES CONVERSE, educator; b. Quincy, Ill., Oct. 11, 1910; s. Charles Dewey and Louise Christine (Pecinovsky) C.; B.S., Knox Coll., 1922; M.A., U. Wis., 1938, Ph.D., 1940; m. Elizabeth H. Smart, Nov. 27, 1931; children—Dick Dewey, Karen (Mrs. Michael McGrath), Don Allen, Charles Gale, John David. Mem. faculty Quincy (Ill.) Sr. High Sch., 1932-37, Sch. Bus., U. Mo., 1940-41; dir. Bureau Labor Statistics, N.Y.C., 1942-46; mem. faculty Sch. Bus., U. Wis., Madison, 1946—, prof. bus.-ins., 1949—. Dir. Am. Pub. Life Ins. Co., Nat. Guardian Life Ins. Co.; cons. State Farm Cos., 1963—. Pres. Madison Rotary Club and Found., 1962-63. Bd. dirs. Dane County Cancer Soc., Four Lakes council Boy Scouts Am., Dane County Givers Fund, Huebner Found. at U. Pa. Mem. Am. Risk and Ins. Assn. (pres. 1962-63), Am. Soc. Sci. Mgmt. (hon. 1959—), U. Wis. Faculty Assn. (pres. 1951—), Beta Theta Pi, Delta Sigma Pi. Republican. Mason (32), Rotarian (dist. gov. 1971-72). Editor McGraw-Hill Ins. series, 1958-59). Home: 3518 Blackhawk Dr Madison WI 53705

CEPEDA, ORLANDO, first baseman with Atlanta Braves Profl. Baseball Team; b. Ponce, P.R., Sept. 17, 1937; m. Ana Hilda Pino Valazguez, Dec. 4, 1960. Named Nat. League Rookie Player of Yr. Sporting News, 1958; Nat. League Rookie Yr. Baseball Writers' Assn., 1958; named 1st baseman Sporting News All-Star Maj. League Team, 1959; 1st baseman Sporting News' Nat. League All-Star Team, 1961-62. Address: care Atlanta Stadium Atlanta GA 30312*

CERAM, C. W., see Marck, Kurt W.

CERF, JAY HENRY, found. exec., polit. scientist; b. Chgo., May 17, 1923; s. Nathan Randolph and Blanche (Ruth) C.; B.A. (Residence Halls fellow), U. Wis., 1948, M.A., 1951; postgrad. Heidelberg U. 1949; M.A., Yale, 1952, Ph.D. (Block fellow, Cowles fellow, Falk fellow), 1957; postgrad. (Fulbright fellow), Free U., Berlin, 1953-54, (Penfield fellow) U. Pa., 1956; m. Carol Montgomery McGovern, June 12, 1951; children—Jay Randolph, Christopher David, William Montgomery. Research analyst U.S. Govt., 1949-51; teaching asst. Yale, 1952-53; guest lectr. Russian Reseach Center, Harvard, 1955; legislative asst. U.S. Ho. of Reps., U.S. Senate, 1955-56; dir. Fgn. Policy Clearing House, 1957-61; spl. asst. to sec. commerce, 1961; sec. Pres. Kennedy's Cabinet Trade Policy Com., 1961-62; dep. asst. sec. commerce for internat. affairs, 1962; mgr. internat. group U.S. C. of C., 1962-69, sec. U.S.-Can. com. 1962-63, U.S.- Mexico com., 1962-66, fgn. policy com., 1962-64, fgn. commerce com., 1962-64; sec. U.S. Mgmt. Adv. Com. to OECD, 1962-64; sec. ann. U.S. delegation Japan-U.S. Bus. Leader Confs. Keidanren of Japan and U.S. C. of C., 1962-67; exec. dir. Pathfinder Fund, 1969—. Cons. on population policy Harvard, 1970—. Trustee Internat. Devel. Conf., U.S. Council Internat. C. of C.; bd. advisers Council of Latin Am., India Cultural Center; bd. dirs. Fed. Union, Interlandia Corp., Roadstead Found. Served with USNR, 1943-46. Am. Polit. Sci. Assn. Congl. fellow, 1955-56. Mem. UN Assn. (dir.), Washington Inst. Fgn. Affairs, Am. Polit. Sci. Assn., Soc. for Internat. Devel. Episcopalian. Clubs: Yale, National Press, Federal City, Harvard Faculty. Author: The Intellectual Bases of Nazism, 1951; History of the Free University, 1954; Political Indoctrination of Students in East Germany, 1957; The Alliance for Progress-A Hemispheric Response to a Global Threat, 1965. Editor: Strategy for the '60's, 1961. Contbr. article to N.Y. Times mag. Home: 245 Brattle St Cambridge MA 02183 Office: 850 Boylston St Chestnut Hill MA 02167

CERF, WALTER, educator; b. Leipzig, Germany, May 14, 1907; s. Hermann and Hertha (Cerf) Heymann; Dr.phil., U. Bonn, 1933; Ph.D., Princeton, 1941. Came to U.S., 1936, naturalized, 1943. Instr. Princeton 1945-46; asst. prof. U. Minn., 1946-47; asst. prof. Bklyn. Coll., 1947-52, asso. prof., 1952-57; prof. philosophy City U. N.Y., 1958—; vis. prof. U. Wis., 1965-66. Served with AUS, 1943-45. Mem. Am. Assn. Univ. Profs., Mind, Am. Philos. Assn., Am. Phenomenol. Soc. Author: Existential Interpretation of Sensitivity, 1933; Kant's Analytic of the Beautiful, 1963. Mem. editorial bd. of Philosophy and Phenomenol. Research, 1963—. Contbr. articles profl. jours. Home: RD 2 Brandon VT 05733 Office: Brooklyn Coll Brooklyn NY 11210

CERMAK, JACK EDWARD, educator, engr.; b. Hastings, Colo., Sept. 8, 1922; s. Joseph and Helen (Herman) C.; B.S., Colo. State U., 1947, M.S., 1948; Ph.D., Cornell U., 1959; NATO postdoctoral fellow, Cambridge (Eng.) U., 1961-62; m. Helen Jane Carlson, Dec. 17, 1949; children—Douglas Karl, Jonathan Joel. Mem. faculty Colo. State U., 1948—, prof. charge fluid mechanics program, 1960—, chmn. engring. sci., 1963—, pres., dir. Research Found., 1965—; vis. lectr. U. Tex., Cambridge U., U. Hokkaido; cons. in field. Mem. bd. mems. Univ. Corp. Atmospheric Research, 1966-67; pres., chmn. 10th Midwestern Mechanics Conf., 1966-67; mem. Nat. Air Pollution Control Adminstrn. Air Pollution Research Grants Adv. Commn., 1970—; dir. summer inst. fluid mechanics NSF, 1963, 65, 68; co-chmn. U.S.-Japan Seminar Lab. Simulation of Stratified Shear Flows. Mem. Am. Soc. Engring. Edn. (chmn. mechanics div.), Nat. Acad. Engring. (mem. com. natural disasters), Am. Inst. Aeros. and Astronautics, Am. Meteorol. Soc., Am. Geophys. Union, Brit. Hydromechanics Research Assn., Am. Soc. C.E., Am. Soc. M.E., A.A.A.S., Air Pollution Control Assn., Sigma Xi. Contbr. articles profl. jours. Mem. editorial adv. bd. Inst. Aerodynamics Abstracts. Home: 407 E Prospect St Fort Collins CO 80521

CERNAN, EUGENE A., astronaut; b. Chgo., Mar. 14, 1934; s. Andrew G. Cernan; B.S. in Elec. Engring., Purdue U., 1956; postgrad. U.S. Naval Postgrad. Sch.; m. Barbara Jean Atchley; 1 dau., Teresa Dawn. Joined USN, 1956, advanced through grades to lt.; former mem. attack squadrons 126, 113, Miramar (Cal.) Naval Air Sta.; now astronaut with Manned Spacecraft Center, NASA. Mem. Tau Beta Pi. Address: care Manned Spacecraft Center NASA Houston TX 77058*

CERNICA, JOHN N., educator, civil engr.; b. Romania, May 14, 1932; s. John and Mary (Ignat) C.; came to U.S., 1947, naturalized, 1950; B.S., Youngstown U., 1954; M.S., Carnegie Inst. Tech., 1955, Ph.D. (NSF grantee), 1957; m. Mary Patricia Marinelli, July 25, 1959; children—Mary Kathleen, Mary Judith, Mary Alice, Mary Johanna, Mary Patricia. Asst. prof. civil engring. Youngstown U., 1957-58, asso. prof., 1958- 61, prof., 1961—, acting head dept., 1957, head dept., 1958—; prin. asso., co-owner Cernica-Fok & Assos., cons. engrs., Youngstown, 1958—; owner John N. Cernica, Cons. Engrs. Examiner, Ohio Bd. Registration Profl. Engrs. and Surveyors. Recipient Distinguished Engrs. award State of Ohio, 1964. Registered profl. engr., Ohio, Pa., Ind., Md., N.Y., W.Va., Ky. Mem. Am. Soc. Engring. Edn., Am. Soc. C.E., Am. Concrete Inst., Nat., Ohio, Mahoning Valley socs. profl. engrs., Sigma Xi, Sigma Tau, Phi Kappa Phi, Sigma Phi Epsilon. Author: Reinforced Concrete Fundamentals, 1964: Strength of Materials, 1966. Contbr. articles to profl. jours. Home: 611 Plymouth Dr Youngstown OH 44512

CERNICK, CLIFFORD, govt. ofcl.; b. Cle Elum, Wash., July 14, 1918; s. Frank and Alma (Radosevich) C.: B.A., U. Wash., 1949; m. Patricia Hervey, Feb. 4, 1956; children—Nancy Ann, Clifford. Mng. editor Anchorage Daily News, 1950-58: corr. United Press, 1950-58; corr. N.Y. Times, 1952—; editor Fairbanks Daily News Miner, 1958-62; corr. A.P., 1958-62; pub. affairs officer FAA, Los Angeles, 1962-68, chief employee information div., Washington, starting 1968, now pub. affairs officer Northwest Region, Seattle. Served t/sgt., AUS, 1942-45. Club: Alaska Press (pres. 1953-54, chmn. 1954-56) (Anchorage). Home: 9500 Rainier Av S Seattle WA 98118 Office: 800 Independence Av S W Washington DC 20003

CERNIK, ZDENEK, ambassador, permanent rep. Czechoslovak Socialist Republic to UN. Address: 1109-111 Madison Av New York City NY 10028*

CERNY, ROBERT GEORGE, architect, educator; b. LaCrosse, Wis., June 11, 1908; s. George J. and Helen P. (Salverson) C.; B. Arch., U. Minn., 1932; M.Arch., Harvard, 1933; m. Vivian M. Boucher, Aug. 21, 1934; children—Robert Leon, Susan Mari. Asso. architect TVA, 1934-36; faculty architecture U. Minn.; partner Jones & Cerny, 1937-42, Thorshov & Cerny, architects, Mpls., 1942-60; pres. Cerny Assos., Inc., architects, engrs., planners, Mpls., 1960—. Mem. Mpls. Inst. Arts, Walker Art Center, Downtown Council Mpls. (pres. 1966-67, dir.), Nat. Conf. Christians and Jews; pres. Constrn. Industry Found., 1969—; bd. dirs. St. Mary's Jr. Coll., Mpls., Interfaith Housing Corp. Nelson Robinson, Jr. travelling fellow (Harvard) 1934. Fellow A.I.A. (pres. Mpls. chpt. 1964-65); mem. C. of C., Minn. Soc. Architects, Am. Assn. U. Profs., Am. Hosp. Assn., Soc. Am. Mil. Engrs., Liturgical Arts Soc., U. Minn. Alumni Assn. (dir.). Clubs: Harvard (Mpls.); Campus, Faculty and Alumni (U. Minn.); Minneapolis; Wayzata Country; Town and Country. Contbr. designs, bldgs. to archtl. mags. Home: Linwood Bay Box 291 Route 3 Excelsior MN 55331 Office: First Nat Concourse Bldg Minneapolis MN 55402

CERRONE, WARREN EDWARD, ednl. adminstr., former air force officer; b. N.Y.C., Oct. 5, 1921; s. Edward Joseph and Cecelia (Gardner) C.; student Iona Coll., N.Y., 1947-51; B.S., U. Md., 1958; M.B.A., George Washington U., 1958; m. Barbara Jane Bishop, Sept. 21, 1946; children—Deborah Jane, Lesley Ann. Commd. 2d lt. Air Corps Res., U.S. Army, 1942, advanced through grades to col. USAF, 1967; dep. asst. chief staff 4th Allied Tactical Air Force, NATO, 1961-64; prof. aerospace studies U. Detroit, 1964-68; chief res., guard studies Air War Coll., 1968-70, chief dept. mil. capabilities and employment, 1970-71; asst. dean U. Detroit Coll. Engring. 1971—. Decorated Legion of Merit with oak leaf cluster, D.F.C. with 2 oak leaf clusters, Air medal with 6 oak leaf clusters; Croix de Guerre with silver star (France). Mem. Air Force Assn., Air Force Hist. Found. Club: George Washington University (charter mem.) Home: 294 Linden Rd Birmingham MI 48009 Office: U Detroit 4001 McNichols Rd Detroit MI 48221

CERVAN, ROBERT BRUCE, agrl. and food marketing co. exec.; b. Buffalo, Dec. 18, 1907; s. John Simpson and Bertha (Conrad) C.; ed. pub. schs.; m. Roberta Mickler, Apr. 30, 1932; children—Marion Marcy (Mrs. Leslie Tarr), Robert Dennis. Account exec. Agrl. Advt. & Research, Inc., Ithaca, N.Y., 1934-38; mgr. information service Coop. GLF Exchange Inc., Ithaca, 1938-47, dir. pub. relations, 1949-58, sec., 1958-64; gen. mgr. Rural Radio Network, Newark, 1947-49; sec. Agway Inc., Syracuse, N.Y., 1964-66, v.p. planning, sec., 1966—; dir. Lincoln Nat. Bank & Trust Co., Syracuse, N.Y., Texas City Refining Co., Taterstate Frozen Foods, Am. Agriculturist, Inc., Ithaca. Bd. dirs. Greater Syracuse C. of C., 1965- -, Nat. Far-City Com., 1954—. Mem. exec. bd. Louis Afassiz Fuertes council Boy Scouts Am., 1950—; chmn. Ithaca United Fund drive, 1956. Bd. dirs. Tompkins County Hosp. Assn., Ithaca, 1949-52. Episcopalian (dir.

Found. Diocese Central N.Y.). Club: Century (Syracuse). Home: Bittersweet and Leverett Lane Fayetteville, NY 13066. Office: Box 1333 Syracuse NY 13201

CERVANTES, ALFONSO J., mayor; b. St. Louis, Aug. 27, 1920; ed. St. Louis U. Pres., Cervantes and Assos., gen. ins., St. Louis; mem. St. Louis City Council, 15th ward, 1949-63, pres. bd. aldermen, 1959-63; mayor St. Louis, 1965—. Founder, St. Louis Ambassadors (domestic and fgn. trade promotion orgn., sponsor cultural activities St. Louis), St. Louis Bus. Devel. Commn.; pres. Mo. Municipal League. Named Outstanding Man of Year, St. Louis Jr. C. of C., 1955, also Met. St. Louis C. of C.; recipient numerous citations human rights orgns. local, nat. Mem. Young Presidents Orgn. (past. nat. treas., nat. bd. dirs.). Democrat. Office: City Hall St Louis MO 63103

CERVENKA, ARTHUR FRANK, aircraft co. exec.; b. Bohemia, N.Y., July 8, 1917; s. Frank and Mary (Bernard) C.; B.S. in Mech. Engring., Columbia, 1941; m. Gladys E. Hunt, July 9, 1944. With Grumman Aerospace Corp., Bethpage, N.Y., 1941—, mgr. equipment and process engring., 1959-63, dir. facilities, 1963-65, staff eng. mfg. mgmt., 1965—, mem. corporate operation staff, 1968-69, mem. pres.'s staff, 1969—. Life mem. Am. Soc. Tool and Mfg. Engrs., 1951—, chmn. chpt. 88, 1953-54, chmn. nat. constn. and bylaws com., 1957-60, field editor monthly pub., 1957-69, nat. sec., 1961-62, dir., 1961-69, treas., 1962-63, 4th v.p., 1963-64, 2d v.p., 1965-66, pres., 1967-68, award merit, 1959; Recipient certificate Am. Soc. M.E., 1964. Registered profl. engr., N.Y. Fellow Instn. Prodn. Engrs. London (life); mem. Am. Soc. Quality Control (regional councilor, automotive div. 1970—), Am. Standards Assn. (chmn. com. 25 1956-63), Aerospace Industries Assn. (past co. rep., past chmn. mfg. equipment com.), N.Y. State, Nat. socs. profl. engrs., Columbia Coll. (life), Columbia Engring. Sch. (life) alumni assns., Dowling Coll. Library (hon. charter mem.), Theta Tau. Republican. Home: 435 Vanderbilt Blvd Oakdale NY 11769 Office: Grumman Aerospace Corp Bethpage NY 11714

CESAR, sculptor; b. Marseille, France, Jan. 1, 1921; s. Omer and Lelia (Magnani) Baldaccini; student Beaux-Arts de Marseille, 1935, de Paris, 1943. Exhbns. include Venis Biennial, 1956, expns. Rive Droite Gallery, Paris, 1956, Anvers Biennial, 1957, Creuzevault Gallery, Paris, 1957, Saõ Paulo Biennial, 1957, Hanover Gallery, London, 1957, Biennale de Carrara, Italy, 1957, Internationale du Bronzetto à Padoue, 1957, Biennale d'Anvers, Belgium, 1958, de Bruexelles Pavillon français, 1958. Faculty, Ecole Nationale Supérieure des Beaux Arts Paris. Recipient Prix de la participation étrangère à la Biennale de Carrara, Italy, 1957; 3d prize Carnegie, Inst., 1958. Address: 10 bis rue Roger Paris 14 France

CESAR, JOSE ANTONIO, banker. Exec. mng. dir. Banco De Londres y Mexico, S.A. Office: Bolivar Y 16 De Septiembre Mexico City Mexico*

CESTARO, MICHAEL PAUL, assn. exec.; b. June 25, 1907; m. Jennie Gallo, Sept. 22, 1929; 1 son, Joseph Michael. Vice pres., dir. SarJen, Inc., Boynton Beach, Fla.; past pres., dir., chmn. bd. J.E. Hangen, Inc., J.E. Hanger, Inc. N.Y. past dir., pres. Am. Orthotics and Prosthetics Assn., Washington; past bd. dirs., treas. Am. Bd. Certification Orthotics and Prosthetics, Washington. Home: 300 North Blvd Boynton Beach FL 33435 Office: 40 Patterson St NE Washington DC 20002

CHABAN-DELMAS, JACQUES MICHEL PIERRE, French govt. ofcl.; b. 1915; student Lycee Lakanal (Sceaux France), Ecole Libre des Sciences Politiques (Paris). Inspecteur des Finances, 1943; nat. mil. del. for coordination mil. planning, Resistance, 1944; insp. gen. of Army, 1944; sec.-gen. Ministry of Information, 1945; elected Radical dep. for Gironde, 1946; mayor, Bordeaux, France, 1947; leader Gaulist group (Republicains Sociaux), Nat. Assembly, 1953-56; minister pub. works Mendés-France Cabinet, 1954-55; minister of State Mollet Cabinet, 1956-57; minister nat. def. Gailliard Cabinet, 1957-58; pres. Nat. Assembly of France, 1958-69; premier of France, 1969—. Pres. European Assembly Local Powers. Served with French Army, 1939-40. Decorated comdr. Legion of Honor, Compagnon de la Libération, Croix de Guerre. Home: 57 rue de Varenne 75 Paris VII France

CHABRIER, JACQUES RENE, music pub. co. exec.; b. Nancy, France, Jan. 15, 1921; s. R. Charles and Simone (Huber) C.; B.A., Rennes U., 1939; B.L., U. Paris, 1942; m. Marie Anne Smith, May 27, 1948; 1 dau., Yvonne Vasquez. Came to U.S., 1946, naturalized, 1954. Staff asst. S.N. Pathe Cinema, Paris, France, 1942-43, exec. asst. prodn., studio v.p., 1944-45, Am. rep., 1946-47; pres. Pathe Cinema Corp., 1947-51, Paris Theatre Corp. N.Y., 1948-51; mem. staff investment dept. Hartford Nat. Bank & Trust Co., 1951, supr., 1952-55, asst. trust officer, 1956, trust officer, 1956-58, v.p., 1958-1961, exec. v.p., 1961-68; pres. Chappell & Co., Inc., N.Y.C., 1968—, also dir.; chmn., mng. dir. Chappell & Co. Ltd., London; dir. Famous-Chappell Ltd., Toronto, Ont., Can., Mut. Ins. Co. Hartford, Covenant Ins. Co. Hartford, Ensign-Bickford Co., N.Am. Philips Co.; v.p., dir. Importers Motion Picture Orgn. N.Y., 1950-51. Film adviser French embassy, Washington, N.Y.C., 1948-52. Bd. dirs. Hartford Festival Music; trustee Hartford Coll. for Women, Nat. Health and Welfare Retirement Assn., Edward W. Hazen Found. Served with French Army, 1943-45. Mem. Nat. Music Pubs. Assn. (dir.), A.S.C.A.P., French C. of C. in U.S. (treas. 1949-51). Home: 1000 Park Av New York City NY 10028 also 199 Hurlbutt St Wilton CT 06897 Office: 609 Fifth Av New York City NY 10017

CHABROL, CLAUDE, film writer, producer; b. Paris, France, June 24, 1930; s. Yves and Madeleine (Delabre) C.; licence de Lettres, Sorbonne, 1951, diplome de Civilisation et Litterature Americaine, 1951; m. Stephaine Audran, Dec. 4, 1964; children—Jean Yves, Matthieu, Thomas. Former film critic, pub. relations officer 20th-Century Fox, Paris; dir., producer, 1958—. Recipient Prix Mise en Scene, Locarno, 1958, Berlin, 1959, Venice, 1959, Barcelona, 1964, San Sebastian, 1966. Club: Fines Gueules. Author scripts: Le Beau Serge, 1958, Les Cousins, 1958; A Double Tour, 1960; Les Bonnes Femmes, 1960; Les Godelureaux, 1961; L'Oeil Du Malin, 1962; Landru, 1963; Ophelia, 1963; Sept Peches Capitaux, 1963; Le Tigre Aime La Chair Fraiche, 1964; Marie Chantal Contre Aime La Chair Fraiche, 1964; Marie Chantal Contre Dr. Kah, 1965; Le Togre Se Parfume a La Dynamite, 1965; La Ligne de Demarcation, 1966; Le Scandale, 1966; Les Biches, 1967; La Femme in Fidele, 1968; The Beast Must Die, 1969. Address: 49 Blvd du Chateau Neuilly-sur-Seine 92 France

CHACE, ARNOLD BUFFUM, realty exec.; b. Yarmouth, Mass., July 11, 1914; s. Malcolm Green and Elizabeth (Edwards) C.; student Yale, 1937; m. Evelyn Thayer, Sept. 1, 1943; 1 son, Arnold B. Pres., dir. Realty Operators Corp., Providence, 1946-53; now pres., dir. Fields Point Mfg. Corp.; sec., dir. Wanskuck Co.; dir. Am. Pres. Lines, Ltd., Merrimack Mfg. Co., Abercombe & Fitch. Served to comdr. USNR. Office: Hospital Trust Bldg Providence RI 02903

CHADBOURN, JAMES HARMON, educator; b. Spartanburg, S.C., Dec. 2, 1905; s. Stephen H. and Gertrude L. (Cunningham) C.; A.B., The Citadel, 1926; J.D., U. N.C., 1931; M.A. (hon.), Harvard, 1963; m. Erika Sammeth, Aug. 16, 1940; children—Marianne, Leslie, James Harmon. Prin. Beaufort (S.C.) High Sch., 1926-28; asst. prof. law U. N.C., 1931-36; lectr. law Duke, 1935; asst. prof. law U. Pa., 1936-39, asso. prof., 1939-40, prof., 1940-50; vis. prof. law Stanford, 1939, Yale, 1946, Columbia U., 1948, Texas, 1954, Harvard, 1961; Connell prof. law U. Cal., 1950-68; prof. law Harvard 1963-69, Fessenden prof., 1970—. Faculty Saizburg Seminar In Am. Studies, 1959; research cons. Cal. Law Revision Commn. Mem. Juristic Soc., Order of Coif, Phi Delta Phi, Delta Tau Delta. Democrat. Episcopalian. Author: Lynching and the Law, 1932; (with Roswell Magill) Cases on Civil Procedure, 1939; (with C.T. McCormick) Cases on Federal Courts, 1946; (with T.E. Atkinson) Cases on Civil Procedure, 1948; (with Harvey M. Grossman and Arvo Van Alstyne) California Pleading; (with A. Leo Levin) Cases on Civil Procedure, 1961; (with Maguire, Weinstein and Mansfield) Cases on Evidence, 1965; Chadbourn Revision of Wigmore on Evidence, vols. III, IIIA. Editor of N.C. Law Review, 1932-36. Home: 12 Blakeslee St Cambridge MA 21613

CHADBOURNE, JOSEPH HUMPHREY, Jr., assn. exec.; b. Boston, May 15, 1931; s. Joseph Humphrey and Barbara (Bullard) C.; grad. Phillips Andover Acad., 1948; B.A., Yale, 1952; M.S., U. Conn., 1965; m. Ann Kellogg Hopkins, Sept. 15, 1956; children—Gay Kellogg, Scott Holt. Plant mgr., purchasing agt. Danielson Mfg. Co. (Conn.), 1955-58; sales and marketing Spencer Chem. Co., Kansas City, Mo., 1958-61; product mgr. Moldex Co., Wauregan, Conn., 1961-62; instr. summer sci. projects in environmental edn. Univ. Sch., Shaker Heights, O., 1964-68; intern Washington Internships in Edn., 1968-69; headmaster Tilton (N.H.) Sch., 1969-71; pres. Inst. for Enviromental Edn., Cleve., 1971—. Dir. Ford Found. grant for water pollution tchr. tng., 1969-70; dir. Dept. Interior grant for water pollution tchr. tng. and curriculum devel., 1970-71; dir. NSF Confs. on Environmental Studies, Quincy, Mass., Phila., Cleve., summer 1971. Bd. dirs. Student Achievement Inst., Worcester, Mass. Served with CIC, U.S. Army, 1952-55. Mem. Nat. Assn. Biology Tchrs., Nat. Sci. Tchrs. Assn., Nat. Assn. Ind. Schs. Address: 2803 Scarborough Rd Cleveland Heights OH 44118

CHADBOURNE, RICHARD MCCLAIN, educator; b. Providence, Sept. 19, 1922; s. Alexander McClain and Ruth (Wilbur) C.; B.A., Brown U., 1943; M.A., Yale, 1947, Ph.D., 1950; m. Anna Gisela Golm, July 13, 1946; children—Lawrence McClain, Eric Francis, Eugene Alexander. Instr., then asst. prof. French, Fordham U., 1950-57; asso. prof. French, U. Colo., 1959-61, prof., 1961-71, also chmn. dept.; head Romance studies U. Calgary (Alta., Can.), 1971—. Am. Council of Learned Socs. fellow, 1962-63. Served to sgt., Signal Corps, AUS, 1943-45. Decorated chevalier Order Palms (France). Mem. Am. Assn. Tchrs. French, Modern Lang. Assn Am., Phi Beta Kappa. Author: Ernest Renan as an Essayist (Modern Lang. Assn.-Crofts Cornell prize), 1957; Ernest Renan, 1968. Contbr. articles on 19th Century French writers to jours. Home: 3732 Underhill Dr NW Calgary Alberta Canada

CHADBURN, PHILIP HEMENWAY, Jr., fgn. service officer; b. Petrograd, Russia, Feb. 22, 1917 (parents Am. citizens); s. Philip Hemenway and Esther (Packard) C.; ed. schs. in France and Cal.; A.B., Harvard, 1939; m. Jacqueline Wilson June 24, 1950 (div.); children—Claudia Packard, Cynthia Glen. With Anita J. (Mrs. William D. O'Donovan), Barbara L., John Lamont. Controller, Hamilton Hotel, vice consul, Calcutta, India, 1948, Frankfurt, Germany, 1949, Salzburg, Austria, 1949; pub. affairs officer, Lyon, France, 1951; 2d sec., consul Am. embassy, Paris, France, 1952; chief tng. br. personnel Dept. State, Washington, 1957-59; officer charge Swiss-Benelux affairs, 1959-61; counselor, dep. chief mission Am. embassy, Vientiane, Laos, 1961-64, Rangoon, Burma, 1964-65, Saigon, Vietnam, 1965-66; spl. asst. to asst. sec. state Dept. State, 1966-68; consul gen., Nice, France, 1968, Marseilles, France, 1969—. Served from pvt. to maj. AUS, 1941-46. Decorated Bronze Star; War Cross with gold palm (France), Mentioned in Despatches (Eng.). Editorial bd. Am. Fgn. Service Jour. Office: Dept of State Washington DC 20521

CHADENET, BERNARD, internat. ofcl.; b. Paris, France, Sept. 16, 1915; s. Julien and Genevieve (Malzieux) C.; License of Scis., Sorbonne, Paris, 1938; engring. degree, Ecole Superieure d'electricite, Paris, 1938; Advanced Mgmt. Program, Harvard, 1958; m. Francoise Chne Carrère, Sept. 4, 1944; childrenLaurence, Marie Christine, Virginie-Anne. Engaged in heavy equipment industry, Algeria and France, 1947-54, 58-64; with World Bank, 1954-58, 64—, dir. of projects dept., 1964—. Served with French Army and Underground, 1940, 44. Decorated Chevalier Legion of Honor (France). Home: 4759 Berkeley Terrace N W Washington, DC 20007. Office: 1818 H St N W Washington, DC 20007.

CHADWELL, JOHN TOOLE, lawyer; b. Lexington, Neb., July 13, 1900; s. Pearl T. and Nellie (Toole) C.; A.B., U. Ill., 1922. J.D., 1924; m. Edna Morris, July 21, 1926; childrenConstance (Mrs. John S. Koch), John T. Admitted to the Illinois bar, 1924, since practiced in Chicago; member firm Chadwell Keck, Kayser and Ruggles, Chgo. Mem. Am., Ill., Chgo. bar assns., Am. Coll. of Trial Lawyers, Am. Bar Foundation. Clubs: Chicago (Chgo.), University (Chgo.), Mid-Day (Chgo.); Glen View Club. Home; 31 Woodley Rd Winnetka IL 60093 Office: 135 S LaSalle St Chicago IL 60603

CHADWICK, ALAN WILLIAM, hosp. adminstr.; b. Worcester, Mass., Sept. 1, 1909; s. John F. and Elizabeth (Shore) C.; B.S., U. Mass., 1931; m. Mary D. Goodhue, Aug. 17, 1935; children—Bruce G., Mary Ellen (Mrs. John C. Linderman) C. Instr. instl. mgmt. U. Mass., 1938-39, mgr. coll. dining halls, 1932-39; supt. Hosp. Cottages for Children, Baldwinville, Mass., 1939-42; asst. dir. VA Hosp., Newington, Conn., 1946-53, VA Hosp., West Haven, Conn., 1953-60; dir. VA Center, Hot Springs, S.D., 1960-64, VA Hosp., Rutland Heights, Mass., 1964-65, VA Hosp., Dearborn, Mich., 1965-69, VA Hosp., Syracuse, N.Y., 1969—; asso. prof. adminstrv. medicine State U. N.Y., Upstate Med. Center, Syracuse, 1969—. Pres., Fed. Bus. Assn. S.D., 1964; chmn. interagy. bd. Civil Service Commn. Mich., 1967-69. Served to capt. AUS, 1942-46. Fellow Am. Coll. Hosp. Adminstrs.; mem. Fed. Exec. Assn., Am., Internat. hosp. assns., Am. Legion, Lambda Chi Alpha. Conglist. Mason, Kiwanian. Address: VA Hosp Irving Av and University Pl Syracuse NY 13210

CHADWICK, DONALD ROGER, physician; b. Boston, Aug. 16, 1925; s. Chester Robert and Fay Althea (Billings) C.; student Harvard, 1943-45, M.D., 1949; student Reed Coll., 1954; m. Elizabeth Ann Hulburt, June 3, 1949; children—Deborah H., Douglas B. Intern Lankenau Hosp., Phila., 1949-50; pub. health resident, Chapel Hill, N.C., 1950-51; local health officer, N.C., 1951-53; commd. USPHS, 1953, med. dir. 1959, asst., surgeon gen., 1967; med. officer charge spl. health dist. Savannah River Area, 1953; spl. tng. radiol. health Reed Coll., Sandia Base, Oak Ridge Nat. Lab., 1954-55; with Occupational Health Field Hdqrs., Cin., 1955-56; chief Program service, radiol. health med. program Div. Spl. Health Services, 1956-57; liaison officer radiation Office Surgeon Gen., 1957-58; acting chief div. radiol. health, 1958, chief program operations, 1958-59; exec. sec. Nat. Adv. Com. Radiation, 1958-59; sec. Fed. Radiation Council, 1959-61; chief div. radiol. health USPHS, 1961-66, dir. Nat. Center Chronic Disease Control, 1967-68; dep. dir. Regional Med. Programs Service, Bethesda, Md., 1968-70; area med. adminstr. United Mine Workers Am. Welfare and Retirement Fund, Beckley, W. Va., 1970—; mem. Med. Radiation Adv. Com., U.S. Dept. Health, Edn. and Welfare; mem. W.Va. Comprehensive Health Planning Adv. council. Recipient Arthur Fleming award, 1963. Mem. A.M.A., Am. Pub. Health Assn., Commd. Officer Assn Pub. Health Service. Home: Rt 1 Box 244-B Mount Hope WV 25880 Office: PO Box 1229 Beckley WV 25801

CHADWICK, FRANK G., Jr., banker; b. Bridgewater, Mass., July 14, 1910; s. Frank G. and Elizabeth (MacDonald) C.; extension student Harvard, 1935; student Brown U., 1934, Rutgers U. Grad. Sch. Banking 1954; hon. degree, Sch. Banking, Williams Coll., 1958; m. Doris Redfield, June 21, 1935; children—William H., Ruth W. (Mrs. Preston Spruill). With Universal Credit Co., Boston, 193540; asst. treas. Granite Trust Co., Quincy, Mass., 1940-50; with First New Haven Nat. Bank 1951—, pres., 1968—; dir. Berger Bros. Co., F.D. Garve & Son, Inc. Simkins Industries, Inc. Mem. regional adv. com. U.S. Comptroller Currency. Bd. dirs. Yale-New Haven Hosp., Quinnipiac council Boy Scouts Am. Served with USNR, 1943-45. Mem. New Haven C. of C. (bd. dirs.). Rotarian. Clubs: Brown, Quinnipiack (bd. govs. 1965-68) (New Haven). Home: 47 Featherbed Lane Branford, CT 06405. Office: 1 Church St New Haven CT 06502

CHADWICK, SIR JAMES, physicist; b. Oct. 20, 1891; s. J.J. Chadwick; ed. Univs. Manchester and Berlin; Ph.D., Cambridge U.; M.Sc., Victoria; D.Sc. (hon.) Oxford, Birmingham, Reading, Dublin, Leeds, McGill, Exeter; LL.D., Liverpool, Edinburgh; m. Aileen Stewart- Brown, 1925; twin daus. Lectr., asst. dir. radioactive research Cavendish Lab. (Cambridge); master Gonville and Caius Coll., Cambridge, 1948-58, now fellow, Lyon Jones prof. physics U. Liverpool, 1935-48. Recipient Nobel prize (physics), 1935; created knight, 1945; U.S. Medal for Merit, 1946; Faraday medal, 1950, Franklin medal, 1951; elected to Pontificia Academia Scientiarum, 1961; fgn. mem. German Order of Pour le merite, 1966; companion of honor, 1970. Fellow Royal Soc. (Hughes medal 1932, Copley medal 1950), Am. Phys. Soc. (hon.); fgn. mem. Royal Acad. Brussels, Royal Danish Acad. Sci., Royal Acad. Sci. Amsterdam; corr. mem. Sachsische Akademie der Wissenchaften, Acad. Sci. Leipzig. Author: (with Lord Rutherford, C.D. Ellis) Radiations from Radioactive Substances; 1930; papers on radioctivity. Actively engaged in expts. that led to devel. of atomic bomb; head Brit. delegation to U.S., 1943. Clubs: Athenaeum (London), University (Liverpool). Home: 16 Grange Ct Pinehurst Cambridge CB3 9BD England

CHADWICK, LYNN RUSSELL, sculptor; b. Nov. 24, 1914; s. Verner Russell and Marjorie Brown (Lynn) C.; ed. Mcht. Taylors' Sch.; m. Charlotte Ann Secord, 1942, 1 son; m. 2d, Frances Mary Jamieson, 1959; 2 daus.; m. 3d, Yvonne Eva Reiner, 1965; 1 son. Archtl. draftsman, 1933-39; sculptor, 1948—; exhibited various galleries in London, numerous internat. shows; represented in permanent collections Tate Gallery, Brit. Council, Arts Council Gt. Britain, Victoria and Albert Mus. (all Eng.), Mus. Modern Art, N.Y.C., Carnegie Inst., Pitts., U. Mich., Albright Art Gallery, Buffalo, Art Inst. Chgo., also museums, galleries in Can., France, Holland, Germany, Sweden, Belgium, Italy, Australia, Can., Chile. Served with Fleet Air Arm, 1941-44. Recipient Internat. Sculpture 0rize Venice Biennale, 1956; 1st prize Padua Internat. Competition; named comdr. Brit. Empire. Address: Lyplatt Park Stroud Gloucestershire England

CHADWICK, STEPHEN FOWLER, lawyer; b. Colfax, Wash., Aug. 14, 1894; s. Stephen James and Emma (Plummer) C.; LL.B., Washington and Lee U., 1914; J.D., U. Wash., 1915; m. Margaret Gardiner Tyler, July 2, 1919; children—Mary T. McCracken, Stephen. Admitted to Wash. bar, 1915; mem. firm Chadwick, Chadwick & Mills, 1929-70, Chadwick, Mills & McLaughlin, 1970—. Democratic candidate Congress, 1st Dist., Wash., 1926; candidate Dem. nomination U.S. Senate, 1932; Republican candidate U.S. Senate, 1940. Mem. Seattle Charter Commn., 1925; nat. judge adv. Forty and Eight, 1922-24; civilian aide to sec. war, 1933-47, sec. army, 1947-54; mem. Civilian War Commn., 1942- 46; chmn. U.S.O. Council, 1942-46, Regional Loyalty Bd., 1948-53; pres. Washington div. Am. Cancer Soc., 1947-52, mem. exec. com., 1952—; mem. Mut. Security Adminstrn. evaluation team, Philippines, 1953; del. Atlantic Congress, 1959. Trustee Seattle C. of C., 1931-51, v.p., 1936-38, sr. council, 1951—. Served as 1st lt., inf. AEF, Siberia, 1918-19; capt. Judge Adv. Gen. Res., 1922-32. Decorated comdr. Legion of Honor (France). Recipient Distinguished Service medal Am. Cancer Soc., 1953. Mem. Am. Coll. Trial Attys., Am., Wash. State bar assns., Am. Legion (mem. nat. Am. Com. 1929-38, chmn. 1935-38, nat. com. 1938-39), Seattle Hist. Soc. (pres. 1965- 67), Omicron Delta Kappa, Phi Delta Phi, Kappa Sigma. Republican. Episcopalian. Mason. Club: University, Rainier, Seattle Tennis (Seattle). Home: 1121 41st Av E Seattle WA 98104 Office: Central Bldg Seattle WA 98104

CHADWICK, WALLACE LACY, cons. engr.; b. Loring, Kan., Dec. 4, 1897; s. P. C. and Anna R. (Lacy) C.; student U. Redlands, D.Engring. Sci. (hon.), 1965; m. Beulah Dye, Oct. 15, 1921; children—Isabelle Ruth, Marilynn Joyce, Sandra Louise. Statistician, plant engr. Cal. Alkali Co., 1920-21; draftsman So. Cal. Edison Co., 1922-24, div. engr., 1924-28, constrn. Big Creek-San Joaquin Hydroelectric project, transmission engr., 1928-31, civil engr., chief civil engr., 1937-44, mgr. engring. dept., 1945-50, v.p., 1951-62, dir. design and constrn. Big Creek No. 4 hydroelectric, Vermillion Valley Dam, Redondo No. 1, Redondo No. 2, Etiwanda, El Segundo, Alamitos, Huntington Beach, Mandalay steampower sta. projects and power system expansion, Mammoth Pool Hydroelectric Project; engr., sr. engr. Met. Water Dist. Cal., constrn. Colorado River Aqueduct, 1931-37, spl. assignment, 1938; cons. So. Cal. Edison Co. Bechtel Corp., Parsons-Brinkerhoff-Tudor-Bechtel, Pacific N.W. Power Co., State of Cal., Earth Dams Cons. Bd., U.S. Bur. Reclamation, Consol. Edison Co. N.Y., Inc., Douglas County PUD (Washington), and others on engring. for dams, tunnels, hydro and thermal power plants, electric utility problems, 1962—. Chmn. Joint Research Council Power Plant Air Pollution Control, Los Angeles, 1956- 62; mem. U.S. com. Internat. Congress Large Dams; mem. U.S. Com. on World Power Conf., joint bd. environmental studies Nat. Acad. Sci. and Nat. Acad. Engring., 1965-69. Mem. San Marino City Council. Pres. board trustees U. Redlands, 1965-69; mem. adv. com. Water Resources Center, U. Cal. at Berkeley. Served as pvt., U.S. Army. Recipient 75th Ann. award Cal. sect. Am. Soc. M.E.; 1st Engr. of the Year award Los Angeles Engring. Socs., 1962; Philip T. Sprague award Instrument Soc. Am., 1963; Golden Beaver award, 1969. Fellow Am. Soc. M.E., I.E.E.E., Am. Soc. C.E. (dir. 1951-53, pres. Los Angeles sect.; nat. pres. 1964-65); mem. Am. Acad. Engring., Assn. Edison Illuminating Cos. (past mem. power generation com.), Edison Electric Inst. (chmn. prime movers com., 1954-55, chmn. exec. com. operating and engring. div. 1959-60), Am. Concrete Inst., Pacific Coast Electric Assn. Republican. Baptist. Clubs: Electric, Engineering (Los Angeles); California; Rotary of Los Angeles; San Gabriel Country. Author tech. articles various publs. Home: 1133 Lorain Rd San Marino CA Office: 523 W 6th St Los Angeles CA 90014

CHAET, BERNARD ROBERT, artist, educator; b. Boston, Mar. 7, 1924; s. David and Golda (Benjamin) C.; student Sch. Fine Arts, Boston, 1942-44, 48; B.S., Tufts U., 1950; m. Ninon Lacey, Dec. 14,

1951; 1 dau., Leah. One-man shows, Boston, N.Y.C., White Museum of Cornell U.; group exhbns. Corcoran Gall. of Art, Modern Mus., Bklyn., Los Angeles County, Detroit museums, Art Inst. Chgo., Inst. Contemporary Art, Boston, Am. Drawings traveling show of French Museums, others; group shows Mass. Inst. Tech., U. Ill., U. Neb., Brandeis U. Tchr. Boston Pub. Schs., Inst. Contemporary Art, Boston, 1951—; instr. painting Yale, 1951-56, asst. prof., 1956-59, asso. prof. painting, chmn. dept. art, 1959-62, prof. painting, 1969—, dir. art. div. Summer Sch. Music and Art, 1960—; contbg. editor Arts mag., 1956-59; org. exhbn. 20th Century Drawing, Yale U. Art Gallery, 1955. Represented in perm. colls. Worcester (Mass.) Art. Mus., Bklyn. Mus., DeCordova Mus. (Lincoln, Mass.), Brandeis U., Addison Gallery Am. Art (Andover, Mass.), U. Cal. at Los Angeles, Fogg Mus., Harvard, Mus. Fine Arts Boston, Mus. Art R.I. Sch. Design, Yale Art Gallery, U. Mass., U. Conn., N.Y. U., State U. N.Y. at Cortland, Brown U. Recipient grant Nat. Found. Arts and Humanities, 1966- 67. Author: Artists at Work, 1960; The Art of Drawing, 1970. Home: 141 Coldspring St New Haven CT 06511 Office: Yale U New Haven CT 06520

CHAFE, WALLACE L., educator, linguist; b. Cambridge, Mass., Sept. 3, 1927; s. Albert J. and Nathalie (Amback) C.; B.A., Yale, 1950, M.A., 1956, Ph.D., 1958; m. Mary Elizabeth Butterworth, June 23, 1951; children—Christopher, Douglas, Stephen. Asst. prof. U. Buffalo, 1958-59; linguist Bur. Am. Ethnology, Smithsonian Instn., 1959-62; mem. faculty U. Cal. at Berkeley, 1962—, prof. linguistics, 1967—. Served with USNR, 1945-46. Mem. Linguistic Soc. Am., Am. Anthrop. Assn. Author: Seneca Thanksgiving Rituals, 1961; Seneca Morphology and Dictionary, 1967; Meaning and the Structure of Language, 1970. Home: 112 Los Cerros Av Walnut Creek CA 94598 Office: Dept Linguistics Univ Cal Berkeley CA 94720

CHAFEE, JOHN HUBBARD, U.S. sec. navy; b. Providence, Oct. 22, 1922; s. John S. and Janet (Hunter) C.; grad. Deerfield (Mass.) Acad., 1940; B.A., Yale, 1947; LL.B., Harvard, 1950; LL.D., Brown U., 1964, Providence Coll., 1965, U. R.I., 1965, Jacksonville U., 1970; m. Virginia Coates, Nov. 4, 1950; children—Zechariah, Lincoln, John, Georgia, Quentin. Admitted to R.I. bar, 1950; practice in Providence, 1952-62; mem. R.I. Ho. of Reps. 3d Dist. Warwick, 1957-62, minority leader, 1959-62; gov. R.I., 1963- 69; U.S. sec. navy, 1969—. Chmn., Republican Gov.'s Assn., 1967—. Served to capt. USMCR, 1942-45, 51-52. Chubb fellow Yale, 1965. Mem. R.I. Bar, Fed. Bar Assn. Home: Ives Rd Warwick RI 02886 Office: Pentagon Washington DC 20350

CHAFFEE, EUGENE BERNARD, ret. educator; b. Aurora, Neb., Mar. 10, 1905; s. Elmer Spencer and Grace Grace (Lyman) C.; B.A., Occidental Coll., 1927; M.A., U. Cal., 1931; postgrad. U. Cal., 1932, George Washington U., 1933; hon. Litt.D., Coll. of Ida., 1940; hon. Doctor of Laws, U. Ida., 1964; m. Lois Barton, June 26, 1937; children—Lois Ann, Eugene Barton. Tchr., music supr. pub. schs., Meridian, Ida., 1927; supt., prin. grade and high schs., Ustick, Ida., 1928-30; tchr. Boise Jr. Coll., Inc., 1932-36, pres., 1936-67; pres. emeritus Boise State Coll., 1970—. Pres. bd. dirs. Am. Assn. Jr. Colls.; pres. N.W. Assn. Jr. Colls., 1941-42 and 1946-47; mem. exec. com. Pacific N.W. Conf. on Higher Edn.; mem. exec. com. Nat. Com. Regional Accrediting Agys. U.S.; chmn. Liberal Arts Coll. of Ida.; mem. Ida. Manpower Devel. and Tng. and Area Redevel. Adv. Com.; 2d v.p. and chmn. of higher commn. N.W. Assn. of Secondary and Higher Schs., 1958-64; mem. Ednl. Adv. Council, Nat. Assn. Mfrs., Nat. Commn. Accrediting (exec. com.); dir. YMCA, United Fund, Boise; exec. com. A.R.C. Served as lt. comdr. U.S.N.R., World War II; mem. Enemy Alien Hearing Bd., Ida., 1941-42; Mem. Fgn. Relations, Boise, Am. Legion. Presbyn. (mem. bd. sessions, chmn. bd. trustees). Clubs: Knife and Fork, Exchange (Boise). Author: An Idea Grows (A History of Boise College), 1970; also articles history to profl. jours. Home: history to profl. jours. Home: 3 Mesa Dr Boise ID 83705

CHAFFER, ELIJAH GEORGE, banker; b. Washington, Ill., Oct. 27, 1905; s. Harley E. and Mary (Stormer) C.; student U. Ore., Am. Inst. Banking, Pacific Coast Banking Sch.; m. Ruth E. Hamilton, Nov. 17, 1928; 1 dau., Joyce Ann. With First Security Bank Ida., N.A., Boise, 1927—, exec. v.p., 1965-68, chmn. bd., 1968- -, also dir.; dir. First Security Corp., Salt Lake City, S.W. Ida. Water Devel. Assn. Treas., Ida. Am. Cancer Soc., 1968-69. Mem. Ida. Bankers Assn. (pres. 1962-63). Republican. Presbyn. Elk, Rotarian. Home: 3110 Crescent Rim Dr Boise ID 83704 Office: Box 7069 Boise ID 83707

CHAFFETZ, HAMMOND EDWARD, lawyer; b. Worcester, Mass., July 9, 1907; s. Carroll J. and Celia (Kessler) C.; A.B. cum laude, Harvard, 1927, LL.D. cum laude, 1930; m. Sara Smeerin, Apr. 4, 1951; children—Peter Richard, David Charles. Admitted to D.C. bar, 1930, U.S. Supreme Ct. bar, 1933, Ill. bar, 1951; staff anti-trust div. Dept. Justice, 1930-38; spl. asst. to atty. gen., 1931-38; trustee Coxe Bros. & Co., Hazelton, Pa., for U.S. Dist. Ct., So. Dist. N.Y., 1936-43; resident partner in Washington, Kirkland, Fleming, Green, Martin & Ellis, Chgo., 1938-51, Chgo., 1951— (firm became Kirkland, Ellis, Hodson, Chaffetz & Masters, 1958); dir. Am. Nat. Bank & Trust Co. of Chgo.; exec. com. Am. Nat. Bank, Chgo. Mem. atty. gen. nat. com. to study anti-trust laws, 1953-55. Trustee Ravina Festival Assn.; v.p., trustee Chgo. Orchestral Assn.; bd. overseers com. to visit Law Sch. Harvard Coll., 1961-68. Mem. exec. com. of council Nat. Harvard Law Sch. Assn., 1968—. Served from lt. to lt. comdr. USNR, 1942-45. Fellow Am. Coll. Trial Lawyers, Am. Bar. Found.; mem. Am. Judicature Soc., Am. (council sect. on antitrust law 1958-60, ho. of dels. 1960-61, chmn. antitrust sect. 1962-63), Ill., D.C., N.Y., 7th Fed. Circuit, Chgo. bar assns., Harvard Law Soc. Ill. (pres. 1962-63), Ill. State C. of C. Republican. Clubs: Chicago, Mid-Day, Mid-America, Executives, Harvard (v.p., dir.) (Chgo.); Lake Shore Country (Glencoe, Ill.); National Lawyers, National Press (Washington). Editor: Harvard Law Rev., 1929-30. Contbr. papers to profl. jours. Home: 1310 Forest Glen Dr N Winnetka IL 60093 Office: Prudential Plaza Chicago IL 60601

CHAFFIN, ROBERT NELSON, state ofcl.; b. Avalon, Mo., July 13, 1905; s. Robert Elliel and Mamie (Curtis) C.; A.B., Park Coll., 1927; student U. Wash., 1926-27; LL.B., U. Wyo., 1947; m. Hester Mae Wiltse, Nov. 24, 1932. Parts mgr. Central Garage, Cody, Wyo., 1927-32; sales agt. Standard Oil Co. (Ind.), 1932- 42; admitted to Wyo. bar, 1947, since practiced in Torrington; mem. firm Chaffin & Maier, 1949-61; judge Municipal Ct., Torrington, 1948-60; dist. atty. U.S. Dist. Ct. of Wyo., 1961-70; spl atty. gen. health, welfare and rehab. State of Wyo., Cheyenne, 1970—. Treas. Goshen County March of Dimes, 1949-51; chmn. Goshen County Bd. Pub. Welfare, 1954-60. Mem. Democratic Central Com. of Wyo., 1952-57. Mem. Am. Legion. Democrat. Episcopalian. Mason, Rotarian; mem. Order Eastern Star. Home: Ken Moor Heights Torrington WY 82240 Office: State Office Bldg Cheyenne WY 82001

CHAGALL, MARC, artist; b. Vitebsk, Russia, July 7, 1887; student l'Academie de St. Petersburg; m. Bella Rosenfeld, 1915 (dec.). Ceramist, painter, illustrator, engraver, watercolorist; went to Paris, 1910; painter numerous pictures including, Moi et le Village, 1910-14; exhibited in Berlin, 1914; designer costumes and decorations, also executed murals for Theatre Julif, Moscow, 1919; returned to Paris, 1929, and made engravings for Ames Mortes (Gogol), 1929, Fables de la Fontaine, 1930, Bible; visited U.S., 1941; designer costumes for ballets: Aleko (Tchaikovsky), Firebird (Stravinsky); murals Met. Opera House, Lincoln Center, N.Y.C., 1966; sets Magic Flute, 1967; had retrospective exhbns. Mus. Modern Art (N.Y.C.), Art Inst. Chgo. (all 1946); retrospective exhbn. Musée d'Art Moderne, Paris, 1947; also exhbns. Tate Gallery (London), museums of Amsterdam, Israel, Turin, Zurich, Berne, Basle, Turin, Rome, Milan. Recipient Carnegie prize, 1939; Internat. prize for engraving Biennial at Venice, 1948; comdr. Légion of Honor. Hon. mem. Am. Acad. Arts and Letters. Author, illustrator: Ma Vie, 1931; illustrator: Mille de une nuits; Contes de Bocace. Home: Vence Alpes Maritimes France

CHAILLE, HOWARD ELMER, bus. exec.; b. Indpls., Apr. 8, 1916; s. Howard Theodore and Lola Marie (Patten) C.; student Kenyon Coll., summers 1934-37; B.S., Ind. U., 1937, postgrad., 1938; m. Naomi Agnes Hardwick, Aug. 3, 1941; children—Claudia Marie, Angela Louise. Fire ins. underwriter, 1938; comdt. jr. sch. Briarley Mil. Acad., 1939; shipping, receiving mgr. comml. firm, 1940; communications supr. Brit. Supply Council and Brit. Purchasing Commn., 1940; asst. chief communications and records Bd. Econ. Warfare, 1941; U.S. Dept. State, 1945-70; chief message control center Div. Communications and Records, 1946, asst. chief, 1949-50, chief telegraph br., 1946-49, field operations officer, 1950-52, orgn. and methods examiner, 1952-53, Program Survey Staff, 1953-54, Sec. of State's Pub. Commn. on Personnel, 1954, dir. exec. staff dep. asst. sec. for operations, Washington, 1955-56, consul, sec. in diplomatic corps, 1st sec., consul of embassy, Taipei, Taiwan, 1956-60, Seoul, Korea, 1960-61; chief program mgmt. and analysis staff Office Personnel, Dept. State, 1961-62, chief personnel services div., 1962-65, fgn. service insp., 1965-67; counselor adminstrv. affairs, Am. consul, Vientiane, Laos, 1967-70; v.p. Makai Corp., Hawaii, 1970—. Served as lt., USNR, 1941-46. Mem. Delta Upsilon. Episcopalian. Home: 41-879 Laumilo Rd Waimonola HI 96795

CHAIN, ERNST BORIS, educator, biochemist; b. Berlin, Germany, June 19, 1906; s. Michael and Margarete (Eisner) C.; Ph.D., Friedrich-Wilhelm U., Berlin, 1930, Cambridge (Eng.) U., 1935; D.Phil., Oxford (Eng.) U., 1937; hon. degrees, U. Liege (Belgium), 1946, U. Bordeaux (France), 1947, U. Paris, 1959, U. Turin (Italy), 1954, U. La Piata (Argentine), 1962, U. Cordoba (Argentine), 1962, U. Montevideo (Uruguay), 1962, U. Brasil, 1962, U. Chgo., 1965, Albert Einstein Coll., 1962; m. Anne Beloff, Oct. 6, 1948; children—Benjamin, Daniel, Judith. Research dept. pathology Charity Hosp., Berlin, 1930-33, Sch. Biochemistry, U. Cambridge (Eng.), 1933-35; univ. lectr. Sch. Pathology, U. Oxford, 1935-48; head Internat. Center Chem. Microbiology, Inst. Superiore de Sanita, Rome, Italy, 1948-61; prof. biochemistry Imperial Coll. Sci. and Tech., U. London, 1963—; co- discoverer curative properties penicillin. Created knight, 1969; decorated comdr. Legion of Honor (France), 1946; grand officer Order of Merit (Italy); recipient Nobel prize for physiology and medicine, 1945; Paul Ehrlich Centenary prize, 1954, numerous other awards. Fellow Royal Soc. London; fgn. asso. mem. Acad. Scis. Paris; fgn. mem. Acad. Lincei Italy; corr. mem. Acad. Medicine Paris, Real Acad. Scis. Madrid, N.Y. Acad. Med.; hon. mem. Finnish Biochem. Soc., Weizman Inst.; hon. fellow Royal Coll. Physicians (London), Inst. Biology (Eng.), Royal Soc. Medicine. Home: Residence Dept Biochemistry Imperial Coll London SW 7 England

CHAISSON, JOHN ROBERT, marine corps officer; b. Swampscott, Mass., Sept. 27, 1916; s. Joseph and Annie Josephine (Donovan) C.; A.B. cum laude, Harvard, 1939; m. Marguerite Martin, Feb. 22, 1946; children—Joseph M., Dorothy (Mrs. Robert Jones), Jane, Thomas M Commd. 2d lt. USMC, 1941, advanced through grades to lt. gen., 1971; assigned 1st Marine Div., 1942-45, 53-54; chief staff USMC, 1971—. Decorated D.S.M., Silver Star, Legion of Merit, Bronze Star, Navy Commendation medal. Home: Quarters 2 Marine Barracks 8th and I Sts SE Washington DC 20003 Office: Chief Staff Hdqrs USMC Washington DC 20340

CHAIT, FREDERICK, atty.; b. Newark, Sept. 20, 1913; s. Boris and Clara (Wolpe) C.; A.B., Coll. City of N.Y., 1932; LL.B., Columbia, 1935; m. Helen Sporn, Sept. 22, 1938. Admitted to N.Y. bar, 1935, Pa. bar, 1952, atty., Social Security Bd., Washington, 1936-37; asso. Konta, Kirchwey and Engel, N.Y. City, 1937-42; chief counsel, rationing brs. O.P.A., 1942-44; war legislation litigation and claims div. U.S. Dept. of Justice, 1944-45; gen. counsel UNRRA, 1946-48; counsel Triangle Publs., Inc., 1948-49; counsel The Phila. Inquirer, 1948-69, gen. mgr., 1958-69; pres. Phila. Inquirer and Phila. Daily News; chmn. bd. Newspaper One; dir. Met. Sunday Newspapers, Inc. Officer, Bur. of Advt., Am. Newspaper Pubs. Assn. Mem. Phila. Com. Public Affairs, Citizens Council on City Planning; chmn. allocations com., v.p. United Fund; bd. dirs. Pa. Ballet. Mem. Pa., N.Y.C. bar assns., Co-author: Monopoly vs. Competition, 1935, Legal Controls on Competitive Practices, 1936, Copyright Law, 1939 (legal casebooks). Home: 250 S 17th St Philadelphia PA 19103 Office: 400 N Broad St Philadelphia PA 19130

CHAIT, LAWRENCE G., advt. exec.; b. Scranton, Pa., June 27, 1917; s. Perez and Rebecca (Chait) C.; student pub. schs.; m. Sylvia Levine, June 12, 1938; children—Martha, Pamela, George. Direct mail advt. mgr. Dow Jones Co., Inc., N.Y.C., 1945-49; advt. mgr. Arthur Wiesenberger & Co., mem. N.Y. Stock Exchange, 1950-51; circulation exec. Time, Life, Fortune, 1951-55; v.p. R.L. Polk Co., 1955-58; founder Lawrence G. Chait & Co., Inc., advt. agy., N.Y.C., 1957, pres., 1958-67, chmn., 1968—. Served with U.S. Maritime Service, World War II. Mem. Direct Mail Advt. Assn. (past v.p.), Sales Promotion Execs. Assn. (past v.p.), Assn. Direct Marketing Agys. (founding pres.). Club: Hundred Million (past pres.). Author: Those Little Golden Lists, 1955; Purchasing is Predictable, 1956; Nine priceless Ingredients of Success in Selling to Businessmen by Mail, 1958; How to Advertize and Sell to the Consumer Market by Mail, 1959; The Case for Legal Regulation of Advertising, 1962; Building business By Mail, 1965; Targeted MarketingNew Science of Advertising and Selling, 1966; Six Elements in the Consumer Credit Revolution, 1967; Four Vital Ingredients of the Coming Revolution in Consumer Marketing, 1968; Multimedia Direct Marketing, 1970. Home: 32 Lynwood Dr Valley Stream NY 11580 Office: 641 Lexington Av New York City NY 10022

CHAIT, WILLIAM, librarian; b. N.Y.C., Dec. 5, 1915; s. Max and Mollie (Miller) C.; B.A., Bklyn. Coll., 1934; B.L.S., Pratt Inst., 1935, M.S. in L. S., Columbia, 1938; m. Beatrice L. Faigelman, June 13, 1937; 1 son, Edward Martin. Library asst., br. librarian Bklyn. Pub. Library, 1935-45; service command librarian 2d Service Command, AUS, 1945-46; chief in- service tng., personnel control Milw. Pub. Library, 1946-48; dir. Kalamazoo Pub. Library, 1948-56; dir. Dayton and Montgomery County Pub. Library, 1956—. Mem. Library Mgmt. and Bldg. Cons., Inc. Pres., Kalamazoo Council Social Agys., 1954-55, Dayton City Beautiful Com., 1968-69; treas. Montgomery County Hist. Soc., 1968-69. Fulbright lectr. library sci. U. Tehran, 1969-70. Mem. Pub. (pres. 1964-65), Am. (chmn. personnel adminstrn. sect. 1958-60), Mich. (pres. 1955-56), Ohio (pres. 1964-65) library assns. Kiwanian. Clubs: Torch (pres. 1960-61), Dayton Discussion (pres. 1966). Home: 2931 Ensley Av Dayton OH 45414 Office: 215 E 3d St Dayton OH 45402

CHAIX, ALFRED VALERIEN, arcitect; b. Los Angeles, May 17, 1913; s. Valerien Alfred and Marie (Chaix) C.; student Beaux Art Inst., 1930-32, Los Angeles Jr. Coll., 1932-33, U So. Cal., 1943, U. Cal., Los Angeles, 1946-48; m. Emma T. Wenzl, Dec. 1, 1936; children—Ronald A., Alfred L., Denise (Mrs. Ralph Blanchard), James A. Draftsman, Eugene Weston, Los Angeles, 1930-32; designer Harbin F. Hunter, Los Angeles, 1933-42, 45-48; supr. U.S. Engring. Dept., Los Angeles, 1942-43; designer, supr. Aircraft Wood Products Corp., Vernon, Cal., 1943-45; pres. Chaix & Johnson Assos., Los Angeles, 1948—. Mem. So. Pasadena Mayor's Bd. Appeals, 1969-71, So. Pasadena Zoning Bd., 1971—. Bd. dirs. Our Little Bros. and Sisters Orphanage. Recipient 8 honor awards for excellency in archtl. design A.I.A. Mem. Los Angeles C. of C. Clubs: Serra, Toastmasters (Los Angeles). Home: 730 La Portada South Pasadena CA 91030 Office: 1666 W 3d St Los Angeles CA 90017

CHAKIRIS, GEORGE, actor; b. Norwood, O., Sept. 16, 1934; s. Steven and Zoe (Anastasiadou) C.; ed. pub. schs., Am. Sch. of Dance. Motion pictures include West Side Story, 1961, Flight from Ashiya, 1962, Diamond Head, 1963, King of the Sun, 1963, Is Paris Burning, 1966, Brigadoon, Young Girls of Rocheford. Recipient Acad. award for best male supporting actor, 1962.

CHAKO, NICHOLAS, educator; b. Hotova, Epirus, Albania, Nov. 11, 1910; s. Kyriacus (Qako) Demetrius and Victoria John (Tako) C.; came to U.S., 1929, naturalized, 1935; B.S., U. Paris-Marseille (France), 1928; postgrad. Harvard, 1933-34; Ph.D., Johns Hopkins, 1934; Dr. es Sciences, Sorbonne, Paris, 1966; m. Bernardine van Looy, July 16, 1952; 1 son, Alexander Constatine. Prof., head math. and physics sects. State Gymnasium, Scutari, Albania, 1936-37; mem. staff Cruft Lab., tutor Harvard, 1938-40; mem. staff spectroscopic lab. Mass. Inst. Tech., 1940- 41; lectr. Ill. Inst. Tech., 1941-42; lectr. Brown U., summer 1944; asso. prof. Kan. State Coll., 1946- 47, Ala. Poly. Inst., 1947-49; Fulbright exchange prof. Utrecht (Holland) U., 1950-51; guest prof. Chalmers U. Tech., Gothenburg, Sweden, 1951-52; vis. lectr. Lund (Sweden) U., spring, 1952; research asso. Inst. Math. Scis., N.Y. U., 1953- 56; prof. physics Adelphi Coll., 1955-56; prof. math. Queens Coll., 1956—. Vis. prof. Inst. Space Studies, N.Y.C., summer 1961; invited lectr. Polish Acad. Scis., Athens (Greece) U., summer 1965; guest lectr. French AEC, Saclay, 1965-66; Exchange prof. U. Paris, 1965-66; tech. adviser Signal Corps, 6th Service Command, 1942; cons. OSS, Washington, 1942-45; mathematician, research engr. Russell Electric Co., Chgo., 1942-46. Recipient ann. prize Royal Soc. Engrs. and Chalmers Alumni Assn., 1952. Fellow Inst. Math. and Applications Gt. Britain; mem. Am., Dutch, Polish phys. socs., French, Am. math. socs., N.Y. Acad. Scis., A.A.A.S. Author: Anglo-Saxon Universities, 1937-39; Emperor Anastasius I, 1940; Contribution à la Théorie de Diffraction, 1966; also research papers. Home: 138-10 Franklin Av Flushing NY 11355 Office: Inst Nat des Sciences et Techniques Nucleáires Saclay France

CHALABI, A. FATTAH, educator; b. Mosul, Iraq, Apr. 12, 1924; s. Kasim S. and Khad (Hadid) C.; came to U.S., 1959, naturalized, 1967; M.Sc., U. Mich., 1952, Ph.D. in Engring., 1956; m. Betrice Austin, Oct. 14, 1956. Asst. prof. U. Baghdad (Iraq), 1956-59; mem. faculty Worcester Poly. Inst., 1959—, prof. civil engring., 1966—. Registered profl. engr., Mass. Mem. Am. Soc. Engring. Edn., Am. Concrete Inst., Am. Soc. C.E., Sigma Xi, Chi Epsilon. Home: 3 Rutland Terrace Worcester, MA 01609.

CHALEK, SOL, food co. exec.; b. Proskurov, Russia, Apr. 15, 1897; s. Morris and Sarah (Grovenman) C.; m. Eleanor Odinov, July 3, 1919; childrenAlverne, Morton J. An organizer, later exec. sec., gen. mgr. L.I. Food Dealers Assn., 1931-47; an organizer, gen. mgr. Assos. Food Stores Coop., Inc., 1942-54; pres., chmn., bd. Asso. Food Stores, Inc. 1954-. Active United Jewish Appeal, Histradut, Fedn. Jewish Philanthropies, Nat. Jewish Hosp. at Denver, Nat. Council Christians and Jews, Deborah Hosp., Browns Mills, N.J., Muscular Dystrophy Assn., Nat. Found. Infantile Paralysis, Cerebral Palsy Assn. Trustee local 338 CIO-Retail Food Clerks Retirement Fund. Recipient Coronet medal St. Edward's U., Austin, Tex. Mem. Jamaica, Queensboro chambers commerce Food Industry Alliance N.Y.C., Empire State Coops, Queens Food Dealers Coop., N.Y. State Food Merchants Assn. Mem. B'nai B'rith (past bd. dirs. lodge). Club: Apron (v.p.). (N.Y.C.). Home: 63-50 Wetherole St Rego Park, NY 11374. Office: 179-45 Brinkerhoff Av Jamaica, NY 11433.

CHALIAPIN, BORIS, painter. Address: 38 Central Park S New York City NY 10019*

CHALK, CLAIRE, air line exec. Sec., Trans Caribbean Airways, Inc., N.Y.C. Office: 714 Fifth Av New York City NY 10022*

CHALK, HOWARD WOLFE, advt. exec.; b. N.Y.C., Jan. 15, 1922; s. Maurice and Zara (Philips) C.; student N.Y. U., 1939-41; m. Shirley Fields, June 1, 1947; children—Robyn Robyn Kim, Russell Jay. Account exec. Sterling Advt., N.Y.C., 1947-50, v.p., account supr., dir., 1950-55; exec. v.p., account supr. Altman, Stoller Chalk Advt., Inc., N.Y.C., 1955-68; mng. dir. Chalk, Nissen, Hanft Advt. Inc., N.Y.C., 1968—. v.p. Broadlawn Harbour Assn., 1965- 66, pres., 1966-67; mem. Non-Partisan Citizens Nominating Com., Great Neck, N.Y., 1966-67. Served with inf. AUS, 1942-45; ETO. Decorated Purple Heart, Bronze Star with oak leaf cluster. Hon. fellow Harry S. Truman Library Inst. Mem. UN Assn. U.S.A., Am. Arbitration Assn., Sales Exec. Club N.Y.C., Internat. Platform Assn. Clubs: Men's Garden Clubs: Mem's Garden City (N.Y.) Jewish Center (founder, past pres.); Old Westbury (L.I.) Golf and Country; Sierra. Home: 5 Harbour Rd Great Neck NY 11024 Office: 666 Fifth Av New York City NY 10019

CHALK, O. ROY, transp. co. exec.; b. London, Eng., June 7, 1907; s. Bennett and Sophie (Stern) C.; came to U.S., 1910, derivative citizen; LL.D., Seoul (Korea) U., 1966; m. Claire Cole; 1 dau., Barbara (Mrs. Henry M. Hubshman). Admitted to N.Y. bar, 1932, U.S. Supreme Ct. bar, 1958; practiced in N.Y.C., 1932—; pres., chmn. bd. O. Roy Chalk Realty & Constrn. Corp., 1942—, Trans Caribbean Airways, Inc., 1945-70, D.C. Transit System, Inc., 1956—, Transp. Corp. Am., 1957—, also Capital Transit Co.; chmn. Internat. Rys. of C. Am., 1963-66, pres., 1965-66; pres. Radio San Juan, Tele San Juan; editor, pub. Washington Examiner, El Diaro-La Prensa; chmn. bd. Virginia Lines. Dir. Wash. Bd. Trade, 1957—. Civilian cons. tng. divs. USN Bur. Aeros., USAF, World War II. Nat. chmn. Am. Jewish Com., 1957—; vice chmn. United Negro Coll. Fund. Trustee Virgin Islands Coll., also Finch Coll., N.Y.C., 1955—; vice chmn., dir. Am.-Korean Found., N.Y.C., 1954—; bd. regents, mem. president's council Georgetown U.; mem. council Catholic U. P.R. Chmn. finance com. U.S. Com. for UN. Recipient award of achievement Advt. Club Washington, 1958; merit award USN Bur. Aeros., 1945; named hon. citizen Govt. Korea, 1957. Fellow Inst. Aero. Scis. Knight of Malta (Supreme Council 71—). Home: 1010 Fifth Av New York City NY 10028 Office: 714 Fifth Av New York City NY 10019

CHALKER, WILLIAM ROGERS, chem. co. exec.; b. Atlanta, Feb. 17, 1920; s. Elliott Lamar and Mildred Edna (Crum) C.; A.B., U. S.C., 1942, B.S., 1943; diploma engring. U.S. Naval Acad. Postgrad. Sch., 1945; M.S., Mass. Inst. Tech., 1948, Profl. Engr., 1950; m. Joan Windsor King, Feb. 12, 1955; children—William Rogers, Scott King.

Observor, U.S. Weather Bur., Petersburg, W.Va., 1946; research asst. Mass. Inst. Tech., 1947-50; cons. meteorologist A.H. Glenn & Assos., New Orleans, 1950-51; with E.I. duPont de Nemours & Co., Inc., 1951—, atmospheric dispersion research Savannah River Plant, 1951-53, moved to engr., sr. cons., 1965—. Mem. Del. Air Pollution Authority, 1957-66; mem. tech. adv. com. Del. Water and Air Resources Commn., 1967-70; mem. Air Quality Com. Mfg. Chemists Assn., 1960—; chmn. air control com. Chem. Industry Council N.J., 1964-66. Served to lt. USNR, 1943-46; ETO. Registered profl. engr., Del. Mem. Am., Royal meteorol. socs., Air Pollution Control Assn. (chmn. mid-states sect. 1964-65), Sigma Xi, Omicron Delta Kappa, Sigma Nu, Kappa Sigma Kappa. Republican. Episcopalian. Contbr. articles to profl. jours. Home: 41 Bridle Brook Lane Newark DE 19711 Office: c/o E I du Pont de Nemours & Co Wilmington DE 19898

CHALL, JEANNE STERNLICHT, psychologist, educator; b. Shendishov, Poland, Jan. 1, 1921; d. Hyman and Eva (Kreinik) Sternlicht; came to U.S., 1927, naturalized, 1927; B.B.A. cum laude, Coll. City N.Y., 1941; M.A., Ohio State U., 1947, Ph.D., 1952; M.A., (hon.) Harvard, 1965; m. Leo P. Chall, June 8, 1946 (div. 1964). Asst., Inst. Psychol. Research, Tchrs. Coll., Columbia, 1943-45; research asst. Ohio State U. Bur. Ednl. Research, 1945-47, research asso., instr., 1947-49; instr. to prof. City Coll., City U., 1950-65; vis. asso. prof. edn. Harvard Grad. Sch. Edn., Cambridge, 1963, prof., 1965—; mem. faculty Tchrs. Coll., Columbia, summers 1958, 60; mem. Nat. Adv. Com. on Dyslexia and related reading disorders, 1968—. Fellow Am. Psychol. Assn., A.A.A.S.; mem. N.Y. Acad. Sci., Am. Ednl. Research Assn., Nat. Soc. for study Edn. (dir.), Internat. Reading Assn. (past dir.), Nat. Conf. on Research in English (past pres.), Nat. Reading Council, Pi Lambda Theta, Beta Gamma Sigma, Phi Delta Kappa. Author: (with Edgar Dale) A Formula for Predicting Readability, 1948; Readability: An Appraisal of Research and Application, 1958; Learning to Read: The Great Debate, 1967. Mem. editorial bd. Reading Research Quarterly, 1966-68. Home: 1558 Massachusetts Av Cambridge MA 02138

CHALLANS, MARY, see Renault, Mary.

CHALLENER, RICHARD DELO, educator; b. Pitts., Jan. 15, 1923; s. William Albert and Winifred (Delo) C.; grad. Hill Sch., Pottstown, Pa., 1940; A.B., Princeton, 1947; A.M., Columbia, 1948, Ph.D., 1952; m. Martha Louise Coate, June 10, 1947; childrenCatherine Louise, Elizabeth Jane, Daniel Delo. Mem. faculty Princeton, 1949—, asso. prof. history, 1959-64, prof. history, 1964—, chmn dept., 1970-71, asso. dean coll., 1961-66. Mem. advanced placement com. Coll. Entrance Exam. Bd., 1959-62. Trustee St. George's Sch., Newport, R.I., Hun Sch., Princeton, N.J. Served with AUS, 1943-46. Mem. Am. Hist. Assn., Am. Mil. Assn., Phi Beta Kappa. Presbyn. (elder). Author: The French Theory of the Nation in Arms, 1866-1939, 1955; (with G.B. Turner) National Security in the Nuclear Age, 1960. Editor: From Isolation to Containment. 1970. books. Home: 569 Riverside Dr E Princeton, N.J. 08540

CHALLIS, JOHN, harpsichord builder; b. South Lyon, Mich., Jan. 9, 1907; s. Charles and Alice D. (Callen) C.; student Eastern Michigan Univ., 1924-26, Arnold Dolmetsch Haslemere, Eng. (Dolmetsch Found. scholarship), 1926- 30, U. Mich., 1933; M.Ed. (hon.), E. Michigan Univ., 1953; H.H.D. (hon.), Wayne State U., 1958. Harpsichord builder, Ypsilanti, Mich., 1930-46, Detroit, 1946-65, N.Y.C., 1966—; developed nonwearing, split proof tuning pin blocks, complete aluminum frame, moisture resistant jacks, metal bridge and soundboard for keyboard instruments. Mem. Am. Musicol. Soc. Address: 133 Fifth Av New York City, NY 10003

CHALMERS, BRUCE, metallurgist; b. London, Eng., Oct. 15, 1907; s. Stephen Drummond and Clara (Rosenhain) C.; grad. Stationers Cos. Sch., London. 1916-26; B.Sc., U. London, 1929; Ph.D., 1931. D.Sc., 1941; A.M. (hon.), Harvard, 1953; m. Gladys Ema Arnouts, July 1, 1938; children—Stephen P., Carol A., Jane H., Alison F., Heather C. naturalized, 1959. Lectr., U. London, 1932- 38; physicist Tin Research Inst., London, 1938-44; head metall. div. Royal Aircraft Establishment, 1944-46, Atomic Energy Research Establishment, Harwell, 1946-48; prof. phys. metallurgy U. Toronto, 1948- 53; Gordon McKay prof. of metall., Harvard, 1953—, master of John Winthrop House, 1964—. Recipient Sauveur award Am. Soc. Metals, 1960; Klamer medal from Franklin Inst., 1965. Fellow Inst. Physics, Inst. Metallurgists, Am. Acad. Arts and Scis.; mem. Inst. Metals. London, Iron and Steel Inst. (London), Am. Inst. Mining & Metall. Engrs., Am. Soc. Metals, Sociét é Française de Metallurgie (hon.), Sigma Xi. Author: Physical Examination of Metal, Vol. 1, 1939, Vol. 2 (with A. G. Quarrell). 1941: Structure and Mechanical Properties of Metals, 1951; Physical Metallurgy, 1959; Energy, 1963; Principles of Solidification, 1964: (with J. G. Holland, K. A. Jackson, R. B. Williamson) Introduction to Crystallography, pub. 1965. Editor: Progress in Materials Science, 1949—, Acta Metallurgica, Scripta Metallurgica. Home: 966 Memorial Dr Cambridge MA 02138 Office: Pierce Hall Harvard University Cambridge MA 02138

CHALMERS, EDWIN LAURENCE, Jr., univ. adminstr.; b. Wildwood, N.J., Mar. 24, 1928; s. Edwin Laurence and Carolyn (Smith) C.; A.B., Princeton, 1948, M.A., 1950, Ph.D., 1951; m. Mary Ann Bealler, Feb. 4, 1950; children—Edwin Laurence III, Thomas Henry. Instr. psychology Princeton, 1951-52; research psychologist USAF, Denver, 1952-53, 56-57; mem. faculty Fla. State U., 1957-69, prof. psychology, dean Coll. Arts and Scis., 1964-66, v.p. acad. affairs, 1966- 69, chancellor U. Kan., Lawrence, 1969—. Served to 1st lt. USAF, 1953- 56. Mem. Am. Assn. U. Profs., Phi Beta Kappa, Sigma Xi, Omicron Delta Kappa, Phi Kappa Phi. Contbr. profl. jours. Home: Lilac Lane Lawrence, KS 66044.

CHALMERS, GORDON HALL, univ. athletic dir.; b. Cranford, N.J., Feb. 24, 1911; s. William Hall and Marguerite (Perdue) C.; B.S., Franklin and Marshall Coll., 1935; m. Helen Marie Schermerhorn, Mar. 29, 1941; children—Margo Annette, Donna Lee. Time study engr. Foster Wheeler Corp., 1936-37, Western Electric Co., 1937-38; sales supr. Tidewater Oil Co., 1938-40; swimming coach Lafayette Coll., 1940-41, Lehigh U., 1941; swimming coach, asst. dir. athletic U.S. Mil. Acad., 1946-59; dir. athletics Ia. State U., Ames, 1959-67; dir. of athletics Ind. State U., Terre Haute, 1967—. Dir. Olympic com. Nat. Collegiate Athletic Assn. Served to lt. comdr. USNR, 1941-46; PTO. Mem. Nat. Gymnastics Fedn. (pres.), Coll. Swimming Coaches Assn., Nat. Athletic Dirs. Assn. (dir.), Phi Kappa Sigma. Elk. Home: 550 Gardendale St Woodridge, Terre Haute, IN 47803.

CHALMERS, HARVEY, II, author; b. Amsterdam, N.Y., Sept. 11, 1890; s. Arthur Augustus and Emma Appleton (Curtin) C.; A.B., Yale, 1913; m. Ruth Elizabeth Warren, Sept. 11, 1914; children—Arthur A., Shirley (Mrs. George H. Carter). Pres., Harvey Chalmers & Son Inc. Cons. N.Y. State Dept. Edn. Served to 2d lt. U.S. Army, World War I. Mem. of Beta Theta Pi. Republican. Episcopalian. Clubs: N.Y. Fencers, Yale (N.Y.C.); Corinthian Yacht (Marblehead, Mass.); Antlers Country (Amsterdam). Author: West to the Setting Sun, 1943; Drums Against Frontenac, 1949; Joseph Brant; Mohawk, 1955; Birth of the Erie Canal, 1960; Last Stand of the Nez Perce; Destruction of a People, 1962; How the Irish Built the Erie, 1964; Tales of the Mohawk, 1967. Contbr. to Northeast Sportsman, Field & Stream, Am. Field, Nat. Sportsman, Hunting and Fishing, Outdoors, Field and Stream Reader, 1935-42. Lectr. on N.Y. State, N.E. history, Indian wars, govt. and way of life, Mohawk Valley. Recs. of stories of pioneer days. N.Y. State Edn. Dept. Home: 439 Guy Park Av Amsterdam NY 12010

CHALMERS, JOHN, coll. dean; b. Fitchburg, Mass., May 25, 1916; s. James Anderson and Bertha Eulalia (Whitcomb) C.; A.B., Middlebury (Vt.) Coll., 1938; Rhodes scholar, Oxford (Eng.) U., 1938-39; Ph.D., Cornell U., 1943; m. Carol Bloom, July 13, 1940; children—James A., Carolyn, Virginia. Instr., Cornell U., 1940-43; asst. prof. Middlebury Coll., 1946-47; asso. prof. econs. Kenyon Coll., 1947-53; Fulbright prof. econs. U. Philippines, 1951-52; successively asso. prof., prof., chmn. div. social scis. Harpur Coll., State U. N.Y., 1953-61; dean acad. affairs and arts and scis. U. Wyo., 1961-63; dean Coll. Arts and Scis., Kan. State U., Manhattan, 1963- -, v.p. acad. affairs. 1969—. Tax research specialist N.Y. Tax Commn., 1946-47; v.p. econs. div. Ohio Coll. Assn., 1948-50; cons. econ. edn. workshops in Ohio, N.J., N.Y. and Kan., 1952—; pres. Council Colls. Arts and Scis., 1968—; mem. Commn. Arts and Scis., 1967- 70. Served to lt. (j.g.) USNR, 1943-46. Mem. Am. Econ. Assn., Beta Gamma Sigma. Home: 1009 Karla Lane Manhattan, KS 66502.

CHALMERS, RENE, minister of foreign affairs of Haiti. Address: Office Minister Fgn Affairs Port-au-Prince, Haiti.*

CHALMERS, THOMAS CLARK, physician, research adminstr.; b. Forest Hills, N.Y., Dec. 8, 1917; s. Thomas Clark and Elizabeth (Ducat) C.; student Yale, 1936-39; M.D., Columbia, 1943; m. Frances Crawford Talcott, Aug. 31, 1942; children—Elizabeth Ducat (Mrs. Daniel G. Wright), Frances Talcott, Thomas Clark, Richard Matthew. Intern Presbyn. Hosp., N.Y.C., 1943-44; research fellow N.Y.U. Malaria Research Unit, Goldwater Meml. Hosp., N.Y.C., 1944-45; resident Harvard Med. Services of Boston City Hosp., 1945-47; asst. physician Thorndike Meml. Lab., 1947-53; chief med. services Lemuel Shattuck Hosp., Boston, 1955-68; asst. chief med. dir. for research and edn. VA, Washington, 1968-70; asso. dir. clin. care NIH, also dir. clin. center NIH, Bethesda, Md., 1970—; lectr. medicine Harvard; prof.medicine George Washington U. Dir. New Eng. Home for Little Wanderers, 1960-65. Served as capt., M.C., AUS, 1953-55. Diplomate Am. Bd. Internal Medicine. Mem. Am. Assn. Study Liver Diseases (pres. 1959), Am. Clin. and Climatol. Assn., A.C.P., Am. Fedn. Clin. Research, Am. Gastroenterol. Assn. (pres. 1969), A.M.A., Am. Soc. Clin. Investigation, Am. Soc. Clin. Pharmacology and Therapeutics, Assn. Am. Physicians, Acad. Medicine Washington, Eastern Gut Club. Club: Cosmos (Washington). Contbr. numerous articles profl. jours. Home: 1007 Turkey Run Rd McLean VA 22101 Office: Nat Institutes Health Bethesda MD 20014

CHALMERS, WILLIAM SCOTT, clergyman, educator; b. Edinburgh, Scotland, Nov. 20, 1907; s. Robert Scott and Adele Winifred (Burnet) C.; brought to U.S., 1909; student Howe Mil. Acad., 1921-25; A.B., Princeton, 1929, A.M., 1930; student Gen. Theol. Seminary, 1930-33; m. Grace C. Griswold, 1949. Ordained priest Protestant Episcopal Church, Nov. 1934; became mem. Order of the Holy Cross (monastic order of P.E. Ch.), 1937; acting headmaster, Kent (Conn.) Sch., 1940, headmaster, 1941-49; became headmaster Harvard Sch., North Hollywood, Cal., 1949; prior Am. Coll. of the Oratory of the Good Shepherd; sec. to the Kent School Corp. Contbr. to (book) This Holy Fellowship, 1939; also to Holy Cross Mag. and The New Start (newspaper for youth). Address: The Harvard School North Hollywood CA 90028

CHAMALES, CHRISTOPHER JOHN, architect; b. Chgo., Nov. 11, 1907; s. John Christopher and Calliope (Stavros) C.; B.S., Mass. Inst. Tech., 1930, M.A., 1931; diploma Fontainebleau (France) Sch. Fine Arts, 1930; traveling fellow Mass. Inst. Tech., 1932-34; fellow Cranbrook Acad. Art, Bloomfield Hills, Mich., 1939-41; m. Margaret Goehst, Mar. 4, 1954. Owner Christopher Chamales & Assos., Chgo., 1945—; cons. archtl. design and planning other archtl. firms; cons. Chgo. Bd. Edn. Pres. Bellevue Place Assn., 1965—; works include master plans for Athens, Greece, and its port, City of Piraeus, 1939-40, Nat. Transport Terminal, 1950. Served to capt. AUS, 1941-45. Fellow Inst. Arts and Letters (Geneva); mem. A.I.A., Am. Soc. Planning Ofcls., Nat. Council Archtl. Registration Bds., Scarab, Frieze and Cornice. Clubs: Arts, Saddle and Cycle, Yacht (Chgo.). Home: 58 E Bellevue Pl Chicago IL 60611 Office: 11 S LaSalle St Chicago IL 60603

CHAMBERLAIN, ADRIAN RAMOND, univ. adminstr.; b. Detroit, Nov. 11, 1929; s. Adrian and Leila (Swisher) C.; B.S., Mich. State U., 1951; M.S., Wash. State U., 1952; Ph.D., Colo. State U., 1955; m. Virginia E. Webster, June 18, 1954; children—Curtis, Tracy, Thomas. Research engr. Phillips Petroleum Co., 1955; research coordinator, civil engr. Colo. State U., 1956-57, chief civil engr. sect., 1957-61, dean engring., 1959-61, v.p., 1960-66, exec. v.p., treas., governing bd., 1966-69, pres., 1969—. Chmn. bd. dirs. University Nat. Bank, 1964-69. Chmn. NSF Commn. Weather Modification, 1964-66; mem. Nat. Air Quality Criteria Adv. Com., 1967-70. Pres., chmn. trustee Colo. State U. Research Found.; pres., bd. dirs. Colo. Cystic Fibrosis Assn.; regional trustee Nat. Cystic Fibrosis Research Found., 1971-73; trustee University Corp. for Atmospheric Research. Fulbright student U. Grenoble, 1955-56. Mem. Am. Soc. Engring. Edn., Internat. Commn. Irrigation and Drainage, Am. Soc. C.E., A.A.A.S., Sigma Xi, Sigma Tau, Tau Beta Pi, Phi Kappa Phi, Chi Epsilon. Rotarian. Home: 645 S Shields St Fort Collins CO 80521

CHAMBERLAIN, ALEXANDER SCOTT, oil refining exec.; b. Pitts., July 4, 1900; s. George Dixon and Jessie (Dunbar) C.; B.S., Yale, 1922; m. Dorothy May Monroe, June 18, 1927; children—Alexander Scott II, Frank Monroe, Ann C. Mellon. Partner Emerson Cons., 1930-38; with Ashland Oil & Refining Co., 1938—, v.p. 1952-66, cons., 1962—; pres. Louisville Refining Co., 1960-67; dir. Louisville Trust Co. Chmn. Ky. Port and River Development Commission, 1966—; also Ohio River Valley Water Sanitation Commn., 1946-48, chmn. petroleum industry committee, 1965-70; pres. Ohio Valley Improvement Assn., 1953-55, 67-68, trustee, 1953-70; dir. Nat. Waterways Conference; regional adminstr. Emergency Petroleum and Gas Adminstrn., U.S. Dept. Interior; chmn. Ky. Personnel and Merit Council, 1959-60; gen. campaign chmn. Louisville and Jefferson County United Appeal, 1964-65. Bd. overseers U. Louisville, 1965—; dir. Internat . Center U. Louisville, 1962—; dir. Art Center Assn. Louisville; chmn. Ky. Ind. Coll. Found. Pres. Ky. Tax Research, 1957-60. Mem. Ky. (dir. 1962-70), Louisville (dir.) C. of C. Louisville Labor-Mgmt. Com., Miss. Valley Assn. (dir.), Ky. Travel Council (chmn. 1961-63). Clubs: Pendennis, Rotary, Louisville Country. Home: 18 River Hill Rd Louisville, KY 40207. Office: Ashland Oil & Refining Co P O Box 1915 Louisville KY 40201

CHAMBERLAIN, BETTY, writer, editor; b. East Orange, N.J., Feb. 10, 1908; d. John Payson and Elizabeth Jennings (Webster) Chamberlain; student Columbia, 1927-28; A.B., Smith Coll., 1929; postgrad. Sorbonne, 1932-33; divorced. Librarian pub. libraries, 1924-25, summer 1926-28; with Met. Mus. Art, 1929-32, Am. Cyanamid Co., 1934-37, Mus. Modern Art, 1940-42, Time mag., 1940-42; librarian Phila. Mus. Art, 1939-40; staff OWI, Washington, N.Y.C., 1942-43; reporter on war labor Time mag., 1943-44; shipyard labor relations U.S. Maritime Commn., Washington, 1944-45; writer, editor King's Crown Press, Physicians' Forum, Art News, Mag. Art, Richardson Wood, Inc., 1945-48; publicity dir. Mus. Modern Art, 1948-54; mng. editor Art News, 1954-56; head community devel. office and publicity dept. Bklyn. Mus., N.Y., 1956-59; pres. Betty Chamberlain Assos., Inc., 1959—; dir. Art Information Center, Inc., N.Y.C., 1959—. Assisted fund raising, clearances for entry of artists in France, 1940-42; campaign worker nat. health ins. fed. law Phys. Forum N.Y. Mem. adv. council Mus. Am. Folk Art, N.y. Sec., Democratic Town Com., Cornwall, Conn.; justice of peace, Cornwall. Mem. Am. Civil Liberties Union, Ams. for Dem. Action. Author: The Artist's Guide to His Market; also articles in profl. jours. Home: Cornwall Bridge CT 06754 also 850 2d Av New York City NY 10017 Office: 189 Lexington Av New York City NY 10016

CHAMBERLAIN, CHARLES ERNEST, congressman; b. Ingham County, Mich., July 22, 1917; s. Orson W. and Clara Adella (DaFoe) C.; B.S. in Commerce, U. Va., 1941, LL.B., 1949; m. Charlotte Mary Craney, Dec. 2, 1943; children—Charlotte Ellen, Christine Clark, Charles Ernest. Agt. Internal Revenue, Treasury Dept., 1946-47; admitted to Va. bar, 1949, Mich. bar, 1949; pvt. practice of law, Lansing, Mich., 1950—; asst. pros. Ingham County, 1950; city atty. East Lansing, 1953-54; legal counsel Mich. Senate Judiciary Com., 1953-54; pros. atty., 1955-56; mem. 85th-92d Congresses, 6th Dist. Mich., mem. ways and means com. Served as officer USCG, World War II. Mem. Mich. Bar, Am. Bar Assn., S.A.R. Republican. Kiwanian. Home: East Lansing MI 48823 Office: Lansing MI 48901

CHAMBERLAIN, CHARLES JAMES, railroad labor union exec.; b. Ashton, Ill., Aug. 7, 1921; s. Charles Hubert and Katherine (Reitz) C.; student pub. schs.; m. Joyce Lois Swanson, June 27, 1942; children—Richard B., Charles M. With signal dept. C.&N.-W. Ry., 1938-57; grand lodge rep. Brotherhood of R.R. Signalmen, 1957-61, sec.-treas., 1961-67, pres., 1967—. Alderman, DeKalb (Ill.) City Council, 1949-57. Mem. Ry. Labor Execs. Assn. (chmn. 1970—). Lutheran. Home: 610 Jon Lane Des Plaines IL 60016 Office: 2247 W Lawrence Av Chicago IL 60625

CHAMBERLAIN, DAVID SMITH, civil engr., air force officer; b. Akron, O., Apr. 8, 1921; s. Smith Frank and Violet Alice (Washabaugh) C.; B.S., U.S. Mil. Acad., 1943; M.S. in Civil Engring., U. Ill., 1947; M.S. in Bus. Adminstrn., George Washington U., 1964; m. Audrey June Baker, June 4, 1943; children—Christine Ann, Sandra Ann. Commd. 2d lt. USAAF, 1943, advanced through grades to brig. gen. USAF, 1967; resident engr. charge airfield design and constrn., China Mainland, 1943-46; civil engr. instr., Boston, 1947-50; civil engr. staff officer, Washington, 1950-54; dir. constrn. airfields, Eng., 1954-57; dir. civil engring. design Titan ICBM, Los Angeles, 1957-61; dir. civil engring. electronic systems, Boston, 1961-63; dir. civil engring. Air Force Systems Command, Washington, 1964-66, Air Force Tactical Air Command, Hampton, Va., 1967-69; Civil engr. Pacific Air Command, Honolulu, 1969—; engr. charge airfield design and constrn., Vietnam, 1966-67. Decorated Legion of Merit with 3 oak leaf clusters, Bronze Star, Commendation medal with 2 oak leaf clusters. Registered profl. engr., Mass., Md. Mem. Am. Soc. C.E., Nat. Soc. Profl. Engrs., Soc. Am. Mil. Engrs. Home: 701 Signer Blvd Hickam Field Honolulu HI 96553 Office: DCS/Civil Engineer US Air Force Hickam Field Honolulu HI 96553

CHAMBERLAIN, DONALD FRANK, govt. ofcl.; b. Wayzata, Minn., July 14, 1914; s. Harry Thomas and Anna Caroline (Olsen) C.; B.Chem. Engring. with distinction, U. Minn., 1936, Ph.D. in Chem. Engring. and Organic Chemistry, 1940; m. Phyllis M. Barnard, Mar. 30, 1940; children—David A., Denis O., Douglas E., Donna I., Deborah K. Teaching asst. chem. engring. U. Minn., 1936-40; research engr. Nat. Aniline div. Allied Chemical & Dye Corp., 1940-46; part time instr. ESMWT, Cornell U., 1943-44; asst. prof. Washington U., 1946-47, asso. prof., 1947-49, prof., 1949-56, vice chmn. dept. chem. engring., 1952-55; adminstr. sci. personnel CIA, Washington, 1955—, Nat. War Coll., Ft. McNair, Washington, 1960-61; dir. office sci. intelligence CIA, Washington , 1963—; cons. various industries. Mem. Am. Inst. Chem. Engrs. (chmn. St. Louis sect.), Am. Chem. Soc., Am. Assn. U. Profs., Am. Soc. Engring. Edn., Engrs. Joint Council of St. Louis, Sigma Xi, Alpha Chi Sigma, Tau Beta Pi, Phi Lambda Upsilon. Club: Cosmos (Washington). Home: 9712 DePaul Dr Bethesda MD 20034 Office: CIA Washington DC 20505

CHAMBERLAIN, ELWYN, artist; b. Mpls., May 19, 1928; s. L. Wynn and Nell Sherman (Moody) C.; B.A., U. Ida., 1949; M.A., U. Wis., 1951; m. Sally Stokes, Sept. 7, 1965. Asst. instr. art U. Wis., 1950; guest instr. painting U. Ida., spring 1955; guest lectr. modern art Bard Coll., 1966-67; one man show, Hewitt Gallery, N.Y.C., 1954, 57, Gallery G, N.Y.C., 1959, Nordness Gallery, N.Y.C., 1961, Fischbach Gallery, N.Y.C., 1965 and 1966; exhbns. include Walker Art Center, Mpls., 1951, 54, Breslar Galleries, Milw., 1951, Pa. Acad., 1953, Hewitt Gallery, 1954. De Cordova Mus., Lincoln, Mass., 1954, Colorado Springs Fine Arts Center, 1955, 61st Western Annual at Denver Art Mus., 1955, Yale Gallery, 1955, Whitney Annual, 1955, Art Alliance, Phila., 1957, Lane Galleries, Los Angeles, 1957, Spoleto (Italy) Festival, 1957, R.I. Sch. Design, 1958, Deefield Acad., Northhampton, Mass., 1958, Provincetown (Mass.) Art Festival, 1958, Chrysler Mus., Provincetown, 1958; rep. permanent collections Whitney Mus. Am. Art, Sara Roby Found., N.Y.C., Johnson Collection-Art Now U.S.A. (traveling). Producer off-Broadway show Conquest of the Universe, 1967. Author: Art Voices (bibliography) 1966. Home: 222 The Bowery New York City NY 10012 also The Quadrangle Staatsburg NY 12580

CHAMBERLAIN, GEORGE RICHARD, actor; b. Los Angeles, Mar. 31, 1935; s. Charles and Elsa Chamberlain; B.A., Pomona Coll., 1956; studied voice Los Angeles Conservatory Music, 1958; studied dramatics with Jeff Corey. Participated coll. dramatics, appeared in King Lear, Arms and the Man, The Lady's Not for Burning; TV roles in Gunsmoke, Bourbon Streeet Beat, Thriller, Mr. Lucky, Alfred Hitchcock Presents, TV series Dr. Kildare, Hamlet, 1970; motion pictures include Secret of Purple Reef, 1950, Thunder of Drums, 1961, Twilight of Honor, Joy in the Morning, 1965; TV singing debut on Hollywood Melody, 1962; recordings include Theme Music from Dr. Kildare, A Kiss to Build A Dream On, Rome Will Never Leave You, Joy In the Morning, April Love, also albums. Served to sgt., AUS, 1956-58. Named favorite male performer TV Guide poll, 1963. Address: care MGM-TV 1540 Broadway New York City NY 10036

CHAMBERLAIN, JAMES MORTIMER WILLS, cons.; b. Akron, O., July 19, 1905; s. John and Elizabeth (Wills) C.; B.S., Mass. Inst. Tech., 1927; m. Florence Scott, 1928; 1 dau., Cynthia Scott; m. 2d, Roberta Wunderlich, June 2, 1945; 1 son, Craig. Devel. engr. Goodyear Tire & Rubber Co., 1927-28, Goodyear Zeppelin, 1928-30; gen. mgr. U.S. Stoneware Co., Akron, 1930-36, chmn., pres., 1936-66; chmn. bd. Intervest, Inc.; pres. Chamberlain Investment Corp., Ensine Corp.; v.p. Hamilton Kent Mfg. Co., Flexlock Corp., Republic Lead Equipment Co.; sec. Hamilton Kent, Ltd., Can., Hamilton Kent of Atlanta, Hamilton Kent of Kan., Freeport Rubber, Freeport, Grand Bahama Islands. Mem. Am. Soc. of M.E., Am. Inst. Chem. Engrs., Nat. Soc. Profl. Engrs., Am. Chem. Soc., Am. Ceramic Soc. Clubs: Aviation Executives (Washington); Union League, Nat. Aviation,

Wings, Chemist (N.Y.C.); Portage Country (Akron). Congress Lake Country. Home: 3333 W Bath Rd Akron, OH 44313. Office: 1013 Portage Trail Cuyahoga Falls OH 44221

CHAMBERLAIN, JOHN, sculptor; b. Rochester, Ind., Apr. 16, 1927; student Art Inst. Chgo., U. Ill., also Black Mountain Coll. Exhbt. in Sao Paulo, Brazil, Chgo., N.Y.C., also Mus. Modern Art; exhibited at Venice Biennial, 1964, Met. Mus., 1969, Guggenheim Mus., 1971; pioneer use automobile metal and color Mus., 1969, Guggenheim Mus., 1971; pioneer use automobile metal and color processes in sculpture. Guggenheim fellow, 1966. Address: care Leo Castelli Gallery 4 E 77th St New York City NY 10021

CHAMBERLAIN, JOHN R., business exec. Exec. v.p. Thomas Industries, Inc., Louisville. Office: 207 E Broadway Louisville KY 40202*

CHAMBERLAIN, JOHN RENSSELAER, staff writer; b. New Haven, Oct. 28, 1903; s. Robert Rensselaer and Emily (Davis) C.; Ph.B., Yale, 1925; m. Margaret Sterling, Apr. 22, 1926 (dec.); children—Elizabeth and Margaret; m. 2d, Ernestine Stodelle, June 29, 1956; 1 son, John. Advertising writer, 1925; report N.Y. Times, 1926-28, daily book columnist, 1933-36; editor of Fortune Mag., 1936-41; asso. prof. Columbia Sch. of Journalism 1941-44; asst. editor N.Y. Times Book Review, 1928-33; asso. editor Saturday Review of Literature, 1933; book editor Scribners Mag., 1936-38; book editor Harper's Mag., 1939-47; lecturer Columbia Sch. Journalism, 1934- 35, New Sch. for Social Research, 1935, Columbia U. Summer Sch., 1937. Contbg. daily book columnist, New York Times, 1942-44; editor, Life mag., 1945-50, The Freeman (rev. politics, econs., arts), 1950-52; asso. editor Barron's Magazine, 1953-55; became staff writer Wall St. Jour., 1955; now daily columnist King Features Syndicate, N.Y.C. Author: Farewell to Reform, 1932; The American Stakes, 1940; MacArthur; 1941- 1951 (with General Charles Willoughby) 1954; The Roots of Capitalism, 1959; The Enterprising Americans: A Business History of the U.S., 1963. Contbr. to the Critique of Humanism, 1930; Challenge to the New Deal, 1934; After the Genteel Tradition, 1937; Books That Changed Our Minds, 1939; America Now and leading mags. Home: 840 N Brooksvale Rd Cheshire CT 06410 Office: King Features Syndicate 235 E 45th St New York City NY 10017

CHAMBERLAIN, JOSEPH MILES, educator, astronomer; b. Peoria, Ill., July 26, 1923; s. Maurice Silloway and Roberta (Miles) C.; B.S., U.S. Mcht. Marine Acad., 1944; B.A., Bradley U., 1947; A.M., Tchrs. Coll. Columbia, 1950, Ed.D., 1962; m. Paula Bruninga, Dec. 12, 1945; children—Janet Ann, Susan Louise, Barbara Jean. Instr. Columbia Jr. High Sch., Peoria, Ill., 1943; instr. navigation War Shipping Adminstrn., 1944-45; boys sec. YMCA, Peoria, 1946-47; instr. U.S. Mcht. Marine Acad., Kings Point, N.Y., 1947-50, asst. prof., 1950-52; asst. curator Am. Museum-Hayden Planetarium, N.Y.C., 1952-53, gen. mgr., chief astronomer, 1953-56, chmn., 1956-64; asst. dir. Am. Mus. Natural History, 1964-68; dir. Adler Planetarium, Chgo., 1968—; prof. astronomy Northwestern U., 1968- -; also professorial lectr. U. Chgo. Led eclipse expdns. to Can., 1954. Ceylon, 1955, astro-geodetic expdns. to Can., 1956, 57, Greenland, 1958; dean council of Sci. staff Am. Museum Nat. History, 1960-62. Active Boy Scouts of Am. Served to lt. USNR, 1945- 46; staff Naval Res. Officers Sch., N.Y.C., 1953-54. Fellow Royal Astron. Soc.; mem. A.A.A.S., Inst. Nav., Am. Astron. Soc., Am. Polar Soc., Am. (mem. council 1965—, v.p. 1971), N.Y. State assns. museums, Phi Delta Kappa, Phi Kappa Phi, Kappa Delta Pi. Republican. Presbyn. (elder). Clubs: University, Tavern, Quadrangle (Chgo.), Dutch Treat. Co-author: Planets, Stars and Space, 1957. Author: Time and the Stars, 1964; also articles on popular astronomy. Home: 1500 Oak Av Evanston IL 60201 Office: Adler Planetarium 900 E Achash Bond Dr Chicago IL 60605

CHAMBERLAIN, JOSEPH WYAN, astronomer; b. Boonville, Mo., Aug. 24, 1928; s. Gilbert Lee and Jessie (Wyan) C.; A.B., U. Mo., 1948, A.M., 1949; M.S., U. Mich., 1951, Ph.D., 1952; m. Marilyn Jean Roesler, Sept. 10, 1949; children—Joy Anne, David Wyan, Jeffrey Scott. Project sci. aurora and airglow USAF Cambridge Research Center, 1951-53; research asso. Yerkes Obs., Chgo., 1953-55, asst. prof., 1955-59, asso. prof., 1959-60, prof., 1961-62, asso. dir., 1960-62; asso. dir. planetary scis. div. of Kitt Peak Nat. Obs., 1962-70, astronomer, planetary scis. div., 1970-71; dir. Lunar Sci. Inst., Houston, 1971—; cons. President's Sci. Adv. Com., Space Sci. Tech. Panel, Inst. Def. Analyses, Los Alamos Sci. Lab. Recipient Warner prize Am. Astron. Soc., 1961; Alfred P. Sloan research fellow, 1961-63. Fellow Royal Astron. Soc., A.A.A.S., Am. Geophys. Union; mem. Am. Astron. Soc. (chmn div. planetary scis. 1969-71), Am. Phys. Soc., Internat. Astron. Union, Internat. Union Geodesy Geophysics, Internat. Sci. Radio Union, Nat. Acad. Sci. Author: Physics of the Aurora and Airglow, 1961. Mem. editorial bd. Ioarus, Planetary Space Sci. Office: 3303 NASA Rd 1 Houston TX 77058

CHAMBERLAIN, LLOYD BAXTER, paperboard co. exec.; b. Hudson Falls, N.Y., Oct. 10, 1915; s. Lloyd Oliver and Dorothea (Harvey) C.; B.S. in Sci., N.Y. State Coll. Forestry, Syracuse, N.Y., 1940; m. Margaret Snow Roach, June 8, 1917; children— Lloyd Michael, Mary Margaret. With Container Corp, Am., 1940-65, div. gen. mgr. Midwest mills, 1960-65; v.p. Fed. Paperboard Inc., 1965-68, sr. v.p. paperboard div., 1968—; pres. Toga Paper Stock, Inc., 1969- -. Bd. dirs. Boxboard Research and Devel. Assn., 1968, Fibre Conservation, 1969—; mem. nat. exec. com. Paper Stock Conservation, 1968—, chmn. eastern div., 1968—. Pres. United Fund and Community Services, Wabash, Ind., 1957. Bd. dirs. Syracuse Found., 1968—. Recipient Dist. Service award Hoya, Western Germany, 1960. Mem. Am. Paper Inst. (exec. com.), Nat. Paperboard Assn. (chmn. Western div. 1964-65, T.A.P.P.I., Paper Industry Mfg. Assn., Holy Name Soc. (pres. Wabash 1957). Catholic. Home: 73 Foxedge Rd Saddle River NJ 07458 Office: 75 Chestnut Ridge Rd Montvale NJ 07645

CHAMBERLAIN, MARK MUNROE, coll. pres.; b. Pawtucket, R.I., Dec. 10, 1931; s. Merle D. and Lois (Munroe) C.; B.S., Franklin and Marshall Coll., 1953; Ph.D., U. Ill., 1956; m. Miriam C. Ewing, May 30, 1953; children—David, Douglas, Matthew. From instr. to vice provost for student services Western Res. U., 1956-69; pres. Glassboro State Coll., 1969—. Commnr., East Cleveland, O., 1967-69. Mem. Am. Chem. Soc. (councilor, chmn. chem. safety), Am. Assn. U. Profs., A.A.A.S., Nat. Fire Protection Assn., Sigma Xi. Home: Holly Bush Whitney Av Glassboro NJ 08028

CHAMBERLAIN, NEIL CORNELIUS WOLVERTON, educator; b. Charlotte, N.C., May 18, 1915; s. Henry Bryan and Elizabeth (Wolverton) C.; A.B., Western Res. U., 1937, M.A., 1939; Ph.D., Ohio State U., 1942; m. Mariam Kenosian, June 27, 1942 (div. June 1967); m. 2d, Harriett Feigenbaum, Aug. 9, 1968. Research fellow Brookings Instn., 1941-42; research dir. Labor and Mgmt. Center, Yale, 1946-49, asst. dir., 1949-54; asst. prof. econs. Yale, 1947-49, asso. prof., 1949-54, prof. econs., 1959-67; prof. econs. Columbia, 1954-59, 67—; dir. program in Econ. Devel. and Adminstrn., Ford Found., 1957-60. Bd. dirs. Salzburg Seminar in Am. Studies, 1957—. Served from ensign to lt. USNR, 1942-46. Mem. Am. Econ. Assn., Indsl. Relations Research Assn., (exec. bd. 1955-58, pres. 1967), Phi Beta Kappa. Author: Collective Bargaining Procedures, 1944; The Union Challenge to Management Control, 1948; Management in Motion, 1950; Collective Bargaining, 1951; Social Responsibility and Strikes, 1953; The Impact of Strikes, 1954; A General Theory of Economic Process, 1955; Labor, 1958; Source-book on Labor, 1958; The Firm: Micro- Economic Planning and Action, 1962; The West in a World Without War, 1963; The Labor Sector, 1965; Private and Public Planning, 1965; Enterprise and Environment, 1968; Beyond Mathus, 1970. Editor: Contemporary Economic Issues, 1969; Business and the Cities, 1970. Co-editor: Cases on Labor Relations, 1949, A Decade of Industrial Relations Research, 1958, Frontiers of Collective Bargaining, 1968; mem. editorial board, editorial cons. Mgmt. Internat., 1960-70; bd. editors Am. Econ. Rev., 1957-59. Cons. editor: Basic Books. Home: 39 Claremont Av New York City NY 10027

CHAMBERLAIN, RICHARD HALL, physician, educator; b. Jacksonville, Fla., May 25, 1915; s. William Douglas and Lucille (McKowen) C.; A.B., Centre Coll., 1934; M.D., U. Louisville, 1939; postgrad. U. Pa., 1940-42; m. Merle Johnson, Aug. 23, 1941. Asst. instr. radiology U. Pa., Phila., 1940-46, instr., 1946-47, asso., 1947-48, asst. prof., 1948-50, asso. prof. 1950-52, prof., 1952—, chmn. dept. radiology, 1961—; cons. in radiology USPHS, 1968—. Mem. nat. adv. council radiation USPHS, 1958-60, chmn. x-ray x-ray adv. com., 1964-68; chmn. radiology tng. com. Nat. Inst. Gen. Med. Scis., 1966-69; mem. com. on pathologic effect of atomic radiation NRC-Nat. Acad. Sci., 1957-63; mem. Internat. Commn. on Radiol. Units, Nat. Council Radiation Protection; cons., internat. lectr. WHO, 1962—, mem. expert adv. panel radiation, 1964—; U.S. ofcl. del. UN Sci. Com. on Effects Atomic Radiation, 1963—. Trustee Asso. Univs., Inc., 1963-70. Diplomate Am. Bd. Radiology, Fellow Am. Coll. Radiology (v.p. 1964-65, Gold medal 1969); mem. A.M.A., Radiol. Soc. N. Am., Am. Radium Soc., Am., Phila. (past pres.) roentgen ray socs. Home: 8327 Germantown Av Philadelphia PA 19118 Office: 3400 Spruce St Philadelphia PA 19104

CHAMBERLAIN, SAMUEL, etcher, author; b. Cresco, Ia., Oct. 28, 1895; s. George Ellsworth and Cora Lee (Summers) C.; student U. Wash., 1913-15, Mass. Inst. Tech., 1915-16, 19-20, Royal Coll. Art, London, 1926-27, M. Edward Léon, Paris, 1925; M.A. (hon.), Marlboro (Vt.), Coll., 1968; m. Narcissa Gellatly, Apr. 27, 1923; children—Narcisse, Stephanne. Architect, 1919-25; asst. prof. architecture U. Mich., 1925-26; dir. Am. Scene. Represented in Brit. Mus., Bibliotheque Nationale (Paris), Library of Congress, Boston Mus. Fine Arts, Art Inst. Chgo., N.Y. Pub. Library. Served as ambulance driver with French Army, 1917-19; served to maj. USAAF, World War II. Decorated Legion of Merit, Bronze Star medal (U.S.); chevalier Legion d'Honneur, Croix de Guerre (France); Italian Star of Solidarity. Recipient hon. mention Paris Salon, 1925, bronze medal, 1928; Field Service traveling fellow, 1923; Guggenheim Meml. fellow, 1926; Kat W. Arms prize Soc. of Am. Etchers Exhbn., 1933, John Taylor Arms prize, 1936; ann. award New Eng. Soc. N.Y., 1955. Fellow Am. Acad. Arts and Scis.; mem. A.I.A. (hon.), Photog. Soc. Am. (asso.), Nat. Acad. (Academician 1945), Société de la Gravure Originale en Noir (Paris), Phi Delta Theta. Democrat. Episcopalian. Author: Tudor Homes in England, 1929; A Small House in the Sun, 1936; Cape Cod in the Sun, 1937; Open House in New England, 1937; Beyond New England Thresholds, 1937; Longfellow's Wayside Inn, 1938; Historic Salem in Four Seasons, 1938; Historic Boston in Four Season, 1938; Gloucester and Cape Ann, 1938; Lexington and Concord, 1939; Nantucket, 1939; New England Doorways, 1939; Old Marblehead, 1940; Portsmouth, N.H.; A Camera Impression, 1940; France Will Live Again, 1940; Martha's Vineyard, A Camera Impression, 1941; The Cast of Maine, 1941; Fair Is Our Land, 1942; Historic Cambridge in Four Seasons, 1942; Ever New England, 1944; Springtime in Virginia, 1947; Behold Williamsburg, 1947; Six New England Villages, 1948; Fair Harvard, 1948; Princeton in Spring, 1950; The Yale Scene, 1950; Salem Interiors, 1950; Old Sturbridge Village, 1951; (with Henry N. Flynt) Frontier of Freedom, 1952; (with Mark A. deWolfe Howe) Who Lived Here, 1952; Bouquet de France, 1952; Soft Skies of France, 1953; The Berkshires, 1956; Southern Interiors (with Narcissa Chamberlin), 1956; Italian Bouquet, 1958; Mystic Seaport, 1960; The Flavor of France (with Narcissa and Narcisse Chamberlain), 1960; The New England Image, 1962; British Bouquet, 1963; Etched in Sunlight, 1968; A Stroll through Historic Salem, 1969; numerous on Am., European architecture. Editor: This Realm, This England, 1941. Address: 5 Tucker St Marblehead MA 01945

CHAMBERLAIN, THOMAS GASSNER, lawyer; b. Auburn, Calif., June 25, 1892; s. Louis Lee and Sarah (Gassner) C.p A.B., Univ. of Calif., 1915; J.D., California School of Jurisprudence, Berkeley, 1917; m. Gertrude Geoghegan, Oct. 21, 1944. Asst. to United States commissioner of reclamation conduction land settlement investigation, Calif. 1915; teaching fellow in polit. science, U. of Calif., 1915-17; admitted to Calif. bar, 1917, and began practice as San Francisco; now member of firm of Chamberlain and Willi. Served as 2d lt., 1st lt. and capt. U.S. Army, 1917-18; with 1st Div. Arty., A.E.F., at Verdun, Chateau-Thierry, etc.; settled in N.Y. City, 1919; with ex-President William H. Taft in speaking tour of U.S. for League to Enforce Peace, discussing foreign policy of U.S., 1919-20; also conducted tour of Calif. for Hoover campaign, later nat. tour for Pro-League Republicans, 1920; incorporator of cotton coöperative marketing assns. throught South, negotiating loans of over A0,000,000 from banks and War Finance Corp., 1922-23; mem. Finance Com. of Nat. Republican Com., 1928; speaking tour U.S.; gen. counsel and dir. Pacific Egg Producers Coöperative, Inc., Tabler & Co., Inc., Sunrise Egg Producers Coöperative, Inc., Am. Lyric Theater, Inc.; Mark Twain Co.; gen. counsel. trustee N.Y. Infirmary, Booth-Ferris Found., Estate of Samuel L. Clemens (Mark Twain); counsel Sun-Maid Raisin Growers, Washington Coop. Egg and Puoltry Assn., Sunland Sales Coöp. Assn., Calif. Peach & Flg Growers Assn., Poultry Producers of Central Calif., Gordon Baking Co. Dir. League of Nations Assn.; mem. Internat. Com. of Y.M.C.a. Mem. American Bar Assn., New york Law Institute, Phi Delta Phi, Bar Assn., N.Y. Law Inst., Phi Delta Phi, and Kappa Sigma. Episcopalian. mason. Clubs: The Pilgrims; Lawrence Lawrence Beach; Everglades (Palm Beach, Fla.); Skytop (Pennsylvania); Univ. Club, University, 1937; asso. editor Time, 1938-45; lit. editor Newsweek, 1949-54; Country, Downtown Athletic, Metropolitan Opera Club, Rotary of N.Y. Author: Land Settlement Conditions in California (article), 1915; Why We Fought, 1919; The Geneva Institute of International Relations (article), 1925; Disarmanent, The International Debts. Contbr. to Scripps Howard Newspapers. Home: 870 Fifth Av New York City 21, NY Office: 55 Liberty St New York City 5, NY

CHAMBERLAIN, WALTER CASE, advt. exec.; b. Greenwich, Conn., Mar. 7, 1922; s. Lawrence and Edna (Owens) C.; A.B., Yale, 1942; grad. exec. program bus. adminstrn., Columbia, 1961; m. Joan Schoellkopf, Feb. 4, 1944; children—Lee, Sandra, Christine, Walter Case, Alfred Scott. With Young & Rubicam, Inc., N.Y.C., 1946-69, mgmt. supr., 1963-65, sr. v.p., dir. marketing services, 1965-68, exec. v.p., 1968-69; mgmt. cons., 1969—. Served to lt. (j.g.) USNR, 1943-46. Presbyn. (deacon 1963-66). Clubs: New Canaan Country, Winter (New Canaan); Adirondack League (Old Forge, N.Y.). Home: 198 W Hills Rd New Canaan CT 06840 Office: 198 W Hills Rd New Canaan CT 06840

CHAMBERLIN, GEORGE LEONARD, paper co. exec.; b. Churchville, Pa., Jan. 20, 1915; s. John Elbert and Josephine (Nestor) C.; grad. George Sch., 1933; A.B., U. Pa., 1937; m. Helen Kramer, July 14, 1939; children—Craig Frederick, Holly. Financial and Gen. mgmt. Gen. Electric Co., 1937-61; v.p. Bell & Howell Co., 1961-65; v.p., controller Scott Paper Co., 1965—, Brunswick Pulp & Paper Co., 1966—. Mem. Financial Execs. Inst., Am. Paper Inst., Pa. C. of C. (dir.), Phi Beta Kappa. Home: 130 Springton Lake Rd Media PA 19063 Office: Scott Paper Co Internat Airport Philadelphia PA 19113

CHAMBERLIN, JOHN STEPHEN, mfr. home furnishings; b. Boston, July 29, 1928; s. Stephen Henry and Olive Helen (McGrath) C.; A.B. cum laude, Harvard, 1950, M.B.A., 1953; m. Mary Katherine Leahy, Oct. 9, 1954; children—Mary Katherine, Patricia Ann, Carol Lynn, John Stephen, Liane Helen, Mark Joseph. Lampsalesman, Gen. Electric Co., N.Y.C., 1954-57, mgmt. cons., 1957-60, mgr. product planning TV receiver dept., Syracuse, N.Y., 1960-63, mgr. marketing gen. mgr. radio receiver dept., Utica, N.Y., 1963-70; exec. v.p., dir. Lenox, Inc., Trenton, N.J., 1970—. Clubs: Harvard (N.Y.C.); Trenton. Home: RD 2 Woodhill Rd Newtown PA 18940 Office: Lenox Inc Prince and Meade Sts Trenton NJ 08605

CHAMBERLIN, JOSEPH WEBB, newspaper exec.; b. Dallas, Feb. 16, 1913; s. Charles and Marie (Lamb) C.; A.B., Stanford, 1934; m. Jean Richardson, Oct. 28, 1944; children—Carol Jill, Joseph Scott, Leslie, Wendy. Sales engr. E. I. duPont de Nemours & Co., Inc., 1935-39; partner Fitzpatrick and Chamberlin, pubs. advt. reps., 1940-54; account exec. Young & Rubicam, advt., 1954-61; pres., chief exec. officer, dir. Million Market Newspapers, Inc., N.Y.C., 1961—. Mem. endowment fund raising com. Stanford. Cal. dir. Wilkie Volunteers, 1940. Served to lt. (s.g.) USNR, 1942-45. Decorated Bronze Star. Mem. Am. Mgmt. Assn. Clubs: Sky (N.Y.C.); Wee Burn Country (Darien, Conn.). Home: 84 Rings End Rd Darien CT 06820 Office: 6 E 43d St New York City NY 10017

CHAMBERLIN, THOMAS WILSON, educator; b. Gays, Ill., May 23, 1914; s. Frank Wilson and Lotty (Ferguson) C.; B.Edn., E. Ill. State Coll., 1936; M.A. in Geography, Clark U., 1937, Ph.D., 1946; Pd.D. (hon.), Eastern Ill. State Coll., 1956; m. Ruby Stallings, Dec. 26, 1936; children—Thomas Wilson, Susan I. Asst. prof. geography Eastern Tenn. State Tchrs. Coll., 1938-42; asst. prof. No. Ill. State Tchrs. Coll., 1946-47; asst. prof. geography, head dept. U. Minn., Duluth, 1947-48, asso. 54, prof., academic dean, 1954-70, spl. asst. to provost, prof. geography, 1970-71, prof. geography, 1971—. Mem. exec. bd. Lake Superior council Boy Scouts Am.; chmn. Duluth Human Resources Planning Coalition; mem. bd. Duluth City Library, Duluth Community Action Program. Served from lt. (j.g.) to lt. comdr., USNR, 1942-45. Mem. Assn. Am. Geographers, Nat. Council Geog. Edn., Am. Assn. for Higher Edn. (life), Am. Geog. Soc., N.E.A., Minn. Council Social Studies, Minn. Acad. Sci., Minn. Council Geog. Edn., Minn. Edn. Assn., Am. Assn. U. Profs. Duluth C. of C., Phi Delta Kappa, Kappa Delta Pi, Phi Sigma Epsilon. Gamma Theta Upsilon, Alpha Phi Omega. Home: 3800 London Rd Duluth MN 55804

CHAMBERLIN, WALDO, educator; b. Rockford, Ill., Oct. 13, 1905; s. Daniel U. and Elizabeth (Coggeshall) C.; A.B., U. Wash., 1927, A.M., 1936; Ph.D., Stanford, 1939; M.A. (hon.), Dartmouth, 1962; m. Kathryn Rogers, Aug. 2, 1940; children—John R., David W. In shipping bus., Seattle, San Francisco, Alaska 1928-36; mem. research staff, Hoover Library, Stanford, 1937-40; fellow Library of Congress in Naval History, 1941-48 (in residence 1941-42) in documentation of Internat. Orgns., 1949—; mem. research staff U.S. Dept. State, Washington, 1942-44; exec. officer Pacific Coast Maritime Industry Bd., 1944-45; chief documents officer U.N. Conf. Internat. Orgn., San Francisco, 1945, U.N. Prep. Commn., London, 1945, U.N., London, N.Y.C., 1946, dep. dir. documents and sales div. UN, 1947, dir. documents, control staff, 1948; prof. govt. N.Y.U., 1949-61; dean summer programs Dartmouth, Hanover, N.H., 1961-69, prof. history, 1969-71, emeritus, 1971—. Chmn. N.Y. regents com. on internat. understanding, 1950—; mem. staff Brookings Instn., 1951-53; adv. council World Affairs Center N.Y., 1958-60. Mem. Nat. Council Religion in Higher Education. Mem. Dept. Internat. Affairs of Nat. Council of Chs. of Christ in Am., 1961. Trustee Manhasset Pub. Library, 1956-61. Conglist. Author: Memorandum concerning the conduct of the bus. of the Gen. Assembly of the UN, 1949; Enabling Instruments of Members of the UN, 1951; A Chronology and Fact Book of the United Nations 1941-1961, 1961; co-author: A Guide to the Use of UN Documents, 1962. Co- editor: Annual Review of UN Affairs, 1954, 1957-59. Contbr. to various periodicals. Home: 14 Conant Rd Hanover NH 03755

CHAMBERLIN, WELLMAN, cartographer; b. Phila., Feb. 15, 1908; s. Leroy and Rose Charlton (Wellman) C.; B.A., Antioch Coll., 1932; m. Anne Carter Waller, Oct. 8, 1938; children—Robert Wellman, John Charlton, David Waller. With Nat. Geog. Soc., 1935—, chief cartographer, 1964—; originator Chamberlin trimetric projection, 1947. Club: Cosmos (Washington). Author: The Round Earth on Flat Paper, 1947. Inventor Nat. Geog. world globe, 1961. Home: Waterford VA 22190 Office: Nat Geog Soc 17th and M Sts Washington DC 20036

CHAMBERS, ALBERT ARTHUR, bishop; b. Cleve., June 22, 1906; s. Arthur S. and Eleanor (Terbrack) C.; A.B., Hobart Coll., Geneva, N.Y., 1928, S.T.D., 1957; S.T.B., Gen. Theol. Sem., N.Y.C., 1932, S.T.D., 1961; D.D., Nashotah House, 1963; m. Frances H. Davis, June 18, 1934; children—Frances H. (Mrs. Robert B. Street), Sally Ann (Mrs. Donald Goldberg). Ordained priest Episcopal Ch., 1932; diocesan missionary Western N.Y. State, 1931- 33; sr. canon St. Paul's Cathedral, Buffalo, also diocesan dir. youth work 1933-36; rector St. Thomas Ch., Neenah-Menasha, Wis., 1936-42, St. Peter's Ch., Auburn, N.Y., 1942-49, Ch. of Resurrection, N.Y.C., 1949- 62; bishop Episcopal Diocese, Springfield, Ill., 1962—. Chmn. dept. Christian edn. Diocese Fond-du-lac, also chmn. bd. examining chaplains, 1938-42; mem. council Diocese Central N.Y. State, 1944-48, chmn. dept. promotion, 1952-56, mem. com. reorgn. Diocese N.Y.C., 1952, mem. council, chmn. dept. promotion, 1952-56, mem. standing com., 1957-61, pres. com., 1961, dean chmn. dept. promotion, 1952-56, mem. standing com., 1957-61, pres. com., 1961, dean Manhattan Convocation, 1961; pres. alumni council Gen. Theol. Sem., 1944- 48, chmn. com. theol. edn. Sunday offering, 1948-52; council, mem. exec. bd. Am. Church Union, 1950—. pres., 1968—. An organizer, 1st pres. Council Social Agys. Neenah-Menasha, 1938; an organizer Fox River Valley regional council Girl Scouts U.S.A., 1937; vice chmn. Cayuga County chpt. A.R.C., also field rep. Sampson Air Base council, 1942-46. Mem. Pilgrims U.S., Kappa Alpha. Home: 1190 Williams Blvd Springfield IL 62704 Office: 821 S 2d St Springfield IL 62704

CHAMBERS, ARTHUR WOODBURNE, Jr., lawyer, chem. co. exec.; b. New Haven, Nov. 26, 1917; s. Arthur Woodburne and Winifred (Smith) C.; A.B., Yale, 1939, LL.B., 1942; m. Margaret Hannah Till, Dec. 30, 1942; children—Winifred Hale, Margaret Ellen. Admitted to Conn. bar, 1942, N.Y. State bar, 1958; asso. firm Chambers & Grimes, New Haven, 1946-50, mem. firm, 1950-51; with Hooker Chem. Corp., Stamford, Conn., 1953—, asst. sec., asso. counsel, 1958-64, sec., asso. counsel, 1964—, also sec. subsidiaries.

Served with USNR, 1942- 45, 52-53; ETO, PTO. Mem. Am. Soc. Corporate Secs. Home: 7 Outlook Dr Darien CT 06820 Office: 1515 Summer St Stamford CT 06905

CHAMBERS, CARL COVALT, educator; b. Phila., May 8, 1907; s. George Gailey and Anna B. (Covalt) C.; B.S., Dickinson Coll., 1929; D.Sc., U. Pa., 1934; m. Margaret Morrison, June 14, 1930; children—Jane Nancy, James Morrison, Elizabeth Gailey. Tech. test dept. Radio Corp. of Am., 1929-30, Victor engring. dept., 1930-32, Bartol Research Found., 1932-33; instr. Moore Sch. Elec. Engring., U. Pa., 1933-37, asst. prof., 1937-42, asso. prof., 1942-47, prof. elec. engring., 1947—, v.p. for engring. affairs, 1953—, dean, 1949-53; cons. Brooke Engring. Co., Phila., 1934-56; cons. dir., research Edward Stern & Co., Phila., 1936-51, Hazeltine Service Corp., N.Y.C., 1939-41; dir. research Internat. Resistance Co., 1944-47, cons., 1947-52. U.S. del. to Com. of Experts on Radio Interference and Com. on Elec. and Magnetic Units of Internat. Electrotech. Commn., London, 1946, Lucerne, 1947, Paris, 1950, Opatija, Yugoslavia, 1953, Phila., 1954, Munich, 1956, Brussels, Belgium, 1956, Stockholm, Sweden, 1958, Madrid, Spain, 1959; Bucharest, Rumania, 1962, Aix-les-Bains, 1964, Prague, Czechoslovakia, 1967, Teheran, Iran, 1969, Washington, 1970, chmn. com. elec. and magnetic magnitudes and units; cons. to asst. sec. Def. for research & devel. bd., Washington. Trustee Dickinson Coll., Carlisle, Pa. Named Engr. of Yr., Del. Valley, 1966. Fellow I.E.E.E., A.A.A.S.; mem. Nat. Soc. of Profl. Engrs., Am. Phys. Soc., Franklin Inst., Am. Soc. Engring. Edn. (pres. 1968-69), Nat. Acad. Engring., Phi Beta Kappa, Tau Beta Pi, Sigma Xi, Eta Kappa Nu, Phi Delta Theta, Pi Mu Epsilon. Republican. Methodist. Clubs: Union League, Engineer's (Phila.). Contbr. articles on conduction of elec. current, vacuum-tube oscillators in 3 publs. Home: Hampton House 1600 Hagy's Ford Rd Narberth PA 19072

CHAMBERS, CURTIS ALLEN, editor, clergyman; b. Damascus, O., Sept. 24, 1924; s. Binford Vincent and Margaret Esther (Patterson) C.; Th.B., Malone Coll., 1946; A.B., Marion Coll., 1947; B.D., Asbury Theol. Sem., 1950; postgrad., Oberlin Grad. Sch. Theology, 1951-53; S.T.M., Temple U., 1955, S.T.D., 1960; D.D. (hon.), Lebanon Valley Coll., 1967; m. Anna June Winn, Aug. 26, 1946; children—David Lloyd, Curtis Allen II, Deborah Ann, Charles Cloyde. Ordained to ministry Evang. United Brethren Ch., 1954; pastor 1st Ch., Cleve., 1951-53, Rockville Ch., Harrisburg, Pa., 1953-59; editor adult publs. Evang. United Brethren Ch., 1959-65; asso. editor Ch. and Home mag., Dayton, O., 1963-66, editor, 1967-69; asst. editorial dir. Together and Christian Advocate, Meth. Pub. House, Nashville, 1969, editor Together mag., 1969—; acting editorial dir. gen. periodicals United Meth. Ch., 1971—. Book editor Evang. United Brethren Ch., 1965-68; co-editor Plan of Union, United Meth. Ch., 1965-68, Book of Discipline, 1968, chmn. staff com. long range planning, 1969—, mem. commn. on ch. union, 1965-68; dir. radio-TV relations gen. confs. Evang. United Brethren Ch., 1958, 62, 66, United Meth. Ch., 1966, 68. Chmn. commn. on ednl. media Nat. Council Chs., 1965-66, chmn. com. on audio visual and broadcast edn., 1962-65; served as capt. (chaplain) Civil Air Patrol, 1960-65. Recipient Distinguished Alumni award Malone Coll., 1967; named 1 of 12 editors sent to Middle East on fact-finding trip, 1969. Mem. Aircraft Owners and Pilots Assn., United Meth. Press Assn. (v.p. 1968—), Asso. Ch. Press. Clubs: United Methodist Executive (v.p. 1971—) (Chgo.); Torch (Dayton). Contbr. articles religious lit. Home: 406 W Burr Oak Dr Arlington Heights IL 60004 Office: 1661 N Northwest Hwy Park Ridge IL 60068

CHAMBERS, DAVID LAURANCE, Jr., investment co. exec.; b. Indpls., Nov. 14, 1912; s. David Laurance and Nora (Taggart) C.; A.B., Princeton, 1934; LL.B., Harvard, 1938; m. Estelle Burpee, June 8, 1939; children—David Laurance III, Diana Rauh. Admitted to Ind. bar, 1938; pvt. practice, Indpls., 1938-42, 46-53; asst. to pres., gen. counsel Indpls. Stockyards Co., Inc., 1953-56, pres., 1956-68; chmn. bd. Highland Investment Corp., Indpls., 1968—; dir., mem. trust com. Merchants Nat. Bank & Trust Co.; dir. Wright- Bachman Lumber Co., Bessire & Co., Inc. Mem. exec. com. Marion County Citizens Juvenile Ct. Bi-Partisan Com.; past chmn. State Scholarship Commn. Bd. dirs. United Fund Greater Indpls., Indpls. Hosp. Devel. Assn. Served to lt. (s.g.) USNR, 1942-45; PTO. Mem. Ind., Indpls. bar assns. Episcopalian. Clubs: Woodstock, Dramatic, Crooked Strick Golf (Indpls.); Little (Delray Beach, Fla.). Home: 3740 Governors Rd Indianapolis IN 46208 Office 4343 W 71st St Indianapolis IN 46268

CHAMBERS, DAVID SMITH, educator, assn. exec.; b. Clarksville, Tex., Jan. 26, 1917; s. Clifton A. and Eva Ellen (Smith) C.; B.A. in Math., U. Tex., 1939, M.B.A. in Statistics, 1947; grad. student math., U. Mich.; m. Mary Othella Parsons, Feb. 22, 1941. Instr. aero. engring. U. Tex., 1941-42, applied math. and astronomy, 1942-46, bus. statistics, 1946-47; asst. prof. statistics U. Tenn., 1947-48, asso. prof., 1948-58, prof. statistics, 1958—. Quality control cons. to AID, Dept. State, 1962—. Mem. Am. Soc. Quality Control 1947—, bd. dirs., 1953-56, 65—, exec. sec., 1959-61, chmn. exec. bd. Inst. Edn. and Tng., 1960-63, chmn. examining com. Tenn. sect., 1958—, fellow 1954—, chmn. textile and needle trades div., 1967-68, treas. chem. div., 1967-68, chmn. chem. div., 1969-70. Recipient E.L. Grant award for edn. in quality control, 1970, pres., 1971—. Fellow A.A.A.S.; mem. Am. Soc. for Testing and Materials (com. E-11, 1969—), Am. Statis. Assn., Phi Beta Kappa, Phi Eta Sigma, Beta Gamma Sigma. Author papers in field. Home: 3304 Bunker Hill Dr Knoxville TN 37920

CHAMBERS, EARL DENTON, banker; b. Norwalk, Conn., June 14, 1925; s. Earl Henderson and Florence (Denton) C.; A.B., Dartmouth, 1948; m. Ann Elizabeth Keating, Sept. 9, 1950; childrenSarah A., Lydia D. With R.I. Hosp. Trust Co., Providence, 1953-65; with Marine Midland Trust Co., Rochester, N.Y., 1965-70, exec. v.p., 1967-70; v.p. Marine Midland Banks, Inc., 1969—; v.p. Marine Rochester. Served as ensign USNR, 1943-46. Chartered financial analyst, 1966. Mem. Rochester Soc. Investment Analysts (exec. com. 1968-69). Club: Genesee Valley (bd. govs.) (Rochester). Home: Lowther Point Riverside CT 06878 Office: 140 Broadway New York City NY 10015

CHAMBERS, FRANK GEORGE, engring. co. exec.; b. Salt Lake City, June 7, 1916; s. George Brower and Vilate Ellen (Schofield) C.; B.S., U. Utah, 1937; M.B.A., Harvard, 1939; m. Jean Snodgrass; children—Allison-Dede, Leslie. A founder Magna Engring. Corp., 1947; pres. Continental Capital Corp.; dir. Guardian Packaging Corp., Inc., Data Products Corp., James Dole Corp., Optical Coating Labs., Golden Gateway Parking Corp. Chief office priorities and controls, Munitions Bd., Dept. of Def., 1951. Served as lt. col., A.U.S., 1940-45; with Office of Under Sec. of War, 1940-42; staff Comdg. Gen., A.S.F., 1942-45. Mem. Phi Kappa Phi. Clubs: Harvard (N.Y.C.); University, Bohemian (San Francisco). Office: Bank of America Center San Francisco CA 94104

CHAMBERS, FRANK WILSON, oral surgeon; b. Star City, Ark., Mar. 29, 1925; s. Elbert Earl and Vivian (Norton) C.; D.D.S., Washington U., St. Louis, 1951; M.Dental Surgery, U. Cal., 1956; m. Dorothy LaVerne Mabry, Dec. 1, 1957 (div. Jan. 1971); children—Thomas Mabry (adopted), Scott Wilson, Shanna Sue, Christine Harriett. Teaching fellow U. Cal., 1954-56; practice oral surgery, Los Angeles, 1956-58, Garden Grove, Cal., 1960; individual practice, Santa Ana, Cal., 1961—; mem. staff Palm Harbor Gen. Hosp., Garden Grove, 1960—, Santa Ana Community Hosp., 1961—, St. Joseph Hosp., Orange, Cal., 1962—, Doctors' Hosp., Santa Ana, 1963—, Martin Luther Hosp., Anaheim Cal., 1964—; head oral surgery sect. Children's Hosp. Orange County, 1966-69, Orange County Med. Center, 1967- -. Instr. oral surgery U. So. Cal. Sch. Dentistry, 1957-60; asst. prof. oral surgery Loma Linda (Cal.) Sch. Dentistry, 1967—. Diplomate Am. Bd. Oral Surgery. Mem. Orange County Dental Soc. (pres. 1965-66), Am., So. Cal. socs. oral surgeons, So. Cal. Acad. Oral Pathology (pres. 1965). Kiwanian. Contbr. articles, papers to profl. lit., also several surg. motion pictures. Home: 12352 S W Ranchwood Rd Santa Ana, CA 92705. Office: 1125 E 17th St Santa Ana CA 92701

CHAMBERS, FRED, govt. ofcl.; b. Carbon Hill, Ala., Feb. 17, 1912; s. Bunnier Greater and Zora (McCollum) C.; B.S. in Elec. Engring., Auburn U., 1930; grad. student Mass. Inst. Tech., 1930-31; m. Margaret Armstrong, Nov. 29, 1933; 1 son, Fred. With Gen. Electric Co., 1930-32, Asso. Gas and Electric Co., Elmira, N.Y., 1932, Tenn. Electric Power Co., 1933-39, Chattanooga Electric Power Bd., 1939; with TVA, 1939—, asst. mgr. power, 1970—. Served with USNR, 1943-45. Registered profl. engr., Tenn. Fellow I.E.E.E.; mem. Chattanooga Engrs. Club, Internat. Conf. Large High Tension Electric Systems, Tenn. Soc. Profl. Engrs. (named Engr. of Decade, Chattanooga chpt. 1970). Democrat. Episcopalian. Author tech. papers. Office: care Bovay Engrs Inc PO Box 8098 5009 Caroline St Houston TX 77004

CHAMBERS, JACK H., lawyer; b. Clothier, W.Va., Nov. 12, 1930; s. Julian H. and Omega (McClung) C.; A.B., Duke, 1951, LL.B., 1953, divorced; 1 son, Matthew Alan. Admitted to Fla. bar, 1957, since practiced in Jacksonville; mem. firm Malhoney, Madlow, Chambers & Adams, 1957-. Trustee So. Fed. Tax Inst. Dir. Barnett Banks of Fla., Inc. Counsel, Duval County Local Govt. Study Commn., 1965-66; mem. Mayor Jacksonville Select Com. Consol., 1967-68; chmn. Jacksonville Housing Authority, 1969-70. Served lt. USNR, 1954-57. Mem. Fla. Bar (bd. govs. 1966-67, pres. young lawyers sect. 1966-67). Presbyn. Home: 3500 Townsend Blvd Jacksonville, FL 32211. Office: Barnett Bldg 100 Laura St Jacksonville FL 32202

CHAMBERS, JAMES FLOYD, Jr., newspaperman; b. Houston, May 13, 1913; s. James Floyd and Elizabeth (Troutman) C.; student Terrill Prep. Sch. for Boys, 1932; m. Elizabeth Valerie Moore, Jan. 4, 1915; children—James Floyd III, Elizabeth Valerie. Copy boy, reporter Dallas Dispatch (later Dallas Dispatch- Jour.), 1934-35, telegraph editor, 1935-36, asst. sports editor, 1936- 38, asst. city editor, 1938-39, city editor, 1940-41; pub. relations dir. Dallas C. of C., 1941-42, N. Am. Aviation Corp., 1942-45; exec. news dir. Dallas Times Herald, 1945, mng. editor, 1946—, dir., 1952—; v.p., gen. mgr. Times Herald, 1952-60, pres., 1960—; chmn., chief exec. officer Times Herald Printing Co., pub. Dallas Times Herald: mem. bd. Times Mirror Co., Republic Nat. Bank; covered atom bomb test at Bikini, 1946; ghost writer for several nat. sports figures, including Byron Nelson and Doak Walker. Mem. Bur. Advt. N.Y. (chmn.), Tex. Daily Newspaper Assn. (past pres.), Sigma Delta Chi. Methodist (steward). Clubs: Preston Trail Golf (founder); Brook Hollow, City, Dallas Country (Dallas). Home: 5319 Castlewood Dallas TX 75229 Office: Dallas Times Herald Dallas TX 75201

CHAMBERS, JAMES ROBERT, French hornist, educator; b. Trenton, N.J., Dec. 15, 1920; s. Melville and Amelia (Neumann) C.; diploma, Curtis Inst. Music, 1942; m. Marjorie Evelyn Weiss, June 3, 1944; children—Robert, Michael, Carol, Patricia. Toured S.A. with All Am. Youth Orch., 1940, toured U.S., 1941; solo hornist Phila. Orch., 1942-46, N.Y. Philharmonic, 1946—; faculty Curtis Inst. Music, 1942-46, Juilliard Sch. Music, 1946—, Manhattan Sch. Music, 1958-64; faculty, artist in residence Aspen (Colo.) Music Sch., 1957-58; woodwind coach, condr. Stratford Shakespearean Festival, Stratford, Ont., Can., 1966; soloist concertos for French horn Phila. Orch., 1945, Robin Hood Dell Orch., 1945, N.Y. Philharmonic, 1946, U.S. Marine Band, 1958; clinician Am. Symphony Orch. League; featured recording artist RCA, Columbia, Mercury, Capitol; personnel mgr. New York Philharmonic, 1969—. Mem. Nat. Sch. Orch. Assn., Nat. Acad. Recording Arts and Scis., Am. Assn. U. Profs. Pioneer, Chambers Model French horn for Reynoldo Mus. Instrument Co. Home: 205 West End Av New York City NY 10023 Office: NY Philharmonic 65th and Broadway New York City NY 10023

CHAMBERS, JOHN CRAWFORD, former hotel exec.; b. Bayonne, N.J., July 12, 1918; s. Percival Watson and Emilie (Esler) C.; B.A., Mich. State U., 1940; m. Lillian Marie Dinelli, July 1, 1941; children—John J., Laura J. Owner, Jo-Etts, Boston, 1961- 65; former mgr. Hilton Hotels, Washington. Bd. dirs. No. Va. Community Coll. Served with AUS, 1943-45: MTO. Decorated Purple Heart. Mem. Kappa Sigma, Sigma Gamma Epsilon. Home: 4301 Massachusetts Av NW Washington DC 20016

CHAMBERS, JUSTICE MARION, consultant; b. Huntington, W.Va., Feb. 2, 1908; s. Arthur Faye and Dixie (Justice) C.; student Marshall Coll., 1925-27, LL.D., 1954; student George Washington U., 1927-30; LL.B., Nat. U., 1933; m. Barbara Claire Fornes, Sept. 25, 1965; children—Patricia, John Arthur, Justice Marion, Peter, Paul. Commd. 2d. lt. USMC, 1932, advanced through grades to col., 1946; served with 5th Marines, 1st Marine Raider Bn., 1941-42, 3d Bn., 25th Marines, 1943-45, ret. 1946; asst. commr. U.S. Maritime Commn., 1936-37; asst. chmn. Fed. Personnel Council, 1946-47; profl. staff adviser U.S. Senate Armed Services Com., 1947-50; asst. adminstr. Fed. Civil Def. Adminstrn., 1950-52, exec. asst. adminstr. 1952-54; asst. exec. dir. Res. Officers Assn., 1954-55; organizer, head J.M. Chambers & Asso., 1955-62; dep. dir. Office Emergency Planning, Exec. Office of Pres., 1962-64; pres. J.M. Chambers, Inc., Washington, 1964—; dir. Greg-Gary Internat., Inc., Oztemel Corp., N.Y.C., Meadows Coal & Constrn. Co., Rush, Ky. Dir. Civil Def., Rockville, Md., 1950-51. Decorated Congl. Medal of Honor, Silver Star, Legion of Merit, Purple Heart (3). Mem. Marine Corps Res. Officers Assn., 1st Raider Bn. Assn. (pres. 1949), Ret. Officers Assn., 1st Marine (1st v.p. 1967), 4th Marine (pres. 1949-50) div. assns., Congl. Medal Honor Soc. (exec. v.p. 1959-61), Sigma Phi Epsilon, Phi Kappa Nu. Club: Army-Navy (Washington). Home: 140 S Adams St Rockville MD 20850 Office: 2300 Calvert St NW Washington DC 20008

CHAMBERS, MADELAINE (Mrs. Alexander Herenchak), operatic soprano; b. N.Y.C., Oct. 16, 1927; d. Anthony and Helen (Wiewiurka) Chemerys; B.S., N.Y.U., 1948; student Columbia Tchrs. Coll., 1948-49; m. Alexander Herenchak, March 8, 1958; childrenValerie A., Gregory A. Made operatic debut in Europe, at Teatro Nuovo, Milan, Italy, 1953, in U.S. at City Center Opera, N.Y.C., 1954; debut Met. Opera House, 1956. Recipient award Music Edn. League, 1951, Friday Morning Music award. Washington, 1952, Fulbright award to Italy, 1952; winner Internat. Competition for Opera Singers, Lausanne, Switzerland, 1953, Internat. Competition in Verviers, Belgium, 1953; Marion Anderson award, 1953, Chgo. Theatre of Air award, 1954, Met. Auditions of Air award, 1955. Mem. Kosciuszko Found., Am. Guild Musical Artists, Actors Equity. Home: 2734 Kennedy Blvd Jersey City NJ 07306

CHAMBERS, MAURICE RIPLEY, shoe mfr.; b. St. Louis, July 14, 1916; s. M. R. and Ruth E. (Brooks) C.; m. Mae Mildred Bartlett, June 30, 1937; 1 dau., Cynthia Ruth. Salesman Tweedie Footwear Corp., Jefferson City, Mo., 1931-39; buyer, mdse. Mgr. Montgomery Ward, N.Y.C., 1939-49; mdse. mgr. Internat. Shoe 1956-62, pres., 1962-66; chmn. bd., chief exec. officer, pres. Interco, Inc., 1966—. Home: 6025 Lindell Blvd St Louis MO 63112 Office: 1509 Washington Av St Louis MO 63166

CHAMBERS, MELBER, lawyer; b. N.Y.C., July 20, 1901; s. Walter Albert and Evangeline (Bowers) C.; A.B., Cornell U.; LL.B., Harvard; m. Katherine Audley Heigho, Aug. 4, 1933; children—Ann Audley (Mrs. Ann C. Sparks), Robert Alan. Admitted to N.Y. bar; mem. firm Sage, Gray, Todd & Sims, N.Y.C., 1926—. Dir. Jersey Central Power & Light Co., 1940-44, Am. Radio Co., 1948—, Concel, Inc., 1965—. Pres. Correctional Assn. N.Y., 1958—. Trustee Goddard Coll. Club: Down Town Assn. (N.Y.C.). Home: 66 E 79th St New York City NY 10021 Office: 140 Broadway New York City NY 10005

CHAMBERS, MERRITT MADISON, educator; b. Knox County, O., Jan. 26, 1899; s. Rufus Ward and Etta Amelia (Miller) C.; student U. Fla., Harvard; B.A., Ohio Wesleyan U., 1922; M.A., Ohio State U., 1927, Ph.D., 1931. Tchr., prin. high schs., 1922-26; with Am. Council on Edn., 1935-42, 45-51; cons. U.S. Office Edn., 1952-53; owner-operator Lafayette Farms, Mt. Vernon, O., 1955- 58; vis. prof. higher edn. U. Mich., 1958-63; exec. dir. Mich. Council State Coll. Presidents, 1961-62; prof. higher edn. Ind. U., 1963-69; prof. ednl. adminstrn., cons. on higher edn. Ill. State U., Normal, 1969—. Participant surveys of higher edn., Mass., Ill., 1949, Conn., Wis., Ia., 1950, N.Y.C., 1961, Ky., 1962, Md., 1963; cons. Com. on Govt. and Higher End., 1957; chmn. Long-Range Study Higher Edn. Ky., 1965-66; cons. So. Ill. U. and Mich. State Bd. Edn., 1966. Served to maj. USAAF, 1942-46. Fellow A.A.A.S.; mem. Knox County Farm Bur. (pres. 1957-58), N.E.A. (life), Delta Sigma Rho, Phi Delta Kappa, Alpha Sigma Phi. Author: Youth-Serving Organizations, rev. edit., 1947; The Campus and the People, 1960; Voluntary Statewide Coordination in Public Higher Education, 1961; Chance and Choice in Higher Education, 1962; Financing Higher Education, 1963; The Colleges and The Courts Since 1950, 1964; Freedom and Repression in Higher Education, 1965; Bibliography of Higher Education, 1966; The Colleges and the Courts, 1962-66, 1967; Higher Education: Who Pays? Who Gains?, 1968; Higher Education in the Fifty States, 1970; Above High School, 1970; The Developing Law of the Student and His College, 1970. Editor various works including: Charters of Philanthropies, 1948; Universities of the World Outside U.S.A., 1950. Contbr. articles to ednl., legal publs. Office: Dept Ednl Adminstrn Illinois State Univ Normal IL 61761

CHAMBERS, PAUL LAURENCE DUNBAR, Jr., jazz bassist; b. Pitts., Apr. 22, 1935; s. Paul Laurence Dunbar and Margaret (Eccles) C.; m. Ann Williams, June 20, 1952 (div. 1961); children—Eric, Renee, Pierre; m. 2d, Myra Greenspan, Feb. 24, 1962. Tech. dir. Cass Tech. High Sch., Detroit, 1951; bassist for Paul Quinichette Quartet, 1954, Benny Green Quintet, 1954, Miles Davis Quintet, 1955-61, Wynton Kelly Trio, 1961-65; recording artist for Columbia, Riverside, Blue Note, Vee-Jay records. Recipient New Star award Downbeat mag., 1957; 1st place Jazz Poll, 1958.‡

CHAMBERS, RICHARD H., U.S. circuit judge; b. Danville, Ill., Nov. 7, 1906; s. William R. and Lida J. (Spencer) C.; A.B., U. Ariz., 1929; LL.B., Stanford, 1932; m. 2d, Mary Martin, November 24, 1945; children by prev. marriage—Martha A. (Mrs. Charles R. Froese), Janet L. (Mrs. John B. Crews). Admitted to Ariz. bar, 1932; practice law in Tucson, 1932-41, 45-54; judge Ct. of Appeals, 9th Circuit, Tucson, 1954—. Served from capt. to maj. USAAF, 1942-45. Mem. Am. Law Inst., Am. Bar Assn., Phi Gamma Delta. Republican. Mason, Elk. Club: Old Pueblo (Tucson). Home: 333 S Alvernon Way Tucson AZ 85711 Office: U S P O and Court House Tucson AZ 85701

CHAMBERS, ROBERT LEROY, pollution control co. exec.; b. Salt Lake City, Sept. 9, 1918; s. George B. and Vilate (Schofield) C.; B.A., U. Utah, 1939; M.A., Fletcher Sch. Internat. Law and Diplomacy, 1940; student Harvard Grad. Sch. Bus., 1940- 42; m. L. June Musser, June 21, 1940; children—Pamela, Penelope, James Henry. Pres. Magna Power Tool Corp., Menlo Park, Cal., 1947-58; pres., dir. BSP Corp., San Francisco, 1959—; v.p., dir. Bangor Punta Corp., N.Y.C., 1962-69; chmn. bd., chief exec. officer, dir. Envirotech Corp., Palo Alto, Cal.; dir. Herrick Corp., Hayward, Cal., Kusan, Inc., Nashville. Trustee Midwest Research Inst., Kansas City, Mo., 1962-. Mem. Young Pres. Orgn. (nat. pres. 1958-59). Clubs: Bohemian, Family (San Francisco); Union (Cleve.); Metropolitan (N.Y.C.); Menlo Country (Woodside, Cal.).‡

CHAMBERS, SIR STANLEY PAUL, ret. chem. co. exec.; b. London, Eng., Apr. 2, 1904; s. Philip Joseph and Catherine Chambers; student City of London Coll.; B.Com., M.Sc., London Sch. Econs., London U.; D.Sc., Bristol U., 1963; LL.D., U. Liverpool, 1967; Dr. Tech., Bradford U., 1967; m. Dorothy Alice Marion Copp, 1926; m. 2d, Edith Lamb, Sept. 23, 1955; children—Naomi Katherine, Sarah Penelope. Mem. Indian Income Tax Enquiry Com., 1935-36; income tax adviser Govt. of India, 1937-40; sec., commr. Bd. Inland Revenue, 1942-47; chief finance div. Control Commn. for Germany, Brit. Element, 1945-47; mem. com. for review orgn. customs and excise, 1951- 53, mem. com. departmental records, 1952-54, chmn. com. on inquiry into London Transport, 1953-55; chmn. Imperial Chem. Industries, Ltd., London, 1960-68; dir. Nat. Westminster Bank, Ltd., Westminster Fgn. Bank Ltd.; chmn. London and Lancashire Ins. Co., Ltd., Royal Ins. Co. Ltd., Liverpool & London & Globe Ins. Co., Ltd. Decorated companion of Indian Empire, 1941, companion of Bath, knight comdr. Order Brit. Empire. Hon. fellow London Sch. Econs.; mem. Nat. Inst. Econ. and Social Research (past pres.), Inst. Dirs. (pres. 1964-68), Brit. Shippers Council (pres. 1963-68). Clubs: Athenaeum; Reform. Home: 1A Frognal Gardens Hampstead London N W 3 England Office: Bow Bells House Bread St London E C 4 England

CHAMBERS, STANLEY W., clergyman; b. Columbus O., July 20, 1915; s. George C. and Blanche (Dailey) C.; grad. Central High Sch., Columbus, 1933; m. Catherine Strepka, Sept. 7, 1940; children—Jean (Mrs. William O. Cowell), Judith (Mrs. Robert L. Bentley), Lawrence Stanley, Jerolyn Marie. Bookkeeper, Propellair, Inc., Springfield, O., 1936-38; sec., bookkeeper Oliver & McClellan, Inc., N.Y.C., 1939-43; ordained to ministry Pentecostal Ch.; pastor in Hazleton, Pa., 1943-45; gen. sec.-treas. United Pentecostal Ch., St. Louis, 1945-67, gen. supt., 1967—. Home: 201 Beverly Lane Collinsville, IL 62234. Office: 3645 S Grand Blvd St Louis MO 63118

CHAMBERS, WALTER LOUIS, educator, landscape architect; b. Hanging Rock, O., Apr. 9, 1907; s. Ulysses Gaylord and Terrena (Bernthold) C.; B.L.A., Ohio State U., 1929; M.L.A., Harvard, 1932; m. Eileen Wilson, 1931 (div. Jan. 1949); m. 2d, Virginia Hodson Howe, July 1949. Instr. landscape architecture Grad. Sch. Design, Harvard, 1933-38, asst. prof., 1938-42, acting chmn. dept., 1940-41, asso. prof., 1942-55, prof. landscape architecture, 1955-58, chmn. dept., 1956-58; profl. practice landscape architecture, 1938-48; instr. landscape engring. Lowthorpe Sch., 1938-41; cons. site planning TVA, 1941; lectr. landscape architecture Grad. Sch. Architecture and Landscape Architecture, Smith Coll. 1941-42; landscape architecture, planning, site engring. Chambers & Moriece, Cambridge, Mass., 1948-56, Chambers & Moriece, Inc., 1956-57; prof. landscape archhitecture U. Mich., 1958—; chmn. dept., 1958-69; dir. Nicholas Arboretum 1958-69; cons. architect, 1957—. Recipient award (with others) for Wellesley Housing Project, Archtl. Forum; citation for Country Sch., Weston, Mass., Progressive Architecture; Centennial Distinguished Alumnus award Ohio State U., 1970. Fellow Am. Soc. Landscape Architects; mem. Am. Hort. Soc., Nat. Audubon Soc., Mich. Acad. Sci., Arts and Letters, Nat. Council State Garden Clubs, mem. Tau Sigma Delta. Author articles profl. publs. Home: 2301 SE 8th St Pompano Beach FL 33062

CHAMBERS, WILLIAM ELY, Jr., advt. agy. exec.; b. N.Y.C., June 2, 1919; s. William Ely and Hazel (Nesbitt) C.; B.A., Harvard, 1942; student Grad. Sch. Bus. Adminstrn., N.Y.U., 1946-48; m. Eleanor Virginia Neill, Mar. 6, 1943; childrenWilliam Ely III, Thomas Neill. Advt. mgr. Nat. Sugar Refining Co., N.Y.C., 1947-48, gen. sales mgr. Arbuckle Sugars div., 1948-50; sr. account exec. Benton & Bowles, N.Y.C., 1950-55; v.p., account supr. Foote, Cone & Belding, N.Y.C., 1956-61, v.p., gen. mgr. N.Y. office, 1962, exec. v.p., 1968-69, chmn. exec. com., 1968-69, also chmn. com., until 1969; exec. v.p. D'Arcy, MacManus, Intermarco, N.Y.C., chmn., Greenwich, 1960; Conn. Rep. Congl. del., 1962. Bd. dirs. Greenwich Health Assn., 1959-63, Brunswick Sch., Greenwich, 1960-63. Served to capt. USAAF, 1942-45. Clubs: Field (Greenwich); Belle Haven (Conn.) Beach; Stanwich (Greenwich, Conn.); Harvard, Racquet and Tennis Upland Dr Greenwich CT 06830

CHAMBERS, WILLIAM NISBET, educator; b. Joplin, Mo., Nov. 30, 1916; s. William Lionel and Lucy (Matthews) C.; B.S. magna cum laude, Harvard, 1939; Ph.D., Washington U., St. Louis, 1949; m. Susan Jane Ross, Apr. 16, 1941; children—Mary Reid, William David, Catherine Jane. Lectr. to prof. polit. sci. Washington U., 1949-65, prof. history, chmn. dept., 1965-67, Edward Mallinckrodt Distinguished U. prof., 1968—; vis. fellow gen. edn. Harvard, 1956-57; vis. asso. prof. history Columbia, 1959; vis. scholar Center for Advanced Study in Behavioral Scis., 1960. Co-founder, dir., bd. dirs., chmn. personnel com. New City Sch., St. Louis. Served with AUS, 1944-46. Recipient research and other grants Carnegie Corp., Ford Found., Am. Philos. Soc., Am. Council Learned Socs., 1952-59. Sr. research award in govtl. affairs Social Sci. Research Council, 1962-63, research award in constl. democracy Rockefeller Found., 1963-64. Fellow Charles Warren Center for Studies in Am. History, Harvard, 1967-68. Mem. Am. Hist. Assn., Orgn. Am. Historians, Am. Polit. Sci. Assn., Phi Beta Kappa, Pi Sigma Alpha, Omicron Delta Kappa. Democrat. Author: Old Bullion Benton: Senator From the New West 1782-1858, 1956; Democracy in the Mid-Twentieth Century: Problems and Prospects, 1960; Political Parties in a New Nation: The American Experience 1776-1809, 1963; The Democrats 1789-1964: A Short History of a Popular Party, 1964; The American Party Systems: Stages of Political Development, 1967; The Image Campaign: Parties and the Election of 1840 in Arthur Schlesinger Jr. and Fred L. Israel eds. Presidential Elections, 1971; The First Party System: Federalists and Republicans, 1971. Contbr. articles profl. jours. Home: 265 Union Blvd St Louis MO 63108

CHAMBLESS, JOHN ROBERT, confection co. exec.; b. Georgetown, Ga., July 13, 1911; s. Jesse Eugene and Geraline (Hatfield) C.; student pub. schs.; m. Frances Eugenia Haines, June 2, 1932; children—Robert Eugene, James Louis. With Tom 1944-58, v.p. charge finance, sec., 1958—, sec.-treas. Muscogee Sales Corp., Columbus, 1951-; dir., sec.-treas. Dixie Confections Inc. Columbus, 1944-47; mem. adv. Columbus Bank & Trust Co., 1961. Sec.- treas. Walter Alan Richards Found., Inc., Columbus, 1956-. Mem. Nat. Assn. Accountants, Ga., Columbus chambers commerce. Methodist. Clubs: Lions, Columbus Country, Executives (Columbus). Home: 2705 Auburn Av Columbus, GA 31906. Office: 8th St and 9th Av Columbus GA 31902

CHAMBLISS, JOHN RANDOLPH, physician; b. Rocky Mt., N.C., Apr. 9, 1920; s. John Randolph and Janet Jeffries (Austin) C.; B.S., U. N.C., 1942; M.D., Harvard, 1944. Resident Boston City Hosp., Lakeside Hosp., Cleve., 1944-50; mem. Boice Willis Clinic, Rocky Mt., N.C., 1950—; clin. prof. medicine U. N.C. Sch. Med. at Chapel Hill, 1967—. Dir. N.C. Regional Med. Program. Served to capt. M.C., AUS, 1945-57; 1953, Korea. Recipient Distinguished Service award, U. N.C. Sch. Med., 1968. Diplomate Am. Bd. Internal Medicine. Fellow Am. Coll. Physicians: mem. Am. Soc. Internal Medicine, A.M.A., Am. Heart Assn. Home: 1036 Sycamore St Rocky Mount NC 27801 Office: 100 Nash Medical Arts Mall Rocky Mount NC 27801

CHAMBLISS, ROLLIN, educator; b. Plains, Ga., July 17, 1902; s. James R. and Henrietta L. (Davison) C.; A.B., U. Ga., 1927, M.A., Harvard, 1941, Ph.D., 1943; m. Amy Carlson, May 21, 1939; children—Carlson, John. Asso. prof. U. Ga., 1946-48, prof., 1948-62; prof. sociology U. Hartford, 1962—; Fulbright visiting prof. Finland, 1955-56, Pakistan, 1959. Served with AUS, 1936-39, 41-46. Fellow Am. Sociol. Assn.; mem. So. Sociol. Soc. (v.p.), Phi Beta Kappa, Phi Kappa Phi. Author: Social thought from Hammurab: to Comte, 1954; the Nature of Man, 1961; Meaning for Man, 1966. Contbr. articles profl. jours. Home: 74 Sunny Reach W Hartford CT 06117

CHAMBRE, PAUL L., educator; b. Kassel, Germany, Aug. 7, 1918; s. Ernest and Minna (Rothenberger) C.; came to U.S., 1937, naturalized, 1942; B.S., U. Cal. at Berkeley, 1941, Ph.D., 1951; M.S., N.Y. U., 1947; m. Jane C. Miller, June 26, 1943 (dec. Mar. 1964); children—Erika Anne, Suzanne, Marianne. Research engr. Airesearch Mfg. Co., Los Angeles, 1943-44; research scientist Jet. Propulsion Lab., Cal. Inst. Tech., 1944-45, Project Squid, N.Y. U., 1945-47; research scientist low pressure research group U. Cal. at Berkeley, 1947-51, mem. faculty, 1951—, prof. math. and engring. sci., 1962—. Mem. Sigma Xi, Pi Mu Epsilon. Author: Flow of Rarefied Gases, 1961; also articles. Office: Univ California Berkeley CA 94720

CHAMERLAIN, OWEN, nuclear physicist; b. San Francisco, July 10, 1920; A.B., Dartmouth, 1941, Cramer fellow, 1941; Ph.D., U. Chgo., 1949; m. 1943; 4 children. Inst. Physics U. Cal. at Berkeley, 1948-50, asst. prof., 1950-54, asso. prof., 1954-58, prof., 1958—; civilian physicist Manhattan Dist., Berkeley, Los Alamos, 1942-46; Guggenheim fellow, 1957-58; Loeb lectr. at Harvard U., 1959. Recipient Nobel prize (with Emilio Segré) for physics, for discovery anti-proton, 1959. Fellow Am. Phys. Soc.; mem. Nat. Acad. Scis. Address: Physics Dept U Cal Berkeley CA 94720

CHAMETZKY, JULES, educator; b. Bklyn., May 24, 1928; s. Benjamin and Anna (Zweig) C.; B.A., Bklyn. Coll., 1950; M.A., U. Minn., 1952, Ph.D., 1958; m. Anne Halley, Feb. 21, 1953; children—Matthew, Robert, Peter. Teaching asst., then instr. U. Minn., 1951-56; instr. humanities Boston U., 1956-58; faculty U. Mass., Amherst, 1958—, asso. prof. English, 1964-69, prof., 1969—. Fulbright prof. Am. lit. U. Tübingen (Germany), 1962-63, Zagreb (Yugoslavia) U., 1966-67; guest prof. Free U. Berlin, 1970-71. Bd. dirs. Coordinating Council Lit. Mags., 1967—. Mem. Assn. Lit. Mag. Am. (pres. 1965—), Am. Studies Assn. (sec. New Eng. sect. 1967-68). Editor: Faulkner Studies, 1953-54, (with Sidney Kaplan) Black and White in American Culture, 1969. mem. editorial bd. Mass. Rev., 1958—, mng. editor, 1961-62, co-editor, 1963-69, 71—. Home: 244 Amity St Amherst MA 01002

CHAMLIN, MAX, physician; b. Loev, USSR, Dec. 21, 1908; s. Jacob and Mary (Segal) C.; brought to U.S., 1910, naturalized, 1915; B.A., Columbia, 1930; M.D., Univ. and Bellevue Hosp. Med. Coll., 1934; postgrad. Coll. Phys. and Surg. Columbia, 1941-42, N.Y. Eye, Ear Infirmary, 1941-42; m. Jeanette Arzt, June 29, 1934; children—Matthew David, Richard Mark. Intern Forham Hosp., N.Y.C., 1935-37; gen. practice medicine, N.Y.C., 1937-41, specialist in ophthalmology, N.Y.C., 1941—; asst. ophthalmologist Forham Hosp., 1937-47, Montefiore Hosp., 1943—; dir. ophthalmology Bronx Mcpl. Hosp., 1954-69, attending ophthalmologist, 1969—; cons. ophthalmologist Bronx VA Hosp., 1954—, N.Y. Eye & Ear Infirmary, 1969—; asst. prof. ophthalmology N.Y. U., 1947-54; prof. Albert Einstein Coll. Medicine, 1954—, chmn. dept., 1956-69. Diplomate Am. Bd. Ophthalmology (asso. examiner). Fellow N.Y. Acad. Medicine (chmn. eye sect. 1965-66), A.C.S., Am. Acad. Ophthalmology and Otolaryngology; mem. N.Y. Soc. Clin. Ophthalmology (pres. 1956-57), Assn. Research in Ophthalmology, Harvey Cushing Soc. (asso.). Inventor Chamlin Perimeter for visual field studies, 1954. Contbr. profl. jours. Home: 37 Oxford Rd New Rochelle NY 10804 Office: 25 Central Park West New York City NY 10023

CHAMPION, GEORGE, banker; b. Normal, Ill., Feb. 8, 1904; s. George and Emily (Moore) C.; B.S., Dartmouth Coll., 1926; m. Eleanor Stevens, Sept., 1928; children—George, Stevens (dec.), Emily Jean (Mrs. Carl W. Knobloch, Jr.). Began with Nat. Bank of Commerce, N.Y.C., 1926; asst. sec. Equitable Trust Co., 1930; v.p. Canal Bank and Trust Co., 1931; 2nd v.p. Chase Nat. Bank, 1933, v.p., 1939, sr. v.p., 1949-55, exec. v.p. merged Chase Manhattan Bank, 1955-57, pres., 1957-61, chmn. bd. dirs., 1961-69, now dir.; dir. Discount Corp, N.Y., Pepsi Co, Inc., Internat. Paper Co., Am. Smelting and Refining Co., Kellogg Co. Chmn. nat. indsl. adv. council Opportunities Industrialization Center. Dir. Freedoms Found., Valley Forge, Pa.; adv. com. Tuck Assos.; mem. Am. Found. Religion and Psychiatry; mem., vice chmn. 1966 Campaign Greater N.Y. Fund; pres. and chmn. Econ. Devel. Council N.Y.C. Mem. Pilgrims of U.S., Psi Upsilon. Clubs: Alfalfa (Washington); Blind Brook (Port Chester, N.Y.); Nat. Golf Links (Southampton, N.Y.); Economic, River, Links, University (N.Y.C.); Augusta (Georgia) National Golf (mem. bd.); Round Hill Club. Home: Wilshire Rd Greenwich CT 06830 also 435 E 52nd St New York City NY 10022 Office: 1 Chase Manhattan Plaza New York City NY 10015

CHAMPION, GOWER, choreographer, dancer; b. Geneva, Ill., June 22, 1921; s. John W. and Beatrice (Carlisle) C.; stud. pub. schs.; Los Angeles; m. Marjorie Cleste Belcher, Oct. 5, 1947; 1 son, Gregg. Early dancing appearances with Jeanne Tyler as Gower and Jeanne, west coast nigh clubs, also N.Y.C.; appeared Broadway mus. revues including Streets of Paris, Lady Comes Across, Count Me In, 1939-41; under contract Metro- Goldwyn Mayer; appeared with Marjorie Bell (Marjorie Celeste Belcher) as Gower and Bell, Montreal, Can., 1947, N.Y.C. debut in Hotel Plaza, 1947; night club tours, 1948; staged dances for Broadway revue Small Wonder; choreographer Lend an Ear, Hollywood, film Girl Most Likely, 1956; TV Chevy Show, Jack Benny Show, Screen Dirs. Playhouse, G.E. Theatre: weekly show Admiral Broadway Revue, Dumont NBC-TV Network, 1949; appeared with Bing Crosby in motion picture Mr. Music, Paramount, 1950; movies include Show Boat, Lovely to Look At, Everything I Have is Yours, 1952, Give the Girl a Break, 1952; various nightclub, TV appearances, including TV show Toast of the Town, 1953, GE Theatre, 1957. Dinah Shore Show, 1958, Telephone Hour, 1959, We Four, 1960; appeared in Three for Tonight; stage dir. Hemingway and All Those People, Indpls., 1958; choreography and directing Bye, Bye, Birdie, Hello, Dolly (Tony award 1963), Three Bags Full. Served with the USCG, World War II; transport duty, also toured with mus. show Tars and Spars. Recipient Donaldson, Dance mag., Antoinette Perry awards for creation best dances on Broadway: Tony award for best dir. musical, choreographer The Happy Time, 1967-68. Mem. Screen Dirs. Guild.*

CHAMPION, JOHN E., educator, accountant; b. Chipley, Ga., May 11, 1922; s. Jesse and Fannie Lou (Stripling) C.; B.B.A., U. Ga., 1942, M.B.A., 1949; student Ind. U., 1949-50; Ph.D., U. Mich., 1960; m. Mary Lanier, June 4, 1955; children—Sally, John. C.P.A., Ga., 1952; asst. prof. U. Ga. at Athens, 1948-54, asst. prof., 1954-56; asso. prof. Fla. State U., Tallahassee, 1956-60, asst. dean Sch. Bus., prof., 1960-62, v.p. for adminstrn., 1962-65, pres., 1965-69, prof. accounting, 1969—. Mem. Gov.'s Commn. on Quality Edn., 1966-67. Served to capt., AUS, 1943-46. Named Outstanding Alumnus, Sch. Bus., U. Ga., 1966: recipient grand cross Order Vasco Nunez de Balboa (Panama), 1966. Mem. Am. Accounting Assn., Am. Inst. C.P.A.'s, Tallahassee C. of C., Gold Key, Phi Beta Kappa, Phi Kappa Phi, Beta Gamma Sigma, Delta Sigma Pi, Beta Alpha Psi, Alpha Phi Omega, Kappa Delta Pi, Omicron Delta Kappa. Presbyn. Republican. Rotarian. Author: Accounting in Business Decisions (with Homer A. Black), 1961. Home: 2214 Killarney Way Tallahassee FL 32303

CHAMPION, MARGE, (Marjorie Celeste Belcher), actress, dancer, b. Los Angeles, Sept. 2; d. Ernest and Gladys (Basquette) Belcher; student pub. schs., Los Angeles; m. Art Babbitt (div.); m. 2d, Gower Champion, Oct. 5, 1947; 1 son, Gregg. Stage debut Los Angeles Civic Opera, 1936; movie debut (under name Marjorie Bell), The Castles, 1938; model for cartoon heroines in Snow White, blue fairy in Pinocchio, Walt Disney prodns., 1938; appeared Broadway musicals Dark of the Moon, Beggar's Holiday, 1947; first profl. appearance with Gower Champion as Gower and Bell, Montreal, Can., 1947, N.Y. debut in Hotel Plaza, 1947; night club tours, 1948; weekly show Admiral Broadway Review, Dumont and NBC TV Network, 1949; appeared with Bing Crosby in movie Mr. Music, Paramount Pictures, 1950; with husband staged dances for revue Make A Wish, Broadway, 1951; now under contract Metro-Goldwyn Mayer; movies include Show Boat, Lovely to Look At, Everything I Have is Yours, 1952, Give the Girl a Break, 1952; various nightclub, TV appearances, including TV show Toast of the Town, 1953; Three for Tonight, 1955; Jupiter's Darling, 1954, Shower of Stars, 1956, GE Theatre, 1957, Dinah Shore Show, 1958, Telephone Hour, We Four, 1960; stage debut Hemingway and All Those People, Indpls., 1958. Toured, title role Sabrina Fair, 1960.*

CHAMPION, ROBERT L., engr.; b. 1913; ed. U. Ill. and Stanford. Engring. tchr. U. Ill., 1937- 39, Mich. State Coll., 1939-41, Northwestern U., 1941-42; staff research and devel. div. War Plans, Bur. Docks, 1942-43; project engr. Amchitka Fido installation, 1943; with landing aids sect. Bur. Aero., fog disposal liaison officer, 1943-44; Bur. Aero. liaison officer RAF Fido Projct and Petroleum Warfare Dept., London, 1944; became pres. Internat. Sci. Corp., 1946—, Internat. Sci. Found., 1954—. Tech. dir. Associacao de Fomento da Aviacao Ltda., 1949-50; dir. Coop. Research Inst., 1950—; asst. dir. office internat. relations Nat. Acad. Scis., San Francisco Bay Area Internat. Sci. Center; cons. U.S. Army Ballistic Missile Agy., Johns Hopkins Operations Research Office, also firms. Mem. Am. Soc. C.E., Cal. Acad. Scis. Address: World Trade Center Ferry Bldg San Francisco CA 94111

CHAMPLIN, CHARLES DAVENPORT, writer, critic; b. Hammondsport, N.Y., Mar. 23, 1926; s. Francis Malburn and Katherine (Masson) C.; A.B. cum laude, Harvard, 1947; m. Margaret Frances Derby, Sept. 11, 1948; children—Charles Davenport, Katherine (Mrs. William B. Karman, Jr.), John, Judith, Susan, Nancy. Reporter, Life mag., 1948-49, corr., Chgo., 1949-52, Denver, 1952-54, writer, N.Y.C., 1954-59; corr. Time mag., Los Angeles, 1959-62, London, Eng., 1962-65; entertainment editor, columnist Los Angeles Times, 1965—, prin. film critic, 1967—; commentator KCET-TV, Los Angeles, also ETV Network, 1969—. Served with inf. AUS, 1944-46. Decorated Purple Heart. Mem. Sigma Delta Chi. Author: (with C. Sava) How to Swim Well, 1960; also numerous articles. Home: 2169 Linda Flora Dr Los Angeles CA 90024 Office: Los Angeles Times Times-Mirror Sq Los Angeles CA 90053

CHAMPLIN, KEITH SCHAFFNER, educator, elec. engr.; b. Mpls., Aug. 20, 1930; s. Glenn Martin and Martha (Schaffner) C.; B.Sc., U. Minn., 1954, M.Sc., 1955, Ph.D., 1958; m. Marian D. Staebler, Sept. 4, 1954; childrenJudson Keith, Michelle Graham. Mem. faculty U. Minn., 1958-, prof. elec. engring., 1966-; exchange prof. U. Paris (France), 1963; cons. to industry, 1960-. Served with AUS, 1951-52. Recipient Distinguished Teaching award U. Minn., 1963, Mem. I.E.E.E., Am. Phys. Soc., Sigma Xi, Tau Beta Pi, Eta Kappa Nu, Gamma Alpha. Research microwave properties semiconductor materials. Contbr. profl. jours. Home: 5437 Elliott Av S Minneapolis, MN 55417.

CHAMPLIN, MALCOLM MCGREGOR, municipal judge; b. San Francisco, Apr. 13, 1911; s. Charles Chaffee and Maude (Fraser) C.; B.S., U.S. Naval Acad., 1934; J.D., U. Cal., 1939; grad. U.S. Naval War Coll., 1944; m. Betty Mee Champlin, Dec. 1943 (div.); children—Sarah, William Bradford, Mimi Lisette; m. 2d, Virginia Pearson, Dec. 2, 1955. Commd. ensign USN, 1934; served in USN, 1934- 37; admitted to Cal. bar, 1940; practiced in Oakland, 1940, 45-67; spl. agt. FBI, 1941; partner firm Stark & Champlin, 1947-67; municipal ct. judge, Oakland, 1967—. Vice pres., dir. Ventura Processors, Inc., 1949-53. Gen. chmn. fund drive Knowland Park Zoo, 1963. Chmn., Speaker's Com. Republican Party, Alameda County, 1949-50; del. Nat. Rep. Conv., 1960-64; chmn. Vets for Eisenhower, Alameda County, 1952, 56. Served as comdr. USNR, 1941-45. Decorated Navy Cross, Army Silver Star. Recipient George Washington Honor Medal award Freedoms Found. at Valley Forge, 1964. Mem. Am., Cal., Alameda County bar assns., Am. Legion (past comdr. 10th Dist., judge adv. dept. of Cal. 1953-54, state comdr. 1954-55, Cal. mem. nat. exec. com. 1956-58), Res. Officers Assn., Phi Delta Phi. Conglist. Mason. Clubs: Commonwealth (San Francisco), Athenian-Nile. Contbr. to Sea Power mag. Home: 485 Ellita Av Oakland, CA 94610. Office: Hall of Justice 600 Washington St Oakland CA 94612

CHAMSON, ANDREW LOUIS J., gen. dir. French Archives; b. Nimes (Gard), France, June 6, 1900; s. Jean and Madeleine (Adelbert) C.; student Sorbonne, Paris, also Chartes Sch.; Paleographic Archivist, 1925; Docteur H.C., U. Laval, Quebec; m. Lucie Alix Mazauric, Aug. 20, 1900; 1 dau., Frederique. Asst. curator Versailles Palace, 1933-39; chief curator Musee du Petit-Palais, 1945-59; gen. dir. French Archives, 1959—. Served as maj. Alsace- Lorraine Brigade, 1st French Army, 1939-40, maj., 1944-45. Decorated Grand Croix Legion of Honor, Croix de Guerre, Resistance medal. Mem. French Acad. Author: Roux the Bandit, 1925; The Road, 1927; The Crime of the Just, 1928; Heritages, 1932; The Year of the Conquered, 1934; A Mountain Boyhood, 1935; The Inn of the Abyss, 1935; Nothing but Testimony, 1937; (pseudonym of Lauter) The Wells of Miracles, 1946; The Last Village, 1946; The Man who Marched Before Me, 1948; Snow and the Flower, 1951; The Number of our Days, 1956; Our Ancestors the Gauls, 1958; Le rendez-vous des Espérances, 1961; Comme une pierre qui tombe, 1964; La petite Odyssée, 1965; La Superbe, 1967; La tour de Constance, 1970; others. Home: 60 rue Mirabeau Paris 16 France

CHAN, SHAU WING, educator; b. Canton, China, Apr. 4, 1907; s. Chan Chi-Tong and Tui Wan- Ying; A.B., Lingnan U., China, 1927; A.M., Stanford, 1932, Ph.D., 1937; m. Anna Mae Chan, July 27, 1935; childrenWayne Lyman, Loren Briggs. Instr. English, Nat. Sun Yat-Sen U., Canton, China, 1927-30; lectr. Chinese, Kwangtung Provincial Normal Sch. for Women, Canton, 1928-30; U. fellow in English, Stanford, 1932-34; apptd. prof. English Nat. U. Shantung, Taingtao, China, 1937; spl. lectr. Utah State Agrl. Coll., summer 1941; vis. prof. U. Utah, summer 1944; Pomona Coll., summers 1945, 1946, 1950, 1951; instr. in Chinese lang. and lit. Stanford, 1938- 39, asst. prof. Chinese and English, 1939-42, asst. prof. Chinese and humanities, 1942-45, asso. prof. Chinese and humanities, 1945-50, prof. Chinese, 1950—, acting exec. head Dept. Asiatic and Slavic exec. head dept. Asian langs., 1958-62; dir. human relations area files China Research Project, Stanford, 1955-56; cons. hist. research Com. for Free Asia, 1951-52; cons. Stanford Research Inst., 1951-53; established soldier-training program in Chinese, Stanford, 1943, dir., 1943-45, dir. Chinese Japanese Lang. and Area Center, 1956—, research asso. Hoover Instn. Lang. cons. Internat. Secretariat, UN Conf., San Francisco, Chmn. bd. library trustees City of Menlo Park. Mem. Am. Oriental Soc., Phi Delta Kappa. Conglist. Clubs: Commonwealth California, Kiwanis. Author: Chinese Reader for Beginners, 1942; Concise English-Chinese Dictionary, 1946; Elementary Flash Cards, 1944; Elementary Chinese, 1951, 2d edit., 1961. Co-author China's Men of Letters Yesterday and Today. Home: 751 Live Oak Av Menlo Park CA 94025 Office: Stanford University Stanford CA 93107

CHAN, SHU-PARK, educator; b. Canton, Cina, Oct. 10, 1929; s. Chi-Tong and Shui-Ying (Mok) C.; B.E.E., Va. Mil. Inst., 1955; M.E.E., U. Ill., 1957, Ph.D., 1963; m. Stella Yok-Sing Lam, Dec. 28, 1956; children—Charlene Li-Hsiang, Yau-Gene. Came to U.S., 1951, naturalized, 1965. Instr. elec. engring. and math. Va. Mil. Inst., 1957-59; instr. elec. engring. U. Ill., 1960-61, research asso., 1961-62, asst. prof. math., 1962-63; asso. prof. elec. engring. U. Santa Clara, 1963-68, prof., 1968—, chmn. elec. engring. dept., 1969—; prin. investigator NSF, Nat. Aeronautics and Space Adminstrn. Univ. fellow U. Ill., 1959-60. Mem. I.E.E.E., Am. Soc. Engring. Edn., Sigma Xi, Tau Beta Pi, Eta Kappa Nu, Pi Mu Epsilon, Phi Kappa Phi. Author: introductory Topological Analysis of Electrical Networks, 1969; (with others): Analysis of Linear Networks and Systems - A Matrix-Oriented Approach with Computer Applications, 1972. Home: 2085 Denise Dr Santa Clara CA 95050

CHAN, STANLEY HONG, educator; b. Canton, China, Dec. 25, 1903; s. Chi-tang and Ying (Tsu) C.; A.B., Lingnan U., Canton, 1927; A.M., Stanford, 1930; J.D., Southwestern U., 1954; LL.D., China Acad. Nationalist China, 1967; m. Lily Luella Lum, July 22, 1933; childrenElizabeth Mae, Adora Kay. Came to U.S., 1928, naturalized, 1943. Prof. polit. sci., Nat. U. of Peking, Peiping, China, 1933-38; lecturer in govt. and Oriental affairs Pomona Coll. and Claremont

Colls., 1938-40; asso. prof. Loyola U., Los Angeles, 1943-46, prof. polit. sci., 1946—, chmn. dept., 1945—. Dir. edn. Chinese Cath. Center in Los Angeles, 1940—. Citizenship chmn. Chinese-Am. Citizens Alliance. Mem. Am. Polit. Sci. Assn., Am. Soc. Internat. Law, Phi Sigma Mu. K.C. Contbr. articles profl. jours. Lectr. internat. subjects. Home: 1259 S Windsor Blvd Los Angeles, CA 90019.

CHAN, SUNNEY IGNATIUS, chemist; b. San Francisco, Oct. 5, 1936; s. Sun and Hip-For (Lai) C.; B.S. in Chem. Engring., U. Cal. at Berkeley, 1957, Ph.D. in Chemistry, 1960; m. Irene Yuk-Hing Tam, July 11, 1964; 1 son, Michael Kenneth. Asst. prof. chemistry U. Cal. at Riverside, 1961-63; mem. faculty Cal. Inst. Tech., 1963—, prof. chem. physics, 1968—; cons. in field. Guggenheim fellow, 1968-69; Sloan fellow, 1965-67; NSF Postdoctoral fellow, 1960-61. Mem. A.A.A.S., Am. Chem. Soc., Am. Phys. Soc., Am. Soc. Biol. Chemists, Am. Inst. Chemists, N.Y. Acad. Scis., So. Cal. Chinese Engrs. and Scientists Assn., Chinese Collegiate Colleagues So. Cal. (v.p. 1970-71), Phi Beta Kappa, Sigma Xi, Tau Beta Pi, Alpha Chi Sigma, Phi Tau Phi. Author numerous articles in field. Home: 420 Parkman St Altadena CA 91001 Office: Cal Inst Tech Pasadena CA 91109

CHAN, WING-TSIT, educator; b. Kwangtung, China, Aug. 18, 1901; s. Yeung-wang and Sze- chook (Lee) C.; A.B., Lingnan U., Canton, China, 1924; A.M., Harvard, 1927, Ph.D., 1929; A.M. (hon.), Dartmouth, 1943; m. Wai-hing Lei, Sept. 1, 1928; children—Jean Chi-yuen, Lo-yi Chang-yuen, Gordon Kun-yuan. Prof. philosophy, dean of faculty Lingnan U., 1929-36; prof. Chinese instns. and phil. U. Hawaii, 1936-42, chmn. dept. philosophy, 1940-42; prof. Chinese culture and philosophy Dartmouth Coll., 1942-66, emeritus, 1966—, chmn. div. humanities, 1951-55; co-director Comparative Studies Center, 1965-66; Anna D. R. Gillespie prof. phiosophy Chatham Coll., 1966—; adj. prof. of Chinese thought, Columbia U., 1965-67, faculty asso., 1964—; sr. fellow China Acad.; Haskell Found. lectr. U. Chgo., 1950. Chinese del. to World Fedn. Ednl. Assns. Conf., Geneva, 1929, to Far Eastern Higher Edn. Conf., Manila, 1934, to Eastern and Western Philosophers Conf., Hawaii, 1939, 49, 59, 64; mem. Conf. Sci., Philosophy & Religion, N.Y.C., 1944, 45, Guggenheim fellow, 1948-49; Rockefeller Found. grantee, 1955-56, 63, Am. Council Learned Soc. grantee, 1955-60, Social Sci. Research Council grantee, 1963, Am. Philos. Society grantee, 1963. Sr. fellow The China Acad. Mem. Am. Soc. for Study of Religion, Am. Council Learned Socs. (com. Far Eastern Studies 1950-53), Am. Oriental Soc., Assn. for Asian Studies, Am. Assn. U. Profs, Assn. Asian and Comparative Philosophy. Author: Religious Trends in Modern China, 1953, 70; An Outline and an Annotated Bibliography of Chinese Philosophy, 1959, 69; Historical Charts of Chinese Philosophy, 1955; Source Book in Chinese Philosophy, 1963; Instructions for Practical Living, and other Neo- Confucian Writings by Wang Yang-ming, 1963; The Way of Lao Tzu, 1963; The Platform Scripture, 1963; Chinese Philosophy, 1949-63, 1967; Reflection on Things at Hand, 1967; Great Asian Religions, 1969; Neo-Confucianism, 1969. Editor: Essentials of Buddhist Philosophy, 1941; (with W. T. de Bary and B. Watson) Sources of Chinese Tradition, 1960. Contributor to China, 1946; Philosophy East and West, 1944; Essays in East-West Philosophy, 1951; The Chinese Mind, 1967; Self and Society in Ming Thought, 1969; Encyclopaedia Brit., 1960-69, Ency. Philsophy, 1967; Revue Bibliographique de Sinologic; Biographies and bibliography song Project. Home: 228 Sharon Dr Pittsburgh PA 15221

CHANCE, BRITTON, educator; b. Wilkes Barre, Pa., July 24, 1913; s. Edwin M. and Eleanor (Kent) C.; B.S. and M.S., U. Pa., 1936, Ph.D., 1940 (E.R. Johnson Found. fellow 1939-40); Ph.D., U. Cambridge, 1942, D.Sc., 1952; M.D. (hon.) Karolinska Inst., Stockholm; m. Jane Earle, Mar. 4, 1938 (div.); children—Eleanor, Britton, Jan. Peter; m. 2d, Lilian Streeter Lucas, Nov. 1956; children—Margaret, Lilian, Benjamin, Samuel; stepchildren—Ann Lucas, Gerald B. Lucas, A. Brooke Lucas, William C. Lucas. Asst. prof. biophysics U. Pa., 1940-48, prof., chmn., 1949—, acting dir. Johnson Found., 1940-41, dir., 1949—; Eldridge Reeves Johnson prof. biophysics and phys. biochemistry, 1949—; staff Mass. Inst. Tech., 1941-46; Guggenheim fellow, Stockholm, Sweden, 1946-48. Cons. NSF, 1952-55; mem. Pres.'s Sci. Adv. Com., 1959-60. Harvey lectr., 1954, Phillips lectr., 1955, 65, Pepper lectr. 1957. Recipient Paul Lewis award for enzyme chemistry, 1950; Pres.'s Certificate of Merit for services, 1941-45, as staff mem. Radiation Lab. of M.I.T., 1950. Exchange scholar to USSR, 1963; Genootschapps medal Dutch Acad. Scis., 1965, Heineken medal, 1970; Keilin medal Brit. Biochem. Soc., 1966; Harrison Howe award, 1966; Franklin medal, 1966; Overseas fellow Churchill Coll., 1966; Herter lectr. N.Y. U., 1968; Pa. award for excellence in life scis., 1968; Nichols award N.Y. sect. Am. Chem. Soc., 1970, Phila. sect. award, 1969; Redfearn lectr., 1970. Fellow Am. Phys. Soc., I.E.E.E. (Morlock award 1961), A.A.A.S.; mem. Chem. Soc., Royal Soc. Arts, Biochem. Soc. Eng., Am. Soc. Biol. Chemists, Am. Philos. Soc., Am. Acad. Arts and Sci., Nat. Acad. Sci., Am. Physiol. Soc., Soc. Gen. Physiologists (council 1956), Am. Inst. Physics, Am. Inst. Chemists, Swedish Biochem. Soc., Royal Swedish Acad. Scis., Royal Acad. Arts and Scis., Sweden, Bavarian Acad. Scis., Harvey Soc., Sigma Xi, Tau Beta Pi. Clubs: Corinthian Yacht (Phila.); St. Anthony, N.Y. Yacht. Author: Waveforms (with F. C. Williams, V. Hughes, E. F. McNichol, David Sayre), 1949; Electronic Time Measurements (with R. I. Hulsizer, E. F. McNichol F. C. Williams), 1949; Energy-linked Functions of Mitochondria, 1964; (with Q. H. Gibson, R. Eisenhardt, K. K. Lonberg-Holm) Rapid Mixing and Sampling Techniques in Biochemistry, 1964; (with R. W. Estabrook, J. R. Williamson) Control of Energy Metabolism, 1965; (with R. W. Estabrook, T. Yonetani) Hemes and Hemoproteins, 1966; (with others) Probes of Structure and Function of Macromolecules and Enzymes, 1971; rev. articles Advances in Enzymology, Vo. 12, 1951, Vol. 17, 1956; Ann. Rev. of Biochemistry, 1952; The Enzymes, Vol. II. Part 1, 1952; Ann. Rev. Plant Physiology, 1958, 68. Bd. editors Physiol. Revs., 1951-54. Contbr. articles to Am., Brit., Swedish, German and Japanese Jours. Holder numerous patents on automatic steering devices, also radar circuitry. Gold medal winner (yachting) 1952 Olympics. Home: 4014 Pine St Philadelphia PA 19104

CHANCE, FRANCIS GANO, former mfg. exec.; b. Centralia, Mo., Feb. 14, 1905; s. A. Bishop and Frances I. (Gano) C.; student Central Coll.; A.B., U. Mo., 1929, B.S. in Chem. Engring., 1929; m. Anna Lee Toalson, June 28, 1930; children—Phillip Gano, John Hardin. Vice pres., asst. gen. mgr. A. B. Chance Co., Centralia, Mo., 1931, pres., 1939-60, chmn. bd., 1949-70, ret. Mem. bd. Mo. Pub. Expenditure Survey (v.p. 1958-59). Trustee Chance Found. Mem. U.S. (nat. councillor), Mo. (pres. 1944-46, dir.), Centralia C.'s of C., Asso. Industries Mo. (pres. 1954-55, 55-56). So. States Indsl. Council (bd. 1957, v.p. 1956-), N.A.M. (bd. 1953-60), Engring. Alumni Assn. U. Mo. (v.p. 1954—), Alpha Chi Sigma, Alpha Tau Omega (nat. found. chmn. 1957—). Member Baptist Ch. Clubs: Missouri Athletic, Discussion, St. Louis (St. Louis); Kiva (Phoenix); Centralia Country, Rotary (Centralia). Home: 510 S Jefferson St Centralia MO 65240

CHANCE, HENRY MARTYN II, engring. exec.; b. Pottsville, Pa., Jan. 16, 1912; s. Edwin M. and Eleanor (Kent) C.; grad. Haverford Sch., 1930; B.S. in Civil Engring., U. Pa., 1934; m. Suzanne Sharpless, June 12, 1934; children—Edwin M. Suzanne, Barbara; m. 2d, Elizabeth Reese, Aug. 19, 1944; children—Steven K., James M., Henry Martyn III, Mark Raymond. Chemist, assayer Am. Smelting & Refining Co., 1934-36; with United Engrs. & Constructors, Inc., Phila., 1936—, Girard Co., Girard Trust Bank, Badger Co., Inc., pres., 1954—; dir. Penwalt Corp. Trustee, mem. exec. bd. U. Pa.; pres. Haverford School, 1962-70, mem. bd., 1970—; bd. mgrs. emeritus Franklin Inst. Named Engr. of Year, Del. Valley, 1964. Registered profl. engr., 14 states and D.C. Mem. Am. Iron and Steel Engrs., Am. Soc. M.E., Am. Soc. C.E. Clubs: Engineers (Phila., N.Y.C.); New York Yacht; Racquet, Union League (Phila.); Duquesne (Pitts.); University (N.Y.C.). Home: Warren Av Malvern PA 19355 Office: 1401 Arch St Philadelphia PA 19103

CHANCELLOR, SIR CHRISTOPHER, industrialist; b. Cobham, England, Mar. 29, 1904; s. Lt. Col. Sir John and Elsie (Thompson) C.; student Eton Coll.; M.A., Trinity Coll., Cambridge (1st class in history); m. Sylvia Paget, 1926; 2 sons, 2 daus. Gen. mgr. Reuters, Ltd., 1944-59; now chmn. The Bowater Paper Corp. Ltd. 1960—. Decorated Companion of Order of St Michael and St. George. Clubs: St. James, Garrick. Home: Hunstrete House Pensford Somerset England Office: 1 Edinburgh Gate SW1 London England

CHANCELLOR, JOHN WILLIAM, correspondent; b. Chgo., July 14, 1927; s. Estil Marion and Mollie (Barrett) C.; student DePaul Acad., Chgo., U. Ill.; m. Constance Herbert; 1 dau., Mary; m. 2d, Barbara Upshaw, Jan. 25, 1958; children—Laura, Barnaby. Reporter, Chgo. Sun-Times; staff NBC News, 1950- 65, newswriter, gen. assignment reporter U.S., 1953-58, Vienna Corr., 1958, with London bur., 1959-60, Moscow Corr., 1960-61, staff N.Y.C. office, 1961-63, Brussels corr., 1963-65; communicator TV program Today, 1961-62, staff corp., 1962-65; dir. Voice of Am., Washington, 1966-67; network nat. affairs corr. NBC, 1967—.

CHANDLER, ALBERT BENJAMIN, lawyer, ex-gov.; b. Corydon, Ky., July 14, 1898; s. Joseph and Callie (Sanders) C.; A.B., Transylvania Coll., 1921, LL.D., 1936; student Harvard, 1921-33; LL.B., U. of Ky., 1924, LL.D., 1937; m. Mildred Watkins, November 12, 1925; children—Marcella (Mrs. Thomas D. Miller), Mildred (Mrs. James J. Lewis), Albert Benjamin, Joseph Daniel. Began Law practice Versailles, Kentucky, 1924; appointed master commr. Circuit Ct., Woodford County, 1928; elected mem. State Senate, Ky., 22d Ky. Dist., 1929; lt. gov. of Ky., term 1931-35; gov. of Ky., 1935- 39, 55-59; resigned, Oct. 1939 and was appointed U.S. senator to fill vacancy caused by death of Marvell Mills Logan; elected, Nov. 1940, to fill remainder of term of to Jan. 1943, re-elected for full 6 year term, Nov. 1942; high commr. of baseball, 1945-51; pres. Internat. Baseball Congress, Wichita; commr. Continental Profl. Football League, 1965—, Global Internat. Baseball League; v.p., dir. First Flight Golf Co., Chattanooga; dir. Coastal States Life Ins. Co. of Georgia. Receiver for Inter- Southern Life Ins. Co., Louisville, 1932; an organizer Ky. Home Life. Ins. Co., Louisville, 1932. Served in the U.S. Army, 1918; capt. (Reserves) Judge Advocate Gen.'s Dept. (ret.). Was one of five Senators designated by the U.S. Senate to visit world battle fronts in 1943, at which time they made the first landplane flight ever made across the Indian Ocean from Ceylon to Australia. Chmn. Woodford County Dem. Exec. Com. Trustee Ty Cobb Found.; mem. bd. trustees U. Ky.; chmn. Transylvania Coll. Bd. Trustees and Fund Raising Com. Dem. Nat. Committeeman for Ky. Named Kentuckian of the Year, Ky. Press Assn. and Ky. Broadcasters Assn.; recipient Bishop's medal Episcopal Ch., 1959; Cross of Mil. service United Daus. of Confederacy, 1959. Mem. Am. Legion, Forty and Eight, Pi Kappa Alpha. Dem. Episcopalian. Mason (32, K.T., Shriner). Clubs: Ky. Mountain (hon.), Lexington Country, Idle Hour Country (Lexington). Football coach Centre Coll., Danville, Ky., 1922- 27. One of 1st 10 named to Ky. Sports Hall of Fame, 1957. Home: Versailles KY 40383

CHANDLER, ALFRED DUPONT, Jr., educator, historian; b. Guyencourt, Del., Sept. 15, 1918; s. Alfred Dupont and Carol (Ramsay) C.; grad. Phillips Exeter Acad., 1936; A.B., Harvard, 1940, A.M., 1947, Ph.D., 1952; A.M., U. N.C., 1951; m. Fay Martin, Jan. 8, 1944; children—Alpine Douglass, Mary Morris, Alfred Dupont III, Howard Martin. Research asso. Mass. Inst. Tech., 1950-51, from instr. to prof., 1951-63; prof. history Johns Hopkins, 1963-71, chmn. dept., 1966-70, dir. Center Study Recent Am. History, 1964-71; Straus Prof. Bus. History, Harvard Bus. Sch., 1971—. Cons. U.S. Naval War Coll., 1954, to Alfred P. Sloan, Jr. on writing My Years with General Motors, 1956-59; mem. Nat. Adv. Council on Edn. Professions Devel., 1970—. Chmn. adv. hist. com. U.S. AEC, 1969. Trustee Park Sch., Brookline, Mass., 1957-63, chmn. bd., 1961-63; trustee Brookline Pub. Library, 1959-65, Roland Park Sch., Balt., 1964-70, Johns Hopkins. Served to lt. comdr. USNR, 1940-45. Guggenheim fellow, 1958-59; Research fellow Harvard, 1953. Mem. Econ. History Assn. (trustee 1966-70, pres. elect 1970), Am. Hist. Assn., Am. Acad. Arts and Scis. Episcopalian. Clubs: Guana Island (British Virgin Islands); St. Botolph (Boston); Nantucket (Mass.) Yacht; Harvard (N.Y.C.); Hamilton Street (Balt.). Author: Henry Varum Poor, 1956; Strategy and Structure (Newcomen award 1964), 1962; Giant Enterprise, 1964; The Railroads, 1965; (with Stephan Salsbury) Pierre S. duPont, 1971. Editor: Papers of Dwight D. Eisenhower, 5 vols., 1970; asst. editor The Letters of Theodore Roosevelt, 4 vols., 1950-53. Home: 211 Highfield Rd Baltimore MD 21218

CHANDLER, ALVIN DUKE, naval officer, coll. pres.; b. Richmond, Va., Aug. 18, 1902; s. Julian Alvin Carroll and Lenore Burten (Duke) C.; student William and Mary Coll., 1918, LL.D., 1963; U.S. Naval Acad., 1923; grad. Imperial Def. Coll., London, Eng., 1950; LL.D., U. Pa., 1955, Brandeis U., 1958; m. Mary Louise Michaels, Sept. 25, 1926. Commd. ensign USN, 1923, advanced through grades to vice adm., 1951; served Nicaraguan campaign, 1927; comdr. div., squadron, Atlantic and Pacific, World War II; staff comdr. in chief U.S. Fleet, 1945; comdr. U.S.S. Des Monies, 1948-49; dir. logistic plans. div. Navy Dept., 1951; pres. Coll. William and Mary in Va., 1951-60, chancellor, 1962—, chancellor Colls. of William and Mary in Va., 1960-62, also v.p. Endowment Assn. Dir. Peninsula Bank & Trust Co. Trustee Jamestown Corp.; adv. dir. Jefferson Davis. Found. Decorated Star of Solidarity (Italy); Legion of Merit with gold star, Bronze Star, Presdl. Unit Citation. Mem. S.A.R., Navy League U.S., Theta Delta Chi. Clubs: Rotary; Army and Navy, Army and Navy Town (Wash.); Virginia Beach (Va.) Sports; Commonwealth (Richmond, Va.). Co-author of textbooks on torpedoes, 1935. Contbr. to mags. Home: 1128 Hill Rd Virginia Beach VA 23451

CHANDLER, B. J., univ. dean; b. Bluffton, Ark., July 23, 1921; s. J. V. and Edna (McCreight) C.; B.A., U. Tex., 1948, M.Ed., 1949; Ed.D., Columbia, 1951; m. Marjorie Barger, Mar. 7, 1942; children—Brenda (Mrs. Thomas Dexter Barbour), Robert W. N., Cynthia. Asst. prof. edn. U. Va., Charlottesville, 1951-54, asso. prof., 1954-56; asso. prof. edn. Northwestern U., 1956-59, prof. edn., 1959—, dean Sch. Edn., 1963—; ednl. cons. State Farm Ins. Cos., 1953—. Co-chmn. Gov.'s Com. on Literacy and Learning, 1963-67. Chmn. adv. council, mem. bd. trustees, Aerospace Edn. Found., 1964-69; mem. adv. council Kellogg Found., 1963-65; mem. Gov.'s Task Force on Edn., 1965-67; pres. Ill. Council on Econ. Edn., 1969—. Trustee Chgo. Y Community Coll., Evanston Roycemore Sch. Served with USAAF, 1942-44. Mem. Internat. Platform Assn. Author: Education and the Teacher, 1961; Education in Urban Society, 1962; (with Lindley J. Stiles and John I. Kitsuse) Personnel Management in School Administration, 1955; (with Daniel Powell and William Hazard) Education and the New Teacher, 1971. Gen. editor: Introduction to Teaching, 1969—. Contbr. articles profl. jours. Home: 2322 Central Park Evanston IL 60201

CHANDLER, CAROLINE A., physician, writer juvenile books; b. Ford City, Pa., Dec. 7, 1906; d. Andrew Hartupee and Lucile Isobel (Brown) C.; student U. Pitts., 1924-27; B.A., Barnard Coll., Columbia, 1929; M.D. cum laude, Yale, 1933. Research fellow pediatrics Harvard Med. Sch., asst. med. service Children's Hosp., Boston, 1934-36; asst. in bacteriology and immunology Harvard Sch. Pub. Health, 1936-37; asst. in bacteriology, research fellow obstetrics Harvard Med. Sch., vol. asst. in bacteriology, Boston Lying-In Hosp., 1937-39; research fellow pediatrics Johns Hopkins, 1939-41, instr. preventive medicine, 1941-43; asst. dispensary pediatrician Johns Hopkins Hosp., 1939-41, asst. dispensary pediatrician, 1939-41, asst. visiting pediatrician, 1941-43, asst. prof. preventive medicine, instr. pediatrics Med. Sch., 1946-53, asst. prof. pediatrics 1953—, instr. mental hygiene, 1960—; cons. community mental health Nat. Inst. Mental Health, NIH; med. counselor Coll. Notre Dame of Md., 1951-56; med. dir. Family and Children's Soc., Balt., 1954-57; chief Div. Maternal and Child Health, Md. Dept. Health, 1957-59, chief Office Mental and Child Health, 1959—; chief demonstrations sect. Nat. Inst. Mental Health, 1963, chief child mental health sect. community research and services br., 1964-66, chief Center for Studies Mental Health of Children and Youth, Bethesda, Md., 1966-68; cons. infant rearing study Children's Hosp., Washington, 1968—. Cons. project head start Office Child Devel., 1968—, Plays for Living, N.Y.C., 1968—; staff Children's Bur., Dept. Labor, 1943-44; med. columnist Cath. Woman's World, 1939-42. Commd. surgeon (Res.) USPHS, 1944, sr. surgeon, 1949, med. dir., 1965—. Lena Lake Forest fellow. Nat. Fedn. Bus. and Profl. Women's Clubs for research on influenzal meningitis, 1936. Diplomate Nat. Bd. Med. Examiners U.S., Am. Bd. Pediatrics, Am. Bd Preventive Medicine and Pub. Health. Fellow Am. Acad. Pediatrics, Soc. for Pediatric Research, Am. Pub. Health Assn., Am. Coll. Preventive Medicine, Royal Soc. Health (Gt. Britain), Am. Orthopsychiat. Assn.; mem. Am. Psychiat. Assn., Balt. Urban League, Authors League Am., Md. Assn. for Mental Health, St. Clement Soc., Phi Beta Kappa, Sigma Xi. Democrat. Roman Catholic. Clubs: 16 East Hamilton St., Johns Hopkins. Author: Susie Stuart, M.D., 1941; Susie Stuart, Home Front Doctor, 1943; (with Marion L. Faegre) Your Child From One to Six, rev. edit., 1945; Dr. Kay Winthrop, Intern. 1947; Famous Men of Medicine, 1950; Famous Modern Men of Medicine, 1965, (with others) Early Child Care-The New Perspectives, 1968, (with Sharon H. Kempf) Nursing as a Career, 1970. Contbg. editor child health Farm Jours., Farmer's Wife, editorial bd., Yale Jour. Biology and Medicine, 1931-33. Contbr. World Book Ency., sci. and med. jours. Address: RD 1 Glen Arm MD 21057

CHANDLER, CHARLES JEROME, banker; b. Medicine Lodge, Kan., Nov. 15, 1902; s. Charles Quarles and Olive Frances (Thayer) C.; student Centre Coll., Danville, Ky., 1921-24; m. Alice E. Cromwell, Apr. 12, 1925; children—Charles Quarles, Jerome Lewis. Cashier, First State Bank, Gage, Okla., 1924-28; v.p. First Nat. Bank, Wichita, Kan., 1928-44, pres., 1948-58, chmn. bd., 1958—; v.p., dir. Kan. Bankers Surety Co.; dir. Gas & Electric Co. Chmn. Kan. Crippled Children Commn., 1944-68; dir. Kan. Soc. Crippled Children; mem. adv. council Fed. Res. Bd., 1953-55; Fed. Jury Commr. Trustee Ottawa U. Mem. Sigma Alpha Epsilon. Presbyn. Mason. Clubs: Wichita, Wichita Country, Rotary (Wichita). Home: 235 South Terrace Dr Wichita KS 67218 Office: First National Bank Wichita KS 67202

CHANDLER, DANIEL BROOKS, life ins. co. exec.; b. Chattanooga, Dec. 8, 1914; s. Daniel Prescott and Mary (Hays) C.; A.B., U. Chattanooga, 1935; m. Miriam Virginia Lamoreaux, Oct. 7, 1939; children-Virginia (Mrs. Alan G. Arthur), Margaret (Mrs. L.L. Smith), Daniel Lamoreaux. With Hamilton Nat. Bank, Chattanooga, 1935-57; with Provident Life & Accident Ins. Co., Chattanooga, 1937—, life underwriter, 1937-41, group underwriter, 1941- 48, group exec., 1948-66, corporate exec., 1967—. Mem. Ins. Econs. Soc. (exec. com.), Life Ins. Assn. Am., Am. Life Conv., Health Ins. Assn. Am. Republican. Clubs: Mountain City, Lookout Mountain-Fairyland, Lookout Mountain Golf (all Chattanooga). Contbg. author Group Ins. Handbook, 1965. Contbr. articles profl. publs. Home: 800 Lee Av Lookout Mountain TN 37350 Office: Fountain Sq Chattanooga TN 37402

CHANDLER, DOROTHY BUFFUM, newspaper exec.; b. Lafayette, Ill.; d. Charles Abel and Fern (Smith) Buffum; student Stanford, 1919-22; L.H.D. (hon.), U. Judaism, U. Redlands, U. Cal.; LL.D., Occidental Coll., Mount St. Mary's Coll.; D.F.A. (hon.), U. Portland, Pepperdine Coll.; Dr. Arts (hon.), Otis Art Inst. Los Angeles County; m. Norman Chandler, Aug. 30, 1922; children—Camilla, Otis. Dir., asst. to chmn. The Times Mirror Co. Hon. life chmn. So. Cal. Symphony- Hollywood Bowl Assn. Chmn. bd. govs. Performing Arts council Music Center Los Angeles; hon. life trustee Occidental Coll. Home: 455 S Lorraine Blvd Los Angeles CA 90020 Office: Times Mirror Sq Los Angeles CA 90053

CHANDLER, EDGAR HUGH STORER, clergyman, religious assn. ofcl.; b. Providence, Aug. 17, 1904; s. Henry Joseph and Christiana (Toms) C.; B.S., Boston U., 1928, D.D., 1961; postgrad. U. London, 1928-31; B.D., Andover Newton Theol. Sch., 1933; postgrad. Harvard Div. Sch., 1933-35; D.D., Northland Coll., 1952; LL.D., Loyloa U., 1965, Ia. Wesleyan Coll., 1967; laureate Lincoln Acad., 1966; m. Ruth Doggett, Apr.. 18, 1927; children—Hugh S., Marjorie Ann, Constance Elsie, Christopher Norris, David Luscombe. Ordained to ministry Conglist. Ch., 1927; pastor, Jamaica Plain, Boston, 1933-42; dir. Conglist. Service Com., 1946-49, Refugee Service, World Council Chs., 1949-60; exec. dir. Ch. Fedn. Greater Chgo., 1960-69; exec. dir. Worcester (Mass.) Area Council Chs., 1969—; adviser religious affairs USIA, 1960—; lectr. Chgo. Theological Sem., 1962-63. Pres. Internat. Conf. Vol. Agys. Working for Refugees, 1956-60; mem. Citizens Com. on Family Ct., Joint Youth Devel. Com.; exec. com. Conf. on Religion and Race; observer del. Vatican 11, 1966; mem. bd. John XXIII Centre for Ecumenical Studies, 1966. Served as comdr. Chaplains Corps, USNR, 1942-46. Decorated Order Brit. Empire, grand cross Order of Merit (Western Germany), gold cross Royal Order King George of Greece, knight-officer Order of Orange Nassau (Netherlands); named Chicagoan of Year in Religion, 1964; Thomas Wright award City of Chgo., 1965, medal of merit City of Chgo., 1969. Author: The High Tower of Refuge, 1960. Contbr. numerous articles to religious jours. Address: 63 Machusett St Worcester MA 01609

CHANDLER, GEORGE, actor; b. Waukegan, Ill., June 30, 1898 s. George William and Abigail Mary (Beck) C.; B.S., U. Ill., 1922; m. Catherine Marie Ward, Jan. 15, 1936 (dec. 1963); children—George Gary, Ward Leslie, Michael Charles; Chatauqua, vaudeville, stock cos.; appeared numerous motion pictures, 1927-, including The Virginian, Jessie James, Across the Wide Missouri, Island in the Sky, High and Mighty; performed as Uncle Petrie in Lassie TV series; TV role Ichabod and Me, CBS, guest star numerous TV shows. Pres. bd. trustees Screen Actors Guild Producers Pension and Welfare Plan, 1962; pres. permanent charities com. Motion Picture Industry, 1963; chmn. Hollywood overseas com. U.S.O., 1965-70; adv. bd. Motion

Recipient Achievement award U. Ill., 1962. Mem. Screen Actors Guild (pres. 1960-63, 1st v.p. 1964-65), Delta Upsilon, Beta Gamma Sigma, Alpha Kappa Psi, Pierrots. Home: 12188 Laurel Terrace Dr Studio City CA 91604 Office: 7750 Sunset Blvd Hollywood CA 90028

CHANDLER, GEORGE GARVIN, lawyer; b. Tacoma, Wash., Aug. 23, 1890; s. George Garvin and Joan Alice (Christie) C.; grad. Haverford Sch., 1907; A.B., Yale, 1912, Larned fellow in English, 1913; LL.B., Harvard, 1917; m. Ann G. Howell, May 11, 1935; children—Alice Christie, George Garvin III. Admitted to Pa. bar, 1919; asso. Roberts & Montgomery, 1919-29; partner Montgomery, McCracken, Walker & Rhoads, Phila., 1929—; prof. torts Temple U., 1924- 27; asst. to Hon. Owen J. Roberts, 1924-30; spl. atty. Commonwealth of Pa., 1930-32, 52-55. Trustee Haverford Sch., 1950-63. Served with AEF, 1917-19, lt. col. AUS, 1943-45. Decorated Legion of Merit. Mem. Am., Pa., Phila. bar assns., Harvard Law Sch. Assn. Phila. (pres. 1953-54), Mil. Order Fgn. Wars (comdr. Pa. 1954-55), Phi Beta Kappa, Psi Upsilon Beta. Clubs: Union League (Phila.); Merion Cricket (Haverford, Pa.). Home: Box 117 Whitford-Exton PA 19341 Office: 1421 Chestnut St Philadelphia PA 19102

CHANDLER, HARRISON, financial adminstr.; b. Los Angeles, Feb. 12, 1903; s. Harry and Marian Otis) C.; A.B., Stanford, 1926; m. Martha Marsh; 1 dau., Mrs. Samuel Haskins. Joined Times Mirror Co., 1927, now dir.; pres. Times Mirror Press, 1960-68, spl. adviser, 1968-; pres., chmn. bd. Chandis Securities Co. Clubs: California, Sunset, Twilight. Home: 801 Singing Wood Dr Arcadia CA 91006 Office: Chandis Securities Co 550 S Flower Los Angeles CA 90017

CHANDLER, HENRY PORTER, lawyer; b. Indian Orchard, Mass., Mar. 19, 1880; s. John Henry and Abbie White (Smith) C.; student Leland Stanford Jr. U., 1896-98; A.B., Harvard, 1901; J.D., U. Chgo., 1906; m. Helen Firman Mack, Mar. 24, 1907 (dec. Nov. 23, 1930); 1 dau., Margaret Mack (Mrs. Myles F. Gibbons) m. 2d, Olive Hull, Nov. 28, 1931. Instr. English, U. Chgo., 1901-04, sec. to pres., 1904-06; admitted to Ill. bar, 1906; in practice law, 1906-39; mem. law firm Tolman & Chandler, 1931-39; dir. Adminstrative Office U.S. Cts., 1939-56, ret.; cons. territorial cts. Hawaii, 1957; cons. judical adminstrn., ct. systems, 1957—; 1st ct. adminstr. State of Ill., 1959-60. Mem. permanent commn. on inter-ch. relations Presbyn. Ch. U.S.A., 1938-53. Mem. Am. Law Inst., Am. (chmn. municipal law sect. 1938-39), Ill. Chgo. (pres. 1938-39), Fed. bar assns., Phi Delta Phi. Clubs: Union League (pres. 1932-33), City (pres. 1923-25), Chicago Literary (Chicago); Cosmos (Washington). Author: Some Major Advances in the Federal Judicial System, 1922-1947, 1963. Contbr. to legao periodicals. Home: 5703 McKinley St Bethesda, MD 20034.

CHANDLER, JAMES BARTON, govt. ofcl.; b. Conway Springs, Kan., May 27, 1922; s. James Perry and Bessie (Stone) C.; A.B., U. Kan., 1947, M.A., 1949; student U. Mich., 1949-52; m. Madeleine Racoux, July 27, 1946; children—Paul Alain, Peter Racoux, Michele Anne. Instr. Mich. State Normal Coll., 1952-55; lang. edn. adv. Okla. State U. (Ethiopia), 1955-57; asst. prof., fgn. student adv. Eastern Mich. U., 1957-58; tchr. edn. adv. Southeast Asian Regional English Project U. Mich., Laos, 1958-60; edn. adv. AID, Laos, 1960-63, Tunisia, 1963-65, asst. dir. manpower devel., Laos, 1965-68, dep. dir. mission, 1968—. Sec.-treas. Tunisia Sch. Bd., 1964, Laos Sch. Bd., 1959-63; chmn. Laos Boy Scout Commn., 1966-69. Served to capt. AUS, 1943-47. Decorated Bronze Star. Mem. Lao Am. Assn. (dir. 1970—), Linguistic Soc. Am., Am. Soc. Pub. Adminstrn., Nat. Assn. Fgn. Student Advisors, Am. Fgn. Service Assn., Phi Beta Kappa, Pi Kappa Phi. Home: 567 Hunt Pl Ypsilanti MI 48197 Office: Agency Internat Development Washington DC 20523

CHANDLER, JAMES E., banker; b. Keene, N.H., July 2, 1924; s. Harold I. and Blanche Chandler; B.S., Wharton Sch. of U. Pa., 1945; grad. Stonier Grad. Sch. Banking, Rutgers U., 1954; m. Christine L. Wilder, Feb. 25, 1945; children—Carolyn, Harold I. With Keene Nat. Bank, 1945, Phila. Nat. Bank, 1945, First Nat. Bank Phila., 1953; with Indian Head Nat. Bank, Nashua, N.H., 1953—, exec. v.p., 1956-58, pres., 1958—; pres. N.H. Bankshares, Inc., Indian Head Nat. Bank, Manchester, N.H.; dir. Gregg Cabinets, Ltd., Edgcomb Steel New Eng., Allen-Rogers Corp., Asso. Grocers of New Eng., Pole & Wood Treating Co., Indsl. Devel. Authority. Chmn. bd. Crotched Mountain Found.; mem. adv. council Daniel Webster council Boy Scouts Am. Mem. Nashua C. of C., New Eng. Council, Stonier Grad. Sch. Banking Alumni Assn., Gen. Alumni Assn. U. Pa., Newcomen Soc. Clubs: Kataska (Que., Cana.); Nashua Country; Manchester Country. Home: Town Crier Rd Amherst NH 03031 Office: 146 Main St Nashua NH 03060

CHANDLER, JOHN WESLEY, coll. pres.; b. Mars Hills, N.C., Sept. 5, 1923; s. Baxter Harrison and Mamie (McIntosh) C.; student Mars Hill Coll., 1941-43; A.B., Wake Forest Coll., 1945; L.H.D. (hon.); B.D., Duke, 1952, Ph.D., 1954; LL.D. Hamilton Coll., 1968, Colgate U., 1968; L.H.D., Wake Forest U., 1968; m. Florence Gordon, Aug. 25, 1948; childrenAlison, John Wesley, Jennifer, Patricia. Instr. philosophy Wake Forest Coll., 1948-51, asst. prof., 1954-55; asst. prof. religion Williams Coll., 1955-60, asso. prof., chmn. dept., 1960-65, Cluett prof. religion, 1965-68, acting provost, 1965-66, dean faculty, 1966-68; pres. Hamilton Coll., 1968-. Mem. com. on resolutions, mem. com. on faculty responsibility, mem. Williams Coll., 1969-. Fulbright fellow, India, 1963; Kent fellow. Mem. Am. Acad. Religion, Soc. for Sci. Study Religion, Phi Beta Kappa. Mem. United Ch. of Christ. Clubs: University, Williams (N.Y.C.); Fort Schuyler (Utica, N.Y.). Contbg. author: Miscellany of American Religion, 1963; Masterpieces of Religious Literature, 1963. Office: Hamilton Coll Clinton NY 13323

CHANDLER, KENNETH ASHTON, educator, psychologist; b. Fitchburg, Mass., Feb. 11, 1921; s. Luther S. and Cora (Cross) C.; A.B., Clark U., 1948, A.M., 1949, Ph.D., 1953; m. Helen A. Hammond, Nov. 1, 1942; children—Kendra, Hilarie. Asst. prof. U. Del., 1953-54; chmn., asso. prof. U. Bridgeport, 1954-58; post-doctoral fellow Yale and West Haven (Conn.) VA Hosp., 1958-60; asst. prof. dept. psychiatry Yale, 1960-65; vis. asso. prof. So. Conn. State Coll., 1962; lectr. vis. scientist program Am. Psychol. Assn., 1961-67; asso. prof. Vassar Coll., Poughkeepsie, 1965-68, prof. psychology, 1969—; cons. psychologist Crippled Children's Workshop, Bridgeport, Conn., 1962-63; cons. Laurel Heights Hosp., Conn. Dept. Health, 1963—; cons. clin. psychology New Britain Meml. Hosp., 1966—. Bd. dirs. Fairfield County Speech and Hearing Clinic, 1958-63. Served with CWS, AUS, 1943-45. Certified psychologist, Conn., N.Y. Mem. Am., Eastern, New Eng., Conn. psychol. assns., A.A.A.S., Am. Assn. U. Profs., Sigma Xi. Office: Vassar Coll Dept Psychology Poughkeepsie NY 12601

CHANDLER, LEN HUNT, Jr., poet, composer, singer, musician; b. Akron O., May 27, 1935; s. Len Chandler and Vonciel (Autry) C.; B.S., U. Akron, 1957; M.A., Columbia Tchrs. Coll., 1958; D.D., Ch. of Universal Brotherhood; m. Nancy Sparrow, 1958. Formerly landscaper, post office clk., elevator operator, children's counsellor St. Barnabas House, N.Y.C.; player oboe, English horn Akron Symphony Orch., 1956-57, Greenwich Village and Riverside orchs.; vocal soloist N.J. Symphony Orch., 1965; concerts at Carnegie and Town halls, Judson Hall, Newport Folk Festival, 1964-65, 69, Phila. Folk Festival, 1965-66, Mariposa (Can.) Folk Festival, 1967; performed nat. convs. Presbyns., 1968, Unitarians., 1968, Episcopalians, 1969, Congress of African People author songs for TV documentaries; appeared sta. WXYZ-TV,-Detroit, 1959, then sta. KRLA, Los Angeles, KCET, Newsical Muse Show, Los Angeles, KLAC, others; author lyrics, music off-Broadway prodn. Psychedelic Burlesque, 1968; active singer, organizer civil rights and peace movements; coast-to-coast tour with Dick Gregory, 1965; lectr. black experience Swarthmore Coll., U. So. Cal., R.I. U., Spellman Coll., Morehouse Coll. Mem. Broadcast Music Inc., Am. Guild Authors and Composers. Served with USMC, 1957. Mem. Free Theatre Assn.; founder, leader Alternative Chorus. Rec. artist for Columbia, Folkways, Brodside, FM, Blue Thumb. Poems pub. in anthologies. Author civil rights songs. Asso. editor Umbra Poetry Anthology, Groits Works; contbg. editor Broadside. Address: 943 N Palm Av Los Angeles CA 90069

CHANDLER, LESTER VERNON, economist; b. Geuda Springs, Kan., Sept. 2, 1905; s. Lloyd Winfield and Lucille (Foote) C.; A.B., U. Mo., 1930, A.M., 1931, LL.D., 1967; Ph.D., Yale, 1934; m. Elizabeth Rider Costenbader, Sept. 8, 1934; children—John Winfield, Jean Elizabeth. Instr. econs. Dartmouth Coll., 1933-35, Princeton U., 1935-37; asst. prof. econ. Amherst Coll., 1937-39, asso. prof., 1939-42, prof., 1942-50; Gordon S. Rentschler prof. of econs. Princeton, 1950-69, chmn. dept. econs. and sociology, 1955-61, 66-68; price exec. OPA, 1943-46; mem. research adv. bd. Com. Econ. Devel., 1953-55; class C dir. Fed. Res. Bank of Phila., 1954-59, dep. chmn., 1958-59; bd. dirs. Atlantic City Electric Co. Mem. Am. Econ. Assn. (v.p. 1954), Am. Finance Assn. (pres. 1958), Nat. Tax Assn., Phi Beta Kappa, Alpha Kappa Psi. Author books, latest being: Inflation in the United States, 1951; Economics of Money and Banking, 1948, 53, 59, 69; Benjamin Strong, Central Banker, 1958; America's Greatest Depression, 1970; American Monetary Policy, 1971; also articles in field. Home: 88 Westerly Rd Princeton NJ 08540 ☆

CHANDLER, MARGARET KUEFFNER, educator; b. St. Paul, Sept. 30, 1922; d. Otto Carl and Marie (Schaedlich) Kueffner: B.A. in Polit. Sci., U. Chgo., 1942, M.A. in Econs., 1944, Ph.D. in Sociology, 1948; m. Louis Chandler, Apr. 8, 1943. Mem. faculty U. Ill., at Urbana, 1947-62, asso. prof. sociology and indsl. relations, 1954-62; asso. prof. sociology U. Ill. at Chgo., 1962- 63, prof., 1963-65; prof. bus. Columbia, 1965—; Fulbright research prof. econs. Keio U., Tokyo, Japan, 1963-64; lectr. Rutgers U., 1958, McGill U., 1963, Emory U., 1966, Columbia, 1962. Labor arbitrator nat. labor panel Am. Arbitration Assn., 1965—, mem. collective bargaining methods study group. 1964—; asso. mem. Center Advanced Study, U. Ill. Grad. Coll., 1964-65; asso. dir. Program Managing Complex Techs., 1967- -. Postdoctoral fellow statistics Yale, 1953-54; Ford Found. Faculty research fellow social sci. and bus. U. Chgo., 1960-61; Ford Found. grant, 1967—; recipient Recognition award Ill. Nurses Assn., 1960. Fellow Am. Sociol. Assn., Soc. Applied Anthropology; mem. Am. Statis. Assn., Am. Econ. Assn., Indsl. Relations Research Assn. (editor research vol. 1960). Author: Labor Management Relations in Illini City, vols. 1 and 2, 1953, 54; Management Rights and Union Interests (McKinsey Found. Book award 1965), 1964; Managing Large Scale Systems, 1971. Address: Uris Hall Grad Sch Business Columbia New York City NY 10027

CHANDLER, MARVIN, utility exec.; b. Boston, Mar. 12, 1910; s. Thomas Evans and Lesley (Hill) C.; student Phillips Exeter Acad., 1927-28; A.B., Dartmouth, 1932; M.B.A., Harvard, 1934; LL.D., St. Procopius Coll., 1963; m. Carmen children—Thomas Marvin, Richard Hill. Security analyst Chas. D. Barney & Co., N.Y.C., 1934-37, Barrett Assos., Inc., 1937-42; mgr. N.Y. office Cayuga Constrn. Corp., 1942-44; v.p., sec., dir. Reis & Chandler, Inc., 1945-54; pres., dir. No. Ill. Gas Co., Aurora, 1954-66, chmn., pres., dir., 1966-69, chmn., dir., 1969-71, chmn. exec. com., dir., 1971—; dir. DuKane Corp., LaSalle Nat. Bank, Interlake, Inc., Nat. Can Corp. Pres. Met. Housing Devel. Corp. Hon. trustee Inst. Gas Technology; trustee U. Chgo., Nat. Opinion Research Corp.; bd. dirs. Central DuPage Hosp.; mem. citizens com. Univ. Ill.; citizens bd. U. Chgo.; bd. dirs., 1st v.p. John Crerar Library; v.p. bd. dirs. Protestant Found. Greater Chgo. Mem. Newcomen soc. N.A., Am. Mgmt. Assn., Am. Gas Assn., N.Y. Soc. Security Analysts (pres. (1952-53), Nat. Fedn. Financial Analysts Socs. (v.p., dir. 1952-53), Am. Finance Assn. Clubs: Chicago, Economic, Executives, Commercial (Chgo.); Glen Oak Country Ill.). Contbr. articles profl. and trade jours. Home: 626 Forest Av Glen Ellyn IL 60137 Office: East-West Tollway at Route 59 PO Box 190 Aurora IL 60507 ☆

CHANDLER, NORMAN, newspaper exec.; b. Los Angeles, Sept. 14, 1899; s. Harry and Marian (Otis) C.; A.B., Stanford U., 1922; LL.D., Occidental Coll., U. So. Cal.; m. Dorothy Buffum, Aug. 30, 1922; children—Camilla, Otis. With Los Angeles Times, 1922—; chmn. exec. com., dir. Times Mirror Co.; vice pres., dir. Chandis Securities Co., Chandler-Sherman Corp.; mem. adv. bd. Am. Mut. Fund, Inc.; dir. Safeway Stores, Inc., Security Pacific Nat. Bank of Los Angeles, Buffums' Dept. Store (Long Beach), Santa Fe Industries, Inc. Trustee Cal. Inst. Tech. Mem. Delta Kappa Epsilon. Rep. Clubs: Bohemian (San Francisco); California. Home: 455 S Lorraine Blvd Los Angeles CA 90020 Office: Times Mirror Sq Los Angeles CA 90053

CHANDLER, OTIS, publisher; b. Los Angeles, Nov. 23, 1927; s. Norman and Dorothy (Buffum) C.; grad. Andover Acad., 1946; B.A., Stanford, 1950; m. Marilyn Brant, June 18, 1951; children—Norman Brant, Harry, Cathleen, Michael, Carolyn. Joined Times Mirror Co., 1953, now vice chmn., dir.; pub. Los Angeles Times, 1960—; dir. A.P., Pan Am. World Airways, TRW, Unionamerica. Pres. bd. trustees Los Angeles Times Fund. Served to 1st Lt. USAAF, 1951-53. Mem. Am. Newspaper Pubs. Assn. (dir.). Club: California. Home: San Marino CA 91108 Office: Times Mirror Sq Los Angeles CA 90053

CHANDLER, PORTER RALPH, lawyer; b. Buffalo, May 11, 1899; s. Porter and Mary (Wadsworth) C.; grad. St. Mark's Sch., 1917; A.B., Harvard, 1920; B.A., Oxford U., 1923, B.C.L., 1924, M.A., 1950; LL.D., St. John's U., 1952, Manhattan Coll., 1956; m. Gabrielle Chanler, July 8, 1924 (dec. Oct. 1958); children—Joseph, Mrs. Judith Chandler Houston, David, Mrs. Mary Chandler Jackson. Admitted to N.Y. State bar, 1924; spl. asst. to the atty. gen. U.S., 1924-26; asst. U.S. atty. So. Dist. N.Y., 1926-28; with law firm Davis Polk & Wardwell, N.Y.C., 1929—, partner, 1938—. Mem. bd. higher edn., N.Y.C., 1952-70, chmn., 1966-69. Served as pvt. U.S. Army, 1918; lt. col. USAAF, 1942-45. Mem. Assn. Bar City N.Y., Am. Bar Assn., N.Y. County Lawyers Assn., Guild of Catholic Lawyers (past pres.). Republican. Roman Catholic. Knight of Malta. Home: 31 E 79th St New York City NY 10021 Office: 1 Chase Manhattan Plaza New York City NY 10005

CHANDLER, REUBEN CARL business exec.; b. Lawrenceville, Ga., Oct. 25, 1917; s. Reuben C. and Florine (Doster) C.; grad. Marist Coll., Atlanta, 1935; student Ga. Inst. Tech., 1935-37; A.B., Emory U., 1941; student Atlanta Law Sch., 1946-48; D.Sc. (hon.) in Bus. Adminstrn., Detroit Inst. Tech., 1960; m. Sarah Megee, Oct. 27, 1940; children—Carla Evalynee (Mrs. Gurkin), Robert Megee, David Pratt, Craig D. Sales rep. Gen. Motors Acceptance Corp., Atlanta, 1941-42; asst. dir. tng. Southeastern Shipbldg. Corp., Savannah, Ga., 1942-43; prodn. Mgr. Mead-Atlanta Paper Co., 1946-49; salesman Union Camp Corp. (formerly Union Bag & Camp Paper Corp.) 1949-50, dist. sales mgr. Trenton, N.J., 1950-51, eastern div. sales mgr., 1951-52, dir. corrugated container and board sales, N.Y.C., 1952, v.p. sales, 1952-55; chmn., chief exec. officer, chmn. exec., finance coms. Standard Packaging Co., N.Y.C., 1955-66; chmn. bd. Crowell-Collier Pub. Co., N.Y.C., 1957; ltd. partner Elliott & Co., investment bankers, N.Y.C., 1960-62; chmn bd. J.D. Jewell, Inc., Gainesville, Ga., 1962—. also pres., 1969—, chmn. exec. com., dir.; dir. Am. Agy. Life Ins. Co., Atlanta, Blums, Inc., San Francisco; Berry Steel Corp., Edison, N.J., Marshall Farms, Greenville, S.C., Uncle John's Restaurants, Inc., Santa Barbara, Cal. Trustee Detroit Inst. Tech., 1960—, Christ Ch. Sch., Short Hills, N.J., 1963—, Brenau Coll., 1968—, Ga. Found. for Ind. Colls., 1969—. Served as lt. (s.g.), USNR, 1943-46. Lt. col. aide de camp Govs. staff, Ga., 1951- 52. Recipient Man of Year award Am. Jewish Com., 1964; Horatio Alger award, 1965; Achievement award Delta Tau Delta, 1966. Mem. Savannah Jr. C. of C. (v.p. 1942-43), Gainesville C. of C., Navy League (life), Def. Orientation Conf. Assn., Am. Pulp and Paper Mill Supts. Assn. (life), Emory U. Alumni Assn. (pres. 1965, Honor award 1968), Ga. Tech. Nat. Alumni Assn. (nat. adv. bd. 1964 —), Ga. Poultry Fedn. (mem. round table 1970—), Tenn. Wesleyan Coll. Parents Assn. Delta Tau Delta (life), Alpha Delta Sigma, Omicron Delta Kappa. Baptist. Mason. Elk. Clubs: Atlanta Athletic, Commerce (Atlanta); N.Y. Area Emory (pres. 1964), Sky, University, Economic (N.Y.C.); Chattahoochee Country (Gainesville). Address: Gainesville GA 30501

CHANDLER, ROBERT FLINT, Jr., research exec.; b. Columbus, O., June 22, 1907; s. Robert F. and Harriet Clark (Loring) C.; B.S., U. Me., 1929, LL.D., 1951; Ph.D., U. Md., 1934; postgrad (NRC fellow) U. Cal. 1935; m. Eunice Copeland, May 22, 1931 (div. 1955); children—David, Ralph Hewitt, Sara Eunice; m. 2d, Muriel Boyd, Oct. 4, 1957. State horticulturist Me. Dept. Agr., 1929-31; grad. asst. U. Md., 1931-34; asst. prof. forest soils Cornell U., 1935-41, asso. prof., 1941-46, prof., 1946-47; dean coll. agr. U. N.H., 1947-50, pres., 1950-54; asst. dir. div. natural scis. and agr. Rockefeller Found., N.Y.C. 1954-57, asso. dir. agrl. scis., 1957—. Vis. prof. agronomy Tex. A. and M. Coll., summer 1940; soil sci. Rockefeller Found., Mexico, 1946-47. Bd. dirs. Internat. Rice Research Inst., Manila, P.I.; trustee Filipinas Found., Manila. Recipient Gold medal award Govt. India, 1966; Sitara-I-Imtiaz award Govt. Pakistan, 1968. Fellow Am. Acad. Arts and Scis.; mem. Am. Soc. Agronomy, Crop Sci. Soc. Am., Soc. for Internat. Devel., A.A.A.S., Newcomen Soc., S.A.R. Club: Manila Polo. Home: Los Baos Philippines Office: Internat Sci. Research Inst P O Box 583 Manila Philippines

CHANDLER, STEPHEN S., judge; b. Blount County, Tenn., Sept. 13, 1899; s. Stephen Sanders and Evelyn Amelia (Johnson) C.; student. U. Tenn., 1917-18, J.D., U. Kan., 1922; m. Margaret Patterson, 1922 (dec.); children—Frances Patterson (Mrs. Sim K. Sims), Stephen Sanders III, Frank Patterson. Private law practice in Oklahoma City, 1922-43; U.S. Dist. judge for the Western Dist. of Oklahoma, 1943—. Recipient Hatton Sumners award in 1961; mem. Okla. Hall of Fame, 1960. Mem. various bar and other legal assns., Sigma Alpha Epsilon, Phi Delta Phi, Order of the Coif. Democrat. Methodist. Mason (Shriner). Clubs: Oklahoma City Golf, Tower, Petroleum, Rotary (pres. 1940-41). Home: Oklahoma City OK 73101 Office: US Court House Oklahoma City OK 73101

CHANDLER, WALLACE LEE, tobacco co. exec.; b. Mecklenburg County, Va., Oct. 18, 1926; s. Joseph Beale and Esma (Clement) C.; A.B., Elon Coll. (N.C.), 1949; LL.B., Smithdeal Coll. Law, Richmond, Va., 1953; m. Virginia Juanita Hodnett, Feb. 25, 1950; children—Elizabeth Hardy, Brenda Lee, Jacqueline Blair. With Universal Leaf Tobacco Co., Inc., Richmond, 1949—, sec., counsel, 1963-66, gen. counsel, dir., 1966-69, v.p., gen. counsel, dir., 1969—; admitted to Va. bar, 1954. Trustee Madison Coll., Harrisonburg, Va., Elon College (N.C.). Served with AUS, 1944-46; ETO. Mem. Am., Va., Richmond (exec. com. corp. counsel sect. 1964-68) bar assns., Tax Execs. Inst., Elon Coll. Alumni Assn. (bd. dirs. 1960-66), Alpha Phi Delta. Democrat. Baptist (chmn. bd. adminstrn., chmn. finance com.). Clubs: Willow Oaks Country (bd. dirs.), Country of Va., Commonwealth (Richmond). Home: (Richmond). Home: 2 Raven Rock Rd Richmond VA 23229 Office: Hamilton at Broad St Richmond VA 23260

CHANDLER, WILLIAM REEDER, oil co. exec.; b. Butte, Mont., Feb. 10, 1913; s. William Blaine and Mabel (Reeder) C.; B.S. in Civil Engring. magna cum laude, U. Wash., 1938; m. Clair Good, Aug. 12, 1940; children—Barbara Ann, Gail Marilyn, William Blaine II. Various positions in engring. dept. Standard Oil Co. of Cal., 1938-43; pipe line supt., later project mgr. Canol Project, Standard Oil Co., Alaska, 1943-45; various positions Trans-Arabian Pipe Line Co., Beirut, Lebanon, 1946-48, asst. gen. mgr., 1948-50, asst. to pres., 1950-55, v.p., 1955, exec. v.p., 1956-63, pres., chief exec. officer, 1963—; dir., 1958—; dir. Aramco Overseas Co., Arabian Am. Oil Co. Decorated Order of Merit (Lebanon), 1955. Mem. Am. Soc. C.E. Home: Du Rafford Bldg Rue de Paris Corniche Beirut Lebanon Office: Box 1348 Beirut Lebanon

CHANDLEY, JOHN STOTHERS, newspaper editor; b. Ellis, Kan., Aug. 26, 1908; s. John Lovejoy and Ella Moore (Stothers) C.; B.S. in Indsl. Journalism, Kan. State U., 1929; m. Edythe Jones, Sept. 6, 1930 (div. June 1963); 1 dau., Barbara Ann; m. 2d, Marjorie G. Bell, May 9, 1964 (dec. Sept. 1964); m. 3d, Eleanor M. Wilson, Aug. 10, 1967. Reporter, Manhattan (Kan.) Mercury, 1927-29; mem. staff Kansas City (Mo.) City Times, 1929—, city editor, 1947-60, mng. editor, 1960—. Pres., Kansas City Star Pub. Activities Assn. Mem. bd. Greater Kansas City chpt. A.R.C. Mem. Sigma Delta Chi, Kappa Sigma. Presbyn. Club: Kansas City Press (pres. 1970). Home: 9943 Walnut Dr Kansas City MO 64114 Office: 1735 Grand Av Kansas City MO 64108

CHANDRASEKHAR, B. S., educator, physicist; b. Bangalore, India, May 24, 1928; s. B.M. Sivaramiah and Lalita (Dasappa) C.; B.Sc. with honors, U. Mysore (India), 1947; M.Sc., U. Delhi (India), 1949; D.Phil (Rhodes scholar 1949-52), U. Oxford (Eng.), 1952; m. Sara Elizabeth Yanason, Dec. 21, 1955; children—Ashok Jai, Jai Kamal. Part-time demonstrator physics Oxford U., 1951-52, vis. scientist, 1954-55; research asso. Univ. Illinois, 1952-54; research physicist Westinghouse Research Labs., 1955-59, fellow physicist, 1959-61, mgr. cryophysics sect. 1961- 63, cons., 1963-64; sr. vis. research fellow Imperial Coll. Sci. and Tech., London, Eng., 1961; mem. faculty Case Western Res. U., and predecessor, 1963—, co-chmn. dept. physics, 1967, Perkins prof. physics, 1967—, also dean of sciences, since 1969—; cons. to Bell Telephone Labs., summers, 1965-66, Argonne Nat. Lab., 1965—, Lewis Research Center, 1966. Fellow Am. Phys. Soc., Phys. Soc. (London), Inst. Physics (London); mem. Am. Assn. U. Profs., Cleve. Physics Soc. (pres. 1965-66), Sigma Xi (pres. Case Western Res. U. chpt. 1966-67). Research in superconductivity, liquid helium, metals. Home: 2558 Derbyshire St Cleveland Heights OH 44106 Office: Dept Physics Case Western Res Univ Cleveland OH 44106

CHANDRASEKHAR, SUBRAHAMANYAN, theoretical astro-physicist; b. Lahore, India, Oct. 19, 1910; M.A., Presidency Coll., Madras, 1930; Ph.D., Trinity Coll., Cambridge, 1933, Sc.D., 1942; Sc.D. (hon.), U. Mysore (India), 1961, Northwestern U., 1962,

U. Newcastle Upon Tyne (Eng.), 1965, Ind. Inst. Tech., 1966, U. Mich., 1967, U. Liege (Belgium), 1967; m. Lalitha, Madras, India. Sept. 1936. Came to U.S., 1936; naturalized, 1953. Govt. India scholar in theoretical physics Cambridge, 1930-34; fellow Trinity Coll., Cambridge, 1933-37; research asso. Yerkes Obs., Williams Bay and U. Chgo., 1937, asst. prof., 1938-41, asso. prof., 1942-43, prof., 1944-47, Distinguished Service prof. 1947—, Morton D. Hull Distinguished Service prof., 1952—. Nehru Meml. lectr. Padma Vibhushan, India, 1968. Recipient Bruce medal Astron. Soc., Pacific, 1952, gold medal Royal Astron. Soc. (London), 1953; Rumford medal Am. Acad. Arts and Scis., 1957; Nat. Medal of Sci., 1966. Fellow Royal Soc. (London, Royal medal 1962); mem. Nat. Acad. Scis. (Henry Draper medal 1971), Am. Philos. Soc., Am. Acad. of Arts and Scis., Cambridge Philos. Soc., Am. Astron. Soc., Royal Astron. Soc. Club: Quadrangle (U. of Chgo.). Author: An Introduction to the Study of Stellar Structure, 1939; Principles of Stellar Dynamics, 1942; Radiative Transfer, 1950; Hydrodynamic and Hydromagnetic Stability, 1961; Ellipsoidal Figures of Equilibrium, 1969. Mng. editor The Astrophysical Jour., 1952-71. Contbr. various sci. periodicals. Address: Lab for Astrophysics and Space Research 933 E 56th St Chicago IL 60637

CHANE, GEORGE WARREN, cons. engr.; b. Gloucester, Mass., June 15, 1910; s. Daniel T. and (MacDonald) C.; B.S. in Mech. Engring., Tufts Coll., 1934; m. Frances D. Howard, June 22, 1940; children—Peggy Howard, George Warren. Indsl. engr. Boston Woven Hose & Rubber Co., 1934-38, Eastman Kodak Co., Rochester, N.Y. 1938-42; mgr. mgmt. services div. Eastern dist. Ernst & Ernst, 1942-58; v.p. finance and mgmt. engring. RCA, 1958-60, v.p. finance and adminstrn., 1960-62; exec. v.p. finance Olin Mathieson Chem. Corp., 1962-65, also dir.; financial v.p. Uniroyal, Inc., N.Y.C., 1965-70, also dir., mem. operating policy com.; pres. George W. Chane, Inc., cons. engrs., 1970—; dir. Rubicon Chems., Inc., Tex.-U.S. Chem. Co., Uniroyal, Ltd., Montreal, Uniroyal, Ltd., London. Bd. dirs. Deafness Research Found. Mem. Financial Execs. Inst., Nat., Conn., Tex., N.Y. State socs. profl. engrs., Operations Research Soc., Air Force Assn., Am. Soc. M.E., Profl. Golfers Assn. (mem. adv. com. 1960—). Clubs: Wings, University (N.Y.C.); Greenwich (Conn.) Country. Author: Motion and Time Study, 1940. Home: Dewart Rd Greenwich CT 06830 Office: 551 Fifth Av New York City NY 10017

CHANEY, DAVID WEBB, univ. dean; b. Cleve., Dec. 19, 1915; s. Newcomb Kinney and Elsie (Webb) C.; student Carleton Coll., Northfield, Minn., 1934-35; A.B., Swarthmore Coll., 1938; M.S., U. Pa., 1940, Ph.D., 1942; m. Faith Hambly Barsalow, Sept. 10, 1938; 1 son, Stephen Gifford. Research chemist Am. Viscose Corp., 1942-46, asst. sect. leader, 1946-51; sr. group leader Chemstrand Corp., 1952-53, asst. dir. research, 1953-58, exec. dir. research, 1958- 60; v.p., exec. dir. Chemstrand Research Center, 1960-65, v.p., tech. dir. new products and basic research, 1965-67; dean Sch. Textiles, N.C. State U., Raleigh, 1967—. Mem. Gov. N.C. Council Econ. Devel., 1966-68. Trustee Textile Research Inst., Princeton, N.J. Mem. Am. Chem. Soc., A.A.A.S., Am. Inst. Chemists, Am. Assn. Textile Chemists and Colorists, N.Y. Acad. Scis., Am. Soc. Engring. Edn., Sigma Xi. Contbr. articles to profl. jours. Home: 4312 Union St Raleigh NC 27609

CHANEY, VINCENT VERLANDO, lawyer; b. Elkins, W. Va., June 12, 1913; s. Thomas Hughes and Anna Gertrude (Merge) C.; A.B., W. Va. U., 1936, LL.B., 1938; m. Caroline O'Neale, Oct. 21, 1939; children—Caroline Stuart, Patricia Saunders, Michael Thomas, Malcolm Lindsay. Admitted to W. Va. bar, 1938, since practiced in Charleston; mem. firm Kay, Casto & Chaney, and predecessors, 1953—. Trustee Charleston General Hosp.; bd. dirs. Kanawha Valley Dental Health Found.; vis. com. W. Va. U. Coll. Law. Served to lt. col., inf., AUS, 1941-46. Mem. Am., W. Va. State Bar (bd. govs. 1956-59, pres. 1961-62), Am. Judicature Soc. (dir. 1969—), Am. Law Inst., W. Va. U. Alumni Assn. (exec. council 1967—, pres. 1971—), Phi Beta Kappa, Order of Coif, Phi Delta Phi. Home: 1209 Williamsburg Way Charleston WV 25314 Office: 1616 Charleston National Plaza Charleston WV 25301

CHANEY, WILLIAM ALBERT, educator; b. Arcadia, Cal., Dec. 23, 1922; s. Horace Pierce and Esther (Bowen) C.; A.B., U. Cal. at Berkeley, 1943, Ph.D., 1961. Mem. faculty Lawrence U., Appleton, Wis., 1952—. George McKendree Steele prof. Western culture, 1966—,' chmn. dept. history, 1967-71; vis. prof. Mich. State U., summer 1958. Jr. fellow Harvard Soc. Fellows, 1949-52; grantee Am. Council Learned Socs., 1966-67. Mem. Am. Hist. Assn., Mediaeval Acad. Am., Am. Soc. Ch. History, Modern Lang. Assn., Conf. British Studies, Am. Assn. U. Profs., Archael. Inst. Am. Episcopalian. Author: The Cult of Kingship in Anglo-Saxon England: The Transition from Paganism to Christianity, 1970. Contbr. profl. jours., encys. Home: 215 E Kimball St Appleton WI 54911

CHANG, CHEN CHUNG, mathematician, educator; b. Tientsin, China, Oct. 13, 1927; s. P.C. and S.T. (Tsai) C.; came to U.S., 1944, naturalized, 1959; B.A., Harvard, 1949; M.A., U. Cal. at Berkeley, 1950, Ph.D., 1955; m. Marjorie Galvan, Aug. 1, 1951; children—Ann, Alice, Peter, Julia. Instr., Cornell U., 1955-56; asst. prof. U. So. Cal., 1956-58; asst. prof. math. U. Cal. at Los Angeles, 1958-61, asso. prof., 1961-64, prof., 1964-; cons. to industry. Sr. postdoctoral fellow NSF, 1962-63; sr. Fulbright research scholar Oxford (Eng.) U., 1966-67, also vis. fellow All Souls Coll. Mem. Am. Math. Soc., Assn. Symbolic Logic, Phi Beta Kappa, Sigma Xi, Pi Mu Epsilon. Contbr. articles profl. jours. Cons. editor Jour. Symbolic Logic, 1968—; editor Annals of Mathematical Logic, 1969—, Algebra Universalis, 1971—. Home: 521 Veteran Av Los Angeles CA 90024

CHANG, CHIEH CHIEN, engring. educator; b. Peiping, China, July 21, 1913; s. Nan Chung and Chow (Mei) C.; came to U.S., 1940, naturalized, 1954; B.S. in Mech. Engring., Nat. Northeastern U., 1932; M.S., Cal. Inst. Tech., 1941, Ph.D., 1950; m. Than-Chie Chang, Aug. 8, 1937; children—William, David, Nancy. Instr., research fellow Nat. Tsing Hua U., Peiping, 1934-40, supr. wind tunnel project, 1935-37; lectr. Chinese Air Force Acad., 1939- 40; research asst. Cal. Inst. Tech., 1940-42; design engr. U.S. Plywood Corp., 1942-43; successively asst. design engr., research aerodynamist, research engr. Glenn L. Martin Co., 1943-47; asso. prof. aero. Johns Hopkins, 1947-52; research prof. Inst. Fluid Dynamics and Applied Math., U. Md., 1952-54; prof. fluid mechanics U. Minn., 1952-62; on leave as head theoretical mechanics dept., sr. staff scientist Phys. Research Labs., Aerospace Corp., 1961-62; summer lectr. magnetohydrodynamics and plasma physics U. Cal. at Los Angeles, 1962-63; vis. prof., dir. Plasma Space Sci. Lab., Cath. U. Am., 1962-63, chair prof. space sci. and applied physics, also head dept., 1963-70, prof. aerospace and atmospheric scis., 1970—; cons. in field, 1951—. Co. recipient 1st Nat. award Inst. Chinese Engrs., 1936; Guggenheim fellow, 1952-53; recipient gold medal award Chinese Govt., 1967. Academican China Acad., 1968. Mem. Acad. Sinica; asso. fellow Am. Inst. Aero. and Astronautics (council. Nat. Capital sect. 1966-68), Combustion Inst., Am. Phys. Soc., A.A.A.S., Am. Geophys. Union, Am. Assn. U. Profs., Am. Soc. M.E., Am. Meteorol. Soc., Sigma Xi, Lambda Beta Pi. Mem. editorial bd. Jour. Aero. Sci., 1947-55. Author: Proceedings of Plasma Space Science Symposium, 1965. Contbr. profl. jours. Patentee, inventor in field of tornado and hurricane models. Home: 2122 Gatewood Pl Silver Spring MD 20903 Office: Cath Univ Am Washington DC 20017

CHANG, CLARENCE HOO YUEN, banker; b. Honolulu, Dec. 7, 1931; s. Shar Chong and See Moi (Chun) C.; B.B.A., U. Hawaii, 1953; m. Irene S.H. Choy, May 25, 1958; 1 son, Duane H. Asst.v.p. Finance Factors, Ltd., Honolulu, 1956-62; sr. v.p. Am. Security Bank, Honolulu, 1962—. Pres. Hawaiian Lenders Exchange, 1970; v.p. Consumer Credit Counseling Service Hawaii, 1970. Treas. Hawaii div. Am. Cancer Soc., 1970. Served to 1st lt. USAF, 1954-56. Mem. Chinese C. of C. Home: 1350 Ala Moana 1801 Honolulu HI 96814 Office: 1108 Keeaumoku St Honolulu HI 96814

CHANG, DAVID PING-CHUNG, architect; b. Shanghai, China, Dec. 10, 1929; s. Hsin-Hai and Siang-Mei (Han) C.; came to U.S., 1941, naturalized, 1956; grad. Hotchkiss Sch., 1947; A.B., Princeton, 1951, M.F.A., 1953; m. Lorna Mickle, Jan. 22, 1955; children—Pamela R., Christopher R., David R., Jennifer R. Pvt. practice architecture, N.Y.C., 1956-59, San Juan, P.R., 1959-68; v.p. Levitt & Sons, Inc., N.Y.C., 1969-71; pres. ESI Assos., Inc., N.Y.C., 1971—; guest lectr. seminar indsl. housing Mass. Inst. Tech., 1971; dir. Environmental Systems Internat., Inc. (Los Angeles), Huntington Comprehensive Service Center; prin. works include Academia San Jose (P.R.), WAPA-TV Studios and Offices (P.R.). Asso. dir. Mt. St. Mary Coll., Newburgh, N.Y., 1967-69. Recipient 1st prize U. P.R. indsl. design seminar, 1961, 1st prize for best comml. bldg. Urbe award, P.R., 1966, 1st prize best ednl. bldg. Urbe award, P.R., 1971. Mem. A.I.A., N.Y. State Architects Assn., Colegio de Ingenieros de P.R. Democrat. Clubs: Colonial (Princeton); Winter (Huntington). Contbg. editor Jour. Indsl. Designers Soc. Am., 1969-70. Home: 88 Jennings Rd Cold Spring Harbor NY 11724 Office: 130 Cutter Mill Rd Great Neck NY 11021

CHANG, HSIN-HAI, educator, author; b. Shanghai, China, June 24, 1900; s. Tung-sen and Shen (Shen-shib) C.; student Tsinghua Coll., 1916-18; A.B., John Hopkins, 1919; M.A. Harvard, 1920, Ph.D., 1923; m. Siang-mei Han, Feb. 28, 1927; children—Yi-an (Mrs. Wenchung Chou), David Ping-chung. Came to U.S., 1941, naturalized, 1964. Prof. Tsinghua Coll. and Nat. U., Peking, 1923- 26; prof., chmn. dept. Western lit., dean coll. Liberal Arts, Nat. Central U., Nanking, 1926-27; prof. v.p. Kwanghua U., 1927-28; sr. counsellor, dir. European and Am. Dept., Chinese Ministrv Fgn. Affairs 1928-33; envoy extraordinary, minister plenipotentiary Republic of China to Portugal, Poland and Czechoslovakia, 1933-37; prof. Western lit. Kwanghua U., 1937-40; lectr. in U.S. on China's war effort. 1941-45; spl. asst. to Chinese Fgn. Minister, 1943; research prof. L.I. U., 1950- 53; vis. prof. Adelphi Coll., 1954-56; prof. English lit. and Asian culture Fairleigh Dickinson U., 1956-69, prof. emeritus, 1969—. Dir. China Inst. London. del. to Universal Postal Congress 1933; dir. Chinese UN Assn., 1947-48; China's chief del. Congress World Fedn. UN Assn., Geneva, 1948; participant as faculty for Pacific-Asia Seminar sponsored by Inst. on Man and Sci. and East-West Center, Honolulu, 1966; invited by Senate Fgn. Relations Com. to testify on U.S.-China relations, 1966. Trustee Tsinghua U., Peking, 1927. Decorated Order of the Nile (Egypt). 1933; Order of the Briliant Jade (China), 1936. Mem. Royal Asiatic, Social and Political Sci., Am. Oriental Soc., Acad. Soc., Am. Acad. Polit. Sci., Am. Assn. Asian. Studies. Club: Harvard (N.Y.C.) Author: Letters form a Chinese Diplomat, 1941; The Fabulous Concubine (novel) 1956 (transl. into French, German, Swedish); Within the Four Seas, 1958; America and China; A New Approach to Asis, 1966 (transl. into Italian); Matthew Arnold and the Humanistic View of Life. Contbr. articles to scholarly jours. Home: 220 Schenck Av Great Neck NY 11021 Office: Fairleigh Dickinson U Teaneck NJ

CHANG, KAWANG-CHIH, anthropologist, educator; b. Peiping, China, Apr. 15, 1931; s. Wo-chün and Hsin-hsiang (Lo) C.; B.A., Nat. Taiwan U., 1954; Ph.D., Harvard, 1960; m. Hwei Li, May 17, 1957; children-Julian Po-keng, Nora Chung-chi. Came to U.S., 1955, naturalized, 1970. Lectr. anthropology Harvard, 1960- 61; instr. anthropology Yale, 1961-63, asst. prof., 1963-66, asso. prof., 1966-69, prof., 1969—, dir. grad. studies anthropology, 1966-69, chmn. dept. anthropology, 1970—. Fellow Am. Anthrop. Assn.; mem. Assn. for Asian Studies (dir.). Author: The Archaeology of Ancient China, 1963, rev. edit., 1968; Rethinking Archaeology 1967; Settlement Archaeology, 1968; Fengpitou, Tapenkeng and the Prehistory of Taiwan, 1969. Home: 37 Lansdowne Av Hamden CT 06517 Office: 51 Hillhouse Av New Haven CT 06520

CHANG, KEY YOUNG, pres., pub. Seoul dailies Hankook Ilbo (Korean lang.), Korea Times (English lang.), five other publs.; former gov. Bank of Korea; former dep. premier-econ. planning minister Korea. Mem. Internat. Olympic Com.; pres. Asian Games Fedn. Mem. Internat. Press Inst. Address: Office: IPO Box 3290 Seoul Korea

CHANG, NGEE-PONG, educator; b. Singapore, Dec. 24, 1940; s. Chow-Hee and Mui-Han (Lim) C.; came to U.S., 1957; B.A. in Physics, Ohio Wesleyan U., 1959; Ph.D., Columbia, 1963; m. Mabel Tean-Neo Lim, June 6, 1965; children—Belinda, Eugene. Research asso. Columbia, 1962-63; research fellow Inst. for Advanced Study, Princeton, 1963-64; research asso. Rockefeller U., N.Y.C., 1964-65; vis. prof. physics City Coll. N.Y., 1965-66, prof., 1966—. Mem. Am. Phys. Soc., Phi Beta Kappa, Sigma Xi. Research in high energy physics, field theory.‡

CHANG, SHELDON SHOU LIEN, educator, elec. engr.; b. Peking, China, Jan. 20, 1920; s. Hsiang Ping and Lucy (Tao) C.; B.S., Nat. Southwestern Asso. U., Kunming, China, 1942, M.S., 1944; Ph.D., Purdue U., 1947; m. Bridget Hsiao Mei Chou, Feb. 6, 1965; children—Theodore Ching-Chien, Kathleen Ching Hsin, Andrew Ching-Hung, Edward Ching Hsing, Ingrid Jeanette. Came to U.S., 1945, naturalized, 1954. Design engr. Central Radio Works, Kunming, China, 1943-45; research and devel. engr. Robbins & Myers, Inc., Springfield, O., 1946-52; from asst. prof. to prof. elec. engring. N.Y. U., 1952-63; prof. elec. engring., chmn. dept. State U. N.Y. at Stony Brook, 1963—; cons. to industry, 1952—. Fellow I.E.E.E. (Fellow award 1962); mem. Sigma Xi (N.Y.U. lectr. 1963), Tau Beta Pi, Eta Kappa Nu. Author: Synthesis of Optimum Control Systems, 1961; Energy Conversion, 1963; also articles. Spl. research feedback communications systems, optimum control theory. Home: 5 Bluetop Rd Setauket NY 11785 Office: State Univ New York Stony Brook NY 11790

CHANG, TE LIN, architect; b. Canton, China, Oct. 8, 1919; s. Pei Ye and Yu-Cheun (Chen) C.; B.Arch., Hangchow (China) Christian U., 1943; m. Shih Wei Yen, Jan. 15, 1950. Chief, Lab. Med. Equipage, 1953-58; chief engr. Vets. Gen. Hosp., 1958-62; head dept. med. engring. Nat. Def. Med. Center, 1962-66; principal architect T.L. Chang & Assos., Architects-Engrs., 1966— (all Taipei, Taiwan, China). Served to col. Chinese Army, 1946-66. Decorated Precious Star medal, Royalty and Diligence medal, Pieh-Liang medal. Fellow A.I.A. (hon.); mem. Inst. Architects (china; pres., 1969-70), Am. Soc. Heating Refrigerating and Air-Conditioning Engrs. Principal works include Chen Hsing Rehab. Center for Children, 1966, Alfred Kohlberg Meml. Med. Research Lab., 1963, Dr. George K. C Yeh residence, 1970 (all Taipei). Home: 7 Alley 25 Lane 24 Roosevelt Rd Sect 4 Taipei Taiwan Office: 3 Roosevelt Rd Sect 1 Taipei Taiwan Republic of China

CHANG, WILLIAM SHEN CHIE, educator, elec. engr.; b. Nantung, Kiangsu, China, Apr. 1, 1931; s. Tung Wu and Phoebe Y.S. (Chow) C.; B.S.E., U. Mich., 1952, M.S.E., 1953; Ph.D., Brown U., 1957; m. Margaret Hwachen Kwei, Nov. 26, 1955; children—Helen Nai-yee, Hugh Nai-hen, Hedy Nai-ling. Lectr., research asso. elec. engring. Stanford, 1957-59; asst. prof. elec. engring. Ohio State U., 1959-62, asso. prof., 1962-65; prof., chmn. dept. elec. engring. Washington U., St. Louis, 1965—. Mem. Am. Optical Soc., Am. Phys. Soc., Am. Assn. Univ. Profs., I.E.E.E., Am. Soc. Engring. Edn. Author: Principles of Quantum Electronics, 1969. Contbr. articles profl. jours. Research on quantum electronics and optics. Home: 7840 Laton Pl St Louis MO 63130

CHANNER, EARLE ADARE, mfg. co. exec.; b. Evanston, Ill., Aug. 18, 1918; s. Earle Adare and Ethel (Lee) C.; student Kenyon Coll., 1937-39; m. Isabelle Johnson, Dec. 25, 1942. With H.M. Harper Co., 1939-63, v.p. charge sales, 1956-63; pres., dir. Harper Everlasting Fastenings Ltd., 1960-63, H.M. Harper Internat., S.A., 1961-63, Anti-Corrosive Metal Products Co., 1961-63; pres., chmn. bd. Fastening Service Center Mass., 1961-63; dir. Communications Systems Corp., 1962-63; pres., dir. Nat. Screw & Mfg. Co., Cleve., 1963-68; v.p., dir. Monogram Industries, Inc., Los Angeles, 1967-68; pres., dir. Channer, Inc., 1969—; dir. Hadco Chem. Co., So. Athletic Service Co., Union Commerce Bank. Industry specialist NPA, 1953. Bd. dirs. Jr. Achievement, Vocational Guidance and Rehab. Center; trustee Community Chest; adv. com. Cleve. Plan; gen. bd. A.R.C. Served to 2d lt., pilot, USAAF, 1943-45. Mem. Fasteners Research Council (past chmn., dir.), Indsl. Fasteners Inst. (exec. com.), Alpha Delta Phi. Episcopalian. Clubs: Everglades (Palm Beach, Fla.), Union, Kirtland Country (Cleve.); Pepper Pike; Bluecoats, Inc. Home: 13901 Shaker Blvd Cleveland OH 44120 Office: Union Commerce Bldg Cleveland OH 44115

CHANNICK, BERTRAM J., physician; b. Phila., Sept. 14, 1925; s. Maurice and Rose (Rosenberg) C.; B.A., Princeton U., 1947; M.D., Boston U., 1949; m. Beverly Jaslow, Jan. 8, 1955; children—Richard Neal, Steven Andrew. Intern Germantown Hosp., Phila., 1949; fellow in endocrinology Phila. Gen. Hosp., 1954; prof. medicine Temple U. Med. Sch., 1965—, head sect. endocrinology Health Scis. Center, 1965—. Served to lt. USNR, 1950-52. Decorated Purple Heart. Fellow A.C.P.; mem. Nat. Endocrine Soc., A.M.A., Am. Fed. Clin. Research. Home: 321 Hidden River Rd Narberth PA 19072 Office: 3701 N Broad St Philadelphia PA 19140

CHANNING, CAROL, actress; b. Seattle, Wash., Jan. 31, 1923; d. George and Adelaide (Glaser) Channing; student Bennington Coll.; m. Charles F. Lowe, Sept. 5, 1956; 1 son, Channing George. Appeared Broadway prodns. No for an Answer, Let's Face It, So Proudly We Hail, Lend an Ear; star of Gentlemen Prefer Blondes, Wonderful Town, The Vamp, Hello Dolly!; actress with RKO Studios, Hollywood, Cal., pictures include First Traveling Saleslady; appeared in Thoroughly Modern Millie, 1967; TV prodns., Svengali and the Blonde, Three Men on a Horse, Crescendo, also guest star appearances. Recipient Theatre World award, Critics Circle award for play, Lend an Ear; award for Best Night Club Act of 1957; 1963 Tony award as starring actress in Hello Dolly!; Golden Globe award as best supporting actress in Thoroughly Modern Millie, 1967; Tony award, 1968. Christian Scientist. Home: 8749 Sunset Blvd Hollywood CA 90046

CHANNING, MARK GUNTHER, mgmt. cons.; b. Berlin, Germany, July 5, 1925; s. Jacob and Maria (Pilger) C.; came to U.S., 1941, naturalized, 1943; B.S., Columbia, 1950, M.A., 1952; m. Lila Lang, Apr. 12, 1951; children—Candace Leslie, Stacey Lisa. Various financial positions Ford Motor Co., Dearborn, Mich., 1953-56; managerial positions in finance and planning, dir. market rep. Chrysler Corp., Highland Park, Mich., 1956-61; v.p. Pratt & Whitney Co., Inc., West Hartford, Conn., 1961-64; v.p. finance Precision Instrument Co., Palo Alto, 1964-65; treas. Am. Comml. Lines, 1965-68; exec. v.p. Computer Applications, Inc., N.Y.C., 1968-70; pres. Channing Assos., Inc., Westport, Conn. and N.Y.C., 1970—. Mem. Am. Mgmt. Assn., Am. Econ. Assn. Home: 14 Side Hill Rd Westport CT 06880 Office: 666 Fifth Av New York City NY 10022 also 14 Side Hill Rd Westport CT 06880

CHANNOCK, RAYMOND E., mfg. co. exec.; b. Cleve., 1906. Former pres., chief exec. officer, now dir. Acme- Cleve. Co.; dir. Society Corp., Scott & Fetzer, Cleve. Home: 15724 Edgecliffe Av Cleveland OH 44111 Office: 170 E 131st St Cleveland OH 44108

CHANTREY, JACK ARTHUR, mfg. exec.; b. Lake Forest, Ill., June 2, 1922; s. Frederick A. and Rae Lillian (Crane) C.; A.B. in Econs., Oberlin Coll., 1947. Sub-accountant Nat. City Bank N.Y., N.Y.C., 1947-52; traveling auditor Standard-Vacuum Oil, N.Y.C., 1952-56; analyst Ford Motor Co., Dearborn, Mich, 1956-59; became treas. Bucyrus-Erie Co., Milw., 1960—, v.p., 1963, also dir.; now exec. v.p. finance N. Am. Car Corp., Chgo.; dir. Home State Bank, South Milwaukee, Wis. Adv. bd. Trinity Meml. Hosp., Cudahy, Wis., 1961—; bd. dirs. Wis. Blue Cross Plan. Served to 1st lt., AUS, 1943-46. Home: 1321 N Prospect Av Milwaukee WI 53202 Office: 586 E Spruce Av Lake Forest IL 60045

CHAO, KWANG-CHU, educator, chmn. engr.; b. Chunging, China, June 7, 1925; s. Chung-Pu and Jui-Pu (Chou) C.; B.S., Nat. Chekiang U., 1948; M.S., U. Wis., 1952, Ph.D., 1956; m. Jiun-Ying Su, May 2, 1953; children—Howard Honshun, Albert Honchi, Bernard Honwei. Came to U.S., 1954, naturalized, 1969. Chem. engr. Taiwan Alkali Co., 1948-51, 52-54; research engr. Chevron Research Co., Richmond, Cal., 1957-63; asso. prof. Ill. Inst. Tech., Chgo., 1963-64; asso. prof. Okla. State U., 1964-68; prof. Purdue U., West Lafayette, Ind., 1968—; cons. to industry, 1964—. Mem. Am. Inst. Chem. Engrs. (sec.-treas. Central Okla. sect., 1966-67, vice chmn., 1967- 68, panelist, session chmn. Nat. Meetings), Am. Chem. Soc., Am. Assn. U. Profs., Sigma Xi, Omega Chi Epsilon. Home: 2909 Henderson Av West Lafayette IN 47906

CHAO, YUEN REN, ret. educator; b. Tientsin, China, Nov. 3, 1892; s. Heng Nien and Lai Sun (Feng) C.; brought to U.S., 1910; A.B., Cornell, 1914; Ph.D., Harvard, 1918; Litt.D. (hon.), Princeton, 1946; LL.D., U. Cal. at Berkeley, 1962; L.H.D., Ohio State U., 1970; m. Buwei Yang, June 1, 1921; children—Rulan, Nova, Lensey, Bella. Instr. physics Cornell, 1919-20; instr. philosophy and Chinese Harvard, 1921-24, lectr., 1941-46; prof. Chinese Nat. Tsing Hua U., 1925-29; chief sect. linguistics Academia Sinica since 1929; vis. prof. U. Hawaii, 1938-39, Yale, 1939-41; prof. oriental langs. and linguistics U. Cal., 1947-52, Agassiz prof. Oriental langs. and lit., 1952-60, prof. emeritus, 1960—, Faculty Research lectr., 1967. Linguistics Soc. Am. chair Linguistic Inst., U. Mich., 1967; China Found. chair on linguistics Nat. Taiwan U., 1959; Fulbright research scholar Kyoto U., 1959. Mem. com. on unification nat. lang., com. music edn. Chinese Ministry Edn.; cons. Bell Telephone Labs.; del. to UNESCO confs. Fellow Am. Acad. Arts and Scis.; mem. Academia Sinica, Sci. Soc. of China, Am. Anthrop. Assn., Am. Oriental Soc. (pres. 1960), Phil. Sci.

Soc., Hist. Sci. Soc., Linguistic Soc. Am. (pres. 1945), Comité International Permanet de Linguistique, Acoustical Soc. Am., A.A.A.S. Author: New Book of Rhymes, 1923; Studies in the Modern Wu Dialects, 1928; Phonetics of Yao Folksongs, 1929; Love Songs of the Sixth Salai Lama (with Yu Dawchyuan), 1929; The Chunghsiang Dialect, 1939; Cantonese Primer, 1947; Concise Dictionary of Spoken Chinese (with L.S. Yang), 1947; Mandarin Primer, 1948; Problems in Linguistics, 1960; Language and Symbolic Systems, 1968; Grammar of Spoken Chinese, 1968; Readings in Sayable Chinese, 3 volumes, 1969. Composer: Songs of Contemporary Poems, 1928; Children's Festival Songs, 1934; Translations into Chinese and English. Contbr. to bulls., jours. and encys. Home: 1059 Cragmont Av Berkeley CA 94701

CHAPANIS, ALPHONSE, educator, psychologist; b. Meriden, Conn., Mar. 17, 1917; s. Anicatas and Mary (Barkevich) C.; B.A., U. Conn., 1937; M.A., Yale, 1942, Ph.D., 1943; m. Marion Rowe, Au. 23, 1941 (div. 1960); children—Linda and Roger (twins); m. 2d, Natalia Potanin, Mar. 25, 1960. Psychologist, Tenn. Dept. Pub. Health, 1939-40; asst. psychologist Aero. Med. Lab., Wright Air Devel. Center, 1942-43; asst. prof., research fellow Johns Hopkins, 1946-49, asso. prof., 1949-56, research contract dir., 1952-53, 1955—, prof. psychology, indsl. engring., 1956-63, prof. psychology, 1963—; mem. tech. staff Bell Telephone Labs., 1953-54. Cons. exec. council Joint Services Human Engring. Guide to Equipment Design, 1953-60; mem. panel on tng., com. on undersea warfare NRC, 1953-57; adv. panel behavioral scis. research Air Force Office Sci. Research, 1956-59; sci. liaison officer Am. embassy, Office Naval Research Br. Office, London, Eng., 1960-61. Served from 2d lt. to capt. USAAF, 1943- 46. Recipient Franklin V. Taylor award, 1963. Fellow A.A.A.S., Am. Psychol. Assn., Soc. Engring. Psychologists (pres. 1959-60), Optical Soc. Am., mem. Am. Inst. Physics, Eastern Psychol. Assn., Soc. Exptl. Psychologists, Ergonomics Research Soc., Internat. Ergonomics Assn. (mem. council 1967—), Sigma Xi. Author: (with W.R. Garner, C.T. Morgan) Applied Experimental Psychology; Human Factors in Engineering Design, 1949; The Design and Conduct of Human Engineering Studies, 1956; Research Techniques in Human Engineering, 1959; Man-Machine Engineering, 1965. Corr. editor Jour. Applied Psychology, 1955-60; Co-editor Human Engineering Guide to Equipment Design, 1963; editorial adv. bd. Jour. Systems Engring., 1969—. Contbr. articles to profl. jours. Address: Johns Hopkins U Baltimore MD 21218

CHAPDELAINE, PAUL, cement co. exec.; b. Montreal, Can., Aug. 18, 1916; s. Joseph Rene and Blanche (Gauthier) C.; chartered accountant, Mt. St. Louis Coll., Montreal, 1927; student U. Montreal m. Anne Marie Jarry, May 15, 1943; children—Guy, Luc, Jean, Diane. Auditor, Riddell, Stead, Graham & Hutchinson, Montreal, 1946-50; internal auditor Canadair Ltd., Montreal, 1950-53; with St. Lawrence Cement Co., 1953—, exec. v.p., gen. mgr., 1961-63, pres., 1963-. Mem. Canadian Inst. Chartered Accountants, Portland Cement Assn., Canadian Good Roads Assn., Canadian C. of C. Home: 633 Laird Blvd Mount Royal Quebec Canada Office: St Lawrence Cement Co 50 Cremazie Blvd Montreal 11 Quebec Canada

CHAPEL, DEWEY ELBERT, univ. dean; b. Murfreesboro, Ark., Mar. 31, 1917; s. Horace Jewel and Alva (Womack) C.; B.A., Henderson State Tchrs. Coll., 1946; M.Ed., East Tex. State Coll., 1952; Ed.D., North Tex. State U., 1965; m. Dorothy Jean Goynes, May 20, 1938; children—Dan, Mark. Rural schs. supt. of schs., Bismarck, Ark., 1946-60; tchr., counselor, Hot Springs (Ark.) High Sch., 1961-63; rehab. counselor, Hot Springs, 1960; prof., dean Grad. Sch., dir. tchr. edn. Ouachita Bapt. U., 1963—. Served to capt. USAAF, 1941-45; CBI. Decorated D.F.C., Air Medal. Mem. Ark. Edn. Assn., N.E.A., Higher Edn. Assn., Assn. Supervision and Curriculum Devel., Phi Delta Kappa. Home: Rt 1 Bismarck AR 71929 Office: Ouachita Baptist Univ Box 1068 Arkadelphia AR 71923

CHAPELLE, HOWARD IRVING, ret. marine architect; b. Tolland, Mass., Feb. 1, 1900; s. Irving and Sarah (Hardy) C.; ed. pub. schs., New Haven and Waterbury, Conn., Webb Inst., N.Y. City; m. Alice Zayma Connolly, July 16, 1935. Draftsman and designer, 1919-25 and 1937-31 (at sea 1936). Chmn. tech. com. Restoration of the Niagara (Perry's flagship). Cons. (naval architect) FAO of UN to Turkey, 1956-57; curator transp. U.S. Nat. Mus., Smithsonian Instn., Washington, 1957-67, sr. historian Mus. History, Washington, 1957-67, sr. historian Mus. History and Tech., 1967-71. Commd. capt. U.S. Army Transp. Corps, 1943, maj., Aug. 1944, lt. col., Sept. 1946; chief, marine br. Research and Devel. div. Army Transp. Corps, April 1945-46; Guggenheim Fellowship Marine Hist. Research, 1950; est. initial research and devel. program for marine transport equipment for U.S. Army. Recipient secretary's exceptional service award, 1970. Mem. Am. Naval Hist. Found., Soc. Naval Archs. and Marine Engrs. Mem. Western hemisphere com. Internat. Fishing Vessel Congress. Author books including: History of American Sailing Navy, 1949; American Small Sailing Craft, 1951; The National Watercraft Collection, 1962; The Bark Canoes and Skin Boats of North America, 1964; Search for Speed Under Sail, 1967; The Constellation Story, 1970. Home: Wilson Towers also Tolland Cambridge MD 21613 ☆

CHAPIN, ALDUS HIGGINS, art mus. and sch. adminstr.; b. Boston, Oct. 6, 1930; s. Vinton and Elizabeth (Higgins) C.; A.B., Harvard, 1952; M.A., Johns Hopkins, 1953; postgrad. Boston U., 1955-56; m. Nancy Newell Daniels, Apr. 7, 1956; children—Elizabeth Rexford, Nancy Higgins, Aldus Newell. Polit. analyst African affairs, State Dept., 1956-61; asst. dean Johns Hopkins Sch. Advanced Internat. Studies, Washington, 1961-68; chmn. bd. govs., exec. v.p. bd. trustees Corcoran Gallery Art and Art Sch., Washington, 1968—. Mem. at large Milton Acad. Grad. Council, 1967—. Bd. dirs., chmn. exec. com. Washington Performing Arts Soc.; bd. dirs. Washington Area Tennis Patrons Found.; trustee Potomac Sch., McLean; bd. dirs. Asso. Harvard Alumni, mem. com. to nominate overseers, since 1916—. Served with AUS, 1953-55. Democrat. Unitarian. Club: Harvard (1st v.p., mem. exec. com.) (Washington). Home: 9100 Falls Run Rd McLean VA 22101 Office: Corcoran Gallery Art Washington DC 20006

CHAPIN, BRADLEY, educator; b. Silver Creek, N.Y., Apr. 13, 1924; s. Erwin M. and Mildred (Yonk) C.; B.A., 1948; M.A., 1950; Ph.D., Cornell., 1952; m. Nancy Newton, Oct. 23, 1942; children—Michael, Penelope, Andrew, Susan, Bradley. Head dept. history Park Sch., Buffalo, 1951-59, bus. mgr., 1956- 59; faculty State U. N.Y. at Buffalo, 1958-66, dean Univ. Coll., 1959- 66, prof. history, 1965-66, chmn. Inst. Am. Studies at Paris, 1965-66; prof. and chmn. history dept. Ohio State U., Columbus, O., 1966—. Served with USAAF, 1942-45. Mem. Am. Hist. Assn., Phi Beta Kappa. Author: The Origins of the American Law of Treason. Home: 4987 Sharon Hill Dr Worthington OH 43085 Office: Ohio State U Columbus OH 43215

CHAPIN, CORNELLA VAN A., sculptor; b. Waterford, Conn.; d. Lindley Hoffman and Cornelia Garrison (Van Auken) Chapin; ed. pvt. schs.; unmarried. Has exhibited since 1930; studied with Mateo Hernandez, Paris. Exhibited Internat. Expn. Art and Technique, Paris, 1937 (won 2d Grand Prize, class stone sculpture), World's Fair, New York, 1939-40, San Francisco Golden Gate Internat. Expn., 1939, Brooklyn (N.Y.) Museum, Modern Museum (Washington), Art Centre (Oganquit, Me.), Salon des Tuileries, Salon d'Automne, Paris, Fairmont Park Art Assn., Internat. Sculpture Show, Phila. Museum, Pa. Acad. (Philadelphia), San Francisco Art Museum, Montclair (New Jersey) Museum, Springfield Art Museum; private collections Paris, London, New York, Philadelphia, Washington; "Christ the King," high altar of Cathedral St. John the Divine, N.Y. City; "Giant Frog," Rittenhouse Square, Phila. Mem. sculpture jury Contemporary Art Exhibit N.Y. World's Fair, 1939; sculpture chmn. N.Y. Met. Area, National Art Week, 1941; work invited for 3d Internat. Exhbn. of Sculpture, Philadelphia, 1949; sculptor mem. N.Y.C. Art Commission, 1951-53. Works in leading museums and national parks. Fellow National Sculpture Soc. (sec. 1942-45; chmn. library and research com. of council), Academician National Academy Design; mem. Soc. Salon d'Autmore, Paris, 1936, Allied Artists Am., Inc., Artists for Victory (Sculpture chmn., 1942). Dir. Kips Bay Boys' Club, N.Y. City. Lectures widely on Carving Direct from Life, Some Tales and Tools. Clubs: Cosmopolitan, National Arts, Architectural League of New York. Address: Wells Hill Rd Lakeville CT 06039

CHAPIN, EDWARD YOUNG, banker; b. Chattanooga, Aug. 10, 1897; s. Edward Young and Elise (Hutcheson) C.; B.S. in Econs., U. Pa., 1918; m. Dorris Inman Carter, Dec. 6, 1921; children—Edward Young III, Mary Lynn (Mrs. W.T. Patten), Dorris (Mrs. J.R. Wells). With Am. Nat. Bank & Trust Co., 1919—, pres., 1948-57, chmn. exec. com., 1957—, also dir.; dir. Tonya Corp.; v.p., dir. Rock City Gardens; dir. Coca-Cola Bottling Works (Thomas), Inc., Coca-Cola Bottling Co. (Thomas), Inc., Coca-Cola Bottling Works Third, Modern Maid, Inc. Trustee Benwood Found., Crystal Found., Maclellan Found., Chattanooga Tb Sanitorium Assn., Forest Hills Cemetery Assn., Caldwell Found. Mem. Beta Theta Pi. Presbyn. Clubs: Lookout Mountain Fairyland, Mountain City, Lookout Mountain Golf; Royal Poinciana Golf (Naples, Fla.), Naples Yacht. Home: 120 Fairy Trail Lookout Mountain TN 37419 Office: 750 Market St Chattanooga TN 37405

CHAPIN, FREDERIC LINCOLN, fgn. service officer; b. N.Y.C., July 13, 1929; s. Selden and Mary Paul (Noyes) C.; grad. St. Paul's Sch., Concord, N.H., 1946; student Stanford, 1948-49; B.A., Harvard, 1950; m. Cornelia Bonner Clarke, Aug. 2, 1952; children—John Clarke Noyes, Anne Cornelia, Grace Selden, Edith Clarke. Econ. analyst ECA, Paris, France, 1950-52; joined U.S. Fgn. Service, 1952; assigned Vienna, Austria, 1952-55, State Dept., 1956-59, Managua, Nicaragua, 1959-61; charge d'affaires embassy, Fort Lamy, Chad, 1961; assigned State Dept., 1962-63; spl. asst. to under-sec. for polit. affairs, 1963-65; exec. sec. AID, 1965-66; Fgn. Service examiner, 1966-67; Fgn. Service insp., 1967; country dir. for Bolivia and Chile, 1968-70; dep. asst. sec. for mgmt., 1970—. Dir. Erie City Iron Works (Pa.), 1962-66; sec.-treas. Am. Fgn. Service Protective Assn., 1970—. Mem. Phi Beta Kappa. Mem. editorial bd. Fgn. Service Jour., 1962-66. Home: 116 New St New Brunswick NJ 08901 Office: Dept of State Washington DC 20520

CHAPIN, HUGH A., lawyer; b. Whitesville, N.Y., Sept. 3, 1925; B.C.E., Cornell U., 1948; LL.B., Harvard, 1951. Admitted to N.Y. bar, 1951; now mem. firm Kenyon, Kenyon, Reilly, Carr & Chapin, N.Y.C.; prof. patent law N.Y.U., 1957-59. Mem. Tau Beta Pi. Office: 59 Maiden Lane New York City NY 10038*

CHAPIN, RICHARD, coll. pres.; b. Boston, Dec. 25, 1923; s. Vinton and Elizabeth (Higgins) C.; grad. Milton Acad., 1942; S.B., Harvard, 1944, M.B.A., 1949; m. Maryan Gainor Fox, Nov. 3, 1956; children—Aldus Higgins II, Margery Rodman, Marya Marsh, Richard Dickinson. Asst. to treas. Anderson, Davis & Platt, Inc., 1946-47; journeyman machinist Yale & Towne Co., 1947; research asst. Harvard Grad. Sch. Bus. Adminstrn., 1949-50, asst. to dean, 1950-54, asst. dean, 1954-67, adminstrv. dir. middle mgmt. program, 1955-57; dir. corp. fund raising for Harvard Coll., 1958; exec. dir. Informal Com. on Corp. Aid to Am. U., 1958; dir. student personnel Harvard Grad. Sch. Bus. Adminstrn., 1963-64, tchr. written analysis cases dept., 1962-64, adminstrv. dir. master's program, 1964-66, dir. ednl. planning, 1966-67; pres. Emerson Coll., Boston, 1967-. Dir. Easton Car & Constrn. Co. (Pa.), 1964—. Cons. regional office Social Security Adminstrn., 1955- 66, Morgan Guaranty Trust Co., 1965-68; pres. Back Bay Ednl. Council, 1967-68. Pres. Cambridge Community Services, 1965-67. Bd. dirs. Mass. Com. for Prevention of Blindness, Douglas A. Thom Clinic, Drug Abuse Found. Boston. Served with USNR, 1942-46. Mem. Assn. Ind. Colls and Univs. of Mass. (v.p. 1970—), Delta Kappa Epsilon. Clubs: Delphic (mem. grad. bd. 1966-70), Hasty Pudding (grad. pres. 1968—) (Harvard); N.Y. Yacht; Manchester (Mass.) Yacht; Union (Boston); Quisset Harbor Yacht. Home: 13 Kennedy Rd Cambridge MA 02138 Office: 148 Beacon St Boston MA 02116

CHAPIN, RICHARD EARL, librarian; b. Danville, Ill., Apr. 29, 1925; s. Harry W. and Lula May (Briggs) C.; A.B., Wabash Coll., 1948; M.S., U. Ill., 1949, Ph.D., 1954; m. Eleanor Jane Lang, Aug. 15, 1949; children—Robert Lang, David Brian, Rebecca Anne. Reference asst. Fla. State U., 1949-50; library asst. U. Ill., 1950-53, vis. prof., 1957; asst. dir., asst. prof. U. Okla. Sch. Library Sci., 1953-55; asso. librarian, asso. prof. Mich. State U., 1955- 59, dir. libraries, prof. journalism, 1959—; cons. Mich. State U. adv. group, Saigon, Vietnam, 1958; field research reader U.S. Office Edn., 1958-60; cons. to Nat. Agr. Library, 1962, Office of Tech. Services, 1963, Kellogg Found., 1967, EDUCOM, 1968. Mem. East Lansing (Michigan) Human Relations Commn., 1966-69, chmn., 1969; mem. East Lansing Bd. Edn., 1970—. Served to lt. (j.g.) USNR, 1943-46. Mem. Am. (chmn. univ. libraries sect. 1959-60), Mich. (pres. 1967) library assns., Assn. of Coll. and Research Libraries (bd. dirs. 1959-60), Sigma Chi, Blue Key. Author: Mass Communications, A Statistical Analysis, 1957. Editor Southwest Library Assn. Newsletter, 1955. Contbr. articles library periodicals and encys. Home: 614 Camelot Dr East Lansing MI 48823

CHAPIN, ROBERT M., JR., cartographer; b. Washington, D.C., Apr. 5 1910; s. Robert Macfarlane and Louise W. (Mulford) C.; B.S. in Architecture, University of Pennsylvania, 1933; m. Pauline May Sell, Feb. 27, 1938; 2 sons, Bruce, James. Architect, designed and built private houses, New York, Ga., Conn., 1933-35; cartographer, Newsweek magazine, 1935-37, Time mag. since 1937; lecturer on cartography, Grad. Sch. Geography, Clark U., 1943. Designed and executed maps for various publs. including: The History of Our World; This is America's Story; The Making of Modern America; A History of the United States. Member of the Am. Geog. Soc., Psi Upsilon. Home: Tan Fat Hill Sharon CT 06069 Office: Time Inc Rockefeller Center New York City NY 10020

CHAPIN, ROY DIKEMAN, Jr., business exec.; b. Detroit, Sept. 21, 1915; s. Roy Dikeman and Inez (Tiedeman) C.; A.B., Yale, 1937; m. Ruth Mary Ruxton, Oct. 29, 1927 (div.); children—Roy D., Christopher K., William, Cicely; m. 2d, Louise Baldwin Wickser, July 19, 1965; children—Alexandra, Robert L., Loise B., Hope B. With Hudson Motor Car Co., and Hudson Sales Corp., Detroit, 1938-54, dir., 1946-54; asst. sales mgr. Hudson div. Am. Motors Corp., 1954-55; asst. treas., dir. Am. Motors Corp., 1954-55, v.p., treas., 1955, exec. v.p., 1956-66, internat. exec. v.p., gen. mgr., 1966-67, chmn., chief exec. officer, 1967—; chmn., dir. Jeep Corp., Am. Motors (Can.), Ltd.; dir. Rambler Motors Ltd. (England). v.p., trustee Roy D. Chapin Found., 1948—; mem. exec. council Boy Scouts of Am.; mem. adv. bd. Leader Dogs for Blind; dir. Econ. Devel. Corp. Greater Detroit, World Wildlife Fund. Mem. Hwy. Users Fedn. (dir.), Internat. Road Fedn. (dir.), N. Am. Wildlife Found. (trustee), Auto Mfrs. Assn. (dir.), Chi Psi. Clubs: Elihu Soc. (New Haven); Links, Racquet and Tennis (N.Y.C.); Country, Grosse Pointe, Fontinalis, Detroit; Pacific Union (San Francisco). Home: 411 Country Club Lane Grosse Pointe Farms MI 48236 Office: Am Motors Corp Detroit MI 48202

CHAPIN, SAMUEL DALE, former forging co. exec.; b. N.Y.C., Aug. 30, 1919; s. Alfred H. and Julia (Neil) C.; grad. Taft Sch., 1938; m. Barbara J. Combs, Nov. 24, 1945; children—Samuel Dale, Scott Lathrop, Dale Dorothy. With Moore Drop Forging Co., Springfield, Mass., 1938-70, v.p., 1955-63, pres., 1963-70, chmn., until 1970, dir.; dir. 3d Nat. Bank Hampden County, Springfield, Mass., Mut. Life Ins. Co.; trustee Springfield Instn. for Savs. Dir. Mass. Taxpayers Found.; past pres., dir. Springfield Boys' Club: trustee Bay Path Jr. Coll. Home: 201 Porter Lake Dr Springfield MA 01106

CHAPIN, SAMUEL M., lawyer; b. N.Y.C., June 30, 1902; LL.B., Columbia, 1925. Admitted to N.Y. bar, 1926; now sr. partner firm Parker, Chapin and Flattau, N.Y.C. Mem. Assn. Bar City N.Y., Am. Bar Assn. Address: 530 Fifth Av New York City NY 10036*

CHAPIN, SLOCUM, travel agy. exec.; b. Quincy, Mass., May 12, 1913; s. Charles Mathews and Helen Marguerite (Slocum) C.; student Peoples Acad., Morrisville, Vt., 1928-30, Tilton (N.H.) Sch., 1930-32, Dartmouth, 1932-35; m. Elaine Hunt, Oct. 20, 1933; 1 son, John; m. 2d, Joan Igou, Aug. 18, 1937; children—David (dec.), Joan, Michele; m. 3d, Jane Daly, March 4, 1961. Guest relations, NBC, N.Y.C., 1933-35; pres. Broadcast Builders, Inc., Hanover, N.H., 1935-36; asst. sales promotion mgr., World Broadcasting System, Inc., N.Y.C., 1936-37; salesman Radio Station WOC, Davenport, 1937-41; sales mgr., Radio Station WKBN, Youngstown, O., 1941; gen. mgr. Radio Station WSTC, Stamford, Conn., 1941-42; with Am. Broadcasting Co. (then Blue Network, Inc.), 1942-66, Eastern sales mgr. for TV, 1948-51, v.p. charge ABC owned TV Stas. 1951, v.p. charge sales TV Network, 1954, v.p. charge sales Western div., 1958-64, v.p. exec. relations, 1964- 66; pres. Adventures Unlimited, agts. for travel at Abercrombie & Fitch, N.Y.C., 1966—. Mem. Camp Fire Club Am., Broadcast Pioneers, Psi Upsilon. Club: Explorers. Home: 500 E 77th St New York City NY 10021 Office: Adventures Unlimited 19 E 45th St New York City NY 10017

CHAPIN, WILLIAM ARTHUR, fgn. service officer; b. Chgo., May 23, 1920; s. Arthur Barber and Elizabeth Margaret (Mann) C.; A.B., U. Chgo., 1942, postgrad., 1947- 49; m. Catherine Wall, May 4, 1945; childrenEthan Paul, Arthur Wall, Margaret. Joined U.S. Fgn. Service, 1949; resident officer U.S. High Commr. for Germany, Bavaria, 1950-52; 2d sec. Am. embassy, Saigon, Vietnam, 1952-54, Brussels, 1955-58; staff Office Spl. Asst. for Atomic Energy Affairs, Dept. State, 1958-60, Bur. African Affairs, 1960-63; assigned Sr. Seminar Fgn. Service Inst., 1963; chief polit. sect. Am. embassy, Laos, Vientiane; research fellow for Far Eastern affairs Inst. for Strategic studies, London, 1966-67; 1st sec. Far Eastern affairs Am. embassy, London, 1967-69; assigned office of sec. Dept. Transp., 1969-70, bur. internat. sci. and technol. affairs Dept. State, 1971—. Served with USAAF, 1943-45. Home: 213 S Lee St Alexandria VA 22314

CHAPIN, WILLIAM SELLEW, adminstrv. engring. exec.; b. Chicopee, Mass., Dec. 29, 1903; s. Clinton G. and Corinne (Sellew) C.; B. Civil Engring., Northeastern U., 1927; D. Engring., 1962; LL.D., Niagara U., 1962; m. Dorothy Powell, May 5, 1928; children—Richard C., Caroline (Mrs. Richard M. Lash), Robert W. Civil engr. N.Y. State Dept. Pub. Works, 1927-40; chief engr. Pitts. Regional Planning Assn., 1940-42; cons. engr. Triborough Bridge and Tunnel Authority, 1945-54; with Power Authority N.Y. State, 1954—, gen. mgr., constrn. and operations St. Lawrence, Niagara, other power projects, also chief engr., 1958-69, cons., 1969—. Served to lt. col., C.E., AUS, 1942-45; CBI. Decorated Bronze Star; recipient Distinguished Attainment citation Northeastern U., 1960. Registered profl. engr., N.Y., Pa. Fellow Am. Soc. C.E.; mem. N.Y. State Soc. Profl. Engrs. (Engr. of Year award 1958). Republican. Methodist. Home: 4 Duffin Av West Islip NY 11795 Office: 10 Columbus Circle New York City NY 10019

CHAPLIN, CHARLES SPENCER, actor, writer, composer; b. London, England, April 16, 1889; both parents in theatrical bus., student pub. schs., London; m. Mildred Harris; m. 2d, Lita Grey; children—Charles Spencer, Sydney; m. 3d, Paulette Goddard (div. 1942); m. 4th Oona O'Neill, June 16, 1943; children—Geraldine, Michael, Josephine, Victoria, Jane, also 3 additional children including 2 sons. Identified with theater at 7 years old, employed in vaudeville and legitimate playhouses; first appearance was as Billy with William Gillette, in "Sherlock Holmes"; came to U.S. with vaudeville act, 1910. Screen debut, 1914, with Keystone Film Co.; with Essanay Co., 1915; Mutual Film Corp., 1916; signed with new First Nat. Exhibitors' Circuit to make eight two-reel pictures for $1,000,000, 1917; began as producer with construction of own motion picture studios at Hollywood, Calif., starring in and directing productions of his own creation; now playing and producing own pictures, distributed by United Artists Corp. of which he is a founder member; latest productions Limelight, 1952, Monsieur Verdoux, 1947; directed film Great Dictator, 1940, A Countess from Hong Kong, 1967; also revived musical and sound version The Gold Rush, 1942. Mem. Société des Beaux Arts, Paris, France, A.S.C.A.P. Decorated Chevalier Legion of Honor (France). Co-recipient (with Dmitri Shostakovich) of world peace prize of World Peace Council, 1953. Clubs: Lambs (New York); Tuna (Catalina). Author: Charles Chaplin: My Autobiography, 1964.*

CHAPLIN, GEORGE, editor; b. Columbia, S.C., Apr. 28, 1914; s. Morris and Netty (Brown) C.; B.S., Clemson Coll., 1935; Nieman fellow Harvard, 1940-41; m. Esta Lillian Solomon, Jan. 26, 1937; children—Stephen Michael, Jerry Gay. Reporter, later city editor Greenville (S.C.) Piedmont, 1935-42; mng. editor Camden (N.J.) Courier-Post, 1946-47. San Diego (Cal.) Jour., 1948-49; mng. editor, then editor New Orleans Item, 1949-58; asso. editor Honolulu Advertiser, 1958-59, editor, 1959—. Pulitzer prize juror, 1969; mem. selection com. Jefferson fellowships, U. Hawaii. Chmn., Gov.'s Conf. on Year 2000. Bd. dirs. U. Hawaii Research Corp., Aloha council Boy Scouts Am., Inst. for Religion and Social Change. Served as capt. AUS, 1942-46, editor, officer-in-charge, mid- Pacific edit. Stars and Stripes. Decorated Star Solidarity (Italy). Recipient award Overseas Press Club, 1961; Headliners award, 1962. Mem. Soc. Nieman Fellows, Honolulu Symphony Soc. (dir.), Pacific and Asian Affairs Council (dir.), Am. Soc. Newspaper Editors (dir.), Nat. Conf. Editorial Writers, Friends of East-West Center, Sigma Delta Chi. Clubs: Pacific; Waialae Country. Home: 4437 Kolohala St Honolulu HI 96816 Office: care Honolulu Advertiser Advertiser Sq Honolulu HI 96802

CHAPLIN, HUGH, Jr., physician, educator; b. N.Y.C., Feb. 4, 1923; A.B., Princeton, 1943; M.D., Columbia, 1947; m. Alice Dougherty, June 16, 1945; 4 children. Intern, Mass. Gen. Hosp., Boton, 1947-48, resident, 1948-50; fellow in hematology Brit. Postgrad. Med. Sch.,

London, 1951-53; physician in charge Clin. Center Blood Bank, NIH, Bethesda, Md., 1953-55; Commonwealth Fund fellow Wright Fleming Inst. Microbiology, London, 1962-63; instr. in medicine Washington U. Sch. Medicine, St. Louis, 1955-56, asst. prof. medicine and preventive medicine, 1956-62, asso. dean, chmn. admissions com., 1957-62, asso. prof., 1963-65, prof., 1965, William B. Kountz Prof. preventive medicine, 1965—; dir. IWJ Inst. of Rehab., St. Louis, 1964—. Mem. Am. Standards Com. for Blood Transfusion Equipment; mem. subcom. on transfusion problems NRC, 1959-62, mem. com. on blood and transfusion problems, 1963—; chmn. ad hoc blood program research com. A.R.C., 1967—. Served with USNR, 1942-45. Diplomate Am. Bd. Internal Medicine, Nat. Bd. Med. Exam. Mem. Am. Fedn. for Clin. Research, Central Soc. for Clin. Research, Am. Soc. for Clin. Investigation, Am. Soc. Hematology, Internat. Soc. Hematology, Brit. Med. Research Soc., Brit. Royal Soc. Medicine, Am. Assn. Blood Banks (sci. program com. 1959-60), Phi Beta Kappa, Alpha Omega Alpha, Sigma Xi. Asso. editor Transfusion, 1960-61; contbg. editor Vox Sanguinis, 1960-65. Office: Washington U Sch Medicine St Louis MO 63103

CHAPLIN, JAMES PATRICK, educator; b. Santa Monica, Cal., Jan. 6, 1919; s. William and Mary (Mahoney) C.; B.A., U. N.M., 1940, M.S., 1941; Ph.D., U. Ill., 1947; m. Madeline Wright, Oct. 23, 1940; 1 son, Paul W. Teaching fellow U. N.M., 1940-41; research asst. U. Ill., 1941-42; asst. prof. psychology U. Vt., 1947-50, asso. prof., 1950-54, prof. psychology, 1956-70, vis. prof. psychology, 1970—; prof. psychology, chmn. dept. St. Michael's Coll., Winooski, Vt., 1970—. Served with USAAF, 1942-45. Mem. Sigma Xi. Author: Rumor, Fear and the Madness of Crowds, 1959; The Unconscious, 1960; (with T. S. Krawiec) Systems and Theories of Psychology, 1960, rev. edit., 1968; Dictionary of Psychology, 1968. Home: 1741 Spear St Burlington VT 05401

CHAPLIN, MAXWELL, fgn. service officer; b. Tsinan, China, Sept. 28, 1926 (parents Am. citizens); s. Maxwell and Edith (Kingman) C.; A.B., U. Cal. at Berkeley, 1948; postgrad. U. Mich., 1957; m. Cynthia Klein, July 2, 1949. Joined U.S. Fgn. Service 1951, vice consul, Kobe, Japan, 1952-54; 3d sec., Caracas, Venezuela, 1954-56; 2d sec., Bogota, Colombia, 1957-59; 1st sec., La Puz, Bolivia, 1964-66; assigned State Dept., 1959-64, 66—, country dir. for Mexico, 1968; assigned Nat. War Coll., 1969-70; counselor, Quito, Ecuador, 1970—. Served with Am. Field Service, 1944-45. Home: 3 Buena Vista Rd Carmel Valley, CA . 93924. Office: care Dept of State Washington DC 20520

CHAPMAN, ALAN JESSE, educator; b. Los Angeles, June 22, 1925; s. Wallace Webster and Isabel (Smith) C.; B.S. in Mech. Engring., Rice U., 1945; M.S., U. Colo., 1949; Ph.D., U. Ill., 1953; m. Marjorie Bray, June 8, 1950; children—Alan Jesse, Katherine Lynn. Faculty Rice U., 1946—, prof. mech. engring., 1954-69, chmn. dept. mech. and aerospace engring. and materials sci., 1954-69, v.p., 1969-70; cons. to Manned Spacecraft Center, NASA, Houston, 1961—. Pres. S.W. Athletic Conf., 1965-67; mem. council Nat. Collegiate Athletic Assn., 1968—. Served with USNR, 1942-45. Registered profl. engr., Tex. Asso. fellow Am. Inst. Aero. and Astronautics; mem. Am. Soc. M.E., Am. Soc. Engring. Edn., Sigma Xi, Tau Beta Pi. Author: Heat Transfer, 2d edit., 1967; Introductory Gas Dynamics, 1970. Home: 10031 Doliver Houston TX 77042

CHAPMAN, ALBERT L., physician; b. Port Richmond, N.Y., Nov. 28, 1905; s. Newton David and Lucy (Lyon) C.; A.B., Cornell U., 1927; M.D., L.I. Coll. Medicine, 1937; M.P.H., Johns Hopkins, 1941; D.Sc., New Eng. Coll. Pharmacy, 1960; m. Margaret Pillo, Nov. 22, 1945; children—Lyon J., Lynne M. Interne U.S. Marine Hosp., Stapleton, N.Y., 1938-39; staff USPHS, 1939—; regional med. dir., N.J. Dept. Health, Wrightstown, N.J., 1941-43; dir. div. communicable disease control Del. Health Dept., 1943; dep. state health commr. State of W.Va., Charleston, 1944-45; health commr., Norfolk, Va., 1946; asst. chief, states relations div. USPHS, 1948, chief, div. chronic diseases, 1949-51, regional med. dir. Region III, 1951- 54, Region I and II, N.Y.C., 1954-56; chief div. spl. health services, 1956-61, chief div. accident prevention, 1961- 62; asst. surgeon gen., rank rear adm. lower half, 1957-62; dir. Bur. Planning, Evaluation and Research, Dept. Health, Harrisburg, 1962—. Dir. Pa. Health Research Inst., Inc., 1970—. Tech. adviser Commn. Chronic Illness, 1950-51; chmn. com. on research, home safety conf. Nat. Safety Council, 1949-50, bd. dirs., 1957-62; mem. adv. council President's Com. Traffic Safety; mem. med. adv. com. Presidents Com. on Employ Physically Handicapped, 1956-62; bd. dirs. Pa. Health Council, 1970—. Served as capt., M.C., U.S. Army Res., 1937-39. Diplomate Am. Bd. Preventive Medicine and Pub. Health, Nat. Bd. Med. Examiners. Fellow Am. Pub. Health Assn. (chmn. com. on accident prevention 1956-61). Royal Sanity Inst. (Eng.); mem. A.M.A., Gerontology Soc., Assn. Mil. Surgeons, Royal San. Soc. (Eng.), Am. Med. writers Assn., Assn. Am. Pub. Health Physicians (charter), Automotive Physicians Assn. (hon.), Assn. State and Territorial Dirs. and Coordinators of Research (pres. 1963-65, v.p. 1965-66), Nu Sigma Nu. Mem. editorial bd. Pub. Health Reports, 1959- 62. Contbr. articles in med. jours. Home: 20 W Lawn Circle Wormleysburg PA 17043

CHAPMAN, ALFRED KING, educator; b. Portland, Me., Apr. 29, 1904; s. Wilford Gore and Tinnie A. (Drummond) C.; A.B., Colby Coll., 1925, L.H.D., 1968; M.A., Harvard, 1928; postgrad. Columbia, 1939-40. Clk., Am. Can Co., 1925-27; faculty Colby Coll., 1928-69, prof. English, 1952- 69, chmn. dept., 1953-66, Roberts prof. English, 1959-69, Roberts prof. English lit. emeritus, 1969—. Served with USAAF, 1942-45. Mem. Modern Lang. Assn., Am. Assn. U. Profs., Keats- Shelley Assn., Phi Beta Kappa, Delta Kappa Epsilon. Home: 33 Averill Terrace Waterville ME 04901

CHAPMAN, ALGER BALDWIN, lawyer; b. Hempstead, L.I., N.Y., Nov. 2, 1904; s. Hannibal Hamlin and Lotta Lulia (Proctor) C.; A.B., Williams Coll., Williamstown, Mass., 1926; LL.B., Columbia, 1930; LL.D., Adelphi College, 1957, St. Lawrence U., 1964; D.Pub. Service, Brigham Young U., 1968; m. Elizabeth Ives, Aug. 20, 1929 (dec.); children—Alger, Carol, William, Hilda; m. 2d, Catherine C. Hubbard. Admitted to D.C. bar, 1932, N.Y. bar, 1940; atty. legislative counsels' office U.S. Senate, 1930-32; mem. firm Donovan Bond & Alvord, Washington, 1932-34; partner firm Alvord & Alvord, 1934, partner in charge N.Y.C. office, 1939-45; commr. taxation and finance, pres. State Tax Commn., N.Y., 1945-48 (except 6 mos. in 1946); with Chapman & Bryson, and successor firm Chapman, Walsh and O'Connell, N.Y.C., 1948-59, partner successor firm Hawkins, Delafield & Wood, 1959-64; chmn. bd., chief exec. officer, pres. Beech-Nut Life Savers, Inc. (name changed to Squibb Beech-Nut, Inc. 1968) 1958-68, chmn. bd., 1968—; dir. Am. Broadcasting Cos., Inc., Adams Express Co., Bank N.Y.; trustee Bowery Savs. Bank. Life mem. bd. trustees Adelphi Coll., 1949—, chmn. bd., 1949-57; exec. dir., trustee Edward John Noble Foundation; trustee, treas., pres., chmn. finance com. YMCA Greater N.Y.; chmn. Tax Found.; past pres. Nat. Assn. Tax Adminstrn.; past trustee N.Y. State U. 1946, 50, Campaign mgr. Republican candidate for gov., N.Y., 1946, 50; state campaign mgr. Rep. candidate for pres., 1948, 52, 56; treas. N.Y. Rep. State Com., 1950-58. Mem. Am., N.Y. State bar assns., Sigma Phi. Clubs: Metropolitan, Wall Street, Cloud (N.Y.C.); Fort Orange (Albany, N.Y.); Columbia Country, Nat. Press (Washington); Blind Brook (Port Chester, N.Y.); Siwanoy Country (Bronxville, N.Y.); Nat. Links Am. (Southampton, N.Y.); Mid-Ocean (Bermuda). Home: 900 Palmer Rd Bronxville NY 10708 Office: care Squibb Beech-Nut 460 Park Av New York City NY 10016

CHAPMAN, ALGER BALDWIN, Jr., bus. exec.; b. Portland, Me., Sept. 28, 1931; s. Alger Balwin and Elizabeth (Ives) C.; A.B., Williams Coll., 1953; LL.B., Columbia, 1957; m. June S. Danziger, Mar. 1, 1963; children—Alger Baldwin III, Samuel, Andrew, Henry. Admitted to N.Y. bar, 1957; atty. Securities and Exchange Commn., 1957-58, legal asst. to commr., 1958-59; mem. staff N.Y. Stock Exchange, 1959-67, v.p. civic and govtl. affairs, 1963-65, v.p legal, civic and govtl. affairs, 1965-67; v.p. Shearson, Hammill & Co., 1967-68, exec. v.p., 1968-70, pres., chief adminstrv. officer, 1970—, also dir. Treas. Police Athletic League, N.Y.C. Mem. Am., N.Y. State bar assns., Investment Bankers Assn. (v.p., mem. bd., mem. exec. com.), Assn. Stock Exchange Firms (mem. bd.), Nat. Tax Assn., Sigma Phi, Phi Delta Phi. Home: 525 E 86th St New York City NY 10028 Office: 14 Wall St New York City NY 10005

CHAPMAN, ALVAH HERMAN, Jr., newspaper exec.; b. Columbus, Ga., Mar. 21, 1921; s. Alvah Hermann and Wyline (Page) C.; B.S., The Citadel, 1942; m. Betty Bateman, Mar. 22, 1943; children—Dale Page (Mrs. Dennis Webb), Chris Ann. Bus. mgr. Columbus Ledger, 1945-53; v.p., gen. mgr. St. Petersburg (Fla.) Times, 1955-57; pres., pub. Morning News and Evening Press, Savannah, Ga., 1957- 60; pres. Savannah News-Press, Inc., 1957-60; exec. Knight Newspapers, Miami, Fla., 1960—, exec. com., 1960—, exec. v.p. Knight Newspapers, Inc., 1967—; v.p., gen. mgr. The Miami Herald, 1962-70, pres., 1970—; lectr. Am. Press Insts., Columbia. Served from 2d lt. to maj. USAAF, World War II. Decorated D.F.C. with 2 oak leaf clusters, Air medal with 5 clusters (U.S.); Croix de Guerre; named one of five outstanding young men in Ga., 1951, Outstanding Young Man, Columbus Jr. C. of C., 1952, Dade County's Outstanding Citizen of 1968-69. Mem. Am., So. newspapers pubs. assns. Methodist. Kiwanian. Home: 4255 Lake Rd Miami FL 33137 Office: Miami Herald Miami FL 33101

CHAPMAN, ARTHUR BARCLAY, geneticist, educator; b. Windermere, Eng., Oct. 25, 1908; s. William Daniel and Nora (Moss) C.; came to U.S., 1925, naturalized, 1936; B.S., Wash. State U., 1930; M.S., Ia. State U., 1931; Ph.D., U. Wis., 1935; m. Winifred Mary Rollin, Sept. 1, 1934; children—Barbara Nora (Mrs. William Joseph Vaughan), Winifred Nell (Mrs. Douglas James Baker), Mary Jane. Teaching fellow Ia. State U., 1930-31; research asst. U. Wis., Madison, 1931-36, instr., 1937-39. asst. prof., 1939-46, asso. prof., 1946-47, prof. genetics, 1947—; NRC fellow Ia. State U. and U. Chgo., 1936-37; Fulbright Research fellow and Guggenheim fellow, New Zealand, 1966-67. Fellow A.A.A.S. (mem. council 1967-68); mem. Am. Soc. Animal Sci. (pres. 1964-65, recipient Animal Breeding and Research award 1969), Am. Dairy Sci. Assn., Genetic Soc. Am., Brit., N.Z. socs. animal prodn., Biometric Soc., Am. Inst. Biol. Scis., Genetics Assn., Sigma Xi. Alpha Zeta, Gamma Alpha, Gamma Sigma Delta, Phi Sigma. Asso. editor Jour. Animal Sci., 1958-60, editor, 1960-63. Contbr. research articles to biol. jours. Home: 1117 Risser St Madison WI 53705

CHAPMAN, BERTRAM DOUGLAS, pub. co. exec.; b. Ashkum, Ill., Feb. 16, 1914; s. Mark M. and Amanda (Goetzelman) C.; student Art Inst. Chgo., 1933-34, Northwestern U., evenings 1934-38, Columbia, 1944-45; m. Helen Marie Bushell, Nov. 25, 1936 (dec.); children—Judith Jean (Mrs. Joseph J. Kane), Douglas Moore, Martha Jane. Sports writer, editor Sheldon (Ill.) Jour., 1934-35; copywriter Meyer-Both Advt., Chgo., 1935-36; prodn. asst. Time and Life mags., 1936- 41; prodn. supr. Army-Navy publs. prepared by Time, Inc., 1941-44; prodn. operations mgr. Time, 1944-63, also Sports Illus. mag., 1962-63; v.p., prodn. dir. Newsweek mag., 1963—, lectr. in field, 1948—. Active local fund raising drives, Community Fund, Boy Scouts Am., Cardinal's Edn. Campaign; entertainment chmn. Arthur Manor Assn., Scarsdale, N.Y., 1945, Wilmot Manor Assn., Scarsdale, 1946—. Mem. Assn. Publ. Prodn. Mgrs. (pres. 1951-52). Clubs: Bonnie Briar Country (sec. bd. govs., chmn. entertainment com. 1966-67) (Larchmont, N.Y.); Rockefeller Center, Western Univ. (N.Y.C.). Author articles in field. Home: 32 Homestead Av Scarsdale NY 10583 Office: 444 Madison Av New York City NY 10022

CHAPMAN, BILL VAN, wholesale grocery co. exec.; b. Oklahoma City, Aug. 1, 1924; s. James L. and Alice (Hurt) C.; B.C. in Accounting, Oklahoma City U., 1949; m. Leita E. Cornett, Sept. 5, 1942; children—Shelly Lynn, Bill Van. With Fleming Co., Inc., Topeka, 1949—, controller, asst. sec., 1965—, officer dir. subsidiary corps. Served with USNR, 1942-45. Club: Shawnee Country (pres. 1967, bd. dirs. 1966-69) (Topeka).‡

CHAPMAN, CARLETON BURKE, physician, educator; b. Sycamore, Ala., June 11, 1915; s. John G. and Mary (Anderson) C.; A.B., Davidson Coll., 1936; B.A. in Physiology (Rhodes scholar), Oxford (Eng.) U., 1939, M.A., 1950; M.D., Harvard, 1941, M.P.H., 1944; M.A. (hon.), Dartmouth, 1968; LL.D., Davidson Coll., 1968; m. Ruth Horine, Aug. 30, 1940; children—Nancy C. (Mrs. Jack A. Collins), John G., Mary A. (Mrs. Robert E. Shoun). Intern 2d and 4th med. services Boston City Hosp., 1941-42, asst. resident, then resident, 1942-44; intern Mallory Inst. Pathology, Boston City Hosp., 1946; asst. medicine Harvard Med. Sch., 1946; faculty U. Minn., 1947-53, asso. prof. medicine, 1950-53; prof. medicine U. Tex. Southwestern Med. Sch., 1953-66; dean Dartmouth Med. Sch., Hanover, N.H., 1966—; spl. research cardiovascular physiology, human exericse; mem. staff Parkland Hosp., Dallas, 1953—; cons. VA and USAF hosps. Mem. com. 50, So. Methodist U., 1963; adviser Bishop Coll., 1962-63. Served with USPHS, 1944-46. Rockefeller fellow, 1944-46; recipient Career Professorship award USPHS, 1963; Guggenheim fellow, 1964. Diplomate Am. Bd. Internal Medicine. Fellow A.C.P., Am. Coll. Cardiology, Am. Heart Assn. (pres. 1964-65); mem. Am., Tex. med. assns., Dallas County Med. Soc., A.A.A.S., Soc. Exptl. Biology and Medicine, Central, So. socs. clin. research, Am. Fedn. Clin. Research, Am. Soc. Clin. Investigation, Assn. Am. Physicians, Am. Physiol. Soc., Am. Acad. Arts and Scis. Author articles in field. Editor Am. Oxonian, 1963-64; editorial bd. Archives Internal Medicine, 1963-68. Home: Thetford VT 05074 Office: Dean's Office Dartmouth Med Sch Hanover NH 03755

CHAPMAN, CECIL WHEELER, former govt. ofcl.; b. Garfield, Ga., Sept. 4, 1911; s. John Albert and Mettie (Chapman) C.; B.S. in Agrl. Engring., U. Ga., 1932; m. Claudia Wheeler, June 11, 1938; children—Suzanne (Mrs. John H. Jackson, Jr.), Cecilia, Claudia, Linda. With Dept. Agr., 1933-71, with Soil Conservation Service, 1934-71, conservationist for Ga., 1954-71, ret. Served to lt. col. AUS, 1941- 46; ETO. Decorated Silver Star, Bronze Star, Purple Heart; recipient Superior Service award Dept. Agr., 1958; named Man of Yr. in Service to Ga. Agr., Progressive Farmer, 1968. Fellow Soil Conservation Soc. Am. (pres. 1967); mem. Am. Soc. A.E. Baptist. Rotarian, Elk, Mason. Home: 175 University Dr Athens GA 30601

CHAPMAN, CEIL, fashion designer; b. N.Y.C., Feb. 19, 1912; d. William and Elizabeth (Doyle) Mitchell; student parochial schs.; m. Samuel Chapman (div.); 1 son, Peter; m. 2d, Thomas G. Rogers, Dec. 1, 1951. Vice pres. Samuel Chapman Inc.; pres. Ceil Chapman Enterprises. Received Mademoiselle merit award, 1946; Am. Fashion Critics' award, 1946; named one of ten best designers Fashion Trade; recipient Foley's Golden Year Designer award; Wilshire Award, May Col; awards for fashion design John Wanamaker, Strawbridge & Clothier, Phila. Fashion Group, others. Home: 230 E 73d St New York City NY 10021 Office: 530 7th Av New York City NY 10018

CHAPMAN, CHARLES EDWARD, coll. pres.; b. Artesia, Cal., Dec. 19, 1915; s. Frederick L. and Georgina (Needham) G.; B.S. magna cum laude, Rocky Mountain Coll., 1947; M.A., State U. Ia., 1949; Ed.D., U. Cal., 1959; m. Naoma Clydine Ledbetter, Jan. 1, 1944; children—Diana (Mrs. Robert L. Smith), David Clyde, Cynthia Denise. Instr. polit. sci. and history Rocky Mountain Coll., 1947; adminstrv. dean Black Hawk Coll., Moline, Ill., 1948-52; dean student personnel services Diablo Valley Coll., Concord, Cal., 1952-60; pres. Barstow (Cal.) Coll., 1960-62; pres. Cuyahoga Community Coll., Cleve., 1962—. Cons., examiner North Central Assn. Colls. and Secondary Schs.; cons. Acad. Ednl. Devel.; cons. in adminstrn. and curriculum devel. to colls. Served from pvt. to maj., USAAF, 1941-46. Recipient Ohio gov.'s edn. award, 1969. Mem. Am. Assn. Jr. Colls. (pres., past dir.), Phi Delta Kappa. Mem. Disciples of Christ. Mason. Contbr. articles profl. jours. Home: 3601 Eldorado Dr Rocky River OH 44116 Office: 2123 E 9th St Cleveland OH 44115

CHAPMAN, CHARLES HICKERSON, Jr., mem. Republican Nat. Com., former constrn. co. exec.; b. Dothan, Ala., Apr. 17, 1920; s. Charles Hickerson and Florrie (Malone) C.; B.S., Washington and Lee U., 1941; m. Martha Farmer, Dec. 30, 1943; children—Charles Hickerson III, Davis F., Florrie Lou. Pres. Chapman Constrn. Co., Dothan, 1946—; chmn. bd. Malone Industries, Inc.; dir. First Nat. Bank Dothan, Dothan Oil Mill Co. Chmn. Houston County Heart Fund, 1965. Mem. Rep. Nat. Committeeman for Ala., 1964—. Served to lt. USNR, 1942-45. Mem. Dothan C. of C. (dir., past chmn. indsl. com., govtl. affairs com.). Home: Enterprise Hwy Dotham AL 36301 Office: PO Drawer 220 Dothan AL 36301

CHAPMAN, CHARLES JARVIS, former metals co. exec.; b. Brookline, Mass., Feb. 22, 1908; s. Charles Jarvis and Marguerite (Rumery) C.; B.A., Dartmouth, 1933; m. Eleanor Waterman, Aug. 28, 1937; children—Charles Jarvis IV, Lawrence Waterman, Sarah Rumery (Mrs. Henry L Strickland); m. 2d, Dorothy Williams, Feb. 23; children—Charles Joseph, Marguerite Elizabeth. With IBM Corp., 1933-36; with Union Carbide Corp., became exec. vice pres. mining and metals div., 1966—. Chmn. Darien Gen. Sch. Planning and Bldg. Com., 1958—. Mem. Am. Iron and Steel Inst., Assn. Iron and Steel Engrs., Am. Mgmt. Assn., Beta Theta Phi. Clubs: Executive (N.Y.C.); Dartmouth Alumni of Darien and Norwalk (pres. 1966—). Home: 733 Silvermine Rd New Canaan CT 06840

CHAPMAN, CHRISTIAN ADDISON, fgn. service officer; b. Paris, France, Sept. 19, 1921; s. Percy Addison and Marthe Aline (Simon) C.; grad. Phillips Exeter Acad., 1939; A.B., Princeton, 1948; postgrad. Sorbonne, 1946-47, U. Cal. at Berkeley, 1948; m. Anita Ioas, Apr. 2, 1960; children—Catherine, Hillary, Jennifer. Fgn. service officer, 1950—; vice consul, Casablanca, Morocco, 1951-53; 3d sec., Beirut, Lebanon, 1953; 2d sec., Tehran, Iran, 1953-56; 2d sec., acting, chief polit. sect., Saigon, Viet Nam, 1957; 2d sec., chief polit. sect., Vientiane, Laos, 1958-59; officer-in-charge Laos affairs, Dept. State, 1959-61; mem. Viet Nam Task Force, chief Far East placement br. personnel, 1962-63; assigned to Nat. War Coll., 1963-64; counselor, dep. U.S. rep. High Authority European Coal and Steel Community, 1965- 66, chargé d'affaires Am. Embassy, Luxembourg; dep. asst. sec. general political affairs NATO, Paris, France, 1966-67, Brussels, Belgium, 1968; now assigned State Dept. Decorated Legion of Honor, Mil. Medal, Croix de Guerre, Medal of the Resistance, (France); Meritorious Service award Dept. of State, 1960. Mem. Am. Fgn. Service Assn. Club: University (N.Y.C). Home: 1527 33d St NW Washington DC Office: care State Dept Washington DC 20525

CHAPMAN, CONRAD, conservationist; b. N.Y.C., Dec. 24, 1896; s. John Jay and Minna (Timmins) C.; grad. St. Paul's Sch., 1915; A.B. cum laude, Harvard, 1919; M.A., Oxford U., 1923; Doc.-es-L., U. Sorbonne, 1926; certificate, Mass. Inst. Tech., 1942; m. Judith Daphne Kemp, Aug. 25, 1937; children—Mary Audrey (Mrs. James M. Forbes), Geoffrey Williams, John Francis Hewitt. Head Chateau Neuvic Sch., also Chateau Laroche Sch., 1927-30; mem. Joint Samaria Palestine Archaeol. Expdn., 1931; head history dept. Ashburnham Sch., 1940-42; mem. bd. govs. Nature Conservancy, Washington, 1950-66; v.p. Mass. Forest and Park Assn., Boston, 1966—. Chmn. Mass. Conservation Council, 1967-69; pres. Nat. Econ. Council, N.Y.C., 1970; mem. com. Latin-Am. Natural Areas, Washington, 1968—; hon. pres. Amigos de la Naturaleza (Madrid). Trustee French Library, Boston, 1967—. Served to lt. (s.g.) USN, 1917-20. Recipient Grand Cordon d'Art et Esthetique, Brussels, 1968. Mem. Am. Geog. Soc., Mediaeval Acad., Trustees of Reservations (Mass.), Am. Church History Soc. Club: Royal Societies (London). Author: Michel Paleólogue, 1926; also articles. Home: 17 W Cedar St Boston MA 02108

CHAPMAN, DAVE, indsl. designer; b. Gilman, Ill., Jan. 30, 1909; s. Arms Spaford and Minnie (Cross) C.; B.S., Armour Inst. Tech., 1932; m. Eileen Ryan, June 24, 1939; children—Nancy Eileen, Carol Elizabeth. Planning, design Century of Progress, Chicago, 1932-33; product design div. Montgomery Ward & Co., 1933-35; sr. partner, Dave Chapman, Indsl. Design, 1935-58; pres. Design Research, Inc., 1955-; pres. Dave Chapman, Inc., indsl. design, 1958—. Recipient Design Award medal Indsl. Designers Inst., 1954, 60. Benjamin Franklin fellow, Royal Soc. Arts, London. Fellow Internat. Inst. Arts and Letters, Soc. Indsl. Designers (dir., past pres.), S.A.R. Clubs: Tavern (dir.); N.Y. Yacht; Chicago Yacht. Home: 3240 Lake Shore Dr Chicago IL 60657 Office: 35 E Wacker Dr Chicago IL 60601

CHAPMAN, DONALD D., lawyer, ret. navy officer; b. Thalia, Tex., Dec. 9, 1917; s. William Gardner and Bertha (Brown) C.; B.A., Tex. Tech. Coll., 1939; LL.B., U. Tex., 1942; grad. Army Judge Adv. Sch., 1959; m. Norene Vernetta Elam, Dec. 30, 1942; children—Ronald Warren, Randall Douglas. Admitted to Tex., Va. bars; commd. ensign U.S. Navy, 1942, advanced through grades to rear adm., 1968; gen. line duty, 1942-45; comdg. officer U.S.S. PC 792, 1945- 46; asst. dist. legal officer Hdqrs. 8th Naval Dist., New Orleans, 1946- 49; staff legal officer to comdr. Amphibious Force, U.S. Pacific Fleet, 1949-51; atty. Mil. Justice div. Office Judge Adv. Gen., 1951-55; staff legal officer to comdr. in chief U.S. Atlantic Fleet, 1955-58; dir. adminstrv. law div. Office Judge Adv. Gen., 1959-63; dist. legal officer Hdqrs. 14th Naval Dist., Pearl Harbor, Hawaii, 1963-66; chmn. bd. rev. Office Judge Adv. Gen., 1966-67, dir. adminstrv. law div., 1967-68, dep. judge adv. gen., 1968—. Decorated Legion of Merit and numerous service and area ribbons; recipient Distinguished Alumnus award Tex. Tech. Coll., 1968. Mem. Tex State Bar, Judge Advocates Assn., Am., Fed., Inter-Am. bar assns. Home: 3400 N Piedmont St Arlington VA 22207 Office: 2060 14th St N Arlington VA 22201

CHAPMAN, DWIGHT WESTLEY, Jr., psychologist; b. South Bend, Ind., June 4, 1905; s. Dwight Westley and Carrie Ethel (Carpenter) C.; A.B., Harvard, 1927, Ph.D., 1930; Sheldon Traveling fellow U. Leipzig, 1927-28; m. Harriet Nye, Sept. 27, 1930; m. 2d, Elisabeth Halsted Bowie, June 30, 1942; children—David Dwight, Judith Carpenter, Michael Beverley. Instr., tutor psychology Harvard,

1930-36; psychologist statistician, psychopathic clinic Recorder's Ct., Detroit, 1936-37; instr. psychology Columbia, 1937-38; tchr. psychology Bennington (Vt.) Coll., 1938-42; study dir., div. program surveys Dept. Agr., 1942, research dir., 1943-44; personnel assessment staff OSS, 1945; dir. nat. surveys div. Office Civilian Requirements, 1946; asst. research dir. Washington Post, 1946-47; asso. Washington Sch. Psychiatry, 1947-51; prof. psychology, chmn. dept., Vassar Coll., 1952-68, prof. emeritus psychology, 1968—; vis. prof. psychology U. Mich., 1951-52; panel dir. com. on human resources Research and Devel. Bd., 1947- 48, dep. exec. dir., 1949, exec. dir., 1950-52; co-chmn. com. on Disaster Studies, NRC, 1955-57. Mem. Am. Psychol. Assn., Soc. Psychol. Study Social Issues. Phi Beta Kappa. Author: (with G.W. Baker) Man and Society in Disaster, 1962. Home: 100 College Av Poughkeepsie NY 12603

CHAPMAN, EDMUND HAUPT, educator; b. West Haven, Conn., Aug. 14, 1906; s. Herman Haupt and Alberta (Pineo) C.; Ph.B., Yale, 1928, A.M., 1930; Ph.D., N.Y.U., 1950; m. Affa Gray, Sept. 15, 1930; children—Frederic Kimball, Greatl. Instr. U. Colo., 1930-35, asst. prof., 1935-37; asst. prof. Goucher Coll., 1939- 42; asso. prof. Case Western Res. U., 1946-56, prof., 1956—, chmn. dept. art and architecture, 1954—. Served as lt. comdr. USNR, 1942-46. Mem. Am. Assn. U. Profs., Coll. Art Assn., Soc. Archtl. Historians (past sec., dir.), Am. Soc. Aesthetics. Author: Cleveland: Village to Metropolis, 1964. Home: 11406 Fowlers Mill Rd Chardon OH 44024 Office: Case Western Res U Cleveland OH 44106

CHAPMAN, EDWARD ARNOLD, former ednl. adminstr.; b. Shelbyville, Ind., Mar. 24, 1906; s. Ira Edward and Bura Ann (Waltz) C.; B.S. in Mech. Engring., U. Mich., 1930, B.L.S., 1934, M. Library Sci., 1936; m. Mary Alice More, Sept. 10, 1930; 1 son, Edward Arnold. Asst. librarian Ind. State Library, 1936-38; dir. library assistance program WPA, 1938-42; asst. dir. div. program and review War Pub. Services, 1942; exec. asst. to asst. commr. Fed. Works Agy., 1942-43; chief copyright adminstrn. sect. U.S. Office Alien Property Custodian, 1943-45; asst. mgr. J.W. Edwards Pub., Ann Arbor, 1945-46, also sec. bd. dirs. Edwards Bros., Inc.; librarian Rensselaer Poly. Inst., Troy, N.Y., 1946-70, asst. to provost, 1970-71. Chmn. individual gifts div. United Community Services, 1967. Bd. dirs. Troy (N.Y.) Boys' Club, 1956-71, pres., 1960-66; bd. dirs. Troy Pub. Library, 1968-71. Mem. Am. Library Assn., Am. Soc. Engring. Edn., N.Y. Library Assn., Assn. Coll. and Research Librarians, Am. Assn. U. Profs., Spl. Libraries Assn., Pi Delta Epsilon, Beta Theta Pi. Author: Library Systems Analysis Guidelines, 1970. Contbr. articles profl. jours. Compiler and co-author procedural manuals, 1940-44. Home: 2200 Gulf Shore Blvd N Apt R-1 Naples FL 33940

CHAPMAN, ETHAN ALLEN, ret. army officer; b. Houston, May 24, 1910; s. Ray Montcalm and Lucy Adele (Swetland) C.; B.S., U.S. Mil. Acad., 1933; m. Svava Louise Magnuson, Aug. 6, 1955; children—Richard Allen (previous marriage), Robert Michael. Commd. 2d lt. U.S. Army, 1933, advanced through grades to maj. gen., 1961; assigned tactical arty. units C.A. and Anti-aircraft, Panama and Cal., Tex. and P.R., 1933-42; Anti-Aircraft Sch., 1942-44, 1st Air Force, 1944, Hdqrs. MTO, Italy, 1945-47, gen. staff Hdgrs. Dept. Army, 1948-50, Armed Forces Staff Coll., 1950, SHAPE, 1951-53; comdr. 17th Arty. Group, Balt., 1954-55; with gen. staff Hdqrs. Dept. Army, 1955-56; assigned Hdqrs. 8th Army, also comdg. gen. 7th Div. Arty., Korea, 1957- 58; assigned Hdqrs. N.Am., Air Def. Command, 1959-61, XII Army Corps, 1961-63; chief staff U.S. Forces, Japan, 1964-66; comdr. gen. Western Norad region, Cal., 1966-67; chief staff Hdgrs., NORAD, Colorado Springs, Colo., 1967-69; retired, 1969. Decorated D.S.M., Legion of Merit; Italian war cross; Mil. Order Ulchi (Korea); 2d Order Sacred Treasure (Japan). Mem. Mil. Order World Wars (past comdr. Atlanta chpt.), Res. Officers Assn., Assn. U.S. Army. Rotarian. Home: 32 Penrose Blvd Colorado Springs, CO . 80906

CHAPMAN, G. ARNOLD, educator; b. Fresno, Cal., June 26, 1917; s. George Arnold and Marie (Homsy) C.; A.B., Fresno State Coll., 1939; M.A., U. Wis., 1941; Ph.D., U.Wis., 1946; m. Marguerite M. Nickerson, Aug. 7, 1957; children—John, Anna, Mary. Instr. Romance langs. Oberlin Coll., 1945-46; from instr. to prof. Spanish, U. Cal., at Berkeley, 1946—. Mem. Instituto Internacional de Literatura Iberoamericana, Am. Assn. Tchrs. of Spanish and Portuguese, Am. Comparative Literature Assn., Philol. Assn. Pacific Coast. Author: The Spanish American Reception of United States Fiction, 1920-1940, 1966. Contbr. articles profl. jours. Home: 231 Yale Av Kensington CA 94708 Office: Univ California Berkeley CA 94720

CHAPMAN, GILBERT W., bus. exec.; b. Woodmere, L.I., May 24, 1902; s. Henry Otis and Harriet M. (Murphey) C.; B.S., Sheffield Sci. Sch., Yale, 1924; LL.D., Roanoke Coll., 1959; m. Katherine Bright, Mar. 21, 1925 (dec. 1949); children—Harriet W. (Mrs. H. Worthington Kalt), Gilbert W.; m. 2d, Elizabeth Fuller (former Mrs. Charles B. Goodspeed), Oct. 28, 1950. With engring. staff of Am. Water Works & Electric Co. 1924-27, asst. treas., 1927- 35, treas., 1935-43, v.p., 1943-47, pres., 1947-48; v.p. charge finance Yale & Towne Mfg. Co., 1948-49, pres., 1949-60, ret., 1960; now pres., dir. Sutton Place South Corp., Pinnacle Press, Inc.; dir. DeLaval Separator Co. Bd. dirs. Lincoln Center Performing Arts; vice chmn., trustee N.Y. Pub. Library; mem. Nat. Book Com., Inc. Clubs: Racquet and Tennis (N.Y.C.); St. Anthony's (Yale U.). Home: One Sutton Pl S New York City NY 10022 Office: 125 E 57th St New York City NY 10022

CHAPMAN, GORDON WARNER, labor union ofcl.; b. Tomah, Wis., Sept. 5, 1907; s. Allie H. and Dora (Parshall) C.; B.S., U. Wis., 1931; m. Ferne Everhardt, June 28, 1935; children—Bruce, Terry, Cherie. Propr. advt. firm, 1932-34; asst. dir. Surplus Commodity Distbn., Wis., 1934-36; spl. asst. to sec. state, 1961- 62; sec.-treas. Am. Fedn. State, County and Municipal Employees, 1937- 45, 48-61, exec. asst. to pres., 1945-48, became internat. sec.-treas., 1963. Mem. Delta Sigma Pi. Conglist. Home: 10937 Amherst Av Wheaton MD 20802 Office: 1155 15th St NW Washington DC 20005

CHAPMAN, HARMON MARBOLD, former, educator; b. Richmond, Mo., Mar. 9, 1901; s. Frank Thomas and Pauline (Miller) C.; A.B., Ohio State U., 1922; A.M., U. Ore., 1926; postgrad. U. Bern (Switzerland), 1929, U. Munich, 1930, U. Freiburg, 1930-31; Ph.D., Harvard, 1933; m. Louise MacDonald, June 24, 1932; children—Pauline, Mary, Harmon Marbold. Asst., Harvard, 1931-33; asst. prof. philosophy N.Y. U., 1934-50, asso. prof., 1950-55, prof., chmn. dept., 1955-66, prof. emeritus, 1970—, dir. gen. studies Coll. Engring., 1955-61, chmn. elected senate, 1959-61; dir. Ford Found. MA-3 program U. Coll., 1962-66; lectr. Berkeley Div. Sch., New Haven, 1953-57. Served with USN, 1918-21. Mem. Am. Philos. Assn., Am. Assn. Realistic Philosophy, Metaphysical Soc. Am., Am. Soc. Engring. Edn., Am. Assn. U. Profs., Phi Beta Kappa. Episcopalian (lay reader 1953—, sr. warden 1957-60). Contbg. author: Realism and Phenomenology, 1953; Sensations and Phenomenology, 1966; Man and World, 2, 3, 1969; Aesthesis and Aesthetics, 1970. Home: 50 Cow Hill Rd Clinton CT 06413

CHAPMAN, HELEN, (Mrs. Theodore Stillman Chapman), clubwoman; b. Coldwater, Mich., Apr. 20, 1904; d. Francis X. and Jeanette (Morrison) Busch; A.B., U. Wis., 1926; M.A., U. Chgo., 1936; LL.D., Blackburn U., 1955; m. Theodore Stillman Chapman, June 28, 1939. Instr. Crane Coll., Chgo., 1933-34; high sch. tchr., Chgo., 1934-38, instr. Monticello Coll., Godfrey, Ill., 1938-39. Pres. Ill. Fedn. Women's Clubs, 1945-47; pres. Gen. Fedn. Women's Clubs, 1954-56, now hon. pres.; mem. correctional services adv. bd. Ill. Youth Commn., 1950- 64; mem. council Ill. Citizens Edn. Com.; mem. Nat. Adv. Food and Drug Council, FDA, 1965-68; mem. com. of 100, Ch. Women United, 1962-66; program asst. Nat. Presbyn. Center; mem. nat. com. Am. Mus. Immigration; mem. adv. bd. Berea in Korea; mem. consumer com. Ill. Status of Women Commn., 1966-68; mem. Ill. Citizens Edn. Council; mem. nat. sponsoring com. UN Assn., 1954-60; mem. gen. sponsoring com. Christian Children's Fund 1954-60; mem. nat. com. Am. Mus. Immigration. Trustee Monticello Coll., 1943-66, Mary Thompson Hosp., Chgo., 1960-68, Blackburn U.; trustee, vice chmn. Allied Youth, Inc.; nat. bd. dirs. Women's Med. Coll. Pa. Decorated by King of Greece, 1956; recipient Distinguished Service award Monticello Coll., 1955; citation for pub. service U. Chgo., 1955; Centennial award Berea Coll., 1955; Freedoms Found. at Valley Forge award, 1955. Mem. P.E.O., D.A.R., Washington Forum, Delta Kappa Gamma, Alpha Gamma Delta. Presbyn. (trustee). Home: 4530 Connecticut Av NW Washington DC 20008

CHAPMAN, HIRAM WENDELL, former steel co. exec.; b. Beaver Dam, Ky., Nov. 14, 1911; s. Talbert Luther and Minnie (Richardson) C.; student U. Ky., 1929-32; B.S. in Physics, Western Ky. State U., 1934; m. Katherine Marie Elliott, Feb. 6, 1942; 1 son, Barry L. High Sch. tchr., Ohio County, Ky., 1934-42; with Am. Steel Foundries, 1942-70, v.p., 1961-66, pres., 1966-70. Named Ky. col., 1960. Mem. Nat., Am. mgmt. assns., Steel Founders Soc. Am. Clubs: Chgo. Athletic Assn.; Lansing (Ill.) Sportsmans. Home: 14205 W 81st Dr Dyer IN 46311

CHAPMAN, HUGH MCMASTER, banker; b. Spartanburg, S.C., Sept. 11, 1932; s. James Alfred and Martha (Marshall) C.; B.S. in Bus. Adminstrn., U. N.C., 1955; certificate Stonier Grad. Sch. Banking, Rutgers U., 1966; m. Anne Allston Morrison, Dec. 27, 1958; children-Anne Allston, Rachel Buchanan, Mary Morrison. With Citizens & So. Nat. Bank S.C., 1958—, v.p., exec. officer, Camden, 1962-65, exec. v.p. charge Eastern area S.C., 1965-68, asst. pres. Columbia, 1968—. Chmn. United Fund Drive, Camden, 1963, pres., 1964; pres. Carolinas United Community Services, 1966, chmn., 1967. Bd. assos. Wofford Coll., Spartanburg. Served to 1st lt. USAF, 1955-57. Named Young Man of Year, Camden Jr. C. of C., 1967. Mem. Camden C. of C. (pres. 1966), Zeta Psi. Presbyn. Home: 5033 Wittering Dr Columbia SC 29206 Office: PO Box 727 Columbia SC 29402

CHAPMAN, IONE MINERVIA, former librarian; b. Parke County, Ind. Apr. 20, 1900; d. Alfred William and Josa (Rutter) Chapman; A.B., U. Ill., 1925, M.S. in L.S., 1944; M.A., Columbia Tchrs. Coll., 1928. Tchr. rural and high schs., Ind., Ill., Ky., 1918-34; dean women Adrian (Mich.) Coll., 1934-40; head residence Russell Sage Coll., 1940-41; librarian Adrian Coll., 1941-42, Western State Coll., Gunnison, Colo., 1944-46, Morehead (Ky.) State U., 1946-70, asst. dir., until 1970. Mem. Ky. Gov.'s Planning Com. Libraries, 1967-68. Trustee treas. Rowan County Pub. Library, 1953- -. Mem. Am., Southeastern, Ky. (pres. 1960-61), library assns., Am. Assn. U. Women, Beta Phi Mu. Club: Morehead Womens. Home: 405 Wilson Av Morehead KY 40351

CHAPMAN, JAMES ALFRED, Jr., textile mfg. co. exec.; b. Inman. S.C., Sept. 30, 1921; s. James Alfred and Martha (Marshall) C.; B.S. in Chemistry, Davidson Coll., 1943; m. Martha LeNoir Cloud, June 2, 1945; children—Mary Chambless (Mrs. Larry D. Zoerner), Martha Marshall, Dorothy Dryer, James Alfred IV. Trainee, Inman Mills (S.C.), 1943-44; indsl. engr. Pacific Mills, Columbia, S.C. and Rhodhiss, N.C., 1944-46; with Riverdale Mills, Enoree, S.C., 1946-53, v.p., 1953-54; v.p. Inman Mills, 1954-64, pres., treas., 1964—, also dir.; dir. Textile Hall Corp., Greenville, S.C.; mem. adv. bd. Citizens & So. Nat. Bank S.C. Moderator, Enoree Presbytery, 1963. Trustee Presbyn. Coll., Clinton, S.C., 1964—, chmn., 1970—; trustee Spartanburg County Found., 1964—, chmn., 1970; trustee Inman-Riverdale Found., 1948—, vice chmn., 1964—; trustee J. E. Sirrine Textile Found., 1964- -. Mem. So. Textile Assn. (pres. 1955-56), S.C. Textile Mfrs. Assn. (bd. dirs. 1963-66, 68-69, v.p. 1970-71), Am. Textile Mfrs. Inst. (dir. 1968-70), N.A.M. (dir. 1968-71), Phi Delta Theta, S.C. C. of C. (pres. 1964-65). Presbyn. (ruling elder). Clubs: Spartanburg Country (v.p. 1958, treas. 1957), Piedmont (Spartanburg); Poinsett (Greenville, S.C.); Biltmore Forest (Asheville, N.C.); Red Fox Country (Landrum, S.C.); University (N.Y.C.). Home: 837 Glendalyn Av Spartanburg SC 29302 Office: Inman Mills Inman SC 29349

CHAPMAN, JAMES EDWARD, lawyer; b. Wadsworth, O., Apr. 27, 1927; s. Horace V. and Sarah L. (Thompson) C.; B.S., Ohio State U., 1952, J.D. summa cum laude, 1954; m. Anita Esbenshade, July 3, 1954; children—Ann Frances, Thomas Marshall, David Abram. Admitted to Ohio bar, 1954; asso. Baker, Hostetler & Patterson, Cleve., 1954-64, partner, 1964—. Dir. Cleve. Inst. Electronics, Inc., Euclid Industries, Inc., Freeway Washer & Stamping Co., Hough Bakeries, Inc., Prachar & Miller Machinery Co.; sec. Preformed Line Products Co., Hough Bakeries, Inc. Dir. Nat. Assn. Mental Health, 1965—, pres., 1970-71; trustee Mental Health Fedn., 1958—, pres., 1965-67; trustee Cleve. Mental Health Assn., 1958-67, 69—, pres., 1963-64. Mem. nat. council Ohio State U. Coll. Law, 1969—. Served with AUS, 1945-47. Mem. Am., Ohio, Cleve. bar assns. Republican. Presbyn. Mason (32, Shriner). Home: 22870 S Woodland St Cleveland OH 44122 Office: Union Commerce Bldg Cleveland OH 44115

CHAPMAN, JANET CARTER GOODRICH, (Mrs. John William Chapman, Jr.), educator, economist; b. Bklyn., May 26, 1922; d. Carter and Florence (Nielsen) Goodrich; B.A., Swarthmore Coll., 1943; M.A., Columbia, 1951, Ph.D., 1963; m. John William Chapman, Jr., Feb. 10, 1943; 1 dau., Hazel Perry. Analyst Nat. War Labor Bd., Phila., 1943; economist Bd. of Govs. Fed. Res. System, 1945-46; cons. econ. dept. RAND Corp., Santa Monica, Cal., 1949-69; asso. prof. U. Pitts., 1964-67, prof. econs., 1967—, chmn. com. Russian and East European studies, 1965—, dir. Russian and E. European studies program, 1970—; vis. lectr. econs. Swarthmore Coll., 1962-63; vis. fellow Australian Nat. U., 1964. Recipient Hannah Leedom fellowship Swarthmore Coll., 1946-47, Garth fellow Columbia, 1946-47, Russian Inst. grant, 1947-48, N.Y. State fellow Am. Assn. U. Women, 1948-49. Mem. Am. Econ. Assn., Assn. Advancement Slavic Studies, Assn. Study Soviet-Type Economics, Phi Beta Kappa. Author: Real Wages in Soviet Russia Since 1928, 1963; Wage Variation in Soviet Industry: The Impact of the 1956-60 Wage Reform, 1970. Contbr. to Economic Trends in the Soviet Union, 1963, The Soviet Economy: A Book of Readings, 1966, 70. Contbr. articles profl. jours. Home: 223 Gladstone Rd Pittsburgh PA 15217

CHAPMAN, JOHN ARTHUR, journalist; b. Denver, June 25, 1900; s. Arthur and Lillian Mathewson (Eddy) C.; student U. Colo, 1916-17, Columbia, 1919-21; H.H.D. (hon.), U. Denver; m. Georgia Christina Anderson, July 31, 1923; 1 dau., Karin. Reporter Denver Times, 1917-19, The News, N.Y., 1920-23; mgr. Paris bur. Pacific and Atlantic Photos, 1924-26; reporter The News, 1926-29, dramatic editor 1929—; condr. of column Mainly about Manhattan, 1931-40; Hollywood corr., 1940-42; drama critic, 1943—; lectr. drama N.Y. U., 1956-57. Mem. N.Y. Drama Critics Circle (pres. 1949-71), Sigma Phi Epsilon. Clubs: Dutch Treat (past pres.), Silurians (N.Y.C.). Editor: Best Plays and Yearbook of Drama, 1947-53; Theatre, 1953-56; Broadway's Best, 1957-60; Tell It to Sweeney, a History of the N.Y. Daily News. Co-editor: Best Plays of 1895- 1899. Home: 57 Kings Hwy Westport CT 06880 Office 220 E 42d St New York City NY 10017

CHAPMAN, JOHN WILLIAM, Jr., govt. ofcl.; b. Chgo., Jan. 21, 1921; s. John William and Eva (Richolson) C.; student U. Chgo., 1938-39, U. Ia., 1940-41; m. Barbara Jane Franklin, Sept. 1, 1961; children—John William III, Sherry Lynn, James Dana, Philip Webb, Linda Ann, Stephen Craig. Regional adminstr. Gen. Services Adminstrn., Chgo., 1955-61; asst. commr. Pub. Bldgs. Service, 1962-69; dep. adminstr. Gen. Services Adminstrn., 1969—. Served to lt. col. AUS, 1943-46. Recipient Meritorious Service award Gen. Services Adminstrn., 1966. Elk, Mason. Club: Argyle Country (Silver Spring). Home: 14505 Gilpin Rd Silver Spring, MD . 20906. Office: Gen Services Adminstrn 18th and F Sts N W Washington DC 20405

CHAPMAN, JOSEPH EDGAR, Jr., lawyer; b. Columbus, Ga., Sept. 6, 1902; s. Joseph Edgar and Eula (Averett) C.; A.B. magna cum laude, U. Ga., 1923; pvt. law tutoring, 1923-24; m. Mary Edwina Smenner, June 8, 1927; children—Joseph Edgar III, Daniel McNeil, Mary Edwina (Mrs. Charles L. Dodds, Jr.). Admitted to Ga. bar, 1924; practiced with father, 1924-42; partner firm Swift, Pease, Davidson & Chapman, Columbus, 1942—. An organizer, Pres. appeals rev. bd. United Givers, Columbus, 1951-52; defendant in civil rights voting case Primus King Vs. Chapman et al, 1941. Chmn. Muscogee County Democratic Com., 1944-56. Mem. Am. Ga. bar assns., Am. Judicature Soc., Am. Coll. Probate Counsel, Columbus Lawyers Club (pres. 1936), Columbus Execs. Clubs (charter), Columbus C. of C. (bd. dirs. 1953), Phi Beta Kappa. Mason, Lion (pres. 1952-53). Presbyn. (elder 1958). Home: 1423 Forest Av Columbus GA 31906 Office: 1043 3d Av Columbus GA 31901

CHAPMAN, LAURA BERNICE, nursing educator; b. Wayne, Neb., Sept. 23, 1909; d. William Henry and Lorena Augusta (Curtis) Chapman; diploma Grinnell (Ia.) Community Hosp., 1930; B.S. in Nursing Edn., U. Minn., 1935; M.A., Columbia, 1952. Staff nurse Community Hosp., Grinnell, 1930-32; sci. instr. Jennie Edmundson Hosp., Council Bluffs, Ia., 1935-38; nursing arts instr. Abbott Hosp., Mpls., 1938-42; sci. instr. Broadlawns Hosp., Des Moines, 1942-43; clin. instr. Wesley Meml. Hosp., Chgo., 1943-48, asst. dir. Sch. Nursing, 1949- 51; asst. prof. Sch. Nursing, U. Ill., 1952-54; dean Coll. Nursing Brigham Young U., 1954-61; dean Coll. Nursing, Rutgers, The State U., Newark, 1964—. Mem. Am., N.J. nurses assns., Nat. League for Nursing, Am. Assn. U. Women, Tchrs. Coll. Alumni Assn., Kappa Delta Pi, Sigma Theta Tau. Home: 555 Mt Prospect Av Newark, NJ 07104. Office: 87 Halsey St Newark NJ 07102

CHAPMAN, LEONARD F., Jr., marine corps officer; b. Key West, Fla., Nov. 3, 1913; grad. U. Fla., 1935; m. Emily Ford; children—Leonard F. III, Walton F. Commd. 2d lt. USMC, 1935, advanced through ranks to gen., 1969; comdr. officer Marine Barracks, Washington, 1956-58; comdg. gen. Force Troops, Fleet Marine Force, Atlantic, 1958-61; asst. chief staff G-4, Hdqrs. Marine Corps, 1961-64, chief of staff, 1964-68; commdt. U.S. Marine Corps, 1968- -. Decorated Legion of Merit (2). Office: Chief of Staff Hdqrs Marine Corp Washington DC 20380

CHAPMAN, MARGARET LOUISE, librarian; b. New Bern, N.C., Apr. 6, 1916; d. Kena King and Louise (Lane) Chapman; A.B., Greensboro Coll., 1938; B.S. in L.S., U. N.C., 1945, M.A., 1956. Librarian, New Bern Pub. Library, 1940-43, Barbour Boat Works, New Bern, 1943-44; asst. in cataloging U. N.C. Library, 1945, cataloger, 1947-51; alumni recorder U. N.C. Alumni Office, 1945-47; cataloger Fla. State U. Library, 1951-54; cataloger, asst. law librarian U. N.C. Law Library, 1954-56; head bibliography room U. Fla. Library 1956-58; librarian P.K. Yonge Library of Fla. History, U. Fla., 1958-62; spl. collections librarian U. S. Fla., Tampa, 1962-71; dir. library Queens Coll., Charlotte, N.C., 1971—. Bd. dirs. Hillsborough County Hist. Commn., 1963-71. Mem. A.L.A., Southeastern, N.C., Fla. (pres. 1965-66) library assns., Fla. Hist Soc. (dir. 1960-62, exec. sec. 1962-70, v.p. 1970-72), Phi Alpha Theta. Democrat. Methodist. Editor: Florida Breezes (Ellen Call Long), 1962. Reviewer adult books, Fla. Libraries, 1969—. Home: 201 N Canterbury Rd Charlotte NC 28211 Office: Everett Library Queens Coll Charlotte NC 28207

CHAPMAN, MARSHALL FULLER, marketing research co. exec.; b. Chetek, Wis., Feb. 18, 1912; s. Charles McCoy and Alma (Fuller) C.; Ph.B., U. Wis., 1934; m. Lucy Porter, Dec. 17, 1935; children—Patricia (Mrs. Donald Ritter), Cynthia (Mrs. Edward Seagroatt), Marshall Fuller II, Pamela Bash. With A. C. Nielsen Co., N.Y.C., 1934—, field auditor, 1934-37, dist. field mgr., 1937-40, regional field mgr., 1940-43, client service exec., 1943-46, v.p., 1946-69, exec. v.p., 1969—. Mem. Phi Gamma Delta. Republican. Club: Scarsdale Golf. Home: Chateau Lafayette Scarsdale NY 10583 Office: 1290 Av of Americas New York City NY 10019

CHAPMAN, MARVIN ALVIN, govt. ofcl.; b. Washington, July 31, 1914; s. Harmon Alvin and Pearl (Duckett) C.; student U. Mich., 1932-35, U. Ala., 1935-36; m. Evelyn Byrd Traxler, Dec. 2, 1939; 1 dau., Mary Alice. With U.S. Govt., 1936—; with VA, 1946—, dir. VA Center, Hampton, Va., 1962—, now dir. VA Hosp., Danville, Ill. Bd. dirs. Tidewater Fed. Execs. Assn., Va. Bd. Civil Service Examiners. Served to maj. USMCR, World War II and Korea. Mem. Mil. Order World Wars (comdr. Hampton Roads (Va.) chpt. 1965, Va. dept. 1966), Am. Legion, Marine Corps Res. Officers Assn., Assn. U.S. Army, Alpha Sigma Phi, Triangle. Clubs: Rotary (pres. Hampton 1966-67); A (U. Ala). Address: Directors Quarters VA Hosp 1900 E Main St Danville IL 61832

CHAPMAN, MARY ILSLEY, (pen name Maristan Chapman), author; b. Chattanooga, Tenn., Sept. 10, 1895; d. John Henry and Mary (Hamilton) Ilsley; privately educated; m. John Stanton Higham Chapman, Feb. 26, 1917. Has been successively missionary, lectr., engring. technician, and has traveled widely; novelist, 1928—. Mem. Mediaeval Acad. Am. P.E.N. Democrat. Episcopalian. Co-author: (with John Stanton Higham Chapman) numerous books including adventure books for young people, biographies, hist. novels and chronicles of mediaeval times, latest being, Trial of the Cheery Cows, 1958; Doubloons, 1959; The Helpful Treasure, 1959; Devorguilla; A 13th Century Chronicle. Additional pen names, Arran Hamilton, R. De L'isle, Stanton Blake, Dent Ilsley, Hamilton Greenwood, Jane Selkirk. Address: 1903 Old Mission Dr Solvang CA 93463 ☆

CHAPMAN, MCLEOD PALM, govt. ofcl.; b. Rangiora, New Zealand, Jan. 14, 1919; s. Robert Henry and Edith (Cunningham) C.; B.Com., Canterbury U. Coll., Christchurch, New Zealand, 1949; m. Tui June Cliff, July 22, 1948; 1 dau., Estella (Mrs. Clayton McElwee). With New Zealand Pub. Services, 1937-40, 45-54; vice consul, N.Y.C., 1954-56; sr. adminstrn. officer Dept. External Affairs, Wellington, New Zealand, 1956-60; counsellor, dep. high commr. New Zealand High Commn., New Delhi, India, 1960-62, Kuala Lumpur, Malaya, 1962-63; consul gen. New Zealand, San Francisco, 1963-65, Los Angeles, 1965—. Served with New Zealand Expeditionary Force, 1940-45. Mem. New Zealand Soc. Accountants, Los Angeles World Affairs Council. Home: 10561 Sunset Blvd Los Angeles CA 90024 Office: 510 W 6th St Los Angeles CA 90014

CHAPMAN, ONIS GERALD, clergyman; b. Warrick County, Ind., Jan. 19, 1914; s. Clarence Alva and Alma Ellen (Bruner) C.; A.B., Oakland City (Ind.) Coll., 1936, Th.B., 1942, D.D. (hon.), 1951; B.D., So. Baptist Theol. Sem., 1949; m. Pauline Louise Holder, June 18, 1932. Ordained to ministry Bapt. Ch., 1934; pastor in Owensville, Ind., 1937-44, Oakland City, 1945-60; pres. Oakland City Coll., Ind., 1955-65; pastor 1st Bapt. Ch., Ft. Madison, Ia., 1965-69; pastor Grace Bapt. Ch., Kansas City, Mo., 1969—. Moderator Gen. Assn. Gen. Baptist, 1954; sec. minister's aid bd. Gen. Bapt. Denomination, 1944-53, bd. religious edn., 1942-43, chmn. social issues com., 1953-60. Mason (K.T.), Kiwanian (pres. Oakland City 1956). Contbr. church periodicals. Home: 5161 Chouteau Trafficway Kansas City MO 64119

CHAPMAN, OSCAR LITTLETON, former sec. of interior; b. Omega, Va., Oct. 22, 1896; s. James Jackson and Rosa Archer (Blount) C.; ed. Randolph-Macon Acad., Bedford, Va., 1918, U. Denver, 1922-24, U. N.M., 1927-28; LL.B., Westminister Law Sch., Denver, 1929; LL.D., Colo. State Coll. of Edn., Augustana Coll., Howard U., 1949, U. Denver, 1951, Western State Coll. Colo., 1961; m. Olga Pauline Edholm, December 21, 1920 (dec.); m. 2d, Ann Kendrick, Feb. 24, 1940; 1 son, James. Asst. chief probation officer Juvenile Ct., Den., 1922-24, chief, 1924-27; admitted to Colo. bar, 1929; apptd. asst. sec. of interior, 1933; apptd. under sec. of interior, 1946; sec. of interior, 1949- 53; mem. law firm Chapman, Duff & Lenzini, Washington. Served with U.S. Navy, 1918-20. Mem. Am. Legion, Phi Alpha Delta. Democrat. Methodist. Home: 4975 Hillbrook Lane N W Washington DC 20016 Office: Chapman Duff & Lenzini: Pennsylvania Bldg Washington DC 20004

CHAPMAN, PHILIP KENYON, physicist, astronaut; b. Melbourne, Australia, Mar. 5, 1935; s. Colin Robison and Phyllis (Kenyon) C.; came to U.S., 1961, naturalized, 1967; B.Sc. in Physics, Sydney (Australia) U., 1956; S.M. in Aero. and Astronautics, Mass. Inst. Tech., 1964, Sc.D. in Instrumentation, 1967; m. Pamela Gatenby, Dec. 4, 1959; children—Peter Hume, Kristen de Querilleau. Electronic engr. Philips Electric Indsl. Pty. Ltd., Sydney, 1956-57; auroral physicist Australian Nat. Antarctic Research Expdn., Mawson, 1958-59; electro-optical engr. Canadian Aviation Electronics Ltd., Montreal, 1960; staff physicist Exptl. Astronomy Lab., Mass. Inst. Tech., 1961-67, former research asso.; scientist-astronaut NASA, 1967—; electro-optical cons., 1963-67. Recipient British Polar medal. Mem. A.A.A.S., Brit. Interplanetary Sco., Am. Astron. Soc. (sr.), Am. Inst. Aero. and Astronautics, Australian Nat. Antarctic Research Expdns. Club. Office: Code CB NASA Manned Spacecraft Center Houston TX 77058

CHAPMAN, REID GILLIS, broadcasting co. exec.; b. Indpls., July 27, 1920; s. Arthur Reid and Esther Mary (Gillis) C.; student Butler U., 1938-40; m. Janet K. Passwater, Oct. 20, 1942; children—Arthur II, Martha (Mrs. Linwood Shull), Mark, Rosalie, James With radio sta. WAOV, Vincennes, Ind., 1943; with WISH, WISH-TV, Indpls., 1943-56; mgr. WANE Radio, Ft. Wayne, Ind., 1956-58, v.p., gen. mgr. WANE-TV, 1958—; v.p., dir. Ind. Broadcasting Corp., Ft. Wayne, 1959—. Chmn. mercantile div. United Fund, 1962-63; hon. chmn. Cancer Crusade Month, 1971; mem. Com. of 24, 1967—. Bd. dirs. United Community Services, Conv. Bur., Parkview Meml. Hosp., Martin Luther King Meml. Fund, Asso. Chs. Ft. Wayne, YMCA, Legal Aid Soc.; bd. dirs. Jr. Achievement Ft. Wayne, 1958—, pres., 1962-64; bd. dirs., v.p. Better Bus. Bur., 1962-65; bd. dirs. Goodwill Industries, 1959-65, v.p., 1964-65. Mem. Ft. Wayne Advt. Club (past pres., Silver medal award 1971), Ft. Wayne Press Club (past pres., roastmaster and chmn. Gridiron Show), Ft. Wayne C. of C. (past v.p., dir.), Ind. Broadcasters Assn. (past pres.), Broadcast Pioneers, Presbyn. (ruling elder, mem. div. mass media). Mason (Shriner). Clubs: Summit, Ft. Wayne Country, Quest (Ft. Wayne). Home: 2906 Shady Oak Dr Fort Wayne IN 46806 Office: 2915 W State Blvd Fort Wayne IN 46808

CHAPMAN, RICHARD PALMER, banker; b. Chester, Ia., May 9, 1905; s. C. A. and E. Blanche (Smith) C.; A.B., Carleton Coll., 1925; M.B.A., Harvard, 1927; LL.D., Wheaton Coll., 1964, Northeastern U., 1966, Boston Coll., 1967; m. Mary Elizabeth Smith, Mar. 26, 1932; children—Richard P., Ann Churchill. With New Eng. Mchts. Nat. Bank, Boston, 1927—, successively as statistician, 1927-35, asst. v.p., 1935-38, v.p., 1938- 47, exec. v.p., 1947-52, pres., 1952-64, chmn. bd., 1964-70, dir., 1945—; dir. Reece Corp., L.G. Balfour Co., Bird & Son, Inc., N.E. Mutual Life Ins. Co., Bird Machine Co., Amoskeag Co., Fieldcrest Mills, Inc., J.P. Maguire & Co., Inc.; Franklin Savs. Bank of Boston; dir. N.E. Enterprise Capital Corp., Fieldcrest Mills, J.P. Maguire & Co., Lumber Mut. Fire Ins. Co., Boston Mfr. Mut. Fire Ins. Co., Mut. Boiler and Machinery Ins. Co., Tampa Electric Co.; chmn. bd. trustees Wm. Underwood Co.; treas. Widows Soc. Boston; incorporator Mass. Meml. Hosps.; dir. Fund Med. Edn. Trustee Boys and Girls Camps, Boston Symphony Orch.; treas. Affiliated Hosps. Center, Inc.; chmn. bd. trustees Peter Bent Brigham Hosp.; dir. United Fund of Met. Boston; trustee Mus. Fine Arts, Boston, Carleton Coll., Northeastern U., Mass. Eye and Ear Infirmary; vis. com. bd. overseers Harvard Bus. Sch.; trustee emeritus Wheaton Coll.; bd. dirs. Boston Coll.; mem. trustee council Boston U. Med. Center. Fellow Am. Acad. Arts and Scis.; mem. Nat. Indsl. Conf. Bd. (sr. mem. corp.). Republican. Conglist. Clubs: Knickerbocker (N.Y.C.); Somerset, Union, The Country (Brookline). Contbr. banking mags.; lectr. on investment and trust subjects. Home: 311 Warren St Brookline MA 02146 Office: 28 State St Boston MA 02109

CHAPMAN, ROBERT B. II, defense co. exec.; b. Balt., May 12, 1917; s. Robert B. and Mary (McCord) C.; B.Engring. with honors, Johns Hopkins, 1930; m. Audrey Lee Frank, Apr. 5, 1941; children—Linda Lee (Mrs. Russell W. Fabiszak), Robert B. IV. Structural engr. John E. Greiner Co., Balt., 1938-41; structural engr., missile project mgr., bus. mgr. spl. weapons sales Glenn L. Martin Co., Balt., 1941-50; chief contracts AAI & Corp Balt., 1950-52, dir., 1952—, pres., chief exec. officer, 1967—. Mem. exec. bd. Balt. Area council Boy Scouts Am.; chmn. Md. Commn. on Dyslexia; chmn. indsl. adv. council Opportunities Industrialization Central Balt.; mem. bd. strategy Presbytery Balt., United Presbyn. Ch.; mem. exec. bd. Johns Hopkins Fund. Served to lt. col. USAAF, 1941-46. Registered profl. engr. Md. Mem. Nat. Security Indsl. Assn. (chmn. bd. trustees), Am. Ordnance Assn. (asso. fellow), Am. Inst. Aero. and Astronautics, Greater Balt. C. of C. (bd. dirs.), Orton Soc. (bd. dirs.), Md. Horse Shows Assn. (registered steward), Alpha Tau Omega. Presbyn. (ordained elder). Clubs: Johns Hopkins (Balt.); Army/Navy Town (Washington). Home: 1505 Cranwell Rd Luthersville MS 21092 Office: Box 6767 Baltimore MD 21204

CHAPMAN, ROBERT HETT, textile mfg. co. exec.; b. Middlesboro, Ky., Feb. 13, 1895; s. James Alfred and Rachel (McMaster) C.; M.E., Cornell U., 1917; dr. Textile Industries Clemson Coll., 1951; m. Sarah Elizabeth Lipscomb, June 29, 1918 (dec. Aug. 1947); chilren—Sarah Elizabeth (Mrs. Thomas Samuel Means, Jr.), Robert Hett; m. 2d, Laura Noell Carr, Sept. 2, 1948. Partner charge mech. engring. dept. J.E. Sirrine & Co., Greenville, S.C., 1919- 37; v.p., asst. treas. Inman Mills (S.C.), 1937-64, dir., 1937—, chmn. bd. dirs., 1965—; dir. Citizens and So. Nat. Bank of S.C. Chmn. bd. Inman-Riverdale Found. Served as ensign USNR, 1917-19. Registered profl. engr., S.C. Mem. Am. Soc. M.E., Chi Psi. Democrat. Presbyn. Clubs: Piedmont, Spartanburg Country. Home: 1010 Glendalyn Circle Spartanburg, SC . 29302. Office: Inman Mills Park Rd Inman SC 29349

CHAPMAN, WILLIAM REMINGTON, banker; b. Yonkers, N.Y., Feb. 14, 1907; s. Henry T. and Irma (Remington) C.; ed. high sch., Mpls.; m. Evelyn F. Post, June 3, 1929; children—Majorie (Mrs. Rodney A. Jenkins), William Remington. With Midland Nat. Bank, Mpls., 1926—, asst. cashier, 1938-44, v.p., 1944-58, sr. v.p., 1958, pres., 1959-70, chmn. bd., 1970—; faculty Sch. Banking, U. Wis.; adv. council N.W. Bancorporation. Bd. dirs., pres., United Fund Mpls. Area; treas. United Negro Coll. Fund campaign; bd. dirs. Asbury Meth. Hosp. Mem. Robert Morris Assos. (past nat. pres.), Assn. Res. City Bankers, Asso. Industries Mpls. (dir., treas.), Am. Inst. Banking, Am. Arbitration Assn. (regional adv. council). Methodist. Rotarian. Home: 2711 Kipling Av Minneapolis MN 55416 Office: 401 2d Av S Minneapolis MN 55480

CHAPPEL, NELSON THOMAS, Christian edn. exec.; b. Minesing, Ont., Can., July 14, 1902; s. Joseph and Harriet (Pattenden) C.; student U. Toronto, 1923-24; B.A., U. Alberta, 1927, B.D., 1932; Testamur, St. Stephen's Theol. Coll., Edmonton, Alberta; A.M., U. Chgo., 1929; D.D., Ind. Central Coll., 1958, St. Stephen's Coll., Edmonton, 1959; m. Mabel Naomi Nix, Sept. 4, 1929; children—John Nelson, Charlotte Ruth (Mrs. S. A. Sayre), Sheila Harriet (Mrs. D. Leaf), Naomi Lynn (Mrs. P. Gaaserud). Ordained to ministry United Ch. of Can., 1928; pastor, Grand Prairie, Alberta, 1930-35, Crescent Heights United Ch., Calgary, Alberta, 1935-37, Westminster United Ch., Saskatoon, Sask., 1937-41; gen. sec. Religious Edn. Council of Can., 1946-47; sec. dept. Christian edn. Canadian Council Chs., 1947-50; gen. sec. John Milton Soc. for Blind, 1950-53, dir., 1957-71; gen. sec. World Council Christian Edn., 1953-65, emeritus, 1966—; spl. cons. All-India Conf. on Sunday Sch. Curriculum, 1955, All-Africa, 1956. West Indies, 1959. Mem. nat. boys work com. Canadian YMCA, 1947-50, nat. youth program com., 1951-58. Served as squadron leader, Chaplain's Corps, Royal Canadian Air Force, 1941-45. Mem. Canadian Assn. Adult edn. (exec. com. 1947-50), Nat. Council Chs. Christ U.S. (exec. bd. div. Christian edn. 1954-66). Editor Canadian Mentor, 1946-49. Founder John Milton Talking Book Mag. for Blind, 1951, editor, 1951-53. Home: 3434 Eglinton Av E Scarborough 708 Ontario Canada Office: 154 University Av Toronto Canada

CHAPPELL, AMEY, physician; b. Providence, Nov. 5, 1900; d. Elwin and Mary Maria (Manchester) Chappell; student Oglethorpe U., 1924-26; M.D., Tulane U., 1930. Intern Touro Infirmary, New Orleans, 1930-31; house physician N.E. Hosp. for Women and Children, Boston, 1931-32; pvt. practice medicine, Atlanta, 1933-69. Dir. Atlanta YWCA, 1940-52, 64—, pres., 1971—; trustee Piedmont Coll. Named Woman of Yr. in Atlanta, 1968. Diplomate Nat. Bd. Med. Examiners. Mem. Internat. Women's Med. Assn., Am. Med. Women's Assn. (pres. 1951- 52), Am., Ga., Fulton County Med. Assns., Soc. Study Sterility, Chi Omega. Conglist. (chmn. bd. trustees 1968-69). Home: 3750 Peachtree Rd N E Atlanta GA 30319 Office: 1293 Peachtree St NE Atlanta GA 30309

CHAPPELL, CLOVIS GILLHAM, Jr., lawyer; b. Waverly, Tenn., Sept. 13, 1911; s. Clovis Gillham and Cecil (Hart) C.; student Southwestern at Memphis, 1929-30; B.A., So. Meth. U., 1934, LL.B., 1936; m. Pauline Mikell LaRoche, Oct. 28, 1938; children—Carolyn (Mrs. D.W. Light III), Polly (Mrs. F. Ferrell Davis), Marian. Landman, Humble Oil & Refining Co., 1938-44; admitted to Tex. bar, 1936; atty. Baker, Botts, Shepherd & Coates, Houston, 1944-50; partner Stubbeman, McRae, Sealy & Laughlin, Midland, 1950-59, now Lynch, Chappell, Allday & Culp, 1959—. Sec., dir. Tex. Am. Oil Corp., Midland; dir. Comml. Bank & Trust Co., Midland. Past mem. bd. visitors So. Meth. U. Law Sch. Mem. Am., Tex., Midland County bar assns., Pi Kappa Alpha. Methodist. Contbr. articles profl. jours. Home: 1605 Bedford Dr Midland TX 79701 Office: Wall Towers East Midland TX 79701

CHAPPELL, RICHARD ARCHIBALD, educator; b. Jeffersonville, Ga., Dec. 23, 1901; s. William Thomas and Nancy (Storey) C.; A.B., Mercer U., 1926, LL.B., LL.D.; m. Annette Richardson, Oct. 7, 1934; children—Mariann (Mrs. Fred W. Evans), Nancy (Mrs. Robert Denson Martin, Jr.). Admitted to Ga. bar, 1928, D.C. bar, 1948; chief probation officer U.S. Dist. Ct., 1928-37; supr. probation U.S. Dept. Justice, 1937-40; chief probation Adminstrv. Office U.S. Cts., 1940-53; mem. U.S. Parole Bd., 1953-65, chmn., 1961-65; asst. prof. Inst. Govt., U. Ga., Athens, 1965—. Lectr. family law and criminology; cons. on probation U.S. High Commn. for Germany, 1950. Served from lt. to comdr. USNR, 1944-46; comdr. Res. Recipient Roscoe Pound award Nat. Council on Crime and Delinquency, 1970. Mem. Am. Bar Assn., Nat. Probation Assn., Am. Correctional Assn. (dir.). Club: Cosmos. Editor: Fed. Probation Quar., 1938-53; Decisions Interpreting the Federal Probation Act. Contbr. articles to profl. jours. Home: 389 West View Dr Athens GA 30602

CHAPPELL, VERE CLAIBORNE, educator; b. Rochester, N.Y., Mar. 22, 1930; s. Vere Chambers and Edyth (Brown) C.; B.A., Yale, 1951, M.A., 1953, Ph.D., 1958; student U. Heidelberg (Germany), 1953-54; m. Sally Anderson, June 7, 1951 (div. June 63); children—Jennifer Helen, Jonathan Claiborne, David Lincoln; m. 2d Sheryl Berglund, July 31, 1963; children—Vere Chambers II, Melissa, Addison Ward; step-children—Clayton Scott Templin, Jaime Allison Templin. Instr. Yale, 1954-57; instr. U. Chgo., 1957-61, asst. prof., 1961-63, asso. prof., 1963-68, prof. philosophy, 1968-70, acting chmn. philosophy dept., 1964-65; prof., head philosophy U. Mass., 1970—; vis. prof. Ind. U., 1967, U. Ill. at Chgo., 1967, U. Ill. at Urbana, 1968, Notre Dame U., 1969, U. So. Cal., 1969-70. Fulbright fellow, 1953-54; Nat. Endowment for the Humanities fellow, 1970. Mem. Am. Philos. Assn., Metaphys. Soc. Am., Soc. Philosophy and Pub. Policy, Aristotelian Soc., Mind Assn., Royal Inst. Philosophy. Editor: The Philosophy of Mind, 1962; The Philosophy of David Hume, 1963; Ordinary Language, 1964; Hume, 1966. Mng. editor Review of Metaphysics, 1954-56; asst. editor Ethics, 1958-61; asst.-treas. Philos. Quarterly, 1959-69; cons. editor Random- House-Knopf, 1963—. Home: Harkness Rd Pelham MA 01002 Office: Philosophy Dept U Mass Amherst MA 01002

CHAPPELL, WILLIAM D., business exec. Vice pres., controller Ferroxcube Corp., Saugerties, N.Y. Office: Mt Marion Rd Saugerites NY 12477*

CHAPPELL, WILLIAM VENROE, Jr., congressman; b. Kendrick, Fla., Feb. 3, 1922; s. William Venroe and Laura (Kemp) C.; B.A., U. Fla., 1947, LL.B., 1949, J.D., 1967; m. Marguerite Gutshall, Mar. 26, 1944; children—Judith Jane (Mrs. Taylor), Deborah Kay, William Venroe 3d, Christopher Clyde. Admitted to Fla. bar, 1949; mem. firm Sturgis and Chappell, and predecessors, Ocala, Fla., 1949—; prosecuting atty. Marion County, 1950-54; mem. Fla. Ho. of Reps. from Marion and other counties, 1954-64, 66-68, speaker, 1961-63; mem. 91st-92d congresses from 4th Dist. Fla. Served with USNR, 1942-46. Named Most Valuable Mem. Fla. Ho. Reps., 1967, Most Effective in Debate, 1967. Mem. Am., Fla., Marion County, Inter-Am. bar assns., Am. Trial Lawyers Assn., Acad. Fla. Trial Lawyers, Am. Legion. Democrat. Methodist. Mason (Shriner), Lion, Elk. Home: 1910 SE 12th St Ocala FL 32670 Office: Longworth House Office Bldg Washington DC 20515

CHAPPELLET, CYRIL, aerospace mfr.; b. Oakland, Cal., Jan. 10, 1906; s. Felix and Mabel C. (Dimon) C.; student Stanford U.; m. Sybil B. Kane, 1930. Sr. adviser, dir. Lockheed Aircraft Corp., Burbank, Cal., also mem. exec. com. dir. Am. Mut. Fund, Inc. Hon. trustee Pomona Coll. Office: care Lockheed Aircraft Corp Burbank CA 92373

CHAR, RENE, poet; b. L'Isle-sur-Sorgue, Vaucluse, France, June 14, 1907; s. Emile and Marie (Rouget) C.; ed. Lycée d'Avignon. Served as capt. Resistance Movement, 1940-45. Decorated Legion of Honor, Croix de Guerre, Medaille de la Resistance; Diplome l'Honneur des Alliés. Author: Le Marteau sans Maitre, 1934; Fureur et Mystere, 1948; Les Matinaux, 1950; La Parole en archipel, 1961; Recherche de la base et du sommet, 1965; Trois coups sous les arbres, 1967. Home: Les Busclats L'Isle-sur-Sorgue Vaucluse France Office: Editions Gallimard 5 rue Sébastien-Bottin Paris 7e France

CHARANIS, PETER, educator; b. Lemnos, Greece, Aug. 15, 1908; s. George and Chresanthy (Stroumtsos) C.; B.A., Rutgers U., 1931; Ph.D., U. Wis., 1935; postgrad. U. Brussels (Belgium), 1936-38; m. Madeleine Schitz, Aug. 5, 1939; children—Alexandra, Anthony. Faculty, Rutgers U., 1938—, prof., 1949-63, Voorhees prof. history, 1963—, chmn. dept., 1964-66. Vis. prof. U. Wis., 1950-51; vis. scholar Harvard at Dumbarton Oaks, 1956-57, mem. bd. scholars Dumbarton Oaks Research Library; mem. Am. Nat. Com. Byzantine Studies, 1963—; editorial staff Byzantinoslavica; mem. com. Gennadeion, Am. Sch. Classical Studies, Athens. Trustee Holy Cross Greek Orthodox Theol. Sch. Guggenheim fellow, 1956-57. Recipient Distinguished Research award Adv. Bd. Research and Grad. Edn.; Lindback Found award for distinguished teaching. Mem. Soc. Macedonian Studies (hon.), Am. Hist. Assn., Medieval Acad. Am. Soc. Ch. History. Author monographs on history Byzantine Empire and medieval Near East. Editorial adv.bd. Greek-Roman and Byzantine Studies, 1956-68, The Greek Orthodox Theological Rev., Neo-Hellenika; cons. editor Comparative Studies in Society and History; gen. editor Rutgers Byzantine series. Home: 105 N 7th Av Highland Park NJ 08904 Office: Rutgers U New Brunswick NJ 08903

CHARBONNET, PIERRE NUMA, Jr., naval officer; b. San Francisco, Dec. 12, 1919; s. Pierre N. and Blanche (Rogers) C.; grad. Hotchkiss Sch., 1937; B.S., U.S. Naval Acad., 1941; grad. Nat. War Coll., 1960, Advanced Mgmt. Program, Harvard, 1964; m. Mary Amelia Wheat Dutton, June 30, 1942; children—Hildegarde (Mrs. John S. Leffen, Jr.), Louise (Mrs. John A. McIver), Michelle, Pierre Numa III, Suzanne. Commd. ensign U.S. Navy, 1941, advanced through grades to rear adm., 1966; various assignments on ships and land, 1941-48; officer charge Flight Instr. Sch., Naval Air Sta., Pensacola, Fla., also personnel and adminstrv. officer naval air tng. bases, 1948-51; exec. officer Air Devel. Squadron 3, 1951-53; assigned Test Pilot Sch., 1953; head carrier aircraft br., flight test and tactical test divs., Naval Air Test Center, Patuxent River, Md., 1953-55; comdr. Attack Carrier Air Group 8, 1955-56; mem. staff comdr. naval air force U.S. Atlantic Fleet, 1956-58; exec. officer U.S.S. Forrestal, 1958-59; head aviation plans DCNO (air) mil. requirements, aviation, 1960-62; comdg. officer U.S.S. Marias, 1962-63, U.S.S. Pawcatuck, 1963, U.S.S. Coral Sea, 1964-65; chief staff, aide Carrier Div. 7, 1965; comdt. 8th Naval Dist., 1965-68; comdr. Carrier Div. 6, also strike force for 6th fleet, 1968-69; dir. Fleet Operations Office CNO, 1969—. Bd. dirs. Navy Mut. Aid Assn. Decorated D.F.C. (2), Air medal (7), Legion of Merit (3). Mem. Soc. Exptl. Test Pilots, Mil. Order World Wars, Naval Acad. Alumni Assn. Roman Catholic. Clubs: Boston (New Orleans); Ponte Vedre Country (Jacksonville, Fla.); Army Navy Country (Arlington, Va.). Home: Rockcliffe Farm Upperville VA 22176 Office: Comdr Fleet Air Mediterranean/CDRASW Force 6th Fleet FPO NY 09521

CHARBONNIER, PIERRE, painter; b. Vienne, France, Aug. 24, 1897; s. Pierre and Marie-Amelie (Gros) C.; student Sch. Fine Arts Lyon (France), 1915. Ranson Acad., Paris, 1919; m. Annette Natanson, June 8, 1920; 1 son, Jean Philippe; m. 2d, Regina Centellas, Oct. 2, 1950. Numerous exhbns. France and abroad; participation biennials of Venice, Sao Paulo, Santiago, also showings French art in London, Tokyo, Turin, Italy, Eastern countries, U.S., Scandinavia; rep.permanent collections Mis. Modern Art, Paris, Nat. Center Contemporary Art, Paris, Valencia, Spain, Tokyo, Sao Paulo. Rio de Janeiro, Marseille, France, St. Etienne, France, Turin, Arles, Frances, others; films produced include Ode. 1928, Contact 1930, Ce Soir A Huit Heures, 1932, Pirates du Rhone, 1933, Bracos de Sologne, 1934. La Fortune Enchantee, 1935; set designs for films include Affaires Publiques, 1936, Le Journal d'un Cure de Campagne, 1950, Un Condemne a mort s'est echappe, 1956, Bobosse, 1958, Pickpocket, 1959. Les Mauvairs Coups. 1960. Process of Jeanne d'Arc, 1961, Au hasard Balthazar, 1965, Une Femme douce, 1968; Quatre nuits d'im reveur, 1970; spl. works include large mural paintings for Auguste Perret, 1926, etching for Chateaubriand, 1926, wedding copies for Andre Salmon 1927, four bewitched ones for Rene Char, window for Francis Ponge, 1955. Decorated knight Legion of Honor, Mem. Drome Acad. Arts and Letters. Home: 7 Quai de la Republique Samois-sur-Seine France also La Roche de Glum Drome France Office: 359 rue Saint-Martin Paris 3 France

CHARD, CHESTER STEVENS, educator, archeologist; b. N.Y.C., Sept. 15, 1915; s. Walter Goodman and Kathleen (Stevens) C.; A.B., Harvard, 1937; Ph.D., U. Cal. at Berkeley, 1953; m. Bernadine Smith, Jan. 20, 1953; children—Carleton S., Kenneth W., Frederick H., Robert L., Alan D., Susan L. Vis. lectr. anthropology U. Wash., 1954-56; faculty U. Wis., 1958—, prof. anthropology, 1963—, chmn. dept., 1962-64; founder, 1962, since editor Arctic Anthropology; cons. Russian translation program Arctic Inst. N.Am., 1960- -. Served to lt. USNR, 1942-46. Fellow Am. Anthrop. Assn., A.A.A.S., Royal Anthrop. Inst.; mem. Prehistoric Soc., Soc. Am. Archaeology, Arctic Inst. N.Am., Far Eastern Prehistory Assn., Sigma Xi. Author: Kamchadal Culture, 1961; Preceramic Japan, 1961; Man in Prehistory, 1969. Office: Dept Anthropology U Wis Madison WI 53706

CHARD, ROLAND TURNER, banker; b. Falmouth, Eng., Oct. 7, 1907; s. Edward Turner and Ethel (Reader) C.; came to U.S., 1908, naturalized, 1918; student Rutgers U., 1925-26; m. Kathleen Mabel Cottell, Aug. 31, 1931; children-John T., David E., Kathleen Susan. With Nat. State Bank, Elizabeth, N.J., 1928—, v.p., 1956—, dir., 1959—, also cashier; pres., dir. Rosedale & Linden Cemetery, Linden, N.J.; sec.-treas., dir. Central Dist. Holding Co., Elizabeth; dir. Nat. State Corp., United Armored Carrier. Mem. Bd. Edn., Roselle, N.J., 1954-65, pres., 1959-60; mem. Commn. Recreation, Roselle, 1958-63; treas., dir. Elizabeth Community Action for Econ. Opportunity, 1964-67; treas. United Fund, Elizabeth, 1964-69, pres., 1969—. Vice pres. bd. mgrs. St. Elizabeth Hosp. Clubs: Suburban Golf (Union, N.J.); Elizabeth Town and Country; Elmora Country (Elizabeth). Home: 219 W 6th Av Roselle NJ 07203 Office: 68 Broad St Elizabeth NJ 07207

CHARGAFF, ERWIN, educator, chemist; b. Austria, Aug. 11, 1905; s. Hermann and Rosa C.; Dr. Phil., U. Vienna, 1928; m. Vera Broido; 1 son, Thomas. Came to U.S., 1928, naturalized 1940. Research fellow Yale, 1928-30; asst. U. Berlin (Germany), 1930-33; research asso. Inst. Pasteur, Paris, France, 1933-34; faculty Columbia, 1935—, prof. biochemistry, 1952- -, chmn. dept. biochemistry, 1970—; vis. prof. Sweden, 1949, Japan, 1958, Brazil, 1959, Coll. de France, 1965, Naples, Palermo, Cornell, 1966, Stazione biologica, Naples, 1969. Guggenheim fellow, 1949, 58; recipient Pasteur medal Soc. Biol. Chemistry, Paris, 1949; Neuberg medal Am. Soc. European Chemists, 1958; Bertner Found. award Houston, 1965; C. L. Mayer prize French Acad. Scis., 1963; Dr. H.P. Heineken prize Netherlands Acad. Scis., 1964. Fellow Am. Acad. Arts and Scis.; mem. Nat. Acad. Scis.; fgn. mem. Royal Swedish Physiographic Soc., German Acad. Scis. Leopoldina. Author: Essays on Nucleic Acids, 1963; other books, articles in field. Home: 350 Central Park W New York City NY 10025

CHARIGNON, JOHN MICHAEL, univ. dean; b. Stanley, N.D., Aug. 7, 1910; s. Jean Paul and Amalie (Gros Burdet) C.; B.S. in Mech. Engring., N.D. state Coll., 1932, B.S. in Elec. Engring., 1933; M.E., 1951; M.S., U. Pitts., 1952, Ph.D., 1960; m. Margaret Gallego, 1964; children—John Joseph and Michelle Jeanne (twins). Service mgr. indsl. stokers Auburn Engring. Co., 1933-37; gen. foreman steam generators Republic Steel Corp. 1937- 51, power engr., 1941-50; prof. mech. engring., dean Engring. Sch., Youngstown U., 1950—, also head indsl. engring. dept. Served to Col., inf., AUS, 1941-46; CBI. Decorated Legion of Merit; crest Order Yun Hui with ribbon (China). Mem. Am. Soc. M.E., Am. Inst. Indsl. Engrs., Sci. Research Soc. Am. Sigma Xi, Mu Pi Epsilon, Kappa Delta Pi, Sigma Tau. Author articles. Home: Metz Rd RD 1 Box 148A New Waterford OH 45445

CHARISSE, CYD (Tula Ellice Finklea), actress, dancer; b. Amarillo, Tex., Mar. 8, 1923; d. Ernest E. and Lela (Norwood) Finklea; student Hollywood Profl. Sch.; m. Nico Charisse, Aug. 12, 1939 (div. 1947); 1 son, Nicky; m. 2d, Tony Martin, May 9, 1948; 1 son, Tony. Toured U.S. with Ballet Russe, also in Europe; dancer in motion picture, Something to Shout About, Columbia Pictures, 1942; other films include: Mission to Moscow, 1943, Ziegfeld Follies, Harvey Girls, 1945; Three Wise Fools, Fiesta, The Unfinished Dance, Till the Clouds Roll By, 1946, On an Island With You, 1947, Words and Music, 1948, The Kissing Bandit, East Side West Side, 1949, Tension, Adventures of Don Renegade, Singin' in the Rain, The Wild North, Sombrero, 1952, The Band Wagon, 1953; Silk Stockings, 1957; Black Tights, 1962; Two Weeks in Another Town, 1962; The Silencers, 1966. Elected Star of Tomorrow, 1948. Home: Beverly Glen Los Angeles CA 90024 Office: care Metro-Goldwyn Mayer Studios 10202 W Washington Blvd Culver City CA 90230

CHARLAND, JACQUES, wholesale co. exec.; b. Bromptonville, Que., Can., Mar. 1, 1932; s. Joseph Adelard and Florida (Carrier) C.; M.Sc.C., Laval U., 1954; m. Monique Cameron, June 23, 1956; children—Pierre, Ann, Andree, Brigitte. Sr. clk. Belanger, St. Jacques, Sirois et Associes, C.A., Sherbrooke, Que., 1955-64; accountant Denault, Ltd., Sherbrooke, 1964-66, chief accountant, sec., 1966-70; sec., comptroller Provigo (Sherbrooke), Inc., Sherbrooke, Que., 1970—(name changed from Denault Ltd. 1970). Home: 295 Rioux Sherbrooke Quebec Canada Office: 1025 Cabana Sherbrooke Quebec Canada

CHARLAP, E. PAUL, business machine co. exec.; b. Phila., Dec. 3, 1924; s. Harold M. and Nan (Hirshman) C.; A.B., U. Pa., 1945; m. Corinne Brout, Dec. 15, 1945; children—Susan Crettol, Marco Crettol, Peter Marc. Salesman, Jacques Kreisler Co., North Bergen, N.J., 1947-51; pres. Nyast Chem. Corp. (later acquired by Seeman Bros.), Phila., 1951-53; dir. marketing Seeman Bros. Nat. Products, N.Y.C., 1953-58; pres. Savin Bus. Machines Corp., N.Y.C., 1958-68, chmn. bd., chief exec. officer, 1968—. Home: 215 Hommocks Rd Larchmont NY 10583 Office: Columbus Av Valhalla NY 10595

CHARLES, (Phillip Arthur George), Prince of Wales; b. Nov. 14, 1948; s. Prince Philip, Duke of Edinburgh and Queen Elizabeth II; heir apparent throne of U.K. Created Knight of the Garter, 1958. Address: Buckingham Palace London SW 1 England

CHARLES, ALLAN E., lawyer; b. Palo Alto, Cal., May 31, 1903; A.B., Stanford, 1925, J.D., 1927; student Harvard. Admitted to Cal. bar, 1927; practice in San Francisco; mem. firm Lillick, McHose, Wheat, Adams & Charles. Dir. Pacific Ins. Co. Commr. Civil Service, San Francisco, 1945-47, commr. pub. welfare, 1947-49; dir. San Francisco Bay Area Rapid Transit Dist., 1960-68. Mem. Am. Bar Assn., State Bar Cal., Maritime Law Assn. U.S. Office: 311 California St San Francisco CA 94104

CHARLES, ERNEST, composer, tenor; b. Mpls., Nov. 21, 1895; s. William Bruno and Louise Augusta (Baker) Grosskopf; ed. pub. schs., Mpls.; studied harmony, U. So. Cal., summer, 1922; m. 2d, Mrs. Maurice Willard Ames, Sept. 1, 1940; 1 son (by 1st marriage), William Kenniston. Has appeared as tenor with Pro Musica Soc., San Francisco; recitals in N.Y.C., Pitts., Los Angeles, Wichita, San Diego; pres. Ecco Music, Inc. Formerly asst. exec. sec. Am. Guild of Musical Artists. Served with 1st Minn. F.A., 1916. Fellow Am. Inst. Fine Arts; mem. Am. Soc. Composers, Authors and Publishers, Nat. Patron of Delta Omicron Sorority, 1941. Hon. mem. Phi Mu Alpha Sinfonia, nat. musical fraternity, U. of Neb., 1941. Republican. Mem. Episcopal Ch. Clubs: Riviera Country (Pacific Palisades, Cal.); Authors (Hollywood); Bohemians (New York). Composer: Clouds, Let My Song Fill Your Heart, When I Have Sung My Songs, Spendthrift, My Lady Walks in Loveliness, Hymn to U.S. Navy (dedicated to class of 1944, U.S. Naval Acad., accepted by them, 1943), The White Swan, Night; Remembrance; Save Me Oh God; Ballet a la Vienna, Miniature quartet for strings; Twenty- Third Psalm; Psalm of Exaltation; Christmas Song; The Greatness of the Lord (Choral); God is Our Strength (Choral); Spring in Vienna (Solo); Long, Long Ago; Nay, Do Not Weep. Home: 1210 Benedict Canyon Dr Beverly Hills CA 90210

CHARLES, HERMAN EDWARD, supt. schs.; b. Hillsboro, Tenn., Apr. 11, 1906; s. James Henry and Ida (Williams) C.; B.A., Abilene Christian Coll., 1935; M.A., Tex. Western Coll., 1947; LL.D., N.M. State U., 1963; m. Lois Dean Hook, Aug. 19, 1926; childrenGuilda Faye (Mrs. Stancil Tipton), Rheda Lanelle (Mrs. Jerome Lattimer). Tchr., prin. various schs., Tex., 1927-28, 29- 30, 31-32; supt. Dowell Pub. Schs., Rotan, Tex., 1932-37; practice law, Rotan, 1937-39; retail oil bus., Encino, N.M., 1939-41; prin. Kirtland (N.M.) High Sch., 1941-42; with U.S. Immigration Service, El Paso, Tex., 1942-43; tchr. Crockett Elementary Sch., El Paso, 1945-47; asst. prin. Bowie High Sch., El Paso, 1947-48; prin. Bell Elementary Sch., El Paso, 1948-50; personnel dir. El Paso pub. schs., 1950-53, asst. supt., 1953- 56, acting supt., 1956-57, supt., 1957-. Mem. exec. bd. Yucca council Boy Scouts Am. Served with AUS, 1943-45. Mem. State Bar Tex., Tex. Tchrs. Assn., Am., Tex. assns. sch. adminstrs., Tex. Assn. Sch. Bus. Ofcls. Lion (past pres. East El Paso). Home: 406 Lombardy El Paso TX 79922 Office: P O Box 1710 El Paso, TX 79999.

CHARLES, JOHN FREDRICK, educator; b. Kalamazoo, Mich., Aug. 19, 1909; s. Fred and Georgia (Jacobs) C.; A.B., Oberlin Coll., 1932; A.M., U. Chgo., 1937, Ph.D., 1938; m. Margaret Ellen Harry, Mar. 16, 1935; children—Elizabeth Ann (Mrs. Rudolf S. Amann), John Wilson. Asst. prof. classics and French, asst. dir. Alfred U. Extension, Jamestown, N.Y., 1938-40; asst. prof. classics Wabash Coll., 1940-46, asso. prof., 1946-50, Lafayette prof. Greek and history, chmn. dept. classics, 1950—, also dean personal devel. program. Awarded Daniel L. Shorey travelling fellowship in Greek, 1935; Am. Council Learned Socs. fellowship in Arabic, 1942; Ford Faculty fellowship, 1951-52; McLain Distinguished Teaching award, 1966. Mem. Mediaeval Acad. Am., Archaeol. Inst. Am., Classical Assn. Middle W. and S., Phi Beta Kappa (pres. E. Central dist.). Author articles on ancient naval affairs in classical jours. Home: Gronert Lane Crawfordsville IN 47933

CHARLES, PHILIPP LAMBERT, lawyer; b. Manila, P.I., Jan. 17, 1909 (parents Am. citizens); s. Oscar Henry and Caroline Deborah (Lambert) C.; A.B., Otterbein Coll., 1929; student, Ohio State U., 1929-30; LL.B., George Washington Univ., 1933; m. Dorothea Montgomery Flickinger, Oct. 18, 1930; children—Richard, Mary Ann Eschbach, David Montgomery. Clerk, U.S. Dept. of State, Washington, 1930-33; admitted to D.C. bar, 1933, practiced in Washington, 1933-34; law clerk, Tenn. Valley Authority, Knoxville, Tenn., 1935; supervisor of pub. reference, U.S. Securities and Exchange Commn., 1935-37, asst. chief, budget and accounts, 1938, chief, records div., 1938-41 (developed and initiated 1st microfilm records program, 1941), dir. of personnel, 1942-46; sec., Philippine War Damage Commn., Manila, 1946- 51; dir. personnel OPS, Washington, 1951-53; asst. regional commr. (adminstrn.) Cin. Regional Office, Internal Revenue Service, Treasury Dept., 1953-55; dist. dir. Internal Revenue for W. Va., 1955-59, Cin., 1960-65; sr. adviser tax adminstrn. Govt. India on staff United States Agy. Internat. Devel., 1965-68; pvt. practice law, Cincinnati, 1968-69; dep. commr. revenue and taxation, 1969—. Asst. prof. corporate finance, business orgn. and mgmt. evening sessions, Columbus U., Washington, 1940-42; asst. prof. pub. personnel adminstrn., eve. sessions, Temple U., Phila., 1944-45; vis. lectr. Fla. State U., 1954. Trustee, Otterbein Coll. Mem. Fed. (past chpt. pres.), Am. bar assns., Pi Kappa Delta. Kiwanian. Democrat. Episcopalian. Home: PO Box 2424 Agana GU 96910 Office: Govt of Guam PO Box 2796 Agana GU 96910

CHARLES, RAY, (Ray Charles Robinson), musician, singer, composer; b. Albany, Ga., Sept. 23, 1930; s. Bailey and Reather R.; student music at sch. for blind, St. Augustine, Fla. Played with bands in South; organized trio, played on TV in Seattle; formed own band, 1954; recording artist for Atlantic Records, 1954-59, ABC-Paramount, 1960-62, Tangerine Records, 1962—. Recipient New Star award Down Beat Critics poll, 1958, 61-64; named number 1 male singer 16th Internat. Jazz Critics Poll, 1968; Grammy awards. Address: RPM Internat Inc 2107 W Washington Blvd Los Angeles CA 90018

CHARLES, RAYMOND ALANSON, ins. co. exec.; b. Knoxville, Ill., Mar. 3, 1919; s. John H. and Leona (Lotts) C.; A.B summa cum laude, Knox Coll., 1941; postgrad. Mass. Inst. Tech., 1942; M.B.A., U. Chgo., 1947; m. Lois D. Sekora, Oct. 6, 1951; children—Margaret Anne, Alanson J. With bond dept. Prudential Ins. Co. Am., 1947-50; mem. finance staff Ford Motor Co., 1950-56; mem. securities investment dept. Equitable Life Assurance Soc., N.Y.C., 1956- 58; with bond dept. Prudential Ins. Co. Am., 1958—, v.p., 1962-65, sr. v.p., 1965—. Trustee Knox Coll., 1966. Served with USAAF, 1943-46. Mem. Am. Econ. Assn., Am. Finance Assn., Phi Beta Kappa, Beta Gamma Sigma, Tau Kappa Epsilon. Presbyn. (mem. bd. pensions U.P. Ch. U.S.A.). Home: 16 Hilltop Circle Morristown, NJ 07960. Office: Prudential Plaza Newark NJ 07101

CHARLES, ROBERT HORNE, corp. exec.; b. St. Louis, Sept. 14, 1913; s. Benjamin Hynes and McCandless (Horne) C.; grad. St. Louis Country Day Sch., 1931; A.B., Yale, 1935; LL.B., 1938; m. Elizabeth Olive Sewall, July 9, 1938; children—Robert Horne, Ellena, Sumner Sewall, McCandless, Elizabeth. Admitted to Mo., Fed. bars, 1938; with Thompson, Mitchell, Thompson & Young, St. Louis, 1938-41; with McDonnell Aircraft Corp., St. Louis, 1941-60, asst. sec., 1943-45, sec., 1945-52, dir., 1948-60, mem. exec. com., 1949-60, v.p., 1952-53, exec. v.p. 1953-60; exec. v.p., mem. exec. com., dir. Universal Match Corp., 1960-61; cons. to adminstr. NASA, Washington, 1962-63; asst. sec of Air Force, 1963-69; v.p. Textron, Inc., Procidence, 1970—; dir. Hamilton Shoe Co., St. Louis, Gateway Fund, St. Louis. Bd. dirs., pres. Geo-Transport Found. of New Eng., 1970—; bd. mgrs. Central Inst. for Deaf, 1958-62; trustee St. Louis Country Day Sch., 1953-56. Mem. St. Louis County C. of C. (dir. 1958-62), Am. Bar Assn., Mo. Bar, Am. Ordnance Assn. (pres. St. Louis 1961-62). Episcopalian. Clubs: Knickerbocker, Yale (N.Y.C.); Racquet, St. Louis Country, Yale (pres. 1961-62) (St. Louis); Burning Tree, Chevy Chase, Metropolitan (Washington). Home: 3529 R St NW Washington DC 20007 Office: 1000 Connecticut Av Washington DC 20036

CHARLES, WILLIAM HAMILL, lawyer; b. St. Louis, Sept. 14, 1913; s. Benjamin Hynes and Nancy McCandless (Horne) C.; A.B., Yale, 1935, L.L.B., 1938; m. Ann Stoughton, June 21, 1941; children—William Hamill, Ann Stoughton. Admitted to Mo. bar, 1939, since practiced in St. Louis; partner firm Bryan, Cave, McPheeters & McRoberts, 1952—. Chmn. com. Health and Welfare Council St. Louis, 1948-60, Jefferson Nat. Expansion Meml. Assn., 1964—. Bd. dirs. Girls Home, 1954-60, Wesley House Assn., 1949-55, Edgewood Children's Center, 1961-67, Planned Parenthood Assn. St. Louis, 1947—; sec. St. Louis Country Day Sch., 1950-52, bd. dirs., 1947-52; pres. Mary Inst., 1963-64, bd. dirs., 1959-64; mem. exec. com. Yale Alumni Bd., 1968—. Served to capt. AUS, 1942-46. Decorated Bronze Star. Mem. Am., Mo. bar assns., Bar Assn. St. Louis, Mo. Hist. Soc. (pres. 1965-68). Episcopalian. Clubs: St. Louis Country, Noonday, Yale (pres. 1965), Yale Law (pres. 1962—), Deer Creek (St Louis). Home: 2 Upper Ladue Rd St Louis, MO 63124. Office: 314 N Broadway St Louis MO 63102

CHARLESWORTH, JAMES CLYDE, educator; b. nr. Greensburg, Pa., May 21, 1900; s. James and Priscilla (Hawkins) C.; student Carnegie Inst. Tech., 1919-23; A.B., U. Pitts., 1926, A.M., 1927, Ph.D., 1932; postgrad. Harvard, 1928; m. Dorothy Louise Coy, Aug. 14, 1928 (dec. Sept. 1945); children—Audrey Elaine, Sylvia Jean; m. 2d, Berenice Lucille Steward, July 6, 1946 (dec. Dec. 1969); children—Pamela Steward, Rodney J. Asst. chief engr. Miller Machine Co. Pitts., 1922-24; mem. faculty U. Pitts., 1926-39; faculty U. Pa. 1930—, prof. polit. sci. 1945—, dir. grad. div. Wharton Sch., 1942-43, supr. ednl. program Inst. Local and State Govt., 1939-55. Sec. adminstrn. Commonwealth Pa., 1955-56; exec. dir. Pa. Reorgn. Commn., 1956; comdg. officer Strategic Intelligence Unit, U. Pa., 1946-47; dir. personnel and tng. Phila Regional Civilian Def. Council, 1942. Served from maj. to lt. col. AUS, 1943-46. Decorated Legion of Merit. Mem. Am., Western, So. polit. sci. assns., Am. Soc. for Pub. Adminstrn. (pres. Phila. region 1947-49), Am. Acad. Polit. and Social Sci. (asso. editor Annals 1949-53, acting editor 1950-51, pres. 1953—), Nat. Parks Assn. (dir.), United World Fedn., Phi Beta Kappa. Author: Governmental Administration, 1951; Governmental Reorganization of the Commonwealth of Pennsylvania, 1957. Editor: American Civilization and Its Leadership Needs, 1959; Behavioralism in Political Science, 1962; Mathematics and the Social Sciences, 1963; Leisure in America, Blessing or Curse? 1964; Ethics in America; Norms and Deviations, 1966; A Design for Political Science, 1966; Contemporary Political Analysis, 1966; The Changing American People: Are We Deteriorating or Improving?, 1968; The Theory and Practice of Public Administration, 1968; Harmonizing Technological Development and Social Policy in America, 1970; America's Most Challenging Objectives, 1971. Contbr. articles to profl. jours. Home: 7125 Penarth Av Upper Darby PA 19082 Office: Am Acad Polit and Social Sci 3937 Chestnut St Philadelphia PA 19104

CHARLOT, JEAN, muralist; b. Paris, France, February 8, 1898; s. Henri and Anna (Goupil) C.; educated pub schs. and art schs.; D.F.A. (hon., Grinnell Coll., 1946; LL.D., St. Marys Coll., 1956; m. Dorothy Zohmah Day, May 26, 1939; children—Ann Maria, John Pierre, Martin Day, Peter Francis. Mural painting for Mexican gov., 1922-26; archeol. studies in Yucatan, Carnegie Instn., Washington, 1926-29; painter, lectr. and art tchr., U.S., 1929—; held more than 100 one-man shows murals in N.J., Ia., N.C., Ga.; recent murals, Notre Dame U., St. Mary's Coll., Ind., Des Moines Art Center, Christ the Good Shepherd Ch., Lincoln Pk., Mich., St. Sylvester Ch., Kilauea Kauai, Hawaiian Village Hotel, Walkiki, Des Moines (Ia.) Art Center; sculpture includes, statue, Hanalei, panels for chapel doors Punahou Sch., bas-reliefs St. John's Evangelist Ch., Mililani, Oahu, ceramic statue Ala Moana Hotel, Honolulu; instr. Art Students League, Ia. U., U. Cal., Columbia, U. Ga., Black Mountain Coll., Smith Coll.; head Fine Arts Sch., Colo. Springs, 1947-50; prof. art U. Hawaii, 1949-66, now emeritus, sr. specialist East- West Center, 1967—. Ryerson lectr., Yale, 1948; summer tchr. U. Notre Dame, Indiana, 1955-56. Served as artillery officer, World War I. Recipient award of merit Honolulu chpt. Nat. Soc. Arts and Letters. Fellow in perpetuity Met. Mus. Art; Guggenheim Fellow, 1945- 47. Nat. dir. Artists Equity. Mem. Am. Inst. Graphic Arts (v.p. 1947), Soc. Am. Etchers, Gravers, Litho., Woodcutters, Hawaiian Hist. Soc. Author books including: Art-Making from Mexico to China, 1950; Dance of Death, 1951. Illustrator many books. Contbr. articles to mags. and periodicals in Mexico and U.S. Executed over 35 murals since 1922, latest being Ch. St. Francis Xavier, Naiserelagi, Fiji, 1962-63, Jefferson Hall, East West Center, Honolulu, 1967, Grace Episcopal Ch., Hoolehua, Molokai, 1967, United Pub. Workers Bldg., Honolulu, 1970. Author or illustrator of over sixty-five books, latest being Mexican Art and the Academy of San Carlos, 1875-1915, 1963; Mexican Mural Renaissance, 1963; Three Plays of Ancient Hawaii, 1963; Jean Charlot: Posada's Dance of Death, 1964; The Timid Ghost (by Anita Brenner), 1966; The Art of Salad Making (by Carol Truex), 1968; Mowentihke Chalman, 1969; Spoken Hawaiian (by Samuel H. Elbert), 1970; An Artist on Art, 1971. Home: 4956 Kahala Av Honolulu HI 96815

CHARLOTTE, GRAND DUCHESS OF LUXEMBOURG, b. Chateau de Berg, Luxembourg, Jan. 23, 1896; d. Guillaume, Grand Duke of Luxembourg and Marie-Anne of Braganca; m. Felix, Prince of Bourbon- Parma, Nov. 6, 1919 (dec. Apr. 1970); children—Jean, Elizabeth, Adelaide, Gabrielle, Charles, Alix. Succeeded to Throne (after abdication of elder sister), Jan. 15, 1919; left country after German invasion, 1940, spent years, 1940-43 in U.S. and Can., returning after liberation of Grand Duchy by U.S. Army; abdicated in favor of son, Jean, 1964. Address: Grand Ducal Palace Luxembourg

CHARMAN, FREDERICK MONTAQUE, artist, educator; b. London, Eng., Apr. 6, 1894; s. Frederic William and Lilly Marie (Ings) C.; ed. pub. schs., Eng.; art edn. Hammersmith Sch., London, and from Sidney Haward; m. Jessie Harris Bone, June 24, 1925. Came to U.S., 1923, naturalized, 1933. Prof. design, Coll. Fine Arts, Syracuse U., 1925-60, prof. design emeritus, 1960—, vis. prof., 1962; designer (fabric and indsl.), 1920—, painter oil and water colors 1922—; work in permanent collections mus., and art galleries; exhibitor annually prin. nat. and regional exhibitions, 1925—; exhibited by invitation: Chgo. Internat., 1936; Water Color Exhibit, N.A.D., 1948; Balt. water color Nat. Ann., 1948; Syracuse Mus. Fine Arts, Cedar City (Utah) Ann. Nat., Springville (Utah), Munson-Williams-Proctor Inst., Utica, N.Y., 1959; also one-man shows, Syracuse, N.Y., Ogden, Salt Lake City, 1956, Cazenovia (N.Y.) Coll., 1961, N.Y. Telephone Co. Lobby Gallery, 1965, Muggleton Galleries, Auburn, N.Y., 1965. Recipient 1st prize for water color Syracuse Regional Exhbn., 1963. Mem. Am., Phila. water color socs., Audubon Artists, Asso. Artists Syracuse (Gordon Steele Meml. award 1967; dir.), Cooperstown Art Assn., Eight Syracuse Watercolorists, Phi Kappa Phi, Tau Sigma Delta, Alpha Xi Alpha. Author: (article) Water Color Demonstrated, 1945; Articles for American Artist. Home: 571 Cumberland Av Syracuse NY 13210

CHARMOLI, TONY, choreographer; b. Minn.; grad. magna cum laude St. Thomas Coll.; dance student Jacob's Pillow, 1946, Am. Theater Wing, 1947. Presently stage, TV choreographer. Served with Am. armed forces, to 1946. Recipient TV Emmy, George Foster Peabody award, others. Choreographer TV shows including: Your Hit Parade, The Dinah Shore Show, The Danny Kaye Show, The Julie Andrews Show, also numerous TV specials. Office: Desilu-Gower Studios Thomas-Spelling Prodns 780 Gower St Hollywood CA 90038

CHARNAUX-GRILLET, RAYMOND PAUL, former mfg. co. exec.; b. Pontarlier, France, Nov. 1, 1922; s. Henry G. and Mary (Bourgeois) Charnaux-G.; B.Sc., U. Besancon (France), 1941, certificate physics, 1943; M.B.A., U. Toronto, 1954; m. Helga Haas, Oct. 26, 1957; children—Hubert, Elizabeth, Lisa-Anne. Came to U.S., 1954, naturalized, 1960. Vice chmn., dir. Joy Mfg. Holding, SA, Luxembourg; former v.p. Joy Mfg. Co., Pitts.; pres. Joy Internat., S.A., Panama; dir. Joy-Sullivan Ltd., London, Eng., Joy-Ville-Gozet, S.A., Paris, France. Mem. I.E.E.E.*

CHARNES, ABRAHAM, educator. Formerly organizer, dir. mgmt. scis. research group Purdue U., also naval operations research group in World War II; now research prof. depts. math., econs., engring. scis., indsl. engring. and mgmt. scis. Applied Math. Center and Bio-Med. Engring. Center, Northwestern U. Fellow Operations Research Soc. Am., Econometric Soc., A.A.A.S.; mem. Inst. Mgmt. Scis. (founding mem., past pres.). Author numerous articles in field, also co-author three books translated into Russian, Japanese and Czechoslovakian. Address: Technology Inst Northwestern Univ Evanston IL 60201*

CHARNEY, JULE GREGORY, meteorologist; b. San Francisco, Jan. 1, 1917; s. Ely and Stella (Litman) C.; A.B., U. Cal. at Los Angeles, 1938, M.A., 1940, Ph.D., 1946; postgrad. (NRC fellow), U. Oslo, Norway, 1947-48; D.Sc., U. Chgo., 1970; children—Nicolas, Nora, Peter. Instr., lectr. physics-meteorology U. Cal. at Los Angeles, 1942-46; research asso. U. Chgo., 1946-47; mem., dir. meteorology project Inst. Advanced Study, Princeton, N.J., 1948-56; prof. meteorology Mass. Inst. Tech., 1956—, Alfred P. Sloan prof., 1966—. Chmn. U.S. com. for Global Atmospheric Research Program, Nat. Acad. Sci., 1968-71. Recipient Robert M. Losey award Inst. Aero. Scis., 1957, Symons Meml. gold medal Royal Meteorol. Soc., 1961, Hodgkins medal Smithsonian Instn., 1968, Internat. Meteorol. Orgn. prize, 1971. Fellow Am. Geophys. Union (pres. meteorol. sect. 1970—), Am. Meteorol. Soc. (Meisinger award 1949, Carl-Gustav Rossby medal 1964), Nat. Acad. Scis., Am. Acad. Arts and Scis., Am. Civil Liberties Union, Royal Swedish (fgn. mem.), Norwegian acads. scis., Phi Beta Kappa. Author articles dynamic meteorology, oceanography. Home: 80 Monmouth St Brookline MA 02146 Office: Mass Inst Tech Cambridge MA 02139

CHARNEY, NICOLAS HERMAN, publisher; b. St. Paul, May 11, 1941; s. Jule G. and Elinor K. (Kesting) C.; B.S., Mass. Inst. Tech., 1961; Ph.D., U. Chgo., 1966; m. Ann Perkins, Mar. 10, 1966; 1 dau., Sarah Camille. Mem. faculty U. Cal., San Diego, 1966-67; founder CRM, Inc., also Psychology Today mag., Del Mar, Cal., 1967, chmn., editor-in-chief, 1967-71; publisher, part-owner Sat. Rev., 1971—. Home: RFD 113 Del Mar CA 92014 Office: 162 E 64th St New York City NY

CHARNLEY, MITCHELL VAUGHN, educator; b. Goshen, Ind., April 9, 1898; s. William Herbert and Louise (Carmien) C.; B.A., Williams Coll., 1919; M.A. in Journalism, U. Wash., 1921; m. Margery A. Lindsay, September 12, 1922 (div. Feb. 1936); 1 son, Donn; m. 2d, Jean Clifford, July 24, 1937; children—Deborah, Blair. Reporter Honolulu Star-Bull., 1921; news editor Walla Walla Bull., 1922; reporter Detroit News, 1922-23; editorial asst. The American Boy, Detroit, 1923-24, asst. mng. editor, 1924-26, acting mng. editor, 1926; asst. editor Short Stories, N.Y., 1927-28; asst. editor Am. Boy, 1928-30; asst. prof. journalism, Ia. State Coll., 1930-31, asso. prof., 1931-34; asst. prof. journalism, U. Minn., 1934-37, asso. prof., 1937-40, prof. 1940-66, William J. Murphy prof. journalism, 1966- 68, prof. emeritus, 1968—, acting chairman dept. journalism, 1937-38, asst. dean Arts Coll., 1958-65, asso. dir. univ. relations, 1969, spl. asst. to dean Arts Coll., 1970-72. Fulbright lectr. journalism and mass communications, U. Florence, Italy, 1952-53; editorial cons. to newspapers and mental health enterprises, 1968-70; editorial cons. Mpls. Tribune, 1969-71. Mem. Council Radio-TV Journalism, 1944-58, chmn. 1948-49. Recipient Tchr. of Year award Sigma Delta Chi, 1968. Mem. Radio-TV News Dirs. Assn. (Distinguished Achievement award 1963), Am. Civil Liberties Union, Assn. for Edn. in Journalism (pres. 1959), Nat. (dir.), Minn. (pres. 1959- 60) assns. mental health, Phi Gamma Delta, Sigma Delta Chi (nat. historian, 1924-26; alumni sec., 1933-35; v.p. 1935-37; chmn. research com., 1937-42). Author books including: News by Radio, 1948; Reporting, 1959. Editor and also compiler of various works; mng. editor Journalism Quarterly, 1935-45, acting editor, 1937-38; contbg. editor The Quill, 1928-50. Contbr. articles, fiction, verse and book revs. to mags. Home: 88 Orlin Av SE Minneapolis MN 55414

CHARPENTIER, ARTHUR ALDRICH, law librarian; b. Waterbury, Conn., Aug. 13, 1919; s. Donat Arthur and Mary Belle (Aldrich) C.; B.S., Springfield (Mass.) Coll., 1941; LL.B., Boston U., 1948; m. Phyllis Eugenia Smith, May 29, 1943; children—Meredith J., Susan A., Peter A., Nancy D. Admitted to Mass. bar, 1948; librarian Boston U. Sch. Law, 1948-50; asst. librarian Assn. Bar City N.Y., 1950-57, librarian, 1957-67; law librarian Yale Law Sch., 1967-70, asso. dean, librarian, 1970—. Mem. library services com. Am. Bar Found.; library adv. com. Am. Arbitration Assn. Served to capt. F.A., AUS, 1941-46. Mem. Am. Assn. Law Libraries (exec. bd. 1962-65, pres. 1965-66), Am. Bar Assn., Internat. Assn. Law Libraries (v.p. 1968-71), Law Library Assn. Greater N.Y. (pres. 1957-58), Kappa Delta Pi. Conglist. Home: 96 Carmalt Rd Hamden CT 06517 Office: Yale Law School New Haven CT 06520

CHARPIE, ROBERT ALAN, physicist; b. Cleve., Sept. 9, 1925; s. Leonard Asbury and Dorothy (McLean) C.; B.S. with honors, Carnegie Inst. Tech., 1948, M.S., 1949, D.Sc. in Theoretical Physics, 1950; D.H.L., Denison U., 1965; D.Sc., Alderson-Broaddus College, 1967; m. Elizabeth Downs, July 12, 1947; children—Richard Alan, Carol Elizabeth, David Wayne, John Robert. With Westinghouse Electric Corp., 1947-50; with Oak Ridge Nat. Lab., 1950-51, tech. asst. to research dir., 1952-54, asst. research dir., 1954-58, dir. reactor div., 1958-61; mgr. adv. devel. Union Carbide Corp., 1961-63, gen. mgr. devel. dept. 1963-64, dir. tech., 1964-66, pres. electronics div., 1966-68; pres. Bell & Howell Co., Chgo., 1968-69; pres., dir. Cabot Corp., Boston, 1969—. Panel oceanography Pres.'s Sci. Adv. Com.; adv. com. UN sci. activities State Dept., 1961—; panels civilian tech. and Pakistan, Pres.'s Sci. Adv. Com., 1961—; sec. gen. adv. com. AEC, 1959-63; mem. Nat. Sci. Bd., 1969—; sci. sec., editor-in-chief proc., author preliminary agenda, also asst. U.S. mem. 7 nation adv. com., 1st Internat. Conf. Peaceful Uses Atomic Energy, 1955, coordinator U.S. fusion research exhibit, 2d Conf., 1958; chmn. invention and innovation panel U.S. Dept. Commerce, 1965-67. Mem. Oak Ridge Bd. Edn., 1957-61; pres. Byram Hills Central Sch. Dist., 1966-68. Trustee Carnegie Inst. Tech., 1962—. Named one of Ten Outstanding Young Men, U.S. Jr. C. of C., 1955; recipient Alumni Merit award Carnegie Inst. Tech., 1957. Fellow Am. Phys. Soc., Am. Nuclear Soc. (bd. dirs.); mem. N.Y. Acad. Sci., Sci. Research Soc. Am., Sigma Xi, Tau Beta Pi, Phi Mu Epsilon. Gen. editor Internat. Monograph Series on Nuclear Energy, 1955-60; editor Progress Series in Nuclear Energy, 1955-60; editor Jour. Nuclear Energy, 1955-60. Office: 125 High St Boston MA 02110

CHARRIN, PAUL JACQUES, oil well cons.; b. Paris, France, Sept. 26, 1901; s. Jacques and Jenny (Des Barrieres) C.; B.A., B.S., U. Paris, 1919, M.S., 1921, LL.B., 1923; Mining Engr., Paris Sch. Mines, 1924; m. Gilberte Denise Moulliere, June 4, 1935; children—Jacques Rene, Pierre Henri, Monique Jeanne. Came to U.S., 1936, naturalized, 1943. From engr. to gen. mgr. Societe de Prospection Electrique, Paris, 1926-36; v.p. Schlumberger Well Surveying Corp., Houston, 1936-45; pres. Pan Geo Atlas Corp., Houston, 1946-65, chmn. bd., 1966-68; pres., dir. Pan Geo Atlas Can., Ltd., 1949-66, Servicios Technicos Atlas, C.A., Venezuela, Bolivia, 1955- 66, Servicios Tecnicos Atlas, S.A., Argentina, 1960-66, PGAC Internat. Corp., 1960-70; pres. Dresser Atlas (France) S.A., Algeria, Libya, Nigeria, Tunisia, 1960-70; spl. cons. to petroleum and mining group Dresser Industries, Inc., 1968-70, cons., 1971—. Mem. Am. Assn. Petroleum Geologists, Am. Inst. Mining and Metall. Engrs., Soc. Exploration Geophysicists, Am. Petroleum Inst., Assn. Francaise des Techniciens du Petrole, Societe des Ingenieurs Civils de France. Home: 11902 Cobblestone Dr Houston TX 77024 Office: 3130 Southwest Freeway Houston TX 77006

CHARRON, ANDRE, investment co. exec.; b. Montreal, Can., Dec. 10, 1923; s. Ernest and Antionette (Champagne), C.; B.A., Coll. Ste.-Marie, 1944; LL.B., U. Montreal, 1947; m. Louise Mongeau, June 14, 1956; children—Andre, Caroline, Guy-Philippe, Fannie, Nicolas. Called to bar Province Que., 1948, created Queen's counsel, 1964; mem. firm Brais, Campbell & Assos., 1947-48, Andre Charron, 1948-58, Charron & Mercier, 1958-63; v.p., dir. Indsl. Life Ins. Co.; pres. Mont Tremblant Lodge (1965) Inc.; dir. Nat. Canadian Bank, Ciments Lafarge (Que.) Ltee., Nat. Trust Co. Ltd., Canadian Arena Co., Steinberg's Ltd. Mem. Nat. Adv. Com. Fitness and Amateur Sport. Treas. Hosp. Marie-Enfant. Roman Catholic. Clubs: St.-Denis; de Reforme; Montreal, Montreal Athletic Amateur Assn. Home: 164 Springrove Crescent Outremont Montreal 1953 Quebec Canada Office: 360 St James St Montreal 126 Quebec Canada

CHARTERIS, LESLIE, author; b. Singapore, May 12, 1907; student Cambridge U., 1926; studied art in Paris; m. Pauline Schishkin, 1931 (div. 1937); 1 dau., Patricia Ann; m. 2d, Barbara Meyer, 1938 (div.); m. 3d, Elizabeth Bryant Borst, 1943 (div.); m. 4th, Audrey Long, 1952. Naturalized U.S. citizen, 1946. Fellow Royal Soc. Arts; mem. Mensa. Clubs: Savage, Yacht de Cannes. Author numerous books from Meet the Tiger, 1928, to Saint to the Rescue, 1959; Trust the Saint, 1962; The Saint in the Sun, 1963; Vendetta for the Saint, 1964; The Saint on TV, 1968; The Saint Returns, 1968; The Saint Abroad, 1969; The Saint in Pursuit, 1971. Contbr. to numerous mags.; also written several motion picture plays. Office: Box 2614 Palm Beach FL 33480

CHARTERS, ALEXANDER NATHANIEL, univ. v.p.; b. Verdant Valley, Alberta, Can., Aug. 22, 1916; s. Alexander Allen and Louisa Magdalena (Kern) C.; B.A., U. B.C., 1938; Ph.D., U. Chgo., 1948; m. Margaret Anne MacNaughton, Mar. 29, 1952; children—Alexander W., David W., John C., Louisa A. Came to U.S., 1948, naturalized, 1957. Tchr. pub. schs., Fernie, B.C., 1939-41, Vancouver, 1941-42; asst. to dean Univ. Coll., Syracuse U., 1948-50, asst. dean, 1950-52, dean, 1952-64, asst. prof. Sch. Edn., 1950-54, asso. prof., 1954-59, prod., 1959—; univ. v.p. continuing edn., 1964—; vis mem. faculty U. Chgo., summer 1958. Mem. bd. Center Study Liberal Edn. Adults, 1957-67; chmn., 1964-65; treas. Internat. Congress U. Adult Edn., 1962-67; mem. N.Y. State Adv. Bd. on Continuation Higher Edn. Mem. exec. com. Met. Syracuse Council Arts and Scis. Mem. com. of 99, chmn. priorities com. Community Chest and Council; dir. Chautaqua Inst., Laubach Literacy Found., Syracuse World Affairs Com., U.S. Nat. Com. UNESCO. Bd. visitors U. Pitts., Washington U., St. Louis. Served with Royal Can. Naval Vol. Res., 1942-45. Mem. Assn. U. Evening Colls. (pres. 1957-48), Adult Edn. Assn., Nat. U. Extension Assn. (pres. 1965-66), Beta Theta Pi. Presbyn. (clk. of session). Clubs: Rotary; University (Syracuse). Contbr. articles to profl. publs. Home: 216 Lockwood Rd Syracuse NY 13214

CHARTERS, ROBERT MICHAEL, lawyer; b. Lincoln, Neb., Jan. 9, 1909; s. Robert W. and Nellie (Houston) C.; A.B., U. Neb., 1931, LL.B., 1934; m. Gerry Thomas, Jan. 7, 1942; children—Mary K., Susan A. Admitted to Neb. bar, 1933, N.Y. bar, 1946; practiced in Lincoln, 1933-41; dist. supr. HOLC, 1935-41; trust, escrow officer Cal. Trust Co., 1941-42; atty. Fed. Pub. Housing Authority, Chgo., 1942; with firm Rogers, Hoge & Hills, N.Y.C., 1945-48; sec., gen. counsel Assn. Stock Exchange Firms, N.Y.C., 1948-56, exec. dir., gen. counsel, 1957—; partner Carlisle and Jacquelin, N.Y.C., mem. N.Y. Stock Exchange, 1963—; ltd. partner Carlisle Decoppet & Co. Served as lt. comdr. USNR, 1942-45. Mem. Am., Neb., N.Y. County bar assns., Assn. Bar City N.Y., Alpha Tau Omega, Phi Delta Phi. Republican. Lion. Clubs: University of Neb. Alumni (pres. N.Y.C. 1957); N.Y. Stock Exchange Luncheon (N.Y.C.); Huntington Country; Midday Lunch. Home: Bacon Rd Old Westbury NY 12123 also 2565 S Ocean Blvd Palm Beach FL 33403 Office: 2 Broadway New York City NY 10004

CHARTERS, WILLIAM ALLEN, mortgage and investment banker; b. Norfolk, Va., Feb. 26, 1894; s. Charles Linwood and Elizabeth Frances (West) C.; student Norfolk pub. schs.; m. Emma Jane Mercer, July 12, 1924. With Norfolk Bank for Savs. & Trusts (later Trust Co. of Norfolk), 1912-27; with Investment Corp. of Norfolk, 1927—, successively sec.-treas., v.p., 1927-50, pres., dir., 1950-64, chmn. bd., 1964—; pres., dir. Investment Corp. of Va., 1960- 64, chmn. bd., 1964—; pres., dir. Lakewood, Inc., Norfolk; chmn. bd. Norfolk-Justice Ins. Corporation. Chairman of the Employees' Retirement System of Norfolk; mem. bd. review Real Estate Assessments Norfolk. Trustee Leigh Meml. Hosp. Served with USNRF, World War I. Mem. Norfolk C. of C. (past director), N.Y., Am. (asso. mem.), Phila.- Balt. stock exchanges. Episcopalian. Clubs: Virginia; Pyramid; Norfolk Yacht and Country. Home: 1302 Harmott Av Norfolk VA 23509 Office: 215 E Plume St Norfolk VA 23514

CHARTON, MARVIN, chemist, educator; b. Bklyn., May 1, 1931; s. William and Elsie (Halpern) C.; B.S., Coll. City N.Y., 1953; M.A., Bklyn. Coll., 1956; Ph.D., Stevens Inst. Tech., 1962; m. Barbara Israel, Aug. 28, 1955; children—Michael, Sarah, Deborah. Instr. chemistry Pratt Inst., Bklyn., 1956-61, asst. prof., 1961-64, asso. prof., 1964-67, prof., 1967—, chmn. dept., 1969—. Fellow Intrasci. Research Found.; mem. Am. Chem. Soc., Royal Chem. Soc. London, N.Y. Acad. Scis., A.A.A.S., Sigma Xi. Contbr. articles profl. jours. Home: 1 Grace Ct Brooklyn NY 11201

CHARUSATHIRA, PRAPAS, dep. premier Thailand; b. 1912; ed. Chulachomklao Royal Mil. Acad., also Nat. Def. Coll. Mem. Thailand Army, 1932—; apptd. gen., 1960; minister interior, 1957—; dep. prime minister, 1963—; army dep. comdr. and dep. supreme comdr., 1963-64, supreme comdr., 1964—. Rector Chulalongkorn U., 1961—. Decorated Crown Thailand (highest class). Author: The Role of the Ministery of Interior in the Development of National Security; The Role of the Ministry of Interior in Maintenance of National Peace and Order. Address: 132-5 Suan Puttan Residence Bangkok Thailand*

CHARWAT, ANDREW FRANCISZEK, educator; b. Talin, Estonia, Feb. 10, 1925; s. Franciszek and Wanda (Niec) C.; came to U.S., 1945, naturalized, 1952; student U. Paranaense, Curitiba, Brazil, 1945; M.E. with distinction, Stevens Inst. Tech., 1948; M.S., U. Cal. at Berkeley, 1949, Ph.D., 1952; m. Halina Maria Stieglitz, Aug. 10, 1948; 1 dau., Danuta Karen. Teaching asst., then instr. mech. engring. U. Cal. at Berkeley, 1948-52; faculty U. Cal. at Los Angeles, 1955—, prof. engring., 1961—, head high speed aerodynamics and propulsion lab., 1957—; asso. prof. Faculte des Scis., U. Paris (France), 1961-63. Vis. lectr. Tng. Center Exptl. Aerodynamics, NATO, 1959; lectr. USIS, Paris, 1962; cons. to govt. and industry, 1954- -. Chmn. Heat Transfer and Fluid Mechanics Inst., 1964-65; mem. com. basic research Nat. Acad. Scis.-NRC, 1965—. Fulbright fellow, 1961-62; Guggenheim fellow, 1962-63; recipient Distinguished Teaching award Engring. Students' Soc., U. Cal. at Los Angeles, 1965. Asso. fellow Am. Inst. Aeros. and Astronautics; Sr. mem. Am. Rocket Soc. (chmn. Western regional student-faculty conf. 1958); mem. Combustion Inst. (vice chmn. Western sect. 1957-58), Soc. Francaise d'Astronautique, Sigma Xi, Tau Beta Pi. Author numerous research papers. Home: 219 Glenroy Pl Los Angeles, CA 90049.

CHARYK, JOSEPH VINCENT, bus. exec.; b. Canmore, Alberta, Can., Sept. 9, 1920; s. John and Anna (Dorosh) C.; B.Sc. in Engring. Physics, U. Alberta, 1942, LL.D., 1964; M.S., Cal. Inst. Tech., 1943, Ph.D., 1946; m. Edwina Elizabeth Rhodes, Aug. 18, 1945; children—William R., Joseph J., Christopher E., Diane E. Came to U.S., 1942, naturalized, 1948. Sect. chief Jet Propulsion Lab., Cal. Inst. Tech., 1945-46, instr. aero., 1945-46; asst. prof. aero., Princeton, 1946-49, asso. prof., 1949- 55; dir. aerophysics and chemistry lab., missile systems div. Lockheed Aircraft Corp., 1955-56; dir. aero. lab., Aeronutronic Systems, Inc., subsidiary Ford Motor Co., 1956-58, gen. mgr. space tech. div., 1958-59. Cons. Sci. Adv. Bd. USAF, 1957-58, mem. 1958-59; asst. AF Sec. Research and Devel., 1959; under secretary of Air Force, 1960-63; pres., dir. Communications Satellite Corp., 1963—. Fellow Am. Inst. Aeros. and Astronautics; mem. Internat. Acad. Astronautics, Nat. Inst. Social Scis., Internat. Broadcast Inst., Newcomen Soc., Sigma Xi. Clubs: 1925 F Street, Federal City, Congressional Country, Chevy Chase; Nat. Space. Asso. editor, gen. editor High Speed Aerodynamics and Jet Propulsion (12 vols.), 1954-58. Contbr. articles to tech. jours. Home: 5126 Tilden St NW Washington DC 20016

CHARYN, JEROME, author; b. N.Y.C., May 13, 1937; s. Sam and Fannie (Paley) C.; B.A. cum laude, Columbia, 1959. Former recreation leader Dept. Parks, N.Y.C.; English tchr. High Sch. Music and Art, Sch. Performing Arts, N.Y.C., 1962-64; asst. prof. English, vis. writer Stanford, 1965-68; asst. prof. English, Herbert Lehman Coll., City U. N.Y., 1968—. Mem. P.E.N., Phi Beta Kappa. Author: Once Upon a Droshky, 1964; On the Darkening Green, 1965; The Man Who Grew Younger, 1967; Going to Jerusalem, 1967; American Scrapbook, 1969; Eisenhower, My Eisenhower, 1971; also short stories. Editor: The Single Voice, 1969; The Troubled Vision, 1970; co-editor The Dutton Review, 1970—. Home: New York City NY Office: Dept English Herbert Lehman Coll Bedford Park Blvd W Bronx New York City NY 10468

CHASE, ALLEN, investment banker; b. Los Angeles, Sept. 11, 1911; s. Edward Tilden and Lenna (Prather) C.; B.S., U. Cal. at Los Angeles, 1933; postgrad. London Sch. Econs., U. London (Eng.), 1934; children—Charlene (Mrs. Alan Kreiger), Diane (Mrs. Jerome Randolph). Salesman, Chase Securities Co., Los Angeles, 1934-39; pres. Standardized Aircraft Co., Los Angeles, 1939—; chmn. bd. dirs. Esperence Plains Pty. Ltd., Australia, 1956—, Agra Paraguay, 1967—; pres. Allen Chase & Co., 1964—; dir. Trans World Financial Co., Allied Pastoral Co. Pty. Ltd., Australia, San Fernando Valley Bank, Los Angeles, Yokine Pastoral Co. Pty. Ltd., Australian. Pres., So. Cal. and Nev., Confrerie de la Chaine des Ratisseurs. Conceived establishment over one million virgin acres to agr. in single area by pvt. enterprise. Home: Riviera Country Club Pacific Palisades CA 90272 Office: 1250 Capri Dr Pacific Palisades CA 90272

CHASE, ANTHONY GOODWIN, govt. ofcl.; b. San Francisco, Feb. 15, 1938; s. Goodwin and Gudrun M. (Mack) C.; B.A., U. Wash., 1960; J.D., Georgetown U., 1967; m. Karen Zeissler, June 18, 1960; children—Elizabeth Marie, Whitney Marie, Goodwin Samuel. Nat. bank examiner U.S. Treasury Dept., 1962-65; asst. U.S. Comptroller of the Currency, 1965-67; admitted to D.C. bar, 1967, Wash., bar, 1969; pvt. practice law, 1967-69; asst. to U.S. Sec. of Commerce, 1969-70; gen. counsel Small Bus. Adminstrn., Washington, 1970-71, dep. adminstr., 1971—; adj. prof. corporate problems Georgetown U., mem. faculty Practicing Law Inst. Sec. Nat. Adv. Com. on Banking Policies and Practices, 1966; mem. Adminstrv. Conf. U.S., Fed. Adv. Council Regional Econ. Devel., Under Sec.'s Group of U.S. Domestic Council; fed. state programs coordinator State of Wash., 1967. Trustee Pierce County March of Dimes, 1969-70; mem. nat. devel. com. Georgetown U., 1970—; mem. bd. control U. Wash., 1960. Served as lt. USMC, 1960-62. Named outstanding young man of year Wash. Jr. C. of C., 1968; recipient fed. silver medal for meritorious service, 1970. Mem. Am., Fed., D.C., Wash. bar assns., Am. Judicature Soc., Nat. Lawyers Club, U.S. Navy League. Republican. Clubs: University, National Press, National Aviation (Washington), Tacoma Country and Golf, Tacoma Lawn Tennis. Contbr. articles profl. jours. Home: 4 Carvel Circle Washington DC 20016 Office: 1441 L St Washington DC 20416

CHASE, AURIN MOODY, Jr., educator; b. Syracuse, N.Y. June 2, 1904; s. Aurin Moody and Bertha (Bucklin) C.; A.B., Amherst Coll., 1926, A.M., 1929; Ph.D., Columbia, 1935; m. Osmunde Olcott Phillips, Dec. 31, 1937; 1 dau., Elise Phillips (Mrs. Tom R. Dennis). Asst. biology Amherst Coll., 1926-28; asst. biophysics Columbia, 1929- 34, instr., research asst. 1934-38; research asso. biology Princeton, 1939-45, asst. prof. biology, 1945-48, asso. prof., 1948-61, prof., 1961-67, prof. biology emeritus, 1967—. Instr., Marine Biol. Lab., Woods Hole, Mass., summers 1945-46, mem. corp., (trustee, 1950-58, 59-67, sec. bd. trustees 1956-58); mem. corp. Bermuda Biol. Sta. Fellow A.A.A.S., N.Y. Acad. Scis.; mem. Am. Physiol. Soc., Am. Soc. Zoologists, N.J. Acad. Scis., Soc. Gen. Physiologists (exec. council 1951-53, treas. 1957-59), Am. Soc. Biol. Chemists, Am. Soc. Cell Biology, Sigma Xi. Episcopalian. Club: Nassau (Princeton, N.J.). Contbr. articles to profl. books, jours. Research on gen. physiology, biochemistry of vision and bioluminescence, human blood storage, enzyme action. Home: 31 Adams Dr Princeton NJ 08540

CHASE, CHARLES HENRY, ret. army officer; b. Portland, Me., Aug. 14, 1910; s. Frank Cushing and Lena Ernestine (Crocker) C.; B.S., U.S. Mil. Acad., 1933; M.S., George Washington U., 1969; grad. Armed Forces Staff Coll., 1947, Army War Coll., 1951, Naval War Coll., 1953; m. Elizabeth Elois Cummings, Aug. 23, 1936; children—Astrid, Frank Charles. Commd. 2d lt. U.S. Army, 1933, advanced through grades to maj. gen., 1961; served with 101st Airborne Div., ETO, World War II, asst. div. comdr., 1956-57; chief staff XVIII Airborne Corps, 1957-59; chief Mil. Assistance Adv. Group, Cambodia, 1959-61; comdg. gen. 2d Inf. Div., 1961-62; chief staff U.S. Strike Command, 1962-64; dep. chief staff Allied Forces Central Europe, 1964- 66; chief staff U.S. Army, Europe, 1967-68; lectr. mgmt. sci. Fla. Inst. Tech., Melbourne. Decorated D.S.M., Silver Star, Legion Merit with oak leaf cluster, Bronze Star with 2 oak leaf clusters, Commendation ribbon; decorated by France, Belgium, Holland, Republic of Korea. Mem. Assn. U.S. Army, 10th Airborne, 2d Inf., 25th Inf. div. assns. Rotarian. Home: 12 Brookside Lane Portland ME 04103 Office: Fla Institute Technology Melbourne FL 32901

CHASE, CHARLES MILLS, banker; b. Kalamazoo, Mich., May 7, 1904; s. Edmund W. and Mabel C. (Mills) C.; A.B., U. Mich., 1927; m. Mary Case, Sept. 5, 1953. Pres. Home Savs. Bank of Kalamazoo, 1947-63; sr. v.p. Am. Nat. Bank & Trust Co., Kalamazoo, 1963—; dir. KVP Sutherland Paper Co., Kalamazoo Laundry Co., Wheeler Roll Co., Club: Park. Home: 1456 Woodlure Dr Kalamazoo MI 49001 Office: PO Box 946 Kalamazoo MI 49005

CHASE, CORNELIUS THURSTON, educator; b. Bklyn., Apr. 20, 1904; s. Cornelius Thurston and Lena Louise (Tyler) C.; grad. Phillips Acad., 1920; A.B., Williams Coll., 1924, M.A. (hon.), 1942; postgrad. Columbia, 1927; L.H.D., Am. Internat. Coll., 1962; m. Lucille Hildreth Keep, Mar. 5, 1927 (div.); children—Cornelius Thurston IV, Anne Audenreid (Mrs. Marion Cheshire Manderson), Allen Keep, Oliver Stuart, John Terry; m. 2d, Susan Talbot Macpherson, Mar. 9, 1956. Tchr. Berkshire Sch., 1923-24, Peekskill Mil. Acad., 1927, Eaglebrook Sch., Deerfield, Mass., 1924-25, part-time 1926, 27, headmaster, 1928-69, emeritus, 1969—, also trustee; ednl. cons., V.I., 1969—; mem. staff Whim Greathouse and Landmarks Soc. Mus., V.I. Mem. adv. council Coll. V.I. Mem. Alumni Ednl. Policy Group Williams Coll., 1943-45, also chmn. scholarship com.; mem. Phillips

Acad. Andover Alumni Ednl. Policy Com., 1949-56; independent schs. adv. com. Ednl. Records Bur. Trustee Good Hope Sch., St. Croix, V.I. Recipient Centennial award for advancement of secondary edn. Shattuck Sch., 1958. Mem. Nat. Assn. Ind. Schs. (mem. ednl. practices com., 1951-52), Psi Upsilon. Clubs: Williams, Univ. (N.Y. City). Contbr. profl. publs. Traveled in Eng., Europe, Caribbean, U.S. Home: Cain Carlton Route 00863 Frederiksted St Croix VI 00840 Office: Care Landmarks Soc Box 242 Christiansted VI 00820

CHASE, DARYL, educator; b. Nephi, Utah, Jan. 15, 1901; s. James and Emma Dale (Draper) C.; A.B., U. Utah, 1927; M.A., U. Chgo., 1931, Ph.D., 1936; Dr. Humanities, Coll. So. Utah, 1969, Utah State U., 1971; m. Alice Koford, June 1, 1935; 1 son, James P. Farmer. Rancher and poultryman 1920—; prin. Franklin Sem., Preston, Ida., 1927-30, Granite Sem., Salt Lake City, 1932-33; instr. Latter Day Saints Bus. Coll., Salt Lake City, 1933-35; dir. Latter Day Saints Inst., Ida. State Coll., 1935-36, U. Wyo., 1936-39, U. Ariz., 1939-43, Utah State Agrl. Coll., 1943-45; dean students Utah State Agrl. Coll., 1945-51, dir. Coll. So. Utah, Cedar City, 1951-54; pres. Utah State U., Logan, 1954-68, pres. emeritus, 1968—, now prof. history, dir. Center for Study Causes War and Conditions for Peace, dir. Mus. of Man and His Daily Bread. Mem. Nat. Commn. on Accreditation Service Experiences, Am. Council on Edn. Vice pres. Utah Sci. Research Found., 1954-68; bd. overseers Coll. V. I. Decorated Order of Crown (Iran); recipient Outstanding Civilian Service award U.S. Army, 1968; Service award Utah Bd. Aeros., 1967; various other awards and citations, including citation for devel. internat. edn. and agrl. programs U. San Simon and Autonomous U. San Juan Misael Saracho (Bolivia), Utah State U., 1968. Fellow A.A.A.S.; mem. Am. Council Edn., Assn. State Univs. and Land-Grant Colls. (mem. senate 1955-68), Assn. Bibl. Instrs., Am. Soc. Ch. History, Western Personnel Inst., Am. Coll. Personnel Assn., N.E.A. Cache Valley C. of C., Cache Valley Civic Music Assn. (pres. 1944-45, 71), Phi Kappa Phi, Phi Alpha Theta, Phi Eta Sigma. Clubs: Faculty Men's (pres. 1946), Knife and Fork, Rotary. Author: Christianity Through the Centuries, 1944; Joseph, The Prophet, 1944. Travelled Europe, Middle East, Orient, Latin Am. Home: 1740 E 1030 N Logan UT 84321

CHASE, EDWARD FULLER, advt. agy. exec.; b. Somerville, Mass., Dec. 4, 1913; s. Leon Grover and M. Louise (Hilliard) C.; student Bowdoin Coll., 1934-38; m. Barbara Halliday Stone, June 24, 1939; children—Ann Halliday (Mrs. W. Ray Worthington), Edward Fuller, Leon Grover III. Account exec. Harold Cabot & Co., Inc., Boston, 1943-45, v.p., account supr., 1945-55, exec. v.p., 1955-58, pres., 1958—; dir. N.E. Fed. Savs. & Loan Assn. Mem. Belmont Town Meeting, 1950-68. Bd. dirs. Advt. Research Found., Mass. Taxpayers Found.; trustee Belmont Hill Sch. Republican. Episcopalian. Clubs: Bowdoin, Union (Boston); Laurel Brook (Uxbridge, Mass.); Menauhant Yacht (Falmouth, Mass.). Home: 156 School St Belmont MA 02178 Office: 10 High St Boston MA 02110

CHASE, EDWARD PAYSON, lawyer, co. exec.; b. Concord, Mass., Mar. 4, 1908; s. Edward N. and Lillian (Hillman) C.; A.B., Harvard, 1931, M.B.A., 1933; LL.B., Northeastern U., 1939; m. Hope E. Dudgeon, June 30, 1934 (dec. Oct. 1969); children—Elizabeth A. (Mrs. Cornelius Searle Hurlbut IV), Edward N., Samuel P.; m. 2d, Audrey W. Hildreth, July 3, 1971. With USM Corp., Boston, 1933-71, asst. treas., 1942-71, sec., 1951-71; corporator Middlesex Instn. Savs.; admitted Mass. bar, 1941. Chmn. bd. appeals, Concord, Mass., 1948-54, 60- 66, bd. selectmen, Concord, 1954-60, chmn., 1954-55. Republican town committeeman, 1946—, 1st Concord rep. Minute Man Nat. Historic Park; sec., dir. Concord River Improvement Assn., Inc., 1946—; corporator Emerson Hosp., 1963—; charter mem. Northeastern U. Nat. Council, 1965- . Served USNR, 1943-46. Mem. Am. Soc. Corporate Sec., Inc., Boston Bar Assn., Louisa H. Alcott Assn., Concord Players. Mass. Soc. Mayflower Descendants. Episcopalian (past vestryman). Clubs: Harvard Varsity, Concord Country. Home: 324 Main St Concord MA 01742

CHASE, FRANCIS SEABURY, educator; b. White Stone, Va., Oct. 2, 1899; s. Francis Seabury and Bettie Landon (Carter) C.; B.S., U. Va., 1927, M.S., 1931; Ph.D., U. Chgo., 1951; L.D., N.Y. U. 1965; m. Sue Wilbourne Elder, Sept. 14, 1922; children—Francis Seabury, III, Sue Wilbourne (Mrs. George H. Gernhardt), James Staton. Prin. Colonial Beach (Va.) elementary and high schs., 1921-26, Suffolk (Va.) High Sch., 1927- 39; exec. sec. Va. Edn. Assn., 1939-45, also editor Va. Jour. Edn.; dir. Rural Editorial Service, 1945-51; lectr. edn. adminstrn. U. Chgo., 1948-51, prof. edn., 1951-68, prof. edn., emeritus, 1968—, dir. Center for Tchr. Edn., 1954-56, chmn. dept. edn., 1954- 64, dean Grad. Sch. Edn., 1958-64; vis. prof. N.Y. U., 1965-66; dir. Midwest Adminstrn. Center, 1950-57; pres. Edn. Communications Service, 1951-56; cons. NSF Office Internat. Sci. Activities, 1966-67, Office Edn., Bur. of Research, 1966-67, Ala. Human Resources Research Council, 1968-69, S.E. Ednl. Devel. Lab., 1969; vis. prof. Ohio State U., 1969; Sandiford vis. prof. Ont. Inst. for Studies in Edn., 1969-70; resident cons. U. Tex. Research and Devel. Center for Tchr. Edn. and S.W. Ednl. Devel. Lab., 1970. Dir. research Council of State Govts. Study on Edn., 1948-49; ednl. adviser to Govt. Pakistan, 1957, 59, 62; examiner Swedish ednl. planning and policy OECD, 1966-67; chmn. nat. adv. com. ednl. labs., 1966-68; chmn. Pres.'s Com. Pub. Higher Edn. in D.C., 1963-64. Pres. Old Dominion area council Boy Scouts Am., 1931- 33; 2d v.p., chmn. budget com. Va. Cancer Fedn., 1943-45. Served with SATC, World War 1; mem. wartime commn. U.S. Office Edn., World War 11. Mem. Nat., Va. (spl. citation for distinguished service to edn. 1945) edn. assns., Am. Assn. Sch. Adminstrs. (yearbook commn. 1955), Nat. Soc. Study Edn., A.A.A.S., Am. Ednl. Research Assn. (editorial bd. 1955), Phi Delta Kappa. Episcopalian. Club: Quadrangle (U. Chgo.). Author: Education Faces New Demands, 1956; (with Edgar T. Morphet) The Forty-eight State School Systems, 1949; also chpts. in books, articles profl. jours. Co- editor: The High School in a New Era, 1958; The National Program of Educational Laboratories, 1968. Home: 1524 E 59th St Chicago IL 60637

CHASE, FRANK BARKER, dept. store exec.; b. Newport, R.I., Sept. 21, 1908; s. John Franklin and Maude (Willis) C.; B.S., Sheffield Sci. Sch., Yale, 1930; m. Beatrice Jean Moore, May 19, 1939; children—John B., Daniel McF., Addison B. Began with L. Bamberger & Co., Newark, N.J., 1930-38; with James McCreery Co., N.Y. City, 1938-47, v.p., 1944-47, dir., 1946; v.p. Bloomingdale Bros., N.Y.C., 1947-61; pres., gen. mgr. Kaufmann's, Pitts., 1961-70; pres., gen. mgr. G. Fox Co., Hartford, Conn., 1970—. Rep. Clubs: Yale, Blue Hill Troupe, University (N.Y.C.). Office: G Fox Co Hartford CT

CHASE, GILBERT, writer, educator; b. Havana, Cuba, Sept. 4, 1906 (parents U.S. citizens); s. Comdr. Gilbert P. and Edelmira (Culmell) C.; student Columbia, 1926; B.A., U. N.C., 1950; D. Litt. (hon.), U. Miami, 1955; pvt. studies music with Max Wald, Paris; m. Kathleen Barentzen, Dec. 27, 1929; children—Paul, Peter John. Music critic Continental Daily Mail, Paris, 1929-35; asso. editor Internat. Cyclopedia of Music and Musicians, N.Y.C., 1936-38; editor G. Schirmer, Inc., N.Y.C., 1939-40; Latin Am. specialist music div. Library of Congress, 1940-43; music supr. NBC U. of the Air, 1943-48; mgr. edn. dept. RCA Victor, Camden, N.J., 1948-49; cultural attache Am. Embassy, Lima, Peru, 1951-53, Buenos Aires, 1953-55; dir. Sch. of Music, U.. Okla., 1955-56; acting dean, Coll. Fine Arts, 1956-57; cultural attaché Am. Embassy, Brussels, Belgium, 1958- 60; prof. Latin Am. studies Tulane U., 1960-66, dir. Inter-Am. Inst. for Musical Research, 1961-69. Paris corr. Mus. America, N.Y.C., 1930-35, Mus. Times, London, 1931-35; adviser, reviewer Book of Month Club, 1936-49; lectr. history Am. music Columbia, 1946-48. Mem. adv. com. on music U.S. Dept. of State, 1943-45; mus. cons. Pan Am. Union, 1943-45; cons. for music loan libraries in Latin Am., Library of Congress, 1944- 46; mem. U.S. Adv. Com. on Cultural Information, 1957-58. Hon. prof. faculty philosophy, letters U. Buenos Aires. Mem. Am. Musciol. Soc., Soc. for Ethnomusicology (1st v.p. 1963-65), Inter-Am Music Council (pres. 1960-63), Latin Am. Studies Assn. (constituent mem.), Société Francaise de Musicologie, Instituto Espaol de Musicología, Music Library Assn. Author: Cities and Souls: Poems of Spain, 1929; The Music of Spain, 1941, 2d rev. edition, 1959; A Guide to Latin American Music, 1945, 2d rev. edit., 1962; America's Music: From the Pilgrims to the Present, 1955, 2d revised edit., 1966; The American Composer Speaks, 1966; A Concise History of Latin American Culture, 1966; Contemporary Art in Latin America, 1970; Music in Latin America; An Introduction, 1971. Editor: Music in Radio Broadcasting, 1946; music editor Handbook of Latin American Studies, 1963-67, The Inter-American Mag., 1940-43; editor yearbook for Inter-Am. Mus. Research, 1964—; contbg. editor Arts in Society, 1965—. Office: Sid W Richardson Hall U Texas Austin TX 78712

CHASE, GOODWIN, banker; b. Los Angeles, June 30, 1911; s. Goodwin and Laurene G. (Crosthwaite) C.; student U. So. Cal., 1930-31, Inst. Econs., Brookings Instn., 1933-34; m. Gudrun M. Mack, May 9, 1936; children—Anthony G., Christine M. (Mrs. Payne Kenyon Kellogg), Stephen M. With Wash. Nat. Bank, Ellensburg, 1939-58, v.p., 1940-56, pres., 1957-58; with Nat. Bank of Wash., Tacoma, 1958-70, exec. v.p., 1958, pres., chmn., 1959-70; pres., dir. Pacific Nat. Bank of Wash. (consolidation of Nat. Bank of Wash. and Pacific Nat. Bank of Seattle 1970), 1970—; pres. Central Wash. Broadcasters, Inc., 1947-58, N.W. Chems., Inc., 1951-55; mem. adv. com. to comptroller currency, 1962-63. Mem. Western Internat. Trade Group, Dept. Commerce, 1966—, Pres.'s Nat. Citizens Com. on Community Relations, 1964-66; chmn. Wash. State Council on Higher Edn., 1969—, chmn., 1969-70; chmn. Wash. council Nat. Council Crime and Delinquency, 1964—, chmn., 1965-67; mem. Seattle Regional Export Expansion Council, 1962—, chmn. 1967-69; mem. Pacific N.W. Ballet Assn., chmn., 1966-69. Bd. dirs. Adlai E. Stevenson Inst. Internat. Affairs, 1966—, United Good Neighbor Fund Pierce County, 1964—, Tacoma Gen. Hosp., United Arts Council Puget Sound, 1968—; trustee Tacoma Art Mus., 1959—, pres., 1959- 61; trustee Wash. State Internat. Trade Fair, 1960—, Tacoma Athletic Commn., 1960—, Tacoma Community Coll. Trust Fund, 1967—, Tacoma Philharmonic, Inc., 1960—; bd. regents Pacific Lutheran U., 1970—; mem. vis. com. Coll. Arts and Scis., U. Wash., 1962—; mem. lay adv. bd. St. Jospeh's Hosp., 1966—. Recipient Distinguished Service award Ellensburg Jr. C. of C., 1945, Sigurd S. Larmon award Nat. Council on Crime and Delinquency, 1969. Mem. Am., Wash. bankers assns. Clubs: Rainier (Seattle); Tacoma, Tacoma Country and Golf. Home: 11415 Gravelly Lake Dr SW Tacoma WA 98499 Office: 1123 Pacific Av Tacoma WA 98402 also PO Box Tacoma WA 98401

CHASE, HERMAN BURLEIGH, educator; b. New Hampton, N.H., May 7, 1913 s. Edwin Elmer and Ada Mabel (Burleigh) C.; A.B., Dartmouth, 1934; Ph.D., U. Chgo., 1938; m. Elizabeth Studley Brown, Aug. 30, 1937; children—Elizabeth Studley, Burleigh Brown (dec.), Anne Louise, Catharine Marie; m. 2d, Anne McKee, January 27, 1968; children—John Burleigh, Brian McKee. Teaching asst. zoology U. Chgo., 1935-38; instr. zoology U. Ill., 1938-44, asst. prof., 1944-48; asso. prof. biology Brown U. 1948-52, prof., 1952—, R.P. Brown prof. biology, 1960—, chmn. biology dept., 1963-67, dir. Inst. Life Scis., 1967—. Mem. Am. Soc. Zoologists, Genetics Soc. Am., Am. Soc. Human Genetics, A.A.A.S., Soc. Study Evolution, Soc. Study Growth and Devel., Am. Soc. Naturalists, Radiation Research Soc., N.Y. Acad. Sci., Am. Assn. U. Profs., Sigma Xi, Phi Beta Kappa. Contbr. papers to profl. jours. Home: 175 Ferris Av Rumford RI 02916 Office: Biomed Div Brown U Providence RI 02912

CHASE, ILKA author, actress; b. N.Y.C., d. Frank D. and Edna (Allaway) Chase; ed. pvt. schs., nr. N.Y.C. and Paris; m. Louis Calhern, 1926 (div.); m. 2d, William B. Murray, July 13, 1935 (div.); m. 3d, Norton Sager Brown, 1946. Has appeared in over 20 Broadway productions, including The Animal Kingdom, Revenge with Music, The Women; motion pictures, including Miss Tatlock's Millions, Johnny Dark, Big Knife, Ocean's 11. Author: Past Imperfect, 1942; In Bed We Cry, 1943; I Love Miss Tilli Bean, 1946; Free Admission, 1948; New York 22, 1951; Always in Vogue (with Edna Woolman Chase), 1954; The Island Players, 1956; Three Men on the Left Hand, 1960; The Carthaginian Rose, 1961. Elephants Arrive at Half-Past Five, 1963; Second Spring and Two Potatoes, 1966; Straight from the Laundry, 1967; Varied Airs of Spring, 1969; Around the World and Other Places, 1970. Radio programs, Luncheon at Waldorf, Penthouse Party guest star appearance; Ilka Chase program, 1945; writer syndicated weekly newspaper column; TV appearances Glamour-Go-Round, Fashion Magic; guest appearance on dramatic programs.‡

CHASE, JOHN DAWSON, naval officer; b. Washington, Apr. 4, 1919; s. Roy Everett and Margaret Edwina (Dawson) C.; B.S., U.S. Naval Acad., 1940; M.S., Mass. Inst. Tech., 1948; postgrad. Armed Forces Staff Coll., 1953-54, Indsl. Coll. of Armed Forces, 1959-60; m. Elouise Dowling Roper, Apr. 13, 1942; 1 son, John David. Commd. ensign USN, 1940, advanced through grades to rear adm., 1969; comdg. officer U.S.S. Boston, 1965-66; comdg. officer Naval Weapons Lab., Dahlgren, Va., 1968-69; comdr. Cruiser-Destroyer Flotilla Four, Norfolk, Va., 1969-70; dep. comdr. Mil. Sealift Command, Washington, 1970—. Decorated Sec. Navy Commendation medal with two gold stars; Govt. of China medal of merit. Mem. Sigma Xi. Presbyn. Home: 7709 Bridle Path Lane McLean VA 22101 Office: Dep Comdr Mil Sealift Command Navy Dept Washington DC 20390

CHASE, JOHN PEIRCE, investment counsel; b. Milton, Mass., June 12, 1906; s. Philip Putnam and Anna Cornelia (Wigglesworth) Chase; grad. Milton Acad., 1923, Phillips Exeter Acad., 1924; A.B. magna cum laude, Harvard, 1928; D.C.S., Suffolk U.; m. Barbara Stone, June 27, 1928 (div.); children—Barbara, George Wigglesworth, Anna Gregg, John Peirce, Sarah Baldwin, Laura Dennison; m. 2d, Gisele Parenty; children—Louise E., Willard P. Research analyst Lee Higginson Co., 1928; head research and statis. dept. Lee Higginson Trust Co., 1929-32; treas., dir. John P. Chase, Inc., investment counsel, Boston, 1932—, pres., 1932-58, chmn. bd., 1959—; pres., treas., dir., mem. corp. Josiah Willard Hayden Recreation Centre, Inc.; chmn. bd., dir. Boston Capital Corp., 1960—; chmn. bd. Income and Capital Shares, Inc.; chmn. bd., dir. Chase Frontier Fund, Inc.; pres. Allied Research & Service Corp.; dir. Bertman Gas & Oil Corp., Blue Bird Food Products Co.; v.p., dir. Community Broadcasting Boston, Inc.; incorporator Suffolk Savs. bank; trustee Shareholders' Trust Boston; trustee, mem. exec. com. Consol. Investment Trust. Treas., dir. Rogerson House; mem. corp. Perkins Inst., Mass. Sch. for Blind; dir. Buffalo Creek Land Co.; dir., treas. Robert B. Brigham Hosp.; v.p. Blood Research Inst., Inc.; trustee Chase Fund of Boston; trustee, chmn. adv. com. Bus. Sch., Suffolk U.; dir., exec. com. Japan Fund. Mem. Canton Sch. Bd., 1936-51, chmn., 1937-45; trustee Hwy. Safety Found., Canton Pub. Library, 1930-51, chmn. Canton Pub. Safety Com., 1942-44; trustee, mem. finance com. Woods Hole Oceanographic Instn. Asso. dir. Am.-Brit. Lab., Div. NDRC, with assimilated rank of col., 1944-45; chmn. regional Econ. Stblzn. Com., Office Emergency Preparedness. Awarded Certificate of Merit, Purple Heart. Independent Rep. Unitarian. Clubs: Madison Square (bd. dirs.); (sec., Harvard (pres. 1968-70) (Boston); Harvard (N.Y.); Country (Brookline); Harvard Varsity (sec.- treas.), Owl (Harvard Coll.); Dedham Country and Polo; Manchester Yacht; Essex Country. Head coach Harvard hockey, 1943-51; capt. U.S. Olympic Hockey, 1932. Home: Wilsondale St Dover MA 02030 Office: Chase Bldg 535 Boylston St Boston MA 02116

CHASE, LUCIUS PETER, corp. exec., lawyer; b. Rochester, N.Y., Jan. 1, 1902; s. Lucius A. and Beatrice (Tucker) C.; A.B., U. Wis., 1923, J.D., 1925; m. Virdelle Simpson, June 13, 1925. Spl. asst. to Atty. Gen. of U. S.; gen. counsel, dir., sr. v.p. Kohler Co. (Wis.); sr. v.p., dir. Kohler Can., Ltd., Kohler de Mexico; dir. Citizens Bank of Sheboygan (Wis.). Trustee YMCA U. Wis., Lakeland Coll., Sheboygan. Served as col. AUS, World War II. Decorated Silver Star, Legion of Merit with oak leaf cluster, Purple Heart; Croix de Guerre with palm (France); officer Order of Leopold (Belgium). Mem. Am., Wis., Sheboygan County bar assns., U.S. C. of C., Am. Legion, V.F.W., Mil. Order Purple Heart, Order of Coif, U. Wis. Alumni Assn. (nat. dir.), Scabbard and Blade, Alpha Sigma Phi, Gamma Eta Gamma. Methodist (trustee). Rotarian. Clubs: Country (Sheboygan); University (Milw.). Contbr. articles profl. jours. Home: 315 Ridge Way Kohler WI 53044 Office: Kohler Co Kohler WI 53044

CHASE, LUCIA, ballet dancer; b. Waterbury, Conn., Mar. 24, 1907; d. Irving Hall and Elizabeth Hosmer (Kellogg) Chase; student St. Margaret's Sch., Waterbury, Theatre Guild Sch., N.Y.C.; m. Thomas Ewing, Jr., Dec. 28, 1926; children—Thomas III, Alexander Cochran. Ballerina Mordkin Ballet 1937-39; ballerina The Ballet Theatre, N.Y.C., 1940-60, co-dir., 1945—. Recipient 17th ann. Capezio Dance award, 1968. Home: 720 Park Av New York City NY 10021 Office: Am Ballet Theatre 1619 Broadway New York City NY 10019

CHASE, MARY COYLE, dramatist; b. Denver, Colo. Feb. 25, 1907; d. Frank Bernard and Mary (McDonough) Coyle; ed. public schools, Denver, Colo.; student Denver Univ., 1921-23, Univ. of Colo., 1923-24; Litt.D., University of Denver, 1947; m. Robert Lamont Chase, June 7, 1928; children—Michael Lamont, Colin Robert, Barry Jerome. Began as newspaper reporter, 1924; reporter, Rocky Mountain News, Denver, Colo., 1928-31; free-lance corr., Internat. News Service and United Press, 1932-36; publicity dir., N.Y.A., Denver, Colo., 1941-42, Teamsters Union, 1942-44. Recipient William MacLeod Raine award from Colo. Authors League, 1944. Pulitzer Drama Award for Play Harvey, 1944-45. Member Dramatist Guild. Author: (plays) Now You've Done It, 1937; Sorority House (produced as motion picture 1938); Too Much Business, 1938; Harvey (produced by Brock Pemberton), 1944; Next Half Hour; Mrs. McThing, 1952; Bernardine, 1952; Loretta Mason Potts, 1958; Midgie Purvis, 1961. Home: 505 Circle Dr Denver CO 80206

CHASE, MARY ELLEN, author, educator; b. Blue Hill, Me., Feb. 24, 1887; d. Edward Everett and Edith (Lord) C.; B.A., U. of Me., 1909; M.A., U. of Minn., 1918, Ph.D., 1922; Litt.D., U. of Maine, 1929, Bowdoin College, 1933, Northeastern U., 1948, Smith College, 1949, Wilson Coll., 1957; LL.D., Goucher Coll., 1960; L.H.D., Colby College, 1937. Inst. English, Univ. of Minn., 1918-22, asst. prof., 1922-26; asso. prof. English lit. Smith Coll., 1926-29, prof. 1929-55, prof. emeritus, 1955—. Mem. Phi Beta Kappa. Episcopalian. Author numerous bks. including: Dawn in Lyonesse, 1938; Jonathan Fisher; Maine Parson, 1948; The Plum Tree, 1949; Abby Aldrich Rockefeller, 1950; Readings from the Bible, 1952; Recipe for a Magic Childhood, 1952; The White Gate, 1954; Life and Language in the Old Testament, 1955; The Edge of Darkness, 1957; Sailing the Seven Seas, 1958; Donald McKay and the Clipper Ships, 1959; The Lovely Ambition, 1960; The New England Fishing Fleets, 1961; The Psalms for the Common Reader, 1962; The Prophets for the Common Reader, 1963; The Edge of Darkness, 1964; A Journey to Boston, 1965. Contbr. stories and reviews to New York Times, N.Y. Herald Tribune, Atlantic Monthly, Yale Review, etc. Home: 16 Paradise Rd Northampton MA 01060

CHASE, MERRILL WALLACE, educator, immunologist; b. Providence, Sept. 17, 1905; s. John Whitman and Bertha H. (Wallace) C.; A.B., Brown U., 1927, Sc.M., 1929, Ph.D., 1931; m. Edith Steele Bowen, Sept. 5, 1931 (dec. 1961); children—Nancy Steele (Mrs. William W. Cowles), John Wallace, Susan Elizabeth; m. 2d, Cynthia Hambury Pierce, July 8, 1961. Instr. biology Brown U., 1931-32; staff mem. Rockefeller Inst. Med. Research, 1932-65; prof. immunology and microbiology head lab. immunology Rockefeller U., 1956—; mem. sci. and ednl. council Allergy Found. Am., 1955—; cons. NIH, 1959—. Hon. fellow Am. Acad. Allergy, Am. Coll. Allergists; mem. Am. Assn. Immunologists (pres. 1956- 57), Soc. Investigative Dermatology, Am. Soc. Microbiology (program chmn. 1959-61), A.A.A.S., Harvey Soc., N.Y. Acad. Scis., Am. Assn. Lab. Animal Sci. Republican. Universalist-Unitarian. Editor: (with C. A. Williams) Methods in Immunology and Immunochemistry, Vol. 1, 1967, Vol. 11, 1968, Vol. III, 1970. Spl. research hypersensitivity to simple chem. allergens, studies Kviem antigen in sarcoidosis. Office: Rockefeller U 66th St and York Av New York City NY 10021

CHASE, MORRIS, internat. mgmt. cons.; b. N.Y.C., May 19, 1918; s. Samuel and Bessie (Rabinowitz) Cherkasky; B.B.A., Coll. City N.Y., 1939; student econ. sci., U. Paris, 1959; m. Claire Pernitz, Mar. 14, 1942; children—Sylvia, Viviane. Mem. staff several C.P.A. firms, 1939-42; asst. to dir. finance and accounting Am. Joint Distbn. Com., 1946-48; dep. controller Marshall Plan mission to France, 1949; controller, finance officer U.S. spl. econ. mission to Cambodia, Laos and Vietnam, 1950; controller U.S. spl. econ. mission to Yugoslavia, 1951; economist Office U.S. Rep. in Europe, Paris, 1952-53; chmn. Internat. Bd. Auditors for Infrastructure, NATO. Paris, 1954-60, dir. infrastructure program, 1961-68, chmn. defense installations com., 1966-68, chmn. payments and progress com; cons. NATO Air Def. Ground Environment Consortium, 1968—. Served from pvt. to capt., USAAF, 1942-46; maj. Res. C.P.A., N.Y. State. Mem. Am. Inst. C.P.A.'s, N.Y. State Soc. C.P.A.'s, Fed. Accountants Assn. (pres. Paris 1961-62), Fed. Govt. Accountants Assn. Paris (pres. 1964-65), Beta Gamma Sigma. Home: Flaminia C Crans-sur-Sierre Valais Switzerland also 163 Av Winston Churchill Brussels 1180 Belgium Office: NATO Air Def Ground Environment Consortium 98 The Centre Feltham Middlesex England also NATO Satellite Consortium Sel Stuttgart- Zufferhausen West Germany

CHASE, NICHOLAS JOSEPH lawyer, educator; b. Windsor, Conn., Jan. 9, 1913; s. Michael and Lucy A. (Sinsigalli) C.; A.B., Catholic U. Am., 1933, A.M. (Columbian fellow), 1934; student Brookings Instn., 1935; LL.B. magna cum laude Georgetown U., 1940; m. F. Louise Dooley, Dec. 27, 1936; children—Stephen Edward, Mary Ann, Michael Dooley, Clare Lucia, Martha Louise. Admitted to D.C. Bar, 1939, U.S. Ct. Appeals and Ct. Claims bars, 1940, Supreme Ct. bar, 1943, Md. bar, 1950; practiced in Washington, 1939—; adminstrv. asst. PWA 1935-40; prof. law Columbus U.,

1943-45, Georgetown U., 1946—. Mem. D.C. Council Law Enforcement, 1958-59; arbitrator Am. Arbitration Assn., 1970—. Chmn. bd. trustees Hawthorne Sch., Washington. Mem. Am. Bar Assn., Bar Assn. of D.C. (1st v.p., dir. 1958-63), Georgetown Alumni Assn. (bd. govs. 1958-62), Catholic U. Alumni (pres. 1952-54), Columbia Hist. Soc. (chmn. memls. and plaques com.), Phi Delta Phi. Clubs: Congressional Country, Nat. Press, Counsellors (founder), Touchdown (founder) (Washington); Kenwood Country, Rehoboth Country. Contbr. articles on trials, tax and real estate law and practice in law jours. Home: 5205 Oakland Rd Chevy Chase MD also Rehoboth DE 19971 Office: Wyatt Building Washington DC 20005

CHASE, NORMAN ELI, educator, radiologist; b. Cin., June 29, 1926; s. Oscar and Irene (Gindy) C.; student Ohio U., 1946; B.S., U. Cin., 1950, M.D., 1953; m. Joan Salkover, Oct. 1, 1954; children—Stephen Owen, Diana Stephanie. Intern Kings County Hosp., Bklyn., 1953-54; resident radiology Columbia Presbyn. Med. Center, 1956-58, instr., asso., 1959-61; asst. prof. N.Y.U. Med. Center, 1961-64, asso. prof., 1964-67, prof. radiology, 1967—, chmn. dept. radiology, 1969—; dir. radiology Bellevue Hosp. 1965—; sr. cons. radiology Manhattan VA Hosp. 1965—. Served with USAAF, 1944-45. Mem. A.M.A., Harvey Soc., Assn. Univ. Radiologists, Am. Coll. Radiology, Am. Soc. Neuroradiology (pres. 1971). Research and publs. cerebrovascular disease. Home: 145 Hudson Terrace Yonkers NY 10701 Office: 550 1st Av New York City NY 10016

CHASE, PAUL J. lawyer; b. N.Y.C., Mar. 8, 1916; s. Oscar Jerome and Ella (Stein) C.; grad. Choate Sch.; B.A., Yale; LL.B., U. Va.; m. Mary Brewster Jennings, June 20, 1948; children—Caroline P., Brewster Jennings, Susan Ayres. Admitted to N.Y. bar, and since practiced in N.Y.C.; partner firm Casey, Beinecke & Chase, 1949-52, Olwine, Connelly, Chase, O'Donnell & Weyther, 1952—. Dir. Lionel Corp., Standard Spray & Chem. Corp., Computing Efficiency, Inc., Dynaiad, Inc., Spacerays, Inc., Oceanics, Inc. Served as ensign USNR. World War II. Clubs: Brook, Link, Piping Rock, Meadowbrook Island, Seminole Golf, 29. Home: High Farms Rd Glen Head NY 11545 Office: 299 Park Av New York City NY 10017

CHASE, RANSOM W., lawyer; b. Los Angeles, Nov.21, 1904; s. Lucius K. and Maria E. (Watkins) C.; A.B., U. Cal., 1926, LL.B., 1929; law student Yale; m. Virginia Sevier, May 9, 1931; 1 son, Laurence R. Admitted to Cal. bar, 1929, since practiced in Los Angeles; mem. firm Chase, Rotchford, Drukker & Bogust. Dir. Central Figueroa Properties Co., Coypass Land Co. Dir. Met. Water Dist. So. Cal., 1947—. Mem. Am., Los Angeles bar assns., State Bar Cal. Home: 212 S Woodburn Dr Los Angeles CA 90049 Office: 411 W 5th St Los Angeles CA 90013

CHASE, RICHARD, author; b. Huntsville, Ala., Feb. 15, 1904; s. Robert Collier and Emma Florence (Chase) C.; B.S. in Botany, Antioch Coll., 1929. Story-teller of Anglo-Celtic Am. tales at various schs., colls., univs., clubs, libraries throughout U.S., 1944—. Recipient So. Cal. Council on Lit. award for Distinguished Contbn. to Field of Folklore for Children and Young People, 1970. Author: The Jack Tales, 1943; Grandfather Tales, 1948; Singing Games and Playparty Games, 1967; American Folk Tales & Songs, 1971. Address: 715 Blanchard Claremont CA 91711

CHASE, ROBERT ARTHUR, surgeon, educator; b. Keene, N.H., Jan. 6, 1923; s. Albert Henry and Georgia Beulah (Bump) C.; B.S. cum laude, U. N.H., 1945; M.D., Yale, 1947; m. Anne Crosby Parker, Feb. 3, 1946; children—Deborah Lee, Nancy Jo, Robert N. Intern New Haven Hosp., 1947-48, asst. resident, 1949-50, sr. resident surgery, 1952-53, chief resident surgeon, 1953-54; mem. faculty Yale Sch. Medicine, 1948-54, 59-62, asst. prof. surgery, 1959- 62; mem. faculty U. Pitts., 1957-59, resident plastic surgeon, also teaching fellow, 1957-59; attending surgeon VA Hosp., W. Haven, Conn., 1959-62; attending surgeon Grace New Haven Community Hosp., 1959-63; prof., exec. dept. surgery Stanford Sch. Medicine, 1963—; cons. plastic surgery Christian Med. Coll. and Hosp., Vellore, S. India, 1962. Served to maj., M.C., AUS, 1949-57. Recipient Francis Gilman Blake award Yale Sch. Medicine, 1962. Diplomate Am. Bd. Surgery, Am. Bd. Plastic Surgery, Am. Bd. Med. Examiners. Fellow A.C.S.; mem. Am. Soc. Plastic Surgery, Col. Acad. Medicine (pres.), San Francisco Surg. Soc., Am. Surg. Assn., Santa Clara County, Conn. med. socs., Am. Soc. Surgery Hand, Am. Soc. Cleft Palate Rehab., Am. Assn. Surgery Trauma, Plastic Surgery Research Council, A.M.A., Soc. Clin. Surgery, Western Surg. Assn., Pacific Coast Surg. Soc., Am. Assn. Plastic Surgery, Am. Cancer Soc. (clin. fellowship com.), Found. Am. Soc. Plastic and Reconstructive Surgery (dir.), Soc. Univ. Surgeons, Inst. Med., Nat. Acad. Scis., Sigma Xi. Mem. editorial bd. Surgery. Contbr. articles to profl. jours. Home: 839 Northampton Dr Palo Alto CA 94303

CHASE, ROBERT LAMONT, former newspaperman; b. Sutherland, Neb., Feb. 16, 1905; s. Albert Lamont and Clara (Coates) C.; student U. Notre Dame, 1926-27; m. Mary Coyle, June 7, 1928; children—Michael Lamont, Colin Robert, Barry Jerome. Reporter, Denver Express, 1922-26; telegraph editor South Bend (Ind.) News-Times, 1926-27; reporter, city editor, news editor Rocky Mountain News, Denver, 1927-45, mng. editor and columnist, 1945-51, asso. editor, 1951-70. Home: 505 Circle Drive Denver CO 80206

CHASE, ROBERT WILLARD, fgn. service officer; b. Marlboro, Mass., Sept. 2, 1921; s. Willard Linwood and Hazel (Spinney) C.; grad. Taft Sch., 1940; A.B., Harvard, 1944; postgrad. George Washington U., 1965; m. Shirley Irene Gustafson, June 6, 1947; children—Kristenna Penney, Willard Linwood II, Ragnar Taft, Ruth Mikkels, Robin Maria, Mark Eastman. Fgn. service officer of U.S., 1951—, positions in The Hague, Montreal, Beirut, Rabat, 1951-64; officer charge Moroccan affairs Dept. State, 1964-66; polit. chief Damascus, 1966-67, Jerusalem, 1967-69; counselor of Embassy charge d'Affaires Mbabane, Swaziland, 1969—. Mem. corp. Proctor Acad., Andover, N.H. Served with USAAF, 1942-45. Decorated Purple Heart, Air medal with 10 oak leaf clusters, Croix de Guerre with palm (French). Clubs: Royal St. Lawrence Yacht (Montreal); Yacht de Maroc (Morocco); Harvard (Boston); Royal Swazi Golf; Mbabane; Swaziland Automobile. Home: Monhegan Island ME 04852 Office: American Embassy Mbabane Swaziland

CHASE, STEPHEN U., educator. Prof. math. Cornell U., Ithaca, N.Y. Office: Grad Sch Phys Scis Cornell U Ithaca NY 14850*

CHASE, STUART, writer; b. Somersworth, N.H., Mar. 8, 1888; s. Harvey Stuart and Aaronette (Rowe) C.; Mass. Inst. Tech., 1907-08; S.B. cum laude, Harvard, 1910; Litt.D., Am. U., 1949; H.H.D., Emerson Coll., 1970; m. Margaret Hatfield, July 5, 1914; children—Robert Hatfield, Sonia Hatfield; m. 2d, Marian Tyler, 1930. Partner, Harvey S. Chase Co., C.P.A.'s, Boston, until 1917; investigating the meat industry and the packers, under the Federal Trade Commn., 1917-22; with Labor Bur., Inc., 1922-39; cons. Nat. Resources Com., 1934, Resettlement Adminstrn., 1935; SEC, 1939; TVA, 1940-41; UNESCO, 1949. Mem. Nat. Inst. Arts and Letters, Phi Gamma Delta, Phi Beta Kappa. Club: Harvard. Author: The Tragedy of Waste, 1925; Your Money's Worth (with F. J. Schlink), 1927; Men and Machines, 1929; ProsperityFact or Myth, 1930; The Nemesis of American Business, 1931; MexicoA Study of Two Americas (with Marian Tyler), 1931; A New Deal, 1932; The Economy of Abundance, 1934; Government in Business, 1935; Rich Land, Poor Land, 1936; The Tyranny of Words, 1938; The New Western Front, 1939; Idle Money, Idle Men, 1941; A Primer of Economics, 1941; The Road We Are Traveling, 1942; Goals for America, 1942; Where's the Money Coming From?, 1943; Democracy Under Pressure, 1945; Men at Work, 1945; Tomorrow's Trade, 1945; For This We Fought, 1956; The Proper Study of Mankind, 1948, rev. edit., 1956; Roads to Agreement, 1951; Power of Words, Guides to Straight Thinking, 1956; Some Things Worth Knowing, 1958; Live and Let Live, 1960; American Credos, 1962; Money to Grow On, 1964; The Most Probable World, 1968; DangerMan Talking, 1969. Contbr. to mags. and periodicals. Home: PO Box 422 Georgetown CT 06829

CHASE, THOMAS GEORGE, lawyer; b. Memphis, Sept. 28, 1911; s. James P. and Fanny (George) C.; B.S., U. Ark., 1934, LL.B., 1936, JD., 1969; m. Ellender Stribling, Oct. 23, 1941; children-Thomas George, Daris Stribling, James P., III. Admitted to Ark. bar, 1936, Tenn bar, 1937, Tex. bar, 1956; practice law Memphis, 1936-41; pres. Chase Beverage Co., Waco, Tex., 1945-56; partner Naman, Howell, Smith & Chase, Waco, 1956—. Pres. Runnymeda Land & Cattle Co., Valley Mills, Tex., 1967—. Pres. Friends Waco Pub. Library, 1967. Chmn. exec. com. Republican Party, McLennan County, 1954. Bd. commrs. Waco-McLennan County Library; mem. bd. dirrs. Waco Legal Aid Clinic. Served with USNR, 1942-45. Mem. Am., Waco-McLennan County (pres. 1965) bar assns., State Bar Tex., Assn. Ins. Atty., Internat. Assn. Ins. Attys., Tex. Assn. Def. Counsel (dir. 1968—), Kappa Alpha. Episcopalian. Rotarian. Ridgewood Country, Ridgewood Yacht (Waco). Home: 3524 Carondolet Dr Waco TX 76710 Office: First Nat Bldg Waco TX 76701

CHASE, WALTER FREDERICK, banker; b. Lowell, Mass., June 26, 1909; s. Cyrus Edgar and May Ellen (Campbell) C.; diploma Northeastern U., Boston, 1934; postgrad. Grad. Sch. Bank, Rutgers U., 1952; m. Helen May Olsen, Oct. 6, 1934; children-Robert F., Richard O., Cynthia (Mrs. Peter T. Thorstensen). With Nat. Shawmut Bank, Boston, 1929—, teller, mgr. deposit accounting, methods analyst, v.p. charge personnel, 1957-69, sr. v.p., 1969—. Dir. Boston Council on Alcoholism, 1960-67, pres., 1965-67. Bd. dirs. Nat. Council Northeastern U. Served to lt. USNR, 1944-46; PTO. Mem. Boston C. of C., Personnel Mgrs. Club Boston. Baptist (trustee). Home: 10 Lancaster Av Chelmsford MA 01824 Office: Nat Shawmut Bank 40 Water St Boston MA 02106

CHASE, WILLIAM EATON BROWER, railroad labor union ofcl.; b. Waltham, Mass., Nov. 13, 1903; s. Wallace Fairbanks and Margaret (Margeson) C.; ed. high sch.; m. Dorothy Annie MacRae, Oct. 4, 1936; children—Bruce F., William Colin (dec.). Yard service Grand Trunk Western Ry., 1923-36; local lodge officer Brotherhood of Railroad Trainmen, 1936-43, dep. pres., 1943-47 member of the exec. bd., 1946-47, v.p., 1947-60, gen. sec., treas., 1960- - Methodist. Mason (Shriner, 32), Elk. Home: RD 1 Tee Lake Lewiston MI 49756 Office: 666 Euclid Av Cleveland OH 44114

CHASE, WILLIAM HOWARD, mgmt. counsel, pub. affairs exec.; b. Omaha, Jan. 30, 1910; s. Charles Herbert and Pauline (Kottal) C.; A.B., U. Ia., 1932; postgrad. London Sch. Econs., 1932-33, Harvard, 1934-36; Ph.D. (hon.), Dong-Guk U., Seoul, Korea, 1968; m. Elizabeth Coykendall, Oct. 25, 1935; children—Anne Coykendall, Alison Howard, Thomas Howard. Instr. internat. relations Harvard, 1935-36; editorial writer Des Moines Register & Tribune, 1936-39; exec. Am. Retail Fedn., Washington, 1939-40; editor Whaley-Eaton Letter Washington, 1941; dir. dept. pub. services Gen. Mills, Mpls., 1941-45; dir. dept. pub. relations Gen. Foods, N.Y.C., 1945-52; v.p., gen. exec. McCann-Erickson; pres. Communications Counselors, Inc.; pres. Howard Chase Assos., 1959-68, chmn., 1965—; chmn. Council Mgmt. Change, Inc., 1965—; pub. Innovation and Mgmt. of Change Letter, 1965- -; v.p. pub. affairs Am. Can Co., N.Y.C., 1970—; chmn. Partners for Growth, Inc., 1968-70. Cons. to sec. commerce, asst. to dir. Office Def. Moblzn., 1950-51. Mem. dental adv. com. NIH, 1962-65; mem. nat. com. on community health Health, Education and Welfare, 1965—; information policy cons. Pres.'s Food for Peace Council; exec. res. USIA. Trustee, Wellesley Coll., 1946-58; bd. dirs. Mannes Coll. Music, N. Conway Inst. Vice chmn. Nat. Citizens for Eisenhower campaign, 1952. Recipient Profl. Proficiency award Pub. Relations Soc. Am., 1948; named One of Ten Distinguished Young Men of Year, U.S. Jr. C. of C., 1943. Mem. N.Y. Council Fgn. Relations, Acad. Polit. Sci., Pub. Relations Soc. Am. (past pres.), Phi Beta Kappa, Alpha Tau Omega. Clubs: Fifth Avenue, Harvard (N.Y.C.); Metropolitan (Washington), Ridgewood (N.J.). Author: Public Relations-An Operating Philsophy, Human Relations-Key to Corporate Survival; Public Relations of Protestant Church; By Any Other Name. Home: E Saddle River Rd Ho-Ho-Kus NJ 07423 Offices: American Lane Greenwich CT 06830 also 100 W 12th St New York City NY 10011

CHASE, WILLIAM ROWELL, corp. exec.; b. Brookline, Mass., Jan. 22, 1904; s. Harry Everett and Florence Ardelia (Rowell) C.; A.B., Harvard, 1926, M.B.A., 1928; m. Katherine Knox Kingsbury, Feb. 15, 1936; children—Harry Rowell Kingsbury, Alison Mason. Mdse. mgr. Sears, Roebuck & Co., 1928-30, asst. retail store mgr., 1930-31; with Procter & Gamble, 1931-70, mgr. brand promotion div., 1936-51, advt. mgr., 1951-54, gen. advt. mgr., 1954-55; v.p. charge advt., 1955-57, v.p. charge soap products div., 1957-60, exec. v.p., 1960-70, dir., 1957-60; v.p. Kingsbury Inc., Phila., 1945-70, chmn., 1970—. Trustee Cin. Summer Opera Assn.; dir. Cin. Planned Parenthood Assn., pres., 1949; trustee Cin. Nature Center, Shakertown at Pleasant Hill. Mem. Asso. Harvard Alumni (v.p. 1965-67), N.A.M. (hon. v.p. 1968—). Clubs: Commonwealth Harvard, Commercial, Country, Queen City (Cin.); Harvard (N.Y.C.). Home: 3424 Paxton Rd Cincinnati OH 45208 Office: Federal Reserve Bank Bldg 105 W 4th St Cincinnati OH 45202

CHASEMAN, JOEL, broadcasting exec.; b. Trenton, N.J., Feb. 18, 1926; s. M.H. and Eva (Pondfield) C.; A.B., Cornell U., 1948; m. Marlene Meyerson, Sept. 11, 1955; children—Martha Hope, Michael, Jeanne Amy. Dir. advtt., pub. relations, and pub. service sta. WAAM-TV, Balt., 1953-55; program mgr. sta. WJZ-TV, Balt., 1957-60; v.p.-gen. mgr. WBC Prodns., N.Y.C., 1961-62, Los Angeles, 1962-63; gen. mgr. sta. WINS, N.Y.C., 1964-66; pres. radio div. Westinghouse Broadcasting, N.Y.C., 1967-70, sr. v.p. programming and prodrn. radio-TV, 1970—, also dir.; dir. Cornell Radio Guild. Pres. L.I. div. Am. Jewish Com., 1966-67. Served with USNR, 1944-45. Recipient Brotherhood award Nat. Conf. Christians and Jews. Mem. Internat. Radio and TV Soc. Am. Acad. TV Arts and Scis. Home: 70 Arleigh Rd Great Neck NY 11021 Office: 90 Park Av New York City NY 10016

CHASEN, ROBERT EFRAYIM, communications co. exec.; b. Newark, July 3, 1916; s. Julius and Mary (Horland) C.; B.C.S., Benjamin Franklin U., 1943; postgrad. Columbia, N.Y. U.; m. Laura Etta Brown, Apr. 15, 1962; children—Julie, Ellie. Spl. agt. FBI, 1943-52; asst. to v.p. indsl. relations TTT, 1952-55; dir. indsl. relations Fed. Telephone & Radio Corp., 1955-57, v.p. adminstrn., 1958-63; exec. v.p., gen. mgr. ITT Kellogg Communications Systems div. ITT, Chgo., 1963-64; chmn. bd., chief exec. officer Fed. Electric Corp., world wide subsidiary ITT, Paramus, N.J., 1964—; chmn. bd., chief exec. officer ITT Fed. Support Services, Inc., 1956—; pres. Intelex Systems, Inc., 1964—; v.p. Internat. Tel. & Tel. Corp. Dir. Nat. Council Tech. Service Industries, 1968—. Mem. Exec. Assn. Grad. Sch. Bus. Columbia, Soc. Former Spl. Agts. FBI. Home: 540 Upper Blvd Ridgewood NJ 07450 Office: 500 Washington Av Nutley NJ 07110

CHASINS, ABRAM, pianist, composer, author; b. N.Y.C., Aug. 17, 1903; s. Saul L. and Elizabeth (Hochstein) C.; student Ethical Culture Sch., 1914-18, Columbia, 1920- 22; m. Constance Keene, 1949. Toured Europe, Am. in recital, also orchestral-soloist, 1925-46; featured performer, recording artist, speaker nat. radio networks, Chasins Music Series, 1932-38; faculty Curtis Inst., 1926-35, Berkshire Center, 1939-40; dir. music N.Y. Times radio sta. WQXR, 1943-65; composer over 100 pub. works performed by leading orchs., soloists; dir. Annual Music Edn. projects, judge internat. competitions; now writer, lectr. Mem. A.S.C.A.P. Clubs: Bohemians, Musicians, Manhattan Chess. Author: Speaking of Pianists, 1957; The Van Cliburn Legend, 1959; The Appreciation of Music, 1966; Music at the Crossroads, 1972. Contbr. articles Sat. Rev., N.Y. Times, McCall's, Ladies' Home Jour., Hi-Fidelity. Address: 200 E 78th St New York City NY 10021

CHASSLER, SEYMOUR MURRAY, editor; b. Bklyn., Nov. 8, 1919; s. David and Henrietta (Becker) C.; B.A., N.Y. U., 1941; M.A., Columbia, 1942; m. Natalie Elizabeth Goldfarb, Apr. 2, 1943; children—Joseph Holland, Philip Isaac, Deborah Louise. Writer, March of Time (film), 1942-45; asso. editor Coronet mag., 1945- 48; picture editor Pageant mag., 1948-50, mng. editor, 1955-57, exec. editor, 1957-59; asso. editor, picture editor Collier's mag., 1950-55; v.p. Hillman Periodicals, Inc., 1959; editorial dir. This Week mag., 1959-60; exec. editor Redbook mag., 1960- 65, editor, 1965—; v.p. McCall Pub. Co., 1965—. Mem. joint com. Mag. Pubs. Assn.-N.E.A. Recipient Graflex award for contbns. photo-journalism in color, 1952. Mem. Am. Soc. Mag. Editors (mem. exec. com.), Child Study Assn. Home: 51 Villa Rd Larchmont NY 10538 Office: 230 Park Av New York City NY 10017

CHASTAIN, ELIJAH DENTON, Jr., educator; b. Pickens, S.C., Sept. 26, 1925; s. Elijah D. and Ida (Hendricks) C.; B.S., Clemson U., 1947; M.S., Cornell U., 1948; postgrad. Va. Poly. Inst., 1950, Duke, 1961, U. Chgo., 1964; Ph.D., Purdue U., 1956; m. Dr. Marian B. Faulkner, Aug. 25, 1956; children—Gwen Caroline, Philip William. Asso. prof. Va. Poly. Inst., 1949-56; research asst. Purdue U., 1954-56; asso. prof. econs. Auburn U., 1956-63, prof., 1963—, dir. grad. studies Sch. of Bus., 1967-70, chmn. Gen. Faculty and Univ. Senate, 1970-71; econ. and managerial cons. Mem. Am., So. econs. assns., Am. Agrl. Econ. Assn., Ala. Acad. Sci. (v.p.), Sigma Xi, Omicron Delta Epsilon, Delta Sigma Pi, Gamma Sigma Delta, Phi Delta Kappa. Editor Jour. Ala. Acad. Sci., 1962-65. Contbr. articles profl. jours. Home: 1104 S Gay St Auburn AL 36830

CHASTAIN, WILLIAM HOYT clergyman; b. Jonestown, Ga., May 20, 1914; s. James Asbury and Daisy (Querry) C.; M. English Bible and Bible Langs., Missionary Baptist Sem., Little Rock, 1944; m. Ruby May Veazey, Sept. 15, 1935; children—James Hoyt, Joyce Ruth, William Ben. Ordained to ministry Bapt. Ch., 1933; pastor, Ark., 1939-40, 45-60, in Ky., 1941-44, Norwalk (Cal.) Missionary Bapt. Ch., 1960—; organizer Seminary Press, Little Rock, 1944-45; editor, pub. The Bapt. Informer, 1941-44, Bapt. Digest, 1947-48, Midnight Hour, 1949-50; asso. editor Missionary Bapt. Searchlight, 1944- 46; editor Cal. Bapt. Sentinel, 1960—; frequent radio speaker. Asst. clk. Cumberland River (Ky.) Bapt. Assn., 1943; pres. Saline (Ark.) Bapt. Assn., 1949, 55-57; adv. council Bapt. Young Peoples State Orgn., 1951- 60; v.p. Ark. Bapt. Assn., 1951-53, pres., 1954-55, publicity dir., 1957- 60; pres. Coop. Assn. Missionary Bapt. Chs., Cal., 1961-62, now publicity dir.; pres. So. Cal. Missionary Bapt. Coop. Assn., 1961-62; v.p. Cal. Missionary Bapt. Sem. Welfare Bd., 1956-60; pres. Am. Bapt. Assn., 1959-60, now chmn. N.T. translating council; pres. Assn. of Schs. and Sems. Mason (K.T.), Rotarian. Home: 10460 Greenhurst Dr Bellflower CA 90706 Office: Box 848 Bellflower CA 90706 Box 848 Bellflower CA 90706

CHATELAIN LEON, Jr., architect; b. Washington, Mar. 8, 1902; s. Leon and Bertha (Aeschbacker) C.; student George Washington U., 1927; m. Mary Wysong, Feb. 14, 1945; children—Leon, Jo Ann (adopted), Edward Russell (adopted). Asso. Waddy B. Wood, 1927-30; pvt. archtl. practice, Washington, 1930-56; partner Chatelain, Gauger & Nolan, 1956-70, Chatelain, Samperton & Nolan, Washington, 1970—. Pres., D.C. Bd. Registrars and Examiners of Architects, 1962-65; chmn. Nat. Commn. Archtl. Barriers, 1966-68. Chmn., Nat. Employ the Physically Handicapped Week; pres. Crippled Children's Soc., 1955, Met. Police Boys' Club, 1954; chmn. D.C. Council on Human Relations, 1958-60, Benjamin Franklin Found., 1957—; mem. exec. com. Pres.'s Com. Employ the Handicapped; pres. Nat. Soc. Crippled Children and Adults, 1967-69; sec. Heroes. Bd. dirs. YMCA, Washington. Recipient medal Conseil Superior, award for community service Wash. Pub. Relations Soc., 1962; F. Stuart Fitzpatrick medal, 1966; Benjamin J. Latrobe Outstanding Architect award, 1966; Pres.'s Distinguished Service award; Das Grosse Verdienstkreuz (West Germany), 1968. Fellow Constrn. Specifications Inst., Royal Archtl. Inst. Can. (hon.), Philippines (hon.), New Zealand (hon.), Am. (past pres. Washington chpt., nat. treas. 1954-46, nat. pres. 1956-58, chmn. finance com.) Insts. architects; mem. Archtl. Soc. Colombia (hon.), Royal Inst. Brit. Architects (hon.), Ch. Archtl. League Am., Bldg. Research Inst. (gov., pres. 1961), Nat. Acad. Scis.-NRC, N.Y. Archtl. League, Wash. Bldg. Congress (pres. 1945-46), Wash. Bd. Trade (pres. 1948-49, Man of Year award 1962). Mason (Shriner), Kiwanian. Clubs: Union Interalliee (Paris, France); Cosmos (Gold Medal), Columbia Country, Capitol Hill, City Tavern, Arts, Congressional Country, University. Home: 1823 23d St NW Washington DC 20008 Office: 1632 K St Washington DC 20006

CHATFIELD, GEORGE IRVING, broadcasting and pub. exec.; b. Mpls., May 1, 1905; s. Franklin and Alice May (Pease) C.; student U. Minn., 1923-24; B.S., Mass. Inst. Tech., 1928; spl. courses Dunwoody Inst., Mpls., Harvard; m. Marie Walters, Apr. 28, 1934; children—Donald Franklin, Susan Morse Chatfield (Mrs. Millard). Owner of printing bus., also amateur radio sta., 9BTL. Mpls., 1921-24; asst. to advt. mgr. Lever Bros. Co., Cambridge, Mass., 1928-39, advt. mgr. Rinso and Lifebuoy, 1939-46; v.p., mem. planning bd. Kenyon & Eckhardt, advt. agy., N.Y.C., 1947-48; v.p., group head, Compton Advt., Inc., N.Y.C., 1949-51; exec. v.p. William Esty Co., Inc., N.Y.C., 1952- 58; sr. v.p., dir. Benton & Bowles, Inc., N.Y.C., 1959-62; owner, pres. WFGL, Inc., WFMP-FM, Music Service Corp., 1962—; pub. Montachusett Rev.; adv. dir. Worcester County Nat. Bank; corporator Fitchburg Savs. Bank; owner amateur radio sta. KIUIL. Bd. dirs. local YMCA, Jr. Achievement. Mem. Lambda Chi Alpha Alumni Assn. Episcopalian (vestryman). Clubs: Mass. Inst. Tech.; Northfield Associates; Rotary (v.p. Fitchburg); Fay. Home: 204 Northfield Rd Lunenburg MA 01462

CHATFIELD, WILLIAM D., educator; b. Slaterville Springs, N.Y., Feb. 7, 1916; s. David A. and Hazel (Card) C.; B.S., Oswego State Coll., 1939; postgrad. Cornell U., summer 1939-40; M.S., N.Y. U., 1946; Ph.D., U. Conn., 1955; m. Mildred R. King, Mar. 29, 1943; children—William D., Cheryl A., Janet E., Mary Lyn. Tchr. Lake George (N.Y.) High Sch., 1939-40; prof. indsl. arts Central Conn. State Coll., New Britain, 1946—, dir. admissions and registrar, 1956, dean students, 1964-69. Pres., sec. Office Econ. Opportunity, New Britain; pres. United P.T.A., New Britain, 1958. Mem. Nat., Conn. edn. assns., Conn. Guidance and Personnel Assn., Sheldon Forum, Phi Beta Kappa. Lion (pres. New Britain 1965). Home: 2414 Stanley St New Britain CT 06050

CHATHAM, JAMES RAY, educator; b. Caryville, Fla., Nov. 11, 1931; s. Clifton Lee and Sadie (McMinn) C.; B.A., Fla. State U., 1953, M.A., 1956, Ph.D., 1960; postgrad. U. Madrid (Spain), 1956-57; m. Nina McCoy, May 27, 1961; 1 dau., Nina Stephanie. Instr., asst. prof. Miss. State U., 1957-63, prof. fgn. langs., head dept., 1964—; asso. prof. U. Ala., 1963-64. Served with AUS, 1953-55. Inst. Internat. Edn. fellow U. Madrid, 1956-57; Nat. Def. Edn. Act fellow U. Tex., 1962. Mem. Am. Council Teaching Fgn. Langs., Miss. Modern Lang. Assn. (pres. 1968-70). Co-author: Dissertations in Hispanic Languages and Literatures, 1970. Home: 605 Lakeview Dr Starkville MS 39759 Office: Drawer FL State College MS 39762

CHATLAND, HAROLD systems analysis cons.; b. Hamilton, Ont., Can., Nov. 13, 1911; s. Albert and Sarah (Hewitt) C.; A.B., McMaster U., 1934; M.S., U. Chgo., 1935. Ph.D., 1937; m. Alice Young, Dec. 28, 1937; children—Anne Young, Clare Lillian, Marilyn Lee. Instr. math. Mont. State U., 1937-41, asst. prof., dept., also dean Coll. Arts and Scis., 1954-56, dean faculty, 1956-57, acad. v.p., 1957-59; asst. prof. Ohio State U., 1946-49; engring. specialist Sylvania Electric Products Co., Moutain View, Cal., 1959-63; prof. math., acad. dean Western Wash. State Coll., Bellingham, 1963-64; mgr. propagation research dept. Electronic Def. Labs., Mountain View, Cal.; cons. in systems analysis. Chmn. aero. com. State of Mont., 1945-46. Mem. Am. Math. Soc., Am. Math. Assn. Address: 10566 Blandor Way Los Altos Hills CA 94022

CHATMAN, ABRAHAM DAVID, union ofcl.; b. Russia, Feb. 16, 1896; s. David and Norene (Brightman) C.; student pub. schs., N.Y.; m. Gertrude Kadish. Aug. 19, 1926; children—Norine Doris (Mrs. Bernard Selby), Arthur Sheldon. Came to U.S., 1914, naturalized, 1926. Tailor Hickey Freeman Co., 1916-24; mgr. Rochester joint bd. Amalgamated Clothing Workers Am., 1924—, v.p., 1926- -. dir. orgn. Western N.Y., 1933, also exec. com. of gen. exec. bd.; dir. Amalgamated Bank of N.Y., Amalgamated Ins. Fund. Mem. N.Y. State Apprenticeship Council; pub. policy adv. com. Advt. Council Rochester, Inc.; mem. Rochester Regional Hosp. Planning Council; mem. finance com., dir. Sidney Hillman Found.; mem. bd. Community Chest, Jewish Home for Aged, Urban League Rochester; mem. Friends of Rochester Pub. Library; with SSS, 1940-46. Home: 2650 Highland Av Rochester NY 14610 Office: 476 Clinton Av N Rochester NY 14605

CHATMAN, PETER, see Memphis Slim. Chaudhry, Anand Parkash oral pathologist; b. W. Punjab, India, Oct. 19, 1922; s. Jagdish C. and K. (Devi) C.; B.S., Punjab (India) U., 1942, B.D.S., 1947; M.S. in Oral Surgery, U. Mich., 1953; Ph.D. in Pathology, U. Minn., 1956; m. Barbara Lois Christiansen, Aug. 12, 1957; children—Anita, Rajan Andrew, Tina. Came to U.S., 1950, naturalized, 1963. Cancer research fellow U. Minn., 1954-56, mem. faculty, 1956-61, prof. pathology, 1959-61; prof. path., chmn. dept. Sch. Dentistry, U. Pitts., 1961-66; prof. pathology Sch. Medicine, State U. N.Y. at Buffalo, 1966—. Mem. Am. Acad. Oral Pathology, Chalmers Lyons Acad. Oral Pathology, Internat. Assn. Dental Research, Sigma Xi, Omicron Kappa Upsilon. Home: 441 Hopkins Rd Amherst NY 14226 Office: Capen Hall Sch Medicine State U N Y at Buffalo Buffalo NY 14214

CHAUNCEY, HENRY, educator; b. Bklyn., Feb. 9, 1905; s. Egisto Fabbri and Edith Lockwood (Taft) C.; grad. Groton (Mass.) Sch., 1923; student Ohio State U., 1923- 24; A.B., Harvard, 1928, student Grad. Sch. Arts and Sci., 1929-31; D.Sc. (hon.), Tufts U., 1952; Litt. D., Rider Coll., 1966; LL.D., Ohio State U., 1968; m. Elizabeth Phalen, June 4, 1932 (div. 1953); children—William Egisto, Henry, Ann, Donald Robertson; m. 2d, Lucy Lawrence Worcester, July 22, 1954; children—Susan Taft, Caroline Train, Deborah, Sarah K. Tchr. history William Penn Charter Sch., Phila., 1927- 29, asst. dean Harvard Coll., 1929-43, asst. to dean faculty, also chmn. com. scholarships, 1943-45; asst. dir. army-navy coll. qualifying tests Coll. Entrance Exam. Bd., 1943-44, asso. sec., then acting exec. sec., 1945-46, dir., 1946-48; pres. Ednl. Testing Service, Princeton, N.J., 1948-70; pres. Interuniv. Communications Council, Inc., Princeton, 1970—; vis. lectr. psychology Princeton, 1950-68. Dir., Variable Annuity Life Ins. Co. of Am. Mem. adv. com. fgn. service exams. State Dept., 1945-52; mem. teaching and testing methods adv. panel Service Acad. Bd., 1949-50; mem. working group army research on officer selection Army Sci. Adv. Panel, 1956-57; mem. Phys. Scis. Study Com., 1956-60; edn. panel President's Sci. Adv. Com., 1957; visited Soviet Union under auspices U.S. Office Edn., 1958; adv. com. of planning commn. Fla. Bd. Control for State U. at Boca Raton, 1960-61; mem. overseers com. to visit psychology Dept. Harvard Coll., 1955-57, to visit social relations dept., 1957-61, to visit social relations, psychology and psychol. labs., 1961-64, chmn. com. to visit Grad. Sch. Edn., mem. bd. overseers, 1966—; trustee Inst. Ednl. Devel., Mercer County (N.J.) Community Coll.; cons. to com. on sch.-coll. relations Nat. Assn. Secondary Sch. Prins., 1963-64; mem. Mercer County (N.J.) Tercentenary Com., 1964; trustee N.J. Citizens Com. for Public Schools, 1956-60; exec. com. Princeton unit Recording for Blind, 1957-63; mem. Commn. on Human Resources and Advanced Tng.; mem. N.J. Adv. Com. Civil Rights, 1958-59; vice chmn. Am. Council on Edn., 1969-70. Trustee Monticello Coll., Alton, Ill., Barnard Coll., Columbia; mem. corp. Ednl. Devel. Center; mem. hon. bd. fellows New Coll., Sarasota, Fla.; bd. visitors Sch. Edn., U. Pitts. Fellow Am. Psychol. Assn.; mem. Am. Acad. Polit. and Social Sci., Eastern Psychol. Assn., N.J. Acad. Sci., Psychonomic Soc., Psychometric Soc., Am. Assn. Sch. Adminstrs., A.A.A.S., Am. Coll. Personnel Assn., Met. Mus. Art, Am. Personnel and Guidance Assn., Am. Ednl. Research Assn., Harvard Alumni Assn. (dir. 1959-62), Groton Sch. Alumni Assn. (pres. 1958-60). Episcopalian. Clubs: Century Assn., Harvard (N.Y.C.): Cosmos (Washington); Nassau (Princeton). Home: RD 1 Ringoes NJ 08551 Office: Interuniversity Communications Council Inc PO Box 364 Princeton NJ 08540

CHAUNCEY, THOMAS WEBSTER, radio-TV exec.; b. Houston, Jan. 20, 1913; s. Brinkley and Lucille Dunn (Weber) C.; student pub. schs.; m. Dorothy Atwater Wrigley, Feb. 27, 1959; children—Karen (Mrs. Donald Blomo), Sharen, Thomas; step-children—Helen (Mrs. Robert Wood), Dorothy, George. Owner, Tom Chauncey Jeweler, 1940-61; mng. dir. Radio Sta KPHO, 1941-48; pres., gen. mgr. KOOL Radio-TV, Inc., 1955—; pres., mng. dir. Old Pueblo Broadcasting Co. (KOLD and KOLD-TV), Tucson, 1955-69; farmer, rancher, Flagstaff, Mayer, Ariz.; former chmn. bd. CBS TV Network Affiliates. Grand marshal J.C. World Championship Rodeo and Parade, 1963; past Ariz. chmn. Radio Free Europe; spl. ambassador, Nigeria, 1960; gen. campaign chmn. Greater Phoenix-Scottsdale United Fund Campaign; mem. Citizen's Action Com.; voting mem. Ariz. State U. Found.; chmn. Ariz. com. A.R.C.; past dir. at large for Ariz. Am. Cancer Soc.; past dir. Community Council; exec. v.p., mem. bd. Barrow Neurol. Inst.; past nat. chmn. Broadcaster's adv. com. U.S. Savs. Bonds; past dir. United Cerebral Palsy Assn. Central Ariz.; past mem. Phoenix All-Am. City Com.; chmn. Ariz. Motion Picture Adv. Bd. past chmn. adv. bd. on radio and TV, Ariz. State U. Mem. Ariz. (pres.), Met. Phoenix (past pres., dir.) broadcasters assns., Nat. Acad. television Arts and Scis. (past Ariz. bd. govs.), Ariz. Quarterhorse Breeders Assn., Ariz. State Horseman's Assn., TV Pioneers, Navy League, Newcomen Soc. N.Am. Elk. Clubs: Phoenix Country; Cloud; Paradise Valley Racquet; Cowmen's Executives; Rancheros Vistadores. Office: 511 W Adams St Phoenix AZ 85003

CHAUT, ROBERT, investment banker; b. N.Y.C., Nov. 12, 1925; s. Abraham and Rita (Abramowitz) C.; B.S., City Coll. N.Y., 1945. Exec. v.p. M.A. Schapiro & Co., Inc., N.Y.C., 1963-65, pres. 1965-68; v.p. Kidder, Peabody & Co., Inc., N.Y.C., 1968—; dir. Manhattan Life Ins. Co., N.Y.C. Home: 311 E 71st St New York City NY 10021 Office: 20 Exchange Pl New York City NY 10005

CHAVAN, YESHWANTRAO BALWANTRAO finance minister India; b. Devrashtre, Maharashtra, India, Mar. 12, 1913; B.A., Rajaram Coll., Kolhapur, 1938; LL.B., Law Coll. at Poona, 1941; m. Venutai. Practice of law, Karad; dir. underground activities Indian independence; imprisoned by British, 1944-45; mem. Bombay state legislative assembly, apptd. parliamentary sec., 1946; mem. Bombay minister's council, charge state dept. civil supplies and later local self-govt. and forests, 1952; chief minister Bombay state, 1956-60, Maharashtra state, 1960-62; minister def. nat. govt. India, succeeding Krishna Menon, 1962-66, minister of home affairs, 1966-70, minister finance, 1970—. Founder Satara Dist. Central Coop. Bank, Marathi weekly Lok Kranti; founded (with others) Prakash, Marathi lang. daily newspaper, 1948. Pres., Inst. Applied Manpower Research, Indian Cancer Soc., Inst. Def. Studies and Analyses. Address: 1 Race Course Rd New Delhi India

CHAVANON, CHRISTIAN, counsellor state; b. Pontivy, Morbihan, Mar. 12, 1913; s. Hippolyte and Jeanne (d'Haucourt) C.; LL.D., Coll. Law Bordeaux; m. Marguerite Enselme, Feb. 22, 1941; children—Yves, Anne. Lawyer Ct. Bordeaux, 1933-41, auditor, 1941, master petitions Council State, 1946, counsellor state, 1963, juridical counsellor Nat. Coal-mines, 1945-46; dir. cabinet E. Claudius-Petit (minister reconstn.), 1951-53; prof. Nat. Sch. Adminstrn., Inst. Polit. Studies Paris; pres.-gen. mgr. Nat. Soc. Press Enterprises, 1953, hon. pres., 1955; juridical counsellor Electricity France, 1946-58; dir. cabinet Sec. State Civil Service, 1957; sec. gen. Information, 1958, gen. mgr. French radio broadcasting-TV, 1958-60; v.p. European Union Radio Broadcasting, 1958—; pres.-gen. mgr. Havas Agy., 1960—; pres. Co. Havas-Council, 1969; adminstr. Univas, 1968—; hon. pres. Nat. Confedn. French Publicity, 1967—, pres. Co. Publicity Agys., 1967-68; chmn. Agence Havas; adminstr. Luxemburg Co. Telecasting. Decorated Officer Legion Honor, Officer Agrl. Merit. Home: 18 bd Maillot 92 Neuilly-sur-Seine France Office: 62 rue de Richelieu Paris 2e France

CHAVARRIA-AGUILAR, O. L., coll. dean; b. San Jose, Costa Rica, Aug. 25, 1922; s. Ricardo Chavarria Flores and Adela Aguilar Mathe; came to U.S., 1927, naturalized, 1942; B.A., U. Cal. at Berkeley, 1949; Ph.D., U. Pa., 1952; m. Frances Bachenheimer, Feb. 28, 1947; children—Nicholas, Leon, Marco. Dir. English lang. inst. Am. U., Cairo, Egypt, 1956-57; from lectr. to prof. linguistics U. Mich., 1957-67; prof. Sanskrit and linguistics, chmn. dept. langs. and linguistics, also dir. S. Asia lang. and area center, U. Rochester, 1967-71; dean Coll. Liberal Arts and Sci., City Coll. of City U. N.Y., 1971—. Adviser Indian Inst. Tech., Kanpur, India, 1962- 64; collaborator ednl. TV program for U. Mich., 1960-67. Trustee, World Edn., Inc. Served with USAAF, 1942-45. Social Sci. Research Council fellow, 1952-53; Rockefeller fellow, 1953-54. Mem. Linguistics Soc. Am., Linguistic Soc. India, Am. Oriental Soc., Phi Beta Kappa. Author: Pashto Basic Course, 1962; A Basic Course in Hindi, 1966. Editor: Traditional India, 1965. Office: Coll Liberal Arts and Science City Coll of City U of NY New York City NY 10010

CHAVE, GEORGE P., life ins. co. exec.; b. N.Y.C., Dec. 8, 1909; s. George P. and Anne (Reynolds) C.; m. Elizabeth C. Badeau, June 15, 1931; children—Virginia (Mrs. Wilmarth), George P., Peter F. Mgr. claims dept. Equitable Life Assurance Soc., 1953-54, 2d v.p., 1954-61, v.p. charge home office adminstrn., 1961—. Exec. bd. Boy Scouts, Manhattan. Home: 100 W 57th St New York City NY 10019 Office: 1285 Av of the Americas New York City NY 10019

CHAVES, JOSE MARIA, educator, lawyer; b. Bogota, Colombia, Aug. 19, 1922; Bachiller, Bogota, 1939, certificate in anthropology, 1942, J.D., 1945; D.Sc. (hon.), U. Antioquia, 1948; M.A., Columbia, 1951, Ph.D., 1953; LL.D., U. Popayan, 1957; m., 2 children. Editor-in-chief Revista Colegio del Rosario, arts and letters mag., Colombia; gen. legal duties specializing pub. adminstrn.; asst. atty. gen. Colombia, Bogota, 1942- 45, instr. Romance langs. Columbia, 1945-48, 50-51; founder, 1st dean faculty U. Andes, Bogota, 1948-49; head area studies Queens Coll., N.Y. U., 1951-53; counselor Colombian embassy, Washington, 1953-55; prof. internat. law U. Colombia, 1955-58, U. Paris, 1957; guest prof. internat. law and relations Brit. Council, various univs. Eng., Scotland, 1957; dir., chief exec. Am. Found. for Cultural Popular Action, Inc., pvt. internat. orgn. for mass edn. by radio, N.Y.C., 1958—; dir. Center Latin Am. Studies, City U. N.Y. Editor in chief Grolier Spanish Universal Ency.; permanent del Iberoam. Bur. Edn. to UN. Organizer, dir. tech. assistance mission Unitarian Service Com. in Latin Am.; author Chaves Plan for settlement religious conflict between Caths. and Protestants in Latin Am.; dir. gen. Nat. U. Fund, Colombia, 1955-58. Decorated Legion of Honor (France); gran cruz Order of St. Constantine the Gt.; knight comdr. Alfonso El Sabio (Spain); recipient medaglia universitaria U. Pro Deo. Rome, 1957; medalla de los Andes, U. Andes, 1958; grand cross Vaseo Nuez de Balboa, Panama, 1970; grand cross Juan P. Duarte, Dominican Republic, 1970. Mem. Internat. Law Assn., Inter-Am. Bar Assn., Acad. Polit. Sci., Modern Lang. Assn., Academia Hispano Americana, Phi Delta Kappa. Clubs: Coveleigh Country (Rye, N.Y.); Metropolitan, Columbia U. (N.Y.C.). Author: Francisco de Vitoria. Founder International Law, 1945; Intergroup relations in the Spain of Cervantes, 1953; University Reform in Colombia, 1957. Home: 26 Autenrieth Rd Scarsdale NY 10583 Office: 515 Park Av New York City NY 10022

CHAVEZ, CESAR, (Estrada), labor union organizer; b. Yuma. Ariz., Mar. 31, 1927; m. Helen Chavez; eight children. Gen. dir. Commun. Service Orgn., 1958-62; found. Nat. Farm Workers Assn., 1962; leader United Farm Workers Organizing Com., AFL-CIO. CIO. 1966—. Served with USNR, 1944-45. Address: PO Box 62 Keene CA 93531

CHAVEZ, CHARLES conductor, composer; b. Mexico, June 13, 1899. Has served as head of Dept. of Fine Arts of Mexico and as dir. Nat. Conservatory, Mexico; founder Symphony Orchestra of Mexico City, 1928, and since conductor; has been guest conductor of many major orchestras in United States; Charles Eliot Norton prof. poetry Harvard, 1958-59. Decorated many fgn. govts. Hon. mem. Am. Acad. Arts and Scis., Nat. Inst. Arts and Letters. Author: Toward a New Music, 1937; Musical Thoughts, 1960. Composer: Sinfonia Antigona, Sinfonia India, music for ballet symphony, H.P. (the initials standing for Horse Power), 4th Symphony, Romántica, 1959, Soli Number I for Wind Quartet, 5th Symphony for Strings, 6th Symphony, 7th Symphony, 3 string quartets, violin and cello sonatinas, Sonata for Four Horns, Toccata for Percussion, and many other leading works. Address: Av Pirineos 775 Lomas de Chapulltepec Mexico 10 DF Mexico*

CHAVEZ, EDWARD A., artist; b. Wagonmound, N.M., Mar. 14, 1917; s. Charles and Beatrice (Martinez) C.; student Colo. Springs Fine Arts Center, 1935-38; pvt. instrn. Frank Mechau, Boardman Robinson, Peppino Mangravite, Arnold Blanch; m. Jenne Magafan, July 28, 1941; m. 2d, Eva Van Rijn, 1962; 1 dau., Maya. Instr. drawing and painting Art Students League N.Y., 1954, summer sch., 1955-58; vis. prof. art Colo. Coll., 1959; asst. prof. art Syracuse U., 1960-61; instr. art Dutchess Community Coll., Poughkeepsie, 1963; executed murals, post offices, service clubs, schs., hosps.; one-man shows Denver Art Mus., 1938, Asso. Am. Artists N.Y., 1948-49, Ganso Gallery, N.Y.C., 1950, 52-54. Il Camino Gallery, Rome, Italy, 1951, Mus. N.M., 1954, Alexandre Rabow Gallery, San Francisco, 1954, Annie Werbe Galleries, Detroit, 1957, John Heller Gallery, N.Y.C., 1955, 56, 58, 59, 60, N.Y. State Coll. Tchrs., Albany, 1960; exhibited Chgo. Art Inst., N.A.D., Nat. Inst. Arts and Letters, Whitney Mus., Met. Mus., N.Y.C., Pa. Acad. Art, Carnegie Inst., Pitts., Corcoran Bienniel, Washington, others; represented in collections Mus. Modern Art, N.Y.C., Newark Mus. Art, Library of Congress Print Collection, other museums, galleries and pvt. collections. Recipient Pepsi-Cola art prize, 1947, Lathrop prize, Print Club of Albany, 1948, Louis Comford Tiffany $2000 fellowship, 1948. Fulbright grantee, Italy, 1951, Hermine Kleinert award, 1952; Childe Hassam Purchase award, 1953; 1st prize Albany Inst. History and Art, 1966. Mem. Nat. Soc. Mural Painters (hon.), Woodstock Art Assn. (sec). Home: 32 Plochman Lane Woodstock NY 12498

CHAVEZ, IGNACIO, physician; b. 1897; ed. Nat. U. of Mexico; hon. degrees univs. Paris, Montpellier, Lyon, Mexico, Sao Paulo, Oxford, Bologna, Praga, others; children—Ignacio Chávez Rivera, Celia Chávez de Garcia Terrés. Clin. prof. Nat. U. of Mexico, 1923-50, dir. Faculty Medicine, 1933-34, prof. cardiology Sch. Grads., 1946-61, rector Nat. U., 1961-66. Founder, hon. dir. Nat. Inst. Cardiology Mexico; founder, mem. Colegio Nacional. Hon. rector U. Michoacan; hon. prof. univs. Guadalajara, Guatemala, San Salvador, Rio de Janeiro, others. Recipient Palmes Academiques. Decorated Legion of Honor, Order Pub. Health (France); comdr. Order Finlay (Cuba); Order Quetzal (Guatemala); Order Cruzeiro do Sul (Brazil); Medal of Civil Merit, (Mexico); Order Nassau (Holland); Merito (Italy); Polonia Restituta; Roi Leopold (Belgium); recipient Scientific prize of Mexico. Mem. Inter-Am. Soc. Cardiology (hon. pres.), Internat. Soc. Cardiology (hon. pres.), Acads. Medicine of Mexico, N.Y., Buenos Aires, France, Rome, others. Author 6 med. books, book on history medicine, book on art, numerous articles on medicine and edn. Home: Paseo de la Reforma 1310 Lomas de Chapultepec Mexico 10 DF Mexico Office: Av Nuevo León 78 Mexico DF Mexico

CHAVEZ, SIMON JOSEPH, educator; b. LaJara, Colo., Apr. 4, 1916; s. Simon M. and Emeteria (Marquez) C.; A.B., Adams State Coll., Alamosa, 1938; M.Ed., U. Colo., 1947, D.Ed., 1952; m. Anna Marie Lobato, Aug. 17, 1945; children—Joan (Mrs. William Slonaker, Jr.), Peggy, Buddy, Annette, Michele. Instr. Spanish, U. Colo., 1946-50; chief ednl. specialist USAF, Pinecastle and Palm Beach, Fla., 1952-54; prof. edn. U. Dayton, 1954—, chmn. dept. elementary edn., 1963—; vis. prof. U. Colo., summer 1963, N.M. Highlands U., summers 1960, 61; cons. visual edn., 1963-65, Pflaum Pub. Co., 1964-66. Served to 1st lt. USAAF, 1942-45. Mem. Assn. Supervision and Curriculum Devel., Assn. Am. Coll. Tchr. Edn., Phi Delta Kappa. Author: (4 filmstrips) Dramatize Your Teaching, 1962; (record) Collection of Spanish Songs for Children, 1965. Contbr. profl. jours. Home: 4725 Shady Hill Lane Dayton OH 45429.

CHAYEFSKY, PADDY, writer; b. N.Y.C., Jan. 29, 1923; s. Harry and Gussie (Stuchevsky) C.; B.S., Coll. City N.Y., 1943; m. Susan Sackler, Feb. 24, 1949; 1 son, Dan. Writer TV dramas, 1952—; writer, asso. producer films Marty, 1955, Bachelor Party, 1957, The Goddess, 1958, Middle of the Night, 1959, The Americanization of Emily, 1964; writer-producer The Hospital, 1971; Broadway dramas, including; Middle of the Night, 1958, The Tenth Man, 1959, The Passion of Josef D., 1964, The Latent Heterosexual, 1968; writer, co-producer Broadway play Gideon, 1961—; pres. Carnegie Prodns., 1957, S.P.D. Corp., 1959, Sudan Corp., 1956—, Sidney Prodns.. Inc., 1967—, Simcha Prodns., 1971—. Served as pfc, AUS, World War II. Decorated Purple Heart. Mem. Dramatists Guild, Screenwriters Guild Am., Writers Guild Am., Screen Actors Guild, Am. Guild Variety Artists. Author: (anthology) Television Plays by Paddy Chayefsky, 1955; The Goddess, 1958; Middle of the Night, 1958; The Tenth Man, 1960; Gideon, 1960; The Passion of Josef D., 1964; (play and book) The Latent Heterosexual, 1968. Address: 850 7th Av New York City NY 10019

CHAYES, ABRAM, educator, lawyer; b. Chgo., July 18, 1922; s. Edward and Kitty (Torch) C.; A.B., Harvard, 1943, LL.B., 1949; m. Antonia Handler, Dec. 24, 1947; children—Eva, Abigail, Lincoln, Sarah Prudence, Angelica. Admitted D.C. bar, 1953, Conn. bar, 1950, Mass. bar, 1958; legal adviser to Gov. of Conn., 1949-50; gen. counsel Pres.'s Materials Policy Commn., 1951; law clk. to Justice Felix Frankfurter, 1951-52; with Covington & Burling, Washington, law firm, 1952-55 Gingburg & Feldman, Washington, 1964-65.; asst. prof. law Harvard, 1955-58, prof., 1958-61, 65—. Staff dir. Democratic Platform Com., 1960. Legal adviser, asst. sec. Dept. of State, 1961-64. Carnegie Corp. reflective year grant, 1965-66. Served from sgt. to capt., F.A., AUS, 1943-46. Decorated Bronze Star. Fellow Am. Acad. Arts and Scis. Author: (with others) The International Legal Process, 2 vols., 1968; ABM, An Evaluation of the Decision to Deploy an Antiballistic Missile System, 1969. Home: 3 Hubbard Park Cambridge MA 02138

CHAYES, FELIX, petrologist; b. N.Y.C., May 10, 1916; s. Nat and Hilda Gretchen (Hoffmann) C.; B.A., N.Y. U., 1936; M.A., Columbia, 1939, Ph.D., 1941; m. Irene Hendry, Dec. 14, 1941. Petrographer, U.S. Bur. Mines, 1942-46; with metallurgy dept. Mass. Inst. Tech., 1946-47; petrologist Geophys. Lab., Carnegie Instn., Washington, 1947—; vis. prof. Cal. Inst. Tech., 1955. Mem. exec. com., div. earth scis. NRC, 1963-66. Fellow Geol. Soc. Am., Mineral. Soc. Am. (councillor 1954-57, pres. 1966-67), Am. Geophys. Union (sec. volcanology sect. 1950-56). Author: Petrographic Modal Analysis, 1956; Ratio Correlation, 1971; also numerous articles. †

CHAYKIN, STERLING, educator; b. N.Y.C., Sept. 18, 1929; s. Frank David and Ruth (Berman) C.; A.B., N.Y. U., 1950; Ph.D., U. Washington, 1954; m. Elaine Loeb, June 13, 1954; children—Ronald Scott, William Lawrence, Janet Gail, Nancy Elizabeth. Postdoctoral fellow chem. dept. Harvard, 1956-59; asst. prof. U. Cal., Davis, 1959-64, asso. prof., 1964-69, prof. biochemistry, 1969—, chmn. dept. biochemistry and biophysics, 1968-70, asso. dean resident instrn., 1970—. Served with AUS, 1954-56. Damon Runyon fellow, 1956-59; Fulbright fellow, 1966-67; Guggenheim fellow, 1966-67. Mem. Am.

Soc. Biol. Chemists, A.A.A.S., Am. Chem. Soc., Sigma Xi. Author: Biochemistry Laboratory Techniques, 1966. Office: U Cal Davis CA 95616

CHAZANOW, GEORGE, mfg. co. exec.; b. Russia, Aug. 13, 1908; s. Frank and Jennie (Krakow) C.; came to U.S., 1912, naturalized, 1929; student Baylor U.; Ph.B. in Econs., U. Chgo., 1929; m. Sibylle Greenberg, Dec. 24, 1931; children—Barbara Ann (Mrs. Charles P. Cohen), Elaine Merl (Mrs. Bernard A. Rotman). With Stone Container Corp., Chgo., 1948—, treas., 1959—, sr. v.p., 1962—, also dir.; dir. S.C. Industries, Inc. Vice pres., dir. Stone Found.; bd. govs. Citizens Greater Chgo. Mem. Financial Execs. Inst., Am. Paper Inst., Phi Epsilon Pi. Jewish religion. Clubs: Standard, Ravisloe Country. Home: 777 N Michigan Av Chicago IL 60611 Office: 360 N Michigan Av Chicago IL 60601

CHE, YIN-SHOU Chinese diplomat; b. Kiangsi, China, Feb. 1, 1922; s. Yun-long and Feng- ying (Chou) C.; grad. Nat. Chengchi U., Chungking, China, 1945; research student N.Y.U., 1954-58; m. Yungchen Chou, Apr. 16, 1947; children—Sophie, Tessie, Mitchell, Maggie. Chief sect. UN affairs Ministry Fgn. Affairs, Republic China, 1949-53; tech. counselor Chinese delegation 6th, 8th-13th sessions UN Gen. Assembly, 1951-58; 1st sec. Chinese permanent Mission to UN, 1953-58; consul gen. of China in Vancouver, B.C., Can., 1958-62, in San Francisco, 1962-68. Served with Chinese Army, 1944-48. Home: 20 Manzanita Ct Millbrae CA 94030 Office: 557 Montgomery St San Francisco CA 94111

CHEADLE, VERNON IRVIN, chancellor; b. Salem, S.D., Feb. 6, 1910; s. Henry Melvin and Inez Eleanor (Engleman) C.; student S.D. State Coll., 1927-28; A.B., Miami U., 1932, LL.D. 1964; A.M., Harvard U., 1934, Ph.D., 1936; LL.D. U. R.I., 1964; m. Mary Jenkins Low, Dec. 23, 1939; 1 son, William Gerald. Agr. agt., U.S.D.A., summers 1928-31; field supr. barberry eradication, S.D., 1931; Austin teaching fellow Harvard, 1933-36; instr., botany, R.I. State Coll., 1936-41, asst. prof. botany, 1941-42, prof., head dept. botany, 1942-52, dir. grad., div. 1943-52; prof. botany, botanist Expt. Sta., U. Cal. at Davis, 1952- 62, chmn. dept., 1952-60, acting vice chancellor, 1961-62; chancellor U. Cal. at Santa Barbara, 1962—; tech. cons., Fish and Game Div., R.I., summers 1948, 49. Served to lt. U.S.N.R., 1944-46. Recipient Certificate of Appreciation, Lambda Chi Alpha, 1950; Certificate of Merit, Bot. Soc. Am.; Fulbright fellow, 1959; Outstanding Civilian Service medal, 1965. Fellow A.A.A.S., Am. Acad. Arts and Scis., Cal. Acad. Scis., mem. Am. Soc. Plant Taxonomists, Internat. Soc. Plant Morphologists (asso. editor jour. 1955-59, councillor 1970—), Bot. Society Am. (chmn. membership com., 1946-49; chmn. gen. sect., 1949; alternate del. Nat. Research Council 1948-50, editorial com. jour. 1953-55, pres. 1961), Torrey Bot. Club, Soc. Study of Growth and Devel., Soc. Study of Evolution, Am. Assn. U. Profs., Am. Soc. Naturalists, Am. Inst. Biol. Scis., Grange, Phi Beta Kappa, Sigma Xi, Phi Delta Theta, Phi Kappa Phi. Presbyn. Clubs: Santa Barbara; Commonwealth of California. Author: Discussion Manuals I and II (with E. A. Palmatier), 1949, 50. Editor and part author: New England Museums of Importance in Graduate Study, 1950. Contbr. tech. articles. Home: 543 Channel Islands Rd U Cal Santa Barbara CA 93106.

CHEATHAM, ELLIOTT EVANS, educator; b. Savannah, Ga., July 13, 1888; s. Elliott Evans and Sarah Frances (Swoll) C.; A.B., U. Ga., 1907; LL.B., Harvard, 1911; LL.D., Boston U., 1942, Oglethorpe U., 1951, Columbia, 1960, Emory U., 1966; D.C.L., U. N.B., 1954; m. Ida May Blount, May 20, 1914. Practiced law Atlanta, 1911-14, 1919-24; faculty Atlanta Law Sch., 1913-14; atty. dept. justice, asst. U.S. atty., 1914-17; prof. law Emory U., 1921-24, U. Ill., 1924-26, Cornell U., 1926-29, Columbia, 1929-57; vis. prof. law U. Istanbul, 1957-58, Harvard, 1958- 59; prof. law Hastings Coll. Law, 1959-60; prof. law Vanderbilt U., Nashville, 1960-68, research prof. law, 1968—. Lectr., Hague Acad. Internat. Law, 1960; Carpentier lectr. Columbia, 1963. Mem. Am. Bar Assn., Assn. Am. Law Schs. (pres. 1942). Democrat. Author: A Lawyer When Needed, 1963; (with Samuel D. Thurman, Ellis L. Phillips, Jr.) Cases on the Legal Profession, 1970; (with Maurice Rosenberg, Erwin N. Griswold, Willis L.M. Rease) Cases on Conflict of Laws, 5th edit., 1964; (with L. Ray Patterson) The Profession of Law, 1971. Contbr. articles various law revs. Home: 2823 Hillside Dr Nashville TN 37212.

CHEATHAM, JOHN MCGEE, textile mfr.; b. Easley, S.C., May 15, 1913; s. John Henry and Janye (Jackson) C.; student Furman U., 1930-32, Ga. Tech., 1932-33; m. Elizabeth Mathis, June 15, 1939; children—John McGee, Elizabeth M., Harvey M., Jackson Kelley. With Dundee Mills, Griffin, Ga., 1933—, successively clk., jr. salesman, asst. to pres., v.p. 1941-50, pres., 1950—; pres., treas. Rushton Cotton Mills. Griffin, Hartwell Mills (Ga.); dir. Trust Co. Ga. Trustee, Ga. Bapt. Found. Served as lt. (j.g.) USNR, 1944-46. Mem. Am. Textile Mfrs. Inst., Inc. (pres. 1960- 61). Baptist. Rotarian. Home: 435 E College St Griffin GA 30223 Office: Dundee Mills Inc Griffin GA 30223

CHEATHAM, JULIAN NORTH, corp. exec.; b. Concord, Va., Sept. 8, 1911; s. Walter B. and Sallie (Franklin) C.; B.S., Va. Poly. Inst., 1933; m. Alyce Roberts, June 14, 1947; children—Alyce Thayer, Julian North, Sallie Franklin. With Western Union Telegraph Co., N.Y.C., 1933-35; v.p. lumber sales and export Georgia-Pacific Corp., now exec. v.p., dir. Served as capt. AUS, 1942-45. Republican. Presbyn. Clubs: Arlington, Waverley Country (Portland, Ore.); Augusta (Ga.) Nat. Golf. Home: Portland OR 97219 Office: 900 SW 5th Av Portland OR 97204

CHEATLE, ESTHEL L., educator, physician. Prof. pathology U. Ill. Med. Center, Chgo. Office: Dept Pathology Coll Med U Ill 1853 W Polk St Chicago IL 60612*

CHEATUM, EVELYN LEONARD, educator; b. Lerado, Kan., Oct. 31, 1909; s. Jasper William and Clara Grace (Wright) C.; student So. Meth. U., 1929-32; A.B., U. Mich., 1934, M.S., 1937, Ph.D., 1947; m. Hortelle Goodwin, June 15, 1939; children—Linda Sue, William Goodwin. Asso. prof. biology Tarleton Coll., Stephenville, Tex., 1937-38, S.W. Tex. State Tchrs. Coll., San Marcus, summer 1938; wildlife pathologist N.Y. State Conservation Dept., 1939-44, 46-50, chief bur. of game, 1952-59, asst. div. dir. fish and game, 1959-64, asst. commr. for fish and game, 1964-68; dir. Inst. Natural Resources, U. Georgia, 1968—, also prof. Sch. Forest Resources; leader Mont. Coop. Wildlife Research Unit, U.S. Fish and Wildlife Service, Missoula, 1950-52. Spl. cons. environmental scis. tng. com. USPHS. Sec. N.Y. State Fish and Wildlife Mgmt. Bd.; mem. State Exec. Com. Parks and Recreation; mem. Ga. Ocean Sci. Center of the Atlantic Commn., 1969, Ga. Sci. and Tech. Commn., 1969—. Mem. com. Ft. Orange council Boy Scouts Am. Served to capt. AUS, World War II; S. Pacific. Decorated Bronze Star; recipient Nash Motors Conservation award, 1954. Mem. Wildlife Soc. (pres. 1960-62; award for achievement wildlife research N.E. sect. 1950). Wildlife Disease Assn. (a founder), Soil Conservation Soc. Am., A.A.A.S., Am. Inst. Biol. Scis., Ga. Conservancy. Baptist. Co-author: The Deer of North America, 1956; Careers in Conservation. Home: 100 Torrey Pine Pl Athens GA 30601.

CHECCHI, VINCENT economist; b. Calais, Me., Nov. 25, 1918; s. Arthur R. and Dina I. (Pisani) C.; A.B., U. Me., 1940; postgrad. Harvard, 1941; M.A., George Washington U., 1942; m. Mary E. Pate, Aug. 2, 1941; children—Dina Ann, Mary Jane, Vincent Arthur. Statistician-economist WPB, 1941-45; dep. dir. requirements br. Allied Mil. Govt. in Italy, 1945-46; dir. program coordination UNRRA, Italy, then asst. to chief mission in China, 1946- 47; loan officer Internat. Bank Reconstrn. and Development, 1947; dir. China econ. br., later dir. East-West trade br., ECA, 1947-49, spl. rep. in Philippines, 1950-51; econ. editor Reporter mag., 1950; founder, 1951, since pres., chmn. bd. Checchi and Co., Washington, also dir. various subsidiaries; dir. Coop. Americane e Italiane, Investment Devel. Corp., Trans-Philippines Investment Corp., Checchi-Pacific Corp. Co-author: Honduras, A Problem in Economic Development. Home: 9206 Watson Rd Silver Spring MD 20910 Office: 815 Connecticut Av NW Washington DC 20006

CHECKER, CHUBBY (Ernest Evans), recording artist; b. Phila., Oct. 3, 1941. Appearances on TV, in theatres, movies. Mem. A.S.C.A.P. Address: care Cameo Records 1405 Locust St Philadelphia PA 19102

CHECKLEY, DAVID MILTON, architect; b. Mattoon, Ill., Aug. 26, 1917; s. Horace R. and Mildred L. (Lemert) C.; B.S. in Architecture and Bus. Adminstrn. with honors, U. Ill., 1940; m. Dorothea Stinson, Oct. 18, 1941; children—Leslie Ruth, David Milton, Elizabeth. Archtl. designer, Chgo., 1940-41; indsl. engr. N.Am. Aviation, Inc., 1941-44; project mgr., v.p., gen. mgr. J. Gordon Turnbull, Inc., cons. engrs., Cleve., 1944-54; gen. mgr. indsl. div. Arthur G. McKee & Co., Cleve., 1954-59; pres. Vitro Engring. Co., N.Y.C., 1959-61; pvt. cons. practice, 1961-64, 70—; mng. dir. John Graham & Co., Seattle, 1964-69, pres., 1969-70. Mem. Am. Inst. Architects, Newcomen Soc., Am. Watercolor Soc., Puget Sound Group N.W. Painters. Episcopalian. Clubs: Engineers (N.Y.C.); American (London, Eng.); Rainier (Seattle). Home: 678 W Prospect Seattle WA 98119

CHEEK, JAMES EDWARD, univ. pres.; b. Roanoke Rapids, N.C., Dec. 4, 1932; s. King Virgil and LeeElla (Williams) C.; B.A., Shaw U., 1955; B.D., Colgate Rochester Div. Sch., 1958; Ph.D., Drew U., 1962, LL.D., 1971; L.H.D., Trinity Coll., 1970; H.H.D., Shaw U., 1970; LL.D., A and T U., 1971; m. Celestine Juanita Williams, June 14, 1953; children—James Edward, Janet Elizabeth. Teaching asst. hist. theology Drew Theol. Sch., Madison, N.J., 1959-60; instr. Western history Union Jr. Coll., Cranford, N.J., 1959-61; vis. instr. Christian history Upsala Coll., East Orange, N.J., summer 1960; asst. prof. N.T. and hist. theology Sch. Religion, Va. Union U., Richmond, 1961-63; pres. Shaw U., 1963-69, Howard U., 1969—. Dir. First Nat. Bank Washington. Cons. to Pres. U.S. on black colls. and univs., 1970. Mem. Pres.'s Commn. on Campus Unrest, 1970, policy council Common Cause, pres.'s devel. council Wilberforce U., nat. adv. council Ind. Found., Washington Home Rule, Inc., VOICE, nat. selection com. Sealantic Fund, adv. com. Woodrow Wilson Internat. Center for Scholars, nat. adv. council Peace Corps, steering com. Nat. Urban Coalition, nat. council U.S. People's Fund for UN, com internat. edn. Coll. Entrance Exam. Bd. Bd. dirs. Nat. Assn. Equal Opportunity Higher Edn., Greater Washington Ednl. TV Assn., Nat. Council Educating Disadvantaged, Downtown Progress, Ednl. Policy Center, Joint Center for Polit. Studies, Nat. Lab. Higher Edn., Washington Urban League, nat. capital area council Boy Scouts Am., Fund Advancement Theol. Edn.; trustee Colgate Rochester Div. Sch., Internat. Council Ednl. Devel., Fed. City Council, Fund Edn. in World Order, Washington Center for Met. Studies, U. Miami. Served with USAF, 1951-52. Colgate Rochester grad. fellow, 1958; Lily Found. fellow, 1958, 59; Rockefeller fellow, 1960. Mem. Soc. Bibl. Lit. and Exegesis, Am. Soc. Ch. History, Nat. Assn. Bibl. Instrs., Am. Assn. U. Profs., Am. Acad. Religion, Religious Research Assn., L.Q.C. Lamar Soc., Internat. African C. of C. (dir.), Am. Assn. Higher Edn. (trustee), Am. Assn. Colls. for Tchr. Edn., Middle States Assn. Colls. and Secondary Schs. (trustee), Internat. Platform Assn., Am. Mgmt. Assn., Nat. Assn. Black Adult Educators (nat. adv. com.), Sigma Pi Sigma, Alpha Theta Nu, Alpha Kappa Delta, Alpha Phi Alpha. Bd. editors Jour. Black Studies. Home: 8035 16th St NW Washington DC 20012 Office: Howard Univ Washington DC 20001

CHEEK, KING VIRGIL, Jr., coll. pres., lawyer; b. Weldon, N.C., May 26, 1937; s. King Virgil and Lee Ella (Williams) C.; A.B., Bates Coll., Lewiston, Me., 1959, LL.D., 1970; M.A. (Jessie Smith Noyes scholar), U. Chgo., 1960, postgrad., 1960-61, J.D., 1964; LL.D., Del. State Coll., 1970; m. Annette Walker, Aug. 10, 1968. With Midwest Inter-Library Loan Center, Chgo., 1959-64; asst. prof. econs. Shaw U., Raleigh, N.C., 1964-65, acting dean of coll., 1965-66, dean, 1966-67, v.p. acad. affairs, 1967-69, lectr. Citizenship Lab., 1968-69, pres., 1969-71; Pres. Morgan State Coll., Balt., 1971; admitted to Ill. bar, 1964, N.C. bar, 1965; practice in Raleigh, 1965-71; cons. U.S. Office Edn., 1967, Instl. Studies Commn. Kittrell (N.C.) Coll., 1967; cons., program evaluator U.S. Office Edn. and U.S. Office Econ. Opportunity. Mem. Mayor's Com. on UN Observance, 1967-71; mem. Task Force, The Vital Univ. sponsored by Sci. and Soc. Program, N.C. State U., 1968-69; chmn. N.C. Adv. Com. to U.S. Civil Rights Commn., 1969-70; mem. adv. council N.C. Regional Med. Program, 1968-69; mem. Md. adv. com. to U.S. Civil Rights Commn. Bd. dirs. GROW, Inc., Ednl. Resources Inst., East St. Louis, Ill., Balt. Urban League, Good Samaritan Hosp., Balt. Mus. Art; mem. adv. bd. W.H. Trentman Mental Health Center of Wake County. Mem. New Eng. Forensic Championship Team, 1967-68. Mem. N.C. Assn. Colls., Assn. Eastern N.C. Colls., Acad. Polit. and Social Sci., Raleigh Bus. and Profl. League, Southeastern Lawyers Assn., Delta Sigma Rho. Address: Morgan State Coll Baltimore MD 21212

CHEESMAN, WILLIAM JAMES mfg. co. exec.; b. Barrie, Ont., Can., July 26, 1921; s. James Walter and Fern (Hutton) C.; B.A.Sc., U. Toronto, 1943; m. Suzanne Grasett, Dec. 1, 1945; children—Judith (Mrs. Gary Bray), Pamela, James, Margaret. Lab. engr. Canadian Gen. Electric Co., 1946-47; research engr. Ont. Hydro Commn., 1947-51; gen. mgr. Canadian Westinghouse Co. Ltd., 1951- 61; gen. mgr. ITT, Can., 1961-64, RCA Victor, 1964-65; with Canadian Westinghouse Co. Ltd., 1965—, pres., 1967—. Bd. govs., mem. senate McMaster U.; bd. dirs. Hamilton United Appeal. Served with Royal Canadian Navy, 1943-45. Mem. Canadian Nuclear Assn. (v.p., bd. dirs.). Clubs: Hamilton, Hamilton Officers. Home: 1338 Wakefield Ct Burlington Ontario Canada Office: PO Box 510 Hamilton Ontario Canada

CHELLGREN, WILBUR E., oil co. exec.; b. Bridgeport, Conn., Oct. 22, 1915; s. Wilhelm E. and Tekla (Janson) C.; B.B.A., U. Minn., 1938; m. Kathryn L. Berquist, Nov. 22, 1941; children—Paul W., Karin L. (Mrs. Larry Lewis), Jon D., Lynn Ann, Mark R., Susan K. Supervising accountant Price, Waterhouse & Co., C.P.A.'s, Pitts., 1939-47; controller Freedom-Valvoline Oil Co. (Pa.), 1947-53; with Ashland Oil, Inc. (Ky.), 1953—, controller, 1969—. Active Boyd County Cancer Soc. Served with AUS, 1941-46. Decorated Bronze Star. C.P.A., Ky. Mem. Am. Inst. C.P.A.'s, Ky. Soc. C.P.A.'s. Home: 2814 Ranch Rd Ashland KY 41101 Office: 1409 Winchester Av Ashland KY 41101

CHELLMAN, JOHN, ednl. adminstr.; B.S., Slippery Rock State Coll., Ed.M., U. Pitts.; Ed.D., George Peabody Coll. Tchrs. Dean, Sch. Health Services Ind. U. of Pa. Office: Sch Health Services Ind U of Pa Indiana PA 15701*

CHEN, CHUAN FANG, educator; b. Tientsin, China, Nov. 15, 1932; s. Kwang Yuan and Chin Han (Wang) C.; came to U.S., 1950, naturalized, 1963; B.Sc., U. Ill., 1953, M.Sc., 1954; Ph.D., Brown U., 1960; m. Frances Ya-Kiang Liu, Aug. 10, 1957; children—Peter Peishan, Paul Peichuan, Philip Peihai. Asst. to chief engr. Hydronautics, Inc., Laurel, Md., 1960-63; asst. prof. mech. and aerospace engring. Rutgers U., New Brunswick, N.J., 1963-66, asso. prof., 1966-69, prof., 1969—; cons. Vitro Labs., Silver Spring, Md., Hydronautics, Inc., Laurel, C.R. Bard, Inc., Murray Hill, N.J. Am. Soc. Engring. Edn.-NASA fellow, summers 1968, 69; Rutgers Research Council Faculty fellow, 1971-72. Asso. fellow Am. Inst. Aeros. and Astronautics; mem. Am. Assn. U. Profs., Am. Phys. Soc., Am. Soc. Engring. Edn., Sigma Xi, Tau Beta Pi, Pi Tau Sigma. Contbr. articles profl. jours. Home: 46 Abbott Rd Somerset NJ 08873

CHEN, KUN-MU, educator; b. Taiwan, China, Feb. 3, 1933; s. Tsa-Mao and Che (Wu) C.; came to U.S., 1957, naturalized, 1969; B.S., Nat. Taiwan U., 1955; M.S., Harvard, 1958, Ph.D., 1960; m. Shun-Shun Chen, Feb. 22, 1962; children-Margaret, Katherine, Kenneth, George. Research asso. U. Mich., 1960-64; vis. prof. Chao-Tung U., Taiwan, 1962; asso. prof. elec. engring. Mich. State U., 1964-67, prof., 1967—. C.T. Loo fellow, 1957; Gordon McKay fellow, 1958-60; Sr. mem. I.E.E.E.; mem. Am. Assn. U. Profs., A.A.A.S., Sigma Xi. Contbr. articles electromagnetic radiation, plasma physics. Home: 4608 Tacoma Blvd Okemos MI 48864 Office: Dept Elec Engring Mich State U East Lansing MI 48823

CHEN, KUO-TSAI, educator, mathematician; b. Chekiang, China, July 15, 1923; s. Sheng-Hai and Yah-Su (Yu) C.; B.S., S.W. Asso. U., 1946; Ph.D., Columbia 1950; m. Julia Tse-Yee Fong, Dec. 22, 1953; children—Matthew, Lydia, Lucia. Came to U.S., 1962, naturalized, 1969. Instr., Princeton, 1950-51; research asso. U. Ill., Urbana, 1951-52, prof., 1967—; lectr. U. Hong Kong 1952- 58; asso. prof. Instituto Technologico de Aeronautic, Brazil, 1958-60, prof., 1960-61; asso. prof. Rutgers U., 1962-63, prof., 1963-65; prof. State U. N.Y., Buffalo, 1965-67. Mem. Inst. for Advanced Study, Princeton, N.J., 1960, 62. Mem. Am. Math. Soc. Home: 403 Evergreen Ct Urbana IL 61801

CHEN, MING MAO, educator; b. China, Apr. 23, 1919; s. Kwang C. and Liao (Shih) C.; B.S.M.E., Nat. Wu-han U., 1941; M.S., U. Ill., 1948; M.S. in aerospace engring., U. Wash., 1952; Ph.D., U. Ill., 1952; m. Frances Cheng, Dec. 22, 1948; children—Elizabeth F., Leon L. Came to U.S., 1947, naturalized, 1963. Research engr. Rep. Aviation Corp., 1952-53; mem. research staff Mass. Inst. Tech., 1953-60; asso. prof. Boston U., 1960-66, prof. aero. engring. 1966—; vis. prof. Cheng-Kung U., Taiwan, 1966-67; acting dean acad. affairs Engring. Sci. Research Center, Taiwan, 1967, chmn. dept. aero. engring., 1968—; cons. Dunn Engring., Inc., Borg-Warner Machines (Fremont, O.). Recipient Generalissimo Chiang Kai-shek scholarship, 1939-41. Mem. Am. Inst. Aeros. and Astronautics, Am. Soc. Engring. Edn., A.A.A.S., N.Y. Acad. Sci., Boston Mus. Sci., Greater Boston Chinese Cultural Assn. (pres. 1962), Sigma Xi. Methodist. Contbr. articles profl. jours. Home: 6 Redcoat Lane Lexington MA 02173 Office: 110 Cummington St Boston MA 02215

CH'EN, SHANG YI, educator; b. Hopei, China, Mar. 4, 1910; s. Tzi W. and M. (Ma) C.; B.S., Yenching U., 1932, M.S., 1934; Ph.D., Cal. Inst. Tech., 1940; m. Ruth Pan, Dec. 27, 1930; children—Betty (Mrs. H.C. Chon), Chorng (Mrs. C.H. Liang), Daniel R., Jane (Mrs. E. Mak), Eugene. Came to U.S., 1949, naturalized, 1955. From lectr. to prof. physics and chmn. dept. Yenching U., 1939-46; research prof. Inst. Physics, Nat. Acad. Peiping, 1946-49; asso. prof. physics U. Ore., 1949-54, prof., 1954—. Vis. scientist Lab. High Pressure, Centre Nat. de la Recherche Sci., Bellevue, France, 1960-61, Clarendon Labs., Oxford (Eng.) U., 1968; chmn. Gordon Research Conf. on Spectral Line Shapes, 1966. Fellow Am. Phys. Soc.; mem. Sigma Xi, Phi Tau Phi, Sigma Pi Sigma. Contbr. articles profl. jours. Home: 3715 Potter St Eugene OR 97405

CHEN, WEN CHAO, educator; b. Shansi, China, Oct. 14, 1919; s. Teh L. and May (Lee) C.; came to U.S., 1945; B.A., Grinnell Coll., 1947; M.A., St. Louis U., 1949, Ph.D., 1951; M.L.S., U. Chgo., 1957; m. Lilia C.J. Chao, Dec. 21, 1950; children—Michael W., Philip E. Instr. polit. sci. Kalamazoo Coll., 1950-53, asst. prof., 1953-58, asso. prof., 1955-57, prof., 1958—, librarian, 1953-70, dean spl. services, 1967-70, v.p., 1970—. Served to capt. Chinese Nationalist Army, 1943-45. Mem. Am. Polit. Sci. Assn., Am. Soc. for Pub. Adminstrn., Am. Library Assn., Am. Assn. U. Profs. Home: 133 Bulkley St Kalamazoo MI 49007 Office: 1200 Academy St Kalamazoo MI 49001

CHEN-CHI, artist; b. Wusih, China, May 2, 1912; s. Shih-Pei Chen and Shih Tsai; ed. in China; m. Alice Zu-Min Huang, Oct. 5, 1962. First one-man exhbn., Shanghai, China, 1940; faculty art St. John's U., Shanghai, 1942-46, Pa. State U., summers 1959-60; artist-in-residence, Odgen, Utah, 1967; one-man exhbns. U.S. museum, art galleries including Allentown (Pa.) Art Mus., Miami Beach Art Center, Portland Art Mus.; group exhbns. Met. Art Mus., Nat. Acad., N.Y.C., Springfield (Mo.) Art Mus., Brooklyn Mus., 1947—, Whitney Mus. Am. Art, many others; painter series Am. city scenes, Collier's, other publs., 1947—; works represented in permanent collections. Jury selection and awards Butler Inst. Am. Art, Frye Mus. Seattle, Am. Watercolor Soc., Allied Artists, Audubon Artists, sole judge ann. N.W. Coast Art Exhibit, Seattle, others. Recipient numerous awards, gold medals, bronze medal Am. Watercolor Soc., Nat. Arts Club. Audubon Artist, Phila. Watercolor Club. Salmagundi Club, Knickerbocker Artists, gold medal ann. watercolor exhbn. Nat. Arts Club. 1954, Adolph and Clara Obrig prize N.A.D., 1955; Spl. $1000 award for watercolor 88th Exhbn. Am. Watercolor Soc., 1955; 1st watercolor prize, Butler Inst. Art, 1955. also Chautaugua Art Assn., 1955; Gold Medal for Watercolor, 14th ann. Audubon Artists, 1956, spl. $1000 award 21st ann. exhbn.; $1500 grant Nat. Inst. Arts and Letters; gold medal honor, 47th ann. Allied Artists Am., 1960; John Singer Sargent Meml. award Springfield Art Mus.; medal honor Nat. Arts Club, 1966; 99th Ann. $600 Grand award and gold medal of honor Am. Watercolor Soc.; Winslow Homer Meml. award Watercolor U.S.A., Springfield Art Mus.; Gold Medal Honor, Nat. Arts Club, 1967, Audubon Artists, 1968; Thomas Hart Benton award, 1968. Mem. Internat. Inst. Arts and Letters, N.A.D., Am. Watercolor Soc. (hon.), Nat. Arts Club, Audubon Artists, Allied Artists. Club: Dutch Treat, Salmagundi. Author: Watercolors by Chen Chi. 1942; Chen Chi-Paintings, 1965; Two or Three Lines from Sketchbooks of Chen Chi, 1969. Home: 23 Washington Sq N New York City NY 10011 Studio: 15 Gramercy Park S New York City NY 10003

CHENAULT, PAUL GEUE, investment co. exec.; b. Alton, Ia., Sept. 12, 1933; s. Stanley H. and Mildred (Bass) C.; B.A. in Polit. Sci., State U. Ia., 1957; grad. student finance, U. Wis., 1962; m. Susan Elizabeth Heikkinen, July 3, 1965; children—Sara Elizabeth, Laura Ann. Criminal statistic clk. FBI, 1951-52; sr. group underwriter Bankers Life Ins. Co., 1957-59; with Sentry Companies, Stevens Point, Wis.,

1960—, v.p., treas., 1968—; pres. Sentry Investment Mgmt., Inc., 1969—; dir. Dairyland Ins. Co., Dairyland Services Co., Sentry Life N.Y., Sentry Plan, Inc., Sentry Agy., Intermed Corp. Mem. investment conf. com. Am. Mut. Ins. Alliance. Bd. dirs. Dairyland Found. Served with AUS, 1953-55. Mem. Milw. Financial Analysts Soc., Acacia. Republican. Lutheran. Clubs: Stevens Point Country, Stevens Point Curling. Home: 18 River Bend Rd Plover WI 54467 Office: 1421 Strongs Av Stevens Point WI 54471

CHENEY, ELLIOTT WARD, educator; b. Gettysburg, Pa., June 28, 1929; s. Elliott Ward and Carleton (Pratt) C.; B.A., Lehigh U., 1951; Ph.D., U. Kan., 1957; m. Elizabeth Jean Helsley, Sept. 5, 1952; children—Margaret, Elliott, David. Instr. U. Kan., 1954-56; research engr., design specialist Convair-Astronautics, San Diego, 1956-59; mem. tech. staff Space Tech. Labs., Los Angeles, 1959-61; asst. prof. Ia. State U., 1961-62; asst. prof. U. Cal. at Los Angeles, 1962-64, asso. prof., 1964-65; vis. asso. prof. math. U. Tex., 1964-65, asso. prof., 1965-66, prof., 1966—; vis. prof. Lund U. (Sweden), 1966-67, Mich. State U., 1969-70; cons. aerospace industry. Mem. Am. Math. Soc., Math. Assn. Am., Soc. Indsl. and Applied Mathematics. Author: Introduction to Approximation Theory, 1966. Asso. editor Jour. Approximation Theory, 1968—, S.I.A.M. Jour. Numerical Analysis, 1964—. Home: 2105 Schulle St Austin TX 78703

CHENEY, GEORGE A., indsl. relations cons., arbitrator; b. Bowling Green, O., Dec. 6, 1900; s. George W. and Suzanna (Avery) C.; A.B., Ohio Wesleyan U., 1922; A.M., Bowling Green State U., 1939; m. Marguerite Riegle, Jan. 1, 1923; 1 son, Franklin. Impartial arbitrator 90 different types industry throughout U.S., 1940—; arbitration cons. U.S. Dept. Labor. Pacific Coast, 1940-47; chmn. Maritime War Emergency Bd., 1949-50; referee Rules Controversy between prin. r.r.s U.S. and Brotherhood R.R. Trainmen, 1951; mem. numerous Presdl. emergency bds., bds. inquiry, 1948—; spl. dep. county counsel San Bernardino County, Cal., 1965. Mem. State Bar Cal., Ohio, Am. bar assns., Am. Arbitration Assn., Delta Sigma Rho. Phi Delta Phi, Sigma Chi. Home: 157 W Buena Vista Barstow CA 92311 Office: 1109 E Main St Barstow CA 92311

CHENEY, HORACE BELLATTI, soil agronomist; b. Emerson, Ia., Dec. 15, 1913; s. Harold F. and Annie (Bellatti) C.: B.S. in Agronomy, Ia. State U. 1935; Ph.D., Ohio State U., 1942; m. Dorothy Remsen, Sept. 3, 1940; children—Roberta, Katharine Ann, Harold Remsen. Soil surveyor Soil Conservation Service in Mo., Ia., Wis., 1935-37; extension agronomist Ia. State U., 1937-39, asst. prof., asso. prof., prof. agronomy and chmn. extension sect., 1949- 52; soil research Ohio Agrl. Expt. Sta., 1939-42; head dept. soils Ore. State U., Corvallis, 1952—. Fellow Am. Soc. Agronomy, A.A.A.S.; mem. Soil Sci. Soc. Am. (pres.), Soil Conservation Soc. Am., Western Soil Sci. Soc. (pres.), Pacific N.W. Sci. Soc., Farm House, Alpha Zeta, Gamma Sigma Delta, Epsilon Sigma Phi, Phi Mu Epsilon, Sigma Xi. Rotarian. Home: 3744 NW Van Buren St Corvallis OR 97330

CHENEY, JAMES SPIERS, air force officer, lawyer; b. Tucson, Aug. 13, 1918; s. Jean Alvin and Ella (Spiers) C.; LL.B., Atlanta Law Sch., 1950; m. Yvonne Irene Parsons. Feb. 27, 1950; children—James Spiers, Frederick K. Commd. 2d lt. USAAF, 1942, advanced through grades to maj. gen., 1969; group navigator 8th Air Force. World War II; with Judge Adv. Gen. Dept., 1946 —, judge adv. gen., 1969—. Mem. adv. bd. Nat. Capitol area Boy Scouts Am. Decorated Legion of Merit with 2 oak leaf clusters, D.F.C., Air medal with 6 oak leaf clusters, Commendation medal; Croix de Guerre with gold star (France). Mem. Am., Ga., Fed., Inter-Am. bar assns., Judge Adv. Assn., Delta Theta Phi. Home: 2411 N Quincy St Arlington, VA 22207. Office: USAF (AFNA) Washington DC 20330

CHENEY, RALPH HOLT, biologist; b. Maynard, Mass., June 3, 1896; s. Levi Raymond and Mary Elizabeth (Billington) C.; B.S., Boston U., 1918, A.M., 1919; M.S., Harvard, 1922, Sc.D., 1923; Sc.D. (hon.), L. I. U., 1962; m. Agnes Lyford Gray, June 11, 1924. Teaching fellow, biology, Boston U., 1918-21; asst. instr., zoölogy and botany, Radcliffe Coll. and Harvard, 1921-22; instr. Western Res. U., 1923; asst. prof. biology N.Y. U., 1923-29; prof. and chmn. biology dept. L.I. U., 1929-46; asso. prof. biology Bklyn Coll., 1946-48, prof., 1949-66; prof. biology Bklyn. Coll. Pharmacy, 1932-66; prof. biology Richard L. Conolly Coll., L.I. U., 1966-68; dir. biology grad. seminars, 1966-68; prof. Alfred U., summer 1927; resident investigator economic plants, Brooklyn Botanic Garden, 1930-51, hon. asso., 1951—; investigator in physiology and pharmacology, also mem. corp. Marine Biol. Lab., Woods Hole, Mass., also the Bermuda Biol. Sta. for Research. Cons. applied physiology and pharmacology, 1925—. Physiologist in U.S. Army Med. Corps, 1918. Chmn. coffee genetics sect. of 6th Internat. Congress of Genetics, 1932. Fellow A.A.A.S. (council life mem.) N.Y. Acad. Sci. (v.p. and chmn. biol. sect.; council mem.); mem. Soc. Gen. Physiologists, Soc. for Cell Biology, Am. Soc. for Pharmacology and Exptl. Therapeutics, Soc. for Exptl. Biology and Medicine, Am. Soc. Zoöl., Bot. Soc. Am., Am. Soc. Plant Physiology, Torrey Bot. Club (life; pres. 1967, council), Am. Inst. Biol. Scis., Am. Fern Soc., Am. Tree Assn., Am. Nature Assn., Sullivant Moss Soc., Boston Soc. Natural History, Am. Genetic Assn., New Eng. Soc. City of N.Y. (life), Bklyn. Inst. Arts and Scis., Am. Inst. City N.Y. (bd. mgrs., trustee, treas.), Am. Pharm. Assn., Nat., N.Y. socs. med. research, Phi Beta Kappa Assos. (life mem.), Phi Beta Kappa, Sigma Xi, Phi Alpha Mu. Republican. Methodist. Clubs: Harvard (N.Y.C.); Knickerbocker Field, Phi Beta Kappa Alumni, N.Y. (pres., 1955-56). Adv. editor Econ. Botany, 1947-57; Am. Collaborator Acta Phytotherapeutica, 1952—; Am. editor Quar. Jour. Crude Drug Research, 1961—. Wrote monograph, Coffee, 1925. Contbr. scientific jours. Home: 612 Ocean Av Brooklyn NY 11226

CHENEY, SHELDON WARREN, author; b. Berkeley, Cal., June 29, 1886; s. Warren and May Lucretia (Shepard) C.; A.B., U. Cal., 1908; m. Maud Meurice Turner, Apr. 2, 1910 (dec. Feb. 1934); children—John Turner, Elizabeth, Michael Sheldon; m. 2d, Martha Candler, Nov. 27, 1934. Dramatic and art critic various newspapers and mags., 1910-16; founder Theatre Arts Mag., 1916, editor, 1916-21; freelance writer, 1921- 22, 1926-68, contbr. numerous mags.; with Equity Players (The Actors' Theatre), New York, 1922-25. Served in War Camp Community Service, 1918-19; Hon. fellow in Art, Union Coll., 1937-40. Lectr. univs. and art museums, 1935-47. Fellow Royal Soc. Arts, London, Eng. Mem. Authors League of Am., Soc. Am. Historians. Club: The Players (N.Y.). Author: The New Movement in the Theatre, 1914; The Open Air Theatre, 1918; A Primer of Modern Art, 1923; The Art Theatre, 1925; Stage Decoration, 1927; The TheatreThree Thousand Years of Drams, Acting and Stagecraft, 1929, rev. and enlarged edition, 1952; The New World Architecture, 1930; Expressionism in Art, 1934; Art and the Machine (with Martha Candler Cheney), 1936; A World History of Art, 1937; The Story of Modern Art, 1941; Men Who Have Walked With God, 1945 (published in German as Von Mystishen Leben); A New World History of Art, 1956; Sculpture of the World: A History, 1968; collected and edited Isadora Duncan's papers, published as The Art of the Dance. Contbr. Ency. Brit., The New Caravan, other encys. and symposia. Home: 12 Stony Hill Rd New Hope PA 18938

CHENG, HSIEN KEI, educator; b. Macau, South China, June 13, 1923; B.Sc., Chiao Tung U., 1947; M.Sc., Cornell U., 1950, Ph.D. in Aero. Engring., 1952; married; 1 child. Naturalized Am. citizen. Aerodynamic engr. Bell Aircraft Corp., 1952-56; research aerodynamicist Cornell Aero. Lab. Inc., Cornell U., 1956-57, prin. aerodynamicist, 1957-63; lectr. Stanford, 1963-64; spl. lectr. aerospace engring. U. So. Cal., 1964-65, now prof., chmn. dept. aerospace engring. Cons. Missile and Space div. Douglas Aircraft Co. Cal. Mem. Am. Inst. Aeros. and Astronautics. Office: Dept Aerospace Engring U So Cal Los Angeles CA 90007*

CHENG, SIN-I, educator; b. Changchow, China, Dec. 28, 1921; s. Mou-yi and Sho-jen (Hsu) C.; B.S. in Mech. Engring. magna cum laude, Chiaotung U., Shanghai, 1946; M.S. in Aero, Engring., U. Mich., 1949; M.A., Princeton, 1952, Ph.D., 1952; m. Jean Sing, Oct. 25, 1950; children—Andrew, Thomas, Irene. Came to U.S., 1948. Fellow Ministry Edn. of China for study in U.S., 1947-49; Guggenheim Jet Propulsion fellow Princeton, 1949-51, mem. faculty univ., 1952-, prof. aero. engring., 1960-; cons. AVCO Mfg. Corp., Boeing Sci. Research Lab. Asso. fellow Inst. Aerospace Scis.; mem. Am. Rocket Soc., Combustion Inst. Home: 379 Prospect Av Princeton NJ 08540

CHENG, WEN YU, educator; b. Chengtu, China, June 28, 1920; s. Mon-chou and Hsang-yoon (Yan) C.; B.A., Nat. Wuhan U., China, 1943; A.M., U. Chgo., 1951, Ph.D., 1954; m. Helen Kuomei Huang, Aug. 27, 1947; children—Chosen Tien-chun, DeWitt Tien-wei, Marietta Nien-hwa, Elaine Mon-hwa. Came to U.S., 1945, naturalized, 1958. Sr. interpreter Chinese Govt. Interpreters Service, 1943-44; econ. researcher Hochuan Petroleum Refineries, Chungking, China, 1944-45; instr. Marietta (O.) Coll., 1948-52, asst. prof., 1952- 55, asso. prof., 1955-60, prof., 1960—, head dept. econs., 1967-70; econ. cons. Ohio River Co., Cin., summer 1965. Mem. Marietta City Charter Commn., 1958-60. Bd. dirs. Washington County chpt. A.R.C. Fellow Found. for Econ. Edn., 1965. Mem. Ohio Assn. Economists and Polit. Scientists (pres. 1971-72), Alpha Sigma Phi, Tau Pi Phi (nat. gov.), Omicron Delta Kappa (nat. treas.). Lion. Club: Marietta Senior Reading. Contbr. chpts. to Money and Banking, 1957, Principles of Economics, 1960. Home: 928 Glendale Rd Marietta OH 45750

CHENOWETH, ALICE DREW, physician; b. Albany, Mo., Feb. 21, 1903; d. John William and Ruby (Wheatley) Chenoweth; A.A., Palmer Coll., 1922; B.S., Northwestern U., 1924, M.A., 1926; M.D., Vanderbilt U., 1932; m. John Ralston Pate, Feb. 12, 1942; 1 son, John Ralston. Instr. history Huntingdon Coll., Montgomery, Ala., 1926-28; intern Strong Meml. Hosp., Rochester, N.Y., 1932-33, Johns Hopkins Hosp., 1933-34; asst. chief resident Children's Hosp., Phila., 1934-36; research fellow Phila. Pediatric Soc. at U. Pa., 1936-38; pvt. practice medicine, specializing in pediatrics, Rosemont, Pa., 1938-42; dir. div. maternal and child health Ky. Dept. Health, 1942-49; research pediatrician Children's Bur., Dept. Health, Edn. and Welfare, Washington, 1949-52, med. tng. cons., 1952-54, pediatric cons., 1954-58, chief program service br. div. health service, 1958-70, now with Maternal and Child Health Service, Health Services and Mental Health Adminstrn., Pub. Health Service. Recipient Superior Service award Dept. Health, Edn. and Welfare, 1967. Diplomate Am. Bd. Pediatrics. Fellow Am. Acad. Pediatrics, Am. Pub. Health Assn. (sec. Maternal and child health sect. 1959-62), Am. Sch. Health Assn.; mem. Am. Med. Women's Assn. (pres. 1968), A.M.A., Women's Med. Soc. D.C. (rec. sec. 1960-62), A.A.A.S. Am. Assn. for Maternal and Infant Health, Am. Eugenics Soc., Pediatric Ambulatory Soc., Alpha Omega Alpha, Phi Beta Kappa. Episcopalian. Home: 1503 N Jefferson St Arlington VA 22205 Office: Maternal and Child Health Service Health Services and Mental Health Adminstrn Pub Health Service Dept Health Edn and Welfare 5600 Fishers Lane Rockville MD 20852

CHENOWETH, MAURICE GENE, educator; b. nr. Lynn, Ind., Mar. 15, 1932; s. Morris Clyde and Marietta (Abner) C.; B.A., Earlham Coll., 1954; M.A., U. Minn., 1957, Ph.D., 1965; postgrad. Cornell U., 1966-67; m. Mary Frances James, Aug. 15, 1954; children—Christopher Evan, Johnathan Neil, Amy Elizabeth. Instr. social sci. program dept. interdisciplinary studies Coll. Sci., Lit. and the Arts, U. Minn., Mpls., 1958-60, research asso. Sch. Pub. Health, 1959; vis. instr. dept. govt. Beloit (Wis.) Coll., 1960-61; instr., asst. prof., asso. prof., chmn. dept. politics and govt. Ohio Wesleyan U., Delaware, 1961-69; prof., chmn. dept. polit. sci. Bucknell U., Lewisburg, Pa., 1969—; N.Y. State regents grant, faculty seminar on internat. politics S.E. Asia, Cornell U., 1965; instr. Lewisburg Fed. Penitentiary, 1970—. Chmn. Union County Jail Inspection Body, 1970. Recipient Sherwood Dodge Shanklin Teaching award Ohio Wesleyan U., 1966. Mem. Am. Assn. U. Profs. (past chmn. Ohio Wesleyan chpt.). Mem. Soc. of Friends. Home: RD 1 Lewisburg PA 17837

CHENOWETH, TOM, city manager; b. Kansas City, Mo., Sept. 11, 1908; s. Edwin Wilson and Carrie (Murray) C.; B.S. in Civil Engring., U. Kan., 1930; m. Lois Mildred, Nov. 8, 1939; children—Don Wilson, Richard Edwin. Asst. to city mgr., Kansas City, Mo., 1945-51; city mgr., Hutchinson, Kan., 1951-55, St. Louis Park, Minn., 1955-60, Springfield, Mo., 1960-64, Des Moines, 1964—. Pres. Kan. Local Govt. Research Corp., 1954, Mo. Assn. City Mgrs., 1962; v.p. Internat. City Mgrs. Assn., 1964-66. Mem. Am. Soc. Pub. Adminstrn., Municipal Finance Officers Assn., Am. Pub. Works Assn., Nat. Soc. Profl. Engrs., Am. Soc. Planning Ofcls. Home: 1911 Willowmere Dr Des Moines IA 50315. Office: Municipal Bldg Des Moines IA 50309

CHEN YI Chinese govt. ofcl.; b. nr. Chengtu, Szechwan, China, 1902; student U. Communications, Shanghai; govt. scholarship for study chemistry in France; m., 2 children. While student in France, assisted formation Paris br. Chinese Communist Party, regular mem. Communist Party, 1923-, now mem, central com.; adjutant Szechwan warlord, also magistrate; founder Chungkin newspaper; mem. polit. br. Chinese Army, 1927, comdr. 1st detachment New Fourth Army, 1938-41, acting comdr., 1941-46, comdr., 1946; head People's Liberation Army of Eastern China, 1947, reorganized forces as Third Field Army, 1949, comdr., 1949, also comdg. gen. East China Mil. Area; mayor of Shanghai, 1949-58; mem. Chinese Communist delegation 19th Soviet Party Congress, 1952; marshall, mem. Nat. People's Congress, 1955, later vice premier of the republic; delivered policy speech 8th Party Congress of Chinese Communists, 1956, full mem. Politburo, 1956; dep. chmn. Nat. Def. Council, 1956-58; fgn. minister Communist China, 1958-. Pres. Nat. Assn. for Eliminating Illiteracy in China, 1956. Address: Ministry of Foreign Affairs Peiping, China.*

CHER, see Bono, Cher.

CHERASKIN, EMANUEL, educator; b. Phila., June 9, 1916; s. Herman and Celia (Homes) C.; A.B., U. Ala., 1939, M.A., 1941, D.M.D., 1952; M.D., U. Cin., 1943; m. Carol Elizabeth Elwood, Sept. 23, 1944; 1 dau., Lisa. Intern, Hartford (Conn.) Municipal Hosp., 1943-44; resident St. Mary's Hosp., Evansville, Ind., 1946-47; gen. practice medicine, Moundville, Ala., 1947-48; instr. anatomy U. Ala. Med. Center, 1948-50, asst. prof. physiology, 1950-52, asso. prof., chmn. dept. oral medicine, 1952-56, prof., chmn. div. oral surgery, 1956-62, prof., chmn. dept. oral medicine, 1962—. Served to capt. M.C., AUS, 1944-46. Recipient Samuel Charles Miller Meml. Lectr. award Am. Acad. Dental Medicine, 1964. Mem. A.M.A., Am. Dental Assn., Am. Acad. Dental Medicine. Author: Diagnostic Stomatology, 1961; (with L.L. Langley, R. Sleeper) Dynamic Anatomy and Physiology, 1958; (with W.M. Ringsdorf Jr. and J.W. Clark) Diet and Disease, 1968, Diet and the Periodontal Patient, 1970; (with W.M. Ringsdorf Jr.) New Hope for Incurable Diseases, 1971. Home: Capri Apts 1316 S 27th Pl Birmingham AL 35205 Office: U Ala Med Center Birmingham AL 35233

CHERBERG, JOHN ANDREW, lt. gov. Wash.; b. Pensacola, Fla., Oct. 17, 1910; s. Fortunato and Annie (Rand) C.; B.A., U. Wash., 1933; m. Elizabeth Ann Walker, Aug. 17, 1935; children—Kay Elizabeth (Mrs. Ray Cohrs), Barbara Jean (Mrs. Dean Tonkin), James Walker. Hign sch. tchr., athletic coach, 1934 ' 46; football coach U. Wash., 1946-56; lt. gov., Wash., 1957—. Chmn. Nat. Conf. Lt. Govs., 1968-69. Mem. N.E.A., A.F.T.R.A., Nat. Acad. TV Arts and Scis., Wash. State Assn. Broadcasters (hon. life), Sigma Nu. Club: Variety. Home: 505 Howe St Seattle WA 98109 Office: Legislative Bldg Olympia WA 98504

CHERBONNIER, EDMOND LABEAUME, educator. Chmn. religion dept. Trinity Coll., Hartford, Conn. Office: Dept Religion Trinity Coll Hartford CT 06106*

CHERENKOV, PAVEL ALEKSANDROVICH, Soviet physicist; b. Voronezh, Guberniya, July 15, 1904; grad. Voronezh U., 1928; postgrad. Physics Inst., USSR Acad. Scis., 1930-35, Cand. Natural Sci., 1935, D. Natural Sci., 1940. Prof., asso. Inst. Phys. Problems, USSR Acad. Sci. Recipient Stalin prize, 1946, Nobel prize in physics (with I.E. Tamm and I.M. Frank), 1958. Mem. USSR Acad. Sci. (corr.). Research and publs. composition of matter; discoverer Charenkov-Vavilov effect; research generated new studies cosmic rays, high-energy sub-atomic particles; research used in devel. rockets. Address: care Inst Phys Problems USSR Acad Sciences Moscow USSR*

CHERESKIN, ALVIN, advt. exec.; b. Bklyn., May 16, 1928; s. Benjamin and Jessie (Levine) C.; student Pratt Inst., 1947-48, Parsons Sch. Designing, 1948, Art Students League, 1948-50; m. Susan Baracas, June 3, 1956; children—Jessica, Benjamin, Sara. Asst. to Joseph Binder; art asst. Hockaday Assos., Inc., 1950-55, v.p., creative dir., 1955-60, pres., 1960-65; established AC & R, 1965-66 (wholly-owned subsidairy of Ted Bates, Inc.), 1966—. Active anti-smoking campaign Am. Cancer Soc., Jewish Fedn. Philanthropies, 1970. Served with AUS, 1945-47. Home: 170 E Rockaway Rd Hewlett NY 11557 Office: 437 Madison Av New York City NY 10022

CHERIN, CARL, lawyer; b. Beedersburg, Ind., Oct. 13, 1917; s. Samuel and Mary (Glusker) C.; A.B., U. Wis., 1937; LL.B., Harvard, 1942; m. Miriam Marcus, Aug. 14, 1941; children—Alan, Steven. Admitted to Pa. bar, 1946, since practiced in Pitts.; partner firm Eckert, Seamans & Cherin, 1958- -; mem. planning con. Pa. Tax Inst., 1958—. Lectr. tax insts. Served to 1st lt. AUS, 1942-45; PTO. Decorated Bronze Star. Mem. Am., Pa., Allegheny County bar assns., Pitts. Tax Club. Home: 217 S Dallas Av Pittsburgh PA 15208 Office: H K Porter Bldg Pittsburgh PA 15219

CHERINGTON, PAUL WHITON, educator; b. Cambridge, Mass., June 16, 1918; s. Paul Terry and Marie Louise (Richards) C.; grad. Phillips Exeter Acad., 1936; B.S., Harvard, 1940, D.B.A., 1956; grad. student Columbia, 1940-41; m. Rita Mary Van Dusen, Jan. 20, 1945 (div.); children—Charlotte Lund, Alexander Whiton, Paul Van Dusen; m. 2d, Dorothea B. Edwards, Aug. 26, 1971. With Pan Am. Airways Africa, Ltd., Brit. West Africa, 1942; econ. analyst, surplus property sub-com. U.S. Senate Mil. Affairs Com., 1946; liaison officer Civil Aero. Bd., Washington, 1947-48, exec. asst. to chmn., 1948-50; asst. prof. Harvard Bus. Sch., 1950-53, asso. prof., 1953-58, prof., 1958-63, James J. Hill prof. trans., 1963—; asst. sec. policy and internat. affairs Dept. Transp., 1969-70; dir. research Aero. Research Found., 1956-58; dir., cons. United Research, Inc., Cambridge, Mass., 1958-67; cons. Harbridge House, Inc., Boston, 1966-69; pres. Transp. Research Found., 1965-67; chmn. bd. Temple, Barker & Sloane Inc., 1970—; trustee B. & M.R.R., 1970—. Mem. Mass. Bd. Econ. Advisers, 1965-67. Served from 2d lt. to maj., USAAF, 1943-45. Mem. Am. Econ. Assn., Am. Statis. Assn., Signet Soc. Author: Airline Price Policy, 1958; (with Ralph Gillen) The Business Representative in Washington, 1962 (with Lewis Schneider), Transportation and Logistics Education, 1967. Clubs: Cosmos, Nat. Aviation (Washington); Harvard (Boston) (N.Y.C.). Home: 63 Atlantic Av Boston MA 02110 also Meriden NH Office: Harvard Bus Sch Soldiers Field Boston MA 02163

CHERKASKY, MARTIN, physician; b. Phila., Oct. 6, 1911; s. Samuel and Sarah (Kosharsky) C.; M.D., Temple U., 1936; m. Sarah Griffin, Feb. 3, 1941; children—Marny, Michael. Pvt. med. practice, Phila., 1939-40; exec. home care dept. Montefiore Hosp., 1947, dir. Med. Group, 1948-51, chief div. social medicine, 1950; dir. Montefiore Hosp. and Med. Center, 1951—; Atran prof. chmn. dept. community health Albert Einstein Coll. Medicine, also asso. dean community affairs, 1970. Cons. N.Y. State Joint Hosp. Survey and Planning Council; cons. to commr. hosps. N.Y.C. Dept. Hosps., 1961—; exec. com. Health Research Council of N.Y.C., 1969-70; regional health adv. bd. Region II, Dept. Health, Edn. and Welfare, 1970-73; chmn. med. adv. com. Joint Distbn. Com., N.Y.C., 1969—; com. of 100 for Nat. Health Ins., 1968—; dir. Asso. Hosp. Service, 1969-71; mem. Gov.'s Steering Com. Social Problems, 1970. Served as lt. col., M.C., AUS, 1940-46. Fellow N.Y. Acad. Medicine; mem. Am. Pub. Health Assn., Am., Greater N.Y. (past pres.) hosp. assns., Assn. Am. Med. Colls. Editorial bd. jour. Chronic Diseases, 1957—, Commonwealth and Internat. Library Sci. Tech. and Engring. Contbr. articles to various publs. Lectr. Home: 150 E 210th St New York City NY 10467 Office: 210th St and Bainbridge Av New York City NY 10461

CHERKASSKY, SHURA, pianist; b. Odessa, Russia, Oct. 7, 1911; s. Isaac and Lydia (Schlemenson) C.; brought to U.S., 1922, naturalized, 1928; grad. Curtis Inst. Music, Phila., 1936; m. Genia Ganz, Jan. 1946 (div. Jan. 1948). Debut in music at age 12, Balt.; concert tours abroad, 1927—, Australia, 1928, 71, South Africa, 1929, 31, 56, Germany, other European countries, 1946, Singapore, 1959, 71; other European countries, 1946, concert tour U.S., 1960; appearance Salzburg Festival, 1960, 63, 65; world tour, 1963—, S. Africa tour, 1963, 67; Latin Am., 1971; rec. artist. Address: care Ibbs & Tillett 124 Wigmore St London W 1 England

CHERMAYEFF, IVAN, graphic designer; b. London, June 6, 1932; s. Serge Ivan and Barbara Maitland (May) C.; grad. Phillips Acad., Andover, 1950; student Harvard, 1950-52, Ill. Inst. Tech., 1952-54; B.F.A., Yale, 1955; m. Sara Anne Duffy, July 15, 1956; children—Catherine, Alexandra, Maro. Asst. to Alvin Lustig, designer, 1955; asst. art dir. Columbia Records, 1956; partner Brownjohn, Chermayeff & Geismar Assos., 1956-59, Chermayeff & Geismar Assos., Inc., N.Y.C., 1959—, Cambridge Seven Assos.,

1965—. Vice pres. Internat. Design Conf., Aspen; trustee Mus. Modern Art, N.Y.C. Recipient awards Art Dirs. Club, N.Y., Am. Inst. Graphic Arts, Type Directors Club: Indsl. Arts, medal A.I.A., 1967, Gold medal Phila. Coll. Art, 1971. Mem. Am. Inst. Graphic Arts (pres. 1963- 64, dir.), Nat. Soc. Indsl. Designers, Alliance Graphique Internat., Royal Soc. Arts (Benjamin Franklin fellow). Clubs: Harvard (N.Y.C.); SPEE (Cambridge, Mass.). Home: 347 E 62d St New York City NY 10021 also East Chestnut Hill Rd Litchfield CT 06759 also Cadaques Spain Office: 830 3d Av New York City NY 10022

CHERMAYEFF, SERGE, architect, artist; b. Caucasus, Oct. 8, 1900; ed. Harrow Sch., Cambridge (Eng.); m. Barbara M. May, Mar. 28, 1928; children—Ivan, Peter. Came to U.S., 1940, naturalized, 1946 Archtl. practice, Eng., 1928-40, in U.S. since 1940; prof., chmn. dept. of designs, Brooklyn Coll., 1942-46; pres. Inst. of Design. Chgo., 1946-51; prof. architecture Harvard, 1953-62; prof. emeritus architecture Yale, 1963—. Fellow Royal Inst. Brit. Architects, Royal Soc. Arts. Paintings exhibited at Art Inst. Chgo., Met. Mus., etc. Author: (with C. Alexander) Community and Privacy, 1963; (with Alexander Tzonis) Shape of Community, 1971. Home: New Haven CT 06501

CHERN, SHIING-SHEN, mathematician, educator; b. Kashing, Cheklang, China, Oct. 26, 1911; s. Lien Ching and Mei (Han) C.; B.S., Nankai U., Tientsin, China, 1930; M.S., Tsing Hua U., Peiping, 1934; D.Sc., U. Hamburg (Germany), 1936; LL.D. honoris causa, Chinese U. Hong Kong, 1969; D.Sc. (hon.), U. Chgo., 1969; m. Shih-ning Chern, July 28, 1939; children—Paul May. Prof. math. Nat. Tsing Hua U., China, 1937-43; mem. Inst. Advanced Study, Princeton, N.J., 1943-45; acting dir. Inst. Mathematics, Academia Sinica, China, 1946-48; prof. math. U. Chgo., 1949-60, U. Cal. at Berkeley, 1960—. Mem. Am. Math. Soc., Nat. Acad. Scis., Am. Acad. Arts and Scis., Academia Sinica. Home: 8336 Kent Ct El Cerrito CA 94530

CHERNE, LEO, economist; b. N.Y.C., Sept. 8, 1912; s. Max and Dora (Bailin) C.; grad. N.Y. U., 1931; LL.B., N.Y. Law Sch., 1934; LL.D., Parsons Coll., Fairfield, Ia., 1951; LL.D., Pace Coll., 1967, N.Y. Law Sch., 1967; m. Julia Rodriguez Lopez, June 7, 1936 (div. 1967); 1 dau., Gail (Mrs. Richard Gambino); m. 2d, Phyllis Abbott Brown, Apr. 13, 1968. Admitted N.Y. bar, 1934; exec. dir. the Research Inst. Am., Inc. Hon. mem. faculty, mem. bd. advisers Indsl. Coll. of Armed Forces; lectr. New Sch. for Social Research, 1946-52; chmn. bd. dirs. Internat. Rescue Com., 1953—; adviser on taxation and fiscal policy to Gen. MacArthur, 1946; chmn. bd. Lawyers Co-op. Pub. Co. Bd. dirs. Wilckie Meml.; bd. dirs., chmn. exec. com. Freedom House, 1946—; mem. select commn. Western Hemisphere Immigration, 1967-68; mem. U.S. Adv. Commn. on Internat. Ednl. and Cultural Affairs. Decorated Comdr.'s Cross of Order of Merit (Fed. Republic of Germany); Kim Khanh Medal (Vietnam); Nat. Order Legion Honor (French Republic). Mem. Hudson Inst. Author: Adjusting Your War, 1939; M-Day and What it Means to You, 1940; The Rest of Your Life, 1944. Sculptor: Bronze of John F. Kennedy, Berlin Germany, bronze portrait Lyndon B. Johnson at Lyndon Baines Johnson Library, bronze of Abraham Lincoln, White House, represented at the Smithsonian Instn., Phoenix Art Mus., Sibelius Mus., Helsinki, U. Cal. at Los Angeles, U. Bahia (Brazil), Lincoln Mus., Washington, Presdl. Palaces, New Delhi, India, Mexico City, U.S. Pavilion, N.Y. World's Fair, 1964-65, Winston Churchill Meml., Fulton, Mo. Mem. Nat. Sculpture Soc. (adviser). Office: 589 Fifth Av New York City NY 10017

CHERNEY, COLBURN GEORGE, chem. co. exec.; b. Indpls., Dec. 28, 1916; s. Charles and Gertrude Ethel (Colburn) C.; A.B., U. Mich., 1939; LL.B., Harvard, 1942; student U. Va., 1945, Northwestern U., 1944; m. Frances Terrell, Feb. 10, 1945; children—Mary Sue (Mrs. John Ramer), Colburn T., Linda, Melissa. Admitted to Ill. bar, 1942, Wis. bar, 1947; asst. dist. atty. Brown County, Wis., 1949-50; individual practice law, Green Bay, Wis., 1950-71; gen. counsel Ansul Co., Marinette, Wis., 1963-66, dir., 1966-71, chmn. bd., 1967—. Wis. del. Uniform Law Commn., 1956-60. Chmn. All-County Chmn. Wis. Republican Party, 1954-61; chmn. campaign com. Rep. candidate gov. Wis., 1960, 62. Mason. Contbr. articles legal publs. Home: 190 Rosemont Dr Green Bay WI 54301 Office: Miwahan Bldg Green Bay WI 54301

CHERNIN, MILTON, educator; b. Mar. 9, 1910; s. Max and Pearl (Dickman) C.; student Columbia, 1925-26; A.B., U. Cal. at Los Angeles, 1929; M.A., U. Cal. at Berkeley, 1930, Ph.D., 1937; m. Gertrude Chemnick, May 5, 1935. Research asst. Bur. of Pub. Adminstrn., U. Cal., 1932-35, research asso., 1936-39; research staff State Relief Adminstrn. of Cal., 1935-36, dir. planning and research, 1939; asst. prof. U. Cal. at Berkeley, 1940-42, asso. prof., prof., dean sch. social welfare, 1946—, asst. to chancellor, 1958-60; vis. prof. U. Bologna, Italy 1958. Acting dir. Bureau Pub. Adminstrn. 1955-57; asst. chief, western hemisphere div. Bd. Econ. Warfare, Washington, 1942. Office Fgn. Relief and Rehab. Operations, 1943; past mem. Cal. State Board Social Welfare. Served from pvt. to 1st lt. AUS, 1943- 46. Decorated Legion of Merit. Mem. Nat. Assn. Social Workers, Nat. Conf. Social Work, Am. Soc. Pub. Adminstrn., Phi Beta Kappa, Phi Delta Kappa, Pi Sigma Alpha. Club: Faculty. Home: 1835 San Ramon Av Berkeley CA 94707

CHERNISS, HAROLD F., prof., b. St. Joseph, Mo., Mar. 11, 1904; s. David B. and Theresa (Hart) C.; A.B., U. of Cal., 1925, Ph.D., 1929; student U. of Göttingen, Berlin, 1927-28; L.H.D., U. Chgo., 1950, Johns Hopkins U., 1965; m. Ruth Meyer, Jan. 1, 1929. Asso. in Greek, U. of Cal., 1928-29; instr. in classics, Cornell U., 1930-33; asso. in Greek, Johns Hopkins U., 1933-36, asso. prof., 1936-42; prof. of Greek, U. of Cal., 1946-48; prof., Inst. for Advanced Study, Princeton 1948—; lectr. in Greek, Johns Hopkins U., 1932; lectr. on Sather Found., U. Cal., 1942; mem. managing com. Am. Sch. Classical Studies, Athens. Served as pvt. to capt., AUS, 1942-46. Corr. fellow Brit. Acad., Royal Acad. Arts and Scis. of Göteborg, Académie Royale Flamande des Scis., Lettres et Beaux Arts de Belgique; mem. Am. Acad. Arts and Scis., Am. Philol. Assn., Am. Philos. Soc., Classical Assn. (Great Britain). Author books. Asst. editor Am. Jour. of Philology, 1936-40, editor, 1940-42. Contbr. articles to profl. jours. Address: Institute for Advanced Study Princeton NJ 08540 ☆

CHERNOFF, HOWARD LEONARD, newspaperman, broadcasting exec.; b. Cleve., Dec. 11, 1907; s. Morris Jacob and Hermine (Leichtman) C.; student John Carroll U., Cleve., 1925- 26, U. Cin., 1926-28; m. Melvina Hunt Graham, June 27, 1938. Reporter, Lorain (O.) Jour., 1928-31, mem. advt. dept., 1931-33; advt. mgr. Mansfield (O.) News-Jour., 1933-36; advt. dir. Clarksburg (W.Va.) Exponent-Telegram, 1936-38; gen. mgr. Kenco Enterprises, newspaper, radio and TV, W.Va., Cal., and S.D., 1938-63; dep. dir. operations USIA, 1965-68; commr. gen. U.S. Pavilion Japan 1970 World Expn., 1968-; U.S. to Japan World Expn., 1969-70; ambassador first ind. radio corr. ETO, World War II; broadcast first account siege of Brest, France. Pres. San Diego Zoo, 1960-63, San Diego chpt. Am. Cancer Soc., 1953-54; chmn. San Diego Citizens Charter Rev. Com., 1962-. Recipient Peabody award outstanding service by radio in U.S., 1943; Variety award for expanding radio's social usefulness, 1944; founder Great Plains Zoo, Sioux Falls, S.D., 1956; hon. consul of Guatemala in San Diego, 1959. Author: Anybody Here From West Virginia?, 1944. Address: PO Box 3863 San Diego, CA 92103.

CHERNOW, DAVID A., distillery exec.; b. N.Y.C., Mar. 10, 1922; s. James and Rose (Rothstein) C.; A.B., Coll. City N.Y., 1941; M.B.A., Harvard, 1946; m. Shirley Kalman, Apr. 11, 1948. Faculty dept. econs. Coll. City N.Y., 1941-42; sec.-treas. Sunrise Curtain Co., Inc., 1946-50; sec. Ky. Distilling Co., Inc., 1950-54; with Schenley Industries, Inc., 1954—, v.p., 1958-65, v.p. finance, 1965-69, exec. v.p., 1969—, also dir. Grad. adv. bd. Bernard M. Baruch Coll., City U. N.Y. Served to lt. USNR, 1942-46; lt. comdr. Res., ret. Mem. Am. Finance Assn., Am. Mgmt. Assn., Phi Beta Kappa, Beta Gamma Sigma. Clubs: Harvard (N.Y.C.); Key Biscayne (Fla.) Yacht. Home: 203 E 72d St New York City, NY 10021. Office: 888 7th Av New York City NY 10019

CHERPACK, CLIFTON, educator; b. New Britain, Conn., Nov. 4, 1925; s. Andrew Nicholas and Olive (Anderson) C.; B.A., Trinity Coll., Hartford, Conn., 1950; M.A., Johns Hopkins, 1951, Ph.D., 1953; m. Margaret Grace Bryan, Jan. 30, 1948; children—Mark, Peter. Asst. prof. Romance langs. Johns Hopkins, 1954-58; mem. faculty Duke U., 1958-67, 68-70, prof. Romance langs., 1968- 70; prof. Romance langs. Wesleyan U., Middletown, Conn., 1967-68, U. Pa., Phila., 1970—;cons., lectr. in field, 1954-. Served with AUS, 1944-46; PTO. Mem. Modern Lang. Assn., Am. Assn. Tchrs. French. Author: The Call of Blood in French Classical Tragedy, 1958; An Essay on Crebillon Fils, 1962; also articles. Home: 218 Windermere Av Wayne PA 19087 Office: Dept Romance Langs U Pa Philadelphia PA 19104

CHERRIER, JAMES FULLER, newspaper syndicate exec.; b. Sherbrooke, Que., Can., July 6, 1930; s. Adolphe George and Lois Marguerite (Fuller) C.; student Carelton U., Ottawa, Can., 1948-50, 52-53; m. Marilyn G. Ireland, June 9, 1956; children—Kimberly Anne, Jill Patricia. With FAO of UN, Rome, Italy, 1950- 52; prodn. controller Torrington Mfg. Co. Can., 1953-55; sales rep. Toronto Star Syndicate, 1955-59, mgr., from 1959. Capt., Canadian Militia Res. Mem. Anglican Ch. Home: 1144 Lynbrook Rd Oakville Ontario Canada

CHERRINGTON, BEN MARK, educator; b. Gibbon, Neb., Nov. 1, 1885; s. George Whittington and Laura Ida (Frick) C.; A.B., U. Neb., 1911, LL.D., 1946; M.A., U. Cal., 1922; Ph.D., Columbia, 1934; Ps.D, U. Denver, 1953; m. Edith Mary Harper, June 28, 1924; children—Anne Mary, Stevens, Benjamin Mark. Gen sec. U. Cal. YMCA, 1911-17; coach, U. Cal., 1915-17; nat. sec. student YMCA, 1919-26; dir. Social Sci. Found., U. Denver, 1926-51; prof. internat. relations, 1926—, chancellor, 1943-46; dir. Denver Regional office Inst. Internat. Edn., 1951-68; cons., 1968—. Adviser to U.S. delegation 8th Internat. Conf. of Am. States, Lima, Peru, 1938; chief Div. of Cultural Relations, Dept. of State, 1938-40; asso. cons. to U.S. delegation UN Conf., San Francisco, 1945; mem. U.S. Nat. Commn., UNESCO matters, 1946-51, vice chmn., 1951. Trustee Carnegie Endowment for Internat. Peace, 1943—. Recipient citation U.S. Dept. of State, 1967; Malcolm Glenn Wyer award, Denver Adult Edn. Council, 1965; Civis Princeps award, Regis Coll., 1969. Named hon. mem. Order Brit. Empire, 1956. Fellow Colo.-Wyo. Acad. Sci. (pres. 1949-50); mem. Am. Polit. Sci. Assn. (exec. council, 1948-50), Colo.-Wyo. Social Sci. Assn., Council Fgn. Relations, Am. Acad. Polit. Sci., N.E.A., Am. Assn. for Adult Edn. (pres. 1950-51), Delta Sigma Rho, Kappa Delta Pi, Phi Beta Kappa, Phi Kappa Psi. Conglist. Clubs: Mile High, Country, Rotary (Denver); Cosmos (Washington). Author: The British Labor Movement, 1921; Methods of Education in International Attitudes, 1933. Co-author: Role of Higher Education in World Affairs, 1950; Outlook for FreedomThen and Now-1926-51; others. Contbr. to religious, social sci. and ednl. jours. Home: 909 Lafayette Denver CO 80218 ☆

CHERRINGTON, ERNEST HURST, Jr., educator, astronomer; b. Westerville, O., Sept. 10, 1909; s. Ernest Hurst and Betty Clifford (Denny) C.; A.B. magna cum laude, O. Wesleyan U., 1931, M.S., 1932; Ph.D., U. Cal., 1935; m. Ann McAfee Naylor, June 25, 1933; children—Robert Naylor, Ernest Hurst. Lab. asst. astronomy Ohio Wesleyan U., 1928-31, teaching fellow, 1931-32; teaching fellow U. Cal., 1932-33; Lick Obs. research fellow U. Cal. 1933-35, Alexander F. Morrison research fellow, 1935; instr. mathematics and astronomy Syracuse U., 1935-36; asst. astronomer Perkins Obs., 1936- 46; instr. astronomy and physics Ohio State and Ohio Wesleyan univs., 1936-40, asst. prof., 1940-46 (mil. leave, 1942-46); asst. dean of coll. and asso. prof. physics Centenary Coll. of La., 1946-47, dean of coll., also prof. and head dept. physics and astronomy, 1947-48; dean Buchtel Coll. of Liberal Arts, U. Akron, 1948-60, prof. astronomy, 1948- 67, dir. grad. studies, 1955-60, dean grad. div., 1960-67; prof. astronomy Hood Coll., Frederick, Md., 1967—. Chmn. Eastern dist. com. Akron Area council Boy Scouts Am., 1959-61. Served with USAAF, 1942-46; disch. as maj. Mem. Ohio Acad. Sci. (chmn. trustees of research fund 1961-62), Am. Astron. Soc., Astron. Soc. Pacific, Royal Astron. Soc. Can., Phi Beta Kappa, Sigma Xi, Omicron Delta Kappa, Sigma Pi Sigma, Pi Mu Epsilon, Phi Delta Theta. Republican. Presbyn. Club: Torch (pres. 1960-61) (Akron. O.). Author: Exploring the Moon Through Binoculars, 1969; also 77 monographs tech. papers, popular articles. Address: Williams Obs Hood Coll Frederick MD 21701 also RD 5 Jefferson Frederick MD 21701

CHERRINGTON, HOMER VIRGIL, educator; b. nr. Gallipolis, O., Jan. 21, 1891; s. Lozier L. and Suzan (Drummond) C.; A.B., Ohio U., 1914; A.M., U. Mich., 1921; A.M., Harvard, 1922, Ph.D., 1940; m. Maria Grover, Sept. 1, 1926. Tchr., Athens (O.) High Sch., 1914-16; asst. prof. English, Ohio U., 1917-18, asst. prof. English, econs., 1919-21, prof. econs., 1925-29, prof. finance, 1956-61, emeritus prof., 1961; prof. econs. Cornell Coll., Mt. Vernon Ia., 1922-25; prof. commerce State U. Ia., 1929-47; vis. prof. Northwestern U., summer 1945, prof. finance, 1947-56, prof. emeritus, 1956; Cameron distinguished prof. bus. Trinity U., San Antonio, 1961-62. Vis. prof. finance Stanford, summers 1956-58, 60; lectr. mortgage banking seminars, Chgo.; ednl. cons. Mortgage Bankers Assn. Am., 1954-56, faculty Sch. Mortgage Banking, jointly with Northwestern U., 1954-59. Served as 2d lt. AUS, 1918. Recipient certificate of merit Ohio U. Alumni Assn., 1957. Mem. Am. Econ. Assn., Phi Beta Kappa, Delta Sigma Pi, Tau Kappa Alpha, Beta Gamma Sigma. Methodist. Author: The Investor and the Securities Act, 1942; Business Organization and Finance, 1948. Co-editor: Mortgage Banking, 1953. Home: 1 Strouds Run Athens OH 45701

CHERRINGTON, VIRGIL ARTHUR, univ. prof., bacteriologist; b. Des Moines, Ia., Jan 24, 1905; s. Charles and Helen (Miller) C.; B.S., Ia. State Coll., 1928, Ph.D., 1941; Ph.D., 1941; M.S., U. of Ida., 1930; m. Maurine Merwin, Dec. 24, 1928. Successively instr., asst. prof., asso. prof., U. of Ida., 1929-42, prof. and head dept. of bacteriology, 1946—. Served as 1st lt., capt., and maj., Sanitary Corps, U.S. Army, 1942-46. Mem. Am. Acad. Microbiology, Am. Soc. for Microbiology, Idaho Public Health Assn., Ida. Acad. Sci., Am. Pub. Health Assn., Sigma Xi, Phi Sigma, Alpha Epsilon Delta. Methodist. Home: 404 N Blaine St Moscow ID 83843

CHERRIX, JOHN ELDER, paper co. exec.; b. Nassawadox, Va., Nov. 1, 1929; s. Eldred J. and Viola W. (Hill) C.; B.S., U. Md., 1956; m. Monica Donoghue, July 8, 1961; 1 son, James Christopher. Accountant, Price Waterhouse & Co., Washington, 1956-67; asst. treas. Brown Co., N.Y.C., 1967-68, treas., Los Angeles, 1968—. Served with AUS 1950-52. C.P.A., Md., Va., D.C. Mem. Financial Execs. Inst., Am. Inst. C.P.A.'s Tax Execs. Inst., Omicron Delta Kappa, Beta Gamma Sigma, Phi Kappa Phi, Beta Alpha Psi, Delta Sigma Pi. Home: 5165 Gould Av La Canada CA 91011 Office: 251 S Lake St Pasadena CA 91101

CHERRY, DONALD E., trumpeter; b. Oklahoma City, Nov. 18, 1936; played with Ornette Coleman's quintet, N.Y.C., 1959, with Sonny Rollins, 1963; later led own quintet in Europe; recordings with Coleman, Coltrane, Rollins and Steve Lacy. Address: care Blue Note Records 43 W 61st St New York City NY 10023*

CHERRY, EDWARD EARL, architect; b. Greenville, N.C., Dec. 4, 1926; s. Jasper and Velma (Smith) C.; B.Arch., Howard U., 1953; m. Mary Jean Jordan, July 18, 1953; children—Edward Earl, Todd Jordan. With Polak & Sullivan, architects, New Haven, 1953-63; pvt. practice architecture, Hamden, Conn., 1963—; vis. critic dept. Art and Architecture, Yale; cons. architect Neighborhood Model Cities Corp., New Haven; bd. govs. Black Workshop. Dir. Arts Council Greater New Haven, TCB, Econ. Devel. Corp. of Model Cities Corp. Served with AUS, 1945-46. Mem. A.I.A. (past dir.), Conn. Soc. Architects, Greater New Haven Bus. Mens Assn. (founder), Am., New Eng. (past pres.) tennis assns., Omega Psi Phi. Democrat. Mason (32). Important works include Dixwell Community House/Neighborhood Facilities Bldg., Winter Gardens Townhouses, New Haven, Barbour Arms Apts., Hartford, Conn., 1st Bapt. Ch., Stratford, Conn., Goffe St. Townhouses, New Haven. Home: 22 Pine Ridge Rd Woodbridge CT 06525 Office: 60 Connolly Pkwy Hamden CT 06514

CHERRY, JERRIE, physician, educator; b. Dallas, Nov. 12, 1928; s. Henry Armistead and Mattilee (Straus) C.; B.A., U. Va., 1951; M.D., Johns Hopkins, 1955; m. Carol Hughes Urban, Jan. 19, 1963; children—John Mason, Henry Armistead. Intern, Union Meml. Hosp., Balt., 1955-56; resident otolaryngology Johns Hopkins, 1958-62; resident gen. surgery Balt. City Hosp., 1960-64; asst. prof. otolaryngology Johns Hopkins, 1965-68; prof., chmn. dept. otolaryngology Vanderbilt U., Nashville, 1968—; dir. Bill Wilkerson Hearing and Speech Center, Nashville, 1968—. Served to capt. M.C., AUS, 1956-58. Mem. Am. Acad. Otolaryngology and Ophthalmology, Soc. U. Otolaryngologists, Am. Bronchosophology Assn., A.M.A., So. Med. Assn. Contbr. articles to profl. jours. Home: 409 Leake St Nashville TN 37205 Office: Vanderbilt Hosp Garland Av Nashville TN 37203

CHERRY, RALPH WALTER, educator; b. nr. Maysville, Ga., Jan. 28, 1909; s. Hugh Graves and Rena (Heikens) C.; A.B., Maryville (Tenn.) Coll., 1930; A.M., U. Ky., 1938; Ed.D., Tchrs. Coll., Columbia, 1942; m. Anne Dedman, Nov. 14, 1936; children—Pauline, Elizabeth. Dir. of census and attendance city schs., Lexington, Ky., 1937-39, dir. secondary instrn., 1940-42; asso. prof. edn. U. Ky., 1946, prof. edn., 1947-49, chmn. div. ednl. adminstrn., 1947-49; supt. of schs., Owensboro, Ky., 1949-54; prof. ednl. adminstrn., dir. office of sch. surveys and studies U. Tex., 1954- 56; prof. edn., dir. summer session U. Va., 1956—, dean sch. edn., 1956-68. Dir., cons. various sch. surveys; cons., div. of sch. bldgs. and grounds Ky. State Dept. Edn., 1947-49. Co-chmn. So. States Work Conf. project on improvement of ednl. leadership, 1948-49. Served from 2d lt. to lt. col. Signal Corps, U.S. Army, 1942-45, ETO. Mem. Am. Assn. Sch. Adminstrn., N.E.A., Nat. Conf. Profs. Ednl. Adminstrn., Am. Assn. Summer Session Dirs., Am. Assn. Colls. for Tchr. Edn. (exec. com.), Phi Delta Kappa, Kappa Delta Pi. Democrat. Presbyn. Clubs: Colonnade, Torch. Contbr. Am. Sch. and U., also profl. jours. Home: 1411 Rugby Rd Charlottesville VA 22903

CHERRY, WILLIAM WALLACE, ins. co. exec.; b. Hopkinsville, Ky., Feb. 7, 1909; s. Wallace Roy and Mallie (Dickenson) C.; student U. of South, 1929-30, La. State U., 1930- 31; m. Naomi Speakman, May 9, 1935; children—William Speakman, Frederick Wallace. With Am. Nat. Ins. Co., Galveston, Tex., 1931-, v.p., 1960-62, sr. v.p., dir., 1962—; exec. v.p., dir. Comb Agys., 1969; dir. Commonwealth Life & Accident Ins. Co.; St. Louis. Co-chmn. Galveston United Fund, 1961, dir. security mgmt. and research, 1969. Mem. Life Ins. Agy. Mgmt. Assn., Life Insurers Conf., Kappa Sigma. Episcopalian. Mason (K.T., Shriner), Kiwanian. Home: 5024 Woodrow St Galveston TX 77550 Office: 21st and D Sts Galveston TX 77550

CHERTOK, JACK, theatrical producer; b. Atlanta, Georgia; son of Isadore and Annie (Rouglin) C.; m. Florence Murray, July 14, 1933; childrenVivian, William Irving, Mary Barbara (Mrs. Lewis M. Terman II). Exec. producer all short subjects Metro-Goldwyn-Mayer, Culver City, Cal., 1925-42; short subjects produced include Robert Benchley series, Pete Smith series, The Passing Parade, Historical Mysteries, also Crime Does Not Pay; feature motion pictures produced at Metro-Goldwyn-Mayer and Warner Bros. include Joe Smith, American, Eyes in the Night, The Corn is Green, also Northern Pursuit; formed own prodn. company in Hollywood, 1945, which produced The Strange Woman and Dishonored Lady; producer films for TV, 1948-; series include Lone Ranger, Sky King, Cavalcade series, Private Secretary, Western Marshall, The Lawless Years, My Favorite Martian, also My Living Doll; pres. Jack Chertok TV, Inc., 1949-, Apex Film Corp., 1945-. Recipient Acad. award, 1935, 36, 37 (2), 38, 40 (2), 41 (2), 43. Home: 415 S Beverly Glen Blvd West Los Angeles CA 90024 Office: 1040 N Las Palmas St Hollywood, CA 90038

CHESAREK, FERDINAND JOSEPH, business exec., former army officer; b. Calumet, Mich., Feb. 18, 1914; s. Joseph and Mary (Pontello) C.; B.S., U.S. Mil. Acad., 1938; M.B.A., Stanford, 1950; grad. Nat. War Coll., 1956. Advanced Mgmt. Program, Harvard, 1958; m. Martha Jayne Rullman, Sept. 1, 1938; 1 son, John Laymon. Commd. 2d lt. U.S. Army, 1938, advanced through grades to lt. gen., 1966; comdg. officer 28th F.A. Battalion, 8th Inf. Div., ETO, World War II, 5th Arty. Group, Korean War; comdg. gen. 4th Logistical Command. Europe, 1959-62; asst. dep. chief staff logistics Dept. Army, 1962-66; comptroller of army, 1966—; asst. vice chief staff Army, 1967-68, comdg. gen. U.S. Army Materiel Command, 1968-70; ret., 1970; now owner Chesarek Cons., Inc.; pres. Consol. Investment & Devel. Corp., Luxembourg. Decorated Silver Star, Legion of Merit, Bronze Star, Commendation medal, Air medal, Purple Heart, D.S.M.; Legion of Honor, Croix de Guerre (France); Croix de Guerre (Luxembourg); Order Ulchi (Korea); Order of Republic (Italy). Home: 25706 Elena Rd Los Altos Hills CA 94022

CHESHIRE, MAXINE, (Mrs. Herbert W. Cheshire), columnist; b. Harlan, Ky., Apr. 5, 1930; d. M.F. and Sylvia (Cornett) Hall; student Union Coll., Barbourville, Ky., 1951-52, U. Ky., 1949-50; m. Herbert W. Cheshire, Apr. 25, 1954; children—Marc, Hall, Paden, Leigh. Reporter, Knoxville (Tenn.) News-Sentinel, 1951-54; reporter Washington Post, 1954-65, columnist, 1965—. Contbr. articles popular mags. Home: 2011 White Oaks Dr Alexandria VA 22306 Office: 1515 L St NW Washington DC

CHESKIN, BERNARD SAMUEL, lawyer, elec. equipment mfg. co. exec.; b. Phila., July 16, 1928; s. Nathan and Betty (Goldberg) C.; B.S., Temple U., 1950, LL.B., 1955; m. Rheta S. Freeman, Sept. 25, 1958;

children—Abbe Beth, Susan, Bruce. Admitted to Pa. and D.C. bars, 1955; trial atty. U.S. Dept. Justice, criminal div., 1955-57; asst. city solicitor City of Phila., 1957-60; partner Weiner, Basch, Lehrer & Cheskin, 1960-68; sec., gen. counsel Fed. Pacific Elec. Co., Newark, 1968—. Active YMCA. Mem. Phila. Bar Assn. Club: Suburban Racquet (Valley Forge, Pa.). Author: The Philadelphia Home Rule Charter and Annotations, 1958. Home: 1412 June Lane Narberth PA 19072 Office: 1201 Chestnut St Philadelphia PA 19107

CHESKIN, LOUIS, marketing and motivational research co. exec.; b. Kiev, Russia, Feb. 19, 1909; s. Joseph and Mary (Bugendler) C.; came to U.S., 1921, naturalized, 1921; M.A., Lewis Inst.-Ill. Inst. Tech., 1932; m. Vivian Martin, Aug. 14, 1948; 1 dau., Bonnie Lynn. Instr., Lewis Inst.; dir. arts div., exptl. projects on psychol. effect design and color Chgo. Bd. Edn., 1935-40; dir. Color Research Inst., Chgo., 1945—; pres. Louis Cheskin Assos., Chgo., 1950—. Pres., Greater Chgo. Adult Edn. Council, 1962-65. Mem. Midland Authors, Chgo. Assn. Commerce and Industry, Ill. C. of C., Am. Inst. Mgmt., Internat. Platform Assn., Am. Acad. Polit. and Social Sci. Unitarian. Clubs: Cliff Dwellers, Executives (Chgo.); Directors (London). Author 12 books, 1940—, latest being Secrets of Marketing Success. Contbr. articles to profl. publs. Home: 1040 N Lake Shore Dr Chicago IL 60611 Office: 11 E Adams St Chicago IL 60603

CHESLEY, HARRY WOOLFORD, Jr., advt. exec.; b. Towson, Md., Feb. 4, 1909; s. Harry W. and Mary F. (Gunsaulus) C.; student Chgo. Coll. Commerce, 1927-29; m. Dorothy E. Todd, Oct. 2, 1937; children—Stephen T., Christopher G. Nat. sales mgr. Pabst Sales Co., 1938-42; partner Chesley & O'Connell, wholesale distbrs., 1946-49; v.p. nat. sales Pepsi-Cola Co., 1949-52; v.p. marketing Philip Morris Co., 1952-56; exec. v.p. D'Arcy Advt. Co., St. Louis, 1956-59, pres., 1959—, chairman, 1967-70; chmn. D'Arcy Internat., 1971—. Bd. dirs. St. Louis Municipal Theatre Assn. Served as lt. col. USAAF, 1942-46; ETO, PTO. Decorated Bronze Star. Mem. Sales Execs. Club N.Y.C. Clubs: Racquet, Media (dir.), Old Warson Country (dir.), Bogey Golf (St. Louis); Chicago Athletic Assn.; Wianno (Osterville, Mass.). Home: 8 Denny Lane St Louis MO 63131 Office: Missouri-Pacific Bldg St Louis MO 63103

CHESLOCK, LOUIS, composer; b. London, Eng., Sept. 25, 1898; s. Jacob and Rebecca (Neumark) C.; to U.S., 1901, naturalized, 1913; certificate violin, Peabody Conservatory Music, 1917, certificate Harmony, 1919, Artist diploma, 1921; D. Musical Arts, Peabody Inst., 1964; m. Elise Brown Hanline, May 31, 1926; 1 son, Barry. Violinist, Balt. Symphony Orch., 1916-37, guest condr., 1928, 1944, 1950, asst. concert master, 1932-37; instr. violin Peabody Conservatory Music, 1916-70, instr. composition, counterpoint and orchestration, 1922—. chmn. dept. theory, 1950-68. Premiere of opera The Jewel Merchants (play by James Branch Cabell) Balt., Feb. 26, 1940. Premier ballet Cinderella, Balt., 1946, enlarged version, 1958; premiere of string quartet Pan Am. Union, Washington, D.C., 1957; performances of orchestral prize works, Washington, 1935, San Diego, Cal., Rochester N.Y., 1936, Akron, O., 1942, Guatemala, 1950, Israel, 1955, P.I., 1955, Belgium, 1956, Puerto Rico, 1956, Chile, Argentina and Panama, 1961, Singapore and Bombay, 1967, Boston, 1970, Washington, 1971, Portugal, 1971. Recipient Peabody alumni prize 1921, Chgo. Daily News prizes for compositions for piano, violin, violoncello and orchestra, 1923, 24; prize Nat. Composers' Clinic Contest for choral composition, 1942; hon. mention Chicago Theatre symphonic contest, 1923; hon. mention N.Y. Women's Symphony Orch. contest, 1938; elected to Balt. City Coll. Hall of Fame, 1960. Wrote: Introductory Study on Violin Vibrato, 1931; Graded List of Violin Music, 1948; H.L. Mencken on Music, 1961. Composer of symphonic, operatic and ensemble works; also compositions for violin, piano, voice, etc. Home: 2318 Sulgrave Av Baltimore MD 21209

CHESNEY, SAMUEL MELVIN, ins. co. exec.; b. Balt., 1905; ed. Johns Hopkins, 1926. Former pres., dir. Calvert Fire Ins. Co., Vehicle Underwriting Co., Eastern Ins. Co.; dir. Am. Health & Life Ins. Co., Auto Fleet Leasing, Inc. Home: 604 Wilton Rd Towson MD 21204 Office: 300 St Paul Pl Baltimore MD 21202

CHESNUT, FRANKLIN GILMORE, clergyman; b. Bowling Green, Ky., Mar. 2., 1919; s. Walter Franklin and Fannie (Meador) C.; student W. Ky. State Tchrs. Coll., Bowling Green, 1937-39; B.A., Bethel Coll., 1941; B.D., Cumberland Presbyn. Theol. Sem., 1943; m. Laurelyn Travillian, Aug. 19, 1950; children—Franklin Gilmore, Kathryn Lynne. Ordained to ministry Presbyn. Ch., 1940; pastor in Brunswick, Tenn., 1943-44; denominational youth dir., 1944-53; mgr. Cumberland Presbyn. Book Store, Memphis, 1953-54; pastor, Callco Rock, Ark., 1954-58, Russellville, Ark., 1958—. Moderator Logan Presbytery, Ky. Synod, 1941, White River and Ewing presbyteries, Ark. Synod, 1956, 59, 61, 64, W. Tenn. Synod, 1945, Cumberland Presbyn. Gen. Assembly, 1963-64; stated clk. Ark. Synod, 1956—. Trustee Cumberland Presbyn. Children's Home, 1962-71. Address: 1311 N Boston Av Russellville AR 72801

CHESROWN, MELVA ANITA, pub. relations cons.; b. Watauga, S.D., Aug. 12, 1911; d. Joseph Dodge and Mathilda Pauline (Mielke) Chesrown; student U. Minn., 1930-38; m. Robert E. Laffin, Aug. 22, 1942 (div. Nov. 1947). Sec., asst. publicity dir. Minn. Petroleum Industries Com., 1936-40; dir. women"s programs Tax Found., 1940-42; pub. relations dept. Gen. Motors Corp., 1942-44, Fred Eldean Orgn., 1944-53; owner Melva Chesrown Orgn., N.Y.C., 1960—. Pres. Nantucket Devel. Bd., 1964—. Mem. Nat. Home Fashions League, Am. Inst. Decorators, Pub. Relations Soc. Am. (chmn. edn. com. 1954-55, chmn. publicity com. 1957, treas., mem. bd. 1961—), Com. Women in Pub. Relations (chmn. 1953-54). Republican. Presbyn. Address: 11 S Water St Nantucket MA 02554

CHESS, EDWIN RALPH, air force chaplain; b. Chgo., Feb. 12, 1913; s. Charles W. and Anna (Zdonek) C.; B.A., St. Mary of Lake Sem., Mundelein, Ill., 1937; postgrad. student, DePaul U., 1946-48. Ordained priest Roman Catholic Ch., 1937; commd. 1st lt. USAAF, 1942, advanced through grades to maj. gen., 1966; various assignments, U.S., ETO, Italy, Africa and France, 1942-45; pastor St. Benedict's Ch., Blue Island, Ill., also St. Bridget's Ch., Chgo., 1946-48; recalled to active duty, 1948; assigned 3565th Air Base Wing, Waco, Tex., 1948-50, 6332d Air Bombardment Wing, Okinawa, 1950-51, 67th Tactical Reconn. Wing, Korea, 1951, 5th Air Force, Korea, 1951-52, 3510 Combat Crew Tng. Wing, Randolph AFB, Tex., 1952, 3525th Pilot Tng. Wing, Williams AFB, Ariz., 1952-53, Hdqrs. Air Tng. Command, Scott AFB, Ill., 1952-56, Hdqrs. Spain Air Materiel Area, 1956, 7602d Air Bombardment Group Spain, 1957, Hdqrs. USAF Europe, Wiesbaden, Germany, 1957-59, Hdqrs. 12th Air Force, Waco, 1959-60, Hdqrs. USAF Security Services, Kelly AFB, Tex., 1960-62; dep. chief chaplains Hdqrs. USAF, 1962-66, chief chaplains, from 1966. Decorated Bronze Star, Air medal, Commendation medal with 2 oak leaf clusters. Home: 3900 Watson Pl NW Washington DC 20016

CHESS, PHILLIP, recording co. exec.; b. Poland, Mar. 27, 1921; s. Joseph and Celia (Pullick) C.; student Western Ky. State Tchrs. Coll., 1940- 42; m. Sheva Jonesi, Feb. 12, 1944; children—Terry, Pamela, Kevin. Co-owner, Mocamba Lounge, Chgo., 1945-47, Chess Records, Chgo., 1947—; v.p. L & P Broadcasting Corp., Chgo., 1963—. Served with AUS, World War II. Mem. B'nai B'rith. Home: 112 Ravinoak Lane Highland Park IL 60035 Office: 320 E 21st St Chicago IL 60616

CHESTER, ALLAN GRIFFITH, educator; b. Phila., Jan. 13, 1900; s. Howard Griffith and Laura (White) C.; A.B., U. Pa., 1922, A.M., 1924, Ph.D., 1930; m. Ama June Warder, June 15, 1933 (dec. May 1943); m. 2d, Florence Foerderer Koch, Feb. 8, 1946. With dept. English, U. Pa., 1923—, successively instr., asst. prof., asso. prof., prof., 1953—, Felix E. Schelling prof. English lit., 1967-70, emeritus, 1970—, chmn. grad. dept., 1946-48, 54-56, 60-62, chmn. dept. English, 1962-66, dir. Navy V-12 English program, 1943-45. Mem. Modern Lang. Assn. (editorial cons.), Modern Humanities Research Assn., Mediaeval Acad. Am., Renaissance Soc. Am. (adv. council), Nat. Council Tchrs. Eng., Phila. Council Tchrs. English (pres.), Shakespeare Soc. Am., Phi Beta Kappa, Sigma Nu. Club: Franklin Inn (Philadelphia). Author: Thomas May, Man of Letters, 1595-1650, 1931; Hugh Latimer, Apostle to the English, 1954; (with C.C. Butterworth) George Joye, Translator of the Scriptures, 1960. Editor: The Bible: Selections from the Old and New Testaments, 1953; Shakespeare, Henry IV, Part II (The Pelican Shakespeare), 1956; The Sermons of Hugh Latimer, 1965. Contbr. articles to profl. jours. Home: 975 Mayberry Rd Gulph Mills Conshohocken PA 19428 Office: Bennett Hall U Pa Philadelphia PA 19104

CHESTER, GIRAUD, TV exec.; b. N.Y.C., Apr. 4, 1922; s. Harry and Minnie (Lachman) C.; B.A., Bklyn. Coll., 1942; M.A., U. Wis., 1943, Ph.D., 1947; m. to Marjorie J. Fatt, 1962; children—Christopher, Katherine. Asst. prof. speech Cornell U., 1947-49, U. Mich., summers 1947-49, Queens Coll., 1949-53; gen. program exec. NBC-TV, 1954-57; asso. Sylvester L. Weaver, Jr., 1957; dir. new TV program devel. Ted Bates & Co., Inc., 1958; v.p. charge network daytime programming ABC-TV, 1958-62; v.p. charge network program adminstr. NBC-TV, 1962-64; exec. v.p. Goodson-Todman Prodns., N.Y.C., 1964—. Ford Found. fellow, 1953-54. Served to lt. (j.g.) USNR, 1943-46. Mem. Am. Assn. U. Profs., Speech Communications Assn., Internat. Radio and TV Soc., Acad. TV Arts and Scis. Clubs: City Athletic, East Hampton Tennis. Author: Embattled Maiden: The Life of Anna Dickinson, 1951; (with G. R. Garrison) Radio and Television, 1950, Television and Radio, 1956; (with G. R. Garrison and E. E. Willis) Television and Radio, 1963, 1971; The Ninth Juror, 1970; also articles. Asso. editor: Quarterly Jour. of Speech, 1948-54. Home: 1010 Fifth Av New York City NY 10028 Office: 375 Park Av New York City NY 10020

CHESTER, WILLIAM MERRILL, Jr., motor vehicle mfg. co. exec.; b. Milw., Mar. 5, 1925; s. William Merrill and Alice Chapman (Miller) M.; B.S. in Engring., Princeton, 1947; M.B.A., Harvard, 1949; m. Priscilla Penfield, June 10, 1949; children—Helen Penfield, Caroline Alice, Mary Penfield, Sarah. With Heil Co., Milw., 1949—, v.p., 1965—, sec., 1964—, also dir.; dir. T.A. Chapman Co., Milw., Wis. Securities Co., Clement Constrn. Co., Evanston Bus Co., Sandusky Foundry & Machine Co. Bd. dirs. Hosp. Area Planning Com., Wis. Humane Soc., Chgo. Symphony Orch. Concerts in Milw., Zool. Soc. Milwaukee County, World Affairs Council, Milw.; bd. dirs. St. Luke's Hosp., Milw., 1961—, pres., 1966-68. Served with USNR, 1944-46. Mem. Milw. World Trade Club, Phi Beta Kappa. Clubs: University (N.Y.C. and Milw.). Home: 2527 N Wahl Av Milwaukee WI 53211 Office: 3000 W Montana St Milwaukee WI 53201

CHESTNUT, HAROLD, elec. engr.; b. Albany, N.Y., Nov. 25, 1917; s. Harry and Dorothy Schulmann C.; B.S. in Elec. Engring., Mass. Inst. Tech., 1939, M.S., 1940; D.E. (hon.), Case Western Res. U., 1966; m. Erma Ruth Callaway, Aug. 24, 1944; children—Peter Callaway, H. Thomas, Andrew T. With Gen. Electric Co., 1940—, cons. systems engr., aeros. and ordnance dept. Advanced Tech. Lab., Schenectady, 1956-66, mgr. Research and Devel. Center, 1966-71; editor Systems Engring. and Analysis, John Wiley and Sons, 1965—. Fellow I.E.E.E. (v.p. tech. activities 1970—, exec. com. 1967—), Internat. Fedn. Automatic Control (pres. 1957-58), Am. Automatic Control Council (pres. 1962-63). Author: Servomechanism and Regulating Systems Design, Vol. I, 1951, Vol. II, 1955; Systems Engineering Tools, 1965; Systems Engineering Methods, 1967. Editor Jour. Automatica, 1961-67. Home: 1266 Waverly Pl Schenectady NY 12308 Office: 1 River Rd Schenectady NY 12345

CHESTNUTT, GEORGE ALEXANDER, Jr., investment co. exec.; b. Helena, Mont., July 16, 1914; s. George Alexander and Edna (Mueller) C.; student Mont. State Coll., 1933-35, 37- 38; m. Sara Marchiano, Jan. 20, 1953; children by previous marriage—Mark M. (adopted), Karen (Mrs. Jon J. Driessen). With Mont. Power Co., 1935- 37, 38-46; gen. partner Mansfield Mills Co., investment adviser, Larchmont, N.Y., 1946-51, Am. Investors Co., Larchmont, 1951-60; pres., dir. Am. Investors Corp., Larchmont, 1961-66, Am. Investors Fund, Inc., Greenwich, Conn., 1957—, Chestnutt Corp., Greenwich, 1966—; editor weekly publ. Am. Investors Service, 1951—; originator geometric stock market averages. Mem. Greenwich C. of C. Republican. Rotarian (past pres. Larchmont, N.Y.). Author: Stock Market Analysis, Facts and Principles, 1952—. Home: 944 Lake Av Greenwich, CT 06830. Office: 88 Field Point Rd Greenwich CT 06830

CHESTON, CHARLES EDWARD, educator; b. Princeton, N.J., Nov. 23, 1911; s. Byron Major and Lula Augusta (Smalley) C.; B.S., N.Y. State Coll. Forestry, 1933; M.F., Yale, 1940; m. Catherine Goe, Sept. 6, 1938; children—Mary Catherine, Lawrence Byron. Jr. forester U.S. Forest Service, also Dept. Interior, 1933-39; asst. state forester N.J., 1940-42; chmn. dept. forestry U. of South, 1942—, prof., 1948—, Annie B. Snowden prof., 1948—. Sec. Keep Tenn. Green Assn., 1956—, also editor publ. and chmn. publications com.; mem. Forest Protection Com., 1958—; mem. Tenn. Conservation Commn., 1963-69. Pres. Sewanee Civic Assn., 1946—. Adv. com. Sewanee Research Center, 1956—. Mem. Soc. Am. Foresters (chmn. Ky.-Tenn. sect. 1964-65), Tenn. Forestry Assn. (pres. 1971), Alumni Assn. Yale Sch. Forestry (sec. 1940 class), Franklin County C. of C. (chmn. ednl. com.), Robin Hood, Ecce Guam Bonum Club, Yale Alumni Bd., Sigma Pi Sigma, Xi Sigma Pi, Sigma Nu, Theta Pi. Episcopalian. Co-author: Rehabilitation of Hurricane Damaged Forests in New England, 1940; also papers. Home: 1 Florida Av Sewanee TN 37375

CHESTON, FRANK CULVER, Jr., telephone co. exec.; b. Woodstock, Ont., Can., Mar. 15, 1914; s. Frank Culver and Charlotte E. (Laedlein) C.; A.B., Princeton, 1935; LL.B., Harvard, 1938; m. Cecile Hallingby, Nov. 17, 1943; children—Sharon, Frank Culver III, Richard P., Christopher H. Admitted to N.Y. bar, 1939, N.M. bar, 1963, N.J. bar, 1968; asso. White & Case, N.Y.C., 1938-42, 46-51, 52-53; atty., asst. gen. solicitor Western Electric Co., N.Y.C., 1953-62, 66-67; gen. atty., sec., treas. Sandia Corp., Albuquerque, 1962-66; sec., gen. counsel Bell Telephone Labs., Summit, N.J., 1967—. Served to capt., Judge Adv. Gen.'s Corps, AUS, 1942-46, U.S. Army, 1951-52. Mem. Am., N.M., N.J., Union County bar assns. Home: 21 Little Wolf Rd Summit NJ 07901 Office: 600 Mountain Av Summit NJ 07974

CHESTON, GEORGE MORRIS, lawyer; b. Phila., Aug. 18, 1917; s. Radcliffe, Jr. and Sydney (Ellis) C.; grad. St. Mark's Sch., 1935; A.B., Harvard, 1939, LL.B., 1947; m. Winifred Dodge Seyburn, May 5, 1955; 1 dau., Sydney. Admitted to Pa. bar, 1947, since practiced in Phila.; atty. firm Ballard, Spahr. Andrews & Ingersoll, Phila., 1947-52; farmer, Bryn Mawr, Pa., 1961—. Treas. Nat. Citizens for Eisenhower, 1955-56. Pres., Phila. Soc. to Protect Children; trustee United Fund, Phila., 1958-69; bd. dirs. Pa. Mental Health Soc., Phila. World Affairs Council; trustee Phila. Mus. Art, 1962—, pres., 1968—. Served to lt. comdr. USNR, 1941-46; PTO. Mem. Carolina Plantation Soc. Home: Wynnewood PA 19096 Office: Phila Nat Bank Bldg Philadelphia PA 19107

CHESTON, MORRIS, lawyer; b. Phila., Sept. 4, 1904; s. Radcliffe and Eugenia (Morris) C.; A.B., Princeton, 1925; LL.B., U. Pa., 1928; m. Caroline Ashton, Feb. 18, 1928; children—Mary Lincoln (Mrs. F. Woodson Hancock, Jr.), Caroline (Mrs. Charles B. Burkhart), Elizabeth (Mrs. Christopher A. Forster), Morris, Charlotte M., (Mrs. Raul Betancourt, Jr.). Admitted to Pa. bar, 1928, since practiced in Phila.; partner firm Ballard, Spahr, Andrews & Ingersoll, 1934—. Dir. Smith Kline & French Labs., Provident Nat. Corp., Provident Nat. Bank, Stock Ins. Co. of Green Tree; trustee Mut. Assurance Co. Mem. bd. mgrs. Pa. Hosp. Mem. Am., Pa., Phila. bar assns. Home: Whitpain Farm Ambler PA 19002 Office: Land Title Bldg Philadelphia PA 19110

CHESTON, WARREN BRUCE, ednl. adminstr.; b. Rochester, N.Y., Mar. 15, 1926; s. George L. and Clara (Hoesterey) C.; B.S., Harvard, 1947; Ph.D., U. Rochester, 1951; m. Roberta Bohrod, Nov. 1, 1950; children—Stephen, Rebecca, Dena, Nicolas. Asst. prof. Washington U., St. Louis, 1951-53; mem. faculty U. Minn., 1953-71, prof. physics, 1961-71, dir. Space Sci. Center, 1965-68, dean Inst. Tech., 1968-71; chancellor U. Ill. at Chgo. Circle, 1971—; sci. attache Am. Embassy, London, Eng., 1963-65; Fulbright prof. U. Utrecht (Netherlands), 1958- 59. Bd. dirs. Mpls. Center Opera Co., 1965-71. Civic Orch. Mpls., 1966-67. Served with AUS, 1944-46. Fellow Am. Phys. Soc. Author: Elementary Theory of Electric and Magnetic Fields, 1964. Home: 1235 N Astor St Chicago IL 60610

CHETKOVICH, MICHAEL N., accountant; b. Angels Camp, Cal., May 7, 1916; s. Nick M. and Anna (Metkovich) C.; B.S., U. Cal. at Berkeley, 1939, M.S., 1940; m. Alice Virginia Roosma, Mar. 20, 1947; children—Carol, Mark, John, Kathryn. With McLaren, Goode & Co., C.P.A.'s, San Francisco, 1940-52; partner with Haskins & Sells, San Francisco and N.Y. City, 1952—, now mng. partner of firm. Instr. extension div. U. Cal., 1947-49. Mem. Santa Clara County Grand Jury, 1963. Served to lt. USNR, 1942-46. C.P.A., Cal., N.Y., Utah, Washington, Ill., others. Mem. Am. Inst. C.P.A.'s, Cal. Soc. C.P.A.'s (v.p. 1965-66), N.Y. State Soc. C.P.A.'s Am. Accounting Assn., Fgn. Policy Assn., UN Assn. U.S.A., U. Cal. at Berkeley Alumni Assn., Accountants Club Am., N.Y.C. C. of C., Phi Beta Kappa, Beta Gamma Sigma, Beta Alpha Psi. Clubs: Recess (Detroit); Stock Exchange, Family (San Francisco); Union League, Harbor View (N.Y.C.); Greenwich (Conn.) Country. Home: Calhoun Dr Greenwich CT 06830 Office: 2 Broadway New York City NY 10004

CHEVALIER, DOUGLAS, news photographer; b. Moutier, Switzerland, Aug. 21, 1919; s. Henry G. and Rachel (Jeanmaire) C.; came to U.S., 1923, naturalized, 1928; student Syracuse U., 1937-38, Kenyon Coll., 1947-49; B.A., George Washington U., 1951; m. Helen Werner, Dec. 23, 1950; children—Kimberly Ann, Michael Douglas, Tracy Rose. Reporter with Mansfield (O.) News-Jours., 1949-50; reporter-photographer Neenah (Wis.) News-Record, 1950-51; Washington photographer Washington Post, 1952—. Recipient 1st prize photography competition, White House Photographers, 1954, 3d pl., 1953, 56, 69; two 2d prizes White House competition, 1960; two 1st prizes photographic competition Wash. Newspaper Guild, 1960. Mem. U.S. Senate Press Photographers Gallery (sec.-treas.), White House News Photographers Assn. (sec. 1960-61), Nat. Press Photographers Assn., Washington Newspaper Guild. Home: 7325 Blair Rd NW Washington DC 20012 Office: Washington Post 1515 L St NW Washington DC 20005

CHEVALIER, ELIZABETH PICKETT, author; b. Chgo., Mar. 25, 1896; d. Montgomery and Alma (Osborne) Pickett; A.B., Wellesley Coll., 1918; Litt.D., Transylvania Coll., 1943, Occidental Coll., 1966; m. Stuart Chevalier, October 17, 1936. Publicity dir. A.R.C. Nursing Service, Washington, 1918-19; hist. research, writing, 1919-23; author, dir. scenics and short subjects Fox Studios, N.Y.C., 1923-24, Hollywood, Cal., 1925-28; scenarist, writer original stories Fox West Coast Studios, 1926-28; author, scenarist, asso. producer first Am. full length color motion picture Redskin, starring Richard Dix, released by Paramount, 1928. Mem. bd. incorporators Am. Nat. Red Cross, 1944-47 (dissolution), mem. nominating com. for 1947 Red Cross Nat. Conv., mem. adv. com. on orgn., 1946; mem.- at-large bd. govs., 1947-52, woman mem. bd. govs. com. nat. blood program, 1947-51; pub. adviser U.S. delegation 15th World Health Assembly, UN; mem. Cal. Welfare Study Commn., 1961-63. Trustee Occidental Coll. and Southwest Mus.; Cal. dir. Robert E. Lee Meml. Found., 1954-65. Mem. Nat. Soc. Colonial Dames Am. (nat. chmn. patriotic services Com. 1954-56), P.E.N. Democrat. Presbyn. Clubs: Sulgrave (Washington); Cosmopolitan, Pen and Brush (N.Y.C.); Town (Pasadena, Cal.). Author: Official History of American Red Cross Nursing Service World War I; The American National Red Cross: Its Origin, Purposes and Service, 1922; Redskin, 1928; (novel) Drivin' Woman, 1942. Home; 865 Comstock Av Los Angeles CA 90024

CHEVALIER, HAAKON MAURICE, author: b. Lakewood, N.J., Sept. 10, 1902; s. Emile and Therese (Roggen) C.; student Stanford U., 1918-20; A.B., U. Cal., 1923, A.M., 1925, Ph.D., 1929; m. Ruth Bosley, 1922 (div. 1931); 1 son, Jacques Anatole; m. 2d, Barbara Lansburgh, 1931 (div. 1950) children—Suzanne Andrée, Haakon Lazarus; m. 3d, Carol Lansburgh, 1952; 1 dau., Karen Anne. Prof. French, U. Cal., 1929-46, French interpreter U.N. Conf., San Francisco, 1945, War Criminals Trials, Nurnberg, 1945-46, U.N., Lake Success, N.Y., 1946. Mem. P.E.N., Authors League Am., Assn. Internationale des Interprètes de Conférence, Assn. Francaise de Traducteurs. Author: The Ironic Temper; Anatole France and His Time, 1932; For Us the Living, 1949; The Man Who Would be God, 1959; Oppenheimer: The Story of a Friendship, 1965; The Last Voyage of the Schooner Rosamond, 1970. Translator of following: Andre Malraux's Man's Fate, 1934; Days of Wrath, 1936; Louis Aragon's Bells of Basel, 1936; Louis Aragon's Residential Quarter, 1938; The Secret Life of Salvador Dali, 1942; Vladimir Pozner's The Edge of the Sword, 1942; First Harvest, 1943; Gontran de Poncins' Home is the Hunter, 1943; André Maurois' Seven Faces of Love, 1943; Salvador Dali's Hidden Faces, 1944; Joseph Kessel's Army of Shadows, 1944; Denis de Rougemont's Devil's Share, 1944; Vercors' Three Short Novels, 1947; Simon Gantillon's Vessel of Wrath, 1947; Salvador Dali's 50 Secrets of Magic Craftmanship, 1948; Salvador Dali: On Modern Art, 1957; Stendhal's A Roman Journey, 1957; René Grousset's Chinese Art and Culture, 1959; Michel Seuphor's The Sculpture of This Century, 1960; Aragon's Holy Week, 1961; Michel Seuphor's Abstract Painting, 1962; Henri Michaux's Light Through Darkness, 1962; Michel Seuphor's Abstract Painting in

Flanders, 1963; Bob Claessen's and Jeanne Rousseau's Our Bruegel, 1969; others. Contbr. to various mags. Home: 19 rue du Mont-Cenis Paris 18 France

CHEVALIER, MAURICE, (Auguste), stage and film actor, entertainer; b. Paris, Sept. 12, 1888; s. Victor Charles and Josephine (Vanden-Boosche) C.; ed. schs. in Paris; m. 1926 (div. 1935). Made debut at 12 yrs. of age as singer-entertainer in cafes, concert and music halls, Paris; later toured in provinces; appeared with Mistinguette at Folies-Bergeres, Paris, 1909; made London debut in revue, 1919; dir. Alhambra-Maurice Chevalier, Paris, 1956; has appeared in revues, operettas and in one-man show in important theatres, Paris and London, and on tour in Argentina, United States, Canada, Scandinavia, and throughout Europe, 1919—; in one-man show, Songs and Impressions, N.Y.C., 1958, 63, 65, 68; has introduced songs, made records, appeared on radio and television programs. Actor in Am. films including: The Love Parade, The Playboy of Paris, One Hour With You, The Beloved Vagabond, Folies Bergéres, Love in the Afternoon, Gigi (1958); Count Your Blessings, Can- Can, Pepe, Fanny, also acted in The Castaways and Monkeys Go Home; starred in French films including: With a Smile, 1939; Man of the Hour, 1940; Le Silence est d'Or (shown in U.S. under title, Man About Town), 1947 and film Black Tights which was produced in 1962. Decorated Chevalier Legion of Honor, Croix de Guerre with palm (France), Order of Leopold (Belgium), Officer Legion of Honor, Officer Merite Nat.; recipient spl. award for contbn. to show business, Acad. of Motion Picture Arts and Scis., 1959; spl. Tony award, in 1968. Served with French Army, World War I; in retirement in Paris during German Occupation, World War II. Mem. Academie des Vins de Bordeaux. Author: Ma Route et Mes Chansons (autobiography); With Love, 1960; I Remember It Well, 1970. Home: "La Louque" Marnés-La-Coquette Hauts-De-Seine France

CHEVERIE, CARROLL LEROY, advt. exec.; b. Eastport, Me., Sept. 19, 1909; s. Carroll H. and Iva M. (Hunt) C. student Northeastern U., 1931; B.B.S., Bentley Coll., 1933; m. Virginia Howard, July 24, 1937; children—Jean (Mrs. David A. Lundquist), Carroll Leroy, Gina (Mrs. David Wick III), Richard H., William H. (dec.). Asst. cashier Frontier Nat. Bank, Eastport, 1926-29; sr. accountant Chase Harris Forbes Corp., Boston and N.Y.C., 1929-33; asst. treas. Washington & Suburban Cos., Boston, 1933-41; treas. Consol. Investment Trust, Boston, 1941-52; treas., dir. H.B. Humphrey, Boston and N.Y.C., 1951-59; treas. Clinton E. Frank, Inc., Chgo., 1959—, sr. v.p., 1965—, also dir., mem. exec. com.; dir. Hartford Plaza Bank, Chgo., Market Measurements, Inc., Chgo. Trustee CEF Found.; bd. dirs. Am. Acad. Art, Chgo. Mason. Clubs: International (Chgo.); Shrine (Glenview). Home: 1435 Evergreen Terrace Glenview IL 60025 Office: 120 S Riverside Plaza Chicago IL 60606

CHEVINS, ANTHONY CHARLES, advt. exec.; b. Frackville, Pa., Apr. 1, 1921; s. Charles A. and Mary (Swade) C.; A.B. magna cum laude, Syracuse U., 1947; postgrad. Columbia, 1948-49; m. Margaret Macy, Sept. 18, 1948; childrenCheryl L., Christopher M., Cynthia A. Writer, Batten, Barton, Durstine & Osborn, advt., 1948-51; with Cunningham & Walsh, 1951—, sr. v.p., 1959-61, creative dir., 1958-61, exec. v.p., 1961-68, pres., 1968—. Served to lt. USNR 1941-45. Mem. Phi Beta Kappa, Alpha Delta Sigma. Home: 135 Nearwater Lane Darien CT Office: 260 Madison St New York City NY 10016

CHEVOOR, WILLIAM ALBERT, govt. ofcl.; b. Boston, Dec. 31, 1916; s. Albert Bedros and Mary (Bovaj) C.; married to Claris Lorris, December 8, 1950; children—Adrienne, David, Michael. Credit manager Snider Fuel Corporation, Boston, 1939-42, 45-47; budget, fiscal officer U.S. Forces, Vienna, Austria, 1948-50, asst. to controller U.S. Operations Mission to Turkey, Ankara, 1950-52, controller U.S. Operations Mission to Netherlands, The Hague, 1952-55, U.S. Operations Mission to Italy, Rome, 1955-57, U.S. Operations Mission to Yugoslavia, Belgrade, 1957-60, Peru, Lima, 1961-65, U.S. AID, Santo Domingo, Dominican Republic, 1965-68; financial mgr. AID, Washington, 1969-70; asst. dir.-controller AID, Seoul, Korea, 1970—. Served with AUS, 1942-45. Decorated Croix de Guerre (France). Home: 76 Putnam St Watertown MA 02172 Office: US AID Seoul Korea

CHEVRIER, LIONEL, lawyer; b. Cornwall, Ont., Can., Apr. 2, 1903; s. Joseph E. and Malvina (DeRepentigny) C.; grad. Collegiate Inst., Cornwall, Ont., 1917; B.A., U. Ottawa, 1924, Ph.B., LL.D.; Law Sch., Osgoode Hall, Toronto, 1928; LL.D., Laval U., 1952, Queens' U., 1956, U. Ottawa, 1946; D.C.L., Bishop's U., 1964; m. Lucienne Brulé, Oct. 22, 1932; children—Lucie (Mrs. Pierre Thomas), Robert, Jean, Bernard, Adele (Mrs. Jean Besner), Marie. Called to Ont. bar, 1928, Que. bar, 1957; appointed K.C., 1938; mem. Chevrier, Latchford & Fitzpatrick, 1928-45; elected to Parliament 1935, 40, 45, 49, 53, 57, 58, 62, 63; Dep. Chief Govt. Whip, 1940; chmn. sub-com. Prodn. and Munitions Contracts (Parliamentary War Expenditure Com. 1942); parliamentary asst. Minister of Munitions and Supply, 1943; minister of transport Govt. Can., 1945-54; pres. Privy Council, 1957; minister of justice, atty. gen. Can., 1963; high commr. for Can. in U.K. 1964-68, ret., 1968; now mem. law firm Geoffrion & Prud'homme, Montreal, Que., Can.; commr. gen. for royal and state visits during Canada's centennial year, 1967; freeman City of London, Eng., 1965; pres. St. Lawrence Seaway Authority, 1954-57. Del. Empire Parliament Assn., Washington, 1943, Breton Woods Conf., 1945; del. UN Gen. Assembly, Paris, 1948. Sec. Bd. of Trade, Cornwall, Ont., 1928-34; sec. Cornwall Centennial Com., 1932. Decorated companion Order of Can. Mem. Phi Delta Phi. Liberal. Roman Catholic. Clubs: St. James (Montreal); Rideau (Ottawa). Author: The St. Lawrence Seaway. Address: 500 Place d'Armes Montreal Quebec Canada

CHEW, GEOFFREY FOUCAR, educator, physicist; b. Washington, June 5, 1924; s. Arthur Percy and Pauline Lisette (Foucar) C.; B.S., George Washington U., 1944; Ph.D., U. Chgo., 1948; m. Ruth Elva Wright, June 16, 1945 (dec. Apr. 1971); children—Berkeley Arthur and Beverly Randall (twins). Research asst. Los Alamos Atomic Bomb project, 1944-46; asst. prof. physics U. Cal. at Berkeley, 1949-50; asso. prof., then prof. U. Ill., 1951-56; prof. physics U. Cal. at Berkeley, 1957—; mem. staff Lawrence Radiation Lab., 1957—, dir. theoretical group, 1966—. Fulbright lectr. Les Houches, France, 1953, 60, 65; Rouse Ball lectr. U. Cambridge, (Eng.), 1963, Overseas fellow Churchill Coll., 1962-63. Received Ernest O. Lawrence Meml. award, 1969. Fellow Am. Phys. Soc. (Hughes prize 1962); mem. Nat. Acad. Scis., Fedn. Am. Scientists (chmn. passport com. 1952-60), Am. Acad. Arts and Scis., Phi Beta Kappa, Sigma Xi, Sigma Alpha Epsilon. Author: S-Matrix Theory of Strong Interactions, 1961; The Analytic S-Matrix; A Basis for Nuclear Democracy, 1966; also articles. Home: 10 Maybeck Twin Dr Berkeley CA 94708 Office: Dept Physics U Cal Berkeley CA 94720

CHEW, JOHN LOUIS, ret. naval officer; b. Annapolis, Md., Sept. 22, 1909; s. John Lee and Rosalyn (Sylvester) C.; B.S., U.S. Naval Acad., 1931; student U.S. Naval Postgrad. Sch., 1938-39; m. Helen Loughan, June 4, 1938 (dec. Sept. 1954); children—Margaret Adams, John Louis; m. 2d, Julia Pierson Wilcox, May 18, 1960; stepchildren—Virginia Edith, Thomas Wharton, Stanley Carter. Commd. ensign U.S. Navy, 1931, advanced through grades to rear adm., 1959; served in battleships, cruisers and destroyers prior to World War II; served in U.S.S. Helena (sunk Battle Kula), 1939-43; assigned Naval Acad., 1944; exec. officer U.S.S. Helena, 1945-47; comdg. officer U.S.S. Stickell, 1947-48; head leadership dept., exec. officer Bancroft Hall, Naval Acad., 1948-51; mem. staff comdr.-in-chief U.S. Naval Forces Eastern Atlantic and Mediterranean, 1951-53; assigned Office Chief Naval Operations, 1953-56, 58-59; comdr. U.S.S. Pawcatuck, 1956-57, U.S.S. Roanoke, 1957-58; dep. comdr. Mil. Sea Trans. Service, 1959-60; comdr. Destroyer Flotilla 4, 1960—, also comdr. Project Mercury Recovery Force; assigned Office Joint Chiefs Staff, 1962-64; comdr. Naval Forces Japan, 1964-65; comdr. Anti-sub Warfare Forces, Pacific, 1965-67; vice adm., 1965—; comdr. U.S. Taiwan Def. Command, 1967-70, ret., 1970. Decorated Navy Unit Commendation ribbon, Letters of Commendation with ribbon and combat V, D.S.M., Legion Merit, also numerous service and area ribbons. Mem. U.S. Naval Inst. Home: 15 Southgate Av Annapolis MD 21401

CHEW, WOODROW WILSON, coll. prof.; b. Burlington, Okla., Jan. 29, 1913; s. Newton Clyde and Mabel Jeannette (Elliott) C.; student Northwestern State Coll., Alva, Okla., 1931-34; B.S., N.M. Coll Agr. and Mech. Arts, 1936; M.S., Okla. A. and M. Coll., 1938; m. Ellen Lorraine Black, May 20, 1939; 1 son, Woodrow Wilson. Grad. asst. Okla. A. and M. Coll., 1936-38; jr. engr. and asst. engr., P.W.A., Ft. Worth, Tex., 1938-39; instr. chemistry and physics Northeastern Jr. Coll., Miami, Okla., 1939-40; asst. prof. and head chem. engring. dept., La. Poly. Inst., 1940-45, asso. prof. and head chem. engring. dept. 1945-47, prof. and head chem. engring. dept., 1947—; chem. engr. Monsanto Chem. Co., Anniston, Ala., Mar.-Nov. 1945, Magnolia Petroleum Co., Dallas, June-Aug., 1952. Registered prof. engr., chem. engring., La. Fellow Am. Inst. Chemists; mem. La., N.Y., acads. sci., Soc. Investigating Recurring Events, Nat. Soc. Prof. Eng., Am. Inst. Chem. Engrs., Am. Chem. Soc., Am. Soc. Engring. Edn., Am. U. Profs., Phi Lambda Upsilon, Theta Xi, Tau Beta Pi. Democrat. Presbyn. Mason. Home: Westwood Hills Ruston LA 71270

CHEWNING, LEWIS GARLAND, ret. box co. exec.; b. Spotsylvania County, Va., Feb. 14, 1905; s. Lynn P. and Kate (Waller) C.; student Hampden-Sydney Coll., 1923-24, U. Richmond, 1924-25; LL.D., Hampden-Sydney Coll., 1968; m. Mary Beverly Chenery, June 14, 1928; 1 dau., Mary Beverly (Mrs. Frank Talbott III). Propr. Lewis G. Chewning, Inc., realtor, Richmond, 1934- 50; pres. Va. Folding Box Co., Inc., subsidiary W.Va. Pulp and Paper Co., 1950-70, ret., 1970, also dir.; hon. dir., exec. com. Life Ins. Co. Va.; dir., mem. exec. and trust coms. Va. Trust Co. Mem. Richmond Planning Commn., 1942- 49, Va. Hosp. Bd., 1955-56; campaign gen. Richmond Area Community Chest, 1944; campaign chmn. Richmond chpt. A.R.C., 1945. Bd. trustees Hampden- Sydney Coll., 1947—, chmn., 1958-69, chmn. finance com., 1969—; finance com. Union Theol. Sem., Richmond, 1948—; bd. trustees Richmond Meml. Hosp., 1950—, Richmond chpt. A.R.C., 1960—. Va. Found Ind. Colls., 1960—; mem. bd. trustees, mem. exec. com. Richmond Corp; bd. dirs. Richmond Found., 1943—. Mem. Va. (past dir.), Richmond (past pres.) C.'s of C. Soc. Colonial Wars Va., Omicron Delta 1946. Presbyn. (elder, trustee). Clubs: Commonwealth (past bd. govs.), Country of Virginia (past bd. govs.) (Richmond). Home: 15 Lexington Rd Richmond, VA 23226.

CHEYNEY, WILLIAM JAMES, research found. ofcl.; b. Phila., Oct. 14, 1900; s. Algernon Roberts and Lila Pancoast (James) C.; A.B., George Washington U., 1920; A.M., Rutgers U., 1932; grad. Westtown Sch. (Friends), 1917; m. Ruth Bryan Hall, Dec. 27, 1925 (dec. Oct. 19, 1951); 1 son, William James II; m. 2d, Mrs. Elizabeth Archer Lank, Aug. 8, 1952. With Chase National Bank, 1920-24; residential and indsl. bldg. and finance bus., under own name, 1923-29; prof. econs. banking and finance and head dept. bus. adminstrn. Rider Coll., Trenton, N.J., 1929-33; economist Nat. Retail Furniture Assn., 1933-36, v.p., 1936-42; counsel for trade relations Am. Retail Fedn., 1938-41; exec. dir. Retail Credit Inst. of Am., 1942-51; exec. v.p. Nat. Found. Consumer Credit (following merger), 1951-67, life mem. bd. trustees, 1967—. Mem. retail adv. com. to the Secretary of Commerce, 1946-53; mem. Nat. Distbn. Council, 1954-67; mem. retail adv. com. Office Defense Mobilization, 1954-60; adv. com. Office Emergency Planning, 1960-67; mem. Central Council Nat. Retail Assn., chmn., 1954-57; cons. ICA, 1954-67. Mem. Am. Retail Fedn. (exec. com. 1954-57), Am. Soc. Assn. Execs., Am. Retail Assn. Execs., Am. Marketing Assn., Am. Econs. Assn., U.S. C. of C. (domestic distbrn. com. 1954-57, 61-62), Delta Sigma Pi. Mem. Soc. of Friends; Methodist (adminstrn. bd., lay leader, chmn. council ministeries). Clubs: University, Exchequer (chancellor 1967-68, steering com. 1964-69). Author: A Handbook for Trade Relations, 1938; The Growth of an Idea, 1952; Using Our Credit Intelligently (textbook), 1956, rev., 1959, 62, 64, 67; Plans and Working Suggestions for Consumer Credit Counseling Services (industry handbook), 1964, 65, 67; also many articles nat. mags. Home: 3711 Cumberland St NW Washington DC 20016 Office: 1819 H St NW Washington DC 20006

CHEZEM, CURTIS GORDON, educator; b. Eugene, Ore., Jan. 28, 1924; s. Clinton Daniel and Vera Veneta (Forrester) C.; B.A. in Math., U. Ore., 1951, M.A. in Physics, 1952; Ph.D., Ore. State U., 1960; m. Margo Linda Stephan, Mar. 7, 1960; children—Joanne, David. Flight radio officer Pan Am. World Airways, Seattle, San Francisco, 1942-44; chief radio officer Hammond S.S. Lines, San Francisco, 1944-45; telegrapher Western Union, Eugene, Ore., 1946; announcer, engr. KUGN-KASH Eugene, 1946-51; staff physicist Los Alamos Sci. Lab., 1952-67; br. chief AEC, 1967-69; head, nuclear engring. dept. Kan. State U., Manhattan, 1969—, Black & Veatch prof. nuclear engring., 1971—; partner Casa Tlaloc, Los Alamos, 1960-68, Manhattan, 1969—; supr. reactor program U.S. Atoms for Peace program, Bogota, Colombia, 1963; vis. prof. Tex. A. and M. U., 1966-67; adj. prof. U. N.M., 1962-65.; Kan. State U. rep. Atomic Indsl. Forum, 1969—; chmn. profl. tng. com. Inst. Nuclear Materials Mgmt., 1968-70, chmn. profl. standards and certification, 1970—; instr. airplane and instrument flight, 1966—. Del. Assembly Border States U.S.-Mexico, Santa Fe, 1966; mem. Kan. Nuclear Energy Council, 1969—. Bd. control Tau Kappa Epsilon, Kan. State U. Served with Ore. N.G., 1939-40, USNR, 1945-46. Mem. Am. Nuclear Soc., Washington Acad. Sci., N.Y. Acad. Sci., Am. Soc. Engring. Edn., Nat. Sci. Tchrs. Assn., Kan. Assn. Tchrs. Sci., Am. Acad. Polit. and Social Sci., Kan. Engring. Soc., Aircraft Owners and Pilots Assn., Sierra Club, Sigma Xi, Pi Mu Epsilon, Sigma Pi Sigma, Tau Kappa Epsilon. Editor: (with W.H. Kohler) Coupled Reactor Kinetics, 1967. Contbr. articles profl. jours. Home: 1621 Virginia Dr Manhattan KS 66502

CHI, NGUYEN HUU, Vietnamese diplomat; b. Son Tay, North Vietnam, Oct. 1, 1914; s. Nguyen Thuan Hy and Nguyen Thi Nhan; M.Laws, Hanoi Law Sch., 1934; m. Trinh Thi Mai, 1938; children—Nguyen Trinh Thiva, Nguyen Thi Ngoe Quyen, Nguyen ngoe Boi, Nguyen bau Khanh. With Ministry of Fgn. Affairs, Vietnam, 1955-62, dir. of cabinet, 1965-67; sr. editor Que Hunng, 1962-63; chief of cabinet Ministry of Information; dir. of cabinet, spl. asst. to dep. prime minister in charge cultural and social affairs, 1964; sec.-gen. Inter-Departmental Com. for Relief and Rehab. Flood-Stricken Areas, 1964-65; permanent observer, ambassador E. and P. to UNI, N.Y.C., 1967—. Del., Colombo Plan Confs., 1955, 56, 58, 60; mem. good-will mission, Australia, 1956, Can., 1958. Home: 5 Phanke Binh St Saigon South Vietnam Office: 866 UN Plaza New York City NY 10017

CHIANG KAI-SHEK, GENERALISSIMO, (Chiang Chung-Cheng), pres. Republic of China; b. Feng-hua, Chekiang Province, Oct. 31, 1887; s. Chiang Suan; ed. Nat. Paoting Mil. Acad., N. China, and Tokyo Mil. Acad. Coll., Japan; m. Soong Mayling, 1927; 2 sons by previous marriage. Met Dr. Sun Yat-sen (founder Chinese Republic) in Japan, 1906; mem. revolutionary party, 1907-11; joined revolutionary army and displayed mil. ability at capture of Shanghai, 1911; attached to Gen. Hdqrs., Canton, 1917-20; studied mil. and social system in Soviet Russia, 1923; founder and prin. Whampoa Mil. Acad., Canton, 1924; became mem. Central Exec. Com. of Kuomintang and chmn. of mil. affairs commn., 1926; comdr. in chief Northward Expeditionary Forces, 1926; chmn. State Council and Generalissimo of all Chinese fighting forces, 1928; resigned all govt. offices in interest of conciliation of groups at Canton and Shanghai, 1931; pres. of Exec. Yuan, 1935-38; chmn. Nat. Mil. Affairs Council, 1932-46; chmn. People's Polit. Council, 1939-40; dir.-gen. of Kuomintang Party, Republic of China, 1938-; pres. of China, 1948- (except Jan. 1949-Mar. 1950). Supreme comdr. Allied Forces in China Theater, World War II. Author: China's Destiny, 1943; The Collected Wartime Messages of Generalissimo Chiang Kai-shek: Soviet Russia in China, 1957; Social Welfare, Education, Health and Happiness, others. Address: Taipei Taiwan Republic of China

CHIANG KAI-SHEK MADAME (Mayling Soong Chiang), Chinese sociologist; b. Shanghai, China, 1899; d. C. J. Soong; ed. Wellesley Coll.; L.H.D., John B. Stetson U., Bryant, Hobart, William Smith colls.; LL.D., Rutgers, Loyola (Los Angeles) univs., Goucher, Wellesley, Russell Sage, Hahnemann Med., Wesleyan (Macon, Ga.) Colleges, University of Michigan, Bob Jones U., U. Hawaii; m. Chiang Kai-shek, 1927. Engaged in social service work in China; first women mem. Child Labor Commn.; inaugurated Moral Endeavor Assn.; established schs. in Nanking for orphans of Revolutionary Soldiers; former mem. Legislative Yuan; served as sec.-gen. Chinese Commn. on Aero. Affairs; dir.-gen. and chmn. women's Adv. council New Life Movement; founder, dir. Nat. Chinese Women's Assn. for War Relief, Nat. Assn. for Refugee Children, Chinese Women's Dept. of Kuomintang. First Chinese woman to be decorated by Nat. Govt. of China, recipient highest mil. and civil decorations: Medal of Honor, N.Y.C. Fedn. Women's Clubs; YWCA Emblem; gold medal N.Y. So. Soc.; Chi Omega nat. achievement award for 1943; gold medal for dist. services Nat. Inst. Social Scis.; Dist. service award Altrusa Internat. Assn.; Churchman 5th ann. award, 1943. Hon. pres. Am. Bur. Med. Aid to China; patroness Internat. Red Cross Com.; hon. pres. Com. for Promotion of Welfare of Blind, University of the Seven Seas, Whittier, Cal.; hon. pres. bd. trustees Wego Orphanage; chmn. bd. trustees Huashing Children's Home. Hon. pres. Nurse's Assn. of China, Am. U. Club, Anti-Tb Assn. of China. Life mem. San Francisco Press Club, Asso. Country women of World; mem. Phi Beta Kappa (hon. Eta chpt.), Tau Zeta Epsilon, Phi Delta Gamma (hon.). Author: Sian: A coup d'Etat, 1937; China in Peace and War, 1939; China Shall Rise Again, 1939; This is Our China, 1940; We Chinese Women, 1941; Little Sister Su, 1943; Album of Reporduction of Paintings, Vol. I, 1952, Vol. II, 1962; The Sure Victory, 1955; Madame Chiang Kai-shek Selected Speeches, 1959. Address: The President's Residence Taipei, Taiwan, Republic of China

CHIAPPETTA, MICHAEL, educator; b. Tacoma, May 23, 1921; s. Vincent and Mary (Greco) C.; student Wayne State U., 1938-40; A.B., U. Mich., 1942, M.A., 1947, Ph.D., 1950; m. Violet Grace Funk, Sept. 7, 1944; children—Vincent Funk, Michael Funk. Prof. internat. and comparative edn. Ariz. State U., 1950- 52, U. Cal. at Berkeley, 1952-53, Pa. State U., 1953-59; prof. internat. and comparative edn. Ind. U., Bloomington, 1965—, dir. Center for Innovations in Human Resource Devel., 1969—. Vis. prof. summers U. Mich., 1952, U. Colo., 1950, U. Ill., 1953; Smith- Mundt. lectr., Mexico, 1956; Fulbright lectr., Peru, 1959; ednl. adviser AID, Peru, 1960-63; regional ednl. adviser AID, 1963-64; ednl. cons. AID Latin Am. Bur., 1968—; dir. multilateral policy planning staff State Dept., 1964-65; program advisor Ford Found., Colombia, 1968—. Served to 2d lt. USAAF, 1942-46. Mem. N.E.A., Ind. Tchrs. Assn., Phi Beta Kappa, Phi Delta Kappa, Phi Kappa Phi. Democrat. Unitarian. Home: Woodridge Rd Marlin Hills Bloomington IN 47401

CHIARELLA, PETER RALPH, cosmetic co. exec.; b. Bklyn., Dec. 6, 1932; s. C. Ralph and Catherine (Zinzi) C.; B.B.A., St. John's U., 1957; m. Frances Crane, Oct. 10, 1953; children—Ralph, Thomas, John, Karen. Sr. accountant Peat, Marwick, Mitchell & Co., N.Y.C., 1957-61; asst. controller Bonwit Teller, N.Y.C., 1961-62; financial coordinator internat. div. Merck & Co., N.Y.C., 1962-63; accounting mgr. plastics div. Celanese Corp., Newark, 1963-67; v.p., controller Clairol, Inc., N.Y.C., 1967—; lectr. Am. Mgmt. Assn. Mem. budget com. United Fund, Stamford, Conn., 1970—. Served with USN, 1952-54. C.P.A., N.Y. Mem. Am. Inst. C.P.A.'s, N.Y. State Soc. C.P.A.'s, Financial Execs. Inst., Delta Mu Delta. Home: 7 Little Brook Rd N Darien CT 06820 Office: 345 Park Av New York City NY 10022

CHIARELLI, JAMES JOSEPH, architect; b. Spokane, July 3, 1908; s. Joseph and Josephine (DeMaties) C.; B. Arch., U. Wash., 1934; m. Patricia Alice Bradwell, May 3, 1947; children—Randall Gennaro, Diana Maria, Mark Angelo, Teresa Allegra. Pvt. practice architecture, Seattle, 1945—. Chmn. Bd. Adjustment Seattle Planning Commn., 1959-60; chmn. Citizens Recreation and Park Com. King County, Wash., 1957-58; chmn. Performing Arts div. Cultural Arts Bd. for Century 21 Seattle World's Fair, 1960-62. Trustee St. Martin's Coll. Fellow A.I.A. (pres. Wash. State chpt. 1956-58); Mem. Tau Sigma Delta. Architect Seattle Center Opera House, 1961, Thomas Burke Meml., Wash. State Museum, 1962, Hertl-Ner Tamid Conservative, Sanctuary, Social Hall and Offices, 1970. Home: 6500 NE Windermere Rd Seattle WA 98105 Office: 1717 E Pine St Seattle WA 98122

CHIARENZA, FRANK JOHN, univ. acad. dean; b. New Britain, Conn., Dec. 10, 1926; s. Sebastian X. and Josephine (Spoto) C.; A.B., Yale, 1949, Ph.D. in Medieval Lit., 1956; M.A. in English, Rutgers U., 1950. Lectr. English, U. Conn., 1954-55; instr. English, Hillyer Coll., Hartford, Conn., 1955-57; from asst. prof. to prof. chmn. dept. English, U. Hartford, 1958-67, acad. dean Sch. Arts and Scis., 1967—. Cons., reader English, Coll. Entrance Exam. Bd., 1959—; reader advanced placement tests Ednl. Testing Service, Princeton, N.J. 1961—; chmn. for Conn., Nat. Council Coll. Pubns. Advisers, 1966-67. Served with USNR, 1944-46. Fulbright grantee U. Rome, 1953-54. Mem. Modern Lang. Assn., Am. Assn. U. Profs. (pres. Hartford 1962-64), Am. Assn. Higher Edn., N.E.A., Am. Conf. Acad. Deans, Am. Council Edn. Club: Yale (New Britain). Author articles. Home: 80 Crestview Dr Newington CT 06111 Office: Univ Hartford West Hartford CT 06117

CHIARULLI, PETER, educator; b. Bklyn., Nov. 8, 1921; s. Dominick and Pauline (Verni) C.; B.A., Bklyn. Coll., 1942; M.S., Brown U., 1944, Ph.D., 1949; m. Mary Leonora Santulli, Sept. 1, 1947; children—Linda Jean, Michael Verne. Jr. physicist NACA,

1943; asst. prof. math. Carnegie Inst. Tech., 1949-52; asst., asso. prof. applied math. Brown U., 1952-55; mathematician Nat. Bur. Standards, 1955-56; prof. mechanics, chmn. dept. Ill. Inst. Tech., 1956-70, dean engring. and phys. scis., 1970—. Served as sgt. USAAF, 1944-46. Decorated Bronze Star medal. Mem. Am. Soc. M.E., Am. Soc. Engring. Edn., Soc. Natural Philosophy, A.A.A.S., Soc. Engring. Scis., Sigma Xi, Pi Mu Epsilon. Home: 810 N Woodbine Oak Park IL 60302 Office: Ill Inst Tech 33d and Federal Chicago IL 60616

CHICHESTER, SIR FRANCIS, author, air and sea navigator; b. Sept. 17, 1901; ed. Marlborough Coll. Emigrated to New Zealand, 1919; dir. Godwin Chichester Aviation Co., Ltd., 1927-30; 2d person to fly solo Eng. to Australia, 1929; first East to West solo flight from New Zealand to Australia across Tasman Sea, 1931 (Johnston Meml. trophy for navigation); 1st long distance solo seaplane flight, New Zealand to Japan, 1931; cruising flight in Puss Moth with one passenger, Sydney to London via Peking, 1936; chmn. Francis Chichester Ltd., map and guide pubs., 1945-; dir. Straight Aviation Tng. Ltd., 1946-49; record solo East-West Crossing, Plymouth to N.Y.C., 1962; 2d in 2d solo trans-Atlantic yacht race, 1964; solo cruise So. Atlantic route in Gypsy Moth, 1967, Warden Guild Air pilots and Air Navigation, 1960; first true circumnavigation of world via Cape of Good Hope, Cape of Leewin, Cape of Horn, 1966-67; one-stop global circumnavigation at record speed in Gypsy Moth IV, 1967; record speed solo sailing in Gypsy Moth V, 1971; v.p. Inst. Navigation, 1964. Trustee Nat. Maritime Mus., 1965-70. Comdr. Order British Empire, 1964; created knight, 1967; winner 1st singlehanded trans-Atlantic Yacht race, 1960; recipient Yachtsman of Year trophy, 1960; Blue Water medal Cruising Club Am., 1960, 67; Gold medal Brit. Inst. Navigation, 1961, Silver Globe award, 1967; Gold medal Australian Inst. Navigation, 1967; Gold medal Guild Yachting Writers, 1967; Superior Achievement award Am. Inst. Navigation, 1967; Gold medal Royal Geog. Soc., 1967; Marconi Meml. Gold medal Vet. Wireless Operators Assn., N.Y.C., 1967; Hon. life mem. Royal Yacht Squadron (spl. bronze medal 1967); mem. Royal Geog. Soc. (v.p. 1970). Author of: Navigation Notes for Instructor and Students, 1941-43; Solo to Sydney, 1930; Seaplane Solo, 1932; Ride on the Wind, 1937; The Spotters Handbook, 1940; Astro Navigation, 1940; Pinpoint the Bombers, 1941; Star Recognition, 1941; The Star Compass; The Sun Compass; Alone Across the Atlantic, 1962; Atlantic Adventure; The Lonely Sea and the Sky, 1964, Along the Clipperway; The Romantic Challange; Gipsy Moth Circles the World, 1967; How to Keep Fit, 1969. Clubs: Royal Aero; Royal Air Force Yacht; Yacht (hon., spl. centenary award) (France); Royal Ocean Racing; Ocean Cruising; Royal Cruising (medal for seamanship); Royal Western Yacht (Plymouth); Royal London Yacht; Royal Thames Yacht. Address: 9 St James Pl London SW England

CHICHESTER-CLARK, JAMES DAWSON, prime minister No. Ireland; b. Feb. 12, 1923; s. J.L.O. Chichester-Clark and Mrs. C.E. Brackenbury; ed. Eton; m. Moyra Maud Haughton Morris, 1959; 2 daus., 1 stepson. Joined Brit. Army, 1942; wounded, Italy, 1944; aid de camp to gov.-gen. Can., 1947-49; student Staff Coll., 1956; retired as maj., 1960; mem. Parliament for S. Derry, also mem. Parliament No. Ireland, 1960—, asst. whip, 1963, chief whip, 1963-69; minister of agr., 1967-69; leader of House, 1966-69; prime minister, 1969—. Club: Guards. Address: Moyola Park Castledawson County Derry North Ireland •

CHICHIZOLA, CARLOS, Peruvian diplomat; b. Lima, Peru, Mar. 6, 1941; s. Carlos and Susana (Guimet) C.; B.A., Catholic U. Peru, 1959, LL.B. sumun laudum, 1964; postgrad. Diplomatic Acad. Peru, 1963-64; m. Gladys Montes, Apr. 10, 1965; 1 son, Carlos A.M. 3d sec. Peruvian Fgn. Service, 1965; vice consul of Peru in Mexico, 1965; 3d sec. Peruvian embassy in Mexico, 1965-68, 2d sec., 1968-70; 2d sec. Peruvian embassy in U.S., Washington, 1970-71, 1st sec., 1971—. Pres. Law Federate Center Catholic U. Peru, 1964. Decorated comendador El Aguila Azteca, 1970. Research work on right of asylum; investigation studies on Peruvian lit. Home: 5500 Prospect Pl Chevy Chase MD 20015 Office: Embassy of Peru 1320 16th St NW Washington DC 20036

CHICK, ROBERT WILLIAM, univ. dean; b. Rich Hill, Mo., Apr. 5, 1918; s. Charles H. and Edna (Williams) C.; B.S., U. Mo., 1946, M.Ed., 1950; Ed.D., U. Denver, 1960; m. Ramon D. Day, Sept. 24, 1949. Dean students Ore. State U., Corvallis, 1962—. Served as pilot USAAF, World War II; lt. col. Res. Mem. Am. (exec. council), N.W. (pres. 1966-67) coll. personnel assns., Coll. Student Personnel Inst. (pres. elect 1968), Am. Personnel Guidance Assn., Omicron Delta Kappa, QEBH, Phi Delta Kappa, Phi Kappa Phi, Blue Key. Home: 3340 Firwood Way Corvallis OR 97330

CHICKERING, ALLEN LAWRENCE, Jr., lawyer; b. Oakland, Cal., Apr. 20, 1907; s. Allen L. and Alma (Sherman) C.; A.B., U. Cal., 1929; student Harvard, 1929-30; LL.B., Hastings Coll. Law, 1933; m. Caroline C. Rogers, May 23, 1931; children—Caroline (Mrs. George A. Fish), Joan (Mrs. Richard C. Volberg), Howard Allen. Admitted to Cal. bar, 1934, since practiced in San Francisco, mem. Chickering & Gregory; chmn., dir. Am. Cement Corp.; dir. Hawaiian Cement Corp., Leslie Salt Co., Dillingham Corp.; Ransome Co. Bd. govs. U.S.O., bd. dirs. Nat. Travelers Aid Assn. Mem. Am., Cal. State, San Francisco bar assns., Delta Kappa Epsilon. Republican. Clubs: Bankers, California, Pacific Union. Home: 300 Family Farm Dr Woodside CA 94062 Office: 111 Sutter St San Francisco CA 94104

CHIDLAW, BENJAMIN W., ret. air force officer; b. Cleve., Dec. 18, 1900; s. William Matson and Margaret May Chidlaw; B.S., U.S. Mil. Acad., 1922; grad. Air Corps Flying Sch., 1924, Air Corps Engring. Sch., 1931, Air Corps Tactical Sch., 1936, Command and Gen. Staff Sch., 1937; rated pursuit pilot, command pilot, sr. combat observer (11000 flying hours); m. Lillian Marie Braun, May 1, 1923; 1 son, Ben Evan. Commd. 2d lt. Air Service, 1922, advanced through grades to gen., 1951; served in Philippine Islands, 1924-26; flying instr. and check pilot, Air Corps Tng. Center, San Antonio, 1927-30; aircraft design and aero. engring., Wright Field, 1931-35; with 2d Bombardment Group, Langley Field, Va., 1937-39; tour G.H.Q., Air Forces Staff, 1939; chief of Materiel Div., Air Staff, Hdqrs. Army Air Forces, 1942; dep. comdg. gen. Mediterranean Theatre, 1944, for operations of Air Materiel Command, Wright-Patterson AFB, 1945-49, comdg. gen., 1949-51; comdr. Air Def. Command, Ent AFB, Colo., 1951 comdr.-in-chief Continental Air Def. Command, 1954-55; ret. as gen., 1955. Decorated D.S.M., Legion of Merit, Air medal, Bronze Star. Mem. Quiet Birdmen. Clubs: Cheyenne, Garden of the Gods, Cooking (Colorado Springs). Home: 1 Upland Rd Broadmoor Colorado Springs CO 80906

CHIEN, JAMES C.W., educator; b. Shanghai, China, Nov. 4, 1929; s. Chu Tsu and Tsen Ming (Poo) C.; B.S., St. John's U., 1949; B.A., Wayland Coll., 1950; M.S., U. Ky., 1951; Ph.D., U. Wis., 1954; m. Stella Lee, Aug. 8, 1953; children—Lisa Christine, Mark L., Nadine Carol. Came to U.S., 1949, naturalized, 1960. Research asso. U. Wis., 1954-55; research chemist Hercules Inc., 1955-60, sr. research chemist, 1960-69, now cons.; prof. chemistry, prof. polymer sci. and engring. U. Mass., 1969—. Mem. Am. Chem. Soc., N.Y. Acad. Scis., Sigma Xi, Phi Lambda Upsilon. Home: 15 Coach Lane Amherst MA 01002

CHIERI, PERICLE ADRIANO CARLO, educator, mech. and aero. engr. naval architect; b. Mokanshan, Chekiang, China, Sept. 6, 1905; s. Virginio and Luisa (Fabbri) C.; D.Engring., U. Genoa, Italy, 1927; M.E., U. Naples, Italy, 1927; Dr. Aero. Engring., U. Rome, 1928; m. Helen Etheredge, Aug. 1, 1938. Came to U.S., 1938, naturalized, 1952. Naval architect, mech. engr. research and exptl. divs., submarines and internal combustion engines Italian Navy, Spezia, 1929-31; naval architect, marine supt. Navigazione Libera Triestina Shipping Corp., Libera Lines, Trieste, Italy, 1931-32. Genova, Italy, 1933-35; aero. engr., tech. adviser Chinese Govt. commn. aero. affairs, Nat. Govt. Republic of China, 1935-37; engring. exec., dir. aircraft materials test lab., supt. factory's tech. vocational instrn. SINAW Nat. Aircraft Works, Nanchang, Kiangsi, China, 1937-39; aero. engr. FIAT aircraft factory, Turin, Italy, 1939; aero. engr. and tech. sec. Office Air Attache, Italian embassy, Washington, 1939-41; prof. aero. engring. Tri-State Coll., Angola, Ind., 1942; aero. engr. helicopter design Aero. Products, Inc., Detroit, 1943-44; sr. aero. engr. ERCO Engring. & Research Corp., Riverdale, Md., 1944-46; asso. prof. mech. engring. U. Toledo, 1946-47; asso. prof. mech. engring., faculty grad. div. Newark Coll. Engring., 1947-52; prof., head dept. mech. engring. U. Southwestern La., Lafayette, 1942—; research engr. adv. devel. sect., aviation gas turbine div. Westinghouse Electric Corp., South Philadelphia, Pa., 1953. Instr. water safety A.R.C. Nat. Aquatic Schs., summers 1958-67. Bd. dirs. Lafayette Parish chpt. A.R.C. Registered profl. engr., Italy, N.J., La., S.C. Asso. fellow Am. Inst. Aeros. and Astronautics; life mem. Royal Instn. Naval Architects London; mem. A.A.A.S., Am. Assn. U. Profs., Am. Soc. Engring. Edn., Am. Soc. M.E., Soc. Automotive Engrs., La., N.Y. acads. scis., Instrument Soc. Am., Soc. Exptl. Stress Analysis, Nat. Soc. Profl. Engrs., Soc. Naval Architects and Marine Engrs., A.A.H.P.E.R., La. Engring. Soc., La. Tchrs. Assn., Commodore Longfellow Soc., Pi Tau Sigma (hon.), Phi Kappa Phi. Home: 142 Oak Crest Dr Lafayette LA 70501

CHIGAS, VESSARIOS GEORGE, electronics co. exec.; b. Athens, Greece, June 8, 1922; s. George V. and Aristea (Rhangos) C.; came to U.S., 1925, naturalized, 1940; B.S. in Elec. Engring., Northeastern U., 1944; m. Filitsa Papathanasiou, Apr. 19, 1960; children—Diana V., Daphne V. With Sylvania Electric Products, Inc., Burlington, Mass., founder Microwave Assos., Inc., Burlington, Mass., 1950, chmn. exec. com.; pres. Microwave Assos. Internat., Inc., 1962—; also dir.; dir. Microwave Assos. Ltd., Luton, Eng. Mem. corp. Northeastern U., Boston, adv. bd. Center Mgmt. Devel., 1965-68, also dir. nat. council; chmn. exec. com., trustee Pierce Coll., Athens, Greece; trustee Belvidere Sch., Chelmsford, Mass.; mem. corp. Goodwill Industries, Boston. Mem. Am. Mgmt. Assn., Beta Kappa Nu (hon.). Rotarian. Home: 62 Bartlett St Chelmsford MA 01824 Office: Microwave Assos Inc Burlington MA 01803

CHIH, CHUNG-YING, physicist, cons.; b. Yuki, Fukien, China, Dec. 11, 1916; s. Lai Sui and Sung- Yee (Lin) C.; B.Sc., Nat. Tsing Hua U., Peking, China, 1937; Ph.D., U. Cal. at Berkeley, 1954; m. Alice Yuen, Aug. 15, 1955. Came to U.S., 1948, naturalized, 1962. Instr. physics Fukien Med. Coll., 1937-40; instr., then asso. prof. Fukien Tchrs. Coll., 1940-44; asso. prof., then prof. physics Nat. Chi-Nan U., 1944-45; prof. physics Kiang-su Coll., 1945-48; physicist Radiation Lab., U. Cal at Berkeley, 1953-54, summer 1956; mem. faculty Middlebury (Vt.) Coll., 1954-68, prof. physics, 1966- 68; sci. cons., Bridgeport, Conn., 1968—. Grantee NSF, 1957-60. Mem. Am. Phys. Soc., Am. Assn. U. Profs., Sigma Xi. Address: PO Box 2556 Noble Station Bridgeport CT 06608

CHILCOTE, LUGEAN LESTER, architect; b. Oklahoma City, Jan. 14, 1929; s. Mark H. and Myrita A.J. (Lugeanbeal) C.; B.Arch., U. Ark., 1951; m. Clara Bernice Dudis, Dec. 18, 1953; children—Martin L., Frederick M., David L., Bradley R. Designer, draftsman Ken Cole, Jr., Architect, 1953-54; architect Swaim & Allen Architects, 1954-58; architect/partner Erhart, Eichenbaum, Rauch & Blass, 1958— (all Little Rock). Judge City Beautiful Commn., 1967-68. Mem. com. Ark. Art Festival, 1968, West Little Rock Y.M.C.A., 1969; mem. Ark. Arts Center 1965—. Served to capt. USAF, 1951-53. Mem. A.I.A. (pres. Ark. chpt., 1967, trustee ednl. endowment fund, 1970—; gen. chmn. gulf states regional conf., 1966, nat. del., 1967), Phi Eta Sigma, Theta Tau. Mem. Christian Ch. Club: Pleasant Valley Country (Little Rock). Prin. works include First Christian Ch., 1962, Continental bldg., 1969, Main Toll and Dial bldg. Southwestern Bell Tel. Co., 1968, Bapt. Med. Center, 1971 (all Little Rock); U.S. Post Office and Courthouse, Pine Bluff, Ark., 1967. Home: 7620 Harmon Dr Little Rock AR 72207 Office: Erhart Eichenbaum Rauch & Blass Continental Bldg Little Rock AR 72201

CHILCOTE, SANFORD MARSHALL, lawyer; b. Nanty-Glo, Pa., May 3, 1905; s. Philip John and Annie (Peters) C.; A.B., Allegheny Coll., 1928; LL.B., U. Pitts., 1931; m. Mildred Vaughn Gilmore, Sept. 2, 1933; 1 son Sanford Marshall. Admitted to Pa. bar, 1934, since practiced in Pitts.; sr. partner firm Dickie, McCamey & Chilcote, 1944—. Adv. dir. Pitts. Nat. Bank. Mem. Civil Service Commn., Oakmont, Pa., 1940-44. Bd. dirs. George Washington Masonic Nat. Meml., Washington, 1962—. Fellow Am. Coll. Trial Lawyers, Internat. Acad. Trial Lawyers; mem. Internat. Assn. Ins. Counsel, Fedn. Ins. Counsel, Am., Pa., Allegheny bar assns., Delta Tau Delta, Delta Theta Phi. Methodist. Mason (33). Clubs: Duquesne, Pittsburgh Athletic Assn., (Pitts.); Oakmont Country; Seaview Country (Absecon, N.J.); Country of Florida, Village of Golf (Delray Beach, Fla.). Home: 1190 Hulton Rd Oakmont PA 15139 Office: Grant Bldg Pittsburgh PA 15219

CHILD, ARTHUR HENRY, educator; b. Deming, N.M., Apr. 21, 1913; s. Arthur Henry and Martina Avila (Long) C.; A.B., U. Cal. at Los Angeles, 1934, M.A., 1935, Ph.D., Berkeley, 1939; m. Mary Fullerson, June 21, 1941. Research asso. philosophy U. Chgo., 1946-47, instr. philosophy, 1947-49, asst. prof., 1949-52; asso. prof. philosophy U. Cal. at Davis, 1952-58, prof., 1958—, chmn. dept. philosophy and fine arts, 1952-58, dept. philosophy, 1958- 63, Guggenheim fellow, 1958-59. Mem. Am. Philos. Assn., Am. Soc. Aesthetics, Internat. Phenomenological Soc. Author: Interpretation, a General Theory, 1965. Contbr. articles profl. jours. Home: 647 Miller Dr Davis CA 95616

CHILD, ARTHUR JAMES EDWARD, food co. exec.; b. Guildford, Eng., May 19, 1910; s. William Arthur and Helena (Wilson) C.; B.Commerce, Queen's U., 1931; grad. Advanced Mgmt. Program, Harvard, 1956; M.A., U. Toronto, 1960; m. Mary Gordon, Dec. 10, 1955; chief auditor Can. Packers Ltd., 1938-52, v.p., 1952-60; pres. Intercontinental Packers Ltd., 1960-66; pres., chief exec. officer Burns Foods Ltd., Calgary, Alta., 1966—; v.p., dir. Continental Discount Corp., LaVerendrye Industries. Ltd.; chmn., dir. Palm Dairies Ltd., Scott Nat. Co., Ltd.; pres., dir. Rivercrest Ranches Ltd.; dir. Allendale Ins. Co., Siebens Oil & Gas Ltd., Pool Packers Ltd.; Canadian Dressed Meats Ltd., Western Canadian Seed Processors Ltd., Dominion Bridge Co. Ltd.; asso. prof. U. Sask., 1964-65. Fellow Chartered Inst. Secs.; mem. Meat Packers Council Can. (pres.), Inst. Internal Auditors (past pres.), Am. Mgmt. Assn., Inst. for Strategic Studies. Author: Economics and Politics in United States Banking, 1965; (with B. Cadmus) Internal Control, 1953. Home: 1320 Baldwin SW Calgary Alberta Canada Office: PO Box 1300 Calgary Alberta Canada

CHILD, CHARLES G., 3d, surgeon; b. N.Y.C., Feb. 1, 1908; s. Charles G. and Helen (Francis) C.; grad. Philips Exeter Acad., 1926; A.B., Yale, 1930; M.D., Cornell U., 1934; m. Margaret MacC. Austin, June 14, 1941; children—Caroline W., Margaret F., Helen D., Cleland G., Charles A., Elizabeth M. Intern, asst. resident and resident surgeon N.Y. Hosp., 1934-42; instr., asst. clin. prof. surgery, asso. clin. prof. surgery Cornell Med. Coll., 1942-52; surgeon-in-chief New Eng. Center Hosp., Boston, 1952-54; prof. surgery, chmn. dept. Tufts U. Med. Sch., 1952-58; dir. first surg. service Boston City Hosp., 1954-58; prof. surgery chmn. dept. U. Mich. Med. Sch., Ann Arbor, 1959—; dir. surgery Wayne County Gen. Hosp., Eloise, Mich., 1966-68, now cons.; cons. VA Hosp., Ann Arbor, 1961—. Mem. transplant com. United Health Found., 1968—. Served as lt. M.C., USNR, 1944-46. Fellow A.C.S. (grad. edn. com. at-large 1968—); mem. Am. Surg. Soc. (ad hoc com. on grad. edn. 1969—), Soc. U. Surgeons, Soc. Clin. Surgery (chmn. com. on admissions 1968), Nat. Acad. Scis. (bd. medicine 1967—). Author articles profl. jours. Editor: Jour. Surg. Research, 1960-66. Home: 3202 N Maple Rd Ann Arbor MI Office: U Mich Med Center Ann Arbor MI 48104

CHILD, FRANK CLAYTON, educator, economist; b. Salt Lake City, Aug. 21, 1921; s. Charles William and Alveretta Gertrude (Clayton) C.; B.A., U. Utah, 1941; M.A., Stanford, 1947, Ph.D., 1954; m. Eva Lorraine Clough, Sept. 22, 1948; children—Charles William, Matthew Daniel, Tracy, Suzanne. Instr. econs. Stanford, 1950, Williams Coll., 1950-52; asst. prof. Pomona Coll., 1952- 56; asst. prof., asso. prof. econs. Mich. State U., 1956-59, adviser Mich. State U. Adv. Group Saigon, Viet Nam, 1959-61; vis. asso. prof. econs. Stanford, 1961-62; from asso. prof. to prof. U. Cal. at Davis, 1962—, chmn. dept., 1963—; on leave as economist Pakistani Inst. Devel., Karachi; econs. cons., Sabah, Malaysia, 1965, Pakistan, 1966; sr. economist, mission to Vietnam, Devel. and Resources Corp., 1967; research adviser Yale-Pakistan project, Karachi, 1967-69. Served from 2d lt. to capt., AUS, 1942-46. Decorated Bronze Star; Croix de Guerre (France). Mem. Am. Econ. Assn. Author: Theory and Practice of German Exchange Control, 1958; Toward a Policy for Economic Growth (in Viet Nam), 1963. Contbr. articles profl. jours. Home: 1014 Vassar Dr Davis CA 95616

CHILD, IRVIN LONG, psychologist, educator; b. Deming, N.M., Mar. 11, 1915; s. Arthur Henry and Martina Avila (Long) C.; B.A., U. Cal. at Los Angeles, 1935; Ph.D., Yale, 1939; m. Alice Dukes Blyth, Mar. 29, 1941; children—Richard Blyth, Pamela Colman. Instr. psychology Harvard U. and Radcliffe Coll., 1939-41; with Yale, 1941—, successively Latin-Am. research fellow, asst. prof., asso. prof., prof. psychology, 1954—. Mem. Am., Eastern psychol. assns., Conn. State Psychol. Soc., Am. Soc. for Aesthetics, Internat. Assn. for Empirical Aesthetics, Assn. for Humanistic Psychology, Phi Beta Kappa, Sigma Xi. Author: Italian or American? The Second Generation in Conflict, 1943; Child Training and Personality: A Cross-Cultural Study (with J. W. M. Whiting), 1953. Home: 2 Cooper Rd North Haven CT 06473 Office: 333 Cedar St New Haven CT 06510

CHILD, JULIA MCWILLIAMS, (Mrs. Paul Child), TV performer; b. Pasadena, Cal., Aug. 15, 1912; d. John and Julia Carolyn (Weston) McWilliams; B.A., Smith Coll., 1934; m. Paul Child, Sept. 1, 1945. With advt. dept. W. & J. Sloane, N.Y.C., 1939-40; with OSS, Washington, also Ceylon, China, 1941-45; condr. TV program The French Chef, WGBH-TV, Boston, 1962—. Recipient Peabody award, 1964, Emmy award, 1966. Author: (with Simone Beck and Louisette Bertholle) Mastering the Art of French Cooking, 1961; The French Chef Cookbook, 1968; (with Simone Beck) Mastering the Art of French Cooking, Vol. II, 1970. Office: WGBH 125 Western Av Boston MA 02134

CHILDERS, KENAN CLARK, Jr., naval officer; b. Clovis, N.M., Mar. 27, 1917; s. Kenan Clark and Katie (Hamilton) C.; B.S., U.S. Naval Acad., 1939; M.S. in Aero. Engring., Cal. Inst. Tech., 1946; student Naval Postgrad. Sch., 1945; m. Elizabeth Woodard Dodson, Jan. 27, 1943; children—Kenan Clark III, Virginia (Mrs. James Muldoon), Susan E. Commd. ensign U.S. Navy, 1939, advanced through grades to rear adm., 1967; asst. dir. ship installation div. Bur. Aero., 1950-53; missile test officer Naval Missile Center, Point Mugu, Cal., 1953-55; Polaris project head field officer, Patrick AFB, Fla., 1956-61; comdr. Naval Missile Center, Point Mugu, 1961-64; dep. project mgr. F- 111B/Phoenix, Dept. Navy, 1965-67; asst. comdr. material acquisition Naval Air Systems Command, 1967-69. Decorated Silver Star, Legion of Merit, Navy Air medal with gold star, Commendation medal. Mem. Am. Ordnance Assn., Am. Inst. Aero. and Astronautics. Home: Quarters SP 24 Naval Air Sta Norfolk VA 23511 Office: Naval Air Sta Norfolk VA 23511

CHILDERS, NORMAN FRANKLIN, educator; b. Moscow, Ida., Oct. 29, 1910; s. Lucius Franklin and Frances M. (Norman) C.; B.S. in Horticulture, U. Mo., 1933, M.S. in Horticulture (Gregory scholar 1933-34), 1934; Ph.D. in Pomology, Cornell U., 1937; m. Virginia Leming, June 23, 1967; 1 child, 4 children by previous marriage. Grad. asst. pomology. Cornell U., 1934-37; asst. prof. horticulture, asst. research specialist Ohio State U. and Ohio Agr. Expt. Sta., 1937-39; asso. in research Ohio Agr. Expt. Sta., 1939-44; asst. dir., sr. plant physiologist fed. expt. sta., U.S. Dept. Agr., Mayaguez, P.R., 1944-47; prof. horticulture, research specialist Rutgers U., New Brunswick, N.J., 1948—, chmn. dept., 1948-66, Maurice A. Blake distinguished pro., 1966—. Councilman, Milltown, N.J. 1953-56. Fellow Am. Soc. Hort. Sci. (L.M. Ware Distinguished Teaching award in hort. 1969); mem. N.J. State Hort. Soc. (pres. 1971), Publisher, co-author six horticulture books. Home: Cranbury Gardens 363 Cranbury Rd East Brunswick NJ 08816 Office: Rutgers U Nichol Av New Brunswick NJ 08903

CHILDRES, ROBERT, educator; b. Williamsville, Miss., Aug. 15, 1934; s. William F. and Ela Fay (Hanna) C.; B.A., U. Miss., 1957, LL.B., 1960; B.C.L., Oxford U., 1960; m. Clare Fraser Fooshee, May 28, 1963; children—Christopher Fooshee, Nathaniel Ashley. Admitted to Miss. bar, 1960, N.Y. bar, 1960; lawyer Dewey, Ballantine, Bushby, Palmer & Wood, N.Y.C., 1960-62; asst. prof., asso. prof. law N.Y.U. Sch. of Law, N.Y.C., 1962-67; vis. asso. prof. law Northwestern U. Sch. of Law, Chgo., 1967-68, prof., 1968—. Rhodes scholar, 1958-60. Mem. Assn. Am. Rhodes Scholars, Chgo. Council Lawyers, Miss., N.Y. bar assns., Am. Civil Liberties Union. Democrat. Author: Equity, Restitution and Damages, 1969. Contbr. articles profl. jours. Home: 2805 Girard Av Evanston IL 60201 Office: 357 E Chicago Av Chicago IL 60611

CHILDRESS, ALICE, writer, actress, dir.; m. Nathan Woodard; 1 dau., Jean Lee. Author: Gold Through the Trees; Trouble in Mind (Obie award 1956); Like One of the Family. Home: 800 Riverside Dr New York City NY 10032 Office: care Flora Roberts Inc 130 E 59th St New York City NY 10022

CHILDRESS, FRANCIS BROWN, investment banker; b. Valdosta, Ga., July 18, 1897; s. Parks Monroe and Judson (Jones) C.; student pub. schs.; m. Miranda Watson Yerkes, Nov. 30, 1926; 1 dau., Frances Ann (Mrs. Lewis S. Lee). Various positions Citizens Bank, Valdosta, Ga., Fed. Res. Bank of Atlanta, Treasury Dept. 6th Fed. Res. Dist., Atlanta, 1914-17; with Atlantic Nat. Bank, Jacksonville, Fla., 1919-32, v.p., 1925-32, pres. investment affiliate Atlantic Nat. Co., 1928-32; propr. Childress & Co., investment banking, Jacksonville, 1932—. Chmn. finance and financial adv. subcom. Jacksonville Com. of One Hundred, 1952-61; pres. Francis and Miranda Childress Found. Bd. dirs., mem. exec. com. St. Luke's Hosp., 1961—; bd. dirs. Jacksonville area Community Chest-United Fund; bd. dirs. Children's Home Soc. of Fla., 1930—, v.p., 1939-63. Served with USNRF, World War I. Mem. Investment Bankers Assn. Am. Episcopalian. Clubs: Seminole (pres. 1946-47), Timuquana Country, Florida Yacht, River, Ponte Vedra, Friars, Ye Mistic Revelers (Jacksonville, Fla.); University. Home: 3775 Ortega Blvd Jacksonville, FL 32210. Office: Fla Bank Bldg Jacksonville FL 32201

CHILDRESS, JACK RAYMOND, univ. dean; b. East St. Louis, Ill., Jan. 13, 1918; s. Thurman Ray and Ada Elizabeth (Pinkstaff) C.; B.Ed., Ill. State Normal U., 1941; M.S., U. Illinois, 1945; Ph.D., Northwestern U., 1950; m. Virginia Ruth Dunmire, June 21, 1942; children—Vickie Lynn, Mary Sue. High sch. tchr. in Ill., 1941-47; mem. faculty Northwestern U., 1947-62, prof. edn., 1958-62, dir. Univ. Coll., 1951-54, asst. dean Sch. Edn., 1954-62; dean Sch.Edn., Boston U., 1962—. Chmn. Nat. Conf. Professors Ednl. Adminstrn., 1958; v.p. Adult Edn. Council Greater Chgo., 1952-54; cons. bd. dir. Ill. Assn. Sch. Adminstrs., 1957-62; mem. Ill. Commn. Advancement Sch. Adminstrn., 1960-62; research program cons. Supts. Round Table No. Ill., 1960; conductor annual salary study Supts. Study Club No. Ill., 1954-62; bd. dirs. New Eng. Commn. Advancement Sch. Adminstrn., 1962—, pres., 1966—; chmn. advisory com. Boston Public Schs., 1966—; chmn. task force Mass. State Bd. Edn. Study on Racial Imbalance in Pub. Schs. of Massachusetts, 1964-65. Pres. bd. Morton Grove (Ill.) Pub. Library 1958- 59. Bd. dirs. Center for Study Liberal Edn. for Adults, 1967—; trustee Edn. Associates, 1965-66. Mem. N.E.A., Am. Assn. Sch. Adminstrs., Lambda Chi Alpha, Phi Delta Kappa, Kappa Delta Pi. Presbyn. (past elder, clk. of session, pres. trustees). Mason. Co-editor: Education in an Era of Transition, 1949; Opportunities for Education in the Next Decade, 1951. Home: 88 Edgewater Dr Needham MA 02192 Office: 765 Commonwealth Av Boston MA 02215

CHILDRESS, RICHARD JEFFERSON, educator; b. Erlanger, Ky., Jan. 31, 1922; s. Henry F. and Kathleen (Foley) C.; B.S., St. Louis U., 1947, postgrad., 1949, 1951; J.D., U. Cin., 1949; student Washington U. Sch. Law., 1948, Harvard Law Sch., 1959-60; m. Marianne Miller, June 2, 1947; children—Richard Jefferson II, Mary Kathleen. Admitted to Mo. bar, 1958; news reporter Cin. Times- Star, 1942; lectr. philosophy St. Louis U., 1946-47, instr. law, 1949- 50, asst. prof. law, 1950-56, asso. prof., 1956-59, prof., 1959—, asso. dean, 1962-69, dean, 1969—; pres. Conf. Jesuit Law Schs., 1954. Spl. asst. circuit atty. City St. Louis, 1958; vice-chmn. St. Louis County Traffic Commn., 1957-61; mem. Civil Def. adv. com., St. Louis, 1963-65, mem. Commn. Human Rights Archdiocese St. Louis, 1964—, chmn., 1967-69; bd. dirs., exec. com. Urban League St. Louis, 1968—; dir. Inter-religious Center Urban Affairs, 1968-70; mem. St. Louis Conf. Religion and Race, 1963-67, chmn., 1965-66; mem. St. Louis Council on Human Relations. Bd. dirs. Soc. Helpers of the Holy Souls, 1955-59, Nursery Found. of St. Louis, 1971—. Served with USAAF, 1943-46. Decorated Bronze Star. Mem. Am., St. Louis County bar assns., Bar Assn. St. Louis, St. Louis Lawyers Assn., Mo. Bar (com. individual liberties, com. criminal law, com. legal edn.), AFTRA. Democrat. Roman Catholic. Home: 4711 Prague Av St Louis MO 63109 Office: St Louis U Sch Law St Louis MO 63108

CHILDS, ALAN DOUGLAS, paint co. exec.; b. Phila., Mar. 16, 1930; s. Geoffrey S. and Olivia (Waelchli) C.; B.A., Mich. State U., 1952; J.D., John Marshall Law Sch., Chgo., 1963; m. Lucy Lindsay, June 21, 1954; children—Janna, Martha, Carolyn, Stephen. Admitted to Ill. bar, 1963, Ohio bar, 1965; asst. dir. indsl. relations Sherwin-Williams Co., Cleve., 1964-66, asst. gen. counsel, 1966-67, gen. counsel, sec., 1967—. Mem. Rocky River Sch. Bd., 1970—. Served with USNR, 1952-54. Mem. Am., Ill., Ohio, Cleve. bar assns., Am. Soc. Corporate Secs., U.S. Trademark Assn. Republican. Club: Cleveland Athletic. Home: 19680 Beach Cliff Blvd Rocky River OH 44116 Office: 101 Prospect Av N W Cleveland OH 44115

CHILDS, BARTON, educator, physician; b. Chgo., Feb. 29, 1916; s. Robert William and Katherine Sayles (Barton) C.; A.B., Williams Coll., 1938; M.D., Johns Hopkins, 1942; m. Eloise L. B. MacKie, Mar. 29, 1950; children—Anne Lloyd, Lucy Barton. Successively intern, asst. resident, resident pediatrics Johns Hopkins Hosp., 1942-43, 46-48; research fellow Children's Hosp., Boston, 1948-49; Commonwealth Fund fellow Univ. Coll., London, Eng., 1952-53; mem. faculty Johns Hopkins Sch. Medicine, 1949—, prof. pediatrics, 1962—. Mem. NIH Cons. Coms., 1959-63, 63-67, 67-69, 69—; research adv. com. United Cerebral Palsy Found., 1960-63. Served to capt., M.C., AUS, 1943-46. John and Mary Markle scholar, 1953-58; Grover F. Powers Distinguished scholar, 1960-62; recipient Research Career award NIH, 1962, Meade Johnson award pediatrics, 1959. Mem. Am. Pediatric Soc., Soc. Pediatric Research, Am. Acad. Pediatrics, Am. Soc. Human Genetics, Genetics Soc. Am. Home: 1019 Winding Way Baltimore MD 21210

CHILDS, BREVARD SPRINGS, educator; b. Columbia, S.C., Sept. 2, 1923; s. Richard A. and Reaux (Jones) C.; B.A., U. Mich., 1946, M.A., 1948; B.D., Princeton, 1950; D.Theol., U. Basel (Switzerland), 1955; m. Ann Taylor, Aug. 7, 1954; children—John, Catherine. Ordained to ministry Presbyn. Ch., 1958; prof. O.T., Mission House Sem., Plymouth, Wis., 1954-58, Yale, New Haven, 1958—. Served with AUS, 1943-45. Guggenheim fellow, 1963-64. Author: Myth and Reality in the Old Testament, 1960; Memory and Tradition in Israel, 1962; Isaiah and the Assyrian Crisis, 1967; Biblical Theology in Crisis, 1970. Home: Amity Rd Bethany CT 06525 Office: 409 Prospect St New Haven CT 06511

CHILDS, HARWOOD LAWRENCE, educator; b. Gray, Me., May 1, 1898; s. Herman Andrew and Eudora (Whittemore) C.; A.B., Dartmouth, 1919; M.A., 1921; Ph.D., U. Chgo., 1928; m. Willa Patricia Whitson, June 28, 1922; children—Elizabeth Ann (Mrs. Arthur Edward Rowse), Margaret Frances (Mrs. Richard Stoll Armstrong), Martha (Mrs. Lyman Edwin Sproul, Jr.). Instr. pub. speaking, Dartmouth Coll., 1919-20, instr. econs., 1920-21; asst. prof. econs. Syracuse U., 1922-24; asso. prof. govt., Coll. of William and Mary, 1925-27; prof. govt. and head dept. polit. sci. Bucknell U., 1928-31; asso. prof. politics Princeton, 1932-46, prof. 1946—; on leave as regional specialist, Overseas Br., O.W.I., Washington, 1943-45; lectr. Sch. Pub. Adminstrn., Rio de Janeiro, 1953-54; vis. lectr. on Haynes Found., U. So. Cal., spring 1957. Research asst. Nat. Industrial Conf. Bd., N.Y.C., 1924; Social Science Research Council fellow for study in Germany, 1931-32; Guggenheim fellow for study in Germany, 1937; founder, 1st editor Public Opinion Quar., pub. Princeton U., 1937-41, editor, 1964-67. Mem. Enemy Allen Hearing Bd., Dist. of N.J., 1942-43. Alumni trustee, Tilton Sch. Served with U.S. Navy, 1918. Mem. Am. Assn. Univ. Profs., Am. Polit. Sci. Assn., Alpha Chi Rho, Delta Sigma Rho, Phi Beta Kappa. Author: Public Opinion Nature, Formation, Role, 1965. Author, editor, translator various publs.; contbr. articles. Home: 51 Lake Lane Princeton NJ 08550 ☆

CHILDS, HOMER A., wholesale grocery exec.; b. Great Falls, Mont., July 7, 1916; s. Homer A. and Charlotte (Milner) C.; B.S. in Law, U. Minn., 1938, LL.B., 1940; m. Charlotte Vera Hilton, May 9, 1942; children—Douglas M., Elizabeth Mary. Practiced law, 1941; spl. agt. FBI, 1942-45; with Red Owl Stores, Inc., Hopkins, Minn., 1946-52; with Super Valu Stores, Inc., Hopkins, 1952—, now v.p., sec. Home: 4801 Wilford Way Edina MN 55435 Office: 101 Jefferson Av S Hopkins MN 55343

CHILDS, JAMES RIVES, ret. fgn. service officer; b. Lynchburg, Va., Feb. 6, 1893; s. John William and Lucy Howard, (Brown) C.; student Va. Mil. Inst., 1909-11; B.A., Randolph-Macon Coll., 1912, H.H.D. (hon.); M.A., Harvard, 1915; grad. Army War Coll., 1917; m. Georgina de Brylkine, Aug. 13, 1922 (dec. Nov. 1964). Newspaper reporter Balt. Am., 1912; 1st O.T.C., Ft. Myer, Va., 1917; apptd. 2d lt., 318th Inf., a.d.c. comdg. officer, 80th Div., Camp Lee, Va., trans, Mil. intelligence, Gen. Staff, 1917; in charge of decipherment of German ciphers, G.H.Q., A.E.F., France, 1918, serving as liaison officer of Radio Intelligence with French and British War Offices, 1st lt., 1918; with Am. Commn. to Negotiate Peace, Paris, 1918-19, Am. Relief Adminstrn., Yugoslavia, 1919, A.P., Washington, 1919-21, Am. Relief Adminstrn., Russia, 1921-23; entered Am. Consular Service, 1923; consul at Jerusalem and Bucharest; 2d sec. Am. Legation, Cairo, 1930, then at Teheran and again at Cairo; Div. Near Eastern Affairs, 1937-40; charge d'affaires, Am. Legation, Tangier, 1941-45; Am. del. Internat. Conf. on Tangier, Paris, 1945; apptd, E.E. and M.P. to Kingdom Saudi Arabia, also to Kingdom Yemen, 1946; A.E. and P., Saudi Arabia, 1949-50; A.E. and P. to Kingdom Ethiopia, 1951-53; vis. Walter Hines Page scholar Randolph-Macon Coll., 1963, scholar in residence, 1966-71. Conseil d'adminstrn. Inst. Am. Univs., Aix-en-Provence. Mem. Huguenot Soc. Founders of Manakin, Va., 1699, Brit. Pvt. Libraries Assn. (pres. 1965-68), Phi Delta Theta, Sigma Upsilon; hon. Phi Beta Kappa. Author books including: American Foreign Service, 1948; Restif de la Bretonne: Ses Critiques et sa Bibliographie (in French), 1949; Casanoviana, 1956; Giacomo Casanova de Seingalt (in German), 1960; Casanova, A Biography Based on New Documents, 1961; Casanova (in Italian), 1961, Casanova (in French), 1962; Diplomatic and Literary Quests, 1963; Casanova (in Japanese), 1968; Collector's Quest: The Correspondence of Henry Miller and J. Rives Childs, 1947-1965, 1968; Farewell to Foreign Service: Thirty Years in the Near East, 1969. Editor: Casanova Gleanings. Home: Chateau des Beaumettes, Nice, France

CHILDS, JAMES WILLIAM, lawyer; b. Muncie, Ind., Sept. 20, 1935; s. Dexter William and Marcelle (Mericle) C.; student Denison U., 1953-55; A.B., U. Mich., 1957, J.D., 1960; m. Louanne Schafer, Aug. 29, 1959; children-Elizabeth, Anne, James William II. Admitted to Ohio bar, 1960, since practiced in Van Wert; mem. firm Beard and Childs, 1962—. Mem. N.W. Ohio Water Devel. Adv. Council, Ohio Water Commn. Dept. Natural Resources, 1966—. Dir. Springfield Beauty Supply Inc. Mem. Starr Commonwealth Adv. Bd., 1962—; pres., 1970; mem. Van Wert County Hosp. Assn., 1963—; trustee Van Wert County Communities for Progress Com., 1961—. Bd. dirs. Van Wert County Heart Assn., Jr. Achievement Van Wert. Mem. Am., Ohio, Northwestern Ohio, Van Wert County (pres. 1969-71) bar assns., Van Wert, Van Wert Jr. chambers commerce. Republican. Methodist (lay leader 1966-70). Kiwanian (pres. Van Wert 1968), Mason. Home: 1009 Rosemont Dr Van Wert OH 45891 Office: First Fed Savs Bldg Van Wert OH 45891

CHILDS, JOHN FARNSWORTH, banker; b. N.Y.C., Nov. 24, 1909; s. Albert Ewing and Amelia (McGraw) C.; B.S., Trinity Coll., Hartford, Conn., 1931, M.S., 1932; M.B.A., Harvard, 1933; LL.B., Fordham U., 1946; m. Mary Elizabeth Cardozo, Apr. 21, 1950; 1 dau., Susan Elizabeth. Admitted to N.Y. bar, 1946; analyst Dick & Merle-Smith, N.Y.C., 1935-40; sr. v.p., head corporate services div. Irving Trust Co., N.Y.C., 1941—; dir. Fla. Power Corp. Treas., trustee Lenox Sch. Served to lt. comdr. USNR, World War II. Mem. Am. Mgmt. Assn. (bd. dirs.), Atomic-Indsl. Forum (bd. dir.), N.Y. Soc. Security Analysts. Clubs: Harvard Business School (past pres) (N.Y.C.); Nantucket (Mass.) Yacht; Pine Valley Golf (Clementin, N.J.). Author: Navy Gun Crew; Long-Term Financing, 1961; A Practical Introduction to Public Utility Security Analysis; Profit Goals and Capital Management, 1968; Earnings Per Share and Management Decisions, 1971. Contbr. articles profl. publs. Home: 15 Washington Pl New York NY 10003 Office: 1 Wall St New York NY 10015

CHILDS, KENNETH DUANE, savs. and loan exec.; b. Herington, Kan., Apr. 13, 1901; s. Charles Fremont and Olive (Noret) C.; student U. Mo., 1919-20, U. Wash., 1920; B.A., U. Kan., 1923; m. Margaret Atherton Clarken, June 22, 1938; childrenKenneth Duane, Timothy Alan, Stephen Anthony. Mgr. retail yard Bowman Hicks Lumber Co., LeGrande, Ore., 1923-25; real estate broker with Harry H. Kem & Co., Ltd., Beverly Hills, Cal., 1925-42, 46-49; exec. v.p. Home Savs. and Loan Assn., Los Angeles, 1949-56, pres., 1957- 64; pres., chmn. bd., dir. So. Cal. Financial Corp., So., Cal. Savs. & Loan Assn., 1964-69, chmn. bd., dir., 1969—; dir. City Investing Mortgage Group, Motel 6. Served to maj. USAAF, 1942-46. Mem. U.S. Savs. and Loan League (dir.), Kappa Sigma. Republican. Clubs: Los Angeles Country; Beach (Santa Monica, Cal.). Home: Office: 9100 Wilshire Blvd Beverly Hills CA 90212

CHILDS, MARQUIS WILLIAM, journalist; b. Clinton, Ia., Mar. 17, 1903; s. William Henry and Lilian Malissa (Marquis) C.; A.B., U. Wis., 1923, Litt.D., 1966; A.M., U. Ia., 1935, Litt.D., 1969; LL.D., Upsala Coll., 1943; m. Lué Prentiss, August 26th, 1926 (dec.); children—Prentiss, Malissa (Elliott); m. 2d, Jane Neglan McBaine. With U.P.I., 1923, 25-26; with St. Louis Post-Dispatch, 1926-44, spl. corr., 1954-62, chief Washington corr., 1962-68. Columnist, United Feature Syndicate, 1944- 54; made 3 mos. tour battlefronts, 1943; lectr. Columbia Sch. Journalism; Eric W. Allen Meml. lectr. U. Ore., 1950. Decorated Order of North Star (Sweden); recipient Sigma Delta Chi award for best Washington corr., 1944; award for journalism U. Mo. Mem. Kappa Sigma, Sigma Delta Chi; Pulitzer prize for commentary (1st), 1969. Clubs: Overseas Writers (pres. 1943-45); Century (N.Y.C.); Washington Press, Gridiron (pres. 1957), Metropolitan, Cosmos (Washington). Author: SwedenThe Middle Way, 1936; They Hate Roosevelt, 1936; Washington Calling, 1937; This Is Democracy, 1938; This Is Your War, 1942; I Write From Washington, 1942; The Cabin, 1944. Editor, writer evaluation new edit. Brooks Adams' America's Economic Supremacy, 1947; The Farmer Takes a Hand, 1952; Ethics in Business Society (with Douglass Cater), 1954; The Ragged Edge, 1955; Eisenhower, Captive Hero, 1958; The Peacemakers, 1961; A Taint of Innocence, 1967. Co-editor: Walter Lippmann and His Times, 1959. Home: 2703 Dumbarton Av NW Washington DC 20007 Office: 1701 Pennsylvania Av NW Washington DC 20036

CHILDS, ORLO ECKERSLEY, educator, petroleum geologist; b. Loa, Utah, Mar. 28, 1914; s. DeVere and Alice (Eckersley) C.; student Weber Coll., 1931-33; B.S., U. Utah, 1935, M.S., 1937; Ph.D., U. Mich., 1945; m. Elizabeth Catharine Swisher, Oct. 31, 1945; children—Bradley, Barry, Elizabeth. Instr., Weber Coll., 1937-42; geologist Sinclair Wyo. Oil Co., 1945-46; asst. prof. Colgate U., 1946-48, U. Wyo., 1948-49; dir. exploration project Phillips Petroleum Co., Denver, 1949-62; marine geologist U.S. Geol. Survey, 1962-63; pres. Colo. Sch. Mines, Golden, 1963-70; v.p. research and spl. programs Tex. Technol. U., Lubbock, 1970—. Mem. regional bd. White House Fellows; mem. Colo. Fulbright Com. Mem. Geol. Soc. Am., Am. Inst. M.E., Intermountain Assn. Petroleum Geologists, Am. Assn. Petroleum Geologists (past pres.), Am. Inst. Profl. Geologists, Rocky Mountain Assn., Geologists, Sigma Xi. Author articles in field. Editor: Backbone of America, 1961. Home: 4617 10th St Lubbock TX 79416

CHILDS, RICHARD SPENCER, orgn. exec., publicist; b. Manchester, Conn., May 24, 1882; s. William Hamlin and Nellie (Spencer) C.; grad. Poly. Preparatory School, Bklyn., 1900; B.A., Yale, 1904; m. Grace P. Hatch, June 15, 1912 (dec. 1961); children—Virginia, Mary, Nancy Jane (dec.). With The Erickson Co., N.Y., 1904-18; gen. mgr. Bon Ami Co., 1911-20; dept. mgr. A. E. Chew Co., 1921-28, asst. to pres., 1928-47; dir. Am. Cyanamid Co.; executive v.p. Lederle Laboratories, Inc., 1935-44; chmn. Nat. Municipal League, 1947—. Served as asst. U.S. War Dept., 1918. Mem. Nat. Municipal League (past pres.), Am. Proportional Representation League (past pres.), Citizens Union, (chmn. 1943-40), Inst. Pub. Adminstrn. (chmn. 1948-60), Am. Museum Health (pres. 1947-48), Phi Gamma Delta. Republican. Presbyn. Club: City (pres. 1928-40). Author: Short Ballot Principles, 1911; Civic Victories, 1953; First 50 Years of the Council, Manager Plan, 1965. Initiator city manager plan and short ballot movement. La Guardia Meml. Assn. award, 1954; Am. Judicature Soc. Jubilee award, 1964. Home: 166 Columbia Heights Brooklyn NY 11201 Office: 47 E 68th St New York City NY 10021

CHILDS, THOMAS WARREN, business exec.; b. Butler, Mo., Nov. 21, 1906; s. Edward Bruglar and Gertrude (Clay) C.; B.S. in Engring. summa cum laude, Princeton, 1928; Rhodes Scholar, Oxford, 1928-31, B.A., 1930, B.C.L. and M.A., 1938; J.S.D., Yale, 1932; m. Isabel Lockward, Jan. 30, 1934; children—Thomas Warren, Henry Clay, William Arthur Purvis. Admitted to N.Y. State bar, 1932, practiced with Sullivan & Cromwell, N.Y.C. 1932-40, Paris, 1937-38; gen. counsel to Brit. Supply Council in N.A. and exec. asst. to minister resident in U.S., Washington, 1940-45; asso. Lazard Freres, N.Y.C., 1943-48; with Am. Metal Climax, Inc., N.Y.C., 1948-62, v.p., 1953-62, dir., 1961-62; chmn. Internat. Nickel Ltd. (formerly Internat. Nickel Co. (Mond) Ltd.), London, Eng., 1963-68; v.p. Internat Nickel Co. of Can., Ltd., 1963-68; pres. Internat. Nickel Projects Ltd., 1969—. Served as gen. counsel for Brit. Govt. War Supply Orgn. in U.S. and mem. Anglo-Am. Patent Com., 1940-45. Decorated comdr. Order Brit. Empire. Mem. Phi Beta Kappa. Republican. Episcopalian. Clubs: Royal Bermuda Yacht; Pilgrims; St. James (London, Eng.). Home: Stancombe Paget Bermuda Office: PO Box 1560 BETCO Bldg Hamilton Bermuda

CHILDS, WYLIE JONES, corp. exec; b. Columbia, S.C., Feb. 25, 1922; s. Richard Austin and Reaux (Jones) C.; B.Metall. Engring., Rensselaer Poly. Inst., 1943, M.Metall. Engring., 1945, Ph.D., 1948; m. Nancy D. Sadler, Apr. 1, 1950; 1 dau., Rebecca Jones. Research metallurgist Mass. Inst. Tech., 1948-49; asso. prof., then prof., head dept. metall. engring. Lafayette Coll., 1949-57; mem. faculty Rensselaer Poly. Inst., 1957-70, prof. metall. engring., 1960-70; cons. to industry, 1948—; tech. rep. Duffers Assos., Inc., Troy, 1962-70; v.p. Reel Vortex, Inc., Troy, N.Y., 1968—, Air Cushion Vehicles, Inc., Troy, 1969—. NSF fellow U. Birmingham (Eng.), 1959. Mem. Am. Inst. Mining and Metall. Engrs., Am. Soc. Metals, Am. Foundrymen's Soc., British Inst. Metals, Iron and Steel Inst., Sigma Xi, Tau Beta Pi, Phi Lambda Upsilon. Home: 1381 Regent St Schnenectady, NY 12309. Office: Air Cushion Vehicles Inc Troy NY 12180

CHILES, EARLE ALTON, retail chain store exec.; b. Baker City, Ore., Sept. 9, 1904; s. Ira and Eva (Charfield) C.; B.S., U. Ore., 1927; M.B.A., Harvard, 1931; m. Virginia Hughes, July 7, 1931; 1 son, Earle Meyer. With Fred Meyer, Inc., Portland, Ore., 1931-70, sales clk., cashier, merchandiser of delicatessen, grocery and drug-variety operations, 1931- 52, gen. mgr., 1952-70, pres., 1954-70, also dir. Mem. Nat., Western (pres. 1959-60) assns. food chains. Republican. Clubs: Harvard of Ore., University, Arlington, Multnomah Athletic, Aeronautic. Home: 2424 SW Arden Rd Portland OR 97201 Office: 721 SW 4th Av Portland OR 97204

CHILES, HARRELL EDMOND, petroleum engr.; b. Itasca, Tex., May 11, 1910; s. Harsh Edmonds and Jewell (Files) C.; B.S. in Petroleum Engring., U. Okla., 1934; m. Wilma Klein, Oct. 12, 1935; children—Carol Ann, Jerry Edmond. Trainee, Reed Roller Bit Co., Houston, 1934, field engr., Ada, Okla., 1934-35, sales engr. Rodessa Oil Field, La., 1935-37, chief rock bit engr., Houston, 1937-39; organizer Western Co., Midland, Tex., 1939, pres., 1939—, chmn. bd. Mem. adv. bd. Tex. Indsl. Commn.; mem. City Council Midland, 1949-51. chmn. March of Dimes, 1954; mem. Ft. Worth Civil Service Commn., U. Okla. Research Inst.; mem. adv. youth council Ft. Worth YMCA. Bd. dirs. Midland Co. Community Chest, Tex. Research League, Austin. Mem. Am. Mgmt. Assn. (dir.), Young Pres.'s Orgn. (pres. 1954-55), Ind. Petroleum Assn. Am. (dir.), Tex. Ind. Producers Royalty Assn. (dir.), Tex., Gen. (dir.) mid-continent oil & gas assns., Am. Petroleum Inst., Am. Inst. Mining & Metall. Engrs., Am. Assn. Oil Well Drilling Contractors, C. of C., Tex. Soc. Profl. Engrs. (Engr. of Year 1953 Permian Basin chpt.), Chief Execs. Forum, Ft. Worth C. of C. (dir.), Sigma Alpha Epsilon, Sigma Tau, Pi Epsilon Tau. Presbyn. Home: 1300 Shady Oaks Lane Fort Worth TX 76107 Office: PO Box 186 Fort Worth TX 76101

CHILES, JOHN HENRY, army officer; b. Buckner, Mo., Nov. 9, 1912; s. Henry Perrin and Virginia (Ragan) C.; student William Jewell Coll., 1930-31; B.S., U.S. Mil. Acad., 1936; postgrad. Command and Gen. Staff Coll., 1942, Armed Forces Staff Coll., 1948, Army War Coll., 1952; Litt.D., Kyung Hee U., Seoul, Korea, 1966; m. Lucille Hall, Mar. 12, 1938; children—Lucylee, Joy, John Hall. Commd. 2d lt. U.S. Army, 1936, advanced through grades to maj. gen., 1964; comdg. officer 23d Inf. Regt., 2d Inf. Div., 1945- 46; sec. gen. staff Far East Command, 1949-50; operations officer X Corps, Korea, 1950-51; comdg. officer 23d Inf. Regt., 2d Inf. Div., 1951; faculty Army War Coll., 1952-55; exec. officer MAAG, Spain, 1955- 58; chief Middle East div. joint staff Joint Chiefs of Staff, 1958-60; chief U.S. Army Mission to Argentina, 1961-62; asst. div. comdr. 1st Armored Div., 1962-63; Army attache to Mexico, 1963-64; comdg. gen. 2d Inf. Div., Ft. Benning, Ga., 1964-65, Korea, 1965-66; dep. comdg. gen. Fifth Army, Chgo., 1966—. Decorated D.S.C., Silver Star medal with oak leaf cluster, Legion of Merit with oak leaf cluster, Bronze Star medal with two oak leaf clusters, Air medal with oak leaf cluster, Purple Heart with two oak leaf clusters, Combat Inf. badge; Legion of Honor, Croix de Guerre (French); Croix de Guerre (Luxembourg), Korean Order of Merit, Belgian Fourragere. Mem. Kappa Sigma. Rotarian. Address: 128 N Leonard Liberty MO 64068

CHILES, LAWTON MAINOR, U.S. senator; b. Lakeland, Fla., Apr. 3, 1930; s. Lawton Mainor and Margaret (Patterson) C.; B.S., U. Fla., 1952, LL.B., 1955; m. Rhea May Grafton, Jan. 27, 1951;

children—Tandy M., Lawton Mainor III, Edward G., Rhea Gay. Admitted to Fla. bar, 1955, since practiced in Lakeland; U.S. senator from Fla., 1971—. Mem. Fla. Ho. of Reps., 1958-66, Fla. Senate, 1966-70. Trustee U. Fla. Law Center, 1968-70. Served as 1st lt. AUS, 1952-54. Recipient Gov.'s award for conservation, 1964, Wildlife Conservation award Nat. Wildlife Fedn., 1965; named Outstanding Young Man, Lakeland Jr. C. of C., 1959. Mem. Fla., Polk County, Lakeland bar assns., Phi Delta Phi, Alpha Tau Omega. Presbyn. Kiwanian. Home: 840 Lake Hollingsworth Dr Lakeland FL 33803 Office: New Senate Office Bldg Washington DC 20510

CHILGREN, ARTHUR DEWEY, lawyer; b. Sauk Rapids, Minn., Oct. 7, 1901; s. Gustave Arthur and Lucy (Dewey) C.; B.A., Northwestern U., 1923, J.D., 1925; m. Jean Howell, Sept. 15, 1925; 1 dau., Lucy (Mrs. David Dalvey Peterson). Admitted to Ill. bar, 1925, since practiced in Chgo.; asso. Chapman & Cutler, 1925- 36; partner Gardner, Carton, Douglas, Chilgren & Waud, 1936—. Dir. Gardner-Denver Co. Mem. Am., Chgo. bar assns. Republican. Episcopalian. Clubs: The Law, University (Chgo.); White Lake Golf (Whitehall, Mich.): Indian Hill (Winnetka, Ill.). Home: 1410 Sheridan Rd Wilmette IL 60091 Office: 1 1st National Plaza Chicago IL 60670

CHILKOVSKY, NADIA, educator, choreographer; b. Ukraine, Jan. 8, 1908; d. Morris and Bella (Segalova) Chilkovsky; came to U.S., 1914, naturalized, 1926; B.S., Temple U., 1944; postgrad. Am. Dalcroze Inst.; pvt. study with Martha Graham, Hanya Holm and Irma Duncan; pre-doctoral student anthropology U. Pa.; Mus.D., Combs Coll. Music, 1971; m. Nicholas Nahumck, Mar. 22, 1941. Founder, dir. Phila. Dance Acad., 1946—; faculty Acad. Vocal Arts, 1958—, Curtis Inst. Music, 1946-66, Temple U., 1944-45, Swarthmore Coll., 1958- 60, Combs Coll. Music, 1964—; editor Dance Notation Record, 1956-58; research asso. U. Pa. Mus., 1964—; lectr. Arts Sch. Allied Health Scis. Jefferson Med. Coll., 1969; founder Performing Arts Sch. for acad. grades 1-12, 1962. Master notator Dance Notation Bur., 1955—, pres. Phila. br., 1963—; del Nat. Council Arts in Edn. 1964-65; del. conf. dance div. Am. Assn. Health, Edn. and Welfare, 1965; mem. fine arts adv. bd. Pa. Dept. Pub. Instrn., 1968-70. Pres. bd. dirs. Phila. Dance Acad.; dance adv. panelist Pa. Arts Council; bd. dirs. Found. Modern Dance. Grantee Mrs. Efrem Zimbalist for dance research; U.S. office Edn., 1965, Wenner-Gren Found. Fellow Internat. Council for Kinetography Laban; mem. Soc. Ethnomusicology (council), Nat. Dance Tchrs. Guild (3d vice chmn.), Nat. Com. Dance Research. Choreographer numerous works, 1929—, including Snow Queen, 1959, Vision of America (commd. Phila. Civic Ballet Co.), 1960, Bagatelles (commd. Contemporary Music Guild), 1961, Tendrils, 1961, Sprig of Lilac, 1963; No Hiding Place, part 1, 1967, part 2 (commd. Phila. Little Symphony), 1969. Author: Ten Dances in Labanotation, 1955; My First Dance Book, Three R's For Dancing, Books I-III; Short Modern Dances in Labanotation, American Bandstand Dances, 1955-62; Comprehensive Curriculum in Dance for Secondary Schools, 1970. Contbr. articles to profl. jours., book revs. Address: 1035 Spruce St Philadelphia PA 19107

CHILLIDA, JUANTEGUI EDUARDO, artist, sculptor; b. San Sebastian, Spain, Jan. 10, 1924; s. Pedro and Carment (Juantegui) C.; student architecture U. Madrid; m. Pilar Belzunce de Carlos, July 28, 1950; children—Guiomar, Pedro, Ignacio, Carmen, Susana, Maria, Luis, Eduardo. One man shows include Clan Gallery, Madrid, 1934, Maeght Gallery, 1956, 61, 64, McRoberts and Tunnard Gallery, London, 1965, Fine Arts Mus., Houston, 1966, Wilhelm Lehmbruck Mus., Germany, 1966, Gallery Buchholz, Munich, 1966, Munsons-Williams-Proctor Inst., Utica, N.Y., 1967; exhibited group shows including Salon de Mai, 1949, 50, Les Mains Eblouies exhbn. at Maeght Galleries, 1950, Denise Rene Gallery, Paris, sculptures and drawings Salomon Guggenheim Mus., 1958; documents, Kassel, 1939, European Art Today, Graham Found., Chgo., 1959, sculpture contemporaine Gallery Claude Bernard, Paris, 1959, Three SpaniardsPicasso, Miro, Chillida, at Houston Mus., 1961, Art Since 1950 Mus. of Seattle, 1962, retrospective exhbn. Grand Prix de la Biennale, Venice, 1962, Paintings and Sculpture of a Decade, Tate Gallery, London, 1964. Pres. commd. arts Mus. San Talmeo, San Sebastian, 1960—; pres. Grupo Aranzadi Natural Sci., 1962—. Recipient diploma of honor Milan Triennial, 1954; prize Commune of Venice for Sculpture, 1958; Scuplture prize Graham Found., 1958; Kandinsky prize, 1960; prize Providence Arts Clubs, 1962; Carnegie prize Pitts. Internat., 1964; Nord-Rhein Westfalen prize for sculpture, 1966. Address: Villa Paz Alto de Miracruz San Sebastian Spain

CHILLMAN, JAMES, Jr., educator, museum dir., architect; b. Phila., Pa., Dec. 24, 1891; s. James Henry and Clara Emma (Miller) C.; B.S., U. of Pa., 1913, M.S., 1914; student Pa. Acad. of Fine Arts, 1915-16, Am. Acad. in Rome, 1919; m. Dorothy Dawes, July 2, 1923; children—Helen, Dawes. Instr. in drawing, U. of Pa., 1914-16; instr. in architecture, Rice Univ., Houston, Tex., 1916—19, asst. prof., 1922-45, asso. prof., 1945-47, prof., 1947-61, trustee prof., 1961—, Agnes Cullen Arnold prof. fine Arts, 1970—; dir. Mus. Fine Arts, Houston, 1924-53, emeritus, 1953—, also life trustee; also cons. architect, Houston, 1924—; lectr. arch., Summer Sch., U. Pa., 1925-29; past lectr. Intercollegiate Tours, Boston; lectr. Woman's Inst. of Houston. Past mem. staff of art lectrs. The Bur. of Univ. Travel, spending 14 summers in Europe and 8 in Mex. Chmn. archtl. com., Tex. Med. Center, Houston. Decorated Stella della Solidarieta (Italy), 1956; Brown award for excellence in teaching, Rice U. Fellow in arch., Am. Acad. Rome, 1919-22, A.I.A., 1950. Fellow emeritus A.I.A.; mem. Tex. Fine Arts Assn. (past pres.; v.p., dir.), So. States Art League (past pres.), Am. Assn. Museums, Am. Fedn. Arts, Archtl. Soc. U. Pa., Am. Assn. Art Mus. Dirs. Houston Philos. Soc. (past pres.). Presbyn. Kiwanian. Clubs: Faculty (Rice Inst.); University (Houston). Contbr. to art and architecture publs. Holder of Carl Schurz Memorial Foundation Fellowship for research work in German speaking countries of Europe, summer of 1936. Radio program Art is Fun, sta. KTRH, Houston, 1950-59. Home: 2242 Stanmore Dr Houston TX 77019 Office: Rice University Houston TX 77001

CHILLRUD, FRANKLIN CHESTER, Jr., mfg. co. exec.; b. Atlanta, June 20, 1930; s. Franklin C. and Ella (Gardner) C.; B.A., Union Coll., Schenectady, 1954; m. Tatiana Padwa Hunold, Jan. 26, 1963; 1 stepson, Michael S. Hunold; 1 dau., Joanna. Investment mgr. bond dept. Prudential Ins. Co. Am., 1954-65; v.p., dir. finance operations bowling products group AMF Inc., 1965-67, group exec. finance services group, 1967-70, v.p., treas., 1970—; dir. N.A.M. Capital Corp., N.Y.C. Home: 820 West End Av New York City NY 10025 Office: AMF Inc 261 Madison Av New York City NY 10016

CHILLSON, CHARLES WHITE, aerospace engr.; b. Los Angeles, Mar. 12, 1910; s. Charles Foster and Mary Boone (White) C.; B.S., Stanford, 1931; postgrad. Cal. Inst. Tech., 1931-35; m. Rosa Grey deWaard, Oct. 23, 1944. Design, test, controllable pitch propellers Green Assos., Los Angeles, 1931-36; with propeller div. Curtiss Wright Corp. 1936-71, chief engr. in rocket dept., 1945-50, tech. dir. Curtiss div. (formerly propeller div.), 1963-71; on leave to assist tech. monitoring mil. satellite program U.S. Dept. Def., Inst. Def. Analysis, Advanced Research Projects Agy., Washington, 1959-60; aerospace cons. engr., 1971—. Served as col. a/s Tech. Intelligence Corps, USAAF, 1945. Fellow Am. Inst. Aeros. and Astronautics (nat. dir. Am. Rocket Soc. 1950-52, pres. 1952, dir. N.Y. sect. 1953-56, pres. 1955). Patentee propellers, multi-engine synchronizers, rocket engines, other aircraft components. Home: 4 Sloping Hill Terrace Wayne NJ 07470

CHILSON, OLIN HATFIELD, U.S. judge; b. Pueblo, Colo., Nov. 22, 1903; s. Leonard and Annie (Mills) C.; LL.B., U. Colo., 1927; m. Marian Cole, Aug. 18, 1929; 1 son, John Hatfield. Admitted to Colo. bar, 1927; practiced in Greeley, Loveland and Denver, 1927-36; city atty., Estes Park, 1928-56, Loveland, 1931-36; dist. atty. 8th Jud. Dist. Colo., 1940-48; mem. firm Grant, Shafroth, Tell, Chilson & McHendrie, Denver, 1959-60; U.S. dist. judge Colo., Denver, 1960—. Mem. Colo. Bd. Law Examiners, 1951-54. Organizer, sec. Big Thompson Soil Conservation Dist., 1940-47; asst. sec. pub. land mgmt. Dept. Interior, 1956-57, under sec. interior, 1957- 58; dir. No. Colo. Water Conservancy Dist., 1951-55; legal cons. Colo. Water Conservation Bd., 1954-56; mem. Loveland Sch. Bd., 1945-55. Trustee Boettcher Found. Mem. Am., Colo. (past pres.), Larimer County (past pres.) bar assns., Alumni Assn. U. Colo. (past pres.), Phi Alpha Delta, Alpha Tau Omega. Methodist. Mason, Rotarian. Club: Denver Country. Home: 660 S Altion Way Denver CO 80231 Office: US Courthouse Denver CO 80202

CHILTON, ARTHUR BOUNDS, educator; b. Montgomery, Ala., Sept. 22, 1918; s. Arthur Bounds and Fannylu (Wheeler) C.; B.S., U.S. Naval Acad., 1939; B.Civil Engring., Rensselaer Poly. Inst., 1942, M.Civil Engring., 1943; student U.S. Naval Postgrad. Sch., 1949; M.S., Ohio State U., 1951, Ph.D., 1953; m. Charlotte Ann Presler, Sept 5, 1942; children—Stephen P., Sara D., Geoffrey P. Commd. ensign U.S. Navy, 1939, advanced through grades to capt., 1958; dir. research Bur. Yards and Docks, 1957-59; dir. U.S. Naval Civil Engring. Lab., 1959-62; retired, 1962; mem. faculty U. Ill. at Urbana, 1962—, prof. civil and nuclear engring., 1965; cons. to govt. and industry, 1962—. Mem. adv. com. civil def. Nat. Acad. Sci.- Nat. Acad. Engring.-NRC, 1960-68, chmn. subcom. radiation shielding, 1965-68. Fellow Am. Nuclear Soc. (chmn. shielding div. 1968-69, bd. dirs. 1970—); mem. Am. Phys. Soc., Health Physics Soc., Sigma Xi, Chi Epsilon, Tau Beta Pi, Sigma Pi Sigma. Author articles in field. Co-editor: Engineering Compendium on Radiation Shielding, 1968. Home: 805 W Michigan Av Urbana IL 61801

CHILTON, CECIL HAMILTON, engineer, economist; b. N.Y.C., Sept. 25, 1918; s. Claudius Lysias and Clara Caroline (Weidmann) C.; B.S., Auburn U., 1939; M.S., Carnegie- Mellon U., 1940; m. Florence Edna Zitzman, Oct. 1, 1941; children—Edward Morgan, Margaret Arnold (Mrs. W. Owen BeMent). Chem. engr. Mobil Oil Corp., 1940-41, E.I. duPont de Nemours & Company, 1941-50; editor McGraw-Hill, Inc., 1950-66, editor-in-chief Chem. Engring., 1959-66; tech. economist Battelle Meml. Inst., Columbus, 1966—. Recipient Am. Bus. Press editorial achievement award, 1966. Mem. Am. Inst. Chem. Engrs. (dir. 1971—), Am. Assn. Cost Engrs. (award of merit, pres. 1962-63), Am. Society for Engring. Edn. Mem. Ch. of Nazarene. Editor: Cost Engineering in the Process Industries, 1960; co-editor: Chemical Engineers' Handbook, 1963. Home: 3511 Schirtzinger Rd Columbus OH 43220 Office: 505 King Av Columbus OH 43201

CHILTON, ROBERT CARTER, food co. exec.; b. Bklyn., Apr. 12, 1921; s. William Carter and Abigail (McCloskey) C.; B.B.A. cum laude St. John's U., 1945; M.B.A., N.Y.U., 1950; m. Elizabeth Nan Dean, Aug. 9, 1947; children—William Reeve, Elizabeth Carter, Susan Gail. Staff accountant Price Waterhouse & Co., 1946-50, asst. controller Girl Scouts U.S.A., 1952-58 (both N.Y.C.); corporate controller Avien, Inc., Woodside, N.Y., 1958-61; exec. v.p. Computer Diode Corp., Fair Lawn, N.J., 1961-68; treas. Savannah Foods & Industries, Inc., Ga., 1968—. Instr. Rutgers U., New Brunswick, N.J., 1950-55. Treas., trustee Candler Gen. Hosp., Savannah, 1970—; treas., dir. Savannah council Girl Scouts U.S.A., 1969—. Served with USNR, 1942-45. Mem. Am. Inst. C.P.A.'s, Nat. Assn. Accountants, Am. Accounting Assn., N.Y., Ga. socs. certified pub. accountants. Presbyn. (elder). Home: 5615 Sweetbrier Circle Savannah GA 31406 Office: Savannah Foods & Industries Inc PO Box 339 Savannah GA 31402

CHILTON, SAMUEL BLACKWELL, clergyman; b. Lakota, Va., May 27, 1900; s. Charles Blackwell and Harriet (Hamilton) C.; student Va. Poly. Inst., 1918-20, U. Va., 1920- 21; B.D., P.E. Theol. Sem. in Va., 1926, D.D., 1957; m. Harriet Harrington McMillan, Sept. 3, 1925; children—Harriet Hamilton (Mrs. Alexander B. Vaughan, Jr.), Charles Alexander, Thomas Harrington. Ordained to ministry Episcopal Ch., 1924; pastor in Hanover, Va., 1924- 41, New Kent, Va., 1928-37; editor So. Churchman mag., 1938-40; sec.- treas. Episcopal Diocese Va., 1940-54, archdeacon, 1954-60, suffragan bishop, 1960-70. Trustee St. Paul's Coll., Lawrenceville, Va., 1960—; mem. trustees of funds Protestant Episcopal Ch. in Diocese Va., 1946—; mem. meml. trustees Va. Diocesan Center, 1963—; bd. dirs. Council Chs. Greater Washington, 1967-70; pres. Diocesan Missionary Soc., Va., 1970—. Mem. Magna Carta Barons. Democrat. Address: 4800 Fillmore Av Alexandria VA 22311

CHILTON, ST. JOHN POINDEXTER, educator; b. Phila., Feb. 3, 1909; s. St. John P. and Helen Frances (McGloin) C.; B.S., La. State U., 1935, M.S., 1936; Ph.D., U. Minn., 1938; m. Alice Pleasance Hunter, Mar. 2, 1935. Agt. plant pathology U.S. Dept. Agr., 1938-40; faculty La. State U., 1940—, prof., 1948—, chmn. dept. botany and plant pathology, 1950-70; plant pathologist, head dept. plant pathology La. Agr. Expt. Sta. 1950—; rep. div. biology and agr. NRC, 1952-57; pres., dir. LaPlace Enterprises, Inc.; pres. Esperanza Farms, Inc.; cons. Nicaraque Sugar Estates, Ingenio San Antonio. Fellow A.A.A.S.; mem. Am. Phytopath. Soc. (ex-counselor), Internat. (vice chmn. 10th congress), Am. (past pres.) socs. sugarcane technologists, S.A.R. (past pres. Phil Thomas chpt.), La. Acad. Sci. (past pres.), Am. Sugarcane League U.S. (life). Rotarian. Home: 3617 Hyacinth Av Baton Rouge LA 70808

CHILTON, THOMAS HAMILTON, chem. engr.; b. Greensboro, Ala., Aug. 14, 1899; s. Claudius Lysias and Mabel Cecilia (Pierce) C.; student Starke's U. Sch., Montgomery, Ala., 1910-13, Lanier High Sch., Montgomery, Ala., 1914-15, U. Ala., 1915-16, Columbia U., 1917-22. Chem. Engr., 1922; D.Sc. (hon.) U. Del., 1943; m. Cherridah McLemore, June 29, 1926 (dec. Mar. 1969); children—Thomas McLemore, Daniel Tanner; m. 2d, Elizabeth Crafs Rinehart, Jan. 2, 1971. Research chemist F.J. Carman, N.Y.C., 1922-25; chemist, chem. dept. Exptl. Sta., E.I. du Pont de Nemours & Co., Wilmington, Del., 1925-30, group leader, chem. engring. research, 1930- 35, asst. div. head, tech. div., engring. dept., 1935-38, dir. tech. div., 1938-45, mgr. devel. engring. div., 1945-46, tech. dir. devel. engring. div., 1946-58, tech. adviser, 1958-59; Regent's prof. U. Cal. at Berkeley, 1959-60; Fulbright lectr. Japan, 1960-61; vis. prof. U. New S. Wales, Australia, 1961, U. Del., 1963-64, Cal. Inst. Tech., 1965, U. Va., 1965-66, Birla Inst. Tech., Pilani, Rajasthan, India, 1967, U. Wash. at Seattle, 1968, U. Ala., spring 1969, U. Mass., Amherst, fall 1969, U. P.R., spring 1970, U. Natal, Durban, South Africa, fall 1970; Fulbright lectr. France, 1961-62; Neely vis. prof. Ga. Inst. Tech., 1962-63. Recipient Presdl. Certificate of Merit, 1948; Chandler medal Columbia, 1939, Univ. medal, 1950; Egleston medal Columbia Engring. Sch. Alumni Assn., 1943; Founders award Am. Inst. C.E., 1958. Mem. adv. bd. for books in chem. engring. John Wiley & Sons, 1939-59. Mem. Am. Inst. Chem. Engrs. (pres. 1951), Am. Chem. Soc. (bd. editors Monographs 1938-57), Am. Soc. Engring. Edn., A.A.A.S., Sons of Am. Revolution, Automobile License Plate Collectors Assn., Nat. Acad. Engring., Sigma Xi, Tau Beta Pi, Phi Lambda Upsilon, Omega Chi Epsilon. Presbyn. (elder 1944-50). Clubs: University and Whist (Wilmington, Delaware); Chemists (N.Y.C.). Author: Strong Water, 1968. Section editor for Indsl. Chemistry, Chem. Abstracts, 1945-51. Contbr. profl. publs. Address: 22 Cragmere Rd Wilmington DE 19809

CHILTON, WILLIAM EDWIN III, journalist; b. Kingston, N.Y., Nov. 26, 1921; s. William Edwin and Louise (Schoonmaker) C.; B.A., Yale, 1950; H.H.D. (hon.), W.Va. State Coll., 1966; m. Elizabeth Easley Early, Apr. 5, 1952; 1 dau., Susan Carroll. Promotion mgr. Charleston Gazette, 1952-55, asst. to pub., 1955- 61, pub., 1961—; pres. Daily Gazette Co., 1961—; gen. mgr. Newspaper Agy. Corp., 1962-68, chmn. bd., 1968—. Mem. W.Va. Ho. of Dels., 1952-60. Mem. W.Va. Centennial Commn., 1956-64; chmn. W.Va. Lincoln-Kennedy Meml. Commn.; mem. Kanawha County Library Bd., 1957—, Kanawha County Salvation Army Bd., Kanawha County Parks and Recreation Commn., 1967—, Citizens Adv. Commn. on W.Va. Legis., 1967—, Worth Bingham Meml. Found.; W.Va. dir. Crusade for Freedom, 1958. Trustee Morris Harvey Coll. W.Va. del. at large Democratic Nat. Conv., 1960; mem. Dem. nat. platform com., 1964. Served with USAAF, 1941-45; CBI. Mem. Chi Phi. Episcopalian. Elk. Clubs: Press, Edgewood. Home: 1 Scott Rd Charleston WV 25314 Office: 1001 Virginia St E Charleston WV 25330

CHIMENTI, DAN, mfg. co. exec.; b. Chgo., June 8, 1912; s. Sam and Pia (Galligani) C.; student Northwestern U., 1929-33, 58, Armour Tech. U., 1933-36; m. Laura Evelyn Magrini, Nov. 28, 1934; 1 son, Norman. With Internat. Harvester Co., 1932—, v.p., 1964—, also dir. subsidiaries. Active Chgo. Crusade Mercy, Jr. Achievement Chgo. Mem. N.A.M., Soc. Automotive Engrs. Roman Catholic. Club: Edgewood Valley Country dir. (La Grange, Ill.). Home: 144 Hillcrest Av Hinsdale IL 60521 Office: 401 N Michigan Av Chicago IL 60611

CHINARD, GILBERT, educator; b. Chtellerault, France, Oct. 17, 1881; s. Hilaire and Marie (Blanchard) C.; student Collège de Ch#87tellerault, Lycée de Poitiers, Université de Bordeaux, Sorbonne; B.L., Poitiers, 1899, Licencié ès lettres, 1902; LL.D., St. John's, 1934; L.H.D., Princeton, 1959; m. Emma Blanchard, 1908 (dec. Feb. 1967); children—Lucienne, Francis. Instr. French, Coll. City N.Y., 1908, Brown U.; 1908-12, U. Chgo., summer 1912; asso. prof., prof. French, U. Cal., 1912-19, Columbia, summer 1919; prof. French, comparative lit. Johns Hopkins, 1919-36; became mem. Walter Hines Page Sch. Internat. Relations, 1925; faculty U. Cal., 1936-37; Pyne prof. French lit. Princeton, 1937-50, emeritus, 1950—. Mem. Inst. for Advanced Study, Princeton, 1950. Newberry Guggenheim fellow, 52—; Laureate de l'Académie Francaise, 1914; Laureate de l'Institut, 1951; comdr. Legion of Honor; Guggenheim fellow, 1956. Mem. Am. Acad. Arts and Scis., Am. Antiquarian Soc., Modern Lang. Assn. (pres. 1956), Am. Philos. Soc., Philol. Assn. Pacific Coast, Société des Américanistes de Paris, Phi Beta Kappa; corr. mem. L'Institut Academie des Scis. Morales et Politiques. Club: Century Assn (N.Y.C.). Author books, 1911—; L'Apothéose de Benjamin Franklin, Paris, 1955. Editor numerous vols. including Morelly, Code de la Nature, 1950; Ode'rahi, 1950. Editor: Institute Francais de Washington, 1928—, French Am. Rev., 1948—. Home: 93 Mercer St Princeton NJ 08540 ☆

CHING, JOHN FREDERIC, educator; b. San Francisco, Dec. 9, 1901; s. John James and Maud (Ekins) C.; B.S., U. Cal. at Berkeley, 1923, M.A., 1927, Ed.D., 1932; m. Gertrude Ellen Hatch, June 15, 1926; children—Donald Frederic, Barbara Ellen (Mrs. John Ottone), Kendrick Ekins. Tchr., prin., dir. research Vallejo (Cal.) pub. schs., 1926-27; asst. dir. research and curriculum Oakland (Cal.) pub. schs., 1927-32, dir. research, curriculum and guidance, 1932-34, prin. high schs., 1934-47; supt. Salinas (Cal.) city schs., also Salinas Union High Sch. Dist., 1947-57; pres. Hartnell Coll., Salinas, Cal., 1957-66, pres. emeritus, 1966—; lectr. Colo. State Coll. of Edn., 1940-41; instr. San Francisco State Coll., 1946; guest lectr. U. Cal. at Berkeley, 1939, Stanford, 1954. Mem. Bd. Edn. Diocese Monterey, 1968—. Pres. Salinas YMCA, 1962-64, Salinas Area Community Chest, 1967-69, also the No. Cal. Industry-Edn. Council, 1965-67; v.p. Industry and Edn. Councils of Am., 1970—; treas. Monterey County Indsl. Devel., 1965-69. Bd. dirs. Golden Gate Internat. Exposition, San Francisco, 1939-41, Childrens Hosp. East Bay, Oakland, 1939-42, Oakland Symphony Orch. Assn., 1937-42, Salinas Valley Memorial Hosp., 1969—, Mid-coast Comprehensive Health Planning Assn., 1970—; mem. nat. council YMCA, 1965-70. Life mem. N.E.A.; mem. Cal. Tchrs. Assn., Am. Assn. Sch. Adminstrs., Cal. Assn. Sch. Adminstrs., Cal. Jr. Coll. Assn., No. Cal. Jr. Coll. Presidents Assn. (pres. 1963-64), Oakland Jr. C. of C. (pres. 1934), A.I.M. (pres.'s council), Phi Delta Kappa. Republican. Methodist. Kiwanian (pres. Salinas 1964), Elk. Contbr.: Cal. Bus. Edn. Jour., Vocational Guidance Quar. Home: 429 College Dr Salinas CA 93901

CHINIFOROUSH, HABIB, Iranian diplomat; b. Shiraz, Iran, May 19, 1931; s. Mahmood and Zaman Chiniforoush; B.S., Tehran U., 1962, M.S., 1965, postgrad., 1965; m. Shamsi Atay, June 2, 1959; children—Behrooz, Behnaz. With Ministry Economy Iran, Tehran, 1962-69. dep. Export Promotion Center Iran, 1966-68; comml. counselor, Washington, 1969—; econ. editor daily newspapers Kayhan, 1955-64, Bourse, 1965-66, Ettelaat, 1967-68, Decorated Homayoon, 1969, Coronation, 1969, Golden Feather, 1962. Author: Carpet Weaving in Iran, 1964; Economic Results of the White Revolution, 1964; Twenty Five Years of Economic Fluctuation of Iran, 1962. Home: 4515 Willard Av Chevy Chase MD 20015 Office: 5530 Wisconsin Av Washington DC 20015

CHINITZ, BENJAMIN, economist, educator; b. N.Y.C., Aug. 24, 1924; s. Abraham and Mollie (Resnick) C.; A.B., Yeshiva U., 1945; A.M., Brown U., 1951; Ph.D., Harvard, 1956; m. Ethel Kleinman, Oct. 15, 1950; children—Adam, Michael, Instr., Dartmouth, 1954-55, Brown U., 1955-56; sr. staff mem. N.Y. Met. Region Study, 1956-59; asso. dir. Pitts. Regional Econ. Study, 1959-62; prof., chmn. dept. econs., asso. dir. Center for Regional Econ. Studies, U. Pitts., 1962-65; dep. asst. sec. commerce for econ. devel., 1965-66; prof. econs. Brown U., Providence, 1967—, chmn. dept., 1967-69. Cons. Pres.'s Appalachian Regional Commn., Rand Corp., Conn. Devel. Commn., Council Econ. Advisers. Mem. adv. bd. area devel. com. Com. Econ. Devel.; mem. Pres.'s Task Force on Transp. Policy, 1964; chief UNDP Mission to Romania, 1970. Trustee, mem. research com. Transp. Research Found., Washington. Mem. Am. Econ. Assn., Regional Sci. Assn. (pres. 1970). Author: Freight and the Metropolis, 1960; (with Barbara Berman, Edgar M. Hoover) Projection of a Metropolis, 1961; (with Edgar M. Hoover) The Role of Accounts in the Economic Study of the Pittsburgh Metropolitan Region, 1961; (with others) Region in Transition, 1964; City and Suburb: Economics of Metropolitan Growth, 1965. Home: 42 Intervale Rd Providence RI 02906

CHINLUND, EDWIN CHRISTIAN, ret. accountant; b. Chgo., Aug. 3, 1909; s. Edwin F. and Lillian (Otto) C.; B.A., Dartmouth, 1929; m. Pauline Lillian Case, Dec. 17, 1960; childrenPhyllis (Mrs. Thomas P. Johnson, Jr.), Jennifer K. With Nat. City Bank of N.Y.,

N.Y.C., 1929-30; accounting staff Price Waterhouse & Co., C.P.A.'s, N.Y.C., also Pitts., 1930-46, partner Pitts., 1946-70. Campaign audit chmn. United Fund of Allegheny County, 1963, major corporate gifts work, 1965. Trustee, chmn. finance com. Kiski Sch., Saltsburg; trustee Winchester-Thurston Sch., Pitts. Mem. Greater Pitts. C. of C. (treas., dir. 1963-), Beta Alpha Psi. Presbyn. Clubs: Field (dir. 1954-, pres. 1961-63), Duquesne (Pitts.). Home: 1605 Powers Run Rd Pittsburgh, PA 15238.

CHINN, HERMAN ISAAC, biochemist; b. Connellsville, Pa., Apr. 8, 1913; s. Alex and Anna (Blumberg) C.; B.S., Pa. State Coll., 1934; M.S., Northwestern U., 1935, Ph.D., 1938; m. Rowena Carter, July 22, 1945; children—Philip, Susan, Stephen, Nancy. Instr. Northwestern U. Med. Sch., 1938-42; prin. chemist Fla. Bd. Health, 1946-47; chief dept. pharmacology Sch. Aviation Medicine, 1947-55; sci. liaison officer Office Naval Research, London, 1955-57; chief biol. scis. Air Force Office Sci. Research, 1957-60; dep. sci. attache Am. embassy, Bonn, Germany, 1960-63; science officer Office Internat. Sci. Affairs, State Dept., Washington, 1963-65; sci. attache Am. embassy, Tehran, Iran, 1965-67; science officer State Dept., 1967-71; sci. attache Am. embassy, Stockholm, Sweden, 1971—. Served to major AUS, 1942-46; col. USAF Res. Recipient Sir Henry Wellcome award; Dist. Civilian award USAF; Commendation medal U.S. Army; Superior Honor award, Department State. Mem. Am. Soc. Pharmacology, Biochem. Soc., Am. Physiol. Soc., Am. Chem. Soc., A.A.A.S., Soc. Exptl. Biology and Medicine, Sigma Xi. Home: 27 Ringvägen Enebyberg Sweden Office: Am Embassy Stockholm Sweden

CHINN, JOSEPH WILLIAM, Jr., banker; b. Warsaw, Va., June 5, 1904; s. Joseph W. and Sarah (Douglas) C.; student Episcopal High Sch., Alexandria, Va., 1917-21; B.L., U. Va., 1928; m. Katherine Brown, Apr. 16, 1931; children—Margery Ann, Sally Douglas, Katherine. Admitted to Va. bar, 1928; asso. office Christian & Lamb, Richard, 1928-30; asst. trust officer Wilmington Trust Co. (Del.), 1930-37, asst. v.p., 1938-43, v. p., 1943-48, v.p., sec., 1949, v.p., trust officer, 1949-58, dir., v.p., 1958-67, chmn., 1967-70; now dir.; dir. U.S. Rubber Co., W.T. Grant Co. chmn., Del. Racing Commn. Trustee Episcopal High Sch., Alexandria, Va., U. Va. Endowment Funds, P.E. Ch. Diocese of Del., Haskell Research Fund. Mem. Nat. Assn. State Racing Commrs. (v.p.), Soc. Colonial Wars. Democrat. Episcopalian. Clubs: Wilmington, Wilmington Country. Home: 900 Cecil Rd Westover Hills Wilmington DE 19807 Office: Wilmington Trust Co Wilmington DE 19801

CHINNOCK, RONALD JOHN, realtor; b. Grand Rapids, Mich., Oct. 5, 1903; s. Fred Charles and Margaret S. (Sullivan) C.; grad. Northwestern, 1926; m. Barbara Farr, Oct. 12, 1929 (dec.); children—John Farr, Margot; m. 2d, Mary Swain, Dec. 29, 1948; children—Christine, Michael, Peter, Mary. With Grace Line, 1926-28; chmn. bd. Chinnock & Doughty, Inc., Chgo.; Des Plaines dir. Trust & Savs. First Fed. Savs. & Loan Assn. Chgo., Chgo. Short Line Ry., Bank & Trust Co. Arlington Heights, Northwest Trust & Savs. Bank. Mem. citizens bd. U. Chgo.; dir. State Ill. Housing Bd.; pres. U.S.O. 1966-68. Chgo., Trustee Chgo. Child Care Soc., Kemper Hall Sch. Girls. Lincoln Meml. U. Served as capt. USNR, 1942-46. Decorated Legion of Merit. Mem. Chgo. Real Estate Bd. (pres. 1942), Ill. Assn. Real Estate Bds. (pres. 1947, dir.), Nat. Inst. Real Estate Brokers (dir.), Res. Officers Naval Services (dir. Chgo. chpt.), Chgo. Assn. Commerce and Industry (dir.), Ill. (pres. 1947, dir.), Nat. (pres.) assns. real estate bds., Soc. Residential Appraisers, Am. Soc. Real Estate Counselors, Northwestern U. Assos., Am. Legion, Soc. Indsl. Realtors, Navy League U.S. (dir.), Chgo. Hist. Soc., Art Inst. Chgo. (life). Chgo. Zool. Soc. (gov. mem.), Com. Econ. Devel., Acad. Polit. Sci. Clubs: Mid Day. University, Realtors Forty. Realty (Chgo.); Army-Navy (Washington); John Evans (Northwestern U.). Home: 1104 Michigan Av Evanston IL 60202 Office: 104 S Michigan Av Chicago IL 60603

CHINOWSKY, WILLIAM, educator; b. Bklyn., Feb. 24, 1929; s. Max and Mary (Ruderman) C.; A.B., Columbia, 1949, A.M., 1951, Ph.D., 1955; m. Joan A. Steinberg, Nov. 22, 1950; children—Alan E., Jane I. Physicist Brookhaven Nat. Lab., Upton, N.Y., 1955-61; asso. prof. physics U. Cal. at Berkeley, 1961-67, prof., 1967—. Guggenheim fellow Oxford U., 1966-67. Home: 453 Michigan Av Berkeley CA 94707

CHINOY, ELY, educator, sociologist; b. Newark, Sept. 5, 1921; s. Solomon and Bella (Traskanoff) C.; B.A., U. Newark, 1942; Ph.D., Columbia, 1953; m. Helen Krich, June 6, 1948; children—Michael, Claire Nicole. Instr., Newark Coll. Engring., 1942-44; instr. N.Y. U., 1945-46; lectr. U. Toronto (Ont., Can.), 1947-51; instr. sociology Smith Coll., Northampton, Mass., 1951- 53, asst. prof., 1953-57, asso. prof., 1957-61, prof., 1961—, Mary Huggins Gamble prof. sociology, 1969—; Fulbright vis. prof. U. Leicester (Eng.), 1963-64; Fulbright lectr., Philippines, summer 1971. Mem. Am. Sociol. Assn., Eastern Sociol. Soc., Am. Assn. U. Profs., Am. Civil Liberties Union. Author: Sociological Perspective, 2d edit., 1968; Society: An Introduction to Sociology, 2d edit., 1967; Automobile Workers and the American Dream, 1954. Cons. editor Atherton Press, 1964—. Asst. editor Am. Sociol. Rev., 1957-60, asso. editor, 1961-64. Home: 230 Crescent St Northampton MA 01060

CHIPMAN, DONALD J., newspaper exec. Pres., gen. mgr. Jour., Twin City Sentinel, Jour. Sentinel, Winston-Salem, N.C. Office: Piedmont Pub Co Inc 416-20 N Marshall St Winston Salem NC 27101*

CHIPMAN, ROBERT KENNETH, educator; b. N.Y.C., Nov. 16, 1931; s. Sidney Shaw and Christene (Fatherley) C.; A.B., Amherst Coll., 1953; M.S., Tulane U., 1958, Ph.D., 1963; m. Geraldine Ann Dietl, July 15, 1954; children—Robert Kenneth, Clay DeWitt. Asst. prof. State U. Coll., Pittsburgh, N.Y., 1961-62; asst. prof. U. Vt., 1962-66, asso. prof., 1966-68, asst. dean grad. coll., 1967-68; prof., chmn. dept. zoology U. R.I., 1968—. Served with AUS, 1953-55. Mem. Am. Soc. Zoologists, A.A.A.S., Sigma Xi. Contbr. articles profl. jours. Home: Box 95 Kingston RI 02881

CHIRELSTEIN, MARVIN ASCHER, legal educator; b. Chgo., Oct. 8, 1928; s. Harry and Rose (Esrig) C.; A.B., U. Cal. at Berkeley, 1950; J.D., U. Chgo., 1953; m. Ellen Katzman, Sept. 4, 1955; childrenAlexander, Paul. Admitted to N.Y. bar, 1955; mem. legal adv. staff Treasury Dept., 1955-56; practice law, N.Y.C., 1956-59; mem. faculty Rutgers U. Law Sch., 1960-65; mem. faculty Yale Law Sch., 1965—, prof. law, 1965—. Contbr. legal pubs. Home: 178 E Rock Rd New Haven CT 06520.

CHIRIAEFF, LUDMILLA, choreographer, artistic dir.; b. Riga, Latvia, Jan. 10, 1924; d. Alexander and Catherine Abramoff (Radziwill) Gorny; grad. Russian-German High Sch., Berlin, 1939; m. 2d, Uriel Luft, Aug. 9, 1962; children—Anastasia, Avde, Glebe, Ludmilla, Catherine. Debut, Ballets Russes du Colonel de Basil. 1936; soloist Berlin Opera Ballet, 1939-41; prima ballerina, choreographer Municipal Theatre, Lausanne, Switzerland, 1947-48. Theatre Des Arts, Geneva, Switzerland, 1948-51; founder Les Ballets Chiriaeff, Montreal, Can., 1952-58; founder, 1958, since artistic dir. Les Grands Ballets Candiens, Montreal. Recipient award best prodn. ballets on TV in Montreal, Canadian Broadcasting Co., 1955; award contbn. field ballet in Can., Montreal Ballet Assn., 1957; medal Order of Can. Mem. Inst. Internat. du Theatre, Union des Artistes, Actors Equity Assn. Office: 4848 Blvd St Laurent Montreal Quebec Canada

CHIROVSKY, NICHOLAS L., educator, author; b. W. Ukraine, Aug. 5, 1919; s. Nicholas and Zenobia (Zarycky) C.; J.S.D., M.A., U. Graz (Austria), D.Pol.Econ., Ukranian Free U.; m. Iwanna Smishkevich, Sept. 21, 1947; children—Leo, George, Andrew, John. Came to U.S., 1949, naturalized, 1955. Instr., Ukranian Grad. Sch. Econs., Munich, Germany, 1947-49; faculty Seton Hall U., South Orange, N.J., 1949—, prof. econs., 1955—, chmn. dept., 1963—, chmn. M.B.A., program, 1952-62. Mem. Am. Econ. Assn., Cath. Econ. Soc., Shevcheko Sci. Soc. Author: The Economic Factors in the Growth of Russia, 1957; The Old Ukraine, 1963; The Ukranian Economy, 1964; An Introduction to Russian History, 1967; Ukraine on the European Cross-roads, 1971. Contbr. numerous articles to profl. jours. Home: 292 Eastern Pkwy Newark NJ 07106 Office: Seton Hall U South Orange NJ 07079

CHIRURG, JAMES THOMAS, advt. co. exec.; b. Boston, July 22, 1906; s. Michael and Martha Mabel (Ames) C.; B.S., Mass. Inst. Tech., 1927, M.S., 1929; postgrad. Harvard Sch. Bus. Adminstrn., 1928; m. Ruth E. French, Dec. 27, 1951; children—James Thomas, Jane Ames. Organizer, partner K.R. Sutherland Co. (now Sutherland-Abbott Co.), Boston, 1931-33; organizer James Thomas Chirurg Co., Inc., Boston, N.Y.C., 1933, pres., 1937-55, chmn. bd. dirs., 1956-60; vice chmn. Chirurg & Cairns, Inc., N.Y.C., Boston, Hartford, Conn., 1960-67, chmn., 1968-69, dir., 1969—; chmn. CMC & C, Inc., N.Y.C., 1964-69. Asso. advt. faculty Simmons Coll., 1948; trade adviser U.S. Dept. Commerce Trade Mission, Egypt, 1960. Founder, James Thomas Chirurg Advt. Fellowship, Harvard Grad. Sch. Bus. Adminstrn., 1953; study reduction war factory absenteeism Brit. Govt., 1942; advt. agy. chmn. Mass. Gov.'s Council on Oil Conservation, 1948; chmn. publicity Community Fund, Greater Met. area, 1946; vice chmn. bd. govs. council Worcester Disaster Relief. 1953; chmn. Danvers Indsl. Devel. Com., 1956. Recipient Jacobs award as Boston's Outstanding Advt. Man, Jr. Advertising Club, Boston, 1957. Mem. Am. Assn. Advt. Agys. (adv. bd., nat. com. pub. relations 1952), Nat. Indsl. Advertisers Assn. (pres. Boston 1949), U.S. C. of C. (nat. com. pub. relations, 1953), Lambda Chi Alpha (Achievement award for leadership in advt and pub. relations 1968). Republican. Conglist. Mason. Clubs: Advertising University (Boston): Union League (N.Y.C.): Salem (Mass.) Country. Author: So You're Going to Choose an Advertising Agency. Home: 15 Winthrop St Danvers MA 01923 Office: Chirurg Bldg 824 Boylston St Chestnut Hill MA 02161 also 641 Lexington Av New York City NY 10022

CHISHOLM, ALEXANDER FIELD, former oil co. exec.; b. N.Y.C., July 17, 1899; s. Alexander Prenctice and Maude (Field) C.; student Westminster Sch.; A.B., Amherst Coll., 1923; m. Elizabeth Gardiner Wisner, Sept. 28, 1925. Chmn. bd. First Nat. Bank, Laurel, Miss.; v.p., dir. Laurel Royalty Co., Central Oil Co.; dir. Green Lumber Co., Miss. Investment Co., Pasagagoula Hardwood Co. Dir., past pres. Miss. Econ. Council Served as comdr. USNR, World War II. Decorated Bronze Star. Mem. Ind. Petroleum Assn. Am. (v.p.), Delta Kappa Epsilon. Clubs: Augusta (Ga.) National Golf (dir.); Boston (New Orleans); Blind Brook (Portchester); Royal and Ancient Golf (St. Andrews). Home: 726 5th Av Laurel MS 39440

CHISHOLM, DANIEL C., corp. exec.; b. 1917; LL.B., Boston Coll., 1952; C.P.A., Mass.; married. With Lybrand, Ross Bros. and Montgomery, C.P.A.'s 1945-50; with Sanders Assos., Inc., 1951—, now v.p. finance, also dir.; dir. Nashua Trust Co. Address: Daniel Webster Hwy S Nashua NH 03060*

CHISHOLM, ROBERT FERGUSON, business exec.; b. Battleford, Sask., Can., Oct. 16, 1904; s. R.F. and Eva (Kitson) C.; B.Commerce, U. Toronto (Ont. Can.), 1926; m. Rosemary Fennell; children—Judie, Janet. Indsl. engr. J.D. Woods & Co., Ltd., Toronto, 1934-37; v.p., gen. mgr. Gordon Mackay & Co., Ltd., 1937-56; exec. v.p. Dominion Stores, Ltd., Toronto, 1957-69; now chmn. bd. Thompson Paper Box Group Cos., Toronto, William Mara Co. Ltd., Toronto; pres. Japan Fund Can. Ltd., Toronto; dir. Confedn. Life Assn., Toronto, R.L. Crain, Ltd., Ottawa, Ont., Benson & Hedges Ltd., Montreal, Capital Growth Fund, Toronto, Supermarket Inst., Chgo. Chmn., Varsity Fund. Pres., bd. dirs. Toronto Symphony; bd. dirs. Victoria U.; bd. govs. U. Toronto. Decorated Order Brit. Empire. Mem. Canadian Council Distbn. (dir.), Boston Conf. Distbn. (dir.). Home: 79 Highland Crescent Willowdale Ontario Canada Office: William Mara Co Ltd 234 Eglinton Av E Toronto 12 Ontario Canada

CHISHOLM, RODERICK MILTON, educator; b. North Attleboro, Mass., Nov. 27, 1916; s. Alpin and Irma (Gardner) C.; A.B., Brown U., 1938; A.M., Harvard, 1940, Ph.D., 1942; m. Eleanor Parker, Oct. 18, 1943; childrenYeddy, Roderick M., Jonathan Parker. Instr., Barnes Found., Merion, Pa., 1946; asst. prof. U. Pa., 1947; mem. philosophy dept. Brown U., 1947—, chmn. dept., prof., 1951-64, Romeo Elton prof. natural theology, 1958—. Vis. lectr. Harvard, 1950, 60; vis. prof. U. So. Cal., 1955, Princeton, 1961-62, U. Cal., Santa Barbara, 1964, U. Ill., 1966, U. Alta., 1965, U. Chgo., 1967, Harvard, 1969; Nellie Wallace lectr. Oxford U., 1967. Exec. dir. Franz Brentano Found.; pres. 5th Interam. Congress Philosophy, 1957. Fulbright grantee U. Graz, Austria, 1959-60. Served with AUS, 1942-46. Mem. Am. Philos. Assn. (exec. com. 1953-56, v. p. Eastern div. 1962, div. pres. 1968, Carus lectr. 1967), Assn. for Symbolic Logic (exec. com. 1950- 53), Sociedad Interamericana de Filosofia (sec. 1956-57), Am. Acad. Arts and Scis., Metaphys. Soc. Am. (councillor), Phi Beta Kappa. Author: Perceiving Philosophical Study, 1957; Realism and the Background of Phenomenology, 1960; Theory of Knowledge, 1966 (Italian transl. 1968. Dutch transl. 1968, Chinese 1967, Japanese 1970). Asso. editor Philosophy and Phenomenological Research; cons. editor Am. Philos. Quar., Metaphilosophy, Southwestern Jour. Philosophy. Home: 170 Adams Point Barrington RI 02806 Office: Brown U Providence RI 02912

CHISHOLM, SHIRLEY ANITA ST. HILL, congresswoman; b. Bklyn., Nov. 30, 1924; d. Charles Christopher and Ruby (Seale) St. Hill; B.A. cum laude, Bklyn. Coll.; M.A., Columbia; LL.D. (hon.), Talladega Coll. (Ala.), Hampton Inst. (Va.); D.H.L. (hon.), N.C. Central Coll., Wilmington Coll. (O.); m. Conrad Chisholm, Oct. 8, 1949. Former nursery sch. tchr., dir. nursery sch.; ednl. cons. Div. Day Care, Bur. Child Welfare, N.Y.C. mem. N.Y. State Assembly, 1964-68; mem. 91st-92d Congresses 12th Dist. N.Y. Named Alumna of Yr. Bklyn. Coll. Alumni Bull., 1957; recipient award for outstanding work in field of child welfare Women's Council of Bklyn., 1957, Key Woman of Yr. award, 1963, Woman of Achievement award Key Women, Inc., 1965. Mem. Nat. Assn. Coll. Women, Bklyn. Coll. Alumni League Women Voters. Methodist. Home: 1028 St Johns Pl Brooklyn NY 11213 Office: House Office Bldg Washington DC 20515

CHISHOLM, WILLIAM HARDENBERGH, paper mfr.; b. N.Y.C., Apr. 24, 1917; s. Hugh J. and Sara Clark (Hardenbergh) C.; A.B., Yale, 1940; m. Alice Jensen, Nov. 7, 1942; children—Barbara Maud (Mrs. Chisholm Young), Margo Jensen. With Oxford Paper Co. (div. Ethyl Corp.), N.Y.C., 1940-, asst. to pres., 1946-50, v.p., dir., 1950-56, pres., 1956—; exec. v.p., dir. Ethyl Corp. 1967-71; vice chmn. bd. Kennebec River Pulp and Paper Co., 1971—; dir. Phelps Dodge Corp.; mem. trust bd. 1st Nat. City Bank, N.Y.C. Dir. nat. council Paper Industry for Air and Stream Improvement. Bd. dirs. Boys' Clubs Am.; pres. bd. dirs. Animal Med. Center; chmn. bd. dirs. U. Me. Pulp and Paper Found. Dep. dir. pulp and paper div. NPA, Washington, 1951. Mem. Am. Paper Inst. (dir., mem. exec. com., chmn. govt. relations com.). Home: Stornoway Rd Cumberland Foreside Portland ME 04110 Office: 100 Park Av New York City NY 10017

CHISM, OLIN, journalist; Music editor Dallas Times-Herald. Office: 1101 Pacific St Dallas TX 75202*

CHITIEA, ANDREW J., corp. exec.; b. Salem, O., Dec. 25, 1924; s. Andrew Nicin and Elizabeth (Canja) C.; B.B.A., Ohio State U., 1948; m. Joan Ellen Klepinger, June 20, 1949; children—Andrew David, Bruce Alan, Joel Thomas, Matthew Justin. With Price Waterhouse & Co., CPA's, N.Y.C., 1949-52; mgr. financial analysis Lincoln-Mercury div. Ford Motor Co., Detroit, 1952-57; comptroller, treas. Chrysler Australia, Ltd., subsidiary Chrysler Internat., Adelaide, South Australia, 1957-60; mgr. financial analysis General Dynamics Corp., N.Y.C., 1960-61, controller Convair div., San Diego, 1962-63; dir., sr. v.p. finance Whittaker Corp., Los Angeles, 1963-70; dir., sr. v.p. financial adminstrn. The Signal Cos., Los Angeles, 1971—. Bd. dirs. Cal. Lutheran Homes, Alhambra. Served to master sgt., 34th Inf. Div., AUS, 1943-45. C.P.A., N.Y. Mem. Financial Execs. Inst., Am. Inst. C.P.A.'s, Beta Alpha Psi. Home: 2908 Roscomare Rd Los Angeles CA 90024 Office: 1010 Wilshire Blvd Los Angeles CA 90017

CHITTENDEN, FAYETTE DUDLEY, rubber co. exec.; b. New Haven, Aug. 11, 1902; s. George Dudley and Ellen (Rossiter) C.; B.S., Yale, 1923, Ph.D., 1926; m. Helen Dickinson, Nov. 11, 1932; children—Ann (Mrs. Cunningham), Jane (Mrs. Harry P. Hopkins, Jr.). Mem. staff research center U.S. Rubber Co., Passaic, N.J., Providence plant, 1926-42, staff Naugatuck (Conn.) chem. div., 1942-60, co. v.p., gen. mgr. chem. div., 1960-64, sr. v.p. tech. and mfg., 1964-68; with Oxford Mgmt. and Research Center, Uniroyal Inc., Middlebury, Conn., 1968—. Mem. Am. Chem. Soc. Clubs: Graduate (New Haven); Pine Orchard (Conn.) Yacht and Country. Home: Yowago Av Branford CT 06405 Office: Uniroyal Inc Oxford Mgmt & Research Center Middlebury CT 06749

CHITTICK, RALPH JAMES, life ins. co. exec.; b. Stuart, Neb., May 27, 1912; s. Robert E. and S. Lorena (Sturdevant) C.; student U. Neb., 1929-31, LL.B., 1936; student Neb. State Tchrs. Coll., Wayne, 1931-32, U. Minn., 1938-39, Am. Inst. Banking, 1937-38; m. Gerayne C. Crawford, Oct. 10, 1935; children—James Rollie, Stephanie Ann. Admitted to Neb. bar, 1936, C.Z. bar, 1942; pvt. practice, Stuart, 1936; with First Nat. Bank & Trust Co., Mpls., 1937- 39, Pure Oil Co., 1939-40, Carnegie Dock & Fuel Co., 1940-42; atty., acting judge Panama Canal and Panama R.R. Co., 1942-45; pvt. practice, Blair, Neb., 1945-46; judge Magistrates Ct., Balboa, C.Z., 1946-51; with Conn. Mut. Life Ins. Co., Hartford, 1951—, now v.p., counsel; dir. Hartford Homes, Inc., 1960-68, v.p., 1963-68; instr. bus. law C.Z. Jr. Coll., 1947-48. Chmn., West Hartford Charter Revision Commn., 1963. Mem. West Hartford Town Council, 1959-63, v.p., 1961-63. Bd. govs. Panama Canal Employees Assn., 1946-51; chmn. Pacific com. Boy Scouts Am., 1950-51; mem. Chpt. Cathedral St. Luke Ancon, C.Z., 1946-51. Mem. Greater Hartford C. of C., Assn. Life Ins. Counsel, Am. Life Conv., Am. Neb., C.Z. (pres. 1949) bar assns., Pi Gamma Mu, Alpha Tau Omega. Republican. Episcopalian. Mason (Shriner). Home: 25 Clover Dr West Hartford, CT 06110. Office: 140 Garden St Hartford CT 06115

CHITTIM, RICHARD LEIGH, mathematician, educator; b. Easthampton, Mass., Dec. 2, 1915; s. Harry and Lulu (Hodges) C.; A.B., Bowdoin Coll., 1941; postgrad. Princeton, 1941-42, U. London, 1961-62; B.A. (Rhodes scholar), Merton Coll., Oxford U., 1950, M.A., 1954; m. Mary Elizabeth Young, July 22, 1949; children—David Bateman, Wendy, Nancy Hodges. Faculty math. Bowdoin Coll., Brunswick, Me., 1942—, prof., 1963—, clk. faculty, 1966—, dir., faculty NSF Summer and In- Service Insts., 1959—. Mathematician-programmer U.S. Geol. Survey, summers 1952-55, 57, IBM, summer, 1956. Troop committeeman Boy Scouts Am., 1952-53; campaign worker A.R.C. NSF sci. faculty fellow, 1961-62. Mem. Am. Math. Soc., Am. Assn. Rhodes Scholars, Assn. Tchrs. Math. in Me., Nat. Council Tchrs. Math., Phi Beta Kappa, Theta Delta Chi. Episcopalian (past vestryman). Home: 9 Wilson St Topsham ME 04086 Office: Seth Adams Hall Bowdoin Coll Brunswick ME 04011

CHITTY, ARTHUR BENJAMIN, assn. exec.; b. Jacksonville, Fla., June 15, 1914; s. Arthur Benjamin and Hazel T. (Brown) C.; B.A., U. of South, 1935; M.A., Tulane U., 1952; m. Elizabeth Nickinson, June 16, 1946; children—Arthur Benjamin III, John Abercrombie Merritt, Em Turner, Nathan Harsh Brown. Vice pres., sales mgr. Chitty & Co., Jacksonville, 1935-45, chmn. bd., 1962-67; mem. exec. com. Assn. Episcopal Colls., N.Y.C., 1964—, pres., 1965—. Pres. Sewanee (Tenn.) Civic Assn., 1948-49; historian Franklin County, Tenn., 1965-69; nat. bd. dirs. Camp Fire Girls, 1969. Trustee Fla. Episcopal Coll., 1968. Served with USNR, 1942-45. Mem. Asso. Alumni of U. of South (dir. pub. relations, exec. dir. 1946-66, historiographer 1954—), Church Hist. Soc. (dir. 1964—), St. George's Soc., Brotherhood St. Andrew (exec. com., nat council 1963-64, 66—, nat. v.p. 1969), Sigma Nu (chmn. Ednl. Found. 1969), Phi Beta Kappa, Phi Gamma Mu, Sigma Upsilon, Phi Alpha Theta. Club: Century (N.Y.C.). Author: Reconstruction at Sewanee, 1954. Contbr. articles to profl. jours. Home: 100 South Carolina Av Sewanee TN 37375 Office: 815 2d Av New York City NY 10017

CHITWOOD, JULIUS RICHARD, librarian; b. Magazine, Ark., June 1, 1921; s. Hoyt Mozart and Florence (Umfrid) C.; A.B. cum laude, Quachita Bapt. Coll., Ark., 1942; M.Mus., Ind. U., 1948; M.A., U. Chgo., 1954; m. Aileen Newsom, Aug. 6, 1944. Music supr. Edinburgh (Ind.) Pub. Schs., 1946-47; music and audiovisual librarian Roosevelt Coll., Chgo., 1948-51; humanities librarian Drake U., 1951-53; spl. cataloger Chgo. Tchrs. Coll., 1953; asst. circulation librarian Indpls. Pub. Library, 1954-57, coordinator adult services, 1957-61; dir. Rockford (Ill.) Pub. Library, 1961—, No. Ill. Library System, Rockford, 1966—. Chmn. subcom. library system devel. Ill. Library Adv. Com., 1965—; adv. com. U. Ill. Grad. Sch. Library Sci., 1964-68; program adv. com. Sauk Valley Jr. Coll., 1967; cons. in field, participant workshops. Mem. history com. Ill. Sesquicentennial Commn.; mem. Mayor Rockford Com. for UN, 1962—; sect. chmn. Rockford United Fund, 1966-; exec. bd. Rockford Civic Orch. Assn., 1962—. Served to maj., inf. AUS, 1942-45; ETO. Mem. Am. (chmn. subcom. revision standards of materials, pub. library div. 1965-66, pres. bldg. and equipment sect. library adminstrn. div. 1967-68, chmn. staff devel. com. personnel adminstrn. sect., library adminstrv. div. 1964-68, pres. library adminstrn. div. 1969—), Ill. (v.p. 1964-65, pres. 1965-66) library assns., Rockford area C. of C. Unitarian (pres. 1965-67). Rotarian (exec. bd. Rockford 1965-66). Club: Rockford University. Home: 2134 Oxford St Rockford, IL 61103. Office: 215 N Wyman St Rockford IL 61101

CHIU, ALFRED KAIMING, librarian; b. Chinhai, Chekiang, China, Mar. 11, 1898; s. Lienfang and Feng (Wang) C.; A.B., Boone U., 1922, A.M., 1927; Ph.D., Harvard, 1933; m. Hui-chun Huang, July 1, 1923; 1 dau., May-i; m. 2d, Katherine Yu Tseng, Aug. 24, 1939; children—Chuang-i, Hsuan-i, Hua-i, Wei-i. Librarian, Amoy U., 1922-24; custodian Chinese and Japanese books Harvard, 1927-30; chief research fellow Peiping Inst. Social Scis. Academia Sinica, 1930-31; librarian Chinese-Japanese library Harvard- Yenching Inst., 1931-65, hon. curator rare books Harvard-Yenching Library, 1965—, lectr. Chinese lit., 1936-65; univ. librarian, prof. Chinese U. Hong Kong, Kowloon, 1966-70. Vis. prof., curator Oriental collection Walter Library, U. Minn., 1965-66; cons. East Asian library material Boston Mus. Fine Arts, 1940-64, Far Eastern books U. Cal. Library, Berkeley, 1947, cataloging Far Eastern books A.L.A., 1954-68. Mem. Am. Oriental Soc., Far Eastern Assn., Spl. Libraries Assn. Author textbooks on classification; also section in China (MacNair, UN series). Contbr. articles to profl. mags., publs. Home: 37 Gorham St Cambridge MA 02138 Office: Harvard-Yenching Library 2 Divinity Av Cambridge MA 02138

CHOATE, ARTHUR O., Jr., investment banker; b. N.Y.C., Nov. 15, 1911; s. Arthur O. and Anne Hyde (Clarke) C.; grad. St. Mark's Sch., 1930; A.B., Harvard, 1934; m. Eloise Weld, Dec. 9, 1931; 1 son, Arthur B. Staff J.P. Morgan & Co., N.Y.C., 1934-39; fgn. rep. Clark Dodge & Co., N.Y.C., 1939-40, gen. partner, 1940—. also chmn. exec. com., dir.; dir. Dominion Equity Investments, Ltd., Montreal, Que., Can., Am. Sci. & Investments, Ltd. Montreal, Am. Sci. & Engring., Inc., Cambridge, Atcor Inc., Hawthorne, N.Y., Bowles Engring Corp., Silver Spring, Md., Istel Fund, N.Y.C., Nassau Fund, Princeton, Unitrode Corp., Watertown, Mass. Vice pres., dir. Lenox Hill Neighborhood Assn.; dir. bd. incorporators Diabetes Found. Served as lt. comdr. USNR, World War II. Decorated Bronze star medal. Club: Bond (N.Y.C.). Home: 162 E 66th St New York City NY 10021 Office: 140 Broadway New York City NY 10005

CHOATE, JOSEPH, lawyer; b. Santa Ana, Cal., Jan. 14, 1900; s. Walter Addison and Nellie E. (Jurd) C.; A.B., LL.B., U. So. Cal., 1925; LL.M., Harvard, 1936; postgrad. intramural session Oxford U., Internat. Law Seminar. U. Mich., 1937; LL.D., Salem Coll., W.Va., 1937; m. Dorothy Drew, 1939; 1 son, Joseph. Admitted to Cal. bar, 1927, U.S. Supreme Ct. bar, 1935; dep. dist. atty. Los Angeles County, Cal., 1927-34; in gen. practice of law, Los Angeles, pvt. internat. law. Public panel mem. War Labor Bd. Mem. Am., Los Angeles County, Internat. bar assns., Japan-Am. Soc. So. Cal., Am. Soc. Internat. Law, U.S. Naval Inst., S.R. (life), Delta Theta Phi. Presbyn. Mason (Shriner, K.T.). Clubs: Lincoln (Los Angeles); Harvard of California. Author: Qualifying for Destiny, 1937; also numerous legal articles. Home: 450 S Serrano Av Los Angeles CA 90005 Office: City Nat Bank Bldg Los Angeles CA 90014

CHOATE, ROBERT ALONZO, educator, musician; b. Anna. Ill., Oct. 22, 1910; s. Robert Melvin and Mary Ellen (Coffman) C.; student U. Ill., 1928-30; Mus. B. Cornell, Mt. Vernon, Ia., Mus. D., 1953; Mus.M., Northwestern U., 1939; student Wash. State Coll., 1940-42; Ed.D. Stanford, 1950; study music with Harold Baltz, Horace Whitehouse, Walter Stulz, Horace Miller; m. Helen Lucille LeMaster, Aug. 5, 1939; children—Mary Lucie, Robert Benjamin, John Gardner. Tchr. music pub. schs., Toledo, Ia., 1935-37; supr. music pub. schs., Polo. Ill., 1936-38; minister music First Presbyn. Ch., Spokane, Wash., 1939-42; dir. music edn. pub. schs., Spokane, 1939-42, Oakland Cal., 1942-50, Evanston, Ill., 1950-52; minister music St. John's Presbyn. Ch., Berkeley, Cal., 1942-50; mem. editorial bd. Music Educators Jour., 1948-50, chmn. bd. 1950-54; vis. prof. Northwestern U., chmn. dept. music edn., dir. placement sch. music, 1950-52; summer faculty U. Cal., Stanford; dean coll. music Boston U., 1952-54, dean school of fine and applied arts, 1954-60, also prof. music. Dir., cons. Manhattanville Music Curriculum project, 1964—; dir. Tanglewood Symposium, 1967, New Eng. Opera Theatre, 1953; mem. Boston com. Friends of Albert Schweitzer, 1953-60; chmn. music com. Boston Arts Festival, 1955-59. Trustee, mem. exec. com. Boston Opera Group; bd. dirs. Mass. Council for Humanities. Mem. Wash. Music Educators Assn. (pres. 1940-42), Cal. Sch. Suprs. Assn. (chmn. 1944-48), Music Educators Nat. Conf. (com. Latin Am. music, com. internat. relations. bd. dirs. 1946-50, exec. com. 1948-50 pres. 1954-56, chmn. publs. com. 1964—), Nat. Assn. Schs. Music (grad. commn.), Oakland Symphony Assn. (bd. dirs.). N.E.A., Am. Musicological Soc., Am. Assn. U. Profs., Am. Guild Organists, Boston Chamber Music Soc. (pres. 1963-66), Phi Delta Kappa, Phi Mu Alpha, Pi Kappa Lambda. Presbyn. Mason. Co-author: Music of Our Time, 1969; sr. author Music Texts-New Dimensions in Music, 1970. Editor; Music of China, 1947; Music of Latin America, 1947; Music In American Society, 1968; editorial bd. Jour. Aesthetic Edn., 1966—. Contbr. profl. publs. Home: 38 Otis St Newtonville MA 02160 Office: Sch Fine and Applied Arts Boston U Boston MA 02215

CHOATE, ROBERT BURNETT, civic worker, writer; b. Boston, Nov. 6, 1924; s. Robert B. and Katherine S. (Crosby) C.; grad. Phillips Exeter Acad., 1943; student Harvard, 1943- 44; B.S. in Civil Engring., U. Cal. at Berkeley, 1949; m. Audrey Evans, 1945 (div. 1953); m. 2d, Laura Jean Emery, Dec. 1956. Engring. positions with constrn., engring. cos., 1949- 53; Western regional mgr. Preload Constrn. Corp., San Francisco, 1953-54; civil engr. Sika Chem. Corp., 1955; pub. Reveille mag., Phoenix, 1965-66; officer real estate investments corp., 1957—. Founder, Careers for Youth, Phoenix, 1958, bd. dirs., 1958-66; cons. Pres. Kennedy's Nat. Service Corp., 1965, Citizens Crusade Against Poverty, 1967-68, Dept. Health, Edn., Welfare, 1969, Senate Com. on Labor and Pub. Welfare, 1970; chmn. Council on Children, Media, Merchandising, 1970—; program asso. Nat. Inst. Pub. Affairs, Washington, 1966-69; adminstrv. staff White House Conf. on Food, Nutrition and Health, 1969; food industry and advt. witness Senate Com. on Commerce, 1970; witness House Small Bus. Com., 1971; witness, cons. Senate Select Com. on Nutrition and Human Needs, 1971; witness FTC Hearings on Advt., 1971; bd. mem. Nat. Com. for an Effective Congress, 1966—, ALCOR, Alice Lloyd Coll., Pippa Passes, Ky., 1969—; participant Nat. Conf. on Citizens' Rights in Broadcasting, 1970, A.A.A.S., 1969. program asso. Nat. Inst. Affairs, Washington, 1966-69. Grantee Ford Found., 1964, Pres.'s Com. on Juvenile Delinquency, 1963. Registered profl. civil engr., Ariz.

CHODOROV, JEROME, playwright, dir.; b. N.Y.C., Aug. 10, 1911; s. Harry and Lena (Simmons) C.; student pub. schs.; m. Rhea Grand, Nov. 19, 1932; 1 dau., Susan. Playwright, dir., 1933—; dir. plays Gazebo, 1958-59, Make a Million, 1958-59; author screenplays (with Joseph Fields) My Sister Eileen, Louisiana Purchase, Tunnel of Love, 1958, (co-author) Happy Anniversary, 1959; author plays (with Joseph Field) My Sister Eileen, 1940, Junior Miss, 1941, Wonderful Town, 1952 (Antoinette Perry award, N.Y. Drama Critics award 1953), Anniversary Waltz, 1954, The Ponder Heart, 1957; (co-author) Tunnel of Love, 1957, 3 Bags Full, 1966; book for mus. comedy I Had a Ball, 1964; writer Los Angeles Civic Light Opera: The Great Waltz, 1965; The Student Prince, 1966; (musical) Dumas & Son, 1967; dir. Blood, Sweat and Stanley Poole, 1961. Served as capt. USAAF, 1942-44. Mem. Dramatists Guild Am. (past mem. council), Authors League Am. Home: 150 West End Av New York City NY 10023

CHODOROW, MARVIN, educator, physicist; b. Buffalo, July 16, 1913; s. Isidor and Lena (Cohen) C.; B.A., U. Buffalo, 1934; Ph.D., Mass. Inst. Tech., 1939; m. Leah Ruth Turitz, Sept. 19, 1937; children—Nancy Julia, Joan Elizabeth. Research asso. Pa. State Coll., 1940-41; instr. physics Coll. City N.Y., 1941-43; sr. project engr. Sperry Gyroscope Co., 1943-47; faculty Stanford, 1947—, prof. applied physics and elec. engring., 1954—, dir. microwave lab., 1959—, chmn. dept. applied physics, 1962-69. Cons. Def. Dept., Rand Corp.; vis. lectr. Ecole Normale Superieure, Paris, France, 1955-56; vis. research asso. U. Coll. London, 1969-70; designed 1st klystron for microwave relay systems, 1946, 1st megawatt klystron, 1949, 1st pulsed high power traveling-wave tubes, 1952-57. Fulbright fellow Cambridge (Eng.) U., 1962-63. Fellow I.E.E.E. (W.R.G. Baker award 1962), Am. Phys. Soc.; mem. Nat. Acad. Scis., Nat. Acad. Engring., Am. Assn. Physics Tchrs., A.A.A.S., Am. Assn. U. Profs., Phi Beta Kappa, Sigma Xi. Co- author: Fundamentals of Microwave Electronics, 1964. Contbr. articles to profl. jours. Home: 247 La Cuesta Dr Menlo Park CA 94025 Office: Microwave Lab Stanford U Stanford CA 94305

CHOGUILL, ORLO, clergyman; b. Humboldt, Kan., Jan. 14, 1904; s. Lewis G. and Effie (Ladd) C.; A.B., Coll. Emporia, 1926, D.D. (hon.), 1940; postgrad. McCormick Theol. Sem., 1929, U. Chgo., 1930; m. Berneice Morgan, June 25, 1929; children—Mary Alice (Mrs. Halverson), Catherine (Mrs. Goldsmith). Ordained to ministry Presbyn. Ch., 1929, pastor Flossmoor (Ill.) Community Ch., 1928-29, Ellsworth (Kan.) Presbyn. Ch., 1930-35, First Presbyn. Ch., Emporia, Kan., 1935-45, First Presbyn. Ch., Topeka, 1945-56, Tabernacle Ch., Indpls., 1956-64; minister 1st Presbyn. Ch., Hays, Kan., 1964-70; spl. asst. First Presbyn. Ch., Topeka, 1970—. Mem. synod com. Nat. Bd. Missions Presbyn. Church U.S.A., chmn. com. Christian edn. Synod Ind., 1959-64; mem. capital funds com. Presbyn. Gen. Assembly, 1963; lectr. Louisville Presbyn. Sem., 1963. Bd. dirs. McCormick Theol. Sem.; past gov. Menninger Found., Topeka; mem. bd. Kan. Childrens' Service League, Westminster Found., Kan Synod. Active YMCA. Mem. C. of C., Pi Kappa Delta. Mason (K.T., 32), Lion. Club: Contemporary, Author: Let Every Heart. Contbr. articles to profl. jours. Home: 4017 W 28th Terrace Topeka KS 66614

CHOKISKI, EARL L., city ofcl.; b. San Antonio, Apr. 22, 1920; s. Charles Steven and Gertrude (Benfer) C.; student Harvard; m. Claire Edith Steffens, July 21, 1949. With El Paso (Tex.) Police Dept., 1946—, now chief of police. Served with Armed Forces, 1939-45. Decorated Bronze Star. Mem. Tex. Police Assn., Internat. Assn. Chiefs Police, First Cav. Assn. Mason (32). Home: 3620 Comstock Ct El Paso TX 79904 Office: 500 E San Antonio El Paso TX 79901

CHOLLAR, ROBERT GANUN, found. exec.; b. Syracuse, N.Y., Feb. 10, 1914; s. Walter Edward and Estelle Augusta (GaNun) C.; student Dartmouth, 1931-32; B.S., Antioch Coll., 1933-34; m. Thelma Lucille Holt, Sept. 22, 1934; children—Charles Edward, Brian Holt, Richard Robert. Joined Nat. Cash Register Com., Dayton, O., 1933, analytical chemist, research chemist, head chem. research dept., dir. research, v.p. research, 1954-59, v.p. research and devel., 1959-64, v.p., group exec. research and devel., mfg., 1964-71; pres., chmn. bd. C.F. Kettering Found., Dayton, 1971—; dir. Dayton Power & Light Co. Mem. tech. adv. com. Cox Coronary Heart Inst.; mem. exec. com. Dayton-Miami Valley Consortium, Engring. and Sci. Inst. Dayton; nat. commn. coop. edn. Thomas Edison Found.; commerce tech. adv. bd. U.S. Dept. Commerce; mem. sci. adv. council Ohio Bd. Regents. Mem. Am. Chem. Soc., Indsl. Research Inst. (pres. 1960-61), Bus. Equipment Mfrs. Assn. (chmn. adv. com. plans and policy 1962-63, TC 97 sec. 1961—, dir.), N.A.M., Tau Beta Pi, Chi Phi. Clubs: Engineers' Dayton (past pres.), Moraine Country, Ohio Commodore. Patentee fields synthetic rubber, plastics, printing. Home: 4472 Lotz Rd Dayton OH 45429 Office: Charles F Kettering Found Dayton OH 45429

CHOLVIN, NEAL ROBERT, educator; b. Chippewa Falls, Wis., Sept. 8, 1928; s. Elmer Frank and Olympia (Elkow) C.; B.S., Wayne State U., 1949; D.V.M., Mich. State U., 1954, M.S., 1958; Ph.D., Ia. State U., 1961; m. Valerie Perkins, June 25, 1957; children—Brooke Diane, Craig Steven, Mark Douglas. From instr. to asso. prof. dept. vet. surgery and medicine Mich. State U., 1955-63; mem. Faculty Ia. State U., 1959- -, USPHS postdoctoral research fellow, 1960-61, prof. vet. physiology and pharmacology, 1963—, chmn. biomed. engring. program, 1963—. USPHS spl. research fellow U. Wash., 1971-72. Mem. Am. Physiol. Soc., A.A.A.S., Am. Soc. Artificial Internal Organs, Am. Vet. Med. Assn., Sigma Xi. Asso. editor: Lab. Animal Sci., 1967—. Research artificial heart control mechanisms. Home: 215 Hickory Dr Ames IA 50010

CHOMSKY, AVRAM NOAM, educator; b. Phila., Dec. 7, 1928; s. William and Elsie (Simonofsky) C.; B.A., U. Pa., 1949, M.A., 1951, Ph.D., 1955; D.H.L. (hon.), U. Chgo., 1967, Loyola U. Chgo., 1970, Swarthmore Coll., 1970, Bard Coll., 1971; D.Litt. (hon.), U. London (Eng.), 1967; m. Carol Doris Schatz, Dec. 24, 1949; children—Aviva, Diane, Harry Alan. Faculty, Mass. Inst. Tech., 1955—, prof. modern langs., 1961—, Ferrari P. Ward prof. modern lang. and linguistics, 1966—. Vis. prof. Columbia, 1957-58; mem. Inst. Advanced Study, Princeton, 1958-59; Linguistic Soc. Am. prof. U. Cal. at Los Angeles, summer 1966; Beckman prof. U. Cal. at Berkeley, 1966-67; John Locke lectr. Oxford, 1969. Jr. fellow Soc. Fellows, Harvard, 1951-55, research fellow Harvard Cognitive Studies Center, 1964-67. Fellow A.A.A.S.; mem. Am. Acad. Arts and Scis., Linguistic Soc. Am., Am. Philol. Assn., Assn. Symbolic Logic, Am. Acad. Polit. and Social Sci., Aristotelian Soc. Gt. Britain. Author: Syntactic Structures, 1957; Current Issues in Linguistic Theory, 1964; Aspects of the Theory of Syntax, 1965; Cartesian Linguistics, 1966; Topics in the Theory of Generative Grammar, 1966; (with Morris Halle) Sound Pattern of English, 1968; Language and Mind, 1968; American Power and the New Mandarins, 1969; At War with Asia, 1970; Problems of Knowledge and Freedom, 1971. Home: 15 Suzanne Road Lexington MA 02173 Office: Mass Inst Tech Massachusetts Av Cambridge MA 02139

CHON, MYRON EDWARD, advt. exec.; b. Chgo., Dec. 12, 1901; s. Benjamin W. and Anna (Bransky) C.; A.B., U. Mich., 1923; m. Bernice Larson, July 30, 1937 (dec. 1959). Copywriter, J. Walter Thompson Chgo., 1923-25; copy dir. William H. Rankin Co., Chgo., 1926-33; exec. creative dir. Arthur Meyerhoff Assos., Inc., Chgo., 1934—, exec. v.p., 1962—. Mem. A.S.C.A.P. Composer musicals, compositions and commls. Home: 1209 Astor St Chicago IL 60610. Office: 410 N Michigan Av Chicago IL 60611

CHOO, YOUNGHAN, former Korean diplomat; b. Hai An Myun, Yang Koo, Kang Won Do, Korea, Dec. 12, 1894; s. Hark Sang and no Soon (Shin) Choo; grad. Korean Central Inst., Honolulu, T.H., 1915; student Los Angeles Bible Inst., 1918-19, Taylor U., Upland Ind., 1920-22; m. Ida Margarete Hirt, June 23, 1935. Naturalized Am. citizen, 1963. Pub. weekly newspaper Minon (People Speak), in Korean, Los Angeles, 1919-20; asst. mgr. cafeteria Central YMCA, Cleve., 1923-28; propr. New Korean Kitchen, Cleve., Akron, O., 1929-49; pub. Korean Open Letter, monthly English and Korean, 1943—; consul gen. Korean Consultate, San Francisco, 1949-60, sub-dean San Francisco Consular Corps, 1958-60; chief procurement officer for Korea, in U.S. west of Miss. River, 1952-60. With Korean Commn., Washington, 1924; govt. rep. 1st World Congress Flight, Nev., 1959. Hon. v.p. 1st World Congress Flight, Nev., 1959. Hon. v.p. Dong Ji Hoi N.Am.; chmn. bd. dirs. Sung Ae Boyuk Won Orphanage, Yang Ku Korea; founder. chmn. bd. Young Han High Sch., Hai Ahn Myun, Korea. Pres., N. San Mateo County Republican Assembly, 1966, precinct capt., 1964. Recipient citation for outstanding achievements and patriotism Pres. Syngman Rhee, Korea, 1952; named hon. col. Okla., hon. citizen Tex., Dallas, Ft. Worth, Mpls.; citations, plaque Korean Army, Korean Marine Corps, Chief Naval Operations; bronze plaque Dong Ji Hoi N.Am. for outstanding service Republic Korea and Dong Ji Hoi; medal, bar for 10 year govt. service Republic Korea, 1960. Mem. Serra Highland Improvement Assn. (civic chmn. 1961-62, pres., 1962-63), Dong Ji Hoi (ofcl.), Dong Ji Hoi N.Am. (chmn. trustees), Nat. Geog. Soc., Internat. Platform Assn., Korean Bible Soc., Cal. Automobile Assn. Methodist. Rotarian Clubs: Top Flight, Seoul Country (Korea): Commonwealth of California (chmn. African problems sect. San Francisco 1966—); 26 Million. Founder, Young Han Ch., Hai Ahn Myun, Kang Won Do, Korea. Address: 351 Newman Dr South San Francisco CA 94080

CHOOKASIAN, LLLI, Contralto; studied in Chgo.; pupil of Rose Ponselle, Tchr. singing Northwestern U.; debut as Azucena in Il Trovatore, Balt. Civic Opera, 1960; N.Y.C. debut with N.Y. Philharmonic in Alexander Nevsky, 1961; debut with Met. Opera as La Cieca in La Gioconda, 1962; appeared as Herodias in Salome at Festival of Two Worlds, Spoleto, Italy. Address: 25 Sussex Rd Tenafly NJ 07670*

CHOONICK, HARRY, physician. Supt., Southeast Ohio Mental Health Center, Athens. Office: Southeast Ohio Mental Health Center Athens OH 45701*

CHOPE, HAROLD DELOS, ret. physician, educator; b. King City, Cal., Mar. 25, 1904; s. John Edward and Nellie M. (Rickard) C.; A.B., Stanford, 1926, M.D., 1931; M.P.H. cum laude, Harvard, 1933, Dr. Pub. Health cum laude, 1940; m. Marjorie Ann Campbell, Aug. 3, 1929; children—Cecille (Mrs. Raymond Whittle) (dec.), Peter. Intern Stanford Hosp., 1930-31, resident, 1931-32; practice medicine, specializing in preventive medicine, San Mateo, Cal., 1948-70; research instr. dept. preventive medicine Stanford, 1929-31, instr., 1931-32, clin. prof. Sch. Medicine, 1955-69, emeritus, 1969—; chief Bur. Epidemiology, St. Louis City Health Dept., 1933-34; asst. dir. Cal. Health Dept., 1934-35; health officer, Newton, Mass., 1935-40; dir. field tng. unit, instr. dept. pub. health adminstrn. Harvard, 1935-40, asso. pub. health adminstrn. Sch. Pub. Health, 1940-41; lectr. Simmons Sch. Pub. Health Nursing, 1936-41; mem. staff Internat. Health div. Rockefeller Found., Sao Paulo, Brazil, 1941-44; asst. dist. health officer San Joaquin Dist., Stockton, Cal., 1944-48; lectr. Pub. Health Adminstrn. U. Cal. at Berkeley, 1947—; dir. Dept. Pub. Health and Welfare, San Mateo, 1948-70. Pres. Cal. Conf. Local Health Officers, 1955; pres. Cal. Conf. Local Mental Health Dirs., 1960-61; mem. Regional Water Pollution Control Bd., 1949-51; mem. State Hosp. Adv. Council, 1950-61; chmn. health, hosp. adv. bd. County Suprs. Assn., 1956-69; cons. community services com. Nat. Inst. Mental Health, 1959-60, chmn., 1961, chmn. tng. com., 1963—; chmn. Bay Area Regional Health Facilities Planning Com., 1962-64; mem. State Adv. Com. Pub. Med. Care for Children, 1962—; mem. Gov.'s Adv. Com. Mental Health, 1963-65; mem. Gov.'s Study Commn. Mental Retardation, 1963-65; mem. Nat. Com. Community Health Services, 1963—. Bd. dirs. Nat. League Nursing. Recipient Bronfman prize for pub. health achievement, 1963. Diplomate Am. Bd. Preventive Medicine. Mem. Am. Assn. Pub. Health Ofcls., Am. Cancer Soc. (dir. San Mateo County chpt.), Cal. Acad. Medicine, Cal. Med. Assn., San Mateo County Med. Soc., Western Hosps. Assn., Phi Beta Kappa, Alpha Omega Alpha, Delta Omega. Bd. editors: Pub. Health Reports, 1957-60. Contbr. articles to profl. Jours. Home: 1509 Pine Knoll Dr Belmont, CA 94002.

CHOPE, HENRY ROY, inventor, engr.; b. Louisville, July 19, 1921; s. Henry Roy and Amelia (Gutermuth) C.; B.E.E., Ohio State U., 1948; M.S., Cal. Inst. Tech. 1948; S.M., Harvard, 1950; m. Lois Elizabeth Sherman, June 11, 1954; children—Elizabeth Ann, David Roy, Amelia Louise, Charles Sherman. Electronic scientist rocket devel. USAF, 1949-50; atomic scientist, 1950-53; exec. v.p., dir. Indsl. Nucleonics Corp., Columbus, O., 1952—; v.p., dir. Accu Ray (U.K.) Ltd., Accu Ray Can. Ltd. Mem. labor-mgmt. adv. com. AEC, 1965—, adv. com. isotopes and radiation devel., 1966-67; mem. Ohio Atomic Energy Adv. Bd.; mem. adv. com. innovation Pres.'s Office Sci. and Tech., 1964; mem. adv. com. state tech. services Ohio Bd. Regents; mem. adv. com. on health care Am. people A.M.A. Trustee, sec., mem. exec., finance coms. Riverside Meth. Hosp., Columbus; trustee Riverside Meth. Hosp. Med. Research Found., Ohio Wesleyan U., Delaware; bd. dirs. Ohio State U. Research Found. Recipient Dist. Alumnus award Ohio State U., 1961, Alumni Centennial award, 1970. Registered profl. engr., Ohio. Fellow A.A.A.S.; sr. mem. I.E.E.E. (Morris E. Leeds award 1967), Instruments Soc. Am., Am. Nuclear Soc.; mem. Nat. Soc. Profl. Engrs., U.S. (dir., chmn. sci. and tech. com. 1968-70), Ohio (dir.), Columbus (dir.) chambers commerce, Newcomen Soc. N.Am., Tau Beta Pi (pres., chmn. exec. com. 1966-70), Eta Kappa Nu, Theta Tau, Pi Kappa Alpha. Clubs: Scioto Country (Columbus); Harvard (N.Y.C., Central Ohio). Patentee nuclear energy, instrumentation, process control. Contbr. tech. papers to profl. lit. Home: 3885 Woodbridge Rd Columbus OH 43220 Office: 650 Ackerman Rd Columbus OH 43202

CHOPE, WILBERT EARL, corp. exec.; b. Louisville, June 11, 1923; s. Henry R. and Amelia (Gutermuth Laufer) C.; student Vanderbilt U., 1941-42; B.E.E., Ohio State U., 1948; M.S., Mass. Inst. Tech., 1949; D.Sc. (hon.), Muskingum Coll., 1966; m. Joanne Begg, Feb. 26, 1955; children—Douglas Begg, Katherine Begg. Pres. Indsl. Nucleonics Corp., Columbus, O., 1950-67, chmn. bd., 1967-70, cons., 1970—; pres., dir. AccuRay Corp., AccuRay Can., Ltd., AccuRay (U.K.), Ltd.-AccuRay Europe U.S.A. Trustee Found. Instrument Edn. and Research; chmn. bd. trustees World Neighbors, Inc. Served as 1st lt., Signal Corps, AUS, 1942-46. Recipient Distinguished Service award for Columbus and Ohio, U.S. Jr. C. of C., 1952, named one of ten outstanding young men, 1957. Mem. I.E.E.E., Instrument Soc. AM., Def. Orientation Conf. Assn., Young President's Orgn., Nat. Soc. Profl. Engrs., Ohio State U., Mass. Inst. Tech. alumni assns., Pi Kappa Alpha, Tau Beta Pi, Eta Kappa Nu (outstanding young elec. engr. 1955). Patentee in field. Home: 12750 Red Rd Coral Gables FL 33156 Office: 100 Edgewater Dr Coral Gables FL 33133

CHOPER, JESSE HERBERT, educator; b. Wilkes-Barre, Pa., Sept. 19, 1935; s. Edward and Dorothy (Resnick) C.; B.S., Wilkes Coll., 1957, D.H.L., 1967; LL.B., U. Pa., 1960; m. Sonya Rae Schwartz, June 27, 1961; 1 son, Marc Steven. Admitted to D.C., 1961; instr. Wharton Sch., U. Pa. 1957-60; law clk. Chief Justice Earl Warren, 1960-61; asst. prof. U. Minn. Law Sch., 1961-62, asso. prof., 1962-65; prof. U. Cal. Law Sch. at Berkeley, 1965—; vis. prof. Cath. U. Law Sch., 1967, Harvard, 1970-71. Mem. Am. Assn. U. Profs., Order of Coif. Democrat. Jewish religion. Author: Constitutional Law, Cases-Comments-Questions, 3d edit., 1970; The American Constitution, Cases and Materials, 3d edit., 1970; Constitutional

Rights and Liberties, Cases and Materials, 3d edit., 1970; Corporations, Cases and Materials, 1966. Contbr. articles profl. jours. Home: 115 Alvarado Rd Berkeley CA 94705

CHOPPIN, GREGORY ROBERT, chemist, educator; b. Eagle Lake, Tex., Nov. 9, 1927; s. Gilbert P. and Nellie (Guidroz) C.; B.S., Loyola U., New Orleans, 1949, D.Sc. (hon.), 1969; Ph.D., U. Tex., 1953; m. Ann M. Warner, June 9, 1951; children—Denise, Suzanne, Paul, Nadine. Research scientist Lawrence Radiation Lab., U. Cal., Berkeley, 1953-56; mem. faculty Fla. State U., Tallahassee, 1956—, prof. chemistry, 1963—, chmn. dept. chemistry, 1968—; vis. scientist Centre D'Etude Nucleaires, Mol-Donk, Belgium, 1962-63; Fulbright-Hayes lectr. Uruguay, 1965, Portugal, 1969. Chmn. sub-com. on radiochemistry com. on nuclear sci. Nat. Acad. Sci.-NRC, 1966—. Named Young Man of Year, El Cerrito (Cal.) Jr. C. of C., 1956. Mem. Am. Chem. Soc., A.A.A.S., Phi Beta Kappa, Sigma Xi. Author: Experimental Nuclear Chemistry, 1961; Nuclei and Radioactivity, 1964; (with B. Jaffe) Chemistry The Science of Matter, Energy and Change, 2d edit. 1970; (with R.H. Johnson) Introductory Chemistry, 1971. Contbr. articles profl. jours. Home: 3290 Longleaf Rd Tallahassee FL 32304

CHORAFAS, DIMITRIS N., engring., mgmt. cons., educator; b. Athens, Greece, Mar. 25, 1926; s. Nicolas and Chryssi (Sissini) C.; Dr. Math., U. Paris, 1958; M.S., U. Cal. at Los Angeles, 1954; M.E.E., Nat. Tech. U., Athens, 1953; postgrad. U. Denver, 1953, George Washington U., 1956. Faculty, Sch. Engring. and Architecture Cath. U. Am., 1956-62; vis. prof. information sci., bus. adminstrn. Wash. State U., 1965-67; chmn. dept. information sci. Centre d'Etudes Industrielles, U. Geneva, 1967-69; vis. prof. information sci. Ga. Inst. Tech., 1968-69, Tech. U., Karlsruhe, Germany, 1970—; systems engr. IBM, Corp., 1957-60; dir. mgmt. information systems Booz, Allen & Hamilton Internat., Inc., Paris and Zurich, 1960-61. Served with Greek Army, 1944-45, 49-51. Mem. Assn. Computing Machinery, Soc. Indsl. and Applied Math., Tech. Chamber Greece. Author: Operations Research for Industrial Management, 1958; Statistical Process and Reliability Engineering, 1960; The Functions of Research in the Enterprise, 1960; Computer Theory, 1960; Computer Applications in Industry and Commerce, 1961; Programming Systems for Electronic Computers, 1962; Industrial Strategy, 1962; New Methods of Economic Analysis, 1963; The Influence of the Computer on the Organization, 1964; Systems and Simulation, 1965; Control Systems Functions, 1966; An Introduction to Product Planning, 1967; Sales Engineering, 1967; Managing Industrial Research For Profits, 1967; La Direction des Nouveaux Produits, 1967; Developing The International Executive, 1967; Selecting The Computer System, 1967; Programmiersysteme fur Electronische Rechenanlogen 1967; The Knowledge Revolution, 1968 (transl., pub. in 14 countries); How to Manage Computers for Results, 1969; Overcoming the Communications Barrier in International Business; Computer Erfolgreich Einseteen, 1970; Introduction to Computing, 1971; Programming Languages, 1971; Executive Development, 1971; Information Systems Design, 1971. Home: Domaine Valmer 06 Saint Laurent d'Eze AM France Office: 11 rue Arc de Triomphe Paris France

CHORBAJIAN, HERBERT GHEVONT, banker; b. Albany, N.Y., Sept. 4, 1938; s. Ghevont and Anna (Bedian) C.; B.S., Boston U., 1959; m. Linda Joyce Postoian, Oct. 30, 1966; 1 son, Gilbert. Staff auditor S.D. Leidesdorf & Co., N.Y.C., 1959-61, 61-62; staff auditor Peat, Marwick, Mitchell & Co., Albany, 1962-67, supr., 1967-68, mgr., 1969; asst. controller State Bank Albany, 1969-70, controller, 1970—. Served with AUS, 1961. C.P.A., N.Y. Mem. Am. Inst. C.P.A.'s, N.Y. Soc. C.P.A.'s, Bank Adminstrn. Inst., Am. Inst. Banking, Armenian Students Assn. (auditor 1968-69), Albany C. of C., Beta Gamma Sigma. Mem. Armenian Apostolic Ch. (auditor). Clubs: University Exchange (past pres., dir.) (Albany). Home: 21 Timberland Dr Loudonville NY 12211 Office: 69 State St Albany NY 12201

CHORNOCK, ORESTES P., head bishop Am. Carpatho-Russian Orthodox Greek Catholic Ch. Address: 2302 Nicholas Av Stratford CT 06497*

CHORON, JACQUES, philosopher; b. Shavli, Russia, Jan. 8, 1904; s. Naum and Anna (Landesberg) Choron-Zicky; U. Berlin (Germany), 1922-25; Ph.D., U. Leipzig (Germany), 1928; D.Social Sci., New Sch. Social Research, 1960; 1 dau., Victoria. Came to U.S., 1941, naturalized, 1946. Faculty, New Sch. Social Research, 1958-64; fellow Los Angeles Suicide Prevention Center, 1965-66; vis. prof. dept. psychiatry U. So. Cal., Los Angeles, 1965-66; dist. fellow Center Studies Suicide Prevention, Nat. Inst. Mental Health, 1967-69; adviser at large Found. Thanatology. Hon. fellow Am. Suicidology; mem. Am. Philos. Assn., Internat. Assn. Suicide Prevention. Author: La doctrine bolcheviste, 1935; L'Impasse, 1936; Romance of Philosophy, 1964; Death and Western Thought, 1963; Modern Man and Mortality, 1964; Suicide, 1972; also papers. Home: 21 W 86th St New York City NY 10024

CHOTINER, MURRAY M., lawyer; b. Pitts., Oct. 4, 1909; s. Albert H. and Sarah (Chass) C.; student U. Cal. at Los Angeles, 1925-26; LL.B., Southwestern U., 1929; 1 son, Kenneth L. Admitted to Cal. bar, 1931; practiced in Newport Beach, Beverly Hills and Los Angeles, 1931-69, Washington, 1971—; gen. counsel Office Spl. Rep. for Trade Negotiations, Exec. Office Pres., 1969-70; spl. counsel to Pres. Nixon, 1970-71. Office: 1701 Pennsylvania Av NW Washington DC 20006

CHOU, KUO-PING, educator; b. Ningpo, China, Aug. 2, 1908; s. T.S. and P.T. (Chang) Chou; Student Yenching U., Peking, China, 1931-33; B.A., Pembroke Coll., 1935; M.A., Yale, 1947; Ph.D., U. Mich., 1952. Came to U.S., 1946, naturalized, 1954. Faculty, U. Wis., Madison, 1952—, prof. Chinese linguistics, Chinese, 1963—. Mem. Linguistic Soc. Am., Assn. for Asian Studies, Modern Lang. Assn., Chinese Lang. Tchrs. Assn. Home: 3319 Harvey St Madison WI 53705

CHOU, SHELLEY NIEN-CHUN, medical educator; b. Chekiang, China, Feb. 6, 1924; s. Shelley P. and Tse-tsun (Chao) C.; B.S., St. John's U., Shanghai, China, 1946; M.D., U. Utah, 1949; M.S., U. Minn., 1954, Ph.D., 1964; m. Jolene Johnson, Nov. 24, 1956; children—Shelley T., Dana, Kerry. Resident, U. Minn. Hosps., 1950-55; practice medicine, specializing in neurosurgery, Salt Lake City, 1955-58, Bethesda, Md., 1959, Mpls., 1960—; clin. asst. Coll. Medicine U. Utah, 1956-58; vis. scientist Nat. Insts. Neurol. Diseases and Blindness NIH, 1959; mem. faculty U. Minn., 1960—, asso. prof. neurosurgery, 1965-68, prof. neurosurgery, 1968—. Diplomate Am. Bd. Neurosurgery. Mem. A.M.A., A.C.S., Congress Neurol. Surgery, Soc. Neurol. Surgeons, Soc. Nuclear Medicine, Harvey Cushing Soc., Neurosurg. Soc. N.Am., N.Y. Acad. Medicine, Forum U. Neurosurgeons, A.A.A.S., Phi Rho Sigma. Contbr. numerous articles to profl. jours. Publs. on studies of intracranial lesions using radioactive angiography techniques; malformations of cerebral vasculature; neurol. dysfunctions of urinary bladder. Home: 2 Otter Lane North Oaks MN 55110 Office: B-590 Mayo Meml 412 S E Union St Minneapolis MN 55455

CHOU, WEN-CHUNG, composer; b. Chefoo, China, June 29, 1923; s. Chung-chieh and Shou-hsien (Fu) C.; came to U.S., 1946, naturalized, 1958; B.S., Nat. Chungking U., 1945; student New Eng. Conservatory Music, 1946-49; M.A., Columbia, 1954; student composition with Edgard Varèse, 1949-54; m. Yi-an Chang, June 23, 1962; children—Luyen, Sumin. Dir. research program classical Chinese music Columbia, 1955-57; panelist music and dance 6th Nat. Conf. UNESCO, 1957; composer-in-residence U. Ill., 1958-59, Festival of Arts of This Century, East-West Center Honolulu, 1967; lit. executor Varèse's music and papers, 1965—; chmn. music div. Sch. Arts Columbia University; prin. speaker UNESCO Internat. Music Symposium, Manila, Philippines, 1966; composer-in-residence Koussevitzky Composers Studio, Tanglewood, 1970; guest tchr. Berkshire Music Center, 1970. Mem. selection com. Am. Music Center Publn. award, 1961, student composers award Broadcast Music, Inc., 1961, 64, 66, 67, 69, 70, 71; sec., bd. dirs. Composers Forum, 1964—. Recipient commn. Louisville Orch., 1954; grantee Rockefeller Found., 1955-57; Guggenheim fellow, 1957-58, 59-60; commn. Am. Wind Symphony Orch., 1961, 64; award Nat. Inst., Arts and Letters, 1963, William and Noma Copley Found., 1966. Mem. Internat. Soc. Contemporary Music (bd. dirs. U.S. sect. 1960-64, 67-70), Am. Composers Alliance (bd. govs. 1963—, chmn. admissions com. 1963, chmn. editorial bd. 1963-65, exec. com. 1964-69), Am. Soc. Univ. Composers, Soc. Asian Music (bd. dirs. 1967). Composer: (for orch.) Landscapes, 1949, All in the Spring Wind, 1952-53, And The Fallen Petals, 1954, In The Mode of Shang, 1956; (for harp and flute) Three Folksongs, 1950; (for harp and wind quintet) Suite, 1951; (for high voice and instrumental ensemble) Seven Poems of T'ang Dynasty, 1951-52; (for chamber ensemble) Two Miniatures From T'ang Dynasty, 1957; (for piano) The Willow Are New, 1957; (for clarinet with strings) To A Wayfarer, 1958; (for trumpet with brass and percussion ensemble) Soliloquy of a Bhiksuni, 1958; Poems of White Stone, 1958-59; (for wind symphony orch.) Metaphors, 1961, Riding the Wind, 1964; (for flute and piano) Cursive, 1963; (for piano, percussion and strings) The Dark and The Light, 1964; (for 9 players) Yu Ko, 1965; (chamber concerto for piano, winds and percussion) Pien, 1966; Yun for winds, two pianos, and percussion, 1969. Editorial bd. Asian Music, 1968—. Pres. Composers Redordings Inc., 1970—. Author: articles in field. Address: 22 E 10th St New York City NY 10003

CHOU EN-LAI, premier and foreign minister Chinese People's Republic; b. 1898; ed. Nankai U., Tientsin; m. Teng Ying-chao. Active in work of Communist Party, 1921—; became sec. and chief of polit. dept. Whampoa Mil. Acad., 1924; became polit. commissar First Army (under Chiang Kaishek); joined Communist insurrectionists against First Army, at Shanghai; acted as liaison man between Communists, Nationalists and representatives of Western nations, Chungking, China, 9 yrs.; mem. People's Polit. Council, 1945—; premier, fgn. minister Chinese People's Republic, 1949—; rep. of Chinese People's Republic at Geneva Conf., 1954.

CHOULES, GEORGE THOMAS, lawyer; b. Driggs, Ida., Mar. 16, 1928; s. Albert and Rula S. (Wilson) C.; student Brigham Young U., 1946-47, 1950; U. Utah, 1950-52; LL.B., Ia. State U., 1956; m. Ida Louise Blair, July 15, 1964; children-Eric Thomas, Michele Lynn, Heather Kristin. Admitted to Ia. bar, 1956, Ariz. bar, 1958; law clerk Ariz. Supreme Ct., 1957-58; mem. firm Westover, Mansfield, Westover & Copple (now Westover, Keddie & Choules), Yuma, 1958—. Mem. Com. Fourteen, Yuma, 1965—, Western States Water Council, 1970—. Mem. Nat. Water Resources Assn. (resolutions com.) Ia., Ariz., Am., Yuma County bar assns., Caballeros de Yuma (pres. 1965), Yuma County C. of C. (bd. dirs. 1963-65), Yuma Fine Arts Assn. (bd. dirs. 1965—), Yuma County Hist. Soc. (bd. dirs. 1968—). Mem. Ch. Jesus Christ of Latter Day Saints (1st counselor Yuma Stake presidency, 1969- -). Club: Golf and Country (pres. 1966), (Yuma). Home: 1483 Gateway Yuma AZ 85364 Office: 190 Madison Av Yuma AZ 85364

CHOVER, JOSHUA, educator, mathematician; b. Detroit, Mar. 26, 1928; s. Abraham S. and Yetta (Weine) C.; B.S., U. Mich., 1949, Ph.D., 1952, m. Flora Lewin, Feb. 3, 1952; children—Daniel B., David A. Research mathematician Bell Telephone Labs., 1951-55; mem. Inst. Advanced Study, Princeton, 1955-56; mem. faculty U. Wis., 1956—, prof. math., 1965—. Mem. Am. Math. Soc. (asso. editor Proc.), Soc. Indsl. and Applied Math., Phi Beta Kappa, Sigma Xi, Phi Eta Sigma. Contbr. articles in field. Editor: Markov Processes and Potential Theory, 1967. Home: 202 Du Rose Terrace Madison, WI 53705.

CHOW, BACON FIELD, educator; b. Foo Chow, China, July 22, 1909; s. Yu-Sing and Su-Fong (Liu) C.; came to U.S., 1927, naturalized, 1942; B.S., U. Ill., 1929; Ph.D., Harvard, 1932; m. Idella Tong, June 30, 1931; children—Jean (Mrs. Vernon Wong), Bryant. Asst., Harvard, 1931-33; fellow Rockefeller Hosp., N.Y.C., 1933-35; asso. prof. Peking Union Med. Coll., 1935-38; head phys. chemistry and nutrition dept. Squibb Inst. Med. Research, 1938-48; prof. biochemistry Sch. Hygiene, Johns Hopkins, 1948. Mem. Am. Inst. Nutrition, Am. Assn. Immunologists, Soc. Internal Secretions, Am. Soc. Clin. Nutrition, Am. Soc. Biol. chemists, Am. Pub. Health Assn., Parlorian Soc. Home: 4518 Arabia Av Baltimore MD 21214.

CHOW, GREGORY CHI-CHONG, educator, economist; b. Macau, S.China, Dec. 25, 1929; s. Tin-Pong and Pauline (Law) C.; came to U.S., 1948, naturalized, 1963; B.A., Cornell U., 1951; M.A., U. Chgo., 1952, Ph.D., 1955; m. Paula K. Chen, Aug. 27, 1955; children—John S., James S., Jeanne S. Asst. prof. Mass. Inst. Tech., 1955-59; asso. prof. Cornell U., 1959-62, vis. prof., 1964-65; staff mem., mgr. econ. models IBM Research Center, Yorktown Heights, N.Y., 1962-70; prof. Princeton, 1970—, also dir. econ. research program; adj. prof. Columbia, 1965—; vis. prof. Harvard, 1967, Rutgers U., 1969. Fellow Econometric Soc., Academia Sinica; mem. Am. Econ. Assn., Am. Statis. Assn., Inst. Math. Statistics. Author: Demand for Automobiles in the United States: A Study in Consumer Durables, 1957. Bd. editors: Am. Econ. Rev., 1970—. Contbr. to The Demand for Durable Goods, 1960; also articles profl. jours. Home: Hardy Dr Princeton NJ 08540

CHOW, KAO LIANG, neuropsychologist, educator; b. Tientsin, China, Apr. 21, 1918; s. Su Tau and Tau Yu (Tsau) C.; B.S., Yenching U., China, 1943; Ph.D., Harvard, 1950; m. Margaret W.C. Zee, May 2, 1964. Came to U.S., 1946, naturalized, 1963. Staff, Yerkes Lab. Primate Biology, Orange Park, Fla., 1947-54, research asso., 1947-54; faculty U. Chgo., 1954-61; mem. faculty Stanford Med. Sch., Palo Alto, Cal., 1961—, prof. neurology, 1965—. Mem. Internat. Brain Research Orgn., N.Y. Acad. Scis., Am. Physiol. Assn., A.A.A.S., Sigma Xi. Contbr. articles profl. jours. Home: 101 Alma St Palo Alto CA 94301

CHOW, SHU-KAI, Chinese diplomat; b. Hupeh, China, Aug. 21, 1913; s. Ching-Shih and Mao (Tso-chen) C.; B.A., Nat. Central U., Nanking, China, 1935; research student U. London (Eng.), 1939-42; m. Lily Chang; children—Shirley, Franklin. Chinese consul, Manchester, Eng., 1944-45; asso. prof. internat. relations U. Nanking, 1946-47; dep. dir. information dept. Ministry Fgn. Affairs, 1947-49; minister, charge d'affairs embassy, Manila, Philippines, 1953-55; chief del. to ECAFE, UN, 1953; vice minister fgn. affairs, 1956-60; cabinet minister, chmn. overseas Chinese affairs, 1960-62; spl. envoy to independence celebrations of Madagascar and Malta, 1960, 64; rep. China to 16th-19th sessions UN Gen. Assembly; Chinese ambassador to Spain, 1963-65, to U.S.A., 1965—. Home: 3225 Woodley Rd NW Washington DC 20008. Office: 2311 Massachusetts Av NW Washington DC 20008

CHOW, TSE-TSUNG, educator, author; b. Kiyang, Hunan, China, Jan. 7, 1916; s. P'eng-Chu and Ai-Ku (Tsou) C.; B.A., Cheng-Chih U., 1942; M.A., U. Mich., 1950, Ph.D., 1955; m. Nancy H.N. Wu; children—Lena Jane, Genie Ann. Editor-in-chief New Understanding monthly, Chungking, China, 1942-43; dir. dept. research and supervision Chungking Municipal Govt., 1943-44; editor-in-chief City Govt., monthly, 1943-44; editor New Critic monthly, 1945; dean Chungking Coll. Pub. Adminstrn., 1944; sec. to Pres. Republic China, 1945-47; research asst. U. Mich., 1955; research fellow Harvard, 1956-60, research asso., 1961-62; vis. lectr. U. Wis., Madison, 1963, asso. prof., 1964-65, prof., 1966—. Recipient medal honor Chinese Govt., 1946. Guggenheim fellow, 1966-67. Mem. Modern Lang. Assn., Assn. Asian Studies, Island Soc. Singapore (hon. pres.). Author: Election, Initiative, Referendum and Recall: Charter Provisions in Michigan Home Rule Cities, 1958; The May Fourth Movement: Intellectual Revolution in Modern China, 1960; Research Guide to The May Fourth Movement, 1963; Hai-yen (Stormy Petrel) (collected poems), 1961; A New Study of the Broken Axes in the book of poetry, 1969; An Index to Mathews' Chinese-English Dictionary with a New Method of Arranging Chinese Words, 1971. Editor: Wen-Lin: Studies in the Chinese Humanities, 1968; On Wang Kuo-wei's Tz'u Poetry, 1971; Chinese transl. Rabindranath Tagore's Fireflies, 1971; Stray Birds, 1971. Home: 1101 Minton Rd Madison WI 53711

CHOW, VEN TE, educator, engring. cons.; b. Hangchow, China, Aug. 14, 1919; s. Chung Tan and Chin Yu (Young) C.; B.S., Nat. Chiao Tung U., 1940; M.S., Pa. State U., 1948; Ph.D., U. Ill., 1950; m. Lora Y. Shu, June 3, 1961; children—Margot, Marana. Came to U.S., 1947, naturalized, 1962. Head instr. engring Gt. China Sch., Shanghai, 1940-41; instr. civil engring. Universitato Utopio, Shanghai, 1941-43; asst. prof. China Agrl. and Textile Engring. Coll., Shanghai, 1943-45; civil engr. Bur. Pub. Works, Taiwan, 1945-46; asso. prof. civil engring. Nat. Chiao Tung U., Shanghai, 1946-47; research asst. Pa. State U., 1947-48; research asst. U. Ill., Urbana, 1948-50, postdoctoral research scholar, 1951, asst. prof. civil engring., 1951-55, asso. prof. hydraulic engring., 1955-58, prof. hydraulic engring., 1958—, asso. mem. Center for Advanced Study, 1962- 63. Freeman Meml. lectr., 1972. Univ. del. Univs. Council on Water Resources, 1963—; dir. NSF Watershed Experimentation System, 1963—, mem. Water Resources Center adv. panel, 1964—; hydrologist Ill. Water Survey, 1951; cons. City and County Honolulu, 1959, 65-66, 68-69; spl. adviser Harza Engring. Co., Chgo., 1968; cons. Control Data Corp., 1968; adv. bd. Tex. Water Devel. Bd., 1968- -; cons. Union Carbide Corp., 1970; mem. U.S. Com. Irrigation, Drainage and Flood Control Internat. Commn. on Irrigation and Drainage, 1961; mem. U.S. Nat. Com. for Internat. Hydrological Decade, 1965—, mem. steering com., 1966—, chmn. working group on standardization problems, 1966-70, chmn. subcom. on information and supporting services, 1967-70; mem. Nat. Acad. Sci. adv. com. U.S. Geol. Survey on use of spacecraft and remote sensing, 1967—; mem. Nat. Acad. Scis. study group for NASA space application, 1967-68; hon. cons. UNESCO, 1966-67; distinguished cons. UN Secretariat, 1968; mem. adv. panel to U.S. Dept. Interior Water Resources Sci. Information Center, 1968—; UNESCO cons. to establish Centre Applied Hydrology Brazil, 1968; Ford Found. cons. Inst. Internat. Edn., 1969; cons. adviser Mexican Fed. Power Commn., 1969; dir. 1st Internat. Seminar for Hydrology Profs., 1969; UNESCO cons., Costa Rica, Peru, 1969; AID expert to India, 1970; lectr., cons. in N.Am., S.Am., Europe, Africa, Asia. Recipient Epstein award, 1955; Chinese Inst. Engrs. N.Y. Achievement award, 1965; named Hon. Tex. citizen, 1971. Academician, China Acad.; mem. N.Y. Acad. Scis., A.A.A.S., Am. Soc. Engring. Edn., Am. Geophys. Union (past com. chmn., vis. scientist 1965—), Am. Soc. C.E. (Research prize 1962), Internat. Assn. Hydraulic Research, Univs. Council on Water Resources (founder forerunner orgn. 1962), Am. Acad. Mechanics (founder 1970), Sigma Xi, Phi Tau Phi, Phi Kappa Phi (Mid-Am. chpt. pres. 1965-66), Phi Kappa Epsilon. Author: Open-Channel Hydraulics. Editor- in-chief: Handbook of Applied Hydrology; editor: Advances in Hydroscience, 1964—; asso. editor Jour. Water Resources Research, 1965- 67; cons. editor McGraw-Hill Book Co., N.Y.C., 1962—; editor Jour. Hydrology, 1969—; editorial bd. Remote Sensing of Environment-An Interdisciplinary Jour., 1967—, Geophys. Surveys-An Internat. Jour., 1971—. Contbr. articles to profl. jours. Home: 2014 S Anderson St Urbana IL 61801

CHOW, WEL-LIANG, mathematician, educator; b. Shanghai, China, Oct. 1, 1911; s. Min Dah and Wuan Chuen (Yu) C.; A.B., U. Chgo., 1931, A.M., 1932; Ph.D., U. Leipzig, 1936; m. Margot Victor, July 10, 1936; children—Marian, Margaret, Barbara. Prof. math. Nat. Central U., Nanking, China, 1936-37, Nat. Tung-Chi U., Shanghai, 1946-47; asso. prof. Johns Hopkins, 1948-50, prof. math., 1950—, also chmn. dept. Mem. Am. Math. Soc., Sigma Xi. Home: 8821 Wolverton Rd Baltimore MD 21234

CHRENCIK, FRANK, chem. mfg. exec.; b. Osage, Ia., Jan. 6, 1914; s. Tom and Agnes (Walashek) C.; B.S. in Chem. Engring., State U. Ia., 1937; grad. Advanced Mgmt. Program Harvard, 1955; m. Edith Jo Phelps, July 27, 1935; children—Charles Frank, James Phelps, Plant engr., prodn. and constrn. supr. gen. chem. div. Allied Chem. & Dye Corp., 1937-40; mgr. various plants Diamond Shamrock Chem. Co., Cleve., 1946-56, gen. mgr. electrochems. div., 1956-60, co. v.p., sr. officer, 1960—; dir., chmn. exec. com. Terra Chem. Internat., Inc., Sioux City, Ia., 1969—; bd. govs. Gulf Coast Devel. Co., Pasadena, Tex., 1955. Mem. adv. council Coll. Engring. State U. Ia. Bd. dirs. Chlorine Inst.; trustee Nat. Homephilia Found., N.Y. Served to lt. col. Chem. Corps, AUS, 1940-46. Mem. Am. Inst. Chem. Engrs., Mfg. Chemists Assn., N.Y. Chemists Club, State U. Ia. Alumni Assn., Cleve. C. of C. Club: Cleveland Athletic. Home: 4920 Countryside Lane Cleveland OH 44124 Office: Union Commerce Bldg Cleveland OH 44114

CHRETIEN, JEAN, Canadian govt. ofcl.; b. Shawinigan, Que., Can., Jan. 11, 1934; s. Wellie and Marie (Boisvert) C.; law degree Laval (Que.) U., 1958; m. Alice Chaine, Sept. 10, 1957; children—France, Hubert, Michel. Called to Que. bar, 1959; mem. firm Lafond, Chretien, Landry & Deschenes: mem. Canadian Ho. of Commons from St. Maurice, 1963—; Parliamentary sec. to prime minister, 1965, to minister of finance, 1966; minister without portfolio, 1967, of nat. revenue, 1968. of Indian affairs and No. devel., 1968—. Mem. Shawinigan Sr. C. of C. (bd. dirs. 1962). Mem. Liberal Party. Home: 3832 Guillemette St Shawinigan Quebec Canada Office: House of Commons Ottawa Ontario Canada

CHRISMAN, ALLEN SIMPSON, physician; b. Greensboro, N.C., July 18, 1906; s. John Riley and Jane (Watlington) C.; B.S. in Medicine, U. N.C., 1928; M.D., Harvard, 1930; grad. Submarine Sch., 1931, Naval War Coll., Newport, R.I., 1951; m. Eleanore Meta Krekeler, Dec. 21, 1935; children—Jane, Allan. Commd. lt. (j.g.) M.C., USN, 1930, advanced through grades to rear adm., 1958;

submarine med. officer, 1931-38; staff Submarine Force Atlantic, 1944-45, 51-52; exec. officer naval hosps., Bainbridge, Md., 1945-46, Camp Lejeune. N.C., 1947-50; dir. personnel Bur. Medicine and Surgery, Washington, 1952-56; comdg. officer Naval Hosp., San Diego, 1956-61, dep. surgeon gen. USN, 1961-64; asso. med. officer Am. Nat. Red Cross, Washington, 1964-67, sr. med. officer, 1967—. Diplomate Am. Bd. Preventive Medicine. Fellow Am. Coll. Preventive Medicine; mem. A.M.A., Phi Beta Kappa, Phi Kappa Sigma, Phi Chi. Home: Bethesda MD 20014 Office: Hdqrs Am Nat Red Cross Washington DC 20006

CHRISNEY, JUDSON CLARK, instl. exec.; b. Indpls., June 30, 1923; s. Garland Edward and Lillian Mabel (Clark) C.; A.B., Swarthmore Coll., 1951; m. Carol Ann MacIntyre, Sept. 16, 1950; children—Brian, Ann Clark, Martin; m. 2d, Marilyn Renfro, Nov. 11, 1961; children—Adam, Meghan. Radio, newspaper writer, Ind., 1946-48; with Am. Ethical Union, 1951-55; dir. fund raising, pub. relations Lenox Hill Neighborhood Assn., 1955; dir. fund raising Fgn. Policy Assn., 1956-60; dir. devel. Nat. Planning Assn., 1960-62; asst. dir. Atlantic Council U.S., 1962-65; cons., San Francisco, 1965-66; dir. long range instnl. planning Nat. Planning Assn., Washington, 1966-69; dir. L.S.B. Leakey Found. for Research, Los Angeles, 1968-69; sec. nat. organizing com. Spokesmen for Interracial Understanding; mgr. corp. relations Standard Sci. Systems, Van Nuys, Cal., 1971—. Founder, dir. Morgan Park Summer Music Festival, Glen Cove. L.I.; mem. Willkie World Coll. Com. (exec. sec. Ind. 1946). Served USNR, 1943-46. Home: 1215 N Vista St Los Angeles CA 90046 Office: 15110 Keswick St Van Nuys CA 91405

CHRIST, CARL FINLEY, educator, economist; b. Chgo., Sept. 19, 1923; s. Jay Finley and Maud (Trego) C.; student Colo. Coll., 1940-42; B.S. in Physics, U. Chgo., 1943; Ph.D. in Econs., 1950; m. Phyllis Tatsch, Mar. 16, 1951; children—Alice Trego, Joan Elizabeth, Lucy Martha. Jr. physicist Manhattan Project, 1943-45; instr. physics Princeton, 1945-46; research asso. Cowles Commn. Research Econs., 1949-50; asst. prof., asso. prof. polit. economy Johns Hopkins, 1950-55; asso. prof. econs. U. Chgo., 1955-61; prof. polit. economy Johns Hopkins, 1961—, chmn. dept., 1961-66, 69-70. Vis. prof. U. Tokyo (Japan), 1959; Keynes vis. prof. econs. U. Essex (Eng.), 1966-67. Chmn., Univs.-Nat. Bur. Com. for Econs. Research, 1967—; mem. Md. Gov.'s Council Econ. Advisers, 1969—. Sr. Fulbright research scholar U. Cambridge (Eng.), 1954-55; fellow Center Advanced Study Behavioral Scis., Palo Alto, Cal., 1960-61. Fellow Econometric Soc., Am. Statis. Assn.; mem. Am. Econ. Assn., Royal Econ. Soc. Author: Econometric Models and Methods, 1966. Bd. editors Am. Econ. Rev., 1969—. Address: Political Economy Dept Johns Hopkins Baltimore MD 21218

CHRISTENBERRY, GEORGE ANDREW, coll. pres.; b. Macon, Ga., Sept. 3, 1915; s. Thomas Edwin and Jessie Gertrude (Earnhardt) C.; B.S., Furman U., 1936; A.M., U. N.C., 1938, Ph.D., 1940; m. Elizabeth Reid, Sept. 4, 1937; children—Becky Anne, George A., John Reid, Mem. faculty Meredith Coll., Raleigh, N.C., 1940-43, prof. biology and head dept., 1942-43; mem. faculty Furman U., Greenville, S.C., 1943-44, 46, prof. biology, dean men's coll., 1948-53, adminstrv. dir., 1958-64; pres. Shorter Coll., Rome, Ga., 1953-58; prof., chmn. dept. biology Ga. Coll. at Milledgeville, 1964-65, dean coll., 1965-70; pres. Augusta (Ga.) Coll., 1970—. Served as lt. USNR, as radar officer board attack transport, 1944-46. Active A.R.C. campaigns; pres. bd. dirs. Traveler's Aid Soc., 1950; chmn. edn. commn. Ga. Bapt. Conv.; mem. exec. com. Bapt. World Alliance, 1965-70. Mem. A.A.A.S., Assn. Mycol. Soc. Am., Assn. Ga. Colls. (pres. 1957-58), Ga. Edn. Assn. (pres. dept. higher edn. 1955-56), Assn. Southeastern Biologists, S.C. Acad. Sci., C. of C., Am. Inst. Biol. Scis., Ga. Acad. Scis. Democrat. Baptist (deacon) Clubs: Torch (pres. Western S.C. 1952-53), Rotary (pres. 1968-69). Contbr. papers on mycology. Home: Augusta College 2500 Walton Way Augusta GA 30904

CHRISTENBERRY, HERBERT WILLIAM, former U.S. judge; b. New Orleans, Dec. 11, 1897; s. Herbert Aden and Anna (Schmitt) C.; student Soule Coll.; LL.B., Loyola U., 1924; postgrad. N.Y. U., 1927; m. Anna Born, Aug. 5, 1924; children—Carolyn Ann, Herbert William. Pvt. practice, 1924-33; asst. atty. Bd. Commrs. Port of New Orleans, 1933-35; dep. commr. La. Debt Moratorium Commn., 1935; asst. dist. atty. Parish of Orleans, 1935- 37; asst. U.S. atty. Eastern Dist. La., 1937-42, U.S. atty. 1942-47; U.S. dist. judge, 1947-69. Instr. Loyola U. of South Sch. of Law. Mem. bd. commrs. City Park, New Orleans. Mem. Fed., La., New Orleans bar assns., Democrat. Club: Young Men's Business. Home: 4300 St Ann St New Orleans LA 70118 Office: PO Bldg New Orleans LA 70150

CHRISTENBERRY, ROBERT KEATON, ret. bus. exec.; b. Huntingdon, Tenn., Jan. 27, 1899; s. William Calvin and Rebecca Arminta (Keaton) C.; ed. by pvt. tutors; student George Washington U.; m. Edna Joan LeRoy, Aug. 14, 1929; children—Robert Keaton, Sally Joan. Entered Foreign Service, State Dept., as vice consul, Vladivostok, Siberia, 1919, later at Santo Domingo, Dominican Republic, then mem. staff Washington (D.C.) Herald and Florida Times Union, dep. hotel commr., State of Fla., 1926-29; public relations dir. Hotel Winton, Cleveland, 1929-31; dir. of sales and promotion Book-Cadillac Hotel, Detroit, 1931-32; manager Jefferson Hotel, Peoria, 1932-34; gen. mgr. Hotel Roosevelt, Pittsburgh, 1934-35; v.p. Hotel Astor, N.Y.C., 1935-44, pres., mng. dir., 1944-45; chmn. bd. Clinton Trust Co., 1946- 47; v.p., mng. dir. Sheraton Astor Hotel to 1955; cons. Webb & Knapp, Inc., real estate developers, 1954-55; pres., chmn. bd. Ambassador hotel, N.Y.C., 1955-64, Ambassador Internat. Corp., 1957—. Postmaster City of New York, 1958-66. Chairman ECA Mission to Ireland, 1950; spl. ambassador of President of U.S. to inauguration of Pres. Storessner of Paraguay, 1954. Chmn. bd. Damon Runyon Meml. Fund of Cancer Research; chmn. N.Y. State Athletic Commn., 1951-54. USMC, World War I, and served overseas with 1st and 2d divs.; civilian cons. on recreation and housing facilities in Germany, Austria and Italy, France, also cons. food and beverage operations, World War II; maj., N.Y. State Guard, 1943-44. Mem. Nat. Assn. Postmasters, Nat. League Postmasters, Com. Econ. Devel., Disabled Am. Vets., Hotel Greeters Assn., Am. Legion, Vets. Fgn. Wars, Fla. State (hon.), Ft. Lauderdale (hon.) hotel and motel assns., Hotel Assn. N.Y.C. (hon. mem., dir.), Broadway Assn. (past pres.), Catholic Actors Guild. Republican. Presbyn. Mason. Clubs: Lambs, Ye Hosts Square (past pres.), (N.Y.C.); National Press Tavern (Washington); Le International. Address: 3430 Galt Ocean Dr Fort Lauderdale FL 33308

CHRISTENSEN, ALBERT SHERMAN, U.S. judge; b. Manti, Utah, June 9, 1905; s. Albert H. and Jennie (Snow) C.; student Brigham Young U., intermittently 1923-27; J.D., Nat. U., 1931; m. Lois Bowen, Apr. 4, 1927; children—A. Kent, Karen D., Krege B. Asst. bus. specialist U.S. Dept. Commerce, 1930-32; admitted to D.C. bar, 1932, Utah bar, 1933, practiced in Provo, 1933-42. 45-54; U.S. dist. judge, Salt Lake City, 1954—. Mem. com. on revision laws Jud. Conf. U.S., 1960-68, com. on ct. adminstrn., 1969—; mem. bd. Utah Bar Examiners, 1939-42. Republican congl. candidate, 1939. Served from lt. to lt. comdr. USNR, 1942-45. Mem. Am., Utah (pres. 1951-52), Utah Jr. (pres. 1937-38), Utah County (pres. 1936-37, 47-48) bar assns., Bar Assn. D.C. Mem. Ch. of Jesus Christ of Latter-day Saints. Home: Bonneville Tower Apts 777 E Temple St Salt Lake City UT 84102 Office: US Ct House Salt Lake City UT 84102

CHRISTENSEN, ALLEN DERBIDGE, constrn. and mining co. exec., real estate developer; b. Salt Lake City, Utah, May 31, 1907; s. Andrew Hyrum and Olive (Derbidge) C.; student U. Utah, 1923-25; B.S., Stanford, 1927, C.E., 1929; m. Carmen Morton, Oct., 30, 1940; children—Carmen Diane, Craig Morton, Karen Kim. With Utah Constrn. & Mining Co. (formerly Utah Constrn. Co.), San Francisco, 1931-61, successively supt., project mgr., dist. mgr., Salt Lake City, v.p., 1944, v.p., gen. mgr., 1950, exec. v.p., gen. mgr., 1951, pres., gen. mgr. 1954, pres., 1958-61; pres. Marcona Mining Co., Peru, 1952-61, Cia. San Juan, S.A., Panama, 1952-61; pres., dir. Texada Mines, Vancouver, B.C., 1952-67, So. Cross Mines, Ltd. , Palo Alto, Cal., 1967—; mng. dir. Texada Mines Pty. Ltd., Perth, Western Australia, 1965—; dir. Kaiser Cement & Gypsum Corp., also dir. Permanente Cement Co. Clubs: The Family, World Trade (San Francisco); Alta (Salt Lake City); Mining (N.Y.C.). Home: 95 Faxon Rd Atherton CA 94025 Office: 780 Welch Rd Palo Alto CA 94304

CHRISTENSEN, BERNHARD MARINUS, former educator; b. Porterfield, Wis., Oct. 21, 1901; s. Nels and Inger (Kristensen) C.; A.B., Augsburg Coll., Mpls., 1922; postgrad. Augsburg Sem., 1922-25; Th.B., Princeton Theol. Sem., 1927, Th.M., 1927; postgrad. univs. Berlin, Göttingen, 1927-28; Ph.D., Hartford Sem. Found., 1929; spl. study U. Oslo (Norway), 1959; Litt.D., Luther Coll., 1962, Coll. St. Thomas, 1965; m. Lilly Gracia Gundersen, Aug. 6, 1935; children—Nadia Margaret, Naomi Grace (dec. 1967), Mary Thorynne, Marina Kirsten, Sonya Ruth. Tchr. Bible, history Oak Grove Sem., 1925-26; asst. pastor Trinity Luth. Ch., Bklyn., 1928-30; prof. philosophy, theology Augsburg Coll. and Sem., 1930-38, pres., 1938-62; prof. theology Luther Theol. Sem., 1963-67. Pres., Nat. Luth. Ednl. Conf., 1944; mem. exec. com. Am. Luth. Conf., 1934-54. Chmn., Mayor's Council on Human Relations, Mpls., 1948-50; mem. Minn. UNESCO Com., Citizen's Club. Decorated knight 1st class Royal Order of St. Olav, Norway. Mem. Am. Assn. for UN. Club: Skylight. Author: Fire Upon the Earth, 1941; He Who Has No Sword, 1964; also religious booklets. Editor: The Presence, 1929, Luth. Messenger, 1931-34, asso. editor Jour. Am. Luth. Conf., 1938-43. Home: 1545 Fulham St Paul MN 55108

CHRISTENSEN, BERT EINAR, educator; b. Duluth, Minn., Oct. 20, 1904; s. Olaf B. and Lena (Hansen) C.; B.S., Wash. State U., 1927; Ph.D., U. Wash., 1932; m. Emelyn M. Burke, Aug. 31, 1932; children—Gerald R., Robert L., Joyce E. With Ore. State U., 1931—, successively instr., asst. prof., asso. prof., 1931- 42, prof. chemistry, 1942-70, chmn. dept., 1956-70; ret. 1970. Mem. A.A.A.S., Corvallis C. of C., Am. Chem. Soc., Am. Assn. U. Profs., Sigma Xi, Phi Lambda Upsilon, Phi Kappa Phi. Clubs: Toastmasters; Triad. Author, co-author papers sci. jours. Home: 337 N 23d St Corvallis OR 97330

CHRISTENSEN, CARLO MOLLER, Danish diplomat; b. Copenhagen, Denmark, Dec. 22, 1903; s. Hans and Lucia (Jensen) C.; L.H.D., Dana Coll., 1966; m. Elizabeth Futtrup, Nov. 1, 1925; 1 dau., Inge Futtrup. Farmer, gardener, free lance writer, chief Danish-Am. Press Servie, Copenhagen, 1936-42, asst. Ministry Fgn. Affairs, Copenhagen, 1942-45, consul, cultural counselor Embassy of Denmark, dean of cultural and ednl. officers Embassies, Washington, 1956—. Mem. Danish Resistance Movement, 1940-45. Decorated knight Order Dannebrog; recipient citation for brave conduct in Danish Resistance Movement, Gen. Eisenhower, 1945, Howard U. award, Internat. Cultural Relations award, 1952; Isaiah award of human relations Am. Jewish Com., 1968. Mem. Danish Authors Soc., Am. Scandinavian Found. N.Y. Club: Cosmos (Washington). Author: Collection of poems: Oest og vest, 1928; Collection of poems: Eventyret kaldts, 1932; History of Occupation: Under Jorden i Borgergade, 1945; History About the First Danes in New York: De foerste Danske i New York, 1953: History from the Virgin Islands: Peter von Scholten, 1955. Home: 2122 Massachusetts Av NW Washington DC 20008 Office: 3200 Whitehaven St NW Washington DC 20008

CHRISTENSEN, CARL ROLAND, educator; b. Tyler, Minn., Aug. 17, 1919; s. Thomas P. and Marie (Dahm) C.; A.B., U. Ia., 1941; M.B.A., Harvard, 1943, D.C.S., 1953; m. Dorothy Isabell Smith, Dec. 26, 1943; children—Philip, Steven, Ann, Joan. Instr. to asso. prof. Harvard Bus. Sch., 1946-58, prof. Harvard Grad. Sch. Bus., 1958—, George F. Baker, Jr. prof. bus. adminstrn., 1963—. Vis prof. Stanford, 1955, Imede, Lausanne, Switzerland, 1963-64; dir. Internat. Register Co., Chgo., Cabot Corp., Boston, New Eng. Mchts. Nat. Bank, Boston, Arthur D. Little, Inc., Cambridge, Mass. Mem. finance com. Town of Lexington, Mass. Served from cpl. to captain AUS, 1943-46. Mem. Am. Soc. Pub. Adminstrn., Acad. Polit. Sci., Soc. Applied Anthropology, Am. Sociol. Soc., Phi Beta Kappa. Author: Management Succession in Small and Growing Enterprise, 1953; (with G.A. Smith, Jr.) Policy Formulation and Administration, 1955, rev. 1968; (with A. Zaleznick, F. J. Roethlisberger) Motivation, Productivity and Satisfaction of Workers, 1959; (with E.P. Learned, K.R. Andrews) Problems in General Management; (with others) Business Policy: Text and Cases, 1965, rev., 1969. Home: 4 Oakmount Circle Lexington MA 02173 Office: Harvard Bus Sch Boston MA 02163

CHRISTENSEN, CLYDE MARTIN, educator; b. Sturgeon Bay, Wis., Aug. 8, 1905; s. Peter Karl and Christine Ann (Christensen) C.; B.S., U. Minn., 1929, M.S., 1930, Ph.D., 1937; postgrad., U. Halle, Halle an der Salle, Germany, 1932-33; m. Katherine Wallace Barry, Sept. 27, 1935; children—Sarah Ellen (Mrs. William R. Nelson), Melanie Barry, Jane Martin (Mrs. Garry Thompson Vance). Instr. U. Minn., 1929-37, asst. prof., 1937-46, asso. prof., 1946-48, prof. plant pathology, 1948—. Cons. various grain storage and processing firms. Fellow Am. Phytopath. Soc., Am. Coll. Allergists (hon.); mem. Am. Soc. Microbiology, Mycol. Soc. Am., Sigma Xi. Author: Common Edible Mushrooms, 1943. Common Fleshy Fungi, 1946, The Molds and Man, 1953; (with H.H. Kaufmann) Grain Storage: The Role of Fungi in Quality Loss, 1969; also articles. Home: 2350 Carter St Paul MN 55108

CHRISTENSEN, EARL PERRY, accountant; b. Detroit, July 19, 1921; s. Hans and Sarah Ann (Perry) C.; B.S.C., Detroit Inst. Tech., 1943; m. Virginia Quinn Miller, May 6, 1944; children—John, David, Philip, Paul, Jeffry. Accountant, Price Waterhouse & Co., C.P.A.'s, 1941—, partner, Stamford, Conn., 1961—. Served to 1st lt. USAAF, 1943-46; to capt. USAF, 1951-53. Mem. Am. Inst. C.P.A.'s, Stamford Assn. C.P.A.'s, Nat. Assn. Accountants. Clubs: Midtown (Stamford); Woodway Country (Darien, Conn.). Home: 70 Braeburn Dr New Canaan CT 06840 Office: 986 Bedford St Stamford CT 06905

CHRISTENSEN, ERNEST EDWARD, naval officer; b. Falmouth, Me., July 31, 1913; s. Rasmus and Agusta (Lunt) C.; B.S., U.S. Naval Acad., 1934; student ordnance engring. Post Grad. Sch., 1941-43; grad. Naval War Coll., 1952; m. Marjorie Holcomb, Oct. 30, 1936; childrenCarol Lee (Mrs. James M. Elster), Ernest Edward. Commd. lt. U.S. Navy, 1934, advanced through grades to rear adm., 1962; designated naval aviator, 1937; various assignments in ships and squadrons, 1934-44; comdg. officer U.S.S. Rehoboth, 1944-45, Naval Air Stas. in Traverse City, Mich. and Mojave, Cal., 1945-47; assignments at sea in U.S.S. Pine Island and U.S.S. Norton Sound, 1947-49; with div. plans and aircraft weapons research Bur. Ordnance, 1949-51; mem. staff comdr. in chief N. Atlantic and Mediterranean, 1953-54; dir. aviation weapons research, research div. Bur. Ordnance, 1955-57; asst. chief staff plans staff comdr. chief Pacific Fleet, 1957-59; comdg. officer U.S.S. Hornet, 1959-60; chief joint reconnaissance center Joint Staff, Joint Chiefs Staff, 1960-62; comdr. Carrier Div. 18, 1962-63; asst. chief staff fleet readiness, asst. chief staff plans and programs Bur. Weapons, 1963-66; plans, programs, comptroller Naval Air Systems Command, 1966-67; chief naval air tech. tng., Memphis, 1967-70; asst. dep. chief naval operations Army Navy (Washington). Home: 1836 Cove Point Rd Annapolis MD 21401 Office: Asst Deputy Chief of Naval Operations (Development)

CHRISTENSEN, EVERETT EUGENE, govt. ofcl.; b. Badger, S.D., Dec. 15, 1922; s. John Gayhart and Matie (Marquardt) C.; B.S., U.S. Mil. Acad., 1946; M.S., U. Mich., 1950; student Harvard Bus. Sch., 1961; m. Mary Frances French, June 5, 1946; childrenKathryn E., Karen M., Everett Eugene, Edward K. Commd. 2d lt. U.S. Army, 1946, advanced through grades to capt. USAF, 1952; resigned, 1953; base mgr. Lockheed Aircraft Corp., Holloman AFB, N.M., 1953-56, asst. flight test engr., missile systems div., Van Nuys, Cal., 1956-57; test mgmt. and operations, fleet ballistic missile weapons system (Polaris) Lockheed Missiles & Space Co., Sunnyvale, Cal., 1957-59, Polaris product support mgr., 1959-61; staff assignments Lockheed Missiles & Space Co., 1961-63, devel. test mgr., 1963-64, spl. asst. to mission operations dir., 1964-67; staff assignments Lockheed Missile & Space Co., 1967-. Home: 25265 LaLoma Dr Los Altos Hills CA 94022 Office: 3251 Hanover St Palo Alto CA 94304

CHRISTENSEN, GEORGE BOWERS, lawyer; b. Oshkosh, Wis., Apr. 12, 1905; s. Martin L. and Nina A. (Bowers) C.; A.B., Lawrence Coll., 1926; J.D., U. Mich., 1929; m. Genevieve Hyde, Feb. 8, 1930; children—Genevieve Ann, Peter George. Admitted to Ill. bar, 1929, since practiced in Chgo.; partner firm Winston, Strawn, Smith & Patterson, and predecessors, 1941—. Faculty, John Marshall Law Sch., Chgo.; guest lectr. law schs. on labor law. Mem. Sch. Bd. Glencoe, Ill., 1950-57, pres., 1956-57. Mem. Am., Ill., Chgo. bar assns., Am. Coll. Trial Lawyers, Chgo. Assn. Industry and Commerce, S.A.R., Ill. C. of C. Republican. Methodist. Clubs: University, Law (Chgo.); Skokie Country (Glencoe). Home: 710 Bluff St Glencoe IL 60022 Office: 1 First Nat Plaza Chicago IL 60607

CHRISTENSEN, GEORGE CURTIS, educator; b. N.Y.C., Feb. 21, 1924; s. Carl Lee and Marie (Larsen) C.; D.V.M., Cornell U., 1949, M.S., 1950, Ph.D., 1953; m. Janeth M. Reid, July 19, 1947; children—Curtis Lee, Joyce Janeth, William George, Cheryl Reid. Instr. vet. anatomy Cornell U., 1949-53; asso. prof. vet. anatomy Ia. State U., 1953-58; prof. vet. anatomy, head dept. Purdue U., 1958-63; dean Ia. State U. Coll. Vet. Medicine, Ames, 1963-65, v.p. acad. affairs Ia. State U., Ames, 1965—, chmn. council on internat. programs examiner N. Central Assn. Colls. and Secondary Schs.; chmn. Ia. Instnl. Com. Ednl. Coordination; mem. com. on edn. and research Nat. Acad. Sci.-NRC. Vice pres. Ia. Bd. Health. Bd. dirs. Quad Cities Grad. Center, State Hygienic Lab. Ia., Center for Research Libraries. Served with AUS, 1942-43. Mem. Am. Assn. Anatomists, Am. Assn. Vet. Anatomists, Am. Vet. Med. Assn. (chmn. council on edn.), Nat. Assn. for Higher Edn., A.A.A.S., Mid-Am. State Univs. Assn. (governing council) Conf. Research Workers Animal Diseases, Nat. Assn. State Univs. and Land Grant Colls. (council acad. affairs), Sigma Xi, Phi Kappa Phi, Phi Zeta, Lambda Chi Alpha, Alpha Psi, Gamma Sigma Delta, Cardinal Key. Lutheran. Rotarian. Co-author: Anatomy of the Dog, 1964. Research numerous pubs. cardiovascular system, genito-urinary system, history vet. med. edn., higher edn. Home: 1025 Gaskill Dr Ames IA 50010

CHRISTENSEN, GLENN JAMES, educator; b. Canton, O.; Dec. 15, 1907; s. James Garfield and Emma Emma (Lynch) C.; B.A., Coll. of Wooster, 1935; Ph.D. in English, Yale, 1939; LL.D., Coll. Notre Dame of Md., 1966; m. Mildred Balmer, Sept. 8, 1931; 1 son, Gregory Balmer (dec.). Instr. English, Lehigh U., Bethlehem, Pa., 1939-42, asst. prof., 1942-46, asso. prof., 1946-55, prof., asso. dean Coll. Arts and Sci., 1955, dean, 1956-62, v.p., provost, 1962-69, Univ. Distinguished prof., 1969—; pres. Lehigh Valley Ednl. TV Corp., 1962-66, now dir. Vis. Carnegie asso. prof. English, Columbia, 1951-52; dir. Research Better Schs., Inc., 1966- 67. Mem. Commn. on Higher Edn., 1960-66. Chmn. bd. trustees Northampton County Area Community Coll., 1966—. Mem. Middle States Assn. (pres. 1968-69), Phi Beta Kappa. Home: 452 N New St Bethlehem PA 18018

CHRISTENSEN, HALVOR NIELS, educator; b. Cozad, Neb., Oct. 24, 1915; s. Niels and Matena (Smidt) C.; B.S., Neb. State Tchrs. Coll., 1935; M.S., Purdue U., 1937; Ph.D., Harvard, 1939; m. Mayme Matthews, Aug. 28, 1939; children—Haldan, Carl, Karen. Asst. chemistry Purdue U., 1935-37; asso. chemistry Harvard, 1939- 40; biochemist Lederle Labs., 1940-42; instr. biol. chemistry Harvard Med. Sch., 1942-44, asst. prof., 1947-49; biochemist Mary Imogene Bassett Hosp., 1944-47; dir. dept. chem. research Children's Hosp., Boston, 1947-49; prof., head dept. biochemistry and nutrition Tufts Coll. Med. Sch., 1949-55; prof. biol. chemistry U. Mich. Med. Sch., Ann Arbor, 1955—, head dept., 1955-70. Guggenheim fellow Carlsberg Lab., Copenhagen, 1952; Nobel guest prof. U. Uppsala (Sweden), 1968-69; cons. USPHS. Mem. Unitarian Service Com. Med. Mission to Germany, 1950. Mem. Am. Soc. Biol. Chemists, Am. Chem. Soc., Am. Acad. Arts and Scis., Biophys. Soc., Am. Inst. Nutrition, Sigma Xi. Author: Diagnostic Biochemistry; Body Fluids and the Acid-Base Balance; PH and Dissociation, (with G. Palmer) Enzyme Kinetics; Neutrality Regulation in the Living Organism; (programmed texts); Biological Transport. Home: 2200 Devonshire Rd Ann Arbor MI 48104

CHRISTENSEN, HAROLD, corp. ofcl.; b. Chgo., Apr. 8, 1916; s. Ludwig and Emma (Reinhold) C.; student Northwestern U.; m. Gladys Distad, Mar. 12, 1938; children—Linda Jean (Mrs. Malcolm S. Graham), Lorna Gladys (Mrs. Dameron M. Black). With Bows & Elman, Chgo., 1934-39, Burke, James & Burke, Chgo., 1939-40; with IBM Corp., 1940-49; sec. IBM World Trade Corp., N.Y.C., 1949—. Bd. dirs. African-American C. of C. Mem. Am. Australian Assn. Club: Union League (N.Y.C.); Siwanoy Country (Bronxville); Pine Tree Golf (Delray Beach, Fla.). Home: 6 Midland Gardens Bronxville NY 10708 Office: 821 UN Plaza New York City NY 10017

CHRISTENSEN, HAROLD TAYLOR, sociologist; b. Preston, Ida., Mar. 10, 1909; s. Henry Oswald and Nettie (Taylor) C.; student Ricks Coll., Rexburg, Ida., 1926-27, 1928- 29; B.S., Brigham Young U., 1935, M.S., 1937; Ph.D., U. Wis., 1941; m. Alice Spencer, June 5, 1935; children—Carl, Boyd, Janice, Larry, Gayle. Elementary sch. tchr., Hibbard, Ida., 1927-28; instr. sociology Brigham Young U., 1935-38, asst. prof., 1938-40, asso. prof., 1940-41, prof. sociology, 1941-47, chmn. dept., 1940-47; leader, div. farm population and rural life Bur. Agrl. Econs., Northeastern region, U.S. Dept. Agr., 1944-45; prof., head dept. sociology Purdue U., 1947-62, prof. sociology, 1962—; vis. prof. U. Hawaii, Spring 1965. Grad. fellow in sociology U. Wis., 1938-39. Chmn. Provo Civic Welfare Com., 1941-44. Fulbright research scholar to Denmark, 1957-58; recipient Burgess

Research award, 1967. Fellow Am. Sociol. Assn.; mem. Nat. Council Family Relations (pres. 1960-61), Ind. Council Family Relations (pres. 1950-52), Ohio Valley Sociol. Soc. (pres. 1953-54), Sociol. Research Assn. Democrat. Author: Marriage Analysis, 1950, rev. 1958; Handbook of Marriage and the Family (editor), 1964; (with Kathryn Johnsen) Marriage and the Family, 1971. Editor: Marriage and Family Living, 1957-59. Contbr. articles to profl. jours. Home: 2167 Tecumseh Park Lane West Lafayette IN 47906 Office: Purdue U Lafayette IN 47907

CHRISTENSEN, HARVEY DEVON, educator, aerospace and mech. engr.; b. Challis, Ind., Apr. 6, 1920; s. Haireld H. and Ethel S. (James) C.; B.S. in Mech. Engring., U. Wash., 1943; M.S., Ore. State U., 1950; Ph.D., Stanford, 1960; m. Dolores M. Spelbrink, June 9, 1951; childrenJeannette Marie, Karen Cozette, Denise Annette, Christopher Benton, Amy Elizabeth. Prof. aerospace and mech. engring. U. Ariz., Tucson, 1958—, head dept., 1958-70. Cons. to industry, 1948—; spl. research individual paced interactive ednl. systems, nonlinear mechanics, structures, exptl. stress analysis, engring. mechanics, applied math. Registered profl. engr., Ariz., Ore. Asso. fellow Am. Inst. Aeros. and Astronautics; mem. Am. Soc. Engring. Edn., Am. Soc. M.E., Soc. Exptl. Stress Analysis, Am. Soc. Profl. Engrs., Sigma Xi, Pi Tau Sigma. Contbr. articles to profl. jours. Home: 5714 E S Wilshire St Tucson AZ 85711

CHRISTENSEN, IRA LOGAN, pub. utility exec.; b. Brodhead, Wis., Mar. 30, 1918; s. Marius and Mary (Nelson) C.; B.B.A., U. Wis., 1947; postgrad. U. So. Cal., 1947-51; m. Sylvia Holmes, June 21, 1949; children—Roger, Linda, Nancy. With Gen. Telephone Co. Cal., 1947—, asst. sec., asst. treas., 1949-59, treas., 1959—; v.p., dir. Cal. Water & Telephone Co., 1966-67. Served to capt. AUS, 1941-46; maj. Res. ret. Mem. Am. Soc. Corporate Secs., Financial Execs. Inst., Tax Execs. Inst., Am. Arbitration Assn., Town Hall. Home: 1014 Bienveneda Av Pacific Palisades CA 90272 Office: 2020 Santa Monica Blvd Santa Monica CA 90404

CHRISTENSEN, IVAR, restaurant exec.; b. Kristiansand S, Norway, July 18, 1922; s. Karsten and Gusta Elizabeth (Olsen) C.; came to U.S., 1945, naturalized, 1955; B.A., Syracuse U., 1948; m. Sally Elizabeth Quimby, Feb. 26, 1949; children-Kathryn Elisabeth, Melanie Gail, Linda Louise, Hans Andrew. With, Internat. Refugee Orgn., 1949-50; with ARA Services, Inc., 1950—, now v.p., pres. Davre's div., Pres. Grace Lutheran Christian Day Sch., Broomall, Pa., 1962—. Trustee, v.p. bd. trustees Germantown Lutheran Acad. Phila., 1969—. Served with Norwegian Army 1940-45. Mem. Pa. Soc. Clubs: Bankers (San Francisco); Broomall Lake Country (Media, Pa.); Blue Line, Epicurean (Phila.). Home: 819 Meredith Dr Media PA 19063 Office: ARA Services Inc Independence Sq Philadelphia PA 19106

CHRISTENSEN, KENNETH CHESTER, former utility co. exec.; b. Palo Alto, Cal., Mar. 3, 1908; s. Christian Hansen and Jessie May (Herriford) C.; A.B., Stanford, 1930; m. Anne Alexina McDonald, May 4, 1946. Engring. asst., asst. treas., treas. Pacific Gas & Electric Co., San Francisco, 1931-57, v.p., treas., 1958-62, v.p. charge finance, 1962-65, sr. v.p. finance, 1965-69, also dir., until 1970; now financial cons. Home: 3965 Washington St San Francisco CA 94118

CHRISTENSEN, KENNETH SERENUS, fgn. service officer; b. Rock Island, Ill., Feb. 19, 1908; s. Clarence Serenus and Signe (Person) C.; student Augustana Coll., 1928-29; B.E., U. Ill., 1931; m. Ann Therese Tramuta, Dec. 25, 1936; children—Kenneth Willard, Clarence Serenus, Paul Norman. Educator, 1935-38; with Dept. Justice, 1938-41; staff Civil Service Commn., 1941-50; dep. regional enforcement dir. OPS, 1951-53; with Dept. State, 1953—, fgn. assistance staff, 1953-56, regional insp. Middle East, Beirut, Lebanon, 1956-58, for S.E. Asia, Saigon, Vietnam, 1959-61, dep. chief investigations mgmt. inspections staff, 1961-66; insp. charge inspections and investigations staff AID, Am. Consulate Gen., Frankfurt-am-Main, Germany, 1966-68; fgn. assistance inspector AID, Washington, 1968-70, cons. to AID, 1971—. Served with CIC, AUS, 1943-45. Decorated Bronze Star. Mem. Nat. Geog. Soc. Club: Clipper Pan American Airways. Home: 3411 Alba Pl Fairfax VA 22030 Office: AID Dept State Washington DC 20523

CHRISTENSEN, LEIF, wholesale co. exec. Comptroller, Oshawa Wholesale Ltd., Toronto, Ont., Can. Office: 125 Queensway Toronto Ontario Canada*

CHRISTENSEN, LEW, dancer, choreographer, ballet dir.; b. Brigham City, Utah, 1909; student dance with L. P. Christensen; student Sch. Am. Ballet, N.Y.C.; m. Gisella Caccialanza. Appeared in vaudeville with bros.; mem. Am. Ballet, 1935, danced title role Appollo, Met. Opera House, N.Y.C.; choreographer, ballet master, soloist, Ballet Caravan, 1936-40; soloist Dance Players, 1941-42; ballet master, dancer Ballet Soc., 1946-48; faculty Sch. Am. Ballet, N.Y.C., 1946-48; ballet master N.Y.C. Ballet, 1948-55; dir., prin. choreographer San Francisco Ballet, from 1955, also former ballet master San Francisco Opera; now dir. Royal Winnipeg (Man., Can.) Ballet. Served with AUS, World War II. Works choreographed include: Charade, Filling Station, Pocahontas, Encounter (Ballet Caravan); Jinx (Dance Players); Blackface (Ballet Soc.); Con Amore, The Nutcracker, Beauty and the Beast, Danses Concertantes, Shadows, Lady of Shalott, Original Sin, Jest of Cards, Sinfonia, Divertissement d'Auber (San Francisco Ballet). Address: 322 Smith St Winnipeg Manitoba Canada*

CHRISTENSEN, PAUL WALTER, mfg. exec.; b. Phila., Aug. 14, 1901; s. John C. and Marie (Jensen) C.; B.S. in Mech. Engring., Purdue U., 1923; m. Lucy M. Sickler, Oct. 6, 1923; 1 son, Paul Walter. Time study engr. Cin. Milling Machine Co., 1923; with Cin. Gear Co., 1924-, pres., 1941-58, chmn., 1958-; pres. Cin. Steel Treating Co., 1958-; dir. Cin. & Suburban Bell Telephone Co., Lukenheimer Co., Gen. Air Conditioning Corp. Bd. dirs., v.p. Boys' Clubs Cin., Inc.; bd. dirs. Bethesda Hosp., United Appeal; chmn. bd. Cin. Symphony Orchestra; trustee Dean Herman Schneider Found. Mem. Am. Gear Mfrs. Assn. (past pres.). Home: 4610 Burley Hills Dr Cincinnati OH 45243. Office: Colonial Center Bldg Cincinnati OH 45227.

CHRISTENSEN, PAUL WALTER, Jr., gear mfg. co. exec.; b. Cin., Jan. 31, 1925; s. Paul Walter and Lucy (Sickler) C.; B.S. in Mech. Engring., Cornell U., 1945; m. Sarah Ernst, Nov. 22, 1947; children—Delle, Sarah, Lucy. With Cin. Gear Co., 1946—, v.p., 1947-58, pres., 1958—; chmn. bd. Cin. Steel Treating Co., 1961-68, pres., 1968—; dir. Ohmart Corp., Potter Shoe Co., Central Trust Co., Natmar, Inc., Eagle Picher Industries, Inc., Central Bancorp., Cin. br. Fed. Res. Bank Cleve. Bd. dirs., exec. com. Cin. area chpt. A.R.C.; mem. adv. bd. Greater Cin. Airport. Mem. Am. Gear Mfrs. Assn. (dir.), Ohio Mfrs. Assn. (pres.). Clubs: Cincinnati Country, Queen City, Commonwealth, Camargo, Commercial (Cin.). Home: 6 Madison Lane Cincinnati OH 45208 Office: Cincinnati Gear Co Wooster Pike Cincinnati OH 45227

CHRISTENSEN, RAY RICHARDS, lawyer; b. Salt Lake City, July 7, 1922; s. E.R. and Carrie (Richards) C.; LL.B., U. Utah, 1944; m. Carolyn Crawford, July 9, 1954; children—Carlie, Paul Ray, Joan, Eric. Admitted to Utah bar, 1944; enforcement atty. OPA, 1946; clk. to Utah Supreme Ct. Justice Wolfe, 1947-48; practice in Salt Lake City, 1949—; partner firm Christensen and Jensen, and predecessor, 1949—. Mem. Utah Bar Commn., 1963-66. Bd. dirs. Salt Lake City Jr. C. of C., 1949-53, v.p., 1950-52. Served with AUS, 1943-46. Fellow Am. Coll. Trial Lawyers; mem. Am. (mem. council jr. bar conf. 1952-56, ho. of dels. 1966-68, mem. council bar activities sect. 1967-70), Utah (pres. 1965-66), Salt Lake County bar assns., Western States Bar Conf. (pres. 1969-70), Internat. Assn. Ins. Counsel, Fedn. Ins. Counsel, Phi Eta Sigma, Phi Kappa Phi. Home: 86 Monument Park Circle Salt Lake City UT 84108 Office: Continental Bank Bldg Salt Lake City UT 84101

CHRISTENSEN, WILLIAM HAROLD, gas transmission co. exec.; b. Wilmot, S.D., Aug. 26, 1909; s. Albert Rasmus and Emma Elenora (Christensen) C.; student Dublin U., Trinity Coll., 1950-51; m. Flora M. MacRae, June 30, 1938; children—Jon Alexander, William James, Kerry MacRae. Clk., Am. consulate, Winnipeg, Can., 1926-40; vice consul, Barbados, B.W.I., 1940-43, Toronto, 1943, Sarnia, 1943; vice consul, officer charge Am. consulate, Antigua, B.W.I., also Curacao and Martinique, 1944; consul, Martinique, F.W.I., 1945, Marseilles, France, 1947; 2d sec., consul Am. embassy, Dublin, Ireland, 1950; assigned staff Dept. State, Washington, 1952-56, desk officer Ireland and Caribbean; dep. chief mission counselor Am. embassy, Luxembourg, 1956- 58, also charge d'affairs; consul gen. St. John's Newfoundland, Can., 1958-60; consul gen. Am. consulate gen., Port of Spain, Trinidad, W.I., 1961, counselor of embassy, dep. chief mission Am. embassy, Port of Spain, 1962-63; assigned State Dept., 1963; consul gen. for Alta., Calgary, 1963-64; ret., 1964; exec. Great Lakes Gas Transmission Co., Detroit, 1965—. Adviser U.S. delegation 15th Session Caribbean Commn., 5th Session West Indian Conf., Montego Bay, Jamaica, 1952, 20th Session Caribbean Commn., 6th Session West Indian Conf., San Juan, P.R., 1955; mem. commn. for selection sculptor and design statue of Commo. James Barry, for gift to people of Ireland, 1953; mem. Detroit area Council on World Affairs; mem. adv. council U. Windsor Seminar on Canadian-Am. Relations. Recipient Silver medal City of Sete, Herault, France, 1948; Meritorious Service award, Dept. State, 1960; decorated comdr. Oak Crown Luxembourg, 1958. Mem. Am. Fgn. Service Assn., Diplomatic and Consular Officers Ret. Club: Economic (Detroit). Lutheran. Home: 717 Sunningdale Dr Grosse Pointe Woods MI 48236 Office: 1 Woodward Av Detroit MI 48226

CHRISTENSEN, WILLIAM ROZELLE, physician, educator; b. Salt Lake City, Nov. 20, 1917; s. Niels Christian and DeVere (Rozelle) C.; B.A., U. Utah, 1938; M.D., Harvard, 1942; m. Mary Beeley, June 24, 1942; children—William B. (dec.), Ellen Ann, Eric Peter. Intern, Mass. Gen. Hosp., Boston, 1942-43; research fellow Harvard Med. Sch., 1946-48; resident radiology Peter Bent Brigham Hosp., Boston, 1948-51; prof. radiology, chmn. dept. U. Utah Coll. Medicine, Salt Lake City, 1952—; radiologist-in-chief Salt Lake City Gen. Hosp., 1952-65, U. Hosp., 1965—. Cons. U.S. Army, VA. Served to maj. M.C., AUS, 1943-46. Fulbright scholar, U.K., 1951-52. Fellow Am. Coll. Radiology; mem. Am. Roentgen Ray Soc., Am. Radium Soc., Assn. U. Radiologists, A.M.A., Radiol. Soc. N.Am., A.A.A.S., Phi Beta Kappa, Phi Kappa Phi, Phi Delta Theta. Contbr. articles to profl. jours. Home: 1469 Harvard Av Salt Lake City UT 84105

CHRISTENSON, CARROLL LAWRENCE, economist; b. Viroqua, Wis., May 9, 1902; s. Christian A. and Louise (Larson) C.; Ph.B., U. Chgo., 1924, Ph.D., 1931; m. Cornelia Vos, June 11, 1929; children—John Martin, Ann Louise. Instr. econs. Ind. U., Bloomington, 1925-27, became asst. prof. econs. 1932, asso. prof., 1935-37, prof., 1937—, emeritus, 1969—, chmn. dept. econs.; 1945-50, on leave 1933-34 to act as econ. adviser NRA, on leave to serve with OPA, 1941-43, loaned to Republic of Costa Rica to aid in adminstrn. price control and rationing, 1944; vis. prof. (summer), U. Wis., 1947, U. So. Cal., 1949. Has served as impartial arbitrator under various trade agreements, and as panel chmn. War Labor Bd. Fellow, Am. Scandinavian Found., 1931-32; Ford Found. research fellow, 1956. Mem. Am. Econ. Assn., Mid-West Econ. Assn. (pres. 1947). Author books including: Economic Redevelopment in Bituminous Coal, 1962; (with Richard Myren) Wage Policy Under Walsh Healey Public Contracts Act, 1966. Contbr. tech. articles to jours. Home: 2965 Ramble Rd Bloomington IN 47401

CHRISTENSON, CHARLES JOHN, educator; b. Chgo., Sept. 25, 1930; s. John Edward and Ethel Dagmar (Osterberg) C.; B.S., Cornell U., 1952; M.B.A., Harvard, 1954, D.B.A., 1961; Mem. faculty Harvard Grad. Sch. Bus., 1957-58, lectr., 1959-61, asst. prof., 1961-63, asso. prof., 1963-68, prof., 1968—, Dir. Falco Corp., Raleigh, N.C., 1962—, Frank Foods Inc., Greenwich, Conn., 1970—; prin. Mgmt. Analysis Center, Inc., Cambridge, 1966—. Served with AUS, 1955-57. Mem. Inst. Mgmt. Scis. Author: (with N.E. Harlan and R.F. Vancil) Managerial Economics: Text and Cases, 1963; Strategic Aspects of Competitive Bidding for Corporate Securities, 1965. Home: 1 Chauncy Lane Cambridge MA 02138 Office: Soldiers Field Boston MA 02163

CHRISTENSON, CLIFFORD C., lawyer; b. Grand Rapids, Mich., Jan. 31, 1915; A.B., U. Mich., 1937, LL.B., 1939. Admitted to Mich. bar, 1939; asst. city atty., Grand Rapids, 1939-40, dep. city atty., 1941-44; civil counsel, Kent County, Mich., 1952-57; mem. firm Varnum, Riddering, Wierengo & Christenson, Grand Rapids. Mem. Am., Grand Rapids bar assns., State Bar Mich. Office: Old Kent Bldg Grand Rapids MI 49502*

CHRISTHILF, STUART MACDONALD, Jr., physician and surgeon; b. Balt., Aug. 18, 1916; s. Stuart MacDonald and Eloise (MacNeal) C.; B.A., St. John's Coll., 1938; M.D., Johns Hopkins, 1942; m. Marion Frances Fromen, Apr. 6, 1942; children—Stuart MacDonald III, Anthony, Deborah, Mark, Nicholas, Geoffrey, Raab, Malcolm, Lucinda. Intern Johns Hopkins Hosp., 1942-43; fellow pathology Washington U., St. Louis, 1946-47; asst. resident N.Y. Hosp., N.Y.C., 1947-48; resident Franklin Sq. Hosp., Balt., 1948-49; pvt. practice specializing in obstetrics and gynecology, Annapolis, Md., 1949—; founder, 1953, sr. partner Christhilf, Sheehan, Riley and Monias Med. Group, 1953-63; cons. Maternal-child health program Anne Arundel and Calvert counties, also Calvert County Hosp., 1949—; mem. staff Anne Arundel Gen. Hosp., 1949—, chief obstetrics, 1954-56; member of the staff North Arundel Hosp.; part-time asst. Johns Hopkins Med. Sch., 1949—, mem. adv. com. stdy prematures Sch. Hygiene, 1954—. Mem. Md. Commn. on the Capital City. Served to lt. (s.g.), M.C., USNR, 1943-46; PTO. Diplomate Am. Bd. Obstetrics and Gynecology. Fellow A.C.S., Am. Coll. Obstetrics and Gynecology; mem. N.Y. Acad. Scis., A.M.A., Med. and Chirugical Faculty Md., Anne Arundel County (past v.p.). Johns Hopkins med. socs., Obstet. and Gynecol. Soc. Md. (pres. 1968-69), alumni assns. St. Johns Coll., Johns Hopkins, Annapolis C. of C., Hist. Soc. Md., Hist. Annapolis, Soc. War 1812, Soc. Colonial Wars. Clubs: Maryland; Annapolis Yacht. Contbr. articles med jours. Home: Melvin Point Box 385 RFD 3 Annapolis MD 21404 Office: 69 Franklin St Annapolis MD 21401

CHRISTIAN, CHARLES CLIFFORD, govt. ofcl.; b. nr. Guthrie, Mo., Oct. 22, 1927; s. Emir Lynes and Lella C. (Wilson) C.; B.A., Westminster Coll., 1950; grad. Indsl. Coll. Armed Forces, 1971—; student George Washington U., 1970-71; m. Hilgerth Elizabeth Saari, Apr. 25, 1959; children—Charlisa Carole, Craig Colin. With Price Waterhouse & Co., St. Louis, 1950-53, Olin Mathieson Chem. Corp., 1954-61; with AID, Dept. of State, 1961—, overseas controller, 1964—. C.P.A., Am. Inst. C.P.A.'s. Served with AUS, 1946-48. Mem. Am. Fgn. Service Assn., Indsl. Coll. Armed Services Assn. Mason. Home: 6502 Lakeview Dr Falls Church VA 22041 Office: Agency Internat Devel Washington DC 20523

CHRISTIAN, CHARLES LEIGH, physician, educator; b. Wichita, Kan., July 10, 1926; s. Robert V. and Anna (Vezie) C.; B.S., U. Wichita, 1949; M.D., Western Res. U., 1953; m. Diane Collings, Nov. 13, 1954; children—Victoria Anne, Jennifer Diane. Mem. faculty Columbia Coll. Phys. and Surg., 1958-70, asso. prof. medicine, 1964-69; prof. medicine, 1969-70; prof. medicine Cornell U. Sch. Medicine, 1970—; adj. prof. Rockefeller U., 1970—; physician-in-chief Hosp. Spl. Surgery. Served with USNR, 1944-46. Research in immunology. Editor Arthritis and Rheumatism. Home: 149 Cedar St Englewood NJ 07631 Office: Cornell U Sch Medicine 1300 York Av New York City NY 10021

CHRISTIAN, DAVID ELWYN, govt. ofcl., diplomat; b. Woodland, Mich., Apr. 4, 1915; s. Forest B. and Nora (Witwer) C.; B.A., Mich. State U., 1937; m. Yolande Shell, July 4, 1940. With War Manpower Commn., 1942-47, Council Econ. Advisors, 1947-50, Nat. Security Resources Bd., 1950-51, Dept. State, 1951-54, Dept. Labor, 1955-68; dep. asst. sec. labor for manpower, 1962-64, asst. manpower adminstr., 1964-66; mem. U.S. Mission to Orgn. Econ. Coop. and Devel., head social affairs div., Paris, France, 1968—; cons. econ. planning to Malaysia and Brazil. Home: 70 rue des Belles Feuilles Paris 16 France Office: OECD 2 rue Andre-Pascal Paris 16 France

CHRISTIAN, DELOS HORACE, life ins. co. exec.; b. Scarville, Ia., June 15, 1920; s. Gilbert Frank and Tena (Drugsvold) C.; B.A., U. Ia., 1942; postgrad. N.Y. U., 1942, U. Richmond, 1957; m. Veloa D. Montgomery, Oct. 3, 1942; childrenKen Arden, Rose Ann, Dale Allen, Cheryl Lynn. Mathematician, Equitable Life Assurance Soc., 1946-52; with Life Ins. Co. Va., Richmond, 1952—, asst. to pres., 1961-63, sr. v.p., 1963-64, 1st v.p., 1964-65, exec. v.p., 1965—, also dir.; pres., dir. First Fund Va., First Va. Mgmt. Co; exec. v.p., dir. Richmond Corp.; Leatherby Ins. Co., Equivest. Served to maj. USAAF, 1942-46. Decorated Air medal. Fellow Soc. Actuaries; mem. Mid Atlantic Acturial Club (pres. 1959), Phi Beta Kappa. Presbyn. (elder). Home: 802 Coleridge Lane Richmond VA 23229 Office: 914 Capitol St Richmond VA 23219

CHRISTIAN, DONALD DALE, educator; s. Richard A. and Irence Marie (Christian) C.; A.B., Hiram Coll., 1950; M.Ed., U. Pitts., 1951, Ed.D., 1962; m. Doris Kathryn Scherer, Nov. 26, 1952; children—Paul Matthew, Karen Jean, Dean Arthur. Tchr. chemistry, math. and physics Franklin Area Schs., Murraysville, Pa., 1951-62; prin. jr. high sch., Franklin Area Schs., Murraysville, 1962-63; asso. prof. edn. U. Cin., 1963-69; prof. edn., chmn. edn. dept. Waynesburg (Pa.) Coll., 1969—. Cons. High Sch. Geography Project Unit 4. Troop com. mem., chmn. Boy Scouts Am., 1964—, chmn. camping and activities Greene County, 1970—; chmn. bd. mgmt. YMCA, 1965-66. Served with USNR, 1944-46. Mem. Am. Assn. U. Profs., Phi Delta Kappa. Presbyn. (tchr. Sunday sch.). Home: 90 N Richhill St Waynesburg PA 15370

CHRISTIAN, FLOYD THOMAS, state ofcl.; b. Bessemer, Ala., Dec. 18, 1914; s. Henry Clayton and Mabel Blanche (Jones) C.; A.B. in Edn., U. Fla., 1937, M.A., Sch. Adminstrn. and Supervision, 1950; m. Margaret Littlejohn, Aug. 27, 1938; children—Vera Ellen (Mrs. Claude Leiby), Floyd Thomas, Robert Rick. Tchr., athletic dir., head coach Clearwater (Fla.) High Sch., also Ft. Myers (Fla.) High Sch., 1937-41; adminstr. charge Fla. Dept. Vets Affairs, 1946-48; supt. schs. Pinellas County, Fla., St. Petersburg, 1948-65; state supt. pub. instrn. State Fla., 1965-69, now commr. edn. State of Fla., Tallahassee. Dir., Central Plaza Bank & Trust Co., St. Petersburg. Mem. Pinellas County Juvenile Welfare Bd., Pinellas County License Bd., Fla. Children's Com.; cons. ednl. TV, Internat. Trade Fair, Turin, Italy, 1961. Bd. regents State Fla., 1965- . Recipient Good Govt. award St. Petersburg Jr. C. of C., 1957. Mem. Fla. Assn. County Supts. (past pres.), Fla. (past pres.), Nat. (life) edn. assns., Am. Assn. Sch. Adminstrs., Fla. Ednl. TV Commn., Fla. W. Coast Ednl. TV, Nat. Assn. Ednl. Broadcasters (exec. bd.). Mason, Rotarian. Home: 2609 Lotus Dr Tallahassee FL 32303. Office: The Capitol Tallahassee FL 32304

CHRISTIAN, FRANK SHARP, banker; b. Phila., Apr. 6, 1906; s. Frank Sharp and Gertrude (Eisenhart) C.; grad. William Penn Charter Sch., 1926, George Sch., 1927; B.A., Swarthmore Coll., 1931; D.S.C., Suffolk U., 1967; m. Martha Merion Wood, Aug. 1931; children—Anne C. (Mrs. John Tedeschi), Michael Wood. Store mgr. Electric, Inc., Phila., 1931-34; sales mgr. Eastern zone Firestone Tire & Rubber Co., 1934-41; v.p., dir. H.B. Humphrey Alley & Richards, Inc., Boston, 1941-55; exec. v.p. Herman Stevens Agy., Inc., Boston, 1955-56; v.p., N.E. regional mgr. Kenyon & Eckhardt, Inc., advt. agy., Boston, 1956-62; sr. v.p., dir. marketing New Eng. Mchts. Nat. Bank, Boston, 1964—; dir. Anderson Power Products, Inc., Parker, Eldridge & Sholl, Inc. Bd. dirs. Mass. Bay United Fund, United Community Services Met. Boston; bd. dirs., mem. exec. and finance coms. Boston chpt. A.R.C.; mem. corp., trustee, chmn. exec. com. Simmons Coll.; bd. advisers Suffolk U. Coll. Bus. Adminstrn.; trustee New Eng. Aquarium Corp., Eastern States Expn., Children's Hosp. Med. Center Mass. Eye and Ear Infirmary; chmn. bd. mgrs. Vis. Nurse Assn. Recipient New Boston award Boston U., 1963; named Advt. Man of Year, 1960. Mem. Greater Boston C. of C. (past pres., hon. v.p., dir.), Am. Inst. Banking. Club: Advertising of Boston (dir., past pres.). Died Jan. 12, 1971. Home: 40 Branch St Boston MA 02108 Office: Prudential Center Boston MA 02199 also 52 Powder Point Av Duxbury MA 02332

CHRISTIAN, GEORGE EASTLAND, bus. exec.; b. Austin, Tex., Jan. 1, 1927; s. George Eastland and Ruby (Scott) C.; B. Journalism, U. Tex., 1949; m. Elizabeth Anne Brown, July 30, 1950 (dec. 1957); m. 2d, Jo Anne Martin, June 20, 1959; children—Elizabeth, Susan, George Scott, Robert Bruce, John, Brian. Sports editor Temple (Tex.) Daily Telegram, 1949; corr. Internat. News Service, 1949-56; asst. to Senator Price Daniel, Washington, 1956, to Gov. Price Daniel, Austin, 1957-63, to Gov. John Connally, Austin, 1963- 66; press sec., spl. asst. to Pres. Johnson, Washington, 1966-69; chmn. bd. Christian, Miller & Honts, Inc. Served with USMCR, 1944-46. Mem. Sigma Delta Chi. Democrat. Episcopalian. Clubs: Citadel, Headliners (Austin); Federal City (Washington). Author: The President Steps Down. Home: 6800 Rockledge Cove Austin TX 78731 Office: 1st Nat Life Bldg Austin TX 78701

CHRISTIAN, JOHN DESPARD, mining co. exec.; b. Edmonton, Alta., Can., Sept. 19, 1914; s. John Russell Ligertwood and Kathleen Imogene (Despard) C.; B.A. Sc. in Mining, U. Toronto, 1937; m. Catherine Elizabeth Robertson, Sept. 1, 1945; 1 son, Peter Jr. engr. Teck-Hughes Gold Mines, Ltd., 1937-39; mgr. Teck Exploration Co., Toronto, 1945-51; cons. mining engr. Teck-Hughes Hold Mines, Ltd., also Lamaque Gold Mines, 1948-51; cons. engr. Conwest Exploration Co., Ltd., Toronto, 1951-54, dir., 1953—, exec. v.p., 1964-70; gen. mgr. Cassiar Asbestes Corp., Ltd., Toronto, 1954-63, pres., gen. mgr., 1963-68, pres., 1968—; dir. Central Patricia Gold Mines, Ltd. Served to brig. gen. Royal Canadian Engrs., 1939-45. Registered profl. Ont.

Mem. Assn. Profl. Engrs. Ont. Home: 279 St Leonards Av Toronto 12, Ontario Canada Office: 85 Richmond St W Toronto 1 Ontario Canada

CHRISTIAN, JOHN EDWARD, educator; b. Indpls., July 12, 1917; s. George Edward and Okel Kandus (Waltz) C.; B.S., Purdue U., 1939, Ph.D., 1944; m. Catherine Ellen Spooner, July 23, 1948; 1 dau., Linda Kay. Control chemist Upjohn Co., 1939-40; faculty Purdue U., Lafayette, Ind., 1940—, prof. pharm. chemistry, 1950- 59, head dept. radiol. control, 1956-59, prof. bionucleonics, head dept., 1959—, chmn. adminstrv. com. Trace Level Research Inst., 1960—, dir. Inst. for Environmental Health, 1965—; prof. radiation therapy Ind. U., Sch. Medicine, 1970—. Harvey Washington Meml. lectr. Purdue U., 1955; Edward-Kremers Meml. lectr. U. Wis., 1956; vis. lectr. U. Tex., 1959, Taylor U. Ann. Sci. Lecture Series, Upton, Ill., 1960; Julius A. Koch meml. lectr. U. Pitts., 1961. Mem. revision com. U.S. Pharmacopeia, 1950-60, now mem. adv. panel on radioactive drugs; adv. com. isotope distbn. AEC, 1952-58, mem. med. adv. com., 1967—; mem. radiation and chem. def. sect. Ind. Dept. Civil Def., 1954—; vice chmn. Radiation Control Adv. Commn. Ind., 1958—; mem. exec. com. Ind. Comprehensive Health Planning Council; mem. adv. com. radiopharms. FDA, 1970—; mem. Ind. Gov.'s Pesticide Council. Alumni research councilor, mem. adv. com. Purdue Research Found. Recipient award Chilean Iodine Ednl. Bur., 1956; Julius Sturmer award Phila. Coll. Pharmacy and Sci., 1958. Fellow A.A.A.S. (past sec. pharm. sci. sect., mem. council), Acad. Pharm. Scis., Ind. Acad. Sci.; mem. Am. Assn. Colls. Pharmacy (past mem. exec. com., chmn. conf. tchrs., chmn. conf. grad. study and grad. tchrs., chmn. com. study grad. edn. in pharmacy), Am. Chem. Soc. (past chmn. Purdue sect.), Am. Pharm. Assn. (Ebert medal 1957, Justin L. Powers Research Achievement award 1962, past chmn. sci. sect.), Acad. Pharm. Scis., Ind. Pharm. Assn., Am. Pub. Health Assn., A.M.A. (spl. affiliate), Am. Nuclear Soc., Am. Soc. Bacteriology, Health Phys. Soc., Am. Assn. U. Profs., Sigma Xi (past pres. Purdue chpt., award Purdue chpt. 1950), Rho Chi, Phi Lambda Upsilon, Sigma Pi Sigma. Asso. editor Radiochem. Letters. Home: 1301 Woodland Av West Lafayette IN 47906 Office: Bionucleonics Dept Purdue U Lafayette IN 47907

CHRISTIAN, JOSEPH RALPH, physician; b. Chgo., June 15, 1920; s. Ralph F. and Anna M. (Across) Co; A.A., U. Chgo., 1941; M.D., Loyola U., Chgo., 1944; m. Marcia Pomeroy, Sept. 25, 1944; children—Patricia Ann, Joseph Ralph. Intern Cook County Hosp., Chgo., 1944-45, resident, 1945-46, 48-49; faculty Stritch Sch. Medicine, Loyola U., Chgo., 1948-61, prof. pediatrics, 1957-61, exec. com. chmn. dept., 1960-61; attending pediatrician Loyola Service at La Rabida Sanitarium, 1948-61; chmn. dept. pediatrics Mercy Hosp., 1960-61; chief pediatrics Lewis Meml. Maternity Hosp., 1951-61; chmn. dept. pediatrics Rush Presbyn.-St. Luke's Med. Center, Chgo., 1961—; prof. pediatrics U. Ill. Coll. Medicine, Chgo., 1961-70, Rush Med. Coll., Chgo., 1970—; sr. attending pediatrician children's div. Cook County Hosp., 1959-65. Chmn. poison control com. Chgo. Bd. Health, 1961-69; chmn. med. com. Infant Welfare Soc. Chgo., 1958-61; chmn. 9th Ill. Congress Meternal and Infant Health, 1962. Chmn. bd. trustees Holy Cross Hosp., Chgo., 1970—. Served to capt. M.C., AUS, 1946-47. Recipient Clin. Faculty award Stritch Sch. Medicine, 1954, 57. Diplomate Am. Bd. Pediatrics. Fellow Am. Coll. Chest Physicians, Am. Acad. Pediatrics (chmn. film rev. com. 1963—, chmn. com. residency fellowships 1964-67), Am. Pub. Health Assn., A.C.P.; mem. A.M.A., Am. Fedn. Clin. Research, Am. Heart Assn., Am. Assn. Poison Control Centers, Am., Ill. (pres. 1964) assns. maternal and infant health, Chgo. Pediatric Soc. (pres. 1964-65), Midwest Soc. Pediatric Research, Am. Soc. for Clin. Pharmacology and Therapeutics, N.Y. Acad. Scis. Editor: Pediatrics Digest. Mem. editorial bd. Childcraft, 1963—. Contbr. articles to med. jours. Home: 1031 Keystone Av River Forest IL 60305 Office: 1753 W Congress Pkwy Chicago IL 60612

CHRISTIAN, MURRAY, oil co. exec.; b. Moberly, Mo., Feb. 27, 1907; s. Robert Emmett and Cecelia B. (Murray) C.; LL.B., St. Louis U., 1931; m. Virginia Guignon, Oct. 28, 1939; childrenAnn, Mary. Admitted to Mo. bar, 1931, Tex. bar, 1933, Miss. bar, 1945; atty. Shell Oil Co., 1931-41; with Superior Oil Co., 1941-, gen. counsel, dir., 1962-, v.p., 1968-; dir. McIntyre Porcupine Mines Ltd., Western Platinum Ltd. Served to lt. (s.g.) USNR, 1942-44. Mem. Am., Tex., Miss., Mo. bar assns. Clubs: Petroleum, Serra (Houston). Home: 3665 Piping Rock Lane Houston TX 77027. Office: Superior Oil Co First City Nat Bank Bldg Houston TX 7701.

CHRISTIAN, PERCY WILLIS, educator; b. Viborg, S.D., Jan. 8, 1907; s. John Willis & Tillie Victoria (Peterson) C.; B.A., Broadview Coll., 1926; B.S., Lewis Inst., Chgo., 1928; M.A., Northwestern U., 1929, Ph.D., 1935; LL.D., Walla Walla Coll., 1967; m. Evelyn Anna deVries, June 25, 1931; 1 son, John Willis. Instr. history Chgo. Acad., 1926-28, Broadview Coll., 1931-33; asst. prof. history Walla Walla Coll., 1933-35, asso. prof., 1935-38, prof., 1938-43, pres., 1955- 64; dean Pacific Union Coll., Angwin, Cal., 1943-45, pres., 1945-50, prof. history, 1964—; pres. Emmanuel Missionary Coll., 1950-55; vis. prof. Eastern Wash. Coll. Edn., summer 1934, State Coll. Wash., summer 1942, Loma Linda U., summer 1962, Andrews U., summer 1966, Seminaire Adventists, Collonges, France, 1968-69. Mem. Am. Hist. Assn., Orgn. Am. Historians. Seventh-day Adventist. Home: 160 White Cottage Rd Angwin CA 94508

CHRISTIAN, RICHARD CARLTON, advt. exec.; b. Dayton, O., Nov. 29, 1924; s. Raymond A. and Louise (Gamber) C.; B.S. in Bus. Adminstrn., Miami U., Oxford O., 1948; M.B.A., Northwestern U., 1949; postgrad. Denison U., The Citadel, Biarritz Am. U.; m. Audrey Bongartz, Sept. 10, 1949; children—Ann Carol, Richard Carlton. Sr. marketing analyst Nat. Cash Register Co., Dayton, 1948, Rockwell Mfg. Co., Pitts., 1949-50; exec. v.p. Marsteller, Rickard, Gebhardt & Reed, Inc. (firm name now Marsteller Inc.), Chgo., 1951-60, pres., 1960—; dir. Wilmette State Bank. Lectr. marketing Northwestern U.; speaker, author marketing, sales mgmt., marketing research and advt. Trustee Northwestern U., Nat. Coll. Edn., Evanston, Ill., Bapt. Grad. Student Center U. Chgo. Chmn. exec. com. James Webb Young Fund for Edn., U. Ill., 1962-68. Served with inf. AUS, 1942-46; ETO. Decorated Bronze Star medal, Purple Heart. Mem. Am. Marketing Assn., Indsl. Marketing Assn. (founder, chmn. 1951), Assn. Indsl. Advertisers (life mem. Chgo., pres. Chgo. 1954-55, nat. v.p. 1955-58), Northwestern U. Bus. Sch. Alumni Assn. (founder, pres.), Am. Mgmt. Assn., Am. Assn. Advt. Agys. (dir., vice chmn. Central region 1968-70), Northwestern U. Alumni Assn. (nat. pres. 1968-70), Chgo. Assn. Commerce and Industry, Alpha Delta Sigma, Beta Gamma Sigma, Delta Sigma Pi, Phi Gamma Delta. Baptist (trustee). Clubs: Sky (N.Y.C.); Mid-America, Executives, Economic (Chgo.); Kenilworth; Westmoreland Country (Wilmette, Ill.). Home: 132 Oxford Rd Kenilworth IL 60043 Office: 1 E Wacker Dr Chicago IL 60601

CHRISTIAN, ROBERT HENRY, architect; b. Cin., Feb. 28, 1922; s. Richard Dudley and Lillian Emma (Huber) C.; B.S. in Architecture, U. Cin., 1952; m. Marjorie Ann Ruff, Apr. 12, 1947; children—Carol Ann, Robert Alan. Color matcher Interchem. Corp., Cin., 1945-46; draftsman various cos., 1946-54; asso. architect Sullivan, Isaacs & Sullivan, Cin., 1954-62; asso. architect L.P. Cotter & Assos., Cin., 1962-67, partner, 1967—. Mem. Hamilton County Regional Planning Commn., Cin., 1963—; active Boy Scouts Am.; artist and archtl. rep. Cin. Archdiocesan Liturgical Commn., 1970—; tech. adviser to Village Woodlawn, O., 1963—, mayor Village, 1957-63. Mem. Edgecliff Coll. Acad. Fine Arts Found., 1961-69, chmn., 1963-66. Served with USAFF, 1942-45. Mem. A.I.A., Nat. Rifle Assn., Scrab. K.C. (4). Home: 626 Glenway Wyoming Cincinnati OH 45215 Office: 3329 Glenmore Cincinnati OH 45211

CHRISTIAN, ROBERT VERNON, Jr., chemist, educator; b. Wichita, Kan., Mar. 1, 1919; s. Robert Vernon and Anna (Vezie) C.; B.S., U. Wichita, 1940; Ph.D., Ia. State Coll., 1946; m. Mary Elizabeth Morton, July 7, 1944; children—Robert Vernon III, John Alan, Ann Elizabeth, Karen Sue. Prof., chmn. dept. chemistry Wichita State U., 1946—. Research engr. Boeing Co., summers 1954-55; staff mem. NSF Summer Inst. Colo. Coll., 1963; vis. staff mem. Los Alamos Sci. Lab., 1965, 67, 68. Mem. Am. Chem. Soc., A.A.A.S., Sigma Xi, Alpha Chi Sigma, Phi Lambda Upsilon. Rotarian. Home: 1736 Harvard St Wichita KS 67208

CHRISTIAN, SHERRIL DUANE, educator; b. Estherville, Ia., Sept. 28, 1931; s. Carl B. and Elverna E. (Kuhlman) C.; B.S. in Math., Ia. State U., 1952, Ph.D. in Phys. Chemistry, 1956; m. Dolores L. Gabriel, Jan. 7, 1956; children—Dale Warren, Ian Mark, Lani Aloha. Asst. prof. chemistry U. Okla., 1956-60, asso. prof., 1960-65, prof., 1965-69, George Lynn Cross research prof., 1969—, asst. dean Coll. Arts and Scis., 1963-66, chmn. chemistry dept., 1963, 68-69. Participant, Oak Ridge Inst. for Nuclear Studies (Tenn.), summer 1956; employed summers at research div. Hawaiian Dole Pineapple Co., Honolulu, 1957, IBM Glendale Lab., Endicott, N.Y., 1959; guest prof., research asso. U. Oslo, Norway, 1966-67. Recipient U. Okla. Found. Research award, 1956, U. Okla. Research Inst. Project Dirs.' Research award, 1966; Fulbright fellow U. Ceylon, 1961; Norwegian Council for Sci. and Indsl. Research fellow, 1966. Mem. Am. Chem. Soc., Am. Assn. U. Profs., Norman Tennis Assn., Norman Jr. Tennis League (dir.), U.S. Lawn Tennis Assn., Chem. Soc. London, Sigma Xi (Faculty Research award 1968), Phi Kappa Phi, Phi Lambda Upsilon, Pi Mu Epsilon. Contbr. articles sci. jours. Home: 1432 24th St SE Norman OK 73069

CHRISTIAN, WILLIAM ARMISTEAD, educator; b. Mobile, Nov. 1, 1905; s. William Armistead and Edith (Dyche) C.; A.B., Davidson Coll., 1927; B.D., Union Theol. Sem., Va., 1930; postgrad. U. Edinburgh (Scotland), 1930, Mansfield Coll., Oxford (Eng.) U., 1931, Chgo. Theol. Sem., 1932-33; Ph.D., Yale, 1942; m. Rena Grubb, June 27, 1933; children—Louise (Mrs. Gary B. Rundle), Edith (Mrs. Richard H. Minear), William Armistead. From instr. to asso. prof. religion Smith Coll., 1937-51; faculty Yale, 1951—, prof. religious studies, 1962—. Vis. asso. prof. philosophy and religion Swarthmore Coll., 1946-47; vis. prof. philosophy of religion U. Chgo., summer 1948; Mem. Am. Philos. Assn., Aristotelian Soc., Am. Theol. Soc. Conglist. Author: An Interpretation of Whitehead's Metaphysics, 1959; Meaning and Truth in Religion, 1964. Home: 191 Ridgewood Av Hamden CT 06517 Office: Yale New Haven CT 06520

CHRISTIANA, FELIX J., banker; b. N.Y.C., Oct. 19, 1922; s. Mark and Marie (Martire) C.; B.S., Fordham U., 1947; M.B.A., N.Y. U., 1956; m. Blanche Martino, Feb. 7, 1948; children—Margaret, Mark. With Dollar Savs. Bank of N.Y., 1947—, asst. comptroller, 1961-64, auditor, 1964-70, v.p., auditor, 1970—; mem. faculty N.Y. and Westchester Am. Inst. Banking. Mem. County of Westchester Grand Jury; mem. Mayor's Citizens Adv. Com. for Community Improvement, Mt. Vernon, N.Y., 1964. Trustee Am. Inst. Banking, 1966—. Served with AUS, 1944-46; ETO. Mem. N.Y. State Savs. Bank Auditors and Comptrollers Forum. Home: 465 Rich Av Mt Vernon NY 10552 Office: 2530 Grand Concourse New York City NY 10458

CHRISTIANO, JOSEPH FRANCIS, fgn. service officer; b. Geneva, N.Y., Oct. 17, 1923; s. Francis R. and Adeline (Scalise) C.; B.A., Yale, 1945; m. Theodora van den Oever, Apr. 15, 1950; children—Lawrence Joseph, Dorothea Francesca, Thomas Dominic. Joined U.S. Fgn. Service, 1948; vice consul, Rotterdam, Holland, 1948- 59, Algiers, 1951-53, Geona, Italy, 1954-55, Trieste, 1955-56; 2d sec., Brussels, 1956-58; consul, Amsterdam, 1958-61; 2d sec., Bucharest, 1962-64; mem. staff Dept. State, Washington, 1964-68; counselor embassy and dep. chief mission, Bamako, Mali, 1968-71; dep. dir. Africa div. Dept. Commerce, Washington, 1971—. Mem. Am. Fgn. Service Assn. Roman Catholic. Clubs: Yale of Washington; Lakewood Country (Rockville, Md.) Home: 12015 Whippoorwill Lane Rockville MD 20852 Office: American Embassy Bamako Republic Mali

CHRISTIANSEN, EDWARD SMITH, IV, metal mfr.; b. Northampton, Mass., June 19, 1909; s. Edward Smith and Mary Ethel (Oldham) C.; A.B., Case Western Res. U., 1933; m. Mary Catherine Badger, May 21, 1938; children—Karen Christiansen Davis, Edward Smith V, William Earl. Mem. sales dept. Stewart Die Casting Corp., Chgo., 1933- 34; sales mgr. Nat. Smelting Co., Cleve., 1935-38; organizer, v.p., dir. Aluminum and Magnesium, Inc., Sandusky, O., 1939-41; v.p., sales mgr., dir. Apex Smelting Co., Chgo., 1941-44; organizer, pres., chmn. bd. Magnesium Co. Am., E. Chicago, Ind., 1944-62, Christiansen Corp., Oak Park, Ill., 1944-62, Indsl. Smelting Corp., Chicago Heights, Ill., 1949- 62, Aluminum Alloyer's Can., Ltd., 1952-62, Magcoa, Ltd., 1954-62; chmn. bd. Equipment Co. Am., Hialeah, Fla., 1962—; consul for Sweden, Miami, Fla., 1956-63. Founder, pres. Magnesium Assn., 1943-46. Bd. dirs. Met. Miami YMCA; bd. govs. Com. of 100, Miami Beach, Fla.; past bd. dirs. United Fund, Mental Health Soc., Cancer Inst., Opera Guild, Hist. Assn. So. Fla.; adv. bd. Fla. Meml. Coll. Named Man of Year in Light Metals Industry, 1951. Mem. Execs. Assn. Greater Miami, World Bus. Council, Delta Kappa Epsilon. Mason (32, Shriner) Clubs: Coral Reef Yacht (founding commodore 1955), Two Hundred (Miami); Century (past bd. govs.) (Coral Gables). Home: 4811 Orduna Dr Coral Gables FL 33146 Office: 1075 Hialeah Dr Hialeah FL 33010

CHRISTIANSEN, ERNEST BERT, educator; b. Richfield, Utah, July 31, 1910; s. Ernest C. and (Nielsen) C.; B.S., U. Utah, 1937; M.S., U. Mich., 1939, Ph.D., 1945; m. Susan Mann, Sept. 6, 1935; childrenDavid Ernest, Susan Catherine, Gale Ann, Alan Grant, Philip Arne, Richard Lee, Lisa Beth. Chem. engr. E.I. DuPont de Nemours Co., 1941-46; prof. head dept. chem. engring U. Ida., 1946-47, U. Utah, 1947—. Registered profl. engr., Utah. Mem. Am. Inst. Chem. Engrs., Am. Chem. Soc., Am. Soc. Engring. Edn., Tau Beta Pi, Sigma Xi, Phi Kappa Phi. Contbr. articles to profl. jours. Home: 3025 S 1935 E St Salt Lake City UT 84106.

CHRISTIANSEN, FRANCIS WYMAN, educator; b. Richfield, Utah, Feb. 19, 1912; s. Ernest C. and Sarah (Nielsen) C.; B.S., U. Utah, 1935, M.S., 1937; Ph.D., Princeton U, 1948; m. Alta Bates, Sept. 1, 1933; children—James, Jean (Mrs. Kent Johnson), Joan (Mrs. Don A. Winn), Colleen (Mrs. Gordon Freeman), William J., Kathleen Jill. Mining geologist Sierra Consol. Mining Co., Reno, 1937-38; instr. U. Utah, 1939-40; teaching asst. Princeton, 1940-42, instr., 1942; mineral specialist Fed. Govt., Washington, 1942-46; asst. prof. econ. and structural geology U. Utah, 1946-51, asso. prof., 1951-55, prof., 1955—; cons. to industry. Merit badge adv. E. Mill Creek council Boy Scouts Am., 1956-71. Fellow Geol. Soc. Am., Am. Inst. Mining and Metall. Engrs., A.A.A.S.; mem. Sigma Xi. Research structural geology. Home: 2320 Neffs Lane Salt Lake City UT 84109

CHRISTIANSEN, JERALD EMMETT, engr., former educator; b. Hyrum, Utah, Apr. 9, 1905; s. Jerry and Emily (Israelsen) C.; student Ida. State U., 1923-25; B.S., Utah State U., 1927; M.S. in Civil Engring., U. Cal., 1928; C.E., 1935; m. Rebecca Nelson, July 17, 1929; children—Jerald Nelson, Henry Nelson. Jr. irrigation engr., asst. irrigation engr. U. Cal. Coll. Agr., 1928- 42; irrigation and drainage engr. U.S. Regional Salinity Lab., U.S. Dept. Agr., Riverside, Cal., 1942-46; dean sch. engring. and tech. Utah State Agrl. Coll. (now Utah State U.), Logan, 1946-57, prof. civil and irrigation engring., 1957-70, prof. emeritus, 1970—. Irrigation engr. FAO, Uruguay, 1957, water resources cons. Rome, Mediterranean countries, 1958; vis. prof. irrigation U. Cal., Davis, 1957-58; irrigation cons. ICA, Spain, 1960-61; cons. FAO, Argentina, 1961, Ford Found., Nigeria, 1962- 63, N.C. agrl. mission to Peru, 1964, Utah State U.-OAS, Venezuela, 1965-71, Argentina, 1967, 68, Uruguay, 1969, Colombia, 1970, 71, El Salvador, Ecuador, 1971, FAO to Peru, 1968, Rockefeller Found., Columbia, 1966. Fellow Am. Soc. C.E. (life); mem. Am. Soc. Agrl. Engrs., Am. Soc. Engring. Edn., Nat., Utah (pres. 1965-66) socs. profl. engrs., Sons Utah Pioneers, Phi Kappa Phi, Sigma Tau, Sigma Xi. Mem. Ch. of Jesus Christ of Latter-day Saints. Kiwanian. Home: 544 E 500 N Logan UT 84321

CHRISTIANSEN, KENNETH ALLEN, educator, biologist; b. Chgo., June 24, 1924; s. Christian Peder and Ethel (Robinson) C.; B.A., Boston U., 1948; Ph.D., Harvard, 1951; m. Phyllis Jean Smith, June 7, 1947; children—Karen, Eric, Paula, Diane. Teaching fellow Harvard, 1949-51; asst. prof. biology Am. U. Beirut, Lebanon, 1951-54; instr. zoology Smith Coll., 1954-55; faculty Grinnell (Ia.) Coll., 1955—, prof. biology, 1962—. Instr., Harvard Summer Sch., 1956, 59; vis. researcher Le Lab. Souterrain, Moulis, France, 1962, 67-68. Served with AUS, 1942-45. Decorated Bronze Star with oak leaf cluster; research grantee Sigma Xi, 1950-55, Bache Fund, 1955, Am. Philos. Soc., 1957, NSF, 1957-70. Fellow A.A.A.S.; mem. Soc. for Study Evolution, Soc. Systemic Zoology, Internat. Soc. Soil Zoology, Am., Cambridge entomol. socs., Nat. Speleological Soc., Mus. of Paris (corr.), Phi Beta Kappa, Sigma Xi. Contbr. articles to profl. jours. Home: 1402 Main St Grinnell IA 50112

CHRISTIANSEN, PAUL JOHN, lawyer, corp. ofcl.; b. Orange, N.J., June 22, 1906; s. William F. and Marie (Erdmann) C.; LL.B., Rutgers U., 1927; m. Mary A. Musk, Dec. 29, 1932; children—Carol S. (Mrs. George L. Polley), Gail M. (Mrs. C. David Witherington). With McCarter & English, counsellors-at- law, Newark, 1927-36; pvt. practice law, Newark, 1936-41; legal staff, then gen. counsel, sec. Thomas A. Edison, Inc., 1941-57; v.p. Thomas A. Edison Industries div. McGraw-Edison Co., 1957, pres., 1957-71; partner Christiansen, Jube & Keegan, Newark, 1971—; bd. mgrs. U.S. Savs. Bank (Newark); adv. bd. Nat. State Bank Orange, N.J.; dir. Automatic Switch Co., Colonial Life Ins. Co. Am. Mem. N.J. State Bd. Edn. Bd. dirs. YMCA, Oranges and Maplewood, N.J.; trustee Thomas Alva Edison Found., Inc.; bd. overseers Found. Advancement Grad. Study Engring., Newark Coll. Engring.; pres. The Brook Found. Mem. N.J. C. of C. (dir.), Essex County Bar Assn. Home: West Rd West Orange NJ 07052 Office: 51 Lakeside Av West Orange NJ 07052

CHRISTIANSEN, ROBERT LESTER, advt. exec.; b. Chgo., July 2, 1927; s. Clarence Martin and Leta (Covey) C.; B.S., Northwestern U., 1949, student Law Sch., 1949-50; m. Annemarie Gabor, Sept. 7, 1952 (dec.); children—Eric Robert, Clarence Martin II; m. 2d, Joy Flodin, Jan. 23, 1965. Sec.-treas. C. M. Christiansen Co., Phelps, Wis., 1949-51, pres., 1957—; with Cramer-Krasselt Co., advt., Milw., 1951—, exec. v.p., 1961-68, pres., 1968—, chief exec. officer, 1971—, also dir.; v.p. Sylvan Products Corp., Phelps, 1959—, Hess & Evenson, Inc., Phelps, 1958—. Former mem. adv. bd. trustees YWCA Greater Milw.; mem. art bd. Milwaukee County War Meml. Center; mem. Greater Milw. Com.; mem. adv. bd., pub. relations chmn. St. Michael Hosp.; v.p., dir. Florentine Opera Co., Milw.; asso. chmn. 1966 Milw. United Fund; gen. chmn. 1960 Bal du Lac. Trustee Milw. Art Center; bd. corp. Milw. Boys Clubs, Univ. Sch., Milw. Symphony Orch., Wis. Coll.-Conservatory, Milw., Lakeside Children's Center; bd. dirs. Better Bus. Bur., Milw.; governing bd. St. Joseph's and St. Michael Hosps.; bd. regents Northwestern U., 1971. Mem. Am. Assn. Advt. Agys. (gov. central region, mem. com. on agy. mgmt.). Clubs: Milwaukee, Milwaukee (Milw.); Chippewa (Iron Mountain, Mich.); Confrerie des Chevaliers du Tastevin. Home: 9370 N Lake Dr Milwaukee WI 53217 Office: 733 N Van Buren St Milwaukee WI 53202

CHRISTIANSON, ALDEN HENIG, can co. exec.; b. Winchester, Wis., Nov. 24, 1916; s. George and Gusta (Frederickson) C.; B.A. in Commerce, U. Wis., 1938; m. Ardis Rattunde, Aug. 5, 1939; 1 son, John Alden. Jr. accountant Haskins & Sells, C.P.A.'s, Chgo., 1938-41; sr. accountant Arthur Andersen, C.P.A.'s, Chgo., 1941-44, audit mgr., Milw., 1946-54; asst. to controller, then controller Marathon Corp., Neenah, Wis., 1954-64; comptroller Am. Can Co., 1964-66, vp., comptroller, 1966—; v.p. asst. treas. Marathon Corp. Can. Ltd., 1960-67; treas. Marathon Packages Can. Ltd., 1960-67; v.p. finance, dir. Meridian & Bigbee R.R., 1960—; treas., dir. Sumter & Choctaw Ry. Co., 1961-67; treas. Marathon So. Corp., 1960-66. Sect. leader Milw. Community Chest, 1951-54; mem. budget com. Neenah (Wis.) Community Chest, 1955, chmn., 1957, bd. dirs., 1959- 61. Bd. dirs. Neenah-Menasha Taxpayers Assn., 1960. Served to lt. (j.g.) USNR, 1944-46. C.P.A., Wis., Ill., Ohio. Mem. Financial Execs. Inst., Am. Inst. C.P.A.'s, Nat. Assn. Accountants. Home: 235 Mill Rd New Canaan CT 06840 Office: American Lane Greenwich CT 06830

CHRISTIANSON, EDWARD GEORGE, oil co. exec.; b. Chgo., Aug. 4, 1916; s. Oren Alfred and Gusta (Dishmaker) C.; B.S. in Mining Engring., U. Wis., 1937; m. Olive Yvonne Bayne, Mar. 15, 1940; children—George B., Mary Karen, Charles E. With Shell Oil Co., 1938-70, v.p., Houston, 1964-67, exec. v.p., dir., N.Y.C., 1967-70; exec. v.p., dir. Amerada Hess Corp., N.Y.C., 1971—. Mem. Mid-Continent Oil and Gas Assn. (dir. 1966), Am. Petroleum Inst. Mason. Clubs: Economic, University (N.Y.C.); Winged Foot (Mamaroneck, N.Y.). Home: 815 Silvermine Rd New Canaan CT 06840 Office: 51 W 51st St New York City NY 10019

CHRISTIANSON, JOHN REES, educator, sociologist; b. Wales, Utah, Aug. 17, 1927; s. ElRay Lavar and Lewella (Rees) C.; B.S., Utah State U., 1949, M.S., 1952; Ph.D., U. Wis., 1955; m. Lucele Kartchner, Sept. 10, 1951; children—David, Steven, ElRay, Carol, Daniel. Asst. rural sociologist U. Ky., 1954-55; social sci. analyst Dept. Agr., 1955-57; mem. faculty Brigham Young U., 1957—, prof. sociology, 1963—; vis. prof. Tex. A. and M. U., 1963-64, Mich. State U., 1969 U. Wis., 1970-71; collaborator Dept. Agr., 1963-65; cons. Teamwork Found., 1967—. Served with USNR, 1945-47. Fellow Am. Social Assn.; mem. Nat. Council Family Relations, Rural Sociol. Soc., Sigma Xi, Pi Kappa Alpha, Alpha Kappa Delta. Kiwanian. Author: Introductory Sociology, 1963; also monographs, articles. Bull. index editor Rural Sociology, 1969—. Home 1161 Holly Circle Provo UT 84601 Office: Dept Sociology Brigham Young Univ Provo UT 84601

CHRISTIANSON, LLOYD FENTON, mgmt. cons.; b. Watertown, S.D., Jan. 6, 1914; s. Charles J. and Pearl Ellen (Auchampach) C.; B.S., Kan. U., 1935, Chem.E., 1940; postgrad. Harvard, 1941, Mass. Inst. Tech., 1942; m. Sergie A. Dannenberg, Dec. 25, 1935; children—George Fenton, Charles John, Lloyd Fredrick, Sergie Ann. Asst. chemist Kan. Bd. Health, Lawrence, 1933-35; petroleum engr. U.S. Bur. Mines, Bartlesville, Okla., 1935-41; pres. Electronic Assos., Inc., 1945-70; now mgmt. cons.; dir. N.J. Nat. Bank, Trenton; bd. mgrs. Howards Savs. Instn. Past pres. Monmouth County United Fund; mem. Ft. Monmouth Adv. Com., Citizens Com. Higher Edn. N.J., N.J. Council Econ. Devel. Bd. dirs. Monmouth County Boy Scouts Am., YMCA; vice chmn., trustee Monmouth Coll. Served to capt. Signal Corps, AUS, 1941-45. Mem. Am. Mgmt. Assn., Armed Forces Communications and Electronics Assn., Long Branch C. of C. (past pres.), Newcomen Soc., U.S. Army Assn., Theta Tau. Rotarian (past pres.). Address: 99 Rumson Rd Rumson NJ 07760

CHRISTIANSON, ROBERT JAMES, lawyer; b. Robbinsdale, Minn., Nov. 22, 1908; s. Theodore and Ruth (Donaldson) C.; B.A., LL.B., U. Minn., 1934; m. Louise Brown, Aug. 8, 1936; children—Robert James, Jean Louise (Mrs. Bruce D. Grussing). Admitted to Minn. bar, 1934, since practiced in Mpls.; mem. firm Faegre & Benson, and predecessors, 1944—. Dir. Title Ins. Co. Minn., Northwest Bancorp., Red Wing Shoe Co., Inc., Buhler Corp., Butter-Kernel Products, Inc., Minnetonka Boat Works, Inc., Leslie Paper Co. Mem. Order of Coif, Psi Upsilon, Phi Delta Phi. Republican. Conglist. Clubs: Minneapolis, Minikahda (Mpls.). Pres., recent case editor U. Minn. Law Rev., 1933-34. Home: 23 Woodland Rd Edina MN 55424 Office: Northwestern Bank Bldg Minneapolis MN 55402

CHRISTIE, AGATHA MARY CLARISSA, author; b. Torguay; d. Frederick Alvah Miller; m. Col. Archibald Christie, 1914 (div. 1928); 1 dau.; m. 2d, Max Edgar Lucien Mallowan, 1930. Decorated Comdr. Order Brit. Empire; 1956, dame Brit. Empire, 1971. Fellow Royal Soc. Lit. Author 80 books including: Murder of Roger Ackroyd, 1926; Mystery of the Blue Train, 1928; Thirteen at Dinner, 1933; Death Comes as the End, 1945; The Hollow, 1946; A Murder Is Announced, 1950; They Came to Baghdad, 1951; Mrs. McGinty's Dead, 1952; Murder With Mirrors, 1952; Funerals are Fatal; A Pocketful of Rye, 1954; So Many Steps to Death, 1955; Hickory Dickory Death, 1955; Dead Man's Folly, 1956; What Mrs. McGillicuddy Saw, 1957; The Pale Horse, 1962; The Clocks, 1964; A Caribbean Mystery, 1965; Third Girl, 1966; At Bertram's Hotel, 1966; Crooked House, 1950; Easy to Kill, 1939; And Then There Were None, 1940; Endless Night, 1968; (plays) Alibi, Appointment with Death, Black Coffee, Go Back for Murder, The Hollow Love from a Stranger, The Mousetrap, Murder at the Vicarage, Murder on the Nile, Peril at End House, Witness for the Prosecution, Rule of Three. Address: Greenway House Churston Ferrers S Devon England

CHRISTIE, ALDEN BRADFORD, architect; b. Montclair, N.J., Apr. 3, 1935; s. John Alden and Elizabeth (Hubbell) C.; A.B., Harvard, 1957, M.Arch., 1961; m. Jane Elsie Tyler, June 21, 1958. Prin., Cambridge Seven Assos., Inc., architects (Mass.), 1962-67; asso. RTKL, Inc., architects and planners, Balt., 1968-70; prin. Alden B. Christie, cons. architect, Balt., 1971—; asst. in graphics Harvard Grad. Sch. Design, 1963-65, asst. prof. architecture, 1965-67. Recipient Alpha Rho Chi medal in architecture, 1961, Progressive Architecture Ann. Design awards, 1964, 65. Mem. A.I.A. Exhibit architect U.S. Pavilion, Expo 67, Montreal. Important works include Abt Assos. Office Bldg., Cambridge Community Services Bldg. Address: 2850 N Charles St Baltimore MD 21218

CHRISTIE, AMOS, physician, educator; b. Eureka, Cal., Aug. 13, 1902; s. Frederick and Edna (Davis) C.; B.S., U. Wash., 1924; M.D., U. Cal., 1929; m. Margaret Cunningham Clarke, July 14, 1934; 1 dau., Linda Davis. Rotating intern Alameda County Hosp., 1928-29; pediatric intern Babies Hosp., Coll. Phys. and Surg. Columbia, 1929-30; vis. pediatrician San Francisco Juvenile Ct. and Infant Shelter, 1931-35; research asso. Johns Hopkins, 1936-37, asst. vis. pediatrician and obstetrician, 1936-37, also specialist in pediatrics Children's Bur., U.S. Dept. Labor, Washington, 1936-37; asst. prof. pediatrics U. Cal., 1937-39, lectr. pub. health, 1938-39, asso. prof. pediatrics, 1939, acting head dept., 1940; asst. dir. med. and health services Nat. A.R.C., Washington, 1942- 43; prof. pediatrics Vanderbilt U., Nashville, 1943—, Harvie Branscomb Distinguished prof., 1964. Mem. Cal. State Bd. Health, 1940-42. Recipient John Phillips Meml. award A.C.P., 1958; Abraham Jacobi award, pediatric sect. A.M.A., 1971. Diplomate Am. Bd. Pediatrics. Mem. Soc. Pediatric Research, Am. Acad. Pediatrics, Am. (v.p. 1955), Tenn. (pres. 1953-54), Nashville (pres. 1954) pediatric socs., Am. Pub. Health Assn., Nashville Acad. Medicine, Assn. Am. Physicians, So. Med. Assn. (chmn. pediatric sect. 1954), Sigma Xi, Alpha Omega Alpha. Contbr. profl. jours. Home: 4312 Esteswood Dr Nashville TN 37212 Office: Vanderbilt University Hospital Nashville TN 37203

CHRISTIE, DAN EDWIN, educator, mathematician; b. Dover-Foxcroft, Me., Oct. 11, 1915; s. Dan Foss and Blanche (Hamlin) C.; A.B., Bowdoin Coll., 1937; postgrad. (Henry fellow) St. John's Coll., Cambridge (Eng.) U., 1937-38; A.M., Princeton, 1940, Ph.D., 1942; m. Eleanor Wilson, Aug. 31, 1940; 1 son, Mark Edwin. Instr. math. Princeton, 1939-42; faculty Bowdoin Coll., Brunswick, Me., 1942—, prof. math. and physics, 1955-65, chmn. math. dept., 1964—, Wing prof. math., 1965—. Lectr., USAAF, 1943-44. USN, 1944-46; cons. math. D.C. Heath & Co., 1965-70. Mem. com. advanced math. grad. record exam. Ednl. Testing Service, 1964-65; mem. panel undergrad. math. edn. Com. Support Research Math. Scis., 1966-68; dir. summer insts. and seminars in math. NSF, 1959—; mem. Com. Undergrad. Program Math., 1963-66, mem. panel coll. tchr. preparation, 1965-69; adv. bd. Sch. Maths. Study Group, 1967- -; mem. com. undergrad. edn., div. math. scis. NRC, 1970—. Mem. Bowdoinham Sch. Bd., 1954-59. Ford Found. faculty fellow, 1953-54. Mem. Am. Math. Soc., A.A.A.S., Am. Assn. Physics Tchrs., Math. Assn. Am. (chmn. N.E. sect. 1960-61, nat. bd. govs. 1966-67, 70—), Nat. Council Tchrs. Math., Phi Beta Kappa, Sigma Xi. Author: Intermediate College Mechanics, 1952; Vector Mechanics, 1964. Home: 4 Atwood Lane Brunswick ME 04011

CHRISTIE, EDWARD JOHN, mut. fund exec.; b. N.Y.C., Jan. 17, 1906; s. Edmund J. and Anna Von (Sitler) C.; student Am. Inst. Banking; m. Matilda Fredericks, Dec. 24, 1931; children—June, Arthur. With Nat. Securities & Research Corp., N.Y.C., 1937—, v.p., 1962—, sr. v.p. Lutheran. Elk. Home: 54 Rottkamp St Valley Stream NY 11580 Office: 120 Broadway New York City NY 10005

CHRISTIE, GEORGE THOMAS, corp. exec.; b. Chgo., Jan. 23, 1912; s. George and Marie (Anderson) C.; B.S., U. Ill., 1933, J.D., 1935; m. Evelyn K. Sligoe, Sept. 11, 1937 (div. Sept. 1965); 1 dau., Patricia A.; m. 2d, Bonnie J. Thompson, May 24, 1969. Admitted to Ill. bar, 1935; asso. Kixmiller, Baar & Morris, Chgo., 1935-42; gen. atty., asst. gen counsel Greyhound Corp., Chgo., 1942-64, sec., 1965—, also sec. subsidiaries. Asst. prof. Chgo. Kent Coll. Law, 1939-42. Mem. Am. Bar Assn., Am. Soc. Corporate Secs., Phi Sigma Kappa. Club: Wigwam (Litchfield Park, Ariz.). Co- author: Foundation Guide for Payroll Taxes, 1940. Home: 1067 Seqovia Dr E Litchfield Park AZ 85340 Office: Greyhound Tower Phoenix AZ 85077

CHRISTIE, HANS FREDERICK, utility exec.; b. Alhambra, Cal., July 10, 1933; s. Andreas B. and Sigrid E. (Falck-Jorgensen) C.; B.S. in Business and Finance, U. So. Cal., 1957, M.B.A. in Mgmt., 1964; m. Susan E. Earley, June 16, 1957; children—Brenda Lynn, Laura Jean. With So. Cal. Edison Co., 1957—, treas., 1970—; v.p., treas. Electric Systems Ci., Energy Services, Inc., Mono Power Co.; treas. Asso. So. Investment Co. Dir. scholarship adminstrn. Los Angeles Jr. C. of C. Bd. dirs. Welfare Planning Council; bd. dirs., treas. Arthritis Found., Dollars for Scholars; bd. dirs., chmn. finance com. Angeles Girl Scout Council. Mem. Pacific Coast Elec. Assn., Nat., Los Angeles socs. financial analysts. Home: 6508 Nancy Rd Miraleste CA 90732 Office: 2244 Walnut Grove Av Rosemead CA 91770

CHRISTIE, JOHN ALDRICH, educator; b. Northampton, Mass., Apr. 12, 1920; s. Ralph A. and Isabel C. (Sutherland) C.; A.B., Oberlin Coll., 1942; A.M., Wesleyan U., Middletown, Conn., 1943; M.A., Yale, 1946; Ph.D., Duke, 1955; m. Dorothy Sexton, Aug. 22, 1946; children—David Brooks, John Sutherland, Roderick Graham. Asst. oral English dept. Wesleyan U., 1942-43; instr. English, U. Ill., 1943-44; mem. faculty Vassar Coll., 1946—, prof. English, 1965—; Fulbright prof. Am. lit. Delhi (India) U., summer 1966, Am. Studies Research Centre, Hyderabad, 1968. Cons. Nyack (N.Y.) High Sch., 1958-65; mem. adv. com. internat. exchange persons Fulbright Commn., 1966—. Trustee Poughkeepsie Day Sch., 1964-67. Mem. Am. Assn. U. Profs. (nat. council 1964-67, chmn. com. profl. ethics, 1967—). Author: Thoreau as World Traveler, 1965. Address: Vassar Coll Poughkeepsie NY 12601

CHRISTIE, JOHN MCDOUGALL, educator, geologist; b. Calcutta, India, Dec. 4, 1931; s. John and Anne (Logie) C.; B.Sc., U. Edinburgh, 1953, Ph.D., 1956; m. Helen Clark Herd, Aug. 24, 1957; children—Catherine M., John D., Ann M. Came to U.S., 1956. Instr. Pomona Coll., 1956-58; asst. prof. U. Cal. at Los Angeles, 1958-64, asso. prof., 1964-68, prof. geology, 1968—. Guggenheim fellow, 1964-65. Fellow Geol. Soc. Am.; mem. Am. Geophys. Union, A.A.A.S., Sigma Xi. Contbr. articles profl. jours. Home: 15861 Seabec Circle Pacific Palisades CA 90272 Office: U Cal Geology Bldg Los Angeles CA 90024

CHRISTIE, JOHN MILTON, banker; b. Corry, Pa., Aug. 14, 1910; s. Leslie Merle and Elvene (Curtis) C.; A.B., George Washington U., 1935; certificate, Rutgers U. Grad. Sch. Banking, 1940; m. Dorothy Anna Farrell, Sept. 12, 1936. Messenger clk. W.B. Hibbs & Co., investment bankers, 1927-35; with Riggs Nat. Bank, Washington, 1935—, v.p., 1952-65, sr. v.p., 1965-69, pres., 1969—, also dir.; dir. Govt. Employees Ins. Cos.; trustee Mortgage Investors Washington. Treas. Republican Nat. Com., 1969—. Bd. dirs. Boys Club Met. Police, D.C., past pres.; bd. dirs. Washington Heart Assn., Washington chpt. A.R.C.; treas., bd. dirs. Am. Forestry Assn.; trustee Am. U.; adv. bd. Nat. Capital div. Salvation Army, past pres., chmn. Served to lt. USNR, 1942-47. Mem. D.C. Bankers Assn. (pres.), Assn. Res. City Bankers. Episcopalian. Rotarian. Clubs: Columbia Country (past pres.) (Chevy Chase, Md.); Metropolitan (Washington); Burning Tree (Bethesda, Md.). Home: 9519 W Stanhope Rd Kensington MD 20795 Office: 1503 Pennsylvania Av NW Washington DC 20013

CHRISTIE, JULIE FRANCES, actress; b. Assam Province, India, Apr. 14, 1940; d. Frank St. John and Rosemary (Ramsden) C.; student Brighton (Eng.) Tech. Coll., 1957-58, Central Sch. Speech and Drama, London, Eng., 1958-61. Motion picture appearances include Crooks Anonymous, 1962; The Fast Lady, 1962-63; Billy Liar, 1963; Darling (best actress award British Film Acad., Oscar award 1965 as best actress for Darling) 1964; Young Cassidy, 1964; Dr. Zhivago, 1965; Fahrenheit 451, 1966; Far From the Madding Crowd, 1966; Petulia, 1967; In Search of Gregory, 1969; mem. Birmingham (Eng.) Repertory Group, 1960, Royal Shakespeare Theatre, Stratford-upon-Avon, 1963; TV appearances include A for Andromeda, 1962, Dangerous Corner, 1963, The Saint, 1963. Address: 11 Hanover Sq London W 1 England.

CHRISTIE, MARION FRANCIS, coll. dean; b. Emerson, Ark., Dec. 10, 1922; s. Scott T. and Milbra (Pafford) C.; B.A., Hendrix Coll., 1944; B.D., So. Meth. U., 1947, M.A., 1947; Ph.D. (Carre fellow, Hillel fellow), Vanderbilt U., 1952; m. Joann Finley, Aug. 23, 1944; children—Catherine Ann, Christine, John Finley. Instr. phys. edn. So. Meth. U., 1944-45, instr. religion, 1946-49; tchr. English, Terrill Prep. Sch., Dallas, 1945-46; prof. religion Birmingham-So. Coll., 1951-57; dean Simpson Coll., Indianola, Ia., 1957-59; head dept. philosophy and religion Mt. Union Coll., Alliance, O., 1959-60, dean 1960-65; acad. dean Hendrix Coll., Conway, Ark., 1965—. Dean acad. affairs Graz (Austria) Center, summers 1970, 71; vis. lectr. Bible, Candler Sch. Theology, Emory U., Div. Sch. Vanderbilt U. Ordained to ministry Meth. Ch., 1947; chmn. N. Ala. Conf. Commn. Christian Vocations, 1955-57. Mem. Blue Key, Alpha Psi Omega. Contbr. articles to profl. jours. Home: Route 4 Box 42 Conway AR 72032

CHRISTIE, RONALD VICTOR, former med. educator; b. Edinburgh, Scotland, June 4, 1902; s. Dugold and Elizabeth (Inglis) C.; M.B., Ch.B., U. Edinburgh, 1925, M.D., 1935, D.S.C., 1970; M.Sc., McGill U., 1933; D.Sc., U. London, 1943; Sc.D., Dublin (Ireland) U., 1960; m. Joyce Mary Ervine, July 23, 1933; children—Janet Ellen (Mrs. John Seely), Dugold Ervine. Intern, Royal Infirmary, Edinburgh, 1925-26; asst. resident Hosp. Rockefeller Inst. Med. Research, 1926-28; resident Royal Victoria Hosp., Montreal, Que., Can., 1928-29; prof. medicine London U. and St. Bartholomews Hosp., 1938-55; prof. medicine McGill U., Montreal, 1955-68, emeritus prof., 1968—, chmn. dept., 1955-65, dean faculty, 1964-68. Spl. research respiratory function in disease. Fellow Royal Coll. Physicians, A.C.P., Royal Coll. Physicians Can., Royal Coll. Physicians Edinburgh; mem. Assn. Physicians Am.; hon. mem. Assn. Physicians Gt. Britain. Home: 1230 MacGregor St Montreal Quebec Canada

CHRISTIN, ROBERT ERNEST, coll. pres.; b. Detroit, June 25, 1921; s. Robert Ernest and Edith (Hickey) C.; student U. Detroit, 1939-40; B.A., Ohio State U., 1947, M.A., 1949, Ph.D., 1958; m. Dorothy Mary Dunn, June 1, 1946; children—Robert, George, Michael, Matthew, Rita, Joseph, Edward, Mary, John. Instr. English, Ohio State U., 1949-52; instr. St. Ambrose Coll., Davenport, Ia., 1952-53; asst. prof., asso. prof., dir. freshman English, U. Notre Dame, 1953-65; dir. Inst. for Services to Edn., Washington, 1965-67; dir. Ednl. Projects, Inc., Washington, 1967; pres. Ednl. Assos., Inc., Washington, 1967-69; pres. St. Norbert Coll., West De Pere, Wis., 1969—; cons. Ednl. Services, Inc., Boston, 1964-65. Served with USNR, 1942-46. Recipient Thomas Madden award for teaching U. Notre Dame, 1964. Roman Catholic. Home: 840 S Monroe St Green Bay WI 54301 Office: St Norbert Coll West De Pere WI 54178

CHRIST-JANER, ALBERT WILLIAM, artist, educator; b. Appleton, Minn., June 13, 1910; s. William Henry and Bertha Wilhelmina (Beckman) C.-J.; B.A., St. Olaf Coll., 1931, A.F.D., 1963; postgrad. Sch. Chgo. Art Inst. 1931-32, Yale Div. Sch., 1932-33; M.A., Yale, 1934; postgrad. Harvard, 1939-40; A.F.D., Lake Erie Coll., 1956; m. Virginia Morgan Carpenter May 28, 1941. Instr. art Stephens Coll., 1934-36, head art dept., 1937-42, dir. summer art school, 1936-39; prof. art Northwestern U., summer 1937; head art dept. Mich. State Coll., 1942-45; dir. mus. and library Cranbrook Acad. Art, 1945-47; dir. humanities devel. U. Chgo., 1947-51; dir. Arts Center Assos., Inc., 1951-52, office ednl. planning N.Y. U., 1952-56; dir. sch. of arts, prof. art Pa. State U., 1956-58; dean Art Sch., Pratt Inst., Bklyn., 1958-68, dir. Pratt Manhattan Center, 1968-70; Fuller E. Callaway Found. prof. art U. Ga., Athens, 1970—. Internat. Cons. Inst. Internat. Edn. Guggenheim award, 1950, 60. Represented in permanent collections Cranbrook Mus., Whitney Mus., Brooklyn Mus., Phillips Gallery, Washington, New Pub. Library, Library of Congress, Art Inst. Chgo., Met. Mus. Served in AUS, 1942-43. Mem. Phi Beta Kappa. Club: Century Association. Author: George Caleb Bingham of Missouri, 1940; Boardman Robinson, 1945; Eliel Saarinen, 1948; (with Mary Mix Foley) Modern Church Architecture, 1962; Forms, 1968. Contbr., articles to profl. jours. Home: River Ct Forest Heights Athens GA 30601

CHRIST-JANER, ARLAND FREDERICK, educator; b. Garland, Neb., Jan. 27, 1922; s. William Henry and Bertha Wilhelmina (Beckman) C.-J., B.A., Carleton Coll., 1943; B.D., Yale, 1949; J.D., U. Chgo., 1952; LL.D., Coe Coll., 1961, Carleton Coll., 1967, Colo. Coll., 1971; L.H.D., Monmouth Coll., 1967; m. Rebecca Irene Butler, Sept. 6, 1944. Asst. to pres. Lake Erie Coll., Painesville, O., 1952-53; asst. to pres. St. John's Coll., Annapolis, Md., 1953-59, tutor, treas., 1954-59, v.p., tutor, 1959-61; pres. Cornell Coll., Mt. Vernon, Ia., 1961-67, Boston U., 1967-70, Coll. Entrance Exam. Bd., N.Y.C., 1970—. Mem. nat. adv. council Peace Corps; chmn. adv. com. Inst. for Coll. and U. Adminstrs.; chmn. Commn. for Study Selected Health Ednl. Programs. Trustee Carleton Coll., Ednl. Testing Service. Served with USAAF, 1943-46. Mem. Am. Acad. Arts and Scis. Clubs: Harvard, (Boston); Century Assn. Yale, University (N.Y.C.); St. Botolph. Exhibiting artist.

CHRIST-JANER, VICTOR FREDERICK, architect, educator; b. Waterville, Minn., Mar. 27, 1915; s. William Henry and Bertha Wilhelmina (Beckman) C.-J.; student St. Olaf Coll., 1933-35; B.F.A. with honors, Yale, 1940; B.Arch., 1947; A.F.D., Lake Erie Coll., 1967; m. Elizabeth Coolidge Whiting, Dec. 20, 1944; childrenKatherine, Karen. Asso. dir. Summer Art Sch., Stephens Coll., 1937-39; vis. critic Yale Sch. Architecture, 1949; prof. grad. design Columbia Sch. Architecture, 1958—; Danforth Found. lectr., 1963-64, 64-65, 67-68, 69-70; lectr. numerous colls. and univs. chief graphic designer for Nelson Rockefeller, Office Am. Affairs, 1941- 42; asso. Nemeny and Geller, 1946-48; designer IBEC, 1948-49; propr. Victor Christ-Janer and Assos., 1955-; prin. works include campus design and all bldgs. in plan Lake Erie Coll., Painesville, O.; St. Mary's Abbey, Morristown, N.J.; plan for Carthusian Found. Am., Arlington, Va.; St. Meinrad (Inds.) Abbey: United Ch. Christ, West Conn.; 10th Ch. Christ Scientist, N.Y.C.; Ch. of the Master, Harlem, N.Y.C.; Unitarian Universalist Ch., Rochester, Minn.; McGraw Chaapel, partner Christ-Janer, Johansen & Kouzmanoff in plan for Nassau campus State U. N.Y., 1966—. Served with AUS, 1942-45. Mem. A.I.A. (award of merit 1961, Reynolds award 1967). Clubs: Yale (N.Y.C.). Home: Frogtown Rd Office: 10 Forest St New Canaan CT 06840

CHRISTMAN, HENRY MAX, author, city ofcl.; b. Kansas City, Mo., Jan. 21, 1932; s. Henry Max and Irene Blanche (McBride) C.; B.A. in History and Govt., U. Mo., 1953; Ph.D., U. Belgrade, 1971. Pub. information cons. Fund for Republic, 1956-62; editorial cons. Macmillan Co.; N.Y. editor Progressive mag.; dir. city record City N.Y., 1966—. Mem. com. candidates Citizens Union City N.Y., 1961-66; com.-at- large Liberal Party. Decorated Star Yugoslavia 1st class, 1970. Mem. Am. Ethical Union, Soc. Am. Historians, Authors League Am., Internat. Typog. Union, League Indsl. Democracy (dir., nat. council 1969—), Ams. for Democratic Action (N.Y. State vice chmn. 1963-67, dir., chmn. Greenwich Village chpt. 1965-66), Deadline Club, P.E.N. Club, Phi Alpha Theta, Pi Gamma Mu, Sigma Delta Chi. Club: Overseas Press (N.Y.C.). Author: The Public Papers of Chief Justice Earl Warren, 1959; The Mind and Spirit of John Peter Altgeld, 1960; A View of the Nation, 1960; Walter P. Reuther-Selected Papers, 1961; This is our Strength- Selected Papers of Golda Meir, 1962; Walt Whitman's New York, 1963; Peace and Arms-Reports from the Nation, 1964; The South As It Is, 1965; One Hundred Years of the Nation, 1965; The Essential Works of Lenin, 1966; The American Journalism of Marx and Engels, 1966; Communism in PracticeA Documentary History, 1969; The State Papers of Levi Eshkol, 1969; The Essential Tito, 1970. Editor: (Myers) The History of Bigotry in the United States, 1960; (La Guardia) The Making of an Insurgent, 1961; (Garland) A Son of the Middlle Border, 1962; also articles. Home: 453 Franklin D Roosevelt Dr New York City NY 10002 Office: Municipal Bldg New York City NY 10007

CHRISTMAN, LUTHER PARMALEE, univ. dean; b. Summit Hill, Pa., Feb. 26, 1915; s. Elmer and Elizabeth (Barnicott) C.; grad. Pa. Hosp. Sch. Nursing for Men, 1939; B.S., Temple U., 1948, Ed.M., 1952; Ph.D., Mich. State U., 1965; m. Dorothy Mary Black, Dec. 5, 1939; children—Gary, Judith, Lillian. Cons., Mich. Dept. Mental Health, Lansing, 1956-63; asso. prof. psychiat. nursing U. Mich., 1963-67; research asso. Instl. Social Research, U. Mich., 1963-67; prof. nursing and sociology, also dean nursing Vanderbilt U., 1967—; cons. community services and research br. Nat. Inst. Mental Health, 1963-66, psychiat. research project So. Regional Edn. Bd., 1964-67. Chmn. planning com. 1st Midwest Conf. Psychiat. Nursing, Mpls., 1956; mem. team to survey mental health facilities of Colo., Nat. Inst. Mental Health, 1962, of Ga., 1964; mem., workshop leader White House Conf. on Children, 1970; mem. nursing panel Nat. Commn. for Study Nursing and Nursing Edn., 1968-70; mem. regional med. programs rev. com. Health Services and Mental Health Adminstrn., Dept. Health, Edn. and Welfare, 1968—; cons. dept. medicine and surgery VA Central Office, 1968—; mem. panel nurse consultants to com. on nursing A.M.A., 1971; mem. health services adv. com. Am. Assn. Med. Colls., 1971—; mem. action com. pub. health Am. Health Found., 1970—; participant numerous confs. in field; mem. S.D. Bd. Nursing, Tenn. Bd. Nursing. Mem. Am. (3rd v.p.), Mich. (pres. 1961-65) nurses assns., Am. Nurses Assn., Am. Sociol. Assn., Soc. Gen. Systems Research, A.A.A.S., Soc. Applied Anthropology, N.Y. Acad. Scis. Biomed. Engring. Soc., Sigma Theta Tau, Alpha Kappa Delta. Author numerous articles in field. Home: 6013 Andover Rd Nashville TN 37215

CHRISTMAN, THOMAS JACKSON, mil. officer; b. Seattle, Mar. 6, 1922; s. Milton Valentine and Ella (Grundler) C.; student U. Fla., 1939-40; B.S. in Naval Sci., U.S. Naval Acad., 1944; E.E., Mass. Inst. Tech., 1950, S.M. in Indsl. Mgmt. (Sloan fellow), 1959; m. Katherine Aiken Martin, Oct. 2, 1946; children—Thomas J., Patricia K., Susan V. Commd. ensign USN, 1943, advanced through grades to rear adm., 1969; service in destroyers, World War II; tech. mgr. guided missiles, 1950-58; tech. mgr. Polaris Missile Program, 1959-67; comdg. officer Naval Ammo Depot, Crane, Ind., 1967-68; dep. comdr. Logistics Support, Naval Ordnance Systems Command, Washington, 1968—. Scoutmaster, Boy Scouts Am., 1951, v.p. local council, 1967-68. Mem. U.S. Naval Inst., Am. Ordnance Assn., Research Soc. Am.

Toastmasters, I.E.E.E. Club: Army Navy Country (Arlington, Va.). Home: 7011 Girard St McLean VA 22101 Office: Code Ord 04 Naval Ordnance Systems Command Navy Dept Washington DC 20360

CHRISTO, JAVACHEFF VLADIMIROV, artist; b. Gabrovo, Bulgaria, June 13, 1935; s. Vladimir Ivan and Tzveta (Dimitrova) C.; student Acad. Fine Arts, Sofia, Bulgaria, 1952-56, Acad. Fine Arts, Vienna, Austria, 1956-57; m. Jeanne-Claude de Guillebon, Nov. 28, 1959; 1 son, Cyril. Came to U.S., 1964. Exhibited Galerie H., Lauhus, Cologne, Germany, 1961, Galerie J. Paris, France, 1962, Galerie Schmela, Düsseldorf, Germany, 1963-64, Gallerie Apollinaire, Milan, Italy, 1963, Galerie del Leone, Venice, Italy, 1963- 64, Galerie La Salita, Rome, Italy, 1963, Galerie and Libitum, Antwerp, Belgium, 1964, Galerie Sperone, Torin, Italy, 1964, Eindhoven (Holland) Stedelijk van Abbemuseum, 1966, Leo Castelli Gallery, N.Y.C., 1966, Galerie der Spiegel, Cologne, 1967, W.W. Space Gallery, Antwerpen, 1967, Mus. Modern Art, N.Y.C., 1968, Inst. Contemporary Art, Phila., 1968, galleries in Kassel, 1968, Spoleto, Italy, 1968, Australia, 1969, Krefeld, 1971, Mus. Contemporary Art, Chgo., 1969; numerous groups exhbns., 1960—. Recipient William and Noma Copley award, 1966. Address: 48 Howard St New York City NY 10013

CHRISTOFF, BORIS, opera singer, basso; b. Plovdiv, Bulgaria, May 19, 1919; s. Kyril and Raina (Teodorova) C.; law degree U. Sofia; student Riccardo Stracciari, Rome; scholarship Mozarteum, Salzburg; m. Franca de Rensis. Basso, Bulgarian Gusla choir, later became soloist, also mem. Sofia Cathedral choir; profl. debut Aceademia Santa Cecilia, Rome, 1946; appeared in opera La Boheme, 1946; operatic debut La Scala, Milan, also Covent Garden, London; appeared Salzburg, Edinburgh festivals; Am. debut with San Francisco Opera Co.; prin. roles include: Boris Godunoff, Dossiteus, Galitzky, Konchak, Phillip II, Don Quixote, Ivan the Terrible. Served with Cav. Bulgarian Army, prior to World War II. Decorated comdr. Order of Italian Republic, Order San Pietro e Paolo de Rio de Janeiro; recipient Académie du Disque Francais, 1953, Académie Charles Cros, 1953, 59; Edison prize, 1964; prize Am. Acad. Arts and Scis., 1964. Numerous recs. opera, Russian folk songs and religious selections. Address: Via Bertloni 1 Rome Italy

CHRISTOPH, JAMES BERNARD, educator; b. Waukesha, Wis., Aug. 17, 1928; s. Floyd Howard and Esther (Orvis) C.; B.A., U. Wis., 1950; postgrad. Harvard, 1950-51; M.A., U. Minn., 1952, Ph.D., 1956; postgrad. London Sch. Econs. and Polit. Sci., 1953-54; m. Natalie Ann Kunz, Dec. 22, 1955; children—Lesley Schafer, Ian Howard, Alison Hunt, Nancy Kunz, Megan Campbell. Instr. to prof. polit. sci. Ohio State U., 1955-67, postdoctoral fellow, 1957-58, asst. dean Coll. Arts and Scis., 1959-61; prof., chmn. polit. sci. Ind. U., Bloomington, 1967—; Fulbright fellow to U.K., 1953-54; Social Sci. Research Council faculty research fellow, 1962-63; Fulbright prof. Johns Hopkins Sch. Advanced Internat. Studies, Bologna, Italy, 1966-67. Recipient Pi Sigma Alpha award Am. Polit. Sci. Assn., 1965. Mem. Am., Midwest polit. sci. assns., Hansard Soc. Parliamentary Affairs, Am. Assn. U. Profs., Phi Beta Kappa. Democrat. Author: Capital Punishment and British Politics, 1962; Britain At the Crossroads, 1967. Editor: Cases in Comparative Politics, 1965, 69. Contbr. articles profl. jours. Home: Route 12 Box 209 Bloomington IN 47401

CHRISTOPH, JOHN RONALD, pub. utility exec.; b. Oshkosh, Wis., Mar. 31, 1917; s. John Fred and Alice (Durant) C.; B.S., Marquette U., 1939; m. Marjorie Ruth Steltz, May 3, 1941; children—Jill (Mrs. Daniel T. Elwing), Jane (Mrs. Stanley Caldwell, Jr.), John. With Wis. Telephone Co., 1939—, gen. mgr., 1962-65, v.p., comptroller, 1965- -. Bd. mgrs. Vols. Am. Children Day Care Center, Milw., 1966-70; bd. mgrs. YMCA-Central Met. Milw., 1967-71. Served with USAAF, 1943-45. Mem. Financial Execs. Inst., Met. Milw. Assn. Commerce. Club: Milwaukee Athletic; Westmoor Country. Home: 2330 N 91st St Wauwatosa WI 53226 Office: 722 N Broadway Milwaukee WI 53202

CHRISTOPH, VAN FRANCIS, educator; b. Seattle, Oct. 23, 1904; s. George Joseph and Barbara (Stauber) C.; A.B., M.A., Gonzaga U., 1934; Ph.D., Cath. U. Am., 1949. Joined Soc. of Jesus, 1928, ordained priest Roman Cath. Ch., 1940; lectr. Cath. U. Am., 1943-45; faculty Gonzaga U., Spokane, Wash., 1946—, prof. social psychology, chmn. dept., 1946—, also trustee. Bd. dirs. Antonian Sch., Spokane, Spokane Family Counselling Service. Mem. Nat. Council Family Relations, Am. Sociol. Soc. Author: (all with John Evoy) Personality Development in Religious Life, 1963, Maturity in Religious Life, 1965, Christ and Women, 1967. Home: Gonzaga Univ Spokane WA 99202

CHRISTOPHER, GEORGE, dairy distbr.; b. St. Peter, Greece, Dec. 8, 1907; s. James and Mary (Koines) C.; came to U.S., 1911, naturalized, 1929; B.C.S., Golden Gate Coll., 1932, also LL.D.; m. Tula Sarantitis, June 23, 1935. Sole owner Christopher Dairy Farms, San Francisco, 1939—. Nat. co-chmn. Nat. Conf. Christians and Jews, 1970—. Mem. bd. suprs. City and County of San Francisco, 1945-55, pres., 1948-55; mayor of San Francisco, 1956-63. Trustee, Golden Gate Coll. Decorated for pub. contbns. to Internat. Goodwill countries of France, Italy, Sweden, Denmark, Greece. Home: 55 Stonecrest Dr San Francisco CA 94132 Office: 555 Fulton St San Francisco CA 94105

CHRISTOPHER, J. GEORGE, banker. Vice chmn. bd. Citizens First Nat. Bank, Ridgewood, N.J. Office: 54 E Ridgewood Av Ridgewood NJ 07451*

CHRISTOPHER, PAUL REVERE, labor union exec.; b. Easley, S.C., Feb. 14, 1910; s. Clarence Erasker and Mary Jane (Hemphill) C.; student Clemson Coll., 1930-32; m. Mary Elizabeth Lybrand, Aug. 13, 1932; children—Patricia Ellen (Mrs. Newman), Sarah Jane (Mrs. Jones). Organizer, United Textile Workers Am., AFL, Shelby, N.C., 1933-37; rep. Textile Workers Organizing Com., CIO, Charlotte, N.C., 1937-39; v.p. Textile Workers Union Am., CIO, Spartanburg, S.C., 1939-41; regional dir. CIO, Knoxville, Tenn., 1940-55; regional dir. AFL-CIO, Knoxville, 1955—. Dir. Knox Fed. Savs. & Loan Assn., Knoxville. Life fellow So. Regional Council, Atlanta, 1969—; cabinet mem. United Fund Appeal, 1965-70; mem. Dulin Gallery Art, Knoxville, 1960—. Mem. Democratic Exec. Com. Knox County, 1948—. Mem. Am. Civil Liberties Union, Indsl. Relations Research Assn. Unitarian. Elk. Home: 445 Circle Hill Dr Knoxville TN 37919 Office: 705 Broadway NE Knoxville TN 37917

CHRISTOPHER, ROBERT COLLINS, mag. exec.; b. Thomaston, Conn., Mar. 3, 1924; s. Gordon Newton and Ruth Mignon (Adams) C.; B.A. with exceptional distinction, Yale, 1948; m. Rita Joan Goldstein, May 17, 1970; children by previous marriage—Ulrica Boyd, Thomas Adams, Valerie, Nicholas. Staff, Investment Dealers Digest, 1949-50; with Time mag., 1950-63, asso. editor, 1956-61, sr. editor U.S. and world bus. sects., 1961-63; dir. fundamental econ. research Corning Glass Works, N.Y.C., 1963; fgn. editor Newsweek mag., 1963-69, exec. editor, 1969—. Trustee Corning Glass Works Found. Served with AUS, 1942-46, 51-52; CBI. Mem. Council on Fgn. Relations, Phi Beta Kappa. Episcopalian. Clubs: Overseas Press, Fifth Ave. (N.Y.C.); Elizabethan (New Haven). Home: 230 E 73d St New York City NY 10021 Office: 444 Madison Av New York City NY 10022

CHRISTOPHER, RUSSELL LEWIS, baritone; b. Grand Rapids, Mich., Mar. 12, 1930; s. Russell Stewart and Violet (Jurewicz) C.; A.A., Grand Rapids Jr. Coll., 1950; Mus.B., U. Mich., 1953, Mus.M., 1954; m. Gail B. Eldredge, Aug. 24, 1963; 1 son, Russell Frederick. Music librarian NBC, N.Y.C., 1955-58; prin. artist N.Y.C. Opera Co., 1958-60, San Francisco Opera Co., 1962, 63, Met Opera Assn., N.Y.C., 1963—; soloist Los Angeles, Montreal, Chgo., Richmond symphony orchs., 1963—; sang role Maecenas in world premiere Antony and Cleopatra at new Met. Opera House, 1966; also appeared with Miami Beach Symphony, Hollywood Bowl, Balt. Civic Opera, Central City Opera, Dayton Opera Assn., Phila. Lyric Opera Assn. Recipient award Martha Baird Rockefeller Fund for Music, 1961, auditions winner Am. Opera, 1962, Met. Opera, 1963, Frederick K. Weyerhaeuser award, 1963, Distinguished Alumni award Grand Rapids Jr. Coll., 1964. Home: 240 West End Av New York City NY 10023 Office: Met Opera Assn Lincoln Center Plaza New York City NY 10023

CHRISTOPHER, SYBIL BURTON, business exec. Address: Arthurs' E 59th St and 3d Av New York City NY 10022*

CHRISTOPHER, THOMAS ALOYSIUS, naval officer; b. Perth Amboy, N.J., May 24, 1911; s. Thomas Aloysius and Estelle Lavinia (Rankin) C.; B.S., U.S. Naval Acad., 1933; postgrad. Naval War Coll., 1954-55; m. Catherine Anne Coleman, Mar. 1, 1938; childrenThomas Aloysius, Charles D., Mary L., James B., John M. Commd. ensign USN, 1933, advanced through grades to rear adm., 1961; mem. staff Supreme Allied Comdr., Atlantic, 1955-57; comdr. U.S.S. Essex, 1957-58; dir. naval recruiting Bur. Naval Personnel, 1958-61; comdr. Carrier Div. 17, Pacific, 1961-62; comdr. naval forces, Marianas, 1962-64; comdr. Key West Force/comdr. Naval Base/comdr. Fleet Air Key West, 1964-. Dist. chmn. Boy Scouts Am., Monroe City, Fla., 1965-67; pres. Guidance Clinic Fla. Keys Mental Health, 1966-67. Decorated Navy Cross with star, Air medal with two stars. Home: Quarters SP-23 Breezy Point Norfolk VA Office: CTF-140 Bldg Sp-71 Naval Air Sta Norfolk VA 23511

CHRISTOPHER, THOMAS WELDON, univ. dean; b. Duncan, S.C., Oct. 8, 1917; s. William Arthur and Ruby (Thomas) C.; A.B., Washington and Lee U., 1939; LL.B., U. Ala., 1948; LL.M., N.Y.U., 1950, J.S.D., 1957; m. Evelyn Montez Hawkins, Oct. 25, 1950; 1 son, Thomas Heflin. From asst. prof. to prof. law Emory U. Law Sch., 1950-61, asso. dean, 1954-61; admitted to Ala. bar, 1948, Ga. bar, 1955, N.Y. bar, 1961, N.C. bar, 1963, N.M. bar, 1968; atty. Corn Products Co., 1959-60; prof. law U. N.C., 1961-65; dean U. N.M. Law Sch., 1965-71; dean, also prof. U. Ala. Sch. Law, 1971—. Mem. nat. adv. food and drug and council Dept. Health, Edn. and Welfare, 1968—. Served with USAAF, World War II. Mem. Am. Bar Assn. Author: (with Dunn) Special Federal Food and Drugs Laws Annotated, 1951; (with others) Georgia Procedure and Practice, 1957; Constitutional Questions in Food and Drug Law, 1960; Cases and Materials on Food and Drug Law, 1966. Home: 7 Pinehurst St Tuscaloosa AL 35401 Office: Univ Ala Sch Law University AL 35486

CHRISTOPHER, WARREN MINOR, lawyer; b. Scranton, N.D., Oct. 27, 1925; s. Ernest W. and Catharine Anna (Lemen) C.; student U. Redlands, 1942-43; B.A. magna cum laude, U. So. Cal., 1945; LL.B., Stanford, 1949; m. Marie Josephine Wyllis, Dec. 21, 1956; children—Lynn, Scott, Thomas, Kristen. Admitted to Cal. bar, 1949, U.S. Supreme Ct. bar; law clk. U.S. Supreme Ct. Justice William O. Douglas, Washington, 1949-50; practice in Los Angeles, 1950-67, 69—; mem. firm O'Melveny & Myers, 1950-67, 69, partner, 1958-67, 69—; dep. atty. gen. U.S., Washington, 1967-69. Spl. counsel to Gov. Cal., 1959; cons. Office Under Sec. State, 1961-66; mem. bd. bar examiners State Bar Cal., 1967-68. Mem. Cal. Coordinating Council for Higher Edn., 1960-67, pres., 1963-65; vice chmn. Gov.'s Commn. on Los Angeles Riots, 1965-66; chmn. U.S. delegations to U.S.-Japan Cotton Textile Negotiations, 1961, Geneva Conf. on Cotton Textiles, 1961; civilian aid to sec. army So. Cal. area, 1962-66; spl. rep. sec. state for Wool Textile Meetings, London, Rome, 1964, Tokyo, 1965. Trustee Occidental Coll. Served to lt. (j.g.) USNR, 1943- 46. Fellow Am. Bar Found., Am. Coll. Trial Lawyers; mem. Am. (past com. chmn.), Cal., Los Angeles County bar assns., Am. Law Inst., Order of Coif, Phi Kappa Phi. Home: 455 N June St Los Angeles CA 90004 Office: 611 W 6th St Los Angeles CA 90017

CHRISTOPHER, WILFORD SCOTT, assn. exec.; b. Enid, Okla., Feb. 8, 1916; s. W. Scott and Mary Elizabeth (Heaton) C.; B.A., Phillips U., 1938; M.A., U. Ia., 1941; m. Marjorie Lois Lester, Dec. 30, 1941; 1 son, Scott Douglas. Asst. prof. speech Phillips U., 1939, asso. prof. sociology, 1940-42; pub. relations dir. Miami (Fla.) C. of C., 1946-51; gen. mgr. Greater Tampa C. of C., 1951-64, exec. v.p., 1964—. Chmn. Nat. Adv. Council Urban Devel., 1959- 60; mem. adv. council U. Tampa, 1966-69; mem. tech.-occupation adv. com. Hillsborough Jr. Coll., 1969—, chmn. advanced mgmt. curriculum com., 1958-59; mem. Adv. Group on Continuing Edn. for Urban Leadership, 1967-68. Bd. dirs. Tampa Philharmonic Orch. Assn., Tampa Oral Sch. for Deaf. Trustee U. South Fla. Found., 1959-65; trustee Berkeley Prep. Sch., 1963, v.p., 1965—. Mem. Fla. C. of C. Execs. Assn. (pres. 1954), Southeastern Inst. C. of C. Execs. (pres. 1956), So. Assn. C. of C. Execs. (pres.-elect 1971), Inst. Orgn. Mgmt. (bd. regents), Am. C. of C. Execs. (sec.-treas., v.p. 1960, pres. 1961-62, chmn. nat. panel on exec. certification 1966). Clubs: Tampa Exchange (pres. 1955), Executive (past pres.), University (dir.), Tampa Yacht and Country; Ye Mystic Kreme of Gasparilla. Contbr.: Chamber of Commerce Administration. Home: 10701 Carrollwood Dr Tampa FL 33618 Office: 801 E John F Kennedy Blvd Tampa FL 33601

CHRISTOPHER, WILLIAM RODOLPHUS, artist; b. Columbus, Ga., Mar. 4, 1924; s. Ira and Grace (Anglin) C.; student Sorbonne, Paris, France, 1946-47, Acad. Julian, Paris, 1946-48, Ecole des Americaines, Fontainbleau, France, 1947; pupil Ossip Zadkine, Paris, 1947, Amedee Ozenfant, N.Y.C., 1948-50, Hans Hoffman, N.Y.C., 1950. One-man exhbns. include Gallerie du Dragon, Cahier D'Art, Paris, 1947, Palais de Fontainebleau, 1947, Roko Gallery, N.Y.C., 1952, Nexus Gallery, Boston, 1957, 59, 60, Joan Peterson Gallery, Boston, 1961, 62, 65, 66, Amel Gallery, N.Y.C., 1961, Boston Archtl. Center, 1963, Dartmouth, 1964-66, Boston U., 1964, Addison Gallery Am. Art, 1966, Larcada Gallery, N.Y.C., 1968, Drew U., 1968, catalog Kennedy Library, 1968, Nat. Mus. Contemporary Art, Madrid, Spain, 1971, Nat. Mus. Modern Art, Borcelona, Spain, 1971; group exhbns. include Whitney Mus., N.Y.C., Bklyn. Mus., Mus. Modern Art, N.Y.C., Fogg Mus., Boston Mus. Fine Arts, Inst. Contl. Arts, Boston, Northeastern U., Boston, Smith Coll., Norfolk Mus., Smithsonian Instn., Corcoran Galleries, Harvard, Providence Mus., Am. Fedn. Arts traveling exhbns., DeCordova Mus., Lincoln, Mass., Am.-Soviet Printmakers, N.Y.C., Larcada Gallery, Joan Peterson Gallery, Park Bernet Gallery, Terrain Gallery, Art at U.S. embassies Program, Boston U., Newport (R.I.) Art Assos., Wellesley Coll., Silvermine Artists Guild, R.I. Sch. Design, Wadsworth Atheneum, N.A.D., U. Tenn., Va. Mus. Art, Inst. Arts and Letters, Swain Sch.; rep. permanent collections Boston Mus. Fine Arts, Whitney Mus., DeCordova Mus., Boston U. Libraries, U. Mass., Dartmouth, Addison Gallery Am. Art, Chase Manhatten Bank, Carroll Reece Mus., U. Tenn., Seattle Art Mus., Wichita Art Mus., Yale, Inst. Contemporary Arts Library, London, Eng., also numerous pvt. collections; tchr. Bklyn. Poly. Inst., 1956-61, Dartmouth, 1966, 68, 69; instr. Dartmouth, 1970-71. Served with USNR, 1941-44. Schmitz-Hille Found. grantee, 1946-48. Recipient Rosenthal Found. award, 1953-55; Shiva award for drawing Bklyn. Mus., 1956; award for painting Silvermine Arrtists Guild, 1962; Gold medal merit Boston Arts Festival, 1964; Frank C. Kirk Meml. prize painting N.A.D., 1968; 1st Purchase award Carroll Reece Mus., 1968; award Inst. Arts and Letters, Am. Acad. Arts and Letters, 1969; Childe Hassam Fund purchase award Inst. Arts and Letters, 1968. Mem. So. Christian Leadership Conf., N.A.A.C.P., Address: Hartland VT 05048

CHRISTOPHERSON, EINOR HUGO, physician; b. Mt. Pleasant, Utah, Oct. 24, 1902; s. Martin Einor and Naomi D. (Mariger) C.; student U. Utah, 1919-22; M.D., Washington U., 1925; m. Mary Grace Cunkle, May 1, 1926; childrenWarren H., Marian (Mrs. David M. Sellgren). Resident, Mo. Bapt. Hosp., 1925-26, St Louis Children's Hosp., 1926-27; physician Am. Smelting & Refining Co., Garfield, Utah, 1927-30; pvt. practice of pediatrics, San Diego, Cal., 1930-42, 46-50; exec. sec. Am. Acad. Pediatrics, Evanston, Ill., 1951- 59; clin. asst. prof. pediatrics U. Ill. Coll. Medicine, 1951-69; clin. prof. pediatrics Sch. Medicine U. Cal. San Diego. Exec. dir. Am. Acad. Pediatrics, 1959-67, chmn. com. internat. child health, 1968-70. Mem. Nat. Com. for Children and Youth, 1965—; chmn. Council of Nat. Orgns. for Children and Youth; chief Bur. Maternal and Child Health Cal. Dept. Pub. Health, cons.; cons. to U. Cal. Sch. Pub. Health; mem. Joint Commn. Mental Health Children. Served from capt. to lt. col. M.C., AUS, 1942- 46; chief Brazilian field party, dept. health and sanitation Office Inter-Am. Affairs, 1943-45, asst. dir. div. health and sanitation, 1945- 46. Recipient Cruzeiro de Sul, Medalia de Guerra (Brazil). Mem. Phi Beta Pi, Alpha Omega Alpha, Sigma Nu. Home: 12246 Casero Ct San Diego CA 92128.

CHRISTOPHERSON, FRED CARL, editor; b. Toronto, S.D., May 13, 1896; s. Christian Theodore and Mathilda (Frankson) C.; student Luther Coll., Decorah, Ia., 1914-15, U. S.D., 1916-17; m. Marie Cilley, Feb. 13, 1926. Reporter, Sioux Falls (S.D.) Press, 1917, Kansas City Star, 1920-21; mng. editor Sioux Falls Press, 1922-26, pub., 1927; exec. editor Sioux Falls Argus-Leader. 1928-45, editor, 1945- 61, contbg. editor, 1962—. Vice-pres., trustee Sioux Valley Hosp., Mt. Rushmore Nat. Meml. Soc.; trustee Crazy Horse Meml. Found. Pres., Karl Mundt Hist. and Ednl. Found. Served to 2d lt. U.S. Army Air Service, 1917-18, Res. Corps, 1919-24, 1st lt., 1924-29. Recipient St. Olav medal King Haakon of Norway, 1947. Mem. Am. Soc. Newspaper Editors (dir.), S.D. Press Assn. (pres. 1942), Am. Legion, Sioux Falls C. of C. (pres. 1950), Sigma Delta Chi. Rotarian. Club: Minnehaha Country. Home: 1005 S Lake Av Sioux Falls SD 57105 Office: 200 S Minnesota Av Sioux Falls SD 57102

CHRISTOPHERSON, PAUL, lawyer; b. Long Prairie, Minn., Aug. 12, 1902; s. Conrad H. and Effie (Jacobsen) C.; B.A., Carleton Coll., 1923; B.A. in Jurisprudence (Rhodes scholar), Oxford (Eng.) U., 1926, B.C.L., 1927, M.A., 1953; student U. Minn. Law Sch., 1927-28; m. Edna M. Belgum, Jan. 11, 1945; childrenPaul Conrad, David Lee, John Alfred. Admitted to Minn. bar, 1928, since practiced in Mpls.; partner firm Faegre & Benson, 1935-. Dir. Munsingwear, Inc., Mpls., Northfield and So. Ry. Co., Northwestern Nat. Life Ins. Co., Pillsbury Co., N. Atlantic Ins. Co., N.Y.C., Hoerner Waldorf Corp., St. Paul. Pres. Minn. Orchestral Assn.; bd. dirs. Guthrie Theatre Found.; trustee Minn. Episcopal Found.; trustee Carleton Coll., 1951-68. Spl. asst. Office Surgeon Gen., War Dept., 1943-44. Mem. Am., Minn. bar assns., Inner Temple (London), Phi Beta Kappa, Phi Delta Phi. Republican. Episcopalian (sr. warden). Clubs: Minneapolis, Minneapolis Athletic, Minikahda (Mpls.). Home: 2250 W Lake of Isles Blvd Minneapolis MN 55405 Office: Northwestern Bank Bldg Minneapolis MN 55402

CHRISTOPHERSON, WESTON, food chain co. exec.; b. Walum, N.D., May 5, 1925; s. Carl and Ermie Marion (Larsen) C.; B.S., U. N.D., 1949, J.D., 1951; m. Myrna Louise Christensen, June 8, 1951; children—Mia Karen, Mary Louisa, Kari Marie. Admitted to N.D. bar, 1951, Ill. bar, 1952; with Jewel Cos., Inc., Chgo., 1951—, v.p., 1963-70, pres., 1970—, also dir.; dir. Ill. Tool Works, Midco, S.A., Mexico City, G.B. Enterprises, Belgium. Mem. alumni bd. dirs. U. N.D., mem. adv. com. U. Ill. Sch. Bus. Lutheran. Clubs: Economic, Chicago, Knollwood. Home: 1696 S Oak Knoll Dr Lake Forest IL 60045 Office: 5725 E River Rd Chicago IL 60631

CHRISTOPHERSON, WILLIAM MARTIN, educator, physician; b. Salt Lake City, July 2, 1916; s. George Walter and Myrtle (Jack) C.; student U. Utah, 1938; M.D., U. Louisville, 1942; m. Kathryn Donley, July 24, 1943; 1 son, George Walter II. Intern Akron (O.) City Hosp., 1942-43, resident, 1946-48; resident U. Louisville Hosp., 1948-49; fellow pathology Meml. Hosp., N.Y.C., 1949-50; mem. faculty U. Louisville Grad. Sch., 1950—, prof. pathology, chmn. dept., 1956—; spl. cons. Nat. Cancer Inst., bur. state service USPHS, adv. com. cancer control program, 1963-67; cons. Oak Ridge Inst. Nuclear Studies, 1956-68, Louisville VA Hosp. Pres., bd. dirs. Ky. div. Am. Cancer Soc., 1960—; mem. at large bd. dirs. Nat. Am. Cancer Soc., 1967—, exec. com., 1968—. Served to capt. AUS, 1943-46. Mem. Am. Soc. Cytology (pres. 1966-67), Am. Assn. Cancer Edn. (pres. 1967-68), Soc. Exptl. Pathology, Internat. Acad. Pathology (pres. 1971-72), Internat. Acad. Cytology, Pathol. Soc. Gt. Britain and Ireland, European Soc. Pathology, Assn. Pathologists and Bacteriologists, Am. Soc. Clin. Pathology, Sigma Xi, Alpha Omega Alpha. Mem. editorial bd. Yearbook of Cancer, Am. Jour. Clin. Pathology, Acta Cytologica, Cancer. Home: 2211 Cherokee Pkwy Louisville KY 40204

CHRISTY, ARTHUR HILL, lawyer; b. Bklyn., July 25, 1923; s. Francis Taggart and Catherine Virginia (Damon) C.; A.B., Yale, 1945; LL.B., Columbia, 1949; m. Muriel Alexandra Horgan, Oct. 26, 1951; children—Duncan Hill, Muriel Alexandra. Admitted to N.Y. bar, 1950; asso. firm Baldwin, Todd & Lefferts, N.Y.C., 1950-52; spl. asst. atty. gen. Saratoga Investigation (N.Y.), 1952-53; asst. U.S. atty. So. Dist. N.Y., 1953-54; chief prosecutor spl. asst. atty. gen. Saratoga and Columbia County Investigations, 1954-55; asst. atty. gen. N.Y., 1955; chief criminal div. U.S. Atty.'s Office, So. Dist. N.Y., 1955-57, chief asst. U.S. atty., 1957-58, U.S. atty., 1958-59; partner firm Christy, Frey & Christy, and predecessor, N.Y.C., 1959—. Spl. asst. to Gov. Rockefeller, 1959-61. Trustee Bklyn. Savs. Bank. Trustee Bklyn. Hosp., Community Service Soc. Served as lt. USNR, 1944-46. Mem. Am., N.Y. State, Fed. bar assns., Assn. Bar City N.Y. (chmn. exec. com. 1966-67), Am. Coll. Trial Lawyers. Republican. Episcopalian. Clubs: Century Assn., Rockefeller Luncheon, University (N.Y.C.); Manursing Island (Rye, N.Y.); Mastigouche Fish and Game (Que., Can.). Home: 161 E 79th St New York City NY 10021. Office: 45 Rockefeller Plaza New York City NY 10020

CHRISTY, FRANCIS TAGGART, lawyer; b. Scranton, Pa., July 23, 1897; s. Arthur H. and Annie S. (Taggart) C.; B.S., Dartmouth, 1918; LL.B., Harvard, 1921; m. Catherine Virginia Damon, June 14, 1922; children—Arthur Hill, Francis Taggart. Admitted to N.Y. bar, 1923, since practiced in N.Y.C.; partner Murray, Aldrich & Webb, 1930-31,

Milbank, Tweed, Hope & Webb, 1931-34, Christy & Perkins, 1944-60, Christy, Perkins & Christy, 1960-63, partner Christy, Bauman & Christy, 1963-65, Christy Bauman, Frey & Christy, 1965-68, Christy, Frey & Christy, 1968—. Sec., dir. Rockefeller Center, Inc., 1928-39, v.p., 1934-39; v.p., sec., dir. Underel Holding Corp., 1929-39; pres. dir. Center Restaurants, Inc., 1933-39, Rockefeller Center Warehouses, Inc., 1936-39; pres., dir. Dodeca, Inc.; dir. Ameaster Internat. Corp., Am. Eastern Corp., Am. Eastern S.A.I., Barr. & Barr, Inc., North Am. Philips Corp., PEPI, Inc. Trustee Bklyn. Inst. Arts and Scis.; trustee YWCA, Bklyn.; nat. bd. YWCA; dir. Heart Fund; dir. N.Y. Heart Assn., Inc., Community Blood Council of Greater N.Y., Community Funds, Inc.; mem. N.Y.C. Art Com., 1955-68; mem. dist. com. New York Community Trust. Decorated officer Order of Oranje Nassau (Netherlands). Mem. Am., N.Y. State bar assns., Assn. Bar City of N.Y., Am. Soc. Internat. Law. Republican. Unitarian. Clubs; University, Rembrandt, Rockefeller Center Luncheon, Century, Netherland (N.Y.C.); Mastigouche F. & G. (Can.). Author: The Transfer of Stock, 1929, 4th edit., 1967. Home: 14 Trails End Rd Wilton CT 06897 Office: 45 Rockefeller Plaza New York City NY 10020

CHRISTY, JUNE, singer; b. Springfield, Ill., November 20, 1925; m. Bob Cooper, Jan. 14, 1947; one son Shay Christy. With local bands, 1938, later society bands vicinity of Chicago, including Boyd Raeburn, Benny Strong, Denny Beckner; with Stan Kenton, 1945-49, concert tours including Europe, 1953; toured Europe with Bob Copper, 1956, Europe and South Africa, 1958; toured U.S. with Ted Heath Show, 1957, 58; recordings include Tampico, Nat Meets June, with Metronome All Stars. Recipient Down Beat award as top female band vocalist. 1946-48, 50, Met. poll award, 1947. Address: 3548 Stonewood Dr Sherman Oaks CA 91413*

CHRISTY, MYRON M., r.r. exec.; b. Seattle, May 26, 1917; s. Harold V. and Elsie A. (Jensen) C.; student U. Wash.; B.B.A., U. Minn., 1948; post grad. Harvard Bus. Sch., 1955; m. Mary J. Deeds, Dec. 28, 1945; children—Susan Ellen (Mrs. Michael Battles), John Harold. With Gen. Electric Supply Corp., 1935-38, Alaska Electric Light & Power Co., 1938-41; with Mchts. Motor Freight, 1946-48; traveling accountant W.P. R.R. Co., San Francisco, 1949, auditor payroll accounts, asst. to gen. auditor, 1950, exec. asst., 1950- 54, exec. asst. to pres., 1960-62, exec. v.p., 1962-65, gen. mgr., 1964- 65, formerly pres., now dir.; pres., dir. Sacramento No. R.R.; pres., mem. exec. com., dir. Tidewater So. R.R. Co.; v.p., dir. Alameda Belt. Line; pres., dir. Oakland Terminal R.R.; dir. Central Cal. Traction Co.; v.p., dir. Standard Realty & Devel. Co., Salt Lake City Union Depot & R.R. Co.; dir. Bank Cal. Trustee San Francisco Bay area Council, Golden Gate Coll. Served to lt. col. AUS, 1941-45. Mem. Federated Employers of Bay Area (bd. govs.), Am. Assn. R.R. Supts., Cal. C. of C., Beta Gamma Sigma. Republican. Clubs: Detroit; Pacific Railway, Sutter (Sacramento); Bohemian, Commercial (San Francisco). Home: 36 Via Cheparro San Rafael CA 94904 Office: 526 Mission St San Francisco CA 94105

CHRISTY, NICHOLAS PIERSON, physician; b. Morristown, N.J., June 18, 1923; s. Leroy and Elizabeth (Baker) C.; A.B., Yale, 1945; M.D., Columbia, 1951; m. Beverly Vairin Morris, June 21, 1947; children—Nicholas Pierson, Martha Vairin. Vis. physician Delafield Hosp., N.Y.C., 1955-66, vis. physician, 1966—; asst. vis. physician 1st med. div. Bellevue Hosp., N.Y.C. 1958-66; asso. attending physician Presbyn. Hosp., N.Y.C., 1962-65; dir. med. service Roosevelt Hosp., N.Y.C., 1965—; faculty Columbia Coll. Phys. and Surg., N.Y.C., 1956—, asso. prof. medicine, 1962-65, asso. clin. prof., 1965-67, clin. prof. medicine, 1967-71, prof. medicine, 1971—. Cons. NIH. Recipient Borden award, Joseph Mather Smith prize Columbia; John and Mary R. Markle scholar. Diplomate Am. Bd. Internal Medicine. Mem. Harvey Soc., A.A.A.S., Soc. Exptl. Biology and Medicine, Am. Soc. Clin. Investigation, Am. Fedn. Clin. Research, N.Y. Acad. Scis., Laurentian Hormone Conf., Am. Physiol. Soc., Royal Soc. Medicine (affiliate), Am. Assn. Study Liver Diseases, Endocrine Soc., N.Y. Medicine, N.Y. Med. and Surg. Soc., Am. Clin. and Climatol. Assn., Assn. Am. Physicians. Clubs: Elizabethan, Berzelius (Yale); Century Assn., University. Editor, co-author: The Human Adrenal Cortex, 1971. Editor-in-chief Jour. Clin. Endocrinology and Metabolism, 1963-67; asso. editor Cecil-Loeb Textbook Medicine, 1968—. Contbr. numerous papers to profl. lit. Home: 8 Peter Cooper Rd New York City NY 10010 Office: Roosevelt Hosp New York City NY 10019

CHRISTY, RALPH LAWRENCE, Jr., naval officer, physician; b. Kansas City, Mo., Oct. 2, 1913; s. Ralph Lawrence and Louise (Rodgers) C.; A.B., U. Colo., 1936, M.D., 1940; m. Mary Lou Sweet, Mar. 17, 1941; children—Ralph Lawrence III, Charles Whistler, James Grier, Daniel Mark; m. 2d, Louise Meyer, July 28, 1966. Intern, resident Colo. Gen. Hosp., 1940-42; commd. lt. (j.g.) USN, 1942, advanced through grades to capt., 1955; assigned U.S.S. Wasp, also U.S.S. Manila Bay, 1942-44; mem. staff ComFAIR West Coast Tng., 1944-45, Sch. Aviation Medicine, Pensacola, Fla., 1945-46, Office Naval Research, 1946-52; sr. med. officer U.S.S. Franklin D. Roosevelt, 1942-54; chief BUMED and ADDU office Chief Naval Operations, 1954-58; with U.S. Naval Hosp., 1958-61; head neuropsychiatry br. in aviation medicine BUMED, 1961-68; spl. asst. for med. dept. spl. projects, Washington, 1968—. Dept. Def. Rep. Nat. Adv. Mental Health Council, 1962—. Decorated Legion of Merit, Navy Commendation medal; recipient Eric Liljencranz award, Aerospace Med. Assn., 1964, William C. Porter lecture award Assn. Mil. Surgeons, 1963. Diplomate Am. Bd. Preventive Medicine. Fellow Aerospace Med. Assn. (pres. 1970), Am. Psychiat. Assn.; mem. Internat. Acad. Aviation and Space Medicine, Assn. Mil. Surgeons, A.M.A. Contbr. articles profl. jours. and textbooks. Home: 5826 Conway Rd Bethesda MD 20034 Office: 23d and E Sts NW Washington DC 20390

CHRISTY, ROBERT FREDERICK, inst. ofcl., physicist; b. Vancouver, B.C., Can., May 14, 1916; s. Moise Jacques and Hattie Alberta (McKay) C.; A.B., U. B.C., 1935, A.M., 1937; Ph.D., U. Cal., 1941; m. Dagmar Elizabeth Lieven, May 31, 1941 (div. 1971); children—Thomas E., Peter R. Came to U.S., 1938, naturalized, 1945. Research, metall. lab. U. Chgo., 1942-43, Los Alamos, 1943-45; asst. prof. physics U. Chgo., 1946; asso. prof., prof. physics Cal. Inst. Tech., Pasadena, 1946—, exec. officer for physics, chmn. faculty, 1969—, v.p. inst., provost, 1970—. Recipient Eddington medal Royal Astron. Soc., 1967. Fellow Am. Phys. Soc., Am. Acad. Arts and Scis.; mem. Am. Astron. Soc., Internat. Astron. Union, Nat. Acad. Scis. Home: 1330 S Euclid Av Pasadena CA 91106

CHRISTY, ROBERT WENTWORTH, educator, physicist; b. Chgo., Nov. 2, 1922; s. Walter Christian and Ruth Adele (Seifried) C.; A.A., U. Chgo., 1942, M.S., 1949, Ph.D., 1953; m. Cynthia Park, May 7, 1955. Mem. faculty Dartmouth, 1953-, prof. physics, 1962-, chmn. dept. physics and astronomy, 1963-67; cons. Motorola, Inc., 1952-53, TRW Systems, since 1958-. Served to lt. (j.g.) with USNR, 1943-46. Mem. Am. Phys. Soc., Am. Assn. Physics Tchrs., A.A.A.S, Sigma Xi, Alpha Delta Phi. Author: (with A. Pytte) Structure of Matter, 1965. Home: Bragg Hill Rd Norwich, VT 05055. Office: Wilder Physics Lab Dartmouth Coll Hanover, NH 03755.

CHROUST, ANTON-HERMANN, educator; b. Würzburg, Germany, Jan. 28, 1907; s. Anton Julius and Johanna (Sander) C.; J.U.D., U. Erlangen (Germany), 1929; Ph.D., U. Munich (Germany), 1931; S.J.D., Harvard, 1933; came to U.S., 1932, naturalized, 1941. Research asst. Harvard, 1934; mem. faculty U. Notre Dame, Law Sch., Grad. Sch., Mediaeval Inst., also history dept., 1946—, Univ. grad. research prof., 1968—. Author: Socrates, Man and Myth, 1957; Aristotle, Protrepicus, 1964; The Rise of the Legal Profession in America, 2 vols., 1965; also numerous articles. Home: 110 Peashway South Bend IN 46517 Office: Univ Notre Dame Law Sch Notre Dame IN 46556

CHRUDEN, HERBERT JEFFERSON, educator; b. Roswell, N.M., Oct. 3, 1918; s. Lawrence B. and Elizabeth (FitzGerald) C.; A.B., San Diego State Coll., 1940; M.B.A., Stanford, 1947, Ed.D., 1949; m. Marie Schwartz, Sept. 9, 1944; 1 dau., Mary Beth. Tchr., Cajon Valley Union Sch., El Cajon, Cal., 1940-41; faculty N. Tex. State U. Sch. Bus., 1949-52; faculty Sacramento State Coll., 1952—, prof. bus. adminstrn., 1961—, chmn. div. bus. adminstrn., 1963-64; mgmt. cons., 1955—. Bd. dirs. Sacramento Zool. Soc. Served to lt. comdr. USNR, 1941-45. Mem. Am. Arbitration Assn. (labor panel), Cal. Conciliation Service (labor panel), Acad. Mgmt., Sacramento Personnel Assn., Beta Gamma Sigma, Delta Sigma Pi. Co- author: Personnel Management, 1959, 4th edit., 1972; Readings in Personnel Management, 1961, 3d edit., 1972. Home: 251 Bancroft Way Sacramento CA 95825

CHRYSLER, WALTER P., Jr., art collector; grad. Dartmouth; m. Marguerite Sykes, Apr. 29, 1938 (div.); m. 2d, Jean Esther Outland. Organizer York Pub. House, 1926; pres., chmn. bd. Cheshire House, Inc., Pubs., N.Y.C., 1930; pres. Chrysler Bldg., N.Y.C., 1937; began collecting art at age 14 with Renoir landscape, later small Picasso; paintings and sculpture in collection show in Richmond, Va. and Phila., 1941; pres. Chrysler Mus., Norfolk. Address: care Chrysler Art Mus Norfolk VA 23510

CHRYSSA, VARDA, sculptor; b. Athens, Greece, 1933; student Academie de la Grande Chaumiere, Paris, France, 1953-54, Cal. Sch. Fine Arts, 1954-55. One man shows include Guggenheim Mus., N.Y.C., 1961, Cordier and Ekstrom Gallery, N.Y.C., 1962, Betty Parsons Gallery, N.Y.C., 1961, Mus. Modern Art, N.Y.C., 1963, Inst. Contemporary Arts, Phila., 1965, Pace Gallery, N.Y.C., 1966, 68, Walker Art Center, Mpls., 1968, Harvard U., 1968, Obelisk Gallery, Boston, 1969, Gallery der Spiegel, Cologne, Germany, 1969, Gallery Rive-Droite, Paris, 1969; group shows include exhbns. at Whitney Mus. Am. Art, N.Y.C., 1960, 61, 62, 64, 66, 69, Mus. Modern Art, 1960-61, 63, 64, 66, 67, Carnegie Instn., 1961, 64, Seattle World's Fair, 1963, VII Biennial, Sao Paolo, Brazil, 1963, 1963, Stedjlik van Abbemuseum, Eindhoven, Holland, 1966, Inst. Contemporary Art, Boston, 1966, Art Inst. Chgo. , 1966, Yale U. Art Gallery, 1967, Los Angeles County Mus., Phila. Art Mus., 1967, Documenta, Kassel, Germany, 1968; represented in permanent collections Mus. Modern Art, Whitney Mus., Guggenheim Mus., Chase Manhattan Bank (all N.Y.C.); Albright-Knox Gallery, Buffalo, Walker Art Center, Mpls., Boise Cascade Corp., Boise, Ida.

CHRYSTAL, ALBERT FRANCIS, lawyer; b. N.Y.C., Apr. 20, 1899; s. Joseph Hall and Fannie Lozier (Moore) C.; A.B., Columbia, 1923, LL.B., 1925; m. Jean Perley, Nov. 9, 1935 (dec.): 1 dau. Joan Margaret. Admitted N.Y. bar, 1927; practiced law, N.Y.C., 1927-36, 64—; asst. sec. Moore-McCormack Lines, Inc., N.Y.C., 1936-44, v.p., 1944-45, v.p., 1955-64, sec., 1955-61, counsel, 1944-64. Bd. mgrs. Seamen's House YMCA, N.Y.C., 1940—, treas., 1945-54. Served with U.S. Army, 1918-19. Mem. S.R., Internat. Law Assn. N.Y. State, N.Y. County bar assns., Maritime Law Assn. Clubs: National Propeller, Downtown Athletic (N.Y.C.). Home: 30 Sutton Pl New York City NY 10022.

CHU, KUANG-HAN, structural engr., educator; b. Kashan, Chekiang, China, Nov. 13, 1919; s. Chih Hsien and Mary (Chang) C.; B.S., Nat. Central U., China, 1942; M.S., U. Ill., 1947, Ph.D., 1950; m. Janie Lee, Aug. 18, 1962. Came to U.S., 1946, naturalized, 1962. Structural designer Ammann & Whitney, N.Y.C., 1950-51, D.B. Steinman, 1951-55; acting asso. prof. civil engring. State U. Ia., 1955-56; asso. prof. dept. civil engring. Ill. Inst. Tech., 1956-63, prof., 1963—. Cons. structural analysis, 1958—. Fellow Am. Soc. C.E. (Collingwood prize 1953); mem. Am. Concrete Inst., Internat. Assn. for Bridge and Structural Engring., Am. Soc. Engring. Edn., Sigma Xi. Contbr. articles profl. jours. Home: 60 E 32d St Chicago IL 60616

CHU, LAN JEN, engr., educator; b. Hweiying, Kiangsu, China, Aug. 24, 1913; s. Shao Wen and Ken C; came to U.S., 1934, naturalized, 1952; B.S., Chiao Tung U., 1934; S.M., Mass. Inst. Tech., 1935, Sc.D., 1938; m. Grace Yu Ping Feng, Aug. 12, 1939; children—Yuan Bo, Yuan Hou, Yuan Ming. With Mass. Inst. Tech., 1934—, prof. elec. engring., 1951—. Recipient Presdl. Certificate of Merit. Fellow Inst. Radio Engrs., Am. Phys. Soc.; mem. Eta Kappa Nu. Home: 18 Oakmount Circle Lexington MA 02173

CHUBB, JOHN EVERSON, former railroad ofcl.; b. Edgewood, Pa., July 12, 1912; s. Lewis Warrington and Mary Porter (Everson) C.; student Carnegie Inst. Tech., 1931-32; B.C.E., Ohio State U., 1935; m. Ida Anita Straube, July 20, 1936; children—John Everson, William St. John II. With Pa. R.R. (name changed to Penn Central), 1935-71, v.p. 1967-71; pres., chmn. bd. Detroit, Toledo & Ironton R.R., Ann Arbor R.R., Manistique & Lake Superior R.R., 1963-67; v.p., chief engr., dir. Strasburg R.R. Co., 1957- 71; pres., chmn. bd. No. Central Rwy. Co., 1970-71. Chmn. bd. trustees Detroit Inst. Tech., 1966-70. Mem. Am. Ry. Engring. Assn., Newcomen Soc., Soc. Cin., Sigma Xi, Tau Beta Pi. Episcopalian. Clubs: Eastern Shore Yacht and Country; Out-of-Town (Cape Charles). Home: Yeardley Point Eastville VA 23347

CHUBB, PERCY, 2d., ins. exec.; b. East Orange, N.J., Apr. 1, 1909; s. Hendon and Alice (Lee) C.; student St. Pauls Sch., 1922-27; Ph.B. (Timothy Dwight fellow), Yale, 1931; m. Corinne Roosevelt Alsop, May 28, 1932; children—Hendon II, Percy III, Corinne R.R. (Mrs. Zimmerman), Joseph A., James P., L. Caldecot. Asso. Chubb & Son, Inc. (formerly Chubb & Son), ins. underwriters, N.Y.C., 1931, partner, 1935-41, 45-59, pres. dir., 1959- 65, chmn., 1965-70, also dir.; chmn., dir. Chubb Corp., 1968-70, chmn. exec. com., also dir., 1970—; dir. Fed. Ins. Co., 1945—, pres., 1948—, chmn. bd., 1964-70, chmn. exec. com., 1970—; dir., chmn. exec. com. Vigilant Ins. Co., 1970—; dir. Colonial Life Ins., Pacific Indemnity Co., Bellemead Devel. Corp. Joined U.S. Maritime Commn. in Wash. to establish war risk ins. orgn., 1941; dir. Wartime Ins. War Shipping Adminstrn., 1942- 43, asst. dep. administr. for fiscal affairs, 1943-45, asst. dep. administr., fiscal and shipping relations, 1945. Headed U.S. delegation to Planning Com. of United Maritime Authority in London, England, 1944. Trustee, pres. Victoria Foundation, Inc.; trustee St. Pauls Sch., Concord, N.H. Awarded Presdl. Certificate of Merit, 1947. Mem. N.Am. Yacht Racing Union. Clubs: India House, Downtown Associations, New York Yacht, Links (New York City); Metropolitan (Washington); Pacific Union (San Francisco). Author: From 60 North to 60 North, 1951; Cruising Guide for the Windward and Leeward Islands of the Eastern Caribbean, 1961. Home: RFD Chester NJ 07930 Office: 90 John St New York City NY 10038

CHUBB, ROBERT WALSTON, lawyer; b. Bklyn., May 13, 1894; s. Percival and Louise (Walston) C.; A.B. cum laude, Harvard, 1915; LL.B., Columbia, 1920; m. Irene Sylvester, May 18, 1918 (dec. 1953); children—Louise, Robert Walston, Elliott; m. 2d, Louise Langenohl, Dec. 4, 1953. Admitted to bar Mo., 1917, N.Y., 1920; asst. gen. counsel War Finance Corp., 1921-24; spl. counsel RFC, 1932; practice in N.Y.C., 1920-21, St. Louis, 1924—; partner firm Lewis, Rice, Tucker, Allen & Chubb, 1929—. Trustee St. Louis Merc. Library Assn., World Affairs Council St. Louis. Served as capt. U.S. Army, 1917-19; AEF, France. Recipient Profl. Merit award Columbia Law Sch. Alumni Assn., 1970. Mem. Am., St. Louis bar assns., Fgn. Policy Assn. (nat. council), Phi Delta Phi. Democrat. Clubs: Algonquin Golf, Noonday, Missouri Athletic (St. Louis); Crystal Downs Country (Frankfort, Mich.). Home: 43 Godwin Lane St Louis MO 63124 Office: 611 Olive St St Louis MO 63101

CHUBB, TALBOT ALBERT, physicist; b. Pitts., Nov. 5, 1923; s. Charles F. and Mary Clare (Albert) C.; A.B., Princeton, 1944; Ph.D., U. N.C., 1950; m. Martha Capps, Oct. 24, 1947; children—Mary Carroll, Nancy Henderson, Talbot Spence, Constance Lamont. Physicist, U.S. Naval Research Lab., 1950-58, head upper air physics br., 1958—. Recipient Elisha Mitchell Soc. award U. N.C., 1951, E.O. Hulbert award Naval Research Lab., 1963, Pure Sci. award Naval. Research Lab.-Research Soc. Am., 1970. Fellow Am. Geophys. Union, Am. Phys. Soc.; mem. Am. Astron. Soc. Spl. research on sun and stars from rockets, solar flare x-rays, x-ray stars, UV aurora. Home: 5023 N 38th St Arlington VA 22207 Office: US Naval Research Lab Washington DC 20390

CHUBB, THOMAS CALDECOT, author; b. East Orange, N.J., Nov. 1, 1899; s. Hendon and Alice Margaret (Lee) C.; B.A., Yale, 1922; m. 2d, Caroline Parker Smith, June 22, 1929 (dec.); m. 3d, Edith Onions, July 1, 1938; children—Russell Parsons, Mary Alice Victoria (Mrs. Gerald Wolsfelt), Rosamond Caldecot (Mrs. Hillyer M. Young). Editorial positions, various mags., 1923-24; with N.Y. Times, 1925-29; dir. Greenwich (Conn.) Broadcasting Co. Mem. Merritt Pkwy. Commn., 1955-59, sec., 1957-59; mem. Conn. Commn. on Arts, 1965—; v.p. Chubb Found., Victoria Found., Inc., Rosemary Hall Found., Yale Library Assos.; vice chmn. Conn. chpt. Com. to Defend Am., 1940-41, chmn. Greenwich chpt., 1941; mem. Greenwich Bd. Estimate and Taxation, 1960-64. Mem. Greenwich Democratic Town Com., 1953-64; Conn. mem. Dem. Nat. Finance Com. 1960; del. Dem. Nat. Conv., 1956, 60. Served with USNRF, 1918; with OSS, 1942- 45; chief port sect., 1944, cons., 1944-45. Fellow Timothy Dwight Coll., Yale. Recipient John Masefield prize, 1920, Albert Stanborough Cook prize, 1921 (both Yale). Fellow Am. Geog. Soc.; mem. Poetry Soc. Am. (exec. bd. 1956), Alpha Delta Phi. Clubs: Indian Harbor Yacht, Royal Bermuda Yacht, Belle Haven, Florida-Georgia Field Trial, Yale, New York Yacht (N.Y.C.); Elizabethan, Chi Delta Theta (New Haven). Author: The White Gold and Other Poems, 1920; Kyrdoon (poem), 1921; The Life of Giovanni Boccaccio, 1930; Ships and Lovers (verse), 1933; Cliff Pace and Other Poems, 1936; Aretino: Scourge of Princes, 1940; My Daughter's World, 1941; A Time to Speak (verse), 1943; Cornucopia: Poems 1919-53; If There Were No Losses, 1957; The Byzantines, 1959; The Months of the Year (verse), 1960; Slavic Peoples, 1962; The Northmen, 1964; Dante and His World, 1967; The Letters of Pietro Aretino, 1967; The Venetians; Merchant Princes, 1968; The Sonnets of a Handsome and Well-Mannered Rogue, 1970; Prince Henry the Navigator, 1970. Contbr. to mags. Address: Porchuck Rd Greenwich CT 06830 also Springwood Plantation Thomasville GA 31792

CHUBBUCK, RAYMOND DANIEL, educator; b. Waterville, Me., Apr. 1, 1909; s. Alfred S. and Eva (Shackley) C.; B.S., U. Conn., 1931; M.A., Yale, 1947, Ph.D., 1951; m. Elsa Thompson, May 2, 1935; children—Betsy (Mrs. Charles Orlando), James Shackley, Pamela (Mrs. Philip Bescher). Instr., Choate Sch., 1931-34; tchr. Woodrow Wilson High Sch. Middletown, Conn., 1934-45; supt. schs., Cromwell, Conn., 1945-50; supt. rural schs., Conn., 1950-53; supt. schs., Glastonbury, Conn., 1953-56, Darien, Conn., 1956-62; Dana prof. edni. adminstrn. U. Bridgeport (Conn.), 1962—. Vis. prof. Mont. State U., 1952, So. Conn. State Coll., 1950-51. Mem. N.E.A. (life), Am. Assn. Sch. Adminstrs., Conn. Edn. Assn., Am. Assn. U. Profs., Conn. (pres. 1961-62), New Eng. assns. sch. supts., Comparative Edn. Assn., New Eng. Ednl. Conf., Phi Delta Kappa. Author pamphlets; contbr. articles to profl. jours. Home: 67 Old Kings Hwy N Darien CT 06820 Office: Fones Hall U Bridgeport Bridgeport CT 06602

CHUCKER, HAROLD, journalist; Editorial writer Mpls. Star. Office: 5th and Portland Sts Minneapolis MN 55415*

CHUDD, CLETUS CHARLES, educator; b. Cleve., May 5, 1911; B.S. in Edn., U. Dayton, 1935; M.S. in Chemistry, Western Res. U., 1948, Ph.D. in Chemistry, 1952. Mem. Soc. Mary, Roman Cath. Ch., 1931-; high sch. tchr. St. Louis Coll., Honolulu, 1935-45; mem. faculty U. Dayton, 1947-; prof. chemistry, 1961- , chmn. dept., 1955-64. Mem. Am. Chem. Soc., A.A.A.S., Sigma Xi. Address: Univ Dayton Dayton OH 45409

CHUKHRAI, GRIGORI NAUMOVICH, film producer, dir.; b. 1921; ed. All-Union State Inst. of Cinematography. Producer, dir. Mosfilm, 1955-64; dir. Exptl. Film Studio, Moscow, USSR, 1965-. Served with Soviet Army, 1939-45. Named Honoured Art worker Russian Soviet Federative Socialist Republic; recipient Lenin prize, 1961, Order of Red Star, Order of Patriotic War. Mem. Communist Party of Soviet Union. Films include: The 41st, 1956; Ballad of a Soldier, 1959; The Clear Sky, 1961; There Lived an Old Man and An Old Woman, 1964. Address: Care Exptl Film Studio Moscow, USSR.*

CHULAKI, MIKHAIL IVANOVICH, Russian composer; b. Simferopol, Crimea, Jan. 19, 1908; ed. Leningrad Conservatoire. Tchr., Leningrad Conservatoire, 1933, Moscow Conservatoire, 1948—; sec. Union Soviet Composers USSR, 1948-57; vice chmn. com. for arts affairs USSR Council Ministers, 1951-53; dep. chief dept. for arts affairs USSR Ministry of Culture, 1953-55; dir. Bolshoi Theatre, 1955-59, 63—. Composer 3 symphonies, 1934, 45, 59; (ballets) The Story of the Priest and his Servant Balda, 1939, The Imaginary Bridegroom, 1946; Youth, 1947; (cantata) On the Banks of the Volhov River, 1943; A Symphony Cycle of Songs and Dances of Old France, 1959; Lenin is with us, 1960; Russian Festival (for violin ensemble), Romances on Whitman's verses, 1962; others. Address: Bolshoi Theatre Sverdlov Square Moscow USSR*

CHUNG, AN-MIN, educator; b. Tientsin, China, May 24, 1921; s. Daniel M. and Alice (Sun) C.; B.S. in Elec. Engring., Nat. S.W. Asso. U., Kunming, China, 1943; M.B.A., U.Pa., 1949, Ph.D., 1953; m. Tsu-shan Mei, July 15, 1950; children—Jacqueline, Jayson, James, Jeffrey, Janice. Came to U.S., 1946, permanent resident, 1957. Instr. Haverford (Pa.) Coll., 1950-51; mem. faculty Drexel U., Phila., 1951—, asso. prof. mgmt. and operations research, 1957-59, prof., 1960—, head dept., 1965—; vis. asst. prof. Carnegie-Mellon U., 1956-57; vis. prof. Lingnan Inst. Bus. Adminstrn., Chinese Univ. of Hong Kong, 1970; cons. C-E-I-R Inc., Washington, 1955-56, electronic instruments div. Burroughs Corp., summers 1956-57, Space Sci. Labs. Gen. Electric, 1971-72; mathematician RCA Service Corp., 1961-62. Co-founder Rho Psi Found., Inc., 1965, now bd. dirs.

Decorated Civilian Meritorious Service award U.S. Army, 1944. Mem. Am. Econ. Assn., Inst. Mgmt. Scis., Operations Research Soc. Am., Acad. Mgmt., Phi Kappa Phi, Beta Gamma Sigma, Rho Psi. Author: Linear Programming, 1963. Home: 120 Deerfield Rd Broomall PA 19008 Office: Drexel Univ 32d and Chestnut Sts Philadelphia PA 19104

CHUNG, KAI LAI, educator; b. Shanghai, China, Sept. 19, 1917; s. Po Chen and Jin Hwai (Shen) C.; came to U.S., 1945, naturalized, 1955; Ph.D., Princeton, 1947; m. Lilia Hernandez, Aug. 11, 1961; children—Daniel, Marilda, Corinna. Mem. faculties Princeton, Cornell U., Columbia, Syracuse U., U. Chgo., 1947-61; prof. math. Stanford, 1961—; G.A. Miller vis. prof. U. Ill., 1970-71. Fellow Inst. Math. Statistics. Author 4 books, numerous research papers. Editor math. jours. Home: 903 Lathrop Dr Stanford CA 94305

CHUNG, PAUL MYUNGHA, educator, mech. engr.; b. Seoul, Korea, Dec. 1, 1929; s. Robert N. and Kyungsook (Kim) C.; came to U.S., 1947, naturalized, 1956; B.S. in Mech. Engring., U. Ky., 1952, M.S., 1954; Ph.D., U. Minn., 1957; m. E. Jean Judy, Mar. 8, 1952; children—Maurice W., Tamara P. Asst. prof. mech. engring. U. Minn., 1957-58; aero. research scientist Ames (Ia.) Research Center, NASA, 1958-61; head fluid physics dept. Aerospace Corp., San Bernardino, Cal., 1961-66; prof. fluid mechanics U. Ill. at Chgo. Circle, 1966—; cons. to industry, 1966—. Bd. govs. Redlands (Cal.) YMCA, 1965-67. Mem. Sigma Xi, Tau Beta Pi, Pi Tau Sigma. Author numerous papers in field. Home: 2003 E Lillian Lane Arlington Heights IL 60004 Office: Univ Ill Chicago Circle Chicago IL 60680

CHUNN, CALVIN ELLSWORTH, state ofcl.; b. Jonesboro, Ark., Apr. 8, 1915; s. John Calvin and Sally Gelena (Kirby) C.; B.A., U. Ark., 1937; M.S., Northwestern U., 1938; Ph.D., U. Mo., 1950; m. Florence Jenkins, Oct. 19, 1945; children—Adele Gelena, Lawrence Jenkins. With Jonesboro (Ark.) Daily Tribune, A.P., Internat. News Service; asso. prof., acting head dept. journalism U. Tulsa, 1946-48; asst., asso. prof. journalism U. Mo., 1949-50; dir. pub. relations Tex. Christian U., 1950-53; edn. dir. So. div. N.A.M., 1953-58; dir. Okla. State U. Sch. Communications, 1958-59; dir. health edn. Am. Acad. Pediatrics, 1959-62; editor research publs. Cal. Dept. Mental Hygiene, Sacramento, 1962-65; chief bur. textbooks Cal. Dept. Edn., 1965—. Served as major Inf., AUS, 1941-46. Decorated Silver Star, Purple Heart with two oak leaf clusters, Bronze Star with one cluster, Combat Inf. Badge. Mem. Cal. State Employees Pilots Assn. (pres.), Nat. Assn. State Textbook Adminstrs. (pres. 1970-71), S.A.R., Mil. Order World Wars, Alpha Kappa Psi, Kappa Tau Alpha, Sigma Delta Chi, Alpha Delta Sigma, Kappa Alpha Mu, Kappa Sigma, Phi Delta Kappa, Phi Eta Sigma, Pi Delta Epsilon. Methodist. Mason (Shriner), Elk, Rotarian. Author: Of Rice and Men, 1946; Okla. Publications Law, 1948; The Publication Laws of Okla., A Digest, 1950; Not to the Strong Alone, 1963; The Man Who Invented Baseball, 1967; Blood Under the Sun, 1967; also short stories, mag. articles. Home: 7740 Palmyra Dr Fair Oaks CA 95628 Office: 721 Capitol Mall Sacramento CA 95814

CHUPP, EDWARD LOWELL, educator; b. Lincoln, Neb., May 14, 1927; s. William W. and Marie (Moller) C.; A.B. with honors, U. Cal., 1950, Ph.D., 1954; m. Mary Christine Miklos, Dec. 15, 1950; children—Timothy Edward, Christine Anne, Geoffrey Lowell. Staff mem. Lawrence Radiation Lab., Livermore, Cal., 1954-59; chief geospace physics unit Boeing Co., Seattle, 1959-62; asso. prof. physics U. N.H., 1962-67, prof., 1967—; cons. solar physics NASA, NCAR Balloon Panel (Palestine, Tex.); mem. Gov. N.H. Council Radiation Safety. Trustee B.V.A. Low-Beer Meml. Trust Fund. Served with USNR, 1945-56. NATO sr. fellow in sci., 1970. Mem. Am. Phys. Soc., Am. Assn. Physics Tchrs., Am. Geophys. Union, Am. Astron. Soc., Am. Assn. Univ. Profs., Phi Beta Kappa, Sigma Xi. Contbr. articles profl. jours. Home: 44 Mill Pond Rd Durham NH 03824

CHURCH, ALONZO, educator; b. Washington, June 14, 1903; s. Samuel Robbins and Mildred Hannah Letterman (Parker) C.; A.B., Princeton, 1924, Ph.D., 1927; D.Sc., Case Western Res. U., 1969; m. Mary Julia Kuczinski, Aug. 25, 1925; children—Alonzo, Mary Ann, Mildred Warner. Faculty, Princeton, 1929-67, prof. math., 1947-67; prof. math. and philosophy U. Cal. Los Angeles, 1967—. Mem. Am. Acad. Arts and Scis., Assn. Symbolic Logic, Am. Math. Soc., A.A.A.S., Brit. Acad. (corr.), Circolo Matematico di Palermo. Editor: Jour. Symbolic Logic, 1936—. Author: Introduction to Mathematical Logic, vol. I, 1956. Contbr. articles to math. jours. Address: Dept Philosophy U Cal Los Angeles CA 90024

CHURCH, ALOYSIUS STANISLAUS, psychiatrist; b. Detroit, Feb. 4, 1909; s. James J. and Josephine (Suchy) Kostielney; B.A., Wayne State U., 1932, M.B., 1936, M.D., 1937; postgrad. Cath. U. Am.; m. Elizabeth Kormend Kuttner, Sept. 11, 1937; children—Elizabeth Maria, Aloysius Stanislaus, Michael Joseph. Intern, Wayne County Gen. Hosp., Eloise, Mich., 1936-37, resident psychiatrist, 1937-38; fellow psychiatry Child Center (auspices Nat. Com. Mental Hygiene, Rockefeller Found.), Washington, 1938-41; med. dir. Lincoln Hall, Westchester County, New York, 1941-45; med. dir. St. Joseph's Retreat, Dearborn, Mich., 1945-62; psychiatrist Recorder's Ct., Psychiat. Clinic, City of Detroit, 1962—; adminstrv. psychiatrist Detroit Pub. Sch. System, 1945—; cons. psychiatrist, bd. dirs. Sobriety House; cons. Cath. Family Center, Detroit, 1945-53, Youth Service Bur., 1945-53; mem. staff Jennings Meml. Hosp., asso. staff Detroit Meml., Lynn hosps. Mem. Mich. Bd. Alcoholism Dept. Pub. Health; mem. bd. Greater Detroit Council on Alcoholism; mem. internat. council on alcoholism WHO. Mem. Nat. Council on Crime and Delinquency; Active Detroit Mus. Art Founders Soc., Detroit Symphony Orch. Trustee Detroit Com. Alcoholism. Fellow Am. Psychiat. Assn., Acad. Psychosomatic Medicine, Am. Geriatric Soc.; mem. Mich. Soc. Gerontology, Am. Soc. Med. Psychiatry, Mich. Soc. Neurology and Psychiatry, Nat. Acad. Religion and Mental Health, Wayne County, Mich. med. socs., A.M.A., Am. Pub. Health Assn., Internat. Council for Exceptional Children, Mich. Soc. Mental Hygiene, Electroshock Research Assn., Med. Correctional Assn., Nat. Conf. Cath. Charities, Guild Cath. Psychiatrists, Nat. Acad. Religion and Mental Health (charter), Am. Forestry Assn., Am. Rocket Soc., Internat. Oceanographic Found., Internat. Brotherhood Magicians, Nat. Med. and Dental Arts Assn., N.Y. Acad. Medicine, Cath. Physician's Guild, Wayne State U., Cath. U. Am. alumni assns., Am. Acad. Polit. and Social Sci., Detroit Players, MacKenzie Honor Soc., Phi Chi. Rotarian. Contbr. articles to profl. jours. Home: 19570 Bretton Dr Detroit MI 48223

CHURCH, AUSTIN HARRIS, educator; b. Mauch Chunk, Pa., Jan. 20, 1906; s. I. Monroe and Harriet (Carpenter) C.; M.E., Cornell, 1928; M.S., N.Y.U., 1934; m. Ruth A. Parry, Sept. 10, 1932; children—Ruth (Mrs. Ralph Stuart), A. Monroe, Elizabeth (Mrs. Byron C. Gibbs). Jr. engr. Westinghouse Electric Corp., 1928-31; instr. machine design Cooper Union, 1931-37; engr. DeLaval Steam Turbine Co., Trenton, N.J., 1937-40; mem. faculty N.Y.U., 1940—, prof. mech. engring., 1946—, chmn. dept., 1946-63. Profl. engr., N.Y. State. Fellow Am. Soc. M.E.; Mem. Am. Soc. E.E., Sigma Xi, Tau Beta Pi, Tau Kappa Epsilon, Pi Tau Sigma. Author: Centrifugal Pumps and Blowers, 1944; Kinematics of Machines (with Guillet), 1950; Mechanical Vibrations, 1963. Home: 56 Buena Vista Dr Hastings-on-Hudson NY 10706 Office: NYU New York City NY 10003

CHURCH, C. HOWARD, artist, educator; b. South Sioux City, Neb., May 1, 1904; s. Charles Cyrus and Della (Pilgrim) C.; B.F.A., Sch. Art Inst. Chgo., 1935; student with John Norton, Wm. P. Welsh, Boris Anisfeld, 1928-32; A.B., U. Chgo., 1938; M.A., Ohio State U., 1939, postgrad., 1939-40; m. Ila Hamer, 1933. Executed mural project for Morgan Park Mil. Acad., Chgo., 1932-36; exhibited group and one-man shows, 1932—; one man print exhbn. Hackley Gallery, Muskegon, Mich., Mich. State U. Gallery, 1970. Free-lance artist, 1928-33; dir. Morgan Park Sch. Art, Chgo., 1933-36: head dept. art and dir. Mulvane Art Mus., Washburn U., Topeka, 1940-45; head dept. art Mich. State U., East Lansing, 1945-60, prof. art, 1960-72. Mem. Mich. Gov.'s Cultural Commn. 1960-68. Recipient prizes Kansas Artists, 1940-41, Six State Exhbn. Omaha, 1941, 42; Print Purchase award Mich. Artists Exhbn., Mich. Edn. Assn., 1969, 70. Mem. Mich. Acad. Sci., Arts and Letters (Fine Arts medal 1963, 1st pruchase award mems. exhbn. 1966), Midwestern Coll. Art Assn. (pres. 1959-60), Am. Assn. U. Profs., Phi Beta Kappa. Home: 271 Lexington Av East Lansing MI 48823

CHURCH, DONALD, (Eisenbrey), govt. ofcl.; b. Reno, Feb. 25, 1904; s. James Edward and Florence (Humphrey) C.; A.B., U. Nev., 1926; A.M., U. Cal., 1929; Ph.D., U. Mich., 1939; postgrad. Columbia; m. Pearl Dee Friedman, June 16, 1929; 1 son, Russell Miller. Asst. labor commr. State Nev., Carson City, 1926-27; bus. research analyst Bur. Bus. Research, Met. Life Ins. Co., N.Y.C., 1929-34; research fellow Brookings Instn., Washington, 1936-37; head statistics dept. Ohio U. Coll. Commerce, Athens, 1937-41; prin. analyst transp. div. Bur. Fgn. and Domestic Commerce, Washington, 1941; chief transp. sect. Office Civilian Supply, WBP, 1941-42; chief research and statistics br. hwy. div. Army Transp. Corps, 1942-44; chief research and analysis sect., processed foods br. OPA, 1944-45, chief supply and requirements div. sugar br., 1945-47; cons. on transp. P.O. Dept., 1947; transp. economist in charge transp. research Bur. Agrl. Econs., 1947-51; chief transp. div. Bur. Census, 1951—. Professorial lectr. geography George Washington U., Washington, 1962—; planner, dir. 1st census of transp. in U.S., 1963. Recipient award Nat. Assn. Travel Orgns., 1958; Silver medal for meritorious fed. service for planning and directing 1st census transp. U.S. Dept. Commerce, 1965; Research award for pioneering research Efforts in Census Transp., Travel Research Assn., 1968. Mem. Am. Statis. Assn., Am. Marketing Assn., Transp. Research Forum, Hwy. Research Bd. Author: Speed Methods of Statistics, 1940. Home: Harbour Sq 560 N St S W Washington DC 20024 Office: Bur Census Dept Commerce Washington DC 20233

CHURCH, FRANK, U.S. senator; b. Boise, Ida., July 25, 1924; s. Frank Forrester and Laura (Bilderback) C.; B.A., Stanford, 1947, LL.B., 1950; student Harvard, 1948; m. Bethine Clark, June 21, 1947; children—Frank Forrester, Chase. Admitted to Ida. bar, 1950, practiced in Boise until 1956; U.S. senator from Ida., 1957—. Chmn. fgn. relations subcom. on Western hemisphere affairs; chmn. interior subcom. on pub. lands; chmn. Spl. Com. on Aging. Mem. U.S. Mission to UN, 1966. Ida. chmn. Crusade for Freedom, 1954, 55. State chmn. Ida. Young Democrats, 1952, 54, keynoter state conv., 1952, nat. conv., 1960. Bd. overseers Coll. of V. I. Served as 1st lt. M.I., AUS, World War II. Recipient nat. award Am. Legion Oratorical Contest, 1941, Joffre Debate medal Stanford, 1947; One of Ten Outstanding Young Men award Nat. Jr. C. of C., 1957. Mem. Am., Ida. bar assns., Am. Legion, V.F.W., Soc. Mayflower Descs., Phi Beta Kappa. Elk. Home: Boise ID 83707 Office: Senate Office Bldg Washington DC 20510

CHURCH, FREDERICK LEWIS, Jr., banker; b. Washington, Nov. 28, 1915; s. Frederick Lewis and Catharine (Brehaut) C.; B.S., Am. U., 1943; m. Alma Bessie White, Aug. 1, 1936; children—Lawrence Brehaut, James Frederick. With Riggs Nat. Bank, Washington. 1936—, sr. v.p., trust exec. officer, 1966—. Trustee Washington Hosp. Center. Home: 4018 N 27th St Arlington, VA 22207. Office: 800 17th St NW Washington DC 20013

CHURCH, GEORGE LYLE, botanist, educator; b. Boston, Dec. 19, 1903; s. William R. and Anna Marie (Lind) C.; Sc.B., U. Mass., 1925; A.M., Harvard, 1927, Ph.D., 1928; m. Margaret Fobes, June 16, 1934; 1 son, Robert Fobes. Mem. faculty Brown U., 1928—, prof. botany, curator of herbarium, 1951-59, Stephen T. Olney prof. natural history, 1959—, chmn. dept. botany, 1958-65. Fellow A.A.A.S.; mem. Bot. Soc. Am., Growth Soc., Soc. Study of Evolution, New Eng. Bot. Club, Soc. Am. Plant Taxonomists, Sigma Xi, Phi Kappa Phi, Alpha Gamma Rho. Contbr. profl. jours. Home: 278 Doyle Av Providence RI 02906.

CHURCH, I.W., lawyer; b. Menomonee Falls, Wis., Aug. 23, 1884; A.B., Lawrence U., 1906; LL.B., Columbia, 1911. Admitted to Mont. bar, 1911; now partner firm Church, Harris, Johnson & Williams, Great Falls, Mont. Mem. Selective Service Bd., World War I; appeal agt. Selective Service, World War II. Mem. Bd. Sch. Trustees, Cascade County, 1932-42, chmn., 1937-42. Mem. Mont., Cascade County bar assns., Phi Alpha Delta, Delta Sigma Rho. Rotarian (gov. 1928-29). Office: Great Falls Nat Bank Bldg Great Falls MT 59401*

CHURCH, JAMES MARION, educator; b. Worcester, Mass., Sept. 25, 1903; s. Frank LeGrand and Mary (Andrews) C.; B.A., William Jewell Coll., 1925; postgrad. Harvard, 1925-27; Ph.D., Pa. State U., 1933; m. Dorothy Borden, June 3, 1933; children—Larry Borden, Thomas Marion, James Andrews. Lab. asst. in chemistry William Jewell Coll., 1923-25; Austin teaching fellow Harvard, 1925-27; instr. chemistry Allegheny Coll., 1927-28, Drexel Inst., 1928-30; chemist and devel. engr. Monsanto Chem. Co., St. Louis, 1932-40; mem. faculty Columbia, 1940—, successively asst. prof., asso. prof. 1940-53, prof., 1953—, acting chmn. dept. chem. engineering, 1970-71; vis. scientist Stanford Research Inst., Menlo Park, Cal., 1968. Mem. Bd. Edn., Tenafly, N.J., 1959-65, pres., 1964-65. Recipient Distinguished Alumni award William Jewell Coll., 1955. Mem. Am. Chem. Soc. (chmn. I. & C.E. div. 1959, councillor 1958-62, 64—; Scroll of Honor, I. & C.E. div. 1963), Am. Inst. Chem. Engrs., Soc. Plastics Engrs., Sigma Xi, Alpha Chi Sigma, Phi Kappa Phi, Phi Lambda Upsilon (nat. sec. 1945-54, nat. pres. 1954-57). Presbyn. (elder). Author articles profl. jours. Contbr. to tech. books. Patentee in field. Home: 6 Kenwood Rd Tenafly NJ 07670 Office: Dept Chem Engring Columbia U New York City NY 10027

CHURCH, JOHN TRAMMELL, retail stores co. exec.; b. Raleigh, N.C., Sept. 22, 1917; s. Charles Randolph and Lela (Johnson) C.; student Catawba Coll., 1936-37; B.S., U. N.C., 1942; m. Emma Thomas Rose, Dec. 31, 1943; children—John Trammell, Elizabeth Howard. With Rose Co., Henderson, N.C., 1945—, asst. sec., dir., 1948-49, buyer several depts., 1949-54, v.p., sec., 1954-57, mdse. mgr. Rose's Stores Inc., 1957—, sr. v.p., 1963—; dir. Peoples Bank and Trust Co. Mem. Tax Study Commn., 1968-72, State Art Mus. Bldg. Commn., 1968-72, Morehead Scholarship Selection Com., 1965, Henderson (N.C.) City Council, 1965-66; chmn. Kerr Lake Devel. Reservoir Commn., 1967; pres. United Fund, 1955; mem. exec. com. Carolinas United, 1955-59; mem. adv. bd. Salvation Army, 1959-65; v.p., mem. exec. bd. Occoneechee Council Boy Scouts Am., 1955-69, pres., 1969-70. Mem. N.C. Ho. of Reps., 1967-69; mem. N.C. Senate, 1971—. Trustee Boys Home N.C., Maria Parham Hosp., U. N.C., Chapel Hill, Vance County Tech. Inst.; vice chmn. bd. trustees Louisburg Coll.; chmn. bd. visitors Peace Coll., Raleigh; bd. dirs. U. N.C. Bus. Found. Served to capt. USMCR, 1942-45. Decorated D.F.C. (three), ten Air medals; recipient Silver Beaver award; named Tarheel of the Week, 1962. Mem. N.C. Mchts. Assn. (pres. 1962-63), Am. Retail Fedn. (vice chmn. 1965), Am. Legion, Henderson C. of C. (dir. 1959-63), Jr. C. of C. (pres. 1950-51). Democrat. Methodist. Mason (Shriner), Elk, Rotarian (pres. Henderson Club 1964-65), Club: Henderson Country (pres. 1956-57). Home: 420 Woodland Rd Henderson NC 27536 Office: Garnett St Henderson NC 27536

CHURCH, KENNETH ROBERT, mfr. gas turbine engines; b. Ottawa, Ont., Can., Mar. 20, 1921; s. George Alexander and Ethel (Turley) C.; B. Comm., Queen's U., 1942; m. Elsie May Chambers, Dec. 9, 1944; children—Kenneth Edward, Thomas Robert. Chartered accountant Price Waterhouse & Co., Toronto, Ont., 1942-50; chief accountant A.V. Roe Can. Ltd., 1950-51; comptroller, v.p. finance Orenda Engines Ltd., Toronto, 1952-60; finance mgr. Hawker Siddeley Can. Ltd., Toronto, 1961-66; treas. Orenda Ltd., Toronto, 1967—. Mem. Univ. Council Queen's U., 1969—. Mem. Air Industries Assn. Can. Club: Weston Golf and Country (Toronto). Home: 30 Cedarland Dr Islington Ontario Canada Office: Box 6001 Toronto Internat Airport Ontario Canada

CHURCH, MARGUERITE STITT, former congresswoman, lecturer and writer; b. N.Y.C., Sept. 13, 1892; A.B., Wellesley Coll., 1914; A.M., Columbia, 1917; LL.D., Russell Sage Coll., Troy, N.Y., 1958, Lake Forest Coll., 1960, Northwestern U., 1962; D.H.L., Nat. Coll. Edn., 1963; m. Ralph E. Church (Evanston lawyer; U.S. congressman 1935-40, 1943-50), Dec. 21, 1918 (dec.); children—Ralph Edwin, Jr., William Stitt, Marjory (Mrs. Church Wood). Instr., Wellesley Coll., 1915; formerly cons. psychologist State Charities Aid Assn., N.Y.C.; mem. 82d to 87th Congresses, 13th Ill. Dist.; lectr., writer. U.S. del. to Gen. Assembly UN, 1961; mem. planning bd. White House Conf. on Aging, 1971. Del. Republican Nat. Conv., 1964. Mem. U.S. Capitol Hist. Soc. (v.p.), Nat. Alumnae Assn. Wellesley Coll. (pres. 1940-42), Bus. and Profl. Women's Club, Phi Beta Kappa, Delta Kappa Gamma, Beta Sigma Phi. Republican. Clubs: Zonta, Congressional (pres. 1948-50), 1925 F St., Sulgrave (Washington); Women's Athletic Glenview, Sheridan Shore Yacht (Chgo.). Home: 300 Church St Evanston IL 60201

CHURCH, PHIL EDWARDS, educator; b. Berwyn, Ill., Apr. 8, 1902; s. Harry Victor and Katherine (Edwards) C.; B.S., U. Chgo., 1923; A.M., Clark U., 1932, Ph.D., 1937; m. Loretta Leidel, Oct. 9, 1933; children—Frances Ellen, Loretta Jean, Katherine Louise, Barbara Helen. Sci. tchr., Streator (Ill.) Twp. High Sch., 1925-30; research asst. Woods Hole Oceanographic Instn., Mass., summers 1931, 33; tchr. Evanston (Ill.) Twp. High Sch., 1934-35; vis. instr. Northwestern, summer 1935; instr. meteorology U. Wash., 1935-37, asst. prof., 1937-43, asso. prof., 1943-48, prof., 1948—, exec. officer dept. atmospheric scis., 1947-67, staff oceanographic labs., 1936-50; research asso. Inst. Meterology., U. Chgo., 1941-44, meteorologist Metall. Lab., 1943-44; meteorologist E.I. DuPont (Hanford Engr. Works), 1944, cons., 1944-46, 1946—; mem. rev. com., radiol. physics div. Argonne U. Assn., 1969—. Trustee Univ. Corp. Atmospheric Research, 1960-67. Mem. Am. Meteorol. Soc. (councilor 1941-43, 54-57, v.p. 1964-65), A.A.A.S. (pres. Pacific div. 1963-64). Geophys. Union (chmn. lakes com. 1946-48, pres. meteor sect. 1953-56), Chi Psi. Presbyn. Contbr. research articles to profl. jours. Home: 3040 134th N E Bellevue WA 98005

CHURCH, RICHARD CASSIUS, musician, educator; b. Belvidere, Ill., May 14, 1907; s. Cassius M. and Minnie E. (Adams) C.; B.A., U. Wis., 1927, Mus. B., 1936, M.A. in Music, 1940; m. Agatha G. McCaffery, June 21, 1928; children—Kathleen Kirwan (Mrs. Stuart W. Wirth), Meredith Ann (Mrs. Joseph L. Rousseau), Julie Adams Bieger, Richard Anthony. Tchr., orch. condr. Janesville (Wis.) High Sch., 1927-28; dir. instrumental music Central High Sch., Madison, Wis., 1928-30, West High Sch., Madison, 1930-44; faculty dept. music U. Wis., Madison, 1944—, prof., 1957—, condr. U. Wis. Symphony Orch., 1944-66, mus. dir. Wis. Players Mus. Prodns., 1935-65. Guest condr. various symphony orchs.; music adjudicator; lectr.; bassoonist, violist Madison Symphony Orch. Recipient citation for excellence in teaching Midwest Program for Airborne Television Instrn. Mem. Music Educators Nat. Conf., Wis. Edn. Assn., Nat. Collegiate Players, Phi Mu Alpha (Sinfonia), Alpha Kappa Lambda. Developer 1st systems approach to teaching violin with film cartridges and manual. Home: P O Box 271 Lodi WI 53555

CHURCH, RUSSELL MILLER, educator; b. N.Y.C., Dec. 24, 1930; s. Donald E. and Pearl (Friedman) C.; B.A., U. Mich., 1952; M.A., Harvard U., 1954, Ph.D., 1956; m. Ruth Kutz, Apr. 4, 1954; children—Kenneth, Emily. Mem. faculty Brown U., 1955—, prof. psychology, 1965—; asso. editor Learning and Motivation; cons. editor Jour. of Comparative and Physiological Psychology. Fellow Am. Psychol. Assn. Editor (with E.E. Boe) Punishment: Issues and Experiments, 1968; editor (with B.A. Campbell) Punishment and Aversive Behavior, 1969. Home: 20 Abbotsford Ct Providence RI 02912

CHURCH, WILLIAM FARR, educator; b. Monmouth, Ill., Dec. 13, 1912; s. Henry Ward and Helen (Farr) C.; A.B., Allegheny Coll., 1934; M.A., Harvard, 1935, Ph.D., 1939; m. Margaret Kathleen Lovelock, Aug. 4, 1947; children—Barbara Monica, David Edmund. Instr. history Gettysburg Coll., 1940-41; instr. history U. Ky., 1941-42, asst. prof., 1946; faculty Brown U., 1947—, prof., 1951—, Munroe, Goodwin, Wilkinson prof. history, 1959—. Guggenheim fellow, 1946-47, 54; Nat. Endowment for Humanities sr. fellow, 1967. Served with AUS, 1942-45. Mem. Am. Hist. Assn., Soc. French Hist. Studies, Am. Assn. U. Profs., Phi Beta Kappa. Author: Constitutional Thought in Sixteenth Century France, 1941. Editor: The Greatness of Louis XIV: Myth or Reality?, 1959. Editor: The Influence of the Enlightenment on the French Revolution: Creative, Disastrous or Non- Existent?, 1964; The Impact of Absolutism in France, 1968. Contbr. profl. jours. Home: 17 Huntington Dr Rumford RI 02916 Office: Dept History Brown U Providence RI 02912

CHURCHILL, EDWARD DELOS, surgeon; b. Chenoa, Ill., Dec. 25, 1895; s. Ebenezer Delos and Maria A. (Farnsworth) C.; B.S., Northwestern U., 1916, A.M., 1917; M.D. cum laude, Harvard, 1920; Dr. Honoris Causa, of Algiers, 1944; D.Sc., Princeton, 1947, U. Ala., 1959, Harvard, 1961; LL.D., Queen's U., 1954; m. Mary Lowell Barton, July 7, 1927; children—Mary Lowell, Frederick Barton, Edward Delos, A. Coolidge. Student intern Faulkner Hosp., Boston, 1919-20; surg. intern Mass. Gen. Hosp., 1920-22, resident, 1922-23, chief West Surg. Service, 1931-48, chief Gen. Surg. Services, 1948—; asso. surgeon and dir. Surg. Research Lab., Boston City Hosp., 1928-30; asst. in surgery Harvard, 1922-23, Alumni asst. in surgery, 1923-24, instr. surgery, 1924-28, Moseley traveling fellow, 1926-27, asso. prof. surgery, 1928-31, John Homans prof. surgery, 1931-62, emeritus, 1962—. Adv. med. bd. Am. Hosp., Paris, 1957—; mem. adv. council Shiraz Med. Center, Nemazee Hosp., Iran, 1957—; charter mem. sci. adv. bd. Walter Reed Inst. Research, Washington, 1958. Served in Med. Res., U.S. Army, 1918, 1st lt., 1924-29; col. M.C., cons. surgeon N. African and Mediterranean theatres, 1943-46. Decorated Legion of Merit, 1944; European Theater Service medal with 4 bronze battle stars; Cross of Knight Legion of Honor, 1953; War medal of Brazil; comdr. Order Crown of Italy; hon. officer Mil. Div. Order Brit. Empire, 1945; D.S.M., 1946; officer de l'Ordre National du Cedre (Lebanon). Chmn. med. adv. com. to sec. of war, 1946-48; vice chmn. task force, Fed. Med. Services, Commn. on Orgn. Exec. Br. Govt., 1948-49, 1953-55; mem. Armed Forces Med. Adv. Com. to Sec. Def., 1948-51; chmn. com. on surgery NRC, 1946-49; sr. civilian cons. in thoracic surgery to Surgeon Gen., 1953—; cons. to Surgeon Gen., 1954-55; mem. edit. bd. Annals of Surgery. Fellow Royal Coll. Surgeons Eng. (hon.), Royal Coll. Univ. Surgeons Denmark (hon.), Am. Acad. Arts and Sci.; lectr. Royal Coll. Physicians and Surgeons (Can.); mem. Am. Assn. for Thoracic Surgery (pres. 1948-49), Am. Bd. Surgery Founders' Group (mem. bd., 1937-49), A.C.S., A.M.A., Am. Soc. for Clin. Investigation (emeritus 1941—), Am. Surg. Assn. (pres. 1946-47), Assn. Mil. Surgeons U.S., Internat., New Eng. Boston, Excelsior (hon.) surg. socs., Halsted Club, Mass. Med. Soc., No. Pacific Surg. Assn. (hon.), Soc. Clin. Surgery (pres. 1949-50), Soc. U.S. Med. Cons. in World War II, Trudeau Soc., Korean Communications Zone Med. and Dental (hon.), 38th Parallel Med. Soc. of Korea (hon.), So. Honshu Med. Soc., Alpha Omega Alpha, Sigma Xi, Delta Tau Delta; hon. mem. U.S. and fgn. surg. socs. Presbyn. Clubs: Tavern, Century Assn., Harvard (Boston and N.Y.C.), Aesculapian. Home: 269 Prospect St Belmont MA 02178 ☆

CHURCHILL, EDWARD JAMES, former business exec.; b. Syracuse, N.Y., June 28, 1895; s. Edward James and Olive (Blanshan) C.; m. Marjorie Craig, Apr. 26, 1927; children—Michael Blanshan, Thomas Marshall, Mary Jane. Vice Pres. Paul Cornell Co., 1928-32; pres. Donahue & Coe, Inc., 1932-61, chmn. bd., 1958-63, chief exec. officer, 1958-62; chmn. bd. Ariz. F.M. Inc., owner radio sta. KRFM. Clubs: Paradise Valley Country, Phoenix Country (Phoenix). Home: 7138 Sandy Mountain Rd Scottsdale AZ 85253

CHURCHILL, EDWARD PERRY, zoologist; b. Allerton, Ia., July 19, 1882; s. Edward Payson and Flavilla Ann (Kellogg) C.; A.B., State U. Ia., 1907; Ph.D., Johns Hopkins, 1916; m. Nellie Arlene Lewis, Aug. 12, 1908; adopted dau., Marjorie C. (Mrs. Marjorie C. Fibikar). Prin. high schools in Iowa, 1907-12; asst. in zoölogy State U. Ia., 1912-13, Johns Hopkins U., 1913-15, fellow in zoölogy, 1915-16; in charge shellfish investigations U.S. Bur. Fisheries, 1916-20; asst. prof. zoölogy U. S.D., 1920-22, prof., 1926—. Mem. S.D. Acad. Scis., Am. Soc. Zoölogists, Soc. Colonial Wars, Phi Beta Kappa, Sigma Xi. Republican. Conglist. Mason (K.T., 32). Author: Life History of Blue Crab, 1919; Zoeal Stages of Blue Crab, 1942; The Least of These; (with W.H. Over) Fishes of South Dakota, 1933; Three Thousand Coyotes and I (memoirs), 1961. Home: 415 S University St Vermillion SD 57069

CHURCHILL, GAIL WINSTON, assn. exec.; b. Bedford, Ia., Jan. 29, 1903; s. William H. and Artie (Adams) C.; B.S., Ia. State Coll., 1926; m. Marjorie Mahaffa, June 15, 1935; children—Maren Gail, Lee Ellen. Copy reader, reporter, state editor Des Moines Register and Tribune, 1926-35; state editor, photo editor A.P. Des Moines, N.Y.C., Washington, 1935-43; picture editor Life mag., N.Y.C., 1943-51; mag. editor Nashville Tennessean, 1951-65, asso. pub., 1965-70. Vice pres.; dir. Tenn. Mental Health Assn., 1970—. Recipient Sprague Meml. award Nat. Press Photographers Assn., 1966. Mem. Am., So. newspaper pubs. assns., A.P. Mng. Editor's Assn. (chmn. color com. 1958-59, news enterprise com. 1961-62, vice chmn. freedom of information com. 1962-63, dir.), Tenn. A.P. Assn. (pres. 1953-54), Tenn. Press Assn. (chmn. journalism edn. com. 1964), Sigma Delta Chi, Delta Tau Delta. Methodist. Lion. Home: 3706 Woodmont Blvd Nashville TN 37215

CHURCHILL, GORDON, lawyer; b. Coldwater, Ont., Can., Nov. 8, 1898; s. John W. and Mary E. (Shier) C.; student United Coll., Winnipeg, U. Man., m. Mona M. McLachlin, Aug. 9, 1922; 1 dau., Noni (Mrs. Cusson). Elementary sch. tchr., 1922-26; high sch. tchr., 1926-28; high sch. prin., 1928-38; called to Canadian bar; mem. firm Haig & Haig, Winnipeg, 1949—; mem. Man. Legislature, 1946-49, Canadian Parliament, 1951-68, Canadian minister trade and commerce, 1957-60; minister Vets.' Affairs, chmn. Privy Council Com., 1960-63, minister nat. def., 1963; practice law with firm D'Arcy, Irving, Haig & Smethurst, Winnipeg, 1968—. Served with Canadian Army, World War I and II. Decorated Distinguished Service Order. Home: 954 Palmerston Av Winnipeg 10 Manitoba Canada Office: 300-286 Smith St Winnipeg Manitoba Canada

CHURCHILL, IRVING LESTER, educator; b. Madison, Wis., Apr. 9, 1901; s. Herman and Cora Mae (Boyce) C.; B.S., R.I. State Coll. (now U. R.I.), 1922; A.M., Yale, 1927, Ph.D., 1932; m. Kathryn M. Hughes, July 27, 1935; children—Malcolm Hughes, Margaret Elizabeth. Instr. Northbridge High Sch., Whitinsville, Mass., 1922-23; instr. English, U. N.H., 1923-25, U. Rochester, 1927-30; asst. prof. English, R.I. State Coll., 1932-34, Bucknell U., 1934-37; prof. English, Coe Coll., 1937-69, emeritus, 1969—, asst. to pres., 1958, head dept., 1937-55, 59-66, chmn div. lang. and lit., 1946-54, acad. dean, 1951-53; Fulbright vis. lectr. in English, Silliman U., Dumaguete, Philippines, 1955-56; vis. prof. English, Tunghai U., Taichung, Taiwan, 1964-65; prof. English, Warren Wilson Coll., Swannanoa, N.C., 1969—. Recipient Silver Beaver award Boy Scouts Am., 1955. Mem. Am. Assn. U. Profs. Modern Lang. Assn., Coll. English Assn., Phi Kappa Phi, Sigma Alpha Epsilon. Conglist. Club: Rotary. Contbr. articles to lit. jours. Address: Warren Wilson Coll Dept English Swannanoa NC 28778

CHURCHILL, MAC MILO, advt. exec.; b. Peoria, Ill., Sept. 28, 1939; s. Milo Albert and Evna (Wyllys) C.; student U. Ill., 1957-61; m. Judy Jeanette Hall, Apr. 20, 1963. With Young & Rubicam Inc., Chgo., 1961-63, Edward H. Weiss Inc., Chgo., 1964-65, Leo Burnett Co. Inc., Chgo., 1965; partner, creative dir. Hurvis, Binzer & Churchill Inc., Chgo., 1965—; dir. Alameda Broadcasting Co., Inc., Fremont, Cal. Served with AUS, 1962-63. Named one of Chicago's Top Ten Copywriters, 1964. Mem. Sigma Phi Epsilon (pres. 1961), Alpha Delta Sigma (sec. 1960). Home: 2030 N Mohawk Chicago IL 60614 Office: 520 N Michigan Av Chicago IL 60611

CHURCHILL, NEIL CENTER, educator; b. Bismarck, N.D., Sept. 6, 1927; s. Neil Orr and Helen (Center) C.; B.S., U. Cal. at Los Angeles, 1951, M.B.A., 1954; Ph.D., U. Mich., 1962; m. Marjorie Ann Shipman, June 28, 1952; children—Neil T., Gregory S., Christopher S. Staff accountant Haskins & Sells, C.P.A.'s, Los Angeles, 1951-53; instr. San Diego State Coll., 1954-56; asso. prof. Carnegie Mellon U., 1958-67; prof. Harvard Grad. Sch. Bus. Adminstrn., 1967—, Royal Little prof. bus. adminstrn., 1970—. Tech. adviser Data Architects and Applied Decision Systems, Boston. Served with USNR, 1945-46. C.P.A., Cal. Mem. Am. Inst. C.P.A.'s, Inst. Mgmt. Sci., Assn. Computing Machinery, Am. Accounting Assn. Author: (with others) Auditing, Management Games and Accounting Education, 1964; (with others) Computer-Based Information Systems in Management, 1968. Home: 61 Temple St West Newton MA 02165 Office: Harvard Bus Sch Boston MA 02163

CHURCHILL, RUEL VANCE, mathematician; b. Akron, Ind., Dec. 12, 1899; s. Abner C. and Meldora (Friend) C.; B.S., U. Chgo., 1922; M.S., U. Mich., 1925, Ph.D., 1929; m. Ruby F. Sicks, 1922; children—Betty Churchill (Mrs. Paul R. McMurray), Eugene S. Faculty, U. Mich., Ann Arbor, 1922—, prof. math., 1942-65, emeritus, 1965—. Vis. lectr. U. Wis., 1941; research U. Freiburg (Germany), 1936, Cal. Inst. Tech., 1949. Part-time supr. project Engring. Research Inst., U. Mich., 1946-49, 53-54; research specialist USAAF, 1944; mem. NRC, 1947-50. Mem. Am. Math. Soc. (council 1946-49, mem. com. on applied math. 1948-49, 51-54, chmn. editorial com. Procs. Symposia in Applied Math. 1949), Math. Assn Am. (asso. editor Am. Math. Monthly 1952-56, v.p. 1956-57, gov. 1959-61), Phi Beta Kappa, Sigma Xi. Author books including: Complex Variables and Applications, 1948, rev. edit. 1960, Spanish edit., 1965: Operational Mathematics, 1944, rev. edit. 1958, Japanese edit. 1950; Fourier Series, 1941, 2d edit., 1963, Japanese edit., 1960, Spanish edit., 1966. Contbr. articles to sci. jours. Home: 1231 Wisteria Dr Ann Arbor MI 48104

CHURCHILL, RUSSELL J., educator; B.E., N.S. Tech. Coll.; M.S., U. Birmingham (Eng.); Ph.D., U. Liverpool (Eng.). Prof. elec. engring. Colo. State U., Fort Collins, also chmn. dept. elec. engring. Office: Coll Engring Colorado State U Fort Collins CO 80521

CHURCHILL, STUART WINSTON, educator, chem. engr.; b. Imlay City, Mich., June 13, 1920; s. Howard Heenan and Faye Erma (Shurte) C.; B.S. in Math., U. Mich., 1942, B.S. in Chem. Engring., 1942, M.S., 1948, Ph.D., 1952; m. Donna Belle Lewis, Feb. 22, 1946 (div.); children—Stuart Lewis, Diana Gail, Cathy Marie, Emily Elizabeth. Technologist, Shell Oil Co., 1942-46; tech. supr. Frontier Chem. Co., 1946-47; mem. faculty U. Mich., 1949-67, prof. chem. engring., 1957-67, chmn. dept. chem. and metall. engring., 1962-67; Carl V.S. Patterson prof. chem. engring. U. Pa., 1967—. Chmn. region 2 edn. and accreditation com. Engrs. Council Profl. Devel., 1961-65, mem. nat. council, 1965-71, exec. com., 1968-71; cons. heat transfer and combustion. Fellow Am. Inst. Chem. Engrs. (nat. council 1962-64, pres. 1966; Profl. Progress award 1964, William H. Walker award 1969); mem., Am. Chem. Soc., Combustion Inst., Sigma Xi, Phi Kappa Phi, Phi Lambda Upsilon (award U. Mich. chpt. 1961), Tau Beta Pi. Unitarian. Home: 2101 Chestnut St Philadelphia PA 19103

CHURCHMAN, CHARLES WEST, educator; b. Phila., Aug. 29, 1913; s. Clarke Wharton and Norah (Fassitt) C.; A.B., U. Pa., 1935, M.A., 1936, Ph.D., 1938; m. Gloria King, Sept. 27, 1950; 1 son, Daniel Wharton. Instr. philosophy U. Pa., 1937-42, head dept., asst. prof. philosophy, 1945-48; asso. prof. philosophy Wayne U., 1948-51; prof. engring. adminstrn. Case Inst. Tech., 1951-58; prof. bus. adminstrn. U. Cal. at Berkeley, 1958—, research philosopher space scis. lab., 1963-70; head math. sect. U.S. Ordnance Lab. Frankford Arsenal, 1942-45; co-founder Inst. Exptl. Method (research city planning), Phila., 1945-48; dir. research System Devel. Corp., 1962-63. Fellow A.A.A.S., Operations Research Soc. Am.; mem. Inst. Mgmt. Scis. (pres. 1962), Philosophy of Sci. Assn. (governing bd.), Am. Philos. Assn., Assn. Symbolic Logic, Am. Statis. Assn. Author: Elements of Logic, 1940; Theory of Experimental Inference, 1948; Methods of Inquiry (with R.L. Ackoff, 1950; Prediction and Optimal Decision, 1961. Co-editor: Measurement of Consumer Interest, 1946; Introduction to Operations Research, 1957; Measurement: Theories and Definitions, 1959; Systems Approach, 1968; Challenge to Reason, 1968; On the Design of In1uiring Systems, 1971. Editor Philosophy of Science (quar.), 1948, Management Science (quar.), 1954—. Home: 657 Lovell Av Mill Valley CA 94941 Office: Bus Adminstrn Dept U Cal Berkeley CA 94720

CHURCHWELL, CHARLES DARRETT, librarian; b. Dunnellon, Fla., Nov. 7, 1926; s. John Dozier and Leeannah (DeLaughter) C.; B.S., Morehouse Coll., 1952; M.S., Atlanta U., 1953; Ph.D., U. Ill., 1966; m. Yvonne Ransom, Aug. 25, 1957; children—Linda Louise, Cynthia Diane. Instr. library sci. Prairie View (Tex.) A. and M. Coll., 1953-57; reference librarian circulation dept. N.Y. Pub. Library, 1959-61; asst. circulation librarian U. Ill., 1965-67; asst. dir. libraries U. Houston, 1967-69; dir. libraries Miami U., Oxford, O., 1969—. Served with USAAF, 1945-47. Mem. Am. (life), Ohio library assns., So. Assn. Colls. and Univs., N.A.A.C.P. (life). Democrat. Home: 1221 Albert Circle Oxford OH 45065 Office: Miami U Libraries Oxford OH 45056

CHUTE, ANDREW LAWRENCE, univ. dean, physician; b. India, May 31, 1909; s. Jesse Edmund and Pearl (Smith) C.; B.A., U. Toronto, 1931, M.A., 1932, M.D., 1935; Ph.D., Univ. Coll., London, 1939; m. Helen Evans Reid, Oct. 6, 1939; children—Judith Omond (Mrs. Alden Redfield). Douglas Lawrence. Intern Toronto Gen. Hosp., 1935-36; resident pediatrics Hosp. Sick Children, Toronto, 1936- 37; Beit Meml. research Scholar Univ. Coll. Hosp., London, 1937-39; resident extern New Eng. Deaconess Hosp. 1945-46; prof. pediatrics, chmn. dept. U. Toronto, 1951-66, dean medicine, 1966—. Served to lt. col., M.C., Canadian Army, 1942-46. Decorated officer Order Brit. Empire. Fellow Royal Coll. Phys. and Surg. Can., Am. Acad. Pediatrics: mem. Assn. Canadian Med. Colls., Am. Acad. Pediatrics, Canadian Pediatric Soc. Home: 330 Spadina Rd Toronto 178 Ontario Canada

CHUTE, BEATRICE JOY, author: b. Mpls., Jan. 3, 1913; d. William Young and Edith Mary (Pickburn) Chute: extension student U. Minn., 1931-33. Asso. in English, Barnard Coll., N.Y.C., 1964-66, adj. asso. prof., 1966—. Fiction judge for Nat. Book Awards, 1960, children's book judge, 1971. Vol. worker Civilian Def., Police Athletic League, N.Y.C., 1942—. Recipient award Bur. Intercultural Edn., 1947. Mem. P.E.N. (pres. Am. Center 1959-61), Authors League, League Women Voters. Democrat. Author: Blocking Back, 1938; Shattuck Cadet, 1940; Camp Hero, 1942; Shift to the Right, 1944; Teen- Age Sports Parade, 1949; The Fields Are White, 1950; The End of Loving, 1952; Greenwillow, 1956; The Blue Cup and Other Stories, 1957; Journey to Christmas, 1958; The Moon and the Thorn, 1961; One Touch of Nature, and Other Stories, 1965; The Story of a Small Life, 1971; also short stories in mags. Address: 450 E 63d St New York City NY 10021

CHUTE, MARCHETTE, author; b. Wayzata, Minn., Aug. 16, 1909; d. William Young and Edith Mary (Pickburn) Chute; A.B., U. Minn., 1930; Litt.D. Western Coll. for Women, 1952, Carleton Coll., 1957, Dickinson Coll., 1964. Author: Rhymes About Ourselves, 1932; The Search for God, 1941; Rhymes About the Country, 1941; The Innocent Wayfaring, 1943; Geoffrey Chaucer of England, 1946; Rhymes About the City, 1946; The End of the Search, 1947; Shakespeare of London, 1950; An Introduction to Shakespeare, 1951; Ben Jonson of Westminster, 1953; The Wonderful Winter, 1954; Stories from Shakespeare, 1956; Around and About, 1957; Two Gentle Men: The Lives of George Herbert and Robert Herrick, 1959; Jesus of Israel, 1961; (with Ernestine Perrie) The Worlds of Shakespeare, 1963; The First Liberty: A History of the Right to Vote in America, 1619-1850, 1969; The Green Tree of Democracy, 1971. Exec. com. Nat. Book Com.; judge non-fiction Nat. Book Awards, 1952, 59. Recipient Author Meets the Critics award for best non-fiction of 1950; Chap-Book award Poetry Soc. Am., 1954; N.Y. Shakespeare Club award, 1954; Secondary Edn. Bd. book award, 1954; Outstanding Achievement award U. Minn., 1957. Fellow Royal Soc. Arts, Soc. Am. Historians; mem. Am. P.E.N. (pres. 1955-57), Nat. Inst. Arts and Letters, Renaissance Soc. Am., Phi Beta Kappa. Home: 450 E 63d St New York City NY 10021

CHUTIKUL, PAYONG, diplomat of Thailand; b. Supanburi, Thailand, Apr. 15, 1919; s. Yoo and Chon (Malithong) C.; B.A., U. Yokohama (Japan), 1940; M.A., U. Kyushu, 1943; student Fgn. Relations, London, 1948; grad. Nat. Def. Coll. Thailand, 1969; m. Momrajwongse Loeslaksana, Mar. 11, 1949; children—Kobsak, Sirilaksana, Sarakit. 3d sec. Royal Thai embassy, Tokyo, 1950-53; chief econ. div. Fgn. Ministry, 1954-55; 1st sec., London, 1956-61; chief diplomatic div. Fgn. Ministry, 1961-62, chief news div., 1962-63; consul-gen., Singapore, 1963-65, counselor, charge d'affaires, 1965-67; econ. adviser Econ. Dept., 1968-70; minister-counselor, dep. chief of mission Royal Thai embassy, Washington, 1970—; lectr. Nat. Def. Coll. Thailand. Club: Royal Turf (Thailand). Home: 9715 Kingston Rd Kensington MD 20795 Office: 2300 Kalorama Rd NW Washington DC 20008

CHWOROWSKY, MARTIN PHILIP, educator; b. San Antonio, Tex., Jan. 28, 1900; s. Frederick J. and Marie (Sussnitz) C.; A.B., Harvard, 1922, LL.B., 1926; A.M., U. Pittsburgh, 1936, Ph.D., 1937; m. Eleanor Weeks, Aug. 21, 1926 (dec. 1965); 1 dau., Jane Lee; m. 2d, Eleanor Dunwoody, July 9, 1966. Began career as teacher at Indian Mt. School, Lakeville, Conn., 1926-29, Community Sch., Pittsburgh, 1929-30; prin. Falk Sch., lectr. in edn., U. Pittsburgh, 1931-39; asso. prof. edn. and psychology, Carnegie Inst. Tech., 1939-46; became prof. edn., coordinator, inter-group relations program. Columbia Teachers Coll., 1948; research prof. human relations U. Pa., Phila., 1951-61, prof. human relations, dir. A. M. Greenfield Center for Human Relations, 1951-66, prof. emeritus, 1968—; prof. social work Va. Commonwealth U., 1966-67, prof. sociology, 1967-70. Mem. nat. bd. parish edn. United Luth. Ch. Am.; bd. dirs. Luth. Found. Phila., Christian Children's Fund, Phila. Fellowship Commn.; vice chmn. chpt. Nat. Council Christians and Jews, Phila. Mem. Am. Arbitration Assn. Contbr.: Year Book of Edn., 1955; Adult Leadership. Home: 17 Wistar Rd Paoli PA 19301

CIAMPAGLIA, CARLO, mural painter; b. Italy, Mar. 8, 1891; s. Natale and Benelde (Delmonaco) C.; diploma Cooper Union, N.Y.C., 1917; student N.A.D., N.Y.C., 1909-15; m. Annette Paltrinieri, Sept. 7, 1920 (dec.); m. 2d, Rosalie Woodbury, May 22, 1969. Came to U.S. 1891, naturalized, 1919. Mural painter, 1924—; made designs for Masonic Temple, Scranton, Pa., ceiling Chgo. Tribune Bldg., niches and ceilings Slovak Girls Acad., Danville, Pa.; decorations Ct. House, Sunbury, Pa., residence Frank Potter, Rome, N.Y.; decorations in mosaic Fairmont Mausoleum, Newark, in tiles Green Hill Farm swimming pool, Phila.; murals in residence David Milton, N.Y.C., Tex. Centennial Expn., 1936, Dallas, in Adminstrn., Transp., Foods, Agr. and Live Stock bldgs.; designed murals Foods Bldg., N.Y. World's Fair, 1939, residence Theodore Kiendl, Bronxville, N.Y., Anzio (Italy) Meml. for Am. Battle Monuments Commn.; painting purchased by Cranbrook Found., Bloomfield Hills, Mich., 1939; painted mural Isaly Dairy Plant, Youngstown, O., 1940. Former instr. in life class Cooper Union Art Sch., life drawing Traphagen Sch. Fashion, N.Y.C. Am. Acad. in Rome fellow in painting. Recipient portrait prize at Plainfield Exhbn., 1951. Academician, N.A.D.; mem. Allied Artists Am., Alumni Am. Acad. in Rome. Address: Middle Valley NJ 07853

CIAMPI, MARIO JOSEPH, architect; b. San Francisco, Apr. 27, 1907; s. Guido and Palmira (Divita) C.; grad. Harvard, Sch. Architecture, 1932; m. Loretta Keane, Sept. 26, 1939. Licensed architecture Cal., 1935; design critic San Francisco Archtl. Club, 1935-40; archtl. practice Mario J. Campi y Assos., San Francisco, 1945—; travelled, studied architecture Europe, S.Am., Orient, Middle East, 1950-66; urban cons. San Francisco Market St. Devel. Plan, 1963—; lectr. various univs. Mem. adv. EFL, sch. planning lab. Stanford. Recipient numerous awards including 1st honor awards, state and nat. A.I.A. Honor Awards Programs; Collaborative medal of honor, 1960, Gold medal of honor, 1962, Archtl. League N.Y.; winner Nat. Competition Arts Center U. Cal., 1965. Fellow A.I.A.: mem. San Francisco Symphony Assn., San Francisco Mus. Art. Clubs: Harvard, Olympic, Serra. Work pub. in U.S., Europe. Home: 85 San Pablo Av San Francisco CA 94127 Office: 425 Bush St San Francisco CA 94108

CIARDI, JOHN, poet, educator; b. Boston, June 24, 1916; s. Carmin and Concetta (di Benedictis) C.; student Bates Coll., 1934-36; A.B. magna cum laude, Tufts Coll., 1938, D. Litt., 1960; M.A., U. Mich., 1939; H.D., Wayne U., 1963; LL.D., Ursinus Coll., 1964; L.H.D., Kalamazoo Coll., 1964; L.H.D., Bates Coll., 1970, Washington U., 1971, Ohio Wesleyan Coll., 1971; m. Myra Judith Hostetter, July 28, 1946; children—Myra Judith, John Lyle, Benn. Instr. English, U. Kansas City, 1940-42, 46; instr. Harvard, 1946-48, Briggs Copeland asst. prof., 1948-53; lectr. Am. Poetry Salzburg Seminar in Am. Studies, 1951; staff lectr. poetry Bread Loaf Writers Conf., 1947—, dir., 1955—; lectr. English, Rutgers U., 1953-54, asso. prof. English, 1954-56, prof. English, 1956-61; poetry editor Sat. Review, 1956—. Recipient Avery Hopwood award in Poetry, 1939; Blumenthal prize Poetry mag., 1944, Eunice Tietjens award, 1945, Levinson prize, 1947, Harriet Monroe Meml. award, 1955; Prix de Rome, Am. Acad. Arts and Letters, 1956. Served with USAAF, 1942-45. Fellow Am. Acad. Arts and Scis., Nat. Inst. Arts and Letters; mem. Nat. (dir. 1955-57, pres. 1958-59), N.E. (past dir.) coll. English assns., Phi Beta Kappa. Author: Homeward to America, 1940; Other Skies, 1947; Live Another Day, 1949; Mid-Century American Poets (anthology), 1950; From Time to Time, 1951; The Inferno of Dante (translation), 1954; As If, Poems New and Selected, 1955; I Marry You, 1958; The Reason for the Pelican, 1959; 39 Poems, 1959; How Does a Poem Mean?, 1959; Scrappy the Pup, 1960; (children's poems) I Met A Man, 1961, The Man Who Sang the Sillies, 1961, You Read to Me, I'll Read to You, 1962, Someone Could Win a Polar Bear, 1970; (poems) In the Stoneworks, 1961, In Fact, 1962, this Strangest Everything, 1966, Lives of X, 1971; (translation) Dante's Purgatorio, 1961, Dante's Paradiso, 1970; (story for children) The Wish-Tree, 1962; (poems for children) J.J. Plenty and Fiddler Den, 1963; (poems for children) You Know Who, 1964; (critical essays) Dialogue with an Audience, 1963; (poems) Person to Person, 1964; (for children) The Monster Den; (for children) The King Who Saved Himself From Being Saved, 1965; (poems) An Alphabestiary, 1966. Home: 359 Middlesex Av Metuchen NJ 08840 Office: Saturday Review 380 Madison Av New York City NY 10017

CIBORSKI, JOHN MICHAEL, metals co. exec.; b. Bklyn., Dec. 1, 1915; s. John and Helen (Szablewski) C.; B.S. in Chem. Engring., Purdue U., 1939; M.S., Harvard, 1940; m. Gula Marguerite Keesling, Sept. 1, 1940; children—Helen Elisabeth (Mrs. Richard Ort), Michael Gene. Mgr. nuclear service dept. Nat. Lead Co., 1956-63; with Titanium Metals Corp. Am., 1963—, v.p. operations and engring., 1967, pres., 1967—; instr. metallurgy Purdue U., 1942-43. Served with USNR, 1944-46. Methodist (trustee). Clubs: Downtown Athletic, Harvard (N.Y.C.). Home: 24 Bradwahl Dr Convent Station NJ 07961 Office: 195 Clinton Rd West Caldwell NJ 07006

CICCOLINI, ALDO, pianist; b. Naples, Italy, Aug. 15, 1925; studied with Paolo Denza, Naples Conservatory. Debut in Naples, 1942; toured France, Spain, S. Am.; made Am. debut with N.Y. Philharmonic, 1950. Address: care Angel Records 1750 N Vine St Hollywood, CA 90028.*

CICCONE, PASQUALE JOSEPH, hosp. dir.; b. Little Falls, N.J., Aug. 19, 1914; s. Vito and Diega (Sperazza) C.; B.A., N.Y. U., 1936; M.D. cum laude, Middlesex U., Waltham, Mass., 1942; m. Anne Daratani, Aug. 15, 1942; children—Barbara M., Joseph M. Intern St. Peter's Hosp., Bklyn., 1942-44; commd. USPHS, 1944, advanced through grades to capt., 1964; adminstr. War Shipping Program, Miami, Fla., 1944-48; chief med. officer Fed. Corrections, Instn., Denver, 1948-51; resigned, 1951; pvt. practice, Springfield, Mass., 1952-60; rejoined USPHS, 1960; chief med. officer Fed. Reformatory, Chillicothe, O., 1960-63; clin. dir. U.S. Med. Center, Springfield, Mo., 1963-65, dir., 1965—. Mem. A.M.A., Mass., Greene County med. socs., Med. Correctional Assn., Am. Correctional Assn., Clin. Soc. USPHS, Am. Acad. Hosp. Adminstrs., Springfield C. of C. K.C. Address: U S Med Center Springfield, MO 65802.

CICOGNANI, AMLETO GIOVANNI, sec. state Pope Paul VI; b. Brisighella, Ravenna, Italy, Feb. 24, 1883; s. William and Ann (Ceroni) C. Ordained priest Roman Catholic Ch., 1905; Ph.D., theology, canon and civil (Roman) law. Adviser, Sacred Roman Rota; ofcl. Sacred Congregation of Sacraments, 1910-14; minutante Sacred Consistorial Congregation, 1914-23, under-sec., 1923- 28; assessor Sacred Congregation for Oriental Ch., sec. Commn. for Codification Oriental Canon Law, 1928-33; titular archbishop Laodicea, apostolic del. U.S., 1933-58; consecrated in Rome, 1933; created cardinal, 1958; sec. Sacred Congregation for Oriental Ch., Vatican, 1960-61; sec. state to His Holiness Pope John XXIII, 1961-63; sec. state to Pope Paul VI, 1963—. Address: Vatican City

CIECIWA, ADAM J., banker. Vice pres., sr. auditor Central Nat. Bank Chgo. Office: La Salle and Monroe Sts Chicago IL 60603*

CIELEWICH, DONALD EUGENE, banker; b. Medina, N.Y., Feb. 4, 1923; s. John W. and Mary (Crowley) C.; (degree comml. banking,) Rutgers U., 1958; m. Ruth M. Feltz, Nov. 25, 1947; children—Scott Paul, Donald Eugene. With Marine Midland Bank- Western, Buffalo, 1950—, v.p., asst. to sr. v.p., 1963-64, v.p., asst. sr. loan officer, 1964-68, sr. v.p. charge retail banking depts., 1968- -; dir., mem. exec. com. Niagara Frontier Housing Devel. Corp. Faculty Consumer Bankers Sch., U. Va., 1966—. Mem. N.Y. State finance com. Am. Cancer Soc., 1967—, unit rep. Assembly Erie County, 1968—; gen. chmn. bus. div. United Fund, 1970; mem. citizens adv. group Assembly Subcom. on Econ. Devel. N.Y. State, 1970—. Mem. adv. bd. Rosary Hill Coll., Trocaire Coll. Served to 1st lt. USAAF, 1942-45; ETO. Mem. Buffalo Area C. of C., Am. (chmn. adv. bd. installment credit com. 2d Fed. Res. Dist.), N.Y. State (mem. exec. com.) bankers assns., Clarence C. of C., Consumer Bankers Assn. (bd. govs., mem. exec. com., com. chmn.), Robert Morris Assos. Home: 8740 Wenner Rd Williamsville NY 14221 Office: 241 Main St Buffalo NY 14203

CIEPLINSKI, MICHEL, former govt. ofcl.; b. Sosnowiec, Poland, Aug. 17, 1906; s. Konstanty and Josephine Cieplinski; diploma econs. Export Acad. Vienna, 1929; M.Polit.Sci., U. Bern, 1932; m. Anna Hanczakowska, July 26, 1934; 1 son, Richard. Came to U.S., 1939, naturalized, 1947. Bus. mgr. newspaper pub. concern, Krakow, Poland, 1930-39; advt., bus. mgr. Nowy Swiat Pub. Co., N.Y.C., 1940-48; pres. Champalain Advt. Co., N.Y.C. 1948-61, Inter-Racial Press Am., 1955-61; dep. and acting adminstr. Bur. Security and Consular Affairs, State Dept., 1961-63, dep. asst. sec. state for adminstrv. affairs, 1963-68. Adviser to U.S. Senator Green, 1948-60; commr. inter-group relations N.Y.C., 1954-61. Mem. Am. Fgn. Service Assn. Clubs: Overseas Press (N.Y.C.); National Press, International (Washington). Office: Dept of State Washington DC 20525

CIERESZKO, LEON STANLEY, educator; b. Holyoke, Mass., July 31, 1917; s. Albert Wojciech and Valerie Ann (Keller) C.; B.S. in Chemistry magna cum laude, Mass. State Coll., 1939; Ph.D. in Physiol. Chemistry, Yale, 1942; m. Esther Wynona Martin, May 1, 1943; 1 son, Leon Stanley. Research biochemist med.-research div. Sharp & Dohme, 1942-45; instr. biol. chemistry U. Utah Sch. Medicine, 1945-46; instr. chemistry U. Ill., 1946-48; mem. faculty U. Okla., Norman, 1948—, prof., 1956—, chmn. dept. chemistry, 1969-70; research participant Oak Ridge Inst. for Nuclear Studies, 1951-52; vis. research asso. Brookhaven Nat. Lab., summmer 1953; ofcl. participant U.S. Program in Biology, Internat. Indian Ocean Expdn., 1963; cons. prof. U. Okla. Sch. Medicine, 1967; vis. research prof. Coll. V.I., 1971; vis. investigator various marine labs. Lalor fellow Marine Biol. Lab., Woods Hole, Mass., 1951-52; Fulbright fellow Stazione Zoologica, Naples, Italy, 1955-56; recipient Regents' award U. Okla., 1967. Fellow A.A.A.S., Chem. Soc. (London), N.Y. Acad. Scis., Okla. Acad. Sci.; mem. Am. Chem. Soc., Geochem. Soc., Sigma Xi, Phi Kappa Phi, Phi Sigma, Lambda Tau, Phi Lambda Upsilon. Research and publs. in comparative biochemistry of marine invertebrates, chemistry of coelenterates, biogeochemistry of coral reefs. Home: 639 S Lahoma Av Norman OK 73069

CIKOVSKY, NICOLAI, artist; b. Pinsk, Province of Minsk, Russia, Dec. 10, 1894; s. Stephan Alexei and Olga (Ivanovna) C.; student Vilna Art Sch. (Russia), 1910-14, Penza Royal Art Sch., 1914-18, Moscow Higher Tech. Art Inst., 1921-23; m. Hortense Hilbert, Sept. 9, 1932; 1 son, Nicolai. Instr., Ekaterinenburg Higher Tech. Art Inst. (Russia), 1919-21, St. Paul Sch. of Art, summer 1934-35, Cin. Art Acad., 1935-36, Chgo. Art Inst., 1937. Represented in permanent collections including Art Inst. Chgo., Kansas City Art Mus., Wheaton (Mass.) Coll., Smithsonian Inst., U. Syracuse, U. Rochester. Recipient Art Inst. Chgo. bronze medal, 1930; Evening Star prize for best painting Washington Soc. Painters, 1941; La Tausca prize; Purchase prize Ranger Fund N.A.D., 1960; others. Nat. Inst. Arts and Letters grantee, 1962. Mem. Am. Soc. Artists Equity; asso. Nat. Acad. Home: 500 W 58th St New York City NY 10019 also Southampton LI Studio 30 E 14th St New York City NY 10003

CIMICHELLA, ANDRE, Cath. aux. bishop Montreal. Address: 2000 Sherbrooke St W Montreal 109 Quebec Canada*

CIMON, CHARLES, lawyer; b. Que., Que., Can., Sept. 2, 1931; B.A., Jesuites Coll., 1954; LL.L., Laval U., 1958. Admitted to Que. bar, 1958; partner firm Flynn, Rivard, Jacques, Cimon, Lessard & Le May, Que. Mem. Que., Canadian Bar Assns. Office: 2 Av Chauveau Quebec 4 Quebec Canada*

CINNATER, JOSEPH HENRY, aerospace co. exec.; b. St. Louis, Jan. 16, 1910; s. William and Cecilia (Braun) C.; student LaSalle U., Chgo., 1934-36, U. Houston, 1941-43; m. Margaret Marie Poston, Nov. 29, 1934; children—Margaret (Mrs. D.S. LaMure), Kathleen, Mary Jo, Nancy. Pub. accountant, St. Louis, 1936-40; with United Gas Pipe Line Co., Houston, 1940-44, Harrison-Abercrombie Oil Co., 1944, Lybrand, Ross Bros. & Montgomery, C.P.A.'s, St. Louis, 1944-48; with McDonnell Aircraft Corp., 1948-67, asst. treas., 1951-52, treas, 1952-67; treas. McDonnell-Douglas Corp., St. Louis, 1967-70, corporate v.p., treas., 1970—. Instr., Mo. Inst. Accountancy and Law, 1946-48. Chmn. auditing div. United Fund St. Louis, 1956-57. C.P.A., Tex. Mem. Mo. Soc. C.P.A.'s, Nat. Security Indsl. Assn., Financial Execs. Inst. (past pres. St. Louis). Home: 501 High Hampton Rd St Louis MO 63124 Office: P O Box 516 St Louis MO 63166

CIOCCO, ANTONIO, biostatistician; b. Columbus, O., May 1, 1908; s. Michael and Gelsomina (Ferraro) C.; Sc.D. (econs.), U. Naples (Italy), 1930; Sc.D. (hygiene), Johns Hopkins, 1936; m. Augusta Kershaw, Feb. 16, 1942; 1 dau., Angela. Research asso. otology Johns Hopkins Sch. Medicine, 1930-35, asso. biology Sch. Hygiene and Public Health, 1936-39; biometrician, pub. health adminstr. USPHS, Washington, 1939-49; prof., head dept. biostatistics U. Pitts. Grad. Sch. Pub. Health, 1949-69, prof. biostatistics, 1969—; sometime cons. USPHS, U.S. Children's Bur., Rockefeller Found., War Manpower Commn., Nat. Security Resources Bd. Mem. Am. Pub. Health Assn., Biometrics Soc., Soc. Research in Child Devel., Am. Soc. Human Genetics, A.A.A.S. Roman Catholic. Author monographs, contbr. articles various jours. dealing with investigations fields deafness, phys. growth and devel., human genetics, etc. Home: 5125 5th Av Pittsburgh PA 15232

CIPOLLARO, ANTHONY CAESAR, physician; b. N.Y.C., Aug. 5, 1900; s. Enrico and Maria (Maucione) C.; B.S., Dartmouth, 1924; M.D., Columbia, 1927; m. Rose Sullivan, July 2, 1925; children—Patricia (Mrs. Joseph Harper), Michael. Intern N.Y. Postgrad. Hosp., 1928-30; practice of dermatology and syphilology, N.Y.C., 1930—; attending dermatologist Mother Cabrini Hosp., 1934-49, cons., 1949-64; asst. prof. medicine Cornell U., 1948- 53, asso. prof., 1953-60; clin. prof., 1961-66, prof. emeritus, 1966—; prof., dir. dept. dermatology and syphilology N.Y. Polyclinic Med. Sch. and Hosp., 1949-60; dir. dept. dermatology Columbus Hosp., 1940-49, cons., 1949—; asst. attending physician dept. medicine N.Y. Hosp., 1948-60, asso. attending, 1960-65, attending physician, 1965-66, cons. physician, 1966—; cons. dermatologist Saranac Lake (N.Y.) Hosp., St. Joseph's Hosp., Far Rockaway, N.Y., 1940-67. Mem. nat. com. on radiation protection U.S. Dept. Commerce, Nat. Bur. Standards, 1947-55; mem. research and grants com., mem. bd. dirs., chmn. com. edn. N.Y.C. cancer com. Am. Cancer Soc., 1950-60, pres., 1960-62, chmn. exec. com., 1962-64. Recipient bronze medal Am. Cancer Soc. for outstanding contbns. to control of cancer, 1959; Clement Cleveland award for contbg. to cancer control N.Y.C. Cancer Com. of Am. Cancer Soc., 1961. Diplomate Am. Bd. Dermatology and Syphilology (pres. 1952). Fellow A.C.P.; mem. A.M.A. (mem. council phys. medicine and rehab. 1936-56, council on med. physics 1956-61; past chmn. dermatology sect.; editorial bd. archives of dermatology 1949-62), Am. Acad. Dermatology and Syphilology (pres. 1959, dir.), N.Y. State Med. Soc. (past chmn. dermatology sec.), Am. Dermatol. Assn. (pres. 1965-66, dir.), N.Y. (pres. 1958-59), R.I. (hon.), Manhattan dermatol. socs., N.Y. Acad. Medicine (past chmn. sect. dermatology and syphilolgy, chmn. com. on admissions 1960-61, sec. 1963-66); hon. mem. Australian, Venezuelan, Italian dermatol. socs.; corr. mem. Swedish, French dermatol. socs. Roman Catholic. Author: Cutaneous Cancer and Precancer (with G.M. MacKee), 1937; Skin Diseases in Children, rev. edit. 1946; X-Rays and Radium in the Treatment of Diseases of the Skin (with G.M. MacKee), rev. edit., 1946, 5th edit. (with Paul C. Crossland), 1967. Contbr. articles, chpts. med. publs. Home: 200 E 66th St New York City NY 10021 Office: 40 E 61st St New York City NY 10021

CIPRIANO, ANTHONY, sculptor; b. Buffalo, Sept. 30, 1937; s. Anthony and Luisa (Ciocca) C.; student Syracuse U., 1954, under Ivan Mestrovic, U. Notre Dame, 1955-58, George Grosz, Art Students League, 1958-59; fellow Fontaineblau (France) Sch. Painting and Sculpture, 1960, Kokoschka Sch., Salzburg, Austria, 1961. Exhibited in one-man shows Encore Gallery, Buffalo, 1955; exhibited group shows Nat. Inst. Arts and Letters, 1963, Salmagundi Club Exhbn., 1966; rep. permanent collection Bass Mus., Miami, Fla., Gallery Modern Art, N.Y.C., Huntington Hartford Collection, pvt. collections. Recipient 1st prize Salmagundi Club Exhbn., 1966. Leopold Schrepp Found. grantee, 1956; named Artist of Year, Am. Profl. Artists League, 1963. Studio: 24 W 56th St New York City NY 10019

CIRESI, ANTHONY SALVATORE, architect; b. Cleve., Jan. 12, 1906; s. Salvatore and Rosina (Rizzo) C.; B.Arch., Western Res. U., 1929, M.A., 1933; diploma Ecole des Beaux Arts Americaine, Fontainbleau, France, 1931, Beaux Arts Inst. Design, 1933; m. Gertrude M. Ceruti, June 22, 1940; children—Salvatore, Rosemary. Practice architecture, Cleve., 1932—; projects include: St. Rose of Lima Cath. Ch., Cleve., St. Michael Cath. Ch., Independence, O., St. Basil the Gt. Cath. Ch., Brecksville, O., Fire Tng. Sch., Cleve., Villa St. Rose Elderly Apts., Cleve. Critic archtl. design, water color, lectr. theory West Res. U., 1931-53. Mem. fine arts adv. com. City Plan Commn. Cleve. Recipient 1st prize archtl. design and water color painting Ecole des Beaux Arts Americaine, Fontainbleau, 1931; winner archtl. competition Gt. Lakes Expn., 1936. Registered architect, Ohio, N.Y., Pa., Va., Fla., Tex. Fellow A.I.A.; mem. Holy Name Soc., Epsilon Delta Rho. Roman Catholic. Home: 7643 Treelawn Dr Brecksville OH 44141 Office: 3030 Euclid Av Cleveland OH 44115

CISLER, WALKER LEE, elec. power exec.; b. Marietta, O., Oct. 8, 1897; s. Louis H. and Sara S. (Walker) C.; M.E., Cornell U., 1922; Eng.D., U. Mich., Stevens Inst. Tech., S.D. Sch. Mines and Tech.; LL.D., U. Detroit, Wayne State U., Marietta Coll., U. Akron, No. Mich. U., Mich. State U., Detroit Coll. of Law; D.Sci., U. Toledo, Ind. Tech. Coll., Mich. Technol. Inst.; D.Pub. Service, Detroit Inst. Tech., 1966; m. Gertrude Demuth Rippe, July 28, 1939; adopted children—Richard Rippe, Jane Rippe (Mrs. Albert J. Eckhardt, Jr.). Various engring. positions Pub. Service Electric & Gas Co., Newark, 1922-41; with WPB, Washington, 1941-43; chief engr. power plants Detroit Edison Co., 1945-47, exec. v.p., 1948-51, pres., 1951-64, chmn. bd., chief exec. officer, 1964—, also dir.; chmn. bd. Freuhauf Corp.; pres. Power Reactor Devel. Co., Atomic Power Devel. Assos., Inc.; dir. Detroit Bank & Trust Co., Burroughs Corp., Nat. Steel Corp.; adv. bd. internat. Chem. Bank N.Y. Trust Co. Cons. AID. Mem. bus. council Pres.'s Fund for peaceful Atomic Devel., Thomas Alva Edison Found.; chmn. internat. com. World Energy Conf.; mem. Nat. Acad. Scis.-Nat. Acad. Engring. Adv. Com. to U.S. Dept. Housing and Urban Devel. Hon. trustee U. Detroit; trustee emeritus Cornell, Cranbrook Inst. Sci., Com. Econ. Devel., Marietta Coll., No. Mich. Univ. Devel. Fund; hon. dir. Atomic Indsl. Forum. Served to col. AUS, 1943-45. Decorated by several fgn. govts., U.S. Fellow I.E.E.E. (Edison medal 1965); mem. Am. Soc. M.E. (pres. 1960, hon. mem.), Assn. Edison Illuminating Cos. (exec. bd.), Res. Officers Assn., Nat. Acad. Scis. (adv. com. for emergency planning), Am. Ordnance Assn., Soc. Am. Mil. Engrs. (pres. 1961), Edison Electric Inst. (pres. 1964, adv. bd.), Engrs. Joint Council (pres. 1964, dir.), Newcomen Soc. N.Am. Clubs: Detroit Economic (chmn.), Country, Athletic (Detroit); Metropolitan (Washington); Engineers, University, Fifth Avenue, Cornell, Brook (N.Y.C.). Home: 1071 Devonshire Rd Grosse Pointe Park MI 48230 Office: 2000 2d Av Detroit MI 48226

CISZEK, WALTER JOSEPH, clergyman, author; b. Shenandoah, Pa., Nov. 4, 1904; s. Martin and Mary (Mika) C.; M.A., St. Mary's (Mich.) Coll., 1928; student theology, Gregorian U., Rome, Italy, 1934-38. Joined Soc. of Jesus, 1928, ordained priest Roman Cath. Ch., 1937; missionary work in Eastern Poland, 1938- 39, USSR, 1939-41. Soviet Prison and camps, 1941-55. Author: (with D. L. Flaherty) With God in Russia-My 23 Years as a Priest in Soviet Prisons and Labor Camps and in Siberia, 1964. Address: John XXIII Center Fordham Univ Bronx NY 10458

CITRON, MINNA, artist; b. Newark, N.J., Oct. 15, 1896; d. Simon and Lena (Tobias) Wright; student Bklyn. Model Sch., Manual Tng. High Sch., Bklyn. Inst. Arts and Scis., Coll. City of N.Y., N.Y. Sch. Social Research; Art Students League; made 3 study trips to Europe; m. Henry Citron, Mary 22, 1916; 2 sons, Casper Henry, Thomas Wright. Held numerous one-man exhbns. including: Corcoran Gallery of Art Washington, 1941; Galerie Lydia Conti, 1947, Galerie R. Grenze, 1951 (both Paris France), El Lyceum, Havana, Cuba, 1949, 52, 56, Instituto Nacional de Cuba, 1957; Delacorte Gallery, N.Y.C., 1957, Museum de Arte Moderna, Saõ Paulo, Brazil, 1954, others in U.S.; tchr. life drawing at Bklyn. Mus., 1943-46. Lectr. Art Student's League, N.Y.C., 1949, 59. Received hon. mention Soc. of Am. Etchers ann. exhbns., 1942,43. Recipient oil painting award Norton Gallery and Sch. Art, West Palm Beach, Fla., 1948; purchase prize, 1st Dallas Print Assn., 1952, 2d Internat. Grenchen, Switzerland, 1960, Am. Color Print Soc., Phila., 1962, 3rd Invitational Print Ann., Brooks Meml. Art Gallery, Memphis, 1962; artist-in-residence grant Ford Found., 1965. Represented in permanent collections including Metropolitan Mus., Library of Congress; Modern Museum, N.Y.C., Chgo. Art Inst., Museu de Arte Moderna, Saõ Paulo, others. Executed murals depicting TVA activities U.S. Post Office, Newport, Tenn., mural for U.S. Post Office, Manchester, Tenn. Lectr. various univs. and colls. Mem. Soc. Am. Etchers, Art Students League, Am. Fedn. Arts, Artists Equity Am. Democrat. Citron Monograph (text by Jean Casson), Paris, 1947; (text by Jose Gomez, Sicre, Karl Kün, Wm. Lieberman), 1952; Gustave von Groschurtz, 1959; author articles. Home: 21 E 9th St New York City NY 10027

CIVIN, W. HAROLD, physician; b. Omaha, Oct. 28, 1916; s. Maurice and Yetta (Kaplan) C.; B.S., U. Neb., 1938; M.D., 1940; M.S. in Pathology, U. Minn., 1950; m. Dorothy Phyllis Louis, Sept. 2, 1946; children—Elaine Merry, Barbara Gail, Laurel Ann. Asst. pathologist Queen's Hosp., Honolulu, 1950-52, pathologist, 1952-64; chmn. dept., prof. med. lab. U. Cin. Coll. Medicine, 1964-71; sr. attending clin. pathologist William Beaumont Hosp., Royal Oak, Mich., 1971—. Pres. Hawaii Cancer Soc., late 1950's; mem. Med. Library Com., Honolulu, 1953-63. Served with AUS, 1942-45. Mem. Coll. Am. Pathologist (standards com. 1966-70), Sigma Nu, Alpha Omega Alpha. Contbr. articles to med. jours. Home: 2505 Twigwood Lane Cincinnati OH 45237 Office: William Beaumont Hospital Royal Oak MI 48072

CIZAUSKAS, ALBERT CHARLES, fgn. service officer; b. Bklyn., Mar. 1, 1920; s. Michael and Anna (Akelaitis) C.; B.A., Manhattan Coll., 1942; M.A., Notre Dame U., 1945, Yale, 1957; m. Genovaite Ambraziejus, Sept. 17, 1949; children—Albert Charles, Robert Paul, Thomas Joseph, Carol Anne, Richard Michael. Grad. asst. English, Notre Dame U., 1942; high sch. instr., Bklyn., 1944-45; joined U.S. Fgn. Service, 1945; vice consul, Karachi, Brit. India, 1945-46, Batavia, Netherlands Indies, 1946; vice consul, Surabaya, Indonesia, 1950-51, officer in charge, 1951-52; vice consul, Milan, Italy, 1952-55, consul, 1955; assigned German econ. affairs Bur. European Affairs, State Dept., 1957-60; 2d sec. embassy, Bonn, Germany, 1960-63, 1st sec., 1963-66; financial economist Dept. State, Washington, 1966—. Mem. Am. Fgn. Service Assn. Roman Catholic. Home: 2339 Walnut St Falls Church VA 22046 Office: Office Internat Financial and Devel Affairs Dept State Washington DC 20523

CIZEK, EUGENE DARWIN, architect; b. Alexandria, La., Nov. 20, 1940; s. Darwin and Matilda (Fabianek) C.; B.Arch. and Urban Design, La. State U., 1964; M. City Planning and Urban Design, Mass. Inst. Tech., 1966; engr. city planning, Delft Technische Hogeschool, Holland, 1967; Ph.D., Tulane U., 1972. Asst. prof. landscape architecture La. State U., 1968-70; vis. prof. architecture and planning Tulane U., 1971—, also planner New Orleans Community Improvement Agy., 1970—; archtl. planning cons. U.S. and Europe; planning cons. Rapides Parish Council of Local Govt. Bd. dirs. Metrolink Community Design Center of New Orleans; exhibiting graphic artist. Sears Found. fellow, 1964-66; Mass. Inst. Tech. Found. fellow, 1964-66; Fulbright scholar to Holland, 1966-67. Mem. A.I.A., Am. Inst. Planners (asso.), Am. Assn. Univ. Profs., La. Landmarks, Friends of the Cabildo, Phi Eta Sigma, Phi Kappa Phi, Tau Beta Pi, Phi Gamma Delta, Omicron Delta Kappa. Contbr. articles profl. jours. Home: 928 Kerlerec St New Orleans LA 70116

CIZIK, ROBERT, mfg. co. exec.; b. Scranton, Pa., Apr. 4, 1931; s. John and Anna (Paraska) C.; B.S., U. Conn., 1953; M.B.A., Harvard, 1958; m. Jane Morin, Oct. 3, 1953; children—Robert Morin, Jan Catherine, Paula Jane, Gregory Alan, Peter Nicholas. Accountant, Price Waterhouse & Co., C.P.A.'s, N.Y.C., 1953-54, 56; financial analyst Standard Oil Co., N.J., 1958-61; with Cooper Industries, Inc. Mt. Vernon, O., 1961—, exec. asst. corporate planning, treas., controller, 1963-67, v.p. for planning, 1967-69, exec. v.p., 1969—, also dir.; dir. Growth Fund Am. Served to 1st lt. USAF, 1954-56. Clubs: Lakeside Country, Houston Petroleum (Houston); Harvard (N.Y.C.). Home: 534 Ramblewood Rd Houston TX 77024 Office: 1st City Nat Bank Bldg Houston TX 77002

CLAAR, JOHN BENNETT, univ. adminstr.; b. Watson, Ill., Aug. 9, 1922; s. Harry Burnett and Ollie (Bryant) C.; student Blackburn Coll., 1939-40; B.S., U. Ill., 1947, M.S., 1948, Ph.D., 1959; m. Charlotte Lucille Wismer, Feb. 18, 1946; childrenNancy Jill, Bonnie Gail (Mrs. Thomas Bennett III), Richard Corbin. Engaged in farm mgmt. service Sangamon Valley Assn., 1948-51; farm mgmt. specialist U. Ill. at Urbana, 1951-55; chief farm mgmt. br. Fed. Extension Service, Dept. Agr., 1955-58, adminstrv. field rep., 1958-60; asso. dir. Coop. Extension Service, U. Ill., 1960-65, dir., 1965; asso. dean Coll. Agr., U. Ill. at Champaign, 1965, also exec. officer U. Ill. Peoria regional office, 1970; vis. prof. U. Wis., 1957. Cons. AID projects in India and Africa; chmn. extension com. orgn. and policy Nat. Assn. State Univs. and Land Grant Colls., 1968. Mem. Nat. 4-H Found. Served with USAAF, 1943-45. Recipient award Farm Credit System, 1968. Mem. Am. Assn. Agrl. Econs., Phi Kappa Phi, Gamma Sigma Delta, Epsilon Sigma Phi. Contbg. author: Goals and Values in Argiculture Policy, 1963; Cooperative Extension Service in the U.S., 1965. Home: 3329 Stonybrook Dr Champaign, IL 61820.

CLABAUGH, SAMUEL FRANCIS, business cons.; b. Birmingham, Ala., Mar. 6, 1890; s. John Henry and Martha Hinton (Graves) C.; A.B., U. Ala., 1909, A.M., 1910, LL.B., 1919; m. Mary Bacon Duncan, Oct. 30, 1913; children—Samuel F. (dec.), Mary (Mrs. Arthur F. Wright), Elizabeth (Mrs. John G. Johnson), Jean (Mrs. Henry C. Hiles), Doris (Mrs. Ivan Jadan); m. 2d, Maitland Thompson Linney, Mar. 17, 1948. Pub., Tuscaloosa (Ala.) News, 1917; v.p., cashier City Nat. Bank, 1919-26; pres. Ala. Nat. Life Ins. Co., 1926-27; pres. Protective Life Ins. Co., 1927-37, chmn. bd., 1937-39; chmn. bd. Fed. Home Loan Bank of Winston-Salem, 1939; pres.

Atlantic Life Ins. Co., 1939-41; govt. ofcl., 1949-53; bus. cons. indsl. moblzn. and indsl. def.; research cons. Center for Strategic Studies, Georgetown U.; pres. Westchester Corp., Washington, 1959. Exec. com. Life Ins. Sales Research Bur. (vice chmn.), 1931-32. Served to col. U.S. Army, 1940-49, faculty Indsl. Coll. of Armed Forces, 1947-49. Awarded Legion of Merit. Mem. Alumni Soc. U. Ala. (past pres.), Tuscaloosa C. of C. (past pres.), Druid City Hosp. (past pres.), Birmingham C. of C. (past pres.), Phi Beta Kappa, Beta Gamma Sigma, Sigma Alpha Epsilon. Methodist. Kiwanian (past internat. treas.). Clubs: Army and Navy, Cosmos (Washington). Co-author: East-West Trade: Its Strategic Implications, 1964; Trading with the Communists: A Research Manual, 1968. Contbr. on econ. warfare to Ency. Brit. Address: Westchester Apts Washington DC 20016

CLABAUGH, STEPHEN EDMUND, educator; b. Carthage, Tex., Apr. 2, 1918; s. Edmund Cumberland and Cosette (Hawthorn) C.; B.S., U. Tex., 1940, M.A., 1941; postgrad. U. Wis., 1941-42; Ph.D., Harvard, 1950; m. Patricia Sutton, Mar. 24, 1945: children—Catherine Neal, Cynthia Loyd, Deborah Jean. Geologist, U.S. Geol. Survey, 1942-46; asst. prof. U. Tex., Austin, 1947-51, asso. prof., 1951-55, prof., 1955—, chmn. dept. geology, 1962-66; cons. Zonolite Corp., summer 1951, Dow Chem. Co., summer 1952; tchr. spl. geology course Shell Oil Co., summers 1954-56; geologic editorial cons. Internat. Ency., 1959-61. Named Piper prof. geology for 1958. Mem. Geol. Soc. Am. (mem. council 1966-69, chmn. South Central sect. 1966-67), Mineral. Soc. Am., Soc. Econ. Geologists, Sociedad Geologia Mexicana, Am. Geophys. Union, Geochem. Soc., Mineral. Soc. Can., A.A.A.S., Tex. Acad. Sci., Sigma Xi. Asso. editor: Am. Mineralogist, 1963-67. Contbr. articles profl. jours. Home: 2316 Enfield Rd Austin TX 78703

CLAFF, C. LLOYD, mfr., banker, scientist; b. Perry, N.Y., Oct. 15, 1895: s. Mark Benedict and Mary Rose (Hameson) C.; student Bowdoin Coll., 1914-47, A.B., 1920, Sc.D., 1958; Harvard O.T.C., 1918; m. Frances Marion Staska, May 10, 1930; 1 son, Mark Mathias. Salesman paper box industry, N.Y.C., 1920-21; supt. M.B. Claff & Sons, Inc., Claffbox for shoes and printers, Randolph, Mass., 1921-29, pres., 1928—; v.p., dir. Randolph Trust Co., 1928—; pres., dir. Image Transfer, Inc., 1944—; pres., dir. Mark Co., 1956—; chmn. bd. Norfolk Industries, Brockton, Mass.; pres. Claffbox of P.R., Eldorado Beach, P.R., 1966—; treas. Single Cell Research Found., Inc., Randolph, Mass., Gen. Biol. Supply House, Turtox, Chgo., 1951—. Pres., Randolph Central Cemetery Assn. Trustee, clk. corp. Marine Biol. Lab., Woods Hole, 1945-65; mem. corp. Woods Hole Oceanographic Inst.; research asso. biology Brown U., 1938-39, Boston U. Grad. Sch., 1956—; research asso. surgery Harvard Med. Sch., 1945-65; research asso. physiology Albert Einstein Sch. Medicine; trustee Falmouth Hosp. Served as lt. (j.g.) USNR, 1917-19. Recipient Bronze Meritorious Service medal Am. Heart Assn., 1964. Fellow N.Y. Acad. Scis., A.A.A.S.; mem. Soc. Gen. Physiologists, N.E. Paper Box Mfg. Assn., Am. Soc. Protozoologists, Am. Biol. Photog. Assn., Am. Legion (past post comdr.), Sigma Xi. Mason (32, Shriner). Clubs: University, Harvard (Boston). Contbr. to biol. pubs. Patentee paper boxes, paper box machinery, candy and shoe stock control, membrane oxygenator for open heart surgery. Home: 5 Van Real Rd Randolph MA 02368 also Windy Pasture Woods Hole MA 02543 Office: 506 N Warren Av Brockton MA 02401

CLAFLIN, AVERY, composer, ret. bus. exec.; b. Keene, N.H., 1898; grad. Phillips Exeter Acad.; grad. Harvard; studied piano with John P. Marshall, composition with Archibald T. Davison. Business Career with French Am. Banking Corp., rising to pres.; now ret. Served with French Red Cross, World War I. Composer: (operas) The Fall of Usher, 1921, Hester Prynne, 1932, La Grand Breteche, 1947; Moby Dick Suite, 1929; (oratorio) Mary of Nazareth; (for orch.) Fishhouse Punch; (for string orch.) Teen Scenes; Four Pieces for Orchestra; (for string orch.) Larghetto and Shuffle; (chorus) Lament for April 15, also symphonies, piano concerto, ballet, chamber music, Hon. dir. Composers Recordsings, Inc. Address: 100 Stonehedge Dr N Greenwich, CT 06830.

CLAFLIN, ROBERT MALDEN, educator; b. Flint, Mich., Nov. 11, 1921; s. Robert Hugh and Kathryn Elizabeth (Ruhl) C.; D.V.M., Mich. State U., 1952; M.S., Purdue U., 1956, Ph.D., 1958; m. Barbara Ellen Garrison, June 21, 1957; children—Deborah Ann, Blair Lawrence, Kathryn Elizabeth. Faculty Purdue U., Lafayette, Ind., 1952—, prof. vet. pathology Sch. Vet. Sci. and Medicine, 1959—, head dept. vet. microbiology, pathology and pub. health, 1959—. Mem. Am. Vet. Med. Assn., Internat. Acad. Pathology, Conf. Research Workers Animal Diseases N.A., Sigma Xi, Phi Zeta, Phi Kappa Phi. Home: 706 Carrolton Blvd West Lafayette IN 47906 Office: Purdue U Lafayette IN 47907

CLAFLIN, WILLIAM H., III, investment banker; b. Boston, Jan. 27, 1920; s. William H., Jr. and Helen (Atkins) C.; A.B., Harvard, 1941; m. Nancy Allis, Feb. 23, 1942; children—William H. IV, Josephine D., Prentice W., Edward A., Elaine Y. Engaged as security salesman, 1946-48; partner Tucker, Anthony & R. L. Day, Boston, 1949—; dir. Tucker, Anthony Mgmt. Corp., Boston & Providence R.R. Corp., Soledad Sugar Co.; trustee Suffolk Franklin Savs. Bank. Trustee Boys' Clubs Boston; pres., bd. dirs., mem. exec. com. Mass. Eye and Ear Infirmary; trustee, mem. finance com. Wheaton Coll., Coll. Retirement Equities Fund; treas. Belmont Hill Sch.; bd. govs. Mus. Sci., N.Y. Stock Exchange. Served to maj. AUS, 1941-45. Mem. Nat. Assn. Security Dealers (dist. com. 1956-59, nat. gov., 1959-61, chmn. 1961-62). Clubs: Somerset (Boston); The Country (Brookline, Mass.). Home: 283 Prospect St Belmont MA 02178 Office: 74 State St Boston MA 02109

CLAGETT, MARSHALL, historian, educator; b. Washington, Jan. 23, 1916; s. M. Brice and Claire (Manning) C.; student Cal. Inst. Tech., 1933-35; A.B., George Washington U., 1937, A.M., 1938; Ph.D., Columbia, 1941; m. Susan M. Riley, Feb. 2, 1946; children—Kathleen A., Dennis M., Michael R. Instr. history Columbia, 1946-47; asst. prof. history of sci. U. Wis., 1947-49, asso. prof., 1949-54, prof., 1954-64; prof. Inst. Research in Humanities, 1959-64; mem. Inst. Advanced Study, Princeton, 1958-59, 63, prof., 1964—. Fellow Am. Acad. Arts and Scis., Medieval Acad. Am.; mem. History of Sci. Soc. (1st v.p. 1958-62, pres. 1962-64), Am. Philos. Soc. (v.p. 1969-71), Acad. Internat. History Sci. Author: Giovanni Marliani and Late Medieval Physics, 1941; (with Ernest Moody) The Medieval Science of Weights, 1952; Greek Science in Antiquity, 1956; Mechanics in the Middle Ages, 1959; Archimedes in the Middle Ages, 1964; Nicole Oresme and the Medieval Geometry of Qualities, 1969. Home: 147 Crestview Dr Princeton, NJ 08540.

CLAGETT, OSCAR THERON, surgeon; b. Jamesport, Mo., Oct. 19, 1908; s. Oscar Frederic and Effie (Stevens) C.; M.D., U. Colo., 1933, D.Sc., 1962; M.S., U. Minn., 1938, postgrad. 1935-40; m. Alicia M. Eames, Nov. 3, 1934; children—Mary Alice, Nancy Jane, Barbara Joan, Martha Eleanor, James Stevens, Robert Scott. Intern Colo. Gen. Hosp., Denver, 1933-34; practice medicine, Glenwood Springs, Colo., 1934-35; fellow in surgery Mayo Found. Grad. Sch., 1935-38; asst. surgeon Mayo Clinic, 1938-40; head sect., div. of surgery, 1940, prof. surgery Mayo Found. Grad. Sch. U. Minn., 1951—; vis. prof. surgery Johns Hopkins Hosp., 1957. Recipient Norlin medal, U. Colo., 1947; Clement Price Thomas award Royal Coll. Surgeons Eng., 1968. Past sec.-treas. Am. Bd. Thoracic Surgery. Fellow A.C.S., Am. Assn. for Thoracic Surgery (past pres.), Am. Central, Western (past pres.) surg. assns., Mexican Nat. Acad. Surgery, Royal Coll. Surgeons Eng. (hon.); hon. mem. Royal Australasian Coll. Surgeons, Royal College Surgeons in Ireland, Thoracic Soc. (Eng.), Soc. Thoracic Surgeons Gt. Britain and Ireland, Royal Coll. Surgeons Eng., Societa Italiana di Chirurgia (corr.). Home: 1611 Merrihills Dr Rochester MN 55901 Office: Mayo Clinic Rochester MN 55901

CLAGUE, EWAN, economist; b. Prescott, Wash., Dec. 27, 1896; s. John and Eleanor Christian (Cooper) C.; A.B., U. Wash., 1917, A.M., 1921; Ph.D., U. Wis., 1929; m. Dorothy Vermilya Whipple, May 29, 1923; children—Ewan (dec.), Anne Vermilya, Llewellyn Whipple, Christopher Karran. Instr. in econs. U. Wash., 1919-21, U. Wis., 1921-26; commr. of conciliation Bur. Labor Statistics, U.S. Dept. Labor, 1926-28; research asst. Bus. Research Bur., Met. Life Ins. Co., 1928-29; research asst. Inst. Human Relations, Yale, 1930; dir. research and prof. social research Pa. Sch. Social Work, Phila., 1931-36; asso. dir. Bur. Research and Statistics and Social Security Bd., 1936-37, dir., 1937-40; dir. Bur. Employment Security, Social Security Bd., 1940-46; commr. labor statistics Dept. Labor, 1946-54, 55-65, spl. asst. to sec. of labor, 1954-55, cons. to sec. of labor, 1966-68; sr. asso. Leo Kramer, Inc., Washington, 1968—. Mem. U.S. nat. com. on UNESCO. Served in U.S. Army, 1917-19. Named one of top ten govt. career men in fed. govt. Nat. Civil Service League, 1958. Mem. Am. Statis. Assn., Am. Econ. Assn. Author: the Bureau of Labor Statistics, 1968; (with others) An All-Volunteer Army, 1970; the older Worker and the Union, 1971. Home: 3821 Woodley Rd NW Washington DC 20016 Office: Leo Kramer Inc 1835 K St NW Washington DC 20006 ☆

CLAIBORNE, JERRY DAVID, coll. football coach; b. Hopkinsville, Ky., Aug. 26, 1928; s. James Johnson and Kathrine (Trimmer) C.; B.A., U. Ky., 1950; m. Anne Faye Hooks, June 30, 1951; children—Jerry David. Jonathan Edward, Kathrine Trimmer, Eileen Glen. Head football and basketball coach Augusta Mil. Acad., Ft. Defiance, Va., 1950-52; asst. football coach U. Ky., 1952-54, U. Ala., 1958-61, Tex. A. and M. Coll., 1954-57, U. Mo., 1957; head football coach Va. Poly. Inst., 1961-71; asst. head football coach U. Colo., Boulder, 1971—. Named So. Conf. Coach of Year, 1963; Dist. Coach of Year, Am. Football Coaches Assn., 1966. Home: 195 Inca Pkwy Boulder CO 80303

CLAIBORNE, JOHN WELLONS, Jr., physician, hosp. exec.; b. Dyersburg, Tenn., June 1, 1908; s. John Wellons and Ella (Bowen) C.; B.A., Vanderbilt U., 1929, M.D., 1932; m. Jennie Cocke, Feb. 4, 1934; children—Constance (Mrs. Philip Putney), John Wellons III. Intern Harper Hosp., Detroit, 1932-33, resident, 1933; commd. 1st lt., M.C., U.S. Army, 1933, advanced through grades to col., 1944; resigned, 1947; dir. VA Hosps., Jefferson Barracks, 1949-52, St. Louis, 1953-63, Houston, 1963—; mem. clin. faculty Coll. Medicine Baylor U. Sch. Dentistry U. Tex. at Houston. Bd. dirs. Houston United Fund, U.S.O., A.R.C. Decorated French Croix de Guerre with gold star. Fellow Am. Coll. Hosp. Adminstrs.; mem. A.M.A., Houston Area Hosp. Assn. (pres. 1966-67), Res. Officers Assn., Houston Fed. Bus. Assn. (pres. 1969—), Phi Beta Pi. Presbyn. Mason (32). Home: 2002 Holcombe Blvd Houston TX 77025 Office: VA Hosp Houston TX 77031

CLAIBORNE, RANDOLPH ROYALL, Jr., bishop; b. Farmville, Va., Nov. 7, 1906; s. Randolph Royall and Mary Thomas (Clark) C.; B.A., U. Va., 1928; B.D., Va. Theol. Sem., 1931, D.D., 1950; D.D., U. of South, 1949; m. Clara Virginia Kinney Stribling, 1955. Ordained to ministry, P.E. Ch., 1931, rector St. James Ch., Macon, Ga., 1931-38; also priest-in-charge St. Andrews Ch., Fort Valley, Ga., St. Luke's Ch., Scoftsboro, Ala., 1938-49; rector Ch. of Nativity, Huntsville, Ala., 1938-49; consecrated suffragen bishop P.E. Ch. Diocese Ala., 1949-53; bishop P.E. Ch., Diocese of Atlanta, 1953—. Home: 108 17th St NE Atlanta GA 30309 Office: 2744 Peachtree Rd NE Atlanta GA 30305

CLAIN-STERANELLI, VLADIMIR, museum curator; b. Czernowitz, Austria, Jan. 2, 1914; s. Wilhelm Klein and Theodora Stefanelli; M.A., U. Carol II, 1936; Ph.D., 1938; m. Elvira Olinescu, Dec. 29, 1938; 1 son, Alexander. Came to U.S., 1951, naturalized, 1956. Librarian, Seminar for South-East European History, 1932-37; asst. Seminar Greek and Roman Epigraphy, in charge coin collections Carol II U., Cernauti-Czernowitz, 1936-38; asst. in temporary charge excavations at Mangalia, 1936-37; museum asst. Museul Regele Carol II, 1937-38; charge Greek Coin Corpus, Prussian Acad. Scis., 1939; cons. coins and medals, firms in Rome and N.Y.C., 1949-56; durator div. numismatics U.S. Nat. Mus., Smithsonian Instn., 1956—. Adviser div. continuing edn. Roosevelt U., 1966; adviser on status gold coins Dept. Treasury. Recipient Prix de Rome, 1939-40. Fellow Royal Numis. Soc. (London); mem. Am. Numis. Assn. (hon. life mem.), Archaeol. Inst. Am., Internat. Inst. Conservation Historic and Artistic Works, Internat. Bank Note Soc., Washington, Md. numis. socs., Ga. Numis. Assn. (hon.). Contbr. papers on numismatics to tech. lit. Home: 2608 N Nelson St Arlington VA 22207 Office: Smithsonian Instn Washington DC 20560

CLAIR, ARNOLD VIRGIL, musician, educator; b. Moline, Ill., Apr. 13, 1907; s. Gust A. and Anna M. (Peterson) C.; student Knox Coll., 1925-26, diploma in violin Juilliard Sch. Music, 1932; M.A., U. Ia., 1934; student U. Minn., 1940; m. Loretta Jane Kenyon, June 20, 1949. With Claremont Quartet, N.Y.C., 1930-32; asst. condr., violin soloist Youngstown Symphony Orch., 1927- 29; with Bklyn. Symphony Orch., 1929-32; instr. Kan. Wesleyan U., 1934- 35, Buena Vista Coll., 1935-36, U. Mont., 1936-40, State Tchrs. Coll., Potsdam, N.Y., 1940-46; prof. U. R.I., 1946-, head music dept., dir. music, 1950-, dir. High Sch. Music Camp, 1949-60. Mem. bd. dirs. R.I. Philharmonic Orch.; adjudicator, condr. Music Educators Nat. Conf. All- State groups. Served with AUS, 1942-45. Mem. Music Educators Nat. Conf. (state pres. chmn. com. on higher edn.), Am. String Tchrs. Assn., R.I. Fedn. Music Clubs (pres. 1958-69), Am. Assn. U. Profs., Coll. Music Soc., Music Tchrs. Nat. Assn., Am. String Tchrs. Assn., Amateur Chamber Music Players, Fphi Mu Alpha Sinfonia. Home: 39 Cherry Rd Kingston RI 02881

CLAIR, MILES NELSON, cons. civil engr.; b. Lickdale, Pa., Sept. 7, 1900; s. Harry Monroee and Victoria (Sussana) C.; B.S. in Engring., Drexel Inst Tech., 1921, D.Eng. (hon.), 1960; S.M. in Civil Engring., Mass. Inst. Tech., 1923; m. Carolyn Florence Green, June 16, 1928; children—Cynthia Yorke (Mrs. Stan Norkin), Valerie de Luce (Mrs. John D. Stelling), Ardith Monroe. Positions with constrn. orgn. in field and office, 1919-22; asst. instr. Mass. Inst. Tech., 1923-24; instr. civil engring. Drexel Inst. Tech., 1924-25; with Thompson & Lichtner Co., Inc., Brookline, Mass., 1925—, pres., 1949—; projects include civilian and mil. airports; spl. lectr. Mass. Inst Tech., Northeastern U., Harvard. Mem. Am. Com. on Large Dams; mem. bldg. code com. City of Boston, 1936-65; air transp. com. New Eng. Council, 1958-62; adv. com. bldg. U.S. C. of C., 1960—; mem. mayor's adv. com. on pub. bldgs., Newton, Mass., 1960-64. Adv. bd. South End Boys Club, Boston, 1940—; nat. councillor U.S.O., 1957—; pres. Salvation Army Assn. Greater Boston, 1958-61; mem. Mass. Com. on Children and Youth, 1964—. Recipient Bronze Keystone medal Boys Club Am., 1958; citation of achievement City of Phila., 1961; Man and Boy award Boys Club Am. and Salvation Army, 1963; Ralph W. Horne Fund award Boston Soc. Civil Engrs., 1966; Howard Coonley medal U.S.A. Standards Inst., 1968; named hon. col. Salvation Army Assn., 1967. Fellow Am. Soc. C.E. (pres. New Eng. sect. 1948; chmn. standards com.); mem. S.A.R., Am. Soc. for Testing Materials (pres. 1961-62), Am. Concrete Inst. (dir. 1940), Am. Standards Assn. (v.p. 1961-62, bd. dirs.), Boston Soc. Civil Engrs. (Herschel prize 1950, pres. 1954-55), Boston Aero. Club, Nat. Aero. Assn., S.A.R., Phi Kappa Phi, Tau Beta Pi. Mason. Author numerous tech. papers, contbr. articles to tech. publs. Pioneered devel. ready-mixed concrete, light-weight aggregates, precast concrete, constrn. quality control use of compacted fills for bldg. founds. Home: 17 Dorset Rd Waban MA 02168 Office: 8 Alton Pl Brookline MA 02146

CLAIR, REGIS DAVID, ins. co. exec.; b. Pitts., Mar. 21, 1907; s. John Joseph and Elizabeth (Foley) C.; student U. Pitts., 1925-26; m. Matilda Katherine Niemeyer, Jan. 19, 1936; 1 son, Robert David. With N.Y. Life Ins. Co., N.Y.C., 1927-, adminstrv. asst., 1946-48, asst v.p., 1948-54 2d v.p., 1954-59, v.p., 1959-. Republican. Roman Catholic. Home: 25 Homewood Av Allendale NJ 07401 Office: 51 Madison Av New York City NY 10010

CLAIR, RENE, motion picture writer, dir.; b. Paris, France, Nov. 11, 1898; student Lycee Montaigne, Lycee Louis le Grand, Paris; Dr. honoris causa, Cambridge U. (Eng.), 1956, Royal Coll. Art (Eng.), 1967; m. Bronja Clair, 1925; 1 son, Jean Francois. Writer, newspaperman, 1919-22, writer, dir. motion pictures, including: Paris oui dort, 1923; Entr'acte, 1924; The Italian Straw Hat, 1928; Sous les Toits de Paris, 1930; Le Million, 1931; A Nous la Liberte, 1932; The Ghost Goes West, 1936; I Married a Witch, 1942; Le Silence est D'or, 1947; Les Belles de Nuit, 1953; Les Grandes Manoeuvres, 1955; Porte des Lilas, 1957; Les Ftes Galantes, 1965; and others. Served with French Red Cross, 1917. Decorated Legion of Honor (France). Mem. Academie Francaise. Author: Adams, 1926; Reflexion Faite, 1951; La Princesse De Chine, 1951; Comedies et Commentaires, 1959; Cinema d'Hier Cinema d'aujourd'hui, 1970. Address: 11 bis av de Madrid 92 Neuilly sur Seine France

CLAIRMONT, M.M., corp. exec.; b. Rumania, 1906. Chmn., pres. Lee Nat. Corp.; pres., dir. Chesterfield Realty Corp.; pres., treas., dir. Clairdale Enterprises, Inc., Kershaw Corp. Home: 1016 Fifth Av New York City NY 10028 Office: 545 Madison Av New York City NY 10022

CLAMANN, HANS GEORG, physiologist; b. Gross-Schwuelper, Germany, Aug. 21, 1902; s. Martin and Hilma (Schick) C.; student U. Güttingen, Munich U.; M.D., U. Heidelberg, 1929; m. Maria Catherine Mueller, Oct. 1, 1937; childrenHans Peter, York Hilmar, Carin Catherine. Came to U.S., 1947, naturalized, 1955. Dep. dir. Inst. Aviation Medicine, Berlin, Germany, 1943-45; prof. biophysics USAF Air U., 1958; chief dept. physiology and biophysics USAF Sch. Aviation Medicine, 1959; chief dept. space medicine Aerospace Med. Center, Brooks AFB, Tex., 1960-68; chief scientist Hdqrs., Aerospace Medical Divison, Brooks Air Force Base, Texas, 1968-. Recipient of Lilienthal plaque for personal research pertaining to oxygen poisoning, explosive decompression, 1939. Mem. Am. Physiol. Soc., N.Y. Acad. Scis., Instrument Soc. Am., A.A.A.S., Soc. Exptl. Biology and Medicine. Contbr. articles profl. publs. Home: 310 S Sequin Rd Converse TX 78109 Office: Hdqrs AMD (AMGS) Brooks AFB, TX 78235.

CLAMP, JESSE CARL, Jr., mfg. co. exec.; b. Helena, Ark., Sept. 29, 1920; s. Jesse Carl and Ethel May (Dunlap) C.; A.B., Duke, 1942; student Mass. Inst. Tech., 1942-43, 46-48; m. Kate Claywell Gantt, Dec. 27, 1941; children—Jesse Carl III, Stephen Claywell, Helen Dunlap. Teaching and research asst. econs. Mass. Inst. Tech., 1942-43, 46-48; instr. econs. Duke, 1948-49; asst. prof. econs. Fla. State U., 1949-51; regional dir. case analysis Wage Stblzn. Bd., 1951-53; personnel mgr. Armour & Co., 1953-58; dir. corp. planning and devel. Gen. Mills, Inc., 1958-63; v.p. corp. planning Allis-Chalmers Mfg Co., Milw., 1963-66, sr. v.p., 1966—, also dir.; dir. Internat. Gen. Ins. Co., Milwaukee County Bank. Served with USAAF, 1943-46. Mem. Assn. Corp. Growth, Nat. Assn. Bus. Economists, Ind. Devel. Research Council, Am. Econ. Assn., Indsl. Relations Research Assn., Phi Beta Kappa, Omicron Delta Kappa, Delta Sigma Pi, Kappa Kappa Psi, Sigma Phi Epsilon. Methodist. Clubs: University, Milwaukee Country, Town (Milw.); Chemists (N.Y.C.). Home: 7855 N Club Circle Fox Point WI 53217 Office: Allis-Chalmers Mfg Co Milwaukee WI 53201

CLANCY, DONALD DANIEL, congressman; b. Cin., July 24, 1921; s. James and Margaret (Headley) C.; student Xavier U., 1939-43; LL.B., U. Cin., 1948; m. Betty Mangeot, Nov. 23, 1949; children—Kathleen, Patricia, Donald Daniel. Admitted to Ohio bar, 1948, since practiced in Cin.; former mem. firm Clancy, Martino & Wrassman. Mem. city council, Cin., 1951-57, mayor, 1958-60; member 87th-92d Congresses 2d District, Ohio. Mem. Am. Legion. K.C. Club: Hamilton County Republican (pres. 1955-56). Home: 7403 Green Farms Dr Cincinnati OH 45224 Office: Longworth House Office Bldg Washington DC 20515

CLANCY, HAROLD EUGENE, publisher; b. Quincy, Mass., Sept. 2, 1920; s. Eugene and Lillian M. (Casey) C.; J.D., Boston Coll., 1961; D. Journalism, Suffolk U., 1969; m. Ernestine Morrill, June 4, 1948; children—Michael, Garrett, Ann, Stephen, Mark, Katherine, Paul, Peter. Sports reporter Quincy Patriot Ledger; radio news writer United Press, 1946-48, night bur. mgr., Boston, 1948; city editor, then exec. news editor Boston Herald-Traveler Corp., 1952-56, mng. editor, 1956-61, 1st v.p., asst. pub., dir., 1964-68, pres., pub., 1968—; pres. WHDH, Inc., AM-FM-TV, 1968—. Admitted to Mass. bar, 1961; practice of law, Boston, 1961-64. Sponsor United Negro Coll. Fund; pres. Boston council Boy Scouts Am., 1969-70. Bd. dirs. Boston Better Bus. Bur., United Community Services. Served as 1st lt., inf. AUS, World War II. Decorated Bronze Star, Silver Star, Purple Heart, Combat Infantryman's badge; recipient Asso. Press Reporting award, 1956, Am. Heritage Found. award; named one of 10 Outstanding Young Men of Mass., Boston Jr. C. of C., 1950. Mem. Greater Boston C. of C. (dir. 1970—), Sigma Delta Chi. Contbr. articles to popular mags. Home: 8 Conant Rd Weston MA 02193 Office: 300 Harrison Av Boston MA 02106

CLANCY, JAMES HARVEY, educator, theatrical dir.; b. 1912; A.B., San Jose State Coll.; M.A., Ph.D., Stanford. Formerly mem. faculty San Jose State Coll.; vis. prof. Stanford, 1948, 50; asst. editor Ednl. Theatre Jour., 1954; asso. editor, 1955-56, editor, 1957—; prof. drama State U. Ia., 1958-61; dir. theatre, prof. drama lit. Stanford, 1961-62; dir. theatre, prof. English, Dartmouth, Hanover, N.H.; now prof., dir. theatre Cornell U., also chmn. theatre dept. Served with USAAF, 1942-45. Ford Found. grantee, 1959. Contbr. articles profl. jours. Home: 107 Ellis Hollow Creek Rd Ithaca NY 14850

CLAPP, ALFRED COMSTOCK, lawyer; b. N.Y.C., June 8, 1903; s. Alfred Chapin and Anna (Roth) C.; Ph.B., U. Vt., 1923, LL.D., 1957; J.D., Harvard, 1927; m. Catharine Shotwell, June 11, 1932; children—Alfred Comstock, Edward Shotwell, John Wells, Roger Stewart. Admitted to N.J. bar, 1927, since in active practice; faculty Mercer Beasley Law Sch., Newark, 1929-30; dep. surrogate, adv. master orphan's ct. Essex County, 1939-47; counsel on drafting state constn. N.J. Legislature, 1944; prin. draftsman rules civil procedure, cts. of N.J., 1947-48; drafted revision N.J. statutes on adminstrn. justice, 1950-53; faculty law sch. N.Y. U., 1947-52; prof., dean law sch. Rutgers U., 1951-53, lectr., 1971—; presiding judge, appellate div. Superior Ct. of N.J., 1953-58; sr. partner Clapp & Eisenberg, Newark, 1958—. Chmn. Inst. Continuing Legal Edn., 1961—; rep. N.J. at U.S. Atty. Gen.'s Conf. Ct. Congestion, 1960; chmn. N.J. Supreme Ct.'s Rules Com. 1959—; mem. State Constl. Conv., 1947, 66. Republican state committeeman Essex County, 1958-59; state senator from Essex County 1948-53; del. Rep. Nat. Conv., 1960; state chmn. Rep. candidate for U.S. senator, 1960; state campaign mgr. Rep. candidate for gov., 1961. Pres., Brookside Sch., Montclair, 1945-47; past pres. Family Welfare Soc., Montclair; regent Am. Coll. Probate Counsel, 1969—. Mem. Am., N.J., Essex County (past pres.), Newark bar assns., Am. Law Inst., Am. Judicature Soc., Inst. Practicing Lawyers N.J. (pres.), Constl. Conv. Assn. (pres. 1959), Phi Beta Kappa (past pres. North Jersey), Sigma Nu, Phi Delta Phi. Presbyn. (elder). Author: Wills and Administration (3 vols.), 3d edit., 1962; Will Service Manual of New Jersey, 1964. Editor: N.J. Law Jour., 1942-53, 70—. Home: 244 S Mountain Av Montclair NJ 07042 Office: 744 Broad St Newark NJ 07102

CLAPP, EUGENE HOWARD, II, mfg. exec.; b. Brookline, Mass., Sept. 22, 1913; s. George Allen and Sarah Lillian (Clapp) C.; B.S., Lafayette U., 1936; m. Maud Millicent Greenwell, Apr. 10, 1943; children—Eugene Howard III, Candace Millicent. With Penobscot Co., Great Works, Me., 1937-68, treas., 1946-50, pres., 1950-65, chmn. bd., 1960-67, dir., 1946-68, also gen. mgr.; with Tileston & Hollingsworth Co., Mattapan, Mass., 1946-67, treas., 1946-53, chmn. bd., 1953-68, dir., 1946-68; pres., dir. Penobscot Capital Investment Co., Pine Tree Land Co.; treas., dir. King Spruce Co.; dir. Arkwright Boston Mfrs. Mut. Ins. Co., Am. Mut. Ins. Co., Am. Mut. Ins. Co. Boston, AM Life Ins. Co., Am. Mut. Corp. Justice of peace. Bd. dirs. Mass. Taxpayers Found., Douglas A. Thom Clinic for Children; bd. dirs., treas. U. Me. Pulp & Paper Found.; bd. dirs. Asso. Industries Mass., Newton-Wellesley Hosp., Mass. div. Am. Cancer Soc.; trustee Children's Hosp. Med. Center, Lafayette Coll.; bd. mgrs., v.p. Roxbury Home for Aged Women. Served with OSS, 1942-46. Mem. Phi Gamma Delta (chmn. bd. trustees). Republican. Episcopalian. Mason. Home: 78 Arnold Rd Wellesley Hills MA 02181 Office: 10 High St Boston MA 02110

CLAPP, JAMES FORD, Jr., architect; b. Cambridge, Mass., Nov. 18, 1908; s. James Ford and Leonora (Fanshawe) C.; A.B., Harvard Coll., 1931; M.Arch., Harvard Grad. Sch. Design, 1935; m. Grace G. FitzGerald, June 3, 1933; children—James Ford III, Susan Fanshawe, Deborah FitzGerald. Architect firm Coolidge Shepley Bulfinch & Abbott, Boston, 1953; asso. architect Shepley, Bulfinch Richardson & Abbott, Boston, 1953-60, partner, 1960—; archtl. cons. Acadia U., also to Keyes D. Metcalf for book Planning Academic and Research Library Buildings, 1965; pres. Boston Archtl. Center, 1955-56. Mem. Cambridge Hist. Commn., 1969—; permanent sec. John Worthington Ames Scholarship, 1966—. Fellow A.I.A.; mem. Boston Soc. Architects (sec. 1957, centennial chmn. 1967), Mass. State Assn. Architects (v.p. 1958-59), Boston Numismatic Soc. (pres. 1949-50), New Eng. (pres. 1956-57), Am. (gen. chmn. 1960) numismatic assns. Home: 20 Bellevue Av Cambridge MA 02138 Office: 1 Court St Boston MA 02108

CLAPP, LEALLYN BURR, educator; b. Paris, Ill., Oct. 13, 1913; s. Ivan Burr and Blanche (Tate) C.; B.Ed., E.Ill. U., 1935, Pd.D. (hon.), 1956; M.A., U. Ill. at Urbana, 1939, Ph.D., 1941; LL.D. (hon.), R.I. Coll., 1964; m. Florence Cottingham, Aug. 28, 1940; children—Peter, Jean. Tchr. math. Paris (Ill.) High Sch., 1935-38; mem. faculty Brown U., 1941—, prof. chemistry, 1956—; lectr. chemistry, Chile, 1961, Nigeria, 1962, India, 1965, 68, 71, Uruguay, 1967, Pakistan, 1970. Mem. New Eng. Assn. Chemistry Tchrs. (sec. 1952-57, pres., 1961-63), Am. Chem. Soc. (vis. scientist 1956—; com. prof. tng. 1958-67; chmn. div. chemistry edn. 1959-60; award western Conn. sect. 1969). Author: Chemistry of the Covalent Bond, 1957; Chemistry of the OH Group, 1967 (Japanese 1968, French 1969). Home: 125 Congdon St Providence RI 02906

CLAPP, M. ROGER, mfg. co. exec.; b. 1910; B.S. in Mech. Engring., Tex. Tech. U.; M.S. in Mech. Engring., Purdue U., married. Mem. faculty Case Inst. Tech., 1938- 40; with Lubrizol Corp., 1941—, pres., chief exec. officer, 1966—, also dir.* 3701 Greenwood Dr Cleveland OH 44124*

CLAPP, NORMAN MOSES, govt. ofcl.; b. Ellsworth, Wis., Oct. 28, 1914; s. Rufus Newell and Jane (Erdman) C.; B.A., Lawrence Coll., 1937; m. Analoyce Elkington, Dec. 26, 1936; children—David Allen, William Reynold, Douglas Edwin. Staff asst. to U.S. Senator Robert M. LaFollette, Jr., 1935-37, 39-42; investigator, mediator Wis. Labor Relations Bd., 1937, 38-39; staff employee NLRB, 1939; minority expert finance com. staff U.S. Senate, 1942-44; editor, pub. Grant County Ind., Lancaster, Wis., 1944-58; partner Muscoda Pub. Co. (Wis.), 1953-58; exec. dir. Democratic Party of Wis. in Western Wis., 1959-60; adminstr. Rural Electrification Adminstrn., 1961-69; mgmt. and pub. relations cons., Washington, 1969-71; sec. Wis. Dept. Transp., Madison, 1971—. Democratic candidate for U.S. Congress 3d Dist. Wis., 1956-58, 60; del. Dem. Nat. Conv., 1956. Mem. Phi Beta Kappa, Sigma Delta Chi. Conglist. Mason; mem. Order Eastern Star. Home: 1214 Brookwood Rd Madison WI 53711 Office: Wis Dept Transp 25 W Main St Madison WI 53703

CLAPP, NORTON, lumber co. exec.; b. Pasadena, Cal., April 15, 1906; s. Eben Pratt and Mary Bell (Norton) C.; A.B., Occidental Coll., 1928, LL.D., 1958; Ph.B., U. Chgo., 1928, J.D., 1929; D.C.L., Coll. Puget Sound, 1958; m. Mary Cordelia Davis, July 8, 1929 (dec.); children—James Hayes, Matthew, Ralph (dec.), Roger (dec.); m. 2d, Evelyn Beatrice Booth, Jan. 15, 1941 (dec.); children—William Hayes, Stephen Gilbert; m. 3d, Jane Bumiller, Apr. 19, 1952. Admitted to Cal., Wash. bars, 1929, practiced in Tacoma, 1929-42; chmn. Met. Bldg. Corp., Seattle 1954—; pres. Pelican (Alaska) Cold Storage Co., 1947-60, chmn., 1960—; pres. Boise (Ida.) Payette Lumber Co., 1949-55; pres. Laird, Norton Co., Winona, Minn., 1950-60, chmn., 1960—; v.p. Weyerhaeuser Co., 1956-57, chmn. bd., 1957-60, 66—, pres., 1960-66; dir. VRW United Corp., Safeco Corp., Seattle-First Nat. Bank. Mem. nat. exec. bd., pres. nat. council Boy Scouts Am. Bd. dirs. Episcopal Ch. Found., N.Y.; chmn. bd. trustees U. Puget Sound, Tacoma; life trustee U. Chgo. Served at lt. comdr. USNR, 1942-46. Mem. Seattle C. of C. (pres. 1970-71). Republican. Episcopalian. Clubs: Harbor, Rainier, University, Overlake Golf and Country, Tennis, Yacht (Seattle); Tacoma, Country and Golf, Yacht (Tacoma). Home: P O Box 99 Medina WA 98039 Office: Tacoma Bldg Tacoma WA 98402

CLAPP, ROBERT TEMPLE, univ. dean; b. Cambridge, Mass., Oct. 3, 1908; s. Clifford Blake and Edith Temple (Horne) C.; student Pomona Coll., 1925-27; B.A., U. Pa., 1929; M.F., Yale, 1933; m. Marianne Josephine Blakeslee, June 28, 1934; children—Robert Gardner, Roger Clifford. Instr., Yale Sch. Forestry, 1934-36, asst. prof., dir. Yale forests, 1937-43; mem. faculty Miss. State U., 1946—, prof. forestry, 1948-50, head dept., 1950-57, dir. Sch. Forest Resources, 1957-58, dean, 1961—. Mem. coop. forestry research adv. bd. U.S. Dept. Agr., 1969—; mem. Council Forestry Sch. Execs. Served to lt. (s.g.) USNR, World War II; lt. comdr. Res. ret. Mem. Assn. State Coll. and Univ. Forestry Research Orgns., Miss. Forestry Assn. (dir.), Forest Farmers Assn., Soc. Am. Foresters (chmn. Gulf States sect. 1963-64). Episcopalian. Home: 919 Barnett Dr Starkville MS 39759 Office: P O Drawer FR State College MS 39762

CLAPP, ROGER HOWLAND, advt. exec.; b. Scarsdale, N.Y., May 11, 1928; s. Kenneth John and Louise (Allen) C.; B.A. cum laude, Amherst Coll., 1954; m. Patricia Anne Townshend, June 26, 1954; children—Roger Howland, Georgia Louise, Sarah Townshend. Vice pres., asso. media dir. Benton & Bowles, Inc., N.Y.C., 1954-67; v.p., media dir. Rumrill-Hoyt, Inc., N.Y.C., 1967—. Served with USNR, 1948-52. Mem. Am. Assn. Advt. Agys. (chmn. newspaper com. 1969—), Theta Delta Chi (trustee Theta Delta chpt. Amherst,). Home: 195 Palmer Hill Rd Old Greenwich CT 06870 Office: 380 Madison Av New York City NY 10017

CLAPP, VERNER WARREN, librarian; b. Johannesburg, Union South Africa (parents Am. citizens), June 3, 1901; s. George Herbert and Mary Sybil (Helms) C.; A.B., Trinity Coll., 1922; postgrad. Harvard, 1922-23; m. Dorothy Devereaux Ladd, Aug. 24, 1929; children—Nancy Priest (Mrs. Joseph H. Roe, Jr.), Verner Warren, Judith Ladd (Mrs. James F. Bromley). With Library of Congress, Washington, 1922-56, dir. adminstrv. dept., 1940-43, dir. acquisitions dept., 1943-47, chief asst. librarian, 1947-56; pres. Council on Library Resources, 1956-67, cons., 1967—; dir. Forest Press, Inc., 1954—, pres., 1962—. Librarian, UN Conf. Internat. Orgn., San Francisco, 1945; chmn. U.S. Library Mission to Japan, 1947-48; mem. Nat. Adv. Commn. on Libraries, 1966-67. Decorated Order of the Sacred Treasure (Japan), 1968. Mem. A.L.A. (Lippincott medal 1960), Spl. Libraries Assn., Canadian, D.C. library assns., Bibliog. Soc. Am., Bibliog. Soc. Can., Am. Inst. Graphic Arts, Phi Beta Kappa, Sigma Nu. Clubs: Grolier; Cosmos (Washington). Author: United Nations Educational, Scientific Cultural Organization Report Bibliog. Services, 1950: The Future of the Research Library, 1963, Copyright-A Librarian's View, 1968. Contbr. articles, reports to profl. jours. Home: 4 W Irving St Chevy Chase MD 20015 Office: 1 Dupont Circle Washington DC 20036

CLAPP, WALTER E., banker; b. Malden, Mass., 1898. Vice chmn. bd. Gt. Western Bank & Trust Co., Phoenix; sec., dir. Gt. Western Corp.; dir. Pima Savs. & Loan Assn. Home: 8020 Tanque Verde Rd Tucson AZ 85715 Office: 3443 N Central Av Box 2012 Phoenix AZ 85001*

CLAPP, WILLIAM JACOB, utility cons.; b. Greenville, S.C., Sept. 27, 1903; s. Crawford and Caroline (West) C.; B.S., Clemson U., 1923; m. Hazel Quigg, Sept. 30, 1926; 1 son, Jack C. With Fla. Pub. Service Co., 1925-45, gen. supt., 1938-43, merger with Fla. Power Corp., 1946, prodn. engr., 1946-47, prodn. supt., 1947-50, v.p., 1950-51, exec. v.p., 1952-67, pres., chmn. bd., 1967-68, cons. engr., 1968—. Former chmn. Fla. Commn.; mem. Fla. Worlds Fair Authority. Chmn. bd. overseers Setson Coll. Law, St. Petersburg, Fla.; trustee Stetson U., DeLand, Fla. Served from capt. to maj. C.E., AUS, World War II. Recipient Outstanding Citizen award St. Petersburg Jr. C. of C., 1954, Fla. Econ. Devel. award First Research Corp., 1958, Mgmt. Achievement award Soc. Advancement Mgmt. of U. Fla., 1958. Mem. Am. Inst. E.E., Am. Soc. M.E., Southeastern Electric Exchange (dir., past pres.), Edison Electric Inst. (past pres., past chmn. policy com. on atomic power), So. Mil. Engrs., Am. Legion, Res. Officers Assn., Com. of 100 St. Petersburg, Sigma Tau, Beta Gamma Sigma. Methodist. Home: 650 Pinellas Point Dr S St Petersburg FL 33705 Office: 1st Fed Bldg St Petersburg FL 33701

CLAPPER, HOMER WALTER, corp. exec.; b. Swissvale, Pa., May 12, 1916; s. Homer Linhart and Marie Cecilia (Thaynor) C.; M.E., Rutgers U., 1938, postgrad. bus. adminstrn., aero., 1942; m. Betty M. Stagg, May 16, 1941; 1 dau., Barbara. With Curtiss-Wright Corp., 1938-46, Reeves Internat. Inc., 1946-48; with Bergen Wire Rope Co., 1948-69, former chmn. bd. dirs.; with Reeves Industries, Inc., 1952-70, pres., 1965-70; pres. Mercury Industries, 1970—, Conveyors & Dumpers (both Park Ridge, N.J.), Chatham Labs. Inc., 1970—; v.p. Conti Causeway Ford, Mercury and Lincoln, Toms River Lincoln Mercury; dir. Ramapo Bank. Registered profl. engr., N.J. Mem. Soc. Automotive Engrs., Am. Inst. Banking. Home: 152 Pines Lake Dr E Wayne NJ 07472 Office: Chatham Labs Inc Industrial Rd Riverdale NJ 07457

CLAPSADDLE, CLARENCE WILLIAM, Jr., land and municipal devel. co. exec.; b. Roanoke, Va., Apr. 10, 1917; s. Clarence W. and Violet (Carper) C.; B.S., U.S. Mil. Acad., 1940; M.P.A., Syracuse U., 1948; student Columbia U., 1949-51; m. Martha Jean Kohl, Nov. 24, 1943; children—Martha Susan (Mrs. Thomas E. Faley Jr.), Peter William. Commd. 2d lt. U.S. Army, 1940, advanced through grades to brig. gen.; ret., 1970; v.p. pub. adminstrn. Ingersoll Republic Corp., Colorado Springs, Colo., 1970—. Decorated Distinguished Service medal, Bronze Star. Mem. Internat. City Mgmt. Assn. Republican. Mem. Christian Ch. Home: 1701 Sundown Dr Colorado Springs CO 80906 Office: 4525 Northpark Dr Colorado Springs CO 80907

CLAPSADDLE, GERALD LEON, clergyman; b. Union County, O., Nov. 10, 1913; s. Harley Clifford and Gertie (Moore) C.; student Marion (Ind.) Coll., 1933-36; Th.B., Taylor U., Upland, Ind., 1936-37, D.D., 1952; B.D., Garrett Theol. Sem., 1943; m. Sara Ester Sprinkle, Dec. 24, 1939; children—Joseph Merrill, Connie Beth. Ordained to ministry Methodist Ch., 1940; pastor chs. in Ind., 1934-57; supt. Indpls. dist. Meth. Ch., 1957-62; gen. sec. bd. missions Meth. Ch., 1962-68, asso. gen. sec. Program Council, 1968—; chmn. bd. Friendship Press, 1963-69. Vice pres. div. Christian edn. Nat. Council Chs., 1963-69, chmn. dept. edn. for mission, 1963-69, mem. gen. planning and program com., 1970—; del. World Council Chs. gen. assembly, Evanston, Ill., 1954. Trustee DePauw U., 1957-62, Meth. Hosp., Indpls., 1957-62, Meth. Theol. Sch. in Ohio, 1960-62. Mem. Acad. Polit. and Social Sci., Internat. Platform Assn. Editor: Technology and Human Values, 1967. Home: 414 Grantham Dr Englewood OH 45322 Office: 601 W Riverview Dayton OH 45406

CLARE, CARL PETER, elec. engr.; b. Rossland, B.C., Can., May 25, 1903; s. Peter and Hattie (Stenson) C.; student U. Mich., 1921-24; B.Sc. in Elec. Engring., U. Ida., 1927, D.Sc., 1962; grad. advanced mgmt. program, Harvard, 1956; D.Engring., S.D. Mines and Tech., 1970; m. Ethel May Johnson, Jan. 22, 1926; 1 dau., Valdine (Mrs. Richard A. Cameron). Engr., Automatic Electric Co., Chgo., 1927-32, Automatic Electric Labs., Chgo., 1932-37; founder C.P. Clare & Co., Chgo., 1937, pres., chmn. bd., 1937—; pres., chmn. bd. C.P. Clare Internat. NV, Tongeren, Belgium; chmn. bd. C.P. Clare Canada, Ltd., Toronto, Ont., pres., dir. C.P. Clare de Mexico S.A. de C.V., Nogales; dir. Clare- Elliott, London, Clare-Pendar Co., Gen. Instrument Corp. Mem. Northwestern U. Assos. Mem. bd. U. Chgo. Cancer Research Found.; bd. dirs. Clearbrook Sch. Retarded Children, Presbyn. Home, Evanston, Ill., Coll. Engring. U. Ida.; trustee McCormick Theol. Sem., Irving Park YMCA, Dickinson Coll., Carlisle, Pa., Northwest Community Hosp., Arlington Heights, Ill. Registered profl. engr., Ill. Fellow Am. Inst. E.E.; mem. Am. Soc. Metals, Newcomen Soc., Western Soc. Engrs., Nat. Assn. Relay Mfrs., Sigma Tau, Sigma Chi (grand trustee). Presbyn. (trustee). Mason (Shriner). Clubs: Union League, Mid-Am., Executives, Harvard, Rotary (Chgo.); Bob O'Link Country (Highland Park, Ill.); Medinah (Ill.) Country; University of Mich. Home: 625 Newbury Pl Arlington Heights IL 60005 Office: 3101 Pratt Blvd Chicago IL 60645

CLARE, DAVID ROSS, mfg. co. exec.; b. Perth, Amboy, N.J., July 21, 1925; s. Robert L. and Helen (Walsh) C.; S.B. in Mech. Engring., Mass. Inst. Tech., 1945; m. Margaret Corcoran, July 5, 1947; children—Lynne, Carol, David II, Christopher. With Johnson & Johnson, 1946—, prodn. mgr. Eastern surg. dressings and Permacel operations, 1960-61, dir. mfg., 1961—, v.p., 1961-64, exec. v.p. operations, 1964—. Served with USNR, World War II. Home: 791 Knollwood Terrace Westfield NJ 07090 Office: 501 George St New Brunswick NJ 08901

CLARENBACH, FRED A., educator; b. Jefferson City, Mo., Apr. 27, 1909; s. Louis Adolph and Julia (Schaper) C.; B.A., U. Mo., 1930, M.A., 1932; Ph.D., Cornell U., 1941; m. Laura Belle McGaffey, Aug. 28, 1930; children—Ann Louise (Mrs. Gerald B. Skutt), Lois Elinor (Mrs. Michel C. Oksenberg). Instr., Jefferson City (Mo.) Sr. High Sch., 1934-36; instr. econs. Cornell U., 1936-39; economist Dept. Agr., 1939-45; asso. prof. agrl. econs. U. Conn., 1944; mem. faculty U. Wis., 1945—, prof. polit. sci., 1951-62, prof. regional planning, 1962—, chmn. water resources mgmt. program com. Grad. Sch., 1964-68; cons. to govt. and instns., 1948—. Mem. Am. Econ. Assn., Am. Polit. Sci. Assn., Am. Soc. Planning Ofcls., Phi Beta Kappa. Democratic. Unitarian. Home: 5009 Risser Rd Madison WI 53705

CLAREY, BERNARD AMBROSE, naval officer; b. Oskaloosa, Ia., May 4, 1912; s. Stephen Bernard and Jennie Agatha (O'Hearn) C.; student William Penn Coll., 1929-30; B.S., U.S. Naval Acad., 1934; grad. Nat. War Coll., 1956; m. Jean Webster Scott, May 29, 1937; children—Stephen Scott, Michael O'Hearn. Commd. ensign USN, 1934, advanced through grades to adm., 1968; service in ships, 1934-41; exec. officer submarine U.S.S. Dolphin, 1941-42, submarine U.S.S. Amberjack, 1942-43; navigator submarine U.S.S. Peto, 1943; comdg. officer submarine U.S.S. Pintado, 1943-45; assigned Navy Dept., 1946-47; staff Comdr. Submarines Atlantic, 1947-49; assigned Bur. Naval Personnel, 1949-51; exec. officer U.S.S. Helena, 1951-52; comdr. Submarine Div. 52, 1952-53; assigned Office Chief Naval Operations, 1953-55, Nat. War Coll., 1955-56; chief staff Comdr. SubForce Pacific, 1956-58; comdg. officer U.S.S. Hassayampa, 1958; dir. mil. personnel Office Sec. Def., 1958-62; comdr. submarine force U.S. Pacific Fleet, 1962-64, dep. comdr. in chief Pacific Fleet, 1964-66; comdr. 2d Fleet, Atlantic, 1966-67; dir. program planning Office Chief Naval Operations, Washington, 1967-68, vice chief naval operations, 1968-70; comdr. in chief Pacific Fleet, 1970—. Decorated Distinguished Service medal (4), Navy Cross (3), Silver Star medal, Legion of Merit, Bronze Star medal. Mem. U.S. Naval Inst., Holy Name Soc. K.C., Lion. Club: Oahu Country (Honolulu). Home: Quarter 37 Makalapa Dr Honolulu HI 96818 Office: Comdr in Chief US Pacific Fleet FPO San Francisco CA 96610

CLAREY, WILLIAM ANDREW, coll. dean; b. Oskaloosa, Ia., June 10, 1924; s. Stephen Bernard and Jennie Agatha (O'Hearn) C.; student Ia. State Coll., 1942-43, 1946-47, Mont. Sch. Mines 1943-44, U. Wis., 1944-45; B.S., Bradley U., 1948, M.A., 1950; postgrad. U. Chgo., 1951-52; m. Mary Magdalene Laffey, Sept. 18, 1948; children—Susan, Stephen, William, Timothy, Sharon. Faculty Bradley U., 1952—, successively instr., asst. prof., asso. prof. 1952-55, prof. bus. adminstrn., econs., dean Coll. Bus. Adminstrn., 1955—. Served as seaman 1st class USNR, 1943-46. Mem. Am., Midwest econ. assns., Phi Gamma Delta, Alpha Kappa Psi, Zeta Pi, Omicron Delta Epsilon. Rotarian. Home: 808 W Kensington Peoria IL 61614

CLARIE, T. EMMET, U.S. judge; b. 1913; Ph.B., Providence Coll.; LL.B., Hartford Coll. Law. Admitted to bar, 1940; now U.S. dist. judge Conn. Mem. Am. Bar Assn. Address: Danielson CT*

CLARK, ALBERT EDWIN, newspaperman; b. Chatham County, N.C., May 12, 1915; s. Walter B. and Mary Hughes (Burns) C.; student Campbell Coll., Buie's Creek, N.C., 1935- 37, U. N.C., 1939-40; m. Naomi Ruth Rouse, Aug. 22, 1942; children—Albert E., George B., Carolyn (dec.). Reporter Daily News, Greensboro, N.C., 1940-45, The Evening Sun, Balt., 1945; reporter Wall Street Jour., Washington, 1945-53, chief corr., Washington bur. chief, 1953-60; exec. asst. U.S. News and Report, 1960-66, adminstrv. editor, 1966—. Mem. pres.'s council advisers Campbell Coll., 1968—. Mem. Sigma Delta Chi. Club: Nat. Press (Washington). Home: 6535 Copa Ct Falls Church VA 22044 Office: 2300 N St NW Washington DC 20037

CLARK, ALBERT PATTON, air force officer; b. Hawaii, Aug. 27, 1913; s. Albert P. and Mary (Gannon) C.; B.S., U.S. Mil. Acad., 1936; m. Carolyn Pierpont Wilbourn, Oct. 8, 1937; children—Carolyn (Mrs. H.A. Homan), Albert Patton, Mary Gannon (Mrs. Y.T. Walker). Commd. 2d lt. U.S. Army, 1936, advanced through grades to lt. gen. USAF, 1965; rated mil. aviator, 1937; fighter pilot ETO, World War II; grad. Nat. War Coll., 1952; assigned Europe, Middle East, also Far East, 1955-65; vice comdr. Tactical Air Command, USAF, 1965-68; comdr. Air U., USAF, 1968-70; supt. USAF Acad., Colo., 1970—. Home: Qrtrs 6776 USAF Academy CO 80840 Office: Superintendent USAF Academy CO 80840

CLARK, ALFRED, chemist; b. Beverly, Mass., Aug. 5, 1909; s. John Thomas and Elinor (Howarth) C.; student Brown U., 1926-28; B.S., Purdue U., 1930; M.S., State U. Mich., 1932; Ph.D., U. Ill., 1935; m. Winifred Gardner, Aug. 25, 1935; 1 son, Alfred. Research chemist N.Am. Rayon Corp., 1935-36; research engr. Battelle Meml. Inst., 1936-43; head catalysis dept. Publicker Comml. Alcohol Co., 1943-44; sr. scientist Phillips Petroleum Co., 1944-. Recipient Modern Pioneer award N.A.M., 1965. Fellow Am. Inst. Chemists; mem. Am. Chem. Soc. (E.V. Murphree award 1967), Sigma Xi, Alpha Chi Sigma, Phi Lambda Upsilon. Elk. Research in Catalysis, polyethylene process. Home: 1901 Crestview Dr Bartlesville, OK 74003.

CLARK, ANDREW HILL, geographer, educator; b. Fairford, Man., Can., Apr. 29, 1911; s. Jeremiah S. and Belle (Pratt) C.; B.A., McMaster U., 1930; student U. Man., 1931-32; M.A., U. Toronto, 1938; Ph.D., U. Cal. at Berkeley, 1944; m. Louise Sassmann, Dec. 28, 1940; children—Charles D., John R. and Stephen P. (twins), Mary E. Came to U.S., 1938, naturalized, 1945. With actuarial dept. Mfrs. Life Ins. Co., Toronto, 1932-35; instr. U. Toronto, 1935-38; asst. Dominion Geol. Survey Can., 1936, 37; extension lectr. U. Cal. at Berkeley, 1940; lectr. Canterbury U., Christchurch, New Zealand, 1941, 42; instr. USAAF, Berkeley, 1943, ASTP, Johns Hopkins, 1943-44; geographer OSS and Dept. of State, 1944-46; asso. prof. geography Rutgers U., 1946-49, prof., chmn. dept., 1949-51; prof. geography U. Wis., Madison, 1951-64, research prof., 1964-66, Vernor Clifford Finch research prof. geography, 1966—, chmn. dept., 1958-61; fellow in Am. studies U. Dundee, Scotland, 1971-72. John Simon Guggenheim Meml. fellow and Fulbright Research scholar, 1961-62; S.S.R.C. fellow, 1962. Chmn. com. hist. geography NRC, 1949-53. Mem. Am. Geog. Soc., Assn. Am. Geographers (hon. pres. 1961-62, editor Monograph series 1961-63), Canadian Assn. Geographers, Internat. Geog. Congress (chmn. hist. geography sect. 1964), Agrl. History Soc. Author: The Invasion of New Zealand by People, Plants and Animals, 1949; Three Centuries and the Island,

1959; Acadia: The Early Geography of Nova Scotia to 1760, 1968; (with others) Canada: A Geographical Interpretation, 1968; New Zealand, 1947, American Geography, Inventory and Prospect, 1954. Contbr. to monographs, jours. in field. Address: Dept Geography Univ Wis Madison WI 53706

CLARK, ANDY EARL, Jr., coll. dean; b. Tulsa, June 28, 1920; s. Andy Earl and Eunice L. (Ray) C.; B.Music Edn., U. Tulsa, 1941; M.Ed., 1952, specialists degree sch. adminstrn., 1955; m. Jean E. Potts, Oct. 4, 1941; children—Andy Earl III, Jan Elizabeth. Dir. instrumental music Strang (Okla.) pub. schs., 1941-42, Nowata (Okla.) pub. schs., 1946-52; prin. high sch., Nowata, 1952-56; head secondary edn. dept. Kan. State Tchrs. Coll., Emporia, 1956-58; dean instrn. Northwestern State Coll., Alva, Okla., 1958—. Served to capt. AUS, 1942-46. Mem. N.E.A. (life), Assn. Higher Edn., Am. Assn. Coll. Tchrs. Edn., Northeastern Okla. Secondary Sch. Prins. Assn. (past pres.), Nowata County (past pres.), Woods County (Okla.) (past pres.) edn. assns., Phi Belta Kappa, Kappa Delta Pi, Kappa Kappa Psi. Home: 1503 Murray Dr Alva, OK 73717.

CLARK, ANN NOLAN, writer, edn. cons.; b. Las Vegas, N.M., 1898; d. Patrick Francis and Mary (Dunn) Nolan; student Highlands U., Las Vegas; m. Thomas Patrick Clark, Aug. 6, 1919 (dec.); children—Thomas Patrick (killed in action World War II). Formerly asst. English tchr. Highlands U., also with U.S. Indian Service as tchr. No. Pueblos; formerly materials specialist Inst. Inter-Am. Affairs, and a U.S. del. to UNESCO Conf., Brazil; head preparation materials dept., adult edn. Bur. Indian Affairs, until 1962; ednl. cons. Latin Am. br. Internat. Coop. Adminstrn.; now writer and lectr. Recipient Distinguished Service award Dept. Interior, 1962; Regina medal Catholic Library Assn., 1963. Mem. Mark Twain Soc. (hon.). Author: In My Mother's House (N.Y. Herald Tribune Spring Festival award), 1941; Little Navajo Bluebird, 1943; Magic Money, 1950; Looking for Something (N.Y. Herald Tribune Spring Festival award), 1952; Secret of the Andes (Newbery medal), 1953 (these five books all Jr. Lit. Guild selections); A Child's History of New Mexico, 1944 (with others); Buffalo Caller, 1942; Blue Canyon House, 1954; Santiago; Third Monkey; A Santa for Pasqalita, 1959; World Song, Desert People; Paco's Miracle; Tia Maria's Garden; Medicine Man's Daughter; Father Kino, Priest to the Pima; Brother Andre of Montreal, 1967; Summer is for Growing, 1968; Arizona for Young People, 1968; Along a Sandy Trail, 1969; Journey to the People, 1969; Circle of Seasons, 1970; These Are the Vallant, 1970; others also textbooks, numerous publs. of Indian Service; articles in mags. Home: P O Box 164 Cortaro AZ 85230

CLARK, ANTHONY MORRIS, museum dir.; b. Phila., Oct. 12, 1923; s. Theobald Forstall and Dorothy (Nevin) C.; B.S., Harvard, 1945; student painting in N.Y.C., Italy, Greece, Denmark, Switzerland and Eng., 1945-54. Faculty asst. Salzburg Seminar of Harvard, 1950; conservation asst. Mus. Art, R.I. Sch. Design, 1953; field worker Byzantine Inst., Istanbul, 1954; sec. of mus., editor Mus. Notes, Mus. Art, R.I. Sch. Design, 1955-59; David E. Finley fellow Nat. Gallery Art, 1959-61; curator paintings and sculpture Mpls. Inst. Arts, 1961-63, acting dir., 1963, dir., 1963—; paintings exhibited Phila. Art Alliance, 1948, Mus. Art, R.I. Sch. Design, 1954; spl. research 18th century paintings in Rome, Roman Baroque and Neoclassical art. Art adv. panel Internal Revenue Service. Decorated comdr. Order Royal North Star (Sweden). Mem. Socio Benemerito of Amici dei Musei di Roma, Assn. Art Mus. Dirs., Archaeol. Inst. Am., Am. Assn. Museums, Coll. Art Assn. Am. (dir. 1970—), Intermus. Conservation Assn. (pres. 1966-67, 70—), Am. Fedn. Arts, English Speaking Union, UN Assn. Minn., Minn. Arts Forum, Minn. Arts Council (adviser), Mpls. Aquatennial Assn. Club: Harvard (Minn.). Author: The Age of Canova, 1957; also numerous articles, mus. publs. Mem. consultative com. Art Quar. Home: 2443 3d Av S Minneapolis MN 55404 Office: 201 E 24th St Minneapolis MN 55404

CLARK, ARTHUR BRYAN, II, seedsman; b. Orange, Conn., Feb. 5, 1907; s. Arthur B. and Glenna (Hostetter) C.; grad. Hotchkiss Sch., 1925; B.A., Yale, 1929; M.B.A., Harvard, 1932; m. Mary Ferguson, June 12, 1930 (div. 1958); children—Katharine (Mrs. Charles A. Kallander), Arthur Bryan III; m. 2d, Ellen Fairweather, Dec. 1958; children—Robert Fairweather, David Bryan Scott. With Asgrow Seed Co. (formerly Asso. Seed Growers, Inc.), New Haven, 1932-, staff sales dept., charge sales branches, 1933-42, pres., treas., 1942-70, chmn. bd., 1970—; dir. Union Trust Co., So. Conn. Gas Co. Mem. nat. adv. council on seeds to U.S. Office Price Adminstrn., 1943-46; pres. Vegetable Seed Inst., 1950-51. Nat. dir. YMCA, 1949-59, vice chmn. exec. com. nat. bd., 1957-58, v.p. nat. council, 1957-58; chmn. trustees New Haven YMCA; pres. Conn. YMCA, 1956-59; gen. campaign chmn. United Fund Greater New Haven, 1960; pres. Central Services Bldg., Inc., New Haven, 1962-63; trustee Edward W. Hazen Found., 1949-67; bd. dirs. Grace New Haven Hosp., 1952-62. Mem. Am. Seed Trade Assn. (pres. 1963-64, hon. life mem.), Nat. Planning Assn. (mem. nat. council), Zeta Psi. Home: 24 Hickory Rd Woodbridge CT 06525 Office: care Asgrow Seed Co Orange CT 06477

CLARK, ARTHUR LEROY, electric utility exec.; b. Norfolk, Va., Sept. 5, 1911; s. Arthur L. and Esther (Murphy) C.; student U. Richmond Evening Sch. Bus., 1939; m. Mildred Love Walker, Aug. 20, 1938; children—Jacqueline L. (Mrs. Charles D. Jackson, Jr.), Arthur LeRoy III. With Va. Electric & Power Co., 1928—, dist. accountant, Suffolk, Va., 1937-38, v.p., Richmond, 1961-69, sr. v.p., 1969—. Bd. dirs. YMCA, Boy Scouts Am., Cerebral Palsy Center, Crippled Childrens Hosp.; trustee Randolph-Macon Coll. Mem. Edison Electric Inst., Southeastern Electric Exchange, Pub. Utilities Assn. Va., So. Indsl. Relations Conf. Methodist. Home: 306 Burnwick Rd Richmond VA 23227 Office: Va Electric & Power Co 700 E Franklin St Richmond VA 23209

CLARK, ARTHUR WATTS, ins. co. exec.; b. Seattle, Nov. 28, 1922; s. Irving Marshall and Nell (Watts) C.; A.B., U. N.C., 1943; M.A., U. Cal., 1948; m. Mary Dick Cannon, Nov. 21, 1942; children—Dr. Arthur Watts, Claiborne Marshall, Johnston Jewell. Dir. planning Home Security Life Ins. Co., Durham, N.C., 1952-58, v.p., 1959-63, exec. v.p., 1964-67, pres., 1967—. Mem. N.C. Health Ins. Adv. Bd., 1966-70. Treas. Research Triangle Regional Planning Commn., 1959-63. Served with USAAF, 1942-46, with USAF, 1950-52. Mem. Nat. Assn. Flight Instrs., Phi Beta Kappa, Sigma Xi. Home: 3540 Rugby Rd Durham NC 27707 Office: 505 W Chapel Hill St Durham NC 27701

CLARK, BARTHOLOMEW ALBERT, educator; b. Bklyn., Oct. 13, 1919; s. Rollin Edmund and Margaret (Hanrahan) C.; B.A., Cath. U. Am., 1940, M.A., 1953, Ph.D., 1955; postgrad. Fordham U., 1947-50, Seattle U., 1966, Sophia U. (Tokyo), 1969; M.A., Manhattan Coll., 1945. Joined Bros. of Christian Schs., 1936; tchr. De LaSalle Inst., Cardinal Hayes High Sch., Bishop Loughlin High Sch., 1940-52; instr. Cath. U., 1952-55; from asst. prof. to prof. religious studies Manhattan Coll., 1955—; editorial cons. W.H. Sadlier Publs., Inc., 1956—. Mem. N.Y. Archdiocese Ecumenical Commn., 1970—. Recipient Thomas Finn Travel-Study Scholarship award Middle East, 1966, Orient, 1969. Mem. Religious Edn. Assn. Am. (local pres. 1965-69), Cath. Theol. Soc. Am., Coll. Theology Soc., Phi Kappa Theta. Author: Religious and Moral Pre-Induction Program for Armed Service, 1955. Contbr. articles periodicals. Address: Manhattan Coll Bronx NY 10471

CLARK, BENJAMIN PRESTRIDGE, hosp. supt.; b. Longton, Kan., Apr. 4, 1910; s. William Elmer and Mamie (Prestridge) C.; B.S., M.D., U. Okla., 1934; m. Edith Lucille Davis, Mar. 2, 1934; children—Carol Edith (Mrs. Russell Laster, Jr.), Benjamin Prestridge. Intern Erlanger Hosp., Chattanooga, 1934-35; resident Children's Hosp., Chattanooga, 1935-36, Children's Hosp. Milw., 1946-47; practice pediatrics, Gadsden, Ala., 1947-58; chief pediatrics Meml. Hosp., Whitesburg, Ky., 1958-64; supt. State Sch. and Hosp., Hamburg, Pa., 1965-68. Served to col. USAAF, World War II. Diplomate Am. Bd. Pediatrics. Fellow Am. Acad. Pediatrics; mem. Am. Assn. Mental Deficiency. Lion (zone chmn., dept. dist. gov. 1962-64). Address: State Sch and Hosp White Haven PA 18661

CLARK, BENJAMIN SCHUYLER, investment banker; b. Englewood, N.J., Feb. 16, 1908; s. Harold Benjamin and Dorothy Q. (Pardee) C.; grad. St. Paul's Sch., 1927; A.B. cum laude, Harvard, 1931; m. Charlotte Lyman, Mar. 10, 1934; children—Charlotte Lyman, Benjamin Schuyler, Ella Lowell, Elizabeth Van Cortlandt. Studied banking, London, 1934-35; with White, Weld & Co., N.Y.C., 1935—, gen. partner, 1941—; dir. Pardee-Curtin Lumber Co.; trustee Franklin Savs. Bank. Trustee Am. Mus. Natural History, 5 Points House, Greenwood Cemetery; bd. govs. Soc. of N.Y. Hosp. Served as master sgt. G-2, 18th Airborne, AUS, 1942-45. Mem. St. Nicholas Soc. Clubs: Racquet and Tennis, Lunch (N.Y.C.); Somerset (Boston). Home: Route 2 Box 136 Pound Ridge NY 10576 Office 20 Broad St New York City NY 10005

CLARK, BIRGE MALCOLM, architect; b. Palo Alto, Cal., Apr. 16, 1893; s. Arthur B. and Grace (Birge) C.; A.B., Stanford, 1914; B. Arch., Columbia, 1917; m. Lucile Townley, June 15, 1922; children—Richard Townley, Dean Townley, Birge Gaylord, Malcolm Mallory. Practicing architect, 1921—; vice chmn. bd. Palo Alto-Salinas Savs. & Loan Assn.; lectr. in architecture Stanford, 1950—. Served to capt. USAAF, 1917-18; comdg. officer 3d Balloon Co. Decorated Silver Star. Fellow A.I.A. Kiwanian. Home: 1490 Edgewood Dr Palo Alto CA 94301 Office 3200 Hanover St Palo Alto CA 94304

CLARK, BLAIR, journalist; b. E. Hampton, N.Y., Aug. 22, 1917; s. William and Marjory (Blair) C.; grad. St. Marks Sch., Southborough, Mass., 1935; A.B., Harvard 1940; children—Timothy Blair, Cameron. Reporter, St. Louis Post- Dispatch, 1940-41; pub. N.H. Sunday News, Manchester, 1946-48; editorial writer Boston Herald-Traveler, 1950-52; fgn. corr. CBS News, Paris, France, 1953-56, N.Y.C., 1957-60, gen. mgr., v.p. CBS News, 1961-64; asso. pub. N.Y. Post, 1965-66; campaign mgr. for Senator Eugene J. McCarthy, 1968; treas. Com. for Pub. Justice. Trustee Harvard Radio Broadcasting (WHRB), Harvard Crimson. Member Assn. Radio and TV News Analysts (past pres.). Home: 229 E 48th St New York City NY 10017

CLARK, BLAKE, mag. editor, author, bus. exec.; b. Howell, Tenn. July 11, 1908; s. Thomas B. and Ethel (Harris) C.; B.A., Vanderbilt U., 1929, M.A., 1930, Ph.D., 1938; student U. London, 1933-34; m. Deena Speliakos; 1 dau., Nikia. Instr. U. Hawaii, 1930-34, asst. prof., 1934-42; information officer U.S. Office Civilian Def., Washington, 1942-43, OSS, 1943-46; roving editor Reader's Digest, 1946—. Pres., Bay Volkswagen, Watergate Ins. Co., Comml. Rentals. Clubs: Metropolitan, University, Chevalier de Tastevin, Cosmos (Washington); Burning Tree (Bethesda, Md.). Author: Oriental England, 1939; Omai, First Polynesian Ambassador to England, 1940; Paradise Limtied, 1941; Remember Pearl Harbor, 1942; Advertising Smoke Screen, 1943; (with George Tweed) Robinson Crusoe, USN, 1945; (with Nicol Smith) Into Siam, 1945; Hawaii, The 49th State, 1947; (with Morris Frank) First Lady of the Seeing Eye, 1957. Contbr. articles popular mags. Home: 2440 Kalorama Rd NW Washington DC 20008

CLARK, BRONSON PETTIBONE, orgn. exec.; b. Cleveland Heights, O., Oct. 6, 1918; s. Sheldon P. and Hazel (Baker) C.; A.B. in Polit. Sci., Antioch Coll., 1941; m. Eleanor Meanor, Dec. 21, 1940; children—Mallory (Mrs. George Waldman, Jr.), Jennifer (Mrs. Stephen Roland), Melissa, Alison. New Eng. sec. Fellowship of Reconciliation, 1941-42; served in U.S. penitentiaries as conscientious objector, 1943-44; with Am. Friends Service Com., 1945-50, 61—. Mem. nat. bd., 1964-67, program asso. Spl. Vietnam Effort, 1967- 68, exec. sec., 1968—; sec.-treas. Community Devel., Inc., 1951-60; v.p. Gilford Instrument Labs., Inc., Oberlin, O., 1964-67, dir., 1958- 64; Charter mem. Bus. Execs. Move for Vietnam Peace, 1967. Mem. Germantown Monthly Meeting of Friends, Coulter St. 1967—. Mem. Am. Civil Liberties Union, Fellowship of Reconciliation. Mem. Soc. Friends. Co-author: Peace in Vietnam: a New Approach in Southeast Asia, 1966. Home: Awbury Philadelphia PA 19138 Office: 160 N 15th St Philadelphia PA 19102

CLARK, BRUCE BUDGE, educator; b. Georgetown, Ida., Apr. 9, 1918; s. Marvin E. and Alice (Budge) C.; B.A., U. Utah, 1943, Ph.D., 1951; M.A., Brigham Young U., 1948; m. Ouida Raphiel, Nov. 7, 1946; children—Lorraine, Drexel, Robert, Jeffrey, Shawn, Sandra. Teaching fellow Brigham Young U., 1946-47, U. Utah, 1947-50; asst. prof. Brigham Young U., 1950-55, asso. prof., 1955-58, prof., 1959—, dir. humanities program, 1958-60, chmn. dept. English, 1960-65, dean Coll. Humanities, 1965—. Served with AUS, 1944-46. Mem. Nat. Council Tchrs. English, Modern Lang. Assn., Rocky Mountain Modern Lang. Assn., Coll. Conf. on Composition and Communications. Mem. Ch. of Jesus Christ of Latter-day Saints. Author: The Spectrum of Faith in Victorian Literature, 1966; The Challenge of Teaching, 1966; Oscar Wilde: A Critical Biography, 1968; Romanticism through Modern Eyes, 1968. Editor anthology (Out of the Best Books, vol. 1, 1964, vol. II, 1966, vol. III, 1967, vol. IV, 1968, vol. V, 1969). Home: 365 E 1655 South St Orem UT 84057 Office: Brigham Young U Provo UT 84601

CLARK, BURTON ROBERT, educator; b. Pleasantville, N.J., Sept. 6, 1921; s. Burton H. and Cornelia (Amole) C.; B.A., U. Cal. at Los Angeles, 1949, Ph.D., 1954; m. Adele Halitsky, Aug. 31, 1949; children—Philip Neil, Adrienne. Asst. prof. sociology Stanford, 1953-56; research asso., asst. prof. edn. Harvard, 1956-58; asso. prof., then prof. edn. and asso. research sociologist, then research sociologist U. Cal. at Berkeley, 1958-66; prof. sociology Yale, 1966—, chmn. dept., 1969—. Served with AUS, 1942-46. Mem. Am., Eastern sociol. assns., Am. Assn. U. Profs., Soc. Study Social Problems. Author: Adult Education in Transition, 1956; The Open Door College, 1960; Educating the Expert Society, 1962; The Distinctive College, 1970. Home: 1501 Ridge Rd North Haven CT 06473 Office: Dept Sociology Yale Univ New Haven CT 06520

CLARK, BYRON BRYANT, pharmacologist; b. Temple, Tex., Apr. 5, 1908; s. Oscar W. and Ida (Hansen) C.; B.A., Baylor U., 1930; M.S., State U. Ia., 1932, Ph.D., 1934; m. Gladys Lawson, Jan. 26, 1931; children—Barbara (Mrs. Edward Riter), Jack, Kenneth. Instr. physiology, pharmacology Albany Med. Coll., 1936-39, asst. prof., 1939-40, asso. prof., 1940-47; became prof. pharmacology, chmn. dept. Med. Sch. Tufts U., 1947; dir. pharmacology and chemotherapy Mead Johnson Research Center, Evansville, Ind., 1957-62, v.p., 1962-68; dir. pharmacology-toxicology program Nat. Inst. Gen. Med. Scis., NIH, Bethesda, Md., 1968—; cons. pharmacologist N.E. Center Hosp.; mem. com. on drug safety, drug research bd. Nat. Acad. Scis.-NRC. Fellow A.A.A.S.; mem. Am. Soc. Pharmacology and Exptl. Therapeutics, Soc. Exptl. Biology and Medicine, Soc. Toxicology, N.Y. Acad. Scis. Contbr. chpts. in books, articles profl. jours. Home: 5101 River Rd Bethesda MD 20016 Office: NIH Bethesda MD 20014

CLARK, C. KENNETH, ret. lawyer; b. Mt. Jackson, Pa., Mar. 23, 1897; s. Robert Sherer and Nannie (Imbrie) C.; student Westminster Coll., 1916-17, Ohio U., 1919-20, Ohio State U., 1921; LL.B., Youngstown Coll. Law, 1923; m. Katharine Griswold, June 30, 1926; 1 son, C. Kenneth. Admitted to Ohio bar, 1924, practiced law in Youngstown, 1924-69; mem. firm Harrington, Huxley & Smith, until 1969; lectr. law Am. Inst. Banking, 1926-30, 42-44; prof. law Youngstown Coll. Law, 1942-45. First chmn. Supreme Court Commn. on Grievances and Discipline, 1957, mem. 1958-63. Trustee Ohio Legal Center Inst.; patron Internat. Bar Assn. Mem. Nat. Assn. R.R. Trial Counsel, Mahoning County (pres. 1947), Am. (chmn. Ohio com. on jud. adminstrn. 1954-55, mem. ho. of dels. 1956-70, adv. com. jud. adminstrn., mem. pres.'s conf., fellow found.), Ohio (chmn. constl. amendment com. jud. selection and tenure 1956-63, co-chmn. modern cts. com. 1963-69, mem. exec. com. 1948-51, chmn. legal ethics and profl. conduct com. 1951-52, v.p. 1952, pres. 1953, del. 1964-65), Inter-Am. bar assns., Nat. Assn. R.R. Counsel, Am. Judicature Soc., Internat. Assn. Ins. Counsel, Youngtown Legal Aid Soc. (past pres.). Republican. Presbyn. (ruling elder 1940-52). Clubs: Youngstown, Exchange (past pres.), Torch (past pres.), Execs. (past pres.) (Youngstown). Home: 657 59th Av S St Petersburg FL 33705

CLARK, CAMERON, Jr., business exec.; b. Sept. 28, 1922; s. Charles Cameron and Agnes (Selkirk) C.; B.S., Yale, 1945; m. Lucetta Warner, Oct. 5, 1946; children—Cameron Warner, Timothy Warner, Ann Warner. With Gen. Electric Co., 1946-49; formerly with Warner Bros. Co., Bridgeport, Conn.; now exec. v.p. Warnaco, Inc., Bridgeport. Mem. Yale Alumni Bd. Mem. adv. com. Fairfield Community Chest, A.R.C. Bd. dirs. Jr. Achievement of Bridgeport; trustee Fairfield Country Day Sch. Served with USNR, 1943- 45. Mem. Am. Inst. Graphic Arts, Am. Mgmt. Assn., Bridgeport C. of C. (dir.), Folding Paper Box Assn. Am. (pres. N.Y. group, nat. dir.). Clubs: Yale of Eastern Fairfield County (dir.), Fairfield Country, Algonquin, Pequot Yacht. Home: 1001 Hillside Rd Fairfield CT 06431 Office: 350 Lafayette St Bridgeport CT 06604

CLARK, CARL ARTHUR, educator, psychologist; b. Oak Park, Ill., Sept. 20, 1911; s. Alfred H. and Mary (Geist) C.; B.A. cum laude, Colo. Coll., 1948, M.A., 1951; Ph.D., State U. Ia., 1954; m. Janet Picquet, Aug. 10, 1946 (div. 1964); 1 son, Peter. Tchr., Colorado Springs (Colo.) High Sch., 1948-50; research asst. State U. Ia., 1951-53; research asso. U. Chgo., 1953-54; tchr. Chgo. Tchrs. Coll. (now Chgo. State Coll.), 1954-56, asso. prof. psychology, 1956-62, prof. psychology, 1956—, chmn. dept., 1966—; research evaluator Chgo. Great Cities Sch. Improvement Porgram, 1963-65. Served with AUS, 1942-45. Mem. A.A.A.S., Am. Assn. U. Profs., Am. Psychol. Assn., Ill. Edn. Assn., Nat. Council Measurement in Edn., Sigma Xi. Contbr. profl. jours.

CLARK, CARL HERITAGE, educator; b. Los Angeles, Nov. 18, 1925; s. E. Russell and Mary (Swing) C.; B.S., Washington State U., 1947, D.V.M., 1947; M.S., Ohio State U., 1949, Ph.D., 1953; m. Dorothy Joan Longman, Sept. 1, 1948; 1 son, Kenneth W. Research asst. Wash. State U., 1946-47; instr. Ohio State U., 1948-53; prof., head dept. physiology and pharmacology Auburn U., 1953—, asso. head dept. animal disease research, 1953-68, chmn. radiol. safety com., 1957-67. Mem. Gov.'s Bd. Radiation, 1967-70, radiol. safety officer, 1970—. Mem. Am. Soc. Vet. Physiologists and Pharmacologists (pres. 1961-62), Am. Vet. Med. Assn., Sigma Xi, Tau Kappa Epsilon, Alpha Zeta. Contbr. articles profl. jours. Home: Route 3 700 Kuderna Acres Auburn AL 36830

CLARK, CARROLL D., sociologist; b. Minneapolis, Kan., Jan. 10, 1898; s. Rolla M. and Elva (Chapin) C.; A.B., U. Kan., 1922, M.A., 1925; Ph.D., U. Chgo., 1931; m. Pearl L. Holland, July 18, 1923; children—Chapin D., DeEtta Jean, Ruby Lorain. Taught school, Ashland, Kan.; supt. schs., Wakefield, Kan., 1922-24; sociol. cons. to Gov. Alfred M. Landon's State Planning Bd., 1933-36; prof. and chmn. dept. sociology U. Kan., 1933-62, prof. sociology, 1962-68, prof. emeritus, 1968—. Research fellow in Human Relations, Harvard 1945-56 (on sabbatical leave from U. Kan.); vis. prof. various summer sessions Cornell U., U. Ore., U. Ida.; condr. weekly broadcast on sociomusicology of jazz music over KANU, Univ. Kan. FM Sta., 1957-59. Served with U.S. Army, 1917, 53d Regt. Coast Arty., in France; as capt. 1942, maj., 1944, USAAF. Fellow Am. Sociol. Assn.; mem. Kan. Conf. Social Work (pres. 1934), Soc. Study Social Problems, S.W. (pres. 1939), Mid-West (pres. 1941) sociol. socs., N.Y. Acad. Scis., Kan. Adult Edn. Assn., Am. Assn. U. Profs., Phi Beta Kappa, Phi Delta Kappa, Phi Mu Alpha. Club: Old and New (Lawrence, Kan.). Author books: also articles in various sociol. jours. Home: 643 Indiana St Lawrence KS 66044

CLARK, CELIN GRANT, economist; b. Eng., 1905; s. James and Marion Nellie (Jolly) C.; M.A., Oxford U., 1931; Sc.D., U. Milan (Italy), 1957; D.Litt., Oxford, 1971; m. Marjorie Tattersall, July 27, 1935; children—Gregory, Nicholas, Christopher, Antony, Bernard, Maurice, Oliver, David, Cecily. Research asst. London Sch. Econs., 1928-29; dep. dir. Social Survey of Liverpool, 1929-30; asst. sec. econ. adv. council Cabinet Offices, London, 1930-31; univ. lectr. statistics Cambridge U., 1931-37; vis. lectr. univs. Sydney and Melbourne, 1937-38; econ. adviser Govt. Queensland, state under-sec. for labor and industry, 1938-52; vis. prof. U. Chgo., 1952; dir. Agrl. Econs. Research Inst., U. Oxford, 1953-69; research fellow Monash U., Clayton, Victoria, Australia, 1969—; supr. research Econometric Inst. N.Y., 1958-61. Mem. Internat. Statis. Inst., Econometrics Soc., Royal Statis. Soc. Club: Johnsonian (Brisbane, Australia). Author: Conditions of Economic Progress, rev. edit., 1957; Australian Hopes and Fears, 1958; Welfare and Taxation, 1954; (with M. R. Haswell) Econ. of Subsistence Agriculture, 1964; Economics of Irrigation, 1967; Population Growth and Land Use, 1967. Home: 8 Parker St Clayton Victoria 3168 Australia

CLARK, CHAMP, mag. editor; b. St. Louis, Aug. 24, 1923; s. Bennett Champ and Miriam (Marsh) C.; grad. Kent Sch., 1940; student U. Mo., 1940-42, 46-47; m. Mizzell Phillips, Feb. 2, 1949; children—Genevieve, Jane, Champ, Julia. Reporter, Kansas City (Mo.) Star, 1947-51; writer Time mag., 1951—, sr. editor, 1960—, Chgo. bur. chief, 1969—. Served with USMCR, 1942-46. Mem. Sigma Chi. Home: 338 Kenilworth Av Kenilworth IL 60043 Office: Time Magazine 401 N Michigan Av Chicago IL 60602

CLARK, CHARLES LESTER, educator; b. San Jose, Cal., Nov. 17, 1917; s. Charles James and Minnie Bethiah (Lester) C.; student San Jose State Coll., 1935-38; A.B., Stanford, 1939, A.M., 1940; Ph.D., U. Va., 1944; m. Jean Show, Sept. 8, 1940; children—Charles Dennis, Robert Keith, Jeffrey Craig. Instr. math. U. Va., 1942-44, vis. prof., 1955-56; from asst. prof. to prof. Ore. State Coll., 1944-57; prof. math.

Cal. State Coll. at Los Angeles, 1957—, head math. dept., 1957-64, 71—, dir. instl. research, 1964—, dir. coll. computing center, 1961—, chmn. acad. senate, 1968-69; cons. edn., industry, 1958—. Royall Victor fellow Stanford, 1940-41; du Pont fellow U. Va., 1941-42. Mem. Am. Math. Soc., Math. Assn. Am., A.A.A.S., Assn. Computing Machinery, Am. Assn. U. Profs., Phi Beta Kappa, Sigma Xi. Home: 414 Terrill Av Los Angeles CA 90042

CLARK, CHARLES MARTIN, Jr., investment banker; b. Summit, N.J., Nov. 2, 1905; s. Charles Martin and Bessie (Milligan) C.; grad. Hotchkiss Sch., 1924; B.S., Harvard, 1928; hon. diploma U.S. Mcht. Marine Acad., 1945; m. Valerie Graham, Aug. 1, 1939; children—Ann Valer (Mrs. Albert F. Gordon), Cecily Martin, John Sheldon. Reporter, Bradstreet Co., 1928-29; statistician Second Nat. Bank, Boston, 1930-33; pres. Martin Co., printers, Boston, 1934-35; partner Charles Clark & Co., mems. N.Y. Stock Exchange, 1937-47; engaged in estate mgmt. and directorship cos., 1948-61; partner Sullivan & Co., mems. N.Y. Stock Exchange, 1962-64; ltd. partner Estabrook & Co., 1965-69, chmn. bd. Eastabrook & Co., Inc., 1970—; v.p., dir. Sherwood Investors, Inc.; dir. Dun & Bradstreet, Inc. U.S. adviser N. Atlantic Planning Bd. Ocean Shipping, 1952. Chmn. bd. Kips Bay Boys Club, N.Y.C.; trustee Hewitt Sch., N.Y.C.; trustee Am. Mcht. Marine Library Assn. Served to lt. (s.g.) U.S. Maritime Service, 1942-44. Presbyn. Clubs: Down Town Assn. (N.Y.C.); Piping Rock (Locust Valley, L.I.); Seawanhaka Corynthian Yacht (Oyster Bay); Jupiter Island (Hobe Sound, Fla.); Union (N.Y.C.). Home: E Main St Oyster Bay NY 11771 Office: 80 Pine St New York City NY 10005 also 15 State St Boston MA 02109

CLARK, CHARLES WENDELL, metalworking co. exec.; b. Cambridge, O., Nov. 21, 1923; s. Charles W. and Lettie (Pyle) C.; B.S. in Metallurgy, Case Inst. Tech., 1944; m. Gladys Irene Vanek, Feb. 14, 1945; 1 son, James. With Cleveland Twist Drill Co. (O.), subsidiary Acme-Cleve. Corp., 1946-70, gen. supt., 1962- 65, v.p. mfg. and engring., 1965-70; pres. mgr. machine tools div. Nat. Acme div. Acme-Cleve. Corp., Cleve., 1970—. Trustee Southwest Gen. Hosp., Berea, O. Served with USNR, 1943-46. Mem. Am. Assn. Indsl. Mgmt. (pres. Cleve. 1969-70, bd. dirs. 1964-70), Cleve. Engring. Soc., Sigma Xi, Tau Beta Pi, Phi Kappa Psi. Patentee extrusion. Home: 179 Manning Dr Berea OH 44017 Office: National Acme 170 E 131st St Cleveland OH 44108

CLARK, CHESTER WILLIAM, ret. army officer, research exec.; b. San Francisco, July 18, 1906; s. Harry Benton and Gertrude Anita (Fisher) C.; B.S. in Chemistry, U. Cal. at Berkeley, 1927, M.S. in Chemistry and Physics, 1929; Ph.D., in Physics, U. Leiden (Netherlands), 1935; m. Jessie May Clark, Feb. 19, 1930; children—Anthony Wayne, Adri Marijke (Mrs. Jack Peacock). Commd. 2d lt. U.S. Army Res., 1927, advanced through grades to maj. gen., 1962; dep. G-4 8th U.S. army Korea, 1954-55; dir. missile research and devel., Ordnance Corps, 1955-59, asst. chief ordnance research and devel., 1958-62; dir. research U.S. Army, 1962-63; vice chmn. NATO Army Adv. Group, 1963; comdg. gen. U.S. Army, Japan, 1963-65; ret., 1965; v.p. research Research Triangle Inst., 1965—. Mem. weapons adv. group U.S. Army, mem. aviation sci. adv. group. Trustee Human Resources Research Orgn. Mem. Nat. Inventors Council, 1962-63. Mem. Am. Phys. Soc., Assn. U. S. Army, Am. Ordnance Assn., N.C. Marine Sci. Council. Rotarian. Club: Cosmos (Washington). Home: 520 Lake Shore Lane Chapel Hill NC 27514 Office: P O Box 12194 Research Triangle Park NC 27709

CLARK, CLARE CLYDE, lawyer; b. Conway, La., Mar. 13, 1888; s. Edward Levin and Susan Hibernia (Mayo) C.; A.B., La. State U., 1911, LL.B., 1913, J.D., 1968; m. Mary Collins Thatcher, Jan. 14, 1922. Admitted to La. bar, 1913, since practiced in Shreveport; pvt. practice, 1914-15; partner firm Cook, Clark, Egan, Yancey & King, and predecessors, 1957—. Mem. exec. bd. La. Bapt. Conv., 1935-41; exec. com. So. Bapt. Conv., 1956-61; mem. Shreveport Municipal Fire and Police Civil Service Bd., 1944-47. Trustee M.E. Dodd Found., 1930-41. Served as 2d lt. F.A., U.S. Army, 1918. Mem. Am., La., Shreveport bar assns., Am. Legion, Phi Delta Phi. Democrat. Baptist (deacon 1927—, chmn. bd. 1930-64). Mason (Shriner). Clubs: Shreveport, Shreveport Country. Home: 920 Ockley Dr Shreveport LA 71106 Office: PO Box 77 Shreveport LA 71102

CLARK, CLARENCE C, ednl. cons.; b. Owensboro, Ky., Aug. 1894; s. Lee and Eleanor (Johnson) C.; B.S., U. Ky., 1917; M.S., U. Chgo., 1924; Ph.D., N.Y. U., 1932; student L. I. Biol. Lab., summer 1933; m. Berenice Bodenhofer Wheeler, Dec. 1924. In charge physics and chemistry courses Owensboro (Ky.) High Sch., 1919-20, instr. physics Wash. Sq. Coll., N.Y. U., 1926- 29, instr. gen. sci. Sch. Commerce, 1929-32, asst. prof., 1932-36, asso. prof., 1936-40, in charge sci. courses, 1938-59, prof., 1940-59, chmn. Gen. Course Group, 1951-59; prof. sci., chmn. phys. sci., U. So. Fla., 1960-66, prof. emeritus, 1966; adminstrv. cons. Fla. Tech. Univ. 1966—; research sci. E.E. Free Labs., 1930-39; chief biol. Rainbow Bridge Expdn., summers 1934-37; cons. on slot machine N.Y. Police Dept., 1936-37; cons. on pin game machines, Teaneck (N.J.) Municipal Govt., 1940; cons. and TV programs artist NBC, 1938-39; presented sci. TV programs Du Mont TV System, 1946-47; mem. bd. Sunstate Builders, Inc. Served as lt., F.A., U.S. Army, 1918-19; major, U.S.A.A.F. 1942-45; lt. col. USAF Res., 1947-54, comdg. officer Communications Squadron, 1949-52, group tng. officer, 1952-54, ret. 1954. Fellow A.A.A.S.; member Am. Assn. Physics Tchrs., Armed Forces Communications Assn., Florida Acad. Scis. (mem. council 1962—, pres. 1968-69), Phi Delta Kappa (pres. Rho chpt., 1938-39), Alpha Phi Sigma, Beta Gamma Sigma. Presbyn. Author books. Contbr. articles to profl. mags. Home: 11105 Carrollwood Dr Tampa FL 33618 Office: 4202 Fowler Av Tampa FL 33620

CLARK, CLIFFORD DALE, educator; b. Moulton, Ia., Feb. 26, 1925; s. Artie Seymour and Myrtle (Severs) C.; B.A., U. Kan., 1948; M.A., U. Chgo., 1951, Ph.D., 1953; m. Margery Blair Miller, June 19, 1949; children—Geoffrey Blair, Kathryn Dale. Fgn. affairs officer C.I.A., 1951-55; asst. prof. econs. N.C. State U., 1955-57, asso. prof., 1957-62, prof., 1962-68, dir. research, 1963-64; asso. dean N.Y.U., 1964-65, vice dean, 1965-68; dean Sch. Bus., prof. econs. U. Kan., 1968—. Cons. to Com. Econ. Development, 1962-63; research dir. Rockefeller Com. to Review Adminstrn. Workman's Compensation in N.Y., 1962; cons. unemployment ins. N.Y. State Legislature, 1964-68. Pres. bd. trustees Woodward Sch., Bklyn., 1967-68. Served as sgt. inf., AUS, 1943-46; ETO. Decorated B.S.M. Mem. Am. Econ. Assn., Am. Finance Assn., Am. Assn. Collegiate Schs. of Bus. Author: (with others) Theory and Measurement of Rent, 1961; Review of Workman's Compensation in New York State, 1962; Wage Theory, Wage Rates and Productivity, 1958. Contbr. articles profl. jours. Home: 2604 Stratford Rd Lawrence KS 66044

CLARK, CLIFTON BOB, educator, physicist; b. nr. Fort Smith, Ark., July 8, 1927; s. Clifton Breckenridge and Coly (Stroud) C.; B.A., U. Ark., 1949, M.A., 1950; Ph.D., U. Md., 1957; m. Sue Magruder, Sept. 1, 1950; children—Carol Jane, Charles Brian, Richard Thomas. Asst. prof. sci. Florence State Tchrs. Coll., 1950-51; asst. prof. physics U.S. Naval Acad., 1951-55; asso. prof., 1956-57; physicist U.S. Naval Research Lab., 1955-56; asso. prof. physics So. Meth. U., Dallas, 1957-61, prof., 1961-65; physicist, prof., head dept. U. N.C., Greensboro, 1965—. Served with USNR, 1945-46. Mem. Am. Assn. Physics Tchrs., Am. Phys. Soc., A.A.A.S., Am. Assn. U. Profs., N.C. Acad. Sci., Phi Beta Kappa, Sigma Xi, Sigma Pi Sigma, Pi Mu Epsilon, Kappa Mu Epsilon, Omicron Delta Kappa. Home: 800 Montrose Dr Greensboro NC 27410

CLARK, DANE, (Barney Zanville), actor, b. Bklyn., Feb. 18, 1913; B.A., Cornell U.; law degree, St. John's U. Began career on stage in Of Mice and Men, other prodns. include Dead End, Golden Boy, Broadway shows The Number, Fragile Fox; numerous motion pictures include Action in the North Atlantic, Destination Tokyo, The Very Thought of You, God is My Co-Pilot, Go Man Go, Blackout, Paid to Kill, Thunder Pass, Port of Hell, Toughest Man Alive; TV series Bold Adventure, also numerous others. Home: 1680 Old Oak Rd Los Angeles CA 90049*

CLARK, DAVID, musician; b. Tottenham, London, Eng., Dec. 15, 1942. Started dance craze in England called Philip Blues; now leader Dave Clark five. Recipient Personality Milkman award Nat. Dairy Council Eng. Address: care Epic Records 51 W 52d St New York City NY 10019*

CLARK, DAVID DELANO physicist; b. Austin, Tex., Feb. 10, 1924; s. David Lee and Grace (Delano) C.; student U. Tex., 1941-42, 46; A.B. in Physics, U. Cal. at Berkeley, 1948, Ph.D. (AEC predoctoral fellow 1950-52), 1953; m. Gladys Braunstein, Dec. 27, 1949; children—Marcia Susan, Gordon Richard, Janet Mirella. Research asso. Brookhaven Nat. Lab., 1953-55, vis. scientist summers, 1957, 58; mem. faculty engring. physics Cornell U., 1955—, asso. prof., 1958-65, prof., 1965—, dir. Nuclear Reactor Lab., 1960—; cons. Gen. Atomic Co., summer 1959. Served with USAAF, 1942-46. Euratom fellow Euratom Research Center, Ispra, Italy, 1962; Guggenheim Found. fellow Niels Bohr Inst., 1968-69. Mem. Am. Phys. Soc., Am. Nuclear Soc., Fedn. Am. Scientists, Phi Beta Kappa, Sigma Xi. Contbr. articles profl. jours. Home: 105 Needham Pl Ithaca NY 14850

CLARK, DAVID LOUIS, univ. dean; b. Binghamton, N.Y., Nov. 14, 1929; s. Ralph Keeler and Catherine (Hartigan) C.; B.A., N.Y. State Coll. Tchrs., Albany, 1951, M.A., 1952; Ed.D., Columbia Tchrs. Coll., 1954; m. Elsie Edith Shaw, June 28, 1952; children—Patricia, Michael, Timothy, Catherine. Research asst. N.Y. State Tchrs. Assn., 1954-56; asst. to supt. Garden City (N.Y.) pub. schs., 1956-58; dir. coop. research program U.S. Office Edn., 1958- 62; asso. dean, prof. edn. Ohio State U., 1962-66; prof. edn., dean Sch. Edn., Ind. U., 1966—. Mem. Am. Ednl. Research Assn., N.E.A., Am. Assn. Sch. Adminstrs., Phi Delta Kappa. Author (with others) Organizing Schools for Effective Education, 1962; (with John E. Hopkins) Educational Research, Development, and Diffusion Manpower, 1969; also reports in field. Home: 1243 Matlock Rd Bloomington IN 47401

CLARK, DEAN ALEXANDER, physician; b. St. Paul, Feb. 7, 1905; s. Charles Alexander and Georgia (Dean) C.; A.B., Princeton, 1927; B.A., Oxford U. (Rhodes Scholar), 1929, B.S., 1930; M.D., Johns Hopkins, 1932; m. Katherine Goldthwaite Dorr, July 12, 1937 (div. 1962); children—Anna Jane, Stephen Higginson, Rosalind Carden, William Dean; m. 2d, Harriet Fidler Jones, 1962. Intern medicine Johns Hopkins Hosp., 1932-33; asst. resident medicine and neurology N.Y. Hosp., N.Y.C., 1933-34; NRC fellow medicine and neurophysiology Cornell, 1934-35; intern, asst. resident Henry Phipps Psychiat. Clinic, Johns Hopkins Hosp., 1935-37; intern Trudeau (N.Y.) Sanatorium, 1938; study med. care in Appalachian bituminous coal fields, 1939; passed asst. surgeon (res.) USPHS, 1939-41, surgeon (res.), 1941-44, sr. surgeon (res.), 1944-45, sr. surgeon (regular) 1945, med. dir. (res.), 1945—, surveys med. care; former asso. prof. pub. health practice Columbia; med. dir. Health Ins. Plan Greater N.Y., 1945-49; gen. dir. Mass. Gen. Hosp., Boston, 1949-62; clin. prof. preventive medicine Harvard Med. Sch., 1953-62; research prof. med. and hosp. adminstrn. Grad. Sch. Pub. Health, U. Pitts., 1962—; mem. staff John J. Kane Hosp., 1970—. Fellow Am. Pub. Health Assn., N.Y. Acad. Med.; mem. A.M.A. Contbr. sci. jours. Home: 1158 Murray Hill Av Pittsburgh PA 15217 Office: Grad Sch Pub Health 130 DeSoto St Pittsburgh PA 15213

CLARK, DICK, performer; b. Mt. Vernon, N.Y., Nov. 30, 1929; grad. Syracuse U., 1951. Summer announcer sta. WRUN, 1950; then staff announcer sta. WOLF; rejoined sta. WRUN, then joined sta. WKTV; announcer sta. WFIL-Radio, Phila., 1952; host Am. Bandstand; Dick Clark Beech-Nut show; Dick Clark's World of Talent; Miss Teenage Am. pageant; The Object Is; Missing Links. Formed Dick Clark Prodns., 1956; producer Shebang, Where The Action Is, Swinging Country, Happening, Get It Together, Music Bag, Roger Williams Special, Mantrap, It's Happening; films include Because They're Young, 1960; The Young Doctors, 1961; Psych-Out, 1968; The Savage Seven, 1968; Killers Three, 1969. Author: Your Happiest Years, 1959; To Goof or Not to Goof, 1963; also articles on teenage problems for nat. publns. Address: care Dick Clark TV Prodns Inc 9125 Sunset Blvd Los Angeles CA 90069*

CLARK, DONALD ROBERT, ins. co. exec.; b. Chgo., Jan. 19, 1924; s. Sherman Fred and Frieda (Grossklags) C.; student Northwestern U., 1941-43, U. Wis., 1943-44; m. Lora Marie Steiner, Aug. 11, 1945; children—Gregory Wayne, Sharon Louise. With div. Kemper Ins. Cos., 1941—; now treas. Am. Motorists Ins. Co., Am. Mfrs. Mut. Ins. Co., Kemper Security Ins. Co., Food Industries Fedn. Mut. Ins. Cos., Kemperco Reins Co., Fed. Mut. Ins. Co., Kemperco, Inc., Fed. Kemper Life Assurance Co., Fidelity Life Assn., Lumbermens Mut Casualty Co.; asst. treas., asst. sec. Ia. Kemper Mt. Ins. Co., Sequoia Ins. Co.; asst. treas. Economy Fire & Casualty Co.; dir. Ia. Kemper Mut. Ins. Co. Former adviser Chgo. Jr. Achievement. Mem. Ins. Accounting and Statis. Assn. (pres. 1968-69). Lutheran (past chmn. congregation and finance com.). Contbr. Insurance Accounting Fire and Casualty, 2d edit., 1965. Home: 1771 Sherwood Rd Des Plaines IL 60016 Office: 4750 Sheridan Rd Chicago IL 60640

CLARK, DONALD SHERMAN, educator; b. Springfield, Mass., Dec. 27, 1906; s. Webster Clifton and Lilla (Sherman) C.; B.S., Cal. Inst. Tech., 1929, M.S., 1930, Ph.D., 1934. Mem. faculty Cal. Inst. Tech., 1934—, prof. phys. metallurgy, 1951—, dir. placements, 1934—; cons. in field, 1934—; spl. research dynamic properties metals and alloys. Mem. Am. Soc. Metals (pres. 1956, trustee 1938-40, 55-58; Edward DeMille Campbell lectr. 1953), Am. Soc. Testing and Materials (Templin award 1949, Dudley medal 1951), Western Coll. Placement Assn. (dir. 1963-66), Am. Soc. M.E., Am. Welding Soc., Am. Foundrymen's Soc., Brit. Iron and Steel Inst., Inst. Metals, Am. Assn. U. Profs., Am. Soc. Engring. Edn., Sigma Xi, Tau Beta Pi (pres. 1962-66), Pi Tau Sigma. Author: Engineering Materials and Processes, 3d edit., 1959; (with W.R. Varney) Physical Metallurgy for Engineers, 2d edit., 1962. Home: 1066 San Pasqual St Pasadena CA 91106

CLARK, DUNCAN WILLIAM, med. educator; b. N.Y.C., Aug. 31, 1910; s. William H. and Lillian (Keating) C.; A.B., Fordham U., 1932; m. Carol Dooley, Jan. 30, 1943; children—Carol Ann, Duncan William, James Fenton. With L.I. Coll. Medicine, Bklyn., 1936, dir. student health, 1942-49, dean, 1948-50; asst. prof. medicine, 1948-50, prof., chmn. dept. environmental medicine and community health, State U. Coll. of Medicine at N.Y.C., 1951—; intern Bklyn. Hosp., 1926-38, also cons. physician, medicine; resident in medicine, coll. div., Kings County (N.Y.) Hosp., 1938-40, now vis. physician, medicine; cons. USPHS, 1961—, NIH, 1961-65, NRC, 1965-68; chmn. health services research tng. com. USPHS, 1965-69; research scientist and fellowship rev. com. Nat. Center for Heath Services Research and Devel.; WHO traveling fellow, 1952; vis. prof. Med. Sch., U. Birmingham (Eng.), 1961. Dir. Health Ins. Plan of N.Y.C., 1953-71; chmn. N.Y. Study Com. Research Accident Prevention in Children, 1958-60, Assn. Aid Crippled Children; chmn. Nat. Adv. Com. on Local Health Depts., 1960-61. Recipient Fordham Alumni award, 1958, Fordham Coll. Encaenia award, 1962. Diplomate Am. Bd. Internal Medicine, Am. Bd. Preventive Medicine. Fellow Am. Pub. Health Assn., N.Y. Acad. Medicine, A.C.P.; mem. N.Y. Pub. Health Assn. (pres. 1954-55), Conf. Profs. Preventive Medicine (chmn. 1953-54), Assn. Tchrs. Preventive Medicine (pres. 1954-55, editor Newsletter 1959-70), Com. to Protect Our Children's Teeth (pres. 1957-60), A.A.A.S., Kings County Med. Soc., Harvey Soc., N.Y. Acad. Sci., Internat. Epidemiological Assn., Alpha Omega Alpha (faculty counsellor). Roman Catholic. Editor, co-author Textbook of Preventive Medicine, 1967. Contbr. articles on med. edn., public health and medicine. Home: 35 Prospect Park W Brooklyn NY 11215 Office: 450 Clarkson Av Brooklyn NY 11203 ☆

CLARK, EARL, ins. co. exec.; b. Enid, Okla., Mar. 22, 1917; s. Owen Earl and Imogene (Timmons) C.; B.S., Kan. State U., 1939; m. Albertine Bernice Putnam, June 23, 1941; children—Kathleen Ann (Mrs. Alexander S. Yankovich), Robert Hamilton, Cynthia Susan. With Occidental Life Ins. Co. of Cal., Los Angeles, 1940—, v.p. charge agencies, 1959-63, pres., 1963—, chief exec. officer, 1965—, also dir.; chmn. bd. Am. Life N.Y. Group v.p., dir. Trans Am. Corp.; chmn. bd. Transam. Life Ins. and Annuity, Occidental Life Ins. Co. Can.; dir. Canadian Surety Co., Trans Internat. Airlines, Transam. Actuarial Cons., Inc., Transam. Investment Mgmt. Co. bd. dirs., mem. exec. com. Better Bus. Bur.; bd. dirs. Central City Assn., Inst. Life Ins. C.L.U., 1956. Mem. Pasadena Tournament Roses, Life Ins. Assn. Am. (dir.), Los Angeles C. of C. (dir.; chmn. dirs. com. for urban affairs). Clubs: Jonathan (Los Angeles); San Gabriel (Cal.) Country; California, San Francisco Golf. Home: 3541 San Pasqual Pasadena CA 91107 Office: 1150 S Olive St Los Angeles CA 90015

CLARK, EARL WESLEY, maritime cons., polit. scientist; b. Cadwell, Ill., Aug. 10, 1901; s. Charles Wesley and Mary Comfort (Harding) C.; A.B., Eureka Coll., 1928; A.M., U. Ill., 1931; m. Mary Eudora Bracken, June 28, 1922; 1 dau., Mrs. Joanne C. Hoover. High School instr., El Paso, Ill., 1928-32; vocational dir. Bur. Pub. Welfare, Chgo. and Cook County, Ill., 1933; dist. and later state rep. Ill. Emergency Relief Comm., 1934-35; Peoria dist. dir., regional exec. officer, dep. regional adminstr., regional adminstr. (covering Ill., Wis., Minn., Neb., Ia., S.D., N.D.), Chgo. OPA Region, 1943-46; asst. and later nat. commr. OPA, 1947; mem. War Contracts Price adjustment Bd., 1947; nat. liquidation officer, Office of Temporary Controls (included OPA, Civilian Prodn. Adminstrn., Office War Mblzn. and Reconversion, Office Econ. Stblzn., 1947; dir. div. of liquidation Dept. Commerce (included OPA, Civilian Prodn. Adminstrn., Office War Mobilization and Reconversion, Office Econ. Stblzn., Office Temp. Controls, Fgn. Econ. Adminstrn.), 1947-48, chief deptl. moblzn. staff, office of industry cooperation, 1948-49; chmn. bd. appeals-employee grievances Dept. Commerce also pub. hearing officer Office of Industry Cooperation; spl. asst. to sec. of commerce, 1949-50; dep. maritime adminstrn. Maritime Administrn., 1950-53; pres. N.Y. & Cuba Mail S.S. Co.; maritime cons. Mem. Nat. Cargo Bur., Inc., 1954; co-dir. Labor-Mgmt. Maritime Com., 1955—; lectr. Fla. State U., 1952; mem. nat. adv. bd. Operation Ship Shape, Inc., 1968—. Mem. adv. com. on requirements Dept. Commerce, 1949; adv. com. on tech. assistance Dept. State, 1949-50; industry adviser Intergovtl. Maritime Consultatory Orgn. of UN, London, 1965. Red Cross div. chmn., 1947, Com. Fund div. chmn., 1947. Mem. Gt. Lakes Pilotage Adv. Com. 1960-70. Bd. dirs., chmn. fgn. relations com. United Seamans Service. Recipient Spl. award United Seamen's Service, 1969; Recognition plaque P.R. Propeller Club, 1970. Mem. Soc. Naval Architects and Marine Engrs., Nat. Def. Transp. Assn., Navy League, Pi Kappa Delta, Lambda Chi Alpha. Episcopalian. Club: Propeller (pres. Washington 1964-66, chmn. position com. of U.S. 1964—; mem. nat. exec. com). Author: O.P.A. reports, Div. of Liquidation reports, Industry Voluntary Agreements Reports, 1949; Program Imperatives for Strengthening the U.S. Merchant Marine, 1965; Bread Upon the Waters, 1970; Reply to the Rockefeller Report, 1970. co-author: State Pilotage in America, 1960; Medical and Hospital Care for Merchant Seamen, 1964; A Dialogue on Maritime Policy, 1966; The U.S. Merchant Marine Today, 1970; The American Passenger Ship Fleet, 1970; Dual U.S.-Foreign Flag Shipping Interests, 1970. Home: 3209 Wood Av Burtonsville MD 20730 Office: 100 Indiana Av NW Washington DC 20001

CLARK, EARNEST HUBERT, Jr., tool co. exec.; b. Birmingham, Ala., Sept. 8, 1926; s. Earnest Hubert and Grace May (Smith) C.; B.S. in Mech. Engring., Cal. Inst. Tech., 1946, M.S., 1947; m. Patricia Margaret Hamilton, June 22, 1947; children—Stephen D., Kenneth A., Timothy R., Daniel S., Scott H., Rebecca G. With Baker Oil Tools, Inc., Los Angeles, 1947—, v.p., asst. gen. mgr., 1958-62, pres., chief exec. officer, 1962-69, pres., chmn. bd., 1969—; div. v.p., also dir. Baker Transworld, Inc.; v.p., dir. Herramientas Interamericanas, S.A., Baker Internat., Baker Argentina; dir. Kobe, Inc., Tech. Oil Tool Corp., Galigher Co., Cementaciones Estimalaciones y Pruelas, S.A. Bd. dirs. Downey (Cal.) YMCA, YMCA for Met. Los Angeles; mem. nat. council YMCA. Served with USNR, 1944-46, 51- 52. Mem. Am. Inst. M.E., Am. Petroleum Inst. (dir.), Am. Ordnance Assn., Petroleum Equipment Suppliers Assn. (dir.), Am. Mgmt. Assn., Mchts. and Mfrs. Assn. (dir.), Tau Beta Pi. Home: PO Box 2274 Terminal Annex Los Angeles CA 90051 Office: 7400 E Slauson Av Los Angeles CA 90040

CLARK, EDWARD, lawyer, banker, former ambassador; b. San Augustine, Tex., July 15, 1906; s. John David, Leila (Downs) C.; B.A., Tulane U., 1926; LL.B., U. Tex., 1928; LL.D., Southwestern U., 1966; m. Anne Metcalfe Dec. 27, 1927; 1 dau., Leila Downs (Mrs. Douglas C. Wynn). Admitted to Tex. bar, 1928; county atty. San Augustine County, 1929-30; asst. atty. gen. Tex., 1931-34; pvt. practice law, Austin, 1939—; sr. partner firm Clark, Thomas, Harris, Denius & Winters, 1939—; chmn. bd. Capital Nat. Bank, Austin, 1960—; pres. First Nat. Bank, San Augustine, 1959—; U.S. ambassador to Australia, Canberra, 1965-68; fed. commr. for HemisFair, San Antonio, 1968; Am. exec. dir. Inter-Am. Devel. Bank, Washington, 1968-69; dir. Telecom Corp., Houston San Benito Bank & Trust Co. (Tex), Employers Casualty Ins. Co., Dallas, Employers Nat. Life Ins. Co., Delhi Internat. Oil Co., Dallas. Sec. to gov. Tex., 1935-36; sec. of state, Tex., 1937-39. Trustee U. Tex. Law Sch. Found. Served to capt. AUS, World War II. Mem. Am. Bar Assn., State Bar Tex., Tex. Philos. Assn., Texas Hist. Assn., S.A.R., Knights San Jacinto, Sons Republic Tex., Kappa Sigma, Phi Delta Phi. Episcopalian. Clubs: Austin (Austin); Ramada (Houston). Collector Tex. books and documents. Home: Cambridge Apts 1801 Lavaca St Austin TX 78701 Office: Capital Nat Bank Bldg PO Box 1148 Austin TX 78701

CLARK, EDWARD FERDNAND, lawyer; b. Delaware, O., May 10, 1921; s. Daniel John and Lillian (Holdgreve) C.; J.D., Ohio No. U., 1953;; m. Helen Ruth Swick, Feb. 10, 1945; children—Pamela Ann (Mrs. James R. Hanser), Michael E., Steven J., Philip J., Joseph W.,

Edward C., Nicholas J. Claims examiner Central Mut. Ins. Co., Van Wert, O., 1954-63; admitted to Ohio bar, 1953; asso. firm Lindeman-Shenk-Clark, Delphos, 1963—. Sec., treas. M.I. Clark, Inc. Past pres. Citizens for Delphos Com.; mem. exec. com. Mental Health and Retardation Bd. Van Wert, Mercer and Paulding Counties; pres. St. John's Parochial Sch. Bd. Served to capt. AUS, 1942-47. Mem. Van Wert County (sec. treas.), Allen County, Ohio, N.W. Dist. bar assns., Delphos C. of C., V.F.W., Am. Legion, Am. Fedn. Musicians (v.p. local 1949-50), Home and Sch. Assn. (pres. 1959). Democrat. Roman Cath. Kiwanian (pres. Delphos 1964-65), K.C. (4). Home: 425 N Clay St Delphos OH 45833 Office: Peoples Nat Bank Bldg Delphos OH 45833

CLARK, EDWARD FRANCIS, univ. chaplain, clergyman; b. N.Y.C., Oct. 11, 1914; s. James Edward and Belle (Hartley) C.; A.B., Georgetown U., 1938; Ph.L., Woodstock Coll., 1939, S.T.L., 1946; M.A., U. Minn., 1951. Entered Soc. Jesus, 1932, ordained priest Roman Catholic Ch., 1945; instr. Latin, Greek, English, Canisius High Sch., Baffalo, 1939-41; instr. Latin, Englsh, Fordham U., 1941-42, acad. v.p., 1956-60, univ. chaplain, 1965—; circulation mgr. Nat. Cath. Weekly, also lectr., 1947-48; instr. philosophy and theology St. Peter's Coll., Jersey City, 1948-49, dean, 1951-56, pres., 1960-65. Decorated Stella Della Solidarieta Italiana Di Prima Classe. Mem. Nat., Jesuit, Nat. Cath. edn. assns., Phi Beta Kappa. Address: Fordam U Bronx New York City NY 10007

CLARK, EDWARD FRANK, Jr., lawyer; b. N.Y.C., Apr. 24, 1907; s. Edward Frank and Grace E. (MacEvoy), C.; A.B. cum laude, Harvard, 1928, LL.B., 1931; m. Mary de Peyster Charles, Dec. 21, 1931; children—Christopher, Michael; m. 2d, Rosemary Reddick, Sept. 17, 1947; children—Raymond E., Celia R., Andrew E. Admitted to N.Y. bar, 1931, since practiced in N.Y.C.; with Carter, Ledyard, Milburn, 1931—, mem. firm, 1946—. Pres., sec., dir. Marineland of Fla.; sec., dir. Tropical Gas Co., Inc., Tropigas Tankers, Inc., Internat. Trading & Transport Co., Inc., Lockwood, Kessler & Bartlett, Inc.; dir. Gordon Jewelry Corp., Marineland of Pacific. Served to 1st lt., inf. AUS, 1944-46. Mem. Am., N.Y. State, N.Y.C. bar assns., Assn. U.S. Army, Vets. 7th Regiment, New Eng. Soc. N.Y., Nat. Rifle Assn. (Outstanding War Service award 1946), Baker St. Irregulars. Clubs: Metropolitan, Players, Harvard, Broad Street, Downtown Athletic (N.Y.C.). Contbr. articles to profl. jours. Home: 520 E 86th St New York City NY 10028 Office: 2 Wall St New York City NY 10005

CLARK, ELIAS, educator; b. New Haven, Aug. 19, 1921; s. Charles Edward and Dorothy (Gregory) C.; grad. Phillips Acad., Andover, Mass., 1939; B.A., Yale, 1943, LL.B., 1947, M.A., 1958; m. Ann Paxton Atkins, Apr. 22, 1947; children—Charles Elias, Katherine Ann, Susan Gregory, Robert Treat, Dorothy Gregory, Ann Atkins, William Rogers. Admitted to N.Y. bar, 1948, Conn. bar, 1950; asso. firm Cleary, Gottlieb, Friendly & Cox, N.Y.C., 1947-49; faculty Yale Law Sch., 1949—, prof. law, 1958-68, Lafayette S. Foster prof. law, 1968—, master Stilliman Coll., 1962- -. Mem., former chmn. Conn. Bd. Mental Health. Served to 1st lt. USAAF, 1943-45; ETO. Decorated Air medal with one cluster. Mem. Am. Judicature Soc., Conn. Bar Assn., Phi Beta Kappa, Order of Coif. Democrat. Contbr. articles to profl. jours. Home: 71 Wall St New Haven CT 06511

CLARK, ELLOT CANDEE, artist; b. N.Y.C., Mar. 27, 1883; s. Walter and Jennie (Woodruff) C.: ed. pub. and high schs., N.Y.; self tought in art; m. Elizabeth Trowbridge Egleston, Apr.5, 1922; m. 2d, Margaret Winslow Fowler, July 1944. Formerly tchr. Art Students' League, N.Y.C. Represented in N.Y. Water Color Club at 9 and in Nat. Acad. at 13 years of age: residence and travel abroad, 1904-06; painting trip in Painted Desert in Ariz., 1926, 35, in Himalayas, travel and study in India, 1937-38. Splty. landscape; exhibited in important annual exhbns.; represented in Md. Inst., Muncie (Ind.) Inst., Dayton (O.) Mus., Fort Worth Mus., Met. Mus., N.Y.C., others; "Rolling Country," purchased by Woodrow Wilson; "Winds of Destiny, " Ranger Fund Purchase, N.A.D., 1922. Represented in several permanent collections; recipient Third Hallgarten prize N.A.D., 1912; Edgar Davis prize San Antonio, 1929 Nat. Academician, 1944; Burton Bush prize Allied Artists, 1950; Spl. exhbn. Paintings of India, Iranian Inst., N.Y.C., 1947. Mem. council India Inst.; mem. council N.A.D., 1946-48, corr. sec.. 1948-56, pres., 1956-59, mem. awards jury, 1962; ex-officio trustee Met. Mus., 1956-59 Bd. dir. City Center Art Gallery, N.Y., Fine Arts Fedn. N.Y. Fellow Met. Mus., pres. Allied Artists Am., 1948-52; N.Y. Soc. Painters; chmn. adv. com. Fine Arts East and West Assn.; mem. Internat. Inst. Arts and Letters, N.Y. Water Color Club, Am. Watercolor Soc. (pres. 1921-23, hon. pres. 1967—), League N.Y. Artists, Artists' Fund Soc., Conn. Acad. Fine Arts, Union Internationale des Beaux Arts et des Lettres; Nat. Sculpture Soc. (hon.), Civic League Charlottesville and Albemarle County. Clubs: Century Assn., Salmagundi Club (hon. mem.), Nat. Arts of N.Y. (life mem; gov., mem. exec. com., 1942-; chmn. com. on painting); Savannah Art. Author: Alexander Wyant (2 vols.), 1916; John Henry Twachtman, 1924; J. Francis Murphy, 1927; Theodore Robinson; History of the National Academy of Design, 1954. Contbr. articles to mags.; N.Y. art critic of studio London.. Home and studio: R D 5 Charlottesville VA 22901 ☆

CLARK, ELMER J., coll. dean; b. Wixom, Mich., Dec. 17, 1919; s. Elmer E. and Ella S. (Decker) C.; A.B., U. Mich., 1941, M.A., 1943, Ph.D., 1949; children—Janet Elizabeth, Thomas Allen; m. 2d. Grace Ella Cruse, Nov. 9, 1968. Tchr., Pontiac (Mich.) pub. Schs., 1941-43; grad. asst. U. Mich., 1946-48; asso. prof. edn. Central Mo. State Coll., 1948-49; asst., then asso. prof. edn. Ind. State Coll., Terre Haute, 1949-55, dean grad. studies, prof. edn., 1955-64; dean Coll. Edn., So. Ill. U., Carbondale, 1964-. Served with USAAF, 1943-46. Mem. Nat. Soc. Coll. Tchrs. Edn., N.E.A., Am. Ednl. Research Assn., Am. Psychol. Assn., Nat. Soc. Study Edn. Democrat. Contbr. articles profl. jours. Home: Rural Rt 1 Anna IL 62906

CLARK, EMERY T., mfg. corp. exec.; b. 1905; married. Gen. contractor, Chgo.; contractor, 1929-33; with Clark Oil and Refining Corp., 1933—, chief exec. officer, dir., 1934-50, sec., treas., now chmn., chief exec. officer, also dir. Address: 8530 W National Av Milwaukee WI 53227*

CLARK, EUGENE, coll. dean; b. Ann Arbor, Mich., July 21, 1917; s. Fred Emerson and Carrie (Patton) C.; B.A., Swarthmore Coll., 1939; M.A., Harvard, 1941, Ph.D., 1949; m. Natalie Marion Fairchild, Sept. 5, 1942; children—Douglas Fairchild, Lawrence Patton, Andrew Nichols, Steven Fifield, Nancy Marion. Economist WPB, 1942, Dept. Commerce, 1943-45; instr. Tufts Coll., 1945-46; asst. prof. econs., bus. adminstrn. Ohio Wesleyan U., 1946-49, asso. prof., 1950-54, prof., 1954-57; cons., economist to bd. govs. Fed. Res. System, 1956-57; dean Coll. Econs. and Bus., prof. econs. Wash. State U. (formerly State Coll. Wash.), 1957—. Mem. Gov.'s Adv. Com. on Salaries, 1957-70; gen. chmn. Pacific Northwest Conf. Banking, 1957-61; mem. Regional Export Expansion Council. Mem. Pullman Federated Drive Bd., 1963-66. Mem. Am., Western econ. assns., Am. Marketing Assn., Royal Econ. Soc., Am. Assn. U. Profs. (mem. standards com. 1966-69, chmn. 1968-69, mem. exec. com.), Am. Assn. Collegiate Schs. of Bus. Club: Rotary (Pullman). Author: (with others) Values and Policy in American Society (rev. edit.), 1954; Problems in Social Policy, 1954; (with Blaine E. Grimes, David H. Jennings) Goals of American Foreign Policy, 1955; (with Blaine E. Grimes) Goals of Economic Policy, 1955; (with R.D. Tousley) Principles of Marketing, 1962; The American Economy, 1962; also articles in profl. jours. Co-editor: Readings in Social Policy, 1954. Contbr. to Ency. Brit. Home: 414 Garfield St Pullman WA 99163

CLARK, EUGENIE, zoologist; b. N.Y.C., May 4, 1922; B.A., Hunter Coll., 1942; M.S., N.Y.U., 1946, Ph. D. (Pacific Sci. Bd. fellow 1949), 1950; m. Hideo Umaki, 1942; m. 2d, Ilias Konstantinu, 1949; 4 children; m. 3d, Chandler Brossard; m. 4th, Igor Klatzo, 1969. Research asst. in ichthyology Scripps Instn. Oceanography, 1946-47; with N.Y. Zool. Soc., 1947-48; research asst. in animal behavior Am. Museum Nat. History, N.Y.C., 1948-49, research asso., 1950-54; instr. Hunter Coll., 1954; exec. dir. Cape Haze Marine Lab., Sarasota, Fla., 1955-67; asso. prof. biology City U. N.Y., 1966-67; asso. prof. zoology U. Md., 1968—; spl. research reproductive behavior fishes, morphology and taxonomy marine fishes, isolating mechanisms poecillid fishes. Recipient Myrtle Wreath award in sci. Hadassah, 1964; Nogi award in art Underwater Soc. Am., 1965; Dugan award in aquatic sci. Am. Littoral Soc., 1969. Fellow AEC, 1950; Fulbright scholar, Egypt, 1951; Saxton fellow, 1952; Breadloaf Writer's fellow; recipient Alumnae award Hunter Coll. Mem. Am. Soc. Icthyology and Herpetology, Soc. Women Geographers, Internat. Soc. Profl. Diving Scientists, Am. Littoral Soc., A.A.A.S. Author: Lady with a Spear, 1953; The Lady and the Sharks, 1969. Home: 7817 Hampden Lane Bethesda MD 20014 Office: Dept of Zoology Univ of Md College Park MD 20742

CLARK, FAITH, ret. govt. ofcl.; b. Canton, O., June 1, 1911; d. Alexander Bierce and Faith (Fogle) Clark; grad. Emma Willard Sch., 1929; student Smith Coll., 1929-30; A.B., Wooster Coll., 1933; M.S., U. Chgo., 1934, Ph.D., 1952. Engaged in food econs. research U.S. Dept. Agr., Washington, 1936—, dir. consumer aand food econs. research div. Agr. Research Service, 1957-70. Mem. Am. Home Econs. Assn., Am. Farm Econs. Assn. Contbr. articles to profl. jours. Author govt. bulls. Home: 5510 Surrey St Chevy Chase MD 20015

CLARK, FRANK DONALD, coll. dean; b. Wellington Kan., July 15, 1913; s. Frank Dan and Nan (Daugherty) C.; student Friends U., Wichita, Kan., 1931-32; B.S., Kan. State Tchrs. Coll., 1936; M.A., State U. Ia., 1938; postgrad. U. Mich., 1941; m. Evelyn Lorene Madison, June 28, 1939; 1 dau., Candy Sue. Actor, Globe Theatre Repertory Co., Dallas summer 1936; instr. speech and drama Kan. State Tchrs. Coll., 1936-38; instr. speech and drama Parsons (Kan.) Jr. Coll., 1938-40; head speech and drama dept. Amarillo (Tex.) Coll., 1940-44; radio news editor KFDA, Amarillo, 1944-46; asst. prof. broadcasting U. Okla., Norman, 1946-55, asso. prof. drama, 1955-61, acting dean Coll. Fine Arts, 1959-61, dean, prof. drama, 1961—. Pres. S. W. Theatre Conf., 1961-62; coordinator adv. panels Okla. Arts and Humanities Council, 1964—. Mem. Nat. Council Fine Arts Deans (past chmn.), Nat. Council Arts in Edn. (dir.). Home: 505 Foreman Av Norman OK 73069.

CLARK, FRANK MONROE, congressman; b. Bessemer, Pa., Dec. 24, 1915; s. Walter and Leila (Davidson) C.; student pub. schs. of Bessemer, Pitts. Sch. Aeros; m. Patricia Loy, 1941; children—Frank Monroe, Kelly. Chief of police, Bessemer, 1945-55; mem. 84th-92d U.S. Congresses, 25th Pa. Dist., mem. pub. works, Mcht. Marine and fisheries coms. Del. NATO Parliamentary Conf., 1956, 65, 66; del. to visit German Govt. as guest of Germans, 1957; del. Internat. Christian Leadership Peace Conf., Hague, 1958. Del. Nat. Rds. Conf. S.A. 1959, Internat. Road Conf., S.Am., 1965, inspection tour NATO bases, 1960, 61, 64, Internat. Road Fedn. Pacific Regional Conf., Sydney, Australia, 1961, NATO Conf., Brussels, 1967, 68, Internat. Rds. Conf., Sydney, 1968, Coast Guard Loran Sta., Mediterranean, 1968, 69, NATO Conf., Brussels, Belgium, 1969. Mem. Bessemer Vol. Fire Dept. Served as glider pilot USAF, World War 11; maj. USAF Res. Mem. Am. Legion (past comdr.), 40 and 8, V.F.W. (past comdr.), Chief of Police Assn. Pa. Presbyn. Mason (Shriner), Odd Fellow, Moose. Home: Bessemer PA 16112 Office: House of Representatives Washington DC 20525

CLARK, FRANK RINKER, Jr., pipe line co. exec.; b. Washington, May 4, 1912; s. Frank Rinker and Theresa Louise (Burton) C.; student Northwestern U., 1930-33, U. Tulsa, 1933-35, Harvard Law Sch., 1935-36, U. Okla. Law Sch., 1936-38, U. Tulsa, 1939-42, 45-47; m. Evelyn Crews, June 27, 1943; children—Theresa Lynn, Frank Robert. Claims adjuster Travelers Ins. Co., 1938; trainee Helmerich & Payne, Tulsa, 1938-39; law clk. Settle, Monnet & Clammer, Tulsa, 1939-42; prodn. planning Douglas Aircraft Co., 1942-45; tax accountant Interstate Oil Pipe Line (named changed to Humble Pipe Line Co. 1961), 1945-50, tax atty., 1950-63, sec., 1955—, treas., 1958-61, 63—; treas. Dixie Pipeline Co., 1966—. Admitted to Okla. bar, 1938, also U.S. Supreme Ct. Mem. Am., Okla. bar assns., Am. Soc. Corporate Secs., Houston Soc. Financial Analysts, U.S., Houston chambers commerce, Am. Petroleum Inst., Mid-Continent, Rocky Mountain oil and gas assns., Tax Research Assn. Houston (adv. dir.), Petroleum Club Houston, Sigma Chi. Republican. Presbyn. (elder). Club: East Ridge Country (Shreveport, La.). Home: 11621 Monica Lane Houston TX 77024 Office: 800 Bell Av Houston TX 77001

CLARK, FRANK WINSLOW, Jr., dept. store exec.; b. Los Angeles, Nov. 17, 1917; s. Frank Winslow and Inez Bell (Roberds) C.; B.S. in Bus. Adminstrn. with honors, U. Cal. at Los Angeles, 1939; LL.B., Hastings Coll. Law, 1946; m. Jean Fox, Mar. 19, 1960. Admitted to Cal. bar, 1946, since practiced in Los Angeles; partner firm Parker, Milliken, Kohlmeier Clark & O'Hara; exec. v.p., gen. counsel, dir. May Dept. Stores Co. Served to lt. comdr. USNR, 1941-46. Mem. Zeta Psi. Club: Los Angeles Country. Home: 567 Comstock Av Los Angeles CA 90024 Office: 606 S Olive St Los Angeles CA 90014

CLARK, FRED GEORGE, found. exec.; b. Cleve., Nov. 2, 1890; s. Frederick George and Mary Angeline (Winter) C.; student Kenyon Coll., Gambier, O., 1909-13; LL.D., Morningside Coll., Sioux City, Ia.; m. Margaret L. Moore, June 26, 1915 (div. Dec. 1931); m. 2d, Sibyl Young Hine, Jan. 16, 1932 (div. Sept. 1948); m. 3d, Diana M. Brodie, Dec. 18, 1948. Oil tester Fred G. Clark Co., oil refining, Cleve., 1913, office mgr., 1914-16, salesman, 1916-17, v.p., 1920-24, pres., 1924-32; pres. Conewango Refining Co., Warren, Pa., 1926-32; pres. Clark, Curtin & Norton, Inc., ins., N.Y., 1932-65; organizer, nat. comdr. Crusaders against Nat. Prohibition, 1929-33; nat. radio broadcaster for econ. enlightenment, 1933-36; established, chmn. bd. Am. Factfinders, 1936; founder, chmn. bd. Am. Econ. Found., ednl. research, 1939—; moderator radio program, Wake Up Am., 1939-46. Served as capt. U. S. Army, in charge all lubricating oil purchases for U. S. Army, 1917-18. Mem. Soc. Colonial Wars, Huguenot Soc., Colonial Lords of Manors in Am., Nat. Inst. Social Scis., Psi Upsilon. Clubs: Racquet and Tennis, Sky, River (N.Y.C.); Atlantic Beach (L.I.). Author: Magnificent Delusion, 1940: (with Richard S. Rimanoczy) How We Live, 1944; Money, 1946; How To Be Popular Though Conservative, 1948; How to Think About Economics, 1952; What Every Supervisor Should Know About the Principles of Economics, 1960; Where the Money Comes From 1961; editorials. Composer, Wake Up America, 1932. Lectr. Home: 45 Sutton Pl S New York City NY 10022 Office: 51 E 42d St New York City NY 10017

CLARK, GEORGE ALFRED, educator; b. Winburne, Pa., May 21, 1910; s. John Elmer and Mary Jane (Nail) C.; A.B., Ursinus Coll., 1931; M.A., Rutgers U., 1939; Ph.D., U. Pa., 1950; m. Emily Elizabeth Fox, Aug. 26, 1935; 1 son, George Alfred. Instr. secondary schs., N.J., 1931-42; instr. Monmouth (N.J.) Jr. Coll., 1946-47; asst. instr. U. Pa., 1947-48; faculty Lafayette Coll., 1948—, chmn. dept. philosophy, 1951—, James Renwick Hogg prof. philosophy, 1958—. Field dir. A.R.C., 1943-46; acting chmn. Easton-Phillipsburg Area Commn. Human Relations, 1960; mem. Hawk Mt. Sanctuary Assn., 1955—. Served with AUS, 1942-43. Mem. Am. Philos. Assn., Am. Assn. U. Profs. (pres. Lafayette 1952-43), N.A.A.C.P., Cape May (N.J.) Geog. Soc. (pres. 1960-62). Contbr. profl. jours. Home: 159 Parker Av Easton PA 18042

CLARK, GEORGE E., banker; b. Evanston, Ill., 1918; ed. Loyola U., Chgo., 1939, U. Mich., 1941. Exec. v.p. Ind. Nat. Bank, Indpls. Home: 9125 Spring Mill Rd Indianapolis IN 46260 Office: 1 Indiana Sq Indianapolis IN 46204

CLARK, GEORGE EVANS, ret. bus. exec.; b. St. Paul, Oct. 30, 1905; s. R. W. and Margaret (Haines) C.; student St. Paul Acad.; B.S., Princeton, 1929; m. Margery Jarvis, Sept. 20, 1940; children—Margery (Mrs. Bernhard J. Peters), George. With Tri-Continental Corp., N.Y.C., 1930-37; with Adams Express Co., N.Y.C., 1937—, treas., 1939, asst. to pres., 1940, v.p. 1941, exec. v.p., 1943, dir. 1941—, pres., 1948-71; dir. Am. Internat. Corp., N.Y.C., 1945—, pres., 1948-71; dir. Petroleum Corp. Am., N.Y.C., 1940—, pres., 1944-71; adv. com. Marine Midland Grace Trust Co. N.Y. Clubs: Country of Fairfield (Conn.); Kittansett Golf, Beverly Yacht, Sippican Tennis (Marion, Mass.); Wall Street, Princeton, University (N.Y.C.); Nassau (Princeton); Princeton Elm; Riomar Country, Johns Island Country, Riomar Bay Yacht (Vero Beach, Fla.). Home: PO Box 3465 510 River Dr Vero Beach FL 32960 also 159 Allen's Point Rd Marion MA 02738

CLARK, GEORGE MCMURRY, banker; b. Christiana, Tenn., Oct. 8, 1902; s. Henry Harvey and Bessie Robinson (Jacobs) C.; student Branham-Hughes Mil. Acad., 1918-21, Vanderbilt U., 1921-22; Cumberland U., 1924; m. Mary Evans Shelton, Feb. 28, 1931; 1 son, George McMurry, Jr. Prin., Murray High Sch., Rutherford County, Tenn., 1922-23; cashier Pioneer Bank, 1924-30; exec. sec. Morris Plan Bankers Assn., 1930-34; exec. v.p. Pioneer Bank, 1934- 36, pres., 1937-59, chmn. bd., 1959—; pres. Consumer Bankers Assn., 1947-50. Mem. Yacutan Exploring Soc. (pres. under water archeology), Pi Kappa Alpha. Presbyn. Ch. Clubs: Mountain City, Fairyland, Golf and Country. Originator Efficiency Audit, technique for measuring bank effciency (while chmn. Com. on Operatons of Consumer Bankers Assn., 1947; orginator and financer of artificial insemination program in dairy devel. (while mem. Agrl. Com. Chattanooga C. of C.). Home: 31 Minnekahda Pl Chattanooga TN 37405 Office: Pioneer Bank Chattanooga TN 31402

CLARK, GEORGE ROBERTS, banker; b. Cynwyd, Pa., Jan. 12, 1910; s. Percy H. and Elizabeth (Roberts) C.; A.B., Harvard, 1932, M.B.A., 1934; m. May Denckla Howe, Sept. 18, 1937. With Corn Exchange Nat. Bank & Trust Co., Phila., 1935-51, asst. cashier, 1939-43, asst. v.p. charge consumer credit, 1946-47, v.p., spl. asst. to pres., 1947-49, v.p. charge personnel and operations, 1949-50, exec. v.p., dir., 1951; sr. v.p. comml. and banking dept. Girard Trust Corn Exchange Bank, Phila., 1951-60, also vice chmn. bd. Girard Trust Bank, 1950—; dir. Gen. Coal Co., Westmoreland Coal Co., Whitehall Cement Mfg. Co. Trustee Acad. Natural Scis. Phila. Mem. Am. Philos. Soc. (chmn. finance com.), Pa. Hort. Soc. (pres.). Clubs: Philadelphia, Harvard, Rabbit (Phila.); Fly (Cambridge, Mass.). Home: 519 Auburn Av Chestnut Hill PA 19118 Office: Girard Trust Bank Broad and Chestnut Sts Philadelphia PA 19101

CLARK, GEORGE WHIPPLE, educator, physicist; b. Evanston, Ill., Aug. 31, 1928; s. Robert Keep and Margaret (Whipple) C.; B.A., Harvard, 1949; Ph.D., Mass. Inst. Tech., 1952; m. Elizabeth Kister, Dec. 18, 1954; children—Katherine, Jacqueline. Instr. physics Mass. Inst. Tech., 1952-54, asst. prof., 1954-60, asso. prof., 1960-65, prof., 1965—. Mem. Am. Acad. Arts and Scis. Research on cosmic ray physics and high energy astronomy. Home: 133 Rawson Rd Brookline MA 02146 Office: Mass Inst Tech Cambridge MA 02139

CLARK, GERALD ROBERT, physician, educator; b. Parr, Alta., Can., Mar. 17, 1918; s. Alfred Francis and Florence Harriet (McRae) C.; student U. Alta., 1936- 38; B.A., U. Ore., 1942, M.D., 1945; M.P.H., Harvard, 1951; m. Beverly Byrniss Colwell, Nov. 2, 1951; children—Gary S., Christy, Linda, Jeffrey Jay, Terry, Gregg R. Came to U.S., 1938, naturalized, 1943. Intern, 1946- 52, dir. Tb and communicable disease control Ariz. Health Dept., Phoenix, 1947-48; pub. health cons. ECA, Athens, Greece, 1949-50; dir. Clackamas County Health Dept., Oregon City, Ore., 1952-53; health commr. N.M. Dept. Health, Santa Fe, 1953-55; mem. psychiat. staff Norristown (Pa.) State Hosp., 1955-58; supt. Somerset (Pa.) State Hosp., 1958-59; dir. Psychiatry Clinics, Jefferson Med. Coll., Phila., 1959-61, asso. prof. psychiatry, 1965-66; asso. prof. psychiatry and pediatrics U. Pa., 1967—; sr. physician Childrens Hosp. Phila., 1967—; supt. Elwyn Sch. and Hosp., Media, Pa., 1960-66; commr. mental retardation Commonwealth Pa., 1966; pres. Elwyn (Pa.) Inst., 1966—, M.H.R. Assos., Inc., 1969—. Diplomate Am. Bd. Preventive Medicine, Am. Bd. Neurology and Psychiatry. Mem. A.M.A., Am. Pub. Health Assn., Am. Psychiat. Assn., Am. Assn. on Mental Deficiency, Am. Coll. Preventive Medicine, Am. Coll. Hosp. Administrs. Nat. Assn. Pvt. Psychiat. Hosps. (chmn. publs. com.), N.E.A., Coll. Physicians Phila., Am. Hosp. Assn. (chmn. governing council psychiat. hosp. sect.). Home: 77 Washington Rd Elwyn PA 19063 Office: Elwyn Inst Elwyn PA 19063

CLARK, GILBERT EDWARD, U.S. ambassador; b. Thompson Ridge, N.Y., Jan 15, 1917; s. Theodore Gilbert and Kathryn Cornelius Morgan (Jones) C.; B.A., Syracuse U., 1938, M.A., 1940; m. Lyla Elaine Sween, Apr. 7, 1943; children—Bonnie Lee, Theodore Edward, George Kirsten. Reporter Middletown (N.Y.) Times Herald, 1937; grad. asst. instr. Syracuse U., 1938-39; prodn. mgr. Whitney Graham Pub. Co., Buffalo, 1940-41; asst. prof. Syracuse U., 1946; with Dept. of State, 1946—; information officer, vice consul, Am. consulate gen., Bombay, India, 1946-49, consul, 1949-51; pub. affairs staff Bur. Near Eastern, South Asia and African Affairs, Dept. of State, 1951-53; 2d sec., consul, 1st sec. Am. Legation, Tangier, Morocco, 1953-56; detailed to Exec. Office of Pres., Bur. of Budget, 1956-57, Dept. of State, 1957-58; assigned to Nat. War Coll., 1958-59; Am. consul gen. Amsterdam, Netherlands, 1959-61; counselor of embassy, dept. chief of Mission Am. Embassy, Pretoria, Transvail, Republic South Africa, 1961-65; dir. Office West Africa Affairs, Dept. State, 1965-66, country dir. So. Africa Affairs, 1966-68; ambassador to Mali, 1968-70, to Senegal and The Gambia, 1970—. Served as lt. col. Signal Corps, AUS, 1941-45; CBI. Decorated Bronze Star. Mem. Am. Fgn. Service Asso., Sigma Delta Chi, Alpha Phi Omega. Episcopalian. Home: Am Embassy Dakar Senegal Office: Dept State Washington DC 20521

CLARK, GLYNN E., ednl. ofcl.; b. Barnhart, Mo., Mar. 14, 1912; s. Edward C. and Eunice E. (Wade) C.; A.B., Washington U., St. Louis, 1934, A.M., 1935, Ed. D., 1957; m. Carolyn I. Humboldt, Aug. 28,

1939; children—Carol Beth, Douglas Paul. Psychol. examiner St. Louis pub. schs., 1936-38; tchr. counselor S.W. High Sch., St. Louis, 1938-41; dir. guidance services St. Louis pub. schs., 1941-55; prin. Soldan High Sch., St. Louis, 1956-57; pres. Harris Tchrs. Coll., St. Louis, 1957-62; campus dir., v.p. Jr. Coll. Dist. St. Louis-St. Louis County, 1962—; pres. Meramec Community Coll. Pres. of Council North Central Jr. Colls., 1968-69. Served to lt. col. USMCR, World War II; lt. col. Ret. Mem. Am. Psychol. Assn. (diplomate counseling psychology), Assn. Higher Edn., Mo. Tchrs. Assn., Sigma Xi, Phi Delta Kappa (chpt. pres. 1966-67), Kappa Delta Pi, Omicron Delta Kappa. Home: 802 Couch Av Kirkwood MO 63122

CLARK, GORDON HADDON, educator; b. Phila., Aug. 31, 1902; s. David Scott and Elizabeth Yates (Haddon) C.; A.B., U. Pa., 1924, Ph.D., 1929; D.D., Ref. Episcopal Sem., 1966; m. Ruth Schmidt, Mar. 28, 1929; children—Lois Antoinette, Nancy Elizabeth. Instr. philosophy U. Pa., 1924-36; lectr. Reformed Episcopal Sem., Phila., 1932-36; asso. prof. philosophy Wheaton Coll., 1936-43; ordained to ministry Presbyn. Ch., 1944; prof. philosophy, chmn. dept. Butler U., 1945—. Moderator Gen. Synod Reformed Presbyn. Ch., 1961. Mem. Am., Ind. philos. assns., Evang. Theol. Soc., Phi Beta Kappa. Author: (with T.V. Smith) Readings in Ethics, 1931; Selections from Hellenistic Philosophy, 1940; (with others) A History of Philosophy, 1941; A Christian Philosophy of Education, 1946; A Christian View of Men and Things, 1952; What Presbyterians Believe, 1956, rev. as What Do Presbyterians Believe?, 1965; Thales to Dewey, 1956; Dewey, 1960; Religion, Reason and Revelation, 1961; Karl Barth's Theological Method, 1963; The Philosophy of Science and Belief in God, 1964; Peter Speaks Today-A Commentary on I Peter; The Philosophy of Gordon H. Clark, 1968; Biblical Predestination, 1969. Home: 345 Buckingham Dr Indianapolis IN 46208

CLARK, H. SOL, lawyer; b. Savannah, Ga., Dec. 29, 1906; s. Sam and Ella (Raskin) C.; A.B., Cornell U., 1928, LL.B., 1930; m. Matilda Shapiro. May 14, 1933; children—Fred Stephen, Janet (dec.). Admitted to Ga. bar, 1929; practice of law, Savannah, 1930—, mem. Brannen Clark & Hester, 1945-70, Brannen & Clark, 1970—; asst. city atty., Savannah, 1944-47. Mem. Ga. Indsl. Loan Adv. Bd., 1955-59; founder Savannah Legal Aid Office, 1946; mem. Chatham County Civil Service Bd., 1968-70. Trustee Telfair Art Acad., 1959-62. Recipient Reginald Heber Smith Legal Aid award, 1961, Arthur von Briesen Legal Aid award, 1970, plaque Harvard Law Sch. Assn. Ga., 1971. Fellow Am. Bar Found., Internat. Acad. Trial Lawyers (dean 1969-70, dir. 1970—), Am. Coll. Probate Counsel; mem. Am. Judicature Soc. (dir. 1960-64), Savannah Bar Assn. (pres. 1952), Nat. Legal Aid Assn. (dir. 1960-64), Scribes. Jewish religion. Mason. (33). Compiler Ga. Masonic Code, 1954. Home: 109 E 44th St Savannah GA 31405 Office: First Bank Bldg 140 Bull St Savannah GA 31401

CLARK, HARLAN BENDELL, fgn. Service officer; b. Brookfield, O., Jan. 5, 1913; s. James and Lillian Maude (Bendell) C.; A.B., Mich. State Coll., 1935; A.M., Fletcher Sch. Law and Diplomacy, Medford, Mass., 1936; m. Mary Patricia Maginn, Jan. 18, 1947; children—Susan Jennifer, Paul Jesson. Apptd. fgn. service officer, vice consul of career, and sec. in diplomatic service, 1937; consul, Aden, 1944-46; administrv. officer Spl. Diplomatic Mission U.S. to Kingdom of Yemen, 1946; 2d sec. legation and consul, Jidda; 1946-47; 2d sec. legation and consul, Sana's, in addition to duties at Jidda 1947; Beirut (for Arabic lang. study), 1947-48; staff Dept. of State, Washington, 1948-51, officer in charge Syria, Lebanon, Iraq Affairs, 1949; assigned acting dep. Office of Near Eastern Affairs, 1950; 1st sec. of embassy, Damascus, Syria, 1951-53, counselor embassy, Damascus, 1953-54; spl. asst. to asst. sec. state for personnel and adminstrn., dep. dir. personnel Dept. State, 1954-56; assigned Nat. War Coll., 1956-57; 1st sec. embassy, Tokyo, 1957, counselor polit. affairs, chief polit. div., 1958-59; consul gen., Alexandria, UAR, 1959-64; charge d'affaires-minister U.S. embassy, Taiz, Yemen, 1964-66; diplomatic adviser to comdt., U.S. Army War Coll., Carlisle Barracks, Pa., 1967—. Sr. fellow Grad. Sch. Internat. Studies, U. Denver, 1966-67. Mem. Internat. House, Tokyo, Japan, Central Asian Soc., Internat. Studies Assn., Am. Acad. Polit. Sci., Rocky Mountain Social Sci. Assn., Assn. U.S. Army, Phi Kappa Phi, Pi Kappa Delta. Contbr. on Arabia to nat. mags. Home: P O Box 64 Brookfield OH Office: PO Box 255 Carlisle Barracks PA 17013

CLARK, HAROLD FLORIAN, educator, economist; b. Lancaster, Ky., Aug. 29, 1899; s. William Leslie and Cora (Dunn) C.; A.B., Asbury Coll., 1920, LL.D., 1939; A.M., Columbia, 1922, Ph.D., 1933; postdoctoral London Sch. Econs., 1926-27; m. Anne Beth Price, Dec. 25, 1931; 1 son, William Price. Asst. prof. ednl. finance, Ind. U., 1923-25, asso., prof., 1925-27, prof., 1927-38; prof. ednl. econs. Columbia, 1928-65; prof. econs. Trinity U., San Antonio, 1965-66; Vernon Taylor prof. econs., chmn. dept., 1966—; cons. to spl. asst. for Air Force Acad. Matters, also to Nat. Manpower Council, Teloprograms, Inc., School Exec. mag. econ. cons. Challenge mag.; study of edn. costs for Ford Found., 1957. Co-chmn. Bogota Conf. Edn. and Econ. Devel. Latin Am. for OAS; chmn. exec. bd. "Social Education" apptd. by Am. Hist. Assn., 1929-41; dir. and v.p. Am. Provident Soc.; chmn. Com. on Coöps., N.E.A., 1941-43; mem. exec. com. Nat. Occupation Conf., 1932-39; co-ordinator Sloan project in applied econs., to get exptl. evidence of what schs. can do to improve econ. conditions in low income communities, 1939-49. Pres. Am. Assn. Gifted Children, 1948; mem. adv. com. and co-ordinating com. Consumer div. N.Y. Civilian Def. Vol. Office, 1942-43. Served in U.S. Army, World War I; mem. 51st Regt., N.Y. Guard, World War II. Fellow A.A.A.S. (v.p., chmn. Sect. Q., 1941, 42), Royal Econ. Soc., Nat. Council Edn.; mem. N.E.A., Am. Assn. Sch. Adminstrs. (mem. yearbook commn. on sch. curriculum 1947), Am. Ednl. Research Assn., Am. Econ. Assn., Nat. Council for Social Studies, Nat. Soc. Coll. Tchrs. Edn., Consumer Edn. Assn. (chmn. college div., pres. 1941, 42), Phi Kappa, Delta Kappa. Democrat. Author books including: Economics, 1948, rev. 1951; Classrooms in the Factories, 1958; Classrooms in the Stores, 1961; Classrooms in the Military, 1964; Classrooms on Main Street, 1966; Cost and Quality in Edn. Co-author: Yearbook of Am. Assn. of Sch. Adminstrs., 1947; Financing Higher Education, 1959. Editor Yearbook Econ. Edn. for Nat. Council for Social Studies; co-editor Social Backgrounds of Education, contbr. to Ency. Social Scis., Compton's Ency., Ency. Ednl. Research, Ency. Vocational Guidance, Ency. of Edn.; author many tech. articles. Address: Trinity U San Antonio TX 78212

CLARK, HAROLD GLEN, educator; b. Mesa, Ariz., June 11, 1902; s. Joseph William and Mary (Noble) C.; certificate, Tempe Normal Sch., 1923; B.S., Brigham Young U., 1928; M.S., U. So. Cal., 1934; Ed.D., George Washington U., 1942; m. Virginia Driggs, June 26, 1929 (dec. Mar. 1950); children—Carol Jean, Mary Louise, Donald Driggs, Virginia Lynn, Joseph William; m. 2d, Mary Deane Gilbert, Dec. 20, 1950; children—Paul Gilbert, Lark Gilbert, Rebecca. Pres. West Pa. Conf., Pitts. Ch. of Jesus Christ of Latter-day Saints, 1925-26; pub. sch. teacher, Mesa, Ariz., 1926-33; prin. Solomonville pub. schs., 1933-37; sec. to Congressman John R. Murdock, Washington, 1937-42; tng. officer, U.S. Dept. Agr., 1942-46; dir. of extension, prof. edn. Brigham Young U., Provo, Utah, 1946—, dean adult edn. and extension services, 1956-64, dean div. continuing edn., 1964-71. Mem. Utah State Bd. for UNESCO, 1949-50; chmn. publicity and adult edn. dept. Utah Conf. Higher Edn., 1948-49. Recipient Spl. Service award Brigham Young U., 1969; Julius Nolte award for outstanding leadership, 1971. Mem. N.E.A., Nat. U. Extension Assn., Nat. Congress Parents and Tchrs. (Ariz. bd. 1934-37), Utah Edn. Assn., Utah Acad. Arts and Scis., Provo C. of C., Phi Delta Kappa (pres. Washington chpt. 1939-40). Mem. Church of Jesus Christ of Latter-day Saints (bishop Washington 1942-46; mem. gen. bd. Young Men's Mut. Improvement Assn., 1949-60; high councilman 1967-69, patriarch 1969-70, pres. temple). Author: Meetings. a Guide and Source Book, 1946; Millions of Meetings: The Art of Governing Zion. Home: 2195 N 1220 E Provo UT 84601

CLARK, HAROLD WHITE, investment banker; b. Sparta, Tenn., Sept. 1, 1922; s. William F. and Eula Pearl (Barlow) C.; B.A., Vanderbilt U., 1943; m. Gloria Gambill, July 20, 1946; children—Carol B. (Mrs. Roy O. Elam III), Harold White, Gloria C. Salesman, J.C. Bradford & Co., Nashville, 1946-48; v.p. Clark, Landstree & Kirkpatrick, Inc., Nashville, 1948-62; pres. Cherokee Securities Co., Nashville, 1962—; dir. Cherokee Equity Corp. Trustee Harpeth Hall Sch., Montgomery Bell Acad. Served to lt. USNR, 1943-46. Mem. Investment Bankers Assn. (bd. govs., municipal div. council), Vanderbilt Alumni Assn. (pres.), Sigma Chi, Omicron Delta Kappa. Presbyn. Clubs: Belle Meade Country, Cumberland (Nashville). Home: 312 Walnut Dr Nashville TN 37205 Office: 95 White Bridge Rd Nashville TN 37205

CLARK, HARRY WITTENMYER, banker; b. Gulfport, Miss., Mar. 24, 1917; s. Harry W. and Aileen (Foxworth) C.; B.S., Bowling Green Coll. Commerce, 1938; certificate Nat. Inst. Comml. and Trade Orgn. Execs., Northwestern U., 1940; m. Margie Baker, Mar. 29, 1946 (div. 1967); children—Marshall, Nancy; m. 2d, Ethel Harris, 1968. Mgr. Okolona and Clarksdale (Miss.) C. of C., 1938-41; new industries rep. Miss. Power Co., Gulport, 1946-51; exec. dir. North Miss. Indsl. Devel. Assn., West Point, 1951-56, Com. 100, Wilmington, N.C., 1956-58; v.p. Fantus Area Research, 1958; indsl. cons. Tex. Power Co., 1958-60; dir. indsl. devel. T. & P. Ry., Dallas, 1960-62; exec. dir. Tex. Indsl. Commn., Austin, 1962-68; v.p. econ. devel. 1st Nat. Bank, Midland, Tex., 1968—. Served with AUS, 1941-45; ETO. Decorated Bronze Star; created mem. Order Brit. Empire; named Tex. World Trade Man of Year, 1967. Fellow Am. Indsl. Devel. Council (pres. 1957-58); mem. So. (pres. 1954; Tex. dir. 1961-62, v.p. 1971) indsl. devel. councils, Dallas Area Indsl. Devel. Assn. (chmn. 1961). U.S. Jr. C. of C. (v.p. 1950-51). Methodist. Lion (dist. gov. 1951). Home: 601 George St Midland TX 79701 Office: 1st Nat Bank Midland TX 79701

CLARK, HENRY BENJAMIN, Jr., food co. exec.; b. Chevy Chase, Md., Oct. 8, 1915; s. Henry Benjamin and Lena (Sefton) C.; B.C.S., Northwestern U., 1937; M.B.A., Harvard, 1940; m. Geraldine D. Putman, July 25, 1942; children—Putman D., Sefton R. Analyst, Castle & Cooke, Inc., Honolulu, 1946-50, asst. sec., 1950-58, asst. treas., 1956-58, treas., 1958-70, v.p., 1962-70, exec. v.p., 1970—; dir. Hawaiian Telephone Co., Honolulu Gas Co., Pacific Resources, Inc., Hawaiian Ind. Refinery, Inc., Hawaiian Airlines, Cal. & Hawaiian Sugar Co., Bay & River Nav. Co. Mem. Gov.'s Com. Employment of the Handicapped; state com. Nat. Council on Crime and Delinquency. Bd. dirs. Honolulu YMCA, Palolo Chinese Home; chmn. Hawaii Prep. Acad. Served to lt. comdr. USNR, 1940-45. Mem. C. of C., Phi Kappa Psi. Clubs: Pacific, Pacific-Union. Home: 3060 Noela Dr Honolulu HI 96815 Office: PO Box 2990 Honolulu HI 96802

CLARK, HENRY TOOLE, Jr., med. adminstr.; b. Scotland Neck, N.C., Oct. 13, 1917; s. Henry Toole and Cornelia Justice (Josey) C.; A.B., U. N.C., 1937; M.D. (Henry C. Buswell fellow), U. Rochester, 1944; m. Blanche Evelyn Burrus, Oct. 1, 1946; children—Laura Irwin, Henry Toole III, Anne Lovelace. Student intern Trudeau Sanatorium (N.Y.), 1940-41, Lawrason Brown fellow pulmonary physiology, 1942; fellow pathology U. Rochester Sch. Medicine, 1944-45; intern medicine Duke U. Hosp., 1945-46; adminstrv. asst., asst. dir. Strong Meml. Hosp., Rochester, N.Y., 1946-48; dir. Vanderbilt U. Hosp., 1948-50; vice chancellor health affairs U. N.C., 1950-65; resident adviser on long range planning U. Leiden (The Netherlands) Med. Center, 1966; dir. Conn. Regional Med. Program, 1966—; vis. prof. pub. health (med. care), Yale, 1966—; vis. prof. gen. medicine U. Conn., 1966—. Spl. cons. to P.R. Med. Center, 1956-69; cons. AID, 1965-68; spl. cons. to dir. NIH, 1965-66, to pres. Tuskegee Inst., 1960-70. Mem. USPHS Gen. Clin. Research Center Com., 1961-64, Mountain States Med. Edn. Adv. Com., 1963-64, state adv. council regional edn.; mem. Gov's Com. on Nuclear Energy; mem. Christian med. council Nat. Council Chs., 1968—; mem. rev. com. Nat. Library Medicine Biomed. Library, 1969—; mem. exec. council Episcopal Diocese N.C., 1960-63; chmn. local Community Chest, 1960-61. Dir. Am. Nurses Found., 1956-61; mem. Gov.'s Med. Center Study Commn., 1964-66; mem. Nat. Adv. Council on Edn. Health Professions, 1964-66; trustee U. of South, 1963-66; sec.-treas. N.C. Tennis Found., 1961-66. Rockefeller Found. Travel fellow, U.S.A., 1953, Western Europe, 1958. Mem. Am. Hosp. Assn. (council profl. practice 1959- 62, chmn. council on research and edn. 1962-64), A.M.A., Am. Pub. Health Assn., Conn., County med. socs., Soc. Med. Adminstrs., Med. Adminstrs. Conf. (sec.-treas. 1960-64, pres. 1964-66), Eastern Carolina (pres. 1959-60), N.C. (pres. 1960-61) tennis assns., Southern Lawn Tennis Assn. (mem. exec. com. 1960-62), Phi Beta Kappa, Alpha Epsilon Delta, Sigma Nu, Phi Chi, Alpha Omega Alpha. Rotarian. Clubs: Chapel Hill Country, New Haven Lawn. Contbr. sci. journs. Home: 36 Indian Trail Woodbridge CT 06525 Office: 272 George St New Haven CT 06510

CLARK, HERBERT MOTTRAM, educator; b. Derby, Conn., Sept. 3, 1918; s. Herbert and Anne (Mottram) C.; B.S. with honors, Yale, 1940, Ph.D., 1944. Instr., Yale, 1942-46, mem. staff Manhattan Project, 1943-46; research asso. Monsanto Chem. Co., Clinton Labs., Oak Ridge, 1946-47; faculty Rensselaer Poly. Inst., 1947—, prof. phys. and nuclear chemistry, 1961—; cons. AEC, 1963-70. Mem. spl. mission to Korea for Internat. Atomic Energy Agy., 1960; mem. subcom. radiochemistry Nat. Acad. Scis., 1961—; mem. radiol. health study sect. USPHS, 1967-69. Fellow N.Y. Acad. Sci., A.A.A.S.; mem. Am. Chem. Soc., Am. Phys. Soc., Am. Soc. Engring. Edn., Phi Beta Kappa, Sigma Xi. Author: (with R. T. Overman) Radioisotope Techniques, 1960; (with others) Principles of Chemistry, 1966; also articles. Patentee in field. Home: 2404 21st St Troy NY 12180

CLARK, HERVEY PARKE, architect; b. Detroit, Apr. 23, 1899; s. LeVert and Mary Eliza (Parke) C.; grad. cum laude, Lawrenceville Sch., 1917; A.B., Yale, 1921; B.A., U. Pa. Archtl. Sch., 1926; m. Isabel Alston Pringle, Jan. 14, 1933; children—Hervey Parke, Antonia. Trained in the office of Raymond Hood, Godley & Fouilhoux, N.Y.C.; practice of architecture, San Francisco, 1933-70, partner Clark & Beuttler, 1946-66, Clark and Morgan, 1966-70; archtl. projects include West Coast Meml. Am. Battle Monuments Commn., San Francisco, Pacific Telephone in Nev., Cal., also U. Cal. and Stanford U. bldgs.; U.S. Consulate Building, Fukuoka, Japan (with G. T. Rockrise), 1958; 6 brs. Citizens Fed. Savs. & Loan Assn., 1953-61, head office, San Francisco, 1964, chs. Lectr., Stanford, 1954—. Bd. dirs. San Francisco Heart Assn., 1960-66, San Francisco Planning and Urban Renewal Assn., 1959. Mem. alumni bd. Yale, 1956-61. Asso. C. F. Gromme, F.E. Lloyd, war housing projects U.S. Govt., shore installations USN, World War II. Recipient nat. honor awards architecture, 1939-40, 52-55, 61,64, 65; Gold Medal Design and Craftsmanship, Archtl. League N.Y., nat. competition, 1960, Henry Hering medal, Nat. Sculpture Soc., 1965. Fellow A.I.A. (achievement archtl. design; pres. No. Cal. chpt. 1947, dir. 1961); mem. San Francisco Planning and Housing Assn. (pres. 1945-46, adv. com. 1969—), Zeta Psi. Clubs: Pacific Union (San Francisco). Home: 524 Moore Rd Woodside CA 94062 Office: 552 Mission St San Francisco CA 94105

CLARK, HOWARD HEWLETT, clergyman; b. Ft. Macleod, Alberta, Can., Apr. 23, 1903; s. Douglass and Florence Lilian (Hewlett) C.; student St. Catherine's Collegiate Inst.; B.A., U. Toronto, 1932; D.D., Trinity Coll., Toronto, others; D.C.L., Bishop's U., others; LL.D., U. Man.; m. Anna Wilson, June 3, 1935; children—Howard, Mary, Esther, Elizabeth. Asst. curate St. John's Norway, Toronto, 1930-32; curate Christ Ch. Cathedral, Ottawa, 1932- 39, rector, 1939-41, canon, 1941-45, dean, 1945; bishop of Edmonton, 1954; archbishop of Edmonton, 1959-61; primate Anglican Church of Can., 1959-70; archbishop Rupert's Land, 1961-69. Decorated companion Can. Home: 252 Glenrose Av Toronto 7 Ontario Canada

CLARK, HOWARD LONGSTRETH, lawyer, bus. exec.; b. Pasadena, Cal., Mar. 14, 1916; s. W.D. and Florence (Longstreth) C.; A.B., Stanford, 1937; LL.B., Harvard, 1942; m. 2d, Jean Beaven; 9 children. Admitted to N.Y. bar, 1942; practiced law with firm Sullivan & Cromwell, N.Y.C., 1941; v.p. Am. Express Co., 1948- 49, sr. v.p., dir., 1952-56, exec. v.p., dir., 1956-60, pres., chief exec. officer, 1960-68, chmn., chief exec. officer, 1968—, also mem. exec. and finance coms.; dir. Chrysler Corp., Lehman Corp., Cluett, Peabody & Co., Stone & Webster, Inc., Fireman's Fund Ins. Co.; trustee U.S. Trust Co. N.Y. Bd. dirs. N.Y. Conv. and Visitors Bur.; trustee Wooster Sch.; bd. govs. Fed. Hall Meml. Assos., Inc. Mem. Internat. Golf Assn. (bd. dirs.), Harvard Law Sch. Assn. Downtown Lower Manhattan Assn. (bd. dirs.), Chi Psi. Clubs: Links, Recess, Wall Street, Madison Square Garden, River, Sky (N.Y.C.); Augusta (Ga.) Nat. Golf: Blind Brook (Port Chester, N.Y.); Stanwich (Greenwich, Conn.); Seminole Golf (Riviera Beach, Fla.); Royal and Ancient Golf of St. Andrews (Fife, Scotland); The Presidents. Home: 607 Riversville Rd Greenwich CT 06803 Office: 65 Broadway New York City NY 10006

CLARK, J. KENT, educator; b. Blue Creek, Utah, Sept. 29, 1917; s. Ernest E. and Adelaide (Kent) G.; A.B., Brigham Young U., 1939; Ph.D., Stanford, 1950; m. Ora Christensen, Sept. 15, 1939; children—Karen Mrie, Marie, Jeffrey Kent, Don Alan. Instr. English, Stanford, 1942-43, 46-47; instr. English, Cal. Inst. Tech.,Pasadena, 1947-50, asst. prof., 1950-54, asso. prof., 1954- 60, prof., 1960—, chmn. faculty com. on programs, 1967. Mem. edn. com. Pasadena Art Mus., 1968—. Served to 1st lt. USAAF, 1943-46; PTO. Life mem. P.T.A., 1957. Author: The King's Agent, 1958; Dimensions in Drama, 1964; (musicals) Take Your Medicine, 1958, Organization Woman, 1962. Home: 473 Fillmore St Pasedena, CA 91106.

CLARK, JAMES BENTON, railroad exec.; b. Sweetwater, Tenn., Jan. 3, 1914; s. John Edgar and Nancy Ella (Webster) C.; B.S., U. Tenn., 1937; grad. transp. course Northwestern U., 1959; m. Maxine Jeanette Butcher, Oct. 14, 1939; children—Diana (Mrs. Thomas K. Hudgens), Sylvia (Mrs. J. Michael Pulliam). Coop. student Bur. Pub. Roads, 1934-36; with L. & N. R.R., 1937—, asst. dir. personnel, 1955-59, chief engr., 1959-69, asst. v.p. personnel and labor relations, 1969—. Registered profl. engr., Ky. Mem. Am. Ry. Engring. Assn. (dir. 1965-68, v.p. 1969), Nat. Ry. Labor Conf. (mem. Southeastern carriers conf. com.), Roadmasters and Maintenance of Way Assn., Ry. Systems and Mgmt. Assn., Am. Mgmt. Assn., Chi Epsilon. Mem. Christian Ch. Home: 3070 Beals Branch Dr Louisville KY 40206 Office: 908 W Broadway Louisville KY 40201

CLARK, JAMES GORDON, cons. engr., author; b. Kansas City, Mo., Dec. 23, 1913; s. John Arthur and Stella (Wright) C.; A.S., Kansas City Jr. Coll., 1933; B.S. with honors, U. Ill., 1935, M.S., 1939; m. Jeannette Hazel McKinstry, May 8, 1937; children—Nannette, Diana; m. 2d, Janice Elizabeth Winters, Nov. 28, 1952; children—Mary, Jane, James. Instr. civil engring. Ore. State Coll., 1935; jr. engr. U.S. Bur. Reclamation, Denver, 1936; from instr. to prof. civil engring. U. Ill., 1936-56; asso. Harry Balke Engrs.; owener James G. Clark, cons. engr.; partner Clark, Daily & Dietz, cons. engrs., 1957-62; pres. Clark, Daily, Dietz & Assos., 1962-63, Clark, Dietz, Painter & Assos., Urbana, Carlyle, Waukegan (Ill.), Memphis, 1963-65, Leffler, Clark, Dietz & Assos., Sanford, Fla., 1963—, Clark, Dietz and Assos., engrs., 1965—; partner Clark, Daily, Smith & Assos., 1962-63, Clark, Altay & Assos., structural engrs., architects, 1963—; interim profl. work in structural engring. Am. Bridge Co., Bethlemen Steel Co., Howar, Needles, Temmen & Bergendoff, Curtiss Wright Corp., Consol. Vultee Aircraft Corp.; partner Balke & Clark; asso. Harry Balke Engrs. Mem. Profl. Engrs. Examining Com., State Ill. Chmn. James F. Lincoln Arc Welding Found. Award Programs. Trustee Ill. Bapt. Student Found., 1954-67. Mem. Nat., Ill. socs. profl. engrs., Am. Soc. C.E. (past pres. Central Ill. sect.), Am. Soc. Engring. Edn., Am. Ry. Engring. Assn., Am. Welding Soc., Am. Ry. Bridge and Bldg. Assn., Ill. Assn. Cons. Engrs., Am. Soc. Testing Materials, Hwy. Research Bd., Greater Champaign-Urbana Devel. Assn. (chmn.), Sigma Xi, Tau Beta Pi, Chi Epsilon. Author: Elementary Theory and Design of Flexural Members, 1950; Welded Deck Highway Bridges, 1950; Welded Highway Bridge Design, 1952; Comparative Bridge Designs, 1954; Welded Interstate Highway Bridges, 1959. Home: 716 W Florida Urbana IL 61801 Office: 211 N Race St Urbana IL 61801

CLARK, JAMES H., exec.; b. El Paso, Tex., Aug. 29, 1909; s. John Milton and Esther (Compton) C.; student Washington and Lee U., 1927-29, U. Fla., 1929- 30, U. N.Y., 1930-31; m. Lillian Bell, May 18, 1935; 1 son, James H. Asso. Lee Higginson Co., N.Y.C., 1930-32, Lawrence Marks & Co., 1932-39; partner Duff & Phelps, 1940-50; asso. Murchison Bros., Dallas, 1951-58; chmn. finance com. Phila. Suburban Water Co., Bryn Mawr, Pa.; chmn. exec. com. Phila. Suburban Corp., Bryn Mawr, Pa.; dir. Tex. Industries, Inc., Dallas, Keebler Co., Elmhurst, Ill., State Securities, Inc., Santa Fe, N.M.; trustee Bankers Life Ins. Co. Neb. Trustee Dallas Mus. Fine Arts, U. Neb. Found., U. Neb. Endowment Fund for Distinguished Teaching. Served as lt. comdr. USNR. Clubs: Brook Hollow Golf, Petroleum (Dallas). Home: 4606 St John's Dr Dallas TX 75205 Office: 3303 Lee Pkwy Dallas TX 75219

CLARK, JAMES INGRAHAM, educator, architect; b. Independence, Mo. Feb. 7, 1918; s. Ned R. and Helen (Bangs) C.; B. Arch., U. Mich., 1939; M. City and Regional Planning, (grad. Fellow) U. So. Cal., 1960; Ph. D. (Werner Hegemann Fellow) N.Y. U., 1964; m. Sinikka Marja-Liisa Kouvo, Apr. 7, 1961; children—Cathaerine, Kenyon, Kathleen, Caroline, Kathryn. With Waid & Corbett, architects, N.Y.C., 1940, ARMCO Steel Co., 1941, Runnells, Clark, Waugh & Matsumoto, architects-planners, Kansas City, Mo., 1947-48, James Ingraham Clark, architect-planner, Kansas City, Mo. and Corpus Christi, Tex., 1950-56, R. Newell Waters, Clark and Tomlinson, architects, Corpus Christi and Weslaco, Tex., 1956-57; asst. prof. architecture Tex. Tech. Coll., Lubbock, 1958-59; instr. U. So. Cal., 1959-60; vis. prof. Finland Inst. Tech., Helsinki, 1961; instr. planning N.Y. U., 1962-64; dir. Sch. Architecture, Ohio U., 1964-67; dean Sch. Architecture and Fine Arts, Auburn U., 1967-69; head grad. program regional planning Penn State U., 1969—; vis. lectr. planning cons., 1947—. Mem. Ala. Bd. Archtl. Registration, 1967—. Mem. Ala. Bd. Community and Tech. Services, 1967—. Bd. dirs. Auburn Found., Ala. Council Continuing Edn. Served to maj. USMCR, World War II. Recipient Nat. award for residence Progressive Architecture, 1947, hon. mention for sch., 1960; Safe Pilot award, 1970. Mem. Ala. Council Architects (treas. 1969), A.I.A. (dir. Corpus Christi chpt. 1955-58, pres. Ohio Valley chpt. 1966, Auburn chpt. 1969), Assn. Collegiate Schs. Architecture (continuing edn. com. 1964-67), Am. Soc. Planning Ofcls., Am. Soc. Photogrammetry, Nat. Council Archtl. Registration Bds., Nat. Pilots Assn., Phi Delta Theta, Sigma Delta Psi. Author: An Evaluation of Aesthetic Expression in Urban Design, 1960; A Critical Evaluation of Some Electronic Computer Uses for Urban Design, 1964. Home: 116 Sand Rd Hershey PA 17033

CLARK, JAMES MOTT, coffee mcht.; b. Kansas City, Mo., Jan. 27, 1916; s. Alexander Sidney and Mary (Mott) C.; B.A., Rice Inst., 1936; Consejero Cientifico y Tecnico, U. Bogota (Colombia), 1956; m. Nanine Howard Ferris, Oct. 5, 1937; children—James Mott, Carol Morgan. Sec.-treas. Southeastern Compress & Warehouse Co., Atlanta, 1940-43; v.p., treas. Gulf Atlantic Warehouse Co., Houston, 1944-46; treas., asst. mgr. Anderson, Clayton & Cia, Ltd., Sao Paulo, Brazil, 1947-50, mgr. coffee div., 1951-52; mgr. coffee div. Anderson, Clayton & Co., N.Y.C., 1952-55, v.p., 1955—; v.p. Ranger Ins. Co., N.Y.C., 1955—, also dir.; partner Anderson, Clayton & Felming, N.Y.C., 1955—; dir. Assn. Commodity Clearing Firm, Inc. Rep., atty. cotton warehousing industry OPA, 1943-46. Mem. N.Y. Coffee and Sugar Exchange (pres. 1965-67, bd. mgrs. 1967—), Nat. Coffee Assn. (vice chmn., chmn. 1968-69, dir. 1960—), N.Y. Produce Exchange, N.Y. Cotton Exchange, Green Coffee Assn. (bd. chmn. 1958-60), N.Y., London cocoa mchts. assns., London Cocoa Terminal Market, N.Y. Cocoa Exchange (dir. 1966, 68), London Sugar Terminal Market, London Sugar Market Assn., Pan Am. Soc. U.S. (dir. 1955—). Clubs: India House (N.Y.C.); Water Mill Rod and Gun. Home: Westbourne Bronxville NY 10708 also Flying Point Rd Water Mill NY 11976 Office: 120 Wall St New York City NY 10005

CLARK, JAMES WILFRED, univ. dean; b. Cleveland, Tenn., Oct. 11, 1920; s. Harley Ransom and Amy Angeline (Lawson) C.; A.B. in Philosophy, U. Tenn., 1941; postgrad. Tulane U., 1941-42; M.A. in Philosophy, U. Mich., 1946, Ph.D. (So. Fellowships Fund grantee), 1956; m. Kathryn Lee Bullington, Dec. 13, 1942; children—Lawrence James, David Bullington. News editor A.P. bur. office, Nashville, 1945; mem. faculty U. Ala., Tuscaloosa, 1947—, asso. prof., 1959-65, prof., 1965—, asst. dean Coll. Arts and Scis., 1961-69, asso. dean, 1969—. Served with USMCR, 1942-45. Recipient Rush Strong Essay medal U. Tenn., 1938. Mem. Am. Philos. Assn., So. Soc. Philosophy and Psychology, Ala. Philos. Soc. (pres. 1965-66), Am. Coll. Personnel Assn. (mem. commn. on acad. affairs adminstrn. 1965-71), Southeastern Acad. Affairs Adminstrs. (pres. 1969-70). Home: 99 Woodridge St Tuscaloosa AL 35401 Office: Box 2926 University AL 35486

CLARK, JOE THOMAS, coll. adminstr.; b. Okolona, Ark., Feb. 24, 1929; s. Joe Grady and Julia Mae (Reid) C.; B.A., Henderson State Tchrs. Coll., Arkadelphia, Ark., 1951; Fulbright student Victoria U., Manchester, Eng., 1951-52; M.Ed., U. Ark., 1955, Ed.D. (Kellogg fellow 1958-59); 1959; m. Earnestine Carroll, June 17, 1951; childrenCarol, Linda, Christy. High sch. prin., Ava; Mo., 1955-58; dean students U. Ark. Med. Center, 1959-64; v.p. instrn. Henderson State Tchrs. Coll., 1964-. Served with AUS, 1952-54. Mem. Nat., Ark. edn. assns., Phi Delta Kappa, Phi Alpha Theta, Kappa Delta Pi. Mason. Home: 1911 Center St Arkadelphia AR 71923.

CLARK, JOHN ALDEN, educator; b. Ahmednagar, India, Aug. 27, 1907 (parents Am. citizens); s. Alden Hyde and Mary (Whitcomb) C.; A.B., Amherst Coll., 1929; M.A., Harvard, 1930, Ph.D., 1935; m. Mary Ann Scott, May 5, 1943; children—Alice (Mrs. Jayant L. Chhaya), Evelyn (Mrs. Marvin R. Farbman), Alden Lee. Instr. philosophy Carleton Coll., Northfield, Minn., 1933-35; asst. prof. Earlham Coll., Richmond, Ind., 1937, asso. prof., 1937-39; asso. prof. U. N.C., Greensboro, 1939-41; mem. faculty Colby Coll., Waterville, Me., 1946—, prof., 1952—, chmn. dept. philosophy and religion, 1952-71; researcher Columbia, 1941-42, U. Edinburgh (Scotland), 1954-55. Served to 1st lt. AUS, 1942-46. Fulbright lectr. Ahmednagar Coll., U. Poona (India), 1961-62. Mem. Am. Philos. Assn., Soc. Religion Higher Edn. Democrat. Mem. United Ch. Christ. Editor: The Student Seeks and Answer, 1960. Contbr. profl. jours. Home: 24 Morrill Av Waterville ME 04901

CLARK, JOHN CONRAD, investment banker; b. N.Y.C., Feb. 19, 1913; s. John C. and Marie (Sparnect) C.; student N.Y. U., 1930-33; m. Lillian Fischer, Dec. 17, 1949; 1 son, Roger Scott. Municipal bond trader Shields & Co., N.Y.C., 1935-40; pres. John C. Clark & Co., N.Y.C., 1946-47; asst. mgr. bond dept. Chase Manhattan Bank, N.Y.C., 1947-51; mgr. bond dept. Wachovia Bank, Winston-Salem, N.C., 1951-55, v.p., mgr., 1955-63, sr. v.p., mgr. bond dept., sr. v.p., mgr. pub. finance, 1967-69; dir. Export-Import Bank U.S., Washington, 1969—. Vice chmn. bd. N.C. Municipal Council, 1961-67; sec. N.C. Securities Adv. Com. to Banks in N.C., 1962-67. Served to lt. col. AUS, 1941- 46; ETO. Recipient certificate of award comptroller of currency, 1963. Mem. Investment Bankers Assn. Am. Rotarian. Clubs: University (Washington); Forsyth Country (Winston-Salem). Contbg. author: Bankers Handbook, 1966. Home: 4141 River St Arlington VA 22207 Office: Export-Import Bank Washington DC 20571

CLARK, JOHN DESMOND, educator; b. London, Eng., Apr. 10, 1916; s. Thomas John Chown and Catherine (Wynne) C.; B.A. Hons., Cambridge U., 1937, M.A., 1942, Ph.D., 1950; m. Betty Cable Baume, Apr. 30, 1938; children—Elizabeth Ann (Mrs. David Miall Winterbottom), John Wynne Desmond. Came to U.S., 1961. Dir. Rhodes-Livingstone Mus., No. Rhodesia, 1938-61; prof. anthropology U. Cal. at Berkeley, 1961—. Served with Brit. Army, 1941-46. Decorated Companion Order Brit. Empire; comdr. Nat. Order Senegal. Fellow Am. Acad. Arts and Scis., Brit. Acad., Royal Soc. S. Africa, Soc. Antiquaries London, A.A.A.S.; mem. Pan-African Congress Prehistory, Geog. Soc. Lisbon, Istituto Italiano di Preistoria e Protostoria, Body Corporate Livingstone Mus. Zambia. Author: The Stone Age Cultures of Northern Rhodesia, 1950; The Prehistoric Cultures of the Horn of Africa, 1954; The Prehistory of Southern Africa, 1959; Prehistoric Cultures of Northeast Angola, 1963; Distribution of Prehistoric Culture in Angola, 1966; The Atlas of African Prehistory, 1967; Kalambo Falls Prehistoric Site, Vol. I, 1968; The Prehistory of Africa, 1970. Office: Dept Anthropology U Cal Berkeley CA 94720

CLARK, JOHN FULMER, scientist, govt. ofcl.; b. Reading, Pa., Dec. 12, 1920; s. John F. and Edith Dix (Long) C.; B.S. in Elec. Engring with honors, Lehigh U., 1942, E.E., 1947; M.S. in Math., George Washington U., 1946; Ph.D. in Physics, U. Md., 1956; m. Virginia Anne Bell, Oct. 2, 1943; children—Linda J., James C. Electronic engr. Naval Research Lab., 1942-47, physicist, atmospheric electricity br. head, 1948-58; asst. prof. elec. engring. Lehigh U., 1947-48; dir. physics and astronomy programs NASA, 1958-63, dep. asso. adminstr. space sci. and applications (scis.), 1963-65, chmn. space sci. steering com., 1963-65, dir. Goddard Space Flight Center, 1965—. Part-time lectr. math. George Washington U., 1957-58, part-time cons. research Grad. Council, 1960-66; part-time lectr. physics U. Md., 1958; mem. indsl. and profl. adv. council Pa. State U., 1963-65; mem. vis. com. physics Lehigh U., 1966—. Pres. Indian Springs Citizens Assn., Silver Spring, Md. Recipient NASA medals for Distinguished Service, Outstanding Leadership, Exceptional Service. Mem. Am. Geophys. Union, Am. Physics Tchrs., Philos. Soc. Washington, Internat. Sci. Radio Union, Sci. Research Soc. Am., Phi Beta Kappa, Sigma Xi, Pi Mu Epsilon, Tau Beta Pi, Sigma Phi Epsilon, Sigma Pi Sigma. Club: Nat. Space (bd. govs.) (Washington). Patentee electronic circuits and systems. Author numerous articles in field. Office: NASA Goddard Space Flight Center Greenbelt MD 20771

CLARK, JOHN HALLETT, III, cons. engr.; b. Bristol, Va., Oct. 31, 1918; s. John Hallett, Jr. and Shirley (Winston) C.; student Williams Coll., 1937-38, Colo. Coll., 1938- 42; B.S. in Civil Engring., U. Ky., 1948; m. Suzanne North Hazelet, Sept. 19, 1942; children—Craig Winston (Mrs. David W. Hill), John Hallett IV, Philip Winston. Jr. engr. Austin Co., 1942; with Hazelet & Erdal, Louisville, 1942-43, 47—, partner, 1956—; co-designer major hwy. and bridge projects. Mem. Louisville and Jefferson County Planning and Zoning Commn., 1957-64, vice chmn., 1962-64; bd. dirs. Better Bus. Bur. Louisville, 1965-68. Mem. town council, Anchorage, Ky., 1969—. Registered profl. engr., Ky., Miss., D.C., S.C.; registered land surveyor, Ky. Fellow Am. Soc. C.E. (pres. Ky. 1954); mem. Am. Inst. Cons. Engrs. (councilor 1970—), Am. Rd. Builders Assn. (dir. engring. div. 1958, 65-68, 69- 72), Internat. Assn. Bridge and Structural Engrs., Nat., Ky. socs. profl. engrs., Cons. Engrs. Council U.S. (bd. dir. from Ky. 1968-70, pres. Ky. 1967), Delta Kappa Epsilon. Episcopalian. Clubs: Red Lantern (Colo. Coll.); Harmony Landing Country (Goshen, Ky.); Tavern (Louisville). Home: 11404 Ridge Rd Anchorage KY 40223 Office: Commerce Bldg Louisville KY 40202

CLARK, JOHN J., educator; b. N.Y.C., June 21, 1924; s. John J. and Mary E. (Taylor) C.; B.B.A. magna cum laude, St. John's U., 1948; M.B.A., City Coll. N.Y., 1950; Ph.D., N.Y. U., 1959; grad. Indsl. Coll. Armed Forces, 1965; m. Margaret T. Norton, July 1, 1965; 1 dau., Patricia Ann. Faculty Coll. Bus. Adminstrn., St. John's U., 1950-69, prof. econs., 1961-69, chmn. dept., 1959-61, dean, 1962-70; now prof. finance and Statistics Drexel U., Phila.; lectr. econs. Bklyn. Poly. Inst., 1954-58; cons. in field, 1957—. Mem. Borough Pres.'s Planning Com., Queens County, N.Y.C., 1964-69; economist joint legislative com. banking law, N.Y. State Legislature, 1965-68. Mem. Am. Econ. Assns., Am. Finance Assn., U.S. Naval Inst. (medal 1969), Beta Gamma Sigma, Delta Mu Delta, Omicron Delta Kappa. Author: Institutionalism, 1962: (with Dr. Blaise J. Opulente) The Impact of the Foundation Reports on Business Education, 1963; (with Morris Cohen) Business Fluctations, Growth and Economic Stabilization, 1963; The New Economics of National Defense, 1966; also numerous articles. Editor: (with B.J. Opulente) Business and The Liberal Arts, 1962. Professional Education for Business, 1964. Home: 1704 Brigantine Av Brigantine NJ 08203 Office: Coll Bus Adminstrn Drexel U Philadelphia PA 19104

CLARK, JOHN LEWIS, univ. dean; b. Mason, Nev., Mar. 30, 1919; s. Warren William and Laura (Edwards) C.; B.A., U. Wis., 1946, M.A., 1946. Ph.D., Stanford, 1955; m. Darlene Rebhausen, Aug. 6, 1944; 1 dau., Laura Jill Clark. Instr. drama U. Buffalo, 1946-47; asst. prof. drama Beloit Coll., 1947-49; from asst. prof. to prof. English, San Francisco State Coll., 1951-65, prof. drama, chmn. dept., 1965-68; dean faculty Sonoma State Coll., 1968-70; dean univ. Ill. Wesleyan U., Bloomington, 1970—; actor- dir. San Francisco Actors Workshop, 1952-60. Served to maj. USAAF, 1941- 45. Mem. Am. Assn. U. Profs., Am. Ednl. Theatre Assn., Speech Assn. Am. Home: 1302 N East St Bloomington IL 61701

CLARK, JOHN MAGRUDER, chem. engr.; b. Chgo., Sept. 21, 1907; s. Eugene B. and Laura (Wolfe) C.; B.Chem., Cornell U., 1929, Ph.D., 1933; m. Emily Blood, Oct. 25, 1930 (div. 1966); children—John M., Charles B.; m. 2d, Ruth H. Frey, Aug. 6, 1966. With E.I. duPont de Nemours & Co., Wilmington, Del., 1933- 69, gen. mgr. photo products dept., 1956-63, gen. mgr. electro- chems. dept., 1963-69; dir. Pa. Indsl. Chem. Co., Clairton; dir., mem. exec. com. Clark Equipment Co., Buchanan, Mich. Pres., Health Planning Council, Wilmington. Trustee Cornell U., 1963-67. Home: 701 Beaver Valley Rd Wilmington DE 19803

CLARK, JOHN RUSSELL, airplane mfg. co. exec.; b. Rockport, Mass., Sept. 21, 1908; s. John Franklin and Florence (Ellis) C.; B.S. in Aero. Engring., Mass. Inst. Tech., 1929; m. Dorothy Virginia Auger, July 30, 1930; children—John Russell, Mary A. (Mrs. Richard Ryder, Jr.), Dorothy A. (Mrs. Allan E. Kemp). Aircraft design engr. N.Am. Aviation Co., 1933-35; chief project engr. Sikorsky VS-300 helicopter United Aircraft Corp., 1935-40, Corsair fighter airplane, chief design Chance Vought div. of corp., 1940-45, transonic aircraft XF7U-1, XF-6U-1 of div., 1946-48, asst. chief engr. aircraft and missiles, exptl. mfg. and flight test of div., 1949-52; asst. chief engr., chief designer supersonic Crusader airplane Chance Vought Corp., 1952-57, chief engr. aircraft, 1957-58, dir. engring. aircraft and missiles, 1958-60, gen. mgr. astronautics div. producing Scout space vehicle, also v.p. corp., 1961-64; gen. mgr. Vought aero. div., also corporate v.p. LTV Aerospace Corp., 1964—, sr. v.p., tech., 1969—. Chmn. Mass. Inst. Tech. Ednl. Council, Dallas, 1956-67, hon. sec. inst., 1958—. Mem. subcom. high speed aerodynamics NACA, 1954-58; mem. USAF Sci. Adv. Bd., 1967—. Fellow Am. Inst. Aero. and Astronautics (guided missile council 1961—); mem. Am. Astronautical Soc., Am. Rocket Soc., Soc. Automotive Engrs. (tech. bd.), U.S. Air Force Assn., U.S. Army Assn., Navy League (life). Clubs: Mass. Inst. Tech. (pres. 1958-66) Royal Oaks Country (Dallas); Mass. Inst. Tech. (N.Y.C.). Home: 6615 Norway Rd Dallas TX 75230 Office: P O Box 5003 Dallas TX 75222

CLARK, JOHN WALTER, Jr., shipping co. exec.; b. Mobile, Oct. 21, 1919; s. John Walter and Mae (Kappner) C.; grad. U.S. Mcht. Marine Acad., 1940; student Tulane U., 1952-54; m. Evelyn Ruth Hamilton, Aug. 29, 1941; children—Ann Hamilton, Ruth Kappner, Susan Jay. Served from cadet to master mariner U.S. Mcht. Marine, 1936-46; port capt., then spl. rep. in West Africa, Delta Steamship Lines, Inc., 1946-50, asst. to pres. New Orleans, 1950-53, v.p., 1953-59, pres., 1959—, also dir.; dir. Liberian Devel. Corp., TCO Industries, Inc. (Holiday Inns). First v.p. New Orleans Internat. Trade Mart; dir. Information Council Ams., Am. Inst. Mcht. Shipping; vice chmn. Council Ams. chmn. central region Nat. Maritime Council; mem. exec. com. Mississippi Valley World Trade Council. Bd. dirs. New Orleans Met. Area Com.; trustee Cordell Hull Found., New Orleans. Decorated knight Order of Crown of Belgium, Order of Star of Africa (Liberia), Order of So. Cross (Brazil), comendador de la Orden de Mayo (Argentina); named Maritime Man of Year, Port of New Orleans Propeller Club, 1965. Mem. New Orleans S.S. Assn. (dir.), U.S. Mcht. Marine Acad. Alumni Assn. (past dir.), New Orleans C. of C. (past dir.). Methodist. Clubs: Plimsoll, New Orleans Country, Southern Yacht, Pickwick, Circumnavigators, Internat. House (New Orleans), Bay-Waveland Yacht (Bay St. Louis, Miss.); Pass Christian (Miss.) Isles Golf. Home: New Orleans LA Office: Internat Trade Mart New Orleans LA 70130

CLARK, JOHN WHITCOMB, diagnostic radiologist; b. Walkerton, Ind., Aug. 14, 1918; s. John and Minnie (Whitcomb) C.; student U. Chgo., 1936-39; M.D., Harvard, 1943; m. Mary Louise Dormady, Apr. 15, 1961. Intern Presbyn. Hosp., Chgo., 1943-44, resident radiology, 1946-49, asst. attending radiologist, 1949-50, asso. attending, 1950-55; attending radiologist div. radiology and nuclear medicine Presbyn.- St. Luke's Hosp., Chgo., 1955-70, attending radiologist, 1970—, head radioisotope dept., 1955-65, chmn. radioisotope com., 1956-70; mem. faculty U. Ill. Sch. Medicine, Chgo., 1948-70, prof. radiology, 1963-70; prof. radiology Rush Med. Coll., Chgo., 1970—; cons. in field. Asso. scientist div. biol. and med. research Argonne Nat. Lab., Lemont, Ill., 1952-56, cons. scientist, 1956-62; mem. radiation study sect. NIH, 1962-66; mem. com. community health Inst. Medicine, Chgo., 1968—. Served to capt. AUS, 1944-46. Diplomate Am. Bd. Radiology. Fellow Am. Coll. Radiology; mem. Radiol. Soc. N.Am., Chgo. Roentgen Soc. (pres. 1963-64), Radiation Research Soc., Inst. Medicine Chgo., A.M.A., Am. Roentgen Ray Soc. Author numerous articles in field. Mem. editorial staff Radiology Jour., 1966—. Patentee ultrasonic rapid sector scan imaging system. Home: 3740 N Lake Shore Dr Chicago IL 60613 Office: 1753 W Congress Pky Chicago IL 60612

CLARK, JOHN WILLIAMS, educator; b. Excelsior, Minn., Dec. 23, 1907; s. Harry Oscar and Gertrude (Williams) C.; B.A., U. Minn., 1928, Ph.D., 1941; M.A., Harvard, 1929; m. Lucile Ann Bayer, Sept. 6, 1930. Instr. English, Rensselaer Poly. Inst., 1929-30; from instr. to asso. prof. U. Minn., 1930-53, prof., 1953—, chmn. dept. English, 1958-69. Mem. examiner- cons. corps North Central Assn. Colls. and Secondary Schs. Served with USAAF, 1944-46. Mem. Modern Lang. Assn. Am., Am. Dialect Soc., Council Basic Edn., Phi Beta Kappa. Author: (with M.B. Carr) An ABC of Idiom and Diction, 1937; (with Eric Partridge) British and American English Since 1900, 1951; Early English, 1957, rev. edit., 1967. Home: 403 Oak Grove Minneapolis MN 55403

CLARK, JOHN WOOD, civil engr.; b. Jacksonville, Ill., July 17, 1922; s. Samuel Nye and Helen (Wood) C.; B.S., Purdue U., 1946, M.S., 1947; Ph.D., U. Pitts., 1954; m. Lois M. Snyder, July 30, 1949 (dec. 1966); children—Meredith J., Judith W., Douglas S.; m. 2d, Gloria Rae Linkins, Nov. 23, 1968. Research engr. engring. design div. Alcoa Research Labs., New Kensington, Pa., 1947-58, asst. chief, 1958-70, chief, 1970—. Mem. exec. com. Column Research Council. Mem. adv. group profl. personnel Home Health div. Miners Clinic, Inc. Served with inf. AUS, 1943-45. Recipient Distinguished Service citation Ill. Coll., 1967; named Distinguished Engring. Alumnus, Purdue U., 1966. Registered profl. engr., Pa. Mem. Am. Soc. C.E. (Rowland prize 1957, Research prize 1958, Croes medal 1966, chmn. engring. mechanics div. 1963-64), Soc. for Exptl. Stress Analysis, Sigma Xi, Tau Beta Pi, Chi Epsilon, Theta Alpha Phi, Phi Kappa Sigma. Club: Hill Crest Country (Newkensington). Contbr. articles profl. jours. Home: 217 Glenview Dr New Kensington PA 15068 Office: Alcoa Research Labs Box 772 New Kensington PA 15068

CLARK, JOSEPH S., former U.S. senator; b. Phila., Oct. 21, 1901; s. Joseph S. and Kate R. (Avery) C.; student Chestnut Hill Acad.; grad. Middlesex Sch., 1919; B.S. magna cum laude, Harvard, 1923; LL.B., U. Pa., 1926; LL.D., Temple U., Harvard, 1952, Drexel Inst., 1957, U. Pa., 1963, Haverford Coll., 1966, Franklin and Marshall Coll., 1967; D.C.L., Susquehanna U., 1961; L.H.D., Lincoln Coll., 1961; m. Iris Richey; children (by previous marriage)—Joseph S., Noel C. Miller. Admitted to Pa. bar, 1926, practiced in Phila., 1926-51; city controller, Phila., 1949-51, mayor, 1952-56; U.S. senator from Pa., 1957-68. Pres. World Federalists U.S.A., 1969-71; chmn. Coalition on Nat. Priorities and Mil. Policy, 1969—. Mem. bd. overseers Harvard, 1953-59. Served to col. USAAF, 1941-45; CBI, 1943-45. Recipient Bok award, Phila., 1956. Fellow Am. Acad. Arts and Scis.; mem. Am. Acad. Polit. and Social Scis. (v.p.), Phi Beta Kappa. Author: The Senate Establishment, 1963; Congress: The Sapless Branch, 1964. Home: 440 Rex Av Chestnut Hill Philadelphia PA 19118

CLARK, JULIAN JEROME, banker; b. Clarkton, N.C., Mar. 7, 1907; s. Eric Conrad and Margaret (Cromartie) C.; A.B., Davidson Coll., 1927; student Stonier Grad. Sch. Banking, Rutgers U., 1945; m. Mary Mackey Hough, Aug. 10, 1936; children—Julian Jerome, William M. Formerly with N.C. Nat. Bank (formerly Am. Trust Co.), Charlotte, asst. treas., 1941, asst. sec., 1942-46, asst. v.p., asst. sec., 1946-47, v.p., asst. sec., 1947-56, sr. v.p., 1956-57, pres.; dir. Am. Comml. Agy., Charlotte, Am. Bank & Trust Co., Monroe, N.C., Bus. Devel. Corp. of N.C. Mem. John Motley Morehead Scholarship Dist. Com. Bd. commrs. Charlotte Meml. Hosp.; bd. dirs. YMCA, Goodwill Industries of Charlotte; trustee Davidson Coll. Mem. Robert Morris Assos. (nat. dir.), N.C. Bankers Assn. (legislative com.). Presbyn. (elder). Club: Charlotte City (dir., pres.). Home: 1309 Providence Rd Charlotte NC

CLARK, KENNETH BANCROFT, educator and psychologist; b. Canal Zone, July 24, 1914; s. Arthur Bancroft and Miriam (Hanson) C.; A.B., Howard U., 1935, M.S., 1936; Ph.D., Columbia, 1940; m. Mamie Phipps, Apr. 14, 1938; children—Kate Miriam, Hilton Bancroft. Staff psychology dept. Coll. City N.Y., 1942—, prof., 1960—, Distinguished U. prof., 1970—; vis. prof. psychology Columbia, summer 1955, U. Cal. at Berkeley, summer 1958, Harvard, summer 1965; research dir. Northside Center for Child Devel., 1946—; social sci. cons. legal and ednl. div. N.A.A.C.P., 1950—; cons. personnel div. U.S. Dept. State, mem. com. on fgn. affairs personnel, 1961-62. Pres. Met. Applied Research Center Corp., 1967—; dir. Harper & Row. Bd. dirs. N.Y. State Urban Devel. Corp., N.Y. Found., Council on Founds.; trustee Howard U., Washington, Antioch Coll., U. Chgo. Recipient Springarn medal, 1961; Kurt Lewin award, 1965. Fellow Am. Psychol. Assn. (dir. 1969, pres. 1970-71); mem. Soc. Psychol. Studies Social Issues (council 1954—, pres. 1949-50), Century Assn., Phi Beta Kappa, Sigma Xi. Protestant Episcopal. Author: Desegregation: An Appraisal of the Evidence, 1953; Prejudice and Your Child, 1955; Dark Ghetto, 1965; A Relevant War Against Poverty, 1968. Home: 17 Pinecrest Dr Hastings-on-Hudson NY 10706 Office: MARC Corp 60 E 86th St New York City NY 10031

CLARK, KENNETH EDWIN, psychologist, dean; b. New Madison O., Dec. 18, 1914; s. Harry H. and Nellie B. (Tremps) C.; B.S., Ohio State U., 1935, M.A., 1937, Ph.D., 1940; m. Helen Titelmaier, June 29, 1942; children—Patricia Storm, Virginia, Joyce Marie. Tchr., Astabula County (O.) Schs., 1935-37; asst. dept. psychology Ohio State U., 1937-40; instr. U. Minn., 1940-42, asst. prof., prof., 1946-60, chmn. dept. psychology, 1957-60, asso. dean Grad. Sch., 1960; dean U. Colo. Coll. Arts and Scis., Boulder, 1961-63; dean U. Rochester (N.Y.) Coll. Arts and Scis. 1963—. Mem. Pres.'s Com. on Nat. Medal of Sci., 1962-64; cons. Office Sci. and Tech., 1961-69; mem. Army Sci. Adv. Panel, 1966—. Trustee Am. Psychol. Found., 1966—. Served with USAAF, 1942-44; lt. (j.g.) USNR, 1944-46. Mem. A.A.A.S., Am., Midwestern psychol. assns., Am. Statis. Assn., Am. Bd. Examiners in Profl. Psychology (pres. 1959- 63), Psi Chi, Phi Delta Kappa, Phi Beta Kappa. Author: America's Psychologists, 1957; Vocational Interests of Nonprofessional Men. 1961; (with G.A. Miller) Psychology, 1970. Editor: Journal of Applied Psychology, 1961-70. Home: 3500 Elmwood Av Rochester NY 14610

CLARK, KENNETH JEROME, banker; b. Seattle, Aug. 3, 1914; s. Edward J. and May (Coyle) C.; B.A., U. Wash., 1937, LL.B., 1939; grad. Pacific Coast Banking Sch., 1951, Banking Sch. South, 1959; m. Josephine Lathrop Jennison, July 20, 1942; children—Kenneth Jerome, Rexford Jennison, Bruce Alfred. Admitted to Wash. bar, 1939; with Nat. Bank Commerce, Seattle, 1934—, v.p., cashier, 1956—; sec. Marine Bancorp., 1963—, Internat. Bank Commerce, 1964—; dir. King County Bldg. Co., Seattle. Bd. dirs. Central Assn. Seattle, 1965-66. Served to maj. AUS, 1941-46; PTO. Mem. Wash., Seattle- King County bar assns., Wash. Bankers Assn., Seattle Transp. Club. Episcopalian (sr. warden 1964-66). Club: Seattle Yacht. Home: 8246 Avalon Dr Mercer Island Seattle WA 98040 Office: Nat Bank of Commerce 2d and Spring St Seattle WA 98124

CLARK, KENNETH SEARS, architect; b. Lamont, Okla., Jan. 21, 1909; s. Allen Sears and Alice (Lumsden) C.; B.Arch., Okla. State U., 1932, M.A., 1933; m. Ellen Montgomery, Feb. 15, 1963; children—Bridget Sharon, John Brion. With U.S. Coast and Geodetic Survey, 1933-35; asst. state architect N.M. W.P.A., 1935-38; pvt. archtl. practice, Santa Fe, 1938—; works include missile research structures White Sands Missile Range (N.M.). Pres. Santa Fe United Fund, 1964. Served to capt. C.E., AUS, 1942-45. Recipient civilian service award Dept. Army, 1960. Fellow A.I.A.; mem. Am. Arbitration Assn., Am. Soc. Testing and Materials, Soc. Am. Mil. Engrs., Bd. Examiners Architects N.M., N.M. Soc. Architects (pres. 1968), Santa Fe C. of C. (dir. 1953-54). Methodist (trustee). Club: Santa Fe Kiwanis (lt. gov. S.W. dist. 1957). Home: 600 Armenta St Santa Fe NM 87501 Office: 208 Delgado St Santa Fe NM 87501

CLARK, KENNETH WILLIS, educator; b. N.Y.C., Jan. 11, 1898; s. Willis Henry and Jennie (Knapp) C.; grad. cum laude Peddie Sch. (valedictorian), 1920; A.B. (Runk scholar 1920-21), Yale, 1924; B.D., Colgate-Rochester Div. Sch., 1927; Ph.D. (fellow in N.T.), U. Chgo. 1931; D.D., U. Glasgow, 1968; m. Adelaide Emeline Dickinson, July 23, 1925. Ordained to ministry No. Bapt. Conv., 1926; pastor, Holley, N.Y., 1926-27, Webster, 1927-28; instr. N.T., div. sch. Duke, 1931-37, asst. prof., 1937-42, asso. prof., 1942-45, prof., 1945—, Junaluska summer sch. (affiliated with Duke), 1936-39, 41; vis. prof. Shaw U., 1941-42, Garrett Bibl. Inst., summer 1945, Duke, summers 1944, 46, 47, 52, U. Manchester (Eng.), 1954-55; Fulbright scholar to Eng., 1954-55, Greece, 1961-62; lectr. John Rylands Library, 1954, U. Salonica, U. Thessaloniki, 1961-62; acting dir., ann. prof. Am. Sch. Oriental Research, Jerusalem, 1949-50; dir. microfilm expdn. Greek Patriarchal Library, Jerusalem, 1949-50; gen. editor expdn. to St. Catherine's Monastery, Mt. Sinai, 1950; cons. Library of Congress, 1950-52. Del. Pauline Pilgrimage in Greece, 1951, Meth. Ecumenical Conf. in Oxford, Eng., 1951; guest lectr. Studiorum Novi Testamenti Societas in Oxford, 1951, Brit. Soc. for O.T. Studies, 1952, Internat. Congress on Four Gospels, Oxford, 1957, Internat. Conf. Patristic Studies, Oxford, 1959, Internat. Congress Orientalists, Moscow, 1960, Internat. Congress Byzantine Studies, Ochrid, 1961; exec. com. Internat. Greek N.T. Project, co-dir., exec. editor; lectr. U. Marburg, 1955; rep. World Methodist Conf., 1956; tech. adviser Office Chief Chaplains USAF. Mem. Studiorum Novi Testamenti Societas (Gt. Britain), Western N.C. Meth. Conf., Soc. Bibl. Lit. and Exegesis (pres. 1964-65), Conf. Secs. of Am. Council Learned Socs., So. Humanities Conf., Am. Acad. Religion, Archaeol. Inst. Am. (lectr. 1951), Am. Assn. U. Profs., Conf. Pres. Deans and Profs. Meth. Theol. Schs., Phi Beta Kappa, Pi Gamma Mu, Beta Theta Pi. Methodist. Author: Codex 2401—The Theophanes Praxapostolos, 1934; A Descriptive Catalogue of Greek New Testament Manuscripts in America, 1937; Eight American Praxapostoloi, 1941; New Testament Manuscript Studies (in collaboration), 1950; Checklist of Manuscripts in St. Catherine's Monastery, 1952; Checklist of Manuscripts in the Greek Orthodox Patriarchate and the Armenian Patriarchate in Jerusalem, 1953. Adv. bd. editor The New Peak Commentary. Mem. editorial bd. Novum Testamentum, Jour Bibl. Lit. Contbr. scholarly and religious publs., including Interpreter's Bible, Interpreters Dictionary of Bible, Peake's Commentary. Home: 1308 W Markham Av Durham NC 27705

CLARK, LEIGH MALLET, lawyer; b. Auburn, Ala., May 16, 1901; s. George Samuel and Mary Gertrude (Little) C.; student Ala. Poly. Inst., 1917-19; A.B., U. Ala., 1921, LL.B., 1923; m. Evelyn Staggers, Aug. 8, 1928; 1 dau., Eva Jean (Mrs. Frank C. Marshall, Jr.). Admitted to Ala. bar, 1923; practice in Tuscaloosa, 1923-25, Birmingham, 1925-43, 51—; circuit judge 10th Jud. Circuit Ala., 1935-51; mem. firm Cabaniss, Johnston, Gardner & Clark, and predecessor, 1951—. Instr., Birmingham Sch. Law, 1927—. Served to lt. col. AUS, 1943-45; col. Res. Fellow Am. Coll. Trial Lawyers; mem. Am., Ala., Birmingham bar assns., Ala. Assn. Circuit Judges (past pres., hon. life), Phi Alpha Delta. Democrat. Mem. Ch. of Christ (elder). Mason (Shriner). Home: 1332 45th St Bellview Heights Birmingham AL 35208 Office: First Nat Bldg Birmingham AL 35203

CLARK, LELAND CHARLES, Jr., educator, research scientist; b. Rochester, N.Y., Dec. 4, 1918; s. Leland Charles and Helen (Foote) C.; B.S., Antioch Coll., 1941; Ph.D., U. Rochester, 1944; m. Eleanor Wilbur Wyckoff, Dec. 28, 1939; children—Susan Lee (Mrs. O.W. Wooley), Joan Irene, Linda Kay, Rebecca Anne. Mem. faculty Antioch Coll., 1944-58, prof. biochemistry, 1956-58, dir. biochem. research at Fels Inst., 1944-58; established, dir. research, open heart surgery unit Children's Hosp., Cin., 1956-58; prof. biochemistry in dept. surgery Med. Coll. Ala., 1958—, also established, dir. open heart surgery labs.; prof. research pediatrics U. Cin. Coll. Medicine; cons. USAF, NIH, Battelle Meml. Inst., Children's Hosp., Cin., Nat. Heart Inst. Ala. chmn. scientists and engrs. Johnson-Humphrey campaign, 1964. Fellow NRC, 1941-44; Research career prof. NIH, 1962—. Fellow N.Y. Acad. Scis.; mem. Am. Chem. Soc., A.A.A.S., Am. Physiol. Soc., Am. Soc. Artificial Internal Organs, Am. Assn. U. Profs. (pres. Birmingham 1962-63), Am. Civil Liberties Union, Sigma Xi. Spl. research cardiovascular physiology, surg. monitoring, electrochem. diagnostic methods, oxygen supply, biochem. analytical methods, enzyme activity, polarography, breathing organic fluids, pharmacology aromatic and indole amines; inventor artificial heart-lung machine, oxygen measuring devices. Home: 346 Compton Hills Dr Cincinnati OH 45215 Office: Elland Av and Bethesda Cincinnati OH 45229

CLARK, LESTER WILLIAM, lawyer; b. Hallowell, Me., Oct. 24, 1911; s. Harlan Eugene and Maude (Ordway) Keyes; B.S. in Elec. Engring., George Washington U., 1937; J.D., U. Conn., 1947; m. Etta Marie Stephenson, Jan. 24, 1935; children—Arthur Keyes, Mary Elizabeth (Mrs. Roland L. Roehrich). Admitted to Conn. bar, 1947, N.Y. bar, 1950; examiner U.S. Patent Office, 1938-39; patent agt. Honeywell, Inc., 1939-43; patent atty. Chandler-Evans div. Colt Industries, 1943-47, Union Switch div. Westinghouse Air Brake Co., 1947-49; atty. George H. Corey, N.Y.C., 1949- 52; mem. firm. Cooper, Dunham, Henninger & Clark, N.Y.C., 1952—. Mem. Am. Bar Assn., N.Y. Patent Law Assn., N.Y. County Lawyers Assn., I.E.E.E., A.A.A.S., Licensing Exec. Soc., Phi Eta Sigma, Sigma Tau. Clubs: Sleepy Hollow Country (Scarborough, N.Y.); Adirondack League (Old Forge, N.Y.); Sixty East (N.Y.C.). Home: 9 Birch Close North Tarrytown NY 10591 Office: 330 Madison Av New York City NY 10017

CLARK, LORD KENNETH MCKENZIE, writer; b. London, Eng., July 13, 1903; s. Kenneth McKenzie and Margaret Alice (McArthur) C.; student Winchester Coll., 1917-22; M.A., Trinity Coll., Oxford U., 1925, D. Litt; LL.D., Glasgow U.; D. Litt., Columbia; m. Elizabeth Winifred Martin, Jan. 10, 1927; children—Alan, Colin, Colette. With Bernard Berenson, Florence, Italy, 1926-27; keeper dept. fine art Ashmolean Mus. Oxford, 1931-33; dir. Nat. Gallery, 1934-45; surveyor King's Pictures, 1934-44; dir. film div., then controller home publicity Ministery Information, 1939-41; Slade prof. fine art Oxford, 1946-50, 61-62; chmn. Arts Council Gt. Britain, 1953-60. Chmn. Ind. TV Authority, 1954-57, adv. council Victoria and Albert Mus., Conseil des Musics Nationaux; bd. Nat. Art Collections Fund, 1961-62; trustee British Mus., Nat. Galleries Scotland. Decorated Companion of Honour, Knight Commander of the Bath; comdr. Legion of Honor (France); comdr. Lion of Finland; Prder of Merit, Grand Cross, 2d Class (Austria); recipient medal for distinguished Service to edn. in art Nat. Gallery Art, 1971. Fellow Brit. Acad., Royal Soc. Ltd.; mem. Swedish Acad., Spanish Acad. Club: Saint James (London, Eng.). Author: The Gothic Revival, 1929; Landscape into Art, 1949; Piero della Francesca 1951; Leonardo da Vinci (rev. edit.), 1952; Moments of Vision, 1954; The Nude, 1956; Looking at Pictures, 1960; Rembrandt and the Italian Renaissance; Ruskin Today, 1964; Civilization, 1970; others. Home: B 5 Albany Piccadilly London W1 England

CLARK, MARGUERITE SHERIDAN, writer, editor; b. Madison, Wis.; d. Andrew Jackson and Louise (Davis) Sheridan; B.A., Columbia, 1924; m. William Alexander Clark, Nov. 23, 1926. Med. editor Newsweek mag., N.Y.C. 1941-61; writer-editor Cornell U. Med. Coll., 1961-65; sci. writer Cybertek, Inc., N.Y.C., 1965—. Recipient Headliner's award for consistently accurate and informative reporting in field of medicine, 1947. Mem. Nat. Assn. Sci. Writers (pres.), Theta Sigma Phi. Episcopalian. Clubs: Cosmopolitan, Pen and Brush (N.Y.C.). Recipient Nat. Headliners award for consistently accurate and informative reporting in the field of medicine, 1947. Author: Medicine on the March, 1949; After the Doctor Leaves, 1954; Medicine Today, A Decade of Progress, 1960; Why So Tired? The Whys of Fatigue and the Ways of Energy, 1962. Contbr. articles to nat. publs. Home: 249 E 48th St New York City NY 10017

CLARK, MARK WAYNE, former army officer, former mil. coll. pres.; b. Madison Barracks, N.Y., May 1, 1896; s. Charles Carr and Rebecca C.; B.S., U.S. Mil. Acad., 1917; grad. Inf. Sch., 1925; Command and Gen. Staff Sch., 1935; Army War Coll., 1937; LL.D., Pa. Mil. Coll., Loyola U., Clemson Coll., U. So. Cal. Oberlin Coll., U. San Francisco, U. S.C., U. Akron, Belmont Abbey Coll., Butler U., the Citadel; D.P.S., U. Vienna, U. Naples; D.C.L., Oxford U.; D. Sc., U. Florence; L.H.D., Newberry Coll.; m. Maurine Doran, May 17, 1924 (dec.); children—Patricia (Mrs. Gordon H. Oostring) (dec.), William Doran; m. 2d, Mary Millard Applegate, Oct. 17, 1967. Commd. 2d lt. inf. U.S. Army, 1917, advanced through grades to gen., 1945; comdg. gen. Fifth Army, Fifteenth Army Group, Italy, 1943-45; comdr.-in-chief U.S. Occupation Forces in Austria, U.S. high commr., 1945; U.S. mem. Allied Commn. for Austria; dep. U.S. Sec. of State, 1947, with Council of Fgn. Ministers negotiating a treaty for Austria; head 6th Army, 1947-49; Western Area rep. Sec. Def. for Unification of Facilities and Services, 1948-49; chief Army Field Forces, Ft. Monroe, Va., 1949-52; comdr. in chief UN Command in Korea; comdg. gen. U.S. Army Forces in Far East; gov. Ryukyu Islands 1952; signed armistice terminating Korean conflict; ret., 1953; pres. The Citadel Mil. Coll. of S.C. 1954-66. pres. emeritus, 1966—. Recipient many mil. decorations. Episcopalian. Author: Calculated Risk, 1950; From the Danube to the Yalu, 1954. Address: Francis Marrin Hotel Charleston SC 29402

CLARK, MARTIN, journalist; b. Beaumont, Tex.; s. John Franklin and Katherine (Hooper) C.; B.A., U. Tex.; postgrad. San Francisco Conservatory Music; m. Nancy Linda Grayson, Dec. 26, 1958 (div. 1970). Tenor, San Francisco Opera, 1946-48; recitalist in personal appearances, also on radio, 1949-51; mng. editor Sandy (Ore.) Post, 1951-53; wire service Enterprise-Courier, Oregon City, Ore., 1953-55; staff writer United Press Internat., Portland, 1955- 56; music editor, daily columnist Ore. Jour., Portland, 1956—; radio talk show sta. KLIQ-AM-FM, Portland, 1966-70. Served with AC, amphibious forces USNR, 1942-46; PTO. Home: 3461 N W Thurman St Portland OR 97210 Office: Oregon Journal 1320 SW Broadway Portland OR 97201

CLARK, MATT, magazine editor, sci. writer; b. Chgo., Feb. 3, 1930; s. Matthew and Kathryn (Speckman) C.; grad. Hill Sch., 1947; A.B., Wesleyan U., Middletown, Conn., 1951; m. Ellen Ann Mitchell, Aug. 23, 1952; children—Thomasin, Geoffrey Beach, Douglas Mitchell. Reporter, Boston Traveler, 1953-56, sci. editor, 1956-58; writer Med. News, N.Y.C., 1958- 61; medicine editor Newsweek mag., 1961—; free-lance contbr. to publs. in field, 1958—. Served with USNR, 1951-53. Recipient Albert Lasker Med. Journalism award, 1964, 67; Howard W. Blakeslee award Am. Heart Assn., 1965, 68; Editorial award Assn. Advancement Med. Instrumentation, 1967; Penney-Mo. mag. award in health, 1967; med. journalism award A.M.A., 1969. Mem. Am. Public Health Assn., Nat. Assn. Sci. Writers, A.A.A.S. Home: 1 Oneida St Rye NY 10580 Office: 444 Madison Av New York City NY 10022

CLARK, MILDRED N., (Mrs. Joel H. Clark), securities co. exec.; m. Joel H. Clark, 1954 (dec. Feb. 1968). Stockbroker, Clark & Clark Securities, Inc., Dallas, 1953-67, pres., 1967—; mem. Midwest Stock Exchange, 1968. Office: Republican Nat Bank Tower Dallas TX 75201

CLARK MINVIL L., clergyman; b. Dixon, Ky., Feb. 8, 1910; s. Henry N. and Sarah E. (Winters) C.; part-time student Western Ky. Tchrs. Coll., 1929-35; B.A., Oakland City (Ind.) Coll., 1947; postgrad. Ky. Wesleyan Coll., 1961; B.Th., Clarksville Sch. Theology, 1967; m. Ethel M. Thomas, Mar. 31, 1930; children—Barbara (Mrs. Percy Morgan), Mac Warren. Primary, secondary sch. tchr., Ky., 1930-43, 56-62; ordained to ministry Bapt. Ch., 1940; missionary Saipan, leper colony Thinian, Marianas Islands, 1949-52; denominational rep. Gen. Bapt. Fgn. Mission Bd. in U.S., 1952-53; mem. Gen. Bapt. Home Mission Bd., 1942-49, 53-64; moderator Gen. Assn. Gen. Bapts., 1948, 63; exec. dir. Christian Edn. and Publs., Inc., 1964—. Pres., Webster County (Ky.) Citizens League, 1963- 64. Bd. dirs. Christian Civic Found. Mem. Poplar Bluff C. of C. Lion, Mason. Home: Route 3 Inman Acres Poplar Bluff MO 63901 Office: Box 79O Poplar Bluff MO 63901.

CLARK, MONTAGUE GRAHAM, Jr., coll. pres.; b. Mecklenburg County, N.C., Feb. 25, 1909; grad. Ga. Inst. Tech., 1930; LL.D., Drury Coll., Mo., 1957; m. Elizabeth Hoyt, May 2, 1933; children—Elizabeth (Mrs. Joe Embser), Alice (Mrs. Harold Davis). Margaret (Mrs. William Miller), Julia (Mrs. Cecil Hampton). Vice pres. W.R. Hoyt & Co., Atlanta, 1933- 46; v.p. Sch. of Ozarks, Point Lookout, Mo., 1946-52, pres., 1952—; ordained to ministry Presbyn. Ch., 1950. Moderator, Lafayette Presbytery, 1947, Synod of Mo., 1957. Chmn. fund raising campaign Mo. Heart Assn., 1957-70, bd. dirs., 1957—; chmn. fund raising adv. and policy com. Am. Heart Assn., 1959-70, bd. dirs., 1961—, past chmn., past v.p. Great Plains region; mem. Wilson's Creek Battlefield Nat. Park Commn., 1961—. Sec. bd. trustees Sch. of Ozarks; bd. dirs. Ozarks Empire Area council Boy Scouts Am., mem. nat. council; adv. bd. Automobile Club Mo.; bd. dirs. Springfield Bapt. Hosp. Col. staff gov. Mo., 1961-65; named Ark. Traveler, 1962. Mem. Order of Founders and Patriots Am., Soc. Colonial Wars, Branson C. of C., DeMolay Legion of Honor, S.A.R. (nat. trustee, citizenship medal 1965), Navy League, Mo. Jr. Coll. Assn. (past pres.), N. Central Assn. Colls. and Secondary Schs. Mason (33, Shriner, K.T.), Rotarian (past pres., dir. Branson, gov. dist. 1966-67). Address: Sch. of Ozarks Point Lookout MO 65726.

CLARK, MRS. MEREDITH PLIER, mem. Republican Nat. Com.; b. Oconto Falls, Wis., Jan. 14, 1927; d. Arnold W. and Herasa (Boyce) Plier; B.A. in Psychology, Lawrence U., 1948; postgrad. N.Y. Sch. Social Work, 1949; m. Philip Cannady Clark, June 24, 1950; children—James William, Meriweather Kaye. Head stock dept. Saks Fifth Av., N.Y.C., 1948-49; psychiat. social worker Bklyn. State Hosp., 1949-50; clk. U.S. Govt., 1951-53; clk.-typist V.I. Telephone Co., St. Croix, 1956, V.I. law firm, 1956-57. Treas. St. Croix br. Rep. Party V.I., 1963-65; mem. Rep. Territorial Com. V.I., 1964—, sec., 1964-68; charter mem. V.I. League Women Voters, 1969; mem. task force V.I. Comprehensive Health Planning Council, 1969, V.I. Inauguration Com. for Pres. Nixon, 1969; V.I. publicity chmn. 17th Ann. Rep. Women's Conf., 1969; mem. Rep. Nat. Com. for V.I., 1968—; adviser inaugural com. 1st elected Gov. V.I., 1971. Mem. Nat. Fedn. Bus. and Profl. Women's Club, St. Croix Arts Council, St. Croix Diving Assn., Kappa Delta (pres. Lawrence U. chpt. 1946-47). Methodist. Clubs: St. Croix Tennis; Capitol Hill. Home: Estate the Sight P O Box 788 Christiansted St Croix VI 00820

CLARK, MURPHY L., lawyer; b. Pebworth, Ky., May 20, 1937; s. Wallace E. Martens and Geneva Steele Clark; student U. Ore., 1954-57; LL.B., U. Wash., 1961; m. Marcia Julene Hancock, Sept. 23, 1966; children-Guy C., Laresa Lee, Tara Kaylene. Admitted to Alaska bar, 1962 since practiced in Anchorage; asso. Hughes, Thorsness & Lowe, 1962-64; partner Hughes, Thorsness, Lowe, Gantz & Clark, 1964—. Dir. Alaska Central Bank & Trust Co., 1969. Mem. Anchorage Planning Commn., 1964-65; mem. Greater Anchorage Borough Planning and Zoning Commn., 1967-68, chmn., 1969. Mem. Am., Alaska, Anchorage bar assns. Club: Alaska Big Game Trophy (pres., past trustee). Home: 3737 Mt Blanc Crescent Anchorage AK 99504 Office: 807 G St Anchorage AK 99501

CLARK, PAUL GORDON, educator, economist; b. Chgo., Oct. 26, 1922; s. Cecil S. and Helen (Bulkley) C.; B.A. summa cum laude, U. Colo., 1943; Ph.D., Harvard, 1950; m. Sara Flanders, June 8, 1943; children—Deborah, Judith, Eleanor, Stephen. Faculty Williams Coll., 1949—, prof. econs., 1960—, dir. research Center for Devel. Econs., 1959-63, chmn., 1965-67, 69—; asst. adminstr. AID, 1968-69; dir. econ. research East African Inst. Social Research, Kampala, Uganda, 1963-65; dep. chief program div. Mut. Security Agy. mission to Italy, 1951-53; economist RAND Corp., 1957-59. Mem. Am. Econ. Assn., Econometric Soc. Author: Development Planning in East Africa, 1965; American Aid for Development, 1971. Co-author: Structure and Growth of the Italian Economy, 1953; Interindustry Economics, 1959. Home: Cluett Dr Williamstown MA 01267

CLARK, PAUL RICHARD, restaurant exec.; b. Orrville, O., Apr. 15, 1915; s. Albert Adam and Laura (Southwood) C.; B.A., Ohio Wesleyan U., 1939; m. Janet Harper, June 29, 1940; children—Paul Richard, Dana Harper, Janet Elizabeth. Sr. accountant Brubaker, Helfrich & Taylor, C.P.A.'s, 1939-42; partner Clewel M. Smith & Co., 1946-50, Conner & Clark, C.P.A.'s, 1950-55; sec., controller Standard Packaging Corp., N.Y.C., 1956-57, v.p., controller, dir., 1957-60, sr. v.p., dir., 1960-63; v.p., treas. Gen. Baking Co., 1963-65, pres., dir., 1965-67; chmn. bd. John Shaw Co., Inc., investment consultants, 1969-71; chmn. bd., dir. Exec. Food Service, Inc., Ft. Worth, 1971—; dir., mem. exec. com. J.D. Jewell, Inc. Mem. N.Y. Soc. C.P.A.'s, Ohio Soc. N.Y., Delta Tau Delta. Clubs: Beacon Hill (Summit, N.J.); Mission Valley Golf and Country (Venice, Fla.). Home: 3752 Casey Key Rd Nokomis FL 33555 Office: 2840 Bryan Ft Worth TX 76107

CLARK, PAUL THOMAS, glass mfg. exec.; b. Corning, N.Y., Dec. 18, 1913; s. John L. and Lena (Barker) C.; B. Chem., Cornell U., 1934; m. Eleanor Lindstrom, June 26, 1940; children—Carolyn, Robert. With Corning Glass Works, 1934—, beginning as glass analyst, successively lab. asst. works control lab., foreman processing, asst. mgr. decorating plant, mgr. finishing, supt. hand made prodn., plant prodn. supt., plant mgr., mgr. mfg. tech. products div., gen. mgr. tech. products div., 1934-57, v.p., gen. mgr. tech. products div., 1957—, lighting products div., 1965—, staff v.p., 1971—, mem. exec. com., 1966—, also dir.; dir. 1st Bank & Trust Co. Corning (N.Y.). Chmn. bd. trustees Corning Community Coll. Clubs: University (N.Y.C.); Elmira Country, Corning Country. Home: 75 E 5th St Corning NY 14830 Office: Houghton Park Corning NY 14830

CLARK, PEGGY, theatrical lighting designer; b. Balt., Sept. 30, 1915; d. Eliot Round (M.D.) and Eleanor (Linton) Clark; A.B. cum laude, Smith Coll., 1935; M.F.A., Yale, 1938; m. Lloyd R. Kelley, Jan. 28, 1960. Designer theatrical costumes, 1938—; instr. lighting Lester Polakov Studio & Forumn, Inc., 1965—; lectr. lighting design Smith Coll., 1967-69, Yale U. Drama Sch., 1969-70; designer settings and lighting Gabrielle, 1941, High Ground, 1951, Curtain Going Up, 1952, Agnes de Mille Dance Theatre, 1953-54; designer stage lighting numerous plays, including Beggar's Holiday, 1946, Song of Norway, 1952, Peter Pan, 1954, Will Success Spoil Rock Hunter, 1955, Kiss Me Kate, 1955, No Time for Sargeants, 1956; designer decor Stage Door Canteen; tech. dir. Lunchtime Follies, Am. Theatre Wing; lighting and tech. dir. other plays including Connecticut Yankee, 1942, Brigadoon, 1946, High Button Shoes, 1947, Along Fifth Avenue, 1948, Gentlemen Prefer Blondes, 1949, Pal Joey, 1951, Mr. Wonderful, Auntie Mame, Bells Are Ringing, 1956, N.Y.C. Center Musical Revivals, 1956-58, 63-68, Say Darling, 1957; prodns. Carousel, Susannah, Wonderful Town, at Brussels Internat. Expn., 1958; lighting tech. supr. Flower Drum Song, Juno, Goodbye Charlie, 1959, Bye Bye Birdie, Unsinkable Molly Brown, Under the Yum Yum Tree, 1960, Show Girl, Mary Mary, 1961, Sell Away, 1961, Romulus, 1962, Girl Who Came to Supper, 1963, Around the World in 80 Days, 1963-64, Bajour, Poor Richard 1965, The Rose Tattoo, 1966; designer lighting Darling of the Day, 1968, South Pacific, 1968, Rosalinda, 1968, Jimmy, 1969, Last of the Red Hot Lovers, 1969, Sound of Music, 1970, How The Other Half Loves, 1971. Bd. counselors Smith Coll., 1961-69, pres. class of 1935, 1970—. Mem. adv. com. Internat. Theatre Inst. Mem. United Scenic Artists (rec. sec. 1942-47, trustee, 1948-51, pres. 1968-69), U.S. Inst. Theatre Tech., ANTA, Illuminating Engring. Soc., Yale Drama Alumni Assn. (Eastern v.p. 1970—). Clubs: French Bull Dog of Am. (v.p.), Smith (Bklyn. and N.Y.C.). Home: 36 Cranberry St Brooklyn NY 11201

CLARK, PENDLETON SCOTT, architect; b. Lynchburg, Va., Feb. 21, 1895; s. John Robert and Bessie B. (Scott) C.; student Augusta Mil. Acad., 1911-12; grad. U. Pa., 1917; m. Alice S. Fleming, Oct. 26, 1922; children—Pendleton Scott, Elizabeth (Mrs. William M. Roberts, Jr.), Katherine (Mrs. Bryant Hare, III). In practice as Pendleton S. Clark, architect, 1920-56, Clark, Nexsen & Owen, architects and engrs., 1956—; engaged in collegiate, instl., schs., housing, banks, comml. architecture, and def. work; dir. Imperial Colliery Co., Co-op. Bldg. & Loan, Langhorne Rd. Apts., Inc. Former mem. adv. council on naval affairs 5th Naval Dist.; former chmn. Lynchburg Planning Commn., Bldg. Code Com. Served as ensign USN, 1917-19, Atlantic Fleet; comdr. USNR, 1942-45. Decorated Bronze Star medal, Naval Res. medal, Victory medal with Atlantic Fleet clasp, others. Fellow A.I.A. (former dir., pres. Va. chpt.); mem. C. of C. (dir. 1935-36, 53), Lynchburg Hist Soc. (charter mem., dir. 1934), Kappa Alpha Soc. Presbyn. (elder, trustee). Clubs: Kiwanis (pres. Lynchburg 1929), Boonsboro Country, Bob White Lodge. Author various archtl. publs. Prin. collegiate works in Va. at Sweet Briar Coll., Washington and Lee U., Hampden-Sydney Coll., Va. Mil. Inst., Randolph Macon Womans Coll., Mary Baldwin Coll. Home: 104 Lee Circle Lynchburg VA 24505

CLARK, PERCY HAMILTON, Jr., banking exec.; b. Ventnor, N.J., Aug. 27, 1908; s. Percy H. and Elizabeth (Roberts) C.; grad. St. Paul's Sch., 1926; A.B., Harvard, 1930; student U. Pa. Law Sch., 1930-33; m. Edith Earle, Oct. 12, 1946; children—Mary Evans, P. Hamilton, Edith Earle. Br. mgr. First Pa. Banking & Trust Co., Phila., 1937-41; dist. sales mgr. Continental Can Co., Devon. Pa., 1946-57; pres. Ibenco, Inc., Linden, N.J., 1957-60; dir. sales Tenco, Inc., Linden 1960-62; sec., sr. v.p. Provident Nat. Bank & Trust Co., Phila.; dir. Sanib Corp., (N.Y.C.). Bd. dirs. United Fund Phila.; pres. bd. trustee St. Timothy's Sch., Stevenson, Md., Charles E. Ellis Sch. bd. mgrs., v.p. Phila. Soc. to Protect Children. Served as lt. comdr. USNR, World War II. Decorated Purple Heart. Mem. Welsh Soc. Episcopalian. Home: 265 Hothorpe Lane Villa Nova PA 19085 Office: Provident Nat Bank Broad and Chestnut Sts Philadelphia PA 19101

CLARK, PETER BRUCE, newspaper exec.; b. Detroit, Oct. 23, 1928; s. Rex Scripps and Marion (Peters) C.; B.A., Pomona Coll., 1952; M.P.A., Syracuse U., 1953; Ph.D., U. Chgo., 1959; m. Lianne Schroeder, Dec. 21, 1952; children—Ellen, James. Research asso., then instr. polit. sci. U. Chgo., 1957-59; asst. prof. polit. sci. Yale, 1959-61; with Evening News Assn., Detroit, 1960—, v.p., 1961-63, pres., pub. Detroit News, 1963—, also dir.; chmn. bd. govs. Detroit br. Fed. Res. Bank Chgo. Bd. dirs. United Found. Met. Detroit, Met. Detroit Sci. Fair; trustee Founders Soc. Detroit, Inst. Arts. Served with AUS, 1953- 55. Mem. Am. Newspaper Pubs. Assn. (dir.), Am. Polit. Sci. Assn., Am. Soc. Newspaper Editors, Adcraft Club Detroit, Econ. Club Detroit. Clubs: Detroit Country, Detroit, Detroit Athletic. Office: 615 W Lafayette Detroit MI 48226

CLARK, PETULA, singer; b. Epson, Surrey, nr. London, Eng., Nov. 15, 1934; d. Leslie Clark; m. Claude Wolff, 1961; children—Barbara Michele, Catherine Natalie. Formerly child star in Eng., then in Europe; recordings in four langs., best known being Downtown (Grammy award), also Don't Sleep in the Subway, Darlin', I Couldn't Live Without Your Love, My Love, A Sign of the Times, Round Every Corner, I Know A Place (Grammy award); numerous concert, nightclub and TV appearances; appeared in motion pictures Finian's Rainbow, 1968, Goodbye, Mr. Chips, 1969; also appeared in 25 films in Eng. Recipient France's Bravos du Music Hall award for outstanding woman in show bus., 1965. Address: care Warner Bros 4000 Warner Blvd Burbank CA 91503*

CLARK, RALPH EWING, Jr., lawyer; b. Cin., Nov. 23, 1914; s. Ralph Ewing and Gladys Dorothy (Baker) C.; A.B., Yale, 1936; LL.B., U. Cin., 1940; m. Margaret Ellen Bartholomay, Dec. 28, 1938; children—Ralph Ewing III, William Langhorst, Bonnie Jean. Admitted to Ohio bar, 1940, since practiced in Cin. Pres., Cin. Travelers Aid Soc., 1966-67; pres. Travelers Aid-Internat. Inst. Cin., 1968; bd. dirs., sec., pres. Cin. Legal Aid Soc.; trustee Ohio State Bar Assn. Found.; gov. mem., trustee Cin. Mus. Natural History. Served to maj. AUS, 1941-45; SW Pacific. Fellow Am. Bar Found., Ohio Bar Found. (trustee); mem. Am., Ohio (exec. com. 1st Dist. 1950—), Cin. (pres. 1960-61) bar assns., Am. Judicature Soc., U. Cin. Law Sch. Alumni Assn. (past pres.), S.A.R. (past treas., dir. Cin.), Soc. May Festival Assn., Phi Delta Phi, Book and Bond (Yale). Episcopalian. Clubs: Cincinnati Country, University, Miami (Cin.); Adirondack Mountain, Antique Automobile Am. Home: PO Box 8 Crested Butte CO 81224

CLARK, RALPH LEIGH, telecommunications cons.; b. East Jordan, Mich., June 2, 1908; s. Earl H. and Ethel M. (Nowland) C.; B.S., Mich. State Coll., 1930; m. Dorothy Fay Webster, Dec. 24, 1930; children—Roy E., Ruth E. (Mrs. Charles Michael Garverick), David W., Dale A. Radio insp. Dept. Commerce, Fed. Radio Commn., FCC, 1930-35; radio engr. FCC, 1935-41; partner Ring & Clark, cons. engrs., 1941-42; dir. programs div. research, devel. bd. Dept. Def., 1946-49; cons. govt. agys., 1949-57; mgr. Washington office Stanford Research Inst., 1957-59; asst. dir. def. research, engring., communications, data processing Dept. Def., 1959-62; spl. asst. to dir. telecommunications mgmt. Exec. Office Pres., Washington, 1962-70; owner Ralph Clark Assos., Telecommunications Consultants, Arlington, Va., 1970—. Served from lt. to comdr. USNR, 1942-46. Fellow A.A.A.S., mem. Council Fgn. Relations, Am. Acad. Polit. and Social Sci., Armed Forces Communications and Electronic Assn., Lambda Chi Alpha, Tau Beta Pi, Phi Lambda Tau. Address: 4307 N 39th St Arlington VA 22207

CLARK, RAMSEY, lawyer; b. Dallas, Dec. 18, 1927; s. Tom C. and Mary (Ramsey) C.; B.A., U. Tex., 1949; A.M., J.D., U. Chgo., 1950; m. Georgia Welch, Apr. 16, 1949; children—Ronda Kathleen, Thomas Campbell. Admitted to Tex. bar 1951, U.S. Supreme Ct. bar, 1956. D.C. bar, 1969; N.Y. bar, 1970; pvt. practice law, Dallas, 1951-61; asst. atty. gen. U.S. Dept. Justice, 1961-65, dep. atty. gen., 1965-67, atty. gen. U.S., 1967-69; partner firm Paul, Weiss, Goldberg, Rifkind, Wharton & Garrison, N.Y.C., Washington, 1969—. Adj. prof. Howard U. Served with USMCR, 1945-46. Recipient Sidney Hillman Found. award, 1971. Author: Crime in America. Home: 3 W 12th St New York City NY

CLARK, RANDOLPH LEE, surgeon, educator; b. Hereford, Tex., 1906; s. Randolph Lee and Leni (Sypert) C.; B.S., U.S.C.; M.D., Med. Coll. Va., 1932, D.Sc. (hon.), 1954; M.Sc. in surgery U. Minn., 1938; postgrad. U. Paris, 1934; m. Bertha Margaret Davis Clark, June 1932; children—Jo Lynn, Randolph Lee III. Intern Garfield Meml. Hosp., Washington, 1933, Am. Hosp., Paris, France, 1933-34, chief resident, 1934-35; fellow surgery Mayo Clinic, 1935-37, 1st asst. surgeon, 1938, emergency surgeon, staff mem., 1939; dir., surgeon-in- chief U. Tex. M.D. Anderson Hosp. and Tumor Inst., 1946-68, pres., 1968—; acting dean post-grad. sch. medicine U. Tex., 1948-50, prof. surgery, 1948-65, prof. surgery Grad. Sch. Biomed. Scis., 1965—; cons. med. div. Oak Ridge Inst. Nuclear Studies, 1950-56; cons. to surgeon gen. USAF, 1948-53. Mem. clin. studies panel Cancer Chemotherapy Nat. Service Center, 1957-61, Nat. Adv. Cancer Council, 1961-65, Pres.'s Commn. Heart Disease, Cancer, Stroke, 1964-65; co-chmn. Senate Panel Cons. for Conquest Cancer, Labor and Pub. Welfare Com., 1970—. Served to lt. col. M.C., AUS, 1942-46. Diplomate Am. Bd. Surgery. Fellow A.C.S. (chmn. com. on cancer 1959-64); mem. A.M.A., Assn. Cancer Inst. Dirs. (pres. 1951-52), Am. Assn. Cancer Research, So. Surg. Soc., Western, Southwestern surg. assns., Aero Med. Assn., Soc. U.S. Medical Cons. World War II, James Ewing Soc., Alpha Omega Alpha. Editor: The Book of Health; directing med. editor: The Cancer Bull.; editor The Heart Bull; co-editor: Year Book of Cancer, 1945—. Home: 1600 Holcombe Blvd Houston TX Office: MD Anderson Hosp Houston TX 77025

CLARK, RICHARD COLEMAN, educator; b. Phila., Oct. 12, 1919; s. William Samuel and Elisabeth (Hannah) C.; B.A., Temple U., 1942; Ph.D., U. Pa., 1954; m. Christine Harris, June 18, 1949; children—Leeann Elizabeth, Layne Kay, Linda Jean. Dir. lang. lab. U. Pa., 1959-62, asst. chmn. German dept., 1960-61, undergrad. chmn. German dept., 1961-62, asst. prof., 1958-62; prof. German, chmn. dept. modern langs. Kan. State U., Manhattan, 1962-68; chmn. German dept. Macalester Coll., St. Paul, 1968-71. Fulbright scholar, Netherlands, 1951-52; recipient award for excellence in teaching U. Pa., 1958. Served to 1st lt. USAAF, 1942-46; lt. col. Res. Mem. Modern Lang. Assn. Am. (bibliography publs. com. 1956-62), Am. Assn. Tchrs. German, Kan. Hist. Soc. (life), Delta Phi Alpha (sec.-treas. 1959-61). Presbyn. Home: 127 Amherst St Paul MN 55105

CLARK, RICHARD SHAW, archtl. engr.; b. Winnetka, Ill., Aug. 1, 1924; s. Neil M. and Pearl (Himmelman) C.; student Antioch Coll., 1942-43, 46-48; B.S. in Archtl. Engring., U. N.M., 1953; m. Julia Blaine Cocks, June 23, 1948; children—Hannah Blaine, Anne Mc Cullough. Draftsman Burwinkle & Milner, Albuquerque, 1953-59; architect Kenneth S. Clark, 1959-64, McHugh & Kidder, 1964-68 (both Santa Fe); architect-engr. Philmont Scout Ranch, Cimarron, N.M., 1968—. Flutist, Albuquerque Civic Symphony, 1940-42, 48-59, Santa Fe Orch., 1961-63. Served with USNR, 1943-46. Mem. A.I.A. (past officer Santa Fe chpt.), Nat. Soc. Profl. Engrs., Sigma Tau. Toastmaster. Prin. works include Dailey Bldg., Albuquerque, Continental Divide Electric Coop., Grants, N.M., addition to Episcopal Ch. of Holy Faith, Santa Fe, addition to Espanola (N.M.) Hosp. Address: Philmont Scout Ranch Cimarron NM 87714

CLARK, ROBERT ARTHUR, educator, mathematician; b. Melrose, Mass., May 3, 1923; s. Arthur Henry and Persis (Kidder) C.; student Colo. Coll., 1940-42; B.A., Duke, 1944; M.S., Mass. Inst. Tech., 1946, Ph.D., 1949; m. Jane Burr Croft Kinder, June 25, 1966. Instr., research asso. Mass. Inst. Tech., 1946-50, vis. asst. prof., 1956-57; faculty Case Inst. Tech. (now Case Western Res. U.), Cleve., 1950—, prof. math., 1964—; vis. mem. U.S. Army Math. Research Center, Madison, Wis., 1961-62. Mem. Am. Math. Soc., Math. Assn. Am., Soc. Indsl. and Applied Math., A.A.A.S., Am. Assn. U. Profs., Phi Beta Kappa, Sigma Xi. Spl. research asymptotic integration theory of differential equations and theory thin elastic shells. Office: Dept Math Case Western Reserve Univ Cleveland OH 44106

CLARK, ROBERT BICKERTON, pharm. co. exec.; b. Arlington, Mass., Dec. 2, 1913; s. Harry Bickerton and Edna (Wales) C.; B.S. in Chemistry, Harvard, 1934, M.S. in Chemistry, 1935; LL.B., Bklyn. Law Sch., 1938; m. Jacqueline Snell, Aug. 5, 1939. Admitted to N.Y. bar, 1938; patent atty. Allied Chem. & Dye Corp., 1935-39, 41-47, Nopco Chem. Corp., Newark, 1939-41, Warner-Hudnut Co., N.Y.C., 1947-49; sec. Warner-Lambert Pharm. Co., Morris Plains, N.J., 1949-58, v.p., 1958-67; sr. v.p. Warner-Chilcott Labs., Morris Plains, 1958-60, exec. v.p., 1960, pres., 1960-68, sr. v.p., parent co., 1967-68; exec. v.p. Hoffmann-LaRoche, Inc., Nutley, N.J., 1968—. Bd. dirs. N.J. Assn. Mental Health. Clubs: University (N.Y.C.); Madison Golf; Harvard of N.J. Home: 8 Highview Terrace Madison NJ 07940 Office: Hoffman-LaRoche Inc 340 Kingsland Dr Nutley NJ 07110

CLARK, ROBERT DONALD, coll. pres.; b. Frontier County, Neb., Mar. 30, 1910; s. Earl N. and Kathryn (Jewel) C.; A.B., Pasadena Coll., 1931; M.A., U. So. Cal., 1935, Ph.D., 1946; LL.D., U. Santa Clara (Cal.), 1968; m. Opal Routh, Sept. 6, 1932; children—Roberta Suzanne, Virginia Ruth, Laurelle Jean. Instr., asst. prof. English, Pasadena Coll., 1931-39; instr., asst. prof. speech Stockton Jr. Coll., 1939-43; asst. prof. Coll. Pacific, 1943; asst. prof. U. Ore., 1943-46, asso. prof., 1946-50, prof., 1950-64, asst. to dean Coll. Liberal Arts, 1949- 51, asst. dean, 1951-55, acting dean, 1955-56, dean, 1956-61, dean of faculties, 1961-64, chairman dept. speech, 1954-55; pres. San Jose (Cal.) State Coll., 1964-69, U. Ore., 1969—. Guggenheim fellow, 1950-51. Mem. Western Speech Assn. (editor jour. 1939-42, pres. 1947), Speech Assn. Am., Am. Soc. Ch. History, Orgn. Am. Historians, Am. Assn. U. Profs. Author: Life of Matthew Simpson, 1956. Home: 2315 McMorran St Eugene OR 97403

CLARK, ROBERT EDWIN, investment banker; b. Springfield, Mass., Oct. 9, 1907; s. James Parker and Katherine Louise (Warren) C.; A.B., Williams Coll., 1929; m. Eleanor Chapman, Oct. 3, 1931; children—Chapman, Katharine, Jonathan Chapin. With Calvin Bullock, Ltd., N.Y.C., 1929-69, became v.p., 1940, exec. v.p., 1956-66, pres., 1966-69; dir. Carriers and Gen. Corp., Nation-Wide Securities Co., Dividend Share, Inc., Bullock Fund, Ltd. Vice pres., dir. Community Fund, Bronxville, 1941-43, 48-51; pres. Pub. Health Nursing Orgn., Eastchester, N.Y., 1947-48. Trustee Bronxville Public Library, 1957-65, pres., 1958-65; trustee Lawrence Hosp., Bronxville, 1965-71, Internat. Execs. Service Corps (Singapore), 1970. Served as lt. USNR, 1943-45, dep. security officer OSS. Mem. Investment Co. Inst. (pres. 1956-57, gov. 1953-59, 62-69), Investment Bankers Assn. Am. (chmn. investment co. com.), New Eng. Soc., Pilgrims of U.S., Williams Alumni Assn. (mem. exec. com. 1953-56), Nat. Inst. Social Scis., Chi Psi. Mem. Reformed Ch. Contbr. articles financial publs. Home: 19 Beech Tree Lane Bronxville NY 10708

CLARK, ROBERT EUGENE, savs. and loan exec.; b. Lansing, Mich., Apr. 6, 1926; s. Roy William and Ruth M. (McCall) C.; B.A., Mich. State U., 1950; m. Anne A. Abbott, June 16, 1950; children—Linda, Thomas, David, Robert. Trainee, Sun Oil Co., Lansing, 1951; with Capital Savs. and Loan Assn., Lansing, 1951—, exec. v.p., 1965-69, pres., 1969—. Adviser Woldamar Wild Life Res., 1969-70; vol. Community Chest, 1962-66; treas. Mich. Tb and Respiratory Disease Assn., 1970-71. Served with USAAF, 1944-46. Mem. Mich. Savs. and Loan League (dir. 1969—, v.p. 1971), C. of C. (dir. 1968-70, treas. 1970), Downtown Bus. Assn. (treas. 1966-69). Mem. Peoples Ch. (elder 1965-68). Mason, Elk, Rotarian. Home: 1714 Cooper Lansing MI 48910 Office: 112 E Allegan Lansing MI 48901

CLARK, ROBERT LINCOLN, economist; b. North Stratford, N.H., June 12, 1903; s. John Lew and Lena Sophia (Frederiksen) C.; grad. Phillips Exeter Acad., 1924; A.B., Dartmouth, 1932; m. Pauline Keysar, July 5, 1935; children—Carol Ann, Robert Lincoln, Christopher John. Asst. to dir. admissions Phillips Exeter Acad., 1932-34; asst. supr. cost of living survey N.H. Dept. Labor, 1934-35; sr. interviewer, mgr. N.H. Employment Service, 1935-40; asst. to chief field mgmt. div. Social Security Bd., 1941- 42; chief employment service div. War Manpower Comm., 1943-44; prin. budget examiner, asst. chief labor welfare br. Bur. Budget, 1944-49; dir. manpower office NSRB, 1949-50, dir. human resources office, 1950- 53; exec. dir. Pres.'s Com. on Scientists and Engrs., 1956-58; head div. sci. and tech. personnel OEEC, 1958-61; manpower adviser to Govt. of India, 1961-65; vis. scholar Resources for Future, 1965-66; exec. dir. Study Internat. Migration Talent, Edn. and World Affairs, Washington, 1967-69. Mem. Spl. Mexican-U.S. Commn. on R.R. Wage Claims, 1944. Adviser to Am. delegation 30th Session of Internat. Labor Conf., Geneva, 1947. Mem. Am. Econ. Assn., Soc. for Internat. Devel., Am. Polit. Sci. Assn., Soc. Pub. Adminstrn. Home: Governor's Rd Wakefield Sanbornville NH 03872

CLARK, ROBERT M., investment banker; b. Evanston, Ill., 1923. Partner, Blunt Ellis & Simmons, Chgo.; dir. Samuel Harris & Co. Mem. Investment Bankers Am. (gov., chmn. Central States Group). Home: 10 Winfield Dr Winnetka IL 60093 Office: 111 W Monroe St Chicago IL 60603

CLARK, ROBERT PHILLIPS, newspaper editor; b. Randolph, Vt., Dec. 3, 1921; s. James S. and Gladys M. (Phillips) C.; A.B., Tufts U., 1942; M.A., U. Mo., 1948; m. Jeanne Orr Rice, Dec. 14, 1949; children—Patricia Orr, Elizabeth Phillips. Reporter, Owensboro (Ky.) Messenger & Inquirer, 1948-49; reporter, sci. writer Courier-Jour., Louisville, 1949-62, Washington corr., 1958; mng. editor Louisville Times, 1962-71; exec. editor Courier-Jour. and Louisville Times, 1971—. Sec. bd. trustees Louisville Presbyn. Theol. Sem.; bd. dirs. Presbyn. Community Center. Served to capt. AUS, World War II. Nieman fellow, Harvard, 1960-61. Decorated Bronze Star. Mem. Am. Soc. Newspaper Editors, A.P. Mng. Editors Assn. (dir.), Sigma Delta Chi, Delta Tau Delta. Democrat. Presbyn. Home: 5811 Brittany Valley Rd Louisville KY 40222 Office: 525 W Broadway Louisville KY 40202

CLARK, ROBISON, metals co. exec.; b. Mineola, N.Y., Nov. 18, 1917; s. Paul E. and Emma (Robison) C.; B.A., Lehigh U., 1939; m. M. Margaret Beal, Oct. 7, 1939 (dec.); children—Sally E. (Mrs. F.W. Masek), Jane E. (Mrs. P.R. Cockrel), Douglas R.; m. 2d. Lillian M. Middleton, Sept. 27, 1969; step-children—John M. Smith, Ellen T. Smith. Controller internat. div. Standard Brands, Inc., N.Y.C., 1947-54; controller, sec. Reeves Bros., Inc., N.Y.C., 1954-57; controller Link Aviation, Binghamton, N.Y., 1957-60; asst. comptroller Gen. Dynamics Corp., N.Y.C., 1960-66; v.p., controller Howmet Corp., N.Y.C., 1966—. Served as lt. (j.g.) USNR, 1944-46. Mem. Financial Execs. Inst., Nat. Assn. Accountants, Beta Theta Pi. Home: 17 Ramsey Dr Summit NJ 07901 Office: 475 Steamboat Rd Greenwich CT 06830

CLARK, RUSSELL N., corp. exec.; b. Cin., Mar. 23, 1921; s. Walter Bruce and Marie (Giewe) C.; B.S., Xavier U., 1942; M.S., U. Detroit, 1942-44; Ph.D., Ia. State Coll., 1946; m. Margaret Suer, Aug. 26, 1942; children—Edward T., Frederick C., Suzanne L., James R., Cherianne L., Kenneth R., Michael S. Research chemist Ia. State Coll., 1944-46; research chemist E.I. duPont de Nemours & Co., Inc.; 1946-49, prodn. devel. supr., 1949-53, tech. mgr., 1953, asst. mgr., 1953-55, tech. supt., 1955-60; v.p., tech. dir. Celanese Corp., 1960-66; v.p. research and comml. devel. Inmont Corp., 1966-69, formerly exec. v.p. Mem. Am. Chem. Soc., Am. Inst. Chem. Engrs., Soc. Plastic Engrs., Am. Mgmt. Assn., Soc. Plastics Industry, Plastics Pipe Inst., Mfg. Chemists Assn., Industry Research Inst. Home: 2170 Bayberry Lane Westfield NJ 07090

CLARK, SAM LILLARD, Jr., educator, physician; b. St. Louis, June 9, 1926; s. Sam Lillard and Nettie Lee (Petrie) C.; student Vanderbilt U., 1943-44, Duke, 1944-45; M.D., Harvard, 1949; m. Elizabeth Morse Jones, Sept. 9, 1950; children—Susan Crockett, David Holmes, Jeffrey Battle. Intern Mass. Gen. Hosp., 1949-50; Nat. Research Council fellow med. scis. Vanderbilt U., 1950-52; instr. anatomy Washington U., 1954-57, asst. prof., 1957-63, asso. prof., 1963-68; prof., chmn. dept. anatomy U. Mass., 1968—; cons. NIH, NSF. Served with USNR, 1944-46, 52-54. Mem. A.A.A.S., Am. Assn. Anatomists, Am. Soc. Cell Biology, Am. Soc. Exptl. Pathology, Internat. Soc. Cell Biology, Pan Am. Assn. Anatomy, Assn. Anatomy Chairmen, Assn. Am. Med. Colls., Sigma Xi, Alpha Omega Alpha. Home: 83 Wit's End Rd Concord MA 01742 Office: 419 Belmont St Worcester MA 01604

CLARK, SAMUEL FRIEND, educator; b. Danville, Ky., Jan. 16, 1914; s. Friend Ebenezer and Emma May (Hanna) C.; A.B., W.Va. U., 1934, M.S., 1937; postgrad. Johns Hopkins, 1936-37; Ph.D., U. N.C., 1939; m. Ann Follansbee, May 4, 1946; children— Martha Ann, Robert Watson. Employed as research chemist Union Carbide Chems. Co., 1939-42, group leader devel. dept., 1942- 46; asso. prof. chemistry U. Miss., 1946-48, prof., 1948-63, chmn. dept., 1955-63, coordinator ann. workshop for jr. coll. sci. faculty, 1958-60, dir. Nat. Sci. Found. summer sci. camp at univ., 1960-62, 63; prof., chmn. dept. chemistry, Fla. Atlantic U., Boca Raton, 1963-66, 68—. Dir. NSF in-Service Inst., 1964-66, 69—, Summer Inst., 1970, Coop. Coll.-Sch. Sci. Program, 1970-72; regional chemistry specialist Consjo Superior Universitario Centro- americano NSF, 1967-68; cons. Colegio Regional de Cayey U. P.R., 1967, Instituto Pedagugico de Carcas, Instituto Pedagogica Exptl. de Barquisimeto, Simon Bolivann U. U.S. AID/Venezuela, 1969; chmn. Fla. Coll. Conf. on Chem. Articulation, 1971. Mem. Miss. Adv. Com. on Sci. Edn. Chmn. Lafayette County (Miss.) Red Cross Blood Program, 1950-52; sec. Lafayette County Soc. Crippled Children and Adults, 1950-54. Mem. Am. Chem. Soc. (chmn. Memphis 1955-56, councilor 1960-63, alternate councilor Fla. 1964, chmn. elect 1967, chem. liaison rep. 1967-68), Fla. Acad. Scis., Phi Beta Kappa, Sigma Xi, Phi Kappa Phi, Phi Lambda Upsilon, Phi Kappa Psi. Office: Florida Atlantic U Boca Raton FL 33432

CLARK, SAMUEL INGALLS, educator; b. Oak Park, Ill., June 3, 1923; s. Lincoln R. and Ellen N.F. (Lethin) C.; A.B in Polit. Sci., U. Chgo., 1943, Ph.D., 1949. Faculty Western Mich. U., 1948—, prof. polit. sci., 1961—, dir. honors coll., 1962—, pres. faculty senate, 1971-72; co-dir. seminars in India, 1963, 67. Mem. exec. com. nat. Collegiate Honors Council, 1971—, chmn. com. on internat. programs. Commr. Mich. Crippled Children Commn., 1958-65. Democratic candidate for U.S. Congress, 1956, 60. Served with AUS, 1943-44. Fulbright fellow U. Louvain (Belgium), 1950-51; Ford Found. fellow, India, 1957- 58; Fulbright prof., Japan, 1961. Mem. Am. Polit. Sci. Assn., Assn. Asian Studies, Am. Assn. U. Profs., Midwest Polit. Sci. Assn., Internat. House Japan. Roman Catholic. Author: (with Jerome Manis) Man and Society, 1961. Home: 1819 Greenlawn St Kalamazoo MI 49007

CLARK, SIR GEORGE NORMAN, historian; b. Halifax, Eng., Feb. 27, 1890; s. James Walker and Mary (Midgley) C.; M.A., Balliol Coll., Oxford, 1915, D. Litt., 1947; LL.D., Aberdeen U., 1936; Litt.D., U. Utrecht, 1936, U. Dublin, 1950. Durham U., 1950, Sheffield U., 1951, Columbia, 1954, Hull U., 1955; Litt.D. (hon.) Cambridge U., 1961; m. Barbara Keen, 1919. Fellow, All Souls Coll., Oxford 1912-19; 31-43; fellow Oriel Coll., 1919-31, provost, 1947-57; prof. econ. history Oxford. 1931-43; Regius prof. modern history, fellow Trinity Coll., Cambridge, 1943-47. Former trustee Brit. Mus. Served capt. 8th London Regt., Royal Army, 1914-19; staff various govt. depts., 1939-45. Decorated Comdr. Order Orange-Nassau, created Knight, 1953. Hon. fellow Balliol and Oriel colls. Oxford Trinity Coll., Cambridge, Trinity Coll., Dublin; fellow All Souls Coll., Oxford, 1912-19, 61—. Fellow Royal Coll. Physicians (hon.); mem. Am. Hist. Assn. (hon.), Brit. Acad. (pres. 1854-58), fgn. mem. Royal Danish Acad., Netherlands Acad., Am. Acad. Arts and Scis. Author: The Seventeenth Century, rev. edit., 1947; The Later Stuarts, rev. edit., 1955; Science and Social Welfare in the Age of Newton, rev. edit., 1970; History of the Royal College of Physicians, Vol. 1, 1964, Vol. 2, 1966; English History, a Survey, 1971. Home: 7 Ethelred Ct Dunstan Rd Headington Oxford England

CLARK, STEPHEN CARLTON, Jr., mfg. co. exec.; b. Woodmere, N.Y. June 29, 1911; s. Stephen Carlton and Susan (Hun) C.; grad. St. Mark's Sch., Southborough, Mass., 1929; B.S., Yale, 1933; m. Jane Forbes Clark, May 26, 1943; children— Susan C., Jane F. Vice pres. Clark Estates, mgmt., N.Y.C., 1960—; dir. Singer Mfg. Co., 1962-71. Vice pres. Nat. Steeplechase and Hunt Assn., 1956-63. Bd. dirs. Clark Found., Scriven Found., N.Y. State Hist. Assn., Nat. Baseball Hall of Fame and Mus. Served with AUS, 1940-45. Home: Cooperstown NY 13326 Office: 30 Wall St New York City NY 10005

CLARK, STEPHEN PATRICK, mayor; b. Florence, Kan., Nov. 19, 1923; s. Stephen Peter and Gertrude (Fisher) C.; grad. U. Miami (Fla.); m. Faye Knowles, June 8, 1947; children—Peter, James, Theresa, John, Cecile, Paul. Formerly Vice pres. Clark Constrn. Co., Miami; dir. Airline and Travel Agy. Sch., U.S. Internat., Inc. Mem. bd. commrs. City of Miami, 1967; mayor, Miami, 1967—. Mem. Interam. Center Authority; mem. adminstrv. bd. Biscayne Coll. Bd. dirs. Jr. Achievement Greater Miami. Served with USAF. Mem. Am. Legion. Democrat. K.C., Moose, Elk. Home: 3051 NW 4th St Miami FL 33125 Office: City Hall Miami FL

CLARK, SYDNEY PROCTER, Jr., educator, geophysicist; b. Phila., July 26, 1929; s. Sydney Procter and Isabella Lee (Mumford) C.; A.B., Harvard, 1951, M.A., 1953, Ph.D., 1955; m. Elizabeth Frey, Jan. 12, 1963; children—Edward, Jordan, Elizabeth, Christina. Research fellow geophysics Harvard, 1955-57; geophysicist Geophys. Lab., Carnegie Instn., Washington, 1957-62; Sidney James Weinberg prof. geophysics Yale, 1962—. Fulbright scholar Australian Nat. U., 1962. Fellow Am. Geophys. Union. Home: Sunset Circle Woodbridge CT 06525 Office: Dept Geology Yale Univ New Haven CT 06520

CLARK, TEUNISON CARY, Jr., govt. ofcl.; b. Ruth, Miss., July 1, 1918; s. Teunison Cary and Annie Elizabeth (Rawls) C.; B.A., Miss. Coll., 1940; M.A., George Peabody Coll., 1947; Ed.D. (Kellogg fellow), Tchrs. Coll., Columbia, 1953; m. Margaret Culpepper, Dec. 26, 1942; children—Marianne, Cary Owen. Dir. Bapt. Student Union, Auburn, Ala., 1940-42; dir. student affairs Auburn U., 1947-51; grad. asst. Tchrs. Coll., Columbia, 1951-53, asst. in adminstrn., 1953-54, asst. provost, asso. prof. edn., 1955-58; asso. exec. sec. Assn. for Higher Edn., N.E.A., Washington, 1958-60; adviser higher edn. AID, State Dept., S.Vietnam, 1960-63, chief edn. adviser, Indonesia, 1963-65, Thailand, 1965, adviser higher edn. Far East Bur., Washington, 1966-67, chief, edn. div., 1967-69, asst. dir. for edn., S.Vietnam, 1969—. Cons. tchr. edn. Ford Found., 1955. Served to lt. comdr. USNR, 1942-46. Mem. N.E.A., Am. Ednl. Research Assn., Phi Delta Kappa, Kappa Delta Pi, Phi Eta Sigma, Alpha Phi Omega. Home: The Westchester 4000 Cathedral Av NW Washington DC 20016 Office: AID/Education APO San Francisco CA 96243

CLARK, THOMAS DIONYSLUS, historian; b. Louisville, Miss., July 14, 1903; s. John Collingsworth and Sallie (Bennett) C.; A.B., U. Miss., 1928; postgrad. U. Va., 1928; M.A., U. Ky., 1929; Ph.D., Duke, 1932; D.Litt., Lincoln Meml. U., 1949, Washington and Lee U., 1963; LL.D., U. Louisville, 1964, U. Ky., 1969; D.H.L., Berea Coll.; m. Martha Elizabeth Turner, June 10, 1933; children—Thomas Bennett, Ruth Elizabeth. Tchr. history Western State Teachers Coll., Memphis, 1930; vis. instr. U. Tenn., 1931; vis. prof. U. Rochester, Duke, U. N.C., U. Chgo., Claremont Grad. Sch., U. Vienna; faculty U. Ky., 1931-68, instr., asst. prof., asso. prof., 1939-42, prof. history, 1942-65, Hallam prof., 1965-68, head dept., 1942-65, now fellow; Sesqui-centennial prof. Am. history Ind. U., 1966, distinguished prof. history, 1968—, U. prof., 1971—; vis. prof. U. Wis. Trustee U. Ky. Guggenheim fellow, 1963-64. Recipient Distinguished Teaching award and Research award, U. Ky., 1968; Ind. Author's award, 1971. Mem. Am., So. (pres. 1947) hist. assns., Orgn. Am. Historians (exec. sec. 1970—), Phi Beta Kappa, Phi Pi Phi, Phi Alpha Theta (nat. hon. mem., nat. pres. 1957-59), Omicron Delta Kappa. Democrat. Baptist. Kiwanian. Clubs: Filson (Louisville); Bradford (Lexington). Author books, latest being Pills, Petticoats and Plows, 1944; The Southern Country Editor, 1948; The Rural Editor and the New South, 1948; The Bluegrass Cavalcade, 1956; Frontier America, 1959; The Emerging South, 1961; (with A.D. Kirwan) The South Since Appomattox; Gold Rush Diary; (with Gerald Hamm) Pleasant Hill and Its Shakers; Three American Frontiers; Indiana University, Mid-Western Pioneer, 1970. Editor: Southern Travel Series, 1950-56; Three Paths to the Modern South, 1965. Mng. editor. Jour. of So. History, 1948-54. Contbr. to hist. jours. Home: 2623 E 2d St Bloomington IN 47401

CLARK, THOMAS GARIS, rubber products mfr.; b. Norristown, Pa., Jan. 30, 1925; s. George W. and Esther (Garis) C.; A.B., Gettysburg Coll., 1947; M.B.A., U. Pa., 1949; m. Dolores M. Debolt, Feb. 18, 1956; children—Kimberley, Valerie. Gen. accountant Firestone Tire & Rubber Co., Akron, O., 1949-57; successively supr., gen. accountant, asst. sec.-treas., sec.-treas., v.p., sec.-treas. Rubbermaid, Inc., Wooster, O., 1957—; dir. subsidiaries Rubbermaid, Inc., 1st Fed. Savs. & Loan Assn. Served from ensign to lt., USNR, 1944-61. Mem. Am. Soc. Corporate Secs., Ohio Mfrs. Assn. (trustee), Cleve. Treasurers' Club, Phi Beta Kappa, Beta Gamma Sigma, Phi Sigma Kappa. Republican. Presbyn. Mason, Rotarian. Home: 1743 Saunders Dr Wooster OH 44691 Office: 1255 E Bowman St Wooster OH 44691

CLARK, THOMAS MCKINSTRY, newspaper exec.; b. Elkhart, Ia., Aug. 22, 1910; s. Ralph Atherton and Bethania (McKinstry) C.; student Drake U., 1929-30; m. Vivian Irene Lewis, Mar. 26, 1937; children—Thomas R., Frank R., Elizabeth D., John A. With Des Moines Register & Tribune, 1929—, market reporter, 1932-42, market, financial, bus. editor, 1942—. Mem. bd. Elkhart Town Council. Bd. dirs. Ia. Council Chs., Ia. unit Ch. World Service. Republican. Mem. Christian Ch. Home: Elkhart IA 50073 Office: 715 Locust St Des Moines IA 50309

CLARK, THOMAS T., Jr., newspaper exec. Pres., gen. mgr. Ariz. Star and Citizen. Office: Tucson Newspaper Inc 208 N Stone St Tucson AZ 85703*

CLARK, TOM C., ret. asso. justice U.S. Supreme Ct.; b. Dallas, Sept. 23, 1899; s. William H. and Jennie (Falls) C.; ed. Va. Mil. Inst., 1917-18; A.B., U. Texas, 1921, LL.B., 1922; hon. degrees from 25 Am. colls. ang univs.; m. Mary Ramsey, Nov. 8, 1924; children—William Ramsey, Mildred (Mrs. Thomas R. Groniund), Tom C., Jr. (dec.). Admitted to Tex. bar and Tex. Supreme Ct., 1922, U.S. Supreme Court, 1932; asso. Clark & Clark, Dallas, 1922-27; became civil dist. atty. Dallas County, Tex., 1927; asst. atty. gen. charge antitrust div. Dept. Justice, 1943, asst. atty. gen. charge criminal div., 1943-45; atty. gen. U.S., 1945-49; asso. justice U.S. Supreme Ct., 1949-67. Mem. at large nat. council Boy Scouts Am. Pres. Inst. Jud. Adminstrn., 1966-67; bd. dirs. Fed. Jud. Center, 1968-69. Served with 153 Inf. U.S. Army, World War I. Recipient Silver Buffalo award, 1960, Silver Beaver award, 1962, Boy Scouts Am.; Gold medal Am. Bar Assn., 1962; 1st Ann. award Am. Judicature Soc., 1962; President's Key, Loyola U., Chgo.; Distinguished Alumnus awards Ex-Students Assn. U. Tex., 1962, U. Tex. Sch. Law, 1964; award merit N.Am. Judges Assn.; 1970. Fellow Am. Coll. Trial Lawyers (hon.); mem. Am. Judicature Soc. (chmn. bd. dirs. 1967-69), Nat. Coll. State Trial Judges (chmn. 1963-71), State Bar Tex., Am. (chmn. sect. jud. adminstrn. 1958-59, chmn. joint com. for effective adminstrn. of justice), Dallas, Fed. (pres. 1944) bar assns., Am. Legion, V.F.W., Order of Coif, Phi Alpha Delta (supreme vice justice 1964-68), Delta Tau Delta (pres. 1966-68). Democrat. Presbyn. Mason (33, Shriner). Eagle. Clubs: University, Chevy Chase, Exchange, Alfalfa, Burning Tree, National Lawyers (Washington). Home: 2101 Connecticut Av NW Washington DC 20008

CLARK, TRUMAN BROUSE, mfr.; b. Boston, Oct. 21, 1920; s. Irving W. and Rachel B. (Brouse) C.; student Ohio State U., 1938-41; m. Joan E. Balliett, Aug. 8, 1942; children—Christianne, Susan, Janet (Mrs. James B. Kerr II), Andrea, Steven, Peter, Sally, Lisa. Aero. engr. Bell Aircraft, Buffalo and Marietta, Ga., 1942-45; with The Tappan Co., Mansfield, O., 1946—, beginning as field salesman, successively mgr. war products, dir. engring., works mgr., exec. v.p. O'Keefe and Merritt, pres., 1963-66, pres. Tappan div., 1966—; v.p., dir. The Tappan Co. Vice pres. Johnny Appleseed council Boy Scouts Am.; dir. North Central Ohio Jr. Achievement. Mem. Gas Appliance Mfrs. Assn. (pres. 1970-71, dir.). Republican. Conglist. (trustee). Patentee ranges, aircraft refrigerators. Home: 1105 Devonwood Rd Mansfield OH 44907 Office: 250 Wayne St Mansfield OH 44902

CLARK, WALTER BUSH, univ. dean; b. Niwet, Colo., Sept. 2, 1906; s. Bush David and Minnie (Peterson) C.; student So. Missionary Coll., 1925-27, Andrews U., 1930- 31; B.A., Pacific Union Coll., 1943; m. Lucile Cherrie White, July 29, 1928; 1 dau., Syliva June (Mrs. M. Jerry Davis). Ordained to ministry Seventh-day Adventist Ch., 1945; instr. printing So. Missionary Coll., 1927-29, dean men, 1929-36; dean men Pacific Union Coll., 1936-38, 40- 45, bus. mgr., 1945-47; asst. adminstr. St. Helena Sanitarium and Hosp., 1938-40; dean students Loma Linda (Cal.) U., 1947-65, dean admissions, 1965-71. Mem. Assn. Collegiate Registrars and Admission Officers. Republican. Home: 11422 Iris St Loma Linda CA 92354

CLARK, WALTER VAN TILBURG, writer; b. East Orland, Me., Aug. 3, 1909; s. Walter Ernest and Euphemia Murray (Abrams) C.; A.B., U. Nev., 1931, M.A., 1932; M.A., U. Vt., 1934; Litt.D., Colgate U., 1958, U. Nev., 1969; m. Barbara Frances Morse, Oct. 14, 1933; children—Barbara Ann, Robert Morse. Tchr. English, dramatics and sports in pub. sch., Cazenovia, N.Y., 1935-45; was asso. prof. English, Mont. State U., lectr.; past tchr. English, coach Va. City High School; prof. English, San Francisco State Coll.; writer in residence U. Nev., Reno, 1962—. Fellow in fiction Center Advanced Studies, Wesleyan U., Middletown, Conn., 1960-61. Winner O. Henry Short Story award, 1945. Mem. Am. Civil Liberties Union, Western History Assn., Western Lit. Assn. (hon. life), Sierra Club, Phi Kappa Phi. Author: The Ox Bow Incident, 1940 (produced as movie); The City of Trembling Leaves, 1945; The Track of the Cat, 1949 (produced as movie 1954); The Watchful Gods, 1950. Contbr. to periodicals, including Atlantic Monthly, Accent, New Yorker, The Nation, Sat. Evening Post. Yale Rev., Va. Quar. Rev., others. Home: Virginia City NV 89440 Office: English Dept U Nev Reno NV 89502

CLARK, WESLEY CLARKE, univ. dean; b. Cleve., Sept. 17, 1907; s. William Chester and Mabel Ruth (Clark) C.; A.B., Marietta Coll., 1930; M.A., U. Pa., 1937, Ph.D., 1942; m. Frances Grace Stiles, Oct. 9, 1931 (dec. Sept. 1969); children—Sally Lee (Judd), William Standish. Reporter, Marietta Times, 1930, Phila. Evening Bull., 1930-41; instr. polit. sci. Wharton Sch. U. Pa., 1937-41; asst. prof. Syracuse U., 1941-43, prof., 1947—, asso. dean sch. journalism, 1950-52, acting dean, 1951-52, dean, 1952—, pres. Syracuse University Press, 1954-55; asst. to Sec. of Interior, 1943-46; research dir. H.L. Ickes, 1946-47; v.p., treas. Skaneateles Press (N.Y.), 1963-69. Pub. relations cons. Inst. State and Local Govt., Phila., 1937, Gov.'s com. for investigation disenfranchisement in Phila., 1938, Caribbean Commn., 1950; mem. Gov.'s Com. on Employment Minority groups in News Media, 1968-69. Mem. Assn. Schs. and Depts. Journalism (v.p. 1956), Assn. Edn. in Journalism, Am. Acad. Polit. and Social Sci., Pub. Relations Soc. Am. Clubs: University (Syracuse); Cosmos (Washington). Author: Some Economic Aspects of a President's Popularity, 1942; El Derecho a la Information, 1966. Editor: Journalism Tomorrow, 1959. Contbr. profl. publs. Home: 18 North St Marcellus NY 13108 Office: Syracuse U Syracuse NY 13210

CLARK, WILBER DALE, former banker; b. Fillmore, Mo., Apr. 26, 1892; s. Samuel Milton and Catherine Laney (Sayres) C.; ed. high sch., St. Joseph, Mo.; m. Ethel Johnston, Aug. 31, 1915; (died July 24, 1955); children—Russell D., Jessie E., Walter W.; m. 2d, Katherine Doorly Young, Nov. 29, 1958. With 1st National Bank, St. Joseph, 1908; assistant cashier, 1st National Bank, Tarkio, Missouri, 1913-15; cashier, Stock Yards National Bank, Denver, Colo., 1915-19; vice-pres. Omaha Nat. Bank, 1919-29, pres., 1929-49, chmn. bd., 1949-62; dir. World Pub. Co., 1960—; Omaha Br. Fed. Reserve Bank, Kansas City, 1933-39; mem. fed. adv. council Fed. Res. Banks, 1941-43; dir. Union Pacific R.R., since 1940. Pres. Omaha Community Chest, 1935-36; dir. U.S. Chamber Commerce, 1935-36; mem. Omaha Chamber Commerce (pres. 1932); mem. business advisory council, Dept. of Commerce, 1938-42; pres. bd. regents Municipal U. Omaha to 1944; chmn. Neb. War Finance Com., 1943-46. Republican. Methodist. Mason (33, Shriner). Clubs: Omaha, Omaha Country. Home: 327 S 73d St Omaha NB 68114 Office: 1620 Farnam St Omaha NB 68102

CLARK, WILFRID LE GROS, anatomist; b. Hemel Hempsted, Eng., June 5, 1895; s. Edward Travers and Ethel (May) C.; D.Sc., London U.; M.A., Oxford; D. Sc. (hon.), Durham, U. Manchester, Edinburgh; M.D. (hon.), Melbourne, U. Oslo; LL.D. (hon.), U. Malaya; m. Freda Constance, Dec. 20, 1923 (dec.); 2 daus. Prin. med. officer, Sarawak, 1920-23; prof. anatomy U. London, 1924-36; prof. anatomy Oxford U., 1934-62; dir. med. research council unit on climate and working efficiency, 1949-62; Penrose lectr. Am. Phil. Soc., 1959, Condon lectr. Oregon U., 1959. Served as capt. Royal Army Med. Corps, 1916-19. Recipient Viking medal, 1955. Fellow Zool. Soc. London, Royal Anthrop. Inst. London (v.p. 1939-52); mem. Physiol. Soc. Eng., Anatomy Soc. Gt. Britain, Am. Philos. Soc., Nat. Acad. Scis. Internat. Congress Anatomy (pres. 1950), Royal Soc. (mem. council 1942-44), Med. Research council Norwegian Acad. Arts and Sci., N.Y. (hon. life), Nat. (fgn. asso.) acads. scis., Royal Soc. New Zealand. Author: Practical Anatomy, rev. edit., 1949: The Fossil Evidence for Human Evolution, 1965; The Tissues of the Body, rev. edit., 1971; The Antecedents of Man., 1969. Contbr. papers sci. jours. Home: 16 Park Close Templar Rd Oxford England

CLARK, WILLIAM GEORGE, lawyer; b. Chgo., July 16, 1924; s. John S. and Ita (Kennedy) C.; student Loyola U., Chgo., 1942-43, 44; J.D., DePaul U., 1946; J.D. (hon.), John Marshall Sch., Chgo., 1962; m. Rosalie Locatis, Nov. 28, 1946; children—Merrilee, William George, Donald, John Steven, Robert. Admitted to Ill. bar, 1947; mem. firm Crane, Kearney, Korzen, Phelan & Clark, and predecessor, Chgo., 1947-56; atty. for Pub. Adminstr. Ill., 1949-53; mem. Ill. Ho. of Reps. from Austin Dist. of Chgo., 1952-54, 56-60, mem. Senate, 1954-56, majority leader, 1959; atty. gen. Ill., 1960-69; partner firm Arvey, Hodes & Mantynband, Chgo. Served with AUS, 1942-44. Mem. Am., Fed., Ill., Chgo., West Suburban bar assns., AMVETS, Celtic Legal Soc., Am. Legion, Ancient Order Hibernians, Irish Fellowship Club (pres. 1961-62), Catholic Lawyers Guild Chgo., Am. Judicature Soc., Delta Theta Phi. Moose, Elk, K.C. Clubs: Nat. Lawyers, Chicago Athletic Assn. Home: 1420 N Lake Shore Dr Chicago IL 60610 Office: 1 N LaSalle St Chicago IL 60602

CLARK, WILLIAM JUDKINS, chem. co. exec.; b. Savannah, Ga., July 21, 1924; s. Reuben G. and Katharine L. (Judkins) C.; grad. Woodberry-Forest Sch., 1942; B.A. in History, Yale, 1948; m. Mary D. Thompson, Sept. 4, 1950; children—William Judkins, Catherine Judkins, Mary Hamilton. With Owens- Corning Fiberglas Corp., 1948-64, sales mgr. textile products div., 1958- 59, v.p. advt., 1959-61, v.p., mgr. reinforced plastics div., 1961- 64; with CIBA Products Co. div. CIBA Corp., Summit, N.J., 1964-70, pres., 1966-70; sr. v.p. plastics and additives div. CIBA-Geigy Corp., 1970—. Served from pvt. to 1st lt., pilot USAAF, World War II; PTO. Mem. Skull and Bones, Torch Honor Soc., Whiffenpoofs, Delta Kappa Epsilon. Clubs: Yale (N.Y.C.); Wee Burn Country (Darien, Conn.). Home: 363 Rowayton Av Rowayton CT 06853 Office: CIBA-Geigy Corp Ardsley NY 10502

CLARK, WILLIAM NEWPORT, newspaperman; b. Chgo., Apr. 2, 1919; s. Samuel Nye and Helen (Wood) C.; A.B., Ill. Coll., 1940; m. Barbara Ormsbee, Feb. 15, 1941; children—John, William, Thomas, Jennifer. Reporter, City News Bur., Chgo., 1940-41; financial news reporter Chgo. Tribune, 1941-51, asst. financial editor, 1951-56, financial editor, 1956-59, asst. to pub., 1969—. Chmn. bd. trustees Ill. Coll. Served with 43d Inf. Div., AUS, 1941-45. Clubs: Press, Mid-Day (Chgo.); Michigan Shores; Executives; Economic. Commentator, broadcast programs on bus. Home: 726 Washington Av Wilmette IL 60091 Office: 435 N Michigan Av Chicago IL 60611

CLARK, WILLIAM STRATTON, physician; b. Dayton, O., Nov. 24, 1914; s. Clyde Melvin and Hazel Marie (Walker) C.; B.S., U. Dayton, 1932; M.D., St. Louis U., 1938; m. Evelyn Fiala, Oct. 9, 1935 (div. Nov. 1952); children—William Stratton, Judith Ann; m. 2d, Joan Drummond Pennell, Dec. 27, 1952 (div.); children—Robin Walker, James Pennell; m. 3d, Vivien Ranschburg, June 25, 1971. Intern, Miami Valley Hosp., Dayton, 1938-39; gen. practice medicine, Dayton, 1939-44; asst. in pathology Tulane U., 1944-45; clin. fellow medicine Mass. Gen. Hosp., 1945-48; research, tchr. Mass. Gen. Hosp., Med. Sch. Harvard, 1948-53; asst. prof. medicine Western Res. U., 1953-56, asso. prof. medicine, 1956-58; dir. med. dept. Nat. Found., 1958-64; pres., chief exec. officer Arthritis Found., N.Y.C., 1964-70, cons., 1970—; asso. prof. medicine Columbia Coll. Phys. and Surgeons, 1971—. Diplomate American Bd. Internal Medicine. Fellow A.C.P.; mem. A.M.A., Am. Fedn. Clin. Research, Am. Rheumatism Assn., Am. Pub. Health Assn. Episcopalian. Former editor-in-chief: Arthritis and RheumatismOfcl. Jour. Am. Rheumatism Assn. Contbr. articles profl. jours. Home: 1349 Lexington Av New York City NY 10028 Office: 72 E 86th St New York City NY 10028

CLARK, WILLIAM T., ins. co. exec.; b. Cleve., Feb. 23, 1920; B.S., Yale, 1941; M.B.A., Harvard, 1947. Formerly with Glens Falls Ins. Co., financial v.p., 1961- 66, sec., sr. v.p. investment; v.p., dir. Kansas City Fire & Marine Ins. Co., 1961—; v.p., sec., dir. Glenway Corp., 1962- -; sec., dir. Glenplan Corp., 1964—; dir. First Nat. Bank Glens Falls. Mem. Boston Security Analysts Socs., Delta Psi. Home: 18 Broadacres Rd Glens Falls NY 12801 Office: 291 Glen St Glens Falls NY 12801*

CLARK, WILLIAM VAN ALAN, Jr., electronics co. exec.; b. Phila., Jan. 21, 1920; s. William Van Alan and Edna (McConnell) C.; grad. Loomis Sch., 1937; A.B., Williams Coll., 1941; S.M., Mass. Inst. Tech., 1942; m. Mary F. Harris, June 21, 1947; children—William Van Alan III, Caroline Helen, Stephen, Lucy, Hannah. Instr., Mass. Inst. Tech. Sch. Indsl. Mgmt., 1946-47, asst. prof., 1947- 52, asso. prof., 1952-57, asst. dean, 1956-58; pres. Sippican Corp., Marion, Mass., 1958—; chmn. bd. Gen. Electronics Labs., Boston, 1964—; dir. Avon Products, Inc., N.Y.C., Tibbetts Industries, Camden, Me., Electronic Engring. Co. of Cal., Siliconix, Inc., Sunnyvale, Cal. Mem. corp. Woods Hole Oceanographic Inst. Served to lt. USNR, 1943-46. Mem. Acad. Mgmt. Clubs: University, N.Y. Yacht (N.Y.C.); St. Botolph (Boston); Beverly (Mass.) Yacht. Home: Ram Island Marion MA 02738 Office: Sippican Corp Barnabas Rd Marion MA 02738

CLARKE, ALFRED CARPENTER, educator, sociologist; b. Milford, Conn., June 26, 1921; s. Stanley Newton and Madge (Haviland) C.; A.B. cum laude, Marietta Coll., 1948; M.A., Ohio State U., 1950, Ph.D., 1955; m. Daisy Jackson, Aug. 29, 1948; children—Kenneth Carpenter, James Alfred. Research asst. dept. sociology, anthropology Ohio State U., Columbus, 1949-50, instr., 1951- 57, asst. prof., 1957-60, asso. prof., 1960-64, prof., 1964—, vice chmn. dept., 1967-70, acting chmn., 1970-71; dir. research projects Grad. Sch.; dir. research projects Sch. Aviation Medicine, Randolph Field, Tex. Served with F.A., AUS, 1942-46; ETO. Fellow Am. Sociol. Assn.; mem. Am. Assn. U. Profs. (past pres.), Ohio Valley Sociol. Soc., Ohio (past pres.), Nat. councils family relations, Ohio Acad. Sci., Alpha Kappa Delta, Beta Gamma Sigma. Author: (with Russel Dynes, Simon Dinitz, Iwao Ishino) Social Problems; Dissensus and Deviation in an Industrial Society, 1964; (with Dynes, Dinitz) Deviance: Studies in the Process of Stigmatization and Societal Reaction, 1969. Contbr. articles to profl. jours. Home: 4016 Windermere Rd Columbus OH 43220

CLARKE, ALLEN BRUCE, educator; b. Saskatoon, Sask., Can., Sept. 8, 1927; s. Arthur Roy and Florence (Clarke) C.; B.A. with honours, U. Sask., 1947; M.Sc., Brown U., 1949, Ph.D., 1951; m. Florence Myres, Sept. 14, 1949; children—David John, Richard Neil, Deborah Lynn. Came to U.S., 1947, naturalized, 1953. From instr. to prof. U. Mich., 1951-67; Fulbright lectr. U. Turku and U. Abo, Finland, 1959-60; prof., chmn. dept. math. Western Mich. U., 1967—; cons., lectr. probability and random processes. Mem. Math. Assn. Am. (sect. chmn. 1969-70), Am. Math. Soc., Inst. Math. Statistics, Nat. Council Tchrs. of Mathematics, Am. Assn. Univ. Profs., A.A.A.S., Am. Civil Liberties Union. Author: Elementary Statistics, 1961; (with R.L. Disney) Probability and Random Processes for Engineers and Scientists, 1970. Contbr. articles profl. jours. Home: 2016 Greenbriar Dr Kalamazoo MI 49008

CLARKE, ARTHUR CHARLES, author; b. Minehead, Eng., Dec. 16, 1917; s. Charles Wright and Norah (Willis) C.; B.Sc. with 1st class honours, King's Coll., London, 1948; m. Marilyn Mayfield, June 15, 1953 (div. 1964). Auditor, Exchequer and Audit Dept., 1936-41; asst. editor Physics Abstracts, 1949-50; lectr., author, 1951—; engaged in underwater photography on Gt. Barrier Reef of Australia and coast of Ceylon, 1955—; numerous TV, radio appearances. Served to flight lt. RAF, 1941-46. Recipient Kalinga prize UNESCO, 1961, Stuart Ballantine medal Franklin Inst., 1963. Mem. Royal, Ceylon (pres. 1960—) astron. socs., British Interplanetary Soc. (chmn. 1946-47, 50-53), Internat. Acad. Astronautics, World Acad. Art and Sci., Am. Inst. Aero. and Astronautics, Assn. Brit. Sci. Writers, Brit. Sub-Aqua Club, Brit. Astron. Assn., Soc. Authors, Am. Astronautical Assn. Author: (non fiction) Interplanetary Flight 1950; The Exploration of Space, 1951; Going Into Space, 1954; (with R. A. Smith) The Exploration of the Moon, 1955; The Coast of Coral, 1956; The Making of a Moon, 1957; The Reefs of Taprobane, 1957; Voice Across the Sea, 1958; The Challenge of the Spaceship, 1959; The

Challenge of the Sea, 1960; (with Mike Wilson) The First Five Fathoms, 1960; Boy Beneath the Sea, 1958; Indian Ocean Adventure, 1961; The Treasure of the Great Reef, Indian Ocean Treasure, 1964; Profiles of the Future, 1962; (with the editors of Life mag., Man and Space, 1964; Voices from the Sky, 1965; The Promise of Space, 1968; Report On Planet Three, 1971; (fiction) Prelude to Space, 1951; Islands in the Sky, 1952; Against the Fall of Night, 1953; The Sands of Mars, 1953; Childhood's End, 1953; Expedition to Earth, 1953; Earthlight, 1955; Reach for Tomorrow, 1956; The City and the Stars, 1956; Tales from the White Hart, 1957; The Deep Range, 1957; The Other Side of the Sky, 1958; Across the Sea of Stars, 1959; A Fall of Moondust, 1961; From the Ocean, From the Stars, 1962; Tales of Ten Worlds, 1962; Dolphin Island, 1962; Glide Path, 1963; (with Stanley Kubrick) 2001: A Space Odyssey (novel and screenplay), 1968; The Nine Billion Names of God, 1967; The Lost Worlds of Zool, 1971. Address: 47/5 Gregory's Rd Colombo 7 Ceylon also care Scott Meredith 580 Fifth Av New York City NY 10036

CLARKE, BEVERLY LEONIDAS, sci. communications cons.; b. Nashville, Sept. 30, 1900; s. Thomas Hopkins and Ida Clyde (Gallegher) C.; B.S. in Chemistry, George Washington U., 1921 (fellow of Chemists Club, N.Y.C., 1919-21); traveling fellow Am.-Scandinavian Found., Nobel Inst., Stockholm, Copenhagen, Sorbonne, Paris, U. Vienna; M.S., Columbia, 1923, Ph.D., 1924; m. Katharine Vander Roest, Apr. 30, 1924 (div. 1930); m. 2d, Ruth Johnston, Sept. 2, 1930; children—Thomas Beverly, James Johnston. Tech. asst. to spl. U.S. comml. attaché, Paris and London, 1922; mem. faculty Coll. City N.Y. and Columbia U., 1923-24; spl. research on colloid chemistry of vital processes Carnegie Inst. of Washington, 1924; NRC fellow in phys. chemistry Stanford, 1925-26; mem. tech. staff Bell Telephone Labs., N.Y.C., 1927-46; materials chemist, 1938-45, anal. res. chem., 1945-46; dir. chem. control Merck & Co., Inc., Rahway, N.J., 1946-59, asst. to v.p. operations, 1959-61; gen. cons. to exec. sec. Am. Chem. Soc., Washington, 1961; adminstrv. officer Fedn. Am. Socs. for Exptl. Biology, Bethesda, Md., until 1966, research officer, 1966-68; dir. surveys and spl. studies Herner & Co., Washington, 1968-70; pvt. cons. in sci. communications, Washington, 1970—; cons. to Dept. State, 1943-45, Dept. Def., 1948. Served as non- commd. officer U.S. Navy, 1918; lt., N.Y. Guard, 1941-43. Recipient Army- Navy certificate for Civilian Work, World War II. Fellow A.A.A.S., Am. Chem. Soc. (dir. N.Y. sect. 1940-41, chmn. 1944-45, Anal. div. 1951-52), Micro Chem. Soc. (pres. 1936-37), Am. Pharm. Assn., Am. Soc. Statis. Control, N.Y. Acad. Sci., Am. Arbitration Assn., Soc. Chem. Industry. Clubs: Canoe Brook Country (Summit, N.J.); Chemists' (v.p., N.Y.C.); George Washington University (Washington). Author: The Romance of Reality, 1927; Marvels of Modern Chemistry, 1932. Co-author: The Doctor Looks at Murder, 1937. Asso. editor Industrial and Engineering Chemistry, also Microchimica Acta (Vienna). Contbr. to Sci. Monthly, Sci. American, N.Y. World, others. Deviser of method of separating certain rare earths. Home and office: 4600 Connecticut Av NW Washington DC 20008

CLARKE, BOWMAN LAFAYETTE, educator; b. Meridian, Miss., Sept. 19, 1927; s. Alvin Merritt and Mamie Edna (Blakeley) C.; B.A., Millsaps Coll., 1948; B.D., Emory U., 1951, M.A., 1952, Ph.D., 1961; M.A., U. Miss., 1957. Ordained to ministry Methodist Ch., 1952; minister to Methodist students Ga. State Coll. for Women, 1953-54, U. Miss., 1954-57; instr. philosophy U. of South, 1959-60; asst. prof. philosophy U. Ga., Athens, 1961-65, asso. prof. philosophy, 1965-67, prof., 1967—. Recipient Danforth grant, 1957, Cokesbury award, 1958, Research grant Ella Lyman Cabot Trust Fund, 1960. Mem. Am. Philos. Assn., Am. Acad. Religion, Soc. for Philosophy of Religion (dir.), Soc. for Sci. Study Religion, So. Soc. for Philosophy and Psychology. Author: Language and Natural Theology, 1966. Asso. editor Internat. Jour. Philosophy Religion, 1970. Contbr. articles profl. jours. Home: 171 Soule St Athens GA 30601

CLARKE, BRUCE COOPER, ret. army officer; b. Adams, N.Y., Apr. 29, 1901; s. Matthew John and Isola Veneta (Stevens) C.; B.S., U.S. Mil. Acad., 1925; C.E., Cornell U., 1927; LL.B., LaSalle Extension U., 1936; grad. Engr. Sch., 1928, Command and Gen. Staff Sch., 1940, Armored Sch., 1949; LL.D., Baylor U., 1961; Dr. Internat. Law, Parsons Coll., 1963; m. Bessie Mitchell, June 12, 1925; children—Bruce Cooper, David Arthur, Gordon Mitchell, Elisabeth Jean. Commd. 2d lt. U.S. Army, 1925, advanced to gen. (temporary), 1958, promoted to gen. (permanent), 1962; mem. Gen. Staff Corps, 1942-43; combat comdr. 7th and 4th Armored Divs., 1943-45; mem. staff Hdqrs. Army Ground Forces, 1945-48; asst. comdt. The Armored Sch., 1948-49; comdg. gen. 2d Constabulary Brigade, 1949-51, 1st Armored Div., 1951-53; comdg. general I and X Corp and dep. 8th Army comdr. in Korea, 1953-54; comdg. gen. U.S. Army, Pacific, 1954-56, 7th U.S. Army, Europe, 1956- 58, U.S. Continental Army Command, hdqrs. Fort Monroe, Va., 1958-60; comdr. in chief U.S. Army in Europe, 1960-62; ret. Mem. exec. council Boy Scouts Am. Decorated D.S.C., D.S.M. with 2 oak leaf clusters, Silver Star with 2 oak leaf clusters, Legion of Merit, Bronze Star with 2 oak leaf clusters and V, Air medal, Conspicuous Service Cross and medal N.Y. (U.S.); Companion of Bath (Gt. Britain); comdr. Legion of Honor, Croix de Guerre with palm (France); Croix de Guerre with palm grand officer Order of the Crown (Belgium); D.S.M. with 2 Silver Stars, Order Service Merit Medal, 1st Class (Korea); Meritorious medal (Colombia); Grand Cross Order Merit (Fed. Republic Germany); various other medals and citations; named hon. senator U. Heidelberg (Germany). Mem. 4th Armored Div. Assn. (past pres.), 1st Armored Div. Assn. (hon. pres.), Nat. Sojourners, Scabbard and Blade, Tau Beta Pi, Lambda Chi Alpha. Mason (33, K.T.). Home: 4026 N Tazewell St Arlington VA 22207

CLARKE, CHARLES GALLOWAY, lectr., author, cinematographer; b. Potter Valley, Cal., Mar. 19, 1899; s. Charles Edwin and Anna Electa (Millington) C.; ed. pub. schs., Los Angeles; m. Marian Nora Bowden, Apr. 25, 1931; 1 dau., Mary Millington (Mrs. David W. Fleming). Dir. photography Hollywood studios, 1920-61; lectr. advanced cinematography U. Cal. at Los Angeles, 1961-65; motion pictures filmed include Viva Villa, 1934, Miracle on 34th Street, 1947, Carousel, 1956, The Barbarian and the Geisha, 1958. Served with F.A., U.S. Army, World War II. Mem. Am. Soc. Cinematographers (pres. 1950-54, treas. 1966—), Acad. Motion Picture Arts and Scis. Clubs: Zamorano, Adventurer's (Los Angeles); Bell-Air Bay (Santa Monica, Cal.). Author: Professional Cinematography, 1964; The Men of the Lewis and Clark Expedition, 1970. Address: 328 S Bedford Dr Beverly Hills CA 90212

CLARKE, CLIFFORD MONTREVILLE, indsl. assn. exec.; b. Ludowici, Ga., July 20, 1925; s. Clifford Montreville and Lelia Bertrue (Hightower) C.; A.B. in Polit. Sci., Emory U., 1951. Radio engr., announcer WSAV, Savannah, 1941-43; pub. relations dir. Ga. dept. Am. Legion, 1945-47; instr. Armstrong Coll., Savannah, 1947-48; asst. supt. Savannah Park and Tree Commn., 1951; instr., supr. tng. dept. Lockheed Aircraft Corp., Marietta, Ga., 1951-52, mgr. employee services dept., 1952-53; exec. v.p. Asso. Industries, Ga., 1953-68; pres. Ga. Bus. and Industry Assn., Atlanta, 1968—; mem. Am. Soc. Execs., 1955—, bd. dirs., 1958- 67, mem. exec. com., 1960-67, treas., 1962-64, sr. v.p., 1964-65, pres., 1965-66; pres. Ga. Soc. Assn. Execs., 1958-60; v.p., chmn. state assn. group Nat. Indsl. Council, 1970—. Mem. Ga. Intergovtl. Relations Commn., 1966, Ga. Ednl. Improvement Council, 1964—, Pres.'s Com. on Employment Handicapped; manpower adv. council Coastal Plains Regional Commn., 1968—, State Planning Bur., 1968—. Mem. policy com. U. Ga. Grad. Sch. Bus.; adv. bd. Ga. Vocational Rehab. Bd. dirs. Arthritis Found. Ga., Atlanta Community Services to Blind, Coop. Services for Blind, Atlanta Sch. Art; trustee Am. Soc. Assn. Execs. Found., Chartered Assn. Exec. Chartering Bd. Served with inf. AUS, World War II. Decorated Purple Heart with 2 oak leaf clusters. Mem. Pub. Relations Soc. Am. Home: 1115 Beechhaven Rd NE Atlanta GA 30324 Office: 181 Washington St SW Atlanta GA 30303

CLARKE, DAVID ANDREW, Jr., educator, agrl. economist; b. Milford, Conn., Feb. 26, 1919; s. David Andrew and Hazel (Munson) C.; B.S., U. Conn., 1940, M.S., 1942; Ph.D., U. Cal. at Berkeley, 1951; m. Dorothy Stoddard Burnap, July 18, 1942; children—Marilyn (Mrs. Donald Bristow), David Alan, Sandra S. (Mrs. Steven A. Smith), Margaret Ann. Grad. asst. U. Conn., 1940-42, research instr., 1942-44; faculty U. Cal. at Berkeley, 1946—, prof. agrl. econs., 1960—, chmn. dept., 1968—, dir. Giannini Found. Agrl. Econs., 1968—. Served to 1st lt. AUS, 1944-46. Mem. Am. (award of merit 1957), Western agrl. econs. assns. Democrat. Conglist. Contbr. profl. jours. Home: 36 Owl Hill Rd Orinda CA 94563 Office: Giannini Hall Univ of California Berkeley CA 94720

CLARKE, DONALD DUDLEY, educator; b. Kingston, Jamaica, B.W.I., Mar. 20, 1930; s. Izett Dudley and Ivy (Burrowes) C.; came to U.S., 1948, naturalized, 1961; B.S., Fordham U., 1950, M.S., 1951, Ph.D., 1955; m. Marie B. Burrowes, Sept. 5, 1953; children—Carol, Stephen, Paula, David, Ian, Sylvia, Peter. Postdoctoral research fellow U. Toronto, 1955-57; sr. research scientist N.Y. Psychiat. Inst., N.Y.C., 1957-62; research asso. biochemistry dept. Columbia, 1959-61; adj. asso. prof. Fordham U., N.Y.C., 1961-62, asso. prof., 1962-70, prof. biochemistry, 1970—. Recipient research grant Nat. Inst. Neurol. Disease and Stroke, 1967. Mem. Am. Chem. Soc. (chmn. organic discussion group, dir. N.Y. sect.), Am. Soc. Biol. Chemists, Biochemical Soc. (London), A.A.A.S., N.Y. Acad. Sci., Internat., Am. socs. for neurochemistry, Soc. for Applied Spectroscopy, Sigma Xi, Phi Lambda Upsilon. Democrat. Roman Catholic. K.C. Contbr. articles profl. jours. Home: 2528 Grand Av New York City NY 10468

CLARKE, EDMUND WILLCOX, ins. co. exec.; b. Bakersfield, Cal., Apr. 25, 1918; s. Dwight Lancelot and Edna Marie (Wilcox) C.; A.B. with great distinction, Stanford, 1939; m. Mary Patricia Lucas, May 29, 1948; children—Donald Alan Garrard, Dwight Lancelot II, Edmund Wilcox, Patricia Ann, Gerald Lucas, Marianne Patrice. Br. mgr. E. F. Hutton and Co., Bakersfield, 1947-60; v.p. Transam. Corp., 1960—; pres., dir. Transam. Ins. Co., 1962-67, chmn. bd., dir., 1967—; chmn. bd. Riverside Ins. Co.; dir. Premier Ins. Co., Am. Life Ins. Co. N.Y., Canadian Surety Co., Surety Fire Ins. Co., Wolverine Ins. Co. Bd. dirs. Transam. Research Corp., Transam. Investment Counselors; mem. exec. com. Western Ins. Information Service. Served to maj. USMCR. Home: 1553 Rancho View Dr Lafayette CA 94559 Office: 701 Montgomery St San Francisco CA 94111

CLARKE, EDWARD NIELSEN, educator; b. Providence, Apr. 25, 1925; s. Edward O.A. and Edith (Nielsen) C.; B.S., Brown U., 1945, Ph.D., 1951; M.S., Harvard, 1947, M.Engring. Sci., 1948; m. Vivian Constance Bergquist, July 23, 1949; children—Sandra J., David E., Allan R., Jeffrey B. Mem. tech. staff, sect. head for semiconductors, physics lab. Sylvania Electric Products Co., Bayside, N.Y., 1950-56; group head for research Sperry Semiconductor div. Sperry Rand Corp., Norwalk, Conn., 1956-59; v.p. operations Nat. Semiconductor Corp., Danbury, Conn., 1959-65; asso. dean faculty, dir. research Worcester Poly. Inst., 1965—. Dir. Meditech Energy & Environmental Corp. Served with USNR, 1943-46. Mem. Research Soc. Am. (past br. pres.), I.E.E.E., Am. Phys. Soc., A.A.A.S., Am. Soc. Engring. Edn., Sigma Xi (past chpt. pres.), Tau Beta Pi. Lutheran. Rotarian. Club: Torch (Worcester). Home: 85 Richards Av Paxton MA 01612 Office: Worcester Poly Inst Worcester MA 01609

CLARKE, EDWIN CAMERON, coll. pres.; b. Beaver Falls, Pa., Oct. 30, 1913; s. Robert and Bernice Mehard (Wilson) C.; B.A., Geneva Coll., 1935; postgrad. Princeton, 1935-37, U. Colo., summer 1938; Ph.D., U. Pitts., 1949; m. Agnes Currie Thorburn, Feb. 29, 1944; children—Robert Thorburn, Carolyn Wilson. Faculty Geneva Coll., 1937—, asso. prof. econs. and bus. adminstrn., acting head dept., 1947-49, prof., head dept., 1949-56, v.p., 1950-56, pres., 1956—. Bd. dirs. Beaver County Heart Assn., Beaver County br. Pa. Assn. for Blind. Served with AUS, 1941-46. Named Man of Year, Beaver Falls Jr. C. of C., 1953. Mem. Am. Econs. Assn., Pa. Edn. Assn., Beaver Falls C. of C. Mem. Reformed Presbyn. Ch. (elder). Kiwanian. Home: 3320 4th Av Beaver Falls PA 15010

CLARKE, ELLIS EMMANUEL INNOCENT, diplomat Trinidad and Tobago; b. Trinidad, Dec. 28, 1917; s. Cecil E. I. and Elma (Pollard) C.; student St. Mary's Coll., Trinidad; LL.B., Univ. Coll., London, Eng., 1940; Barrister-at-Law, Gray's Inn, London, 1940; m. Eyrmyntrude Hagley, June 29, 1952; children—Peter Clarke, Margaret-Ann. Called to Trinidad bar; solicitor gen. Trinidad and Tobago, 1954, dep. colonial sec., 1956, atty. gen., 1957, chief justice, 1961; constl. adviser to cabinet, Trinidad and Tobago, 1961; ambassador to U.S., 1962—; permanent rep. Trinidad and Tobago rep. UN, 1962-66, ambassador to Mexico, 1966—; ambassador, rep. of Trinidad and Tobago on council OAS, 1967—. Chmn., Brit. West Indian Airways, 1968—, Leeward Islands Air Transport, 1970—. House scholar London U., 1932; recipient Jerningham Silver medal, 1933; Book prize, 1934; Island Scholar in math., 1936; Jerningham Gold medal, 1936; Trinity Cross, 1969; decorated comdr. Order St. Michael and St. George, 1960; created knight, 1963. Roman Catholic. Home: 7530 17th St NW Washington DC 20012 Office: 2209 Massachusetts Av Washington DC 20008

CLARKE, FRANK ELDRIDGE, govt. ofcl.; b. Brunswick, Md., Dec. 26, 1913; s. Frank Dorsey and Mary J. (McKenzie) C.; A.B. in Chemistry with honors, Western Md. Coll., 1935; M.S. equivalent in Phys. Chemistry, U. Md., 1942; m. Doris Mae Booth, Aug. 20, 1934; children—Virginia Mary (Mrs. G. Robert Blakley), Ernest Eldridge. With U.S. Naval Engring. Expt. Sta., 1941-61; with U.S. Geol. Survey, 1961-71, asst. dir., 1968-71; dep. under sec. for sci. engring. Dept. Interior, 1971—. Cons. in corrosion field, 1961- -. Recipient Gordon research certificate of award, 1966; Dept. Interior Distinguished Service award, 1971. Mem. Am. Soc. Testing and Materials (bd. dirs., v.p. water com. D-19, award of merit 1961, Max Hecht award 1964), Am. Chem. Soc. (certificate merit 1953), Am. Geophys. Union, Am. Inst. Chem. Engrs., A.A.A.S. Lutheran (pres. 1957-63). Elk. Club: Cosmos (Washington). Patentee in field. Home: 165 Williams Dr Annapolis MD 21401 Office: Dept Interior Washington DC 20242

CLARKE, FREDERICK JAMES, army officer; b. Little Falls, N.Y., Mar. 1, 1915; s. Edward J. and Grace (Joller) C.; B.S., U.S. Mil. Acad., 1937; M.S. in Civil Engring., Cornell U., 1940; postgrad. Harvard Advanced Mgmt. Sch.; m. Isabel M. Van Slyke, Sept. 15, 1938; children—Warren E., Isabel V., Nancy S. Commd. 2d lt. C.E., U.S. Army, 1937, advanced through grades to lt. gen., 1969; served with troops and staff, World War II; area mgr. Hanford (Wash.) operations, 1945-47; dist. engr., Pakistan, 1957-59; engr. commr. D.C., 1960-63; dir. mil. constrn. U.S. Army, 1963-65; comdg. gen. U.S. Army Engr. Center, comdt. U.S. Army Engr. Sch., Ft. Belvoir, Va., 1965-66; dep. chief engrs. U.S. Army, Washington, 1966-69, chief of engrs., 1969—. Mem. U.S., Internat. coms. on large dams; mem. D.C. Pub. Utility Commn., 1960-63; chmn. Washington Met. Area Transit Commn., 1962-63. Mem. exec. bd. Nat. Capitol area council Boy Scouts Am., 1960—. Decorated D.S.M., Legion of Merit. Registered profl. engr., D.C. Fellow Am. Soc. C.E.; mem. Soc. Am. Mil. Engrs., Nat. Soc. Profl. Engrs., Am. Pub. Works Assn., Am. Soc. M.E., Permanent Internat. Assn. Nav. Congresses. Home: Quarters 5 Ft McNair Washington DC 20024 Office: Office Chief Engrs Washington DC 20314

CLARKE, GILBERT CAMPBELL, merchandising exec.; b. Ottawa, Ont., Can., Aug. 31, 1911; s. Thomas E. and Marie (Rhodes) C.; B.A., U. Western Ont., 1933; m. Margaret R., Aug. 7, 1937. Pres., gen. mgr., dir. Standards Brands Ltd., 1961—; v.p., dir. Best Yeast Ltd., Dr. Ballard's Animal Foods Ltd., Planters Nut & Chocolate Co., Ltd., Ingersoll Cheese Co., Ltd. Home: 360 Revere Av Mount Royal Quebec Canada Office: 550 Sherbrooke St W Montreal 2 Quebec Canada

CLARKE, GILMORE DAVID, cons. engr., landscape architect; b. N.Y.C., July 12, 1892; s. Gilmore and Johanna F. (Knubel) C.; student Dwight Sch. (N.Y.), 1907-09; B.S., Cornell U., 1913; L.H.D., Yale, 1940; m. Emma Elizabeth Vought, Aug. 16, 1917; children—Elizabeth Nelson (Mrs. Peter Tower), Edward Perry, Doris Jean (Mrs. Maurice C. Bond); m. 2d, Mary Elizabeth Sprout, July 11, 1941 (dec. Sept. 1962); m. 3d, Dolores Nancy Bedford, Apr. 5, 1968. Practiced as landscape architect, 1913—; landscape architect Westchester County Park Commn., 1923-35; cons. engr., landscape architect numerous local, state, fed. commns., spl. constrn. authorities; mem. bd. archtl.-engring. consultants UN Hdqrs., N.Y.C.; mem. bd. design Met. Life Ins. Co. Housing Projects, 1938-49, chmn., 1945-49; prof. Coll. Architecture, Coll. Engring. Cornell U., 1935-50, dean Coll. Architecture, 1938-50, prof. landscape architecture emeritus, 1963—; practice landscape architecture, also civil engring. Clarke & Rapuano, 1935-62, pres., 1962—. Cons. landscape architect N.Y. World's Fair, 1964-65. Mem. Nat. Commn. Fine Arts, 1932-50, chmn. 1937-50; mem. Art Commn. City N.Y., 1950-53; mem. N.Y. State Planning Council, 1935-41; mem. Bd. Design N.Y. World's Fair, 1939; landscape architect mem. Adv. Bd. Architects, U.S. Capitol, 1956—; cons. N.Y. State Power Authority; mem. adv. com. on Arts, Dept. State; mem. Smithsonian Art Commn., 1940—. First scout commr. Borough of Bronx, N.Y.C., Boy Scouts Am., 1916- 17. Trustee, mem. exec. com. Am. Acad. in Rome, 1931-46, chmn. jury in landscape architecture, 1932-37; chmn. bd. trustees Bayard Cutting Arboretum, now, emeritus; trustee Am. Mus. Natural History, 1948-57. Adv. com. Grad. Sch. Design Harvard, 1932-44. Served from lt. to capt. 6th Engrs., 3d Div. U.S. Army, World War, 1917-19. Decorated Silver Star medal, Order of Purple Heart. Recipient Medals of Honor, Archtl. League N.Y., 1931, Nat. Sculpture Soc., 1970; Frank P. Brown medal Franklin Inst., 1945. Fellow Am. Soc. Landscape Architects (pres. 1949-50), Royal Soc. Arts; mem. Am. Acad. Arts and Letters, Nat. Inst. Art and Letters, Am. Soc. Cons. Engrs., Am. Soc. C.E., hon. mem. A.I.A., N.A.D., Société Francaise D'Architecture de Jardins, Tau Beta Pi. Republican. Presbyn. Clubs: Century (N.Y.C.); Cosmos (Washington); Sleepy Hollow Country. Author: Sonnets-1949-1962; Sonnets-1963-1966; A Septet of Sonnets, 1967, 68, 70. Home: 480 Park Av New York City NY 10022 Office: 830 3d Av New York City NY 10022

CLARKE, HARRISON, investment banker; b. Savannah, Ga., May 13, 1917; s. Hagood and Dorothy (Harrison) C.; student U. Ga., 1935-36; m. Betty C. Dameron, May 14, 1954; children—Elizabeth Ann, Harrison, James Porter. With Citizens & So. Nat. Bank, Atlanta, 1936-37; with Johnson, Lane, Space & Co., Inc., Atlanta, 1937—, exec. v.p., 1958—, also dir. Pres. Ga. Security Dealers Assn., 1961; chmn. So. group Investment Bankers Assn. Am., 1961, bd. govs., 1962-64; allied mem. N.Y. Stock Exchange. Pres. Harrison Clarke Found. Served to capt. USAAF, 1942-46; ETO. Decorated Air medal. Mem. Am. Legion, Chi Phi. Presbyn. Clubs: Cherokee Country, Commerce (Atlanta). Home: 4020 Randall Mill Rd NW Atlanta GA 30327 Office: Johnson Lang Space & Co Inc Commerce Bldg Atlanta GA 30303

CLARKE, HARRY JOSEPH, former metal plate structures co. exec.; b. Wallinford, Conn., Mar. 7, 1904; s. Richard and Ida (Steele) C.; C.E., Rensselaer Poly. Inst., 1926; m. Ruth Studholme, July 27, 1929; children—Phyllis (Mrs. Ronald Perrin), Marilyn (Mrs. Dayton K. Sippy). With Chgo. Bridge & Iron Co., 1927-68, v.p. field constrn., 1952- 61, sr. v.p. operations, 1961-62, pres., chief exec. officer, 1962-68. Trustee Village of Hinsdale, Ill., 1957-61. Clubs: Hinsdale Golf; Hole in the Wall, Port Royal Beach (Naples, Fla.); Royal Poinciana Golf. Home: 980 Nelsons Walk Naples FL 33940

CLARKE, HELEN ELIZABETH, coll. dean; b. Edmondton, Alta., Can., Nov. 28, 1920; d. Clarence C. and Ethel (Moore) Clarke; came to U.S., 1928, naturalized, 1946; B.S., U. Mich., 1943; certificate phys. therapy, Mayo Clinic, 1946; M.A., U. Ill., 1951; Ed.D., Columbia Tchrs. Coll., 1960. Recreational dir. U.S. Govt., Germany, 1949-50; resident counselor Ind. U., 1951-52; asso. dean students Lake Forest (Ill.) Coll., 1953-58; asst. dean students U. Cal., Berkeley, 1958-60; dean women U. Md., College Park, 1960-66, asso. dean students, 1966—. Mem. def. adv. com. Women in Services; adviser ednl. policies commn. N.E.A. of U.S. and Am. Assn. Sch. Adminstrs. Mem. Nat. Assn. Women Deans and Counselors (treas. 1965-67), Internat. Platform Assn., Am. Personnel and Guidance Assn., N.E.A., Am. Assn. U. Women, Pi Lambda Theta, Kappa Delta Pi, Alpha Lambda Delta, Kappa Delta. Episcopalian. Club: Soroptimist. Contbr. articles to profl. jours. Home: 3429 Duke St College Park MD 20740

CLARKE, HENRY LELAND, educator, composer; b. Dover, N.H., Mar. 9, 1907; s. Ward Robinson and Annie Leland (Barber) C.; A.B., Harvard, 1928, M.A., 1929, Ph.D., 1947; student of Nadia Boulanger, 1929-31; m. Julia Newbold Keasbey, June 24, 1937; children—Anne Newbold (dec.). Asst., N.Y. Pub. Library, 1932-36; teaching asst. Bennington Coll., Vt., 1936-38; chmn. grad. faculty Westminster Choir Coll., Princeton, N.J., 1938-42; lectr. U. Cal. at Los Angeles, 1947-48; asst. prof. Vassar Coll., 1948-49, U. Cal. at Los Angeles, 1949-58; asso. prof. U. Wash., Seattle, 1959—. Served with AUS, 1944. John Harvard Traveling fellow, 1929-30; Am. Council Learned Socs. grantee, 1936; recipient Wash. Music Educators prize award, 1964. Mem. Bohemians of Los Angeles, Am. Cmposers Alliance, Am. Musicol. Soc. (past chpt. pres.), Am. Soc. Aesthetics (past chpt. pres.), Coll. Music Soc. (past v.p.), Phi Mu Alpha. Unitarian. Club: Harvard (N.Y.C.). Composer: The Loafer and the Loaf, 1951; Lysistrata, 1969; Monograph, 1948; No Man Is an Island (chorus and band), 1951; A Game That Two Can Play (flute and clarinet), 1959. Home: 6500 57th Av NE Seattle WA 98115

CLARKE, JACK ALDEN, educator, librarian; b. Bay City, Mich., Feb. 20, 1924; s. Harry and Olivia (Bence) C.; B.A., Mich. State U., 1949; postgrad. U. Poitiers (France), 1949; M.A., U. Wis., 1950, M.A. in L.S., 1952, Ph.D. in History, 1954; m. Anna Holler, Feb. 1, 1951; children—David, Cynthia. Intern, Library of Congress, 1952-53; dir. Washington Cathedral Library, 1953-55, Doane Coll. Library, 1955-56; asst. librarian U. Wis., 1956-62; dir. libraries, chmn. dept.

library sci. Wis. State U., Eau Claire, 1962- 66; asst. dir. U. Wis. Grad. Sch. Library Sci., Madison, 1966-68, acting dir., 1968-69, 70-71, prof., 1967- -. Mem. Am. Assn. U. Profs., Am., Wis. (chmn. coll. sect. 1963-64) library assns., Assn. Coll. Reference Librarians. Author: Huguenot Warrior, The Life and Times of Henri de Rohan, 1579-1638; Gabriel Naudé 1600- 1653. Contbr. articles to profl. jours. Compiler: Research Materials in the Social Sciences, 1967. Home: 4326 Herrick Lane Madison WI 53711

CLARKE, JACK WELLS, corporation exec.; b. Abingdon, Va., June 26, 1914; s. James Sydnor and Ottie B. (Wells) C.; A.B., Williams Coll., 1935; postgrad. N.Y. U., 1935- 37; m. Dorothy Irelan, Mar. 24, 1938. Bond analyst, statistician, N.Y.C., 1935-37; asst., mgr. budget and statis. dept., asst. to pres., asst. to chmn. bd., dir. pub. relations Lion Oil Co., 1938-51; dir. pub. relations Tex. Eastern Transmission Corp., 1951-55; exec. v.p. Freestate Indsl. Devel. Co., 1955-56, pres., dir., 1956-68; pres., dir. North Shreveport Devel. Co. (La.), 1956-68; ind. developer, investor, Shreveport, 1968—; dir. Curry Sanders Aircraft Co., Freestate Drugs, Inc.; co-owner shopping centers. Mem. Shreveport-Bossier Found., Urban Land Inst., Am. Indsl. Devel. Council, Internat. Council Shopping Centers; adv. com. Nat. Rivers and Harbors Congress. Bd. dist. Holiday in Dixie, Shreveport Mental Health Center; dir., mem. governing bd. Shreveport YMCA. Mem. La. State Democratic Central Com.; chmn. Caddo Parish Dem. Assn. Served to lt. USNR, 1942-45. Mem. Am. Ordnance Assn., Res. Officers Assn., Pub. Affairs Research Council La. (trustee), Shreveport C. of C. (dir.), Internat. Assn. Assessing Officers, Bossier City C. of C. Shreveport Com. 100, Navy League, Phi Delta Theta. Episcopalian. Clubs: Ambassadors; Williams, (N.Y.C.); Shreveport, Shreveport Country. Home: 708 Azalea Dr Shreveport LA 71107 Office: PO Box 7776 Shreveport LA 71107

CLARKE, JAMES SPENCER, educator, physician; b. Chgo., June 28, 1918; s. James Cunningham and Gladys Aileen (Spencer) C.; B.S., Harvard, 1940, M.D., 1943; m. Maxine Yvonne Taylor, Apr. 9, 1949; children—Nancy Lynn, Mary Kathryn. Intern, U. Chgo. Clinics, 1944, resident surgery, 1945-46, 48-53; mem. dept. surgery U. Chgo., 1953-56; chief surg. service VA Hosp., Los Angeles, also mem. dept. surgery U. Cal. at Los Angeles Med. Center, 1956-63; prof. surgery U. N.M. Sch. Medicine, 1963-68, U. Cal. Los Angeles Med. Center, 1968—; chief surgery Bernalillo County Indian Hosp., 1963-68; cons. VA Hosp., Albuquerque, 1963-68. Served to capt. M.C., AUS, 1946-48. Diplomate Am. Bd. Surgery. Fellow A.C.S.; mem. Soc. U. Surgeons, Am., Pacific Coast, Western surg. assns., Am. Gastroent Assn., Soc. Surgery Alimentary Tract, Phi Beta Kappa, Sigma Xi, Alpha Omega Alpha. Home: 13620 Sunset Blvd Pacific Palisades CA 90272

CLARKE, JOHN FREDERICK GATES, entomologist; b. Victoria, B.C., Can., Feb. 22, 1905; s. Robert Wilson and Ida Charlotte (Gates) C.; came to U.S., 1916, naturalized, 1934; student U. Wash., 1923-24; Ph.C. in Pharmacy, Wash. State U., 1926, B.S. in Zoology, 1930; M.S. in Entomology, 1931, postgrad., 1935- 36; postgrad. U. Paris (France), 1945-46; Ph.D. in Entomology, U. London (Eng.), 1953; m. Thelma Blanche Canterbury Miesen, June 14, 1929; children—John Frederick Gates, Carol Canterbury. Pharmacist, Offerman Drug Co., Bellingham, Wash., 1926-29; instr. biology Wash. State Coll., 1931-35; entomologist Dept. Agr., 1936-54; curator div. insects U.S. Nat. Mus., Smithsonian Instn., 1954-62, chmn. dept. entomology, 1963-65, sr. entomologist Smithsonian Instn., 1965—. Field expdns. to Pacific Islands, Micronesia, 1952-53, W.I., V.I., 1956, 58, Eng., Austria, 1957, 60, S.Am., 1958-59, Yucatan, 1960, S. Pacific, Polynesia, 1961, Tahiti, Raivavae, Tubuai, Rapa, Fiji, 1963, Dominica, 1965, Marquesas Islands, Tuamotus Islands, 1968; vis. prof. entomology Ore. State U., 1970. Dept. Agr. del. 8th Entomol. Conf., Stockholm, Sweden, 1948; presented papers numerous internat. confs. Served to capt. AUS, 1942-46; ETO. Decorated Bronze Star. Grantee, NRC, 1934, 35, Smithsonian Instn., 1947, Am. Philos. Soc., 1950, NSF, 1958, 61, Office Naval Research, 1961, 62, Smithsonian Research Found., 1967-68. Fellow Royal Entomol. Soc., Entomol. Soc. Am. (chmn. com. proposal establish Nat. Inst. Entomology 1957); mem. Lepidopterists Soc., Entomol. Soc. Washington (chmn. program com. 1955-58, pres., mem. exec. com. 1960), Soc. Brit. Entomology, Biol. Soc. Washington, Washington Biologists Field Club, Sigma Xi, Phi Kappa Phi, Rho Chi, Phi Sigma, Phi Delta Theta; hon. mem. Soc. Crucena de Ciencias Naturales (Bolivia), Entomol. Soc. Peru. Clubs: Cosmos, Biologists Field (Washington). Author: Giant Golden Book on Butterflies, 1963. Contbr. numerous articles to profl. jours. Inventor philatelic tool. Home: 5115 72d Av Glenridge Hyattsville MD 20784 Office: Dept Entomology US Nat Mus Smithsonian Instn Washington DC 20560

CLARKE, JOHN HENRIK, editor, educator, writer; b. Union Springs, Ala., Jan. 1, 1915; s. John and Willella (Mays) C.; student N.Y. U., 1948-52, New Sch. Social Research, 1956-58; L.H.D., U. Denver, 1970; m. Eugenia Evans, Dec. 24, 1961; 1 dau., Nzingha Marie. Book rev. editor Negro History Bull., 1947-49; co-founder, asso. editor Harlem Quar., 1949-51; occasional tchr. African, Afro-Am. history New Sch. Social Research, 1956-58, a developer African Study Center, 1957-59, asst. to dir., 1958-60; asso. prof. dept. Black and Puerto Rican studies Hunter Coll., City U. N.Y., 1970—; Carter G. Woodson distinguished vis. prof. African history Africana Studies and Research Center, Cornell U., Ithaca, N.Y., 1969—. Extensive travel through W. Africa, 1958-59; feature writer Pitts. Courier, 1957-58, Ghana Evening News, 1958; research dir. 1st African Heritage Expn., 1959; editor mag. African Heritage, 1959; asso. editor Freedomways mag., 1961—; a developer TV series Black Heritage; The Story of Afro-Americans, 1968-69. Bd. dirs. Langston Hughes Center Child Devel. Adv. bd. Martin Luther King Library Center, Atlanta, 1969—. Served with USAAF, 1941-45. Recipient Carter G. Woodson award for distinguished and outstanding work in teaching history African-Am. Hist. Assn., 1971; NATRA citation for meritorious achievement in ednl. TV, Nat. Assn. TV and Radio Announcers, 1969. Mem. Am. Acad. Polit. and Social Sci., Black Acad. Arts and Letters (a founder), Assn. Study Negro Life and History (v.p. 1949-55), African Heritage Studies Assn. (pres. 1969). Author: Rebellion in Rhyme, 1948; The Lives of Great African Chiefs, 1958; Harlem, A Community in Transition, 1964; Harlem, U.S.A., 1965; American Negro Short Stories (anthology), 1966; William Styron's Nat Turner; Ten Black Writers Respond, 1968; Harlem: Voices from the Soul of the Black Community (anthology), 1970. Editor: (with staff of Freedomways) Black Titan: W.E.B. DuBois, 1970; (with Vincent Harding) Slavery and the Slave Trade, 1970. Home: 223 W 137th St New York City NY 10030 Office: 799 Broadway New York City NY 10003

CLARKE, JOHN L., coll. pres.; b. American Fork, Utah, May 14, 1905; s. James Hill and Bertha Harrison (Jackson) C.; A.B., A.M., Brigham Young U., 1932, D.Pub. Service (hon.), 1969; postgrad. U. Cal. at Los Angeles, 1937, U. So. Cal. m. Fay Christensen, Dec. 9, 1931 (dec. Feb. 1970); children—Fay Renee (Mrs. Richard Gordon Scott), Catherine Ann (Mrs. Peter O. Thompson III), John Robert; m. 2d, LaRae Pickett King, Oct. 14, 1970; stepchildren—William Christopher, Laurel Lyn, Kay Tamara. Missionary, Ch. of Jesus Christ of Latter- day Saints, Gt. Britain, 1928-30; instr. American Fork High Sch., 1933; head social sci. dept. Uintah (Utah) High Sch., 1933-35; prin. Lovell-Cowley (Wyo.) Sem., 1935-36, Moroni (Utah) Sem., 1936-38, Juab Sem., Nephi, Utah, 1938- 39; dir. Latter-day Saints Inst. Religion, Thatcher, Ariz., 1939-42, St. George, Utah, 1942-44; pres. Ricks Coll., Rexburg, Ida., 1944—. Pres., Monarch Mining Co., American Fork, 1948—. Adv. bd. Targhee Nat. Forest, mem. Rexburg Planning Bd., 1950- 58; hon. mem. nat. council Boy Scouts Am., 1960. Trustee Idaho Falls (Ida.) Hosp. Recipient Distinguished Service award Brigham Young U., 1952. Mem. C. of C. (dir.) Am., Western polit. sci. assns., Am. Acad. Polit. and Social Sci., N.E.A., Ida. Edn. Assn., Northwest Assn. Jr. Colls. (pres. 1965-66), Delta Phi, Lambda Delta Sigma. Democrat. Rotarian (dir., pres. 1962-63). Home: 264 E Main St Rexburg ID 83440

CLARKE, JOHN RICHARD, outboard motor mfg. co. exec.; b. St. Paul, Apr. 15, 1913; s. John Richard and Anne (Murphy) C.; A.B., U. Puget Sound, 1938; M.S. in Psychology, Purdue U., 1939; m. Opal Emmons, Dec. 16, 1939; children—Carol, John, Dale, Richard, Susan. With B.F. Goodrich Co., 1939-45; with Stewart-Warner Corp., 1945-60, dir. indsl. relations, 1955- 60; v.p. indsl. relations Outboard Marine Corp., 1960—; dir. 1st Fed. Savs. & Loan Assn., Waukegan. Mem. adv. bd. St. Therese Hosp., Coll. Lake County. Bd. dirs. United Community Services of Lake County, Indsl. Mgmt. Inst. of Lake Forest, Coll. Hosp. Planning Council Lake County, Lake County Urban League. Mem. Am. Psychol. Assn., Ill. (dir.), Waukegan chambers commerce. Home: 726 Montesano St Waukegan IL 60085 Office: 100 Sea Horse Dr Waukegan IL 60085

CLARKE, KENNETH KINGSLEY, elec. equipment co. exec.; b. Miami, Fla., June 7, 1924; s. Kenneth Kingsley and Mary (Coffin) C.; student Cornell U., 1941-43; M.Sc. in Elec. Engring., Stanford, 1948; D.Elec.Engring., Bklyn. Poly. Inst., 1959; m. Nona Nelme, Sept. 15, 1945; 1 son, Kenneth Stephen. Research fellow Bklyn. Poly. Inst., 1949-50; asst. prof. Madras (India) Inst. Tech., 1950-52; lectr. U. Ceylon, Colombo, 1952-54; asst. prof. Clarkson Coll. Tech., Potsdam, N.Y., 1954-55; faculty Bklyn. Poly. Inst., 1955-69, prof. elec. engring., 1965-69, dir. grad. elec. engring. div., 1967-69; pres. Clarke-Hess Communication Research Corp., N.Y.C., 1969—. Cons. to govt., industry, 1952—; vis. prof. Middle East Tech. U., Ankara, Turkey, 1961-62; dir. Julie Research Labs., 1966—. Served to 2d lt. USAAF, 1943-46. Mem. I.E.E.E., Am. Assn. U. Profs., A.A.A.S., Sigma Xi, Tau Beta Pi. Author: (with M.V. Joyce) Transistor Circuit Analysis, 1961; (with D.T. Hess) Communication Circuit Analysis, 1971. Co-inventor frequency locked loop. Home: 300 Riverside Dr New York City NY 10025 Office: 43 W 16th St New York City NY 10011

CLARKE, KENNETH SPEARMAN, (Kenny Clarke), musician; b. Pitts., Jan. 9, 1914; s. Charles Spearman and Grace (Scott) C.; ed. Ecole Normale de Musique de Paris; m. Daisy Dina Wallbach, May 26, 1962; 1 son, Laurent. Drummer; mem. Leroy Bradley Orch., 1933, Edgar Hayes Orch., 1936-37, Teddy Hill Orch., 1938-39, Louis Armstrong Orch., 1941, Ella Fitzgerald Orch., Minton's Playhouse, Birth of Modern Jazz, 1941-42; has appeared with Dizzy Gillespie, Charlie Parker, Th. Monk, others; prof. percussion Conservatory de St. Germain-en-Laye, France; mem. Clarke-Boland Orch. Served with AUS, 1944-46; ETO. Mason. Research field of percussion; creator modern conception of drumming; coordinated Independence style for drummers. Home: 142 bis rue de Rosny Montreuil s/bois 93 France Office: 18 rue de la Fontaine au Roi Paris 11 France

CLARKE, L. FLOYD, coll. dean; b. Newton, Utah, June 21, 1906; s. David R. and Martha (Cooley) C.; B.S., Utah State Agr. Coll., 1927, M.S., 1931; Ph.D., U. Chgo., 1935; postgrad. U. Rochester, 1933-34, U. Utah, 1940; m. Nina Robinson, June 16, 1927; children—Lucille (Mrs. Richard S. Dumbrill), Evelyn (Mrs. James Skordas), David. High sch. tchr., Laketown, Utah, 1927-29; jr. entomologist Utah State Expt. Sta., Duchesne and Delta, 1930-31; instr. br. Agrl. Coll. Utah, Cedar City, 1934-35; mem. dept. zoology U. Wyo., Laramie, 1935—, prof. zoology, 1945—, asso. dean Coll. Health Scis., 1968—, head zoology, 1945-68; dir., curator Jackson Hole Biol. Research Sta., 1953-. Mem. Laramie City San. Bd., 1949-; mem. adv. bd. Jackson Hole Wildlife Park, 1947-53; Wyo. certifying officer Western Interstate Commn. for Higher Edn. Served as aviation physiologist USAAF, Randolph Field, 1943-44. Recipient G.D. Humphrey Distinguished Faculty award, 1965. Mem. A.A.A.S., Am. Soc. Zoologists, Colo.-Wyo. Acad. Sci., Sigma Xi, Phi Kappa Phi, Alpha Epsilon Delta. Mem. Ch. of Jesus Christ of Latter-day Saints. Rotarian (pres. 1950-51). Home: 830 S 8th St Laramie WY 82070

CLARKE, NORMAN FORD, educator, librarian; b. St. Paul, May 7, 1928; s. Norman Edward and Katharine (Hall) C.; A.B., Ind. U., 1950; M.S. in L.S., M.A. in Polit. Sci., U. Minn., 1955; m. Mary Evelyn Porter, July 15, 1951; children—Jean Marie, Christina, Katharine. Spl. asst. to asso. dir. libraries U. Minn., 1953-55; document librarian U. Omaha, 1955-56; head librarian Jamestown (N.D.) Coll., 1956-62; asst. prof. library sci. U. Ky., 1963-65; prof. library sci., chmn. dept. Ind. State U., Terre Haute, 1965-71; dir., prof. Kan. Grad. Library Sch., Kansas State Tchrs. Coll., Emporia, 1971—. Mem. exec. bd. Mountain Plains Library Assn., 1958-60; pres. N.D. Library Assn., 1961-62, Ohio Valley Group Tech. Service Librarians, 1966- 69. Pres., N.D. Council U.P. Men. 1957-59; treas. Ind. State U. United Campus Christian Fellowship Exec. Bd., 1967-69. Served with AUS, 1951-53. Decorated Purple Heart. Carnegie Library fellow U. Mich., 1962-63. Mem. Am., Ind. (chmn. library edn. com. 1967- 69) library assns., Spl. Libraries Assn., Am. Soc. Information Sci., Am. Civil Liberties Union. Presbyn. (elder 1967—). Rotarian (sec. Terre Haute 1968-70). Office: Kan Grad Library Sch Kan State Tchrs Coll Emporia KS 66801

CLARKE, OLDHAM, lawyer; b. Falmouth, Ky., Mar. 28, 1904; s. Ernest Swope and Mary Virginia (Oldham) C.; LL.B., Washington and Lee U., 1928; m. Louisa Hoge, May 4, 1929; children—Ernest Hoge, Louisa C. Robb. Admitted to Ky. bar, 1928, since practiced in Louisville; with Beckham, Hamilton & Beckham, 1928-29, Woodward, Hamilton & Hobson, 1929-35; 1st asst. U.S. dist. atty., Louisville, 1935-37; faculty Jefferson Sch. Law U. Louisville, 1936-51; partner Allen & Clarke, 1937-42, McElwain, Dinning, Clarke & Winstead, 1942-69, Stites & McElwain, 1969—. Mem. Fiscal Ct. of Jefferson County, Ky., 1943; spl. judge Circuit Ct. of Oldham County, 1948-49; mem. Ky. Constl. Rev. Commn., 1949-50. Bd. dirs. Louisville YMCA, Ky. Easter Seal Soc. for Crippled Children and Adults. Mem. Am., Ky. (pres. 1954-55), Louisville (pres. 1951-52) bar assns., Phi Delta Theta, Phi Delta Phi. Democrat. Mem. Christian Ch. Clubs: Louisville Country, Lawyers, Pendennis (Louisville). Home: 458 Swing Lane Louisville KY 40207 Office: Kentucky Home Life Bldg Louisville KY 40202

CLARKE, OWEN FREDERICK, r.r. ofcl.; b. St. Maries, Ida., Oct. 22, 1913; s. William Francis and Sarah Jane (Davies) C.; J.D., U. Wash., 1936; m. Ruth Ann Moreland, June 20, 1938; 1 son, Owen Frederick. Admitted to Wash. bar, 1936, practiced in Yakima, 1936-43; pros. atty. Yakima County, 1946-48; chmn. Wash. Pub. Service Commn., 1949-51; mem. ICC, 1953-58, chmn., 1957-58; v.p. C. & O. Ry., 1958—, B. & O. R.R., 1964—; dir. Chesapeake Realty Devel. Corp., Western Pocahontas Corp., Cin. Union Terminal Co., Cin. Inter-Terminal R.R. Co. Adminstr., Def. Transport Adminstr., 1954-55. Republican nominee state atty. gen., 1948. Mem. Wash. Toll Bridge Authority, 1949-51. Trustee Am. Mus. Safety. Served as lt. (j.g.) USNR, 1943-46. Mem. Am., Fed., Wash. State bar assns., Transp. Assn. Am. (dir.), Delta Theta Phi, Phi Gamma Delta. Clubs: Congressional Country, Burning Tree (Washington); Canterbury Golf (Cleve.). Home: 13415 Shaker Blvd Cleveland OH 44120 Office: 3500 Terminal Tower Cleveland OH 44101

CLARKE, PHILIP REAM, Jr., banker; b. Chgo., Feb. 10, 1914; s. Philip Ream and Louise (Hildebrand) C.; A.B., U. Chgo., 1937; m. Valerie Mead, Oct. 20, 1939 (dec. Sept. 1965); children—Barbara Foster, Philip Ream III; m. 2d, Jan Finan, Dec. 2, 1967. With Glore, Forgan & Co., Chgo., 1937-42; with City Nat. Bank & Trust Co. Chgo., 1946-57, asst. v.p., 1947-51, v.p., 1951-57; with Lehman Bros., Chgo., 1957-65, mgr. indsl. dept., 1959-62, dir. new bus., 1962-66; v.p., treas., dir. Hinsdale Cemetery Co., 1946-66; sr. v.p., dir. Chgo Corp., 1965—, mem. exec. com., 1968—; dir. Sun Electric Corp., 1st Fed. Savs. & Loan Assn. Chgo., Hollymatic Corp., Property Owners Service Corp. Mem. Midwest Stock Exchange, 1954-56. Pres., treas., dir. Bronswood Cemetery, 1966—; bd. dirs., exec. com. Cook County Sch. of Nursing, 1958-68, v.p., 1965-68; treas., dir. Chgo. Com. on Alcoholism, 1952-56, v.p., 1957, exec. v.p., 1958, pres., 1959, chmn., 1960-61; vice chmn. Chgo. Non Partisan Com. Mem. Republican Nat. Conv., 1959-60; treas. Citizens Com. to Bring Republican and Democratic convs. to Chgo., 1952, 56; bd. govs. Hinsdale Community House, 1968-70, vice chmn., 1969, chmn., 1970; trustee, chmn. finance com. Village of Clarendon Hills, Ill., 1956-60, pres., 1961-65, dep. village treas., 1965-68; bd. dirs. United Rep. Fund of Ill., 1948—, treas., 1948-62, v.p., exec. com., 1955-69; trustee U. Chgo. Alumni Found., 1958-61, citizens bd., 1955—. Served as lt. comdr. USNR, 1942-45. Mem. Chgo. Assn. Commerce and Industry (treas. 1952-53), Citizens of Greater Chgo., Chgo. Zool. Soc. (governing mem. 1956-69), Nat. Council on Alcoholism (v.p. 1959-62), Alpha Delta Phi. Republican. Episcopalian. Clubs: Chicago, Executives (dir.), Bond (Chgo.); Ruth Lake Country; Hinsdale Golf; Coleman Lake (Wis.). Home: 125 Eastern Av Clarendon Hills IL 60514 Office: 208 S LaSalle St Chicago IL 60603

CLARKE, RICHARD WARNER, investment banker; b. Utica, N.Y., Dec. 25, 1896; s. Charles Patrick and Agnes Sinclair (Warner) C.; student Utica Acad., Amherst Coll., 1919, also U.S. Naval Acad.; m. Catherine B. Cartan, Aug. 27, 1927; children—Henry Cartan, Richard Warner, Michael (dec.). Pres. Richard W. Clarke Corp., investment bankers, 1924-; sr. partner Richard W. Clarke & Co., mem. N.Y. Stock Exchange, asso. mem. Am. Exchange. Served with U.S. Navy, 1917-19; from ensign to lt. comdr. USNR, 1941-45. Mem. S.R., Soc. Colonial Wars (counsel), The Pilgrims, New Eng. Soc. (dir.), Alpha Delta Phi. Clubs: Knickerbocker, Down Town Assn., N.Y. Yacht, Racquet and Tennis (N.Y.C.); Bedford Golf and Tennis. Home: The Meadows Katonah NY 10536 Office: 535 Fifth Av New York City NY 10017

CLARKE, ROBERT W., lawyer; b. Needham, Mass., Apr. 4, 1916; A.B., Bowdoin Coll., 1938; LL.B., Harvard, 1941. Admitted to N.Y. bar, 1946; now mem. firm Wood, Oviatt, Gilman, Sturman & Clarke, Rochester. Mem. N.Y. State, Monroe County bar assns. Office: Central Trust Bldg 44 Exchange St Rochester NY 14614*

CLARKE, SAMUEL EUGENE, banker; b. Washington, Kan., Dec. 5, 1922; s. Oscar Lundy and Zoe (Nims) C.; B.A., Doane Coll., Crete, Neb., 1947; postgrad. Pacific Coast Banking Sch., U. Wash., 1964-66; m. Janet Verna Johnson, Aug. 24, 1946; children—Zoe Verna, Jack Lundy. Owner, mgr. Franklin Press, Beatrice, Neb., 1947-53; teller to asst. trust officer Bank Am., Santa Barbara, Cal., Los Angeles, 1953-63; with trust investments and adminstrn., operations City Nat. Bank, Beverly Hills, Cal., 1963-66, v.p., trust officer, div. head, 1966-69, sr. v.p., trust officer, 1969—, also mem. exec. com., trust investment and adminstrn. coms. Served to 2d lt. USAAF, 1943-46; ETO. Mem. Am. Legion, V.F.W. Democrat. Episcopalian. Lion, Elk. Clubs: Woodland Hills (Cal.) Country; Beverly Hills. Home: 26239 Adamor Rd Calabasas CA 91302 Office: 404 N Roxbury Dr Beverly Hills CA 90213

CLARKE, SHIRLEY, film director; b. N.Y.C., Oct. 2, 1927; d. Samuel N. and Florence (Rose) Brimberg; student Stephens Coll., Bennington Coll., Columbia, U. N.C., Johns Hopkins; m. Bert L. Clarke, Aug. 1944 (div. 1963); 1 dau., Wendy Elizabeth. Modern dancer with Hanya Holm, Doris Humphrey, Martha Graham, also Anna Sokolow, 1943-53; tchr. film making Northwestern U., summer 1959, Columbia, summer 1960, N.Y. U., winter 1965; lectr. univs., colls. and museums throughout U.S.; dir. films; Dance in the Sun, 1953; Bullfight (award Edinburg Festival), 1954; Paris Parks, 1955; Moment in Love, 1956; Loops, 1958; Skyscraper (1st prize documentary Venice Festival, also 1st prize Oberhauzen Festival San Francisco Festival and Acad. award nomination), 1958; Bridges Go Round (Bruxelles Exptl. Festival film), 1959; Scarytime (for UNICEF), 1959; The Connection (Critics prize Cannes Festival, best dir. prize Lacarno Festival), 1960; Cool World (spl. invitation Venice Festival), 1963; Love Letter to the 526 W 27th St Hays KS 67601 (Expo 67); Portrait of Jason (feature film), 1967. chmn. bd. Nat. Dance Assn., 1951; mem. bd. Ind. Film Makers Assn., 1954, Screen Dirs. Internat. Guild, 1963-64, Filmmakers Distbn. Center. Mem. Dirs. Guild Am., Dirs. Unit of Actors Studio. Address: Hotel Chelsea New York City, NY 10011.

CLARKE, STEPHEN R., corp. exec.; b. Hackensack; N.J., 1919; ed. U. Notre Dame, 1941. Formerly asst. treas., now treas., dir. Hercules, Inc. Home: 1406 Jan Dr Wilmington DE 19803 Office: 910 Market St Wilmington DE 19899*

CLARKE, THOMAS HAL, lawyer, govt. ofcl.; b. Atlanta, Aug. 10, 1914; s. James Caleb and Mary Cox (DeSaussure) C.; LL.B., Washington and Lee U., 1938; m. Mary Louise Hastings, July 12, 1951; children-Thomas Hal, Mary Katherine, Rebecca DeSaussure. Admitted to Ga. bar, 1939; practiced in Atlanta, 1946-69; mem. firm Mitchell, Clarke, Pate & Anderson, 1948-69; mem. bd. Fed. Home Loan Bank, Washington, 1969—. Pres., bd. dirs. Atlanta Hist. Soc.; bd. visitors Emory U.; mem. alumni bd. Washington and Lee U. Served with USNR, 1942-46; ETO. Mem. Am. Sec. sect. corp., banking and bus. law, Ga., Atlanta bar assns., Am. Law Inst., Atlanta Lawyers Club (past pres.), Selden Soc., English Speaking Union (past pres., chmn. bd.). Clubs: Piedmont Driving, Commerce (Atlanta). Home: 186 15th St NE Atlanta GA 30309 Office: 101 Indiana Av Washington DC 20552

CLARKE, THOMAS HOWARD, physician, surgeon; b. Ottawa, Can., June 30, 1909; s. Thomas Enoch and Marie (Rhodes) C.; B.A., U. Western Ont., 1931, M.D., 1935; m. Thelma Dow, Aug. 17, 1940; children—John Thomas, Paul Howard, Gilbert Byron, Robert Burton. Came to U.S., 1937, naturalized, 1942. Fellow pathology U. Western Ont., 1935-36, research asst. pathology, 1937; intern Royal Victoria Hosp., Montreal, Que., Can., 1936-37; resident surgery, asst. dept. U. Chgo. Med. Sch., 1938-41; faculty Northwestern U. Med. Sch., 1941-71, prof. surgery, 1964-71; faculty U. Ill. Med. Sch., Chgo., 1971—; sr. attending staff Chgo. Wesley Meml. Hosp., 1941-71, cons., 1971—; cons. staff VA Research Hosp., Chgo.; civilian cons. U.S. 5th Army, 1959-71; dir. med. affairs Ill. Masonic Med. Center, 1969—. Trustee U. Western Ont. Found.; bd. dirs. Am. Cancer Soc.; bd. regents Luther Coll., Decorah, Ia. Served to lt. col. M.C., AUS, 1942-46. Fellow A.C.S. (gov.); mem. A.M.A., Central, Western surg. assns., Chgo.

(pres. 1964), Ill. surg. socs., Ill., Chgo. med. socs., Am. Thyroid Assn. Contbr. papers to profl. lit. Home: 999 N Lake Shore Dr Chicago IL 60610 Office: 836 Wellington Av Chicago IL 60657

CLARKE, W.A., banker. Pres., Bank N.M., Albuquerque. Office: 320 Gold Av SW Albuquerque NM 87103*

CLARKE, WILLIAM NORRIS, educator; b. N.Y.C., June 1, 1915; s. Richard Henry and Frances (Chew) C.; Ph.L., Coll. St. Louis, Jersey, Eng., 1939; M.A., Fordham U., 1940; Th.L., Woodstock Coll., 1946; Ph.D., Louvain U., 1949. Instr. philosophy Woodstock Coll., 1949-52; asst. prof. philosophy Bellarmine Coll., Plattsburg, N.Y., 1952-55; asst. prof. Fordham U., Bronx, N.Y., 1955-60, asso. prof., 1960-66, prof. philosophy, 1966—. Mem. Metaphysical Soc. Am. (pres. 1967), Am. Cath. Philos. Assn. (pres. 1968), Jesuit Philos. Assn. (pres. 1960), Soc. of Jesus. Founder, editor-in-chief Internat. Philos. Quart., 1961. Contbr. articles profl. jours. and chpts. to books. Address: Fordham U Bronx NY 10458

CLARKE, WILLIAM WETZEL, pulp and paper co. exec.; b. Yakima, Wash., July 23, 1912; s. Charles William and Louise Adella (Wetzel) C.; B.S. in Chem. Engring., U. Wash., 1933; grad. Advanced Mgmt. Program, Harvard, 1959; m. Edna Murphy, Sept. 19, 1936; children—Barrie Louise, Linda Jean, Charles William. With Longview Fibre Co. (Wash.), 1933—, asst. resident mgr., Longview, 1957- 60, v.p. prodn. and mill mgr., 1960-, also dir. Mem. Paper Industry Mgmt. Assn. (chmn. Pacific Coast), T.A.P.P.I. Elk, Elwanian. Home: 1644 25th Av Longview WA 98632

CLARKIN, DONALD J., ins. co. exec.; b. Mpls., 1929; ed. U. Minn. Vice pres., treas. Am. Casualty Co., Valley Forge Ins. Co.; asst. v.p. Continental Casualty Co.; asst. treas. Valley Forge Life Ins. Co. Home: 512 Wellington Av Lincoln Park PA 19609 Office: 412 Washington St Reading PA 19601*

CLARKSON, ELLIS HUTCHINSON, ins. exec.; b. Blair, Okla., June 23, 1908; s. William Hutchinson and Elizabeth Deva (Ellis) C.; B.S., U. Okla., 1929; m. Mary Juliet Pruitt, Feb. 10, 1934; children—William Ellis, John Pruitt. Fieldman, Nat. Fire Ins. Co. of Hartford, Conn., 1938, agy. supt., Hartford, 1939, asst. sec., 1940-46, sec., 1946-52, v.p., sec., 1952-58; exec. v.p., dir. Nat. Fire & Transcontinental Ins. Co., 1958-59, pres., 1959—; sr. v.p. Continental Casualty Co., Chgo.; v.p. CNA Finance Corp.; dir. Underwriters Salvage Co., Chgo., Gen. Adjustment Bur. N.Y. Pres., Oil Ins. Assn., 1966-67. Served as lt. USNR, 1943-46. Mem. Kappa Sigma. Conglist. Clubs: Hartford (Conn.) Golf; Sunset Ridge Country (Winnetka, Ill.); Blue Goose International; Union League (Chgo.). Home: 210 Abingdon Av Kenilworth IL 60043 Office: 310 S Michigan Av Chicago IL 60604

CLARKSON, JESSE DUNSMORE, ret. historian; b. Bklyn., Aug. 6, 1897; s. William Kemble and Mary Augusta (Brown) C.; A.B., Williams Coll., 1918; A.M. Columbia, 1920, Ph.D., 1925; m. Mary Griffiths, Nov. 25, 1922; children—Myfanwy G., William K. Mem. faculty Coll. City N.Y., 1922-30; faculty Bklyn. Coll., 1930-67, prof. history, 1945-67, emeritus, 1967—, chmn. dept. history, 1937-50, sec. faculty council, 1938-50; sometime vis. prof. history Russian Inst. Columbia U., 1952-63; vis. prof. U. Cal. at Berkeley, 1962, Columbia, 1963; lectr. O.W.I. tng. program, 1944-45, staff officers European studies course, 1945-46. Mem. Am. Assn. U. Profs., Am. Hist. Assn. (exec. com. Slavic conf.), Am. Acad. Polit. Sci., Am. Acad. Polit. and Social Sci., Econ. History Assn., Soc. Am. Historians, Phi Beta Kappa. Club: Union League (Bklyn.). Author: Labour and Nationalism in Ireland, 1925; A History of Russia, 1961. Bd. editors Jour. Modern History. Contbr. articles to profl. jours. Translator and editor various works. Home: 32 Awixa Av Bay Shore NY 11706

CLARKSON, JOHN DONALD, educator, artist; b. Pitts., Jan. 25, 1916; s. James H. and Mary Agnes (Hollihan) C.; B.F.A. in Painting and Design, Carnegie Inst. Tech., 1939; M.A. in Art, U. Pitts., 1950; m. Mary Lou Campbell, Apr. 26, 1943. Asst. mgr. display Kaufmann's Dept. Store, 1939-46; instr. Art Inst. Pitts., 1946-48; faculty W.Va. U., Morgantown, 1948—, prof. art, 1961—, chmn. dept., 1961-67, dir. art acquistions, curator Creative Arts Center; one man shows include Pitts. Playhouse, 1950, Two Arts and Crafts Center, Pitts., 1946-62, W.Va. U., 1951-61, Madison Gallery, N.Y.C., 1961; group exhbns. include Asso. Artists Pitts., 1943-63, Ind. State Tchrs. Coll. (1st Purchase prize), 1945, Butler Art Inst., 1948-51, Met. Print and Graphic Nat., 1950, Allied Artists W.Va. (twice prize winner), 1957-60, Morgantown Art Assn. (Best in Show award), 1960-61, Latrobe Art Exhibit (Purchase prize), 1946-52, Huntington Exhibits, 1961-63. Recipient Clarksburg prize, 1960-62; Critics Choice Playhouse Exhibit, 1958; Jurors Choice prize, Huntington, 1961; Peaks of Progress award, 1959; Carnegie Summer Invitational award, 1946. W.Va. Found. fellow in humanities, Europe, 1960. Mem. Asso. Artists Pitts., Allied Artists W. Va., Morgantown, Eastern, Coll. art assn. Home: 643 Lashley St Morgantown WV 26505

CLARKSON, MARK H., educator; b. Lafayette County, Mo., Sept. 27, 1917; s. Julius A. and Frances (Anderson) C.; B.S. in Aero. Engring., U. Minn., 1939; M.S., U. Tex., 1948, Ph.D., 1953; m. Florence Johnston, Mar. 14, 1941; children—David, Michael, Linda. With Douglas Aircraft Co., 1939-41, Consol. Vultee Co., 1942-45; research engr., research mathematician Def. Research Lab., U. Tex., 1945-53; supr. theoretical aerodynamics Chance Vought Aircraft Corp., 1953-59, supr. aerophysics, 1959-61; prof. aerospace engring., chmn. dept. U. Fla., 1961-; mem. part-time grad. faculty So. Meth. U., 1954-59; cons. to industry, 1961—. Asso. fellow Am. Inst. Aero. and Astronautics; mem. Am. Soc. Engring. Edn. (chmn. aerospace div. 1968), Sigma Xi. Contbr. profl. jours. Home: 2400 NW 18th Pl Gainesville FL 32601

CLARKSON, MAX BOYDELL ELLIOTT, printing co. exec.; b. Lenzie, Scotland, Oct. 14, 1922; s. George Elliott and Helene (Mannaberg) C.; B.A., U. Toronto, 1945, M.A., 1946; m. Madeleine Earls, June 5, 1948; children—Max Adam, Helene Edith. Vice pres. Tech. Charts, Inc., Buffalo, 1947-50; pres. Clarkson Press Inc., Buffalo, 1950-57, Graphic Controls Corp., Buffalo, 1957—; dir. Niagara Frontier Bank of N.Y., Graphic Arts Mut. Ins. Co. Pres. Printing Industries Am., 1962-63. Chmn., Mayor Buffalo Citizens Adv. Com. on Community Improvement, 1964—; pres. Allentown (N.Y.) Assn., 1963—. Bd. dirs. Buffalo Fine Arts Acad., Value Line Devel. Capital Fund. Served to lt. Royal Canadian Navy, 1942-45. Mem. Buffalo C. of C. (bd. dirs.). Clubs: Buffalo; Metropolitan (N.Y.C.); Bath (London, Eng.). Episcopalian. Home: 180 Summer St Buffalo NY 14222 Office: 189 Van Rensselaer St Buffalo NY 14210

CLARKSON, MERTON ROBERT, assn. exec.; b. Ferndale, Wash., July 25, 1908; s. Joseph and Mary Belle (Farnsworth) C.; B.S., State Coll. Wash., 1930, D.V.M., 1930; LL.B., Georgetown U., 1942; m. Eva Marie Petterson, Oct. 6, 1930; children—Kathleen Mary, Laura Ellen, Jill Marie. With Fed. Meat Inspection, U.S. Dept. Agrl. Bur. of Animal Industry, 1930-47, asst. chief, 1945-47, chief inspection and quarantine, 1947-51; mem. Mexican- U.S. Commn. for Prevention of Foot-and-Mouth Disease, 1949—; asst. to administr. Agrl. Research Adminstrn., charge def. activities, 1951, dep. adminstr. Agrl. Research Service, 1952-59, asso. adminstr. 1959- 64; dir. Bur. Vet. Medicine, FDA, Washington, 1966; exec. v.p. Am. Vet. Med. Assn., Chgo., 1966—; trustee A.M.V.A. Group Ins. Trust, 1967—, Profl. Liability Ins. Trust, 1966—, dir. Profl. Exam. Service, 1970—, also sec. Found. Cons., health resources office NSRB, 1950-51; mem. com. on animal health Nat. Acad. Scis.-NRC, chmn., 1963-69; mem. agrl. board Nat. Acad. Scis.-NRC, vice chmn., 1965-70. Recipient distinguished service award Dept. of Agr., 1956, 12th Internat. Vet. Congress prize, 1962. Fellow A.A.A.S.; mem. Am. (pres. 1964), Ill., Chgo. vet. med. assns., U.S. Animal Health Assn., Am. Bar Assn., Ill. Assn. Professions, Conf. Research Workers Animal Diseases, Am. Soc. Animal Sci., Nat. Assn. Fed. Veterinarians, Am. Animal Hosp. Assn. Alpha Gamma Rho, Alpha Psi, Phi Zeta, Presbyn. (elder). Club: University of Chicago. Home: 400 E Randolph St Chicago IL 60601 Office: 600 S Michigan Av Chicago IL 60605

CLARKSON, PHILIP BAYARD, educator; b. Garden City, N.Y., July 29, 1924; s. William Bayard and Enid (Clute) C.; grad. Lawrenceville Sch., 1943; student U.S. Mil. Acad., 1943; B.A., Wesleyan U., 1946; M.A., Columbia, 1950; postgrad. Alliance Francaise, 1954-55, Central Sch. Speech Tng. and Dramatic Arts, London, Eng., 1955; Ph.D., Stanford, 1963, grad. Radio-TV Inst., 1960; m. Lola June Jacobs, Dec. 28, 1959. Adminstrv. asst., teaching asst. English, Wesleyan U., Middletown, Conn., 1946-47; instr. English, Worcester Poly. Inst., 1947-49; asst. prof. English, dir. drama Norwich U., Northfield, Vt., 1950-54; asso. prof. speech and drama, head dept. Morningside Coll., Sioux City, Ia., 1956-59; prof. speech and drama, chmn. dept. Ripon (Wis.) Coll., 1963—, acting dean, v.p. coll., 1968-69. Bus. rep. Westchester Lighting Co., 1947; research cons. Corcoran Gallery Art, 1956; asst. dir. Mt. Airy (N.C.) Title III Fine Arts Project, summer 1968. Trustee Ripon Pub. Library, 1966-69, pres., 1969. Recipient Uhrig Found. award for excellence in teaching Ripon Coll., 1967, Severy award for excellence in teaching, 1970. Mem. Speech Communication Assn., Am. Assn. U. Profs. (pres. Ripon chpt. 1967-68), Alpha Delta Phi (pres. Wesleyan chpt. 1944-45), Alpha Psi Omega, Pi Kappa Delta. Conglist. Home: 23 Lawndale Av Ripon WI 54971

CLARSON, JOHN JULIUS, plywood co. exec.; b. N.Y.C., Feb. 27, 1921; s. John F. and Martha (Nichols) C.; B.B.A., Pace Coll., 1953; m. Ruth Ann Beck, Apr. 28, 1945; children—Dorothy, John, Donna, Patrick. With U.S. Plywood Corp., N.Y.C., 1949—, treas., 1961—. Served with AUS, 1942-45. Mem. Tax Execs. Inst. Home: 77 Nottingham Dr Springdale CT 06907 Office: 777 3d Av New York City NY 10017

CLARY, HOWARD LEONARD, corp. ofcl.; b. Wilkinsburg, Pa., Jan. 14, 1910; s. Ernest G. and Edna (Dryden) C.; student Carnegie Inst. Tech., 1928-32; m. Lois Strang, Mar. 24, 1940; children—Sandra Lynne, Mary Lois. Sales rep. Ludwig Hommel & Co., elec. appliance wholesalers, Pitts., 1927-42; dept. head WPB, Washington, 1942-45; sales promotion mgr. Norge div. Borg-Warner Corp., Detroit, Chgo., 1945-46, gen. sales mgr., 1946-50, v.p. in charge sales, 1950-53; v.p. Affiliated Gas Equipment, Inc., Cleve., 1953— (merger with Carrier Corp. 1955); v.p. Carrier Corp., Syracuse, 1955-56; v.p., gen. sales mgr. Bryant Mfg. Co. div. Carrier Corp., Indpls., 1956-59; pres., chmn. McElwain Clary, Inc., Jacksonville, Fla., 1961—; dir. Bryant Indsl. Products Corp., Cleve. Mem. C. of C. Mason (Shriner). Club: Deerwood. Home: 3915 Sierra Madre Dr Jacksonville FL 32217 Office: 14th and Market Sts Jacksonville FL 32206

CLARY, THOMAS J., judge; b. Seneca Falls, N.Y., Aug. 31, 1899; A.B., Cornell U., 1920; LL.B., Georgetown U., 1924. Admitted to Pa. bar, 1924, practiced in Phila.; asso. with Walter B. Gibbons; chief judge Eastern Dist. of Pa. Member Am., Pa. and Phila. bar assns., Delta Theta Phi. Address: care Office of the Clerk U S District Court Philadelphia PA

CLARY, WILLIAM WEBB, lawyer; b. Northfield, Minn., Oct. 15, 1888; s. Smith B. and Anna (Lathrop) C.; B.A., Pomona Coll., 1911, M.A., 1917, LL.D., 1956; pvt. law studies; D.H.L., Claremont Grad. Sch., 1964; m. Elizabeth A. Foss, June 20, 1914; children—William Webb, Everett Burton, Mary Virginia (Mrs. Garry W. Meeker). Admitted to Cal. bar, 1912; dep. pub. defender Los Angeles County, 1914-18, dep. county counsel, 1918-20; spl. counsel Los Angeles County Flood Control Dist., 1920-21; asst. atty. Cal. R.R. Commn., 1921-23; with O'Melveny & Myers, Los Angeles, 1923—, partner, 1925-56, of counsel, 1956—; v.p., dir. Clary Corp. Spl. asst. atty. gen. State of Cal., 1945-47; mem. Cal. Code Commn., 1944-55. Mem. bd. fellows Claremont U. Center, 1928—, chmn., 1953-63, hon. mem., 1963—, acting pres., 1963. Trustee Pomona Coll., 1952-62, hon. trustee, 1962—; trustee Harvey Mudd Coll., 1955-64, hon. trustee, 1964—; trustee Pitzer Coll., 1963-65, hon. trustee, 1965—; bd. dirs. Friends of Huntington Library, 1939—, pres., 1940-50. Mem. Am., Cal., Los Angeles county bar assns. Clubs: Lincoln (dir., pres. 1956-58), California, Sunset, Zamorano (Los Angeles, Cal.); Twilight (Pasadena, Cal.). Author: B. Franklin, Printer and Publisher, 1935; Japan: The Warnings and Prophecies of Lafcadio Hearn, 1943; How Abe Lincoln Went to Oxford, 1948. Contbr. articles to mags. Established at Honnold Library, Claremont Coll., collection of 4000 books on Oxford U. and its colls. Home: 555 Orange Grove Circle Pasadena CA 91105 Office: care O'Melveny & Meyers 611 W 6th St Los Angeles CA 90017

CLAS, ANGELO ROBERT, architect; b. Milw., Feb. 13, 1887; s. Alfred Charles and Louise (Wick) C.; grad. E. Div. High Sch., Milw., 1905; B.S. in Architecture, Harvard, 1909; m. Norma Huette, Oct. 12, 1910 (dec. 1963); 1 dau., Mary Louise (Mrs. Delmar W. Holloman); m. 2d, Alice Beier Nicholson, 1965. Began as architect in Milw., 1908; engaged in mfg. business, Sheboygan, Wis., also Toledo, 1909-23; manufactured truck and tractor motors and shells during World War; traveled abroad, 1924; partner D.H. Burnham & Co., architects, Chgo., 1924-26, W.W. Ahlschlager, 1927-29, Holabird & Root, 1929-34; apptd. mem. housing div. Fed. Emergency Adminstrn. of Pub. Works, Washington, 1934, dir. of housing, 1935-36; asst. adminstr. pub. works, 1936-37; now cons. Clas, Riggs, Owens & Ramos. Recent work: Fed. Loan Agy., Internat. Bank for Reconstrn. and Devel., YMCA Addition, Washington Statler Hotel, Wyatt Bldg. (winner 1952 Archtl. award of Merit); large scale housing devels. in Md., Va., Pa. and Tenn.; office bldg. Govt. of India, also Nat. Rifle Assn., Philip Murray, IMF bldgs. of Washington (winner 1959 Archtl. award of Merit). Recipient Bronze award for outstanding contbns. to architecture of Nat. Capitol, Bldg. Stone Inst.; bronze medal Am. Heart Assn., 1965. Fellow A.I.A.; mem. Washington Bldg. Congress, Honolulu Acad. Arts, Delta Upsilon. Mason. Methodist. Club: Harvard, Outrigger Canoe. Home: 1001 Wilder Av Honolulu, HI 96822.

CLASEN, EARL A., food co. exec.; b. South Milwaukee, Wis., Jan. 10, 1918; s. Elmer F. and Emelia (Sjogren) C.; B.A., Gustavus Adolphus Coll., 1939; grad. Exec. Devel. Program Stanford, 1955; m. Doris Jean Day, June 12, 1941; children—Judy, Mark, Nancy. Tchr., Atwater (Minn.) High Sch., 1939-40; clk. W.H. Barber Oil Co., Mpls., 1940-44; v.p. Pillsbury Co., Mpls., 1944—; dir. Valspar Corp. Bd. dirs. Gustavus Adolphus Coll. Mem. Assn. Nat. Advertisers (vice chmn. bd. dirs.). Home: 5809 Hidden Lane Minneapolis MN 55436

CLASS, CALVIN MILLER, educator, physicist; b. Baltimore County, Md., Jan. 27, 1924; s. Edwin H. and Anna (Miller) C.; A.B., Johns Hopkins, 1943, Ph.D., 1951; m. Bernice Lutz, Dec. 27, 1948; 1 dau., Martha Ann. Physicist, NACA, 1944- 46; research asst. nuclear physics Johns Hopkins, 1951-52; faculty Rice U., Houston, 1952—, prof. physics, 1963—, master Mary Gibbs Jones Coll., 1957-65; sr. research asso. Cal. Inst. Tech., 1963. Guggenheim fellow, 1955-56. Fellow Am. Phys. Soc.; mem. Italian Phys. Soc., Houston Philos. Soc., Sigma Xi (pres. Houston 1964-65), Sigma Phi Epsilon (hon.). Democrat. Unitarian. Contbr. research papers to profl. lit. Home: 5669 Bordley Dr Houston TX 77027

CLASS, MAURICE MORRISSEY, civil and mil. engr.; b. Morristown, N.J., Nov. 9, 1898; s. John B. and Ellen (Morrissey) C.; grad. U.S. Army Engr. Schs., Chaumont, France, 1918- 19, Geiger Field, Washington, 1943; m. Evelyn A. Topping Oct. 7, 1924; children—Joan E. (Mrs. Orrin P. Daniels), Shellmerdene M. (Mrs. Joseph P. Leo), Maurice Morrissey II. Chief of party Malcomb White, civil engr., Morristown, 1916-17, Clyde Potts, cons. engr., N.Y.C., 1920-21; resident engr. Young & Wintermute, civil and mining engrs., Wilkes-Barre, Pa., 1922, Clyde Potts, 1922-24, City of Newark, 1925-26, Consol. Edison Co., N.Y.C., 1927; pres., chief engr. Navesink Constrn. & Engring. Corp., Red Bank, N.J., Newark, 1927-33; area engr. Fed. Works Agy., N.J., 1933-42; dir. prodn. and utilities SCAP, Tokyo, Japan, 1947-52; cons. engr. Maurice M. Class, Tokyo, Washington, FSO, 1952-56; with internat. staff NATO, Paris, France, 1956-58; engr. adviser to program evaluation officer U.S. Operations Mission to Laos, 1958-60. Served with U.S. Army, 1917-19; AEF in France; from capt. to col. C.E., AUS, 1942-47, 50-53; ETO, PTO. Decorated Bronze Star medal, Air medal, Purple Heart. Named chevalier du Tastavin. Registered profl. civil engr., N.J. Mem. Am. Soc. C.E., Nat. Soc. Profl. Engrs., Soc. Am. Mil. Engrs., Japan-Am. Soc., S.A.R. Clubs: Army and Navy (Washington); American, Kogena Golf (Tokyo, Japan). Address: 2 Hamilton Rd Morristown NJ 07960

CLASSEN, JOHN NEWELL, educator, surgeon; b. Balt., Nov. 11; s. Henry W. and Mary Ward (Rayner) C.; A.B., Princeton, 1938; M.D., Johns Hopkins, 1942; m. Margaret Taylor Speer, June 20, 1958; children—Henry Ward, John Barthelow, Taylor Speer. Intern Union Meml. Hosp., 1942-43, surg. resident, 1946-49; surg. fellow Lahey Clinic, 1949-50; mem. staff Union Meml. Hosp., Balt., now chief surgery, 1964—; asst. prof. Johns Hopkins Sch. Medicine, 1963—. Served with M.C., USNR, 1942-46. Decorated Purple Heart, Bronze Star. Diplomate Am. Bd. Surgery. Mem. Eastern, So. surg. assns. Home: Montrose Av Baltimore MD 21212 Office: 5820 York Rd Baltimore MD 21212

CLATWORTHY, HARRY WILLIAM, Jr., physician, educator; b. Denver, Oct. 2, 1917; s. Harry William and Freda Althea (Miller) C.; B.S., Stanford, 1939; M.D., Harvard, 1943; M.Sc., U. Minn., 1950; m. Rovena Louise Conn, Aug. 31, 1940 (div.); children—Harry William III, Diana Ro, John Conn, Susan Honor; m. 2d, Betty Jones (dec. 1960); m. 3d, Nancy Moore Krueger, Dec. 1961. Student asst. children's pathology Boston Children's Hosp., 1942, surg. intern, 1943-44, asst. resident surgery, 1946-47, chief surg. resident, 1947-48; asst. surgery Harvard Med. Sch., 1946-48; sr. surg. fellow Univ. Hosp. U. Minn. Med. Sch., 1948-50; asst. prof. pediatric surgery Ohio State U. Coll. Medicine, 1950-52, asso. prof., dir. div. pediatric surgery, 1952- 60; prof. pediatric surgery, 1960—; attending surgeon U. Hosp., 1950-52; attending surgeon Children's Hosp., Columbus, 1950-52, chief surg. service, 1953—; Felton Bequest vis. prof. Royal Children's Hosp., Melbourne, Australia, 1964. Chmn. 27th Ross Pediatric Conf. Bd. dirs. Ohio Crippled Children. Served as capt. M.C., AUS, 1944-46, Diplomate Am. Bd. Surgery. Fellow A.C.S., Am. Acad. Pediatrics; mem. Am., Ohio med. assns., Ohio, Columbus, Central, Am. surg. assns., Brit. Assn. Pediatric Surgeons, Soc. U. Surgeons, Am. Assn. Thoracic Surgery, Am. Pediatric Surg. Assn. (pres. elect 1971-72), Sigma Xi, Phi Gamma Delta. Episcopalian. Contbr. prof. jours., chpts. books. Asso. editor Am. Jour. Surgery. Home: Fireside Farm Rural Rt 3 Delaware OH 43015 Office: Childrens Hosp Columbus OH 43205

CLATWORTHY, WILLIAM ROBERT, art dir.; b. Redlands, Cal., Dec. 31, 1911; s. William E. and Lois Edith Edith (Field) C.; student Choinard Art Inst., Los Angeles; m. Ruth Joy Summers, Sept. 28, 1940; children—Pamela, Diane. Designer motion pictures setting for Paramount Pictures, David O. Selznick, also Universal Pictures, 1933-44; art dir. Universal Pictures, Paramount Pictures, also Walt Disney Prodns., 1944-63; prodn. designer Stanley Kramer Prodns., 1964—. Mem. Acad. Motion Picture Arts and Scis. (Oscar award for black and white art direction Ship of Fools 1965), Soc. Motion Picture Art Dirs. (trustee 1963—).

CLAUDE, INIS LOTHAIR, Jr., educator, polit. scientist; b. Yellville, Ark., Sept. 3, 1922; s. Inis Lothair and Parilla Jane (Pledger) C.; B.A. with high honors, Hendrix Coll., 1942; M.A., Harvard, 1947, Ph.D. (Chase prize), 1949; m. Marie Stapleton, Aug. 1, 1943; children—Susan, Robert Burr, Cathy. Instr., then asst. prof. govt. Harvard, 1949-56; asso. prof. polit sci. U. Del., 1956-57; asso. prof. polit. sci. U. Mich., 1957-60, prof., 1960- 68; Edward R. Stettinius Jr. prof. govt. and fgn. affairs U. Va., Charlottesville, 1968—, mem. Center Advanced Study, 1968—. Vis. research scholar Carnegie Endowment Internat. Peace, 1960-61; faculty chmn. course internat. relations Inst. Social Studies, The Hague, 1964- 65. Mem. exec. com. Center Research Conflict Resolution, 1959-63; chmn. com. internat. orgn. Social Sci. Research Council, 1962-69; mem. research group UN financial problems Brookings Instn., 1962-63, adv. com. UN policy study program, 1963—, occasional lectr. Nat., Army, Navy war colls., UN Fgn. Service Tng. Seminar; cons. Dept. State, 1962—, mem. adv. com. fgn. relations publs., 1968—. Served with AUS, 1942-46. Faculty fellow Fund Advancement Edn., 1951-52; Rockefeller research grantee, 1958-59; Horace H. Rackham Grad. Sch. research grantee, 1963; Guggenheim fellow, 1964-65; Fulbright research grantee, 1964-65. Recipient Distinguished Alumnus award Hendrix Coll., 1968. Mem. Am. (Woodrow Wilson Found. award 1963), Internat. (rapporteur gen. internat. orgn. 1964) polit. sci. assns., Am. Soc. Internat. Law, Commn. Study Orgn. Peace (exec. com. 1957-66), Am. Assn. U. Profs., Am. Civil Liberties Union. Author: National Minorities: An International Problem, 1955; Swords Into Plowshares: The Problems and Progress of International Organization, 4th edit., 1971; Power and International Relations, 1962; The Changing United Nations, 1967. Bd. editors Internat. Orgn., 1960—; chmn. bd. editors Jour. Conflict Resolution, 1961-63; cons. editor internat. affairs Random House, Inc., 1962—. Home: 103 Melissa Pl Charlottesville VA 22901

CLAUDEL, HENRI, French govt. ofcl.; b. Frankfort/on-Main, Germany, Aug. 24, 1912; s. Paul and Reine Ste. Marie (Perrin) C.; m. Christine Diplarakos, Apr. 29, 1936; children—Marie S. (Mrs. Christopher James), Paul, Francois, Marie H. Mem. Free French Delegation, 1941-43; with French embassy, Washington, 1943-48, Ministry Fgn. Affairs, Paris, France, 1948-52; 1st counsellor in Brussels, 1952-61; consul gen., Naples, Italy, 1961-64; head NATO press service, 1965-66; consul gen., Tangier, 1966-69; consul gen., N.Y.C., 1969—. Decorated chevalier Legion of Honor, officer French Nat. Order Merit. Address: 934 5th Av New York City NY 10021

CLAUDON, CHESTER JOSEPH, lawyer; b. Fairbury, Ill., June 17, 1922; s. Chester Joseph and Leona (James) C.; B.A., Coll. of William and Mary, 1943; LL.B., U. Va., 1948; m. Martha Ann Soldwedel, June 20, 1952; children—Chester Joseph III, Ann Rueling, Thomas James, Timothy James. Admitted to Ill. bar, 1948, since practiced in Canton; city atty., Canton, 1948; partner Claudon & Taylor, 1960-62; partner Claudon, Elson & Lloyd, 1962—. Chmn. bd. Community Bank & Trust Co.; dir. Illini Developers, Inc., Mid Am. Credit, Inc., Scripps McCartney Co., Mut. Savs. & Loan Assn., Kage, Ltd. Mem. Gov. Ill. Adv. Council, 1969. Pres. Community Concert Assn., Canton Friendship Festival, Salvation Army, Community Chest, Canton YMCA; pres., bd. dirs. Spoon River Coll. Found. Served to lt. (j.g.) USNR, 1943-46. Mem. Am. Legion, 40 and 8. Mason (32, Shriner), Elk, Lion. Club: Canton Country (past pres.). Home: 62 Redwood Circle Canton IL 61520 Office: 121 W Elm St Canton IL 61520

CLAUNCH, JOHN M., pres. George Peabody Coll. Address: care George Peabody Coll Nashville TN 37203*

CLAUS, CARL, mfg. exec.; b. Berlin, Germany, Mar. 16, 1909; s. Carl and Elsie (Regling) C.; brought to U.S., 1910; B.S., Lehigh U., 1931; m. Ruby Miller, Aug. 29, 1935; 1 son, Carl Miller. With Babcock & Wilcox Co., 1931—, asst. supt. Bayonne (N.J.) works, 1937, supt. Augusta (Ga.) works, 1938-53, exec. asst., 1953-55, dir. staff, 1955-58, v.p., 1958-; dir. Lincoln Securities Corp., Bound Brook, N.J. Mem. Republican Com., Town of Newcastle, Chappaqua, N.Y., 1957—. Mem. C. of C., Newcomen Soc. N. Am., Am. Mgmt. Assn., Omicron Delta Kappa, Delta Upsilon, Tau Beta Pi, Pi Delta Epsilon. Clubs: Cloud, Engineers (N.Y.C.); Rotary; Whippoorwill (Armonk, N.Y.). Home: Paulding Dr Chappaqua NY 10514 Office: 161 E 42d St New York City NY 10017

CLAUSEN, ALDEN WINSHIP, banker; b. Hamilton, Ill., Feb. 17, 1923; s. Morton and Elsie (Kroll) C.; B.A., Carthage Coll., 1944, LL.D., 1970; LL.B., U. Minn., 1949; m. Mary Margaret Crassweller, Feb. 11, 1950; children—Eric David, Mark Winship. Admitted to Minn. bar, 1949, Cal. bar, 1950; with Bank of Am., N.T. & S.A., 1949-, pres., chief exec. officer, 1970—, vice chmn., 1969-70, chmn. gen. finance com., 1969-70. Bd. dirs. Ind. Colls. No. Cal., 1968; vis. com. Harvard Bus. Sch.; trustee Carthage Coll. Served to 1st lt. USAAF, 1943-46. Mem. Am. mgmt. Assn., Presidents Assn., State Bar Cal., Res. City Bankers Assn., Transp. Assn. Am. (bd. dirs.), Am. Bankers Assn. Clubs: Bankers, Burlingane Country, Villa Tavern, Commonwealth, Stock Exchange, World Trade (San Francisco); The Links (N.Y.). Home: 510 Ravenscourt Rd Hillsborough CA 94010 Office: Bank of America Center San Francisco CA 94120

CLAUSEN, BARTON RANDOLPH, med. agy. exec.; b. Syracuse, N.Y., Feb. 11, 1924; s. Bernard Chancellor and Elizabeth (Darnell) C.; student Colgate U., 1943-44, 47-48, Western Res. U., 1953-55; m. Lodoska Kent, Jan. 4, 1945; children—Peter Bernard, Kristen Psyche, Karen Elizabeth, Lauren, Kurt Chancellor. Propr. bldg. supply and constrn. co., Weston, Vt., 1948-53; editorial dir. Sta. KYW- TV and radio, Cleve., 1956-64; pres. Community Project Consultants, Cleve., 1964-65; asst. to sec. U.S. Dept. Interior, Washington, 1965-66; dir. dept. urban renewal and housing City of Cleve., 1966-68; dir. dept. information and edn. Am. Civil Liberties Union; now exec. dir. Abnaki Health Council, Claremont, N.H. Mem. Weston Bd. Edn., 1950-53, chmn., 1953. Bd. dirs. Pace Assn., Cleve., 1962-66, Cleve. Devel. Found., Cleve. Growth Corp.; trustee Cleve. Legal Aid Soc. Cleve. Civil Liberties Union, Sigma Delta Chi. Democrat. Clubs: Cleveland Press, City (pres. 1963-64) (Cleve.). Home: RFD 1 Chester Depot VT 05144 Office: 109 Pleasant St Claremont NH 03743

CLAUSEN, DONALD NEATH, lawyer; b. Racine, Wis., Aug. 30, 1898; s. Christian F. W. and Josephine (Burkert) C.; student U. Ill., 1917-18; U. Chicago, 1918-20; LL.B., Chgo. Kent. Coll. Law, 1923; m. Henrietta Underwood, Sept. 3, 1938; children—Catherine (dec.), Karen Neath, Henrietta Carol, Barbara Jean. Admitted to Ill. bar, 1925, since engaged in gen. civil practice specializing in trial of cases; sr. partner firm Clausen, Hirsh & Miller 1936-58, Clausen, Hirsh, Miller & Gorman, 1958—. Vice pres., dir. Tablet & Ticket Co. Fellow Internat. Acad. Trial Lawyers, Am. Coll. Trial Lawyers; mem. Internat. Assn. In Counsel, Am., Ill., Chgo. bar assns., Bar Assn. U.S. Cts. of Appeals of 7th Circuit, Phi Delta Phi, Chi Psi. Episcopalian. Clubs: Executives, Skokie Country, Chicago Athletic, Union League, Internat., Wine and Food Soc. (Chgo.). Home: 650 Blackthorn Rd Winnetka IL 60093 Office: 135 LaSalle St Chicago IL 60603

CLAUSEN, DON HOLST, congressman; b. Ferndale, Cal., Apr. 27, 1923; s. Henry August and Marine Sorine (Holst) C.; student San Jose State Coll., 1940, Cal. Poly. Inst., 1943, Weber Coll., 1943, St. Mary's (Cal.) Coll., 1943; m. Ollie Piper, Jan. 16, 1949; children—Beverly, Dawn Marie. Engaged in ins. bus. as Clausen Assos., Crescent City, Cal., 1954- -; pres. Air Ambulance Service, Crescent City, 1946—, Clausen Flying Service, Crescent City, 1946—; mem. 88th-92d congresses First Dist. Cal. Bd. suprs. Del Norte County, Cal., 1955-63; pres. suprs. unit Redwood Empire Assn., 1962. Served as carrier-pilot USNR, World War II; PTO. Mem. Del Norte County C. of C., Del Norte County Suprs. Assn. Republican. Home: Crescent City CA 95531 Office: House Office Bldg Washington DC 20525

CLAUSEN, JOHN ADAM, sociologist; b. N.Y.C., Dec. 20, 1914; s. Adam Peter and Mary (Blum) C.; A.B., Cornell U., 1936, M.A., 1939; Ph.D., U. Chgo., 1949; m. Suzanne Ravage, June 2, 1939; children—Christopher John, Peter Anthony, Bruce Martin, Michael Allen. Research asso. Va. Planning Bd., 1941-42; study dir. troop attitude research War Dept., 1942-46; asst. prof. sociology Cornell U., 1946-48, social sci. research cons. Nat. Inst. Mental Health, Bethesda, Md., 1948-51, chief lab. sociol. environmental studies, 1951-60, research career award com., 1960-64, social sci. research rev. com., 1967—. Mem. com. on internat. centers NIH, 1961-63; prof. sociology, dir. Inst. Human Devel., U. Cal. at Berkeley, 1960-65, research sociologist, prof. sociology, 1965—; vis. prof. sociology U. N.C., 1968-69. Mem. com. social sci., psychiatry Social Sci. Research Council, 1952-57, chmn. com. social structure and socialization, 1960-68, also dir.; mem. com. disaster studies NRC, 1954-57. Research adv. com. Cal. Dept. Mental Hygiene, 1964-66; research com. Cal. Dept. Corrections, 1962-65, mem. spl. med. adv. group VA, 1965-70, also mem. council on extended care, 1967—; mem. Adv. Com. on Abuse of Depressant and Stimulant Drugs, FDA, 1965-69; mem. Scottish Rite Joint Com. Schizophrenia Research, 1965—; social sci. research rev. com. Nat. Inst. Mental Health, 1967-71; mem. council Assn. Aid Crippled Children. Center Advanced Study Behavioral Scis. fellow, 1957-58. Fellow Am. Sociol. Assn. (exec. com., council 1957-61, chmn. com. on certification in social psychology 1961-64, chmn. sect. social psychology 1960-61, chmn.-elect sect. med. sociology 1970-71), Gerontol. Soc., A.A.A.S.; mem. Am. Psychopath. Assn. (council 1969), Soc. Research in Child Devel. (council 1969—), Am. Pub. Health Assn. (com. on pub. health and behavioral scis. 1958-60), Internat. Sociol. Assn. (chmn. research com. on psychiat. sociology 1970—), Sociol. Research Assn. (pres. 1964). Unitarian. Author: Sociology in the Field of Mental Health, 1956; (with others) Measurement and Prediction, 1950; Explorations in Social Psychiatry, 1957; Socialization and Society, 1968. Editor: (with R. Strauss) Medicine and Society, 1963; asso. editor Sociometry, 1956-59, editor, 1959-61; editorial bd.: Am. Jour. Orthopsychiatry, 1956-59, Psychosomatic Medicine 1962—, Jour. Psychiat. Research, 1963—; regional editor Social Sci. and Medicine, 1966-68. Contbr. articles to profl. jours. Home: 1963 Yosemite Rd Berkeley CA 94707 Office: Inst Human Devel U Cal Berkeley CA 94720

CLAUSEN, WENDELL VERNON, educator; b. Coquille, Ore., Apr. 2, 1923; s. George R. and Gertrude (Johnson) C.; A.B., U. Wash., 1945; Ph.D., U. Chgo., 1948; A.M. (hon.) Harvard, 1959; m. Corinna Slice, Aug. 20, 1947; children—John, Raymond, Thomas; m. 2d, Margaret W. Woodman, June 19, 1970. Mem. faculty Amherst Coll., 1948-59, asso. prof. classics, 1955- 59; prof. Greek and Latin, Harvard, 1959—. Fellow Am. Acad. in Rome, 1952-53, Am. Council Learned Sos., 1962-63; fellow commoner Peterhouse, Cambridge. Fellow Am. Acad. Arts and Sciences; mem. Am. Philol. Assn., Phi Beta Kappa. Editor: Persius, 1956; Persius and Juvenal, 1959. Contbr. articles in classical philology. Home: 8 Kenway St Cambridge MA Office: Harvard U Cambridge MA 02138

CLAUSER, FRANCIS H., educator; b. Kansas City, Mo., May 25, 1913; s. Claude H. and Celeste (Horton) C.; B.S., Cal. Inst. Tech., 1934, M.S., 1935, Ph.D., 1937; m. Catharine McMillan, July 30, 1937; children—Caroline, John. Research aerodynamicist Douglas Aircraft Co., Santa Monica, Cal., 1937-46; chmn. dept. aeros. Johns Hopkins, 1946- 60, prof. mechanics, 1960-64; asst. vice chancellor U. Cal. at Santa Cruz, 1965-66, vice chancellor sci. and engring. 1966-68, prof. applied sci., 1968-69; Clark B. Millikan prof. aeros., chmn. div. engring. and applied sci. Cal. Inst. Tech., Pasadena, 1969—. Fellow Am. Inst. Aeros. and Astronautics, Am. Phys. Soc., Am. Acad. Arts and Scis.; mem. Nat. Acad. Engring., Sigma Xi, Tau Beta Pi. Contbr. articles to tech. publs. Office: Cal Inst Tech Pasadena CA 91109

CLAUSER, MILTON U., ednl. adminstr.; b. Kansas City, Mo., May 25, 1913; s. Claude H. and Celeste U. (Horton) C.; B.S., Cal. Inst. Tech., 1934, M.S., 1935, Ph.D., 1937; D.Engring., Purdue U., 1967; m. H. Virginia Randall, July 30, 1937; children—Milton John, Marilyn Ann. Engr. Douglas Aircraft Co., Cal., 1937-50; prof. head Purdue U. Sch. Aeros., 1950-54; dir. aerodynamics and structures guided missile research div. Ramo Wooldridge Corp., 1954-55, v.p., dir. phys. research lab. Space Tech. Labs., 1955-60; pres., chmn. bd. Clauser Tech. Corp., Torrance, Cal., 1960-62, cons., 1962-65; dir. research and engring. support div. Inst. Def. Analysis, Arlington, Va., 1965- 66; dir. internat. devel. Communication Satellite Corp., Washington, 1966; dir. Lincoln Lab., Mass. Inst. Tech., 1967-70; provost, acad. dean Navy Postgrad. Sch., Monterey, Cal., 1970—. Cons. aircraft nuclear propulsion Gen. Electric Co.; cons. Nat. Engring. Sci. Co., Draper, Gaither & Anderson, Emerson Electric Mfg. Co., St. Louis, Communications Satellite Corp., Hughes Research Lab., Litton Systems in Cal.; tech. adv. panel on aeros. asst. sec. def.; sci. adv. bd. USAF, 1956-59; mem. research com. elec. energy systems NASA, 1959-62; cons. ARO, Inc., 1950-54, USN, MIT Operations Evaluation Group, 1961-64; mem. rev. com., reactor engring. div. Argonne Nat. Lab., 1961-64; mem. Mercury ad hoc com. Pres.'s Sci. Adv. Com., 1961, mem. space sci. panel, 1961-63; mem. adv. com. Project Agile, Advanced Research projects Agy., 1967- 69; mem. observers, div. adv. group Air Force Electronics Systems Div., 1967-70; mem. adv. bd. for regional conf. New Eng. Econ. Research Found., 1970; mem. lab adv. bd. for air warfare Naval Research Adv. Com., 1969-70. Fellow Am. Inst. Aeros. and Astronautics (mem. ground testing com., council)); mem. Am. Acad. Arts and Scis., A.A.A.S., Internat. Astronautics Fedn., Tau Beta Pi, Sigma Xi, Sigma Gamma Tau. Mem. editorial bd. Jour. Def. Research, 1968—. Contbr. articles to tech. publs. Home: Quarters M Naval Postgrad Sch Monterey CA 93940

CLAUSING, RICHARD BURNS, lawyer; b. Cushing, Okla., June 8, 1918; s. Walter F. and Bertha (Burns) C.; A.B., Wichita U., 1939; J.D., Washburn U., 1942; m. Nancy Green Hunter, Apr. 15, 1944; children—Carroll (Mrs. Michael Cunningham), Nancy Jane (Mrs. Thomas J. Little), Richard B., Mary Ellen, Kurt Frederick, Jamie Louise. Admitted to Kan. bar; asso. Ratner & Allen, 1946-49; partner McClintock & Clausing, 1950, Yankey, Alkire, McClintock & Clausing, 1952-54; dir. F.H.A., Topeka, Kan., 1954-55; sr. partner Alkire, Clausing, Wichita, 1956—. Dir. Instrument Flight Research Corp., Inc. Mem. nat. legacies com. UN Assn. of U.S.A., 1967-68. Rep. precinct committeeman, 1958-62. Served with USNR, 1942-46, 51-52; capt. Res. Mem. Kan., Sedgwick County (past gov.) bar assns., Naval Res. Assn. (past pres. Wichita), Res. Officers Assn. (pres. Wichita chpt.), Navy League, V.F.W. Presbyn. (ruling elder). Home: 376 Brunswick St Wichita KS 67212 Office: 4th National Bank Bldg Wichita KS 67202

CLAUSON, ANDREW GUSTAF, Jr., banker; b. Staten Is., N.Y., July 1, 1895 s. Andrew Gustaf and Maria (Olson) C.; A.A.S., State U. N.Y., 1947; LL.D., Upsala Coll., 1948, Wagner Coll., 1950; m. Esther Larsen, Sept. 25, 1920; children—Ralph Andrew, Barbara C. Accountant, Richmond Light and R.R. Co., 1913-17; with Haskins & Sells, C.P.A's, 1919-23; comptroller J.H. Schroeder Banking Corp., 1924-27, United Wallpapers, Inc., 1928; founder, partner firm Bayer & Clauson, C.P.A.'s, 1929-64; retired, 1964; chmn. bd. Richmond County Savs. Bank, S.I., 1967—, pres., 1968—; chmn. bd. Sika Chem. Corp.; pres. Obelisk Trading Corp.; sec., treas. Sika Chem. Can., Ltd.; sr. v.p., treas. Sika Panama, S.A.; dir. New Brighton-S.I. Savs. and Loan Assn., Richmond County Savs. Bank. Mem. N.Y.C. Bd. Edn., 1945- 61, pres., 1946-49, 51-53. Chmn. bd. trustees S.I. Hosp.; treas. Wagner Coll.; v.p. Wingate Meml. Found. Served to ensign U.S. Navy, 1917-19. Decorated Legion of Honor (France); knight 1st class Royal Order N. Star (Sweden); recipient Distinguished Citizenship award Wagner Coll., 1948. C.P.A., N.Y. State. Mem. N.Y. State Soc. C.P.A.'s, Am. Inst. C.P.A.'s, Naval Order U.S., Am. Legion, N.Y. Acad. Pub. Edn., S.I. Inst. Arts and Scis., S.I. Hist. Soc., S.I. Tchrs. Assn. (life), Am.-Scandinavian Found., LaGuardia Meml. Found., Richmond County Grand Jurors Assn., John Erickson Soc., S.I. C. of C. (bd. dirs.), Tall Cedars of Lebanon, Beta Alpha Psi, Tau Phi Sigma. Conglist. Mason. Clubs: Lawyers (N.Y.C); Richmond County Country; Manasquan River Golf (Brielle, N.J.). Home: 171 Bertha Pl Staten Island NY 10301 Office: 1214 Castleton Av Staten Island NY 10310

CLAUSON, JAMES WILSON, furniture mfg. co. exec.; b. N.Y.C., Aug. 2, 1913; s. James Earl and Bertha Vivian (Stickney) C.; B.A., Amherst Coll., 1934; postgrad., N.Y. U., 1936-37; m. Mary Penelope Parrish, Oct. 6, 1939; children—James W., Judith P., Andrew S. Pub. accountant Price, Waterhouse & Co., N.Y.C., 1934-41; with United Aircraft Corp., 1941-45, Heyer Industries, Inc., 1945-51; v.p., treas. S. P.R. Sugar Co., 1951-69; treas. Baumritter Corp., N.Y.C., 1969—. Mem. Am. Inst. C.P.A.'s, N.Y. State Soc. C.P.A.'s, Newcomen Soc. N.Am. Mem. Delta Kappa Epsilon. Club: Montclair Golf. Author: Investments and Taxes, 1968. Home: 8 Erwin Park Montclair NJ 07042 Office: 205 Lexington Av New York City NY 10016

CLAUSS, ALFRED, architect; b. Munich, Germany, Aug. 23, 1906; s. Walter and Clara (Osburg) C.; B.S., Munich Archtl. Sch., 1926; m. Jane West, Dec. 22, 1934; children—Peter Otto, Carin Ann, Carl Alex. Came to U.S., 1930, naturalized, 1936. Chief design architect, partner Bellante & Clauss, Phila., 1947-67, Bellante, Clauss, Miller & Nolan, 1968—; chief architect Clauss & Nolan, Trenton, N.J., 1956. Asso. prof. Yale, 1950. Mem. A.I.A. Contbr. numerous articles profl. jours. Home: 314 Copples Lane Wallingford PA 19086 Office: Widener Bldg-Concourse Chestnut St at Broad Philadelphia PA 19107

CLAUSS, ROBERT RIDER, soft drink co. exec.; b. Cin., Apr. 18, 1924; s. William A. and Clara (Wehrmann) C.; student U. Cin., 1942, Miami U., Oxford, O., 1946-47; B.S., Washington and Jefferson Coll., 1949; m. Patricia Gene Davis, Dec. 21, 1946; children—Robert Rider, Kathleen R. (Mrs. Thomas Curtis), Theresa Annette, Allen Davis. Salesman, engr. Am. Steel & Wire Co., Cleve., 1949-52; dist. mgr. P.R. Mallory Co., Indpls., 1952-57; dist. mgr. CBS, N.Y.C., 1957-60; cons. actuary McLauren & Co., Jacksonville, Fla., 1960-64; asst. treas. Asso. Coca-Cola Bottling Co., Inc., Daytona Beach, Fla., 1964-68, sec., 1969—. Served with AUS, 1942-46. Mem. Soc. Corporate Secs. Home: 107 Imperial Heights Dr Ormond Beach FL 32074 Office: 320 Orange Av Daytona Beach FL 32015

CLAVAN, IRWIN, architect; b. Newport News, Va., Feb. 1, 1900; s. Harry E. and Rachel (Holzweig) C.; B.Arch., U. Pa., 1921, M.Arch., 1922; m. Virginia Moschak, Jan. 18, 1952; 1 son, Peter. Projects- mgr. Shreve, Lamb & Harmon, architects, 1926-33, including Empire State Bldg., 1930-31; pvt. practice, 1934—; asso. architect, Parkchester, N.Y.C., 1937-39; architect Stuyvesant Town, Riverton and Peter Cooper Village, N.Y.C. 1946-48; architect devel. and 1st sect. Gateway Center, Pitts., 1950-52; cons. architect Equitable Life Bldg., San Francisco, Met. Life Ins. Co. Recipient medal Société des Architectes Diplomes, Governement Francais, 1922. Registered profl. architect, N.Y. Mem. A.I.A. Club: Sleepy Hollow Country. Home: 420 E 51st St New York City NY 10022 Office: 355 Lexington Av New York City NY 10017

CLAVELL, JAMES, author; b. Eng., Oct. 10, 1924; s. Richard Charles and Eileen (Collis) C.; student Birmingham U., 1946-47; m. April Stride, Feb. 20, 1951; children—Michaela, Holly. Came to U.S., 1953, naturalized, 1963. Screenwriter, dir., producer (films) The Fly, 1956, Watussi, 1957, Five Gates to Hell, 1957, Walk Like A Dragon, 1958, The Great Escape, 1962, 633 Squadron, 1963, The Satan Bug, 1963, To Sir With Love, 1966, Where's Jack, 1968, The Last Valley, 1970; dir. various TV programs. Served to capt. Royal Arty., 1941-46. Recipient award for screenplay The Great Escape, Writers Guild, 1963. Author: (novels) King Rat, 1962; The Children's Story, 1962; Taipan, 1966; (play) Countdown at Armegeddon, 1966; also poetry.

CLAVERIE, LOUIS BARBOT, lawyer; b. New Orleans, Apr. 27 1904; s. Auguste Joseph and Gilberte Leonie (Rey) C.; B.A., Tulane U., 1925, J.D., 1927; m. Viola Aimee Schlegel, Apr. 17, 1937; 1 son, Philip deVilliers. Admitted to La. bar, 1927, since practiced in New Orleans; partner firm Phelps, Dunbar, Marks, Claverie & Sims, and predecessor, 1941—; asso. prof. corp. law Tulane U. Law Sch., 1944-48, spl. lectr. legal ethics, 1949-51, prof. law legal ethics, 1952-69. Mem. exec. com. Mayor's Adv. Com. Housing Rehab., 1953-67, Mayor's Adv. Community Improvement, 1967-69, Citizens' Housing Council, 1964—; mem. Mayor's Adv. Com. City Planning, 1966—; Bd. dirs. Social Welfare Planning Council, New Orleans, 1948-55, v.p., 1951-53, pres., 1953-55; trustee New Orleans United Fund, 1961-68, pres., 1964-65; bd. dirs. Family Service Soc., New Orleans, 1959-65, pres., 1962, 63; bd. dirs. Legal Air Bur., New Orleans, 1933—, pres. 1943-48; bd. dirs. Orleans Neighborhood Center, 1958-61, Cultural Attractions Fund, 1967-69; bd. dirs. New Orleans Philharmonic Symphony Soc., 1961- -, v.p., 1968—; bd. dirs. New Orleans Community Chest, 1947-48, 68—; Com. on Alcoholism, New Orleans, 1960-63; trustee Metairie Park Country Day Sch., 1948-54, v.p., 1949-51, pres., 1951-53. Mem. Am., La., New Orleans (pres. 1967-68) bar assns., Am. Law Inst., Am. Judicature Soc., Am. Coll. Probate Counsel, Nat. Planning Assn. (council 1969—), Order of Coif, Phi Delta Theta, Phi Delta Phi, Sigma Upsilon. Clubs: Pickwick, Plimsoll, Stratford, International House (New Orleans). Home: 81 Audubon Blvd New Orleans LA 70118 Office: Hibernia Bank Bldg New Orleans LA 70112

CLAWSON, DAVID KAY, orthopedic surgeon; b. Salt Lake City, Aug. 8, 1927; s. David J. and Elva (Gundry) C.; student U. Utah, 1944-45, 47-48; M.D., Harvard, 1952; m. Janet Dorothy Smith, June 1, 1952; children—Kim Debra, David Roger. Intern Stanford U. Hosp., 1952-53, resident gen. surgery, 1953-54; resident orthopedic surgery Stanford U. Hosp., also San Francisco City and County Hosp., 1954-57; fellow in orthopedics Nat. Found. Infantile Paralysis, 1955-58; hon. sr. registrar Royal Nat. Orthopedic Hosp., London, Eng., 1957-58; asst. prof. U. Cal. at Los Angeles Med. Sch., 1958; asst. prof. surgery, head div. orthopedic surgery U. Wash. Med. Sch., 1958-61, asso. prof. surgery, head div. orthopedic surgery, 1961- 65, prof., chmn. dept. orthopedics, 1964—. Served with USNR, 1945-46. Exchange fellow Am. Orthopedic Assn., 1967. Diplomate Am. Bd. Orthopedic Surgery. Mem. Am. Acad. Orthopedic Surgeons, Assn. Bone and Joint Surgeons, Seattle Surg. Soc., Wash. Med. Assn., King County Med. Soc. Contbr. med. jours. Mem. editorial bd. Clin. Orthopedics and Related Research, 1964—. Home: 4827 NE 85th St Seattle WA 98115

CLAWSON, DELWIN MORGAN, (Del) congressman; b. Thatcher, Ariz., Jan. 11, 1914; s. Charles Moses and Edna (Allen) C.; student Gila Coll., Thatcher, 1934; m. Marjorie Anderson, Oct. 19, 1934; children—Delwin L., James B. Salesman, bookkeeper, 1934-41; interviewer U.S. Employment Service, 1941-42; mgmt. adviser Fed. Pub. Housing Authority, Ariz., Cal., 1942-47; 88th-92d Congresses, 23d Dist. Cal., appropriations com. Mgr., Mut. Housing Assn., Compton, Cal., 1947-63; dir. Los Angeles County Sanitation Dists. 1, 2 and 8, 1957-63; mem. Compton Park and Recreation Commn., 1950-53, City Council, 1953-57, mayor, 1957-63. Chmn., Compton campaigns for Community Chest, A.R.C., Boy Scouts Am.; exec. bd. Los Angeles area council Boy Scouts Am., also mem. nat. council. Mem. Republican Congl. Com. Mem. Ch. of Jesus Christ of Latter-day Saints (missionary 1931-33, bishop 1948-54). Kiwanian (past lt. gov.). Home: 9117 Manzanar Av Downey CA 90240 Office: House Office Bldg Washington DC 20515

CLAWSON, ELDON RICHARD, moving and storage co. exec.; b. Tucson, May 15, 1926; s. Leslie Vern and Ethel (Skousen) C.; LL.B., U. Arix., 1952; LL.M., Columbia, 1955; m. Luana W. Willis, June 14, 1950; children—Byde W., Reed Eldon, Leslie Ann, Ross Willis, Bruce Arthur. Admitted to Cal. bar, 1955, Ariz. bar, 1952; clk. to Ariz. Supreme Ct. justice, 1952-53; asst. atty. gen. Ariz., 1953-54; pvt. practice, Los Angeles, 1955-57; with Bekins Moving & Storage Co., 1957—, exec. v.p. legal, sec., 1966—. Bd. dirs. Am. Movers Conf., Cal. Trucking Assn., Los Angeles chpt. Am. Soc. Ins. Mgmt. Served with USNR, 1944-46. Mem. Am., Cal., Ariz., Los Angeles bar assns. Home: 1222 Via del Sol San Dimas CA 91773 Office: 1335 S Figueroa St Los Angeles CA 90015

CLAWSON, JAMES HAROLD, former utilities co. exec.; b. Providence, Utah, Apr. 18, 1899; s. Charles Curtis and Rosetta (Thorpe) C.; B.S., Utah State U., 1920; M.B.A., Harvard, 1922; m. Leora Gibbs, Sept. 23, 1925; children—Harold Darcy, John Gibbs, Charles Curtis. Auditor, Stone & Webster, Inc., 1922-33; with Puget Sound Power & Light Co., Seattle, 1933-69, pres., 1959-62, chmn.

chief exec. officer, 1962-69, former chmn. finance com. dir. Pay'n Save Drugs, Inc., Seattle. Home: 138 W Lake Sammamish Blvd S E Bellevue WA 98004 Office: Stuart Bldg Seattle WA 98101

CLAWSON, MARION, economist; b. Elko, Nev., Aug. 10, 1905; s. William Ennes and Agnes (Thompson) C.; B.S. (Agr.), U. Nev., 1926, M.S., 1929; postgrad. U. Cal., summer 1928, Am. U., 1932; Ph.D., Harvard, 1943; m. Clara Partridge, Jan. 1, 1931 (div. 1947); children—Robert Marion, Nancy Agnes; m. 2d, Mary Montgomery, Sept. 27, 1947; children—Daniel Conness, Patrick Lyell. Agrl. economist, expt. sta. U. Nev., 1926-29, U.S. Dept. Agr. Bur. Agrl. Econs., Washington and Berkeley, Cal., 1929-47; head U.S. Dept. Agr. research and planning studies Columbia basin irrigation project, 1940-42, Central Valley irrigation project, Cal., 1942-45; regional adminstr. Bur. Land Mgmt., U.S. Dept. Interior, San Francisco, 1947-48; dir. Bur. Land Mgmt., Washington, 1948-53; mem. econ. adv. staff Jerusalem, Israel, 1953-55; dir. land use and mgmt. program Resources for Future, Inc., 1955—. Fellow Am. Agrl. Econ. Assn. (v.p. 1947); mem. Western Agrl. Econ. Assn. (pres. 1945-46), Am. Soc. for Range Mgmt., Soc. Internat. Devel. (exec. sec. 1959-62, v.p. 1963-66). Democrat. Author: (with John Black, C.R. Sayre, Walter W. Wilcox) Farm Management 1947; Western Range Livestock Industry, 1949; Uncle Sam's Acres, 1951; (with Burnell Held) The Federal Lands: Their Use and Management, 1957; (with Held, C.H. Stoddard) Land for the Future, 1960; Land for Americans, Land and Water for Recreation, 1963; Man and Land in the United States, 1964; (with Held) Soil Conservation in Perspective 1965; (with Charles L. Stewart) Land Use Information-A Critical Survey of U.S. Statistics Including Possibilities for Greater Uniformity, 1966; (with Jack L. Knetsch), Economics of Outdoor Recreation, 1966; The Land System of the United States, 1968; Policy Directions for U.S. Agriculture—Long Range Choices in Farming and Rural Living 1968; Federal Lands Since 1956—Recent Trends in Use and Management, 1967; The Bureau of Land Management, 1971; The Agricultural Potential of the Middle East (with Hans Landsberg, Lyle T. Alexander), 1971; Suburban Land Conversion in the United States; An Economic and Governmental Process, 1971. Editor: Natural Resources and International Development, 1964; (with Landsberg) Desalting Seawater—Achievements and Prospects, 1971; others. Contbr. articles to profl., govt. publs. Home: 6918 Maple Av Chevy Chase MD 20015 Office: 1755 Massachusetts Av NW Washington DC 20036

CLAXTON, ALVIE JACOB, bus. exec.; b. Hinsdale, Ill., Oct. 1, 1901; s. Allen Enes and Mary Jane (Casey) C.; B.S., U. Ill., 1923; m. Earlene Carrie Nees, May 7, 1924; children—Robert Franklin, Mary Lou, Richard Allen. With Champaign Ice Cream Co. (Ill.), 1919-23, Mattoon Ice Cream and Dairy Co. (Ill.), 1924-30; with Beatrice Foods Co. (formerly Beatrice Creamery Co.), 1930—, nat. dir. trade relations, Chgo., 1958—, also mem. nat. operating com., cons. European operations; v.p., dir. Beatrice Foods Co. of Chgo., also dir. several Eastern subsidiaries; supr. Beatrice Foods operations in Belgium; mgr. Meadow Gold Dairies, Inc., Pitts., 1940-43, pres., 1945-57, dir.; mem. adv. bd. Peoples First Nat. Bank. Pres. Retail Council; chmn. joint com. on taxation Dairy Industry; mem. expert adv. com. U.S. Dept. State. Del. to World Council Chs.; trustee Pitts. Conf. Methodist Ch.; bd. dir. Pitts. Hosp., Children's Civic Theatre; pres. Dairy Remembrance Fund, 1962—, Milk Industry Found., 1963—. Mem. Internat. (dir.), Pa. (pres.) assns. ice cream mfrs., Am. Dairy Sci. Assn., Inst. Food Technologists, Better Milk Assn., Nat. (dir. 1957—, v.p. 1961-63), Pitts. (pres.) dairy councils, Dairy Products Improvement Inst. (v.p.), Grocery Mfrs. Am. (mem. agr. com.), U.S.C. of C. (mem. agr., internat. affairs, policy coms., dir.), Dairy Soc. Internat. (pres. 1962-64), Cream Improvement Inst. (dir.), Pa. Assn. Milk Dealers (dir.), Pa., Del. and N.J. Ice Cream Assn. (pres.), Pitts. Milk Exchange (dir.), Scabbard and Blade. Methodist. Rotarian. Clubs: Sales Executives (dir.), Athletic Assn., Longue Vue, University (Pitts.); University (Washington); Pinehurst Country, Tin Whistles (v.p.), Country of N.C. (Pinehurst, N.C.), Royal and Ancient Golf of St. Andrews (Scotland). Contbr. numerous articles on dairy mgmt. to trade jours. Speaker before trade assn. groups, religious and civic orgns. Home: Box 948 Pinehurst, NC Office: 120 S LaSalle St Chicago IL 60603 ☆

CLAXTON, JOHN WILBERT, clergyman; b. Richmond, Ont., Can., June 30, 1901; s. Edwin and Eva Nina (Graham) C.; B.A., Queen's U., Kingston, Ont., 1923; M.A., McGill U., Montreal, 1927; B.D., United Theol. Coll., Montreal, 1927; fellow Union Theol. Sem., N.Y.C., 1927-28; D.D., Defiance Coll., 1940; m. Elizabeth Field Laughton, June 6, 1933; children—Edwin John and George Laughton (twins). Ordained to ministry United Ch. of Can., 1927; asst. minister Asbury M.E. Ch., Watertown, N.Y., 1928-29; asso. minister First Congl. Ch., Detroit, 1929-31; minister First Congl. Ch., Manistee, Mich., 1931-36; pres. Defiance (O.) Coll. 1936-43; minister Union Congl. Ch., Green Bay, Wis., 1943-52, Plymouth Congl. Ch., Lansing, Mich., 1952; asso. sec. Nat. Assn. Congl. Chs., 1962-70, dean, exec. sec. Congl. Found. for Theol. Studies; interim minister First Congl. Ch., Los Angeles, 1970—. Pres., Congl. Summer Assembly, Frankfort, Mich.; minister (summer) Little Stone Ch., Mackinac Island, Mich., 1948—; mem. com. on ministry Mich. Congl. Conf.; chmn. Lansing Christmas Parade Com.; v.p. Greater Lansing Council Chs.; pres. Lansing Ministerial Assn., mem. Nat. Commn. on Ministry Congl. Chs., 1948-54; moderator Central Assn. Congl. Chs.; mem. chmn. publs. Nat. Assn. Congl. Chs. Mem. Gov.'s Commn. Hwy. Safety. Bd. dirs. Lansing YMCA. Republican. Rotarian. Author: Facets of Our Faith. Contbr. articles to mags. Home: Mackinac Island MI 49757 Office: 540 S Commonwealth Av Los Angeles CA 90020

CLAXTON, PHILANDER PRIESTLEY, Jr., govt. ofcl.; b. Washington, Dec. 11, 1914; s. Philander and Mary Hannah (Johnson) C.; A.B., U. Tenn., 1934; M.A., Princeton, 1935; LL.B., Yale, 1938; m. Mary Ann Elizabeth Watkins, Apr. 8, 1943; children—Philander Priestley III, Mary Isabelle, Elizabeth Argyle Gettys, Ann Emily Julia Johnson, Kathleen Watkins, Caroline. Admitted to Tenn. bar, 1938; spl. atty. anti-trust div. Dept. Justice, 1938-39; mem. enforcement unit Fair Labor Standards Act, 1939; sr. atty., counsel power dept. TVA, 1939-43; chief standards of living div., asst. dir. Occupied Areas Directorate, State-War-Navy Coordinating Com., 1946; spl. asst. to asst. sec. state occupied areas, 1946-49; spl. asst. to dir. bur. Far Eastern affairs, State Dept., 1949; spl. asst. to asst. sec. state congl. relations, 1949- 59, dep. asst. sec. congl. relations (mut. security affairs), 1959-62; assigned sr. seminar fgn. policy State Dept., 1962-63, multilateral force negotiating team, 1963-64; spl. asst. to sec. state, 1965—, spl. asst. for population matters, 1966—. Mem. Pres. Com. on Population and Family Planning, 1968. Served with USNR, 1943-46; comdr. Res. Mem. Phi Kappa Phi. Democrat. Conglist. Clubs: Kenwood Country (Bethesda, Md.); Nat. Capital Democratic. Home: 5837 Osceola Ct Washington DC 20016 Office: Dept of State Washington DC 20525

CLAXTON, R. ALLEN, corp. exec.; b. Davenport, Ia., Aug. 12, 1931; s. Alvie J. and Earlene C. (Nees) C.; A.B., Duke, 1953, J.D., 1962; m. Cornelia Ann Barnes, June 26, 1956; children—Pamela Ann, Richard A., Jennifer Carrie. Ins. broker Babb & Co., Pitts., 1953-54; asst. ins. mgr. Beatrice Foods Co., Chgo., 1956-59; asst mgr. casualty dept. Asso. Casualty & Surety Cos., N.Y.C., 1962-65; admitted to N.Y. bar; sec.-counsel Purolator, Inc., Rahway, N.J., 1965-70, sec., counsel, 1967-70; sec., counsel RPS Products, Inc., Balt., 1971—. Served to 1st lt. USAF, 1954-56. Mem. Am. Bar Assn., N.Y. County Lawyers Assn., Am. Soc. Corp. Secs. Home: 3924 Noyes Circle Randallstown MD 21133 Office: RPS Products Inc 1700 S Caton Av Baltimore MD 21227

CLAY, ALBERT GREENE, banker; b. Mt. Sterling Ky., May 27, 1917; s. William Caldwell and Kathryn (Greene) C.; B.A., Duke, 1938; M.B.A., Harvard, 1939; m. Lorraine Case Newlin, Oct. 28, 1939; children—Robert Newlin, John William II, Charlotte Newlin. Pres., Farmers Tobacco Warehouse and Growers Tobacco Warehouse; owner Clay's Tobacco Warehouse; pres. Clay Tobacco Co., Mt. Sterling; sec.-treas. Burley Belt Fertilizer Co., Lexington, Ky.; pres. Burley Auction Warehouse Assn., 1946-65, chmn. bd., 1965—; dir. Fed. Res. Bank Cleve., 1964—, chmn. bd., 1968—. Mem. Nat. Tobacco Adv. Com., 1962—; sec. Tobacco Tax Council, Burley and Dark Leaf Tobacco Export Assn., 1957-69, Am. Horse Council, 1969—; mem. adv. com. on horse industry Internal Revenue Service Commr., 1970—. Active Boy Scouts Am.; chmn. exec. com. U. Ky., 1969—, vice chmn. bd. trustees; mem. bd. curators Transylvania Coll., Lexington, 1969—. Served to lt. USNR, 1939-42. Mem. Ky., Mt. Sterling chambers commerce, Montgomery County Farm Bur., Am. Legion, Am. Horse Council, Alpha Tau Omega. Christian Scientist. Home: Fairway Farm Mt Sterling KY 40353 Office: Fed Res Bank-Cleve PO Box 6387 Cleveland OH 44101

CLAY, CASSIUS, (Muhammad Ali), profl. boxer; b. Louisville, Jan. 18, 1942; s. Marcellus Clay; ed. pub. schs., Louisville, Amateur boxer, 1954-60; profl. boxer, 1960- 67; refused to be drafted, 1967; now engaged in acting and TV appearances, Winner 6 Golden Gloves titles in Ky., nat. Golden Gloves title, 1959, 60; Amateur Athletic Union light heavyweight championship, 1959, 60; Olympic championship, 1960; World Heavyweight championship, 1963. Mem. Black Muslims. Address: 3302 Grand Av Louisville KY*

CLAY, FRANK BUTNER, army officer; b. Auburn, Ala., Feb. 26, 1921; s. Gen. Lucius D. and Marjorie (McKeown) C.; student Valley Forge Mil. Acad., 1935-37, Millard Prep. Sch., Washington, 1937-38; B.S., U.S. Mil. Acad., 1942; grad. U.S. Army Armor Sch., 1950, Command and Gen. Staff Coll., 1952, Command Mgmt. Sch., 1958, Nat. War Coll., 1961; m. Patricia A. Casey, Jan. 12, 1946; children—Frank B., Cathleen, Christine. Commd. 2d lt. AUS, 1942, advanced through grades to maj. gen. U.S. Army, 1970; platoon leader to exec. officer 13th Tank Bn., 1st Armored Div., Tunisia and Italy, World War II; assigned Hdqrs. U.S. Forces, ETO, 1945-47; mem. staff Dept. Army, Washington, 1947-49; comdt. NCO Acad. of 2d Armored Div., comdr. 57th Tank Bn., Europe, 1952-55; sr. armor instr. Arty. Sch., Ft. Sill, Okla., 1955-57; mil. asst. to under sec. army, 1957-58; mil. sec. Office Joint Chiefs Staff, 1958-60; sr. advisor 7th Vietnam Inf. Div., 1961-62; staff officer Dept. Army, 1962-63; exec. officer Office Spl. Asst. for Tactical Mobility, 1963, chief air mobility test and evaluation div., 1963-64; comdr. 2d Armored Cavalry Regt., Europe, 1964-65; asst. dep. chief staff logistics U.S. Army, Europe, 1965-67; chief staff Hdqrs. U.S. Army Communications Zone, Europe, 1967; asst. div. comdr. for operations 101st Airborne Div., Ft. Campbell, Ky., 1967, comdr. advance party, Vietnam, 1967; asst. chief staff personnel Hdqrs. U.S. Mil. Assistance Command, Vietnam, 1968-69; dep. comdt. U.S. Army Command and Gen. Staff Coll., Ft. Leavenworth, Kan., 1969-70; dep. dir. joint staff Orgn. Joint Chiefs of Staff, Washington, 1970—. Decorated D.S.M., Silver Star with 2 oak leaf clusters, Legion of Merit, D.F.C., B.S.M. with V and 2 oak leaf clusters, Air Medal with V and 14 oak leaf clusters, Joint Service Commendation medal, Army Commendation medal, Purple Heart with oak leaf cluster (U.S.); Nat. Order Merit 5th Class, Distinguished Service Order 1st Class, Cross of Gallantry with palm, Cross of Gallantry with silver star, Air Service medal Hon. Class, Personal Fourragere for Heroic Actions (Vietnam); Order of Nat. Security Merit (Republic of Korea). Home: 1209 Colonial Rd McLean VA 22101 Office: Joint Chiefs Staff The Pentagon Washington DC 20301

CLAY, GEORGE HARRY, bank exec., lawyer; b. Kansas City, Kan., Feb. 14, 1911; s. G. Harry and Linnie Winn (Phillips) C.; A.B., LL.B., U. Mo., 1934; m. Harriett Hawley, Feb. 17, 1940; children—Constance Lucille (Loosli), Martha Linnie (Wood), Charles Hawley, Catherine Louise, James Nicholas. Admitted to Mo. bar, 1934; gen. practice law Borders, Borders & Warrick, 1935, Parker & Knipmeyer, 1935- 40, Winger, Reeder & Barker, 1940-44; exec. asst. Trans World Airlines, Inc., Kansas City, Mo., 1944-47, sec., 1947-54, v.p., sec., 1954-57, v.p. adminstrv. service, 1957-58, dir., 1956-58; v.p., gen. counsel Fed. Res. Bank Kansas City, 1958-61, pres., 1961—. Pres., Regional Health and Welfare Council, 1965-67. Bd. dirs. Kansas City (Mo.) YMCA, 1950-58, 61—, pres., 1955-56; bd. dirs. Starlight Theatre Assn., U. Mo.- Columbia Devel. Fund, United Funds; bd. govs. Am. Royal Live Stock and Horse Show; trustee Conservatory Music (chmn.), Midwest Research Inst. Mem. Am., Mo., Kansas City bar assns., Chancery, Phi Gamma Delta. Presbyn. (elder), Rotarian. Clubs: Kansas City; Mission Hills Country. Home: 1008 W 63d St Kansas City MO 64113 Office: Fed Reserve Bank 10th and Grand Av Kansas City MO 64198

CLAY, GRADY EDWARD, editor; b. Ann Arbor, Mich., Nov. 5, 1916; s. Grady Edward and Eleanor (Solomon) C.; A.B., Emory U., 1938; M.S., Columbia U., 1939; Nieman fellow Harvard U., 1949; m. Nanine Irwin Hilliard, Apr. 25, 1941; children—Grady Edward III, Theodore Hilliard, Peter Maitland. Pub., St. Simons (Ga.) Star, 1938; reporter Louisville Times, 1939-41; rotogravure editor Courier-Jour., Louisville, 1941-42, reporter, 1946-48, real estate editor, 1949-60, urban affairs editor, 1964-66; editor Landscape Architecture Quar., Louisville, 1961—; cons. urban jour. center Northwestern U., 1966-68; mem. faculty Salzburg Seminar in Am. Studies, 1968. Mem. Citizens Met. Planning Council, 1956—; mem. adv. bd. Envirionic Found. Inc., 1971—. Served with AUS, 1942-46. Mem. A.I.A., Am. Soc. Landscape Architects, Soc. Nieman Fellows, Urban Writers Soc., Nat. Assn. Real Estate Editors. Democrat. Episcopalian. Clubs: Louisville Country; Tavern; Salmagundi; Cosmos (Washington). Home: 344 S Peterson Av Louisville KY 40206 Office: 1500 Bardstown Rd Louisville KY 40205

CLAY, H.D., gas co. exec.; b. Emlenton, Pa., Sept. 12, 1910; s. Ralph D. and Jessie V. (Moore) C.; B.S., Pa. State U., 1932; m. Henrietta Louise Johnston, June 10, 1939. Engr., United Natural Gas Co., Oil City, Pa., 1933-43; with Iroquois Gas Corp., Buffalo, 1946—, exec. v.p., 1957-59, pres., controller, 1959—; pres. Nat. Fuel Gas Co., N.Y.C.; dir. Marine Midland Bank-Western, Buffalo. Bd. dirs. Deaconess Hosp., Blue Cross Western N.Y., Children's Aid and Soc. Prevention Cruelty to Children, Greater Buffalo Devel. Found., Nat. Conf. Christians and Jews, Western N.Y. Traffic Safety Council; trustee Buffalo-Niagara Indsl. Devel. Corp., United Fund Buffalo and Erie County, Inst. Gas Tech. Served to lt. USNR, 1943-46. Mem. Buffalo C. of C., Am. Gas Assn. (2d vice chmn.). Presbyn. Rotarian. Clubs: Buffalo Athletic, Buffalo, Park Country (Buffalo). Home: 94 Dawnbrook Lane Buffalo NY 14221 Office: 10 Lafayette Sq Buffalo NY 14203

CLAY, HENRY JONES, lawyer; b. Jamaica, N.Y., July 13, 1915; s. George H. and Amelia S. (Jones) C.; A.B., Union Coll., Schenectady, 1939; LL.B., U. Va., 1942; m. Mary Belle Trent, Aug. 14, 1948 (div.); children—Marcia, Henry Jones, Jonathan. Admitted to N.Y. bar, 1946, D.C. bar, 1952, Vt. bar, 1964; practiced in N.Y.C.; gen. partner Abberley, Kooiman, Marcellino & Clay, also mem. firm DeWitt, Lockman & DeWitt; asst. atty. gen. N.Y. State, 1947-48; gen. counsel Workman's Compensation Bd. State N.Y., 1948-50. Dir. Pandick Press, Advanced Design Products, Manchester Printing Co. Exec. dir. N.Y. State Labor Relations Bd., 1950-52; acting chmn. Internat. Claims Commn. U.S., 1954; mem. Fgn. Claims Settlement Commn. U.S., 1954-59; enforcement commr. Nat. Enforcement Commn. of Fed. Wage Stblzn. Bd., 1953. Served from ensign to lt. comdr. USNR, 1941-46. Mem. Am., Internat., N.Y., Vt. bar assns., Assn. Bar City N.Y., Am. Arbitration Assn. (panel). Republican. Episcopalian. Mason. Clubs: Union, Brook (N.Y.C.); University, Army and Navy (Washington); Landsdowne (London). Contbr. articles to profl. jours. Home: 1050 Park Av New York City NY 10028 also Madison CT 06439 Office: 521 Fifth Av New York City NY 10017

CLAY, HERBERT D., gas co. exec.; b. Emlenton, Pa., Sept. 12, 1910; s. Ralph D. and Jessie V. (Moore) C.; B.S., Pa. State U., 1932; m. Henrietta Louise Johnston, June 10, 1939. Engr., United Natural Gas Co., Oil City, Pa., 1933-43; with Iroquois Gas Corp., Buffalo, 1946—, v.p., 1953-57, exec. v.p., 1957-59, pres., 1959-71; pres., dir. Nat. Fuel Gas Co., N.Y.C.; dir. Marine Midland Banks Western, Buffalo, Bd. dirs. Deaconess Hosp., Blue Cross Western N.Y.; trustee Inst. Gas Tech. Served to lt. USNR, 1943-46. Mem. Buffalo C. of C., Am. Gas Assn. (2d vice chmn.). Presbyn. Rotarian Clubs: Buffalo Athletic, Park Country. Home: 94 Dawnbrook Lane Buffalo NY 14221 Office: 10 Lafayette Sq Buffalo NY 14203 also 30 Rockefeller Plaza New York City NY 10020

CLAY, JOHN WILLIAM, banker; b. nr. Americus, Ga., Dec. 5, 1913; s. Charles Clifford and Zerelda (Martin) C.; B.A., Vanderbilt U., 1937; m. Eleanor Eakin Reed, Oct. 2, 1939; children—John William, James Reed. With Third Nat. Bank, Nashville, 1937—, v.p., 1951-63, sr. v.p., 1963-65, exec. v.p., 1965-70, pres., 1970—. Co-chmn. Nashville Com. for Am. Industry Nat. Fund for Med. Edn., 1956- 64; gen. chmn. Middle Tenn. Heart Assn. campaign, 1951, dir., 1954-57; gen. chmn. United Givers Fund for Nashville and Davidson County campaign, 1958-59, also trustee; gen. alumni reunion chmn. Vanderbilt U., 1962, chmn. Nashville Living Endowment Program, 1964-66, nat. chmn., 1968-69. Trustee Nashville Meml. Hosp. Mem. Am. Bankers Assn. (task force on econ. edn. 1970—), Tenn. Taxpayers Assn. (exec. com. 1969—), Assn. Res. City Bankers, Nashville Area C. of C. (past pres., dir., mem. exec. com.), Vanderbilt U. Alumni Assn. (past trustee, mem. exec. com.), Sigma Alpha Epsilon. Methodist. Clubs: Belle Meade Country (past dir.), Cumberland (Nashville). Home: 4422 Harding Pl Nashville TN 37205 Office: 201 4th Av N Nashville TN 37219

CLAY, LUCIUS DUB., ret. army officer, corp. exec.; b. Marietta, Ga., Apr. 23, 1897; s. Alexander Stephen and Frances (White) C.; B.S., U.S. Mil. Acad., 1918; m. Marjorie McKeown, Sept. 21, 1918; children—Lucius D., Jr., Frank B. Commd. 2d lt. U.S. Army, 1918, advanced through grades to gen., 1947; instr. Officers Tng. Sch. (Engrs.), 1918; with Engr. troops, 1918-24; instr. in civil and mil. engring. U.S. Mil. Acad., 1924-28; river and harbor assignments; represented U.S. at Permanent Internat. Nav. Conf., Brussels, 1934; on Gen. MacArthur's staff in Philippines, 1937; in charge of constrn. Red River Dam, Denison, Tex., 1938-40; in charge of def. airport program CAA, 1940-41; asst. chief of staff for Materials Service of Supply; apptd. dep. dir. for war programs, Dec. 1944; dep. to Gen. Eisenhower, 1945; dep. mil. gov. Germany (U.S.), 1946; comdr. in chief U.S. Forces in Europe and mil. gov. U.S. Zone, Germany, 1947-49, ret., 1949. Former chmn. bd. Continental Can Co., dir., mem. exec. com. until 1970; sr. partner Lehman Bros., 1963- -; dir. Lehman Corp., Lehman Bros., Inc., Chase Internat. Investment Corp.; chmn. bd. Fed. Nat. Mortgage Assn., 1970—. Personal rep. of President Kennedy in Berlin, 1961. Trustee Presbyn. Hosp., Tuskegee Inst. Mem. Am. Soc. C.E. (Hoover medal), Soc. Am. Mil. Engrs., Permanent Internat. Nav. Congress. Clubs: Army and Navy, Links, University, Blind Brook, Pinnacle, Bohemian, Eastward Ho! Country. Home: 680 Madison Av New York City NY 10021 Office: 1 William St New York City NY 10004

CLAY, LUCIUS DUBIGNON, Jr., air force officer; b. Alexandria, Va., July 6, 1919; s. Lucius DuBignon and Marjorie (McKeown) C.; B.S., U.S. Mil. Acad., 1942; grad. Flying Sch., 1942; m. Betty Rose Commander, Dec. 16, 1943; children—Lucious DuBignon III, Charles Commander, Carla Lynn, Colin McKeown. Commd. 2d lt. U.S. Army 1942, advanced through grades to gen. USAF, 1970; various assignments U.S. and ETO, 1942-44; asst. operations officer 344th Bomb Group, ETO, 1944; operations officer, later comdr. 495th Bomb Squardon, ETO, 1944-45; dep., later comdr. 344th Bomb Group, ETO, 1945- 46; dep. comdr., later dep. for base services 43 Air Depot, Germany, 1946-47; div., dep. chief staff operations for atomic energy, 1948-49; project officer, tech. services evaluation div., Air Univ. evaluation staff Air War Coll., 1949-51, devel. officer, aero. and tech. div., evaluation staff, 1951-52; air force mem. joint strategic plans group Office Joint Chiefs Staff, 1952-54; chief joint plans br., war plans div., dep. chief staff operations Hdqrs. USAF, 1954-56; dep. comdr. 72 Bomb Wing, Ramey AFB, P.R., 1956-58; chief plans div., directorate plans SAC, 1958-61; mem. joint war games control group, joint staff Office Joint Chiefs Staff, 1961-62, dep. dir. operations, 1962-64; vice comdr., 12th Air Force, Tactical Air Command, Waco, Tex., 1964-66, comdr., 1966; dir. plans, dep. chief staff plans and operations Hdqrs. USAF, 1966-67; dir. aerospace programs, later dep. chief staff programs and resources hdqrs., 1967-69; dep. chief staff plans and operations, 1969-70; comdr. 7th Air Force, Southeast Asia, 1970—. Decorated Legion of Merit, D.F.C., Bronze Star, Air medal with 2 silver clusters, Purple Heart; Croix de Guerre with silver star. Home: 313 Vassar Rd Alexandria VA 22314 Office: Comdr 7th Air Force AOI San Francisco CA 96307

CLAY, WILLIAM DANE, lawyer; b. Fort Smith, Ark., Feb. 1, 1928; s. W. Wesley and Ina (Stephens) C.; A.A., Fort Smith Jr. Coll., 1947; LL.B. (J.D.), U. Ark., 1951; m. Mary Ann Smith, Nov. 5, 1961. Admitted to Ark. bar, 1951; asso. firm Rose, Barron, Nash, Williamson, Carroll & Clay, Little Rock, 1953- 58, partner, 1958-70, sr. partner, 1970. Dir., gen. counsel Modern Am. Mortgage Corp., Little Rock. Served to 1st lt., Judge Advocate Gen. Corps, USAF, 1952-53. Mem. Little Rock Philharmonic Assn. (pres. 1961), Am. Contract Bridge League (nat. goodwill, charity coms., pres. Ark. 1962-64), Phi Alpha Delta, Omicron Delta Kappa. Democrat. Home: 12010 Fairway Dr Little Rock AR 72207 Office: 720 W 3rd Little Rock AR 72201

CLAY, WILLIAM LACY, congressman; b. St. Louis, Apr. 30, 1931; s. Irving C. and Luella (Hyatt) C.; B.S. in Polit. Sci., St. Louis U., 1953; m. Carol A. Johnson, Oct. 10, 1953; children—Vicki, Lacy, Michelle. Real estate broker, 1964—; mgr. life ins. co., 1959-61; alderman 26th Ward, St. Louis, 1959-64; bus. rep. state, county and municipal employees union, 1961-64; edn. coordinator Steamfitters local 562, 1966-67; mem. 91st Congress 1st Dist. Mo. Dist. chmn. Friends of Scouts. Bd. dirs. Narcotics Anonymous. Served with AUS, 1953-55. Mem. N.A.A.C.P. (past exec. bd. mem. St. Louis), CORE, St. Louis Jr. C. of C. Democrat. Home: 5146a Minerva St St Louis MO 63108 Office: Cannon House Office Bldg Washington DC 20515

CLAY, WILLIAM MARION, educator; b. Myers, Ky., Oct. 3, 1906; s. George Washington and Katie (Clark) C.; A.B., Transylvania Coll., 1927; postgrad. U. Ky.; M.A., U. Mich., 1934, Ph.D., 1937; m. Lucille Naff, May 25, 1929; children—Doris Lee (Mrs. Michael deLaval Landon), Nelson Marion; m. 2d, Katherine Montgomery, Oct. 31, 1942. Instr. biology Transylvania Coll., 1927-29, asst. prof., 1929-32; asst. zoology U. Mich., 1932-36; faculty biology U. Louisville, 1936—, prof., 1950—, head dept., 1956-63, Tom Wallace prof. conservation, 1963—. Exec. dir. Potamological Inst., 1960-63, ichthyologist, sr. research asso., 1963—. Mem. Am. Soc. Ichthyologists and Herpetologists (gov. 1957-62, sec. treas. S.E. sect. 1958-60, pres.), Am. Fisheries Soc., Herpetologists League, Soc. for Study Evolution, Ky. Acad. Sci. (editor 1949-55, pres. 1957- 58), Soc. Systematic Zoology, Ky. Soc. Natural History (pres. 1939), Phi Kappa Phi, Tau Kappa Epsilon, Sigma Xi (chpt. pres. 1957-58). Clubs: Torch, Propeller. Author: Field Manual of Kentucky Fishes. Contbr. sci. papers to profl. lit. Home: 4532 Southern Pkwy Louisville KY 40214

CLAYCOMB, CECIL KEITH, biochemist, educator; b. Twin Falls, Ida., Oct. 19, 1920; s. Cecil R. and Frilla E. (Reams) C.; B.S., U. Ore., 1947, M.S., 1948, Ph.D., 1951; m. Elizabeth Jane Gregg, Mar. 10, 1943; children—John K., Mary E. Prof., head dept. biochemistry Dental Sch. U. Ore., Portland, 1951—, also chmn. admissions com., 1959-69. Served to 1st lt. AUS, 1943-46. Mem. Am. Chem. Soc., Internat. Assn. Dental Research, A.A.A.S., Res. Officers Assn., Sigma Xi. Mem. dental bd. N.S.W. Scholar, Sydney, Australia, 1970. Contbr. articles to sci. jours. Home: 3324 SW 13th Av Portland OR 97201 Office: 611 S W Campus Dr Portland OR 97201

CLAYDON, JOHN FREDERICK, abrasives co. mfg. exec.; b. Red Wing, Minn., Mar. 22, 1912; s. Percy H. and Elizabeth (Johnson) C.; B.S. in Chem. Engring., U. Minn., 1935; grad. Advanced Mgmt. Program Harvard, 1945; m. Mary Ellen Haas, Dec. 31, 1941; children—Marilyn, Richard. With Carborundum Co., Niagara Falls, N.Y., 1935—, plant engring. and prodn. staff, indsl. sales exec., dist. sales mgr. New Eng., dist. sales mgr., Mich., 1935-54, gen. sales mgr. coated abrasives div., 1954-56, gen. mgr. coated abrasives div., 1957-58, gen. mgr., v.p., 1959-63, group v.p. abrasives, 1963-68, sr. v.p., 1969—. Bd. dirs. Niagara Coalition. Mem. Coated Abrasive Mfrs. Inst. (dir.). Clubs: Niagara, Niagara Falls Country. Home: 5238 Lewiston Rd Lewiston NY 14092 Office: Carborundum Co Niagara Falls NY 14302

CLAYDON, SISTER MARGARET, coll. pres.; b. N.Y.C., July 19, 1923; d. George Thomas and Susan (Murray) Claydon; A.B., Trinity Coll., 1945; M.A., Cath. U. Am., 1953, Ph.D., 1960; postgrad. Oxford U., summer 1958; L.H.D., Georgetown U. Tchr. Latin St. Hubert's High Sch., Phila., 1948-51, Trinity Prep. Sch., Ilchester, Med., 1951-52; faculty dept. English, Trinity Coll., Washington, 1952-59, pres., 1959—; exchange lectr. English, Notre Dame Coll., Glasgow, Scotland, 1958-59. Mem. Commn. on Instl. Affairs, A.A.C. Trustee Greater Washington Ednl. TV Assn.; mem. exec. com., trustee Middle States Assn. Coll. and Secondary Schs. Mem. N.E.A., Nat. Cath. Edn. Assn. (pres. coll. and univ. dept., 1968-70). Address: Trinity Coll Washington DC 20017

CLAYTON, CARL CLEVELAND, Jr., chem. co. exec.; b. Texarkana, Tex., May 23, 1919; s. Carl Cleveland and Mary Louise (Heath) C.; student Texarkana Coll., 1937-39; B.S. in Chem. Engring., U. Tex., 1942; m. Hazel Maxine Aaron, Oct. 13, 1951; 1 dau., Carol Louise. Chem. engr. devel. dept. PPG Industries, Corpus Christi, Tex., 1942-44, project leader, 1946-51, group leader econ. evaluations, 1953-66, sr. project engr., 1966—. Served with USNR, 1944-46, 51-53. Mem. Am. Assn. Cost Engrs. (founder 1956; nat. sec. 1963-66, pres. S. Tex. sect. 1971), Nat. Spelcological Soc. Patentee in field. Home: 4701 Bonner Dr Corpus Christi TX 78411 Office: PO Box 4026 Corpus Christi TX 78408

CLAYTON, CHARLES CURTIS, journalist; b. Cambridge, Neb., June 3, 1902; s. Curtis Stanton and Clara Clyde (Richardson) C.; student U. Neb., 1919-22; B.J., U. Mo., 1925; m. Elizabeth Elliott, June 3, 1925; children—Carol Roma (Mrs. William G. Hill), Charles Stephen. Reporter St. Louis Globe Democrat, 1925-29, asst. city editor, 1929-39, lit. editor, 1937-39, city editor, 1939-40, editorial writer, 1940-54, exec. asst. to publisher, 1954-55; prof. journalism So. Ill. Univ., 1956—, on leave to establish Sch. Journalism and Mass Communications Center at Chinese U. of Hong Kong, 1965-66; lectr. journalism Washington U., St. Louis, 1928-29, Webster Coll., 1937-40, Lindenwood Coll., St. Charles, Mo., 1940-52, sch. journalism U. Mo., 1947-50; chmn. publ. bd. Quill, 1951-53, editor The Quill, 1956-61; vis. prof. journalism, grad. sch. journalism Nat. Chengchi U., Taipei, Formosa, 1961-62, 70-71, hon. prof. for life; dir. Yenching Inst., 1970-71. Bd. dirs. Walter Williams Found. in Journalism, 1936-38. Recipient U. Mo. Honor Medal for distinguished service to journalism, 1952. Mem. U. Mo. Journalism Alumni Assn. (pres. 1936-38), Sigma Delta Chi (exec. council 1947—, chmn. 1952-53, nat. pres. 1951-52), Kappa Tau Alpha, Alpha Epsilon Rho. Rotarian. Club: Circumnavigators. Author books including: Newspaper Reporting Today, 1947; Fifty Years for Freedom, 1959; Little Mack: Joseph McCullah of the St. Louis Globe-Democrat, 1969; also mag. articles. Home: 805 Taylor Dr Carbondale IL 62901

CLAYTON, CHARLES TRUEHEART, ins. co. exec.; b. Birmingham, Ala., Jan. 10, 1910; s. William W. and Titelle (Trueheart) C.; student U. Ariz., 1925-27; m. Betty Hudson, Mar. 24, 1932; children—Lella (Mrs. Frank H. Bromberg, Jr.), Trueheart (Mrs. Morton L. Carl, Jr.), Charles Trueheart. Agt., Nat. Life Ins. Co. Vt., 1927-29; with Liberty Nat. Life Ins. Co., 1929—, mgr., Memphis, 1933-47, div. mgr. for Tenn., 1947-49, v.p., Birmingham, 1949-59, exec. v.p., 1960—, also dir.; dir. Brown-Service Funeral Homes Co., Inc., Service Ins. Co. Ala. Mem. Birmingham council Boy Scouts Am.; pres. Crippled Children's Hosp., 1959-60. Trustee Crippled Children's Clinic. Recipient Silver Beaver award Boy Scouts Am. Mem. Nat. Assn. Life Underwriters, Gen. Agts. and Mgrs. Conf., Life Ins. Agy. Mgmt. Assn. (dir.), Ala. Life Ins. Cos., Sigma Nu. Presbyn. Kiwanian, Mason (Shriner). Clubs: Birmingham Country, Mason (Shriner). Clubs: Birmingham Country, Club, Relay House (Birmingham). Home: 3758 Country Club Dr Birmingham AL 35213 Office: 301 S 27th St Birmingham AL 35233

CLAYTON, DONALD DELBERT, astrophysicist, nuclear physicist, educator; b. Shenandoah, Ia., Mar. 18, 1935; s. Delbert Homer and Avis (Kembery) C.; B.S., So. Meth. U., 1956; Ph.D., Cal. Inst. Tech., 1962; m. Mary Lou Keesee, Dec. 18, 1954; children-Donald Douglas, Devon Charles. Research fellow in physics Cal. Inst. Tech., 1961-63; staff scientist Aerospace Corp., El Segundo, Cal., 1961-63; mem. faculty Rice U., Houston, 1963—, asso. prof. physics and space sci., 1965-69, prof. physics and space sci. and faculty asso. Brown Coll., 1969—; vis. asso. physics Cal. Inst. Tech., 1966-67. Sloan fellow, 1966-70. Fellow Am. Phys. Soc.; mem. Am. Astron. Soc., Am. Geophys. Union, A.A.A.S., Phi Beta Kappa, Sigma Xi. Contbr. articles profl. jours. Office: Dept Space Sci Rice U Houston TX 77001

CLAYTON, GLENN LOWELL, coll. pres.; b. Brookville, O., Oct. 31, 1910; s. Sherman and Lottie (Erbaugh) C.; B.S., Miami U., 1932; M.A., Ohio State U., 1937, Ph.D., 1948; LL.D., Central Mich. U., 1958; m. Janet Stutz, June 11, 1938; children—John M., Glenn L. II. Tchr. high sch., New Lebanon, O., 1932-38, prin., 1938-40, supt. schs., 1940-45; instr. Ohio State U., 1945-48; pres. Ashland (O.) Coll., 1948—. Adv. com. Ohio Bd. Regents; exec. com. Ohio Council on Econ. Edn. Bd. dirs. Ohio Found. Ind. Colls., 1957-63, chmn., 1962. Mem. Pres. Assn., Ohio Pres. and Deans Assn., Ohio C. of C. (dir.), Phi Beta Kappa, Kappa Phi Kappa, Kappa Delta Pi, Beta Pi Theta. Republican. Mem. Brethren Ch. (pres. Nat. Laymens Orgn. 1946-48, trustee, moderator Nat. Conf. 1948-49). Rotarian (citation as citizen of year 1959). Home: 1320 Center St Ashland OH 44805

CLAYTON, HUGH NEWTON, lawyer; b. Ripley, Miss., Aug. 22, 1907; s. Ira L. and Nancy (McCord) C.; A.B., U. Miss., 1929, J.D., 1931; m. Cathryn Rose Carter, June 26, 1939; children—Rose (Mrs. Thad Cochran), Hugh Carter. Admitted to Miss. and Tenn. State bars, 1931; practiced in Memphis, 1931-33, Ripley, 1933-36, city atty., Ripley, 1933-36; city atty., New Albany, Miss., 1937—. Dir., Bank of New Albany. Served from lt. to lt. comdr. USNR, 1942-45, served as acting comdg. officer Naval Air Sta., New Orleans, 1945. Chmn. Union Co. chpt. A.R.C., 1945-51, nat. com. on internat. operations, 1946-47, chmn. nat. conv., 1959, mem. nat. exec. com. and chmn. nat. chpt. relations com., 1954- 56; vice chmn. and parliamentarian, 1948, nat. conv.; chmn. area adv. com. Southeastern U.S., 1949-51; nat. bd. govs., 1950-56, vol. field cons., 1956—, chmn. nat. conv., 1959, chmn. state conv., 1961; mem. exec. bd. Yacona Area council Boy Scouts Am., 1955—, chmn. com. on advancements, 1956-57, chmn. com. on orgn. and extension, 1958- 60, chmn. Region 5 com. on trust fund promotion, 1968—, mem. nat. council, 1959—, pres. Yacona Area council, 1963-65, mem. regional exec. com., 1966—, mem. nat. ann. meeting com., 1970—; pres. Union Co. Tb Assn., 1937-40, New Albany Planning Com., 1945-49; mem. nat. conf. Commrs. on Uniform State Laws, 1956—. Mem. state exec. com. Dem. Party, 1952-56, mem. nat. com., 1956-60; mem. exec. com. Nat. Dem. Com., 1959-60; mem. Democratic Nat. Adv. Council, 1959-60. Founder, 1st pres. Miss. Jr. Bar, 1936. Recipient Silver Beaver award Boy Scouts Am., 1962, Silver Antelope award Boy Scouts Am., 1968. Fellow Am. Coll. Trial Lawyers, Miss. Bar Found. (trustee), Am. Bar Found., Am. Coll. Probate Counsel, Internat. Acad. Law and Sci.; mem. Am. Judicature Soc. (dir. 1962-65), Internat. Platform Assn., Internat. (patron), Fed., Am. (mem. various coms., mem. ho. dels. 1966—, chmn. communications com. 1967-68) bar assns., Miss. Bar Found. (trustee 1963-65, pres. 1965-66), Miss. State Bar (1st v.p. 1958-59, pres. 1959-60), 3d Miss. Circuit Bar Assn. (pres. 1963-68), Jud. Conf. U.S. 5th Circuit, U. Miss. Alumni Assn. (dir. 1962—, founder, 1st pres. law alumni chpt. 1964- 65), Am. Acad. Polit. and Social Sci., Miss. Assn. Meth. Ministers and Laymen (pres. 1958), Inst. Jud. Adminstrn., Am. Legion, Omicron Delta Kappa, Phi Delta Theta, Phi Alpha Delta, Tau Kappa Alpha. Sigma Upsilon, Scribes (dir. 1969—). Democrat. Methodist (treas. N. Miss. Conf. bd. missions 1938-60, trustee N. Miss. Conf. 1960—, treas. Lewis Meml. Hosp. Fund Miss. 1938-49, nat. emergency com. 1940). Mason, Rotarian (dist. gov. 1965-66). Clubs: Pine Hill Country (Ripley, Miss.); Oaks Country (New Albany, Miss.); Rivermont (Memphis). Editor: Miss. Law Jour., 1931; asso. editor; New Orleans Christian Advocate, 1941-42. Contbr. articles to profl. publs. Home: 258 Reeves New Albany MS 48652 Office: Clayton Bldg PO Box 157 New Albany MS 48652

CLAYTON, JEAN PAUL, pub. utilities; b. Sterling, Ill., Oct. 3, 1888; s. Gilbert Oliver and Mary Adeline (Robinson) C.; B.Engring., Tulane, 1909, D.Engring., 1942; M.E.E. (research fellow), U. Ill., 1911; m. Helen Electa Burbank, June 2, 1915; children—Jean Paul, Hugh Burbank, Helen Ruth. With Central Ill. Pub. Service Co., Mattoon, Ill., 1912-32, v.p., 1919- 32, pres., 1932; asst. to pres. Super-Power Co. Ill., 1928-32; v.p. in charge operations Middle West Utilities Co., 1932; chief system officer Commonwealth Edison Co., Pub. Service Co. of No. Ill., Western United Gas & Electric Co., Ill. No. Utilities Co., Chgo. Dist. Electric Generating Corp., 1932-49; v.p. Power Dispatchers Equipment Co., 1952—. Mem. Ill. Legislature Commn. on Future Rd. Program, 1931-33; chmn. Com. on Elimination of Grade Crossings, Springfield, Regional Hwy. Com. for Springfield and Sangamon County, 1930-32. Fellow Am. Inst. E.E.; mem. Am. Soc. M.E., Western Soc. Engrs. (chmn. awards com. 1941-45, Octave Chanute medal 1938), Ill. State Electric Assn. (past pres.), Springfield C. of C. (pres. 1926-27), Ill. C. of C. (pres. 1930-32, chmn. bd., 1932-35), Sigma Xi. Club: Union League (Chgo.). Discoverer, developer new analysis of cylinder performances of reciprocating engines; compiler Illinois-Its Resources-Development and Possibilities. Home: 714 Oak St Winnetka IL 60093

CLAYTON, JOE TODD, educator; b. Etowah, Tenn., Oct. 2, 1924; s. Joe Madison and Onye (Rymer) C.; B.S. in Agrl. Engring., U. Tenn., 1949, postgrad., 1949-50; M.S., U. Ill. Urbana, 1951; Ph.D. (NSF sci. faculty fellow), Cornell U., 1962; m. Helen Deane Harris, Aug. 30, 1946; children—Jeffrey Todd, Jill Elaine, Joel Harris. Instr. U. Ill., Urbana, 1951-54, asst. prof., 1955-57; asst. prof. U. Conn., 1954-55; asso. prof. U. Mass. at Amherst, 1957-61, prof. agrl. engring., 1961-66, prof., head dept. food and agrl. engring., 1966—; vis. prof. bioengring., NATO sr. fellow sci. U. Reading (Eng.), 1971—. Served with AUS, 1943-46. Registered profl. agrl. engr., Ill., Mass. Fellow A.A.A.S.; mem. Am. Soc. Agrl. Engrs. (sr. mem.), Inst. Food Technologists, Internat. Soc. Biometeorology, Sigma Xi, Gamma Sigma Delta. Contbr. numerous articles profl. jours. Home: N Silver Lane Sunderland MA 01375

CLAYTON, PRESTON COPELAND, lawyer; b. Eufaula, Ala., Sept. 21, 1903; s. Lee Johnston and Caroline E. (Copeland) C.; B.A., U. Ala., 1924; LL.B., Jones Law Sch., 1935; m. Jewel Gladys Robinson, July 20, 1933; children-Mary Elliott (Mrs. Robert Mack Dixon), Sarah Hunter (Mrs. Thos. S. Lawson, Jr.), Preston Copeland. Cotton mcht., Quanah, Tex., 1927-32; admitted to Ala. bar, 1931; pvt. practice in Clayton and Eufaula, 1932—; asso. justice Supreme Ct. Ala., 1953-54; instr. econs. U. Ala., 1923-24; dir., atty. Clayton Banking Co., 1946-53; organizer, atty. Pea River Electric Coop., 1937-53, Wiregrass Electric Coop., 1938-42. Breeder Arabian horses. City atty., Clayton, 1933-39; Mem. Ala. Bd. Vets. Affairs, 1946-50. Chmn. Barbour County Democratic Exec. Com., 1937-53; mem. Ala. Senate, 1938-53. Pres. Ala. Cattlemens Assns. Served to lt. col. AUS, World War II. Episcopalian. Rotarian. Contbr. articles on Arabian and Barb horses of No. Africa to mags. Home: 1 mile South of Clayton AL 36016 Office: 210 E Broad St Eufaula AL 36027

CLAYTON, RAYMOND BRAZENOR, educator; b. Manchester, Eng., Sept. 16, 1925; B.Sc., U. Manchester, 1949, M.Sc., 1950, Ph.D. in Chemistry, 1952; married; 2 children. Research fellow in organic chemistry U. Manchester, 1952-53; fellow in biochemistry U. Chgo., 1953-54; fellow in chemistry Harvard, 1954-55, 59-63; Imperial Chem. Industry fellow in biochemistry Oxford (Eng.) U., 1955-56; research dir. Manchester Cancer Research Trust Fund, 1956-58; asso. prof. biochemistry dept. of psychiatry Stanford, 1963-69, prof., 1969—. Hon. lectr. U. Manchester, 1956-58. Mem. A.A.A.S., Am. Soc. Biol. Chemistry, Brit. Chem. Soc., Brit. Biochem. Soc. Office: Stanford U Stanford CA 94305*

CLAYTON, ROBERT NORMAN, educator, chemist; b. Hamilton, Ont., Can., Mar. 20, 1930; s. Norman and Gwenda (Twist) C.; B.Sc., Queens U., 1951, M.Sc., 1952; Ph.D., Cal. Inst. Tech., 1955; m. Cathleen Shelburne, Jan. 30, 1971. Came to U.S., 1952. Research fellow Cal. Inst. Tech., 1955-56; mem. faculty Pa. State U., 1956-58; mem. faculty U. Chgo., 1958- -, prof. chemistry and geochemistry, 1966—. Mem. Am. Geophys. Union, A.A.A.S., Sigma Xi. Research distbn. stable isotopes of light elements in nature, Application to problems in geology. Home: 5201 S Cornell Av Chicago IL 60615

CLAYTON, ROBERT WILLIAM, mfr.; b. Hightstown, N.J., Sept. 24, 1922; s. William Henry and Eleanor Ann (Dilts) C.; B.S., Rider Coll., 1943; m. Marjorie Ruth Bradley, Aug. 23, 1947; children—Carol, Robert William. Sr. accountant Price Waterhouse & Co., Phila., 1947-55; controller Permacel div. Johnson & Johnson, New Brunswick, N.J., 1955-61, asst. controller, 1961-62; div. controller Ducommun Inc., Los Angeles, 1962-66, corporate controller, 1966-69; v.p., controller Avery Products Corp., San Marino, Cal., 1969—. Mem. Hightstown Bd. Edn., 1955-61. Served to 2d lt., USAAF, 1943-45. C.P.A., N.J. Mem. Nat. Assn. Accountants (v.p. Los Angeles chpt.), Am. Mgmt. Assn. Club: Lions. Home: 1849 Hillside Dr Glendale CA 91208 Office: 415 Huntington Dr San Marino CA 91108

CLAYTON, RODERICK KEENER, biophysicist, educator; b. Tallinn, Estonia, Mar. 29, 1922 (parents Am. citizens); s. John Heber and Helena (Mullerstein) C.; B.S., Cal. Inst. Tech., 1947, Ph.D., 1951; m. Betty Jean Compton, June 28, 1944; children—Roderick Dale, Ann Keener. Merck postdoctoral fellow Stanford, 1951-52; asso. prof. physics U.S. Naval Postgrad. Sch., Monterey, Cal., 1952-57; NSF sr. postdoctoral fellow, Oxford, Eng., Trondheim, Norway, 1957-58; sr. biophysicist Oak Ridge Nat. Lab., 1958-62; vis. prof. microbiology Dartmouth, 1962-63; sr. investigator C.F. Kettering Research Lab., Yellow Springs, O., 1963-66; prof. biology, biophysics Cornell U., Ithaca, N.Y., 1966—. Instr., Marine Biol. Lab., Woods Hole, Mass. Pres., Carmel P.T.A., 1955-56, Willowbrook P.T.A., Oak Ridge, 1960-61. Served to 1st lt. USAAF, 1942-46. Decorated Air medal with oak leaf cluster. Fellow Am. Acad. Arts and scis., A.A.A.S.; mem. Am. Soc. Biol. Chemists, Biophys. Soc., Soc. Gen. Physiologists, Am. Soc. Plant Physiologists, Sigma Xi. Author: Molecular Physics in Photosynthesis, 1965; Light and Living Matter, 1970. Contbr. articles to profl. jours. Home: 111 Brandon Pl Ithaca NY 14850

CLAYTON, RUSSELL ADELBERT, cattle rancher; b. Elko, Nev., July 12, 1918; s. Charles A. and Carrie (Prunty) C.; B.S., U. Cal., 1942; m. Marie Urrusuno, Aug. 17, 1940; children—William C., Kathleen M. With various Kaiser Cos., 1942—, accountant-clk. Kaiser Co., Inc., Oakland, Cal., 1942-45, adminstrv. asst. Henry J. Kaiser Co., Oakland, 1945-46, with Kaiser Aluminum & Chem. Corp., Oakland, 1946—, chief accountant, 1946-50, controller, 1950-56, v.p. charge finance, 1957-61, pres. internat. div., 1961-67, v.p., 1967-72; cattle rancher XL Ranch, Nampa, Ida., 1972—. Address: Route 2 Box 2153 Nampa ID 83651

CLAYTON, WILBUR DORSEY, (Buck), musician; b. Parsons, Kan., Nov. 12, 1911; s. Simeon Oliver and Aritha (Dorsey) C.; student pub. schs., Parsons; m. Patricia Roberta DeVigne, Sept. 25, 1946; children—Candice, Steven. Began as musician, 1932; musician, Shanghai, China, 1934-36; with Count Basie's Band, 1936-43; toured Europe, 1949, 1953; contract musician Columbia Records, Inc., 1953--; trumpet soloist motion picture Benny Goodman Story. Served as staff sgt. AUS, 1943-46. Home: 145-31 Glassboro Av Jamaica NY 11435

CLAYTOR, HELEN NATALIE, civic worker; b. Mpls., Apr. 12, 1907; d. Madison S. and Amy B. (Wood) Jackson; B.A. cum laude, U. Minn., 1928; H.H.D., Eastern Mich. U., 1968; m. Earl W. Wilkins, Aug. 19, 1929 (dec. Jan. 1941); 1 son, Roger W.; m. 2d, Robert W. Claytor, Oct. 2, 1943; children—Judith Amy, Sharon Ann. Girl res. sec. Trenton (N.J.) YWCA, 1928-30; case worker Kansas City (Mo.) Provident Assn., 1939-32, Jackson County (Mo.) Emergency Relief Service, 1932-35; group work sec. Kansas City (Mo.) YWCA, 1935-40; race relations specialist nat. bd. YWCA, N.Y.C., 1940-44; pres. Grand Rapids (Mich.) YWCA, 1949-51; nat. pres. YWCA U.S., 1967—. Pres., Grand Rapids Community Health Service, 1957-59. Recipient Outstanding Achievement award U. Minn., 1968. Mem. Phi Beta Kappa, Alpha Kappa Alpha. Author: (with Juliet Bell) Study of Interracial Practices in Community YWCAs, 1943. Home: 2032 Coit Av NE Grand Rapids MI 49505

CLAYTOR, ROBERT BUCKNER, r.r. ofcl.; b. Roanoke, Va., Feb. 27, 1922; s. William Graham and Gertrude Harris (Boatwright) C.; grad. Mercersburg (Pa.) Acad., 1940; A.B. cum laude, Princeton, 1943; J.D., Harvard, 1948; m. Frances Tice, Sept. 25, 1943; children—Jane Gordon, Robert Harris, John Preston. Admitted to Mass. bar, 1948, N.Y. bar, 1949, Va. bar, 1952; atty. Am. Tel.&Tel. Co., 1948-51; solicitor N.&W. R.R., Roanoke, 1951-54, asst. gen. solicitor, 1954-56, asst. gen. counsel, 1956-60, gen. solicitor, 1960- 64, v.p. law, 1964-68, sr. v.p., 1968-70, exec. v.p., 1970—, also dir.; dir. Del. & Hudson Ry. Co., Dereco, Inc., Norfolk, Franklin & Danville Ry. Co., Richardson- Wayland Elec. Corp. Chancellor, Episcopal Diocese Southwestern Va., 1969- -, trustee diocese funds. Trustee Hollins Coll., VPI Ednl. Found., Burrell Meml. Hosp., Roanoke. Served to 1st lt. AUS, 1943-46. Mem. Am., Va., St. Louis, Roanoke bar assns., Phi Beta Kappa. Episcopalian. Clubs: Princeton (N.Y.C.); Metropolitan (Washington); Norfolk (Va.) Yacht and Country; Shenandoah (Roanoke). Home: 836 Wildwood Rd S W Roanoke VA 24014 Office: 8 N Jefferson St Roanoke VA 24011

CLAYTOR, WILLIAM GRAHAM, Jr., lawyer, r.r. ofcl.; b. Roanoke, Va., Mar. 14, 1912 s. William Graham and Gertrude Harris (Boatwright) C.; grad. Riverdale Country Sch., 1930; B.A., U. Va., 1933; LL.B. summa cum laude, Harvard, 1936; m. Frances Murray Hammond, Aug. 14, 1948; children—Frances Murray, William Graham III. Admitted to N.Y. bar, 1937, D.C. bar, 1938; law clk. U.S. Judge Learned Hand, 1936-37, Mr. Justice Brandeis, 1937-38; asso. firm Covington & Burling, Washington, 1938-47, partner, 1947-67; v.p. law So. Ry. Co., 1963-67, pres., 1967—, also dir.; chief exec. officer, dir. Central of Ga. R.R. Co., Ala. Gt. So. R.R. Co., Cin., New Orleans & Tex. Pacific Ry. Co., Ga. So. & Fla. Ry. Co., various other companies comprising So. Ry. System; dir. Fla. E. Coast Ry. Co., Richmond, Fredericksburg & Potomac R.R. Co., Richmond-Washington Co., Morgan Guaranty Trust Co., Penn Va. Corp. R.R., So. Ga. Ry. Co., Atlanta & E. Carolina Ry. Co., Interstate R.R. Co., Ala. Indsl. Realty Co., St. Johns River Terminal Company, Ga. Indsl. Realty Co.; dir. Fredericksburg and Potomac R.R. Co., Richmond- Washington Co., Fla. E. Coast Ry. Co., Riggs Nat. Bank, Penn Va. Corp. Dir., mem. exec. com. Assn. Am. Railroads. Trustee Episcopal Home Children, Washington, 1960-65, v.p., 1960-63; bd. govs. Beauvoir Sch., Washington, 1958- 61, St. Albans Sch., Washington, 1961-67. Served to lt. comdr. USNR, 1941-46. Mem. Am. Bar Assn., Am. Law Inst., Am. Judicature Soc. Democrat. Episcopalian. Clubs: Metropolitan, City Tavern Assn. (bd. govs. 1961-64) (Washington); Chevy Chase (Md.); Gibson Island (Md.); Shenandoah (Roanoke). Pres. Harvard Law Rev., 1935-36. Home: 2912 N St NW Washington DC 20007 Office: 920 15th St Washington DC 20005

CLEAGE, ALBERT B., Jr., pastor Central United Ch. of Christ, Detroit; named ch. Shrine of Black Madonna; leads congregation in worship of black Messiah. Founder Freedom Now Party, 1964. Address: 7625 Linwood Detroit MI 48206*

CLEAR, ALBERT F., Jr., hardware mfg. co. exec.; b. N.Y.C., June 9, 1920; s. Albert F. and Edna (Coyle) C.; B.S., Mass. Inst. Tech., 1942; M.B.A., Harvard, 1948; m. Jeanne Posselt, Aug. 7, 1947; children—Geoffrey-Posselt, Gregory Stuart. Vice pres., mgr. Mallory div. John B. Stetson Co., Danbury, Conn., 1948- 57; mng. asso. Booz-Allen & Hamilton, N.Y.C., 1957-65; v.p., gen. mgr. hardware div. Stanley Works, New Britain, Conn., 1965-69, v.p. consumer group, chmn. European operations, 1967-69, exec. v.p., 1969—; dir. Stanley Works, New Britain, Conn., Barden Corp., Denbury, Conn. Vice chmn. Mass. Inst. Tech. Center of N.Y., 1965; dir. Danbury chpt. A.R.C., 1953. Served to capt. AUS, 1942-46. Mem. Builders Hardware Mfrs. Assn. (exec. com.), Danbury (pres. 1954), New Britain (dir. 1967-69) chambers commerce. Rotarian. Home: 344 Westmont West Hartford CT 60117 Office: Stanley Works 195 Lake St New Britain CT 06050

CLEARY, CATHERINE BLANCHARD, trust co. exec.; b. Madison, Wis., Dec. 19, 1916; d. Michael J. and Bonnie (Blanchard) Cleary; A.B., U. Chgo., 1937; LL.B., U. Wis., 1943; LL.D., Ripon Coll., 1955, Alverno Coll., 1970. Apprentice Shady Hill Sch., Cambridge, Mass., 1937-38, tchr., 1938-39; tchr. New Canaan (Conn.) Country Sch., 1939-40; admitted to Wis. bar, 1943, Ill. bar, 1945; legal dept. Kohler Co. (Wis.), 1943-44; asso. Defrees, Fiske, O'Brien & Thomson, Chgo., 1944-47; with First Wis. Trust Co., Milw., 1947—, asst. trust officer, trust officer, exec. v.p., now pres. and dir.; dir. Wis. Telephone Co., First Wis. Bankshares Co.; trustee Northwestern Mut. Life Ins. Co. Asst. treas. U.S., 1953; asst. to sec. treasury, 1953-54. Mem. Am., Wis. (ho. of govs. 1951-52, chmn. com. fed. legislation 1952-53), Milw. bar assns. Clubs: University; Woman's of Wis.; Milwaukee Country. Home: 929 N Astor Milwaukee WI 53202 Office: 735 N Water St Milwaukee WI 53213

CLEARY, EDWARD JOHN, cons. engr.; b. Newark, June 16, 1906; s. Daniel A. and Bertha (Geiges) C.; B.S., Rutgers U., 1929, M.S., 1933, C.E., 1935, Sc.D., 1959; m. Adelaide Rogers, June 16, 1934; children—Edward R., Kathleen S., Daniel H., Adelaide Ellen. Field engr. Utilities Power & Light Corp., Chgo., 1929-31; mem. editorial staff Engr. News Record (pub. McGraw Hill Co.), 1935—, exec. editor, 1945-49; exec. dir., chief engr. Ohio River Valley Water Sanitation Commn., Cin., 1949-67, cons., 1967—. Adj. prof. environmental health U. Cin., 1967—. Bd. dirs. Resources for Future, Washington. Registered profl. engr., N.Y., Ohio, N.J. Diplomate Am. Acad. Environmental Engrs. Mem. Am. Pub. Health Assn., Am. Soc. C.E., Water Pollution Control Fedn. (hon.), Engring. Soc. Cin., Brit. Inst. Pollution Control (hon.), Am. Pub. Works Assn. (pres.), Am. Water Works Assn. (hon.), Inter Am. Assn. San. Engring., Nat. Acad. Engring., Sigma Xi, Tau Beta Pi, Delta Upsilon. Roman Catholic. Club: Cosmos. Co-author: Bulldozers Come First, 1944. Author: The Orsanco Story, 1967. Home: 421 Bond Pl Cincinnati OH 45206 Office: 414 Walnut St Cincinnati OH 45202

CLEARY, EDWARD WILLIAM, diversified forest products co. exec.; b. Sergeant Bluff, Ia., May 21, 1919; s. Edward D. and Laura Helen (Rich) C.; B.A., DePauw U., 1941; B.S.C., Ohio State U., 1947; m. Arita Louise Hefferan, June 12, 1946; children—John William, Kathryn Louise, Patricia Jane. Sr. accountant Price Waterhouse & Co., Portland, Ore., 1947-53; treas., controller Nat. Hosp. Assn., Portland, 1953-55; treas., controller Valsetz Lumber Co., Portland, 1955-60; asst. comptroller Boise Cascade Corp. (Ida.), 1960-63, comptroller, 1963-68, v.p., comptroller, 1968, v.p., treas, 1968—. Mem. Pacific N.W. Area council YMCA, 1967-70; mem. exec. com. Boise United Fund, 1966-69, chmn. budget com., 1966-69; pres., bd. dirs. YMCA, 1967-69; bd. dirs. Ida. Blue Cross Hosp. Assn. Served with AUS, 1941-42, USNR, 1942-46. Mem. Am. Inst. C.P.A.'s, Ida. Soc. C.P.A.'s, Financial Execs. Inst., Nat. Assn. Accountants (past pres. Boise chpt., past nat. dir.), Stuart Cameron McLeod Soc. Home: 2018 N Beach St Boise ID 83704 Office: PO Box 200 Boise ID 83701

CLEARY, FRANK JOSEPH, brewing exec.; b. Phila., July 6, 1930; s. Frank and Rebecca (Carbrey) C.; B.S., Wharton Sch., U. Pa., 1952; M.B.A., Rutgers U., 1957. Asst. to controller Curtiss-Wright Co., Woodridge, N.J., 1954-59; dir. corporate systems Aerojet Gen. Corp., Los Angeles, 1959-67; asst. comptroller ITT Gilfillan, Los Angeles, 1967-69; v.p. finance, treas. Lucky Breweries, Inc., San Francisco, 1969—; v.p., treas. Capital Estates Corp., Premium Brands Corp.; asst. prof. Sacramento State Coll., 1961, U. Cal. At Los Angeles, 1966-68. Mem. Cal. Electronic Data Processing Policy Bd., 1967—, Cal. Adv. Com. Higher Edn., 1968; chmn. edn. sect. Gov.'s Survey Efficiency and Cost Control, 1967. Served to 1st lt. AUS, 1952-54; maj. Res. Mem. Los Angeles Assn. Systems Mgmt. (pres. 1967), Am. Inst. Indsl. Engrs., Financial Execs. Inst. Contbr. articles profl. jours. Home: 817 N Humboldt St San Mateo CA 94401 Office: 2601 Newhall St San Francisco CA 94124

CLEARY, GEORGE EDWARD, lawyer; b. Platteville, Wis., Nov. 7, 1890; s. Thomas L. and Ada Jane (Grindell) C.; B.A., U. Wis., 1911, LL.B., 1914; m. Lulu M. Rundell, Nov. 21, 1915; 1 dau., Elizabeth Ann; m. 2d, Frances Power, July 2, 1936; 1 son, George Edward. Assessor incomes, Platteville, 1914-16; prof. law U. Mont., 1916-18; sec. adv. tax bd. Bur. Internal Revenue, 1919; mem. firm Root, Clark, Buckner & Ballantine, N.Y.C., 1926-45; mem. firm Cleary, Gottleib, Steen & Hamilton, N.Y.C. 1946—. Mem. Commerce and Industry Assn. N.Y. (dir.), Order of Coif, Phi Beta Kappa, Beta Gamma Sigma. Republican. Roman Catholic. Clubs: City Midday, University (N.Y.C.). Home: 784 Park Av New York City NY 10021 Office: 1 State St Plaza New York City NY 10004

CLEARY, JAMES ROY, lawyer; b. Springville, Ala., July 16, 1926; s. Bereman Leroy and Bertie (Jones) C.; B.A., Birmingham-So. Coll., 1948; J.D., Northwestern U., 1951; m. Miriam Voncille James, Apr. 10, 1960; children—Johanna, Susan. Admitted to Ala. bar, 1951; practice in Huntsville, 1956—; atty. Dept. Army, Redstone Arsenal, 1951-55; mem. firm Bell, Richardson, Cleary, McLain & Tucker, 1955—. Vice pres. Security Fed. Savs. Assn.; dir. Am. Nat. Bank, Huntsville. Sec., trustee Birmingham-So. Coll. Named Young Man of Year, Huntsville, 1957. Mem. Ala. Jr. C. of C. (past v.p.). Club: Alabama-Mississippi Dist. Optimist International (past lt. gov.). Home: 1709 Mont Dale Rd SE Huntsville AL 35801 Office: PO Box 2008 408 Franklin St Huntsville AL 35801

CLEARY, JAMES W., coll. pres.; b. Milw., Apr. 16, 1927; Ph.B., Marquette U., 1950, M.A., 1951; Ph.D. (univ. fellow 1954-55), U. Wis.; married 1950. Instr., dir. forensics high sch., Wis., 1949-51; instr. speech, head coach debate Marquette U., 1951-53; from instr. to prof. speech U. Wis., then vice chancellor acad. affairs, 1956-69; pres. San Fernando Valley State Coll., 1969—. Served to 2d lt. AUS, 1945-47. Mem. Speech Communication Assn. Author books in field including Robert's Rules of Order Newly Revised. Co-editor: Bibliography of Rhetoric and Public Address. Address: 18111 Nordhoff St Northridge CA 91324*

CLEARY, JOHN JOSEPH, journalist; b. Cleve., Mar. 7, 1905; s. John Joseph and Susan Ann (MacLain) C.; L.H.B., Cath. U. Am., 1927. Asst. financial editor Cleve. News, 1928-36, marine editor, 1936-46, bus. editor, 1946-49, financial editor, 1949-60, columnist, 1946-60; gen. bus. editor Cleve. Plain Dealer, 1960—. Served to 1st lt. AUS, 1942-46. Mem. Sigma Delta Chi (pres. Cleve. chpt. 1957-58). Home: 12506 Edgewater Dr Lakewood OH 44107 Office: 1801 Superior Av Cleveland OH 44114

CLEARY, JOHN VINCENT, electric utility exec.; b. Liberty, N.Y., Oct. 15, 1901; s. John P. and Sarah Jane (Tracy) C.; B.S., Cooper Union Coll., 1925; spl. courses, N.Y.U., 1925-28; m. Lillian Dacey, June 1, 1926; children—John V., Thomas J. Asst. controller Consol. Edison Co. of N.Y., Inc., N.Y.C., 1936-46, sr. asst. controller, 1946-52, controller, 1952-57, v.p., chief accounting officer, 1957-62, sr. v.p., 1962-65, pres., 1965—. Mem. Financial Execs. Inst., Edison Electric Inst., Am. Gas. Assn. Roman Catholic. Clubs: Manhattan; Leewood Golf (Crestwood, N.Y.). Home: 1225 Midland Av Bronxville NY 10708 Office: 4 Irving Pl New York City NY 10003

CLEARY, JOHN WASHINGTON, lawyer; b. Milw., Feb. 22, 1911; s. Peter A. and Mathilda A. (Borning) C.; J.D., Marquette U., 1933; m. Alice M. Shinners, Jan. 15, 1938; children—Terrence P., Mary E., Peter J., Margaret A., John T., Catherine A. Admitted to Wis. bar, 1933, since practiced in Milw.; partner firm Erbstoeszer, Cleary & Zabel, 1936—. Sec. Hopkins Savs. & Loan Assn., Milw., 1936-65, pres., 1965—. Faculty Savs. and Loan Inst., Milw., 1961- 63. Vice chmn. Milw. Commn. Community Relations, 1959-63; savs. and loan commr. Wis., 1963-65. Bd. dirs. Greater Milw. chpt. A.R.C., pres. 1961-63; trustee Marquette U. High Sch.; gov. nat. A.R.C. Mem. Wis. Legislative Council, Milw. Savs. and Loan Council (pres. 1948-50), Wis. (pres. 1954-55), U.S. (bd. dirs. 1962-63) savs. and loan leagues. Home: 2728 N 98th St Milwaukee WI 53222 Office: 7901 W Burleigh St Milwaukee WI 53222

CLEARY, JON, author; b. Sydney, Australia, Nov. 22, 1917; s. Matthew and Ida (Brown) C.; ed. pub. sch., Sydney. Formerly journalist Australian Govt. Bur., London and N.Y.C.; full-time writer, 1945—. Co-winner 1st prize Australian Broadcasting Commn.'s Nat. Play award, 1944; 2d prize Sydney Morning Herald Nat. Novel contest, 1946; Crouch gold medal for best Australian Novel, 1950; co-winner Australian sect. N.Y. Herald Tribune World Story contest, Author: These Small Glories, 1946; You Can't See Around the Corners, 1947; The Long Shadow, 1950; Just Let Me Be, 1951; The Sundowners, 1952; The Climate of Courage, 1954; Justin Bayard, 1955; The Green Helmet, 1958; Black of Sunset, 1959; North From Thursday, 1961; The Country of Marriage, 1962; Forests of the Night, 1963; Sundowners, 1965; High Commissioner, 1966; Season of Doubt, 1968; Remember Jack Hoxie, 1969; Helga's Web, 1970; also film and TV scripts. Home: Riverview Rd Clareville Beach New South Wales Australia*

CLEARY, ROBERT EDWARD, univ. dean; b. East Orange, N.J., Feb. 27, 1932; s. Charles A. and Mary J. (Solomon) C.; B.A. in Social Sci., Montclair (N.J.) State Coll., 1953; M.A. in Polit. Sci., Rutgers U., 1959, Ph.D., 1962; m. Marilyn F. Jacoby, Apr. 21, 1956; children—Barbara, Kevin, Charles. Asst. dir. secondary sch. project Eagleton Inst. Politics, Rutgers U., 1959-61; asst. prof. polit. sci. Geroge Peabody Coll. for Tchrs., 1961-64; asst. dir. Am. Polit. Sci. Assn., 1966-67; asso. prof., asso. dean Sch. Govt. and Pub. Adminstrn., Am. U., Washington, 1965-70, prof. govt., dean acad. devel., 1970—. Mem. Am. Polit. Sci. Assn. (Congl. fellow 1964-65), Nat. Council Social Studies. Contbr. articles to profl. jours. Home: 9208 Adelaide Dr Bethesda MD 20034

CLEARY, WILLIAM EDWARD, assn. exec.; b. Bklyn., July 20, 1906; s. Philip H. and Rose (McMullen) C.; B.S. magna cum laude, Georgetown U., 1929; B.B.A., Browne Bus. Coll., Bklyn., 1930; D.Sc., Cleary Coll., 1955. Asso., Cleary Bros., Inc., N.Y.C., 1930-44, pres., chmn. bd., 1940- 44; gen. mgr. Jacobus Transp. Co., Inc., 1944-51; pres. N.Y. Tow Boat Exchange and Harbor Carriers Port of N.Y., 1952—; exec. sec. N.Y. State Waterways Assn., sec.-treas., dir. Am. Waterways Operators, Inc., 1952—. Cons., adviser N.Y.C., N.Y. State Civil Def. authorities on N.Y. Harbor; mem. civil def. adv. panel USCG on N.Y. Harbor; handled labor negotiations for marine transp. industry, N.Y. Harbor, 1952—. Vice pres., trustee Victory Meml. Hosp., Bklyn., 1956—; trustee Cleary Coll., Ypsilanti, Mich.; bd. chmn. Holy Family Home for Aged, Bklyn. Named Man of Week, Bklyn. Community Councils, 1953. Mem. Canal Hist. Soc. N.Y. State (pres., dir.), Soc. Naval Architects and Marine Engrs., Propeller Club U.S., Naval Inst. Clubs: Whitehall, Downtown Athletic (N.Y.C.). Home: 74 Gatling Pl Brooklyn NY 11209 Office: 17 Battery Pl New York City NY 10004

CLEAVELAND, CHARLES H., gas co. exec.; b. 1908; B.S., Lehigh U., 1931; LL.B., St. John's U. 1953. With Bklyn. Union Gas Co., 1931—, treas., 1962—. Address: 195 Montague St Brooklyn NY 11201*

CLEAVELAND, FREDERIC NEILL, educator; b. Phoenix, Oct. 30, 1915; s. John Frederic and Zelma (Bailey) C.; A.B., Duke 1937, M.A. in History, 1942; M.A. in Politics, Princeton, 1950, Ph.D., 1951; m. Barbara Ann Henry, Dec. 28, 1940; children—Marilyn Ruth (Mrs. John F. Lundberg), Barbara Ann (Mrs. Stephen McNees), Kenneth David. Field tng. supr. A.R.C., 1942-43, field dir., 1943-44; instr. govt. Washington Sq. Coll., N.Y. U., 1950-51; faculty U. N.C., Chapel Hill, 1951-71, prof. polit. sci., 1957-71, chmn. dept. 1958-70, research asso. Inst. Research Social Sci., 1957-58, research prof., 1958- 71, chmn. faculty, 1967-70; prof. polit. sci., provost Duke, 1971—. Vis. prof. polit. sci. U. Cal. at Berkeley, 1959-60; vis. sr. staff mem. govtl. studies Brookings Instn., 1964-66. Mem. adv. com. govt. programs in behavioral scis. Nat. Acad. Scis., 1967-69. Mem. Chapel Hill Planning Bd., 1955-59, 62-63, 66-70. Served with med. dept. AUS, 1944-46. Mem. Am., So. (pres. 1964-65) polit. sci. assns., Am. Soc. Pub. Adminstrn., Nat. Acad. Pub. Adminstrn. (research dir. edn. programs 1970-71), Nat. Inst. Pub. Affairs (pres. 1971), Phi Beta Kappa. Author: Science and State Government, 1959. Editor: Congress and Urban Problems: A Casebook on the Legislative Process, 1968. Contbr. profl. jours. Home: 1822 N Lakeshore Dr Chapel Hill NC 27514

CLEAVER, J. BENJAMIN, lawyer; b. Dixon, Ill., Sept. 2, 1898; s. Joseph Brierton and Violet May (Canfield) C.; student U. Ill., 1922-23; LL.B., Chgo.-Kent Coll. Law, 1926; m. Helen Louise Haas, Sept. 25, 1926; children—Helen Louise (Mrs. Robert K. Smither), Joseph B. Admitted to Ill. bar, 1926; practiced in Chgo., 1929-70; ret. as partner firm Kirkland, Ellis, Hodson, Chaffetz & Masters, Chgo. Mem. Am., Ill., Chgo. bar assns., Delta Theta Phi. Republican. Presbyn. Clubs: Mid-Am. (Chgo.); Exmoor Country (Highland Park). Home: 1854 Somerset Lane Northbrook IL 60062

CLEAVER, LEROY ELDRIDGE, author, Black militant; b. Wabbaseka, nr. Little Rock, 1935; s. Leroy and Thelma Cleaver; m. Kathleen Neal, Dec. 27, 1967; 1 son, Antonio Maceo. Author: Soul on Ice, 1968; Post-Prison Writings and Speeches, 1969. Asst. editor Ramparts. Spokesman for Black Panthers. Address: 301 Broadway San Francisco CA 94133*

CLEAVER, WILLIAM PENNINGTON, sugar refining co. exec.; b. Newark, Nov. 13, 1914; s. Chester H. and Mildred (Day) C.; A.B., Princeton, 1937; m. Virginia Whaley, Apr. 15, 1938; children—Jane P. With Amstar Corp. (formerly Am. Sugar Co.), N.Y.C., 1937—, raw sugar buyer, 1954-57, v.p., 1957—. Presbyn. Home: 38 Manor Av Cranford NJ 07016 Office: 1251 Av of Americas New York City NY 10020

CLEAVES, HERBERT MARTIN, assn. exec.; b. Lowell, Mass., Feb. 27, 1911; s. William S. and Blanche (Blake) C.; A.B., Harvard, 1933; m. Barbara Morrison, March 6, 1936 (dec. Mar. 1963); children—Deborah, Craig, Linda; m. 2d, Madolyn Wood, May 16, 1964; With the sales dept. Aetna Life Ins. Co., 1933-34, Am. Tissue Mills., 1934-36; with Gen. Foods Corp., 1936—, beginning in sales areas. successively nat. sales mgr. Diamond Crystall Salt div., marketing mgr. asso. products div., gen., v.p.-marketing, 1961-64, sr. v.p., 1964-71, dir., 1960-71; vice chmn. Council Better Bus. Burs., N.Y.C., 1970—. Dir., trustee Nutrition Founds., Inc., 1965-70; chmn. nat. marketing adv. com. Dept. Commerce, 1969-70. Mem. Grocery Mfrs. Am. (dir. 1960-70), Newcomen Soc. Clubs: Harvard (New Canaan, Conn.); Norwalk (Conn.) Yacht; Harvard (N.Y.C.); Portland (Me.) Yacht; International (Washington). Home: 22 Intervale Rd Darien CT 06820 Office: Council of Better Business Bureaus Inc 845 3d Av New York City NY 10022

CLEAVINGER, HOWARD CARSON, editor; b. Wallace, Ida., July 25, 1910; s. George Walter and Helga (Berg) C.; grad. high sch.; m. Mary Lou Weatherton, May 17, 1932. With Wallace Press-Times, 1928-34; reporter Spokane (Wash.) Daily Chronicle, 1934-41, city editor, 1941-47, mng. editor, 1947—. Mem. A.P. Mng. Editors Assn., Am. Soc. Newspaper Editors, Sigma Delta Chi. Conglist. Clubs: Spokane, Spokane Country. Home: N 8909 Mountain View Lane Spokane WA Office: Spokane Daily Chronicle Spokane WA 99204

CLEBORNE, GUY MILLER, steel co. exec.; b. Bridgeport, Conn., Jan. 20, 1927; s. Edmund B. and Mary (Miller) C.; grad. Phillips Exeter Acad., 1944; B.S., Yale 1947; m. Ruth Larrabee, Nov. 29, 1952; children—Keith D., Guy E., Rockwell J. With Wallingford Steel Co. (Conn.), 1948-65, v.p. gen. mgr. sales, 1960-65; treas. Allegheny Ludlum Steel Corp., Pitts., 1965—. Originator, dir. 1st United Fund, Wallingford, 1959; mem. nat. adv. council United Fund, 1960-65; past head fund drives A.R.C., Am. Cancer Soc., YMCA, Wallingford. Mem. Wallingford Bd. Finance, 1958-61. Served to capt. USMCR, 1944-46, 51-52. Named Man of Year, Wallingford Jr. C. of C., 1961. Mem. Am. Iron and Steel Inst. Home: 8 N Pasadena Dr Pittsburgh PA 15215

CLEBSCH, WILLIAM ANTHONY, educator; b. Clarksville, Tenn., July 27, 1923; s. Alfred and Julia (Wilee) C.; B.A., U. Tenn., 1946; B.D., Theol. Sem. Va., 1946, S.T.M., 1951; Th.D., Union Theol. Sem., N.Y.C., 1957; M.A. status, Clare Coll., Cambridge U., 1959-60; m. Betsy Berkeley Birchfield, June 10, 1944; children—William Ernst, Sarah Elizabeth. Lectr. religion, Episcopal chaplain Mich. State U., 1946-49; instr., asst. prof. ch. history Theol. Sem. Va., 1949-56; asso. prof., prof. history Theol. Sem. of S.W., 1956-64; asso. prof. religion Stanford, 1964-67, prof. religion and humanities, 1967—, chmn. humanities spl. programs, 1967—, vice chmn. Faculty Senate, 1968-69, chmn., 1969—; cons. on religion World Book Ency. Sr. fellow Nat. Ednowment for Humanities, 1971-72. Fellow Am. Assn. Theol. Schs., Soc. Religion in Higher Edn.; mem. Ch. Hist. Soc. (dir.), Am. Soc. Ch. History (dir.), Am. Acad. Religion, Soc. for Reformation Research, Am. Assn. U. Profs., Nat. Humanities Faculty (dir.). Democrat. Author: (with C.R. Jaekle) Pastoral Care in Historical Perspective, 1964; England's Earliest Protestants, 1964; From Sacred To Profane America, 1968; Christian Interpretations of the Civil War, 1969. Home: 847 Mayfield Av Stanford CA 94305

CLEERE, ALBERT EUGENE, banker; b. Ellis County, Tex., Mar. 11, 1905; s. Thomas Moore and Mary Frances (Sugg) C.; student Houston Jr. Coll., Am. Inst. Banking; m. Edna Mae Tompkins, Nov. 17, 1924; children—Barbara Ellen (Mrs. J. Wright Wilson), Patricia Lynne (Mrs. Robert Strybos). With First City Nat. Bank, Houston, 1920—, auditor, 1942-45, comptroller, 1945-47, v.p., comptroller, 1947-56, sr. v.p., 1956—; pres., dir. Gulfgate State Bank, Houston, 1958-69, Harrisburg Bank, Houston, 1964—, Heights State Bank, Houston; chmn. bd. La Porte State Bank (Tex.), 1960- -; v.p., dir. First State Bank of Clear Lake City, 1964—; sec.-treas., dir. Pearl Beer Distbrs., Houston, 1958—; dir. Clear Lake Savs. Assn. Instr., Tex. Bankers Assn. ednl. conf., Austin, 1955-58; mem. exec. com., trustee NABAC Sch. Bank Audit, Control and Operations, 1966—. Mem. Gulf Coast (past pres.), Nat. (dir.-at-large, nat. dir., v.p. Tex.) assns. bank auditors and comptrollers, Financial Execs. Inst. (past dir., v.p. Houston), Gulfgate Bd. Trade (dir.). Clubs: Houston, Executive, Variety (Houston); Bayshore, Houston Yacht (La Porte, Tex.); Lakewood Yacht (Seabrook). Home: Route 1 Box 582 Seabrook TX 77585 Office: First City Nat Bank Houston TX 77002

CLEERE, ROY LEON, pub. health physician; b. Madisonville, Tex., Dec. 20, 1905; s. James Lee and Florence (Randolph) C.; B.S., Tex. A. and M., 1927; M.D., U. Tex., 1929; M.P.H., Johns Hopkins, 1936; m. Alice Stemmons, July 10, 1931. Intern Kansas City Gen. Hosp., Kansas City, Mo., 1929-30; Presbyn. Hosp., Denver, 1930-31; pvt. practice, Denver, 1931- 35; sec. Colo. Bd. Health and exec. dir. Colo. Dept. Pub. Health, 1935—. Fellow Am. Pub. Health Assn.; mem. A.M.A., Denver City and County, Colo. State med. socs. Mem. Christian Ch. Home: 1266 Bellaire St Denver CO 80220 Office: 4210 E 11th Av Denver CO 80220

CLEGG, ANTHONY, hotel exec.; b. Eng., Feb. 14, 1921; s. Arthur Markland and Margery (Evelyn) G.; ed. Taunton (Eng.) Sch.; m. Joyce Valerie Mills, Aug. 30, 1953. Gen. mgr. Royal Tehran Hilton, 1962-64, Tokyo Hilton, 1964-68; area dir. Hilton Internat., Co., Africa and W. Asia, 1968—; chmn. Nairobi Hilton (Kenya), Ltd. Mem. Hotel and Catering Inst. Home: Mau Park Rd Nairobi Kenya Office: P O Box 30680 Nairobi Kenya

CLEGG, CHARLES MYRON, Jr., author, editor, corp. exec.; b. Youngstown, O., June 29, 1916; s. Charles Myron and Ruth (Standish) C.; spl. photog. student J. Ghrislain Lootens. Editor, v.p. Territorial Enterprise, Virginia City, Nev., 1952-61; pres. Nev. Alvarado Corp., 1965—; splty. r.r. photogrphy, history Western Am., Am. transp. Bd. chmn. Lucius Morris Beebe Meml. Found., 1966—. Mem. Internat. Platform Assn., Ry. and Locomotive Hist. Soc., Nat. Ry. Hist. Soc. Author (with Lucius Beebe): U.S. West, the Saga of Wells Fargo, 1949; Virginia and Truckee, A Story of Virginia City and Comstock Times, 1949; Legends of the Comstock Lode, 1950; Cable Car Carnival, 1951; Hear the Train Blow: A Pictorial Epic of America, 1952; The American West, The Pictorial Epic of a Continent, 1955; Steam Cars to the Comstock, 1957; The Age of Steam, Classic of American Railroading, 1957; Narrow Gauge in the Rockies, 1958; (with Lucius Beebe) Great Railroad Photographs, U.S.A., 1964, The Trains We Rode, Vol. I, 1965, vol. II, 1966. Editor: (with Lucius Beebe) Dreadful California, 1948. Pictorial collaborator (with Lucius Beebe): Highball, A Pageant of Trains, 1945; Mixed Train Daily, A Book of Short Line Railroads, 1947; Narrow Gauge in the Rockies, 1959, San Francisco's Golden Era: A Picture Story Before the Fire, 1960; Rio Grande, Mainline of the Rockies, 1962; When Beauty Rode the Rails, A Pictorial Album of Old-time Railroading, 1962. Compiler, editor: (with Duncan Emrich) The Lucius Beebe Reader, 1967. Contbr. articles to various mags. Address: Union and A Sts Virginia City NV 89440

CLEGG, COURTNEY GEE, former naval med. officer; b. Greenville, Tex., June 10, 1902; s. Edwin Booth and Lucie Gowan (Gee) C.; A.B., U. Cal., 1924, M.D., 1928; m. Margaret Walker children—James Courtney, Mary Jane. Commd. lt. (j.g.) M.C., USN, 1927, advanced through grades to rear adm., 1955; assigned various naval hosps., U.S. also various ships; fleet surgeon staff Comdr. in Chief, U.S. Pacific Fleet, Pearl Harbor, Hawaii, 1958, 60; dist. med. officer 9th Naval Dist., Great Lakes, Ill., 1960-62; dir. med. edn. French Hosp., San Francisco, 1962-66; now disability determination program cons., Oakland, Cal. Decorated Legion of Merit. Diplomate Am. Bd. Surgery. Fellow A.C.S., Phila. Acad. Surgeons; mem. Phi Chi. Mason (32, Shriner). Home: 654 Funston Av San Francisco CA 94118 Office: 1111 Jackson St Oakland CA 94607

CLEGHORN, REESE, editor; b. Lyerly, Ga., Apr. 9, 1930; s. John Storey and Nona (Reese) C.; M.A. in Pub. Law and Govt., Columbia, 1956; B.A., Emory U., 1950; m. Gwendolyn Michael, Dec. 28, 1954; children—Nona Elizabeth, John Michael. Gen. assignments reporter Atlanta Jour., 1950-54, 52-54; reporter editor A.P., 1954-58; editor, co-pub. Cal. Courier, Fresno, 1958-60; asst. city editor, state news editor Atlanta Jour., 1960-63, editorial writer, 1963- 64, asso. editor, 1964-69; dir. Leadership Project, So. Regional Council, editor South Today, 1969—; part-time tchr. journalism Ga. State U., 1963-65. Mem. Mayor Atlanta Housing Resources Com., 1968—. Bd. dirs. Acad. Theatre, Atlanta, 1968—. Served with USAF, 1951-52. Mem. Sigma Delta Chi (pres. Atlanta 1966), Omicron Delta Kappa, Chi Phi. Presbyn. Club: Atlanta Press. Author: (with Pat Watters) Climbing Jacob's Ladder, 1967; also articles. Home: Atlanta GA Office: So Regional Council 5 Forsyth St N W Atlanta GA 30303

CLEGHORN, ROBERT ALLEN, educator, psychiatrist; b. Cambridge, Mass., Oct. 6, 1904; s. Allen Mackenzie and Edna (Cartshore) G.; M.D., U. Toronto, 1928; D.Sc. in Physiology, Marischal Coll., Aberdeen, Scotland, 1932; m. Sheena Marnoch, Apr. 2, 1932; children—Mhairi, Jane (Mrs. Z.M. Santiago), Ailie M. (Mrs. B.D. Fletcher), John M. Rotating intern Toronto Gen. Hosp., 1928-29; asst. physiology Marischal Coll., Aberdeen, Scotland, 1929-32; asst. attending physician Toronto Gen. Hosp., 1933-46; dir. lab. exptl. therapeutics Allan Meml. Inst., Montreal, 1946-64; psychiatrist-in-chief Royal Victoria Hosp., 1964-70; prof., psychiatry McGill U., 1960—, chmn. dept., 1964-70. Fellow Royal Coll. Physicians and Surgeons, Am. Coll. Psychiatrists; mem. Am. Psychosomatic Soc. (past pres.), Que. Psychiat. Assn. Author numerous articles in field. Home: 3160 St Sulpice Rd Montreal Quebec Canada

CLEINO, EDWARD HENRY, music educator; b. Rolla, Mo., Jan. 29, 1917; s. Henry and Lulu (Phariss) C.; B.S., S.E. Mo. State Coll., 1938; M.A., George Peabody Coll., 1940, Ed.D., 1958; m. Elizabeth Anne White, Mar. 7, 1943; children—Anne Louise (Mrs. James Ivy), William Henry, Jeanne Marie, (Mrs. Edward Darling), Catherine Elizabeth, Barbara Claire. Prin. percussionist St. Louis Philharmonic, 1933-35; tchr. music New Madrid (Mo.) High Sch., 1938-39; dir. music Vanderbilt U., 1939-42; mem. music staff George Peabody Coll., summers 1939-41; chmn. dept. fne arts edn. U. Ala., University, 1949—. Served with USAAF, 1942-45. Named Ky col. Mem. Soc. Research Music Edn., Music Educators Nat. Conf. (life, pres. So. div. 1970—), Pi Kappa Lambda, Kappa Delta Pi, Phi Delta Kappa, Phi Mu Alpha. Episcopalian (lay reader). Contbr. articles to profl. jours. Home: 7 Hickory Hill Tuscaloosa AL 35401 Office: Box 1912 University AL 35486

CLELAND, GEORGE L., ednl. adminstr.; b. Hoyt, Kan., Feb. 9, 1904; s. Frank Estel and Laura Elizabeth (White) C.; A.B., Baker U., 1926, Pd.D., 1959; A.M., Columbia, 1935; Ed.D., Kan. U., 1958; m. Virginia Penick, July 27, 1930; children—John David, Joseph Le. Country sch. tchr., Whiting, Kan., 1922-24; math. tchr., coach, Effingham, Kan., 1926-31; dir. extra class activities, Atchison, Kan., 1931-35; prin. Atchison Jr.-Sr. High Sch., 1935-52; became dir. secondary curriculum Kan. Dept. Edn., 1952, now asst. commr. edn. Vis. lectr. Kan. State Coll., Manhattan, summer 1948-49; mem. Nat. Com. on Secondary Edn., 1965—. John Hay fellow U. Ore., 1962. Mem. Kan. State (legislative council 1944-48), Kan. (bd. control 1952) activities assn., Kan. Prins. Assn. (pres. 1949), Nat. Assn. Secondary Sch. Prins. (exec. com. 1952-58, pres. 1956-57), N.E.A., Nat. Com. Devel. Sci. and Engrs., Council Advancement Secondary Edn., Nat. Com. Exptl. Projects Secondary Edn., Phi Delta Kappa, Kappa Sigma. Republican. Methodist. Mason, Kiwanian (lt. gov. 1948). Club: Educators. Contbr. articles to profl. publs. Address: 1256 Wayne Av Topeka KS 66604

CLELLAND, RICHARD COOK, educator; b. Camden, N.Y., Aug. 23, 1921; s. Ford John and Beryl (Cook) C.; B.A., Hamilton Coll., 1944; A.M., Columbia, 1949; Ph.D., U. Pa., 1956; m. Anne Chapin Buel, June 16, 1963; children—Richard Buel, Susan Elizabeth. Asst. prof. U. Pa., Phila., 1956-61, asso. prof., 1961-66, prof., chmn. dept. statistics and operations research, 1966-71, acting dean Wharton Sch., 1971—; statis. cons. to bus., govt. and research orgns. Served with Signal Corps, AUS, 1944-46. Mem. Operations Research Soc. Am., Math. Assn. Am., Am. Statis. Assn., Inst. Math. Statistics, Am. Assn. U. Profs. Author: (with M.W. Tate) Nonparametric and Shortcut Statistics, 1957; (with J.B. O'Hara) Effective Use of Statistics in Accounting and Business, 1964; (with others) Basic Statistics with Business Applications, 1966. Home: 422 S 47th St Philadelphia PA 19143

CLELLAND, ROD, hosp. adminstr.; b. Imperial, Cal., Oct. 17, 1916; s. George Andrew and Laura (Miller) C.; B.F.A. with high distinction, U. Ariz., 1937; M.B.A., Ariz. State U., 1966; Ph.D. candidate U. Ga., 1970-73; m. Nathel Stapley, Dec. 21, 1936; children—Velda Jean (Mrs. Brian Hutchings), Rick A., Michael Dow, Marty Kathleen (Mrs. Michael Abercrombie), Jacquelyn Dee (Mrs. David McDonald), Christine Anne (Mrs. Lynn Archer), Jeffrey George, Shelly Gay. Exec. sec. Ariz. Council Assns., Phoenix, 1947-52; bus. adminstr. Ariz. State Hosp., Phoenix, 1952-64; adminstr. Maryvale Community Hosp., Phoneix, 1964-67; asst. supt. adminstrv. Central State Hosp., Milledgeville, Ga., 1967—. Mem. bd. Bapt. Hosp., Scottsdale, Ariz., 1962-63. Served with USNR, World War II. Fellow Am. Coll. Hosp. Adminstrs.; mem. Assn. Mental Hosp. Adminstrs. (past pres., past chmn. bd. govs.), Nat. Assn. Hosp. Purchasing Agts. (past pres.), Am. Hosp. Assn., Nat. Assn. Purchasing Agts. (past dir.), Am., Ga. pub. health assns., Baldwin County Mental Health Assn., Iota Sigma Alpha, Alpha Mu Gamma, Delta Psi Omega. Mem. Ch. of Jesus Christ of Latter-day Saints. Kiwanian. Contbr. articles profl. jours. Home: 1732 Columbine Rd Milledgeville GA 31061 Office: Central State Hospital Milledgeville GA 31061

CLEMENCE, GERALD MAURICE, astronomer; b. Greenville, R.I., Aug. 16, 1908; s. Richard R. and Lora E. (Oatley) C.; Ph.B., Brown U., 1930; Sc.D., Case Inst. Tech., 1954; Dr., Univ. de Cuyo (Argentina), 1961; m. Edith M. Vail, Aug. 17, 1929; children—Gerald V., Thedore G. Jr. astronomer Naval Obs., 1930-37, asst. astonomer, 1937-40, astronomer, 1940- 42, sr. astronomer, 1942-45, head astronomer and dir. Nautical Almanac, U.S. Naval Obs., Washington, 1945-58; sci. dir. Naval Obs., 1958-63; sr. research asso., lectr. astonomy Yale 1963-66, prof. astronomy, 1966—. Chmn. div. phys. scis. NRC, 1963-66; vis. prof. astronomy Columbia, 1958. Adviser Internat. com. on weights and measures Assn. Royal Astron. Soc., 1952, gold medal, 1965. Recipient USN award for distinguished achievement, 1963, superior achievement, 1964. Mem. A.A.A.S. (sect. chmn., v.p. 1954); mem. Inst. Nav. (charter mem., councillor 1945-57), Internat. Astron. Union (pres. commn. on clestial mechanics 1948-55, pres. commn. on ephemrides 1946-67), Academia Nacional de Ciencias Exactas, Fiaicas y Naturales de Buenos Aires (Argentina), Bur. Geophysics, Am. Astron. Soc. (councillor 1949-52, v.p. 1952-54, pres. 1958-60), Am. Acad. Arts and Scis., Nat. Acad. Scis., Paine Brook Assos. (dir.), Royal Astron. Soc. Can. (hon.), Sigma Xi. Author: First-order Theory of Motion of Mars; Standards of Time and Frequency. Joint author: Coordinates of Five Outer Planets 1653-2060; Methods of Celestial Mechanics; Spherical Astronomy. Asso. editor Astron. Jour., 1949-63, joint editor, 1963-66, editor, 1966. Contbr. articles to astron. jours., obs. publs. Address: Yale U Observatory Box 2023 Yale Station New Haven CT 06520

CLEMENCE, MAURICE LUCIAN, mfg. co. exec.; b. Southbridge, Mass., Aug. 31, 1912; s. Elliot M. and Helen (Potter) C.; A.B., Brown U., 1934; M.B.A., Harvard, 1936; m. Gwendolyn Monroe, June 20, 1936; children—Judith, Cynthia. With Dennison Mfg. Co., Framingham, Mass., 1936-41; with Kendall Co., Boston, 1941—, asst. treas., 1951-54, treas., 1954—, v.p., 1965—, dir.; dir. Allendale Mut. Ins. Co., NEL Mut. Funds. Sch. com. Town of Wellesley, 1955-61. Trustee emeritus Brown U.; trustee, chmn. bd. Wheaton Coll., Norton, Mass.; trustee Kendall Co. Found., Newton Wellesley Hosp.; bd. dirs. Mass. Taxpayers Assn. Mem. Phi Beta Kappa. Republican. Conglist. Clubs: Commercial of Boston, Boston Economics, Downtown; Wellesley Country. Home: 2 Jackson Rd Wellesley Hills MA 02181 Office: 225 Franklin St Boston MA 02110

CLEMENCE, RICHARD VERNON, economist; b. Greenville, R.I., Oct. 13, 1910; s. Richard R. and Lora Eliza (Oatley) C.; Ph.B., Brown U., 1934, A.M., 1936; M.A., Harvard, 1940, Ph.D., 1948; m. Eleanor Prescott, Dec. 5, 1942; 1 dau., Melissa. Instr. econs. Boston U., 1937-38; asst. econs. Mass. Inst. Tech., 1939- 42; research asso. Nat. Bur. Econ. Research, 1942-43; head dept. econs. Pine Manor Jr. Coll., 1945-47; faculty Wellesley Coll., 1947—, prof. econs., 1958—, chmn. dept., 1956—, A. Barton Hepburn prof. econs., 1966—, also dir. program economic edn. Cons. economist New Eng. Econ. Edn. Council, Kingston Ins. Agy. Dir. Benjamin Chase Co.; dir. fgn. operations div. Paine Brook Assos. Served with AUS, 1942-44. Life fellow Royal Econ. Soc., Nat. Assn. Bus. Economists (dir. internship program in econs.); mem. Am. Econ. Assn., Am. Finance Assn., Econ. History Assn., Am. Statis. Assn., Econometric Soc., Paine Brook Assos. (dir.), Internat. Mark Twain Soc. (hon.), Phi Beta Kappa. Author: The Schumpeterian System, 1950; Income Analysis, 1951; The Economics of Defense, 1953; also numerous articles. Filler editor The Enterprise. Home: 61 Beverly Rd Wellesley MA 02181

CLEMENS, MICHAEL JOSEPH, lawyer; b. Bklyn., June 26, 1920; s. Emil Joseph and Louise (Mayo) C.; student Bluefield (Va.) Jr. Coll., 1937-39; B.S., U.S. Naval Acad., 1942; LL.B., Loyola U., Los Angeles, 1948, J.D., 1951; m. Irene A. Horden, Feb. 3, 1946; children-Kathleen Louise (Mrs. Charles C. Lawler, Jr.), Patricia Ann, Barbara Jean. Jr. screen writer Columbia Pictures, 1947-48; admitted to Cal. bar, 1952; pvt. practice in Beverly Hills, 1953—; dep. atty. gen. Cal., 1952-53; spl. prosecutor San Diego County, 1955. Dir. Cal Pine Foods, Inc., Stanco Mfg. & Sales, Inc. Bd. govs. Loyola Law Sch. Served to lt. U.S. Navy, 1943-46; PTO. Mem. Am., Cal., Beverly Hills bar assns., Am. Judicature Soc., Am. Trial Lawyers Assn., Loyola Law Sch. Alumni (past pres.), Navy Youth Found. (past pres.), U.S. Naval Acad. Alumni Assn. (trustee), Phi Delta Phi, Phi Theta Kappa. Club: Bel-Air (Cal.) Country. Home: 1101 Stradella Rd Los Angeles CA 90024 Office: 9418 Wilshire Blvd Beverly Hills CA 90212

CLEMENS, PAUL LEWIS, artist; b. Superior, Wis., Oct. 29, 1911; studied under Oscar Gagen and at Art Inst. Chgo.; A.B., U. Wis. Exhibited, 1937-, in well known galleries and museums throughout U.S., including Art Inst., Chgo., Carnegie Inst., Corcoran Gallery Art, World's Fair N.Y., N.A.D., Pa. Acad. Fine Art, Los Angeles Co. Mus. Art, Whitney Mus. Modern Art. Represented in collections of museums, including Mus. Modern Art, Milw. Art Inst., Los Angeles Co. Mus. Art, Nelson Gallery (Kansas City, Mo.). Recipient purchase prize Milw. Jour., 1937, medal Milw. Art Inst., 1937; Altman Prize N.A.D., 1942, prize N.A.D., 1944. Mem. Portraits, Inc., Address: 620 N Beverly Dr Beverly Hills CA 90210*

CLEMENT, BESSE ALBERTA, educator; b. Norman, Okla., Nov. 10, 1902; d. Thomas Egbert and Daisy Alberta (Armstrong) Clement; student Nat. Park Coll., 1920-21; Franco- Am. exchange scholar Lycée de Jeunes Filles, St.-Germain-en-Laye, France, 1922-23; B.A., U. Okla., 1925, M.A., 1928; postgrad. Columbia, 1934; Ph.D. (Univ. Grad. scholar 1938-39), Stanford, 1947. Asst. modern langs. Ouachita Coll., Arkadelphia, Ark., 1925-26; mem. faculty U. Okla., Norman, 1926—, prof. Romance langs., 1958-63, David Ross Boyd prof. Romance langs., 1963-. Recipient Teaching award U. Okla., 1955. Mem. Modern Lang. Assn., Am. Assn. Tchrs. French, S. Central Modern Lang. Assn., Phi Beta Kappa (past pres. U. Okla. chpt.), Delta Delta Delta. Translator: (Roger Le Tourneau) Fez in the Age of the Marinides, 1961. Home: 1108 Chautauqua St Norman, OK 73069.

CLEMENT, DALE EUGENE, univ. dean; b. Tarkio, Mo., Aug. 1, 1933; s. Wilbur Sterling and Crystal Marie (Johnson) C.; S.B., Tarkio Coll., 1954; M.A., U. Neb., 1959, Ph.D., 1965; m. Barbara Jean Hughes, June 19, 1962; children-Crystal Ann, James Russell. Instr., Tingley (Ia.) High Sch., 1954; grad. asst., then asst. prof. Midland Coll., Fremont, Neb., 1957-61; grad. asst. U. Neb., 1961-63; mem. faculty U. S.D., 1961—, prof. finance, 1967—, dean Sch. Business, 1968—. Dir. United Nat. Bank, Vermillion. Bd. dirs. S.D. Joint Council Econ. Edn.; mem. adv. council Small Bus. Adminstrn. Clay Country chmn. Gunderson for Congress, 1970. Bd. dirs. United Fund Vermillion, U. S.D. Found. Served with AUS, 1955-57. Mem. Am. Finance Assn., Financial Analysts Soc., Beta Gamma Sigma, Delta Sigma Pi. Mason (Shriner) Author articles in field. Home: 854 Valley View Vermillion SD 57069

CLEMENT, HOWARD WHEELER, lawyer; b. Greencastle, Ind., Apr. 27, 1917; s. John A. and Clara Caroline (Wheeler) C.; B.A., U. Ill., 1938, J.D., 1942; m. Carol L. Ege, Aug. 22, 1942; children—John Jeffrey, Patricia Louise, Martha Anne. Admitted to Ill. bar, 1942; asso. Wilkinson, Huxley, Byron & Hume, 1946- 51, partner, 1952-56; partner Byron, Hume, Groen & Clement, Chgo., 1957- 63, Hume, Groen, Clement & Hume, 1964-66; pres. Hume, Clement, Hume & Lee, Ltd., 1967—. Mem. grad. faculty John Marshall Law Sch., 1955-60. Tech. adv. bd. Dept. Commerce, 1964-65; mem. Pres.'s Commn. on Patent System, 1965-67; mem. Ill. Bd. Higher Edn., 1959-71. Trustee U. Ill., 1959-71, pres. 1962-67; Served 1st lt. USAAF, 1942-45. Decorated Air medal. Mem. Am., Ill., Chgo. (chmn. profl. ethics com. 1957, bd. mgrs. 1968-70) bar assns., Am., Chgo. patent law assns., Am. Judicature Soc., Phi Gamma Delta, Phi Delta Phi. Democrat. Unitarian. Clubs: Law, University, Mid-Day, Mid-Town Tennis (Chgo.); Lake Delavan (Wis.) Yacht; Big Foot Country (Lake Geneva, Wis.). Home: 355 Stratford Rd Des Plaines IL 60016 also Turtle Point S Shore Dr Delavan WI 53115 Office: 1 First Nat Plaza Chicago IL 60670

CLEMENT, JOSEPH DALE, educator; b. Kalamazoo, Jan. 7, 1928; s. William S. and Bernadette C. (Rynne) C.; B.S., Western Mich. U., 1949; M.S., U. Wis., 1953, Ph.D. (Knapp fellow), 1957; m. Elizabeth Viola Boyd, July 28, 1956; children—Steven Louis, Mark Robert. Sr. scientist Westinghouse Bettis Atomic Power Lab., Pitts., 1957; supervisory engr. Martin Co., Balt., 1959-60; sr. scientist Westinghouse Astronuclear Lab., Pitts., 1960-62; mgr. nuclear engring. dept. Nuclear Materials & Equipment Corp., Apollo, Pa., 1962-65; asso. prof. nuclear engring. Ga. Inst. Tech., Atlanta, 1965-68, prof., 1968—. Dir., Sci., Tech. & Research, Inc.; cons. Nuclear Assurance Corp. Served with U.S. Army, 1953-55. Recipient McCraken award in chemistry Western Mich. U., 1949. Mem. Am. Nuclear Soc., Sigma Xi. Contbr. articles profl. jours. Patentee in field. Home: 2484 Burnt Leaf Lane Decatur GA 30033 Office: Sch Nuclear Engring Ga Inst Tech Atlanta GA 30332

CLEMENT, KARL GUSTAV, printing co. exec.; b. St. Paul, Nov. 10, 1906; s. Henry and Ida (Mueller) C.; grad. Shattuck Sch., 1924; B.S. in Bus., U. Minn., 1928; m. Mavis W. Poole, Feb. 28, 1945; children—Ronalie (Mrs. Thomas Peterson), Karla. With Nat. Park Bank, comptroller, asst. to pres. Vick Chem. Co., 1933-48; comptroller Port of N.Y. Authority, 1949-53; comptroller R.H. Donnelley Corp., 1953—, 1953-60, v.p. adminstrn., 1960—; asst. to pres., 1969—; dir. Vierhand Reclamediensten, N.V., Holland. Served as col. USAAF, World War II; ETO. Mem. Financial Execs. Inst. (bd. dirs. N.Y.C.), Beta Gamma Sigma, Alpha Tau Omega. Episcopalian. Clubs: Executives, Cloud (N.Y.C.); Bath (Redington Beach); University (N.Y.C., Chgo.); Lyford Cay (Bahamas); Nassau Country (Glen Cove). Home: 89 Fruitledge Rd Brookville LI NY 11545 Office: 825 3d Av New York City NY 10022

CLEMENT, KENNETH WITCHER, surgeon; b. Pittsylvania County, Va., Feb. 24, 1920; s. Harry Leonard and Inez (Mae) C.; A.B. (Amos Miller scholar), Oberlin Coll., 1942, LL.D., 1968; M.D. with honors (W.K. Kellogg scholar), Howard U., 1945; LL.D., Central State U., 1968; m. Ruth Doss, Aug. 22, 1942; children—Michael Craig, Leslie Denise, Lia Deborah. Intern, N.Y.C. Hosp., 1945-46; intern Cleve. City Hosp., 1945, resident surgeon, 1946-50, chief resident surgeon, 1950-51; pvt. practice, Cleve., 1953—; mem. staff St. Luke's, Forest City, Marymount hosps.; asst. vis. surgeon Met. Gen. Hosp.; sr. clin. instr. surgery Western Res. U., 1959- 66, asst. clin. prof., 1966—. Dir. Mt. Pleasant Med. center, Inc., 912 Galatin Corp., Bardun Investment Corp. Mem. Cleve. Mayor's Com. Employment Physically Handicapped, 1958—; mem. Nat. Adv. Com. Social Security, 1963-65, med. adv. com. disability operation, 1965—; mem. Hosp. Ins. Benefit Adv. Council, 1965—, Nat. Selective Service Bd., 1966—; cons. Office Tech. Coop. and Research AID, State Dept.; Cleve. Adv. Com. Urban Renewal, 1961—; com. community resources nursing edn. Cleve. Hosp. Council, 1961—; mem. Cleve. Community Relations Bd., 1963-66. Team capt. United Appeal Cleve., 1952-63; gen. campaign chmn. Cleve. YMCA, 1959; co-chmn. life membership com. Cleve. and Ohio N.A.A.C.P., 1957—, v.p. Cleve. br., 1962—. Bd. dirs. Cleve. Christian Community Center, Greater Cleve. Equal Opportunity Act, Nat. Urban League; bd. dirs., pres. Cleve. Urban League, Cleve. N.A.A.C.P., 1955—, Cleve. Bapt. Assn., 1956—, Cleve. and Ohio br. Am. Civil Liberites Union, 1962—, Served to maj., M.C., USAF, 1951-53. Recipient Jesse Green award surgery Howard U., 1945, John Hale award surgery Winston Salem (N.C.) Med. Sch., 1950; merit award for med. bldg. Cleve. C. of C., 1958; Distinguished Service award Cleve. Med. Assn., 1962, 64, Nat. Med. Assn., 1965; New Frontiers award Ams. for Democratic Action. Diplomate Am. Bd. Surgery. Fellow A.C.S.; mem. Am., Nat. (chmn. com. health care aged 1960—, pres. 1963-64), Ohio med. assns., Aero-Space Med. Assn., Assn. Mil. Surgeons, Howard U. Sch. Medicine (exec. com. 1962-65), Howard U. (pres. 1965-67) alumni assns., Kappa Pi. Democrat. Baptist. Club: City (Cleve.). Contbr. articles to profl. jours. Home: 2 Bratenahl Pl Bratenahl OH 44108 Office: 13815 Kinsman Rd Cleveland OH 44120

CLEMENT, MEREDITH OWEN, educator, economist; b. Colusa, Cal., June 7, 1926; s. Eldon Wilfred and Lillian (Ohm) C.; student Yuba Coll., Marysville, Cal., 1946-48; B.S., U. Cal. at Berkeley, 1950, Ph.D., 1958; m. Jacqueline Parker, Apr. 10, 1955; children—William Christopher. Research economist CIA, 1954-56; mem. faculty Dartmouth, 1956-, prof. econs., 1967-; vis. asst. prof. U. Cal. at Berkeley, 1961-62; Brookings research prof. Brookings Instn., 1964-65; Fulbright lectr. Robert Coll., Instanbul, Turkey, 1969-70. Served with USMCR, 1944-46. Mem. Am., So. econ. assns., Royal Econ. Soc., Econometric Soc. Unitarian. Author: (with others) Theoretical Issues in International Economics, 1967; An Economic Evaluation of the Federal Grant-in-Aid Programs in New England, 1961; also articles. Home: Star Route Etna NH 03750 Office: Dept Econs Dartmouth Coll Hanover NH 03755

CLEMENT, PAUL AUGUSTUS, educator; b. Atlanta, Feb. 26, 1906; s. Paul A. and Irene (Lewis) C.; A.B., U. N.C., 1926; Ph.D., Johns Hopkins, 1930; m. Harlotte Cole Taylor, Oct. 5, 1926; 1 son, Paul Augustus III. Asso. prof. Greek, Coll. William and Mary, 1930-32; fellow U. Brussels (Belgium), 1932-33; asso. fellow Am. Sch. Classical Studies, Athens, Greece, 1933-34, vis. prof., 1967-68, mem. mng. com.; asso. Johns Hopkins, 1934-38; mem. Inst. Advanced Study, Princeton, N.J., 1938- 49, 52-53, 56; mgr. editor publs. Am. Sch. Classical Studies, Princeton, 1939-49; asst. prof. classics and classical archaeology U. Cal. at Los Angeles, 1949-52, asso. prof., 1952-58, prof., 1958—, acting chmn. dept., 1961, chmn., 1962-65. Co-dir. Isthmia excavations, Corinth, Greece, 1966-67, dir., 1968—. Guggenheim fellow, 1960. Mem. German Archaeol. Inst., Am. Philol. Assn., Archaeol. Inst. Am., Soc. Promotion Hellenic Studies, Soc. Promotion Roman Studies, Assn. Guillaume Bude, Phi Beta Kappa. Contbr. several chpts. to archeol. books; articles, revs. to profl. jours. Home: 1556 Wellesley Av Los Angeles CA 90025 also 54 Souidias St Athens 140 Greece

CLEMENT, PRESTON RIVELY, educator; b. Kansas City, Mo., Oct. 12, 1925; s. Ben F. and Mary (Rively) C.; B.S., U. Kan., 1946, M.S., 1948; Ph.D., Princeton, 1950. Instr. elec. engring. U. Kan., 1946-48; asst. prof., then asso. prof. Princeton, 1951-64; prof. elec. engring., head dept. Stevens Inst. Tech., Hoboken, N.J., 1964-66, dean faculty, 1966—, provost, 1968—. Sr. engr. N.Am. Aviation Co., 1956; cons. Johnsville Naval Air Devel. Center, 1957-61, IBM Corp., 1960-61. Served with USNR, 1943-46, 52-54. Higgins postdoctoral fellow Princeton, 1960-61. Sr. mem. I.E.E.E.; mem. Am. Assn. U. Profs., A.A.A.S., Soc. Indsl. and Applied Math., Am. Soc. Engring. Edn., Sigma Xi, Tau Beta Pi, Sigma Tau, Pi Mu Epsilon. Club: University (N.Y.C.). Author: (with W.C. Johnson) Electrical Engineering Science, 1960. Contbr. articles to profl. jours. Home: 245 Varsity Av Princeton NJ 08540 Office: Stevens Inst Tech Hoboken NJ 07030

CLEMENT, RICHARD FRANCIS, business exec.; b. Chgo., Nov. 29, 1906; s. Robert Fawne and Jennie (Halvorson) C.; B.S., U. Wis., 1928; m. Margaret Buchanan, Aug. 11, 1934; children—Richard Bradley, Jane Elizabeth, Charles Frederic. Men's furnishings merchandiser Wilson Bros., Chgo., 1935-39; sportswear merchaniser Ely & Walker, St. Louis, 1939-47, v.p., 1949-65, dir. sales, 1954-63, dir. marketing and planning, 1963-65; partner Yates & Co., investments, St. Louis, 1965-69, Newhard, Cook & Co., investments, St. Louis, 1970—; chmn. Clement & Benner, Inc., Los Alamos; dir. Financial Data Systems, Inc., Leadville Corp. Mem. Alpha Tau Omega. Conglist. Clubs: Algonquin; St. Louis. Home: 324 Jackson Rd Webster Groves MO 63119 Office: 400 Olive St St Louis MO 63102

CLEMENT, WILLIAM ALEXANDER, life ins. co. exec.; b. Charleston, S.C., May 6, 1912; s. Arthur John and Sadie (Jones) C.; student Talladega Coll., 1934; m. Josephine Dobbs, Dec. 24, 1941; children—Alexine C. (Mrs. Aaron G. Jackson), William Alexander II, Wesley Dobbs, Arthur John, Kathleen O., Josephine M. With N.C. Mutual Life Ins. Co., Durham, N.C., 1934—, agy. dir., 1961-62, v.p., 1962-66, v.p. charge field operations, 1966, agy. v.p., 1967-69, sr. v.p., 1969—; vis. prof. N.C. Coll., 1960. Chmn. dist. Boy Scouts Am., v.p. Occoneechee council, 1971—, spl. dep. grand master, 1959—; pres. Durham United Fund, 1970. Recipient Silver Beaver award, 1966. Mem. Life Ins. Agy. Mgmt. Assn. (bd. 1970), Durham C. of C., (bd. 1970), Am. Coll. Life Underwriters (dir.), Am. Soc. Chartered Life Underwriters, Sigma Pi Phi, Alpha Phi, Alpha. Baptist. Mason. Home: 206 Pekoe St Durham NC 27707 Office: 411 W Chapel Hill Durham NC 27701

CLEMENTE, CARMINE DOMENIC, educator; b. Penns Grove, N.J., Apr. 29, 1928; s. Ermanno and Caroline (Friozzi) C.; A.B., U. Pa., 1948, M.S., 1950, Ph.D., 1952; postdoctoral fellow U. London, 1953-54; m. Dorothy Warren, Dec. 19, 1955 (div.); m. 2d, Juliette Vance, Sept. 19, 1968. Asst. instr. anatomy U. Pa., 1950- 52; faculty U. Cal. at Los Angeles, 1952—, 53, prof., chmn. dept. anatomy, 1963—. Hon. research asso. Univ. Coll., U. London, 1953-54; cons. Sepulveda VA Hosp., NIH. Mem. med. adv. panel Bank Am.-Giannini Found. Mem. Pavlovian Soc. N.Am. (Ann. award 1968, pres. 1972), Brain Research Inst., Am. Physiol. Soc., Am. Assn. Anatomists (v.p. 1970-72), Am. Acad. Neurology, Am. Acad. Cerebral Palsy, Biol. Stain Commn., Internat. Brain Research Orgn., Med. Research Assn. Cal., N.Y. Acad. Sci., Nat. Acad. Sci. (mem. com. neuropathology, BEAR coms.), Sigma Xi. Democrat. Methodist. Author: Aggression and Defense: Neurol Mechanisms and Social Patterns, 1967; Physiological Correlates of Dreaming. Asso. editor Experimental Neurology, Anatomical Record, Conditional Reflex. Contbr. articles to sci. jours. Home: 11737 Bellagio Rd Los Angeles CA 90049

CLEMENTE, ROBERTO WALKER, profl. baseball player; b. Carolina, P.R., Aug. 18, 1934; student Julio Coronado Bezcarrondo Coll.; m. Vera Zahala, Nov. 14, 1964. Mem. Pitts. Pirates Profl. Baseball Team, 1955—. Named as outfielder Sporting News Nat. League All-Star Team, 1961, 64, 66; Nat. League Most Valuable Player, 1966; Nat. League Player Yr. Sporting News, 1966; Most Valuable Player World Series, 1971; recipient Gold Glove award as outstanding Nat. League fielder in outfield, 1961, 62, 63, 64, 65, 66. Address: care Forbes Field Pittsburgh PA 15213*

CLEMENTS, CHARLES L., banker; b. Berrien County, Ga., s. David C. and Martha (Baskin) C.; student Ga. A. and M. Coll; m. Lena Pafford, 1915; children—Bertha Virginia, Frances Marian, Charles L. Sec., Valdosta Drug Co. (Ga.), 1923-26; cashier, v.p. Miami Beach Bank & Trust Co. (now Merc. Nat. Bank), (Fla.), 1926-33; pres. Chase Fed. Savs. & Loan Assn., 1933-64, chmn. bd., 1964—; chmn. Community Nat. Bank of Bal Harbour, Miami Beach; propr. C.L. Clements Ins. Agy., Inc., 1943—. Former pres. Community Chest Dade County, Fla. Mem. U.S. Savs. and Loan League (past pres.), Miami Beach C. of C. (past pres.), Com. of One Hundred (dir.). Rotarian. Clubs: Bath, Surf (bd. govs.), LaGorce Country, Biscayne Bay Yacht, Indian Creek Country (Miami Beach). Home: 5170 Pine Tree Dr Miami Beach FL 33139 Office: 1100 Lincoln Rd Miami Beach FL 33139

CLEMENTS, CHARLES LANE, Jr., banker; b. Miami Beach, Fla., Sept. 19, 1929; s. Charles Lane and Salena (Pafford) C.; grad. Philips Acad., Andover, Mass., 1947; B.A., Harvard, 1951; m. Nancy Horne Dickinson, Jan. 14, 1956; children—Charles Lane III, Nancy Dickinson II, Thomas Ehrhart, Virginia Eleanor. Pres., Chase Fed. Savs. & Loan Assn., Miami Beach, Fla., 1964—; vice chmn. bd. Community Nat. Bank & Trust Co., Bal Harbour, Fla., 1963—. Past pres. Comprehensive Health Planning Council S. Fla.; mem. Orange Bowl Com. bd. mem. Greater Miami Coalition. Mem. Greater Miami C. of C. (v.p.-treas.). Home: 1830 W 24th St Sunset Island 3 Miami Beach FL 33140 Office: 1100 Lincoln Rd Mall Miami Beach FL 33139

CLEMENTS, GEORGE L., chain store exec.; b. Chgo., Feb. 24, 1909; s. Fred and Ina (Small) C.; student U. Ill., 1926; m. Ruth Howell, Sept. 1, 1933; children—Lynne, John. Asso. with Jewel Cos., Inc., Chgo., 1929—, dir. 1948—, pres., 1951-65, chmn. bd., 1965-70, chmn. exec. com., 1970—; dir. No. Ill. Gas Co., Universal Oil Products. Dir., mem. exec. com. Nat. Assn. Foods Chains. Chmn. Ill. State Bd. Higher Edn. Home: 3 S 574 N Adams Rd Hinsdale IL 60521 Office: 1955 W North Av Melrose Park IL 60160

CLEMENTS, SIR JOHN, actor, producer, dir.; b. London, Eng., Apr. 25, 1910; s. Herbert William and Mary Elizabeth (Stevens) C.; ed. St. John's Coll., Cambridge U.; m. Kay Hammond, Aug. 21, 1946. Debut at Lyric Hammersmith, London, 1930; founder intimate theatre in N. London, 1935; appeared opposite wife, also produced and directed numerous plays in London, 1943—, including Private Lives, 1944, The Kingmaker, 1946, Marriage a la Mode, 1946, The Beaux Stratagem, 1949, Man and Superman, 1951, The Happy Marriage, 1952, Pygmalion, 1953, The Little Glass Clock, 1954, The Rivals, 1956, The Way of the World, 1956, The Rape of the Belt, 1957, Gilt and Ginger Bead, 1958, Marriage Go Round, 1959; appeared with Old Vic in London as Coriolanus, 1947, Petrichio, 1947, Dunois, 1947, in N.Y.C. as Macbeth, 1962, Warwick, 1962; appeared in London in The Affair, 1961-62, The Tulip Tree, 1962-63; producer, dir., appeared in the Masters, 1963; motion pictures include Knight Without Armour, 1936, South Riding, 1927, Four Feathers, 1938, Convoy, 1940, Ships With Wings, 1941, Silent Enemy, 1959, The Mind Benders, 1962; dir. Chichester Festival Theatre, 1966—. Decorated comdr. Brit. Empire, 1956. Club: Garrick (London). Home: 7 Royal Cresent Brighton Sussex England

CLEMENTS, JOHN J.A., former pub. co. exec.; b. Walnut, Kan., Jan. 5, 1901; s. George Hanson and Emma Catherine (Mills) C.; m. Stasia Mayer, June 29, 1949. With Hearst Corp., N.Y.C., 1920-68, pub. relations dir., 1939-68; editor Am. Mercury, 1953-57. Clubs: Advertising, New York Athletic (N.Y.C.); Nat. Press (Washington); Copper Hill Golf; Raritan Country; Overseas Press. Office: 959 8th Av New York City NY 10019

CLEMENTS, JOY soprano; b. Dayton, O.; d. Verne Brent and Lulu Frances (Day) Albrecht; student Acad. Vocal Arts, Phila., 1951, U. Miami (Fla.), 1954-56; m. L.D. Clements, Dec. 29, 1957; children—Lori Elena, Matthew David. Debut in La Boheme, Opera Guild Miami, 1956; mem. N.Y.C. Opera, 1959-62, Met. Opera Assn., 1962—; leading soprano Copeland's The Tender Land, N.Y. Philharmonic, 1965; rec. artist Columbia Records; solo appearances Israel Philharmonic, Tel Aviv, Lewissohn Stadium, N.Y.C., N.Y.C. Opera, also operas in Cin., Duluth, Minn., Houston, Tulsa, and Central City, Colo.; guest appearance White House, 1967; appeared as Gretel in Hansel and Gretel, 1967-68. Created role of Mary Warren in opera The Crucible.

CLEMENTS, R. CANON, banker; b. Plainview, Tex., 1913; B.B.A., Tex. Tech. Coll., 1933; M.B.A., Harvard, 1935; B.L.H. (Rhodes scholar), Oxford U., 1938. Exec. v.p., dir. J. Henry Schroder Banking Corp., Schroder Trust Co., until 1966; vice chmn., dir. Nat. Bank N.Am., 1966—; v.p., dir. Clements Properties Inc., Clements Corp.; dir. Am. Export Industries Inc., Barth-Spencer Corp., Pan Am. Trade Devel. Corp. Mem. Fgn. Policy Assn. (treas., dir.). Home: 309 Carter St New Canaan, CT 06840 Office: 44 Wall St New York City NY 10005

CLEMENTS, REX STOWERS, clergyman; b. Lisbon, N.Y., Aug. 13, 1902; s. Henry G. and Anna (Stowers) C.; A.B., Colgate U., 1926; B.D., Yale, 1929; Ph.D., Edinburgh U., 1931; S.T.D. U. Pa., 1942; D.D., Occidental Coll., 1942, Ursinus Coll., 1942; Litt.D., Trinity U. (Tex.). 1944; LL.D., Temple U., 1955; m. Marian K. Hutchinson, June 29, 1933; children— Richard Hutchinson, Rex Stowers. Ordained to ministry Presbyn. Ch., 1929; asst. minister Fifth Av. Presbyn. Ch., N.Y.C., 1931-32; pastor Ch. of Convenant, Boston, 1932-37, Bryn Mawr (Pa.) Presbyn. Ch., 1937-62; exec. sec. council on theol. edn. U.P. Ch. in U.S., 1962-67. Pres., Presbyn. Bd. Christian Edn., 1941-49; v.p. U.P. Found.; pres. Phila. Council Chs., 1950-51. Mem. Phi Beta Kappa, Sigma Nu, Phi Alpha. Republican. Clubs: Union League, Merion Cricket, Adelphi. Home: 230 Steeplechase Rd Devon PA 19333

CLEMENTS, ROBERT JOHN, educator; b. Cleve., Oct. 23, 1912; s. Earl W. and Mildred (Warner) C.; A.B., Oberlin, 1934; Ph.D. U. Chgo., 1939; postgrad. U. Bordeaux, U. Florence, Harvard; Litt. D., U. Rome (Italy), 1961; H.H.D., Alethia Coll., Can., 1966; m. Helen Louise Card, Sept. 3, 1940 (div.); children—Caird Robert, Cleveland Warner. Instr., U. Chgo., 1937-39, U. Ill., 1939-40; instr., asst. prof. Harvard, 1940-47; prof., chmn. dept. Romance langs., lits. Pa. State U., 1947-54; prof. Romance langs., lits. grad. sch. N.Y. U., 1954—, also dir. comparative lit. dept., grad. sch. Lectr., U. Madrid, 1953; univ. asso. Columbia, 1955; Fulbright Research scholar, Rome, 1960-61; Mellon prof. lit. U. Pitts., 1968; screening com. for langs. and lit. Fulbright office, Washington, 1965-68; adv. modern lang. editor Ginn & Co., Boston, 1944-57; cons. Juilliard Sch., 1971—. Co-organizer, Civil Affairs Tng. Program, Harvard, 1940-44. Mem. Phi Beta Kappa Assos. (nat. bd. 1954-62), Lang. and Lit. (v.p. 1962—), Modern Lang. Assn. Am. (chmn. French, Italian, Portuguese, Romance sects.), Am. Council Learned Socs. (mem. editorial bd., Renaissance com. 1944—), Société des Amis du Louvre, Dante Alighieri Soc., Mazzini Soc., Mediaeval Acad., Am. (sec. pub. 1940-47), Am. Assn. Tchrs. Italian (pres. 1960-62), Phi Beta Kappa. Author: Critical Theory and Practice of the Pléiade, 1942 (rev. as Critical Theory of Pléiade 1968); co- author Pennsylvania Curriculum Revision for Modern Languages, 1952; co- author Platonism in French Renaissance Poetry; The Peregrine Muse; Studies in Renaissance Comparative Literature, 1959, rev. 1968; Picta Poesis, Literary and Humanistic Theory in Renaissance Emblem Books, 1960; Michelangelo's Theory of Art, 1960; Michelangelo, A Self-Portrait, 1962 (rev. as Michelangelo, Self Portrait 1968); co- author Michelangelo Scultore, 1964; The Poetry of Michelangelo, 1964. Corr. editor Boletín de Filología Espaola, Madrid, Romantisches Jahrbuch, Hamburg; asso. editor Gotham Library, 1962—. Contbr. chpts. to books and bibliographies, many articles, revs. to profl. periodicals, newspapers. Columnist: Literary Scene in Europe, Saturday Rev., 1964—. Home: 8 E 8th St New York City NY 10003

CLEMENTS, THOMAS, cons. geologist; b. Chgo., June 7, 1898; s. George Henry and Caroline Barbara (Nathan) C.; E.M., Tex. Sch. Mines, 1922; M.S., Cal. Inst. Tech., 1929, Ph.D., 1932; m. Lydia Pryce Brooks, Oct. 14, 1922; 1 dau., Anne. Metallurgist Compaia Minera de Peoles. S.A., Torreòn, Mexico, 1922-25; engr. Security Title Ins. & Guarantee Co., Los Angeles, 1925- 28; teaching fellow Cal. Inst. Tech., 1928-29; teaching staff U. So. Cal., Los Angeles, 1929-64, Hancock prof. geology, 1945-64, head dept., 1933-63, chmn. com. research Hancock Found., 1952-60; curator of mineralogy and petrology Los Angeles County Mus., 1955-60; condr. research in Mexico on source of ancient Mexican jade, 1957—; geologist Los Angeles County Mus. Expdn. to Lake Chapala, Jalisco, Mexico, 1956, Nat. Geog. Soc. archeol. site, Calico, Cal., 1964—. Cons. mining engr., geologist, 1930—; cons. geologist Dept. Petroleum, Ministerio de la Economia Nacional, Bogotá, Colombia, 1939. Mem. geol. hazards com. City Los Angeles, 1957-63; mem. cons. bd. Bldg. and Safety Commn., 1963- -, pres. Qualifications Bd. Engring. Geologists, 1960-70. Served USN, 1917-19. Fellow Geol. Soc. Am., So. Cal. Acad. Scis.; mem. Sociedad Geológica Mexicana, Death Valley Fortyniners (dir., past pres. 1955), Soc. Econ. Geologists, Am. Inst. Mining and Metall. Engrs., Am. Assn. Petroleum Geologists, Am. Inst. Profl. Geologists, Sigma Xi, Phi Kappa Phi, Sigma Delta Pi (asso.), Sigma Gamma Epsilon (asso.) Acacia. Author: Geological Story of Death Valley, 1954. Contbr. tech. articles to sci. jours. Home: 2171 Vista del Mar Av Hollywood CA 90068 Office: 2323 W 3d St Los Angeles CA 90057

CLEMENTS, WILLIAM DENNEY, Jr., life ins. co., exec.; b. Dover, Del., Mar. 16, 1920; s. William Denney and Jesse (Palmatary) C.; ed. pub. schs.; m. Doris Kruse, Feb. 28, 1942; children—William Denney III, Jeffrey, Andrew, Martha, Matthew, Frances. Engaged in life ins. bus., 1947—; with Franklin Life Ins. Co., 1952—, v.p., 1960-61, agy. v.p., 1961—, also dir. Bd. dirs. Jr. Achievement, Springfield, Ill. Served with USNR, World War II. Mem. Nat. Assn. Life Underwriters. Republican. Presbyn. (trustee). Mason (Shriner). Clubs: Sangamo, Illini Country (Springfield). Home: 2001 Willemoore St Springfield IL 62704 Office: Franklin Life Ins Co Springfield IL 62705

CLEMENTS, WOODROW WILSON, beverage co. exec.; b. Tuscaloosa, Ala., July 30, 1914; s. William Houston and Martha (Christian) C.; student Howard Coll., Birmingham, Ala., 1932-33, U. Ala., 1933-35; m. Eloise Davis, Mar. 20, 1937; 1 son, Wayne Wilson. Began as route salesman advancing to sales mgr. Dr. Pepper Bottling Co., Tusculoosa, 1935-42; with Dr. Pepper Co., 1942—, successively dist. mgr., sales promotion mgr., asst. mgr. bottler service, gen. sales mgr., 1942-49, 49-51, v.p., gen. sales mgr., 1951-58, v.p. marketing, 1958-67, exec. v.p., dir., 1967-68, pres., 1969—, chief exec. officer, 1970—; exec. v.p. Roanoke Dr. Pepper Bottling Co., 1949; v.p. Dr. Pepper Finance Corp. Mem. Sales and Marketing Execs. Internat. (regional v.p., pres. 1968-69, chmn. bd. 1969-70), S.W. Sales Execs. Council (pres.), Dallas Sales Exec. Club (pres. 1957). Rotarian. Clubs: Glen Lakes Country; Dallas Country. Home: 3712 Centenary St Dallas TX 75225. Office: 5523 E Mockingbird Lane Dallas TX 75222

CLEMINSHAW, CLARENCE HIGBEE, astronomer; b. Cleve., Jan. 15, 1902; s. William Holbrook and Mary Emma (Higbee) C.; A.B., Cornell U., 1923; LL.B., Harvard, 1926; M.S., Case Sch. Applied Sci., Cleve., 1931; Ph.D., U. Mich., 1934; m. Dixie Jean Borton, June 25, 1932; children—Marian Borton, Carol Borton. Admitted to Ohio bar, 1926; practiced law with Thompson, Hine & Flory, 1926-30; research asso. in astronomy U. Pa., 1935-36; asst. dir. Griffith Obs. and Planetarium, Los Angeles, 1936-58, dir., 1958-69, dir. emeritus, 1969—; asso. prof. astronomy U. So. Cal., 1936-46. Mem. Am. Astron. Soc., Phi Beta Kappa, Sigma Xi. Kiwanian. Home: 1941 N New Hampshire Av Los Angeles CA 90027

CLEMINSHAW, FRANK FOSTER, electronic co. exec.; b. Bklyn., July 21, 1911; s. Frank V. and Virginia (Foster) C.; student St. Thomas Coll., 1928-30, Columbia, 1931-36; grad. Advanced Mgmt. Program Harvard, 1957; m. Gertrude Niclas, Feb. 21, 1934; children—Lenore (Mrs. Walter J. Lekki), Theresa, Catherine; m. 2d, Corinne Bernstein, 1971. Various positions U. R.I. Tabulating Corp., N.Y.C., 1938-40; mgr. data processing, cost accounting Am. Car & Foundry Co., N.Y.C., 1940-48, dir. methods, 1948-52, asst. comptroller, 1952-54, comptroller, 1954-59; v.p., gen. mgr. Diebold Assos., N.Y.C., 1959-60; cons. mgmt. controls Internat. Paper Co., N.Y.C., 1960-61; v.p., treas. Gen. Instrument Corp., Newark, 1961—; dir. Beckley Mfg. Corp. (W.Va.), T.S. Farley, Ltd., Watt Elec. Products Co., Gen. Instrument Can., Ltd., (all Waterloo, Ont., Can.), Pyramid Realty Co., Newark, Gen. Electronics Apparatus Corp., Jersey City, F.W. Sickles, Inc., Chicopee, Mass., Taiwan Electronics Corp., Taipei, C.P. Clare Co., Chgo., others. Mem. Financial Execs. Inst., Harvard Advanced Mgmt. Assn. Episcopalian. Clubs: Cornell (N.Y.C.); Harvard (Boston); Mensa (London and N.Y.C.); Essex County Country (West Orange, N.J.). Home: Scotchwood Scotch Plains NJ 07076 Office: Gen Instrument Corp 65 Gouverneur St Newark NJ 07104

CLEMMER, ROBERT LEE, architect; b. Stanley, N.C., June 19, 1903; s. Lester Dean and Kathleen (Morris) C.; A.B., Lenoir Rhyne Coll., 1926; m. Mildred Klutz Wilfong, Aug. 17, 1926; children—Betty Jean (Mrs. John H. Charles), Dorothy Ann (Mrs. William L. McCord Jr.), Mildred (Mrs. Charles H. Shuford). Draftsman, office clk. Herman-Sipe & Co., Conover, N.C., 1926-27; draftsman Reynolds Tobacco Co., Winston-Salem, N.C., 1927-28; draftsman, estimator R. M. Perry, Hickory, N.C., 1928-32; asso. M. R. Marsh, Charlotte, N.C., 1932-34; pvt. practice architecture, Hickory, N.C., 1934-65; prin. firm Clemmer, Horton, Bush Assos. Inc., Hickory, N.C., 1965—; mem. N.C. chpt. A.I.A. adv. com. new sch. architecture U. N.C.; dir. Hickory Devel. Corp. Vice-chmn. Hickory Urban Redevel. Commn., 1965—; mem. N.C. Bd. Architecture, 1965-70. Fellow A.I.A. (pres. N.C. 1959-61); mem. N.C. Assn. Professions (dir. 1963—). Lutheran. Kiwanian. Home: 827 9th Av NW Hickory NC 28601 Office: 226 2d St NW Hickory NC 28601

CLEMO, RICHARD FREDERICK, educator; b. Ontario, Ore., Sept. 23, 1920; s. Frederick James and Emma (McGivern) C.; A.B. magna cum laude, U. Portland, 1941; M.A., Columbia, 1948, postgrad., 1948-50; postgrad. New Sch., 1964-66. Tchr., Portland (Ore.) Pub. Schs., 1941-42, 45; asst. prof. speech and drama U. Portland, 1945-48; lectr. speech and rhetoric Tchrs. Coll., Columbia, 1948-50; asst. prof., asso. prof., prof. speech and dramatic art Adelphi U., Garden City, N.Y., 1950-70, prof. performings arts, 1970—, dean Sch. Gen. Studies, 1956-67, dean Coll. Arts and Scis., 1967—. Cons. group techniques L.I. labor unions; curriculum cons. pvt. schs. and colls. Pres. L.I. Television Council, 1967; bd. dirs. Nat. Council Christians and Jews, Nassau Reference Library; treas., bd. dirs. L.I. Arts Assn. Served with AUS, 1942-45. Decorated Bronze Star medal, Silver Star medal with oak leaf cluster, Purple Heart; recipient Paul Dawson Eddy award for distinguished service to Adelphi U., 1970. Richard F. Clemo scholarship for students in bus. and econs. Columbia Soc. Real Estate Appraisers. Author: Discussion Methods, 1950; Play Production: A Handbook, 1952. Contbr. articles profl. jours. Home: 257 Buckram Rd Locust Valley NY 11560 Office: Adelphi U Garden City NY 11530

CLEMONS, LESTER STANLEY, lawyer; b. Eau Claire, Wis., Aug. 28, 1904; s. Homer D. and Etta (Stanley) C.; student Wis. State Coll., Eau Claire, 1921-23; J.D., U. Wis., 1926; m. Elizabeth Ditto, June 30, 1931; children—Thomas A., Margaret E., Cynthia A. Admitted to Wis. bar, 1926, since practiced in Milw.; partner Quarles, Herriott, Clemons, Teschner & Noelke, 1942-. Dir., chmn. exec. com. Bucyrus-Erie Co.; dir., mem. exec. com. Kearney & Trecker Corp., W.H. Brady Co.; dir. Marshall & Ilsley Bank, Wis. Tower, Inc., Madison Twentieth Century Theatre Corps. Bd. dirs., exec. com., pres. U. Wis. Found.; bd. dirs. Bucyrus-Erie Found., Kearney & Trecker Found., W.H. Brady Found. Mem. Am., Wis., Milw., 7th Circuit bar assns., U. Wis. Law Alumni Assn., Met. Milw. Assn. Commerce (dir.), Phi Delta Phi. Methodist (trustee Wis. conf.). Rotarian. Clubs: Athletic, University (Milw.). Home: 1407 E Goodrich Ct Fox Point WI 53217 Office: 780 N Water St Milwaukee WI 53202

CLENDENEN, RICHARD JOHN, legal educator; b. La Porte, Ind., Mar. 16, 1915; s. Max Perry and Grace Marie (Condra) C.; A.B., Ind. U., 1941; M.S.W., Western Res. U., 1947; m. Ann Marie Speakes, Sept. 4, 1960; children—Barry James, Charles Condra, Kathleen Dorothy. Tchr., Ind. Boys Sch., Plainfield, 1941-45; with Lakeside Childrens Center, Milw., 1947, childrens bur. Dept. Health, Edn. and Welfare, 1947-53; mem. staff U.S. Senate, 1953-55; prof. social work Ohio State U., 1957-60; commr. Ky. Dept. Child Welfare, 1960-65; prof. criminal law U. Minn. Law Sch., 1965—. Cons. Youth Devel. and Delinquency Prevention Adminstrn.; pres Nat. Council State Coms. for Children and Youth. Mem. Am. Pub. Welfare Assn., Nat. Council Crime and Delinquency, Council Social Work Edn. Home: 1928 Glen Paul Av St Paul MN 55112 Office: Fraser Hall Univ Minn Minneapolis MN 55455

CLENDENIN, THOMAS FAUNTLEROY, investment counsel; b. St. Louis, Mar. 6, 1927; s. Edward Hume and Janet (Fauntleroy) C.; student Amherst Coll., 1945-46, Duke, 1948; m. Maria Kimball Lyons, May 28, 1965; children—Lawrence Hume, Bruce Edward, Maria Braden, Thomas Fauntleroy, William Hart. With U.S. Maritime Service, 1945; joined AUS, 1945, advanced through grades to capt. U.S. Army, 1954; Advanced Course Inf. Sch., Ga., 1952, Staff and Faculty Inf. Sch., Ft. Benning, Ga., 1954, Command and Gen. Staff Coll., Ft. Leavenworth, Kan., 1957; resigned 1957; account exec. Merrill & Lynch, 1957-63; with Acacia Mut. Life Ins. Co., 1963-67, treas., 1967-68; founder Clendenin Corp., 1968; investment counsel, 1963—; dir. Summation Systems Inc., Pow-Met, Inc., Solid Power, Sudinan Internat., Ltd. Decorated Bronze Star, Purple Heart, Combat Inf. badge. Mem. Washington Soc. Investment Analysts (pres. 1969), Municipal Finance Forum, Nat. Economists Club, Financial Analysts Fedn. Club: Metropolitan (N.Y.C.). Address: 13705 Wendover Rd Silver Spring MD 20904

CLENDENON, DONN ALVIN, profl. baseball player; b. Neosho, Mo., July 15, 1935; B.A., Morehouse Coll.; m. Deanna Marriott, Aug. 7, 1965. First baseman with N.Y. Mets Profl. Baseball Team. Named Most Valuable Player Sally League, 1960. Address: care Shea Stadium Roosevelt Av and 126th St Flushing NY 11368*

CLENDINEN, JAMES AUGUSTUS, newspaper editor; b. Eufaula, Ala., Dec. 1, 1910; s. Thomas A. and Katherine M. (Powell) C.; student U. Fla., 1929-30; m. Barbara Harrison, May 22, 1943; children—James Dudley, Melissa Louise. Reporter, then mng. editor Clearwater (Fla.) Evening Sun, 1930-35; mem. staff Tampa (Fla.) Tribune, 1935-42, 46—, editor, 1958—. Pres., Nat. Conf. Editorial Writers, 1966. Mem. Pulitzer Prize Jury, 1967, 68. Served with USAAF, 1942-45. Recipient 1st prize for editorial writing Fla. Daily Newspaper Assn., 1953, 57, 58, 60, 64, 66, 68, 70, 71; Freedoms Found. award for editorial writing, 1961, 62; traveling fellow to study conditions in Spain, So. Assn. Nieman Fellows, 1953; Fla. Edn. Assn. award, 1963; Nat. Headliners Club award, 1964; Pub. Service award Fla. Bar, 1965. Mem. Am. Soc. Newspaper Editors (dir.), Fla. Soc. Editors (founder, 1st pres. 1955), Sigma Delta Chi (award editorial writing 1962), Phi Kappa Tau. Episcopalian. Clubs: Tampa Yacht and Country, University, Exchange (Tampa), Gasparilla Krewe. Home: 3000 Schiller Av Tampa FL 33609 Office: Tampa Tribune 507 Kennedy Blvd Tampa FL 33601

CLEPPER, HENRY EDWARD, forester; b. Columbia, Pa., Mar. 21, 1901; s. Martin Neil and Charlotte (Keech) C.; B.Forestry, Pa. State Forest Acad. (Pa. State U.), 1921; m. Clorinda McFerren, Aug. 14, 1921; children—Charlotte Mae, Albert Lynn. Forester, Pa. Dept. Forests and Waters, 1921-36; forest service U.S. Dept. Agr., 1936-37; mng. editor jour. Forestry, 1937-66; exec. sec. Soc. Am. Foresters, 1937-66; dir. Am. forestry history project Forest History Soc., Inc., 1966—. Tech. cons. (lumber) WPB, 1942-44; U.S. del. World Forestry Congress, 1960, 66. Recipient Gifford Pinchot medal, 1957. Fellow A.A.A.S., Soc. Am. Foresters; hon. mem. Am. Forestry Assn., Canadian Inst. Forestry, Natural Resources Council Am., Soil Conservation Soc. Am. Club: Cosmos (Washington). Author: (with A.B. Meyer) World of the Forest, 1965; Origins of American Conservation, 1966. Author, editor: American Forestry; Six Decades of Growth, 1960; Careers in Conservation, 1963; Leaders of American Conservation, 1971; Professional Forestry in the United States, 1971. Home: 1206 N Buchanan St Arlington VA 22205

CLERKIN, JAMES JOSEPH, Jr., telephone co. exec.; b. New Britain Conn., June 4, 1923; s. James Joseph and Lillian (Seinel) C.; B.S. in Mech. Engring., Worcester Poly. Inst., 1944; M.B.A., Harvard, 1947; m. Theresa D. Vadnais, June 30, 1945; 1 dau., Patricia Ann. With Theo. Gary & Co., and subsidiaries, 1947-56; v.p., dir. Continental Telephone Co. and subsidiaries, 1952-56; with Comptometer Corp., 1956-61; pres. Gen. Telephone & Electronics Internat. Corp., N.Y.C., 1961-64; exec. v.p. telephone operations Gen. Telephone and Electronics Corp., 1964—, also dir.; dir. Allied Products Corp. Trustee Worcester Poly. Inst. Served with USNR, 1944-45. Mem. Harvard Bus. Sch. Assn., Worcester Poly. Inst. Alumni Assn. Clubs: Harvard of New York; Wee Burn Country (Darien, Conn.); University (N.Y.C.). Home: Winding Lane Darien CT 06820 Office: 730 3d Av New York City NY 10017

CLEVELAND, FORREST FENTON, educator, physicist; b. Pendleton County, Ky., Jan. 10, 1906; s. George Edwin and Flora (Wyatt) C.; A.B., Transylvania Coll., 1927; M.S., U. Ky., 1931, Ph.D., 1934; postgrad. summers U. Chgo., 1932, 33, 39, U. Mich., 1939; m. Marguerite Ewalt, Aug. 17, 1929. Sci. tchr. Middlesboro (Ky.) High Sch., 1927-28; physics tchr. Henry Clay High Sch., Lexington, Ky., 1928-30; instr. physics U. Ky., 1930-34; sci. tchr. Highland Jr. High Sch., Louisville, 1934-35; prof. physics and math., chmn. dept. Lynchburg (Va.) Coll., 1935-39; faculty Ill. Inst. Tech., Chgo., 1939—, prof. physics, 1943—; Vis. prof. physics Ohio State U., summer 1947; Transylvania Coll., summer 1929. Co-recipient Research prize Va. Acad. Sci., 1939. Fellow Am. Phys. Soc., A.A.A.S.; mem. Am. Assn. U. Profs., Am. Assn. Physics Tchrs., Soc. Applied Spectroscopy (hon.), Sigma Xi, Sigma Pi Sigma. Editor, pub. Spectroscopia Molecular, 1952—; asso. editor Jour. Chem. Physics, 1950- 53. Author physics manuals, numerous articles. Home: 1633 E Hyde Park Blvd Chicago IL 60615

CLEVELAND, GEORGE GILBERT, banker; b. Malden, Mass., Oct. 18, 1907; s. Charles G. and Anna (Haverty) C.; B.B.A., Boston U., 1935; m. Grace Halliday Macdonald, Oct. 15, 1938; 1 dau., Susan E. With Provident Instn. Savs., Boton, 1928- -, sr. v.p., corporator, 1969—; v.p. Bankers Data Processing, Inc., Boston, 1962—. Served with AUS, 1943-45. Home: 352 York St Canton MA 02021 Office: 36 Temple Pl Boston MA 02105

CLEVELAND, GERALD ARTHUR, ednl. adminstr.; b. Syracuse, N.Y., Jan. 9, 1916; s. Arthur Bryon and Henrietta (Weigand) C.; A.B., Syracuse U., 1938, M.S. in Edn., 1939, Ed.D., 1961; m. Mildred Antes, Nov. 23, 1939; children—Roger, Linda. Grad. asst. Syracuse U., 1938-39, 40-41; with Syracuse City Sch. Dist., 1939—, jr. high and sr. high tchr., elementary tchr. and adult evening sch. prin., elementary jr. high prin., asst. supt. elementary edn., 1949-55, asst. supt. curriculum and elementary edn., 1955-63, acting supt., 1962-63, asst. supt. instrn., 1964-70, asst. supt. elementary edn., 1970—, dir. instructional survey, 1963—. Cons. coop. program rev. N.Y.C. schs., 1962; bd. dirs. Ednl. TV Council, Empire State F.M. Sch. of Air, 1963-68, treas., 1964, pres., 1967-68; mem. exec. and policy coms. Vocational Survey Onondaga and Oswego counties, N.Y., 1964-66; vice chmn. office ednl. relations Syracuse and Onondaga County chpt. A.R.C., 1964-66; mem. com. instrn. and innovation N.Y. State Council Sch. Supts., 1964-67; mem. com. on econs. in curriculum N.Y. State Assn. Supervision and Curriculum Devel. N.Y. State Council on Econ. Edn., 1968. Bd. dirs. Mental Health Assn. Onodaga County. Mem. N.E.A., N.Y. State (pres. 1961-62), assns. supervision and curriculum devel. N.E.A. (life), N.Y. State Tchrs. Assn., N.Y. State Council City and Village Supts., Am. Assn. Sch. Adminstrs., Phi Beta Kappa, Pi Gamma Mu. Presbyn. (supt. ch. sch. 1951-70, elder), Kiwanian. Office: 409 W Genesee St Syracuse NY 13202

CLEVELAND, GERALD LLOYD, educator; b. Conde, S.D., Apr. 18, 1931; s. Lloyd Edward and Frances (Miesen) C.; B.S. summa cum laude, U. S.D., 1953; M.B.A., U. Minn., 1957; D.B.A., U. Wash., 1965; m. Ramona June Morgan, Sept. 11, 1952; children—Debra Jean, Linda Kay, Sara Beth. Asst. prof., asso. prof. Sch. Bus., U. S.D., 1956-61; lectr., asst. prof. Sch. Bus. Adminstrn., U. Wash., 1962-67; asso. prof. Sch. Bus., Seattle U., 1967-69, prof., dean Sch. Bus., 1969—. Sec.-treas. R.E. Chase & Co., Inc. Chmn. N.W. Area, Accounting Careers Council, 1968-69. Served to lt., Finance Corps, U.S. Army, 1954-56. Mem. Am. Accounting Assn., Financial Execs. Inst., Phi Eta Sigma, Beta Alpha Psi, Beta Gamma Sigma, Alpha Kappa Psi. Office: Sch Bus Seattle U Seattle WA

CLEVELAND, JAMES COLGATE, congressman; b. June 13, 1920; s. Mather and Susan (Colgate) C.; student Deerfield Acad., 1933-37; B.A. magna cum laude, Colgate U., 1941; LL.B., Yale, 1948; m. Hilary Paterson, Dec. 9, 1950; children—Cotton Mather, James Colby, David Paterson, Lincoln Mather, Susan Slater. Admitted to N.H. bar, 1948; practice law, Concord, New London, 1949—; sr. partner Cleveland, Waters & Bass, on leave, 1960—; mem. 88th-92d Congresses, 2d dist. N.H. Organizer, incorporator, officer, dir. New London Trust Co. Rep. 7th Dist. to N.H. Senate, 1950-62, twice majority floor leader. Served with AUS, World War II, Korean War. Decorated Bronze Star. Mem. Am. Legion, Grange, Phi Beta Kappa. Rotarian, Elk, Mason, Eagle, Moose. Club: New London Outing. Co-author: We Propose A Modern Congress, 1966. Home: New London NH 03257 Office: House Office Bldg Washington DC 20525

CLEVELAND, JAMES HARIAN, univ. pres.; b. N.Y.C., Jan 19, 1918; s. Stanley Matthews and Marian Phelps (Van Buren) C.; grad. cum laude, Phillips Acad., Andover, Mass., 1934; A.B. with high honors in politics, Princeton, 1938; Rhodes scholar, Oxford U., 1938-39; LL.D., Rollins Coll., 1956, Franklin and Marshall Coll., 1960, Middlebury Coll., Kent State U., 1962, Ariz. State U., 1968; L.H.D., Alfred U., 1958, Kenyon Coll., 1966; D.C.L., Am. U., 1966; Litt.D., U. Pitts., 1968; m. Lois W. Burton, July 12, 1941; children-Carol Zee, Anne Moore, Alan Thorburn. Intern, Nat. Inst. Pub. Affairs, 1939-40; writer information div. Farm Security Adminstrn., Washington, 1940-42; ofcl. Bd. Econ. Warfare and its successor, Fgn. Econ. Adminstrn., Washington, 1942-44; exec. dir. econ. sect. Allied Control Commn., Rome, Italy, 1944-45; mem. U.S. delegation, 3d session UNRRA Council, London, 1945; acting v.p. in charge econ. sect. Allied Commn., Rome, 1945-46; dept. chief of mission UNRRA Italian Mission. Rome, 1946-47, dir. China office, Shanghai, 1947-48; dir. China program. ECA, Washington, 1948-49, dept. asst. adminstr., 1949-51; asst. dir. for Europe, Mut. Security Agy., 1952-53; exec. editor Reporter, N.Y.C., 1953-56, pub., 1955-56; dean Maxwell grad. sch. citizenship and pub. affairs Syracuse U., 1956-61; asst. sec. for internat. orgn. affairs Dept. State, 1961-65; U.S. ambassador, rep. to NATO, 1965-69; pres. U. Hawaii, Honolulu, 1969—. Trustee Expt. in Internat. Living, New Sch., N.Y.C. Awarded Medal of Freedom, U.S. Army, 1946; grand knight officer Order of Crown of Italy (Italian govt.), 1946; gold star Order Brilliant Star (China), 1948; Woodrow Wilson award Princeton, 1968. Mem. Am. Polit. Sci. Assn., Am. Soc. for Pub. Adminstrn., Phi Beta Kappa. Clubs: Century (N.Y.C.); International (Washington); Ravenstein Golf (Brussels). Author: The Obligations of Power, 1966. Co-author: The Overseas Americans, 1960. Editor: The Promise of World Tensions, 1961. Co-editor: The Art of Overseasmanship, 1957; The Ethic of Power, 1962; Ethics and Bigness, 1962. Home: 2234 Kam Av Honolulu HI 96822

CLEVELAND, KING D., banker. Pres., Nat. Bank Ga., Atlanta. Office: 34 Peachtree St NW Atlanta GA 30301*

CLEVELAND, ROBERT GRAN, found. exec.; b. Seattle, Aug. 21, 1910; s. Henry Davenport and Helen (Gran) C.; A.B., Rollins Coll., 1932; m. Mary Adams Manning, Jan. 22, 1944; children—Mary Manning, (Mrs. Roberts), Frances, David. Engaged in pvt. business, N.Y.C., 1932-40; with WPB, Washington, 1940-42; exec. dir. Office Fgn. Liquidation Commr., Dept. State, 1946-47; apptd. fgn. service officer, 1947, 1st sec. and consul Am. legation, Bucharest, Rumania, 1947-48, 1st sec., consul Am. embassy, Paris, 1948- 52; fgn. service officer, Washington, 1952-54; Am. consul, Sydney, Australia, 1954-56; counselor Am. embassy, Bangkok, Thailand, 1956; dep. dir. S.E. Asian Affairs, Dept. of State, Wahington, 1958-62; dir. U.S. AID mission, counselor Am. embassy, Belgrade, Yugoslavia, 1962-65; dir. Office Pub. Services, Dept. State, Washington, 1965-70; v.p. Meridian House Found., Washington, 1970—. Served with USN, 1942-46, ETO; disch. to Res. as comdr. Clubs: Chevy Chase (Md.); Metropolitan (Washington). Home: 2911 Garfield St N W Washington DC 20008 Office: Meridian House Found 1630 Crescent Pl NW Washington DC 20009

CLEVELAND, STANLEY MATTHEWS, fgn. service officer; b. Madison, Wis., May 20, 1923; s. Stanley Matthews and Marian Phelps (Van Buren) C.; grad. Phillips Acad., 1940; A.B., Princeton, 1943; m. Sally Taishoff, June 29, 1946; children—Thomas Reid, Michael Lambert, Carole Lee; m. 2d, Sieta Kooiman, 1963; children— Cybèle, Irina. U.S. fgn. service officer, 1946—; assigned Sofia, Bulgaria, 1947-49, Paris, France, 1949-55, Washington, 1955-58; chief polit. sect. Am. embassy, Brussels, Belgium, 1958-61, spl. asst. to under sec. of state, Washington, 1961-62; dir. Office of Atlantic Polit.-Econ. Affairs, Dept. State, 1962-63; minister for econ. affairs Am. embassy, Paris, 1963-68; minister for econ. affairs, London, Eng., 1968-71; dep. chief mission, Brasilia, Brazil, 1971—. Mem. U.S. Fgn. Service Assn. (dir. 1956-58), Am. C. of C. France (cons. dir.). Address: American Embassy Brasilia Brazil

CLEVELAND, THERON CLAIR, Jr., banker; b. Greenville, S.C., Nov. 19, 1915; s. Theron Clair and Elizabeth (Davis) C.; student Furman U., 1932-33; A.B., Duke, 1935, LL.B., 1938; m. Elizabeth Linley; children—Elizabeth Linley, Theron Clair III, Susan Davis. Admitted to S.C. bar, 1938, Tenn. bar, 1946; pvt. practice law Greenville, S.C., 1938-41; lawyer Poore, Kramer & Overton, Knoxville, Tenn., 1945-46; trust officer S.C. Nat. Bank, Greenville, 1947-52, v.p. charge Greenville office, 1952-56, regional v.p. Western region, 1956-63, exec. v.p., 1963—. Mem. Total Devel. Com. Greenville County. Mem. bd. Greenville County Home, 1949-62. Served to capt. AUS, 1941-45. Presbyn. Clubs: Greenville Country, Green Valley Country. Home: 24 Dogwood Lane Cleveland Forest Greenville SC 29607 Office: 13-15 S Main St Greenville SC 29602

CLEVENGER, CURTIS HAROLD, retail foods co. exec.; b. Sterling, Kan., Oct. 19, 1919; s. William R. and Stella (Buchanan) C.; student Okla. State U., 1937-40; m. Dorothy May Pendleton, Mar. 28, 1938; children—Robert A., Barbara (Mrs. Larry Gusman), Beverly (Mrs. Wayne Morris). With Humpty-Dumpty, Oklahoma City, Okla., 1938-65, v.p., div. mgr., 1963-65; v.p., div. mgr. Wrigley Food Stores, Detroit, Mich., 1965-67; with Allied Supermarkets, Inc., Detroit, Mich., 1968—, corp. v.p., div. mgr., Atlanta, Ga., 1968—. Bd. dirs. Frontier ouncil Boy Scouts Am., 1963-65. Served with USNR, 1943-46. Mem. Sales and Mktg. Execs.-Atlanta Inc. Home: 3546 Old Chamblee-Tucker Rd Atlanta GA 30340 Office: 1677 Tully Circle NE Atlanta GA 30329

CLEVENGER, JOHN COWGILL, educator; b. Belleville, Kan., Mar. 20, 1913; s. James A. and Gladys A. (Cowgill) C.; B.S., Colo. A. and M. Coll., 1936; M.E., 1948; Ed.D., Stanford, 1951; m. Valeria Ann Dorsey, Aug. 1, 1936; children—James D., David L. Tchr. vocational agr., Julesburg, Colo., 1936-38, Centerville, Cal., 1938-40; alumni sec. Colo. A. and M. Coll., 1940-43, asst. to pres., 1946, dean students, 1947; now v.p. for student affairs Wash. State U., Pullman. First chmn. Council Student Personnel Assns., 1963-64; mem. State Dept. Higher Edn. Survey Team to South Vietnam, 1967. Mem. nat. council YMCA, mem. Pacific Northwest bd. Served to lt. USNR, 1943-46. Mem. Am., N.W. coll. personnel assns., Nat. Assn. Student Personnel Adminstrs. (pres. 1962), Am. Council Edn. (commn. acad. affairs), Coll. Student Personnel Inst. (past chmn. acad. council), Alpha Zeta, Alpha Tau Alpha, Pi Delta Epsilon, Sigma Phi Epsilon. Office: Wash State U Pullman WA 99163

CLEVENGER, JOSEPH R., lawyer, author, editor, pub.; b. nr. Excelsior Springs, Mo., May 13, 1884; s. Gordon and Sarah (Sisk) C.; A.B., U. Mo., 1905, LL.B., 1907. Admitted to N.Y. bar, 1912, tried and won N.Y. City Savs. and Loan Fraud cases, 1916-19. Author: Annual Practice of New York, 1922-56; Criminal Law and Practice, 1928-53; Parol Evidence, 1928; Applied Law of Automobiles, 1929; Clevenger-Huddy Cyclopedia of Automobile Law, 1932; Automobile Trials, 1935; Annulment of Marriage, 1946; Supreme Court Practice, 1921; Rules of Civil Practice, 1922; Surrogate's Court Practice, 1922; New York City Court and Municipal Court Practice, 1922; total 92 vols. Editor: Gulbert-Bliss Civil Practice, 1940-56; Nichols- Cahill Annotated Civil Practice Acts, 1950-56; pub. propr. Am. Law Pubs. 1922-50. Staff editor Corpus Juris (1908-12). Home: 14 Monroe St New York City, NY 10002.

CLEVENGER, RAYMOND CHARLES, banker; b. Williamsburg, Kan., Apr. 2, 1910; s. Raymond Charles and Era (Poage) C.; student Kan. U., 1928-30; D.Bus. Adminstrn. (hon.), Washburn U., 1961; m. Mary Margatet Ramsey, Nov. 26, 1932; children—Thomas R., Raymond Charles III, John N. Asst. cashier Nat. Bank Topeka, 1936-38, v.p., 1939-42, exec. v.p., 1942-49, pres., 1949-57; pres, First Nat. Bank Topeka (merger Central Nat. Bank and Nat. Bank Topeka), 1957—, also dir.; dir. Kan. Power & Light Co., Security Benefit Life Ins. Co., Kan. Bankers Surety Co. (Topeka), A.T.&S.F. Ry. Trustee Kan. U. Endowment Assn., Menninger Found., Kan. Pub. Employees Retirement System. Served with USAAF, World War II. Mem. Topeka C. of C. (pres. 1960), Kan. Bankers Assn. (pres. 1963). Home: 1540 Westover Rd Topeka KS 66604 Office: 535 Kansas Av Topeka KS 66603

CLEVENGER, RAYMOND FRANCIS, lawyer; b. Chgo., June 6, 1926; s. James Harold and Rose Ann (Fontaine) C.; student London (Eng.) Sch. Econs. and Polit. Sci., 1948-49; A.B., Roosevelt U., 1949; J.D., U. Mich., 1952; m. Francile M. Corbat, Aug. 22, 1948; children—Philip, Diane, Jeffrey, John, Sue Ann. Admitted to Ill. bar, 1952, Mich. bar, 1953; practice in Sault Ste. Marie, 1953-61, 63-64; research asso. Legislative Research Center, U. Mich., 1952-53; commr. Mich. Corp. and Securities Commn., 1961-63; mem. 89th Congress 11th Dist. Mich.; chmn. Gt. Lakes Basin Commn., 1967-68; partner law firm Forsythe, Campbell, Vandenberg & Clevenger. Served with AUS, 1944-46. Home: 1616 Harding Rd Ann Arbor MI 48104 Office: 111 S Main St Ann Arbor MI 48108

CLEVENGER, THEODORE, Jr., educator; b. Kansas City, Mo., Dec. 2, 1929; s. Theodore and Alice (Dorsett) C.; student Phillips U., 1947-49; B.A., Baylor U., 1951, M.A., 1952; Ph.D., Fla. State U., 1958; m. Charlotte Ruth Dorrill, Apr. 19, 1951; children—Theodore III, Ruth Alice, Frederick William, Elizabeth Anne. Tchr. Henderson State Coll., 1953-54, U. Ill., 1957-59, U. Wis., 1959-62, U. Pitts., 1962-65; prof. U. Tex., 1965-67; prof. chmn. dept. communication Fla. State U., 1967—. Pres. Fox Chapel P.T.A., 1965. Mem. A.A.A.S., Am. Psychol. Assn., Soc. Psycho-physiol. Research, Internat. Communication Assn., Speech Communication Assn. (1st v.p. 1971). Club: Tallahassee Kennel (pres. 1970). Author: Audience Analysis, 1966; (with Huber Ellingsworth) Speech and Social Action, 1968; (with Jack Matthews) The Speech Communication Process, 1971. Editor of Jour. Communication, 1965-67. Home: 9300 Mahan Dr Tallahassee FL 32301

CLEVERDON, ERNEST GROVE, former banker; b. Marlow, Ala., Sept. 28, 1900; s. Walter I. and Millicent (Grove) C.; B.A., U. Ala., 1924; m. Marian Hauser, Oct. 8, 1927; children—John Hauser, Walter Irving. With Mchts. Nat. Bank Mobile, 1929—, cashier, 1938-65, exec. v.p., 1963-68, ret., 1968, dir. until 1968, hon. dir., 1968—. Pres., America's Jr. Miss. Scholarship Found., 1963—; dir., past pres. Mobile Symphony and Civic Music Assn.; pres. Mobile County Found. Pub. Higher Edn., 1961—. Bd. dirs., past pres. Mobile chpt. A.R.C., Jr. Achievement Mobile; bd. dirs., past 1st v.p. Mobile Better Bus. Bur.; bd. dirs. Group Aid for Retarded Children, Ala. Motorist Assn., Birmingam; v.p., trustee, chmn. exec. com. U. of S. Ala.; treas., bd. dirs. Am.'s Jr. Miss Pageant, 1970—; v.p., bd. dirs. Ala. Council on Econ. Edn., U. Ala., 1970—. Named Educator of Year, Phi Delta Kappa, 1965, Mobilian of Year, 1962; recipient Civic award Alpha Kappa Psi, 1969, First Alumni Assn. Service award U.S. Ala., 1970. Mem. English Speaking Union, Mobile C. of C. (chmn. edn. com. 1957-70), Beta Gamma Sigma. Methodist (trustee, treas.). Lion (past pres. Mobile). Clubs: Mobile Country; Isle Dauphine Country. Home: 1860 Dauphin St Mobile AL 36606 Office: P O Box 2527 Mobile AL 36601

CLEW, WILLIAM JOSEPH, newspaper editor; b. Middletown, Conn., June 28, 1904; s. Timothy J. and Anne (Taylor) C.; student Wesleyan U., Middletown, 1926-27; m. Mona Gallivan, Oct. 12, 1928; children—William Taylor, Harvey Taylor and Carole (Mrs. Edwin A. Hoey) (twins), Elizabeth Barrow. Reporter, Middletown Press, 1923-25; mem. staff Hartford (Conn.) Courant, 1925—, asst. mng. editor, 1949-66, mng. editor, 1966—; mem. expdn. Operation Deep Freeze to S. Pole, 1964; search expdn. for lost bomber Lady Be Good, 1960. Mem. Middletown Bd. Edn., 1945-49, Haddam (Conn.) Bd. Edn., 1956-60. Served as capt. AUS, 1942-43. Mem. New Eng. A.P. News Execs. Assn. (pres. 1965-66), Res. Officers Assn., A.P. Mng. Editors Assn., Sigma Delta Chi. Clubs: Explorers, Overseas Press (N.Y.C.); Kiwi (New Zealand); Antarctica Press (McMurdo, Antarctica). Author articles. Home: Middlesex Turnpike Haddam CT 06438 Office: 285 Broad St Hartford CT 06101

CLEWELL, DAYTON HARRIS, oil co. exec.; b. Berwick, Pa., Dec. 15, 1912; s. H. Bert and Emma (Kile) C.; B.S., Mass. Inst. Tech., 1933, Ph.D. in Physics, 1936; m. Jean Rapp, June 25, 1938; children—Don B., Nancy H. Research physicist C.K. Williams Co., Easton, Pa., 1935-38; with Magnolia Petroleum Co., 1938-56, dir. research, 1952-56; with Mobil Oil Corp. Inc., 1956—, gen. mgr. research and engring., 1962-64, sr. v.p., 1964—. Spl. research color pigments, devel. gravity measuring instruments for petroleum prospecting, electronic instrumentation, geophysics N.Y.C. Mayor's Sci. and Tech. Adv. Council, 1966—; mem. vis. com. div. engring., applied physics Harvard, 1962-68; mem. corp. Mass. Inst. Tech., 1965-70, mem. devel. com., 1970—. Fellow I.E.E.E.; mem. Am. Phys. Soc., Dirs. Indsl. Research, Am. Assn. Petroleum Geologists, Soc. Exploration Geophysicists, Indsl. Research Inst., Nat. Security Indsl. Assn. (chmn. ocean sci. and tech. adv. com. 1969—), Am. Petroleum Inst. (vice chmn. div. sci. and tech. 1962- 63), N.Y. Acad. Sci. Conglist. (deacon). Clubs: Pinnacle (N.Y.C.); Tokeneke (Darien, Conn.). Home: 34 Driftway Lane Darien CT 06820 Office: 150 E 42d St New York City NY 10017

CLEWETT, RICHARD MONROE educator; b. San Diego, Cal., Feb. 1, 1911; s. George E. and (Rees) C.; B.A., U. Nev., 1934; M.A., U. Pa., 1942, Ph.D., 1948; m. Mary Jane Roby, Dec. 24, 1941; children—Richard Monroe, Barbara Jane. With Universal Credit Co., 1934-36, Gen. Motors Acceptance Corp., 1936-37; asst. econs. U. Cal., 1937-39; inst. marketing U. Pa., 1939-42, 45-48; asst. prof. sch. bus. Northwestern U., 1948-51, asso. prof., 1951-54, prof., 1954—, chmn. dept. marketing, 1953-58, 65—; faculty Internat. Inst. Mgmt., Lucerne. Participant, Pres.'. Conf. on Tech. and Distbn. Research for Small Business, 1957; cons. Orgn. European Econ. Cooperation, 1958-59. Served with USNR, 1942-45. Mem. A.A.A.S., Econ. Assn., Am. Marketing Assn., Am. Inst. Baking (dir.; ednl. adv. com., 1963—), Phi Kappa Phi, Delta Sigma Pi, Beta Gamma Sigma. Baptist. Club: Univ. Author: Marketing Channels for Manufactured Products, 1953. Co-author: Cases in Marketing Strategy, 1958, rev. edit., 1964. Co-editor; Contemporary American Marketing, 1957, rev. edit.,1963. Editorial staff Jour. Marketing, 1950-58. Home: 1401 Lincoln St Evanston IL 60201

CLIBURN, VAN, (Harvey Lavan, Jr.), concert pianist; b. Shreveport, La., July 12, 1934; s. Harvey Lavan and Rildia Bee (O'Bryan) C.; studied music with mother, 1937-51; grad. with highest honors (Frank Damrosch scholar), Julliard Sch. Music, 1954; H.H.D. (hon.), Baylor U., 1958. Pub. appearances, Shreveport, 1940; debut Houston Symphony Orch., 1947; appeared with Dallas Symphony Orch., 1952, N.Y. Philharmonic Orch., Carnegie Hall, 1954, 58; concert pianist on tour U.S., 1955-56, Soviet Union, 1958; recs. RCA Victor; guest TV shows; concert with Symphony of the Air, Carnegie Hall, 1958, concert Brussels Fair, Belgium, 1958, other appearances include Phila., Chgo., Hollywood, Denver, London, Amsterdam, Paris; nation-wide tour U.S., 1958—. Recipient Tex. State prize, 1947, Nat. Music Festival award, 1948, G.B. Dealy award, Dallas, 1952, Kosciuszko Found. Chopin award, 1952; grand Olga Samaroff Found., 1953; 1st pl. Julliard Concerto concert, 1953; Edgar M. Leventritt Found. award, 1954; Carl M. Roeder Meml. award Julliard Sch. Music, 1954; 1st prize Internat. Tschaikovsky Piano Competition, Moscow, Russia, 1958; citation Am. Assn. Sch. Adminstrs., 1959; named number in classical field Top Artists on Campus Poll (album sales), 1968. Mem. Am. Guild Mus. Artists. Baptist. Clubs: Thespian (pres. Kilgore, Tex.); Rotary (hon.), Lotus (life). Composer classical music. Office: care S Hurok 730 Fifth Av New York City NY 10019 also Salisbury Hotel 123 W 57th St New York City NY 10019

CLIETT, CHARLES BUREN, educator; b. Montpelier, Miss., July 10, 1924; s. James Thomas and Sally Lou (Saul) C.; B.S. in Aero. Engring., Ga. Inst. Tech., 1945, M.S. in Aero. Engring., 1950; m. Grace Holland Campbell, Dec. 25, 1946; children—Susan Marie, Charles Buren. Faculty Miss. State U., 1947—, prof. aero. engring., 1957—, chmn. dept., 1960—. Served to lt. (j.g.) USNR, 1943-46. Registered profl. engr., Miss. Mem. Am. Soc. Engring. Edn., Am. Inst. Aeros. and Astronautics, Am. Legion, Nat., Miss. socs. profl. engrs., Tau Beta Pi, Mem. Christian Ch. (elder). Home: 638 Commerce St West Point MS 39773 Office: P O Drawer A State College MS 39762

CLIFCORN, LAVERNE EDWARD, former chemist; b. Rockford, Ill., Aug. 28, 1906; s. Edward Franklin and Wilhelmina Gertrude (Mulder) C.; B.A., U. Wis., 1928, M.A., 1930, Ph.D., 1934; m. Bernice Edna Dengel, Sept. 16, 1930; children—Joan Bernice, Charlene LaVerne. Chemist, State of Wis., 1928-36; staff research div. Continental Can Co., 1936-55, dir. fundamental research div., 1950-55, asso. dir. research, metal div., 1955; supr. container utilization, research div. Am. Can Co., 1955-58; mgr. research dept. Nat. Can Corp., 1958-61; dir. research Crown Cork & Seal Co., Phila., 1961-67, mgr. tech. service, Chgo., 1967- 70. Cons. Dept. Def., 1962—; v.p. Agrl. Research Inst. NRC, 1955; chmn. Nat. Chem. Expn., Chgo., 1948; chmn. panel on food Research and Devel. Bd., Dept. Def., 1952-53; chmn. gen. com. on foods NRC, 1960-66. Mem. Am. Chem. Soc. (chmn. div. agrl. and food chemistry 1950), Sigma Xi, Alpha Chi Sigma, Phi Lambda Upsilon. Mason. Contbr. articles to profl. publs. Patentee in field. Home: 115 N Ela Rd Barrington IL 60010

CLIFF, EDWARD P., govt. ofcl.; b. Heber City, Utah, Sept. 3, 1909; s. Edward Parley and Geneva Rachel (Bergener) C.; B.S., Utah State U., 1931, D.Sc., 1965; m. Kathryn Mitchell, Apr. 2, 1931; children—Carolyn, Jane. Jr. range examiner Wenatchee Nat. Forest, Washington, U.S. Forest Service, 1931-34, range examiner in charge wildlife mgmt. Pacific N.W. Region, Portland, Ore., 1934-39, supr. Siskiyou Nat. Forest, Grants Pass, Ore., 1939-41, Fremont Nat. Forest, Lakeview, Ore., 1942-44, asst. chief div. range mgmt., Washington, 1944-46, asst. regional forester in charge div. range and wildlife mgmt. Intermountain Region, Ogden, Utah, 1946-49, regional forester Rocky Mountain Region, Denver, 1950-52, asst. chief in charge nat. forest adminstrn., Washington, 1952- 62, chief Forest Service, 1962—. Chmn., N.Am. Forestry Commn., 1964-65, 69—; mem. U.S. Bd. Geog. Names, 1952-67, chmn., 1962-65; alternate mem. Adv. Council Historic Preservation, 1967—. Recipient Distinguished Service award Utah State U., 1958; Distinguished service award Dept. Agr., 1962; Nat. Civil Service League's Career Service award, 1968. Mem. Soc. Am. Foresters, Wildlife Soc. (charter), Am. Soc. Range Mgmt. (charter), Am. Forestry Assn., Wilderness Soc. Mem. Ch. of Jesus Christ of Latter-day Saints. Mason. Clubs: Cosmos, Boone and Crockett. Author: (with W.A. Dayton, others) Range Plant Handbook, 1937. Contbr. articles to govt. publs. Home: 221 N Royal St Alexandria VA 22314 Office: Forest Service Dept Agr Washington DC 20250

CLIFFORD, SISTER ADELE, coll. pres., biologist; b. Chillicothe, O., Aug. 29, 1906; d. Timothy and Ellen (Murphy) Clifford; A.B., Coll. Mt. St. Joseph (O.), 1933; M.S., Fordham U., 1946, Ph.D., 1949. Grade sch. tchr., Cleve., 1930-33; grade sch. prin., Royal Oak, Mich., 1933-35; high sch. tchr., Cin., 1935-42; instr. biology Coll. Mt. St. Joseph, 1942-67, pres., 1967—. Bd. advisers Cin. Montessori Soc., 1967—. Research Marine Biol. Lab., Woods Hole, Mass., 1946-48, summers 1961-67. Mem. Am. Inst. Biol. Ohio Scis., Bot. Soc. Am., Coll. Biology Tchrs. Conf. (sec. 1966-67), Am. Soc. Zoologists, A.A.A.S., Ohio Acad. Sci., Am. Genetic Assn., Assn. Am. Colls. Club: Zonta (Cin.). Home: College Mount St Jospeh Mount St Joseph OH 45051

CLIFFORD, ALAN FRANK educator; b. Natick, Mass., June 8, 1919; s. Arthur Woodbury and Elva (Buck) C.; A.B., Harvard, 1941; M.S., U. Del., 1947, Ph.D., 1949; m. Shirley Catherine Mittleman, Aug. 20, 1949; children—Abbie Louise, Philip Alan. Chemist, Kankakee Ordnance Works, Joliet, Ill., 1941-43; research chemist Manhattan Project U. Chgo.-Oak Ridge-Richland, Wash., 1943-45; instr. chemistry dept. U. Del., 1947-49; asst. prof. Ill. Inst. Tech., 1949-51; Guggenheim fellow Cambridge U., 1951-53; asst. prof., asso. prof. Purdue U., 1953-66; prof., head chemistry dept. Va. Poly. Inst. and State U., Blackburg, 1966—. Fellow N.Y. Acad. Scis.; chmn. NAS-NRC com. on Inorganic Nomenclautre. Mem. Am. Chem. Soc. (com. chmn.), Faraday Soc., Chem. Soc. (London), Am. Assn. U., Profs., Sigma Xi, Alpha Chi Sigma, Phi Lambda Upsilon, Pi Kappa Alpha, Triangle, Author: Inorganic Chemistry of Qualitative Analysis, 1961. Home: 860 Hutcheson Lane Blacksburg VA 24060

CLIFFORD, ALFRED HOBLITZELLE, educator; b. St. Louis, July 11, 1908; s. Arthur Morton and Judith (Hoblitzelle) C.; A.B., Yale, 1929; Ph.D., Cal. Inst. Tech., 1933; m. Alice Colt, June 20, 1942; 1 son, Karl Hoblitzelle. Asst. to Hermann Weyl, Inst. Advanced Study, Princeton, 1936-38; instr. math. Mass. Inst. Tech., 1938-42; asso. prof. math. Johns Hopkins, 1946-50, 52-55; prof. math. Tulane U.-Newcomb Coll., 1955—, head dept. Newcomb Coll., 1955—, univ. chmn., 1959-61. Served to lt. comdr. USNR, 1942-46, 50-52. Mem. Am. Math. Soc. (editorial bd. transactions 1956-57), Math. Assn. Am. Author: (with G.B. Preston) The Algebraic Theory of Semigroups, Vol. 1, 1961, Vol. 2, 1967. Contbr. articles profl. jours. Home: 1207 Exposition Blvd New Orleans, LA 70118.

CLIFFORD, CLARK MCADAMS, lawyer; b. Fort Scott, Kan., Dec. 25, 1906; s. Frank Andrew and Georgia (McAdams) C.; LL.B., Washington U., St. Louis, 1928; m. Margery Pepperell Kimball, Oct. 3, 1931; children—Margery Pepperrell (Mrs. William H. Lanagan, Jr.), Joyce Carter (Mrs. Richard D. Barett), Randall (Mrs. Edward I. Wight). Asso. firm Holland, Lashly & Donnell, St. Louis, 1928-33; with Holland, Lashly & Lashly, 1933-37; partner Lashly, Lashly, Miller & Clifford, 1938-50, sr. partner Clifford & Miller, Washington, 1950-68; sec. def. Def. Dept., Washington, 1968-69; sr. partner Clifford, Warnke, Glass, McIlwain & Finney, Washington, 1969—. Spl. counsel to Pres. U.S., 1946-50. Served from lt. (j.g.) to capt. USNR, 1944-46; naval aide to Pres. U.S., 1946. Recipient medal of Freedom. Mem. Fed., Am., Mo., D.C., St. Louis bar assns., Kappa Alpha. Clubs: Racquet (St. Louis); Burning Tree, Metropolitan, Chevy Chase (Washington). Home: 9421 Rockville Pike Bethesda MD 20014 Office: 815 Connecticut Av Washington DC 20006

CLIFFORD, D.W., Jr., banker. Exec. v.p. So. Ariz. Bank, Tucson. Office: 150 N Stone Av PO Box 1871 Tucson AZ 85701*

CLIFFORD, EARLE WINCHESTER, Jr., univ. adminstr.; b. Rutland, Vt., Sept. 12, 1925; s. Earle Winchester and Florence U. (Phillips) C.; student U. Me., 1943; diploma with highest honors, Rutland Jr. Coll., 1948; A.B. magna cum laude, Syracuse U., 1950, M.S., 1951, postgrad., 1951—; LL.D., St. Peter's Coll., 1968; m. Marie T. Mondella, Nov. 15, 1952; children—Karen, Philip. Mem. staff Syracuse U., 1952-57, 61-63, dean men, 1961-63, instr. citizenship dept., 1954-57, 62-63; dean men U. Vt., 1957-61, instr. evening div., 1958-61; dean student affairs, 1963-70, v.p. for student affairs, 1970—; lectr. sociology dept. and Grad. Sch. Edn., Rutgers U., New Brunswick, N.J., 1963—. Mem. Gov. Vt. Com. Youth Fitness, 1958-60; div. chmn. govt. and edn. Burlington (Vt.) United Fund, 1960-61; chmn. ednl. div. United Hosp. Appeal; chmn. New Brunswick Adv. Com. on Recreation. Bd. dirs. Burlington Boys Club, 1959-61, v.p., 1960-61; bd. dirs. New Brunswick chpt. A.R.C., Saint Peter's Hosp. Served with AUS, 1943-46. Mem. Am. Acad. Polit. and Social Sci., Nat. Assn. Student Personnel Adminstrs. (exec. com., pres. 1970), Am. Personnel and Guidance Assn., Am. Coll. Personnel Assn. (chmn. resolutions com.), Phi Beta Kappa, Kappa Phi Kappa (nat. councillor 1950-52), Phi Delta Kappa, Pi Gamma Mu, Alpha Phi Omega (mem. nat. bd. dirs.), Alpha Delta Kappa, Tau Theta Upsilon. Republican. Conglist. Mem. editorial bd. Guidance Research Group, also Nat. Assn. Student Personnel Adminstrs. Jour. Contbr. articles to learned publs. Home: 18 Bishop Pl New Brunswick NJ 08901

CLIFFORD, EDWARD LAMBERT, banker; b. Evanston, Ill., Dec. 23, 1905; s. Edward and Anne Watson (Lambert) C.; B.S., Princeton, 1927; M.B.A., Harvard, 1932; m. Emelie Bennet Terry, June 25, 1946. With Hornblower & Weeks, investment bankers, N.Y.C., 1928-30; with R.I. Hosp. Trust Co., Providence, 1932- 50, v.p., 1946-50; pres. Worcester (Mass.) County Nat. Bank, 1950-70, cons., dir., 1971—; dir. Worcester Mut. Fire Ins. Co., Crompton & Knowles Corp., Wyman-Gordon Co., Guarantee Mut. Assurance Co.; trustee Worcester Co. Inst. for Savs. Treas., dir. Worcester Bus. Devel. Corp. Chmn., dir. Mass. Taxpayers Found.; adv. trustee Assumption Coll., Worcester; trustee Meml. Hosp., Worcester. Served to lt. comdr. USNR, 1942-45. Mem. Mass. Fed. Taxpayers (trustee). Republican (treas. R.I. State Central Com., 1946-48). Episcopalian. Clubs: Worcester, Tatnuck Country, Worcester Country (Worcester). Home: 1 Bancroft Tower Rd Worcester MA 01609 Office: 446 Main St Worcester MA 01608

CLIFFORD, FRANCIS, writer; b. Bristol, Eng., Dec. 1, 1917; s. George Bell and Agnes (Evans) Thompson; student Christ's Hosp., Horsham, Eng., 1928-35; 1 son by previous marriage, Peter; m. 2d, Josephine Bridget Devereux, Sept. 17, 1955; 1 son, Mark Bell. Served with Brit. Army, 1939-45; Burma, U.K. Decorated Distinguished Service Order. Mem. Author's League Am. Author: Honour the Shrine, 1953; The Trembling Earth, 1955; Overdue, 1957; Something to Love, 1958; Act of Mercy, 1960; A Battle is Fought to be Won, 1960; Time is an Ambush, 1962; The Green Fields of Eden, 1963; The Hunting Ground, 1964; The Third Side of the Coin, 1965; The Naked Runner, 1966; All Men Are Lonely Now, 1967; Spanish Duet, 1966; Another Way of Dying, 1969; The Blind Side, 1971. Address: Brook House Eriswell Crescent Burwood Park Walton-on-Thames Surrey England

CLIFFORD, FRANK RICHARD, univ. adminstr.; b. Bklyn., Jan. 13, 1923; s. James Vincent and Maude (Schuler) C.; B.A., Cornell U., 1950; m. Jean Marie Goodell, June 23, 1951; children—Richard H., Mark F., John R. Dir. coll. union and residence halls, asst. dean students State U. N.Y. Coll. Edn., Brockport, 1951-56; asst. dir. ann. giving, asso. dir. devel., dir. univ. assos. Cornell U., 1956-63; v.p. devel. Western Res. U., 1963-67; dir. alumni relations Cornell U., Ithaca, N.Y., exec. sec. Cornell Univ. Alumni Assn., 1967—. Served to lt. (j.g.) USNR, 1942-45. Decorated D.F.C., Air medal (2). Mem. Am. Coll. Pub. Relations Assn., Am. Alumni Council, Phi Kappa Sigma. Roman Catholic. Clubs: Cornell (N.Y.C.); Country of Ithaca, Savage of Ithaca. Home: 112 Salem Dr Ithaca NY 14850

CLIFFORD, FREDERICK BURR, coll. dean; b. Samaria, Mich., June 3, 1914; s. Frederick Jesse and Genevieve Clara (Burr) C.; A.B., No. Mich. Coll., 1935; M.A., U. Mich., 1937, Ph.D., 1943; B.D., Oberlin Coll., 1946; m. Doris Jean Jones, Aug. 26, 1943; children—John Frederick, David Burr, Jeanne Ellen. Ordained to ministry Methodist Ch., 1943; pastor in Dearborn, Mich., 1943-47; prof. English Adrian (Mich.) Coll., 1947-53; asso. prof. humanities Emory-at- Oxford, Emory U., 1953-58; prof. English, chmn. dept. Southwestern U., 1958-62, dean Coll. Arts and Scis., 1962—. Mem. Central Tex. Conf. Meth. Ch., Am. Philol. Assn., Classical Assn. Middle West and South, Nat. Council Tchrs. English. Home: 1407 Hutto Rd Georgetown TX 78626

CLIFFORD, JACK CARL, broadcasting co. exec.; b. Gary, Ind., Sept. 13, 1933; s. Jack Charles and Pauline Rose (Arndt) C.; B.A., Western Mich. U., 1956; postgrad., Harvard Bus. Sch., 1970; m. Marguerite Eileen Seeds, Oct. 24, 1958; children—Jack Jay, Kristin Leigh. Announcer, WKMI Radio, Kalamazoo, Mich., 1955-57; sports dir. KTUK-TV, Phoenix, 1957-59, sales rep., 1958-62; sales rep. KTAR-TV, Phoenix, 1962-68, v.p., gen. sales mgr., 1968-70, pres., gen. mgr., 1970—. Pres. television for Combined Communications Corp., Phoenix, 1970—. Mem. Pub. relations com. YMCA, 1971—. Mem. A.P. Radio/Television Assn. (dir. 1970—), Met. Phoenix Broadcasters Assn. (dir. 1971—), Nat. Assn. Television Arts and Scis., Ariz. Broadcasters Assn., Newcomen Soc. N.Am., Young Pres.'s Orgn. Kiwanian. Home: 4121 N 52d Pl Phoenix AZ 85018 Office: 1101 N Central Av Phoenix AZ 85001

CLIFFORD, JAMES LOWRY, ret. educator; b. Evansville, Ind., Feb. 24, 1901; s. George S. and Emily (Orr) C.; A.B., Wabash Coll., 1923, L.H.D., 1956; B.S., Mass. Inst. Tech., 1925; Ph.D., Columbia, 1941; Litt.D. (hon.), Evansville Coll., 1955; L.H.D., Ind. U., 1963; m. Virginia Iglehart, Aug. 31, 1940; children—Emily Orr, James Townley, Joseph Holt. Gen. mgr. Young Car Co., Evansville, 1926-28; English master Evans Sch., Tucson, 1929-32; Cutting traveling fellow Columbia, 1935-36; from English instr. to asso. prof. Lehigh U., 1937-44; asso. prof. English, Barnard Coll., 1945-46; prof. English, Columbia, 1946-69, William Peterfield Trent prof. English, 1964-69, emeritus, 1969—. Guggenheim fellow 1951-52, 65-66; research in Eng. during year 1958-59. Editor of Johnsonian News Letter; sec. English Inst. 1946; chmn. 18th century groups Modern Lang. Assn., 1944, 46. Fellow Royal Soc. Lit., Royal Soc. Arts (both London); mem. Johnson Soc. (pres. Lichfield, Eng. 1958-59; hon. v.p. London), P.E.N., Phi Beta Kappa, Phi Gamma Delta. Presbyn. Author: Hester Lynch Piozzi (Mrs. Thrale), 1941; Young Sam Johnson, 1955; From Puzzles to Portraits: Problems of a Literary Biographer, 1970. Editor: Dr. Campbell's Diary, 1947; Johnsonian Studies 1887-1950. A Survey and Bibliography, 1951, rev. and expanded (with D.J. Greene), 1970; Eighteenth Century English Literature: Modern Essays in Criticism, 1959; (with Louis A. Landa) Pope and His Contemporaries, 1949; Biography as an Art, 1962; Peregrine Pickle (Tobias Smollett), 1964; Man Versus Society in Eighteenth-Century Britain, 1968. Adv. editorial bd. Yale Boswell edit., also Wesleyan U. edit. Works of Henry Fielding, Yale Johnson edit. Contbr. articles to profl. jours. Home: 25 Claremont Av New York City NY 10027

CLIFFORD, JOHN MCLEAN, lawyer; b. Salt Lake City, Dec. 9, 1904; s. William Ernest and Margaret M. (McLean) C.; student U. Utah, 1923-25; LL.B., Southwestern U., 1930; m. Lucetta Penrose Brown, June 10, 1925; 1 dau., Patricia Lou (Mrs. Frank Jordan). Admitted to Cal. bar, 1930, D.C. bar, 1939; v.p. NBC, Inc., N.Y.C., 1953-54, adminstrv. v.p., 1954-56, exec. v.p., 1956-61, staff v.p. RCA, 1961-62; exec. v.p. Curtis Pub. Co., Phila., 1962-64, pres., dir., 1964-68; dir. Camden First Nat. Bank & Trust Co. (N.J.), Beehive Med. Electronics, Inc., Salt Lake City. Mem. D.C., Cal. bar assns. Home: 965 Via Fruteria Hope Ranch Park Santa Barbara CA 93105 Office: 125 E Victoria St Santa Barbara CA 93104 also 114 Oakdene Teaneck NJ 07666

CLIFFORD, PATRICK JOSEPH, banker; b. Bklyn., Nov. 10, 1912; s. William Edward and Mary (Aylward) C.; m. Mary Gorman, Mar. 16, 1942; children—William, Patricia. With Catham Phoenix Nat. Bank & Trust Co., Mfrs. Trust Co., N.Y.C., 1928-45; exec. v.p., dir. Franklin Nat. Bank, N.Y.C., 1946-66; pres., dir. Security Nat. Bank L.I., Huntington, 1966-69, chmn., dir., 1969—; dir., mem. salary and compensation com. Glen Alden Corp.; dir. McCrory corp. L.I., Masters, Inc., Utilities & Industries Corp. Bd. dirs. L.I. Assn. Mem. adv. Council L.I. Better Bus. Bur., 1966—; mem. Suffolk County council Boy Scouts Am., 1966—. Served to 1st lt. USAAF, World War II. Mem. Robert Morris Assos., N.Y. State (past pres.), Am. (exec. council, chmn. comml. lending com.) bankers assns. Home: 500 E 77th St New York City NY 10021 Office: 350 Main St Huntington NY 11743

CLIFFORD, PAUL CLEMENT, educator; b. Bismarels, N.D., Nov. 23, 1910; s. Stephen S. and Catherine (Cronin) C.; B.A., Columbia, 1931, M.A., 1934; m. Katherine Corbett, July 16, 1936; children—Denis, Joanne, Steven, Gregory, Douglas, Cathy, Justin. Instr. math. Columbia, 1932-35; mem. faculty Montclair (N.J.) State Coll., 1935—, prof. math., 1957—, chmn. dept., 1963—; lectr. N.Y. U., 1944-45, Newark Coll. Engring., 1946-47, Rutgers U., 1948-64, U. Mich., 1957-70, U. Wis., 1962—, indsl. cons., 1942—. NBC Continental Classroom, 1961-62; cons. UN, 1953-54, UN Orgn. Indsl. Devel., 1966, ICA, 1954-59, AID, 1959—. Class chmn. Columbia Coll. Fund, 1964-70; mem. Montclair Community Com., 1964-71. Fellow A.A.A.S. (mem. coop. com. on teaching sci. and math. 1967—), Am. Statis. Assn., Am. Soc. Quality Control (Shewhart medal 1965; dir. ednl. and tng. 1959- 64); mem. Math. Assn. Am. (bd. govs. 1970—, C.U.P.M. panel on statistics 1967—), Am. Soc. Testing Materials (com. on statis. methods 1967—). Initiator European Orgn. Quality Control, 1954. Home: 39 Norman Rd Upper Montclair NJ 07043

CLIFFORD, STEWART HILTON, physician; b. Grand Forks, N.D., Sept. 12, 1900; s. Alvin Prescott and Katherine (Stewart) C.; student U. N.D.; M.D., Harvard, 1925; m. Ellinor Burnett, Oct. 19, 1927; children—Stewart B., Paul B., Frederic M., Donald J. Assigned East med. service Mass. Gen. Hosp., 1926-27; pediatric intern Children's and Infants Hosp., Boston, 1928-29; practice pediatrics, Boston, 1929-59; former pediatrician-in-chief Boston Lying -In Hosp.; also former project dir., co-investigator collaborative perinatal study; physician Children's Hosp., Boston; hon. pediatrician Boston Hosp. for Women; asso. clin. prof. pediatrics emeritus Harvard. Mem. exec. com. bd. dirs. Monumental Corp. of Balt.; dir. Monumental Life Ins. Co., Balt. Diplomate Am. Bd. Pediatrics. Mem. A.M.A., Mass. Med. Soc., Am., New Eng. pediatric socs., Am. Acad. Pediatrics (pres. 1957-58, exec. bd.), Soc. Pediatric Research. Contbr. articles to med. jours. Home: 33 Water St Duxbury MA 02332 Office: 221 Longwood Av Boston MA 02115

CLIFFORD, THOMAS JOHN, univ. pres.; b. Langdon, N.D., Mar. 16, 1921; s. Thomas Joseph and Elizabeth (Howitz) C.; B.C.S., U. N.D., 1942, J.D., 1948; M.B.S., Stanford, 1957, Stanford exec. fellow, 1958; m. Florence Marie Schmidt, Jan. 25, 1943; children—Thomas John, Stephen Michael. Instr. accounting U. N.D., 1946-47, counselor men, 1947-49, head accounting dept., 1948-49, dean sch. commerce, 1950-71, pres. univ., 1971—. C.P.A., 1949—; dir. Red River Nat. Bank, Grand Forks, N.D. Served from 2d lt. to maj. USMC, 1942-45. Decorated Purple Heart, Bronze Star medal, Silver Star. Mem. N.D. C.P.A. Soc. (pres. 1953-54), A.I.M., Am. Inst. Accountants, Am. Bar Assn., Beta Gamma Sigma, Beta Alpha Psi, Phi Eta Sigma, Kappa Sigma, Blue Key, Order Coif. K.C. Home: 521 Harvard St Grand Forks ND 58201

CLIFT, ARNOLD, Brit. diplomat; b. London, Eng., Apr. 15, 1935; s. Arnold and Dorothy (Hooper) C.; student Magdalene Coll. Cambridge U., 1956-59. Adminstrv. asst. Greater London Council, 1960; asst. prin. Brit. Treasury, 1960-64, pvt. sec. to permanent sec., then econ. sec., 1962-64, prin., 1964-68; banking student Bank of Eng., 1967-68; 1st sec. British embassy, Washington, 1968—. Served as 2d lt. Royal Army Ordnance Corps, 1954-56. Home: 2939 Van Ness St Washington DC 20008 Office: 3100 Massachusetts Av Washington DC 20006

CLIFT, DAVID HORACE, librarian; b. Mason Co., Ky., June 16, 1907; s. Charles Lawson and Mary E. (Tomlin) C.; B.S., U. Ky., 1930; B.S. in L.S., Columbia, 1931; m. Eleanore Flynn, Nov. 4, 1933. Student asst. U. Ky. Library, 1927-30, Lexington (Ky.) Pub. Library, summer 1930, Columbia U. Libraries, 1930- 31; reference asst. N.Y. Pub. Library, 1931-37; asst. to dir. libraries Columbia, 1937-42; dep., later acting chief Library of Congress Mission to Germany, 1945-46; asso. librarian Yale, 1945-51; instr. New Haven State Tchrs. Coll., summer 1948; exec. sec. Am. Library Assn., 1951-58, exec. dir., 1958—. Head delegation U.S. Librarians to Soviet Union, 1961; study tour libraries Fed. Republic Germany, 1963; bd. visitors Duke U. Library, 1964; mem. Librarian of Congress Liaison Com.; del. Internat. Fedn. Library Assns., 1964—. Hon. trustee Am. Library, Paris, 1969—. Served from pvt. to 1st lt. OSS, AUS, 1942-45. Recipient U. Ky. Founders' Day award for distinguished achievement in librarianship, 1957, Joseph W. Lippincott award for notable achievement in librarianship, 1962; Distinguished Alumni Centennial award, U. Ky., 1965. Mem. Conn. Library Assn. (pres. 1950-51; hon. mem.), A.L.A. Clubs: N.Y. Library (pres. 1941-42); Tavern (Chgo.). Home: 3054 Hartzell Evanston IL 60201 Office: American Library Association 50 E Huron St Chicago IL 60611

CLIFT, WILLIAM ORRIN, oil co. exec.; b. Flint, Mich., Mar. 27, 1914; s. M. William and Eliza (Denham) C.; B.S. with honors in Geology, U. Mich., 1938; Ph.D., Columbia, 1956; grad. Advanced

Mgmt. Program, Harvard, 1962; m. Lorraine Marie Badu, Mar. 28, 1951; children—Eliza Eugenia, William Denham. Paleontologist, Venezuelan Petroleum Co., Caracas, 1946-49; with Sinclair Petroleum Co., dir. Dawa, Ethiopia, 1949-56, gen. supt., 1953- 56; mgr. Sinclair Somal Corp., Mogadiscio, Somalia, 1956-59, pres., dir., 1962—; pres. Sinclair and BP Explorations Co., N.Y.C., 1959-62; former v.p. Sinclair Internat. Oil Co., N.Y.C., coordinator marketing, expln., prodn. Eastern hemisphere; pres., dir. Libyan Oil Co., 1962- dir. Sinclair Mediterranean Petroleum Co. Served to lt. USNR, 1942-45. Mem. Geol. Soc. Am., Paleontol. Soc. Am., Am. Assn. Petroleum Geologists, N.Y. Acad. Scis., Sigma Xi, Phi Kappa Sigma, Sigma Gamma Epsilon. Republican. Roman Catholic. Author paper. Home: 168 Av de Tervuereh Brussels 15 Belgium Office: Sinclair Internat Oil Co 137 Av Louise Brussels Belgium

CLIFTON, CHESTER VICTOR, Jr., pub. relations exec., ret. army officer; b. Edmonton, Alta., Can., Sept. 24, 1913; s. Chester Victor and Minnie (Corbett) C.; student U. Wash., 1931-32; B.S., U.S. Mil. Acad., 1936; M.A., U. Wis., 1948; grad. Nat. War Coll., 1954; m. Anne Bodine, Oct. 16, 1937. Newspaper reporter Seattle Post Intelligencer, 1930-32, N.Y. Herald Tribune, summer 1936; commd. 2d lt. U.S. Army, 1936, advanced through grades to maj. gen., 1961; operations officer Hdqrs. 22d F.A. Group, Ft. Bragg, N.C., 1942-43; comdg. officer 193d F.A. Group, 1943, 698th F.A. bn., Ft. Bragg, then Italy, France, Germany, 1943-45; pub. relations officer Hdqrs. Army Ground Forces, Washington, 1945-47; asst. sec. Gen. Staff, Office Chief of Staff, Washington, 1948-49, asst. to chmn. Joint Chiefs Staff, 1949-53; exec. officer Hdqrs. 2d Armored Div. Arty., Germany, 1954-55; chief joint plans J-3 Div., European Command, Germany, 1955-56; dep. chief, then chief of information Dept. Army, 1956-61; mil. aide to Pres. Kennedy, 1961-63, Pres. Johnson, 1963-65; pres. Thomas J. Deegan Co., Inc., 1965-67, Clifton-Raymond Assos., Inc., 1967-68, Clifton Counselors, Inc., Washington, 1968—. Mem. Sigma Delta Chi. Delta Upsilon. Clubs: National Press, Federal City (Washington). Contbr. articles to mags.; Korean War history in Ency. Brit. Home: 2339 Massachusetts Av NW Washington DC 20008 Office: Ring Bldg Washington DC 20036

CLIFTON, ERNEST SMITH, educator; b. Darlington, S.C., July 31, 1914; s. Thomas and Rosa (Smith) C.; B.A., U. Va., 1935; M.A., La. State U., 1937, Ph.D., 1940; student U. Cologne, Germany, 1938, U. Heidelberg, 1939; m. Eula Clyde Miller, Aug. 7, 1940; children—Frank, Ernest, Gail, Patricia. Sch. prin., Johnsonville, S.C., 1935-36; tchr. English, North Tex. State U., Denton, 1939-49, dir. dept. English, 1950—, chmn. div. humanities, 1957- 65. Mem. Tex. Folklore Soc. (past v.p.), Tex. Conf. Coll. Tchrs. English (pres. 1969), South-Central Modern Lang. Assn. (chmn. gen. liguistics sect.), Modern Lang. Assn. Am., Am. Assn. U. Profs., Nat. Council Tchrs. English, Coll. English Assn., Conf. Coll. Composition and Communication, Phi Beta Kappa, Phi Kappa Phi. Home: 2224 Houston Pl Denton TX 76201

CLIFTON, G. ELEANOR, ret. coll. dean; b. Chgo., Sept. 20, 1904; d. William and Harriett (Yauney) Clifton; A.B., Goucher Coll., 1926; A.M., Columbia, 1944. Sec. to pres. Goucher Coll., 1934-43, dir. admissions, 1947-49; dir. students N.J. Coll. for Women (now Douglas Coll.) 1944-46; field dir., Camp Fire Girls, Inc., 1946-47; dean Simmons Coll., Boston, 1949-70, dean emerita, mem. alumnae council, hon. alumna, 1970—. Mem. bd. Greater Boston council Camp Fire Girls; trustee Women's Ednl. and Indsl. Union, Boston. Mem. Nat. Assn. Women Deans and Counselors, Mass. Assn. Deans Women (pres. 1960-62), Mass. Soc. for U. Edn. of Women (v.p.), Pi Lambda Theta, Kappa Delta Pi. Club: College (Boston). Home: 27 Oxford Rd Wellesley MA 02181

CLIFTON, JOSEPH WENDEL, govt. ofcl.; b. Brunswick, Neb., July 30, 1913; s. Kem A. and Pauline (Hoscheit) C.;student Neb. U., 1930-31; m. Helen Mach, Oct. 4, 1941. Tchr., Boyd County (Neb.) rural schs., 1931-34; clk., field supr. Boyd County A.A.A., U.S. Dept. Agr., 1934-36; farmer, Boyd County, 1937-38; supr. Neb. Office Prodn. and Marketing Adminstrn., 1938-42, 46-48; adminstrv. officer Fed. Crop Ins. Corp., Washington, 1949-51; staff asst. Prodn. and Marketing Adminstrn., Washington, 1951-57, dep. dir. aerial photograhy div. Agrl. Stblzn. and Conservation Service, U.S. Dept. Agr., Washington, 1957-61, dir., 1961-69, asso. dir. compliance and appeals div., 1969—, also coordinator aerial photog. work U.S. Dept. Agr.; dir. Shenandoah Retreat Land Corp. Served with AUS, 1942-45; ETO. Decorated Purple Heart, Bronze Star medal; recipient Certificate Merit, Dept. Agr., 1962, 64, 66, 68, 69, 70. Mem. Am. Soc. Photogrammetry, Orgn. Profl. Employees Dept. Agr. Democrat. Mason (Shriner). Home: 1301 Elsinore Av McLean VA 22101 Office: US Dept Agr 14th and Independence Washington DC 20250

CLIFTON, LUDWIG HAROLD, corp. exec.; b. Krakow, Poland, Jan. 22, 1916; s. Andrew and Mary (Olson) C.; B.S., Ind. U., 1938; J.D., Harvard, 1949; m. Margaret Evelyn Lyness, Sept. 11, 1948; children—Claudia Mary, Bryan Terence, Howard Allen. Mem. staff Arthur Andersen & Co., C.P.A.'s, Chgo., 1938- 40; comptroller, dir. subsidiaries Pan Am. Tel. and Tel. Co., Colombia, S.A., 1941-46; with Telephone Bond & Share Co., Asso. Tel. and Tel. Co., 1949-55; asst. treas. Gen. Telephone Corp., N.Y.C., 1956; v.p., comptroller Pan-Am. Grace Airways, Inc., N.Y.C., 1956-61; treas. Worthington Corp., Harrison, N.J., 1962-67; treas. Worthington Internat., Inc.; treas. Electric Machinery Mfg. Co., Mpls., 1963-67; v.p. Studebaker-Worthington, Inc., N.Y.C., 1967-69; v.p., treas. Doubleday & Co., Inc., N.Y.C., 1969—. Admitted to Ill. bar, 1950. Pres. Greenridge Assn., Greenburgh, N.Y., 1960-61. Councilman, Borough of Madison, 1966-71. C.P.A., Ill. Mem. Chgo. Bar Assn., Beta Gamma Sigma. Republican. Presbn. Clubs: Madison Golf, Pond; Harvard of N.Y. Home: 37 Cross Gates Rd Madison NJ 07940 Office: 277 Park Av New York City NY 10017

CLIMENHAGA, ARTHUR MERLIN, clergyman, sem. dean; b. Grantham, Pa., Feb. 21, 1916; s. John Arthur and Emma Light (Smith) C.; B.S.L., Upland (Cal.) Coll., 1936; B.A. magna cum laude, Pasadena Coll., 1937; M.A. in Theology, Taylor U., 1938; postgrad. Claremont Grad. Sch., 1942-43; S.T.D., Los Angeles Baptist Theol. Sem., 1944; LL.D., Houghton Coll., 1965; m. Arlene Brubaker, Aug. 27, 1937 (dec.); m. 2d, Lona Brubaker, Sept. 27, 1969. Ordained to ministry Brethren in Christ Ch., 1938; religious dir. Upland Coll., 1938-39, pres., 1939-44; dist. supt. Wanezi mission, So. Rhodesia, Africa, 1945-50; bishop Brethren in Christ Ch. (Rhodesia), gen. supt. missions in So. and No. Rhodesia, 1951-60; pres. Messiah Coll., Grantham, 1960-64; exec. dir. Nat. Assn. Evangelicals, Wheaton, Ill., 1964-67; bishop Western confs. Brethren Christ Ch., 1967-72; dean Western Evangelical Seminary, Portland, Ore., 1972—. Treas. bd. young people's work Brethren in Christ Ch., 1941-44, mem. bd. adminstrn., 1960—; sec. So. Rhodesia Missionary Conf., 1948-50; pres. So. Rhodesia (Africa), Christian Conf., 1954-60. Mem. Pa. Gov.'s Prayer Breakfast Com., 1962-64. Bd. dirs. Rhodesia Christian Press, 1956- 60, Council for Advancement Small Colls., 1960-64; mem. So. Rhodesia Edn. Adv. Bd. 1952-60, mem. standing exec. com., 1954-60. Mem. Phi Delta Kappa. Republican. Rotarian. Author: (with Frank McConnell) Draw Nigh Unto God, 1952. Contbr. to Facing Facts in Modern Mission, 1963; Further Insights into Holiness, 1963; The Word and The Doctrine, 1965. Address: Western Evangelical Seminary Portland OR

CLIMENKO, JESSE, lawyer; b. N.Y.C., Apr. 3, 1904; s. Hyman and Rose (Busky) C.; B.A. magna cum laude, Harvard, 1924, LL.B., 1927; m. Pearl Siegel, July 3, 1929; 1 dau., Jane (Mrs. Bernard Gottschalk). Admitted to N.Y. bar, 1927, since practiced in N.Y.C.; mem. firm Shea, Gallop, Climenko & Gould, and predecessors, 1944-; spl. asst. to atty. gen. U.S., 1943-44, 48. Mem. Am., Fed. bar assns., Assn. Bar City N.Y., N.Y. County Lawyers Assn., Am. Law Inst. Home: 190 E 72d St New York City, NY 10021. Office: 330 Madison Av New York City, NY

CLINARD, MARSHALL BARRON, educator; b. Boston, Nov. 12, 1911; s. Andrew Marshall and Gladys (Barron) C.; B.A., Stanford, 1932, M.A., 1934; Ph.D., U. Chgo., 1941; m. Ruth Blackburn, Aug. 28, 1937; children—Marsha (Mrs. Richard L. Schacht), Stephen Andrew. Instr., U. Ia., 1937-41; chief criminal statistics U.S. Bur. Census, 1941-43; chief analysis report, enforcement dept. OPA, 1943-45; asso. prof. Vanderbilt U., 1945-46; mem. faculty U. Wis., 1946—, prof. sociology, 1951—; Fulbright research prof. U. Stockholm (Sweden), 1954-55; vis. prof. Makerere U. Coll., Kampala, Uganda, 1968-69. Cons. urban community devel. Ford Found., India, 1958-60, 62-63; UN expert Asian Seminar Urban Community Devel., Singapore, 1962; rapporteur 3d UN Congress Prevention Crime and Treatment Offenders, Stockholm, 1965, panel expert 4th UN Congress, Kyoto, 1970; cons. Dept. Labor, 1966-67. Recipient Sutherland award Am. Soc. Criminology, 1970. Mem. Soc. Study Social Problems (exec. com. 1959-60, 62-63, 65-67, pres. 1961- 62), Midwest Sociol. Soc. (pres. 1965-66), Am. Sociol. Assn. (council mem. at large 1966-68). Author: The Black Market: A Study of White Collar Crime, 1952; Sociology of Deviant Behavior, 3d edit., 1968. Editor, contbr.: Anomie and Deviant Behavior: A Discussion and Critique, 1964; Slums and Community Development: Experiments in Self-Help, 1966; (with Richard Quinney) Criminal Behavior Systems: A Typology, 1967. Home: 6022 Green Tree Rd Madison WI 53711

CLINCH, HARRY ANSELM, bishop; b. San Anselmo, Cal., Oct. 27, 1908; s. Henry Joseph and Mary (McLaughlin) C.; student St. Joseph Sem., Mountain View, 1928-30, St. Patrick's Sem., Menlo Park, Cal., 1930-36. Ordained priest Roman Catholic Ch., 1936; founder, dir. Camp Santa Teresita Youth Camp, 1937-41; diocesan dir. Soc. for Propagation of Faith, 1936-48; editor Central Cal. Register, 1939-48; pastor, Taft, Cal., 1948-58, Mission Carmel, Cal., 1958—; consecrated bishop, 1957, aux. bishop Diocese Monterey-Fresno; bishop Diocese of Monterey, 1967—. Past mem. bd. dirs. Fresno and Taft chpts. A.R.C. Kiwanian. Office: 580 Freemont Blvd Monterey CA 93940

CLINCH, JOHN HOUSTOUN MCINTOSH, lawyer; b. Danville, Ill., Aug. 18, 1902; s. John Houston McIntosh and Edna L. (Wilber) C.; student U. Ill., 1920-22, John Marshall Law Sch., 1942; A.B., U. Chgo., 1924; m. Frances S. Bell, June 25, 1927; children—Frances B. (Mrs. Richard I. Stearns, III), J. Houstoun M. With Chgo. North Shore & Milw. Ry. (now Susquehanna Corp., 1925- 57, pres., 1948-57; pres. Consol. Mgmt. Co., 1957—; v.p. Middle West Service Co., 1963-64; partner Clinch and Boden, Attys. Lectr., instr. Grad. School Bus., U. Chgo., 1958-63; spl. asst. atty. gen. State of N.M., 1969-70. Cons. Ill. Commerce Commn.; spl. counsel Ia. Commerce Commn., Minn. Pub. Service Commn., 1971. Mem. Winnetka Caucus Com. Mem. Am., Ill., Chgo. bar assns., Sigma Alpha Epsilon. Episcopalian. Clubs: University (Chgo.); Sheridan Shore Yacht (Wilmette, Ill), Skokie Country (Glencoe, Ill.); Bird Key Yacht (Sarasota, Fla.). Home: 707 Ardsley Rd Winnetka IL 60093 also 623 N Owl Dr Bird Key Sarasota FL 33577 Office: 1 First National Plaza Chicago IL 60670

CLINCHY, EVERETT ROSS, educator; b. N.Y.C., Dec. 16, 1896; s. James Hugh and Lydie (Staff) C.; student Wesleyan U., Middletown, Conn., 1916-18, D.D., 1950; B.S., Lafayette Coll., 1920, D.D., 1951; postgrad. Union Theol. Sem., 1920-21, Yale, 1922-23; M.A., Columbia, 1921; Ph.D. in Edn., Drew U., 1934; LL.D., Fla. So. Coll., 1946, Washington U., 1955; L.H.D., Missouri Valley Coll., 1949, Wilberforce Coll., 1958; L.H.D., Hartwick Coll., 1959; m. Winifred Marcena Mead, Sept. 21, 1918; children—Everett Ross, Eleanor Marcena, Barbara Rex. Ordained to ministry Presbyn. Ch., 1921; pastor Ch. of Christ, Wesleyan U., 1923-28; sec. Fed. Council Chs. of Christ Am., 1928-33; pres. Nat. Conf. Christians and Jews, 1928-58; pres. Council on World Tension, World Brotherhood; v.p., exec. dir. Roger Willaims Straus Found.; mem. extension winter faculty U. Cal. at Riverside, 1968- -. Mem. Joint Army and Navy Com. on Welfare and Recreation, Washington. Originated "Seminar" confs. for study Cath.-Protestant-Jewish relations; dir. Williamstown Inst. Human Relations, summers, 1935, 37, 39, 41; founder, pres. Inst. Man and Sci., Rensselaerville, N.Y., 1963—; founder Oliver Wendell Holmes Assn. Served as 2d lt. F.A., U.S. Army, World War I. Mem. Council on Fgn. Relations, Am. Sociol. Soc., Am. Acad. Polit. Sci., Alpha Delta Phi. Clubs: Cosmos (Washington); Yale (N.Y.C.). Author: All in the Name of God, 1934; The World We Want to Live In, 1942; A Handbook on Human Relations, 1949; Intergroup Relations Center, 1950. Contbr. articles to religious, ednl. publs. Home: Rensselaerville NY 12147 Office: 325 E 41st St New York City NY 10017

CLINE, ARTHUR RAYMOND, lawyer; b. Barr Mills, O., Aug. 20, 1898; s. Alvin Arthur and Clara (Froelich) C.; student Coshocton County (O.) Normal Sch., 1916-17; A.B., Ohio State U., 1923, J.D., 1925; m. Christine D. Wippel, Sept. 2, 1924. Tchr. rural schs., Ohio, 1917-18; brakeman Pa. R.R., 1920; supt. maintenance and repair Athens County (O.) Dept. Hwys., 1925-28; admitted to Ohio bar, 1925; practice in Toledo, 1928—; mem. firm Cline, Bischoff and Cook, 1941—. Sec., dir. Dundee Truck Line, Inc., Funk Motor Transp., Inc., Auto-Tonic Control Co., Dundee Motor Express, Inc., Airport Mobile Homes, Inc.; v.p., dir. Progress Nat. Bank, Toledo. Chmn. Toledo Citizens Com. Lake Erie Water Works, 1938, mem. citizens adv. com. constrn., 1938-41, exec. chmn. dedication com., 1941; mem. Toledo City Plan Commn., 1937—, chmn., 1941—; mem. Lucas County (O.) Plan Commn., 1941—, chmn., 1942—; chmn. coordination com. Toledo Regional Plan for Action, 1963—. Trustee U. Toledo, 1967—. Served with U.S. Army, 1918-19. Mem. Am., Ohio (v.p. 1942-44), Toledo (past pres.), Lucas County (past pres.) bar assns., Ohio State U. Alumni Assn. (life) Toledo C. of C., Am. Legion, Sphinx, Gamma Eta Gamma. Methodist. Mason (33, Shriner). Clubs: Toledo, Maumee River Yacht (Toledo); South Side Toledo Exchange (past pres.). Home: 2720 Medford St Toledo OH 43614 Office: Cline Bischoff and Cool Securitity Bldg Toledo OH 43604

CLINE, CLARENCE LEE, educator; b. Belton, Tex., Jan. 6, 1905; s. William Edwin and Permilla (Mitchell) C.; B.A., Baylor U., 1926; M.A., U. Tex., 1931, Ph.D., 1938; m. Henriette Fechenbach, June 12, 1933; children—Patricia (Mrs. James R. Holmes, Jr.), Judith (Mrs. J. H. Harrison IV). Mem. faculty U. Tex., 1938—, prof. English, 1952—, chmn. dept., 1949-52, 62-68, Ashbel Smith prof. English, 1971—; vis. asso. prof. Harvard, summer 1952. Mem. Modern Lang. Assn., Am. Assn. U. Profs., S. Central Modern Lang. Assn., Coll. Conf. Tchrs. English, Nat. Council Tchrs. English, Modern Humanities Research Assn. Author: Byron, Shelley and Their Pisan Circle, 1952; also articles, chpts. in books. Editor: Rinehart Book of Short Stories, 1952; Rinehart Book of Short Stories, alternate edit., 1964; The Letters of George Meredith, 1971; The Ordeal of Richard Feverel (George Meredith), 1971. Home: 1401 Hardouin Av Austin TX 78703

CLINE, EARL, lawyer; b. Weeping Water, Neb., Dec. 18, 1886; s. William T. and Emma F. (Meloy) C.; student Peru State Tchrs. Coll., 1905-07, U. Neb. Coll. Law, 1910-12, U. Mich. Coll. Law, 1916; LL.D., U. Neb., 1966; m. Mildred Holland, Sept. 4, 1919. Tchr. high sch., 1907; prin. high sch., Sidney, Neb., 1907-09; supt. schs., Geneva, Neb., 1913-15, Nebraska City, Neb., 1915-16; with law firm Pitzer, Cline & Tyler, Nebraska City, 1917-22; mem. Hall, Cline & Williams, Lincoln, 1922-42, Cline, Williams & Wright, 1942-51, Cline, Williams, Wright & Johnson, 1951—, now Cline, Williams, Wright, Johnson & Oldfather. Mem. bd. regents, U. Neb., 1925-37. Trustee U. Neb. Found., pres., 1954-55. Served as capt. 89th Div., U.S. Army, 1917-19; wounded in action St. Mihiel offensive, 1918. Decorated Order of Purple Heart. Recipient Distinguished Service award U. Neb., 1946. Mem. Am., Neb., Lincoln bar assns., Am. Legion (state comdr., 1919), Phi Kappa Psi, Phi Delta Phi. Republican. Methodist. Mason. Club. Country (Lincoln). Home: Sky Park Manor 1301 J St Lincoln NB 68508 Office: First Nat Bank Bldg Lincoln NB 68508

CLINE, GEORGE IRICK, U.S. atty.; b. Carter County, Ky., Jan. 16, 1915; s. George Thomas and Elsie Mae (Adams) C.; student Morehead (Ky.) State Coll., 1933-36; LL.B., U. Louisville, 1941; m. Mary Katherine Stidham, May 31, 1941; children—Karen Rae, Mary Ann, Martha Nelle. Admitted to Ky. bar, 1941; with engring. dept. E. I. duPont de Nemours & Co., Inc., 1941-45; gen. practice law, Morehead, Ky., 1945-26; city atty., Morehead, 1948-60; asst. U.S. atty. Eastern Dist. Ky., 1962-63, U.S. atty., 1963-71; pvt. practice, Morehead, 1971—. Mem. Ky. Legislature from Rowan County, 1948; Democratic candidate for judge Ky. Ct. Appeals, 1958. Mem. Morehead C. of C. (pres. 1956-57), Fed. Jud. Conf. 6th Circuit (life), Ky. Bar Assn. Disciple of Christ (elder). Mason (Shriner), Kiwanian (lt. gov. Ky.-Tenn. 1953). Home: 210 Knapp Av Morehead KY 40351 Office: 151 E Main Morehead KY 40351

CLINE, JOHN HENRY, ret. newspaperman; b. Washington, Dec. 14, 1904; s. Sheldon Scott and Mary Marjorie (Brigham) C.; student Ohio State U., 1924-25 and 1927; LL.B., Columbus U., 1936; m. Frances Elizabeth Butterworth, Feb. 21, 1935; children—Elizabeth Hughes, Sheldon Scott, Jr. and John Brigham (twins) (both dec.), John Brigham. Reporter, Detroit News and Ohio State Jour., Columbus; with Washington Star, 1928-69, editorial writer, 1938, chief editorial writer, 1940-48, editor editorial page, until 1969. Mem. bar of U.S. Ct. for D.C., also U.S. Ct. of Appeals. Mem. Am. Soc. Newspaper Editors, Delta Tau Delta. Club: Nat. Press. Home: 315 Little Falls St Falls Church VA 22046

CLINE, JOHN WESLEY, surgeon; b. Santa Rosa, Calif., 1898; A.B., U. Cal., 1921; M.D., Harvard, 1925; D.Sc. (hon.), California Coll. Medicine, 1962; m. Edith Corde, 1925; children—John W. III, Robert C., Janet. Intern, Mass. Gen. Hosp., Boston, 1925-27; resident surgeon Cornell Div., Bellevue Hosp., 1927-29; surgeon Hosp. for Children; Stanford Service, San Francisco Hosp.; surg. cons. Biggs-Gridley Meml. Hosp.; expert med. cons. to Surgeon Gen. USAF and USN, 1950-54; cons. for cancer control to surgeon gen. USPHS; asso. clin. prof. Stanford U. Sch. Med.; dir. Citizens Fed. Savs. and Loan Assn. Trustee St. Francis Meml. Hosp.; mem. Council on Med. Edn. and Hosps., 1952-59. Diplomate Am. Bd. Surgery. Fellow A.C.S. (chmn. commn. on cancer); mem. AMA (del. to World Assn. 1948, 49; pres. 1951-52; chmn. sect. gen. surgery 1964-65), Soc. Head and Neck Surgeons, Cal. Med. Assn. (chmn. cancer commn.), Am. Pacific Coast surg. assns., Cal. Acad. Medicine, San Francisco Surg. Soc., San Francisco County Med. Soc., Am. Cancer Soc. (dir. 1957-59, chmn. med. and sci. com. 1958-59, pres. 1960-61), S.A.R. Clubs: Bohemian, Family, St. Frances Yacht (San Francisco). Author papers on surg. subjects. Address: 490 Post St San Francisco CA 94102

CLINE, LEWIS MANNING, educator; b. Duncan, Okla., Sept. 25, 1909; s. Edgar Betel and Leila (Sims) C.; B.S., U. Tulsa, 1931; M.S., U. Ia., 1934, Ph.D., 1935; m. Grace Ellen Shaw, Nov. 27, 1935; children—Ellen Sperling, Catherine Arlene, Charles Harry. Instr. geology U. Tulsa, 1931-32; research asst. U. Ia., 1932-35; instr. Tex. A. and M. Coll., 1935-36; instr. Ia. State Coll., 1936-37, asst. prof., 1938-42; dist. geologist Standard Oil Co. Tex., 1943-45; faculty U. Wis., Madison, 1946—, prof. geology, 1947—, chmn. dept., 1960-65. Mem. Ia. Geol. Survey, summers 1936-42; cons. Natural Gas Pipeline Co. Am., 1940-42, Ia. Ins. Commn., 1939-41, Mobil Oil Research Lab., 1957-61, other cos.; Distinguished prof. Tex. Technol. Coll., 1952-53. Recipient Lew Wentz prize U. Tulsa, Lowden prize U. Ia. Fellow Geol. Soc. Am. (rep. Am. Stratigraphic Commn. 1957-60, chmn. publs. com. 1965, mem. council 1966-69, chmn. tech. program 1970); mem. Paleontol. Soc. Am. (chmn. nominating com. 1962), Am. Geol. Inst. (geol. orientation study 1962-63, chmn. publs. com. 1966-68), Internat. Assn. Sedimentology, Am. Assn. Petroleum Geologists (dist. rep. 1958-59, Distinguished lectr. 1965), Soc. Econ. Paleontologists and Mineralogists (pres. 1965, chmn. publs. com. 1965, editor Jour. Sedimentary Petrology 1961-64), Sigma Xi (sec.-treas. Ia. State Coll. 1940-42, pres. U. Wis. chpt. 1965-66), Gamma Alpha (v.p. U. Ia. 1934-35). Republican. Methodist. Rotarian (chmn. fellowship com. Madison 1951, Uthrotar com. Madison 1959, v.p. chpt. 1964-65). Author: Late Paleozoic Rocks of the Ouachita Mountains, 1960. Editor, contbr.: Guidebook to Ouachita Mountains, 1956; co-editor, contbr.: Geology of Ouachita Mountains, a symposium, 1959. Died Mar. 10, 1971.

CLINE, MARJORIE ANN, editor; b. Washington, Mar. 9, 1920; d. Sheldon Scott and Mary Marjorie (Brigham) C.; student Strayer's Bus. Coll., 1939-40, George Washington U., 1943-44, Dunbarton Coll., 1945-46. Secretarial worker Nat. Wildlife Fedn. WPA, 1941-43; with Evening Star Newspaper Co., Washington, 1943—, asst. women's editor, 1961—, also society editor. Home: 9823 Old Georgetown Rd Bethesda MD 20014 Office: 225 Virginia Av SE Washington DC 20003

CLINE, MARLIN GEORGE, educator, soil scientist; b. Bertha, Minn., Dec. 31, 1909; s. Sampson and Amy (Smith) C.; B.S., N.D. State Coll., 1935, D.Sc., 1965; Ph.D. (grad. fellow 1938-41), Cornell U., 1942; D.Sc., Trinity Coll., Dublin, Ireland, 1965; m. Agnes Irene Israelson, Augl 17, 1936; children—Richard George, Mary E. (Mrs. Harold H. Harris), Carol Jean (Mrs. William Powers). Soil scientist Dept. Agr., 1936-38, 41-42, 44—; mem. faculty Cornell U., 1942- -, prof. soil sci., 1947—, head dept., 1964-70, univ. project leader to U. Philippines, 1954-56; cons. Brit. Colonial Office, Africa, 1949; exchange scientist USSR, 1958; spl. research soil genesis, classification and geography. Recipient Service award N.Y. Agrl. Soc., 1963. Fellow Am. Soc. Agronomy; mem. Soil Sci. Soc. Am., Internat. Soc. Soil Sci., Brit. Soc. Soil Sci., A.A.A.S. Author: Soil Survey of Hawaii, 1950; also articles. Home: 27 Main St Freeville NY 13068 Office: Dept Agronomy Cornell U Ithaca NY 14850

CLINE, RAY STEINER, govt. ofcl.; b. Anderson, Ill., June 4, 1918; s. Charles and Ina May (Steiner) C.; A.B., Harvard, 1939, M.A., 1941, Ph.D., 1949; Henry prize fellow, Balliol Coll., Oxford (Eng.) U., 1939-40; m. Marjorie Wilson, June 4, 1941; children—Judith, Sibyl. Jr. fellow Harvard, 1941-42; with OSS, 1943-46, Office Chief Mil. History, Dept. Army, 1946-49, CIA, 1949- 51; attache Am. embassy, London, Eng., 1951-53; with CIA, 1954-58; dir. U.S. Naval Aux. Communications Center, Taipei, 1958-62; dep. dir. for intelligence CIA, 1962-66; spl. adviser Am. embassy, Bonn, Germany, 1966-69;

dir. Bur. Intelligence Research, 1969—. Mem. Oxford Soc., Phi Beta Kappa. Club: Federal City (Washington). Author: Washington Command Post, 1951. Home: 4601 N 41st St Arlington VA 22207

CLINE, THOMAS WILLIAM, shelter industry exec.; b. Flint, Mich., Oct. 17, 1932; s. Leo D. and Helen (Wolohan) C.; B.S., U. Detroit, 1954, J.D., 1956; m. Joanne Greiner, July 18, 1959; children—Robert Arthur, Thomas John, Mary Elizabeth. Admitted to Mich. bar, 1957; gen. atty. Wickes Corp., Saginaw, Mich., 1958-61, sec., gen. counsel, 1961-69, sr. v.p., gen. counsel, 1969-71, sr. v.p. corporate devel., 1971—, dir., 1964—; dir. Vac-Hyd Processing Corp. Chmn. finance com. Diocese of Saginaw, 1970—; chmn. Saginaw Cath. Schs. Study Com., 1969. Pres., bd. dirs. St. Vincents Home; bd. dirs. Cath. Charities Saginaw Diocese; trustee Saginaw Gen. Hosp. Assn., 1971—. Served with U.S. Army, 1956-58. Mem. Am., Mich., Saginaw County bar assns., Blue Key, Delta Sigma Pi, Beta Alpha Psi, Delta Theta Phi. Clubs: Bay City (Mich.) Country; Saginaw Serra of Saginaw County (pres., dir.). Home: 1893 Avalon St Saginaw MI 48603 Office: 515 N Washington St Saginaw MI 48607

CLINESMITH, BRUCE CARLISLE, oil co. exec.; b. Wakita, Okla., Aug. 2, 1917; s. Fred Lawrence and Avis (Garrett) C.; student N. Okla. Jr. Coll., 1934-36; B.S., Okla. State U., 1938; postgrad. Harvard, 1955; m. June Evelyn Suttle, Dec. 28, 1939 (dec.); children—Larry Lee, Cathe Lynn; m. Ruth M. Sanford, June 8, 1970. With Standard Oil Co. (N.J.), 1938- 66, accountant, div. head, N.Y.C., 1946-57, asst. comptroller, 1957-58, dep. comptroller, 1958-66; vice chmn. adv. bd. Port Charlotte Bank, 1969, dir., 1969—; dir. Cox Plastics Corp., Buffalo. Chmn., Charlotte County Charter Commn., 1969-71. Dir., chmn. finance com. U.P. Home for Aged, 1964; mem., chmn budget com. Nat. Council U.P. Men, 1964; sr. v.p. N.Y. State Synod Council U.P. Men, 1964; pres. U.P. Men United Presbyn. Ch. in U.S.A., 1965; mem. gen. council Gen. Assembly U.P. Ch., 1965-69; treas. Presbytery W. Fla. United Presbyn. Ch., 1969, mem. exec. com., treas. Synod Fla., 1969-71. Bd. dirs. United Fund Charlotte County, Fla. 1968—, pres., 1970; bd. dirs. Presbyn. Social Ministries West Fla.; trustee Pikeville (Ky.) Coll. Mem. Financial Execs. Inst. Home: 258 Beeney Rd SE Port Charlotte FL 33952

CLINGER, A. W., oil co. exec. b. Oil City, Pa., Mar. 15, 1906; s. William T. and (Pressy) C.; student Lehigh U., 1924-28; m. Elizabeth Bloss, Oct. 9, 1933; childrenArthur William, Suzanne (Mrs. Sherman B. Kellar). With Pennzoil Co., 1928-, v.p. wholesale sales, 1950-60, sr. v.p., gen. sales mgr., 1960-62, sr. v.p., coordinator refining and marketing, now v.p. marketing nat. accounts. Mem. exec. council Diocese of Erie, Episcopal Ch. Mem. Nat. Petroleum Refiners Assn., Am. Petroleum Inst., Chi Psi. Clubs: Oil City (past pres.), Wanango Country (past pres.), Franklin. Home: 546 Bouquin Circle Oil City PA 16301 Office: Pennzoil Co Drake Bldg Oil City PA 16301

CLINGERMAN, JOHN RUFUS, fgn. service officer; b. Doniphan County, Kan., May 9, 1931; s. Charles E. and Nell (Taylor) C.; B.A., Mich. State U., 1953, M.A., 1957; m. Ruth Mary Muilenburg, Sept. 1953. Joined U.S. Fgn. Service, 1957; assigned State Dept., 1957-59; vice consul, econ. officer Am. embassy, Katamandu, 1959-61; econ. officer Am. embassy, Leopoldville, Congo, 1962; consul, Stanleyville, Congo, 1963-64; officer charge Congo, State Dept., Washington 1964-65, charge Ghanaian affairs, 1965; assigned African Studies, Sorbonne, Paris, 1965-66; dep. chief mission, Cotonou, Dahomey, 1966-69; polit. officer Am. embassy, Brussels, Belgium, 1969—. Recipient Distinguished Honor award State Dept., 1965; decorated officer L'Ordre National du Dahomey. Mem. Am. Fgn. Service Assn. Rotarian. Home: 1710 High St Lansing, MI 48906. Office: Am Embassy 27 Blvd du Regent Brussels Belgium

CLINK, STEPHEN H., lawyer; b. Muskegon, Mich., Jan. 26, 1911; A.B., U. Mich., 1933, J.D., 1936; LL.M. in Taxation, N.Y.U., 1949. Admitted to Mich. bar, 1936; pros. atty., Muskegon County, 1939-41; judge of probate, Muskegon County, 1941-48; now mem. firm Landman, Hathaway, Latimer, Clink & Robb, Muskegon. Teaching fellow N.Y.U., 1948-49. Mem. com. of visitors U. Mich. Law Sch., 1963-64. Fellow Am. Coll. Probate Counsel (regent 1967-70); mem. Am., Muskegon County (pres. 1952-53) bar assns., State Bar Mich. (chmn. taxation sect. 1958-59, chmn. council 1968-69, ethics com. 1958-70), Am. Judicature Soc. Contbr. articles to profl. jours. Office: Hackley Union Nat Bank Bldg Muskegon MI 49443*

CLINTON, FRANK MARK, civil engr.; b. Bisbee, Ariz., May 11, 1908; s. John and Delia (Varley) C.; B.S., U. Ariz., 1934, C.E., 1957; m. Mary Foudy, Aug. 23, 1938 (dec. 1967); children—Mary Frances, Elizabeth Delia, Michael John, Mark, Roseanne, Patrick Anthony, Terrance Joseph; m. 2d, Alice Dahlin, Sept. 1968. Rodman, Ariz. Hwy. Dept., 1934; jr. engr. Geol. Survey, 1934-37; instrumentman, insp. U.S. Bur. Reclamation, Barlett Dam, Ariz., 1937-39, engr. charge planning surveys Big Horn River Basin, Mont.-Wyo., 1939-42, detailed study on water supply, Snake River, Ida., 1942-44, asst. regional planning engr., 1944- 49, asst. regional dir., Boise, Ida., 1949-54, regional dir., Billings, Mont., 1954- 60, Salt Lake City, 1960-65; chief project engr. Met. Water Dist. So. Cal., 1965-67, asst. gen. mgr., 1967-71, gen. mgr., 1971—. Mem. Am. Soc. C.E., Am. Water Works Assn. Home: Bunker Hill Towers Apt 510 800 W First St Los Angeles CA 90012 Office: PO Box 54153 Los Angeles CA 90054

CLINTON, GORDON STANLEY, lawyer; b. Medicine Hat, Alta., Can., Apr. 13, 1920; s. John H. and Gladys (Hall) C.; A.B. in Polit. Sci., U. Wash., 1942, J.D., 1947; spl. student Harvard Grad. Sch., 1945; LL.D., Coll. Puget Sound, 1957, Seattle Pacific Coll., 1961; m. Florence H. Vayhinger, Dec. 19, 1942; children—Barbara H., Gordon Stanley, Deborah. Spl. agt. FBI, 1942-44; admitted to Wash. bar, 1947; pvt. practice, Seattle, 1949—; firm Clinton, Moats, Andersen and Fleck; dep. pros. atty. King County, 1947-49; judge pro-tem Municipa; Court Seattle, 1949-52; spl. atty. City Council of Seattle, 1954, mayor, 1956-64. Chmn. exec. com. Japan-Am. Conf. Mayors; adv. bd. U.S. Conf. Mayors, 1956-64; mem. Presdl. Commn. Intergovtl. Relations; v.p. Western region, civic com. People to People; chmn. of Kobe-Seattle Affiliation Com., Marine Employees Commn.; chmn. Wash. Bd. Edn., 1969—. Trustee Seattle Pacific Coll., 1964-70; bd. dirs. YMCA, Wesley Found., 1968—, Town Affiliation Assn.; pres. Asso. Methodist Home, 1969. Del., Gen. Conf. Meth. Ch. Served appretice seaman to lt. (j.g.) USNR, 1944-46. Recipient Silver Beaver award, Distinguished Service award Chief Seattle council Boy Scouts Am.; Distinguished Grad. award Roosevelt High Sch., 1960; Newsmakers of Tomorrow award Time Mag. and Seattle C. of C., 1953; citation of honor Wash. State chpt. A.I.A., 1957; Human Relations award Seattle Civic Unity Commn., 1963; citation Nat. Conf. Christian and Jews, 1964; outstanding Pub. Ofcl. award Municipal League, 1964. Mem. Am. Municipal Assn. (mem. exec. com. 1957—, pres. 1962), Am. Wash. State, Seattle bar assns., Nat. Conf. Christians and Jews. Phi Delta Phi. Republican. Methodist (bd. missions). Mason (32, Shriner). Home: 7733 58th Av NE Seattle WA 98115 Office: Third-Lenora Bldg Seattle WA 98121

CLINTON, JOHN HART, lawyer; b. Quincy, Mass., Apr. 3, 1905; s. John Francis and Catherine Veronica (Hart) C.; A.B., Boston Coll., 1926; LL.B., Harvard, 1929; m. Helen Alice Amphlett, Feb. 18, 1933 (dec. 1965); children—Mary Jane, Mary Ann (Mrs. Christopher Gardner, Jr.), John Hart; m. 2d, Mathilda A. Schoorel van Dillen, Feb. 22, 1969. Admitted to Cal. bar, 1930, since practiced in San Francisco; asso. firm Morrison, Foerster, Holloway, Clinton & Clark, and predecessor, 1939—, partner, 1941—. Vice pres., gen. counsel Indsl. Employers and Distbrs. Assn., San Francisco, 1944—; pres. Leamington Hotel, Oakland, Cal., 1933-47, Amphlett Printing Co., San Mateo, Cal., 1943—; pub. San Mateo Times, 1943—, editor, 1960—. Mem. San Francisco Archdiocesan Com. Cath. Charities; exec. com. San Mateo County council Boy Scouts Am. Bd. dirs. United Bay Area Crusade, Bay Area Social Planning Council, Cal. Jockey Club Found.; bd. regents Notre Dame Coll., Belmont, Cal. Mem. FCC, Am., San Francisco, San Mateo County bar assns., State Bar Cal., Am. Judicature Soc., Nat. Lawyers Club, Am. Law Inst., San Mateo County Devel. Assn (pres. 1963-65), San Mateo County Hist. Assn. (pres. 1960-64), Cal. Press Assn. (pres.), Cal. Newspapers Pubs. Assn. (pres. 1969), Food and Wine Soc., Confrerie de la chaine des Rotisseurs, Assn. Cath. Newsman, Nat. Press Photographers Assn., Internat. Platform Assn. Rotarian, Elk. Clubs: Commonwealth (past pres.), San Francisco Commercial, Bohemian (San Francisco), Executives (San Mateo). Home: 131 Sycamore Av San Mateo CA 94402 Office: Crocker Plaza San Francisco CA 94104

CLIPP, ROGER WILLIAM, broadcasting co. exec.; b. Sharpsburg, Md., Sept. 20, 1903; s. William H. and Helen A. (Schamel) C.; B.S., Wharton Sch., U. Pa., 1925; m. Marjorie F. Allerton, Sept. 4, 1925; children—Elizabeth A. (Mrs. A. Roy Auchinachie, Jr.), Samuel W. With Hagerstown Trust Co. (Md.), 1925-29; with sta. relations dept. NBC, 1929-33, asst. mgr. owned and operating stas., 1933-35; with WFIL, Phila., 1935-46, v.p., 1941-43, pres., 1943- 46; WFIL purchased by Triangle Pub. Co., Inc., 1946, gen. mgr., 1946-55; v.p. newly organized co. radio TV div. Triangle Publs., Inc., 1955-69; v.p. WSER, Inc., Elkton, Md.; pres. Broadcast Mgmt. Inc., WAYK, Lehigh Acres, Fla.; dir. Bellevue Stratford Co. Dir. Robin Hood Dell Concerts, 1965—. Mem. broadcast adv. com. U.S. Information Agy.; chmn. promotion activities com. 3d War Loan Dr., v.p. chmn. 4th, 5th, 6th, 7th Victory drives. Bd. govs. Phila. Heart Assn.; trustee U. Pa.; campaign chmn. 1951, Phila. March of Dimes; pres. Chestnut Hill Center, United Cerebral Palsy Assn., 1953-54; bd. dirs. Eagleville Sanitorium; chmn. bd. Phila. Civic Center, 1968—. Mem. Nat. (chmn. code rev. bd. 1958; chmn. finance com.; mem. NAB (bd. dirs. 1966-68), Pa. (pres. 1952-53) assns. broadcasters, TV Bur. Advt. (chmn. dir.), Phila. Bd. Trade, Radio Exec. Club N.Y.C., Md. Soc. of Pa., U. Pa. Wharton Sch. Alumni Soc. (pres. 1954-55), U.S. C. of C. (dir.. 1953- 55), Phila. Conv. and Visitors Bur. (dir., v.p. 1945—), Radio Advt. Bur. (dir. 1964, chmn. 1968—). Episcopalian. Clubs: Union League, Racquet, Poor Richard (pres. 1945-46), City Business, Variety (Phila.); University (Phila. and N.Y.C.); Merion (Pa.) Golf. Home: 172 Whitemarsh Rd Ardmore PA 19003

CLIPPINGER, FRANK WARREN, educator; b. Warrensburg, Mo., Apr. 17, 1895; s. Edward Warren and Haddie (Bunger) C.; A.B., Wabash Coll., 1916; M.A., U. Ill., 1917; Ph.D., 1941; LL.D., Westminster Coll., 1965; L.H.D., Drury Coll., 1965; m. Emmylou Brietstadt, June 22, 1922; 1 son, Frank Warren. Instr. English, U. Ill., 1919-24; prof. Lawrence Coll., 1924-39; prof., head dept. English, Drury Coll., 1941, dean of men, 1942-54, dean of coll., 1954- 65, acting pres., 1967-68. Co-ordinator commn. liberal arts studies N. Central Assn., 1945-54. Bd. dirs. Springfield Civic Symphony, 1959-68. Served to sgt. U.S. Army, World War I. Mem. Nat. Council Tchrs. English, Coll. Coll. English Assn., Conf. Acad. Deans (exec. com. 1959-63), Phi Beta Kappa, Omicron Delta Kappa, Phi Eta, Beta Theta Pi. Presbyn. Rotarian. Home: 1851 S Kings St Springfield MO 65804

CLIPPINGER, JOHN HENRY, lawyer; b. Cin., Aug. 21, 1897; s. Walter Welty and Helen L. (Glidden) C.; student Western Res. U., 1915-19; LL.B., U. Tex., 1922; m. Jane B. Becker, June 9, 1928; children Jane J. (Mrs. David Chavchavadze), Sarah G. (Mrs. Michael P. Hamilton), John Henry. Admitted to Ohio bar, 1922-, since practiced in Cin.; asso. firm Taft, Stettinius & Hollister, 1929- , sr. partner, 1942-; asst. prosecutor Hamilton County, 1927-28, spl. asst. prosecutor, 1929-30, 33; spl. asst. city solicitor, Cin., 1930-31; an incorporater, 1941, Village Indian Hill, O., 1st city solicitor, 42. Pres., dir. S.A. Gerrard Co., Cin., 1934-48; pres. Shawnee Estates, Inc., Cin., 1953-, Midham Corp., 1939-; dir. L. B. Wilson, Inc., Ohio Valley Financial Corp., Buckeye Loan & Bldg. Co. Cons., dir. Cin. Crime Commn., 1934-38; pres. Health Care Mut. Assn., Cin., 1960-; chmn. disaster com. bd. dirs. Cin. and Hamilton County chpt. A.R.C., 1940-50, chmn. chpt., 1951-52; pres., mem. exec. com. Hosp. Care Corp. (Cin. Blue Cross Assn.) 1961-62, trustee, 1959—; pres. elect Greater Cin. Hosp. Council, 1964-65. Treas. Robert A. Taft for Senate Com., 1938; mem. policy com. Hamilton County Republican Party, 1942-. Mem. bd. Cin. Central YMCA; trustee, exec. com., sec. bd. dirs. Childrens Hosp. Cin.; trustee Cin. Widows and Old Men's Home, Thomas J. Emery Meml. Found. Served with U.S. Army, 1917-19; AEF in France. Mem. Am., Ohio, Cin. bar assns., Cincinnatus Assn. (pres. 1934-36), Phi Alpha Delta, Alpha Tau Omega. Clubs: City (sec. 1919-20), Commonwealth (sec. 1947), Cin. Country, Cin. Athletic, Queen City (dir.) (Cin.); Camargo Country, Camargo Hunt (mast fox hounds 1954-) (Indian Hill, O.). Home: 1263 Hayward Av Cincinnati OH 45226 Office: Dixie Terminal Bldg Cincinnati OH 45202

CLIPSHAM, GEORGE FREDERICK, utility exec.; b. Liverpool, Eng., 1897; grad. Manchester U. (Eng.), 1922. Sec., Lincoln Electric Co., Cleve. Home: 1389 Westover Rd Cleveland OH 44118 Office: 22801 St Clair Av Cleveland OH 44117

CLISSOLD, PAUL EDWARD, former publisher; b. Morgan Park, Ill., May 1, 1906; s. Edward T. and Mina (Swartwout) C.; B.S., Denison U., 1928; m. Sarah Smith, June 28, 1930 (dec. July 1955); children—June (Mrs. James R. Arnold), Edward T., Henry R.; m. 2d, Elizabeth Scudder, Sept. 28, 1957 (div. 1965). With Clissoid Pub. Co., 1928-71, circulation mgr., 1931-38, v.p., 1938-43, pres., 1943-64, chmn., 1964-71. Trustee Denison U., 1951-58, permanent pres. class of '28. Mem. Am. Soc. Bakery Engrs., Asso. Bus. Publs. (past chmn.), Chgo. Bus. Publs. (past pres.), Am. Inst. Baking (dir. 1947-61), Phi Mu Alpha, Beta Theta Pi. Mason (K.T., Shriner). Clubs: Westmoreland Country; Rotary (Chgo.); Bakers (N.Y.C.). Home: 112 Lawndale Wilmette IL 60091

CLITHEROE, LORD, (Sir Ralph Assheton), banker, industrialist; b. nr. Clitheroe, Eng., Feb. 24, 1901; s. Sir Ralph and Mildred (Master) Assheton; M.A. with honours in history, Christ Church, Oxford U., 1923; m. Sylvia Hotham, Jan. 24, 1924; children—Bridget (Mrs. Marcus Worlsey), Ralph John, Nicholas. Called to bar Inner Temple, 1925; M.P. for Rushcliffe, City of London, Blackburn, 1934-55; mem. House of Lords, 1955—; privy counsellor, 1944—; financial sec. Treasury Dept., 1942-44; chmn. Borax Holdings, 1958-69, Mercantile Investment Trust, 1956-71; vice chmn. John Brown & Co., 1959-71, Tube Investments, 1961—; former dep. chmn. Nat. Westminster Bank; dir. U.S. Borax and Chem. Corp., 1956-70, also Coutts & Co., 1955-71, Nat. Mut. Life Assn. Australia, English & Calddonian Investment Trust, Union Miniere, Rio Tinto Zinc Corp., Ltd., 1968-71, Tanganyika Concessions Ltd., others. Lord lt. County Lancashire, 1971—, justice of peace, 1934—. Created Lord Clitheroe, 1955; High Steward of Westminster, 1962. Fellow Soc. of Antiquaries. Home: Downham Hall Clitheroe England also 17 Chelsea Park Gardens London SW 3 England Office: Winchester House London Wall London EC2 England

CLIVE, JOHN LEONARD, educator; b. Berlin, Germany, Sept. 25, 1924; s. Bruno and Rose (Rosenfeld) C.; came to U.S., 1940, naturalized, 1943; student Buxton Coll., Derbyshire, Eng., 1937-40; A.B., U. N.C., 1943; M.A., Harvard, 1947, Ph.D., 1952. From teaching fellow to asst. prof. history Harvard, 1948-60, prof. history and lit., 1965—; asst. prof., then asso. prof. history U. Chgo., 1960-65. Served to 2d lt. AUS, 1943-46. Mem. Am. Hist. Assn., Phi Beta Kappa. Author: Scotch Reviewers: The Edinburgh Review, 1802-1815, 1957. Gen. editor: Classics of British Historical Literature. Home: 38 Fernald Dr Cambridge MA 02138

CLOAK, FRANK THEODORE, educator; b. Detroit, Aug. 13, 1904; s. Frank V.C. and Harriet A. (White) C.; B.A., Wesleyan U., Middletown, Conn., 1925; M.A., Northwestern U., 1927; hon. fellow, Yale, 1937-39; M.F.A., Lawrence U., 1969; m. Loe Comer, June 11, 1930; children—Frank Theodore, Andrea Louise (Mrs. Raymond Mihok), Nathaniel Healy; m. 2d, Evelyn Campbell, Jan. 8, 1965. Prodn. mgr. Evanston Childrens Theatre, 1925-26; instr. theatre Northwestern U., 1926-28; tchr. speech and theatre Benton Harbor (Mich.) High Sch., 1928-29; asst. prof. theatre Lawrence U., Appleton, Wis., 1929-35, asso. prof., 1935-40, prof., 1940—, Evangeline Bergstrom prof. fine arts, 1966—, founder, dir. Berkshire Playhouse Drama Sch., summers 1932-42. Served with OSS, 1943-45. Recipient Rockefeller Found. grants for study, 1938-39, 45-46, 57. Author: Allardyce Nicoll Forbidden Fruit and Other Plays, 1940. Home: 1515 S Alicia Dr Appleton WI 54911

CLOAR, CARROLL, artist; b. Earle, Ark., Jan. 18, 1913; s. Charles W. and Eva (David) C.; A.B., Southwestern Coll., Memphis, 1934; student Memphis Acad. Art, 1935, Art Students League, N.Y.C., 1936-40. One man shows include Alan Gallery, N.Y.C., 1956, 58, 60, 62, 64, 66, Memphis, 1955, Atlanta, 1959, San Francisco, 1967, Little Rock, 1956; exhbns. includes Pitts. Internat., 1955, Whitney Annual, 1960, Phila. Annual, 1962; retrospective exhbn. N.Y. State U., 1968; represented in permanent collections Met. Mus., Mus. Modern Art, Whitney Mus., Corcoran Gallery, Library of Congress, Wadsworth Atheneum, others, also pvt. collections. Trustee Brooks Meml. Gallery Art, Memphis. Served with USAAF, 1942-45, Guggenheim fellow, 1946; named Ark. traveller, 1956. Hon. mem. Phi Beta Kappa. Contbr. to Esquire, Delta Rev. Address: 235 S Greer St Memphis, TN 38111.

CLOCK, CHARLES PHILIP, UN ofcl.; b. Redlands, Cal., Aug. 30, 1915; s. Charles Henry and Muriel Adelaide (Beamer) C.; grad. Webb Prep. Sch., Claremont, Cal., 1933; A.B., Stanford, 1937, LL.B., 1940; student U. Hawaii, summer 1935, U. Lingnan, Canton, China, 1935-36; grad. Nat. War Coll., 1958; student Brookings Instn., 1958; m. Audrey Marie Brumfield, Feb. 15, 1941; children—Charles Henry, Barbara, Frederick Timothy. Admitted to Cal. bar, 1946; mem. firm Clock, Waestman & Clock, Long Beach, 1940-41; fgn. service officer, 1947-68; treaty and claims, then polit. officer Am. Legation, Budapest, 1947-49; polit. officer, liaison officer with Internat. Ct. Justice, Embassy, The Hague, 1949-52; mem. U.S. delegation UN Gen. Assembly, N.Y.C., 1952; charge econ. and comml. sect. Consulate Gen., Singapore, 1953-55; mem. U.S. delegation ECAFE Conf., Hong Kong, 1955; charge polit. sect. Embassy, Tehran, 1955-57; spl. asst. to under-sec. of state, Washington, 1958-61, dep. chief of mission, U.S. Embassy, Panama, 1961-62; counselor polit. affairs Am. Embassy, Ankara, Turkey, 1962-65; dep. chief mission Am. Embassy, Monrovia, Liberia, 1966-68; dep. regional rep. UN Devel. Program, 1968—, dep. regional rep., Malaysia. Dept. representative U.S. Army Logistical Exercise, Ft. Lee, Va., 1959. Served from pvt. to maj., AUS, 1941-46. Decorated Bronze Star medal. Mem. State Bar of Cal., Phi Delta Phi, Beta Theta Pi. Clubs: Swiss, Rotary (Singapore); Tehran, Iran (Tehran); Chevy Chase (Md.) Country; Army and Navy, Fort McNair Officers, University (Washington); Ankara Golf; International (Washington); Royal Selanger Golf (Kuala Lumpur, Malaysia); De Golf Sotogrande (Spain). Home: No 7 Jalan Kenny Tengah Kuala Lumbur Malaysia Office: UNDP PO Box 2544 Kuala Lumpur Malaysia

CLOCK, JOHN G., lawyer; b. Hampton, Ia., Feb. 26, 1896; s. Henry A. and Susan M. (Reeve) C.; student U. So. Calif. Law Sch., 1915-19; m. Blanche Dorsett, Sept. 30, 1922; children—Rosemary (Mrs. John Sadler), Carolyn (dec.). Admitted to Cal. bar, 1920, since practiced in Long Beach; mem. Clock, Waestman and Clock. Served in United States Army, 1917- 19. Fellow Am. Bar Found.; mem. of American, Los Angeles County (bd. trustees 1939-42) and Long Beach (pres. 1943) bar assns., Am. Judicature Soc., Am. Counsel Assn., State Bar Calif. (bd. govs. 1945-48; v.p. 1948), Am. Coll. Probate Counsel (pres. 1950- 51, regent), So. Calif. Golf Assn. (dir. 1941-50, pres. 1946), Calif. Golf Assn. (sec.-treas. 1946, pres. 1950), U.S. Golf Assn. (exec. com.; pres. 1960- 61), Delta Theta Phi. Mason (32). Republican. Clubs: Royal and Ancient Golf (St. Andrews, Scotland); Virginia Country (pres. 1950); Thunderbird Country (Palm Springs). Home: 525 Devon Pl Long Beach CA 90807 also 1214 Sandpiper Palm Desert CA 92260 Office: 4047 Long Beach Blvd Long Beach CA 90807

CLODIUS, ROBERT LEROY, educator, economist; b. Walla Walla, Wash., Mar. 10, 1921; s. Hans Frederick and Emma (Wellman) C.; student Whitman Coll., 1938-40, LL.D., 1970; B.S., U. Cal. at Berkeley, 1942, Ph.D., 1950; m. Joan Elizabeth Coyle, Aug. 27, 1949; children—Catherine, Mark. Lectr. econs. U. Cal. at Berkeley, 1949-50; mem. faculty U. Wis., 1950—, prof. agrl. econs., 1958—, chmn. dept., 1960-62, v.p. univ., 1964—, acting pres., 1970; vis. asso. Harvard Bus. Sch., 1954; lectr. Am. Council Edn., Inst. Coll. and U. Adminstrs. State Dept. specialist in S.Am., 1961; cons. dept. Agr., 1961; mem. com. agr. scis. to sec. agr., 1961-69; cons. Rockefeller Found., 1963-67; adviser U. E. Africa, 1963-67; chmn. Com. Instnl. Coop., 1968; mem. exec. bd. commn. colls. and univs. N. Central Assn.; v.p. Midwest Univs. Consortium Internat. Activities, Inc., 1964-70, chmn. bd., 1970—; mem. Commn. on Higher Edn., Govt. Sierra Leone, 1969. Bd. dirs. Univ. Corp. Atmospheric Research, 1962-67, Center for Research Libraries, 1969—. Served to lt. USNR, 1942-46. Decorated Commendation medal; recipient Kiekhofer Teaching award U. Wis., 1953. Mem. Am. Econs. Assn., Am. Agrl. Econs. Assn. (v.p. 1960; Thesis award 1951), Am. Assn. U. Profs. (pres. Wis. 1957), Phi Beta Kappa, Alpha Zeta, Phi Kappa Phi. Author articles, monographs, chpts. in books. Editor Jour. Farm Econs., 1958-60. Home: 3435 Edgehill Pkwy Madison WI 53705

CLOETE, STUART, author; b. Paris, France, July 23, 1897; s. Laurence and Edith Margaret (Park) C.; student Paris schs. and Lancing Coll.; Sussex, Eng.; m. Mildred Ellison, Apr. 6, 1940. Served in Brit. Army as mem. Coldstream Guards, 1914-25, and wounded in action, 1916 and 1918; ranching in South Africa, 1925-35; visited U.S., 1937; writing for several yrs., publishing first novel in 1937. Trustee South Africa Found. Mem. Internat. Platform Assn. Mem. Ch. of Eng. Clubs: Guards, Savage (London); Coffee House, Explorers, Nat. Arts (N.Y.C.). Author: Turning Wheels, 1937; Watch For the Dawn, 1939; Yesterday is Dead, 1940; The Hill of Doves, 1941; The Young Men and the Old, 1941; Congo Song, 1943; Against

These Three; The Third Way; Curve and the Tusk, 1952; The African Giant, 1955; Mamba, 1956; The Mask, 1957; Gazella, 1958; The Soldier's Peaches and Other African Stories, 1959; The Fiercest Heart, 1960; The Silver Trumpet, 1961; West With the Sun, 1962; Rags of Glory, 1963; The Looking Glass, 1963; The Thousand and One Nights of Jean Macque, 1965; The Honey Bird, 1965; The Abductors, 1966; The Writing on the Wall, 1967; South Africa Land and People, 1968; How Young They Died, 1969; Three White Swans, 1971; A Son of Queen Victoria, 1971. Contbr. to mags. Home: Box 3164 Hermanus South Africa Office: care John Cushman Asso 24 E 38th St New York City NY 10016

CLOKE, HARVEY WALTON, pub. relations and advt. exec.; b. Hazelton, Pa. Aug. 12, 1919; s. Harvey Raymond and Viola Mary (Walton) C.; A.B., Bucknell U., 1942; m. Janet Alden House, July 24, 1943; m. 2d, Marjorie Mitchell, Dec. 1960. Mng. editor Lewisburg (Pa.) Jour., 1940-42; financial writer, legislative corr. Asso. Press, 1943-45; financial corr. N.Y. Times, Phila. and Washington burs., 1945-50; coordinator pub. relations Kaiser Industries Corp. and affiliates, 1950-63; sr. v.p. Barnet and Reef Assos., Inc., N.Y.C., 1963-64; v.p. pub. relations and advt., corporate officer Am. Can Co., N.Y.C., 1964- 68; v.p. pub. relations and advt., also corporate officer N.Am. Rockwell Corp., El Segundo, Cal., 1968—; Washington editor of Finance mag., 1948-50. Past exec. bd. U.S. nat. com UNESCO. Mem. Pub. Relations Soc. Am. (past pres., mem. accreditation bd.), Am. (past pres.), Internat. pub. relations assns., Assn. Nat. Advertisers (dir.), Pub. Relations Found. (dir.), N.A.M. (pub. relations council), Aerospace Industries Assn. (exec. com., pub. affairs council), Lambda Chi Alpha, Sigma Tau Delta, Phi Delta Epsilon. Clubs: Nat. Press, Internat., Nat. Aviation, Kenwood Country (Washington); Overseas Press, Pinnacle (N.Y.C.); Bel Air Country (Los Angeles). Home: Pittsburgh PA 15230 Office: Fifth and Wood Sts Pittsburgh PA 15222

CLOKEY, SAMUEL JOSEPH, steel co. exec.; b. Washington, Pa., May 20, 1914; s. Samuel J. and Maude (Munce) C.; B.S., Washington and Jefferson Coll., 1936; Metall. Engr., Carnegie Inst. Tech., 1942; m. Dorothy Skinner. Feb. 20, 1941; children—Carol Anne, Rebecca Louise. With Firestone Tire & Rubber Co., 1936-39, Mut. LIfe Ins. Co., 1939-40; with Jessop Steel Co., Washington, Pa., 1940—, v.p. comml., 1957-65, sr. v.p. comml., 1965- -; v.p. Jessop Steel Internat. Corp.; pres. Steel Warehousing Corp. Mem. Am. Iron and Steel Inst., Am. Soc. Tool Engrs., Pa. Soc., Am. Ordnance Soc., Canadian, Washington chambers commerce Pa. Soc., Newcomen Soc. Presbyn. (trustee). Mason, (Jester). Clubs: Valley Brook Country (Canonsburgh, Pa.); Duquesne, University (Pitts.). Home: 4 LeMoyne Av Extension Washington PA 15301 Office: Jessop Steel Co Washington PA 15301

CLONEY, WILLIAM THOMAS, Jr., investment co. exec.; b. Boston, Oct. 29, 1911; s. William T. and Elizabeth Anne (McLaughlin) C.; A.B., Harvard, 1933, student Grad. Sch. Edn., 1934-35; m. Arline Patricia Lynch, June 29, 1937; children—Mary E. (Mrs. William D. Benjes, Jr.), Kathleen (Mrs. N. Phillips Dodge III), Martha (Mrs. W. Brooke Hamilton, Jr.), William Thomas (killed in action). With Boston Herald, 1930-53; sports editor Boston Post, 1953-56; jr. master Roxbury Latin Sch., 1935- 36; instr. to asso. prof. English and journalism Northeastern U. 1937- 53; pub. relations counsel, 1956-59; asst. to pres. Keystone Custodian Funds, 1956-62, v.p., 1962—; pres. Boston Athletic Assn. indoor games and Boston Marathon, 1946—. Served as lt. to lt. col. AUS, 1942-46. Author: The Story of a New England Industrialist, James Lorin Richards, 1952. Author mag. articles. Home: 30 Lantern Lane Milton MA 02186 Office: 50 Congress St Boston MA 02109

CLOONEY, ROSEMARY, singer, actress; b. Maysville, Ky., May 23, 1928; d. Andrew and Frances (Guilfoyle) Clooney; student pub. schs.; m. José Ferrer, 1953; children—Miguel, Maria, Gabriel, Monsita, Rafael Francisco. First solo rec. I'm Sorry I Didn't Say I'm Sorry When I Made You Cry Last Night, 1946; other recs. include Come On-a My House, Half as Much; Botcha-me; Tenderly; Hey, There; This Ole House; Mambo Italiano; Fancy Meeting You Here (with Bing Crosby, album in stereo); Clap Hands Here Comes Rosie; Rosie Solves The Swinging Riddle; The Wonderful Season of Love; TV, radio, 1946—, Rosemary Clooney TV Show, 1957—, starring Lux Show, 1958—; night club, theater singing engagements, 1949-; motion pictures include The Stars are Singing, Here Come the Girls, Red Garters, White Christmas. Home: 1019 N Roxbury Dr Beverly Hills CA 90210 Office: 6430 Sunset Blvd Los Angeles CA 90028

CLOOS, ERNST, geologist, educator; b. Saarbrücken, Germany, May 17, 1898; s. Ulrich and Elisabeth (Heckel) C.; student univs. Freiburg and Göttingen; Ph.D., U. Breslau, 1923; m. Margaret Spemann, Dec. 27, 1923; children—Gisela, Veronica. Came to U.S., 1929, naturalized 1938. Geologist, Seismos Co., Hannover, Germany, 1924-29, in charge geophys. exploration in Tex., 1924-26, Eng., 1927, Germany and Iraq, 1927-28; conducted investigation Sierra Nevada granites, 1929-30; lectr. Johns Hopkins U., Balt., 1931-37, asso. prof., 1937-41, prof., 1941-68, prof. emeritus, 1968—. Chmn. Commn. Md. Geol. Survey, 1962. Guggenheim fellow, 1956-57, Fellow Geol. Soc. London; mem. Nat. Acad. Scis., Geol. Soc. Am. Geophys. Union, A.A.A.S., Am. Philos. Soc., Geol. Soc. Finland, Geologists Assn., Phi Beta Kappa, Sigma Xi. Condr. research expdns. Mesopotamia, Persia, Cal. and Tex. Research in structural geology of Appalachians and Petrofabrics. Home: 610 Fairway Dr Towson MD 21204 Office: Johns Hopkins University Baltimore MD 21218

CLOPTON, JOHN RAYMOND, biochemist, educator; b. Bozeman, Mont., Oct. 5, 1908; s. John Wentworth and Lorena (Holt) C.; B.S., Mont. State Coll., 1935; M.S., Columbia, 1939; Ph.D., Pa. State U., 1943; m. Margaret Louise Davis, June 14, 1934 (div.); children—John C., Louise Elizabeth; m. 2d, Amelia M. Broughton, Sept. 1, 1965; children—Raymond, William. Group leader chem. research Armour Research Found., Chgo., 1943-45; group leader chem. research U.S. Dept. Agr., N. Regional Research Lab., Peoria, Ill., 1945-47; head biochem. and analysis div. Tex. Research Found., Dallas, 1947-49; prof. biochemistry U. Colo., Boulder, 1950—, past chmn. basic sci. program, past dir. Acad. Year Inst. and Summer Inst. Tchrs., past head biochem. div. chemistry dept.; research and indsl. cons. to food processing and florists industries, 1951—. Fellow Am. Inst. Chemists, A.A.A.S.; mem. Am. Chem. Soc., Am. Oil Chemists Soc., N.Y. Acad. Sci., Sigma Xi, Phi Lambda Upsilon. Home: 2060 Kohler Dr Boulder CO 80302

CLORE, CHARLES, co. dir.; b. Dec. 24, 1904; ed. in London, Eng.; m. Francine R. Halphen, 1943 (div.); 1 son, 1 dau. Chmn. Sears Holdings, Ltd., Sears Engring. Ltd., Brit. Shoe Corp. Ltd., Bentley Engring. Group Ltd., Taylor & Lodge Ltd., Furness Shipbldg. Co. Ltd., B.S.C. Footwear Ltd., Sears Industries Inc., Lewis' Investment Trust Ltd., Selfridges Ltd., Mappin & Webb Ltd., Scottish Motor Traction Co. Ltd., Kaye & Stewart Ltd., Princes Investments Ltd.; dir. Orange Free State Investment Trust Ltd., Hill, Samuel & Co. Ltd., other pub. companies. Address: 22 Park St Park Lane London W 1 England

CLOSE, CHARLES MOLLISON, engring. educator; b. Ilion, N.Y., Mar. 15, 1927; s. Charles M. and Marion (Young) C.; B.S., Lehigh U., 1950; M.S., Stevens Inst. Tech., 1953; Ph.D., Rensselaer Poly. Inst., 1962; m. Ann V. Hasbrouck, June 8, 1957; children—Douglas A., Kimberly A., Scott C. Devel. engr. Westinghouse Electric Corp., 1950-52; grad. asst. Stevens Inst. Tech., 1952-54; mem. faculty Rensselaer Poly. Inst., 1954—, prof. elec. engring., 1967—. Served with USNR, 1945-46. Mem. I.E.E.E., Am. Soc. Engring. Edn., Phi Beta Kappa, Sigma Xi, Tau Beta Pi, Eta Kappa Nu, Pi Mu Epsilon. Republican. Episcopalian. Author: (with others) State Variables for Engineers, 1965; The Analysis of Linear Circuits, 1966. Home: 12 Petticoat Lane Troy NY 12180

CLOSE, ELIZABETH SCHEU, (Mrs. Winston A. Close), architect; b. Vienna, Austria, June 4, 1912; d. Gustav and Helene (Riesz) C.; came to U.S., 1932, naturalized, 1938; student Technische Hochschule, Vienna, 1931-32; B.Arch., Mass. Inst. Tech., 1934, M.Arch., 1935; m. Winston A. Close, Apr. 11, 1938; children—Anne Miriam (Mrs. Milton Ulmer), Roy Michel, Robert Arthur. Draftsman Oscar Stonorov, Architect, Phila., 1935-36; designer Magney & Tusler, Mpls., 1936-38; partner, architect Close & Scheu (changed to Close Assos., Inc., 1969), Mpls., 1938—; instr. Mpls. Sch. Art, 1936-37; instr. design U. Minn. Sch. Arch., 1938-39. Bd. dirs. Civic Orch. Mpls., 1951-68; bd. dirs., exec. com. Center Opera Co.; sec. New Friends Chamber Music, 1968—. Recipient Honor award Pub. Housing Adminstrn., 1964; hon. mention F.D. Roosevelt Meml. competion, 1960. Fellow A.I.A. (dir. Mpls. chpt., 1964-69); mem. Minn. Soc. Architects. Principal works include Garden City Devel., Brooklyn Center, Minn., 1957; Duff House, Wayzata, Minn., 1959; variety structures Met. Med. Center Complex, 1960—, Golden Age Homes, 1960, both Mpls.; Peavey Tech. Center, Chaska, Minn., 1970. Home: 1588 Fulham St St Paul MN 55108 Office: Close Assos Inc 3101 E Franklin Av Minneapolis MN 55406

CLOSE, FREDERICK JACOB, aluminum mfg. exec.; b. Pitts., June 21, 1905; s. Clarence William and Lyda (Bushfield) C.; B.A., Pa. State U., 1928; m. Lillian Roberts, Aug. 30, 1930; 1 son, Frederick Jacob III. With Aluminum Co. of Am., 1929—, beginning as mem. archtl. sales dept., N.Y.C., successively staff collapsible tube, screw machine products, impact extrusions depts., Edgewater, N.J., mgr. forge shop, Cleve., industry mgr. archtl. sales, mgr. market devel., gen. mgr. sales devel. and comml. research, 1929-59, v.p., gen. mgr. industry sales and sales devel., 1959- 62, v.p. charge marketing, 1962-63, exec. v.p., 1963-66, chmn. bd., 1966- 70, now dir.; dir. Alcoa Service Corp. Devel. aluminum pressed forgings, aluminum windows, increased use of aluminum as bldg. material; gen. adv. com. Harmarville (Pa.) Rehab. Center. Mem. Pa. State U. Alumni Assn., Beta Theta Pi, Blue Key. Clubs: Duquesne, University, Pittsburgh Athletic Assn., Fox Chapel Golf (Pitts.); Sky (N.Y.C.); Rolling Rock, Laurel Valley Golf, Madison (O.) Golf and Country. Home: Washington Plaza Pittsburgh PA 15219 Office: Alcoa Bldg Pittsburgh PA 15219

CLOSE, GORDON RALPH, lawyer; b. Chgo., Aug. 18, 1906; s. D. Ralph and Helen E. (Withrow) C.; student U. Ill., 1924-26; diploma in commerce Northwestern U., 1929; LL.B., John Marshall Law Sch., 1932; m. Ruth H. Kernwein, June 19, 1935; children—Gordon Ralph, Karen E. Admitted to Ill. bar, 1933; asso. Lord, Bissell & Brook, Chgo., 1930-40, partner, 1940—. Mem. legal adv. com. U.S. Dept. Transp., 1968—. Bd. govs. Hinsdale Community House, 1956-59. Trustee John Marshall Law Sch. Served to capt. USAAF, 1942-45. Fellow Am. Coll. Trial Lawyers, Am. Bar Found.; mem. Chgo. Bar Assn. (bd. mgrs. 1958-60, pres. 1964-65), Internat. Assn. Ins. Counsel (exec. com. pres. 1968-69), Soc. Trial Lawyers (pres. 1949), Nat. Assn. R.R. Trial Attys. (sec. exec. com. 1959- 60), Law Club Chgo. Episcopalian (warden). Clubs: Mid-America, Mid-Day (Chgo.); Hinsdale Golf. Home: 127 E 5th St Hinsdale IL 60521 Office: 135 S LaSalle St Chicago IL 60603

CLOSE, HUGH WILLIAM, textile mfg. exec.; b. Phila., Nov. 18, 1919; s. Hugh William and Marian Lucy (Crandall) C.; B.S., U. Pa., 1942; grad. Exec. Program, U. N.C., 1959; LL.D., (hon.), U. S.C., 1967; m. Anne Kingsley Springs, Nov. 23, 1946; children—Lillian Crandall (Mrs. Erskine B. Bowles), Frances Allison, Leroy Springs, Patricia, Elliott Springs, Hugh William, Derick Springsteen, and Katherine Anne Close. Employed with Springs Mills, Inc., N.Y.C., 1946—, beginning as mem. sales staff, Fort Mill, S.C. Succesively apprentice Springs Cotton Mills, asst. supt., asst. mgr. Fort Mill plant, gen. supt. card and spinning, asst. gen. mgr., asst. to pres., v.p., 1946-59, pres., dir. Springs Mills, Inc., 1966-69, chmn., 1969—; pres., dir. Lancaster Trust Co., Ft. Mill Trust Co., Bank of Lancaster, Springmaid of Can., Inc. Kanawha Ins. Co., Lancaster & Chester R.R., Leroy Springs & Co.; dir. The Springs Co., Carolina & Northwestern Ry. Co. Commr. 5th dist. S.C. Dept. Parks, Recreation and Tourism. Pres., dir. Elliott White Springs Found., Inc.; dir. Elliott White Springs Meml. Hosp., Lancaster, S.C. Bd. dirs. U. S.C. Devel. Adv. Council, J.E. Sirrine Found.; trustee S.C. Coll. Council, Inc. Served as pvt. with AUS, 1942; ensign to lt. (s.g.), USNR, 1942-46. Named Textile Man of Year, N.Y. Bd. Trade, 1963. Mem. Am. Textile Mfrs. Inst., Inc. (dir., v.p.), S.C. Textile Mfrs. Assn., Newcomen Soc. N. Am., Phi Gamma Delta, Beta Gamma Sigma. Episcopalian. Club: Lions (Fort Mill). Home: Fort Mill SC 29715 Office: Springs Mills Inc Fort Mill SC 29715

CLOSE, JAMES WILLIAM, lawyer; b. Denver, Apr. 3, 1909; s. Henry Francis and Rose (Youk) C.; Ph. B., Regis Coll., Denver, 1931; LL.B., Cath. U. Am., 1934; m. Jane Winburn, Dec. 29, 1934; children—Henry, Mary Jane, Betty Anne, Nancy Lou, Jeannie, John, Patricia. Admitted to D.C. bar, 1934, Ill. bar, 1944; counsel RFC, 1934-44; gen. counsel War Damage Corp., 1942-44; partner Wilson & McIlvaine, Chgo., 1944—; dir. Hibbard, Spencer, Bartlett Trust, Evanston, Ill. Mem. Am., Ill., Chgo. bar assns. Home: 103 Broadway Wilmette IL 60091 Office: 135 S LaSalle St Chicago IL 60603

CLOSE, WINSTON ARTHUR, architect; b. Appleton, Minn., Apr. 27, 1906; s. Arthur Edwin and Clara (Michel) C.; B.Arch., U. Minn., 1927; M.Arch., Mass. Inst. Tech., 1935; m. Elizabeth Hilde Scheu, Apr. 11, 1938; children—Ann Miriam (Mrs. Milton Ulmer), Roy Michel, Robert Arthur. Draftsman and designer, 1927-38; partner firm Elizabeth and Winston Close, Mpls., 1938- -; prof. architecture U. Minn., 1946-71, adv. architect, 1950-71; prin. works include Duluth campus U. Minn., 1949; coordinator planning W. Bank campus U. Minn., Mpls., 1956-61. Pres. bd. Civic Orch. Mpls.; bd. dirs. New Friends Chamber Music, Mpls.; past mem. bd. Walker Art Center, Mpls. Fellow A.I.A. (past pres. Mpls.); mem. Assn. U. Architects (past pres.), Minn. Soc. Architects (sec.), Sigma Phi Epsilon, Grey Friars, Scarab. Home: 1588 Fulham St St Paul MN 55108 Office: 3101 E Franklin Av Minneapolis MN 55406

CLOSE, WINTON RALPH, ret. air force officer; b. Columbus, O., Dec. 12, 1917; s. Ralph and Sadie J. (Harris) C.; B.A., Stanford, 1938; grad. USAAF Flying Sch., 1939; m. Marion Joan Millsop, June 12, 1943. Commd. 2d lt. USAAF, 1939, advanced through grades to maj. gen. USAF, 1964; heavy bombardment squadron comdr., 1942-45; air attache, Yugoslavia, 1946; heavy bombardment wing comdr., Korea, 1952, 57-62; heavy bombardment div. comdr., 1962-64; dir. plans SAC, 1964-66; became comdr. Joint Task Force Two, Joint Chiefs Staff, 1966. Decorated D.S.M., Legion of Merit with 2 oak leaf clusters, D.F.C. with 1 oak leaf cluster, Bronze Star medal, Air medal with six oak leaf clusters. Home: 29 Baynard Park Rd Hilton Head SC 29928

CLOSS, GERHARD LUDWIG, chemist, educator; b. Wuppertal, Germany, May 1, 1928; s. Ludwig and Maria (Pfeiffer) C.; student U. Würzburg, 1949-52; Ph.D., U. Tubingen, 1955; m. Liselotte Else Pohmer, Aug. 17, 1956. Came to U.S., 1955, naturalized, 1966. Research fellow Harvard, 1955-57; asst. prof. chemistry U. Chgo., 1957-61, asso. prof., 1961-63, prof., 1963—. Editorial adviser for chemistry Ency. Brit., 1964—. A.P. Sloan Found. fellow, 1962-66. Mem. Am. Chem. Soc., A.A.A.S., Chem. Soc. (London). Contbr. articles phys. organic chemistry profl. jours. Home: 5532 South Shore Dr Chicago IL 60637

CLOTHIER, FLORENCE, (Mrs. George B. Wislocki), see Wislocki, (Mrs. George B.),

CLOTHIER, GEORGE BALL, lawyer; b. Wynnewood, Pa., Feb. 12, 1905; s. Walter and Edith (Ball) C.; grad. Haverford Sch., 1922; A.B., Swarthmore Coll., 1926; LL.B., Harvard, 1929; m. Helen Louise Taylor, Feb. 24, 1933 (div.); children—Ann (Mrs. Lenssen), Birchard T., Helen L. (Mrs. William F. Hoffman), Sandra (Mrs. David R. Singer); m. 2d, Jane Corfield, Apr. 25, 1969; children—Adrian, John. Admitted to Pa. bar, 1929, practiced in Phila.; asso. Obermayer, Rebmann, Maxwell & Hippel (and predecessor cos.), 1929-37, partner, 1937—. Dir. Title Ins. Corp. Pa. Trustee Phila. Mus. Art; bd. mgrs. Swarthmore Coll. Mem. Am., Pa., Phila. bar assns., Phi Beta Kappa, Phi Kappa Psi. Home: 108 Bloomingdale Av Wayne PA Office: Packard Bldg Philadelphia PA 19102

CLOTWORTHY, JOHN HARRIS, recreational co. exec.; b. Balt., Mar. 23, 1924; s. Harris A. and Violet (Klein) C.; B.E.E., U. Va., 1946; certificate Harvard Bus. Sch., 1956; m. Martha D. Wilson, Mar. 22, 1947; 1 son, John S. With Westinghouse Electric Corp., 1948-67, v.p. def. and space center, gen. mgr. underseas div., 1963-67; chmn. div. ocean engring. U. Miami (Fla.), 1967-68; cons. to oceanographic industry, 1967-68; founder, pres. Oceans Gen., Inc., Miami, 1968-71; dir. Office Congl. and Legislative Affairs Nat. Oceanic and Atmospheric Adminstrn., Washington, 1971—. Sec., v.p. Oak Bldg. & Savs. Assn., 1946-56. Bd. govs. Va. Engring. Found., 1965-68. Registered profl. engr., Md. Mem. Marine Tech. Soc. (founding mem., dir. 1966-69), Nat. Oceanography Assn. (pres. 1966-69), U.S. C. of C., Am. Guild Organists, I.E.E.E., Am. Ordnance Assn., Inst. Naval Engrs., Alpha Tau Omega. Club: Annapolis (Md.) Yacht. Mem. editorial bd., contbr. Oceanology Internat. mag. Home: 7225 Van Ness Ct McLean VA 22101 Office: 14th and Constitution Washington DC 20230

CLOUD, BRUCE BENJAMIN, constrn. co. exec.; b. Thomas, Okla., Feb. 15, 1920; s. Dudley R. and Lillian (Sanders) C.; B.S. in Civil Engring., Tex. A. and M. U., 1940; m. Virginia Dugan, June 5, 1944; children—Sheila Marie (Mrs. Mark Kiselis), Karen Susan (Mrs. Anthony Padilla), Bruce Benjamin, Deborah Ann, Virginia Ann. With H.B. Zachry Co., San Antonio, 1940-42, 55—, exec. v.p., 1963—, also dir.; partner Dudley R. Cloud & Son, constrn., San Antonio, 1946-55. Served to lt. col. C.E., AUS, 1942-46; ETO. Recipient Pro Deo Et Juventute award Nat. Council Catholic Youth. Registered profl. engr., Tex. Mem. Tex. Asso. Gen. Contractors (past dir. hwy. and heavy br.), Am. Concrete Paving Assn. (v.p., dir.), Nat. Asphalt Paving Assn., San Antonio Livestock Assn. (life), Nat., Tex. socs. profl. engrs., Holy Name Soc. (v.p. 1962-63), Noctural Adoration Soc. K.C. (3). Home: 209 Calumet Pl San Antonio TX 78209 Office: PO Box 21130 San Antonio TX 78285

CLOUD, LUTHER ATWOOD, physician; b. Wilmington, Del., Aug. 21, 1920; s. Luther Atwood and Mary Gertrude (Eldridge) C.; B.A., N.Y.U., 1942, M.D., 1949; m. Kathleen Goodwin, Nov. 21, 1954. Intern Charity Hosp., New Orleans, 1949-50; resident Bellevue Hosp., N.Y.C., 1950-51; pvt. practice medicine, Montgomery, W.Va., 1951-54; chief supervisory physician N.Y. Telephone Co., 1955-57; sr. asso. med. dir. Equitable Life Assurance Soc. of U.S., N.Y.C., 1957—; mem. med. staff Gracie Sq. Hosp., N.Y.C.; staff physician Preventive Medicine Inst., N.Y.C.; lectr. Menninger Found., Topeka, 1968, Rutgers U. Sch. Alcohol Studies, 1969-71. Pres. Nat. Council on Alcoholism, Inc., 1969-71, now mem. bd. dirs., exec. com.; mem. founding com., bd. dirs. N.Y. Council on Alcoholism; mem. adv. council on alcoholism Health Service Adminstrn., N.Y.C.; mem. Gov. N.Y. Adv. Council Alcoholism; exec. com. Alcohol Recovery Inst., N.Y.C. Served with AUS, 1942-45. Fellow Indsl. Med. Assn. (chmn. com. on alcoholism 1964-69), Acad. Psychomatic Medicine; mem. A.M.A., N.Y. State, N.Y. County med. socs., Am. Acad. Occupational Medicine (pres. 1963-65), N.Y.C. Med. Soc. on Alcoholism, N.Y. Acad. Scis. (chmn. Conf. on Food and Alcoholism in Health and Disease 1966, editor conf. proc.). Home: 316 W 90th St New York City NY 10024 Office: 1285 Av of Americas New York City NY 10019

CLOUD, PRESTON, biogeologist; b. West Upton, Mass., Sept. 26, 1912; s. Preston E. and Pauline L. (Wiedemann) C.; B.S., George Washington U., 1938; Ph.D., Yale, 1940; children—Karen, Lisa, Kevin. Instr. Mo. Sch. Mines and Metallurgy, 1940-41; research fellow Yale, 1941-42; geologist U.S. Geol. Survey, 1942-46, 48-61, chief paleontology and stratigraphy br., 1949-59; research geologist, 1959-61; asst. prof. curator invertebrate paleontology Harvard, 1946-48; prof. dept. geology and geophysics U. Minn., 1961-65, chmn., 1961-63; Mem. Pacific Sci. Bd. NRC, 1952-56, 62-65, mem. exec. com., div. earth sci., 1953-56, del. internat. sci. congresses. Recipient A. Cressey Morrison prize natural history, 1941; Rockefeller Pub. Service award, 1956; U.S. Dept. Interior Distinguished Service award, 1959. Fellow Am. Acad. Arts and Scis.; mem. Nat. Acad. Scis. (mem. com. on sci. and pub. policy 1965-69, chmn. com. on resources and man 1965-69), Geol. Soc. Am., Soc. Systematic Zoologists, Am. Soc. Limnology and Oceanography, Paleontol. Soc. Am. (medal 1971), Paleontol. Soc. India (hon.), A.A.A.S., Am. Soc. Naturalists, Am. Assn. Petroleum Geologists, Geochem. Soc., Soc. for Study Evolution, Am. Geophys. Union, Phi Beta Kappa, Sigma Xi, Sigma Gamma Epsilon. Club: Cosmos (Washington). Author: Terebratuloid Brachiopoda of the Silurian and Devonian, 1942; (with Virgil E. Barnes) The Ellenburger Group of Central Texas, 1948; (with others) Geology of Saipan, Mariana Islands, 1957; (with others) Environment of Calcium Carbonate Deposition West of Andros Island, Bahamas, 1962; (with others) Resources and Man; also articles. Editor: Adventures in Earth History. Office: Dept of Geol Scis U Cal Santa Barbara CA 93106

CLOUD, WILLIAM R., union ofcl; Sec.-treas. Internat. Typographical Union AFL-CIO. Office: PO Box 157 Colorado Spring CO 80901*

CLOUDMAN, HARRY HOWARD, Jr., book publisher; b. Oklahoma City, July 23, 1917; s. Harry Howard and Maebelle (Burnell) C.; B.A. Letters, U. Okla., 1939, M.A., 1941; m. Hazel Marcellus Clay, June 1, 1947; 1 dau., Ruth Howard. Grad. asst. English, U. Okla., 1940-42; coll. rep. Macmillan Co., 1942, 46-52, editor coll. dept., 1952-55, asst. dir. coll. dept., 1955-59, dir. coll. dept., 1959-61, dir. of co., 1957-60, 66-69, dir. coll. and profl. div.,

1961-69, sr. v.p., 1965-69, pres. div., 1969—. Served from pvt. to staff sgt. AUS, 1942-46. Mem. Coll. Pubs. Group (chmn. 1962-63), Delta Upsilon. Unitarian. Club: The Players (N.Y.C.). Home: 56 Carthage Rd Scarsdale NY 10583 Office: 866 3d Av New York City NY 10022

CLOUDY, CHARLES LESTER, lawyer; b. Ketchikan, Alaska, May 26, 1924; s. Charles Lester and Doris (Wells) C.; student San Bernardino (Cal.) Jr. Coll., 1946-47; LL.B., Willamette U., 1952; m. Marjorie Jean Peihl, Aug. 19, 1948; children-Candace Marie (Mrs. Paul Perry), Charles Lester. Admitted to Alaska bar, 1952, since practiced in Ketchikan. Vice pres. S.E. Alaska Area council Boy Scouts Am., 1955-61. Trustee Willamette U. Law Found. Served with USAAF, 1943-45. Mem. Am., Alaska (past mem. bd. govs.), Ore. bar assns., Alaska (past pres.), Ketchikan (past pres.) chambers commerce. Elk. Editor: Willamette Series Legal Handbooks, 1951-52. Home: Route 1 Box 327 Ketchikan AK 99901 Office: Box 979 Ketchikan AK 99901

CLOUGH, MERRILL H., pub. co. exec.; b. Sharpsburg, Ia., Feb. 21, 1919; s. Raymond S. and Helen (King) C.; student Drake U., 1939-40, N.Y. U., 1941-42; B.B.A., U. Tex., 1948; m. Louise Henry, Nov. 24, 1940; childrenThomas N., Nancy J. Vice pres., controller Cowles Communications, Inc., N.Y.C., 1948-, dir., 1967-. Served to 1st lt. USAAF, 1943-45. Methodist. Clubs: Huntington Yacht; Lloyd Harbor (N.Y. Yacht. Home: 148 Maple Hill Rd Huntington, NY 11743. Office: 488 Madison Av New York City NY 10022

CLOUGH, RALPH NELSON, research scholar; b. Seattle, Nov. 17, 1916; s. Ray William and Mildred (Nelson) C.; A.B., U. Wash., 1939; student Lingnan U., 1936-37; M.A., Fletcher Sch. Law and Diplomacy, 1940; m. Mary Lou Sander, Nov. 1, 1941 (dec. Mar. 1950) m. 2d, Awana Alene Stiles, Sept. 5, 1952; children—Frederick William, Marshall Sander, Laurie, Drusilla. Vice consul, Toronto, Ont., Can., 1941-42; 3d sec. embassy, vice consul, Tegucigalpa, Honduras, 1942-45; vice consul, successively Kunming, Chungking, Peiping, China, 1945-47, 3d sec. embassy, vice consul, Nanking, China, 1947-49, 2d sec., consul, 1949-50; consul, Hong Kong, 1950-54; assigned Nat. War Coll., 1954-55; dep. dir. office Chinese affairs, Dept. of State, 1955-57, dir., 1957-58; counselor Am. embassy, Bern, Switzerland, 1958-59; 1st sec. Am. embassy, London, Eng., 1959-61; became dep. chief of mission Am. embassy, Taipei, Taiwan, 1961, also consul gen. until 1965; fellow Center for Internat. Affairs, Harvard, 1965-66; mem. policy planning council Dept. State, 1966-69; sr. fellow Brookings Instn., Washington, 1969—. Mem. Phi Beta Kappa, Theta Delta Chi. Rotarian (Hong Kong). Home: 4540 N 41st St Arlington VA 22207 Office: 1775 Massachusetts Av Washington DC 20036

CLOUGH, RAY WILLIAM, Jr., educator; b. Seattle, July 23, 1920; s. Ray William and Mildred (Nelson) C.; B.S. in Civil Engring., U. Wash., 1942; M.S., Cal. Inst. Tech., 1943; S.M., Mass. Inst. Tech., 1947, Sc.D., 1949; m. Shirley Claire Potter, Oct. 30, 1942; children—Douglas Potter, Allison Justine, Meredith Anne. Faculty, U. Cal. at Berkeley, 1949—, prof. civil engring., 1959—, chmn. div. structural engring. and structural mechanics, 1967-70. Cons. in field, 1953—. Mem. Nat. Acad. Scis.-Nat. Acad. Engring. adv. com. Environmental Sci. Services Adminstrn., 1967- 70; mem. dynamics panel Nat. Acad. Scis. adv. bd. on hardened electric power system, 1964-70; mem. U.S. C.E. Structural Design Adv. Bd., 1967—. Served to capt. USAAF, 1942-46. Fulbright fellow Ship Research Inst., Trondheim, Norway, 1956-57; Churchill fellow Churchill Coll., Cambridge (Eng.) U., 1963-64. Registered profl. engr., Wash. Fellow Am. Soc. C.E. (chmn. engring. mechanics div. 1964-65; Research award 1960, Howard award 1970); mem. Structural Engrs. Assn. No. Cal. (dir.), Earthquake Engring. Research Inst. (dir. 1957-60, 70—), Seismol. Soc. Am. (dir. 1970—), Nat. Acad. Engring. Home: 975 Leneve Pl El Cerrito CA 94530 Office: Davis Hall U Cal Berkeley CA 94720

CLOUGH, RICHARD HUDSON, educator; b. Springer, N.M., Aug. 25, 1922; s. Richard Buckley and Minnie (Caldwell) C.; B.S. in Civil Engring., U. N.M., 1943; M.S. in Civil Engring., U. Colo., 1949; Sc.D., Mass. Inst. Tech., 1951; m. Ethel J. Lamb, Oct. 19, 1945; children—Kenneth Richard, Janet Louise. Mem. faculty civil engring. U. N.M., 1946-49; researcher Mass. Inst. Tech., 1949-51; exec. v.p. Lembke, Clough & King, Inc., gen. contrators, Albuquerque, 1951-57; faculty civil engring. U. N.M., 1957-60, dean Coll. Engring., 1960-68, dir. Bur. Engring. Research, 1960-68, prof. civil engring., 1968—. Served with USNR, 1943-46; PTO. Registered profl. engr., N.M.. Mem. Am. Soc. C.E., Nat. Soc. Profl. Engrs., Am. Soc. Engring. Edn., Sigma Xi, Sigma Tau, Chi Epsilon. Mason (Shriner). Rotarian. Author: Construction Contracting, 1960, 2d edit., 1969. Home: 1025 Pueblo Solano NW Albuquerque NM 87107

CLOUGH, SHEPARD BANCROFT, ret. educator, historian; b. Bloomington, Ind., Dec. 6, 1901; s. Clarence Edward and Mary Ellen (Shepard) C.; A.B., Colgate U., 1923; postgrad. Sorbonne, 1923-24, U. Heidelberg, 1924; Ph.D., Columbia, 1930; m. Rose Trillo, Jan. 5, 1926; children—Shepard Anthony, Peter Nelson. Instr. history, Columbia, 1928-37, prof. history and mem. faculty polit. sci., 1937-70, sec. faculty, 1938-42 (on leave 1942-45); dir. Casa Italiana, Columbia U. Mem. research staff Mut. Life Ins. Co., N.Y.C., 1941-42; mem. div. econ. studies U.S. Dept. State, 1942-43; lectr. Sch. Mil. Govt., Charlottesville, Va., 1942-43, Office Fgn. Relief and Rehab., 1943-44; vis. prof. Institut d'Etudes Politiques, U. Paris, 1952, Faculté de Droit, U. Grenoble, 1952, Inst. European Studies, Turin, 1955-56; vis. lectr. Free U. Berlin, also univs. Turin, Genoa and Rome, 1952-53; NATO prof. to Italy, 1966-67. Asso. editor Jour. Econ. History, 1941-43. Mem. Hist. Service Bd., Adv. Council on War History, Social Sci. Research Council, 1943-52, sec., 1946-50. Com. N.Y. Bus. Records, 1944-49; mem. adv. bd. Indsl. Coll. Armed Forces, NATO fellow, 1958; Rockefeller fellow, 1961-62. Decorated officer knight of Order of Merit of Italian Republic. Mem. Am. Hist. Assn., Storia del Risorgimento, Econ. History Assn. (sec.-treas., trustee, 1940-43, 46-48, 68—, pres. 1968-69), Internat. Econ. History Assn. (exec. com.), Am. Econ. Assn., Soc. Modern History (France), English Econ. History Soc., Soc. French Hist. Studies (pres. 1964-65), Acad. Polit. Sci., Phi Beta Kappa, Delta Upsilon. Club: Columbia Men's Faculty (N.Y.C.). Author books including: A Century of American Life Insurance, 1946; Rise and Fall of Civilization, 1951 (French and German transls. 1952); Histoire économique des Etats Unis, 1952; Basic Values in Western Civilization, 1960; The Econimic History of Modern Italy, 1964; (with others) European Economic History, Documents and readings, 1965; (with others) History of Italy, 1968; The Economic Basis of American Civilization, 1968; Economic History of Europe, 1968; (with others) European Past, 1970. Contbr. to jours. Home: East Peacham VT 05862 also 319 Puritan Rd West Palm Beach FL 33405

CLOUSE, ROGER ROY, banker; b. Apple Creek, O., Dec. 18, 1907; s. Charles W. and Eleanor Lake (Graham) C.; B.S., Coll. Wooster, 1929; M.B.A., Northwestern U., 1931, J.D., 1934; student grad. sch. banking, Rutgers U., 1946; m. Mary Elinor McCabe, Nov. 25, 1937; children—Janet, Dorothy, Linda. Asst. to pres. Comml. Wall Paper Mill, Hammond, Ind., 1929-30; admitted to Ohio bar, 1934; asso. Garfield, Daoust, Baldwin & Vrooman, Cleve., 1934-42; lectr. Western Res. U. 1937—; sec. Fed. Res. Bank Cleve., 1943- 46, 53—, asst. v.p., 1945-49, v.p., 1949—. Acting dir. 5th region Office Civilian Def., 1942-43. Corporate trustee Cleve. Hearing and Speech Center; trustee Chautauqua Instn., 1955-65, Salvation Army. Mem. Cleve. Bar Assn., Cleve. Council on World Affairs, Newcomen Society N.Am. Cleve. Engring. Soc., Delta Theta Phi, Delta Sigma Pi, Beta Gamma Sigma. Presbyn. Mason. Rotarian (past pres., dir. Cleve.). Home: 2362 Woodmere Dr Cleveland Heights OH 44118 also 6 Vincent Av Chautauqua NY 14722 Office: 1455 E 6th St Cleveland OH 44101

CLOUTIER, DANIEL RAYMOND, educator; b. Skowhegan, Me., Feb. 24, 1924; s. Alfred J. and Odila (Villeneuve) C.; A.B. magna cum laude, Bates Coll., 1949; M.P.A., U. Mich., 1951; Ph.D., U. Ala., 1961; m. Nancy Shelton Cosman, June 1969; children—Jeffrey, Kelly, Jill, Daniel Raymond, Suzanne, Paul. Program officer for European Tech. Assistance Program of Mut. Security Agy., Paris, 1951-53; asso. dir. Com. to Revise Tax Laws of Ala. Legislature, 1955-57; prof., chmn. dept. pub. adminstrn. George Washington U., 1961—. Served with AUS, 1943-46. Mem. Am. Soc. polit. sci. assns., Am. Soc. Pub. Adminstrn. Contbr. articles profl. jours. Home: 4841 Broadbrook Dr Bethesda MD 20014 Office: George Washington Univ Washington DC 20006

CLOVIS, PAUL CURTIS, business exec.; b. Griswold, Ia., Sept. 5, 1902; s. Curtis Brady and Pearl Grace (Salisbury) C.; B.A., Grinnell Coll., 1924; J.D., U. Ia., 1927; m. Lucille Kepford, Sept. 6, 1924; 1 son, Paul Curtis. Admitted to Ill. bar, 1927; with Butler, Lamb, Foster & Pope, 1927-31; v.p. Twentieth Century Press, Inc., Chgo., 1931-38, dir., 1938—, pres., 1938- -; dir., pres. Graphic Arts Assn. Ill., Inc., 1949-52; dir., exec. com. Printing Industry Am. Inc., 1951-54; dir. Lumbermens Mut. Casualty Co., Ill. Mfrs. Co. Co-chmn. gen. campaign Community Fund Chgo., 1947. Former trustee Chgo. Wesley Meml. Hosp., Evanston Hosp. Mem. Am., Ill., Chgo. bar assns., Order of Coif. Clubs: Chicago, Commercial, Mid-Am., Commonwealth, University (Chgo.); Old Elm, Glen View (Winnetka, Ill.). Home: 76 Hibbard Rd Winnetka IL 60093 Office: 320 S Jefferson St Chicago IL 60606

CLOW, ARTHUR PLUMB, communications equipment mfg. co. exec.; b. Terryville, Conn., May 16, 1907; s. Harry C. and Carrie (Plumb) C.; A.B., Dartmouth, 1929; m. Marjorie Churchill Holmes, May 16, 1931; children—Arthur Plumb, Stanley H., Richard C. With Western Electric Co., 1929-60, 63—, employee relations, 1929-49, works comptroller, 1950-53, gen. mgr., 1956-57 (all Kearney Works, N.J.), dir. personnel, 1954-56, v.p. personnel, pub. relations, 1957-60, exec. v.p., 1963— (all N.Y.C.); v.p., dir. Chesapeake & Potomac Tel. Cos., 1960-63; dir. Western Electric Co., Inc., Sandia Corp., Bellcomm, Inc., First Jersey Corp., First Jersey Nat. Bank. Mem. Nat. Security Indsl. Assn. (chmn. bd. trustees 1970-71), Electronic Industries Assn. (bd. govs. 1963—), New Eng. Soc. N.Y.C., Newcomen Soc. N.Am. Episcopalian. Clubs: Metropolitan (Washington); Baltusrol Golf (Springfield, N.J.). Home: 45 Joanna Way Short Hills NJ 07078 Office: Western Electric Co 195 Broadway New York City NY 10007

CLOWARD, RICHARD ANDREW, educator; b. Rochester, N.Y., Dec. 25, 1926; s. Donald Bernard and Esther (Fleming) C.; B.A., U. Rochester, 1948; M.S.W., Columbia, 1950, Ph.D., 1958; m. Ethelmarie McGaffin, Mar. 25, 1951; children—Leslie Anne, Mark, Kevin, Keith. Mem. faculty Columbia, 1954—, prof. social work, 1961—; dir. research Mblzn. for Youth, N.Y.C., 1958-65. Trustee Abbott House for Children, N.Y.C., 1965-69, Northside Center Child Devel., N.Y.C., 1964-68, Citizens Crusade Against Poverty, Washington, 1964—, Poverty/Rights Action Center, Washington, 1966—; bd. dirs. N.Y. Civil Liberties Union, 1968—. Served with USNR, 1944-46; as officer AUS, 1951-54. Mem. Nat. Assn. Social Workers, Am. Sociol. Assn., Am. Assn. U. Profs. Author: Social Perspectives on Behavior, 1958; Delinquency and Opportunity (Dennis Carroll award Internat. Soc. Criminology 1965), 1960; Regulating the Poor: The Functions of Public Welfare, 1971. Home: 85 Miles Av White Plains NY 10606 Office: 622 W 113th St New York City NY 10025

CLOWES, GEORGE HENRY ALEXANDER, Jr., educator, surgeon; b. Buffalo, May 3, 1915; s. George Henry Alexander and Edith Whitehill (Hinkel) C.; B.S., Harvard, 1937, M.D., 1941; M.A. in Physiology, U. Toronto, 1951; m. Margaret Gracie Jackson, June 27, 1942; children—Margaret Allen (Mrs. Francis P. Bowles), Alexander Whitehill, Thomas Jackson, Jonathan Jackson, Edith Whitehill. Intern Harvard Surg. Service, Boston City Hosp., 1941-43; resident surgeon Mass. Gen. Hosp., Boston, 1946-48, Cushing VA Hosp., Framingham, Mass., 1948-49; fellow surgery, research asso. U. Toronto, 1949-51; from sr. instr. to asso. prof. surgery Western Res. U., 1951-62; prof. surgery, chmn. dept. Med. Coll. S.C., Charleston, 1962-65; clin. prof. surgery Harvard Med. Sch., 1965—; surgeon charge thoracic surg. services Cleve. Met. Gen. Hosp., 1951-62; asso. vis. surgeon Univ. Hosp., Cleve., 1951- 62; chief surgery Med. Coll. Hosp., Charleston, 1962-65; dir. of research Sears Surg. Labs., 1968—; surgeon Harvard Surg. Service, Boston City Hosp., 1965—. Mem. adv. com. metabolism of trauma Surgeon Gen. U.S. Army, 1962-71; mem. surg. study sect. NIH, 1963-68; spl. research physiology and biochemistry extracorporeal circulation and cardiac surgery, devel. membrane artificial lung, relationship circulatory and respiratory function to metabolic state in illness. Trustee Cleve. Area Heart Assn., 1958-62, S.C. Heart Assn., 1962-65, S.C. chpt. Am. Cancer Soc., 1962-65, Charleston Symphony Soc., 1962-65, Marine Biol. Lab., Woods Hole, Opera Co. Boston; overseer Boston Symphony Orch.; bd. overseers com. on biology Harvard, 1962-65. Mem. Am. Assn. Thoracic Surgery, A.C.S., Am. Heart Assn., A.M.A., Am. Physiol. Soc., Am. Soc. Artificial Internal Organs (pres. 1958), Am. Surg. Assn., Soc. Exptl. Biology and Medicine, Soc. Univ. Surgeons, Soc. Vascular Surgery (v.p. 1964), Sigma Xi. Club: Cruising of Am. (fleet surgeon 1970—). Author papers, monographs, chpts. in books. Home: Pegan Lane Dover MA 02030 Office: Harvard Surgical Unit Boston City Hosp Boston MA 02118

CLOWES, MOLLY (Mrs. Jacques Willy Walsh), former newspaper editor; b. Brimingham, Eng., 1906; d. William Henry and Margaret L. (Devine) Clowes; m. Jacques Willy Walsh, May 15, 1943. Editorial writer Louisville Courier-Jour., 1940-66, became editor editorial page. Home: 547 Dover Rd Louisville KY 40206

CLOYD, ROYAL HARRISON, educator; b. Watseka, Ill., May 21, 1925; s. Roy Nelson and Gwen (Harrison) C.; student Am. U., Biarritz, France, 1946; A.B., U. Ill., 1949, M.A., 1953; m. Nancy Jean Evans, Aug. 28, 1948; children—Jay Raymond, Aaron, Bronwen. With Bur. Instl. Research, U. Ill., 1950-51; edn. dir. Chanute AFB, Ill., 1952-58; dir. adult programs Council Liberal Chs., 1958-61; dir. adult programs, information and coll. centers Unitarian-Universalist Assn. N.Am., 1961-70; New Eng. exec. dir. Unitarian-Universalist Assn., Boston, 1970—. Mem. corp. Boston Ednl. Services and Tng. Center, 1967; chmn. participation com. Council Nat. Orgns., 1961-63. Pres., South End Fedn. Citizens Orgns., 1967—; chmn. Community Arts Theatre, Champaign, Ill., 1955-58; chmn. South End Urban Redevel. Com., 1961-64; mem. corp. South End Settlements, 1965—, pres. Boston Center for Arts, 1970—. Bd. dirs. Boston Ams. for Democratic Action. Served with AUS, 1943-46. Recipient Citizen award S. End Planning Council, 1963; Citizen award Nat. Conf. Christians and Jews, 1964. Mem. Adult Edn. Assn. U.S. (nat. exec. com. 1966-70), Nat. Council Crime and Delinquency, Mass. Adult Edn. Assn., Internat. Inst., United World Federalists, World Affairs Council, Phi Delta Kappa, Alpha Sigma Phi. Unitarian. Club: St. Botolph, Boston Press. Contbr. articles to profl. jours., also plays, scripts and programs. Home: 42 Union Park Boston MA 02118 Office: 555 Tremont St Boston MA 02118

CLUBB, BRUCE EDWIN, lawyer; b. Blackduck, Minn., Feb. 6, 1931; s. Ernest and Abigail (Gordy) C.; B.B.A., U. Minn., 1955, LL.B. cum laude, 1958; m. Martha Lucia Trapp, Dec. 19, 1954; children—Bruce Allen, Christopher Wade. Admitted to D.C. bar, 1959; atty. Covington & Burling, 1958-61, Devel. Loan Fund, 1961-62, Chapman, DiSalle and Friedman, 1962-67; commr. U.S. Tariff Commn., 1967-71; of counsel to Baker & McKenzie, Washington, 1971—. Served with AUS, 1952-54. Mem. D.C. Bar Assn., Am. Judicature Soc., Order of Coif. Republican. Contbr. law revs. Home: 8700 Greystone Pl Alexandria VA 22309 Office: 815 Connecticut Av NW Washington DC 20006

CLUBB, JAMES EARL, mgmt. cons.; b. Morris, Man., Can., Mar. 27, 1911; s. James and Jennie (Morrison) C.; Chartered Accountant, U. Man., 1936; m. Phyllis Bronson, June 29, 1944; children—James B., Gordon F., H. Norman, Julia Ann. Partner in charge Ottawa office Price Waterhouse Assos. Mem. Inst. Chartered Accountants Que. Clubs: Rideau, Royal Ottawa Golf. Home: 124 Springfield Rd Ottawa Ontario Canada

CLUETT, W. SCOTT, sr. v.p., dir. Drexel Harriman Ripley, Inc., N.Y.C.; v.p., dir. Middlebrook Farm, Inc. Mem. Investment Bankers Assn. Am., Nat. Assn. Securities Dealers (gov.). Club: Bond (N.Y.C.). Office: 60 Broad St New York City NY 10004

CLUFF, LEIGHTON EGGERTSEN, educator, physician; b. Salt Lake City, June 10, 1923; s. Lehi Eggertsen and Lottie (Brain) C.; student U. Utah, 1941-44; M.D. with distinction, George Washington U., 1949; m. Beth Allen, Aug. 19, 1944; children—Claudia Beth, Patricia Leigh. Intern Johns Hopkins Hosp., 1949- 50, asst. resident, 1951-52; asst. resident physician Duke Hosp., 1950- 51; vis. investigator, asst. physician Rockefeller Inst. Med. Research, 1952-54; fellow Nat. Found. Infantile Paralysis, 1952-54; mem. faculty Johns Hopkins Sch. Medicine, staff Johns Hopkins Hosp., 1954-66, prof. medicine, 1964-66, physician, head div. clin. immunology, allergy and infectious diseases, 1964-66; prof., chmn. dept. medicine U. Fla., 1966—. Mem. commn. streptococcal and staphylococcal diseases, also commn. epidemiological survey Armed Forces Epidemiology Bd.; mem. council drugs A.M.A.; mem. NRC-Nt. Acad. Sci. Drug Research Bd.; mem. expert adv. panel bacterial diseases (coccal infection) WHO; mem. nat. adv. allergy and infectious diseases council Nat. Inst. Allergy and Infectious Diseases NIH; cons. FDA; tng. grant com. NIH, 1964-68; com. continuing edn. NRC, 1965-68. Markle scholar med. scis., 1955-62; recipient Career Research award NIH, 1962. Mem. Am. Soc. Clin. Investigation, Assn. Am. Physicians, Soc. Exptl. Biology and Medicine, Am. Assn. Immunologists, Am. Fedn. Clin. Research, Harvey Soc., N.Y. Acad. Sci., Am. Acad. Allergy, So. Soc. Clin. Investigation, A.C.P. (Mead-Johnson postgrad scholar 1954-55, Ordronaux Ward med. scholarship 1949), Infectious Disease Soc., Am. Clin. and Climatological Assn., Assn. Profs. Medicine, Alpha Omega Alpha. Contbr. articles to profl. jours. Home: 3217 NW 18th Av Gainesville FL 32601

CLUGSTON, PAUL L., lawyer; b. Waynesboro, Pa., Feb. 8, 1893; s. Frank Howard and Jennie (Notley) C.; Ph.B., Lafayette Coll., 1915; LL.B., Harvard, 1921; m. Vola Kathryn Price, Aug. 31, 1928. Admitted to N.Y. bar, 1926, since practiced in N.Y.C.; sr. partner firm Thacher, Proffitt, Prizer, Crawley & Wood, and predecessor, 1951—. Dir. of Albany Ins. Co., Motorships, Inc., Motorships P.R., Inc., Motorships Chartering Corp., Cargo Service Corp., Nordstrom Freighting Corp., No. Feather Works, Inc., China Java Co., Inc. Mem. Am. Bar Assn., Maritime Law Assn. U.S., N.Y. County Lawyers Assn., Harvard Law Sch. Assn., Phi Beta Kappa, Sigma Nu. Theta Nu Epsilon. Republican. Roman Catholic. Clubs: Harvard, India House (N.Y.C.); Scarsdale (N.Y.) Golf: Lake Placid (N.Y.); Skytop (Pa.). Home: 6 Leith Pl White Plains NY 10605 Office: 40 Wall St New York City NY 10005

CLUMECK, JACK REGINALD, business exec.; b. Singapore, Nov. 22, 1913 (parents Brit. citizens); s. Victor and Marie (Frankel) C.; student Stanford, 1933; m. Lois Lees, May 30, 1934; children—Jack Reginald, Jill Marie (Mrs. J. Friedenrich). Exec. v.p. Hunt Foods & Industries, Inc., 1956-61, dir., vice chmn. finance com., 1961-68; partner L.C.L. Co., real estate and investments, 1948—; dir., mem. finance com. Norton Simon, Inc., 1968—, chmn. finance com., 1970—. dir. GRT Corp. Home: PO Box 116 Ross CA 94957 Office: 582 Market St San Francisco CA 94104

CLURMAN, HAROLD EDGAR, stage dir.; b. N.Y.C., Sept. 18, 1901; s. Samuel M. and Bertha (Saphir) C.; student Columbia, 1921; degree in letters, U. Paris (Sorbonne), 1923; LL.D., Bard Coll., 1951; D.F.A. (hon.), Carnegie Inst. Tech., 1963; m. Stella Adler, 1943 (div. 1959); 1 stepdau., Ellen; m. 2d, Juleen Compton, 1959. Actor, stage mgr. Theatre Guild, Jed Harris and John Golden, 1924-29; play reader, 1929- 31; founder dir. Group Theatre, 1931-41; motion picture producer, dir., 1941-45. Producer of Men in White by Sidney Kingsley; Awake and Sing, Golden Boy, Rocket to the Moon by Clifford Odets; My Heart's in the Highlands by William Saroyan; staged The Autumn Garden, 1951. Dir. Awake and Sing, Paradise Lost, Golden Boy, Gentle People, The Russian People, Deadline at Dawn, RKO, 1945; The Whole World Over by Konstantin Simonov, 1947; Eugene O'Neill's Desire Under the Elms, Arthur Laurent's Time of the Cuckoo, 1952; The Member of the Wedding, 1950; Mademoiselle Colombo, 1954; William Inge's Bus Stop, 1955; Tiger at the Gates, 1955; Pipe Dream, 1955; Waltz of the Toreador, Orpheus Descending, 1957; directed Eugene O'Neill's A Touch of the Poet, 1958; Heartbreak House, by Bernard Shaw, 1959; Incident at Vichy, by Arthur Miller, 1965; co- producer of All My Sons by Arthur Miller, 1947; staged A Shot in the Dark, 1961. Contbr. Monthly column on arts, Tomorrow Mag., 1946-51. Drama critic The Nation, 1953. Exec. cons. Repertory Theatre Lincoln Center, 1963—. Decorated Order Chevalier, Legion of Honor (France); recipient George Jean Nathan Drama Criticism award, 1961. Mem. Acad. Arts and Scis. Author: The Fervent Years (group theatre in 30's), 1945; Lies Like Truth, Essays on Theatres, 1958.

CLURMAN, RICHARD MICHAEL, journalist; b. N.Y.C., Mar. 10, 1924; s. Will N. and Emma (Hertzberg) C.; Ph.B., U. Chgo., 1946, postgrad., 1946-47; m. Marilyn Miller, 1947 (div.); children—Susan Emma, Carol Mae; m. 2d, Shirley Potash, Apr. 13, 1957; 1 son, Richard Michael. Asst. editor Commentary mag., 1946-49; press editor Time mag., 1949-55, dep. chief corrs. Time and Life Mag., N.Y.C., 1958-60, chief, 1960-69; editorial dir. Newsday, 1955-58; v.p. Time Inc., 1969—; chmn. bd. Time-Life Broadcast, 1971—. Chmn. bd. N.Y.C. Center Music and Drama, Inc.; pres. N.Y. Found. for Arts,

Inc., 1971—; bd. dirs. Sch. Am. Ballet, 1970—. Served with AUS, 1942-46. Home: 19 E 72d St New York City NY 10021 Office: Time Inc Time & Life Bldg Rockefeller Center New York City NY 10020

CLUTE, EDWARD T., banker; b. Curwensville, Pa., 1907; ed. U. Pa., 1931. v.p. treas. Girard Trust Bank, Phila. Mason. Home: 25 Pine Valley Rd Broomall, PA 19008. Office: Broad and Chestnut St Philadelphia PA 19101.*

CLUTE, HENRY LANSING, former banker; b. Montclair, N.J., Jan. 15, 1906; s. Frank T. and Charlotte (Pierce) C.; student Antioch Coll., 1924-25, Columbia, 1930-31, Princeton, 1931-32; m. Genevieve Marian Speer, Nov. 23, 1932. With First Nat. City Bank, N.Y.C., 1927-70, mgr. Salvador, Brazil br., 1950-55, asst. cashier Brazilian dist. at main office, N.Y.C., 1955-61, v.p. overseas operations and personnel, 1961-65, sr. v.p., dep. charge operating div., 1966-69, former exec. v.p., v.p., cashier Internat. Banking Corp., N.Y.C., 1959-64. Mem. Cloister Inn. Home: 300 E 51st St New York City NY 10022

CLUTTERBUCK, THOMAS E., banker; b. Latonia, Ky., 1909. Sr. v.p. Cleve. Trust Co.; dir. Brewer Greetings, Cowgill Printing, Watson Realty Co., Schloz Plumbing & Heating Co., Howard S. Bissell, Inc.; pres., dir. Anis Co., City & Suburban Co.; v.p., dir. Nat. Officer Bldg Co. Treas. Lake Erie council Girl Scouts Am. Home: 98 Skyview Dr Seven Hills OH 44131 Office: 916 Euclid Av Cleveland OH 44115*

CLUXTON, HARLEY ERNEST, Jr., physician; b. Columbia, Tenn., Dec. 6, 1914; s. Harley Ernest and Ellen Mae (Catinna) C.; A.B., Washington and Lee U., 1937; student pathology Vanderbilt U., 1939; M.D., Johns Hopkins, 1941; M.S., U. Minn., 1949; m. Elizabeth Parsons King, Dec. 31, 1940; childrenElizabeth King, Harley Ernest. Spl. study endocrinology Mass. Gen. Hosp., Boston, 1940; staff internal medicine Balt. City Hosps., 1941-42; fellow internal medicine Mayo Found., Rochester, Minn., 1942-44, 1947-49, first asst. endocrinology Mayo Clinic, 1943, first asst. rheumatic disease, 1944; dir. med. research Armour Labs., Chgo., 1950-51; pvt. practice internal medicine, Chgo., 1951—; attending physician Passavant, Meml. Hosp., 1951—, dir. health service, 1951-54; dir. med. sch. clinics, chmn. internal med. sect. Northwestern U., 1952-54, asso. medicine, 1952—. Served as maj. M.C., U.S. Army, 1944-47, chief gen. medicine Army-Navy Gen. Hosp., Hot Springs, Ark. Decorated Army Commendation medal. Diplomate Am. Bd. Internal Medicine. Fellow A.C.P.; mem. A.M.A., Chgo. Med. Soc., Chgo. Soc. Internal Medicine, Endocrine Soc., Am. Diabetes Assn., Am. Rheumatism Assn., Am. Fedn. Clin. Research, N.Y. Acad. Sci., Am. Geriatrics Soc., Mississippi Valley Med. Soc., World Med. Assn., Sigma Xi, Phi Beta Kappa, Phi Chi, Sigma Chi. Episcopalian. Mason. Club: Racquet, Yacht, Rotary (Chgo); Onwentsia (Lake Forest, Ill.). Author articles on endocrinology. Home: Office: 700 N Michigan Av Chicago IL 60611

CLYDE, NORMAN ASA, explorer western mountains; b. Phila., Apr. 8, 1885; s. Charles and Isabelle (Purvis) C.; A.B., Geneva Coll., Beaver Falls, Pa., 1909, Sc.D., 1939; postgrad. U. Wis., 1910, U. Cal., 1911-13; postgrad. in English, U. Cal. at Berkeley, 1923-24, in edn. U. So. Cal., 1926. Tchr. high schs. N.D., Utah, Ariz., Cal., 1898-10; engaged in solitary mountaineering, exploring (over 1000 ascents, 200 1st ascents including new routes), 1910—, in various mountain ranges and peaks including Sierra Nevadas (Cal.), Cascades (Wash. and Ore.) Selkirks (B.C., Can.), Canadian Rockies (Alta., B.C. and Yukon, Can.), Tetons (Wyo.), Colo. Rockies, Wasatch Mountains (Utah), Sawtooth Range (Ida.), Sierra Madre (So. Cal.), Mt. Whitney, North Palisade (both in Sierra Nevadas), Beartooth Range (Mont.), Wind River Range (Wyo.), Salmon Alps (Cal.), Sierra San Pedro Martir (Baja, Cal.); much individual exploratory climbing in Glacier Park, Mont. (36 peaks in 36 days), 1926; cons. A.C., U.S. Army, on various occasions; collector zool. specimens U. Cal.; guide, climbing leader Sierra Club base camp, summers; ascents with Sierra Club (Glacier Park, Canadian Rockies), Seattle Mountaineers (Canadian Rockies, No. Cascades of Wash. State), Alpine Club Can. (Selkirks). Recipient Distinguished Service award Geneva Coll., 1962. Mem. Nat. Rifle Assn., Cal. Acad. Scis. (wildlife observer 1943—). Clubs: Sierra (San Francisco); American Alpine; Appalachian (corr.). Expert on high altitude flora and fauna (Hudsonian and Arctic Alpine zones of Sierra Nevada), geol. history and structure of mountain ranges of Western U.S., ski mountaineering. Classical scholar, linguist. Author: Close Ups of the Sierra, 1961; also over 300 articles on various phases of mountains, trout fishing, camping, wild life, other subjects, pub. in various mags., newspapers including Field and Stream, Touring Topics, Westward, Sierra Club Bull., Am. Alpine Jour., Nat. Motorist, Sports Afield. Made several rescues of lost mountain climbers, dead and alive, locating them by knowledge of the terrain, sometimes after other searchers had given up. Numerous mountain features in the Sierra named after him including Clyde's Minaret, Clyde's Spires, Clyde's Ledge, Clyde Meadow, Clyde Peak. Address: Big Pine Inyo County CA 93513

CLYNE, CHARLES TERENCE, advt. exec.; b. Phila.; s. Charles T. and Mary (Reall) C.; A.B., Amherst (Mass.) Coll., 1928; m. Frances Donelon, Oct. 6, 1946; children-Terence Donelon, Michael John. v.p. Free & Peters, Inc., 1937-46; exec. v.p. The Biow Co., Inc., N.Y.C., 1946-54; vice chmn. bd. McCann-Erickson, Inc., 1954-61; chmn. bd. M.E. Prodns., 1954-61; exec. v.p. Maxon, Inc., 1962-64, pres., 1964; pres. Clyne-Maxon, Inc., 1965—; chmn. bd. Coral Telurnen Corp., 1965—. Served as col. with Eighth Air Force, World War II. Decorated Bronze Star with oak- leaf cluster, Legion of Merit, Croix de Guerre. Clubs: Maidstone, Devon Yacht (East Hampton, N.Y.); N.Y. Athletic, Amherst (N.Y.C.); Bridgehampton, Greenwich Country; Palm Bay, Bath and Tennis, Jockey (Miami, Fla.); Racquet, Tennis (Palm Springs, Cal.). Home: 59 E 64th St New York City NY 10021 Office: 245 Park Av New York City NY 10017

CLYNE, JAMES, supt. schs., clergyman; b. Hartford, Conn., June 12, 1921; s. Thomas Joseph and Alice E. (Fogarty) C.; B.A., St. John's Maj. Sem., 1947; M.A., Ph.D., Catholic U. Am. Ordained priest Roman Cath. Ch., 1947; head Latin dept. St. Anthony's High Sch., Long Beach, Cal., 1947-50; vice prin. Bishop Conaty High Sch., Los Angeles, 1953-54; prin. St. John Vianney High Sch., Los Angeles, 1954-56; asst. supt. Roman Cath. schs., Los Angeles, 1966-. Instr. edn. Mt. St. Mary's Coll., Los Angeles, Immaculate Heart Coll.; chmn. Religious Sponsored Schs., Los Angeles, 1960-. Bd. dirs. Harlan Shoemaker Clinic, Los Angeles. Mem. Nat. Cath. Edn. Assn. (pres. elementary dept. 1965-, gen. exec. bd. 1965-). Home: 1440 W Imperial Hwy Los Angeles, CA 90047. Office: 1520 W 9th St Los Angeles CA 90015

CLYNE, JAMES FRANCIS, Jr., cement co. exec.; b. Bklyn., Mar. 1, 1927; s. James Francis and Mildred deS. (Cogan) C.; B.A. cum laude, U. Notre Dame, 1949; LL.B., N.Y. U., 1953, student Grad. Sch. Bus. Adminstrn., 1953-54; m. Eileen T. O'Shea, Aug. 5, 1950; children—James Francis III, Kathleen Ann, Michael Eugene, Patricia Eileen, Elizabeth Mary, Moira Jean. Admitted to N.Y. bar, 1954; with firm Chadbourne, Parke, Whiteside & Wolff, N.Y.C., 1953; with Lone Star Cement Corp., Greenwich, Conn., 1953—, asst. sec., 1958-61, corp. sec., 1961—, gen. counsel, dir., officer subsidiaries. Served with USNR, 1945-46. Mem. Am. Soc. Corp. Secs., Shareholders Relations Soc. Home: 66 Broadway Rockville Centre NY 11570 Office: 1 Greenwich Plaza Greenwich CT

CLYNE, JOHN VALENTINE, lawyer, corp. exec.; b. Vancouver, B.C., Can., Feb. 14, 1902; s. Henry and Martha A. (Dillon) C.; B.A., U. B.C., 1923; postgrad. student law London Sch. Econs., King's Coll., London; m. Betty V. A. Somerset, Dec. 14, 1927; children—Valentine, (Mrs. Anthony W. Gamage), J. Stuart. With E. P. Davis & Co., Vancouver, 1923-25, 27, Blake & Redden, legal firm, London, Eng., 1925-27, William & Mason, lawyers, Prince Rupert, Can., 1928-29; called to Canadian bar, 1927; partner firm Macrae, Duncan & Clyne, Vancouver, 1929-46, Campney, Owen, Clyne & Murphy, Vancouver, 1929-46, Campney, Owen, Clyne & Murphy, Vancouver, 1947-50; judge Supreme Ct. B.C., 1950-57; chmn. bd. MacMillan, Bloedel and Powell River (company name now MacMillan Bloedel Ltd.), 1960—, also chief exec. officer; pres. Park S.S. Co. (Crown Co.), 1945-50; dir. Canadian Imperial Bank of Commerce, Canadian Pacific Ry. Co., B.N.A. Holdings Ltd.; Vancouver adv. bd. Can. Trust-Huron & Erie. Royal commr. Land Expropriation in B.S., 1961. Chmn. The Canadian Maritime Commn., 1947-50; rep. Can. sub-coms. UN and NATO dealing with shipping; chmn. preparatory com. inter-govtl. Maritime Consultative Orgn., Lake Success, 1948-50; royal commnr. to investigate Whatshan Power House Disaster, 1954; royal commnr. on Milk Inquiry, 1954- 55; chmn. adv. group Compensation Pub. Service. Trustee Archives Soc. Vancouver, Indsl. Relations Counsellors Service, Inc.; former mem. senate U.B.C.; past provincial pres. St. John Ambulance Assn.; bd. mem. Nat. Indsl. Conf. Bd., Can., 1961—, Nat. Indsl. Conf. U.S., 1962—. Decorated comdr. Order Knights St. John. Mem. Canadian Bar Assn., Law Soc. B.C. , Canada-Japan Soc. Vancouver. Clubs: The Vancouver, University, The Shaughnessy Golf and Country (Vancouver); Union (Victoria, B.C.); Rideau (Ottawa). Home: 3738 Angus Dr Vancouver 9 British Columbia Canada Office: 1075 W Georgia St Vancouver 5 British Columbia Canada

CMICH, STANLEY A., mayor; b. Glencampbell, Pa.; student Ohio State U. Agt. charge 18 counties Ohio Dept. Liquor Control, 1949-51; safety dir. City of Canton (O.), 1952-57, mayor, 1963-; gen. prodn. mgr. A. G. Stafford Co., Canton, 1958-63. Bd. dirs. Stark County Constrn. Council. Served with AUS, World War II. Named Outstanding Young Man of Year, U.S. Jr. C. of C., 1952; recipient distinguished Service award Ohio Jr. C. of C., 1952; Man of Year award Canton Jr. C. of C., 1952; Young Republican Orgn. award, 1965, Gold Service award Canton Kiwanis Club, 1965; V.F.W. World War I award, 1965; plaque Stark County Rep. Council, 1965. Mem. Stark County Hist. Soc., Ex-Newsboys Assn., Am. Legion, Old Timers Assn., V.F.W., D.A.V. Roman Catholic. Eagle, Moose. Home: 138 20th St NE Canton OH 44714

COAD, WILLIAM JAMES, Jr., former corp. exec.; b. Omaha, Mar. 26, 1910; s. William James and Helen (O'neil) C.; student Phillips Exeter Acad., Lawrenceville Sch., 1925-29, Princeton, 1930; m. Ethel Worthington, Oct. 22, 1938 (div.); children —William James, III, John Worthington; m. 2d, Jane Hopkins Hatch, Apr. 29, 1958; 1 son, Douglas Hopkins. Began with Ramo, Inc. (formerly Omar, Inc.), 1930, successively gen. purchasing agt., bakery mgr., treas., v.p. and gen. mgr. mill div., exec. v.p., former pres., treas., dir. Mem. C. of C. Republican. Roman Catholic. Clubs: Racquet (Chgo.); Omaha Omaha Country, Plaza (Omaha); Minnesouri Angling (Alexandria, Minn.); University Cottage (Princeton). Home: 400 N Elmwood Rd Omaha NB 68132

COAKLEY, JOSEPH CHARLES, lawyer; b. Cleve., June 10, 1928; s. John A. and Marie (Beckman) C.; B.S., John Carroll U., 1948; LL.B., Cleve. State U., 1951; m. Patricia Hunkin, July 6, 1949; children—Patricia H., Joseph Charles, M. Sean, Lisa F. Admitted to Ohio bar, 1951; pvt. practice law, Cleve., 1951—; partner firm Squire, Sanders & Dempsey, Cleve., 1961—. Chmn. bd. dirs. Union Commerce Corp.; dir. Union Commerce Bank; Minster Machine Co.; v.p., dir. Marjon Co.; pres. M-F Securities Inc.; v.p. Cleve. Industries Inc. Trustee, v.p. Henry Beckman Coakley Found.; trustee Musical Arts Assn., John Carroll U., St. Vincent Charity Hosp. Clubs: Union, Kirtland, Skating, Tavern (Cleve.); Brook (N.Y.C.). Home: 8341 Chillicothe Rd Mentor OH 44060 Office: Union Commerce Bldg Cleveland OH 44115

COAKLEY, MICHAEL, newspaper correspondent. Washington correspondent Chgo. Today. Office: Chgo Today 441 N Michigan Av Chicago IL 60611*

COAKLEY, THOMAS, former judge; b. Oakland, Cal., Mar. 30, 1905; s. James and Emma A. (Curley) C.; A.B., U. Cal., 1929, J.D., 1933; m. Katharine W. Torney, Feb. 5, 1934; children—Peter Torney, Jeannette Wright (Mrs. Robert Bruce Stewart), Katharine Mitchell (Mrs. Thomas C. Hoyle III), Joseph Michael. Admitted Cal. bar, 1933, practiced San Francisco 1933-53; judge superior ct., Mariposa County, 1953-69; asso. justice Ct. Appeal 5th Appellate Dist., Fresno, Cal., 1969-71. Pres., Bd. State Harbor Commrs., San Francisco, 1946-48, Pacific Coast Assn. Port Authorities, 1947-48, Cal. Assn. Port Authorities, 1945-46. Gov. State Bar Cal., 1951- 53. Trustee Cal. Heritage Council. Mem. Am. Bar Assn., Bar Assn. San Francisco (pres. 1948), San Francisco C. of C. (dir.), Bay Area Council (dir.), Cal. (trustee), Mariposa County (pres. 1957-60) hist. socs. Club: Family (San Francisco). Home: Mariposa CA 95338

COALE, ANSLEY JOHNSON, educator; b. Balt., Nov. 14, 1917; s. James Johnson and Nellie Ansley (Johnson) C.; B.A., Princeton, 1939, M.A., 1941, Ph.D., 1947; m. Sarah Hamilton Campbell, Oct. 18, 1941; children—Ansley Johnson, Robert Campbell. Research asst. Office Population Research, Princeton, 1941-42; sec. com. social implications atomic energy Social Sci. Research Council, 1946-47; faculty Princeton, 1947—, prof. econs., 1959—, dir. Office Population Research, 1959—, U.S. rep. UN Population Commn., 1961- 67, Social Sci. Research Council-Nat. Sci. Research Council fellow Inst. Advanced Study, 1947-49. Served with USNR, 1942-46. Fellow Am. Statis. Assn.; mem. Population Assn. Am. (pres. 1967-68), Am. Econ. Assn., Am. Philos. Soc., Internat. Population Union, Am. Acad. Arts and Scis. Author: The Problems of Reducing Vulnerability to Atomic Bombs, 1947; (with Edgar M. Hoover) Population Growth and Economic Development in Low Income Countries, 1958; (with Melvin Zelnik) New Estimates of Population and Births in the United States, 1963; (with Paul Demeny) Regional Model Life Tables and Stable Populations, 1966; also articles. Home: 155 Edgerstoune Rd Princeton NJ 08540

COALTER, GEORGE W., banker. Sr. v.p., treas. Bronx Savs. Bank. Office: Tremont & Park Avs Bronx NY 10457*

COAN, ERNEST WORTH, ins. co. exec.; b. Hurley, N.M., Jan. 9, 1914; s. Ernest Garfield and Tot Belle (Spafford) C.; grad. high sch. Salesman, Titche-Goettinger & Co., Dallas, 1931-37, Southwestern Life Ins. Co., Dallas, 1937-42; sr. v.p. Occidental Life Ins. Co. of Cal., Los Angeles, 1946—. Served with USAAF, 1942-46. Home: 333 N San Marino Av San Gabriel CA 91775 Office: Occidental Center Olive at 12th St Los Angeles CA 90054

COAN, HILLARD JEROME, supermarket exec.; b. N.Y.C., Dec. 14, 1916; s. Arthur I. and Jeanette (Goodman) C.; student Lehigh U., 1933-34; m. Janet Bensinger, Jan. 24, 1945; children—Peter, Peggy, Michael. Buyer, Montauk Wholesale Grocer Co., Farmingdale, N.Y., 1934-37, gen. mgr., treas., 1937; gen. mgr. Mid Island Markets, Farmingdale, 1937-55; pres. Hills Supermarkets, Farmingdale, 1955-65; chmn. bd. E. J. Korvette, N.Y.C., 1965-66; pres. First Nat. Stores, Somerville, Mass., 1966—; dir. Superior Surg. Mfg. Co; mem. adv. com. Bankers Trust Co. Served with USNR, 1942-46. Home: 1010 Memorial Dr Cambridge MA 02138 Office: 5 Middlesex Av Somerville MA 02145

COASE, RONALD HARRY, educator, economist; b. Willesden, Eng., Dec. 29, 1910; s. Henry Joseph and Rosalie (Giles) C.; B. Commerce, London (Eng.) Sch. Econs., 1932, D.Sc. in Econs., 1951; m. Marian Ruth Hartung, Aug. 7, 1937. Came to U.S., 1951. Sir Ernest Cassel Travelling scholar, 1931-32; asst. lectr. Dundee Sch. Econs., 1932-34, U. Liverpool, 1934-35; asst. lectr., lectr., then reader London Sch. Econs., 1935-51; prof. U. Buffalo, 1951- 58, U. Va., 1958-64, U. Chgo., 1964—. Statistician, then chief statistician Central Statis. Office, Offices War Cabinet, Eng., 1941-46. Rockefeller fellow, 1948, fellow Center for Advanced Study Behavioral Scis. Mem. Am. Econ. Assn., Royal Econ. Soc., Mont Pelerin Soc. Author: British Broadcasting, A Study in Monopoly, 1950. Editor Jour. Law and Econs., 1964—. Home: 5401 Hyde Park Blvd Chicago IL 60615

COATES, ALBERT, educator; b. Johnston County, N.C., Aug. 25, 1896; s. Daniel Miller and Nancy (Lassiter) C.; A.B., U. N.C., 1918; LL. B., Harvard, 1923; LL.D., Wake Forest Coll., 1960, Duke U., 1971; m. Gladys J. Hall, June 23, 1928. Teaching fellow English, U. N.C., 1919-20, asst. prof. law, 1923-25, asso. prof. 1925-27, prof., 1927-62, prof. emeritus, 1962—, founder, dir, Inst. Govt., 1931-62. Served as 2d lt. U.S. Army, 1918. Recipient Gardner award U. N.C., 1952; N.C. award for pub. services state of N.C., 1967; Di-Phi award U. N.C., 1951. Mem. N.C. State Bar Assn. (Parker award 1964), Tau Kappa Alpha, Sigma Upsilon, Order of Coif, Phi Delta Phi. Democrat. Methodist. Author: What the University of North Carolina Meant to Me, 1969; Talks to Students and Teachers, The Structure and Workings of Government in the Cities and the Counties and the State of North Carolina, 1971. Editor: Popular Government (mag.), 1931-62. Contbr. articles to profl. jours. Home: 508 Hooper Lane Chapel Hill NC 27514

COATES, CLARENCE LEROY, Jr., educator, research engr.; b. Hastings, Neb., Nov. 5, 1923; s. Clarence Leroy and Mildred (Creighton) C.; B.S. in Elec. Engring., U. Kan., 1944, M.S., 1948; Ph.D., U. Ill., 1954; m. Henrietta Hoff, Jan. 1, 1943; children—Catherine Anne, Christopher John; m. 2d, Lila M. Mustola, Mar. 5, 1969; 1 son, Randall Lee. Instr. elec. engring. U. Kan., 1946-48; instr., then asso. prof. elec. engring. U. Ill., 1948-56; research scientist Gen. Electric Research Labs., 1956-63; prof. elec. engring. U. Tex., 1963-71, chmn. dept., 1964-66, dir. Electronics Research Centre, 1967-71; dir. Coordinated Sci. Lab., prof. U. Ill., 1971—. Cons. NSF, 1969-70. Served as officer USNR, 1944- 46. Sr. mem. I.E.E.E. (v.p. publ. activities, mem. bd. dirs.); mem. Am. Math. Assn., Soc. Indsl. and Applied Math., Assn. Computing Machinery, Sigma Xi, Phi Kappa Phi, Tau Beta Pi, Eta Kappa Nu, Sigma Tau. Author: Threshold Logic. Cons. editor Blaisdell Pub. Co., 1968-70. Contbr. articles in field to profl. jours. Home: 2118 Plymouth Dr Champaign IL 61820

COATES, FRANCIS GRAHAM, lawyer; b. Balt., Oct. 31, 1893; s. George William Pennock and Edwin (Graham) C.; B.A., Yale, 1916; LL.B., Tex. U., 1920; m. Emily Fairfax Davis, Oct. 4, 1930; children—Emily Fairfax, Cynthia Pennock, Francis Graham, Merrick. Admitted to Tex. bar, 1920; practice law, Ft. Worth, 1920-29; asst. state atty., 1922-24; spl. counsel City Ft. Worth, 1925-29; partner Coates & Mastin, 1924-29, Baker, Botts, Shepherd & Coates, and predecessor firms, Houston, 1929—. Co-organizer Hedcroft Clinic, Houston. Life trustee U. Tex. Law Sch. Found. Served as capt. F.A., U.S. Army, World War I. Mem. Tex., Houston bar assns., Am. Horse Show Assn. (dir.) U.S. Equestrian Team, Tex. Hunter and Jumper assn. (co-founder). Episcopalian. Clubs: Bayou, Eagle Lake Rod and Gun (Houston); Links, Yale (N.Y.C.). Home: 3711 San Felipe Rd Houston TX 77027 Office: Esperson Bldg Houston TX 77002

COATES, GOEFFREY EDWARD, chemist, educator; b. London, Eng., May 14, 1917; s. Joseph Edward and Ada (Finney) C.; student Clifton Coll., 1929-34; B.A., Queens Coll., Oxford U., 1938, B.S., 1939, M.A., 1942; D.Sc., Bristol U., 1954; m. Winifred Jean Hobbs, Mar. 28, 1951; children—Helen Mary, Anthony Peter. Research chemist Magnesium Metal Corp., Swansea, U.K., 1940-45; lectr. chemistry Bristol U., 1945-53; prof., head chemistry dept. Durham U., 1953-68; head chemistry dept. U. Wyo., Laramie, 1968—; sci. adviser for civil def. No. Region U.K., 1955-67. Mem. Chem. Soc. (past mem. council), Am. Chem. Soc., N.Y. Acad. Sci., Am. Inst. Chemist, Faraday Soc., Royal Inst. Chemistry, Sigma Xi. Author: Organometallic Compounds, 1956; (with others) Principles of Organometallic Chemistry, 1968. Contbr. articles profl. jours. Home: 1801 Rainbow Av Laramie WY 82070

COATES, JAMES OTIS, lawyer; b. Cin., Feb. 13, 1914; s. Charles Houston and Bessie Lee (Becraft) C.; A.B., Princeton, 1935; J.D., Harvard, 1938; postgrad. Columbia, 1958; m. Shirley Jane Ripley, Sept. 4, 1937; children—James Houston, Thomas Ripley, Virginia Lee. Admitted to Ohio bar, 1939, since practiced in Cin.; asso. firm Dinsmore, Shohl, Sawyer & Dinsmore, 1938- 43, partner, 1946-61; sr. partner Dinsmore, Shohl, Barrett, Coates & Deupree, 1961-67, Dinsmore, Shohl, Coates & Deupree, 1967—; counsel Procter & Gamble Co., dist. atty. L. & N. R.R. Co. Dist. chmn. United Appeal 1958-59; pres. local chpt. Am. Field Service, 1962-64, treas., 1964—; trustee Legal Aid Soc. Cin., 1970—; adviser to registrants Draft Bd. Served to lt. (j.g.) USNR, 1943-46. Decorated Bronze Star medal. Mem. Am., Ohio, Cin. bar assns., Nat. Assn. R.R. Trial Counsel. Princeton Alumni Assn. So. Ohio, Am. Acad. Polit. Sci., Am. Soc. Internat. Law, Harvard Law Sch. Assn., Phi Beta Kappa. Episcopalian. Clubs: Torch, University, Coldstream Country. Home: 2954 Alpine Terrace Cincinnati OH 45208 Office: 2100 Fountain Sq Plaza Cincinnati OH 45202

COATES, JESSE, educator; b. Baton Rouge, Mar. 12, 1908; s. Charles Edward and Ollie (Maurin) C.; B.S., La. State U., 1928; postgrad. Mass. Inst. Tech., 1930- 31; M.S., U. Mich., 1932, Ph.D., 1936; m. Judith Mills Williams, Apr. 16, 1938; children—Judith Mills, Jesse, Victor Maurin (dec.). Chemist, treating engr. Nat. Lumber & Creosoting Co., 1928; chemist Internat. Paper Co., 1928-29. Meeker Sugar Refinery, 1930-31, Punta Alegre Sugar Co., 1931; chem. engr. Tex. Pacific Coal & Oil Co., 1932- 33, United Gas Pub. Service, 1933-36; asst. prof. chem. engring. La. State U., Baton Rouge, 1936-42, asso. prof., 1942-47, prof., 1947—, chmn. dept., 1955-67, 69-70, Alumni prof., 1969—. Cons. chem. engr. Mem. La. Bd. for Registration Profl. Engineers. Recipient Technol. Accomplishment medal La. Engring. Soc., 1958; Charles E. Coates meml. award Am. Chem. Soc.-Am. Inst. Chem. Engrs. 1958; named Man of Month, Chem. Engring. mag., Apr. 1958. Fellow Am. Inst. Chemists; mem. Am. Chem. Soc., Am. Inst. Chem. Engrs., Am. Soc. Engring. Edn.,

La. Acad. Scis., Sigma Xi, Phi Kappa Phi, Alpha Chi Sigma, Phi Lambda Upsilon, Kappa Alpha. Episcopalian. Contbr. articles to profl. jours. Home: 2320 Terrace Av Baton Rouge LA 70806

COATES, JOHN BOYD, Jr., physician, army officer; b. Glenside, Pa., Dec. 30, 1911; s. John Boyd and Florence (Kerper) C.; B.S., Ursinus Coll., 1932, D.Sc. (hon.), 1968; M.D. U. Pa., 1936; grad. Army Med. Sch., 1938; honor grad Med. Field Service Sch., 1939, Command and Gen. Staff Coll., 1941, Army War Coll., 1954; m. Margaret Huff Fonville, Oct. 23, 1937; children—John Boyd III, Margaret Jane. Commd. 1st lt. Med. Res. Corps, U.S. Army 1936, 1st lt. M.C., U.S. Army, 1937, advanced through grades to brig. gen., 1969; intern Walter Reed Gen. Hosp., 1936-37, resident, 1937-38; co. comdr., bn. comdr., regtl. staff officer 1st Med. Regt., 1939-41; asst. corps surgeon III Corps, 1941-42; bn. comdr. 99th Inf. Div., 1942; med. exec. officer, dep. army surgeon Third Army, 1943-45, surgeon, 1945; exec. officer, dir. profl. tng. Walter Reed Gen. Hosp., 1946-49; comdg. officer Rodriguez Gen. Hosp., P.R., 1949-51; surgeon U.S. Army Forces, Antilles, 1949-51; dep. surgeon, later surgeon Fifth Army, 1951-53; editor-in-chief, ofcl. history med. dept. U.S. Army in World War II (50 vols.), also ofcl. history Army Med. Service in Korean War, dir. Hist. unit Office Surgeon Gen., Hdqrs. Dept. of Army, Washington, 1954-64; dep. surgeon U.S. Army, Europe, 1964-66; comdg. officer Valley Forge Gen. Hosp., 1966, comdg. gen. Madigan Gen. Hosp., Tacoma, 1966—. Trustee J. Boyd Coates Meml. Found.; dir. United Fund Tacoma, Boy Scouts Am., Mt. Rainier Council. Decorated Legion of Merit with oak leaf cluster, Bronze Star medal (U.S.), Croix de Guerre with palm (France); recipient citation for exhibit A.C.S., 1959, Am. Acad. Orthopedic Surgeons, 1958; Skinner gold medal U.S. Army, 1939; Distinguished Service award Am. Med. Authors, 1963. Fellow A.M.A., Am. Geriatric Soc., Am. Med. Writers Assn. (dir. 1957-60), Am. Med. Authors; mem. Assn. Mil. Surgeons U.S. (dir. 1962-64), Assn. U.S. Army, Am. Assn. History of Medicine, A.A.A.S., Am. Pub. Health Assn., Am. Acad. Gen. Practice (asso.), Med. Soc. D.C. (Asso.) Soc. Med. Cons. to Armed Forces (asso.) Acad. Medicine Washington, Tacoma C. of C. (dir.). Republican, Mason (Shriner). Mem. adv. editorial bd. Armed Forces Inst. Pathology. Address: Madigan Gen Hosp Tacoma WA 98431

COATES, JOHN MERCER, bus. exec.; b. Wausau, Wis., Aug. 4, 1906; s. Joseph William and Jeannette (Mercer) C.; student Va. Mil. Inst., 1923-24; Ph.B., U. Wis., 1927; LL.B., Harvard, 1932; m. Mary E. Abbott, Aug. 21, 1937; children—Robert Mercer, William Abott, Catherine Forseman. Practiced law Chgo., 1932-39; with Masonite Corp. 1939—, dir. 1944—, v.p. operations, 1947-52, pres. 1952—, also chmn. bd., chief exec. officer; pres., dir. Marsh Wall Products Co.; dir. Allis Chalmers Co., Masonite Co. of Can., Ltd., Gulf, Mobile & Ohio R.R. Mem. Am., Chgo. bar assns., Alpha Delta Phi. Clubs: Legal, Harvard (Chgo.). Home: 350 N Cumrock Rd Inverness Countryside Palatine IL 60067 Office: 29 N Wacker Dr Chicago IL 60606

COATES, LEONIDAS DIXON, aerospace engr.; b. Fresno, Cal., Oct. 24, 1907; s. Leonidas D. and Beatrice (Williams) C.; B.S., U.S. Naval Acad., 1930, student Postgrad. Sch., 1936-38; M.S. in Aero. Engring., Cal. Inst. Tech., 1939; grad. Advanced Mgmt. Program, Harvard, 1950; m. Farley Fane Ullrich, Mar. 19, 1939; children—Carolyn (Mrs. D.W. Kiess), Patricia (Mrs. T.L. Poe): m. 2d, Evelynne Gummel Friend, Nov. 28, 1961; 1 dau., Onica Friend. Commd. ensign USN, 1930, advanced through grades to rear adm., 1956, ret., 1964; designated naval aviator, 1934, aero. engr., 1941; research and devel., 1941-64; asst. chief research and devel., bur. aeros. Dept. of Navy, Washington, 1957-61, chief of naval research, 1961-64; program mgr. anti-submarine warfare-ocean systems Lockheed Cal. Co., Burbank, 1964—. Mem. Am. Inst. Aeros. and Astronautics, Armed Forces Communications and Electronics Assn., Navy League. Home: 4002 Mary Ellen Av Studio City CA 91604 Office: Lockheed Cal Co Burbank CA 91505

COATES, ROBERT MYRON, writer, art critic; b. New Haven, Conn., Apr. 6, 1897; s. Frederick and Harriet (Davidson) C.; B.A., Yale, 1919; m. Elsa Kirpal, Feb. 3, 1927 (div. Jan. 1946); m. 2d, Astrid Peters, June 14,, 1946. Mem. Internat. Art Crítics Assn., Nat. Inst. Arts and Letters. Clubs: P.E.N., Century Assn. Author: The Eater of Darkness, 1929; The Outlaw Years, 1930; Yesterday's Burdens, 1933; All the Year Round, 1943; The Bitter Season, 1946; Wisteria Cottage, 1948; The Farther Shore, 1955; The Hour After Westerly, 1957; The View From Here, 1960; Beyond the Alps, 1961; The Man Just Ahead of You, 1963; South of Rome, 1965. Contbr. to Whither, Whither, a Symposium, 1930; The American Caravan IV, 1931; also articles and fiction to The New Yorker, others. Home: Old Chatham NY 12136 Office: 25 W 43d St New York City NY 10036

COATES, STANLEY E., theatrical dir.; b. Dublin, Ireland, 1926; m. Myra Coates; 1 son Robert. Formerly mem., dir. Abbey Theatre and Gaiety Theatre, Dublin; charter mem. Irish Ballet company; physiotherapist London Festival Ballet company; also associated with Ballets de France de Jainne Charrat and Am. Ballet Theatre; founder, adviser Council Irish Arts, 1967. Recipient Fels Ceoil Dramatic award, 1949. Address: 18 W 236th Buckingham St Villa Park IL*

COATNEY, GEORGE ROBERT, pharmacologist, malariologist; b. Falls City, Neb., May 3, 1902; s. Edward Ernest and Ida Virginia (Banner) C.; A.B., Grand Island (Neb.) Coll., 1925; A.M., U. Neb., 1926, Sc.D. (hon), 1963; Ph.D., la. State U., 1932; Sc.D., Bowling Green (Ohio) State U., 1958; m. Eva Mae Rice, May 2, 1929; children—Cathryn Ann, John Edward. Faculty Grand Island Coll., 1926-30, Neb. Wesleyan U., 1931-33, Peru (Neb.) State Coll., 1933-38; with NIH, 1938-68, sr. protozoologist, 1942-45, sec. malaria study sect., 1946-48, head chemotherapy sect. Lab. Tropical Disease, 1947-57, asst. chief, 1955-58, acting chief, 1958; chief Lab. Parasite Chemotherapy, 1959-66; lectr. tropical pub. health Harvard, 1955-70; vis. prof. preventive medicine and pub. health Howard U., 1959—; prof. pharmacology La. State U. Med. Sch., New Orleans, 1966- 69; vis. prof. pharmacology Tulane U. Med. Sch., 1968—. Commd. scientist (lt. comdr.) regular corps USPHS, 1945, sr. scientist, 1947, scientist dir., 1949. U.S. del. to VI Internat. Congress Tropical Medicine and Malaria, Lisbon, 1958; mem. expert com. malaria WHO, 1948, 49, 60, 65, list of experts on malaria, 1949—; mem. Commn. on Malaria Armed Forces Epidemiology Bd., 1964—. asso. dir. commn. malaria, 1965-68, mem. commn. parasitic diseases, 1965-69; mem. Sci. Adv. Council and Liberian Inst. Am. Found. Tropical Medicine. Recipient Army-Navy Certificate of Appreciation, 1947, Dept. of Army Certificate of Appreciation, 1953; Darling Found. medal and prize, 1954, Gorgas medal and prize, 1954, Alumni Merit award la. State U., 1956, Distinguished Service medal USPHS, 1966, Le Prince medal, 1970. Hon. fellow Royal Soc. Health Gt. Britain; fellow N.Y. Acad. Sci.; mem. A.A.A.S., Am. Soc. Parasitologists. Royal, Am. (pres. 1962) socs. tropical medicine and hygiene, Tropical Medicine Assn. Washington (pres. 1961). Am. Acad. Tropical Med., Am. Acad. Microbiology, Am. Pub. Health Assn., Assn. Mil. Surgeons U.S., Acacia, S.W. Assn. Parasitologists (pres. 1968), Sigma Xi, Phi Kappa Phi, Author: (with others) Survey of Antimalarial Agents, 1952, Chemotherapy of Malaria, 1955; The Primate Malarias, 1971. Contbr. sci. papers to tech. jours. Home: 5012 Wickford Way NE Atlanta GA 30338 ☆

COATS, DONALD LEROY, organist; b. Moberly, Mo., Aug. 15, 1909; s. LeRoy Joel and Estella (Tedford) C.; Mus.B., Washburn Municipal Coll., 1933; student Northwestern U., 1930-31; M.Sacred Music, Union Theol. Sem., N.Y.C., 1937; m. Bernice Vosburg, July 28, 1934; children—Caroline (Mrs. Lee O. Snow), Elizabeth (Mrs. Joseph V. Sullivan). Head organ dept. Washburn Municipal U., organist-choirmaster Grace Episcopal Cathedral, Topeka, 1934-42; organist, choirmaster St. Paul's Episcopal Cathedral, Los Angeles, 1942-53; acting head organ dept. U. So. Cal., 1950-51; organist-choirmaster St. James' Episcopal Ch., N.Y.C., also tchr. organ Sch. Sacred Music, Union Theol. Sem., 1953—. Chmn. music commn. Episcopal Diocese Los Angeles, 1951-52; mem. music commn. Los Angeles Ch. Fedn., 1950-53. Bd. dirs. Union Theol. Sem., 1962-70, mem. alumni council, 1961- 64. Mem. Am. Guild Organists (dean Kan. chpt. 1940-41, Los Angeles chpt. 1944-46, N.Y.C. chpt. 1960-62, mem. nat. council 1954-57, 62-65, nat. chmn. conv. and expansion com. 1966-70), Phi Delta Theta, Phi Mu Alpha, Clubs: St. Wilfred, Church (N.Y.C.). Home: 955 Lexington Av New York City NY 10021 Office: 865 Madison Av New York City NY 10021

COATS, EDWIN ALBERT, psychiatrist; b. Chgo., Apr. 23, 1906; s. Albert James and May (Jeary) C.; student U. Neb., 1923-26; M.D., U. Mich., 1932; m. Pauline Calvelage, June 4, 1944; children—Pamela, Michael. Intern, Los Angeles County Gen. Hosp., 1933-34; resident Kern Gen. Hosp., 1934; resident psychiatrist Hastings State Hosp., 1938-41, staff psychiatrist, 1941-48; asst. supt. Logansport State Hosp., 1948; asst. supt. Ind. Village for Epileptics, 1948-50; psychiatrist State Hosp., Madison, Wis., 1950-53; psychiatrist Lincoln (Neb.) Regional Center, 1953-57, asst. supt. 1957-65, supt., 1965—; asst. clin. prof. psychiatry and neurology Creighton Med. Sch., 1965—. Served to 1st lt. AUS, 1935-36. Fellow Am. Psychiat. Assn.; mem. A.M.A., Am. Assn. Med. Supts. Mental Hosp., Am. Med. Writers Asst. Home: 6321 Sumner St Lincoln NB 68506 Office: Box 271 Lincoln NB 68501

COATS, WENDELL JOHN, army officer; b. Sterling, Colo., July 28, 1915; s. Elbert W. and Hannah Grace (Castleberry) C.; B.S., U.S. Mil. Acad., 1940; M.A., U. Wis., 1949; grad. Command and Gen. Staff Coll., 1952, Army War Coll., 1956; fellow Center Internat. Relations Harvard, 1961-62; Ph.D., Georgetown U., 1963; m. Benny Lee Smith, 1946; children—Wendell John, Nathan B., Wilson C. Commd. 2d lt. U.S. Army, 1940. Advanced through grades to maj. gen., 1968; assigned 39th F.A. Bn., 1940-42, Hdqrs. 3d Inf. Div., 1942-43, 39th F.A. Bn., 1943-45; mem. staff and faculty F.A. Sch., 1945-47, 49-51; assigned Hdqrs. TRUST, Free Territory Trieste, 1952-53, Allied Mil. Govt., 1953-54; sec. to gen. staff Hdqrs. U.S. Army Europe, 1954-55; dep. chief orgn. and tng. div. Office Dep. Chief Staff Logistics Dept. Army, 1956-58, Office Internat. Affairs, Office Sec. Army, 1958-60; exec. officer div. arty. 1st Cav. Div., U.S. Army Pacific, 1960-61; asst. to chief information, Dept. Army, 1962-63; exec. officer Office Asst. Sec. Def. Internat. Security Affairs, 1963-64; dep. dir. J-4 Hdqrs. U.S. European Command, 1964-67; dep. comdg. gen. U.S. Army Tng. Center, Ft. Polk, La., 1967; dep. chief information Dept. Army, 1967, chief information, 1967-69; comdg. gen. 2d Armored Div., Fort Hood, Tex., 1969-71; chief staff Hdqrs. U.S. Readiness Command, MacDill AFB, 1971—. Dir. United Services Automobile Assn., U.S. AA Life Ins. Co., Decorated D.S.M., Silver Star, Legion of Merit with 2 oak leaf clusters, Bronze Star, Army Commendation medal with 2 oak leaf clusters; Croix de Guerre, Fourragere of Colors. Mem. Assn. U.S. Army, Am. Polit. Sci. Assn., Armor Assn., Pi Sigma Alpha. Author: Armed Force as Power, 1966; also articles. Home: 402 Staff Loop MacDill AFB FL 33621 Office: Chief Staff US Readiness Command MacDill AFB FL 33608

COATSWORTH, ELIZABETH, (Mrs. Henry Beston), author; b. Buffalo, May 31, 1893; d. William T. and Ida (Reid) Coatsworth; prep. edn., Buffalo Sem.; A.B., Vassar, 1915; M.A., Columbia, 1916; Litt.D., U. Me., 1955; L.H.D., New Eng. Coll., 1958; m. Henry Beston, June 18, 1929; children—Margaret Coatsworth (Mrs. Dorik Mechau), Catherine Maurice (Mrs. Richard Barnes). Recipient Newbery medal, 1931, Golden Rose award New Eng. Poetry Club, 1967. Fellow Internat. Inst. Arts and Letters; mem. Phi Beta Kappa. Author: Country Poems, Night and the Cat, Summer Green, and 7 other books of verse; Here I Stay, The Enchanted, Mountain Bride, and 4 other novels, 3 books essays, numerous childrens books including: Newbery Medal Book, The Cat Who Went to Heaven, the 5 Sally books beginning with Away Goes Sally, Horses, Dogs and Cats, 1957; book of collected verse 1957; (novel) The White Room, 1958; The Peaceable Kingdom, The Cave, 1958; Indian Encounters, 1960; Lonely Maria, 1960; Desert Dan, 1960; The UNICEF Christmas Book, 1960; The Noble Doll, 1961; Ronnie and the Chief's Son, 1962; The Princess and the Lion, 1963; Jock's Island, 1963; Cricket and the Emperors Son, 1965; The Secret, 1965; The Hand of Apollo, 1965; The Sparrow Bush (poetry), 1966; The Fox Friend, 1966; The Place, 1966; (with Henry Beston) Chimney Farm Bedtime Stories, 1966; Maine Memories, 1968; Bess and the Sphinx, 1968; Lighthouse Island, 1968; George and Red, 1969; Indian Mound Farm, 1969; Grandmother Cat and the Hermit, 1970; Good Night, 1971; The Wanderers, 1971. Books pub. in England, Germany, Norway, Sweden, other countries. Editor: Henry Beston's Especially Maine, 1970. Home: Chimney Farm Nobleboro ME 04555 ☆

COBB, CULLY ALTON, editor, printing corp. exec.; b. Prospect, Tenn., Feb. 25, 1884; s. Rev. Napoleon Bonaparte and Mary Agnes (Woodward) C.; B.S., Miss. Agrl. & Mech. Coll. (now Miss. State U.), 1908; D.Sc., Clemson U., 1937; m. Byrdie Ball, Dec. 23, 1910 (dec.); children—Cully Alton, David Alexander; m. 2d, Lois Dowdle, Aug. 24, 1934. Supt. high sch. Buena Vista, Miss., 1908-10; state agt. Miss. Agrl. and Mech. Coll., in charge boys' agrl. club work, 1910-19, also asst. dir. extension work in Miss.; editor and dir. So. Ruralist, 1919-30; pres. Ruralist Press, Inc., Atlanta. Dir. cotton div. AAA. 1933; served as mem. printing industry com. WPB. Mem. agr. com. U.S. C. of C. Bd. govs. Agrl. Hall of Fame, 1964. Mem. Ash Kahn Crew (hon. soc. printing industry Am.); recipient Distinguished Service award Printing Industry of Atlanta, 1958, citation for distinguished service Printing Industry Am., 1962; Patron Excellence award Miss. State U., 1965. Mem. Nat. Boys' and Girls' Club Com. 1923—, "Unit of Value" Stabilization Com. created by Am. Farm Bureau Fed. Mem. Atlanta C. of C. (chmn. agrl. com., livestock com.), Ga. Printers Assn. (pres.), Atlanta Master Printers Club (pres. 1944), Am. Agrl. Editors Assn. (pres. 1923-28), Country Life Assn. (dir.), Printing Industry Am. (past pres. union employer sect.), Omicron Delta Kappa (hon.). Democrat. Baptist. Mason (32), Rotarian. Organized first sch. of Miss. system of agrl. high schs., and first internat. stock judging contests; as pres. Am. Agrl. Editors' Assn., conducted agrl. study tours to Europe, Can. and Mexico. Home: 2632 Fox Hill Dr Decatur GA 30033 Office: 713 Glenn St SW Atlanta GA 30310

COBB, DUDLEY MANCHESTER, Jr., physician, surgeon; b. Cleve., Aug. 13, 1907; s. Dudley Manchester and Maude (Van Wyck) C.; B.S., Andrews U., 1935; M.D., Loma Linda U., 1937; m. Alethea May Usborne, Aug. 20, 1929 (dec. Apr. 1971); 1 son, Dudley Manchester III. Rotating intern White Meml. Hosp., Los Angeles, 1937-38; practice in Los Angeles, 1937—; sr. staff mem. Cal. Luth. Hosp., 1947-72, chmn. gen. practice sect., 1963-64; sr. cons. staff Resthaven Psychiat. Hosp., 1963- 67; med. dir. Los Angeles County Sheriff's Dept., 1970—. Mem. area 5186 FCDA, 1946—; chmn. med. div. Los Angeles Community Chest, 1959; mem. exec. bd. Cancer Prevention Soc., 1958-67. Diplomate Nat. Bd. Med. Examiners. Mem. Am. (chmn. sect. gen. practice 1964-65, chmn. physicians adv. com. TV, radio and motion pictures 1963-65, alternate del. 1961-68, del. 1970—), Cal. (del. 1960-63, 67-68, 70—, chmn. uniform ins. claims com. 1960, 63, 67-68, mem. reference com. C, 1971), Los Angeles County (pres. sect. gen. practice 1956, councillor 1957, 1st pres. met. area dist. 1, 1959, chmn. cancer quackery com. 1957-59) med. assns., Am. (chmn. TV, radio and motion pictures subcom. 1961-65, del.), Cal. (pres. 1968-69, ho. of dels., bd. dirs. acads. gen. practice, Cal. Physicians Service (trustee 1957-63, exec. com. 1957-63, chmn. med. Policy com. 1959-61, chmn. editorial com. 1962), Alumni Assn. Loma Linda U. Sch. Medicine (pres. 1971-72), Los Angeles World Affairs Council, Los Angeles C. of C., Res. USPHS Assn. Ret. Surgeons (life), Nat. Rifle Assn. (life), Navy League, Clubs: Jonathan, Breakfast, Town Hall, Press, Los Caballeros (charter) (Los Angeles). Home: 3500 W Manchester Blvd Inglewood CA 90305 Office: Vermont Knoll Profl Bldg 8015 S Vermont Av Los Angeles CA 90044

COBB, EMERSON GILLMORE, chemist, educator; b. Slaughters, Ky., Nov. 28, 1907; s. Jess and Sarah Jane (Ramsey) C.; B.A., Union Coll., Ky., 1928; M.S., U. Ky., 1931; Ph.D., U. N.C., 1941; L.H.D., Union Coll., 1961; m. Edith Kendrich Cheap, May 25, 1929; children—John, Benjamin. Tchr., Ky. high schs., 1928-40; asst. prof. chemistry La. Poly. Inst., 1940-42; prof., chmn. dept. chemistry Dakota Wesleyan U., 1942-48; spl chem. investigator Pratt & Whitney Aircraft, Hartford, Conn., summer 1944-45; prof., chmn. dept. chemistry U. Pacific, 1948—; Fulbright vis. lectr. U. Peshawar, Pakistan, 1961-62; advisor summer study program in chemistry Sci. Found. of India at U. Poona, summer 1967. Mem. Am. Chem. Soc. (councillor), Sigma Xi, Phi Kappa Phi, Alpha Epsilon Delta, Alpha Chi Sigma. Methodist. Kiwanian. Author: Science Series for Elementary Schools, 1946-47. Research on polyhydroxy compounds, carcinomic agts., chem. edn.; inventor impregnants for porous castings. Home: 632 Lexington St Stockton CA 95204

COBB, GEORGE HAMILTON, oil, mineral, research exec.; b. St. Louis, Aug. 16, 1911; s. George H. and Julia L. (Middleton) C.; student Okla. State U., 1929-30, U. Neb., 1934; B.S., U. Kan., 1939; m. Esther Victoria Preston, Nov. 30, 1957; children—Carolyn Rozella Palamar, David Dean. Petroleum engr. Kerr-McGee Corp., Oklahoma City, 1939-41, prodn. supt., 1942-47, prodn. mgr., 1948-53, asst. to pres., 1953-56, v.p. exploration, 1959-60, v.p. minerals div., 1960-63, v.p. exploration research, 1964-67, sr. v.p., 1968-71, exec. v.p., 1968—, chmn. operating com., 1968—; exec. v.p. Kermac Nuclear Fuels Corp., Oklahoma City, 1956—, asso. dir.; v.p., dir. Community Nat. Bank of Warr Acres, Oklahoma City. Registered profl. engr., Okla., Tex. Mem. Am. Inst. M.E., Am. Petroleum Inst., Am. Assn. Petroleum Geologists, N.M., Colo. mining assns. Home: 1506 Buttram Rd Oklahoma City OK 73120 Office: Kerr-McGee Bldg Oklahoma City OK 73102

COBB, HENRY NICHOLS, architect; b. Boston, Apr. 8, 1926; s. Charles Kane and Elsie Quincy (Nichols) C.; grad. Phillips Exeter Acad., 1943; A.B., Harvard, 1947, M. Arch., 1949; m. Joan Stewart Spaulding, June 5, 1953; children—Sara, Quincy, Emma Trow, Pamela Codman. Designer in office Hugh Stubbins, 1949-50; mem. archtl. div. Webb & Knapp, Inc., 1950-55; partner I.M. Pei & Partners, 1955—. Vis. critic Yale, 1963-66, U. Pa., 1965; vis. lectr. Washington U., St. Louis, 1963, Columbia, 1965; prin. works include May-D&F Dept. Store, Denver, 1958, Pl. Ville Marie, Montreal, Can., 1962, acad. center and residence halls State U. Coll., Fredonia, N.Y., 1967. John Hancock Tower, Boston, 1969. Served with USNR, 1944-46. Mem. A.I.A. Club; Knickerbocker (N.Y.C.). Patentee insulated metal curtain-wall system. Home: 830 Park Av New York City NY 10021 Office: 600 Madison Av New York City NY 10022

COBB, HENRY VAN ZANDT, univ. adminstr.; b. East Orange, N.J., Feb. 22, 1909; s. Sanford Ellsworth and Margaret Brown (Macleish) C.; A.B., Pomona Coll., 1930; Ph.D., Yale, 1936; m. Florence Ruth Crozier, Aug. 3, 1932; children—Margaret Alice, Judith Helen, Catherine Macleish, Peter Van Zandt, David Crozier. Acting prof. psychology andd philosophy Furman U., Greenville, S.C., 1934-35; instr. philosophy Carleton Coll., Northfield, Minn., 1936-41, asst. prof., 1941-44; prof. philosophy and psychology, head dept. U. S.D., 1946-58, prof., chmn. dept. psychology, 1958-67, dean Coll. Arts and Scis., 1967-69, v.p. acad. affairs, acting dean Grad. Sch., 1969—; vis. prof. edn. Tchrs. Coll. Columbia U., 1964-65; with Florence R. Cobb, weekly radio program Our Children, 1952- 53; faculty study fellowship Ford Found., 1953. Mem. Gov.'s Com. on Mental Health S.D., 1954; mem. S.D. Gov.'s Com. Mental Retardation, 1962; councilor Internat. League Socs. for Mentally Handicapped, 1963- 65, pres., 1966-70; bd. dirs. Joint Commn. on Mental Health of Children, 1966-70; chmn. Joint Commn. Internat. Aspects Mental Retardation, 1970—. Served with USNR, 1944-45; assigned duty on U.S.S. Wichita. Mem. A.A.A.S., Am. Assn. U. Profs., Am. Philos. Assn., Am. Psychol. Assn., Soc. Religion in Higher Edn., Nat. (pres. 1964-65), S.D. (pres. 1954) assns. retarded children, Am. Assn. Mental Deficiency, Sigma Xi, Phi Beta Kappa. Author: Man's Way, 1942. Contbr. articles and revs. to profl. jours. Home: 1211 Valley View Vermillion SD 57069

COBB, HUBBARD HANFORD, mag. editor; b. N.Y.C., Aug. 5, 1917; s. Frank I. and Margaret Hubbard (Ayer) C.; grad. Avon (Conn.) Prep. Sch., 1936; m. Elizabeth Youngblood Simon, Feb. 6, 1954. Bldg. editor Am. Home mag., 1952-61, editor, 1961-69; editor Cal. Home, New Home Jour.; author syndicated column home problems, 1946-50; condr. radio program home and house bldg., 1947-54. Served with USAAF, World War II. Mem. Author's Guild. Author: How to Build Your Dream House, 1948; Home Handyman's Guide, 1949; Homeowners Guide to Remodeling, 1950; Complete Homeowner, 1965; The Dream House Encyclopedia, 1970. Home: Main St East Haddam CT 06423

COBB, JACOB ERNEST, univ. dean; b. Morganton, N.C., Feb. 14, 1910; s. Edgar W.S. and Lizzie (Shore) C.; A.B., U. N.C., 1929; M.A., Duke, 1938; Ph.D., George Peabody Coll., 1947; m. Peggy Eloise Vanstrom, Dec. 31, 1943; children—William Jacob, Katharine, Frederick Vanstrom. Tchr., adminstr. pub. schs., N.C., 1929-41; asso. div. instrl. services N.C. Dept. Edn., 1941-42; cons. psychologist Rohrer, Hibler & Replogle, Atlanta, 1950-51; mem. faculty Ind. State U., Terre Haute. 1946—, prof. edn. and psychology, 1950—, dean Sch. Grad. Studies, 1964—. Mem. exec. com. Council Grad. Schs. U.S., 1968—; mem. Govs. Commn. Mental Health-Mental Retardation, 1970—. Served to lt. comdr. USNR, 1942- 46. Mem. Am., Ind. psychol. assns., Phi Delta Kappa, Kappa Delta Pi. Methodist. Rotarian. Author: A Study of Functional Reading, 1948. Home: 814 Collett Av Terre Haute IN 47804

COBB, JAMES OUTTERSON, naval officer; b. Albany, N.Y., Jan. 9, 1911; s. Charles Sherman and Frances Elizabeth (Monty) C.; B.S., U.S. Naval Acad., 1933; grad. Naval War Coll., 1948; postgrad. George Washington U., 1956; m. Enid Eileen Walker, Aug. 16, 1935 (dec. 1954); children—David Ayrton, Peter Carroll, Michael Sherman; m. 2d, Yvonne Keller, Jan. 28, 1955; children—Claudia Ann, James Monte. Commd. ensign USN, 1933, advanced through grades to rear adm., 1961; with U.S.S. Colorado, 1933-35, Aleutian Island expdn., 1935-36; NAS, Pensacola, Fla., 1936; naval aviator Fighter Squadron One, 1937; with U.S.S. Saratoga, Pacific Fleet, 1938-39, U.S.S. New Orleans, 1939-41, Patrol Bomber Squadron 11, 1941-42; comdg. officer Patrol Squadron 91, 1942-43; combat operations Central and South Pacific; exec. officer U.S.S. Salerno Bay, 1944-46; staff Naval War Coll., 1947-51; staff Comdr. Naval Air Force Pacific Fleet, Korean War, 1951-53; staff Comdr. in Chief So. Europe, Naples, Italy, 1953-55; with Joint Staff, Washington, 1955-57; comdr. officer U.S.S. Yorktown, 1957-58; sec. Joint Chiefs Staff, 1958-60; chief staff Carrier Div. 5, Pacific Fleet, 1960-61; comdr. Carrier Div. 19, 1961-62; dep. chief naval personnel, 1962-64; comdr. Carrier Div. 2, Atlantic and Mediterranean, 1964-65; dir. joint staff Joint Chiefs of Staff, 1966-68; chief Joint U.S. Mil. Group, Spain, 1968-70, comdt. 5th Naval Dist., Norfolk, Va., 1970—. Pres., Pentagon Officers Athletic Center, 1963-64, Fed. Exec. Assn. Tidewater Area Va. Bd. dirs. Navy Mut. Aid Assn.; trustee Navy-Marine Residence Found. Club: American (Madrid, Spain). Home: 6120 Beachway Dr Falls Church VA 22041 Office: Naval Sta Norfolk VA 23511

COBB, JEWEL PLUMMER, educator, cell physiologist; b. Chgo., Jan. 17, 1924; A.B., Talladega Coll., 1944; M.S., N.Y.U., 1947, Ph.D. in Biology, 1950; div., 1 child. Fellow Nat. Cancer Inst., 1950-52; instr. anatomy U. Ill. Coll. Medicine, 1952-54; research surgery Postgrad. Med. Coll., N.Y.U., 1955, asst. prof., 1955-60; Cancer Research Found. prof. biology Sarah Lawrence Coll., 1960-69; prof. zoology, dean Conn. Coll., 1969—; spl. research on tissue culture studies human neoplasms, change produced by promising chemotherapeutic agts., mechanisms normal and abnormal pigment cell metabolism. Mem. New London Conservation Commn., Conn. Health and Edn. Facilities Authority; bd. dirs. Nat. Center Resource Recovery. Regent U. Hartford; trustee Hartt Coll. Music. Fellow Cancer Research, Tissue Culture Assn.; Sigma Xi. Home: 740 Williams St New London CT 06320 Office: Conn Coll New London CT 06320

COBB, LEE J., actor; b. N.Y.C., Dec. 9, 1911; s. Benjamin Jacob and Kate (Neilecht) C.; student City Coll. N.Y.; m. Helen Beverly, February 6, 1940; m. 2d, Mary Hirsch, July 1957. Actor, dir. Pasadena Community Playhouse, 1931-33; mem. Group Theatre, N.Y.C., 1935-37, appeared Group prodn. Golden Boy, London, Eng., 1938; appeared in title role Broadway prodn. Death of a Salesman, The Emperor's Clothes; on screen 1937—; motion pictures include: The Moon is Down, 1943; Song of Bernadette, 1945; Anna and the King of Siam, 1946; Boomerang, 1947; Captain from Castile, 1948; Call Northside 777, 1948; But Not For me, 1959; The Trap, 1959; Green Mansions, 1959; Exodus, 1960, How the West Was Won; Come Blow Your Horn, 1963; appeared on TV series The Virginian, now appearing TV series the Young Lawyers. Mem. Actors Equity Assn., Screen Actors Guild, Am. Fedn. Radio Artists, Nat. Aero. Assn., Aircrafts Pilots and Owners Assn., Civil Air Patrol. Address: 1037 S Odgen St Los Angeles CA 90019*

COBB, LLOYD JOSEPH, lawyer; b. New Orleans, July 19, 1904; s. William Holmes and Katherine Mary (Salter) C.; LL.B., Tulane U., 1924; m. Mireille LeBreton, 1934; 1 dau., Mary. Admitted to La. bar, 1924; asso. Milling, Godchaux, Saal & Milling, 1924-26; pvt. practice, New Orleans, 1928-; partner Cobb & Wright, 1949-; asst. to gen. counsel Pan Am. Petroleum Corp., 1926-28, gen. counsel, 1928, and to successor firm Pan Am. So. Corp., 1948-; founder Marydale Products Co., Inc.; pres. New Orleans Internat. Trade Mart. Recipient Thomas A. Cunningham award, 1952; hon. consul Dominican Republic, 1956, 57. Club: Internat. House (pres. 1949-51). Pioneered dehydration sweet potatoes for cattle feed, for food for mil. use, World War II; developer model grassland farming operation Marydale Farm nr. St. Francisville, La., 1944. Home: 500 Woodvine Av New Orleans LA 70120 Office: Whitney Bldg New Orleans LA 70130

COBB, NATHAN A., lawyer; b. Portland, Me., June 27, 1905; A.B. cum laude, Bowdoin Coll., 1926; LL.B. cum laude, Harvard, 1929. Admitted to Minn. bar, 1930; now mem. firm Richards, Montgomery, Cobb & Bassford, Mpls. Mem. Am., Minn. State, Hennepin County bar assns., Am. Judicature Soc., Maritime Law Assn. U.S., Phi Beta Kappa. Office: Richards Montgomery Cobb & Bassford Dain Tower Minneapolis MN 55402*

COBB, RAYMOND, W., ins. exec.; b. Rutland, Vt.; July 10, 1910; s. Irving Cassius and Mabel (Ruggles) C.; B.S. in C.E., U. Vt., 1932; m. Helen Elizabeth Baker, June 19, 1937; children—Jeremy, Betsey, Jonathan, David. With Prudential Ins. Co. of Am. 1932—, 2d v.p., 1954-61, sr. v.p. 1962—, sr. v.p. charge Central Atlantic operations, 1969—. Home: 2 Campbelton Circle Princeton NJ 08540 Office: Prudential Ins Co Fort Washington PA 19034

COBB, RICHARD NEIL, educator; b. Portland, Me., June 15, 1911; s. William Lord and Fannie (Gray) C.; A.B., Bowdoin Coll., 1932; A.M., Harvard, 1933; postgrad. Lehigh U., 1936-39, 54-55; m. Barbara Damon, June 27, 1936; children—Suzanne, Richard Damon. Instr. math. Williston Acad., 1934; teaching fellow math. and physics Bowdoin Coll., 1934-35; instr. math. Los Alamos Ranch Sch., 1935-36; grad. asst. math. Lehigh U., 1936-39; instr. math. Deering High Sch., Portland, Me., 1939-45, head dept., 1940-45; instr. math. Worcester Poly. Inst., 1946- 60, head dept., 1957-60, Sinclair prof. math., 1960—. Mem. Math. Assn. Am., Nat. Council Tchrs. Math., Assn. Tchrs. Math. in N.E., Phi Beta Kappa, Pi Mu Epsilon, Kappa Sigma. Home: 5 Suburban Rd Worcester MA 01602

COBB, ROGER BURNHAM, utility exec.; b. Kingston, R.I., July 21, 1914; s. George Robert and Ethel (Burnham) C.; B.A., St. John's Coll., Annapolis, Md., 1933; B.E., Johns Hopkins, 1935; m. Millicent Allen, June 14, 1939; 1 son, Allen R. Engr. Iroquois Gas Corp., Buffalo, 1937-43, supt., 1944-53, v.p., 1953-63, sr. v.p., 1963—, dir., 1965—; v.p., dir. Producers Gas Co. (Olean, N.Y.); dir. Direct Approach Methods, Inc. (Hamburg, N.Y.). Dir. Jr. Achievement, 1958—, pres., 1960; dir. United Taxpayers League, 1962—; mem. Buffalo Bd. Safety, 1963-66. Mem. Buffalo Area C. of C., Ellicott Club Assn., Automobile Club Buffalo (dir. 1964-67). Club: Buffalo Athletic (dir. 1967-70). Home: 410 Ashland Av Buffalo NY 14222 Office: 10 Lafayette Sq Buffalo NY 14203

COBB, WILLIAM BALLINGER, lawyer, govt. ofcl.; b. Kansas City, Kan., Dec. 3, 1894; s. Alfred H. and Carrie (Lee) C.; A.B., U. Wyo., 1916; LL.B., Kan. U., 1920, J.D., 1968; m. Olivine Steffens, Aug. 19, 1939; children—Stephen Henry, Stephanie Marguerite, William Ballinger, Marjorie; m. 2d, Lee Ann Koth, Sept. 12, 1959. Admitted to Wyo. bar, 1920, Hawaii bar, 1948; practice law, Casper, Wyo., 1920-41; surplus property officer Dept. Interior for Hawaii, 1945-47; practice law, Hawaii, 1948—; now mem. firm Cobb & Gould, Honolulu; referee in bankruptcy Dist. Ct., Hawaii, 1962—. Mem. Wyo. state legislature, 1925-29; arbitrator industries and Internat. Longshoreman's and Warehousemen's Union Sugar, Pineapple and Longshore Unions; dir. Civil Def. Agy., Hawaii, 1950-53; pub. mem., chmn. Hawaii Employment Relations Bd.; chmn. Territorial Traffic Safety Com., 1958-64. Candidate for del. to congress, 1950. Served with U.S. Army, 1917-19, 1941-46; col. Judge Adv. Gen. Corps, 1954. Decorated Legion of Merit. Mem. Am. Legion, V.F.W., Res. Officers Assn., Am. Bar Assn., Bar Assn. Hawaii (chmn. unauthorized practice com.). Ret. Officers Assn., Assn. U.S. Army, Mason (Shriner), Elk, Kiwanian. Home: 3059 Felix St Honolulu HI 96816 Office: AMFAC Bldg Honolulu HI 96813

COBB, WILLIAM LYMAN, ins. exec.; b. Sutherland, Ia., May 31, 1909; s. Burt L. and Carrie Louise (Dollman) C.; student Des Moines U., 1928-30; m. Ruth Arlene Mountain, July 14, 1934; children—Carolyn Ann, William Lyman. Pres., chief exec. officer, chmn. exec. com. Financial Gen. Bankshares, Inc.; dir. Internat. Bank Washington; dir., chmn. exec. com. Bradford Speed Packaging & Devel. Corp.; chmn. bd. Globe Industries, Inc.; dir. Foster Wheeler Corp.; Intermediate Credit Corp., Kliklok Corp., Amforge, Inc., H.G. Smithy Co., Bankers Financial Life Co., Northeastern Ins. Co., Hartford, Hawkeye-Security Ins. Co., United Security Ins. Co., United Services Life Ins. Co., Bankers Security Life Ins. Soc., Central Nat. Bank & Trust Co., Des Moines, Am. Nat. Bank Md., Silver Spring, Pullman Bank & Trust Co., Standard Bank & Trust Co. (both Chgo.), Nat. Bank of Ga., Atlanta, Valley Fidelity Bank & Trust Co., Knoxville, Tenn., Bank of Commerce, N.Y.C. Served as lt. USNR, 1943-46. Mem. Washington Bd. Trade, Nat. Lawyers Club Washington, Phi Sigma Chi. Club: Congressional Country (Bethesda, Md.). Home: 1220 N Nash St Arlington VA 22209 Office: 1701 Pennsylvania Av NW Washington DC 20006

COBB, WILLIAM MONTAGUE, anatomist, phys. anthropologist; b. Washington, Oct. 12, 1904; s. William Elmer and Alexzine E. (Montague) C.; A.B. (Blodgett scholar), Amherst Coll., 1925, Sc.D., 1955; M.D., Howard U., 1929; Ph.D., Western Res. U., 1932; certificate in embryology Marine Biol. Lab., Woods Hole. Mass.; student U.S. Nat. Museum, Washington U.; LL.D., Morgan State Coll., 1964; m. Hilda B. Smith, June 25, 1929; children—Carolyn (Mrs. R.S. Wilkinson, Jr.), Hilda Amelia (Mrs. L. C. Gray). Intern Freedmen's Hosp., Washington, 1929-30; instr. embroyology Howard U., 1928-29, asst. prof. anatomy, 1932-34, asso. prof., 1934-42, prof. anatomy, 1942-69, head dept., 1947- -69, distinguished prof. anatomy, 1969—; jr. med. officer U.S. Dept. Agr., 1935; mem. Pub. Health Adv. Council of D.C., 1953-61, chmn., 1956-58. Chief med. examiner Freedman Hosp. Bd., D.C. SSS, 1941; civilian cons. to surgeon gen. U.S. Army, 1945. Mem. exec. com. White House Conf. Health, 1965. Fellow in anatomy Western Res. U., 1933-39, asso. anatomy, 1942-44; Rosenwald fellow, 1941-42; recipient citations from Opportunity mag., 1947, Chgo. Defender, 1948, Washington Afro-Am., 1948; distinguished service award Medico-Chirurg. Soc. D.C., 1952; D.S.M., Nat. Med. Assn., 1955; meritorious service award Med. Soc. of D.C., 1968. Fellow Am. Anthrop. Assn., Gerontol. Soc., A.A.A.S.; mem. Am. Assn. Anatomists, Am. Assn. Phys. Anthropologists (v.p. 1948-50, pres. 1957-59), Am. Eugenics Soc. (dir. 1957-68), Anat. Soc. Gt. Brit. and Ireland, Nat. Med. Assn. (state v.p. 1943, editor, 1949—, chmn. council on med. edn. and hosps. 1948- 63, nat. pres. 1964-65), Nat. Urban League (health specialist, 1945-47), N.A.A.C.P. (chmn. nat. med. com., 1950, dir. 1949—) Am. Soc. Mammalogists, Am. Assn. History of Medicine, Assn. Study of Negro Life and History, Anthrop. Soc. Washington (pres. 1949-51), Medico-Chirurgical Soc., D.C. (rec. sec., 1935-41, pres. 1945-47), Omega Psi Phi (chmn. scholarship com., 1939-48), Sigma Xi, Alpha Omega Alpha. Club: Cosmos (Washington). Presbyn. Founder Bull. of Medico-Chirurg. Soc. D.C., 1941, editor, 1945—; editor Jour. Nat. Med. Assn., 1949—. Author monographs, articles. Home: 1219 Girard St NW Washington DC 20009

COBB, WILLIAM WARREN, army officer; b. Dallas, Aug. 15, 1917; s. Luther Leon and Edna (Daugherty) C.; student U.S. Army Command and Staff Coll., 1951-52, U.S. Army War Coll., 1958-59; A.B., U. Kan., 1960; m. Frances Bowman, Feb. 13, 1946; children—William Warren, Betsy B. Commd. 2d lt. U.S. Army, 1941, advanced through grades to maj. gen., 1970; spl. asst. to high commr. and dep. civil adminstr. Ryukyu Islands, 1962-65; comdt. U.S. Army Armor Sch., 1967-69; comdg. gen. 4th Armored Div., Germany, 1970-71; U.S. comdr. Berlin, 1971—. Decorated Silver Star, Legion of Merit with two oak leaf clusters, D.F.C. Home: 14-16 Pacellialle Berlin Germany Office: US Comdr Berlin APO NY 09742

COBBLE, JAMES WIKLE, educator; b. Kansas City, Mo., Mar. 15, 1926; s. Ray and Crystal Edith (Wikle) C.; student San Diego State Coll., 1942-44; B.A., No. Ariz. U., 1946; M.S., U. So. Cal., 1949; Ph.D., U. Tenn., 1952; m. Margaret Ann Zumwalt, June 9, 1949; children—Catherine Ann, Richard James. Chemist, Oak Ridge Nat. Lab., 1949-52; research asso. U. Cal., Berkeley, 1952-55, instr. dept. chemistry, 1953; asst. prof. dept. chemistry Purdue U., Lafayette, Ind., 1955-58, asso. prof., 1958-61, prof., 1961—. Adv. editor chemistry Macmillan Co., 1967—; cons. in field. Served to lt. (j.g.) USNR, 1943-45. Recipient E.O. Lawrence award U.S. AEC, 1970; Guggenheim fellow, 1966; Robert A. Welch Found. lectr., 1971. Fellow Am. Inst. Chemists, Am. Phys. Soc.; mem. Am. Chem. Soc., Sigma Xi, Phi Kappa Phi, Alpha Chi Sigma, Phi Lambda Upsilon. Contbr. articles to sci. publs. Home: 312 Fernleaf Dr West Lafayette IN 47906

COBBLE, JAMES WILLIAM, coll. dean; b. Millersville, Mo., Apr. 13, 1920; s. Walter Ray and Mary Annie (Seabaugh) C.; student Southeast State Coll., Cape Girardeau, Mo., summers 1937-40; B.S., U. Mo., 1947, M.A., 1948, Ph.D., 1951; m. Mildred Lorene Crowe, Oct. 1, 1940; children—Carolyn (Mrs. David Eastwood), Kaye Lynne. Elementary sch. tchr., Millersville, 1937- 38, Conran, Mo., 1939-40; jr. high sch. tchr., Conran, 1940-41; with Mo. Social Security Commn., 1941; asst. instr. U. Mo., also supt. ofcl. dairy testing for Mo., 1947-50; instr. U. Mo., 1950-51; mem. faculty U. R.I., 1951—, prof., chmn. animal and dairy sci. dept., 1953-60, asso. dean Coll. Agr., also asso. dir. R.I. Agrl. Expt. Sta., 1959-62, dean Coll. Resource Devel., dir. Agrl. Expt. Sta., also dir. Co-op. Extension Service, 1962—; adminstr. AID team to S. Korea, 1971-72. Served with USCGR, 1941-45. Mem. Am. Dairy Sci. Assn., Am. Animal Products Soc., Nat. Milk and Food Sanitarians, Am. Assn. Land-Grant Colls. and Univs., N.E.A., Sigma Xi, Phi Kappa Phi, Sigma Gamma Delta, Gamma Alpha, Alpha Zeta. Lion. Home: 41 Linden Dr Kingston RI 02881

COBBOLD, CAMERON FROMANTEEL, (1st baron Cobbold) Brit. govt. ofcl.; b. Sept. 14, 1904; s. Clement Cobbold; student Eton; Kings Coll., Cambridge; D.Sc. (Econ.), London U., 1963; LL.D. McGill U., Montreal Can., 1963; m. Lady Margaret Hermione Millicent Bulwer-Lytton, 1930; children—two sons, one dau. Adviser to Bank of Eng., 1935-38, exec. dir., 1938-45; dep. gov., 1945-49; gov. Bank of Eng., London, 1949-61; bd. dirs. Brit. Petroleum Co., Ltd., Guardian Royal Exchange Assurance, Hudson's Bay Co.; mem. internat. adv. bd. Chem. Bank N.Y. Trust Co. Her Majesty's Lt. for City of London. High sheriff County of London, 1946- 47; apptd. member Her Majesty's Privy Council, Jan. 1959; lord chamberlain Her Majesty's household, 1963—. Chmn. bd. govs. Middlesex Hosp., 1963. Created Baron of Knebworth, 1960; decorated knight of Garter, knight grand cross Royal Victorian Order. Clubs: The Athenaeum, White's. Home: Knebworth House Hertfordshire England also St James Palace London SW1 England

COBBS, JOHN LEWIS, magazine editor; b. Washington, Sept. 10, 1917; s. John Lewis and Jessie (Ware) C.; student U. N.C., 1935-36; B.A. with great distinction, Stanford U., 1939, M.A., 1940; postgrad. Harvard, 1940-41; m. Phyllis Conway White, Dec. 27, 1941; children—John Lewis, Nicholas Hamner. Research asst. Nat. Indsl. Conf. Bd., 1941-42; finance editor Bus. Week mag., N.Y.C., 1942-43, Washington corr., 1943-45, bus. policy editor, 1945-50, asst. mng. editor, 1950-63, mng. editor, 1963-66, editor, 1966—. Trustee Chappaqua (N.Y.) Pub. Library, 1967—. Recipient school bell award N.E.A., 1958, distinguished service award Sigma Delta Chi, 1959. Mem. Phi Beta Kappa, Phi Gamma Delta, Sigma Delta Chi. Republican. Episcopalian. Club: Harvard (N.Y.C.). Contbr. articles mags. Home: 20 Leroy Pl Chappaqua NY 10514 Office: 330 W 42d St New York City NY 10036

COBBS, SUSAN PARKER, former coll. dean; b. Anniston, Ala., Dec. 9, 1905; A.B., Randolph-Macon Women's Coll., 1927; A.M., N.Y.U., 1930; Ph.D., U. Chgo., 1937. Tchr., Latin High Sch., Alexandria, Va., 1927-28, Phillips High Sch., Birmingham, Ala., 1928-29, Randolph-Macon Woman's Coll., 1930-31, 1932- 39, adj. prof., 1939-49; tchr. St. Catherine's Sch., Richmond, Va., 1931- 32, Shipley Sch., Pa., 1940-41; asst. prof. Latin and Greek, Agnes Scott Coll., Decatur, Ga., 1941-45; dean Swarthmore Coll., 1945-69, also prof. classics. Mem. Philol. Assn., Nat. Assn. Deans of Women. Address: Box 147 Greensboro AL 36744

COBERLY, CAMDEN ARTHUR, educator; b. Elizabeth, W.Va., Dec. 21, 1922; s. James G. Blaine and Edith Luella (Simpson) C.; B.S., W.Va. U., 1944; M.S., Carnegie Inst. Tech., 1947; Ph.D., U. Wis., 1949; m. Lenore McComas, June 14, 1946; children—Catherine (Mrs. George D. Manson), Elizabeth Ann, Charles Owen, Robert Olaf. Chem. engr. Mallinckrodt Chem. Works, 1949-55, chief engr., 1955-64; prof. chem. engring., asso. dir. Engring. Expt. Sta. of U. Wis., 1964-68, chmn. dept. chem. engring., 1968-71, asso. dean Coll. of Engring., 1971—; cons. Lakeside Labs. Served to lt. (j.g.) USNR, 1944-46. Mem. Am. Inst. Chem. Engrs., Am. Chem. Soc., Am. Soc. Engring. Edn., Am. Soc. C.E., A.A.A.S., Sigma Xi, Tau Beta Pi, Phi Lambda Upsilon, Sigma Gamma Epsilon. Home: 4114 N Sunset Ct Madison WI 53705

COBERLY, WILLIAM BAYLEY, Jr., cotton oil corp. exec.; b. Tucson, May 8, 1908; s. William Bayley and Winifred (Wheeler) C.; A.B., Stanford, 1930; m. Aileen Dorsey, Dec. 10, 1934 (dec. Nov. 1948); children—Sheryl (Mrs. John S. Griffith, Jr.), Aileen (Mrs. John H. Hadley, Jr.), William 3d; m. 2d, Victoria Nebeker Mudd, Sept. 16, 1969. Asso., Cal. Cotton Oil Co., predecessor firms, 1930—, dir., asst. gen. mgr., 1945-51, v.p., gen. mgr., 1951—, pres., 1956—; v.p., dir. Coberly-West Co., Bakersfield, Cal., 1951-57, pres., dir., 1957—; dir. Kobe, Inc., So. Cal. Edison Co., Forest Lawn Co., Am. Security & Fidelity Corp. Trustee Found. Econ. Edn., Irvington, N.Y., Inst. for Humane Studies, Menlo Park, Cal., Harvey Mudd Coll., Claremont, Cal. Mem. Nat. Cottonseed Products Assn. (pres. 1952-53, dir., hon. mem.), Chi Psi. Republican. Conglist. Clubs: California, Beach, Sunset, Lincoln (Los Angeles). Home: 800 W 1st St Los Angeles CA 90012 Office: 626 Wilshire Blvd Los Angeles CA 90017

COBEY, RALPH, industrialist; b. Sycamore, O., Aug. 15, 1909; s. Harry and Minnie (Silverman) C.; student mech. engring. Carnegie Inst. Tech., 1928-30; D.Sc., Findlay Coll., 1958; m. Hortense Kohn, Feb. 28, 1944; children—Minnie, Susanne Yetta. With Perfection Steel Body Co., Galion, O., 1930-65, successively mech. engr., plant mgr., sales mgr., asst. gen. mgr., gen. mgr., sec.-treas., pres., 1950-65; pres. Eagle Crusher Co., 1954—, Philips-Davies Co., Kenton, 1965-70, O., Cobey, Co., Galion, 1950-70, Perfection-Cobey, Co., Galion, 1965-70, Crawford County Land Co., Galion, World Wide Investment Co., Fredericktown, Marion County Land Co.; pres., chmn. bd. Imco, Inc., Crestline, O.; dir. 1st Nat. Bank, Galion, Aide in preparation of prodn. and design of Army tanks OPM, 1940-42. Mem. contbg. com. Nat. Conf. Christians and Jews, 1951-55, now area chmn. spl. gifts com.; founder, pres. Harry Cobey Found.; area chmn. U.S. Savs. Bonds; mem. pres.'s adv. council for devel. Ashland Coll.; mem. Ohio Gov.'s Citizens' Task Force on Environmental Protection mem. U.S. Pres.'s Tax Com., 1962-66; pioneer chaplain services in indsl. plants; mem. Ohio Expns. Commn., 1961, Radio Free Europe Com., Internat. Platform Com.; mem. Ohio Gov.'s Citizens' Task Force on Environmental Protection. Mem. Ohio Rep. Finance Com. Bd. dirs., chmn. long range planning com. Johnny Appleseed Area Council Boy Scouts of Am.; bd. dirs. Galion Community Center; trustee Hillel Found. at Ohio State U., Galion City Hosp. Found. Bd.; chmn., founder Minnie Cobey Meml. Library; founder, chmn. bd. trustees Louis Bromfield Malabar Farm Found.; bd. overseers Jewish Theol. Sem. of Am.; mem. bd. Galion United Appeals; mem. nat. council Am. Jewish Com. Served as capt. USAAF, 1942-46, 51, Korea, Commendation for contrbn. to B-29 bomber, World War II. Mem. Nat. Safety Council, Nat. Assn. Foreman, Nat. Assn. Credit Men (dir. North Central Ohio div.), N.A.M., A.I.M. (pres. council), Am. Ordnance Assn., Am. Legion, United Comml. Travelers, Nat. Assn. 4-H Clubs, Future Farmers Am., Navy League U.S., Newcomen Soc. N.Am., United Comml. Travelers, U.S. C. of C. (mem. taxation, fgn. affairs, labor relations coms.), Acad. Polit. Sci. Beta Sigma Rho (trustee). Jewish religion. Mason. Elk. Club: Galion Country. Home: RFD 2 Galion OH 44833 Office: Eagle Crusher Co Inc Rt 2 Box 72 Galion OH 44833

COBHAM, CHARLES JOHN LYTTELTON, ex-gov.-gen. New Zealand; b. London, Eng., Aug. 8, 1909; s. John Cavendish Cobham and Violet Yolande (Leonard) C.; B.A. in Law with Honors, Trinity Coll., Cambridge U., 1933; hon. law degree, U. New Zealand, 1961; m. Elizabeth Alison Makeig-Jones, Apr. 30, 1942; children—John William Leonard, Juliet Meriel, Elizabeth Catherine, Christopher Charles, Richard Cavendish, Nicholas Makeig, Lucy and Sarah (twins). Vice capt. M.C.C. touring cricket team to Australia and New Zealand, 1935-36; capt. Worcestershire County Cricket Team, 1936-39; dir. Asso. Elec. Industries Ltd., 1954-65; pres. M.C.C., 1954; gov.-gen. New Zealand, 1957-62. Justice of peace, 1936; chmn. West Midland Region Lloyds Bank, 1962—; dir. Eagle Star Ins. Co.,Monks Investment Trust, Nat. Bank New Zealand, Dennis Motor Holdings, Ltd. Chmn. bd. govs. Worcester Coll. for Blind; chmn. Outward Bound Trust. Lord-lt. County of Worcester, 1963. Served with Brit. Army, 1939-45. Became peer, 1949, Knight of St. John, 1957, Knight of Garter, Knight Grand Cross St. Michael and St. George. Mem. Royal Agrl. Soc. (pres. 1969). Clubs: Marylebone Cricket (London). Address: Hagley Hall Worcestershire England

COBIN, MARTIN THEODORE, educator; b. N.Y.C., Oct. 20, 1920; s. Joseph Bernard and Rose (Lubin) Cohen; student Coll. City N.Y., 1938-40; B.F.A., Ohio U., 1942; M.A., U. Wis., 1947, Ph.D., 1953; m. June Peterson, June 27, 1944; children—Lyn Marie (Mrs. William Gullette), Gail Louise (Mrs. David Cowdrey), Karen Thea (Mrs. Garett Warner), Peter Martin. Asst. prof. W.Va. U., 1947-55; asst. prof. to asso. prof. U. Ill., 1955-61; from asso. prof. to prof. and chmn. dept. communication and theatre U. Colo., 1961—. Play dir. Colo. Shakespeare Festival, 1965, 67, 69. Served with AUS, 1942-46. Mem. Speech Communication Assn., Am. Ednl. Theatre Assn., Assn. Asian Studies. Mem. Soc. of Friends. Author: Theory and Technique of Interpretation, 1959; (with Therrel B. Fest) Speech and Theater, 1963; From Convincement to Conversion, 1964. Research on Japanese theater. Home: 825 Dellwood Av Boulder CO 80302

COBLENTZ, STANTON ARTHUR, author; b. San Francisco, Aug. 24, 1896; s. Mayer and Mattie (Arndt) C.; A.B., U. Cal., 1917, A.M., 1919; m. Flora Bachrach, 1922. Mem. staff San Francisco Examiner, 1919-20; book reviewer N.Y. Times, N.Y. Sun, N.Y. Herald, Internat. Book Rev., 1920—. Mem. Authors' League Am., Poetry Soc. Am. Winner Peace Poetry Contest, San Francisco Chronicle, 1918, Star Poem Contest, The Poetry Rev., London, 1924; 1952 award Lyric Found. for Traditional Poetry, N.Y. Author books including: An Editor Looks at Poetry, 1947; The Sunken World, 1948; Unseen Wings (anthology), 1949; Garnered Sheaves (verse), 1949; New Poetic Lamps and Old, 1950; Into Plutonian Depths, 1950; After 12,000 Years, 1950; Time's Travelers, 1952; From Arrow to Atom Bomb, 1953; From a Western Hilltop (verse), 1954; Under the Triple Suns, 1954; The Rise of the Anti-Poets, 1955; The Pageant of Man, 3d edit., 1957; Villains and Vigilantes, 1957; Magic Casements, 1957; The Blue Barbarians, Out of Many Songs, The Long Road to Humanity, 1959; My Life in Poetry, 1960; Next Door to the Sun, 1960, Atlantis and other Poems, 1960; The Runaway World, 1961; The Swallowing Wilderness, 1961; Redwood Poems, 1961; Next Door to the Sun, 1961; The Generation That Forgot to Sing, 1962; The Moon People, 1964; The Last of the Great Race, 1964; The Lizard Lords, 1964; Avarice: A History, 1965; Ten Crises in Civilization, 1965; Demons, Witch Doctors and Modern Man, 1965; The Paradox of Man's Greatness, 1966; Lord of Tranerica, 1966; The Poetry Circus, 1967; The Crimson Capsule, 1967; The Pageant of the New World, 1968; Aesop's Fables (rhymed versions), 1968; The Day the World Stopped, 1968; The Power Trap, 1970; The Militant Dissenters, 1970. Compiler: Modern American Lyrics, 1924; Modern British Lyrics, 1925; The Music Makers, 1945; Unseen Wings, 1949; Poems to Change Lives, 1960. Editor: Wings A Quarterly of Verse, 1933-60. Contbr. newspapers and mags. Book reviewer Los Angeles Times. Address: P O Box 1354 Los Gatos CA 95030 ☆

COBLENTZ, WILLIAM KRAEMER, lawyer; b. San Francisco, July 28, 1922; s. Zach B. and Fritze (Levy) C.; B.A., U. Cal. at Berkeley, 1943; LL.B., Yale, 1947; m. Jean Berlin, Nov. 27, 1952; children—Wendy K., Andrew S. Admitted to Cal. bar, 1947; exec. dir. Am. Com. United Europe, 1950-51; spl. asst. to atty. gen. Cal., 1951-53; spl. counsel to gov. Cal., 1959-61; mem. firm Jacobs, Sills & Coblentz, San Francisco, 1953—. Cons. to sec. state, 1962. Dir. Bay Area Ednl. TV; regent U. Cal. Bd. dirs. Mount Zion Hosp. and Medical Center, N.A.A.C.P. Legal Def. Fund, Am. Assn. for UN, San Francisco Airports Commn. Served to Capt. AUS. Mem. Am., Cal., San Francisco bar assns., Am. Law Inst., Assn. Bar City N.Y. Contbr. articles to legal jours., mags. Home: 10 5th Av San Francisco CA 94117 Office: Bank of Am Center San Francisco CA 94104

COBLEY, GEORGE GORDON, physician, assn. ofcl.; b. Sumas, Wash., Aug. 6, 1919; s. William Henry and Anne (Myers) C.; B.S., U. Wash., 1941; M.D., Columbia, 1944; m. Mildred Overheu, May 16, 1946; children—George Gordon II, Candice Ann, Intern King County Hosp., Seattle, 1944-45; resident pediatrics Childrens Hosp., Los Angeles, 1945-47; practice pediatrics, Santa Monica, Cal., 1947—; clin. instr. pediatrics U. Cal. at Los Angeles Sch. Medicine, 1954-62, asst. clin. prof. pediatrics, 1963-66, clin. prof. pediatrics, 1966—. Mem. Optimist Internat., 1948—, v.p., 1959-60, internat. pres., 1963-64. Bd. dirs. Boys Clubs Santa Monica, Santa Monica Community Chest. Served to capt., M.C., AUS, 1951- 53. Named Young Man of Year, Santa Monica, 1954. Fellow Am. Acad. Pediatrics; mem. Los Angeles County Med. Assn. (v.p. Bay Dist. br. 1962), A.M.A., Delta Upsilon. Home: 1124 N Amalfi Dr Pacific Palisades CA 90272 Office: 2021 Santa Monica Blvd Santa Monica CA 90404

COBURN, HAYWARD HOBEN, lawyer; b. Deadwood, S.D., Nov. 8, 1907; s. George Hayward and Helen (Hoben) C.; grad. Hebron (Me.) Acad., 1924; A.B. summa cum laude, Bowdoin Coll., 1928; A.M., Harvard, 1929; pvt. study law, 1934-39; m. Margaret Phinney, June 22, 1929; children—Carol M. (Mrs. J. Eliot Woodbridge), Alan H. Chemist Hercules Powder Co., Wilmington, Del., 1929- 33; patent atty. Busser & Harding, Phila., 1933-41; admitted to Pa. bar, 1939; asso. Drinker, Biddle & Reath, Phila., 1941-48, partner, 1948-63, mng. partner, 1963—. Mem. nat. bd. YMCA, mem. exec. com. Nat. Budget and Cons. Com. Past chmn. bd. trustees Meadville Theol. Sch. Mem. Am., Pa., Phila. bar assns., Phi Beta Kappa. Unitarian. Home: 665 Conestoga Rd Villanova PA 19085 Office: Phila Nat Bank Bldg Philadelphia PA 19107

COBURN, JAMES, actor; b. Neb.; married; children—James IV, Lisa. Appeared in movies The Magnificent Seven, The Great Escape, The Americanization of Emily, Our Man Flint, 1966; In Like Flint; owner Panpiper Prodns., Hollywood, Cal., producers The President's Analyst; produced Waterhole No. 3. Address: Panpiper Productions Hollywood CA 90028*

COBURN, JOHN BOWEN, clergyman; b. Danbury, Conn., Sept. 27, 1914; s. Rev. Aaron Cutler and Eugenia Bowen (Woolfolk) C.; A.B. with high honors, Princeton, 1936, D.D., 1960; B.D. cum laude, Union Theol. Sem., 1942; D.D., Amherst Coll., 1955, Harvard, 1964, Huron Coll., 1964, Middlebury Coll., 1969, Bucknell U., 1970; S.T.D., Berkeley Div. Sch., 1958; D.D., Hobart Coll., William Smith Colls., 1967; D.Canon Law, Kenyon Coll., 1968; D.S.T., Gen. Theol. Sem., 1968; m. Ruth Alvord Barnum, May 26, 1941; children—Thomas, Judith, Michael, Sarah. Tchr., English and biology Robert Coll., Istanbul, Turkey, 1936- 39; ordained to ministry Protestant Episcopal Ch., as deacon, 1943, as priest, 1943; asst. minister Grace Ch., N.Y.C., 1942-44; rector Grace Ch., Amherst, Mass., chaplain Amherst Coll., 1946-53; dean Trinity Cathedral, Newark, 1953-57, Episcopal Theol. Sch., Cambridge, Mass., 1957-68; tchr. St. Acad., Urban League, Harlem, N.Y.C., 1968-69; rector St. James' Ch., N.Y.C., 1969—. Bd. dirs. Corning Glass Works Found. Center. Mem. Joint Commn. on Ecumenical Relations P.E. Ch.; del. Anglican Congress, 1954, Gen. Conv., 1955, 61, 64, 67, pres. house deps., 1967—. Trustee Princeton, Wooster Sch., Ethel Walker Sch. Union Theol. Sem. Served to lt. (s.g.), Chaplains Corps, USNR, 1944-46. Club: Century (N.Y.C.). Author: Priests in a Pagan Community, 1950; Professors are People; Prayer and Personal Religion, 1957; One Family in Christ, 1958; Minister, 1963; Anne and the Sand Dobbies, 1964; Twentieth Century Spiritual Letters, 1967. Editor: (with Norman Pittenger) Viewpoints, 1959. Home: 4 E 72d St New York City NY 10021 Office: St James' Ch 865 Madison Av New York City NY 10021

COBURN, JULIA CLARK, educator; b. Kansas City, Mo.; d. James Mitchell and Mary Van Valkenburg (Lewis) Coburn; A.B., Vassar Coll., 1918; m. Dante Antolini, 1953 (dec. 1968). Asst. advt. mgr. Lasalle & Koch Co., Toledo, O., 1919-20, mgr., 1920-24, publicity dir., 1924-27; promotion mgr. Harper's Bazaar, 1927-31; dir. fashion bur. Hearst Newspapers, 1931-32; fashion editor Ladies' Home Jour., 1932-37; co- founder Tobé-Coburn Sch. for Fashion Careers Ltd., 1937, pres., 1937-68, chmn. adv. council, 1968—, vice chmn. sales promotion div. Nat. Retail Dry Goods Assn., 1923-24; pres. Women's Advt. Club of Toledo, 1925-26; pres. The Fashion Group, Inc., 1940-42. Vocational lectr. schs. colls. Mem. retail bus. mgmt. adv. com. Dutchess Community Coll., 1971—. Decorated Comdr. in Order of Merit Italian Republic, 1967. Republican. Club: The Fashion Group. Conglist. Contbr. articles on fashion subjects to mags., reference books. Home: 1 Vassar Lake Dr Poughkeepsie NY 12601

COBURN, MELVILLE BROWN, army officer; b. Utah, Sept. 6, 1912; ed. Mil Acad., Okla.; B.S., U.S. Mil. Acad., 1935; grad. Command and Gen. Staff Coll., 1948, Armed Forces Staff Coll., 1950, Nat. War Coll., 1955. Commd. 2d lt. U.S. Army, 1935, advanced through grades to maj. gen., 1965. Decorated Silver Star, Legion of Merit with 2 oak leaf clusters. Bronze Star medal, Air medal, Commendation ribbon. Address: care Office Adj Gen US Army Washington DC 20310*

COBURN, MORTON, librarian; b. Chgo., Dec. 28, 1921; s. Henry and Kate (Bronstein) C.; B.S. in Edn., U. Ill., 1949, M.S. in Library Sci., 1950. Reference librarian U. Kan., 1950-51; librarian acquisitions dept. Ohio State U. Library, 1951-56; dir. libraries Edmonton (Alta., Can.) Pub. Library, 1956—. Bd. dirs., mem. exec. com. Edmonton Welfare Council, 1958-64. Served with AUS, 1943-45. Mem. Am., Canadian, Alta., Edmonton library assns., Kappa Delta Pi. Rotarian. Office: Edmonton Pub Library 7 Sir Winston Churchill Sq Edmonton 15 Alberta Canada

COBURN, RICHMOND CASH, lawyer; b. Oregon, Mo., May 5, 1902; s. Alexander Royal and Mary Auvergne (Cash) C.; A.B., U. Mo., 1923, LL.B., 1925; m. Ruth Wharton, July 11, 1936; children—Mary Judith, Richmond Wharton. Admitted to Mo. bar, 1925, since practiced in St. Louis; partner Coburn, Croft, Shepherd & Derzog, 1949—. Chmn. Fellows Am. Bar Found., 1964. Trustee So. Meth. U., trustee Barnes Hosp., St. Louis, 1956- -. Served with USNR, 1942-45. Mem. C. of C. Met. St. Louis (chmn. 1955- 57), Gen. Alumni Assn. U. Mo. (past pres.), Am. (bd. govs. 1956—), Mo. (pres. 1951-52) bar assns., Bar Assn. St. Louis (pres. 1947-48), Phi Beta Kappa, Phi Alpha Delta, Phi Delta Theta, Order of Coif. Republican. Methodist. Clubs: Noonday, Bogey, Old Warson Country, St. Louis (St. Louis). Home: 10040 Litzinger Rd St Louis MO 63124 Office: 411 N 7th St St Louis MO 63101

COBURN, ROBERT CRAIG, educator; b. Mpls., Jan. 25, 1930; s. William Carl and Esther (Rudd) C.; B.A., Yale, 1951; D.B., U. Chgo., 1954; M.A., Harvard, 1958, Ph.D., 1958; m. Patricia Lee Eddy, Oct. 7, 1961. Instr. philosophy Ohio State U., 1958-59, Dartmouth, 1959-60; asst. prof. philosophy U. Chgo., 1960- 65, asso. prof., 1965-68, prof., 1968—; vis. asso. prof. Cornell U., 1966; vis. prof. philosophy U. Wash., 1970. Mem. Am. Philos. Assn., Am. Assn. U. Profs., Soc. for Religion in Higher Edn., Phi Beta Kappa. Home: 6019 S Ingleside Av Chicago IL 60637

COBURN, ROYAL LEONARD, lawyer, banker; b. Upper Sandusky, O., July 12, 1902; s. Raymond Clinton and Bertie (Howdeshell) C.; student Ohio Wesleyan U., 1920-23; LL.B., Washington U., 1926; m. Muriel Knight Moore; 1 son, Robert. Admitted to Mo. bar, 1926, D.C. bar, 1962; gen. practice law, St. Louis, 1926-53; gen. counsel Fed. Deposit Ins. Corp., Washington, 1953- 62; minority counsel Banking and Currency Com. U.S. Ho. of Reps., 1962; v.p. Suburban Trust Co., Hyattsville, Md., 1963- -. Pres., Clayton (Mo.) Library Bd., 1946-52; adv. bd. St. Louis Coll. Pharmacy. Mem. Am., Mo., Fed. St. Louis bar assns. (Washington). Home: 10201 Grosvenor Park Rockville MD 20852 Office: 6495 New Hampshire Av Hyattsville MD 20783

COCA, IMOGENE, comedienne; b. Phila.; d. Joe and Sadie (Brady) Coca; m. Bob Burton, 1935; m. 2d King Donovan, Oct., 1960. Made first appearance as tap dancer in N.Y.C. vaudeville at age of 11; debut as comedienne, New Faces of 1934; appeared with husband in Straw Hat Revue, 1939; played in summer shows, Pa., 1938-42; first appearance with Sid Caesar on TV in Broadway Revue, 1949; on Your Show of Shows, NBC-TV, 1950; TV series Grindl, 1963. Address: care Nat Broadcasting Co 30 Rockefeller Plaza New York City

COCCHIA, NEAL, journalist; Editorial page editor Newark Star-Ledger. Office: Court and University Sts Newark NJ 07101*

COCHRAN, ALEXANDER RUSSELL, Jr., mech. engr.; b. Santurce, P.R., Aug. 24, 1916; s. Alexander Russell and Beatrice (Thomes) C.; grad. Suffield Acad., 1934; Bachelor Engring., Yale, 1938; m. Beryl Sprouse, Jan. 1942; children—Beryl V. Beatrice, Claudia, Alexander Russell III. Engr. Houston refinery Shell Oil Co., 1938-42, 45-47, asst. chief engr. charge maintenance, 1948-51; plant engr. Celanese Corp. Am., Bishop, Tex., 1951—, chem. div. engr., 1952, mgr. mfg. chem. div., 1953-56, v.p. mfg. and engring., 1957-64, group v.p. for chems. and plastics, 1965-66, sr. v.p., 1966—. Served as 1st lt. USAAF, 1942-45; cadet, instr., 8th AF pilot. Profl. engr., Tex. Mem. Am. Soc. M.E. Home: Birch Hill Rd Weston CT 06880 Office: 522 Fifth Av New York City NY 10036

COCHRAN, ALEXANDER SMITH, architect; b. Balt., Jan. 22, 1913; s. William Francis and Nina (Gill) C.; student Gilman Country Sch., Balt., 1921-31; A.B., Princeton, 1935; postgrad. Sch. Fine Arts, Yale, 1935-37; M.Arch., Harvard, 1939; m. Caroline Sizer, June 5, 1937; children—Alexander Smith, Theodore Sizer, Gill, Caroline Foster (Mrs. James S. Boynton). Draftsman for archtl. firms, 1940-41; constrn. insp. E.I. duPont Co., 1941; project planner U.S. Housing Authority, Washington, 1941-42; pvt. practice architecture, 1945—; with Cochran, Stephenson & Donkervoet, Inc. and predecessor firms, 1954—, also chmn. bd.; v.p. Sherwood Forest Co., 1945-59; prof. architecture U. Md., part-time 1968. Mem. Balt. Planning Commn., 1958-60, 63-70. Trustee Peabody Inst., Balt. Mus. Art, Goucher Coll. Served from ensign to lt., C.E. Corps, USNR, 1942-45. Recipient Cochran Residence award of merit, A.I.A., 1951. Fellow A.I.A. (pres. Balt. chpt. 1962); mem. Nat. Soc. Architects (dir. 1969). Episcopalian (lay reader Diocese Md. 1952). Clubs: Sailing of the Chesapeake; Century Assn. (N.Y.); Fourteen West Hamilton Street; Maryland; Elkridge; Cosmos (Washington). Home: 901 W Lake Av Baltimore MD 21210 Office: 925 N Charles St Baltimore MD 21201 ☆

COCHRAN, BLAKE, fgn. service officer; b. Wilmot, Kan., June 25, 1910; s. Hilton B. and Alma Hope (Jones) C.; A.B., Southwestern Coll., 1932; M.A., Columbia, Tchrs. Coll., 1939, Ed.D., 1941; m. Claire Atwood, Mar. 6, 1944; 1 son, Charles H. Tchr. high schs., 1932-37; research asst. Am. Council on Edn., 1939-42; writer, dir. documentary and ednl. films Ency. Brit., 1945-48; with USIA, 1949—, assignments in Athens, Greece, 1949-52, Cairo, Egypt, 1952-55, Amman, Jordan, 1955-57, Madras, India, 1960; dir. Voice of Am. Arabic Program Center, Rhodes, Greece, 1963-67, dir. African Program Center, Monrovia, Liberia, 1967-68; now with USIA. Served with USNR, 1942-45. Home: 7502 Lynn Dr Chevy Chase MD 20015 Office: Voice of Am (USIA) 330 Independence Av SW Washington DC 20003

COCHRAN, BURT, advt. exec.; b. Metroplis, Ill., Feb. 5, 1898; s. William Phares and Sarah Effie (Jones) C.; A.B., U. Kan., 1921; m. Jessie-Lee Wyatt, Jan. 14, 1922; 1 son, Burt. Ad writer, salesman Dallas News and Evening Jour.; asst. advt. mgr. Foreman & Clark, 1921; copywriter, account exec. Ferry-Hanley Advt. Co., 1922-26; account exec. H. K. McCann Co. (now McCann-Erickson, Inc.), San Francisco, 1926-27, mgr. Seattle office, 1927-36, Chgo. office, 1936-38, mgr. So. Cal. operations, 1941-59; v.p. McCann-Erickson, Inc., 1945-59; exec. v.p., partner Stebbins & Cochran, advt., Los Angeles, 1958; partner McNeil, McCleery & Cochran, 1959-61; Burt Cochran, Advt., marketing communications service, 1961—; dir. Bell Brand Foods, Ltd., Los Angeles. Mem. pub. relations com. John Tracy Clinic, also Boy Scouts Council of Greater Los Angeles. Served as 2d lt. inf., U.S. Army, World War I, Mem. Am. Assn. Advt. Agencies (past mem. bd., vice chmn. So. Cal. chpt.). Friends of Huntington Library, So. Cal. Symphony Assn., Pasadena Art Mus., Conquistadores del Cielo, Sigma Nu, Alpha Delta Sigma, Sigma Delta Chi. Clubs: Greater Los Angeles Advertising (past mem. bd.), California, Men's Garden, Sales Execs. (Los Angeles). Home: 4415 Hobbs Dr La Canada CA 91011 Office: 1010 S Flower Los Angeles CA 90017

COCHRAN, DWIGHT M., corp. exec.; b. Lexington, Ill., Aug. 16, 1904; s. William and Elizabeth Ann (Jones) C.; B.S., U. Chgo., 1927; m. Stella Catherine Adams, Feb. 22, 1936; children—Dwight M., Stella Ann. With I.C. R.R., Chgo., 1922- 23, White Weld & Co., 1927-30; asst. sales mgr. Kroger Co., Cin., 1931- 38; dir. Eastern sales Joseph Schlitz Brewing Co., 1938-43; with Safeway Stores, Inc., 1943-56, v.p., 1951-56, dir., 1952-56; dir. Kern County Land Co., 1956-68, exec. v.p., 1957-59, pres., 1959- 68, chief exec. officer, 1960-68; dir. Lockheed Aircraft Corp., Fireman Fund Am. Cos., Watkins-Johnson Co.; hon. dir. United Cal. Bank. Life trustee U. Chgo. Mem. Delta Upsilon. Republican. Presbyn. Clubs: San Francisco Golf, Pacific-Union, Bohemian (San Francisco); Burlingame (Cal.) Country; Cypress Point (Pebble Beach, Cal.). Home: 711 Eucalyptus Av Hillsborough CA 94010 Office: 235 Montgomery St San Francisco CA 94104

COCHRAN, GEORGE MOFFETT, judge; b. Staunton, Va., Apr. 20, 1912; s. Peyton and Susie (Robertson) C.; grad. Episcopal High Sch., Alexandria, Va., 1930; B.A., U. Va., 1934, LL.B., 1936; m. Marion Lee Stuart, May 1, 1948; children—George Moffett, Harry Carter Stuart. Admitted to Md. bar, 1936, Va. bar, 1935; asso. firm Parker, Carey & Doub, Balt., 1936-38; partner firm Peyton Cochran and George M. Cochran, Staunton, 1938-64, Cochran, Lotz & Black, Staunton, 1964-69; justice Supreme Ct. Appeals Va., Richmond, 1969—. Pres., Planters Bank & Trust Co., Staunton, 1963-69. Chmn., Woodrow Wilson Centennial Commn. of Va., 1952- 58, Va. Cultural Devel. Study Commn., 1966-68; mem. Va. Commn. on Constl. Revision, 1968-69, Jud. Council of Va., 1963-69. Mem. Va. Ho. of Dels., 1948-66, Va. Senate, 1966-68. Chmn. bd. dirs. Stuart Hall; bd. visitors Va. Poly. Inst., 1960-68; trustee Mary Baldwin Coll. Served to lt. comdr. USNR, 1942-46. Mem. Am., Va. (pres. 1965-66), Augusta County (past pres.) bar assns., Phi Delta Phi, Beta Theta Pi. Episcopalian. Clubs: Staunton Country (Staunton); Commonwealth (Richmond); Boar's Head (Charlottesville, Va.). Home: 219 Williams St Staunton VA 24401 Office: Masonic Temple Bldg Staunton VA 24401 also: Supreme Ct of Appeals Bldg Richmond VA 23210

COCHRAN, HAMILTON, author; b. Phila., Sept. 9, 1898; s. Rev. Joseph Wilson and Helen V. (Scudder) C.; student Swarthmore Prep. Sch., 1914-17; A.B., U. Mich., 1922; m. Enid C. D. Slee, Apr. 18, 1925; children—Enid Clare (Mrs. R.N. Taylor), Susan H. (Mrs. S.C. Swanson), Margaret Ellen (Mrs. Garret C. Miller). Engaged in advt. and editorial work, including 2 years in Eng. handling advt. for Am. and Brit. firms, 1931-32; commr. pub. welfare for islands of St. Thomas and St. John, govt. Virgin Islands of U.S., 1932-33; advt. work for Standard Oil Co. N.J., 1933-36; sales promotion and sales tng. work for Tradeways, Inc., N.Y.C., 1936-40; advt. work for R. H. Donnelley Corp., N.Y.C., 1940-44; automotive marketing mgr. Saturday Eve. Post, Phila., 1944-60; advt. dir. Curtis Circulation Co., 1960-62; v.p. Stanley Pub. Co., Chgo., 1962-64, cons., free-lance writer, 1965—. Served in USCG, 1917-19. Decorated World War medal. Fellow Co. Mil. Historians; mem. Centro Studi e Scambi Internationalli (Rome), Am. Legion, S.A.R., Delta Sigma Pi. Republican. Episcopalian. Author books including: Rogue's Holiday, 1947; Blockade Runners of the Confederacy, 1958; Pirates of the Spanish Main, 1961; Dram Tree, 1962; Noted American Duels, 1963; Freeboters of the Red Sea, 1965. Contr. 3 anthologies poetry; articles and fiction. Established native handicraft industries in Virgin Islands and created markets for them in U.S. Home: 4 Kershaw Rd Wallingford PA 19086 ☆

COCHRAN, HAROLD WAID, tin plate co. exec.; b. Mobile, June 18, 1915; s. Harold W. and Marie (Kribbs) C.; A.B. cum laude, Washington and Lee U., 1937; m. Lora Jane Ladd, Apr. 4, 1941; children—Carol, Mary Ellen, Virginia, Barbara. With Caspers Tin Plate Co., 1938—, exec. v.p., 1962-64, pres., 1964—, also dir.; v.p. sales Lafayette Steel & Aluminum Corp., 1957-60, pres., 1964—. Active Hinsdale (Ill.) Community Chest, Hinsdale chpt. A.R.C., Hinsdale Sanitarium and Hosp. fund raising campaign. Served with USNR, 1943-46. Mem. Ill. C. of C., Beta Theta Pi, Omicron Delta Kappa. Home: 433 E 3d St Hinsdale IL 60521 Office: 4100 W 42d Pl Chicago IL 60632

COCHRAN, JACQUELINE, (Mrs. Floyd B. Odlum), aviatrix; b. Pensacola, Fla.; m. Floyd B. Odlum, May 11, 1936. With cosmetics industry since age 14; owner of cosmetic mfg. co., 1935-63; received pilot's license after 3 weeks tng., Roosevelt Field, L.I., 1932; additional tng. in Cal. for 1 yr., equal to U.S. Navy course in groundwork and flight; has flown comml., transport and army pursuit planes and bombers; only Am. woman entrant in McRobertson London-Melbourne race, 1934; 1st woman to fly in Bendix transcontinental race, 1934; winner 1st place in women's div. and 3d place against field of men in Bendix race, 1937; winner of Bendix race, 1938, 2d place, 1946, and third place, 1948 1st woman to pass sonic barrier and exceed speed of sound in Sabre jet F-86, 1953; holder internat., U.S. 2,000 Kilometer records and numerous other speed, distance and altitude records including flights in 1964 at more than twice the speed of sound; piloted bombing plane across the North Atlantic, June 1941; took group of Am.women pilots to Eng., Mar. 1942, for service with Brit. Air Transport Aux., in which she held rank of flight capt.; apptd. dir. Women Pilots, U.S. Air Force, July 1943, after having headed Woman Pilot Tng. program of Army Air Force for several months; commd. lt. col. in USAF Res., 1948, col., 1969. Dir. Northeast Airlines. Cons. NASA. Mem. Cal. State and Riverside County Republican Central Com. Trustee George Washinggton U., 1962—. Decorated Distinguished Service medal, D.F.C. with two oak leaf clusters, Legion of Merit; Order Legion Honor (France); Pionierkette Winderose (W. Germany); recipient of the Clifford Burke Harman trophy of Internat. League of Aviators, 1937, 38, 39, 46, 50 (for years 1940-49), 53; Air Force Assn. Award for Distinguished civilian service, 1948; Mitchell Award for gen. serial achievements, 1937; McGough Meml., 1940; D.S.M. (only civilian woman to receive this award); Gold medal, Fedn. Aeronautique Internationale, 1953; Zonta Achievement award, 1957. Pres. Ninety-Nines (internat. orgn. of women pilots), 1942-43; sr. v.p. Fedn. Aeronautique Internationale, 1956-47, pres. 1959—. Pres., trustee Air Force Village Found., Air Force Acad. Found. Mem. Internat. Acad. Astronautics (hon. life), Bus. and Profl. Womens' Clubs Cal., Nat. Aero. Assn. (hon. pres.). Club: Zonta. Author: The Stars at Noon, 1954. Address: Cochran Odlum Ranch Indio CA 92201

COCHRAN, JOHN ARTHUR, educator; b. Des Moines, Sept. 25, 1921; s. Arthur John and Lena (McCowin) C.; A.B., Drake U., 1943; certificate U. Exeter (Eng.), 1945; M.A., Harvard, 1948, Ph.D., 1949; m. Mary Leffler, July 10, 1943; children—Jacquelyn Sue, Cynthia Elizabeth, Catherine Edna. Teaching asst. Mass. Inst. Tech., 1947-48; teaching fellow Harvard, 1948-49; asst. prof. econs. U. Ill. at Urbana, 1949-56; monetary economist Fed. Res. Bank N.Y., 1956-57; asso. prof. econs. So. Ill. U., 1957-62; prof. econs. Ariz. State U., 1962—, chmn. dept., 1962-67, chmn. faculty assembly and faculty senate, 1970-71; vis. prof. U. Colo., summer 1965. Sec.- treas. Midwest Econ. Assn., 1960-62. Mem. Ariz. Acad., sponsors Ariz. Town Halls for Ariz. leaders, 1962—. Served with AUS, 1943-46, 51-52. Mem. Phi Beta Kappa, Phi Kappa Phi, Beta Gamma Sigma. Presbyn. (trustee 1964-67). Author: Money, Banking and the Economy, 1967, 2d edit., 1971; also numerous articles. Home: 412 Loyola Dr Tempe AZ 85281

COCHRAN, JOHN DANIEL, lawyer; b. Pitts., Aug. 12, 1917; s. Ray Clifton and Vida (Gentsch) C.; A.B., U. Pitts., 1938; J.D., Harvard, 1941; m. Doris Alleen Prothro, Mar. 24, 1944; children—John Daniel, Thomas R., David L., Celinda L. Admitted to Pa. bar, 1942, N.Y. bar, 1942, Ind. bar, 1946; asso. LeBoeuf, Machold & Lamb, N.Y.C., 1941-42; asso. Baker & Daniels, Indpls., 1945-51, partner, 1952—. Dir. Weimer Typesetting Co., Inc., A.B. Cochran & Son, Inc. Active United Fund Greater Indpls., 1960-69. Mem. standing com. Episcopal Diocese Indpls. Served to capt. AUS, 1942-45. Mem. Am., Ind., Indpls., 7th Circuit bar assns., Am. Judicature Soc., Indpls. Lawyers Club, Estate Planning Council Indpls., Newcomen Soc. U.S. Home: 4205 Washington Blvd Indianapolis IN 46205 Office: Fletcher Trust Bldg Indianapolis IN 46204

COCHRAN, KENDALL PINNEY, educator; b. Newton, Kan., Oct. 12, 1924; s. William Walter and Enid (Pinney) C.; B.A. cum laude, U. Tex., 1949, M.A., 1950; Ph.D., Ohio State U., 1955; m. Beverly Ray Bradbury, July 11, 1969. Instr. economics Ohio State U., 1953-55, asst. prof., 1955-57; asso. prof. North Tex. State U., 1957-59, prof., 1959—, chmn. dept. econs., 1969—; dir. NSF Economics Inst., 1964-69; vis. prof. Bishop Coll., 1969; asso. editor Southwestern Social Sci. Quar., 1962-64; editorial bd. North Tex. Business Studies, 1961-67; asso. editor Southwestern Jour. Social Education, 1970. Pres. Denton Credit Union, 1968-69, dir., 1961-69. Served with USAF, 1942-44. Mem. Am., Southeastern (pres. 1965) economic assns., Assn. for Evolutionary Economics (mem. exec. com. 1964), Tex. Assn. Coll. Tchrs. (coordinator research 1960-64), Am. Assn. U. Profs. (mem. nat. council 1967-70). Democrat. Home: 1911 Whippoorwill Lane Denton TX 76201

COCHRAN, LEWIS W., univ. ofcl., physicist; b. Perryville, Ky., Oct. 12, 1915; s. Ernest Beeler and Mayme (Martin) C.; B.S., Morehead (Ky.) State Coll., 1936; M.S., U. Ky., 1939, Ph.D., 1952; m. Carolyn Wilson, Nov. 20, 1940; children—Sue Carol, Phillip. Instr. physics Morehead State Coll., 1939-40, 41, asst. prof., 1946; instr. physics Cumberland U., 1941; radio engr. Lexington Signal Depot, 1942; faculty U. Ky., 1946—, prof. physics, 1957—, acting head dept., 1956-58, asso. dean Grad. Sch., 1963- 65, provost, 1965-70, acting dean Grad. Sch., 1966-67, dean Grad. Sch., v.p. univ. research, 1967-70, v.p. acad. affairs, 1970—; research physicist Oak Ridge Nat. Lab., summers 1949, 50, 53, 59-60; spl. research low energy nuclear physics, gaseous electronics, neuron physics. Bd. dirs. Spindletop Research, Inc., Oak Ridge Asso. Univs., U. Ky. Research Found.; trustee Lees Coll. Served to maj. AUS, 1942-46. Mem. Am. Phys. Soc., Am. Assn. Physics Tchrs., Health Physics Soc., Sigma Xi, Sigma Pi Sigma, Omicron Delta Kappa. Presbyn. (elder). Home: 1581 Beacon Hill Rd Lexington KY 40506

COCHRAN, ROBERT GLENN, educator; b. Indpls., July 12, 1919; s. Lucian Glenn and Daisy P. (Wachstetter) C.; B.A., Ind. U., 1948, M.S., 1950; Ph.D., Pa. State U., 1957; m. Mary Olive Worland, Mar. 1945; 1 son, Robert Glenn. Physicist, Ohio State Health Dept., 1950; physicist, group leader Oak Ridge Nat. Lab., 1950-55; dir. research reactor, asso. prof. Pa. State U., 1955-59; prof., head dept. nuclear engring. Tex. A. and M. U., College Station, 1959—; cons. USAF, U.S. AEC. Served with USNR, 1942-45. Mem. Am. Nuclear Soc., Am. Phys. Soc., Am. Soc. Engring. Edn., Sigma Xi, Phi Kappa Phi. Mason. Contbr. articles profl. jours. Home: Route 4 Box 90A Bryan TX 77801 Office: Tex A and M U College Station TX 77843

COCHRAN, THOMAS CHILDS, author, educator; b. Bklyn., Apr. 29, 1902; s. Thomas and Ethel Vaughan (Childs) C.; B.S., N.Y. U., 1923; grad. study, N.Y. U., and Columbia U., 1924-26; Ph.D., U. of Pa., 1930; m. Rosamond Beebe, May 26, 1938. Harrison fellow in history, U. of Pa., 1927; instr. in history, N.Y. U., 1927-36, asst. prof. 1936-43, asso. prof. 1943-44, prof. 1944-50; prof. U.S. history, U. Pa., 1950-68, Benjamin Franklin prof., 1968—; grad. chmn. dept. Am. Civilization, 1951, chmn. dept. history, 1953-55, 63-65. Mem. historiography com. Social Sci. Research Council, 1943-45, 48-60, dir., exec. com., 1962-65; treas. N.Y. Com. on Bus. Records, 1943-49; del. Am. Council Learned Socs.; chmn. Com. on Research Econ. History, 1954-55; Walgreen lectr., U. Chgo., 1957; dir. Nat. Bur. Econ. Research, 1949-52; Pitt prof. Cambridge (England), 1965-66; chmn. bd. Benjamin Franklin Papers; vis. fellow St. Anontony's Coll., Oxford, Eng., 1970. Mem. Selective Service Bd. No. 1, N.Y.C., 1940. Pres., chmn. Nat. Records Mgmt. Council, 1948-51. Mem. Am. Hist. Assn., (sec. program com. 1940, same com. 1941, chmn. com. on bus. records 1946, chmn. arr. com., 1946, rep. on bd. Am. Year Book 1944-51, former mem. council), Econ. History Assn. (pres. 1958-60), Hist. Soc. Pa. (mem. council 1960—), Am. Philos. Soc., Am. Acad. Arts and Sci., Soc. Am. Studies, Orgn. Am. Historians (pres. 1966-67), Am. Assn. of U. Profs., Phi Beta Kappa, Psi Upsilon. Episcopalian. Author books including: New York in the Confederation, 1932; A History of the Pabst Brewing Company, 1948; History of City of Greater New York (with others), 1949; Railroad Leaders 1845-1890, 1953; The Social Sciences in Historical Studies (with others), 1954; The American Business System, 1957; The Puerto Rican Businessman, 1959; A Basic History of American Business, 1959; (with William Miller) The Age of Enterprise, 1961; (with Ruben Reina) Entrepreneurship in Argentine Culture, 1962; The Inner Revolution, 1965; The Great Depression and World War II, 1968; Social Change in Industrial Society, 1971. Editor: New York University Business History Series, 1945-50; Journal of Economic History, 1945-55; adv. editor Direction Mag. 1938-43. Contbr. revs. and articles to publs. Home: Radnor PA 19087 Office: University of Pa Philadelphia PA 19104 ☆

COCHRAN, THOMAS CUNNINGHAM, Jr., lawyer, corp. exec.; b. Mercer, Pa., June 4, 1920; s. Thomas Cunningham and Olive Belle (Pierson) C.; A.B., Haverford Coll., 1942; M.B.A., Harvard, 1946; LL.B., U. Mich., 1949; m. Helen L. Kent, June 3, 1950; children—Thomas A., Stephen K., Anne L. Admitted to Pa. bar, 1950; counsel, asst. sec. Koppers Co., Inc., 1956-66, v.p., secretary, gen. counsel, 1966—; dir. Lone Star Gas Co. Served to lt. (s.g.) USNR, 1943-46. Mem. Am., Pa., Allegheny County, Mercer County bar assns., Am. Judicature Soc. Clubs: Duquesne, University (Pitts.); South Hills Country. Home: 40 Standish Blvd Pittsburgh PA 15228 Office: Koppers Bldg Pittsburgh PA 15219

COCHRAN, WILLIAM GEMMELL, educator; b. Rutherglen, Scotland, July 15, 1909; s. Thomas and Jeanie W. (Gemmell) C.; M.A., Glasgow U., 1931, LL.D., 1970; M.A., Cambridge U., 1938; m. Betty Mitchell, July 17, 1937; children—Elizabeth, Alexander, Teresa. Came to U.S., 1939, naturalized, 1946. Statistician Rothamsted Exptl. Sta., 1934-39; prof. math. statistics Ia. State Coll., 1939-46; asso. dir. Inst. Statisties, U.N.C., 1946-48; prof. biostatistics, Sch. Hygiene Johns Hopkins, 1948-57; prof. statistics Harvard, 1957—. Mem. Am. Statis. Assn., (pres. 1953), Inst. Math. Statistics (pres. 1946), Internat. Statis. Inst. (pres. 1967-71). Author Experimental Designs (with G.M. Cox), 1950; Sampling Techniques, 1953; (with G.W. Snedecor) Statistical Methods, 1957; Home: 2 Ardley Place Winchester MA 01890 Office: Harvard U Cambridge MA 02138

COCHRAN, WILLIAM WATTS, ins. underwriting exec.; b. Kuling, China, June 6, 1907; s. Dr. Samuel and Margaret (Watts) C.; student North China Am. Sch., 1921-23, Hotchkiss Sch., 1923-25, Princeton, 1925-29; m. Mary Vanderpool, Sept. 18, 1930; children—Cornelia (Mrs. Allen M. Daley), William W., Lois (Mrs. Wayne Marshall). With Dominick & Dominick, N.Y. State Exchange brokers, 1929-38; asst. treas. Am. Ins. Co., Newark, 1938-42, asst. sec., 1945-50; v.p. Reins. Corp. of N.Y., 1950-58, pres., 1958-65, now vice chmn. bd., mem. exec. com., also dir.; bd. mgrs. Howard Savs. Instn., Newark; dir. Am. Nat. Bank & Trust Co. (N.J.). Mgr. Morristown Meml. Hosp., 1938-41. Served 2d lt. to lt. col., Gen. Staff Corps, USAAF, 1942-45. Decorated Bronze Star medal, Presdl. Unit citation. mem. St. Andrews Soc. Clubs: Downtown Assn. (N.Y.C.); Pine Valley Golf (Clemonton, N.J.); Cap and Gown (Princeton, N.J.); Morris County Golf (bd. govs. 1933-55) (Convent, N.J.). Home: Canfield Rd Convent NJ 07961 Office: 99 John St New York City NY 10035

COCHRANE, ALEXANDER PAUL chemist, educator; b. Chicago, 1928; B.S. in Physics, Yale, 1950; Ph.D. in Chemistry, Harvard, 1956; m. Sally Ann Jones, July 5, 1957; children--Kenneth J., Nancy A. Chemist, Acme Chem. Co., Blue Island, Ill., 1950-51; director of Research Lab., Indsl. Chemicals Corp., Cambrige, Mass., 1956-60; project coordinator environmental sect. Steinmetz Assos., Chgo., 1960-61; v.p. for research Bauer Bros. Chem. Co., Inc., Memphis, 1961-64; asst. prof. chemistry Washington U., St. Louis, 1964-66, asso. prof., 1966-70, prof., 1970--, head of chemistry dept., 1970-71. Vis. prof. So. Ill. U., summer 1967, U. of Ore., 1969. Bd. dirs. Rest Haven Home for Elderly, 1960-61; trustee of the Lutheran Hosp., 1965-71. Served from lt. to capt., AUS, 1951-53. Mem. Am. Chem. Soc., Sci. Research Soc. Am. (chpt. treas. 1967), Sigma Xi. Author: (with others) Basic Inorganic Chemistry, 1971. Home: Fairfax Apts 7291 Windermere Dr University City MO 63105 Office: Dept Chemistry Washington University St Louis MO 63130

COCHRANE, HUGH VICTOR HUNTER, dept. store exec.; b. Balt., Aug. 6, 1932; s. Laurence Victor and Dorothy (Ryan) C.; student U. Va., 1955; B.S. in Econs., U. Pa., 1959; m. Alice Elizabeth Haggerty, July 13, 1962; children—Laurence Victor II, Hugh Victor Hunter, Allan Ryan. Pub. accountant Touche, Ross, Bailey & Smart, Balt., 1959-63; asst. treas. Stewart & Co., Balt., 1963-67; controller Joseph Horne Co., Pitts., 1967-69, treas., 1969-71, v.p., treas., 1971—; pres., dir. Pitts. Credit Bur., Inc.; treas., dir. Service Engraving, Inc. Served with U.S. Army, 1953-55. Home: Dilworth Rd RD 3 Sewickley PA 15143 Office: Penn and Stanwix Sts Pittsburgh PA 15222

COCHRANE, VINCENT WINNER, educator; b. Plainfield, N.J. Aug. 21, 1916; s. Ira Leigh and Florence Lillian (Winner) C.; B.S. Cornell U., 1939, Ph.D., 1943; M.A. (hon.) Wesleyan U., Middletown, Conn., 1957; m. Jean Elizabeth Conn, Mar. 31, 1945; children—Nancy Jean, Bruce Joel. Microbiologist, Lederle Labs., 1943-45; asst. plant pathologist Conn. Agrl. Expt. Sta., 1945-47; faculty Wesleyan U., Middletown, 1947—, prof. biology, 1957—, Daniel Ayres prof. 1960—. Pres. Telluride Assn., 1947-49. Fellow Am. Phytopathological Soc.; mem. Am. Assn. Advancement Sci., Am. Soc. Microbiology, Mycological Soc. Am., Bot. Soc. Am., Sigma Xi, Phi Kappa Phi. Author: Physiology of Fungi, 1958; also articles. Home: 61 Prospect St Portland CT 06480 Office: Wesleyan U Middletown CT 06457

COCHRANE, WILLARD WESLEY, economist; b. Frenso, Cal., May 15, 1914; s. Willard Wesley and Clara (Chambers) C.; B.S., U. Cal. at Berkeley, 1937; M.S., Mont. State Coll., 1938; M.P.A. (Littauer fellow), Harvard, 1942, Ph.D., 1945; LL.D., Mont. State U., 1967; m. Mary Herget, Aug. 23, 1942; children—Willard Wesley III, Stephen A., James M., Timothy S. Economist, Dept. Agr., 1939-41, 43-47, dr. agrl. econs., 1961-64; with FAO, 1947- 48; prof. Pa. State U., 1948-51; prof. U. Minn., 1951-59, prof. agrl. econs., 1964-65, 70—, dean internat. programs, 1965-70. Vis. prof. U. Chgo., 1958-59. Chmn. gov.'s study commn. on agr. Minn., 1958; cons. Commodity Credit Corp., U.S. Dept. Agr., Ford Found.; mem. Presdl. Commn. on Food and Fiber, 1965. Served as ensign USNR, 1942-43. Fellow Am. Farm Econ. Assn. (past pres.); mem. Am. Econ. Assn. Democrat. Presbyterian. Club: Cosmos (Washington). Author: (with W. Wilcox) Economics of American Agriculture, 1951; (with Carolyn Bell) Economics of Consumption, 1955; Farm PricesMyth and Reality, 1958; The City Man's Guide to the Farm Problem, 1965; The World Food Problem: A Guardedly Optimistic View, 1969. Home: 2225 Folwell Saint Paul MN 55108

COCHRANE, WILLIAM HENRY, corp. ofcl.; b. Norfolk, Va., Apr. 3, 1912; s. William F. and Gretchen (Schneider) C.; student Princeton, 1931-32; m. Elizabeth J. Ballantine, Aug. 3, 1935; children—William Henry, Elizabeth J., Susan B., Peter B. Successively chemist, salesman, dist. mgr., mgr. market and sales analysis, mgr. detergent project U.S. Indsl. Chems. Co., 1932- 52; gen. mgr. indsl. div. Lever Bros. Co., 1952-57; exec. v.p. Neptune Meter Co., 1957-58, pres., 1958-69, chmn. 1966—, also dir.; dir. Los Angeles Soap Co., Neptune Meters Ltd., (Can.) Alcolae Inc., Revere Corp. Am., Neptune Measurement, Ltd., Eng. Served from lt. (j.g.) to lt. USNR, 1944-46. Mem. Am. Waterworks Assn. Nat. Planning Assn., Soc. Chem. Industry, Newcomen Soc., Societe Chemie Industrille. Clubs: Economic, Princeton (N.Y.C.); Nassau, Seaview (N.J.) Country; Los Angeles Country; Pine Valley Golf (N.J.); Baltusrol Golf; Mountain Lake, (Fla.). Home: Mountain Lake Wales FL 33853 Office: 6990 Lake Ellenor Dr Orlando FL 32809

COCKAYNE, THOMAS WILLIAM, sugar co. exec.; b. Sheffield Eng., July 14, 1906; s. Sam and Alice (Hollingsworth) C.; brought to U.S., 1914; student bus. coll.; m. Mary Morris, July 14, 1934; children—Joan (Mrs. Frederick F. DeMetrovich), Thomas William, Nancy Ann,David, Janet. With Utah-Ida. Sugar Co., 1923- -, asst. mgr., Toppenish, Wash., 1942-45, sec., Salt Lake City, 1945—, treas., 1951—, v.p., 1955—, mem. exec. com. 1959—, also dir.; dir., V.P., sec-treas. Layton Sugar Co., Salt Lake City, 1959—; v.p., sec- treas. Gunnison Sugar Co., Salt Lake City, 1955—; dir. Gunnison Sugar, Inc., Desert Fed. Savs. & Loan Assn. Mem. finance com. Salt Lake City Republican Com. Mem. Salt Lake City C. of C. Mem. Ch. of Jesus Christ of Latter-day Saints. Home: 930 S 12th St E Salt Lake City UT 84105 Office: 47 W S Temple St Salt Lake City UT 84110

COCKCROFT, JOHN DENISON, corp. exec.; b. Yorkshire, Eng., June 24, 1902; s. Ernest E. and Annie (Denison) C.; chartered accountant, London, Eng., 1924; m. Emily Mary Smith, July 16, 1928; children—David D., Elizabeth A., Joan Mary. Came to U.S., 1932. With J & J Colman, Norwich, Eng., 1926-32; treas. R. T. French Co., Rochester, N.Y. 1932-43; v.p. 1943-45, dir., 1943—, pres. 1945—; dir. Reckitt & Colman Holdings Ltd., Hull, Eng., 1957—; Lincoln Rochester Trust Co., Rochester, Rochester Gas & Electric Corp. Mem. Inst. Chartered Accountants (England), C. of C. Clubs: Genesee Valley, Rotary, University, Rochester Country (Rochester, N.Y.). Home: 12 Elmwood Hill Lane Rochester NY 14610 Office: 1 Mustard St Rochester NY 14609

COCKE, BARTLETT, architect; b. Floresville, Tex., Oct. 10 1901; B.Arch., U. Tex., 1922; postgrad. Mass. Inst. Tech., 1922-24. Partner Eickenroht & Cocke, 1927-31; with Bartlett Cocke & Assos. San Antonio, 1931—; prin. works include Alamo Nat. Bank, Motor Bank & Parking Garage, 1961, Bapt. Meml. Hosp. projects, 1949, 62, M&S Tower, 1964 (all San Antonio), Joske's Retail Stores, San Antonio and Houston, Basset Shopping Center, El Paso, Hancock Shopping Center, Austin, Sears, Roebuck & Co., San Antonio, El Paso, Galveston, Laredo, Fellow A.I.A. (pres. San Antonio 1940); mem. Tex. Soc. Architects (pres, 1944-45). Address: 3501 Broadway San Antonio TX 78209

COCKE, ERLE, Sr., banker, railway exec.; b. Lee County, Ga., June 26, 1895; s. Isaac Perry and Minne (Huff) C.; grad. Dawson (Ga.) High Sch., 1911; B.S., U. Ga., 1915; m. Elise Meadows, Dec. 9, 1917; children—Aline (Mrs. Eugene P. Cofeld, Jr.), Erle. Banking, mfg. and farming, Dawson and Macon, Ga., 1920-31; state senator, 11th Ga. dist., 1927-28; sec-treas. and exec. officer, bd. regents, Univ. System of Ga., 1932-33; mgr. Atlanta agy., R.F.C., 1934-38, R.F.C. Mortgage Co., Atlanta area, 1936-38, C.C.C., Atlanta area 1934-39; gen. chmn. Roosevelt Homecoming, 1935; state dir. Nat. Emergency Council, 1936-38; v.p. Fulton Nat. Bank, 1938-42, exec. v.p., 1942-45, pres., 1945-54, vice chmn. bd., chmn. exec. com., 1954-57; pres. Atlanta Clearing House, 1947, 51; dir. Fed. Deposit Ins. Corp., 1957-60, chmn., 1960- 63, dir.; v.p., dir. Central of Ga. Ry. Co.; cons. So. Ry. Systems; dir. Citizens Bank Md., Am. Bank Atlanta, Gen. Acceptance Corp., financial observer Bretton Woods Conf. inaugurating World Bank & World Fund, del. ann. meetings, 1958, 61. Trustee Com. for Econ. Devel. Served as lt. A.E.F., World War I. Mem. Am. Legion (nat. vice comdr., 1922-23), Ga. (chmn. fed. legislative com., other offices), Am. (v.p. 1955-56, pres. 1956-57) bankers assns., Nat. Indsl. Conf. Bd., Soc. Indsl. Realtors (award bd.), Nat. Planning Assn. (nat. council), Newcomen Soc., Ga. Agrl. and Indsl. Devel. Bd.(adv. com. 1944-45), Internat. C. of C. (trustee U.S. council), Alpha Tau Omega. Baptist. Clubs: Capital City, Piedmont Driving (Atlanta); Nat. Press (Washington). Home: 2637 Peachtree Rd NE Atlanta GA 30305 Office: 127 Peachtree St NE Atlanta GA 30303

COCKE, ERLE, Sr., banker, railway exec.; b. Lee County, Ga., June 26, 1895; s. Isaac Perry and Minne (Huff) C.; grad. Dawson (Ga.) High Sch., 1911; B.S., U. Ga., 1915; m. Elise Meadows, Dec. 9, 1917; children—Aline (Mrs. Eugene P. Cofeld, Jr.), Erle. Banking, mfg. and farming, Dawson and Macon, Ga., 1920-31; state senator, 11th Ga. dist., 1927-28; sec-treas. and exec. officer, bd. regents, Univ. System of Ga., 1932-33; mgr. Atlanta agy., R.F.C., 1934-38, R.F.C. Mortgage Co., Atlanta area, 1936-38, C.C.C., Atlanta area 1934-39; gen. chmn. Roosevelt Homecoming, 1935; state dir. Nat. Emergency Council, 1936-38; v.p. Fulton Nat. Bank, 1938-42, exec. v.p., 1942-45, pres., 1945-54, vice chmn. bd., chmn. exec. com., 1954-57; pres. Atlanta Clearing House, 1947, 51; dir. Fed. Deposit Ins. Corp., 1957-60, chmn., 1960- 63, dir.; v.p., dir. Central of Ga. Ry. Co.; cons. So. Ry. Systems; dir. Citizens Bank Md., Am. Bank Atlanta, Gen. Acceptance Corp., financial observer Bretton Woods Conf. inaugurating World Bank & World Fund, del. ann. meetings, 1958, 61. Trustee Com. for Econ. Devel. Served as lt. A.E.F., World War I. Mem. Am. Legion (nat. vice comdr., 1922-23), Ga. (chmn. fed. legislative com., other offices), Am. (v.p. 1955-56, pres. 1956-57) bankers assns., Nat. Indsl. Conf. Bd., Soc. Indsl. Realtors (award bd.), Nat. Planning Assn. (nat. council), Newcomen Soc., Ga. Agrl. and Indsl. Devel. Bd.(adv. com. 1944-45), Internat. C. of C. (trustee U.S. council), Alpha Tau Omega. Baptist. Clubs: Capital City, Piedmont Driving (Atlanta); Nat. Press (Washington). Home: 2637 Peachtree Rd NE Atlanta GA 30305 Office: 127 Peachtree St NE Atlanta GA 30303

COCKE, JOHN B., banker. Sr. v.p., trust officer First Nat. Exchange Bank Va. Office: 201 S Jefferson St Roanoke VA 24010*

COCKE, JOSEPH GARBER, hosp. supt.; b. Livingston, Ala., Sept. 21, 1905; s. William Thompson and Bessie (Browder) C.; B.A., U. Ala., 1926; M.D., Jefferson Med. Coll., Phila., 1930; m. Violet Delaplane Hoile, June 5, 1933; children—Joseph Garber, William Browder. Intern, Employees' Hosp., Tenn. Coal, Iron & R.R. Co., Fairfield, Ala., 1930-31, resident 1931-33; commd. 2d lt., M.C., U.S. Army, 1933, advanced through grades to col., 1944; staff surgeon U.S. Army Command at retirement; ret., 1961; ward physician San Antonio State Hosp., 1961-67, asst. supt., 1967-69, acting supt., 1969-70, supt., 1970—; adminstrv. cons. Sid Peterson Meml. Hosp., Kerrville, Tex., 1962-64. Bd. dirs. Mental Health Assn. Bexar County. Decorated Legion of Merit with two oak leaf clusters, French Croix de Guerre with palm. Mem. A.M.A., Tex. Med. Assn., Bexar County Med. Soc., Bexar County Psychiat. Soc., Am. Psychiat. Assn. (asso.), Theta Kappa Psi, Alpha Omega Alpha, Alpha Epsilon Delta (founder mem.). Home: 422 Laramie St San Antonio TX 78209 Office: 5900 S Presa St San Antonio TX 78223

COCKER, JOHN R., banker. Vice pres., cashier Riggs Nat. Bank, Washington. Office: 1503 Pennsylvania Av NW Washington DC 20013*

COCKETT, JAMES HARRISON, resort hotel mgr.; b. Maui, Hawaii, Dec. 16 1924; s. J. Pia and Mary (Kekahu) C.; grad. Kamahameha Sch. Boys, 1944; m. Darlene Mae Brimhall, Jan 9, 1953; children—James Randall, Wendy Malia. Asst. mgr. Royal Hawaiian Hotel, 1956-59; catering and sales mgr. Moana Surfrider Hotel, 1959-62; exec. asst. mgr. Sheraton Maui Hotel, 1962-64; mgr. Moana Surfrider Hotels, 1964—, Mem. Hawaii Hotel Assn. Mem. Ch. of Jesus Christ of Latter-day Saints, Rotarian. Address: 2635 Kalakaua Av Honolulu HI 96815

COCKLE, JOHN ROBINSON, lawyer; b. Omaha, June 2, 1921; s. Albert L. and Eda (Marquardt) C.; A.B., U. Neb., 1942; LL.B., Creighton U., 1947; m. Barbara York, Feb. 19, 1943; children—Sally Y., John Robert, Laura L., Mary T. Admitted to Neb. bar, 1947; asso. firm Brown, Crossman, West, Barton & Quinlan, Omaha, 1947-50; partner firm Neely, Otis & Cockle, Omaha, 1950-53; with trust dept. Omaha Nat. Bank, 1953-67, v.p., 1960-67; v.p. charge trust dept. Marine Nat. Exchange Bank, Milw., 1968-70, sr. v.p., 1970—. Served with USAAF, 1942-46. Mem. Am., Wis., Milw. bar assns., Wis. Trustees Assn. Rotarian. Clubs: Milw. Country, Univ. (Milw.). Home: 9515 N Sequoia Dr Milwaukee WI 53217 Office: 1 Marine Plaza Milwaukee WI 53201

COCKREL, CLEMENT LEE, editor; b. Elfie, Ky., Oct. 29, 1925; s. Allison and Lou (Smith) C.; B.A., U. Ky., 1950; m. Margaret L. Ferrell, June 15, 1952; children—Edward Lee, Christopher Bryan, Martha Ann. Radio-television broadcasting prior to 1966; marketing specialist Watt Pub. Co., Mt. Morris, Ill., 1966-67; editor Tenn. Farmer mag. So. Farm Publs., 1967-68, editor Tenn. Farmer and N.C. Grower, 1968-69, editor Tenn. Farmer and Ky. Farmer, 1969-70, editor Tenn. and Ky. Farmer, mng. editor So. Farm Publs., Nashville, 1970—. Crusade chmn. Warren County chpt. Am. Cancer Soc., 1964-65, Ky. bd. dirs., 1965-66. Served with USNR, 1944-46; PTO. Named Ky. col. Republican. Baptist. Mason, Kiwanian. Home: 1531 Ridgecrest St Bowling Green KY 42101 Office: 3405 West End Av Nashville TN 37212

COCKRELL, JAMES O., utility exec.; b. 1921; student William and Mary Coll.; B.S., U. N.C., 1941; married. Sr. asst. accountant Haskins & Sells, 1951-53; accountant Piedmont Natural Gas Co., Charlotte, N.C., 1953-58, asst. sec., asst. treas., 1958-65, treas., 1965-70, controller, 1970—. Served with USAF, 1941-45. Office: 4301 Yancey Rd Charlotte NC 28210*

COCKRILL, JOHN LONG, electronics firm exec.; b. Quincy, Ill., Aug. 6, 1920; s. Lowell E. and Anna Josephine (Lillard) C.; B.A., State U. Ia., 1941, J.D., 1942; m. Ellen Virginia Schocke, Aug. 22, 1942; children—Joanne (Mrs. Paul K. Vetterick), John Lawrence. With Wilson & Co., Inc., Chgo., 1943-67, v. p. law, tax, real estate and ins., indsl. relations, casualty, med., retirement and group ins. divs., 1959-63, v.p. plant operating, engring., quality control, indsl. relations, casualty, med., retirement and group ins. divs., 1963-65, exec. v.p. adminstrn., 1965-67; v.p. adminstrn. Ling-Temco Vought, Inc., 1967-69; pres., chief exec. officer LTV Ling Altec, Inc., 1969—, also dir.; dir. Staco, Inc.; chmn., dir. Tamar Electronics Industries, Inc., 1969—. Admitted to Ia. bar, 1942, Ill. bar, 1945. Mem. S.W. regional manpower adv. com. U.S. Dept. Labor, Health, Edn. and Welfare, 1969-71; adv. council tech.- vocational edn. State Tex., 1969—. Mem. Nat. Alliance Businessmen (regional exec. 1968), Delta Chi. Presbyn. Mason. Clubs: Preston Trails Golf, Lancers (Dallas); Midlothian Country. Home: 5832 Lupton Dr Dallas TX 75225 Office: First Bank and Trust Bldg Richardson TX 75080

CODD, LEE A., assn. exec.; b. Balt., Apr. 20, 1895; s. John and Amelia (Dittmar) C.; A.B., Loyola, 1916; A.M. Georgetown U., 1923, LL.B., 1922, LL.M., 1923, L.H.D., 1964; m. Gertrude Jane Callahan, Dec. 27, Asst. sec. Am. Ordnance Assn., 1923, sec., 1928, exec. v.p., 1940-64; editor Ordnance mag., 1928-65, contbg. editor, 1965—; instr., Georgetown Coll, 1917, Cyrus Fogg Brackett lectr., Princeton, 1937. Served as chemist, Ordnance Dept., U.S. Army, World War 1; exec. asst. to chief of ordnance, AUS, World War 11; capt., Ordnance Res., 1920, col. 1943—. Decorated Legion of Merit. Mem D.C., Md. bar assns. Roman Catholic. Clubs: Army and Navy (Washington); University (N.Y.). Author: American Industry and the National Defense, 1937. Lectr. in U.S., Can. and Eng. Home: 1637 35th St NW Washington DC 20007 Office: Transp Bldg Washington DC 20006

CODDINGTON, EARL ALEXANDER educator, mathematician; b. Washington, Dec. 16 1920; s. Cyrus Alexander and Lillian (Dezarn) C.; Ph.D., Johns Hopkins, 1948; m. Susan Klaber, Nov. 17, 1945; children—Alan Alexander, Robert Henry, Claire Helen. Instr., Johns Hopkins, 1948-49; instr. Mass. Inst. Tech., 1949-50, C.L.E. Moore instr.,1950-52; mem. faculty U. Cal. at Los Angeles, 1952- -, prof. math., 1959—, chmn. math. dept., 1968-71; Fulbright lectr. U. Copenhagen (Denmark), 1955-56, vis. prof., 1963-64; vis. asso. prof. Princeton 1957-58. Mem. sci. adv. com. Cal. State Coll. at Fullerton, 1964—. Mem. Am. (coop. editor proc. 1952-55, coop. editor trans. 1957-62), Danish math. socs., Math. Assn. Am., Am. Assn. U. Profs., A.A.A.S., Phi Beta Kappa, Sigma Xi. Author: (with N. Levinson) Theory of Ordinary Differential Equations, 1955; An Introduction to Ordinary Differential Equations, 1961. Cons. editor math. Holden-Day, Inc., 1960—. Home: 764 Wildomar St Pacific Palisades CA 90272 Office: Math Dept Univ California Los Angeles CA 90024

CODDINGTON, GILBERT HAROLD, architect; b. Conover, O., Feb. 6, 1907; s. C. Harvey and Maude (Wolcott) C.; B.Arch., B.Archtl. Engring., Ohio State U., 1931; student Lake Forest Found. Arch. and Landscape Arch., 1931; M. Arch., Columbia, 1932; m. Loise Hazen, Apr. 28, 1937 (dec. Nov. 1969); 1 son, Thomas Tucker; m. 2d, Mary Elizabeth Ackerman, May 30, 1970. Designer, delineator Lloyd Morgan Yost, 1945; designer Daniel Karmichael, 1946; with firm Brooks & Coddington, architects, Columbus, O., 1946-68; prin. archtl. works include the Dresser Industries, Inc. exhbn. bldg. for Internat. Petroleum Expn., Tulsa, 1958, St. Stephens Episcopal Ch., Columbus, 1950, Garfield Elementary Sch., 1953, St. Marks Episcopal Ch., 1955, Vorys Bros., Inc., warehouse office, 1956, Bell Sound div. Thompson Ramo Wooldridge, Inc., factory and office bldg., Worthington, O., 1961, also 1st Congl. Ch., Ohio High Sch. Athletic Assn. Office bldg., Pres.'s house Ohio Wesleyan U., Delaware, 1961—. Trustee Urbana Coll. Fellow A.I.A. (pres. Columbus chpt. 1949); mem. Architects Soc. Ohio (pres. 1961), Tau Beta Pi, Tau Sigma Delta. Club: Torch (Columbus, O.) Home: 286 W Southington Av Worthington OH 43085

CODE, ARTHUR DODD, educator; b. Bklyn., Aug. 13 1923; s. Lorne Arthur and Jessica (Dodd) C.; M.S., U. Chgo., 1947; Ph.D. in Astronomy and Astrophysics, 1950; m. Mary Ella Guild, Oct 9, 1943; children—Alan D., Douglas Merritt, Edith Louise, David Arthur. Research asst. Yerkes Obs., 1946-49; inst. astron. U. Va., 1949-50; faculty U. Wis. 1951-56, 58—, prof. astronomy, chmn. dept., 1958-70, Joel Stebbins prof. astronomy, 1970—, dir. Washburn Obs. of univ., 1958—; asso. prof. astronomy Cal. Inst. Tech., also mem. staff Mt. Wilson and Palomar Obs., 1956-58; spl. research photoelectric spectrophotometry of stars and galaxies, space astronomy. Served with USNR, 1943-46. Recipient Pub. Service award NASA, 1970; Profl. Achievement award U. Chgo. Alumni Assn., 1970. Mem. Am. Astron. Soc., A.A.A.S., Nat. Acad. Sci., Sigma Xi. Home: 2813 Mason St Madison WI 53705

CODE, CHARLES FREDERICK, educator; b. Winnipeg, Man., Can., Feb. 1, 1910; s. Abraham and Gertrude Casilda (Drewry) C.; prep. edn. St. John's Coll. Boys' Sch., Winnipeg, 1918-26; B.Sc., M.D., U. Man., 1934; Ph.D., U. Minn., 1940; m. Gwendolyn Irene Bond, Dec. 30, 1935; children—Gwendolyn D., Carla Radford, Allan. Came to U.S., 1934. Fellow in physiology and clin. med., Mayo Found., Rochester, Minn., 1934-37, 1st asst. in exptl. surgery and physiology, 1937; lectr. physiology, U. Coll., U. London, Eng., 1935, 36; instr. in physiology, U. Minn. Med. Sch.; faculty Mayo Found.-U. Minn., 1939—, successivley asst. prof., 1939, asso. prof., 1942, prof. physiology, 1946—. Cons. physiology Mayo Clinic, 1940—, dir. med. edn. and research, 1966—, past mem. bd. govs. clinic. Engaged in War Aviation Medical Research, 1943-46. Recipient Physiol. Research prize and gold medal U. Man., 1930; Bayliss-Starling meml. scholar U. London 1936; Theobald Smith medal and award in med. science A.A.A.S., 1938. Mem. Am. Physiol. Soc., Physiol. Soc. Eng., Am. Soc. Clin. Investigation, Soc. Exptl. Biology and Medicine, Am. Fedn. Clin. Research, Central Soc. Clin. Research, Assn. Am. Physicians, Am. Gastroent. Assn. (pres. 1964-65), Sigma Xi, Zeta Psi. Episcopalian. Clubs: Royal Lake of the Woods Yacht (Kenora, Ont); Campus University of Minnesota; Balboa (Mazatlan, Mexico). Co-author: Atlas of Esophagial Motility in Health and Disease; Contbr. sci. papers in field. Address: The Mayo Foundation 200 First St SW Rochester MN 55901

CODE, JAMES A., Jr., telephone co. exec., ret. army officer; b. San Francisco, Jan 17, 1893; s. James Arthur and Katherine (Shaw) C.; B.S., U.S. Mil. Acad., 1917; M.S., Yale, 1920, E.E., 1933; postgrad. Ohio State U., 1920-23, U. Cal., 1934-38; m. Isabelle Elizabeth Black, Jan. 17, 1929. Commd. 2d lt., C.A.C., U.S. Army, 1917, and advanced to capt., 1930; maj. S. C., 1932, lt. col., 1940, col., 1941; brig. gen., dep. chief signal officer, 1942, maj. gen., asst. chief signal officer, 1942-45; chief signal officer, ETO (France), 1945; ret. 1945. Chmn. bd. Telephone Services, Inc.; dir., v.p. Asso. Tel. & Tel. Co. (Wilmington, Del.); chief exec. Gary Group; v.p., dir. Anglo-Canadian Telephone Co., Automatic Elec. Co. (1946), Internat. Automatic Elec. Corp., Pan-Am. Tel. & Tel. Co., Continental Telephone Co., Dominican Dir. Co., Can., Tex., Home and Citizens Telephone Cos., Allied Syndicate, Inc., Gen. and Telephone Investments, Inc., Ohio Consol., Ill. Telephone Co.; v.p., dir. Gary Services and Investment Co., Tel. Bond & Share Co., Linwood Investment Co., Antel Services, Ltd., Asso. Telephone Services Ltd.; dir. various other telephone cos.; v.p., trustee Pt. Roberts & Gulf Telephone Co.; cons. Automatic Electric Co., Diablo Labs., 1963, Lenkurt Electric Co., 1959. Decorated Bronze Star medal, D.S.M.; Croix de Guerre, L'Ordre de la Legion d'Honneur (France), Commandeur de l' Ordre de la Couroune (Belgium). Asso. mem. Am. Inst. E.E.; sr. mem. Inst. Radio Engrs.; mem. Armed Forces Commn., Am. Soc. Legion of Honor, West Point Soc., Yale Alumni Assn., Army Athletic Assn., Assn. Grads. U.S.M.C., Am. Signal Corps Assn., Am. Legion, Mil. Order of World Wars, S.A.R., Scabbard and Blade, Pi Tau, Pi Sigma. Republican. Episcopalian. Clubs: Olympic; Army and Navy; Lake Shore; South Shore Country; Chicago; University. Address: 1386 Dana Av Palo Alto CA 94301 ☆

CODE, WILLIAM E., lawyer; b. Gadsby, Alta., Can., Nov. 20, 1932; B.A., U. Alta., 1953, LL.B., 1956. Admitted to Alta. bar, 1957; partner firm Fenerty, McGillivray, Robertson, Prowse, Brennan, Fraser, Bell & Code, Calgary, Alta. Mem. Law Soc. Alta., Canadian, Clagary bar assns. Office: 1500 Guinness House Calgary 2 Alberta Canada*

CODER, RALPH VERNON, ret. educator; b. La Belle, Mo., Aug. 19, 1904; s. James T. and Margaret Ann (Dailey) C.; A.B., William Jewell Coll., 1926; M.A., U. Ia., 1936, Ph. D., 1941; m. Virginia Hall, Aug. 6, 1930 (dec. Oct. 9, 1936); m. 2d, Edna B. Triplett, Apr. 5, 1943. Prin., supt., instr. small schs., Ia., 1929-39; chmn., instr. English dept. Ft. Hays (Kan.) State Coll., 1941-52, chmn. grad. div., 1950-69, chmn. humanities div., 1946-62. Served as capt. AUS, 1943-45. Mem. N.E.A., Kan. State Tchrs. Assn., Nat. Council Tchrs. English, Kan. Assn. English Tchrs., Phi Gamma Delta. Rotarian. Home: 526 W 27th St Hays KS 67601

CODER, SAMUEL MAXWELL, educator, clergyman; b. Straight, Pa., Mar. 25, 1902; s. Emmanuel Miller and Abbie Mary (Bailey) C.; student Evang. Theol. Coll., Dallas, 1932- 35; B.S., Temple U., 1938; Th.B., Dallas Theol. Sem. 1938; Th.M., 1940; D.D., Bible Theol. Sem. of Los Angeles, 1949; m. Elizabeth Maria Dieterle, Feb. 20, 1932; children—Margaret Elizabeth (dec.), Maxine Joyce, Donald Maxwell. Bus. exec., 1928-32; ordained to ministry Presbyn. Ch., 1938; pastor, Grace Ch, Camden, N.J. 1935-38, Chelsea Ch., Atlantic City, N.J., 1938-43, Evangel Ch., Phila., 1944-45; mem. faculty Moody Bible Inst., Chgo., 1945, v.p. and dean edn., 1947-69, now emeritus, editor in chief, Moody Press, 1946, also gen. editor, The Wycliffe Series of Christian Classics 1950—. Republican. Author: Youth Triumphant, 3 vols., Moody Corr. Course, 1946; Dobbie, Defender of Malta, 1946; God's Will for Your Life, 1950; Jude: the Acts of the Apostates, 1955. Editor: Memoirs of McCheyne, 1947; Our Lord Prays for His Own, 1950; The World to Come, 1954. Contbr. to religious jours. Home: 1860 Sherman Av Evanston IL 60201 Office: 820 N La Salle St Chicago IL 60610

CODERE, HELEN FRANCES, educator, anthropologist; b. Winnipeg, Can., Sept. 10, 1917; d. Charles Francis and Mabelle (Prosser) Codere; came to U.S., 1919, naturalized, 1924; B.A. summa cum laude, U. Minn., 1939; Ph.D., Columbia, 1950. Instr., Vassar Coll, 1946-50, asst. prof., 1951-53, asso. prof. 1955-57, prof., 1958-63; vis. lectr. anthropology U.B.C., 1954-55, Northwestern U., winter 1963; mem. faculty Bennington Coll., 1963-64; prof. anthropology Brandeis U., 1964—; anthrop. fieldwork Kwakiutl Indians of B.C., 1951-55, Rwanda, Africa 1959-60. Faculty fellow Vassar Coll., 1956; Social Sci. Research Council fellow, 1956, 62-63; Guggenheim fellow, 1959-60. Fellow Am. Anthrop. Assn. (exec. council 1966-69), A.A.A.S., African Studies Assn., N.Y. Acad. Scis., Phi Beta Kappa. Author: Fighting with Property; a study of Kwakiutl Potlatching and Warfare, 1792-1930, 1950; also articles. Editor: Kawkiutl Enography (Franz Boas), 1966. Office: Dept Anthropology Brandeis U Waltham MA 02154

CODERRE, GERARD MARIE, bishop; b. St. Jacques de Montcalm, Que., Can., Dec. 19 1904; s. Ovide and Marie Louise (Beliveau) C.; B.A., U. Montreal, 1927, L.Th., 1931, Bachelier en droit Canon, 1931, certificat en Historie Universelle et en langue grecque, 1933. Ordained priest Roman Catholic Ch., 1931; bishop of St. Jean, Que., Can., 1955—. Home: 210 Labonté Longqueuil Quebec Canada Office: 1530 Blvd Tremblay Longqueuil Quebec Canada

CODNER, BERNARD, business exec.; b. 1928; B.A., M.B.A., Coll. City N.Y.; married. With Big Apple Supermarkets Inc., until 1969; v.p., controller Allied Maintenance Corp., 1969—. Office: Allied Maintenance Corp Pennsylvania Plaza New York City NY 10001*

CODRARO, LAWRENCE FREDERICK, watch co. exec.; b. Bklyn., Apr. 27 1926; s. Natale and Frances (Cerasuolo) C.; B.S., Fordham U., 1946, J.D., 1950; LL.M., N.Y. U., 1961. Admitted to N.Y. bar, 1950; atty. N.Y. Ordnance Dist., 1951-56, Mergenthaler Linotype Co., 1956-58; with Bulova Watch Co., Inc., 1958—, asst. counsel, 1958—, corp. sec. 1967—. Mem. Kings County Republican Law Com., 1968—. Served with AUS, 1946-47. Home: 149 Marine Av Brooklyn NY 10029 Office: 630 Fifth Av New York City NY 10020

CODRESCU, ANDREI, author: b. Sibiu, Transylvania, Rumania, Dec. 20, 1946; s. Julius Szegety and Eva (Geller) C.; B.A. in Math., U. Rome, 1966; m. Alice Terril Henderson, Sept. 19, 1969; 1 son, Lucian. Came to U.S., 1966, naturalized, 1971. Narrator revolutionary mysteries. Mem. Dada Council for World Revolution. Author: License to Carry A Gun, 1970 (winner Big Table award for Younger Poets, 1970), 7 Romanian Poets, 1971; editor (with Tom Veitch) Planet News, bi-monthly jour., 1970—. Address: 119 Lowell St San Francisco CA 94112

CODVILLE, BRUCE H., business exec. Pres., Codville Distbrs., Ltd., Winnipeg, Man., Can. Office: 140 Otter St Winnipeg Manitoba 19 Canada*

CODY, DONALD DAVID, actuary; b. Hartford, Conn., Aug. 10, 1913; s. David J. and Ellen (Murphy) C.; A.B. summa cum laude in Math., Harvard, 1934, courses in electronics Columbia; m. Thamas Eve Ritchie, Oct. 12, 1940; children—Susan Eve (Mrs. Robert Wrenn Freeman), Diane Margot (Mrs. Alan Loyd Beaurline). Asso. actuary Equitable Life Assurance Soc., 1934-50; 2d v.p. N.Y. Life Ins. Co., N.Y.C., 1951-62, group actuary, 1951-64, v.p., 1961-67; sr. v.p. New Eng. Mut. Life Ins. Co., ind. ins. operation, 1967- -. With NDRC, 1942, Naval Ordnance Plant, Indpls., also Naval Ordnance Test Sta., Cal., 1943-45. Vis. com. math. dept. Harvard, 1969—; exec. mgmt. program Columbia U., 1968—. Recipient Naval Ordnance Devel. award for exceptional service, 1945. Fellow Soc. Actuaries; mem. N.Y. Health Ins. Assn. (chmn. actuarial com. 1963-66), Phi Beta Kappa. Club: Actuaries of New York (pres. 1966-67). Home: Walpole St Dover MA 02030 Office: 501 Boylston St Boston MA 02117

CODY, HIRAM SEDGWICK, Jr., mfg. co. exec.; b. Evanston Ill., Nov. 1, 1915; s. Hiram Sedgwick and Harriett Mary (Collins) C.; B.S. cum laude, Yale, 1937, LL.B., 1940; m. Mary Vaughn Jacoby, Oct. 4, 1941; children—Margaret Vaughn, Harriett Mary, Hiram Sedgwick III, Henry Jacoby, William Collins. With Western Electric Co., Inc., 1946-71, regional mgr. engring. and installation, Chgo., 1961-64, dir. orgn. planning, N.Y.C., 1964-65, sec., treas., 1965-71; asst. treas. Am. Tel. & Tel. Co., N.Y.C., 1971—. Admitted to N.C. bar, 1940. Vice pres. Morris- Sussex council Boy Scouts Am., Mountain Lakes (N.J.) Pub. Library. Mem. Zoning Bd. Adjustment Mountain Lakes; boro councilman, Mountain Lakes, N.J. 1960-61. Served to comdr. USNR, 1941-46. Mem. Am. Soc. Corporate Secs. (treas. N.Y. chpt. 1968-69), N.C. State Bar, Telephone Pioneers Am. (v.p. 1969-71, treas. 1971—), Tau Beta Pi. Home: 50 Dartmouth Rd Mountain Lakes NJ 07046 Office: 195 Broadway New York City NY 10007

CODY, JOHN CARDINAL, Clergyman; Ordained, 1931; aux. bishop Diocese St. Louis, 1947-54; co- adjutor with right of succession to bishop of St. Joseph, Mo., 1954; bishop of St. Joseph, 1955; coadjutor to Archbishop-Bishop of Kansas City-St. Joseph, Aug., 1956; bishop of Kansas City-St. Joseph, Oct. 1956; coadjutor with right of succession to Archdiocese New Orleans, 1961, apostolic adminstr., 1962-64; archbishop New Orleans 1964; archbishop Chgo., 1965—, elevated to Sacred Coll. of Cardinals, 1967. Mem. Congregation for Divine Worship, Sacred Congregation for Evangelization Nations, Sacred Congregation Clergy; chancellor Cath. Ch. Extension Soc.; nat. chaplain Nat. Cath. Soc. Foresters; high spiritual dir. Cath. Order Foresters. Mem. regional bd. Boy Scouts Am. Mem. N.Am. Coll. Alumni Assn., Nat. Conf. Cath. Bishops. Address: 1555 N State Pkwy Chicago IL 60610

CODY, JOSEPH JULIUS, Jr., air force officer; b. San Antonio, Feb. 13, 1918; s. Joseph J. and Hazel E. (Wright) C.; B.S., St. Mary's U., 1940; m. Elizabeth Lorraine Burns, July 13, 1956; children—Patricia Ann, Mary Catherine. Commd. 2d lt. USAAF, 1940, advanced through grades to maj. gen. USAF, 1965; with 70th Fighter Wing, 1942-46; assigned U.S. bases, 1946-50; chief spl. projects 1009th Spl. Weapons Squadron, 1950-52; assigned Hdqrs. ARDC, 1952-56, 58; student Air War Coll, 1956-57; comdr. 6595th Aerospace Test Wing, 1958-63; vice comdr., space systems Div. AFSC, 1963-64; chief staff AFSC, 1964-65; dep. chief staff systems Hdqrs. AFSC, 1965- 67; chief staff Hdqrs. AFSC 1967-68; comdr. Electronic Systems Dir., Bedford, Mass., 1968—. Decorated Legion of Merit with 3 oak leaf clusters, Bronze Star, Air medal, Commendation medal with oak leaf cluster. Mem. Soc. Am. Mil. Engrs. Home: Andrews Rd Hanscom Field Bedford MA 01730 Office: Hdqrs Electronic Systems Dir (AFSC) Hanscom Field MA 01730

CODY, MORRILL, radio cons.; b. Lake Forest, Ill., Apr. 10, 1901; s. Sherwin and Marian Theresa (Hurley) C.; A.B., Amherst Coll, 1921; m. Frances Ryan, Mar. 2, 1922 (div.); 1 son Peter Malcolm; m. 2d, Marian Holbrook, Jane 1, 1935 (dec.); 1 dau., Judith Alden (Mrs. Larry Gleeson); m. 3d, Verna Feuerhelm, Feb. 7, 1953 (dec.); m. 4th, Jane Hoster, Nov. 3, 1960; 1 dau., Gabrielle. Fgn. corr., 1924-34; editor, 1934-41; cultural attache, Asuncion, Paraguay, 1941-45, Buenos Aires, 1945-46; cultural attache, 2d sec., Mexico City, 1946-48; assigned Dept. State Wash., 1948-50; information liaison officer Am. embassy, Paris, 1950-53; pub. affairs officer, Stockholm, 1951; 1st sec. Am. embassy, Madrid, Spain, 1953-55; counsellor Am. embassy for pub. affairs, Paris, 1955-61; asst. dir. USIA, Washington, 1961-63; con. Radio Liberty, N.Y., Paris, 1963-65, bur. mgr. Paris office, 1965—. Served with U.S. Army, 1918. Club: Overseas Press (N.Y.C.). Author: This Must be the Place, 1934; Passing Stranger, 1936; Hemingway's Paris, 1965; The Favorite Restaurants of an American in Paris, 1966. Home: 185 rue de Vaugirard Paris, France. also Wanakena NY 13695 Office: 122 rue de Rennes Paris France

CODY, PETER MALCOLM, fgn. service officer; b. Paris, France, July 30, 1925; s. Morrill and Frances (Ryan) C. B.A., Yale, 1947, M.A., 1948; m. Rosa Maria Alatorre, Jan. 28, 1957; children—Michael Peter, William Ryan, Peter Malcolm, Cornelia Francisca, Cecilia Lenor. Instr. econs. Yale, 1948-50; economist Fed. Res. Bd., 1950-54; with fgn. aid program State Dept., 1954—; program economist, Mexico, 1954-57; program officer, El Salvador, 1957-59; Laos affairs officer, 1959-61; dep. dir., Cambodia, 1961-64, Laos, 1965-67; dir. Office Vietnam Affairs, 1964-65; dir., Paraguay, 1967-71, Ecuador, 1971—. Bd. dirs. Am. Sch., Vientiane, Laos, 1965-67, Am. Sch., Asuncion, Paraguay, 1969-71, BiNat. Cultural Center, 1968-70. Served to ensign USNR, 1943-46. Fellow Yale, 1946-50. Mem. Am. Econs. Assn., Am. Fgn. Service Assn. Club: Quito Tennis. Home: Francisco Andrade Marin 281 Quito Ecuador Office: Quito ID State Dept Washington DC 20521

CODY, WELBORN BUTT, lawyer; b. Atlanta, 1899; s. William Butt and Leila (Butt) C.; A.B., LL.B., U. Ga., 1922; postgrad. law Columbia; m. Marjorie Lewis, Aug. 12, 1942; 1 dau., Carolyn. Admitted to Ga. bar, 1921; partner Kilpatrick, Cody, Rogers, McClathay & Regenstein, Atlanta, 1936—; dir. Fox Mfg. Co. Trustee Westminster Schs. Mem. Phi Delta Phi, Kappa Sigma. Democrat. Presbyn. Clubs: Piedmont Driving, Capital City (Atlanta). Home: 3543 Woodhaven Rd NW Atlanta GA 30305 Office: 1045 Hurt Bldg Atlanta GA 30303

COE, BENJAMIN PLAISTED, vol. orgn. exec.; b. Long Beach, Cal., Aug. 24, 1930; s. Benjamin and Mary Plaisted (Ricker) C.; A.B., Bowdoin Coll., 1953; B.S., Mass. Inst. Tech., 1954; m. Margaret Jane Butler, Sept. 5, 1953; children—Benjamin B., Elizabeth C., Mary Susan, Margaret Jane. With silicone products dept. Gen. Elec. Co., Waterford, N.Y., 1953-65, process econs. engr., 1955-65; exec. dir. Vols. for Internat. Tech. Assistance, Schenectady, 1965-68, U.S.A. div., 1969—. Dir. Schenectady Symphony, 1969. Licensed profl. engr., N.Y. Mem. Am. Inst. Chem. Engrs. (chmn. N.E. N.Y. sect. 1965), Nat. Assn. Community Devel., Phi Beta Kappa, Sigma Xi, Tau Beta Pi. Episcopalian. Club: Rotary (Schenectady). Home: 1169 Ardsley Rd Schenectady NY 12308 Office: VITA Inc Union College Campus Schenectady NY 12308

COE, CHARLES NORTON, coll. adminstr., educator; b. Rahway, N.J., Apr. 29, 1915; s. Maxwell Alanson and Ethel May (Norton) C.; B.A. cum laude, Amherst Coll., 1937; M.A., Trinity Coll. (Conn.), 1940; Ph.D., Yale, 1950; m. Elizabeth Brown, July 11, 1953; children—Timothy Maxwell, Dorothy Elizabeth. Instr. English and Latin, Williston (Mass.) Acad., 1937-39; asst. English, Trinity Coll., 1939-47; headmaster Williston Jr. Sch., 1947-48; asst. prof. English, U. Ida., 1948-51, asso. prof., 1951- 54, prof., head dept. humanities,

1954-59; prof. English, dean Grad. Sch. No. Ill. U. 1959-64; prof. English, provost Monmouth Coll., West Long Branch, N.J., 1964-66, v.p., acad. affairs, 1966—. dir. grad. programs, 1967—. Served with AUS, 1943-46. Mem. Nat., N.J. edn. assns., Modern Lang. Assn., Nat. Council Tchrs. English, Coll. English Assn., Phi Beta Kappa, Alpha Phi Omega, Phi Kappa Psi, Phi Delta Kappa. Episcopalian. Author: Wordsworth and the Literature of Travel, 1953; Shakespeare's Villains, 1957; Demi-devils; The Character of Shakespeare's Villains, 1963. Home: 3 Southern Dr New Shrewsbury NJ 07701 Office: Monmouth Coll West Long Branch NJ 07764

COE, FRED HAYDEN, TV and theatre producer, film dir.; b. Alligator, Miss., Dec. 23, 1914; s. Frederick Hayden and Annette (Harroll) C.; student Peabody Coll. for Tchrs.; student fine arts, Yale; children—John Hayden, Laurence Anne, Sue Anne, Samuel Hayden; m. 2d, Joyce Beeler, Aug. 1, 1952. Producer, dir. NBC-TV, 1947-57, Philco-Goodyear Playhouse, Mr. Peepers, Producer's Showcase, CBS-TV, Playhouse 90, 1957-60; theatrical prodns. (N.Y.C); 1945—; Trip to Bountiful, Two For the Seesaw, The Miracle Worker, All The Way Home, Gideon, A Thousand Clowns, Wait Unitl Dark; motion picture prodns.: The Left Handed Gun, The Miracle Worker, A Thousand Clowns (also dir.), Me Natalie (also dir.). Recipient Peabody award, 1952-53. Office: 667 Madison Av New York City NY 10021

COE, MICHAEL DOUGLAS, anthropologist, educator; b. N.Y.C., May 14, 1929; s. William Rogers and Clover (Simonton) C.; A.B., Harvard, 1950, Ph.D., 1959; m. Sophie Dobzhansky, June 5, 1955; children—Nicholas, Andrew, Sarah, Peter, Natalie. Asst. prof. U. Tenn., 1958-60; mem. faculty Yale, 1960—, prof. anthropology, 1968—. Adviser, Robert Woods Bliss Collection Pre- Columbian Art, Dumbarton Oaks, Harvard, 1963—. Fellow Royal Anthrop. Soc., Am. Anthropol. Assn., A.A.A.S.; mem. Soc. Am. Archaeology. Author: La Victoria, An Early Site on the Pacific Coast of Guatemala, 1961; Mexico, 1962; The Jaguar's Children: Pre-Classic Art of Central Mexico, 1965; The Maya, 1966; (with Kent V. Flannery) Early Cultures and Human Ecology in South Coastal Guatemala, 1967; America's First Civilization, 1968. Contbr. articles profl. jours. Home: 376 St Ronan St New Haven CT 06511

COE, PAUL FRANCIS, demographer, economist; b. Horton, Kan., Oct. 29, 1909; s. Clarence Griffin and Laura (Blakely) C.; Ph.B., U. Chgo., 1932, postgrad., 1933-34; m. Evelyn Marie Eseman, Sept. 24, 1933; children—Lynn (Mrs. Malcolm E. Rhodes), Jean (Mrs. Charles A. Lacina), Laura (Mrs. Elvan L. Alyea). Complaint adjuster Mandel Bros., Chgo., 1932; office mgr. pvt. bus., Chgo., 1933-34; research asst. Fed. Emergency Relief Adminstrn., also WPA., Washington, 1934-37; economist FHA, Washington, 1938-39, economist and asst. chief Operating Statistics, 1939-42, economist. chief Operating Statistics, 1942-47, economist, analytical statistician, demographer, editor, 1947-65; dir. research Population Reference Bur., Washington, 1965-57; pvt. cons., 1967-69; statistician, spl. asst. housing div. Census Bur., Washington, 1969—. Mem. fed. com. standard met. statis. areas Exec. Office of Pres., 1950-65, participant interagy, adv. com. population and housing censuses of 1950, 60; mem. tech. com. on area definitions, 1960-65; mem. Population and Housing Census Users Conf., 1966. Chmn. U. Chgo. Arlington Alumni Fund dr., 1962, 63. Mem. Population Assn. Am., Lambda Alpha, Alpha Kappa Psi, Phi Kappa Sigma. Methodist (exec. com. 1960-62). Mason. Author: FHA Homes in Metropolitan Districts, 1934-40, 1942; numerous articles on econs., statistics, housing demography, marketing, Home: 601 N Buchanan St Arlington VA 22203 Office: Housing Division Census Bureau Washington DC 20233

COE, RICHARD LIVINGSTON, drama and film critic; b. N.Y.C., Nov. 8 1916; s. Elmer James Secor and Lillie Isabel (Musgrave) C.; student George Washington U., 1934-38; m. Christine Sadler, May 4, 1946. Radio editor asst. drama- film critic Washington Post, 1938-42, drama editor, film critic 1946—; critic for WRC-TV (NBC), 1969—; special US corr. Reynolds News, London, Eng., Egyptian Gazette, Cairo, Egypt, Guest lectr. Am. U., Cairo, Egypt; drama panel ANTA; staff Pres.'s Program for Cultural Exchange. Served as staff sgt. AUS, 1942-46; columnist, editor Middle East edit. Stars and Stripes. Recipient pub. service award Newspaper Guild, 1949; achievement award Gen. Fedn. Women's Clubs, 1957; award Washington Bd. Trade, 1957. D.C. Theater, 1957; Critic of Year award Dirs. Guild Am., 1963. Mem. Am. Newspaper Guild. Clubs: Nat. Press, Variety (Washington); Overseas Press, The Players (N.Y.C.). Home: 2713 Dumbarton Ave Washington DC 20007 Office: 1515 L St NW Washington DC 20005

COE, ROBERT NORMAN, utility exec.; b. Colton, Cal., Apr. 26 1911; s. George Lyman and Nellie (Archibald) C.; Elec. Engr., Internat. Corr. Schs., 1936; student Cal. Inst. Tech., 1942, 53, U. Cal. at Los Angeles, 1954, 60, U. So. Cal., 1956; m. Rhoda Moore, July 15, 1928; children—Robert E., Shirley (Mrs. William D. Hand). With So. Cal. Edison Co., 1929—, mgr. operations, 1957-65, v.p., 1965—. Pres. San Gabriel (Cal.) Valley Shrine Found., 1964—. Mem. I.E.E.E., Edison Electric Inst., Los Angeles C. of C. Mason (Shriner, Jester). Clubs: Los Angeles Electric, Glendora Country. Home: 540 N Segovia Av San Gabriel CA 91775 Office: 601 W 5th St Los Angeles CA 90017

COE, VINCENT, accountant; b. Youngstown, O., May 22, 1923; s. Harry Dean and Katherine (Edmunds) C.; B.S. in Bus. Adminstrn. cum laude, Ohio State U., 1947; m. Marybelle Semple, July 15, 1943. With Price Waterhouse & Co., C.P.A.'s 1947—, partner, 1960, with Tokyo, Japan br., 1961—, Served with AUS 1942-45; prisoner of war in Germany. Decorated Purple Heart. Bronze Star (2). Mem. Am. Inst. C.P.A.'s, La. Soc. C.P.A.'s, Fgn. C.P.A. Assn. Japan (exec. sec.), Am. C. of C. in Japan (chmn. taxation com. 1962-64, bd. govs. 1964—, pres. 1970), Beta Gamma Sigma, Beta Alpha Psi, Phi Delta Theta. Republican. Methodist. Club: Big Ten Univ. (pres. 1956-57), (New Orleans). Home Pine Manor 1-Ichigaya Nakanocho Shinjuku Tokyo Japan Office: Sempaku Shinko Bldg 35 Shiba Kotohira-cho Minatoku Tokyo Japan

COE, WILLIAM CHAMBERLAINE, investment banker; b. Newburg, N.Y., May 25, 1901; s. Frank Winston and Anne Dillard (Chamberlaine) C.; B.A., U.S. Mil. Acad., 1920; m. Katherine Keith Donnellan, Feb. 16, 1934; children—Anne (Mrs. Lambert Heyniger), Katherine (Mrs. Edmund S. Ruffin III), Linda C. Commd. 2d lt. U.S. Army, 1920, advanced through grades to 1st lt.; ret., 1926; mgr. Washington office Brooke, Stokes, 1930-39; partner Mackall & Coe, Washington, 1939—. Asso. mem. N.Y. Stock Exchange, 1949—. Mem. Assn. Stock Exchange Firms (regional gov.), Washington Bond Club (pres. 1949- 50). Office: 738 15th St Washington DC 20005

COE, WILLIAM ROGERS, found. exec.; b. N.Y.C., Mar. 22, 1901; s. William Robertson and Mai Huttleston (Rogers) C.; student U.S. Naval Acad., 1924; LL.D., U. Wyo., 1956; m. Clover Simonton, Mar. 31, 1923; children—William Robertson, II, Michael Douglas. With J.A. Sisto & Co., N.Y.C., 1923-24; r.r. security analyst Nat. City Co. of N.Y.C., 1923-34; head r.r. buying dept. Harriman Ripley & Co (formerly Brown, Harriman & Co.), 1934-41; v.p., dir. treas. Va. Ry. Co., N.Y.C., 1942-56, chmn. exec. com., 1956-60; pres. Planting Fields Found.; pres., trustee Coe Found. Clubs: Piping Rock (L.I.): Seawanhaka-Corinthian Yacht. Home: Shutter Lane Oyster Bay NY 11771 Office: Coe Found 225 E 57th St New York City NY 10022

COEN, ARTHUR BROWN, utilities exec.; b. Hazlehurst, Miss., Oct. 4, 1908; s. Claude C. and Mary (Hooker) C.; student Bowling Green Bus. U., 1925-26; m. Eva Simpson, Oct. 14, 1934; 1 son, Arthur Brown. With Ark. Power & Light Co., Pine Bluff, 1926—, asst. treas., 1960-62, treas., sec., 1962-71, v.p., 1966-71, treas., Little Rock, 1962-71; dir. Simmons First Nat. Bank. Mason (Shriner). Home: 1215 Beech St Pine Bluff AR 71601 Office: 9th and Louisiana Sts Little Rock AR 72203

COEN, ELEANOR, artist; b. Normall, Ill., Oct. 21 1916; d. John and Roslyn (Fritz) Coen; B.F.A., Art Inst. Chgo., 1941; m. Max Kahn, Dec. 4, 1942; children—Katie, Noah. Exhibited Art Inst. Chgo., Library of Congress, Smithsonian Inst., Bklyn., Phila., Carnegie and San Francisco museums, also traveling shows in Europe, Middle East, Japan, U.S.; works in permanent collections Art Inst. Chgo., Library of Congress, Carnegie Inst., Phila., Bklyn. and San Francisco museums. Mus. Modern Art (Brazil), Nat. Mus. (Sweden). Recipient awards San Francisco Mus., 1943, 46, Phila. Print Club, 1946, 48, 53, 56. Bklyn. Mus., 1948, 49, Northshore Art League, 1948, 52. Old N.W. Territory Exhbn., 1948, 49, 52, Library of Congress, 1951, 55, Am. Color Print Soc., 1951, 53, U. Ill., 1956, Print Club, 1952, Art Inst. Chgo., 1946, 47, 48, 49, 50, 51, 64; blue ribbon 2d Union League Art Competition 1957; Logan medal and 1st prize No-Jury Chgo. Show, 1957; Logan medal and 1st prize Chgo. and Vicinity Show, 1960. Address: 1759 N Cleveland St Chicago IL 60614

COEN, M.J., investment broker; b. Afton, Ia., Apr. 20, 1917; s. H. Vane and Violet (Gibson) C.; student St. Joseph Jr. Coll., 1936-38; B.S., Okla. State U., 1940; m. Dorothy Dodd, Apr. 22, 1949; children—Carolyn (Mrs. Jerome Bellinger), Eleanor Ann. Pres., owner Midland Securities Co., Inc., Kansas City, Mo., 1956-71; pres. First California Co., Inc., San Francisco and Kansas City, Mo., 1970—; chmn. bd. Golconda Corp.; chmn. bd. Fortuna Corp. Trustee Midwest Research Inst. Servd with USAAF, 1941-45. Mem. Kansas City C. of C. Mason (Shriner). Home: 1015 W Meyer Blvd Kansas City MO 64118 Office: 10 Main Center Upper Plaza Kansas City MO 64105

COERR, WYMBERLEY DERENNE, govt. ofcl.; b. N.Y.C., Oct. 2, 1913; s. Frederick Huntington and Audrey (DeRenne) C.; B.A., Yale, 1936, student, 1936-37; m. Janet Hill, Jan. 1, 1937; children—Susan DeRenne, Stanton Paine; m. 2d, Eleanor Page Hicks, June 10, 1965. Vice consul, Montreal, 1940; student Fgn. Service Sch., 1941; vice consul, La Ceiba 1941-43; 3d sec., vice consul, Mexico City, 1943; mgr. edn. dir. consumer coop. corps., Catasauqua, Pa., New Haven, 1944-46; assigned Dept. State, 1947; vice consul, Suva, 1947, Batavia, 1948, consul, 1949; 2d. sec., consul, Djakarta, 1950; assigned Dept. State, Office Philippine and Southeast Asian Affairs, 1950-53; first sec., Tegucigalpa, 1954, then dep. chief of mission, counselor of Am. Embassy, La Paz, Bolivia; dir. Office West Coast Affairs, Bur. Inter-Am. Affairs. Dept. of State, 1959-60, dep. asst. sec., Bur. Inter-Am. Affairs, 1960-62; ambassador to Uruguay, 1962-65; A.E. and P. to Ecuador, 1965-67; dir. Office Research and Analysis for Latin Am. Reps., 1969—. Conglist. Home: 5 Recard Lane Holl in Hills Alexandria VA 22307 Office: care State Dept Washington DC 20520

COERVER, HARRISON F., pres. Mercantile Trust Co. Nat. Assn. Address: 721 Locust St Saint Louis MO 63166

COES, KENT DAY, artist; b. Chgo., Feb. 14, 1910; s. Harold Vinton and Agnes Wickfield (Day) C.; student Grand Central Sch. Art, N.Y.C., 1928-32; Art Students League, N.Y.C., 1930-34, N.Y.U., 1935-38; m. Helen Elizabeth Stoll, May 29, 1937. Numerous group shows galleries and museums, U.S., Mexico City, Mex., and London, Eng., 1935—; represented watercolors permanent collections U. Pa., St. Vincent Coll., Latrobe, Pa., U. Scranton (Pa.), U. Wyo., Montclair (N.J.) Art Mus., Norfolk (Va.) Mus. Arts and Scis., Charles and Emma Frye Mus., Seattle, Holyoke (Mass.) Mus. Art, others, also pvt. and indsl. collections; mem. art staff publs. div. McGraw-Hill, Inc., 1947—; tchr. Montclair Art Mus., 1955, 60, E. Orange (N.J.) High Sch. Adult Edn. div., 1959, Bloomfield Art League, 1971. Served with F.A., AUS, 1943-46; ETO. Recipient awards watercolors Am. Watercolor Soc., N.J. Watercolor Soc., Balt. Watercolor Club, Acad. Artists Assn., Nat. Arts Club, N.Y.C.; Gold medal honor, Allied Artists Am., Hudson Valley Art Assn.; Rosenthal award Salmagundi Club. A.N.A. Mem. Am. (chmn. pub. relations com. 1956—), N.J. (founder-mem., pres. 1947-48) watercolor socs., Artists Fellowship (dir. 1961-65), Allied Artists Am. (v.p. 1961-63), Grand Central Galleries, Knickerbocker Artists, Acad. Artists Assn., Hudson Valley Art Assn., Am. Artists Group. Republican. Unitarian. Club: Salmagundi (N.Y.C.). Home: 463 Valley Rd Upper Montclair NJ 07043 Office: 330 W 42d St New York City NY 10036

COEY, JOHN SMILEY, chemist; b. Youngstown, O., July 17, 1914; s. Stewart Clark and Elizabeth Fyfe (Davidson) C.; grad. Deerfield Acad., 1933; B.A. cum laude, Amherst Coll., 1937; m. Florence F.W. Whitehead, June 24, 1939; 1 dau., Kathleen Clark; m. 2d, Marion Garden Robinson, July 3, 1945; children—John Smiley III, Edward Clark; m. 3d, Marian Emerson Allen, Oct. 3, 1959. With Hooker Chem. Corp., Niagara Falls, N.Y., 1939- -, successively supr. process study group, mgr. sales devel., Eastern sales mgr., 1939-58, v.p. Eastern chem. sales, 1958-59, v.p., gen. mgr. Eastern Chem. Div., 1959-65, group v.p., 1965—; dir. Chlorine Inst., Asso. Industries N.Y. State, Inc. Mem. Coml. Chem. Devel. Assn., Mfg. Chemists Assn. (pub. relations com.), Psi Upsilon. Presbyn. Clubs: Chemists (N.Y.C.); Manhattan; Silver Spring Country; Niagara Falls Country. Home: 85 Laurel Rd New Canaan CT 06840 Office: 1515 Summer St Stamford CT 06905

COFER, CHARLES NORVAL, psychologist; b. Cape Girardeau, Mo., June 1, 1916; s. Charles Norval and Ernestine (Osterloh) C.; A.B., S.E. Mo. State Coll., 1937; M.A., U. Ia., 1937; Ph.D., Brown U., 1940; m. Justine Marie Donnelly, Aug. 3, 1940; children—Thomas Michael, Jonathan Charles. Faculty George Washington U., 1941-47, asst. prof., 1946-47; faculty U. Md., College Park, 1947-59, prof. psychology, 1951-59; prof., dir. grad. studies in psychology N.Y.U., 1959-63; vis. prof. U. Cal. at Berkeley, 1962-63; prof. Pa. State U., University Park, 1963-67; prof., chmn. dept. psychology U. Md., College Park, 1967-68; prof. Pa. State U., 1968—. Mem. Am., D.C. (past pres.), Md. (past pres.), Eastern (past pres., dir. 1965-68) psychol. assns., Psychonomic Soc. (bd. govs. 1965-70), A.A.A.S. (council 1970—), Sigma Xi. Author: (with M.H. Appley) Motivation: Theory and Research, 1964; also numerous articles. Editor Psychol. Rev., 1965-70. Research in verbal learning and verbal behavior, basic associative processess, structure lang. as factor in relation to problem solving and thinking. Home: 439 Hillcrest Av State College PA 16801 Office: Psychology Bldg University Park PA 16802

COFFEE, JOSEPH DENIS, Jr., coll. adminstr.; b. Glens Falls, N.Y., Dec. 8, 1918; s. Joseph Denis and Kathryne Grace (Dwyer) C.; A.B., Columbia, 1941; m. Margaret Mary Jennings, Oct. 7, 1941; children—John Allan, James Jennings, Mary Joyce , Barbara Grace, Matthew Brian, Margaret Erin, Ann Ellen. Asst. to gen. sec. Columbia, 1946-50, dir. devel. Columbia Coll., N.Y.C., 1950- 60, asso. dean, 1959-60, asst. pres. for alumni affairs, 1960-66; v.p. Eisenhower Coll., Seneca Falls, N.Y., 1966-69, exec. v.p., 1969—. Dir. scholarship program Joint Industry Bd., Elec. Industry of N.Y.; exec. sec. Com. for Corporate Support Am. Univs., 1962-64; chmn. March Dimes campaign, Closter, N.J., 1953; active Boy Scout Am. treas., dir. Anglo-Am. Hellenic Bur. Edn.; cons. Nat. Center Citizens in Edn. Bd. dirs. Seneca County United Found.; trustee Teaneck Bd. Edn., 1961-64, 65-68; bd. dirs. Citizens Care Com., N.Y.C. Chmn., Teaneck Polit. Assembly, 1967-68. Served from ensign to lt. comdr. USNR, 1941-46; Mem. Seneca Falls Hist. Soc. (trustee), Psi Upsilon. Roman Catholic. Rotarian. Club: Columbia University (past pres.). Home: 83 Cayuga St Seneca Falls NY 13148

COFFEY, FRANCIS ALEXANDER, Irish diplomat; b. Waterford, Ireland, Dec. 28, 1920; s. Alexander and Margaret (Dawson) C.; student Waterpark Coll., Waterford; m. Marion Wolberg, Apr. 15, 1950; children—Brian J., Daniel S., Mary Alexandra. With Dept. of Def., Ireland, 1938-47; with Dept. External Affairs of Ireland, 1947—; 2d sec. Irish embassy, Washington, 1948-55, 1st sec., London, Eng., 1960-62; consul gen. in N.Y.C., 1966-70.

COFFEY, GILBERT HAVEN, Jr., physician, govt. ofcl.; b. Lackawanna, N.Y., Nov. 27, 1926; s. Gilbert Haven and Josephine (Caesar) C.; B.A., U. Buffalo, 1952, certificate in phys. therapy, 1955; M.D., Meharry Med. Coll., 1963; m. Madelyn Elizabeth Brewer, June 19, 1963; 1 dau., Denise E. Phys. therapist, chief Wayne County Gen. Hosp., Eloise, Mich., 1956-59; intern Wayne County Gen. Hosp., Eloise, Mich., 1963-64; resident VA Hosp., Buffalo, 1964-67, asst. chief phys. medicine and rehab. service, 1967-69, chief phys. medicine and rehab. service, 1969-70; chief policy, program devel., phys. medicine and rehab. Central Office VA, Washington, 1970—; clin. prof. U. Buffalo Med. Sch., 1968-70, Howard U. Med. Sch., Washington, 1971—, asst. dir. prof. George Washington U. Med. Sch., 1971—. Commr. Parks and Recreation, Inkster, Mich., 1958-59. Served with AUS, 1946-47. Diplomate Am. Bd. Phys. Medicine and Rehab. Mem. Am. Acad. Phys. Medicine and Rehab., Am. (award 1969), Nat. med. assns., Am. Congress Rehab., Alpha Phi Alpha. Republican. Mason (32, Shriner). Contbr. articles profl. jours. Home: 611 Hillsboro Dr Silver Spring MD 20902 Office: Central Office VA 810 Vermont Av Washington DC 20420

COFFEY, HARRY GERALD, ret. machinery builder; b. Willard, O., June 21, 1904; s. Charles A. and Bertha (Tanner) C.; student Oberlin Coll., 1922-23; m. Mary Lucretia Dillon, Feb. 20, 1932; children—Gerald D., Charles A. Sales dept. Aetna- Standard Engring. Co., Pitts., 1926-40, mgr. sales, 1940-43, v.p., 1943- 56, pres., 1956-60; sr. v.p., gen. mgr. Aetna-Standard div. Blaw-Knox Co., 1959-68, sr. v.p. Blaw-Knox Co., 1969-70, cons., 1970-71. Mem. Newcomen Soc. N.Am. Clubs: Duquesne, Pittsburgh Field. Home: Windsor Rd Fox Chapel Pittsburgh PA 15215

COFFEY, JAMES WILLIAM, lawyer; b. Chgo., July 19, 1907; s. Daniel David and Sophia (Klarkowski) C.; B.S., Northwestern U., 1929, J.D., 1932; m. Esther Nielsen, Jan. 19, 1934; children—Patrick, Terry Angelina (Mrs. Don Angelina), Kathleen (Mrs. Keith J. Bane). Admitted to Ill. bar, 1932; with firm Poppenhusen, Johnson, Thompson & Cole, Chgo., 1932-37; asst. atty. Bd. Edn. City Chgo., 1937-61, atty., 1961—. Home: 3742 N Lowell Av Chicago IL 60641 Office: 228 N LaSalle St Chicago IL 60601

COFFEY, JOHN G., lawyer; b. Providence. Aug. 24, 1912; s. Michael Leo and Effie M. (Gately) C.; Ph.B., Providence Coll., 1933; LL.B., Harvard, 1936; m. Madeline L. Struck, Dec. 2, 1939; children—John G., Harry C., Robert N., Catherine M., Richard N. Admitted to R.I. bar, 1937, practiced in Providence; partner firm Coffey, Ward, McGovern & Novogroski, 1945—. Dir. Providence Washington Ins. Co., Providence Washington Life Ins. Co.; trustee Old Stone Mortgage & Realty Trust. Mem. R.I. Ho. Senate from E. Providence, 1948-52. Home: 1330 Warwick Neck Av Warwick RI 02889 Office: 15 Westminster St Providence RI 02903

COFFEY, RAY LEONARD, mfg. co. exec.; b. Dallas, May 12, 1918; s. Ray L. and Lela (Gannon) C.; B.A., Coll. City N.Y., 1946; LL.B., N.Y.U., 1943; m. Theresa Wahl, Jan. 21, 1945; children—George L., Nancy J. Admitted to N.Y. bar, 1946; asso. firm Rogers, Hoge & Hills, N.Y.C., 1946-53, partner, 1953-66; v.p., gen. counsel AMF Inc., N.Y.C., 1966—. Served to lt. USNR, 1943-46. Mem. Am., N.Y. State bar assns., Assn. Bar City N.Y. Office: 261 Madison Av New York City NY 10016

COFFEY, RAYMOND RICHARD, journalist; b. Racine, Wis., Mar. 31, 1929; s. Raymond Francis and Catherine (Costello) C.; B.A., Marquette U., 1951; m. Holly Schroeder, Nov. 26, 1955; children—Brigid, Brendan, Erin, Ellen, Clare, Amy, Nancy. With U.P.I., 1953-61, bur. mgr., Detroit, 1959-61, corr. Chgo. Daily News, 1961—, named fgn. corr., Saigon, Vietnam, 1966, now nat. corr., Chgo. Served with AUS, 1951- 53. Recipient Nat. Headliners award nat. reporting, 1963. Address: care Chicago Daily News 401 N Wabash Av Chicago IL 60611

COFFEY, ROBERT JAMES, surgeon, educator; b. Elmira, N.Y., Nov. 14, 1908; s. Jeremiah J. and Mary (McElligott) C.; B.S., St. Bonaventure U., 1928; M.D., Georgetown U., 1932; M.S. in Medicine, U. Minn., 1937, Ph.D. in Surgery, 1938; m. Mary Catherine Mundell, Sept. 1939; children—Maureen, Robert James, Christine, Anne, Joseph J. Prof. exptl. surgery Georgetown U., 1938- 1941, prof. surgery, chmn. dept., 1946—; cons. surgery U.S. Naval Med. Center, NIH, VA. Served to lt. comdr. USNR, World War II. Mem. A.C.S. (bd. govs.), Am., So. (pres. 1968) surg. assns., A.M.A., Internat. Soc. Surgery, D.C. Med. Soc. (pres. 1966), Southeastern Surg. Congress (pres.). Club: Chevy Chase (Md.) Golf. Contbr. articles to numerous publs. Home: 4936 Loughboro Rd NW Washington DC 20016 Office: Georgetown U Hosp 3800 Reservoir Rd Washington DC 20007

COFFEY, RUFUS, clergyman; b. Amherst County, Va., Nov. 15, 1926; s. Early B. and Gertie (Davis) C.; B.A. in Religion, Bob Jones U., Greenville, S.C., 1951; postgrad. Vanderbilt U., 1952-53; m. Maude Janelle Felder, Feb. 13, 1952; children—Raymond, Rebecca, Reuel. Ordained to ministry Baptist Ch., 1949; pastor in Timmonsville, S.C., 1949-51, Nashville, 1951-54, Darlington, S.C., 1954-57, Florence, S.C., 1957-62; exec. Nat. Assn. Free Will Bapt. Fgn. Missions, 1962-67; exec. sec. Nat. Assn. Free Will Baptists, 1967—. Served with USNR, 1944-46. Editor mag. Contact, 1967- -. Home: 653 River Rouge Dr Nashville TN 37209 Office: 1134 Murfreesboro Rd Nashville TN 37217

COFFEY, THOMAS FRANCIS, Jr., city ofcl., journalist; b. Walthourville, Ga., Feb. 14, 1923; s. Thomas Francis and Julian (Bacon) C.; grad. high sch.; student Am. Press Inst., Columbia, 1964, Program for Urban Execs., Mass. Inst. Tech., 1970; m. Mary Corley, Apr. 6, 1946; 1 dau., Mary Cynthia Smith. Reporter, Savannah (Ga.) Eve. Press, 1940-42; civilian pub. relations dir. AUS, Camp Stewart, Ga., 1942; asst. city editor, sports editor Savannah Eve. Press, 1945-55, city editor, 1960- 64, managing editor, 1964-67; news dir. sta. WSAV-TV, Savannah, 1955-57; sports editor Savannah Morning News, 1957-60, mng. editor, 1967-69; asst. city mgr. City of

Savannah, 1969—. Bd. dirs. Family Counseling Center Savannah. Served with AUS, 1943-45. Decorated Bronze Star, Purple Heart. Mem. Ga. Heart Assn. (dir. 1st dist.), Ga. A.P. News Council, Greater Savannah Hall Fame Assn. (pres. 1969), Internat. City Mgmt. Assn., Am. Legion Sigma Delta Chi. Republican. Episcopalian (lay reader). Clubs: Savannah Lions; Am. Business (past pres. Savannah chpt.). Home: 209 Kensington Dr Savannah GA 31405 Office: City of Savannah City Hall Savannah GA 31402

COFFEY, WILLIAM VINCENT, oil co. exec.; b. Spencer, Neb., Mar. 2, 1911; s. Cornelius J. and Mary Anna (Dailey) C.; student St. Marys (Kan.) Coll., 1927-28, St. Edwards U., Austin, Tex., 1928-30; m. Elizabeth Sue Hines, Oct. 26, 1935; children—Nancy Jo (Mrs. John M. Montgomery), Timothy Michael. Office mgr. Horitz & Oldom, Wichita Falls, Tex., 1937-43, Jack Grace Drilling Co., P.M. Grace, Grace & Wood, Barrow, Grace, Grace & Wood, also Henry Grace Prodn. Co. (all Wichita Falls), 1941-43; asst. to chmn. bd. New Enamel Corp., Chgo., 1943-47; sec.-treas. New Enamel Oil Operating Co., 1943-47; v.p., gen. mgr. Star Oil Co., Dallas, 1947-50; v.p. Mars Drilling Corp. and Jupiter Oil Co., Dallas, 1947-50, Katy Oil Co., Dallas, 1950-51; office mgr., tax cons. F. Kirk Johnson, Ft. Worth, 1951-65; v.p., dir. Kleinjo Oil Co., 1951-65; treas., dir. Ehrhart Oil Co., 1952-53, pres., 1955; treas. Texota Oil Corp., 1952-53; treas., dir. Ute Royalty Corp., 1953-55; asst. sec., asst. treas. Texota Oil Co., 1953-58; pres., dir. South Coast Oil Co., 1954-55; sec.-treas., dir. Kirk Basin Uranium Corp., 1954-58, pres., 1958; v.p., treas. Ambassador Oil Co., 1954-55; treas., dir. Johnson-Gadgois Drilling Co., 1954-65; v.p., dir. Petroleum Exploration Cons., Inc., also Anvil Oil Co., and Johnson Oil Co., 1954-55, Fgn. Car Co., 1956-65, Engineered Air Balance Co., Inc., 1957, Trans Atlantic Motors, Inc., 1958-59; treas. Beneficiadora de Jales, S.A., 1957-65; treas., dir. Imported Motor Cars, Inc., 1957-58, Electromation Co., 1957-59. Amkirk Petroleum Corp., also Italian S.W. Car Co., 1958-65, Ambassador Petroleum Co. Colombia, 1959-65; v.p., treas. Tad McGhee Motor Co., 1958-63; v.p., treas., dir. Ambassador Oil Corp., Ft. Worth, 1956-62, exec. v.p., dir., 1962-66; sec.-treas. Murjo Oil & Royalty Co., Mid-States Italian Motors, Inc.; financial vice pres. King Resources Co., Denver, 1966-68, exec. v.p., 1968-70; asst. sec.-treas. Franklin River Livestock Co.; sec., dir. Overseas Motors Corp. Bd. dirs. Arlington Heights Athletic Council, 1957- 65; chmn. bd. Tarrant County Heart Assn. Mem. Ind. Petroleum Assn. Am. (dir. 1960, v.p. 1962), Petroleum Accountants Soc. Ft. Worth (dir. 1958, pres. 1960). Home: 3236 Cherryridge Rd Englewood CO 80110 Office: Security Life Bldg Denver CO 80202

COFFIELD, WILLIAM HOWARD, educator; b. Lee County, Ala., Aug. 3, 1923; s. William James and Cora (Dyess) C.; B.S., Troy (Ala.) State Coll., 1948; M.A., George Peabody Coll., 1951; Ph.D., State U. Ia., 1954; m. Jeanette Cooper, Aug. 21, 1948; children—Walter Michael, James Leonard, Tchr. chemistry secondary sch., Mobile, 1948-50, elementary sch. prin., 1950-52; asst., then asso. prof. edn1. adminstrn. Auburn U., 1954-58; staff research asso. Columbia Tchrs. Coll., 1958; asso. dir. Univ. Council Ednl. Adminstrn., Ohio State U., 1959-61; prof. edn., head dept. No. Ill. U., DeKalb, 1961-63; prof. edn., dean Sch. Edn., Kan. State U., Manhattan, 1963-67; dean of univ. Youngstown (O.) State U., 1967-68, v.p. acad. affairs, 1968-70; vis. prof. Ohio State U., 1961, Ariz. State Coll., 1965. Served with USAAF, 1942-46. Mem. N.E.A., Assn. Higher Edn., Am. Assn. Sch. Adminstrs., Am. Ednl. Research Assn., Phi Delta Kappa. Presbyn. Rotarian. Author: (with others) Elementary School Administration, 1963; also numerous articles. Editor: (vith J. Culbertson) Simulation in Administrative Training, 1960. Contbr. to books. Home: 10420 Pinedale Dr Concord TN 37720

COFFIN, DAVID DOUW, former missile mfr.; b. W. Bedford, Mass., May 18, 1901; s. Freeman Clarke and Janet Agnes (Lighthall) C.; A.B., Harvard, 1922, B.S. in Elec. Engring., 1923; postgrad in Charlottenburg, Berlin, Germany, 1926-27; m. Hilda Ann Spross, Jan. 1, 1928; children—Nancy, David Douw. With Raytheon Co., 1934-62, group v.p. govt. equipment and systems, 1959-62; mgmt. responsibility with achieved interception of drone by guided missile, 1950, destruction of drone by guided missile, 1951, destruction of ballistic missile by another missile (Honest John by Hawk), 1960; v.p. Sanders Assos., Inc., Nashua, N.H., ret., 1969. Recipient certificate of commendation Navy Dept., 1949. Mem. Am. Inst. E.E. (asso.), Harvard Engring. Soc. Home: Hildreth Lane Concord MA 01742

COFFIN, DAVID ROBBINS, educator, art historian; b. N.Y.C., Mar. 20, 1918; s. H. Errol and Lois (Robbins) C.; A.B., Princeton, 1940, M.F.A., 1947, Ph.D., 1954; postgrad. Yale, 1940-41; m. Nancy Merritt Nesbit, June 10, 1947; children—Elizabeth, David Tristram, Lois, Peter. Instr. fine arts U. Mich., 1947-49; lectr. art and archaeology Princeton, 1949-54, asst. prof., 1954-56, asso. prof., 1956-60, prof. art and archaeology, 1960- 66, Marquand prof. art and archaeology, 1966-70, Howard Crosby Butler Meml. prof. history architecture, 1970—, chmn. dept. of art and archaeology, 1964-70; editor in chief Art Bull., 1959-62. Fulbright research award to Italy, 1951-52; McCosh Faculty fellowship, also Am. Council of Learned Socs. fellowship, 1963-64; Alice Davis Hitchcock book award Society of Archtl. Historians, 1960. Mem. Coll. Art Assn. Am. (dir. 1957-61), Soc. Archtl. Historians (dir. 1968-70, treas. 1970-71), Renaissance Soc., Phi Beta Kappa. Author: Villa d'Este at Tivoli, 1960. Home: 143 McCosh Circle Princeton NJ 08540

COFFIN, FRANK MOREY, judge; b. Lewiston, Me., July 11, 1919; s. Herbert Rice and Ruth (Morey) C.; A.B., Bates Coll., 1940, LL.D., 1959; postgrad. indsl. adminstrn., Harvard, 1943, LL.B., 1947; LL.D., U. Me., 1967, Bowdoin Coll., 1969; m. Ruth Ulrich, Dec. 19, 1942; children—Nancy, Douglas, Meredith, Susan. Admitted to Me. bar, 1947; law clk. Fed. Judge, Dist. of Me., 1947-49; engaged in practice, Lewiston, Me., 1947-52; Verrill, Dana, Walker, Philbrick & Whitehouse, Portland, Me., 1952-56; mem. 85th, 86th Congresses, 2d Dist. Me., mem. House Com. Fgn. Affairs; mng. dir. Devel. Loan Fund, Dept. of State, Washington, 1961, dep. adminstr. AID, 1961-64; U.S. rep. devel. assistance com. Orgn. Econ. Coop. and Devel., 1964-65; judge 1st circuit U.S. Ct. Appeals, 1965—. Chmn. Me. Democratic Com., 1954-56. Trustee Overseas Devel. Council, Bates Coll.; bd. dirs. Fed. Jud. Center, World Peace Found. Served from ensign to lt. USNR, 1943-46. Mem. Am. Acad. Arts and Scis. Author: Witness for Aid, 1964. Home: 1 Ocean Rd South Portland ME 04106 Office: 156 Federal St Portland ME 04112

COFFIN, LEWIS CHARLES, ret. librarian; b. Ashland, Me., Feb. 15, 1909; s. Laurence Smith and Katherine Morrell (Trafton) C.; A.B., Bowdoin Coll., 1930; J.D., George Washington U., 1934; m. Elizabeth Van Brakle, Oct. 15, 1938; 1 dau., Elizabeth Louise. Admitted to D.C. bar, 1935, asst. Dept. Justice, 1930-31; with Library of Congress, 1931-71, asso. dir. processing dept., 1958-64, law librarian, 1964-71, gen. counsel, 1964-70. Served to lt. comdr. USNR, 1942-46; PTO. U.S. mem. meetings internat. exchange publs. UNESCO, Paris, France, 1948, 56; a U.S. mem. spl. intergovtl. com. to draft new convs. for internat. exchange publs., Brussels, Belgium, 1958; chief teams to establish Am. book procurement centers, Egypt, 1961, Israel, 1963. Mem. Am., Fed. bar assns., A.L.A., Am., Internat. (1st v.p. 1965-68, pres. 1968-71) assns. law libraries, Phi Delta Psi, Alpha Tau Omega. Mem. Ch. of Saviour. Home: 6432 Barnaby St NW Washington DC 20015 Office: 110 1st St NE Washington DC 20002

COFFIN, ROBERT EDMONDSTON, army officer; b. Bellingham, Wash., June 15, 1917; s. Leslie Roland and Fanny (Johnson) C.; B.A., Stanford, 1939; postgrad. U. Wash., 1939, George Washington U., 1956; grad. Command and Gen. Staff Coll., 1950, Armed Forces Staff Coll., 1955, Nat. War Coll., 1959; m. Joan Nelson, Nov. 2, 1940; children—Barbara Joan (Mrs. John S. Kittle), Lynne, James John. Commd. 2d lt., arty., U.S. Army, 1940, advanced through grades to maj. gen., 1963; with 3d Inf. Div. in invasion of Africa, 1942; instr. Command and Gen. Staff Coll., 1950-53; battalion comdr. in Korea; comdr. 1st Missile Command, Italy, 1960-61; asst. commdr. 2d. Inf. Div., 1963- 64; assigned planning div. SHAPE, 1965-67; became dep. chief army research and devel., 1967. Vice pres. Transatlantic council Boy Scouts Am., 1966—. Decorated Legion of Merit, Bronze Star; Croix de Guerre (France). Mem. U.S. Army Assn., Am. Ordnance Assn., Delta Tau Delta. Catholic. Contbr. profl. jours. Office: OCRD Dept of Army The Pentagon Washington DC 20310

COFFIN, ROY RIDDELL, investment exec.; b. Phila., May 10, 1898; s. Harry Morse and Sarah Louise (Young) C.; grad. Germantown Acad., 1915; B.S., Lehigh U., 1919; m. Catharine Marie Pfingst, Nov. 17, 1930; children—Roy Riddell, Evelyn Osborne (Mrs. Dale A. Hoffman), Gail Barthold (Mrs. Grant R. Grissom). Salesman Studebaker Corp., 1920, Kieckhefer Paper Co., 1921-22, H.M. Coffin & Co., wool importers, 1923-24, Samuel McCreery & Co., investments, 1925-32, E.W. Clark & Co., investments, 1932-39; partner Coffin, Betz & Co., investments, 1940-53; partner Fahnestock & Co., investments, 1953-69, ltd. partner, 1969—; pres., dir. Phila. Fund, Inc., until 1969; pres., dir. Rainbow Corp., Eastern Banker, Reqenbogen Corp. Trustee Germantown Acad. Served as g.m. USNRF, 1918-19. Mem. Delta Tau Delta. Episcopalian. Clubs: Philadelphia Country, Germantown Cricket, Union League (Phila.); Pine Valley Golf (N.J.); Portland (Me.) Country; Coral Beach and Tennis (Bermuda). Home: 513 Revere Rd Merion Station Merion PA 17235 Office: 2 Penn Center Plaza Philadelphia PA 19102

COFFIN, TRISTRAM, author; b. Hood River, Ore., July 25, 1912; s. Clarence Eugene and Lenora (Smith) C.; A.B., DePauw U., 1933; m. Margaret Avery, June 26, 1933; children—Lynne (Mrs. Williard M. Cronyn), Stephen Avery. Reporter, Indpls. Times, 1933-37; asst. to gov. Ind., 1937-41; with Office Facts and Figures, OWI, 1941-44; White House corr. CBS, 1945-47; newspaper columnist, 1948-51; free-lance writer and broadcaster, 1951—; author Washington Watch Newsletter, 1968—. Mem. P.E.N. Author: Missouri Compromise, 1947; Your Washington, 1954; Not To The Swift, 1961; The Passion of the Hawks, 1964; Mine Eyes Have Seen the Glory, 1964; The Sex Kick, 1966; Senator Fulbright, 1966. Address: 5601 Warwick Pl Chevy Chase MD 20015

COFFIN, TRISTRAM POTTER, educator; b. San Marino, Cal., Feb. 13, 1922; s. Tristram Roberts and Elsie Potter (Robinson) C.; B.S., Haverford Coll., 1943; M.A., U. Pa., 1947, Ph.D., 1949; m. Ruth Anne Hendrickson, Feb. 15, 1944; children—Patricia L., Mark T., Priscilla R., Jonathan P. From instr. to asso. prof. English, Denison U., 1949-58; asso. prof. English and folklore U. Pa., 1958-64, prof. English and folklore, 1964- -, vice dean Grad. Sch. Arts and Scis., 1965-68. Guggenheim fellow, 1953. Fellow Am. Folklore Soc. (sec.-treas. 1960-65); mem. Ohio Folklore Soc. (pres. 1956-58), Modern Lang. Soc., Phi Beta Kappa, Delta Upsilon. Author: British Traditional Ballad in North America, 1950; An Analytical Index to the Journal of American Folklore, 1958; (with Flanders and Nettl) Ancient Ballads Traditionally Sung in New England, vol. 1, 1960; Uncertain Glory, 1971; The Old Ball Game, 1971. Editor: Indian Tales of N. America, 1961; (with Leach) The Critics and the Ballad, 1961; (with Cohen) Folklore in America, 1966; Our Living Traditions, 1968. Home: Box 89 Wakefield RI 02880 Office: U Pa Philadelphia PA 19104

COFFIN, WILLIAM SLOANE, Jr., clergyman; b. N.Y.C., June 1, 1924; s. William Sloane and Catherine (Butterfield) C.; grad. Phillips Acad., Andover, Mass., 1942; student Yale Sch. Music, 1942-43, Union Theol. Sem., N.Y.C., 1949-50; B.A., Yale, 1949, B.D., 1956; D.D. (hon.), Wesleyan U.; m. Eva Anna Rubinstein, Dec. 12, 1956; children—Amy Elizabeth, Alexander Sloane, David Andrew. With CIA, 1950-53; ordained to ministry Presbyn. Ch., 1956; acting chaplain Phillips Acad., 1956-57; chaplain Williams Coll., 1957-58; univ. chaplain Yale, 1958—. Bd. dirs. Pres.'s Adv. Council Peace Corps, Operation Crossroads Africa, Am. Freedom of Residence Fund. Recipient Conn. Valley B'nai B'rith award for Americanism. Served with AUS, 1943-47. Author sermons in books, 1962. Home: 66 Wall St New Haven CT 06511

COFFMAN, AMOS JAMES, govt. ofcl.; b. Dallas, S.D., Dec. 30, 1911; s. Marshall and Sarah Gilliland (Ward) C.; B.A., Neb. Wesleyan U., 1933; J.D., U. Mich., 1938; m. Jeanne Edna Stringfellow, June 6, 1936; children—Amos James, Carolyn Ann, Kathleen Jean. High Sch. tchr., Unadilla and DeWitt, Neb., 1934-36; admitted to N.Y. bar, 1939, Ill. bar, 1947; asso. Cravath, de Gersdorff, Swaine and Wood, N.Y.C., 1938-41; enforcement atty. OPA, Washington, 1941-42, regional enforcement exec., Dallas, 1942-45, regional atty., regional enforcement exec., Chgo., 1945; pvt. practice law, Chgo., 1946-52; regional atty., acting chmn., mem. bd. Chgo. Regional Renegotiation Bd., 1952-57; asst. gen. counsel Renegotiation Bd., Washington, 1957-62; dep. asst. postmaster gen., Post Office Dept., 1962- -. Ill. rep. Nat. Council YMCA, 1955-58; gen. chmn. finance campaigns Hyde Park YMCA, Chgo., 1955-57, chmn. bd., 1956-57. Recipient Distinguished Service award P.O. Dept., 1967. Mem. Am., Fed. bar assns., Nat. Lawyers Club. Presbyn. (elder). Home: 6324 Anneliese Dr Falls Church VA 22044 Office: PO Dept Washington DC 20260

COFFMAN, CHARLES DEWITT, hotel exec.; b. Richmond, Va., July 10, 1909; s. William Harnsberger and Rosina (Brennan) C.; Ph.B., Georgetown U., 1931; m. Katharine Luttrell, Jan. 10, 1933 (dec.); 1 son, Michael; m. 2d, Suzanne Gregoire, Feb. 11, 1961. Sales mgr. Mayflower Hotel, Washington, 1938-47; pres. C. DeWitt Coffman, hotel reps., Washington, also N.Y.C., 1947-52; exec. dir. Phila. Conv. and Visitors Bur., 1952-54; gen. mgr. Woodner Hotel, Washington, 1954-55; pres. Hotel Sales Engring., 1955-56; gen. mgr. McAllister Hotel, Miami, Fla., 1956-60; v.p. Schine Hotels, Miami, 1956- 60; v.p. The Futterman Corp., N.Y.C., 1960-65; pres. Internat. Hotel Mgmt. Co., Miami, Fla., 1965—. Served as lt. comdr. USNR, 1942-45. Mem. Hotel Sales Mgmt. Assn. Internat. (pres. 1948, original mem. Hall of Fame) Inter-Am., Am., Fla., Greater Miami hotel assns., Miami-Dade County C. of C., Downtown Bus. Council (dir.), Better Bus. Bur. (dir.), Am. Soc. Travel Agts., Nat. Assn. Travel Orgns. Roman Catholic. Kiwanian (pres. Washington 1952). Author: Profits Through Promotion, 1950; The Full House, 1964; The Keyhole, 1971; Marketing for a Full House, 1971. Mgmt. editor Hospitality. Contbr. tech. articles trade periodicals. Home: 1352 Blue Rd Coral Gables FL 33146 Office: 169 Miracle Mile Coral Gables FL 33134

COFFMAN, L. DALE, lawyer, educator; b. Delta, Ia., Aug. 28, 1905; s. Ralph Gideon and Georgia (Green) C.; B.A. State U. Ia., 1926, J.D., 1928; LL.M., Harvard, 1929, S.J.D., 1935; m. Helen Crouch, Dec. 31, 1925; 1 dau., Georganne. Practiced law with Sargent Gamble & Read, DesMoines, Ia., 1928- 31; prof. law U. Neb., 1931-37; counsel Gen. Electric Co., Schenectady, 1937-46; dean Sch. of Law, Vanderbilt U., 1946-49; dean Sch. of Law, U. Cal., Los Angeles, 1949-57, prof. of law, 1957—; chief cons. Commn. on Govt. Security, 1956-57; arbitrator in labor-mgmt. disputes, Fellow Am. Bar Assn.; mem. Phi Delta Phi, Phi Beta Kappa, Kappa Sigma, Order of Coif. Rep. Conglist. Mason. Clubs: Harvard, Lincoln, Riviera Country, Los Angeles Athletic, Pacific Coast Club, Rotary (past pres.). Editor: Cases on Nebraska Trial Practice, 1933. Contbr. articles to law publs. Home: 730 S Amalfi Dr Pacific Palisades CA 90272 Office: Law Sch U of Cal Los Angeles CA 90024

COFFMAN, MAX, dept. store exec.; b. Quincy, Mass., 1910; Asst. mgr. Enterprise Dept. Store, Inc., Quincy, 1924-33; from buyer to supr. Food Fair Market, Inc., Boston, 1933-38; store mgr. Economy Store Co., Cambridge, Mass., 1938-40; with Pub. Food Market Inc., Boston, 1942-45; operator retail store, 1944-45; chmn. bd., pres., chief exec. officer, Mammoth Mart, Inc., West Bridgewater, Mass., 1946—. Home: 25 Braemoor Rd Brockton MA 02401 Office: 321 Manley St West Bridgewater MA 02379

COFFMAN, PAUL BROWN, former mgmt. cons.; b. Columbus, O., Dec. 20, 1900; s. Elmer and Helen (Brown) C.; B.S., Ohio State U., 1923; M.B.A., Harvard, 1926; m. Ruth Marcella Hudson, Oct. 14, 1922 (div. Apr. 1960); children—Louise Joan, Earle Merritt Wesley; m. 2d, Christine Mary Araman, Aug. 12, 1960. Mem. faculty Northeastern U., also Boston U., 1923-26, Coll. William and Mary, 1926- 27, Harvard, 1927-35; exec. v.p., gen. mgr. Poor's Pub. Co., N.Y.C., Wellesley, Mass., 1930-32; v.p., dir. Standard Statistics Co., N.Y.C., 1935-40, Standard and Poor's Corp., 1941-44, mem. exec. com., 1941-66; pres., dir. Standard Research Cons., Inc., N.Y.C., 1944-66, chmn. bd., 1944-66; pres., dir. Overseas Cons. Inc., 1950-57, Standard Research Cons. Internat., 1957-61; chmn. exec. com. Squier, Schilling & Skiff, Newark, 1944-61. Pres. West Barnstable (Mass.) Civic Assn., 1969—; mem. Water Commn., West Barnstable, Mass., 1968—; rep. West Barnstable, 1970—. Mem. corp. Cape Cod Hosp., 1968—. Fellow Am. Soc. Appraisers (life mem., chmn. manual editorial bd., 1956-61, editor Appraisal and Valuation Manual 1956-61, pres., 1959-61); mem. A.I.M. (charter, pres. council 1951-66), Assn. Consulting Mgmt. Engrs., Inc., Newcomen Soc., Aircraft Owners and Pilots Assn., Nat. Mus. Arts, Iran-Am., N.Y.C. chambers of commerce, Acad. Polit. and Social Sci. (life), Japan Soc., Acad. Polit. Sci., Beta Alpha Psi. Methodist. Mason. Clubs: Harvard (Boston); University, Harvard, India House (N.Y.C.); Hyannis (Mass.) Yacht; Craigville Beach (Centerville, Mass.). Author: (with Arthur Hanson) Problems in Auditing, 1930; (with Thomas Saunders) Problems in Industrial Accounting, 1930; (with Dr. Ralph E. Badger) A Complete Guide to Investment Analysis, 1967; also writer columns on bus. evaluation to profl. jours; mem. adv. council The Executive, pub. Harvard Bus. Sch., 1957-64. Home: Twelve Acres West Barnstable MA 02668

COFFMAN, ROBERT J., corp. exec.; b. Columbus, O., 1921; grad. Ohio State U., 1943, LL.B., 1951. Treas., Ametek Corp. Home: 6O Nottingham Rd Short Hills NJ 07078 Office: 233 Broadway New York City NY 10007 *

COFFMAN, STANLEY KNIGHT, Jr., educator; b. Huntington, W. Va., Dec. 30, 1916; s. Stanley Knight and Werneth (Brockmeyer) C.; A.B., Haverford Coll., 1939; M.A., Ohio State U., 1940, Ph.D., 1948; m. Ann Channing Wrentmore, Dec. 27, 1942; children—Ann Channing, Stanley Knight III, Eric Ewing. Part-time instr. English, Ohio State U., 1946-48; faculty U. Okla., 1948-62, prof. English, 1956-62, asst. dean Univ. Coll., 1954-62; prof. English, chmn. dept. Bowling Green (O.) State U., 1962—, acting dean Grad. Sch., 1967-68, v.p. acad. affairs, 1968—. Served with AUS, 1942-46; lt. col. Res. Mem. Modern Lang. Assn. Am., Am. Assn. U. Profs., Phi Beta Kappa, Omicron Delta Kappa. Presbyn. (past elder). Author: Imagism, 1951. Contbr. articles to profl. jours. Home: 319 N Prospect St Bowling Green OH 43402

COGAN, DAVID GLENDENNING, physician, educator; b. Fall River, Mass., Feb. 14, 1908; s. James Joseph and Edith (Ives) C.; A.B., Dartmouth, 1929, med. student, 1930- 31; M.D., Harvard, 1932, travelling fellow, 1937-38; m. Frances Capps, July 14, 1934; children—Christy (dec.), Frances, Ann, Priscilla. Intern U. Chgo. Clinics, 1931-32; resident Mass. Eye and Ear Infirmary, Boston, 1932-34, asso. surgeon, 1943-54, surgeon, 1954-60, chief ophthalmology, 1963-68; practiced medicine, Boston, 1934—; dir. Howe Lab. Ophthalmology, Harvard, 1940—, asso. prof. ophthalmic research, 1943—, prof. ophthalmology Harvard Med. Sch., 1955—, chmn. dept., 1963-68, Henry Willard Williams prof., 1963-70. Mem. council Nat. Inst. Neurologic Diseases and Blindness, Council Nat. Eye Inst., NIH. Recipient Warren Triennial prize Mass. Gen. Hosp., 1944; Proctor award, 1954; Knapp prize A.M.A., 1955; Howe medal Am. Ophthal. Soc. 1965, Research to Prevent Blindness award, 1969. Mem. Am. Acad. Arts and Sci., Am. Ophthal. Soc., Am. Soc. Clin. Research, Nat. Soc. Prevention Blindness (dir.). Author: Neurology of the Ocular Muscles, 1946, rev. edit., 1958; Neurology of the Visual System, 1966. Editor-in-chief Archives of Ophthalmology, 1960-66; cons. editor, 1966-70. Home: 30 Clark St Belmont MA 02178 Office: 243 Charles St Boston MA 02114

COGAN, DAVID HAROLD, corp. exec.; b. nr. Barton, Vt., Jan. 10, 1909 s. Bened and Annie (Grant) C.; student Northeastern U., 1926-30; m. Martha Sharp, 1957; 1 son, Bruce M. Sales engr. Hytrom Corp., Salem, Mass., 1930, sales mgr. 1931; pres., dir. Air King Products Co., Inc., Bklyn., 1946-54, Royal Wood Products Co., Inc., 1946-54, King Assoc., Inc., 1946-54, CBS-Columbia, Inc., 1951-54, Seymour Chevrolet Sales, Inc., 1954-67, Continental Discount Fund, Inc., 1955-64, Tri-Continental Realty Corp., 1960-67, Victoreen Instrument Co., 1957—; pres. treas., dir. D.H. Cogan, Inc., 1952-65, Pathe Radio Corp., 1942-54, Ravac Electronics Corp., 1942-57, Continental Holding Corp., 1954-61; v.p. dir. Hytron Radio & Electronics Corp., 1931-54, CBS, Inc., 1951-54, CBS-Hytron, 1951-54; treas., dir. Atlantic Realty, Inc., 1952-57, Continental Holding Corp. 1954-61; dir. Gilchrist Co., Premier Microwave; chmn. bd. Mirawal Corp., 1955-56, Victoreen Instrument Co., 1955—, Phaostron Instrument & Electronic Co., 1966—, Bohn Bus. Machines, Inc., 1964-68; chmn. bd., pres. Nuclear Electronics Ohio, Inc., 1955-59; dir., chmn. exec. com. Estey Organ Co., 1956-64; chmn. bd. dirs. Colonial Press, Inc., 1967—. Vice pres., sec., dir. L. Peter Cogan Found.; pres., treas., dir. David H. Cogan Found. Bd. dirs. Northeastern U. Mem. N.A.M., Radio Electronic Television Mfrs. Assn. Clubs: Stamford Yacht; Williamsburg Yacht. Home: 1 Rogers Rd Stamford CT 06902 Office: 18 E 80th St New York City NY 10121 also 1374 E 51st St Cleveland OH 44103

COGAN, DAVID JOSEPH, theatrical producer; b. Rumania, July 24, 1923; s. Morris and Helen (Meyers) C.; came to U.S., 1923, naturalized, 1928; B.B.S., St. John's U., 1945; m. Ferne Cogan, 1946; children—Sharon Ann, Carol Lynn. Producer: (film) Run Across the River, 1954; (stage plays) A Raisin in the Sun, 1958, Midnight Sun, 1959, In the Counting House, 1961, Does the Tiger Wear a Necktie; co-producer (stage play) Odd Couple, 1965; owner legitimate theatre Biltmore Theatre, N.Y.C., 1960—, Eugene O'Neill Theatre, N.Y.C., 1964—, Plaza Theatre, N.Y.C., Viking Theatre, Phila.; partner firm Cogan, Bell & Co., N.Y.C., 1955—; pres. David J. Cogan Agy., Inc., theatrical agy. and mgmt. firm, N.Y.C., 1955-; bus. mgr. numerous theatrical notables, 1956—; tchr. prodn. and theatrical mgmt. New

Sch. Social Research Grad. Sch., 1971; pres. Cogan Mgmt., Inc., 1968—. Treas., mem. bd. Family Inst., N.Y.C., 1961—; chmn. legitimate theatre sect. N.Y. chpt. A.R.C., 1964—. Bd. dirs. Young Childrens Music Sch. and Dance, N.Y.C., 1959—, Berkshire Theatre Festival. Recipient Critics award for A Raisin in the Sun, 1959; TV Emmy award, 1970. Mem. Nat. Soc. Pub. Accountants, Actors Studio, League N.Y. Theatres, N.Y. Theatre Owners Assn. Author magazine articles. Office: 350 Fifth Av New York City NY 10001

COGAN, EDWARD J., educator, author; b. Milw., Jan. 18, 1925; s. Leo J. and Elizabeth (Berman) C.; B.A., U. Wis., 1946, M.A., 1948; Ph.D., Pa. State U., 1955; m. Frances Bernstein, Aug. 3, 1947; 1 dau., Deborah. Instr. math. Pa. State U., 1948-55, Dartmouth, 1955-57; mathematician IBM Corp., summer 1957; mem. faculty sci. and math. Sarah Lawrence Coll., 1957—, dir. Inst. Sci. and Math. Tchrs., 1958—, co-dir. Upward Bound summer residence program, 1966. Mem. Am. Math. Soc., Math. Assn. Am., Assn. Symbolic Logic, Am. Assn. U. Profs., A.A.A.S. Author: A Formalization of the Theory of Sets from the Point of View of Combinatory Logic, 1955; Foundations of Analysis, 1962; also articles. Home: 1 Wilgarth Rd Bronxville NY 10708

COGAN, JERRY ALBERT, oil co. exec.; b. Canon City, Colo, July 29, 1910; s. Jeremiah J. and Quintina (Penney) C.; B.A., Colo. Coll., 1930; S.M., Mass. Inst. Tech., 1932; m. Genevieve Engel, Oct. 14, 1933; children—Jerry Albert, Jane, Jacqueline. Chem. engr. Standard Oil Co. La., 1932-34; tech. analyst Standard Oil Co. N.J., 1934-42; mem. staff Petroleum Industry War Council, N.Y.C., 1942-43; asso. dir. program div. Petroleum Adminstrn. for War, Washington, 1943-45; mem. coordination and econs. dept. Standard Oil Co. N.J., 1945-54, mgr., 1947-54; asst. gen. mgr. mfg. Imperial Oil, Ltd., Toronto, Can., 1954-56; dir., 1956—, also sr. v.p.; dir. Interprovincial Pipeline Co. Bd. dirs. Toronto Symphony. Member Mil. Petroleum Adv. Bd., 1947-54, Fgn. Petroleum Supply Com., 1952-54; vice chmn. Middle East Emergency Com., 1956-57. Mem. Phi Beta Kappa, Phi Gamma Delta. Home: 90 Cortleigh Blvd Toronto 12 Ontario Canada Office: 111 St Clair Av W Toronto 7 Ontario Canada

COGAN, JOHN BERNARD, corp. exec.; b. San Luis Obispo, Cal., Jan. 19, 1921; s. John Francis and Mary (Uzzell) C.; B.A., U. So. Cal., 1958; m. Grace Louella Landis, Apr. 2, 1946; children—John Kevin, Kerry Michael. Vice pres. finance Longren Aircraft Co., Torrance, Cal, 1954-58; treas. Litton Industries, Beverly Hills, Cal., 1954-65, v.p., 1965-67; became sr. v.p. Ogden Corp., N.Y.C., 1964; dir. Independence Bank, Canoga Park, Cal., Avondale Shipyards, New Orleans, New World Fund, Los Angeles, Charles Luckman & Assos., Los Angeles. Served with CIC, USAAF, 1945-48. Home: 1910 Toledo St Palm Springs CA 92262

COGAN, JOHN FRANCIS, Jr., lawyer; b. Boston, June 13, 1926; s. John Francis and Mary (Galligan) C.; A.B. cum laude, Harvard, 1949, LL.B., 1952; m. Mary T. Hart, May 1, 1951; children—Peter G., Pamela E., Jonathan C., Gregory M. Admitted to Mass. bar, 1952, since practiced in Boston; partner firm Hale and Dorr, 1957—. Pres. Pioneer Fund, Inc., Boston, 1963—, Fund Research and Mgmt., Boston, 1963—, Pioneering Mgmt. Corp., Boston, 1963—; dir. Seatrain Lines, Inc., 1959-65; sec. Cabot, Cabot & Forbes Co., 1963—, Ritz-Carlton Hotel Co., Boston, 1964—; corporator Boston 5 Savs. Bank, 1961—; chmn. exec. com., dir. Pioneer Western Corp., 1968—; sr. v.p., dir. Western Res. Life Assurance Co. Ohio, 1968—; dir. Spaulding & Slye Corp., N.Am. Fund Mgmt. Corp. Ltd., Noram Secured Income N.V. Treas. Lexington (Mass.) Counseling Service, 1964-69; v.p., trustee Univ. Hosp., Boston, 1965—. Treas. Friends of Harvard Track, 1964-66; mem. Lexington Capital Expenditures Com., 1967—. Mem. Mass. Democratic State Com., 1968—. Bd. dirs. Wendell P. Clark Meml. Assn., Walker Home for Children. Served with USNR, 1944-46. Mem. Internat. Am., Inter-Am., Boston bar assns., Boston Estate and Bus. Planning Council (past pres.), Boston Probate and Estate Planning Forum (sec.). Home: 29 Patterson Rd Lexington MA 02173 Office: 28 State St Boston MA 02109

COGAN, ROBERT DAVID, composer; b. Detroit, Feb. 2, 1930; s. Leon and Merrium (Gottschalk) C.; B.Mus. with distinction, U. Mich., 1951, M. Mus., 1952; student composition Berkshire Music Center, 1953; M.F.A., Princeton, 1956; composition Staatliche Hochschule für Musik in Hamburg, Germany, 1958- 60; m. Pozzi Escot, July 1, 1959. Teaching asst. theory and composition U. Mich., 1951-52; teaching asst. music Princeton, 1954-55; participant Salzburg (Austria) Seminar Am. Studies, 1950, European Cultural Found., Copenhagen, Denmark, 1961; lectr., vis. cultural affairs office USIA, Bonn, Germany, 1960-61; pvt. teaching composition, N.Y.C., 1961-63; chmn. theoretical studies New Eng. Conservatory Music, 1963—; program head, mem. Eastern regional exec. bd. Inst. for Music in Contemporary Edn., 1966—; guest composer Berkshire Music Center, 1968; lectr. 1st internat. seminar Composers N. and S. Am., Ind. U., 1965. Mem. Ford Found.-Music Educators Nat. Conf. panel on teaching composition, theory, music history in the univ., 1965. Recipient Young Composers Radio award Broadcast Music, Inc., 1952; Fulbright scholar, Brussels, Belgium, 1952-53; Chopin scholar in composition Kosciuszko Found. 1954; fellow MacDowell Colony, 1958, 62-65; German Govt. grantee for study in Hamburg, 1958-59, 59-60; fellow European Cultural Found., 1960; fellow Reemstsma Found., Hamburg, 1960-61; Paderewski Fund commn. for symphonic work, 1964-65; Guggenheim fellow, 1968-69. Mem. Internat. Soc. Contemporary Music (dir. U.S. sect.), Phi Beta Kappa. Composer: Fantasia for Orchestra, 1951; Songs on Texts by Ezra Pound, 1952-54; Two Compositions for String Trio, 1956-59; Sounds, and variations for Piano, 1959-61; Spaces and Cries for Five Brasses, 1962- 64 (performed Jordan Hall, Boston 1965); Whirl...ds I, 1967. Author: Space Time and Sound-Musical Language and Gesture, 1969. Contbr. articles to profl. jours. Home: 24 Avon Hill St Cambridge, MA 02140. Office: 290 Huntington Av Boston MA 92115

COGEN, CHARLES, educator; b. N.Y.C., Oct. 31, 1903; s. Joseph and Bessie (Wishnick) C.; A.B., Cornell U., 1924; LL.B., Fordham U., 1927; M.A., Columbia, 1931; m. Tess Schnittkramer, Feb. 9, 1930; children—Joel, Edward. Tchr. pub. schs., N.Y.C., 1924-30, 33-64; chmn. social studies dept. Bay Ridge High Sch., Bklyn., 1952-64; admitted to N.Y. bar, 1927; practice in N.Y.C., 1930-33; pres. United Fedn. Tchrs., N.Y.C., 1952-64; pres. Am Fedn. Tchrs., Washington, 1964-68; tchr., dir. Hudson Shore Labor Sch., 1948- 51; lectr. New Sch. Social Research, N.Y.C., 1958; instr. Met. dist. Cornell Univ. Sch. Indsl. and Labor Relations, 1969—; v.p. indsl. union dept. AFL-CIO, 1966-68, mem. exec. bd., 1964-68, del. N.Y.C. Central Labor Council, 1952-64, del. convs., 1961, 63, 65. Candidate N.Y.C. Council, 1958; bd. dirs. Ams. For Democratic Action, League Indsl. Democracy. Hon. vice chmn. Am. Trade Union Council, Nat. Council for Labor Israel. Author: (with Albert Sayer) Review Materials in Economics, 1935; (with Albert Sayer and Sidney Nanes) Economics in Our Democracy, 1950. Mem. editorial adv. bd. Educators Negotiating Service, 1967—, Integrated Education 1964—. Contbr. prof. jours. Home: 185 Park Row New York City NY 10038

COGGAN, BERNARD FREDERICK, aircraft, missiles mfr.; b. Gary, Ind., Apr. 18, 1918; s. Bernard and Blanch (Brown) C.; B.S. in Elec. Engring., Mich. State U., 1939; postgrad. AAC Radar and Electronics Inst., Dayton, O., Air Force and Navy war colls.; m. Bonita Creagan, Nov. 21, 1940; children—Barry B., Sandra B. Elec. engr. Gen. Motors Corp., 1939-41, supt. B-25 aircraft program, 1941-43, chief design engr. B-29, P-75 aircraft programs, 1943-45, gen. master mechanic, 1945-48, plant supt., Detroit, 1948-51; asst. to exec. v.p. Convair Corp., 1952, Convair div. mgr., 1952-56, v.p., div. mgr. Convair div. Gen. Dynamics Corp., San Diego, Cal, 1956-63; v.p. operations Douglas Aircraft Corp., Santa Monica, Cal., 1963-65, v.p. marketing, adminstrn. and finance, 1965-67; v.p. marketing N.Am. Rockwell Corp., 1967—; pres. Econ. Devel. Corp., San Diego, 1970—; pres. B.F. Coggan Assos., Inc.; chmn. bd. Douglas Aircraft Can. Ltd., 1964-67; v.p. West Coast Financial Corp.; pres. Internat. Devel. Corp., 1970—; dir. Wynn Oil Co., U.S. Financial Corp. Spl. cons. Dept. Def., 1966—; sr. inter-regional adviser UN, 1966—. Commr., San Diego Harbor Commn.; chmn. San Diego Indsl. Devel. Commn.; pres. San Diego Bd. Edn. Vice pres. A.R.C., 1946—; bd. dirs. Santa Monica Indsl. Devel. Commn., Nat. United Funds and Councils Am., 1947—, Greater San Diego Area YMCA; exec. com. United Fund; trustee Scripps Clinic and Research Found., La Jolla, Cal., 1947—, Santa Monica Salvation Army; chmn. bd. Council Chs. Homes, Inc., San Diego Sr. Citizens, Inc. Mem. Pres.'s White House Conf., 1963; sr. cons. Dept. Def., 1963—. Served as 2d lt. C.A., AUS, 1939-43. Decorated Knight of Holy Sepulchre (Jerusalem). Mem. U.S. (atomic energy com.), Cal. (atomic energy com.), San Diego, Los Angeles (dir.) chambers commerce, Electronics Industries Assn. (nat. dir.), Nat. Security Industries Assn. (chmn. bd.), Am. Inst. Astronautics and Aeros. (pres.), Am. Ordnance Assn. (chmn. bd. Los Angeles 1969—), Nat. Acad. Sci. (nat. materials adv. bd.), Am. Inst. E.E., Council Chs. (dir.), Soc. Advancement Mgmt. Rotarian (dir. San Diego). Home: 6436 Camino de la Costa La Jolla CA 92037 also 11740 Wilshire Blvd Los Angeles CA 90025 Office: US National Bank Bldg 2d at Broadway San Diego CA 92101 also UN Bldg New York City NY 10017 also The Pentagon Washington DC 20301

COGGAN, FREDERICK DONALD, archbishop of York; b. London, Eng., Oct. 9, 1909; s. Cornish Arthur and Fanny Sarah (Chubb) C.; grad. Wycliffe Hall, Oxford U., 1934; M.A., St. John's Coll., Cambridge U., 1935; B.D., U. Toronto, 1941; D.D. (hon.), Wycliffe Coll., Can., 1944, Lambeth D.D., 1957, U. Leeds, 1958, Cambridge (Eng.) U., 1962, U. Aberdeen, also Toronto, Saskatoon, Huron, Tokyo, Hull, 1963; H.H.D., Westminster Choir Coll., 1966; D.Litt., Lancaster, 1967; S.T.D., Gen. Theol. Sem., 1967; m. Jean Braithwaite Strain, Oct. 17, 1935; children—Dorothy Ann, Ruth Evelyn. Ordained to ministry Ch. of Eng., 1934; asst. lectr. Semitic langs. and lit. Manchester U., 1931-34; curate St. Mary, Islington, London, 1934-37; prof. N.T., Wycliffe Coll., Toronto, 1937-44; prin. London Coll. Div., 1944-56; bishop of Bradford, 1956-61; archbishop of York, 1961—; pres. United Bible Socs.; chmn. Coll. of Preachers; Pro- chancellor Univ. York, 1962, Univ. of Hull, 1968. Prelate Order St. John Jerusalem, 1967—. Author: The Ministry of the Word, 1945; The Glory of God, 1950; Stewards of Grace, 1956; Five Makers of the New Testament, 1962; Christian Priorities, 1963, The Prayers of the New Testament, 1967; Sinews of Faith, 1969; Word and World, 1971. Address: Bishopthorpe York 21QE England

COGGESHALL, IVAN STODDARD, engr. former communications co. exec.; b. Middletown, R.I., Sept. 30, 1896; s. Benjamin Bateman and Minnie Louise (Stoddard) C.: student Worcester Poly. Inst., 1914-17, D.Eng. (hon.), 1951; m. Ada Louise Crowe, Oct. 23, 1920; 1 dau., Lynette Louise (Mrs. John T. Miller). With Western Union Telegraph Co., N.Y. C., 1920-59, gen. traffic mgr., 1946, dir. internat. communications, 1951-58, asst. v-p., 1959; mgr. tech. operations Am. Inst. E.E., 1960-62. Served as ensign, USNRF, World War I; lt. comdr. UNSR, bd. war communications, submarine cables, World War II. Fellow I.E.E.E. (pres. 1951); mem. Tau Beta Pi. Republican. Editor: Elec. Engring. Contbr. articles on telegraph and radio, Ency. Brit. Home: 670 Maywood Av Maywood NJ 07607

COGGESHALL, JAMES, Jr., investment banker; b. N.Y.C., June 4, 1896; s. James and Hannah Elizabeth (Harrington) C.; B.S., Harvard, 1918, student law sch.; m. Esther Clarke, Aug. 15, 1918; children—John Clarke (dec.), Timothy, Caroline Frothingham (Mrs. Joseph Clark Segar), James Wells, Clarke. With First Boston Corp. 1919—, pres., 1947-62, now dir.; dir. Colonial Equity Fund. Bd. dirs. Colonial Fund, Boston; adv. com. Colonial Growth Fund, Colonial Income Fund, Boston; trustee Cape Cod Hosp. Clubs: Bond, Harvard (N.Y.). Home: Barnstable MA 02630 Office: The First Boston Corp 20 Exchange Pl New York City NY 10005

COGGIN, WALTER ARTHUR, clergyman; b. Richmond, Va., Feb. 10, 1916; s. Walter Arthur and Mary Veronica (Moshy) C.; student Belmont (N.C.) Abbey Jr. Coll., 1934-36, Belmont Abbey Sem., 1939-43; A.B., St. Benedict's Coll., Atchison, Kan., 1939; postgrad U. N.C., 1942; M.A., Cath. U., 1948, Ph.D., 1954. Became Benedictine Monk, 1936; ordained priest Roman Catholic Ch., 1943; vicar Belmont Abbey Monastery, 1956-60, abbot-ordinary of Belmont Abbey Nullius, 1960-70; tchr. philosophy Belmont Abbey Coll., 1970—. Mem. 2d Vatican Council, 1962-65. Mem. N.C. Philos. Soc. (pres. 1955-56), Am. Cath. Philos. Assn. Address: Belmont Abbey Belmont NC 28012

COGGIN, WILLIAM C., mfg. co. exec.; b. 1911; B.S. in Physics and Math., Alma Coll., 1933; B.S. in Elec. Engring., U. Mich., 1935, M.S. in Elec. Engring., 1936; postgrad. Harvard, 1965; married. With plastics dept. Dow Chem. Co., 1936-67; pres., chief operations officer Dow Corning Corp., 1967—, chmn., 1971—, also dir. Address: Box 592 Midland MI 48640*

COGGINS, JACK BANHAM, author, artist; b. London, Eng., July 10, 1914; s. Sidney George and Ethel May (Dobby) C.; student Grand Central Sch. Art, 1931-33, Art League, 1933-34; m. Alma Woods, Jan. 15, 1948. Came to U.S., 1923, naturalized, 1943. Free-lance comml. artist doing work for Life mag., U.S. Steel, Elec. Boat Co., Brown & Bigelow, others, 1940-53; mem. faculty art dept. Hunter Coll., N.Y.C., 1948-53; instr. fine arts Wyomissing (Pa.) Inst. Fine Arts, 1959—; author, illustrator, 1957—. Mem. adv. bd. Phila. Maritime Mus., 1968—. Served with AUS, 1943-45; ETO. Recipient Am. Revolution Round Table award for best book on Am. Revolution, 1969. Mem. Am. Ordnance Assn., U.S. Naval Inst., Nat. Rifle Assn. Author, illustrator: Illustrated Book of Knights, 1957; Arms and Equipment of Civil War, 1962; Horsemen of World, 1963; Flashes and Flags, 1963; Nets Overboard, 1965; Hydrospace, 1966; Horseman's Bible, 1966; The Fighting Man, 1966; By Star and Compass, 1967; Prepare to Dive, 1971; Boys in Revolution, 1967; Ships and Seamen of American Revolution, 1969; The Campaign for Guadalcanal, 1972. Address: Stonewalls Hill Church RD 1 Boyertown PA 19512

COGHILL, CALVIN EDWARD, metals exec.; b. Roanoke, Va., Mar. 4, 1906; s. Henry Hancock and Ida (Austin) C.; m. Marjorie Harding, Jan. 9, 1926; children—Thomas Ellis, Donald Edward. Treas., Reynolds Metals Co., Richmond, Va., 1949-56, v.p., treas., 1956-61, financial v.p. 1961—, also dir.; dir. So. Bank & Trust Co., Richmond, United Va. Bank Internat., Norfolk, Va. Mem. Va. Soc. Pub. Accountants, Controllers Inst. Methodist. Clubs: Metropolitan (Washington); Country, Commonwealth, Deep Run Hunt (Richmond, Va.); New York Athletic (N.Y.C). Home: Krafton River Rd Richmond VA 23229 Office: 6601 W Broad St Richmond VA 23230

COGLEY, JOHN, editor; b. Chgo., Mar. 16, 1916; s. John Francis and Anne (Geenty) C.; A.B., Loyola U., Chgo., 1947; Licentiate in Philosophy, U. Fribourg (Switzerland), 1949; L.D.Litt. (hon.), St. Martin's Coll., 1962; m. Theodora Schmidt, Apr. 6, 1942; children—Terence, Ann Sturmo, Christopher, Joan, Paul, Mark. Editor, Today Mag., 1946-48; exec. editor Commonwealth, 1950-55; mem. religious news editor N.Y. Times, 1955-56; exec. staff Fund for the Republic, 1956-64; editor The Center Mag., 1967—; sr. fellow Center for Study of Democratic Instns., 1967—. Vis. lectr. U. Cal. at Santa Barbara, 1970; mem. selection bd. Dept. State, 1962. Mem. campaign staffs John F. Kennedy, 1960, Eugene McCarthy, 1968. Trustee Council on Religion and Internat. Affairs, 1956-70. Served with USAAF, 1942-45. Recipient award for coverage of Vatican Council, Catholic Press Assn., 1965. Author: Report on Blacklisting, 1956; Religion in a Secular Age, 1969. Editor: Religion in Am., 1958; Natural Law and Modern Society, 1963. Contbr. to Ency. Britannica, Perspectives, New Cath. Ency. Office: The Center Mag Box 4068 Santa Barbara CA 93103

COGSWELL, ANDREW COLVILLE, ret. univ. dean; b. Livingston, Mont., Dec. 10, 1904; s. William F. and Mabel (Allen) C.; B.A. in Journalism, U. Mont., 1927; M.A., U. Minn., 1943; m. Pauline Rachel Swartz, Aug. 15, 1931; 1 son, William Burchard. Publicity writer Mont. State Fair, summer, 1927; reporter Anaconda (Mont.) Standard, 1927; ships reporter Honolulu Star-Bull., 1928; telegraph editor Daily Northwest, Missoula, Mont., 1928; publicity writer Yellowstone Nat. Park, summer, 1929; asst. city editor Mont. Standard. Butte, 1929; writer Portland Cement Assn., 1930-31; mem. staff U. Mont. Sch. Journalism, 1931—, prof., 1946-70, dir. pub. service div., 1946-55, dean students, 1955-70, dean, prof. emeritus, 1970—; a founder U. Mont. Found., 1950. Bd. dirs. Western Mont. Council Alcoholism, 1961-62. Mem. Nat. Assn. Student Personnel Adminstrs., U. Mont. Alumni Assn. (sec. 1945-55), Sigma Delta Chi. Kiwanian (pres. Missoula 1947). Home: 404 Pattee Canyon Dr Missoula MT 59801

COGSWELL, ARNOLD, financial mgmt. exec.; b. Albany, N.Y., Feb. 15, 1924, s. Ledyard, Jr. and Dorothy Treat (Arnold) C.; B.A., Yale, 1950; m. Jessie Batcheller, July 11, 1953; children—Arnold, Jessie Jackson, Elizabeth Ledyard. Treas. Aire Island Inc., Albany, 1949—, pres., 1954—; chmn. bd. Pitts. Tube Co., Rensselaer Research Corp., Pitts.-Internat. Corp.; dir. Nat. Comml. Bank & Trust Co., Albany, Fiduciary Equity Assos., Inc., Air Cushion Vehicles, Inc., First Comml. Banks, Inc. Pres., bd. govs. Albany Med. Center Hosp.; trustee Rensselaer Poly. Inst.; incorporator Am. Sch. for Deaf, Hartford, Conn.; trustee, v.p. Albany Med. Coll.; gov., treas. Union U.; trustee Hudson-Mohawk Assn. Colls. and Univs., Brooks Sch.; pres., treas. Albany's Hosp. Incurables. Served with AUS, 1943-46. Home: 99 Old Niskayuna Rd Loudonville NY 12211 Office: PO Box 4087 Albany NY 12204

COGSWELL, DOROTHY MCINTOSH, educator; b. Plymouth, Mass., Nov. 13, 1909; d. Clarence H. and Ruth (McIntosh) Cogswell; B.F.A., Yale, 1933, M.F.A., 1939. Instr. Mt. Holyoke Coll., 1939-44, asst. prof., asso. prof., 1947-59, prof., 1959- -, chmn. dept. art, 1960-69, dir. art collection, 1970—. One man shows G.W.V. Smith Mus., Springfield, Albany Inst. History and Art, U. Mass., Elmira Coll., Rutgers U.; exhibited group shows N.Y. World's Fair, N.Y. Watercolor Soc., Conn. Acad., New Haven Paint and Clay Club; rep. permanent collection Springfield Mus. Fine Arts, Newport Assn., Holyoke Mus.; murals Mt. Holyoke Coll. Recipient 1st watercolor prize Eastern States, 1941; Fulbright grant for lectureship Nat. Art. Sch., Sydney, Australia, 1957-58. Mem. Springfield Art League (pres. 1942-43), Mt. Holyoke Friends of Art (chmn. 1947-60), Coll. Art Assn., New Haven Paint and Clay Club, Am. Assn. Museums, Soc. Archtl. Historians. Conglist. Home: 23 Jewett Lane South Hadley MA 01075

COGSWELL, GLENN DALE, lawyer; b. nr. Kingman, Kan., Feb. 1, 1922; s. Carl Clifford and Susie (Schisler) C.; student U. Kan., 1940; A.B., Washburn U., 1943, LL.B., 1947, J.D., 1969; children by previous marriage-Carolyn, David; m. 2d, Judith Hahn; children-Michael Christian, Dia Michelle, Niki Lynn, Shea Lara. Admitted to Kan. bar, 1947, since practiced in Topeka; judge Ct. of Topeka, 1949-51; judge Shawnee County Probate and Juvenile Cts., 1951- 57; partner Goodell, Casey, Brinan, Rice & Cogswell, 1965—. Dir. Topeka Morris Plan Co. State chmn. Kan. Young Republican Fedn., 1955-57; del. Rep. Nat. Conv., 1956; Rep. nominee lt. gov. Kan., 1958. Served to lt. (j.g.) USNR, 1943-46. Recipient Distinguished Service award Kan. Jr. C. of C., 1955, DeMolay Legion of Honor, 1956. Mem. Am., Kan., Topeka bar assns., Am. Legion, Native Sons Kan. (past pres.), Kan. Probate Judges Assn. (past pres.), Phi Delta Theta, Delta Theta Phi. Episcopalian. Mason (Shriner). Home: 3719 W 31st St Topeka KS 66614 Office: 215 E 8th St Topeka KS 66603

COGSWELL, WILTON W., dental surgeon; b. Kansas City, Mo. Sept. 6, 1913; s. Asa Ferris and Bina (Haldeman) C.; D.D.S., Kansas City (Mo.) Dent. Coll. 1913; m. Dawn Frances James, Jan. 14, 1913; children—Wilton W., Walter Ferris, Kenneth James. Practiced in Kansas City, Mo., 1913-18; practiced oral surgery, Colorado Springs, Colo.; mem. attending staff Glockner Sanatorium and Hosp., vis. lectr., clin. instr. oral surgery U. Kansas City Sch. Dentistry. Oral surgery cons. USAF Acad., Colorado Springs, Fitzsimons Army Hosp., Denver, surgeon USAF Air Def. Command, Colorado Springs; originator, builder oral surgery clinic Cogswell Clinic, comprising more than 300 wax models on permanent exhbn. Pres., Colo. State Bd. Dental Examiners, 1929-35, Nat. Dental Examiners Assn., 1932. Recipient award for distinguished public service. U.S. Dept. Def. 1968. Fellow Am. Coll. Dentists; mem. Am. Soc. Oral Surgeons and Exodontists, Colo. Dental Assn. (pres. 1943-44), Delta Sigma Delta, Omicron Kappa Upsilon. Club: Cheyenne Mountain Country. Author: Dental Oral Surgery, 1932; Surgery of the Oral Cavity, 1959. Home: 16 Berthe Circle Broadmoor CO 80906 Office: Exchange Nat Bank Bldg Colorado Springs CO 80902

COHAN, AVERY BERLOW, educator; b. Boston, July 12, 1914; s. Max Joseph and Elizabeth (Berlow) C.; A.B., Cornell U., 1934; A.M., Columbia, 1942, Ph.D., 1959; m. Margaret Ann Kelley, Jan. 20, 1948; children—Beth Neal, Judith Kelley, Kevin Berlow, Peter Marshall. Research asst. Nat. Bur. Econ. Research, 1943; research asso. N.A.M., 1944-45; attache Dept. State, Berne, Switzerland, 1945-48, Stockholm, Sweden, 1949-51; resident rep. Econ. Com. Europe, Geneva, Switzerland, 1951-53; sales Top Co., Boston, 1953-56; teaching asso. Harvard, 1956-57; mem. faculty U.N.C., 1957—, prof. finance, 1961—, chmn. grad. studies bus. adminstrn., 1962-67; on leave as chief ins. br., cons. UN Conf. Trade and Devel., Geneva, Switzerland, 1968-69; cons. Nat. Bur. Econ. Research, 1961-69; vis. prof. IMEDE Mgmt. Devel. Inst., Lausanne, Switzerland, 1964-65. Bd. govs. Durham Acad., 1967-69. Mem. Am., So. econ. assns., Inst. Mgmt. Scis., Am. Statis. Assn., Beta Gamma Sigma. Club: Chapel Hill Country (treas. 1963). Author: Cost of Flotation of Long Term Corporate Debt Since 1935, 1961; Yields on Corporate Debt Directly Placed, 1967; Financial Decision-Making—Theory and Practice, 1971; Case Problems in Financial Decision Making, 1972; also articles. Home: Kings Mill Rd Chapel Hill NC 27514

COHANE, TIM, educator, writer; b. New Haven, Feb. 7, 1912; s. Sylvester T. and Margaret (Hogan) C.; B.A. Fordham U., 1935; m. Margaret U. Hill, Dec. 29, 1936; children—Margaret Mary, Lorraine Elizabeth, Timothy, Peter, Rosemary, Ellen, Mary Therese. Dir. athletic publicity Fordham U., 1935- 40; mem. sports dept. N.Y. World-Telegram, 1940-44; sports editor Look mag., 1944-65; editor Sunrise mag., Boston, 1965-67; prof. journalism Boston U., 1968—. Contbr. sports articles nat. mags., 1940-44. Adviser, Bud Wilkinson for U.S. Senate, 1964. Mem. Football Writers Assn. Am., U.S. Basketball Writers Assn., Authors League, Sycamore Tribe Okla. (hon.). Club: Touchdown (N.Y.C.). Author: Gridiron Grenadiers, The Story of West Point Football, 1948; The Yale Football Story, 1951; (with Earl H. Blaik) You Have to Pay the Price, 1960; Bypaths to Glory, 1963. Home: 90 Undine Rd Brighton MA 02135 Office: 640 Commonwealth Av Boston MA 02116

COHART, EDWARD MAURICE, physician, educator; b. Bklyn., Dec. 8, 1909, s. Maurice Abraham and Emma (Chess) C.; A.B., Columbia, 1928, M.D. 1933, M.S. in Pub. Health, 1947; m. Mary Schleifer, Oct. 19, 1933; children—Paul, Diana. Pvt. practice medicine, 1935-42; cancer control cons. USPHS, Dist. 1, 1947- 48; asso. prof. pub. health Yale U. Med. Sch., 1948-56, on leave, 1955-56, prof., 1956-61, Charles-Edward A. Winslow prof. pub. health, 1961- -, chmn. dept. pub. health 1966-68; dep. commr. Dept. Health, N.Y.C.; cons. pub. health Inst. Pub. Adminstrn, N.Y., 1955-56. Diplomate Am. Bd. Preventive Medicine Fellow Am. Coll. Preventive Medicine; mem. A.M.A., Assn. Schs. Pub. Health (sec.-treas, 1965-68), Am., New Eng. (pres. 1966-67), Conn. pub. health assns., A.A.A.S., Assn. Tchrs. Preventive Medicine, Conn. Acad. Preventive Medicine, Phi Beta Kappa, Sigma Xi. Home: 625 Ellsworth Av New Haven CT 06511

COHEE, GEORGE VINCENT, geologist; b. Indpls., Feb. 4, 1907, s. Frank Lloyd and Estella Jane (Holsapple) C.; B.S. in Geology, U. Ill., 1931, M.S. in Geology, 1932; B.S. in Edn., 1933, Ph.D. in Geology, 1937; m. Vera French, Aug. 14, 1930. Asst. geologist oil and gas div. Ill. Geol. Survey, 1936-42; asst. state geologist Ind. Geol. Survey, 1942-43; petroleum analyst Petroleum Adminstrn. for War, 1943; supervising geologist fuels br. U.S. Geol. Survey, 1943-49, sr. geologist fuel br., 1949-51; research asso. geology U. Mich., 1947-49; chmn. dept. geology U. Ark., 1951-52; chmn. geologic names com., also chief geologic names rev. staff U.S. Geol. Survey, 1952—. Pres. for N.Am. subcommn. tectonic map of World, Internat. Geol. Congress, 1960-66; mem. Internat. Commn. Stratigraphic Nomenclature, 1954—, Am. Commn. Stratigraphic Nomenclature, 1953-55, 57—. Fellow Geol. Soc. Am.; mem. Am. Assn. Petroleum Geologists (sec.-treas. 1960-62, chmn. tectonic map com. 1955-61; hon. mem.), Soc. Econ. Pal. and Mineralogy, Geochem. Soc., Geol. Soc. Washington (pres. 1965). Club: Cosmos (Washington). Author articles in field. Co-editor: Possible Future Petroleum Provinces of North America, 1957. Home: 5508 Namakagan Rd Washington, DC 20016. Office: US Geol Survey Washington DC 20242

COHEE, ROBERT NATHAN, librarian; b. Greenwood, Del., May 10, 1927; s. Henry H. and Mabel (Barwick) C.; B.A., U. Del., 1950; M.S. in L.S., Drexel Inst. Tech., 1954; m. Marilyn Goodis, Sept. 18, 1954; children—Karen, Susan, Wendy, Laura. Circulation head U. Del. Library, 1954-58; librarian Elkins Park (Pa.) Free Library, 1958-59, Hazelton (Pa.) Pub. Library, 1959-62; readers service librarian Elizabethtown (Pa.) Coll. Library, 1962-63; librarian Scranton (Pa.) Pub. Library, 1963-69; dist. librarian Pocono Library Dist., 1963-69; library dir. Luzerne County (Pa.) Community Coll., Wilkes-Barre, 1969—. Mem. Citizens Participation in Community Devel. Com., Scranton, 1966-69; mem. cultural com. region M, Elementary and Secondary Edn. Act program, 1966—; mem. Scranton UN Com., 1963-69; mem. Com. of 100,000 Pennsylvanians, 1965—; sec. Scranton Mayors Flag Display Com., 1968-69. Served with USNR, 1945-46, AUS, 1952-53. Mem. Pa. Library Assn. (pres. Northeastern chpt. 1960-61), Scabbard and Blade, Phi Kappa Tau. Home: 700 Harrison Av Scranton PA 18510 Office: Luzerne County Community Coll Wilkes-Barre PA 18702

COHELAN, JEFFERY, med. plans assn. exec.; b. San Francisco, June 24, 1914; A.B., U. Cal. at Berkeley; Fulbright research scholar U. Leeds and Oxford U., 1953-54; m. Evelyn Elizabeth Ellis, Feb. 10, 1939; children—Pamela (Mrs. David Benson), Catherine, Timothy D., Terrence D. Became sec.-treas. Milk Drivers and Dairy Employees Local 302, Alameda and Contra Costa counties, Cal., 1942; mem. Berkeley Welfare Commn., 1949-53, Berkeley City Council, 1955. Mem. 86th-91st Congresses, 7th Cal. Dist., mem. Appropriations Com., former mem. Armed Services Com., D.C. Com.; exec. dir. Group Health Assn. Am., 1971—. Democrat. Club: Commonwealth. Home: Berkeley CA 94701

COHEN, ALAN NORMAN, service co. exec.; b. Clifton, N.J., Dec. 19, 1930; s. Samuel and Ida (Phillips) C.; student Dartmouth, 1948-49; A.B., Columbia, 1952, LL.B., 1954; m. Joan Meryl Fields, Nov. 25, 1953; children—Laurie Elizabeth, Gordon Geoffrey. Admitted to N.Y. bar, 1954; asso. firm Cahill, Gordon, Reindel & Ohl, N.Y.C., 1954; asso. firm Paul, Weiss, Goldberg, Rifkind, Wharton & Garrison, N.Y.C., 1957-63, partner, 1964-70; sr. v.p., dir., mem. exec. com. Kinney Service, Inc., N.Y.C., 1970—. Mem. exec. com. lawyers' div. Anti-Defamation League, 1964-68; mem. Montclair (N.J.) Bd. Adjustment, 1970—. Served with AUS, 1955-57. Mem. N.Y.C., N.Y. State bar assns. Home: 77 Myrtle Av Montclair NJ 07042 Office: 10 Rockefeller Plaza New York City NY 10020

COHEN, ALBERT DIAMOND, merchandising exec.; b. Winnipeg, Man., Can., Jan. 20, 1916; s. Alexander and Rose (Diamond) C.; grad. St. Johns High Sch., Winnipeg, 1930; m. Irena Kankova, Nov. 6, 1953; children—Anthony Jan, James Edward, Anna Lisa. Pres. Gen. Distbrs., Ltd., Winnipeg, 1953—; pres., chief exec. officer, Gen. Distbrs. Can. Ltd., 1968—; chmn. bd. Met. Stores of Can., Ltd., Winnipeg, 1961—, Greenberg Stores Ltd.; sec., treas., dir. Saan Stores Ltd.; dir. Cam-Gard Supply Ltd., Consol. Supply Co. Ltd. Pres. Man. Theatre Centre. Served with Royal Canadian Navy, 1942-45. Home: 305 Park Blvd Tuxedo 29 Manitoba Canada Office: 1370 Sony Pl Winnipeg 19 Manitoba Canada

COHEN, ALEXANDER H., theatrical and television producer; b. N.Y.C., July 24, 1920; s. Alexander H. and Laura (Tarantous) C.; ed. N.Y.U.; m. Jocelyn Newmark, Jan. 12, 1942; 1 dau., Barbara Ann; m. 2d, Hildy Parks, Feb. 24, 1956; children— Gerald Parks, Christopher Alexander. Producer plays, 1941—, starting with Angel Street; other prodns. include: The Duke In Darkness, King Lear, The First Gentleman, At The Drop of a Hat, An Evening with Yves Montand, Victor Borge's Comedy in Music, An Evening with Mike Nichols and Elaine May, Beyond the Fringe, Maurice Chevalier at 77, The School for Scandal, Hamlet (Richard Burton), Baker Street, The Devils, A Time for Singing, Ivanov, At the Drop of Another Hat, The Homecoming, Black Comedy, Little Murders, The Unknown Soldier and His Wife, Halfway Up the Tree, Marlene Dietrich, Dear World, Home; also numerous plays presented in West End of London (Eng.), including The Doctor's Dilemma, Man and Boy, Ivanov, You Never Can Tell, Season of Goodwill, The Merchant of Venice, Halfway Up the Tree, The Rivals, Plaza Suite, The Price, Come as You Are, 1776, The Happy Apple, Who Killed Santa Claus?; for television has produced The Antoinette Perry (Tony) awards show, 1967-71, A World of Love, 1970, CBS-TV Spl. for UNICEF, 1970. Bd. govs. League N.Y. Theatres; mem. bd. Council of Living Theatre, Ind. Booking Office; trustee Actors Fund Am. Served with inf. AUS, 1943-44. Clubs: Lambs, Friars, Players. Home: Trinity Pass Pound Ridge NY 10576 Office: Shubert Threatre 225 W 44th New York City NY 10036 also Queens Theatre Shaftesbury Av London W1 England

COHEN, ARTHUR, educator; b. Bklyn., May 23, 1933; s. Ezra and Ernestine (Salzman) C.; B.A., Bklyn. Coll., 1955; M.A., Columbia, 1957, Ph.D., 1963; m. Anita Kern, Aug. 18, 1957; children—Richard, Elizabeth. Asst. to asso. prof. Rutgers U., New Brunswick, N.J., 1963-68, prof., chmn. dept. applied and math. statistics, 1968—. Served with USPHS, 1957-59. NSF research grantee, 1965—. Mem. Inst. Math. Statistics, Am. Statis. Assn., Royal Statis. Soc. Contbr. numerous articles math. jours. Home: 6 King Rd Somerset NJ 08873

COHEN, ARTHUR ALLEN, author, pub.; b. N.Y.C., June 25, 1928; s. Isidore Meyer and Bess (Junger) C.; B.A., U. Chgo., 1946, M.A., 1949; fellow Jewish philosophy Jewish Theol. Sem. Am., 1951-53; m. Elaine Firstenberg Lustig, Oct. 14, 1956; 1 dau., Tamar Judith. Co-founder Noonday Press, N.Y.C., 1951; founder, pres., exec. editor Meridian Books, Inc., N.Y.C., 1955 (acquired by World Pub. Co., 1960), pres. Meridian Books, v.p. World Pub. Co., 1961; dir. religious pub. Holt, Rinehart, and Winston, Inc., 1961-64, editor-in-chief gen. book div., v.p., 1964-68; cons. editor E.P. Dutton, mng. editor Documents 20th Century Art, Viking Press, 1968—; cons. project on religion and free soc. Fund for Republic, 1957-61. Adv. council Inst. Advanced Judaic Studies, Brandeis U.; adv. council B'nai B'rith com. adult Jewish edn. Author: Martin Buber, 1958; The Natural and the Supernatural Jew; An Historical and Theological Introduction, 1963; The Carpenter Years, 1967; The Myth of the Judeo-Christian Tradition, 1970; A People Apart—Hasidism in America, 1970. Contbr. Am. Catholics: A Protestant-Jewish View, 1959; Christianity: Some Non-Christian Appraisals, 1964; Sacramentum Mundi, 1964; others. Editor: Anatomy of Faith, 1960; Humanistic Education and Western Civilization, 1964; Arguments and Doctrines: A Reader in Jewish Thinking, 1970; Judaism, 1969—. Contbr. articles religious publs. Mem. publ. com. Congress Bi-Weekly, Judaism. Home: 160 E 70th St New York City NY 10021 Office: 25 E 69th St New York City NY 10021

COHEN, ARTHUR LEROY, educator; b. Newport News, Va., Jan. 22, 1916; s. Benjamin Herman and Florence (Gerson) C.; student Bakersfield (Cal.) Jr. Coll., 1933-34; A.B., Stanford, 1937; M.A., Harvard, 1939, Ph.D., 1940; m. Julia Silberberg, June 12, 1944; children—Florence Rebecca, Philip, Theodore, Gilbert. Austin fellow Harvard, 1940-41; research fellow Cal. Inst. Tech., 1942-47; prof. biology Oglethorpe Coll., 1947- 62; dir. Electron Milcroscope Center, prof. botany and biol. scis. Wash. State U., Pullman, 1962—; vis. prof. anatomy Yale Med. Sch., 1971. Guggenheim fellow Technische Hogeschool, Delft, Holland, 1956-57. Recipient travel award NSF, 1954. Mem. Bot. Soc. Am., Electron Miscroscope Soc. Am., France, Japan, Soc. Gen. Microbiologists, Protozoological Soc., Mycol. Soc. Am. Home: Box 92A Route 1 Pullman WA 99163

COHEN, BENJAMIN BERNARD, educator; b. Balt., May 30, 1922; s. Louis I. and Lillie (Laken) C.; A.B., U. Md., 1943, M.A., 1944; Ph.D., Ind. U., 1950; m. Lucian Anderson, July 29, 1952. Instr., Wayne U., 1948-52; asst. prof. Ga. Inst. Tech., 1953-55; asst. prof. Ind. State Tchrs. Coll., Terre Haute, 1955-57; asso. prof. Jacksonville (Ala.) State Tchrs. Coll., 1957-59; asso. prof. Oglethorpe U., 1959-60; asso. prof., prof. Wichita State U., 1960-68; prof. English, U. Mo., St. Louis, 1968—. Recipient Excellence in Teaching award Wichita State U., 1968. Am. Council Learned Socs. research scholar Yale, 1952-53. Mem. Modern Lang. Assn., Midwest Modern Lang. Assn., Nat. Council Tchrs. English, Conf. on Coll. Composition and Communication. Author: Writing About Literature, 1963; Working for Literary Understanding, 1966. Editor: The Recognition of Nathaniel Hawthorne, 1969; Guide to Nathaniel Hawthorne, 1970. Contbr. articles profl. jours. Home: 7433 Overbrook Dr St Louis MO 63121 Professional: University of Missouri St Louis 8001 Natural Bridge Road St Louis MO 63121

COHEN, BENJAMIN VICTOR, lawyer; b. Muncie, Ind.; Sept. 23, 1894; s. Moses and Sarah (Ringold) C.; Ph.B., U. Chicago, 1914, J.D., 1915; S.J.D., Harvard, 1916; LL.D., Dropsie Coll., 1952, Ball State U., 1969. Admitted to Ill. bar, 1916; sec. to U.S. circuit judge, 1916-17; atty. U.S. Shipping Bd., 1917-19; counsel Am. Zionists, Peace Confs., London, Paris, 1919-21; pvt. practice N.Y.C., 1922- 33; asso. gen. counsel PWA, 1933-34; gen. counsel Nat. Power Policy Com., 1934-1941; spl. asst. to U.S. atty. gen., concerned with pub. utility holding co. litigation, 1936-38; adviser Am. ambassador to Gt. Britain, 1941; asst. to dir., Office Econ. Stblzn., 1942-43; gen. counsel Office of War Moblzn., 1943-45; counselor Dept. State 1945-47. Assisted Congl. coms. in drafting Securities Act 1933, Securities and Exchange Act 1934, Utility Holding Co. Act 1935, Fair Labor Standards Act 1937; legal adviser Internat. Monetary Conf., Breton Woods, N.H., 1944; mem. Am. delegation Dumbarton Oaks Conf., 1944; Berlin Conf., 1945; Council of Fgn. Ministers, London, 1945, Moscow, 1945, 47, Paris, 1946, N.Y.C., 1946; Paris Peace Conf., 1946; sr. adviser Am. delegation UN Gen. Assembly, London, N.Y., 1946, mem. delegation, Paris, 1948, 51, N.Y.C., 1949, 50, 52; U.S. rep. before Internat. Ct. Justice, The Hague, 1950; U.S. rep. on UN Disarmament Commn., 1952. Oliver Wendell Holmes lectr. Harvard Law Sch., 1961; David Miles Meml. lectr. Hebrew U. of Jerusalem, 1965; mem. adv. panel internat. law Dept. State, 1968. Recipient Isaiah award, Washington chpt. Am. Jewish Com., 1969. Mem. Phi Beta Kappa. Author: The United Nations Constitutional Development, Growth and Possibilities, 1961. Home: 1727 Massachusetts Av NW Washington DC 20036 ☆

COHEN, BERNARD CECIL, educator, polit. scientist; b. Northampton, Mass., Feb. 22, 1926; s. Lous Mark and Lena (Slotnick) C.; B.A., Yale, 1948, M.A., 1950, Ph.D., 1952; m. Laura Mae Propper, Sept. 1, 1947; children—Barbara Ellen (Mrs. Steven L. Christopherson), Janie Louise. Research asst. Yale, 1950-51; research asst., then research asso. Princeton, 1951-59, asst. prof., 1957-59; mem. faculty U. Wis., 1959—, prof. polit. sci., 1963—, chmn. dept., 1966-69, asso. dean grad. sch., 1971—; vis. research scholar Carnegie Endowment Internat. Peace, 1965-66; mng. editor World Politics 1956-59, mem. bd. editors, 1959-60; mem. bd. editors Internat. Studies Quar., 1966—. Served with AUS, 1944-46. Ford Found. Faculty Research fellow, 1969-70, fellow Center Advanced Study Behavioral Scis., 1961-62, 69-70. Mem. Am., Midwest polit. sci. assns., Internat. Studies Assn. Author: The Political Process and Foreign Policy, 1957; The Press and Foreign Policy, 1963. Editor: Foreign Policy in American Government, 1965. Home: 1034 Seminole Hwy Madison WI 53711

COHEN, BERNARD LEONARD, physicist, educator; b. Pitts., June 14, 1924; s. Samuel and Mollie (Friedman) C.; B.S., Case Inst. Tech., 1944; M.S., U. Pitts., 1948; D.Sc., Carnegie Inst. Tech., 1950; m. Anna Foner, Mar. 30, 1950; children—Donald, Judith, Frederick, Ernest. With Oak Ridge Nat. Lab., 1950-58; prof. physics U. Pitts., 1958—, dir. Sarah Mellon Scaife Nuclear Physicis Lab., 1965—. Fellow Am. Phys. Soc. Home: 5414 Albemarle Av Pittsburgh PA 15217

COHEN, BERNARD P., educator; b. N.Y.C., Jan. 31, 1930; s. Max and Iris (Adler) C.; A.B., Harvard, 1951, Ph.D., 1957; M.A., U. Minn., 1952; m. Elizabeth Asher Ginsburg, Sept. 20, 1953; children—Anita Gail, Lewis Samuel. Lectr. dept. social relations Harvard, Cambridge, Mass., 1956-58; research asso. computer center Mass. Inst. Tech., Cambridge, 1956-57, fellow Inst. Advanced Studies, 1957-58; asst. prof. sociology and social instns. U. Cal. at Berkeley, 1958-59; mem. faculty Stanford, 1959—, dir. lab. social research, asso. prof., 1962-68, prof. sociology, 1968—, also head dept. Cons. Cal. Commn. on Equal Opportunity and Edn., 1965-67. Mem. Santa Clara County Democratic Central Com., 1962-64; local finance chmn. Alan Cranston for Senate U.S. campaign, 1968. Mem. Am., Pacific (v.p.), sociol. assns., Sociol. Research Assn. Author: Conflict and Confomity, 1963; (with others) Types of Formalization in Small Groups Research, 1962. Home: 851 Sonoma Terrace Stanford CA 94305

COHEN, BERTRAM DAVID, educator; b. Bklyn., Jan. 16, 1923; s. Irving and Rose (Rabinowitz) C.; B.A., Bklyn. Coll., 1944; M.A., U. Ia., 1945, Ph.D., 1949; m. Helen Elizabeth Swartley, Aug. 8, 1946; children—Philip S., Sarah L., Matthew A., Michael B., Aaron M., Andrew S. Asst. prof. Ind. U., 1949-52; chief psychologist Iowa City VA Hosp., 1952-56; dir. psychology Lafayette Clinic, Detroit, 1956-62; dir. clin. tng. Rutgers U., 1962-69, prof. psychiatry, Med. Sch., 1965—, chmn. grad. psychology, 1970—. Cons., Nat. Inst. Mental Health, VA, Rutgers Mgmt. Services; mem. certification commn. for psychology state Mich., 1960-62. Mem. bd. profl. advisers Coll. Profl. Psychology, Maplewood,, N.J., 1971—. Trustee Warren Twp. Library Assn. NSF grantee, 1963—, Nat. Inst. Mental Health grantee, 1963-69. Fellow Am. Psychol. Assn. (chmn. sect. 3 div. clin. psychology 1969-70); mem. Am. Coll. Neuropsychopharmacology, Sigma Xi. Asso. editor Jour. Exptl. Research in Personality, 1964—; adv. editor Jour. Cons. and Clin. Psychology, 1964—. Home: 9 Rockage Rd Warren NJ 07060

COHEN, CHARLES L., mfg. exec.; b. Chgo., July 8, 1895; s. Charles and Lena (Broslov) C.; student U. Chgo. 1912-13; LL. B., Webster Coll. Law, 1917; m. Thelma Panama, June 15, 1921; children—Donald, Joann. Admitted to Ill. bar 1917; jr. partner M. Snower & Co., 1913-17, sec., 1917-24, pres., treas., 1924-54; chmn. bd. Opelika Mfg. Corp., 1954—. Sec., dir., MSL Industries, Inc., 1966—. Republican Jewish religion. Mason; mem. B'nai B'rith. Clubs: Standard, Bryn Mawr Country (past pres.); Tamarisk Country (Palm Springs, Cal.) Home: 1325 N State Pkwy Chicago IL 60610 Office: 361 W Chestnut St Chicago, IL 60610.

COHEN, DONALD PANAMA, mfg. co. exec.; b. Chgo., May 8, 1926; s. Charles Leonard and Thelma (Panama) C.; grad. Lake Forest (Ill.) Acad., 1943; B.S., Mass. Inst. Tech, 1949; m. Beverly Axelrod, Feb. 22, 1958; children—Debra Ellen, Ronald Jay, Adrienne. With Opelika Mfg. Corp., Chgo., 1949—, pres., treas., 1962—, also dir. Served with USNR, 1944-46. Jewish religion. Clubs: Standard (Chgo); Bryn Mawr Country (Lincolnwood, Ill). Home: 1040 Lake Shore Dr Chicago, IL 60611. Office: 361 W Chestnut St Chicago IL 60610

COHEN, EDWARD, cons. engr.; b. Glastonbury, Conn., Jan. 6, 1921; s. Samuel and Ida (Tanewitz) C.; B.S. in Engring., Columbia, 1946, M.S. in Civil Engring., 1954; m. Elizabeth Belle Cohen, Dec. 19, 1948; children—Samuel, Libby, James. Asst. engr. Conn. Dept. Pub. Works, 1942-44; structural engr. Hardesry & Hanover, N.Y.C., 1945-47, Sanderson & Proctor, N.Y.C., 1947-49; lectr. architecture Columbia, 1948-51; with Ammann & Whitney, cons. engr., N.Y.C., 1949—, partner, 1963—; v.p. Amman & Whitney, Inc., 1964—, Ammann & Whitney Internat., Ltd., 1963—; cons. to govt. and industry. Recipient Illig medal Columbia, 1946. Registered profl. engr., N.Y., Conn., Fla., Md., N.J., D.C. Fellow Am. Soc. C.E. (Ridgway award 1946), N.Y. Acad. Scis. (Laskowitz research award); mem. Am. Concrete Inst. (dir. 1966-69, v.p. 1970—, chmn. bldg. code requirements for reinforced concrete, Wason medal 1951), Internat. Assn. Bridge and Structural Engrs., Am. Soc. Planning Ofcls., Am. Welding Soc., Am. Nat. Standards Inst. (chmn. minimum design loads for bldgs. and other structures), Reinforced Concrete Research Inst., Performance Full Scale Structures Research Council (chmn. com. long term observations), N.Y. Concrete Constrn. Inst. (chmn. tall bldg. com.), Tau Beta Pi. Jewish religion. Mem. B'nai B'rith. Contbr. manuals profl. assns., articles profl. jours. Home: 15 Holiday Dr Williston Park NY 11596 Office: 111 8th Av New York City NY 10011

COHEN, EDWARD MILTON, furniture co. exec.; b. Uniontown, Pa., Sept. 5, 1909; s. Max and Lillian (Shirk) C.; B.S., U. Pitts., 1931; m. Emily Weinberg, May 28, 1933; children—Lois (Mrs. Howard Sodokoff), Miles. With Cohen Furniture Co., Uniontown, 1932—, v.p., mdse. mgr., 1946-51, pres., 1951—, also dir.; sec., dir. Cohen Furniture Co., Brownsville, Pa., 1946—. Pres., Uniontown Credit Bur., 1959—; treas. Uniontown Parking Authority, 1950- -. Bd. dirs. Uniontown Hosp., Uniontown Indsl. Fund, Uniontown Motor Club; pres. Uniontown Community Chest, 1958, bd. dirs., 1947—. Recipient All Am. Merchant award Cavalier Corp. and furniture industry, 1952; Furniture World Industry award Furniture World mag., 1951; named Uniontown Man of Year, 1959. Mem. Nat. Retail Furniture Assn. (dir., pres. 1961), Pa. Retailers Assn. (dir.), Uniontown C. of C. (pres. 1958- 59), Phi Epsilon Pi. Clubs: Export, Westmoreland Country (Pitts.). Author articles. Home: 5407 Beacon St Pittsburgh PA 15217 Office: 19 Beeson Blvd Uniontown PA 15401

COHEN, EDWIN SAMUEL, lawyer, educator; b. Richmond, Va., Sept. 27, 1914; s. LeRoy S. Cohen and Mirian (Rosenheim) C; B.A., U. Richmond, 1933; LL.B., U. Va., 1936; m. Helen Herz, Aug. 31, 1944; children—Edwin C., Roger, Susan Wendy. Admitted to Va. Bar, 1935, N.Y. bar, 1937; asso. Sullivan & Cromwell, N.Y.C., 1936-49; partner Root, Barrett, Cohen, Knapp & Smith and predecessor firm, N.Y.C., 1949-65, counsel, 1965-69; prof. law U. Va., Charlottsville, 1965-68, Joseph M. Hartfield Prof., 1968-69; asst. sec. treasury for tax policy, 1969—. Mem. and counsel adv. group on corporate taxes Ways and Means Com. Ho. of Reps., 1956-58; spl. cons. on corps. Am. Law Inst. Fed. Income Tax Project, 1949-54, mem. adv. group Fed. Estate and Gift Tax Project, 1964-68; mem. Va. Income Tax Conformity Study Commn., 1970—; cons. Va. Income Tax Study Commn., 1966-68; mem. adv. group Commr. Internal Revenue, 1967-68; mem. adv. com. N.Y. U. Inst. on Fed. Taxation, 1968—. Recipient Alexander Hamilton award Treasury Dept. Mem. Am. Judicature Soc., Am. (chmn. com. on corporate stockholder relationships 1956-58, chmn. spl. com. on substantive tax reform 1962-63, spl. adviser 1963-68), Va., N.Y. State bar assns., Va. Tax Conf. (planning com. 1965-68), Assn. Bar City N.Y., N.Y. County Lawyers Assn., Am. Assn. U. Profs., Am. Law Inst. Order Coif, Raven Soc., U. Va., Phi Beta Kappa, Omicron Delta Kappa, Pi Delta Epsilon, Phi Epsilon Pi (Nat. Achievement award). Clubs: University of Virginia of New York; Broad Street; Colonnade; Boar's Head; Keswick; Nat. Lawyers. Home: 104 Stuart Pl Ednam Forest Charlottesville VA 22901 Office: US Treasury Dept 15th & Pennsylvania Av NW Washington DC 20220

COHEN, ELI EDWARD, youth agy. ofcl.; b. Chgo., Aug. 3, 1912; s. Kalman and Rose (Sirota) C.; B.S., U. Ill., 1933; postgrad. Sch. Social Service Adminstrn. U. Chgo., 1934-37; m. Dorothy Hersh, Feb. 17, 1936 (dec. 1959); children—Robert, Ellen, Katey; m. 2d, Selma Stein Rosenbaum, May 18, 1969. Supr. Marks Nathan Jewish Orphan Home, Chgo., 1933-34; case worker Chgo. Relief Adminstrn., 1934-36; counselor Jewish Vocational Service, Chgo., 1936-39; dir. Phila. Jewish Vocational Service, 1939-40; exec. dir. Jewish Occupational Council, N.Y.C., 1940-51; v.p. Exec. Job Counselors, N.Y.C., 1952-57; exec. sec. Nat. Child Labor Com. and div., Nat. Com. Employment Youth, 1958—; lectr. N.Y.U., 1951, 64; cons. youth employment Dept. Labor, 1961-64, 66, 69. Dir. Am. Parents Com., 1960—, Mental Health Film Bd., 1963—, Nat. Council Agrl. Life and Labor, 1958-64; mem. U.S. steering com. for World Mental Health Year, 1959-60; nat. panel arbitrators Am. Arbitration Assn., 1953—. Sec. Nat. Conf. Jewish Social Welfare, 1950-51; pres. N.Y. Vocational Guidance Assn., 1949-51; mem. Mayor N.Y.C. Com. Youth and Work, 1960-66; cons. White House Conf. Children and Youth, 1960; mem. Pres.'s Com. Youth Employment, 1961-64; task force youth U.S. Employment Service, 1964; mem. nat. com. Citizens Crusade Against Poverty, 1965-69; cons. anti-poverty task force Nat. Council Chs.; chmn. adv. council for occupational edn. N.Y.C. Bd. Edn., 1968—; chmn. Council Nat. Orgns. for Children and Youth, 1971—. Profl. mem. Nat. Vocational Guidance Assn. of Am. Personnel and Guidance Assn., past chmn. young workers sect; mem. Nat. Com. for Children and Youth, 1968—; mem. exec. com. N.Y. State com. for 1970 White House Conf. on Children and Youth. Author articles, contbr. books and encys. Co-editor: Manpower Policies for Youth, 1966. Home: 2109 Broadway New York City NY 10023 Office: 145 E 32d St New York City NY 10016

COHEN, EUGENE ERWIN, univ. adminstr.; b. Johnstown, Pa., Nov. 1, 1917; s. Leory Samuel and Ann (Aronson) C.; B.B.A., U. Miami (Fla.), 1941, M.B.A., 1951; postgrad. U. N.C., Wayne State U.; m. Lee Woodward Edmundson, Dec. 31, 1944; children—William Palmer, Margaret Gene, Ann Woodard. Asst. auditor Embry Riddle Co., 1940-41; mem. faculty and staff U. Miami, 1945—, asso. prof. accounting, 1954-67, prof. accounting, 1967—, treas., 1957- -, v.p., 1958—, also treas. univ. Internat. Research Found. Chmn., pres. Laurel Corp., 1971; dir. Garret & Co.; cons. Greyhound Corp., Plastetics, Inc., Reynolds & Co.; mem.'s rep. Univ. Corp. for Atmospheric Research. Cons. NSF, U.S. Office Edn., So. Assn. Colls. and Schs., NIH; mem. com. taxation Am. Council Edn. Bd. dirs. Miami Goodwill Industries, Dade County Citizens Safety Council, Greater Miami Indsl. Commn., asso. mem. Orange Bowl Com.; chmn. Dade County Higher Edn. Facilities Authority, 1969—; v.p., dir. Nat. Childrens Cardiac Hosp.; dir. Dormitory Housing Assn., Family Services, Miami; trustee United Fund Dade County. Served with USAAF, 1941-45. Mem. Dade County C. of C., Am. Mgmt. Assn., Nat. (dir.), so. (pres. 1963) assns. coll. and univ. bus. officers Coll. and U. Personnel Assn., Coll. and U. Housing Officers Assn., Nat. Assn. Cost Accountants, Financial Execs. Inst. (founder mem. Fla. chpt., chpt. pres. 1963), Econ. Soc. S.Fla., Newcomen Soc., Omicron Delta Kappa, Alpha Phi Omega, Phi Mu Alpha, Alpha Kappa Psi. Clubs: Miami University Yacht, Miami (gov.); Ocean Reef Yacht and Country (Key Largo, Fla.). Author articles in field. Cons. editor Coll. and Univ. Bus., 1959-70. Home: 6700 SW 117th St Miami FL 33156 Office: Ashe Adminstrn Bldg U Miami Coral Gables FL 33124

COHEN, EZECHIEL GODERT DAVID, physicist; b. Amsterdam, Holland, Jan. 16, 1923; s. David Ezechiel and Sophie Louise (de Sterke) C.; B.S. in Math., Physics and Astronomy, U. Amsterdam, 1947, Ph.D., 1957; m. Marina Arnoldina Linnekamp, Apr. 19, 1950; children—Michael Benjamin, Andrea Margaret. Came to U.S., 1963. First asst. U. Amsterdam, 1950-61, asso. prof., 1961-63; research asso. U. Mich., 1957-58, Johns Hopkins, 1958-59; prof., mem. Rockefeller U., 1963—. Fellow Am. Phys. Soc.; mem. Netherlands Phys. Soc. Editor: Fundamental Problems in Statistical Mechanics, vol. I, 1961, vol. II, 1968; Statistical Mechanics at the Turn of the Decade, 1971. Home: 144-15 Charterroad Jamaica NY 11435 Office: Rockefeller U York Av and 66th St New York City NY 10021

COHEN, GEORGE HAYM, educator, artist; b. Worcester, Mass. Sept. 14, 1913, s. Myer and Rose (Glaser) C.; student Sch. Worcester Art Mus., 1933-36, Inst. Design, Chicago, 1949; m. Lois Jean Carl, June 30, 1952; children—Martha, Sarah Rachel. Faculty Smith Coll., 1942—, prof. art 1962—; one man exhbns. include Boston, N.Y.C., Springfield, Mass., Worcester, Smith Coll., U. Conn.; exhbns. include Met. Mus. Art, Mus. Modern Art, Worcester Art Mus., Art Inst. Chgo., Am. Acad. Arts and Letters. Cons. advanced placement in art Coll. Entrance Exam. Bd. Recipient numerous prizes and awards; fellow MacDowell Colony. Mem. Am. Assn. U. Profs., Am. Film Inst., Univ. Film Assn., Am. Soc. Cinematologists, Coll. Art Assn. Home: 15 Washington Av Northampton MA 01060

COHEN, HENNIG, educator; b. Darlington, S.C., Aug. 26, 1919; s. David A. and Hilda (Hennig) C.; A.B., U. S.C., 1941, M.A., 1948; Ph.D., Tulane U., 1951; M.A. (hon.), U. Pa., 1971; m. Merrie Lou Conaway, June 16, 1946; children—David, Mark, Jonathan. News editor Sta. WCOS, Columbia, S.C. 1945-46; dir. pub. relations U. S.C., Columbia, 1946-56; asst. prof. English, U. Pa., Phila., 1957-61; asso. prof., 1961-65, prof., 1965—; vis. lectr. Bryn Mawr Coll., 1962-63, Swarthmore Coll., 1963-64, 65; vis. prof. Stanford, 1968. Served with USAAF, 1941- 45; ETO. Decorated Air medal with five oak leaf clusters; Guggenheim fellow, 1960. Mem. Modern Lang. Assn. Melville Soc. (sec.), Am. Studies Assn. (exec. sec. 1956-61). Jewish religion. Clubs: Franklin Inn; University of Pa. Faculty (Phila.) Author: The South Carolina Gazette, 1953. Editor Am. Quar., 1958-70, chmn. editorial bd., 1970—. Editor: The Battle Pieces of Herman Melville, 1963; Selected Poems of Herman Melville, 1964; (with William Dillingham) Humor of the Old Southwest, 1964; (with T.P. Coffin) Folklore in America, 1966; The American Culture, 1968; The American Experience, 1968; Landmarks in American Writing, 1969. Contbr. articles to profl. jours. Home: 37 Amherst Av Swarthmore PA 19081 Office: Dept English U Pa Philadelphia PA 19104

COHEN, HERBERT ERWIN, lawyer, supermarket exec.; b. Utica, N.Y., Nov. 3, 1932; s. Moe and Mae (Greenbaum) C.; A.B., U. Mich., 1953; J.D., Union U., 1957; LL.M. in Taxation, N.Y.U., 1958; m. Phyllis Simonovitz, July 14, 1957; children—Linda Jean, Michael Howard, David Jonathan. Admitted to N.Y. bar, 1958, also U.S. Supreme Ct., 2d Circuit Ct. Appeals; with Strang, Wright, Combs, Wiser & Shaw, Rochester, N.Y., 1958-59, Marine Midland Corp., Buffalo, 1959-61; pvt. practice law, Albany, N.Y., 1961-64; with Newkirk Assos., Inc., 1964-65; v.p., gen. counsel, sec. Central Markets, Inc. (Golub Corp.), Schenectady, 1965—; lectr. N.Y. State Bar Assn., Practicing Law Inst., Albany Law Sch., Am. Mgmt. Assn. Vice pres. Albany Jewish Family Services, 1971, trustee, 1967—. Trustee Daughters of Sarah Home for the Aged, Troy, N.Y., 1969—. Mem. N.Y. State Bar Assn. Jewish religion (trustee congregation). Home: 19 Pine Tree Lane Albany NY 12208 Office: 501 Duanesburg Rd Schenectady NY 12306

COHEN, HOWARD MARTIN, educator, psychologist; b. N.Y.C., June 6, 1926; s. Bernard and Gertrude (Stecker) C.; student Coll. City N.Y., 1943-44; B.A., George Washington U., 1948, M.A., 1949; Ph.D., N.Y.U., 1957; m. Mildred L. Jones, Oct. 4, 1953; children—Joshua L., Ellen M. Psychologist Stevens Inst. Tech., Hoboken, N.J., 1949-50; psychol. intern Bklyn. State Hosp., 1951-52; clin. psychologist Wallkill Prison, N.Y., 1952-54; chief psychologist Hudson River State Hosp., Poughkeepsie, N.Y., 1954-66; cons. social sci. N.Y. Dept. Mental Hygiene, Albany, 1966-67; prof., chmn. dept. psychology State U. Coll., New Paltz, N.Y., 1967—; tng. cons. Astor Home for Children, Rhinebeck, N.Y., 1957—; mem. Staff Vassar Bros. Hosp., Poughkeepsie, 1971—. Served with USNR, 1944-46, 51. Diplomate Am. Bd. Profl. Psychology. Mem. Am., N.Y. (sec., treas. 1969-72), Eastern psychol. assns. Home: 12 Hornbeck Ridge Poughkeepsie NY 12603

COHEN, I. BERNARD, educator; b. N.Y.C., Mar. 1, 1914; s. Isidor and Blanche (Bernstein) C.; grad. Valley Forge Mil. Acad., 1933; B.S. cum Laude, Harvard, 1937, Ph.D., 1947; LL.D., Poly. Inst. Bklyn., 1964; m. Frances Parsons Davis, June 23, 1944; 1 dau., Frances. Fellow dept. hist. sci. Carnegie Inst., 1938-41; instr. physics Harvard, 1942-46, instr. phys. sci., 1946-47, from instr. to asso. prof. history of sci., 1947-59, prof. history of sci., 1959—. Guggenheim fellow, 1956; NSF Sr. Postdoctoral fellow, 1960-61, Lowell lectr., Boston, 1961; vis. fellow Clare Hall, Cambridge U. Eng., 1965; Wiles lectr. Queens U., Belfast No. Ireland, 1966; Vis. Overseas fellow Churchill Coll., 1968. Chmn. U.S. Com. History and Philosophy Sci., 1961-62. Recipient Bowdoin prize Harvard, 1941. Mem. John Winthrop Soc. (pres. 1939-40). History Sci. Soc. (exec. council 1945-58, pres. 1961-62), A.A.A.S. (v.p. 1959-60), Inst. Early Am. History and Culture (council 1957-60), Internat. Acad. History Sci. (membership com. 1956—, chmn. 1961-62), Mass. Hist. Soc. Am. Assn. History Medicine, Am. Antiquarian Soc., Colonial Soc. Mass., Am. Acad. Arts and Scis. (v.p.), Am. Hist. Assn., Internat. Union History and Philosophy Science (first v.p. 1962-68, prss. 1968—), Club Odd Volumes (council 1965-69) Sigma Xi. Author: Benjamin Franklin's Experiments, 1941; Roemer and the First Determination of the Velocity of Light, 1944; Physical Laboratory Manual, 1944; Science Servant of Man, 1948; Some Early Tools of American Science, 1950; (with F. Watson) General Education in Science, 1952; Benjamin Franklin, His Contribution to the American Tradition, 1953; Isaac Newton's Papers on Natural Philosophy, 1957; Benjamin Franklin's Account of the Pennsylvania Hospital, 1954; Franklin and Newton, 1956; the Birth of the New Physics, 1960; (with H.M. Jones) A Treasury of Scientific Prose, 1963; also articles. Mng. Editor Isis, 1947-52; editor, chmn. editorial com., 1953-58; editorial adv. com. Papers of Benjamin Franklin. Editor: (with Alexandre Koy#83re) Principia (Newton), 1969. Home: 22 Gray Gardens E Cambridge MA 02318

COHEN, IRA STANLEY, univ. adminstr.; b. N.Y.C., Sept. 1, 1922; s. Herbert H. and Minnie (Raden) C.; B.A., Queens Coll., 1948; Ph.D., Ind. U., 1953; m. Nina Taormina, Sept. 1, 1949; children—Rachel, Sarah. Asst. prof. psychology State U. N.Y. at Buffalo, 1952-58, asso. prof., 1958-63, prof., 1963—, acting provost Faculty Social Scis. and Adminstrn., 1968-69, provost, 1969—. Served with AUS, 1942-46. Mem. Am., Eastern psychol. assns., Am. Assn. U. Profs. Home: 159 Morris Av Buffalo NY 14214 Office: State U N Y Buffalo NY 14214

COHEN, ISADORE T., lawyer; b. Savannah, Ga., Jan. 28, 1908, s. Moses G. and Hannah (Katzoff) C.; LL.B., Atlanta Law Sch., 1927; m. Sylvia Gold, Sept. 3, 1929; 1 dau., Barbara (Mrs. William Eugene Schatten). Admitted to Ga., bar, 1927, N.C. bar, 1933; practice in Atlanta, 1927-33, Charlotte, N.C., 1933-39; gen. So. counsel A.S.C.A.P., Atlanta 1939; gen. counsel Tent 21 Variety Club; sr. partner firm Smith, Cohen, Ringel, Kohler, Martin & Lowe, Atlanta. Dir. Fulton Industries, Inc., 1956-68; pres. WIIN, Inc., Atlanta. Bd. govs. Israel Bond Com.; mem. nat. joint distbn. com. United Jewish Appeal. Mem. Am., Ga., N.C. bar assns., Nu Beta. Clubs: Standard, Progressive (Atlanta); Friars (N.Y.C.), Jewish religion (v.p. temple, 1935-37, supt. Sunday Sch. 1935-37). Home: 1371 W Wesley Rd NW Atlanta GA 30327 also Harbour House 2295 S Ocean Blvd Palm Beach FL 33480 Office: First Nat Bank Bldg Atlanta GA 30303

COHEN, JACK CARY, architect; b. Washington, June 13, 1924; s. Harry and Aneta (Yusik) C.; B.S., Catholic U. Am., 1949; m. Marion Goldsmith, June 20, 1948; children—Michael, Claudia, Allison, Maxwell. Prin. partner firm Cohen, Haft & Assos., Silver Spring, Md., 1954—. Served with USAAF, 1943-46. Fellow A.I.A. (chmn. nat. housing com. 1968-70, pres. Potomac Valley chpt. 1961-62), Sigma Xi. Home: 700 Crail Dr Bethesda MD 20034 Office: 814 Thayer Av Silver Spring MD 20910

COHEN, JEROME ALAN, educator; b. Elizabeth, N.J., July 1, 1930; s. Philip and Beatrice (Kaufman) C.; B.A., Yale, 1951; LL.B., 1955; postgrad. U. Lyons (France), 1951-52; m. Joan F. Lebold, June 30, 1954; children—Peter, Seth, Ethan. Admitted to Conn. bar, 1955, D.C. bar, 1957; law sec. to Chief Justice Warren, 1955-56, to Mr. Justice Frankfurter, 1956-57; asso. firm Covington & Burling, Washington, 1957-58; asst. U.S. atty., Washington, 1958-59; cons. U.S. Senate Com. Fgn. Relations, 1959; mem. faculty U. Cal. at Berkeley, 1959-65; prof. Harvard Law Sch., 1964—. Chmn. subcom. Chinese law, joint com. comtemporary China, Am. Council Learned Socs.- Social Sci. Research Council, 1965—; chmn. panel China and world order Soc. Internat. Law, 1967—. Mem. Assn. Asian Studies, Am. Soc. Internat. Law, Am. Assn. U. Profs. Author: The Criminal Process in the Peoples Republic of China, 1949-63, 1968. Editor: Contemporary Chinese Law, 1970; The Dynamics of China's Foreign Relations, 1970. Home: 21 Bryant St Cambridge MA 02138

COHEN, JEROME BERNARD, educator, economist; b. N.Y.C., Jan. 18, 1915; s. Charles Kenneth and Estelle (Bauland) C.; B.S.S., Coll. City N.Y., 1934; A.M., Columbia, 1935, Ph.D., 1947; m. Mina Salmon, June 18, 1941; 1 dau., Carla Lee. Prof. econs. and finance Bernard M. Baruch Coll., City U. N.Y., 1956-71, dean grad. studies, 1968-71; acting pres. Baruch Coll., fall 1970, spring 1971; research asso. Am. Inst. Banking, summer 1937, Brookings Instn., summer 1938; vis. prof. statistics So. Meth. U., summer 1939; vis. prof. econs. State Coll. Wash., summer 1940, U. P.R., summer 1941. Economist, Coordinator Inter-Am. Affairs, 1941- 42; asst. regional adminstr. for tys. and possessions OPA, 1942-43; mem. Tax Mission to Japan, 1949; chief S. Asia br. Office Intelligence Research U.S. Dept. State, 1950-51; research asso. Center of Internat. Studies, Princeton, 1952; research sec. Council on Fgn. Relations, 1952- 53; research asso. Center for Internat. Studies, Mass. Inst. Tech., summer 1953. Served as Japanese specialist with the rank of lt. Intelligence Corps, USNR, 1943-46. Recipient Rockefeller Found. grant for new study of Japan's economy, 1956; Social Sci. Research Council grant, 1963-64. Townsend Harris medal, 1967. Mem. Royal Econ. Soc. Eng., Am. Econ. Assn., Nat. Tax Assn., Am. Finance Assn., Am. Statis. Assn., Council Fgn. Relations, Japan Soc., Asia Soc. Am. Assn. U. Profs., Nat. Assn. Bus. Economists, Phi Beta Kappa (chpt. pres. 1970-71), Phi Beta Kappa Assos., Beta Gamma Sigma. Author: Japan's Economy in War and Reconstruction, 1949; Economic Problems of Free Japan, 1952; (with A.W. Hanson) Personal Finance: Principles and Case Problems, 3d edit., 1964; Japan's Postwar Economy, 1958; (with S.R. Robbins) The Financial Manager, 1966; (with E. Zinbarg) Investment Analysis and Portfolio Management, 1967; also articles in jours. Home: 135 E 74th St New York City NY 10021 Office: 17 Lexington Av New York City NY 10010

COHEN, JOHN, guitarist, banjoist, mandolinist; b. 1933; married. Mem. group New Lost City Ramblers; tchr. music and firm New Canaan (Conn.) Coll. Arts; producer three documentary films including The End of an Old Song*

COHEN, JOZEF, educator, psychologist; b. Brookline, Mass., July 21, 1921; s. David J. and Dora A. (Levin) C.; B.S., U. Chgo., 1942; Ph.D., Cornell U., 1945; m. Huguette Schachnovitch, July 31, 1958. Susan Linn Sage fellow Cornell U., 1942-45; mem. research staff Psycho-Acoustic Lab., Harvard, 1945; mem. faculty Cornell U., 1945-48; mem. faculty U. Ill. at Champaign, 1948—, prof. psychology, 1969—. Fellow Am. Psychol. Assn., A.A.A.S.; mem. Midwestern Psychol. Assn., Psychonomic Soc., Sigma Xi. Democrat. Jewish religion. Author: Eyewitness Series in Psychology, 20 vols., 1969- 71; also articles. Home: 303 Burkwood Ct W Urbana IL 61801 Office: Psychology Bldg Univ Ill Champaign IL 61820

COHEN, JULIUS, educator; b. N.Y.C., Oct. 27, 1910; s. Saul and Mollie (Sidler) C.; A.B., W. Va. U., 1931, A.M., 1932, LL.B., 1937; LL.M., Harvard Law Sch., 1938; postgrad. Columbia U. Sch. Law, 1936; m. Lillian Tyson, Dec. 22, 1945. Instr., dept. govt., W.Va. U., 1935-37. asst. professor, 1938-41; admitted to W.Va. bar, 1937, Neb. bar, 1954; legal and adminstrv. aide to gov., W. Va., 1940-42; adviser, W.Va. Legislative Interim Com., 1939-40; chmn., W. Va. State Election Commn., 1941-43; legal adviser, W.Va., Office of Civilian Def., 1941-43; legal div., War Manpower Commn., 1943-44; legal div., Alien Property Custodian, 1944-45; prof. law U. Neb. Coll. Law, 1946-57; vis. prof. Ind. U. Sch. Law, summers 1950, 53, 54; vis. prof. Rutgers Sch. Law, 1956-57, prof. law, 1957—; vis. prof. law Yale Law Sch., 1958-59; legislative aide U.S. Senate, summer 1949, 51. Guggenheim fellow, 1963-64. Mem. Phi Beta Kappa. Author: Materials and Problems on Legislation, 1949, rev. 2d edit., 1967; (wih Robson and Bates) Parental Authority: The Community and the Law, 1958. Contbr.: Freedom and Authority in Our Time, 1953; Symbols and Values, 1954; Nomos, 1962, 1968; (with Haber) The Law School of Tomorrow, 1968; others. Contbr. to legal and other periodicals. Home: 16 Clover Lane Princeton NJ 08540

COHEN, KARL PALEY, corp. exec., physicist; b. N.Y.C., Feb. 5, 1913; s. Joseph M. and Ray (Paley) C.; A.B., Columbia, 1933, M.A., 1934, Ph.D., 1937; postgrad. U. Paris (France), 1936-37; m. Marthe H. Malartre, Sept. 20, 1938; children—Martine (Madame Jean Claude LeBouc), Elisabeth (Mrs. Allen G. Brown), Beatrix J.M. Research asst. to Prof. H. C. Urey, Columbia, 1937- 40; dir. theoretical div. SAM Manhattan project, 1940-44; physicist Standard Oil Devel. Co., 1944-48; tech. dir. H.K. Ferguson Co., 1948-52; v.p. Walter Kidde Nuclear Lab., 1952-55; cons. AEC, sr. sci. Columbia, 1955-56; mgr. advance engring. atomic power equipment dept. Gen. Electric Co., 1956-65, gen. mgr. breeder reactor devel. dept., 1965-71, mgr. strategic planning, nuclear energy div., 1971—. Fellow Am. Nuclear Soc. (pres. 1968-69, dir.); mem. Nat. Acad. Engring., Am. Phys. Soc., Cactus and Succulent Soc., Phi Beta Kappa, Sigma Xi, Phi Lambda Upsilon. Author: The Theory of Isotope Separation as Applied to Large Scale Production of U-235, 1951. Contbr. articles to profl. jours. Home: 928 N California Av Palo Alto CA 94306 Office: 175 Curtner Av San Jose CA 95125

COHEN, LAWRENCE, physician, educator; b. Leeds, Eng., Nov. 23, 1926; s. Joseph and Millie (Burnstein) C.; B Ch.D., L.D.S., Leeds U., 1949, F.D.S.R.C.S., 1951; L.R.C.P., M.R.C.S., Guys Hosp., 1956; Ph.D., U. London, 1966; m. Gloria Stewart, Dec. 27, 1951; children—Alan Steven, Martin Ian, David Charles. Clin. instr. U. Birmingham, 1949-50; intern, resident oral surgery Middlesex Hosp., 1956-59; sr. resident plastic unit Stoke Mandeville, 1960-61; sr. resident Univ. Coll., 1961-62, lectr. oral pathology, 1962- 63, sr. lectr. oral medicine, 1963-67; prof., head dept. oral diagnosis U. Ill., Chgo., 1967—; dir. dental edn. Ill. Masonic Med. Center, Chgo.; cons. oral diagonis VA West Side Hosp., Chgo. Mem. dental adv. com. Health Edn. Commn., Bd. Higher Edn. State of Ill., 1969—. Served to squadron leader RAF, 1950-52. Fellow Royal Soc. Medicine; mem. Internat. Assn. Dental Research, Am., Brit. dental assns., Sigma Xi. Home: 200 Kilpatrick Av Wilmette IL 60091 Office: 808 S Wood St Chicago IL 60612

COHEN, LEONARD, (Norman), poet, novelist, musician, songwriter; b. Montreal, Can., Sept. 21, 1934; s. Nathan R. and Marsha (Klinitsky) C.; B.A., McGill U., 1955; grad. student, Columbia. With Stranger Music, Inc., N.Y.C. Recipient McGill Lit. award, 1956; Canada Council grant, 1960-61; Quebec Lit. award, 1964. Author: (poetry) Let Us Compare Mythologies, 1956. The Spice Box of Earth, 1961, Flowers for Hitler, 1964, Parasites of Heaven, 1966, Selected Poems, 1956-68, 1968; (novels) The Favorite Game, 1963, Beautiful Losers, 1966; also articles, songs; recording artist for Columbia Records. Address: care Stranger Music Inc 39 W 55th St New York City NY 10019*

COHEN, LEONARD, lawyer; b. N.Y.C., Jan. 19, 1925; s. Alexander and Alice (Bloom) C.; B.S., U. Cal., Los Angeles, 1948; LL.B., Loyola U., Los Angeles, 1951; m. Jean E. Hide, Nov. 21, 1948; children-Jondy, Jamie, Justie, Jennifer. Admitted to Cal. bar, 1951, since practiced in Beverly Hills; partner Ervin, Cohen & Jessup, 1952—; exec. v.p., dir. Nat. Med. Enterprises, 1969—; lectr. U. So. Cal. Law Sch., 1958—. Served with USAAF, 1942-46. C.P.A., Cal. Mem. Am., Cal., Beverly Hills bar assns., Am. Inst. C.P.A.'s Phi Alpha Delta, Zeta Beta Tau. Author: articles in field. Home 489 Dalehurst Av Los Angeles CA 90024 Office: 9171 Wilshire Blvd Beverly Hills CA 90210

COHEN, LEON WARREN, mathematician; b. N.Y.C., Apr. 24, 1903; s. Joseph W. and Sarah (Warren) C.; A.B., Columbia, 1923, A.M., 1925; Ph.D., U. Mich., 1928; m. Isabel Ackerman, June 18, 1927; 1 dau., Amy Judith. Instr. U. Mich., 1926-29; NRC fellow Princeton, 1929-31; prof. U. Ky., 1931-47; lectr. U. Wis., 1942-44; research mathematician Columbia, 1944-45, Brown U., 1945; prof. Ohio State U., Wright-Patterson Field, 1946; prof. Queens Coll., 1947- 54; mem. Inst. Advanced Study, fellow Fund for Advancement Edn., 1952- 53; program dir. math. scis. NSF, 1953-58; mem. div. math. Nat. Acad. Sci.-NRC, 1954-58, now exec. sec. div.; head dept. math. U. Md., 1958-68, prof., 1958—. Fgn. region 5, Nat. Woodrow Wilson Fellowship Found., 1958- 59; exec. dir. Conf. Bd. Math. Scis., 1962-66. Fellow A.A.A.S.; mem. Am. Math. Soc. (asso. sec., mem. council 1951- 54), Math. Assn. Am., Am. Assn. U. Profs. (chpt. pres. 1940), Phi Beta Kappa, Sigma Xi. Home: 3629 Yuma St NW Washington DC 20008 Office: U Md College Park MD 20740

COHEN, LESTER, lawyer; b. Norfolk, Va., Aug. 1935; m. Lydia Goldblatt, Jan. 14, 1936; 1 son, Robert Stephen. Admitted to D.C. bar, 1934, since practiced in Washington; partner firm Hogan & Hartson, and predecessor, 1945—. Chmn. bldg. com. Washington Sch. Psychiatry, 1958—. Mem. Am., D.C., Fed. Communications (chmn. profl. ethics) bar assns., Zeta Beta Tau. Republican. Jewish religion (bd. govs. congregation 1953-56). Club: Woodmont Country (bd. govs. 1955-59, 62-63) (Rockville, Md.). Home: 1818 24th St NW Washington DC 20008 Office: 815 Connecticut Av NW Washington DC 20006

COHEN, LOUIS DAVID, educator; b. Bklyn., Nov. 26, 1912; s. Gutman and Lillie (Kolko) C.; B.S., Bklyn. Coll., 1934; M.A., Columbia, 1936; postgrad. N.Y.U., 1937-39; Ph.D., Duke, 1949; m. Tina Simon, June 28, 1936; children—Myra (Mrs. Jonathan Paul Dey), Beth (Mrs. Herman Bernard Shubert). Head psychologist N.Y.C. Penitentiary, 1936-38; dir. classification, edn. and welfare Ind. State Farm, Greencastle, 1938-42; asso. clin. psychology to prof. psychology and med. psychology Duke, 1946-62; prof., chmn. dept. clin. psychology U. Fla., Gainesville, 1962—; cons. Nat. Inst. Mental Health, VA, Washington. Mem. Fla. Bd. Examiners Psychology, 1965-67. Chmn. Commn. on Mental Illness and Retardation, So. Regional Edn. Bd., 1966-68. Served from lt. to lt. col., AUS, 1942-46. Decorated Army Commendation medal. Fellow Am. Psychol. Assn., Am. Pub. Health Assn.; mem. N.C. (pres.), Southeastern (pres.) psychol. assns. Contbr. articles profl. jours. Home: 1250 NW 61st Terrace Gainesville FL 32601

COHEN, MANUEL FREDERICK, lawyer; b. Bklyn., Oct. 9, 1912; s. Edward and Lena (Kartzmar) C.; B.S. in Social Scis., Bklyn. Coll., 1933; LL.B. cum laude, St. Lawrence U., 1936, LL.D., 1962; LL.D., Babson Inst. Finance, 1968; L.H.D., Hebrew Union Coll. 1969; m. Pauline Grossman, Apr. 20, 1940; children—Susan D. (Mrs. Borman), Jonathan W. Research asso. 20th Century Fund, 1933-34; admitted to N.Y. bar, 1937; pvt. practice, N.Y.C., 1937-42; with SEC, 1942-69, chief counsel div. corp. finance, 1952-59, adviser to commn., 1959-60, dir. div. corp. finance, 1960-61, commr. 1961-69, chmn., 1964-69; mem. Wilmer, Cutler, & Pickering, 1969—. Dir. Internat. Chem. & Nuclear Corp. Lectr. law George Washington U. Law Sch., 1958—; mem. council Adminstrv. Conf. U.S., 1961-69; mem. adv. bd. Bur. Nat. Affairs. Recipient Rockefeller Pub. Service award, 1956, Nat. Civil Service League Career Service award, 1961; Brotherhood award Nat. Conf. Christians and Jews. Mem. Am. Acad. Polit. and Social Sci., Am., Fed., N.Y. bar assns., Am. Soc. Internat. Law, Am. Law Inst., Am. Judicature Soc., Acad. Polit. Sci., Société Royale D'Economic Politique de Belgique, Practicing Law Inst. (nat. bd. advisers). Clubs: Cosmos, Woodmont Country, Nat. Lawyers. Cons. editor Finance Mag. Contbr. articles profl. jours. Home: 6403 Marjory Lane Bethesda MD 20034 Office: 900 17th St NW Washington DC 20006

COHEN, MARSHALL HARRIS, educator, radio astronomer; b. Manchester, N.H., July 5, 1926; s. Solomon and Mollie (Epstein) C.; B.E.E., Ohio State U., 1948, M.S., 1949, Ph.D., 1952; m. Shirley Kekst, Sept. 19, 1948; children—Thelma, Linda, Sara. Research asso. Ohio State U., 1950-54; faculty Cornell U., 1954-66; prof. applied electrophysics U. Cal., San Diego, 1966; vis. asso. prof. radio astronomy Cal. Inst. Tech., Pasadena, 1965, prof. radio astronomy, 1968—. Guggenheim fellow Paris Obs., 1960-61. Fellow A.A.A.S.; mem. Am. Astron. Soc., Internat. Astron. Union (U.S. chmn. Commn. V), Internat. Sci. Radio Union. Contbr. articles profl. jours. Office: 1201 E California Blvd Pasadena CA 91109

COHEN, MARVIN LOU, educator; b. Montreal, Que., Can., Mar. 3, 1935; s. Elmo and Molly (Zaritsky) C.; came to U.S., 1947, naturalized, 1953; A.B., U. Cal., 1957; M.S., U. Chgo., 1958, Ph.D., 1964; m. Merrill L. Gardner, Aug. 31, 1958; children—Mark, Susan. Tech. staff mem. Bell Telephone Labs., Murray Hill, N.J., 1963-64; asst. prof. U. Cal. at Berkeley, 1964-65, asso. prof., 1966-68, prof. physics, 1969—, also prof. Miller Inst. Basic Research in Sci. of U. Cal., 1969-70. Alfred P. Sloan fellow Cambridge U. (Eng.), 1965-67; exchange prof. U. Paris (France), summer 1968. Fellow Am. Phys. Soc.; mem. Sigma Xi. Contbr. articles tech. jours. Home: 666 Woodmont Av Berkeley CA 94708

COHEN, MARVIN SANFORD, lawyer; b. Akron, O., Oct. 16, 1931; s. Norman J. and Faye (Abramovitz) C.; B.A., U. Ariz., 1953, LL.B., 1957; m. Frances E. Smith, June 19, 1953; children—Samuel David, Jeffrey Lee, Rachel Ann. Admitted to Ariz. bar, 1957, since practiced in Tucson; chief civil dep. Pima County atty., 1958-60; 1st asst. Tucson city atty., 1961; spl. asst. to solicitor Dept. Interior, Washington, 1961-63; mem. firm Bilby, Thompson, Shoenhair & Warnock, 1963—; instr. U. Ariz. Coll. Law, 1965. Mem. Tucson Fgn. Relations Com., 1968—; chmn. Ariz. Anti-Defamation League, 1970. Pres. Young Democratic Clubs Ariz., 1960; pres. Democrats for Better Govt., 1964; del. Dem. Nat. Conv., 1964; chmn. Pima County Dem. Central Com., 1960; parliamentarian Dem. Party Ariz., 1970. Pres. Tucson Jewish Community Center; bd. dirs. United Community Campaign, Tucson Urban League Com. Served to 1st lt. USAF, 1953-55. Named Young Man of Year, Tucson Jewish Community, 1966. Mem. Ariz. Civil Liberties Union. Jewish religion (bd. dirs. temple). Home: 4645 E San Carlos Pl Tucson AZ 85716 Office: Valley Nat Bldg Tucson AZ 85701

COHEN, MAXWELL, educator; b. Winnipeg, Man., Can., Mar. 17, 1910; s. Moses and Sarah (Waserman) C.; B.A., U. Man., 1930, LL.B., 1934, LL.D., 1963; LL.M., Northwestern U., 1936; research fellow Harvard Law Sch., 1937-38; LL.D., U. N.B.; D.C.L. (hon.), Bishop U.; LL.D., York U., 1969; m. Isle Alexandra Sternberg; 1 dau., Joanne. Called to Man. bar, 1939; spl. asst., also jr. counsel Combines Investigation Com., 1938-40; with econ. br. Dept. Munitions and Supply, 1941-42; spl. corr. Christian Sci. Monitor, 1941-42; lectr. law McGill U., 1946-47, mem. faculty, 1947—, prof. law, 1952—, Macdonald prof. law, 1964-, dean law, 1964-69. Impartial chmn. Men's Clothing Industry, 1948-51; spl. asst. to dir. gen. Tech. Assistance Adminstrn., UN, 1951; mem. Canadian del. 14th Gen. Assembly UN, 1959-60; dir. dept. external affairs project Royal Commn. Govt. Orgn., 1961-62; chmn. Minister of Justice Spl. Com. on Hate Propaganda, 1965-66; chmn. Spl. Com. on Manpower and Automation in Unloading Grain Vessels, Montreal, 1966-67; chmn. Royal Commn. into Affairs Coll. Militaire Royal, St. Jean, Quebec, 1967-68; spl. counsel on constn. Govt. N.B., 1967-70; chmn. Royal Commn. Labour Legislation, Nfld. and Labrador, 1969-71. Served to maj. Canadian Army, 1942-46. Hon. fellow Consular Law Soc. (N.Y.C.); mem. Internat. Law Assn. (past pres. Canadian br.), Canadian (chmn. constl. and internat. law com. 1964-71), Que., Mont. bar assns., Law Soc. Man., Canadian Inst. Internat. Affairs, Canadian Polit. Sci. Assn., Am. Soc. Internat. Law (mem. exec. council, exec. com. 1961-63), Sigma Alpha Nu. Clubs: University; Faculty; Montefiore; Elm Ridge Country, Elm Ridge Golf; Harvard of Montreal (pres. 1966-67). Home: 519 Victoria Av Montreal Quebec Canada

COHEN, MAYNARD MANUEL, neurologist, neurochemist; b. Regina, Sask., Can., May 17, 1920; s. Aleck and Dora (Pinsk) C.; brought to U.S., 1920, naturalized, 1925; A.B., U. Mich., 1941; M.D., Wayne U., 1944; Ph.D., U. Minn., 1953; m. Doris Rosenshine; children—Deborah, Elena. Intern Woman's Hosp., Detroit, 1944-45, resident pathology, 1945-46; resident pathology U. Minn. and Mpls. VA Hosp., 1948-50, resident neurology, 1949-50; faculty U. Minn., 1950-63, prof. neurology, 1959-63; dir. Center Cerebrovascular Research, 1961-63; prof. neurology, head div. U. Ill., 1963-71, prof. pharmacology, 1963—; chmn. dept. neurology Presbyn.-St. Luke's Hosp., Chgo., 1963—; prof., chmn. dept. neurol. scis., prof. biochemistry Rush Med. Coll., 1971—. Mem. med. adv. bd. Ill. Epilepsy League, Epilepsy Found.; mem. neurol. scis. postgrad. tng. grant com. Nat. Inst. Neurol. Diseases and Blindness, 1959-63; mem. biol. scis. tng. grant com. Nat. Inst. Mental Health, 1968—. Served to capt. M.C., AUS, 1946-47. Fellow Am. Scandinavian Sco., Rikshospitalet, Oslo, Norway and Oslo Community Hosp., 1951-52; NIH fellow Inst., Psychiatry, Maudsley Hosp., U. London (Eng.), 1957-58; recipient Distinguished Service award Wayne State U. Sch. Medicine, 1964, Alumni award Wayne State U., 1970. Mem. Am. Acad. Neurology (v.p. 1967-69), Assn. U. Profs. Neurology (pres. 1967-68), Biochem. Soc., Am. Assn. Neuropathologists, Assn. Research Nervous and Mental Diseases, Sigma Xi, Alpha Omega Alpha. Co- editor: Morphological and Biochemical Correlates of Neural Activity, 1964. Asso. editor Jour. Neurol. Scis., 1963—. Editor: Monographs in Basic Neurology. Home: 1000 Chestnut St Wilmette IL 60091 Office: 1753 W Congress Pkwy Chicago IL 60612

COHEN, MELVIN SAMUEL, mfg. co. exec.; b. Mpls., Jan. 16, 1918; s. Henry Benjamin and Mary (Witebsky) C.; B.S. in Law, U. Minn., 1939, J.D., 1941; m. Eileen Phillips, Aug. 16, 1947; children—Amy Rebecca, Mary-Jo Rose. Admitted to Minn. bar, 1941, U.S. Supreme Ct. bar, 1944; practiced in Mpls. until 1942; with legal div. rationing sect. OPA, Washington, 1942- 43; pub. counsel CAB, 1943-44: with Nat. Presto Industries, Inc., Eau Claire, Wis., 1944—, treas., 1950-51, v.p. adminstrn., treas., 1951-54, exec. v.p., 1954-60, pres., 1960—, also dir.; chmn. bd., dir. Century Metalcraft Corp., Los Angeles, Presto Mfg. Co., Jackson, Miss., World Aerospace Corp., Mpls., 1963—; pres., dir. Master Corp. Tex., Abilene, 1965—, Midwestern Co., Mpls., Jackson Sales & Storage Co. (Miss.), Presto Parts & Service Corp., N.Y.C., Presto Parts & Service, Inc., Los Angeles; dir. Johnson Printing, Eau Claire, Wis., 1st Wis. Nat. Bank, Eau Claire; v.p., dir. Nat. Pipeline Co., Cleve., Nat. Automatic Pipeline Operations, Inc., Escanaba, Mich. Pres., trustee Presto Found., Eau Claire. Mem. industry adv. com. for aluminum industry and internal combustion engine industry, NPA, Korean War. Club: Eau Claire Country. Editor Minn. Law Rev., 1939-41. Home: 1703 Drummond St Eau Claire WI 54701 Office: Presto Area Eau Claire WI 54701

COHEN, MENDEL F., educator; b. Denver, Sept. 13, 1928; s. Sam and Emma (Fisher) C.; student U. Chgo., 1948-49; B.A., U. Colo., 1952, M.A., 1958; Ph.D., U. Ill., 1961; m. Renie Sussman, Feb. 10, 1957; children—Nathan Phillip, Eleanor Judith. Instr. U. Ill., 1960-61; asst. prof. Cornell U., 1961-64; asst. prof. U. Wis., 1964-67, asso. prof., 1967-69; vis. asso. prof. U. Utah, 1969-70, prof., 1970—. Served with AUS, 1946-48. Mem. Phi Beta Kappa. Home: 2321 E 13th S Salt Lake City UT 84108

COHEN, MEYER, rabbi; b. Shatava, Russia, Aug. 15, 1902; s. Samuel and M. (Schendel) C.; student Rabbi Isaac Elchanan Theol. Sem. (now component of Yeshiva U.; m. Henrietta Gershman, Mar. 29, 1932; children—Samuel I., Norma (Mrs. B. Yoselovsky), Jacob S., Harris S. Came to U.S., 1923. Licensed as rabbi, Russia, 1917; rabbi, U.S., 1926; rabbi Congregation Sons of Israel, Asbury Park, N.J., 1927-50; dir. Union Orthodox Rabbis U.S. and Can., 1950—. Chmn. Joint Orthodox Chaplaincy Bd.; pres. Myzrachi Council N.J., mem. exec., adminstrv. coms. Nat. Myzrachi Orgn. Am., 1940-50; dir. Torah Relief Soc., mem. Rabbinical Bd. Greater N.Y.; bd. dirs. Federated Council Israel Instns.; mem. Am. bd. of central com. Am. Com. Israel, Jerusalem; mem. adminstrv. com. Am. Com. for Taharas Hamishpacha, Israel; mem. Greater N.Y. Jewish Sabbath Observance Com.; bd. dirs. Yeshivath Chayei Olam, Jerusalem; mem. Presidium Joint Orthodox Rabbinic Representation for Civic Affairs N.Y.; mem. Rabbinic sponsors com. Kollel Harbozas Hatorah N.Y. Mem. Presidium of Fedn. of Orthodox Synagogues Am. Author: Chelkas Meir. Contbr. articles to religious publs. Home: 1147 49th St Brooklyn NY 11219 Office: 235 E Broadway New York City NY 10007

COHEN, MILTON HOWARD, lawyer; b. Milw., Aug. 9, 1911; s. Louis L. and Rose (Horwitz) C.; A.B., Harvard, 1932, LL.B., 1935; m. Rowna Chaffetz, Sept. 3, 1939; children—Louis R., Mark N., Rosalind. Admitted to Wis. bar, 1935, Ill. bar, 1947, U.S. Supreme Ct. bar, 1960; with SEC, 1935-46, 61-63, dir. spl. study securities markets, 1961-63; partner Schiff, Hardin, Waite, Dorschel & Britton, and predecessor firm, Chgo., 1947-61, 63—; counsel, sec. Chgo. White Sox Baseball Club, 1959-61; counsel, dir. Manpower, Inc., Milwaukee, 1959-61, 63—. Vis. prof. law Harvard Law Sch., 1966-67; mem. adv. com. instl. investor study SEC 1969-71; mem. adv. council U. Pa. Center for Study Financial Instns. Mem. Am. Bar Assn., Am. Law Inst. (cons. fed. securities code project), Nat. Planning Assn., Phi Beta Kappa. Jewish religion. Clubs: Standard, Mid-Day (Chgo.); Nat. Lawyers (Washington). Home: 1440 Lakeshore Dr Chicago IL 60610 Office: 231 S LaSalle St Chicago IL 60604

COHEN, MONTGOMERY mfg. exec.; b. Lima, O., Apr. 1, 1932; B.S., U. San Francisco, 1954; M.S., Stanford University, 1956; m. Rosemarie Lois Brown, May 15, 1955; 1 son, Anthony Robinson. Sales rep. Ames-Brockton Fabricated Products, Akron, O., 1956-58, sales mgr. Coshocton, Ohio, 1959-61, gen. manager plant, 1961-68, v.p. sales, 1968--. Instr. bus. Coshocton Jr. College, 1968-69. Secretary Coshocton YMCA, 1960-61; active Boy Scouts of America. Named Man of Year, Coshocton Junior Chamber of Commerce, 1968. Mem. Coshocton C. of C. (vice president 1967-68, pres. 1969-70), English Speaking Union, Coshocton Sertoma Club, Nat. Assn. Mfrs., Sales Executives Institute, Phi Beta Kappa, Sigma Chi, Phi Mu. Democrat. Mem. Christian Ch. (lay leader). Mason (32, Shriner). Clubs: Coshocton Country, Coshocton City, Running Deer Country. Home: 2d Av Coshocton OH Office: 3d Av Coshocton OH

COHEN, MORLEY, surgeon; b. Winnipeg, Man., Can., Nov. 18, 1923; s. Isaac and Anne (Shore) C.; M.D., U. Man., 1948; Ph. D., U. Minn., 1954; m. Joan Crane, May 3, 1953; childrenEve, James, Patricia, Richard, Charles. Intern, St. Boniface (Man.) Hosp., 1948; resident surgery U. Minn Hosp., 1950-54; instr. surgery U. Minn., 1954; practicing surgeon, Winnipeg, 1955—; instr. surgery U. Man., 1955- 59, asst. prof. surgery, 1959-65, asso. prof. surgery, 1965—; head div. thoracic and cardiovascular surgery, 1966; chmn. cardiopulmonary surg. unit St. Boniface Hosp. Recipient Albert Lasker award USPHS, 1955. Diplomate Am. Bd. Surgery, Am. Bd. Thoracic Surgery. Fellow Royal Coll. Surgeons, Coll. Chest Surgeons; mem. Canadian Assn. Clin. Surgs., Am. Assn. for Thoracic Surgery, Soc. Thoracic Surgeons, Sigma Xi. Home: 295 Dromore Av Winnipeg 9, Canada. Office: Medical Arts Bldg Winnipeg 1, Canada.

COHEN, MORREL HERMAN, educator, physicist; b. Boston, Sept. 10, 1927; s. David and Rose (Kemler) C.; B.S. in Physics, Worcester Poly. Inst., 1947; M.A. in Physics, Dartmouth, 1948; Ph.D. in Physics, U. Cal. at Berkeley, 1952; m. Sylvia Zwein, June 18, 1950; children—Julie, Robert, Daniel, Lisa. Mem. faculty U. Chgo., 1952—, prof. physics, 1960—, prof. theoretical biology, 1968—, acting dir. James Franck Inst., 1965-66, dir., 1968-71; cons. govt. and industry, 1953—; vis. scientist Nat. Research Council Can., 1960. Mem. adv. panel electro-physics NASA, 1962-66; mem. adv. com. Nat. Magnet Lab., 1963-66; mem. rev. com. solid state sci. and metallurgy div. Argonne Nat. Lab., 1964-67, chmn., 1966; chmn. Gordon Conf., 1968, 4th Internat. Conf. Armorphous and Liquid Semiconductors, 1971. Guggenheim fellow, 1957-58; NSF sr. postdoctoral fellow, 1964-65; vis. fellow Clare Hall, U. Cambridge, 1972—. Fellow Am. Phys. Soc.; mem. A.A.A.S., Am. Inst. Physics, Sigma Xi (nat. lectr.). Author articles physics of Solids, liquids, gases, amorphous semiconductors, theoretical biology. Asso. editor Jour. Chem. Physics, 1960-63; mem. editorial bd. McGraw-Hill Co. advanced physics monograph series, 1963-70; publs. bd. U. Chgo., 1969-70; bd. editors Jour. Statis. Physics, 1970—. Home: 1463 E Park Pl Chicago IL 60637

COHEN, MORRIS, educator; b. Chelsea, Mass., Nov. 27, 1911; s. Julius Harry and Alice (Olson) C.; B.S., Mass. Inst. Tech., 1933, Sc.D., 1936; m. Ruth Krentzman, Jan. 24, 1937 (dec.); children—Barbara (Mrs. Willy Nordwind), Joel Alan. Asst. prof. Mass. Inst. Tech., 1937-42, asso. prof., 1942-46, prof., 1946-62, Ford prof. materials sci. and engring., 1962—. Metall. cons.; dir. Addison-Wesley Pub. Co., Reading, Mass. Recipient Mathewson Gold medal Am. Inst. Mining, Metall. Engrs., 1953, Gold medal Japan Inst. Metals, 1970, Chevenard medal French Metall. Soc., 1971. Fellow Am. Acad. Arts and Scis., N.Y. Acad. Scis.; mem. Nat. Acad. Scis.; hon. mem. Am. Soc. Metals (past pres., trustee, Howe medal 1945, 49, Gold medal 1968); hon. mem. Indian Inst. Metals (Kamani Gold medal 1953), Iron and Steel Inst. Japan. Home: 491 Puritan Rd Swampscott MA 01907 Office: Mass Inst Tech Cambridge MA 02139

COHEN, MORRIS, economist; b. Phila., Mar. 27, 1919; s. Meyer P. and Bella (Furman) C.; B.A., U. Pa., 1939; M.A., Pa. State U., 1941; M.P.A., Harvard, 1952, Ph.D., 1958; postgrad. U. Cambridge (Eng.), 1952-53; m. Kathleen E. Shanahan, July 30, 1950; children—Barbara Jeanne, Mark David. Research asst. econs. Pa. State U., 1940-41; economist tax div. Bd. Investigation and Research, Washington, 1942-43, OPA, Washington, 1946; bus. economist Office Bus. Econs., Washington, 1947-50; instr. Sch. Indsl. Mgmt., Mass. Inst. Tech., 1951-52; sr. economist Nat. Indsl. Conf. Bd., N.Y.C., 1953- 60; asso. economist, asso. editor Fortune mag., N.Y.C., 1960-67; dir. bus. research, prof. finance Grad. Sch. Bus., L.I. U. Bklyn., 1967—; cons. economist Schroder, Nuess and Thomas, 1969—; lectr. bus. statistics Grad. Sch., Fairleigh Dickinson U., 1955-57; lectr. econs. Grad. Sch., Coll. City N.Y., Baruch Sch. Bus., 1955-60, Grad. Sch. Bus. L.I. U., Bklyn., 1967—; lectr. bus. statistics Grad. Sch., Fairleigh Dickinson U., 1955-57; lectr. econs. Grad. Sch., Coll. City N.Y., Baruch Sch. Bus., 1955-60, Grad. Sch., St. John's U., 1960-66; tech. cons. Republic Turkey State Planning Orgn. OECD, 1964. Mem. steering group for bus. incentives President's Task Force War Against Poverty, 1964; mem. Bergen County (N.J.) Econ. Resources and Devel. Commn., 1968—. Served with AUS, 1943-46; PTO. Mem. Am., Royal, Met. (pres. 1965-66) econ. assns., Am. Statis. Assn. (program chmn. 1967; chmn. bus., econ. statistics sect. 1968; mem. council 1970-71, mem. steering com. future goals 1970-71, publs. com. 1971-73), Nat. Assn. Bus. Economists (council 1971—), Bus. Economists Council, Am. Finance Assn., A.A.A.S. Jewish religion (trustee temple). Club: Harvard of New York (N.Y.C.). Author: A Critique of the United States National Income and Product Accounts, 1958; The Quality and Economic Significance of Anticipations Data, 1959; Thought Patterns, 1960; Business Fluctuations, Growth and Economic Stabilization, 1963; Fiscal Policy Issues of the Coming Decade, 1965; How Business Economists Forecast, 1966; Markets of the Seventies, 1968; The Unwinding U.S. Economy, 1968. Editor: Business Economics, 1968- -. Contbr. articles profl. jours. Home: 411 Churchill Rd West Englewood NJ 07666 Office: Grad Sch Bus LI U Brooklyn NY 11201

COHEN, MORRIS LEO, educator, librarian, b. N.Y.C., Nov. 2, 1927; s. Emanuel and Anna (Frank) C.; B.A., U. Chgo., 1947; LL.B., Columbia, 1951; M.L.S., Pratt Inst., 1959; m. Gloria Weitzner, Feb. 1, 1953; children—Havi, Daniel Asher. Admitted to N.Y. bar, 1951; pvt. practice, N.Y.C., 1951-58; asst. law librarian Rutgers U. Law Sch., 1958-59, Columbia Law Sch., 1959-61; law librarian, asso. prof. law State U. N.Y. at Buffalo, 1961-63; Biddle law librarian, prof. law U. Pa. Law Sch., Phila., 1963-71; law librarian, prof. law Harvard Law Sch., 1971—; lectr. Drexel Inst. Sch. Library Sci., 1964-70, Columbia Sch. Library Service, 1965—. Mem. exec. bd. Phila. chpt. Am. Civil Liberties Union. Nat. Endowment for Humanities grantee. Mem. A.L.A. (chmn. law and polit. sci. sect. 1967-69), Am. Assn. U. Profs. (pres. U. Pa. chpt. 1966-67), Am. Assn. Law Libraries (pres. 1970-71), Am. Bar Assn., Am. Documentation Inst., Bibliog. Soc. Am., Internat. Assn. Law Libraries. Jewish religion (dir. synagogue). Author: Legal Bibliography Briefed, 1965: Legal Research in a Nutshell, 1968, 2d edit., 1971. Home: 336 Clark Rd Brookline MA 02146

COHEN, MURRY HERBERT, cosmetic co. exec.; b. N.Y.C., Apr. 19, 1917; s. Joseph and Nettie (Waxman) C.; B.S., Mich. State Coll., 1939; m. Helen Baer, June 14, 1941; children—Robert, JoAnn, Cathy. With Joseph E. Seagram & Sons, Inc. and affiliates, 1939-68, chief accountant Prodn. div., 1941-45, head grain dept., 1951-52, bus. mgr. Prodn. div., 1946-48, Louisville plant mgr., 1948-50, 53-57, mgr. systems dept., controller 1958-68, dir., 1962- 68, v.p. finance, 1964-68, controller several distilling subsidiaries, Distillers Corp. Seagram, Ltd.; exec. v.p. finance, treas. Helena Rubinstein, Inc., N.Y.C., 1968-70, exec. v.p., 1970—, dir., 1968—. Past dir. Louisville council Boy Scouts Am., Jr. Achievement, City of Louisville Com. of 100; mem. Louisville adv. bd. for adult edn. Ford Found. Mem. industry adv. bd. on distillers grains OPS. Mem. Distillers Feed Research Council (past v.p.), Louisville Bd. Trade (past pres.), Nat. Assn. Accountants, Soc. Advancement Mgmt., Financial Execs. Inst. Home: 1667 Buckingham Rd Teaneck NJ 07666 Office: 767 Fifth Av New York City NY 10017

COHEN, NATHAN EDWARD, educator; b. Derry, N.H., Sept. 29, 1909; s. David Harry and Ada (Cottler) C.; A.B., Harvard, 1931; M.A., 1932, Ph.D., 1934, Sheldon fellow, 1934-35; m. Sylvia Lee Golden, June 29, 1934; children—David Harris, Edward Richard, Susan Anne. Exec. dir. YMHA, Boston, 1935-37, Jewish Community Welfare Fund and Council, Springfield, Mass., 1937-39; dir. leadership tng. and research Nat. Jewish Welfare Bd., 1939-41, dir. program div. and Jewish Center div., 1941-45; prof. social work N.Y. Sch. Social Work, Columbia, 1945-54, asso. dean, 1955-58; dean sch. applied social scis. Western Res. U., 1958-63, v.p. univ., 1963-64; prof. social welfare U. Cal. at Los Angeles, 1964—, dean Sch. Social Welfare, 1968-69, chmn., prof. doctoral program, 1969—, also associate Institute Govt. and Pub. Affairs; spl. assignment for Peace Corps, India; 1970; vis. prof. Chinese U., Hong Kong, 1966. Mem. liaison com. Nat. Assn. Social Workers to Dept. Health, Edn. and Welfare, 1957; mem. bd. Nat. Planned Parenthood; cons. Nat. Inst. Mental Health, mem. delinquency grants revision com. Mem. Citizens Com. Tax Reduction and Revision, 1964. Recipient Bi-centennial medal Columbia, 1955; spl. award Nat. Assn. Jewish Center Workers, 1956. Mem. Am. Assn. Group Workers (v.p. 1946-50), Nat. Conf. on Social Welfare (pres. 1963-64), Nat. Council Social Work Edn. (chmn. 1949-52, dir. 1954-55), Nat. Assn. Social Workers (pres. 1955-57, mem. fed. relations com. 1962—), Am. Assn. U. Profs. Am. Orthopsychiat. Assn., Nat. Conf. Social Work. Author: Social Work in the American Tradition, 1958. Editor: The Citizen Volunteer, 1960; Social Work and Social Problems, 1964; Los Angeles Riot Study, 1965. Contbr. articles profl. publs. Home: 13288 Chalon Rd Los Angeles CA 90049 ☆

COHEN, NEHEMIAH MYER, merchant; b. Palestine, Jerusalem, Sept. 10, 1890; s. Jehuda and Leah (Dennenberg) C.; ed. Jeusalem; m. Naomi Halperin, Sept. 10, 1908; children—Emanuel, Israel, Lillian (Mrs. Lawrence P. Solomon). Came to U.S., 1915, naturalized, 1921.

Ordained Orthodox rabbi, 1914; mem. clergy in U.S., 1915-21; with Giant Food Inc., 1936—, pres., 1949-64, chmn. bd., gen. mgr., 1964—; pres. Giant Foods Properties, 1957—. Cabinet mem. United Jewish Appeal; mem. bd. United Givers Fund. Home: 2931 Albermarle St NW Washington DC 20008 Office: 6900 Sheriff Rd Landover MD 20785

COHEN, OLLIE AARON, chain dept. store exec.; b. Balt., July 4, 1911; s. Myer Cohen; student Balt. City Coll., U. Md., also bus. extension courses Harvard, Boston U.; m. Eleanor Mervis, Aug. 4, 1932; children—Rhea (Mrs. Martin Reiss), Flois (Mrs. Neil Schwartz). Engaged in merchandising and marketing in retailing, retailing, 1934—; co-founder King's Dept. Stores, self-service chain, Boston, 1955, chmn. bd., chief exec. officer, 1961—; dir. Comml. Bank and Trust Co., Down East Television Co.; pres., dir. King's Bldgs.; trustee Torrey & West Realty Co.; lectr. retailing symposiums. Co-chmn. Heart Fund Campaign Greater Boston; chmn. disaster com. Boston chpt. A.R.C., New Eng. region campaign Jewish Theol. Sem. Am. Trustee Brookline Hosp., New Eng. Hebrew Acad. Donor sci. lab. to Brandeis U., 1963; recipient Nat. Community Service award Jewish Theol. Sem. Am. Mem. U.S. C. of C. Jewish religion (asst. treas., trustee congregation). Mason (Shriner). Author: articles. Originated mobile shopping cart. Home: 4747 Collins Av Miami Beach FL 33139 Office: 150 California St Newton MA 02158

COHEN, PAUL JOSEPH, educator, mathematician; b. Long Branch, N.J., Apr. 2, 1934; s. Abraham and Minnie (Kaplan) C.; student Bklyn. Coll., 1950-53; M.S., U. Chgo., 1954, Ph.D., 1958; m. Christina Martha Karls, 1963; children—Eric, Steven. Instr., U. Rochester, 1957-58, Mass. Inst. Tech., 1958-59; fellow Inst. Advanced Study, Princeton, 1959-61; mem. faculty Stanford, 1961—, prof. math., 1964—. Recipient Fields medal Internat. Math. Union, 1966; Bocher prize Am. Math. Soc., 1964; Research Corp. award Research Corp., 1964; Nat. Medal Sci., 1967. Proved impossibility of demonstrating continuum hypothesis from the axims of set theory. Home: 755 Santa Ynez St Stanford CA 94305 150 New Amsterdam Av Buffalo NY 14216 Office: 70 Niagara St Buffalo NY 14202 also 256 3d St Niagara Falls NY 14303

COHEN, PHILIP FRANCIS, pub. co. exec.; b. Manchester, Eng., July 16, 1911; s. Reuben and Frances (Kneeter) C.; came to U.S., 1928, naturalized, 1928; student Brit. schs., also Columbia, Library Sch.; m. Fay Roytman, Dec. 5, 1943; children—David, Anne, Karen. Acquisition law librarian Columbia Law Library, 1928-42; founder, 1946, since pres. Oceana Publs., Inc., Dobbs Ferry, N.Y. Served with USAAF, 1942-46. Mem. Am. Soc. Internat. Law, Am. Law Library Assn., Am. Assn. Pubs., Vanderbilt Asso. N.Y. U. Law Sch. Author: How To Serve on a Jury, 1953, Legal Status of Women, 1963; (under name Philip Francis) Protection Through the Law, 1964. Export on legal bibliography and evaluation of rare legal material. Home: 15 Bobolink Rd Yonkers NY 10701 Office: 75 Main St Dobbs Ferry NY 10522

COHEN, PHILIP PACY, biochemist, educator; b. Derry, N.H., Sept. 26, 1908; s. David Harris and Ada (Cottler) C.; B.S., Tufts Coll., 1930; Ph.D., U. Wis., 1937, M.D., 1938; m. Rubye Herzfeld Tepper, June 15, 1935; children—Philip T., David B., Julie A., Milton T. Nat. Research Council fellow, Sheffield, Eng., 1938-39, Yale, 1939-40; instr. Yale, 1940-41; intern Wis. Gen. Hosp., 1941-42; asst. prof. clin. biochem. U. Wis., 1942- 45, asso. prof. physiol. chem., 1945-47, prof., 1947—, chmn. dept. physiol. chemistry, 1948—, H.C. Bradley prof., 1968—, acting dean Med. Sch., 1961- 63. Chmn. com. on growth, mem. exec. com. div. med. scis. Nat. Research Council, 1954-56; bd. sci. counselors Nat. Cancer Inst., 1957-59, chmn., 1959-61; mem. physiol. chemistry study sect. NIH, 1959-62, nat. adv. cancer council, 1963-67, mem. adv. com. to dir., 1966-70; mem. Nat. Adv. Arthritis and Metabolic Disease Council, 1970—; adv. com. biology and medicine AEC, 1963-71; mem. biochemistry test com. Nat. Bd. Med. Examiners, 1958-63. Commonwealth Fund fellow Oxford U., Eng., 1958. Fellow A.A.A.S.; mem. Am. Soc. Biol. Chemists (treas. 1951-56), Am. Chem. Soc., Nat. Acad. Scis., Biochem. Soc. (Eng.)., Central Soc. Clin. Research, Harvey Soc. (hon.), Sigma Xi. Home: 1117 Oak Way Shorewood Hills Madison WI 53705

COHEN, RAYMOND, educator; b. St. Louis, Nov. 30, 1923; s. Benjamin and Leah (Lewis) C.; B.S., Purdue U., 1947, M.S., 1950, Ph.D., 1955; m. Katherine Elise Silverman, Feb. 1, 1948; children—Richard Samuel, Deborah, Barbara Beth. Instr. mech. engring. Purdue U., 1948-55, asst. prof., 1955-58, asso. prof., 1958-60, prof., 1960—, asst. dir. Ray W. Herrick Labs., 1970-71, cons., 1971—; cons. to industry. Served as sgt. inf., AUS, 1943-46. N.A.T.O. sr. fellow in sci., 1971. Mem. Am. Soc. M.E., Am. Soc. Engring. Edn., Soc. Exptl. Stress Analysis, Am. Soc. Heating, Refrigerating and Air Conditioning Engrs., Nat. Soc. Profl. Engrs., Internat. Inst. Refrigeration, Sigma Xi, Pi Tau Sigma, Tau Beta Pi. Deptl. editor of Ency. Britannica, 1957-62; editorial bd. of Jour. Sound and Vibration, 1971—. Home: 316 Leslie Av West Lafayette IN 47906 Office: RW Herrick Laboratories Purdue Univ Lafayette IN 47907

COHEN, RICHARD NORMAN, ins. exec.; b. N.Y.C., Oct. 28, 1923; s. Norman M. and Janet (Goldsmith) C.; grad. Phillips Exeter Acad., 1941; B.A., Yale, 1947; m. Judith Peixotto Sulzberger, Jan. 31, 1958; children—Daniel Hays, James Matthew. Salesman, Cohen, Goldman & Co., N.Y.C., 1947-50; mens fashion editor Fawcett Publs., N.Y.C., 1951-52; life ins. broker Mass. Mut. Life Ins. Co., N.Y.C., 1954—; account exec. John M. Riehle, Inc., N.Y.C., 1961-63, v.p., 1963—; dir. The New York Times Co. Bd. dirs. Stamford Museum and Nature Center; bd. dirs. N.Y. Times Found Served to 2d lt. USAAF. 1943-45. C.L.U., 1959. Mem. Am. Coll. Life Underwriters, Million Dollar Round Table, Beta Theta Pi. Rep. Jewish religion. Clubs: Yale (N.Y.C.); Century Country (White Plains, N.Y.). Home: 284 Briar Brae Rd Stamford, CT . 06903. Office: 41 E 42d St New York City NY 10017

COHEN, ROBERT ABRAHAM, physician; b. Chgo., Nov. 13, 1909; s. Ezra Harry and Catherine (Kurzon) C.; B.S., U. Chgo., 1930, Ph.D., M.D., 1935; m. Mabel Jean Blake, Mar. 21, 1933; children—Donald Edward, Margery Jean. Intern, Michael Reese Hosp., Chgo., 1936-37; resident Johns Hopkins, Sheppard-Pratt hosps., 1937-41; pvt. practice, Washington, 1946-48; clin. dir. Chestnut Lodge, Rockville, Md., 1948-53; dir. clin. investigations Nat. Inst. Mental Health, Bethesda, Md., 1953-69, dir. div. clin. and behavioral research, 1969—, dep. dir. intramural research program, 1969—. Bd. dirs. Founds. Fund for Research in Psychiatry, 1960-63, chmn. bd., 1962-63; trustee William Alanson White Psychiatric Found. Served from lt. (j.g.) to comdr., M.C., USNR, 1941-46. Fellow Am. Psychiatric Assn.; mem. Am. Psychoanalytical Assn., Washington Psychoanalytic Soc. (pres. 1951-53), Washington Psychiatric Soc. (pres. 1958-59), Washington Psychoanalytic Inst. (chmn. edn. com. 1953-58, dir. 1959-63), Washington Acad. Medicine. Home: 4514 Dorset Av Chevy Chase MD 20015 Office: 9000 Wisconsin Av Bethesda MD 20014

COHEN, ROBERT L., bus. exec.; b. Sedalia, Colo., Jan. 18, 1929; s. Laurence and Lucile (Draper) C.; B.A., Dartmouth, 1951; M.C.S., Amos Tuck Sch. Bus., 1952; m. Lorraine A. Young, Jan. 21, 1962 (dec.); children—Larry, Stanley David, Frank; m. 2d, Meryle L. Brooks. With Witmer Rumsey Ins. Agy., Crystal Lake, Ill., 1951-52; with Navajo Freight Lines, Inc., Denver, 1953-70, exec. v.p., 1958-64, pres., 1964-70; chmn. bd., pres., dir. Kanco Tech., Inc., 1970—; dir. Alameda Nat. Bank, Columbia State Bank, Jet-X Corp. Mem. adv. com. Gen. Rose Hosp., Denver. Mem. Colo. Motor Carriers Assn. (past pres.). Home: 3925 S Colorado Blvd Englewood CO 80110 Office: 5035 E 39th Av Denver CO 80207

COHEN, ROBERT SONNE, educator; b. N.Y.C., Feb. 18, 1923 s. Mordecai M. and Mabel (Reinschreiber) C.; B.A., Wesleyan U., Middletown, Conn., 1943; M.S., Yale, 1943, Ph.D. (NRC fellow), 1948; m. Robin Gertrude Hirshhorn, June 18, 1944; children—Michael, Daniel, Deborah. Instr. physics Yale 1943-44, inst. philosophy, 1949-51; sci. staff, war research div. Columbia, 1944-46; asst. prof. physics and philosophy Wesleyan U., 1949-57; asso. prof. physics Boston U., 1957-59, prof., chmn. dept., 1959—, acting dean Coll. Liberal Arts, 1971—; chmn. Boston Center for Philos. Sci.; vis. lectr. humanities and philosophy of sci. Mass. Inst. Tech., 1958-59, 61-62; vis. prof. history of ideas Brandeis U., 1959-60; Inst. History and Philosophy of Sci. lectr. Am. U., Washington, summers 1958-68; vis. fellow Polish and Yugoslav Acad. Sci., 1963, Hungarian Acad. Sci., 1964; vis. prof. philosophy U. Cal. at San Diego, 1969. Mem., sec. U.S. Nat. Com. for Internat. Union History and Philosophy of Sci. Trustee Weslyan U., 1968-71. Am. Council Learned Soc. fellow philosophy and sci., 1948-49; Ford faculty fellow, Cambridge, Eng., 1955-56. Trustee Bill of Rights Found. Fellow A.A.A.S. mem. Am. Phys. Soc., Am. Assn. Physics Tchrs., Am. Philos. Assn., History Sci. Soc., Philosophy Sci. Assn. (governing bd.), Am. Assn. U. Profs., Emergency Civil Liberties Com. (mem. nat. council), Am. Civil Liberties Union, Am. Inst. Marxist Studies (chmn.), Fedn. Am. Scientists (nat. council 1967-70), Inst. for Unity of Sci. (exec. com.). Author, editor articles, books and jours. in field. Editor: Boston Studies in Philosophy of Science. Home: 44 Adams Av Watertown MA 02172 Office: 111 Cummington St Boston MA 02215

COHEN, RONALD, educator; b. Canada, Jan. 22, 1930; s. Maxwell B. and Pauline (Golant) C.; came to U.S., 1963; B.A., U. Toronto, 1951; M.Sc., U. Wis., 1955, Ph.D., 1960; m. Diana Barbara Williams, June 21, 1955; children—Paul Yerima, Stephen Benjamin. Lectr. anthropology U. Toronto, 1958-61; asst. prof. McGill U., 1961-63; mem. faculty Northwestern U., 1963—, prof. anthropology and polit. sci., 1968—; cons. Nat. Inst. Mental Health, 1968—. Chmn. African Students Found., Can., 1962. Fellow Am. Anthrop. Assn.; mem. African Studies Assn., Assn. Brit. Social Amthropologists. Author: The Kanuri of Bornu, 1967; Dominance and Defiance, 1970. Editor: (with John Middleton) From Tribe to Nation in Africa, 1970; asst. editor Anthropologica, 1963—, Am. Anthropologist, 1970—. Home: 1040 Michigan Av Evanston IL 60202

COHEN, SAMUEL NATHAN, mcht.; b. Winnipeg, Man., Can., July 9, 1919; s. Alex and Rose (Diamond) C.; ed. Central Collegiate Sch. (Calgary); m. Leatrice Joy, Dec. 12, 1944; children—Charles, Mark, Sheri. With Met. Stores of Can., Ltd., Saan Stores, Ltd., Gen. Distbrs. of Can., Ltd. Chmn. Man. Centennial Citizens Campaign, 1971—. Dir. Winnipeg Symphony Orch., 1968—; gov. Winnipeg Art Gallery, 1971—. Home: 810 Wellington Crescent Winnipeg Manitoba Canada Office: 1370 Sony Pl Winnipeg Manitoba Canada

COHEN, SANFORD, educator; b. Cleve., Sept. 8, 1920; s. Louis J. and Celia (Schoenberg) C.; B.A., Ohio State U., 1943, M.A., 1947, Ph.D., 1951; m. Julia Catherine Beach, June 15, 1955; children—Jon, Elizabeth, Melanie. Asst. prof. econs. Western Res. U., 1953-56; asso. prof., prof. econs. Butler U., Indpls., 1957-62; vis. prof. U. Ill., Champaign, 1962-63; vis. prof. U. Mich., 1964-66; prof. econs. U. N.M., Albuquerque, 1966—, chmn. dept. econs., 1969—; vis. prof. Inter-Am. U., San German, P.R., 1969; examiner NLRB, 1948; br. chief WSB, 1951-52; manpower adviser Govt. of Bolivia, 1963-64; faculty dir. Internat. Manpower Inst., U.S. Dept. Labor, summers 1966, 67, 69; manpower adviser Venezuela, 1970; arbitrator labor-mgmt. disputes. Served with AUS, 1943-45. Mem. Am. Econ. Assn., Indsl. Relations Research Assn., Soc. for Internat. Devel. Author: State Labor Legislation, 1937-47, 1948; Labor in the United States, 1960; Labor Law, 1964; (with others) Management Preparation for Collective Bargaining, 1966. Contbr. articles profl. jours. Home: 3708 Gen Chenault St NE Albuquerque NM 87111

COHEN, SAUL BERNARD, educator, geographer; b. Malden, Mass., July 28, 1925; s. Barnett and Anna (Kaplinsky) C.; A.B., Harvard, 1948, A.M., 1949, Ph.D., 1955; m. Miriam Friederman, June 11, 1950; children—Deborah Fae, Louise Esther. From instr. to prof. geography Boston U., 1952-65; vis. prof. U.S. Naval War Coll., 1957; prof. geography, dir. Grad. Sch. Geography. Clark U., Worcester, Mass., 1965—, dean Grad. Sch., 1967-70. Cons. social sci. div. NSF; mem. U.S. nat. delegation Internat. Geog. Union, 1966-69; chmn. com. geography Nat. Acad. of Scis.-NRC, 1966-69. Fellow A.A.A.S.; mem. Consortium Profl. Assns. (chmn.), Assn. Am. Geographers (exec. officer 1964-65, del. Am. Council Learned Socs. 1964- 66, mem. council 1966-70), Am. Geog. Soc. (mem. council 1970—). Club: Cosmos (Washington, D.C.). Author of: Store Location Research for the Food Industry, 1961; Geography and Politics in a World Divided, 1963; Problems and Trends in American Geography, 1967; also articles. Home: 50 Solon St Newton MA 02161 Office: Clark U Worcester MA 01610

COHEN, SAUL GERALD, educator, chemist; b. Boston, May 10 1916; s. Barnet M. and Ida (Levine) C.; A.B., Harvard, 1937, M.A., 1938, Ph.D., 1940; m. Doris E. Brewer, Nov. 27, 1941 (dec. July 1971); children—Jonathan Brewer, Elisabeth Jane. Research fellow Harvard, 1939-40, 41-43, instr., 1940-41; NRC fellow, lectr. U. Cal. at Los Angeles, 1943-44; research chemist Pitts. Plate Glass Co., 1944-45, Polaroid Corp., 1945-50; with Brandeis U., 1950—, prof. chemistry, 1952—, chmn. Sch. Sci., 1950-55, dean faculty, 1955-59, chmn. dept. chemistry, 1959-66, 68—; vis. prof. Havard Med. Sch., 1965. Fulbright sr. scholar, 1958-59; Guggenheim fellow, 1958-59. Fellow Am. Acad. Arts and Scis. (council), A.A.A.S.; mem. Am. Soc. Biol. Chemists, Am. Chem. Soc., Chem. Soc. London, Am. Assn. U. Profs., Phi Beta Kappa, Sigma Xi. Home: Moon Hill Rd Lexington MA 02173 Office: Dept Chemistry Brandeis U Waltham MA 02154

COHEN, SEYMOUR JAY, rabbi; b. N.Y.C., Jan. 30, 1922; s. Philip J. and Rose (Cohen) C.; B.S.S., Coll. City N.Y., 1942; postgrad. Jewish Theol. Sem., 1942-46, Hebrew U., Jerusalem, 1946-47; M.A. Columbia 1949; Ph. D., U. Pitts., 1953; m. Naomi Greenberg, June 11, 1946; children—Grace, Marc, Leeber, Ordained rabbi, 1946; rabbi Patchogue (N.Y.) Jewish Center, 1947-51, B'nai Israel Synagogue, Pitts., 1951-60, Anshe Emet Synagogue, Chgo., 1961—; instr. industry and econs. U. Pitts., 1954-57. Pres. Synagogue Council Am., 1965-67; chmn. Am. Jewish Conf. on Soviet Jewry, 1965; sec. Rabbinical Assembly, 1962-64; co-chmn. Interreligious Com. Against Poverty, 1966—; pres. Chgo. Bd. Rabbis, 1968-70. Mem. com. medicine and religion A.M.A., 1961-66. Travelling fellow Zionist Orgn. Am., 1946-47. Mem. Phi Beta Kappa. Author: Judaism and the Worlds of Business and Labor, 1961; Negro-Jewish Dialogue, 1963; Religious Freedom and the Constitution, 1968; A Time to Speak, 1968. Translator: Ways of the Righteous, 1969. Home: 3800 Lake Shore Dr Chicago IL 60613 Office: 3760 N Pine Grove St Chicago IL 60613

COHEN, SEYMOUR STANLEY, biochemist; b. N.Y.C., Apr. 30, 1917; s. Herman and Lena (Tanz) C.; B.S., Coll. City N.Y., 1936; Ph.D. in Biol. Chemistry, Columbia, 1941; m. Elaine Pear, July 12, 1940; children—Michael, Sara. NRC fellow Rockefeller Inst., 1941-42; mem. faculty U. Pa., 1943-71, prof. biochemistry in pediatrics, 1954-71, Charles Hayden-Am. Cancer Soc. prof. biochemistry, 1957-71, Hartzell prof., chmn. dept. therapeutic research, Sch. Medicine, 1963-71; prof. microbiology U. Colo. Sch. Medicine, Denver, 1971—. Guggenheim fellow Pasteur Inst., Paris, France, 1947-48; Jesup lectr. Columbia, 1967; guest investigator Institut du Radium, Paris, 1967-68; vis. prof. Collège de France, Paris, 1970. Trustee Marine Biol. Lab., Woods Hole, Mass.; bd. sci. cons. Sloan-Kettering Inst. Recipient certificate war research OSRD, 1945, War Manpower Commn., 1945; War Research medal Columbia, 1943; Eli Lily award and medal Am. Soc. Bacteriology, Immunology and Pathology, 1951; 1st Mead Johnson award Am. Acad. Pediatrics, 1952; medal Soc. de Chimie Biologique (France), 1964; Borden award Am. Assn. Med. Colls., 1967. Fellow A.A.A.S. (Newcomb Cleveland award 1955), Am. Acad. Arts and Scis., Soc. Gen. Physiologists (councilor, pres. 1967-68), Nat. Acad. Scis. Author: Virus-Induced Enzymes, 1968; Introduction to the Polyamines, 1971. Editorial bd. Virology, 1954-59, Jour. Biol. Chemistry, 1959-65, Jour. Call Physiology, 1966-71, Bacteriological Revs., 1969—. Home: 112 Colwyn Lane Bala Cynwyd PA 19004 Office: Univ of Colorado School of Medicine Denver CO 80220

COHEN, SHELDON STANLEY, lawyer; b. Washington, June 28, 1927; s. Herman and Pearl (Jaffe) C.; A.B. with spl. honors, George Washington U., 1950, J.D. with distinction (Charles W. Dorsey scholar), 1952; m. Faye Fram, Feb. 21, 1951; children—Melinda Ann, Laura Eve, Jonathan Adam, Sharon Ruevena. Accountant, 1950-52; admitted to D.C. bar, 1952, U.S. Supreme Ct. bar, 1956; legislative atty. Office Chief Counsel, Internal Revenue Service, 1952- 56; asso. firm Stevenson, Paul, Rifkind, Wharton & Garrison, Washington, 1956-60; asso.-partner firm Arnold Fortas & Porter, Washington, 1960-64; chief counsel Internal Revenue Service, 1964-65, commr. internal revenue, 1965-69; mem. firm Cohen & Uretz, Washington, 1969—. Lectr., Howard U. Law Sch., 1957-58; professorial lectr. George Washington U. Law Sch., 1958—. pres. Am.-Israel Tax Found.; mem. bd. Nat. Jewish Welfare Bd., council Sch. Govt. and Bus. Adminstrn., George Washington U. Bd. dirs. Nat. Found. for Jewish Culture; bd. dirs., v.p. Jewish Community Center Greater Washington; bd. dirs. pres. Jewish Social Service Agy., Washington, Adas Israel, United Jewish Appeal, United Synagogues Am. Spl. tax counsel Democratic Nat. Com., 1969. Served with USNR, 1945-46. Recipient Alumni Achievement award George Washington U., 1965; Arthur Flemming award, 1966; Alexander Hamilton award U.S. Treasury Dept., 1969. C.P.A., Md. Mem. Am., Fed., D.C. bar assns., D.C. Inst. C.P.A.'s (hon.), Order of Coif, Phi Delta Phi, Phi Sigma Delta, Omicron Delta Kappa (hon.). Mason. Editorial, bus. sec. George Washington U. Law Rev., 1952, case notes editor, 1951-52. Home: 5518 Trent St., Chevy Chase MD . 20015. Office: 1730 M St N W Washington DC 20236

COHEN, SIDNEY, physician; b. N.Y.C., June 7, 1910; s. Adolph and Esther (Gordon) C.; Ph.D., Columbia, 1930; postgrad. Coll. City N.Y., 1930-32, Bonn (Germany) U., 1932-38; m. Illse Annalouise Franke, Feb. 27, 1934; children—Dorothy Elizabeth, Richard Sidney. Intern Jamaica (L.I.) Hosp., 1938-40; resident VA Hosp., Los Angeles, 1946-49; chief research Brentwood Hosp., Los Angeles, 1949-59; chief psychosomatic medicine Wadsworth VA Hosp., Los Angeles, 1959-68; chief Center Studies Narcotics and Drug Abuse, Nat. Inst. Mental Health, Chevy Chase, Md., 1968—; asso. clin. prof. medicine U. Cal. at Los Angeles, 1956—; All Univ. lectr. U. Cal., 1965; William Harvey Taylor lectr. Am. Therapeutic Soc., 1964; cons. Suicide Prevention Center, Alcoholism Research Clinic, Central Office Research Psychiatry, Neurology and Psychology. Mem. sci. adv. bd. Am. Schizophrenia Found.; dir. Los Angeles Med. Research Found. Served to col., M.C., AUS, 1941-46. Diplomate Am. Bd. Internal Medicine. Mem. Soc. Biol. Psychiatry, Am., Cal., Los Angeles County med. assns., Los Angeles Soc. Neurology and Psychiatry, Cal. Med. Research Assn. Author: Chemopsychotherapy, 1963; LSD, 1964; The Drug Dilemma, 1968; also numerous articles. Editor-in-chief Mind, Psychiatry in Private Practice, 1963-64; editorial bd. Psychosomatics, 1964—; editor Jour. Psychopharmacology, 1967. Home: 13020 Sky Valley Rd Los Angeles CA 90049 Office: 5454 Wisconsin Av Chevy Chase MD 20203

COHEN, SIMON, author; b. Balt., Feb. 26, 1894; s. Benjamin and Rebecca (Sinsheimer) C.; student Johns Hopkins U., 1910-11; A.B., U. Cin., 1941; rabbi Hebrew Union Coll., 1916, D.D., 1924; m. Dagmar Abramson, Oct. 5, 1944; 1 dau., Marthamae (Mrs. Frank R. Schlow). Rabbi, N.Y.C., 1916-28, 46-51; dir. research Universal Jewish Ency., 1928-43; reference and serial librarian Hebrew Union Coll., 1952-71; cons. posthumous writing Samuel S. Cohon, 1964—. Mem. Soc. Bibl. Lit., Central Conf. Am. Rabbis. Clubs: Cincinnati. Author: Essence of Judaism, 1924; Seven-Branched Light, 1944; Shaaray Tefila, 1945. Editor B.H. Hartogensis, Studies in the History Maryland, 1941. Contbr. articles reference works. Address: 2200 Victory Pkwy Cincinnati OH 45206

COHEN, SYLVAN M., lawyer; b. Phila., July 18, 1914; s. Banjamin and Ray (Cohen) C.; B.A., U. Pa., 1935, LL.B., 1938; m. Alma Orlowitz, Sept 5, 1953; children— Stephen Bruce, Marc Alan. Admitted to Pa. bar, 1939; sr. enforcement atty. OPA, 1941-42; sr. partner firm Cohen, Shapiro, Berger, Polisher & Cohen, Phila., 1939—; pres., trustee Pa. Real Estate Investment Trust; dir. Indsl. Valley Bank & Trust Co., Sci. Resources Corp., Fla. Palm-Aire Corp., Belmont Industries, Inc. Mem. bd. ethics City Phila.; chmn. pension com. Phila. Gas Works. Pres. bd. trustees The Fedn. Jewish Agys. Greater Phila., 1967—; v.p., mem. exec. com., trustee United Fund; v.p. Phila. chpt. Am. Friends Hebrew U.; asso. chmn. bd. govs. Phila. com. State Israel Bonds; chmn. community participation unit Council on Youth Opportunity; co-chmn. resolutions com. United Jewish Appeal study mission, 1968; fund raising chmn. Citizens Com. for Phila. improvement program, 1964—; chmn. U. Pa. coll. ann. alumni giving campaign. 1968- 69. Dir. Police Athletic League Phila., Variety Club Camp for Handicapped Children, Nat. Found. March of Dimes, Technion Soc., Joint Distbn. Com.; trustee, v.p. Albert Einstein Med. Center; trustee The United Israel Appeal. Served with USAF, 1943-46. Mem. Am. Arbitration Assn. (nat. panel arbitrators), Nat. Assn. Real Estate Investment Funds (v.p., gov., chmn. state legistation com.), Socia-Legal Club, Phila. Layers Club, Am., Fed., Pa., Phila. (1st chmn. compulsory arbitration com. 1957-62, mem. judiciary com.) bar assns. Editorial staff: Collier on Bankruptcy. Home: 1000 Serpentine Lane Wyncota PA 19095. Office: 12 S 12th St Philadelphia PA 19107

COHEN, WALLACE MOSES, lawyer; b. Norton, Va., July 11, 1908; s. Jacob Edward and Annie (Hyman) C.: grad. Lake Forest Acad. 1925; S.B., Harvard 1929, postgrad. Law Sch., 1930-31; LL.B., Cornell U., 1932; m. Sylvia J. Stone, Sept. 7, 1932; children—Anne E. (Mrs. Steven A. Winkelman), Edward S., David W. Admitted to Mass. bar, 1932, Md. bar, 1952, D.C. bar, 1946, U.S. Supreme Ct.; practice of law, Boston, 1932-38; staff NLRB, Dept. Labor, Shipbuilding Stablzn. Commn., Adv. Commn. Council Nat. Def.,

OPA, Lend Lease Adminstrn., Fgn. Econ. Assn., 1938-45; dep. administrv. asst. to Pres.; mem. firm Landis, Cohen, Singman & Rauh, Washington, 1951—. Mem. County Housing Authority; mem. adv. bd. Clinch Valley Coll. of U. Va. Fellow Brandeis U. Mem. nat. bd. Am. Jewish Com. Served with USCGR, 1943-45. Mem. Am., Fed., Fed. Communications, D.C., Mass., Md. bar assns. Clubs: Harvard (Boston and Washington); Woodmont Country (Rockville, Md.); Lonesome Pine Country (Norton, Va.); Nat. Capital Democratic, Federal City, International, Nat. Press (Washington); Federal Bar. Home: 2444 Massachusetts Av NW Washington DC 20008 Office: 1910 Sunderland Pl NW Washington DC 20036

COHEN, WILBUR JOSEPH, ex-govt. ofcl., educator; b. Milw., June 10, 1913; s. Aaron and Bessie (Rubenstein) C.; Ph.B., U. Wis., 1934; L.H.D., Adelphi Coll., 1962, Yeshiva U., 1967, Cleve. State U., 1970, Ohio State U., 1970; LL.D., U. Wis., 1966, Yeshiva U., 1967, Brandeis U., 1968, Detroit U., Kenyon Coll., 1969; D.S.S., U. Louisville, 1969; m. Eloise Bittel, Apr. 8, 1938; children—Christopher, Bruce, Stuart. With Com. Econ. Secutiry, 1934-35; with Social Security Adminstrn., 1935-56; dir. div. research and statistics, 1953-56; prof. pub. welfare adminstrn. U. Mich., 1956-61; asst. sec. Dept. Health, Edn. and Welfare, 1961-65, under sec., 1965-68, sec., 1968- 69; prof. edn., dean Sch. Edn., U. Mich., 1969—, co-chmn. Inst. of Gerontology, 1969—, chmn. adv. com. on hwy. safety research, 1969—; vis. prof. U. Cal. at Los Angeles, 1957; lectr. Catholic U., 1961-62. Cons. aging to U.S. Senate Com. Labor and Pub. Welfare, 1956-57, 59, to UN, 1956-57; chmn. Pres.'s Task Force on Health and Social Security, 1960; Adv. Council Pub. Assistance, 1959; chmn. Pres.'s Com. on Mental Retardation, 1968; del. Gen. Assembly Internat. Social Security Assn., Turkey, 1961, U.S., 1964, vice chmn. council, 1964; rep. U.S. Govt. at Internat. Confs. Social Security, Internat. Conf. Social Work, Internat. Labor Conf., chmn. U.S. delegation UN Conf. Ministers Responsible Social Welfare, 1968. Mem. J.F. Kennedy Center Performing Arts, 1968. Recipient Distinguished Service award Dept. Health, Edn. and Welfare, 1956, Group Health Assn., 1956, Florina Lasker award, 1961; Blanche Ittleson award, 1962; award Nat. Assn. Mentally Retarded Children, 1965; award Assn. Phys. Medicine, 1965; Bronfman Pub. Health prize, 1967; Rockefeller Pub. Service award, 1967; Murray-Green award, 1968; Wilbur award Golden Ring Council Sr. Citizens, 1968; Forand award Nat. Council Sr. Citizens, 1969. Mem. Am. Pub. Welfare Assn. (Terry Meml. Merit award 1961, dir. 1962-65), Internat. Assn. Gerontology, Nat. Conf. Social Welfare (Distinguished Service award 1957, pres. 1969), Council Social Work Edn. (ho. of dels. 1959-62), Nat. Assn. Social Workers, Am. Assn. U. Profs., Indsl. Relations Research Assn. (exec. bd. 1969—), Am. Pub. Health Assn. (governing council 1970—), Am. Assn. Higher Edn., Am. Econ. Assn. Author: Retirement Policies in Social Security, 1957; (with William Haber) Readings in Social Security, 1948, Social Security; Programs, Problems and Policies, 1960; co-author Income and Welfare in the United States 1962; also numerous articles. Home: 620 Oxford Rd Ann Arbor MI 48104 also 9819 Capitol View Av Silver Spring MD 20910

COHEN, WILLIAM, educator; b. Scranton, Pa., June 1, 1933; s. Maurice M. and Nellie (Rubin) C.; B.A., U. Cal. at Los Angeles, 1953, LL.B., 1956; m. Betty C. Stein, Sept. 13, 1952; children—Barbara Jean, David Alan, Rebecca Anne. Admitted to Cal. bar, 1961; law clk. to U.S. Supreme Ct. Justice William O. Douglas, 1956-57; from asst. prof. to asso. prof. U. Minn. Law Sch., 1957-60; vis. asso. prof. U. Cal. at Los Angeles Law Sch., 1959-60, mem. faculty, 1960-70, prof., 1962-70; prof. Stanford (Cal.) Law Sch., 1970—. Co-author: The Bill of Rights, a Source Book, 1968. Home: 820 Lathrop Dr Stanford CA 94305

COHEN, YEHUDI ARYEH, educator; b. N.Y.C., June 7, 1928; s. Meyer Benjamin and Nehama (Goldin) C.; B.A., Bklyn. Coll., 1948; Ph.D., Yale, 1953; m. Rhoda Holtz, June 28, 1962; 1 dau., Lisa Ellen. Instr., Conn. Coll., 1952-53, Albert Einstein Coll. Medicine, 1955-59; asso. prof. U. Cal. at Davis, 1964-67; prof. anthropology Rutgers U., New Brunswick, N.J., 1967—; lectr. Columbia, 1956-62, U. Chgo. and Northwestern U., 1962-64; vis. prof. U. Pa., 1971. Served with AUS, 1953-54. Mem. A.A.A.S. (Socio-Psychol. award 1955). Author: Social Structure and Personality: A Casebook, 1961, The Transition from Childhood to Adolescence, 1964; editor Man in Adaptation, 3 vols., 1968-71. Address: Rutgers U Dept Anthropology Tillett Hall New Brunswick NJ 08903

COHN, BERNARD SAMUEL, educator, anthropologist; b. Bklyn., May 13, 1928; s. Nathan and Blanche (Herc) C.; B.A., U. Wis., 1949; Ph.D. (Social Sci. Research Council fellow), Cornell U., Ithaca, N.Y., 1954; m. Rella Israly, Mar. 19, 1950; children—Jenny Miriam, Abigail Catherine, Jacob Israly, Naomi Juliet. Research asso., asst. prof. anthropology U. Chgo., 1956-58, vis. asst. prof. history, 1959-60, prof. anthropology and S. Asian history, 1964—, chmn. dept. anthropology, 1969—; asso. prof., chmn. dept. anthropology U. Rochester, 1960-64. Vis. prof. history U. Mich., 1967. Served with UAS, 1954-56. Rockefeller Found. fellow, 1957-59; Am. Council Learned Socs. fellow, 1962; Guggenheim fellow, 1964; fellow Center Advanced Study Behavioral Scis., 1967-68. Mem. Assn. Asian Studies (chmn. S. Asia com. 1962-64), Royal (Eng.), Am. anthrop. assns., Am. Soc. Ethnohistory (exec. bd. 1968-70). Asso. editor Jour. Asian Studies, 1962- 65; editorial bd. Comparative Studies in Society and History, 1966—, Jour. Social History, 1968—. Home: 5822 S Blackstone Av Chicago IL 60637

COHN, BYRON EMANUEL, ret. educator; b. Chgo., Nov. 2, 1901; s. Nathan D. and Sarah (Schoemann) C.; B.S., U. Denver, 1923, M.S., 1924; Pd.D., U. Chgo., 1931; m. Essie R. White, June 10, 1926 (dec. Mar. 4 1963); m. 2d, Margaret W. Carney, May 25, 1968. Chem. engr. Berkshire Hills Paper Co., Adams, Mass., 1923-25; instr. math. U. Denver, 1925-26, instr. physics, 1926-30, asst. prof., 1930-33, asso. prof., 1933-36, prof., 1936-70, prof. emeritus, 1970—, chmn. dept., 1944-62, dir. NSF summer Sci. Inst., 1958, 59, Esso. Edn. Found. Sat. In-Service Inst., 1958-60. Staff Naval Ordnance Lab., Washington, 1942, 43; chmn. Inter-Univ. High Altitude Labs., 1948—; sci. adv. com. Harvard-Colo. High Altitude Obs., 1951-52; mem. mgmt. com. Research Corp. High Altitude Sta., 1949-53. Mem. Am. Physics Soc., A.A.A.S., Am. Assn. Physics Tchrs., Colo.-Wyo. Acad. Sci. (pres. 1958-59), Phi Beta Kappa, Sigma Xi, Phi Lambda Upsilon, Omicron Delta Kappa, Sigma Pi Sigma, Alpha Epsilon Delta (hon.). Clubs: Teknik, Buchtel, Torch (pres.) (Denver). Contbr. profl. publs. Home: 3202 S Oneida Way Denver CO 80222

COHN, HARVEY, educator, mathematician; b. N.Y.C., Dec. 27, 1923; s. Morris and Leah (Spielmann) C.; B.S., Coll. City N.Y., 1942; M.S., N.Y.U., 1943; Ph.D., Harvard, 1948; m. Bernice Blaufarb, Mar. 8, 1951; children—Anthony, Susan. Teaching fellow Harvard, 1947-48; asst. prof. Wayne U., 1948-54, asso. prof., 1955-56; vis. asso. prof. Stanford, 1954-55; asso. prof., then prof., head computer center Washington, St. Louis, 1956-58; prof. math., U. Ariz., 1958—; summer lectr. math, U. Cal. at Los Angeles, 1960, U. Wis., 1963. Cons. Gen. Motors Corp., AEC computing facility at N.Y.U., Nat. Bur. Standards, Argonne Nat. Labs. Adv. bd. autonamous U. Guadalajara, Mex., 1963—; mem. Inst. for Advanced Study, 1970-71. Served with USNR, 1944-46. Recipient William Lowell Putnam prize Harvard, 1946. Mem. Am. Math. Soc., Math. Assn. Am., Assn. Computing Machinery, Phi Beta Kappa, Sigma Xi. Author: Second Course in Number Theory, 1962; Conformal Mapping on Riemann Surfaces, 1967. Home: Box 827 Route 5 Tucson AZ 85718

COHN, HASKELL, lawyer; b. Concord, N.H., Dec. 4, 1901; s. Abraham I. and Miriam (Caro) C.; A.B., Dartmouth, 1922; LL.B., Harvard, 1925; m. Harriet Segal, Mar. 27, 1928; children—Marjorie (Mrs. William H. Wolf), Susan (Mrs. Arthur M. Hartman). Admitted to Mass. bar, 1926, since practiced in Boston; sr. partner firm Mintz, Levin, Cohn and Glovsky, and predecessor, 1933—. Mem. Gov. Mass. Com. Revision Workmen's Compensation Law, 1960. Bd. dirs. Greater Boston YMCA, 1956—. Fellow Am. Bar Found., Am. Coll. Probate Lawyers; mem. Am. (vice chmn. estate and gift tax com. of tax sect. 1966-68, ho. of dels. 1968—), Boston (mem. council 1958-61, chmn. family law 1959-65, chmn. workmen's compensation 1958-60, pres. 1969- 71) bar associations, Am. Law Inst. (joint com. continuing legal edn. 1965-71), Harvard Law Sch. Assn. (regional v.p., mem. council 1966-70), Dartmouth Alumni Assn. (pres. Boston 1954), Phi Beta Kappa. Clubs: Harvard (Boston and N.Y.C.); Union, Belmont Country. Author articles on taxation. Home: 91 Seaver St Brookline MA 02146 Office: 1 Center Plaza Boston MA 02108

COHN, HERBERT B., lawyer; b. N.Y.C., Oct. 2, 1912; s. Joseph J. and Lillian (Rosing) C.; A.B., Yale, 1933; LL.B. magna cum laude, Harvard, 1936, editor Law Rev., 1934-36; m. Kathryn E. Coe, May 24, 1941; 1 dau., Elizabeth (Mrs. John A. Kark). Admitted to N.Y. bar, 1936; mem. legal staff SEC, 1936-48, dir. op. writ. office SEC, 1942-48; mem. legal staff Am. Electric Power Service Corp., N.Y.C., 1948-67, v.p., dir., chief counsel, 1954-67, exec. v.p. adminstrv. and corporate services, 1967—; dir., mem. exec. com. Am. Electric Power Co., 1966—; v.p., dir. various utility cos.; dir. Twin Br. R.R. Co. Served from lt. (j.g.) to lt. comdr. USNR, 1942-46. Mem. Am. Bar Assn. (chmn. pub. utility sect. 1968-69), Harvard Law Sch. Assn., Edison Electric Inst. (dir. 1965-67, 70—, chmn. legal com. 1962-64). Clubs: Harbor View, Harvard (N.Y.C.); Metropolitan, Lawyers (Washington). Home: 860 UN Plaza New York City NY 10017

COHN, HOWARD, mag. editor; b. N.Y.C., Nov. 1, 1922; s. Morris and Vivian (Siegel) C.; B.A., Am. U., 1947; m. Regina Levy, Apr. 2, 1949; children—Steven B., Robert D. Asso. editor Sportfolio mag., 1947-48; asso. editor, then mng. editor Am. Lawn Tennis mag., 1948-50; asso. editor Quick mag., 1950-51, Collier's mag., 1951-56; freelance writer, 1957-59; articles editor Pageant mag., 1959, exec. editor, 1959-63; mng. editor True mag., 1964- 68; mng. editor Med. World News mag., N.Y.C., 1968, exec. editor, 1968—. Served with AUS, 1943-46. Mem. Soc. Mag. Writers. Home: 35 Shirley Lane White Plains NY 10607 Office: 299 Park Av New York City NY 10017

COHN, HOWARD T., tel. and tel. co. exec.; b. Richmond, Va., 1929; ed. William and Mary Coll., 1949; v.p. internat. Internat. Tel. & Tel. Corp., N.Y.C. Home: 7 Lawrence Rd Madison NJ 07940 Office: 320 Park Av New York City NY 10022*

COHN, JESS VICTOR, psychiatrist; b. Cin., Jan. 1, 1908; s. Samuel L. and Hannah (Pritz) C.; M.D., U. Cin., 1933; m. Norma J. Hana, Sept. 7, 1947; children—Jess Victor, William S., James D. Rotating intern Cin. Gen. Hosp., 1933, resident psychiatry, 1934; resident neurology Bellevue Hosp., N.Y.C., 1935; pres. neuro-psychiat. dept. N. Broward Gen. Hosp., Ft. Lauderdale, Fla., 1961, mem. active staff, 1955-63; cons. psychiatry Meml. Hosp., Hollywood, Fla., 1957-63, Mt. Sinai Hosp., Miami Beach, Fla., 1956-63, mem. active staff N. Broward Provident Hosp., Ft. Lauderdale, 1956-63, Holy Cross Hosp., Ft. Lauderdale, 1957—, Ft. Lauderdale Beach Hosp., 1957—; cons. psychiatry Social Security Adminstrn., 1963-69, Sinai Hosp., Balt., 1964-69, Carroll County Gen. Hosp., 1965-69; asst. supt. Central State Hosp., Indpls., 1948-50; instr. neuro-psychiatry Ind. U. Med. Sch., 1948-50; dir. clerkship in applied practical psychology Butler U., 1949-50; supt. Embreevill (Pa.) State Hosp., 1950-55; asso. psychiatry U. Pa. Med. Sch., 1952-55, asso. psychiatry Grad. Sch. Medicine, 1952-55; asst. prof. psychiatry U. Miami 1957; supt. Springfield State Hosp., Sykesville, Md., 1963-69; asso. prof. psychiatry Johns Hopkins Med. Sch., 1963-69, psychiatrist Johns Hopkins Hosp., 1963-69; mem. faculty U. Md. Med Sch., 1963-69; psychiatrist Univ. Hosp., 1963-69; regional dir. mental health for Western Md. Founding mem., chmn. med. adv. com. Mental Health Assn. S.E. Fla., 1944-48; chmn. Fla. commn. Internat. Congress Mental Health, 1948. Diplomate Am. Bd. Psychiatry and Neurology. Fellow A.C.P.; mem. A.M.A., Assn. Med. Supts. Mental Hosps. (editor newsletter), Am., So. psychiat. assns., Pa., Phila. (chmn. program com.) psychiat. socs., Med. Chirurgical Faculty Md., Broward County Med. Assn. (chmn. med. adv. com. to mental health clinic), Broward County Neuropsychiat. Assn. (founding mem., 1st pres.), Fla. Psychiat. Soc., Delaware Valley Group Psychotherapy Soc. (founding mem., chmn. program com., mem. exec. com.), Am. Acad. Psychotherapists, Eastern Psychoanalytic Assn., Am. Coll. Psychiatrists. Author articles, bulls. in field. Address: 2916 Bayview Dr Fort Lauderdale FL 33306

COHN, MARCUS, lawyer; b. Omaha, Sept. 20, 1913; s. Sam and Rose (Forman) C.; student U. Okla., 1931-34; A.B., U. Chgo., 1935, J.D. cum laude (Bigelow fellow), 1938; LL.M., Harvard, 1940; m. Harryette Evelyn Nightingale, Aug. 20, 1939; children—Lawrence N., Barbara Gale. Chief field and investigation sect. law dept. FCC, 1940-44; individual practice law, 1944-46, 65—; partner Cohn & Marks, Washington; professorial lectr. Grad. Sch. Pub. Law, George Washington U.; resource panelist Aspen Inst. Humanistic Studies; participant U. Colo. Conf. World Affairs, 1964-68. Chmn. nat. campaign cabinet Am. Jewish Com. Chmn. sponsors Cortez A.M. Ewing Found.; bd. visitors, mem. exec. planning com. U. Okla. Wilton Park (Sussex, Eng. fellow, 1967; trustee, exec. com. Greater Washington Ednl. TV Assn. Mem. A.A.A.S. (com. on pub. understanding sci., Order of Coif, Phi Beta Kappa. Clubs: Federal City, Broadcast Pioneers, Nat. Press. Contbr. articles in field to revs. Editorial bd. Ednl. Broadcasting Rev. Home: 4031 Oliver St Chevy Chase MD 20015 Office: 1625 Eye St NW Washington DC 20006

COHN, MELVIN, biochemist; b. N.Y.C., Mar. 28, 1922; s. Isidore and Pauline (Burstein) C.; B.S., Coll. City N.Y., 1940; M.A., Columbia, 1941; Ph.D., N.Y.U., 1949; m. Suzanne H. Bourgeois, June 12, 1963. Merck NRC fellow Pasteur Inst., 1949-55, NSF fellow, 1961-63; prof. microbiology Sch. Medicine Washington U., 1955-58; prof. biochemistry Sch. Medicine Stanford, 1959- 61; sr. fellow Salk Inst., San Diego, 1963-; prof. biology U. Cal., San Diego, La Jolla. Served with AUS, 1940-46; PTO. Recipient Eli Lilly award microbiology, 1957. Mem. Am. Soc. Microbiology, Am. Assn. Immunologists, Am. Inst. Biol. Scis., Sigma Xi. Home: Box 140 Route 1, Del Mar, CA 92014. Office: Box 1809 San Diego CA 92112

COHN, MILDRED, educator; b. N.Y.C., July 12, 1913; d. Isidore M. and Bertha (Klein) Cohn; B.A., Hunter Coll., 1931; M.A., Columbia, 1932, Ph.D., 1938; Sc.D. (hon.), Women's Med. Coll., 1966; m. Henry Primakoff, May 31, 1938; children—Nina, Paul, Laura. Research asst. biochemistry George Washington U. Sch. Medicine, 1937-38; research asso. Cornell U., 1938- 46; research asso. Washington U., 1946-50, 51-58, asso. prof. biol. chemistry, 1958-60; asso. prof. biophysics and phys. biochemistry U. Pa. Med. Sch., 1960-61, prof., 1961—; research asso. Harvard, 1950-51. Established investigator Am. Heart Assn., 1953-59, career investigator, 1964—. Recipient Garvan medal. Mem. Nat. Acad. Scis., Am. Chem. Soc., Harvey Soc., Am. Soc. Biol. Chemists, Am. Acad. Arts and Scis., Phi Beta Kappa, Sigma Xi. Editorial bd. Jour. Biol. Chemistry, 1958-63, 67—. Home: 135 S 18th St Philadelphia PA 19103 Office: U Pa Philadelphia PA 19104

COHN, MILTON SEYMOUR, mfg. co. exec.; b. Bklyn., Oct. 11, 1920; s. Max B. and Dorothy (Zucker) C.; B.S. cum laude, N.Y. U., 1941, J.D. cum laude, 1950; m. Lucille Sanders, May 20, 1945; children—Bonnie L., Judd M. Admitted to N.Y. bar, 1950. Pres. Cerro Wire & Cable Co.; dir. Condec Corp., Spiral Metals Co. Bd. dirs. Beth Israel Hosp., Beth Jacob Schs.; hon. dir. Waldemar Med. Research Found. Mem. Nat. Elec. Mfrs. (chmn., bd. govs.), Young Pres. Orgn., Beta Gamma Sigma. Home: 36 Sunset Rd Kings Point NY 11024 Office: 5500 Maspeth Av Maspeth NY 11378

COHN, NATHAN, engring. co. exec.; b. Hartford, Conn., Jan. 2, 1907; s. Harris and Dora Leah (Levin) C.; S.B., Mass. Inst. Tech., 1927; m. Marjorie Kurtzon, June 30, 1940; children—Theodore Elliot, David Leslie, Anne Harris, Amy Elizabeth, Julie Archer. With Leeds & Northrup Co., Phila., 1927—, mgr. market devel. div., 1955-58, v.p. tech. affairs, 1958-65, sr. v.p. tech. affairs, 1965-67, exec. v.p. research and corporate devel., 1967—, dir., 1963—. Pres., Nat. Electronics Conf., 1950; mem. NRC; exec. bd. Found. for Instrumentation, Edn. and Research, 1962-64; del. congress Internat. Fedn. Automatic Control, 1960, 63, 66, 69, chmn. tech. com. on applications, 1969—; vis. com. libraries Mass. Inst. Tech., 1964—. Bd. dirs. Eagleville Hosp. and Rehab. Center. Fellow I.E.E.E. (Lamme medalist 1968), Nat. Acad. Engring.; Instrument Soc. Am. (v.p. industries, scis. 1960-61, sec. 1962, pres. 1963, Sperry medalist 1968), A.A.A.S.; mem. Engrs. Joint Council (exec. bd.), Indsl. Research Inst., Engrs. Council Profl. Devel. (vis. com. curriculum accreditation), Sci. Apparatus Makers Assn. (exec. bd. 1961-62, 66—, pres. 1969-71), Franklin Inst. (Wetherill medalist 1968), Nat. Soc. Profl. Engrs. (Engr. of Year, Delaware Valley 1968, State Pa. 1969), Engrs. Club Phila., Sigma Xi, Tau Beta Pi, Eta Kappa Nu. Pi Lambda Phi. Jewish religion. Club: Rydal (Phila.). Contbr. articles to profl. jours., chpts. to books, textbook. Home: 1457 Noble Rd Jenkintown PA 19046 Office: Sumneytown Pike North Wales PA 19454

COHN, NORMAN, educator, historian; b. London, Eng., Jan. 12, 1915; s. August Sylvester and Daisy (Reimer) C.; scholar, sr. scholar Christ Ch., Oxford U., 1933- 39; M.A. with 1st class honours, Oxford U., 1936; D.Litt., U. Glasgow (Scotland), 1957; m. Vera Broido, Sept. 3, 1941; 1 son, Nik. Prof. French, U. Durham (Eng.), 1960-63; professorial fellow U. Sussex (Eng.), also dir. Columbus Centre (formerly Centre Research Collective Psychopathology), 1966—; fellow Center Advanced Study Behavioral Scis., 1965-66. Served with Brit. Army, 1940-46. Fellow Royal Hist. Soc.; mem. The Athenaeum, London. Author: The Prusuit of the Millennium, rev. edits., 1961, 70, trans. into French, German, Italian, Spanish and Portuguese; Warrant for Genocide, 1967, rev. edit., 1970, trans. into French, German, Italian, Spanish, Hebrew (Anisfield-Wolf award in race relations). Translator: Gold Khan and other Siberian Legends, 1946. Home: 61 New End London NW 3 England

COHN, ROY BARNETT, surgeon; b. Portland, Ore., 1910; M.D. Stanford, 1933. Intern Mass. Gen. Hosp., Boston, 1932-33; now prof. surgery Stanford, mem. staff Palo Alto-Stanford Hosp. Diplomate Am. Bd. Surgery, Am. Bd. Thoracic Surgery. Office: 300 Pasteur Dr Palo Alto CA 94304

COHN, ROY MARCUS, lawyer; b. N.Y.C., Feb. 20, 1927; s. Albert and Dora (Marcus) C.; B.A., Columbia, 1946, LL.B., 1947. Admitted to N.Y. State bar, 1948; with U.S. dist. atty.'s office, N.Y.C., 1947-52, asst. U.S. atty., 1948-50; confidential asst. to U.S. atty. Saypol, 1950-52; spl. asst. to U.S. atty. gen. McGranery, 1952; chief counsel U.S. Senate Permanent investigations sub-com., 1953-54; counsel to firm Saxe, Bacon & Bolan, and predecessor firm, N.Y.C., 1959—; prof. law N.Y. Law Sch., 1957—; Pres. Am. Jewish League Against Communism. Regent St. Francis Coll., N.Y.C.; bd. dirs. Hebrew Home for Aged, N.Y.C.; trustee Roy M. Cohn Found. Capt., N.Y. State N.G. Recipient annual award lawyers div. Fedn. Jewish Philanthropies, 1952, Americanism award Am. Legion N.Y. State, 1956, Patriotism award Cath. War Vets., 1970. Mem. Am., N.Y. State, Bronx County, Internat. (patron) bar assns., Assn. Bar City N.Y. Clubs: Lafayette Yacht (Norfolk, Va.); Manhattan (N.Y.C.). Author: Mc Carthy, 1968. Address: 39 E 68th New York City NY 10021

COHN, SAMUEL MAURICE, govt. ofcl.; b. Phila., Nov. 11, 1915; s. Herman and Bessie (Weisberg) C.; B.A., U. Pa., 1936, postgrad., 1936, 38-40; m. Alma Cantor, Oct. 2, 1948; children—Anne L., Richard D. Research asst. Wharton Sch. U. Pa., 1938-39, 41-42; research asst., relocation dir. Phila. Housing Authority, 1939-40; econ. analyst Office War Moblzn. and Reconversion, 1946-47; fiscal economist, chief economist, chief fiscal analysis, dep. asst. dir. for budget review, asst. dir. for budget rev. Office Mgmt. and Budget and predecessor agy., Exec. Office President, Washington, 1947—. Served with AUS, USAAF, 1942-45. Recipient Dir.'s Exceptional Service award Bur. of Budget, 1962; Career Service award Nat. Civil Service League, 1968; Pres.'s award for Distinguished Fed. Civilian Service, 1971. Mem. Am. Statis. Assn., Am. Econ. Assn., Econometric Soc., Am. Soc. Pub. Adminstrn. Contbr. profl. jours. Home: 3400 Rose Lane Falls Church VA 22042 Office: Office of Mgmt and Budget Washington DC 20503

COHN, VICTOR EDWARD, journalist; b. Mpls., Aug. 4, 1919; s. Louis and Lillian (Bessler) C.; A.B., U. Minn., 1941; m. Marcella Rigler, Aug. 30, 1941; children—Jeffrey, Deborah, Phyllis. Editor Minn. Daily, U. Minn., 1940- 41; desk man Mpls. Star, 1941-42; copyreader Mpls. Tribune, 1946, reporter, 1946-47, sci. reporter, 1947-67; sci. editor Washington Post, 1968—; incorporator and dir. Council Advancement Sci. Writing, 1960—, v.p., 1967-68; vis. lectr. U. Minn. Sch. Journalism, 1966-67. Served with USNR, 1942-45. Recipient George Westinghouse award A.A.A.S., 1951, 59, Distinguished Reporting award Sigma Delta Chi, 1952, 56, 59; citations for distinguished service to health Minn. Med. Assn., 1955, Minn. Pub. Health Assn., 1966; Albert Lasker med. journalism award, 1958; Howard W. Blakeslee award Am. Heart Assn., 1963; Distinguished Citizen award Phi Beta Kappa Assn., Minn., 1966; James T. Grady award Am. Chem. Soc., 1971. Fellow A.A.A.S.; mem. Nat. Assn. Sci. Writers (pres. 1961-62), Am. Newspaper Guild, Phi Beta Kappa. Jewish religion. Author: 1999 Our Hopeful Future, 1956. Home: 4701 Willard Av Chevy Chase MD 20015 Office: 1515 L St NW Washington DC 20005

COHN, ZANVIL ALEXANDER, physician, educator; b. N.Y.C., Nov. 16, 1926; s. David and Esther (Schwartz) C.; B.S., Bates Coll., 1948; M.D., Harvard, 1953; m. Fern Dworkin, Dec. 19, 1948; children—David Jonathan, Ellen Rachel. Intern, asst. resident Mass. Gen. Hosp., Boston, 1954-55; chief Rickettsial Biology div. Walter Reed Army Inst. Research, Washington, 1955-57; med. research, specializing in cell biology, N.Y.C., 1958—; research asso., prof., sr. physician Rockefeller U., 1958—; mem. com. radiation, infection Armed Forces Epidemiological Bd. Served to capt., M.C. AUS,

1955-57. Recipient Boylston medal Harvard, 1960. Mem. Am. Soc. Clin. Investigation, A.A.A.S., Am. Soc. Microbiology, Am. Assn. Immunologists, Am. Soc. for Cell Biology, Am. Assn. Physicians. Asso. editor Am. Jour. Epidemiology, 1963—, Jour. Clin. Investigation, 1967—, Jour. Exptl. Medicine, 1970—, Cellular Immunology, 1970—. Home: 34 Beacon Hill Rd Port Washington NY 10050 Office: Rockefeller Univ 66th St and York Av New York City NY 10021

COHN-HAFT, LOUIS, educator; b. N.Y.C., Nov. 13, 1919; s. Harry and Goldie (Haft) C.; B.A., Columbia, 1941, M.A., 1949, Ph.D., 1955; m. Athena Capraro, Apr. 23, 1942; children—Hera, Anthony, Mario. Instr. history Columbia, 1950-53; instr. history Smith Coll., Northampton, Mass., 1953-56, asst. prof., 1956-58, asso. prof., 1958-63, prof., 1963—, chmn. dept. history, 1966 69, dir. Nat. Def. Edn. Act. Inst. for High Sch. Tchrs. History, summers 1967-68, Edn. Professions Devel. Act, summer 1969; prof. history Hartford Coll. for Women, 1965—. Chmn. Hampshire County (Mass.) chpt. Am. Civil Liberties Union, 1958-60, mem. exec. com., 1956-66. Served with USAAF, 1942-45. Mem. Am. Hist. Assn., Am. Philol. Assn., Archeol. Inst. Am., History of Sci. Soc., Am. Soc. Papyrology, Am. Assn. U. Profs. (chpt. pres.). Author: Public Physicians of Ancient Greece, 1956; Source Readings in Ancient History: The Ancient Near East and Greece, 1965. Home: 54 Kensington Av Northampton, MA 01060.

COHODES, ELI AARON, ednl. cons.; b. Iron Mountain, Mich., Sept 12, 1927; s. Joseph Harry and Esther Ida (Albert) C.; B.A., Harvard, 1950; m. Phyllis Hersh, Jan. 4, 1953; children—Stephen Eliot, David Bruce, Mitchell Joseph, Paul Andrew. Asso. editor Hosp. Mgmt. mag., 1953-54; mng. editor Hospitals, jour. Am. Hosp. Assn., 1955-59, Trustee mag., 1957-59, Modern Hosp. mag., 1959-63; editor Nation's Schs. mag., Chgo., 1963-68, chmn. editorial adv. bd., columnist, 1968—; v.p. Instructional Dynamics, Inc., Chgo., 1968-70; pres. Teach'em, Inc., Chgo., 1970—, Supts. Only, Inc., Chgo., 1970—; mem. exec. planning com. Ednl. Facilities Center, Chgo., 1970—; lectr. profl. writing U. Chgo., 1959-63. Served with AUS, 1945-46. Mem. Council Ednl. Facilities Planners, Am. Assn. Sch. Adminstrs. Home: 37 Turnbull Woods Highland Park IL 60035 Office: 25 E Chestnut St Chicago IL 60611

COHON, MORRIS, investment broker; b. N.Y.C., June 22, 1904; s. Benjamin and Rachel (Silver) C.; B.S. in Chem. Engring., Mass. Inst. Tech., 1925; postgrad. Law Sch. Columbia, 1926-29; m. Ruth Fidler, June 1938; children—Peter, Elizabeth. Statistician, 1929; established investment firm, 1935; sr. partner Morris Cohon & Co., N.Y.C., 1935—; pres. Hudson & Manhattan R.R. Co., 1949-50; pres. Englewood Antiques Corp. (N.J.). Mem. Nat. Assn. Security Dealers, N.Y. Security Dealers Assn., American-Internat. Charolais Assn. Author: The Broker- Dealer-Customer Problem-A Study of Dealer's Profits, Broker's Commissions and the Trend of Regulation, 1945; A Study of the Dealer- Customer Relationship, 1946; An Analysis of the New Issue Problem, 1960. Home: 90 Booth Av Englewood NJ 07631 Office: 19 Rector St New York City NY 10006

COIE, J. PAUL, lawyer; b. Riverside, Cal. Apr. 12, 1910; s. John S. and Floss (Bond) C.; A.B., Wash. State U., 1930; LL.B., Duke, 1933; m. Evelyn Nobach, June 30, 1931; children—Mary Lynne (Mrs. Stephen E. Connor), John P., Michael J. Admitted to Wash. bar, 1934, since practiced in Seattle; partner firm Perkins, Coie, Stone, Olsen, & Williams, 1942—. Fellow Am. Coll. Trial Lawyers; mem. Am., Wash., Seattle-King County (pres. 1967- 68) bar assns., Delta Sigma Rho, Phi Kappa Phi, Phi Delta Theta, Phi Delta Phi. Clubs: Rainier, Tennis (Seattle). Home: 2110 40th Av E Seattle WA 98102 Office: Washington Bldg Seattle WA 98101

COINER, CHARLES TOUCEY, artist; b. Santa Barbara, Cal., Aug. 20 1898; s. Charles Anderson and Mary (Gasgoigne) C.; student Chgo. Acad. Fine Arts, 1919; m. Mae Howe, Sept. 23, 1924. Designer N.W. Ayer & Son, Inc., Phila., 1924-29, v.p. in charge art, 1929-64. Designer govt. posters and symbols, also Red Feather design, NRA blue eagle; represented in permanent collections Whitney Mus. Nat. Acad. Davenport Mus. Philadelphia Adad. Fine Arts, Pa. Mus., also pvt. collections. Recipient lst award Nat. Assn. Art Dirs. N.A. Mem. Phila. Art Alliance, N.Y., Phila. art dirs. clubs, Nat. Acad. Art, N.A.D. Author articles on art and travel. Home: Mechanicsville PA 18934 Office: care Midtown Gallery 11 E 57th St New York City NY 10022

COINER, RICHARD TIDE, Jr., ret. air force officer; b. Washington, Sept. 2, 1910; s. Richard and Emily (Hall) C.; B.S., U.S. Mil. Acad., 1932; m. Helen Lanier Nix, Feb. 22, 1936; children—Richard Tide III, Beverly Nix, William Lanier. Commd. 2d lt., U.S. Army, 1932, advanced through grades to major gen., 1956; exec. to asst. sec. of war for air, 1941-43; comd. 397th Bomber Group, ETO, 1943-45; RAF Staff Coll., 1946; Hdqrs. U.S. Air Force Europe, 1946-49; div. mil. application AEC, 1949-51; dep. comdr., field command, Armed Forces Spl. Weapons Project, 1951-54; asst. dep. chief of staff Operations for Atomic Energy, Hdqrs. USAF, 1954-58, asst. chief staff, Air and Spl. Operations, SHAPE, 1958-61; comdr. Hdqrs. Ninth Air Force, 1961-63; dir. trans. Hdqrs. USAF, 1963-66; aviation cons.; v.p., dir. Nix Profl. Bldg. Corp., Nix St. Marys Corp. Mem. Nat. Def. Transp. Assn. Episcopalian. Clubs: The Argyle, San Antonio Country (San Antonio); Army and Navy (Washington). Address: 140 Patterson Av San Antonio TX 78209

COIRA, LOUIS EDWARD, ret. air force officer; b. Bloomsburg, Pa., Apr. 25, 1916; s. Louis and Elizabeth (Girton) C.; B.S., U.S. Mil. Acad., 1938; M.A., George Washington U., 1962; grad. Flying Sch., 1939, Air Command and Staff Coll., 1947, Nat. War Coll., 1955; m. Ellen Kathleen Holst, Nov. 28, 1942; children—Christine E. (Mrs. Peter Dinwoodie), Peter Louis, Paul Edward, Mark Emil. Commd. 2d lt. U.S. Army, 1938, advanced through grades to maj. gen. USAF, 1965; comdr. and staff officer Hdqrs. USAF, 1947-50, Office Sec. Def., 1959-62; comdr. USAF Security Service, 1965- 69; vice comdr. U.S. 5th Air Force in Japan, 1969-71, ret., 1971. Bd. dirs. United Services Automobile Assn., USAF Security Service Fed. Credit Union, United Services Automobile Assn. Life Ins. Co. Home: Fuchu Air Station Japan APO San Francisco CA 96525

COIT, ELISABETH, architect; b. Winchester, Mass.; d. Robert and Eliza Richmond (Atwood) Coit; student Radcliffe Coll., 1909-11, Boston Sch. Mus. Fine Arts, 1911- 13; B.Arch., Mass. Inst. Tech.; postgrad. U. Paris, Sorbonne, 1923-24. Designer with Grosvenor Atterbury, architect, 1918-23; pvt. practice of architecture, N.Y.C., 1923-42; architect PHA, Washington, 1942-47; prin. project planner N.Y.C. Housing Authority, 1947-62; cons. U.S. Dept. Housing & Urban Devel., N.Y.C. Mayor's Office for Aging, 1969—. Mem. N.Y.C. Landmarks Preservation Commn., 1970—; Fellow A.I.A. (Pioneer in Architecture N.Y. chpt. 1969); mem. Nat. Assn. Housing and Redevel. Ofcls., Citizens' Housing and Planning Council of N.Y.C. Author: Report on Family Living in High Apartment Buildings, 1965. Editor Required Reading, N.Y. Archtl. Record, 1941- 43; Public Housing Design, 1946. Contbr. profl. jours. Home: 330 W 72d St New York City NY 10023

COIT, MARGARET LOUISE, writer; b. Norwich, Conn.; d. Archa Willoughby and Grace Louise (Trow) Coit; A.B., U.N.C. (Weil scholarships 1940, 41), 1941; Litt.D., Woman's Coll., U. N.C., 1959. With Lawrence (Mass.) Daily Eagle, 1941, Newburyport (Mass.) Daily News, 1944, House in the Pines Jr. Coll., Norton, Mass., 1945, Haverhill (Mass.) Gazette, 1946; book reviewer Greensboro (N.C.) Daily News, N.Y. Times, N.Y. Post, others; mem. staff U. N.H. Writers Conf., 1950-61, U. Colo. Writers Conf., 1958- -; author-in-residence Fairleigh Dickinson U., 1955—, prof. Moderator W. Newbury Town Meeting; Breadloaf fellow, Breadloaf Writers Conf., 1948. Awarded Pulitzer prize for biography, 1950; Book award of Nat. Council of Women U.S., 1958. Vice adm. Confederate Navy of U.S. Mem. Soc. Am. Historians, Phi Beta Kappa. Republican. Episcopalian. Author: John C. Calhoun: American Portrait, 1950; Mr. Baruch (biography), 1957; The Fight for Union, 1961 (Thomas Edison Award); The Growing Years; (with others) The Sweep Westward, 1963, Andrew Jackson, 1965; Massachusetts, 1968. Editor: Calhoun: Great Lives Observed. Contbr. Va. Quar. Rev., N.Y. Times mag., Am. Heritage, Look, Saturday Rev., others. Home: 368 Park Av Rutherford NJ 07070

COKE, HENRY CORNICK, Jr., lawyer; b. Dallas, Aug. 24, 1903, s. Henry C. and Margaret (Johnson) C.; B.A., Yale, 1926; LL.B. magna cum laude, 1929; children—Henry Cornick, Nancy, Alexander; m. Kathleen Walker, Nov. 29, 1967. Admitted to Tex. bar, 1929, since practiced in Dallas; mem. firm Coke & Coke, 1930—; dir. Otis Engring. Corp., Halliburton Co., First Nat. Bank, Dallas. Served as maj. USAAF, 1942-45. Decorated D.F.C., Bronze Star medal, Air medal. Mem. Am., Dallas bar assns., State Bar Tex., Dallas Symphony Soc. (pres. 1941, 42); Dallas Hist. Soc. (pres. 1969—), Tex. Philatelic Soc. Clubs: Southern Yacht (New Orleans); Brook Hollow Golf, Petroleum (Dallas); St. Petersburg Yacht. Home: 4429 Belclaire Dallas TX 75205 Office: First Nat Bank Bldg Dallas TX 75202

COKE, JAMES EARL, banker; b. Downey, Cal., May 28, 1900; s. Walter W. and Minnie E. (Smith) C.; student Pomona Coll., Claremont, Cal., 1919-20; B.S., U. Cal., 1923; D.Sc. (hon.) Clemson Agrl. Coll., 1955; m. Madelene Mary Fulton, Aug. 16, 1922 (dec.); children—James Earl, Thomas Richard; m. 2d, Elizabeth Harrold, Oct. 1, 1955; Asst. farm adviser, Agrl. Extension Service, U. Cal., 1923-27, agonomy specialist, 1928-34; dir., 1949-52, 1954-55; v.p., agriculturist Speckels Sugar Co., 1935-49; asst. sec. agr. U.S. Dept. Agr., 1953-54; dir. C.C.C., 1953-54; v.p. Bank of Am., 1955-65; pres. Consol. Agrl. Industries, Inc., 1965-66; dir. Cal. State Dept. Agriculture, 1967-68; sec. Agr. and Services Agy., 1968- -; asst. to gov. for cabinet affairs, 1969—. Mem. San Francisco C. of C., Am., Western farm econs. assns. Presbyn. Clubs: Commonwealth (San Francisco). Home: 4100 Folsom Blvd Sacramento CA 95819 Office: 1220 N St Sacramento CA 95814

COKER, CHARLES WESTFIELD, mfg. exec.; b. Hartsville, S.C., Aug. 15, 1906, s. Charles Westfield and Carrie (Lide) C.; A.B., U. S.C., 1928, LL.D., 1958; postgrad. Harvard Sch. Bus., 1929-30; m. Elizabeth Howard, Oct. 23, 1931; children—Charles Westfield, Fitzlee Howard. With Sonoco Products Co., 1930—, v.p., exec. v.p., 1934-61, pres., 1961-70, chmn. bd., 1970—; dir. Sonoco Products Co. of Canada, Ltd., Brantford, Ont., Bank of Hartsville, Hartsville Oil Mill, J. L. Coker & Co., Sonoco de Mexico, S.A., Mexico City, T.P.T. Ltd., Romiley, Eng., Coker's Pedigreed Seed Co., Columbia, Newberry & Laurens R.R., S.C. Nat. Bank; Carolinas adv. bd. Am. Mut. Liability Ins. Co. Regional exec. com. Boy Scouts Am.; chmn. bd. trustees Coker Coll. Mem. Composite Can and Tube Inst. (v.p.), N.A.M., Newcomen Soc., Soc. Colonial Wars, Pi Kappa Alpha, Omicron Delta Kappa. Mason, Rotarian. Club: Lotos, Metropolitan (N.Y.C.). Home: Segars Rd Hartsville SC 29550 Office: Sonoco Products Hartsville SC 29550

COKER, CURTIS E., lawyer; b. New Albany, Miss., Sept. 30, 1918; B.S., U. Utah, 1950; J.D., U. Miss., 1952. Admitted to Miss. bar, 1952; now partner firm Daniel, Coker, Horton & Bell, Jackson, Miss. Mem. Am., Hinds County bar assns., Miss. State Bar, Miss. Def. Lawyers Assn., Fedn. Ins. Counsel, Phi Alpha Delta. Office: 405 Tombigbee St at S Congress St Jackson MS 39205*

COKER, ELIZABETH BOATWRIGHT, (Mrs. James Lide Coker), author; b. Darlington, S.C., Apr. 21, 1909; d. Purvis Jenkins and Bessie (Heard) Boatwright; A.B., Converse Coll., 1929; postgrad. Middleburg Coll., 1938; m. James Lide Coker, Sept. 27, 1930; children—Penelope, James Lide. Mem. Hartsville Sch. Bd., 1939-49; sec., dir. Blowing Rock Horse Show Assn., 1943-49; dir. United Cerebral Palsy of S.C. Mem. nat. bd. Womans Med. Coll. Pa.; nat. adv. council I.S.S. Mem. Poetry Soc. Ga., Am. Assn. U. Women, P.E.N., S.C. Poetry Soc., Authors Guild, Nat. Steeplechase and Hunt Assn., Garden Club Am. Republican. Episcopalian. Club: Palmetto Garden. Author: Daughter of Strangers, 1950; The Day of the Peacock, 1952; India Allan, 1953; The Big Drum, 1957; La Belle, 1959; Lady Rich, 1963; The Bees, 1968. Contbr. mag. articles, poems. Home: 1812 W Home Av Hartsville SC 29550

COKER, ROBERT RICHARDSON, business exec.; b. Hartsville, S.C., Sept. 6, 1905; s. David Robert and Jessie Ruth (Richardson) C.; grad. Webb Sch., 1924; B.A., U. S.C., 1928, LL.D., 1970; D.Sc., Clemson U., 1955; m. Lois Walters, Oct. 24, 1936; children—Ione C. Lee, William Chambers. Pres. Coker's Pedigreed Seed Co., Coker's of Florence, J.L. Coker & Co.; v.p. Hartsville Oil Mill; chmn. bd. Bank of Hartsville; dir. Textile Paper Tube Co., Ltd., Romiley, Eng., Sonoco Products Co. Life trustee Clemson U. Named S.C. Man of the Year in Agriculture, Progressive Farmer, 1964. Mem. S.C. Farm Bur. (1st pres. 1944, life mem. bd.), Nat. Cotton Council (chmn. bd. 1964), Alpha Tau Omega, Gamma Sigma Delta. Baptist. Home: 1318 W Carolina Av Hartsville SC 29550 Office: Carolina Av Hartsville SC 29550

COKER, SAMUEL TERRY, univ. dean; b. Evergreen, Ala., Nov. 29, 1926, s. Zollie Watson and Lillie (Anthony) C.; B.S. in Pharmacy, Auburn U., 1951; M.S. in Pharmacology, Purdue U., 1953, Ph.D., 1955; m. Carolyn Sue Ridnour, Aug. 15, 1954; children—Ann Louise, Susan, Blair. Instr. pharmacology, U. Pitts., 1953-54: asso. prof. pharmacology U. Miss., 1955-56, U. Mo., Kansas City, 1956-59; prov. pharmacology, dean Sch. Pharmacy, Auburn U., 1959—. Mem. Acad. Pharm. Scis., Am. Pharm. Assn., Sigma Xi, Rho Chi, Phi Sigma, Kappa Psi, Phi Delta Chi. Club: Toastmasters. Kiwanian. Contbr. articles profl. jours. Home: Route 3 Box 99 Auburn AL 36830

COLAHAN, THOMAS SEERY, ednl. adminstr.; b. N.Y.C., Nov. 25, 1926; s. Thomas Edward and Mabel (Sheeran) C.; B.A., Columbia, 1951, M.A. (Henry Evans fellow 1952-53), 1953, Ph.D., 1962; postgrad. U. London (Eng.), 1953, U. Edinburgh (Scotland), 1952; m. Anne Gibson, Dec. 3, 1949; children—Alexandra, Charity. Asst. dir. admissions Columbia, 1953-55; dir. reception center Asian intellectuals Am. Com. Cultural Freedom, 1955-57; asst. rep. in Korea, Asia Found, 1957-59; asso. dir. admissions Columbia, 1960-64, lectr. history, 1963-69, asso. dean acad. affairs, 1964-67, vice dean, 1967-69; v.p. acad. affairs, prof. history State U. Coll. Arts and Scis., Geneseo, N.Y. 1969—. Trustee Brit. Am. Ednl. Found., 1966, N.Y. State Center for Migrant Edn., 1969—. Served with AUS, 1944-46. Mem. Am. Hist. Assn., Asia Soc., Phi Beta Kappa. Club: University (Rochester, N.Y.). Home: 13 Oak St Geneseo NY 14454

COLAS, ANTONIO ESPADA, educator; b. Muel, Spain, June 22, 1928; s. Pedro Lagunas and Antonia Romeo (Espada) C.; Licentiate, U. Zaragoza, 1951; M.D., U. Madrid, 1953; Ph.D., U. Edinburgh, 1955; m. María Immaculada Martín, Feb. 24, 1955; children—Antonio de Padua, Juan Baptista, María del Pilar, Santiago. Came to U.S., 1962, naturalized, 1968. Prof., U. Salamanca Med. Sch., Spain, 1955-57; prof., head, grad. div. U. del Valle Med. Sch., Cali, Colombia, 1957-62; prof. U. Ore. Med. Sch., 1962-68; prof. U. Wis. Med. Sch., Madison, 1968—. Brit. Council scholar, 1953-55; NIH, Rockefeller Found., Ford Found. grantee, 1957-71. Mem. Biochem. Soc. Gt. Britain, Sociedad Espaola de Ciencias Fisiológicas (Spain), A.A.A.S., Am. Chem. Soc., Div. Biol. Chemists, Sociedad Espaola de Bioquímica (Spain), Endocrine Soc., Am. Soc. Biol. Chemists, Soc. Gynecol. Investigation. Roman Catholic. Research, publs. on studies of biosynthesis and metabolism of steroid hormones.‡

COLAS, EMILE JULES, lawyer; b. Montreal, Que., Can., Oct. 3, 1923; s. Emile and Elise (Pila) C.; B.Eng., McGill U., 1946, B.C.L., 1949, M.C.L., 1950; B.A., Ottawa U., 1947; m. Rejane Laberge, Oct. 25, 1958; children—Bernard, Hubert, Francois. Lectr. Faculty Engring., McGill U., 1946-49; del. Carnegie Endowment for Internat. Peace Conf., Ann Arbor, Mich., 1950; called to bar, Que., 1950, since practiced in Montreal. Sec., v.p., pres. Jr. Bar Montreal, 1952-56; mem. council Bar of Montreal, 1956-57, 1st v.p., pres., hon. pres. Legal Aid Bur., 1956-61, pres. Legal Aid Bur., 1967-68; del. Conf. Commrs. on Uniformity of Legislation in Can., 1956-63, pres., 1969-70; hon. mem., del. Union des Jeunes avocats de France et de la Communaute, Nimes, 1956, Paris, 1959, Bordeaux, 1962; corr. mem. for Can., del. Institut Belge de Droit Internat. et de Droit Compare, Brussels, 1957—. Decorated Liberated France medal Knight Order of Palmes académiques (France). Mem. Corp. Profl.Engrs. Que., Engring. Inst. Can., Bar of Province Que., Canadian (pres., mem. council Que.), Commonwealth (past del.) bar assns., Canadian Inst. Internat. Affairs (past br. sec.), Chambre de Commerce Francaise au Can. (mem. council), Alliance Francaise, Comite France-Amerique, Charity Assn. Bar Montreal (life), Assn. des Anciens du Mont St. Louis (life), Assn. des Anciens de l'Universite d'Ottawa (life), Internat. Union Young Lawyers (past v.p.). Roman Catholic. Club: Touring de France (life). Author: The Judicial Control of Administrative Discretion, 1949; The Concept of Legal Personality and Trade Unions in Canada, 1950; The Labour Tribunals, 1952. Contbr. articles profl. jours. Home: 18 Ainslie Av Outremont Quebec Canada Office: Stock Exchange Tower Place Victoria Montreal 3 Quebec Canada

COLASURD, RICHARD MICHAEL, lawyer; b. Navarre, O., Apr. 1, 1928; s. Michael and Adeline (Manack) C.; A.B., U. Notre Dame, 1950; J.D., Harvard, 1953; m. Bette Rae Cochrane, Nov. 24, 1956; children—Steven Michael, David Gerard, Cathie Marie. Admitted to Ohio bar, 1953; practice in Toledo, 1960—; spl. agt. FBI, 1953-56; asst. U.S. atty. charge Northwestern Ohio, 1956-60; mem. firm Shumaker, Loop & Kendrick, 1960-64; asst. city law dir., Toledo, 1964; mem. firm Mulholland, Hickey & Lyman, 1964—; U.S. commr., 1963-67. Mem. Am., Ohio, Toledo bar assns., Soc. Former Spl. Agts. of FBI. Roman Catholic. Rotarian. Club: Inverness (Toledo). Home: 3250 Cheltenham Rd Toledo OH 43606 Office: Nat Bank Bldg Toledo OH 43604

COLASURDO, LEWIS LIPPINCOTT, banker, mfg. co. exec.; b. Hammonton, N.J., June 1, 1916; s. P. Anthony and Kathryn (Cowperthwaite) C.; student Villanova U., 1934; m. Madeline Reitano, Nov. 30, 1940. Former v.p. Boardwalk Nat. Bank, Atlantic City, 1959; pres. Crescent Corp., N.Y.C., 1965-68. Served to lt. USAAF, 1942-46. Roman Catholic. Home: The Harbour Hammonton NJ 08037 Office: 270 Park Av New York City NY 10017

COLBAUGH, ROBERT CRAWFORD, Jr., steel Co. exec.; b. Pitts., Apr. 19, 1913; s. S. Robert Crawford and Ida L. (Neff) C.; B.S. in Indsl. Engring., Lehigh U., 1935; m. Elizabeth W. Barron, June 22, 1940; children—Nancy, Sally, Edward. Metallurgist, indsl. engr. Carnegie-Ill. Steel Corp., Pitts., 1935-41, plant indsl. engr. Edgar Thomson works, 1941-43, indsl. engring, div., Pitts., 1943-50, asst. to mgr. operations Central Operations, U.S. Steel Corp., 1950-56, asst. v.p. indsl. engring., 1956-60, v.p., Pitts., 1960-69, v.p. long range facility planning, 1969—. Mem. Am. Iron and Steel Inst., Chi Psi. Clubs: Duquesne, Longue Vue (Pitts.) Office: 600 Grant St Pittsburgh PA 15230 †

COLBERG, MARSHALL RUDOLPH, educator, economist; b. Chgo., June 11, 1913, s. Rudolph E. and Elvira (Wester) C.; A.B., U. Chgo., 1934, A.M., 1938; Ph.D., U. Mich., 1950; m. Peggy Lou Dean, Nov. 25, 1942 (dec. 1964); children—Marsha, Daniel; m. 2d, Sarah N. McCoy, Sept. 17, 1966. Economist, WPB, 1940-43, Civilian Prodn. Adminstrn., 1945-46; analyst USAF, 1946-50; mem. faculty Fla. State U., 1950—, prof. econs., 1953—, chmn. dept., 1954-67. Mem. Am. (mem. com. econ. edn.), So. (pres., 1962, chmn. nominating com., 1964) econ. assns., Mt. Pelerin Soc. Author: (with Allen and Buchanan) Prices, Income and Public Policy, 2d edit., 1959; (with Forbush and Whitaker) Business Economics, 1964, 4th edit., 1970; (with M. Greenhut) Factors in the Location of Florida Industry, 1962; Human Capital in Southern Development: 1939-1963, 1965. Home: 1323 Diamond St Tallahassee FL 32301

COLBERT, CHARLES FRANCIS, Jr., corp. exec.; b. Pitts., s. Charles Francis and Philomena (Dischner) C.; ed. Cathedral Sch. Ill., Shurtleff Coll., Ill.; m. Marie Louise Benford, Jan. 12, 1911 (dec. Jan. 1931); children—Jane Elizabeth (Mrs. Eugene Scott), Dorothy Benford (Mrs. Ralph H. Irwin). Richard Gary, Margaret L. (Mrs. William J. Gehweiler) (dec.), Patricia (Mrs. Emmett E. Robinson); m. Mildred Frances Allen, Oct. 27, 1955; 1 son, Charles Francis III. Engaged in coal, coke and alloys bus., Pitts., Charleston, S.C., Calvert, Ky. and Niagara Falls, N.Y., 1908; chmn., cons. Pitts. Metall. Co. div. Air Reduction Co. of N.Y., also dir. parent co.; chmn. adv. bd. Mfrs. & Traders Trust Co., Niagara Falls. Mem. Am. Iron and Steel Inst. Clubs: Duquesne (Pitts.); Niagara Falls; Country, Pinnacle (N.Y.C.); Palm Beach Civic, Beach, Everglades (Palm Beach, Fla.); Youngstown (N.Y.) Yacht. Home: Shore Acres 3881 Lower River Rd Youngstown, NY 14174.

COLBERT, CHARLES RALPH, architect; b. Dow, Okla., June 23, 1921; s. James Eden and Alice (Hendon) C.; B.Arch., U. Tex., 1943; M.S. Columbia, 1947; m. Rosemary Frances Schrafft, Sept. 26, 1946 (dec. May 1954); children—Kathryn H., James Eden III, Thomas M.; m. 2d, Frances B. Stern June 18, 1956 (dec. Apr. 1962). Asst. prof. Tulane U., 1947- 49; pvt. practice architecture and planning, 1949-50, architecture and city planning, New Orleans, 1953—; supervising architect, dir. Office Planning and Constrn., New Orleans pub. schs., 1951-53; dir. architecture div. Tex. A. and M. Coll., 1956-57; dean Sch. Architecture, Columbia, 1960-63. Mem. La. Bd. Edn., 1970—. Served to lt. (s.g.) USNR, 1943-45. Fellow A.I.A.: mem. Royal Soc. Arts, Tau Beta Pi. Home: 510 Woodvine Av Metairie LA 70005 Office: 8522 Freret St New Orleans LA 70118

COLBERT, CLAUDETTE (maiden name Lily Chauchoin), actress; b. Paris, France; d. Georges and Jeanne (Loew) Chauchoin; brought to U.S., 1910; grad. Washington Irving High Sch., 1923; m. Norman Foster, Mar. 13, 1928; m. 2d, Dr. Joel Pressman. Debut as Sibyl Blake in Wild Westcotts, Frazee Theatre, 1924; later appeared in plays including The Marionette Man, Leah Kleschna, High Stakes, The Kiss in a Taxi, The Ghost Train, Pearl of Great Price, Tin Pan Alley, See Naples and Die, Eugene O'Neill's Dynamo; 1st appearance in London, as Lou in the Barker, 1928; left stage for moving pictures, 1929, films include The Lady Lies, Manslaughter, The Smiling Lieutenant, Sign of the Cross, Cleopatra, Private Worlds, Maid of Salem, It Happened One Night, The Gilded Lily, I Met Him In Paris, Bluebeard's Eighth Wife, Zaza Midnight, Drums Along the Mohawk, Skylark, Remember the Day, Palm Beach Story, No Time for Love, So Proudly We Hail, Parrish for Warner Bros.; stage play Marriage-Go-Round; starred in Broadway plays Julia, Jake and Uncle Joe, 1961, The Irregular Verb To Love, 1963. Awarded 1st honors (with Clark Gable) Acad. Motion Picture Arts and Scis. for best acting of the year, 1934. Home: Holmby Hills Los Angeles CA 90058 Office: Paramount Studios Hollywood CA 90028

COLBERT, EDWIN H., paleontologist; b. Clarinda, Ia., Sept. 28, 1905; s. George Harris and Mary (Adamson) C.; student Northwest Mo. State Teachers Coll., 1923- 26; B.A., U. Neb. 1928; A.M., Columbia, 1930, Ph.D., 1935; m. Margaret Mary Matthew, July 8, 1933; children—George Matthew, David William, Philip Valentine, Daniel Lee, Charles Diller. Student asst. U. Museum, U. Neb., 1926-29; univ. fellow, Columbia, 1929-30; research asst., Am. Museum Natural History, 1930-32, asst. curator, 1933-42, acting curator, 1942, curator, 1943, chmn. dept. amphibians and reptiles, 1943-44, curator of fossil reptiles and amphibians, 1945-70, chmn. dept. geology and paleontology, 1958-60, chmn. dept. vertebrate paleontology, 1960-66, curator emeritus, 1970—; lectr. dept. zoology, Columbia, 1938-39; prof. vertebrate paleontology, 1945-69, professor emeritus, 1969—; curator vertebrate paleontology Mus. No. Ariz., Flagstaff, 1970—. Recipient John Strong Newberry prize Columbia, 1931; Daniel Giraud Elliot medal Nat. Acad. Scis., 1935; medal Am. Mus. Natural History, 1970. Fellow A.A.A.S., Geol. Soc. Am., Paleontol. Soc. (v.p. 1963), N.Y. Zool. Soc.; mem. Soc. Vertebrate Paleontology (sec.-treas. 1944-46, pres. 1946-47), Soc. Mammalogy, Soc. Ichthyology and Herpetology, Soc. for Study Evolution (editor 1950-52, v.p. 1957, pres. 1958), Nat. Acad. Scis., Sigma Xi. Author: Evolution of the Vertebrates, 1955; Dinosaurs, 1961; (with M. Kay) Stratigraphy and Life History, 1965: The Age of Reptiles, 1965; Men and Dinosaurs, 1968; also sci. papers and monographs. Home: Flagstaff AZ 86001 Office: Mus No Ariz Flagstaff AZ 86001

COLBERT, JAMES CANFIELD, chemist, educator; b. Canfield, Ark., Sept. 2, 1899; s. Canfield and Alice (Creswell) C.; B.S., U. Ark., 1921; M.S., State U. Ia., 1923, Ph.D., 1925; m. Margaret Amelia Bates, Sept. 10, 1922 (dec. Nov. 1961); 1 son, Thomas Alfred; m. 2d, Lucile Senner Meigs, Aug. 6, 1966. Asst. prof. chemistry U. Okla., 1925-35, asso. prof., 1935-44, prof., 1944-70, chmn. pre-med. adv. com., 1946-71, David Ross Boyd prof. of chemistry, 1955-70, supr. research project for Office Ordnance Research at U. Okla. Research Inst., 1951-54. Mem. Okla. Acad. Sci., Am. Chem. Soc., Sigma Xi, Phi Lambda Upsilon (charter mem. Ia. and Okla. chpts.), Phi Sigma, Alpha Chi Sigma, Alpha Epsilon Delta. Protestant Episcopal. Author: Experiments and Problems for College Chemistry (with James E. Belcher), 1928, 6th edit. (with James E. Belcher and H.H. Rowley), 1961; A Shorter Course in Organic Chemistry, 1931; Laboratory Technique for Organic Chemistry, 1933; Properties and Numerical Relationships of the Common Elements and Compounds (with James E. Belcher), 1930, 6th edit. (with James E. Belcher, H. H. Rowley), 1961; Identification and Properties of the Common Metals and Non-Metals, (with James E. Belcher) 1929; also research papers chem. jour. Home: 319 Merkle Dr Norman OK 73069 Office: U Okla Norman OK 73069

COLBERT, JAMES WILLIAM, Jr., govt. med. dir.; b. N.Y.C., Dec. 14, 1920; s. James William and Mary (Tormey) C.; A.B., Holy Cross Coll., 1942; M.D., Columbia, 1945; m. Lorna Tuck, Aug. 26, 1944; children—James William, Edward, Mary, William, Margaret, Thomas, John, Andrew, Elizabeth, Paul J., Peter, Stephen. Intern Bellevue Hosp., N.Y.C., 1945-46; resident medicine Grace-New Haven Community Hosp., 1948-49, asso. physician, 1950-53; instr. medicine Yale, 1949-50, asst. prof. Sch. Medicine, 1950-53, asst. dean, 1951-53; clin. dir. U.S. Army Hepatitis Center, Munich, Germany, 1949-50; dir. edn. Middlesex Hosp., 1950-53, cons. physician, 1952-53; asst. prof. internat. medicine St. Louis U., 1953-62, dean sch. medicine, 1953-62; asso. dir. Nat. Inst. Allergy and Infectious Diseases, NIH. Bethesda, Md., 1962—. Chmn. Montmery Health and Welfare Council. Mem. Washington Acad. Medicine, Sigma Xi, Alpha Sigma Nu, Delta Epsilon Sigma. Home: 9011 Honey Bee Lane Bethesda MD 20014 Office: Inst Allergy and Infectious Diseases Nat Insts Health Bethesda MD 20014

COLBERT, LESTER LUM, former automobile co. exec., lawyer; b. Oakwood, Tex., June 13, 1905; s. Lum and Sallie (Driver) C.; B.B.A., Tex. U., 1925; LL.B., Harvard, 1929; LL.D., Bethany Coll., 1954; m. Daisy Gorman, Nov. 23, 1928 (dec. Aug. 1970); children—Lester Lum, Sarah (Colbert- Noble), Nicholas, Cotton buyer, Tex., 1921-29; practiced law Larkin, Rathbone & Perry, N.Y.C., 1929-33; with Chrysler Corp., 1933-65, mem. operation com., 1933-61, resident atty., 1933-42, v.p. Dodge div., 1935- 45, operating mgr. Dodge Chicago plant, 1942, gen. mgr., 1943-46, pres. Dodge div., 1946-51, v.p. Chrysler Corp., 1949-50, dir., 1949-61, pres., 1950-61, chmn. 1960-61; chmn. bd., dir. Chrysler Corp. of Can., Ltd., 1961-65; trustee Hanover Bank, N.Y.C., 1955-61; hon. dir. Mfrs. Hanover Trust Co. N.Y.C. Chmn., United Found. Detroit, 1959-60, dir., 1951-62; mem. Nat. Indsl. Conf. Bd., 1958-61; trustee Automotive Safety Found., 1955-61, Com. for Econ. Devel., 1956- 61; dir. devel. bd. U. Tex., 1958—; overseers com. to visit Harvard Law Sch., 1952-58; trustee Nat. Jewish Hosp., 1958-66. Decorated chevalier Legion of Honor (France), 1959; Texan of Distinction award, 1953. Brother-hood award Nat. Conf. Christians and Jews, 1957; award Am. Soc. Tool Engrs., 1958. Mem. Am. Ordnance Assn. (life), Automobile Old Timers (life), Am., Detroit bar assns., Am. Judicature Soc., Automobile Mfrs. Assn. (pres. 1958-61), Soc. Automotive Engrs., State Bar Mich., Beta Gamma Sigma. Methodist. Clubs: Detroit, University, Orchard Lake Country, Detroit Athletic (pres. 1960), Question, Harvard, Recess, Economic, Press (Detroit); Chicago; Twenty Nine (N.Y.C.); Bloomfield Hills (Mich.) Country; Windsor (Ont. Can.); Headliners, Forty Acres (Austin, Tex.); Poor Richard (Phila.) Home: 491 Martell Dr Bloomfield Hills MI 48013 Office: Fisher Bldg Detroit MI 48202

COLBERT, MARVIN JAY, physician; b. Spokane, Nov. 6, 1923; s. John B. and Elizabeth (Peters) C.; student U. Utah, 1940-43; B.S., Yale, 1943-44; M.D., Boston U., 1949; m. Eleanor Ruth Rott, June 2, 1951; children—Janet Lynn, James Lee, Lawrence Jay. Intern Presbyn. Hosp., Chgo., 1949-50, resident, 1949- 50; resident VA Hosp., Boston, 1953-54, U. Ill. Research and Ednl. Hosp., 1954-55; practice internal medicine, Belmond, Ia., 1955-56; with U. Ill., 1956—, dir. health service Med. Center, 1959—, prof. medicine, 1969—. Pres. Hillcrest P.T.A., Downers Grove, Ill., 1960-62, Parent-Tchrs. Group Chiengmai Co-ednl. Center, Thailand, 1965-66. Served to capt. M.C. AUS, 1943-46, 50-52. Recipient Golden Apple instr. award U. Ill., 1958. Diplomate Am. Bd. Internal Medicine. Mem. Am. Assn. Automotive Medicine (dir. 1969-72), Chgo. Soc. Internal Medicine, Am. Fedn. Clin. Research, Am. Coll. Physicians, Am. Coll. Health Assn., Sigma Xi. Home: 5600 Plymouth Ct Downers Grove IL 60515 Office: 840 S Wood St Chicago IL 60612

COLBERT, SISTER MARY COLUMKILLE, ret. coll. pres.; b. Ireland, Mar. 12, 1884; d. Michael and Alice (Kenniry) Colbert; A.B., Catholic U. of Am., 1913, A.M., 1914, Ph.D., 1923; student U. Minn., summer, 1927, Columbia U., summer, 1928, U. Mexico, summer, 1944. Tchr. high school, 1905-11, 1914-17; inst. Latin, Incarnate Word Coll., 1917-21, became pres. and prof. classical langs. 1923, chmn. bd. dirs. Mem. Tex. Edn. Commn., 1930-34, Conf. of Catholic Women's Coll., 1931- 35. Mem. Am. Philol. Assn., Am. Classical League, Nat. Catholic Ednl. Assn. (com. on reorgn. 1934-36; exec. com. of Coll. and Univ. Dept. 1938-42), Tex. State Tchrs. Assn., Texas Council on Tchr. Edn. Author: The Syntax of the De Civitate Dei of St. Augustine, 1923. Address: Incarnate Word Coll San Antonio TX 78209

COLBERT, RICHARD GARY, naval officer; b. Brownsville, Pa., Feb. 12, 1915, s. Charles F. and Marie Louise (Benford) C.; B.S., U.S. Naval Acad., 1937; postgrad. Naval War Coll., 1955-56; m. Prudence Ann Robertson, Nov. 15, 1950; children—Melissa Robertson, Richard Gary, Anthony Jonathan, Christopher Mark. Commd. ensign USN, 1937, advanced through grades to vice adm., 1968; dir. naval command course for Free World Naval Officers at Naval War Coll., Newport, R.I., 1956-58, pres. coll., 1968-71; mem. joint staff Joint Chiefs of Staff, Washington, 1958-60; comdg. officer U.S.S. Altair, 1960-61, U.S.S. Boston, 1961-63; mem. Policy Planning Council U.S. Dept. State, 1963-65; comdr. Cruiser Destroyer Flotilla Six, 1965-66; dep. chief staff, asst. chief staff for policy, plans, operations Supreme Allied Comdr. Atlantic, Norfolk, Va., 1966-68; chief staff Supreme Allied Command Atlantic, Norfolk, 1971—. Decorated Joint Service Commendation medal, Legion of Merit. Clubs: New York Yacht; Army and Navy (Washington); Chevy Chase (Md.); Duquesne (Pitts.); Internat. Sportsmens (London, Eng.). Home: Delaware House Quarters AA US Naval Base Norfolk VA 23511 Office: care of SACLANT US Naval Base Norfolk VA 23511

COLBERT, ROBERT B., Jr., apparel co. exec.; b. Columbus, Ga., Sept. 24, 1921; s. Robert B. and Mae (Hindsman) C.; student Emory U., U. Ga.; m. Margaret Moore, Mar. 22, 1942; children—Margaret, Bert, John. Chmn. bd., pres., dir. Wayne-Gossard Corp., Humboldt, Tenn.; dir. Archer Mills, Inc., Main Street Corp., Mchts. State Bank, Humboldt, King Leathers, Inc., Union Planters Nat. Bank Memphis. Trustee, chmn. bus. and corp. com. devel. council Lambuth Coll., Jackson, Tenn. Served with USNR, World War II. Home: 235 Woodland St Humboldt TN 38343 Office: Gibson Hwy Humboldt TN 38343

COLBORN, THEODORE REYNOLDS, lawyer; b. Oxford, O., Nov. 8, 1914, s. Earl F. and Hazel (Brackett) C.; A.B., Cornell U., Ithaca, N.Y., 1935; LL.B., Harvard, 1938; m. Constance Parry, Sept. 26, 1937; children—Deborah Frum, Theodore Reynolds, Ann Constance, Paul Parry. Admitted to Ohio bar, 1938, since practiced in Cleve.; asso. firm Jones, Day, Cockley & Reavis, 1938-44, partner, 1944—; dir. Hathaway Brown Corp. Trustee Albert A. List Found., Hathaway Brown Sch., Mather Fund. Mem. Am., Cleve. bar assns., Ct. Nisi Prius, Cleve. C. of C. (chmn. fed. taxation com.), Phi Beta Kappa, Sigma Chi. Clubs: Union, Kirtland Country (Cleve.) Home: 2832 Weybridge Rd Shaker Heights OH 44120 Office: Union Commerce Bldg Cleveland OH 44115

COLBOURN, TREVOR, educator, historian; b. Armidale, New South Wales, Australia, Feb. 24, 1927; s. Harold Arthur and Ella Mary (Henderson) C.; came to U.S., 1948 B.A. (Honors), U. London (Eng.), 1948; M.A., Coll. William and Mary,1949; M.A., Johns Hopkins, 1951, Ph.D., 1953; m. Beryl Richards Evans, Jan. 10, 1949; children-Katherine Elizabeth, Lisa Sian Eleanor. From instr. to asst. prof. Pa. State U., 1952-59; from asst. prof. to prof. Am. history Ind. U., 1959-67; dean Grad. Sch., prof. History U. N.H., 1967—. Mem. spl. com. liberal studies Assn. Am. Colls., 1966—. Mem. Am. Hist. Assn., Orgn. Am. Historians. Author: The Lamp of Experience, 1965; The Colonial Experience, 1966; The American Past in Perspective 1970. Home: 8 Ryan Way Durham NH 03824

COLBURN, CHARLES BUFORD, educator, chemist; b. Harrisonville, Mo., July 6, 1923; s. George C. and Nannie (Chinn) C.; B.S., Kan. State U., 1944; Ph.D., U. Utah, 1951; m. L. Joan Pettis, Aug. 31, 1950; children—Catherine Anne, Susan Margaret, Amy Loraine, Marsie Jane, Gordon Andrew. Phys. chemistry group leader Rohm & Haas Redstone Research Labs., Huntsville, Ala., 1952-68; prof., head dept. chemistry Auburn U., 1968—. Dir. Econ. Forecasting Inst., Trident Oceanographic Corp. Served with USNR, 1944-46. Mem. Am. Chem. Soc., Chem. Soc. London, Am. Phys. Soc., Am. Inst. Chemistry, Sigma Xi, Sigma Pi Sigma. Editor: Developments in Inorganic Nitrogen Chemistry, Vol. 1, 1966. Developer field nitrogen-fluorine chemistry. Home: 235 Cary Dr Auburn AL 36830

COLBURN, FRANCIS PEABODY, artist, educator; b. Fairfax, Vt., Oct. 20, 1909; s. John Edward and Florence (Read) C.; Ph.B., U. Vt., 1934; spl. student painting Bennington Coll.; scholar Art Students League, N.Y.C., m. Gladys Laflamme, Dec. 23, 1934; 1 son, David. Resident artist U. Vt., Burlington, 1942—, chmn. art. dept., 1946—; dir. Craftsbury Chamber Players, Inc.; exhibited one-man shows Knoedler, McBeth galleries, N.Y.C., Wood Gallery, Montpelier, Vt., also coll. and univs.; group shows Carnegie Inst., Corcoran Gallery, Whitney Mus. Am. Art, N.A.D., Audubon Artists Assn., Boston Inst. Contemporary Art, Chgo. Art Inst., Pasadena Art Inst., Cordova Mus., Boston, Conn. Acad. Art. Trustee Vt. Symphony Orch. Recipient awards for paintings Springfield (Mass.) Mus. Fine Arts, Boston Inst. Contemporary Art, San Francisco Palace Legion of Honor, Fleming Mus. Mem. Vt. Art Tchrs. Assn. (pres.), So., No. Vt. art assns., Vt. Council on the Arts (Distinguished Service award 1968), Artists Equity, Delta Psi. Episcopalian. Recs. of New Eng. humor. Home: 118 S Willard St Burlington VT 05401

COLBURN, IRVING WALKER, architect; b. Boston, May 21, 1924; s. Frank Lewis and Ann Torrance (McGeorge) C.; student Fontainbleau (France) Acad., 1948; B.Arch., Yale, 1951; m. Frances Haffner, May 21, 1960; children—Clariissa Haffner, Oliver Call. Designer, Schweikher & Elting, Chgo., 1951-53, Sahw, Metz & Dolio, Chgo., 1953-55; pres. I.W. Colburn & Assos., Inc., Chgo., 1955—. Exec. dir. St. Joseph (Mich.) Greater Community Corp., 1960-63; asst. prof. architecture U. Ill., 1958-60, mem. devel. com., 1958-50; mem. men's council Art Inst. Chgo., 1961—, mem. purchase com. decorative arts, 1962—; mem. vis. com. dep. architecture Carnegie Inst. Tech., 1963—; cons. architect U. Chgo., 1963—; dir. Chgo. Flower and Garden Show, Inc., 1964—; pres. Chgo. World Flower Show, 1965; mem. archtl. adv. com. Lake Forest (Ill.). Trustee Lake Forest Open Lands Trust, Pacific Bot. Garden. Principal works include William L. McLennan House, Lake Forest, Ill, 1959, St. Anastasia Ch., Waukegan, Ill., 1962, William D. Gregory II house, Wayzata, Minn., 1963, Robert E. Brooker house, Winnetka, Ill., 1963, John H. Leslie house, Winnetka, Ill., 1963. I.W. Colburn house, Lake Forest, Ill., 1965, Henry Hinds Lab. for Geophys. Scis. bldg. U. Chgo. (award A.I.A. 1970), 1965, Cathedral and Diocesan Center Diocese Western Mich., P.E. Ch., Kalamazoo, 1965. Served with AUS, 1943-45. Registered architect, Ill., Mich., Mass., Fla. Mem. A.I.A. (1st Honor award Homes for Better Living, 1960; Honor award for excellence in architecture, 1965; Honor award for Sonia Shankman Orthogenic Sch. at U. Chgo., 1968; Beaus Arts Scarab, archtl. medal, 1948. Home: 700 N Lake Rd Lake Forest IL 60045 Office: 135 S LaSalle St Chicago IL 60603

COLBURN, JOHN H., editor, publisher; b. Columbus, O., Apr. 13, 1912; s. Stanley W. and Alverta C. (Kundts) C.; student Ohio State U.; m. Margaret MacFaden, Sept. 5, 1936 (div. Jan. 1944); m. 2d, Florence Angier Jackson, June 29, 1945; children—Charlotte Chane, Kristine. Reporter Columbus (O.) Dispatch, 1930-34; staff A.P., Columbus, 1935-42, fgn. staff including London, Stockholm, Paris, 1942-44, dir., sec. A.P., Ltd., London, 1944- 46, exec. asst., gen. mgr. gen. offices, N.Y.C., 1946-48, gen. exec., 1948-49; mng. editor Richmond (Va.) Times-Dispatch, 1949-63; editor, pub. Wichita (Kan.) Eagle & Beacon, 1963—. Mem. A.P. Mng. Editors Assn. (pres. 1959-60), Am. Soc. Newspaper Editors (dir.), Am. Newspaper Pubs. Assn. (dir.), Sigma Delta Chi, Pi Delta Upsilon, Kappa Tau Alpha. Episcopalian. Home: 326 S Brookside Wichita KS 67218 Office: 825 E Douglas Wichita KS 67201

COLBURN, JOSEPH BRADLEY, lawyer; b. Washington, Apr. 10, 1902; s. William Edward and Frances (Augusterfer) C.; LL.B., George Washington U., 1924; m. Grace Harris, Feb. 28, 1931; 1 dau., Carolyn Ann. With U.S. Consular Service, London, Eng. 1919-20; admitted to D.C. bar, 1924; with U.S. Tarriff Commn., 1924-28; pvt. practice law, N.Y.C., Washington, 1929—; partner firm Barnes, Richardson & Colburn, N.Y.C., Washington, 1935—; rep. U.S. Customs Ct. in Matter of Spector, 1959. Mem. Am. (chmn. com. customs law), Inter-Am., Internat. bar assns., Assn. Customs Bar (dir.), N.Y. County Lawyers Assn. (com. customs law). Home: 64 Beacon Hill Port Washington NY 11050 Office: 475 Park Av S New York City NY 10016

COLBURN, RICHARD DUNTON, mfg. and utility exec.; b. Carpentersville, Ill., June 24, 1911; s. Cary R. and Daisy (Dunton) C.; student Antioch Coll., 1929-33; m. Elizabeth Whiting, Dec. 30, 1941; children—Richard Whiting, Carol Dunton, Keith Whiting. Prin. in acquisition, rehab. and mgmt. distressed enterprises, 1944—; Formerly chief exec. officer, dir. Ariz. Power Co., Crucible Steel Casting Co., Mich. Steel Casting Co., Western Foundry Co., Misco Precision Casting Co.; chmn. bd. Consol. Elec. Distbrs., Inc., 1971—; chmn. bd. Rolled Alloys, Inc.; dir. Cerro Corp., STP Corp., Studebaker-Worthington, Inc., Masoneilan Internat., Inc., Wagner Elec. Corp., Pan Am. Sulphur Co., The Susquehanna Corp. Home: 1120 La Collina Rd Beverly Hills CA 90210 Office: 1627 W 20th St Los Angeles CA 90007

COLBY, ANITA (Anita Catherine Counihan) (Mrs. Phalen Flagler), writer, editor; b. Washington, Aug. 5, 1914, d. Daniel and Margaret (McCarthy) Counihan; student St. Agnes Sem., Pratt Inst. Art; m. Phalen Flagler, Mar. 8, 1971. Model for John Power Agy., cover girl, 1936; actress R.K.O., Hollywood, 1937-39; editor Harper's Bazaar; tech. adviser, exploiter, motion picture Cover Girl, 1942; feminine dir. Selznick Studios; exec. asst. to head Paramount Pictures; beauty editor Photoplay mag.; part owner, pres. and editor Women's News Service, 1956-61; organizer Dr. Erno Lazlo's cosmetic co.; spokeswoman Sperry- Hutchinson Co.; TV appearances Dave Garroway Today Show, appeared in motion pictures including Mary, Queen of Scots, The Bride Walked Out. Mem. woman's div. Cancer Fund, Ladies of Charity, Cath. Charities. Voted most popular and typical Am. cover girl, 1936. Roman Catholic. Club: Republican Women's. Author: Anita Colby's Beauty Book. Home: Stockton NJ also 111 E 80th St New York City NY 10021 Office: NBC Rockefeller Plaza New York City NY 10020

COLBY, BARBARA, actress; grad. Bard Coll.; studied with Marcel Marceau, Jean Louis Barrault in Paris. Toured U.S. in repertory; most recent stage appearances include Under Milk Wood, The Insect Comedy, Six Characters in Search of an Author; TV appearances include Armstrong Circle Theatre, Play of the Week, A Day in Court.*

COLBY, CARROLL BURLEIGH, author; b. Claremont, N.H., Sept. 7, 1904; s. Melvin Forrest and Stella Adella (Whitcomb) C.; grad. Sch. Practical Art, Boston, 1925; m. Lila Margaret Thoday, Nov. 29, 1928; children—Susan (Mrs. Robert S. McKanna), Fred Melvin. Free-lance illustrator and author, 1925-37; editor Air Trails and Air Progress mags., 1937-43; aviation editor Popular Sci. Monthly, 1943-46; free-lance writer, author, illustrator, 1946—; camping editor Outdoor Life mag., 1958—; lectr. writing books, mil., space, conservation, camping, wildlife. Past mem. Briarcliff Manor (N.Y.) Bd. Trustees, also Planning Commn.; past fire commr., also mem. hook and ladder and rescue co.; now exec. officer spl. patrolmen Briarcliff Manor Police Dept. Past pres. Briarcliff Manor Library Bd. Mem. USAAF and USAF aux., 1942—. Mem. Aviation Space Writers Assn. (a founder 1937), Outdoor Writers Assn. Am. (past bd. dirs.), Adventurers Club, Camp Fire Club Am., S.A.R., Company Mil. Historians, Soc. Am. Travel Writers, Arctic Circle Club. Author over 100 published books, including Colby Books for Boys. Address: 304 Pine Rd Briarcliff Manor NY 10510

COLBY, DAVID LAWRENCE, banker; b. Mason City, Ia., Feb. 19, 1908; s. William Martin and Mary Agnes (Boyle) C.; grad. Sch. Commerce and Finance, St. Louis U., 1933, Rutgers U. Grad. Sch. Banking, 1952; m. Marcella Reid, Aug. 27, 1926; 1 dau., Susan Colby Vandegrift. Asst. v.p. Boatmen's Nat. Bank of St. Louis, 1938-46, v.p., 1946-65, sr. v.p., 1965—. Mem. bd. regents Rutgers U. Grad. Sch. Banking, 1942-43. Mem. St. Louis Safe Deposit Assn. (pres. 1935-36), Am. Inst. Banking (past nat. pres., mem. exec. council), Am. Bankers Assn. (past mem. exec. council). Home: 640 Greenview Dr St Louis County MO 63122 Office: 300 N Broadway St Louis MO 63102

COLBY, ETHEL, drama and film critic; b. N.Y.C.; d. M. Duckman and (Scharlin) Dallon; student Columbia, 1925-27; m. Julius J. Colby, Sept. 25, 1929; 1 son, Jeffrey Victor. Child actress, vaudeville, Broadway, 1927-38; featured singing, dancing comedienne Student Prince; mem. cast Maytime, Blossom Time, Fabulous Invalid, The Moorings, It Should't Happen to a Dog, others; motion picture actress, 1927-29; radio show, Miss Hollywood, 1948-50; drama, film critic N.Y. Jour. of Commerce and Ridder Papers, N.Y.C., 1940—; producer, star TV shows, C.B.S., 1944-46; condr., star Broadway Matinee, Du-Mont Network TV program 1952—. Mem. Drama Critics Circle, Drama Desk (N.Y.C.) Women Broadcasters and Commentators. Am. Club: N.Y. Newspaperwomen's Home: 10300 West Bay Harbor Dr Bay Harbor Island FL 33154

COLBY, JOSEPH MILTON, mech. engr., former army officer; b. Lake Mills, Ia., Mar. 27, 1904; s. Joseph Eli and Millie J. (Eiel) C.; B.S., U. S. Mil. Acad., 1929; M.S., Mass. Inst. Tech., 1935; m. Margaret Capelle Brisley, Aug. 19, 1929; children—Janice Margaret (Mrs. Michele DeAngeli), Carol Capelle (Mrs. Chen Tung Leong).

Commd. 2d lt. U.S. Army, 1929, advanced through grades to brig. gen., 1954; chief devel. br. Tank Automotive Center, Detroit, 1942-45; chief indsl. operations, chief engring. and mfg. div. Detroit Arsenal, 1945-46, chief devel. and engring. dept., 1946-51; spl. duty mission to Japan and Korea, 1950-51; adviser to sr. U.S. rep. North Atlantic Def. Prodn. Bd., London, Eng., 1951-52; organized, comdr. Ordnance Procurement Center, U.S. Army Europe, 1952-54; exec. officer then comdg. gen. Frankford Arsenal, 1954-57; comdg. gen. Ordnance Ammunition Command, 1957-58; dep. comdg. gen. Army Ordnance Missile Command, Redstone Arsenal, Ala., 1958-59; ret., 1959; v.p. research, devel. Rockwell Mfg. Co., Pitts., chmn. products com., 1959-66; v.p. tech. growth N. Am. Rockwell Corp., 1967-69, ret. 1969. Bd. dirs. Pitts. Opera. Decorated Legion of Merit with two oak leaf clusters, Bronze Star medal (U.S.); Order Brit. Empire Merit; officer Legion of Honor (France); comdr. Royal Order Phoenix (Greece). Mem. Am. Gas. Assn., Am. Ordnance Assn. Am. Petroleum Inst., Am. Soc. M.E., Assn. Grads. U.S. Mil. Acad. (trustee), Pitts. Athletic Assn., Assn. U.S. Army, C. of C. Greater Pitts., Mil. Order World Wars (vice comdr., past pres. Pitts. chpt.), World Affairs Council Pitts., Army Athletic Assn., Soc. Automotive Engrs., Pa. Soc. V.F.W. Clubs: Steel City Retired Officers (past pres.); Duquesne, Pittsburgh Press (Pitts.); Army-Navy (Washington). Contbr. numerous aritcles to profl. jours. Home: The Galleon 4100 Galt Ocean Dr Ft Lauderdale FL 33308

COLBY, KENNETH POOLE, ins. co. exec.; b. Keene, N.H., June 21, 1908; s. Everett Nahum and Grace (Poole) C.; student Clark U., 1927-30; m. Bernece Esther Wilson, July 17, 1933; 1 son, Kenneth P. With Nat. Grange Mut. Ins. Co., Keene, 1930—, successively claims adjuster and underwriter, agy. dir., exec. in charge casualty underwriting, 1930-55, v.p., 1955-63, dir., exec. com., 1957—, exec. v.p., 1963-66, pres., chief exec., 1966—; pres., trustee Keene Savs. Bank. Dir. Am. Mut. Ins. Alliance; past dir. Nat. Assn. of Mut. Ins. Cos.; chmn. bd. dirs. N.H. Ins. Guaranty Assn. Mem. Nat. Grange. Odd Fellow. Club: Keene Country. Home: 71 Greenwood Av Keene NH 03431 Office: 55 West St Keene NH 03431

COLBY, PAUL S., utility exec.; b. Junction City, Kan., 1905; grad. Kan. State U. Sr. v.p., dir. Carolina Power & Light Co., Raleigh, N.C. Home: 1501 Chester Rd Raleigh NC 27608 Office: 336 Fayetteville St Raleigh NC 27602*

COLBY, STARR JOCELYN, missile systems exec.; b. Montclair, N.J., Apr. 1, 1923; s. Whitney Coffin and Elizabeth Whiting (Murphy) C.; B.S., U. Mich., 1944, M.S., 1951; m. Jean Brewster Mackaye, Nov. 4, 1945; children—Stephen M., Peter M., David G., Elizabeth L., Sara S. Aerodynamicist G.L. Martin Co., Balt., 1944-48; instr. Boston U., 1948-49; asst. chief aerodynamics, tech. asst. to engring. v.p., mgr. advt. space systems Douglas Aircraft Co., Santa Monica, Cal., 1951-63; asst. dir. space tech. Office Dir. Def. Research and Engring., The Pentagon, 1963-65; dir. advanced programs research and devel. div. Lockheed Missile & Space Co., Sunnyvale, Cal., 1965-69, dir. spl. programs missile systems div., 1970—; cons. Office Sci. and Tech. Mem. ground warfare panel President's Sci. Adv. Com. Asso. fellow Am. Inst. Aeros. and Astronautics; mem. Am. Astron. Soc., Am. Ordnance Assn., Sigma Xi.‡

COLBY, WILLIAM GEORGE, educator; b. Cornwall Twp., Ill., Feb. 4, 1907; s. William Davis and Fannie Jane (Vail) C.; B.S., U. Ill., 1929; M. Sc., Rutgers U., 1932, Ph.D., 1934; m. Dorothy Axford, Oct. 27, 1934; children—Dorothy Louise, (Mrs. John B. Hall) William George, Jonathan Axford, Thomas Vail. Agronomist, Soil Erosion Service, 1935-36; research prof. agronomy U. Mass., 1936-50, prof., head dept., 1950-64, research prof. agronomy, dept. plant and soil sci., 1964—. Fulbright vis. research prof., Japan, 1965. Mem. Am. Soc. Agronomy, Soil Sci. Soc. Am., Sigma Xi. Rotarian. Home: 115 Blue Hills Rd Amherst, MA 01002.

COLCLASER, H. ALBERTA, govt. ofcl.; b. Turtle Creek, Pa., Feb. 19, 1911; d. Levi A. and Bertha M. (Lear) Colclaser; A.B., Coll. Wooster, 1933, L.L.D., 1965; J.D., Western Res. U., 1936; LL.M., Columbia, 1939. Asso. editor Banks-Baldwin Law Pub. Co., Cleve., 1936-38; asst. to legal adviser Dept. State, 1939-42, with aviation div., 1942-58, chief air transport sect., 1951-56, asst. chief div., 1956-58; indsl. adviser USRO, 1958-59; chief transp. and communications policy sect., civil air attache Am. embassy, Paris, France, 1959-63; policy officer Office Internat. Aviation, Washington, 1963-65; 1st sec. Am. embassy, Ottawa, Ont., Can., 1965-68; policy officer Office Aviation, Washington, 1968, cons., 1969; specialist transp. products div. Dept. Commerce, 1969- -. Mem. U.S. Delegation Paris Peace Conf., 1946, to 3d, 4th, 6th, 7th, 8th, 9th, 10th, 11th, 12th, 14th sessions Legal Com., Internat. Civil Aviation Orgn., ICAO assemblies, 1949, 50, 56, 62, diplomatic conf. pvt. air law, 1952, 55, facilitation div. ICAO, 1948. Mem. Am. Soc. Internat. Law, Phi Beta Kappa, Delta Sigma Rho. Clubs: International (Washington); National Aviation, International Aviatron. Home: 6386 Dockser Terrace Falls Church VA 22041 Office: Bur Domestic Commerce Dept Commerce Washington DC 20230

COLCLOUGH, WILLIAM FREDERIC, former printing co. exec.; b. Elkland, Pa., July 10, 1905; s. William F. and Sara (Guy) C.; A.B., Lehigh U., 1925; J.D., U. Pa., 1930; m. Olga Fabian, May 17, 1947. Admitted to Pa. bar, 1930, N.Y. bar, 1932; with Sullivan & Cromwell, N.Y.C., 1930-40; asst. to pres. Am. Bank Note Co., N.Y.C., 1940-41, 45-49, sec., 1945-49, v.p., 1949-52, pres., 1952-65, chmn., 1957-70, chief exec. officer, 1952-70. Trustee Lehigh U. Served from pvt. to maj. AUS, 1941-45. Decorated Bronze Star medal. Mem. Phi Beta Kappa, Phi Delta Phi, Theta Delta Chi. Episcopalian. Clubs: Bankers of Am., University, Lehigh (N.Y.C.); Woodstock Country. Home: Stafford Box 487 Route 28A West Hurley NY 12491

COLDIRON, WILLIAM HALBERT, lawyer; b. Catlettsburg, Ky., Aug. 12, 1916, s. John Franklin and Virginia (Litteral) C.; A.B., Morehead State U., 1938; LL.B., U. Ky., 1947; m. Margaret Thrailkill, Sept. 23, 1950; children—Steven F., Margaret, John Reeves. Clk., Supreme Ct. 20th Jud. Dist., 1940-41; admitted to Ky. Bar, 1947, Mont. bar, 1948; prof. law U. Mont., 1947, 50, 52, 54, asst. gen. Mont., 1950-51; atty. Mont. Power Co., Butte, 1953- -, v.p., gen. counsel, 1965—. Served to capt., arty., AUS, 1942-46: ETO. Fellow Am. Bar Found.; mem. Am., Mont. (pres. 1963-64) bar assns., Am. Judicature Soc., Edison Electric Inst., Order of Coif. Contbr. articles to profl. jours. Home: 1218 W Platinum St Butte MT 59701 Office: 40 E Broadway Butte MT 59701

COLDWELL, EVERETT S., cons. engr.; b. New London, Conn., Aug. 10, 1893; s. Joseph and Esther (Sharples) C.; B.S., Mass. Inst. Tech., 1915, M.S., 1916; M.S. Harvard, 1916; m. Charlotte Holbert Bates, Sept. 6, 1924 (dec. Jan. 1953) children—Charles W., Robert S.; m. 2d, Verta Mills White, Mar. 19, 1955. Research engr. Westinghouse Lamp Co., Bloomfield, N.J., 1916; indsl. operation and mgmt. various cos., 1917, 19; indsl. operation Columbia Phonograph Mfg. Co., Bridgeport, Conn., 1920-25; Ford, Bacon & Davis, Inc., 1926-59, v.p., 1941, exec. v.p., 1947, pres., 1949-56, dir. 1942- 59 chmn. bd., 1949-59. Mem. Mass. Inst. Tech. Corp., 1952-57; trustee, sec. Roosevelt Hosp., N.Y.C. Served as lt., inf. U.S. Army, 1918. Registered profl. engr., N.Y., Ill., Cal., N.J. Fellow Am. Soc. M.E.; mem. Assn. Cons. Mgmt. Engrs., New Eng. Soc. Nat. Bur. Engring Registration. Republican. Clubs: Siwanoy Country; Harvard, University, Economic, M.I.T., Pilgrims U.S. (N.Y.C.) Home: 2 Stoneleigh Bronxville NY 10708

COLDWELL, PHILIP EDWARD, banker; b. Champaign, Ill., July 20, 1922; s. Montgomery Ian and Donna Clare (Rose) C.; B.A., U. Ill., 1946, M.S., 1947; Ph.D., U. Wis., 1952; m. Norma Elaine Abels, June 1, 1947; children—Douglas Michael, Cameron Iliff. Teaching asst. U. Ill. at Urbana, 1947; instr. Southwestern La. Inst., Lafayette, 1947-48, asst. prof., 1950-51; instr. Mont. State U., 1949-50; research economist Fed. Res. Bank Kansas City, 1951-52; economist, officer Fed. Res. Bank, Dallas, 1952-62, 1st v.p., 1962-68, pres., 1968—; lectr. Banking Sch. South, Baton Rouge, 1958-68; trustee, lectr. Southwestern Legal Found. Served as pilot USNR, 1942-46. Mem. Am. Econ. Assn., So. Finance Assn., Phi Delta Theta. Presbyn. (elder). Club: Economists (founder, 1st pres.) (Dallas). Contbr. articles to profl. jours. Home: 3330 Southwestern Blvd Dallas TX 75225 Office: Fed Reserve Bank Akard and Wood Sts Dallas TX 75222

COLE, ALBERT LESLIE, mag. publisher, B. Chgo., Dec. 12, 1894; s. Albert Channing and Frances M. (Deininger) C.; student pub. schs. N.Y.C.; m. Margauerite N. Haas, Dec. 10, 1921 (dec. July 1968); children—Jean (Mrs. Martin E. Van Buren), Margaret (Mrs. Frederick M. Jennings), Robert Douglas; m. 2d, Margaret Winston, 1969. With Frank A. Munsey Publs., N.Y.C., 1910-15; Popular Sci. Pub. Co., 1915, pres., pub. Popular Sci. Monthly and Outdoor Life, 1929-39, dir. 1924—; dir., gen. bus. mgr. Reader's Digest Assn., Inc., 1930-66, now v.p. Bd. dirs. Boys Clubs Am., Inc., 1947—, chmn. exec. committee, 1954, pres., 1954-69, chmn. 1969—. Served as ensign, USNRF, 1917-18. Clubs: Union League, Sky (N.Y.C.); Blind Brook (Port Chester, N.Y.); Round Hill (Greenwich, Conn.). Home: Round Hill Rd Greenwich CT 06830

COLE, ALTON P., banker; b. Plymouth, Mass., 1918. Formerly chmn. investment bd., pres., trustee Home Savs. Bank, Boston; chmn. bd., dir. Nat. Shawmut Bank, Boston. Mason. Home: 39 Westcliffe Rd Weston MA 02193 Office: 69 Tremont St Boston MA 02108*

COLE, BENJAMIN RICHASON, newspaperman; b. Indpls., July 10, 1916; s. Almon Theodore and Maude (Richason) C.; student Butler U., 1934-35, Ind. State Tchrs. Coll., 1938, Am. Press Inst. of Columbia, 1948; m. Alice Louise Porteous, Sept. 11, 1937; children—Alan Andrew, Amy (Mrs. George E. Martin, Jr.), Benjamin Richason. Reporter, Terre Haute Tribune-Star Pub. Co., 1938-40, Terre Haute Star, 1940-44; with Indpls. Star, 1944—, statehouse reporter, 1945-48, asst. city editor, 1948, city editor, 1948-49, Washington corr., 1949—; corr. Arizona Republic, Phoenix, 1955—. Mem. Sigma Delta Chi. Presbyn. Mason. Clubs: Gridiron, National Press (Washington); Press (Indpls.) Home: 6529 Beverly Av McLean VA 22101 Office: Nat Press Bldg Washington DC 20004

COLE, BENJAMIN THEODORE, educator; b. New Brunswick, N.J., May 24, 1921; s. Frederick and Grace King (Trimmer) C.; B.S. in Zoology, Duke, 1949; M.A., 1951, Ph.D. in Physiology, 1954; m. Leona Todd, May 30, 1943; children—Timothy Theodore, Rebecca Joyce. Instr. physiology Duke, 1953-54; asst. prof. La. State U., Baton Rouge, 1954-59; research participant biology div. Oak Ridge Nat. Lab., 1959-60, cons., 1960—; asso. prof. biology U. S.C., Columbia, 1960-63, prof., 1963—, head dept., 1964—. Served with USAAF, 1942-46. Fellow A.A.A.S.; mem. Am. Physiol. Soc., Soc. for Exptl. Biology, Med. Assn. Southeastern Biologists, S.C. Acad. Sci., Sigma Xi. Home: 3910 Glenfield Rd Columbia, SC 29208.

COLE, BUSTER, lawyer; b. Saltillo, Tex., Nov. 28, 1911; s. Virgil Ester and Nettie (Teer) C.; A.B., Hardin-Simmons U., 1932; m. Lena Mae McClure, Mar. 8, 1936; children—David, Carmen. Admitted to Tex. bar, 1933, since practiced in Bonham; dist. atty. Fannin County, 1935-39; mem. firm Cunningham, Cole & Sutherland and predecessor, 1948—. Dir. First Nat. Bank, Bonham. Tex. commr. Red River Compact, 1960-62; sec.-treas. Sam Rayburn Found., 1950—. Sec., Fannin County Dem. Exec. Com. Served to capt. AUS, 1944-45. Mem. Am. Bar Assn. (com. on edn. against communism), State Bar Tex. (pres. 1964-65). Mason. Home: 822 Lynn St Bonham TX 75418 Office: PO Box 344 Bonham TX 75418

COLE, CHARLES CHESTER, Jr., coll. pres.; b. Altoona, Pa., Sept. 12, 1922; s. Charles Chester and Kathryn Platt (Snyder) C.; A.B., Columbia, 1943, M.A., 1947, Ph.D., 1951; m. Mary Elizabeth Ewald, Apr. 20, 1944; children—Phyllis, Dorothy, Barbara, Elizabeth. Lectr. history Columbia, 1946-49, asst. dean Columbia Coll., 1949-57, asso. dean, 1957-58; instr. history Briarcliff Jr. Coll., 1949; dean Lafayette Coll., 1958-70, provost, 1967- 70; pres. Wilson Coll., Chambersburg, Pa., 1970—. Trustee Ednl. Testing Service, 1968—, Coll. Entrance Examination Bd. 1965-68; cons. coll. entrance exam. bd. State U. N.Y. Served as 1st lt. 8th Air Force, USAAF, 1944-45. Recipient Carnegie Corp. adminstrv. travel grant, NSF grant. Mem. Am. Hist. Assn., Assn. Higher Edn. (exec. com. 1955-58), Phi Beta Kappa, Alpha Phi Omega, Phi Alpha Theta. Presbyn. Author: The Social Ideas of Northern Evangelists, 1826-1860, 1954; Encouraging Scientific Talent, 1956; Flexibility in the Undergraduate Curriculum, 1962. Home: President's House Wilson Coll Chambersburg PA 17201

COLE, CHARLES WOOLSEY, ednl. cons., former coll. pres. and ambassador; b. Montclair, N.J., Feb 8, 1908; s. Charles Buckingham and Bertha Woolsey (Dwight) C.; A.B., Amherst Coll., 1927, L.H.D., 1942, LL.D., 1960; A.M., Columbia, 1928, Ph.D., 1931, LL.D., 1954; LL.D. Wagner Coll., 1946, Wesleyan U., 1946, Williams Coll., 1946, Doshisha U., 1953 Emerson Coll., 1964; Litt.D., Hamilton Coll., 1948; Sc.D., Clarkson Coll., 1948; L.H.D., U. Mass., 1951, Trinity Coll., 1953; LL.D., Am. Internat. Coll., 1952; m. Katharine Bush Salmon, Aug. 29, 1938; children—Elizabeth (Mrs. Hugh M. Hamill, Jr.), Katharine (Mrs. John C. Esty, Jr.). Instr. history Columbia 1929-35; travelling fellow Social Sci. Research Council Paris, 1932-33; asso. prof. econs., Amherst Coll., 1935-37. George D. Olds prof. econs., 1937-40; vis. lectr. econs. Yale, 1938-39; prof. history, Columbia, 1940-46; pres. Amherst Coll., 1946- 60, pres. emeritus, 1960—; v.p. Rockefeller Found., 1960-61; U.S. ambassador to Chile, 1961-64; editor Macmillan Career Books. Chief Service Trades Br. Retail Trade, services div., Office Price Adminstrn., 1942; regional price exec., N.Y. region, Office Price Adminstrn., 1942-43; mem. teaching staff, Navy Sch. Mil. Govt. and Adminstrn., Columbia, 1943-44; lectr. Army Sch. Mil. Govt., Charlottesville, Va., 1943-44; mem. faculty, Manhattan Sch. Music, 1944-46. Mem. Nat. security orgn. com. of Commn. on Orgn. of Exec. Br. Govt., 1948; selective service scientific adv. com., 1948-51. Trustee Charles E. Merrill Trust, Clarke Sch., Northampton, Mass., Hampshire Coll. Decorated grand cross Order of Merit (Chile); grand officer Order of Morazán (Honduras). Mem. Am. Acad. Arts and Scis., Econ. History Assn., Am. Assn. U. Profs., Am. Hist. Assn. (council 1947-50), Council Fgn. Relations, Phi Beta Kappa, Delta Kappa Epsilon, Delta Sigma Rho. Congregationalist. Clubs: Century, Anglers (N.Y.C.). Author French Merchantilist Doctrines Before Colbert, 1931; Colbert and a Century of French Mercantilism, 2 vols., 1939, 64; Economic History of Europe (with S.B. Clough), 1941, French Mercantilism, 1683-1700, 1943; History of Europe (with C. J. H. Hayes and M. Baldwin), 1949; (with C.J.H. Hayes and M. Baldwin) History of Western Civilization, 1962, 67; (with S.P. McCutchen and H.W. Bragdon) A Free People, The United States in the Formative Years, 1970, A Free People, The United States in the Twentieth Century, 1971. Home: Box 66 Amherst MA 01002

COLE, CHESTER FREDERICK, educator; b. Spokane, Wash., Mar. 10, 1916; s. Orin Hale and Hazel (Smith) C.; B.A., Eastern Wash. Coll. Edn., 1937; M.A., U. Wash., 1941; Ph.D., U. Neb., 1951; m. Elaine Helleberg, Aug. 10, 1947 (div. 1966); children—Betty Jean, Jaqueline Rae. Faculty Seattle pub. schs., 1938- 42, 1946; instr. geography U. Neb., 1946-47; with Fresno State Coll., 1947—, asst. prof., 1947-54, asso. prof., 1954-59, prof., 1959—. chmn. dept. geogrpaphy, 1960-70, acting dean Sch. Social Scis., 1970-71; summer vis. prof. geography San Diego State Coll., 1951, 65, U. Vt. 1953, 55, 57, 60, Eastern Wash. Coll. Edn., 1958, Portland State Coll., 1959, 61, 64, 67, U. Victoria, 1970, others. Served from pvt. to capt., AUS, 1942-46. Fellow Am. Geog. Soc., Assn. Am. Geographers, Nat. Council Geog. Edn. (past mem. exec. bd.), Assn. Pacific Coast Geographers (pres. 1963-64), Cal. Council Geog. Edn. (past pres.), Regional Sci. Assn., A.A.A.S., Cal. Employees Assn., Assn. Cal. Coll. Profs., Am. Fedn. Tchrs, Sigma Xi, Phi Kappa Phi. Unitarian. Contbr. articles to profl. jours. Home: 6052 E Townsend St Fresno CA 93702

COLE, CLIFFORD ADAIR, clergyman; b. Lamoni, Ia., Nov. 16, 1915; s. Fayette V. and Mable F. (Adair) C.; student Graceland Coll., Lamoni, 1934-35, 41-42, U. Wyo., 1938; B.S. in Edn., Central Mo. State Coll., 1943; postgrad. U. Ia., 1946; U. Chgo., 1952; M.A. in Edn., U. Mo. at Kansas City, 1957; m. Harriett Lucile Hartshorn, June 28, 1936; children—Aletha Rae (Mrs. Justus S. Allen), Beverly Sue (Mrs. Lloyd G. Hilburn, Jr.), Lawrence Dean. High Sch. tchr., Lamoni, 1943-46, Bellevue, Ia., 1946- 47; ordained to ministry Reorganized Ch. of Jesus Christ of Latter Day Saints, 1939; minister in Ia., 1947-51; dean students Graceland Coll., 1951-53; dir. dept. religious edn. Reorganized Ch. of Jesus Christ of Latter Day Saints, 1955-58, apostle in council twelve, 1958—, pres. council, 1964—. Trustee Sch. Restoration Reorganized Ch. of Jesus Christ of Latter Day Saints. Mem. Phi Sigma Pi, Zeta Kappa Epsilon, Kappa Delta Pi. Author: The Prophets Speak, 1954; Working Together in our Families, 1955; Celebrating Together in our Families, 1955; Faith for New Frontier, 1956; The Revelation in Christ, 1963; Modern Women in a Modern World, 1965. Home: 800 E Manor Rd Independence MO 64055 Office: Reorganized Sch of Jesus Christ Latter Day Saints Auditorium Independence MO 64051

COLE, CLYDE CURTIS, Jr., c. of c. exec.; b. Ft. Smith, Ark., May 4, 1932; s. Clyde Curtis and Alta Mae (Lasater) C.; Asso. in Arts and Scis., Northeastern A. and M. Coll., Miami, Okla., 1952; B.A. in History, Econs. and Polit. Sci., Eastern N.M. U., Portales, 1954; postgrad. U. N.M. Coll. Law, 1954-55, U. Colo., 1965; m. Marcia Anne Johnson, Nov. 25, 1953; children—Clyde Curtis III, Deborah Dianne, Douglas Scott, Mark Johnson. Mgr., Guymon (Okla.) C. of C., 1955-57; asst. dir., exec. dir. Okla. Devel. Council, Oklahoma City, 1957-59; dir. Indsl. Devel. Commn., Columbia, S.C. and mgr. indsl. dept. Columbia C. of C., 1959-61; exec. dir. Greater Enid (Okla.) C. of C., 1961-65; exec. dir. South Bend-Mishawaka Area C. of C., South Bend, Ind., 1965-67; exec. v.p. Met. Tulsa C. of C., 1967—. Pres. Industries for Tulsa, Inc. Mem. faculty Insts. for Orgn. Mgmt., U. Colo., 1964, 65, 69, 70, 71. Mem. Gov.'s Econ. Adv. Council, 1963-65; 1st v.p., bd. dirs. Okla. Good Rds. and Sts. Assn., 1962-65; sec.-treas. So. Indsl. Devel. Council, 1963-64; sec.-treas. Econ. Devel. Commn., Tulsa, 1969—; mem. Tulsa Indsl. Authority, 1969—; mem. Nat. Municipal League, 1968—. Bd. dirs. Ark. Basin Devel. Assn., Indian Nations Council of Govts. Mem. Am. C. of C. Execs. Assn. (mem. bd., sr. counselor), So. Assn. C. of C. Execs. (pres.), Okla. C. of C. Execs. (past pres.). Kiwanian. Home: 7227 S Richmond St Tulsa OK 74135 Office: 616 S Boston Av Tulsa OK 74119

COLE, COZY, see Cole, William R.

COLE, DAN MAURICE, gas co. exec.; b. Dallas, 1917; ed. So. Meth. U. Sr. v.p. adminstrn. Lone Star Gas Co., Dallas, Lone Star Gathering Co., Nipak, Inc.; exec. v.p. adminstrn., dir. Lone Star Producing Co. Home: 9200 Guernsey Lane Dallas TX 75201 Office: 301 S Harwood St Dallas TX 75201*

COLE, DAVID HARRIS, clergyman; b. Lynn, Mass., Apr. 5, 1921; s. Milton N. and Lorena (Campbell) C.; student Northeastern U., 1939-41; A.B., Tufts U., 1947; S.T.B. Crane Theol. Sch., Medford, Mass., 1948; grad. Inst. Pastoral Care, 1950; m. Isabelle T. Jurasek, July 25, 1963; children—Victoria Stephen, Lynda, Karen, Cynthia, Kevin, Gloria. Ordained to ministry Unitarian Universalist Ch., 1948; pastor in Danvers, Mass., 1944-49, Chgo., 1949-59, Urbana Ill., 1959-63. Unitarian Ch., Rockville, Md., 1963-69, West Shore Unitarian Ch., Cleve., 1969—; tchr. sociology Montgomery Jr. Coll., Rockville, 1966-68. Pres. Universalist Youth Fellowship, 1947, Universalist Ministerial Assn., 1956-58, Ill. Universaist Conv., 1952-57, Midwest Universalist Conf., 1958-62; co-pres. Midwest Unitarian-Universalist Conf., 1961-62; pres. Unitarian-Universalist Fellowship for Social Justice, 1965-67, v.p. Ohio-Meadville dist. Unitarian-Universalist Assn., 1970-71, pres., 1971—; sec. Am. Christian Palestine Com., 1950-59; mem. bd. Universalist Service Com., 1949-56. Pres. Ryder Community Center, Chgo., 1954-59, Montgomery County Citizens Com. Human Relations, 1965- 66; chmn. March on Crime. Chgo., 1953, Champaign County (Ill.) Urban League, 1961-63; chmn. bd. Internat. Affairs Inst., Star Is., N.H., 1967; bd. dirs. Meadville Theol. Sch., Chgo., 1962-70. Named Man of the Year, Chgo. B'nai B'rith, 1957. Author articles. Home: 240 Argyle Rd Rocky River OH 44116 Office: 20401 Hilliard Rd Cleveland OH 44116

COLE, DAVID L., lawyer; b. Paterson, N.J., May 1, 1902; s. Nathan and Ethel (Feldman) C.; B.S., Harvard, 1921, LL.B., 1924; LL.D., Fairleigh Dickinson U., 1964; m. Helen M. David, Oct. 8, 1925; children—Elizabeth, Morrill J., Charles T. Admitted to N.Y. bar, 1925, N.J. bar, 1926; practiced, Paterson, 1926—; mem. firm Cole, Berman & Garth, 1932—; city counsel Paterson, 1952. Active in labor relations as counsel for employer groups in textile industry 1926-42; dir., counsel Comml. Nat. Bank, 2d Nat. Bank, Paterson, 1937-49. Chmn., N.J. State Bd. Mediation, pub. mem. 2d region War Labor Board, 1943-45, chmn. steel and iron ore panels 1943; chmn. No. Textile Commn., 1945-46; impartial chmn. numerous labor contracts; arbitrator labor difficulties; chmn. presdl. bd. inquiry Bituminous Coal Industry, 1948, 50, Longshore Industry, 1953, 68; mem. or chmn. Pres.'s Emergency Bd. on dispute between r.r.'s and 16 unions representing non-operating employees, 1948, 52, Ry. Express Co., 1949, Am. Airlines Pilots, 1951, Eastern Air Lines pilots and flight engrs., 1958; gov. Nat. Acad. Arbitrators, 1948-52, pres. 1951-52, chmn. conciliation panel N.Y.C. Transit, 1961-65, transit fact finding bd., 1950, 57, N.J. Gov.'s pub. service electric cases; mem. Pres.'s Steel Industry Bd., 1949; dir. Fed. Mediation and Conciliation Service, 1952-53; chmn. N.J. Gov.'s Com. on Pub. Utility Strike Legislation, 1954; chmn., sec. labor's adv. com. on atomic energy, 1955- -; cons. ILO, Geneva, 1955, 56, 64; mem. Pres.'s Labor-Mgmt. Adv. Com., 1961-65, N.Y. Gov.'s Com. Pub. Employee Relations, 1966-68; N.Y.C. Mayor's rep. newspaper labor dispute, 1966; pub. mem. Kaiser Steel Long-Range Com.; vis. prof. Cornell U., 1954- 55; Kestenbaum lectr. Harvard, 1962. Carnegie Endowment for Internat.

Peace; pres., bd. dirs. Shapiro Found. Recipient N.J. award Nat. Conf. Christians and Jews, 1954; medal Commonwealth of Pa. 1956. Mem. Am. Arbitration Assn. (medal 1955, dir.). Jewish religion. Clubs: Harvard (N.Y.C.); Preakness Hills Country (pres. and trustee 1937-42). Author: The Quest for Industrial Peace, 1963. Home: 15 Overlook Av Paterson NJ 07508 Office: 45 Church St Paterson NJ 07505

COLE, DAVID WILLIAM, coll. dean; b. Albany, Ga., July 19, 1919; s. Frank Thomas and Janetta Minerva (Strevig) C.; A.B., Erskine Coll., 1940; M.A., U. S.C., 1948, Ph.D., 1953; m. Mary Clark Denny, Aug. 10, 1942; children—David William, Carol Denny, Mary Clark, James Franklin. Instr. history U. S.C., 1946- 47; prof. history Lander Coll., 1949-58, Pfeiffer Coll., 1958-62; mem. faculty High Point (N.C.) Coll., 1962—, prof. history, head dept., 1962-64, dean coll., 1963—. Served with USNR, 1942-46. Mem. Delta Sigma Phi. Democrat. Methodist. Club: Emery Wood Country. Home: 1006 Emery Circle High Point NC 27262

COLE, DONALD WILLARD, cons. psychologist; b. San Diego, Jan. 12, 1920; s. Rolland Ames and Genevieve (Bender) C.; student U. Redlands; A.B., Stanford, 1942; B.D., Eastern Bapt. Theol. Sem., 1945; Ed.D., Southwestern Bapt. Theol. Sem., 1952; Ph.D., U. London, 1962; m. Ann Bradford, Sept. 18, 1942; 1 son Timothy Bradford, Ordained to ministry Bapt. Ch., 1945; pastor Linden Bapt. Ch., Camden, N.J., 1944-46; asso. pastor First Bapt. Ch., San Diego, 1946-48; univ. pastor, dir. Bapt. student work, So. Cal., 1948-52; dean, dir. Bapt. confs., camps, coll. and univ. students So. Cal., 1948-52; pres. Cal. Bapt. Theol. Sem. and Coll., 1952-59; Brit. Nat. Health Service fellow, 1959-61; dean students, prof. psychology Fuller Theol. Sem., Pasadena, Cal., 1962-70; pvt. practice cons; clin. psychology, psychotherapy, religion, Monrovia; Cal., 1970—. Fellow Royal Geog. Soc. London; mem. N.E.A., Religious Edn. Assn., Am. Group Psychotherapy Assn., Nat. Assn. Mental Health, Acad. Religion and Mental Health, Am. Psychol. Assn., Am. Assn. Schs. Religious Edn., Western, Cal. State, Los Angeles County psychol. assns., Nat. Council Family Relations, Am. Soc. Psychical Research, Am. Acad. Polit. and Social Sci., U.S. Air Force Assn., Alpha Gamma Nu, Alpha Phi Omega. Republican. Author: The Place of the Question In the Teaching Ministry of Jesus; The Role of Religion In The Development of Personality. Contbr. articles to religious publs. Home: 1826 E Badillo Av West Covina CA 94590 Office: 525 S Myrtle Av Monrovia CA 91016

COLE, EDWARD CYRUS, educator; b. Pawtucket, R.I., Mar 26, 1904; s. Washington Leverett and Fanny Ethel (Nicholson) C.; A.B., Dartmouth, 1926; M.F.A., Yale, 1942; m. Alice Sylvia Crawford, Sept. 6, 1930; children—Ann Frances (Mrs. Ellsworth H. Wheeler, Jr.), James Washington Leverett. Mem. faculty Yale, 1930—, asso. prof., 1946-71, emeritus, 1971—, prodn. mgr. Sch. Drama, 1946- 66, exec. officer, 1959-64, acting dean, 1965-66, sr. faculty fellow, 1966-67, fellow Timothy Dwight Coll., 1959—, Yale Alumni Bd., 1971—; practice as theatre planning cons., 1937—; central com. Am. Coll. Theater Festival, 1962-71, dept. nat. coordinator, 1969-71. Bd. dirs. Yale Alumni Fund, 1962-71, Theatre Haven, Inc. 1970—; bd. govs. Am. Playwrights Theatre, 1963—. Recipient Treasury citation for war bond sales, 1944; award Theta Alpha Phi, 1958. Fellow Am. Ednl. Theatre Assn. (pres. 1958, Merit award 1964); mem. ANTA (dir., exec. com. 1953-69, 2d v.p. 1962, sec. 1967-68), Nat. Council Arts in Edn. (dir. 1962—, exec. sec. 1962-66), U.S. Power Squadrons, Am. Assn. U. Profs., Marine, New Haven Colony, Branford hist. socs., Branford Land Trust, Conn. Forest and Park Assn., Hutmens Assn., U.S. Inst. Theatre Tech., New Haven Power Squadron, Zeta Psi. Episcopalian. Clubs: Yale, Dartmouth (New Haven); Branford Yacht; Appalachian Mountain. Author: (with Harold Burris-Meyer) Scenery for the Theatre, 1938, Theatres and Auditoriums, 1949, 2d edit., 1964. Home: 17 Parker Pl Branford CT 06405 Office: Box 1903-A Yale Sta New Haven CT 06520 ☆

COLE, EDWARD N., automobile mfg. co. exec.; b. Marne, Mich., Sept. 17, 1909; s. Franklin Benjamin and Lucy Catherine (Blasen) C.; student Grand Rapids Jr. Coll., 1927-29; B.S., Gen. Motors Inst., Flint, Mich., 1933; D. Eng., Lawrence Inst. Tech.; D.Sc., Wayne State U.; D.Engring., Mich. State U., U. Mich., PMC Colls.; LL.D., Akron U., Eastern Mich. U.; m. Dollie Ann McVey, Dec. 11, 1964; children—Anne Murray, Robert Michael Joseph, Edward N.; children by previous marriage— David, Martha. With Gen. Motors Corp., Detroit, 1933—, beginning as lab. asst. Cadillac Motor Car div., successively lab. technician, technician and designer, engr., chief design engr., ordnance equipment, asst. chief engr., chief engr., works mgr., plant mgr. Cadillac-Cleve. Tank plant, chief engr. and gen. mgr. Chevrolet Motor div., Detroit, group v.p. charge Car and Truck divs. Gen. Motors, then exec. v.p. corp. charge operations staff, 1965-67, pres., chief operating officer, 1967- -, also chmn. adminstrn. com. Dir., past pres. Detroit Area council Boy Scouts Am.; bd. dirs. Detroit United Found.; trustee Mich. Heart Assn., Detroit Grace Hosp.; chmn. Gen. Motors Inst., 1962-65. Mem. Soc. Automotive Engrs., Nat. Indusl. Pollution Control Council, Nat. Acad. Engring., Am. Soc. Metals (distinguished life mem.), Sigma Xi, Tau Beta Pi, Pi Tau Sigma, Delta Sigma Pi. Clubs: Detroit Athletic, Recess; Bloomfield Hills (Mich.). Office: Gen Motors Bldg Detroit MI 48202

COLE, FRANKLIN ALAN, finance co. exec.; b. Park Falls, Wis., May 20, 1926; s. David A. and Elizabeth (Schwid) C.; B.A., U. Ill., 1947; J.D., Northwestern U., 1950; m. Joan Lauter; children—Todd, Andrew, Robert, Mary, Ellen, Peter. Admitted to Ill. bar, 1950; practice in Chgo., 1950-63; asso. Lederer, Livingston, Kahn & Adsit, 1950-55; partner Cole, Wishner, Epstein & Manilow, 1955-63; exec. Walter E. Heller & Co., Chgo., 1963—, pres., chief exec. officer, 1969—; exec., dir. Walter E. Heller Internat. Corp. Home: 110 Acorn Lane Highland Park IL 60035 Office: 105 W Adams St Chicago IL 60690

COLE, FRED CARRINGTON, acad. adminstr.; b. Franklin, Tex., Apr. 12, 1912; s. Robert Wiley and Elizabeth (Taylor) C.; A.B., La. State U., 1934, A.M., 1936, Ph.D., 1941; LL.D., Union Coll., 1961, Washington and Lee U., 1968; m. Lois Ferguson, Aug. 22, 1937; children—Caroline (Mrs. Elmer Cornwell, Jr.), Fred Carrington, Robert Grey, Taylor Morris. Editorial asso. Jour. So. History, La. State U., 1936-41. mng. editor, 1941-42; co-editor, So. Biography Series, 1938-45; hist. editor. La. State Univ. Press, 1938-42; asso. prof. history Tulane U., 1946-47, prof. 1947-59, dean Coll. Arts and Scis., 1947-55. acad. v.p., 1954-59; pres. Washington and Lee U., 1959-67; pres. Council on Library Resources, Inc., 1967—; asso. editor Mississippi Valley Hist. Rev., 1946- 53. Staff asso. edn. Ford Found., 1954-55; cons. med. research and edn. U.S. Dept. Health, Edn. and Welfare, 1957-58: cons. to Surgeon Gen. on med. manpower, 1958-59; mem. Com. on Internat. Exchange of Persons; trustee United Negro Coll. Fund, George C. Marshall Found.; bd. dirs. Council Library Resources, Ford Motor Co. Fund Scholarship Program; pres. Va. Found. Ind. Colls., 1964-67; chmn adv. com. div. instl. programs NSF, 1957-63; chmn. adv. council coop. research Office Edn.; chmn. hist. adv. com. Dept. Army, 1963-67. Served with USNR, 1942-46. Awarded spl. commendation Surgeon Gen., U.S. Navy. 1945; Outstanding Service award Dept. Army, 1967. Mem. So. Hist. Assn., Am. Hist. Assn., Miss. Valley Hist. Assn., Am. So. polit. assns., Acad. Polit. Sci., Phi Beta Kappa Assos., Phi Beta Kappa (chmn. council nominating com. 1964-67), Sigma Chi, Phi Kappa Phi, Pi Sigma Alpha, Omicron Delta Kappa. Democrat. Baptist. Clubs: Cosmos (Washington); Round Table (New Orleans); Century (N.Y.C.). Home: 3900 Watson Pl NW Washington DC 20016

COLE, G. FRANK, Jr., banker; b. Nashville, June 12, 1909; s. G. Frank and Anne (Zickler) C.; student Rutgers U. Grad. Sch. Banking, 1945-47; m. Corralyn Leavell, Sept. 4, 1936; children-G. Frank III, J. Richard. With First Am. Nat. Bank, Nashville, 1925—, sr. v.p., trust officer, 1965—, also dir.; pres., dir. Bank of Hendersonville (Tenn.); dir. Franklin Builders Supply Co., Franklin Limestone Co., Tennessean Newspapers, Inc., Newspaper Printing Corp. Bd. dirs. So. Baptist Found., Nashville Meml. Hosp., Bapt. Hosp., Belmont Coll. Mem. Am. Inst. Banking, Nashville C. of C. Mason, Kiwanian. Clubs: Belle Meade, Cumberland (Nashville) Bluegrass Yacht and Country, (Hendersonville, Tenn.). Home: 6140 Hillsboro Rd Nashville TN 37215 Office: 326 Union St Nashville TN 37202

COLE, GEORGE JAMES, (Lord Cole), corp. exec.; b. Singapore, 1906; ed. in Singapore and Eng.; m. Ruth Harpham, 1940; 2 children. Bd. dirs. Unilever Ltd., 1948—, vice chmn., 1956-60, chmn., 1960—; vice chmn. Unilever N.V., 1960—. Home: 50 Victoria Rd Kensington London W 8 England Office: Unilever Ltd Unilever House Blackfriars London EC 4 England*

COLE, GORDON HENRY, labor union ofcl., editor; b. Providence, Jan. 11, 1912; s. Albert Jourdan and Margaret Cooper (Ricketts) C.; A.B., Syracuse U., 1934; m. Malvine Gescheidt, Sept. 19, 1939; children—Stephen Adams, Jeremy David; m. 2d, Morag Douglas Macintyre, Dec. 19, 1952; children—Gordon Macintyre, Susan Douglas, Margaret Cooper. Reporter, Syracuse Post-Standard, 1934-35, Griffin News Bur., 1935-37, Wall St. Jour., 1937; asso. editor Labor Relations Reporter, Bur. Nat. Affairs, 1937-39; labor editor U.S. News, 1939-42, Washington bur., newspaper PM, 1942-43; with civilian psychol. warfare br. 12th U.S. Army Group, OSS, 1943-45; commr. conciliation U.S. Dept. Labor, 1946-47; editor The Machinist, pub. relations dir. Internat. Assn. Machinists, AFL-CIO, 1947—. Mem. Clifton (Va.) Vol. Fire Dept. Decorated Medal of Freedom, Croix de Guerre. Mem. Internat. Labor Press Assn. (pres. 1955-57), Am. (v.p. 1943-44), Washington (pres. 1942) newspaper guilds, Aviation Writers Assn., Nat. Press Club, Sigma Delta Chi. Democrat. Presbyn. Author: (with Gertrude Blair) Picnic Meals, 1951. Editor: Right-to-Work Laws: Three Moral Studies, 1955; co-editor Labor's Story, 1961. Home: 12421 Fairfax Station Rd Clifton VA 22024 Office: 1300 Connecticut Av Washington DC 20036

COLE, HAROLD HARRISON, educator; b. Waterloo, Wis., Feb. 11, 1897; s. Clarence E. and Hattie (White) C.; B.S., U. Wis., 1920; M.S., U. Cal. at Davis, 1925; Ph.D., U. Minn., 1928; LL.D., U. Cal., 1965; m. Jessie I. Cliff, May 1, 1929 (dec. 1952); 1 son, Cliff H.; m. 2d, Cynthia Clegg, Mar. 2, 1955; 1 dau., Nancy. Asst. prof. animal husbandry U. Cal. at Davis, 1928-43, prof., 1943—, chmn. dept. 1952-60, faculty research lectr., 1943. Chmn. subcom. bloat Com. Animal Health, 1944-54; com. on beef NRC, 1959-60; range land utilization adv. com. Cal. Bd. Forestry. Recipient Morrison award Am. Soc. Animal Prodn., 1952. Mem. Am. Assn. Anatomists, Soc. Exptl. Biology and Medicine, Endocrine Soc., Am. Dairy Sci. Assn., Am. Soc. Animal Prodn. (asso. editor Jour. 1943-45), A.A.A.S., Soc. Study Reprodn. (editor Biology of Reprodn.), Sigma Xi. Club: Commonwealth (San Francisco). Co- editor: Reproduction in Domestic Animals, 2 vols., 1959, 68. Editor Introduction to Livestock Production, Including Dairy and Poultry, 1962, 66; Gonadotropins: Their Biol. and Chem. Properties and Secretory Control. Contbr. profl. jours. Home: 528 Miller Dr Davis CA 95616

COLE, HAROLD MERCER, lawyer; b. Montclair, N.J., Dec. 10, 1905; s. Harry Mercer and Julie (Young) C.; A.B., Brown U., 1929; LL.B., Harvard, 1932; m. Eleanor Kountze, June 3, 1933; 1 dau., Eleanor Estabrook; m. 2d, Barbara Chisholm Scott, June 30, 1948. Admitted to N.Y. bar, 1932, since practiced in N.Y.C.; partner Cole & Deitz, 1942—; spl. dep. asst. dist. atty. on staff Thomas E. Dewey, 1935-37; asst. dist. atty. N.Y. County, 1938-41; chmn. bd. Allegheny River Mining Co.; dir. Am. Australian Fund, Inc., Amoskeag Co., Exeter Fund, Inc., Exeter Second Fund, Inc., Exeter Third Fund, Inc., W.L. Morgan Growth Fund, Gemeni Fund, Inc., Santa Cruz Industries, Inc., Arthur T. Walker Estate Corp., Winsdor Fund, Inc., First Investors Life Ins. Co., McCandless Corp., Standard-Thomson Corp.; mem. N.Y. adv. com. Am. Mut. Liability Ins. Co. Bd. dirs. Wellington Fund. Served as lt. USNR, 1943- 45. Mem. Assn. Bar City N.Y., Newcomen Soc. Am. Republican (spl. counsel to chmn. nat. com. 1946-48, treas. N.Y. County com. 1949-53). Clubs: National Republican, Union League, Leash Indian Harbor Yacht, Edgartown Yacht, Down Town Assn., River (N.Y.C.). Home: 38 E 37th St New York City NY 10016 Office: 40 Wall St New York City NY 10005

COLE, HARRY, lawyer; b. Birmingham, Ala., Feb. 16, 1929; s. Ellis and Geraldine (Metcalfe) C.; B.A., U. Ala., 1951; LL.B., Jones Law Sch., Montgomery, Ala., 1959; m. Jimmie Rice, Jan. 23, 1951; children—Shelton Cameron, Susan Amanda, Harry. Ins. adjuster Crawford & Co., Greensboro, N.C., 1951-52; ins. adjuster McPhail, Haigler & Cole, Montgomery, Ala., 1952- 59; admitted to Ala. bar, 1959, since practiced in Montgomery; partner Hill, Hill, Stovall, Carter & Franco; lectr. Jones Law Sch. Mem. Am., Ala., Montgomery County (past pres.) bar assns., Internat. Assn. Ins. Counsel, Ala. Def. Lawyers Assn. (past v.p.). Republican. Presbyn. Home: 2721 Fairmont Rd Montgomery AL 36105 Office: Hill Bldg Montgomery AL 36104

COLE, HORACE WELLINGTON, former banker; b. Boston, Jan. 23, 1903; s. Herbert Milton and Dorothy (Snow) C.; grad. Phillips Acad., Andover, Mass., 1922; B.A., Yale, 1926; m. Charlotte D. Fawcett, Oct. 1, 1927; children—Charlotte Deborah (Mrs. John B. French), Herbert Milton. Engaged in investments, 1926-32; with Boston Safe Deposit & Trust Co., 1932-70, v.p., sec., 1948-70, ret., 1970; sec., clk. Boston Co. Inc.; trustee Boston Five Cents Sav. Bank. Treas. Nat. Found. Eye Research; corporator Retina Found. Episcopalian (past vestryman, jr. warden, sr. warden). Clubs: Duxbury (Mass.) Yacht; Country (Brookline). Home: 32 Gypsy Trail Weston MA 02193

COLE, HOUSTON, coll. pres.; b. Fort Payne, Ala., Nov. 24, 1902; s. John and Pollyana (Cash) C.: B.S., M.S., U. Ala., 1927, LL.D., 1948; postgrad U. Chgo. and Columbia; m. Leone Pruett; 1 dau., Beth; m. 2d, Martha Bellenger Graves; 1 stepdau., Alex. Supt. Guntersville (Ala.) schs., 1925-33, Tuscaloosa County (Ala.) schs., 1934-39; prof. edn. U. Ala., 1939-41; state dir. Ala. Civilian Def., 1941-42, OPA, 1942; pres. Jacksonville (Ala.) State U., 1942—. Dir. First Nat. Bank Jacksonville (Ala.), Nat. Educators Life Ins. Co., Fort Worth. Established high sch. Civil Def. councils, forerunner of Victory Corps; Boy Scouts Am. leader; chmn. Gov.'s Adv. Com. on Law and Order. Mem. Phi Beta Kappa, Kappa Delta Pi, Phi Delta Kappa. Democrat. Methodist. Rotarian. (Ala. dist. gov. 1938). Contbr. articles to mags.; pub. speaker. Address: State U Jacksonville AL 36265

COLE, HOWARD WARE, lawyer; b. Marblehead, Mass., June 27, 1898; s. Leland Howard and Mary Abby (Roundy) C.; A.B., Dartmouth, 1919; LL.B., Harvard, 1922; m. Doris W. Enslin, Sept. 15, 1925; children—Rosamonde E. (Mrs. George R. Little), Natalie W. (Mrs. Gordon R. Hamilton, Jr.), Roger E. Admitted to Mass. bar, 1922, since practiced in Boston, 1922—; mem. Brickley, Sears & Cole. Dir. New Eng. Electric System. Del. nat. council YMCA, 1940- 60, chmn. bd. Mass. YMCA, 1957—; bd. mgrs. Am. Bapt. Fgn. Mission Soc., 1936-58. Chmn. bd. trustees Andover Newton Theol. Sch., 1965-69; trustee Bapt. Home Mass., pres. 1970—. Mem. Mass. Bible Soc. (pres. 1965—), Am., Mass., Boston bar assns., Am. Trial Lawyers Assn., Am. Judicature Soc. Home: 36 Washington St Beverly MA 01915 Office: 75 Federal St Boston MA 02110

COLE, IRA WILLIAM, univ. dean; b. Mattoon, Ill., Apr. 21, 1924; s. Harry Ellsworth and Carrie Juliet (Connor) C.; B.S., U. Ill., 1948, M.S., 1952; m. Sally Ann Savage, Jan. 5, 1944; children—Molly Ann, Timothy William. Reporter, Champaign (Ill.) News-Gazette, 1941-43, 46-47; asst. to dir. U. Ill. Sch. Journalism and Communications, 1948-56; dir. Pa. State U. Sch. Journalism, 1956-57; dean Medill Sch. Journalism Northwestern U., 1957- -, dir. Urban Journalism Center, 1966—. Bd. dirs. Christian Century Found. Served from sgt. to 1st lt., Inf. AUS, 1942-45, 51; pub. informtion specialist, hdqrs. UN Command Far East Command. Mem. Assn. for Edn. Journalism, Am. Med. Writers Assn., A.P. Mng. Editors Assn. (research com.), Council for Advancement Sci. Writing, Phi Kappa Psi, Sigma Delta Chi, Kappa Tau Alpha. Clubs: Economic, Tavern (Chgo.). Home: 10 Canterbury Ct Wilmette IL 60091

COLE, JACK, choreographer, dancer, dir.; b. New Brunswick, N.J., Apr. 27, 1914; student with Ted Shawn, Ruth St. Denis, Charles Weidman, Doris Humphrey, others, ethnic dance forms in Brazil, Cuba, Philippines, Ireland. Made debut as dancer in Job, N.Y.C., summer 1931; toured with Denishawn Concert Dancers, 1930-32, Humphrey-Weidman Dance Group, N.Y.C., 1932-33; Broadway debut as dancer in The School for Husbands, 1933, later danced in Thumbs Up, 1934, May Wine, 1935; appeared with own dance group, 1937, in Keep 'Em Laughing, 1942; dancer the Ziegfeld Follies, 1943; choreographer Something for the Boys, 1943, Allah Be Praised!, 1944, Bonanza Bound, 1947, Magdalena, 1948, Alive and Kicking, 1960, Kismet, 1953, Jamaica, 1957, Candide, 1959, Kean, 1961, A Funny Thing Happened on the Way to the Forum, 1962, Foxy, 1964; choreographer, dancer films including Moon Over Miami, 1941, Kismet, 1944, Lydia Bailey, 1952, Designing Women, 1957; choreographer movies including Eadie Was a Lady, 1945, The Jolson Story, 1945, Tars and Spars, 1946, Down to Earth, 1947, On the Riviera, 1951, David and Bathsheba, 1951, The Merry Widow, 1952, Gentlemen Prefer Blondes, 1953, The Farmer Takes a Wife, 1953, Gentlemen Marry Brunettes, 1955, Les Girls, 1957, Some Like It Hot, 1959, Let's Make Love, 1960; choreographer, dancer TV shows including Perry Como Show, Bob Hope Show, Sid Caesar Show; also nightclub work. Recipient award for dancing in Ziegfeld Follies, Dance Mag., 1943; Photoplay award for choreography The Jolson Story, 1945; Donaldson award for choreography and dancing in Alive and Kicking, 1950; Dance mag. award for choreography Three for the Show, 1955.

COLE, JACK WESTLEY, physician; b. Portland, Ore., Aug. 28, 1920; s. Alva Warren and Louise (Shafer) C.; A.B., U. Ore., 1941; M.D., Wash. U., 1944; M.A., Yale, 1966; m. Ruth Adele Kraft, Dec. 22, 1943; children—Deborah, Linda, Douglas, John. Mem. faculty Western Res. U. Sch. Medicine, 1952-63; prof., chmn. dept. surgery Hahnemann Med. Coll. and Hosp., 1963-66; Ensign prof., chmn. dept. surgery Yale Sch. Medicine, 1966—; cons. various hosps. Eleanor Roosevelt Internat. Cancer Research fellow, 1962. Mem. Am. Surg. Assn., Halsted Soc., Soc. Surgery of Alimentary Tract, Am. Soc. Cell Biology, Soc. Cryobiology. Research and publs. on histochemistry, cytochemistry, carcinogenesis; studies dealing with cellular kinetics in normal and abnormal intestinal epithelium. Home: Prospect Court Woodbridge CT 06525 Office: 333 Cedar St New Haven CT 06510

COLE, JAMES F., corp. exec.; b. 1918; B.A., Capital City Comml. Coll., Des Moines; married. With Sherwin-Williams Co., 1942—, treas., 1967—. Address: 101 Prospect Av NW Cleveland OH 44101*

COLE, JAMES WEBB, Jr., chemist, univ. dean; b. Norfolk, Va., July 22, 1910; s. James Webb and Mabel (Stephenson) C.; B.S., U. Va., 1932, M.S., 1935, Ph.D. (DuPont fellow), 1936; m. Katherine P. Smith, Aug. 23, 1936; children—James Webb III, William Marshall. Research chemist, exptl. sta. E. I. DuPont de Nemours Co., 1936-38; asst. prof. U. Va., 1938-46, asso. prof., 1946-57. prof., 1957—, dir. Acad. Year Inst., 1957—, dean Sch. Gen. Studies 1958—; part-time Investigator Nat. Def. Research Commn., 1941-45; program dir. NSF, 1952-53, cons., 1953—; prin. investigator Air Force Research Project, 1953—; spl. instr. engring. sci. mgmt. Def. Tng. Program. Fellow Am. Inst. Chemists, A.A.A.S.; mem. Va. Acad. Sci. (pres. 1967-68), Am. Chem. Soc., Sigma Xi. Rotarian. Club: Farmington Country (Charlottesville). Co- author textbooks on chemistry. Contbr. articles profl. jours. Home: 900 Rosser Lane Charlottesville VA 22903

COLE, JOHN OWEN, banker; b. Forest City, N.C., May 29, 1929; s. Dee Christopher and Fave (Best) C.; B.A., Duke, 1953; m. Katherine Stuart Davidson, June 27, 1953; children—Mark Davidson, D. Matthew, Chapman Stuart, Benjamin Donnell, John Owen II, Jamie Clark, Mary F. with First Nat. Bank Md., Balt., 1956—, pres., dir., 1968—. Bd. dirs. Balt. chpt. A.R.C., 1966—. Served with USMCR, 1953-56. Mem. Res. City Bankers Assn. Home: Route 5 Box 159 Annapolis MD 21401 Office: First Nat Bank Md Light and Redwood Sts Baltimore MD 21203

COLE, JONATHON OTIS, psychiatrist; b. Boston, Aug. 16, 1925; s. Arthur Harrison and Anna (Steckel) C.; student Harvard Coll., 1942-43; M.D., Cornell U., 1947; m. Kathleen Gleason, July 12, 1952; children—Jonathan Patrick, Joshua Peter. Intern Peter Bent Brigham Hosp., Boston, 1947-48; resident psychiatry Payne Whitney Clinic, N.Y.C., 1948-51; asso. prof. Nat. Acad. Scis., Washington, 1953-56; dir. psychopharmacology research br. Nat. Inst. Mental Health, Chevy Chase, Md., 1956-67; supt. Boston State Hosp., 1967—; prof. psychiatry Tufts Med. Sch., 1967—. Served with AUS, 1951-53. Fellow Am. Psychiatric Assn., Am. Coll. Neuropsychopharmacology, Collegium Internationale Neuro-Psychopharmacologicum; mem. Am. Psychopathol. Assn. Editor: Psychopharmacology: Problems in Evaluation. Contbr. numerous articles sci. jours. Home: 78 Powell St Brookline MA 02146 Office: 591 Morton St Boston MA 02124

COLE, JOSEPH EDMOND, mfg. and distbg. co. exec.; b. Cleve., Jan. 4, 1915; s. Solomon and Sarah (Miller) C.; student Ohio State U., 1932, Fenn Coll., Cleve., 1933; m. Marcia Newman, Oct. 31, 1937; children—Jeffrey, Stephan. Salesman, Waldorf Brewing Co., 1933-35; office mgr., then gen. mgr. Nat. Key Shops, Inc., 1935-44; partner, sales dir. Curtis Industries, 1944- 50; pres. Cole Motors, Inc., 1947-54; pres., now chmn. Cole Nat. Corp., Cleve., 1950—; dir. Capital Bank, Cleve. Broadcasting Co., PEC Israel Econ. Corp., Gen. Life Ins. Co.; prin. Terminal Tower Co. Mem. Pres. Kennedy's Com. Internat. Devel., 1962; pres. Pioneers of New Industries, 1960; spl. cons. P.R. Econ. Devel. Adminstrn., 1963. Mem. exec. com. Cleve. council Boy Scouts Am.; divisional and spl. fund chmn. Jewish Welfare Fund, Cleve., 1963-64. Chmn. Ohio Citizens for Kennedy, 1960; mem. Cuyahoga County Democratic Exec. Com., 1960—. Bd. dirs. United Convalescent Hosps. Am., Cleve. chpt. Nat. Conf. Christians and

Jews, Mt. Sinai Hosp.; trustee Albert Einstein Coll. Medicine, Jewish Community Fedn., Cleve., Notre Dame Coll., Cleve.; past chmn. scholarship fund Ohio State Coll.; life mem. Brandeis U. Mem. Cleve. C. of C. Jewish religion (trustee temple). Mason (32, Shriner), Rotarian. Clubs: Beechmont Country, City (Cleve.); Standard (Chgo.); Palm Beach (Fla.) Country, Coral Beach Tennis (Palm Beach); Marco Polo (N.Y.C.). Home: 18595 Parkland Dr Shaker Heights OH 44122 Office: 5777 Grant Av Cleveland OH 44105

COLE, KENDALL MARTIN, lawyer; b. Bangor, Me., Oct. 25, 1922; s. William Spratt and Alice (Lord) C.; A.B. cum laude, Amherst Coll., 1943; LL.B., Harvard, 1948; m. Mary Daintry Malloch, Nov. 12, 1949; children—Robert, Jane. Admitted to Ill. bar, 1949, Pa. bar, 1961, N.Y. bar, 1963; practice in Chgo., 1948-60, Phila., 1960-63, White Plains, N.Y., 1963—; asso. Carney, Crowell & Leibman, 1948-56, partner, 1956-60; asst. gen. counsel Scott Paper Co., 1960-63; asst. gen. counsel Gen. Foods Corp., 1963-64, gen. counsel, 1964—, v.p., 1967—. Dir. General Foods Fund, Inc., Viviane Woodward Corp., W. Atlee Burpee Co. Police magistrate, Bannockburn, Ill., 1959-60. Trustee Food and Drug Law Inst., Brunswick Sch., Greenwich Acad. Served with USNR, 1943-46. Mem. Grocery Mfrs. Am. (chmn. lawyers com.), Alpha Delta Phi. Clubs: Belle Haven; Harvard (N.Y.C.). Home: 7 Deer Lane Greenwich, CT 06830. Office: 250 North St White Plains NY 10602

COLE, KENNETH REESE, Jr., govt. ofcl.; b. N.Y.C., Jan. 27, 1938; s. Kenneth Reese and Laura (Hughes) C.; B.S. in Bus. Adminstrn., Bucknell U., 1959; m. Marilyn Joan Slifer, July 20, 1963; children—Corinne, Megan. Asst. to v.p. operations Elizabethtown Gas Co., Elizabeth, N.J., 1959-61; account rep. J. Walter Thompson Co., N.Y.C., 1965-68; spl. asst. to Pres. Richard M. Nixon, 1969-70, dep. asst. for domestic affairs, 1970—. Mem. Pres.'s Commn. on White House Fellowships. Advance Nat. Nixon-Agnew campaign, 1968. Served to lt. USNR, 1961-65. Republican. Episcopalian. Home: 5705 Marengo Rd Washington DC 20016 Office: White House 1600 Pennsylvania Av Washington DC 20500

COLE, KENNETH STEWART, biophysicist; b. Ithaca, N.Y., July 10, 1900; s. Charles Nelson and Mabel (Stewart) Cole; A.B., Oberlin Coll., 1922; Sc.D. (hon.), 1954; Ph.D., Cornell U., 1926; Sc.D. (hon.), U. Chgo., 1967; M.D. (hon.) U. Uppsala, 1967; m. Elizabeth Evans Roberts, June 29, 1932 (dec. 1966); children—Roger Braley, Sarah C. Main. Fellow NRC, Harvard, U., 1926- 28; research fellow Gen. Edn. Bd., Leipzig, 1928-29; asst. prof. physiology Columbia, 1929-37, asso. prof., 1937-46; cons. physicist Presbyn. Hosp., N.Y.C., 1929-46; fellow Guggenheim Found., Inst. Advanced Study, Princeton, 1941-42; prin. biophysicist, metall. lab., U. Chgo., 1942-46, prof. biophysics and physiology, 1946-49; tech. dir. Naval Med. Research Inst., Bethesda, 1949-54; chief lab of biophysics Nat. Inst. Neurol. Diseases and Blindness, NIH, Bethesda, Md., 1954-66, sr. research biophysicist, 1966—; regents prof. U. Cal. at Berkeley, 1963-64, prof. biophysics, 1965- -; Priestley lectr. Pa. State Coll., 1939; Tennent lectr., Bryn Mawr Coll., 1941. Mem. bd. Lab., Cold Spring Harbor, 1940-45. Trustee Marine Biol. Lab., 1947-55, 56-64, emeritus, 1966—. Decorated Order of So. Cross (Brazil); recipient Nat. Medal of Science, 1967. Fellow Am. Phys. Soc., A.A.A.S., N.Y. Acad. Sci.; mem. Nat. Acad. Scis., Am. Acad. Arts and Scis., Am. Physiol. Soc. (council 1963- 65), Societe philomatique Paris, Soc. Gen. Physiologists, Biophys. Soc. (council 1957-62, pres. 1963), Sigma Xi, Alpha Epsilon Delta (hon.), Epsilon Chi (hon.), Sociedade Brasileira de Biologia (hon.). Club: Cosmos (Washington). Office: NIH Bethesda MD 20014

COLE, LAMONT COOK, educator, ecologist; b. Chgo., July 15, 1916; s. Fay-Cooper and Mabel (Cook) C.; S.B., U. Chgo., 1938, Ph.D., 1944; M.S., U. Utah, 1940; Sc.D., U. Vt., 1969, Ripon Coll., 1971; m. Ann Louise Schuster, Aug. 27, 1940; children—John LaMont, George Frederic. Instr., then asst. prof. Ind. U., 1946-48; faculty Cornell U., Ithaca, N.Y., 1948—, prof. zoology, 1954—, chmn. dept. zoology, 1964-65, chmn. sect. ecology and systematics, 1965-67. Mem. adv. com. environmental biology NSF, 1958-61, mem. scis. information service, 1968; chmn. rev. team math.- statistics NIH, 1963-70; mem. Sec. of Health, Edn. and Welfare com. on pesticides, 1969—. Served with USPHS, 1944-46. Fellow A.A.A.S.; mem. Ecol. Soc. Am. (pres. 1967-68), Am. Inst. Biol. Scis. (gov. bd. 1964—, exec. com. 1965—, pres. 1969), Chi Psi. Republican. Methodist. Contbr. profl. jours. Zool. editor Ecology, 1958- 63. Home: RD 3 Trumansburgh NY 14886 Office: Langmuir Lab Cornell Univ Ithaca NY 14850

COLE, LARRY SNOW, educator; b. Logan, Utah, Aug. 31, 1906; s. Alfred L. and Mabelle (Snow) C.; B.S., U. Utah, 1940; M.S., Utah State U., 1945; D. Eng., Stanford, 1950; m. Lucy Gardner, Sept. 26, 1929; children—Marjorie Louise (Mrs. Wilford Gardner), Richard Gardner. Radio technician, service mgr., 1929- 39; faculty dept. elec. engring. Utah State U., Logan, 1939—, now prof. elec. engring., asso. dean Coll. Engring. Recipient Pub. Service award Utah sect. I.E.E.E., 1968. Registered profl. engr., Utah. Mem. Utah Soc. Profl. Engrs., I.E.E.E. (past sect. chmn.), Am. Soc. Engring. Edn., Logan/Cache C. of C., Sigma Xi, Sigma Tau. Kiwanian. Contbr. articles profl. jours. Home: 696 E 4th North Logan UT 84321

COLE, LOUIS WILLIAM, former mfg. exec.; b. N.Y.C., July 1, 1890; s. Michael and Esther Gertrude (Manne) C.; B.S., Cooper Union, 1912, E.E., 1916; m. Estelle Melnick, June 8, 1920; children—Thomas M., Carol (Mrs. Millard Rothenberg). Draftsman Met. Switchboard Co., N.Y.C., 1905-09; constrn. engr. Tucker Electric Constrn. Co., N.Y.C., 1910-11; comml. mgr. Columbia Metal Box Co., 1911-14, chief emgr., 1914-18; pres., gen. mgr. Fed. Pacific Electric Co., Newark, 1918-50, chmn. bd. 1950-69. Mem. Am. Inst. E.E., Nat. Elec. Mfrs. Assn., Tau Beta Pi. Home: Stratford Rd Harrison NY 10528 Office: 505 Park Av New York City NY 10022

COLE, NED, bishop; b. California, Mo., Feb. 6, 1917; s. Ned and Gladys (Walser) C.; B.A., Westminster Coll., Fulton, Mo., 1939, D.D., 1957; postgrad. U. Mo. Law Sch., 1939-40; B.D., Episcopal Theol. Sch., Cambridge, Mass., 1948; m. Martha Elizabeth Dunlap, Dec. 28, 1950; children—Deborah Anne, Stephen Eberly, Elizabeth Ann, David Brooks. Sec. to Mo. sec. state, 1940-42; ordained ot ministry Episcopal Ch., 1948; curate, Columbia, Mo., 1948-49; rector in Jefferson City, Mo., 1949-56; vicar in Portland, Mo., 1949-56; dean Christ Ch. Cathedral, St. Louis, 1956-64; bishop co- adjutor Diocese Central N.Y., Syracuse, 1963-69, bishop, 1969—. Mem. gen. bd. Nat. Council Chs., 1963-66; mem. com. of nine Episcopal House of Bishops, 1964—; mem. Bd. Theol. Edn., P.E. Ch., 1970—; mem. legislative commn. N.Y. Council Ch., 1964-67; Episcopal rep. to Consultation of Ch. Union, 1968—; rep. exec. council Province II, P.E. Ch., 1967-69; mem. Syracuse div. N.Y. State Commn. Human Rights, 1964-67, Human Rights Commn. Syracuse and Onondaga County, 1965-67, Onondaga Neighborhood Legal Services, 1966-67. Served with USAAF, 1942- 46. Home: 222 Salt Springs St Fayetteville NY 13066 Office: 935 James St Syracuse NY 13203

COLE, ORLANDO, cellist; b. Phila., Aug. 16, 1908; s. Lucius Sylvanus and Rosalia (Winkler) C.; Mus.B., Curtis Inst. Music, 1932; m. Rosamonde Adams, Jan. 15, 1933; children—Timothy, Deborah, David. Cellist, Curtis String Quartet, 1927—; concerts throughout U.S., 1928—, Europe, 1935-37, at The White House, 1934, in London for silver jubilee King George V, 1935; prof. cello New Sch. Music, Phila., 1942—, Curtis Inst. Music, 1952—. Recipient medal achievement Phila. Art Alliance, 1954. Home: 1017 Keystone Av Upper Darby PA 19082 Office: 301 S 21st St Philadelphia PA 19103

COLE, PAUL C., dept. store exec.; b. Bklyn., July 31, 1913; s. Clarence E. and Christine (Freytag) C.; A.B., N.Y. U., 1933; student Columbia Grad. Sch., 1937-39; m. Florence K. Krage, Mar. 11, 1938; 1 son, Garrett P. With R.H. Macy & Co., Inc., 1933—, sr. v.p. corp. operations and expense standards, 1967—. Mem. adv. com. state orgn. Am. Retail Fedn. Served with USAAF, 1941-46. Decorated Legion of Merit. Home: 30 Park Av New York City NY 10016 Office: 151 W 34th St New York City NY 10001

COLE, RALPH BUSTON, Jr., mfg. co. exec.; b. Washington, Oct. 20, 1915; s. Ralph Buxton and Katherine (Thorpe) C.; B.S. in Chem. Engring., Ga. Inst. Tech., 1936; m. Louise Pancoast, Nov. 1, 1941; 1 dau., Deborah Louise. With E.I. duPont de Nemours & Co., Inc., Wilmington, Del., 1936—, treas., 1968—; dir. New Castle Mut. Ins. Co. Clubs: Greenville Country, Vicmead Hunt (Wilmington). Home: 909 Du Pont Rd Wilmington DE 19807 Office: Du Pont Bldg Wilmington DE 19898

COLE, RICHARD, philosopher, educator; b. Evanston, Ill., Oct. 28, 1929; s. Harry and Bertha (Slavitt) C.; B.A. in Math., U. Tex., Austin, 1958; Ph.D., U. Chgo., 1962; m. Marjorie Jean Emerson, May 31, 1958; children—Mark Warren, Wendy Elizabeth, Aletha Jocelyn. Instr., Colo. Coll., 1961-62; asst. prof. Grinnell Coll., 1962-65; asso. prof. philosophy U. Kan., Lawrence, 1965-69, prof., 1969—, acting chmn. philosophy dept., 1969- 70, chmn. com. history and philosophy of sci., 1967-69. Chmn. Kan. U. Judiciary Hearing Div., 1970-71. Served with Signal Corps and Pub. Information, U.S. Army, 1951-53. Mem. Mind Assn., Am. Philos. Assn., Am. Assn. U. Profs., Philosophy of Sci. Assn., S.W. Philos. Soc. (mem. exec. com.). Contbg. author: The Concept of Order, 1968. Mng. editor: Studies in the Philosophy of Logic, 1968—. Contbr. articles profl. jours. Home: 1804 Mississippi St Lawrence KS 66044

COLE, RICHARD CARROLL, copper co. exec.; b. Tacoma, Dec. 24, 1914; s. Floyd Raymond and Minnie (Harm) C.; B.S. in Metall. Engring., U. Wash., 1941; hon. degree Mont. Coll. Mineral Sci. and Tech., 1967; m. Evelyn Virginia Finstad, May 24, 1937; children—Richard Carroll, Janet Elizabeth. With Am. Smelting & Refining Co., 1941-54, asst. to mgr. ore purchasing dept., N.Y.C., 1950- 54; with Vitro Corp. Am., 1954-61, v.p., 1957-58, pres., gen. mgr. div. Vitro Uranium Co., 1958-59, v.p. mfg. divs. Vitro Chem. Co., Vitro Minerals Co., 1959-61; exec. v.p., gen. mgr. White Pine Copper Co. (Mich.), 1961-64, pres., 1964-68; v.p. Copper Range Co., N.Y.C., 1962-68; v.p., gen. mgr. Inspiration Consol. Copper Co., Ariz. Mem. Am. Inst. Mining, Metall. and Petroleum Engrs. (dir. 1960-64, pres. metall. soc. 1963), Canadian Inst. Mining and Metallurgy, Am. Inst. Chem. Engrs., Mining and Metall. Soc. Am., Newcomen Soc. N.Am. Lutheran. Mason (Shriner), Elk, Rotarian (past pres.); Toastmaster. Home: Inspiration AZ 85537 Office: Inspiration Consol Copper Co Inspiration AZ 85537

COLE, ROBERT, advt. and marketing co. exec.; b. Detroit, Jan. 4, 1917; s. S.M. and Estelle (Spater) C.; student Brown U., 1936-39; m. Mary Rose Pennebaker, Jan. 19, 1942; children—Robert Daniel, Karen Christine. Copywriter, McCann-Erickson, Inc., 1940-41; with Grant Advt. Inc., 1945-53, v.p. charge N.Y. Office, 1951-53; dir. advt. and publicity Olin Mathieson Chem. Corp., 1953-56; v.p. McCann-Erickson, Inc., 1956-58, pres. indsl., tech., sci. marketing div., sr. v.p., dir., memb. bd. mgmt., 1963—; pres., dir.-gen. Interpub., S.A., Paris, France; exec. v.p., dir. McCann-Erickson Internat. Corp. Active local Community Chest drives; chmn. N.Y. chpt. Help for Retarded Children, advt. sect., 1965-66; mem. Mayor Cleve. Bond Com., 1960. Served with USNR, 1941-45. Named Brazilian Advt. Man of Year, 1950. Mem. Internat. Assn. Advt. Agys.; Sigma Chi. Club: Nassau Country (Glen Cove, L.I., N.Y.). Home: 3 East View Ct Port Washington NY 11050 Office: 485 Lexington Av New York City NY 10017

COLE, ROBERT BATES, lawyer; b. Scarborough, Eng., Feb. 9, 1911; s. William and Mary Elizabeth (Bates) C.; brought to U.S., 1911, naturalized, 1914; A.B., U. Fla., 1932, J.D., 1935; m. Frances Lee Arnold, June 23, 1937; children—Charles Robert, George Thomas, Richard Phillip. Admitted to Fla. bar, 1935, since practiced in Miami; mem. firm Mershon, Sawyer, Johnston, Dunwody & Cole, Miami Fla., 1946—. Sec. Arvida Corp., 1961—; sec., dir. Arnold Cellophane Corp., 1953—, Major Appliances, Inc., 1953— (all Miami); sec., treas., dir. Fla. Dairy Producers Corp., Orlando, 1962—; dir. Miami Beach First Nat. Bank. Trustee Bapt. Hosp. Miami, Inc. Mem. Nat. Assn. Coll. and U. Attys., Am., Dade County bar assns., Fla. Bar, Phi Delta Phi, Sigma Chi. Baptist. Kiwanian (dir.). Clubs: Miami; Riviera Country (pres., treas., gov.) (Coral Gables, Fla.). Home: 1124 Valencia Av Coral Gables FL 33134 Office: First Nat Bank Bldg Miami FL 33131

COLE, ROBERT HUGH, educator; b. Oberlin, O., Oct. 26, 1914; s. Charles Nelson and Mable (Stewart) C.; A.B., Oberlin Coll., 1935; A.M., Harvard, 1936, Ph.D., 1940; A.M., Brown U., 1952; m. Elisabeth French, Apr. 24, 1943. Instr., tutor Harvard, 1938-41; research supr. Underwater Explosives Research Lab., Woods Hole, Mass., 1941-46; asso. prof. physics U. Mo., 1946-47; asso. prof. chemistry Brown U., Providence, 1947-51, chmn. dept., 1948—, prof., 1951—, now Jesse H. and Louisa D. Sharpe Metacalfe prof. chemistry. Prof. asso. Faculty Scis. d'Orsay, U. Paris, 1969-70. Trustee Woods Hole Oceanographic Instn., 1968—. Fulbright lectr., Guggenheim fellow U. Leiden, 1955-56, Oxford U., 1962; NSF Sr. postdoctoral fellow, 1961-62. Fellow Am. Phys. Soc., mem. Am. Chem. Soc., Am., Acad. Arts and Sci., Sigma Xi, Phi Beta Kappa. Author: Underwater Explosions, 1948; (with J.S. Coles) Physical Principles of Chemistry, 1964. Home: 45 Humboldt Av Providence RI 02906

COLE, ROBERT LEE, corp. exec.; b. Rockport, Mo., May 4, 1929; s. Branchie Ray and Mary (Clevenger) C.; A.A. summa cum laude Fullerton Jr. Coll., 1949; A.B. cum laude, U. Cal. at Berkeley, 1951; m. Bonnie Lou Roseberry, July 1950 (div. Oct. 1965); children—Brenda Lynn, Bradford Lee; m. 2d, Judith Lucina Robinson, Jan. 1968. Asst. to plant mgr., staff indsl. engr. Rheem Mfg. Co., Downey, Cal., 1951-55; asst. to pres., chief prodn. control Longren Aircraft Co., Torrance, Cal., 1955-58; div. mgr. Aerojet-Gen. Corp., Fullerton, Cal., 1960-62, mgr. indsl. engring., Downey, 1962-63, exec. asst. to corp. v.p., gen. mgr., El Monte, Cal., 1963-64; corp. mgr. real estate and constrn. dept. Litton Industries, Inc., Beverly Hills, Cal., 1964-67, treas., 1967-69; v.p. Litton Internat., 1967-69; treas. Litton Industries Found., 1967-69; pres. Litton Power Transmission, West Hartford, Conn., 1969—. Registered profl. engr., Cal. Mem. Am. Inst. Indsl. Engrs., Systems and Procedures Assn., Am. Mgmt. Assn., Am. Ordnance Assn. Elk. Club: Toastmasters (past pres.) (Downey). Home: 11 Reverknolls Avon CT 06001 Office: 41 N Main St West Hartford CT 06032

COLE, ROBERT TAYLOR, educator; b. Bald Prairie, Tex., Sept. 3, 1905; s. Robert Wiles and Elizabeth (Taylor) C.; A.B., U. of Tex., 1925, A.M., 1927; Ph.D., Harvard U., 1936; m. Anne C. Berton, 1935. Instr., asst. prof., asso. prof. govt., La. State U., 1926-29, 1931-33; instr. polit. sci., Harvard U., 1930-31, 34-35; asst. prof. polit. sci., Duke U., 1935-37, asso. prof., 1937-45, prof., 1945-53, James B. Duke prof. polit. sci., 1953—, provost, 1960-68, dir. grad. studies in polit. sci., 1947-49; Ford research prof. govt. Harvard U., 1965; editor Jour. Politics, 1945-49, Am. Polit. Sci. Rev., 1950-53; editorial bd. South Atlantic Quar., 1945-60, 69—; cons. to O.M.G.U.S., Germany, summers 1948, 1949; Guggenheim Fellowship, 1946-47; Fullbright Research fellow, Italy, 1952-53. Mem. Social Sci. Research Council, 1952-58; rapporteur Internat. Polit. Sci. Assn. Meeting, Paris, 1953; chmn. com. on British Commonwealth Studies, 1955-60; mem. Fulbright Com. on Internat. Exchange Persons; council Ahmadu Bello Univ., Nigeria, 1964—. Decorated Medal of Freedom. Mem. Am. Polit. Sci. Assn. (pres. 1958-59), Am. Acad. Arts and Scis., So. Polit. Sci. Assn. (pres. 1951-52), Nat. Acad. Scis., Phi Beta Kappa. Democrat. Baptist. Clubs: Cosmos (Washington); Century Assn. (N.Y.C.). Author books including: The Canadian Bureaucracy, 1949; co-author: The Nigerian Political Scene, 1962. Editor and contbr. European Political Systems, 1953, rev. edit., 1959. Co-editor: Post-Primary Education and Political and Economic Development, 1964. Contbr. to profl. jours. Home: 7 Sylvan Rd Durham NC 27701

COLE, ROGER DAVID, educator, biochemist; b. Berkeley, Cal., Nov. 17, 1924; s. Naylor Elmer and Frances (Slankard) C.; B.S., U. Cal. at Berkeley, 1948, Ph.D., 1954; m. Thelma Bennett, July 11, 1944; children—David Naylor, Miriam Faith, Janice Joy. Jr. research biochemist U. Cal. at Berkeley, 1954-55, faculty, 1958—, prof. biochemistry, 1965—, chmn. dept. biochemistry, 1968—; Nat. Found. Infantile Paralysis fellow Nat. Inst. Med. Research, London, Eng., 1955-56; research asso. Rockefeller Inst. Med. Research, N.Y.C., 1956-58; Guggenheim Meml. fellow Lab. for Molecular Biology, Cambridge, Eng., 1966-67. Com. mem., sect. chmn., lectr. sci. confs., 1955—; cons. numerous pubs., 1960—. Mem. A.A.A.S., Am. Soc. Biol. Chemists, Am. Chem. Soc., Sigma Xi. Mem. editorial bd. Archives Biochemistry and Biophysics, 1965—, Biochimica Biophysica Acta, 1966—, Biochemistry, 1971—. Contbr. articles profl. jours. Home: 109 Villa Ct Lafayette CA 94549 Office: Biochemistry Bldg U Cal Berkeley CA 94720

COLE, SANDFORD STODDARD, cons. engr.; b. Cuba, N.Y., Nov. 24, 1900; s. John Browning and Inez (Bassett) C.; B.S., Alfred (N.Y.) U., 1923, M.S., 1933, Ceramic Engr., 1950; Ph.D., Pa. State U., 1934; m. Frances Halderman, July 11, 1925; children—Sandford Stoddard, David Lee, Stephen Hervey. Fellow Mellon Inst., 1923-32; with titanium div. Nat. Lead Co., 1934-65, asst. mgr. research, 1948-65; cons. engr., 1966—. Trustee Alfred U., 1958-61, Engring. Found., 1962-66, dir. research conf., 1966—; dir. Engrs. Joint Council, 1962-65; adv. bd. N.Y. Coll. Ceramics, 1960-65. Recipient Alumni citation Alfred U., 1952. Registered profl. engr., N.J., Pa. Fellow Am. Ceramic Soc., Am. Inst. Chemists; mem. Soc. Mining Engrs. (bd. dirs. 1960-66, pres. 1964-65), Am. Inst. Mining Metall. and Petroleum Engrs. (dir. 1963- 66, v.p. 1965-66), Am. Chem. Soc., Nat. Inst. Ceramic Engrs., Keramos, Sigma Xi, Phi Kappa Phi. Editorial bd. Indsl. Minerals and Rocks, 3d edit., 1960; author tech. papers. Patentee high temperature phys. chemistry, mineral conversions, smelting titaniferous ores, titanium hydrometallurgy, recovery vanadium values, crystal growth, silica refractories, reactions solid state. Home: 636 S Main St Hightstown NJ 08520 Office: PO Box 219 Hightstown NJ 08520

COLE, STERLING, lawyer; b. Painted Post, N.Y., Apr. 18, 1904; s. Ernest Ethelbert and Minnie (Pierce) C.; A.B., Colgate U., 1925, LL.D., 1954; LL.B., Albany Law Sch., Union U., 1929; D.Sc., Union Coll.; LL.D., Elmira Coll.; m. Mary Elizabeth Thomas, July 3, 1929; children—William Sterling, Thomas Ernest, David Aaron. Teacher pub. schs., 1925-26; began practice at Bath, N.Y., 1930, mem. firm Cole & Cole; mem. 74th to 85th Congresses, 39th and 37th N.Y. Dist.; dir. gen. Internat. Atomic Energy Agy., Vienna, Austria, 1957-61; mem. firm Cole and Norris, Washington, 1962—; v.p., dir. Chemtree Corp., Harriman, N.Y., Cambridge Nuclear Corp. (Mass.), Space Research Corp., North Troy, Vt., Sanders Nuclear Corp., Nashua, N.H. Mem. joint com. atomic energy U.S. Congress, 1947- 57, chmn., 1953-54; fed. rep. So. Interstate Nuclear Bd.; mem. Adv. Council for Internat. Studies, Graz, Austria. Trustee Colgate U., 1945-50, Woodlawn Found., Elmira Coll.; bd. advisers Robins Awards Am. Served to lt. comdr. USNR, 1939-59. Decorated Order of Merit (Italy); Gt. Golden Decoration of Honor for Merits (Austria). Mem. Fed., Am., N.Y. State, Steuben County bar assns., Am. Nuclear Soc., Washington Inst. Fgn. Affairs, Phi Beta Kappa, Sigma Nu, Pi Delta Epsilon, Delta Sigma Rho. Republican. Presbyn. (elder). Mason. Clubs: Nat. Lawyers, Sulgrave, Dacor (Washington). Home: 2201 S Knoll Rd Arlington VA 22202 Office: 1737 H St NW Washington DC 20006

COLE, THOMAS CASILEAR, portrait painter; b. Staatsburgh, N.Y.; s. Thomas Lafayette and Jessie Duncan (Savage) C.; student Riverview Mil. Acad., N.Y., 1900-04; studied Boston Mus., Sch. Fine Arts under Philip L. Hale, Frank W. Benson, Edmund C. Tarbell, 1905-11, Academie Julian, Paris, under J.P. Laurens, 1912-13. Portrait painter 1913—; prin. works include: Woodrow Wilson, Herbert Hoover, Theodore Roosevelt, Sir J. Forbes Robertson, E.H. Sothern, Sir Herbert Tree, Judge Alfred C. Coxe, Fed. Ct., N.Y., John L. Cadwalader, Bar Assn., N.Y., Dr. William S. Halsted, Duke U., Judge Edward P. Pierce, Mass. Supreme Court, Pres. Hore, Newton Theol. Sem., Gov. Stickney, Vt. State Capitol, hist. portrait of Col. Taylor, Battle Abbey, Richmond, Va., Frank Murphy, mayor of Detroit, Dr. R. G. Reese, Med. Center, N.Y., Dr. Francis R. Packard, Phila., Gen. Hugh Scott, Gen. Mills, Col. Morris, Col. Peyton, many other prominent men and women; represented in numerous pub. and private collections; also in exhbns. at Nat. Acad. of Design, Pa. Acad. of Fine Arts (Phila.), Metropolitan Mus. Rochester Mus., Art Inst. Chgo., Albright Art Gallery, Buffalo, San Francisco Art Mus., Boston Mus. Fine Arts, Salon, Paris; painted a hist. portrait of President James K. Polk for Bancroft Hall, U.S. Naval Acad. Commd. by State of Tenn. Has also done work in imaginative painting. Served in U.S. Navy, 1917-19; officer U.S. Naval Camauflage Sect. Design, 1918; apptd. comdr. overseas section, U.S. Naval Camouflage, 1918. Instr. portrait painting Phoenix Art Inst., N.Y., 1930-32, N.Y. Sch. Fine and Indsl. Arts, 1932-35. Mem. Soc. of Descendants of Founders of Hartford, Poetry Soc. Am., Rockport Art Assn. of Mass., Am. Fedn. Arts, Am. Legion, S.A.R. Episcopalian. Address: 939 8th Av New York City NY 10019

COLE, THOMAS WINSTON, Sr., coll. pres.; b. Navasota, Tex., Oct. 24, 1915; s. Joseph and Vada Martha (Lewis) C.; B.S., Wiley Coll., 1934; M.S., U. Wis., 1947; Ed.D., U. Tex., 1955; m. Eva M. Sharp, July 7, 1938; children—JoAnn, Thomas Winston, Eva Marie, Margaret Patricia. Prin., Washington High Sch., Vernon, Tex., 1934-44, Washington Elementary Sch., Bryan, Tex., 1944-50; registrar Wiley Coll., Marshall, Tex., 1950-52, dean, 1952-58, pres., 1958—. Mem. Small Bus. Adminstrn. Adv. Council, Marshall; vice chmn. bd. Community Action Program, Harrison-Panola County; co-chmn. Bi-Racial Com. Marshall; mem. Adv. Com. Developing Instns., 1966; mem. Commn. on Presdl. Scholars, 1969-70; panel on edn. AID, 1964; cons. to Dept. State, Bur. Latin Am. Countries, 1964-65; exec. com. United Negro Coll. Fund chmn. bd. trustees Tex. Assn. Developing Colls. Named hon. adm. Tex. Navy. Mem. Am. Assn. Colls., Nat. Assn. Higher Edn., Internat. Platform Speakers, Am. Assn. Higher Edn. (various coms.), A.I.M. (pres.'s council), Alpha Phi Alpha (nat. pres.), Phi Delta Kappa, Alpha Epsilon Boule, Sigma Pi Phi. Mason. Home: Wiley College Marshall TX 75670

COLE, TODD G., financial co. exec.; b. Coushatta, La., Mar. 5, 1921; s. Ira and Lucie (Tricke) C.; student La. State U., 1935-37; LL.B., Woodrow Wilson Coll., 1947; m. Inez Hamilton, Feb. 9, 1953; children—Michael H., Mrs. Kenneth C. Janusz. With Delta Airlines, 1940-63, exec. v.p. adminstrn., 1959-63; sr. v.p. finance and adminstrn., dir. Eastern Airlines, 1963-67, vice chmn., chmn. finance com., bd. dir., 1967-69; v.p., asst. to pres. C.I.T. Financial Corp., N.Y.C., 1969—, dir., 1970—; dir., mem. exec. com. Gt. Internat. Life Ins. Co.; mem. Rockefeller Center adv. bd. Chem. Bank N.Y. Trust Co. Chmn. met. commerce and industry com. Nat. Multiple Sclerosis Soc., 1968-69. Mem. Ga. Bar Assn. Home: 1080 Fifth Av New York City NY 10028 Office: 650 Madison Av New York City NY 10022

COLE, TOM CHARLES THOMAS, author; b. Paterson, N.J., Apr. 8, 1933; s. David Lawrence and Helen (David) C.; A.B. magna cum laude, Harvard, 1954, M.A., 1958; m. Ellen R. Nurnberg, Oct. 24, 1954 (div. 1969); m. 2d, Joyce Kalina, Dec. 21, 1969; 1 dau., Sarah Rose. Tchr., Commonwealth Sch., Boston, 1959-61; instr. modern langs. Mass. Inst. Tech., 1962-63, lectr. humanities, 1965- 69, asso. prof. lit., 1969—. Trustee Theatre Co. Boston, 1963—. Served with AUS, 1954-57. Recipient Atlantic First award Atlantic Monthly mag., 1961; O'Henry prize, 1962, 66, 70, Rosenthal award for fiction Nat. Inst. Arts and Letters, 1966. Jewish religion. Author: An End to Chivalry, 1965. Contbr. short stories Atlantic Monthly, Sat. Eve. Post, Kenyon Rev. Translator: Letter to a Teacher, 1970. Address: 100 Memorial Dr Cambridge MA 02142

COLE, WENDELL GORDON, eductor; b. Chgo., May 15, 1914; s. Herbert F. and Susan (Richards) C.; A.B., Albion (Mich.) Coll., 1936; A.M., U. Mich., 1937; Ph.D., Stanford, 1951; m. Charlotte Clarice Klein, Dec. 14, 1948. Mem. faculty Alma (Mich.) Coll., 1943-45; mem. faculty Stanford, 1946—, prof. speech and drama 1963—, exec. head dept., 1956-59, 64-65, 67-69, scene designer, 1945-65, acting chmn. dept. speech and drama, 1968-69. Mem. Am. Ednl. Theatre Assn., Soc. Archtl. Historians, U.S. Inst. Theatre Tech. Author: The Elements of Scene Design, 1962; Kyoto in the Momoyama Period, 1967; Theatre Architecture, 1970. Editor: The Story of The Meininger, 1963. Home: 853 Esplanada Way Stanford, CA 94305.

COLE, WILLARD W., merchandising exec.; b. Montclair, N.J., 1908. Dir., Lytton's, Henry C. Lytton & Co., Chgo.; pres., chief operating officer retail stores div. Cluett Peabody & Co., Chgo., N.Y.C.; dir. Santa Cruz Industries, Inc. Home: 620 N Linden Av Oak Park IL 60302 Office: 14 E Jackson Blvd Chicago IL 60604

COLE, WILLIAM EARLE, educator; b. Crandull, Tenn., July 28, 1904; s. William S. and Sallie (Johnson) C.; B.S.A., U. Tenn., 1926; A.M., Cornell U., Ithaca, N.Y., 1928, Ph.D., 1930; m. Beulah A. Atchley, Aug. 26, 1933; children—Glenda Mateel, William E. III. Instr. U. Tenn., Nashville, 1926-27, asst. prof. edn., 1930-33, asso. prof. sociology, 1933-36, prof., 1965—, also head dept., 1963-65, on leave to TVA, 1943-47; research asst. in edn. Cornell U., Ithaca, N.Y., 1928-30. Tchr. sociology George Peabody Coll. for Tchrs., Nashville, summer 1930; teacher sociology Cornell U., summer 1941; cons. Tenn. State Dept. Welfare, 1938-39, TVA, 1940-43; sr. soc. sci. analyst, 1944, chief program review and anal. staff, 1945-47; chmn. adv. com. Tenn. Dept. Pub. Welfare, 1949-56; Phi Kappa Phi lectr. U. Tenn., 1959. Mem. Commn. on Interracial Co-op., 1942-44; exec. chmn. Conf. on Tomorrow's Children; dir. Farmers State Bank (Mountain City, Tenn.), Knoxville Co-Op. Assn., Tenn. Crippled Children's Commn., Save the Children Fund; chmn. Met. Planning Commn., 1956-69; mem. Gov.'s Commn. on Aging, 1960—. Mem. Am. Sociol. Soc., So. Sociol. Soc., Tenn. Conf. Social Work (pres. 1937), So. Sociol. Soc. (pres. 1940-41), Tenn. Maternal Health Assn. (pres. 1940-44), Newcomen Soc. of Eng., Knoxville Tech. Soc., Delta Sigma Phi, Phi Delta Kappa, Alpha Phi Epsilon. Presbyn. Rotarian (pres. 1956-57). Author: Teaching of Biology, 1934; Sociology for Schools (with C. S. Montgomery), rev. edits. 1943, 47, 53, 55; Recent Trends in Rural Planning, 1937; Guidebook in Sociology, (with Marvin Kemp), 1939; Tennessee: A Political Study (with William H. Combs), 1940; (with Clyde B. Moore) Sociology in Educational Practice, 1952; Urban Society, 1957; (with C. S. Montgomery) High School Sociology, 1959, rev., 1967; (with Roy L. Cox) Southern Citizenship Problems, 1960; Introductory Sociology, 1962; (with Charles H. Miller) Social Problems: A Sociological Interpretation, 1965; (with Roy L. Cox) Social Foundations of Education, 1968; The Tennessee Citizen (with Ruby Johnson), 1958, rev., 1964; also textbooks in field; bulls. and jour. articles. Editor Dynamic Urban Sociology, 1954, Tenn. Welfare News, 1937-41. Home: 6508 Sherwood Dr Knoxville TN 37919

COLE, WILLIAM GRAHAM, ednl. adminstr.; b. Jamaica, N.Y., Mar. 7, 1917; s. John D. and Helen (Graham) C.; B.A., Columbia, 1940, Ph.D., 1955; B.D., Union Theol. Sem., 1943; LL.D., Grinnell Coll., 1961; D.D., Colgate U., 1963; L.H.D., Hamilton Coll., 1969; m. Doris Williams, Dec. 20, 1941 (div. Sept. 1969); children—William Graham, Edward Morris, Stephen Salisbury; m. 2d, Sally Kintsarver, July 18, 1970. Ordained to ministry Presbyn. Ch., 1942, demitted ministry, 1970; asst. minister Ch. of Covenant, Cleve., also chaplain and lectr. Western Res. U., 1943-46; vis. chaplain Stanford, 1946; counselor Protestant students Columbia, 1946-48; chaplain, asst. prof. religion Smith Coll., 1948-52; dean freshmen, Cluett prof. religion Williams Coll., 1952-60; pres. Lake Forest (Ill.) Coll., 1960-69; exec. dir. Chgo. Council on Fgn. Relations, 1969-71; v.p. acad. affairs Chgo. State U., 1971—. Chmn., Ill. Commn. on Human Relations; dir. Nat. Merit Scholarship Corp., Council Protestant Colls. and Univs. Recipient silver plaque Nat. Conf. Christians and Jews. Fellow Soc. for Religion in Higher Edn.; mem. Phi Beta Kappa. Clubs: University, Caxton, Wayfarers, Commerical (Chgo.). Author: Sex in Christianity and Psychoanalysis, 1955; Sex and Love in the Bible, 1959; The Restless Quest of Modern Man, 1966. Home: 986 Brittany Rd Highland Park IL 60035

COLE, WILLIAM PENDLETON, mfg. co. exec.; b. Sandusky, O., Aug. 3, 1919; s. Robert MacFarlan and Wertha (Pendleton) C.; A.B., Harvard, 1941; LL.B., Temple U., 1949; m. Hilda K. Zanzig, Sept. 14, 1942; children—James, Katharine, Elizabeth, Susan, Peter. Admitted to Pa. bar, 1949; asso. partner Synnestvedt & Lechner, Phila., 1949-64; pres., dir. Polymer Corp., Reading, Pa., 1964- 70; pres., dir. Carmer Industries, Inc., Hanover, N.J., Polypenco Can., Ltd., Acton, Ont., Can.; chmn., dir. Polypenco, Ltd., Welwyn Garden City, Eng.; v.p., dir. Nippom Polypenco, Ltd., Tokyo, Japan; dir. Polypenco Europa N.V., Almelo, Holland, Bank of Pa., Reading. Mgr. Reading Hosp. Served to capt. USAAF, 1941-46, to maj. USAF, 1951-53. Mem. Soc. of Plastics Industry (dir.-at-large), Am., Phila. bar assns., Am., Phila. patent law assns., Franklin Inst. Clubs: Union League (Phila.); Berkshire Country, Wyomissing (Reading). Home: 17 Hickory Dr Doylestown PA 18901 Office: 15 W Oakland Av Doylestown PA 18901

COLE, WILLIAM, R., (Cozy Cole), musician; b. East Orange, N.J., Oct. 17, 1909; s. Reuben and Carrie (Johnson) C.; student Wilberforce U., 1927-30, Juilliard Conservatory Music, 1941; m. Evalena Kiggins, July 18, 1951. With Benny Carter Orchestra, 1934-37, Cab Calloway Orchestra, 1939-42, Raymond Scott Orchestra, 1942-44; actor stage play Carmen Jones, 1944-47; with Benny Goodman's Band, 1945-47, Louis Armstrong, 1949-52; sec., v.p. Gene Krupa and Cozy Cole Music Sch., Inc., N.Y.C. Recipient citation of merit Muscular Dystrophy Assn. Am., Inc., 1956. Mem. Nat. Jazz Frat. (dir.). Mason. Home: 1326 College St Bronx NY 10456 Office: 261 W 54th St New York City NY 10019

COLE, WILTON DONALD, publisher, lawyer; b. St. Paul, Jan. 23, 1903; s. Wilton Francis and Elizabeth L. (McMahon) C.; A.B., Harvard, 1923, postgrad. in law, 1923-24; M.A. (Rhodes scholar), Oxford U., 1926; LL.B., Fordham U., 1929; Sc.D., Detroit Inst. Tech., 1960; m. Gloria Hermandez, Dec. 24, 1943; children—Patricia Scott, Steven Robert. Admitted to N.Y. bar, 1932; with Imbrie & Co., 1926-31; atty. Menken, Ferguson & Hills, N.Y.C., 1931-33, Port of N.Y. Authority, 1933-36; asst. atty. Union Bag-Camp Paper Corp., N.Y.C., 1936-42, counsel, 1945-56, dir., v.p. charge future planning, 1956-57; dir. Crowell-Collier Pub. Co., 1956-64, chmn. bd., 1957-64; chmn. bd. MacMillan Co., 1960-61; pres. Washington Ednl. Research Assos., Inc., 1966—; dir. J. D. Jewell, Inc. Trustee New Coll., Am. Univ., Cairo, New Sch. for Social Research, Morristown (N.J.) Meml. Hosp. Mem. N.Y. County Lawyers Assn., Assn. Bar City N.Y. Club: University (N.Y.C.). Home: Tucson AZ 85702 Office: 2001 Connecticut Av NW Washington DC 20008

COLEAN, MILES LANIER, cons. economist; b. Peoria, Ill., Aug. 4, 1898; s. William Henry and Frances (Putman) C.; student U. Wis., 1916-17; B. Arch., Columbia, 1922; m. Marion Feltman, Jan. 21, 1925; 1 dau., Mary Katherine (Mrs. E.D. Etherington). Asso. with R.H. Dana, architect, N.Y.C., 1922-24, Holabird & Root, Chgo., 1925-29; mem. Cowles, Colean, Architects, Chgo., 1929-34; tech. dir. Fed. Housing Adminstrn., 1934-37, asst. administr., 1937-40; dir. housing survey Twentieth Century Fund, 1940-42; v.p. Starrett Bros. & Eken, Inc., 1942- 44; cons. constrn., finance, 1944—; chmn. Investors Central Mgmt. Corp., 1956—; econ. adviser Mortgage Banker's Assn. Am., 1945—; adviser Central Mortgage & Housing Corp. Can., 1945-55; dir. Walker & Dunlop, Inc.; trustee ICM Realty Trust. Chmn., Am. delegation 16th Internat. Congress on Planning and Housing, Mexico City, 1938; mem. Central Housing Com., 1936-40; cons. Adv. Com. on Nat. Def., 1940, Nat. Resources Planning Board, 1942; bd. govs. Nat. Assn. Housing Ofcls., 1934-42; adviser on housing Senate and House Postwar Policy and Planning Coms., 1944-46; mem. bus. research adv. com. U.S. Bur. Labor Statistics, 1947-60, chmn., 1953- 54; mem. Adminstrn. Bd. Urban Land Use and Housing Studies of Columbia, 1947-49; mem. adv. com. U.S. Bur. Budget, U.S. Census on constrn., housing statistics, 1949-50; mem. Pres.'s Com. on Housing Policies and Programs, 1953; mem. bldg. research adv. bd. NRC, 1950-57; staff Nat. Bur. Econ. Research. 1947-50; chmn. adv. com. housing inventory Bur. Census, 1956; chmn. adv. com. for 1960 housing census Bur. Census, Dept. Commerce; chmn. adv. com. on constrn. statistics Bur. Census, 1960-68; chmn. Pres.'s Task Force on Urban Renewal, 1969-70. Trustee Fed. City Council, 1954—. Recipient Columbia U. medal, 1943. Fellow A.I.A., A.A.A.S., Am. Statis. Soc.; mem. Conf. Bus. Economists (chmn. 1960). Episcopalian (warden 1954-65, vestryman). Clubs: Metropolitan, Chevy Chase, Cosmos (Washington). Author: Can America Build Houses?, 1938; Housing for Defense, 1940; The Role of the Housebuilding Industry, 1942; American Housing: Problems and Prospects, 1944; Stabilizing the Construction Industry, 1945; Impact of Government on Real Estate Finance in the United States, 1950; (with Robinson Newcomb) Stabilizing Construction: The Record and Potential, 1952; Renewing Our Cities, 1953; Mortgage Companies and Their Place in the Financial Structure, 1962; (with R.J. Saulnier) The Federal Land Bank System and the Real Estate Lending Activities of the Farmers Home Administration, 1962. Editorial adviser Architectural Forum, House and Home mags., 1944-64, House Beautiful mag., 1944-68; contbg. editor Savs. Bank Jour., 1959-61. Contbr. to periodicals. Home: 5001 Macomb St Washington DC 20016 Office: 1707 H St NW Washington DC 20006

COLEE, HAROLD WILFRED, former assn. exec.; b. St. Augustine, Fla., Oct. 11, 1894; s. George B. and Maria Louise (King) C.; student Lawrence Sch., 1812; m. Alice Sheldon Gillespie, Sept. 26, 1917; children—Harold Wilfred, Betty. Mgr. pub. relations Fla. East Coast Ry., 1926-31; exec. mgr. pub. affairs Fla. Motor Lines, 1931-39; pres. Fla. C. of C., Jacksonville, 1935-39, dir., mem. exec. com., exec. v.p., gen. mgr., 1939-69. Hon. consul Republic of Panama, 1947-48; bd. dirs. Fla. Ports and Fgn. Trade Council, 1961—; mem. Fla. Indsl. Devel. Council, 1950, Everglades Nat. Park Commn., 1946-50; Fla. chmn. Crusade for Freedom, 1950; mem. nat. adv. bd. Vols. Am., 1956; mem. Fla. adv. council U.S. Commn. on Civil Rights, 1958—, chmn., 1960—; treas. Fla. Assn. for Mental Health, 1962-63. Trustee Harry-Anna Crippled Children's Commn., Jacksonville U.; Fla. trustee United Student Aid Fund, Inc. Decorated knight 2d class Order of White Rose (Finland); recipient numerous awards for pub. service, most recent being citation for distinguished service Fla. Fedn. Women's Clubs, 1955; Cervantes Gold medal Hispanic Inst. Fla., 1956; award of appreciation State of Fla., 1962; named to Fla. Pub. Relations Assn.'s Hall of Fame, 1961. Mem. St. Augustine and St. Johns County C. of C. (hon. life, pres. 1927), St. Augustine Hist. Soc. and Inst. Sci. (hon life, pres. 1931), Fla. Jr. C. of C. (hon.), Delta Sigma Pi (hon.), U. Fla. Blue Key. Democrat. Roman Catholic. Elk, Moose. Clubs: Saint Johns Dinner, Meninak, Timuquana Country, Seminole. Home: 3517 Pine St Jacksonville FL 32205 Office: PO Drawer 8046 Jacksonville FL 32211

COLEFAX, PETER, bus. exec.; b. London, Eng., Mar. 22, 1903; s. Arthur and Sibyl (Halsey) C.; student Eton Coll., 1916-20; B.A., M.A., Oxford, 1921-24; m. Elda Garbe Cook, Aug. 23, 1957; 1 son by previous marriage, Michael; stepchildren— Barbara (Mrs. Willard E. Fay), Penny (Mrs. William J. Gemar). Came to U.S., 1924, naturalized. With New York Times, 1924- 25, Edward B. Smith & Co. (now Smith, Barney & Co.), N.Y., 1925-29; Am. rep. Guinness Mahon & Co., London, Eng., 1929-32; with Cyrus J. Lawrence & Sons, N.Y.C., 1932-34; with Am. Potash & Chemical Corp., N.Y.C., 1934-45, Los Angeles, 1945-69, dir., 1935-69, sec.- treas., 1935-41, v.p., sec.-treas., 1941-44, v.p., sec., 1944-45, exec. v.p., sec., 1945-46, exec. v.p., 1946- 47, pres., 1947-63, chmn., 1960-68, chief exec. officer, 1963-68; now cons., dir. Kerr-McGee Corp.; dir. Security Pacific Nat. Bank, Diners Club, Inc. Diners Club Gt. Britain, Ltd.; mem. adv. com. Investment Co. Am. Clubs: Bohemian (San Francisco); Union League (N.Y.C.); California (Los Angeles). Home: 1636 Moore Rd Montecito CA 93108

COLEGROVE, KENNETH WALLACE educator; b. Waukon, Ia., Oct. 8, 1886; s. Chauncey Peter and Winifred Della (Mack) C.; diploma Ia. State Tchrs. Coll., 1905; A.B., State U. Ia., 1909; Ph.D., Harvard, 1915; Litt.D., Columbia, 1945; m. Louise Burrows, Jan. 5, 1923; 1 dau., Marian Louise (Mrs. John H. Blankenship). Lectr. history Mt. Holyoke Coll., 1913-16; asst. prof. European history, Syracuse (N.Y.) U., 1916-19; asso. prof. polit. sci. Northwestern U., 1919-26, prof., 1926-52; prof. polit. sci. Queens Coll., 1953-54; editor-in-chief Inst. Fiscal and Polit. Edn., N.Y.C., 1954—; prof. history and polit. sci. C.W. Post Coll., L.I. U., 1959—. Mem. Bd. Personnel Examiners, U.S. Dept. Labor, 1933; chmn. Evanston chpt. Com. to Defend Am. by Aiding the Allies, 1940-41; cons. OSS, 1943-45; polit. cons. Gen. MacArthur Hdqrs., Tokyo, 1946. Trustee Upper Ia. U. Mem. Am. Soc. Internat. Law (exec. council), Am. Council Learned Socs. (del. 1952-55), Am. Hist. Assn., Am. Polit. Sci. Assn. (sec.-treas. 1936-1947), Alpha Pi Zeta. Methodist. Clubs: Mens Faculty, Columbia University (N.Y.C.); University (Evanston). Author several books including: The American Senate and World Peace, 1944; Democracy versus Communism, 1957; (with Hall Bartlett) The Menace of Communism, 1962; also articles to profl. jours. Editor European Economic and Political Survey (Paris), 1929. Address: Butler Hall 88 Morningside Dr New York City NY 10027

COLEMAN, ALMAND ROUSE, educator; b. Smithfield, Va., July 16, 1905; s. Archer Almand and Ruby Booth (Rouse) C.; A.B., Washington and Lee U., 1926, B.S. in Commerce, 1927; M.B.A., Harvard, 1934; m. Clare Merryman Whitfield, April 13, 1940 (dec. Jan. 1961); children—Lisa Crane (Mrs. Frederick E. Rose), William Stephen; m. 2d, Louise Hudson Foster, May 21, 1962; stepchildren—Emily (Mrs. John Pickering), Edmund Palmer Foster, George William Foster; 1 son, Charles Almand. Asst. to treas. Wash. and Lee U., 1926-28; sr. accountant A.M. Pullen & Co., Richmond, Va. 1928-33; acting chief, financial analysis and statis. sec. Farm Credit Adminstrn., Washington, 1934-35; asst. trust officer, asst. cashier State Planters Bank and Trust Co., Richmond, 1935-39; asso. prof. Washington and Lee U., 1939-41, prof. accounting, 1941- 55; vis. prof. accounting Harvard Bus. Sch., 1954- 55; prof. bus. adminstrn. U. Va. Grad. Sch. Bus., Charlottesville, 1955- -; cons. contract pricing Army Ordnance Corps, 1951-62. Served to maj. Ordnance, U.S. Army, 1942-45; lt. col. Res., 1950-54. C.P.A., Va. Mem. Am. Inst. C.P.A.'s, (accounting procedure com. 1953-56), Am. Accounting Assn. (v.p. 1956), Financial Execs. Inst., Raven Soc., Phi Beta Kappa. Episcopalian. Author: Financial Accounting: A General Management Approach, 1970. Editor: Bank Operating Forms and Procedures, 1940. Contbr. to bus. and profl. jours. Home: 1867 Field Rd Charlottesville VA 22903

COLEMAN, AMOSS LEE, educator, sociologist; b. Devereaux, Ga., Jan. 3, 1913; s. John Amoss and Magnolia (Lee) C.; B.A., Emory U., 1937; M.A., U. N.C., 1940; Ph.D., Cornell U., 1949; m. Alberta Louise Nelson, Dec. 11, 1943; children—Nancy Louise, Martha Lee. Research analyst Govtl. Research Inst., St. Louis, 1938-39; social sci. analyst, farm population, rural life br. U.S. Dept. Agr., Atlanta, also Freeport, Ill., 1939-42, 45-46; grad. asst. dept. rural sociology Cornell U., 1946-49; asst. prof. U. Ky., 1949-53, asso. prof., 1953-57, prof., 1957—, head, later chmn. dept. sociology, 1959-66; cons. so. regional council State Commn. on Human Rights; state adv. com. U.S. Civil Rights Commn., 1963-66. Served with AUS, 1942-45. Mem. Am. Sociol. Assn., Rural (pres. 1964-65), So. (pres. 1966-67) sociol. socs. Democrat. Contbr. profl. jours. Home: 316 Cassidy Av Lexington KY 40502

COLEMAN, BEATRICE, apparel mfg. co. exec.; b. Jersey City, 1916; grad. Barnard Coll., 1938; married. Pres. Maidenform, Inc., N.Y.C. Home: 5051 Iselin Av New York City NY 10471 Office: 90 Park Av New York City NY 10016

COLEMAN, BERNARD DAVID, educator, mathematician; b. N.Y.C., July 5, 1930; s. Nathaniel and Pauline (Listain) C.; B.S. cum laude, Ind. U., 1951; M.S., Yale, 1952, Ph.D., 1954; m. Jane Winthrop Candia, Mar. 27, 1965; children—David Augustus, Daniel Nathan. Research chemist E.I. duPont de Nemours & Co., Wilmington, Del., 1954-57; sr. fellow Mellon Inst., Pitts., 1957—; prof. math. Carnegie-Mellon U., 1967—; visitor Istituto Matematico, Università di Bologna (Italy), 1960-61; vis. prof. Johns Hopkins, 1962-63; adj. prof. U. Pitts., 1964-65; vis. lectr. U. Manchester (Eng.), summer 1965, Università di Pisa (Italy), summer 1966-70, Scuola Normale Superiore, Pisa, 1969, 70. Mem. Soc. Natural Philosophy (chmn. 1971-72). Author: (with H. Markovitz, W. Noll) Viscometric Flows of Non-Newtonian Fluids, 1965. Editorial bd. The Archive for Rational Mechanics and Analysis, 1962—. Editor-in-chief Springer Tracts in Natural Philosophy, 1967—. Research, numerous publs. in hydrodynamics of non-classical fluids, founds. of thermodynamics, theory of wave propagation in materials with memory, biophysics; developed gen. theory of fading memory in non-linear materials. Office: 4400 5th Av Pittsburgh PA 15213

COLEMAN, BERTRAM, investment banker; b. Phila., 1920; ed. Yale, 1942. Co-chmn. exec. com. , dir. Drexel-Harriman-Ripley, Inc.; dir. B.V.D. Co., Wyomissing Corp., Western Sav. Bank, Abitibi Paper Co., Ltd., Susan Thomas, Inc., Rockowan Bros.; trustee Greenfield Real Estate Investment Trust. Home: 1054 Rock Creek Rd Bryn Mawr PA 19010 Office: 60 Broad St New York City NY 10004*

COLEMAN, CLARENCE, banker; b. Wichita, Kan., Mar. 24, 1909; s. William Coffin and Fanny Lucinda (Sheldon) C.; student Culver Mil. Acad., 1924-25, U. Kan., 1928-32; m. Emry Begester Inghram, Oct. 2, 1935; children—Rochelle, Pamela, Kathryn Sheldon. With the Coleman Co., Inc., Wichita, Kan., 1932—, v.p. charge mfg., 1944, dir., 1935—, asst. gen. mgr., 1951-54; pres., vice chmn. bd. Union Nat. Bank, Wichita, 1957—; chmn. bd., dir. Cherry Creek Inn, Inc., Denver, Kan. Devel. Credit Corp. Bd. dirs. Inst. Logopedics, 1940—, chmn. bd., 1947-48; bd. dirs. Wichita Symphony Soc.; trustee Wichita Symphony Soc. Found.; bd. dirs. Found. for Study of Cycles, Pitts.; bd. dirs. Wichita Mental Health Assn., 1956—. United Fund Wichita and Sedgewick County, 1957—. Friends U., 1956—; bd. dirs. Wichita Crime Commn., 1953—, pres. 1958; mem. Nat. Budget Com., 1952; chmn. State Mental Health Fund. Kansas, 1953. Mem. bd. incorporators Peddie Sch., Hightstown, N.J. Mem. Mid-Ark. Valley Devel. Assn. (treas.), Wichita C. of C. (pres. 1956, dir. 1947—), Ohio Soc. Advancement of Mgmt., Nat. Assn. Mfrs., Phi Kappa Psi. Rotarian. Home: 530 Broadmoor Ct Wichita KS 67206 Office: 1005 Union Center Wichita KS 67202

COLEMAN, CY, pianist, composer; b. N.Y.C., June 14, 1929; s. Max and Ida (Prizent) Kaufman; diploma N.Y. Coll. Music, 1948; pvt. student with Rudolph Gruen, Adele Marcus, Bernard Wagenaar, Hall Overton. Pianist night clubs throughout U.S. 1948—; TV appearances on Dumont, 1947-48, Date in Manhattan, 1948-51, Kate Smith Show, 1951-52, Art Ford Greenwich Village Party, 1957-58; contbr. music John Murray Anderson's Almanac, 1953; background music to Compulsion, 1957; composer music for Wildcat, 1960, Little Me, 1962, motion pictures Father Goose, The Art of Love, Sweet Charity, N.Y.C., 1965-66, movie version, 1969; rec. artist for Seeco, Jubilee, Westminster, Everest, Capitol, Columbia, M.G.M. records; pres. Notable Music Co., Notable Records Co. Recipient Interborough awards Music Edn. League, 1934, 35, 36, LaGuardia Meml. award, 1961. Composer popular songs: Why Try to Change Me Now, 1952; I'm Gonna Laugh You out of My Life, 1955; Witchcraft, 1957; Firefly, 1958; It Amazes Me, 1958; You Fascinate Me So, 1958; The Best is Yet to Come, 1959; The Rivera, 1959; Play Boy Theme, 1960; Rules of the Road, 1961; Pass Me By, Pussy Cat. Mem. A.S.C.A.P. (dir.), Acad. Motion Picture Arts and Scis., Dramatists Guild. Office: 161 W 54th St New York City NY 10023

COLEMAN, DELBERT WILLIAM, investor; b. Cleve., Sept. 19, 1925; s. Nathan and Rose (Gertzman) C.; A.B., Harvard, 1948; LL.B., U. Pa., 1952; div.; children—Neil S., Susan. Admitted to Ohio, Pa. bars; pres. Enness Realty Corp., Chgo.; part owner Atlanta Braves, Inc. Mem. Am., Akron bar assns., Youg Pres.'s Orgn., Harvard Alumni Assn. Home: 175 E Delaware Pl Chicago IL 60611

COLEMAN, EDMUND BENEDICT, univ. dean; b. Columbia, S.C., Mar. 29, 1926; s. Edmund Benedict and Evelyn (Russell) C.; B.S., U. S.C., 1958; Ph.D., Johns Hopkins, 1961; m. Fumiko Toyoshita, Jan. 1, 1953; children—Merl, John Edmund, Evelyn. Research scientist Humrro, Ft. Bliss, Tex., 1961-62; asso. prof. Sul Ross State Coll., Alpine, Tex., 1962-64, N.M. State U., Las Cruces, 1964- 64; prof. psychology, chmn. dept. U. Tex. at El Paso, 1965-67, grad. dean 1967—, Mem. Am. Psychol. Assn., Internat. Reading Assn., Phi Beta Kappa, Sigma Xi. Spl. research pre-sch. reading. Home: 1001 Baltimore St El Paso TX 79902

COLEMAN, ELLIOTT, educator; b. Binghamton, N.Y., Sept. 26, 1906; s. Benjamin Archibald and Jennie (Galbraith) C.; B.A., Wheaton (Ill.) Coll., 1928; postgrad. Princeton Theol. Sem., 1933; diaconate Gen. Theol. Sem., N.Y.C., 1941. Master, Asheville (N.C.) Sch., 1928-32, 34-40; with Henry Holt & Co., 1942-43, Doubleday & Co., 1944-45; faculty Johns Hopkins, Balt., 1945—, prof. English Writing, 1960—, dir. writing seminars, 1946—. Hon. mem. Phi Beta Kappa. Author: (poems) An American in Augustland, 1940, A Glass Darkly, 1952, 33 Night Sonnets, 1955, Mockingbirds at Fort McHenry, 1963, Broken Death, 1964, Rose Demonics: 1936-66, 1967; (prose) The Golden Angel: Papers on Proust, 1954. Translator: (George Poulet) Studies in Human Time, 1956-59. Editor: Poems of Byron, Keats and Shelley, 1968. Home: 3201 N Charles St Baltimore, MD 21218.

COLEMAN, FRANCIS CARTER, physician; b. Jackson, Miss., May 14, 1915; s. Francis Marion and Emma (Carter) C.; B.A., Miss. Coll., 1935; M.D., Tulane U., 1941; m. Ruth Yvonne Ellzey, Sept. 2, 1937; children-Nancy Ruth, Stephen Carter, John Timothy, Jeanne Laurie. Intern Touro Infirmary, New Orleans, 1941-42, resident pathology, 1942-45; pvt. practice, Des Moines, 1946-64; dir. dept. pathology Mercy Hosp., Des Moines, 1946-64; asst. clin. prof. pathology U. Neb. Coll. Medicine, 1951; clin. prof. pathology U. Ia. Coll. Medicine, 1964-65; pvt. practice, Tampa, Fla., 1964—; dir. Tampa Sch. Med. Tech., 1954—; mem. staff Centro-Asturiano Hosp., Tampa, Centro-Espanol Hosp., Tampa, Tarpon (Fla.) Springs Hosp., W. Pasco Hosp., New Port Richey, Fla., Citrus Meml. Hosp., Inverness, Fla., Leesburg (Fla.) Gen. Hosp., N. Orange Hosp., Apopka, Fla., Jackson Meml. Hosp., Dade City, Fla., Hardee Meml. Hosp., Wauchula, Fla., DeSota Meml. Hosp., Arcadia, Fla. Dir. Patterson Coleman Labs., Tampa. Bd. dirs. Gulf Symphony. Recipient Sci. Products award for outstanding service to pathology, 1965. Diplomate Am. Bd. Pathology. Fellow A.M.A. (chmn. council legislative activities 1963-64, chmn. polit. action com. 1965- 66, chmn. subcom. certification, registration and licansure of counci health manpower 1967—), Coll. Am. Pathologists (pres. 1960-61), Am. Soc. Clin. Pathologists, A.C.P., Am. Coll. Chest Physicians; mem. Am. Assn. Blood Banks (pres. 1968-69), A.A.A.S., Soc. Nuclear Medicine, Am. Soc. Cytology, Fla. Med. Assn. (chmn. com. blood 1969—), Hillsborough County Med. Soc. (ex-council 1965—), Tampa C. of C. (chmn. health and welfare council 1969-70). Rotarian. Home: Box 737 Route 2 Lutz FL 33545 Office: 4600 N Habana Tampa FL 33614

COLEMAN, GEORGE, tenor and alto saxophonist; b. Memphis, Mar. 8, 1935; s. George and Indiana (Lyle) C.; ed. pub. schs.; m. Gloria Bell, Aug. 3, 1959; children—George, Gloria. Mem. Max Roach Quintet, 1958-59, Miles Davis Quintet, 1963- 64, Lionel Hampton Orch., 1965-66, Lee Morgan Quintet, 1969, Elvin Jones Quartet, 1970; cons. Lenox (Mass.) Jazz Sch. Music, 1958—. Selected by Internat. Jazz Critics Poll, 1958; named Artist of Year, Record World Mag., 1969. Writer, arranger mus. shows. Address: 331 E 14th St New York City NY 10003

COLEMAN, HENRY CRIM, banker; b. Columbia, S.C., June 5, 1904; s. Lewis Andrew and Mary Ella (Crim) C.; B.S., Clemson U., 1926; postgrad. Cornell U., 1931-32; m. Sara Goodman McHugh, Aug. 22, 1928; children—Mary Anne (Mrs. David C. Jackson), Henry Crim. Engaged in wholesale and retail oil bus., 1926-29; tchr. Dillon (S.C.) high sch., 1929-33; asst. statistician FCA, 1933-37; with Comml. Bank Daytona Beach (Fla.), and predecessor, 1937—, pres., 1952-60, chmn. bd., 1960—; chmn. bd. Peninsula State Bank Daytona Beach Shore, 1963—; pres. Comco, Inc., Daytona Beach, 1960—; exec. v.p. Nameloc, Inc., Daytona Beach, 1959—; v.p. Exchange Bank Holly Hill (Fla.), 1962—. mem. bd. annuities and relief Presbyn. Ch. of U.S. Pres., Clemson U. Found.; v.p. Fla. Tech. U. Found.; trustee Fla. Presbyn. Coll. Served to lt. col. AUS, World War II. Mem. Fla. Bankers Assn. (past pres.), U. S. (chmn. banking and monetary policy com., v.p., dir.), Fla. (past pres.), Daytona Beach (past pres.) chambers commerce, Daytona Beach Area Execs. Club, Am. Legion, Elk, Rotarian (pres. Daytona Beach). Clubs: Citrus (Orlando); Oceanside Country; River (Jacksonville, Fla.). Home: 415 Revilo Blvd Daytona Beach FL 32018 Office: PO Box 2120 Daytona Beach FL 32015

COLEMAN, HOWARD S., engineer, physicist; b. Everett, Pa., Jan. 10, 1917; s. Howard Solomon and Amy (Ritchey) C.; B.S., Pa. State U., 1938, M.S. in Physics, 1939, Ph.D., 1942; children—Michael Howard, Madeline Frances, Thomas Robert, Carl William; m. 2d, Jeannette Eve Mozes, Dec. 27, 1969. Faculty, Pa. State U., 1934-47, dir. optical inspection lab., 1941-47; with optical research lab., asso. prof. physics U. Tex., 1947-51; with Bausch & Lomb, Inc., 1951-62, mgr., v.p. research and engring., 1954-62; head physics research dept., tech. asst. to v.p. charge research Melpar, Inc., Falls Church, Va., 1962-64; dean U. Ariz. Coll. Engring., prof. elec. engring., 1964-68; dir. Spl. Projects Center, Schellenger Research Labs., U. Tex., El Paso, 1968—. Cons. industry, govt., 1941—; spl. research optical inspection devices; mem. Ariz. Bd. Tech. Registration. Mem. adv. vis. com. electronics U. Rochester, 1952; chmn. vis. com. math. Clarkson Coll. Tech., 1953-63. Recipient Joint Service award, 1942. Registered profl. engr., Va., Ariz. Fellow Optical Soc. Am.; mem. Am. Phys. Soc., Meteorol. Soc., Inst. Aero. Scis., Am. Assn. Physics Tchrs., Am. Soc. Metals, Internat. Commn. Optics, Am. Geophys. Union, Am. Inst. Physics, Am. Soc. Engring. Edn., Nat. Soc. Profl. Engrs. Patentee in field. Home: 6400 Edgemore Blvd El Paso, TX 79925.

COLEMAN, JACK WILBUR, coll. dean; b. Wamego, Kan., Apr. 28, 1923; s. Harold Leslie and Gladys (Cosley) C.; B.S., U. Kan., 1947; M.B.A., U. Mich., 1953; D.B.A., Ind. U., 1958; m. Sara Martha Russell, Aug. 25, 1946; children—Linda Jane (Mrs. Barry Powell), Deborah Ann. Commd. 2d lt. USAF, 1944, advanced through grades to col. 1964; rated command pilot and navigator; controller Hdqrs. Air Force Logistics Command, 1958-62, procurement officer, 1962-65; ret., 1966; head accounting dept. Tex. A. and M. U., 1966-68; dean Sch. Bus. Adminstrn. and Econs., Cal. State Coll., Fullerton, 1968—. Decorated D.F.C., Air medal with two oak leaf clusters; recipient prize for outstanding articles of year Fed. Govt. Accounting Rev., 1960, Outstanding Citizen award Fullerton C. of C., 1969. Mem. Am. Accounting Assn., Am. Econ. Assn., Fed. Govt. Accounting Assn., Financial Execs. Inst., Fullerton C. of C. (dir.), Beta Gamma Sigma, Beta Alpha Psi. Contbr. articles profl. jours. Home: 1269 Miramar Dr Fullerton CA 92631

COLEMAN, JAMES A., hosp. adminstr. Adminstr., Eastern State Hosp., Lexington, Ky. Office: 627 W 4th St Lexington KY 40508*

COLEMAN, JAMES COVINGTON, educator, author; b. Salem, N.H., Oct. 19, 1914; s. J.C. and Mary (Lillie) C.; B.A. with highest honors, U. Cal. at Los Angeles, 1938, Ph.D. in Psychology, 1942; m. Betty Collins, Oct. 28, 1961. Asst. personnel dir., chief psychol. research cons., engring. research div. Douglas Aircraft Co., 1943-45; instr. psychology U. Kan., 1945-47; asst. prof., dir. psychology clinic U. N.M., 1946-47; asst. prof. U. So. Cal., 1948-50; dir. psychology clinic sch., asst., asso., then prof. psychology U. Cal. at Los Angeles, 1950-65, prof. psychology, prof. edn., 1964—; cons. in field, 1942—. Chmn. research com., statewide acad. senate U. Cal., 1970—; cons. children's div. Camarillo State Hosp. Diplomate Am. Bd. Profl. Psychology. Fellow Am. Psychol. Assn.; mem. N.Y. Acad. Scis., A.A.A.S., Am. Acad. Polit. and Social Sci., Nat. Acad. Polit. Sci., Nat. Council Family Relations, Day Care and Child Devel. Council Am., Am. Assn. for Higher Edn., Am. Assn. U. Profs., Western, Cal., Los Angeles psychol. assns., Phi Beta Kappa, Sigma Xi, Pi Gamma Mu, Phi Delta Kappa, Delta Chi. Author: Personality Dynamics and Effective Behavior, 1960; Psychology and Effective Behavior, 1969; co-author Abnormal Psychology and Modern Life, 1950, 4th edit., 1972; Deep Sea Adventure Series, 3d edit., 1967; also research articles. Mem. bd. cons. editors Personality: An Internat. Jour. Home: 20178 Rockport Way Malibu CA 90265 Office: Dept Psychology Univ Coll 405 Hilgard Av Los Angeles CA 90024

COLEMAN, JAMES DANIEL STETSON, financial exec.; b. Macon, Ga., Sept. 29, 1904; s. Samuel Taylor and Edith Dean (Stetson) C.; grad. Phillips Exeter Acad., 1923; A.B., Yale, 1927; M.B.A., Harvard, 1929; m. Dorothy Wooden, Dec. 11, 1944. Chmn. bd. Coleman-Meadows Pate Wholesale Drug Co., Macon, 1949—, Cities Transit Inc. of Fla., Lakeland, 1950—; chmn. finance com. Fannie May Candy Co., Chgo., 1945—; part-owner Los Angeles Angels Baseball Team, 1960—, Los Angeles Rams Football Team, 1961—; chmn. finance com. Gulf Gas Corp., 1966—; finance chmn. Pennzoil United, Inc.; dir. Comml. Solvents Corp. Served to maj. USMCR, 1941-45; PTO. Mem. Chi Psi. Episcopalian. Clubs: Racquet and Tennis, Brook (N.Y.C.); Chevy Chase (Md.); Burning Tree (Washington); Cypress Point (Cal.); Seminole, Indian Creek (Gulf Stream, Fla.); Pacific Union (San Francisco); Links (N.Y.C.). Home: Archwood Farm The Plains VA 22171 Office: 1137 W Jackson Blvd Chicago IL 60607

COLEMAN, JAMES JULIAN, lawyer, banker; b. New Orleans, May 5, 1915; s. William Ballin and Millie (Davis) C.; B.A., Tulane U., 1934, J.D., 1937; m. Dorothy Louise Jurisich, July 30, 1940; children-James Julian, Thomas Blaise, Peter Dee, Dian Judith. Admitted to La. bar, 1937; sr. partner firm Clay, Coleman, Dutrey & Thomson, New Orleans. Pres. Internat. Tank Terminals, Ltd., Internat. Tank Terminals, Ltd., Karachi, W. Pakistan and Chittagong, E. Pakistan; sr. v.p. New Orleans East, Inc.; chmn. bd. Internat. City Bank & Trust Co., Loving Enterprises, Civic Center Devel. Co., Inc.; dir. New Orleans & Lower Coast R.R.Co.; v.p., gen. counsel Internat. Trade Mart. Past pres. New Orleans C. of C.; past bd. dirs. U.S. C. of C.; past mem. exec. com., internat. relations com. Miss. Valley World Trade Council; past chmn. New Orleans coordinating com. NASA; past pres. Jr. Achievement New Orleans. Trustee Principia Coll.; mem. bd., bus. adminstrn. adv. bd. Tulane U.; pres. Adult Edn. Center; trustee Cordell Hull Found., Loving Found., Bradley Family Found.; past bd. dirs. Met. Safety Council, Internat. House, Fed. Relations Assn., La. Civil Service League. Mem. Am., Internat., La., New Orleans bar assns. Christian Scientist (1st reader 1953-56). Home: 10 Audubon Pl New Orleans LA 70118 Office: 321 St Charles Av New Orleans LA 70130

COLEMAN, JAMES PLEMON, U.S. judge; b. Ackerman, Miss., Jan. 9, 1914; s. Thomas A. and Jennie Essie (Worrell) C.; student U. Miss., 1932-35; LL.B., George Washington U., 1939, LL.D., 1960; m. Margaret Janet Dennis, May 2, 1937; 1 son, Thomas Allen. Sec. to Rep. Aaron Lane Ford, Washington, 1935-39; admitted to Miss. bar, 1937, since practiced in Ackerman; dist. atty. 5th circuit Ct., Dist. of Miss., 1940-46, circuit judge, 1946-50; commr. Supreme Ct. of Miss., Sept. 1 to Oct. 23, 1950; atty. gen., Miss., 1950- 56; gov. Miss., 1956-60; mem. Miss. Ho. Reps. from Choctaw County, 1960- 65; judge U.S. Ct. Appeals 5th Circuit, 1965—. Publisher Choctaw Plaindealer, weekly, 1949-56. Trustee Miss. Coll., 1952-56. Democrat (presdl. elector 1944). Baptist. Mason (Shriner). Home: Ackerman MS 39735 Office: 115 E Quinn Av Ackerman MS 39735

COLEMAN, JAMES SAMUEL, educator, sociologist; b. Bedford, Ind., May 12, 1926; s. James Fox and Maurine (Lappin) C.; student Emory and Henry Coll., 1944-46; B.S., Purdue U., 1949; Ph.D., Columbia, 1955; m. Lucille Richey, Feb. 5, 1949; children—Thomas Sedgwick, John Samuel, James Stephen. Research asso. Bur. Applied Social Research, Columbia, 1953-55; fellow Center Advanced Study Behavorial Scis., Palo Alto, Cal., 1955-56; asst. prof. sociology U. Chgo., 1956-59; asso. prof., prof. social relations Johns Hopkins, 1959—. Mem. Am. Sociol. Assn., Nat. Acad. Edn., Am. Acad. Arts and Scis. Author: (with Lipset, Trow) Union Democracy, 1956; Community Conflict, 1957; The Adolescent Society, 1961; Introduction to Mathematical Sociology, 1964; Models of Change and Response Uncertainty, 1964; Adolescents and the Schools, 1965; (with others) Equality of Education Opportunity, 1966. Home: 207 Ridgemede Rd Baltimore MD 21210

COLEMAN, JAMES SAMUEL, Jr., justice; b. Mobile, Ala., June 8, 1906; s. James Samuel and Mary Belle (Peteet) C.; student Marion Inst. Ala.; B.S., U.S. Naval Acad., 1927; postgrad. U. Ala. Law Sch.; m. Eleanor Ruth Montgomery, Sept. 17, 1933 (dec. Oct. 1959); 1 son, James Samuel III; m. 2d, Mary Ruth Morgan Hobbs, Feb. 20, 1965. Admitted to Ala. bar, 1934; practiced in Eutaw, 1934-57; asso. justice Supreme Ct. of Ala., 1957—. Mem. Ala. Senate, 1946-50, 54-56. Served as lt. comdr. USNR, 1942-45. Mem. V.F.W., Am. Legion. Presbyn. Lion. Home: 2803 Woodley Rd Montgomery AL 36111 Office: Jud Bldg Montgomery AL 36104

COLEMAN, JOHN A., stock broker, civic worker; b. N.Y.C., Dec. 24, 1901; s. John A. and Nora (O'Connor) C.; student Holy Trinity Sch., 1907-15; LL.D., Manhattan Coll., Niagara U., St. Anselm's Coll., Notre Dame U., Fordham U., Manhattanville Coll., Marymount Coll., Syracuse (N.Y.) U.; D.C.S., Holy Cross; Ph.D. in Bus. Adminstrn., Providence Coll.; m. Ann Meehan, June 7, 1930; children—John A., Thomas, Mary Ann (Mrs. Harry C. Hagerty, Jr.). Floor page N.Y. Stock Exchange, 1916; mem. N.Y. Curb Exchange, 1923-24; mem. N.Y. Stock Exchange, 1924—, gov. 1938-43, 48—, vice chmn. bd., 1941-43, chmn., 1943-47; partner Adler, Coleman & Co.; dir. Chrysler Corp., Mfrs. Hanover Trust Co., East River Savs. Bank, N.Y. Telephone Co; chmn. exec. com. Am. Broadcasting-Paramount Theatres; dir. Gen. Aniline & Film Corp. Pres. bd. N.Y. Foundling Hosp.; trustee Cath. U. Am., Washington, Altman Found., Alfred E. Smith Meml. Found. Exec. Chmn. Cardinal's Com. of Laity. Trustee Cath. Charities, Inc. Decorated knight St. Gregory the Great; knight of the Order of Malta (pres.-master); Grand Cross Equestrian Order Holy Sepulchure; recipient Cath. Action medal St. Bonaventure's Coll., Saint Vincent de Paul, St. John's U., Bklyn.; Brotherhood award Nat. Conf. Christians and Jews, Papal Chamberlain, 1957. Mem. Friendly Sons of St. Patrick (past pres.). Clubs: Athletic, Manhattan (N.Y.C.); Bathing and Tennis, Spring Lake (N.J.) Golf and Country. Home: 812 Park Av New York City NY 10021 Office: Adler Coleman & Co 20 Broadway New York City NY 10005

COLEMAN, JOHN H., banker; b. Nova Scotia, Can., Mar. 22, 1912; s. William Bartholomew and Rosalie (Comeau) C.; ed. pub. sch.; m. Kathryn Marguerite Mitchell, Sept. 12, 1939; children—Kathryn Claire (Mrs. J.H. Green), Gerald Francis. With Royal Bank Can., 1928—, exec. v.p., 1969—, dep. chmn., exec. v.p., 1970—; dir. Ben's Holdings Ltd., Domco Industries Ltd., Hall Corp. (Shipping) 1969 Ltd., Hunter Douglas Ltd., N.W. Nitro-Chems. Ltd., N.S. Light & Power Co. Ltd., PurOlater Productus (Can.) Ltd., Royal Bank Can. (France), Royal Bank Can. Trust Co., Royal Bank Can. Trust Corp. Ltd., London, Eng., Siebens Oil & Gas Ltd., Trans Can. Pipelines Ltd., Westburne Internat. Industries Ltd. Bd. dirs. Donwood Found., Mt. Allison U., St. Michael's Coll. Found. Home: 561 Avenue Rd Toronto 195 Ontario Canada Office: 20 King St W Toronto Ontario Canada

COLEMAN, JOHN JAMES, Jr., lawyer; b. Montreal, Que., Can., Aug. 10, 1926; s. John James and Mary (Lecky) C.; came to U.S., 1926, student Auburn U., 1944-45; A.B., Duke, 1947, LL.B., 1950; m. Vonceil Oden Foster, Sept. 2, 1954; children-John James III, A. Key. Daniel B., J. Carey. Admitted to Ala. bar, 1950 since practiced in Birmingham, asso. White, Bradley, Arant, All & Rose, 1950- 57; partner Bradley, Arant, Rose & White, 1957—; part-time prof. law Cumberland Law Sch., Samford U., 1966—; chmn. Ala. alumni admissions com. Duke, 1968—, mem. bd. Alumni Council, Duke Law Sch., 1970—. Mem. Am., Ala.,Birmingham bar assns., Am. Judicature Soc., Asso. Indsl. Ala., Newcomen Soc., Phi Delta Phi, Sigma Alpha Epsilon. Republican. Roman Catholic. Clubs: Mountain Brook (Ala.); Relay House (Birmingham). Home: 3844 Glencoe Dr Birmingham AL 35213 Office: Brown-Mark Bldg Birmingham AL 35203

COLEMAN, JOHN PHILLIPS, banker; b. Roanoke, Va., Jan. 21, 1903; s. John William and Sarah Alice (Phillips) C.; B.S., U. Va., 1926; m. Jewell Bowles, Apr. 14, 1934. Credit dept. Bankers Trust Co. of N.Y., 1926-34, asst. treas., 1934-38; asst. v.p. First & Mchts. Nat. Bank, Richmond, Va., 1938-42, v.p., 1942- 52, sr. v.p., 1952-62, pres., chief adminstrv. officer, 1962-66, chmn. bd., chief exec. officer, 1966-68, hon. chmn. bd., 1968-69, dir.; dir. Lea Industries, Inc., Richmond, Brenco, Inc.; adv. dir. Am. Filtrona Corp. Bd. dirs. Va. Bd. Health. Mem. Sigma Phi Epsilon, Delta Sigma Pi, Beta Gamma Sigma. Presbyn. Mason, Kiwanian. Clubs: Commonwealth, Country of Virginia (Richmond). Home: 312 St Davids Lane Richmond VA 23221 Office: First & Mchts Nat Bank Richmond VA 23219

COLEMAN, JOHN ROYSTON, coll. pres.; b. Copper Cliff, Ont., Can., June 24, 1921; s. Richard Mowbray and Mary Irene (Lawson) C.; B.A., U. Toronto, 1943; M.A., U. Chgo., 1949, Ph.D., 1950; LL.D., Beaver Coll., 1963; LL.D., U. Pa., 1968; m. Mary N. Irwin, Oct. 1, 1943 (div. 1967); children—John M., Nancy, Patty, Paul R., Stephen W.; m. 2d, Elizabeth Barrett Terry, June 30, 1970. Came to U.S., 1946, naturalized, 1954. Research asso. U. Chgo., 1947-49; instr. econs. Mass. Inst. Tech., 1949-51, asst. prof., 1951-55; asso. prof., asst. head dept. econs. Carnegie Inst. Tech., 1955-60, prof., head dept. econs., 1960-63, dean div. humanities and social sci., 1963-65; asso. dir. econ. devel. and adminstrn. Ford Found., 1965-66, program officer in charge social devel., 1966-67; pres. Haverford (Pa.) Coll., 1967—. Dir. Fed. Res. Bank Phila. Labor arbitrator, cons., 1953—; cons. indsl. relations research Ford Found. in India, 1960-61; tchr. Am. Economy, CBS-TV, 1962-63. Mem. Commn. on Study of Peace, 1968—. Trustee Com. for Econ. Devel., AFL-CIO Labor Studies Center, Mountain Sch., Vershire, Vt., Meadville Theol. Sch., Chgo., N.A.A.C.P. Spl. Devel. Fund, Carlow Coll.; bd. dirs. Fellowship Commn. Phila., Council on Founds.; overseer William Penn Charter Sch., 1968—; vice chmn. Joint Council Econ. Edn., 1969—. Served with Royal Canadian Navy, 1943-45. Mem. Indsl. Relations Research Assn., Am. Econ. Assn. Unitarian (pres. ch. 1959-60). Author: Goals and Strategy in Collective Bargaining, 1951; Readings in Economics, 1952, 55, 58, 64, 67; Labor Problems, 1953, 59; Working Harmony, 1955; The Changing American Economy, 1967; Comparative Economic Systems, 1968. Mem. editorial adv. bd. World Book Ency., 1968—. Home: 1 College Circle Haverford PA 19041

COLEMAN, JOHN SHERRARD, orgn. exec.; b. Oahu, T.H., Jan. 15, 1914; s. Sherrard and Mary Comstock (Griswold) C.; B.S., Coll. William and Mary, 1935; M.S., Mass. Inst. Tech., 1940; m. Beverly Reynolds Bridge, Dec. 24, 1944; children—Sherrard, Deborah Reynolds. Residential constrn. and design, 1936-38; mem. Nat. Def. Research Com., 1940-43; research asso. Harvard, 1943-44; London rep. OSRD, 1944; div. war research Columbia U., 1945-46; com. underseas warfare NRC, 1947-53; prof. engring. research Pa. State U., 1953; exec. sec. div. phys. scis. Nat. Acad. Scis.-NRC, 1953-65; exec. officer Nat. Acad. Scis., Washington, 1965—. Chmn. acoustics panel Research and Devel. Bd., 1952-53; cons. Air Research and Devel. Command, 1952-53, Office Sec. Def., 1953-55; chmn. Pres.'s Com. for Local Action in Sci. and Engring. Recipient Meritorious Pub. Service award, 1958. Clubs: Fairfax Country, Cosmos. Home: 3010 N Florida St Arlington VA 22207 Office: 2101 Constitution Av NW Washington DC 20025

COLEMAN, JOHN SHIELDS, banker; b. Jasper, Ala., Nov. 13, 1894; s. E.W. and Nancy (Shields) C.; student U. Ala. 1912-23, LL.B. 1915; student spl. session Harvard Grad. Sch., 1929; m. Gertrude Davidson, July 7, 1921 (dec. 1924); m. 2d, May Steiner, Apr. 28, 1928 (dec. 1970); 1 son John Shields; m. 3d, Dorothy H. Morrow, July 14, 1970. Admitted to Ala. bar, 1915; asso. with Tillman, Bradley & Baldwin, 1920-26; mem. Bradley, Baldwin, All & White, 1926-37; pres. Birmingham Trust Nat. Bank, 1937- 58, now mem. bd.; Chmn. banking div. War Finance Com. for Ala.; chmn., dir. Jefferson County chpt. A.R.C. (chmn. drive 1944), Birmingham and Jefferson County Community Chest (Chmn. drive 1941, pres. 1951-52). Served as 2d lt. 7th Div., U.S. Army, 1918; AEF. Mem. Birmingham C. of C. (pres. 1941). Am. Bankers Assn. (exec. com. nat. bank div. 1956-57, chmn. 1957-58, pres. 1959-60), Newcomen Soc. Eng., S.A.R., Soc. Colonial Wars, Delta Kappa Epsilon. Presbyn. Democrat. Mason (32 Shriner). Clubs: Links (N.Y.C.); Redstone, Downtown Birmingham Country, Club. Home: 2800 11th Court S Birmingham AL 35205 Office: Birmingham Trust Nat Bank Birmingham AL 35202

COLEMAN, JOHN WINSTON, Jr., historian, author; b. Lexington, Ky., Nov. 5, 1898; s. John Winston and Mary (Payne) C.; B.S. in Mech. Engring., U. Ky., 1920, M.E., 1929 Litt.D. (hon.), 1947; Litt.D., Lincoln Meml. U., Harrogate, Tenn., 1945; LL.D. Transylvania U., 1969; m. Burnetta Z. Mullen, Oct. 15, 1930. Engaged in engring. work, N.Y., Ky., and other states, 1920-23; organizer and pres. Coleman & Davis, Inc., gen. contractors, engrs. and blds., Lexington, Ky., 1924-36; owner and operator Winburn Farm, specializing in tobacco and hemp, Lexington, Ky., 1936—. Pres. bd. Lexington Cemetery Co. Bd. mgrs. Henry Clay Meml. Found., bd. dirs. George Rogers Clark Meml. Commn.; mem. Kentucky Civil War

Centennial Commn.; trustee Lincoln Meml. U. Served with R.O.T.C. U. of Ky., World War I. Mem. John Bradford Hist. Soc. (pres.), Am. Antiquarian Soc., Miss. Valley, So. hist. assns., S.R. (pres. Ky.), Sigma Nu, Phi Alpha Theta, Omicron Delta Kappa. Presbyterian. Mason (33). Club: Filson, Kiwanis. Author: Masonry in the Bluegrass, 1933; Stage-Coach Days in the Bluegrass, 1935; The Court-Houses of Lexington, 1937; Lexington During the Civil War, 1938; Slavery Times in Kentucky, 1940; A Bibliography of Kentucky History, 1949; The Beauchamp- Sharp Tragedy, 1950; Old Homes of The Blue Grass, 1950; Famous Kentucky Duels, 1953; The Springs of Kentucky, 1955; Historic Kentucky, 1967. Contbr. hist. articles to mags., and collector of rare Kentuckiana. Home: 2048 Blairmore Rd Lexington KY 40502

COLEMAN, LAWRENCE ARVER, lawyer; b. N.Y.C., Aug. 16, 1912; s. Lawrence A. and Florence E. (Miller) C.; A.B. in Chemistry, Cornell U., Ithaca, N.Y., 1933; LL.B., Columbia, 1936; J.S.D., St. Lawrence U., 1941; m. Barbara Baldwin, Oct. 9, 1937; children—Patricia Pond, Lawrence Arver III, Gerry R. Admitted to N.Y. bar, 1936; with firm Whitman, Ransom, Coulson & Geotz, N.Y.C., 1936-41, legal dept. Allied Chem. Corp., 1941-42, 46-51, head legal div., 1951- 57, now gen. counsel; mem. firm Scoll and Coleman, 1965—. Legal com. Indsl. Hygiene Found. Served from capt. to lt. col., AUS, 1942-46. Mem. Am. Bar Assn., Am. Chem. Soc., Cornell Soc. Engrs., Mfg. Chemists Assn. (chmn. food additives com. 1956-59, legal adv. com.). Roman Catholic. Clubs: Lawyers (N.Y.C.); Shenorock Yacht (sec.). Home: 2 Lieb Pl Eastchester NY 10709 Office: 342 Madison Av New York City NY 10017

COLEMAN, LEIGHTON HAMMOND, lawyer; b. Bethlehem, Pa., Sept. 25, 1897; s. Charles Philip and Helen Douglas (Rulison) C.; A.B., Williams Coll., 1919; LL.B., Harvard, 1922; m. Jane Fraser, May 14, 1927; children—Jane (Mrs. William D. Blair, Jr.), Helen (Mrs. William M. Evarts, Jr.), Leighton Hammond, Sally (Mrs. John Gordon Woodworth), Prudence (Mrs. Allen Sperry). Admitted to N.Y. bar, 1924, since practiced in N.Y.C.; mem. firm Davis, Polk & Wardwell, 1934—, now of counsel. Dir. Melville Shoe Corp. Trustee Village-of-the-Harbor, L.I., St. Luke's Internat. Med. Center, Tokyo. Served as lt., AS, U.S. Army, World War I. Mem. Soc. Preservation L.I. Antiquities (dir.), Kappa Alpha. Clubs: Union, Links, N.Y. Yacht, Pilgrims (N.Y.C.) Home: 139 E 66th St New York City NY 10021 also East Farm Stony Brook NY 11790 Office: 1 Chase Manhattan Plaza New York City NY 10005

COLEMAN, MARTIN STONE, safe and vault co. exec.; b. N.Y.C., Oct. 22, 1913; s. Adolph H. and Hannah (Stone) C.; B.S., N.Y. U., 1937; m. Janet Mosler, June 30, 1940; children—Ann, John, Nancy. Vice pres., treas., dir. Mosler Safe Co., N.Y.C., 1952-61, exec. v.p., treas., 1961-66, pres., dir., 1966-67, chmn. bd., 1968—; pres. Bus. Expansion Advisers, Inc., N.Y.C., 1968—. Trustee Hillside Hosp., Glen Oaks, N.Y. Coleman Found.; v.p., bd. dirs. Mosler Found. Cost insp. Bur. Supplies and Accounts, Navy Dept., 1942-45. C.P.A., N.Y. Mem. Am. Inst. C.P.A.'s N.Y. State Soc. C.P.A.'s. Clubs: Sunningdale Country, Harmonie, Racquet, Tamarisk Country. Home: 740 Park Av New York City, NY 10021. Office: 551 Fifth Av New York City NY 10017

COLEMAN, ORNETTE, composer, saxophonist; b. Ft. Worth, Mar. 9, 1930; student Sch. of Jazz, Lenox, Mass., 1959. Played tenor, alto saxophone; appeared with Donald Cherry; toured with Clarence Samuels, 1949; with Pee Wee Crayton, 1950; appeared Newport, Monterey jazz festivals, N.Y.C. Town Hall, 1962; various appearances New Orleans, Los Angeles, Ft. Worth; formerly on contract Atlantic Records; developed new style not based on chord patterns; recordings include Something Else, The Shape of Jazz to Come, Tomorrow is the Question, Free Jazz, Change of the Century, This is Our Music, Ornette!, Ornette on Tenor, John Lewis Presents Jazz Abstractions, Friends and Neighbors, Ornette Live at Prince St. Named number 1 Jazz Man of the Year, Jazz and Pop 3d Ann. Readers Poll, 1968; Guggenheim Found. fellow, 1967.*

COLEMAN, PAUL DARE, educator; b. Stoystown, Pa., June 4, 1918; s. Clyde R. and Catharine (Livengood) C.; A.B., Susquehanna U., 1940; M.S., Pa. State U., 1942; Ph.D., Mass. Inst. Tech., 1951; m. Betty L. Carter, June 20, 1942; children—Susan Dare, Peter Carter. Asst. physics Susquehanna U., 1938-40, Pa. State U., 1940-42; physicist USAF-WADC, Wright Field, O., 1942-46; physicist Cambridge Air Research Center, also grad. research asso. Mass. Inst. Tech., 1946-51; prof. elec. engring. dir. electro-physics lab. U. Ill. at Urbana, 1951—; cons. Argonne Nat. Lab., industry. Recipient meritorious civilian award, USAAF, 1946. Fellow I.E.E.E.; mem. Am. Phys. Soc., Sigma Xi, Pi Mu Delta, Pi Mu Epsilon. Research on millimeter waves, relativistic electronics, far infrared molecular lasers, submillimeter wave beam guides and detecgors, chem. lasers. Home: 710 Park Lane Campaign IL 61820 Office: Univ Illinois Urbana IL 61801

COLEMAN, PHILIP ANNABLE, brass co. exec.; b. Somerville, Mass., Dec. 17, 1908; s. Philip Henry and Bessie (Taylor) C.; student Mass. Inst. Tech., 1928; m. Elinor Gay, Oct. 27, 1934; children—Barbara (Mrs. Richard W. Eller), Bruce T., Carol L., Philip H. With Anaconda Am. Brass Co., 1935-52; Bristol Brass Corp. (Conn.), and subsidiaries, 1952—, pres., 1963- -, also dir.; dir. Accurate Brass Corp., Pres. bd. Bristol Brass Found. Pres. bd. Bristol United Fund, 1961-62; bd. dirs. Bristol Pub. Library; exec. com. Bristol Hosp. Mem. Conn. (dir.), Bristol chambers commerce, Conn. Hosp. Assn. (pres. elect). Clubs: Engineers (N.Y.C.); Farmington (Conn.) Country. Home: 24 Dorset Lane Farmington CT 06032 Office: 580 Broad St Bristol CT 06010

COLEMAN, RALPH PALLEN, Jr., editor, pub., financial exec.; b. Chestnut Hill, Pa., May 26, 1923; s. Ralph Pallen and Florence (Haeberle) C.; A.B., U. Pa., 1946, M.B.A., 1948; m. Jean Louise Kilpatrick, Sept. 10, 1949; children—Ralph Pallen III, Richard Carleton. Editor indsl. publs., 1943-69; founder, editor, pub. Over-The-Counter Securities Rev., 1951—, Listed Securities Jour., 1961—; editor, pub. Over-The-Counter Securities Handbook, 1954- -, Over-The-Counter Spl. Reports, 1958—, Over-The-Counter Newsletter, 1963—, New Issues, 1968—. Founder, pres., treas., dir. Over-the-Counter Securities Fund, Inc., 1955—; pres. Rev. Pub. Co., 1951—; pres., treas., dir. Rev. Mgmt. Corp., 1955—. Chmn., Com. for Pa. Hall of Fame. Served with USCGR, 1944-45. Mem. Huguenot Soc. Pa. Republican. Presbyn. Home: 1916 Hilltop Rd Jenkintown PA 19046 Office: Plymouth and Walnut Avs Oreland PA 19075

COLEMAN, RAY J., lawyer; b. Duell County, Neb., June 19, 1906; s. Arthur E. and Lula R. (Teagarden) C.; A.B., Stanford, 1928, J.D., 1930; m. Hazel R. Kay, Aug. 3, 1934; children—Wade A., Dana K. Admitted to Cal. bar, 1930; with firm Newlin & Ashburn, Los Angeles, 1930-48, partner, 1943-48; sr. partner firm Coleman & McDonald, Los Angeles, 1948-63; v.p., gen. counsel U.S. Borax & Chem. Corp., Los Angeles, 1963-71. Mem. Phi Delta Phi, Delta Kappa Epsilon. Home: 1966 Pepper Dr Altadena CA 91001 Office: 3075 Wilshire Blvd Los Angeles CA 90005

COLEMAN, RAYMOND W., economist; b. Mt. Brydges, Ont., Can., Mar. 3, 1901 (derivative citizenship 1910); s. Angus and Sarah Jeanne (Wilkinson) C.; B.B.A., U. Wash., 1923, M.B.A., 1926; Ph.D., U. Pitts., 1935; m. Essie Bee Pumphrey, Sept. 3, 1927; children—Ellsworth Pumphrey, Bruce Pumphrey. Instr. accounting Ore. State Coll., 1926-27, U. Mich., 1927-28; instr. econs. and accounting Wayne U., Detroit, 1928-29; asst. prof. and asso. prof. mgmt. engring. Carnegie Inst. Tech., Pitts., 1929-42, 46-47; chief extension service U.S. Dept. Commerce, 1947-48; prof., head dept. econs. and bus. adminstrn. W.Va. U., 1948-52, dir. bur. bus. research, 1948-56; dean Coll. Commerce, 1952-61, prof. econs. and mgmt., 1961-63; dean U. Ill. Coll. Bus. Adminstrn., Chgo., 1963-66, prof. econs. and mgmt., 1966-69, prof. emeritus, 1969—. Cons. U.S. Dept. Commerce, Small Def. Plants Adminstrn., Small Bus. Adminstrn., 1949—. Trustee Joint Council on Econ. Edn. Served from capt. to lt. col., USAAF and U.S. Army Service Force, 1942-46. Recipient grant Ford Found., 1961-62. Mem. Am. Econ. Assn., Am. Accounting Assn., Am. Assn. U. Profs., W.Va. Tax Inst. (dir., pres.), Beta Gamma Sigma, Beta Alpha Psi, Alpha Kappa Psi. Author: Elements of Accounting, 1941. Contbr. articles bus. and econ. jours. Home: 4117 Schwalbe Dr Sarasota FL 33580

COLEMAN, ROBERT MARSHALL, educator; b. Bridgton, Me., Sept. 27, 1925; s. Louis Elmer and Helen (Marr) C.; B.S., Bates Coll., 1950; M.S., U. N.H., 1951; Ph.D., U. Notre Dame, 1954; m. Patricia Ann Stocum, Dec. 29, 1947; children—Mary Deborah, Kevin Robert. Faculty Russell Sage Coll., Troy, N.Y., 1954-62, asst. prof. biology, 1956-58, asso. prof., 1958-62; asso. prof. Boston Coll., 1962-68; prof., head dept. biol. scis. Lowell (Mass.) Tech. Inst., 1968—. Cons. AID, NSF, India, 1965, 68, Lowell Tech. Inst., 1964-67. Served with AUS, 1943-46. Mem. Am. Soc. Parasitology, Am. Soc. Tropical Medicine and Hygiene, Am. Soc. Microbiology, N.Y. Acad. Scis., Radiation Research Soc., Sigma Xi, Phi Sigma. Contbr. articles profl. jours. Home: 25 Eaton Rd W Framingham MA 01701 Office: Lowell Tech Inst Biol Scis Dept Lowell MA 01854

COLEMAN, ROBERT VINCENT, educator; b. Iowa City, Ia., Oct. 11, 1930; s. George Hopkins and Leah Estel (Rose) C.; B.A., U. Va., 1953, Ph.D., 1956. Research physicist Gen. Electric Research Labs., 1954; sr. research physicist Gen. Motors Research Labs., 1956-58; research asst. prof. U. Ill., 1958-60; asso. prof. U. Va., Charlottesville, 1960-64, prof., 1964—. Mem. solid state panel NRC-Nat. Acad. Sci. Fellow Am. Phys. Soc.; mem. Phi Beta Kappa, Sigma Xi. Contbr. articles profl. jours. Home: Box 348 Forrest Ridge Rd Earlysville VA 22936 Office: Physics Dept U Va McCormick Rd Charlottesville VA 22901

COLEMAN, ROWLAND HENRY, arms mfg. ofcl.; b. Mystic, Conn., June 7, 1909; s. William Harold and Edna (Wilcox) C.; A.B., Bucknell U., Lewisburg, Pa., 1929. L.L.D. (hon.), 1965; m. Esther Keim, May 31, 1930; children—Rowland Henry, William Harold II. Div. advt. mgr. E. I. duPont de Nemours & Co., Wilmington, Del., 1929-37; advt. mgr. Remington Arms Co., Inc., Bridgeport, 1937-41, dir. sales promotion div., 1941-44, asst. dir. sales, 1944-49, dir. sales, 1949-51, v.p., dir. sales 1951- 54, v.p., asst. gen. mgr., 1954-63, pres., gen. mgr., dir., 1963—; dir. Cartuchos Deportivos de Mexico, S.A., Mexico City, Remington Arms Can. Ltd., Toronto, Ont., Conn. Nat. Bank; trustee People's Savs. Bank. Trustee Bucknell U., chmn. exec. com.; trustee Bridgeport Hosp. Mem. Am. Ordnance Assn. (v.p., dir.), Am. Hardware Mfrs. Assn. (past pres.), Wildlife Mgmt. Inst. (dir.), Sporting Arms and Ammunition Mfrs. Inst. (exec. com.), Nat. Rifle Assn. (patron), Ducks Unltd., Field Trial Gunners Guild, Nat. Skeet Shooting Assn., Amateur Trap Shooting Assn., Sigma Alpha Epsilon, Tau Kappa Alpha. Republican. Conglist. Mason. (32 Shriner). Clubs: Pequot Yacht; Aubichwi Gun, Brooklawn Country of Fairfield; Aspetuck Fish and Game (Bridgeport); Country (Manchester, Vt.); Ocean Reef (North Key Largo, Fla); Yacht, University (N.Y.C.); Cutty Hunk Anglers. Home: Catamount Rd Fairfield CT 06430 Office: Bridgeport CT 06601

COLEMAN, SAMUEL OTHELLO, govt. ofcl.; b. Monrovia, Liberia, Feb. 12, 1928; s. Samuel David and Etta (Melvina) C.; B.A., Am. Internat. Coll., Springfield, Mass., 1953; m. Winifred Walker, Aug. 5, 1960; children—Kathleen, Sandra, Kim, Samuel Othello. Asst. research officer Bur. Econ. Research, Monrovia, Liberia, 1960—; trainee census techniques and analysis Bur. Census, Dept. Commerce; budget analysis Exec. Office Pres., Dept. State; tax course U.S. Internal Revenue Service, 1953-54. Mem. exec. com. Pres. Liberia govt.; Liberian del. Internat. Confs. and Seminars, 1960-64. Served with Liberian Militia, 1947-48. Recipient award World Bank, 1964-66. Club: African (Washington). Author: Manuel for Training Internal Revenue Agents of the Liberian Government, 1963. Home: 4251 Blagden Av NW Washington DC 20011 Office: 1818 H St NW Washington DC 20433

COLEMAN, SHELDON, business exec.; b. Ft. Worth, Nov. 15, 1901; s. William Coffin and Fanny (Sheldon) C.; M.E. Cornell U., 1925; m. Georgia Cleveland, Dec. 20, 1923 (div. 1949); children—Virginia Lee, Carolyn; m. 2d, Galey Dater, May 22, 1951; 1 son, Sheldon. Engr., Coleman Co., Wichita, Kan., 1925-32, gen. works mgr., 1932-40, became exec. v.p. and gen. mgr., 1940, later pres., now chmn. bd., chief exec. officer Coleman Co., Inc.; dir. 4th Nat. Bank, Wichita, Cessna Aircraft Corp., Rockwell Mfg. Co. Mem. nat. central com. A.R.C., past chmn. bd. govs. Sedgwick County chpt. Mem. Am. Gas Assn. (bd.), Nat. Warm Air Heating and Air Conditioning Assn. (bd.), Gas Appliance Mfrs. Assn. (bd., past pres.), Inst. Appliance Mfrs. (pres. bd.), N.A.M. Republican. Baptist. Home: 8 N Hampton Rd Wichita KS 67206 Office: Coleman Co Inc Wichita KS 67201

COLEMAN, SHEPARD DAVID, musician, conductor; b. N.Y.C., Apr. 24, 1924; s. Albert Payson and Etta (Ershowsky) C.; student Inst. Musical Art, N.Y.C., 1939-41; fellowship Juilliard Grad. Sch., 1942-44; m. Gretchen Wyler, June 18, 1956. Concertized as cellist in Europe and U.S.; staff cellist various radio stas., N.Y.C.; mem. N.Y. Philharmonic Orch., 1962; conductor Broadway prodns. Bye Bye Birdie, 1961, Student Gypsey, 1963, Hello Dolly!, 1964, Oh What a Lovely War, 1964. Recipient Antoinette Perry award for mus. direction Hello, Dolly!, 1964. Home: Sleepy Valley Rd Warwick, NY 10990.

COLEMAN, SIDNEY RICHARD, physicist, educator; b. Chgo., Mar. 7, 1937; s. Harold Albert and Sadie (Shanas) C.; B.S., Ill. Inst. Tech., 1957; Ph.D., Cal. Inst. Tech., 1962. Mem. faculty dept. physics Harvard, 1961—, prof., 1969—. Partner, Advent Pubs. Mem. Am. Phys. Soc., Am. Civil Liberties Union, LILAPA. Home: 84 Prescott St Cambridge MA 02138

COLEMAN, SYLVAN CLARENCE, investment co. exec.; b. San Francisco, Aug. 29, 1905; s. William W. and Rose (Loewy) C.; B.S., U. Cal., 1926; M.B.A., Harvard, 1928; m. Louise Macnamara, Oct. 17, 1941. With E.F. Hutton & Co., N.Y.C., 1928—, mgr. research div., 1931-35, mgr. fgn. dept., 1935-38, gen. partner, 1938-62, chmn., chief exec. officer E.F. Hutton & Co., Inc., 1962-70, cons., 1970—; pres., dir. E.F. Hutton & Co. AG (Zurich), 1970—; dir. Am. Home Assurance Corp., Am. Internat. Group, Inc., Commerce and Industry Ins. Co., Petroleum Corp. Am., Am. Internat. Life Assurance Co. of N.Y., Continental Telephone Corp., Real Property Owners, Inc., West Chem. Products, Inc., Transatlantic Reins. Co., Scudder Duo-Vest, Inc., Scudder Duo-Vest Exchange Fund, Inc.; mem. adv. com. Bankers Trust Co. Mem. Navy Dept. and War Dept. Price Adjustment Bd. office undersec. USN, Washington, 1942-45. Bd. dirs. Fountain House Found., Inc.; chmn. exec. com. N.Y. chpt. Am. Cancer Soc., Manhattan Eye, Ear and Throat Hosp., Assos. Harvard Bus. Sch., mem. adv. com. adminstrn.; mem. bd. advisers U.S. Naval War Coll.; trustee Am. Mus. Natural History. Recipient Meritorious Civilian Service award from sec. navy. Mem. Beta Gamma Sigma (nat. exec. com.). Republican. Clubs: Recess, Deepdale. Home: 150 E 69th St New York City NY 10021 Office: One Battery Park Plaza New York City NY 10004

COLEMAN, THOMAS PHILIP, air force officer; b. Middletown, Conn., Mar. 26, 1918; s. Thomas Francis and Kathleen (Sarsfield) C.; student Glendale (Cal.) Jr. Coll., 1938-40; B.S., Ariz. State U., 1942; grad. Advanced Mgmt. program Harvard, 1967; m. Ann Marie Barnett, Dec. 23, 1941; children—Sandra Ann (Mrs. John J. Hyland III), Robert F. Commd. 2d lt. USAF, 1943, advanced through grades to brig. gen., 1969; staff and combat positions with SAC, 1947-57; comdr. Pease AFB, N.H., 1957-58; dir. information 8th Air Force, Westover AFB, Mass., 1958-61; information duties SAC Hdqrs., Neb., 1961-65, dir. information, 1965-67; pub. affairs officer CINCPAC, Hawaii, 1967-69; dep. dir. information Office Sec. Air Force, Washington, 1969—. Decorated Legion of Merit, Bronze Star medal, Air medal. Mem. Air Force Assn. Washington, Order Daedalions. Home: 8337 Queen Elizabeth Blvd Annandale VA 22003 Office: Dep Dir Information Office Sec Air Force Washington DC 20330

COLEMAN, WADE HAMPTON, Jr., former educator; b. Livingston, Ala., June 10, 1904; s. Wade Hampton and Lillian (Jackson) C.; diploma Livingston State Normal Sch., 1923; B.S., U. Ala., 1925, A.M., 1927; postgrad. U. Chgo., summers 1929, 34, 35, 36, 39-41; U. Paris, Sorbonne and Institut de Phonétique, summer 1930; m. Margaret Pauline James, June 3, 1930; children—Ann James (Mrs. John Morgan Sims), Wade Hampton, Elizabeth Ten Eyck (Mrs. Joseph William Ferguson, Jr.). Asst. in Romance langs. U. Ill., 1927-28; instr. Romance langs. U. Ala., Tuscaloosa, 1928-31, asst. prof., 1931-42, asso. prof., 1942-46, prof. Romance langs., 1946-70, ret. Vis. prof. French in coll. U. Chgo., summer 1956; tchr. French courses Ala. Ednl. TV Network, 1956- 60. Served USNR 1942-46, 50-54. Decorated officier Ordre des Palmes Academiques (France); knight of justice Sovereign Order St. John of Jerusalem. Mem. Navy League U.S., Am. Assn. Tchrs. French, S. Atlantic Modern Lang. Assn., Modern Lang. Assn. Am., Ala. Hist. Assn., U.S. Naval Inst., S.A.R. (chpt. pres. 1956, pres., bd. mgrs. Ala. soc.), Am. Legion (post comdr. 1949-50), Ala. Edn. Assn. (permanent sec.-treas. modern langs.), Phi Beta Kappa (past pres.), Phi Delta Kappa, Kappa Delta Pi, Delta Chi. Democrat. Episcopalian (lay reader Diocese Springfield 1927-28, Ala. 1928—). Club: University (gov.). Contbr. articles in field. Home: 28 Pinehurst Tuscaloosa AL 35401

COLEMAN, WILLIAM ARMSTRONG, mfg. co. exec.; b. Spartanburg, S.C., Mar. 13, 1927; s. Armstrong R. and Mattie Day (Vaughan) C.; student U. S.C., 1948-50; m. Terry Miller, June 24, 1953; children—Vaughan, William Armstrong IV, Jane, Miller. With Synalloy Corp., Spartanburg, 1955—, pres., 1970—; dir. Spartanburg br. S.C. Nat. Bank. Served with USAAF, 1945-47. Mem. Kappa Alpha. Home: 7 Montgomery Dr Spartanburg SC 29301 Office: Box 5627 Spartanburg SC 29301

COLEMAN, WILLIAM CARLTON, mfg. and transp. exec.; b. McEwen, Tenn., Sept. 4, 1898; s. William H. and Donna (Daniel) C.; B.S., Southwestern U., Georgetown, Tex., 1919; student U. Tex.; m. Elizabeth Murphy, Oct. 25, 1922; children—William Carlton, James Wilburn, Joan Elizabeth (Mrs. Cushman S. Radebaugh, Jr.), Richard Thomas. Prof. history and English, MacFarren Jr. Coll., Martin, Tenn., 1920-21; salesman So. Coal Co., Memphis, 1921-24; sales mgr. Randall Fuel Co., Atlanta, 1925-29; dist. mgr. Koppers Coal Co., Atlanta, 1929-35, Cin. div., 1936-41; dist. mgr. Northwestern div. Koppers Eastern Gas & Fuel Assn., Chgo., 1941-53; v.p., dir. Milw. & Suburban Transp. Co., 1953—, Indpls. Transit System, Inc.; pres., dir. Mid Empire Corp., 1953—; dir. Monon Coal Co., Chgo. & Indpls. Coal Co., Inc., Monon Realty Co.; dir., exec. com. Monon R.R.; dir. Can. Javelin Ltd., Gateway Industries, Inc., Midland Transp. Corp., Louisville Transit Co. Served as aviator USN, World War I. Home: 2135 N Lake Dr Milwaukee WI 53202 Office: 4212 W Highland Blvd Milwaukee WI 53208

COLEMAN, WILLIAM HOWARD, metal products mfr.; b. Cleve., Feb. 16, 1918; s. Robert Aloysius and Lois Elizabeth (Franks) C.; student U. Notre Dame, 1936-40; m. Isabelle J. Schultze, Nov. 11, 1941; children—Anne Christine, Mary Patricia, William Howard, Thomas Kelly, Michael Franks, Constance Therese, Donna M., Gregory Matthew, Lois E. Founder, Coleman-Pettersen Corp., mfrs. wire products, Cleve., 1941, merged with Fanner Metal Products Co., Cleve., 1952; partner Ball, Burge & Kraus, Cleve., investment bankers, 1952-66; pres. Aero Supply Mfg. Co., Corry, Pa., 1953-55; founder, chmn. Banner Metals, Inc., Los Angeles, 1955; chmn. Alco Standard Corp., Phila., 1956- 65; pres. Twin Industries Corp., Buffalo, 1957-61, merged with Wheelabrator Corp., Mishawaka, Ind., chmn. bd., 1961-70; chmn. Stewart Bolling & Co., Inc., Cleve., 1967—, also dir.; chmn. bd. Intercole Automation, Inc., Cleve., 1969—; dir. Banner Metals, Union Financial Corp., Cleve., E.F. Hauserman Co., Cleve., Everest & Jennings, Los Angeles. Trustee Cath. Charities Corp., Cleve., Huron Rd. Hosp., Gilmour Acad., Cleve. Health Mus., Notre Dame Coll., adv. council U. Notre Dame Coll. Commerce. Clubs: Mayfield Country, Mid-day (Cleve.); Metropolitan (N.Y.C.); Bel-Air Country, Beach of Los Angeles, El Dorado (Los Angeles). Home: 321 Alma Real Dr Pacific Palisades CA 90272 Office: 12011 San Vicente Blvd Los Angeles CA 90049

COLEMAN, WILLIAM LUTHER, lawyer; b. Paris Township, O., Feb. 7, 1914; s. John Henry and Marie (Zacharias) C.; student Ohio No. U., 1934-36; LL.B., Ohio State U., 1939; m. Rose Anna Green, Nov. 23, 1940; children—William Henry, Thomas Hewitt, Charlotte Marie, Stephen Green, Rose Anna, Michael Stuart. Admitted to Ohio bar, 1939, since practiced in Marysville; pros. atty. Union County, 1941-49. Chmn. Ohio Dem. Exec. Com., 1956—, Union County Dem. Exec. Com.; chmn. Nat. Young Dems. Conv., 1947, Bi-annual Conv. League Young Dems., Ohio, 1940, 44, 46, 50, 52; mem. state exec. com. League Young Dems. Clubs, 1939-54; mem. Dem. Nat. Com., 1960-64; Dem. candidate for lt. gov. of Ohio, 1966. Active Boy Scouts of Am. Mem. Am., Ohio, Union County bar assns., Am. Judicature Soc., Heart of Ohio Fish and Game Assn., County Tb and Health Assn. Lutheran. Kiwanian. Home: R D 1 Milford Center OH 43045 Office: 110 S Court St Marysville OH 43040 also Neil House Columbus OH 43215

COLEMAN, WILLIAM SAMUEL EDWARD, educator; b. Parnassus, Pa., June 7, 1926; s. William Robert and Ila (Phillips) C.; B.S., Slippery Rock (Pa.) State Coll., 1949; M.A., Pa. State U., 1953; Ph.D., U. Pitts., 1965; student Va. Mil. Inst., 1944, N.Y.U., 1949; m. Phyllis June Young, Dec. 20, 1957; children—William Samuel Edward, Eric Franklin. Instr. English and journalism Grove City (Pa.) High Sch., 1946-49; asst. prof. speech and English, Slippery Rock State Coll., 1953-55; asso. prof., head dept. speech and theatre Glenville (W.Va.) State Coll., 1955-63; touring dir. W.Va. Centennial

Showboat, summer 1963; dir. Off-Broadway for N.Y. Stage Co., 1965; asst. prof. theatre State U. N.Y., Buffalo, 1965-66; prof., chmn. dept. theatre arts and speech, dir. Univ. Theatre, Drake U., Des Moines, 1966—; drama cons. Des Moines Pub. Schs., 1968; hist. cons. Neb. Game and Park Commn., 1971. Mem. Am. Civil Liberties Union, 1969-71, Mid-Ia. Arts Council, 1970—; drama dir. W.Va. State Folk Festival, summers 1956-62. Served with inf., AUS, 1944-46. Recipient Danforth Tchr. Study grants, 1963-65, State U. N.Y. Found. grant, 1966, four research grants Drake U., 1st prize W.Va. Centennial Folk Play Contest, 1963. Mem. Am. Ednl. Theatre Assn. (asst. adminstrv. v.p.), Speech Communications Assn., Am. Assn. U. Profs. (v.p., pres.-elect Drake chpt. 1971-72), Central States Speech Assn., W.Va. Intercollegiate Speech Assn. (past pres.). Author: (with Ned Bowman and Glorianne Engel) Planning for the Theatre, 1965; also numerous plays. Contbr. articles profl. jours. Home: 1334 31st St Des Moines IA 50311

COLEMAN, WILLIAM SMITH, army officer; b. Iva, S.C., Jan. 29, 1919; s. Clifford Dean and Leon (Smith) C.; B.S., Clemson (S.C.) Coll., 1939; postgrad. Command and Gen. Staff Coll., 1951-52, Army War Coll., 1959-60; M.A., George Washington U., 1966; m. Ruth Ducworth, Dec. 19, 1942; children—Susan C. (Mrs. David A. Fedor), Nancy C. (Mrs. Robert H. Hart), William Smith, Mary L. Commd. 2d lt. U.S. Army, 1942, advanced through grades to maj. gen., 1970; S-3 and exec. officer 1st Bn. 8th Cav. Regt., 1949-50, S-3 and exec. officer 8th Cav. Regt., 1950; comdg. officer 2d Bn., 8th Cav. Regt., 1950-51; instr. tactical dept. Inf. Sch., 1952-55; sr. Army adviser Alaska N.G., 1955-57; mem. Joint Secretariat, Office Joint Chiefs of Staff, 1957-59; staff officer Plans Div., Joint Staff, CINCPAC, 1960-63; comdg. officer 2d Brigade, 1st Armored Div., 1963-64, chief of staff 1st Armored Div., 1964-65; staff officer Inst. Advanced Studies, Army Combat Devels. Command, 1965-66; dir. course I and internat. relations studies, faculty Army War Coll., Carlisle Barracks, Pa., 1966-67; asst. div. comdr. 1st Inf. Div. U.S. Army, Vietnam, 1967-68; dep. asst. chief of staff, J-3, U.S. Army Vietnam and RF/PF, USMACV, 1968, asst. div. comdr. 1st Inf. Div., U.S. Army, Vietnam, 1968; dep. comdg. gen., Ft. Jackson, S.C., 1969-70, comdg. gen., 1970—. Decorated D.S.M., Silver Star medal with 3 oak leaf clusters, Legion of Merit, D.F.C. with oak leaf cluster, Bronze Star medal with V device, Air medal with 38 oak leaf clusters with V device, Joint Service Commendation medal, Army Commendation medal with 3 oak leaf clusters, Combat Inf. badge; Order Brit. Empire; Vietnamese Cross of Gallantry with palm, Republic of Vietnam Armed Forces Honor medal 1st Class. Mem. Greater Columbia C. of C. (dir.), Assn. U.S. Army, Mil. Order World Wars. Mason. Home: 3606 Pershing Rd Columbia SC 29206 Office: Hdqrs USATCI Fort Jackson SC 29207

COLEMAN, WINSON, univ. dean.; b. Oskaloosa, Ia., Sept. 10, 1905; s. Winson and Cassie (Sanford) C.; B.A., Penn Coll., 1928; M.A., Haverford Coll., 1929; Ph.D., U. Chgo., 1950; m. Theodora Dugas, Aug. 29, 1933; children—Grace Mauvene (Mrs. Bobby Edwards), Winson, Edwina Elaine (Mrs. Louis Clark). Mem. faculty Johnson C. Smith U., Charlotte, N.C., 1929—, prof. philosophy, 1950—, acad. dean, 1962—; vis. lectr. U. Colo., summer 1960; editor Quar. Rev. Higher Edn. Among Negroes, 1963—. Gen. Edn. Bd. fellow philosophy U. Chgo., 1947-49, Univ. fellow philosophy, 1949-50. Mem. Am. Philos. Assn., Mind Assn., Am. Conf. Acad. Deans, N.E.A. Presbyn. Author article. Home: 1601 Washington Av Charlotte NC 28216

COLEN, LOUIS MICHAEL, cigar mfg. co. exec.; b. Phila., Jan. 26, 1904; s. Michael and Rebecca (Shatz) C.; B.S. in Econs., U. Pa., 1926; m. Ethel B. Poppel, June 16, 1929; childrenRonny Jane (Mrs. Sheldon G. Altman), Marjorie Sue (Mrs. Ronald A. Smith). Surveyor, Midwest Refining Co., Casper, Wyo., 1921; sec. asst. treas., dir. Congress Cigar Co., N.Y.C. 1924-40; treas. Consol. Cigar Corp., N.Y.C., 1940-65, sec.-treas., 1965- ; v.p., dir. Mich. Peat Corp., N.Y.C., 1945-54. Trustee Nat. Conf. Christians and Jews, Great Neck, N.Y. Co-chmn. United Jewish Appeal N.Y., 1955—; sec. Consol. Cigar Philanthropic Fund, N.Y.C. Republican dist. leader, Newark, 1935. Mem. Nat. Accountants Soc. Club: Lake Success (N.Y.) Country. Home: 4 Ardsley Pl Great Neck NY 11021 Office: 529 Fifth Av New York City, NY , 10017.

COLES, ALBERT LEONARD, lawyer; b. Bridgeport, Conn., Nov. 8, 1909; s. Joseph and Margaret (Lennon) C.; B.A., Yale, 1931, LL.B., 1933; m. Eileen M. Pelath, 1946; children—Kevin A., Matthew A., Brigid M., Albert L., Mary Norah. Admitted to Conn. bar, 1933, also the U.S. Dist. Ct., Ct. Appeals, U.S. Supreme Ct.; practice of law, Bridgeport, 1933—; mem. Coles, O'Connell & Dolan, 1942—; pros. atty. city ct. Bridgeport, 1941-43, judge, 1945-47, 49-51; atty. gen. Conn., 1959-63; judge Conn. Superior Ct., 1963-65. Dir. Unlied Illuminating Co., So. New Eng. Telephone Co. Senator, 22d Dist of Conn., 1939-47, majority leader, 1941; Democratic chmn. Bridgeport, 1952-55. Bd. dirs. Park City Hosp. Mem. Phi Beta Kappa. K.C. Home: 140 Sailors Lane Bridgeport CT 06605 Office: 855 Main St Bridgeport CT 06603

COLES, ANNA B., univ. dean; b. Kansas City, Kan., Jan. 16, 1925; d. Gordon A. and Lillie Mae (Buchanan) Bailey; B.S.N., Avila Coll., 1958; M.S.N., Catholic U. Am., 1960, Ph.D., 1967; m. Herbert Reval Coles, May 19, 1953; children—Margot Ann, Michelle Annette, Gina Antoinette. Instr. VA Hosp., Topeka, Kan., 1950-52; supr. VA Hosp., Kansas City, Mo., 1952-58; asst. dir. in-service edn. Freedmen's Hosp., Washington, 1960-61, adminstrv. asst. to dir. nursing, 1961-66, asso. dir. nursing service, 1966-67, dir. nursing, 1967-69; dean Howard U. Sch. Nursing, Washington, 1968—. Mem. Task Force for Community Planning for Nursing, D.C. Met. Area; profl. adv. com. to Vis. Nurses' Assn. of D.C.; mem. Health Planning Adv. Com. D.C.; mem. adv. bd. Am. Assn. Med. Colls. Bd. dirs. Iona Whipper Home for Unwed Mothers; bd. dirs. Nursing Edn. Opportunity. Mem. Am. Nurses Assn., Freedmen's Hosp. Sch. Nursing Alumni Assn., Alpha Kappa Alpha. Author: Doctoral Education of Nurses in the United States, 1967. Home: 627 G St SW Washington DC 20024

COLES, DONALD EARL, educator; b. St. Paul, Feb. 8, 1924; s. Courtney J. and Lorna (Addison) C.; B.Aero. Engring., U. Minn., 1947; M.S., Cal. Inst. Tech., 1948, Ph.D., 1953; m. Ellen Searight, Sept. 11, 1947; children—Christopher Lee, Elizabeth Anne, Kenneth Spencer, Janet Jacqueline. Research engr. Jet Propulsion Lab., Pasadena, Cal., 1950-53; research fellow Cal. Inst. Tech., 1953-56, mem. faculty, 1953, prof. aeros., 1964—. Cons. to industry, 1954—; mem. Nat. Com. Fluid Mechs. Films, 1960. Served with AUS, 1943-46. Mem. Am. Inst. Aeros. and Astronautics (Lawrence Sperry award 1953), Am. Phys. Soc., Sigma Xi. Producer ednl. film Channel Flow of a Compressible Fluid, 1966. Office: 1201 E California Blvd Pasadena CA 91109

COLES, EMBERT HARVEY, Jr., educator; b. Garden City, Kan., Oct. 12, 1923; s. Embert Harvey and Neva (Blanchard) C.; D.V.M., Kan. State U., 1945, Ph.D. 1958; M.S., Ia. State U., 1946; m. Janis Waterman, July 27, 1946; children—Charles David, Kay Ann. Grad. asst., then instr. Ia. State U., 1945-48; practice vet. medicine, Colby, Kan., 1948-54; mem. faculty Kan. State U., 1954—, prof., head dept. pathology parasitology and pub. health, 1964-67, prof. clin. pathology, head dept. infectious diseases, 1968—; dean Faculty Vet. Medicine, chief of party U.S. AID program Ahmadu Bello U., Zaria, Nigeria, 1970-72. Mem. Am. Vet. Med. Assn., A.A.A.S., Am. Soc. Vet. Clin. Pathologists (pres. 1966), Am. Soc. Animal Sci., Kan. Vet. Med. Assn., Sigma Xi, Phi Kappa Phi, Gamma Sigma Delta, Phi Zeta. Author: Veterinary Clinical Pathology, 1967. Home: 230 Summit St Manhattan, KS 66502.

COLES, HARRY LEWIS, educator, historian; b. Nashville, Apr. 30, 1920; s. Harry L. and Zay (Freeman) C.; A.B. magna cum laude, Vanderbilt U., 1939, Ph.D., 1949; m. Patricia Lockwood Sinnott, Dec. 26, 1959; children—Christopher Desmond, Carl Edward. Archival asst. Nat. Archives, 1942-43; historian Dept. Def., 1943-49; mem. faculty Ohio State U., Columbus, 1949—, prof. history, 1961- -, chmn. dept., 1967—; Ernest J. King prof. maritime history Naval War Coll., 1966-67. Rosenwald research fellow, 1948-49; Mershon post-doctoral fellow, 1959-60; sr. asso. mem. St. Antony's Coll., Oxford U., 1970. Mem. Phi Beta Kappa. Club: Athenaeum (London). Author: (with others) The Public Lands, 1963; (with A. Weinberg) Soldiers Become Governors: Studies in Military Government in World War II, 1964; The War of 1812, 1965; Reinterpretations of Jeffersonian America, 1970; also articles, revs. Editor Total War and Cold War, 1962. Home: 2605 Wellesley Dr Columbus OH 43221

COLES, JAMES STACY, research co. exec.; b. Mansfield, Pa., June 3, 1913; s. Edwin Stacy and Emavieve (Rose) C.; B.S., Mansfield State Coll., 1934; A.B., Columbia, 1936, A.M., 1939, Ph.D., 1941; m. Martha Louise Reed, June 18, 1938; children—Ann Stacy, James Reed, Christopher. Instr. chemistry Coll. City N.Y., 1936-41; instr. later asst. prof. chemistry Middlebury (Vt.) Coll., 1941-43; research group leader, later supr. Underwater Explosives Research Lab., Woods Hole (Mass.) Oceanographic Instn., 1943-46, now trustee; asst. prof. chemistry Brown U., 1946-49, asso. prof., 1949-52, acting dean coll., 1951-52, exec. officer dept. chemistry, 1947- 52; pres. Bowdoin Coll., Brunswick, Me., 1952-67; pres. Research Corp. N.Y., N.Y.C., 1968—; dir. Research-Cottrell, Inc. Civilian technician U.S. Naval Tech. Mission in Europe, 1945; bd. dirs. Chem. Fund. Recipient Pres.'s certificate of merit; certificate of merit OSRD; Bur. Ordnance Devel. award (Navy). Fellow Am. Acad. Arts and Scis.; mem. A.A.A.S., Am. Chem. Soc., N.E. Assn. Chemistry Tchrs., Council on Library Resources (dir.), Sigma Xi. Clubs: Century Assn., University, Skating (N.Y.C.); Walkers Island Yacht; Tavern (Boston). Author: (with Robert H. Cole) Physical Principles of Chemistry, 1965. Home: 1025 Fifth Av New York City NY 10028 Office: 405 Lexington Av New York City NY 10017

COLES, JOHN WILLIAM, banker; b. Olmstead, Ky., Sept. 17, 1905; s. John T. and Nell Elizabeth (Adams) C.; grad. Bowling Green Coll. Commerce, 1925, Am. Inst. Banking, 1933, Grad. Sch. Banking, Rutgers U., 1947; LL.B., YMCA Law Sch., Nashville, 1934; m. Margaret Swaney, Oct. 11, 1934; children—William S., John Read. Admitted to Tenn. bar, 1934; with First Am. Nat. Bank, Nashville, 1926—, v.p., trust officer, head trust dept., 1966—. Past pres. Nashville Estate Planning Council. Mem. Davidson County Bar Assn., Tenn. Bankers Assn. (past pres. fiduciary sect.). Baptist. Mason (33). Club: Richland Country (Nashville). Home: 3749 Whitland Av Nashville TN 37205 Office: 326 Union St Nashville TN 37202

COLES, ROBERT MARTIN, psychiatrist; b. 1929; ed. Harvard, Columbia, U. Chgo.; m. Jane Hallowell, July 4, 1960; children—Robert Emmet, Daniel Agee, Michael Hallowell. Former chief neuropsychiat. service AFB, Biloxi, Miss.; now research psychiatrist Harvard U. Health Services. Recipient Family Life Book award Child Study Assn. Am., 1967; Hefheimer prize for research Am. Psychiat. Assn., 1968. Author: Children of Crisis (Ralph Waldo Emerson award Phi Beta Kappa 1968, Four Freedoms award 1968, Wolf-Anisfield award 1968), 1967; Dead End School, 1968; Still Hungry In America, 1968; (with Maria Piers) The Wages of Neglect, 1969; The Grass Pipe, 1969; The Image Is You, 1969; Uprooted Children, 1970; Drugs and Youth, 1970; Erik H. Erikson: The Growth of His Work, 1970. Contbg. editor New Republic; editorial bd. Am. Scholar, Contemporary Psychoanalysis, Child Psychiatry and Human Development. Home: Coolidge Rd Concord MA 01742 Office: 75 Mt Auburn St Cambridge MA 02138

COLESCOTT, WARRINGTON WICKHAM, artist, educator; b. Oakland, Cal., Mar. 7, 1921; s. Warrington W. and Lydia (Hutton) C.; A.B., U. Cal. at Berkeley, 1942, M.A., 1947; postgrad. Acad. de la Grand Chaumiere, Paris, France, 1950, 53, Slade Sch. Art, U. London (Eng.), 1957; children (from previous marriage)—Louis Moore, Julian Hutton, Lydia Alice; m. 2d, Frances Myers, Mar. 15, 1971. Instr., Long Beach (Cal.) City Coll., 1947- 49; mem. faculty U. Wis., 1949—, prof. art, 1957—, chmn. dept., 1958- 60; exhibited one man exhbn. Asso. Am. Artists Galleries, N.Y.C., 1963, 69; permanent collections Mus. Modern Art, Victoria and Alberta Mus., London, Bibliotechque Nat., Paris, N.Y. Pub. Library, Met. Mus., Chgo. Art Inst., Bklyn. Mus., Phila. Mus. Art, Walker Art Center, Mpls.; vis. prof. printmaking Tyler Sch. Art, Rome, Italy, 1966. Served to 1st lt., inf., AUS, 1942-46. Fulbright fellow, 1957; Guggenheim fellow, 1965; recipient award Okla. Printmakers, 1961, 65; purchase award Wis. Salon Art, 1970; purchase award Colorprint USA, 1971. Mem. Soc. Am. Graphic Arts (award 1963, 64), Midwestern Coll. Art Conf., Phila. Print Club, Boston Printmakers, Am. Colorprint Soc., Coll. Art Assn. Illustrator: Mariposa Poems (by Carl Thayler), 1970; Death in Venice (Thomas Mann), 1971. Home: Hollandale WI 53544

COLETTI, JOSEPH ARTHUR, sculptor; b. San Donato, Italy, Nov. 5, 1898; s. Dominick and Donata (Cardarelli) C.; came to U.S., 1900; student Mass. Art Sch., 1915-17, Northeastern Prep. Sch., 1917-19; A.A., Harvard, 1923; m. Miriam Kerruish Whitney, Sept. 28, 1929 (div. 1943); children—Donata (Mrs. Kirke L. Mechem), Miriam Whitney (Mrs. Peter B. Dow). Pupil, became asst. John Singer Sargent. Numerous works including: baptismal font St. John's Episcopal Ch., Westwood, Mass., Henry B. Washburn Meml., Episcopal Sem., Cambridge, Mass., Lt. William F. Callahan, Jr. Callahan Tunnel Entrance, Boston, Albert Schweizer medal; Ferdinand Gagnon Meml. Seminaire St. Hyacinthe, Que., Can.; Gagnon statue, LaFayette Park, Manchester, N.H.; "Mourning Victory," Lafayette Park, Salem, Mass.; Harvard Glee Club medal in collection Bibliotheque Nationale, Paris, France; Senator David I. Walsh Statue, Esplanade, Boston; Orpheus, Nonquitt, Mass.; Gen. Edward L. Logan statue Logan Internat. Airport, Boston: Father Michael Joseph McGivney statue, Waterbury, Conn.; Boston Arts Festival medal; facade and 11 heroic sized panels for Cathedral of Mary Our Queen, Balt.; St. George statue Nat. Gall. Modern Art, Florence, Italy; Paderewski Centennial medal Mus. Treasures Cathedral Wavel Castle, Cracow, Poland; Admiral Samuel Eliot Morison medallion Vatican Collection; Dr. George P. Berry Meml., Countway Med. Library, Boston, Orphens Fountain, Lowell (Mass.) State Coll., Dante Soc. Am. 7th Centennial medal, Dow Meml., Buffalo, Boston Tea Party coin-medal, George Peabody Gardner Meml., Sci. Bldg. Children's Hosp. Boston. Mem. Nat. Humanities Faculty. Decorated cavaliere ufficiale Nell'Ordine al Merito (Italy); recipient 1st prize medal Boston Tercentenary Fine Arts Exhbn., 1932; traveling fellow fine arts Harvard, 1923, Sachs fellow, 1924-25; vis. fellow Am. Academy Rome, 1924-26. Mem. Boston Hist. Conservation Com.; chmn. Mass. Art Commn., 1960-65; adv. com. Inst. Modern Art; mem. camouflage com. Mass. Com. Pub. Safety, 1939-42; adv. com. Swain Sch. Design. Trustee New Eng. Conservatory Music. Fellow Nat. Sculpture Soc.; mem. Medieval Acad. Am., Am. Federation Arts, Dante Soc. Am., Italian Hist. Soc., Phi Beta Kappa (hon.). Clubs: Saint Botolph, Harvard. Author: Aristide Maillol; articles for Ency. Brit. Address: Fenway Studios 30 Ipswich St Boston MA 02215

COLEY, WILLIAM BRADLEY, educator; b. N.Y.C., Sept. 21, 1923; s. Bradley L. and Phyllis (Macdonell) C.; grad. Pomfret (Conn.) Sch., 1941; A.B., Yale, 1947, M.A., 1951, Ph.D., 1954; A.M. (hon.), Wesleyan U., Middletown, Conn., 1964; m. Katharine Truman Smith, June 17, 1950; children—Phyllis D., Katharine L. Instr., Yale, 1948-49; mem. faculty Wesleyan U., 1952—, prof. English, 1964—, chmn. dept., 1965-67, 69-71; exec. editor Wesleyan edit. works of Henry Fielding, 1967—. Served with AUS, 1942-46. Research fellow Am. Council Learned Socs., 1963-64; Guggenheim fellow, 1967-68. Mem. Modern Lang. Assn. Club: Elizabethan (New Haven). Author: (with A.S. Wensinger) Hogarth on High Life, also articles, revs. Asso. editor College English, 1969—. Home: Maple Shade Rd Middletown CT 06457

COLFLESH, PAUL WILLIAM, life ins. co. exec.; b. Phila., Sept. 14, 1925; s. John Gaul and Pauline (Riegert) C.; B.S., Drexel U., 1950; exec. program Stanford U., 1967; m. Thelma L. Fulton, Jan. 31, 1948; children—Paula, Galen, David. Sales Bankers Life Ia., 1950-57; supt. Eastern region Paul Revere Life Ins. Co., 1957-64; agy. v.p. Pacific Mut. Life Ins. Co., Los Angeles, 1964-69, sr. v.p. individual ins., 1969—. Mem. Los Angeles exec. bd. Boy Scouts Am. C.L.U. Mem. Nat. Assn. Life Underwriters, Am. Soc. C.L.U.'s, Life Ins. Agy. Mgmt. Assn. (dir.), Gen. Agts. and Mgrs. Assn. Los Angeles, Sales and Marketing Execs. Assn. Los Angeles, Stanford Bus. Sch. Assn. Methodist (pres. bd. trustees). Clubs: Lincoln, Jonathan (Los Angeles). Home: 2308 Nottingham Av Los Angeles CA 90027 Office: 523 W 6th St Los Angeles CA 90014

COLGATE, STIRLING AUCHINCLOSS, coll. pres.; b. N.Y.C., Nov. 14, 1925; s. Henry Auchincloss and Jeanette Thurber (Prwyn) C.; B.A. in Physics, Cornell U., Ithaca, N.Y., 1948, Ph.D., 1952; m. Rosemary Williamson, July 12, 1947; children—Henry Auchincloss II, Mary Sarah, Arthur Stirling. With Lawrence Radiation Lab., Berkeley, Cal., 1951-52, Livermore, Cal., 1952-64; engaged in electron and accelerator physics work, devel. nuclear weapons and tests in Eniwetok, 1955, with Controlled Thermonuclear Fusion project, 1955-64; del. 2d Internat. Conf. Peaceful Uses of Atomic Energy, Geneva, Switzerland, 1958; tech. adviser Conf. Discontinuance Nuclear Weapons Tests, Geneva, 1959; part-time lectr. elec. engring. U. Cal. at Berkeley, 1960-64; pres. N.M. Inst. Mining and Tech., Socorro, 1965—; spl. research controlled thermonuclear fusion with toroidal pinches and plasma confinement astrophysics; partner Richard M. Colgate, patent devel., 1958—. Cons. AEC, 1960—; mem. nuclear panel Sci. Adv. Bd., 1959-61; adv. com. fluid mechanics NASA, 1960-62; cons. ballistic missile div. USAF, 1960-62; cons. Def. Atomic Support Agy., 1962-64; mem. adv. com. environmental scis. NSF, 1967. Trustee-at-large Asso. Univ., 1970—. Fellow Am. Phys. Soc.; mem. Am. Astron. Soc., Sigma Xi. Address: New Mexico Inst Mining and Tech Socorro NM 87801

COLGRASS, MICHAEL CHARLES, composer; b. Chgo., Apr. 22, 1932; s. Michael Clement and Ann (Hand) C.; Mus.B., U. Ill., 1956; scholar Tanglewood, 1952, 54, Aspen, 1953; m. Ulla Damgaard, Nov. 25, 1966; 1 son, Neal. Pupil, Paul Price, Eugene Weigle, Darius Milhand, Lukas Foss, Wallingford Riegger, Ben Weber. Free-lance solo percussionist maj. N.Y. mus. orgns., 1956—. Narrator Boston Symphony, 1969, Phila. Orch., 1970; dir. Virgil's Dream, Brighton Festival, Danish Radio Orch., 1965; author, poet own theatre works, 1966—. Served with AUS, 1954-56. Guggenheim fellow, 1964-65, 68-69; recipient Fromm award, 1966; Rockefeller grantee, 1967-69. Composer: Divertimento, 1961; Fantasy Variations, 1961; Wind Quintet, 1962; Light Spirit, 1963; Rhapsody, 1963; Rhapsodic Fantasy, 1965; Sea Shadow, 1966; As Quiet As, 1966, Virgil's Dream, 1967; Three Brothers, 1951; Percussion Music, 1953; Chamber Music for Four Drums and String Quintet, 1954; Chamber Music for Percussion Quintet, 1955; Variations for Four Drums and Viola, 1957; The Earth's a Baked Apple, 1968-69; New People for mezzosoprano, viola, piano, 1969; Nightingale, Inc., comic jazz opera, 1971. Works commd. Boston Symphony, Lincoln Center chamber Mus. Soc., Fromm Found., Corp. for Pub. Broadcasting; works recorded various cos. Recipient Chem. Bank award, 1971. Contbr. articles to publs. Home: 280 Riverside Dr New York City NY 10025

COLI, GUIDO JOHN, Jr., chem. co. exec.; b. Richmond, Va., Sept. 12, 1921; s. Guido and Rena (Pacini) C.; B.A., Va. Poly. Inst., 1941, M.S., 1942, Ph.D., 1949; m. Gloria Ann Bolton, Feb. 1, 1947; children—Pamela, Patricia, Deborah, Richard. Asst. engr. Va. Health Dept. bur. indsl. hygiene, 1941; asso. chemist Naval Research Lab., 1942-43; instr. chem. engring. Va. Poly. Inst., 1947-48; chem. engr. Mobil Oil Co., Paulsboro, N.J., 1949-50; with Allied Chem. Corp., N.Y.C., 1950—, pres. fibers div., 1968, group v.p. corp., 1968—, dir., 1970—. Mem. Gov. Va. Commn. to Establish Urban Univ. in Richmond Area, 1966-67. Served to lt. USNR, 1943-46. Registered profl. engr., N.Y., Va. Fellow Am. Inst. Chemists; mem. Am. Chem. Soc. (chmn. Va. 1957), Am. Inst. Chem. Engrs., Va. C. of C., Sigma Xi, Phi Lambda Upsilon, Tau Beta Pi, Phi Kappa Phi, Alpha Kappa Psi. Club: Lambs (N.Y.C.). Home: 11 Winding Way Madison NJ 07940 Office: 1411 Broadway New York City NY 10018

COLIE, ROSALIE LITTELL, educator; b. N.Y.C., June 18, 1924; d. Frederic Runyon and Rosalie (Hall) Colie; A.B., Vassar Coll., 1944; M.A., Columbia, 1946, Ph.D., 1950. From instr. to asso. prof. Barnard Coll., 1948-61; asso. prof. history Wesleyan U., Middletown, Conn., 1961-63; prof. history and English, U. Ia., 1963-66; prof. English, U. Toronto, 1968-69; Nancy Duke Lewis prof. Brown U., 1969—. Fulbright fellow, 1952, 67-68; Howard fellow, 1958-59; Guggenheim fellow, 1959-60, 67-68; fellow Am. Council Learned Socs., 1948. Mem. Am. Assn. U. Women. Author: Some Thankfulnesse to Constantine, 1956; Light and Enlightment, 1957; Paradoxia Epidemica, 1966; My Echoing Song, 1970. Home: Ferry Rd Old Lyme CT 06371 Office: Marston Hall Brown Univ Providence RI 02912

COLIN, ANDRE, French politician, educator; b. Brest, France, Jan. 19, 1910; s. Pierre and Marie (Soubigou) C.; etudes superieures, Free Sch. of Angers, 1927; grad. Paris Sch. Law, 1931; m. Marguerite Laurent, July 24, 1950; children—Anne-Marie, Pierre, Francoise, and Paul. Began as sec. gen. of the Assn. Catholique Jeunesse Francaise, 1933-36, pres. gen., 1936-39; prof. Free Sch. Law, Lille, 1936-39; officer of marine justice, Beirut, 1940; mem. Nat. Resistance Council, 1944; mem. Provisional Adv. Assembly, 1944-45; dep. from Finistere, 1945-58, senator from Finistere, 1958-; gen. councillor ile d'Ouessant, 1951-; presiding sec. of council Govt. Bidault, 1946; minister of merchant marine, 1948-49; sec. of interior, 1950-53; commonwealth senator to European Parliamentary Assembly, 1958. Sec. gen. Popular Republican Party, 1945-55, nat. pres., 1959—. Decorated chevalier Legion of Honor, Croix de Guerre with palms. Resistance medal with rosettes. comdr0. Merite Maritime. Home: 10 rue Voltaire Brest, Finistère. Office: Palais du Luxembourg Paris b, France.

COLIN, RALPH FREDERICK, lawyer; b. N.Y.C., Nov. 18, 1900; s. William and Elizabeth (Benjamin) C.; A.B., Coll. City N.Y., 1918; LL.B., Columbia, 1921; m. Georgia Talmey, June 2, 1931; children—Ralph Frederick, Pamela Talmey (Lady Harlech). Admitted to N.Y. bar, 1922; asso. with Rosenberg & Ball, New York, 1921, mem. firm, 1926; later mem. firm Rosenberg, Goldmark & Colin; now Rosenman Colin Kaye Petschek Freund & Emil; dir., gen. counsel CBS, 1927—, Columbia Artists Mgmt., Inc.; adminstrv. v.p., gen. counsel Art Dealers Assn. Am.; dir. Carnegie Coating Co., Inc., Maria Bergson Assos., Ltd. Active early devel. art theatres; dir. Provincetown, Greenwich Village, Actors theatres. Dir., trustee, v.p. Philharmonic Symphony Soc. of N.Y., 1942-56; trustee, hon. sec. Baron de Hirsch Fund, 1935-56; trustee, v.p. Mus. Modern Art, 1954-69; vice chmn. Internat. Council; pres. Hosp. Joint Diseases, 1951-52; mem. vis. com. dept. fine arts and Fogg Mus. Harvard, 1951—; bd. visitors Columbia Law Sch.; dir. Shelter Rock Found., Rockmeadow Found., CBS Found. (pres. 1956-69), Am. Fedn. Arts, 1946-56; chmn. radio broadcasting div. Nat. War Fund, 1943-44. Mem. Assn. Bar City N.Y. (exec. com. 1942-46, chmn. spl. com. on pub. and bar relations 1956-59, v.p. 1961-62), N.Y. County Lawyers Assn., Am., Fed. Communications, N.Y. bar assns. Cons. editor Air Law Rev. Contbr. to law reviews. Home 941 Park Av New York City NY Office: 575 Madison Av New York City NY 10022

COLITON, WILLIAM PETER, r.r. exec.; b. Grand Forks, N.D., Jan. 18, 1920; s. Peter J. and Katherine P. (Carroll) C.; B.S., U. Pa., 1942; m. Marjorie L. Dundas, Sept. 13, 1952; children—Margaret, Susan, John, James. Train master, supt. G.N., R.R., 1946-55; v.p. operations, dir. M. & St.L. Ry., Mpls., 1955-60; pres., gen. mgr. Chgo., South Shore & South Bend R.R. Co., 1960-66; v.p. sales Western Md. Ry. Co., 1966-69, pres., dir., 1969—. Served Transp. Corps., AUS, 1942-46. Decorated Legion of Merit. Mem. Nat. Def. Transp. Assn., Nat. Freight Traffic Assn., C. of C. Met. Balt. (dir.). Clubs: Traffic (Balt., Chgo., N.Y.C.); Union League (Chgo., N.Y.C.); Center; Sky; LaCoquille; Seaview Country; Baltimore Country, Maryland. Home: 5400 Springlake Way Baltimore MD 21212 Office: 201 N Charles St Baltimore MD 21201

COLKER, MARVIN LEONARD, educator; b. Pitts., Mar. 19, 1927; s. Philip Marcus and Sarah (Grodner) C.; B.A. summa cum laude, U. Pitts., 1948; Ph.D., Harvard, 1951, postgrad. Sheldon fellow, 1951-52; Fulbright fellow, U. Paris, 1951-52; m. Hazel Robinson, Nov. 28, 1959; 1 son, Philip Ian. Instr. Classics U. Va., 1953-56, asst. prof., 1956-59, asso. prof., 1959-68, prof., 1968—, chmn. dept. Classics, 1963-68; cataloguer Mediaeval manuscripts U. Dublin, Ireland, 1958—, lectr. patristics, Mediaeval Latin, 1962-63; co- director Mediaeval manuscripts course standing conf. Nat. and Univ. Librarians, Dublin, 1968. Grantee Am. Philos. Soc., Trinity Trust Nat. Endowment for Humanities, U. Dublin Fund. Fellow Am. Council Learned Socs., 1962-63. Mem. Am. Philological Assn., Archaeol. Inst. Am., Mediaeval Acad. Am., Classical Assn. Middle West and South, Phi Beta Kappa. Author: Fulcoii Belvacensis Epistolae, 1954, Henrici Augustensis Planctus Evae, 1956, Richard of S. Victor and the Anonymous of Bridlington, 1962. Mem. editorial bd. Medievalia et Humanistica. Home: 105 Westminster Rd Charlottesville VA 22901

COLL, HARRY HILLARD, boat co. exec.; b. Detroit, May 23, 1909; s. Harry H. and Frances (Jarmin) C.; B.S. in Mech. Engring., U. Mich., B.S. in Aero. Engring., 1931; m. Betty Kelley, Dec. 22, 1934; children—Nancy E. (Mrs. J. Kehm), Norman A., Carolyn F. (Mrs. David Nugent). Div. prodn. supr. Murray Corp. Am., 1931-39; div. mgr. Chris-Craft Corp., Holland, Mich., 1939- 55, v.p., 1955-59, pres., 1959-69; v.p., dir. Chris-Craft Industries, until 1969; v.p. indsl. and marine div. N. Am. Rockwell Corp., 1969—; dir. First Nat. Bank Pompano Beach. Mem. Phi Kappa Tau. Episcopalian. Home: 2580 SE 8th St Pompano Beach FL 33062 Office: PO Box 860 Pompano Beach FL 33061

COLL, HELEN F., banker; b. nr. Lovettsville, Va., Dec. 2, 1921; d. Raymond C. and Minnie (Peters) Frye; grad. Washington Sch. Secs., 1940; student George Washington U., 1945-46; grad. Sch. Financial Pub. Relations, Northwestern U., 1963, Stonier Sch. Banking, Rutgers U., 1966; m. Lee Stanley Sherline, Sept. 1, 1940 (div. Feb. 1955); m. 2d, Robert Francis Coll, May 25, 1957. With Nat. Savs. & Trust Co., Washington, 1940—, bookkeeping clk., note dept. clk., collection teller, sec. trust dept., sec. safe deposit dept., head new accounts dept., sec. to pres., 1948-51, asst. sec., 1951-55, sec., 1955—, v.p., sec., 1963—, v.p. sec. bd., 1966—. Mem. Met. Bd. Trade. Mem. Nat. Assn. Bank Women, D.C. Bankers Assn., Bank Marketing Assn. Presbyn. Clubs: City Tavern, Aviation. Home: 1310 29th St NW Washington DC 20007 Office: Nat Savs & Trust Co New York Av at 15th St NW Washington DC 20005

COLLACOTT, ROBERT HOVER, former oil co. exec., child welfare ofcl.; b. Painesville, O., Aug. 30, 1897; s. Harry R. and Mary (Hover) C.; A.B., Cornell U., 1919; m. Margaret Oliver, Sept. 7, 1929; children—May O. (Mrs. Robert S. Targett), Catharine H. (Mrs. Richard DeWitt). With Standard Oil Co., Cleve., 1920- 69, dir. pub. relations, 1955-62, spl. asst. to pres., 1962-69; pres. Jos. Dyson & Sons, Inc.; dir. Akron Nat. Bank, Steere Enterprises, Inc. (both Akron). Chief petroleum products pricing OPA, World War II; mem. Nat. Indsl. Conf. Bd. Pres., Child Welfare League Am., 1962, 64, v.p. 1964—; pres. Cleve. Council World Affairs, 1962-64, chmn., 1964-69; v.p. Family Services Assn. Am., 1956-62; pres. Family Service Assn. Cleve., 1958-60, trustee, 1950—; mem. Cleve. Sr. Council, 1957—; chmn. Cleve. Better Bus. Bur., 1959-61, trustee 1954—; vice chmn. Ohio U. Council Econ. Edn.; mem. adv. council Coll. Arts and Scis., Univ. council, chmn. adminstrv. bd., pres. library assos. devel. com. Cornell U., Ithaca, New York; mem. Clergy-Econ. Edn. Found. Trustee Akron Gen. Hosp., Lake Erie Coll.; bd. dirs. Ohio Citizens Council Health and Welfare, 1958—, Nat. Conf. Social Welfare, 1962—. Mem. N.A.M., Am. Mgmt. Assn., Am. Econ. Assn., U.S., Ohio chambers commerce, Cleve. Engring. Soc., Am. Acad. Polit. and Social Scis., Newcomen Soc. N.A.M., English Speaking Union. Republican. Episcopalian. Clubs: Union, Cornell, Mid-Day, Philosophical (past pres.), University, City (Cleve.); City (Akron); University, Cornell (N.Y.C.). Home: 7645 Little Mountain Rd Mentor OH 44060 Office: Jos Dyson & Sons Inc 33300 Lakeland Blvd Eastlake OH 44094

COLLADO, EMILIO GABRIEL, oil co. exec.; b. Cranford, N.J., Dec. 20, 1910; s. Emilio Gabriel and Carrie (Hansee) C.; student Phillips Acad., Andover, Mass., 1925-27; S.B., Mass. Inst. Tech., 1931; A.M., Harvard, 1934, Ph.D., 1936; m. Janet Gilbert, June 30, 1932; children—Emilio Gabriel, Lisa. With printing and pub. firm, 1931; econ. analyst U.S. Treasury Dept., 1934- 36; economist Fed. Res. Bank N.Y., 1936-38; with Dept. of State, 1938- 46, asst. chief div. Am. Republics, 1940, spl. asst. to under sec. state, 1941-44, exec. sec. Bd. Econ. Operations, 1941-43, asso. adviser internat. econ. affairs, 1943-44, chief div. financial and monetary affairs, 1944-45, dir. Office Financial and Devel. Policy, 1945-46; U.S. exec. dir. Internat. Bank for Reconstrn. and Devel., 1946-47; trustee Export-Import Bank Washington, 1944-45; with Standard Oil Co. (N.J.), 1947—, asst. treas., 1949-54, treas., 1954-60, dir., 1960—, v.p., 1962-66, exec. v.p., 1966—; vice chmn. bd. Adela Investment Co. S.A., Discount Corp., Pvt. Investment Co. for ASIA (PICA); dir. Morgan Guaranty Trust Co. N.Y., J.P. Morgan & Co., Inc. U.S. alternate mem. Inter-Am. Finance and Econ. Adv. Com., 1939-46. Mem. USA/BIAC to Orgn. for Econ. Cooperation and Devel. Mem. bd. visitors Fletcher Sch. Internat. Diplomacy; vice chmn. bd. trustees Long Island U.; trustee, co-chmn. research and policy com. Com. for Econ. Devel.; bd. advisers to pres. Naval War Coll., 1967—; bd. dirs. Spanish Inst., Nat. Bur. Econ. Research. Mem. Am. Acad. Arts and Scis., Am. Econ. Assn., Internat. C. of C. (mem. U.S. council), Council of Americas, Atlantic Council U.S. (bd. dirs.), Council Fgn. Relations, Phi Mu Delta. Clubs: University (N.Y.C.); Metropolitan, Internat. (Washington); Harvard (Boston); Piping Rock; Knickerbocker; Racquet and Tennis; River. Home: 435 E 52d St New York City NY 10022 Office: Standard Oil Co (NJ) 30 Rockefeller Plaza New York City NY 10020

COLLAMORE, HARRY BACON, steel co. exec.; b. Middletown, Conn.; s. Harry N. and Matie (Bacon) C.; A.M., Colby Coll., 1939; m. Dorothy H. Rowe, Oct. 24, 1925; children—Harry Bacon, Wallace Rowe. Examiner, Nat. Fire Ins. Co., 1912- 16, Conn. spl. agt. for gen. agy., 1916-17; fieldman Nat. Fire Ins. Co., Tex. 1918-21, Pa., 1925, agy., supt., Hartford, Conn., 1925- 1926, later asst. sec. advancing to sec. and v.p., dir. and exec. v.p., pres. and chmn. bd., ret. 1956; chmn. bd., dir. Pitts. Steel Co., 1956—; dir. Am. Leasing Co., Conn. Bank & Trust Co., Mechanics Savs. Bank. Trustee Rosenbach Found., Phila., Watkinson Library; bd. dirs. Am. Sch. for Deaf. Served with U.S. Army, 1917-18. Episcopalian. Clubs: Hartford, Hartford Golf, Acorn (Hartford); Duquesne Club (Pitts.); Lotos, Grolier (N.Y.C.). Author: (with Lawrence R. Thompson) E.A. Robinson-Collection of His Works, 1936. Contbr. to Colophon, Lit. Observer. Home: 53 Mountain Brook Rd West Hartford CT 06117 Office: Grant Bldg Pittsburgh PA 15219

COLLEDGE, CHARLES HOPSON, broadcasting cons.; b. Paterson, N.J., June 3, 1911; s. William Arthur and Mary (Hopson) C.; student Newark Coll. Engring., Mass. Inst. Tech., Columbia U.; m. Margaret Whittaker, Sept. 2, 1931; children—Charles Edmund, William Arthur. Engr. NBC, 1933-43, supr. TV operations, Washington, 1947-49; dir. color operations RCA Labs., 1949-50; chief engr. NBC, Washington, 1950-52, dir. spl. events, news operations NBC-TV network, 1952-53, dir. operations and engring. NBC owned stas., 1953-56, v.p. operations, 1956-59, gen. mgr. broadcasting and TV equipment div. RCA, 1959-60, v.p., gen. mgr., broadcast and TV equipment div., RCA, 1960-61, v.p., gen. mgr. Broadcast & Communications Products div., 1961-68; mgmt. and engring. cons., 1968—; dir. St. Michaels Bank (Md.). Served from lt. (j.g.) to comdr. USNR, 1943-47. Profl. engr., D.C. Mem. Nat. Soc. Profl. Engrs., Izaak Walton League Am., TV Pioneers. Mason. Clubs: Radio Amateur Old Old Times; Talbot Country (Easton, Md.); Miles River Yacht; Georgetown (Md.) Racing Fleet; Poplar Island Yacht. Home: Quaker Neck Farm Edgar Cove Bozman MD 21612 Office: Box 175 Bozman MD 21612

COLLENS, WILLIAM S., physician; b. N.Y.C., June 5, 1897; s. Jacob and Rebecca (Skolnick) C.; B.S., Coll. City New York, 1917; M.D., Cornell U., 1921; m. Clara Lerner, May 15, 1930; children—Joanna, Richard. Intern Mt. Sinai Hosp., N.Y., 1921-23, voluntary asst. in physiol. research, Cornell U. Med U. Med. Coll., 1923-25; guest investigator dept. physiol. U. Rochester Med. Sch., 1928; asst. pediatric research, Jewish Hosp., Bklyn., 1925-30; chief diabetic clinic, clinic for peripheral vascular diseases, attending physician, Maimonides Hosp., Bklyn., 1930—; attending physician Jewish Chronic Disease Hosp.; cons. metabolic diseases, Rockaway Beach Hosp., N.Y.; clin. asst. prof. medicine State U. N.Y., N.Y.C. Diplomate Am. Bd. Internal Medicine. Fellow A.M.A., A.A.A.S., N.Y. Acad. Medicine, A.C.P.; mem. N.Y. State, Kings County med. Socs., Am. Heart Assn., Am. Fedn. for Clinic Research, Soc. for Exptl. Biology and Medicine Am. Diabetes Assn., Am. Soc. Study Internal Secretions, Am. Soc. Study Arteriosclerosis. Club: Unity. Author books including: Helpful Hints to the Diabetic, 1947; Peripheral Vascular Diseases. Contributor articles to journals. Inventor of intermittent venous occlusion apparatus for treatment of peripheral circulatory impairment and others. Home: 123A 8th Av Brooklyn NY 11215 ☆

COLLERY, ARNOLD, educator, economist; b. Glen Cove, N.Y., Feb. 1, 1927; s. James Edward and Lillian (Froehlich) C.; B.A magna cum laude, U. Buffalo, 1950; Ph.D., Princeton, 1958; M.A. (hon.), Amherst Coll., 1964; m. Helen Odile Cassily, Feb. 2, 1957; children—Peter Mitchell, Elizabeth Dorsey. Mem. faculty Amherst Coll., 1953—, prof. econs., 1964—, chmn. dept., 1957- 58, 64-66; vis. prof. Mass. Inst. Tech., summers 1965, 68—; mem. adv. council dept. econs. Princeton, 1965—. Cons. to industry. Treas. Hampshire (Mass.) Community Action Commn., 1965-67, mem. bd. dirs., 1965-70. Served with AUS, 1945-47. NSF postdoctoral fellow, 1963-64. Mem. Am. Econ. Assn., Phi Beta Kappa. Author: National Income and Employment Analysis. 1966, rev. edit., 1970. Home: 271 S Pleasant St Amherst MA 01002

COLLET, GEORGES PAUL, educator; b. Biere, Vaud, Switzerland, Apr. 8, 1917; s. Georges and Marguerite (Barth) C.; Doctorat ès lettres, U. Geneva, 1957; m. Violette George, Sept. 19, 1942; children—Claire, Laurent. French lectr. Durham Colls., Eng., 1948-50; prof. French, school interpreters U. Geneva, 1952-59; prof. French UN, Geneva, 1950-59; vis. prof. French U. Tex., 1959-60; prof. French, Tulane U., 1960-63; vis. prof. French, Fla. State U., 1963-64; prof. French, McGill U., 1964—, chmn. dept., 1966—. Decorated chevalier des palmes académiques (France), 1964. Mem. Modern Lang. Assn. Am., Am. Assn. Tchrs. of French, Internat., Canadian comparative literature assns., Société des amis d'André Gide, Anglo-Genevese Soc. (pres. 1952-55), L'Alliance Française (pres. 1963). Author: George Moore et la France, 1957; La Correspondance entre Andre Gide et Jacques-Emile Blanche, in preparation; Jacques-Emile Blanche, peintre-écrivain, in preparation. Home: 73 Churchill Rd Baie d'Urfé Quebec Canada Office: 3460 McTavish St Montreal 112 Quebec Canada

COLLETT, ROBERT ARTHUR, apparel co. exec.; b. Evanston, Ill., Sept. 16, 1922; s. Arthur Barrie and Daisy (Gaunt) C.; student Beloit Coll., 1939-41; B.B.A., Northwestern U., 1947; m. Gwynneth C. Hamilton, Jan. 23, 1951; childrenJohn Frederick, Thomas Arthur, Robert James. Auditor, Touche, Ross, Bailey & Smart, Chgo., 1947-49; auditor, factory comptroller Sears, Roebuck & Co., Chgo., 1949-60, asst. to v.p. in charge mfg., 1960- 62; v.p. finance Kellwood Co., St. Louis, 1962-, treas., 1966-, also dir. Served to capt. USMCR, 1942-45, to maj., 1951-53. Decorated D.F.C. with 6 air medals. Mem. Mo. Amateur Ice Hockey Assn. (pres.), Sigma Chi Episcopalian. Mason. Home: 30 Mason Rd Webster Groves, MO 63119 Office: 9909 Clayton Rd Saint Louis, MO 63124

COLLETTE, ALFRED THOMAS, educator; b. Syracuse, N.Y., Sept. 10, 1922; s. Samuel M. and Pauline (Quint) C.; student W.Va. Wesleyan Coll., 1940-41, Hamilton Coll., 1943- 44; A.B., Syracuse (N.Y.) U., 1947, M.S., 1948, Ph.D., 1952. Asst. prof. Syracuse (N.Y.) U., 1951-54, asso. prof., 1955-59, dual prof. sci. edn. and genetics, 1959—, chmn. div. sci. teaching, 1954—, prof. bacteriology and botany, 1951—, prof., chmn. zoology dept., 1968-70, dir. acad. year program NSF, 1958—, dir. fgn. scientist program, 1959-66. Served to sgt. USAAF, 1942-46. Recipient grants NSF, AEC, A.A.A.S. Mem. Am. Soc. Human Genetics, Nat. Assn. Research Sci. Edn., Am. Genetics Soc., Nat. Sci. Tchrs. Assns., Sigma Xi, Phi Beta Kappa, Kappa Phi Kappa, Phi Kappa Phi, Sigma Pi Sigma, Phi Delta Kappa. Author: Curriculum For The Science Gifted, 1961; Teaching Science in Today's Secondary Schools, 1959, latest edit., 1968; Science Teaching In The Secondary School: A Modern Approach, 1971. Home: 706 Livingston Av Syracuse NY 13210

COLLETTE, WILLIAM MARCELL, flutist, composer; b. Los Angeles, Aug. 6, 1921; s. Willie H. and Goldie (Dorris) C.; grad. pub. schs.; m. Louise Harris, Jan. 24, 1944 (div. 1962); children—William Zan, Cheryl Ann, Veda. With own band, 1940-41, Cee Pee Johnson Orch., 1941-42, Les Hite, 1942, various bands, 1946-50, Chico Hamilton, 1956; mem. Jerry Fielding orch. Groucho Marx Show, 1950-60, Edie Adams Show, Gary Moore Show, others, also Danny Kaye Show; instr. reeds, composing, arranging; pub. appearances include Newport Jazz Festival, 1956, San Remo Jazz Festival, 1961, Monterey Jazz Festival, 1964; composer mus. scores for motion pictures including The Most Important Man, 1963, A Comedy Tale of Fanny Hill, 1964, ECS, 1964, the George Washington Carver Story, Trauma; Composer Blue Sands, Santa Monica Soft Touch, Rooms with Skies (songs); record albums for Ricordi, 1961. Mercury, 1962, World Pacific, 1964, others. Served with USNR, 1942-45. Home: 5177 Pickford St Los Angeles CA 90019

COLLEY, JOHN LEONARD, Jr., educator; b. Wilmington, N.C., Feb. 17, 1930; s. John L. and Icie (Hall) C.; B.S., N.C. State U., 1957; M.S., Yale, 1959; D.B.A., U. So. Cal., 1964; m. Tommie Lancaster, Dec. 14, 1950; children—John Lawrence, Clair Ellen, Thomas Michael. Planning engr. operations and systems analysis Western Electric Co., 1959-62; chief operations analysis Hughes Aircraft Co., 1962-65; group leader Research Triangle Inst., Durham, N.C., 1965-67; also lectr. U. So. Cal., 1963-65; adj. prof. indsl. engring. N.C. State U., 1965-67; prof. bus. adminstrn. Grad. Sch. Bus., U. Va., 1967—; pres. Southeastern Cons. Group, Ltd., 1969—. Served with USAF, 1952-56. Mem. Operations Research Soc. Am., Inst. Mgmt. Sci., Am. Inst. Indsl. Engrs. (program chmn. 1969, dir. product planning and control div. 1970—), Sigma Xi, Tau Kappa Epsilon, Tau Beta Pi, Alpha Pi Mu, Beta Gamma Sigma, Phi Kappa Phi. Club: Farmington (Charlottesville). Home: 1423 Foxbrook Lane Charlottesville VA 22901

COLLEY, WALTER M., clay products mfg. exec.; b. 1922; m. 1949; grad. U. Cal. at Los Angeles. With Arthur Andersen & Co., 1949-51; with Pacific Clay Products, Los Angeles, 1951—, exec. v.p., 1962-65, pres., chief exec. officer, 1965—, also dir., 1969—; dir. PCP Transp. Co.; v.p., dir. Pacific Holding Corp., Anaheim Union Water Co. Home: 801 E Norman Av Arcadia CA 91006 Office: 1255 W 4th St Los Angeles CA 90017

COLLIE, ALBERTO WILLIAM, sculptor; b. Caracas, Venezuela, June 1, 1939; s. Alberto Ronal Collie and Elsa Senior de Collie; came to U.S., 1959; B.F.A., Boston U., 1963; M.A., Harvard, 1966; m. Ruth Elen Sussman, Sept. 24, 1960; children—Noemi Alesamdra, Miguel Alberto, Luis Roberto. One-man exhibits include Mus. Fine Arts, Caracas, 1966, Atelier Chapman Kelly, Dallas, 1963, 66, Nordness Gallery, N.Y.C., 1964, 66, Comara Gallery, Los Angeles, 1964, Pepsi Cola Bldg., N.Y.C., 1966, Pan Am. Union, Washington, 1966, Ward-Nasse Gallery, Boston, 1966, Venezuelan Embassy, Washington, 1966; group exhibits include Contemporary Painting and Sculpture in U.S. at U. Ill., 1967, Albany (N.Y.) Inst. History and Art, 1965, Albany Inst. traveling exhbn., Berkeley, Cal., 1965, Hansen Gallery, San Francisco, 1964, Pitts. Internat., 1964, Venezula Pavillion at N.Y. World's Fair, 1964-65, U. Houston, 1965, Gallery Vendome, N.Y.C., 1964, Ateneo de Valencia (Spain), 1958, New Eng. Contemporary Artists, 1963-65, Sao Paulo (Brazil) Biennal, 1967, Boston U. Sch. Fine and Applied Arts, 1962. Esther Stuttman Gallery, Provincetown, Mass., 1963, CHIA Cartpenter Center, Harvard, 1967; rep. permanent collections Dallas Mus. Fine Arts, Chrysler Mus., Provincetown, Mass., Mus. Fine Arts, Caracus, S.C. Johnson & Son, Inc., Racine, Wis., Carnegie Inst., Irving Sabin Chem. Co., Boston Art for Industry, Weston, Mass., First Nat. Savs. Bank, Dallas Venezuelan Embassy, Washington, also pvt. collections; pres. Terra Internat., environmental research, design and regional resources planning. Guggenheim fellow, 1966-67. Mem. Am. Venezuelan assns. landscape architects. Home: 134 E 70th St New York City, NY 10021 Office: U de Oriente Edo Anzuatesui Puerto La Cruz, Venezuela

COLLIE, MARVIN KEY, lawyer; b. San Antonio, July 16, 1916; s. Marvin Key and Gladys (Stanley) C.; student Washington and Lee U., 1939; B.A., LL.B., U. Tex., 1941; m. Nancy Morriss, Nov. 21, 1942; children—Nancy Gwynne, Marvin Key III, David Wade. Admitted to Tex. bar, 1941, since practiced in Houston; partner Vinson, Elkins, Searis and Smith, partner in charge tax dept.; pres. Nat. Bank of Commerce, Houston, 1958-60. Mem. tax adv. group Ways and Means Com., 85th Congress; adv. com. Commr. Internal Revenue, 1963; mem. Presdl. task force on bus. taxation, 1969-70. Bd. dirs. Meth. Hosp., Houston; mem. devel. bd. U. Tex., Austin; pres. U. Tex. Found., Med. Research Found. Tex.; exec. com., trustee Baylor Coll. Medicine. Served as lt. M.I., AAC, World War II. Fellow Am. Bar Found., Am. Soc. Probate Counsel; mem. Philos. Soc. Tex., Am. Bar Assn., State Bar Tex. (past chmn. taxation sect.), Am. Law Inst. (cons. estate tax project 1965-69), Sigma Alpha Epsilon. Methodist. Home: 3415 Sleepy Hollow Ct Houston TX 77019 Office: First City Nat Bank Bldg Houston TX 77002

COLLIER, ABRAM THURLOW, ins. co. exec., lawyer; b. Billerica, Mass., Oct. 26, 1913; s. Forrest Foster and Lucy Bryant (Foster) C.; A.B. cum laude, Harvard, 1934, LL.B., 1937; m. Eleanor Whitney, Dec. 11, 1937; children—Linda (Mrs. E. H. Kenerson), Debora (Mrs. J.W. Zug), Joyce (Mrs. J.T. Fearnside), Charles W. Admitted to Mass. bar, 1937; practiced in Boston, 1937-39; with John Hancock Mut. Life Ins. Co., 1939-66, vice chmn., 1965-66; pres. New Eng. Mut. Life Ins. Co., 1966—; adv. dir. New Eng. Mchts. Nat. Bank; dir. New Eng. Tel. & Tel. Co., Houghton Mifflin Co. Mem. corp. Northeastern U.; trustee, chmn. bd. overseers Boston Symphony Orch.; vice chmn. bd. trustees Wheaton Coll.; bd. dirs. Babson Coll., Boston Mus. of Sci. Recipient McKinsey award Harvard Bus. Rev., 1960. Mem. Am., Boston bar assns., Assn. Life Ins. Counsel (pres. 1962-63), Am. Coll. Life Underwriters (trustee), Boston C. of C. (pres. 1965-66, mem. bd. dirs.). Clubs: Appalachian Mountain; Somerset, Algonquin, Harvard, Commercial (Boston); The Country (Brookline). Author: Management, Men, and Values, 1962. Home: 80 Westcliff Rd Weston MA 02193 Office: 501 Boylston St Boston MA 02116

COLLIER, BLANTON, former head coach Cleveland Browns Profl. Football Team, ret., 1970. Address: Cleveland Stadium Cleveland OH 44114*

COLLIER, DONALD, mus. curator, anthropologist; b. Sparkill, N.Y., May 1, 1911; s. John and Lucy (Wood) C.; A.B., U. Cal., 1933; Ph.D., U. Chgo., 1954; m. Malcolm Carr, Oct. 18, 1939; children—David, Bruce. Field asst. Mus. Ariz., excavations at Wupatki, Ariz., 1933; fellow dept. anthropology U. Chgo., 1934-35, research fellow, 1938-39, lectr. in anthropology 1949—; fellow Lab. Anthropology Santa Fe, 1935, Inst. Andean Research, archaeol. research in Peru, 1937; instr. anthropology Wash. State Coll.,

1940-41, field supr. Latin Am. Archaeol. Surveys, Ecuadorian Reconnaissance, 1941-42; asso. dir. Columbia Basin Archaeol. Survey, State Wash., 1940; asst. curator S. Am. ethnology and archaeol. Field Mus. Natural History, Chgo., 1941-43, curator, 1943-64, chief curator anthropology dept., 1964—. Rep. Am. Anthrop. Assn. to NRC, 1949-51; archaeol. expdns. to Peru, 1946, 56. Book review editor Am. Anthropologist, 1949-50, Am. Antiquity, 1958- 62. Mem. Am. Anthrop. Assn. (exec. bd. 1965-67), Soc. Am. Archaeology, Inst. Andean Research (chmn. 1956), Central States Anthrop. Soc. (pres. 1953-54), Sigma Xi. Author books including: (with P.S. Martin and G.I. Quimby) Indians Before Columbus, 1947; Indian Art of the Americas, 1959. Home: 5632 Kimbark Av Chicago IL 60636 Office: Field Mus Natural History Chicago IL 60605

COLLIER, DONALD WALTER, electronic mfg. co. exec.; b. Washington, June 5, 1920; s. A. Walter and Helen (Cherry) Collier; B. Applied Chemistry summa cum laude, Cath. U. Am., 1941; A.M., Princeton, 1943, Ph.D., 1944, Chem.E., 1944; m. Janine Louise Robin, May 29, 1948 (div. Jan. 1968); children—Paul Robin, Kathryn Robin. Research chemist, chem. engr. research lab. Sharples Corp., 1944-51; dir. research Thomas A. Edison, Inc., 1951-57, v.p., 1955-57, v.p., dir. research Thomas A. Edison Industries, West Orange, N.J., 1957-59; pres. research lab. Thomas A. Edison, Inc., McGraw Edison Co., West Orange, 1959-60; v.p. research Borg-Warner Corp., Chgo., 1960—; dir. Atomic Instrument Co., 1953-56, Baird-Atomic, Inc., 1956-57, Sci. & Nuclear Fund, Inc., 1954-58. Trustee Rittenhouse Fund, 1958-60; vis. com. John Crerar Library, Chgo., 1963—. Pres. Pines Lake Country Club and Community Assn., Wayne, N.Y., 1959-60; chmn. personnel policy com. Wayne Twp. Bd. Edn., 1956-60; adv. council chem. engring. dept. Princeton, 1955-61, adv. council plastics program, 1968—. Bd. dirs. Chgo. Area Research and Devel. Council. Mem. Am. Inst. Chem. Engrs., A.A.A.S. (v.p. 1968), Am. Chem. Soc., Assn. Research Dirs. (pres. 1958-59), Research Dirs. Assn. Chgo. (pres. 1964-65), Indsl. Research Inst. (pres. 1966-67, dir.), N.A.M. (research com. 1953—), Sci. Research Soc. Am., N.R.C., Dirs. Indsl. Research (chmn. membership com.), Am. Ordnance Assn., Engrs. Joint Council (dir. 1966-67), Sigma Xi, Phi Eta Sigma. Home: 6101 Sheridan Rd E Chicago IL 60626 Office: 200 S Michigan Av Chicago IL 60604

COLLIER, EVERETT DOLTON, newspaper exec.; b. Long Beach, Miss., Feb. 26, 1914; s. Thomas Lee and Elizabeth Naomi (Cruthirds) C.; B.A., Rice Inst., 1937; m. Mary Margaret Chisholm, Mar. 26, 1950; 1 son, Ervin Cornell. Mem. staff Houston Chronicle, 1934—, polit. editor, 1946-52, editorial writer, 1952-57, asst. editor, 1957-59, mng. editor, 1959-65, v.p., editor, bd. dirs., 1965—; dir. Fairbanks State Bank. Bd. dirs. Tex. Soc. Prevention Blindness, 1965-66, Tex. Water Found., United Fund, Salvation Army, Tex. Good Rds. Assn., Houston Harris County Tb Assn., Houston Livestock Show and Rodeo. Mem. Am. Soc. Newspaper Editors, Rice U. Alumni Assn. (pres. 1963), Tex. U.P.I. Editors Assn. (v.p. 1965), Houston C. of C. (dir. 1970—). Methodist (bd. ofcl.). Club: Press (Houston). Home: 4622 Ingersoll Av Houston TX 77027 Office: Houston Chronicle 512-20 Travis St Houston TX 77002

COLLIER, FELTON MORELAND, architect; b. Bessemer, Ala., Mar. 20, 1924; s. Felton and Grace (Moreland) C.; student Birmingham-So. Coll., 1942-43, Howard Coll. (now Samford U.), 1943; B.A., U. N.C., 1945; postgrad. N.C. State U., 1948-50; B.Arch., Auburn U., 1954; m. Elizabeth Pettus Buck, Oct. 22, 1955 (dec. 1966); children—Felton Moreland, Marcus Ashby Moreland. Archtl. experience with firms in Birmingham, Ala. and Durham, N.C., 1949-51, 54-57; architect Felton Moreland Collier, Birmingham, 1958—, Felton Moreland Collier and Carroll C. Harmon, Asso. Architects, Birmingham, 1965—. Chief lectr. Naval Res. Officers Sch., Birmingham, 1957-69. Served with USNR, 1945-46, to lt., 1951-53; Korea. Recipient Regional Merit award A.I.A., 1962, Honor award Birmingham chpt. A.I.A., 1965. Mem. A.I.A. (founding mem., sec. Birmingham chpt. 1963-64, v.p. 1966), Alpha Tau Omega. Democrat (candidate Ala. Ho. Reps. 1970). Episcopalian (vestryman 1969-71). Club: Exchange. Contbr. articles recreational jours.; lit. editor Ala. Architect, 1969-70. Home: 2223 20th Av S Birmingham AL 35223 Office: 1623 S 21st St Birmingham AL 35205

COLLIER, HAMPDEN FISCHER, banker; b. Richmond, Va., Oct. 8, 1920; s. Hampden Fischer and Elsie (Miller) C.; grad. U. Wis. Sch. Banking, 1955; m. Marian Lee Austin, Jan. 23, 1943; children—Marian Jean (Mrs. James Adger Edmunds), Carl Hampden, Bruce Paul, Alan Thomas. With Bank of Va., Richmond, 1938—, v.p. operations, 1968—, cashier, 1970—. Treas., mem. exec. com. Va. Heart Assn., Richmond, 1969—. Served with USNR, 1943-46. Mem. Am. Inst. Banking. Baptist. Club: Sertoma (treas. 1962—). Home: 3516 Margate Dr Richmond VA 23235 Office: 800 E Main St Richmond VA 23214

COLLIER, HAROLD REGINALD, congressman; b. Lansing, Mich., Dec. 12, 1915; s. Joseph H. and Anna (Koener) C.; student Morton Jr. Coll., Cicero, Ill., 1932-33, Lake Forest (Ill.) Coll., 1933-34, 35-37; m. Carol Jean Bangert, Sept. 3, 1938; children—Calvin Joseph, Lynne Ann (Mrs. Terrence R. Kulp), Harold Paul. Suburban newspaper editor and columnist, 1938-42; personnel mgr. Match Corp. Am., Chgo., 1940-52; advt., pub. relations dir. McAlear Mfg. Corp., Chgo., 1952-56. Alderman, City of Berwyn, Ill., 1950-52; Republican candidate sec. state, Ill., 1952; twp. supr. Berwyn, 1953-56; sec.-treas. Cook County Supervisors Assn., 1953- 56; Republican twp. committeeman, 1954-60; chmn. 1st Senatorial Dist. Rep. Com., 1954—; mem. 85th-92d Congresses, 10th Dist. Ill., mem. com. on ways and means. Former mem. Outdoor Recreation Resources Commn.; mem. adv. bd. Nat. Council on Drug Abuse, nat. adv. bd. Am. Security Council. Mem. Ill. Soc. of Washington (v.p.), Quill and Scroll Soc., U.S. Capitol Hist. Soc., Lake Forest Coll. Alumni Assn., Internat. Platform Assn. Methodist. Elk. Clubs: National Rocket, 85th Congressional (Washington). Home: 3819 Howard Av Western Springs IL 60558 Office: Longworth House Office Bldg Washington DC 20515

COLLIER, HERMAN EDWARD, Jr., coll. pres.; b. St. Louis, Mo., Aug. 8, 1927; s. Herman E. and Evelyn (Savill) C.; B.S., Randolph-Macon Coll., 1950; M.S., Lehigh U., 1952, Ph.D., 1955, LL.D., 1971; m. Jerline L. Weston, Mar. 25, 1948; children—Herman Edward III, Michael F., Thomas W. Chmn. dept. chemistry Moravian Coll., 1955-57; research chemist E. I. duPont de Nemours Co., Wilmington, Del., 1957-63; prof. chemistry, chmn. div. natural scis. Moravian Coll., 1963-69, pres., 1969—; chmn. dirs. Lehigh Regional Consortium. Mem. Com. to Employ the Handicapped 1970—. Bd. dirs. United Fund Bethlehem, Historic Bethlehem, Inc.; trustee St. Luke's Hosp. Served with USNR, 1945-46. Mem. Lehigh Valley Assn. Ind. Colls., Pa. Soc. Coll. Chemistry Tchrs., Am. Chem. Soc., Am. Assn. U. Profs., Am. Inst. Chemists, Phi Beta Kappa, Sigma Xi, Kappa Alpha. Patentee mfg. tech. and product quality organo-lead compounds; sodium tetraphenyl boron for potassium detection; periodic table for lecture room, 1953; flame spectra metallic ions from the H-F Flame, 1957. Home: 79 W Church St Bethlehem PA 18018

COLLIER, JAMES ALAN, educator; b. LaCrosse, Ind., Dec. 15, 1925; s. James Vance and Grace Margaret (Wells) C.; B.S., Northwestern U., 1951; M.B.A., Ind. U., 1956; Ph.D., U. Wis., 1966; m. Marilyn Jean Sherwood, Dec. 31, 1951; children—Alan Jay, Cosette Rene. Owner, James A. Collier Agy., gen. ins., LaPorte, Ind., 1951-55; asst. prof. ins. U. N.D., 1956-59; asst. prof. ins. U. Ariz., 1963-67; prof. ins. (Wunderlich chair) Memphis State U., 1967—, chmn. dept. finance, ins. and real estate Coll. Bus., 1968-70. Mem. ins. adv. bd. City of Memphis and Shelby County, 1968—. Served with USNR, World War II. Employers Mut. Casualty Ins. Co. fellow, 1959-61; Northwestern Mut. Life Ins. Co. fellow, 1961-63. Mem. Estate Planning Council Memphis, Am. Soc. Ins. Mgmt., Am. Risk and Ins. Assn., So. Econ. Assn. Author: Capital Planning Problems of Small Mutual Insurance Companies, 1966. Home: 3176 Raleigh-Millington Rd 9 Memphis TN 38128

COLLIER, LOUIS AUGUSTUS, food mfg. co. exec.; b. Barnesville, Ga., Dec. 22, 1914; s. Louis A. and Ezra (Matthews) C.; grad. Gordon Mil. Coll., Barnesville, Ga.; m. Ella McGee, Feb. 15, 1936; children—Louis A., Robert D. With H.J. Heinz Co., 1938—, salesman, sales supr., br. sales mgr., sales promotion mgr., zone sales mgr., 1960-61, v.p. marketing, Pitts., 1961-64, sr. v.p. sales and marketing, 1964-. Served to lt. col., inf. AUS, 1942-46. Mem. Grocery Mfrs. Assn., Am. Marketing Assn., Assn. Nat. Advertisers. Clubs: Pittsburgh Athletic, Duquesne; Highland Country. Home: 143 Beaconview Rd Pittsburgh, PA 15237 Office: Progress St Pittsburgh PA 15212

COLLIER, MARIE ELIZABETH, soprano; b. Ballarat, Australia, Apr. 16, 1927; d. Thomas Robinson and Ann- Marie (Bechaz) C.; grad. high sch.; m. 1952; three sons, 1 dau. Australian debut, 1952; appeared in prin. parts in Italian and Slavic, modern operas at Covent Gardens, 1957, Lincoln Centre, N.Y.C., 1962, 67, also Sadler's Wells, Yugoslavia, Paris, France, Argentina, Austria, Italy, Germany, Canada, S.Africa. Address: Burnt Oak Cookham Rise Berks England*

COLLIER, NEIL REX, former journalist; b. Washington, Sept. 20, 1897; s. Harry Lee and Maude (Hicks) C.; student George Washington U., 1916-18; m. Pauline L. Palmer, Oct. 1, 1919; children—Elaine (dec.), Neil Rex (dec.), William Lee, Jack Wayne. Reporter, Washington Herald, 1919, Washington Post, 1919-20, Evening and Sunday Star, 1920-23, asst. city editor, 1924, asst. to mng. editor, 1939-40, editorial writer, 1940- 62; author syndicated newspaper strip War on Crime, 1938-39; collaborated with Phillips Lord in first authenticated series of radio dramatizations of F.B.I. cases, 1937. Student-officer, U.S. Naval Aviation, 1918, commd. Vol. Naval Res., 1927, active duty, 1942-45; office pub. relations, Navy Dept., and 1st Naval Dist.; capt. USNR, 1945. Mem. U.S. Naval Inst., Am. Mus. Natural History, Internat. Oceanographic Found., Ret. Officers Assn. Home: 4774 Old Dominion Dr Arlington VA 22207 also Route 1 Kilmarnock VA 22484

COLLIER, OSCAR, lit. agt.; b. Waco, Tex., Feb. 26, 1924; s. Hosea Oscar and Percy Virginia (Moore) C.; student Baylor U., 1941-42, U. Ia., 1943, Art Students League, 1945-47, New Sch. Social Research, 1947-48; m. Gertrude Barrer, 1942 (div. 1947); 1 dau., Greer; m. 2d, Gladys Perin Whitridge, 1949 (div. 1970); children—Lisa Whitridge, Sophia Whitridge; m. 3d, Diana Meerwarth, 1970. Artist, writer, 1945-59; one man shows Galerie Neuf, N.Y.C., 1945, Ashby Gallery N.Y.C., 1945; co-editor Iconograph mag., N.Y.C., 1947-48; N.Y.C. corr. Mediarts mag., 1958; editor, asst. to pres. Fleet Pub. Corp., N.Y.C., 1960-63, pres., editor, 1964-67; v.p. Hobbs, Dormann & Co., Inc., N.Y.C., 1967; partner Collier-Hobbs Agy., 1967-68, Seligmann & Collier, N.Y.C., 1968- -. Mem. Soc. Authors Reps. Contbr. articles stories, poems to various publs. Home: 170 West End Av New York City NY 10023 Office: 280 Madison Av New York City NY 10016

COLLIER, PAUL STANLEY, trade assn. cons.; b. Durant, Ia., Mar. 28, 1890; s. Durbin Burton and Lydia (Schreckengast) C.; A.B., U. of Ia., 1911, M.A., 1912; Ph.D., Columbia, 1915; m. Fannie A. Koch, Mar. 6, 1917; children—Gretchen Koch, Paul Stanley. Investigator, N.Y. State Factory Investigating Commn., 1913-15; research N.Y. Bur. Municipal Research, 1915-16; sec. Oneonta (N.Y.) C. of C. and sec.-mgr. Retail Lumber Dealers Assn. of State of N.Y., 1916-21; sec.-mgr. Northeastern Retail Lumbermens Assn., Rochester, N.Y., 1922-49, exec. v.p., 1949-61, cons., 1961—; sec. mgr. Merchandising Council of Retail Lumber Dealer Assns., 1932-38; sec. and councillor Retail Lumber Bldg. Material Code Authority, 1933- 35; sec., treas. Merchandising Inst. of Nat. Retail Lumber Dealers Assn., Inc., 1938-65; treas. Merchandising Inst., Nat. Lumber and Bldg. Material Dealers Assn., Inc., 1965—; dir. Northeastern Homes Found. 1940—; pres. and chmn. adv. bd. Am. Trade Assn. Executives, 1933-35, chmn. com. on ethics and standards, 1935-37. Mem. Rochester C. of C., Chamber of Commerce of U.S., Am. Acad. Polit. and Social Science, Citizens Hist. Assn., S.A.R., Phi Beta Kappa, Delta Sigma Rho. Episcopalian. Mason. Clubs: Rochester, University, Advertising, The Monroe Golf and Country (Rochester, N.Y.); The Rotary. Editor: Hand Book for Lumber and Building Material Dealers, 1920; Decisions Under the Anti-Trust Laws, 1935. Author: Minimum Wage Legislation in Australasia, 1915. Editor and pub. The Lumber Coöperator Jour., 1917-61, chmn. editorial bd., 1961—. Contbr. to jours. and publs. Home: 210 Kilbourn Rd Rochester NY 14618 Office: 339 East Av Rochester NY 14604

COLLIER, ROBERT PERCY, educator; b. Pendleton, Ore., July 18, 1920; s. Percival Meredith and Ruth (Graybill) C.; B.A., Reed Coll., 1942; Ph.D., Stanford, 1955; m. Constance Sayre, Feb. 8, 1943; children—Catherine, Daniel S., Charles S., Hal M., Matthew R. Teaching asst. econs. and accounting Stanford, 1949-51; asst. prof. econs. U. Wash., 1951-52; research coordinator So. Cal. Research Council, 1953-57; asst. prof. econs. Occidental Coll., 1952-57, asso. prof., 1957-58, acting dept. head, chmn. scholarship com., 1953-58; prof. econs. and bus. adminstrn. Utah State U., Logan, 1958—, head bus. adminstrn. dept., 1958-64, dean Coll. Bus. and Social Scis., 1958-68, dean Coll. Bus., 1968—; pres. Los Lagos Ranch, Inc., 1971—; research asst. Rand Corp., 1950. Cons., Joint Council Econ. Edn., 1955-58; chmn. Utah Agr.-Industry Conf., 1959-63; mem. exec. com. Utah Council Econ. Edn., 1961-62, chmn., 1963-65; dir. Utah Sci. Research Found., 1963-65; economist and campus coordinator U.S. AID rural indsl. tech. assistance project, Rio Grande de Norte, Brazil, 1965, acting party chief, summer 1965; cons. indsl. devel. on Indian Reservation, Bur. Indian Services, U. Utah, 1966; visitor faculty econs. and politics U. Cambridge, 1967-68. Mem. Logan City Zoning and Planning Commn., 1962-67. Served with USNR, 1942-46. Recipient Freedom Found. award, 1954; Haynes Found. research fellow, 1957. Mem. Am., Western (past mem. exec. com.) econ. assns., Am. Assn. U. Profs., Utah Edn. Assn., Nat. Assn. State Univs. and Land Grant Colls. (sec. commn. on edn. bus. professions, past mem. exec. com.), Cache C. of C. (dir. 1970—). Presbyn. (trustee). Author: Purchasing Power Bonds and Other Escalated Contracts, 1969. Home: 926 N 15 East Logan UT 84321

COLLIGAN, FRANCIS JAMES, govt. ofcl., educator; b. San Francisco, Dec. 27, 1908; s. Dr. Francis Joseph and Mary Helen (Barrett) C.; A.B., U. San Francisco, 1929; A.M., U. Cal., 1933, Ph.D., 1941; student Latin Am. Inst., Am. Council Learned Socs., 1941; Prof. (hon.), Sch. Letters and Edn., Nat. U. Ecuador, 1944; m. Margaret Clara Haxton, Aug. 1, 1933; 1 son, Francis Sherwin. Jr. employee Bank of Am., 1929; jr. underwriter State Compensation Ins. Fund, 1930; instr. to asst. prof. U. San Francisco, 1931-35; organizer and dir. library services City Coll. San Francisco, 1935-40, chmn. dept. English and speech, 1941; cultural relations attache U.S. Embassy, Quito, Ecuador, 1942-44; sect. chief Div. Cultural Cooperation, Dept. of State, 1944-45, asst. chief Div. Exchange of Persons, 1946, chief Div. Service, 1952-58, also exec. sec. Bd. Fgn. Scholarships, 1948-57; dir. Cultural Planning and Coordination Staff, 1958-60; dir. Ednl. and Cultural Plans and Devel. Staff, 1960-64; dir. Cultural Policy and Review staff, exec. dir. Inter-Agy. Council Internat. Ednl. and Cultural Affairs, 1964-70; sr. policy adviser Ednl. and Cultural Affairs, 1970—; vis. fellow Princeton, fall 1956; U.S. rep. Ad Hoc Com. on Cultural Policy, Southeast Asia Treaty Orgn., 1958; U.S. rep. Commn. on L.S. Rowe Fund, OAS, 1948-50; U.S. mem. com. experts UNESCO, Paris, 1960, 62; U.S. del. Anglo-Am. Conf. on English Lang., Ditchley, 1965; adviser U.S. del. Inter-Am. Cultural Council, Mexico, 1951, P.R., 1959, Inter Am. Conf., Caracas, 1954; del. Geneva Meeting of Fgn. Ministers, 1955. mem. adv. council Sch. of Langs. and Linguistics, Georgetown U. Recipient Rockefeller Pub. Service award, 1955, Superior Service award, U.S. Dept. State, 1966. Mem. Internat. Studies Assn., Internat. Platform Assn., Am. Fgn. Service Assn., Washington Soc. Internat. Devel., Modern Lang. Assn., Medieval Acad. Am. Fgn. Service Assn.; hon. mem. Grupo America, Sociedad Juridico-Literaria (Ecuador), Nat. Assn. Univ. Men of Finland. Roman Catholic. Clubs: Bethesda (Md.) Country; Commonwealth (San Francisco); Cosmos, Internat., Foreign Service (Wash.). Co-author: Fundamentals of Public Speaking, 1935; The Fulbright Program: A History, 1966; articles on cultural relations. Editor: Guide to U.S. Govt. Agencies in Internat. Ednl. and Cultural Activities, 1968. Home: 5200 Oakland Rd Chevy Chase MD 20015 Office: Dept of State Washington DC 20520

COLLIGAN, GEORGE AUSTIN, educator; b. Far Rockaway, N.Y., Sept. 10, 1928; s. George Austin and Mildred (Bradley) C.; B.Metall. Engring., Rensselaer Poly. Inst., 1950; M.S. in Metall. Engring., U. Mich., 1957, Ph.D., 1959, M.A., Dartmouth, 1967; m. Marcia Elizabeth Walsh, Sept. 1, 1951; children—Susan, Catherine, Julia, John, Paul, Patrick. Asst. foundry metallurgist Farrel- Birmingham Co., Ansonia Derby, Conn., 1950-52; foundry metallurgist Gen. Electric Co., 1952-54, project engr. applied research and devel. research lab., 1954-55; instr. chem. and metall. engring. U. Mich., 1955- 59; adj. asst. prof. metallurgy Hartford Grad. Center, Rensselaer Poly. Inst., also sr. research metallurgist research labs. United Aircraft Corp., 1959-62; mem. faculty Thayer Sch. Engring., Dartmouth, Hanover, N.H., 1962—, prof. engring., 1966—, asso. dean, 1967—. Indsl. cons., 1955—; prin. investigator research project metal-refractory reaction studies U.S. Army Materials and Mechs. Research Agy., 1965-69; prin. investigator research project nucleation of undercooled alloys—control of solidification NSF, 1966-70; dir. R.D. Brew & Co., Concord, N.H., 1967—. Chmn. local chpt. N.H. Cath. Charities Fund, 1966- 68; pres. Hanover Confrat. Christian Doctrine, 1966-67. Recipient Thomas W. Pangborn Gold medal Am. Foundrymen's Soc., 1970. Registered profl. engr., N.H. Mem. Am. Foundrymen's Soc. (chmn. editorial bd. Cast Metals Research Jour. 1966-70, mem. tech. council 1964-70, chmn. research com. steel div. 1958-67, mem. exec. com. steel div. 1958-70), Am. Inst. Mining, Metall. and Petroleum Engrs., N.Y. Acad. Scis., Am. Ceramic Soc., A.A.A.S., Am. Soc. Engring. Edn., Sigma Xi, Phi Lambda Upsilon, Alpha Chi Sigma. Author numerous articles and papers. Home: 33 Rayton Rd Hanover NH 03755

COLLIGAN, RICHARD VINCENT, mining co. exec.; b. N.Y.C., June 15, 1916; s. John William and Teresa (Dorr) C.; B.A., Columbia, 1938; M.A., Cornell U., 1940; m. Sadie Alberta Fereira, Dec. 23, 1944; children—Patricia, Maria Teresa, Richard Vincent. Geologist, Cuban Am. Manganese Corp., 1940-42; mine supt. Nicaro Nickel Co., Cuba, 1942, 47, v.p., 1956-60; with Freeport Sulphur Co. (now Freeport Minerals Co.) and subsidiaries, 1947—, v.p., 1960—; pres. Moa Bay Mining Co., 1959-60, Island Exploration Co., 1952—; pres. Freeport Kaolin Co., 1967- -. Mem. Am. Inst. Mining and Metall. Engrs., Am. Assn. Petroleum Geologists, Soc. Econ. Geologists, Phi Beta Kappa. Clubs: Cloud, Wee Burn Country. Home: 250 Hollow Tree Ridge Rd Darien CT 06820 Office: 733 3d Av New York City NY 10017

COLLIN, HARRY E., business exec.; b. Tontogany, O., Dec. 4, 1885; s. Robert J. and Alice E. (Hannah) C.; ed. Ohio State U.; m. Selma G. Gardner, Oct. 8, 1913. With Northern Nat. Bank, Toledo, O., 1906-12; with Citizens Securities Co., 1912-20; sr. partner Collin Norton & Co., Toledo, 1920-64; asso. Clark, Dodge & Co., Inc. (merger with Collin, Norton & Co.), 1964—; dir., mem. exec. com., Canrad Precision Industries, Inc., Owens Ill. Glass Co.; dir. numerous other cos. Mason (33, Shriner). Mem. C. of C. Clubs: Toledo, Country (Toledo); Bankers, (N.Y.); Recess (Detroit); Buttonwood (N.Y.C.). Home: 4215 River Rd Toledo OH 43614 Office: Gardner Bldg Toledo OH 43604 ☆

COLLIN, ROBERT EMANUEL, educator; b. Donalda, Alta., Can., Oct. 24, 1928; s. Knute Emanuel and Hannah (Hanson) C.; B.S. in Engring. Physics, U. Sask. (Can.), 1951; Ph.D., Imperial Coll., U. London (Eng.), 1954; m. Kathleen Patricia Smith, Sept. 15, 1952; children—Patricia Ann, Linda Marie, David Robert. Came to U.S., 1958, naturalized, 1965. Sci. officer Canadian Def. Research Bd., 1954-58; faculty Case Western Res. U., 1958—, prof. elec. engring., 1965—. Recipient Jr. Achievement award Cleve. Tech. Socs. Council, 1964. Mem. I.E.E.E. (sr. mem., chmn. Que. subsect. 1956-57), Sigma Xi (v.p. Case Inst. Tech. chpt. 1966-67), Eta Kappa Nu. Author: Field Theory of Guided Waves, 1960; (with R. Plonsey) Principles and Applications of Electromagnetic Fields, 1961; Foundations for Microwave Engineering, 1966. Contbr., editor: (with F J Zucker) Antenna Theory, 2 vols., 1969. Home: 1041 West Mill Dr Highland Heights OH 44143 Office: 10900 Euclid Av Cleveland OH 44106

COLLINGE, PATRICIA, former actress, writer; b. Dublin, Ireland, Sept. 20, 1894; d. F. Channon and Emmie (Russell) Collinge; ed. in Dublin; m. James Nichols Smith, June 10, 1921. Made first appearance in Garrick Theatre, London, as Ching-a- Ling in "Little Black Sambo and Little White Barbara," Dec. 21, 1904 ; latest stage appearances include Birdie in The Little Foxes, 1939, The Heiress, 1947, I've Got Sixpence, 1952; latest motion picture roles in Teresa, 1950, Shadow of a Doubt, The Nun's Story, 1958; numerous TV appearances. Author: (with Margalo Gillmore) The B.O.W.S., 1945; Small Mosaics of Mr. and Mrs. Engel, 1959. Contbr. to The New Yorker and other mags. Home: 30 Beekman Pl New York City NY 20027 ☆

COLLINGWOOD, CHARLES CUMMINGS, radio, TV commentator; b. Three Rivers, Mich., June 4, 1917; s. George Harris and Jean Grinnell (Cummings) C.; A.B., Cornell, 1939; student New Coll., Oxford, Eng., 1939-40; m. Louise Allbritton, May 13, 1946. War corr. United Press, London, 1939-41; commentator C.B.S., 1941-46. United Nations corr., 1946-48, White House corr., 1948-52, radio, TV commentator, 1952—; chief CBS news bur., 1957-60, chief fgn. corr., 1966—; spl. asst. to dir. Mut. Security Agy., 1952. Received Headliners award, 1942, 1948; Peabody award for best fgn. reporting, 1943, for tour White House with Mrs. John Kennedy, 1963; Alexander Hadden Medal for promoting world understanding, 1954; Better Understanding award, English Speaking Union, 1957; decorated Chevalier, Legion of Honor (France). Mem. Inst. of World

Affairs (mem. bd. dirs.), Assn. Radio News Analysts. Clubs: Century Assn., Players, National Press; Garrick, Savile (London). Author: (novel) The Defector, 1970. Home: 3 Belgrave Pl London SW 1 England Office: CBS News 100 Brompton Rd London W3 England

COLLINGWOOD, CHARLES GILBERT, financial exec.; b. Chgo., Nov. 16, 1925; s. C. Gilbert and Margaret V. (Loomis) C.; B.A., Yale, 1948; m. Ellen S. Boyd, Aug. 26, 1950; children—Michael L., Melissa. With A.G. Becker & Co., 1949-56; dir. financial planning P.R. Indsl. Devel. Co., 1956-60; treas. Air Products & Chems., Inc., 1960-67; v.p. finance Am. Maize Products Co., 1967-69; treas. Phillip Morris, Inc., N.Y.C., 1969—. Mme. dist exec. com. Boy Scouts Am., 1966-67. Bd. asso. Muhlenberg Coll., 1966-67. Served as officer USMCR, 1943-45, 51-53. Recipient Service to Scouting award Boy Scouts Am,. 1967. Home: 160 Ridge Acres Rd Darien CT 06820 Office: 100 Park Av New York City NY 10017

COLLINS, ARTHUR ANDREWS, inventor, mfr.; b. Kingfisher, Okla., Sept. 9, 1909; s. M. H. and Faith (Andrews) C.; student Coe Coll., Cedar Rapids, Ia., 1926-27, Amherst Coll., 1927-28; D.Engring. (hon.), Bklyn. Poly Inst., 1968, So. Meth. U., 1970; spl. study U. Iowa; m. Margaret Van Dyke, Jan. 4, 1930 (dec. Dec. 1955); children—Susan, Michael; m. 2d, Mary Margaret Meis, June 10, 1957; children—Alan, David. Pioneer in devel. high frequency radio communication; founder Collins Radio Co., 1931, propr., 1931-33, pres., 1933—, also chmn.; inventor electronic equipment, including automatic tuned multi-channel radio equipment. Dir. Coe College, 1945-51. Fellow I.E.E.E.; mem. Nat. Acad. Engring. Amateur radio operator; patentee radio electronic inventions. Home: 201 34th St SE Cedar Rapids IA 52403 Office: 5225 C Av NE Cedar Rapids IA 52406

COLLINS, ARTHUR SYLVESTER, Jr., army officer; b. Boston, Aug. 6, 1915; s. Arthur Sylvester and Anne T. (Farrell) C.; B.S., U.S. Mil. Acad., 1938; grad. Command and Gen. Staff Coll., Armed Forces Staff Coll., Army War Coll., 1953; M.A. in Internat. Relations, George Washington U., 1964; m. Naomi Cashmore Wulfsberg, Nov. 20, 1948; children—Dennis Charles, Kevin Arthur, Maureen Ray. Commd. 2d lt. U.S. Army, 1938, advanced through grades to lt. gen., 1967; assigned 13th and 14th inf. regiments, Panama, 1938-41; battalion comdr. 130th Inf., Hawaii, 1942-43; regtl. comdr., New Guinea, Morotai and Luzon, 1944-46; with tactical dept. U.S. Mil Acad., 1948-52; comdr. 1st regt., U.S. Mil. Acad., 1950-52; regtl. comdr. 10th Inf., Germany, 1955- 56; mem. faculty Army War Coll., 1956-59; spl. asst. tng. to chief U.S. Army Adv. Group, also G-3 adviser to 1st Republic Korea Army, 1959-60; J- 5 plans div. Joint Chief Staff, 1960-61; J-1, J-3, chief Staff USSTRICOM, 1961-63; dir. office personnel, Dept. Army, 1963-64, asst. dep. chief staff mil. operations, 1964-65; comdr. 4th Inf. div., Fort Lewis, Wash., and Vietnam, 1965-67; asst. chief staff force devel. Dept. Army, 1967-70; comdr. 1st Field Force, Vietnam, 1970—. Mem. adv. bd. S.W. Wash. State Coll. Com. Decorated Silver Star, Legion of Merit with oak clusters, Bronze Star with 2 oak leaf clusters, Air medal, Combat Inf. badge, D.S.M. Mem. Tacoma C. of C. (bd. dirs.). Kiwanian, Rotarian (hon.). Contbr. articles Army mag. Home: Quarters 11 B Fort Meyer Arlington, VA 22211 Office: 1st Field Force Vietnam APO San Francisco CA 96350

COLLINS, BARNEY WILLIAM, industrialist, assn. exec.; b. Raton, N.M., Jan. 16, 1905; s. Walter W. and Dorothy (Moraskey) C.; student U. Pacific, Stockton, Cal.; A.B., U. America's (Mexico City), 1950; m. Florence Evans, Dec. 7, 1970; children by previous marriage—Debra, Billy, Lori. Salesman of steel to mines in Mexico; organized stock co., presenting mfrs.; builder textile plants in Mexico; real estate, land devel. Mem. Anahuac Masonic Lodge, Mexico, past illustrious master City of Mexico R & S.M., past eminent comdr. Ivanhoe Commandery Anezeh Temple, past i K.T., past venerable master Consistory No. 1, past potentate Anezeh Temple, past dir. Royal Order Jesters; mem. Royal Order of Scotland, Red Cross of Constantine, and the Cabiri; mem. Order Eastern Star, past venerable master Lodge of Perfection, past wise master Rose Croix, past comdr. Council Kadosh; coroneted 33, Supreme Consejo of Mexico, nat. officer Internat. Supreme Council, Order DeMolay; imperial potentat Ancient Arabic Order Nobles of Mystic Shrine for North Am., 1965-66. Chmn. bd. Shriner's Hosp. Crippled Children; bd. dirs. Council Am. Resident Abroad. Mem. Pi Kappa Delta. Home: Paseo de la Reforma No 27 Mexico City Mexico Office: 323 N Michigan Av Chicago IL 60614

COLLINS, BESSIE BARTLETT, univ. dean; b. Norwood, Pa., May 10, 1916; d. Richard Paul and Bessie Lovell (Bartlett) Collins; student Ursinus Coll., 1934-35; B.S., U. Pa., 1938, M.S., 1940, postgrad., 1941—. Instr. grades Illman Sch. for Children, U. Pa. Sch. Edn., 1939-41; asst. dean women, 1941-47, assistantship personnel Sch. Edn., 1947-49, personnel officer, asst. instr., 1949-52; dean women U. Del., Newark, 1952—. Mem. Wesley Found. Trustee, U. Del. Mem. Nat. adminstrv. com. coll. and univ. div. YMCA, 1959- 62; mem. Gov.'s Commn. on Status Women. Mem. Nat. Assn. Women Deans and Counselors (v.p. 1960-62), Am. Council Edn., Regional (sect. v.p. 1954-56), Pa. (sec. 1950-52) assns. deans women, Alumnae Assn. U. Pa. (exec. bd., dir. 1944-47), N.E.A., Del. Edn. Assn., Regional Assn. Women Deans and Counselors (v.p. 1963-65), Am. Assn. U. Women (dir. at large Phila. 1946-48, v.p. Newark 1962-64), Pi Lambda Theta, Delta Kappa Gamma, Delta Delta Delta. Methodist. Soroptimist (hon.). Home: 29 Park Dr Silverbook Newark DE 19711

COLLINS, BLANCHE WALLACE, librarian; b. Visalia, Cal., Feb. 8, 1903; d. William Wallace and Louise (Clarke) Collins; A.B., Mills Coll., 1924; certificate librarianship, Carnegie Inst. Tech., 1925. Mem. staff Long Beach (Cal.) Pub. Library, 1925-59, asst. librarian, 1951-60, city librarian, 1960-69. Sec. bd. Long Beach chpt. Nat. Conf. Christians and Jews; adv. bd. Los Angeles County Dept. Mental Health, Long Beach chpt. UN Assn., Fair Housing Found.; bd. dirs. Los Angeles County Mental Health Assn. Recipient Distinguished Merit citation Nat. Conf. Christians and Jews, 1965. Mem. Cal. Congress Parents and Tchrs. (hon. life mem.), Am., Cal. (pres. pub. libraries sect. 1962) library assns., Pub. Library Execs. Assn. So. Cal. (pres. 1963), Long Beach C. of C., League Women Voters, Am. Assn. U. Women, Libraria Sodalitas, Beta Phi Mu. Club: Altrusa (hon.). Contbr. prof. jours. Home: 4008 E 5th St Long Beach CA 90814 Office: Long Beach Pub Library Long Beach CA 90802

COLLINS, CARR P., Jr., corp. exec.; b. Dallas, Feb. 9, 1918; s. Carr P. and Ruth (Woodall) C.; B.S. in Commerce, So. Meth. U., 1939; grad. bus. study Harvard, 1939-40; LL.D., Howard Payne Coll., 1965; m. Calvert Keoun, Dec. 24, 1941; children—Carr P. III, Richard Howell, Christy Calvert; m. 2d, Yyronne Deakins, Jan. 1, 1968; children—Mark Bond, Brad Bond. Pres. Investment Trust Co., 1949—, S.W. Bank & Trust Co., 1955-56, Nat. Petro-Sonics, Inc., 1968; v.p., dir. Fidelity Union Life Ins. Co., Dallas, 1949—; v.p. Elaboradora Farmaceutica S.A., Nicaragua, 1965-70. Mem. panel arbitrators N.Y. Stock Exchange, 1957—; vice consul for Italy in Dallas, 1962—; mem. U.S. Trade Mission to Pakistan, 1960. Mem. adv. bd. Italian-U.S. Center Jud. Studies, 1965—. Served to maj. USAAF, 1940-45; PTO. Decorated Purple Heart, Air medal; knight officer Order of Merit (Italy); recipient of the Freedom medal Douglas MacArthur Acad. Freedom, 1965. C.L.U. Fellow Am. Soc. for Psychial Research; mem. Phi Delta Theta, Alpha Kappa Psi. Episcopalian. Mason (32, Shriner). Clubs: Idlewild; Petroleum; Brook Hollow Golf. Home: 4801 St Johns Dr Dallas, TX 75205 Office: Fidelity Union Life Bldg Dallas TX 75201

COLLINS, CARR PRITCHETT, ins. co. exec.; b. Chester, Tex., May 12, 1892; s. Vincent Allen and Elizabeth (Hopkins) C.; student S.W. State Tchrs., Coll., San Marcos, Tex., 1909; LL.D., Baylor U., 1952; m. Ruth Woodall, Nov. 21, 1914; children—James Mitchell, Carr Pritchett, Ruth (Mrs. Charles S. Sharp). Chmn. bd., pres. Fidelity Union Life Ins. Co., Dallas, 1927—; founder, pres. Baptist Found. Tex., 1931—; dir. First Nat. Bank Dallas, 1928-65. Donator Carr P. Collins award Tex. Inst. Letters, 1946, Ruth Collins. Hall, Baylor U., 1957, Carr P. Collins Convalescent Care Hosp., Dallas, 1967, Carr P. Collins Chapel, Bishop Coll., 1967, Carr P. Collins Chair Fgn. Affairs, Howard Payne Coll., 1966. Past trustee Baylor U., Bishop Coll., Wadley Blood Research Center, Dallas; bd. dirs. So. Bapt. Conv. Recipient Horatio Alger award, 1964, Douglas MacArthur Freedom medal, 1966, Distinguished Alumnus award S.W. State Tchrs. Coll., 1966, Univ. medal Hardin-Simmons U., 1967, Holden Plate award Am. Acad. Achievement, 1968, Distinguished Am. Citizen award Harding Coll., 1968, Am. Citizen award Harding Coll., 1968. Baptist (deacon 1917—). Home: 5134 Kelsey Rd Dallas, TX 75229 Office: Fidelity Union Life Bldg Dallas TX 75201

COLLINS, CARVEL, educator; b. West Union, O., June 14, 1912; s. John Edgar and Ina (Treber) C.; B.S., Miami U., 1933; M.A., U. Chgo., 1937, Ph.D., 1944; m. Mary Brewster, Nov. 17, 1939 (div. 1956); 1 dau., Lucy Emerson; m. 2d, Ann Green, Oct. 1, 1960. Instr. of English, Colorado State Coll., 1938-39, Stephens Coll., 1939-40; instr. Harvard, 1942-45, asst. dean, 1945, asst. prof., 1946-50; asst. prof. Swarthmore Coll., 1945-46; asso. prof. Mass. Inst. Tech., 1950-56, prof. English, 1956-67; prof. English, U. Notre Dame, Ind., 1967—; vis. lectr. U. Cal., 1949; Salzburg Seminar, 1955; U. d'Aix-Marseille, 1955, U. Tokyo, 1961, U. Colo., 1962. Recipient Library of Congress fellowship, 1946, Am. Philos. Soc. grant, 1963, Fidelis Found. grant, 1963, Bollingen Found. fellowship, 1964-65. Mem. Coll. English Assn., Nat. Council Tchrs. English. Club: St. Botolph (Boston). Author: The American Sporting Gallery, 1949; Literature in the Modern World (with others), 1954. Editor: Sam Ward in the Gold Rush, 1949; William Faulkner's New Orleans Sketches, 1958; William Faulkner, The Unvanquished, 1959; Faulkner's Univeristy Pieces, 1961; Erskine Caldwell's Men and Women, 1961; William Faulkner; Early Prose and Poetry, 1962. Address: Dept English U Notre Dame Notre Dame IN 46556

COLLINS, CHARLES BERTINE, lawyer; b. Portland, Me., July 20, 1904; s. John Lyon and Aimee R. (Brown) C.; A.B., Rutgers Coll., 1927; postgrad. Harvard Law Sch., 1927-30; m. Marjorie Marten Perine, Mar. 12, 1935; children—Patricia, Charles Bertine, Susan (Mrs. Frederick N. Reidenbach), Marcia. Admitted to N.J. bar, 1930, also U.S. Supreme Ct.; practice in Newark, 1959—; sr. partner Carpenter, Bennett & Morrissey. Referee Maplewood Juvenile Conf. Com., 1964—. Trustee, counsel Boys Clubs Newark, 200 Club Newark. Mem. Am., N.J., Essex County bar assns., Am. Judicature Soc., Maritime Law Assn. U.S., Harvard Law Sch. Assn. N.J. (pres. 1966), No. N.J. Estate Planning Council, Am. Arbitration Assn. (arbitrator), Lambda Chi Alpha. Republican. Methodist. Mason, Rotarian. Clubs: Harvard (N.Y.C.); Essex, Down Town (Newark); Rock Spring (West Orange, N.J.); Merriewold (Forestburg, N.Y.). Author: Foreclosure of Mortgages, Skills and Methods, N.J. Practice, 1960. Asso. editor N.J. Law Jour., 1957—. Home: 20 Woodhill Dr Maplewood NJ 07040 Office: 744 Broad St Newark NJ 07102

COLLINS, CHARLES C., lawyer; b. Washington, Jan. 31, 1900; s. Lewis F. and Mary A. (Fitzpatrick) C.; LL.B., Georgetown U., 1922; m. Judith I. Collins, Dec. 14, 1947; 1 dau., Nancy M. Admitted to the D.C. bar, 1922, since practiced in Washington; mem. Collins, Anderson, Ahern, Quinn & Wyland; gen. counsel Am. Automobile Assn.; rep. several ins. cos. as Washington trial counsel. Mem. Am., D.C. bar assns., Am. Coll. Trial Lawyers. Club: Congressional Country. Home: 2538 44th St Washington DC 20007 Office: 1750 Pennsylvania Av NW Washington DC 20006

COLLINS, CHARLES DICKINSON, business exec.; b. Pensacola, Fla., Mar. 24, 1903; s. James Harry and Ginsie N. (Dickinson) C.; B.S.C., Ga. Inst. Tech., 1921; m. Hazel Stamps, Aug. 24, 1929; children—Ginsie Cecil, Carolyn Florence. Salesman Miami (Fla.) Furniture Co., 1925-28; mgr. Rhodes Collins Furniture Co., Valdosta, Ga., 1928-32; with A.G. Rhodes & Son, Atlanta, 1932-48, v.p., 1935-48; 1st v.p. Rhodes, Inc., Atlanta, 1948-52, now chmn. bd. dirs. Mem. Sigma Alpha Epsilon. Episcopalian. Clubs: Capital City, University Yacht, Piedmont Driving (Atlanta); Lake Shore (Chgo.). Home: 330 Argonne Dr NW Atlanta GA 30305 Office: 10 Rhodes Center N Atlanta GA 30313

COLLINS, CHARLES JOSEPH, investment cons.; b. Lake City, Fla., Dec. 7, 1894; s. Thomas Currie and Sarah Frink (Spencer) C.; B.A., Va. Mil. Inst., Lexington, 1916, hon. M.A., 1926; m. Hazel Beatrice Wharton, Dec. 25, 1919; children—Anne Wharton (Mrs. Henry G. Husted), Josephine Spencer (Mrs. John M. Penberthy). Investment analyst E.E. MacCrone & Co., Detroit, 1919-23, partner, 1923-63; chmn., dir. Investment Counsel, Inc., 1930-59, mem. adv. bd., 1962-69; trustee Investment Co. Am. 1927-32; editor, pub. Investment Letters, Inc., 1934-63, dir. Am. Midland Co., 1930-63, Investment Research Corp., 1927-32, Am. Industries Corp. 1929-33, 55-63, Am. Industries Securities Co., 1930-33; mem., N.Y. Stock Exchange, 1929-30. Trustee Va. Mil. Inst. Found., 1964—. Entered the CAC, U.S. Army, 2d lt., 1917, advanced to maj.; served on front with 8th and 4th French armies, 1st and 2d Am. armies; resigned Feb. 1919. Mem. Financial Analysts Soc. of Detroit (pres. 1952, dir. 1951-53), Nat. Fedn. Financial Analyst Socs. (mem. bd. dirs. 1950-52), Va. Mil. Inst. Alumni Assn. (dir. 1937—), Kappa Alpha (Southern). Clubs: Detroit; Country (Grosse Pointe, Mich.). Author: Fortune's Before You, 1937. Contbr. investment articles. Home: 858 Lochmoor Blvd Grosse Pointe Woods MI 48236

COLLINS, CHARLES ROLAND, lawyer, multi-market co. exec.; b. Pitts., Sept. 1, 1931; s. Charles Peyton and Dorothy (Cantley) C.; B.A., U. Cal. at Los Angeles, 1953; LL.B. cum laude, Harvard, 1959; m. Virginia Anne Wright, Feb. 6, 1955; children—Elizabeth Anne, Charles Edward, Walter Bruce, Richard Allen, Catherine Kaye. Admitted to Cal. bar, 1960; practice in Los Angeles, 1960-68; mem. firm Gibson, Dunn & Crutcher, 1959-68; v.p., gen. counsel, sec. Whittaker Corp., Los Angeles, 1968-71; pres. Whittaker Environmental Devel., Inc., Los Angeles, 1970—; dir. Yardney Electric Corp. Served to lt. comdr. USNR, 1953-56. Clubs: Los Angeles Athletic; Balboa Bay (Newport Beach, Cal.); San Diego Yacht. Home: 60 S San Rafael Av Pasadena CA 91105 Office: 10880 Wilshire Blvd Los Angeles CA 90024

COLLINS, CLELLA REEVES, author; b. Omaha, May 23, 1893; d. Jesse and Ida (Compton) Reeves; student U. Ida., 1911, U. Cal., 1913, Northwestern U., 1920, Columbia, 1921, U. Hawaii, 1922, U. Cal. at Los Angeles, 1927; Hum. D., Chungang U., Seoul, Korea, 1965, LL.D.; m. Carter Collins, Aug. 17, 1916; children—Betty, Carter Compton. Woman's financial editor Los Angeles Herald, 1925-26; editor, pub. Sound mag., 1926-31; editor, pub. The Army and Navy Woman's mag., 1943—; asst. to pub. Army-Navy Jour. Mem. Marshall Plan Com., UN Com. Human Rights; mem. U.S. com. UNICEF adv. commn. War Claims Com.; del. Nat. Conf. on Occupied Countries; civilian adv. council Dept. Army, Pacific Coast UNESCO, World Affairs Council Cal.; pub. liaison com. State Dept., Nat. Council of Women. Founder Women's Investment Inst., 1929-30; organized schs. for U.S. Army children Schofield Barracks, Hawaii, 1922; mem. Newton D. Baker com., 1918-19; E and R Div., World War I; mem. nat. bd. UNICEF-UN, KEEP (Japan), Orphans of Italy, Inc.; cons. People to People, Inc., mem. exec. com., trustee, founder, pres. Internat. Family Day; adv. bd. 20th Ann. Comm. UN; mem. White House Conf. on Children and Youth; U.S. dir. Assn. Advancement So. Italy. Recipient citation Korean Govt., 1956; Eisenhower People to People award, 1962, 68; award for internat. relations Cal. Fedn. Women's Clubs, 1965; Intercultural award Christian Fellowship, 1967; Univ. Gold medal Korea, 1968; Named Woman of Yr., B'nai B'rith, 1966. Mem. White House Conf. Edn., Armed Forces Writer's League (nat. bd.), Assn. Army and Navy Wives (founder, past pres.), Asso. Wives of Armed Forces (organizing chmn., pres. emeritus), Cal. Writers Club, A.R.C., Pen Women, YWCA, Am. Assn. UN, Fgn. Policy Assn., Care Book Commn., Am. Acad. Polit. and Social Sci. Author: Woman's Handbook of Financial Facts, 1928; The First Thousand, 1926; Step by Step to Fortune, 1925; Women and Their Money, 1929; Army Wife, Her Rights, Duties and Privleges, 1940; Army Woman's Hand Book, 1942; Navy Woman's Handbook, 1943; When Your Son Goes to War, 1943; When Your Son Comes Home to You, 1944; Welcome Home My Darling, 1945; Veteran's Wife, 1946; So Your Son's in the Service; Around The World with the Army; Words to the Wives, 1953. Home: 1438 Arch St Berkeley CA 94708 Office: care Whittlesey House McGraw Hill Bldg New York City NY 10001

COLLINS, CONRAD GREEN, physician; b. New Orleans, Apr. 23, 1907; s. Charles and Amelie Marie (Haydel) C.; B.S., Tulane, 1926, M.D., 1928, M.S., 1931; m. Louise Carroll, Oct. 9, 1935; children—Louise Carroll, Conrad G., Claudia Elizabeth. Intern Touro Hosp., New Orleans, 1928-29; asst. resident obstetrics and gynecol. Touro Infirmary, 1929-30, and 1930-31; pvt. practice splty., New Orleans, 1931—; sr. vis. surgeon Charity Hosp. of La., 1938—; sr. cons. Hotel Dieu. Vets. Hosp., U.S. Marine Hosp., Flint Goodridge and Sara Mayo hosps. Instr. gynecol. and lab., Sch. Med., Tulane, 1931-32, asst. prof. gynecol., 1932-38, asst. prof. clin., obstet. and gynecol., 1938-45, prof., chmn., 1945-50, chmn. dept. gynecol., 1949-50, prof., chmn. dept. obstet. and gynecol., 1950—; nat. cons. obstet. and gynecol. Surgeon Gen., USAF, 1952-62. Served as maj. U.S.A., 1942-46; Asiatic-Pac. Theatre, 1942-43, Europen Theatre, 1944- 45. Diplomate Am. Bd. Obstetrics and Gynecol. Fellow A.C.S., mem. A.M.A., Am. Assn. Obetetrics and Gynecology, Am. Coll. Obstetricians and Gynecol., Am. Gynecol. Soc., Sigma Psi. Club: American Gynecological; Boston (New Orleans). Home: 1423 State St New Orleans LA 70118 Office: 1430 Tulane Av New Orleans LA 70112

COLLINS, COPP, govt. ofcl.; b. Keokuk, Ia., Dec. 31, 1914; s. Harrie Richards and Elsie (Parsons) C.; B.A., U. Redlands, 1938; m. Frances Cordelia Truax, Sept. 28, 1940; children—Michael Truax, Nicole Elyse, Copp Parsons. Bur. mgr. San Diego bur. United Press, then asst. Los Angeles bur., 1939- 40; comml. sales supr., flight adminstrn. supr. Consol. Vultee Aircraft Corp., 1942-47; owner-dir. Copp Collins Pub. Relations, San Diego and Beverly Hills, Cal., 1948-51; West Coast rep., mgr. information and pub. relations MBS, 1951-53, mgr. pub. relations, N.Y.C., 1953-55; mgr. pub. relations Bahrain Petroleum Co., Ltd., Awali, Persian Gulf, 1955 58; asst. to exec. v.p. Burns & Roe, Inc., N.Y.C., 1958-60; pub. relations cons. Copp Collins Assos., N.Y.C., and Westport, Conn., 1960- 61, pres., cons., 1963-67; v.p., dir. pub. relations Chirurg & Cairns, Inc., N.Y.C., 1961-62; v.p., dir. pub. relations Freind-Reiss Advt., Inc., N.Y.C., 1962-63; president Collins & Lynge, Ltd., N.Y.C. and Norwalk, Conn., 1965-67; dir. marketing, merchandising and promotion N.Am. Soccer League, dir. information Nat. Profl Soccer League, 1967-68; press aide to dir. communications Nixon for Pres., Nixon-Agnew campaign coms.; press aide to dir. communications Office of Pres. Elect, Washington and N.Y.C., 1968-69; asst. to sec. pub. affairs U.S. Dept. Agr., Washington, 1969; cons. pub. affairs State Dept., 1969-70; cons., spl. asst. to dir. Peace Corps, 1970-71; conf. asst. to sec., field rep. S.W. U.S. Dept. Interior, 1971—. Chmn. pub. relations adv. council to So. Conn. chpts. A.R.C., 1955. Press aide Sen. Clifford Case primary campaign, 1959, 60, Ogden Reid for Congress Com., Westchester County, N.Y., 1962, 64, Romeo Petroni for Congress, 5th Dist. Conn., 1966. Mem. U. Redlands Alumni Assn. (past chpt. chmn.), Pi Kappa Delta, Alpha Phi Gamma, Kappa Sigma Sigma. Republican. Home: 6024 Hardwick Pl Falls Church VA 22041 Office: US Dept Interior 517 Gold SW Albuquerque NM 87101

COLLINS, CYRUS STICKNEY, airlines exec.; b. Oak Park, Ill., Oct. 31, 1917; s. Frank S. and Margaret (Stickney) C.; A.B., Amherst Coll., 1939; m. Madeleine Robertson, Sept. 3, 1941; children—Michael, David, Stephen. With W.R. Grace & Co., 1939-42; with Pan-American-Grace Airways, Inc., 1942-66, asst. to pres., asst. v.p., 1952-56, v.p. sales and traffic, 1956-63, v.p. gen. mgmt., 1963-66; regional v.p. Am. Airlines, 1966-67, v.p. pub. affairs, 1967—. Mem. bd. dirs. Children's Village, Dobbs Ferry, N.Y., pres. bd., 1955-58. Decorated Order Nunez de Balboa (Panama). Mem. Argentine Am. C. of C. (v.p. 1961-63, pres. 1963-65). Beta Theta Pi. Clubs: Cloud, Wings (pres. 1970-71) (N.Y.C.); North Fork Country (Cutchogue, L.I.); Old Cove Yacht (L.I.). Home: 20 Sutton Pl S New York City NY 10022 Office: 633 3d Av New York City NY 10017

COLLINS, DAVID EDMOND, health product co. exec.; b. Oak Park, Ill., June 6, 1934; s. Charles Cornelius and Penelope (Jones) C.; B.A. magna cum laude, U. Notre Dame, 1956; LL.B. magna cum laude, Harvard, 1959; m. Judith Elizabeth Thompson, Sept. 16, 1961; children—Patrick, Katherine Ann, Paul, Ann Marie. Admitted to N.Y. bar, 1961, N.J. bar, 1963; asso. Shearman & Sterling, N.Y.C., 1959-62; gen. atty. Johnson & Johnson, New Brunswick, N.J., 1962—, asst. sec., 1964-70, sec., 1970—. Capt., Westfield (N.J.) United Fund, 1968-69. Frederick Sheldon traveling fellow, 1959-60. Mem. Am. Bar Assn. (mem. sects. antitrust, corps., individual rights), N.J. Bar Assn. Home: Oak Knoll Rd Mendham NJ 07945 Office: 501 George St New Brunswick NJ 08903

COLLINS, DONALD LAMAR, lawyer; b. Gadsden, Ala., Sept. 8, 1929; s. Luther Thomas and Mattie (Scarborough) C.; student U. Ala., 1948-49; B.S., Jacksonville State U., 1952; LL.B., J.D., U. Ala., 1957; m. Hannah Case Snellgrove, Aug. 30, 1952; children—Henry Clay, Cynthia Case, Donald Lamar, Hannah Case. Admitted to Ala. bar, 1957, since practiced in Birmingham; partner firm Deramus, Johnston, Barton, Proctor and Swedlaw, 1958-70; law clk. Supreme Ct. Ala., 1957-58. Mem. Ala. Ho. of Reps., 1963-67; Republican nominee for atty. gen. Ala., 1966; Ala. coordinator for Nixon-Agnew, 1968. Served to maj. USMCR, 1965. Mem. Am., Ala., Birmingham bar assns., Am. Judicature Soc., Am. Legion, V.F.W., Phi Alpha Delta, Omicron Delta Kappa. Episcopalian. Clubs: Birmingham Country, Rotary (Birmingham). Asso. editor Ala. Law Rev., 1957. Home: 29 Ridge Dr Birmingham AL 35213

COLLINS, ELSON K., legislator, lawyer; b. Laurel, Miss., Dec. 17, 1911; s. William Thomas and Susanna (Cooley) C.; student Jones County Jr. Coll., Miss. State U.; LL.B., Cumberland U., 1940; m. Grace Easterling, Aug. 19, 1932; children—Peggy R. (Mrs. Joseph S. Gatlin), Sylvia (Mrs. J. Hood Garber). Admitted to Miss. bar, 1940, since practice in Laurel; pros. atty. Jones County (Miss.), 1948-52; sr. partner Collins & Tew, 1959- -; mem. Miss. Senate, 1960—, chmn. judiciary com., 1961—. Mem. nat. adv. com. Kennedy for Pres., 1960; Miss. chmn. Vets. for Johnson, 1964; del. Dem. Nat. Conf., 1960, 64; mem. Dem. Nat. Com. for Miss., 1960—. Served with AUS, 1943-46. Decorated Bronze Star medal. Mem. Am., Jones County (past pres.) bar assns., Miss. State Bar (past commr., certificate of merit 1962), Am. Trial Lawyers Assn. (Miss. pres.), Legislative Leaders Am., Miss. (pres.), Legislative Leaders Am., Miss. State U. Alumni Assn., Cumberland Univ. Alumni Assn., V.F.W. (nat. judge advocate gen. 1957-58). Democrat. Presbyn. Mason (Shriner). Home: PO Box 732 Waynesboro Dr Office: PO Box 732 501 5th Av Laurel MS 39440

COLLINS, EMMONS WILLIAMS, banker; b. Duluth, Minn., Nov. 4, 1906; s. Edwin James and Edith M. (Cook) C.; A.B., Cornell U., 1927; m. Mary Ten Eyck Bradley, June 18, 1932; children—Stephen, Mary (Mrs. John W. Moore), Sarah (Mrs. Willis L. Wyard), Johanna (Mrs. David L. Duclos). With First Am. Nat. Bank and predecessor, Duluth, 1927—, exec. v.p., 1957-63, pres., 1963-68, chmn. bd., 1968—, also dir.; dir. Minn. Power & Light Co.; presdl. adviser N. Central Airlines. Past treas., dir. Govt. Research Bur. Bd. dirs. St. Luke's Hosp., Duluth, Coll. St. Scholastica, Mpls. Ordean Found.; past treas., dir. Duluth Tb and Health Assn., Duluth Multiple Sclerosis Soc. Mem. Theta Delta Chi. Rotarian. Clubs: Northland Country, Kitchi Gammi (past pres., dir.) (Duluth); Moorings Country (Naples, Fla.). Home: 2930 London Rd Duluth MN 55804 Office: 230 W Superior St Duluth MN 55802

COLLINS, EVAN REVERE, coll. pres.; b. Bklyn., Sept. 1, 1911; s. Raymond Revere and Lillian (Jenkins) C.; A.B., Dartmouth, 1933; Ed. M., Harvard, 1938, Ed.D., 1946; Sc.D., Union U., 1967; Dr. h.c., U. Strasbourg, 1968; LL.D., Lehigh U., 1969; m. Virginia Lillard, June 13, 1935; children— Evan Revere, Ann Harriett (dec. Dec. 1949), Marta. Instr., dir. program Tabor Acad., 1933-38; instr., dir. placement Harvard, 1938, asst. dean Harvard Grad. Sch. Edn., 1939-46; dean Ohio U. Coll. Edn., 1946-49; pres. State U. at Albany (N.Y.), 1949-69; prof. higher edn. Boston Coll., 1969—; dir. State Bank of Albany. Dir. Inst. for Coll. and U. Adminstrs., Am. Council on Edn., 1969—. Bd. dirs. N.Y. State Christian Movement, N.Y. State Assn. Crippled Children and Adults, St. Agnes Sch., Dudley Obs. Spl. cons. to asst. sec. Air Forces, 1949. Served as chief operations analysis 2d Army Air Force, 1943-45. Decorated officer l'Ordre des Palmes Academiques. Mem. Inter- Collegiate Assn., Amateur Athletes of Am., Am. Assn. Sch. Adminstrs., Am. Council Edn. (dir.), N.Y. Council Econ. Edn. (dir.), Am. Assn. Colls. Tchr. Edn. (pres., dir.), Casque and Gauntlet, Phi Delta Kappa, Delta Kappa Epsilon. Rotarian (past pres. Albany). Contbr.; Teacher Education and Religion, 1959. Home: 221 Mount Auburn St Cambridge MA 02138 Office: Boston Coll Chestnut Hill MA

COLLINS, FREDERIC WILLIAM, newspaperman; b. Whitman, Mass., Oct. 18, 1906; s. John Thomas and Flora (Hassett) C.; student Phillips Acad., Andover, Mass., 1922-24; Ph.B., Brown U., 1928; m. Margaret V. Kelley, Mar. 9, 1931; children—Susan (Mrs. Lawrence Kinvin Wroth), Martha (Mrs. William Keen, Jr.). Reporter Lowell (Mass.) Sun., 1928-29, Boston Post, 1929; reporter, columnist, editorial writer, Providence (R.I.) News-Tribune, 1930-37, Providence Star-Tribune, 1937- 38; polit. writer and legislative corr., Providence Jour., 1938-42; Wash. corr. Providence Jour., 1942-60; chief, Washington Bur., Providence Jour. and Evening Bull., 1944-60; founder Collins Spl. Corr. Service, 1960; v.p. Clifton Counselors, Inc., pub. relations advisers, 1969-70; staff cons. NSF, Washington, 1971—. Spl. corr. London Sunday Times, Ridder Newspapers; guest commentator Voice Am. Clubs: Gridiron (pres. 1965), Nat. Press Overseas Writer (pres. 1954-55), Metropolitan. Contbr. mags. U.S., Eng., France. Home: 3929 Jenifer St Washington DC 20015 (summer) RFD Narragansett RI 02882

COLLINS, GEORGE BERNARD, lawyer; b. Waseca, Minn., Feb. 28, 1899; s. Robert and Catherine (Burns) C.; student Creighton U., 1920, St. Thomas Coll., S.A.T.C., 1918, Georgetown U., 1919; m. Katherine Leahy, Jan. 25, 1927; children—Mary Dolores, Cathleen Ann, Robert Maurice, Bernard George, Joanne Rae. Admitted to Neb. bar, 1920, Okla. bar, 1927, Kan. bar, 1934; practicing lawyer, Omaha, 1920-26, Wichita, since 1934; atty. Skelly Oil Co., Tulsa, Oklahoma, 1927-31; now mem. firm Collins and Collins; lectr. legal leasing procedure Wichita ext. center U. Kan., 1951-55; lectr. petroleum landwork, ext. div. U. Okla., 1956. Mem. Neb. State Legislature, 1923-24; chmn. Nat. Cath. Community Service, U.S.O., 1942- 46; co-chmn. Nat. Conf. Christians and Jews, Inc., 1943-51; mem. Kan. Bd. Regents, 1958-61. Trustee Sacred Heart Coll. Recipient honor citation in jurisprudence Creighton U., 1959. Mem. Ind. Petroleum Assn., Am., Okla., Kan. Wichita (past pres.) bar assns., Am. Legion, Order of Coif, Gamma Eta Gamma. Democrat (chmn. 4th Dist. Congl. Com., 1946). K.C. Clubs: Rotary (past pres.), Petroleum (dir. 1949-50) (Wichita). Author legal articles. Home: 214 N Bluff Wichita, KS 67208 Office: Wichita Plaza Wichita KS 67202

COLLINS, GEORGE BRIGGS, physicist; b. Washington, D.C., Jan. 3, 1906; s. Guy N. and Christine (Schmidt) C.; student U. Md., 1924-28; Ph.D., Johns Hopkins, 1932; m. Elsa Leser, June 6, 1934; children—Peter, Lucy, Robert. Research in ultraviolet spectroscopy, Johns Hopkins, 1930-33; mem. dept. physics U. Notre Dame, 1933-41; with Mass. Inst. Tech. Radiation Lab., 1941-46; prof. and chmn. dept. physics. U. Rochester 1946- 50; chmn. accelerator project Brookhaven Nat. Lab. 1950—. Trustee Asso. Univs., Inc., 1946-50; mem. council State U. N.Y. at Stony Brook, 1958—. Fulbright fellow, Belgium, 1957. Fellow Am. Phys. Soc.; mem. Phi Beta Kappa, Sigma Xi. Editor and contbg. author Microwave Magnetrons, 1947. Home: 46 Bellport Lane Bellport NY 11713 Office: Brookhaven Nat Lab Upton NY 11973

COLLINS, GEORGE W., congressman; b. Chgo., Mar. 5, 1925; student Northwestern U.; m. Cardiss Robertson; 1 son, Keith. Various positions Cook County Sheriff's Dept., Municipal Ct. System, Bd. Health; pres. Lawndale Youth Commn.; bd. dirs. Greater Lawndale Conservation Commn.; mem. 91st and 92d Congresses from 6th Dist. Ill. Served with C.E., AUS, World War II; PTO. Mem. Profl. and Businessmens Assn. Democrat. Baptist. Address: 3604 W Roosevelt Rd Chicago IL*

COLLINS, HARLAN BARNES, former mfg. exec.; b. Cleve., Oct. 19, 1904; s. Wilford Ellsworth and Emma (Barnes) C.; Ph.B., Yale, 1925; J.D., Western Res. U., 1948; m. Ruth Barlow Denison, Jan. 30, 1937; children—Christopher Hall, Julia Denison. Admitted to Ohio bar, 1928; practiced in Cleve., 1928-38; trial counsel Securities and Exchange Commn., 1938-40; sec., gen. counsel Cleve. Pneumatic Tool Co., 1941-47; asst. to pres. Link-Belt div. FMC Corp., Chgo., 1948-49, sec., 1949-61, sec., v.p., 1961-65, pres., 1965- 69, sr. v.p., dir. 1967-69, ret. Mem. Ann. Fund Bd., Case Western Res. U., 1966-. Mem. Am. Bar Assn., Am. Soc. Corporate Secs., Yale Alumni Assn., Order of Coif, Delta Theta Phi. Clubs: Yale (N.Y.C.); Chicago Yacht, Mid-America. Home: 25 E Delaware Pl Chicago IL 60611 also The Depot Otter Lake Quebec Canada

COLLINS, HENRY BASCOM, anthropologist; b. Geneva, Ala., Apr. 9, 1899; s. Henry Bascom and Anna Sophie (Neville) C.; A.B., Millsaps Coll., 1922, Sc.D. (hon.), 1940; A.M., George Washington U., 1925; m. Carolyn Walker, Nov. 26, 1931; 1 dau., Judith Ann (Mrs. A.L. Pagani). Asst. with the Pueblo Bonito expedition Nat. Geog. Soc., 1922-24; asst. Miss. dept. of Archives and History, 1923; aid, div. ethnology, U.S. Nat. Mus., 1924- 25, asst. curator, 1925-37, asso. curator, 1938-39; sr. ethnologist Bur. Am. Ethnology, 1939-51 sr. anthropologist, 1951—, acting dir., 1963-65; sr. scientist Smithsonian Office Anthropology, 1965—; dir. Smithsonian expeditions to Fla., Miss., La., 1925, 26, 28, 29, Nunivak Island and Bering Sea, 1927, Punuk Island and Bering Strait, 1928, St. Lawrence Island, Norton Sound and Arctic coast, 1929, St. Lawrence Island, 1930; dir. Nat. Geog. Soc.-Smithsonian Expdn., Bering Strait, 1936; dir., Nat. Mus. Canada-Smithsonian expedition to Baffin Island, 1948, Cornwallis Island, N.W.T., 1949, 50, 53. Nat. Geog. Soc.-Nat. Mus. Canada-Smithsonian Expedition to Southampton Island, 1954, 55. Asst. dir. Ethnogeog. Bd., 1943-44, dir., 1944-46; bd. govs., Arctic Inst. N.A., 1944-48, 51-56, 60-65; chmn. bd. 1948; chmn. adv. com. Russian Anthropology Translations Project, 1960—; chmn. directing com. of Arctic Bibliography 1947—; v.p. 2d Internat. cong. Ethnol., Anthrop. Scis., Copenhagen, 1938 (chmn. Am. delegation), mem. permanent council 1952—, v.p. 7th Internat. congress, Moscow, 1964; hon. v.p. 32d Internat. Congress Americanists, Copenhagen, 1956. Served as pvt. U.S. Army, 1918. Recipient gold medal Royal Danish Acad. Sci. and Letters, 1936. Fellow A.A.A.S. (mem. council 1953-60); mem. Am. Anthrop. Assn., Anthrop. Soc. of Washington (pres. 1938, 39), Am. Assn. of Phys. Antrhopologists, Soc. Am. Archeology (v.p., 1942, 52), Washington Acad. Scis., Sigma Xi, Pi Kappa Alpha, Sigma Upsilon. Clubs: Explorers (N.Y. C.); Cosmos (Washington). Author: Prehistoric Art of the Alaskan Eskimo, 1929; Archeology of St. Lawrence Island, Alaska, 1937; Outline of Eskimo Prehistory, 1940; The Arctic Area (Program of the History of America), 1953; The Aleutian Islands, their People and Natural History (with A.H. Clark and E.H. Walker), 1946. Editor: Science In Alaska, 1952. Contbr. anthrop., archeol. papers to sci. jours. Home: 2557 36th St NW Washington DC 20007 Office: Smithsonian Inst Washington DC 20560 ☆

COLLINS, HENRY JAMES III, ins. co. exec.; b. Washington, July 9, 1927; s. Henry James and Genevieve (Downey) C.; B.C.S., Strayers Coll., 1951; m. Josephine Ann McDonald, July 13, 1946; children—Jonathan Alexander, Thomas James, Patricia Ann. With Govt. Employees Ins. Co., Washington, 1945, 46—, treas., 1965—, treas. Govt. Employees Corp., Washington, 1966—, Govt. Employees Financial Corp., Washington, 1966—; asst. treas. Criterion Ins. Co., 1961-70, treas., 1970—. Treas. Oakview Citizens Assn., 1952-53. Served with AUS, 1945-46. Mem. Soc. Ins. Accountants, Ins. Accounting and Statis. Assn., Nat. Assn. Ind. Insureres (com. blanks and uniform accounting 1964—), Izaak Walton League Am. Home: 204 Bluff Terrace Wheaton MD 20902 Office: 5260 Western Av N W Washington DC 20015

COLLINS, JAMES DANIEL, educator, philosopher; b. Holyoke, Mass., July 12, 1917; s. Michael Joseph and Mary Magdalen (Rooney) C.; A.B., Cath. U. Am., 1941, A.M., 1942, Ph.D., 1944; m. Yvonne Marie Stafford, June 6, 1945; 1 son, Michael Leo. Research fellow philosophy Harvard, 1944-45; mem. faculty St. Louis U., 1945—, prof. philosophy, 1956—; Suarez lectr. Fordham U., 1953; Aquinas lectr. Marquette U., 1962; Thomas More lectr. Yale, 1963. Penfield fellow Cath. U. Am., 1944-45; Guggenheim fellow, 1963-64; recipient Cardinal Newman medal Newman Found., 1962; Cath. U. Alumni award, 1962; award for scholarship Nat. Council Cath. Men, 1961; 29th Ann. Christian Culture medal U. Windsor. Mem. Am., Am. Cath. (pres. 1954; Aquinas medal 1965) philos. assns. Metaphys. Soc. Am. (pres. 1962). Author: The Existenialists, 1952; The Mind of Kierkegaard, 1953; A History of Modern European Philosophy, 1954; God in Modern Philosophy, 1959; The Lure of Widsom, 1962; Three Paths in Philosophy, 1962; The Emergence of Philosophy of Religion, 1967; Descartes' Philosophy of Nature, 1971. Editorial bd. Am. Philos. Quar., Internat. Archives History of Ideas, The Modern Schoolman, Jour. History Philosophy. The Philosopher's Index. Home: 5508 Norway Dr St Louis MO 63121

COLLINS, JAMES E., newspaper exec.; b. Buffalo, Jan. 28, 1915; s. James E. and Clara (Rice) C.; student pub. schs.; m. Grace Evelyn Hess, Apr. 28, 1938; children—James C., Karen. Copy boy Buffalo Evening News, 1929, then supt. wire room, stockboard marker, reporter, copy editor, asst. financial editor, financial editor, now business and financial editor. Mason. Home: 226 Stillwell Rd Hamburg Village NY 14075 Office: 218 Main St Buffalo NY 14202

COLLINS, JAMES FRANCIS, former army officer; b. N.Y.C., Sept. 2, 1905; s. Thomas William and Anna Cecilia (Flanagan) C.; B.S., U.S. Mil. Acad., 1927; student Nat. War Coll., 1946-47; m. Marian McLaughlin, June 7, 1932; 1 dau., Patricia Marian (Mrs. Ronald N. Bowman). Commd. 2d lt. U.S. Army, 1927, advanced through grades to gen., 1961; comdg. gen. I Corps Arty., 1945-46; faculty mem., dir. dept. personnel Command and Gen. Staff Sch., 1947-50; faculty mem. Army War Coll., 1950; exec. to asst. sec. def. for manpower and personnel, 1950-53, dep. asst. sec. for manpower and personnel, 1952-53; comdg. gen. U.S. Army, Alaska, 1954, comdg. gen. 71st Div., 1954-56, 2d Inf. div., 1956, dep. chief of staff personnel, 1956-60, comdr. in chief U.S. Army, Pacific, 1961-64; pres. A.R.C., Washington, 1964-70; dir. Am. Security & Trust Co. Decorated D.S.M. with oak leaf cluster, Legion of Merit, Bronze Star medal, Air medal. Clubs: Army-Navy Town, Army-Navy Country, Chevy Chase, Metropolitan (Washington). Home: 4133 N River St Arlington VA 22207

COLLINS, JAMES FRANCIS, hosp. adminstr.; b. Norwood, Mass. Jan. 24, 1912; s. Daniel J. and Nora (Toomey) C.; A.B., Holy Cross Coll., 1937; M.D., Tufts U., 1937; m. Anne C. Sheehan, Apr. 26, 1941; children—Nancy (Mrs. William A. Edwards), Mary Ellen, James Francis. Intern, St. Francis Hosp., Hartford, Conn., 1937-38; med. resident Soldiers Home and Hosp., Chelsea, Mass., 1938-39; pvt. practice medicine, Gloucester, Mass., 1939-41; asst. med. dir. Mass. Vets. Hosp., Chelsea, 1946-50; med. dir. Mass. Vets. Hosp., Holyoke, 1950-52, asso. supt. Boston City Hosp., 1952-54; med. dir. Cambridge (Mass.) City Hosp., 1954-63; supt. Nassau County Med. Center, East Meadow, N.Y., 1963—. Exec. sec.-treas. Meadowbrook Med. Edn. and Research Found.; preceptor hosp. adminstrn. George Washington U.; mem. exec. council Tufts U. Sch. Medicine; mem. Community Health Services Com., Health and Welfare Council Nassau County, L.I. Health and Hosp. Planning Council, Nassau-Suffolk Hosp. Council. Bd. dirs. local A.R.C., Hofstra U. Served to col., M.C., AUS, 1941-46. Decorated Legion of Merit; named Man of Year, Woodward Sch., 1969, L.I. Assn. Children with Learning Disabilities, 1970. Fellow Am. Coll. Hosp. Adminstrs.; mem. Hosp. Assn. State N.Y., Nassau-Suffolk Hosp. Council (chmn. profl. practice com.), Mass. Hosp. Assn. (past pres. elect), Am. Hosp. Assn. (past del.). Roman Catholic. K.C. Author articles. Home: 2201 Hempstead Turnpike East Meadow NY 11554

COLLINS, JAMES MITCHELL, congressman; b. Hallsville, Tex., Apr. 29, 1916; s. Carr P. and Ruth (Woodall) C.; B.S.C., So. Meth. U., 1937; M.B.A., Northwestern U., 1938, Harvard, 1943; C.L.U., 1940; m. Dorothy Dann, Sept. 16, 1942; children—Michael James, Dorothy Colville (Mrs. David R. Weaver), Nancy Miles. Pres. Consol. Industries, Inc., 1954-65, Internat. Industries, Inc., 1954-65, Fidelity Union Life Ins. Co., 1954-65; mem. 90th-91st-92d Congresses 3d Dist. Tex. Active local Greater Dallas Planning Council, Salvation Army, Dallas Council World Affairs. Served to capt., C.E., AUS, World War II. Mem. Am. Legion, V.F.W., Phi Delta Theta. Republican. Baptist. Home: 1525 Hardrock Rd Irving TX 75060 Office: Longworth Office Bldg Washington DC 20515

COLLINS, JANET, concert dancer; b. New Orleans; d. Ernest Lee and Alma (de Lavallade) Collins; student Los Angeles City Coll., Art Center Sch. (Julius Rosenwald fellow). Concert debut, N.Y.C., 1949; lead dancer in Cole Porter's Out of This World, 1950-51; solo concert dancer, 1947—; prima ballerina Met. Opera, 1951—; tchr. modern dance. Sch. Am. Ballet, 1949-52; now teaching dance Marymount Manhattan Coll., Sch. Am. Ballet, Harkness House Ballet Arts. Awarded scholarships study ballet with Madame Toscanini, modern dance with Hanya Holm, choreography with Doris Humphrey. Mem. Am. Guild Mus. Artists (bd. govs.), Screen Actors Guild, Actors' Equity, Am. Guild Variety Artists. Home: 370 Central Park W New York City NY 10025

COLLINS, JOHN FREDERICK, educator; b. Boston, July 20, 1919; s. Frederick B., Margaret (Mellyn) C.; LL.B., cum laude, Suffolk U., 1941; m. Mary P. Cunniff, Sept. 6, 1947; children—Mary P., John Frederick, Thomas, Margaret. Admitted to Mass. bar, 1941, since practiced in Boston; mayor of Boston, 1960-68; prof. urban affairs Alfred P. Sloan Sch. Mgmt., Mass. Inst. Tech., Cambridge, 1968—. Mem. Mass. Ho. Reps., 1947-50, Mass. Senate, 1950-54; councilman, City of Boston. 1956; Suffolk Register of Probate, 1957-59. Served from pvt. to capt. AUS, 1942-46. Mem. Boston Bar Assn., Am. Bar Assn., Am. Legion, D.A.V.K.C. Eagle. Home: 20 Myrtle St Jamaica Plain MA 02130 Office: 50 Memorial Dr Cambridge MA 02139

COLLINS, JOHN LAMONT, publisher; b. Bklyn., Jan. 3, 1919; s. John and Elizabeth (Lamont) C.; B.S. in Econs., U. Pa. Wharton Sch., 1940; m. Dorothea C. Convery, Mar. 24, 1951; children—Joseph, Diane, Stephen, Joanne. With Nat. City Bank N.Y., 1935; mdsg. exec. R.H. Macy & Co., N.Y.C., 1940-41; with Curtis Pub. Co., 1946—, pub. Am. Home mag., 1963—. Served with USNR 1941-46. Recipient citation Chilean Navy, 1943. Mem. Friars Honor Soc., Beta Gamma Sigma, Delta Tau Delta. Club: Port Washington (N.Y.) Yacht. Home: 10 Vanderlyn Dr Manhasset NY 11030 Office: 641 Lexington Av New York City NY 10022

COLLINS, JOSEPH LAWTON, bus. exec.; ret. army officer; b. New Orleans, May 1, 1896; s. Jeremiah Bernard and Catherine (Lawton) C.; student La. State U., 1912-31; B.S., U.S. Mil. Acad. 1917; student Command and Gen. Staff Sch., 1931-33, Army Indsl. Coll., 1936-37, Army War Coll., 1937-38; LL.D., Tulane U., 1953, Georgetown U., 1956; m. Gladys Easterbrook, July 15, 1921; children—Joseph Easterbrook (col. U.S. Army), Gladys May (Mrs. Jerome J. Stenger, Jr.), Nancy Katherine (Mrs. Michael J. Rubino). Commd. 2d lt., U.S. Army, 1917, advanced through grades to gen. 1948; with 22d Inf., N.Y.C., World War I; with 1st Div. and Hdqrs. Am. Forces in Germany, 1919-21; instr. U.S. Mil. Acad., 1921-25, Inf. Sch., 1927-31, Army War Coll., 1938-40; asst. sec. War Dept. Gen. Staff, 1940-41; chief of staff VII Army Corps, Birmingham, 1941-42, Hawaiian Dept., 1941-42; comdr. 25th Div., 1942- 44; comdr. VII Corps, 1944-45; dep. commd. gen. and chief of staff, Army Ground Forces, Washington, 1945; chief Pub. Information, War Dept., 1945-47; dep. and vice chief of staff U.S. Army, 1947-49, chief of staff, 1949-53; U.S. rep. NATO's mil. Com. and Standing Group, 1953-56; spl. rep. of U.S. in Viet Nam, with personal rank of ambassador, 1954-55; dir., vice chmn. Pres.'s Com. for Hungarian Refugee Relief, 1956-57; vice chmn. bd. dirs. Pfizer Internat. subsidiaries, 1957—. Chmn. bd. dirs. Fgn. Student Service Council of Greater Washington, Inc., 1957-58, now hon. chmn.; hon. trustee Inst. Internat. Edn., Inc., N.Y.C., 1965—. Decorated D.S.M. with 3 oak leaf clusters, Silver Star with oak leaf cluster, Legion of Merit with 2 oak leaf clusters; Companion Order of Bath (Eng.); Order of Suvorov 2d Class (2 medals, Russia); Croix de Guerre Palm, Grand Officer Legion of Honor (France); Grand Officer Order of Leopold II, Croix de Guerre with Palm (Belgium); 1950 Laetare medal; recipient Cardinal Gibbons medal Cath. U., 1955. Clubs: Army and Navy (Washington); Chevy Chase (Md.). Home: Scientists Cliff MD 21213 Office: 1700 Pennsylvania Av NW Washington DC 20006 also 4000 Massachusetts Av Washington DC 20016

COLLINS, JUDY MARJORIE, folk singer; b. Seattle, May 1, 1939; d. Charles T. and Marjorie (Byrd) Collins; pvt. study piano, 1953-56; m. Peter A. Taylor, Apr., 1958; 1 son, Clark Collin. Debut as profl. folk singer, Boulder, Colo., 1959, since has appeared in numerous clubs U.S. and Can.; performer concerts including Newport Folk Festival, ann. concerts, 1963—, Orch. Hall, Chgo., 1964, Carnegie Hall, N.Y.C.; also appeared radio and TV; recording artist Elektra albums including A Maid of Constant Sorrow, Golden Apples of the Sun, Judy Collins No. 3, Who Knows Where the Time Goes, Recollections, Whale and Nightingales. Recipient 5 Gold LPs. Office: care Harold Leventhal 200 W 57th St New York City NY 10019

COLLINS, JULIEN H., investment banker; b. Chgo., June 27, 1897; s. Samuel and Anna C. (Thompson) C.; B.S., U. Ill., 1919; m. Bertha Meyer, Aug. 18, 1926; children—Julien H., Claire. Joined Harris Trust & Savs. Bank, 1919; asst. mgr. investment dept., 1927-31, mgr., 1931-35; v.p., dir. Harris, Hall & Co., 1935-45; pres. Julien Collins & Co., Chgo., 1945—; dir. Comml. Discount Corp. Chmn. Chgo. chpt. A.R.C., 1950; chmn., trustee Ravinia (Ill.) Festival Assn.; trustee Chgo. Hearing Soc., U. Ill. YMCA, chmn.; trustee U. Ill. Found., Orchestral Assn. Chgo.; mem. citizen's bd. U. Chgo., Northwestern U. Assos. Served as ensign USN, 1918-19. Chmn. 6th War Loan Drive. Mem. Investment Bankers Assn. Am. (gov. 1940-43, v.p. 1943-47, chmn. edn. com. 1943-47, pres. 1947-48), Am. Finance Assn. (v.p.), Better Govt. Assn., Alpha Delta Phi, Sigma Delta Chi. Mason. Clubs: Bond (pres. 1945), University, Economic, Mid-Day, Indian Hill, Saddle and Cycle Commercial (Chgo.). Co-author: Fundamentals of Investment Banking. Home: 213 Raleigh Rd Kenilworth IL 60043 Office: 230 W Monroe St Chicago IL 60606

COLLINS, KENNETH WILSON, ret. army officer; b. Magnolia, Del., Jan. 4, 1916; s. George W. and Ethel (Mensch) C.; B.S., U.S. Mil. Acad., 1939; grad. Air Force War Coll., 1951, Nat. War Coll., 1960; m. Allie Lou Conner, Oct. 18, 1941; 1 dau., Karen (Mrs. Arthur L. West III). Commd. 2d lt., inf., U.S. Army, 1939, advanced through grades to maj. gen., 1967; bn. comdr. 9th Armored Div., U.S. and Europe, 1942-45; instr. Command and Gen. Staff Coll., 1945-52; with SHAPE, Paris, France, 1952-54; comdg. officer 12th Inf. Regt., 1954-55; chief of staff 1st Div., 1955-56; asst. dir. plans Office Dep. Chief of Staff for Operations, Dept. Army, Washington, 1956-60; chief of staff Korean Mil. Adv. Group, 1960-61; dep. comdt. of cadets U.S. Mil. Acad., 1961-64; dep. chief MAAG, Germany, 1964-65; dep. comdg. gen., comdg. gen. 7th Army Support Command, 1965-67; comdg. gen. Ft. Dix, N.J., 1967-69; ret., 1970. Dist. commr. Boy

Scouts Am., 1966-67. Decorated D.S.M., Silver Star medal, Legion of Merit, Bronze Star medal, Combat Inf. badge, Belgian Croix de Guerre avec palm, Luxembourg Croix de Guerre, Czechoslovakian War Cross. Home: 9 Palmetto Pl Hilton Head SC 29928

COLLINS, LARRY, author, journalist; b. Hartford, Conn., Sept. 14, 1929; s. John Laurence and Helen (Cannon) C.; grad. Loomis Inst., Windsor, Conn., 1947; B.A., Yale University, 1951; m. Nadia Hoda Sultan, Sept. 17, 1966; 1 son, John Lawrence III. With United Press Internat., 1956-59, corr. Middle East, 1957-59; Middle East editor Newsweek mag., 1959-61, chief Paris bur., 1961-64. Served with AUS, 1953-55. Author: (with Doninique La Pierre) Is Paris Burning, 1965, Or I'll Dress You in Mourning, 1967. Address: 64 bis Rue Pergolèse Paris 16 France

COLLINS, LEROY, lawyer, former gov. Fla.; b. Tallahassee, Mar. 10, 1909; s. Marvin H. and Mattie (Brandon) C.; LL.B., Cumberland U., 1931; m. Mary Call Darby, June 29, 1932; children—LeRoy, Jane, Mary Call, and Darby Collins. Admitted to Fla. bar, 1931; Ark., 1931, Tenn. 1931; Leon County rep. to Fla. Legislature, 1934-40, mem. Senate, 1940-54; gov. Fla., 1955-60; pres. Nat. Assn. Broadcasters, 1961- 64; dir. Community Relations Service. Dept. Commerce, 1964-65; undersec. commerce, 1965-66, pvt. practice law, Tampa, Fla., 1966-68; pvt. bus., Miami, 1969; mem. firm Ervin, Pennington, Varn & Jacobs, Tallahassee, 1970—. Former chmn. Nat. Gov.'s Conf., So. Gov.'s Conf.; mem. nat. adv. council Peace Corps. mem. honor corps Nat. Conf. Christians and Jews; chmn. S. Regional Edn. Bd., 1955-57; mem. Commn. on Goals for Higher Edn. in South, 1961- 62. Trustee Randolph Macon Woman's Coll.; bd. govs. Nat. Cathedral Sch. Served as lt. USNR, World War II. Mem. Am. Bar Assn., Nat. Municipal League (governing council). Democrat. Episcopalian. Home: The Grove Tallahassee FL 32301 Office: PO Box 1170 305 S Gadsden St Tallahassee FL 32301

COLLINS, LESTER ALBERTSON, landscape architect; b. Moorestown, N.J., Apr. 19, 1914; s. Lester and Anne (Albertson) C.; grad. Choate Sch., 1933; student Princeton, 1933- 35; A.B., Harvard, 1938, M.L.A., 1942; m. Petronella leRoux, July 8, 1947; children—Abigail Anne, Lester Adrian, Oliver Michael. Chmn. dept. landscape architecture, 1950-53; Fulbright scholar, Japan, 1953- 54; prin. Collins, Simonds and Simonds, Washington, 1955-70, Lester Collins Assos., 1971—. Pres., Innisfree Found. Bd. dirs. Hubbard Endl. Trust; trustee Am. Beautiful Fund Nat. Area Council. Served with Am. Field Service, 1942-45. Fellow Am. Soc. Landscape Architects. Mem. Soc. of Friends. Clubs: Cosmos (Washington); Century Assn. (N.Y.C.). Home: 1619 33d St NW Washington DC 20007

COLLINS, LINTON MCGEE, fed. judge; b. Reidsville, Ga., June 21, 1902; s. Ernest Clyde and Beulah Edna (Rogers) C.; A.B., Mercer U., 1921; M.A. 1922; postgrad. Mercer and Columbia; LL.D., Gallaudet Coll., 1955; m. Josephine Staten Hardman, Jan. 30, 1934: 1 dau., Cynthia Hardman (Mrs. Randolph). Admitted to Ga. bar, 1924, Fla. bar, 1925, D.C. bar, 1947; tchr. English, Lanier High Sch., Macon, Ga., 1922-24, English, history Columbia (S.C.) High Sch., 1924-25, Am. govt., polit sci. U. Miami, Coral Gables, Fla., 1930-32; personnel dir. div. adminstr., pub. agys. div. NRA, 1933-35; 1st asst. Office Dep. Atty. Gen., spl. asst. to atty. gen., acting dep. atty. gen. Dept. Justice, 1935-44; mem. Prison Industries Reorgn. Adminstrn., 1935-38; mem. Nat. Workshop adv. com., 1938-56; mem. Shackleford & Brown, Tampa, Fla., 1925-26, Collins & Collins, Miami, Fla., 1926-30. Kremer & Bingham, Washington, 1944-46, Bingham, Collins, Porter & Kistler, 1946-60, Collins, Robb, Porter & Kistler, 1960-64; pvt. practice law, 1930-33; judge U.S. Ct. Claims, Washington, 1964—. Sec., treas.; dir. Equity Pub. Corp., 1952-54. Mem. Dade County Democratic Exec. Com., 1930-34; sec., treas., Fla. Democratic State Com., 1932-36. Bd. dirs. Gallaudet Coll., 1944, sec., 1950-51, vice chmn. bd., 1952-69; Recipient Congl. Selective Service medal Pres. Truman, 1945. Mem. U.S. C. of C. (nat. adv. council 1950-51, govt. operations and expenditures com. 1952-60), D.C. Bd. Trade (chmn. law and legislation com. 1951-54), gen. counsel 1959-64, chmn. congl. relations com. 1956- 59), U.S. (nat. dir. 1931-34), Miami (pres. 1927-28), Fla. (pres. 1930-31) jr. chambers commerce, Miami C. of C. (dir. 1932-33), Fla. (hon. life), Am., D.C. (hon. life) bar assns., Phi Delta Theta. Baptist. Rotarian. Clubs: Cosmos, Palaver, Columbia Country, Metropolitan, National Lawyers (Washington). Home: 5025 Macomb St NW Washington DC 20016 Office: US Ct Claims 717 Madison Pl NW Washington DC 20005

COLLINS, LOWELL O, investment securities exec.; b. nr. Linn, Kan., Apr. 10, 1900; s. Wesley Taylor and Neona (Outwater) C.; A.B., Colo. Coll., 1922; grad. study U. Toulouse, France, 1923-24; m. Leona J. Siebring, Dec. 23, 1945; children-Lowell O., Roger W. (by former marriage), Michael S., Cynthia Janelle, Kevin T. Pres. Founders Mut. Depositor Corp., Denver, since 1938; v.p. Collins Croke & Co., Denver, 1930-38. Clubs: Denver County Garden of Gods, Univ. (Denver). Home: 5609 E 17th Av Denver CO 80220 Office: 1st Nat Bank Bldg Denver CO 80202

COLLINS, MARCUS WHITFORD, educator; b. Marion, S.C., Mar. 23, 1910; s. Murphy C. and Sallie L. (Capps) C.; B.A., U. Ala., 1929; M.A., George Washington U., 1937; M.A., Ph.D. (Bowdoin Grad. prize), Harvard, 1943. Successively dir. transient homes, Greenville, S.C.; legal contact soil erosion project Dept. Interior, Spartanburg, S.C.; sec. Washington YMCA; met. dir. Nat. Conf. Christians and Jews, N.Y.C.; community service specialist Fed. Council Chs. Christ in Am.; prof. sociology, chmn. dept. Pa. Coll. for Women; vis. prof., lectr. U. St. Louis; asso. prof. sociology Fla. State U.; prof. sociology John B. Stetson U., also Atlanta div. U. Ga.; vis. prof., chmn. dept. sociology Dakota Wesleyan U., U. N.M.; vis. prof. Johns Hopkins, Houston U., Yale Sch. Alcoholic Studies; ednl. specialist Dept. State in Europe; chmn. dept. sociology Wayland Coll., High Point Coll.; prof. sociology, Wayland Coll., High Point Coll.; prof. sociology, chmn. Wis. State Coll., Eau Claire, 1959-64; prof; sociology Knoxville Coll., Tenn., 1964, also chmn. div. social scis; now with Boise (Ida.) Coll.; vs. prof. Atlanta University, also U. S.C. at S.C. State College. Mem. city planning commn., Findlay, O. Delegate Govs. Conference on Aging, 1960, Recipient award for outstanding research Fla. Acad. Sci., 1948; citation work in human relations Internat. Dictionary Biographies; named coll. staff Gov. Ky., also adm staff Gov. Neb. Fellow A.A.A.S., Am. Sociol. Soc.; mem. Am. Acad. Polit. and Social Sci., Am. Assn. U. Profs., So. Sociol Soc., Pi Gamma Mu (Scholarship medal), Phi Alpha Theta (Scholarship medal), Phi Alpha Omega (Faculty Service medal), also numerous others. Masons, Elk, Kiwanian, Rotarian. Author articles minority groups. Address: care Mrs FH Barnhart 852 E Main St Lock Haven PA ☆

COLLINS, MARK FRANCIS, newspaper pub.; b. Mechanicville, N.Y., Oct. 15, 1913; s. John Joseph and Elizabeth (Farley) C.; A.B., U. Ala., 1935; student Union Coll., Schenectady, 1936-37; m. Olive Jameson, Aug. 9, 1943; children—Joseph J., Judith, Mark II, David. Reporter, Saratogan, Saratoga Springs, N.Y., 1939-41; mem. advt. staff Schenectady Gazette, 1941-50; advt. mgr. Albany (N.Y.) Times-Union, 1950-54, asst. pub., advt. dir., 1955-59; advt. dir. Boston Post, 1954-55; asst. pub., advt. dir. Boston Record Am., 1959-64; pub. Balt. News Am., 1964-; v.p., dir. Hearst Consol. Publs., Hearst Pub. Co. Bd. dirs. Greater Balt. Good Will Industries, Bur. Advt., Am. Newspaper Pubs. Assn., Balt. Conv. Bur.; Md. regional bd. Nat. Conf. Christians and Jews; adv. bd. Md. Higher Edn. Com. Served to 1st lt. USMCR, World War II. Mem. Balt. Assn. Commerce (dir.), Advt. Club Balt. (gov.), Md.-Del.-D.C. Press, Asso. Press, C. of C. Met. Balt. (dir.). Clubs: Merchants, Balt. Country, Center (Balt.). Home: 211 Wendover Rd Baltimore MD 21218 Office: Balt News American Lombard and South Sts Baltimore MD 21203

COLLINS, MICHAEL, museum dir., former astronaut; b. Rome, Italy, Oct. 31, 1930 (parents Am. citizens); s. James L. Collins; B.S., U.S. Mil. Acad., 1952; D.Sc. (hon.), Northeastern U., Stonehill Coll.; LL.D., St. Michael's Coll.; m. Patricia Mary Finnegan, 1957; children—Kathleen, Ann Stewart, Michael Lawton. Commd. 2d lt. USAF, advanced through grades to col.; exptl. flight test officer Air Force Flight Test Center, Edwards AFB, Cal., 1960-63; astronaut, pilot Gemini X (nation's 3d space walker), command module pilot Apollo 11, 1963-69; asst. sec. state for pub. affairs, 1970-71; dir. Nat. Air and Space Mus., Smithsonian Instn., 1971—. Decorated D.S.M., D.F.C.; recipient Distinguished, Exceptional Service medals NASA, Hubbard medal, Collier Trophy, Harmon Trophy, Gen. Thomas D. White USAF Space Trophy. Mem. Soc. Exptl. Test Pilots. Office: Nat Air and Space Museum Smithsonian Instn Washington DC 20560

COLLINS, ROBERT JOSEPH, newspaperman; b. Indpls., Jan. 22, 1927; s. Patrick Joseph and Evelyn (Mattingly) C.; student Butler U., 1949; m. Louise Zore, Nov. 28, 1946; children—Kathleen, Carolyn, Cynthia, Mary Louise, Evelyn, Michael, Kevin, Linda. With Indpls. Star, 1948—, columnist, 1960—, sports editor, 1964—. Served with USNR, World War II. Roman Catholic. Club: Indianapolis Press (pres. 1963). Author: The Best of Bob Collins, 1965; (with Mario Andretti) What's It Like Out There, 1970; (with Johnny Rutherford) Championship Trail, 1971. Home: 3450 Sandy Springs Lane Indianapolis IN 46222 Office: 307 N Penn St Indianapolis IN 46206

COLLINS, ROBERT JOSEPH, educator; b. Phila., July 23, 1923; s. Marie J. Collins; student U. Miami, 1940-42; A.B.B., U. Mich., 1947, M.S., 1949; Ph.D., Purdue U., 1953; children—Michael, Martha, Molly, William, Researcher, Bell Telephone Labs., 1953-63, Inst. Def. Analysis, 1962-63; prof. physics and elec. engring. head dept. elec. engring. U. Minn., 1963—. Mem. adv. panel spl. group optical masers Office Sec. Def., 1964—. Served with USAAF, 1943-46. Fellow I.E.E.E.; mem. Am. Phys. Soc., Optical Soc. Am., Sigma Xi. Contbr. profl. jours. Home: 1408 Douglas Av S Minneapolis MN 55403

COLLINS, THOMAS ASA, coll. pres.; b. Rome, Ga., Aug. 31, 1921; s. Earle Strathmore and Hazel (Alverson) C.; B.A., Asbury Coll., Wilmore, Ky., 1941, B.D., 1944; M.Divinity, Emory U., 1944; D.D. (hon.), High Point (N.C.) Coll.; m. Anna E. Galloway, Aug. 17, 1944; children—Faye Anne (Mrs. Cullen B. Rivers), Thomas Asa, Robert Earle, William Ray. Ordained to ministry Methodist Ch., 1944; pastor in Atlanta, 1942-43, Talbot, Ga., 1943-44, Gatesville, N.C., 1944-49, Raleigh, N.C., 1949-53; exec. dir. Meth. Conf. Bd. Missions, 1953-59; 1st pres. N.C. Wesleyan Coll., Rocky Mount, 1959- -; prin., tchr. high sch., Gates County, 1944-46. Dir. People's Bank & Trust Co., Rocky Mount, 1966-69. Del. gen. conf. and jurisdictional confs. Meth. Ch., 1960-64, 68, 70; pres. N.C. Council Chs., 1967-70; mem. bd. Commn. Christian Edn., Nat. Council Chs., 1959-68. Named N.C. Tar Heel of Week, 1959. Mem. Am. Acad. Religion, Am. Assn. Colls. Democrat. Clubs: Ruritan (pres. 1947-49), Kiwanis (pres. 1959) (Rocky Mount). Sermon editor Carolina Cooperator, 1949—. Contbr. religious jours. Home: Wesleyan Coll Station Rocky Mount NC 27801

COLLINS, THOMAS HIGHTOWER, newspaperman, author; b. Cedartown, Ga., Nov. 26, 1910; s. Clifford Augustus and Fannie Lou (Hightower) C.; student U. Ga., 1929-31; Ga. State Coll., 1931-35; m. Beulah Blagden Stowe, Apr. 6, 1946; children—Carol, Kent, Paul, Todd. Reporter, DeKalb New Era, Decatur, Ga., 1932-35; copyreader, picture editor Atlanta Jour., 1935-40; copyreader, writer Louisville Courier-Jour., 1940-42; copyreader Chgo. Daily News, 1942—, feature editor, 1946-59, asst. mng. editor, 1959-60, mng. editor, 1960-61, exec. editor, 1961-62. Served to lt. (s.g.) USNR, 1944- 46. Episcopalian. Author: The Golden Years, An Invitation to Retirement, 1956; The Complete Guide to Retirement, 1970; syndicated column, The Golden Years, 1948—; (pseudo Paul Hightower) syndicated column The Senior Forum, 1952—. Address: 15 Lake Shore Dr Chapel Hill NC 27514

COLLINS, TRUMAN EDWARD, clergyman; b. Advance, Mo., Aug. 22, 1919; s. Edward and Pearl (Shell) C.; diploma Calvary Bible Coll., Kansas City, Mo., 1952; m. Dorothy Virginia Eaker, Dec. 23, 1939; 1 son, Edward Alan. Ordained to ministry Baptist Ch., 1949; pastor Mt. Zion Gen. Bapt. Ch., Granite City, Ill., 1950-64, First Gen. Bapt. Ch., Princeton, Ind., 1964-67, Dover Chapel Gen. Bapt. Ch., Louisville, 1967-69, Southland Bapt. Mission Ch., Louisville, 1969—. Pres. Nat. Sunday Sch. Bd. Gen. Bapt., 1956-63, moderator nat. conv., 1961-62; pres. Gen. Bapt. Publs. and Edn. Bd., Inc., 1964-66; mem. Liberty Presbyter Gen. Bapt. Assn., Ind., 1965-67; mem. Christian Edn. and Publs. Bd., Inc. of Gen. Baptist Denomination, 1963-66, pres. 1964-65; pres. Illmo Assn. Endowment Corp., 1959-64; dir. Illmo Assn. Youth Camp of Gen. Bapt., 1954-64. Pres. Emerson Sch. P.T.A., 1962-63. Mem. Nat. Congress P.T.A., Quad City Ministerial Assn. (treas.), Kentuckana Assn. Gen. Baptist, Greater Louisville Evang. Fellowship (v.p.). Author: Sun Rays In the Sickroom. Address: 2119 Auburn Dr Louisville KY 40216

COLLINS, VINCENT PATRICK, physician, educator; b. Toronto, Ont., Can., Nov. 11, 1912; s. John and Laura (Doyle) C.; M.D., U. Toronto, 1937; J.D., U. Houston, 1964; m. Lois Cowan, Dec. 26, 1942; children—Cowan, Ross, Christopher. Came to U.S., 1940, naturalized, 1945. Intern Toronto Gen. Hosp., 1937-38; demonstrator anatomy, fellow physiology U. Toronto, 1938- 39, research fellow Banting Inst., 1939-40; sr. resident pathology N.E. Deaconess Hosp., Boston, 1940-42; resident surg. pathology, instr. surgery Presbyn. Hosp., Columbia, 1942-43, resident radiology, 1945-47, attending radiologist, 1950-52; instr. radiology Columbia, 1947-49; cons. radiology USPHS Marine Hosp., S.I. 1948-52; asst. prof. Columbia, 1949-50, asso. prof. radiology, 1950-52; chief radiotherapy Francis Delafield Hosp., 1950-52; prof. radiology, chmn. dept. Baylor U., 1952- 68; radiologist-in-chief Jefferson Davis Hosp., Houston, 1952-68, Ben Taub Gen. Hosp., Houston, 1963-68; chief cons. radiology VA Hosp., Houston, 1952-68; attending radiologist Meth. Hosp., Houston, 1955-68; cons. radiology Tex. Children's Hosp., Houston, 1956-68; dir. radiotherapy Rosewood Gen. Hosp.; cons. radiotherapy Ochsner Clinic, New Orleans, 1968—, U. Tex. Med. Br., 1969—; prin. cons. radiology Nat. Inst. Gen. Med. Scis., Bethesda, Md., 1966. Served from 1st lt. to capt., M.C., AUS, 1943-45. Diplomate Am. Bd. Radiology. Fellow Am. Coll. Radiology; mem. Am. Roentgen Ray Soc., Radiol. Soc. N.Am., Tex. Radiol. Soc., James Ewing Soc., Am. Radium Soc., Soc. Nuclear Medicine, Arthur Purdy Stout Soc., Am. Assn. Automotive Medicine, Am. Pub. Health Assn., Internat. Acad. Pathology, Sigma Xi. Home: 105 Shasta Dr Houston TX 77024 Office: 9200 Westheimer Rd Houston TX 77042

COLLINS, WILLIAM FINN, mfg. co. exec.; b. Edgar, Wis., May 5, 1919; s. Francis E. and Mary C. (Finn) C.; A.B., U. Wis., 1942; LL.B., 1942; m. Jacqueline Knee, Jan. 14, 1944; children—Michael, F., Katharine F., Alexis S., Benjamin N., Sarah S. Admitted to Wis. bar, 1945, N.Y. bar, 1947; asso. firm Cravath, Swaine & Moore, N.Y.C., 1945-52; with Revere Copper & Brass, Inc., 1952- -, gen. counsel, 1955—, sec., 1960—, v.p., 1965-67, exec. v.p., dir.; dir. Ormet Corp., Multimetals, Ltd., Treas., bd. dirs. Revere Found. Served to lt. USNR, 1942-45. Mem. Am. Bar Assn., Bar City N.Y., Order of Coif. Home: 136 E Hunting Ridge Rd Stamford CT 06903 Office: 605 3d Av New York City NY 10016

COLLINS, WILLIAM FRANCIS, educator, physician; b. New Haven, Jan. 20, 1924; s. William F. and Jane (Shanley) C.; grad. Choate Sch., 1941; B.S., Yale, 1944, M.D., 1947; m. Gwendolyn Ruth Davis, Dec. 16, 1950; children—William Francis III, Peter Davis, Ruth Ellen. Intern surgery Barnes Hosp., St. Louis, 1947-49, resident neurosurgery, 1951-54; instr. neurosurgery Western Res. U. Sch. Medicine, 1954-57, asso. prof. 1957-63; prof., chmn. dept. neurol. surgery, chmn. dept. Yale Sch. Medicine, 1967—, Cushing prof. surgery, 1970—; fellow Pierson Coll., 1969. Served to capt. M.C., AUS, 1947-49. Mem. Neurosurg. Soc. Am. (sec. 1968-71). Home: 403 St Ronan St New Haven CT 06511

COLLINS, WILLIAM G., banker. Sr. v.p. First Nat. Bank S. Jersey. Office: 1102 Black Horse Pike Pleasantville NJ 08232*

COLLINS, WILLIAM LEIGHTON, engring. educator; b. Highland, Ill., Jan. 8, 1906; s. William Alvin and Clara Lucy (Lauener) C.; B.S., U. Ill., 1928, M.S., 1932; m. Anita Blanche Wood, Feb. 3, 1938; children—Kathryn Janet, William Wood. Structural draftsman Holabird & Root, 1928-29; with theoretical and applied mechs. dept. U. Ill., 1929-65, successively asst., instr., asso., asst. prof., 1929-45, asso. prof., 1945-49, prof., 1949-65, prof. emeritus, 1965—; exec. sec. Am. Soc. Engring. Edn., 1955-71, exec. dir. emeritus, 1971—. U.S. specialist on engring. edn. Paraguay, 1960, Venezuela, 1961; cons. engring. edn. Pres., dir. Champaign County Community Chest, Council Social Agys. Served as capt. AUS, 1942-45. Fulbright-Hays grantee, Venezuela, 1971; recipient Distinguished Alumni award Coll. Engring., U. Ill., 1968. Mem. Am. Soc. C.E., Am. Soc. Testing and Materials, A.A.A.S., Am. Soc. Engring. Edn. (hon.), Sigma Xi, Gamma Alpha (nat. pres.), Chi Epsilon, Alpha Sigma Phi. Rotarian. Author: (with J.O. Draffin) Statics and Strength of Materials, 1950; (with others) The Britannica Review of Developments in Engineering Education, 1970. Contbr. tech. publs. on properties of metals and engring. edn. Author monthly column and comments Jour. Engring. Edn. Home: 4600 Connecticut Av NW Washington DC 20008 Office: One Dupont Circle Washington DC 20036

COLLINS, WILLIAM MURPHY, Jr., corp. exec.; b. Chgo., Nov. 19, 1905; s. William M. and Anna (Henrici) C.; A.B., Princeton, 1927; J.D., Northwestern U., 1935; m. Louise A. Neff, June 12, 1934; children—Deborah (Mrs. R.O. Duff, Jr.), Judy, Kathleen. Chmn. exec. com., dir. John R. Thompson Co. Trustee Presby.-St. Luke's Hosp.; hon. trustee Orchestral Assn. Clubs: Casino, Commonwealth, Old Elm, Commercial (Chgo.). Home: 1530 N State Pkwy Chicago IL 60610 Office: 29 W Randolph St Chicago IL 60601

COLLINS, WILLIAM ROBERT, ret. marine corps officer; b. Washington, Feb. 5, 1913; s. Ralph A. and Maude F. (Fletcher) C.; B.Fgn. Service, Georgetown U., 1935; M.A., George Washington U., 1963; m. Mary Lee Griffith, May 9, 1940; children—Donna (Mrs. Kenneth Neilsen), Sandra (Mrs. Rex Bocher). Commd. 2d lt. USMC, 1935, advanced through grades to maj. gen., 1964; SKY control officer U.S.S. New Orleans, 1940; comdg. officer 5th Tank Battalion, 1944; comdg. gen. 3d Marine Div., 1964-66; asst. chief staff for intelligence Hdqrs., Marine Corps, 1966-68; now with Gen. Electric Co. Decorated Silver Star, Joint Services commendation Presdl. Unit citation. Home: 202 Laurel Hill Dr South Burlington VT 05401

COLLINSON, JOSEPH BRUERD, mfg. co. exec.; b. Raymond, O., Dec.. 11, 1914; s. Alfred O. and Jennifer L. (Bruerd) C.; B.S., Ohio State U., 1938; m. Jean Crayton, May 31, 1939; children—Jeffrey, Jill. Mgr. Arthur Young & Co., Tulsa and Cleve., 1956-57; v.p., treas. Textron, Inc., Providence, 1959-63, exec. v.p. finance and adminstrn., 1963—; v.p., treas. Textron Electronics, Inc., 1960- 63. C.P.A., Okla., Ohio, Illl., Mich. Clubs: Rhode Island Country, Turks Head (Providence). Home: Tallwood Dr Barrington RI 02806 Office: 10 Dorrance St Providence RI 02903

COLLINSON, WILLIAM ROBERT, U.S. judge; b. Chariton, Ia., Aug. 26, 1912; s. William and Julia (Leonard) C.; A.B., Drury Coll., 1933; LL.B., Mo. U., 1935; m. Mary Rosalie Umbarger, Aug. 23, 1934; 1 dau., Rosalie (Mrs. James R. Cook). Admitted to Mo. bar, 1935; practice in Kansas City, 1935-36; Springfield Mo., 1936-41; pros. atty., Greene County, Springfield, Mo., 1941-43; practice in Springfield, 1946-49; circuit judge 31st Jud. Circuit Mo., 1949-65; U.S. dist judge Eastern and Western Dist. Mo., 1965—. Served to lt. USNR, 1944-46; PTO. Mem. Order of Coif. Presbyn. Mason. Home: 1223 W 69th Terrace Kansas City, MO 64113 Office: US Courthouse 811 Grand St Kansas City MO 64106

COLLINSWORTH, EVEN THOMAS, Jr., corp. exec.; b. Knoxville, Tenn., Oct. 11, 1921; s. E.T. and Lillian (Smith) C.; B.S., U. Tenn., 1943; M.B.A., Harvard, 1950; m. Edith Merory, June 5, 1949; children—Even III, Eden, Sean. Sales mgr. Worthington Corp., 1943-48; cons. Arthur D. Little, 1949; dir. bus. research Monsanto Chem. Co., 1950-52; pres., dir. Velsicol Chem. Corp., 1953-59; chmn. bd. Velsicol Internat. Corp., 1955-59; pres., dir. Fansteel Metall. Corp., N. Chgo., 1960-61, pres. chief administrv. officer, 1961- 63; v.p. Armour & Co., Chgo. 1964-66, group v.p. industrial products and agrl. chem. internat., 1966-68, group v.p. indsl. products and grocery products, 1968-69, exec. v.p., 1969—; mng. dir. Fansteel A.G., 1960-63; dir. Carlon Products Corp., Kalium Chem. Co., Can., Armour Hess (Eng.), Armour Indsl. Chem. Co. Ltd., Med. Supply Co., V-R Europa Corp., Bliss & Laughlin Corp. Mem. Chgo. Crime Commn. Mem. citizens adv. com. on econs. and bus. Lake Forest Coll. Trustee Chgo. Library Internat. Relations. Registered profl. engr., N.J. Mem. Am. Agrl. Chem. Assn. (dir. 1957-59), Chicago C. of C., Alpha Chi Sigma, Phi Gamma Delta. Clubs: Economic, Chicago. Home: 368 Circle Lane Lake Forest IL 60045 Office: 111 E Wacker Chicago IL 60601

COLLIS, CHARLES, aircraft co. exec.; b. Bklyn., Aug. 6, 1920; s. Charles and Marie (Barnaby) C.; B.S. in Mech. Engring., Brown U., 1942; m. Margaret Howell, July 11, 1942; children—Jane, Joy. Vice pres. Stratos div. Fairchild Hiller Corp., 1946-65, sr. v.p. Republic Aviation div., 1965- -, exec. v.p. corp., 1967—; pres. Fairchild Hiller-F.R.G. Corp., 1966—. Mem. grad. mgmt. engring. adv. council C. W. Post Coll., L.I. U., 1965-66. Served to lt. USNR, 1942-45. Mem. Am. Inst. Aeros. and Astronautics, Assn. U.S. Army, L.I. Assn. Commerce and Industry (bd. dirs. 1964-66). Clubs: Nat. Aviation, Nat. Space (Washington); Capital Hill; River Bend Country (Va.). Home: 8550 Georgetown Pike McLean VA 22101 Office: Fairchild Hiller Corp Sherman Fairchild Tech Center Germantown MD 20767

COLLIS, JOSEPH FRANCIS, journalist; b. Wilkes-Barre, Pa., Aug. 9, 1905; s. Frank and Anne (Kearney) C.; student Duquesne U., 1926-27; B.S., Villanova Coll., 1933; m. Anne Czuleger, June 5, 1934; children—Joseph James, Rosemary. Reporter Wilkes-Barre Record,

1920-26, asst. mng. editor, 1958-60, mng. editor, 1962—, reporter Pitts. Gazette Times and Sun- Telegraph, 1926-27; v.p. Am. Newspaper Guild, 1945-53, pres., 1953-60. Vice pres. Wyoming Valley Community Chest; dir. Wyo. Valley chpt. A.R.C. Dir. Scranton div. War Manpower Commn. Mem. Internat. Fedn. Journalists (v.p.). Home: 351 Reynolds St Kingston PA 18704 Office: 15 N Main St Wilkes-Barre PA 18701

COLLIS, SIDNEY ROBERT, telephone co. exec.; b. Oak Park, Ill., Mar. 24, 1924; s. Sidney John and Cella (Steele) C.; student Ill. Inst. Tech., 1941-43, U. Santa Clara, 1943-44; B.S. in Elec. Engring., Northwestern U., 1947; m. Lois E. Harding, Feb. 23, 1946; childrenRobert H., Elizabeth A., Gail M., April L. With Ill. Bell Telephone Co., 1947-54, 60-61; with Am. tel. & Tel. Co., 1954-60, 61-62, asst. v.p., 1968-; asst. v.p. N.Y. Telephone Co., 1962-63, v.p., 1963-68. Registered profl. engr., Ill. Mem. I.E.E.E. Home: 70 Fieldstone Dr Basking Ridge NJ 07920 Office: 195 Broadway New York City NY 10007

COLLISON, BERT A., lawyer; b. N.Y.C., 1920; B.A., Johns Hopkins U., 1942; LL.B., U. Md., 1949. Admitted to Md. bar, 1948, N.Y. bar, 1952; now partner firm Nims, Halliday, Whitman, Howes & Collison, N.Y.C. Mem. Wyckoff (N.J.) Bd. Edn., 1958—. Mem. Am. Bar Assn., Assn. Bar City N.Y., Am., N.Y. (sec. 1968—) patent law assns., Delta Theta Phi. Office: 60 E 42d St New York City NY 10017*

COLLMAN, JAMES PADDOCK, educator; b. Beatrice, Neb., Oct. 31, 1932; B.Sc., U. Neb., 1954, M.S., 1956; Ph.D. (NSF fellow), U. Ill., 1958; married. Instr. chemistry U. N.C., Chapel Hill, 1958-59, asst. prof., 1959-62, asso. prof., 1962-67; prof. chemistry Stanford, 1967—. Frontiers in Chemistry lectr., 1964. Mem. N.Y. Acad. Sci., Am., Brit. chem. socs. Office: Stanford U Stauffer 11 Stanford CA 94305*

COLLUM, M.E., Jr., banker. Sr. v.p., exec. officer First Nat. Bank, Jackson, Miss. Office: 248 E Capitol St Jackson MS 39205*

COLLUM, THAD LUMPKIN, constrn. co. exec.; b. Corsicana, Tex., July 24, 1898; s. Simon C. and Pauline (Kelly) C.; C.E., Cornell U., 1921; LL.D., Lemoyne Coll., 1967; m. Anne Boshart, Sept. 4, 1926; children—Edward B., Thad P. Instr. civil engring. Cornell U., 1920-23; cons. engr., 1923-28; treas., dir. Henderson Johnson Co., Inc., Syracuse, N.Y., 1928—, Collum Accustical Co., Inc., Syracuse, 1934—; dir. Paragon Supply Co., Syracuse Transit Corp.; trustee Onondaga County Savs. Bank. Bd. regents U. State N.Y., 1954-67, vice-chancellor, 1961- 67; trustee Community Hosp. Syracuse, Midtown Hosp. Home: Marvelle Rd Fayetteville NY 13066 Office: 918 Canal St Syracuse NY 13210

COLLYER, C.R., pub. utility exec.; b. 1916; B.A., St. John's U., 1941; married. With Haskins & Sells, 1946-53; with Pa. Power & Light Co., 1953—, now treas. Served with AUS, 1942-46. Address: 901 Hamilton St Allentown PA 18101*

COLMAN, CHARLES, III, publisher; b. Phila., June 8, 1914; s. Charles and Eva Ethel (Thompson) C.; B.S., Wharton Sch., U. Pa., 1935; m. Elsie Mae Gilmore, Aug. 8, 1940; children—Meridith Ann (Mrs. Cornelius V.R. Bogert III), Barbara Ellen. With Union Central Life Ins. Co., Phila. and Houston, 1935-38, Horace T. Potts Co., Phila., 1938-42; with Westminster Press, Phila., 1946—, mdsg. mgr., 1952-67, gen. mgr., 1967—. Sec. gen. div. media Bd. Christian Edn. United Presbyn. Ch. U.S.A., 1967—. Served to lt. USNR, 1942-46. Mem. Protestant Ch.-Owned Publishers Assn. (pres. 1971-72, bd. dirs., 1970-72), Assn. Am. Publishers, Inc. Presbyn. (elder). Club: Poor Richard (Phila.). Home: 305 Bethlehem Pike Fort Washington PA 19034 Office: Witherspoon Bldg Philadelphia PA 19107

COLMAN, CHARLES WILSON, educator; b. Brookfield, N.H., Sept. 22, 1909; s. Wilson and Helene (Chamberlain) C.; A.B., Harvard, 1930; certificate U. Bordeaux (France), 1931; Ph.D., Cornell U., 1937; m. Ruth Irene Thompson, Dec. 26, 1935; children—Charlotte Anne (Mrs. William E. Payne, Jr.), Martha Sue (Mrs. Francis E. Ferro, Jr.), Charles Wilson, John Dudley. Mem. faculty Cornell U., 1934-37, U. Ill., 1937-46, U. Miss., 1946-47; prof. French, U. Neb., 1947-64, chmn. dept. romance langs., 1956-64, dir. Nat. Def. Edn. Act. Summer Lang. Inst., 1961, 62; prof., chmn. dept. romance langs. State U. N.Y. Albany, 1964-68, asso. dean Coll. Arts and Scis., 1968-71, dir. internat. programs, 1971—. Dir. Citizens Consultation on Modern Fgn. Langs., 1955. Decorated chevalier Ordre des Palmes Academiques. Mem. Modern Lang. Assn., Am. Assn. Tchrs. French. Author: (with Carter and Nordon) French for Children, 1955. Home: 12 Glenwood St Albany NY 12203

COLMAN, JAMES DOUGLAS, health services exec.; b. N.Y. City, 1910; s. Cecil and Margaret (Plenderleith) C.; M.E., Cornell, 1932; spl. student Johns Hopkins, 1939- 41; m. Ruth E. Baldwin, 1935; children—Ann Elizabeth, Jane Carol. Mgr. med. hosp. and dental div. N.J. Emergency Relief Adminstrn., 1932-35; exec. sec. Hosp. Council of Essex Co., N.J., 1935-37, also exec. dir. Hosp. Service Plan of N.J.; exec. dir. Md. Hosp. Service, Inc. and Md. Med. Service, Inc., 1937-51; v.p. Johns Hopkins U. and Hosp., 1951-57; v.p., sec. Nat. Blue Cross Assn., 1957-60, chmn. exec. com., 1966—; pres. Asso. Hosp. Service of N.Y., 1960—; lectr. pub. health adminstrn. John Hopkins, 1942-59, Columbia, 1958—. Chmn. Nat. Blue Cross Commn., 1947-50; sec.- treas. Commn. Chronic Illness, 1949-52, treas., 1952-56; treas. Nat. Tb Assn., 1957-64; mem. bd. dirs. Nat. Health Council, 1962—, pres., 1967-68; mem. Fed. Hosp. Council, 1967- -; vice chmn. N.Y. Hosp. Rev. and Planning Council, 1966—. Fellow Am. Pub. Health Assn.; mem. Am. Statis. Assn., Am. Hosp. Assn. (trustee, 1963-66; recipient Kimball award 1965). Clubs: University (N.Y.C.), Maryland (Balt.). Home: 59 Drake Rd Scarsdale NY 10583 Office: 80 Lexington Av New York City NY 10016

COLMAN, WILLIAM GERALD, govt. ofcl.; b. Callao, Mo., Nov. 27, 1914; s. Ivy S. and Mabel (Green) C.; B.S., U. Mo., 1937, M.A., 1939; grad. student U. Chgo., 1939-40; m. Marjorie Van Auken, July 30, 1954; 1 son, Robert A. Merit system supr., Mo., 1940-41, La., 1941; dir. Ore. Civil Service Commn., 1946-47; dep. dir. orgn. and mgmt. div., also asst. dir. tech. assistance div., then dep. chief mission to Korea, ECA, 1948-51; dep. dir. field adminstrn. FCDA, 1951-52; cons. ODM, 1952-53, Commn. Intergovtl. Relations, 1954-55; exec. asst. to dir. NSF, 1955-59, spl. cons. to dir., 1960-63; exec. dir. Adv. Commn. Intergovtl. Relations, 1960-70. Mem. President's Commn. on Sch. Finance, 1970-71; chmn. Md. Adv. Council on Comprehensive Health Planning, 1970—; cons. Nat. Urban Coalition, 1970; mem. Montgomery County (Md.) Bd. Edn., 1968—; mem. adv. council Sch. Bus. and Pub. Adminstrn., U. Mo., 1968-70. Trustee, Montgomery Coll., mem. governing bd. U.S. Dept. Agr. Grad. Sch., 1968—. Served to lt. USNR, 1942-46; comdr. Res. Recipient Citation of Merit, U. Mo. Alumni Assn., 1958. Mem. Am. Acad. Polit. and Social Scis., Nat. Acad. Pub. Adminstrn., Internat. City Mgmt. Assn. (hon.). Democrat. Home: 9805 Logan Dr Potomac MD 20854 Office: 1016 16th St NW Washington DC 20036

COLMER, WILLIAM MEYERS, congressman; b. Moss Point, Miss., Feb. 11, 1890; s. Henry and Anna S. (Meyers) C.; student Millsaps Coll., Jackson, Miss., 1910-14; m. Ruth Miner, Sept. 17, 1917; children—William Meyers, James Henry, Thomas Warren. Sch. tchr., 1914; admitted to Miss. bar, 1917; county atty. Jackson County, 1921-27; dist. atty. 2d Dist of Miss., 1928-33; mem. 73d to 92d Congresses, 5th Miss. Dist., chmn. house rules com. Served with U.S. Army, 1918-1919. Mem. Am. Legion, 40 and 8, Pi Kappa Alpha. Democrat. Methodist. Mason, Woodman, Rotarian. Home: Pascagoula MS 39567

COLMERY, HARRY WALTER, Jr., investment banker; b. Topeka, Kan., Jan. 10, 1924; s. Harry Walter and Minerva (Hiserodt) C.; A.B., Dartmouth, 1949; student U. Va. Law Sch., 1949-50; m. Sallie Morphy, Oct. 19, 1955; children—Sarah E., Scott G., Katherine E. Partner, William R. Staats & Co., 1953—; sr. v.p. charge Western div. Glore, Forgan, Wm. R. Staats, Inc., 1965-66, exec. v.p., dir. charge Western div., 1966—; dir. Dymo Industries, Mut. Exploration Funds, Inc. Cal. Financial Corp., Security Savs. & Loan, Pioneer Nat. Life Ins. Co., Regency Life Ins. Co. Bd. govs. Pacific Coast Stock Exchange. Served with USMCR, 1942-46, maj., 1950-52. Decorated D.F.C., Air medal, Clubs: San Francisco Stock Exchange, Los Angeles Athletic, California, Pacific Union (Los Angeles). Home: 707 Rockwood Rd Pasadena CA 91105 Office: 640 S Spring St Los Angeles CA 90014

COLNON, STUART JAMES, coal co. exec.; b. Chgo., June 20, 1903; s. John Edward and Helen (Neemes) C.; m. Rosalie Frances McMahon, June 22, 1940. With John E. Colnon & Co., realtors, Chgo., 1921—, now chmn., dir.; pres. Freeman Coal Mining Corp., 1946-57; pres., dir. Bell & Zoller Coal Co., 1957—; chmn., chief exec. officer Zeigler Coal & Coke Co., 1964—; dir. Ill. State Bank, Chgo. Home: 1430 Lake Shore Dr Chicago IL 60610 Office: 208 S LaSalle St Chicago IL 60604

COLODNY, EDWIN IRVING, airline exec.; b. Burlington, Vt., June 7, 1926; s. Meyer and Lena (Yett) C.; A.B., U. Rochester, 1948; LL.B., Harvard, 1951; m. Nancy Dessoff, Dec. 11, 1965; children—Elizabeth, Mark, David. Admitted to N.Y. bar, 1951, D.C. bar, 1958; with Office Gen. Counsel, Gen. Services Adminstrn., 1951-52, CAB, 1954-57; with Allegheny Airlines, Inc., 1957—, exec. v.p. legal affairs and marketing services, 1969—; sec., treas., dir. Washington Airways, Inc. Served to 1st lt. AUS, 1952-54. Recipient James D. McGill Meml. award U. Rochester. Mem. Am. Bar Assn. Home: 6135 Nevada Av Chevy Chase MD 20015 Office: Hangar 12 Washington Nat Airport Washington DC 20001

COLOMBO, EMILIO, Italian prime minister; b. Apr. 11, 1920; ed. Rome U. Participant in Catholic youth orgns.; former v.p. Italian Cath. Youth Assn.; dep. Constituent Assembly, 1946-48; mem. Parliament, 1948—; under-sec. agr., 1948-51; under-sec. state for pub. works, 1953-55; minister agr., 1955-58; minister fgn. trade, 1958-59; minister industry and commerce, 1959-63; minister treasury, 1963-70; prime minister, 1970—. Pres. Nat. Com. for Nuclear Research, 1961; chmn. Common Market's Ministerial Council. Mem. central com. Christian Democratic party, 1952-53. Address: Palazzo Chigi Rome Italy

COLOMBO, FRANK A., retail dept. store exec.; b. Morenci, Ariz., Sept. 7, 1913; s. Joseph Louis and Caroline (Pessina) C.; B.S. in Bus. Adminstrn., U. Ariz., 1935; M.B.A., Harvard, 1937; m. Josephine M. Garavaglia, Oct. 5, 1940; children—Richard F., Linda Anne, Sandra Jo. With J.L. Hudson Co., Detroit, 1939—, v.p., asst. gen. mgr., 1957-61, exec. v.p., gen. mgr., 1961—, also dir.; vice chmn. bd. Shopping Centers, Inc., also dir.; pres., dir. Detroit Shopping News and Newsplate Engraving Co., 1957—; dir. Asso. Mdsg. Corp., Detroit Bank & Trust Co., Dayton- Hudson Corp. Bd. dirs. Greater Detroit Board Commerce, 1963, 1st vice chairman, 1966. chmn. bd., 1968—; bd. dirs., mem. exec. com. Detroit Conv. Bur., 1957—, pres., 1960-62; mem. exec. com. Central Bus. Dist. Assn., 1958—, pres., 1967, chmn. bd., 1969—. Trustee Grace Hosp., 1966—; bd. dirs. United Found., 1964—. Mem. Detroit Econ. Club, U. Ariz. Alumni Assn. Clubs: Detroit, Detroit Athletic (dir.), Grosse Pointe Yacht; Lochmoor. Home: 611 Lake Shore Rd Grosse Point Shores MI 48236 Office: 1206 Woodward Av Detroit MI 48226

COLOMBO, JOE, architect; b. Chgo., June 29, 1926; s. Robert Albert and Caroline (Longobardo) C.; A.A., E. Los Angeles Coll., 1948; B.A., So. Cal. Coll., 1951, B. Th., 1952; B.Arch., U. So. Cal., 1954; m. Irma A. Colantonio, Aug. 11, 1951; children—Corinne, Joel, Candace, Cynthia, Cara, Charles. Pastor, architect, builder Country Ch., Cypress, Cal., 1954; lectr. on tour eight major cities, 1956; jr. partner Burge, Roach & Colombo, 1957; nat. chmn. Ch. Bldg. & Planning Commn., 1960; pvt. practice architecture, Santa Ana, Cal., 1960—; dean students So. Cal. Coll., Costa Messa, 1957-60. Served with AUS, World War II, 1944-45. Mem. A.I.A., So. Cal. Coll. Alumni (pres. 1965-66). Author: Church Planning Guide, 1957. Architect first Bearing Wall highrise bldg. in Orange County; designer Milti-Learning Hexaplex, 1968. Home: 13691 Yellowstone Dr Santa Ana, CA 92705. Office: 2315 E 17th St Santa Ana CA 92701

COLOMBO, LOUIS JOSEPH, Jr., lawyer; b. Detroit, Apr. 27, 1911; s. Louis J. and Irene (McKinney) C.; A.B., U. Mkch., 1933, LL.B., 1935; m. Elizabeth Monathan, Sept. 11, 1937; children—Louis Joseph III, Alice. Admitted to Mich. bar, 1935, since practiced in Detroit as mem. Colombo, Colombo & Vermeulen. Bd. govs. Detroit chpt. A.R.C., chpt. chmn.; bd. govs. nat. A.R.C., 1948—; bd. govs. William Beaumont Hosp.; trustee Children's Center of Met. Detroit, Mercy Coll., Detroit. Clubs: Bloomfield Hills Country, Bloomfield Open Hunt; University (Detroit). Home: 3635 Lahser Rd Bloomfield Hills MI 48013 Office: Buhl Bldg Detroit MI 48226

COLON, ADRIAN, supermarket co. exec.; b. 1923; B.B.A., U. P.R., 1950; married. Tax insp. Treasury Dept., Commonwealth of P.R., 1949-52; sr. auditor Pal Toro & Co., C.P.A.'s, 1952-56; treas., asst. sec., comptroller Pueblo Internat. Inc. (and predecessors), Hato Rey, P.R., 1956—. Served to 2d lt. AUS, 1943-46. Office: Pueblo Internat Inc Franklin D Roosevelt Av Hato Rey PR*

COLON, CECIL K. J. R., Jr., banker; b. Shreveport, June 21, 1930; s. Cecil Kermit and Marian (Palmer) C.; student U. South, 1947-49; B.B.A., Tulane U., 1951; M.B.A., Harvard, 1957; m. Barbara Marie Guerin, July 9, 1955; children-Jeffrey Palmer, Robert Baker, John Guerin. With Hibernia Nat. Bank, New Orleans, 1957—, sr. v.p., 1965—; Trustee New Orleans Endl. TV Found.; bd. dirs. Isidore Newman Sch. Served with USNR, 1951-55. Mem. Am. Inst. Banking, Assn. Res. City Bankers, Robert Morris Assos., New Orleans C. of C. Home: 1330 Pine St New Orleans La 70118 Office: 313 Carondelet St New Orleans LA 70130

COLONNIER, MARC LEOPOLD, neuroanatomist, educator; b. Quebec, Que., Can., May 12, 1930; s. Jean and Enilda (Bourguignon) C.; B.A., B.Ph., U. Ottawa, 1951, M.D., 1959, M.S., 1960; Ph.D., U. Coll. London, 1963; m. Lise De Gagne, Oct. 24, 1959; 1 son, Jean. Asst. prof. dept. anatomy U. Ottawa, 1963-65; asst. prof. dept. physiology U. Montreal, Quebec, Canada, 1965-67; asso. prof., asso. fellow neurol. scis. group Med. Research Council Can., 1967-69; prof., head dept. anatomy U. Ottawa, 1969—. Recipient Lederle Med. Faculty award, 1966, Charles Judson Herrick award Am. Assn. Anatomists, 1967. Mem. Am., Canadian assns. anatomists. Club Cajal. Home: 2266F Halifax Dr Ottawa Ontario Canada

COLOWICK, SIDNEY PAUL, biochemist, educator, editor; b. St. Louis, Jan. 12, 1916; s. Michael and Frieda (Singer) C.; B.S., Washington U., 1936, M.S., 1939, Ph.D., 1942; m. Grace Shaffel, 1943; 1 son, Frank Shaffel; m. 2d, Maryda Swanstrom, 1951; children—Ann Maryda, Susan, Nancy. Instr. pharmacology Washington U., 1943-44, asst. prof., 1945-46; asso. Pub. Health Research Inst., N.Y.C., 1946-48; asso. prof. biochemistry U. Ill. Coll. Medicine, Chgo., 1948-49; asso. prof. biology Johns Hopkins, 1950-54; prof., 1954- 59; Am. Cancer Soc. prof. microbiology Vanderbilt U., 1959—. Recipient Eli Lilly award, Am. Chem. Soc., 1947. Mem. Am. Soc. Biol. Chemists, Am. Chem. Soc., Internat. Union Biochemistry (enzyme commn.), Am. Acad. Arts and Scis. Editor: Methods in Enzymology (with Nathan O. Kaplan), Vols. I, II, 1955—; exec. editor Archives Biochemistry and Biophysics, 1970—. Home: 709 Crescent Rd Nashville TN 37205

COLPITTS, ROLFE R., cons. engr.; b. Moncton, N.B., Can., 1921; ed. N.S. Tech. Coll. Dir. energy div. Lalonde Girouard Letendre & Assos., Montreal, Que.; v.p. LGM Engring. Ltd., Toronto, Ont., Can., R.R. Colpitts & Son Ltd., Moncton. Home: 356 Beaconsfield Blvd Beaconsfield Quebec Canada Office: 8790 Park Av Montreal 354 Quebec Canada

COLQUHOUN, WILLIAM HENRY, engring. co. exec.; b. Yonkers, N.Y., Dec. 20, 1911; s. William and Florence M. (Stroh) C.; E.E., Rensselaer Poly. Inst., 1934; m. Agnes Reid, June 26, 1937; children—Susan (Mrs. Robert Jon Napier), William Reid. Elec. engr. M.R. Scharff, N.Y.C., 1934-35, 37-39, Ford, Bacon & Davis, N.Y.C., 1935 ' 37; sr. engr. Pub. Service Commn N.Y. State, 1939-40; valuation engr. Duquesne Light Co., 1940, Rochester Gas & Electric Co., 1940-41; with Ebasco Services, Inc. (became div. Boise Cascade Corp. 1969), N.Y.C., 1941—, v.p., 1956-63, pres., chief exec. officer, 1963-69, chmn. bd., 1969—, also dir.; v.p. Boise Cascade Corp., 1969—; pres., dir. Ebasco Corp., 1963—, Ebasco Overseas Corp., 1963—; chmn. bd. Vernon Graphics, Inc., 1964—; v.p., dir. Ebasco Engring. Corp., 1959—, Ebasco India Ltd., 1962—. Chmn. engring. div. U.S.O., N.Y.C. Registered profl. engr., Ariz., Ark., Colo., Conn., Fla., Ida., Mich., N.H., N.Y., N.C., Ore., Wash. Mem. Nat., N.Y. State socs. profl. engrs., Am. Nuclear Soc., Profl. Engrs. Ore., St. Andrews Soc., Newcomen Soc., Commerce and Industry Assn. N.Y. (dir.). Clubs: Manhattan, Engineers (N.Y.C.); Woodway Country. Home: 25 Foxwood Rd Stamford CT 06903 Office: 345 Park Av New York City NY 10022

COLQUITT, LANDON AUGUSTUS, educator, mathematician; b. Fort Worth, Tex., Jan. 25, 1919; s. Fred Augustus and Maude Lena (Pyeatt) C.; B.A., Tex. Christian U., 1939; M.A., Ohio State U., 1941, Ph.D., 1948; postgrad. Cal. Inst. Tech., 1942; m. Betsy Feagan, May 29, 1954; children—Clare E., Catherine A. Asst. instr. math. Ohio State U., 1946-48; mem. faculty Tex. Christian U., 1948—, prof. math., 1955—, chmn. dept., 1962—; sr. nuclear engr. Convair, Fort Worth, summers 1955, 56. Served with USAAF, 1942-46; ETO. Fellow A.A.A.S., Tex. Acad. Scis. (past vice chmn.); mem. Am. Math. Soc., Math. Assn. Am., Soc. Indsl. and Applied Math., Am. Meteorol. Soc., Sigma Xi, Pi Mu Epsilon. Home: 2601 McPherson St Fort Worth TX 76109

COLSON, CHARLES WENDELL, lawyer; b. Boston, Oct. 16, 1931; s. Wendell Ball and Inez (Ducrow) C.; A.B., Brown U., 1953; J.D., George Washington U., 1959; m. Nancy Billings June 3, 1953; children—Wendell Ball II, Christian B., Emily Ann; m. 2d, Patricia Ann Hughes, Apr. 4, 1964. Admitted to D.C. bar, 1961, practiced in Washington, 1961-69; admitted to Va. bar, 1959, Mass. bar, 1964; asst. to asst. sec. Navy, 1955-56; adminstrv. asst. Senator Leverett Saltonstall, U.S. Senate, 1956-61; sr. partner Gadsby & Hannah, 1961-69; spl. counsel to Pres. of U.S., 1969—. Campaign mgr. Saltonstall campaign, 1960. Served to captain USMCR, Korean Conflict. Named Outstanding Young Man of Boston, Jr. C. of C., 1960. Mem. Order of Coif, Beta Theta Pi Republican. Episcopalian. Home: 1350 Ballantrae Lane McLean VA 22101 Office: The White House Washington DC 20500

COLSON, ELIZABETH FLORENCE, anthropologist; b. Hewitt, Minn., June 15, 1917; d. Louis H. and Metta (Damon) Colson; B.A., U. Minn., 1938, M.A., 1940; M.A., Radcliffe Coll., 1941, Ph.D. (Am. Assn. U. Women Traveling fellow), 1945. Asst. social sci. analyst War Relocation Authority, 1942-43; research asst. Harvard, 1944-45; research officer Rhodes-Livingstone Inst., 1946-47, dir., 1948-51; sr. lectr. Manchester U., 1951-53; asso. prof. Goucher Coll., 1954-55; research asso. African Research Program, Boston U., 1955- 59, part-time, 1959-63; prof. anthropology Brandeis U., 1959-63, U. Cal. at Berkeley, 1964—. Fellow Center Advanced Study Behavioral Scis., 1967-68. Fellow Am. Anthrop. Assn., Brit. Assn. Social Anthropologists, Royal Anthrop. Inst.; mem. Phi Beta Kappa. Author: The Makah, 1953; Marriage and the Family Among The Plateau Tonga, 1958; Social Organization of the Gwembe Tonga, 1960, The Plateau Tonga, 1962; The Social Consequences of Resettlement, 1971. Sr. editor: Seven Tribes of British Central Africa, 1951. Office: Dept Anthropology U Cal Berkeley CA 94720

COLSTON, JAMES ALLEN, coll. pres.; b. Quincy, Fla., July 27, 1909; s. Meadie and Anica (Jordan) C.; B.S., Morehouse Coll., 1932, LL.D., 1959; M.A., Atlanta U., 1933; postgrad. Columbia U., summers 1938, 39, 40, U. Chgo., 1945-46; Ph.D., N.Y. U., 1950; LL.D., Monmouth Coll., 1954; L.H.D., Westminster Coll., 1966, Gettysburg Coll., 1969; Litt.D., Knoxville Coll., 1968; m. Wilhelmina Thelma White, Dec. 22, 1935; children—Jean, Alliece. Instr., E. P. Johnson Sch., Atlanta, 1932-33; prin. Rigby Jr. High Sch., Ormond, Fla., 1933-38; dir. Ballard Sch., Macon, Ga., 1938-43; instr. Atlanta U., summer 1941; workshop dir. Hampton Inst., Grad. Study Center, Jacksonville, Fla., summer 1942; pres. Bethune-Cookman Coll., Daytona Beach, 1942-46; dir. public relations Hampton Inst., 1946-47; pres. Ga. State Coll., Savannah, 1947- 49; lectr. in edn. N.Y.U., 1949-50; chmn. dept. edn. A. and T. Coll., Greensboro, N.C., 1950-51; pres. Knoxville Coll., 1951-66, Bronx Community Coll. of City U. N.Y., 1966—. Mem. commn. on curriculum Am. Assn. Jr. Colls.; mem. com. on disadvantages U. State N.Y.; mem. Bronx adv. council State Commn. for Human Rights; mem. exec. bd., chmn. advancement com. Bronx Boy Scouts; mem. N.Y. State Health Planning Adv. Council; mem. council on admissions City U. N.Y.; mem. adv. council to Joint Legislative Com. on Higher Edn.; chmn. Commn. on Theol. Edn. in Southeastern States, U.P. Ch. in U.S.A.; mem. Fordham Rd. Devel. Corp.; mem. adv. com. Bronx Service Center, A.R.C. Greater N.Y. Bd. dirs. A.R.C., Internat. Visitors Center, So. Regional Council, YMCA Greater N.Y., Council of Higher Ednl. Instns., N.Y.C., Gallaudet Coll.; bd. dirs., vice pres. vice chmn. pub. edn. com. Am. Cancer Soc.; chmn. com. ednl. service, bd. dirs. United Negro Coll. Fund; trustee U.P. Found., Princeton Theol. Sem.; chmn. bd. trustees Johnson C. Smith Theol. Sem., Wilmington, Del.; state examinations bd. regents U. State N.Y. Mem. N.C. Tchrs. Assn. (life), Am. Tchrs. Assn., Am. Assn. Sch. Adminstrs., Am. Council on Edn., N.E.A. (dept. higher edn.), Boy Scouts Am., Knoxville C. of C., N.A.A.C.P., New Homemakers of Am. (hon., adv.

com.), Traid-Bus. and Profl. Men, Nat. Geog. Soc., Assn. for Higher Edn., Nat. Council United Presbyn. Men (exec. com., v.p.), Phi Delta Kappa, Alpha Kappa Mu. Presbyn. Mason (scholarship com. State Ga.), Rotarian. Home: 4901 Henry Hudson Pkwy Bronx NY 10471 Office: 120 E 184th St Bronx NY 10468

COLT, THOMAS CLYDE, Jr., museum dir.; b. Orange, N.J., Feb. 20, 1905; s. Thomas Clyde and Florence (Clery) C.; student Blair Acad., Blairstown, N.J., 1920-22; B.S., Dartmouth, 1926; m. Martha Belle Patterson Willingham, June 17, 1933 (div. 1950); children—Thomas Clyde III, Jon Landstreet, Corinne Patterson; m. 2d, Priscilla Crum, Apr. 4, 1950; children—Christopher, Penelope, Susannah. Writer, critic, N.Y., 1926-27; asso. Rehn Galleries, N.Y., 1927-29; trustee Richmond Acad. Arts, 1933-35; sec. Va. Art Alliance, 1934-35; curator (title later changed to dir.) Va. Mus. Fine Arts, 1935-42, 45-48; dir. Portland (Ore.) Art Mus., 1948-56; dir. Art Inst., Dayton, O., 1957—; past pres. Colt Bros. Inc.; exec. com. Ohio Art Council, 1965-70; pres. Intermus. Conservation Assn., 1968-70. Served with USMCR, 1929-31, 42-45; naval aviator, 1930, lt. col. Res. ret. Decorated Star Solidarity 2d class (Italy). Compiler art catalogues, booklets. Mem. Assn. Art Mus. Dirs., Am. Assn. Museums, Internat. Inst. Conservation Mus. Objects. Home: 330 W Schantz Av Dayton OH 45409 Office: Dayton Art Inst Box 941 Dayton OH 45401

COLTON, JOEL, educator; b. N.Y.C., Aug. 23, 1918; s. Philip and Theresa (Cotler) C.; B.A., Coll. City N.Y., 1937, M.S., 1938; M.A., Columbia, 1940, Ph.D., 1950; m. Shirley Baron, May 8, 1942; children—Valerie Beth, Kenneth Richard. Lectr. history Columbia, 1946-47; successively instr., asst. prof., asso. prof., prof. history Duke, 1947—, chmn. dept. history, 1967—; cons. Coll. Entrance Exams. Bd., Advanced Placement Program; mem. Herbert Baxter Adams Prize Com., Koren Prize Com. Served to 1st lt., M.I., AUS, 1942-46; ETO. Recipient Non-Fiction Book award Mayflower Soc. 1967, Guggenheim fellow, 1957-58, Rockefeller Found. fellow, 1961-62, Nat. Endowment for Humanities sr. fellow 1970-71. Mem. Am. Hist. Assn., Soc. for French Hist. Studies, Phi Beta Kappa. Author: Compulsory Labor Arbitration in France, 1936-39, 1951; (with R.R. Palmer) A History of the Modern World, 4th edit., 1971; A Study Guide for a History of the Modern World, 3d edit., 1971; Leon Blum: Humanist in Politics, 1966 (French transl. 1968); Twentieth Century: Great Ages of Man Series, 1968. Bd. editors Jour. Modern History, 1968-71. Home: 1616 Pinecrest Rd Durham NC 27705

COLUM, PADRAIC, poet, dramatist; b. Longford, Ireland, Dec. 8, 1881; s. Padraic and Susanna (MacCormack) C.; Litt. D., Columbia, 1958, Trinity Coll. (Dublin Ireland), 1958; m. Mary Gunning Maguire, 1912 (dec.). Came to U.S., 1914. Mem. Acad. Irish Letters (pres.), Am. Acad. Arts and Letters. Roman Catholic. Author: Wild Earth (poems), 1907; A Boy in Eirinn, 1913; Three Plays, 1916; The King of Ireland's Son, 1916; The Adventures of Odysseus and the Tale of Troy; The Boy Who Knew What the Bird Said, 1918; The Girl Who Sat by the Ashes, 1919; The Children of Odin, 1920; The Boy Apprenticed to an Enchanter, 1920; The Golden Fleece, 1921; The Children Who Followed the Piper, 1922; Castle Conquer, 1923; Dramatic Legends (poems), 1922; The Island of the Mighty, At the Gateways of the Day (Hawaiian Stories), 1924; The Voyagers, The Forge in the Forest, The Bright Islands (Hawaiian Stories), 1925; The Road Round Ireland, 1926; Creatures (verse); The Fountain of Youth, 1927; Balloon, a comedy in four acts; OrpheusStories from the Mythologies of the World, 1929; Poems, 1932; A Half-Day's Ride and A Book of Essays., 1932; The Big Tree of Bunlahy (stories), 1933; The Legend of Saint Columbia, 1935; The Story of Lowry Maen (narrative poem), 1937; Where The Winds Never Blew and the Cocks Never Crew, 1940; The Frenzied Prince, 1943; Anthology of Irish Verse, 1948; A Treasury of Irish Folklore, 1954; The Flying Swans, 1957; Arthur Griffith and the Origins of the Irish Free State, 1958; Our Friend James Joyce, 1958; Legends of Hawaii, 1960; Ourselves Alone, 1960; Poet's circuits (collection of poems of Ireland), 1960; Roofs of Gold (poetry anthology), 1964; The Stone of Victory (anthology own children's poems), 1966. Recipient Acad. Am. Poets award, 1952; Gregory medal Irish Acad. Letters, 1953; Regina medal Cath. Library Assn., 1961; Boston Arts Festival Poet, citation 1961; Georgetown U. 175th Anniversary Medal of Honor, 1964. Address: 415 Central Park W New York City NY 10025

COLVARD, DEAN WALLACE, univ. ofcl.; b. Ashe County, N.C., July 10, 1913; s. W. P. and Mary (Shepherd) C.; B.S., Berea Coll., 1935; M.S., U. Mo., 1938; Ph.D., Purdue U., 1950, D.Agr., 1961; m. Martha Lampkin, July 7, 1939; children—Carol Lampkin, Mary Lynda, Dean Wallace. Instr. agr., farm mgr. Brevard Coll., 1935-37; supt. N.C. Mountain Expt. Sta., 1938-46; head dairy husbandry sect. N.C. State Coll., 1947, head dept. animal industry, 1948-53; dean agr., 1953-60; pres. Miss. State U., 1960-66; chancellor U. N.C. at Charlotte, 1966—; dir. Fed. Res. Bank of Richmond, 1955-60, dep. chmn., 1959-60; dir. Mut. Savs. & Loan. Spl. cons. ICA, Bangkok, Thailand, 1960. Adv. bd. Nat. Agrl. Extension Center for Advanced Study, chmn. 1957-58; chmn. agrl. subcom. Nuclear Energy Adv. Com. for N.C., 1958-60; mem. Gov.'s Research Triangle Devel. Council, 1957-59; co-ordinator Agr. Research Mission in Peru, S. Am., 1954-60. Mem. agr. adv. com. W. K. Kellogg Found., 1954-60; chmn. Miss. Gov.'s Com. on Latin Am. Edn., 1961; exec. com. Southeastern Conf., 1964-66; adv. council grad. edn. agrl. scis. So. Regional Edn. Bd., 1961-65, chmn., 1963-65; chmn. Miss. Rhodes Scholar Com., 1965-66, N.C. Rhodes Scholar Com., 1967; mem. com. Profl. Sch. and World Affairs sponsored by Edn. and World Affairs, Inc., Ford Found., 1965-66; mem. Miss. Jr. Coll. Commn., 1960- 66. Trustee, mem. scholarship com. Cordell Hull Found. for Internat. Edn., 1961-67; bd. dirs., exec. com. U. Research Park, Charlotte, 1966—. Trustee Berea Coll., 1956—, St. Andrews Coll., 1969—. Named Man of Year in Agr. in N.C., 1954; recipient Distinguished Service award N.C. Farm Bur. 1956, Miss. Farm Bur., 1965; Distinguished Service award N.C. Grange, 1958; Outstanding Civilian award U.S. Dept. Army, 1966. Mem Nat. Assn. State Univs. and Land Grant Colls. (co-chmn. joint com. edn. for govt. service 1961-65, chmn. pres.'s council 1966), Am. Council Edn. (commn. internat. edn. 1965—, chmn. com. higher adult edn. 1966—), So. Assn. Colls. and Schs. (commn. colls. 1965-68), Charlotte C. of C. (dir.), Blue Key, Omicron Delta, Sigma Xi, Phi Kappa Phi, Gamma Alpha, Alpha Gamma Rho, Gamma Sigma Delta, Alpha Zeta. Rotarian. Contbr. publs. in animal sci., agrl. econs., ednl. adminstrn. Home: 3066 Stonybrook Rd Charlotte NC 28205 Office: U NC at Charlotte Charlotte NC 28202

COLVER, WARREN CORNELL, lawyer; b. Fenton, Mich., Jan. 19, 1925; s. Howard Sidney and Esther (Cornell) C.; student U. Alaska, 1950-52; B.A., Williamette U., Salem, Ore., 1954, LL.B., 1956; m. Della Elizabeth Kruse, Nov. 10, 1949; children—John Warren, James Cornell, Jane Della. Admitted to Alaska bar, 1956; dep. U.S. Commr., Anchorage, 1956-57; mem. firm Moody & Colver, Anchorage, 1957-59, 60-61; asst. atty., gen. Alaska, also 1st state dist. atty., 3d dist., Anchorage, 1959; U.S. atty. for Alaska, 1961-64, atty. gen. State of Alaska, 1964-66; partner firm Wilson, Wilson & Colver, 1967; now individual practice of law, Anchorage, Alaska. Co- chmn. Alaska, Kennedy for Pres. Com., 1960; pres. Greater Anchorage Dem. Club. 1958. Served with USNR, 1942-45. Mem. Am., Alaska, Anchorage bar assns., Comml. Law League Am., Fed. Bar Assn., Am. Legion (vice comdr. Alaska 1959, judge adv. Alaska 1960-67), Anchorage Athletic Round Table (charter), U. Alaska Alumni Assn. (past pres.), Pi Gamma Mu, Delta Theta Phi. Elk, Lion, Odd Fellow. Home: 6040 Foothill Dr Anchorage AK 99503 Office: 360 K St Anchorage AK 99501

COLVERT, CLYDE CORNELLUS, educator; b. Clarksville, Tex., Sept. 29, 1899; s. Walter H. and Lou Ella (McCain) C.; B.S. in Edn., U. Ark., 1929, M.S., 1930; Ph.D., George Peabody Coll., 1937, m. Lottie Mae Melton, Dec. 25, 1923; 1 dau., Marguerite (Mrs. Charles F. Freeman). Supt. schs., Elliott, Ark., 1917- 18, Marion, 1920-22, DeWitt, 1923-24, Carlisle, 1924-26; instr., dean Central Coll., Conway, Ark., 1926-31; pres. N.E. Jr. Coll., Monroe, La., 1931-44; prof., cons. in jr. coll. edn. U. Tex. since 1944, prof., chmn. dept. edn. adminstrn. 1946-57, dean Coll. of Edn., 1962-64, dir. Jr. Coll. Adminstrv. Tng. Center; vis. prof. U. So. Cal., summer, 1953, 56, Fla. State U., fall 1956-57. Mem. Am. Assn. Jr. Colls. (dir. research 1949-54, pres. 1940-41), So. Assn. Jr. Colls. (pres. 1939-40), N.E.A., Tex. State Tchrs. Assn., Assn. of Tex. Colls. (pres. 1954-55). Mason (32), Kiwanian (lt. gov. div. 5 Tex.-Okla. Dist. 1952). Author: The Public Junior Curriculum, 1939; The Junior Colleges of TexasThe Peoples' College, 1945; A Survey of Public Junior Colleges of Florida (with J.W. Reynolds), 1952; State Survey of the Junior Colleges in Mississippi, 1961; A State Program for Public Junior Colleges in Colorado, 1963; A Financial Program for the Public Junior Colleges in Mississippi, 1963; A Survey of the Junior College Needs-Dallas County, Texas, 1964; Master Plan for Public Junior Colleges in Texas, 1967. Contbr. articles profl. mags. Home: 4511 Edgemont Dr Austin, TX 78731.

COLVIN, HAYWOOD CLAYTON, chem. co. exec.; b. Birmingham, Ala., Dec. 8, 1924; s. Henry Clay and Beatrice (Clark) C.; B.S., Auburn U., 1947; m. Doris Tucker, Jan. 28, 1950; 1 son, John Kim. Asst. dist. sales mgr. Va.-Carolina Chem. Co., Birmingham, 1948-52; v.p. Duval Sales Corp., Houston, 1952-68; exec. v.p. Goodpasture, Inc., Brownfield, Tex., 1968—, also dir. Active Boy Scouts Am. Bd. dirs. United Fund; High Plains Research Found. Served with inf. AUS, 1943-45; ETO. Mem. Fertilizer Inst. (dir. 1970), Delta Sigma Pi. Baptist. Rotarian. Home: 1805 E Buckley St Brownfield TX 79316 Office: 902 W Broadway Brownfield TX 79316

COLVIN, HUGH FRANK, chem. engr.; b. Spokane, Wash., Apr. 25, 1917; s. Frank Leroy and Alice Josephine (Campbell) C.; B.S., Cal. Inst. Tech., 1936; M.B.A., Harvard, 1939; m. Audy Lou Holden, July 2, 1940; children—Carol Ann, Barbara Lynne, Donald Scott, Mary Alice. Engr. Am. Gas Assn., 1936-37; with Wilshire Oil Co., 1939-40, Union Oil Co., 1940-46; treas., asst. to pres. Consol. Electrodynamics Corp., Pasadena, Cal. 1947-53, dir., 1949- 59; v.p., 1953-54, v.p., gen. mgr., 1954-56, pres., 1956-58; treas., dir. Unitek Corp., 1948—, pres., 1963—; dir. Istel Fund, Inc., Inter- Unitek A.G., Computer Communications, Inc., Precision Research Corp., Registered profl. engr., Cal. Mem. Am. Mgmt. Assn., Instrument Soc. Am., Am. Inst. Chem. Engrs., E. Clampus Vitus, Clubs: Athenaeum, University (Pasadena); Harvard (So. Cal.). Home: 336 Sturtevant Dr Sierra Madre CA 91024 Office: 950 Royal Oaks Dr Monrovia CA 91016

COLVIN, MILTON, educator; b. Missoula, Mont., June 20, 1923; s. Howard Milton and Katharine (Ostrander) C.; B.A., Yale, 1948; Ph.D. cum laude, U. Heidelberg, Germany, 1953; m. Maria Countess von Kielmansegg, Sept. 1, 1953; children—Christopher, Alexander, Katharine, Maria-Gabriele, Caroline- Leontine. Mem. White House Commn. on Refugees, 1948-50; asst. prof. anthropology U. Mont., 1954-57; asst. prof., asso. prof. polit. sci. Vanderbilt U., 1957-60; lectr. U. Chgo., 1960-61; asso. prof., prof. politics Washington and Lee U., Lexington, Va., 1961—; vis. prof. Nat. War Coll., Washington, 1965-66. Vol. tchr. Free Sch. Prince Edward County, Va., 1964. Candidate, U.S. Senate, Democratic Primary Va., 1970. Mem. Yale Alumni Bd. Served with AUS, 1942-45. Decorated Silver Star medal, Purple Heart with oak leaf cluster. Mem. Am., So. polit. sci. assns., Am. Assn. U. Profs., Wilderness Soc., Sierra Club, Zeta Psi. Democrat. Roman Catholic. Contbr. profl. jours. Home: Honeysuckle Hill Lexington VA 24450

COLVIN, OTIS HERBERT, Jr., educator, musician; b. El Dorado, Ark., Mar. 18, 1923; s. Otis Herbert and Irene (Hammons) C.; B.A., Baylor U., 1944, B.Mus., 1948; M.Mus., U. Colo., 1950; Ph.D., U. Rochester, 1958; m. Mary Ila Ullom, June 18, 1948; children—Carol Kay, Mary Edith, Susan Elizabeth. Grad. asst. U. Colo., 1948-50; instr. music Tex. Tech. Coll., 1950-55; grad. asst. Eastman Sch. Music, 1955-57; asst. prof. piano Baylor U., 1957-62, chmn. dept., 1958-62, asso. prof. theory, 1962-64, chmn. dept., 1962—, prof., 1964—; concert accompanist; organist 7th and James Bapt. Ch., 1969—; editor choral compositions. Served with USNR, 1944-46; CBI. Mem. Am. Guild Organists (dean Waco chpt. 1958-60, 68-69), Music Tchrs. Nat. Assn., Phi Mu Alpha Sinfonia. Baptist. Mason. (32), Kiwanian. Composer: Organ Voluntaries Based on Early American Hymn Tunes, 1964; Short Pieces for Organ, 1971. Contbr. articles profl. jours. Home: 9121 Pin Oak Dr Waco TX 76710

COLWELL, ARTHUR RALPH, Sr., physician; b. Chgo., July 8, 1897; s. Lewis William and Grace (Stryker) C.; S.B., U. Chgo., 1919; M.D., Rush Med. Coll., 1921; Nat. Research Council fellow, Harvard, 1928-29; m. Jeane Haskins, Sept. 1, 1921; children—Arthur Ralph, John Amory, Elizabeth (dec.), Mary Ann (Mrs. Nitchie). Practice internal medicine, Chgo., 1923-49; chmn. dept. med., Irving S. Cutter prof. medicine Northwestern U. Med. Sch., Chgo., 1950-65, prof. emeritus medicine, 1965—; attending physician Passavant Meml. Hosp., Chgo., 1950—. Trustee Otho S. A. Sprague Meml. Inst. Recipient Banting Meml. award Am. Diabetes Assn., 1968. Fellow A.C.P.; mem. Assn. Am. Physicians, A.M.A., Am. Diabetes Assn. (pres. 1951), Central Soc. Clin. Research, Sigma Xi, Beta Theta Pi, Nu Sigma Nu, Alpha Omega Alpha. Methodist. Clubs: Big Foot Country (Lake Geneva, Wis.). Author: Diabetes in General Practice, 1948; Types of Diabetes Mellitus and Their Treatment, 1949. Home: Route 1 Box 38 Fontana WI 53125 Office: 707 Fairbanks Ct Chicago IL 60611

COLWELL, ERNEST CADMAN, educator; b. Hallstead, Pa., Jan. 19, 1901; s. Ernest and Anna (Lantz) C.; Ph.B., Emory U., 1923, Litt.D. (hon.), 1944; B.D., Candler Sch. Theol. 1927; Ph.D., U. Chgo., 1930; LL.D. (hon.), Colby Coll., 1947; S.T.D. (hon.), Harvard, 1947, Ripon (Wis.) Coll., 1962; L.H.D. (hon.), Claremont Coll., 1966; D.Hum.Litt., Hebrew Union Coll.-Jewish Inst. Religion, 1968; m. Annette Carter, May 7, 1925; children—Elizabeth Ann, Carter Colwell. Instr. English lit. and Bible, Emory U., 1924-28; with U. Chgo., 1930-45, asst. prof. of N.T. lit., 1930-38, asso. prof., 1938-39, prof., 1939-51, dean Div. Sch., 1938-43, dean faculties, 1943-45, v.p. U., 1944, pres., 1945-51; dean faculties, v.p. Emory U., 1951-57; pres. So. Cal. Sch. Theology, Claremont, 1957-68; distinguished prof. N.T., Claremont Grad. Sch., 1968-71; vis. prof. Greek, Stetson U., Deland, Fla., 1969—. Mem. bd. edn. Meth. Ch., vice chmn. commn. ecumenical consultation, 1963; trustee Blaisdell Inst. Claremont, Cal., 1958-70, Interdenominational Theol. Center at Atlanta, 1961—. Pres. Soc. Bibl. Lit. and Exegesis, 1947, Am. Assn. Theol. Schs., 1958-60. Hon. Fellow Am. Coll. Dentistry; mem. Phi Beta Kappa, Omicron Delta Kappa, Sigma Chi. Methodist. Author: The Greek of the Fourth Gospel, 1931; John Defends the Gospel, 1936; The Study of the Bible, 1937, revised edit. and paperback edit., 1964; The Four Gospels of Karahissar, Vol. I, 1936; Elizabeth Day McCormick Apocalyse, Vol. II, 1939; An Approach to the Teaching of Jesus, 1947; What is the Best New Testament?, 1952; The Text and Ancient Versions of the New Testament (in The Interpreter's Bible); (with E. Titus) The Gospel of the Spirit, 1953; Jesus and the Gospel, 1963; (with Ernest W. Tune) A Beginner's Reader- Grammar for New Testament Greek, 1965; Studies in Methodology in Textual Criticism of the New Testament, 1969; New or Old? The Christian Struggle with Change and Tradition, 1970. Editor: (with D. W. Riddle) Prolegomena to the Study of Lectionary Text of the Gospels, 1933; (with E. J. Goodspeed) A Greek Papyrus Reader, 1935; (with J. R. Mantey) A Hellenistic Greek Reader, 1939; (with Ralph Marcus and A. P. Wikgren) Hellenistic Greek Texts, 1947. Contbr. religious jours. Home: 613 Marion Ct Deland FL 32720

COLWELL, FELTON, printer; b. Excelsior, Minn., Aug. 17, 1902; s. Thomas Henry and Harriet Hortense (Felton) C.; B.A., Carleton Coll., 1925; m. Helen Edythe Graham, Oct. 27, 1928; children—Thomas Graham, John Graham, David Graham, Cynthia Felton. With Colwell Press, Mpls., 1920—, pres., 1934-65, chmn. bd. 1965—; pres., treas. Colight, Inc. (formerly Colwell Litho Products, Inc.), 1951-60, chmn. bd., 1960—; dir. Twin City Fed. Savs. & Loan Assn., Mpls., 1950—. Mem. exec. com. Ednl. Council of Graphic Arts Industry, Inc., 1954-60, mem. research and engring. council, exec. com., 1960—; pres. Research and Engring. Council Graphic Arts, Inc., 1956-58. Mem. Bd. Edn., planning commn., Mpls., 1945-51. Alumni trustee Carleton Coll. 1946-54. Gen. campaign chmn. United Fund Hennepin County, 1964; 1st v.p. United Fund Mpls. and Hennepin County, 1965-69; chmn. Mpls. Library Campaign Millage, 1966; del. Minn.-Uruguay Partners Alliance, pres., 1968—, chmn. bd., 1969—. Recipient A.F. Lewis Meml. award as 1957 Man of Year in the Graphic Arts Industry Mem. Lithographic Tech. Found. (dir. 1951-55, v.p. 1960, pres. 1961-63), Printing Industry Twin Cities (pres. 1961-62), Printing Industry Am. (dir. 1960, nat. sec. 1954), Mpls. C. of C. (dir. 1951-54, pres. 1956-58), Carleton Coll. Alumni Assn. (sec. 1927, pres. 1944), Mpls. Soc. Fine Arts. Conglist. (chmn. bd. trustees 1954). Clubs: Advertising (pres. 1931-32), Breakfast (pres. 1948), Kiwanis (pres. 1960, lt. gov. 1965), Minneapolis, Minikahda, 6 O'Clock, Athletic (dir. 1962-65), Thirteen (chmn. 1964), Dunkers (Mpls.); Alexandria (Minn.) Golf. Home: 3430 List Pl Minneapolis MN 55416 Office: 501 S 6th St Minneapolis MN 55415

COLWELL, JOHN BARR, ret. naval officer; b. Pawnee City, Neb., Nov. 26, 1909; s. Clyde George and Mary Bergen (Potts) C.; B.S., U.S. Naval Acad., 1931; postgrad. U.S. Naval Postgrad. Sch., 1937-39; m. Grace Margaret Arent, Sept. 12, 1939; children—John Barr, James Christopher, Margaret Delaney. Commd. ensign U.S. Navy, 1931, advanced through grades to vice adm., 1964; ret., 1969. Decorated D.S.M., Legion of Merit, Bronze Star. Home: 2101 Connecticut Av Washington DC 20008

COLWELL, WILLIAM H., ret. electric co. exec.; b. Paris, Ill., Apr. 4, 1907; s. William H. and Adda (Burnett) C.; A.B., U. Ill., 1928; m. Vera Klintz, Mar. 9, 1929; 1 son, William B. Editor, Chgo. Financial Digest, 1929-33; with Fed. Emergency Relief Adminstrn., and successors, 1933-41, asst. commnr., 1939-41; with Commonwealth Edison Co., and affiliates, Chgo., 1941-70, asst. sec., 1954-65, sec., 1965-70. Mem. Am. Soc. Corp. Secs., Delta Tau Delta, Sigma Delta Chi. Clubs: Press, Headline (Chgo.). Home: 928 S Home Av Park Ridge IL 60068

COLWIN, ARTHUR LENTZ, educator, biologist; b. Sydney, Australia, Jan. 26, 1911; B.Sc., McGill U., 1933, M.Sc., 1934, Ph.D. (Nat. Research Council Can. fellow), 1935-36; Moyse Travelling fellow Cambridge (Eng.) U., 1934-35; Seessel fellow Yale, 1936-37, Royal Soc. Can. fellow, 1937-38; m. Laura North Hunter, June 15, 1940. Came to U.S., 1936, naturalized, 1942. Mem. faculty Queens Coll., 1940—, prof., 1957—; Fulbright research fellow Tokyo (Japan) U., 1953-54; vis. scientist Nat. Inst. Med. Research, London, Eng., 1960; spl. research fertilization, devel. biology, cell contacts and assn., membrane structure and behavior. Trustee Marine Biol. Lab., Woods Hole, Mass., 1962—. Served to capt. USAAF, 1943-46. Fellow N.Y. Acad. Scis.; mem. Internat. Inst. Developmental Biology, Internat. Soc. Cell Biology, Am. Soc. Zoologists, Soc. Study Devel. and Growth, Soc. for Study of Reprodn., Electron Microscope Soc. Am. Contbr. profl. jours. Asso. editor Jour. Exptl. Zoology, 1964-68, Jour. Morphology, 1964-68; editorial bd. Biol. Bull., 1969—, Am. Zoologist, 1970—. Office: Dept Biology Queens Coll Flushing NY 11367

COLYAR, ARDELL BENTON, city health ofcl.; b. Altus, Okla, Mar. 24, 1914; s. Richard N. and Algae (Hughes) C.; student Oklahoma City U., 1935-37; M.D., U. Okla., 1941; M.P.H., Johns Hopkins, 1951; m. Florence Benita Morgan, Sept. 1, 1939; children—Ardell Benita (Mrs. John T. Strauss), Paul Cay, Berrie Dee, Melodie Rae. Commd. officer USPHS, 1943—, med. dir., 1966; rotating intern Broadlawns Gen. Hosp., Des Moines, 1941-42, resident surgery, 1942-43; assigned Okla. Health Dept., 1944-48; div. dir. Venereal Disease Control, 1946-48; clin. investigator Okla. U. Med. Sch., 1945-47; health officer Pittsburg County, Okla., 1949-50; med. cons., 1951-54; dir. Arctic Health Research Center, 1954-65, dep. chief Med. Care Adminstrn., 1966; commr. health Okla., 1966-71; dir. Anchorage Health Dept., 1971—; spl. research epidemiology infections and communicable diseases in Arctic regions; prof. pub. health adminstrn. U. Okla. Sch. Health. Mem. A.A.A.S., Am. Pub. Health Assn., A.M.A., Am. Assn. Pub. Health Physicians. Baptist (deacon). Office: 327 Eagle St Anchorage AK 99501

COLZANI, ANSELMO, baritone; pupil of Corrado Zambelli in Bologna, Italy. Operatic debut as the herald in Lohengrin, Teatro Comunale, 1947; appearances in opera houses throughout Italy, making debut at La Scala, Milan, 1954; Am. debut San Francisco Opera, 1956; debut with Met. Opera in title role in Simon Boccanegra, 1960. Address: care Metropolitan Opera 147 W 39th St New York City NY 10018*

COMAN, DALE REX, pathologist, educator, author, artist; b. Hartford, Conn., Feb. 22, 1906; s. Edward Lokker and Florence Marguerite (Rex) C.; student U. R.I., 1924-26; B.A., U. Mich., 1928; M.D., McGill U., 1933; m. Mona Charity Segal, Dec. 22, 1937; children—Michael Dale, Charity Beth. Asst. to Pathologic Inst., McGill U., 1933-34; resident pathology U. Pa. Hosp., 1934-35, Mass. State Gen. Hosp., Pondville, 1935- 36; instr. pathology N.Y.U., 1936-37; instr. U. Pa., 1937-49, prof. exptl. pathology, 1949—, chmn. dept. pathology, 1954-67. Diplomate Am. Bd. Pathology in path. anatomy. Fellow A.A.A.S.; mem. Internat. Soc. Cell Biology, Am. Assn. Pathologists and Bacteriologists, Am. Soc. Exptl. Pathology, Am. Assn. Cancer Research, Tissue Culture Assn. (past v.p.), Wilderness Soc., Nat. Audubon Soc., Sigma Xi, Alpha Omega Alpha. Club: Sierra. Author: The Technique of Postmortem Examination, 1934. Author, illustrator: Pleasant River. Contbr. articles on cancer research sci. jours.; author essays and chronicles on out-of- doors, natural history to newspapers, to lit. and sporting mags. Home: Garden Court Apts 47th and Pine St Philadelphia PA 19143

COMAR, CYRIL LEWIS, phys. biologist, educator; b. Dudley, Eng., Mar. 28, 1914; s. David and Bertha (Simon) C.; B.S., U. Cal. at Berkeley, 1936, postgrad. food tech., 1937-38; Ph.D., Purdue U., 1940; m. Mildred Cashin, Aug. 7, 1939; children—Anne Patricia, Thomas Allan, Louise Elaine. Came to U.S., 1923, naturalized, 1941. Prof. biophysics U. Tenn., 1948-54, lab. dir., research coordinator U. Tenn.-AEC agrl. research program. Oak Ridge, 1948-54; chief biomed. research Oak Ridge Inst. Nuclear Studies, 1954- 57; dir. lab. radiation biology, prof. radiation biology Cornell U., 1957-60, head dept. phys. biology, 1960—, prof. phys. biology and head dept. N.Y. State Veterinary Coll., Cornell U., Ithaca; cons. biology and medicine div. AEC, Oak Ridge Inst. Nuclear Studies, atomic energy and agr. FAO, also USPHS. Mem. U.S. delegation Conf. on Peaceful Uses Atomic Energy, Geneva, 1955; mem. com. effects atomic radiation on agr. and food supplies Nat. Acad. Sci., 1956; cons. effects atomic radiation UN Sci. Com., 1956-58; cons. FAO to UNESCO Conf. Radioisotopes Sci. Research, Paris, 1957, WHO Conf. on Radiochem. Methods of Analysis, Geneva, 1958; dir. internat. tng. courses on use radiosotopes in biol. research FAO, 1959, 62, 65, 70; cons. Nat. Center Radiol. Health, USPHS, 1967—, Nat. Adv. Radiol. Health Council, 1967; cons. environmental health scis. div., USPHS, 1968—; mem. nat. adv. com. radiation to surgeon gen. Chmn. adv. com. Fed. Radiation Council, 1966—. Recipient Borden award, 1968. Mem. Am. Soc. Biol. Chemists, A.A.A.S., Soc. Nuclear Medicine, Am. Vet. Med. Assn., Am. Chem. Soc., Am. Inst. Nutrition, Soc. Exptl. Biology and Medicine, Radiation Research Soc., Am. Soc. Animal Prodn., Sigma Xi, Phi Lambda Upsilon, Gamma Sigma Epsilon, Gamma Alpha. Author: Radioisotopes in Biology and Agriculture, Principles and Practice, 1955. Editor: Atomic Energy and Agriculture, 1957; (with F. Bronner) Mineral Metabolism, An Advanced Treatise, 3 vols., 1960-69. Author articles profl. jours. Home: 8 Highland Park Lane Ithaca NY 14850

COMAR, JEROME MORTON, automotive, textile machinery mfg. co. exec.; b. Chgo., May 20, 1911; s. Samuel R. and Goldie (Maremont) Cohen; B.S. in Mech. Engring., U. Mich., 1933; m. Gertrude Mintz, June 16, 1937; childrenStephen R., Lois D. With Maremount Corp., Chgo., 1933—, chmn bd., dir. Bd. dirs., past pres. Vocational Research Council; chmn. bd. dirs. Chgo. chpt., bd. govs., nat. exec. com. dir. nat. bd. Am. Jewish Com.; bd. dirs. Council Jewish Fedns. and Welfare Funds; bd. dirs., pres. Jewish Fedn. Met. Chgo.; trustee Chgo. Youth Center. Mem. Am. Mgmt. Assn. Clubs: Standard, Mid-America (Chgo.); Northmoor Country. Home: 889 Private Rd Winnetka IL 60093 Office: 168 N Michigan Av Chicago, IL 60601.

COMAS, EDWIN, tobacco co. exec.; b. Rosebank, N.Y., Feb. 10, 1916; s. Salvador and Johanna (Kunath) C.; C.S., N.Y.U., 1951; m. Rita M. Johnson, Aug. 5, 1971; children by previous marriage—Judith C. (Mrs. Werner Hinz), Richard A., Christine L. With U.S. Tobacco Co., Greenwich, Conn., 1931—, asst. treas., 1961-64, treas., 1964—, also dir.; treas., dir. Cadillac Pet Foods, Inc., Camden, N.J., 1966—, Henry, Leonard & Thomas Inc., Greensboro, N.C., 1969—, House of Windsor, Inc. (Pa.), 1965—, Tuckersharpe Pen Co., Inc., Richmond, Va., 1965—, J.C. Winter & Co., Red Lion, Pa., 1965—. Served with AUS, 1943-46. Mem. Danbury Mineral. Soc. Episcopalian. Club: Greenwich. Office: 100 W Putnam Av Greenwich CT 06830

COMBELLACK, FREDERICK MALCOLM, educator; b. Placerville, Cal., May 30, 1906; s. William Hill and Mary Ellen (Dunstan) C.; A.B. (Royall Victor fellow), Stanford 1928; Christ Church, Oxford (Eng.) U., 1931-32; Ph.D. (Univ. fellow 1934-36), U. Cal. at Berkeley, 1936; m. Clara Rose Brecher, July 2, 1932. Research fellow U. Cal. at Berkeley, 1937; mem. faculty U. Ore., 1937—, prof. Greek lit., 1954—, head dept. classics, Chinese, Japanese, 1964-65, 67—; Horace White Meml. lectr. Bryn Mawr Coll., 1952; vis. prof. Greek. U. Chgo., 1959; vis. prof. classics U. Wash., 1961-62, U. Cal. at Los Angeles, 1967, U. Colo., 1968; vis. Andrew Mellon prof. classics U. Pitts., 1966-67. Guggenheim fellow, 1942-43; fellow Am. Council Learned Societies, 1952-53; Fulbright Sr. Research fellow, Am. Sch. Classical Studies, Athens, Greece, 1954-55. Mem. Am. Philol. Assn. (bd. dirs. 1960-65, pres. 1968), Classical Assn. Pacific State (pres. 1938, 48), Archaeol. Inst. Am., Soc. Promotion Hellenic Studies. Author: The War at Troy; What Homer Didn't Tell, 1967. Home: 3021 Friendly St Eugene OR 94705

COMBELLACK, WILFRED JAMES, educator; b. New Gloucester, Me., June 27, 1915; s. James Henry and Hazel (Marston) C.; A.B., Colby Coll., Waterville, Me., 1937, M.A., 1938; Ph.D., Boston U., 1944; m. Mary Cadwallader, Oct. 2, 1937; children—John P., Jean A. (Mrs. Donald W. Marshall). From instr. to asso. prof. Northwestern U., 1938-48; prof. math. Colby Coll., 1948—, head dept., 1948-70. Mem. Am. Math. Soc., Math. Assn. Am., Am. Assn. U. Profs. Author: Introduction to Elementary Functions, 1962. Home: 7 Noyes Av Waterville ME 04901

COMBER, JOHN W., bishop; b. Lawrence, Mass., Mar. 12, 1906; ed. Boston Coll., also Maryknoll Sem. Ordained priest Roman Catholic Ch., 1931; missionary, Manchuria, 1931-43; in Japanese concentration camp, 2 yrs.; rector Maryknoll Sem., 1944-53, superior gen., 1956—; supr. Maryknoll missionaries, Chile, 1953-56; titular bishop of Foratinana, 1959—; superior gen. Cath. Fgn. Mission Soc. Address: Maryknoll NY 10545*

COMBES, FRANK CHARLES, physician; b. N.Y.C., Aug. 15, 1896; s. Frank and Mary (Mullin) C.; M.D., N.Y.U., 1918; m. Frances Jean Thrasher; children—Gene, Marian, Frank III, Richard. Prof. emeritus dermatology and syphilology N.Y. U. Postgrad. Med. Sch.; dir. dermatology and syphilology Bellvue Hosp., N.Y.C.; attending dermatologist Univ. Hosp.; cons. dermatologist United Hosp., Portchester, New Rochelle Hosp. Vice pres. Com. Promotion Med. Research, Inc. Fellow A.A.A.S., N.Y. Acad. Scis., Am. Med. Authors; mem. Tenn. Nursing Home Assn., Indsl. Med. Assn., Am. Social Hygiene Assn. (dir.), Am. Dermatol. Assn., N.Y. Dermatol. Soc., Manhattan Dermatol. Soc., Internat. Soc. Tropical Dermatology (charter), Am. Acad. Dermatology, N.Y. Acad. Medicine, Am. Acad. Dermatology and Syphilogy, A.M.A. (mem. council on indsl. health), N.Y. Tb and Health Assn. (chmn. social hygiene com.) Sociedad de Dermatologia y Sifilografia (Argentina), Alpha Omega Alpha (hon.), Kappa Sigma, Nu Sigma Nu; corr. Cuban Soc. Dermatology & Syphilology; hon. mem. Sociedad Venezolana de Dermatologia Venereologica y Leprologia. Author: Coal Tar and Cutaneous Carcinogenesis in Industry, 1954; Grenz Ray Therapy, 1954; also articles profl. jours. Editor: N.Y. Physician and American Medicine. Asso. editor Cancer Year Book (U. Tex.). Address: 3518 Cathy Lane East Ridge, TN 37412.

COMBES, JAMES HOMER, business equipment co. exec.; b. Oak Park, Ill., Sept. 17, 1938; s. Homer M. and Virginia (Brand) C.; B.S., Ill. Inst. Tech., 1960; M.B.A., Harvard, 1962; m. Dorothy Anne Dziak, Aug. 29, 1959; children—Candace Suzanne, Cheryl Lynn, Kevin James. With Nat. Cash Register Co., Dayton, O., 1962—, asst. mgr. pricing and program financial mgmt., 1965-66, mgr., dir., 1966-68, controller, 1968—; sec., dir. Intercontinental Investments, Inc., 1967- 69; dir. N. Central Realty Corp. Chmn. Dayton Area comml. div. United Appeal, 1964-65; mem. Citizens Com. for Fair Housing, 1966-67, Jr. Achievement, 1966-67, Recipient NSF research grants, 1959, 60. Mem. Am. Mgmt. Assn. (finance adv. council 1969—), Financial Execs. Inst. (corp. reporting com. 1971—), Nat. Assn. Accountants (past dir. Dayton chpt.), Operations Research Soc. Am., Am. Statis. Assn., Dayton Area Jr. (past finance dir., bd. dirs.), Dayton chambers commerce, Tau Beta Pi, Alpha Phi Omega. Republican. Home: 6501 Reigate Rd Dayton OH 45459 Office: Nat Cash Register Co Main and K Sts Dayton OH 45409

COMBES, WILLARD WETMORE, artist, cartonnist; b. Cleve., Dec. 23, 1901; s. Frank and Jessie Elizabeth (Wetmore) C.; grad. Cleve. Inst. Art. 1924; Gottwalk traveling scholar in Europe, 1924; postgrad. Slade Sch. U. London, also Paris and Madrid, 1924-25, Belgium and Holland; m. Vivian C. Kepler, July 9, 1925; children—Richard W., William K.; m. 2d, Mary Jean McCready, April 26, 1958, two childrenKim Marie and also Frank Byron. Dept. head Cleve. Inst. Art, 1926-44; instr. Western Res. U. Archtl. Sch., 1926-36; editorial cartoonist Cleve. Press, 1934-63; cartoon history series represented in collection Library Congress, Cleve, Mus. Art; water colors exhibited prin. museums, cartoons in maj. univ. schs. of journalism; executed murals for churches, also stained glass art. Recipient Pulitzer award pub. service Cleve. Press, 1938; 1 st prize Nat. Safety Council, 1945; U.S. Treasury citation for war and def. bond programs, 1954; award for best art Cleve. Newspaper Guild. 1955; Cleve. Builders award for best art mosaic mural Luth. High Sch. East. Mem. Cleve. Soc. Artists, Alpha Beta Delta. Mason. Home and studio: 1266 Oakridge Dr Cleveland Heights OH 44121

COMBS, ARTHUR WRIGHT, educator, psychologist; b. Newark, June 3, 1912; s. Arthur Wright and Charlotte (Vyse) C.; B.S., Ohio State U., 1935, M.A., 1942; Ph.D., 1945; m. Mildred Janet Mitchell, Sept. 23, 1934; children—Carol Andrea (Mrs. Jeremy G. Hole), Peter Arthur. Tchr., sch. psychologist Alliance (O.) Pub. Schs., 1935-41; teaching asst. Ohio State U., 1941-43; asst., asso. prof., head personal counseling service, dir. clin. tng. Syracuse U., 1943-54; prof. edn., founds. in edn. dept. U. Fla., 1954—. Recipient Am. Personnel and Guidance Assn. commendation for outstanding research, 1963, John Dewey Soc. award for outstanding contbns. to contemporary edn., 1967. Diplomate Am. Bd. Examiners Profl. Psychology. Fellow Am. Psychol. Assn.; mem. N.E.A., Fla. Edn. Assn., Soc. Psychol. Study Social Issues, Assn. Supervision and Curriculum Devel. (past nat. pres.), Fla. Assn. Sch. Psychologists (past pres.), Sigma Xi, Phi Delta Kappa. Author: (with others) Casebook of Nondirective Counseling, 1947; (with D. Snygg) Individual Behavior: A New Frame of Reference for Psychology, 1949; Individual Behavior: A Perceptual Approach to Behavior, 1959; Human Relations, Instructor's Handbook Including Suggested Discussion Material, 1953; (with R.S. Fisk) Human Relations Training for School Administrators, 1954; Instructor's Handbook for NCO Human Relations Course, 1954; (with D.W. Soper) The Relationship of Child Perceptions to Achievement and Behavior in the Early School Years, 1963; The Professional Education of Teachers; A Perceptual View of Teacher Preparation, 1965; (with D. Avila and W. Purkey) Helping Relationships: Basic Concepts for the Helping Professions, 1971, Helping Relationships Sourcebook, 1971. Editor: Perceiving, Behaving, Becoming: A New Focus for Education, 1962. Contbr. articles profl. jours. Home: 2904 SW 2d Ct Gainesville FL 32601

COMBS, BERT THOMAS, lawyer, former gov. Ky.; b. Manchester, Ky., Aug. 13, 1911; s. Stephen Gibson and Martha (Jones) C.; student Cumberland Coll., 1929-31; LL.B., U. Ky., 1937; m. Mabel Hall, June 15, 1937 (div. 1969); children—Lois Ann (Mrs. William Weinberg), Thomas George; m. 2d, Helen C. Rechtin, Aug. 30, 1969. Admitted to Ky. bar, 1937; pvt. practice law, 1938-41, 46-51, 64—; city atty., Prestonsburg, Ky., 1950; commonwealth atty. 31st Jud. Dist. Ky., 1950-51; judge Ct. Appeals Ky., 1951-55; gov. Ky., 1959-64; judge U.S. Ct. Appeals, 6th Circuit, 1967-70; practice law, Louisville, 1970—. Capt., judge adv. gen. dept. AUS, 1941-46; assisted in investigation and prosecution Japanese war criminals, P.I., 1945-46. Decorated Bronze Star medal; Medal of Merit (P.I.). Fellow Am. Bar Found.; mem. Jr. Bar. Assn. Ky. (pres. 1946-47), Am. Bar Assn., Order of Coif, Phi Delta Phi. Baptist. Mason (32) Home: 715 Alta Vista Rd Louisville KY 40206 Office: Kentucky Home Life Bldg Louisville KY 40202

COMBS, CECIL EDWARD, ednl. adminstr., retired air force officer; b. Dallas, Oct. 21, 1912; s. Nicholas Alexander and Lela Ada (Bridwell) C.; B.S., U.S. Mil. Acad., 1936; M.A., George Washington U., 1958; Ed.D. (hon.), U. Dayton, 1962; m. Beverly Biddle Brown, Oct. 7, 1937; children—Beverly (Mrs. James Bassett), Cecil Kimball. Commd. 2d lt. U.S. Army, 1936, advanced through grades to maj. gen. USAF, 1961; pilot in Philippine Islands, 1938-40; comdg. officer B-17 Squadron, 1941, 19th Bomber Group, Java, 1941-42, 7th Bomber Group, India, 1942, India Air Task Force, 1942-43; dep. chief staff, then chief staff 20th Air Force, 1944-45; dep. comdr. 8th Air Force, 1949-50; comdr. 376th Bomber Wing, 1951-52; comdt. Officer Mil. Schs., Lackland AFB, 1952; dep. comdr. crew tng. USAF, 1954-56; comdt. Air Force Inst. Tech., 1957-65; sr. mem. UN Command, Mil. Armistice Commn., Korea, 1964; asso. provost U. Rochester, N.Y., 1965—, acting dean Coll. Engring. and Applied Sci., 1966—, acting dean Coll. Edn., 1968—. Trustee Rochester Area Ednl. TV Assn., Clarkson Coll. Tech. Decorated Silver Star, Legion of Merit, D.F.C. with 2 oak leaf clusters, Air medal with one oak leaf cluster, Tex. Distinguished Service medal, D.S.M. Mem. Am. Soc. Engring. Edn., Order Daedalians, Tau Beta Pi, Phi Gamma Delta. Clubs: Genesee Valley, Oak Hill Country. Contbr. articles profl. jours. Home: 146 Kilbourn Rd Rochester, NY 14618. Office: Office of the Provost U Rochester Rochester NY 14627

COMBS, CLARENCE MURPHY, anatomist; b. Louisville, Apr. 13, 1925; s. C.H. and Mary (Murphy) C.; A.B., Transylvania Coll., 1946; M.S., Northwestern U., 1948, Ph.D., 1950; m. Virginia Lee Thompson, Aug. 24, 1946 (div. Oct. 1964); children—Jeanne Marie, Stephen Murphy, Nancy Clare. Instr., W.Va. U. Med. Sch., 1948; Ward fellow Northwestern U. Med. Sch., 1946-50, faculty, 1950-66, prof. anatomy, 1963-66; prof., chmn. dept. anatomy Chgo. Med. Sch., 1966—; asso. prof. U. P.R. Med. Sch., 1958-60; chief sect. perinatal physiology Nat. Inst. Neurol. Disease and Blindness, San Juan, P.R., 1958-60, spl. cons., 1958. Spl. lectr. Ill. State Psychopathic Inst., 1954-58. USPHS Sr. Research fellow, 1959-61; recipient Research Career Devel. award USPHS, 1961-64. Mem. Am. Assn. Anatomists, Soc. for Neurosci., Internat. Brain Research Orgn., Am. Assn. U. Profs., A.A.A.S., Biol. Stain Commn., Sigma Xi. Editorial bd. Dorland's Med. Dictionary, 1965. Research, publs. on relationships between cerebellum and other parts of central and peripheral nervous systems, interconnections between cerebral cortex and diencephalon, gross structure of spinal cord segments, neurophysiol. regulation lingual movement. Home: 1706 Washington St Evanston IL 60602 Office: 2020 W Ogden Av Chicago IL 60612

COMBS, LAURENCE ASBURY, mfg. exec.; b. Findlay, Ill., Oct. 7, 1907; s. Joel Asbury and Anna (Hennings) C.; A.B., Central YMCA Coll., 1932; LL.B., John Marshall Law Sch., 1935; m. Dorothy E. Kidd, Apr. 10, 1937; 1 son, James Laurence. Registered to practice patent law, 1931; admitted to Ill. bar, 1936; with Container Corp. of Am., Chgo., 1928—, beginning as sec. to patent atty., successively asst. patent atty., tax atty., asst. sec., dir. indsl. relations, 1928-54, v.p., 1954—. Mem. Indsl. Relations Assn. Chgo., Patent Law Assn. Chgo., Delta Theta Phi. Clubs: Executives, Chicago Tax, Edgewood Valley Country, Mid-Day (Chgo.). Office: 1 First National Plaza Chicago IL 60670

COMBS, LEE, Jr., lawyer; b. Valley City, N.D., Nov. 25, 1905; s. Lee and Mabel (Osher) C.; B.A., Harvard, 1926; J.D., U. So. Cal., 1929; m. Evelyn Hefner, Feb. 25, 1929; children—David (dec.), Donald (dec.), Deanna (dec.), Lee Hefner (dec.), Margaret Evelyn (Mrs. Michael Chumo, Jr.). Admitted to Cal. bar, 1929, also U.S. Supreme Ct.; practice in Los Angeles, 1929-51, Beverly Hills, 1951—. Pres., dir. So. Cal. Com. Olympic Games. Co- founder, trustee Belair (Cal.) Town and Country Sch., 1949-52; pres. Lee Hefner Combs Meml. Found., 1960—, also dir.; trustee Harvard Sch., 1959- 64; asso. U. So. Cal., 1961—. Mem. Am. Judicature Soc., Am., Cal., Los Angeles County, Beverly Hills (bd. govs. 1952-59, pres. 1956) bar assns., U. So. Cal. Alumni Assn., U. So. Cal. Law Alumni Assn. (pres.), Brit. Interplanetary Soc., Am., Cal. (v.p. 1960-61, bd. dirs. 1959-61) revenue assns., Am. Horse Show Assn., Am. Philatelic Assn., Skull and Dagger. Episcopalian. Mason (Shriner). Clubs: Bel Air Bay, Beverly Hills, Exchange (founding pres.), Stock Exchange (Beverly Hills); Flintridge (Cal.) Riding. Home: 264 Tigertail Rd Los Angeles CA 90049 Office: 9601 Wilshire Rd Beverly Hills CA 90210

COMBS, WALTER VINCENT, ret. naval officer; b. N.Y.C., Mar. 27, 1914; s. Walter Vincent and Dorothy (Garrison) C.; B.S. in Elec. Engring., U.S. Naval Acad., 1936; grad. Naval War Coll., 1953, Nat. War Coll., 1961; M.A. in Internat. Affairs, George Washington U., 1963; m. Bernice Louise Cotton, Oct. 15, 1938; children—Walter Vincent III, Michael Cotton. Commd. ensign U.S. Navy, 1936, advanced through grades to rear adm., 1964; assigned various ships, 1936-41, 43-44; mem. staff comdr. Submarines Asiatic Fleet, 1941-42; comdg. officer U.S.S. Harrison, 1944-46; asssigned Bur. Naval Personnel, 1946-49, 50-52; comdg. officer U.S.S. Putnam, 1949, U.S.S. Borie, 1950; comdr. Escort Squadron II, 1953-55; assigned Office Chief Naval Operations, 1955-58; comdg. officer U.S.S. Hamul, 1958-59; U.S.S. Los Angeles, 1959-60; chief staff comdr. Cruiser Force Atlantic, 1961-62; assigned Office Sec. Def., 1962-64; asst. chief naval operations (manpower), 1964-66; comdr. Cruiser-Destroyer Flotilla 3, 1966-68; comdr. service force Pacific Fleet, 1968-70; retired, 1970. Decorated D.S.M., Silver Star, Legion of Merit, Bronze Star with V, Navy Commendation with V. Home: Irish Beach CA

COMBS, WILLIAM HOBART, coll. prof. and adminstr.; b. Bloomfield, Ind., Oct. 5, 1896; s. James E. and Nellie (Mays) C.; A.B., Ind. U., 1924, A.M., 1926; Baldwin fellow, U. of Cincinnati, 1926-27; Ph.D. (Harrison fellow) U. of Pa., 1933; m. Elizabeth J. Edington, Apr. 15, 1916; children—Robert G., Joan E. (Mrs. Wm. Rudman), Hilda Ann (dec.). Tchr. pub. schs. in Ind., 1914- 25; asso. prof. Berea Coll., Ky., 1928-30; instr. U. of Tenn., 1931-38; cons. Tenn. State Dept. of Pub. Welfare, 1938; asst. prof. to asso. prof. history and polit. sci., prof. and head dept. of pub. adminstrn., Mich. State U., 1938-49, adminstrv. asst. to pres. charge acad. affairs and dean all-coll. div., 1949-56, dean univ. services, 1956-67, sec. of faculties, 1959-67, prof. and dean emeritus, 1967, dir. archives, asst. dean continuing edn. Coll. Arts and Letters, part-time, 1967—. Mem. Commn. on Modernization and Reform of Govt. in Mich., 1938-39; mem. Constl. Revision Study Commn., 1942; mem. tech. staff Tax Study Adv. Commn., 1945-46; mem. Mich. Inst. of Local Govt. since 1948; mem. bd. dirs. Midwest Inter-Library Corp., 1949-66, chmn., 1957-58; mem. council Center for Research Libraries, 1966-67; project dir. Mich. Joint Legislative Com. Reorganization State Govt., 1950; staff dir. Mich. Constl. Conv. Prep. Commn., 1961; co-dir. research and drafting Mich. Constl. Conv., 1961-62. Mem. Internat. City Mgrs. Assn., Mich. Acad. Arts, Letters and Sci., Soc. Am. Archivists, Am. Records Mgmt. Assn. (Mid-Mich. chpt.). Conglist. Mason. Club: State College. Author: (with W.E. Cole, A. D. Mueller and C. P. White) Constitutional Problems in Tennessee, 1937; (with W. E. Cole) Tennessee A Political Study, 1940. Contbr. articles to Am. Polit. Sci. Rev., Tenn. Law Rev., Nat. Municipal Rev., Bull. of Nat. Tax Assn. Home: 427 Orchard St East Lansing, MI 48823.

COMDEN, BETTY, writer; b. Bklyn., May 3, 1919; d. Leo and Rebecca (Sadvoransky) Comden; student Bklyn. Ethical Culture Sch., Erasmus Hall High Sch.; B.S., N.Y.U.; m. Steven Kyle, Jan. 4, 1942; children—Susanna, Alan. Performer, writer nightclub act Revuers. Writer book and lyrics (with Adolph Green) Broadway shows On the Town, 1944-45, Billion Dollar Baby, Two on the Aisle, Bells are Ringing, Fade-Out—Fade-In, Subways are for Sleeping; lyrics Wonderful Town, Peter Pan, Say, Darling, Do Re Mi, Hallelujah, Baby!; screen plays Good News, Barkleys of Broadway, Band Wagon, Singing in the Rain, Auntie Mame; screenplay and lyrics for Bells are Ringing, On The Town, It's Always Fair Weather, What a Way to Go; A Party (performed with A. Green in show of their works), 1959; co-author book for Applause, 1970. Recipient Donaldson award and Tony award for Wonderful Town, as co-lyricist best score, 1953; Tony award for Hallelujah, Baby, as co-writer best score, 1968; Tony award for Applause, 1970. Office: care John Springer Assos Inc 667 Madison Av New York City NY 10021

COME, ARNOLD BRUCE, sem. pres.; b. Lansing, Mich., Mar. 9, 1918; s. Edward Peter and Maude (McAllister) C.; A.B., Mich. State U., 1939; Th.B., Princeton Theol. Sem., 1942, Th.D., 1946; m. Elizabeth Leota McClure, Sept. 9, 1942; children—Arnold Bruce, Lee McClure. Ordained to ministry Presbyn. Ch., 1942; pastor Robert Grand Meml. Presbyn. Ch., Phila., 1942-45; teaching fellow Princeton Theol. Sem., 1945-46; prof. philosophy and religion Centre Coll. of Ky., 1946-52; prof. systematic theology San Francisco Theol. Sem., 1952—, pres., 1967—. Mem. dept. on laity World Council Chs., 1960-68; mem. Theol. Commn., World Presbyn. Alliance, 1955-65; mem. bd. Christian edn. United presbyn. Ch., U.S.A., 1968-71, mem. Council on Evangelism, 1967-70. Carnegie research grantee, 1950. Am. Assn. Theol. Schs. fellow, 1959-60. Mem. Phi Kappa Tau, Phi Kappa Phi, Omicron Delta Kappa. Author: Human Spirit, Holy Spirit, 1959; Agents of Reconciliation, 1960; An Introduction to Barth's Dogmatics for Preachers, 1963; Drinking: A Christian Position, 1964; Reluctant Revolution, 1965. Home: 108 Bolinas Av San Anselmo CA 94960

COMER, DAVID B., III, educator. Prof. English, head English dept. Ga. Inst. Tech., Atlanta. Office: English Dept Ga Inst Tech Atlanta GA 30332*

COMER, DONALD, Jr., textile co. exec.; b. Birmingham, Ala., May 18, 1913; s. Donald and Gertrude (Miller) C.; m. Isabel Anderson, Oct. 29, 1936; children—Donald III, Isabel Anderson. With Avondale Mills, Sylacauga, Ala., 1932—, exec. v.p., 1954-70, pres., chief exec. officer, treas., 1970—, also dir.; with Cowikee Mills, Eufaula, Ala., 1943—, treas., pres. 1956-67, chmn. bd., 1967—; dir. First Nat. Bank of Birmingham, 1st Fed. Savs. & Loan Assn., Sylacauga, Home Fed. Savs. & Loan Assn., Birmingham, Am. Mut. Liability Ins. Co., Wakefield, Mass., Asso. Industries Ala.; adv. bd. Chem. Bank N.Y. Trust Co., N.Y.C. Past bd. dirs. Birmingham YMCA; bd. govs. Ala. Assn. Ind. Colls.; pres. Chocolocco council Boy Scouts Am., mem. exec. com. Region V; trustee So. Research Soc., Am. Bible Soc. Mem.

N.A.M. (dir.), Am. Textile Mfrs. Inst. (dir.), Birmingham C. of C. (past dir.). Home: Comer Hill Sylacauga AL 35150 Office: Sylacauga AL 35150

COMER, GORDON V., church ofcl.; b. Frederick, Kansas; s. Will E. and Janet (Monroe) C.; ed. pub. schs., private tutoring; m. Josephine S. Puckett, Apr. 20, 1914; 1 dau., Mary Elizabeth (Mrs. Forrest Cranmer). In real estate business to 1926; entered practice of Christian Science in 1927; reader in branch church (Denver), 1926-29; became tchr. of C.S., 1934; taught and practiced in Denver, 1935-42; first reader, Mother Church, Boston, 1932-35 42-44, lectr., 1944-46, clk., 1946—. Served as com. on C.S. publs., Colo., 1929-32. Home: 145 Pinckney St Boston MA 02114 Office: 107 Falmouth St Boston MA 02115

COMER, JAMES PIERPONT, psychiatrist; b. East Chicago, Ind., Sept. 25, 1934; s. Hugh and Maggie (Nichols) C.; A.B., Ind. U., 1956; M.D., Howard U., 1960; M.P.H., U. Mich., 1964; m. Shirley Ann Arnold, June 20, 1959; children—Brian Jay, Dawn Renee. Served with USPHS, Washington and Chevy Chase, Md., 1961-68; intern St. Catherine's Hosp., East Chicago, Ind., 1960-61; resident Yale U. Sch. Medicine, 1964-67; asso. prof. psychiatry Yale Child Study Center and dept. psychiatry, 1968—; asso. dean Yale Med. Sch., New Haven, 1969—; dir. pupil services Baldwin-King Sch. Project, New Haven; cons. Joint Commn. on Mental Health of Children, Nat. Commn. on Causes and Prevention of Violence, Nat. Inst. Mental Health. Bd. dirs. Dixwell Soul Sta. and Yale Afro-Am. House, Children's TV Workshop; mem. profl. adv. council Nat. Assn. Mental Health; mem. ad hoc adv. com. Conn. Research commn. John and Mary Markle Found. scholar 1969—. Mem. A.M.A., Am. Psychiat. Assn., Am. Orthopsychiatric Assn., N.A.A.C.P., Black Coalition of New Haven, Alpha Phi Alpha. Author: Beyond Black and White, 1971. Mem. editorial bd. Am. Jour. Orthopsychiatry, 1970—, Youth and Adolescence. Contbr. articles profl. jours. Home: 21 Kent Dr North Haven CT 06517 Office: 333 Cedar St New Haven CT 06510

COMFORT, ALEXANDER, writer, biologist; b. Palmers Green, Eng., Feb. 10, 1920; s. Alexander Charles and Daisy (Fenner) C.; Robert Styring scholar, Trinity Coll., Cambridge, 1938-41; M.B., B.Ch., London Hosp., 1944, M.A., 1945, Ph.D., 1949; D.Sc., 1963. House physician London Hosp., 1944; lectr. physiology Med. Sch., 1948-51; Nuffield fellow gerontology Univ. Coll. London, 1951- 63, dir. M.R.C. Group on Aging, 1963-70, dir. research gerontology, 1970—. Mem. Com. of 100, 1962. Mem. Brit. Soc. for Research on Aging (pres. 1968). Author: The Powerhouse, 1944; On This Side Nothing, 1949; Come Out to Play, 1961; Haste to the Wedding (poems), 1961; Aging, the Biology of Senescence, 1964; Nature and Human Nature, 1966; numerous others. Office: Univ Coll London WC 1 England

COMFORT, CHARLOTTE WALRATH, former headmistress; b. Ft. Plain, N.Y., Mar. 22, 1903; d. Alton Alphonso and Charlotte (Barber) Walrath; A.B., Vassar Coll., 1924; m. Lowell R. Comfort, Sept. 8, 1928; children—Joan (Mrs. H. Alden Johnson, Jr.), Robert. Tchr., Warrenton (Va.) Country Sch., 1924-25; with Miss Hewitt's Sch., 1925-69, headmistress, 1942-69. Bd. dirs. Profl. Children's Sch., 1954-58, hon. dir., 1958-69; trustee The Hewitt Sch., 1969—. Mem. Nat. Assn. Prins. Schs. Girls, Headmistresses Assn. East (council 1957-60, pres. 1960-62, hon. mem. 1969—), Guild Ind. Schs. N.Y. (pres. 1956-58). Club: Cosmopolitan (N.Y.C.). Home: Siesta Club 7111 Pine Needle Rd Sarasota FL 33581

COMFORT, EDWIN GUSTAVUS HUNTER, educator; b. Phila., Aug. 12, 1907; s. Joseph C. and Augusta (Hunter) C.; B.S., Northwestern U., 1930, M.A., 1931; Ph.D., Brown U., 1936; m. Roberta Robinson, June 28, 1938; children—Joseph R., Richard E. Instr. math. Tulane U., 1936-37, U. Ark., 1937-46; instr., then asst. prof. Ill. Inst. Tech., 1946-52; mem. faculty Ripon Coll., 1952—, prof. math., 1956—, chmn. dept., 1957—. Served to lt. col. USAAF, 1941-45. Recipient Harold and May Severy award for excellence in teaching Ripon Coll., 1961. Mem. A.A.A.S., Am. Math. Soc., Math. Assn. Am., Nat. Council Tchrs. Math., Am. Assn. U. Profs., Wis. Acad. Arts. Sci. and Letters, Phi Beta Kappa, Sigma Xi. Author: articles book revs. Home: 563 Metomen St Ripon WI 54971

COMFORT, HAROLD WESLEY, food processing co. exec.; b. Brooklyn, N.Y., Nov. 7, 1896; s. Walter R. and Myra (La Due) C.; student Irving Sch., Tarrytown, N.Y., Lawrenceville Sch.; student Yale, 1915-16; student Williams Coll. (class 1920); m. Lillian Whiteley, Oct. 25, 1918; children—Harold W., Robert H., Richard W., John. Salesman, Reid Ice Cream Co., Bklyn., 1919-21, br. mgr., N.Y.C., 1921-24, sales mgr., 1924-28; with Borden Co., 1928—, v.p. Reids's Ice Cream, pres., 1931- 33; v.p. Pioneer Ice Cream Div. of Borden's 1933-35; chmn. Met. Fluid Milk Div. of Borden, 1935-36, gen. mgr. Fluid Milk Div., 1936-37, v.p. Fluid Milk Div., 1937-44, dir., 1938—, exec. v.p., 1944-56, pres. Borden Co., 1956-64, now dir. emeritus; mem. adv. com. to bd. Chem. Bank N.Y. Trust Co.; dir. Moody's Fund, Moody's Capital Fund; trustee Dollar Savs. Bank. Trustee Am. Heritage Found., Roosevelt Hosp. Served in USN, 1918; later officer USNR. Republican. Clubs: Gulf Stream (Fla.) Golf: Gulf Stream Bath and Tennis; Union League, Round Hill, Blind Brook, Pelham, Clove Rod and Gun; Connetquot River (L.I.) Home: Lake Av Greenwich CT 06830 Office: 350 Madison Av New York City NY 10017

COMFORT, HOWARD, former educator; b. Haverford, Pa., June 4, 1904; s. William Wistar and Mary Lawton (Fales) C.; A.B., Haverford Coll., 1924; M.A., Princeton, 1927, Ph.D. in Classics, 1932; fellow classics Am. Acad. in Rome, 1927-29; m. Elizabeth Philbrook Webb, June 3, 1931; children—William Wistar II, Laura Washburn (Mrs. George F. Kesel). Tchr. Latin, Haverford Sch., 1924- 26, Taft Sch., 1927; asst. prof. classics Hamilton Coll., 1929-30; faculty classics Haverford Coll., 1932-69, chmn. dept., 1958-69, coach of cricket, 1914-68, emeritus, 1969—; cons. Prison Industries Reorgn. Adminstrn., Washington, 1936; dir. Rome office Am. Friends Service Com., 1940; staff Human Events mag., Washington, 1944-45; cultural attache Am. embassy, Rome, 1950-51, Bern, Switzerland, 1951-52; mem. Inst. Advanced Study, Princeton, 1956, 60. Founding mem., pres. Rei Cretariae Romanae Fautores, 1957—; mgr. Harcum Jr. Coll., Bryn Mawr, Pa., 1954-55, Moore Coll. Art, Phila., 1960-68, chmn. edn. com., 1965-68; dir. Richard Humphreys Found., 1939-45, Pa. Com. Penal Affairs, 1936- 45, Carl Schurz Found., 1955-58, Osborne Assn., 1936-51, Indian Rights Assn., 1932-45; mem. nat. selections com. Fulbright award of Inst. Internat. Edn., 1954-56. Bd. dirs. Family Soc. Phila., 1938-45, Community Health and Civic Assn., Ardmore, Pa., 1945, Main Line Fedn. Chs., 1945; family sect. budget com. Phila. Community Fund, 1945-48. Fellow Soc. Antiquaries of London; mem. Am. Philol. Assn. (sec.-treas. 1946-49, dir. 1955-59, v.p. 1961, pres. 1962-63), Oriental Club Phila., Phila. Classical Club (pres. 1955-56), Classical Assn. Atlantic States, Archaeol. Inst. Am., Deutsches Archaeol. Inst., Accademia Petrarca Arezzo (corr.), Inst. Studi Liguri Bordighera, Seminario de Arqueología de Santiago de Compostela (hon.), Phi Beta Kappa (pres. Haverford 1957- 59). Mem. Soc. of Friends (clk. Phila. Yrly. Meeting on Worship and Ministry 1958-60). Club: Merion Cricket. Co-author: Corpus Vasorum Arretinorum. Author articles on Roman ceramic archaeology. Home: 754 Millbrook Lane Haverford PA 19041

COMFORT, THOMAS EDWIN, educator; b. Streator, Ill., Apr. 15, 1921; s. Patrick James and Jane (Dickinson) C.; A.B., Northwestern U., 1943; A.M., U. Ill., 1951, Ph.D., 1954; m. Evelyn Lorraine Trotter, Oct. 1, 1945; children—Thomas Edwin, Judith Ann, Patrick James, Kathleen Ann, Michael James. Self-employed as ins. broker, 1945-47; instr. Latin, Greek, French and English, St. Ambrose Coll., Davenport, Ia., 1947-48; instr. French, U. Ill., 1949-54; mem. faculty Tex. A. and M. U., 1954-58, 61, 63-65, asso. prof. French, 1957-65; dir. English lang. program, Morocco, 1958-60; dir. Turkish Air Force Lang. Sch., Izmir, 1961-63; prof. French, head dept. fgn. langs. Ill. State U., Normal, 1965—. Vice pres. Tex. Acad. Sci., 1957. Served to lt. (j.g.) USNR, 1943-46; PTO. Bonbright scholar in langs. and lit., 1942-43. Mem. Am. Assn. Tchrs. French, Am. Council Teaching Fgn. Langs., Modern Lang. Assn., Am. Assn. U. Profs., Phi Beta Kappa, Phi Eta Sigma, Eta Sigma Phi. Home: 2 Turner Rd Normal IL 61761

COMFORT, WILLIAM WISTAR, educator; b. Bryn Mawr, Pa., Apr. 19, 1933; s. Howard and Elizabeth (Webb) C.; B.A., Haverford Coll., 1954; M.S., U. Wash., 1957, Ph.D., 1958; M.A. (hon.), Wesleyan U., Middletown, Conn., 1969; m. Mary Constance Lyon, Mar. 30, 1957; children—Martha Wistar, Howard III. Teaching asst., research asst. U. Wash., 1954-58; B. Peirce instr. Harvard, 1958-61; asst. prof. U. Rochester, 1961-65; instr. NSF Summer Inst., U. Ark., 1965; asso. prof. U. Mass., 1965-67; prof. math. Wesleyan U., Middletown, 1967—, chmn. dept., 1969-70; sr. research asso., dept. math. McGill U., Montreal, Que., Can., 1970-71. Mem. Internat. Congress Mathematicians, Russia, 1966. Recipient Excellence-in-teaching award U. Rochester, 1966. Mem. Math. Assn. Am., Am. Math. Soc., Phi Beta Kappa. Mem. Soc. of Friends. Contbr. articles profl. jours. Home: Main St Higganum CT 06441 Office: Wesleyan U Middletown CT 06457

COMINGS, EDWARD WALTER, dean; b. Phillipsburg, N.J., Feb. 24, 1908; s. Robert Morrow and Nellie (Breen) C.; B.S., U. Ill., 1930; D.Sc. in Chem. Engring., Mass. Inst. Tech., 1934; m. Jeannette Florentine Rice, Nov. 14, 1931; children—Gordon Robert, David Edward, Miriam Louise (Mrs. John J. Lobell). Asst., Mass. Inst. Tech., 1931-33; chem. engr. The Tex. Co., Beacon, N.Y., 1933-35; asst. prof. N.C. State Coll., 1935-36; asst. prof. U. Ill., 1936-43, asso. prof., 1943-47, prof. chem. engring., 1947-51, ofcl. investigator, 1940-43, asst. dir. munitions devel. lab. Nat. Def. Research Commn. and OSRD, 1943-45; head Sch. Chem. and Metall. Engring. Purdue U., 1951-59; dean engring. U. Del., Newark, 1959—. Chmn. Gordon Conf. on High Pressure Research, 1956. Mem. Gov.'s Council on Sci. and Tech. Trustee Del. Inst. Tech. Recipient Naval Ordnance Devel. Award, 1945; William H. Walker award Am. Inst. Chem. Engrs., 1956. Registered profl. engr., Del. Fellow A.A.A.S.; mem. Am. Chem. Soc. (chmn. div. indsl. and engring. chemistry, 1954), Am. Inst. Chem. Engrs., Am. Soc. Engring. Edn., Del. Acad. Sci. (pres. 1966), Sigma Xi, Alpha Chi Sigma, Phi Lambda Upsilon, Tau Kappa Epsilon, Phi Eta Sigma, Omega Chi Epsilon, Tau Beta Pi. Unitarian. Rotarian (pres. Newark 1967-68). Author: High Pressure Technology, 1956; also articles tech. jours. Contbr.; Applications of Chemical Engineering, 1940. Home: 509 Windsor Dr Fairfield Newark DE 19711

COMINOS, ACHILLES, banker; b. Sydney, Australia, Apr. 12, 1911; s. Zachariah Demetrius and Calliope (Symigdalas) C.; grad. State Coll. for Econs., 1932; Dr. in Econs., Berlin U., 1938; m. Betty Papastratos, Mar. 18, 1951; 1 dau., Mina. Requirements analyst UNRRA, Athens, 1944-46; econ. counselor Ministry Coordination Greece, 1946-53; dep. chief Greek permanent delegation OEEC, Paris, 1948-53; dir. Papastratos Cigarettes, Piraeus, Greece, 1953-68; gov. Nat. Bank Greece, Athens, 1968-71; mem. bd. Center Planning and Research, 1965-67; mem. central com. Econ. Devel. Program, 1967-69. Chmn. bd. Greek Line, Dexion (Hellas) Ltd., Colgate Palmolive (Hellas), Ethniki Ins. Co., Hellenic Hulls/Aircraft Ins., Fertilisers Co. No. Greece, Union Greek Banks; dir. several Greek and fgn. companies. Mem. several econ. committees, 1948—; dep. pres. adv. com. on attraction of fgn. investments to Greece, 1953; mem. Greek delegation UNIDO, 1967; pres. with rank of full ambassador Econ. Coop. Com., 1965-67. Dept. chmn. Greek Nat. Art Gallery; bd. dirs. Nat. Research Inst.; chmn. Nat. Bank Found. Decorated golden cross King George; comdr. Order Phoenix. Mem. Am. Econometric Soc., Greek Soc. Econ. Sci. Author: Wäbrungs und Kredit politik der Bank von Griechenland, 1940; others. Contbr. Greek and fgn. press and periodicals. Home: 1 Marasli Athens Greece 140 Office: 86 Aeolou Athens Greece

COMISKEY, JAMES AUGUST, U.S. dist. judge; b. New Orleans, Oct. 16, 1926; s. James Edward and Laura (Arceneaux) C.; B.A., Loyola U., New Orleans, 1948, LL.B., 1951; m. Blanche Catherine Mouledoux, Aug. 20, 1952; children—Margaret, Marian, James, Laura, Michelle, Jeanne, Eileen, Paula, Louise, Elizabeth, Catherine. Admitted to La. bar, 1951; partner firm Comiskey & Schaff, New Orleans, 1951-67; U.S. judge Eastern Dist. La., 1967—. Past dir. Bank of La., Bank of South, Fidelity Bank and Trust Co. Councilman-at-large, New Orleans, also pres. council, 1961-62; del. La. Democratic nat. convs., 1956, 60, 64; candidate for mayor New Orleans, 1962; del. La. Constl. Conv., 1956. Past mem. men's adv. bd. Sara Mayo Hosp.; bd. dirs. New Orleans Floral Trail, Greater New Orleans Police Found.; adv. dir. Volunteers Am. Served with inf. AUS, 1944-46. Mem. Am., La., New Orleans, Fed., Criminal Cts. bar assns., St. Thomas More Catholic Lawyers Assn. K.C. Home: 131 S St Patrick St New Orleans LA 70119 Office: 400 Royal St New Orleans LA 70130

COMISKY, MARVIN, lawyer; b. Phila., June 5, 1918; s. Max and Anna (Levine) C.; B.S.C. summa cum laude, 1938; LL.B. cum laude, U. Pa., 1941, Gowen fellow, 1941- 42; LL.D., Dickinson Sch. Law, 1970; m. Goldie Elving, June 29, 1946; children—Ian Michael, Hope Ann, Matthew James. Admitted to Pa. bar, 1942; law clk. to Judge Charles E. Kenworthy, Pa. Superior Ct., 1942, to Chief Justice Horace Stern, Pa. Supreme Ct., 1946; partner firm Blank, Rome, Klaus & Comisky, Phila., 1959—. Chief counsel Pa. Constl. Conv., 1967-68; chmn. Phila. Law Enforcement Planning Council, 1967; mem. Pa. Criminal Procedural Rules Com., 1959- -. Past chmn. ann. fund raising B'nai B'rith. Bd. dirs. Am. Jewish Com.; past mem. bd. dirs., now trustee Dropsie Coll. Served with AUS, 1942-46. Fellow Am. Internat. Acad. Trial Lawyers, Am. Coll. Trial Lawyers, Am. Bar Found.; mem. Am., Pa. (ho. dels.; pres. 1970), Phila. (chancellor 1965) bar assns., Phila. Bar Found. (pres. 1967), Am. Law Inst., Am. Judicature Soc., Nat. Assn. Def. Lawyers in Criminal Cases, Beta Gamma Sigma. Jewish religion (bd. dirs. temple). Author: Basic Criminal Procedure, 1958; (with L.D. Apothaker) Federal Criminal Procedure, 1963; also articles. Home: 1109 Orleans Rd Cheltenham PA 19012 Office: 4 Penn Center Plaza Philadelphia PA 19103

COMISSIONA, SERGIU, orch. condr.; b. Bucharest, Rumania, June 16, 1928; s. Isaac and Jeanne (Haufrecht) C.; grad. Bucharest Conservatory Music, 1947; m. Robinne Feldstein, July 16, 1949. Came to U.S., 1969, naturalized, 1971. Prin. condr. Rumanian State Opera, 1955-59; music dir. Haifa (Israel) Symphony Orch., 1959, Israel Chamber Orch., 1960, Goteborg Symphony Orch., 1966-70; condr. No. Ireland Orch., 1967; music dir. Balt. Symphony Orch., 1969—. Recipient prize Internat. Competition for Young Condrs., Bescancon, France, 1956, award for contbns. to culture city of Goteborg, 1970. Home: 4000 N Charles St Baltimore MD 21218 Office: 120 W Mt Royal Av Baltimore MD 21201

COMITAS, LAMBROS, educator; b. N.Y.C., Sept. 29, 1927; s. Dennis and Magdaline (Livanis) C.; A.B., Columbia, 1948, Ph.D., 1962; m. Irene Mousouris, Nov. 2, 1952. Instr. dept. anthropology Columbia, N.Y.C., 1958-62, asst. prof., 1962-64, asst. prof. Tchrs. Coll., 1964, asso. prof., 1964-67, prof., 1967—, dir. Center for Edn. in Latin Am., Tchrs. Coll., dir. Center for Urban Studies and Programs, Tchrs. Coll. Cons. on W.Indies, tng. dir. for Jamaica, evaluation and research dir. for Bolivia, Peace Corps, 1961-67. Asso. dir. Research Inst. for Study of Man. Served with Signal Corps, AUS, 1946-47. Recipient Fulbright grant (W.Indies), 1957-58, Office of Edn. grant, 1968-69. Research Inst. for Study of Man fellow, 1962-65, John Simon Guggenheim fellow, 1971—. Fellow Am. Anthrop. Assn., Am. Ethnol. Soc., N.Y. Acad. Scis.; mem. Soc. for Applied Anthropology (pres. 1970-71), Council on Anthropology and Edn. (mem. exec. com. 1969-70), Phi Kappa Psi. Author: Caribbeana 1900-1965: A Topical Bibliography, 1968. Gen. editor Series on Latin America, 1967—; contbg. editor Handbook of Latin American Studies, 1966—; asso. editor Human Organization, 1970—; editorial bd. Estudios Andinos: The World Year Book of Education, 1968—. Contbr. articles profl. jours. Home: 1107 Fifth Av New York City NY 10028

COMLEY, FREDERICK LUQUIENS, lawyer; b. Bridgeport, Conn., Jan. 17, 1916; s. William H. and Maud (Skidmore) C.; grad. Phillips Andover Acad., 1933; B.A., Yale, 1937, LL.B., 1940; m. Jane G. Gilkinson, June 7, 1941; children—Lynn G., Mark H. Admitted to Conn. bar, 1940, since practiced in Bridgeport; mem. firm Pullman, Comley, Bradley & Reeves, 1940—, partner, 1948—. Mem. Conn. Bar Exam. Com., 1964—. Pres. Corp. Asso. Charities, Bridgeport, 1954-58; mem. bd. edn., Weston, Conn., 1959-67, chmn., 1965-67. Trustee Greens Farms Acad., 1967—. Served with USNR, 1940-45. Fellow Am. Coll. Trial Lawyers; mem. Am. Bar Assn., Sigma Xi. Republican. Episcopalian. Home: Godfrey Rd Weston, CT 06880. Office: 855 Main St Bridgeport CT 06603

COMLEY, JOHN MUNSON, ret. judge; b. Bridgeport, Conn., July 1, 1895; s. William Henry and Lucy Isabelle (Nicholson) C.; A.B., Yale, 1917, LL.B. 1920; m. Grace Isabel Aufford, Feb. 14, 1925 (dec. Sept. 1933); children—Mary Elizabeth (Philbrick), John Munson; m. 2d, Frances E. Bruggerhof. Admitted to Conn. bar, 1920; began practice at Bridgeport; mem. firm Pullman & Comley, 1920-24; reporter jud. decisions Conn. Supreme Ct., 1924-29; mem. Durey, Pierson & Comley, 1929-45; judge Superior Ct. of Conn., 1945- 63; asso. justice Conn. Supreme Ct., 1963—, now ret. Sgt. Q.M. Corps, U.S.A., 1918-19. Chmn. founding com., Conn. Bar Jour. (quarterly), 1927, editor, 1927-35. Mem. Am. Law Inst., Am., Conn. State and Stamford bar assns., Phi Beta Kappa, Zeta Psi, Phi Delta Phi, Corbey Court, Order of Coif. Republican. Episcopalian. Editor: Connecticut Reports, Vols. 100-108 1924-29; Index-Digest Conn. Reports, Vols. 98-107, 1928. Home: 98 Hoyt St Stamford CT 06905

COMMAGER, HENRY STEELE, educator; b. Pittsburgh, Pennsylvania, Oct. 25, 1902; s. James Williams and Elisabeth (Dan) C.; Ph.B., U. of Chicago, 1923, A.M., 1924, Ph.D., 1928; student U. of Copenhagen, 1924-25; M.A. (Cantab.); M.A. (Oxon.); hon. fellow Peterhouse; Litt.D., Washington Coll. (Md.), Ohio Wesleyan, 1958. Monmouth Coll., 1959; Doctor of Civil Law (hon.), Alfred U., Litt. D., 1965; Ed.D., R.I. Coll. Edn; LL.D., Brandeis U., 1960, Mich. State U., 1960, Franklin and Marshall Coll., 1962, Marymount Coll., D.Litt., Cambridge U., 1962; L.H.D., U. Hartford, 1962, U. Puget Sound, 1963; D.H.L., Carleton Coll., 1966; m. Evan Carroll, July 3, 1928; children—Henry Steele, Nellie Thomas McColl, Elisabeth Carroll. Instr. of history, N.Y.U., 1926-29; asst. prof., 1929-30, asso. prof., 1930-31, prof., 1931-38; prof. history Columbia, 1939-56, adj. prof., 1956—, now Sperenza lectr.; prof. history Amherst Coll., 1956—; lectr. U. Mexico, 1965. Trustee Am. Scandinavian Found. Liberty and Order. Fellow Am. Scandinavian Soc.; mem. Nat. Acad. Arts and Letters, Am. Historical Society, Mass. Historical Soc., Am. Antiquarian Soc., Century Assn., Phi Beta Kappa. Received Herbert B. Adams award of Am. Hist. Assn., 1929; mem. War Dept. Com. on History of the War; to Britain for War Dept. and OWI, summer 1943; to France, Belgium, Britain for War Dept., 1946. Lecturer in American history Cambridge U., Eng., 1942-43, Bacon lecturer Boston U., 1943, Richards lectr. U. of Va., 1944, Pitt. prof. Am. history Cambridge Univ., Eng., 1947-48, Harmsworth prof. Am. history Oxford U., Eng., 1952-53, Gottesman lectr. Uppsala U., 1953; vis. prof. U. Copenhagen, 1956; lectr. for Dept. of State at German univs., 1954, Israel and Italy, 1955, Trinidad, 1959, Italy, spring 1961, Chilean universities, 1963; Ziskind prof. Brandeis, 1955; Aix en Provence at Nice, 1957; lecturer U. Jerusalem, Israel, 1958; hon. prof. U. of Santiago de Chile. Decorated Knight Order of Dannebrog; Guggenheim fellow, 1960-61. Democrat. Author: The Growth of the American Republic (with S. E. Morison), 1931-42; Theodore Parker, 1936; The Heritage of America (with A. Nevins), 1939; Our Nation (with E. C. Barker), 1941; American; the Story of a Free People (with A. Nevins), 1942; Majority Rule and Minority Rights, 1943; The Blue and the Gray (2 vol.); America, Story of Free Nation, 1950; The American Mind, 1951; Living Ideas in America, 1952; Freedom, Loyalty, Dissent, 1954; Joseph Story, 1954; Europe and America since 1492 (with G. Bruun), 1954; The Great Declaration, 1958; (with R. B. Morris) The Spirit of Seventy- Six, 2 volumes, pub. 1958; The Era of Reform, 1960; The Great Proclamation, 1960; Theodore Parker, an Anthology, published 1960; Crusaders for Freedom, published 1962; Lester Ward and Welfare State, 1965; Nature and Problems of History, published in 1965. Editor: Documents of American Hist., 1934, 40, 50; Tocqueville's Democracy in America, 1946; A St. Nicholas Anthology, 1948; The Second St. Nicholas Anthology, 1950; America in Perspective, 1947; The Rise of the American Nation, 50 vols. (in process); Selected Writings of William Dean Howells' Atlas of Civil War, 1958; Immigration in American History, 1961; Conscience of a Liberal (Chester Bowles), 1962; The Defeat of the Confederacy; History of the English Speaking Peoples (Churchill). Clubs: Century Assn. (N.Y.C.); St. Botolph's (Boston); Athenaeum, Lansdowne (London). Home: 405 S Pleasant St Amherst MA 01002 (summer) Lane's End Linton Cambs England

COMMANDAY, ROBERT, music editor San Francisco Chronicle. Address: 901 Mission St San Francisco, CA 94119.*

COMMERCE, ROBERT E., union ofcl. Pres., Air Line Dispatchers Assn. AFL-CIO. Office: 243 W Maple Av Vienna VA 22180*

COMMON, FRANK BREADON, Jr., Q.C., Lawyer; b. Montreal, Can., Apr. 16, 1920; s. Frank Breadon and Ruth Louise (Lang) C.; diploma in engring., Royal Mil. Coll., 1940; B. Civil Law, McGill U., 1948; created Queen's Counsel, 1959; m. Katharine Ruth Laws, Sept. 7, 1946; children—Katharine Ruth, Anne Elizabeth, Diana Melanie, Ruth Elizabeth, Jane Laws, James Lang. Admitted to Can. bar, 1948; mem. firm Montgomery, McMichael, Common, Howard, Forsyth & Kerr, and successor firms, 1948-68; partner Ogilvy, Cope, Porteous, Hansard; Marler, Montgomery & Renault, chmn. dir. of Montreal Refrigerating & Storage, Ltd., Peterson, Howell & Heather (Can.). Ltd.; v.p., dir. Gulf Trust Corp., Canadian Corps., Ltd.; chmn. finance com., dir. Gleneagles Investment Co., Ltd.; dir. Place Ville Marie Corp., Trizee Corp., Peterson, Howell & Heather, Inc. (Balt.), Canadian Salt Co., Ltd., Canadian Rock Salt Co., Ltd., Schweppes Powell Ltd., Cadbury Schweppes Powell Ltd., Selco Exploration Co. Ltd., Ralston Purina Co. (Can.), N. Am. Car (Can.) Ltd., Ciba-Geigy Can. Ltd., Beneficial Finance Co. Can., Montreal Combined Health and Red Cross Appeal. Gov., past pres., chmn. Douglas Hosp.; gov. Montreal Gen. Hosp. Ex-alderman City of Westmount, P.Q. Exec. com. Can. Red Cross. Founder pres. Can. Found. for Ednl. Devel. Served as officer Royal Can. Engrs., 1940-45. Mentioned in despatches. Mem. Can. Bar Assn. (past mem. council), Canadian Tax Found., Mil. Engrs. Assn. Can. (past pres. of the Montreal branch). Clubs: Seigniory (past pres.) (Montebello, Quebec, Canada); Mount Royal; Brook (New York City) Mount Bruno Shawbridge (P.Q.); Bayou (La.). Home: 3940 Cote des Neiges Rd Montreal 109 Quebec Canada Office: 700 Place Ville Marie Montreal 113 Quebec Canada

COMMON, ROBERT HADDON, educator; b. Larne, No. Ireland, Feb. 25, 1907; s. Robert Hall and Alice (Magill) C.; B.Sc., Queen's U., Belfast, Ireland, 1928, B.Agr., 1929, D.Sc., 1957; Ph.D., London (Eng.) U., 1935, D.Sc., 1944; m. Renate Liselotte Gueterbock, Oct. 16, 1935; children—Alice Edith (Mrs. Donald S. Layne), Christine Dorothy (Mrs. Jagat Singh), Robert Magill, Sonja Haddon, Jennifer Avery, Andrew Ainslie. Asst., then lectr. agrl. chemistry Queen's U., 1929-47; mem. faculty Macdonald Coll., McGill U., 1947—, prof. agrl. chemistry, 1947—. Fellow Royal Inst. Chemistry Great Britain and Ireland, Agrl. Inst. Can., Royal Soc. Can., Chem. Inst. Can. Author papers in field. Address: Box 223 Macdonald Coll 800 Quebec Canada

COMMONER, BARRY, biologist, educator; b. Bklyn., May 28, 1917; s. Isidore and Goldie (Yarmolinsky) C.; A.B. with honors, Columbia, 1937; M.A., Harvard, 1938, Ph.D., 1941; D.Sc., Hahnemann Med. Coll., 1963, Grinnell Coll., 1968, Lehigh U., 1969, Williams Coll., 1970, Ripon Coll., 1971; U. Cal., 1967; m. Gloria C. Gordon, Dec. 1, 1946; children—Lucy Alison, Frederic Gordon. Asst. biology Harvard, 1938-40; instr. biology Queens Coll., 1940-42; asso. editor Sci. Illustrated, 1946-47; asso. prof. plant physiology Washington U., St. Louis, 1947-53, prof., 1953—, chmn. dept. botany, 1965-69, dir. Center for the Biology of Natural Systems, 1965—. Pres. St. Louis Com. for Nuclear Information, 1965-66, bd. dirs., 1958—; mem. Nat. Tb Commn. on Air Conservation, 1966—; co-chmn. Scientists Inst. Pub. Information, 1963- 69, chmn. bd. dirs., 1969—. Served to lt. USNR, 1942-46. Recipient Newcomb Cleveland prize A.A.A.S., 1953; 1st Humanist award Internat. Humanist and Ethical Union, 1970. Fellow A.A.A.S. (chmn. com. on sci. in promotion of human welfare 1958-65, dir. 1967—); mem. Soc. Biol. Chemists, Soc. Gen. Physiologists, Am. Soc. Plant Physiologists, Nat. Parks Assn. (trustee 1968-70), Soil Assn. Eng. (hon. life v.p.), Phi Beta Kappa, Sigma Xi, Editorial bd. World Book Ency., 1967—; mem. adv. bd. Science Year, 1965—, Science and Survival, 1966. Home: 25 Crestwood Dr Clayton MO 63105 Office: Washington U St Louis MO 63130

COMO, PERRY, singer; b. Canonsburg, Pa., May 18, s. Pietro and Lucille (Travaglini) C.; student pub. schs., Canonsburg. With Carlone Band, later Ted Weems, 1937; singer night clubs, Victor Records; screen debut Something for the Boys, 20th Century Fox; motion pictures include: Doll Face, If I'm Lucky; now star Perry Como show NBC-TV. Named best vocalist Motion Picture Daily TV poll, 1952-53; Emmy, Peabody, Christopher awards, 1956; named personality of year Variety Club, 1956; decorated knight comdr. Equestrian Order Holy Sepulchre Jerusalem. Office: 485 Madison Av New York City NY 10022

COMPERE, CLINTON LEE, physician; b. Greenville, Tex., Feb. 17, 1911; s. Edward L. and Clara (Davison) C.; B.S., U. Chgo., 1936, M.D., 1937; m. Katharine Gram, Mar. 31, 1949; children—Clinton Lee, Mary Katherine. Intern Henry Ford Hosp., Detroit, 1938-39; resident Blodgett Meml. Hosp., Grand Rapids, Mich., 1939-40; pvt. practice orthopaedic surgery, Chgo., 1966—; mem. sr. attending staff Chgo. Wesley Meml. Hosp., 1949—, chief staff, 1964-66; acad. dir. Prosthetic Research Center, Chgo., 1955—, Prosthetic- Orthotic Edn., Chgo., 1958—; cons. 5th Army Hdqrs., 1947—; cons. amputee clinics Regional Office VA, 1947—; asso. prof. orthopaedic surgery Northwestern U. Med. Sch., 1954-65, prof., 1965—. Vice chmn. bd. Rehab. Inst. Chgo.; mem. med. adv. com. Ill. Div. Vocational Rehab. Served to lt. col., M.C., AUS, 1940-46. Recipient citation Pres.'s Com. Employment Physically Handicapped, 1959. Diplomate Am. Bd. Orthopaedic Surgery. Mem. Am. Acad. Orthopaedic Surgeons (sec. 1959-62, pres. 1963-64), Ill., Chgo. med. socs., A.M.A., A.C.S., Am., 20th Century orthopaedic assns., Chgo. Orthopaedic Soc., Clin Orthopaedic Soc., Ill. Soc. Med. Research, Internat. Soc. Orthopaedic Surgery and Traumatology, Alpha Omega Alpha. Co-author: Fracture Treatment, 1937; also articles. Home: 2600 Orrington Av Evanston IL 60201 Office: 737 N Michigan Av Chicago IL 60611

COMPERE, EDWARD LYON, orthopedic surgeon; b. Chickasha, Okla., Sept. 7, 1901; s. Edward Lyon and Clara (Davison) C.; student Okla. Bapt. U., 1919-20; B.A., Baylor U., 1922; M.S., U. Chgo., 1924; M.D., Rush Med. Coll., 1926; LL.D., Beloit Coll., 1971; m. Virginia Odell, Aug. 10, 1926; children—Edward Lyon III, John Curtis, James Lawrence. Instr. physiology Loyola Med. Sch., Chgo., 1924-26; instr. surgery U. Chgo. Med. Sch., 1928-30, asst. prof. surgery, 1930-36, asso. prof., 1936-40; attending surgeon, chief div. orthopedic surgery U. Chgo. Clinics, 1931-40; staff Home for Destitute and Crippled Children, Home for Convalescent Crippled Children, 1930-40, Presbyn. Hosp., 1940- 41; cons. orthopedic surgeon Chgo. Meml. Hosp., 1940-55; asso. prof. surgery Rush Med. Goll., 1940; asso. prof. orthopedic surgery Northwestern U. Med. Coll., 1941-52, prof., 1952—, chmn. dept., 1953—; chmn. dept. orthopedic surgery Chgo. Wesley Meml. Hosp., 1941—; attending orthopedic surgeon, chief orthopedic div. Children's Meml. Hosp., Chgo., 1943-53; cons. orthopedic surgery, chmn. dept. VA Research Hosp., Chgo.; Fulbright vis. prof. U. São Paulo, Ribeirão, Preto, Brazil, 1963. Pres. Profl. Life and Casualty Co. Trustee No. Bapt. Theol. Sem., Bapt. Home and Hosp., Beloit Coll. (chmn. 1955-58). Served with S.A.T.C., 1917; spl. cons. surgeon gen. AUS, 1948-49. Fellow A.C.S., Internat. Coll. Surgeons (pres. U.S. sect. 1958-60; pres. 1967-70); mem. A.M.A. (chmn. sect. orthopedic surgery 1956-57), Am. Orthopedic Assn. (pres. 1966-67), Greater Chgo. Churchmen (pres.), Chgo. Orthopedic Soc., Am. Acad. Orthopedic Surgeons, Sigma Xi, Phi Chi. Baptist. Clubs: University (Chgo.); Glendora Country (Cal.). Author: Pictorial Handbook of Fracture Treatment (with Drs. Sam W. Banks and Clinton L. Compere), 1943; Microbes That Cripple (with T. A. Turner), 1944. Editor; Year Book of Orthopedics and Traumatic Surgery, 1947-59; trustee, sec. bd. trustees, asso. editor Jour. of Bone and Joint Surgery, 1954-57. Home: 832 W Huntington Dr Arcadia CA 91006 Office: El Monte Medical Center 3131 Santa Anita Av El Monte CA 91734

COMPTON, CHARLES DANIEL, educator; b. Elizabeth, N.J., Jan. 8, 1915; s. Charles Daniel and Janie (Little) C.; A.B., Princeton, 1940; Ph.D. in Chemistry, Yale, 1943; m. Ida Lightman, Dec. 19, 1953. Research chemist Calco Chem. Co., 1943; instr. Princeton, 1944-46; research asso. Manhattan Dist. Project, Princeton, 1943-44; mem. faculty Williams Coll., 1946—, prof., 1957—, chmn. chemistry dept., 1964—, Halford R. Clark prof. Natural sci., 1966—. Allied Chem. and Dye Co. fellow, 1942-43. Fellow A.A.A.S.; mem. Am. Chem. Soc., Phi Beta Kappa, Sigma Xi. Author: Introduction to Chemistry; also articles. Home: 1 Grandview Dr Williamstown, MA 01267.

COMPTON, JAMES C., jurist; b. Fayetteville, Ark., Dec. 19, 1886; LL.B., Cumberland U., 1908, J.D., 1951; m. Bessie Johnson; children—Helen, James C., Ben. Admitted to N.M. state bar, 1909; served as dist. atty, 9th Jud. Dist. of N.M.; judge 9th Jud. Dist., 1941-47; apptd. to N.M. Supreme Ct., 1947, elected for 8 yr. term, 1948, 56, 64. Home: 501 Armenta St Santa Fe NM 87501 Office: The Supreme Court Sante Fe NM 87501

COMPTON, JOHN JOSEPH, educator; b. Chgo., May 17, 1928; s. Arthur Holly and Betty (McCloskey) C.; B.A., Coll. Wooster, 1949; M.A., Yale, 1951, Ph.D., 1953; m. Marjorie Ann Yaple, July 8, 1950; children—Elizabeth Holly, Catherine Marchus, John Arthur. Mem. faculty Vanderbilt U., Nashville, 1952—, prof. philosophy, 1968—, chmn. dept., 1967—. Bd. dirs. Nashville Community Relations Conf. and Tenn. Council Human Relations, 1960—. Kent Fellow, 1951; Belgian Am. Found. fellow, 1956-57; recipient Harbison award Danforth Found., 1966. Mem. Am. Philos. Assn. (sec.-treas. 1971—), Metaphys. Soc., Soc. Phenomenology and Existential Philosophy, So. Soc. Philosophy and Psychology, Phi Beta Kappa, Omicron Delta Kappa. Author articles in field. Home: 3708 Whitland Av Nashville TN 37205

COMPTON, JOHN ROBINSON, rake co. exec.; b. Elmira, N.Y., Feb. 24, 1923; s. William Randall and Ada (Viele) C.; B.S. cum laude, Syracuse U., 1950; m. Jean Elinor York, Apr. 17, 1943; children—John York, Jan Elizabeth (Mrs. Harriss M. Ganey), Julie Ann. Accountant, factory mgr. York Modern Corp., Unadilla, N.Y., 1947-51, pres., 1969—, also treas., dir.; accountant Brewer-Titchener Corp., Binghamton, N.Y., 1951-52; div. controller Riegel Paper Corp., Riegelwood, N.C., 1953-65, corporate controller, N.Y.C., 1966-69; pres. York Modern Corp., 1969—; Mail-Print, Inc., 1970—. Served to 2d lt. USAAF, World War II. Methodist. Home: RD 2 Bainbridge, NY 13733. Office: 40 S Main St Bainbridge NY 13733

COMPTON, RALPH THEODORE, assn. exec.; b. Avalon, Cal., June 15, 1903; s. Ralph Smith and Henrietta (Treat) C.; A.B., U. Cal., 1924, A.M., 1926; Ph.D., Yale, 1929; m. Ethel Evans, May 5, 1930 (dec.); children—Ralph Theodore, Patricia Jean; m. 2d, Mary B. Brown. Mar. 18, 1961. Instr., Yale, 1926- 29; tax staff Nat. Indsl. Conf. Bd., 1929-30; dir. Governor's Taxation Com. of Ohio, 1930-31; dir. research Asso. Industries of Mo., 1931-41; social security dir. N.A.M., 1941-48; v.p. Asso. Fund, Inc., 1939-41; lectr. St. Louis U., 1939, 40; asst. dir. Nat. Indsl. Council, Washington, 1943-50, exec. dir., 1950-59; v.p. govt. relations div. N.A.M., Washington, 1960-67, v.p., 1967-68, govt. relations cons., 1968- 70; econ. adviser Chevy Chase Bank & Trust Co., 1968—. Adv. council Tax Inst., 1947-51. Mem. Am. Econ. Assn., Nat. Tax Assn., Am., Washington trade assn. execs., Sigma Pi, Artus. Methodist (trustee). Clubs: Yale (N.Y.C.); University, Capitol Hill, Congressional Country (Washington). Author: (compiled with Fred R. Fairchild) Economic Problems, 1928, 30; Fiscal Problems of Rural Decline, 1929; State and Local Taxation of Property, 1930; The Social Security Payroll Taxes, 1940. Home: 10701 Burbank Dr Potomac MD 20854 Office: 918 16th St Washington DC 20006

COMPTON, RANDOLPH PARKER, investment banker; b. Macon, Mo., Mar. 18, 1892; s. William R. and Caroline (Parker) C.; grad. Smith Acad., St. Louis, 1911; LL.B., Princeton, 1915; postgrad. Harvard Bus. Sch., 1943; m. Dorothy Danforth, Oct. 11, 1917; children—W. Danforth (dec.), James Randolph, Ann Randolph (Mrs. Ellis M. Stephens), John Parker (dec.). Vice pres. charge N.Y. office, William R. Compton Co., 1919-29; propr. municipal bond firm, N.Y.C., 1929-34; v.p. charge municipal bond dept. Lazard Freres & Co., N.Y.C., 1934-41, Union Securities Corp., N.Y.C., 1941-42; corp. relations mgr. Republic Aviation Co., Ltd., Farmingdale, L.I., N.Y., 1943-44; v.p. Kidder, Peabody & Co., Inc., Investment bankers, N.Y. C., 1945—. Past treas., trustee Scarsdale (N.Y.) Found.; trustee, mem. bd. Meharry Medical Coll.; chmn. bd. trustees Fund for Peace, N.Y.C. Served as ensign USN, World War I. Mem. United World Federalists (controller). Republican. Conglist (trustee). Clubs: Bond, Recess, Princeton (N.Y.C.); Elm (Princeton); Fox Meadow Tennis, Manursing Island (Scarsdale, N.Y.). Home: 53 Brookby Rd Scarsdale NY 10583 Office: 20 Exchange Pl New York City NY 10005

COMPTON, ROBERT ROSS, educator; b. Los Angeles, July 21, 1922; s. Charles Ross and Hattie (Brown) C.; B.A., Stanford, 1943, Ph.D., 1949; divorced; children—Peter S., Candace B., Andrew R., James D., John S. Mem. faculty Stanford (Cal.) U., 1947—, asso. prof. geology, 1956-61, prof., 1961—; geologist U.S. Geol. Survey, 1943, 50-51, 66— (part time). Served with USNR, 1944-46. NSF postdoctoral fellow, 1955-56; Guggenheim fellow, 1963-64. Fellow Geol. Soc. Am., Geol. Soc. London. Author: Manual of Field Geology, 1962. Asso. editor Bulletin Geol. Soc. Am., 1968—. Office: Dept Geology Stanford U Stanford CA 94305

COMPTON, RUSSELL JOHN, educator, clergyman; b. Peru, Ind., Apr. 5, 1909; s. Wills E. and Effie A. (Overman) C.; A.B., Manchester Coll., 1931; B.D., Garrett Bibl. Inst., 1935; Ph.D., Yale, 1939; m. Susanna Gump Aug. 31, 1935; children—Clyde Douglas, John Willis. Ordained to ministry, Meth. Ch., 1941; prof. religion Wesley Coll., Grand Forks, N.D., 1939-41; prof. religion, head dept. philosophy and religion Hendrix Coll., Conway, Ark., 1941-43, Hamline U., St. Paul, 1943-5l; prof. philosophy DePauw U., 1951—, head dept. philosophy and religion, 1952—. Mem. Am. Philosophy Assn., Nat. Assn. Bibl. Instrs. Home: 114 Northwood Blvd Greencastle IN 46135

COMPTON, W DALE, physicist; b. Chrisman, Ill., Jan. 7, 1929; s. Roy L. and Marcia (Wood) D.; B.A., Wabash Coll., 1949; M.S., U. Okla., 1951; Ph.D., U. Ill., 1955; m. Jeanne C. Parker, Oct. 14, 1951; children—Gayle Corinne, Donald Leonard, Duane Arthur. Physicist, U.S. Naval Ordnance Test Sta., China Lake, Cal., 1951-52, U.S. Naval Research Lab., Washington, 1955-61; prof. physics U. Ill. at Urbana, 1961-70, dir. coordinated sci. lab., 1965-70, dir. chem. and phys. scis., sci. research staff Ford Motor Co., Dearborn, Mich., 1970—. Fellow Am. Phys. Soc., Washington Acad. Scis.; mem. Research Soc. Am. Author: (with J.H. Schulman) Color Centers in Solids, 1962. Editor Interaction of Science and Technology, 1969. Home: 5565 Forman Dr Birmingham MI 48010

COMPTON, WALTER AMES, drug mfg. exec.; b. Elkhart, Ind., Apr. 22, 1911; s. Herman A. and Grace (Cooper) C.; A.B., Princeton, 1933; M.D., Harvard, 1937; m. Phoebe Emerson, June 22, 1935; children—Cynthia, Joan, Phoebe, Walter Ames, Gordon. Intern, Billings Hosp., 1938; med. and research dir. Miles Lab., Inc., Elkhart, Ind., 1939-42, v.p., charge med. and research div., 1946, now pres., chief exec. officer, also dir.; dir. Miles Labs. Ltd. (Eng.), Miles Pan Am., Inc. Served M.C., AUS 1942-46. Mem. Am., Ind. med. assns., Elkart Med. Soc., Royal Soc. of Medicine (Eng.), A.A.A.S., N.Y. Acad. of Science. Presby. Home: 2225 Greenleaf Blvd Elkhart IN 46514 Office: 1127 Myrtle St Elkhart IN 46514

COMPTON, WILLIAM RANDALL, lawyer; b. Elmira, N.Y., July 9, 1902; s. William R. and Helen R. (Tubbs) C.; LL.B., Albany Law Sch., 1928; M.B.A., Harvard, 1931; J.S.D., Cornell U., 1933; m. Norma E. Haynes, Mar. 27, 1946; children—William Randall, Anne. Prof. bus. adminstrn., dean Green Mountain Jr. Coll., Poultney, Vt., 1931-32; admitted to N.Y. bar, 1933, practiced in Elmira until 1935; professorial lectr. law George Washington U., 1935-52; gen. counsel Q.M.C., Dept. of Army, 1943-56; dep. gen. counsel Dept. of Army, 1956-63; professorial lectr. law Am. U., 1963-65; prof. Utah State U., 1965-68. Served from capt. to lt. col. AUS, 1942-45. Decorated Legion of Merit; recipient Exceptional Civilian Service award, Meritorious Civilian Service award. Mem. Order of Coif. Author: Digest of Safe Deposit Custom, 1933. Editor: Cases on Domestic Relations, 1951; 1965 Supplement to Compton Cases and Materials on Domestic Relations. Co-editor: Cases on Domestic Relations (with Madden), 1940. Home: 1135 Annalue Dr Auburn AL 36830

COMROE, JULIUS HIRAM, Jr., educator; b. York, Pa., Mar. 13, 1911; s. Julius Hiram and Mollie (Levy) C.; A.B., U. of Pa., 1931, M.D., 1934; Commonwealth Fund fellow, Nat. Inst. Med. Research, London, 1939; M.D. (hon.), Karolinska Inst., Stockholm, 1968; D.Sc., U. Chgo., 1968; m. Jeanette Wolfson, June 30, 1936; 1 dau., Joan Von Gehr. Interne, Hosp. of U. of Pa., 1934-36; instr. in pharmacology U. of Pa. Med. Sch., 1936-40, asso. in pharmacology, 1940-42, asst. prof., 1942-46; prof. physiology and pharmacology U. of Pa. Grad. Sch. of Medicine, 1946-57; prof. of physiology, dir. Cardiovascular Research Inst., U. Cal. Med. Center, San Francisco, 1957—; chmn. 1st Teaching Inst. (1953), Asso. Am. Med. Colls., also chmn. 1961 Inst.; chmn. Physiology Study Section, 1955-58; mem. bd. sci. counselors Nat. Heart Inst., 1957-61; mem. Nat. Adv. Mental Health Council, 1958-62; mem. Nat. Adv. Heart Council, 1963-67; mem. U.S. National committee I.U.P.S., 1962-68; mem. Nat. Adv. Heart and Lung Council, 1970—; chmn. I.U.P.S. Commn. on Med. Physiology, 1970—. Cons. med. research div. CWS, 1944-46. Recipient Am. Physiol. Soc. Travel award, 1938, Distinguished Achievement award, Modern Medicine, 1961, Research Achievement award Am. Heart Assn., 1968, Coll. medal Am. Coll. Chest Physicians, 1970, Mayo Soley award Western Soc. Clin. Investigation, 1971. Fellow A.C.P., A.A.A.S., Am. Coll. Cardiology, (hon.); mem. Assn. Am. Physicians, Am. Physiol. Soc. (pres. 1960-61), Am. Soc. for Pharmacology and Exptl. Therapeutics (councilor 1953-56), Nat. Acad. Scis. (mem. bd. of medicine 1967), Am. Acad. Arts and Scis., Harvey Soc. (hon. mem.), Am. Soc. for Clin. Investigation, Phi Beta Kappa, Sigma Xi, Alpha Omega Alpha. Author: Physiological Basis for 02 Therapy, 1950; Methods in Medical Research, Vol. 2, 1950; The Lung: Clinical Physiology and Pulmonary Function Tests, 1955, 62; Physiology of Respiration, 1964. Editor: Physiology for Physicians, 1963-66, Circulation Research, 1966-70; Ann. Rev. Physiology, 1971—. Mem. editorial bd. Am. Jour. Physiology, 1954-62, Pharmacological Revs., 1949-51, Jour. Med. Edn., 1955-60, Am. Rev. of Respiratory Diseases, 1959-63. Home: 555 Laurent Rd Hillsborough, CA 94010. Office: Cardiovascular Research Inst U Cal Med Center San Francisco CA 94122

COMSTOCK, EDWARD GARFIELD, advt. exec.; b. Englewood, N.J., June 25, 1907; s. Harry Garfield and Laura (Woolridge) C.; ed. Rutgers U.; m. Anita Inman, July 1, 1932; 1 dau., Janice Inman. With advt. dept. Best & Co., J.C. Penney Co., 1930- 37; asst. prof. econs. U. P.R., 1937-38; with Cunningham & Walsh, Inc., and Newell-Emmett, predecessor firm, 1939—, sr. v.p., dir., chmn. trustees profit sharing trust fund, 1953—. With Office Q.M. Gen., War Dept., 1942-45. Mem. Am. Econ. Assn., S.A.R. Mem. Reformed Ch. Clubs: Union League (N.Y.C.); Siwanoy Country, Field (Bronxville). Home: 22 Sagamore Nest Rd Bronxville NY 10708 Office: 260 Madison Av New York City NY 10016

COMSTOCK, GEORGE WILLS, educator, epidemiologist; b. Niagara Falls, N.Y., Jan. 7, 1915; s. George Frederick and Ella G. (Wills) C.; B.S. with honors, Antioch Coll., 1937; M.D., Harvard, 1941; M.P.H., U. Mich., 1951; Dr.P.H., Johns Hopkins, 1956; m. Margaret Karr, Aug. 29, 1939; children—Gordon F., Lloyd K., Martha W. Intern U.S. Marine Hosp., Balt., 1941-42; commd. officer USPHS, 1941-62; dir. Muscogee County Tb Study, Columbus, Ga., 1946-55; epidemiologist Tb program USPHS, 1956-62; mem. faculty Johns Hopkins Sch. Hygiene and Pub. Health, 1962—, prof. epidemiology, 1966- -; cons. Tb program USPHS, 1962—, disease control study sect. NIH, 1964- 67; dir. Tng. Center Pub. Health Research, 1963—. Diplomate Am. Bd. Preventive Medicine. Fellow Am. Pub. Health Assn.; mem. Am. Thoracic Soc., Am. Epidemiological Soc., Washington County Med. Soc., N.Y. Acad. Scis. Author articles in field. Home: Route 2 Box 273 Smithsburg, MD 21783. Office: Box 2067 Hagerstown MD 21740

COMSTOCK, LYNDON DAVIS, banker; b. St. Joseph, Mich., Feb. 17, 1922; s. Lyndon M. and Margaret M. (Flexman) C.; m. Lillian Gasparac, July 2, 1949; children—Lyndon B., Deborah C., Elizabeth C., Susan L. With Suburban Trust & Savs. Bank, Oak Park. Ill., 1941-42, 46-47; nat. bank examiner Treasury Dept., 1947-56; pres. Hackley Union Nat Bank, Muskegon, Mich., 1956—. Home; 922 Oakmere Dr North Muskegon MI 49445 Office: 289 W Western Av Muskegon MI 49443

COMSTOCK, RALPH ERNEST, educator; b. Spring Valley, Minn., July 19, 1912; s. Charles Roy and Bertha (Drewes) C.; B.S., U. Minn., 1934, M.S., 1936, Ph.D., 1938; m. Helen Agnes Bartel, Aug. 8, 1936; children—Cynthia Pam (dec.), Mary Sue, John Alan. Instr., then asst. prof. animal husbandry U. Minn., 1937-43; asso. prof. animal husbandry and exptl. statistics N.C. state Coll., 1943-46; head dept. animal husbandry P.R. Agrl. Exptl. Sta., 1946-47; prof. exptl. statistics N.C. State Coll., 1947-57; prof. animal husbandry U. Minn., 1957-65, prof. dept. of genetics and cell biology, 1965—, Regent's prof. genetics, 1968—, head dept., 1965-68. Mem. Am. Soc. Animal Sci. (award animal breeding and genetics 1966), Biometrics Soc., Genetics Soc. Am., Am. Soc. Naturalists, Crop Sci. Soc. Am., Soc. Study Evolution, A.A.A.S., Am. Inst. Biol. Scis., Sigma Xi. Home: 1958 Roselawn Av W St Paul MN 55113

COMSTOCK, RALPH J., Jr., banker; b. Rexburg, Ida., Oct. 18, 1917; s. Ralph J. and Gladys (Bassett) C.; student U. Ida., 1935-37; B.S., U. Utah, 1939; grad. Pacific Coast Sch. Banking, U. Wash. 1954; m. Bernice Broomfield, July 3, 1942; children—Ralph J. III, Christine, Robert Stephen. With First Security Bank Ida., N.A., Boise, 1946—, exec. v.p., 1962-65; pres., 1965—, also dir.; v.p., dir., mem. exec. com. First Security Corp., Salt Lake City; v.p., dir. First Security Co., Salt Lake City; dir. Am. Fine Foods, Inc., Payette. mem. regional adv. com. 13th Nat. Bank Region, 1968-69. Treas. Ida. div. Am. Cancer Soc., 1963-68. Bd. dirs. Pacific Coast Sch. Banking, 1966—, chmn. bd., 1970; trustee St. Luke's Hosp., Boise, Boise Jr. Coll. Dist. Served to maj. AUS, 1941-46. Recipient Businessman of Year award Alpha Kappa Psi, Ida. State U., 1970; Distinguished Eagle Scout award Boy Scouts Am., 1970. Mem. Am. (Ida. v.p. 1968), Ida. (pres. 1968) bankers assns., Greater Boise (pres. 1967), Ida. (dir., mem. exec. com., pres. 1970-71) chambers commerce, Asso. Taxpayers Ida. (pres. 1963-65), Am. Legion (past post comdr.), 40 and 8, S.A.R., Sigma Chi, Alpha Kappa Psi (hon.). Mason, Rotarian (pres. Pocatello 1956), Elk. Republican. Clubs: Arid, Hillcrest Country (Boise). Home: 4023 Del Monte Dr Boise ID 83704 Office: PO Box 7069 Boise ID 83707

COMSTOCK, WILLIAM COLLINS, singer, composer; b. Rockbridge, O., Feb. 1, 1924; s. Charles Harrison and Louella (Collins) C.; student Ohio Wesleyan U., 1942, 46-47; m. Susan Gail Siegler, June 25, 1953; 1 son, Geoffrey Charles. Mem. singing group Four Freshmen, 1960—; partner Hornblower Music Internat.; pres. Devonshire Prodns., Inc. Winner Playboy Mag. All-Stars Poll, 1968. Mem. A.S.C.A.P., Nat. Acad. Recording Arts and Scis., Am. Guild Authors and Composers. Composer: Oh Lonely Winter, 1961; Lonely For My Love, 1962; Act III, 1963; Don't Make Me Sorry, 1964; Nashville Blues, 1964; Summer Has Gone, 1965; Napoli, 1966; I've Had One Too Many, 1966; Nowhere To Go, 1966; Terry's Little Tune, 1967; Come Live Your Life With Me, 1968; Christmas Lullaby, 1968. Home: 12526 Woodley Av Granada Hills, CA 91344. Office: 8720 Woodley Av Sepulveda CA 91343

COMTE, GEORGE RICHARD, broadcasting co. exec.; b. Marinette, Wis., June 1, 1913; s. Eugene Arthur and Nellie (Fitzpatrick) C.; B.A. in Polit. Sci., U. Wis., 1935; grad. Command and Gen. Staff Sch., 1944; m. Rita Moran, May 11, 1959; children by previous marriage—Karen (Mrs. Daniel Sullivan), Stephen. Announcer, newscaster radio sta. WTMJ, Milw., 1935-50, asst. sta. mgr., 1950-53, sta. mgr., 1953-56, mgr. radio and TV, 1956-58, gen. mgr. radio and TV, also v.p. Jour. Co., 1958; gen. mgr. Teltron, CATV Div., 1966—, Midwestern Relay, Microwave Div., 1970—. Sec.-treas. NBC-TV Affiliates Com., 1962-67. Mem. Gov.'s Com. Econ. Devel., 1967-71. Corp. mem. United Fund, Milw. Symphony Corp., Boy Scouts Am. Served to lt. col. AUS, 1941-46. Mem. Am. Forestry Assn., Radio Advt. Bur. (dir. 1961—), Nat. Assn. Broadcasters (dir. 1970—), Assn. Broadcasting Engring. Standards (v.p. 1961-65, pres. 1965—), Milw. Ad Club (dir. 1956-64), Wis. Alumni Assn., Res. Officers Assn. Kiwanian (pres. 1963). Clubs: Ozaukee Country (Mequon, Wis.); Curling (dir. 1968—) (Milw.). Home: 403 Alta Loma Dr Thiensville WI 53092 Office: 720 E Capitol Dr Milwaukee WI 53201

CONABLE, BARBER B., Jr., congressman; b. Warsaw, N.Y., Nov. 2, 1922; s. Barber B. and Agnes G. (Gouinlock) C.; A.B., Cornell U., 1942, LL.B., 1948; m. Charlotte Williams, Sept. 13, 1952; 4 children. Admitted to N.Y. bar, 1948; practice in Buffalo, 1948-50, in Batavia, 1952-64; mem. N.Y. State Senate from 53d Dist., 1963-64; mem. 89th-92d Congresses, 37th Dist. N.Y., mem. ways and means com., joint econ. com., chmn. Ho. Republican research com. Pres. Genesee United Fund, Genesee Health Found. Trust. N.Y. Hosp. Rev. and Planning Council. Served with USMCR, 1942-46, 50-51. Republican. Rotarian (pres. Batavia). Editor Cornell Law Quar., 1947-48. Home: 10532 Alexander Rd Alexander NY 14005 Office: House Office Bldg Washington DC 20515

CONANT, FRANK E., real estate exec.; b. Malden, Mass., Oct. 31, 1909; s. Frank E. and Florence (Planta) C.; student Boston U.; grad. Advanced Mgmt. Program, Harvard, 1955; m. Frances Towne, June 19, 1943; 1 son, F. Scott. With First Boston Corp., 1927-38; v.p. Lawrence Warehouse Co., N.Y.C., 1938-48, Irving Trust Co., N.Y.C., 1948-54, Chase Manhattan Bank, N.Y.C., 1954-69; vice chmn. bd., chmn. exec. com. Cushman & Wakefield, N.Y.C., 1969—; dir., mem. exec. com. Metro-Goldwyn-Mayer, Inc., P.R. Mallory Co.; dir. Chgo. Pneumatic Tool Co., Inter-Credit Agy., Inc., Transcontinental Investing Co., Unishops, Inc.; chmn. exec. com., dir. Sterling Nat. Bank, N.Y.C.; dir. P. R. Mallory & Co., Inc. Hon. dep. chief Fire Dept. N.Y.C., 1967—; pres., chmn., dir. Fifth Av. Assn., 1959—; chmn. commerce and industry div. Salvation Army, N.Y.C., 1961-62; vice chmn. spl. gifts com. N.Y.C. council Boy Scouts Am., 1958-63; dir. U.S.O., N.Y.C.; nat. trustee, N.Y. chmn. Ducks Unlimited. Served to maj. USAAF, World War II. Clubs: Union League, Sky (N.Y.C.); Woodway Country (past dir., treas.), Woodway Gun (pres.) (Darien); Harvard (New Canaan, Conn.); U.S. Seniors Golf Assn.; Am. Seniors Golf Assn.; Mid-Ocean (Bermuda). Home: Half Mile Rd Darien CT 06820 Office: 529 Fifth Av New York City NY 10017

CONANT, HOWARD ROSSET, steel co. exec.; b. Chgo., Sept. 30, 1924; s. Louis J. and Fredericka (Rosset) Cohn; B.S., U. Pa., 1947; m. Doris S. Kaplan, Dec. 14, 1947; children—Alison Sue, Howard R., Meredith Ann. Pres., dir. Interstate Steel Co., Des Plaines, Ill., 1947-71, chmn. bd., 1971—; pres., dir. Elliott Paint & Varnish Co. (Chgo.); dir. Argus, Inc., 1964-66, Caspers Tin Plate Co., 1962-65; chmn. bd. dirs. White Products Corp., 1965-67. Discussion leader Center Study of Continuing Edn., 1955-62; dir. Com. for Sane Nuclear Policy, 1964-69; mem. Bus. Execs. Move for Vietnam Peace, 1965—. Served with AUS, 1943-46; PTO. Mem. Young Pres.'s Orgn. Clubs: Arts (Chgo.); Ridge and Valley Tennis (Glenview). Home: 736 Greenacres St Glenview IL 60025 Office: 401 Touhy Av Des Plaines IL 60018

CONANT, HOWARD SOMERS, educator, artist; b. Beloit, Wis., May 5, 1921; s. Rufus P. and Edith B. (Somers) C.; student Art Students League of N.Y., 1944-45; B.S., Wis. State Coll., 1946; M.S., U. Wis., 1947; Ed.D., U. Buffalo, 1950; m. Florence C. Craft, June 18, 1943; children—Judith Lynne, Jeffrey Scott. Instr. art, asst. head housefellow U. Wis., 1946-47; instr. advanced painting Amherst Adult Sch., Snyder, N.Y., 1947-55; asst. prof. art State Coll. for Tchrs., Buffalo, 1947-50, prof. art, 1950-55; moderator weekly TV program, Fun to Learn About Art, WBEN-TV, Buffalo, 1951-55; chmn. dept. art edn. also chmn. art collection, N.Y. U., 1955—, also head div. creative arts; art edn. cons. to NBC-TV, also Girl Scouts Am. tv series, 1958-60, Midwest Program on Airborne TV Instrn., 1960; field reader, also Title III program cons. U.S. Office of Edn.; adviser N.Y. State Council on Arts, 1962-63, Conn. Commn. on Arts, 1967-68; mem. adv. com. Housatonic Community Coll., 1970—; exhibited one man shows, also represented maj. group exhbns. and coll. art collections. State Dept. lectr., India, 1964. Dir. Waukesha County (Wis.) YMCA Art Program, 1946-48. Dir. Children's Creative Art Found., 1959-60; mem. adv. com. Coll. of Potomac, 1966—, Served as lt. USAAF, 1943-46, Recipient medal Nat. Gallery Art, 1966; Distinguished Alumnus award U. Wis., 1968. Mem. N.Y. State. Art Tchrs. Assn., Nat. Art Edn. Assn., Eastern Arts Assn., Nat. Com. art Edn. (council, chmn. 1962-63), Inst. for Study of Art in Edn. (mem. bd. govs., pres. 1965-68), Internat. Soc. Edn. Through Art. Club: Torch (pres. 1965-66) (N.Y.C.). Author: (with Arne Randall) Art in Education, 1959, 63. Author, editor: Vol. 4, Masterpieces of the Arts, New Wonder World Cultural Library, 1963; Seminar on Elementary and Secondary School Education in the Visual Arts, 1965; Art Workshop Leaders Planning Guide, 1958. Author: Art Education, 1964. Contbr. articles profl. publs. Home: 81 Stony Run New Rochelle NY 10804 Office: N Y U Washington Sq New York City NY 10003

CONANT, JAMES BRYANT, educator, former U.S. ambassador; b. Dorchester Mass., Mar. 26, 1893; s. James Scott and Jennet Orr (Bryant) C.; A.B., Harvard, 1913, Ph.D., 1916; also numerous hon. degrees; m. Grace Thaver Richards, Apr. 17, 1921; children—James Richards, Theodore Richards. Prof. chemistry Harvard, 1919-33, pres., 1933-53, now pres. emeritus; U.S. high commr. for Germany, 1953-55; U.S. ambassador to Fed. Republic Germany, 1955-57; condr. study on the American Pub. High Sch., 1957-62, study of the Edn. of Am. Tchrs., 1962-63 (both under grant from Carnegie Corp. N.Y.). Chmn. Nat. Def. Research Com., 1941-46; dep. dir. OSRD, 1941-46; mem. gen. adv. com. AEC, 1947-52; ednl. adviser to Ford Found. in Berlin, Germany, 1963-65. Served CWS, U.S. Army 1917-18. Author: On Understanding Science, 1947; Education in a Divided World, 1948; Science and Common Sense, 1951; Modern Science and Modern Man, 1952; Education and Liberty, 1953; The Citadel of Learning, 1956; Germany and Freedom, 1958; The American High School Today, 1959; The Child, The Parent, and the State, 1959; Education in the Junior High School Years, 1960; Slums and Suburbs; A Commentary on Schools in Metropolitan Areas, 1961; The Education of American Teachers, 1963; Two Modes of Thought, 1964; Shaping Educational Policy, 1964; The Comprehensive High School, 1967; My Several Lives, 1970; (with N. H. Black) a high sch. chemistry textbook; also other textbooks on organic chemistry. Editor: Harvard Case Histories in Experimental Science, 2 vols., 1957. Address: 200 E 66th St New York City NY 10021

CONANT, JOSEPH M., educator; B.A., Columbia, 1934, M.A., 1936, Ph.D., 1953. Prof. classics Emory U., Atlanta. Office: Classics Dept Emory U Atlanta GA 30322*

CONANT, KENNETH JOHN, educator, archaeologist; b. Neenah, Wis., June 28, 1894; s. John Franklin and Lucie Ell (Micklesen) C.; A.B., Harvard, 1915, M.Arch., 1919, Ph.D., 1925; Litt.D. (hon.), Lawrence Coll., 1933; Docteur de l'Université de Dijon (hon.), 1950; D.Litt., U. Ill., 1966; m. Marie A. Schneider, Sept. 1, 1923; children—Kenneth John, John Simon; m. 2d, Isabel Pope, Jan. 14, 1956. Archtl. draftsman, instr. Harvard, 1920-23, faculty instr., later asst. prof., asso. prof., 1923-26, prof., 1936-56, prof. emeritus, 1956—; George A. Miller exchange prof. U. Ill., 1955; exchange prof. The Sorbonne, Paris, France, 1935-36, 50, Nat. U. Mexico, 1942; hon. lectr. U. Buenos Aires, 1947; mem. Carnegie Instn. expedn. to Yucatan, 1926; mem. Nat. Geog. expdn. to N.M., 1926; Guggenheim fellowship, 1927, 55-58; research asso. in archaeology excavating abbey of Cluny, France for the Mediaeval Acad. Am. Served U.S. Army Engrs., World War I; AEF. Recipient Am. Inst. Architects sch. medal Harvard, 1919; Congress medal, Sociét é0française d'Archéologie, 1935; Chevalier Legion of Honor, 1936, Officer Legion of Honor, 1966; named hon. citizen Ville de Cluny, France. Trustee Bur. Univ. Travel, Newton, Mass. Fellow Am. Acad. Arts and Scis. (former officer), Mediaeval Acad. Am., Archaeol. Inst. Am. (former pres., now hon. pres.). Royal Soc. Arts, Soc. Antiquaries of London (hon.), Chevalier du Tastevin; mem. Pilgrim Soc., Colonial Soc. Mass., Soc. Archtl. Historians (past pres., now hon. pres.), Am. Philos. Soc., Boston Soc. Architects, A.I.A. (hon.), Académie de Mcon (hon.), Société des Antiquaires de France (hon.), Académie de Dijon (non- resident mem.), Phi Beta Kappa, Gargoyle, Signet. Republican. Mem. Greek Orthodox Ch. Author books on Romanesque ch. architecture. Adv. editor and contbr. articles on architecture, also sketching and designing including Harvard Tercentenary ware. Address: 274 Grove St Wellesley MA 02181 ☆

CONANT, MIRIAM B., educator; b. Paris, France, Aug. 4, 1931; d. Claude A. and Janine (Wertheimer) Bernheim; B.A., Bryn Mawr Coll., 1951; Ph.D., Columbia U., 1962; m. Francis Paine Conant, Aug. 4, 1952; children—Oliver, Nora. Came to U.S., 1940. Instr. Columbia, 1963-65, asst. prof., 1965-69; prof. Sarah Lawrence Coll., 1969—. Mem. Am. Polit. Sci. Assn., Am. Assn. U. Profs., Am. Acad. Polit. and Social Sci. Research youth and politics. Home: 1261 Madison Av New York City NY 10028 Office: Sarah Lawrence Coll Bronxville NY 10708

CONANT, NORMAN FRANCIS, former educator; b. Walpole, Mass., Mar. 9, 1908; s. Frank Hall and Sarah (Purdy) C.; B.S., Bates Coll., 1930; M.A., Harvard, 1931, Ph.D., 1933, postgrad. Laboratoire de Parasitologie, U. Paris (Sheldon traveling fellow), 1933-34, Army Med. Sch., Washington, 1944, Institute Oswaldo Cruz. Rio de Janeiro, Brazil, 1944, U. Sao Paulo, Faculdade de Medicine, Sao Paulo, Brazil, 1944; m. Sylvia Clare Nute, Dec. 6, 1929; children—Norman Francis, Sylvia Lee (Mrs. Leslie F. Chesson), Linda Ann (Mrs. Ledyard D. Gardner, Jr.), Willa M. (Mrs. Max Pruzan), Laura (Mrs. George P. Varga), Talitha (Mrs. John Martin), Stephen Hayward. Instr. to asso. prof. dept. microbiology, Sch. Medicine Duke, 1935-58, prof., chmn. dept., 1958-68; Lectr. mycology Army Med. Sch, Washington, 1943-46, expert cons. tropical medicine Sec. War, 1943- 46; cons. Communicable Disease Center USPHS, Atlanta, 1947-49; cons. div. research grants and fellowships Nat. Inst. Health, 1948-52; cons. Inst. Allergy and Infectious Diseases. NIH, 1957-60, chmn. tng. grants com., 1960-61; mem. Nat. Adv. Allergy and Infectious Diseases Council, Nat. Insts. Health, 1961-65; referee pathogenic fungi Am. Pub. Health Assn., 1948; mem. subcom. cutaneous diseases, com. medicine. div. med. scis. NRC, 1951-53; adv. panel microbiology Office Naval Research, 1952-57. Recipient award N.C. Acad. Sci., 1940. Diplomate in mycology Am. Acad. Microbiology (gov.) Mem. Mycological Soc. Am., Soc. Exptl. Biology and Medicine, Internat. Soc. Human and Animal Mycology (pres. 1962-67), Med. Mycology Soc. Ams. (pres. 1970), Am. Soc. Microbiology, Internat. Soc. Tropical Dermatology, Phi Beta Kappa, Sigma Xi, Alpha Omega Alpha. Presbyn. (elder). Mason. Home: 5622 Gamitt Rd Durham NC 27707

CONARD, ALFRED FLETCHER, legal educator; b. Grinnell, Ia., Nov. 30, 1911; s. Henry S. and Letitia (Moon) C.; A.B., Grinnell Coll., 1932, LL.D., 1971; student U. Ia., 1932-34; LL.B., U. Pa., 1936; LL.M., Columbia, 1939, J.S.D., 1942; m. Georgia Murray, Aug. 7, 1939; children—Joy L., Deborah J. Admitted to Pa. bar, 1937; Mich. bar, 1967; practice in Phila., 1936-38; asst. prof. U. Kansas City (Mo.) Law Sch., 1939-42, acting dean, 1941-42; atty. OPA, 1942-43, Office Alien Property Custodian, 1945-46; asso. prof., then prof. law U. Ill. Law Sch., 1946-54; prof. law U. Mich. Law Sch., 1954—; lectr. U. Istanbul, 1958-59, Luxembourg, 1959, Mexico, 1963, Brussels, 1965, Salzburg, 1971; chmn. editorial adv. bd. Bobbs-Merrill Co., 1962—. Exec. com. Am. Assn. Law Schs., 1964-65, chmn. research com., 1968-69, pres., 1971. Served OSS, AUS, 1943-45. Decorated Purple Heart; Ordre des Chevaliers de la Couronne (Belgium); recipient Kulp Meml. award Am. Risk & Ins. Assn., 1965. Mem. Am. Assn. U. Profs. (chpt. pres. 1963-64), NRC, Am. Bar Assn. (exec. com. corp. law sect. 1967-71), Am. Judicature Soc., State Bar Mich., Am. Law Inst., Law and Soc. Assn. (trustee), Council for Law Related Studies, Phi Beta Kappa, Order of the Coif. Mem. Soc. of Friends. Rotarian (mem. bd. dirs. Ann Arbor 1962-64). Author: Studies in Easements and Licenses, 1942; Cases on Business Organization, 3d edit., 1965; Automobile Accident Costs and Payments; Studies in the Economics of Injury Reparation, 1964. Editor in chief Am. Jour. Comparative Law, 1968- -; chief editor bus. and pvt. orgns. Internat. Ency. Comparative Law. Home: 16 Heatheridge Ann Arbor MI 48104

CONARD, RAYMOND FOSS, ret. constrn. co. exec.; b. Atlantic Highlands, N.J., Apr. 29, 1911; s. Richard W. and Marion (Morgan) C.; B.S. in Civil Engring., Drexel Inst. Tech., 1934; m. Perry Harlow, June 18, 1938. With U.S. Bur. Pub. Rds., Va., 1935-36, U.S. Geol. Survey, Va., W.Va. and Ga., 1936-41; with Warren Bros. Co., 1946-71, v.p., 1955-71. Served to lt. col. C.E., AUS, 1941-46; PTO. Registered profl. engr., Mass., N.C. Fellow Am. Soc. C.E.; mem. Soc. Am. Mil. Engrs., Newcomen Soc. N.Am. Home: 1060 SW Cypress Way Boca Raton FL 33432

CONAWAY, CHRISTINE YERGES, educator; b. Columbus, O., Nov. 18, 1901; d. Frederick Joseph and Ada May (Crothers) Yerges; A.B., Ohio State U., 1923, A.M., 1942; L.H.D., Otterbein Coll., 1957; m. Samuel Steele Conaway, August 29, 1924 (dec.); children—Patricia Ann (Mrs. Joseph P. Ruddell), Samuel Steele, Lawrence Yerges (dec. 1970). Pub. sch. tchr., Athens, O., 1924; asst. to dean, Coll. Arts and Scis., Ohio State U., 1937-42, acting sec., 1942- 44, dean women, 1944-67, dean women emeritus, 1967. Mem. Grandview Heights Sch. Bd. Edn., 1943-51, v.p., 1945-50. Mem. Community Village Program Com., Continuing Edn. for Women Com.; chmn. Women's Juvenile Bd.; v.p. Childhood League; mem. Florence Crittendon Bd.; bd. govs. Arrowmont Sch., Gatlinburg, Tenn. Mem. Am. Assn. U. Women (past v.p. Columbus br.), Nat. Assn. Women Deans and Counselors (chmn. arrangement com., nat. conv., 1947, publicity chmn. 1948-50. v.p., chmn. regional contacts com. 1950-52), Ohio Assn. Women Deans, Administrs. and Counselors, Nat. Council on Family Relations, N.E.A., Am. Coll. Personnel Assn. (exec. com. 1955-57, 60-62), Am. Personnel and Guidance Assn., U.S. Nat. Student Assn. Adv. Board, Central Ohio Guidance Assn., Nat. Vocational Guidance Assn., Mortar Board, Delta Kappa Gamma, Theta Sigma Phi, Alpha Lambda Delta (nat. council 1948-54, 58-62, editor newsletter 1962-66), Pi Beta Phi, Chimes, Sigma Phi Alpha. Rep. Mem. 1st Community Ch. Clubs: Ohio State University Faculty (mem. bd.), Ohio State University Faculty Women's (pres. 1950-51). Home: 1230 Glenn Av Columbus OH 43212

CONAWAY, HOWARD HAMMOND, lawyer; b. Georgetown, Del., Sept. 26, 1909; s. Harley James and Anna Gooden (West) C.; LL.B., U. Va., 1932; m. Eileen Mitchell, Jan. 7, 1948; children—Howard Hammond, Anne West, Mary Mitchell. Admitted to Md. bar, 1932, since practiced in Balt.; partner firm Frank, Bernstein, Conaway & Goldman, 1940—. Dir. Balt. Aircoil Co., Inc., Lloyd E. Mitchell, Inc. Served with AUS, 1943-46. Decorated Bronze Star. Mem. Am., Md. bar assns., Kappa Alpha, Phi Alpha Delta. Clubs: University, Baltimore Country (Balt.). Home: 201 E Highfield Rd Baltimore, MD 21218. Office: Mercantile Bank & Trust Bldg Baltimore MD 21201

CONCANNON, ROBERT BURTON, cosmetic co. exec.; b. Rock Island, Ill., Apr. 21, 1928; s. Edward B. and Margaret (Arnold) C.; B.S.C., U. Ia., 1951; m. Betty G. Stalder, Aug. 22, 1948; children—William, Joan, Vice pres. finance Honeggers' & Co., Fairbury, Ill., 1957-61; controller Libby, McNeill & Libby, Chgo., 1961-66; controller, treas. Max Factor & Co., Hollywood, Cal., 1966—; dir. Graphic Arts Packaging Corp. Served with AUS, 1946-48. C.P.A., Ill. Home: 3451 Wrightwood Dr North Hollywood CA 91604 Office: 1655 N McCadden Pl Hollywood CA 90028

CONDER, JOSEPH MARTIN, accountant; b. Winslow, Ind., Jan. 27, 1921; s. Joseph H. and Freda (Adler) C.; B.S., Ark. State Coll., 1942; M.B.A., U. Pa., 1947; m. Harriet Lothman, Sept. 8, 1951; 1 dau., Meta Carolyn. With Lybrand, Ross Bros. & Montgomery, C.P.A.'s, 1947—, partner, 1960—, partner charge, Houston, 1964—. Served to maj. AUS, 1942-46; C.P.A., Ind., Ky., Tex., La. Home: 11809 Durrette Houston TX 77024 Office: Americana Bldg Houston TX 77002

CONDER, ROBERT WENDELL, mgmt. cons., educator; b. Indpls., Aug. 25, 1903; s. Earl R. and Edith (Walker) C.; A.B., DePauw U., 1925, L.H.D., 1958; J.D., U. Mich., 1927; m. Katherine Keller, June 29, 1927; children—Richard Keller, Marcia K. (dec.). Admitted to Mich. bar, 1927, and practiced in Detroit, 1927-36; mem. legal staff Chrysler Corp., 1936- 39, dir. labor relations, 1939-51; became dir. indsl. relations, 1951, v.p., 1952-58; prof. Sch. Bus. Adminstrn. Wayne State U., 1959—. Mem. Mich. Bar Assn., Barristers of Mich., Indsl. Relations Research Assn., Phi Kappa Psi, Delta Sigma Rho, Alpha Kappa Psi, Order of the Coif. Republican. Presbyn. Clubs: Detroit Boat, Country of Detroit. Home: 315 Touraine Rd Grosse Pointe Farms MI 48236 Office: Sch Bus Adminstrn Wayne State U Detroit MI 48202

CONDIE, RICHARD PALFREYMAN, musician; b. Springville, Utah, July 5, 1898; s. Gibson Sharp and Esther (Palfreyman) C.; A.B., Brigham Young U., 1923, H.H.D., 1963; grad. New Eng. Conservatory of Music, Boston, 1927; scholar Fontainebleau Conservatory Music, summers 1927-28; m. Blanche Mendenhall, Aug. 31, 1923 (dec. Dec. 1959); children—Richard M., Robert A., Jeanette, Joan C. (Mrs. Charles Stewart), Douglas G.; m. 2d, Manda B. Morrison, July 22, 1963. Tenor role in opera, North Africa, Tunis, Algeria, 1929; asso. prof. music U. Utah, 1957—, now emeritus; asst. condr. Tabernacle Choir, Salt Lake City, 1938-57, Condr., 1957—. Home: 2304 Berkeley St Salt Lake City UT 84109 Office: Mormon Tabernacle Temple Sq Salt Lake City UT 84110

CONDIT, CARL WILBUR, educator; b. Cin., Sept. 29, 1914; s. Arthur Thomas And Gertrude (Pletz) C.; B.S., in Mech. Engring., Purdue U., 1936; M.A., U. Cin., 1939, Ph.D., 1941, L.H.D., (hon.), 1967; hon. fellow history sci., U. Wis., 1951-52; m. Isabel Marion Campbell, June 19, 1943; children—Stephen Campbell, Richard Stuart, Kenneth Arthur. Instr. math. and mechanics ordnance tng. div. War Dept., Cin., 1941, War Prodn. Sch., Cin., 1941-42, Engring. Coll., U. Cin., 1942-44; asst. designing engr. bldg. dept. N.Y.C. R.R., Cin., 1944-45; asst. prof. Carnegie Inst. Tech., 1946-47; from instr. to asso. prof. Northwestern U., Evanston, Ill., 1945-46, 47-61, prof. gen. studies, art and urban affairs, 1961—. Research asso. Smithsonian Instn., 1966-67. Recipient Abbott Payson Usher prize Soc. for History Tech., 1968; Civil Engring. History and Heritage award Am. Soc. C.E., 1971. Mem. Am. Assn. U. Profs., Am. Civil Liberties Union, History Sci. Soc., Soc. Archtl. Historians, Soc. History Tech. (exec. council 1959-63). Author: The Rise of the Skyscraper, 1952; American Building Art; The 19th Centry, 1960; American Building Art; The 20th Century, 1961; The Chicago Sch. of Architecture, 1964; (with others) Technology in Western Civilization, 1967; American Building; Materials and Techniques, 1968. Editor (with Eugene Ferguson) Technology and Culture, 1962—. Home: 9300 Linder Av Morton Grove IL 60053 Office: Northwestern U Evanston IL 60201

CONDIT, ELEANOR LOUISE, mus. supr.; b. Balt., May 7, 1914; d. George Smith and Bessie Blaine (Madeira) Condit; A.B., Vassar Coll., 1935; A.M., Columbia, 1941; m. Frederic G. M. Lange, Sept. 19, 1946. Carnegie grant for study edn. museums of Brit. Isles, Scandinavia, Germany, France, Netherlands, summer 1939; supr. edn. Bklyn. Children's Mus., 1935-42; collaborator H. W. Wilson Co. Ednl. Film guide, 1941-54; supr. Jr. Mus., Met. Mus. Art, 1943-61, asst. dean charge Jr., Mus., 1961-68, asso. in charge Jr. Mus., 1968—. Incorporator Bergen Community Mus., Hackensack, N.J. Mem. Am. Assn. Mus. (council 1957-63, v.p. 1960-63). Museums Council N.Y.C. (sec.-treas. 1960-65). Archaeol. Inst. Am., N.Y. Film Council, Phi Beta Kappa. Home: 1203 Emerson Av Teaneck NJ 07666 Office: Met Mus Art Fifth Av and 82d St New York City NY 10028

CONDIT, GEX PULLEN, Jr., box board mfr.; b. Gary, Ind., Feb. 14, 1926; s. Gex Pullen and Alice (Worden) C.; student Millsaps Coll., 1943-44, Ga. Sch. Tech., 1944-45; B.S., Yale, 1946; M.B.A., Xavier U., 1956; m. Virginia Jones, May 6, 1950; children—Rebecca, Jennifer. Indsl. engr. Nat. Tube Co., div. U.S. Steel, 1946-50; indsl.

engr. Gardner Board & Carton Co., 1950-57 (merged to become Diamond-Gardner, then Diamond Nat. Corp.), pres. subsidiary Manchester Machine Co., 1960-62, pres. Gardner div., 1962-66; v.p. Diamond Nat. Corp., 1963-66; v.p., asst. to pres. Eastex Inc., 1966—; exec. v.p., gen. mgr. Eastex Packaging Inc., subsidiary, 1969-71, pres., 1971—. Past pres. Box Board Research and Devel. Assn. Club: Beaumont Country. Home: 1280 Nottingham Lane Beaumont TX 77706 Office: Eastex Inc P O Box 816 Silsbee TX 77656

CONDIT, PAUL TAYLOR, medical educator; b. N.Y.C., Oct. 27, 1918; s. Kenneth H. and Marjorie W. (Brown) C.; A.B. cum laude, Princeton, 1940, A.M., 1941, Ph.D., 1958; M.D., Johns Hopkins, 1950; m. Mary Louise Winterode, Apr. 18, 1942; children—Nancy P., Paul Taylor, Philip H. II. Sr. investigator Nat. Cancer Inst., Bethesda, Md., 1951-53, 55-58; fellow in medicine Johns Hopkins, 1953-55; asso. head cancer sect. Okla. Med. Research Found., Oklahoma City, 1958-64, head, 1964—; asso. prof. research medicine, biochemistry, radiology U. Okla. Sch. Medicine, 1958—, prof. research biochemistry, 1969—. Fellow A.C.P., Am. Coll. Clin. Pharmacology and Chemotherapy; mem. Am. Chem. Soc., A.M.A., Am. Assn. Cancer Research, A.A.A.S., Am. Soc. Pharm. and Exptl. Therapeutics, N.Y. Acad. Sci. Research, publs. in cancer chemotherapy, mechanism of folic acid antagonists, combination of radiation therapy and chemotherapy. Home: 1605 Norwood Pl Oklahoma City OK 73120

CONDIT, ROSS ROWLAND, Jr., army officer; b. Aumsville, Ore., Oct. 12, 1917; s. Ross Rowland and Emma (McLellan) C.; B.S., U. Md., 1970; grad. Indsl Coll. of Armed Forces, 1963—; m. Katharina Margarete Landler, July 1, 1950; children—Patricia, Howard. Commd. 2d lt. U.S. Army, 1942, advanced through grades to brig. gen., 1967; served in logistics, Europe, World War II, Vietnam, 1965-66, Taiwan, 1955-57; comdg. gen. Combat Devel. Command, personnel and Logistics System Group, Ft. Lee, Va., 1969—. Decorated Legion of Merit with 2 oak leaf clusters, Bronze Star. Mem. Am. Ordnance Assn., Assn. U.S. Army, Sigma Tau. Lutheran. Home: 368 Coral Sea Circle Fort Lee VA 23801 Office: Comdg Gen Combat Devel Command Personnel and Logistics Systems Group Fort Lee VA 23801

CONDLIFFE, JOHN B., economist; b. Melbourne, Australia, Dec. 23, 1891; s. Alfred Bell and Margaret (Marley) C.; ed. Canterbury Univ. Coll., Gonville and Caius Coll., Cambridge; D.Sc. (N.Z.), D. Letters (hon.); 1957; LL.D., Occidental Coll., 1942; m. Olive G. Mills, June 20, 1916; children—John Charles, Peter George, Margaret Mary. Prof. econs. Canterbury Coll., Christchurch, New Zealand, 1920-26; research sec., Inst. Pacific Relations, 1927-30; prof. econs. U. Mich., 1930-31; mem. League of Nations Secretariat, 1931-37; prof. of commerce U. of London, 1937-39; prof. econs. U. Cal., 1940-58, and dir. teaching Inst. of Econs., 1947-52; cons. to Reserve Bank of New Zealand, 1957; asso. dir., Div. of History and Economics, Carnegie Endowment, 1943-48; sr. economist Stanford Research Institute, 1961-67. Rapporteur-general, International Studies Conf., 1937-39; chmn. Geneva Research Center, 1937-39; chairman international research com., Inst. of Pacific Relations, 1942-45. Adviser Indian Nat. Council Applied Econ. Research, 1959-60; Henry E. Howland Mem. prize, Yale U., 1939; Wendell Willkie prize, 1950. Decorated Gold Cross Order of Phoenix (Greece). Mem. Royal Econ. Soc., Am. Econ. Assn., Econ. Society of Australia and New Zealand. Author books including: The Commerce of Nations, 1949; The Welfare State in New Zealand, 1959; The Development of Australia, 1964; Te Rangi Hiroa: The Life of Sir Peter Buck, 1971. Home: 1801 Broadway San Francisco CA 94109

CONDON, ARNOLD CLARION, educator; b. Brodhead, Wis., Sept. 29, 1909; s. Glen and Alice (Arnold) C.; Ed.B., Wis. State Coll., 1934; M.A., Columbia, 1938; Ph.D., N.Y.U., 1946; m. Joyce Blackbourne, Aug. 17, 1945; 1 son, Gregg. Tchr. high sch., Highland Park, Ill., 1934-38; instr. U. Ia., 1938-41, vis. prof., summers, 1945-46, 48-49; vis. prof. Northwestern U., summers 1940-43; asst. prof., acting head dept. U. Ariz., 1941, asso. prof., head dept. secretarial studies, 1945-48, prof., 1948-49; asso. prof. U. Ill., 1949- 54, head dept. bus. edn., prof., 1954-64; prof. business edn. Ill. State U., Normal, 1964—, acting head of dept. bus. edn., 1967-68. Vis. prof. Colo. State Coll., 1961, U. Wis. summers 1961, 63. Recipient Distinguished Alumni Service award Wis. State U., 1970. Mem. Ill., Chgo. Area, Univ. Area bus. edn. assns., Am., Ill. vocational assns., Nat. Bus. Tchrs. Assn. (chmn. secretarial sect. 1947-48; sec. adminstrs. and dept. heads sect. 1955, vice chmn. 1956, chmn. 1957), United Bus. Edn. Assn. (v.p. 1961- 62, pres. Central region 1961-62), Nat. Council Bus. Edn., Nat. Assn. Bus. Tchr. Tng. Instns., Order of Artus, Pi Omega Pi, Delta Psi Omega, Alpha Kappa Psi, Delta Pi Epsilon (chmn. research award com.). Author: (with Rowena Wellman and others) Transcription Method Shorthand Series, 1952, 53; (with Rowena Wellman) Shorthand Modified Series, 1959; (with others) Programmed Gregg Shorthand, The Selection and Use of Multiple- Channel Equipment in the Teaching of Shorthand, 1969, Using Multiple-Channel Equipment To Develop Stenographic Computing, 1969; also articles, editorials, chpts. to books. Typewriting service editor Bus. Edn. Forum, 1959-60, shorthand feature editor, 1960-62. Home: Brodhead WI 53520 Office: Dept Bus Edn Ill State U Normal IL 61761

CONDON, ARTHUR DAVID, lawyer; b. N.Y.C., Mar. 4, 1900; s. David Paulinus and Margaret Gertrude (Farnan) C.; A.B., Coll. City N.Y.; B.S., U.S. Naval Acad., 1920; LL.B., Nat. U.; m. Evelyn Cronin. Served as spl. atty. Bur. Internal Revenue, also U.S. Maritime Commn.; Madrid, 1928; M.A., U. Central, Madrid, 1936; Ph.D., Columbia, pvt. practice law, from 1945; with firm Davies, Richberg, Tydings, Landa & Duff. Served with USN, World War I, World War II. Mem. Am., Fed., D.C. bar assns. Clubs: Metropolitan (Washington); Annapolitan (Md.); Marlboro (Md.) Hunt; Annapolis Yacht. Contbr. articles on taxation. Home: Annapolis MD 21401 Office: 1000 Vermont Av Washington DC 20005 Coll. City N.Y., 1943-44; lectr. Columbia, summer 1939-45;

CONDON, DAVID HOLT, architect; b. Pasadena, Cal., Mar. 14, 1916; s. Holt E. and Marcia (Coolidge) C.; A.B. in Architecture, U. Cal. at Berkeley, 1939; m. Sylvia E. Marquez, Mar. 8, 1947; children—Michael D., Ann M. Asso., architect Charles M. Goodman, 1936-52; architect Keyes, Smith, Satterlee & Lethbridge, Washington, 1952-54, Ronald S. Senseman, Silver Spring, Md., 1954-55; partner Keyes, Lethbridge & Condon, Washington, 1956—; cons. U.S. Pub. Housing Authority, 1962-66. Served to lt. USNR, 1941-45. Recipient Excellence in Architecture award Washington Bd. Trade, 1965, 71; Oliver Owen Kuher award Bethesda-Chevy (Md.) C. of C., 1962; awards Potomac Valley chpt. A.I.A., 1956, 58, 60, 62, 64, 66, 68, 70; Nat. First Honor award A.I.A., 1966. Fellow A.I.A. (chmn. com. exhbns. 1963-65, commr. community Met. chpt. 1968-69); mem. Washington Bldg. Congress. Club: Cosmos (Washington). Prin. works include Tiber Island, redevel. housing, Washington, 1965, Carrollsburg Sq., redevel. housing, Washington, 1967, gen. adminstrn. bldg. NIH, Bethesda, 1969, New Mark Commons, planned residential community, Rockville, Md., 1970, operations control center bldg. Washington Met. Area Transit Authority. Home: 6805 Georgia St Chevy Chase MD 20015 Office: 1320 19th St NW Washington DC 20036

CONDON, EDDIE (Albert Edwin Condon), USIA. Decorated Ordem Nacional do Cruzeiro do Sul; Great Margaret (McGraw) C.; student pub. schs., Chicago Heights, Ill.; m. prize for poetry, Portugal, 1960; named hon. citizen Rio de Janeiro, Hillis Peavey Orchestra, 1923; club dates, Chgo., 1923-27; musician Bath Club, Stork Club, N.Y.C., 1930-33; 1st appearance Town Hall, N.Y.C., 1942; night club owner, N.Y.C., 1946-. Mem. Toots Shor Athletic Club. Author: (with Thomas Sugrue) We Called It Music, 1948; (with Richard (trustee N.Y.) Spanish Inst. N.Y., Phi Beta Kappa, Phi Lambda Home: 27 Washington Sq N New York City NY 10011 Rio de Sonho E Tempo, 1963. Contbr. articles to profl. publs. Home: Office: 47 W 3d Av New York City NY 10012

CONDON, EDWARD MAURICE, retail co. exec.; b. Newark, Oct. 27, 1914; s. William A. and Itala M. (de Vitalis) C.; ed. pub. schs., N.J.; m. Alma Soell, Mar. 19, 1938; children—Linda (Mrs. Francis J. Pitts, Jr.), William Edward, Barbara Alma (Mrs. Alfred Earle); m. 2d, Betty Hall, May 20, 1959. Dept. mgr. The Bon Marche, dept. store, Seattle, 1935-42, mdse. mgr., 1946-49, v.p. mdsg., 1949-52; buyer cosmetics Marshall Field & Co., Chgo., 1942-46; gen. mdse. mgr. Strawbridge and Clothier, Phila., 1952-58; exec. v.p. William Hengerer Co., dept. store, Buffalo, 1958-59, pres., 1959-61; pres. H. & S. Pogue Co., dept. store, Cin., 1961—; v.p. Asso. Dry Goods Corp., 1959—, dir., regional exec. v.p., 1970—; dir. Central Trust Co. Bd. dirs. Cin. Downtown Promotion Council. Mem. Greater Cin. C. of C. (trustee). Clubs: Queen City, Cincinnati Country. Home: 9060 Indian Ridge Road Cincinnati OH 45243 Office: H & S Pogue Co Cincinnati OH 45202

CONDON, EDWARD U., physicist; b. Alamogordo, N.M., Mar. 2, 1902; s. William Edward and Caroline Barr (Uhler) C.; A.B., U. of Calif., 1924, Ph.D., 1926; D.Sc. (hon.), U. Delhi (India), N.M. Sch. of Mines, 1950, Alfred U., Am. U., 1952; m. Emilie Honzik, Nov. 9, 1922; children—Caroline Marie, Paul Edward, Joseph Henry. Nat. Research fellow, Göttingen and Munich, 1926-27; lectr. in physics, Columbia U., spring 1928; asst. prof. physics. Princton U., 1928-29, asso. prof., 1930-37; prof. theoretical physics, U. of Minn., 1929-30; asso. dir. Westinghouse Research Lab., 1937-45; dir. Nat. Bur. of Standards, Washington, 1945-51; dir. research and devel. Corning Glass Works, 1951-54; cons. physicist, 1954—; prof. Washington U. at St. Louis, 1956-63; prof. physics, fellow joint inst. for lab. astrophysics, U. Colo., 1963—; vis. prof. Oberlin (O.) Coll., 1962-63; v.p. Ann. Reviews, Inc.; sci. dir. Air Force financed investigation Unidentified Flying Objects. Mem. NACA, 1945-51; sci. adv., spl. senate com. on atomic energy, 79th congress; pres. Colo. Sci. Devel. Commn., 1966-68. Mem. Am. Philos. Soc., Soc. for Social Responsibility in Sci. (pres. 1968-69), Am. Acad. Arts and Sci., Royal Soc. Arts (London), Societé Francaise de Physique (Paris), Royal Swedish Acad. Enginrg. Sci. (Stockholm), Royal Norwegian Soc. Scis. (Trondheim), Nat. Acad. Scis., Am. Phys. Soc. (pres. 1946), A.A.A.S. (pres. 1953), Am. Assn. Physics Teachers (pres. 1964), Phi Beta Kappa, Sigma Xi. Clubs: University (Boulder, Colo.); Cosmos (Washington). Author: Quantum Mechanics (with P. M. Morse), 1929; Theory of Atomic Spectra (with G. H. Shortley), 1935. Editor: Handbook of Physics (with Hugh Odishaw), 1958. Editor Reviews of Modern Physics, 1957-68. Home: 761 Cascade Av Boulder CO 80302

CONDON, JAMES J., utility co. exec.; b. 1911; student Ill. Inst. Tech., Northwestern U.; m. Virginia Newell Condon, May 4, 1946; children—Susan Marie (Mrs. Robert Reid), Mary Virginia. With Peoples Gas Light & Coke Co., Chgo., 1930—, exec. v.p., 1966—, also dir.; dir. Natural Gas Pipeline Co. Am., North Shore Gas Co. Bd. dirs. Conv. and Tourism Bur. Chgo., Better Bus. Bur. Met. Chgo. Mem. Am. Mgmt. Assn., Am. Gas Assn., Assn. Commerce and Industry, Homebuilders Assn. Chicagoland. Clubs: Beverly Country; Mid-America. Address; 122 S Michigan Av Chicago IL 60603

CONDON, JUSTIN JEROME, machinery mfr.; b. Bklyn., July 21, 1917; s. Jerome Daniel and Peggy (Maides) C.; A.B. in Econs., Cornell U., 1939; M.A. in Indsl. Relations, U. Wash., 1947; postgrad. Harvard Grad. Sch. Bus. Adminstrn., 1948; m. Jean Louise Rodger, Mar. 28, 1942; children—James, Margaret. Sales tng. and personnel supr. Continental Can Co., 1948-56; with Whirlpool Corp., Benton Harbor, Mich., 1956-66, gen. mgr. St. Joseph div., 1959-62, v.p. personnel, 1962-66; v.p. indsl. relations Rex Chainbelt, Inc., Milw., 1967—. Served to lt. col. AUS, 1941-46. Mem, Phi Beta Kappa, Beta Theta Pi. Home: 1475 E Fairy Chasm Rd Milwaukee WI 53217 Office: Rex Chainbelt Inc Marine Plaza Milwaukee WI 53202

CONDON, LESTER PATRICK, govt. ofcl.; b. Mt. Vernon, N.Y., Oct. 13, 1922, s. Lester P. and Eileen V. (Malone) P.; B.Sc., Providence Coll., 1943; postgrad. Georgetown Law Sch., 1947-51, (Ford Found. scholar) U. Chgo., summer 1957; m. Vera Crossley, Apr. 21, 1946; children—Thomas J., John K., Leslie Patricia, Marietta, Lisa Ann. Spl. agt. FBI, 1947-51; asst. chief security OPS, 1951-53; dir. investigation U.S. Ho. of Reps. Com. on Govt. Operations, 1953-54; spl. asst. to adminstr. HHFA, 1954-55, dir. compliance div., 1955-60; dep. commr. FHA, 1960-61, asst. commr. audit and exam. FHA, 1961-62; insp. gen. U.S. Dept. Agr., 1962-69; asst. sec. for adminstrn. U.S. Dept. Housing and Urban Devel., 1969—. Served to lt. (j.g.) USNR, World War II. Decorated Purple Heart; recipient Distinguished Service award HHFA. Mem. Soc. Former Spl. Agts. FBI, Inst. Internal Auditors, Am. Legion, Phi Delta Phi. Roman Catholic. Club: Springfield (Va.) Country. Home: Curri er 1306 Janneys Lane Alexandria VA 23202 Office: US Dept Housing and Urban Devel Washington DC 20410

CONDON, MARTIN J., III, bus. exec.; b. Pelham Manor, N.Y., Dec. 11, 1908; s. Martin J. and Shirley (Cummins) C.; A.B., Princeton, 1932; H.H.D., Southwestern U., 1958; m. Alice Berry, Feb. 22, 1936; children—Alice, Katherine, Louisa, Frances, Martin. Joined Am. Snuff Co. (co. name changed to Conwood Corp.), 1933, pres., 1949, dir. 1940—; dir. Union Planters Nat. Bank, Plough, Inc. (all Memphis), Cavenham Food's Ltd., London, Eng., Gencrate Occidentale, Paris, France. Trustee George Peabody Coll., Nashville, Garrison (Md.) Forest Sch. Served as lt. USNR, 1943-45. Mem. Nat. Indsl. Conf. Bd. (dir.), Nat. Assn. Mfrs. (past v.p., dir.), Tenn. Mfrs. Assn. (past pres., dir.), So. States Indsl. Council (past pres., dir.), Newcomen Soc., Phi Beta Kappa. Episcopalian. Clubs: Brook (N.Y.C.); Memphis Country, Hunt and Polo, Tennessee (Memphis); Ivy (Princeton, N.J.). Home: 806 Sweetbrier Rd Memphis TN 38117 Office: PO Box 217 Memphis TN 38101

CONDON, RICHARD, author; b. N.Y.C., Mar. 18, 1915; s. Richard Aloysius and Martha (Pickering) C.; ed. pub. schs., N.Y.C.; m. Evelyn Rose Hunt, January 14, 1938; children—Deborah (Mrs. Kenneth Jupp), Wendy (Mrs. Davis Bennett). Decorated chevalier La Confrérie du Tastevin, 1968. Author: (play) Men of Distinction, 1953; (children's record albums) The Horse Stories, 1947; (novels pub. 21 langs.) The Oldest Confession, 1958, The Manchurian Candidate, 1959, Some Angry Angel, 1960, A Talent for Loving, 1961, An Infinity of Mirrors, 1964, Any God Will Do, 1966, The Ecstasy Business, 1967; Mile High, 1969; (screenplay) The Summer Music, in 1964; (screen adaptation) A Talent for Loving, 1965. Contbr. nat. magazines. Donor Richard Condon Collection to Boston U. Library, 1965. Address: care A D Peters 10 Buckingham St London WC 2 England

CONDON, VERNER HOLMES, Jr., financial exec.; b. Bloomington, Ill., June 26, 1926; s. Verner Holmes and Lucille (Dennis) C.; B.S., Pa. State U., 1948; M.B.A., Northwestern U., 1949; m. Ann Garman, Sept. 3, 1949; children—Martha, Nancy. Securities analyst Harris Trust & Savs. Bank, Chgo., 1949-51; with Ford Motor Co., 1951-68, controller tractor div., 1961-62, marketing mgr., 1962-68; v.p. finance AMBAC Industries, Inc., Garden City, N.Y., 1968- -. Served with USNR, 1944-46. Mem. Financial Execs. Inst. Home: 57 Whitehall Blvd Garden City NY 11530 Office: 900 Country Rd Garden City NY 11530

CONDREN, FRANK T., corp. exec.; b. N.Y.C., 1933; grad. Fordham U., 1955. Controller, Unexcelled, Inc., N.Y.C. Home: 81 Creeping Hemlock Dr Norwalk CT 06851 Office: 375 Park Av New York City NY 10022*

CONE, CARL BRUCE, educator; b. Davenport, Ia., Feb. 22, 1916; s. Carl S. and Lena (Peterson) C.; B.A., U. Ia., 1936, M.A., 1937, Ph.D., 1940; m. Mary Louise Regan, Dec. 20, 1942; 1 son, Timothy. Instr. history Allegheny Coll., Meadville, Pa., 1940-41; research asst. Ia. Hist. Soc., 1941-42; asst. prof. history La. State U., 1942-47; faculty U. Ky., Lexington, 1947—, prof. history, 1956—, chmn. dept., 1965-70. Summer vis. prof. U. Mo., 1952, La. State U., 1960, Miami U., Oxford, O., 1964. Mem. Lexington Civil Service Commn., 1958-68. Recipient Nat. Book award Phi Alpha Theta, 1965; Sang award U. Ky., 1968. Hallam prof. U. Ky., also Faculty fellow Fund Advancement Teaching, 1951-52; Guggenheim fellow, 1963-64; Am. Council Learned Socs. grant-in-aid, 1971. Mem. Am., So. (chmn. European sect. 1972), Am. Catholic (pres. 1967) hist. assns., So. Conf. Brit. Studies (pres. 1972), Omicron Delta Kappa, Phi Beta Kappa, Phi Alpha Theta. Republican. Roman Catholic. Author: Torchbearer of Freedom, 1952; Burke and the Nature of Politics: The Age of the American Revolution, 1957; Burke and the Nature of Politics: The Age of the French Revolution, 1964; The English Jacobins, 1968; also articles. Home: 474 W 3d St Lexington KY 40508

CONE, CEASER, textile mfr.; b. N.Y.C., Jan. 30, 1908; s. Ceaser and Jeanette (Siegel) C.; A.B., U. N.C., 1928; M.B.A., Harvard, 1930; m. Martha Abercrombie, Nov. 19, 1938; children—Ceaser III, Martha, Lawrence. With Cone Mills Corp., 1930—, treas., dir., 1945-56, pres., dir., 1956-65, chmn. bd., 1965, now dir. Pres. Greensboro United Fund, 1965. Chmn. bd. trustees Oak Ridge Found., 1968. Mem. Am. Textile Mfrs. Inst. (dir. 1956-59, 61-64), N.A.M. (dir. 1966—), Greensboro C. of C. (pres. 1955). Rotarian. Home: 506 Cornwallis Dr Greensboro NC 27408 Office: Cone Mills Corp Greensboro NC 27405

CONE, CLARENCE NEWTON, textile mfr.; b. Asheville, N.C., Sept. 16, 1910; s. Clarence N. and Sadie (Frank) C.; B.S., N.C. State Coll., 1932; m. Elisabeth Gaither, July 29, 1933; children—Nancy C. (Mrs. Bryant M. Hanley, Jr.), Barbara W. (Mrs. Jack H. Fales). With Cone Mills Corp., Greensboro, N.C., 1933—, v.p., 1945—, also dir. Exec. bd. Boy Scouts Am., also mem. adv. com. region 6; mem. adv. bd. Henry Wiseman Kendall Center. Mem. Greensboro C. of C. Home: 910 Sunset Dr Greensboro NC 27408 Office: Cone Mills Corp Greensboro NC 27405

CONE, EDWARD TONER, composer, educator; b. Greensboro, N.C., May 4, 1917; s. Julius Washington and Laura Barbara (Weill) C.; A.B., Princeton, 1939, M.F.A., 1942. Composer numerous compositions, 1 symphony, other works for piano, voice, chorus, orch., chamber combinations, 1939—; asst. prof. dept. music, Princeton (N.J.), 1947-52, asso. prof., 1952-60, prof., prof., 1960—. Guggenheim fellow in composition, 1947-48. Treas. Am. sect. Internat. Soc. Contemporary Music, 1950-52. Mem. Am. Assn. U. Profs. Author: Musical Form and Musical Performance, 1968. Co-editor: Perspectives of New Music, 1965-69, adv. editor, 1969—. Home: 18 College Rd W Princeton NJ 08540

CONE, FAIRFAX MASTICK, adv. agy. exec.; b. San Francisco, Calif., Feb. 21, 1903: s. William H. and Isabelle F. (Williams) C.; U. Cal., 1925; LL.D., Mundelein Coll., 1961; m. Gertrude Kennedy, June 29, 1929; 1 dau., Mary Mastick (Mrs. Richard H. O'Riley). With San Francisco Examiner, 1926-29; copywriter and account exec. Lord & Thomas, advt. agy., San Francisco, 1929-38, v.p. and mgr., 1938-40, v.p. in charge creative work, N.Y.C., 1941, exec. v.p., mgr. Chicago Office, 1942; with Emerson Foote and Don Belding, organized Foote, Cone & Belding Dec., 1942, chmn. exec. com., 1942-48, chmn. bd., 1942-51, pres., 1951-57, chmn. exec. com., 1957-66. Mem. Chgo. Bd. Edn., 1961-63. Dir. Community Fund Chgo., 1940-63; chmn. bd. trustees U. Chgo., 1963-70; trustee Chgo. Ednl. TV, 1961-70, Com. for Econ. Devel.; chmn. 1960 Crusade of Mercy. Berkeley fellow U. Cal. Recipient Distinguished Service in Advt. medal Syracuse U.

CONE, GEORGE SEALY, Jr., banker; b. Falfurrias, Tex., July 7, 1915; s. George Sealy and Odessa (Ludwig) C.; student Schreiner Inst., Kerrville, Tex., 1933-34; m. Bertie C. Ward, Mar. 5, 1939; children—George William, Kendrick Ward. Bookkeeper, Charles Scheiner Bank. Kerrville, 1935-37; clk. Tex.- N.M. Pipeline Co., Midland, Tex., 1937-42, Tex. Pipeline Co., West Columbia, 1944-48; with First Nat. Bank, Midland, 1948-70, exec. v.p., 1960-70, also dir.; pres. Bank of Commerce, Corpus Christi, Tex., 1970—. Past bd. dirs. Midland Community Theatre, Midland Symphony Orch., Midland Community Chest, Midland Salvation Army, Midland YMCA. Served with USNR. 1942-44; PTO. Named Boss of Year, Midland Chpt. Nat. Secs. Assn., 1963. Clubs: Racquet (past pres.). Petroleum (Midland); Corpus Christi Country. Home: 18 Whooping Crane Lane Key Allegro Isle Rockport TX 78382 Office: Drawer 2090 Corpus Christi TX 78403

CONE, SYDNEY M., Jr., ret. bus. exec.; b. Balt., Oct. 19, 1904; s. Sydney M. and Bessie (Skutch) C.; student U. Wis., 1921-23; A.B., Johns Hopkins, 1925; m. Isabel Frank, June 14, 1926; children—Sydney M., III, Donald Frank. With Cone Mills Corp., Greensboro, N.C., 1925-69; v.p., 1940-69, dir., 1940—, pres. Finishing div., until 1960, pres. Research and Devel. div., 1959-69; dir. Otto B. May, Inc.; dir. Texlin Corp., Industry mem., 4th region WLB, 1944-45. Chmn. Greensboro Youth Center, 1947-50, pres. Council Social Agys., 1940-41; pres. Friends Library, 1949-50, 63-65; pres. Greensboro Community Arts Council, 1961-62, hon. chmn., 1963-65; mem. vis. com. Margaret Morrison Carnegie Coll., Carnegie Inst. Tech., 1962-66. Trustee Johns Hopkins, 1961-67; past dir. Apparel Research Found., Inc. Past mem. Textile Research Inst. (pres. 1955-56, exec. com.), Nat. Cotton Council Research, Nat. Assn. Finishers Textile Fabrics (pres. 1952-53, chmn. 1954-55). Am. Assn. Textile Chemists and Colorists (ex-councilor). Author: Aim for a Job in Textiles. Home: 306 Rockford Rd Greensboro NC 27408

CONERLY, RICHARD PUGH, corp. exec.; b. Jackson, Ala., May 6, 1924; s. William L. and Eunice (Pugh) C.; student Howard Coll., Birmingham, Ala., 1942; B.J., U. Mo., 1949; LL.B., Harvard, 1952; m. Iva Jean Brightwell. Aug. 12, 1956; children—William Edward, Robert Andrew, Christopher Brightwell, Elizabeth Anne. Admitted to Mo. bar, 1952; practice in St. Louis, 1952- 68; asso., partner Thompson, Mitchel, Douglas, Neill & Guerri, 1952-65; v.p., gen. counsel, exec. v.p. Peabody Coal Co., St. Louis, 1965-69; pres. Pott

Ind., Inc., St. Louis, 1969—. Served with USAAF, 1942- 46. Home: 339 Hawthorne St Webster Groves, MO 63119. Office: 611 E Marceau St St Louis MO 63111

CONESE, E.P., business exec. Pres., chief exec. officer Irvin Industries, Inc., Lexington, Ky. Office: 1315 Versailles Rd Lexington KY 40504*

CONFER, OGDEN PALMER, feed and flour mill exec.: b. Mpls., Nov. 14, 1921; s. Ogden Armour and Ruth (Palmer) C.; student Westminster Coll. Mo., 1939-40; B.A., U. Minn., 1943; m. Elizabeth McElhenny, Dec. 20, 1941; children—Ogden William, Kay, Richard Palmer, Carol, Mgr. Feed div., v.p. Hubbard Milling Co., Mankato, Minn., 1946-59, pres., 1959-70, chmn. bd., chief exec. officer, 1970—, also dir.; dir. Nat. Citizens Bank Mankato, Kayot Corp. (Mankato), Confer Bros. (Mpls.). Bd. dirs. YMCA. Mem. N.W. (past pres.), Am. (dir., chmn. bd. 1970—) feed mfrs. assns., Millers Nat. Fedn. (past dir.), Mankato C. of C. (past dir.). Presbyn. (trustee). Club: Mankato Golf (past dir.). Home: Rural Route 1 Mankato MN 56001 Office: 424 N Front St Mankato MN 56001

CONFORTI, JAMES ANTHONY, podiatrist; b. N.Y.C., June 10, 1921; s. James M. and Brigida (Conforti) C.; student John Carroll U., 1939-42; D. Podiatric Medicine, Ohio Coll. Podiatry, Cleve., 1944; m. Frances Jeanette Marconi, May 18, 1946; children—James Michael, Stephen Paul, Bruce Charles, Douglas Mark. Clin. intern Ohio Coll. Podiatry, 1944-45; pvt. practice, Bedford, O., 1946- 65; tchr. pub. health Ohio Coll. Podiatry, 1948-67, dir. clinics, 1965—; founder podiatry clinc at Hawthornden State Hosp., Northfield, O., 1950-67, Jenning Hall Home Aged, Garfield Heights, O., 1949, Huron Rd. Hosp., East Cleveland, O., 1957, also extension clinics of Cleve. Foot Clinic; lectr., 1948-. Mem. Nat. Adv. Com. Med., Dental, Optometric and Podiatry Edn. 1966-70. Recipient Mennen Research aWard, 1946, 47, 48. Mem. N.E. Ohio Acad. Podiatry (pres. 1949-50), Am. (exec. council 1955-57, trustee 1957-66, pres. 1964-65), Ohio (pres. 1953-54, chmn. trustees 1954-56; Man of Year award, 1957, Spl. Recognition award 1965) podiatry assns., Am. Soc. Podiatric Dermatology (pres. 1962-63), Am., Ohio pub. health assns., Diabetes Assn. Greater Cleve. Home: 18214 Van Aken Blvd Shaker Heights OH 44122

CONFREY, EUGENE A., research adminstr.: b. Buffalo, Apr. 6, 1922; s. Joseph J. and Mary (Sexton) C.; student Syracuse U., 1940-43; B.A., George Washington U., 1948; M.A., Yale, 1951, Ph.D., 1963; M. Magdalene Santell, Sept. 13, 1946; children—Lyle, Jere. Analytical statistician; tech. editor Office Surgeon Gen., 1951-56; with USPHS, 1956—, asst. chief div. research grants NIH, 1962-63, dir. div., 1963-69, asso. dir. for program planning and evaluation Bur. Health Manpower Edn. Served with AUS, 1943-46. Mem. A.A.A.S., Am. Radio Relay League. Contbr. to Handbook of Social Gerontology. Editor: Administration of Community Health Services, 1961. Home: 6509 Laverock Lane, Bethesda, MD 20034 Office: Nat Insts Health Bethesda MD 20014

CONGDON, JEFFREY DELL, profl. basketball player; b. Whitewater, Wis., Oct. 17, 1943; s. Donald William and Marvel Rose (Moore) C.; student Brigham Young U., 1962-66; m. Julia Marie Anderson Sept. 10, 1966; children—Derek Paul, Cara Marie. Profl. basketball player with Anaheim (Cal.) Amigos, 1967, Denver Rockets, 1967-70, Utah Stars, 1970-71, N.Y. Mets, 1971, Dallas Chaparrals, 1971—. Mem. Am. Basketball Assn. Players Assn. Republican. Mem. Ch. of Jesus Christ of Latter-day Saints. Home: 2127 South 2200 East Salt Lake City UT 84109

CONGDON, WILLIAM, artist; b. Providence. Apr. 15, 1912; s. Gilbert Maurice and Caroline (Grosvenor) C.; grad. St. Marks Sch., Southboro, Mass., 1930, Yale, 1934; studied Dematrious Sch. of Sculpture, 1935, 39, Pa. Acad. Fine Arts, 1935, with Henry Hensche, Provincetown, 1935-36. Exhibited Boston, Carnegie Inst., Whitney Mus., U. Ill., U. Neb., Place of Legion of Honor, San Francisco, Toledo Gallery of Art, R.I. Mus., St. Louis Mus., Mus. Modern Art, Washington Galleria Obelisco, Rome, Walker Art Center, Mpls., Obelisco Gallery, London, 1958. Rome, Jeffress Gallery, London, 1958; Houston, 1954, Contemporary Am. Art Show Tokyo 1952, Venice Biennale, 1952, 58, Carnegie Internat., Pitts., 1952, 58, others; one man show Peggy Guggenheim Mus. Venice, 1957, Betty Parsons Gallery, N.Y.C., 1949, 50, 52-54, 56, 62, 67, Duncan Phillips, Washington, 1952, Santa Barbara Mus., 1954, Mass. Inst. Tech., 1958, Osserratorio Cristiano, Assisi, 1961, Palazzo Reale, Milan, Italy, 1962, R.I. Mus. Art (retrospective), 1965, Cambridge U., Eng., 1968, Galleria Cadario, Rome, Milan, 1969. Represented in collections of Whitney Mus. Am. Art, John S. Newberry, St. Louis Museum, Metropolitan Museum, Boston Mus., U. Ill., R.I. Mus., Mus. Modern Art, Toledo Mus., Detroit Inst. Fine Arts, Carnegie Inst., Wadsworth Atheneum, Contemporary Arts Mus., Houston, Addison Gallery, Andover, Mus. Modern Art (Venice), Ia. State Tchrs. Coll., Pro-Civitate-Christiana, Assisi, private collections including Nelson Rockefeller, Edward Root, Igor Stravinsky. Awarded prizes R.I. Ann., 1948, 49, Temple Gold Medal, Pa. Acad., 1951, purchase award University of Illinois, 1952, W.A. Clark award Corcoran Gallery, Washington, 1953. Roman Catholic. Author: In My Disc of Gold, 1961 (Italy), 1962 (U.S.); Congdon (A Search for Structure in the Work of William Congdon), 1968. Home: Vicolo Bovi 1 Assisi (Perugia) Italy Office: Betty Parsons Gallery 24 W 57th St New York City NY 10019 also Galleria Cadario Milan Italy

CONGER, CLEMENT ELLIS, fgn. service officer; b. Rockingham, Va., Oct. 15, 1912; s. Clement E. and Hallie (Ramsey) C.; grad. Strayer Coll., postgrad George Washington U., 1933-34; grad. Adj. Gen. Officer Candidate Sch., Ft. Washington Md., 1943; m. Lianne Hopkins, May 29, 1948; children—William Ramsay, Jay Alden, Shelley Louise. Asst. finance examiner PWA, 1933-34; officer mgr., corr. Chgo. Tribune, Washington 1934-41; office mgr. U.S. Rubber Co., Washington. 1941-42, pub. relations asst., N.Y.C., 1946-47; staff asst., asst. exec. dir. asst. sec. state for occupied areas Dept. State, 1947-49, staff asst., asst. exec. dir. Bur. German Affairs, 1949-54; asst. chief protocol, 1955-57, dep. chief protocol, 1958-61: spl. asst. to dir., exec. sec. U.S. Arms Control and Disarmament Agy., State Dept., Washington, 1962-69; dep. chief protocol, 1969-70; protocol asst. to chmn. Nixon-Agnew Inaugural, 1968-69; chmn. spl. fine arts com. State Dept., 1962—, White House curator, 1970—. Producer color motion picture travel films, lectr. on diplomatic reception rooms Dept. of State. Mem. Alexandria (Va.) Hist. Restoration and Preservation Commn., 1968—, Com. for Preservation White House, men's adv. com. Gunston Hall Plantation, Va. Trustee Va. Mus. Fine Arts, Richmond, St. Stephen's Sch., Alexandria; bd. dirs. Historic Alexandria Found. Served from 2d lt. to maj. AUS, 1942-46; asst. sec. combined civil affairs com. Combined Chiefs Staff. Episcopalian. Clubs: Metropolitan, Chevy Chase, City Tavern (Washington). Contbr. articles, illustrations to various publs. radio, TV programs. Home: 320 Mansion Dr Alexandria VA Office: Dept State Washington DC 20525

CONGER, JOHN JANEWAY, educator, psychologist; b. New Brunswick, N.J., Feb. 27, 1921; s. John C. and Katharine (Janeway) C.; B.A. magna cum laude, Amherst Coll., 1943; M.S., Yale, 1947, Ph.D., 1949; m. Mayo Trist Kline, Jan. 1, 1944; children—Steven Janeway, David Trist, Asst. prof. Psychology Ind. U., 1949-53; chief staff psychologist U.S. Naval Acad., 1951-52; mem. faculty U. Colo. Sch. Medicine, prof. psychology, 1957—, asso. dean, 1961-63, v.p. for med. affairs, 1963-70, dean, 1963-68; fellow Center for Advanced Study in Behavioral Scis., Stanford, Cal., 1970-71; cons. to NIH, VA, USPHS. Vice chmn. Colo. Bd. Psychology Examiners, 1961-64; mem. Gov. Colo. Com. Mental Health, 1957; chmn. mental health adv. council Colo. Dept. Pub. Health, 1957-61; mem. tng. com. Nat. Inst. Mental Health, 1959-62; mem. Western council mental health research and tng. Western Interstate Commn. Higher Edn., 1959-66; chmn. research com. President's Com. Traffic Safety, 1960- 63; mem. com. road user characteristics Hwy. Research Bd., 1960-63; vice chmn. nat. motor vehicle safety adv. council Dept. Transp. 1967-70; mem. inter-council com. constrn. univ.-affiliated facilities for mentally retarded Dept. Health, Edn. and Welfare, 1967—, mem. Sec.'s adv. com. traffic safety, 1966-69; council research and planning Am. Hosp. Assn., 1965-68; nat. adv. mental health council USPHS, 1965-69; nat. adv. com. John F. Kennedy Center for Research on Edn. and Human Devel., 1965— , chmn., 1970—; mem. adv. com. on undergrad med. edn. A.M.A., 1969- -, adv. com. on casualty ins. Dept. Transp., 1970; mem. Pres.'s Task Force on Hwy. Safety, 1970. Served to lt. USNR, 1944-46, 51-52. Recipient Stearns Alumni medal for extraordinary Service U Colo., 1970. Fellow Am. Psychol. Assn. (mem. policy and planning bd. 1967-70), A.A.A.S., Am. Acad. Polit. and Social Sci.; mem. Denver (hon. mem.), Colo. (Distinguished Service award 1970) med. socs., Phi Beta Kappa, Sigma Xi, Alpha Omega Alpha (hon.). Author: Child Development and Personality, 3d edit., 1969; Readings in Child Development, 1964, 2d edit., 1970; Personality, Social Class and Delinquency, 1965; also articles. Editorial bd. Jour. Med. Edn., Traffic Safety Research Rev. Home: 130 S Birch St Denver CO 80222

CONGER, KYRIL B., surgeon; b. Berlin, Germany, Apr. 11, 1913; s. Seymour Beach and Lucile (Boiley) C.; A.B., U. Mich., 1933, M.D., 1936; m. Joy Springer, June 1, 1945; children—Steven B., Kyril B. II, James W. and William T. (twins). Instr. urology U. Mich. Hosp., 1941; urologist; med. group, Honolulu, 1946-47; prof. urology, dept. head Temple U. Med. Sch. and Hosp., Phila., 1947—; area cons. urology VA Mid-Atlantic State and P.R. Served from lt. to col. M.C., AUS, 1942-46; urology sect., 208th Gen Hosp. Fellow A.C.S.; mem. Am. Urological Assn., Sigma Xi, Nu Sigma Nu. Contbr. articles to profl. jours. Author: Transurethral Prostatic Surgery, 1964. Home: 1636 Lafayette Rd Gladwyne PA 19035 Office: 3401 N Broad St Philadelphia PA 19140

CONGLETON, JAMES EDMUND, educator; b. Slade, Ky., Nov. 16, 1901; s. George Washington and Annie (Wells) C.; A.B., Berea (Ky.) Coll., 1926; A.M., George Peabody Coll. for Tchrs., 1928; postgrad. U. Chgo., 1930; fellow U. N.C., 1934-36, Smith research fellow, 1935, Ph.D., 1937; m. Elizabeth Cunningham, June 11, 1936; 1 dau., Elizabeth Carol. Instr., Van Lear (Ky.) High Sch., 1925-28; prin., Canton (Miss.) High Sch., 1928-31; instr. Tulane U., 1936-37; instr. U. Fla., 1937-41, asst. prof., 1041-44, asso. prof., 1944-46, prof., 1946-59; head dept. English, Findlay (O.) Coll., 1960-61, chmn. div. humanities, 1961, dean Sch. Humanities and Scis., 1962-65, prof., 1965- -; Fulbright prof. Englsih U. Turin, Italy, 1957-58. Mem. Modern Lang. Assn., Am. Soc. for 18th Century Studies, Am. Assn. U. Profs., Nat. Council Tchrs. English, Johnson Society of London, Johnson Soc. Central Region, Johnson Soc. Litchfield, Sigma Tau Delta, Phi Kappa Phi, Phi Delta Kappa. Democrat. Episcopalian. Mng. editor So. Folklore Quarterly, 1943-45, editorial bd. since 1944; editor with introduction: René Rapin's De Carmine Pastorali, 1947; Essays for Better Reading (in collaboration); The Meaning in Reading, 1943 (rev. 1947, 53, 56); Theories of Pastoral Poetry in England, 1684-1798, 1952; College English—The First Year, 1952, rev. 1956. Contbr. articles to encys. and jours. Home: 205 Clifton Av Findlay OH 45840

CONGLETON, RICHARD J., lawyer; b. Newark, July 25, 1905; s. Jerome T. and Jesse (Tobin) C.; B.S., Princeton, 1928; LL.B., Rutgers U., 1931; m. Margaret Hedden, June 23, 1930 (dec.) children—Margaret Jane (Mrs. James R. Lacey), Richard J., William G.; m. 2d, Melba Coutsonikas, Jan, 20, 1968. Admitted to N.J. bar, 1931, D.C. bar, 1969; asso. McCarter & English, Newark, 1931-37; partner Gongleton & McLaughlin, Newark, 1937-42; first asst. prosecutor Essex County, N.J., 1946-48; partner Shanley, Congleton & Fisher, Newark, 1948- 52; prosecutor Essex County, 1950-52; gen. atty. Prudential Ins. Co. Am., Newark, 1952-65, sr. v.p., 1965-70. Served with USAAF, 1942-46. Mem. Am., N.J., Essex County (pres. 1954-55), Fed. bar assns., Assn. Life Ins. Counsel, Rutgers Law Sch. Alumni Assn. (pres. 1952). Home: 2111 Jefferson Davis Hwy Arlington VA 22202 Office: 734 15th St NW Washington DC 20005

CONKLE, DWIGHT HARLEY, banker; b. Winona Lake, Ind., Mar. 27, 1908; s. David I. and Edna (Mellen) C.; student spl. courses Am. Inst. Banking, 1935-41; m. Dorothea F. Dethloff, Aug. 26, 1944 (dec. Feb. 1960); m. 2d, Ruth D. Kleinsmith, Sept. 9, 1967. With Cleve. Trust Co., 1924—, v.p., 1958-70, sr. v.p., 1970—. Served with C.E., AUS, 1942-44. Mem. Cleve. C. of C. Clubs: Cleveland Bond, Mid Day (Cleve.). Home: 30649 Jackson Rd Chagrin Falls OH 44022 Office: 901 Euclid Av Cleveland OH 44101

CONKLIN, CLARENCE ROBERT, lawyer; b. Arcadia, Kan., Aug. 18, 1899; s. Thomas C. and Elizabeth (Yoos) C.; student Phillips U., 1919-1921, Okla, State Coll., 1923; A.B., Drake U., 1925; J.D., U. Chgo., 1928; m. Ellen Gleason Birkhoff, Aug. 20, 1932; children—Dr. Robert D. Birkhoff (stepson), Adrienne Diane (Mrs. Russell F. Stephens. Jr.), Thomas William, Ellen Melissa C. (Mrs. David P. Harmon, Jr.). Admitted to Ill. bar. 1928; with Nat. Surety Corp., claims atty. 1929-1937; with Toplis & Harding, 1937-1945; partner law firm of Heineke & Conklin, and Heineke Conklin & Schrader 1945-67; council various ins. underwriters. Mem. Internat. Assn. Ins. Counsel, Am., Ill., Chgo. bar assns., Am. Judicature Soc., Maritime Law Assn. U.S., Beta Theta Pi, Phi Alpha Delta. Clubs: Traffic, Executives, Union League (Chgo.); Hinsdale (Ill.) Golf; Misquamicut (Watch Hill, R.I.). Home: Central Beach Quonochontaug, RI 02808; also Sanibel Island FL 33957

CONKLIN, E.J., physician. Dir., Long Term Care Hosp., Eloise, Mich. Office: 30712 Michigan Av Eloise MI 48132*

CONKLIN, GEORGE MELVILLE, food co. exec.; b. Roselle Park, N.J., Dec. 29, 1921; s. Melville Guy and Anna Elizabeth (McMahon) C.; B.S., Clarkson Coll. Tech., 1947; M.S., Newark Coll. Engring., 1951; m. Jean Austin Wiley, Feb. 19, 1944; children—Andrea (Mrs. Sidney G. Johnston, Jr.), Blair. Draftsman, Babcock & Wilcox, N.Y.C., 1939-42; indsl. engr. Johns-Manville Co., Manville, N.J., 1945-47; indsl. engr. Western Electric Co., Kearny, N.J., 1950-51, indsl. engring. supr., Bloomfield, N.J., 1951-52; with M & M/Mars, Hackettstown, N.J., 1952—, pres., 1968—; v.p. Mars, Inc. Served with inf. AUS, 1943-45. Decorated Combat Inf. badge. Mem. Chocolate Mfrs. Am., Nat. Confectioners Assn. Clubs: Congressional Country (Bethesda, Md.); Roxiticus Golf (Mendham, N.J.). Home: Summit Rd Brookside NJ 07926 Office: High St Hackettstown NJ 07840

CONKLIN, GEORGE TAYLOR, Jr., ins. co. exec.; b. Merrick, N.Y., Dec. 18, 1914; s. George Taylor and Ellen (Stolworthy) C.; A.B., Dartmouth, 1936, M.C.S., 1937; student columbia 1941-43; Ph.D., N.Y.U., 1943; m. Carol Szecheny, Mar. 28, 1959; children—Sandra Dawn, George Taylor III, Heather Jean, Holly Ellen. With Guardian Life Insurance Company of America, 1939—, successively asst. to pres., asst. to pres. and dir. research, financial v.p., v.p. and dir., 1944-59, sr. v.p. chmn. finance com., 1958-64, exec. v.p., 1964-69, pres., 1969-; mem. downtown adv. com. Bank Trust Co.; trustee Continental Mortage Investors, Hubbard Real Estate Investments; adj. prof. finance N.Y. U. Mem. Lower Midtown adv. bd. Chem. Bank N.Y. Trust Co.; adv. com. Wharton Sch. Finance and Commerce, U. Pa. Trustee, mem. finance com. Tchrs. Ins. and Annuity Assn.; trustee com. on investments Social Sci. Research Council; mem. bd. overseers Amos Tuck Sch., Dartmouth; trustee, finance com. Woodlawn Cemetery; mem. investment adv. com. N.Y. State Tchr.'s Retirement Bd. Mem. Am. Econ. Assn., Am. Finance Assn. (pres. 1963), Am. Statis. Assn., N.Y. State C. of C., Assn. N.Y. State Life Ins. Cos. (sec.-treas., mem. exec. com), Conf. Bus. Economists (vice chmn. 1970), Bus. Economists Council. Home: 20 Summit Rd Port Washington NY 11050 Office: 201 Park Av S New York City NY 10003

CONKLIN, HAROLD COLYER, educator, anthropologist; b. Easton, Pa., Apr. 27, 1926; s. Howard S. and May W. (Colyer) C.; A.B., U. Cal. at Berkeley, 1950; Ph.D., Yale, 1955; m. Jean M. Morisuye, June 11, 1954; children—Bruce Robert, Mark William. From instr. to asso. prof. anthropology Columbia, 1954-62; lectr. anthropology Rockefeller Inst., 1961-62; prof. anthropology Yale, 1962—, chmn. dept., 1964-68; vis. mem. Inst. for Advanced Study, Princeton, 1972; field research in Philippines, 1945-47, 52- 54, 55, 57-58, 61, 62-63, 64, 65, 68-69, 70, Malaya and Indonesia, 1948, 57, Cal. and N.Y., 1951, 52, Guatemala, 1959. Dir., com. problems and policy Social Sci. Research Council, 1963-70; spl. cons. Internat. Rice Research Inst., Los Baos, Philippines, 1962—; book rev. editor Am. Anthropologist, 1960-62; mem. Pacific sci. bd. Nat. Acad. Scis.-NRC, 1962-66. Served with AUS, 1944-46. Fellow Am. Anthrop. Assn. (exec. bd. 1965-68), Royal Anthrop. Soc., N.Y. Acad. Scis. (sec. sect. anthropology 1956), Sigma Xi; mem. Am. Ethnol. Soc. (councilor 1960-62), Koninklijk Inst. voor Taal- Land- en Volkenkunde, Linguistic Soc. Am., Soc. Am. Archaeology, Kroeber Anthrop. Soc., Phila. Anthrop. Assn., Am. Geog. Soc., Am. Oriental Soc., Assn. Asian Studies, Classification Soc., La Société de Linguistique de Paris, Far Eastern Prehistory Soc., Am. Folklore Soc., Soc. Ethnomusicology, Soc. Econ. Botany, Internat. Assn. Plant Taxonomy, A.A.A.S., Phi Beta Kappa. Author articles, reports, monographs. Home: 106 York Sq New Haven CT 06851 Office: 51 Hillhouse Av New Haven CT 06520

CONKLIN, HARVEY HINTON, ins. co. exec.; b. Allentown. O., Sept. 7, 1913; s. Harvey Hinton and Etta (Barney) C.; A.B., Dartmouth, 1935; m. Violet Mary Dowding, Sept. 5, 1936. Research asso. Met. Life Ins. Co., 1935-59; with Life Ins. Co. Va., 1959—, v.p., actuary, 1965-70, sr. v.p., actuary, 1971—, also dir. Fellow Soc. Actuaries; mem. Internat. Congress Actuaries, Am. Acad. Actuaries, Mid-Atlantic Actuarial Club (pres. 1968-69). Methodist. Home: 609 Horsepen Rd Richmond VA 23229 Office: 914 Capitol St Richmond VA 23209

CONKLIN, HUGH RANDOLPH, beverage co. exec.; b. Battle Creek, Mich., Oct. 20, 1911; s. Hugh William and Ida Charlotte (Maier) C.; B.S. in Engring., U. Mich., 1933; m. Mary Alice Kendel, Mar. 12, 1938; children—Hugh Randolph, Drue Kendel. With Gen. Foods Corp., 1933-57, Eastern regional Sales mgr., 1954-55, nat. sales mgr. Post Cereals div., 1955-57; with Lever Bros. Co., 1957—, v.p. sales, 1962-71; v.p. nat. sales Pepsicola Co., Purchase, N.Y., 1971—; dir. Apollo Investments, Inc. Trustee Osteo. Hosp. and Clinic of N.Y., Post Grad. Inst. Osteo. Medicine & Surgery; bd. dirs. Found. for Research, N.Y. Acad. Osteopathy, Wilton Town Assn.; past chmn. trustees 101 Assn. Served to capt., inf. AUS, 1942-46; CBI. Decorated Bronze Star, Combat Inf. badge. Mem. Am. Mgmt. Assn., U.S. C. of C., N.Y. Sales Execs. Club, Delta Kappa Epsilon. Clubs: Saugatuck River (Conn.) Power Squadron; Cedar Point Yacht (Westport, Conn.); University (N.Y.). Office: Pepsicola Co Purchase NY 10577

CONKLIN, MARIE ECKHARDT, biologist; b. Derby, Conn., Sept. 30, 1908; d. Malcolm Moyer and Elizabeth Nancy (McLean) Eckhardt; B.A., Wellesley Coll., 1929; M.S., U. Wis., 1930; Ph.D., Columbia, 1936; m. G. Howard Conklin, June 27, 1931; children—Elizabeth Nancy, George William. Teaching asst. dept. botany Wellesley Coll., 1930-31; research Bklyn. Botanic Garden, 1935-36; research asso. dept. genetics Carnegie Inst. of Washington at Cold Spring Harbor, 1936-41; instr. to prof. Adelphi U., 1943—, chmn. dept. biology, 1953-67; research collaborator Brookhaven Nat. Lab., 1959—. Dir. Adelphi Coll. Nat. Sci. Found. AEC summer insts. and in- service programs for high sch. tchrs. sci., 1959-64. Mem. Genetics Soc. Am., A.A.A.S., Rehab. Research Soc., Am. Inst. Biol. Scis., Bot. Soc. Am., Sigma Xi, Sigma Delta Epsilon, Beta Beta Beta. Home: 12062 Caminito Cadena Rancho Bernardo San Diego CA 92128

CONKLIN, THOMAS ROSCOE, metal products co. exec.; b. Aurora, Ill., May 5, 1924; s. Thomas R. and Jane (Waters) C.; grad. U.S. Mcht. Marine Acad., 1943-44; B.B.A., U. Mich., 1949; m. Grace Ann Robbie, Apr. 8, 1950; children-Robbie, Jane, Edward. With Lyon Metal Products Co., Aurora, 1949—, dir., 1967—, exec. v.p., 1968, pres., chief exec. officer, 1969—; dir. Mchts. Nat. Bank of Aurora. Trustee YWCA; mem. citizens adv. bd. Aurora Coll. Served with U.S. Mcht. Marines, 1943-46. Mem. Delta Kappa Epsilon. Episcopalian. Elk. Clubs: Union League, Aurora Country (Aurora); Economic (Chgo.). Home: 215 LeGrande St Aurora IL 60506 Office: P O Box 671 Aurora IL 60507

CONKLIN, WILLIAM J., architect; b. Hebron, Neb., May 2, 1923; s. J.E. and Wilhelmina C. (Barrett) C.; grad. Phillips Exeter Acad., 1940; B.A., Doane Coll., 1944; M.Arch., Harvard, 1950; m. Barbara Mallon, Apr. 28, 1945; 1 son, Christopher. Project mgr. IBEC Corp., N.Y.C., 1950-51; archtl. designer Mayer Whittlesey & Glass, N.Y.C., 1951-58, asso. partner charge design, 1958-60; partner Whittlesey & Conklin, N.Y.C., 1960-65, Whittlesey Conklin & Rossant, N.Y.C., 1966-67, Conklin & Rossant, N.Y.C., 1967—; adjunct prof. Pratt Inst., 1962-66; lectr. urban design New Sch.; prin. works include New Town of Reston, Va., 2 Charles Center, Balt., Butterfield House, Premier Apt. Houses (both N.Y.C.), Student Activities Bldg. of Upstate Med. Center, Syracuse, N.Y. Mem. Municipal Art Soc., Met. Council Housing, Parks Council, Citizens Union. Fellow Found. for the Arts, Religion and Culture; supporting mem. Textile Mus. (Washington); pres. Harvard Grad. Sch. Design Council, 1966-67; mem. vis. com. and Loeb fellowship program Harvard. Served with USNR, 1943-45. Recipient Ware prize, Harvard, 1949; Wheelwright traveling fellow, 1952. Mem. A.I.A., N.Y. State Assn. Architects. Mem. United Ch. of Christ (trustee). Home: 22 E 51st St New York City NY 10022 Office: 251 Park Av S New York City NY 10010

CONLEY, BINFORD HARRISON, librarian; b. Madison County Ala., Feb. 13, 1933; s. Benjamin Harrison and Effie Lynette (Fowlkes) C.; A.B., Morehouse Coll., 1953; M.S. in L.S., Atlanta U., 1960; m.

Thelma Bond, August 12, 1956; children—Binford Harrison, Elizabeth Binelle. Engaged as a radio announcer with radio station WERD, Atlanta, 1952-54; asst. librarian Atlanta U., 1958-60; chief librarian S.C. State Coll., Orangeburg, 1960- 62, Ala. A. and M. Coll., 1962—. Served with AUS, 1954-57; maj. Res. Mem. Am., Southeastern library assns. Christian Meth. Episcopal (trustee, supt. Sunday Sch.). Home: 112 Whitney Av N E Huntsville AL 35811 Office: Library Ala A and M Coll Normal AL 35762

CONLEY, CARROLL LOCKARD, physician, educator; b. Balt., May 14, 1915; s. Harry Lewis and Harriet (Coulbourne) C.; A.B., Johns Hopkins, 1935; M.D., Columbia, 1940; m. Edith DeYoung, Feb. 27, 1943; children—Anne Marie, Jean Alice. Intern Presbyn. Hosp., N.Y.C., 1940-42; fellow medicine Johns Hopkins, 1946, instr. to asso. prof. medicine, 1947-56, prof. medicine, 1956—, physician in charge hematology clinic Johns Hopkins Hosp., 1947-60, dir. labs., 1956-66; hon. asso. prof. medicine Guy's Hosp. Med. Sch., London, Eng. Cons. USPHS, FDA, Army, VA, WHO. Mem. com. on blood NRC, 1954-63, chmn. subcom. on thrombosis and hemorrhage NRC, 1962-64; chmn. hematology study section NIH, 1962-65. Served from lt. to maj. M.C., AUS, 1942-45. Recipient Bicentennial medal Coll. Physicians and Surgeons, 1967. Fellow A.C.P.: mem. Assn. Am. Physicians, Am. Soc. Clin. Investigation, A.M.A., Am. (exec. com.), European (corr. mem.) socs. hematology, Interurban Clin. Club, Phi Beta Kappa, Alpha Omega Alpha. Editorial bd. Archives of Internal Medicine, 1959-65, Blood, the Jour. of Hematology, 1954-67, Bull. of Johns Hopkins Hosp., 1963-70. Contbr. med. textbooks and profl. jours. Home: 120 E Lake Av Baltimore MD 21212 Office: Johns Hopkins Hosp Baltimore MD 21205

CONLEY, CLARE DEAN, magazine editor; b. Caldwell, Ida., Jan. 22, 1929; s. Claris F. and Gladys (Goodall) C.; student Stanford, 1947-49; B.A., Coll. Ida., 1951; m. Mike Ann Packard, Aug. 4, 1951; children—Brent, Kim, Ted. Newspaper and Freelance writer, 1951-61; mem. staff Field and Stream mag., 1961—, editor-in-chief, 1970—. Named Outstanding Young Alumni of Coll. Ida., 1964, Outstanding Young Man of Am., 1965. Mem. Outdoor Writers Assn. Am., Advt. Sportsmen's Club N.Y., Rod and Gun Editors Assn. Met. N.Y., Aircraft Owners and Pilots Assn. Club: N.Y. Athletic. Author: Guide to Upland Birds, 1966. Home: Hemlock Farms Hawley PA 18428 Office: 383 Madison Av New York City NY 10017

CONLEY, DEAN, mgmt. cons.; b. St. Paul, Minn., July 6, 1905; s. William W. and Josephine (Dean) C.; student St. Thomas Mil. Acad., St. Paul, Minn.; B.B.A., Univ. Minn., 1931; m. Mildred Casey, Aug. 21, 1941; children—Dean, James William. Mem. adminstrv. staff U. Minn. hosps., 1931-35, mgr. students' health service U. Minn., 1935-41; exec. dir. Am. Coll. Hosp. Adminstrs., 1941-65, also editor Hosp. Adminstrn., 1956-66, v.p. research and edn., 1965-66; dir. hosp. relations Merck Sharp & Dohme, 1966-70; mgmt. cons., 1970—. Hon. mem. bd. Chgo. council Camp Fire Girls, Inc.; tustee Health Research and Ednl. Trust N.J. Fellow Am. Coll. Hosp. Adminstrs.; mem. Hosp. Assn. Brazil (hon.), Sao Paulo Hosp. Assn. (hon.). Chgo., Am., Pa. (dir. 1969—) pub. health assns., Am. (hon.), Pa. Hosp. Assn., Delaware Valley Hosp. Forum Am. Med. Colls., Phi Gamma Delta. Roman Catholic. Club: Lake Shore (Chgo.). Home: Hampton House Penn Valley Narberth PA 19072

CONLEY, EUGENE, operatic singer; b. Lynn, Mass., Mar. 12, 1908; s. Reuben Anthony and Josephin (Farnsworth) C.; student pub. schs. Lynn; studied with Ettore Verna; m. Winifred Heidt, Mar. 9, 1948; m. 2d, Alvah Lea, July 9, 1960. Began as ch. soloist; singer local radio stas.; toured with Boston Male Choir; 1st profl. appearance in Robin Hood, Boston Light Opera Co.; sang with Handel-Haydn Soc. in Messiah; soloist Commonwealth Symphony; appeared in radio program NBC Presents Eugene Conley; guest engagements NBC Symphony under Arturo Toscanini and Frank Black; N.Y. operatic debut in Rigoletto, as the Duke, Bklyn. Acad. Music, 1940; toured transcontinentally with San Carlo Opera Co., also with New Opera Co. under Fritz Busch; featured lyric tenor Cin. Summer Opera Co., summers; appeared with Mexico Nat. Opera Co., N.Y.C. Center Opera Co., New Orleans Opera Assn.; toured Europe, singing in numerous opera houses, 1947-48; various concerts, U.S. and Can., 1949-50; also appeared City Center Opera; also soloist with Stokowski and New York Philharmonic in 5 concerts Carnegie Hall; also sang at LaScala Opera House, Milan, Italy. 1949, 50, 51; debut in title role of Faust, Met. Opera; guest artist Stadium Concerts, N.Y.C., summer 1950; appeared in La Boheme, Arena, Verona, Italy, 1950; sang with Netherlands Opera and Holland Festival, 1957; frequent appearances leading network radio and TV programs including Voice of Firestone; soloist Presidential Inauguration, 1953; appeared in 20th-Century-Fox short Of Men and Music: recordings for London FFRR; Am. premiere Stravinskys Rakes Progress, Metropolitan Opera, 1953: artist tenor in residence Sch. Music, N. Tex. State U., 1960—; mem. faculty, soloist Summer Vocal Inst., Am. Inst. Mus. Studies, Graz, Austria, 1971. Mem. Met. Opera Assn., LaScala Opera Co. in Milan, San Francisco Opera Co., New Orleans Opera, N.Y.C. Center Opera Co., Cin. Zoo Opera Co., Chgo. Opera Co., Royal Opera House in Stockholm, Opera Comique in Paris, Nat. Opera of Mexico City, Am. Assn. U. Profs., Nat. Assn. Tchrs Singing, Ft. Worth Opera Co. (bd.). Am. Guild Mus. Artists (life mem. bd.). Home: 108 Forest St Denton TX 76201

CONLEY, JOHN JOSEPH, physician: b. Carnegie, Pa., Juje 1, 1912; s. Phillip B. and Susan (Burns) C.; B.S., U. of Pittsburgh, 1933, M.D., 1937; m. Mary Bradwell; children—John Joseph, Mary B., Anna, Intern. Mercy Hosp., Pitts., 1937-38; res. internal medicine Kings Co. Hosp., N.Y. City, 1938- 39, resident ear, nose and throat-endoscopy, 1939-41; asst. chief plastic surgery, ear, nose and throat Tilton Gen. Hosp., Ft. Dix, N.J., 1941-43, chief plastic surgery, 1943-45, 315th Gen. Hosp., 1945; dir. head and neck dept. Pack Med. Group, N.Y.C.; chief head and neck service St. Vincent's Hosp., N.Y.C.; cons. plastic surgeon Paterson (N.J.) Gen. Hosp.; cons. head and neck surgery United Hosp., Portchester, St. Joseph's Hosp., Yonkers, N.Y.; cons. otolaryngology St. Agnes Hosp., White Plains; cons. otorhinolaryngology Mercy Hosp., Rockville Centre; attending otolaryngologist Presbyn. Hosp.; attending staff Doctors Hosp., courtesy staff Manhattan Eye Ear and Throat Hosp. (all N.Y.C.); consultant otolaryngologist U.S. Army. Clin. prof. otolaryngology Columbia Coll. Phys. and Surg. Diplomate Am. Bd. Otolaryngology. Fellow Triological Soc., A.C.S.; mem. A.M.A., N.Y., N.Y. County med. socs., Am. Laryngological Assn., N.Y. Acad. Med., N.Y. Acad. Scis., James Ewing Soc., Soc. Head and Neck Surgeons, Am. Society for Head and Neck Surgery (pres.), N.Y. Cancer Soc., N.Y. Laryngol. Soc. (chmn. postgrad. course head and neck surgery, president 1966), Am. Acad. Facial Plastic and Reconstructive Surgery (president 1966). Club: N.Y. Atteltic. Author articles on Otolaryngology, plastic and cancer in med. and dental journals. Home: 24 E 78th St New York City NY 10021 Office: 139 E 36th St New York City NY 10016

CONLEY, PATRICK, elec. engr.; b. Roby, Tex., Oct. 10, 1921; s. Bourne Lurl and Mary Esther (Barlow) C.; B.S. in Elec. Engring., Rice Inst., 1942; Sc.M. Communications Engring., Harvard, 1946, Ph.D. Applied Physics, 1948, M.B.A., 1955; m. Lucy Webster, Sept. 26, 1942; children—Christopher, Peter, Molly. With Westinghouse Electric Corp., Pitts., 1948-64, successively staff research labs., dir. devel. to v.p. engring., exec. asst. to v.p. Balt. divs., tech. dir. def. products hdqrs., Washington, 1948-59, gen. mgr. air-arm div., Balt., 1959-61, v.p. industry engring. apparatus, service and indsl. systems, 1961-64; vis. prof. Carnegie Inst. Tech., Pitts., 1964-67; adj. sr. fellow Mellon Inst., 1964-67; sci. adviser to gov. of Pa., 1965-67; v.p. Boston Cons. Group, Boston, 1967—; with exec. office Pres., Office Sci. and Tech., 1964-65. Served lt. comdr. USNR, 1942-45. Mem. I.E.E.E., Am. Orchid Soc. Clubs: Gibson Island (Md.); Manchester Yacht, Essex County (Manchester, Mass.). Contbr. articles electromagnetic acoustic and bus. subjects. Home: Crowhurst Manchester MA 01944 Office: Boston Consulting Group 1 Boston Pl Boston MA 02106

CONLEY, PAUL A., investment banker. President, dir., mem. exec. com. Blyth & Co., Inc.; dir. Hart Schaffner & Marx, Gen. Am. Oil Co. Tex., Pauley Petroleum, Inc., Banque Blyth & Cie., Paris, France. Address: Blyth & Co 14 St New York City NY 10005

CONLEY, PHILIP MALLORY, editor and publisher; b. Charleston, W.Va., Nov. 30, 1887; s. George W. and Alice (Simpson) C.; B.S., W.Va. U., 1914; Litt.D., W.Va. Wesleyan Coll., 1936; LL.D., Concord Coll., 1960; m. Pearl Scott; Aug. 5, 1914 (dec.); 1 adopted dau., Phyllis P. Tchr., supt. pub. schs. 8 yrs.; dir. welfare work Consolidation Coal Co., Jenkins, Ky., 1919-21; editor-in chief The W.Va. Ency., 1929; editor, The West Virginia Review, 1923-46; spl. European corr. Cin. Enquirer, 1950; pres. Edn. Found., Inc.; chmn. bd. Charleston Printing Co. Liaison officer Am. Mission to Greece, 1947-48; spl. assignment by Inst. Inter-Am. Affairs to Latin Am. Countries, 1952; specialist for Dept. of State to Greece, 1955. Past pres. Kanawha Valley Heart Assn; mem. W.Va. Centennial Commission. Commd. 2d lt. U.S. Army, Sept. 13, 1918; chief of ednl. service Mil. Hosp., Markleton, Pa., and Camp Wadsworth, Spartanburg, S.C., 1918-19. Decorated Chevalier Legion of Honor (France), 1937; Gold Cross of Royal Order of George I (Greece), 1962; named W.Va. son of Year W.Va. Soc. D.C., 1964. Mem. Am. Legion (nat. vice comdr. 1937-38), Phi Beta Kappa, Alpha Alumnae Chapter (pres. 1939). Republican. Methodist. Mason (K.T., 32, K.C.C.H., Shriner), Rotarian. Club: Emeritus of U.W. Va. Author: Life in a West Virginia Coal Field (monograph), 1923; Little Stories About West Virginia (series of magazine articles); West Virginia Yesterday and Today, 1931, rev., 1952, 1966; (with Boyd B. Stutler), Beacon Lights of West Virginia History, 1939; Mountain Murder, 1939; Uncle Amos, Politician, 1940; West Virginia, A Brief History of the Mountain State, 1940; Your Country and Mine (textbook on government, with Grace A. Turkington), 1943; Everday Philosophy, 1944; America's Debt to Greece, 1957; The Greatest Century in History, 1958; History of the West Virginia Coal Industry, 1958; As I See It, 1965; West Virginia Reader, Stories of Early Days, 1970; also monographs; contbr. 24 articles on Mining Town Morale to Coal Review, 1922. Home: 2504 S Kanawha Av Charleston WV 25304 Office: 810 Virginia St W Charleston WV 25302

CONLEY, ROBERT FRANCIS, marine corps officer; b. Lansing, Mich., Apr. 9, 1919; s. Robert Frank and Margaret (Thompson) C.; B.A., Muskingum Coll., New Concord, O., 1941; grad. Joint Services Staff Coll., Latimer, Eng., 1956, Air War Coll., Maxwell AFB, Montgomery, Ala., 1961; m. Jane Reed, June 6, 1942; children—Robert Frank (dec.), John Christopher. Commd. 2d lt. AC, USMC, 1942, advanced through grades to brig. gen., 1968; served in combat Guadalcanal, 1942, Okinawa, 1944; comdr. night fighter squadron, Korean conflict; comdr. Marine Air Group, Vietnam, 1965; comdg. gen. Marine Corps Air Sta., Cherry Point, N.C., Marine Bases Eastern Area, 1968-70; comdg. gen. 1st Marine Air Wing (rear), 1970-71; gen. 1st Marine Air Wing, Iwakuni, Japan, 1971—; dir. information Hdqrs. USMC, 1971—. Decorated (2) Legion of Merit with combat V, D.F.C. with 3 oak leaf clusters, Air medal with 3 silver oak leaf clusters; recipient Sec. of Navy award for cost reduction program, 1970, Distinguished Service award New Bern-Craven County C. of C. (N.C.), 1970, certificate of Appreciation Gov. N.C. Mem. Naval Order U.S., Sertoma Internat., Order of Daedalians. Home: 1600 S Eads St Arlington VA 22202 Office: Dir Information Hdqrs Marine Corps Washington DC 20380

CONLEY, WILLIAM H., educator; b. Sharon, Wis., Feb. 13, 1907; s. Stephen E. and Agnes (Kinna) G.; B.S.C., Loyola U., 1930, A.M., 1935; M.B.A., Northwestern University, 1932, Ph.D., 1947; LL.D., Seton Hall, 1953, St. Ambrose Coll., 1962; L.H.D., Manhattan College, 1963; Marvcrest Coll., 1964; LL.D., Fairfield U., 1965, U. Bridgeport, 1967; m. Evelyn McIntyre, June 20, 1936; children—William H., Mary Cecile, Mary Eileen, Stephen E. Instr., Loyola U., 1930-32, asst. dean 1932-35; dean, Wright Jr. Coll. (Chgo. Municipal, 1935-46; dean Loyola U. Sch. of Commerce, 1946-48; specialist higher edn., U.S. Office Edn., 1948-49; chmn. dept. edn., dean U. Coll. Loyola U., 1949-51; v.p. instruction Seton Hall U., 1951-53; ednl. asst. to pres. Marquette U., 1953-63; on leave, dir. Carnegie Study Cath. Edn., U. Notre Dame, 1962-63; pres. Sacred Heart U., Bridgeport, Conn., 1963-71, chancellor, 1971—. Regional rep. consumer div., O.P.A., 1941- 42; dir. publs. Naval Air Tech. Tng. Center, 1942-44; mem. U.S. nat. com. on UNESCO 1956—, mem. exec. com., 1957—; mem. Gov.'s Commn. on Youth; mem. Conn. Commn. in Cooperation with Fed. Authorities in matters pertaining to Higher Edn. Pres. Conn. Fedn. Citizens for Ednl. Freedom; mem. Diocesan Sch. Bd. 1968—. Trustee Coll. Entrance Examination Bd., 1959—; bd. dirs. Center for Study of Liberal Edn. for Adults, 1956. Served as lt. comdr. USNR, officer-in-charge instrn., tng. Service Schs. Bur. of Personnel, Navy Dept., 1944-46. Chmn U.S. Armed Forces Edn. Program Com. 1949-51. Recipient Distinguished Alumni award Loyola U., 1961. Mem. Nat. Catholic Bus. Edn. Assn. (co-chmn. midwest div. 1948), Am. Econ. Assn., N.E.A. (v.p. Assn. for Higher Edn. 1963-64), Am. Assn. Sch. Adminstrs., Am. Ednl. Research Assn., Nat. Cath. Ednl. Assn. (exec. com. 1956—, chmn. mid-west coll. and univ. dept. 1956-57, pres. coll. and univ. dept. 1960-62, v.p. gen. 1966—). Am. Council on Edn., Cath. Com on Intellectual and Cultural Affairs, Assn. U. Eve. Colls. (pres. 1956-57). Serra Internat. Roman Catholic. Clubs: University, Algonquin, Brooklawn. Author ednl. articles. Editor Cath. Sch. Jour., 1961—; Ofcl. Guide to Catholic Educational Instns., 1960—. Home: 58 Cherry Hill Rd Fairfield CT 06604 Office: Sacred Heart Univ Bridgeport CT 06604 ☆

CONLIN, ALFRED THOMAS, food co. exec.; b. Lawrence, Mass., Apr. 18, 1921; s. Alfred A. and Helene (Roy) C.; A.B., Harvard, 1942, student U. Pa., 1946-47, Drexel Inst. Tech., 1947-49; m. Mary McKee Butler, June 29, 1946; Robert Thomas, James Alfred, Nancy Kee. With Campbell Soup Co., 1946-59, supt. can mfg., 1957-59; with Hunt Foods and Industries, Inc., 1959—, v.p. container group, can and glass divs., 1962-64, v.p. indsl. group, container, crushing mill and shellfish divs., 1964—; pres. United Can Co., So. Cotton Oil Co., Inc., So. Shell Fish Co., Inc., Southport Paint Co. Served to lt. USNR, 1942-46. Club: Harvard (So. Cal.). Home: 14857 La Cuarta Whittier CA 90605 Office: 14501 E Artesia Blvd La Mirada CA 90638

CONLIN, EARL EDGAR, tool mfg. exec.; b. Detroit, July 20, 1906; s. James S. and Nellie (Cowing) C.; A.B., U. Mich., 1933, M.B.A., 1934; m. Annette Pauline Fansler, May 29, 1935; children—James, David, Ann. With Ex-Cell-O Corp., Detroit, 1934—, successively statistician and analyst, asst. sec., sec. and asst. treas., sec.-treas., sec., 1934-60, v.p. finance, 1960-67, exec. v.p. group operations, 1967-69, sr. exec. v.p., 1969—, dir., 1955—; officer, dir. affiliated and subsidiary cos. Trustee Citizens Research Council Mich., 1953—; bd. dirs. Mich. Med. Services, dist. v.p.; bd. dirs. United Community Services. Mem. Financial Execs. Inst., Highland Park (dir.), Detroit bds. commerce, N.A.M., Council Tech. Advancement (financial council), Am. Accounting Assn., Corporate Secs. Am., United Community Services Com., Delta Sigma Pi. Clubs: Economic, Detroit Golf (Detroit); Lost Lake Woods. Home: 463 Arlington St Birmingham MI 48009 Office: P O Box 386 Detroit MI 48232

CONLIN, WILLIAM LIVINGSTONE, mfg. co. exec.; b. Rathwell, Man., Can., July 5, 1932; s. Thomas David and Kathleen (Johnston) C.; student U. Toronto, 1953-55; m. Barbara Ann Johnson, May 14, 1960; children—Kelly Ann, Bradley David, Gregory Martin. Comptroller Mallory Battery Co., Toronto, 1955-61; controller P.R. Mallory & Co. Inc., Indpls., 1961—. Club: Optimists Internat. Home: 7638 Camelback Dr Indianapolis IN 46250 Office: 3029 E Washington St Indianapolis IN 46206

CONLISK, JAMES B., Jr., city ofcl.; b. Chgo.; attended Northwestern U.; m. Colette; 2 sons. Bank clk. early in career; joined Chgo. Plice Force, 1946, advancing through grades to capt., 1959, became dep. supt. for field services, 1960, Chgo. police supt., 1967—. Served with USAAF, World War II. Home: 5448 Redwood St Chicago IL 60656*

CONLON, CHARLES FRANCIS, Jr., pub. adminstrn., finance; b. Providence, R.I., June 3, 1910; s. Charles F. and Honora Mary (Nolan) C.; student St. Mary's Acad., Milford, Mass., 1924-28; student Holy Cross Coll., Worcester, Mass. 1928-30; LL.B., George Washington U., 1938; m. Dorothy Irene Tighe, Sept. 15, 1937. Admitted to D.C. bar, 1938; jr. atty. U.S. Govt. Service, 1939; research and asst. dir. Fedn. Tax Adminstrs., Chgo., 1939-41, exec. dir., 1941—; exec. sec. Nat. Assn. Tax Adminstrs., Nat. Tobacco Tax Assn., North Am. Gasoline Tax Conf., 1941—. Tax adviser, Am. mission to Greece, 1947-48. Served with USNR, 1942-46. Trustee Pub. Adminstrn. Service. Mem. Am. Bar Assn., Inst. Urban Life (dir.), Am. Soc. Pub. Adminstrn., Phi Delta Phi, Order Coif. Roman Catholic. Club: National Lawyers. Contbr. profl. periodicals. Home: 5000 Cornell Av Chicago, IL 60615. Office: 1313 E 60th St Chicago IL 60637

CONLON, JACK MARTIN, savs. and loan co. exec.; b. Parsons, Kan., Oct. 8, 1931; s. John Thomas and Alice M. (MacCaskill) C.; B.S., U. Kan., 1957; student U. So. Cal., 1957-59; children—Lisa, Catherine, Julia; m. Elsie Ann Spicer, Jan. 29, 1970. C.P.A., Peat, Marwick, Mitchell & Co., Los Angeles, 1957-59, Kansas City, Mo., 1959-63; pres. Coachella Valley Savs. & Loan Assn., Palm Springs, Cal., 1963—. Dir., treas. Palm Springs United Fund, 1966-67; dir., sec.-treas. Palm Springs Conv. and Visitors Bur., 1967—. Dir. Palm Springs Republican Assembly, 1971. Trustee Palm Valley Sch. Served with USNR, 1951-54. C.P.A., Cal. Mem. Am. Savs. and Loan Inst. (instr.), Soc. Controllers and Finance Officers Savs. Instns. (pres. 1966), Palm Springs C. of C. (pres.), Phi Kappa Psi. Rotarian. Clubs: Palm Springs, Canyon Country. Home: 1315 Verano Dr Palm Springs CA 92262 Office: 499 S Palm Canyon Dr Palm Springs CA 92262

CONLON, JAMES A., govt. ofcl.; b. N.Y.C., Feb. 21, 1921; s. Robert Joseph and Mary (Mulroy) C.; student George Washington U., 1948-52; m. Jill Terese Armandi, Aug. 21, 1943; children—James Allan, Craig Douglas, Jill Ellen, Lynne Susan. With Bur. Printing and Engraving, Treasury Dept., 1942—, dep. dir., 1966-67, dir., 1967—. Chmn. exec. com. Washington Plate Printers, Die Stampers and Engravers, 1952-53. Served to 2d lt. AUS, 1942-46. Recipient High Quality Performance awards Treasury Dept.; Exceptional Service award Sec. Treasury, 1970. Mem. Am. Legion (past post comdr.). Roman Cath. Home: 6605 Lee Chapel Rd Burke VA 22015 Office: Bur Printing and Engraving 14th and C St SW Washington DC 20226

CONMY, PETER THOMAS, pub. library exec.; b. San Francisco, Calif., July 8, 1901; s. Thomas Cherry and Mary Henrietta (Richter) C.; A.B., U. Cal., 1924, M.A., 1927, Ed.D., 1937, B.L.S., 1947; M.A., Stanford, 1941; LL.B., U. San Francisco, 1952; m. Emiliette Constance Storti, July 11, 1928; children—Constance Louise, Thomas Peter. Tchr. jr. high schs., San Francisco, 1926; tchr., counselor, debate coach, evening sch. tchr. evening high sch. registrar and evening high sch. prin., 2 pub. schs., San Francisco, 1927-43, serving at Horace Mann Fr. High Sch., Mission High Sch., Evening High Sch. of Commerce and Galileo Evening High Sch.; apptd. city librarian of Oakland, Cal. 1943, charge Oakland Pub. Library dept. including Oakland Pub. Mus., Snow Mus., Oakland Art Gallery. Mem. Selective Service Bd. No. 100. San Francisco, 1943, chmn., 1944—; city historian, Oakland, 1969—. Named Knight of Saint Gregory, 1963. Mem. A.L.A. Cal. Library Assn. (pres. 1961), N.E.A. Cal. Tchrs. Assn., Cal. Hist. Soc., Am. Polit. Sci. Assn., Native Sons of Golden West (grand pres. 1949-50, dir. hist. research 1954—), Young Men's Inst., Phi Delta Kappa, Phi Delta Kappa. Knight of Columbus (4), Elk. Clubs: Serra (pres. 1952), Rotary (Oakland). Author: History of the Entrance Requirements of the University of California, 1928; Aids to the Study of Government, 1928; History of Public School Finance in California, 1937; Self Determination and the Paris Peace Conference, 1941; Public School-Public Library Relationships, 1945; Studies in English Education during the 18th Century, 1946; The Date of the Founding of San Francisco, 1947; A Centennial Evaluation of the Treaty of Guadalupe Hidalgo, 1848-1948; The Queen of the Avenue, the history of St. Francis Church, 1949; The Public Library and The State, 1962; also numerous articles on Calif. History pub. by Native Sons of Golden West. Home: 1066 Ardmore Av Oakland CA 94610 Office: 2101 Telegraph Av Oakland CA 94612

CONN, HOWARD JAMES, clergyman; b. Fresno, Cal., June 19, 1911; s. William Alexander and Anna (Peabbles) C. student Fresno State Coll., 1928-29; B.A., Stanford, 1932; postgrad. Harvard, 1932-33; B.D., Yale, 1936; D.D., Yankton Coll., 1948; m. Viola Mann, June 26, 1938; children—Mrs. Judith C. Green, Janet Murray. Ordained to ministry Congl. Ch., 1936; asso. minister Union Meml. Ch., Glenbrook, Conn., 1936-41; minister First Congl. Ch., Great Barrington, Mass., 1941-44, Plymouth Congl. Ch., Mpls., 1941-; pres. Minn. Council Chs., 1952-54; summer preacher Nat. Radio Pulpit, 1955; final chaplain Gen. Council Congl. Christian Chs., 1961. Bd. dirs. Ministers Life and Casualty Union, Minn. Protestant Found.; trustee Carleton Coll. Mem. Nat. Assn. Congl. Christian Chs. (past moderator). Author: History of the Congregational Church in Great Barrington, 1944; Symbolism in Stone and Glass, 1949; The Hope That Sets Men Free, 1954; The Dilemma of Congregationalism, 1961; Teilhard and the Phenomenon of Man, 1967. Home: 5420 Southwood Dr Minneapolis, MN 55431. Office: 1900 Nicollet Av Minneapolis MN 55403

CONN, JACK TRAMMELL, banker, lawyer; b. Ada, Okla., Nov. 19 1909; s. Jared Trammell and Carrie (Chaplin) C.; grad. E. Central Coll., Ada, 1931; LL.B., U. Okla., 1940. Admitted to Okla. bar, 1940; practice in Ada, 1940-64, Oklahoma City, 1947-64; mem. firm Conn, Mayhue & Kerr, Ada, 1964—; counsel Kerr Davis, Roberts, Irvine & Burbage, Oklahoma city, 1964—; pres., chmn. bd. Okla. State Bank, Ada, 1951-64; chmn. bd., chief exec. officer Fidelty Nat. Bank & Trust Co., Oklahoma City, Oklahoma, 1964—; mem. exec. com., bd. dirs. Okla. Med. Research Found. Mem. Am. (past pres.), Okla. (past pres.)

bankers assns., Order of Coif, Phi Delta Phi, Sigma Nu. Mason (33, Shriner, Jester). Contbr. profl. jours. Home: 7202 Waverly St Oklahoma City OK 73120

CONN, JEROME W., physician, med. educator; b. N.Y.C., Sept. 24, 1907; s. Joseph and Dora (Kobrin) C; student Rutgers U., 1925-28, D.Sc., 1964; M.D., U. of Mich., 1932; m. Elizabeth Stern, June 17, 1932; children—Phyllis, J. William. Intern, U. Hosp., Ann Arbor, Mich., 1932-33, asst. resident, 1933-34, instr. medicine, 1935-38, asst. prof. medicine, 1938-44, asso. prof., 1944-50, prof. internal medicine 1950-68, Distinguished Univ. prof internal medicine, 1968—, also dir. dept. metabolism and endocrinology, also metabolism research unit, 1943—; cons. to surgeon gen. U.S. Army, 1945-54, surgeon gen. USPHS, 1947-58; holder numerous named lectureships, including Banting Meml. lectr. Am. Diabetes Assn., 1958; Russell lectr. U. Mich., 1961, Gordon Wilson lectr. Am. Clin. and Climatological Assn., 1962. Lawson lectr. Royal Coll. Physicians and Surgeons of Can., 1964; Phillips lectr. A.C.P., 1965; Joslin Meml. lectr. N.E. Diebetes Assn., 1965; Harvey lectr., N.Y.C., 1967; Ramon Guiteras lectr. Am. Urol. Assn., 1967; Ricketts lectr. U. Chgo., 1967; Loeb lectr. St. Louis U., 1970. Mem. com. on metabolism in trauma U.S. Army Dept. Research and Devel., 1953-61; drug research bd. div. med. scis. Nat. Acad. Scis.-NRC, 1963-64; mem. expert adv. panel on chronic degenerative disease WHO, 1964—. Bd. sci. dirs. Center for Research in Diseases of Heart, Recipient Modern Medicine award for achievement in endocrinology, 1957; citation for contbrn. to medicine Mich. Med. Soc., 1962; Banting award Am. Diabetes Assn., 1963; Phillips award A.C.P., 1965; Joslin award New Eng. Diabetes Assn., 1965; Internat. prize Gairdner Found., 1965; Ricketts award U. Chgo., Taylor award Am. Therapeutics Soc., 1967; Stouffer prize, 1969; gold medal Internat. Soc. for Progress in Internal Medicine, Buenos Aires, 1969. Diplomate Am. Bd. of Internal Medicine. Fellow A.C.P., A.C.S. (hon.); mem. Am. Soc. Clin. Investigation (council 1949-52), Central Soc. Clin. Research (v.p. 1953, pres. 1954), Am. Inst. Nutrition, Am. Diabetes Assn. (pres. 1962, chmn. com. research 1964- 65), Nat. Acad. Scis. (charter mem. Inst. Medicine), Assn. Am. Physicians, Endocrine Soc., Sigma Xi, Alpha Omega Alpha, Phi Kappa Phi; hon. mem. Nat. Acad. Medicine Argentina, Endocrine Soc. Colombia, Peruvian Soc. Cardiology, Peruvian Soc. Angiology, Med. Soc. Santiago. Contbr. to books, jours. in field of metabolism and endocrinology. Home: 200 Orchard Hill Dr Ann Arbor MI 48104 Office: University Hospital Ann Arbor MI 48104

CONN, KENNETH SMITH, editor; b. Springfield,O., Sept. 20, 1900; s. Knowles E. and Jessie K. (Smith) C.; grad. Wittenberg Acad., Springfield, O., 1918, Ohio State U., 1922; m. Thelma Lucille Dye, June 3, 1924; children—Frank Knowles, Marilyn Joan. Mng. editor News-Bee, Toledo, 1927-33, Salt Lake City Tribune Telegram, 1933-37, Look mag., 1937-38; editor Santa Barbara News-Press, 1938-41; exec. editor San Jose (Calif.) Mercury and News since 1941. Mem. Am. Soc. Newspaper Editors (dir.), Newspaper Editorial Assn., Cal. Publs. Assn., Sigma Delta Chi (mem. bd. dirs.). Episcopalian. Mason. Clubs: La Rinconada country; Press and Union League (San Francisco); San Jose Country, Sainte Claire, Rotary (San Jose). Home: 19480 Valle Vista Saratoga CA 95070 Office: 750 Ridder Park Dr San Jose CA 95131

CONNABLE, ALFRED BARNES, pvt. trustee; b. Kalamazoo, Feb. 20, 1904; s. Alfred B. and Frances (Peck) C.; student Culver Mil. Acad., 1921; A.B., U. of Mich., 1925; M.B.A., Harvard, 1929; H.H.D., Western Mich. U., 1962; m. Dorothy Jean Malcomson, Apr. 15, 1927; children—Nancy M., Alfred B. III, John Lee. Sales asst. Kalamazoo Vegetable Parchment Co., 1925-28; asst. sec. Selected Securities Corp. of Detroit, 1928-30; successively asst. sec., asst. v.p. and dir. of investment analysis dept. Detroit Trust Co., 1930-43; state price adminstr. for Mich., OPA, 1942-43; state mgr. Wendell L. Willkie presdl. campaign, 1943-44; instr. investments and econs, Detroit Inst. Tech. 1929-30; chmn., dir. Monroe Calculating Co., 1944-58; pres. Lafourche Realty Co., Inc., Kalamazoo; dir. Hayes-Albion Co., Albion Malleable Iron Co. 1945-67, Am. Nat. Bank & Trust Co. of Mich., Kalamazoo Sled & Toys Co., Inc. 1944-68, Bond Supply Co., Kalamazoo Ice and Fuel Co., Hayes Industries, Inc. (Jackson, Mich.) 1947-67, KVP Sutherland Paper Co., 1946-66, Litton Industries, 1958-61. Regent U. Mich., 1942-58, emeritus, 1960; trustee Douglas Community Assn., Western Mich. U.; mem. exec. com. Community Chest; dir., past pres. Kalamazoo Symphony Orch. Soc.; mem. adv. council Assn. Governing Bds. Univs., Colls.; past pres. Assn. of Governing Bds. of State Univs. and Colls., Am. Symphony Orchestra League (dir.), mem. exec. com. Mich. State Council for the Arts. Mem. Pi Delta Epsilon, Alpha Kappa Psi, Delta Kappa Epsilon. Republican. Presbyn. Clubs: Rotary, U. of Mich. (Detroit and Kalamazoo); Harvard (N.Y.); Univ. (Ann Arbor); Lake Placid. Home: 708 W South St Kalamazoo MI 49007 Office: Am Nat Bank Bldg Kalamazoo MI 49006

CONNALLY, BEN C., judge; born Marlin, Texas, Dec. 28, 1909; s. Tom and Louise (Clarkson) C.; A.B., U. of Tex., 1930, LL.B., 1933; LL. M., Harvard, 1934; m. Sarah Nell Allen, Sept. 27, 1937; children—Tom, Louise. Admitted to bar. Tex., 1933; practiced as mem. firm Sewell, Taylor, Morris & Connally, Houston, 1934-42, Butler & Binion, 1945-49; U.S. district judge, southern district of Texas, since 1949. Served with USAAF, 1942-45. Mem. Am., Tex. and Houston bar assns. Methodist. Home: 244 Hedwig Rd Houston TX Office: US Court House Houston TX 77002

CONNALLY, FREDERICK HAROLD, oil co. exec.; b. Dallas, June 5, 1904; s. Walter C. and Eulalie (Hatcher) C.; B.A., U. Tex., 1925; m. Nettie Mae Jones, Nov. 15, 1952; children—Frederick H., Leslie Walter, Lydia Lee. Pub. accountant, 33; chief accountant Gilliland Producing & Refining Corp., 1934-36; controller Gen. Am. Oil Co. of Tex., Dallas, 1936-42, treas., 1942-54, v.p., treas., 1955-60, exec. v.p., dir., mem. exec. com., 1960—; treas., asst. sec., dir. Gen. Am. Oils, Ltd.; treas., asst. sec. Gen. Am. Oils of Spain; v.p., dir. Meadows Bldg. Corp.; v.p., dir. Meadows Bldg. Cafeteria; asst. sec., asst. treas. Fargo Oils Ltd.; asst. sec., asst. treas., dir. Gen. Am. Pipe Line Co. C.P.A., Tex. Mem. Am. Inst. C.P.A.'s, Financial Execs. Inst., Am. Petroleum Inst., Nat. Fedn. Financial Analysts Soc., Mid-Continent Oil and Gas Assn., Tex. Ind. Producers Owners and Royalty Assn., Ind. Petroleum Assn. Am., Dallas Estate Council, Petroleum Accountatns Dallas, Tex. Soc. C.P.A.'s, Phi Beta Kappa, Beta Gamma Sigma, Beta Alpha Psi, Delta Chi. Clubs: Dallas Athletic, Dallas Athletic Country, Engineers, Texas, Petroleum (Dallas). Home: 5373 Wenonah Dr Dallas TX 75209 Office: Meadows Bldg Dallas TX 75206

CONNALLY, HERSCHEL FRANK, Jr., physician; b. Waco, Tex., Nov. 17, 1912; s. Herschel Frank and Clara (Blailock) C.; A.B., U. Tex., 1933, M.D., 1937; m. Frances Louise Eastland, June 9, 1937; children—Herschel Frank III, Seaborn Eastland. Intern, John Sealy Hosp., Hosp., Galveston, Tex., 1937-38; house officer obstetrics and gynecology Royal Victoria Hosp., McGill U., Montreal, Can., 1938-39; asst. resident obstetrics Balt. City Hosp., 1939-40; asst. resident obstetrics and gynecology Johns Hopkins Hosp., 1940-42; pvt. practice specializing obstetrics and gynecology, Waco, 1946-58, 59- -; med. faculty M.D. Anderson Tumor Clinic and Hosp., U. Tex. Med. Br., 1958-59. Dir. Waco Savs. & Loan Co., Citizens Nat. Bank Waco. Mem. Tex. Commn. on Higher Edn., 1955-58, Heart Tex. council Boy Scouts Am., 1955—; pres. Heart Tex. Fair, 1957-58; mem. com. 75 U. Tex., 1957-58, Tex. Finance Adv. Commn., 1960—; mem. Tex. Adv. Council of Higher Edn., 1969—; mem. adv. council to McDonald Obs., U. Tex.; commd. spl. Tex. Ranger, 1969. Mem. City Council Waco., 1951-55, mayor, 1954-55. Bd. regents U. Tex., 1961—; trustee Waco United Fund. Served to capt. M.C., AUS, 1942-46; ETO. Recipient Ashbel Smith Dist. Alumnus award U. Tex. Med. Br., Galveston, 1967. Diplomate Am. Bd. Obstetrics and Gynecology. Fellow A.C.S., Am. Coll. Obstetricians and Gynecologists; mem A.M.A., Tex. Surg. Soc. Continental Gynecol. Soc., Kappa Sigma, Phi Rho Sigma, Alpha Epsilon Delta. Presbyn. (past deacon, elder). Mem. editorial com. Year Book of Cancer, 1960-62. Home: 2508 Lake Oaks Dr Waco TX 76710 Office: 2225 Washington Av Waco TX 76702

CONNALLY, JOHN BOWDEN, govt. ofcl., lawyer; b. Floresville, Tex., Feb. 27, 1917; s. John Bowden and Lela (Wright) C.; LL.B., U. Tex., 1941; m. Idanell Brill, Dec. 21, 1940; children—John Bowden III, Sharon, Mark. Pres., gen. mgr. radio sta. KVET, Austin, Tex., 1946-49; adminstrv. asst. to Senator Lyndon B. Johnson, 1949; mem. firm Powell, Wirtz & Rauhut, Austin, 1949-52; atty. for Sid W. Richardson & Perry R. Bass, ind. oil operators, Fort Worth, 1952-61; sec. U.S. Navy, 1961; gov. of Tex., 1963-69; partner Vinson, Elkins, Searls & Connally, Houston, 1969-71; sec. U.S. Treasury, Washington, 1971—. Mem. U.S. Adv. Council on Exec. Orgn. Recipient Distinguished Alumnus award U. Tex. Ex-Students Assn., 1961. Democrat. Address: US Dept Treasury 15th and Pennsylvania Av NW Washington DC 20220

CONNARE, WILLIAM GRAHAM, bishop; b. Pitts., Dec. 11, 1911; s. James J. and Nellie T. (O'Connor) C.; B.A., Duquesne U.; 1932, Litt.D., 1961; M.A., St. Vincent Coll., Latrobe, Pa., 1934, L.H.D., 1962; LL.D., Seton Hill Coll., 1960. Ordained priest Roman Cath. Ch., 1936; named domestic prelate, 1955; asst. pastor St. Canice, Pitts., 1936-37, St. Paul's Cathedral, 1937-49; adminstr. St. Richard's Ch., Pitts., 1949-55, pastor, 1955-60; chaplain Univ. Cath. Club, Pitts., 1947-60, Cath. Interracial Council Pitts., 1953-60; dir. Soc. Propagation of Faith, 1950-59; vicar for religious as rep. Bishop of Pitts., 1959-60; consecrated bishop of Greensburg (Pa.), 1960—. Bd. dirs., chmn. community services com. Urban League Pitts., 1950-60; mem. Pitts. Commn. Human Relations, 1953-60; mem. Allegheny County Council Civil Rights, 1953-60, bd. dirs., 1958-60; bd. dirs. Pitts. br. N.A.A.C.P., 1959-60; Episcopal chmn. Nat. Cath. Com. on Scouting, Boy Scouts Am., 1962-70; Episcopal moderator div. youth activities U.S. Cath. Conf.,1968-70; mem. Bishop's Commn. for Liturgical Apostolate; chmn. commn. on missions Nat. Conf. Cath. Bishops, 1967-71. Address: 723 E Pittsburgh St Greensburg PA 15601

CONNAUGHTON, CHARLES ARTHUR, former forester; b. Placeville, Ida., May 25, 1908; s. Peter and Nancy Elizabeth (Coonrod) C.; B.S., U. Ida., 1928, Ph.D. (hon.), 1965; M.F., Yale, 1934; m. Myrtle Snyder, Jan. 20, 1932; children—Sharon Sue, Kent Peter. Forest ranger, Ogden, Utah, 1928- 31; forest research technician Fort Collins, Colo. and Ogden, Utah, 1931-38; dir. Rocky Mt. Forest and Range Expt. Sta., Fort Collins, 1938-44, So. Forest Expt. Sta., New Orleans, 1944-51; regional forester charge So. region U.S. Forest Service, 1951-56, Cal. region, 1956-67, Pacific N.W. region, 1967, now ret. Mem. Am. Forestry Assn. (dir., v.p., pres. 1971—), Soc. Am. Foresters (pres. 1959-60, dir.). Contbr. articles profl. jours.

CONNAUGHTON, JAMES FRANCIS, mfg. exec.; b. Hamilton, O., Dec. 22, 1914; s. John B. and Blanche (Collins) C.; B.S. in M.E., U. Cin., 1937; D. Comml. Sci., Duquesne U.; m. Sue Graham, Nov. 26, 1938; children—James Francis, Thomas Alfred, Mary Jane, Stephen Graham. Asst. gen. mgr. Gen. Ordnance Corp., 1940-43, gen. mgr., 1943- 46, asst. to pres., 1946-47; sec. Lima-Hamilton Corp., 1947-51, gen. mgr. Hamilton div., gen. mgr. Lima div., 1951-53, v.p. gen. mgr., dir. Eddystone div., 1953-56; pres. Am. La France Corp. 1956-62; pres., chief exec. officer, dir. Sterling Precision corp., 1958-62; pres., dir. Wheelabrator Corp., 1958—, Bell Intercontinental Corp., 1960-66; chmn., dir. Wheelabrator Corp. Can., First bank & Trust Co., South Bend, Ind.; dir. Wheel Horse Products, Inc., South Bend. Mem. adv. council arts and letters U. Notre Dame. Trustee St. Joseph Hosp., Mishawaka. Roman Catholic. Clubs: Chicago (Chgo.); Metropolitan (N.Y.C.); Detroit Athletic. Home: 1515 E Jefferson Blvd South Bend IN 46617 Office: 400 S Byrkit Av Mishawaka IN 46544

CONNELL, EVAN SHELBY, Jr., author; b. Kansas City, Mo., Aug. 17, 1924; s. Evan Shelby and Elton (Williamson) C.; student Dartmouth, 1941-43, U. Kan., 1946-47, Stanford, 1947-48, Columbia, 1948-49. Editor Contact mag., 1959-65. Served as naval aviator, 1943-45. Eugene Saxton fellow, 1953; Guggenheim fellow, 1963; recipient of Rockefeller Foundation grant, 1967. Author: The Anatomy Lesson and Other Stories, 1957; Mrs. Bridge, 1959; The Patriot, 1960; Notes From a Bottle Found on the Beach at Carmel, 1963; At the Crossroads, 1965; The Diary of a Rapist, 1966; Mr. Bridge, 1969. Address: 2355 Polk St San Francisco CA 94109

CONNELL, FRANK HERMAN, found. exec.; b. Hudson, N.H., Apr. 7, 1905; s. Frank A. and Mary E. (Watts) C.; B.S., Dartmouth, 1928; A.M., U. Cal., 1929, Ph.D., 1931; m. Katherine Chandler Norwood, Sept. 23, 1931; 1 son, John Norwood. Prof. zoology, Dartmouth, prof. parasitology, Med. Sch., 1931-55; parasitologist, Atomic Bomb Casualty Commn., Japan, 1950-51, chief of labs., 1952, asso. dir., 1953, acting dir., 1954; exec. dir. com. on atomic casualties Nat. Acad. Sci., 1954- 55; clin. prof. parasitology Baylor U. Sch. Medicine, 1955-60; head lab. services and parasitology U. Tex.-M. D. Anderson Hosp. and Tumor Inst., 1955-60; asst. dir. China Med. Bd. of N.Y., Inc., 1960-68, asso. dir., 1968—. Served to maj. AUS, 1943-46. Mem. Am. Soc. Tropical Medicine and Hygiene, Assn. Am. Med. Colls., A.A.A.S. Republican. Home: 1155 Sasco Hill Rd Southport CT 06490 Office: China Med Bd of NY 420 Lexington Av New York City NY 10017

CONNELL, FREDERICK MARTIN, mining engr.; b. Spencerville, Ont., Can., Sept. 9, 1884; s. Martin and Sarah (Bennett) C.; B.S., Queen's U., 1906, LL.D., 1950; m. Amy Florence Milne, 1912 (dec.); children—John Martin, Elizabeth (Mrs. John E. Kennedy); m. 2d, Cicely J. Burge, 1950. Chmn., dir. Conwest Exploration Co., Ltd.; chmn. bd., dir. Cassiar Asbestos Corp. Ltd.; pres., dir. Central Patricia Gold Mines, Ltd.; dir. Crown Trust Co. Metals, controller, Can., 1939-45. Decorated Order Brit. Empire. Mem. Assn. Profl. Engrs. Ont., Canadian Inst. Mining and Metallurgy. Mason. Clubs: York, National, Rosedale Golf, Toronto Hunt, Caledon Mountain Trout (Toronto); Mount Royal (Montreal); Mining (N.Y.C.). Home: 53 Russell Hill Rd Toronto 7 Ontario Canada Office: 85 Richmond St W Toronto 1 Ontario Canada

CONNELL, GEORGE W., lawyer; b. N.Y.C., Dec. 12, 1923; LL.B., Rutgers U., 1950. Admitted to N.J. bar, 1951; now mem. firm Pindar, McElroy, Connell, Foley & Geiser, Newark. Mem. Am., N.J. State, Essex County bar assns. Office: Pindar McElroy Connell Foley & Geiser Fed Trust Bldg 24 Commerce St Newark NJ 07102*

CONNELL, GROVER, food co. exec.; b. N.Y.C., Apr. 12, 1918; s. Grover Cleveland and Violet Regina (Connell) C.; B.S. in Bus. Adminstrn., Columbia, 1939; m. Patricia Day, July 31, 1940; children—Ted, Terry, Toni. With Connell Rice & Sugar Co., Inc., Westfield, N.J., 1939—, pres., 1950—. Served to lt. USNR, 1942-46. Democrat. Presbyn. Home: 207 Watchung Fork Westfield NJ 07090 Office: 45 Cardinal Dr Westfield NJ 07090

CONNELL, HUGH PAUL, advt. exec., lawyer; b. Bethlehem, Pa., May 7, 1931; s. Joseph B. and Mary (McFadden) C.; A.B., Moravian Coll., 1953; LL.B., U. Pa., 1956; student Hague Acad. Internat. Law, 1959; LL.M., U. London (Eng.), 1960; m. Susan Richardson Hobbs, July 2, 1965; children—Hugh Richardson, Andrew Warfield. Admitted to Pa. bar, 1956, N.Y. bar, 1963; lectr. internat. law U. London (Eng.), 1960-62; with firm Coudert Bros., N.Y.C., 1962-65; gen. counsel J. Walter Thompson Co., N.Y.C., 1966—, v.p., 1967—. Trustee Moravian Coll., 1967-69, Bedford-Rippowam Sch., 1971—. Served with AUS, 1956-58. Mem. Am., Inter-Am. bar assns., Assn. Bar City N.Y., Am. Soc. Internat. Law, Am. Assn. Comparative Study Law, British Inst. Internat. and Comparative Law, Soc. Pub. Tchrs. Law (U.K.), Alumni Assn. Moravian Coll. (bd. dirs. 1965-67, pres. 1967). Clubs: Bedford Golf and Tennis; Union (N.Y.C.); Wadawanuck (Stonington, Conn.). Home: Maple Av Katonah NY 10536 Office: 420 Lexington Av New York City NY 10017

CONNELL, JAMES CHARLES, judge; b. Cleve., Sept. 20, 1897; s. Thomas F. and Elizabeth (Stoll) C.; LL.B., Cleveland-Marshall Law Sch., 1918, LL.D., 1946, John Carroll U., 1954; m. Cecelia Marie McDonough, Sept. 21, 1921; 1 son, Thomas F. H. Admitted to Ohio bar, 1918; asst. police prosecutor city of Clev., 1922-23; asst. county prosecutor Cuyahoga County, Cleve., 1923-27, chief asst. county prosecutor, 1928; pvt. practice law, 1928- 41; judge Ct. Common Pleas of Cuyahoga County, 1941-54-; judge U.S. Dist. Ct., Cleve., 1954—. Mem. Am., Ohio, Cleve., Cuyahoga County (pres. 1936) bar assns. Home: 22399 Shelburn St Shaker Heights OH 44120 Office: Federal Bldg Cleveland OH 44114

CONNELL, JOHN GIBBS, Jr., govt. ofcl.; b. Atlanta, Sept. 26, 1914; s. John Gibbs and Vena Estelle (Turner) C.; A.A., George Washington U., 1948, A.B., 1952; m. Bernice E. Siewerdsen, Oct. 2, 1941; childrenSharon Elaine, Candace Anne. Employee U.S. Civil Service Commn., 1935-38, U.S. Housing Authority, 1938-40; with War Dept. and Army Dept., 1940—, personnel mgr. Office of Sec. Army, 1942-54, asst. for security and personnel, 1954-62, dep. adminstrv. asst. to sec. army, 1962-66, adminstr. asst. to sec. army, 1966—. Chmn. Army Secutiry Screening Bd., 1953-66; prin. adminstrv. officer Army Loyalty-Security Program, 1950—; mem. Army Bd. Correction Mil. Records, 1947-62; Army Dept. rep. interdepartmental com. to study govt. employee security programs for Pres. Truman, 1951- 52; Army rep. Exec. Officers Group, 1968—; mem. Dept. Def. Concessions com., 1966—, Army rep. Fed. Exec. Bd., 1969—. Bd. dirs. Youth Devel. Inst. Served from pvt. to 2d lt. USAAF, 1943-45, 1st lt. OSS, 1945-46; maj. M.I., Army Res. Mem. Sigma Nu. Presbyn. (elder). Home: Cloverway Alexandria VA 22314 Office: Pentagon Washington DC 20310

CONNELL, KARL, corp. exec.; lawyer; b. N.Y.C., Dec. 4, 1924; s. Karl A. and Frank (Hovey-Roof) C.; student Millbrook Sch., 1938-42, Yale, 1942-43, 46-47; J.D., Columbia, 1950; m. Jean Hampton, June 28, 1965; children—Karl III, Lawrence F., Gioia H. Admitted to N.Y. bar, 1950, Pa. bar, 1970; atty. Chadbourne, Hunt, Jaeckel & Brown, N.Y.C., 1950-53, Chesapeake Industries, Inc., 1953-56, Breed, Abbott & Morgan, N.Y.C., 1956-63; asst. v.p. charge legal and govt. affairs dept. Am. Stock Exchange, 1963-67; v.p., gen. counsel GAC Corp., Allentown, Pa. and Miami, Fla., 1968—; treas., dir. Wintoon Waters, Inc., 1967—. Mem. N.Y. County Com. Republican Party, 1953-54. Pres., bd. dirs. Neversink Assn., Inc.; bd. dirs. Frost Valley YMCA; trustee Millbrook Sch., 1960-63. Served with AUS, 1942-46; PTO. Mem. Am., Fed., N.Y. State, Internat. bar assns., N.Y. Law Inst., Millbrook Sch. Alumni Assn. (pres. 1959-63), Phi Delta Phi. Unitarian. Clubs: Anglers of New York (sec. 1960-62, dir.), Yale (Miami). Author chpt. in Financing A theatrical Production. Compiler, editor: Floor Transactions Handbook, 1965; American Stock Exchange Company Guide, 1967. Home: 910 Andora St Coral Gables FL 33146 Office: 825 S Bayshore Dr Miami FL 33131

CONNELL, LOUIS FRED, Jr., physicist, educator; b. Honey Grove, Tex., June 25, 1914; s. Louis Fred and Hazel (Price) C.; B.A., Tex. Coll. Arts and Industries, 1934; M.A., U. Tex., 1936, Ph.D., 1948; m. Geraldine Jopling, Apr. 30, 1938; children—Fred Jopling, Carolyn, James Richard. Tchr. schs., Tex., 1934- 35, 36-37; instr. physics North Tex. State U., Denton, 1937-41, asst. prof., 1941-42, prof. physics, 1951—, dir. dept., 1951- 69; asst. prof. Tex. U., 1947-51. Research participant Oak Ridge Nat. Lab., summers 1954, 57. Served from lt. (j.g.) to lt. comdr., USNR, 1942- 45. Fellow Tex. Acad. Sci.; mem. Am. Assn. Physics Tchrs. (sec.-treas. Tex. sect. 1954-56, chmn. 1956-57), Am. Phys. Soc., A.A.A.S., Acoustical Soc. Am., Sigma Xi. Presbyn. (elder). Home: 924 Ridgecrest Circle Denton TX 76201

CONNELL, PHILIP FRANCIS, food industry co. exec.; b. Hamilton, Ont., Can., Jan. 20, 1924; s. Maurice W. and Kathleen (Richardson) C.; B.A., McMaster U. (Can.) 1946. With Clarkson Gordon & Co., Hamilton and Toronto, 1946-57; comptroller Canadian Westinghouse Co. Ltd., Hamilton, 1957-67; controller Domtar Ltd., Montreal, 1967-68; v.p. finance George Weston Ltd., Toronto, Ont., 1968—. Vice pres. Hamilton United Appeal, 1967. Chartered accountant, 1950. Mem. financial Execs. Inst. (pres. Hamilton chpt. 1966-67). Clubs: Hamilton, Hamilton Golf and Country. Home: 400 Walmer Rd Toronto Ontario Canada Office: 25 King St W Toronto Ontario Canada

CONNELL, ROBERT JOHN, sch. adminstr.; b. Scranton, Pa., Oct. 17, 1912; s. Robert Charles and Teresa (Nallin) C.; A.B., Brown U., 1938; student lang. course Internat. Corr. Schs., 1948; m. Mary Linen, Jan. 2, 1939; children—Linda, Robert John, Richard Tuthill; m. 2d, Henrietta Gardner. With Bache and Co., 1945-47, Internat. Schs. Co. of Latin Am., Scranton, Pa., 1947—, pres., 1950—, also dir.; exec. v.p. I.C.S. World Ltd., 1954-55, pres., 1955—, chmn. bd., 1964—, also dir.; pres. Centro Espanol de Ensenanza por Corespondencia; Madrid, Spain, 1950—; chmn. I.C.S. Ltd. London, Capetown, Cairo, Bombay, Australia, N.Z.; v.p., dir. Internat. Textbook Co. Served as lt. USNR, 1942-45. Mem. Psi Upsilon. Clubs: Scranton, Scranton (Pa.) Country; Brown University, Canadian (N.Y.C.); Blooming Grove Hunting and Fishing (Hawley, Pa.); Triton Fish and Game (Can.) Home: Route 3 Clarks Summit PA 18411 Office: ICS Pawnee Av and Oak St Scranton PA 18515

CONNELL, TED C., automobile co. exec.; b. Hamlin, Tex., Dec. 5, 1924; s. Albert Austin and Etna (Lawrence) C.; m. Edith Juanette Duty, Nov. 5, 1946; children— Mark Stanley, Carol Juanette. Pres. Connell Chevrolet Co., Inc., Killeen, Tex., 1955—; owner Modern Dry Cleaners & Laundry, Killeen, Connell Ins. Agy., Killeen, T.C. & E. Realty Co., Killeen; dir. First Nat. Bank, Killeen; chmn., v.p. Rio Airways Killeen. Mem. Am. Battle Monuments Commns. Mayor, Killeen, 1962-66; dl., sgt.-at-arms Tex. Democratic Conv., 1948-70. Mem. bd. devel. Sam Rayborn Found., 1965-70. Served with AUS, 1943-45. Named Outstanding Citizen of Tex., Am. Legion, 1966;

recipient Distinguished Service medal V.F.W., 1965. Mem. Tex. Automobile Assn., V.F.W. (past nat. comdr.). Baptist Home: 501 Nolan Av Killeen TX 76541 Office: PO Box 666 Killeen TX 76541

CONNELL, WILLIAM FRANCIS, diversified co. exec.; b. Lynn, Mass., May 12, 1938; s. William J. and Theresa (Keaney) C.; B.S. magna cum laude, Boston Coll., 1959; M.B.A., Harvard, 1963; m. Margot C. Gensler, May 29, 1965; children—Monica Cameron, Lisa Terese, Courtenay Erin. Controller, Olga Co.,Inc., Van Nuys, Cal., 1963-65; asst. treas. Litton Industries, Inc., also pres. div. Marine Tech., Inc., 1965-68; treas. Ogden corp., N.Y.C., 1968-69, v.p. treas., 1969—; dir. various Ogden subsidaries, 1969—. Active fund raising Harvard Bus. Sch., also Boston Coll. Served to 1st lt. AUS, 1959-61. Mem. Beta Gamma Sigma, Alpha Sigma Nu, Alpha Kappa Psi. Republican. Catholic. Clubs: Harvard, Cloud (N.Y.C.); Boston Coll. Downtown (Boston). Home: 11 Harvard Ct Woodcliff Lake NJ 07675. Office: 161 E 42d St New York City NY 10017

CONNELLY, ALBERT RAY, lawyer; b. N.Y.C., Mar. 24, 1908; s. John E. and Julia (Broughey) C.; B.A., Yale, 1929, LL.B., 1932; m. Eleanor Milburn, June 17, 1930; children—Mary (Mrs. Gene Fairly), Jean (Mrs. Alan P. Mooney). Admitted to N.Y. bar, 1933, since practiced in N.Y.C.; partner firm Cravath Swaine & Moore, and predecessors, 1941—. Pres. Five Points House, Pomona, N.Y., 1955—. Chmn. FTC Adv. Council on Rules of Practice and Procedure, 1970—. Trustee Berkshire Sch. Fellow Am. Bar Found., Am Coll. Trial Lawyers; mem. Am., N.Y. State, N.Y. County, bar assns., Assn. Bar City N.Y. Clubs: Union, Down Town Assn, Yale (N.Y. C.); St Andrews Golf (Hastings, N.Y.) Metropolitan (Washington). Home: 36 E 72d St New York City, NY 10021. Office: 1 Chase Manhattan Plaza New York City NY 10005

CONNELLY, CHARLES EDWARD, textile co. exec.; b. Morganton, N.C., Mar. 4, 1911; s. Charles A. and Essie M. (Greene) C.; student Furman U., 1930-32; advanced accounting degree Internat. Accountants Soc., 1942; M. Sara Scott Moore, Feb. 22, 1941; children—Maurice M., Charles Edward. Tax examiner N.C. Dept. Revenue, 1935-42; accountant A.M. Pullen & Co., 1942-50, Cone Mills Corp., Greensboro, N.C., 1950-53, asst. comptroller, 1953-57, comptroller, 1957-63, treas., comptroller, 1963-70, v.p., treas., 1970—, also dir. C.P.A., N.C. Mem. Tax Execs. Inst., Am. Inst. C.P.A.'s, N.C. Assn. C.P.A.'s, Financial Execs. Inst. Presbyn. Club: Greensboro Country. Home: 302 Kimberly Dr Greensboro NC 27408 Office: Cone Mills Corp 4th and Maple Streets Greensboro NC 27405

CONNELLY, JAMES RICHARD, assn. exec.; b. Detroit May 12, 1917; s. James F. and Luella (Werner) C.; A.B., Am. U., 1939; grad. Southeastern U., 1940; m. Wilva Louise Hankinson, Oct. 12, 1940; children—Richard Hankinson, Betty-Brown. Sales mgr. Profl. Bus. Service, Washington, 1930-41; asst. exec. dir. and sec. Med. Soc. D.C., 1946-49, asst. sec. Med. Service D.C., 1948-49; del. Nat. Health Council, 1949—, 1st-7th Congresses Internat. Diabetes Fedn., 1952, 55, 58, 61, 64, 67, 70; exec. dir. Am. Diabetes Assn. Inc., 1949—, exec. editor ADA Forecast also Diabetes, 1952—. Mem. bd. dirs. Nat. Health Council, 1957-58, 62-63; mem. spl. com. on purposes; chmn. com. on pub. information and detection Internat. Diabetes Fedn., 1961- 64; mem. Pres.'s Com. on Employment of Handicapped; mem. Nat. Adv. Com. Local Health Units; adviser to secretariat Internat. Diabetes Found. Fellow Am. Pub. Health Assn.; mem. Am. Assn. Health, Phys. Edn. and Recreation, Am. Camping Assn., Am. Assn. Med. Soc. Execs., Nat. Citizens Com. for WHO, Adult Edn. Assn. U.S.A., Am. Acad. Polit. and Social Sci., Pharm. Advertising Club, Phi Sigma Kappa. Club: Columbia University. Author articles med. subjects profl. jours. Mem. editoral bd. The Executive, 1958-59. Home: 60 Locust Av New Rochelle NY 10801

CONNELLY, JOHN BRUCE, aircraft exec.; b. Sacramento, Feb. 26, 1907; s. John Bruce and Bertha (Gupton) C.; B.A., U. Nev., 1928; m. Evelyn Turner, Aug. 31, 1929 (dec. May, 1952); children—Susan Marie, Sharon Ann; m. 2d, Illis Harper Ferry, July 3, 1953. Pub. accountant, 1929-35; regional auditor U.S. Pub. Works Adminstrn., 1935-40; asst. sec.-treas., adminstry. mgr. Todd- Pacific Shipyards, Inc., 1940-48; asst. controller Boeing Airplane Co., Seattle, 1848-49, dir. contract adminstrn., 1950-55, v.p., gen. mgr. transport div., Renton, Wash., 1956-66, v.p., asst. gen. mgr. comml. airplane div., 1967—. Trustee Helen Bush-Parkside Sch., Seattle, 1953-57. Mem. Sigma Alpha Epsilon. Clubs: University, Seattle Golf, Rainier, Seattle Tennis. Home: 1854 Broadmoor Dr E Seattle WA 98102 Office: Box 707 Renton WA 98055

CONNELLY, JOHN EDWARD, Jr., lawyer; b. N.Y.C., Mar. 4, 1904; s. John Edward and Julia (Broughey) C; grad. Berkshire Sch., Sheffield, Mass., 1922; A.B., Middlebury Coll. 1926; LL.B., Harvard, 1929; m. Troy Stix, Mar. 3, 1959. Admitted to N.Y. bar, 1930, since practiced in N.Y.C.; counsel Olwine, Connelly, Chase, O'Donnell Weyher, and predecessors, 1952—; pres., dir. Seas Shipping Co., Inc.; dir. McGuire Bros., Inc. Bd. dirs. Life Extension Found., Ada Howe Kent Found. Mem. Am., N.Y., N.Y. County lawyers assns., Assn. Bar City N.Y., Chi Psi. Clubs: Harvard, Union (N.Y.C.). Home: 169 E 78th St New York City NY 10021 Office: 299 Park Av New York City NY 10017

CONNELLY, JOHN FRANCIS, industrialist; b. Phila., Mar. 4, 1905; LL.D. (hon.), LaSalle Coll., 1958; m. Josephine O'Neill, Apr. 1938; children—Josephine, Emily, John, Thomas, Judith, Christine. Dir. Crown Cork & Seal Co., Phila., 1956—, chmn., pres., 1957—; pres. Crown Cork Internat. Corp., 1961—, Arden Corp., Chgo.; chmn. Connelly Container, Phila., Nat. Milling and Dehydrating Co., Lamar, Colo. Chmn. Archbishop's laity com. Home: Hilltop and Arden Rds Jenkintown PA 19046 Office: Crown Cork & Seal Co 9300 Ashton Rd Philadelphia PA 19136

CONNELLY, JOHN H., airline exec.; b. N.Y.C., Oct. 10, 1903; s. Arthur J. and Adeline (Von Siefke)C.; student N.Y. U., 1918; m. Dorothy Martin, Oct. 5, 1940; 1 son, Scott. Aeronaut. engr. CAA, Santa Monica, Cal., 1937-39; pres. Pacific Air Lines, San Francisco, 1939-63, Scott, Inc., San Francisco, 1946—. Mem. Aero Tng. Soc. (Washington), Quiet Birdman. Clubs: Newport Harbor Yacht (Newport Beach, Cal.), Burlingame (Cal.) Country; National Aviation (Washington). Home: 6620 Desert Fairways Dr Scottsdale AZ 85251 Office: Pacific Air Lines San Francisco Internat Airport San Francisco CA 94128

CONNELLY, KENNETH AMOR, Jr., educator, critic; b. Billings, Mont., June 28, 1920; s. Kenneth Amor and Mary Kirsten (Hansen) C.; B.A., U. Wash., 1942; student Worcester Coll., Oxford (Eng.) U., 1945-46, U. Chgo., 1947-48; Ph.D., Yale, 1952. Tchr., Coll. William and Mary, 1951, Yale, 1951-57; mem. faculty Smith Coll., Northampton, Mass., 1957—, now prof. English, chmn. dept.; tchr. Bread Loaf Grad. Sch., 1962-67, Aegean Inst., 1969; music critic Yale Rev., 1957-67, poetry reviewer, 1968—. Dir. F.B. Connelly Co., Seattle. Served with AUS, 1942- 45. Decorated Bronze Star medal. Mem. Glapthorne Soc. Home: 450 W 20th St New York City NY 10011 Office: Smith Coll Northampton MA 01060

CONNELLY, LEO B., cable co. exec.; b. 1930; A.B., Fordham U., 1951; LL.B., Columbia, 1956; married. With firm Sullivan, Donovan, Hanrahan, McGovern & Lane, 1956- 58; law asst. appellate div. Supreme Ct. N.Y. State 1958-60; with firm Dewey, Ballantine, Bushby, Palmer & Wood, 1960-66; with Gen. Cable Corp., 1966—, sec., gen counsel, 1967—. Served with AUS, 1951-53. Address: Gen Cable Corp 730 3d Av New York City NY 10017*

CONNELLY, MARC, (Marcus Cook), playwright; b. McKeesport, Pa., Dec. 13, 1890; s. Patrick Joseph and Mabel Fowler (Cook) C.; ed. Trinity Hall, Washington, Pa., 1902-07. Reporter Pitts. newspapers and writer of humorous column Pitts. Gazette Times; contbr. verse, articles and short stories (O. Henry award 1930) to mags; former prof. playwrighting Yale. Past pres. Author's League of Am., Nat. Inst. Arts and Letters; alumnus. Mem. exec. com. U.S. nat commn. for UNESCO. Clubs: Coffee House, Players; Savage (London). Author: The Wisdom Tooth (play), 1926; The Green Pastures (Pulitzer award), 1930; A Souvenir from Qam (novel), 1965; Voices Offstage (memoirs), 1968. Co-author: Dulcy, To the Ladies, Merton of the Movies, Beggar on Horseback, The Farmer Takes a Wife, other plays, several musical comedies. Address: 25 Central Park W New York City NY 10023

CONNELLY, ROBERT LEITH, furniture mfg. co. exec.; b. Morganton, N.C., July 31, 1913; s. Charles A. and Essie (Greene) C.; B.B.A., U. N.C., 1936; m. Miriam Dickinson, Nov. 30, 1940; children—Daphne Leith (Mrs. John S. McKee III), Sarah Melinda, Martha Karen, Robert Leith. With Drexel Enterprises, Inc., 1936- -, treas., dir. mem. exec. com., 1948—, adminstrv. v.p., chief financial officer, 1961-68, exec. v.p., chief operating officer, 1968- -; bd. mgrs. Charlotte br. Wachovia Bank and Trust Co., 1963—. Trustee, treas. Drexel Fund, 1953—; pres. bd. govs. Drexel Found.; bd. govs., treas. Morganton Park and Recreation Found., 1951—; trustee Brevard Coll., 1960—; trustee, treas. Morgantown-Burke Library, 1968—. Home: 106 Pearson Dr Morgantown NC 28655 Office: Drexel Enterprises Inc Drexel NC 28619

CONNER, DOYLE E., farmer, state ofcl.; b. Starke, Fla., Dec. 17, 1928; s. Leon and Ruby (Celmons) C.; B.S. in Agr., U. Fla., 1952; m. Johnnie Bennett, June 28, 1953; children—Doyle E., Kimberly Ann, John Bryant. Gen. farming and ins. bus.; commr. agr. State of Fla., Tallahassee, 1961—. Nat. pres. Future Farmers Am., 1948-49; mem. Nat Food for Peace Com. Former mem., speaker Fla. Ho. of Reps. Named One of 5 Outstanding Men, Fla. Jr. C. of C., 1950, Outstanding Farmer, Bradford County Jr. C. of C., 1958, One of 10 Outstanding Young Men, U.S. Jr. C. of C., 1961. Mem. Nat. (pres.), So. assns. state depts. agr., Fla. Farm Bur., Fla. Cattlemens Assn., Fla., Tallahassee jr. chambers commerce, Fla. Blue Key, Alpha Gamma Rho. Baptist. Mason (Shriner). Home: 2902 Woodside Dr Tallahassee FL 32303 Office: Capitol Bldg Tallahassee FL 32304

CONNER, FORREST E., former assn. exec.; b. Baldwin, Wis., Apr. 12, 1901; s. Ernest E. and Jessie M. (Wilford) C.; A.B., U. S.D., 1923; A.M., State U. Ia., 1933, Ph.D., 1937; m. Florence Adelaide Smiley, June 16, 1927 (dec. Oct. 1959); children—Patricia Conner Williams, John Robert. Coach and prin. Belle Fourche (S.D.) High Sch., 1923-25, supt. schs., 1925-35; prin., Univ. High Sch., Iowa City, 1935-37; dir. secondary edn., Hibbing, Minn., 1937-44; supt. schs., Kenosha, Wis., 1944-49, St. Paul, 1949-63; exec. sec. Am. Assn. Sch. Adminstrs., Washington, 1963-71, ret. Recipient William G. Anderson award A.A.H.P.E.R., 1963. Mem. Phi Delta Kappa, Kappa Delta Pi (laureate mem.), Delta Tau Delta. Conglist. Mason; mem. Order of Eastern Star. Author ednl. publs. Home: 1400 20th St NW Washington DC 20036

CONNER, FREDERICK WILLIAM, univ. adminstr.; b. Rochester, N.Y., May 16 1909; s. William B. and Serene M. (Loper) C.; A.B., U. Rochester, 1930; M.A., U. Pa., 1934, Ph.D., 1944; m. Jane Speese Bronson, Dec. 27, 1935; children—William B. (dec.), James F. From instr. to prof. English, Univ. Fla., Gainesville, 1935-61, asst. dean Grad. Sch., 1957-61, v.p., 1966-67, v.p. acad. affairs, 1967—; prof. English, dean Coll. Arts and Scis., U. Ala., 1961-66. Served to lt. (s.g.) USNR. 1944-46. Mem. Am. Assn. U. Profs., Modern Lang. Assn., Coll. English Assn., Nat. Council Tchrs. English, Am. Studies Assn., Emerson Soc., Omicron Delta Kappa. Presbyn. Kiwanian. Author: Cosmic Optimism: A Study of the Interpretation of Evolution by American Poets From Emerson to Robinson, 1949. Home: 400 N W 32d St Gainesville FL 32601

CONNER, JAMES ELWOOD, educator; b. Pittsylvania County, Va., Jan. 26, 1924; s. Herbert A. and Geogia E. (Logan) C.; B.S., Coll. William and Mary, 1949; M.Ed., U. Va., 1951; Ed. D., U. Md., 1958; m. Margaret A. Walter, Aug. 20, 1948. Elementary sch. tchr., Chaptico, Md., 1948-49; elementary sch. prin. Henrico County (Va.) pub. schs., 1951-53, Montgomery County, Md., 1953- 60; dir. elementary edn., Highland Park, Mich., 1960-62; pres. Wheelock Coll., Boston, 1962-66, specialist for curriculum devel. U.S. Office Edn., Washington; asso. prof. Temple U., 1967-70, dir. Student Teaching Center, 1968-69; curriculum cons. Phila. Sch. Dist., 1967—; edn. dir. U.S. C. of C., Washington, 1970—. Adv. bd. Phila. Opportunities for Women; del. to White House Conf. on Children and Youth, 1970. Served with USAAF, 1943- 45. Mem. Assn. Childhood Edn. Internat., Assn. Supervision and Curriculum Devel., Am. Coll. Pub. Relations Assn., Nat. Council Accreditation Tchr. Edn., World Affairs Council, Am. Acad. Political and Social Science, World Affairs Council. Address: 3900 16th St NW Washington DC 20011

CONNER, JOHN DAVIS, lawyer; b. Seminary Hill, Tex., Feb. 24, 1911; s. Walter Thomas and Blanche Ethel (Horne) C.; A.B., Baylor U., 1933; LL.B., George Washington U., 1938; m. Carolyn Rose Hyatt, Nov. 17, 1934; children—Rose Mary, Jenny Lu, John Davis, Walter Thomas. Admitted to D.C. bar, 1938, since practiced in Washington; mem. firm Sellers, Conner & Cuneo, Washington. Served as lt. USNR, 1943-46. Fellow Am. Bar Found., mem. Am. Judicature Soc. (mem. bd. dirs. 1967-70), Am. (chmn. com. econs. law practice 1959-65), D.C. (chmn. adminstrv. law 1956-67, dir. 1957-58) bar assns. Baptist. Clubs: Metropolitan, University (Washington); Belle Haven Country (Alexandria, Va.). Author: Compilation of Economic Poisons Laws and Regulations; Manual of Chemical Products Liability; Product Liability Trends; Lawyers Handbook, others. Home: 506 W Braddock Rd Alexandria VA 22302 Office: 1625 K St Washington DC 20006

CONNER, NADINE, singer; b. Compton, Cal., Feb.20, , 1913; studied voice with Amado Fernadez; music scholarship U. So. Cal., Euterpe Opera Scholarship; m. Dr. Laurance Heacock; childrenSue Lynn, Loren David. Staff vocalist radio sta. KHJ, Los Angeles; co-star with Nelson Eddy, performer Show Boat hour: staff Los Angeles Opera Co., 1939-41; debut Met. Opera House, 1941; performances include Pamina in the Magic Flute, Micacela in Carmen, Sophia in Der Rosenkavalier, English Version of Hansel and Gretel; appeared in motion picture Of Men and Music, 1950; recording Hansel and Gretel, Columbia Records. Voted best-dressed woman in opera world Fashion Inst. Home: 300 S Poinsettia St Compton CA 90221 Office: care Metropolitan Opera Assn., Inc., 1947 W 39th St New York City NY 10018 *

CONNER, NORVAL WHITE, research dir.; b. Blacksburg, Va., Sept. 18, 1905; s. William George and Virginia (Thomas) C.; B.S., Va. Poly Inst., 1925, M.E., 1926; M.S., Ia. State Coll., 1930; m. Margaret Prentis Miller. Engr., Atlantic Ice Co., Coatesville, Pa., 1926-27, Lukens Steel Co., Coatesville, 1927-28; research engr. Ia. State Coll.; instr. mech. engring. Va. Poly. Inst., Blacksburg, 1928-29, asst. prof. applied mechanics, head of aeronautics, 1930-37; asst. prof. engr. mechanics N.C. State Coll., Raleigh, 1937-38, asso. prof., 1938-44, prof. of fluid mechanics, 1944-47, prof. mech. engring., head of design div. 1947-51, dir. engring. research, 1951-67, assistant dean for research, 1967—. Member American Soc. M.E. (sec.- treas. Raleigh sect.; hon. chmn. student br.; sec. Region IV 2 yrs.), Am. Soc. for Testing Materials (mem. council, vice chmn. Middle Atlantic dist.), Am. Soc. Engring. Edn. (pres. Southeastern sect..), Am. Ordnance Assn. (bd. directors), North Carolina Society Engring., Sigma Xi, Phi Kappa Phi, Tau Beta Pi, Pi Tau Sigma, Sigma Chi. Presbyterian. Clubs: Engineers (Raleigh), Executives. Contbr. to Engineer Experiment Sta. Bull. Home: 3006 Ruffin St Raleigh NC 27607

CONNER, RICHARD H., business exec.; b. Moundsville, W.Va., July 18, 1914; s. Richard H. and Ada (Baumann) C.; grad. high sch.; m. Helene A. Scanlon, Dec. 17, 1945. Asst. city editor H.C. Ogden Newspapers, Weirton, W.Va., 1932-36; W.Va. mgr. editorial, advt. Brush-Moore Newspapers, Steubenville, O., 1937-42; sr. pub. relations staff, Mich. pub. relations mgr. Goodyear Tire & Rubber Co., Akron, O., 1942-48; exec. v.p., dir. pub. relations Ketchum, MacLeod & Grove, Inc., Pitts., 1948—, also dir. Served with AUS, 1943-45. Mem. Pub. Relations Soc. Am., Pitts. Press Club. Clubs: Duquesne, South Hills Country (Pitts.). Home: 204 Beall Dr Pittsburgh PA 15236 Office: 4 Gateway Center Pittsburgh PA 15222

CONNER, TROY BLAINE, Jr., lawyer; b. Moundsville, W.Va., Jan. 23, 1926; s. Troy Blaine and Ethel (Barbour) C.; A.B., W.Va. U., 1945, J.D., 1948; m. Betty Lenore Luzier, Dec. 29, 1953; children—Troy Blaine III, Kimberly Ann, Robert James, David Jefferson. Admitted to W.Va. bar, 1948, D.C. bar, 1969; practice in Morgantown, W.Va., 1948-53; trial atty. criminal and internal security divs. Dept. Justice, 1953-55, head front orgns. unit, internal security div., 1955-58; trial counsel AEC, 1958-70; exec. dir. CAB, 1970-71; partner firm Reid & Priest, N.Y.C., 1971—. Fellow Internat. Acad. Law and Sci., Am. Nuclear Soc.; mem. Am., Fed. bar assns., Atomic Indsl. Forum, W.Va. U. Alumni Assn. (pres. D.C. 1956, 66), Nat. Aero. Assn. (bd. dirs.), Phi Sigma Kappa. Republican. Methodist. Clubs: Aero, Capitol Hill (Washington); Lakeview Country (Morgantown, W.Va.). Asso. editor Lex et Scientia, 1967—. Home: 11503 Farmland Dr Rockville MD 20852 Office: 1701 K St NW Washington DC 20006

CONNERAT, WILLIAM SPENCER, lawyer; b. Savannah, Ga., May 7, 1889; s. Clarence S. and Laura (Spencer) C.; student Univ. Virginia Law Sch., 1910-11; LL.B., U. Ga., 1912; m. Josephine N. Crisfield, Dec. 17, 1927; children—Josephine (Mrs. Fred M. Blanton), William Spencer, Pearce Crisfield, Laura Spencer (Mrs. Freeman N. Jelks, Jr.). Admitted to Ga. bar, 1912, since practiced in Savannah; sr. mem. Connerat, Dunn, Hunter, Houlihan, Maclean & Exley and predecessors, 1946—; secretary Savannah Dist. Authority, 1951-61. Mem. Ga. Legislature, 1945-46. Mem. bd. officer Protestant Episcopal Ch. in Diocese of Ga., treas. Diocese of Ga., 1950—. Served as capt. 320th F.A. 82d Div., U.S. Army, World War I. Cited for exceptional service Meuse-Argonne offensives. Mem. Chi Phi.Clubs: Oglethorpe, Century, Cotillion (Savannah). Home: 20 E 50th St Savannah GA 31405 Office: Savannah Bank & Trust Bldg Savannah GA 31401

CONNERS, WILLIAM JAMES, III, publisher; b. Buffalo, May 31, 1922; s. William James and Corinne (Tilford) C.; student U. Va., 1941; m. Barbara J. Strebel, Feb. 9, 1946; children—William James IV, Robert N., Christine Strebel, Cathy Ann. With Buffalo Courier-Express, Inc., 1945—, pres., pub., 1951—; pres. Niagara Photo Engraving Co. 1951—. Served as staff sgt. AUS, 1941-45. Mem. East Africa Profl. Hunters Assn. (asso.; Nairobi, Kenya). Clubs: Saturn, Buffalo Country, Buffalo Athletic; Cherry Hill Country (Ont., Can.); Palm Beach Gun (Lake Worth, Fla.); Club Metropolitan De Tiro (San Juan, P.R.); Winter Haven (Fla.) Skeet and Trap; Beach (Palm Beach, Fla.). Home: 12 St Catherine's Ct Buffalo NY 14222

CONNERS, WILLIAM R., union ofcl. Sec., Bricklayers, Masons and Plasterers' Internat. Union Am. AFL-CIO. Office: 815 15th St NW Washington DC 20005*

CONNERY, PAUL JOSEPH, international communications company executive; born at Fort Smith, Arkansas, January 14, 1923; s. Arthur James and Ervema (Wolcott) C.; B.S., S.W. Mo. State Coll., 1943; M.B.A., Northwestern U., 1948; m. Audrey Dolores Zimmerman, May 14, 1949; 1 son, Brian Arthur. Accountant Arthur Andersen & Co., 1948-50; asst. treas. Ia. Power & Light Co., 1950-53; sec., treas. Ohio Valley Electric Corp., 1953-57; v.p., comptroller New Haven R.R., 1957-60; v.p. finance Am. Cable & Radio Corp., 1960-62; dir. financial controls Internat. Tel. & Tel., 1962—. Served as capt. inf. AUS, 1942-46. Roman Catholic. Home: 1464 Ridge Rd North Haven CT 06473 Office: 320 Park Av New York City NY 10022

CONNERY, ROBERT HOWE, educator, author; b. St. Paul, Oct. 1, 1907; s. Robert Henry and Nellie Elizabeth (Collins) C.; A.B., U. Minn., 1929, A.M., 1930; Ph.D., Columbia, 1935. Instr. U. Minn., 1930-31, Columbia, 1933-38; asso. prof. Cath. U. Am., Washington, 1939-42, Stanford, 1946-48; prof. U. Ill., 1948-49, Duke., 1949-66; prof. govt. Columbia U., 1966—. Cons. Hoover Commn. on reorgn. exec. br. govt., 1948, Brookings Instn. Survey Adminstrn. U.S. Fgn. Affairs, 1950, Survey NATO and U.N., 1952, Sec. of Def. on NATO, 1951, N.Y. State commn. on govtl. operations of N.Y.C., 1959-60; exec. sec. com. on modern zoning, 1959-60; cons. Nat. Inst. Mental Health, 1961-66; dir. reports Mayor's Office, N.Y.C, 1954-55; dep. city adminstr. N.Y.C., 1965—. Commd. lt. USNR, 1942, advancing to comdr.; on duty Office of Sec. of Navy. Fellow Brookings Instn. Mem. Acad. of Polit. Sci. (pres. 1966—), Am. Polit. Sci. Assn. Roman Catholic. Club: Cosmos (Washington). Author: The Navy and the Industrial Mobilization in World War II, 1951; (with Richard Leach), The Federal Government and Metropolitan Areas, 1960; Forrestal and the Navy (with Robert Albion), 1962; (with others) The Politics of Mental Health, 1968. Editor Teaching Political Science, 1965; Urban Riots, 1968; Governing the City, 1969; The Corporation and the Campus, 1970. Home: 35 Claremont Av New York City NY 10027 ☆

CONNERY, SEAN, actor; b. Edinburg, Scotland, Aug. 25, 1930. Stage debut in South Pacific, 1953; motion picture actor, 1956—; films include Action of the Tiger, Timclick, Hell Divers, Another Time, Another Place, Barby O'Gill and the Little People, Tarzan's Greatest Adventure, The Frightened City, On The Fiddle, The Longest Day, 1962, Dr. No, 1963, From Russia With Love, 1964, Marnie, 1964, Woman of Straw, 1964, Goldfinger, 1964, The Hill, 1965, Thunderball, 1965, A Fine Madness, 1966, You Only Live Twice, 1967, Shalako; TV appearances include Requiem for a Heavyweight, Anna Christie, Boy with the Meataxe, Women in Love, The Crucible, Riders to the Sea, Colombe, Adventure Story, Anna Karenina, McBeth. *

CONNETT, WILLIAM BREWER, Jr., fgn. service officer; b. South Orange, N.J., July 14, 1918; s. William Brewer and Helen (Enger) C.; grad. St. Paul's Sch., 1937; student Georgetown U., 1945-46; m. Bartan Lowell, June 10, 1942. Vice consul, Maracaibo, Venezuela, 1947- 49, 2d sec., Caracas, Venezuela, 1949-52; staff Bur. Inter-Am. Affairs, Washington, 1952-55; 1st sec., Guatemala City, 1955-57, Am. embassy, Paris, France, 1957-61, charge mil. affairs sect., 1958- 61; dep. exec. sec., dir. Operations Center, Washington, 1962; dep. chief mission Am. embassy, Santo Domingo, Dominican Republic, until 1966; State Dept. adviser Armed Forces Staff Coll., Norfolk, Va., 1966-68, consul gen., Guadalajara, Mex., 1968—. Served from ensign to lt. comdr., USNR, 1941-45. Center Internat. Affairs fellow Harvard, 1961. Home: 2469 Paseo de Las Aguilas Guadalajara Mexico Office: Am Consulate Gen Guadalajara Mexico

CONNICK, CHARLES MILO, clergyman, educator; b. Conneaut Lake, Pa., Mar. 23, 1917; s. Walter and Iola Belle (Wintermute) C.; A.B., Allegheny Coll., 1939, D.D., 1960; S.T.B., Boston U., 1942, Ph.D., 1944; Roswell R. Robinson fellow, Harvard, 1942-43; student Edinboro State Coll., 1935-36, Episcopal Theol. Sch., 1942-44; m. Genevieve Shaul, June 7, 1941; children—Joy (Mrs. J. Bruce Parker), Christopher Milo, Nancy. Ordained deacon Meth. Ch., 1941, elder, 1942; asso. minister, Lowell, Mass., 1940-41, Copley Meth. Ch., Boston, 1941- 42; minister to students Harvard Epworth Meth. Ch., Cambridge, Mass., 1943-44; sr. instr. pub. speaking Curry Coll., Boston, 1942-44; head Bible dept. Northfield School, East Northfield, Mass., 1944-46; prof. religion, head dept. philosophy, religion Whittier (Cal.) Coll., 1946—, chmn. social sci. div., 1950, 60, pres. faculty senate, 1970-71, dir. coll. study tour to Europe, Middle East, around the world, summers 1955-69. Danforth asso., 1959—, Danforth sr. asso., 1964—; spl. lectr. Bibl. lit. Sch. Religion, First Congl. Church, Los Angeles, 1947-62; mem. Western Pa. Conf. United Meth. Ch., 1942—. Recipient Distinguished Alumnus award Boston U., 1971. Mem. Am. Civil Liberties Union (pres. Whittier br. 1954-56), Am. Assn. U. Profs., (Whittier pres. 1970—), Pacific Coast Assn. for Religious Studies (exec. com.), Am. Acad. Religion (pres. Pacific Coast sect. 1953- 54), Soc. Bibl. Lit. and Exegesis, Am. Oriental Soc., Am. Christian Assn. for Isreal (mem. nat. adv. com.), Phi Sigma Tau, Kappa Phi Kappa, Chi Delta Sigma. Democrat. Author: Build on The Rock, You and the Sermon on the Mount, 1960; Jesus, the Man, the Mission, and the Message, 1963; The Message and Meaning of the Bible, 1965. Editorial adviser The Dickenson Pub. Co., Inc., 1964—. Contbr. articles to religious jours. and mags. Home: 6249 S Roundhill Dr Whittier CA 90601 Office: 13421 E Philadelphia St Whittier CA 90608 ☆

CONNICK, ROBERT ELWELL, coll. ofcl.; b. Eureka, Cal., July 29, 1917; s. Arthur Elwell and Florence (Robertson) C.; B.S., U. Cal. at Berkeley, 1939, Ph.D., 1942; m. Frances Spieth, Dec. 19, 1952; children—Mary Catherine, Elizabeth, Arthur, Megan, Sarah, William Beach. Faculty U. Cal., Berkeley, 1942—, research Manhattan project, 1943-46, asst. prof. then asso. prof. chemistry, 1945-52, prof., 1952—, chmn. dept., 1958-60, dean Coll. Chemistry, 1960-65, vice chancellor acad. affairs, 1965-69, vice chancellor, 1969—. Guggenheim fellow, 1949, 59. Trustee Mills Coll. Mem. Am. Chem. Soc., Nat. Acad. Scis., Phi Beta Kappa, Sigma Xi, Pi Mu Epsilon. Contbr. articles profl. jours. Home: 50 Marguerita Rd Berkeley CA 94707

CONNIFF, RAY, conductor, composer, arranger; b. Attleboro, Mass., Nov. 6, 1916; s. John Lawrence and Maude (Angela)0 C.; student Julliard Sch. Music; studied with Tom Timothy, Sol Kaplan, Hugo Friedhofer; m. Emily Jo Ann Imhof, Feb. 14, 1938; children—James Lawrence, Jo Ann Patricia; m. 2d, Ann Marie Engberg, Aug. 24, 1947; 1 foster son, Richard J. Bibo. Trombone Player, arranger Bunny Berigan, Bob Crosby, Artie Shaw, Harry James orchestras; arranger, composer, conductor, rec. artist Columbia Records. Home: 17348 Weddington St Encino CA 91316 Office: 17100 Ventura Blvd Encino CA 91316

CONNOLE, ROGER JOSEPH, clergyman; b. Harvey, Minn., Nov. 28, 1900; s. John C. and Agnes (Quinn) C.; A.B., St. Thomas Coll., 1925, LL.D., 1965; grad. St. Paul Sem., 1929; Ph.D., Cath. U. Am., 1937. Ordained priest Roman Cath. Ch., 1929; asst. pastor, St. Paul, 1929-34, archdiocesan supt. schs., 1937-67; staff Coll. St. Thomas, St. Paul, 1967—. Author: Christian Inheritance Religion Series. Home: 1925 Norfolk Av St Paul MN 55116

CONNOLLY, ARTHUR GUILD, lawyer; b. Boston, Nov. 8, 1905; s. George Augustus and Elizabeth Campbell (Burns) C.; B.S., in Chem. Engring., Mass. Inst. Tech., 1927; LL.B., Harvard 1930; m. Gerardine Laffey, Nov. 25, 1936; children—Arthur Guild, Ronald G., Christopher G., Gerardine L., Mary G., Thomas A. Admitted Mass., D.C. bars, 1932, Del. bar, 1940; with legal dept. Universal Oil Products Co., Chgo., 1930-31; patent dept. duPont Co., Wilmington, Del., 1931-42, exec. asst. dir., 1936-42; pvt. practice law, Wilmington, 1942—, sr. partner Connolly, Bove & Lodge and predecessor firms, 1944—. Dirs. Sprague Electric Co., North Adams, Mass. Fellow Am. Coll. Trial Lawyers; mem. Am., Del. bar assns., Am., N.Y., Phila. patent law assns. Clubs: Union League (Chgo.); Canadian (N.Y.C.); Mass. Inst. Technology (N.Y.C.); Harvard of Delaware; Wilmington Country; Cumberland (Portland, Me.). Home: 102 School Rd Alapocas Wilmington DE 19803 Office: Farmers Bank Bldg Wilmington DE 19899

CONNOLLY, BRENDAN, librarian; b. Boston, Feb. 10, 1913; s. Daniel and Mary Ellen (Keane) C.; A.B., Boston Coll., 1937, M.A., 1938; S.T.L., Weston Coll., 1944; B.S. in L.S., Cath. U. Am., 1946; Ph.D., U. Chgo., 1955. Joined Soc. of Jesus, 1931, ordained priest Roman Cath. Ch., 1943; instr. English, Boston Coll., 1938-40; instr. library sci. Cath. U. Am., 1950-51; librarian Weston Coll., 1951-59, asst. prof. theology, 1951-59; dir. libraries Boston Coll., 1959—; chaplain Country Day Sch. Sacred Heart, 1959—. Cons. library adminstrn. and bldg. Mem. Am. Cath., Mass., New Eng. Library assns., N.A.A.C.P., Am. Assn. U. Profs., Jesuit Library Conf. Asso. editor; New Testament Abstracts, 1956-60, Writer religious library articles. Address: Boston Coll Chestnut Hill MA 02167

CONNOLLY, CHARLES HUNTLEY, life ins. co. exec.; b. Denton, Tex., Oct. 27, 1918; s. Otis Allen and LeNora (Harrell) C.; student So. Meth. U., 1935-37; m. Anne Ashburn, Nov. 29, 1947; children—David Lawrence, Carol Eileen, Martin Allen. With Southwestern Life Ins. Co., 1937-70, successively actuarial asst., actuary and mgr. research div., asso. actuary, actuary of co., 1946- 62, v.p., actuary, 1962-70; cons. actuary, 1970—. Served with USNR, 1942-45. Fellow Soc. Actuaries; mem. Actuaries of Southwest (past pres.). Home: 13515 Sprucewood St Dallas TX 75240 Office: 511 N Akard Dallas TX 75201

CONNOLLY, DONALD HILARY, former army officer; b. Fort Mojave, Ariz., Feb. 11, 1880; s. Thomas Worthington and Mary Alice (Kiser) C.; student U. Cal., 1905-06; B.S., U.S. Mill. Acad., 1910; student Engr. Sch. of Application, 1911- 12, Command and Gen. Staff Sch., 1922-23, Army War Coll., 1928-29; m. Grace Hollingsworth Baxter, Sept. 16, 1916 (dec. Sept. 1963); children—Donald Hilary, Thomas Worthington. Joined C.E. U.S. Army, 1910; fgn. service in Canal Zone, Philipines, France, Iran, and Iraq; mem. War Dept. Gen. Staff, 1916-22, in charge Memphis River and Harbor Dist., 1923-28, instr. Command and Gen. Staff Sch., Fort Leavenworth, Kan., 1929-34; in charge Civil Works Adminstrn., Los Angeles, 1934, Chicago River and Harbor Dist., 1934-35, WPA, So. Calif., 1935-39; comdr. 2d Engrs., Fort Logan, Colo., 1939-40, adminstr. civil aeronautics Dept. Commerce, Washington, 1940-41; with Hdqrs. USAAF, Washington, 1942; comdr. Persian Gulf command, 1942-1944; dep. Army-Navy Liquidation Commn., 1945, fgn. liquidation commn., 1945-1948; ret. maj. gen.; dir. Balt. dept. aviation, 1948-56. Decorated D.S.M., Legion of Merit; Order of Suvorov (Russia); Order of Homayoon (Iran); hon. companion Order of Bath (British). Mem. Am. Soc. C.E., Soc. Am. Mil. Engrs., Am. Legion, Newcomen Soc. of Eng. Democrat. Mason. Clubs: Army and Navy, Army, Navy Country (Washington); Gibson Island (Md.). Home: Gibson Island MD 21056

CONNOLLY, EUGENE THOMAS, former lawyer; b. Beverly, Mass., May 1, 1891; s. Stephen J. and Ella H. (Devlin) C.; grad, Philips Exeter Acad., 1908; B.A., Yale, 1912; LL.B., Harvard, 1916; m. Ellen Louise Lane, May 25, 1922; children—Barbara (Mrs. William H. Guild), Ellen Lane, Margaret (Mrs. Edwin F. Hoffman, Jr.), Eugene Thomas, Mary Lane (Mrs. Walter F. Cairns). Admitted to Mass. bar, 1916, since practiced in Boston; partner Herrick, Smith, Donald, Farley & Ketchum, 1926-70, ret., 1970. Dir. Connolly Bros., Inc. Pres., N. Shore council Boy Scouts Am., 1949-54, mem. exec.com. Region 1, 1956-69, mem. region adv. com., 1969—; a founder, pres. Yacht Racing Union Mass. Bay, 1949- 50; chmn. Old and Historic Marblehead Dists. Commn., 1968-70. Bd. dirs. Marblehead Hist. Soc. Served with Signal Corps, U.S. Army, World War I. Recipient Silver Beaver, Silver Antelope award Boy Scouts Am. Mem. N.E. Alumni Assn. Philips Exeter Acad. (pres.), Phi Beta Kappa. Republican. Roman Catholic. Clubs: Eastern Yacht, Pleon Yacht (Marblehead). Home: 8 Lookout Ct Marblehead MA 01945

CONNOLLY, JAMES LOUIS, former bishop; b. Fall River, Mass., Nov. 15, 1894; s. Francis T. and Agnes (Mcbride) C.; student St. Charles Coll., 1918; A.B., St. Mary's Univ., Balt., 1919, A.M., 1920; S.T.B., Sulpician Sem., Washington, 1923; A.M., Cath. U. Am., 1924; Ph.D., Cath. Univ of Louvain (France), 1927; LL.D., Stonehill Coll., 1952, Boston Coll., 1953, St. Michaels Coll., 1954; S.T. D., Providence Coll., 1954. Ordained priest Roman Cath. Ch., 1923; studied abroad, 1924-28; prof. history and philosophy St. Paul (Minn.) Sem., 1928-33, spiritual dir., 1933-40; prof. history and religion Diocesan Tchrs.; Coll., St. Paul, 1929-43, dean studies, 1939-45; rector Nazareth Hall Prep. Sem., 1940- 43; rector The St. Paul Sem., 1943-45; apptd. coadjutor bishop, Fall River, Mass., 1945; consecrated bishop St. Paul Cath., 1945; bishop Fall River, 1951-70, ret. Bd. dirs. St. Thomas Coll., St. Paul, 1942-45, St. Paul Sem., 1943-45, Minn. Soc. for Control of Cancer, 1943-45, Our Lady of Good Counsel Free Cancer Home, 1941-46, Rose Hawthorne Lathrop Home, Fall River, Mass., 1945-46. Mem. Cath. Hist. Soc. St. Paul (editorial bd. 1930-36), Minn. Hist. Soc. (exec. council 1938-46), Cath. Hist. Assn., Fall River Hist. Soc., Medieval Acad. of Am. K.C. Chaplain. Minneapolis Serra Club. Author: John Gerson, Reformer and Mystic, 1928; Catholic Action Conferences, 1932. Home: 394 Highland Fall River MA 02720 Office: 362 Highland Av Fall River MA 02720

CONNOLLY, JAMES R., hosp. supt.; b. Pitts., July 26, 1904; s. James and Brigid (Murphy) C.; B.S,Duquesne U., 1927; M.D., Georgetown U., 1936; m. Kathryn A. Tiegel, June 30, 1936; children—Kathleen Clare (Mrs. Howard Dumire), Robert, James, Michael. Practice medicine, Pitts.; now supt. Ebensburg (Pa.) State Sch. and Hosp. for Retarded. Address: Ebensburg State Sch Ebensburg PA 15931

CONNOLLY, JOHN JAMES, electronics co. exec.; b. Ft. Worth, Mar. 21, 1924; s. John James and Lenore (Moore) C.; student Carnegie Inst. Tech., 1941-43; B.S. in Elec. Engring., Yale, 1944; postgrad. Columbia, Mass. Inst. Tech., Bowdoin Coll., 1945, N.Y. U. Grad. Sch. Bus. Adminstrn., 1948; m. Vera Irene Snow; children—Louise Homer, Jane Allan, Elizabeth Ann, John Nicholas, Cynthia Anne, Ann Marie. With Teleregister Corp., 1947-52, Rand Corp., 1952-55; with Litton Industries, Inc., 1955-69, v.p., 1965-67, sr. v.p., 1967-69; chmn., pres. Cosmodyne Corp., Los Angeles, 1969—. Served to lt. USNR, 1943-46. Mem. Tau Beta Pi. Club: Los Angeles Country. Home: 12838 Marlboro St Los Angeles CA 90049 Office: 12011 San Vicente Blvd Los Angeles CA 90049

CONNOLLY, JOHN JAMES, corp. exec.; b. Ft. Worth, Mar. 21, 1924; s. John James and Lenore C. (Moore) C.; B.S., Yale, 1944; student Carnegie Inst. Tech., 1941-43, Columbia, 1945, Mass. Inst. Tech., 1945, Bowdoin Coll., 1945, N.Y.U., 1948; m. Vera Irene Snow, Apr. 16, 1962; children—Louise Homer, Jane Allan, Elisabeth Ann, John Nicholas, Cynthia Anne, Ann Marie. With Teleregister Corp., 1947-52, Rand Corp., 1952-55; with Litton Industries, Inc., 1955-69, v.p., 1965-67, sr. v.p., 1967-69; pres., chmn. bd. dirs. Cosmodyne Corp., Los Angeles, 1969—. Served as lt. USNR, 1943-46. Mem. Tau Beta Pi. Club: Los Angeles Country. Home: 12838 Marlboro St Los Angeles CA 99049 Office: 12011 San Vicente Blvd Los Angeles CA 90049

CONNOLLY, JOHN JOSEPH, Canadian senator; b. Ottawa, Ont., Can., Oct. 31, 1906; s. Patrick Thomas and Josephine (Macdonald) C.; Ph.D., U. Ottawa, 1931, LL.D., 1956; LL.D., U. Montreal, 1934; LL.D., St. Thomas U., N.B., 1965; m. Ida Bernadette Jones, Aug. 6, 1938; children—Peter Charles, John Macdonald. Prof. philosophy U. Notre Dame, 1928-31; exec. asst. to Canadian minister nat. def. for naval services, 1941-45; called to Que. bar, 1934, Ont. bar, 1935; created Queen's counsel, 1947; counsel to Macdonald & Connolly, Ottawa, 1934-41, 45-64; mem. Canadian Senate for Ont., 1953—, leader of govt., minister without portfolio, 1964-68; mem. Queen's Privy Council for Can., 1964—. Past bd. govs. U. Ottawa. Pres. Liberal Fedn. Can., 1961-64. Officer Order Brit. Empire; knight comdr. with star Order St. Gregory the Great. Mem. bars provinces Ont., Que., Canadian Cath. Hist. Soc., (past pres.), Ont. Cath. Edn. Assn. (past pres.), Canadian Bar Assn. (past mem. council), County Carleton Law Assn. (past pres.), Commonwealth Parliamentary Assn. (chmn. gen. council 1965-66, mem. exec. com. 1967-70). Clubs: Rideau, Royal Ottawa Golf, Le Cerole Universitare D'Ottawa. Home: 281 Roger Rd Ottawa Ontario Canada Office: The Senate of Canada Ottawa Ontario Canada

CONNOLLY, PAUL RAYMOND, lawyer; b. Balt., June 28, 1922; s. Paul Raymond and Loretta (Barry) C.; A.B. cum laude, Loyola Coll., Balt., 1943; LL.B., Georgetown U., 1948, LL.M., 1952; m. Mary Catherine Garvey, June 26, 1948; children—Mary Tressa, Paul Brian, Margaret Carroll, Sheila Barry, Michael Ignatius, Peter Christopher. Admitted to Md. bar, 1948, D.C. bar, 1949; prac. in Wahington, 1948—; partner firm Williams, Connolly & Califano, 1967—; adj. prof. Georgetown U. Law Sch., 1956-65. Mem. adv. council Practicing Law Inst.; mem. Jud. Conf. D.C. Circuit, 1954—. Trustee Pub. Defender Service, D.C., 1969—. Served to lt. (j.g.) USNR, 1943-46. Fellow Am. Coll. Trial Lawyers; mem. Am., D.C. (v.p. 1958, bd. dirs 1959-61), Md. bar assns., Internat. Assn. Ins. Counsel (exec. com. 1967-69), Am. Judicature Soc., Barristers and Counsellors, John Carroll Soc. (chmn. bd. govs. 1967-69, pres. 1969-70), Delta Theta Phi, Alpha Sigma Nu. Democrat. Catholic. Clubs: Metropolitan, George Town, Nat. Lawyers (Washington); Chevy Chase (Md.). Home: 3005 45th St NW Washington DC 20016 Office: 1000 Hill Bldg Washington DC 20006

CONNOLLY, RUSSELL GIRARD, lawyer, oil corp. exec.; b. Pitts., Oct. 14, 1913; s. John Charles and Olive Gertrude (Evans) C.; A.B., U. Pitts., 1936, LL.B., 1939; m. Frances Mae Chambon, Feb. 12, 1947; children—Carolyn (Mrs. James C. McElroy), Steven, Constance, Cheryl, Brian. Admitted to Pa. bar, 1939; asso. law firm Moorhead & Knox, Pitts., 1946-47; with law dept. Gulf Oil Corp., Pitts., 1948—, sec. corp. and domestic subsidiaries, 1955—, v.p., 1968- -. Trustee Carlow Coll., Pitts. Robert Morris Coll., Pitts. Served from pvt. to maj., F.A., AUS, 1941-46. Decorated Bronze Star medal Mem. Am., Pa., Allegheny County bar assns., Phi Alpha Delta, Omicron Delta Kappa. Clubs: Duquesne (Pitts.); The Wildwood Golf (Allison Park, Pa.). Home: Pearce Mill Rd RR 3 Box 1321 Wexford PA 15090 Office: Gulf Bldg Pittsburgh PA 15219

CONNOLLY, SYBIL, dress designer; b. Wales (Irish national), Ja. 24, 1921; d. John and Evelyn Connolly; ed. pvt. tutors; student Convent of Mercy (Waterford, So. Ireland). First visit to Am. to show collection of clothes, Mar. 1953; opened couture house, Dublin, Ireland, 1957; designer of clothes distributed in Am., Australia, Europe. Named Woman of the Year, Great Britain, 1958; one of ten best-dressed women in the world, 1957, 58, 59. Home: 71 Merrion Sq Dublin, Ireland.

CONNOLLY, THOMAS ARTHUR, archbishop; b. San Francisco, Oct. 5, 1899; s. Thomas and Catherine (Gilsenan) C.; ed. St. Patrick's Sem., Menlo Park, Cal., 1915-26, Cath. U., 1930-32 (J.C.D.). Ordained priest Roman Cath. 1926; asst. pastor, 1926- 30; sec. to archbishop, 1934-39; chancellor Archdiocese San Francisco, 1935-48; named domestic prelate, 1936; pastor Mission Dolores Ch., San Francisco, 1939-48; apptd. aux. bishop San Francisco, titular bishop Sila, 1939, consecrated, Aug, 1939; apptd. vicar del. Cath. Chaplains, U.S. Army and Navy, Pacific Coast, 1941: apptd. coadjutor bishop Seattle, 1948, bishop Seattle, 1950; archbishop Seattle, 1951; apptd. asst. at Pontifical Throne, 1959. Author: Appeals in Canon Law, 1932. Home: 1104 Spring St Seattle WA 98104 Office: 907 Terry Av Seattle WA 98104

CONNOLLY, THOMAS FRANCIS, naval officer; b. St. Paul, Oct. 24, 1909; s. Thomas Ignatius and Leona (Gillespie) C.; student U. Cal. at Los Angeles, 1929; B.S., U.S. Naval Acad., 1933; M.S., Mass. Inst. Tech., 1942; m. Margaret Irene Hagy, June 27, 1939; children—Thomas Francis, Susan Loraine. Comnd. ensign U.S. Navy, 1933, advanced through grades to vice adm., 1963; designated naval aviator, 1936; comdr. Patrol Bombing Squadron 13, 1943-44; asst. dir. flight test Naval Air Test Center, Patuxent River, Va., 1944-47; exec. officer U.S.S. Rendova, 1947-48; dir. Test Pilot Sch., 1948-51; comdr. Heavy Attack Squadron 6, 1951-52; exptl. officer rocket project Naval Ordanance Test Sta., China Lake, Cal., 1952-54; assigned strategic plans div. Office Chief Naval Operations, 1954-56; comdr. aircraft carriers U.S.S. Corregidor, 1956-57, U.S.S. Hornet, 1957-58; asst. chief Navy Bur. Aero., 1958-59; asst. chief Bur. Naval Weapons for Pacific Missile Range and Astronautics Matters, 1959-61; comdr. Carrier Div. 7, 1961-62; dir. strike warfare div. Office Chief Naval Operations, 1962-63, dep. chief naval operations (air warfare), 1964—. Decorated Legion of Merit with gold star, D.F.C. with 2 gold stars, Air medal with 2 gold stars. Mem. Soc. Exptl. Test Pilots. Co-author: Airplane-Aerodynamics, 1951. Home: 1703 S Shore Dr Holland MI 49423 Office: Chief Naval Operations Dept Navy Washington DC 20360

CONNOLLY, THOMAS JOSEPH, educator; b. Syracuse, N.Y., Feb. 17, 1923; s. John and Margaret (Lawless) C.; B.Ch.E., Syracuse U., 1943; M.S., Carnegie Inst. Tech., 1947; Ph.D., Cal. Inst. Tech., 1950; m. Helen M. Schetter, Feb. 7, 1953; childrenMark Joseph, Steven Thomas, Mary Karin, James Brian. Chem. engr. Standard Oil Co., Whiting, Ind., 1943-44, 46-48, U. Cal., Los Alamos, 1945-46; instr. to asso. prof. engring U. Cal. at Los Angeles, 1950-59; prof., dir. nuclear engring. div. Stanford, 1959-. Served with AUS, 1944-46. Mem. Am. Nuclear Soc. Home: 855 Lathrop Dr Stanford, CA 94305.

CONNOLLY, VINCENT JAMES PATRICK, investment co. exec.; b. Manchester, Eng., July 2, 1907; s. Frank and Mary (Callan) C.; came to U.S., 1908, naturalized, 1915; grad. Am. Inst. Banking, 1928; hon. certificate Hampton Inst., 1954; m. Margaret M. Malloy, Sept. 9, 1931; children—Peggy Ann (Mrs. Arthur J. Haby), Maureen Ann (Mrs. Henry Deuschell), Kathleen Ann (Mrs. John N. Rosenberger), Patricia Ann. Eileen Ann (Mrs. David M. Murdock). With Guaranty Co. N.Y., 1925-34, Edward B. Smith & Co., N.Y.C., 1934-38; with Smith, Barney & Co., N.Y., 1938—, account exec., 1940—; spl. work in investments for pvt. ednl. instns. Investment adviser Hampton Inst. Active local hosp., sch. and coll. fund drives, 1946—. Home: 519 First St Oradell NJ 07649 Office: 1345 Av of Americas New York City NY 10019

CONNOR, ALBERT OLLIE, army officer; b. Helena, Mont., Aug. 28, 1914; s. Charles Oille and Marguerite (Simon) C.; B.S., U.S. Mil. Acad., 1937; grad. Command and Gen. Staff Coll., 1946, Army War Coll., 1952; m. Betty Schofield Stewart, June 1, 1938; children—John Stewart, Michael James, Cathleen Jane. Commd. 2d lt. U.S. Army, 1937, advanced through grades to lt. gen., 1967; operations officer 3d Inf. Div., also VI Corps. MTO and ETO, World War II; mem. faculty Inf. Sch., 1946-49; comdr. 503d Airborne Inf. Regt., 1951, 27th Inf. Regt., Korea, 1952; dep. chief staff X Corps, Korea, 1953; mem. faculty Army War Coll., 1953-56; chief plans, dep. operations officer U.S. Army, Europe, 1956-58; dep. comdt. cadets U.S. Mil. Acad., 1958-61; dep. comdg. gen. U.S. Army Tng. Center, Fort Dix, N.J., 1961-62; sec. staff SHAPE, Paris, France, 1962-64; comdg. gen. 3d Inf. Div., Germany, 1964-66; chief personnel operations Hdqrs. Dept. Army, 1966-67; dep. chief staff for personnel Dept. Army, 1966-67; now with Hdqrs. Continental Army Command 3d U.S. Army, Fort McPherson, Ga. Decorated Legion of Merit with 2 oak leaf clusters, Bronze Star medal with 2 oak leaf clusters, Purple Heart, Combat Inf. Badge, Croix de Guerre with palm and gold star, Fourragere (France); Ulchi medal with silver star (Korea). Address: Hdqrs US Army Continental Army Command 3d US Army Fort McPherson GA 20330

CONNOR, CHARLES ASHLEY RICHARD, physician; born N.Y. City, Oct. 12, 1905; s. Joseph P. and Octavia (Willis) C.; A.B., Holy Cross Coll., 1927; M.D., Univ. and Bellevue Hosp. Med. Coll., 1931; D.Sc. med., N.Y.U., 1940; m. Elizabeth R. Prial, Aug. 18, 1934; children—Charles Prial, Irene Elizabeth, Intern Bellevue Hosp., 1932-34, resident medicine, 1934-35; pvt. practice limited to cardiovascular diseases, New York City, since 1935; asst. prof. clin. medicine N.Y.U. Coll. Medicine, 1947-58, associate professor of clinical medicine, 1958—; consulting physician cardiovascular diseases Lenox Hill Hosp., 1968—; attending physician, chief cardiovascular service St. Clare's Hosp., 1951—; asso. in cardiology VA, 1956—; cons. physician St. Francis Hosp., Poughkeepsie, N.Y., 1954- -; cons. physician Misericordia Hosp., Bronx, 1961—, Yonker's General Hosp., Yonkers, N.Y., 1966—. Maj. U.S.A.A.F., 1942-45; flight Surgeon instructor School Aviation Med.; 1942-44; cons.

cardiol., 1st A.F., 1944-45; assistant chief medical division Office Air Surgeon, 1945-46. Qualified splist. Am. Bd. Internal Med., Subsplty. Cardiovascular Disease, 1940. Fellow A.C.P., A.M.A., Am. Heart Assn., A.A.A.S., N.Y. Acad. Medicine, Am. Therapeutic Soc. (pres. 1964-65). Roman Catholic. Author med. pubs. on rheumatic fever, heart disease. Home: 1050 Fifth Av New York City NY 10028 Office: 104 E 40th St New York City NY 10016

CONNOR, DAVID EDMUND, banker; b. Omaha, Sept. 23, 1925; s. Edward J. and Eleanor (McGilton) C.; B.A., Yale, 1947; m. Carroll Luthy, Apr. 15, 1950; children—Susan Carroll, Sara Eleanor. With Connor Co., Peoria, Ill., 1947-52; with Comml. Nat. Bank Peoria, 1952—, sr. v.p., 1964-67, pres., 1967—, also dir.; v.p., dir. Peoria Devel. Corp., 1963—, Connor Co., 1952- -; dir. Cohen Furniture Co., Peoria, Central Ill. Light Co. Pres. Heart of Ill. United Fund, 1957-58; v.p., treas. Carver Community Center, 1964- 68; chmn. finance com. Child and Family Service, Peoria, Peoria Players, 1954-57; treas. Urban League. Peoria, 1967-68; vice chmn. Citizens Com. for Quality Edn., Peoria, 1966—. Supr., Peoria County, 1949; bd. dirs. United Republican Fund Ill., 1960—. Served in War II; PTO. Named Outstanding Young Man of Year, Peoria Jr. C. of C., 1956. Mem. Phi Beta Kappa. Presbyn. Rotarian. Home: 4500 Knoxville Av Peoria 61614 Office: 301 SW Adams St Peoria IL 61602

CONNOR, FRANCES PARTRIDGE, educator; b. Bklyn., May, 1919; d. Horace K. and Sybil (Lannon) Partridge; B.A., St. Joseph's Coll. Women, Bklyn., 1940; M.A., Columbia. 1948, Ed.D., 1953; m. Leo E. Connor, June 7, 1952. Tchr. social studies. Havestraw and Congers (N.Y.) high schs., 1940-42; tchr. N.Y.C. Rehab. Hosp., W. Havestraw, 1942-49; lectr. Hunter Coll., 1946-54; spl. class tchr. Ramapo Central Sch., Suffern, N.Y., 1949-53; survey asst. N.Y. Dept. Mental Hygiene, 1953-54; research asso. U.S. Office Edn., 1954-55; mem. faculty Columbia Tchrs. Coll., 1954—, prof. edn., 1960—, chmn. dept. spl. edn., 1962—. Chmn. ednl. adv. com. Nat. Hemophilia Found., 1964—; ednl. adv. com. Assn. Help Retarded Children, 1963—, United Cerebral Palsy Assn., 1963—, N.Y. Assn. Brain Injured Children, 1958—, N.Y. Philanthropic League. 1960—; mem. Pres.'s Com. on Employment of Handicapped. Fellow Am. Assn. Mental Deficiency, A.A.A.S.; mem. Council Exceptional Children (pres. 1963-64), Am. Psychol. Assn., Am. Assn. U. Profs., Internat. Soc. Rehab. Disabled, Am. Ednl. Research Assn. Author: (with R. P. Mackie) Teachers of Children Who Are Crippled and Teachers of Children with Special Health Problems, 1961; (with Fouracre and Goldberg) The Effects of a Pre-School Program Upon Young Educable Mentally Retarded, 1962; Education of Homebound and Hospitalized Children. 1964; (with M. Taibot) An Experimental Curriculum for Young Mentally Retarded Children, 1964. Home: 2626 75th St Jackson Heights New York City NY 11370

CONNOR, GEORGE CARLEY, elec. mfg. exec.; b. Hoquiam, Wash., May 28, 1903; s. John Henry and Anna Mary (Brisel) C.; student U. Wis., 1922-24; m. Helen Loosbrock, July 13, 1933; (dec. July 1960); children—George Carley, Terrance Curtis; m. 2d, Lanelle Nicholson Williams, June 26, 1971. Mgr. br. service Brunswick Radio Corp., Chgo., 1926-30; gen. mgr. Electronic Radio Corp., N.Y.C., 1930-33; sales engr. Sylvania Electric Products, Inc., N.Y.C., 1933-50, gen. sales mgr. photolamp div., 1950-58, v.p. sales photolamp div., 1958-59, v.p. marketing-eastern region, 1959-60, sr. v.p. marketing, 1960-62, sr. v.p., gen. mgr. home and comml. electronics div., Batavia, N.Y., 1962-66, head entertainment products div., 1964-66; pres. Sylvania Rail Data Corp., 1966-68, South Moon Devel. Co., Weirsdale, Fla., 1968—. Fellow Radio Club Am.; mem. Am. Inst. E.E., Photog. Mfrs. and Distbrs. Assn. (dir.), Photog. Soc. Am. (Corner Stone mem.), A.A.A.S., Electronic Industries Assn. Clubs: Silver Springs Shore Golf and Country, Golden Hills Country (Ocala, Fla.); Lake Weir Yacht (East Lake Weir, Fla.). Home: PO Box 528 Weirsdale FL 32695 Office: South Moon Devel Co Weirsdale FL 32695

CONNOR, HAROLD P., corp. exec.; b. Montreal, Que., Can., 1913; grad. Dalhousie U. Chmn., dir. Nat. Sea Products Ltd., Halifax, N.S., Can.; pres., dir. Eastern Can. Savs. and Loan Co.; dir. Royal Trust Co., Phoenix Assurance Co., Ltd., Acadia Life Ins., Halifax Devels. Ltd. Bd. govs. Dalhousie U. Home: 6503 Jubilee Rd Halifax Nova Scotia Canada Office: Scotia Sq Halifax Nova Scotia Canada*

CONNOR, HENRY WILLIAM, indsl. cons.; b. Springfield, Mass., Aug. 11, 1912; s. Timothy E. and Catherine (Cosgrove) C.; A.B., Brown U., 1935; postgrad. Oxford (Eng.) U., 1935-36; m. Pauline E. Kane, Nov. 4, 1937; children—Lawrence H., Susan Cosgrove. Engaged in taxpayers work, 1936-46; dir. Newark Bur. Municipal Research, 1946-67; exec. dir. Greater Newark Devel. Council, 1954-69, Greater Newark C. of C., 1962-69; v.p. Newark Symphony Hall, Inc., 1964-69; sec. Newark Indsl. Devel. Corp., 1964-70. Trustee Urban Coalition, 1968-70; now govt., civic cons. Mem. Soc. Pub. Adminstrn., Nat. Housing Conf. (trustee). Clubs: Essex (Newark); Keyport (N.J.) Yacht. Address: Parkview at Madison Laurence Harbor NJ 08879

CONNOR, HOWARD, Jr., hotel exec.; b. Cleve., Feb. 17, 1925; s. Howard and Anne (Null) C.; student Middlebury Coll., 1943; B.A., Washington and Jefferson Coll., 1949; m. Peggy Morgan Hollis, Feb. 20, 1954; childrenHollis Anne, Morgan James. Resident mgr. Wade Park Manor Hotel, Cleve., 1954-55; dir. personnel Realty Hotels, N.Y. C., 1955-57; resident mgr. Flamingo Hotel, Miami Beach, Fla., 1957-58; gen. mgr. Ritz Tower Hotel, N.Y.C., 1958-70. Hotel Carlyle, N.Y.C., 1970—; gen. mgr. Ritz Assos., Inc., 465 Park Corp., N.Y.C. Mem. Confrerie De La Chaine Des Rotisseurs. Home: 40 Benedict Pl Pelham NY 10803 Office: 465 Park Av New York City NY 10022

CONNOR, JAMES RICHARD, univ. adminstr.; b. Indpls., Oct. 31, 1928; s. Frank Elliott and Edna (Felt) C.; B.A., U. Ia., 1951; M.S., U. Wis., 1954, Ph.D., 1961; m. Zoe Ezopov, July 7, 1954; children—Janet K., Paul A. Asst. prof. history Washington and Lee U., 1956-57, Va. Mil. Inst., 1958-61; asst. dir. Salzburg Seminar in Am. Studies, 1961-62; joint staff mem. Wis. Coordinating Com. Higher Edn., 1962-63; dir. Inst. Analysis, asst. prof. history U. Va., 1963-66; asso. prof. history, asso. provost No. Ill. U., 1966-69; provost, acad. v.p., prof. history Western Ill. U., 1969—. Asso. dir. Va. Higher Edn. Study Com., 1964-65; Am. Council Edn. intern acad. adminstrn. Stanford U., 1965-66; staff dir. Study of Governance of Acad. Med. Center, Josiah Macy, Jr., Found., 1968-70. Served with AUS, 1946-47, 51-53. Woodrow Wilson fellow, 1953-54, So. fellow, 1957-58. Mem. Am. Hist. Assn., Am. Assn. U. Profs., Phi Beta Kappa, Phi Eta Sigma, Phi Kappa Phi, Phi Delta Kappa. Author: Studies in Higher Education, 1965. Contbr. Ency. Britannica. Home: 9 Hickory Bow Macomb IL 61455

CONNOR, JAMES THOMAS, lawyer, educator; b. Wilmington, Ill., Aug. 29, 1905; s. Cornelius B. and Angela (Dillion) C.; student Campion Coll., Prairie du Chien, Wis., 1923-25; A.B., St. Viator Coll., Bourbonnais, Ill., 1927; J.D., Northwestern U., 1930; A.M., Loyola U., New Orleans, 1934; m. Brunilda M. Fransen, June 26, 1935; children—James Thomas, Colleen, Colette. Admitted to Ill. bar, 1931, La. bar, 1942; prof. of law Loyola U., New Orleans, 1931-36, prof. and dean law, 1936-46, lectr. on bus. law, 1946—; gen. practice law in New Orleans; founder, dir. The Connor Sch., New Orleans. Chief legal div. La. S.S.S., 1940-44, dep. state dir. Selective Service for La., 1951-52; mem. Nat. Conf. Commrs. on Uniform Laws; asst. city atty., New Orleans, 1946, mem. civil service commn., 1953. chief treaty analysis sect. war crimes div. Office Judge Advocate Gen., Washington, 1944-45; asst. counsel, office of chief of counsel, Nurnberg, 1945. Commd. capt. Judge Advocate Gen.'s Dept., N.G.U.S., 1939, maj. AUS, 1942, col. 1950. Recipient Army Commendation Ribbon with cluster; decorated chevaller Order Crown (Belgium), 1962. Mem. Am., La., New Orleans bar assns., Am. Law Inst. (councillor), Gamma Eta Gamma. Home: 1926 Napoleon Av New Orleans LA 70115

CONNOR, JOHN F., investment banker; b. Chgo., Aug. 25, 1928; s. Charles H. and Esther M. (Keeley) C.; A.B., Notre Dame U., 1950; student DePaul Law Sch., 1950- 51, 54; m. Alice Sebesta, May 11, 1957; children—Kevin, Mary Therese, Kathleen, Patricia. Spl. agt. FBI, 1955-60; with A.G. Becker & Co. Inc., 1960—, exec. v.p., 1968—, treas., 1970—, also dir. Chmn. services area United Settlement Appeal, Chgo., 1970. Served to capt. USMCR, 1951-53. Mem. Soc. Formers FBI Agts., Chgo. Assn. Commerce and Industry, Municipal Finance Officers Assn. Clubs: Notre Dame, Chgo. Athletic Assn., Bond (Chgo.); N.Y. Athletic. Home: 10633 S California St Chicago IL 60655 Office: 1 First Nat Plaza Chicago IL 60670

CONNOR, JOHN THOMAS, chem. co. exec.; b. Syracuse, N.Y., Nov. 3, 1914; s. Michael J. and Mary (Sullivan) C.; A.B. magna cum laude, Syracuse U., 1936; LL.B., Harvard, 1939; D.Sc., Phila. Coll. Pharmacy, 1959; D.Sc., Hahnemann Med. Coll., 1964; LL.D., Rutgers U., 1964; D.H.L., Ohio No. U., 1965; LL.D., St. Louis U., 1965, Boston Coll., 1965, Syracus U., 1965, Manhattan Coll., 1967, Mt. Mary Coll., 1967, N.J. Coll. Medicine and Dentistry, 1967, St. Peters Coll., 1968; m. Mary O'Boyle, June 22, 1940; children—John Thomas, Geoffrey, Lisa Forrestal. Admitted to N.Y. bar, 1939; asso. firm Cravath, deCersdorff, Swaine & Wood, 1939-42; gen. counsel Office Sci. Research and Devel., 1942-44; counsel Office Naval Research, also spl. asst. to sec. navy, 1945-47; gen. atty. Merck & Co., Inc., Rahway, N.J., 1947, sec., 1947-51, counsel, 1947-53, v.p., 1950-55, pres., dir., 1955- 65; U.S. sec. commerce, 1965-67; pres., chief exec. officer, dir. Allied Chem. Corp., 1967—; dir. Gen. Motors Corp., Gen. Foods Corp., Chase Manhattan Bank. Mem. Bus. Council, Com. Econ. Devel., Council Fgn. Relations. Trustee Syracuse U., Tuskegee Inst. Served to capt. USMCR, 1944-45. Recipient Presidential certificate of merit, 1948; N.J. Brotherhood award Nat. Conf. Christians and Jews, 1959; Jefferson medal N.J. Patent Law Assn., 1962; Harvard Bus. Club award, 1965; named N.J. Bus. Statesman of Year, 1964; recipient Pub. Services award Advt. Council, 1967. Mem. Pilgrims, Phi Beta Kappa. Home: Blue Mill Rd New Vernon NJ 07976 Office: 1411 Broadway New York City NY 10018

CONNOR, JOSEPH GERARD, univ. dean; b. Phila., July 10, 1909; s. James Francis Xavier and Anna Marie (Funk) C.; A.B., St. Joseph's Coll., Phila., 1933, A.M., 1934; Ph.D., Georgetown U., 1957; m. Rosalie Cecilia Ryan, Sept. 27, 1935; children—Joseph Gerard, Gerald Ryan, Terence Gregory, Kyran William. Asst. prof. physics St. Joseph's Coll., Phila., 1939-42, Georgetown U., 1946-47, registrar Coll. Arts and Scis., 1947-56, registrar Grad. Sch., 1956-59, univ. registrar, 1956-62; dean grad. studies Seton Hall U., South Orange, N.J., 1963—. Mem. president's adv. bd. Georgetown Visitation Jr. Coll., Washington; trustee Walsh Coll., Morristown, N.J. Served from lt. (j.g.) to lt. comdr., USNR, 1942-46. Mem. Assn. Higher Edn., Council Grad. Schs. U.S., Am. Assn. Collegiate Registrars, Middle States Assn. Collegiate Registrars (pres. 1956, past sec.-treas.), Am. Studies Assn., Nat. Cath. Edn. Assn., Alpha Sigma Nu. K.C. Home: 315 Cumberland Rd South Orange NJ

CONNOR, LAURENCE R., broadcasting editor; b. North Lewisburg, O., Dec. 19, 1901; s. Thomas C. and Grace (Hunter) Co.; B.J., Ohio State U., 1927, M.A., 1961; m. Marguerite Riel, Feb. 3, 1928 (dec. Jan. 1933); children—Nancy (Mrs. George Walter), William M., Jonathan J.; m. 2d, Gladys Davis, Sept. 19, 1936 (dec. Dec. 1964); children—Larry D., Elizabeth V. Reporter, city editor, chief editorial writer Ohio State Jour., 1922-32; chief editorial writer Dispatch, 1932-60; asso. editor Richmond (Va.) News Leader, 1960-61; editorial editor WBNS, WRNS-TV, 1961—; also Columbus lectr. Ohio State U., 1961—. Mem. Ohio Legislative Corrs. Assn., Nat. Conf. Editorial Writers, Nat. Conf. Editorial Broadcasters, Sigma Delta Chi, Pi Kappa Alpha. Republican. Methodist. Clubs: Press, University (Columbus). Home: 1401 Broadview Av Columbus OH 43212 Office: Denney Hall Ohio State U Columbus OH 43210 also 62 E Broad St Columbus OH 43215

CONNOR, RALPH, chem. mfg. co. exec.; b. Newton, Ill., July 12, 1907; s. Stephen A. and Minnie (Ross) C.; B.S., U. Ill., 1929; Ph.D., U. Wis., 1932; D.Sc. (hon.), Phila. Coll. Pharmacy and Sci., 1954, Poly. Inst. Bklyn., 1967, U. Pa., 1959; LL.D., Lehigh U., 1966; m. Margaret Raef, Sept. 1, 1931; 1 son, Stephen. Instr., Cornell, U., Ithaca, N.Y., 1932-35; asst. prof. U. Pa., Phila., 1935-38, asso. prof., 1938-41; tech. aid, sect. chief and chief div. 8, Nat. Def. Research Com., 1941-45; asso. dir. research Rohm & Haas Co., Phila., 1945-48, v.p. and dir., 1948—, chmn. bd., 1960-70, chmn. exec. com., 1970—. Mem. sci. manpower adv. com. Nat. Security Resources Bd., 1950-53; mem.-at-large div. chemistry and chem. tech. NRC, 1953-57; mem. tech. adv. panel biol. and chem. warfare, 1954-60. Asso. trustee U. Pa. Recipient Gold medal Am. Inst. Chemists, 1963; Chem. Industry medal, 1965; Priestley medal Am. Chem. Soc., 1966, 67; Chem. Pioneer award Am. Inst. Chemists, 1968; Outstanding Civilian Service medal Dept. Army, 1970; Illini Achievement award U. Ill., 1971. Mem. Am. Chem. Soc. (dir. 1954-65, chmn. bd. 1956-58), Theta Chi, Alpha Chi Sigma. Author: Brief Course in Organic Chemistry (with Fuson, Price and Snyder), 1947; also articles in tech. jours. Home: 234 N Bent Rd Wyncote PA 19095 Office: Research Labs Spring House PA 19477

CONNOR, RALPH, farming exec., lawyer; b. Belmont, Mass., Oct. 18, 1909; s. Louis and Selena (Sheffield) C.; A.B. with honors, Swarthmore Coll., 1931; student Harvard Grad. Sch. Edn., 1932-34, U. Va. Law Sch., 1941; LL.B., St. John's U., 1947; m. Jean Webster McKinney, July 17, 1937; 1 dau., Sarah Gordon (Mrs. Alexander M. Hart). Admitted to N.Y. bar, 1947; with firm Duncombe & Pleasants, N.Y.C., 1947-62; owner-operator Tymor Farm, LaGrangeville, N.Y., 1949—; dir. Marine Midland Nat. Bank, Poughkeepsie, N.Y. Chmn. Dutchess County council N.Y. State Commn. Human Rights, 1964-66; pres. Dutchess County Philharmonic Soc., 1962-65; v.p. Dutchess County Community Chest and Council, 1962-65; exec. com. Five Years Meeting of Friends, 1949-65. Treas. Dutchess County Republican Com., 1963-65. Trustee Vassar Coll., 1963—, Vassar Bros. Hosp., 1957- 67, Degenerative Diseases Research Found., 1960-65, Mid Hudson Catskills Mus., 1966-68; pres. trustees Oakwood Friends Sch., Poughkeepsie, 1956- 65; 70—; pres. Fishkill Creek Watershed Assn., 1966-70; bd. dirs. Am. Friends Service Com. Phila., 1959-61. Served to lt. comdr. USNR, World War II. Mem. N.Y., Fed. bar assns., N.Y. County Lawyers Assn., Phi Delta Phi. Home: Innisfree 652 Lake Av Greenwich CT 06830 (summer) Green Island Penobscot Bay ME Office: Tymor Farm LaGrangeville NY 12540

CONNOR, THOMAS BYRNE, physician, educator; b. Balt., Dec. 21, 1921; s. John Stephen and Ann Loretta (McCabe) C.; A.B., Loyola Coll., Balt., 1943; M.D., U. Md., 1946; m. Eleanor Ann Rulis, Oct. 10, 1957; children—Thomas Byrne, Kathyrn McCabe. Intern, Mercy Hosp., Balt., 1946-47, resident medicine, 1949-51; fellow medicine Johns Hopkins Hosp., Balt., 1951-56, asst. physician, 1951-59; asst. prof. medicine Sch. Medicine, U. Md., 1956-59, asso. prof., 1959-67, prof., 1967—, dir. div. endocrinology and metabolism, 1956—; staff physician U. Md. Hosp., Balt., 1956—, dir. Clin. Research Center, 1961—; cons. medicine Loch Raven VA Hosp., 1966—, Mercy Hosp., Balt., 1965—. Served to lt. (j.g.), M.C., USNR, 1947-49. Fellow A.C.P.; mem. Endocrine Soc., Am. Diabetes Assn., A.A.A.S., Am. Fedn. Clin. Research, Balt. City Med. Soc., Am. Clin. and Climatological Assn., Interurban Clin. Club, Alpha Omega Alpha. Editorial bd. Jour., Clin. Endocrinology and Metabolism, 1961-67. Research and publs. in calcium and bone metabolism, parathyroid disorders and hypertension. Home: 112 Croydon Rd Baltimore MD 21212

CONNORS, CHUCK KEVIN JOSEPH, actor; b. Bklyn., Apr. 10, 1921; ed. Seton Hall U.; m. Betty Jane Riddle (div.). Profl. baseball player with Bklyn., N.Y. Yankees, later on West Coast; various TV and motion picture appearances; started in The Rifleman series, ABC-TV, 1958, later in Arrest and Trial; films include Walk the Dark Street, Geronomo. Address: PO Box 1027 Studio City CA 91604

CONNORS, DONALD FRANCIS, educator; b. Bklyn., Oct. 18, 1907; s. Michael F. and Harriet (Reynolds) C.; B.A., Fordham Coll., 1929; postgrad. Harvard Law Sch., 1929-30; M.A., Columbia, 1934, Ph.D., 1961; m. Helen Elizabeth Newman, July 1, 1933; children—Donald F., Thomas, Harriette, Michael, Edward, Helen, Christopher. Prof. English, chmn. dept. Fordham U. at Lincoln Center, 1932—; lectr., pub., editor, cons.; author radio documentaries. Trustee Scarsdale Adult Sch., 1962-69. Mem. Am. Assn. Univ. Profs., N.Y. Acad. Pub. Edn., Modern Lang. Assn. Am., Nat. Council Tchrs. of English, Coll. English Assn. Author: Poems for the Grades, 1939; Poetry in the Classroom, 1940; Freedom Speaks, 1943; The New American Profile, 1954; Thomas Morton, 1969. Contbr. articles and book reviews to profl. jours. Home: 34 Barry Rd Scarsdale NY 10583 Office: Fordham Univ at Lincoln Center New York City NY 10023

CONNORS, EDWARD JOSEPH, hosp. adminstr.; b. Sioux City, Ia., Feb. 23, 1929; s. Edward Thomas and Rose (Shechan) C.; B.S., U. S.D., 1951; M.H.A., U. Minn., 1955; m. Irene O'Connor, Nov. 20, 1951; children—Timothy, Colleen, Bridget, Patrick. Adminstrv. resident, adminstrv. asst. R. I. Hosp., Providence, 1954-55; asst. dir. program in hosp. adminstrn. U. Mich., 1956-60, instr., 1956- 57, asst. prof., 1957-60, research staff mem. Bur. Hosp. Adminstrn. Study Hosp. and Med. Econs.; asso. prof. U. Wis., Madison, 1960-66, prof., 1966—, supr. U. Hosps., 1966—, asst. dir. Med. Center, 1963—. Project dir. study progressive patient care Kellogg Found. grant, 1957-60, Study Wis. Nursing Homes, 1964; study dir., asso. dir. Community Surveys Mich., 1956-61; project dir. USPHS Study Nursing Homes in Wis.; cons. Health Service Adminstrn.; mem. adv. council to div. hosps. W.I. Kellogg Found. Mem. Am. (chmn. adv. council Hosp. Research and Ednl. Trust), Wis. (trustee) hosp. assns. Home: 106 S Rock Rd Madison WI 53706 Office: 1300 University Av Madison WI 53706

CONNORS, EDWARD MICHAEL, supt. schs.; b. Bronx, N.Y., Feb. 23, 1921; s. Edward and Mary (O'Loughlin) C.; B.A., St. Joseph's Coll., Yonkers, N.Y., 1943; student St. Joseph's Sem., Yonkers, 1943-47; M.A., Cath. U., 1949, Ph.D., 1951. Ordained priest Roman Cath. Ch., 1947; mem. staff St. Patrick's Cathedral, N.Y.C., 1950-52; prof. Cathedral Coll., 1952-53; tchr. Cardinal Hayes High Sch., Bronx, N.Y., 1953-59; asso. supt. schs. Archdiocese N.Y., 1959-68, supt. schs., 1968—; ednl. adviser Lincoln Center, 1968—; chaplain Maria Regina High Sch., Hartsdale, N.Y. Trustee N.Y.C. Council Econ. Edn. Mem. Nat. Cath. Ednl. Assn., Am. Assn. Sch. Adminstrs. Author: (with Martin J. Quigley) Catholic Action in Practice, 1964. Address: 31 E 50th St New York City NY 10022.

CONNORS, JAMES JOSEPH, metal products co. exec.; b. Hartford, Conn., Dec. 11, 1926; s. James Joseph and Catherine Elizabeth (Meehan) C.; student Notre Dame, 1944-45; B.S., U.S. Naval Acad., 1949; m. Lorraine Marie Felice, June 11, 1949; children—Dennis Michael, Peter James. Salesman, Container Corp. Am., Phila., 1955-58, sales mgr., 1958-62, marketing mgr., 1962-64, v.p. marketing, 1964-65; exec. v.p. Haveg Industries, Wilmanston, Del., 1966; v.p. marketing Engineered Plastic Products, 1966-67, v.p. operations staff, 1967-68; sr. v.p. Ametek, Inc., N.Y.C., 1969—. Served to capt. USMC. Decorated Navy Commendation medal. Home: 517 Louella Av Wayne PA 19087 Office: Ametek Station Square 2 Paoli PA 19301

CONNORS, JOHN STANLEY, publishing co. exec.; b. Worcester, Mass., July 26, 1925; s. Frank J. and Lucy A. (Kennedy) C.; student Mich. State Coll., 1943, 46-49, U.S. Mil. Acad., 1945-46; m. Anne Marie Burnham, Apr. 19, 1952; children—Susan, Patricia, Kathleen, Richard, Jane, John. With advt. dept. N.Y. Daily News, 1949-53; mdsg. dir. R.W. Orr Assos., Inc., advt., 1953-56; with N.Y. World Telegram and Sun, 1956, Am. Weekly, 1956-59; with Sat. Eve. Post, 1960—, N.Y. sales mgr., 1963, nat. sales mgr., 1963-65, advt. dir., 1965—; pub. Holiday, 1967—; v.p. Curtis Pub. Co., 1964—; v.p., pub. Psychology Today mag., 1968-71; pub. Travel and Leisure mag., exec. v.p. U.S. Camera Pub. Corp., 1971—. Vice chmn. publicity N.Y. State Youth for Eisenhower-Nixon, 1956. Served with AUS, 1943-45. Mem. N.Y.C. Sales Execs. Club, N.Y.C. Mdsg. Execs. Club, Delta Sigma Phi, Alpha Phi Roman Cath. Home: 18 Donellan Rd Scarsdale NY 10583 Office: 18 E 53d St New York City NY 10022

CONNORS, RICHARD J., educator; B.A., Seton Hall U.; M.A., Ph.D., Columbia. Asso. prof. govt., chmn. govt. dept. Seton Hall U., South Orange, N.J. Office: Seton Hall U South Orange NJ 07079*

CONOLE, CLEMENT VINCENT, mgmt. exec.; b. Binghamton, N.Y., Sept. 29, 1909; s. P.J. and Briget (Holleran) C.; B.S., Clarkson Coll. Tech., Potsdam, N.Y., 1931; grad. courses Cornell U., N.Y.U., Yale; M.B.A., Fla. Atlantic U.; m. Marjorie Anable, Sept. 26, 1931; children—Barbara (Mrs. Francis B. McElroy), Marjorie (Mrs. Lee E. Hargrave), Richard, Jacalyn (Mrs. John N. Harman III). Served as engr. for the City of Binghamton, also N.Y. State, 1930-32; partner Richmeyer, Harding and Conole, 1932-33; engr. Dept. of Interior, 1933- 35; dist. dir. Fed. Works Adminstrn.; dist. supt. New York Unemployment Ins. Div. 1936-37; asst. state indsl. commr., N.Y., 1937-39, dep. indsl. commr., 1939-43, dir. indsl. bur. C. of C., Bd. of Trade of Phila., 1943-44, operating mgr., 1945-46, exec. v.p., 1946-52, also editor, pub. Greater Phila. mag., 1945-50; v.p. Bankers Securities corp., 1952-55; pres. Municipal Publications, Inc., 1947-50; pub. relations cons. Phila.-Balt. Stock Exchange, 1947-52; chmn. bd., pres., dir. Hearn Dept. Stores, Inc., N.Y.C., 1952-54; dir. chmn. bd. James McCutcheon & Co., 1956-57; chmn. bd., dir. Bus. Supplies Corp. Am., Skytop, Pa., 1962-65; chmn. bd. dir., pres. Tabulating Card Co., Inc., Princeton, N.J., 1955-62; chmn. bd. dir. Am. Bus. Mgmt. Co., 1955-62, Whiting Paper Co., Inc., 1959-62, Sky Meadow Farms, Inc. 1965-68, Am. Bus. Machines Co., 1958-65, Data Processing Supplies Co., 1959-65, Am. Bus. Execs. Co., 1960-65, Am. Bus. Investment

Co., 1958-62, Gen. Bus. Supplies Corp., 1965—; exec. head. mgmt. engring. div. S.D. Leidesdorf & Co., 1954-55; dir. City Stores Corp., City Stores Merc. Co., Inc., City Specialty Stores Co., Inc., Oppenheim Collins & Co., Franklin Simon Co. (N.Y.C.), R.H. White Co. (Boston), Wise Smith & Co. (Hartford, Conn.). Mem. Broome County Planning Commn., 1936-38, Pa. War Manpower Commn.; chmn. War. Emergency Bd. N.Y. State, 1941; industry mem. appeals com. Nat. War Labor Bd., 1943-45; cons. HOLC and FHA, 1936-39; chmn. Armed Forces Regional Council, Pa. and Del., 1950-52; mem. adv. com. 2d Army. Pres., 175th Anniversary of the Signing of the Declaration of Independence. 1951; pres. Phila. Conv. and Visitors Bur., 1953; dir. Nat. Conf. of Christians and Jews; chmn. of United Com. Fund, Princeton. Apptd. mem. of State Commn. to reorgn. Govt. City N.Y., 1953, Mayor's Adv. Council, chmn. com. on city mgmt. and adminstrn., 1954, Citizens Com. to Keep N.Y. Clean, 1955. Citizens Com. on Cts., 1955; pres. Quiet City Campaign, 1956; vice chmn., sec. Phila. Parking Authority. Mem. bd. trustees William Shelton Harrison Found., Hun School, Princeton, N.J., Clarkson Coll. of Tech. Licensed profl engr. and land surveyor, N.Y., Pa. Mem. Am. Mgmt. Assn., A.I.M. (president's Council. charter mem. adv. bd.), Nat. Retail Research Inst. (dir.), Bronx Bd. Trade (dir. 1954-64), Av. of Americas Assn. (dir. 1952-55). Soc. for Advancement Mgmt., Nat. Assn. Cost Accountants, 4th Naval Dist. Adv. Com., 2d Army Adv. Com., Commerce and Industry Assn. New York (treas., dir., mem. exec. com. 1954-58), Delta Upsilon (trustee). Clubs: Midday, Philadelphia Country, Lake Placid, Skytop, Merion Cricket, Racquet, Poor Richard, Pen and Pencil (Phila.); Economic, Union League (N.Y.C.); Nat. Golf Links of Am. (Southampton, L.I.); Uptown; Springdale Golf, Rotary, Nassau (Princeton, N.J.); Boca Raton, Pinehurst Country, Royal Palm Yacht and Country, P.G.A. National Golf. Address: 875 E Camino Real Boca Raton FL 33432

CONOMOS, WILLIAM G., newspaper pub.; b. Blairsville, Pa., Apr. 29, 1931; s. Van H. and Grace (Hoover) C.; student Orlando (Fla.) Jr. Coll., Rollins Coll., Winter Park, Fla.; m. Dorothy Bradford McGuffin, Mar. 17, 1956; stepchildren—Bradford, Amelia, Joanna Silliman; children—Andrew, Christopher. Pub. newspaper in Orlando. Home: 1223 Ensenada St Orlando FL 32801 Office: 633 N Orange Av Orlando FL 32801

CONOT, ROBERT E., author Ministers of Vengeance, 1964; Rivers of Blood, Years of Darkness, 1968. Address: Banton Books Inc 271 Madison Av New York City NY 10016.*

CONOVER, DONALD P., ins. co. exec.; b. Loveland, O., Jan. 29, 1916; s. Lee E. and Clara (Beckman) C.; B.S., Ohio State U., 1938; m. Velva DeFosset, Apr. 26, 1941; children—Philip Lee, Michael Craig. Formerly state agt. Northwestern Mut. Fire Assn.; state agt. Allied Fire Ins. Co.; exec. v.p., dir. Am. States Ins. Group, Indpls., 1943—; v.p., dir. LNC Equity Sales Corp. Mem. Indpls. C. of C. Home: 7440 Dean Rd Indianapolis IN 46240 Office: 542 N Meridian St Indianapolis IN 46206

CONOVER, HARRY, banker; b. Newark, Jan. 26, 1913; s. Henry and Nell M. (Peach) C.; B.S., N.Y. U., 1934; postgrad. U. Cal., 1934-36; m. Flora Hargrove, Sept. 28, 1941; children—Nancy H., H. Harrison, William. Instr. econs. U. Cal., 1934-36, econ. field supr. Nat. Bur. Econ. Research, 1936-37; research asso. The Brookings Inst., 1937-38; expert U.S. Senate Com. on Labor and Edn., 1938; econ. adviser U.S. Dept. Justice, 1938-44; economist Office Coordinator Inter-Am. Affairs, 1944-45; attache U.S. legation, Bern, Switzerland, 1945-47; chief econ. sect. and consul Am. embassy, Oslo, Norway, 1947-51; 1st. sec. and consul Am. embassy, Paris, France, 1951- 54; counselor econ. affairs Am. embassy, Bangkok, Thailand, 1954- 56; officer charge econ. affairs Office Internat. Econ. and Social Affairs, 1956, later dep. dir. Office Inter-Am. Regional Econ. Affairs, counselor for econ. affairs Am. embassy, Buenos Aires, 1959-63; adviser U.S. Treasury, 1963-64; exec. asst. to pres. Interam. Council Commerce and Prodn., 1964-66; asst. v.p. 1st Nat. City Bank N.Y., 1964-70, v.p. 1970—. Mem. Am. Econ. Assn., Pan Am. Soc., Beta Gamma Sigma. Club: International (Washington). Home: 51 Logan Rd New Canaan CT 06840 Office: 399 Park Av New York City NY 10022

CONOVER, HARVEY, publisher; b. New Rochelle, N.Y., Oct. 23, 1925; s. Harvey and Dorothy (Jobson) C.; B.S., U.S. Naval Acad., 1949; m. June Vlchek; Apr. 12, 1952; children—Harvey III, Stephen, Jeffrey, Cynthia. With Mill & Factory mag., 1953-54, Purchasing mag., 1954-56; dist. mgr. Volumne Feeding mag., 1956-57, sales mgr., 1958-59; pub. Boating Industry mag., 1959-62; exec. v.p. Conover-Mast Publs., Inc., 1962-64, pres., 1964-68; pres. Cahners Pub. Co., Inc., N.Y.C., 1968—. Served to lt. (j.g.) USN, 1949-53. Mem. Am. Bus. Press Assn., Assn. Indsl. Advertisers, Newcomen Soc. N. Am., Yacht Racing Assn. Clubs: Larchmont (N.Y.) Yacht; New York Yacht; Chicago Yacht. Home: 1251 Flagler Dr Mamaroneck NY 10543 Office: 205 E 42d St New York City NY 10017

CONOVER, MILTON, educator; b. nr. Swedesboro, N.J.; s. Samuel S. and Atlantic Dean (Moore) C.; Ph.B., Dickinson Coll., 1913, Sc.D., 1933; M.A. in Polit. Sci., U. Minn., 1916; M.A., Harvard, 1934; postgrad. in politics univs. of Oxford, Munich and Paris (Inst. of Urbanism); LL.B., Vanderbilt U., 1955, J.D., 1969. Corr., Boston Herald, 1908-09; tchr. pub. schs., Swedesboro, N.J., 1909-10, St. Matthew's Episcopal Sch., Burlingame, Cal., 1913-15; admitted to Ind. bar, 1916; bill draftsman Ind. Legislature, 1917; fellow polit. sci. Ind. U., 1916- 17; instr. govt. U. Pa. and Camden YMCA, 1919-20, N.Y. U., 1922-24, 46- 47; mem. faculty govt. Yale, 1924-35, asso. prof., 1930-35; seminarian Princeton U. and Dropsie Coll. for Hebrew and Cognate Learning, Phila., 1938-39; investigated Indian and French communities in Can., 1941-42; resident researcher Cath. U. Am., Washington, 1942-43; research Middle Am. Research Inst., New Orleans, 1943-44; legal practice, Chgo., 1944-45; law adjudicator U.S. VA, Newark, 1946-48; seminarian in law Columbia, 1948-53; lectr. finance Rutgers U., 1949; mem. faculties of social sci. and law Seton Hall U., 1947-68, asso. prof. law, 1955, prof. law, 1960-68, prof. emeritus law, 1968—; exec. sec. N.J. Assn. Pvt. Colls. and Univs., 1958- 60. Served as pvt. 3d N.J. Inf., 1917, later cpl. 104th Engrs., 29th Div.; commd. 2d lt. inf., Camp Lee, Va.; with 42d (Rainbow) Div. in Argonne drive; convoy officer Army of Occupation, Germany; diplomatic courier to Am. Commn. to Negotiate Peace, Paris, operating in Finland, Lithuania, Poland, Czechoslovakia, Italy and Greece; del. Founders' Conv. of Am. Legion, Paris, 1919; mem. staff Inst. for Govt. Research, Brookings Instn., Washington, 1921-22, asso., 1922-32; visited numerous countries and fgn. univs.; mil.-polit. observations in Europe, mid-Asia and Africa, journeying mainly by land from France to Mongolia and Korea via Siberia, 1929-30, Germany to India and Arabia via Khyber Pass, 1935-37, Latin-Am., finishing journey mainly by land from Alaska to Strait of Magellan, 1939-40; studied Negro self-govt. in Haiti, 1940-41; pres. Am. Immigrant Inst. Conn., affillie Nat. Inst. of Immigrant Welfare, 1934-35. Recipient Bernard J. McQuaid Distinguished Service Medal Seton Hall U., 1969. Mem. Royal Soc. Tchrs. (London), Holland Soc. of N.Y., Huguenot Soc. of N.J., Swedish colonial Soc., Soc. Colonial Wars, Am., Fed., Inter- Am. bar assns., Order of Founders and Patriots of Am., Assn. Princeton Grad. Alumni, S.A.R., Delta Theta Phi, Phi Kappa Psi, Grange (7), Oxford Soc. Pi Gamma Mu. Club: Harvard. Author: The General Land Office, 1923; The Federal Power Commission, 1923; The Office of Experiment Stations. 1924; Working Manual of Original Sources in American Government, 1924; co-author Political Theory, 1959. Contbr. to legal and social sci. publs. Home: 17 New St Mullica Hill NJ 08062 Office: Seton Hall U Law Sch 40 Clinton St Newark NJ 07102

CONOYER, JOHN WEEDON, educator; b. St. Charles, Mo., Jan. 6, 1905; A.B., Culver-Stockton Coll., 1936; M.S., Washington U., St. Louis, 1941; married; 3 children. Prof., chmn. dept. geography St. Louis U., 1943—; prof. Classroom on Wheels, 1961—, TV prof. series on modern world in perspective. Cons., William H. Sadlier Coll. Mem. Assn. Am. Geographers, Nat. Council Geog. Edn. Author: The Geography of Missouri; Better Living in Today's World; St. Louis, Gateway to the West. Office: Dept Geography St Louis U St Louis MO 63103*

CONQUEST, GEORGE ROBERT ACWORTH, author; b. Malvern, Eng., July 15, 1917; s. Robert Folger Westcott and Rosamund (Acworth) C.; student Winchester Coll., U. Grenoble, Magdalen Coll.; B.A., Oxford (Eng.) U., 1939; m. Joan Watkins, 1942 (div. 1948); children—John, Richard; m. 2d, Tatiana Mihailova, 1948 (div. 1962); m. 3d, Caroleen Nimmo Macfarlane, Apr. 4, 1964. Fellow, London Sch. Econs., 1956-58, Buffalo U., 1959-60; sr. fellow Columbia, 1964-65. Author: Poems, 1955; Common Sense about Russia, 1960; The Soviet Deportation of Nationalities, 1960; Power and Policy in the USSR, 1961; The Pasternak Affair, 1962; Between Mars and Venus, 1962; A World of Difference. 1964; (with Kingsley Amis) The Egyptologists, 1965; The Great Terror, 1968; Arias from a Love Opera, 1968; The Nation Killers, 1970. Editor: New Lines, 1956; Back to Life, 1958; New Lines II, 1963; (with Kingsley Amis) Spectrum I, II, III, IV, 1961-65. Home: 4 York Mansions London SW 11 England Office: care Scott Meredith 580 Fifth Av New York City NY 10036

CONQUEST, VICTOR, cons. chemist; b. Kan., Feb. 7, 1896; s. Harrison and Amanda (Huffman) C.; student U. Kan., 1916, U. Dijon (France), 1919; m. Ella W. Bensing, May 19, 1920; children—Dorothy Lee (Mrs. Campbell), Victor B., Robert D. Research chemist Armour & Co., Chgo., 1926-31, dir. research, 1931-49, gen. mgr. research div., 1949-51, v.p. research div., 1951, v.p., European rep., 1960-62; dir. Armour-Bezons, Bezons (S. & O.) France, Armour-Hess Chesm., Ltd., Leeds, Eng.; dir. Armour-Erba Pharm. Co., Milan, Italy, 1961, adviser in research mgmt., 1962—. Mem. chem. meats sub-com. Nat. Acad. Scis. Joint Argentine-U.S. Commn. for Study of Foot and Mouth Disease. Recipient Nicholas Anpert medal, 1953; Indsl. Research Inst. medal, 1956. Mem. Am. Chem. Soc., Am. Oil Chemists Soc., Inst. Food Technologists, Phi Tau Sigma. Contbr. articles Profl. publs. Home: 10317 S Bell Av Chicago IL 60643

CONRAD, ALBERT GODFREY, educator; b. Norwalk, O., May 19, 1902; s. Godfrey C. and Margaret (Moroney) C.; B.S. in Elec. Engring., Ohio State U., 1925, M.S., 1927; E.E. Yale, 1931; m. Marion Finch, June 18, 1931; children—Marion (Mrs. Robert G. Crouse), Albert Godfrey. Prin. Gratis (O.) High Sch., 1921-22; instr. Wheelersburg (O.) High Sch., 1922-24; with Gen. Electric Co., Schenectady, 1927-28; instr. elec. engring. Yale, 1928-31, asst. prof., 1931-40, asso. prof., 1940-43, prof., chmn. dept. elec. engring., 1943-62; dean Coll. Engring. U. Cal. at Santa Barbara, 1962-70, dean emeritus, 1970—; dir. Internat. Instruments Inc. Fellow Timothy Dwight Coll. Fellow I.E.E.E., A.A.A.S.; mem. Am. Radio Engrs., I.R.E., Am. Soc. Engring. Edn., Sigma Xi, Tau Beta Pi. Club: Yale (N.Y.C.). Author: (with Puchstein and Lloyd) Alternating Current Machines, 1954. Cons. editor Ency. Sci. and Tech. Contbr numerous articles on elec. engring., engring. edn. Patentee in field of elec. machines and instruments. Home: 4591 Camino del Mirasol Santa Barbara CA 93105

CONRAD, ANTHONY LEE, electronics co. exec.; b. Norwood, Mass., May 3, 1921; s. Charles W. and Flora (Tandy) C.; student Phillips Exter Acad.; B.A., Lafayette Coll., 1943; D.Sc. (hon.), Fla. Inst. Tech., 1970; m. Katherine W. Wolfe, May 23, 1943 (dec. May 1968); children—Catherine F., Anthony Lee, William L.; m. 2d, Nancy Ruth Morrison, Feb. 28, 1969. Pres. RCA Service Co., 1960-68; v.p. edn. systems RCA Corp., N.Y.C., 1968-69, exec. v.p. services, 1969-71, pres., 1971—, also dir.); dir. Banquet Foods Corp., Coronet Industries, Inc., Cushman and Wakefield, Inc., Atlas Chem. Industries, Inc., Chesebrough-Pond's Inc. Trustee, Lafayette Coll. Served to 1st lt., Signal Corps, AUS, 1943-46. Asso. fellow Am. Inst. Aeros. and Astronautics; mem. Phi Kappa Psi. Presbyn. Clubs: Gibson Island (Md.); Philadelphia Cricket; Metropolitan (N.Y.C.). Home: 528 W Moreland Av Philadelphia PA 19118 Office: RCA Corp 30 Rockefeller Pl New York City NY 10020

CONRAD, BARNABY, Jr., author, artist; b. San Francisco, Mar. 27, 1922; s. Barnaby and Helen Upshur (Hunt) C.; student U. N.C., 1940, U. Mexico, 1941; A.B., Yale, 1944; m. Dale Cowgill, Mar. 19, 1949; children—Barnaby III, Winston Stuart, Tani; m. 2d, Mary Slater, May 18, 1962; 1 dau., Kendall. Am. vice consul, Vigo, Malaga, Sevilla, Barcelona, Spain, 1943-46; student bullfighting with Juan Belmonte, 1943-46; bullfighter Spain, Mexico, Peru, 1946; sec. to Sinclair Lewis, 1947. Author, illustrator: The Innocent Villa, 1948; Matador, 1952; La Fiesta Brava, 1953, My Life as Matador, 1956; Gates of Fear, 1957; The Death of Manolete, 1958; San Francisco, 1959; Ency. of Bullfighting, 1961; Tahiti, 1961; Famous Last Words, 1961; Dangerfield, 1961; How to Fight a Bull, 1968; Fun While It Lasted, 1969; also short story Cavetano the Perfect (O. Henry Collection Prize Stories), 1949. Address: 2520 Octavia St San Francisco CA 94123

CONRAD, CHARLES, Jr., astronaut; b. Phila., June 2, 1930; s. Charles and Frances V. (Sargent) C.; B.S. in Aero. Engring., Princeton, 1953; m. Jane DuBose, June 17, 1953; children—Peter, Thomas, Andrew, Christopher. Commd. ensign U.S. Navy, 1953, advanced through grades to lt. comdr., 1964; project test pilot, armaments test div. Navy Dept., 1959-60; flight instr., performance engr. U.S. Naval Test Pilot Sch., 1960-61; flight instr. for F4H, Naval Air Sta., Miramar, Cal., 1961-62; safety flight officer Fighter Squadron 96, 1963; astronaut Manned Spacecraft Center, NASA, Houston, 1964—, pilot Gemini V, 1965, comdg. pilot Gemini XI, 1966. Asso. fellow Am. Inst. Aero. and Astronauties; mem. Soc. Exptl. Test Pilots. Home: 102 Whispering Oaks Seabrook TX 77586 Office: Manned Spacecraft Center NASA Houston TX 77058

CONRAD, CYRIL HARRY, educator; b. Great Falls, Mont., Sept. 9, 1910; s. Oscar G. and Army (Shippam) C.; B.S. in Applied Art, Mont. State Coll., 1934; M.F.A. in Sculpture (Carnegie scholar 1940-41), U. Ore., 1941; student Skowhegan Sch. Painting and Scultpture, 1949, Europe, 1955, 59, 63, Japan, 1957; m. Helen Autry, Aug. 1, 1937; children—Cyril Autry, Terry Eugene, Helen Sue. Art tchr. Great Falls (Mout.) High Sch., 1934-45; grad. asst. sculpture U. Ore., 1940-41; instr. art Mont. State Coll., Bozeman, 1945-47, prof. art., dir. Sch. Art, 1947—. Mem. Danforth Assos., 1952-56. Fellow Mont. Inst. Arts (a founder, art chmn. 194O-49, pres. 1956-58); mem. Mont. Art Edn. Assn. (a founder), Phi Kappa Phi, Phi Eta Sigma, Delta Phi Delta, Kappa Kappa Psi, Kappa Sigma. Home: 503 S 7th St Bozeman MT 59715

CONRAD, EDWIN, lawyer, author; b. Milw., Feb. 18, 1910; s. Jacob and Genevieve (Lewandowski) C.; B.A., U. Wis., 1932, J.D., 1934, M.A., 1938; m. Phyllis A. Legler, July 8, 1933; children—Joseph Edwin, James Stephen. Admitted to Wis. bar, 1934, N.Y. bar, 1959; mem. law firm Aberg, Blake & Conrad, 1937-58; sr. atty. FCC, 1943; lectr. law U. Wis., 1954-61; exec. sec. Wis. Broadcasters Assn., 1950-61; prof. law Syracuse U. Law Sch., 1958-60; city atty., Madison, Wis. Bd. dirs. Univ. YMCA, Madison. Recipient Vilas medal in forensics U. Wis., 1931; named Ky. col. Fellow Am. Acad. Forensic Scis. (sec. jurisprudence sect. 1966-67, program chmn. for acad. 1968-69, pres. elect 1969, now pres.); mem. Am. Law Inst., Order of Coif, Phi Beta Kappa, Phi Kappa Phi, Delta Sigma Rho, Tau Kappa Alpha, Alpha Kappa Delta, Phi Eta Sigma. Author: Wisconsin Annotations, Restatement Trusts, 1941; Wisconsin Evidence, 2 vols., 1949; Modern Trial Evidence, 2 vols., 1956. Contbr. articles profl. jours. Home: 126 S Whitney Way Madison WI 53705 Office: City County Bldg Madison WI 53709

CONRAD, HAROLD EVERETT, educator; b. Woodstock, N.H., Aug. 22, 1905; s. Rev. John Rufus and Mary Elizabeth (Hall) C.; A.B., Brown U., 1927; A.M., Clark U., 1929; Ph.D., U. Toronto, 1935; Carnegie Endowment summer session on Internat. Law, McGill U., 1939; m. Elizabeth Speicher, June 26, 1937; children—John William, David Pennington. Instr. in history and govt. Urbana Jr. Coll., 1929-31; supr. collegiate center under Alfred U., 1935-37; prof. history and polit. sci. and dean of men Ottawa U., 1937-42; prof. polit. sci. and history, Washburn Municipal U., Topeka. Kan., 1942-55; dean of academic planning High Point College (North Carolina), 1963-70, dean emeritus, 1970—, prof. history, 1970—. Vis. prof. history U. Kan., summer 1942, Canadian history Boston U., summers 1941, 47, 48, 52; mem. faculty Midwest Inst. Internat. Relations, Des Moines, 1947; Carnegie Endowment lectr. Internat. Relations Clubs Confs., 1941, 42, 44, 45. Kan. rep. British War Relief Assn., World War II; asso. with Kan. and Topeka UNESCO work, 1947-49; asst. in research on Canadian-Am. Relations under Carnegie Endowment, 1933-34; mem. peace commn. local Am. Friends Service Com.; chmn. Citizens curriculum study com. Pub. Schs., pres. High Point Planning Commn.; bd. dirs. Salvation Army, United Appeal High Point, High Point Pub. Library; chmn. Christian Workers Sch. Meth. Ch. Mem. Am. Assn. Acad. Deans, N.C. Assn. of Summer Sch. Dirs. (pres.), N.C. Coll. Conf., Kan. History Tchrs. Assn. (pres. 1940), Topeka Council Chs. Methodist (ofcl. bd.). Kiwanian (pres. 1941). Contbr. articles to profl. jours. Collector material on Can. Home: 805 E Farris Av High Point NC 27262

CONRAD, HAROLD THEODORE, physician; b. Milw., 1934; M.D., U. Chgo., 1958. Intern, USPHS Hosp., San Francisco, 1958-59; resident USPHS Hosp., Lexington, Ky., 1959-61; chief of psychiatry USPHS Hosp., New Orleans, 1962-67, clin. dir., 1968; chief clin. research center Nat. Inst. Mental Health, Lexington, 1969—. Diplomate in psychiatry Am. Bd. Psychiatry and Neurology. Mem. A.M.A., Am. Psychiat. Assn., Alpha Omega Alpha. Office: Nat Inst Mental Health Clin Research Center Leestown Pike Lexington KY 40507*

CONRAD, IVAN WILLARD, physicist, govt. ofcl.; b. Stilesville, Ind., July 26, 1910; s. Lawrence J. and Leah (Bevars) C.; A.B. with high distinction, Ind. U., 1932, M.A., 1933. Asst. instr. physics Ind. U., 1934; physicist FBI Lab., 1934- 36, spl. agt. FBI, 1936, chief electronics sect. lab., 1941-55, scientific chief lab., 1955-60, asst. dir. charge lab., 1961—; expert witness various phases sci. crime detection; lectr. application sci. to crime detection. Mem. Quarter Century Wireless Assn., Am. Acad. Forensic Scis., Phi Beta Kappa, Sigma Xi. Address: Fed Bureau Investigation Washington DC 20535

CONRAD, LEONARD WALTER, mfg. co. exec.; b. Milw., May 13, 1917; s. Joseph P. and Helen (Lennart) C.; student U. Wis., 1938-41; m. Dale M. Hart, July 10, 1945; children—Steven, Michael, Sally (Mrs. James Walker), Christine, Judith, Marilee, Katherine, William, Joseph, Peter. With Heil Co., Milw., 1935-59, v.p. mfg., 1955-59; exec. v.p. Heil-Quaker Co., Nashville, 1959-62, pres., 1962—. Vice chmn. Catholic Charities Bd.; mem. Nashville Diocesan Cath. Sch. Bd.; mem. exec. com. Boy Scouts Am.; asso. Vanderbilt Grad. Sch. Bus. Served to capt. USAAF, 1942-46. Col. staff Gov. Tenn. Mem. Gas Appliance Mfrs. Assn., Tenn. Mfrs. Assn. (bd. govs.), Nashville C. of C. Home: 1921 Woodmont Blvd Nashville TN 37215 Office: 647 Thompson Lane Nashville TN 37204

CONRAD, PAUL FRANCIS, editorial cartoonist; b. Cedar Rapids, Ia., June 27, 1924; s. Robert H. and Florence G. (Lawler) C.; B.A., U. Ia., 1950; m. Barbara Kay King, Feb. 27, 1954; children—James, David, Carol, Elizabeth. Editorial cartoonist Denver Post, 1950-64, Los Angeles Times, 1964—; cartoonist Register and Tribune Syndicate, Des Moines; lectr. Cooke-Daniels Lecture Tours, Denver Art Mus., 1964. Served with C.E., AUS, 1942-46. PTO. Recipient Editorial Cartoon award Sigma Delta Chi, 1962, 68, 70; Pulitzer prize editorial cartooning, 1964, 71. Overseas Press Club award, 1969. Mem. Phi Delta Theta. Democrat. Roman Catholic. Office: Times Mirror Sq Los Angeles CA 90053

CONRAD, RICHARD, singer, recording artist for London Records. Address: care Decca Record Co Ltd 9 Albert Embkt London SE 1 England*

CONRAD, THEODORE EMANUEL, clergyman, educator; b. Elgin, Ill., Nov. 22, 1905; s. Titus Anderson and Antonia Marie (Rovelstad) C.; B.A., Gustavus Adolphus Coll., 1925; B.D., Augustana Theol. Sem., 1928; Ph.D., U. Chgo., 1942; m. Alice Ingeborg Peterson, June 22, 1928; children—Donald Luther, Dorothy Marie, Norman Theodore, Paul Richard, Sharon Louise, Thomas Yung-Il. Ordained to ministry Luth. Ch., 1928; pastor St. Luke's, Chgo., 1928-37, 1st and Calvary Evang. Luth. chs., Rush City, Minn., 1937-43; asst. prof. Greek, Gustavus Adolphus Coll., 1943-45, asso. prof. Greek, Latin, 1945-1951, prof. Greek, Latin, 1951-55, v.p., 1949-52, acting dean, 1952-55; dean students Augustana Theol. Sem., Rock Island, Ill., 1955-67, asst. prof., 1955-58, asso. prof., 1958-60, prof., 1961-67; prof. registrar, dir. admissions Luth. Sch. Theology, Chgo., 1967-68; asst. pastor Arlington Hills Luth. Ch., St. Paul, 1968—. Bd. dirs. Christian Service Augustana Luth. Ch., Minn., 1939-48, v.p., 1946-48. Mem. Soc. Biblical Lit. Author: The Seymour Gospels, 1942; (with Gustav A. Herbert), The Bible Study Quarterly, vol. 21 1940, vol. 26 (with George F. Hall), 1945. Home: 749 E Hyacinth Av St Paul MN 55106

CONRAD, WALTER ALLAN GRENVILLE, airline exec.; b. Melrose, Ont., Can., Apr. 3, 1920; s. William Walter and Ena Eloise (Trethewey) C.; B.A. in Polit. Sci. and Philosophy, McGill U., 1940; m. Kathleen Horton, Sept. 22, 1945; children—Allan, Brian, Joanne. Came to U.S., 1960. With McLeod, Young, Weir & Co., stock brokers, Montreal, 1946; asst. sec. Internat. Air Transp. Assn., 1947- 49; with Am. Airlines, Inc., 1949-64, v.p. No. region, 1960-64, v.p., gen. mgr. Am. Airlines de Mexico, S.A., 1956-60; v.p. field sales Eastern Airlines, Inc., 1964-70; gen. mgr. N.Am. Olympic Airways, S.A.,

N.Y.C., 1970-71; sr. v.p. sales and services Braniff Internat., Dallas, 1971—. Bd. dirs. Friends of McGill U. Served as fighter pilot RCAF, 1940-45. Decorated D.F.C. and Bar. Home: 5715 Meadow Crest Dr Dallas TX 75230 Office: Braniff Bldg Exchange Park Dallas TX 75235

CONRAD, WILLIAM HENRY, architect; b. Elyria, O., Oct. 10, 1901; s. Frederick and Louise (Smith) C.; B.Arch., Western Res. U., 1929; diplome, Fontainebleau (France) Sch. Fine Arts, 1919; m. Mary T. Riley, Oct. 7, 1931; 1 dau., Mary Elizabeth (Mrs. Andrew P. Bratton). Mem. firm J.L. Weinberg and Conrad & Teare, Cleve., 1930-42; sr. architect Fed. Pub. Housing Authority, 1942-45; mem. firm Ward & Conrad, 1945-61; mem. firm Conrad & Fleischman, Cleve., 1961—; spl. lectr. European architecture Western Res. U., 1930-40; critic in archtl. design John Huntington Poly. Inst., 1930-52. Trustee, Cleve. Music Sch. Settlement. Mem. emeritus A.I.A. Co-designer Lakeview Terrace, Cleve. Home: 1123 Hereford Rd Cleveland Heights OH 44112 Office: 3091 Mayfield Rd Cleveland Heights OH 44118

CONRIED, HANS, actor. Appeared summer stock in Too Young to Kiss, Texas Carnival, Behave Yourself, Rich, Young and Pretty, World in His Arms, Jet Pilot, Three for Bedroom C.; on Broadway in Can-Can; motion pictures include It's A Wonderful World, Duley, The Wife Takes a Flyer, The Falcon Takes Over, Blondie's Blessed Event, Nightmare, Journey into Fear, His Butler's Sister, Senator was Indiscreet, Nancy Goes to Rio, My Friend Irma, Big Jim McClain, Peter Pan, The 5000 Fingers of Dr. T., Affairs of Dobie Gills, You're Never Too Young, Davy Crockett King of the Wild Frontier, Birds and the Bees. Office: care Sid Gold Agy 8961 Sunset Blvd Hollywood CA 90048*

CONRON, CALVIN HALSEY, Jr., lawyer; b. Topeka, Aug. 11, 1904; s. Calvin Halsey and Beatrice (Weber) C.; A.B., Stanford, 1925, J.D., 1927; m. Mary Owen, Feb. 8, 1965; children-Carol Ann (Mrs. Mark O'Leary), Constance Marie (Mrs. D.R. Lundy, Jr.). Admitted to Cal. bar, 1927, since practiced in Bakersfield; partner firm Conron, Heard & James, 1950—. Named Lawyer of Year, Kern County Bar Assn., 1965. Mem. Cal., Am., Kern County bar assns., Am. Arbitration Assn. Rotarian, Elk, Mason (Shriner). Club: Commonwealth (San Francisco). Home: 287 El Cerito Dr Bakersfield CA 93305 Office: Haberfelde Bldg Bakersfield CA 93301

CONROY, EUGENE JOSEPH, former ins. co. exec.; b. Oneida, N.Y., June 9, 1904; s. Daniel J. and Jane (Burke) C.; A.B., Cornell U., 1925, LL.B., 1927; m. Mary Dodds, Nov. 13, 1929; children—Eugene D., Ann, Melissa. Admitted to N.Y. bar, 1927, N.J. bar, 1939; with firm Cadwalader, Wickersham & Taft, N.Y.C., 1927-36; with Prudential Ins. Co. Am., 1936-69, gen. solicitor, 1948-63, gen. counsel, 1963-69; sec., dir. Internat. Match Realization Co., Ltd. (Bermuda), 1936-48, pres., 1949-50. Mem. Internat., Am. (chmn. sec. corp., banking and bus. law 1963-64), N.J., Essex County bar assns., Assn. Life Ins. Counsel, Phi Beta Kappa, Order of Coif, Phi Alpha Delta. Clubs: Essex (Newark); Baltusrol Golf (Springfield, N.J.); Short Hills. Editor Bus. Lawyer, 1962-63. Home: 21 Chestnut Pl Short Hills NJ 07078 Office: 745 Broad St Newark NJ 07102

CONROY, FRANCIS PATRICK, II, lawyer; b. Jacksonville, Fla., Jan. 6, 1912; s. Daniel John and Katharine (Hammond) C.; student Va. Mil. Inst., 1929-30; J.D., U. Fla., 1934; m. Marie Wanda Saunders, Apr. 23, 1965; children by previous marriage—Geraldine (Mrs. Robert Kloeppel III), Cynthia, Katharine, Helen, Claudia. Admitted to Fla. bar, 1934, since practiced in Jacksonville; mng. partner firm Marks, Gray, Conroy & Gibbs, 1946- -; gen. counsel, dir. S.E. First Bank of Jacksonville, Title & Trust Co. Fla., Jacksonville Port Authority. Chmn. Duval County Bd. Pub. Instrn., 1946-47. Bd. dirs. Jacksonville YMCA, 1940-60, pres., 1950-53. Served to capt. AUS, 1942-45. Fellow Am. Coll. Trial Lawyers; mem. Am., Jacksonville bar assns., Fla. Bar, Fedn. of Ins. Counsel, Blue Key, Internat. Assn. Ins. Counsel, Sigma Nu, Phi Delta Phi. Rotarian. Home: 9780 Scott Mill Rd Jacksonville FL 32217 Office: Southeast First Bank Bldg Jacksonville FL 32201

CONROY, FRANK, author; b. N.Y.C., Jan. 15, 1936; s. Francis Philip and Helga (Lassen) C.; B.A., Haverford Coll., 1958; m. Patty Munro Ferguson, Nov. 21, 1958; children—Daniel, Will. Pres., Prose City, Inc., N.Y.C., 1968—. Grantee Nat. Found. Arts and Humanities, 1968, Rockefeller Found., 196O. Mem. P.E.N. Club, Authors Guild, Writers Guild Am. Author: Stop-time, 1967. Home: 80 State St Brooklyn NY 11201 Office: 34 Park Row New York City NY 10038

CONROY, JACK, (John Wesley), author, editor; b. Moberly, Mo., Dec. 5, 1899; s. Thomas Edward and Eliza Jane (McCollough) C.; student U. Mo., 1920-21; m. Elizabeth Gladys Kelly, June 30, 1922; children—Margaret Jean (Mrs. James Walter Tillery), Thomas Vernon (dec.), Jack. Editor, The Robel Poet, 1931-32, The Anvil, 1933-37, The New Anvil, 1939-41; asso. editor Nelson's Ency. and Universal World Reference Ency., 1943-47; sr. editor New Standard Ency., Chgo., 1947-66; dir. Standard Information Service, 1949-55; lit. editor Chgo. Defender, 1946-47, Chgo. Globe, 1950; instr. Fiction writing Columbia Coll., 1962-66. John Simon Guggenheim fellow for creative writing, 1935; recipient James L. Dow award Soc. Midland Authors, 1966; award Literary Times, 1967. Mem. Soc. Midland Authors, Chgo. Council Fgn. Relations, Internat. Platform Assn. Methodist. Author: The Disinberited, 1933, reissued 1963; A World To Win, 1935; (with Arna Bontemps) The Fast Sooner Hound, 1942; They Seek A City, 1945; Slappy Hooper, The Wonderful Sign Painter, 1946; Sam Patch, The High, Wide and Handsome Jumper, 1951; Anyplace But Here, 1966. Editor, Unrest, 1929-31; Midland Humor: A Harvest of Fun and Folklore, 1947. Home: 701 Fisk Av Moberly MO 65270

CONROY, RAYMOND CHANDLER, army officer; b. Chgo., Jan. 17, 1916; s. Joseph Stanley and Annette (Andres) C.; B.S., U. Ore., 1942; M.B.A., U. So. Cal., 1950; grad. Armed Forces Staff Coll., 1954, Command and Gen. Staff Coll., 1945, Indsl. Coll. Armed Forces, 1958; m. Isabel Antoinette Nagorna, Jan. 24, 1945; children—Sandra Veronica, Constance Lynn. Commd. U.S. Army, 1943, advanced through grades to maj. gen., 1966; served transp. field World War II and Korean War; overseas assignments in Middle East, India, N. Africa, Korea and Germany, Vietnam; assigned office Joint Chiefs Staff, 1961, Office Dep. Chief Staff Logistics, 1966; asst. dep. chief logistics, 1967-69; asst. chief staff J-4 U.S. Mil. Assistance Command, Vietnam, 1969-70; dep. chief staff logistics, Europe, 1970—. Decorated Legion of Merit with oak leaf cluster, Army Commendation medal with oak leaf cluster, Joint Service Commendation medal D.S.M. with oak leaf cluster, Bronze Star medal, others. Mem. Nat. Def. Transp. Assn., Lambda Phi Alpha. Home: 28 San Jacinto Dr Partick Henry Village 69 Heidelberg Germany Office: DCS LOG HQ USAREURS and 7th Army APO NY 09403

CONROYD, W. DANIEL, educator, lawyer; b. Oak Park, Ill., Oct. 1, 1920; s. Walter Earl and Lucille Mary (McCabe) C.; B.S. in Commerce, Loyola U., Chgo., 1942; J.D., DePaul U., 1947; m. Margaret Ann McAuliff, Feb. 13, 1943; children—Colleen (Mrs. Michael C. Strening), Maureen (Mrs. Thomas Fitzgerald), Michael, Sheila (Mrs. William Hogan), Alicia. Clk., FBI, 1942-44; wage adminstr. Montgomery Ward & Co., 1944-45; mem. staff Loyola U., Chgo., 1945—, asst. to pres., 1955-59, v.p. devel. and pub. relations, 1959—; admitted to Ill. bar, 1947. Bd. dirs. St. Francis Hosp., Evanston, Ill. Served with USNR, 1943. Mem. Pub. Relations Soc. Am., Am. Coll. Pub. Relations Assn., Am. Alumni Council, Am., Chgo. bar assns., Pub. Relations Clinic, Delta Theta Phi, Tau Kappa Epsilon. Clubs: Economic, Chgo. Athletic Assn., (Chgo.); North shore Country (Glenview, Ill.). Home: 3108 Walden Lane Wilmette IL 60091 Office: 228 N LaSalle St Chicago IL 60601

CONSER, EUGENE POOLE, former assn. exec.; b. Mpls., Jan. 30, 1904; student U. Minn.; B.S., U. Cal. at Los Angeles, 1928; m. Helen Miller, Aug. 7, 1930; children—Richard, Paula. Asst. financial editor Los Angeles Evening Express, 1928-29; partner Pacific Financial Pubs., 1929-32; with Apt. Assn. of Los Angeles County, 1932-46, sec. Cal. State Apt. Conf., 1930-45; exec. v.p. Nat. Apt. Owners Assn., 1943-45; sec. Cal. Real Estate Assn., 1947-55; exec. v.p. Nat. Assn. Real Estate Bds., Chgo., 1955-70; secretary-general International Real Estate Federation, 1957-59, director, 1959-70, hon. life dir., 1970—. Teacher of real estate courses U. Cal. at Los Angeles. Mem. Lambda Alpha, Rho Epsilon, Pi Delta Epsilon, Phi Kappa Psi. Author: Manual of Real Estate Board Operation, 1955; Commentaries on the Code of Ethics, 1958, Realtor Studies In European Countries, 1961, 65; Human Relations and the Realtor, 1963; Historical Background of the Realtor's Position in Race Relations, 1965. Home: 306 Forest St Winnetka IL 60093

CONSIDINE, FRANK WILLIAM, container corp. exec.; b. Chgo., Aug. 15, 1921; s. Frank Joseph and Minnie (Regan) C.; Ph.B., Loyola U., Chgo., 1943; m. Nancy Scott, Apr. 3, 1948; children—Nancy, Carol, Frank, Susan, Lynne, Cathy, Mary, Maureen, Kevin. Partner, F. J. Hogan Agy., entertainment agy., Chgo., 1946-47; asst. to pres. Graham Glass Co., Chgo., 1947-51; owner F.W. Considine Co., Chgo., 1951-55; v.p. Metro Glass div. Nat. Dairy Products Corp., Chgo., 1955-60; exec. v.p., dir. Nat. Can Corp., Chgo., 1961-69, pres., 1969—; dir. Oak Park (Ill.) Nat. Bank. Mem. lay bd. St. Elizabeth's Hosp., Chgo. Served to lt. USNR, 1943-46. Mem. U.S. Brewers Assn. (bd. dirs.), Econ. Club Chgo., Am. Inst. Food Distbrs. (trustee), Food Processing Machinery and Supply Assn. (dir.). Office: 5959 S Cicero Av Chicago IL 60638

CONSIDINE, JAMES WILLIAM, corp. exec.; b. Washington Jan. 24, 1908; s. James Leo and Marie Calfernia (Bell) C.; B.C.S., Benjamin Franklin U., 1928; LL.B., Columbus U., Washington, 1938; m. Carrie Estelle Layton. Feb. 9, 1929; children—Carrie Marie (Mrs. E.L. Haan), Catherine Lee (Mrs. Martin S. Kilsdonk), Jane Myrtle (Mrs. Ralph Lemon), James W., Linda Anne (Mrs. Thomas J. Fitzsimmons III). Admitted to D.C. bar, 1938, also U.S. Supreme Ct. bar; treas. Def. Homes Corp., Washington, 1940-43, Metals Res. Co., 1943-45; asst. treas. Reconstrn. Finance Corp., 1944-47, controller, 1948-50, asst. to dir., 1948; asst. treas. Fed. Nat. Mortgage Assn., 1938-45, controller, asst. to dir., 1948-67, v.p., 1967—; asst. to pres. Gar Wood Industries, Inc., Wayne, Mich., sec.-treas., dir., mem. exec. com., until 1967. Pres. Long Lake Shore Civic Assn. C.P.A., D.C. Mem. Am. Bar Assn., Am. Ordnance Assn., Mich. Soc. C.P.A.'s, Am. Soc. Corporate Secs., Sigma Delta Kappa. K.C. Home: 1630 Courtland Rd Alexandria VA 22306 Office: 451 7th St SW Washington DC 20414

CONSIDINE, JOHN JOSEPH, advt. exec.; b. Jersey City, Sept. 6, 1941; s. Joseph Patrick and Helen (Hrezak) C.; B.S. in Psychology, St. Peter's Coll., 1963; m. Catherine Christine Noone, Nov. 26, 1966; children—Elizabeth Mairead, Laura Bridget. Research analyst Prudential Ins. Co., 1964-66; research mgr. The Mennen Co., 1966-68; research adminstr. Gillette Corp., 1968-69; v.p., corp. dir. research W.B. Doner & Co., Detroit, 1969—. Mem. Am. Marketing Assn., Am. Mgmt. Assn. Home: 7112 Stonebrook Rd Birmingham MI 48010 Office: First Nat Bldg Detroit MI 48226

CONSIDINE, ROBERT BERNARD, newspaperman; b. Washington, D.C., Nov. 4, 1908; s. James William and Sophie (Small) C.; ed. Gonzaga High Sch., George Washington U.; m. Mildred Anderson, July 21, 1931; children—Michael Riley, Robert Barry, Dennis Joel, Deborah Joan. Corr. sports, drama, writer Sunday features Washington Post, 1930-33; sports editor, editorial and feature writer Washington Herald, 1933-37; syndicated sports columnist, trial reporter, feature writer N.Y. Am., during 1937 was transferred to Mirror and Internat. News Service, 1938; war corr. Internat. News Service, England, 1943, C.B.I. theatre, 1945, Korea. 1950. Member Sigma Alpha Epsilon, Sigma Delta Chi. Roman Catholic. Knight of Malta. Clubs Dutch Treat, Overseas Press (past pres.), Nat. Press (Washington) and Artists and Writers. Author: MacArthur the Magnificent, 1942; Thirty Seconds over Tokyo (with Capt. Ted W. Lawson), 1943; Where's Sammy (with Sammy Schulman), 1943; Gen. Wainwright's Story (with Gen. Jonathan M. Wainwright), 1946; The Babe Ruth Story (with Babe Ruth), 1948; Innocents at Home, 1951; Panama Canal, 1952; Man Against Fire, 1955; Christmas Stocking, Jack Dempsey Story (with Bill Slocum); Ask Me Anything-Our Adventures with Khrushchev (with W. R. Hearst, Jr. and Frank Conniff); The Brink's Robbery; It's All News to Me—A Reporter's Deposition; asst. Harold E. Stassen, Stanislaw Mikolajczyk and Robert E. Stribling in prep. their books, 1948; motion picture originals: Church of the Good Thief (MGM), Ladies Day (RKO), The Beginning or the End (MGM), The Babe Ruth Story (Allied Artists), Hoodium Empire (Republic). Contbr. fiction and articles to nat. mags., 1944—. Awarded George R. Holmes Memorial Award, 1947; Catholic Writers Guild and Catholic Inst. of the Press Awards, 1949 Lasker Award 1952; Overseas Press Club awards for best fgn. correspondence, 1957-58. Home: 200 Central Park S New York City NY 10019 Office: 235 E 45th St New York City NY 10017

CONSOLATA, SISTER M., hosp. adminstr. Adminstr. St. Elizabeth Hosp., Youngstown, O. Office: 1044 Belmont Av Youngstown OH 44505*

CONSOLE, F.M., savs. and loan assn. exec. Exec. v.p. Santa Barbara Savs. and Loan Assn. Office: 1035 State St Santa Barbara CA 93102*

CONSOLO, FEDERICO, Italian internat. bank ofcl.; b. Mar. 18, 1906; ed. in Milan and London, also univs. Cambridge and Rome. With Montecatini S.p.S. and Pirelli S.P.A., 1928-43; liaison between Italian govt. and Allied Commn. and subsequently UNRRA, Rome, 1945-47; with Internat. Bank Reconstrn. and Devel. rising to asst. dir. Western Hemisphere Dept., 1947-58; dir.-gen., spl. adviser to commn. EURATOM, Brussels, 1958-64; spl. rep. UN orgns. Internat. Bank Reconstrn. and Devel., 1964—. Address: 4530 Connecticut Av Washington DC 20008*

CONSTABLE, GILES, educator; b. London, Eng., June 1, 1929; s. William George and Olivia (Carson-Roberts) C.; grad. Phillips Acad., Andover, Mass., 1946; B.A., Harvard, 1950, Ph.D., 1957; student Cambridge (Eng.) U., 1952-53; m. Esther Van Horne Young, Jan. 3, 1959; children—Olivia Remie, John Van Horne. Teaching fellow, tutor history Harvard, 1953-55; instr., then asst. prof. State U. Ia., 1955-58; mem. faculty Harvard, 1958—, H.C. Lea prof. Medieval history, 1966—. Lectr., Centre D'tudes Supéricures de Civilization Médiévale Poitiers, 1961; master North House, Radcliffe Coll., 1963-67; sr. fellow Southeastern Inst. Medieval and Renaissance Studies, 1969; acting master Lowell House, Harvard U., 1970. Guggenheim fellow, 1967-68. Mem. Am. Hist. Assn., Mediaeval Acad. Am., Royal Hist. Soc. Author: Monastic Tithes from their Origins to the Twelfth Century, 1964; The Letters of Peter the Venerable, 1967. Editor: (with James Kritzeck) Petrus Venerabilis 1156-1956, 1956. Asst. editor Speculum, 1958—. Home: 25 Mt Pleasant St Cambridge MA 02140

CONSTABLE, ROBERT DALTON, utility exec.; b. Bklyn., Dec. 7, 1904; s. George Edward and Ella (Dalton) C.; ed. pub. schs.; m. Theckla Youngblood, Oct. 12, 1927; children—Theckla (Mrs. Richard F. Ledyard), Robert S., Peter D. Engaged in fire ins. bus., 1921-42; with Niagara Mohawk Power Corp., 1942—, v.p., 1963—; cons., 1970—. Club: Cazenovia. Home: 27 Chenango St Cazenovia NY 13035 Office: 300 Erie Blvd Syracuse NY 13202

CONSTABLE, STUART, architect, landscape architect, pub. ofcl.; b. Columbus, O., Sept. 9, 1900; s. Thomas Gibson and Francis M. (Whiser) C.; B.S., Ohio State U., 1922; M. Landscape Architecture, Harvard, 1927; m. Margaret Joyce Cottingham, Sept. 9, 1922; children—John Stuart, Thomas Gibson II. Pvt. practice St. Petersburg, Fla., and Stamford, Conn., 1924-35; chief designer dept. parks City N.Y., 1936-55, exec. officer, 1955-60; acting commnr. N.Y.C. Planning Commn., 1950-60, N.Y.C. Art Commn., 1949-55; v.p. operations N.Y. World's Fair 1964-65 Corp., 1960-66; pres. C & T Enterprises, Ft. Lauderdale, 1966—; cons. 1st hdqrs. UN, Jones Beach State Pkwy. Authority and N.Y. State Power Authority, also James Found. of St. James, Mo., Dorado, P.R. Winner Bklyn. War Meml. Competition, 1945. Mem. Am. Soc. Testing Materials, Alpha Gamma Rho. Clubs: Ohio Society of New York, The Brook; Surf (Wrightsville Beach, N.C.). Home: The Meed Route 1 Box 3 Hampstead NC 28443 Office: PO Box 381 Pompano Beach FL 32561

CONSTAN, GEORGE NICHOLAS, govt. ofcl.; b. Sparta, Greece, Mar. 24, 1909; s. Nicholas Peter and Starroula (Theophylakes) C.; came to U.S., 1920; naturalized through father; B.S. in Chemistry, Clemson Coll., 1933, S.D. (hon.), 1960; student power and explosives. Ga. Inst. Tech., 1941; m. Louise Stephens, Oct. 8, 1939; children—Nicholas George, Stephen Themis. Engaged mfg. and sales chems. and related products, 1933-41, mfg., prodn., engring., indsl. engring ammunition and ballistic missiles. Ordnance Dept., U.S. Army, 1948-60; with NASA, 1960—. gen. mgr. Michoud operations Marshall Space Flight Center, New Orleans, 1961—. Dep chmn. Intergration Com. Ammunition Loading. 1952-56; govt. cons. Army Ordnance Assn., 1952-60. Served to capt. AUS, 1942-48. Decorated Army Commendation ribon. 1945; recipient Commendation for Meritorious Civilian Service, Dept. Army 1955. Mem. Am. Inst. Aero. and Astronautics. Mason. Home: 215 Tchefuncte Dr Covington LA 70433 Office: Michoud Operations NASA New Orleans LA 70129

CONSTANCE, LINCOLN, educator, botanist; b. Eugene, Ore., Feb. 16, 1909; s. Lewis Llewylin and Ella (Clifford) C.; A.B., U. Ore., 1930; M.A., U. Cal., 1932, Ph.D., 1934; m. Sara Luten, July 12, 1936; 1 son, William Clifford. Instr. botany State Coll. Wash., 1934-35, asst. prof., 1936-37; asso. geobotanist OSS, Washington, 1943, geobotanist. 1943-44, research analyst, 1944-45; vis. lectr. biology, acting dir. Gray Herbarium, Harvard, 1947-48; teaching asst. botany U. Cal., 1930- 34, asst. prof., 1937-43, asso. prof. botany, asst. curator herbarium, 1943-44, 45-47, prof. botany, curator seed plant collections, 1947-65, chmn. dept. botany, 1954-55, dean Coll. of Letters and Sci. at Berkeley, 1955-62, vice chancellor acad. affairs, 1962-65, dir. U. Cal. Herbarium, 1965—. Guggenheim fellow, 1953-54. Mem. Am. Inst. Biol. Scis., Am. Acad. Arts and Scis., A.A.A.S., Am. Soc. Naturalists, Am. Soc. Plant Taxonomists, Biosystematists, Bot. Soc. Am., Cal. Acad. Scis., Cal. Bot. Soc., N.E. Bot. Club, Soc. for Study Evolution, Torrey Bot. Club, Phi Beta Kappa, Sigma Xi, Gamma Alpha. Author articles sci. jours. Home: 47 Alamo Av Berkeley CA 94708

CONSTANGY, FRANK ALAN, lawyer; b. Atlanta, Feb. 23, 1911; s. Harry and Mamie (Cohen) C.; A.B., U. Ga., 1929, J.D., 1930; m. Eleanor Smullyan, Nov. 4, 1931; 1 dau., Carolyn (Mrs. Richard S. Wasser). Admitted to Ga. bar, 1930, since practiced in Atlanta; mem. firm Walker, Kilbridge & Constangy, 1933-35; mem. dress code authority and millinery code authority NRA, 1933-35; S.E. regional atty. Social Security Bd., 1936-38; S.E. regional atty. FSA, 1938-41; regional dir. operations S.E. War Manpower Commn., 1941- 45; chmn. indstry mems. S.E. War Labor Bd., S.E. Wsb, 1944-46; sr. partner Constangy & Prowell, 1945—; prof. constl. law Woodrow Wilson Coll. Law 1933-44; gen. counsel Tufted Textile Mfrs. Assn., Carpet and Rug Inst. Am. Dir. Murray Ohio Mfg. Co. Participant Nat. Labor Relations Conf., 1945; chmn. Bd. of Rev., Employment Security Agy. of Ga., 1950—; mem. Gov.'s staff, Govs. Griffin, Arnall and Sanders of Ga., 1945-50, 62- 66; mem. Adv. Council on employment Security Legislation, 1945—; mem. Ga. Commn. Aging, 1962-70 mem. adv. bd. Vets. Re-employment Rights. Recipient Merit award for war time service Pres. Truman, 1946. Mem. Am. (mem. Ho. of Dels., past chmn. labor relations law sect.) Ga., Atlanta bar assns., Tau Epsilon Phi, Omicron Delta Kappa. Republican. Jewish religion. Clubs: Commerce, Standard (both Atlanta). Contbr. articles profl. jours. Home: 3184 Wood Valley Rd NW Atlanta GA 30327 Office: 1900 Peachtree Center Bldg Atlanta GA 30303

CONSTANT, FRANK WOODBRIDGE, physicist; b. Mpls., June 1, 1904; s. Frank Henry and Annette (Woodbridge) C.; grad. Lawrenceville Sch., 1921; B.S., Princeton, 1925; Ph.D., Yale (Sloane fellow 1925-26, Loomis fellow 1926-28), 1928; Nat. Research fellow Cal. Inst. Tech., 1928-30; m. Elizabeth Bellamy Bass, Jan. 25, 1940. Instr. physics Duke U., 1930-33, asst., prof. physics, 1934-42, asso. prof., 1942-46; Jarvis prof. physics Trinity Coll., Hartford, Conn., 1946—; dir. Dorn-Loomis Summer Sci. Center, 1958-59; research student, Cambridge, Eng., 1933-34. Served as instr. meteorology, civilian pilot tng. program Duke U., 1940-42; ofcl. investigator and research physicist Nat. Def. Research Com., Office Sci. Research and Devel., Duke U. and Ft. Bragg, 1942-46. Fellow Am. Phys. Soc.; mem. Am. Assn. Physics Tchrs., Phi Beta Kappa, Sigma Xi, Sigma Pi Sigma. Clubs: 20th Century, American Alpine, Dublin Lake. Author: Theoretical Physics-Mechanics, 1954; Theoretical Physics Electromagnetism, 1958; Fundamental Laws of Physics, 1963; Fundamental Principles of Physics, 1967. Contbr. articles to profl. jours. Home: Gun Mill Rd Bloomfield CT 06002 also Jubilee Farm Dublin NH 03444 Office: Trinity College Hartford CT 06106

CONSTANT, GEORGE ZACHARY, artist; b. Greece. Apr. 2, 1892; s. Zachary and Zaphire (Argiropoulou) Constantinopoulos; came to U.S., 1910, naturalized, 1936; student fine arts, Washington U., St. Louis, 1912-14, Art Inst. Chgo., 1914-18; m. Calliroe Lekakis, Sept. 18, 1942; 1 dau., Georgette (Mrs. David Preston). Over forty one-man shows, 1927—; numerous group exhbns. including Met. Mus. Art, Chgo. Art Inst., Bklyn. Mus., Va. Mus. Fine Arts, Mus. Modern Art, Carnegie Inst., Whitney Mus., Pa. Acad. Fine Arts, U. Mixico, Los Angeles N.Y. World's Fair, 1939, San Francisco Golden Gate Exbns., 1939, U. Ia., Stedalijk Mus., Amsterdam, Holland, Musee D'art Moderne, Paris France, Corcoran Gallery Art, Walker Art Center, Library of Congress, Salle Franklin, Bordeaux, France, Musee

Cantini, Marseille, France, De Beyard, Breda. Germany, Galleria Nazionale D'arte Moderna Valle Gralia, Rome, Italy, Mus. Fine Arts, Santiago, Chile rep. permanent collections Met. Mus. Art, Andover (Mass.) Mus. Am. Art, Auburn U., Brandeis U., Bklyn. Mus., Balt. Mus. Am. Art, Butler Inst. Am. Art, Dayton (O.) Art Inst., Isaac Delgado Mus. Art, Detroit Inst. Art, Library of Congress, Pa. Acad. Fine Arts, Phila. Mus. Art, Stedlijk Mus., Tel-Aviv (Israel) Mus., U. Neb., Walker Art Center, N.Y. U. Art Collection, Norfolk (Va.) Mus. Arts and Scis., Ball State U., San Francisco Mus., Smithsonian Instn., Whitney Museum of American Art, Guild Hall Mus., Joseph Hirshhorn Mus., Griffiths Art Center, State Dept., instructor at Dayton Art Inst., 1919-21. Recipient Shilling purchase prize, 1939, 43, 56; Frank G. Logan prize and medal Chgo. Art Inst., 1943; Library of Congress purchase prize, 1947; Audubon Artists prize, 1946; first prize Guild Hall, Easthampton, N.Y., 1963, 66; first prize Parrish Art Mus., Southampton, N.Y., 1950, 51; Mark Rothko Found. grant, 1970; decorated Phoenix Cross of Taxiarchs (Greece), 1963. Mem. Fedn. Modern Painters and sculptors (past pres.), Audubon Artists (Emily Lowe award 1968). Address: 187 E Broadway New York City NY 10002.

CONSTANTINE, A., physician. Asst. commr. Met. Hosp. Center, N.Y.C. Office: Met Hosp Center 1901 1st Av New York City NY 10029*

CONSTANTINE, MICHAEL, actor; b. Reading, Pa., May 22, 1927; s. Theoharis and Andromache (Foteadou) Efstration; grad. high sch.; m. Julianna McCarthy, Oct. 5, 1953; children—Thea, Brendan. Broadway debut in Inherit The Wind; understudy to Paul Muni, 1955-57; appeared in Broadway plays The Miracle Worker, Compulsion, The Egg, Arturo Ui; appeared in numerous television plays; motion pictures include The Reivers, Justine, If Its Tuesday This Must Be Belgium, The Hustler, Don't Drink The Water; star TV series Room 222, 1968—. Recipient Emmy award for best supporting actor in comedy series, 1969. Home: 1356 N Stanley Av Los Angeles CA 90046

CONSTANTINE II, KING OF THE HELLENES; b. Athens, Greece, June 2, 1940; s. King Paul and Queen Fredericka; ed. Anavryta Sch., Athens, U. Athens; m. Princess Anne-Marie, Sept. 18, 1964; children—Prince Paul (Crown Prince of Greece), Princess Alexia. Ascended throne, Mar. 6, 1964 following death of father. Served in Greek Army, Navy and Air Force, 1956-58. Recipient Gold medal yachting Olympic Games, Rome, 1960. Mem. Greek Orthodox Ch. Address: care of Greek Embassy Viale Gioacchino Rossini 4 Rome Italy

CONTA, BART JOSEPH, educator; b. Rochester, N.Y., Mar. 29, E1914; s. Joseph and Mary (Dalcin) C.; B.S., U. Rochester, 1936; M.S., Cornell U., 1937; m. Ruth Fletcher, Nov. 26, 1937; childrenFred, Jacquelyn (Mrs. Jefferson Tippett), Susan. Instr., Cornell U., Ithaca, N.Y., 1937-40, asst. prof., asso. mech. engring., 1941-47, 51-; research engr. Texaco Corp., Beacon, N.Y., 1940- 41; prof. mech. engring. Syracuse U., 1947-51. Ford Found. vis. prof. Universidad del Valle, Cali, Colombia, 1964-65. NSF fellow U. Cal. at Berkeley, 1967-68. Registered profl. engr., N.Y. Mem. Am. Soc. Engring. Edn., Am. Assn. U. Profs., Phi Beta Kappa, Sigma Xi, Tau Beta Pi, Pi Tau Sigma, Phi Kappa Phi, Clubs: Statler (past pres.), Yacht (Ithaca). Home: 211 White Park Rd Ithaca, NY 14850.

CONTA, LEWIS DALCIN, educator; b. Rochester, N.Y., Sept. 16, 1912; s. Joseph and Mary Elizabeth (Dalcin) C.; B.S. with highest distinction, U. Rochester, 1934, M.S., 1935; Ph.D., Cornell, Ithaca, N.Y., 1942; m. Hilda Agnes Bowen, Aug. 31, 1935 (div.); children—Jean Patricia (Mrs. Roger Holland), Barbara Ann (Mrs. John Boyer), Robert Lewis; m. 2d, Carolyn H. Conklin. Instr. U. Rochester (N.Y.) 1935-37, prof. mech. engring., chmn. engring. div., 1950-59, asso. dean for grad. studies, 1959-64; on leave as program dir. spl. engring. programs engring. div. NSF., 1967-69; instr. Cornell, Ithaca, N.Y., 1937- 42, asst. prof. mech. engring., 1942-46, instr. diesel engine Naval Tng. 1941-42, asst. supr., 1942-45, supr., 1945-46; research engr. and sect. head Air Reduction Research Labs., Murray Hill, N.J., 1946-48, cons., 1948-60; dean engring., dir. div., also Prof. U. R.I., Kingston, 1969—. Cons. and research Crucible Steel Co., Marquette Metal Products Co., NRC, and others; mem. com. to reorganize Navy Diesel Engine Schs., Washington, Feb.-Apr. 1943. Registered profl. engr., N.Y. Mem. Am. Soc. M.E. (v.p. 1966-68, chmn. Rochester sect. 1956-57), Am. Soc. Engring. Edn. (chmn. New Eng. sect. 1970), Nat. Soc. Profl. Engrs., Am. Assn. U. Profs., Assn. Engring. Colls. N.Y. (pres. 1953-55), Phi Beta Kappa, Sigma Xi, Tau Beta Pi, Phi Kappa Phi, Pi Tau Sigma. Author tech. papers and reports. Patentee in field. Home: 95 Oakwood Dr Peace Dale RI 02879

CONTE, RICHARD, actor; b. Jersey City, Mar. 24, 1916; s. Pasquale and Julia (Fina) C.; scholar Neighborhood Playhouse, N.Y.C.; 1 son, Mark. Appeared on N.Y. stage in Jason and the Family; motion pictures include Guadalcanal Diary, The Purple Heart, Call Northside 777, Cry of the City, House of Strangers, Thieves Highway, Whirlpool. Under the Gun, Sleeping City, Hollywood Story, Raging Tide, The Fighter, Raiders, Desert Legion, Blue Gardenia, Slaves of Babylon, Highway Draget, New York Confidential, Big Combo, Target Zero, Big Tip Off, Bengazi, Case of the Red Monkey, I'll Cry Tomorrow, Full of Life, Brothers Rico, Oceans Eleven. They Came to Cordura, Assault on a Queen, The Greatest Story Ever Told; actor, dir. motion picture Operation Cross Eagle; numerous TV appearances. Address: 340 N Maple Dr Beverly Hills CA 90210

CONTE, SAMUEL DANIEL, computer scientist; b. Lackawanna, N.Y., June 5, 1917; s. Samuel and Amelia (Jiuditta) C.; B.S., Buffalo State Coll., 1939; M.S., U. Buffalo, 1943; Ph.D., U. Mich., 1950; m. Margaret Mary Boyle, Oct. 24, 1970; children—Cheryl, Robert. Prof., Wayne State U., 1946-56; mgr. math. dept. Aerospace Corp., Los Angeles, 1956-62; head computer sci. dept. Purdur U., Lafayette, Ind., 1962—; cons. NSF. Served with AUS, 1943-46. Mem. Am. Math. Soc., Assn. for Computing Machinery, Soc. for Indsl. and Applied Math., Math. Assn. Am. Author: Elementary Numerical Analysis, 1965; Solid State Geometry, 1956; Plasma Dispersion Function, 1961. Contbr. articles profl. jours. Home: 2241 Indian Trails Dr West Lafayette IN 47906

CONTE, SILVIO O., congressman; b. Pittsfield, Mass., Nov. 9, 1921; s. Ottavio and Lucia (Lora) C.; LL.B., Boston Coll., 1949; LL.D., Williams Coll., Hampshire Coll., 1970; m. Corinne L. Duval, Nov. 11, 1947; children—Michele, Sylvia, John, Gayle. Admitted to Mass. bar, 1949, since practiced in Pittsfield; mem. 86th-92d congresses 1st Dist. Mass., mem. appropriations com., house select com. on small bus., migratory bird conservation commn., joint commn. on coinage; mem. Mass. Senate, 1950-58, chmn. coms. on ins., constl. law, jud., chmn. legislative research council, chmn. spl. coms. for investigation health and welfare trust funds. Bd. dirs. Pittsfield Girls Club, Hillcrest Hosp. Named outstanding young man of year, Mass. Jr. C. of C., 1954. Mem. Italian-Am. League Mass., Fed., Mass., Berkshire bar assns., Am. Legion, V.F.W., D.A.V. K.C. Home: Blythewood Dr Pittsfield MA 01201 Office: Berkshire Common Pittsfield MA 01201

CONTI, JAMES JOSEPH, educator, chem. engr.; b. Coraopolis, Pa., Nov. 2, 1930; s. James Joseph and Mary (Smrekar) C.; B.Chem. Engring., Poly. Inst. Bklyn., 1954, M.Chem. Engring., 1956, D. Chem. Engring., 1959; m. Concetta Razziano, May 13, 1961; children—Lori Ann, James R. Sr. engr. Bettis atomic power div. Westinghouse Electric Corp., 1958-59; mem. faculty Poly. Inst. Bklyn., 1959—, prof. chem. engring., 1965—, chmn. dept., 1964-70, provost, 1970—; cons. to industry and govt., 1960—. Mem. Am. Inst. Chem. Engrs., Am. Soc. Engring. Edn., N.Y. Acad. Scis., A.A.A.S., Sigma Xi, Tau Beta Pi, Phi Lambda Upsilon, Omega Chi Epsilon. Author articles, patentee in field Home: 26 Miami Rd Bethpage, NY 11714. Office: 333 Jay St Brooklyn NY 11201

CONTI, SAMUEL FRANCIS, educator; b. Bklyn., Dec. 24, 1931; s. John and Sabina (Fontana) C.; B.S., Bklyn. Coll., 1952; M.S., U. Conn., 1956; Ph.D., Cornell U., 1959; m. Judith Rosenberg, Jan. 27, 1954; children—Deborah, Scott F., Suzanne. Research asso. biology Brookhaven Nat. Labs., 1959-61; from instr. to asso. prof. microbiology Dartmouth, 1961-63; prof., chmn. dept. microbiology U. Ky., 1966, dir. T.H. Morgan Sch. Biol. Sci., 1966—, asso. dean Coll. Arts and Scis., 1966—. Nat. lectr. Found. for Microbiology, 1967-68. Served with AUS. 1954-55. Recipient Career award NIH, 1963-66. Mem. Am. Acad. Microbiology, Am. Soc. Microbiology, Am. Soc. Biol. Chemists, Am. Soc. Plant Physiology, A.A.A.S., Sigma Xi. Mem. editorial bd. Jour. Bacteriology. Home: 500 Clinton Rd Lexington, KY 40502.

CONVERSE, GORDON NOBLE, photo-journalist; b. Medford, Mass., July 16, 1920; s. Stanley C. and Alice (Noble) C.; student Tilton Jr. Coll., 1939-41, N.Y. Inst. Photography, 1941-42; m. Shirley E. Wixon, Sept. 27, 1947; children— Linda J., Deborah J. Photo editor Christian Sci. Monitor, Boston, 1946- -. Oneman show Siembab Gallery, Boston, 1963; exhbt. group shows Principia Coll., Harvard, Boston U., DeCordova Mus., Boston Arts Festival, Boston Mus. Fine Arts Sch. Recipient Brotherhood award Nat. Conf. Christians and Jews, 1955, 60, Newhouse citation Syracuse U. Sch. Journalism, 1961, Nat. Sch. Bell award, 1961, award in photography Freedoms Found., 1964, Yankee Quill award Acad. New Eng. Journalists, 1965. Mem. Nat. (Newspaper-Mag. Photographer of Year 1959. Picture of Year-1st place Presdl. award 1964, 1st place pictorial picture of year 1965, Graflex award Photographer of Year 1965), Boston (recipient over 50 awards) press photographers assns. Home: 67 Pine St Needham, MA 02192. Office: 1 Norway St Boston MA 02115

CONVERSE, JOHN MARQUIS, surgeon; b. San Francisco, Sept. 29, 1909; s. George Marquis and Adele (Clot) C.; student Ecole Gerson, 1920-24; A.B., Lycee Janson de Sailly, 1928; M.D., U. Paris (France), 1935; m. Sheila Paull-Delany, Nov. 12, 1932; 1 son, John Marquis; m. 2d, Veronica Balfe Cooper, June 27, 1964. Surgeon-dir. clinic reconstructive plastic surgery of face Manhattan Eye, Ear and Throat Hosp., N.Y.C., 1952—, chmn. dept. plastic surgery; Lawrence D. Bell prof. plastic surgery N.Y. U. Sch. Medicine, dir. Inst. Reconstructive Plastic Surgery, N.Y.U. Med. Center, 1957—. Cons., VA Hosp., N.Y.C.; med. cons. Armed Forces. Pres., Found. for Med. and Biol. Research, 1970—. Served as maj. French Army, N. Africa, 1943-44, AUS, 1944-46. Decorated Croix de Guerre with palms; comdr. Legion of Honor (France). Diplomate Am. Bd. Plastic Surgery. Fellow A.C.S., Am. Soc. Plastic and Reconstructive Surgery, Am. Acad. Ophthalmology and Otolaryngology, N.Y. Acad. Medicine; hon. fellow Spanish, Venezuelian Uruguayan, Brazilian plastic surgery socs.; mem. Soc. Rehab. Facially Disfigured (v.p. 1951—, founder), Am. Assn. Plastic Surgeons, N.Y. Acad. Scis. Author: (with Dr. V. H. Kazanjian) Surgical Treatment of Facial Injuries, 2d edit., 1959, also numerous profl. articles. Editor: Reconstructive Plastic Surgery, 1964. Home: 700 Park Av New York City NY 10021 Office: 722 Park Av New York City NY 10021

CONVEY, JOHN, Canadian govt. ofcl.; b. County Durham, Eng., Mar. 29, 1910; s. John and Mary (Catterson) C.; B.Sc., U. Alta., 1933, M.Sc., 1936; Ph.D., U. Toronto, 1940; D.Sc., McMaster U., 1965, U. Windsor, 1967; m. Annette Therese Lemieux, Dec. 29, 1940; children—Annette (Mrs. R.T. Spillane), Jacqueline (Mrs. T. Gow), John, Nicole. Prof. physics U. Toronto, 1946-48; dir. Canadian Dept. Mines and Tech. Surveys, Ottawa, 1948—; dir. Royal Canadian Mint. Gov. Notre Dame U. (Nelson, B.C.). Served with Canadian Navy, 1940-46. Recipient Sorby award, Sheffield, Eng., 1942, Blaylock medal Canadian Inst. Mining and Metallurgy, 1956, Centennial award, 1967. Fellow Am. Soc. Metals; mem. Inst. Mining and Metallurgy (G.B.), Canadian Inst. Mining and Metallurgy, Am. Inst. Mining Engrs., Faraday Soc., Canadian Standards Assn. K.C. Editor: Mining in Canada, 1967, The Milling of Canadian Ores, 1967; Mining Geophysics, 1967; Geology of Canadian Ore Deposits, 1967; Canadian Industrial Minerals, 1967. Home: 9 Bayswater Pl Ottawa Ontario K1Y2E1 Canada Office: 555 Booth St Ottawa Ontario Canada

CONWAY, BERNARD JOHN, lawyer; b. Chgo., June 12, 1916; s. David and Mabel (Reagen) C.; LL.B., Loyola U., Chgo., 1949; m. Nona B. Peters, Mar. 17, 1950; children—Peter, Honoreé. Admitted to Ill. bar, 1949, since practiced in Chgo.; atty. Am. Dental Assn., Chgo., 1950—, also sec. Council Sec. Legal Affairs. Instr. bus. law Loyola U., 1950; lectr. Bd. dirs. Loyola U. Law Alumni Fund, Joint Council to Improve Health Care of the Aged, 1958. Served in Signal Corps, AUS, 1941-45. Recipient citation Hoover Commn., 1954. Fellow Am. Coll. Dentists; mem. Am., Ill. bar assns., A.A.A.S., Am. Judicature Soc., Nat. Wildlife Assn., Delta Theta Phi. Contbr. articles to profl. jours., chpts. to book. Home: 211 E Chicago Av Chicago IL 60611 Office: 222 E Superior St Chicago IL 60611

CONWAY, CARL FREDERICK, lawyer; b. Garner, Ia., Sept. 16, 1906; s. Charles Robert and Emma (Hoeft) C.; B.A., Coe Coll., 1929; J.D., U. Ia., 1931; m. Edith Marietta Fisher, July 16, 1941; 1 dau., Roberta. Admitted to Ia. bar, 1931, since practiced in Osage; mem. firm Conway & Casey; county atty. Mitchell County, 1935-58. Dir. Home Savs. & Loan Assn., Osage. Served with AUS, 1942-45; PTO. Mem. Am., Ia. (bd. govs. 1953-58, pres. 1959-60), Mitchell County bar assns., Am. Legion (past post comdr.), Phi Kappa Tau, Phi Delta Phi. Republican. Lutheran. Rotarian (pres. Osage 1948-49). Home: 1021 E Main St Osage IA 50461 Office: 626 / Main St Osage IA 50461

CONWAY, CHARLES MITCHELL, lawyer, former U.S. atty.; b. Texarkana, Ark., May 5, 1925; s. George T. and Mary Cecelia (O'Dwyer) C.; B.S. in Bus. Adminstrn., U. Ark., 1948, LL.D., 1949; m. Hazel Dodson, July 27, 1951; children—Charles Mitchell, Charlotte Melinda, Michael Dodson, Mary Louise. Admitted to Ark. bar, 1949; practice in Texarkana, 1949-61; partner firm Conway & Webber, 1954- 61, Smith, Straud, McClerkin & Conway, Texarkana, 1969—; city atty. Texarkana (Ark.), 1954-58; U.S. atty. Western dist. Ark., 1961- 68. Home: 1822 S 23d Fort Smith AR 72901 Office: State Line Plaza Texarkana AR 75501

CONWAY, DANIEL EDWARD, labor union ofcl.; b. East St. Louis, Ill., Oct. 18, 1911; s. Daniel Patrick and Bertha M. (Fitzgerald) C.; student Los Angeles Jr. Coll., 1930-33, U. Cal. at Los Angeles, 1933-34; m. Kathryn Lenora Muscat, Apr. 15, 1939; children—Daniel Edward, Linda May. Employed in pie shops, Los Angeles, 1935-37; bus. agt. for local Bakery & Confectionery Workers Internat. Union, 1937, internat. rep., 1937-48, internat. v.p., 1948-53, dir. orgn., 1953-55, adminstrv. dir., 1955-57, internat. v.p., 1956-57, sec. con. to preserve integrity of union, 1957, acting pres., sec.-treas. Am. Bakery and Confectionary Workers Internat. Union AFL-CIO, 1957-58, internat. pres., 1958-66, pres. Bakery and Confectionery Workers Nat. Union Am. AFL-CIO, 1966—, sec.-treas. food and beverage trades dept., 1961—; v.p. union label and trades dept. AFL/CIO, 1960—. Chmn. trustees Union and Industry Health and Welfare Fund, Union and Industry Pension Fund; mem. gen. bd. AFL-CIO; inter-Am. com. Internat. Union Food, Drink and Allied Workers Assn., 1959—, v.p. 2d Inter-Am. Conf., 1960; pres. Internat. Union Food and Allied Workers' Assn., Geneva, Switzerland, 1970—. Presbyn. (trustee). Mason. Home: 11901 Greenleaf Av Willerburn Acres Potomac MD 20854 Office: 1828 L St NW Washington DC 20036

CONWAY, EDMUND VIRGIL, banker; b. Montauk, N.Y., Aug. 2, 1929; s. Edmund Virgil and Dorothy (Brandes) C.; B.A. magna cum laude, Colgate U., 1951; LL.B. cum laude. Yale, 1956; m. Elaine Wingate, June 28, 1969; children (by prev. marriage)—Allison Brandes, Sarah Lindner. Admitted to N.Y. bar, 1956; atty. firm Debevoise, Plimpton, Lyons & Gates, 1956- 64; 1st dep. supt. banks N.Y. State, also sec. N.Y. State Banking Bd., 1964-67; exec. v.p., trustee Manhattan Savs. Bank, 1967-68; chmn. bd., pres., trustee Seamen's Bank Savs., N.Y.C., 1969—; trustees Consol. Edison Co., N.Y.C.; dir. Nat. Securities and Research Corp. Mem. adv. com. supervision mut. instns. N.Y. State Supt. Banks, 1969-70; dir., mem. legislative com., mem. exec. com., mem. com. pub. information Savs. Bank Assn. N.Y.; chmn. com. on relations with fed. supervisory authorities Nat. Assn. Mut. Savs. Banks; chmn. temp. State com. to study water supply needs S.E. N.Y.; N.Y. state rep. conf. State Bank Suprs. Del. N.Y. State Republican Conv., 1962, 66, pres. N.Y. Young Rep. Club, 1962-63. Trustee, mem. finance com. Colgate U., sec. class 1951; trustee Packer Collegiate Inst., Plymouth Ch. of Pilgrims, South Street Seaport Mus., Annuity Fund Congl. Ministers, Pension Bds. United Chs. Christ, Citizens Budget Commn.; bd. dirs. Regional Plan Assn.; chmn. South Street Mus. Council. Served with USAF, 1951-53; capt. Res. Mem. Am., N.Y. State bar assns., Assn. Bar City N.Y., Phi Beta Kappa. Clubs: Economic, Bankers, Union League, Downtown Assn. (N.Y.C.); Rembrandt (Bklyn.); Siwanoy (Westchester). Home: 345 Pondfield Rd Bronxville NY 10708 Office: 30 Wall St New York City NY 10005

CONWAY, FRANCIS JOSEPH, corp ofcl.; b. Wis., Mar. 5, 1902; s. Michael Francis and Catherine Ellen (Doyle) C.; m. Philomene Tolford, June 22, 1929; children—Mary Elizabeth, Catherine Ellen, Rosanne, Jane, Connaught. Asst. cashier Lyndon State Bank, Lyndon Station, Wis., 1920-22; with Wis. Banking Dept., 1922-24; cashier Framers Exchange Bank, Thorp, Wis., 1924-32; organizer Thorp Finance Corp., 1925, sec. treas., 1925-59, pres., 1950- 64, chmn., dir., 1964—; chmn., dir. Thorp Loan & Thrift Co., Rochester, Minn., Thorp Sales Co., Rochester, Lyndon Ins. Co., Thorp, ITT Midwestern Life Ins. Corp., Thorp, ITT Aetna Corp., ITT Consumer Services Corp., ITT Financial Services, Inc. Bd. rev. Wis. Banking Dept., Madison, Wis. Consumer Credit Rev. Bd., Madison Pres. Thorp Found., Inc. Mem. Am. Indsl. Bankers Assn. (hon. mem. exec. com., past pres.), Wis. Consumer Finance Assn. (hon., life dir., past pres. Milw.). K.C. Clubs: Milwaukee Athletic; The Madison (Wis.); Wausau (Wis.); Eau Claire (Wis.) Country; Meadowview Country (Owen, Wis.); La-Ho-Go Golf (Holcombe, Wis.). Home: Thorp WI

CONWAY, FRED E., educator; b. St. Louis, Aug. 24, 1900; s. Frederick E. and Georgia (Wallis) C.; student St. Louis Sch. Fine Arts, Washington U., Julian Acad., Paris Academie Moderne, Paris; m. Alice Gaylord, May 7, 1927; children—William Gaylord and Joan Grace; m. 2d, Constance Conway; children—Fred and Helen Busch; m. 3d, Helen Busch, June 22, 1964. Prof. drawing and painting at the St. Louis Sch. Fine Arts, Washington U.; instr. Creative Arts Workshop, U. of Wyo., summer 1950; U. of Miss., summer 1950, Houston U., 1952; prof. painting Syracuse (N.Y.) U. Rep. Grand Central Art Galleries, N.Y.C. Works owned by pub. instns. and mus., including St. Louis Art Mus., Springfield Mus., Denver Art Mus., Mulvane Art Mus., Hallmark Collection, Pepsi-Cola Co. Works have been exhibited throughout the country in institutes and art museums as well as at one man shows; executed murals Mayo Clinic, Rochester, Minn., Brown Shoe Co., Barnes Hosp., Channel 9 TV Sta., St. Louis, Peabody Coal Co., St. Louis, Lowe Art Center, Syracuse, N.Y. Recipient awards from St. Louis Art Mus., St. Louis Artists Guild, various other shows and exhibitions; hallmark award, Am., Internat. awards, Tulsa Mural competition; gold medal for mural painting Archtl. League N.Y., 1956; gold medal Pa. Acad. Hon. mem. Art Dirs. Club, Archtl. League. Home: 265 Union Senate Apt St Louis MO 63108

CONWAY, HARRY DONALD, research engr., educator; b. Chatham, Eng., Dec. 3, 1917; s. John and Ada Frances (Young) C.; B.Sc., London U., 1942, Ph.D., 1945, D.Sc., 1949; M.A., Cambridge (Eng.) U., 1946; m. Dorothy Daphne Adams, Aug. 24, 1946; children—Geoffrey, Peter. Came to U.S., 1947, naturalized, 1956. Sci. officer, research on high temperature properties of metals Nat. Phys. Lab., Teddington, Eng., 1942-45; univ. demonstrator engring. Cambridge (Eng.) U. and dir. studies St. Catharine's Coll., 1946-47; asso. prof. engring. mecs. Cornell U., Ithaca, N.Y., 1947-48, prof. engring. mecs., 1948—. John Simon Guggenheim fellow and vis. prof. Imperial Coll., London U., 1953-54, NSF sr. postdoctoral fellow, 1961-62; Julius F. Stone vis. prof. Ohio State U., 1958-59; Sir Joseph Whitworth scholar, 1941; Sir John Johnson scholar London U., 1941. Author: Aircraft Strength of Materials, 1947; Mechanics of Materials, 1950. Contbr. articles on theoretical analyses of plates and shells, elastic vibrations to profl. jours. Address: Thurston Hall Cornell University Ithaca NY 14850

CONWAY, JACK THOMAS, orgn. exec.; b. Detroit Dec. 20, 1917; s. James B. and Blanche (Harper) C.; B.A., University of Chicago, 1940; married to LuVerne Heger, Sept. 12, 1939; children—Cynthia, Jan, Thomas. Adminstrative asst. to pres. United Auto Workers Union, 1946-61; deputy administrator, HHFA, 1961-63; dept. dir. Office Econ. Opportunity, 1964-65 exec. dir. Industrial Union Dept., AFL-CIO, 1965-68; now pres. Center for Community Change, Washington. Home: 1307 4th St NW Washington DC 20001 Office: 1000 Wisconsin Av NW Washington DC 20007

CONWAY, JOHN HAROLD, Jr., lawyer; b. Tonkawa, Okla., June 11, 1924; s. John Harold and Theresa (Flynn) C.; B.S. in Bus. Adminstrn., U. Notre Dame, 1947; J.D., U. Okla., 1949; m. June Francis Costello, Aug. 23, 1947; children—John Harold III, Margaret Sue. Admitted to Okla. bar, 1949; mgr. tax dept. Tulsa office Arthur Young & Co., C.P.A.'s, 1949-54; partner Martin, Logan, Moyers, Martin & Conway, Tulsa, 1955—. Trustee Cascia Hall Prep. Sch.; bd. dirs. Monte Cassino High Sch., Vianney Sch. for Girls. Served to lt. (j.g.) USNR, 1943-45. Mem. Am., Okla., Tulsa bar assns., Phi Alpha Delta. Republican. Roman Catholic. Club: Tulsa. Home: 2110 Forest Blvd Tulsa OK 74114 Office: Nat Bank Tulsa Tulsa OK 74103

CONWAY, MARTHA BELL, ednl. adminstr.; b. Raleigh, N.C., July 24, 1917; d. Elijah James and Cora (Henderson) Conway; student William and Mary Coll., 1932-35; LL.B., U. Richmond, 1937-39. Admitted to Va. bar, 1940, since practiced in Richmond; registered patent atty., 1945; commr. chancery Hanover County Circuit Ct., 1943-51; real estate broker, Richmond, 1951-55; sec. Commonwealth for Va., 1952-70; adminstr. research grants and contracts Va. Commonwealth U., 1970—. Mem. Va. Bar Assn., Am. Assn. U. Women, Nat. Assn. Secs. of State. Methodist. Democrat. Author: The Compacts of Virginia, 1960. Home: 2500 Grove Av Richmond VA 23219 Office: Virginia Commonwealth Univ 1200 E Broad St Richmond VA 23219

CONWAY, PATRICK JOSEPH, educator; b. N.Y.C., June 14, 1920; s. Timothy Patrick and Anne (O'Driscoll) C.; B.S., Cath. U., 1941; M.S., Fordham U., 1948; J.D., St. John's U., 1953; Ph.D., Stevens Inst., 1965; m. Margaret Hareadon, Dec. 26, 1949; children—Kevin, Dennis. Chief chemist Kuppers Co., Kearney, N.J., 1948-55; faculty Fairleigh Dickinson U., Rutherford, N.J., 1955—, prof. chemistry, chmn. dept., 1968—. Cons. Sel Rex. Co., Nutley, N.J., 1968-70, Bector Dickinson Co., East Rutherford, 1956, Western Electric, N.Y.C., 1965-68. County com. chmn. Democratic party, Rutherford, 1968-71. Elk. Home: 225 Jackson Av Rutherford NJ 07070

CONWAY, THEODORE JOHN, former army officer; b. Valejo, Cal., July 24, 1909; s. Theodore Allen and Ruth Irene (Quinn) Barnwitz; B.S., U.S. Mil. Acad., 1933; student Sorbonne, Paris, France, 1938, Middlebury Coll., 1939; grad. Armed Forces Staff Coll., 1948, Nat. War Coll., 1950; m. Eleanor Mitchell Wright, Nov. 30, 1935; children—Laura Mitchell (Mrs. Nason), Ruth Quinn Mrs. Willms), John Wright. Commd. 2d lt. U.S. Army, 1933, advanced through grades to gen., 1966; instr. lang. and mechs. U.S. Mil. Acad.; amphibious operations, Dieppe, France, Morocco, N. Africa, So. France; acting regtl. comdr. 60th Inf. Regt., Tunisia, exec. officer, Sicily; G-3 of VI Corps, then exec. officer, acting G-3 Fifth Army, Italy and France; staff strategic plans br. operations div. War Dept. Gen. Staff; instr. Armed Forces Staff Coll.; comdr. 188th Airborne Inf. Regt., later chief staff 11th Airborne Div., Ft. Campbell, Ky., 1950-52; spl. weapons adviser to comdr. in chief Allied Forces Central Europe, 1952-55; staff, then dir. research Office Chief Research and Devel., Dept. Army, 1955-60; comdg. gen. 82d Airborne Div., 1961-62; chief joint adv. group, Thailand, 1962-63; dep. comdr. gen. 8th Army, Korea, 1963-65; asst. chief staff Force Devel. Dept. Army, 1965- 66; comdg. gen. 7th Army, Germany, 1966; comdr. in chief U.S. Strike Command, also Middle E., Africa S. of Sahara, So. Asia, 1966. Decorated Legion of Merit with cluster, Bronze Star medal with clusters, Order Brit. Empire; French Legion of Honor, Croix de Guerre with Palm (France); Italian Order of Crown; Czechoslovak Mil. Cross; Polish Gold Cross Merit with Swords; Order Merit (Korea); Order Leopard (Congo). Mem. Nat. Inventors Council, Am. Radio Relay League. Airborne Assn. (v.p.). Address: 2160 Tanglewood Way NE St Petersburg FL 33702

CONWAY, THOMAS JAMES, Jr., lawyer; b. Kansas City, July 20, 1913; s. Thomas James and Neil M. (O'Sullivan) C.; LL.B., Washington U., St. Louis, 1935; m. Eleanor M. Nolan, June 4, 1938; children—Terry N., Bria J., Diana S. Admitted to Mo. bar, 1935; atty. Kansas City Park Dept., 1936-42; asst. city counselor Kansas City, 1942-50, chief trial atty. City Counselor's Office, 1950-59; partner firm Popham, Popham, Conway, Sweeny & Fremont, Kansas City, 1959—. Mem. Am., Mo., Kansas City bar assns., Internat. Soc. Barristers, Pi Epsilon Delta, Kappa Alpha. Roman Cath. K.C. Clubs: Carriage (Kansas City Racquet.) Home: 1227 W 64th Terrace Kansas City MO 64113 Office: Commerce Trust Bldg Kansas City MO 64106

CONWAY, WALTER JOSEPH, cement co. exec.; b. Fort Worth, Mar. 26, 1922; s. Walter M. and Lou Ella (Doyle) C.; student Tex. Wesleyan Coll., Fort Worth, 1940-42; m. Dorothy Erwin, Feb. 1, 1943; children—David Patrick, Robert Adrian. With Thomas Concrete Pipe Co., Corpus Christi, Tex., 1946, Ideal Cement Co., 1947—, Pacific regional sales mgr., San Francisco, 1952-61, v.p. sales, 1961-64, v.p. exec. dept., 1964-65, exec. v.p., 1965-68; v.p., gen. mgr. Trinity div. Gen. Portland Cement Co., Dallas, 1968-70; v.p., gen. mgr. Pacific Western Industries, Inc. subsidiary gen. Portland Cement Co., Los Angeles, 1970—. Served with USNR, 1942-45. Home: 888 Toulon Dr Pacific Palisades CA 90272

CONWAY, WILLIAM FRANCIS, lawyer; b. Albany, N.Y., Mar. 28, 1915; s. William Francis and Lucy A. (McCormack) C.; B.S., Georgetown U., 1936; LL.B., Union U., 1939; m. Elaine R. Lawrence, Apr. 22, 1938; children—William Francis III, Gerard L., John E., Elaine R. (Mrs. Donald McCarthy), Edward P. J., Gayle M., Lawrence C., Mary Lucy, Thomas A., Rita C., Laura G., Christopher M.; m. 2d, Arlene A. Iwaneazho, Oct. 23, 1965. Admitted to N.Y. bar, 1939, since practiced in Albany; mem. firm DeGraff, Foy, Conway & Holt-Harris, 1939—; asst. exec. N.Y. State Bd. Law Examiners. Dir. G & G Erectors, Arrowhead Estates. Mem. adv. bd. Child's Hosp. Mem. Am., N.Y. State bar assns., N.Y. State Trial Lawyers Assn. Clubs: Schuyler Meadows (Loudonville); University (Albany). Home: 15 Old Niskayuna Rd Loudonville, NY 12211. Office: 90 State St Albany NY 12207

CONWAY, WILLIAM GAYLORD, zoologist; b St. Louis, Nov. 20, 1929; s. Frederick Eldridge and Alice Harriet (Gaylord) C.; A.B., Washington U., 1951. Curator birds St. Louis Zool. Park, 1950-56; curator birds N.Y. Zool. Park, N.Y.C., 1956-60, asso. dir., 1960-61, curator birds, 1956-, general director, 1966-. Bd. dirs. Am. Com. Internat. Wildliife Protection, Lab. Ornithology, Caribbean Conservation Corp. Fellow N.Y. Zool. Soc.; mem. Brit. Avicultural Soc., Am. Ornithologists Union (elective), Cooper Ornithol Soc., Internat. Wild Waterfowl Assn. (dir.), Nat. Audubon Soc. (dir.), Wilson Ornithol. Club, Wild Animal Propagation Trust (past pres.), Am. Assn. Zool. Parks and Aquariums (past pres.), Internat. Survival Service Commn., Am. Soc. Ichthyologists and Herpetologists. Contbr. articles to profl. jours. Expdns. to Trinidad, Argentina, Bolivia. Office: NY Zool Park New York City NY 10460

CONWAY, WILLIAM IGNATIUS, lawyer; b. Aledo, Ill., Feb. 10, 1900; s. Patrick J. and Julia A. (Kennedy) C.; A.B., Loras Coll., 1924; LL.B., Georgetown U., 1928; m. Jane S. Steele, Jan. 12, 1952; children—Jane, Mary. Admitted to D.C. bar, 1927, Ill. bar, 1928; spl. agt. F.B.I., 1928-33; chief investigator assigned inquiry involving ofcl. corruption in Bklyn., atty. gen. N.Y., 1938-42; law practice, Chgo., 1933-38, 45—. Served to lt. col. USAAF, 1942-45. Mem. Chgo. Bar Assn. Roman Catholic. Club: Union League (Chgo.). Home: 1132 Fair Oaks Av Oak Park IL 60302 Office: 120 S LaSalle St Chicago IL 60603

CONWELL, HUGH EARLE, orthopaedic surgeon; b. Oakman, Ala., Dec. 29, 1893; s. Thomas and Catherine (Williams) C.; M.D., U. Ala., 1915; m. Mary Lou Perry, Jan. 16, 1949; 1 son, Perry Hooper. Began practice at Birmingham, Ala., 1915; vis. orthopaedic surgeon St. Vincent's Hosp., South Highlands Infirmary, Children's Hospital, Univ. Hospital, and also Bapt. Hosp.; chief Conwell Orthopaedic Clinic, Birmingham; state orthopaedic cons. and mem. med. adv. bd. Ala. Crippled Children's Services. asso. prof. orthopaedic surgery, U. Ala. Med. Coll.; orthopaedic cons. Vets. Hosp. in Tuscaloosa and Montgomery Ala. Capt. Med. Res. Corps. U.S. Army, 1917-19, attached to Brit. Army Med. Corps, base hosps. London. England and Calais, France, 1917-19. Fellow A.C.S. (nat. fracture com.; chmn. Ala. state regional fracture com.), A.M.A. (mem. adv. com. on fractures); mem. A.A.A.S., Ala. Acad. Sci., Birmingham Surg. Soc., Ala. State Med. Assn. (life councillor, also chmn. fracture com.), Jefferson County Med. Soc. (pres. 1936), Am. Med. Editors Assn., Am. Orthopaedic Assn. (chmn. orthopaedic sect. 1932). Clin. Orthopaedic Soc. (sec. 1936-37; pres. 1939-40); Am. Acad. Orthopaedic Surgeons (mem. com. on fractures and traumatic surgery, v.p., 1944-45-46), Assn. of Mil. Surgeons, So. Surg. Assn., Southeastern Surg. Congress, Cattahoochee Valley Med. Assn., Pan-Pacific Surg. Assn., Internat. Soc. Traumatic and Orthopedic Surgery, Am. Bd. Orthopedic Surgeons, Sigma Xi, Theta Kappa Psi. Baptist. Mason (Shriner, Jester). Clubs: Sir Robert Jones, Rotary, The Club. Mountain Brook Country. Author: (with Key) The Management of Fractures, Dislocations and Sprains. Co-author of Text-book The Management of Fractures. Dislocations and Sprains" (textbook). 7th edit., 1961. Asso. editor Southern Surgeon; mem. editorial com. on Progress of Orthopaedic Surgery. Contbr. to Cyclopedia of Medicine, Textbook of Surgery, The Injured Spine, also many papers on fractures. Home: 1407 Windsor Circle Redmont Park Birmingham AL 35205 Office: 2031 11th Av S Birmingham AL 35205

CONWELL, JOSEPH FRANCIS, educator; b. Spokane, Aug. 10, 1919; s. James Urban and Gertrude (O'Malley) C.; A.B., Gonzaga U., 1943, M.A., 1944; S.T.L., Alma Coll., 1951; S.T.D., Gregorian U., 1957. Joined Soc. Jesus, 1937, ordained priest Roman Cath. Ch., 1950; mem. faculty Gonzaga U., 1951—, prof. theology, 1961—, past chmn. dept., grad. dean, 1961-67. Mem. Diocesan Commn. Ecumenism, 1966—. Bd. dirs. Pacific N.W. Council Theol. Edn., 1966—. Mem. Coll. Theology Soc., Cath. Bib. Assn. Am., Cath. Theol. Soc. Author: Contemplation in Action: A Study in Ignation Prayer, 1957. Address: E 502 Boone Av Spokane WA 99202

CONWILL, ALLAN FRANKLIN, lawyer; b. Hutchinson, Kan., Oct. 21, 1921; s. Joseph Dillard and Phyills Ruth (Fuhr) C.; B.S., Northwestern U., 1943, J.D., 1949; m. Arolyn Frances Hodgkins, Aug. 30, 1947; children—Joseph Dillard, Stephen Hodgkins, Michael Francis. Admitted to N.Y. bar, 1949; with firm Willkie, Farr & Gallagher, New York City, 1949-61, partner, 1956-61, 64—; gen. counsel SEC, 1961, dir. div. corp. regulation, 1961-64; prof. law N.Y. Law Sch., 1951-56; lectr. law Columbia, 1964—. Dir. Finevest Services, Inc., Performance Analysis Fund, Inc., Investors Overseas Services Mgmt. Ltd., Fund of Funds, Ltd., Knickerbocker Growth Fund, Northeastern Life Ins. Co. of N.Y. Served to lt. (j.g.) USNR, 1943-46. Decorated Bronze Star medal, Distinguished Unit citation. Mem. Assn. Bar City N.Y. Club: University (N.Y.C.). Author articles. Home: 481 Carlton Rd Wyckoff, NJ 07481.

CONY, EDWARD ROGER, newspaperman; b. Augusta, Me., Mar. 15, 1923; s. Daniel William and Mary (Doyle) C.; B.A. in Polit. Sci., Reed Coll., 1948; M.A., Stanford, 1951; m. Susan Wheat, June 12, 1954; children—Ann, Daniel, Elizabeth, Katharine, Marilyn, Lauren. Reporter, The Oregonian, Portland, 1951-52; with The Wall Street Jour., 1953-70, successively mem. staff San Francisco office, news bur. mgr., Los Angeles, Southeastern news bur. mgr., Jacksonville, Fla., 1953-60, news editor, N.Y.C., 1960-64, asst. mng. editor Pacific Coast edit., 1964-65, mng. editor, 1965-70; exec. editor Dow Jones Publs., N.Y.C., 1970—. Recipient Pulitzer prize for nat. reporting, 1961. Home: 7 Gull's Cove Manhasset NY 11030 Office: 30 Broad St New York City NY 10004

CONYERS, JOHN, Jr., congressman; b. Detroit, May 16, 1929; s. John and Lucille (Simpson) C.; B.A., Wayne State U., 1957, LL.B., (Lamson McElhone labor scholar), 1958. Admitted to Mich. bar, 1959, since practiced in Detroit; sr. mem. firm Conyers, Bell & Townsend, 1960- -; legislative asst. to Congressman Dingell, 1958-61; referee Mich. Workman's Compensation Dept., 1961-64; mem. 89th to 92d U.S. congresses, from 1st Mich. Dist. Mem. Lawyers' Com. for Civil Rights Under Law, 1963. Served with C.E., AUS, 1950-54. Mem. Am. Civil Liberties Union (hon. co-chmn. nat. adv. bd.), Ams. Democratic Action (mem. nat. bd.), Kappa Alpha Psi. Democrat. Home: 19970 Canterbury Rd Detroit MI 48221 Office: Cannon House Office Bldg Washington DC 20515 also Federal Bldg Detroit MI 48226

CONYERS, NATHAN GEORGE, auto dealer, lawyer; b. Detroit, July 3, 1932; s. John James and Lucille (Simpson) C.; LL.B., Wayne State U., 1959; m. Diana Callie Howze, Aug. 25, 1956; children—Nancy, Steven, Susan, Ellen, Peter. Admitted to Mich. bar, 1959; mem. firm Colven, Snowden, Smith & Keith, Detroit, 1960-63; partner Keith, Conyers & Anderson, 1964-67; sr. partner Conyers, Anderson, Brown & Wahls, Detroit, 1967-70; pres. Conyers Ford, Inc., Detroit, 1970—. Spl. asst. atty. gen. State of Mich., 1967-70. Mem. Mich. Bd. State Canvassers, 1967—, chmn., 1971. Served with AUS, 1953-55. Mem. Nat. Black Auto Dealers Assn. (pres.). Office: 2475 W Grand Blvd Detroit MI 48208

CONZE, PETER H., corp. exec.; b. 1920; grad. chem. engring., Princeton, 1942; married. Vice pres. plastic div. Susquehanna Mills Inc., 1946-53; sales mgr. Reeves Bros., 1953-54; partner mfg. div. Midland Textiles Inc., 1954-56; with Celanese Corp., 1956—, exec. v.p. fibers and forest products 1965—, also dir. Address: 522 Fifth Av New York City NY 10036*

CONZEN, WILLIBALD HERMANN, pharm. co. exec.; b. Dortmund, Germany, Aug. 3, 1913; s. Friedrich Wilhelm and Elisabeth (Mathies) C.; abitur degree Kaiserin Augusta Gymnasium, Koblenz, Germany, 1931; m. Salome Bruwer, July 11, 1951; children—Vincent, Elizabeth, Suzanne. Came to U.S., 1952, naturalized, 1959. With Schering A.G., Berlin, Germany, 1931-38; with Scherag (Pty.) Ltd., Johannesburg, S. Africa, 1938-52, gen. mgr., 1941-52; with Schering Corp., U.S.A., Bloomfield, N.J., 1952—, v.p., 1959-65, sr. v.p., 1965-66, pres., chief exec. officer, dir., 1966—; pres., chief exec. officer Schering-Plough Corp., 1971—; N.J. dir. Midatlantic Banks, Inc., Nat. Newark and Essex Bank. Bd. dirs. People-to-People Health Found. Mem. Pharm. Mfrs. Assn. (dir.), Proprietary Assn. Clubs: Union League (N.Y.C.); Montclair (N.J.) Golf; Essex (Newark). Home: 130 Lloyd Rd Montclair NJ 07042 Office: 60 Orange St Bloomfield NJ 07003

COOGAN, CHARLES HENRY, Jr., educator, mech. engr.; b. Boston, Apr. 2, 1908; s. Charles Henry and Katherine Elizabeth (Heffner) C.; B.S. in Mech. Engring. magna cum laude, Tufts Coll., 1930; M.S., Harvard, 1931; M.E., U. Pa., 1937; m. Ruth Evelyn Lawson, July 6, 1934; chidlren—Rhoda Patricia, Katherine Elizabeth. Designer Buerkel & Co., Inc., Boston, summers 1925-30, Electric Ry., Bklyn., summer 1931; instr. mech. engring. U. Pa., 1931- 42; successively asst., asso. prof. mech. engring. U. Conn., 1942-48, head dept., 1947-68, prof., 1948—; cons. engr., sec., mem. Conn. Bd. Registration Profl. Engrs. and Land Surveyors, 1957—; mem. Conn. adv. com. engring., sci. and specialized personnel SSS; mem. Conn. Gov's. Indsl. Research Adv. Com., 1961-65; commr. Conn. Research Commn., 1965—. Profl. engr., Conn. Fellow Am. Soc. M.E. (v.p., mem. council 1958-62); mem. Inst. Aeros. and Astronautics, Am. Soc. Engring. Edn., Nat. Soc. Profl. Engrs., Sigma Xi, Tau Beta Pi, Pi Tau Sigma, Phi Kappa Phi, Sigma Pi Sigma. Republican. Conglist. Contbr. articles profl. publs. Home: RD 1 Box 306 Storrs CT 06268

COOGAN, JOHN LESLIE (Jackie), actor; b. Los Angeles, Oct. 26, 1914; s. John Henry and Lillian Rita (Dolliver) C.; student Santa Clara U., 1931-32, U. So. Cal., 1933-34; m. Dorothea Odetta Hanson, May 27, 1950; children—John Anthony, Joann Dolliver, Leslie Diane, Christopher Fenton. Appeared in numerous motion pictures, 1916—, including Skinner's Baby, 1916, The Kid, 1919, latest being The Actress, 1953, Fine Madness, 1965, Shakiest Gun In The West, 1967, Rogues Gallery, 1967, Little Sister, 1968, Marlo, 1968; appeared on numerous TV shows, 1947—, including Playhouse 90, 1955, Studio One, 1956, Johnny Carson, 1965, Mike Douglas, 1965, Regis Philbin, 1966, Les Crane, 1966, Joey Bishop Show, 1967, U Don't Say, 1967, Truth or Consequences, 1967, Woody Woodbury, 1967, Name of the Game, 1968, 69, 70, Red Skelton, 1970, Jeanie, 1970, Julia, 1970, The Interns, 1970, Partridge Family, 1970, Stump the Stars, 1970, Barefoot in the Park, 1970, Matt Lincoln, 1970; appeared on television series Cowboy G-Men, 1951-53, McKeever and Colonel, 1960s, Addams Family, 1963-65; appeared in stage plays Blue Denim, 1967, Make a Million, 1968, Sweet Bird of Youth, 1968, Odd Couple, 1969, Come Blow Your Horn, 1969; toured U.S. and Europe with Donald O'Connor, 1950; toured U.S. with Ted Cassidy, summer stock 1963-65. Served with USAAF, 1941-45; CBI. Decorated D.F.C., Air medal; recipient Papal medal Pope Pius 10th, 1924, Order of King George, Greek Govt., 1924, Justinian Cross, Greek Orthodox Ch., 1924. Mem. Screen Actors Guild, A.F.T.R.A., Am. Guild Variety Artists, Equity, Acad. Motion Picture and Television Arts and Scis. Author: Jackie Coogan Child Labor Law, 1937. Home: Palm Springs CA Office: care Kitty Davis Box 1305 Hollywood CA 90028

COOGAN, THOMAS JAMES, physician; b. Lincoln, Ill., Nov. 24, 1900; s. Michael J. and Alice (Ryan) C.; B.A. cum laude, Columbia Coll., 1922; M.D., St. Louis (Mo.) U., 1927; Sc.D., Loras College, 1967; m. Evelyn Bermingham, Apr. 13, 1929; children—Mary Alice, Thomas James, Evelyn Renee. Intern, St. Luke's Hosp., Chgo., 1927-29, asst. physician, 1930-36, sr. attending physician 1940-57, v.p. staff, 1947-50, chmn. dept. of medicine, 1956-59; asso. attending physician Cook County Hosp., 1932-37; asso. in medicine, instr. Northwestern U., 1936-57; asso. in medicine, prof. medicine, 1958-61, clin. asso. prof. medicine, 1961-68; clin. prof., 1968—; staff Presbyn.-St. Luke's Hosp., 1957—. Diplomate Am. Bd. Internal Medicine, Nat. Bd. Med. Examiners. Fellow Am. Coll. Chest Physicians (gov. Ill. 1963-69), A.C.P., Am. Therapeutic Soc. (pres. 1947-48), Am. Coll. Cardiology; mem. Ill. Soc. of Internal Medicine, also St. Luke's Hosp. Interns Alumni Assn. (past pres.), Alumni St. Louis U. Sch. of Medicine (past pres.), Am., Chgo. heart assns., Chgo. Soc. Internat Medicine, Ill. State, Chgo. med. socs., Am., Chgo. diabetes assns., World Med. Soc., Internat. Soc. Internal Medicine, Am. Med. Writers Assn., Chgo. Inst. Medicine, Alpha Omega Alpha. Republican. Roman Catholic. Club: Glen View. Home: 1242 Lake Shore Dr Chicago IL 60610 Office: 900 N Michigan Av Chicago IL 60611

COOGAN, THOMAS PHILLIPS, mortgage banker; b. Springfield, Mass., July 27, 1898; s. John Patrick and Helen (Phillips) C.; stud. Mass. Inst. Tech., 1924; m. Helen Harrington Kennelly, June 24, 1922; 1 dau., Jacqueline H. (Mrs. John F. Beatty). Pres., South Fla. Builders Assn., 1945-46, Nat. Assn. Home Builders, 1950, Housing Credit Corp., N.Y.C.; pres. Housing Securities, Inc., N.Y.C., 1950—; chmn. bd. Community Fed. Savs. & Loan Assn., Hialeah, Fla.; housing cons. ICA, 1958—; chmn. bd. Housing Investment Corp., San Juan. P.R. Bd. dirs. Nat. Housing Center, Washington. Asst. to sec. of def., 1952-53; del. Am. Constrn. Indsl. Mission to Soviet Union, 1956; leader Housing Mission to Soviet Union, 1958. Mayor, Surfside, Florida, 1949-50. Served with A.S., USN, 1917-18; Mem. Boston Soc. Civil Engrs., Nat. Assn. Home Builders, Asso. Gen. Contractors. Clubs: Oyster Harbors (Mass.); Surf, Indian Creek, La Gorce. Bal Harbour (Miami Beach); Metropolitan (N.Y.C.). Author: (monthly) Mortgage Market Memo. Home: 10190 Collins Av Miami Beach FL 33154 Office: 250 Park Av New York City NY 10017

COOGLE, JOSEPH MOORE, Jr., advt. exec.; b. Louisville, Jan. 13, 1933; s. Joseph Moore and Dorothy Virginia (Miller) C.; B.S., U. Ky., 1957; M.B.A., U. Chgo., 1958; m. Maryhelen Doty, Jan. 27, 1957; children—Suzanne Grace, Virginia Louise. Grocery products salesman Pillsbury Co., Mpls., 1958-59, marketing research up to sr. research analyst, 1959-62, up to marketing mgr. marketing dept., 1962-65; account exec. Ketchum, MacLeod & Grove, Pitts., 1965-66, account supr., 1966-68, v.p., account mgr., 1968-70, v.p., dir. marketing research and media planning, 1970—. Served with AUS, 1953-55. Mem. Beta Gamma Sigma. Lutheran. Clubs: St. Clair Country (Upper St. Clair, Pa.); Nemacolin Country (Beallesville, Pa.). Home: 2269 Sidgefield Lane Pittsburgh PA 15241 Office: 4 Gateway Center Pittsburgh PA 15222

COOK, A. HALSEY, banker; b. Bayonne, N.J. Aug. 7, 1905; s. William Leigh and Marie Holden (Montford) C.; B.S., Princeton, 1927; m. Margaret Van Doren, Sept. 29, 1934 (died June 27, 1942); 1 dau., Margaret Van Doren. With Bank of Am., 1927-31; v.p. Nat. City Bank of N.Y., 1945-60. v.p. operations, 1960-61, exec. v.p., 1961-69; partner Clark, Dodge & Co., Inc., N.Y.C., 1969—. Mem. finance com. Girl Scouts Am. Republican. Presbyn. Clubs: Apawamis (Rye, N.Y.); Farmington Country (Charlottesville, Va.); Bond, University, Racquet and Tennis (N.Y.C.). Home: 907 Park Av New York City NY 10028 Office: 140 Broadway New York City NY 10005

COOK, BARBARA, actress; b. Atlanta, Oct. 25, 1927; d. Charles Bunyan and Nell (Harwell) Cook; m. David LeGrant, Mar. 9, 1952; 1 son, Adam Maximillian Actress, 1944—; plays include Flahooley, 1951, Oklahoma (revival), 1953, Carousel (revival), 1954, 57, Plain and Fancy, 1955, Candide, 1956, The Music Man, 1957, The King and I (revival), 1960, Gay Life, 1961, She Loves Me, 1963, Something More. 1964, Little Murders, 1967; star role in Any Wednesday, 1965. Recipient Tony award, 1957. Address: care William Morris Agy 1740 Broadway New York City NY 10019

COOK, CECIL NEWTON, lawyer; b. Lufkin, Tex., Feb. 14, 1905; s. William Newton and Mattie (Stanley) C.; LL.B., U. Tex., 1926; m. Donalda Maxine Lamb, Jan. 7, 1944; children—James Randolph, Richard Nash. Admitted to Tex. bar, 1926; practice in Fort Worth, 1926-34, Houston, 1934—; asst. dist. atty., 1926; asso. Coates & Mastin, 1927-28; partner Phillips, Trammell, Chizum, Price & Estes, 1929-34, Cook & Walker, 1935, Kayser, Liddell, Benbow & Butler, 1936-40, Cook, Blake, McCormick & Dickson, 1941-44, Butler, Binion, Rice, Cook & Knapp, 1945—. Lectr., Southwestern Legal Found., Dallas, Am. Bar Assn. N.Y.C. Dir. Gulf States United Telephone Co., Tyler, Tex.; spl. asst. atty. gen. Tex., 1954; pres. Houston Law Rev., 1970—. Pres. bd. Houston Civic Music Assn., 1951. Adv. trustee Houston Bapt. Coll.; trustee Edna Gladney Home, Fort Worth, South Tex. Jr. Coll., S. Tex. Coll. Law. Fellow Am. Bar Found., Tex. Bar Found.; mem. Am., Internat., Tex. (chmn. mineral sect.), Houston (past pres.) bar assns., Am. Law Inst., Selden Soc., Phi

Kappa Psi, Phi Delta Phi. Baptist (deacon). Clubs: Houston Country, Houston Yacht, Petroleum, Ramada (Houston). Home: 2212 Looscan Lane Houston TX 77019 Office: Esperson Bldg Houston TX 77002

COOK, CHARLES DAVENPORT, educator, pediatrician; b. Mpls., Nov. 30, 1919; s. Henry W. and Ellen (Davenport) C.; A.B., Princeton, 1941; M.D., Harvard, 1944; M.A. (hon.), Yale, 1964; m. Sheila Gamble, Mar. 10, 1945; children—Andrew D., Sheila D., Peter G., Charles Davenport II. Intern U. Minn. Hosp., 1944-45; fellow Mayo Clinic, 1945-46; resident Mass. Gen. Hosp., 1948-49; chief resident Children's Hosp., Boston, 1949-51; asso. clin. prof. pediatrics Harvard Med. Sch., 1963-64; prof., chmn. dept. pediatrics Yale Sch. Medicine, 1964. Served with M.C., AUS, 1945-47. Mem. Am. Pediatric Soc. (sec., treas. 1964—). Research pulmonary physiology, fetal and neonatal physiology. Home: 176 Armory St New Haven, CT 06511.

COOK, CHARLES DAVID, lawyer; b. Saginaw, Mich., Apr. 5, 1924; s. Charles Christian and Grace (Robins) C.; A.B., U. Mich., 1947; LL.B., Columbia, 1950, M.A. in Internat. Affairs, 1950; m. Robette Ringland, Oct. 30, 1947; children—Ian Ainsworth, Kendra. Asso. dir. Inst. World Affairs seminar, Twin Lakes, Conn., summer 1950; admitted to N.Y. bar, 1951, D.C. bar, 1965, Fed. Dist. Ct. So. N.Y., 1965, Supreme Ct. U.S., 1967; mem. U.S. Mission to UN, 1950-62, dep. counselor, chief polit. sect., 1956-60, counselor, 1960-62; partner firm Barco, Cook, Patton & Blow, 1962; sr. counsel Gen. Tel & Electronics Internat., 1967—. Counselor U.S. delegations UN Gen. Assemblies, 1958-61; accompanied Ambassador Stevenson on Presdl. mission to S.A., 1961; mem. U.S. delegation Disarmament com., Geneva, Switzerland, 1962; adviser U.S. delegation WHO, Geneva, 1962; spl. cons. Pres. Nixon's Commn. for Observance of 25th Anniversary of UN; bd. dirs. Inst. World Affairs, Afro-Am. Center. Served to ensign USNR, 1943-46. Univ. seminar asso. Columbia, 1961—. Mem. Am. Bar Assn. (African law com. internat. and comp. law sect.), Assn. Bar City N.Y. (com. on lawyers role in search for peace), Am. Soc. Internat. Law (panel on internat. telecommunications policy), Internat. Law Assn., Am. Arbitration Assn. (past arbitrator), Nat. Planning Assn. (mem. nat. council). Club: Columbia University Faculty. Home: 1 Legget Rd Bronxville NY 10708 Office: 909 Third Av New York City NY 10022

COOK, CHARLES REGINALD, accountant, brewery exec.; b. Montreal, Que., Can., Jan. 21, 1919; s. Charles and Edith Mabel (Ironman) C.; Chartered Accountant, McGill U., 1947; student Exec. Devel. Inst., 1954-55; m. Anne Margaret Milton, June 22, 1946; children— Dorothy Louise, Barbara Isabel, Carol Elaine. With Johnson & Johnson, Ltd., Montreal, 1949-65, asst. treas.-controller, 1956-58, sec.-treas., 1958-62, v.p. finance, 1962-65, also dir.; comptroller Molson Breweries, Ltd., 1965—; v.p. finance and adminstrn. Molson Breweries Can. Ltd., 1968—; speaker various seminars, 1954—. Served with RCAF, 1941-45. Mem. Exec. Devel. Inst. Montreal (pres. 1959-60), Am. Mgmt. Assn., Financial Execs. Inst. (chpt. pres. 1968-69), Soc. Indsl. and Cost Accountants. Home: 70 Wicksteed Av Town of Mount Royal Quebec Canada Office: 1555 Notre Dame St E Montreal 24 Quebec Canada

COOK, CHARLES WILKERSON, shoe mfg. exec.; b. Nashville, Sept. 17, 1905; s. William B. and Molly (Wilkerson) C.; LL.B., Vanderbilt U., 1929; m. Virginia Jones, Sept. 6, 1930; children—Charles Wilkerson, William Compton. With Genesco, Inc. (formerly General Shoe Corp.), Nashville, 1931—, dir., 1944—, v.p., 1951—, head Republic div., 1951—. Chmn. campaign United Givers Fund, Nashville, 1955; bd. dirs. Middle Tenn. Heart Assn. Mem. Vanderbilt Alumni Assn. (pres.), Omicron Delta Kappa, Kappa Alpha. Methodist (mem. ofcl. bd.). Clubs: Bellemeade Country, Cumberland (Nashville); Union League (Chgo.). Home: 4409 Chickering Lane Nashville TN 37215 Office: 111 7th Av N Nashville TN 37206

COOK, CHAUNCEY WILLIAM WALLACE, food co. exec.; b. Hugo, Okla., June 22, 1909; s. Chauncey William and Minnie Malona (Cherry) C.; B.S., U. Tex., 1930; postgrad. Columbia, 1930-31; LL.D., C.W. Post Coll., L.I. U., 1967, Babson Inst. Bus. Adminstrn., 1967, Iona Coll., 1968; L.H.D., Pace Coll., 1969; D. Engring., Mich. Tech. U., 1969; m. Ethel Frances Crain, Dec. 27, 1934; children—David William, Frances Ann (Mrs. John A. Cole). Prodn. engr. Procter & Gamble Co., 1931-37, plant engr., 1937-42; chief engr. Gen. Foods Corp., 1942-44, div. mgr. mfg. and engring., 1944-46, div. prodn. mgr., 1946- 51, div. sales and advt. mgr., 1952-53, asst. div. gen. mgr., 1953-55, v.p. corp., gen. mgr. Maxwell House div., Hoboken, N.J., 1955-59, exec. v.p., 1959-62, dir. corp., 1960—, pres. Gen. Foods Corp., 1962-65, pres., chief exec. officer, 1965-66, chmn., chief exec. officer, 1966—; dir. Whirlpool Corp., Chase Manhattan Bank. Mem. exec. com. Business Council, 1968—; mem. N.Y. Gov.'s Steering Com. on Social Problems, 1968—, vice chmn., 1970—; chmn. food sub-council Nat. Indsl. Pollution Control Council, 1970—. Trustee Tuskegee Inst., Rockefeller U., Com. for Econ. Devel., Council of the Americas, The Conf. Bd. chmn., 1970—; bd. dirs. Council of Better Bus. Bureaus, Inc. Recipient Distinguished Engring. grad. award U. Tex., 1963; Distinguished Achievement award U. Tex. Ex-Students Assn. N.Y., 1963; Distinguished Alumnus award Ex-Students Assn. U. Tex., 1965. Mem. Grocery Mfrs. Am., C. of C. U.S., Advt. Council, Pan Am. Soc. U.S., Am.-Philippines Soc. (bd. govs.), Pi Sigma Epsilon (hon.), Tau Beta Pi, Beta Gamma Sigma, Eta Kappa Nu, Delta Chi. Clubs: University (pres. 1956-57) (Larchmont, N.Y.); Blind Brook (Port Chester, N.Y.); Links, Economic (N.Y.C.); Winged Foot Golf (Mamaroneck, N.Y.); Country, Headliners (Austin, Tex.). Home: 2 Larch Lane Larchmont NY 10538 Office: 250 North St White Plains NY 10602

COOK, CLARENCE JOSEPH, banker; b. Union Hill, N.J., Mar. 31, 1912; s. John Henry and Mary (Daly) C.; student Pace Coll., 1934; m. Marion McDonald, Apr. 9, 1941; children—Kathleen, Stephen, Patricia. Vice pres. Eastern Acceptance Corp., Newark, 1955-62, Interstate Ins. Co., Newark, 1955-62, Eastern Life Ins. Co., Newark, 1955-62; v.p. Motor Finance Co., Newark, 1955-62, dir., 1960-62; with First Nat. State Bank N.J., Newark, and predecessor, 1962—, sr. v.p., 1969—. Trustee Garden State Credit Bur., Essex County Automotive Trade Assn. Catholic. Elk. Office: 550 Broad St Newark NJ 07101

COOK, CLARENCE SHARP, educator; b. St. Louis Crossing, Ind., Aug. 18, 1918; s. Clarence C. and Musa Gladys (Sharp) C.; A.B., DePauw U., 1940; M.A. in Physics, Ind. U., 1942, Ph.D. in Physics, 1948; m. Marian Norma Waring, June 19, 1943; children—Sherma Louise, Wayne William. Asst. prof. physics Washington U., St. Louis, 1948-53; head nuclear radiation br. U.S. Naval Radiol. Def. Lab., San Francisco, 1953-60, head nucleonics div., 1960-62, physics cons. to sci. dir., 1962-65, head radiation physics div., 1965-69; lectr. U. Santa Clara (Cal.), 1969-70; prof. chmn. dept. physics U. Tex. at El Paso, 1970—. Chmn. Bd. Civil Service Engrs. for Scientists and Engrs., Pasadena, Cal., 1957-58. Bd. dirs. El Paso Radiation Center Found., 1971—. Served to capt. AUS, 1942-46. Fulbright research scholar Aarhus (Denmark) U., 1961-62. Fellow Am. Phys. Soc., Cal. Acad. Scis.; mem. Am. Assn. Physics Tchrs., Am. Geophys. Union, Meteroritical Soc., Health Physics Soc., Phi Beta Kappa, Sigma Xi. Author: Modern Atomic and Nuclear Physics, 1961; Structure of Atomic Nuclei, 1964. Contbg. author: Van Nostrand's Scientific Encyclopedia. Contbr. articles profl. jours. Home: Box 204 U Tex at El Paso El Paso TX 79968

COOK, CLAUDE TRABUE, educator; b. Portland, Ore., Apr. 10, 1913; s. Claude T. and Bertha M. (O'Neill) C.; A.B., Willamette U., 1934; M.S., U. Ore., 1953; Ed.D., Stanford U., 1957; m. Mabel Eastridge, Aug. 29, 1934; children—Garry M., Penelope Rae. Tchr., coach Ore. high schs., 1934-46; dir. health and phys. edn. Bend (Ore.) Pub. Schs., 1946-55; teaching asst. Stanford U., 1955-57; asst. prof. San Fernando Valley State Coll., 1957-59, asso. prof., 1959-62, prof., 1962—, chmn. dept. health scis., 1959—; cons. cancer epidemiology project U. So. Cal. Mem. Los Angeles Bd. Health Commrs., 1961-64, vice chmn., 1964; mem. Los Angeles County Pub. Health Commn., 1964-70, chmn., 1967-70; mem. commn. Los Angeles County Dept. Pub. Social Service, 1970—; dir. Los Angeles County Tuberculosis and Health Assn., 1963-69; mem. Los Angeles County Health Services Planning Com., 1968—. Travel fellow WHO, 1966-67. Fellow Am. Pub. Health Assn.; mem. Am. Sch. Health Assn., Ore. Assn. Health, Phys. Edn. and Recreation (pres. 1952-53). Republican. Episcopalian. Home: 9007 Etiwanda Av Northridge CA 91324

COOK, DAVID CHARLES III, pub. and editor; b. Elgin, Ill., June 11, 1912; s. David Charles, Jr., and Frances Lois (Kerr) C.; student Occidental Coll., 1930-32; Ph.B., U. Chgo., 1934; Litt.D., Judson Coll., 1965; m. Anna Mae Lawrence, Oct. 3, 1937; children—Margaret Anne, Martha L., Bruce L., Gregory D., Rebecca. Editor, David C. Cook Pub. Co. (founded by grandfather 1875), Elgin, Ill., 1934, pres. and editor-in-chief of its 35 publs., 1935—. Dir. youth study tour Cultural Travel Found., 1955; v.p. Elgin Council Chs., 1954, pres., 1956-57; governing bd. Elgin Community Chest. Pres. David C. Cook Found.; trustee Conf. Point Camp, Judson Bapt. Coll., Laubach Literacy. Mem. Phi Kappa Psi. Methodist (trustee). Author: Walk the High Places, 1964. Home: 32 River Bluff Rd Elgin IL 60120 Office: David C Cook Pub Co Elgin IL 60120

COOK, DAVY CLAY, ins. co. exec.; b. Hillsboro, Tex., Mar. 7, 1897; s. Phineas G. and Roxey (Downs) C.; student Culver-Stockton Coll., 1921; m. Estelle Paulsen, Oct. 20, 1924; children—Darlene Priscilla (Mrs. John D. Erwin), Margretta Jean (Mrs. Charles K. Burke). With Grain Dealers Mut. Ins. Co., 1922—, successively fieldman, exec. spl. agt. N.Y. and N.E., 1922- 47, western mgr., 1947-61, dir., 1953—, v.p., 1958-60, 1st v.p., 1960- 61, pres., 1961-65, chmn. exec. com., 1965-69, (chmn. bd. 1969—; pres., dir. Companion Ins. Co., 1962-65; chmn. bd., 1969; pres. Grain Dealers Mut. Agency, Inc., 1965; dir. Iowa Kemper Mut. Ins. Co. Mem. various nat. mut. and co. agy. orgns. Republican. Methodist. Mason (32, Shriner). Clubs: Rotary, Columbia. Home: 7831 Hoover Rd Indianapolis IN 46260 Office: 1752 N Meridian St Indianapolis IN 46202

COOK, DON, fgn. corr.; b. Bridgeport, Conn., Aug. 8, 1920; s. Paul J. and Nelle Brown (Reed) C.; student pub. schs., Abington, Pa.; m. Cherry Mitchell, Oct. 31, 1943; children—Christopher, Jenifer, Adrienne, Deborah, Caron, Danielle, and Dominique. With St. Petersburg (Fla.) Times, 1938- 40, Jenkintown (Pa.) Times-Chronicle, 1940-41; with Phila. bur., Trans-radio Press Service, 1941, Washington bur., 1941-43; with N.Y. Herald Tribune, Washington, 1943-45, London, 1945-49, corr., West Germany, 1949-52, roving European corr., Paris, 1952-55, chief London bur., 1956-60, chief European corr., Paris, 1960-65; Paris corr. Los Angeles Times, since 1965—. Recipient William the Silent award for journalism, 1956; English Speaking Union award for better understanding, 1957. Mem. Assn. Am. Corr. in London (p.p.), Authors Guild, Anglo- American Press Assn. of Paris, Inst. for Strategic Studies, London. Clubs: Garrick, Lansdowne (London). Author: Floodtide in Europe, 1965. Contbr. popular mags. Office: Los Angeles Times 73 Av des Champs-Elysees Paris VIII France

COOK, DONALD C., corp. pres.; b. Escanaba, Mich.; Apr. 14, 1909; s. Nelson and Edith (Bryant) C.; A.B., U. of Mich., 1932, M.B.A., 1935; J.D., George Washington U., 1939, LL.M., 1940; m. Winnifred V. Carlsen, Dec. 4, 1943; 1 son, Nicholas Bryant. Financial examiner, registration div., SEC, 1935-36, utilities analyst, pub. utilities div., 1937-42, asst. dir., 1943-45; spl. counsel U.S. Ho. of Reps. Com. Naval Affairs, 1943-45; exec. asst. to atty. gen. of U.S., 1945-46; dir. Office of Alien Property, 1946-47; partner Cook and Berger, law offices, 1947-49; commr. SEC, 1949-53, vice chmn., 1950-52, chmn., 1952-53; chief counsel, Preparedness Investigating Subcom., Senate Armed Services Com., 1950-52; with Am. Electric Power Service Corp., 1953—, exec. v.p., 1954-61, pres., 1961—, dir., mem. exec. com. Am. Electric Power Co., 1960—; pres., dir., chief exec. subsidiaries Appalachian Power Co., Ind. & Mich. Electric Co., Ky. Power Co., Kingsport Power Co., Ohio Power Co., Wheeling Electric Co., Central Appalachian Coal Co., Franklin Real Estate Co., Ind. Franklin Realty, Inc., Cardinal Operating Co. South Bend Mfg. Co., Twin Branch Railroad Company, Va. Power Co., Am. Elec. Power Service Corp., Beech Bottom Power Co., Inc., Captina Operating Co., Central Coal Co., Central Ohio Coal Co., Central Operating Co., Kanawha Valley Power Co., 1961—. Trustee, Center Advanced Study Behavioral Scis., Stanford, Cal. Mem. bus. leadership adv. council Office Econ. Opportunity. C.P.A., Md., 1941. Mem. Am., Mich. bar assns., Am. Accounting Assn., Am. Inst. C.P.A.'s, Am. Judicature Soc., Theta Xi, Phi Delta Phi. Democrat. Episcopalian (vestryman). Clubs: University, Harbor View Mining, U. of Michigan, Economic (N.Y.C.); Nat. Capital Democratic, Metropolitan, George Washington U. (Washington); U. of Mich. Presidents. Author articles on legal, financial and accounting subjects. Home: 988 Fifth Av New York City, NY 10021. Office: 2 Broadway New York City NY 10004

COOK, DONALD JACK, educator, chemist; b. Rock Island, Ill., Feb. 12, 1915; s. Herbert Edgar and Daisy (Strupp) C.; A.B., Augustana (Ill.) Coll., 1937; M.A., U. Ill., 1938; Ph.D., Ind. U., 1944; m. Marion McCauley, Sept. 9, 1939; children—Christine Margaret, Hope Ann. With Am. Container Corp., Rock Island, 1939-40; mem faculty Augustana Coll., 1940-41; with Tex. Co., 1941-42, Lubrizol Corp., 1944-45; mem. faculty DePauw U., 1945—, prof. chemistry, 1954—, head dept., 1964—; with div. sci. personnel and edn. NSF, 1961-62; spl. research nitrogen heterocyclics. Purdue U, postdoctoral fellow, 1952-53. Mem. Am. Chem. Soc. Republican. Methodist. Rotarian, Mason. Contbr. profl. jours. Home: 625 E Washington St Greencastle, IN 46135.

COOK, DONALD JEAN, educator; b. Astoria, Ore., Feb. 14, 1920; s. Arthur E. and Ida (Josephson) C.; B.S. in Mining Engring., U. Alaska, 1947, M.E., 1952; M.S., Pa. State U., 1958, Ph.D., 1961; m. Cora Jackinsky, Oct. 26, 1944; children—Wayne, Kenneth, Galen, Donald. Dredge engr. U.S. Smelting Refining and Mining Co., Fairbanks, Alaska, 1947-50; assayer engr. Alaska State Coll., 1950-52; instr. U. Alaska, 1952-54, asst. prof., 1959-61, asso. prof., 1961-64, prof., head dept. mineral engring., 1964—; mining engr. U.S. Smelting Refining and Mining Co., Fairbanks, 1954-57. Vis. prof. Cheng Kung U., Taiwan China, 1971. Served with inf. AUS, 1943-46. Decorated Purple Heart, Combat Inf. Badge; grantee NSF, 1960; U.S. Bur. Mines research grant. Registered mining engr., Alaska. Mem. Am. Inst. Mining and Metall. Engrs., Nat. Soc. Profl. Engrs., Alaska Miners Assn., Alpha Sigma Nu (hon.). Author: (with others) Placer Mining in Alaska, I.C. 1926; Heavy Minerals in Alaska Beach Band Deposits; Magnetic Susceptibility of Principal Minerals of Light Metal Group. Home: Box 5093 College AK 99701

COOK, EARL FERGUSON, univ. dean; b. Belingham, Wash., May 24, 1920; s. Earl Ferguson and Helen (Royer) C.; B.S. in Mining Engring., U. Wash., 1943, M.S. in Geology, 1947, Ph.D. in Geology, 1954; student U. Paris (France), 1945- 46, U. Geneva (Switzerland), 1948-49; m. Jean E. Wiltse, June 21, 1947 (div. 1964.); children—Jeanette, Randall, Cynthia. Instr. geology U. Wash., 1947-48, Stanford, 1948; geologist Geophoto Services, Denver, 1949-51; mem. faculty U. Ida., 1951-64, dean Coll. Mines, prof. geology, 1957-64, also dir. Ida. Bur. Mines, 1957-64; now prof. geology, asso. dean coll. geoscience Tex. A. and M. U., College Station, 1966—. Exec. sec. div. earth scis. Nat. Acad. Scis.-NRC, Washington, 1964—; geologist Gulf Oil Corp., summers 1955, 56. Served with AUS, 1943-46: ETO. Decorated Purple Heart; recipient Award of Merit, Austrian Province of Burgenland, 1966. Mem. Geol. Soc. Am., Am. Inst. Mining, Metall. and Petroleum Engrs., Am. Assn. Petroleum Geologists, Soc. Econ. Geologists, Am. Geophys. Union, Am. Inst. Profl. Geologists, N.W. Sci. Assn. Address: Tex A and M Univ Coll Geosci College Station TX 77840

COOK, EDMOND MAUREL, lawyer; b. Ark., Aug. 14, 1897; s. Reuel B. and Eleanor (Spelletich) C.; LL.B., U. of Ia., 1922; m. Grace Webber Murphy; children—John W., Carol. Gen. practice law as employee and partner Cook & Balluff, Davenport, Ia., 1922-42, counsel for firm and its successor, 1942—; former v.p. and gen. counsel Deere & Co., Moline, Ill.; Served as seaman 2d class, USN, World War I. Mem. Order of Coif. Clubs: Union League (Chgo.); Rock Island (Ill.) Arsenal Golf. Home: 1313 9th St Moline IL 61265 Office: PO Box 357 Moline IL 61265

COOK, EDWARD NOBLE, former physician; b. St. Paul, Aug. 21, 1905; s. Edward and Jessie Gertrude (Noble) C.; B.A., U. Minn., 1926, B.S., 1927, B. Medicine, 1928, M.D., 1929, M.S. in Urology, 1935; m. Jean Elizabeth Moore, June 14, 1934; children—Margaret (Mrs. C.M. Berndt, Jr.), Edward Noble, Nancy. Intern, Kings County Hosp., Bklyn., 1929-30; mem. staff Mayo Found., U. Minn., 1930—, prof. urology, 1958—; staff Mayo Clinic, 1935-70, cons. urology, 1935-70; cons. urology Meth., St. Mary's hosps.; spl. research infections urinary tract, transurethral surgery; ret., 1970. Served as lt. MC., USN, 1939-47. Mem. Am. Urol. Assn., A.M.A. (sec. sect. urology 1946-49), chmn. sec. 1949-50), Societe Internationale de Chirugie, Minn. Med. Assn., Olmsted County Med. Soc., Sigma Xi, Delta Upsilon, Alpha Kappa Kappa. Clubs: Country, University. Contbr. profl. jours. Home: Crocus Hill Salem Rd Rochester MN 55901

COOK, EDWARD WILLINGHAM, bldg. products, cotton and grain exec.; b. Memphis, June 19, 1922; s. Everett Richard and Phoebe (Willingham) C.; grad. Hotchkiss Sch., 1940; A.B., Yale, 1944; m. Nancy Barber, Apr. 29, 1947; children—Edward Willingham, Everett Richard II, Barbara Moore. Pres., Cook & Co., Inc., Memphis, N.Y., Chgo., Kansas City, Los Angeles, Phoenix, Fresno, Cal., Tokyo, Osaka, Japan, Hong Kong, Rotterdam, Paris, 1956—; Cook y Cia. de Mexico, S.A., 1952; dir. First Nat. Bank of Memphis, Frisco R.R., St. Louis, Life and Casualty Ins. Co., Tenn. Mem. Cotton Adv. Com., 1964-68. Bd. dirs. St. Mary's Sch. Served to maj. USAAF, 1943- 45; MTO. Decorated D.F.C., Bronze Star, Air medal with six oak leaf clusters. Mem. So. Cotton Assn. (past pres.), Cotton Council Am. (dir. 1962-65), Cotton Council Internat. (dir. 1964-65), Am. Cotton Shippers Assn., Memphis C. of C. (past dir.), English Speaking Union. Democrat. Episcopalian. Clubs: Memphis Country, Memphis Hunt and Polo; Links (N.Y.C.); Boston (New Orleans). Home: 3155 Cotton Plant Rd Germantown, TN 38038. Office: 131 Gayoso St Memphis TN 38101

COOK, ELTON STRAUS, chemist; b. Oberlin, O., Dec. 24, 1909; s. Edward Monroe and Bertha (Straus) C.; B.A. summa cum laude, Oberlin Coll., 1930; Ph.D., Yale, 1933, postdoctoral fellow chemistry, 1933-34; m. Elizabeth Luck, June 1, 1935; children—Edward Mark, David Charles. Head dept. organic prodn. Wm. S. Merrell Co., Cin., 1934-37; research prof., head div. chemistry and biochemistry St. Thomas Inst. (formerly Institutum Divi Thomae), Cin., 1937—, dean research, 1945- -, v.p., dir., 1955-70, mem., 1970—; formerly dir. Internat. Hormones, Inc., Rookwood Pottery; sec. sci. adv. council Sperti Drug Products Corp., 1966—. Del. 3d, 4th, 5th, 6th, 7th, 8th, 9th Internat. Cancer congresses; mem. Cin. Mayor's Com. Atomic Engergy, 1948. Dir. Mariemont Town Meeting, 1955-58. Alumni bd. Oberlin Coll., 1958-59. Recipient diploma of honor 1st Pan Am. Cancer Cytology Congress, 1957; Ann. Chemist award Cin. sect. Am. Chem. Soc., 1964. Fellow Am. Inst. Chemists (dist. dir. hon. mem. 1969), A.A.A.S., Chem. Soc. London; mem. Am. Chem. Soc. (chmn. Cin. 1958), Am. Pharm. Assn., Biochem. Soc. Gt. Britain, History Sci. Soc., Soc. Exptl. Biology and Medicine, Am. Assn. Cancer Research, N.Y. Acad. Sci., Phi Beta Kappa, Sigma Xi (v.p. Cin. 1955-57). Contbr. numerous publs. to tech. jours. Home: 6503 Park Lane Mariemont Cincinnati OH 45227 Office: 1842 Madison Rd Cincinnati OH 45206

COOK, EVERETT RICHARD, merchant, exporter; b. Indpls., Dec. 13, 1894; s. Jesse Everett and Ollie Belle (Shonacker) C.; ed. Memphis public schs.; LL.D. D. (hon.), Southwestern at Memphis, 1954; m. Phoebe Willingham, June 4, 1919; children—Edward (Willingham), Phoebe (Mrs. John L. Welsch, Jr.). Organized own cotton bus., Marianna, Ark., 1916; pres. Cook and Co., Inc., raw cotton, Memphis; chmn. bd. Cook Industries, Inc., Paris, Rotterdam, Tokyo, Osaka, Hong Kong, Mexico City, 1969—; chmn. bd. Cotton Belt Ins. Co., E.L. Bruce & Co., Terminix Robbins Flooring, Royal Oak Charcoal, Memphis, Marble Decor, Los Angeles, Riverside Industries, Marks, Miss.; dir. Eastern Air Lines, Plough Inc. Adviser wartime econ. affairs Dept. State, 1945, cons., 1945-46; spl. asst. war food adminstr. and sec. agr.; nat. chmn. Agrl. War Bd., 1944-45. Mem. U.S. mission to negotiate Peruvian cotton purchase, 1942; v.p. CCC, 1942; mem. Tenn. Constl. Com., 1953, Rubber Producing Facilities Disposal Commn., 1953. Chmn. Cook Found., Memphis, 1954—; bd. dirs. Falcon Found., US-Air Force Academy, 1966; trustee Air Force Hist. Found. Served as capt., pilot comdg. officer 91st Aero Squadron Army Air Service, France, 1918- 19, col., A.A.F., 1942-44; dep. chief staff, 8th, 12th Air Forces, U.K., N. Africa and Italy, 1942-43; Northwest African Air Force, 1943; U.S. Strategic Air Force, E.T.O., 1944; brig. gen., Air Force Reserve, 1948-53, ret.; mem. Res. Forces Policy Bd. for Dept. of Defense, 1951-52. Decorated D.S.C., Legion of Merit, Silver Star (U.S.); Croix de Guerre palm; Legion of Honor (France); Master of Free Enterprise award Jr. Achievement, 1968. Mem. Am. Cotton Shippers Assn. (pres. 1949), New York Cotton Exchange, New Orleans Cotton Exchange, Memphis Cotton Exchange (pres. 1931) Cotton Council Internat. (pres. 1957-58), Memphis Cotton Carnival Assn. (pres. 1931), So. Cotton Shippers Assn. (pres. 1931-32), Independent. Episcopalian. Clubs: Memphis Country, Memphis Hunt and Polo (Memphis); Metropolitan (Washington); Boston (New Orleans). Home: 232 S Highland St Memphis TN 38111 Office: 131 Gayoso Av Memphis TN 38103

COOK, FREDERICK BISHOP, fgn. service officer; b. Holcomb, Kan., Aug. 28, 1913; s. George H. and Mary A. (Bishop) C.; student George Washington U., 1930-31, 33-34, Wilson Tchrs. Coll., 1932-33, Am. U., 1942-47, Salmon P. Chase Coll. Law, 1948-49; m. Myrtle M. Carr, June 15, 1947; 1 son, Frederick Bishop. With U.S. Govt., 1936-54; joined U.S. Fgn. Service, 1955; assigned New Delhi, India, 1955-56, Amman, Jordan, 1956-60, Manila, Philippines, 1960-65; fgn. service insp., 1965-67; counselor of embassy, Djakarta, Indonesia, 1967—. Served with USNR, 1944-46. Recipient Meritorious Honor award State Dept., 1965, Superior Honor award, 1970. Mem. Am. Fgn. Service Assn. Clubs: Djakarta Golf; Lakewood Country (St. Petersburg, Fla.). Address: Am embassy APO San Francisco CA 96356

COOK, FRED JAMES, journalist, author; b. Point Pleasant, N.J., Mar. 8, 1911; s. Frederick P. and Huldah (Compton) C.; Litt.B., Rutgers U., 1932; m. Julia Barbara Simpson, June 5, 1936; children—Frederick P. II, Barbara J. (Mrs. Michael F. Gallagher). Reporter, Asbury Park Press (N.J.), 1933-36, desk man, city editor, 1938-44; editor N.J. Courier, Toms River, 1936-37; rewriteman, feature writer N.Y. World Telegram and Sun, 1944-59; free-lance writer, 1959—. Recipient Page One award N.Y. Newspaper Guild, 1958, 59, 60; Sidney Hillman Found. award, 1960. Mem. Authors League Am., Am. Acad. Polit. and Soc. Scis., Internat. Platform Assn. Author of numerous books including: The FBI Nobody Knows, 1964; The Corrupted Land, 1966; The Secret Rulers, 1966; The Plot Against the Patient, 1967; What So Proudly We Hailed, 1968; The Nightmare Decade, The Era of Senator Joe McCarthy, 1971. Home: 722 Fernmere Av Interlaken NJ 07712

COOK, FRED S., educator; b. Lima, O., July 17, 1920; s. J. Fred and Ruth (Greenawalt) C.; student Bluffton Coll., 1938-41; B.Sc., Ohio No. U., 1946; M.A., U. Mich., 1948, Ph.D., 1953; m. Betty Jean Samsal, Apr. 6, 1941; children—Linda Jean (Mrs. Russell Hickman), Marcia Diane. Instr. bus. adminstrn. Ohio No. U., 1947-48; teaching fellow, lectr. edn. U. Mich., 1948-52, vis. prof., summers 1953-54; head bus. edn. dept. Coe Coll., Cedar Rapids, Ia., 1952-55; asst. prof. edn. in charge bus. and audio-visual edn. Stanford, 1955-59; asso. prof. bus. and distbn. edn. Wayne State U., 1960-63, prof., 1963—, chmn. dept., 1960-71, dir. div. vocational and applied arts edn., 1971—; dir. research and edn. Nat. Secs. Assn. Internat., 1960-69; lectr. Indsl. Edn. Inst. Chmn. bd. govs. Fund Advancement Bus. Edn., 1959-60; bd. govs. Research and Devel. in Bus. Edn., 1st v.p., 1967—. Served as sgt. AUS, 1944-45. Mem. Cal. Bus. Edn. Assn. (state pres. 1959-60), Nat. Office Mgmt. Assn. (nat. dir. 1959, past chpt. pres.), North Central Bus. Edn. Assn. (2d v.p. 1964-65), Delta Pi Epsilon. Sr. Author: Gregg Junior High Typing, 2d edit., 1965; (with Lenore S. Forti) Professional Secretary's Handbook, 1971. Editor Secretarial Study Guide, 2d edit., 1970; Secretaries on the Spot, 2d edit., 1967; Secretarial Techniques Manual, 1963; Contbr. articles to profl. jours. Home: 1460 Fairholme St Grosse Pointe Woods MI 48236 Office: Coll Education Wayne State Univ Detroit MI 48202

COOK, GEORGE ALVIN, banker; b. El Paso, Tex., Sept. 24, 1920; s. George Alvin and Inez (Lindsey) C.; student Ind. U. Savs. and Loan Grad. Sch., 1955-57; m. Emma A. Bjornson, Apr. 11, 1947; children—George III, Charles, Janice. Tax assessor Hawaii State Govt., 1938-50; loan officer 1st Fed. Savs. and Loan Assn. Hawaii, Honolulu, 1950-67, pres., mng. officer, 1967—; v.p., dir. Honolulu Model Cities Devel. Corp., 1968—, Hawaii Council for Housing Devel. Corp., 1968—; instr. real estate finance U. Hawaii small bus. edn. program, 1966—; dir. Hawaii Bus. Devel. Corp. Bd. dirs. Hawaii Found. Lupus Research, v.p., 1970—. Mem. U.S. (dir. 1967-68, Hawaii (pres. 1964) savs. and loan leagues, Soc. Real Estate Appraisers (pres. Hawaii chpt. 1961), Hawaiian Malacological Soc. (dir. 1971—), Navy League Hawaii. Clubs: Rotary, Outrigger Canoe (Honolulu). Home: 1120 Makaiwa St Honolulu HI 96816 Office: 851 Fort St Mall Honolulu HI 96813

COOK, GEORGE BRASH, life ins. co. exec.; b. Beatrice, Neb., July 20, 1910; s. Daniel W. and Sibbie (Thacker) C.; grad. Wentworth Mil. Acad., Lexington, Mo., 1927, Babson Inst., 1931; student U. Neb., 1927-30; m. Margaret Colman, Oct. 1, 1931; children—Daniel W. III, G. Bradford. With Bankers Life Ins. Co., Lincoln, Neb., 1931—, beginning as clk., successively staff investment dept., mgr. bond dept., investment v.p., exec. v.p. and financial officer, 1931- 58, trustee, 1941—, pres., 1958-69, chmn., chief exec. officer, 1969—; dir. Pickrell State Bank (Neb.), Wymore Nat. Bank (Neb.), Beatrice Nat. Bank, Lincoln Tel. & Tel. Co., Keebler Co., Chgo., Phila. Suburban Corp., Bryn Mawr, Pa., Beatrice State Co. (Neb.), Wymore, Inc., Nat. Health Enterprises, Inc., Milw., Financial Corp. of Ariz., Phoenix, Island Gem Enterprises, Ltd. St. Maarten, Netherlands Antilles, Taunus N.V., St. Maarten. Past pres., bd. dirs. Lincoln Indsl. Devel. Corp.; pres. Lincoln Indsl. Park Mgmt. Bd.; bd. dirs., chmn. bd. U. Neb. Found.; trustee Neb. Ind. Coll. Found. Served to lt. USNR, 1943-45. Recipient Distinguished Service award, Neb. Builder award U. Neb. Mem. Lincoln C. of C. (dir.), U. Neb. Alumni Assn. (past pres.), Phi Kappa Psi. Republican. Presbyn. Mason (32, Shriner, Jester). Clubs: Lincoln University, Lincoln Country. Home: 3070 Sheridan Blvd Lincoln NB 68502 Office: Bankers Life Ins Co of Neb Cotner and O Sts Lincoln NB 68501

COOK, GEORGE ROY, utility co. exec.; b. Springfield, Ill., Sept. 16, 1907; s. William Roy and Marie (Ruch) C.; B.S., U. Ill., 1929. With Central Ill. Pub. Service Co., Springfield, 1929—, asst. treas., 1951-58, treas., asst. sec., 1958-61, v.p., sec., 1961—. Home: 527 E Capitol Av Springfield IL 62701 Office: 607 E Adams St Springfield IL 62701

COOK, GEORGE THOMAS, newspaper exec.; b. Indpls., Apr. 12, 1921; s. James Merkle and Mary (Harp) C.; A.B. in Journalism, U. Ala., 1949; m. Mary Frances Berry, May 3, 1952; children—Frances Ellen, Christopher Alan. Reporter, Birmingham (Ala.) Post-Herald, 1949-62, state editor, 1962-65, city editor, 1965- 66, mng. editor, 1966—. Served to 1st lt., inf., Military Police, Transp. Corps, AUS, 1940-46. Methodist. Home: 1905 Helen Circle Birmingham AL 35226 Office: 2200 4th Ave Birmingham AL 35202

COOK, GLADYS EMERSON, artist; b. Haverhill, Mass.; d. George Ward and Hattie Burson (Emerson) Cook; B.S., Skidmore Coll., 1921; M.S., U. Wis., 1923; studied Art Students League, also with Anthony Thieme. Exhibited one-man shows Heads and Horns Museum, Bronx Zool. Park, 1941, Soc. of Illustrators, 1944; work exhibited at Black, Starr and Gorham, Brentano's, Scribner's Harlow and Co., Kennedy and Co., Grand Central Art Gallery; works in many pvt. collections; drawings have appeared in New York Times, Boston Herald, Christian Sci. Monitor, Boston Transcript; ten originals reproduced in Ringling Brothers circus programs, 1943; lectr. on drawing the cat Met. Mus., 1943; illustrator of animal calendars for Am. Soc. Prevention Cruelty to Animals, 1943-44, Christmas cards for Am. Artist Group, 1940—; illustrator for motion pictures The Yearling and Bob, Son of Battle; dog illustrations for Internat. Corr. Schs.; draws cats for Carter's Ink advt., on TV advt. for Puss in Boots Cat Food; one-man exhibit of horse paintings at Nat. Horse Show, Madison Square Garden, 1954, pastel drawings champion dogs Grand Central Art Gallery. Lithographs in permanent collections Met. Mus., Congl. Library, Cin. Mus. Chosen Artist of Year, Albany Print Club. Fellow Royal Soc. Arts Eng.; mem. Soc. Illustrators, Soc. Am. Etchers, Am. Assn. U. Women, English-Speaking Union, U. Wis. Alumni, Panhellenic Group, Asia House Artists Guild, Bus. and Profl. Women's Club, Mu Phi Epsilon. Club: Skidmore College. Illustrator several cat and dog books, publs. including The Siamese Cat; Cat Stories (James Mason); wrote and illustrated cat book Personal Acquaintances; Big Book of Cats; Portfolio of Cats; How to Draw Cats; Drawing Horses; Circus Clowns on Parade; How to Draw Dogs; Portfolio of Dogs; My Dog; Champion Dogs of the World; All Breeds-All Champions; Drawing Wild Life; drawings Pres. Nixon's 3 dogs. Home: Hotel Wolcott 4 W 31st St New York City NY 10001 Studio: 32 Union Sq New York City NY 10027 ☆

COOK, HAROLD HUNTTING, investment banker; b. N.Y., 1903; s. Ferdinand H. and Mary W. (Aldrich) C.; A.B., Williams Coll., 1926; m. Alice Doyle, Oct. 2, 1928 (div.); children—Joan M., Anne H. (now Mrs. Forbes Durey); m. 2d, Mrs. Catherine Johnson Baehr, Dec. 15, 1961; stepchildren—John J. Baehr, Jr., Carlo Baehr, William Baehr. With Spencer Trask & Co., N.Y.C., 1926-33, 41-68, gen. partner, 1944-68, sr. v.p. Spencer Trask & Co., Inc., 1968-69, cons., 1969—; utility specialist C.W. Young & Co., 1933-35; mgr. bond dept. Reynolds & Co., 1935-37; sec. Reynolds Metals Co., 1937-41. Gov. of N.Y. Stock Exchange, 1962-68. Chmn. alumni fund Williams Coll., 1945-47, mem. alumni exec. com., 1945-47; pres. bd. trustees Collegiate Sch., N.Y.C., 1949-52, Kimberley Sch., Montclair, N.J., 1949-52. Mem. Nat. Assn. Securities Dealers (gov. 1956-59), Investment Bankers Assn. (gov. 1955-58), Pilgrims Soc., Soc. Colonial Wars, Newcomen Soc., S.R. Clubs: Bond of N.Y. (pres. 1958-59); Essex County Country; Downtown Assn.; U.S. Seniors Golf Assn.; Paradise Valley Country. Home: 7625 E Orange Blossom Lane Scottsdale AZ 85252 Office: 60 Broad St New York City NY 10004

COOK, HOWARD, trust co. exec.; b. Mexico, Mo., Nov. 30, 1889; s. Sam B. and Olivia (Hord) C.; student pub. schs.; m. Gertrude Shuman, June 4, 1921; children—Sam B., Howard W. With Central Mo. Trust Co., Jefferson City, 1906—, 2d asst. treas., 1916, 1st asst. treas., 1919, dir., 1919, v.p., 1921, pres., 1931-55, chmn. bd., 1955—. Served to capt. inf., U.S. Army, 1917-18. Home: 1208 Elmarine Av Jefferson City MO Office: Madison and High Sts Jefferson City MO 65101

COOK, HOWARD ALEXANDER, social relations adminstr.; b. New Rochelle, N.Y., Apr. 4, 1915; s. Howard B. and Blanche (Gibbs) C.; B.S., Harvard, 1937; M.A. in Internat. Relations, Stanford, 1947; m. Diana Loring Pattison, Jan. 14, 1942 (div. 1967); children—Anthony Pattison, Lee Winship, Timothy Gibbs, Jennifer Loring, Jonathan Alexander; m. 2d, Diane G.H. Bissell, Sept. 1967. Asst., head financial dept. Haskins & Sells, C.P.A.'s N.Y.C., 1937-40; asst. dir. Cleve. Council on World Affairs, 1946-47; asst. dir. to dir. World Affairs Council of No. Cal., San Francisco, 1948-52; chief pub. services div. Dept. State, Washington, 1952-55; pres. International House, N.Y.C., 1955—. Pres. Nat. Assn. Fgn. Students Advisers, 1962-63; organizer, co-chmn. 1st World Conf. Internat. Houses and Centers, Paris, France, 1961; mem. Youth Activities Com. White House Conf. on Internat. Cooperation. Chmn. exec. Com. chmn. interim bd. of dirs. incorporator English in Action, Inc. Mem. bd. dirs. Morningside Heights, Inc., Manhattanville Community Centers, Inc. Served from 2d lt. to maj., F.A., AUS, 1941-45. Mem. Council Fgn. Relations, Fgn. Policy Assn., Nat. Assn. Fgn. Students Affairs, Episcopalian. Clubs: Harvard (N.Y.C.); Faculty (Columbia); Rotary (1st pres., charter mem. Upper Manhattan). Home: 100 LaSalle St New York City NY 10027 Office: 500 Riverside Dr New York City NY 10027

COOK, HOWARD CARL, lawyer, state senator; b. Toledo, Feb. 20, 1918; s. Henry D. and Caroline (Ackerman) C.; B.A., Wittenberg Coll., 1939; LL.B., Harvard, 1942, J.D., 1969; m. Elizabeth M. Ruch, Nov. 13, 1943; children-Susan E., Howard Carl. Admitted to Ohio bar, 1942, since practiced in Toledo; mem. firm Cline, Bischoff and Cook, 1946—; civil service commnr., Toledo, 1948-52, vice mayor, 1952-53, councilman, 1952-53, 59-67; mem. Ohio Senate, 1967—. Chmn. bd., sec., gen. counsel Progress Nat. Bank, Toledo; dir. Nat. Cement Products Co., Sanders Tool & Prodn. Co., Toledo. Pres. trustees Riverside Hosp., 1961-67. Served with USNR, 1942- 45. Named One of Ten Outstanding Men of Year, Jr. C. of C., 1950-53. Mem. Am., Ohio, Toledo bar assns., Amvets, Am. Legion, Phi Gamma Delta, Tau Kappa Alpha, Theta Alpha Phi. Home: 3818 Beechway Blvd Toledo OH 43614 Office: Security Bldg Toledo OH 43604

COOK, HOWARD NORTON, artist; b. Springfield, Mass., July 16, 1901; s. Frank Chester and Annie (Norton) C.; studied Art Students League, N.Y.C., 1919-21; m. Barbara Latham, May 27, 1927. Commd. to do war industry paintings Office Emergency Adminstrn., Norfolk, Va., 1942; guest prof. art, U. Tex., 1942-43, U. N.M., summer, 1947, U. Cal., 1948; guest instr. Colo. Springs Fine Arts Center, 1949; tchr. painting Mpls. Sch. Art, 1945, guest artist, 1950; leader war art unit C.E., U.S. Army, PTO, 1943; war artist corr. Collier's mag., 1943-44; guest artist Scripps Coll., 1951, Washington U., St. Louis, 1954-55, Highlands (N.M.) U., summer 1957, 60; artist-in-residence Roswell (NM.) Mus. and Art Center, 1967-68. Exhbn. war paintings, watercolors, Rehn Galleries, 1945, oil paintings of N.M., winter 1949; paintings of N.Y., Alexandre Rabow Galleries, San Francisco, 1955; paintings of the City, Grand Central Moderns, N.Y.C., 1956, Grand Central Moderns, Collages exhbn., 1960, 64, Phila. Art Alliance, exhbn. collages, 1961, paintings, collages Colorado Springs Fine Arts Center, 1961, retrospective paintings exhbns. Rosequist Galleries, Tucson, 1962, Raymond Burr Galleries, Beverly Hills, Cal., 1962. Mem. regional and nat. jury "Am. Painting Today," Met. Mus. illustrator in woodcut, pen and ink on Forum (6 years), Harper's Century, Scribner's Survey Graphic, Nation mags.; executed frescoes, 2 tempera murals, U.S. Post Office, Corpus Christi, Tex., 1941; mural paintings; commn. Mayo Clinic, Rochester, Minn., 1952- 53; circuit exhbn. 29 pastels, 20 Museums U.S., 1951, 52, 53; 20 pastels Grand Central Moderns, 1952, oil of New York, 1951; represented by etchings, woodcuts, lithographs, drawings and water colors including Met. Mus., Whitney Mus. Am. Art, Mus. Mod. Art, N.Y. Pub. Library (N.Y.C.), Art Inst. Chgo., Fogg Art. Mus. Work in graphic arts awarded 9 prizes, 1929-37; Mrs. Henry F. Noyes award to Exodus etching Soc. Am. Etchers, 1946; represented in 50 Prints of Year for 5 yrs.; several awards including 6th purchase award, Artists for Victory Exhbn., Met. Mus., N.Y.C., 1942; Painting Purchase award Denver Art Mus., 1950; Fleisher Meml. Purchase Painting, Phila., 1952; Tupperware purchase award, 1956; 1st award oil painting Tucson Art Assn., 1958; purchase awards drawings Mus. N.M., Dallas Museum Fine Arts, Nat. Acad. Design, 1958; 1st purchase award paintings Oklahoma City Art Ann., Am. Ann.; Oakes purchase award, College-Taos Art Assn.; Samuel F. B. Morse Gold medal Nat. Acad. Design; Grand award oil painting N.M. State Fair, 1964; Logan medal in graphics Art Inst. Chgo.; Gold medal mural painting Archtl. League of New York. Mem. Graphic Class N.A.D.; life mem. Art Student's League of N.Y. Contbr. articles to Survey-Graphic, Jr. Red Cross, Forum, Am. Mag. Art, Springfield (Mass.). Republican. Author-illustrator; Sammis Army (juvenile picture book), 1943; Road from Prints to Frescoes (autobiography), 1942. Home: Ranchos de Taos NM 87557 Office: Grand Central Moderns Gallery 1018 Madison Av New York City NY 10027

COOK, IRVING LAWRENCE, sugar refinery co. exec.; b. Bklyn., May 24, 1904; s. Joseph A. and Cornelia (Stillwell) C.; student Columbia, 1931; grad. Advanced Mgmt. Program, Harvard, 1946; m. E. Elizabeth Eydt, Apr. 6, 1957; children—Elizabeth A., Wallace L., Patricia S. With Sucrest Corp., 1958- -, sr. v.p. marketing, N.Y.C., 1967—. Mem. Sales Execs. Club N.Y.C., Candy Execs. Club N.Y.C. Club: Bankers (N.Y.C.). Home: 1015 Spanish River Rd Boca Raton FL 33432 Office: 120 Wall St New York City NY 10005

COOK, JAMES FIELDER, producer-director; b. Atlanta, Mar. 9, 1923; s. George Lindsey and Marion (Fielder) C.; grad. McCallie Sch., Chattanooga, 1942; B.A. cum laude in English Lit., Washington and Lee U., 1947; postgrad. Elizabethan drama U. Birmingham (Eng.), 1948; m. Sarah Eden Chamberlin, Apr. 1, 1950; children—Rebecca Eden, Lindsey Fielder. Dir. Lux Video Theatre, 1950-53; producer-dir. Kraft TV Theatre, 1953-56; exec. J. Walter Thompson, advt., 1950-56; partner Unit Four, producer-dir. Kaiser Aluminum Hour, 1956-57; TV producer-dir. Am. Jewish Com., 1961-62; freelance dir. Studio One, Philco-Goodyear Playhouse, U.S. Steel-Goodyear Playhouse, Playhouse 90, 1957-62; pres. Eden Prodns., Inc., producers-dir. Du Pont Show of Week, 1962-64; dir. motion pictures Patterns, 1956, Home is the Hero, 1958, How To Save A Marriage and Ruin Your Life, 1966, Prudence and the Pill (London), 1965, Eagle In A Cage (Yugoslavia), 1969; dir. theatrical prodn. A Cook for Mr. General, 1961; author original TV plays Zone Four, 1950, The Moment of the Rose, 1953, Throw Me a Rope, 1957. Served to ensign USNR,.1943-46. Mem. Acad. TV Arts and Scis. (bd. govs.), Dirs. Guild Am. (v.p., mem. nat. bd.). Club: Players (N.Y.C.). Home: 1148 Fifth Av New York City NY 10028

COOK, JAMES LEE, banker; b. Beaumont, Tex., Jan. 10, 1907; s. Frank Lee and Julia Theresa (Coleman) C.; student U. Wis. Sch. Banking, 1949-51; m. Tillie Mae Elliott, Aug. 30, 1930; 1 dau., Barbara Colleen (Mrs. J.D. Flickinger). With Fed. Res. Bank of Dallas, 1923—, successively clk., dept. mgr., asst. cashier, cashier Houston br., 1923-51, v.p., cashier, Dallas, 1951-55, v.p. in charge Houston br., 1955-69, sr. v.p., 1969—. Mem. Am. Inst. Banking (pres. Houston 1935-36), Houston World Trade Assn., Houston C. of C. Baptist. Rotarian. Home: 3210 Fairhope St Houston TX 77025 Office: P O Box 2578 Houston TX 77001

COOK, JAMES WHITNEY, cons.; b. Newcastle-on-Tyne, Eng. (parnts U.S. citizens), Aug. 25, 1904; s. Nelson Pingrey and Honora (Gallagher) C.; grad. Phillips Exeter Acad., 1924; A.B., Yale, 1929; m. Frances Gramont Holmes, Sept. 12, 1931; children—Cory (Mrs. John G. Loucks), Langdon Pingrey, William David and Donald Lincoln. Employed N.J. Bell Telephone Co., 1929-41, Am. Tel. & Tel. Co., 1941-44, Pacific Tel. & Tel. Co., 1944-47; v.p. pub. relations Northwestern Bell Telephone Co., 1947-49, v.p., gen. mgr. Neb.-S.D., 1949-51, v.p. operations, 1951-53; v.p. charge rates and revenues Am. Tel. & Tel. Co., 1954-56, v.p. charge marketing, 1956-59, v.p. charge pub. relations, 1959-66; pres., dir. Ill. Bell Telephone Co., 1966-69, chmn., 1969-70; coordinator manpower devel., Ill., 1970-71; pres. Cook, Nelson and Tuthill, Inc., consultants, Chgo., 1971—; dir. Continental Ill. Bank & Trust Co., Sundstrand Corp. Chmn., Ill. Bd. Vocational Edn. and Rehab. Mem. bd. Chgo. Ednl. TV Assn.; trustee Mus. Sci. and Industry, Ill. Inst. Tech.; dir. Michael Reese Hosp. Former mem. Civil Def. Adv. Council; past pres. Leadership Council for Met. Open Communities; former chmn. Better Schs. Com.; former mem. citizens bd. U. Chgo.; former gen. chmn. Yale Alumni Fund. Fellow Timothy Dwight Coll., Yale. Mem. Northwestern U. Assos., George Williams Coll. Assos., Chi Psi. Episcopalian. Clubs: Yale, University (N.Y.C.); Wianno; Commercial, Yale, Old Elm, Indian Hill, Mid America, Chicago. Home: 1200 Whitebridge Hill Winnetka IL 60093 Office: 150 S Wacker Dr Chicago IL 60606

COOK, JAY DEARDOFF, Jr., educator; b. Chester, Pa., Apr. 26, 1921; s. Jay Deardoff and Margaretta (Nelson) C.; B. A., Washington and Lee U., 1943; M.B.A., Wharton Sch., U. Pa., 1948; Ph.D., Ohio State U., 1956; m. Florence Garrett, Dec. 28, 1946; children—Jay Deardoff III, Richard Garrett. Instr., then asst. prof. Denison U., Granville, O., 1948-53; mem. faculty Washington and Lee U., 1953—, prof. accounting, 1962—, chmn. dept., 1962—. Dir. Mental Health Assn. Rockbridge County, 1964-70, pres., 1965; bd. dirs. Rockbridge-Buena Vista Psychiat. Clinic, 1967—. Served to capt. USMCR, 1943-46; PTO, CBI. Decorated Air medal, D.F.C. Mem. Am. Accounting Assn., Am. Econ. Assn. Home: 905 Sunset Dr Lexington, VA 23450.

COOK, JOHN BROWN, mfg. co. exec.; b. Chgo., July 4, 1908; s. Wallace L. and Mary (Lemmon) C.; A.B. in Physics, Dartmouth, 1929; m. Marian Frances Miner, Nov. 17, 1943; children—Morcia (Mrs. William B. Hart, Jr.), Gregory Miner. Pres. Reliable Electric Co., Franklin Park, Ill., 1943-66, chmn. bd., 1966—; pres. Whitney Blake Co., New Haven, 1947-69, chmn., 1970—; pres. Koiled Kords, Inc., New Haven, 1949-69; dir. Mich. Adv. Bank, Chgo. Pres., trustee Library Internat. Relations, Chgo., 1943-47; founding mem. Cook Found., 1952; bd. dirs. New Haven Symphony Orch., 1958-65; trustee Scripps Coll., Claremont, Cal., 1966—, Cate Sch., Carpinteria, Cal., 1966—, Los Angeles Mus. Natural History, 1969—. Mem. Nat. Elec. Mfrs. Assn. (past bd. dirs.), Elec. Mfrs. Club (past bd. dirs.), New Haven C. of C. (past bd. dirs.), U.S. Ind. Telephone Pioneers Assn. (bd. dirs. 1964—, pres. 1967). Soc. Vitieole de Chateau Lascombes (bd. dirs. 1964-71), Confrerie de la Chaine des Rotisseurs (bailli Los Angeles chpt. 1966-70), Soc. Am. Magicians (past v.p.), Internat. Brotherhood Magicians (past v.p.), Sigma Alpha Epsilon. Clubs: Lotus (N.Y.C.); Bohemian (San Francisco); New Haven Country; Bel Air Country (Los Angeles). Author: Gems of Mental Magic, 1947; also numerous articles on magic. Patentee telephony, wire and cable design and mfr. Home: 620 Stone Canyon Rd Los Angeles CA 90024 Office: Reliable Electric Co 11333 Addison Franklin Park IL 60131

COOK, JOHN LOGAN, Jr., librarian, govt. ofcl.; b. Charlotte, N.C., June 30, 1917; s. John Logan and Margaret May (Sloop) C.; B.S. in Edn., Wilson Tchrs. Coll., Washington, 1940; M.L.S., Cath. U. Am., 1952; m. Sara Louise Stoddard, Oct. 18, 1947; children—Kenneth Berryman, Carolyn Elizabeth, Nancy Margaret. Library asst. Library of Congress, Washington, 1940-42; librarian Canadian div. WPB, Ottawa, 1942; battalion librarian 17th Base Post Office, Paris, France, 1946; legal librarian Civilian Prodn. Adminstrn., 1946-47; chief law library AEC, 1947-51; chief tech. library, 1951-61 dir. libraries USAF Inst. Tech., Wright-Patterson AFB, 1961-67, librarian, instr. STINFO course Sch. Systems and Logistics, 1964—, cons. SAC Minuteman Edn. program, 1962-67; dir. libraries Hdqrs. USAF Personnel Center, Randolph AFB, Tex. Instr. library sci. Wittenburg U., 1966-67. Served with AUS, 1942-46: ETO. Mem. Spl. Libraries Assn. (pres. chpt. 1963-64, chmn. mil. librarians div. 1965-66, found. grants com. (1966-68), Am., Tex., S. Western, Bexar library assns. Presbyn. Home: 658 Richfield Dr San Antonio TX 78239 Office: Hdqrs USAF USAFMPC (AFDPMSBRI) Library Sect Randolph AFB TX 78148

COOK, KENNETH LORIMER, educator, geophysicist; b. Middleton, N.H., June 8, 1915; s. Fred Rae and Ella Florence (Moulton) C.; B.S. in Physics, Mass. Inst. Tech., 1939; Ph.D. in Geology and Physics, U. Chgo., 1943; m. Lois Hunter Luke, Sept. 2, 1946; childrenWayne Kenneth, Carla Rae, Shauna Lee. Instr., U. Chgo., 1941-43; geophysicist div. geophys. exploration U.S. Bur.

Mines, 1943-46, geophys. br. U.S. Geol. Survey, 1946-53, part-time, 1953-56; faculty U. Utah, 1952—, prof. geophysics, head dept., 1952-58, now also dir. univ. seismograph stas. Spl. research relative ambundance isotopes, geophys. interpretation, magnetic, gravity, elec. and seismic surveys, studies earth's crust and mantle. Mem. Am. Inst. Mining, Metall. and Petroleum Engrs. (chmn. div. mining, geology and geophysics, dir. 1956-57), A.A.A.S., Am. Assn. Petroleum Geologists, Am. Geophys. Union, Soc. Exptl. Geophysicists, (v.p. 1967-68), European Assn. Exptl. Geophysicists. Geol. Soc. Am., Seismol. Soc. Am., Sigma Xi, Phi Kappa Phi. Contbr. articles to profl. jours. Editor: Cumulative Index Geophysics, 1931-53, 1965, 1931-61, 1963. Home: 1778 Nevada St Salt Lake City, UT 84108.

COOK, LANGDON PINGRY, banker; b. Orange, N.J., June 1, 1938; s. James Whitney and Frances (Holmes) C.; grad. Phillips Exeter Acad., 1956; A.B., Princeton, 1960; m. Lyn Corey Gillmore, Aug. 28, 1965; 1 son, Langdon Cutler. With Morgan Guaranty Trust Co., N.Y.C., 1961—, sr. v.p., head municipal bond dept., 1968—. Clubs: University (N.Y.C.); Round Hill (Greenwich). Home: W Old Mill Rd Greenwich CT 06830 Office: 23 Wall St New York City NY 10015

COOK, LEROY FRANKLIN, Jr., educator, physicist; b. Ashland, Ky., Dec. 12, 1931; s. LeRoy Franklin and Dorothy (Williams) C.; B.A., U. Cal. at Berkeley, 1953, M.A., 1957, Ph.D., 1959; m. Arrelle Janet Rapp, June 16, 1957; children—Nancy Grace, Laura Arrelle, Andrew LeRoy. Instr., Princeton, 1959-62, asst. prof., 1962-65; asso. prof. U. Mass., Amherst, 1965-68, prof. physics, 1968—, acting head physics dept., 1969-71, head physics and astronomy dept., 1971—; cons. Inst. Def. Analyses, Arlington, Va., 1963-67; vis. fellow Clare Hall, Cambridge U., spring 1972. Served with AUS, 1953-55. Fellow Am. Phys. Soc.; mem. A.A.A.S., Am. Assn. U. Profs., Sigma Xi. Contbr. articles profl. jours. Home: 13 Berkshire Terrace Amherst MA 01002

COOK, LOUIS, newspaperman; b. Council Bluffs, Ia., July 5, 1915; s. Louis Harold and Marguerite (Graham) C.; student Drake U., 1933; B.A., U. Ia., 1936; m. Margaret Dorothea Glassburn, June 14, 1938 (div. 1957); children—Sarah (Mrs. Ray Cole), Graham Judson. Reporter, Des Moines (Ia) Register, 1937- 51; reporter, spl. writer Detroit (Mich.) Free Press, 1951- 61, theatre and movie critic, 1961-68, editorial bd., 1968—; free- lance writer arts and automobile industry, 1960—. Served with AUS, 1942- 46. Decorated Bronze Star, Combat Inf. badge. Mem. Am. Newspaper Guild (past pres. locals), Phi Beta Kappa. Home: 508 Marquette Dr Detroit MI 48214 Office: 325 W Lafayette St Detroit MI 48213

COOK, LYLE EDWARDS, health planning cons.; b. Astoria, Ore., Aug. 19, 1918; s. Courtney Carson and Fanchon (Edwards) C.; A.B. in History, Stanford, 1940, postgrad. 1940-41; m. Olive Freeman, Dec. 28, 1940; children—James Michael, Ellen Anita (Mrs. James R. Otto), Mary Lucinda (Mrs. Richard A. Ware), Jane Victoria. Instr. history Yuba Jr. Coll., Marysville, Cal., 1941-42; methods analyst Lockheed Aircraft Corp., 1942-45; investment broker Quincy Cass Assos., Los Angeles, 1945-49; mem. staff Stanford, 1949-66, asso. dean Sch. Medicine, 1958-65; sr. staff mem. Lester Gorsline Assos., Belvedere, Cal., 1966—, v.p., 1967-70, exec. v.p., 1970—. Spl. cons. NIH, 1960-62. Mem. Assn. Am. Med. Colls., A.A.A.S., Assn. Higher Edn., Stanford Assos., Assn. Schs. Allied Health Professions, Soc. for Coll. and U. Planning, Theta Delta Chi. Episcopalian. Home: 1750 Lagoon View Dr Tiburon CA 94920 Office: 1550 Tiburon Blvd Belvedere CA 94920

COOK, M. L., lawyer; b. Scranton, Tex., June 29, 1908; s. John T. and Myrtle (Fleming) C.; student Simmons U., 1925-26; student U. Tex., 1927-28, LL.B. with highest honors, 1931; m. Laurette Virginia Jones, July 17, 1935; children—John Taylor, Robert R., Terry A., Lewis Clark. Admitted to Tex. bar, 1931; with firm Levy and Levy, Galveston, Tex. 1931-36; asst. to gen. mgr. So. Pacific, 1936-38; with Royston, Raysor and Cook, Galveston, also Houston, 1938—, sr. partner, 1942—. Chmn. bd. dirs. Jack and Katherine Pearce Ednl. Found., 1948—. Mem. Maritime Law Assn., Order of Coif, Chancellors, Phi Delta Phi. Clubs: Galveston Artillery (pres. 1949); Houston, World Trade (Houston). Home: Friendswood TX 77546 Office: One Shell Plaza Houston TX 77002

COOK, MARLOW WEBSTER, U.S. senator; b. Akron, N.Y., July 27, 1926; s. Floyd Truman and Mary Lee (Webster) C.; LL.B., U. Louisville, 1950; m. Nancy Elizabeth Remmers, Nov. 22, 1947; children—Christine, Caroline, Nancy, Mary Louise, Marlow Webster. Admitted to Ky. bar, 1950; practice with firm Hottell and Stephenson, Louisville, 1952-61; mem. Ky. Ho. of Rep. from Jefferson County, 1958-59, 60-61; judge Jefferson County, 1961-65, 66- 68; mem. 91st Congress from Ky.; U.S. senator from Ky., 1969—. Served with USNR, 1944-46. Home: 4000 River St North Arlington VA 22207 Office: Old Senate Office Bldg Washington DC 20510

COOK, MELVIN ALONZO, chemist; b. Swan Creek, Utah, Oct. 10, 1911; s. Alonzo Laker and Alice Maud C.; Ph.D. (Loomis fellow), Yale, 1937; m. Wanda Garfield, June 19, 1935; children—Barbara Jean (Mrs. S. Keith Petersen), Melvin Garfield, Virginia (Mrs. Gill O. Saunders), Merrill Alonzo, Krehl Osmond. Research chemist DuPont Co., 1937-47, cons., 1947-52; prof. metallurgy U. Utah, 1947—, Reynolds lectr., 1952, dir. Inst. Metals Explosives Research, 1952-66; pres. IRECO Chems., Salt Lake City; cons. on explosives; cons., expert witness Texas City Com. and Monsanto Co., 1948-50; past mem. adv. council Picatinny Arsenal. Recipient sci. award, Utah Acad. Arts Letters and Sci., 1954, Utah award Salt Lake sect. Am. Chem. Soc., 1961; E.V. Murphree award in indsl. chemistry Am. Chem. Soc., 1968, Nitro Nobel Gold medal, Nobel Found., Stockholm, 1968. Member Am. Inst. Mining, Metall. and Petroleum Engrs., A.A.A.S., Am. Chem. Soc., Am. Phys. Soc., Sigma Xi. Mem. Ch. of Jesus Christ of Latter-Day Saints. Author: Science of High Explosives, 1958; Prehistory and Earth Models, 1966; Science and Mormonism, 1967; also articles on chemistry, physics, geophysics. Home: 631 16th Av Salt Lake City UT 24103 ☆

COOK, MERCER, educator; b. Washington, Mar. 30, 1903; s. Will Marion and Abbie (Mitchell) C.; A.B., Amherst Coll., 1925, LL.D., 1965; tchrs. diploma U. Paris (France), 1926; M.A., Brown U., 1931, Ph.D., 1936, LL.D., 1970; m. Vashti Smith, Aug. 31, 1929; children—Mercer, Jacques. Asst. prof. Romance langs. Howard U., 1927-36, prof., 1945-60; prof. French, Atlanta U., 1936-43; prof. English, U. Haiti, 1943-45; fgn. rep. Am. Soc. African Culture, 1958-60; U.S. ambassador to Niger, 1961-64, to Senegal and Gambia, 1964-66; prof., head dept. Romance langs. Howard U., until 1970, prof. emeritus, 1970—; vis. prof. French, Harvard U., 1969-70. Recipient decorations from Haitian Govt., 1945, Niger Govt., 1964, Senegal, 1966; Palmes Academiques (France). Mem. Assn. Study Negro Life and History, N.A.A.C.P., Am. Assn. Tchrs. French, A.S.C.A.P., Phi Beta Kappa. Roman Catholic. Author: Le Noir, 1934; Portraits americains, 1938; Five French Negro Authors, 1943; Education in Haiti, 1948; Militant Black Writer in Africa and U.S.A., 1969. Translator: (Senghor) African Socialism, 1959; (Mamadou Dia) African Nations and World Solidarity, 1961. Address: 4811 Blagden Av N W Washington DC 20001

COOK, NATHAN HENRY, educator; b. Ridgewood, N.J., Mar. 17, 1925; s. Henry Dyer and Dora G. (Bingham) C.; B.S., Mass. Inst. Tech., 1950, S.M., 1951, M.E., 1954, Sc.D., 1955; m. Alice Winslow Collins, Sept. 13, 1947; children—Nancy G., James B., Richard H., Anne E. Asst. prof. mech. engring. Mass. Inst. Tech., 1953-59, asso. prof., 1959-65, prof., 1965—, head materials processing lab., 1961—, housemaster MacGregor House, 1970—. Pres. Cook, Smith & Assos., Inc., Concord, Mass.; cons. in field; advisor Birla Inst. Tech. and Sci., Pilani, India. Served with USNR, 1943-46. Decorated Purple Heart. Mem. Am. Soc. M.E., Am. Soc. Engring. Edn., Sigma Xi, Tau Beta Pi, Pi Tau Sigma. Author: Manufacturing Analysis, 1966; (with others) Physical Measurement and Analysis, 1963; (with others) Mechanics of Solids, 1959. Contbr. articles profl. jours., Ency. Britannica. Home: 450 Memorial Dr Cambridge MA 02139

COOK, PAUL WENTWORTH, mfg. co. exec.; b. New Bedford, Mass., July 17, 1921; s. Louis deLaittre and Helena (Lindsay) C.; grad. Phillips Acad., Andover, Mass., 1939; A.B., Harvard, 1943; M.B.A., J.D., U. Mich., 1950; LL.M., N.Y.U., 1962; m. Marjory Louise Biggart, Dec. 12, 1944; children—Billie Louise, Paul Wentworth, Elizabeth Stanton, James Rowland. Tax specialist Lybrand, Ross Bros. and Montgomery, C.P.A.'s, N.Y.C., 1950-55; sr. tax accountant ACF Industries, Inc., 1955-57; sr. analyst Mobil Oil Corp., 1957-58; asst. controller Mobil Oil of Can. Ltd., 1958-60, div. controller, 1960-62, mgr. tax adminstrn., 1962-66; with Lever Bros. Co., 1966—, treas., 1968—. Bd. dirs., chmn. com. municipal and County govt. N.J. Taxpayers Assn.; mem. exec. bd. Union council Boy Scouts Am. Served to 1st lt. AUS, World War II. C.P.A., N.Y.; admitted to N.Y. bar, 1952. Mem. Am. Bar Assn. (past chmn. com. excise and employment taxes), N.A.M., Am. Inst. C.P.A.'s, N.Y. State Soc. C.P.A.'s, Financial Execs. Inst., Am. Mgmt. Assn., Phi Kappa Phi, Beta Gamma Sigma. Episcopalian. Home: 105 Cranford Av Cranford NJ 07016 Office: 390 Park Av New York City NY 10022

COOK, PAUL WEST, Jr., educator; b. Evanston, Ill., Nov. 7, 1926; s. Paul West and Mary (Ruminer) C.; B.A., Brown U., 1948; Ph.D., U. Chgo., 1952; LL.D., Butler U., 1967; m. Marian M. Miller, Mar. 19, 1950; children—Peter, John, Catherine. Instr. econs. Northwestern U., 1951; econ. analyst Standard Oil Co. Ind., 1952; asst. prof. bus. U. Chgo., 1952-55; prof. bus. adminstrn. Harvard Bus. Sch., 1955-66; pres. Wabash Coll., 1966-68; dir. analytical studies group Mass. Inst. Tech., 1968—; econ. and edn. cons., 1957—. Mem. Edn. Commn. of States, 1967-70; chmn. High Commr.'s Devel. Coordination Com., U.S. Pacific Trust Ty., 1969. Mem. Am. Econ. Assn. Author (with G. Von Peterfly) Problems of Corporate Power, 1966. Editor: Cases in Antitrust Policy, 1961. Home: 23 Phinney Rd Lexington MA 02173 Office: Mass Inst Tech Cambridge MA 02139

COOK, PETER GEOFFREY, artist; b. N.Y.C., June 10, 1915; s. Thomas G. and Grace (Tracy) C.; grad. St. Mark's Sch., Southboro, Mass., 1933; A.B. in Arch., Princeton, 1937; student Nat. Acad. Sch., 1938-39, Art Student League, 1938-40; m. Joan Baldwin Folinsbee, June 15, 1938; childrenPeter Bigelow, John Folinsbee, Stephen Standish, Paula. Tchr. in Clearwater, Fla., 1940, N.A.D., Sch., 1943-44; one man shows include Princeton, N.J., 1946, 50, 54, 57, 60, 64, Boston, 1950, Richmond, Va., 1952, Palm Beach, Fla., 1950, 52; numerous group shows, 1941—; rep. perm. colls. Princeton, Rutgers, Bradley, Cornell, Temple, Washington univs., Wells Coll., U.S. Supreme Ct., also pvt. collections. Pres., Princeton Art Assn., 1964-66. Recipient Pres.'s prize Clearwater Art Mus., 1941, 1st prize Montclair (N.J.) Art Mus., 1944, 2d Hallgarten prize N.A.D., 1944, Art Center prize Ogunquit, Me., 1951, Figure prize Ogunquit, 1956, Grumbacher award Jersey City, 1956, Bronze medal Nat. Arts Club, 1957, Century Assn. Medal of Honor, 1957, Boston Arts Festival prize, 1961, Portland (Me.) Arts Festival prize, 1961, Gov.'s prize Me. Arts Festival, 1962, Ogonquit Art Center Marine prize, 1963. Pulitzer scholar, 1939. Mem. N.A.D. Club: Century Assn. (N.Y.C.). Home: Heathcote Farm Kingston, NJ 08528.

COOK, RAMONA GRAHAM, (pen name Ramona Graham), author; b. San Miguel, Cal., Jan. 3; d. Oswell M. and Florence (Mead) Graham; student pub. schs., also Cornell Coll. and Thomas Normal Tng. Sch.; m. William R. Cook, Sept. 17, 1924; 1 son, William R. Lit. chmn. Mass. State Fedn., 1948-50; pres. Boston chpt. then pres. Mass. chpt. Nat. League Am. Pen Women, nat. v.p., Washington, 1966-68, nat. pres., 1968-70. Life mem. N.E. Women's Press Assn. Clubs: New England Poetry, Boston Authors. Author: (book of poems) From Boston, 1936; Hills of New England, 1946; What the Heart Crates, 1956; Aeolus Drives, 1969; (non fiction) With Uncle Thomas, 1967; (poems) Ballads From A Cart, 1970; numerous poems pub. in popular mags. and newspapers, including Sat. Evening Post, Am. Scholar, Yankee Mag., N.Y. Times, Advance, Love Story; author short fiction. Home: 12 Woodcliff Rd Wellesley Hills MA 02181

COOK, RAY LEWIS, educator; b. Okemos, Mich., Mar. 10, 1904; s. L.D. and Nellie (Plant) C.; B.S., Mich. State U., 1927, M.S., 1929; Ph.D. (fellow), U. Wis., 1934; m. Carrie St. Clair, Mar. 29, 1930; 1 dau., Jessie (Mrs. R.G. Finch). With Mich. State U., 1927—, beginning as grad. asst., successively research asst., instr., asst. prof., asso. prof., 1927-46, prof., 1946- 53, chmn. soil sci. dept., 1953-69. Soils adviser, Taiwan, 1962; UN devel. program spl. cons. Iran, 1965, Iraq, Thailand, 1966, 70, Chile, 1971; vis. prof. Chung Hsing U., Taiwan, 1969-70. Fellow Am. Soc. Agronomy, Soil Conservation Soc. Am.; mem. Soil Sci. Soc. of Am., Am. Soc. Sugar Beet Tech., Sigma Xi, Phi Kappa Phi, Pi Alpha Xi, Alpha Zeta. Author: Soil Management for Conservation and Production, 1960. Contbr. articles sci. jours., farm mags. Home: 830 Newton Av Lansing MI 48912 Office: Michigan State U East Lansing MI 48823

COOK, RAYMOND AUGUSTUS, lawyer; b. Houston, Dec. 4, 1914; s. William Lawrence and Juliette (Elliott) C.; B.A., Rice Inst., 1935; LL.B., U. Tex., 1938; m. Florence Bryan, Mar. 30, 1942; children—Florence, Frank, Lawrence, Stephen. Admitted to Tex. bar, 1937, since practiced in Houston; partner firm Andrews, Kurth, Cambell & Jones, 1947—. Trustee Amigos de las Americas, Scott and White Meml. Hosp. Served to maj. AUS, 1940-45; col. Res. Mem. Am., Houston bar assns., State Bar Tex., Am. Law Inst., Phi Beta Kappa, Phi Delta Phi, Phi Kappa Psi. Democrat. Methodist. Kiwanian. Clubs: Houston Country, Petroleum, Forest (Houston); Conquistadores Del Cielo. Home: 1936 Sunset Blvd Houston TX 77005 Office: Humble Bldg Houston TX 77002

COOK, REGINALD LANSING, educator; b. Mendon, Mass., Nov. 5, 1903; s. Lyman and Wilhelmina (Rittmann) C.; A.B., Middlebury Coll., 1924, A.M., 1926, Litt.D., 1960; B.A. (Rhodes scholar) Oxford U., 1929; m. L. Juanita Pritchard, Aug. 24, 1929. Instr. English and Am. lit. Middlebury (Vt.) Coll., 1929-31, asso. prof., 1931-32, prof. Am. lit., 1932-69, prof. emeritus Am. lit., 1969—, Abernethy prof. Am. lit., 1965-67, Charles A. Dana prof., 1967—; dir. Bread Loaf School of English, 1946-64. Mem. Thoreau Soc., Melville Soc., Vt. Acad. Arts and Scis. (trustee), Phi Beta Kappa, Kappa Delta Rho. Baptist. Author: Passage of Walden, 1949; The Dimensions of Robert Frost, 1958; Selected Prose and Poetry of Emerson, 1968. Home: Pulp Mill Bridge Rd Weybridge VT 05753

COOK, RICHARD KAUFMAN, physicist; b. Chgo., June 30, 1910; s. William G. and Alice (Kaufman) C.; B.S., U. Ill., 1931, M.S., 1932, Ph.D., 1935; m. Dorothy Sweet, Mar. 17, 1938; 1 son, Michael Faraday. Asst. physics U. Ill., 1930-35; physicist Nat. Bur. Standards, Wash., 1935-66, 71—, chief sect. sound, 1942-66; physicist Environmental Sci. Services Adminstrn., Washington, 1966-71, chief geoacoustics group, 1966-71. Instr. math. U.S. Dept. Agr. Grad. Sch., 1941-50; mem. tech. staff Bell Telephone Labs., 1955-56; adj. prof. elec. engring. Bklyn. Poly. Inst., 1956. Recipient Gold medal Exceptional Service award Dept. Commerce, 1964. Fellow Am. Phys. Soc., Acoustical Soc. Am. (council 1948-51, pres. 1957-58, asso. editor Sound 1962-63), A.A.A.S., Washington Acad. Scis. (Engring. Scis. award 1949, sr. editor 1955, treas. 1966—); mem. Am. Geophys. Union, Sigma Xi, Tau Beta Pi. Editor acoustics sect. Am. Inst. Physics Handbook, 2d and 3d edits. Home: 8517 Milford Av Silver Spring MD 20910 Office: Nat Bur Standards Washington DC 20234

COOK, RICHARD WALLACE, engr.; b. Muskegon, Mich., Aug. 8, 1907; s. Harry James and Rose (Van Dame) C.; B.S., Mich. State U., 1933; m. Helen L. Benson, Dec. 25, 1934. Marine constrn. Gt. Lakes area, 1933-35; resident engr. in charge constrn. Consoer, Townsend & Quinlan, cons. engrs., 1935-40; dep. mgr. Oak Ridge operations A.E.C., 1947-49, mgr., 1949-51, dir. prodn., Washington, 1951; asst. gen. mgr. mfg. A.E.C., Washington, 1954, dep. gen. mgr., 1954-58; dir. adminstrn. govt. products group Am. Machine and Foundry Co., 1958-59, divisional v.p., dep. group exec., also group exec. Atomic Energy Group, AMF, 1959-61, v.p., dep. group exec. Titan program and govt. products group; dir. AMF Atomics Can., Ltd., 1959-61, dir. atomics and adminstrv. divs., 1962, corporate v.p. spl. products Advance Products Group AMF, 1962-64; asst. dir. research and devel. operations, dep. dir. operations, sci. and engring. Marshall Space Flight Center, NASA, Huntsville, Ala., 1964-69, dep. dir. mgmt., 1969—. Served with C.E., Q.M.C. AUS, 1940-47; Decorations include Legion of Merit, Army Commendation ribbon, Meritorious Service Unit Star; recipient Mich. State U. Centennial award, 1955; AEC Distinguished Service award, 1956. Registered profl. engr., Wis., Ill. Mem. Am. Soc. C.E., Phi Kappa Tau, Blue Key, Scabbard and Blade. Elk. Club: Army-Navy (Washington.). Home: 8003 Bengroya Lane SW Huntsville AL 35802 Office: Marshall Space Flight Center Huntsville AL 35812

COOK, ROBERT ANDREW, coll. pres.; b. Santa Clara, Cal., June 7, 1912; s. Charles Alfred and Daisy (Gray) C.; grad. pastor's course, Moody Bible Inst., Chgo., 1930; B.A., Wheaton (Ill.) Coll., 1934; B.D., Eastern Bapt. Sem., 1939; LL.D. (hon.), Northwestern Schs., Mpls., 1950; L.H.D. (hon.), Bob Jones U., 1945; Ped.D. (hon.), Houghton Coll., 1965; m. Coreen Nilsen, Sept. 24, 1935; children—Carolyn (Mrs. Wendell Borrink), Marilyn (Mrs. John Parry), and Lois. Ordained to ministry Baptist Ch., 1931; pastor in Phila., 1934-39, LaSalle, Ill., 1939-44, Chgo., 1944-48; pres. Youth for Christ Internat., 1948-57; v.p. Scripture Press, Wheaton, 1957-61; pres. King's Coll., Briarcliff Manor, N.Y., 1962—. Pres. Nat. Assn. Evangelicals, 1962-64. Mem. N.E.A., Evangelical Theol. Soc., Am. Assn. Higher Edn., Ministerial Assn. Evang. Free Ch. Am. Author: Reaching Youth for Christ, 1944; Now That I Believe, 1949; It's Tough to be a Teenager, 1955; How to Get Along with Christians, 1956; Just Between Us, 1960; Leveling with God, 1966, also articles. Home: 224 Central Dr Briarcliff Manor NY 10510

COOK, ROBERT CARTER, population cons.; b. Washington, Apr. 9, 1898; s. O.F. and Alice (Carter) C.; student Friends Sch., Washington, 1913-14, Tech. High Sch., 1915- 16, George Washington U., 1917-19; pre-med. student U. Md., 1920-21; m. Margaret Brown, Aug. 4, 1921; children—John Robert, Barbara Alice, Victoria Marian; m. 2d, Helen Hall Jennings, Feb. 28, 1944; m. 3d, Annabelle Desmond, August 19, 1946. Sci. aid, U.S. Bur. Standards, 1916-18; mgr. editor The Journal of Heredity 1922-52, editor, 1952-62; dir. Population Reference Bur., 1951-58, pres., 1959- 68, sr. cons., 1968-69, editor Population Bull., 1951-69; professorial lectr. med. genetics, Med. Sch. George Washington U., 1944-63, lectr. biology, 1946-63. Mem. program com., organizer sect. I, Inter-Am. Conf. on Conservation, 1948; mem. adv. com. Conservation Found. Bd. dirs. Assn. for Research in Human Heredity, 1947-50. Recipient Albert and Mary Lasker Found. award in planned parenthood, 1956. Fellow A.A.A.S.; mem. Am. Eugenics Soc. (editor Eugenical News 1942, dir.), Am. Genetic Assn., Genetics Soc. Am., Am. Soc. Human Genetics, Am. Acad. Polit.and Social Sci., Acad. Medicine Washington, Washington Acad. Sci., Nat. Parks and Cons. Assn. (trustee), Nat. Assn. Sci. Writers. Clubs: Cosmos (Washington); Nat Press. Author: Human Fertility: The Modern Dilemma, 1951. Contbr. to popular mags. and tech. jours. Address: 1701 18th St N W Washington DC 20009

COOK, ROBERT CECIL, publisher; b. Fayette, Ala., July 6, 1903; s. James Alfred and Athea (McKelvey) C.; B.S., Miss. State, 1924; A.M., Columbia, 1933, Ed.D., 1942; m. Bonnibel Wood, June 30, 1926; children—Robert Cecil, Rhetta Louise (Mrs. R.T. Dodder). Tchr. and prin. of high schools, 1924- 29; dir. U. High School, dir. tchr. edn., asso. prof. of edn., U. of Miss., 1929-41, dean of Sch. of Edn., dir. the summer session, prof. of secondary edn., 1941-42; pres. Miss. So. Coll., 1945-55; v.p. and gen. mgr. Jackson (Miss.) State Times, 1955; pres. Southeastern Life Ins. Co., 1955-70. dir. Univ. and Coll. Press of Miss., 1970—. Dist. chmn. Boy Scouts Am.; mem. Miss. Econ. Council; Chmn., State Library Commn. Miss. Ednl. TV Commn. Trustee, Insts. of Higher Learning. Served 39th Brigade Coast Arty., Anti-Aircraft, Seattle, Dec. 1942-Oct. 1943; staff officer, A.S.T.P., Stanford U. Oct. 1943-Dec. 1944. Chief, curriculm and advisement sections, Army Education Program. United Kingdom Base Headquarters ETOUSA, 1944-45. Recipient Outstanding Citizen award, Hattiesburg, 1948. Fellow A.A.A.S.; mem. Miss Life Cos. Assn. (pres. 1963-64), Newcomen Society, Phi Delta Kappa, Alpha Tau Omega, Pi Kappa Pi, Omicron Delta Kappa. Presbyn. Mason; Elk, Rotarian. Club: Country. Editor Who's Who in American Education, 1928-68; Current Science Rev., 1926-28; Presidents in American Colleges and Universities, 1934-68; Leaders in American Science, 1953-68. Home: 1915 Ridgeway Lane Hattiesburg MS 39401 Office: Southern Sta Box 5164 Hattiesburg MS 39401

COOK, ROBERT DONALD, cons. co. exec.; b. Chicago Heights, Ill., Nov. 1, 1929; s. Webster Warren and Gladys (Miner) C.; B.S in Bus., U. Md., 1956; m. Maxine Jensen, Nov. 11, 1950; children—Carolyn Jean, Robert Donald II. Audit mgr. Arthur Andersen & Co., C.P.A.'s, Washington, 1956-63; comptroller Peoples Drug Stores, Washington, 1963-68; v.p., comptroller Booz, Allen & Hamilton, Inc., 1968—. Served with U.S. Navy, 1948-52. C.P.A., Md. Mem. Am., D.C. insts. C.P.A.'s, Beta Alpha Psi. Mason (32, Shriner). Home: 119 Whispering Oaks Barrington IL 60010 Office: 135 S Lasalle St Chicago IL 60603

COOK, ROBERT GRANT, educator; b. New Britain, Conn., Dec. 5, 1921; s. Walter Oscar and Lulu May (Grant) C.; B.S., U. R.I., 1949, M.S., 1951; D.B.A., Ind. U., 1958; m. Ruth Isabel Cooper, July 1, 1961. Sr. indsl. engr. Bendix Radio Corp., Towson, Md., 1951-52; faculty lectr. Ind. U., 1953-56; asso. prof. Air Force Inst. Tech., Wright Petterson AFB, O., 1956-58; prof. mgmt. U. Mo., Columbia, 1958—, with Office of Chancellor, 1966-67, asst. dir. research adminstrn. Grad. Sch., 1967-69, chmn. dept. mgmt., 1969—; mgmt.

cons., 1953—. Served with USMCR, 1942-45. Mem. Am. Econ. Assn., Am. Inst. for Decision Scis., Acad. Mgmt., Beta Gamma Sigma, Phi Kappa Phi. Home: 2700 Bayonne Ct Columbia MO 65201

COOK, SAM B., banker; b. Jefferson City, Mo., Apr. 20, 1922; s. Howard and Gertrude (Shuman) C.; grad. Lawrenceville Sch., 1941; student U. Mo., 1941-43; B.A., Yale, 1948; m. Lois McAdam, Dec. 29, 1949; children—Sam Bryan, Cynthia Ann, Sarah, Julia. With Chase-Manhattan Bank, N.Y.C., 1948-50; with The Central Trust Bank, Jefferson City, 1950—, v.p., dir., 1953- 61, pres., dir., 1961—; chmn. bd. First Nat. Bank of Clayton, 1970—; dir. M.P.R.R., Jefferson Bank Mo. Campaign chmn. Jefferson City United Community Fund, 1954; Mo. treas. Crusade for Freedom, 1957; chmn. exec. com. Greater Jefferson City Com.; mem. Gov.'s Task Force on Higher Edn., Mo. Hwy. Commn., 1963. Bd. dirs. William Woods Coll., Salvation Army, 1956; mem. corp. Madeira Sch., Greenway, Va. Served to capt., F.A. AUS, 1943-46. Named outstanding young man, Jefferson City, 1958. Mem. Mo. Bankers Assn. (pres. 1958-59), Mo. Conservation Fedn., Phi Beta Kappa, Phi Delta Theta. Home: 3308 Country Club Dr Jefferson City MO 65101 Office: Central Trust Bank Madison and High Sts Jefferson City MO 65101

COOK, SIDNEY R., publisher. Publisher Springfield Union, News, Republican. Office: Republican Co 32 Cypress St Springfield MA 01101*

COOK, STUART WELLFORD, psychologist, educator; b. Richmond, Va., Apr. 17, 1913; s. Arthur B. and Lois (Leonard) E.; A.B., U. Richmond, 1934, M.A., 1935; Ph.D., U. Minn., 1938; m. Annabelle Hurley, July 14, 1938; children—Jonathan Boyd, Timothy Quinn, Stephen Hurley, Hoanna Helene. Instr. psychology, clin. psychologist Psychiat. Clinic for Children, U. Minn., 1938-41; head Bur. Psychol. Services, State Minn., 1941-42; dir. research Commn. Community Interrelations, Am. Jewish Congress, 1946-50; head dept. psychology N.Y. U., 1950-63, dir. Research Center for Human Relations 1950-57; chairman dept. psychology U. Colo., 1963-68, prof. psychology, 1968—. Psychol. research work USAAF, 1942-46. Mem. Am. (past chmn. edn. tng. bd., mem. bd. of directors), N.Y. (pres. 1955-56), Eastern (pres. 1957-58), psychol. assns. A.A.A.S., Am. Assn. U. Profs., Soc. Psychol. Study Social Issued (pres. 1952), Am. Vets. Com., Am. Assn. for U.N., World Federalists, Sigma Xi, Phi Beta Kappa, Psi Chi, Omicron Delta Kappa. Author: Research Methods in Social Relations (with M. Jaboda and Deutsch), 1951; revised edit., 1959; Human Relations in Interracial Housing (with R.P. Walkey and D.M. Wilner), 1956; Attitudes and Social Relations in the United States (with C. Selltiz, J. Christ, J. Havel), 1963. Editor: Psychological Research in Radar Observer Training, 1947. Home: 1540 Columbine Boulder CO 80302

COOK, THOMAS GEORGE, mfg. co. exec.; b. Washington Island, Wis., Apr. 4, 1927; s. T.G. and Caroline (Swenson) C.; student U. Chgo., 1946; B.B.A., with honors, U. Wis., 1950; m. Beverly Foss, 1950; children—Gary, Debbie, Greg, Brian. With Lybrand Ross Bros. & Montgomery, C.P.A.'s, 1950-57; with Walker Mfg. Co., Racine, Wis., 1957—, treas., 1964—, v.p. 1965—. Served with USNR, 1946-47. C.P.A., Ill. Mem. Am. Inst. C.P.A.'s, Sigma Chi, Phi Eta Sigma, Beta Alpha Psi. Home: 6620 Brook Rd Franksville WI 53126

COOK, THOMAS IRA, polit. scientist; b. Suffolk, Eng., Mar. 31, 1907; s. Frederick and Martha (Pell) C.; student Dover (Eng.) Coll., 1921-25; B.Sc. in Econs., London Sch. Econs., London U., 1928; Ph.D., Columbia, 1937; m. Anne Peloubet, June 21, 1930 (dec.); children—Penelope Anne, Jennifer Taft; m. 2d, Anne Crystal, June 3, 1961. Came to U.S., 1930, naturalized, 1939. Instr. econs., Acadia U., Wolfville, N.S., 1929-30; instr. govt., Columbia, 1930-36; asst. prof. polit. sci. U. Cal. at Los Angeles, 1936-39; asso., later prof. polit. sci. U. Wash., 1939-49; vis. prof. social scis. U. Chgo., 1948-49; vis. prof. polit. sci. Johns Hopkins, 1949-50, prof. polit. sci., 1950-66, chmn. dept., 1961-64; H.Y. Benedict prof. U. Tex. at El Paso, 1966—. Asst. dir. wage stblzn. div. 12th regional W.L.B., 1942-44. Mem. Am. Polit. Sci. Assn. (exec. council 1943-45), Am. Assn. U. Profs., Northwest Polit. Sci. Assn. (acting pres., 1947-48). Author: History of Political Philosophy from Plato to Burke, 1937; Democratic Rights versus Communist Activity, 1954; Power Through Purpose, 1954. Editor: John Locke, Two Treatises of Government, 1947. Mem. editorial bd., Western Political Quarterly, 1948-50. Home: 6421 Cloudview El Paso TX 77912

COOK, THOMAS MARKS, pulp and paper co. exec.; b. Ilion, N.Y., June 24, 1913; s. Ward L. and Martha L. (Marks) C.; B.S., N.Y. State Coll. Forestry, 1936; m. Mary G. Pepitone, July 1, 1940; children—Martha J., Mary E. Chief chemist Racquette River Paper co., Potsdam, N.Y., 1935-38; v.p. Grace paper div. W.R. Grace & Co., 1938-61; with Penobscot Co., Boston, 1961-68, exec. v.p., 1962-65, pres., 1965-68; pres. Newfondland Pulp & Chem. Co., Ltd., N.Y.C., 1968—, also dir. Mem. T.A.P.P.I., C.P.P.A., Am. Chem. Soc., Forest Products Research Soc., Sigma Chi. Home: 293 Boston Post Rd Weston, MA 02193. Office: 90 Park Av New York City NY 10016

COOK, W.A., gas utility exec.; b. Portland, Ore., June 27, 1906; s. Raymond W. and Eva (Fairweather) C.; B.S., Ore. State U., 1931; m. Esther Allen, Jan. 1933; children—Wesley A., Raymond Lee, Caroline Ann (Mrs. Michael C. Hennessy). With Northwest Natural Gas Co., Portland, 1946—, v.p., 1955- 61, sr. v.p., 1961—. Served to lt col. USAAF, 1941-46. Mem. Am. Legion, Mil. Order World Wars, USCG Aux., U.S. Power Squadron, Alpha Chi Rho. Clubs: Portland Yacht, Arlington, Aero. Home: 4911 S E Aldercrest Rd Portland OR 97222 Office: 735 W Morrison St Portland OR 97205

COOK, WALTER MCQUEEN, lawyer; b. Selma, Ala., Jan. 29, 1915; s. Walter Pitts and Mattie Julia (McQueen) C.; student U. Ala., 1933-34, Springhill Coll., 1943; LL.B., J.D., LL.M., George Washington U., 1948; m. Norma Webster Rogers, June 15, 1938; children—Norma McQueen, Julia Webster (Mrs. Robert D. Melson), Walter McQueen, Katharyn Rogers. Examiner, OPA, 1942-47; admitted to Ala., D.C. bars, 1948, since practiced in Mobile; partner law firm Lyons, Pipes & Cook, 1948—; dir. Port City Investment Co., Blackwater Ranch. Pres. Mobile County Wildlife and Conservation Assn., Ala. Wildlife Fedn., Mobile's Azalea Trail, Am.'s Jr. Miss Pageant, Ala. Wildlife Fedn. Endowment. Named Water Conservationist of Year, Ala. Wildlife Fedn. in cooperation with Nat. Wildlife Fedn., 1966. Mem. Am., D.C., Ala., Mobile bar assns., Fedn. Ins. Counsel, Internat. Assn. Ins. Counsel, Delta Kappa Epsilon. Democrat. Episcopalian. Home: 2009 Old Shell Rd Mobile AL 36607 Office: First Nat Bank Bldg Mobile AL 36601

COOK, WALTER R., concrete co. exec.; b. Jackson County, Ill., Sept. 9, 1909; s. Albert Dolph and Edna Laura (Reagan) C.; B.S., U. Ill., 1938, grad. student, 1941-42; m. Doris Lucile Schneider, Aug. 22, 1937; children—Walter Reagan, Robert Stephen, John Michael. With Eastman Kodak Co., 1938-41; instr. mgmt. U. Ill., 1941-42; engaged as bus. cons., home builder, realtor in San Antonio, 1945-48; exec. mgmt. service div., S.W. div. Ernst & Ernst, C.P.A.'s, 1948-55; with Tex. Industries, Inc., Dallas, 1955—, former sr. v.p.; former pres. Athens Brick Co., Athens, Tex. Served with AUS, 1942-45. Mem. Bronze Tablet (U. Ill.), Beta Gamma Sigma, Beta Alpha Psi, Sigma Iota Epsilon. Home: 3412 Allen Av Tyler TX 75701 Office: Athens Brick Co PO Box 70 Athens TX 75751

COOK, WILLIAM BOYD, coll. dean; b. Dallas, July 20, 1918; s. James Monroe and Lucile (Holland) C.; B.A., U. Tex., 1940; M.S., U. Colo., 1942; Ph.D., U. Wyo., 1950; m. Romerta Marie Fox, Sept. 4, 1942; 1 son, Kem Holland. Chemist, analyst Monsanto Chem. Co., 1942-43, research asso., 1943-47; instr., then asst. prof. chemistry U. Wyo., 1949-52; research asso. U. Cal., 1952; vis. prof. Princeton, 1953; asso. prof. Baylor U., 1953-57; prof. chemistry, head dept. Mont. State Coll., 1958-67; dean Coll. Natural Scis., Colo. State U., Fort Collins, 1967—. Vis. prof. Cambridge U., 1962-63; vis. scholar Stanford, 1965-67; program dir. summer insts. NSF, 1957, cons. U.S.-Indo Conf. Chem. Edn. and Research, 1969; exec. dir. Adv. Council Coll. Chemistry, 1965-67; corr. com. teaching chemistry Internat. Union Pure and Applied Chemistry, 1970—; mem. adv. com. grants Research Corp., 1969—; cons. sci. teaching div. UNESCO, 1969; chmn. govt. relations com. Council Coll. Deans, 1969—. Fellow A.A.A.S., Chem. Soc. London; mem. Am. Chem. Soc. (sec. div. chem. edn. 1959-62, chmn. 1969, gov. internat. conf. edn. chemistry 1969), Sigma Xi. Mem. bd. publ. Jour. Chem. Edn., 1959-62, 67-70. Home: 1615 Miramont Dr Fort Collins CO 80521

COOK, WILLIAM HOWARD, architect; s. Clare Cyril and Matilda Hermine (Schuldt) C.; B.A., U. Cal. at Los Angeles, 1947; B.Arch., U. Mich., 1952; m. Nancy Ann Dean, Feb. 1, 1949; children—Robert, Cynthia, James. Chief designer Fabrica de Muebles Camacho-Roldan, Bogota, Colombia, S.Am., 1949-52; asso. architecte Orus Eash, Traverse City, Mich., Ft. Wayne, Ind., 1952-60; partner Cook & Swaim, architects, Tucson, 1961-68; project specialist in urban devel. Banco Interamericano de Desarrollo, Buenos Aires, Argentina, 1968-69; partner Cain, Nelson, Wares, Cook and Assos., architects, Tucson, 1969—. Bd. dirs. Campus Christian Center of U. Ariz. Served to lt. (j.g.) USNR, 1943-46. Mem. A.I.A. (pres. So. Ariz. 1967), Ariz. Soc. Architects (pres. 1970). Presbyn. Rotarian. Home: 7065 Mesa Grande Ct Tucson AZ 85715 Office: 405 W Franklin St Tucson AZ 85705

COOK, WILLIAM WARNER, pub. relations exec.; b. Coldwater, Mich., July 29, 1913; s. William Alfred and Bernice Carrie (Warner) C.; A.B., U. Mich., 1935; M.S., Columbia, 1938; m. Darlys Marilyn Ford, Dec. 28, 1957. Reporter, Royal Oak (Mich.) Daily Tribune, 1935-37; copy editor N.Y. Times, 1938-47; mem. faculty Grad. Sch. Journalism, Columbia, 1946-47; exec. editor Motor Mag., 1947-48; account exec. Hill and Knowlton, Inc., 1951-53; partner Pendray & Cook, 1953-59; mem. faculty Baruch Sch. Bus. and Civic Adminstrn., Coll. City N.Y., 1953-54; dir. pub. relations research U.S. Steel Corp., 1959-69, dir. pub. communications service, 1969—. Pres. Found. for Pub. Relations Research and Edn., 1970—. Served to capt. AUS, 1942-46. Mem Pub. Relations Soc. Am. (treas. 1963-64, pres. N.Y. chpt. 1959-60), Am. Iron and Steel Inst., Sigma Alpha Epsilon. Club: Pittsburgh Press. Home: R D 1 Box 123 Wexford PA 15090 Office: 600 Grant St Pittsburgh PA 15230

COOKE, ALFRED ALISTAIR, journalist, broadcaster; b. Manchester, Eng.. Nov. 20, 1908; s. Samuel and Mary Elizabeth (Byrne) C.; scholar Jesus Coll., Cambridge, 1st class English Tripos, 1929, B.A. summa cum laude, 1930; Commonwealth Fund fellow Yale, 1932-33, Harvard, 1933-34; LL.D., U. Edinburgh, 1969; m. Ruth Emerson; 1 son, John Byrne; m. 2d, Jane White Hawkes; 1 dau., Susan Byrne. Film critic BBC, 1934-37, commentator on Am. affairs, 1938—; London corr. NBC, 1936-37; spl. corr. Am. affairs London Times, 1938- 42; Am. feature writer London Daily Herald, 1941-43; UN corr. (Manchester) Guardian, 1945-48, chief U.S. corr., 1948—; tv emcee Omnibus, 1952-61; host Masterpiece Theatre (TV), 1971—. Peabody award for internat. news reporting, 1952. Clubs: National Press (Washington); Royal and Ancient G.C. (St. Andrews); Savile, Athenaeum (London). Author: Douglas Fairbanks, 1940; A Generation On Trial, 1950; One Man's America, 1952; Christmas Eve, 1952; A Commencement Address, 1954; Talk About America, 1968. Editor: Garbo and the Night Watchmen, 1937; The Vintage Mencken, 1955; The Granta, 1931-32. Address: Nassau Point Cutchogue Long Island NY 11935

COOKE, BLAINE, airlines co. exec.; b. Reedsburg, Wis., Apr. 18, 1918; s. Joseph E. and Gertrude M. (McLyman) C.; B.A., Hamline U., 1938; Ph.D., U. Minn., 1954; m. Ione L. Hals, Nov. 3, 1943; 1 son, Jerry Alan. Instr., Sch. Bus. U. Minn., 1948-50; dir. marketing research, dir. personnel research Standard Oil Co. Ind., 1950-57; mgr. comml. research div. Am. Oil Co., 1957-61; mgr. marketing research dept. Lincoln-Mercury div. Ford Motor Co., 1961-63; v.p. marketing services United Air Lines, 1963-68; v.p. marketing Trans World Airlines, 1968-69, sr. v.p. marketing, dir., 1969—. Mem. marketing adv. com. Dept. Commerce, 1967—, travel adv. bd, 1969—. Bd. edn. sch. dist. 163, Park Forest, Ill., 1959-61. Served with AUS, 1942-46. Mem. Am. Marketing Assn. (chmn. com. ethics and standards 1963, v.p. marketing mgmt. div. 1964-65), Am. Econ. Assn., Am. Statis. Assn. Contbr. articles to profl. jours. Home; 870 UN Plaza New York City NY 10017 Office: 605 3d Av New York City NY 10016

COOKE, C. LESLIE, utility exec.; b. 1909; married. With Community Pub. Service Co., Fort Worth, 1928—, v.p., treas., 1962-65, exec. v.p., 1965-66, pres., 1966-68, pres., chief exec. officer, 1968—, also dir. Office: 501 W 6th St Fort Worth TX 76102*

COOKE, CARL FREDERICK, investment banker; b. Sweet Springs, Va., Aug 18, 1915; s. Porcher M. and Vera E. (Zimmerman) C.; m. Alice Belle Cloud, June 18, 1939; children—Thomas L., Judith E. With E.H. Rollins & Sons, Inc., Phila., 1936-43; with First Boston Corp., N.Y.C., 1943—, v.p., 1959-67, sr. v.p., mem. exec. com., 1967—, also dir., mgr. govt. bond dept. Served with USNR, World War II. Presbyn. (ruling elder). Clubs: Whispering Pines Country (N.C.); Broad Street (N.Y.C.); Fairmount Country (Chatham, N.J.). Home: 2 Coursen Way Madison NJ 07940 Office: 20 Exchange Pl New York City NY 10005

COOKE, DAVID, banker; b. Scotland, 1904. Vice pres., controller Zions First Nat. Bank, Salt Lake City. Home: 1963 Longview Dr Salt Lake City UT 84117 Office: 1 Main St Salt Lake City UT 84110*

COOKE, DENNIS HARGROVE, educator; b. Maiden, N.C., Feb. 23, 1904; s. Avery Little and Alice Medora (Keener) C.; A.B., Duke, 1925, M.Ed., 1928; Ph.D. (Rosenwald fellow), George Peabody Coll. for Tchrs., 1930; m. Gertrude Elizabeth Murray, Dec. 30, 1925; children—Dennis H., Avery Murray. Prin. schs. in N.C., 1922-23, 25-26; supt. Oxford (N.C.) Masonic Orphanage Schs., 1926-28; fellowship asst. Duke, 1928-29; asso. prof. Peabody Coll., 1930-32, prof. ednl. adminstrn., 1932-40, head dept. ednl. adminstrn., 1940-46; pres. East Carolina Tchrs. Coll., Greenville, N.C., 1946-47; dir. summer sessions, head dept. edn., Woman's Coll., U. N.C., 1947-49; pres. High Point (N.C.) Coll., 1949-59, dir. tchr. edn., 1959-69, prof. edn., psychology, 1969—. Served in adv. capacity to large number of univ., coll., and pub. sch. bds., adminstrv. officers, and presidents; on surveys ednl. instns. in Miss., N.C., La., Ky., Ga., S.C., Ark.; state del. White House Conf. on Edn., 1955. Mem. So. Soc. for Philos., Psychology and Edn., Am. Psychol. Assn., Am. Ednl. Research Assn., N.E.A., Am. Assn. Sch. Adminstrs., N.C. Edn. Assn., C. of C. (dir.), Kappa Delta Pi, Phi Delta Kappa. Methodist (ofcl. bd.). Rotarian (pres). Author: The White Superintendent and the Negro Schools in North Carolina, 1930; Minimum Essentials of Statistics, as Applied to Psychology and Education, 1936; (with Hamon and Proctor) Principles of School Administration, 1938; (with Mallory and Loughren) Using Arithmetic: Grades III through VIII, 1941, Key to Using Arithmetic, 1941; Humanizing Educational Adminstration, 1946; others. Gen. editor Ednl. Trends Series of Profl. Books in Edn., 1935—. Contbr. articles ednl. publs. Home: 924 Kingston St High Point NC 27260 ☆

COOKE, DERYCK VICTOR, musicologist; b. Leicester, Eng., Sept. 14, 1919; s. Henry Victor and Mabel (Judd) C.; M.A. in English with honours, Selwyn Coll., Cambridge U., 1944, Mus.B., 1947; diploma Royal Coll. Music, 1937; m. Jacqueline Robert, Oct 25, 1966, With BBC, 1947—, sr. asst. music information, 1965—; free-lance writer, 1959-65. Served with British Royal Arty., 1939-45. Recipient Kilenyi Mahler medal Bruckner Soc. Am., 1964. Asso. Royal Coll. Music, Royal Coll. Organists. Author: The Language of Music, 1959; Mahler 1860-1911, 1960. Arranger performing version Mahler's unfinished 10th Symphony, 1964. Home: 76 Eton Pl Eton Coll Rd London NW 3 England Office: BBC Music Div Broadcasting House London W 1 England

COOKE, DON ALVIN, clergyman; b. St. James, Minn., Mar. 18, 1898; s. George Alfred an Bertha (Case) C.; student Taylor U., Upland, Ind., 1916-17; A.B., Emory U., 1922; S.T.B., Yale 1928; D.D., Fla. So. U., 1952; m. Mabel Priest, June 26, 1930; children—Elizabeth (Mrs. Jack Martin), Dorothy (Mrs. W. Ray Finklea), Florence (Mrs. J. Russell Sackett, Jr.). Ordained to ministry Methodist Ch., 1924; pastor, dist. supt., Miami, 1950-52, Jacksonville, 1952-55; dir. Wesley Found., U. Fla., 1930-38; sec. Southeastern Jurisdictional Conf., 1956-60; gen. sec.-treas. Council World Service and Finance, Meth. Ch., 1961-68; retired, 1968. Sec. Fla. Annual Conf., 1935-60; mem. council secs. Meth. Ch., also mem. gen. conf., 1952, 56, 60, mem. Southeastern gen. conf., 1948, 52, 56, 60. Trustee Meth. Ch. Served as chaplain AUS, 1941-45. Decorated Bronze Star medal. Mem. Mil. Chapalins Assn., World Meth. Council, Ret. Officers Assn., Sigma Chi. Mason (Shriner). Club: Miami Acacia. Address: 750 W 5th St Miami Beach FL 33140

COOKE, HARRISON RICE, banker; b. Honolulu, Oct. 11, 1908; s. Clarence Hyde and Lily (Love) C.; student Yale, 1928-30; m. Dorothea Sloggett, Apr. 7, 1931. With Bank of Hawaii, 1930-34; v.p., sec. Cooke Trust Co., Honolulu, 1934-41; pres. Honolulu Sporting Goods Co., 1946-; chmn. Bank of Hawaii, 1963-; pres. Molokai Ranch Ltd., 1958—, Molokai Electric Co., 1961—. Trustee, v.p. Honolulu Acad. Arts. Served to comdr. USNR, 1941-45. Decorated Bronze Star. Home: 2549 Tantalus St Honolulu, HI 96814. Office: 140 S King St Honolulu, HI 96502.

COOKE, JACK KENT, business exec., publisher; b. Hamilton, Ont., Can., Oct. 25, 1912; s. Ralph Ercil and Nancy (Jacobs) C.; student Malvern Collegiate; m. Barbara Jean Carnegie, May 5, 1934; children—Ralph, John. Joined No. Broadcasting and Publishing Ltd., 1937; partner Thomson Cooke Newspapers, 1937-52; pres. radio sta. CKEY, Toronto, 1944-61; pres. Micro Plastics, Ltd., Acton, Ont., 1955-60, Robinson Indsl. Crafts, Ltd., London, Ont., 1957-63, Precision Die Casting Ltd., Toronto, 1955-60, Toronto Maple Leaf Baseball Club Ltd., 1951-64, Liberty of Can., Ltd., 1947-61; pres. Consol. Frybrook Industries, Ltd., 1952-61, Aubyn Investments, Ltd., 1961-68; Continental Cablevision, Inc., 1965-68; pres. Jack Kent Cooke Inc. Cal. (Cooke Pub. Co. and Am. Cablevision Co.), 1959-68; 1st v.p., pres., treas. Pro-Football, Inc. (Washington Redskins, Nat. Football League), Washington; pres. Cal. Sports, Inc. (Los Angeles Lakers, Nat. Basketball Assn.; Los Angeles Kings, Nat. Hockey League); pres. The Forum of Inglewood, Inc.; dir., chmn. exec. com. H & B Am. Corp.; chmn. bd. Transam. Microwave, Inc., 1965-69. Trustee Little League Found., City of Hope; gov. Arthritis Found. Clubs: National, Royal Canadian Yacht (Toronto); Bel Air Country (Los Angeles). Home: 310 St Cloud Rd Los Angeles CA 90024 Office: The Forum Manchester and Prairie Av Inglewood CA 90307

COOKE, JACOB ERNEST, educator, author; b. Aulander, N.C., Sept. 23, 1924; s. Jacob E. and Myrtle (Basemore) C.; A.B., U. N.C., 1947; Ph.D., Columbia, 1955; m. Jean Gordon, Nov. 3, 1956; children—Jacob Ernest III, Christopher II. Instr., then asst. prof. Columbia, 1953-61; asso. editor Papers of Alexander Hamilton, 1955—; prof. history, head dept. Carnegie Inst. Tech., 1961-62; John Henry MacCracken prof. history Lafayette Coll., 1962—; vis. prof. Columbia, 1969. Served with USAAF, 1941-45. Guggenheim fellow, 1968-69. Mem. Am., Miss. Valley, So. hist. assns. Author: Frederick Bancroft, 1956; The March of Democracy, vols. VI and VII, 1965; The Age of Responsibility, 1965; The Kennedy Years, 1966. Editor: The Federalist, 1961; Reports of Alexander Hamilton, 1964; The Challenge of History, 1965. Home: 172 Shawnee Av Easton PA 18042

COOKE, JAMES, chain store exec.; b. Phila., Nov. 13, 1909; s. Kalman and Ethel (Vinocur) C.; B.S., U. Pa., 1933; m. Lillian Minor, July 31, 1933; children—Molly Ann (Mrs. Beitner), Sally Lynne (Mrs. Rubiner). Asso. with Penn Fruit Co., Phila., 1927-59, beginning as clk., successively advt. mgr., gen. supt. stores, 1927-45, gen.mgr., 1945-52, v.p., gen. mgr., 1952-59, pres., chief exec. officer, 1964—, pres. Allied Supermarkets, Inc. (formerly ACF-Wrigley Stores, Inc.), Detroit, 1959-64, chief exec. officer, 1960-64; pres. Topco Assos., Inc. Bd. govs. Acad. Food Marketing, St. Joseph's Coll. Mem. Nat. Assn. Food Chains (mem. exec. com. 1954, chmn. 1963-64, dir.), Super Market Inst. (v.p., dir.), Pi Gamma Mu. Home: Cedarbrook Hill Apts Wyncote PA 19095 Office: Grant Av and Blue Grass Rd Philadelphia PA 19115

COOKE, JAMES NEGLEY, Jr., drug and pharm. mfr.; b. Pitts., Mar. 12, 1908; s. James Negley and Mary (Miller)C.; grad. Salisbury (Conn). Sch., 1928; student Princeton, 1932; m. Frances Ann Bonfoey, May 2, 1931; children—Diann Bonfoey (Mrs. Peter Coombs), James Negley III; m. 2d. Nancy Reynolds, Dec. 23, 1941; children—Peter Reynolds, Christopher Creighton. Salesman Monroe Chem. Co., Quincy, Ill., 1931-32; mgr. Monroe Chem. Co., Ltd., London, Eng., 1932; sales mgr. Monroe Chem. Co., N.Y.C., 1933-34; gen. mgr. Wells & Richardson Co., Burlington, Vt., subsidiary Sterling Drug, Inc., 1935-40, The Cummer Products Co., also The Molle Co., Bedford, O., subsidiary Sterling Drug Inc., 1940-43; divisional v.p. Sterling Drug, Inc., Brattleboro, Vt., 1950-56, dir. marketing, N.Y.C., 1950-56, v.p., 1956—, dir., 1960—, pres. Glenbrook Labs. div., 1958—; dir. Mad River Corp., Burlington, Vt., Mt. Mansfield Co., Stowe, Vt.; v.p. d'Con Co., Inc., N.Y.C., 1957—. Hon. dir. Brattleboro Meml. Hosp.; mem. bd. Brand Names Found.; trustee Holderness Sch., Plymouth, N.H.; past pres., mem. bd. Proprietary Assn. Mem. U.S. Eastern Amateur Ski Assn. (past dir.; chmn. N.Y. com. U.S. Ski Team Fund 1969—). Clubs: Bedford (N.Y.) Golf and Tennis; Princeton, Amateur Ski N.Y.C.); Mad River Ski (Waitsfield, Vt.); Mt. Mansfield Ski (Stowe, Vt.); Cap and Gown (Princeton, N.J.); Pinnacle (N.Y.C.). Home: 14 North Lake Rd Armonk NY 10504 Office: 90 Park Av New York City NY 10016

COOKE, JOHN DANIEL, educator; b. Beloit, Kan., May 26, 1892; s. Edwin Willis and Sarah Arminda (Shutts) C.; A.B., Stanford U., 1914, A.M., 1915, Ph.D., 1924; m. Grace Steinberger, Aug. 15, 1917 (dec. 1945); 1 dau., Marianne Whitehead; m. 2d, Mariam Bailey Parr, April 15, 1950. Asst. in Greek, Stanford U., 1913-15; instr. English Kan. State Agrl. Coll., 1915-17; instr. comparative and English lit. U. Colo., 1917-19; asst. prof. English Wash. State Coll., 1919-20; asst. prof., prof. English U. So. Cal., 1920—, dept. head, 1930-38, chmn. div. humanities, 1938-59. Ednl. dir., Naval Flight Prep. Sch., 1943; dean summer sessions, 1945-60, now emeritus, acting dean grad. sch., 1956-58. Mem. Am. Assn. U. Profs., Modern Lang. Assn., Am. Pacific Coast Philol. Assn., Phi Beta Kappa (chmn. essay contest Southern Calif. Alumni 1930-36), Phi Delta Kappa, Phi Kappa Phi, Alpha Phi Epsilon. Roman Catholic. Mason. Club: Am. College Quill (high chancellor 1934-36). Editor: Minor Victorian Poets, 1928; (with M.C. Struble) Essays for the New America, 1930; (with Lionel Stevenson) English Literature of the Victorian Period, 1949. Home: San Ismael 666 Jardines de los Arcos Guadalajara Jal Mexico

COOKE, JOHN JOSEPH, pub. co. exec.; b. Bklyn., Nov. 11, 1908; s. John Joseph and Stella DePaul (Kiernan) C.; A.B., Manhattan Coll., 1930; LL.B., St. John's Law Sch., Bklyn., 1935; m. Virginia Norsworthy Humphreys, Aug. 13, 1938; children—Mary H., Jame U., John N., Paul K., Virginia A., Roger A., Hilary F., Linus G. Admitted to N.Y. bar, 1935, practiced in N.Y.C., 1935-40; law sec. to judge N.Y. State Ct. Appeals, 1941-43; with McGraw-Hill Inc., 1943—, now sr. v.p., sec., gen. counsel; sec. Newton Falls Paper Mill, Inc.; trustee Fulton Savs. Bank Kings County, Bklyn.; dir. Shepard's Citations Inc., Colorado Springs, Ednl. Devel. Labs., Huntington, N.Y., Am. Heritage Pub. Co., N.Y.C., Spitz Labs. Inc., Chadd's Ford, Pa., McGraw Hill Book Co. (U.K.) Ltd., McGraw Hill Ryerson Ltd., Toronto. Trustee Manhattan Coll., Riverdale, N.Y. Mem. Am., N.Y. bar assns., Assn. Bar City N.Y., Am. Soc. Corporate Secs. Home: 7 Cathedral Av Garden City NY 11530 Office: 330 W 42d St New York City NY 10036

COOKE, KENNETH LLOYD, educator, mathematician; b. Kansas City, Mo., Aug. 13, 1925; s. Sidney Kenneth and Mildred Blanche (Brown) C.; B.A., Pomona Coll., 1947; M.S., Stanford, 1949, Ph.D., 1952; m. Margaret Sarah Burgess, Aug. 18, 1950; children—Catherine Sarah, Robert K., Susan. Instr., then asst. prof. math. State Coll. Wash., Pullman, 1950-57; mem. faculty Pomona Coll., 1957—, Joseph N. Fiske prof. math., 1963—, chmn. dept., 1961-71; cons. RAND Corp., 1956-65; mathematician Research Inst. Advanced Studies, Balt., 1963-64; NSF sci. faculty fellow Stanford, 1966-67; Fulbright research scholar U. Florence (Italy), 1971-72. Served with USNR, 1944-46. Mem. Am. Math. Soc., Math. Assn. Am., Soc. Indsl. and Applied Math., Am. Assn. U. Profs., Phi Beta Kappa, Sigma Xi. Mem. United Ch. Christ. Author: (with Richard Bellman) Differential-Difference Equations, 1963, Modern Elementary Differential Equations, 2d edit., 1971; (with Richard Bellman and J.A. Lockett) Algorithms, Graphs and Computers, 1970. Home: 654 Northwestern Dr Claremont CA 91711

COOKE, LLOYD MILLER, chem. co. exec.; b. LaSalle, Ill., June 7, 1916; s. William Wilson and Anna (Miller) C.; B.S., U. Wis., 1937; Ph.D., McGill U., 1941; m. Vera E. Schlegel, June 29, 1957; children—Barbara Anne, William E. Lectr., McGill U., 1941-42; sect. leader Corn Products Refining Co., Argo, Ill., 1942-46; group leader food products div. Union Carbide Corp., Chgo., 1946-49, dept. mgr., 1950-54, asst. to mgr. tech. div., 1954-57, asst. dir. research, 1957-65, mgr. market research, 1965-67, mgr. planning, 1967-70, dir. urban affairs, N.Y.C., 1970—. Mem. Community Conf. Bd., Downers Grove, Ill., 1968-70. Trustee Nat. Sci. Bd. Recipient Proctor prize sci. Sci. Research Soc. Am., 1970. Fellow Am. Inst. Chemists (honor scroll Chgo.), N.Y. Acad. Scis.; mem. Am. Chem. Soc., A.A.A.S., Sigma Xi, Phi Kappa Phi, Beta Kappa Chi. Club: Chicago Chemists. Contbr. articles to profl. jours. Home: 1 Beaufort Rd White Plains NY 10607 Office: 270 Park Av New York City NY 10017

COOKE, MERRITT TODD, Jr., banker; b. Phila., Mar. 20, 1920; s. Merritt Todd and Beatrice (Crawford) C.; B.A., Princeton, 1942; M.C.P., Mass. Inst. Tech., 1947; m. Mary T. Cooke, Sept. 24, 1949 (dec.); children—Mary Marshall, Merritt Todd; m. 2d, Margaret S. Groome, Dec. 4, 1965. Exec. dir. Del. County Planning Commn., Media, Pa., 1951-55; c.p. W.A. Clarke Mortgage Co., Phila., 1956-60; asst. v.p. First Pa. Bank, Phila., 1961-65; with The Phila. Saving Fund Soc., 1966—, pres., 1971—. Trustee First Pa. Mortgage Trust. Vice pres. United Fund Phila., 1971—; chmn. bd. Pa. Hosp., Phila. Served with AUS, 1942-46. Mem. Phi Beta Kappa, Lambda Alpha. Home: Greenlands Newton St Rd Media PA 19063 Office: 1212 Market St Philadelphia PA 19107

COOKE, PAUL DENVIR, advt. agy. exec.; b. Phila., Jan. 26, 1920; s. Charles J. and Katharine (Freer) C.; B.A., Yale, 1942; m. Marian K. Spiegel, Oct. 17, 1943; 1 dau., Katharine M. Account exec. Compton Advt., Inc., N.Y.C., 1948, v.p., 1953-63, sr. v.p., 1963-67, exec. v.p., 1967-70, dep. chmn. bd., 1970—, also dir. Served to lt. USNR, 1942-48. Mem. Newcomen Soc. N.Am., Navy League U.S. Club : Yale (N.Y.C.); Hackensack Golf (Oraddell, N.J.). Home: 282 Schley Pl Teaneck, NJ 07666. Office: 625 Madison Av New York City NY 10022

COOKE, ROBERT EDMOND, physician, educator; b. Attleboro, Mass., Nov. 13, 1920; s. Ronald Melbourne and Renee Jeanne (Wuillumier) C.; B.S. Sheffield Sci. Sch., Yale, 1941, M.D., 1944, postgrad. (NIH postdoctorate fellow) Sch. Medicine, 1948-50, (John and Mary R. Markle scholar), 1951-55; m. 2d, Nancy Perry Dwight, Sept 3, 1965; children (by prev. marriage)-Robyn (dec.), Christopher, Wendy, W. Robert, Kim. Intern, asst. resident dept. pediatrics New Haven Hosp., 1944-46; instr. pediatrics Yale, 1950-51, asst. prof. pediatrics, physiology, 1951- 54, asso. prof., 1954-56; resident to asso. pediatrician Grace-New Haven Community Hosp., 1951-56; pediatrician-in-chief Johns Hopkins Hosp.; chmn. dept. Johns Hopkins Sch. Medicine, 1956—; Grover Powers prof. pediatrics Nat. Assn. Retarded Children, 1957-59, Given Found. prof. pediatrics, 1962—. Mem. nat. adv. bd. mental health Jr. C of C.; sci. adv. council Children's Hosp. Research Found.; chmn. med. adv. bd. Kennedy Found.; mem. med. adv. bd. Balt. chpt. Cystic Fibrosis, United Cerebral Palsy Greater Balt., Md. Soc. Mentally Retarded Children, Children's Guild; mem. adv. council Yale U. Sch. Medicine, Colo. Allergy Research Inst. Trustee children's Rehab. Inst. Served from lt. to capt. M.C., AUS, 1946-48. Recipient Mead Johnson award in pediatrics, 1954; Kennedy Internat. award for distinguished service in field mental retardation, 1968. Fellow Am. Acad. Pediatrics; Distinguished fellow Am. Psychiat. Assn.; mem. Am. Pediatric Soc., Soc. for Pediatric Research (pres. 1965-66), Am. Soc. for Clin. Investigation, Md. Med. Soc., A.M.A., Am. Pub. Health Assn., Am. Fedn. Clin. Research, Aurelian Hon. Soc., Phi Beta Kappa, Sigma Xi, Alpha Omega Alpha. Editor, contbr. to pediatric textbooks, profl. jours. Home: 1013 St George's Rd Baltimore MD 21210 Office: Johns Hopkins Hosp Baltimore MD 21205

COOKE, SIDNEY M., Sr., banker. Vice chmn. bd., dir., exec. officer Columbia Union Nat. Bank & Trust Co., Kansas City, Mo. Office: 900 Walnut St Kansas City MO 64106*

COOKE, STRATHMORE RIDLEY BARNOTT, metallurgist; b. Wanganui, N.Z., Jan. 4, 1907; s. Charles Ridley and Lilian Dawn Auckland (Barnott) C.; B.S., U. N.Z., 1928, B.E., 1929; Asso. Otago Sch. of Mines, U. Otago, 1929; M.S., Mo. Sch. Mines, 1930; Ph.D., U. Mo., 1933; m. Helen Ruth Cahill, Oct. 14, 1933; 1 son, S.R. Bruce. Came to U.S., 1929, naturalized, 1941. Research metallurgist Mo. Expt. Sta., 1933-36; asst. prof. Mo. Sch. Mines and Metallurgy, 1936-39; research prof. Mont. Sch. Mines, 1939-46; prof. metallurgy, mineral dressing U. Minn. Sch. Mines, 1946—, head sch. mines and metallurgy, 1957-60, chief dir. metall. engring., 1960-63, prof. metall. engring., 1963-70, prof. Sch. Earth Scis., 1970—; cons. metallurgist. Member Am. Inst. M.E., Am. Chem. Soc., Mineral. Soc. Am., Astron. Soc. Pacific, Brit. Astron. Assn., Sigma Xi, Phi Kappa Phi, Theta Tau, Kappa Sigma, Tau Beta Pi. Contbr. articles in field. Home: 4408 Zenith Av N Robbinsdale MN 55422 Office: Pillsbury Hall U Minn Minneapolis MN 55455

COOKE, TERENCE CARDINAL, bishop; b. N.Y.C., Mar. 1, 1921; s. Michael and Margaret (Gannon) C.; student Cathedral Coll., N.Y.C.; B.A., St. Joseph's Sem., Yonkers, N.Y., 1945; M.S. in Social Work, Cath. U., 1949. Ordained priest Roman Cath. Ch., 1945; asst. pastor St. Athanasius Ch., Bronx, N.Y., also chaplain St. Agatha Home, Nanuet, N.Y., 1946-47; asst. dir. Cath. Youth Orgn., also dir. youth activities, N.Y.C., 1949-54; procurator St. Joseph's Sem., Yonkers, N.Y., 1954-57; sec. to Cardinal Spellman, 1957-58; named papal chamberlain, vice chancellor Archdiocese N.Y., 1958, domestic prelate, chancellor, 1961-65, vicar gen., 1965-68; titular bishop of Summa and aux. bishop N.Y., 1965-68; archbishop of N.Y., 1968—; created cardinal, 1968. Home: 452 Madison Av New York City NY 10022 Office: 451 Madison Av New York City NY 10022

COOKE, WILLIAM BRIDGE, mycologist; b. Foster, O., July 16, 1908; s. William Thomas Hunter and Katharine May (Bridge) C.; B.A., U. Cin., 1937; M.S., Ore. State U., 1939; Ph.D., Wash. State U., 1950; m. Vivian Greenwald, June 12, 1942. Research asso. dept. plant pathology Wash. State U., Pullman, 1950-51; mycologist charge fungus studies Robert A. Taft Water Research Center, U.S. Dept. Health, Edn. and Welfare, Cin., 1952-65; mycologist Advanced Waste Treatment Research Lab., Fed. Water Pollution Control Adminstrn., Dept. Health Edn. Welfare, 1965-66, Dept. Interior, Cin., 1966-69; research asso. botany dept. Miami U., Oxford, O., 1968-70; sr. research asso. Miami Valley Project, U. Cin., asso. with dept. biol. scis., 1970—. Cons. Bur. Solid Waste Mgmt., Environmental Protection Agy. Served Q.M.C., AUS, 1945-46. Recipient Superior Service award Dept. Health, Edn. and Welfare, 1960; Award of Excellence Fed. Water Pollution Control Adminstrn. U.S. Dept. Interior, 1971. Fellow A.A.A.S., Ohio Acad. Sci., Am. Acad. Microbiology (charter); mem. Mycol. Soc. Am. (chmn. foray com.), Ecol. Soc. Am., Am. Inst. Biol. Scis., Bot. Soc. Am., Am. Soc. Plant Taxonomy, Internat. Assn. Plant Taxonomists, Cal. Bot. Soc., Brit. Mycol. Soc., Internat. Soc. Human and Animal Micology, Sierra Club. Author: A Laboratory Guide to Culture and Identification of Sewage Fungi, 1963. Developed techniques demonstrating presence of fungus populations in sewage and polluted waters; research and publs. list of flora and fungi of Mt. Shasta, Cal. Home: 1135 Wilshire Ct Cincinnati OH 45230

COOKE, WILLIAM DONALD, univ. ofcl.; b. Phila., May 15, 1918; s. William Donald and Gertrude (Raith) C.; B.S., St. Joseph's Coll., Phila., 1940; student Mass. Inst. Tech., 1941-42; M.S., U. Pa., 1947, Ph.D., 1949; fellow Princeton, 1949- 51; m. June Marie Orr, Oct. 5, 1946; children—W. Donald, Peter K., Christopher A., Catherine A., M. Timothy, Antonia. Mem. faculty Cornell U., Ithaca, N.Y., 1951—, prof. chemistry, 1957—, dean Grad. Sch., 1964—, v.p. research, 1969—. Served to maj. USAAF, 1942-46; ETO. Mem. Am. Chem. Soc. (chmn. analytical div. 1964-65), Assn. Grad. Schs. (pres. 1971). Contbr. to profl. jours. Home: 215 Dearborn Pl Ithaca NY 14850

COOKE, WILLIAM LATIMER, physician; b. Newport News, Va., Dec. 3, 1906; s. William L. and Martha H. (Turner) C.; student San Diego State Coll., 1923-25; M.D., Med. Coll. Va., 1929; m. Sally Ann Boxley, Feb. 10, 1931. Intern Charleston (W.Va.) Gen. Hosp., 1929-30, resident, 1932-34; resident Pinecrest Sanatorium, Beckley, W.Va., 1930-32; practice medicine, specializing in chest diseases, Charleston, 1934-72; mem. courtesy staff Charleston Gen., Charleston Meml., Kanawha Valley hosps. Chmn. Kanawha-Clay chpt. A.R.C., 1955-56; chmn. United Fund, 1957-58. Served to maj., M.C., AUS, 1942-46. Mem. Nat. Tb Assn. (pres. 1964-65), Kanawha County Med. Soc. (past chmn.), Alumni Assn. Med. Coll. Va. (pres. 1965-66). Kiwanian. Home: 5 Roller Rd Charleston WV 25314

COOKENBACH, JOHN M., banker; b. Phila., 1910; grad. Swarthmore Coll., 1931. Exec. v.p. First Pa. Banking & Trust Co. Home: 811 Oak Ridge Rd Rosemont PA 19010 Office: First Pennsylvania Banking & Trust Co 15th and Chestnut Sts Philadelphia PA 19101

COOKENBOO, JOHN B., gas co. exec.; b. Wharton, Tex., 1910; ed. S. Tex. Coll., 1943. Formerly sr. v.p. adminstrn. and finance Houston Natural Gas Corp., now vice chmn. bd., also dir.; dir. Houston Pipe Line Co., Houston Natural Gas Prodn. Co., H.N.G. Petrochems. Co., Valley Gas Transmission Co., Valley Pipe Lines, Inc., Roden Oil Co., Liquid Carbonic Corp., Mid. La Gas Co. Home: 250 Chimney Rock Rd Houston TX 77024 PO Box 1188 Houston TX 77002

COOKMAN, JOHN E., cigarette co. exec.; b. Englewood, N.J., Sept. 2, 1909; s. Arthur S. and Martha Cookman; grad. Exeter Acad.; 1927, Yale, 1931; m. Anne Mererole 1936. With N.Y. Trust Co., 1933-51; sr. v.p., dir. Phillip Morris, Inc., 1952—. Home: 189 Chestnut St Englewood NJ 07631 Office: 100 Park Av New York City NY 10017

COOKSEY, HOWARD HARRISON, army officer; b. Brentsville, Va., June 21, 1921; s. Paul Jackson and Norma (Young) C.; B.S., Va. Poly. Inst., 1943; M.A., George Washington U., 1964; grad. Command and Gen. Staff Coll., 1954, Armed Forces Staff Coll., 1959, Nat. War Coll., 1963; m. Althea Maitland Hooff, Oct. 5, 1946; children—Paul H., Allison M. Commd. 2d lt. U.S. Army, 1943, advanced through grades to maj. gen., 1970; in No. Philippines and Luzon, World War II; with 7th Inf. Div., Korea, 1954-57; Office Chief of Research and Devel., Washington, 1963-66, Hdqrs. U.S. European Command, 1959-61, 6th Inf. Regt., Berlin, 1961-62, 2d Inf. Div., Korea, 1966-67, U.S. Strike Command, 1967-68, Americal Div., Vietnam, 1968-69; comdg. gen. U.S. Army Tng. Center, Inf., Ft. Dix, N.J., 1970—; asst. prof. mil. sci. Drexel U., 1949-51. Decorated D.S.M., Silver Star, Legion of Merit, Bronze Star, Air medal, Purple Heart. Mem. Brotherhood of St. Andrew, Scabbard and Blade. Home: 9135 N Grant Av Manassas VA 22110 Office: Hdqrs U S Army Tng Center Infantry Fort Dix NJ 08640

COOKSON, FRANK BARTON, univ. dean; b. Wigan, Eng., Sept. 27, 1912; s. William and Hannah (Barton) C.; came to U.S., 1913, naturalized, 1939; B.Mus., Northwestern U., 1935, M.Mus., 1936; Ph.D., Eastman Sch. Music, 1947; m. 2d, Sandra Palmer, June 17, 1961; children by previous marriage—Julie (Mrs. Denis Jones), Christine (Mrs. David Wheelock); 1 son by present marriage, Matthew Barton; stepchildren—Karla Wentzel, Ingrid Wentzel. Mem. faculty Northwestern U., 1939-62, prof., chmn. dept.theory and composition, 1951- 62, mng. editor Ednl. Music mag., 1936-53; organist, choir dir. chs. in Ill., 1934-62; v.p. Ednl. Music Bur., 1953-63; v.p. Frederick Charles Pub. Co., 1959-62; dean Sch. Fine Arts, U. Conn., 1962—. Mem. Conn. Commn. on Arts, 1965—. Mem. bd. edn. Regional High Sch. 11, Conn., 1965- 67. Mem. Nat. Council Fine Arts Deans, Phi Mu Alpha, Pi Kappa Lambda. Co- author, gen. editor: Creative-Analytical Theory of music, vols. 1 and 2, 1948-49. Composer over 60 choral compositions. Home: Westgate Lane Storrs, CT 06268. Office: Sch Fine Arts Univ Conn Storrs CT 06268

COOLBAUGH, FRANK, mining exec., cons. b. Rapid City, S.D., Dec. 21, 1908; s. Melville Fuller and Osie (Smith) C.; E.M., Colo. Sch. Mines, 1933; grad. Advanced Mgmt. Program, Harvard, 1947; m. Dallos Inez Davies, Aug. 17, 1947; 1 son, Melville James. Coal miner U.S. Fuel Co., Mohrland, Utah, 1928-30; from mine helper to asst. mill supt. Climax Molybdenum Co., Climax, Colo., 1933- 42, planning dir., asst. gen. supt., resident mgr., gen. mgr., v.p., 1946-59, pres., 1959-60, dir., 1955-58; pres., dir. Climax Uranium Co.; v.p., Am. Metal Climax, Inc., 1958-60, pres., 1960-65, chmn., chief exec. officer, 1966-67, cons., 1967-68, dir., 1958-68; pres., dir. Coolbaugh Mining Corp., 1969—; mine developer, cons. industry, 1968—; dir. Newmont Mining Corp., Ranchers Exploration & Devel. Corp., N.W. Zinc Co., Ltd. Served to capt., C.E., AUS, 1942-46. Mem. Am. Inst. Mining and Metall. Engrs., Mining and Metall. Soc. Am., Instn. Mining and Metallurgy London, Am. Mining Congress. Presbyn. Home: 1700 Maple St Golden CO 80401 Office: 8700 W 14th Av Lakewood CO 80215

COOLEY, ALBERT M., educator; b. Clarence, Mo., July 26, 1908; s. Albert M. and Margaret (Thompson) C.; B.S., Mont. State Coll., 1930; M.S., U. of N.D., 1931; m. Coen; Margaret Fosmark, June 21, 1939 (dec.); chilren—Albert M. and Stephen A. Began career as chemist with C.F. Burgess Labs., Madison, Wis., 1932-34; instr. chem. engring. U. of N.D., 1934-36, asst. prof., 1936-42, asso. prof., 1942-46, prof. chem. engring. and head dept. chem. engring., 1946—. Mem. Inst. Food Tech Am. Chem. Soc., Am. Inst. Mining, Metall. and Petroleum Engrs., Am. Inst. Chem. Engrs., Am. Soc. Engring. Edn., Sigma Xi, Alpha Chi Sigma, Kappa Sigma, Sigma Tau. Club: Rotary. Home: 405 Cambridge St Grand Forks ND 58201

COOLEY, BERNARD HENRY, hotel developer and cons.; b. N.Y.C., Feb. 8, 1906; s. Anthony Bernard and Annie Katherine (Smith) C.; ed. U.S., Cuba and Eng.; m. Doris J. Liebfried, Aug. 18, 1948; children—Carol E., Brenda J. Fgn. trade counsellor, 1926-34; comml. attache of Republic of Cuba, 1934-42; asst. pres., Brighton Hotel, Atlantic City, N.J., 1947-49; pres., dir. Colony Hotel , Palm Beach, Fla., 1949-59, Hotel Colony, Inc., Palm Beach, 1949-61; cons. supr. devel. El Colony, resort hotel, Isle of Pines, Cuba, 1958; v.p., operational and mgmt. cons. Old Port Village, Fla., 1959-63; v.p. gen. mgr. Lost Tree Country Club, Palm Beach, 1959-63; v.p., dir. Westport Utilities Corp. (Fla.), 1959-63; pres., dir. Salco, Inc., 1957-62; pres., dir. Hotel Consultants & Developers, Inc., Palm Beach, 1960—; exec. dir. Kings Bay Yacht and Country Club, Miami, Fla., 1964—; gen. mgr. Everglades Club, Palm Beach, 1969-70; asst. to pres. FPA Corp., Pompano Beach, Fla., 1970—; dir. Fla. Capital Corp. Commr. 6th Congl. Dist. Fla., Fla. Advt. Commn., 1954- 57; vice chmn. arrangements 20th ann. So. Governors Conf., 1954; dir. resources devel. bd. Palm Beach County, 1950—. Bd. suprs. St. Francis Coll., Loretto, Pa., 1958. Served to maj. AUS, 1942-46. Mem. Fla. (dir. 1953-58), Palm Beach County (pres. 1950-60, dir. 1956-59) hotel assns., Hotel Sales Mgmt. Assn., Fla. Pub. Relations Assn., Am. Automobile Assn. (adv. bd. So. Fla. 1953—), Fraternal Order Police Assos. (pres. Palm Beach 1957-58, trustee 1957-63). Clubs: River (Jacksonville, Fla.); Everglades, Beach (Palm Beach, Fla.). Home: 400 S Ocean Blvd Palm Beach FL 33480 Office: PO Box 207 Palm Beach FL 33480

COOLEY, CHARLES PARSONS, Jr., investment banker; b. Hartford, Conn., June 17, 1903; s. Charles P. and Sarah I. (Whitman) C.; grad. Pomfret Sch., 1922; student Yale, 1922-24; m. Adelaide F. Eberts, June 25, 1930; children—Samuel, Timothy, David E., Robert H. With U.S. Security Trust Co., 1924-26, Thomson Fenn & Co., 1926-30, Francis R. Cooley & Co., 1930-34; sr. partner Cooley & Co., Hartford, 1934-69; ltd. partner Burnham & Co., N.Y.C., 1970—; dir. Aetna Ins. Co., Conn. Gen. Life Ins. Co., Arrow Hart & Hageman Electric Co., Conn. Gen. Ins. Corp. Past gov. N.Y. Stock Exchange. Trustee Hartford Hosp. Mem. Assn. Stock Exchange Firms (past gov.), Nat. Assn. Securities Dealers (past gov.). Home: 18 Westwood Rd West Hartford CT 06117 Office: 100 Pearl St Hartford CT 06103

COOLEY, DAVID WILLIAM, assn. exec.; b. Hendersonville, N.C., Feb. 6, 1929; s. Arthur Guilford and Reina (McNee) C.; m. Diane Clair Miller, Oct. 24, 1953; children—Ann, David William, John Philip, Matthew. Chief exec. officer Greer C. of C. (S.C.), 1951-52, Hendersonville (N.C.) C. of C., 1952-58, Greenville (S.C.) C. of C., 1958-64; chief exec. officer Jacksonville (Fla.) C. of C., 1964-68; now chief exec. officer Memphis C. of C., 1968—. Served with USMCR, 1948-50. Episcopalian. Mason (Shriner), Rotarian. Home: 219 Cherokee Dr Memphis TN 38111 Office: Chamber of Commerce Memphis TN 38103

COOLEY, DENTON, surgeon, educator; b. Houston, Aug. 22, 1920; s. Ralph C. and Mary (Fraley) C.; B.A., U. Tex., 1941; M.D., Johns Hopkins, 1944; m. Louise Goldsborough Thomas, Jan. 15, 1949; children—Mary, Susan, Louise, Florence, Helen. Asso. prof. surgery Baylor U. Coll. Medicine, Houston, 1954-62, prof. surgery, 1962—; chief cardiovascular service St. Luke's Hosp., Tex. Children's Hosp. Dir. Southwestern Savs. Assn., Bank of Tex. Trustee St. Stephen. Episcopal Sch., Austin, Tex. Served as capt., M.C., AUS, 1946- 48. Decorated Condeacoracion Al Merito (Ecuador); recipient Grande Medailile, U. Ghent, Belgium, 1963, Humanitarian award Variety Clubs Internat., 1963, Coronat medal St. Edwards U., 1963, Kappa Sigma Man Yr. award, 1964, Dist. Citizen award Rotary Club Houston, 1965, Billings Gold medal, 1967; named one of ten outstanding Young Men in U.S., U.S. Jr. C. of C., 1955. Diplomate Am. Bd. Surgery, Am. Bd. Thoracic Surgery (bd. 1965—). Fellow A.C.S. (gov. 1965-68); mem. Soc. Thoracic Surgeons, Thoracic Soc., So. Med. Assn., Am. Assn. Thoracic Surgery, Soc. Univ. Surgeons, Am. Coll. Cardiology, Am. Coll. Chest Physicians, Am., Pan- Pacific, Western Surg. assns., Tex. Acad. sci., soc. clin. surgery, Internat. Cardiovascular Soc., Soc. Vascular Surgery, Western, So. surg. assns., Halsted Soc., Tex. Surg. Soc., Internat. Soc. Surgery. Performed numerous heart transplants; implanted 1st artificial heart, 1969. Home: 3014 Del Monte Dr Houston TX 77019

COOLEY, GEORGE RALPH, investment banker; b. Troy, N.Y., May 29, 1896; s. Wallace Willard and Ruby (Webb) C.; student Colgate U., 1921; D.Sc. (hon.), U. of So. Florida; LL.D., Colgate U.; m. Myra Taylor, Oct. 1, 1919; children— Barbara Burroughs (Mrs. Daniel V. McNamee Jr.), Dorothy Read (Mrs. Elbert V. Mulleneaux Jr.), Janet Littlefield (Mrs. William John Sloss), Robin (Mrs. Jerome O. Krivanek). Salesman, Dillon, Read & Co., N.Y.C., 1918-24; pres., dir. George R. Cooley & Co., Inc., Albany, N.Y., 1924—; dir., chmn. finance com. North Am. Cement Corp., 1936-48; dir. Pioneer Fund, Inc., 1962—, Pioneer II, Inc. Research fellow Gray Herbarium, Harvard, 1954-65. Dir. Colgate-Rochester Div. Sch., 1950-70, Pioneer Enterprise Fund; trustee U. South Fla. Found., Tampa,

1959-69. Served as 2d lt. Engrs., U.S. Army, 1918. Mem: Nature Conservancy (v.p., bd. govs.), Sigma Nu, also numerous sci. orgns. Presbyn. (trustee). Clubs: Fort Orange, University (Albany, N.Y.). Home: Rensselaerville NY 12147 Office: 90 State St Albany NY 12207

COOLEY, JAMES AVAS, educator; b. Scottsburg, Ind., Nov. 3, 1901; s. James Louis and Lennie (Morris) C.; student Ind. State Coll., 1919-21; A.B., U. Ill., 1928, A.M., 1929; Ph.D., U. Ill., 1935; m. Bertha M. Hill, Sept. 3, 1930; children—Mary Jane, James Louis. Tchr. high sch. math., Scottsburg, 1921-26, Harrisburg, Ill., 1929-30; grad. asst. U. Ill., 1930-35; instr. math. U. Ida., 1935-38; asso. prof. U. Tenn., 1938- 39, prof. math., 1939-70, prof. emeritus, 1970—, head dept., 1942-61. Mem. Math. Assn. Am., Sigma Xi, Phi Kappa Phi. Presbyn. (elder). Home: Sherwood Dr Knoxville TN 37919

COOLEY, JOHN KENT, journalist; b. N.Y.C., Nov. 25, 1927; s. John Landon and Ruth (Robinson) C.; A.B., Darthmouth, 1952; student U. Zurich, 1948-49, U. Vienna, 1951- 52, New Sch. Social Research, 1954, Columbia, 1964-65; m. Edith Stoegermayer, Apr. 2, 1951 (div. Apr. 1970); 1 dau., Katherine Anne; m. 2d, Eugenie Katelanis, May 30, 1970. With U.S. Depts. State and Def., Vienna, 1949-51; free lance writer, journalist, Europe and North Africa, 1947-64; editorial writer N.Y. Herald Tribune, 1954, UPI, North Africa, and London, 1958-59; Middle East corr. Christian Sci. Monitor, 1965—; contbr. NBC radio and television news, 1961-67; news corr. ABC Radio, 1967—. Served with AUS, 1946-47. Carnegie Fgn. Corr. fellow, Council Fgn. Relations, 1964-65; recipient citation for best newspaper interpretation, fgn. affairs, Overseas Press Club, 1967, 69. Mem. Fgn. Press Assn. Beirut, Authors League Am., Phi Beta Kappa. Club: Overseas Press of America (N.Y.C.). Author: Baal, Christ and Mohammed; Religion and Revolution in North Africa, 1965; East Wind Over Africa; Red China's African Offensive, 1965; The Emergence of Palestinian Nationalism, in The Government and Politics of The Middle East, 1971. Home: 22 Landmark Lane Pigeon Cove Rockport MA 01966 Office: Hotel St George Beirut Lebanon

COOLEY, MARGUERITE BOWERS, librarian; b. Wellington, Kan., Sept. 6, 1909; d. Albert Eugene and Jennie V. (McManis) Bowers; student Ferry Hall Jr. Coll., Lake Forest, Ill., 1927-29; A.B., U. Kan., 1931; M.A., George Peabody Coll., 1951; m. Gerald A. Cooley, June 30, 1931 (div., 1950). Asst. librarian pub. library, Medford, Okla., 1933-38; library clk. VA Hosp., McKinney, Tex., 1948-50; asst. at reference George Peabody Coll. Library, 1951; librarian Ariz. Dept. Library and Archives, Phoenix, 1952-61, dir., 1961- -; reader Recording for Blind. Mem. Am., Ariz. (past pres.) library assns., Am. Assn. U. Women, Gamma Phi Beta. Episcopalian. Club: Altrusa (Phoenix). Home: 922-A W Monterosa St Phoenix, AZ 85013. Office: State Capitol Phoenix AZ 85007

COOLEY, RICHARD PIERCE, banker; b. Dallas, Nov. 25, 1923; s. Victor E. and Helen (Pierce) C.; student Yale, 1944. With Wells Fargo Bank, San Francisco, 1949—, exec. v.p., 1965-66, pres., chief exec. officer, 1966—. Chmn. campaign policy com. United Bay Area Crusade, 1966, gen. campaign chmn., 1965, pres., 1969, chmn., 1970. Bd. dirs. Children's Hosp., San Francisco; bd. regents U. San Francisco. Served to 1st lt. USAAF, 1943-46. Decorated Air medal. Clubs: Pacific Union, Bohemian (San Francisco). Home: 947 Green St San Francisco CA 94133 Office: 464 California St San Francisco CA 94120

COOLEY, ROBERT NELSON, educator; b. Woodlawn, Va., Mar. 12, 1911; s. Elmer Jackson and Elizabeth Lee (Clark) C.; M.D., U. Va., 1934; m. Eula Grace Jarnagin, July 1, 1948; children—Helen Hope, Caroline, Robert Nelson. Intern, Bellevue Hosp., N.Y.C., 1934-36, Mary McClelland Hosp., Cambridge, N.Y., 1936; resident Johns Hopkins Hosp., Balt., 1941-42, 46-48; practice medicine, specializing in radiology, Balt., 1948-53, Galveston, Tex., 1953—; mem. staffs U. Tex. Med. Br. Hosps., Galveston; asst. prof., radiology Johns Hopkins U. Sch. Medicine, Balt., 1948-50, asso. prof., 1950-53; prof., chmn. dept. radiology U. Tex. Med. Br., 1953—. Served from 1st lt. to maj., M.C., AUS, 1942-46. Diplomate Am. Bd. Radiology. Fellow Am. Coll. Radiology; mem. Am. Assn. U. Profs., Am. Heart Assn., Am. Roentgen Ray Soc., A.M.A., Assn. U. Radiologists, Galveston County Med. Soc., Tex. Med. Assn., Tex. Radiol. Soc., Radiol. Soc. N.Am. Presbyn. (elder). Author: (with R.D. Sloan, M.H. Schreiber) Radiology of Heart and Great Vessels, 1956. Contbr. articles profl. jours. Home: 1913 Oaklawn Dr LaMarque TX 77568 Office: 915 Strand St Galveston TX 77550

COOLEY, THOMAS MCINTYRE, II, lawyer, educator; b. Detroit, Mar. 5, 1910; s. Thomas Benton and Abigail (Hubbard) C.; grad. Phillips Exeter Acad., 1928; A.B., U. Mich., 1932; LL.B., Harvard, 1935, grad. fellow, 1935-36; m. Helen Stringham, June 24, 1938; children—Abigail Jane, Harriet Stringham, Hilary Elizabeth. Admitted to Mich., bar, 1936, D.C. bar, Va. bar, 1947, Pa. bar, 1958; asso. firms Dykema, Jones & Wheat, Detroit, 1937-38, Barbour, Garnett, Pickett, Keith & Glassie, Washington, 1948-50, Weaver & Glassie, Washington, 1950-58; instr., asst. prof. law Western Res. U., 1938-41; mem. Bd. Immigration Appeals, Dept. Justice, 1941, asst. dir. alien enemy control, chief alien enemy litigation, 1941-44, 46-47; dep. dir. displaced persons UNRRA, 1944-45; counsel immigration com. U.S. Ho. of Reps., 1945-46, subcom. on labor mgmt. relations U.S. Senate, 1949-50; prof. Ohio State U. Law Sch., summer 1949; dean U. Pitts. Law Sch., 1958- 65, prof. law, 1966—, pres. univ. faculty senate, 1967, chief research div. Health Law Center, 1966-68; prof. law U. Ill. Law Sch., 1965-66. Counsel Citizens Com. on Displaced Persons, 1947-48. Mem. Fed., Pa., D.C., Va., Immigration, Am., Allegheny Co. bar assns., Assn. Immigration and Nationality Lawyers. Contbr. articles revs. legal periodicals. Home: 4644 Filmore St Pittsburgh PA 15213

COOLIDGE, ARLAN RALPH, educator; b. Orange, Mass., Apr. 10, 1902; s. Charles Eugene and Annie Loyise (Herrick) C.; Ph.B., Brown U., 1924; grad. study Juilliard Sch. 1961—; Music, 1929-29, Akademie für Musik, U. Vienna, 1929-30, Jahreszeugnis, 1930; m. Sylvia Clark, June 21, 1934; 1 son, Clark, Violinist, N.Y. Philharmonic Orchestra Stadium Concerts, 1925, Cin. Symphony Orchestra, 1925-27; with Brown U., 1930—, chmn. music dept., 1931-63, successively acting asst. prof., asst. prof., asso. prof., prof., now prof. emeritus; v.p. R.I. Philharmonic Orchestra, 1950—; 1st violin University String Quartet. Acting pres. Providence Pub. Edn. Council, 1953-54; v.p. Providence Community Concert Assn., 1960—; chmn. exec. com. R.I. Chamber Music Concerts, 1954—; pres. R.I. Fine Arts Council, 1965-66 Mem. Music Educators National Conf., Providence Art Club Soc. for Music in Liberal Arts Coll. (chmn. 1954), Music Tchrs Nat Assn., R.I. Fedn. Music Clubs (v.p., 1950-55, 60-64), College Music Soc. (mem. council), Am. Musicol. Soc. (council), Music Library Assn., Am. Fedn. Musicians, Am. String Tchrs. Assn., Am. Assn. U. Profs. Conglist. Mason. Contbr.: International Cyclopedia of Music, 1938. Mem. editorial bd. Musical America, 1960—.

COOLIDGE, CHARLES ALLERTON, lawyer; b. Chgo., Oct. 13, 1894; s. Charles Allerton and Julia (Shepley) C.; prep. edn. Groton (Mass.) Sch., 1908-13; A.B. cum laude, Harvard, 1917, LL.B., 1922, LL.D., 1966; m. Alison Jones, June 14, 1922; children—Charles Allerton, Daniel Jones, Alison R. (dec.). Admitted to Mass. bar, 1922; partner law firm Ropes & Gray, 1928—; dir. H. P. Hood & Sons, Inc.; chmn. bd., Mitre Corp., 1961-67, Eastern Gas and Fuel Assos. Pres. Com. for Central Bus. Dist., Inc., 1962-68. Dep. dir. internat. security affairs Dept. State, 1951; asst. sec. def. legal, legislative affairs, 1951-52, spl. asst. to sec. def., 1955-58; dir. Joint State-Def. Dept. Disarmament Study, 1959. Trustee Groton Sch., 1940-68, Radcliffe Coll., 1959-66, New Eng. Aquarium, Affiliated Hosp. Center, Blood Research Inst., Cambridge Corp.; chmn. bd. Inst. Ednl. Mgmt., 1968-71; trustee Boston Mus. Fine Arts, 1940- 68. Served to capt. inf. AUS, 1917-19; lt. col., Mass. State Guard, 1940-44. Mem. Am. Acad. Arts and Scis., Am., N.Y., Mass., Boston bar assns., Mass. Soc. Cincinnati, Greater Boston C. of C. (pres. 1960-61, hon. v.p., dir.), Phi Beta Kappa (hon.). Republican. Episcopalian. Clubs: Somerset, Tavern, Harvard (Boston) Home: 150 Somerset St Belmont MA 02178 Office: 225 Franklin St Boston MA 02110

COOLIDGE, HAROLD JEFFERSON, zoologist; b. Boston, Jan. 15, 1904; s. Harold Jefferson and Edith (Lawrence) C.; grad. Milton Acad., 1922; student U. Ariz., 1922-23; B.S., Harvard, 1927; Cambridge (Eng.) U. 1927-28; D.Sc., George Washington U., 1959, Seoul Nat. U., 1965, Brandeis U., 1970; m. Helen Carpenter Isaacs, Apr. 25, 1931; children—Nicholas Jefferson, Thomas Richards, Isabella Gardner. Asst. mammalogist Harvard African Expdn. to Liberia, Belgian Congo, 1926-27; leader Indo-China div. Kelley-Roosevelt's Field Mus. Expdn., 1928-29; asst. curator mammals Mus. Comparative Zoology, Harvard, 1929-46, asso. mammalogy, 1946—; exec. dir. Pacific sci. bd. Nat. Acad. Scis.-NRC, 1946-70; collaborator U.S. Nat. Park Service, 1948—. Sec. Am. Com. Internat. Wild Life Protection, 1930—, chmn., 1951-69, hon. chmn., 1969—; cons. Bernice P. Bishop Mus., 1953—; pres. Internat. Union for Conservation Nature and Natural Resources, 1966—, chmn. internat. commn. nat. parks, 1958-63, chmn. Survival Service Commn., 1949-58; sec. gen. 10th Pacific Sci. Congress, Honolulu, 1961; mem. organizing com. XVI Internat. Zool. Congress, 1961-63; chmn. 1st World Conf. on Nat. Parks, Seattle, 1962. Bd. dirs. Chicorua Island Chapel Assn.; corp. Boston Mus. Sci., Squam Lake Sci. Center. Served to maj. AUS, 1943-45. Decorated Mil. Legion of Merit (U.S.); decorations from Ecuadorian, French, Laotian, Cambodian, Belgian govts.; recipient 75th Anniversary medal of merit U. Ariz., 1960; Frances K. Hutchinson medal Garden Club Am., 1963; Conservation award Washington African Safari Club, 1967; Horace Marden Albright Scenic Preservation medal Am. Scenic and Historic Preservation Soc., 1969. Fellow N.Y. Zool. Soc. (gold medal 1969); mem. Am. Soc. Mammalogists, Pan-Am. Soc. N.E. (dir.), Inst. Nat. Parks Belgian Congo (dir.), Nat. Parks and Conservation Assn. (sec. 1946-59, dir. 1959—), Nature Conservancy, Systematic Zoologists, Wilderness Soc., Wild Life Soc., Pacific Sci. Assn. (Pacific sci. council), Monticello Assn., Bishop Mus. Assn., Washington Acad. Scis., Chgo. Mus. Natural History (life), Internat. Inst. Differing Civilizations (Brussels), A.A.A.S., Nat. Audubon Soc., Cerole Zoologique Congolaise (hon., Belgium), Zool. Soc. London (corr.), Sigma Xi. Episcopalian. Clubs: Harvard, Harvard Travelers, Tavern (Boston); Cosmos (Washington); Harvard, Boone and Crockett, Explorers (N.Y.C.). Author: (with Theodore Roosevelt) Three Kingdoms of Indo-China, 1933. Author sci. publs. on primates, internat. conservation. Home: 2500 Virginia Av N W Washington DC 20037 Office: 2101 Constitution Av NW Washington DC 20418 ☆

COOLIDGE, JOHN PHILLIPS, educator; b. Cambridge, Mass., Dec. 16, 1913; s. Julian Lowell and Theresa (Reynolds) C.; student Groton Sch., 1927-31; A.B., Harvard, 1935; Ph.D., N.Y. U., 1948; m. Mary Elizabeth Welch, May 25, 1935; 1 dau., Mary Elizabeth. Instr. art Vassar Coll., 1937-39; asst. prof. art U. Pa., 1946-47; asst. prof. fine arts Harvard, Cambridge, Mass., 1947-48, asso. prof., now prof. fine arts, dir. Fogg Museum, 1948-68. Vice pres. bd. trustees Boston Mus. Fine Arts. Served from ensign to lt. USNR, 1943-46. Mem. Soc. Archtl. Historians, Am. Acad. Arts and Scis., Coll. Art Assn. Author: Mill and Mansion. Home: 24 Gray Gardens W Cambridge MA 02138

COOLIDGE, JOHN WASHBURN, former mfg. exec.; b. Washington, Jan. 15, 1903; s. Louis Arthur and Helen Irene (Pickerill); grad. Milton Acad., 1922; student Williams Coll., 1922-25; m. Helen Seymour, May 28, 1931; children—John Washburn, Hannah Whitney. With United Shoe Machinery Corp., 1925-68, v.p., dir., 1951-68; former dir. Brit. United Shoe Machinery Co., Ltd., United Shoe Machinery Co. de France, Bostik, Ltd., Eng., Bostik S.A., France; dir. Mutinational Bus. Assos., Inc. Mem. Pan-Am. Soc., S.A.R., Vets. Assn. Mass. Organized Militia, Psi Upsilon. Republican. Clubs: Boothbay Harbor Yacht; Coral Reef Yacht. Home: Hodgdon's Island Box 44 Trevett ME 04571

COOLIDGE, LOWELL WILLIAM, educator; b. Sherborn, Mass., Sept. 18, 1906; s. William Hoit and Christine (MacLean) C.; B.A., Boston U., 1927, M.A., 1928; Ph.D., Western Res. U., 1937; m. Dorothy Wilda Dillon, June 6, 1931; 1 dau., Christine (Mrs. Robert A. Jones). Mem. faculty Coll. Wooster, 1928—, prof. English, 1948—, chmn. dept., 1959—; summer tchr. Western Res. U., Bowling Green State U. Mem. Modern Lang. Assn., Milton Soc. Am., Renaissance Soc. Am., Coll. English Assn. Ohio (pres. 1955), Phi Beta Kappa. Episcopalian (lay reader). Co-editor: Complete Prose Works of John Milton, Vol. II, 1959. Home: 404 Bloomington Av Wooster OH 44691

COOLIDGE, SOLLACE B., Jr., paint mfg. exec.; b. Cleveland, June 1, 1902; s. Sollace B. and Mary (Dennison) C.; A.B., Yale, 1924; m. Priscilla Rutherford, Jan. 23, 1932; 1 dau., Ann. Former dir., v.p., The Sherwin Williams Co., Cleve. Mem. Beta Theta Pi. Clubs: Union, Country, Pepper Pike (Cleve.); Naples Yacht, Hole-in-the-Wall Golf (Naples, Fla.); Zanesfield (O.) Rod and Gun. Home: 1 Bratenahl Pl Cleveland OH 44108

COOLIDGE, WILLIAM APPLETON, financier; b. Boston, Oct. 22, 1901; s. Thomas Jefferson and Clara (Amory) C.; student St. Marks Sch., Southboro, Mass., 1914-20; A.B. cum laude, Harvard, 1924; M.A., Balliol Coll., Oxford, 1927; LL.B. cum laude, Harvard, 1936. With Jackson & Curtis, investment bankers, Boston, 1927-33; admitted to Mass. bar, 1936; practiced as asso. Ropes, Gray, Boyden & Perkins, 1936-41; chmn. bd. Nat. Research Corp., 1940-68; dir. Norton Co., Coca-Cola Co., Invest Inc. v.p. Boston Mus. Fine Arts chmn. bd. Mass. Half-Way Houses; life mem. corp. Mass. Inst. Tech., Peter Bent Brigham Hosp.; chmn. vis. com. Harvard Div. Sch.; treas. ch. Soc. for Coll. Work; hon. fellow Balliol Coll., Oxford, Eng. Bd. overseers Harvard; trustee Bishop Rhinelander Found.; pres. bd. trustees Episcopal Theol. Sch., St. Marks Sch.; pres. bd. dirs. Episcopal Ch. Found.; bd. dirs. Boston Theol. Inst.; life mem. corp. Mass. Inst. Tech. Served with USNR, 1941-46. Mem. Am., Mass. bar assns. Republican. Episcopalian. Clubs: Somerset, Tennis and Racquet (Boston); A.D. (Cambridge); Brook, Racquet and Tennis, River (N.Y.C.); Metropolitan (Washington); Myopia Hunt (Hamilton). Home: River Rd Topsfield MA 01983 Office: 70 Memorial Dr Cambridge MA 02142

COOLIDGE, WILLIAM DAVID, physical chemist; b. Hudson, Mass., Oct. 23, 1873; s. Albert Edward and M. Alice C.; B.S., Mass. Inst. Tech., 1896; Ph.D., U. of Leipzig, 1899; D.Sc.(hon.) Lehigh, Union Univ., 1927; M.D. (hon.), U. of Zurich, 1937; LL.D., Ursinus Coll., 1942; Dr. h.c., U. of São Paulo, 1945. Nat. Sch. Engring., U. of Brazil, 1945; D.Sc., Catholic U. of Chili, 1945; D. Eng., Ind. Tech. Coll, 1947; m. Ethel Westcott Woodard, Dec. 30, 1908 (dec. Feb. 20, 1915); children—Elizabeth B., Lawrence D.; m. 2d, Dorothy Elizabeth MacHaffie, Feb. 29, 1916. Faculty, Mass. Inst. Tech., 1897, 1901-05, U. of Leipzig, 1899; research in physical-chemistry Gen. Electric Co., Schenectady, 1905-07, asst. dir. research lab., 1908- 28, asso. dir., 1928-32, dir., 1932-40, v.p., dir. research, 1940-44, cons. X-rays, 1945—. Served with Nat. Def. Research Com., World War II; apptd. to Nat. Acad. Scis. Com. in connection with Atomic Bomb project, 1941, attended firm Bikini test as spl. observer for Manhattan Dist. Mem. Nat. Inventors Council, 1940—. Recipient numerous awards for work in field and on X-ray, including Faraday medal Instn. Elec. engrs. Eng., 1939; Franklin medal, 1944, K.C. Li medal and award Columbia, 1952; Henry Spenadel award, 3rd Dist. Dental Soc., 1953; Roentgen medal, 1963. Fellow Am. Acad. Arts and Sci., A.A.A.S., Am. Philos. Soc., Am. Inst. Chemists, Am. Acad. Oral Roentgenology, Sigma Psi; mem. Am. Acad. History Dentistry (hon.), Société Odontologique de France (hon.), Nat., Washington acads. sci., Edison Pioneers, Soc. Non-Destructive Testing, Am. Chem. Soc., Am. Electrochem. Soc., Am. Phys. Soc., Am. Inst. Elec. Engrs.; hon. or corr. mem. numerous Am., fgn. socs. Unitarian. Clubs: Mohawk(Schenectady); Engineers (Dayton, (O.). Contbr. results original research to sci. publs. Home: 1480 Lenox Rd Schenectady NY 12308 Office: Gen Electric Co Research Lab PO Box 1088 Schenectady NY 12301

COOMBE, GEORGE WILLIAM, Jr., lawyer, automotive co. exec.; b. Kearny, N.J., Oct. 1, 1925; s. George William and Laura (Montgomery) C.; A.B., Rutgers U., 1946; LL.B., Harvard 1949; m. Marilyn V. Ross, June 4, 1949; children—Susan, Donald William, Nancy. Admitted to N.Y. bar, 1950, Mich. bar, 1953, also U.S. Supreme Ct.; practice in N.Y.C., 1949-53, Detroit, 1953-69; pvt. practice, 1949-53; atty., mem. legal staff Gen. Motors Corp., Detroit, 1953-69, asst. gen. counsel, sec., N.Y.C., 1969—. Pres., trustee Birmingham (Mich.) Sch. Bd.; trustee Oakland County (Mich.) Sch. Bd. Served to lt. USNR, 1942-46. Mem. Am., Mich., Detroit, N.Y.C. bar assns., Am. Soc. Corporate Secs., Phi Beta Kappa, Phi Gamma Delta. Presbyn. Home: 26 Fox Meadow Rd Scarsdale NY 10583 Office: 767 Fifth Av New York City NY 10022

COOMBE, PHILIP, banker. Sr. v.p. S. Bklyn. Savs. Bank. Office: Atlantic Av and Court St Brooklyn NY 11202*

COOMBE, V. ANDERSON, valve mfg. co. exec.; b. Cin., Mar. 5, 1926; s. Harry Elijah and Mary (Anderson) C.; B.E., Yale, 1948; m. Eva Jane Romaine, Sept. 26, 1957; children—James, Michael, Peter. Asst. to pres. Wm. Powell Co., Cin., 1953-57, v.p., 1957-63, exec. v.p., 1963-69, pres., treas., 1969—, also dir.; dir. First Nat. Bank Cin., Union Central Life Ins., Lodge & Shipley Co. Episcopalian. Clubs: Camargo, Queen City Cincinnati Country (Cin.). Home: 6 Corbin Lane Cincinnati OH 45208 Office: 2503 Spring Grove Av Cincinnati OH 45211

COOMBES, ETHEL RUSSELL, editor and publisher; b. Plainville, Ill.; d. Albert Alan and Sarah Ann (Haynes) Russell; ed. high schs., by special study and George Washington U., m. David S. Coombes; children—David Russell, Edward Raymond. With American Mining Congress, 1913-37; organized national standardization movement to eliminate waste and promote efficiency and economy in mineral prodn., 1919; organized industrial cooperation div. Am. Mining Congress; editor The Mining Congress Jour., 1923-37; conv. and expn. mgr. annual meetings Am. Mining Congress, 1925-37; est. Mechanization, Inc., 1937, publishers of Mechanization, the Magazine of Modern Coal, and Mechannual, the Book of Mechanization Progress, Utilization, The Magazine of Coal Uses (chmn. bd. publishers). Founder, Energy Reports, 1963. Home: 4008 Rosemary St Chevy Chase MD 20015 Address: Munsey Bldg Washington DC 20004

COOMBS, CHARLES ANTHONY, banker; b. Newton, Mass., Apr. 9, 1918; s. Charles Harold and Florence (Campbell) C.; A.B., Harvard, 1940, M.P.A., M.A., 1942, Ph.D., 1953; m. Ilona Harman, Apr. 5, 1945; 1 dau., Claire. With Fed. Res. Bank N.Y., 1946—, sr. v.p. charge fgn. function, 1959—. Reed. Res. rep. meetings Bank Internat. Settlements, Basle, Switzerland; financial adviser AID mission to Greece, 1947; mem. Presdl. Task Force Promoting Fgn. Investment in U.S., 1963. Served with AUS, 1942-44. Recipient Distinguished Service award Treasury Dept., 1968. Mem. Council Fgn. Relations. Author articles in field. Home: PO Box 38 Green Village NJ 07935 Office: 33 Liberty St New York City NY 10045

COOMBS, EDWARD C., auditor. Auditor, Syracuse Savs. Bank. Office: 102 N Salina St Syracuse NY 13201*

COOMBS, EDWIN SEEGER, Jr., brewery exec.; b. Kansas City, Mo., June 9, 1926; s. Edwin Seeger and Grace Marion (Winegar) C.; student U. N.C., 1945, 46; B.A., U. of South, 1948; m. Georgi Culliton, Mar. 3, 1953; children—Craig Edwin, Carolyn Ainsworth, Scott Michael. Account exec. Ayer Baker Advt., Seattle, 1955-60; div. advt. mgr. Carling Brewing Co., Tacoma, 1961-64, div. sales mgr., 1964, Western div. marketing dir., 1965-67, Western div. v.p., 1967-69; pres. Rainier Brewing Co., Seattle, 1969—; dir., v.p. Rainier Cos., Inc., 1970—. Mem. bus. adv. bd. Pacific Luth. U., 1969—; mem. Puget Sound adv. com. Wash. State U., 1970—. Served with USNR, 1944-46; to lt. (j.g.) USCGR, 1950-51. Clubs: Washington Athletic, Broadmoor Golf (Seattle). Home: 1701 86th St NE Bellevue WA 98004 Office: 3100 Airport Way S Seattle WA 98134

COOMBS, HOWARD ABBOTT, educator; b. Dallas, Apr. 10, 1906; s. Horace Milton and Anola (Sigerfoose) C.; B.S., U. Wash., 1929, Ph.D., 1935; m. Leila P. Ewing, Jan. 1, 1936; 1 dau., Carol Leigh (Mrs. Thomas L. Boeder). Mem. faculty U. Wash., 1935—; prof. geology, 1936—, chmn. dept., 1954-69; engring. geology cons., 1943—. Collaborator for Wash. on Earthquakes, U.S. com. Internat. Commn. Large Dams, 1965—. Fellow Geol. Soc. Am. (nat. sec. engring. div. 1955, chmn. cordilleran sect. 1956, nat. chmn. engring. div. 1971), Seismological Soc. Am. (adv. com. seismology 1955- 56), Assn. Engring. Geologists. Author papers in field. Home: 3856 46th Av NE Seattle WA 98105

COOMBS, JOHN WENDELL, bus. exec.; b. Salt Lake City, Jan. 29, 1905; s. John Hardy and Merle (Halliday) C.; A.B., U. Utah, 1926; LL.B., George Washington U., 1934; m. Norma Druke, June 7, 1929; 1 son, John Wendell. Examiner R.F.C., Washington, 1935-42, asst. to dir., 1945-46; pres. Aeronautical Tng. Soc., Washington, 1943-45; asst. to pres. Transam. Corp., San Francisco, 1946-51, v.p. 1952-57; v.p., sec., dir., Gen. Metals Corp., Oakland, Cal., 1957-63; v.p. Transam. Financial Corp. (formerly Pacific Finance Corp.), 1963-69, dir. 1969—; v.p., dir. Transam. Comml. Corp. (formerly Transam. Financial Corp.), 1963-65, pres., dir., 1965-69; chmn. Bankers Mortgage Co., San Francisco, 1967-70, dir., 1966—; pres. Transam. Devel. Co., 1968-69, chmn., 1969-70, dir., 1966—; pres., dir. Transam. Land Capital, Inc., 1968—; pres. Mortgage Trust of Am., 1969—; chmn. Transam. Mtg. Adv., Inc., 1969-70, dir., 1969—; chmn. Transinternat. Hotel Co., 1969—; v.p. Transam. Corp.,

1968-70. Mem. Security Analysts San Francisco. Home: 229 Rocky Point Rd Palos Verdes Estates CA 90274 Office: 1150 S Olive St Los Angeles CA 90015

COOMBS, PHILIP HALL, economist, educator; b. Holyoke, Mass., August 15, 1915; s. Charles Gilmore and Nellie (Hall) C.; B.A., Amherst Coll., 1937, L.H.D., 1962; LL.D., Brandeis U., 1962, Monmouth College, 1962; grad. study econs. U. Chgo., 1937-39; study Brookings Instn., 1939-40; m. Helena Brooks, Oct. 18, 1941; children—Peter Brooks, Helena Hall. Instr. econs. Williams Coll., 1939, 1940-41; economist OPA, 1941-42; econ. adv. to dir. Office Econ. Stblzn., 1945-46; dep. housing expediter Vets. Emergency Housing Program, 1946-47; prof. econs. Amherst Coll., 1947- 49; econ. adviser to gov. Conn., 1949-50; exec. dir. President's Materials Policy Commn., 1951-52; sec. Fund Advancement Edn. (Ford Found.), 1952-61, program dir. edn. div., 1957-61; asst. sec. of state for ednl. and cultural affairs, 1961-62; guest scholar Brookings Instn., Washington, also fellow Council on Fgn. Relations, 1962-63; dir. Internat. Inst. for Ednl. Planning, Paris, 1963-68, dir. research, 1969—; vis. lectr. Grad. Sch. Edn., Harvard, 1969; vice chmn. Internat. Council for Ednl. Devel., 1970—; vis. prof. Inst. of Social Sci., Yale, 1970-71. Cons. Ministry of Edn., Govt. of India, 1953, 55, Turkey, 1957, Spain, 1969-70; mem. President's Com. on Sci. and Engrng. Manpower, Pres.'s Com. on Edn. Beyond High Sch. Trustee Amherst Coll. Served with OSS, U.S. Army, 1943-45; adviser strategic bombing targets USAAF. Mem. Am. Econ. Assn., Council on Fgn. Relations, Century Assn., Phi Beta Kappa. Democrat. Author: The Fourth Dimension of Foreign Policy-Education and Cultural Affairs, 1964; Education and Foreign Aid, 1964; New Media; Memo to Educational Planners, 1967; The World Educational Crisis: A Systems Analysis, 1968. Contbr. profl. publs. Address: River Rd Essex CT 06426 Office: Internat Council for Ednl Devel 522 Fifth Av New York City NY 10020

COOMES, EDWARD ARTHUR, research physicist; b. Louisville, Ky., June 27, 1909; s. Arthur Grey and Anna Veronica (Fein) C.; B.S. in E.E., U. Notre Dame, 1931; M.Sc., 1933; D.Sc. (Rockefeller Found. scholar), Mass. Inst. Tech., 1938; m. Marie Teresa Shaffer, Aug. 7, 1940; children—Jane Ann, Michael J., Mary Agnes, Thomas E., Martha R. Instr. math., elec. engrng. and physics. U. Notre Dame, 1934-36, asst. prof. physics, 1938-41, asso. prof. 1941-42, prof. physics, 1945—; teaching fellow Mass. Inst. Tech., 1936-37, staff mem. radiation lab., 1942-45. Cons. in field. Fellow Am. Phys. Soc.; mem. Inst. Radio Engrs. (sr.), Sigma Xi. Roman Catholic. Democrat. Home: 1036 N Johnson St South Bend IN 46628

COON, CARLETON STEVENS, anthropologist; b. Wakefield, Mass., June 23, 1904; s. John Lewis and Bessie (Carleton) C.; grad. Phillips Acad., 1921; A.B., magna cum laude, Harvard, 1925. A.M., 1928, Ph.D., 1928; m. Mary Goodale, 1926; children—Carleton S., Charles Adams; m. 2d, Lisa Dougherty Geddes, 1945. Field work, anthrop. research. N. Africa, Balkans, Ethiopia, Arabia, 1925-34, discovering remains of Aterian fossil man, in N. Africa, 1939; began as instr., became asst. prof., asso. prof., prof. anthrop. Harvard, 1934-48 (on leave, 1942-45); curator ethnology, also prof. anthropology Univ. Mus., Phila., 1948-63; research curator in anthropology, 1963—; cons. Scott-Foresman and Co., Chgo.; mem. NSF com. on scientific personnel, 1961-64, Smithsonian com. on fgn. currency, 1965-70; led archeological expdn., Iran, which discovered Hotu man, 1951; expdn. Afghanistan, 1954, Syria, Central Africa, 1955, India, 1956-57, Alakaluf Indians, Chile, 1959, Morocco, 1962-63, discovering Jebel Ighoud man No. 2, Sierra Leone, 1965. Spl. asst. Dept. State, 1942-43. Served to maj. AUS, 1943-45. Decorated Legion of Merit, 1945; Viking Medal in Phys. Anthropology, 1952; Membre d'Honneur, Assn. de la Libération Francaise du 8 Novembre, 1963. Mem. Nat. Acad. Sci., Am. Anthropl. Assn., Am. Assn. Phys. Anthropologists, Am. Acad. Arts and Sci., Phi Beta Kappa, Sigma Xi. Conglist. Clubs: Explorers (fellow) (N.Y.C.); Cosmos (Washington); Franklin Inn (Phila.); Harvard (Boston). Editor: Dixon Meml. Volume for Peabody Mus. (Harvard), 1943. Author: Tribes of Rif, 1931; Flesh of the Wild Ox, 1932; The Riffian, 1934; Measuring Ethiopia, 1935; Races of Europe, 1939; Principles of Anthropology (with Eliot D. Chapple), 1942; A Reader in General Anthropology, 1948; Races (with Garn and Birdsell), 1950; The Mountains of Giants, 1950; Cave Explorations in Iran, 1951; Caravan, 1951; The Story of Man, 1954; The Seven Caves, 1957; The Origin of Races, 1962; The Living Races of Man, 1965; Yengema Cave Report, 1968; The Hunting Peoples, 1971. Contbr. anthrop. jours., mags. Panelist, What in the World, TV show, 1949-64. Address: 207 Concord St Gloucester MA 01930

COON, CARLETON STEVENS, Jr., fgn. service officer; b. Paris, France, Apr. 27, 1927 (parents Am. citizens); s. Carleton Stevens and Mary (Goodale) C.; grad. cum laude, Phillips Acad., Andover, Mass., 1944; B.A. cum laude, Harvard, 1949; m. Janet January Wulsin, June 14, 1949 (dec. 1967); children—William Howard, Katharine, Elizabeth, Ellen, Richard; m. 2d, Jane S. Abell, Jan. 2, 1968. Joined U.S. Fgn. Service, 1949, Kreis resident officer, Germany, 1950-52; 2d sec. embassy, Damascus, Syria, 1952-56, New Delhi, India, 1956-59; served on Cyprus, later India desks State Dept., 1959- 63; consul, prin. officer, Tabriz, Iran, 1963-65, India desk, 1965-68; assigned Nat. War Coll., Ft. McNair, Washington 1968-69; dir. Presdl. appointments staff, 1969-70; counselor, dep. chief mission Am. embassy, Kathmandu, Nepal, 1970—. Home: 3520 Edmunds St NW Washington DC 20007 Office: Am Embassy Kathmandu Nepal

COON, GERALDINE ALMA, educator; b. N. Stonington, Conn., Sept. 13, 1913; d. Frank Eugene and Melissa (Greene) Coon.; B.A., Conn. Coll., 1935; M.S., Brown U., 1937; Ph.D., U. Rochester, 1950. Instr. shop mathematics Scovill Mfg. Co., 1939-44; research mathematical Taylor Instrument Cos., Rochester, N.Y., 1944-58; asst. prof., then asso. prof. U. Conn., 1958-64; mem. Courant Inst., N.Y. U., 1959-60; prof. math. Goucher Coll., 1964—; vis. prof. Brown U., 1967-68. Mem. Am. Math. Soc., Math. Assn. Am., Soc. Indsl. and Applied Math., Assn. Computing Machinery, Phi Beta Kappa, Sigma Xi. Author: (with others) Frequency Response for Process Control, 1959. Home: 6857 Queens Ferry Rd Towson MD 21204

COON, JULIUS MOSHER, educator; b. Liberty, Mo., Oct. 29, 1910; s. Raymond H. and Mayme (Bryan) C.; A.B., in Chemistry, Ind. U., 1932; Ph.D., U. Chgo., 1938; M.D., U. Ill., 1945; m. Mary E. Bond, July 26, 1947; children—James S., Margaret B. Instr. pharmacology U. Chgo., 1939-45, toxicological research, toxicity lab., 1941-45, dir., 1948-51, asst. prof., 1946, asso. prof., 1947-53, dir. USAF Radiation Lab., 1951-53; pharmacologist FDA, 1946, mem. adv. com. protocols for safety evaluation, 1966—; prof. pharmacology, head dept. Jefferson Med. Coll., Phila., 1953—; cons. U.S. Army Chem. Warfare Labs., Army Chem. Center, Md., 1956-58, poison control program Phila. Dept. Health, 1958—. Mem. toxicology study sect. USPHS, 1958-64, chmn. sect., 1962-64; mem. pharmacology test com. Nat. Bd. Med. Examiners, 1954-58; mem. clin. and preclin. pharmacology adv. com. Dept. Army, Walter Reed Army Inst. Research, 1966-70; expert adv. panel food additives WHO, 1966—; mem. adv. com. on research in biol., phys. scis. FDA, 1966-68; mem. food protection com. Nat. Acad. Scis.-NRC, 1952—, chmn. toxicology subcom., 1958—, chmn. subcom. on nonnutritive sweetners, 1968—, mem. com. on radiation preservation of food, 1969—; mem. Food and Agr. Orgn.-WHO Joint Expert Com. on Pesticide Residues, 1966, 1967, chmn., 1966; chmn. FAD-WHO Joint Expert Com. on Food Additives, 1969; chmn. panel on food safety White House Conf. on Food, Nutrition and Health, 1969; mem. com. on admissions Nat. Formulary, 1970—. Hygiene Assn., Radiation Research Soc., Soc. Exptl. Biology and Medicine, Soc. Pharmacology and Exptl. Therapeutics (treas. past com. chmn.), Coll. Physicians Phila., Soc. Toxicology (bd. publs. 1970—), N.Y. Acad. Scis., Phila. Physiol. Soc., Sigma Xi, Alpha Chi Sigma. Bd. editors Clin. Medicine, 1962—, Toxicology and Applied Pharmacology, 1967—. Contbr. articles profl. jours. Home: 130 Summit Av Jenkintown PA 19046 Office: 1020 Locust St Philadelphia PA 19107

COON, MILTON COLWELL, Jr., research exec.; b. Poughkeepsie, N.Y., May 17, 1921; s. Milton Colwell and Lillian (Becker) C.; m. Phyllis Black, Sept. 22, 1945; children—Christopher, Carol Lynn. Washington editor Commerce Clearing House, 1949-56; asst. sec. Tile Contractors Assn. Am., 1956-58; exec. dir. Bldg. Research Inst., Washington, 1958-67, also was exec. v.p.; Home: 2121 Paul Spring Rd Hollins Hills Alexandria VA 22307

COON, ROBERT L., educator; B.A., Dartmouth Coll., M.A., Ph.D., Princeton. Prof. French Sweetbriar Coll. Office: French Dept Sweetbriar Coll Sweet Briar VA 24595*

COON, ROBERT WILLIAM, educator, pathologist; b. Billings, Mont., July 13, 1920; s. Cordon William and Stella (Miller) C.; B.S., N.D. State Coll., 1942; M.D., U. Rochester, 1944; m. Jeanette Chute, Mar. 23, 1947; children—William L., Barbara E., Margaret J. Intern pathology Strong Meml. Hosp., Rochester, N.Y., 1944-45; resident pathology Grady Meml. Hosp., Atlanta, 1945-46; fellow pathology U. Rochester Sch. Medicine, 1947-49; from asst. to asso. prof. Columbia Coll. Phys. and Surg., 1949-55; prof. pathology, chmn. dept. U. Vt. Coll. Medicine, 1955—, asso. dean div. health scis., 1968—; dir. regional med. program heart disease, cancer and stroke, 1966-67. Diplomate Am. Bd. Pathology (bd. trustees 1960—, v.p. 1969—). Mem. Am. Soc. Clin. Pathologists (bd. dirs. 1958- 61, pres. 1963-64), Am. Soc. Exptl. Pathology, N.Y. Acad. Scis., Internat. Acad. Pathology, Am. Assn. Pathologists and Bacteriologists, Coll. Am. Pathologists, A.M.A. Home: 453 S Willard St Burlington VT 05401

COONEN, LESTER PETER, educator; b. Dundas, Wis., Jan. 4, 1907; s. James L. and Nellie (Biese) C.; B.A., St. Norbert Coll., 1933, M.A., 1935; Ph.D., U. Wis., 1938; m. Virginia Goetzman, Aug. 9, 1941; children—Mary, Peter, John, Christopher, Shelley, Kim, Lee, Michael, Katherine, Steven, Erik. Tchr. DeSales Coll., 1938-42; writer Sci. Reader Series, 1942-43; asst. prof., acting dir. biology dept., U. Detroit, 1943-44, asso. prof., 1944- 48, dir. biology dept., 1944-62, prof., 1948—. Mem. A.A.A.S., Am. Genetic Soc., History of Sci. Soc., Mich. Acad. Sci., Arts and Letters, N.Y. Acad. Sci., Alpha Epsilon Delta, Sigma Xi, Phi Sigma. Roman Catholic. Author: Everyday Science, 1945; also other books on sci.; also several articles on history biology. Home: 14707 Abington Rd Detroit MI 48227 ☆

COONEY, BARBARA, illustrator, author; b. Bklyn., Aug. 6, 1917; d. Russell Schenck and Mae Evelyn (Bossert) Cooney; student Great Neck Prep. Sch., L.I., 1929-31; grad. Briarcliff Sch., Briarcliff Manor, N.Y., 1934; B.A., Smith Coll., 1938; student Art Students' League, 1940; m. Guy Murchie, Dec. 1942 (div. Mar. 1947); children—Gretel, Barnaby; m. 2d, Charles T. Porter, July 16, 1949; children—Charles Talbot, Phoebe. Author, illustrator: King of Wreck Island, The Kellyhorns, Captain Pottle's House; illustrator: Oke and his World, American Folk Songs for Children, The Man Who Didn't Wash His Dishes, Animal Folk Songs for Children, The Best Christmas, Read Me Another Story, Where Have You Been, Christmas in the Barn, The Little Fir Tree, City Springtime, Snow Birthday, Friends with God, The American Speller, Le Hibou et la Poussiquette, The Little Juggler, Twenty-five Years A Growing, A White Heron, Mother Goose in French, Snow White and Rose Red, Papillot, Clignot et Dodo, Mother Goose in Spanish, A Garland of Games, Christmas Folk, Dionysos and the Pirates, others. Recipient Caldecott medal for Chanticleer and the Fox, 1958. Home: Pepperell MA 01463

COONEY, JAMES PATRICK, physician; b. Parnell, Ia., Mar. 17, 1903; s. James Francis and Catherine Agnes (Kennedy) C.; B.S., U. Ia., 1925, M.D., 1927; grad. Army Med. Sch., Army Med. Field Service Sch., 1929; m. Irene Kelly, Aug. 4, 1928; 1 son, James P. Commd. 2d lt. M.C., U.S. Army, 1927, advanced through grades to maj. gen., 1955; intern Fitzsimons Army Hosp., Denver; staff Sternberg Hosp., Manila, P.I., Letterman Army Hosp., San Francisco, Mil. Acad. Sta. Hosp., West Point, N.Y., Walter Reed Army Hosp., Washington; chief radiologist Gorgas Gen. Hosp., C.Z., 1940-43; exec. officer, asst. comdt. N.E. Gen. Hosp., Atlantic City, N.J., 1943-45; mem. group to study med. and hospitalization methods, Sweden, 1945; rep. Army Surgeon Gen., Manhattan Engrng. Dist., 1946, later med. dir.; mem. spl. mission to Japan to study A-bomb survivors at Hiroshima; cons. Armed Forces Spl. Weapons Project, dir. spl. projects div. Office Army Surgeon Gen.; radiol. safety officer Eniwetok tests, 1949, 1951; chief radiol. br., div. mil. application AEC, 1951; surgeon Japanese Logistical Command, Yokohama, Japan, 1951-53; spl. asst. to comdg. gen. Walter Reed Army Med. Center, 1953; comdt. Med. Field Service Sch., Brooke Army Medical Center. Ft. Sam Houston, Texas, 1953-55; deputy surgeon gen. Army, 1955-58; chief surgeon, European Command, Germany, 1958-60, ret., 1960; vice pres. med. affairs Am. Cancer Soc., 1960-69; dir. state cancer registration activities Ga. Regional Med. Program, 1969—. Decorated Legion of Merit with cluster, Bronze Star medal, D.S.M. Diplomate Am. Bd. Radiology. Fellow Am. Coll. Chest Physicians, Am. Coll. Radiology; mem. Radiol. Soc. N.Am., Nat. Tb Assn., Radioation Research Soc., A.M.A. Home: 3653 N Stradford Rd NE Atlanta GA 30342 Office: 938 Peachtree St NE Atlanta GA 30309

COONEY, JOAN GANZ, (Mrs. Timothy J. Cooney), TV exec.; b. Phoenix, Nov. 30, 1929; d. Sylvan C. and Pauline (Reardan) Ganz; B.A., U. Ariz., 1951; D.Sc. in Edn. (hon.), Boston Coll., 1970; L.H.D. (hon.), Hofstra U., 1971, Oberlin Coll., 1971, Ohio Wesleyan U., 1971; m. Timothy J. Cooney, Feb. 22, 1964. Reporter, Ariz. Republic, Phoenix, 1952-54; publicist NBC, 1954-55, U.S. Steel Hour, 1955-62; producer Chanel 13/WNDT, pub. affairs documentaries, N.Y.C., 1962-67; TV cons. Carnegie Corp. N.Y., N.Y.C., 1967-68; exec. dir. Children's TV Workshop, producers Sesame Street, N.Y.C., 1968-70, pres. Children's TV Workshop, 1970—, trustee, 1970—; trustee Ednl. Broadcasting Corp., N.Y.C., Am. Film Inst., Washington. Dir. First Pa. Corp., 1971—. Mem. Pres.'s Commn. on Marihuana and Drug Abuse, 1971—, Nat. Reading Council, 1970—. Recipient Emmy for Poverty, Anti-Poverty and the Poor, 1966; also numerous awards for Sesame Street. Mem. Nat. Orgn. Women, Acad. TV Arts and Sci. Home: 201 E 21st St New York City NY 10010 Office: 1 Lincoln Plaza New York City NY 10023

COONEY, JOSEPH PATRICK, lawyer; b. Hartford, Conn., Aug. 30, 1906; s. Jeremiah and Margaret (Dwyer) Cooney; LL.B., Georgetown U., 1929; m. Mary M. Malliet, June 28, 1933; children—Jane (Mrs. V.J. Dowling), Edwina (Mrs. H.T. Gillis), Margaret (Mrs. B.J. Coughlin), Anne. Joseph Patrick, Mary Alice (Mrs. Edgar A. Belden), Barbara (Mrs. Robert G. Oliver). Mem. Conn. State Senate, 2d Senatorial dist., 1931-33, 1st dist., 1937, 1941; mem. Hartford Co. Commn., 1933-39, Hartford Aviation Commn., 1930-31; asst. U.S. dist. atty., 1941-43. Mem. Hartford County Grievance Com., 1961-65. Trustee of Catholic Family Services, St. Agnes Home, St. Joseph Coll.; bd. dirs., St. Francis Hosp., Conn. Hosp. Assn. (pres. 1961-62), Mt. St. Benedict Cemetery, Conn. Inst. for Blind, Hosp. Council Greater Hartford (pres. 1962-63); bd. incorporators Inst. Living, Mt. Sinai Hosp. Recipient John Carrollaward Georgetown U., 1965. Fellow Am. Coll. Trial Lawyers; mem. Internat. Soc. Barristers, Am. (ho. dels. 1966-67), Conn. (pres. 1965-66, chmn. com. on jud. selection), Hartford County (pres. 1946-48) bar assns. Roman Catholic, Knight St. Gregory. Clubs: Pine Orchard Yacht and Country, Wampanoag Country. Home: 820 Prospect Av Hartford CT 06105 Office: 266 Pearl St Hartford CT 06103

COONEY, LLOYD EVERETT, broadcasting exec.; b. Council Bluffs, Ia., June 3, 1923; s. Cecil E. and Vera E. (Williams) C.; B.S., U. Utah, 1949, postgrad. 1949-50; m. Betty Lou Packard, Mar. 4, 1946; children—Shauna, Kevin and Kim (twins). Sales rep. Paul Revere Ins. Co., Salt Lake City, 1949-51; dir. pub. relations Intermountain Hosp. Service (Blue Cross), Salt Lake City, 1951-54; v.p., gen. mgr. sta. KSL-TV, Salt Lake City, 1954-64; pres., gen. mgr. KIRO radio and TV stas., Seattle, 1964—; v.p., dir. Bonneville Internat. Corp., Salt Lake City, 1968—. Bd. dirs. Providence Hosp. Found.; trustee Seattle Salvation Army. Served with 82d Airborne Div., AUS, 1943-46. Named Man of Year, Seattle Variety Club, 1968, Seattle's Salesman of Year, Sales and Marketing Execs., 1969, Media Man of Year Wash. Assn. Realtors, 1969; recipient TV journalism award Sigma Delta Chi, 1970, Americanism medal Am. Legion, 1971. Mem. Wash. State Assn. Broadcasters (bd. dirs.), United CATV (v.p. 1968—), Central Assn. Seattle (v.p. 1970—), Seattle C. of C., Am. Legion (Americanism medal 1971). Rotarian. Clubs: Metropolitan Dinner (bd. dirs.), Washington Athletic (bd. dirs.), Rainier, Variety, Broadmoor Golf (Seattle). Home: 9014 NE 37th Pl Bellevue WA 98004 Office: Broadcast House 3d and Broad Sts Seattle WA 98121

COONEY, ROBERT P.J., ins. co. exec.; b. St. Louis, July 30, 1915; Ph.B., St. Louis U., 1937, LL.M., 1940. Now sec., sr. v.p., gen. counsel Fund Am. Companies, Fireman's Fund Ins. Co., Am. Ins. Co., Am. Automobile Ins. Co., Asso. Indemnity Corp., Fireman's Fund Ins. Co. Tex., Nat. Surety Corp., Nat. Surety Corp. Cal.; v.p., gen. counsel, sec., dir. Firefund Service Corp., Fireman's Am. Life Ins. Co., Fireman's Fund Am. Life Ins. Co. N.Y.; sec., dir. Econ. Security Assn., Inc.; dir. Am. Auto Ins. Co., Am. Ins. Co., Am. Exp. Investment Co., Fund Am. Investment Mgmt. Co. Mem. Am. Bar Assn., Mo. State Bar, Delta Theta Phi, Alpha Sigma Nu. Home: 2618 Buchanan St San Francisco CA 94115 Office: 3333 California St San Francisco CA 94120*

COONROD, ROBERT WINGATE, univ. adminstr.; b. Warrensburg, Mo., Feb. 16, 1921; s. Halbert Floyd and Lula (Wingate) C.; B.S., S.W. Mo. State Coll., 1942; M.A., Stanford, 1947, Ph.D., 1950; student Am. U. Beirut, Lebanon, 1953; fellow coll. adminstrn., Center for Study Higher Edn., U. Mich., 1959-60; m. Virginia Joyce McGill, Dec. 31, 1942; children—Michael McGill, Patrick Floyd, C. Kevin, Kathleen. Supt. schs., Northview, Mo., 1942; instr. history Stanford, 1950-51, 54-55; instr. to asst. prof. history U.S. Mil. Acad., 1951-54; asst. to asso. prof. history Ariz. State U., 1955-60, chmn. dept., 1957-60; dean Coll. Arts and Scis., prof. history U. Mont., 1960-69; acad. v.p. U. Ida., Moscow, 1969—. Rockefeller fellow Slavic studies Hoover Instn., Stanford, 1950; asso. leadership tng. project North Central Assn., Colls. and Secondary Schs., 1958-59, cons. higher edn., 1959—; commr. commn. on higher schs. N.W. Assn. Secondary and Higher Schs., 1967—. Pres. Western Mont. council, mem. regional exec. com. Boy Scouts Am., 1964-69. Mem. Council Colls. of Arts and Scis., Mississippi Valley Deans Group, Am. Hist. Assn., Nat. Assn. State Univs. and Land Grant Colls. (council on acad. affairs), N.Y. State Assn. European Historians (exec. council 1953-54). Contbr. articles profl. publs. Home: 122 S Howard St Moscow ID 83843

COONS, ALBERT HEWETT, med. scientist; b. Gloversville, N.Y., June 28, 1912; s. Albert Selmser and Marion (Hewett) C.; A.B., Williams Coll., 1933, Sc.D., 1960; M.D., Harvard, 1937; Sc.D., Yale, 1961, Emory U., 1969; m. Phyllis Watts, Dec. 27, 1947; children—Elizabeth Schuyler, Susan Wakefield, Hilary, Wendy, Albert Hewett. Engaged as house officer at Mass. Gen. Hosp. Boston, 1937-39; asst. resident physician Thorndike Meml. Lab., Boston City Hosp., 1939-40; research fellow medicine Harvard, 1939- 40, research fellow bacteriology, immunology, 1940-47 (on leave 1942- 46), instr., 1947-48, asso., 1948-50, asst. prof., 1950-53, vis. prof., 1953-70, prof., 1970—; research fellow med. scis. Nat. Research Council, 1940-42; career investigator Am. Heart Assn., 1953—; cons. USPHS, 1956-62; Harvey lectr., 1957. Served to maj. M.C. AUS, 1942-46. Recipient Kimble Methodology award, 1958, Lasker award, Am. Pub. Health Assn., 1959, Paul Ehrlich award (Germany), 1961, Passano award, 1962, T. Duckett Jones Meml. award, 1962, Gairdner Found. award (Can.), 1962; Emil v. Behring prize (West Germany), 1966. Fellow A.A.A.S., Am. Acad. Arts and Scis.; mem. Soc. Am. Bacteriologists, Soc. Exptl. Biology and Medicine, Nat. Acad. Scis., Am. Assn. Immunologists (pres. 1960-61), Am. Rheumatism Soc., Histochem. Soc. (councillor 1952-56, pres. 1964- 65), Sigma Xi, Phi Delta Theta. Clubs: Harvard (Boston); Brookline (Mass.) Country. Asso. editor Jour. Immunology, 1956-61, editor, 1961-65; asso. editor Jour. Histochemistry and Cytochemistry, 1958—; adv. editor Jour. Exptl. Medicine, 1963-70. Home: 132 High St Brookline MA 02146 Office: 25 Shattuck St Boston MA 02115

COONS, CLIFFORD VERNON, corp. ofcl.; b. St. Joseph, Mo., Nov. 13, 1911; s. Edwin and Carrie (Fairhurst) C.; student St. Joseph Coll., 1930-32; m. Delma DeYoung, Aug. 9, 1941; 1 son, Robert. With accounting dept. Rheem Mfg. Co., N.Y.C., 1934, successively purchasing agt., office mgr., tng. sales mgr., plant mgr., sales mgr., gen. sales mgr. v.p., 1935-56, dir., 1950—, exec. v.p., 1956-67, pres., 1967—. Mem. Gas Appliance Mfrs. Assn. (pres. 1957-59, bd. dirs.). Clubs: Westchester Country (Rye, N.Y.); Canadian, Sky (N.Y.C.); Pine Valley (New Jersey) Golf. Home: Pilgrim Rd Rye NY 10580 Office: 400 Park Av New York City NY 10022

COONS, KENNETH WILLIAM, chem. engr.; b. Dodge City, Kan., Aug. 27, 1904; s. William Olin and Flora (Swan) C.; student Sherman County High Sch., Goodland, Kan., 1921- 25; A.B. and B.S., U. of Alabama, 1930; Ph.D., Columbia, 1933; m. Hortense V. Duncan, Sept. 1, 1931 (dec.); children—William Duncan, Kenneth Frederic. Research chemist Bakelite Corp., 1931; chem. engr. in charge hydrogenation, Nat. Anlline & Chem. Co., 1932-35; prof. emeritus U. Ala., head dept. chem. engring., 1935-63; cons. chem. engr., 1938—. Bakelite fellow Columbia U., 1930-31, 1931-32. Registered engr., Ala. Fellow Am. Inst. Chem. Engrs.; mem. Tuscaloosa C. of C., Am. Chem. Soc., Society for the Promotion of Engineering Education. Author: Surface Active Agents, 1945; numerous papers on fluid flow and heat transfer Holder of several U.S. patents. Home: 2901 E 15th St Tuscaloosa AL 35401 Office: University of Alabama University AL 35486

COONTZ, GUSTAF, govt. ofcl.; b. Vienna, Austria, Nov. 7, 1919; s. Max and Friedericke (Wechsberg) Kuntz; came to U.S., 1937; student Worcester Polyt. Inst., 1937-38; B.A., Clark U., 1941; m. Clare Elliot McSheehy, Nov. 19, 1942; children—Robert, Otto, Eric, Raymond, Clare. Supr. order dept. Coppus Engring. Corp., Worcester, Mass., 1946-48, sales engr., 1949-55, dir. indsl. relations, 1956-60, treas. 1961-69, dir., 1956-69; consul, prin. comml. officer, dir. Trade Center, Am. consulate, Frankfurt, Germany, 1970—. Mem. Worcester City Council, 1962-69, vice mayor, 1962-65, 68-69. Bd. dirs. St. Vincent Research Found., 1967-70; trustee Clark U., 1967-70. Served to 1st lt. AUS, 1941-46. Recipient Distinguished Service award Clark U. Alumni Assn., 1970. Mem. Adminstrv. Mgmt. Soc. (pres. Worcester chpt. 1959), Clark U. Alumni Assn. (pres. 1960). Clubs: Rotary, University (Worcester). Home: 18 Am Leonhardsbrunn 6 Frankfurt Main West Germany Office: US Trade Center Am Consulate General APO New York City NY 09757

COOP, FREDERICK ROBERT, govt. ofcl.; b. San Diego, Mar. 1, 1914; s. Ernest Frederick and Hazel (Angier) C.; A.B., U. Cal. at Berkeley, 1935; M.S. in Pub. Adminstrn., U. So. Cal., 1937; m. Jean Haven, Feb. 11, 1939; children—Susan, Robert, Thomas, Elizabeth. Personnel technician Cal. Personnel Bd., 1937-41; personnel dir., Pasadena, Cal., 1941-49; personnel cons. UN, 1947; city mgr., Inglewood, Cal., 1949-56, Fremont, Cal., 1956-58; chief pub. services div. U.S. Operations Mission to Yugoslavia, 1958-61; city mgr., Newport Beach, Cal., 1961-64, Phoenix, 1964-69; regional dir. U.S. Dept. Health, Edn. and Welfare, San Francisco, 1969—. Served to lt. comdr. USNR, World War II. Named Young Man of Year, 1947, Pasadena Jr. C. of C. Mem. Pub. Personnel Assn., Internat. City Mgmt. Assn. (pres. Cal. 1956, regional v.p.), Am. Soc. Pub. Adminstrn. (bd. dirs.), Nat. Acad. Pub. Adminstrn. Home: 3164 Maryola Ct Lafayette CA 94549 Office: 50 Fulton St San Francisco CA 94102

COOPE, GEORGE FREDERICK, dir. Potash Co. America; b. N.Y. City, July 5, 1893; s. Herbert and Catherine (MacDougall) C.; E.M., Columbia U., 1916; m. Jessica Lewis, Dec. 8, 1917; children—George Frederick, Peter McDougall, Robert Lewis. Mining engr. in Nev., Ariz., Chile and N.M., 1916-36; with Potash Co. of America, Denver, 1936-1958, retired as pres. 1958, now dir. Home: Blue Hill ME 04614 Office: 818 17th St Denver CO 80202

COOPER, ABE, distbg. co. exec. Pres., Continental Distbg. Co., Chgo. Office: 700 W Chicago Av Chicago IL 60610*

COOPER, ALBERT HUDIBURGH, engring. educator; b. Knoxville, Tenn., Nov. 6, 1906; s. John Hudibrugh and Rubie (Wallace) C.; B.S. in Chem. Engring., U. Tenn., 1929, M.S. in Chem. Engring., 1930; postgrad. Mass. Inst. Tech., 1930-31; Ph.D., Mich. State U., 1933; m. Louise Kaderly, Feb. 20, 1930. Chem. engr. Aluminum Co. Am., 1926-27; asst. editor Chem. and Metall. Engring. mag., 1929; chem. engr. E.I. duPont de Nemours [Co., 1930; asst. prof. N.C. State Coll., 1935-37; asso. prof. Va. Poly. Inst., 1937-45; chem. engr. U.S. Indsl. Chem. Co., 1945-46; head chem. engring. dept. Bucknell U., 1946- 51; mgr. engring. research and devel. Davison Chem. div. W.R. Grace Co., 1951-52; prof. chem. engring. U. Md., 1952-56; prof., head dept. Pratt Inst., 1955-59; gen. mgr. Am. Indsl. Chem. Co., 1956-59; tech. dir. Waverly Chem. Co., 1959-61; prof. chem. engring., head dept. chem., metall. and nuclear engring. U. Conn., 1959-64; dean grad. sch. Tenn. Technol. U., 1964-68; dir. U. Tenn. Grad. Centers, 1968—; v.p., tech. dir. Chemecon Corp., 1952-60; pres. Pilot Engring. Co., 1947—; mgr. engring. research and devel. D. M. Weatherly Co., 1967-69. Served to capt., CWS, AUS, 1942-45; lt. col. Res. Registered profl. engr., Conn., Md., Pa., Va. Mem. Am. Chem. Soc., Am. Inst. Chem. Engrs., Am. Soc. M.E., A.A.A.S., Am. Soc. Engring. Edn., Am. Assn. U. Profs., Am. Mgmt. Assn., Electrochem. Soc., Sigma Xi, Alpha Chi Sigma, Tau Beta Pi. Contbr. articles profl. jours. Editor Chem. Engring. Edn., 1946-64. Home: PO Box 10883 Knoxville TN 37919

COOPER, BYRON NELSON, geologist; b. Plainfield, Ind., Aug. 19, 1912; s. Frank Landers and Stella Patience (Lynch) C.; A.B., DePauw U., Greencastle, Ind., 1934; M.S., U. of Ia., 1935, Ph.D., 1937; m. Elizabeth Doyne, Sept. 2, 1935; children—John, Patricia Ann. Jr. geologist U.S. Geologic Survey, Denver, 1937; instr. Wichita U., 1937-38, asst. prof. geology, 1938-42; field geologist Va. Geol. Survey, summers 1936- 1938-41, asso. geologist, 1942-45; paleontologist U.S. Nat. Mus., 1945- 46; prof. and head dept. geology Va. Poly. Inst. 1946—, acting dir. of grad. studies 1950, dir. Geology Summer Field Station, asso. dean engring., 1951-52; mem. exec. com. Va. Center for Environmental Studies; cons. geologist on geol. and mineral resources of Va. and Southeastern U.S. 1946—; guest lectr. NSF Geology Summer Insts., U. Miss., 1958, Clemson Coll., 1959, Am. U., 1960, 61, 64, vis. lectr., 1965, 67, 68; lectr. Appalachian geology U. Mo., Rolla, 1966, W. Va., 1969. Dir. Gen. Stone and Materials Corp. Leader Am. Assn. Petroleum Geologists Shenandoah Valley field excursion, 1960, Geol. Soc. Am. Grand Appalachian Excursion, 1961; leader Geol. Soc. Am. field excursion in Appalachians, 1971; engring. geology: Tinker Mountain Water Diversion Tunnel, 1965, Catawba Mountain Water Diversion Tunnel, I-77 Vehicular Tunnel in Walker Mountain, Appomattox Water Supply Impoundment Dam, 1966-68, evaporite deposits in Saltville Dist., all in Va., also deep coal mines in Western Va.; geol. control of runoff. Mem. Am. Commn. on Stratigraphic Nomenclature, 1961-63; NSF project evaluation panelist, 1962. Ednl. cons. East Carolina U., 1969. Del. 21st Internat. Geol. Congress, Copenhagen. Mem. Gov.'s Adv. Commn. on geology, 1953-57; mem. com. on stratigraphical paleontology NRC. Mem. adv. council Va. Economy, 1958-60. Chmn. United Christian Aid, Blacksburg. Fellow of Geological Soc. Am. (councilor 1956-58, chmn. S.E. sect. 1956), Paleontol. Soc., A.A.A.S. (councilor 1956-58; v.p. and chmn. sect. E 1958); mem. Am. Assn. Petroleum Geologists (distinguished lectr. 1956-57), Internat. Platform Assn., Am. Arbitration Assn. (tech. panelist), Va. Acad. Sci. (chmn. geology sect. 1949, councilor 1955-57), Am. Inst. Mining, Metall, and Petroleum Engrs., Am. Inst. Profl. Geologists, Am. Assn. U. Profs., Soc. Econ. Geologists, Va. Assn. Profl. Geologists (pres. 1965-66), Sigma Xi (sec. Va. Poly. Inst.). Presbyn. Clubs: Shenandoah (Roanoke, Va.); Lions. Author articles in geol. survey bulls. and jours. in field. Asso. editor Va. Jour. of Sci., 1954-57; editor Mineral Industries Jour., 1958-60. Died Mar. 26, 1971.

COOPER, CECIL HARRISON, oil and gas co. exec.; b. Lawton, Okla., Dec. 20, 1909; s. Mary Daniels Briscoe; B.S. in Geology, U. Okal., 1933; m. Estelle Lewis, Mar. 21, 1931; 1 dau., Sandra Ann. Gen. oil field laborer Phillips Petroleum Col., 1933-34; jr. engr. Indian Territory Illuminating Oil Co., Bartlesville, Okla., 1934-35, jr. geologist, 1935-36, asst. dist. geologist, Wichita, Kan., 1936-37, staff geologist, 1937-39, dist. geologist, Kan., 1939-40; div. mgr. Oklahoma City, British Am. Oil Producing Co., 1946-49, div. mgr., Midland, Tex., 1949-51; exploration mgr. F. Kirk Johnson-Brooks-Scanlon Co., Ft. Worth, 1951-56; formerly with Ambassador Oil Corp., Ft. Worth; pres., gen. manager Ambassador English Oil Company, London, Ambassador Irish Oil Co., Dublin, Ambassador Italian Petroli; former v.p. Anadarko Production Company, Fort Worth; pres., chief operating officer King Resources Co., Denver, 1971—. Served to major USAAF, 1940-46; PTO. Mem. Am. Assn. Petroleum Geologists, Am. Petroleum Inst., Ind. Petroleum Producers Am. Clubs: Admirals, River Crest Country (Ft. Worth). Office: 100 Seurity Life Bldg Denver CO 80202

COOPER, CHARLES ARTHUR, govt. ofcl.; b. Chgo., Dec. 23, 1933; s. S. Robert and Betty (Greenabaum) C.; B.A., Swarthmore Coll., 1955; Ph.D. in Econs., Mass. Inst. Tech., 1960; student Russian Studies Program, Harvard, 1957-59; m. Janis Starr Stone, Mar. 3, 1966; children—Elizabeth Starr, Melora Christina. With Council Econ. Advisers, Washington, 1961-63; with RAND Corp., Santa Monica, Cal., 1963-66, 68-70; econ. adviser to Robert W. Komer, spl. asst. to pres. for civilian programs in Vietnam, 1966-67; asso. dir. AID, econ. counselor Am. embassy, Saigon, Vietnam, 1967-68; minister-counselor for econ. affairs, 1970—. Served with USAF, 1959-60. Recipient Superior Honor award AID, 1968. Mem. Am. Econ. Assn., Phi Beta Kappa. Editor: Economic Development in the Middle East, 1971.

COOPER, CHARLES ARTHUR, former corp. exec.; b. Bad Axe, Mich., Dec. 31, 1904; s. William H. and Mabel R. (Nichols) C.; student U. Mich., 1922-23, Ohio State U., 1923; J.D., Detroit Coll. Law, 1931; m. Violet F. Mohaske, Sept. 14, 1927; children—Charles Arthur, Peter Mohaske. With N.Am. Rockwell Corp. and predecessor cos., Pitts., 1928-70, gen. mgr. Bossert div., Utica, N.Y., 1953-57, v.p., Rockwell-Standard Corp., 1957-62, dir. 1960-61, exec. v.p., 1962-65, sr. v.p., 1965-67, also group mgr. Indsl. Products Group of parent co., 1967-70, sr. v.p. Comml. Products Group, N.Am. Rockwell Corp., 1967-70; v.p., dir., Kerrigan Iron Works Co., Nashville, 1962-65, Aero Commander, Inc., Pitts., 1964-70, Canadian Motor Lamp Co., Ltd., Windsor, Ont., Compressed Steel Shafting Co., Boston; v.p. Murray Co. of Tex., Inc., Pitts., 1965-70, Standard Property Corp., Pitts., 1964—; dir. Bossert Mfg. Co., Utica, N.Y., 1964-70, Aero. Commander Acceptance Corp., Bethany, Okla., Rockwell-Standard Corp. Can., Ltd., Tilbury, Ont.; v.p. N. Am. Rockwell Internat., El Segundo, Cal., 1968—. Mem. State Bar Mich., Automotive Old Timers, Soc. Automotive Engrs., Delta Theta Phi. Club: St. Clair Country (Pitts.). Home: 1553 Hastings Mill Rd Upper St Claire Pittsburgh PA 15241

COOPER, CHARLES GRAY, business exec., cons.; b. Gloucester, Mass., Sept. 13, 1902; s. Charles Gray and Irene Way (Martin) C.; prep. edn. Fessenden Sch., West Newton, Mass., 1915-18, Hotchkiss Sch., Lakeville, Conn., 1918-21; B.S., Yale, 1926; m. Dorothy Alice Booth, Sept. 7, 1932 (dec. Aug. 1949); 1 son, David Booth; m. 2d, Marguerite Hosack, December 9, 1950. Engr., Chapman Stein Co., Mount Vernon, O., 1928-31; sales engr. Cooper- Bessemer Corp., N.Y.C., 1931-33, dist. mgr. Washington and Southeastern regional office, 1933-57, dir., 1945-67, v.p., 1950—, v.p., internat. dir., 1957-66; v.p., Washington corporate rep. Cooper Industries, Inc., 1966-68; past pres. Cooper-Bessemer, S.A., Cooper- Bessemer Internat. Corp., Cooper-Bessemer (U.K.) Ltd., Cooper- Bessemer of Can., Ltd. Mem. Am. Soc. M.E., Washington Soc. Engrs. (past dir.), Am. Soc. Naval Engrs. (past councilor), Soc. Naval Architects and Marine Engrs. (past councilor), Yale Alumni Assn. (past pres. Wash.), Yale Alumni Bd. (past vice chmn.), Newcomen Soc., Delta Psi. Republican. Mason. Clubs: Chevy Chase, Metropolitan (Washington); Yale, U.S. Sr. Golf Assn. (N.Y.C.); Mt. Vernon (O.) Country; Burning Tree (Washington). Home: 3900 Watson Pl NW Washington DC 20016

COOPER, CHARLES MUHLENBERG, sem. pres.; b. Lima, O., Jan. 7, 1909; s. Frederick Eugene and Rosa Muhlenberg (Richards) C.; A.B. cum laude, Harvard, 1930; B.D. with distinction, Lutheran Theol. Sem., Phila., 1935; Ph.D., Dropsie Coll. for Hebrew and Cognate Learning, 1941; D.D., Muhlenberg Coll., 1954; m. Alta Ernestine Peterson, May 29, 1934; children—Charles (dec.), Jeremy, Catherine (Mrs. Donald A. Millard, Jr.). Ordained to ministry Lutheran Ch., 1933; asst. pastor Trinity Lutheran Ch., Akron, O., 1933-36; instr. O.T., Luth. Theol. Sem., Phila., 1936-41, asst. prof., 1941-45, Norton prof., 1945-53; pres. Luth. Ministerium of Pa. and Adjacent States, 1953-61; pres. Pacific Luth. Theol. Sem., Berkeley, Cal., 1961—. Mem. Joint Commn. on Lutheran Unity, 1956-62; mem. exec. bd. United Luth. Ch. in Am., 1956-62; mem. exec. council Luth. Ch. in Am., 1962-64. Del. 3d Assembly World Council Chs., New Delhi, India, 1961, Luth. World Fedn., Helsinki, 1963. Mem. bd. Grad. Theol. Union. Mem. Soc. Bibl. Lit. and Exegesis, Dropsie Coll. Alumni Assn. (pres. 1951-52), Am. Assn. Theol. Schs. (exec. com. 1964-70). Clubs: Harvard (San Francisco); City Commons (pres. 1971). Author articles, revs., religious jours. Contbg. editor: The Holy Bible: Westminister Study Edition, 1948; Deuteronomy, Old Testament Commentary, 1948; Uniform Lesson Commentary, 1953, 56, 64; The Psalms in Life, 1959; The Old Testament for Us, 1965; Jeremiah, 1971. Home: 22 Acacia Av Berkeley CA 94708 Office: 2770 Marin Av Berkeley CA 94708

COOPER, CHARLES WILLIAM, lawyer; b. Pitts., May 19, 1911; s. Howell Carnahen and Anetta Christina (Heissenbuttel) C.; grad. Phillips Acad., 1929; B.S. in Engring., Lehigh U., 1933; LL.B., Harvard, 1937; m. Martha Stewart Smith, Sept. 13, 1937; children—Carolyn Howell, Barbara Lloyd, Pamela Weir, William Douglas. Admitted to Pa. bar, 1937, N.Y. bar, 1941, also Fed. Cts.; practice of law, Pitts., 1937-41, N.Y.C., 1941—, specializing utility law, 1939—; former dir., v.p., gen. counsel Consol. Natural Gas Co., N.Y.C., exec. v.p., gen. counsel. Mem. Am. Bar Assn., Fed. Power Bar Assn., Tau Beta Pi. Conglist. Home: 71 West Rd New Canaan CT 06840 Office: 30 Rockefeller Plaza New York City NY 10020

COOPER, CHAUNCEY IRA, coll. dean; b. St. Louis, May 31, 1906; s. Ira Luther and Mattie Salina (Horton) C.; B.S. in Pharmacy, U. Minn., 1934, M.S., 1935; D.Sc., Phila. Coll. Pharmacy and Sci., 1970; m. Marie Taylor, June 7, 1937; 1 son, Chauncey M.; foster children, William R. Hyde, Jeanne H. Lofton. Instr. pharmacy Meharry Med. Coll., Nashville, 1927-32; instr. pharmacy Howard U., 1935-38, asso. prof., acting dean Coll. Pharmacy, 1938-41, prof., dean, 1941—. Founder, organizer Nat. Pharm. Assn., pres., 1947, exec. sec., 1950—, editor Jour., 1955—. Recipient award for leadership Washington Pharm. Assn., 1957; Chauncey I. Cooper award established by Nat. Pharm. Assn. Mem. Am. Pharm. Assn., Am. Assn. Colls. Pharmacy, Washington Pharm. Assn., D.C. Pharm. Assn. (pres. 1970), Beta Kappa Chi, Alpha Phi Alpha. Club: Pigskin (Washington). Home: 3800 Montrose Driveway North Chevy Chase MD 20015 Office: Howard University Washington DC 20001

COOPER, DAMON WARREN, naval officer; b. Elizabethtown, Ky., Apr. 27, 1919; s. Damon McCluskey and Mary (McDermott) C.; B.S., U.S. Navy Acad., 1941; M.A., George Washington U., 1963; m. Anne Porter Leverich, Jan. 2, 1943; children—Anne Michele (Mrs. Robert M. Davidson), Mary Patricia, Jeanne Fleetwood, John Rockwell. Commd. ensign U.S. Navy, 1941, advanced through grades to rear adm., 1967; comdr. aircraft squadrons, World War II and Korea; comdr. U.S. Ticonderoga, 1964-65; assigned Bur. Personnel, 1965-66; comdr. Patrol Force 7th Fleet, 1966-68; asst. chief Bur. Naval Personnel, 1968-70; comdr. Task Force 77, 1971—. Decorated Legion of Merit, D.F.C., Bronze Star, Air medal. Roman Catholic. Home: Quarters NAV STA SUBK BAY Philippine Islands Office: Comcar Division 5 FPO San Francisco CA 96601

COOPER, DAN HENRY, educator; b. Lewistown, Mont., Nov. 14, 1913; s. Fred A. and Amelia (Hill) C.; B.S., Northwestern U., 1934; intermittent student Stanford, 1939-42; M.A., U. Chgo., 1938, Ph.D., 1946; m. Annabelle Doke, Feb. 24, 1950; children—Fred Louis, John Scott, Amelia Ann. Tchr., Jefferson County (Ky.) pub. schs., 1934-37; head lower div. Tamalpais (Cal.) Sch. for Boys, 1937-39; prin. jr. high San Mateo (Cal.) pub. schs., 1939-42; asst. to supt. schs. Pitts. pub. schs., 1944-46; asst. prof. edn. U. Chgo., 1946-49; asso. prof. edn. U. Ia., 1949-54; asso. dean Sch. Sci., Edn. and Humanities, also dir. div. edn., prof. edn. Purdue University, 1954-62; prof. of ednl. adminstrn. U. Mich., Ann Arbor, 1962—; spl. work evaluation tchr. merit in city sch. systems, schs. for young adolescents, sch. survey reports. Mem. N.E.A., Am. Assn. Sch. Adminstrs., Am. Ednl. Research Assn., Nat. Council Schoolhouse Constrn., Nat. Conf. Profs. Ednl. Adminstrn., Phi Delta Kappa, Kappa Delta Pi, Acacia. Rotarian. Club: Torch. Home: 6330 Daly Rd Dexter MI 48130

COOPER, DONALD LEE, physician; b. Columbus, Kan., Aug. 11, 1928; s. Calvin M. and J. Pearl (Mullen) C.; A.B., Kan. State Coll., 1949; M.D., U. Kan., 1953; m. Dona Faye Maddux, June 4, 1950; children—Donald Lee, Catherine Susan, Cheryl Lyn, Tad Houston. Intern St. Mary's and Childrens Mercy hosps., Kansas City, Mo., 1953-54; pvt. practice medicine, Manhattan, Kan., 1956-57; team physician, asst. dir. Health Center Kan. State U., 1957-60; dir. health service, team physician Okla. State U. Hosp. and Clinic, Stillwater, 1960—; liaison officer Am. Coll. Health Assn. to Nat. Athletic Trainers Assn., 1963—; Am. chmn. 1st Am.-Soviet Conf. on Student Health, Moscow, Russia, 1967; team physician U.S. Olympic Team, 1967-68. Served to capt. USAF, 1954-56. Mem. A.M.A., Nat. Collegiate Athletic Assn. (med. cons. to football rules com. 1969—), Am. (past pres., mem. exec. com.), Southwestern (past pres.) coll. health assns., Nat. Athletic Trainers Assn., Alpha Omega Alpha, Nu Sigma Nu. Presbyn. Lion. Author: (with others) Standard Nomenclature of Athletic Injuries, 1966. Contbr. articles med. jours. Home: 1001 Liberty Lane Stillwater OK 74074 Office: Okla State U Hosp and Clinic Stillwater OK 74074

COOPER, DOROTHY ANNE, hosp. adminstr.; b. Toledo, Ohio, Aug. 17, 1931; d. Sample Wren and Gertrude (Pinkelman) Cooper; B.S.N., Boston Coll., 1964; M.S.N., Catholic U. Am., 1966. Pediatric supr. St. Peter's Gen. Hosp., New Brunswick, N.J., 1953-57, med.-surg. supr., 1959-61, asso. dir. nursing service, 1961-62; hosp. adminstr. St. John's Hosp., Kabba, Nigeria, W. Africa, 1966-68; asst. adminstr. St. Vincent Hosp. & Med. Center, Toledo, Ohio, 1968-69, adminstr., 1969—; dir. corp. Sisters of Charity of St. Vincent Hosp. and Med. Center Toledo. Mem. Toledo Adv. Council Sisters (treas. 1970-71), Nat. Honor Soc. Nursing. Address: 2213 Cherry St Toledo OH 43608

COOPER, EDWARD BROOKS, physicist; b. Rutland, Vt., Sept. 30, 1908; s. Charles Paine and Julia (Brooks) C.; A.B., Berea Coll., 1930, D.Sc. 1960; M.A., U. Me., 1934; postgrad. Mass. Inst. Tech., 1937-38; m. Nettie West, Aug. 20, 1932; childrenPeter Bradford, Wilson Edward. Tchr. sci. New Eng. high schs., 1930-41; supr., mgr., dir. plastics research labs. E.I. duPont de Nemours & Co., Inc., Arlington, N.J. and Wilmington, Del., 1942-66, mgr. personnel research, 1966—. Head U.S. delegation Internat. Standards Orgn., Turin, Italy, 1952. Mem. exec. com. No. Del. United Fund, 1958-63. Trustee Berea Coll. Mem. Am. Chem. Soc., Am. Phys. Soc., I.E.E.E., Franklin Inst., Soc. Plastics Engrs., Plastics Inst. (Gt. Britain). Lion (pres. Newark 1964). Home: 104 Bent Lane Newark DE 19711 Office: Nemours Bldg Wilmington DE 19711

COOPER, EDWIN LAVERN, educator; b. Utica, Mich., Aug. 31, 1919; s. George Edwin and Ada Anna (Dentel) C.; B.S., U. Mich., 1940, M.S., 1948, Ph.D., 1949; m. Margaret Elizabeth Simmons, Dec. 20, 1941; children—Marilyn, John. Dir., Fishery Research Sta. Mich., 1949-52; chief fishery biologist Wis., 1952-56; prof. zoology Pa. State U., University Park, 1956—; ecol. cons. Served with AUS, 1941-45. Mem. Am. Inst. Fishery Research Biologists (pres.), A.A.A.S., Am. Inst. Biol. Scis., Ecol. Soc. Am., Am. Soc. Limnology and Oceanography, Am. Fisheries Soc. (pres. 1971), Am. Soc. Ichthyologists and Herpetologists, Internat. Soc. Theoretical and Applied Limnology. Editor trans. Am. Fisheries Soc., 1963-66. Home: 1282 Penfield Rd State College PA 16801

COOPER, FRANK EVANS, banker; b. Seattle, Nov. 28, 1928; s. Frank Homer and Marguerite Caroline (Madison) C.; B.A., U. Wash., 1950; M.B.A., Pacific Coast Grad. Sch. Banking, 1958-61; m. Erlene Rose Johnson, June 30, 1951; children—Dawn Rene, Frank Evans. Br. mgr. Comml. Credit Corp., Eugene, Ore., 1951-58; v.p. Puget Sound Nat. Bank, Tacoma, 1958-64; pres. Bank of Tacoma, 1964-68; supr. banking, Wash., 1968-70; sr. v.p. Bank of Hawaii, Honolulu, 1970—. Chmn. Western States Commrs. Banking, 1970; dir. Nat. Assn. Bank Commrs., 1970. Mem. bd. Tacoma Community Coll., 1967-69; mem. adv. bd. Nat. Consumer Finance Assn., 1969. Del. Wash. Republican convs., 1958-68; precinct committeeman, Tacoma, 1950-69; del. Rep. Nat. Conv., 1964, 68; mem. Wash. Ho. of Reps., 1963-64. Bd. dirs. Jessie Dslyn Boys' Ranch, Tacoma, Mary Bridge Children's Hosp., Tacoma; trustee Annie Wright Girls' Acad., Tacoma. Mem. Internat. Platform Assn. Am. Marketing Assn., Hawaii Bankers Assn., Navy League, Sales and Marketing Execs. Honolulu. Mason (Shriner), Elk. Clubs: Oahu Country, Outrigger Canoe (Hawaii). Home: 1039 Waiki St Honolulu HI 96821 Office: 111 S King St Honolulu HI 96813

COOPER, GEORGE BRINTON, educator; b. Phila., Apr. 14, 1916; s. Lloyd W. and Esther L. (Cooper) C.; B.A. in Social Scis. with highest honors, Swarthmore Coll., 1938; Lockwood fellow Univ. Coll., London, Eng., 1938-39; M.A., Yale, 1942, Ph.D., 1948. Mem. faculty Trinity Coll., Hartford, Conn., 1941—, prof. history, 1958—, Northam prof., chm. dept., 1964—; mng. editor Jour. British Studies, 1961—; Am. vice consul, London, Eng., 1944-46. Mem. Hartford Bd. Edn., 1959-65, pres., 1961-62; chmn. Gov. Conn. Bi-Partisan Com. Redistricting Conn. Senate, 1960; nat. adv. cancer council USPHS, 1961-64. Bd. dirs. Hartford Pub. Library, 1964-71. Served with USNR, 1943- 44. Mem. Conf. Brit. Studies, Am. Hist. Assn., Hakluyt Soc. (London), Phi Beta Kappa, Pi Gamma Mu, Delta Upsilon. Democrat. Clubs: 20th Century, University (Hartford). Home: Pomfret's Choice West Simsbury CT 06092 Office: Trinity Coll Hartford CT 06106

COOPER, GEORGE ROBERT, elec. engr., educator; b. Connersville, Ind., Nov. 29, 1921; s. William Russell and Margaret (Frederick) C.; B.S., Purdue U., 1943, M.S., 1945, Ph.D., 1949; m. Helen Elizabeth Conder, Nov. 23, 1949; children—George Michael, David Russell, Susan Rachael, Ann Elizabeth, Steven Robert, Thomas Jonathan. Instr. elec. engring. Purdue U., 1943-49, asst. prof., 1949-51, asso. prof., 1951-55, prof., 1955—; cons. elec. engring. Fellow I.E.E.E.; mem. Am. Soc. E.E., Soc. Indsl. and Applied Math., Sigma Xi, Eta Kappa Nu, Tau Beta Pi, Sigma Pi Sigma. Patentee in field. Home: P O Box 2255 West Lafayette, IN 47906 Office: Sch Elec Engring Purdue U Lafayette IN 47907

COOPER, GRACE ROGERS, museum curator; b. Sharon, Pa., Nov. 22, 1924; d. Byron Alonzo and Wilda Emily (Boyer) Rogers; student Maryville (Tenn.) Coll., 1942-44; B.S., U. Md., 1946; m. Sanford Lee

Cooper, Dec. 15, 1961. Asst. curator textiles U.S. Nat. Mus., Smithsonian Instn., 1948-56, asso. curator, 1956-61, curator, 1961—; cons. in field, 1948—; sr. tech. editor textiles Ency. Britannica, 1959—. Mem. Internat. Inst. Conservation Historic and Artistic Works, Internat. Center Study Ancient Textiles, Am. Assn. Museums. Lutheran. Author: The Invention of the Sewing Machine, 1968; The Copp Family Textiles, 1971. Home: 3114 Wisconsin Av NW Washington DC 20016 Office: Div Textiles Nat Museum History and Tech Smithsonian Inst Washington DC 20560

COOPER, GRANT BURR, lawyer; b. N.Y.C., Apr. 1, 1903; s. Louis Baxter and Josephine (Christensen) C.; student Pace Coll., N.Y.C., 1921; LL.B., Southwestern U., 1926; m. Edna Reynolds, Nov. 21, 1929 (dec. 1934); children—Judith Ann (Mrs. Charles D. Hunt), Natalie Caroline (Mrs. Rollin D. Wallace); m. 2d, Phyllis A. Norton, Apr. 3, 1935; children—Meredith Jane (Mrs. Robert K. Worrell), Grant Burr, John Norton. Admitted to Cal. bar, 1927; with Office Dist. Atty., Los Angeles, 1929-35, 40-42, chief dep. dist. atty., 1940-43; dep. city atty., Los Angeles, 1935-38; pvt. practice, Los Angeles, 1946—. Chief asst. ins. commr., Cal., 1943; pres. Los Angeles Health Commn., 1944. Fellow Am. Bar Found., Am. Coll. Trial Lawyers (past bd. regents, pres. 1962-63); mem. Los Angeles County Bar Assn. (pres. 1960-61, trustee 1951-52, 56- 62), State Bar Cal. (bd. govs. 1953-56, v.p. 1956). Mason (Shriner). Clubs: University, Chancery, Legion Lex (Los Angeles); Tuna (Catalina, Cal.). Home: 335 N McCadden Pl Los Angeles CA 90004 Office: 1880 Century Park E Los Angeles CA 90067

COOPER, GUSTAV ARTHUR, paleontologist; b. College Point, N.Y., Feb. 9, 1902; s. Gustav A. and Lucy I. (English) C.; B.S., Colgate U., 1924, M.A., 1926, D.Sc., 1953; Ph.D., Yale, 1929; m. Josephine P. Wells, June 21, 1930; children—Arthur W., Anne (Mrs. George R. Gay). Research asso. Yale, 1929-30; asst. curator stratigraphic paleontology Smithsonian Instn., 1930-43, curator invertebrate paleontology and paleobotany, 1943-56, head curator geology dept., 1956-67, sr. scientist, 1967—. Recipient Mary Clarke Thompson medal Nat. Acad. Scis., 1958. Fellow Geol. Soc. Am., Paleontol. Soc. (pres. 1956-57, recipient medal 1964); mem. Washington Acad. Scis., Am. Acad. Arts and Scis., Geol. Soc. London (corr. mem.), Geol. Soc. Washington (pres. 1961), Phi Beta Kappa, Sigma Xi, Beta Theta Pi. Club: Cosmos. Contbr. articles profl. jours. Home: 3425 Porter St Washington DC 20016 Office: Smithsonian Institution Washington DC 20560

COOPER, HENRY, lawyer; b. Pitts., Nov. 16, 1909; s. Roy Cummings and Anne (Robinson) C.; grad. Shady Side Acad., 1927; A.B., Princeton, 1931; LL.B., U. Pitts., 1934; m. Lois Anne Watt, Dec. 6, 1962; children—Betty Anne (Mrs. Harry B. Watkins III), Margaret (Mrs. William E. Young), Amy R., Henry II. Admitted to Pa. bar, 1934, also Fed. Cts., 1934; practice of law, 1934-36; with firm Rose, Rose & Houston, Pitts., 1965; partner firm Houston, Cooper, Speer & German, 1965—. Fund-raising counsellor Ketchum, Inc., 1936-41; trust officer Pitts. Nat. Bank, 1941-45; asst. v.p. Mellon Nat. Bank, 1945-53; sec. dir. Allegheny Lime Co., Gateway Marketing Service, Inc., Indsl. Wastes, Inc., Robinson-Indsl. Wastes, Inc., Washington-Indsl. Wastes, Inc., West Penn Products, Inc., Westmoreland- Indsl. Wastes, Inc.; sec. Gardner Assos., Inc., Franklin Advt. Corp., Latrobe Printing & Pub. Co., McShane Contracting Co., Nat. Carbide Die Co., Rohrich Cadillac, Inc., Typecraft Press, Inc. Pres. Pitts. Life Ins. and Trust Council, 1952; chmn. planning com. Pa. Tax Inst., 1964, 65. Chmn. profl. div. Heart Fund, 1964-65. Sec. Young Republicans of Allegheny County, 1935, local dist. committeeman, 1935. Mem. Am., Pa., Allegheny County bar assns., Corporate Fiduciaries Assn. Allegheny County (pres. 1949), Pitts. Tax Club (pres. 1960). Presbyn. Rotarian (pres. 1955-56). Clubs: University (pres. 1950- 51) (Pitts.); Duquesne. Home: 3955 Bigelow Blvd Pittsburgh PA 15213 Office 1330 Oliver Bldg Pittsburgh PA 15222

COOPER, HERBERT KURTZ, orthodontist; b. Brownstown, Pa., Jan. 2, 1897; s. Clayton S. and Caroline Amanda (Kurtz) C.; student Franklin and Marshall Acad., 1914; student Franklin and Marshall Coll., 1916, D.Sc., 1950; D.D.S., U. Pa., 1919, D.Sc., 1953; L.H.D., Moravian Coll., 1955; m. Mercedes Miller, June 2, 1920; children—Caroline Elizabeth (Mrs. Ross E. Long), Herbert Kurtz, John Allan. Practice of dentistry, Lititz, Pa., 1919-25, Lancaster, 1925—, specializing orthodontics, 1925—; cons. Pa. State Hosp. Crippled Children, 1928; orthondontist, dir. dental dept. Milton Hershey Sch., Hershey, Pa., 1933-39; founder, dir. Lancaster Cleft Palate Clinic, 1939—; prof. cleft palate therapy U. Pa., 1945, 47; cons. Lancaster Gen. Hosp., St. Josephs Hosp., Lancaster. Adv. health bd. Pa.; chmn. bd. dirs. Linden Hall Lititz. Recipient Benjamin Rush award Pa. State Med. Soc., 1947, 2d sci. award exhibit. Am. Dental Assn., 1948, ann. award, Elks, 1951, Award of Merit, Dental Alumni Soc. U. Pa., 1952, Moravian Ch. 1952, Spenadel award 1st Dist. Dental Soc. N.Y., 1956, B'nai B'rith award, 1961, Callahan Meml. award, Cin., 1965, Pa. award of excellence in field of life scis., 1967; Albert H. Ketcham meml. award, 1970, William John Gies award, 1970. Diplomate Am. Bd. Orthondontists. Fellow Acad. Internat. Dentistry, N.Y. Acad. Dentists, Am. Coll. Dentists, Internat. Coll. Dentists; mem. Pa. Soc. Crippled Children (bd. dirs.), Feb. Dentaire Internat., Pa. State, N.C. State, Harris dental socs., Phi Sigma Kappa, Psi Xi Phi. Mem. Moravian Ch. Mason, Elk, Contbr. articles profl. publs. Home: Wheatland Arms Apts Marieta Av Lancaster PA 17603 Office: 24 N Lime St Lancaster PA 17602

COOPER, IRVING BEN, U.S. judge; b. London, Eng., Feb. 7, 1902; s. Max and Rachel (Shimansky) C.; LL.B., Washington U., 1925; m. Anita Bennett, Mar. 28, 1929; children—Richard Bennett, Benita H. (Mrs. Theodore Lee Marks). Came to U.S., 1912, naturalized, 1921. Admitted to N.Y. bar, 1927; gen. practice civil law, N.Y.C. 1927-38; investigation Appellate div. N.Y. Supreme Ct., 1928; Counsel bar assns. disciplinary proc., 1928-30; spl. dep. atty. gen. to investigate improper med. practices, 1929; asso. counsel investigation Magistrates courts, 1930-31; asso. counsel to Judge Samuel Seabury in investigation N.Y.C. Govt., 1932-33; spl. counsel Dept. Investigation, N.Y.C., 1934- city magistrate, 1938-39; asso. justice Ct. Spl. Sessions, 1939-51, chief justice, 1951-60; U.S. dist. judge So. Dist. N.Y., 1961—. Asso. counsel ambulance chasing investigation Appellate div. N.Y. Supreme Ct., 1928; counsel bar assns. disciplinary proc., 1928-30; sp. dep. atty. gen. to investigate improper med. practice, 1929; asso. counsel investigation Magistrates Cts., 1930-31; asso. counsel to Judge Samuel Seabury in investigation N.Y.C. Govt., 1932-33; spl. counsel Dept. Investigation, N.Y.C., 1934-37; lectr., cons. program of law and psychiatry Menninger Found. 1960; lectr. criminal law, 1960-61. Hon. pres. Univ. Settlement, N.Y.C.; trustee Nat. Council Crime and Delinquency, chmn. criminal courts sect., adv. counsel of judges, 1954-69; trustee Reconstructionist Found. Recipient Silver Buffalo award Boy Scouts Am., 1965. Mem. Am. Judicature Soc., Assn. of Bar, N.Y. County Lawyers Assn., Am. (chmn. com. on sentencing, probation and parole 1957-61), N.Y. State bar assns. Home: 33 Riverside Dr New York City NY 10023 Office: Foley Sq New York City NY 10007

COOPER, IRVING S., neurosurgeon; b. Atlantic City, July 15, 1922; s. Louis and Eleanor Lillian (Cooper) C.; B.A., George Washington U., 1942, M.D., 1945; M.S., Ph.D., U. Minn., 1951; m. Mary Dan Frost, Dec. 15, 1944; children—Daniel Alan, Douglas Paul, Lisa Front; m. 2d, Sissel Holm, Jan. 31, 1970. Intern U.S. Naval Hosp., St. Albans, N.Y., 1945-46; fellow neurosurgery Mayo Found., 1948-51; mem. faculty N.Y.U. Med. Sch., 1961-64, prof. clin. neurosurgery, 1954-64; research prof. neuroanatomy N.Y. Med. Coll.; dir. neurosurgery St. Barnabas Hosp., N.Y.C., 1954—; spl. research devel., practice, teaching specialized brain operations for treatment Parkinsonism, related diseases, devel. cryogenic surgery. Eliza Savage vis. prof. Australia, 1962. Served to lt. (j.g.), M.C., USNR, 1946-48. Recipient Lewis Harvey Taylor award Am. Therapeutic Soc., 1957, St. Barnabas Hosp. award, 1959, Modern Medicine award, 1960, alumni achievement award George Washington U., 1960, award in medicine N.Y. Philanthropic League, 1960, civic award in medicine Bronx Bd. Trade, 1961, Humanitarian award Nat. Cystic Fibrosis Found., 1962, gold medal Worshipful Soc. Apothecaries, London, 1967, bronze award Am. Congress Rehab. Med., 1967. Diplomate neurology Am. Bd. Neurology and Psychiatry, Am. Bd. Neurol. Surgery. Fellow A.C.S., Am. Geriatric Soc., N.Y. Acad. Medicine, N.Y. Acad. Sci.; mem. Harvey Cushing Neurosurg. Soc., A.M.A. (Hektoen Bronze Medal 1957, 58, Certificate of Merit 1961), Neurosurg. Soc. Am., Am. Acad. Neurology, Soc. Cryobiology (gov.), Soc. Cryosurgery (pres.), Am. Fedn. Clin. Research, Pan Am. Soc. U.S., Am. Congress Phys. Medicine and Rehab., Scandinavian Neurosurg. Soc., Med. Honor Soc., Sigma Xi (hon.), Alpha Omega Alpha; hon. mem. Neurol. and Neurosurg. Soc. Argentina, Egyptian Neurosurg. Soc., Soc. Neurology and Neurosurgery Cuba. Author: The Neurosurgical Alleviation of Parkinsonism, 1956; Parkinsonism: Its Medical and Surgical Therapy, 1961; Involuntary Movement Disorders, 1968. Home: 76 Mount Tom Rd Pelham Manor NY 10803 Office: 4422 3d Av Bronx NY 10457

COOPER, JACKIE, actor; b. Los Angeles, Sept. 15, 1922. Child actor, beginning at age three; motion pictures include Skippy, The Champ, Remains to be Seen, French Leave; Broadway plays include Remains to be Seen, King of Hearts; star People's Choice, NBC-TV, until 1959, Hennessey, 1959; v.p. Screen Gems, Inc. Served with USNR, World War II. Address: care of Screen Gems 1334 N Beachwood Dr Hollywood CA 90028*

COOPER, JAMES LEES, publisher; b. Darwen, Eng., Mar. 6, 1907; s. James William and Alice (Lees) C.; student pub. schs.; m. Ruby Smith, July 16, 1930; 1 dau., Rita (Mrs. W.H. Pickford). Reporter, war corr., editor, editor-in-chief Globe & Mail, Ltd., Toronto, Ont., Can., 1963-65, pub., editor-in- chief, 1965—, also dir.; dir. Imperial Trust, Montreal, Que., Can. Trustee Toronto Gen. Hosp. Served with AUS, 1941-45. Mem. Canadian Daily Newspaper Pubs. Assn., Commonwealth Press Union (chmn. Canadian sect.). Anglican. Office: 140 King St W Toronto 1 Ontario Canada

COOPER, JAMES WAYNE, lawyer; b. New Britain, Conn., May 22, 1904; s. James E. and Elizabeth C. (Wayne) C.; grad. Choate Sch., 1922; B.A., Yale, 1926, LL.B., 1929; m. Louise B. Field, June 26, 1929; children—Field McIntyre, James Nicoll, Peter Brintnall. Admitted to Conn. bar, 1929; law clk. to Judges T.W. Swan, Learned Hand, N.Y.C., 1929-30; instr. Yale Law Sch., 1930-32; asso. Watrous, Hewitt, Gumbart & Corbin, New Haven, 1932-35; partner Tyler, Cooper, Grant, Bowerman & Keefe, and predecessor firm, 1935—. Dir. Second Nat. Bank of New Haven, New Haven Savs. Bank, Whitney Blake Co.; dir., mem. exec. com. Stanley Works. Counsel Anna Fuller Fund; pres. Foote Sch. Assn., Inc., 1947-49; sec. New Haven Found., 1947-67; mem. Yale U. Council, 1954-59, exec. com., 1956-59, pres. 1958-59. Fellow Saybrook Coll.; mem. Am., Conn. (pres. 1957-58), New Haven County (pres. 1948-49) bar assns. Clubs: Lawn, Graduate, Quinnipack (New Haven); New Britain. Home: Clark Rd Woodbridge New Haven CT 06525 Office: 205 Church St New Haven CT 06509

COOPER, JEROME A., lawyer; b. Brookwood, Ala., Jan. 15, 1913; s. Marks Benjamin and Etta (Temerson) C.; A.B., Harvard, 1933, LL.B., 1936; m. Lois Harriet McMillen, Aug. 16, 1938; children—Ellen (Mrs. Benjamin L. Erdreich), Carol (Mrs. James D. Sokol). Admitted to Ala. bar, 1936; practice in Birmingham, 1946—; law clk. U.S. Dist. Judge Davis, 1936-37, U.S. Supreme Ct. Judge Black, 1937-40; regional atty. Solicitors Office, Dept. Labor, 1940-41; partner firm Cooper, Mitch & Crawford, 1950—. Mem. Pres. Kennedy's Lawyers' Com. for Civil Rights Under Law, 1963; mem. Birmingham area Manpower Resource Devel. Planning Bd., 1969—; chmn. community devel. com. Operation New Birmingham. Pres. Jefferson County Assn. Mental Health, Birmingham Jewish Community Center, United Jewish Fund; exec. bd. Birmingham Concentrated Employment Program; sec., exec. bd. Jefferson County Com. Econ. Opportunity. Democratic candidate for Ala. Senate, 1966. Bd. dirs. Birmingham Symphony Assn. Served to lt. comdr. USNR, 1942-45. Mem. Ala. Law Inst. Jewish religion (trustee temple). Mem. editorial adv. bd. The Ala. Lawyer. Home: 42 Fairway Dr Birmingham AL 35213 Office: Bank for Savs Bldg Birmingham AL 35203

COOPER, JOHN A., Sr., business exec. Chmn., John A. Cooper Co. Office: Cherokee Village AR 72542*

COOPER, JOHN ALFRED, Jr., realtor, banker; b. Memphis, Sept. 13, 1938; s. John Alfred and Mildred (Borum) C.; student U. Ark., 1961; m. Pat McInnis, Oct. 23, 1965; children—Mary Virginia, John Alfred III, Borum. With Cherokee Village Devel. Co., Inc., 1962—, exec. v.p., 1967—; pres. Bank of Ash Flat (Ark.); pres. John A. Cooper Co., 1968—. Commr., Cherokee Village Improvement Dist. Bd. dirs. Hot Springs Property Assn. Mem. Ark. Air N.G., 1962-68. Club: Bella Vista Country (pres.). Home: Bella Vista AR 72712 Office: Bella Vista AR 72712

COOPER, JOHN ALLEN DICKS, med. educator; b. El Paso, Tex., Dec. 22, 1918; s. John Allen Dicks and Cora (Walker) C.; B.S. in Chemistry, N.M. State U., 1939; Ph.D. in Biochemistry, Northwestern U., 1943, M.D., 1951; D.Honoris Causa, U. Brasil, 1958; m. Mary Jane Stratton, June 17, 1944; children—Margaret Ann, John Allen Dicks, Patricia Alison, Randolph Arend Stratton. Intern, Passavant Meml. Hosp., Chgo., 1951, mem. attending staff, 1955-69; mem. faculty Northwestern U., 1943-69, prof. biochemistry, 1957-69, asso. dean Med. Sch., 1959-63, dean scis., 1963-69, mem. faculty Grad. Sch., 1955-69; mem. faculty Georgetown U., 1970—; vis. prof. U. Brasil, 1956, U. Buenos Aires, 1958; dir. radioisotope service VA Research Hosp., Chgo., 1954-65, cons. in research, 1954-69; advisor to adminstr. AID, U.S. Department of State, 1966—. Mem. bd. of pub. health advisers Ill., 1962-69; mem. Ill. legis. com. atomic energy, 1964-69; mem. policy adv. bd., Argonne Nat. Lab., 1957-63, mem. review com. divs. biol. and med. research and radiol. physics, 1958-63, chmn. review com., 1958-62; mem. com. on licensure AEC, 1956-58; cons. div. edn. and tng. AEC, 1963; mem. adv. council on health research facilities NIH, 1965-69; chmn. com. sci. exhibits World Conf. Med. Edn., 1958-59; organizing com. Pan Am. Fedn. of Assn. Med. Colls., 1962-64, treas., 1963—; adv. com. personnel for research Am. Cancer Soc., 1962-66; cons. commr. food and drugs FDA, 1965-70; spl. cons. to dir. NIH, 1968-69; cons. to div. physician and health professions edn. Bur. Health Manpower Edn. NIH, 1970—; mem. adv. com. instnl. relations NSF, 1967—. Cons. Nuclear-Chgo. Corp. Mem. alumni council Northwestern U. Mem. bd. higher edn. Ill., 1964-69; chmn. Gov.'s Sci. Adv. Council, State Ill., 1967-69; mem. council Asso. Midwest Univs., 1963-68, v.p., bd. dirs., 1964-65, pres., bd. dirs., 1965-66; v.p., bd. trustees Argonne Univs. Assn. Served to 1st lt., San. Corps, AUS, 1945-47. Recipient Outstanding Alumni award N.M. State U., 1960. John and Mary R. Markle scholar in acad. medicine, 1950- 55. Mem. Am. Soc. Biol. Chemists, Assn. Am. Med. Colls. (del. numerous confs., mem. various coms., pres. 1969—), A.M.A., A.A.A.S., Central Soc. Clin. Research, Inst. Medicine, Chgo., Am. Pub. Health Assn., Asociacion Venezolana Para el Avance de la Ciencia (hon.), Sigma Xi, Alpha Omega Alpha. Clubs: Cosmos (Washington), Tavern (Chgo.). Editor Jour. Med. Edn., 1962—; editorial bd. Health Services Research, Am. Hosp. Assn., 1965-69. Contbr. numerous articles sci. jours., books. Home: 4118 N River St Arlington VA 22207 Office: No 1 DuPont Circle NW Washington DC 20036

COOPER, JOHN CROSSAN, Jr., lawyer; b. Balt., Oct. 16, 1901; s. John Crossan and Louisa Carrel (Jenkins) C.; A.B., Princeton, 1923; LL.B., Yale, 1927; m. Eleanor Chalfant, Jan. 28, 1930; children—John C. III, Louisa J., Harriet W. Partner, Venable, Baetjer & Howard, 1937; dir. Mercantile Safe Deposit & Trust Co., Merc. Bankshares Corp., Balt. Savs. Bank, Baltimore, Louisville & Nashville R.R. Co., Seaboard Coast Line R.R. Co., Seaboard Coast Line Industries, Inc., Canton Co. of Balt., Mt. Vernon Mills, Inc., Glass Crafters, Inc., Cottman Co.; bd. trustees Penn Mutual Life Ins. Co. Trustee Johns Hopkins U., Gilman Sch.; chmn. bd. trustees Johns Hopkins Hosp. Mem. Am., Md., Balt. (pres. 1954-55) bar assns. Democrat. Roman Catholic. Clubs: Maryland, Elkridge (Baltimore); Seminole (Palm Beach, Fla.); Brook (New York). Home: 915 W Lake Av Baltimore MD 21210 Office: 1800 2 Hopkins Plaza Baltimore MD 21201

COOPER, JOHN JOSEPH, lawyer; b. Vincennes, Ind., Oct. 20, 1924; s. Homer O. and Ruth (House) C.; A.B., Stanford, 1950, LL.B., 1951; LL.M., U. So. Cal., 1964; m. Nathalie Brooke, Aug. 8, 1945. Admitted to Cal. bar, 1952; practice in San Francisco, 1951-54, Los Angeles, 1954-61, Palo Alto, 1961—; gen. counsel Varian Assos., 1970—. Served with USNR, 1942-45. Mem. Am., Cal., Santa Clara bar assns. Republican. Contbr. articles profl. jours. Home: 191 Ramoso Rd Portola Valley CA 94025 Office: 611 Hansen Way Palo Alto CA 94303

COOPER, JOHN LEWIS, investment co. exec.; b. Pitts., June 26, 1913; s. Maurice Diehl and Marion (Lewis) C.; student Phillips Acad., Andover, Mass., 1929-31; A.B., Yale, 1935; advanced mgmt. program Harvard Grad. Sch. Bus. Adminstrn., 1953; m. Marie Tudor McCook, Mar. 21, 1942; children—John Lewis, Daniel, Rosamond (dec.), Marianna H. With Bankers Trust Co., N.Y.C., 1935-47; investment research dept. Mass. Investors Trust, Boston, 1947-53, trustee, 1954-69, pres., 1969—; chmn. Mass. Investors Growth Stock Fund; pres. Mass. Financial Services, Inc.; dir. Mass. Income Devel. Fund, Mass. Capital Devel. Fund, Mass. Financial Devel. Fund, New Eng. Mut. Life Ins. Co.; trustee Provident Instn. for Savs. Trustee Children's Hosp., Cabot, Cabot & Forbes Land Trust, Mt. Holyoke Coll., Phillips Acad., overseer Boys' Clubs of Boston, Boston Symphony Orch.; bd. mgrs. Greater Boston Charities Trust. Served to lt. col., Cav. and General Staff Corps, AUS, World War II. Republican. Episcopalian. Clubs: Yale, Recess, Knickerbocker (N.Y.C.); Dedham (Mass.) Country and Polo; Union, Norfolk Hunt, Somerset, Tennis and Racquet (Boston). Home: Needham MA 02191 Office: 200 Berkeley St Boston MA 02116

COOPER, JOHN N., lawyer; b. New Brunswick, N.J., Nov. 30, 1910; A.B., Brown U., 1932; LL.B., Yale, 1935. Admitted to N.Y. bar, 1938; now mem. firm Cooper, Dunham, Henninger & Clark, N.Y.C. Mem. Am. Bar Assn., Assn. Bar City N.Y., New York County Lawyers Assn., N.Y. Patent Law Assn. (pres. 1965-66). Office: Cooper Dunham Henninger & Clark 330 Madison Av New York City NY 10017*

COOPER, JOHN SHERMAN, U.S. senator; b. Somerset, Ky., Aug. 23, 1901; s. John Sherman and Helen Gertrude (Tartar) C.; student Centre Coll., 1918-19, LL.D.; A.B., Yale, 1923, LL.D.; postgrad. Harvard Law School, 1923- 25; LL.D., University Ky., U. Pitts., Georgetown Coll., Berea Coll., Eastern Ky. State Coll.; L.H.D., Lincoln Meml. U.; D.C.L., Nasson Coll.; m. Lorraine Rowan Shevlin, Mar. 17, 1955. Mem. lower ho. Ky. Legislature, 1928-30; judge, Pulaski Co., Ky., 1930-38; circuit judge, 28th Judicial Dist., Ky. 1946; U.S. Senator from Ky., 1946-1948, 52-55, 57—; mem. com. fgn. relations, pub. works, com. rules and adminstrn., member select committee on standards and conduct; apptd. cons. to Sec. State Acheson, 1950; sworn in as U.S. ambassador-at-large; U.S. del. Gen. Assembly, UN, 1949-51; U.S. Ambassador to India, Nepal, 1955-56. Mem. law firm Gardner, Morrison & Rogers, Wash., 1949-51. Congressional adviser to U.S. delegation UNESCO Conf., Paris, France, 1958; mem. President's Commn. to Investigate Assassination of President Kennedy. Served from pvt. to capt., AUS, 1942- 46, ETO, 1944-46, assisted reorgn. German jud. system, Bavaria, after hostilities ceased. Awarded Bronze Star Medal for services, World War II. Trustee U. Ky., 1935-46, Centre Coll. Mem. Yale Council. Mem. Am., Ky., bar assns., Am. Legion, V.F.W., Beta Theta Pi. Republican. Baptist. Rotarian. Home: 503 N Main St Somerset KY 42501 Office: Old Senate Office Bldg Washington DC 20525

COOPER, JOSEPH DAVID, educator; b. Boston, May 25, 1917; s. Samuel and Hinde R. (Bryner) C.; A.B., George Washington U., 1944; M.A., Am. U., 1947, Ph.D., 1951; m. Ruth Zeidner, Feb. 11, 1942; children—Lenore Byron. Employee Fed. Service, 1934-45, 47-58; dep. dir., dir. procedural coordination staff U.N.R.R.A., 1945-47; chief procedural coordination br. State Dept., 1947- 51, exec. dir. Salary Stblzn. Bd., 1951-53; exec. asst. to dep. postmaster gen., 1953-58; dir. Mgmt. Engring. div., Corp. for Econ. and Indsl. Research. Arlington, Va., 1958; now prof. dept. polit. sci. Howard U., also adj. prof. Am. U., Washington; project dir. conf. series on philosophy and tech. drug assessment Interdisciplinary Communications Program, SMithsonian Instn.; asst. to exec. v.p. Emerson Research Labs., Emerson Radio and Phonograph Corp., 1958-60; dir. pub. relations, U.S. Photo Supply Co., Inc., 1961; cons. commn. on research A.M.A., 1965-67. Fellow Royal Soc. Medicine; mem. Am. Soc. Pub. Adminstrn., Am. Polit. Sci. Assn., Am. Acad. Polit. and Social Sci. Author books in field of mgmt., med. econs., also books on photography; How to Communicate Policies and Instructions 1960; The Minox Manual, 1961; The New Ultra-Miniature Photography, 1961; The Art of Decision-Making, 1961; How to Get More Done in Less Time, 1962, rev. edit., 1971; Organization, 1963, The Nikon F Nikkonmat Handbook of Photography, 1968; The Minolta Systems Handbook, 1971, others. Editor: The Economics of Drug Innovation, 1970; Decision-Making on the Efficacy and Safety of Drugs, 1971. Contbr. Modern Photograpphy mag., Med. Tribune; articles on med. sociology, econs. and politics. Home: 2810 Blaine Dr Chevy Chase MD 20015

COOPER, KENNETH EZELLE, lawyer; b. Wynne, Ark., July 7, 1892; s. Coy J. and Cora (Browne) C.; student So. U., Greensboro, Ala., 1911-14; LL.B., U. Ala., 1916; m. Grace McCleskey, Oct. 1, 1916; children—Kenneth M., Elaire (Mrs. Gordon D. Fletcher), Coy Mack, Erlin Cantey, Admitted to Ala. bar, 1916, since practiced in Birmingham; mem. firm Cabaniss & Johnston, 1935—. Chmn. bd.

Methodist Children's Home, Selma, Ala., 1940—; bd. dirs., chmn. exec. com. Carraway Meth. Hosp., Birmingham, 1945—; organizer Meth. Home for Aging, Birmingham, 1956. Named mem. Meth. Hall of Fame, 1954; recipient Boss of Year award Legal Secs. Assn., 1963. Mem. Am., Birmingham bar assns., State Bar Ala., Omicron Delta Kappa (hon.), Kappa Alpha. Kiwanian (pres. Birmingham 1955). Home: 2126 Blue Ridge Blvd Birmingham AL 35205 Office: First Nat Bldg Birmingham AL 35203

COOPER, LEON N., physicist, educator; b. N.Y.C., Feb. 28, 1930; s. Irving and Anna (Zola) C.; A.B., Columbia, 1951, A.M., 1953, Ph.D., 1954; m. Kay Anne Allard, May 18, 1969; children (by previous marriage)—Kathleen Ann, Coralie Lauren. NSF postdoctoral fellow, mem. Inst. for Advanced Study, 1954-55; research asso. U. Ill., 1955-57; asst. prof. Ohio State U., 1957-58; asso. prof. Brown U., Providence, 1958-62, prof., 1962-66, Henry Ledyard Goddard U. prof., 1966—; lectr. Summer Sch. Varenna, Italy, 1955; vis. prof. Brandeis Summer Inst., 1959, Bergen Internat. Sch. Physics, Norway, 1961, Scuola Internatzionali Di Fisica, Erice, Italy, 1965, L'Ecole Normal Supèrieure, Centre Universitaire Internationale, Paris, 1966, Cargèse Summer Sch., 1966; cons. indsl., ednl. orgns. Alfred P. Sloan Found. research fellow, 1959-66, John Simon Guggenheim Meml. Found. fellow, 1965-66. Recipient Comstock prize, Nat. Acad. Scis., 1968. Fellow Am. Phys. Soc., Phi Beta Kappa, Sigma Xi. Author: Introduction to The Meaning and Structure of Phsyics, 1968. Contbr. profl. jours. Home: 31 Summit Av Providence RI 02906

COOPER, LEROY GORDON, Jr., former astronaut, bus. exec.; b. Shawnee, Okla., Mar. 6, 1927; s. Leroy Gordon and Hattie Lee (Herd) C.; student U. Hawaii, 1946-49, European extension U. Md., 1951-53; B.S. in Aero. Engring., Air Force Inst. Tech., 1956; grad. Exptl. Test Pilot Sch., USAF, 1957; m. Trudy B. Olson, Aug. 29, 1947; children—Camala Keoki, Janita Lee. Commd. USAF, 1949, advanced through grades to col., 1965; jet fighter pilot, 1950-54; pilot exptl. flight test engring., 1957-59; astronaut with Project Mercury, NASA, 1959-70; made 22 orbit flight in Faith 7, May 1963; worked with Gemini program of Astronaut Office, made 122 Orbit flight in Gemini V, 1965; worked with Apollo lunar program; now pres. Nat. Exhibits, Inc. Mem. Am. Inst. Aero. and Astronautics, Soc. Exptl. Test Pilots, Am. Astronautical Soc. Mason (Shriner, Jester). Home: 101 Cedar Lane Circle Seabrook TX 77586

COOPER, LOUISE FIELD, author; b. Hartford, Conn., Mar. 8, 1905; d. Francis Elliott and Anna (Dunning) Field; student Miss Porter's Sch., Farmington, 1921-24; m. James Wayne Cooper, June 26, 1929; children—Field, James Nicoll, Peter Brintnal. Author: The Lighted Box, 1942; The Deer on the Stairs; Love and Admiration; Summer Stranger, 1947; The Boys from Sharon, 1950; The Cheerful Captive, 1954; The Windfall Child, 1963; Widows and Admirals, 1964; A Week at the Most, 1967; One Dragon Too Many, 1971. Contbr. short stories to New Yorker mag. Home: Clark Rd Woodbridge New Haven CT 06525

COOPER, MARIO, educator, artist; b. Mexico City, Mexico, Nov. 26, 1905; s. Luis and Maria (Garfias) C.; came to U.S., 1915; student Otis Art Inst., Los Angeles, 1924, Chouinard Art Sch., Los Angeles, 1925, Grand Central Art Sch., N.Y.C., 1927-37; pupil F. Tolles Chamberlin, Louis Treviso, Pruett Carter, Harvey Dunn; m. Aileen Whetstine, Feb. 26, 1927 (div. Apr. 1964); children—Vincent, Patricia; m. 2d, G. Dale Meyers, Oct. 1964. Staff artist Tracey Locke & Dawson, Dallas, 1925, Honig Cooper Advt., San Francisco, 1926; visualizer and layout man Batten, Barton, Durstine & Osborne, N.Y.C., 1927-28; art dir. Lord Thomas, 1929- 31; freelance, Los Angeles, San Francisco, N.Y.C., 1926-27; instr. illustration, advt. art Columbia, 1937-41, Grand Central Art Sch., 1941-45, Art Students League, 1945, Vets. Class, Soc. Illustrators, 1945- 50, Pratt Inst., 1950-57; tchr. watercolor Art Students League, N.Y., 1957—; instr. watercolor Nat. Acad. Sch. Fine Arts, 1959; guest instr. Municipal Mus. Art, Springfield, Mo., 1961, Laguna Beach Art Assn., 1962; lectr. City Coll. N.Y.C., 1962—; art cons. USAF, 1959; on temporary duty for USAF in the Far East, 1954, to Hokkaido, Korea, Formosa, Alaska, 1956; paintings in collection USAF Acad. 1931— for stories by P.G. Woodhouse, Alfred Noyes, Gouverneur Morris, Quentin Reynolds, Clarence Budington Kelland, Agatha Christie, Eric Maria Remarque; represented in collection Adelphi Coll., L.I.; represented in permanent collection Met. Mus. Art, N.Y.C., Library of Congress, Library Royal Soc. Arts (London, Eng.), N.A.D., Butler Inst. Am. Art. Reading (Pa.) Public Mus.; represented at St. Luke's Hosp., Denver, Madonna and Child; exhibited Sculpture: Third Internat. Sculpture Phila., 1949, Pa. Acad., 1948-51, Nat. Acad., 1947, 49, 50, 51, others; exhibited water colors various acads. and soc. shows, Exchange Exhbn. Royal Painters in Watercolour, London, 1962; Ichiban Gallery, Tokyo, Fuji Daimaru Gallery, Kyoto; commd. by NASA to document Apollo 10 and Apollo 11 flights to moon at Cape Kennedy, 1969. Recipient various gold and 1st awards for sculpture; watercolor awards include: Harriet Sanford Stuart purchase prize Am. Watercolor Soc., 1955, awards in soc.'s anns., 1961-63, Emily Lowe award, 1956, Herb Olsen award, 1959, achievement award, 1967, Famous Artists award, Watercolor USA award, 1968, awards, 1969, 70, 71; Bklyn. Soc. Artists award, 1955; Grumbacher award Allied Artists Am., 1956; 1st award N.A.D., 1956, Samuel F.B. Morse medal, 1967; Medal of Achievement Inst. Art Mexico, 1970. Fellow Royal Soc. Arts (London); mem. Audubon Artists (hon. pres. 1954—), N.A.D., Soc. Illustrators (life), Nat. Sculptors Soc., Artists Guild (v.p. N.Y. 1936), Am. Water Color Soc. (pres. 1959—), Casein Painters Soc., Knickerbocker Artists, Tex. Watercolor Soc., N.J. Painters and Sculptors, Allied Artists Am., Cal. Water Color Soc. Clubs: Officers (hon.), Salmagundi (hon.). Author: Flower Painting in Watercolor, 1962; Drawing and Painting the City, 1967. Address: 1 W 67th St New York City NY 10023

COOPER, MARSH ALEXANDER, mining exec.; b. Toronto, Ont., Can., Oct. 8, 1912; s. Frederick W. and Gertrude (Marsh) C.; B.S.C., M.A. Sc., U. Toronto, 1935; postgrad. Harvard, 1938-39; m. Doris Elsie Roos, Sept. 13, 1941. Partner, James, Buffam & Cooper, 1937-67; pres., chief exec. officer McIntyre Porcupine Mines, Ltd., 1967-69, now chmn. bd.; pres., mng. dir. Falconbridge Mickel Mines, Ltd., Toronto, 1969—; dir. Bridge & Tank Co. of Can., Ltd., Canadian Imperial Bank of Commerce, Crown Life Ins. Co., Granby Mining Co., Ltd., Granisle Copper, Ltd., Home Oil, Ltd., Jefferson Lake Petrochemicals Can., Ltd., Mogul of Ireland, Ltd., Natural Resources Growth Fund, Ltd. Tex. Eastern Transmission Corp. Mem. Soc. Econ. Geologists, Assn. Profl. Engrs. Providences of Ont., B.C., Alta., Am. Inst. Mining, Metall. and Petroleum Engrs., Canadian Inst. Mining and Metallurgy, Engring. Inst. Can. Home: 72 Ardwold Gate Toronto 178 Ont Can Office: 7 King St E Toronto 210 Ont Can

COOPER, MERIAN C., motion picture dir., producer, author; b. Jacksonville, Fla., Oct. 24, 1894; s. John C. and Mary (Coldwell) C.; ed. Lawrenceville Sch., U.S. Naval Acad., 1911-14; m. Dorothy Jordan; children—Mary Caroline, Elizabeth T., Richard. Advanced to capt. U.S. Army, World War I, pilot aviation France, later lt. col. Kosciusko Squadron, Poland, traveled widely in Orient, Africa making moving pictures, as newspaper, mag. corr.; exploration in Arabia, Iran; co-dir., co- author, co-producer motion pictures, Grass, Chang, Four Feathers; sole creator, co-producer, co-author King Kong; producer Flying Down to Rio, Last Days Pompeii, Little Women, Lost Patrol, and others; producer (with John Ford); Three Godfathers, Fort Apache, She Wore a Yellow Ribbon, Wagonmaster, Rio Grande, Quiet Man; co-dir., co-producer (with Lowell Thomas) This Is Cinerama; exec. producer The Searchers; dir., co-producer The Best of Cinerama, 1962. Exec. producer with RKO Studios, Hollywood, 2 yrs.; pres. Argosy Pictures Corp., 1946-56, Merian C. Cooper Enterprises, Inc., 1958—; v.p. Cinerama Prodn. Corp. Was early supporter civilian aviation, former dir. Pan Am. World Airways, Western Airlines, Gen. Aviation, others. Served as col. USAAF, 1942-45, staff China Air Task Force, 1942, 5th Air Force, New Guinea, 1943-45; to brig. gen. Air Force, 1950. Clubs: Explorers, Brook, Boone and Crockett (N.Y.C.), Daedalians (San Antonio). Recipient Acad. Motion Picture Arts and Scis. spl. award motion picture innovator, 1952. Author: (with Edward A. Salisbury) The Sea Gypsy, 1924; Grass, 1925; Things Men Die For, 1927; (with Edgar Wallace) King Kong, 1932. Home: 952 E Av Coronado CA 92118

COOPER, OWEN, chem. co. exec.; b. Warren County, Miss., Apr. 19, 1908; s. William S. and Malena (Head) C.; student Culkin Acad., 1925; B.S. in Agr., Miss. State Coll., 1929; M.A., U. Miss., 1936; grad. Jackson (Miss.) Sch. Law, 1938; postgrad. U. So. Cal., 1934; LL.D., Miss. Coll., 1960; m. Elizabeth Thompson, Sept. 2, 1938; children—Nancy (Mrs. Spencer Gilbert), Carolyn (Mrs. Ben Ladner), Owen, Elizabeth, Frances. Tchr. vocational agr., 1930-35; asst. dir. Miss. Planning Commn., 1936-40; exec. dir. Miss. Farm Bur. Fedn., Jackson, 1940-48; exec. v.p. Miss. Chem. Corp., Yazoo City, 1948-60, pres., 1960—; exec. v.p. Coastal Chem. Corp., 1956-60, pres., 1960—; dir. Central Bank for Coops., Fed. Res. Bd. Atlanta. Exec. com. So. Baptist Conv.; v.p. Bapt. World Alliance. Baptist (deacon). Home: 1826 Grand Av Yazoo City MS 39194 Office: Miss Chem Corp PO Box 388 Yazoo City MS 39194

COOPER, RICHARD FOSS, lawyer; b. Strafford, N.H., Aug. 12, 1915; s. Burt Randall and Emily Lillian (Foss) C.; student Phillips Exeter Acad.; A.B., Dartmouth, 1937; LL.B., Harvard, 1940; m. Elizabeth Hall Wentworth, Oct. 19, 1940; children—Candace Wentworth, Randall Foss. Admitted to N.H. bar, fed. dist. cts., 1940; partner Cooper, Hall & Walker since 1946; city solicitor, 1946-50; justice Rochester Dist. Ct.; dir. of Rochester Savs. Bank & Trust Co., Grange Mut. Ins. Co., Eastern Slope Hotel, Inc., Community Television Corp. Chmn. N.H. Bd. of Probation; dep. chmn. Gov.'s Com. on Crime and Delinquency. Served as lt. USNR, 1942-46; capt. Res. Mem. Am., N.H., Strafford County bar assns., N.H. Assn. Municipal and Dist. Ct. Judges (pres.), N.H. Dept. Res. Officers Assn. (pres.), Gamma Delta Chi. Republican (chmn. state com. 1947- 52, 54; mem. nat. com. 1952-60; chmn. finance com. 1953-57). Mason. Home: 1 Dartmouth Lane Rochester NH 03867 Office: 11 Wakefield St Rochester NH 03867

COOPER, RICHARD NEWELL, educator, economist; b. Seattle, June 14, 1934; s. Richard Warren and Lucile (Newell) C.; A.B., Oberlin Coll., 1956; M.Sc. in Econs., London (England) Sch. Econs. and Polit. Sci., 1958; Ph.D., Harvard, 1962; M.A. (hon.), Yale, 1966; m. Carolyn Jane Cahalan, June 5, 1956; children—Laura Katherine, Mark Daniel. Sr. staff economist Council Econ. Advisers, 1961-63; asst. prof. econs. Yale, 1963-65, prof., 1966—; dep. asst. sec. state internat. monetary affairs, 1965-66; lectr. U. Md., 1961-62; cons. to govt. and industry. Mem. Am. Econ. Assn., Royal Econ. Soc., Council Fgn. Relations. Author: Economics of Interdependence, 1968. Contbr. articles to profl. jours. Home: 239 Everit St New Haven CT 06511

COOPER, RITA ANN, pub. exec.; b. Indpls., July 23, 1940; d. Miller L. and Mary Catherine (Lux) Keller; student Purdue U., 1961; m. Vernon K. Cooper, Mar. 23, 1962; children—Vernon Kelley, Catherine Marie. Asst. dir. marketing Stark & Wetzel Co., Indpls., 1964-65; asso. editor Topics Newspapers, Indpls., 1965-66; mng. editor Child Life and Design mags., Indpls., 1967-69, editor, bus. mgr. Child Life, Design, Brownie Reader, 1967-69; pub. Amateur Athlete, Child Life, Brownie Reader, Children's Playmate, Design Rev. Pub. Co., Indpls., 1969—; pub. Golden Mag., Jack and Jill mag. Curtis PUb. Co., 1970—; exec. pub. Holiday mag., asso. pub. Sat. Eve. Post, Curtis Pub. Co., 1971—; dir. SerVass, Inc., SerVass Labs. Precinct finance chmn. Republican Party, 1966-67. Mem. Nat. Writers Assn., Theta Sigma Phi. Clubs: Indianapolis Press; Riviera (Indpls.). Home: 684 Holliday Lane Indianapolis IN 46260 Office: 1100 Waterway Blvd Indianapolis IN 46202

COOPER, ROBERT ELMER, Jr., mfg. exec.; b. Bellingham, Wash., July 13, 1910; s. Robert E. and Mae Gertrude (Redhead) C.; B.S. in Elec. Engring., U. Cal., 1931; m. Margaret F. Johnson, July 2, 1932; children—Anne Lorraine (Mrs. John B. Munson), Robert Bruce. Various positions Montgomery Ward & Co., Oakland, Cal., also Chgo., 1933-56, mdse. mgr. home furnishings, 1952-56; pres., dir. Ingraham Co., Bristol, Conn., 1956-61; exec. v.p., dir. Scantlin Electronics, Inc., Los Angeles, 1961-64; v.p., dir. Istar, Inc. Los Angeles, 1961-63; v.p. Stanadyne, Inc., Elyria, Ohio, 1964—; pres., dir. E. Town Time Corp., Elizabethtown, Ky., Ingraham Canadian Clock Co., Toronto, Can. Chmn. merchandise div. Chgo. Community Fund, 1956. Corporator Bristol Hosp.; founder U. Hartford. Served to col. USAAF, World War II. Decorated Legion of Merit. Mem. N.A.M., Cal. Alumnae Assn., Elyria C. of C. (dir.), Am. Mgmt. Assn., Nat. Indsl. Conf. Bd. Presbyn. Home: 30234 Wolf Rd Bay Village OH 44140 Office: 377 Woodland Av Elyria OH 44035

COOPER, ROBERT ELY, Jr., motor carrier co. exec.; b. Birmingham, Ala., Nov. 9, 1904; s. Robert Ely and Fannie (Morrow) C.; student Kansas City (Mo.) Jr. Coll., 1924; m. Catherine Madorie, Aug. 29, 1928; children—Diane (Mrs. Stephen E. Parker), Karen (Mrs. William D. Baker), Penelope (Mrs. Robert O. Hall). With Washburn, Crosby Milling Co., 1924-25, Frigidaire Corp., 1925-27; treas. Ralph B. Innis, Inc., ins., 1927-34; founder, 1934, Cooper-Jarrett, Inc., Orange, N.J., now chmn., chief exec. officer; dir. N.Y. Equities, Inc., Cooper's Corner, Inc., Clinton Engine Corp. Trustee Kessler Inst. Rehab. Clubs: Rock Spring Golf (W. Orange, N.J.); Spring Lake (N.J.) Country. Home: Claridge House Verona NJ 07044 Office: 23 S Essex Av Orange NJ 07051

COOPER, RUSSELL MORGAN, educator; b. Newton, Ia., Dec. 6, 1907; s. William Reupert and Virginia Steele (Russell) C.; A.B., Cornell Coll., 1928, LL.D., 1953; M.A., Columbia, 1929, Ph.D., 1934; postgrad. L'Institut Universitaire des Hautes Etudes Internat., 1932-33; m. Lucile Trump, June 26, 1930; children—Mary Lee, Donald Russell, Julia Ann, Sarah Ruth. State student sec. YMCA, Mich., 1929-31; prof. history, polit. sci. Cornell Coll., 1934-44; chmn. dept. interdisciplinary studies U. Minn., 1944-59, asst. dean coll. sci. lit. and arts, 1945-59; dean liberal arts coll., U. South Fla., 1959-71, asst. to v.p., 1971—; editor gen. edn. books U.S. Armed Forces Inst., 1943-44. Exec. sec. com. liberal arts edn. North Central Assn., 1940-46, chmn., 1946-59, vice chmn. commn. on research and service, 1955-57, sec., 1957-59; mem. Am. Council on Edn. Commn. on Instrn. and Evaluation, 1953-56. Cons. Civil Information and Edn., S.C.A.P., Japan, 1948. Mem. N.E.A. (mem. exec. com. Assn. Higher Edn. 1956-60, pres. 1958- 59), Am. Acad. Polit. and Social Sci., Am. Polit. Sci. Assn., Am. Assn. U. Profs., Phi Beta Kappa, Tau Kappa Alpha. Author: American Consultation in World Affairs, 1934; Better CollegesBetter Teachers, 1944. Editor: The Two Ends of the Log; Learning and Teaching in Today's College, 1958. Co-editor: Preparation of College Teachers, 1950. Home: 10617 Carrollwood Dr Tampa FL 33618

COOPER, SAMUEL INMAN, architect, engr.; b. Atlanta, Feb. 14, 1894; s. Joseph Walter and Nellie Sue (Inman) C.; student Episcopal Acad., 1906-10; grad. Hotchkiss Sch., 1913; Litt.B., Princeton, 1917; B.Arch., U. Pa., 1921; m. Augusta Skeen, Oct. 14, 1930. Draftsman office A. Ten Eyck Brown, architect, Atlanta, 1922-25; pres. Cooper & Cooper, architects, 1925-42; v.p. Cooper, Bond & Cooper, Inc., architects and engrs., 1945-52, pres., 1952-65; chmn. Cooper, Barrett, Skinner, Woodbury and Cooper, Inc., architects on pub. and residential bldgs., 1965—; pub. bldgs. include sch., coll., libraries, dormitories, gymnasia, pub. housing and office bldgs. A.I.A. del., State Dept. rep. 6th Pan Am. Congress Architects, Lima, Peru, 1947, 7th Pan Am. Congress, Havana, Cuba, 1950, 8th Pan Am. Congress, Mexico City, 1952; A.I.A. del. 12th Pan Am. Congress, Bogota, Colombia, 1968, 13th Congress, San Juan, P.R., 1970; chmn. A.I.A. delegation 9th Pan Am. Congress, Venezuela, 1955, 10th Pan Am. Congress, Buenos Aires, Argentina, 1960; A.I.A. rep. to V Congress, Union Internat. Architects, Moscow, Russia, 1958, to Assembly, Lisbon, Portugal, 1959, VI Congress, London, Eng., 1961; pres. 10th Pan Am. Congress, Washington, 1965; chmn. Atlanta Civic Design Commn., 1967-70. Served to lt. 22d Inf., U.S. Army, 1917-19; to lt. col. C.E., 1942-45. Hon. mem. archtl. faculty U. of Chile. Fellow A.I.A. (chmn. com. on internat. relations 1961-65); mem. Pan Am. Fedn. Assns. Architects (pres. 1960-65), Nat. Soc. Profl. Engrs., Archeol. Inst. Am. (v.p. Ga. chpt. 1951-52), Soc. Colonial Wars in Ga. (dep. gov. 1963), The Newcomen Soc., Atlanta Art Assn. (dir. 1946-48), English Speaking Union, Princeton, U. Pa., alumni assns., Atalnta Hist. Soc. (vice chmn., dir.), U. Pa., Princeton alumni assns.; Phi Kappa Sigma; hon. mem. Brazilian, Chilean, Colombian, Mexican, Venezuelan, Panamanian socs. architects. Presbyn. Mason. Clubs: Charter, Nassau (Princeton); Piedmont Driving, Capitol City, Nine O'Clocks, Commerce (Atlanta); Cosmos (Washington). Home: 1325 Peachtree St NE Atlanta GA Office: 715 Carnegie Bldg Atlanta GA 30303

COOPER, SHELDON GOODALL, lawyer; b. San Francisco, Aug. 25, 1904; s. Edwin Theodore and Mary (Smith) C.; A.B., U. Cal., 1926; LL.B., Harvard, 1930; m. Patricia Tobin, Nov. 18, 1936. Admitted to Cal. bar, 1930, since practiced in San Francisco; with Cooper, White & Cooper, 1930—, partner, 1932—; dir. Hibernia Bank, San Francisco Newspaper Printing Co., Continental Air Lines, Inc., Met. Stevedore Co., Pacific Lighting Corp., Cal.-Western States Life Ins. Co., Cal. Stevedore & Ballast Co., Allied Properties, Inc. Served as maj. USAAF, 1942-45. Clubs: Pacific Union, Burlingame Country. Home: 669 Hayne Rd San Mateo CA 94502 Office: 44 Montgomery St San Francisco CA 94104

COOPER, STANLEY MILLER, former business exec.; b. Hartford, Conn., May 10, 1902; s. Elisha H. and Margaret M.C.; A.B., Yale, 1924; m. Elizabeth Hubbard, Sept. 29, 1925; children—Anthony Ashley, Nancy Hubbard (Mrs. Charles T. Young III). Joined Fafnir Bearing Co., 1924, pres., 1947-55, chmn. bd., 1955-68. With OPM, Washington, 1941, War Dept., 1942, WPB, 1944, WLB, Boston, 1945. Pres. New Britain Gen. Hosp. Mem. Beta Theta Pi. Republican. Conglist. Clubs: Shuttle Meadow (dir., New Britain); Yale (N.Y.C.); Sachem's Head Yacht (Guilford, Conn.). Home: 86 Brookside Rd New Britain CT 06052

COOPER, THEODORE, physician; b. Trenton, N.J., Dec. 28, 1928; s. Victor and Dora (Popkin) C.; B.S., Georgetown U., 1949; M.D., St. Louis U., 1954, Ph.D., 1956; m. Vivian Cecilia Evans, June 16, 1956; children—Michael Harris, Mary Katherine, Victoria Susan, Frank Victor. USPHS fellow St. Louis U. Dept. Physiology, 1955-56; clin. asso. surgery br. Nat. Heart Inst., Bethesda, Md., 1956-58, chief animal lab., surgery br., 1959-60; faculty St. Louis U., 1960-66, prof. surgery, 1964-66; prof., chmn. dept. pharmacology U. N.M., Albuquerque, 1966-68, on leave, 1967-69; asso. dir. artificial heart, myocardial infarction programs Nat. Heart Inst., Bethesda, 1967- 68, dir., 1968—. With USPHS Pharmacology and Exptl. Therapeutics Study sect., 1964-67. Recipient Borden award, 1954. Mem. Am. Soc. Pharmacology and Exptl. Therapeutics, Am. Physiol. Soc., Soc. Exptl. Biology and Medicine, Am. Soc. Clin. Investigation, Am. Fedn. Clin. Research, Am. Soc. Artificial Internal Organs, Internat. Cardiovascular Soc., Am. Coll. Chest Physicians, Am. Assn. U. Profs., Am. Coll. Cardiology, A.A.A.S., Sigma Xi. Author: (with others) Nervous Control of the Heart, 1965, Heart Substitutes, 1966, The Baboon in Medical Research, Vol. II, 1967, Factors Influencing Myocardial Contractility, 1967, Acute Myocardial Infarction, 1968, Advance in Transplantation, Prosthetic Heart Valves, 1969, Depressed Metabolism, 1969. Editorial bd. Jour. Pharmacology and Exptl. Therapeutics, 1965-68, Circulation Research, 1966-71; editor Supplements to Circulation, 1966-71; sect. co-editor for Circulation, Am. Jour. Physiology, Jour. Applied Physiology, 1967-70. Contbr. numerous articles med. jours. Discoverer new techniques of denervating heart which have helped delineate role of nerves in heart, on its ability to function under a wide variety of circumstances, and on its ability to respond to drugs. Home: 5204 W Cedar Lane Bethesda MD 20014 Office: Bldg 31 NIH Bethesda MD 20014

COOPER, THOMAS LUTHER, engraving co. exec.; b. Statham, Ga., Sept. 30, 1917; s. William Henry and Ovelia Jane (Arnold) C.; student Ga. State U., 1938-39, High Mus. Art, Atlanta, 1946; m. Helen Brown, Aug. 30, 1941; 1 son, Thomas Luther. With Constn. Pub. Co., Atlanta, 1936-50, head photoengraving dept., 1947-50; pres. So. Engraving Co., Atlanta, 1950—, Photo Process Engraving Co., Atlanta, 1954—; pres., gen. mgr. So. Photo Process Engraving Co., Atlanta, 1955—; v.p., dir. Bech Engraving Co., Inc., Phila., 1968—; dir. J.M. Tull Metals Co., Inc. Exec. bd. Atlanta Area council Boy Scouts Am. Trustee Shorter Coll., Rome, Ga.; mem. adv. council Ga. State U. Served to capt. USAAF, 1942-45. Recipient Craftsman of Year award Inland Printer and Am. Lithographer mag., 1961. Mem. Internat. Assn. Printing House Craftsmen (pres. 1959-60), Am. (exec. com. 1952-54), Southeastern (pres. 1951-52) photoengravers assns., Nat. Soc. Art Dirs., Printing Industry Atlanta, Advt. Club Atlanta, Mil. Order World Wars, Am. Legion. Baptist. Mason (Shriner), Rotarian. Clubs: Commerce, Capital City (Atlanta). Home: 459 Blanton Rd NW Atlanta GA 30342 Office: 730 Bluff St SW Atlanta GA 30310

COOPER, TOM RICHARDSON, advt. exec.; b. Denver, Nov. 14, 1909; s. Elmer A. and Clara S. (Richardson) C.; A.B., Stanford, 1931; M.B.A., Harvard, 1933; m. Marion T. Dirr, Nov. 26, 1937; children—Peter Dirr, Tom Richardson. Formerly v.p. and mgr. Los Angeles office J. Walter Thompson; pres. Steedman, Cooper & Busse, Inc. Mem. Zeta Psi. Home: 405 Davis Ct San Francisco CA 94111 Office: 333 Pine St San Francisco CA 94104

COOPER, WARREN STANLEY, mfg. co. exec.; b. N.J., Jan. 18, 1922; s. Edwin and Louise (Hartje) C.; B.S., Drexel U., 1947, M.B.A., 1954; m. Joyce Heller, Sept. 15, 1942; children—Susan, Edwin, Scott. Indsl. engr., then office mgr. Container Corp. Am., 1947-50; asst. treas. Pioneer Folding Box Co., 1950- 54; partner Hitchcock & Co., C.P.A.'s, Springfield, Mass., 1954-64; exec. v.p., treas., dir. Standard

Internat. Corp., Andover, Mass., 1964—. Bd. dirs. YMCA, Lawrence, Mass., 1971—. Served to 1st lt. USAAF, 1942-45. C.P.A., Masss. Mem. Am. Inst. C.P.A.'s, Financial Execs. Inst., Lambda Chi Alpha. Home: 7 Turner Circle Andover MA 01810 Office: Standard Internat Corp Elm Sq Andover MA 01810

COOPER, WELDON, educator, govt. ofcl.; b. Kirbyville, Tex., Nov. 12, 1906; s. Robert Jackson and Eliza Jane (Bean) C.; A.B., Abilene (Tex.) Christian Coll., 1926; A.M., U. of Tex., 1932; Ph.D., U. of Chgo., 1939; m. Julia Allen, June 6, 1930. Research asst., Bur. of Research in the Social Scis., 1933-35, asst. dir., Bur. of Municipal Research, 1935-36, acting dir., 1937; instr. dept. of govt. all U. of Tex., 1936; asst. prof. polit. sci., U. of Ala., 1938-40, asso. prof., 1940-41, asst. dir. Bur. Pub. Adminstrn., 1938-41, prof. pub. adminstrn., 1946-47, dir. of research, Legislative Adv. Commn. for the Jefferson County (Ala.) Survey, 1946-47; organ. and methods examiner, U.S. Bur. of the Budget, 1941-44, 1945-46; prof. polit. sci. U. Va., 1957-64, prof. of govt., 1964—, sec. bd. visitors 1958-69, asso. dir. Bur. Pub. Adminstrn., 1947-56, dir., 1956- 64, dir. Inst. Govt., 1964—, adminstrn. asst. to the pres., 1959-69; exec. asst. Gov. of Va., 1950-51; cons. Alaska Constnl. Conv., 1955. Recipient Raven award. Mem. Am. Polit. Sci. Assn (exec. council 1955- 57), Am. Soc. for Pub. Adminstrn., Nat. Municipal League, So. Polit. Sci. Assn, Va. Social Sci. Assn. (pres. 1956-57), Raven Soc., Omicron Delta Kappa. Club: Colonnade (U. Va.) Author: several books since 1936; State and Local Finance in Virginia (with Rowland Egger and Edward S. Overman), 1950. Editor: U. Va. News Letter, 1957—. Home: 2025 Thomson Rd Charlottesville VA 22903 ☆

COOPER, WILLIAM, physician; b. Bklyn., Apr. 23, 1909; s. Isaiah K. and Lena (Strunsky) C.; B.S., N.Y. U., 1929; M.D., L.I. Coll. Medicine, 1933; postgrad. U. Ia., 1936-39; m. Therese I. Sheldon, Apr. 7, 1946; children—Rebecca, James Sheldon. Intern Green Point Hosp., N.Y.C., 1933- 35; resident orthopedic surgery Kings County Hosp., N.Y.C., 1935-36, U. Ia. Hosps., 1936-39; attending orthopedic surgeon Hosp. Special Surgery, N.Y.C.; attending orthopedic surgeon N.Y. Hosp., N.Y.C.; chief orthopedic surgery Montefiore Hosp. (N.Y.C. (resigned 1947); prof. clin. surgery (orthopedics) Cornell U. Med. Coll.; sr. cons. orthopedic surgery Bur. Handicapped Children, N.Y. Dept. Health (resigned 1952); orthopedic cons. N.Y.C. Dept. Health, N.Y.C. Bd. Edn., N.Y.C. Police Dept., New York chpt. Nat. Found., La Guardia Hosp., N.Y. Service for Orthopedically Handicapped; cons. orthopedic surgeon L.I. Jewish Hospital, Beth Israel Hospital; medical director Cerebral Palsy Treatment Center of Nassau; chmn. clin. adv. bd. United Cerebral Palsy Assns.; mem. med. control bd. Health Ins. Plan, N.Y.; research on social effects of crippling diseases. Served as maj. M.C., U.S. Army, 1942-45. Received Gold Medal for sci. exhibit Am. Acad. Orthopedic Surgeons, 1949, Certificate of Merit, 1950. Diplomate Am. Bd. Orthopedic Surgery. Fellow A.C.S.; mem. Am. Acad. Orthopedic Surgeons, Am. Acad. Cerebral Palsy, Am. Orthopedic Assn., World Commn. Cerebral Palsy, Am. Pub. Health Assn., Westhampton Yacht Squadron, Sigma Xi. Club: Lotos. Mem. editorial bd. Jour. Developmental Medicine and Child Neurology. Home: 1120 Park Av New York City NY 10028 Office: Hosp for Spl Surgery New York City NY 10021

COOPER, WILLIAM JOSEPH, utility co. exec.; b. Columbus, Ga., June 13, 1906; s. Cornelius W. and Emily (Maynard) C.; B.S. in Engring., Ga. Inst. Tech., 1928; M.S., Yale, 1929; m. Jessie Arrington, July 23, 1932; children—William J., Tarlton Heath. Coop. student Ga. Power Co., Columbus, 1923-28; with Central Hudson Gas & Electric Corp., Poughkeepsie, N.Y., 1929-40, asst. div. mgr., later dist. supt., Beacon, N.Y., asst. to pres. Line Material Co., Milw., 1940-42; with United Illuminating Co., New Haven, 1942—, supr. purchasing and stores, 1942-43, exec. asst., 1943-47, dir. employee relations, 1947-52, asst. to pres., 1952-53, operating v.p., 1953-56, exec. v.p., 1956-58, pres., 1958-64, chief exec. officer, 1958-71, chmn. bd., 1964—, also dir.; dir. North East Data-Com Inc., New Haven Savs. Bank, 1st New Haven Nat. Bank, Electric Council N.E., Bridgeport Hydraulic Co. Profl. engr., Conn. Mem. I.E.E.E., Am. Soc. M.E., Yale Engring. Assn. (exec. bd.). Club: Quinnipiac (New Haven). Home: Timber Lane Woodbridge CT 06525 Office: 80 Temple St New Haven CT 06506

COOPER, WILLIAM WAGER, univ. dean; b. Birmingham, Ala., July 23, 1914; s. William Wager and Rae (Rossman) C.; A.B., U. Chgo., 1938; postgrad. Columbia, 1940-42; D.Sc., Ohio State U., 1969; m. Ruth Fay West, Sept. 11, 1944. Asst. to comptroller TVA, 1938-40; prin. economist Bur. Budget, 1942-44; asst. prof. econs. U. Chgo., 1944-46; asst. prof. to prof. Carnegie-Mellon U., 1946-68, dean Sch. Urban and Pub. Affairs, 1968—. Fellow Econometric Soc., A.A.A.S.; mem. Inst. Mgmt. Sci. (past pres.). Author: (with A. Charnes) Management Models and Industrial Applications of Linear Programming; (with H. Leavitt, M.W. Shelly) New Perspectives in Organization Research; (with others) Studies in Budgeting. Editorial bd. Mgmt. Sci., Operations Research, Naval Research Logistics Quar. Contbr. articles to profl. jours. Home: Box 232 RD 2 Cheswick PA 15024

COOPERMAN, ALVIN, theatrical exec.; b. Bklyn., July 24, 1923; s. Nathan and Marietta (Steinmann) C.; student N.Y. U., eves. 1939-43; m. Marilyn Frances Fisher; children (by previous marriage)—Karen Lynn, Audrey Joan, Margot Jane. From office boy to asst. booking chief Shubert theatres, N.Y.C., 1939-43, 46-51; unit mgr. Milton Berle's Texaco Star Theatre, 1951-53; producer color team NBC, 1953, first color TV shows with mobile unit, NBC, 1954; devel. and produced Wide Wide World, spl., 1955; mgr. program sales TV network, 1955, exec. producer Producer's Showcase, 1955-56, producer Dodsworth, Rosalinda, Jack and the Beanstalk, also Festival of Music, 1955-56, producer Shirley Temple Storybook, 1956-57; exec. producer Screen Gems, 1957-58; producer Du Pont Show, CBS, 1958-59; exec. producer Roncom Prodns., 1959-62; producer The Untouchables, ABC, 1962-63; exec. dir. charge booking Shubert Theatre Enterprises, 1963-67; v.p. spl. programs, TV network, NBC, 1967-68; exec. v.p., dir. Madison Sq. Garden Corp., N.Y.C., 1968—. Mem. Judy Holliday Meml. Com. for Am. Med. Center, Denver; asso. chmn. N.Y. chpt. Arthritis Found. Trustee Am. Med. Center, Denver; bd. dirs. Roosevelt Raceway. Served with AUS, World War II. Recipient Peabody award, 1957, Christopher award, 1957. Mem. Newcomen Soc. N.Am. Club: Players (N.Y.C.). Composer lyrics for Nixon campaign song. Home: 146 Central Park W New York City NY 10021 Office: 2 Pennsylvania Plaza New York City NY 10001

COOPERMAN, JAMES, fgn. service officer; b. Pitts., Nov. 4, 1912; s. Jacob and Alice (Gordon) C.; B.S. in Chemistry, Carnegie Inst. Tech., 1935, M.S., 1941; m. Tillie Lipsman, Aug. 17, 1941. Chem. engr. U.S. Steel Corp., 1935-42; chief chemist Universal-Cyclops Steel Co., 1942-46; supervising chem. engr. So. Natural Gas Co., 1946-52; chem. engr. Armour Research Found., 1952- 64; chief indsl. devel. div., Am. consulate, New Delhi, India; now with Bur. East Asian and Pacific Affairs Dept. State, Washington. Mem. Am. Chem. Soc., Am. Inst. Chem. Engrs. Office: Bur East Asian and Pacific Affairs Dept State Washington DC 20521

COOPERMAN, PHILIP, educator; b. N.Y.C., Dec. 3, 1918; s. Meyer and Bessie (Wolocizer) C.; B.S., Coll. City N.Y., 1938; M.S., N.Y.U., 1948, Ph.D., 1951; m. Elsie B. Rosenson, Oct. 8, 1950; children—Gene D., Lawrence J. Physicist, USN Dept., Balt., 1941-43; physicist Los Alamos Sci. Labs., 1944-46; physicist Research Corp., Bound Brook, N.J., 1951-56; sr. mathematician Gulf Oil Corp., Hamarville, Pa., 1956-58; asst. prof. U. Pitts., 1958-60; dir. research and devel. Research-Cottrell, Bound Brook, 1960, cons., 1959-60, 61-62; prof. math. Fairleigh-Dickinson U., Teaneck, N.J., 1961—; cons. U.S. Steel Corp., 1959, Precipitoir Pollution Control, Inc., 1967—; tech. editor All Clear Mag., 1969—; reviewer math. revs., 1963-69. Served with C.E., AUS, 1943-46. Mem. Air Pollution Control Assn., I.E.E.E., Am. Math. Soc., Math. Assn. Am., Electrostatic Soc. Am. Contbr. articles profl. jours. Patentee in field. Home: 46 Elizabeth Av Teaneck NJ 07666

COOPERRIDER, LUKE KING, educator; b. Glenford, O., Dec. 2, 1918; s. Luke K. and Lola (King) C.; B.S., Harvard, 1940; J.D., U. Mich., 1948; m. Helen Virginia Harle, Nov. 28, 1945; children—Peter A., Mark W., Carol S. Admitted to Ohio bar, 1949; with Ohio Dept. Taxation, 1940-41; asso. firm Squire, Sanders & Dempsey, Cleve., 1948-52; mem. faculty U. Mich. Law Sch., 1952- -, prof. law, 1958—, chmn. bd. control student publs., 1962-69. Chmn. Ann Arbor Citizens Council, 1967-68. Served to maj., Signal Corps, AUS, 1941-46. Mem. Am. Bar Assn. Home: 3095 Exmoor Rd Ann Arbor MI 48104

COOPERSTEIN, SHERWIN JEROME, medical educator; b. N.Y.C., Sept. 14, 1923; s. Joseph and Bessie (Berger) C.; B.S., Coll. City N.Y., 1943; D.D.S., N.Y.U., 1948; Ph.D. in Anatomy, Western Res. U., 1951; m. Alice Ruth Peskin, June 1, 1947; children—Rhonda Ann, Lawrence Alan. Instr. biology Coll. City N.Y., 1943, 46-48; research asso. physiology N.Y.U., 1946-68; instr. anatomy Western Res. U., 1948-49, fellow anatomy, 1949-51, sr. instr., 1951-52, asst. prof. anatomy, 1952-55, asso. prof., 1955-64, asst. dean, 1957-64; prof., head dept. anatomy, U. Conn. Schs. Medicine and Dental Medicine, Hartford, 1964—. Mem. anatomical scis. tng. com. Nat. Inst. Gen. Med. Scis., 1966-70. Served with AUS, 1943-44. Mem. A.A.A.S., Am. Chem. Soc., Marine Biol. Lab., Am. Assn. Anatomists, Histochem. Soc., Assn. Am. Med. Colls., Am. Soc. Biol. Chemists, Am. Diabetes Assn., Sigma Xi. Contbr. articles profl. jours. Home: 10 Hillsboro Dr West Hartford CT 06107 Office: U Conn 1280 Asylum Av Hartford CT 06105

COORDS, HENRY H., toy mfg. co. exec. Pres., chief exec. officer Fisher-Price Toys, Inc. Office: 606 Girard Av East Aurora NY 14052*

COOTE, COLIN REITH, journalist; b. Fenstanton, Huntingdonshire, Eng., Oct. 19, 1893; s. Howard and Jean Reith (Gray) C.; B.A., Balliol Coll., Oxford, 1914; m. Amalie Marinus, Mar. 29, 1946. M.P., 1917-22; Rome corr. The Times, 1922-25; Parliamentary sketch writer, 1927-30, Times leader-writer, 1930-42; dep. editor Daily Telegraph, 1942-50, mng. editor, 1950-64. Served with Gloucester Regiment, 1914-18; French 26th Inf. div., France and Italy, 1917-18. Decorated companion Distinguished Service Order; Legion of Honor, 1956, Knight Batchelor, 1962. Author: Italian Town and Country Life, 1924; In and About Rome, 1925; Maxims and Reflections of Winston Churchill, 1947; Through Five Generations, 1949; Sir Winston Churchill, A Self-Portrait, 1953; Companion of Honour-A Life of Walter Elliot, 1965; Editorial (personal memoirs), 1965; The Government We Deserve, 1969. Home: 16 Bigwood Rd NW XI London, England

COOTNER, PAUL HAROLD, educator, economist; b. Logansport, Ind., May 25, 1930; s. William David and Rose (Singer) C.; B.S. magna cum laude, U. Fla., 1949, M.A., 1950; Ph.D., Mass. Inst. Tech., 1953; m. Cathryn Mae Marcho, Dec. 2, 1962. Ford teaching intern Brown U., 1955-56; research asso. Resources for the Future, Inc., 1956-59; mem. faculty Mass. Inst. Tech., 1959-70, prof. finance, 1966-70; cons. to govt. and industry, 1959—; Ford Found. distinguished vis. prof. finance Harvard Bus. Sch. 1969-70; C.O.G. Miller prof. finance Grad. Sch. Bus. Stanford (Cal.) U., 1970—. Served with AUS, 1953-55. Ford Found. faculty fellow, 1965-66. Mem. Am. Econ. Assn., Am. Finance Assn. Jewish religion. Editor: The Random Character of Stock Market Prices, 1964. Home: 676 Mayfield Av Stanford CA 94305

COOVER, ROBERT LOWELL, author; b. Charles City, Ia., Feb. 4, 1932; s. Grant Marion and Maxine (Sweet) C.; B.A., Ind. U., 1953; M.A., U. Chgo., 1965; m. Maria del Pilar Sans-Mallafre, June 3, 1959; children—Diana Nin, Sara Chapin, Roderick Luis. Tchr. Bard Coll., 1966 67, U. Ia., 1967-69; writer in residence Wis. State U., Superior, 1968, Washington U., St. Louis, 1969. Served with USNR, 1953-57. Recipient William Faulkner award for best first novel, 1966; citation in Fiction, Brandeis U., 1970. Rockefeller grantee, 1969; Guggenheim fellow, 1971. Author: The Origin of the Brunists, 1966; The Universal Baseball Association, J. Henry Waugh, Prop., 1968; Pricksongs and Descants, 1969; (film) On a Confrontation in Iowa City, 1969; (plays) The Kid, 1968; Love Scene, 1970; Rip Awake, 1971; A Theological Position, 1971. Address: care EP Dutton & Co 201 Park Av S New York City NY 10003

COPE, JAMES, pub. relations exec.; b. Genoa, Italy, Oct. 27, 1904; s. James Canby Biddle and Emilia Stefania (Polesini) C.; m. Martha Lyle Wright, Sept. 4, 1928; children—Joan Charlotte Emilia (Mrs. David L. Sutter), James Roderick, Julia (Mrs. Robertson Brinker). Newspaperman, Asheville (N.C.) Citizen, 1923; with Asso. Press, Montgomery, Ala., Nashville, Washington, 1926-34; spl. asst. to Gen. Hugh S. Johnson, N.R.A., 1934; Washington rep. Automobile Mfrs. Assn., 1935-44, in charge pub. relations, 1938-40; asst. to pres. Chrysler Corp., 1944-52, v.p. pub. relations, 1952-57, mem. adminstrv. com., 1957-58; pres. Selvage & Lee, Inc., pub. relations, N.Y.C., 1958-61, chmn. bd., 1961-69; chmn. Selvage, Lee & Howard, Inc., N.Y.C., 1969—. Vice pres. Detroit Edn. TV Found., 1955-58. Mem. Pub. Relations Soc. Am. (chmn. com. on standards profl. practice 1968). Clubs: Detroit; Metropolitan, Nat. Press. (Washington). Home: 511 E 80th St New York City NY 10021 Office: 500 Fifth Av New York City NY 10036

COPE, KENNETH WAYNE, chain store exec.; b. Rifle, Colo., May 31, 1924; s. William Grant and Mary (Park) C.; B.A., La Sierra Coll., Arlington, Cal., 1948; postgrad. U. Wash., 1948-50; m. Patricia Miller, Feb. 1, 1946; children—Kimberly Ann, Bradley Mark. From staff accountant to mgr. Price Waterhouse & Co., C.P.A.'s Los Angeles, 1950-58, resident mgr., Phoenix, 1959-63; regional controller Lucky Stores, Inc., San Leandro, Cal., 1963-68, v.p., corp. controller, 1968—. Served with AUS, 1943-46. C.P.A., Cal. Mem. Am. Inst. C.P.A.'s, Cal. Soc. C.P.A.'s, Soc. Advancement Mgmt. (v.p. San Francisco 1967-69), Republican. Episcopalian. Home: 1683 Graff Av San Leandro CA 94577 Office: 6300 Clark Av Dublin CA 94566

COPE, OLIVER, surgeon, educator; b. Germantown, Pa., Aug. 15, 1902; s. Walter and Eliza Middleton (Kane) C.; A.B., Harvard, 1923, M.D., 1928; Dr. Honoris Causa, U. Toulouse, 1950; m. Alice DeNormandie, Dec. 28, 1932; children—Robert DeNormandie, Eliza Middleton. Intern, resident surgery Mass. Gen. Hosp., 1928-32, asst. to asso. surgeon, 1934-46, vis. surgeon, 1946-69, acting chief surg. services, 1968-69, mem. bd. consultation, 1969—; travelling fellow Harvard, 1933, instr., later asso., asst. prof. surgery, med. sch. 1934-38, asso. prof. surgery, 1948-63, prof. surgery, 1963-69, prof. surgery emeritus, 1969—, acting head dept. surgery, 1968-69; chief of staff Boston unit of Shriners Burn Inst., 1964-69, chief staff emeritus, 1969—. Responsible investigator Office Sci. Research and Devel. 1942-45; mem. subcom. burns Nat. Research Council, 1943-45; dir. research under contract with Office Naval Research, 1947-52. Diplomate Am. Bd. Surgery. Fellow A.C.S.; mem. Am. Surg. Assn. (pres. 1962- 63), N.E. Surg. Soc., Internat. Soc. Surgery, A.A.A.S., Soc. Clin. Surgery, Soc. Clin. Investigation, Soc. U. Surgeons, A.M.A., Mass. Med. Soc., Am. Acad. Arts and Scis., Boston Surg. Soc. (pres. 1965), Boylston Med. Soc. (pres. 1964). Home: 20 Hubbard Park Cambridge MA 02138 Office: Mass Gen Hosp Boston MA 02114

COPE, SYDNEY RAYMOND, banker; b. London, Eng., May 14, 1907; s. Sydney Charles and Madeline Ethel (Pugh) C.; B.Sc. in Econs., London Sch. Econs., 1937, Ph.D. in Econs., 1947. With Guinness, Mahon & Co., bankers, London, 1923-41, 46- 47, Esso Transp. Ltd., London, 1947; with Internat. Bank Reconstrn. and Devel. 1947—, dir. dept. operations Europe, 1962- 65, dir. Europe and Middle East dept., 1965-67, dir. Europe dept., 1967- 68, dep. chmn. loan com., office of pres., 1968—. Served as squadron leader RAF, 1941-46. Mem. Inst. of Bankers London (asso.). Clubs: Reform (London); Federal City (Washington). Home: 3413 R St NW Washington, DC 20007. Office: 1818 H St NW Washington DC 20433

COPE, THOMAS FREEMAN, former educator; b. Dallas, Nov. 24, 1900; s. Willis Henry and Victoria (Doll) C.; B.S., Tulane U., 1923, M.S., 1925; Ph.D., U. Chgo., 1927; m. Frances Thorndike, June 29, 1929; children—Freeman Widener, Elizabeth Frances, Mary Thorndike. Instr. math. Tulane U., 1923-25, Western Res. U., 1926-27, U. Chgo., 1927-28; NRC fellow Harvard, 1928-29, instr., 1929-30; asst. prof. Marietta Coll., 1930-31, head dept., 1930-37, prof., 1931-37; asst. prof. Queens Coll., 1937-39, asso. prof., 1939-48, prof., 1948-70, prof. emeritus, 1970—, chmn. dept. math., 1937-50, 52-69. Expert cons. math. tests Adj. Gen.'s Office, 1944-46. Fellow A.A.A.S.; mem. Am. Math. Soc., Math. Assn. Am., Phi Beta Kappa, Sigma Xi. Home: Montrose NY 10548

COPE, WILLIAM HENRY, physician, govt. ofcl.; b. Wellsville, O., Nov. 25, 1918; s. William Carl and Mary Ellen (Slavin) C.; B.A., Ohio State U., 1943, M.D., 1947; grad. preventive medicine, Maracay, Venezuela, 1951; M.P.H., Harvard, 1953; m. Dorothy Ann Hargrove, June 10, 1950; children—William Henry, Nancy Ann, Patricia Ann. Intern Nat. Naval Med. Center, Bethesda, Md., 1947-48; mem. Am. mission to Greece, adviser pub. health Greek Govt., 1948-50; pvt. practice Euclid Clinic Found., also chief clin. services U.S. Steel Co., 1955-59; fgn. service officer, U.S. Dept. State adviser pub. health and med. edn. Brazilian Govt., 1959-61; chief pub. health adviser Ministry Health Colombia, Bogota, 1961-62; field dir. Central Am. Health Program, AID, 1962-63; chief Latin Am. office Office Internat. Health, NIH, USPHS, 1963-65; med. dir. USPHS, dep. chief neurol. and sensory disease service program, div. chronic diseases, Washington, 1965-66, acting dir. div. physician manpower, 1967, asst. dir. Bur. Health Services, 1967-68; dir. internat. affairs Health Services and Mental Health Adminstrn., Dept. Health, Edn. and Welfare, 1968—; asst. prof. internat. health Georgetown U. Sch. Medicine. Served to lt. USNR, 1947- 55; comdg. officer U.S. Navy Preventive Med. Unit 2, Norfolk, Va., 1953- 55. Decorated Order King George I (Greece), 1950. Fellow Royal Soc. Tropical Medicine and Hygiene, Indsl. Med. Assn., Am. Acad. Occupational Medicine, Am. Pub. Health Assn.; mem. A.M.A. Contbr. articles in field. Home: 3503 Prince William Dr Fairfax VA 22030 Office: Office of Adminstr Health Services and Mental Health Adminstrn Parklawn Bldg 5600 Fishers Lane Rockville MD 20852

COPE, WILLIAM HENRY, retail co. exec.; b. Toronto, Can., June 7, 1923; s. Henry and Jean (McKain) C.; came to U.S., 1950; B.Sc., U. Mich., 1942; m. Elisabeth Telfer, Feb. 3, 1950; children—William David, Catherine Mary, Margaret Anne. With Asso. Dry Goods Corp., 1950-55, Seneca Corp., 1955-58, B. Forman Co., 1958-60, Can. Trust Co., 1960-63; v.p. retail coordination, Genesco Inc., 1963—; exec. v.p., dir. Bonwit Teller Co.; dir. S.H. Kress & Co., Henri Bendel, Gidding-Jenny Co., Hordy Shoe Co., Interstate Shoe Co., Superior Shoe Co., I. Miller Co., Nationwide Shoe Co., R.A.M. Co., Vaness Co., Henri Bendel, Bell Shoe Co. Home: 175 Saddle Hill Rd Stamford CT 06903 Office: 114 Fifth Av New York City NY 10011

COPELAND, ABBOT JOSEPH, textile co. exec.; b. N.Y.C., Sept. 4, 1905; s. Samuel and Mary (Grotsky) C.; student Cornell U., 1925; m. Nora Grogan, Aug. 4, 1930; children—Michael, Denis. Pres. Cohn-Hall-Marx Co., Inc., 1965—; exec. v.p. United Merchants and Mfgs. Inc., 1960—. Active local Fedn. Jewish Charities, Nat. Conf. Christians and Jews. Mem. Am. Arbitration Assn. (panel mem.), Grand Jury Assn.‡

COPELAND, DONALD EUGENE, educator; b. Mendon, O., Feb. 6, 1912; s. Arland Murlin and Chloe (Severns) C.; A.B., Rochester U., 1935; M.A., Amherst Coll., 1937; Ph.D., Harvard, 1941; m. Marjorie Groves, June 20, 1941; children—Sandra Kay, Jane Hance, Diana Sue. Instr. zoology U. N.C., 1941-42; asst. then asso. prof. zoology Brown U., 1946-51; chief aviation physiologist Office Surgeon Gen., USAF, 1951-53; profl. asso. Nat. Acad. Scis.-NRC, 1953-56; sec. NIH, 1956-59; prof. zoology Tulane U., 1959—, chmn. dept., 1959-65; mem. Marine Biol. Lab., 1948—; research histophysiology and ultra structure salt secreting mechanism fish gills and gas secretion in swim bladders. Mem. morphology and genetics study sect., physiology study sect. NIH 1952- 53. Served to capt. USAAF, 1942-46. Mem. Am. Assn. Anatomists, Am. Soc. Zoologists, Soc. Study Devel. and Growth, Assn. Southeastern Biologists. Home: 2808 Calhoun St New Orleans LA 70118

COPELAND, EDWARD MARION, Jr., educator; b. Los Angeles, Aug. 9, 1925; s. Edward Marion and Myrtle (Evans) C.; B.A. with highest honors, U. Cal. at Berkeley, 1954, M.A., 1958; children—Edward Daniel, David Evans. Research asst. Inst. Asian Studies, U. Cal. at Berkeley, 1955-57; faculty U. Minn., 1957—, prof. Japanese, 1968—, chmn. dept. E. and S. Asian langs., 1966-68, chmn. dept. E. Asian langs., 1968- -; vis. lectr. Stanford, 1961-62; vis. summer prof. Ind. U., 1964, 69, Ohio State U., 1965, U. Wis., 1968. Served with AUS, 1943-47. Mem. Am. Oriental Soc., Assn. Asian Studies, Midwest Conf. Asian Studies. Contbr. papers in field. Home: 6 Barton Av SE Minneapolis MN 55414

COPELAND, FREDERICK CLEVELAND, educator; b. Brunswick, Me., Oct. 9, 1912; s. Manton and Ruth W. (Ripley) C.; B.A. Williams Coll., 1935; postgrad. U. Munich (Germany), 1936; M.A., Harvard, 1937, Ph.D., 1940; m. Caroline Louise Day, June 24, 1939; children—Frederick Cleveland, Winsor Ripley, Emily Day. Instr. biology Trinity Coll., Hartford, Conn., 1940-46, dir. admissions, 1944-46; faculty Williams Coll., 1946—, dir. admissions, 1946—, prof. biology, 1957—. Chmn. standing com. entrance procedures Coll. Entrance Exam. Bd., 1966-68. Trustee Hotchkiss Sch., Lenox Sch., Pine Cobble Sch. Recipient Rogerson cup Williams Coll., 1967. Mem.

New Eng. Assn. Colls. and Secondary Schs. (pres. 1962-63), Beta Theta Pi. Republican. Episcopalian (vestry). Home: Oblong Rd Williamstown, MA 01267.

COPELAND, GEORGE GORDON, former telephone co. exec.; b. East Haven, Conn., Oct. 9, 1905; s. George Hawksley and Rosamond (Bragg) C.; B.C.S., Northeastern U., 1927; m. Thelma Campbell Larrabee, Sept. 23, 1933; childrenPenelope Ruth, Anthony Gordon. With So. New Eng. Telephone Co., New Haven, 1921-, sec.-treas., 1941-70, v.p., 1951-70; dir. Second Nat. Bank New Haven, New Haven Savs. Bank. Bd. dirs. New Haven YMCA; trustee Quinnipiac Coll., New Haven. Mem. Am. Soc. Corp. Secs. Republican. Episcopalian. Clubs: New Haven Country, Quinnipiack (New Haven). Home: 931 Ridge Rd Hamden CT 06517 Office: 227 Church St New Haven 6, CT

COPELAND, GEORGE R., pipeline co. exec. Chmn. bd. Algonquin Gas Transmission Co., Boston. Office: 1284 Soldiers Field Rd Boston MA 02135*

COPELAND, GEORGE WILBUR, mfg. exec.; b. N.Y.C., Nov. 11, 1911; s. Albert E. and Edith (Wilbur) C.; grad. Milw. Country Day Sch., 1929; student Yale; m. Sara Marshall Richardson, Sept. 3, 1932; children—Sally (Mrs. Burke Raynor Field), Cherry (Mrs. William F. Gillespie, III). Engaged as factory worker, time study engr. Hommel & Downing Co., Milw., 1932-36; with Hart & Cooley Mfg. Co. div. Allied Thermal Corp., Holland, Mich., 1936—, successively time study engr., personnel dir., v.p., gen. mgr., now chmn.; v.p. Allied Thermal Corp., New Britain, Conn., 1955-57, pres., 1957—; trustee New Britain Bank & Trust Co. Bd. dirs. New Britain Gen. Hosp., New Britain Meml. Hosp. Republican. Episcopalian. Home: 105 Ten Acre Rd New Britain CT 06511 Office: 215 Warren St New Britain CT 06511

COPELAND, JAMES ISAAC, librarian; b. Clinton, S.C., May 5, 1910; s. William D. and Laura (Vance) C.; B.A., Presbyn. Coll., 1931; B.S. in L.S., George Peabody Coll. Tchrs., 1932, M.A., 1934; postgrad. U. Chgo., summers 1936, 38, 39, 40; Ph.D., U. N.C., 1957. Asst. reference and periodicals Peabody Coll., 1932-35; librarian Furman U., 1936-42, Presbyn. Coll., 1942-45; documents librarian U. N.C., 1947-50; librarian Peabody Coll., 1952-67, also prof. history; dir. So. Hist. Collection, U. N.C. Library, prof. history U. N.C., Chapel Hill, 1967—. Mem. region 4 archives adv. council U.S. Nat. Archives and Records Service, 1971—. Mem. bd. Nashville Council on Human Relations, 1961-63. Mem. Am. (mem. assn. council 1962-65), S.C. (pres. 1942-43), Southeastern (treas. 1960-62), N.C. library assns., So., Am., S.C. hist. assns., Orgn. Am. Historians, Nashville Library Club (pres. 1962-63), Hist. Soc. N.C., N.C. Lit. and Hist. Assn., Kappa Delta Pi, Phi Delta Kappa. Presbyn. Kiwanian. Contbr. to Writing Southern History. Editor: Democracy in The Old South and Other Essays. Home: 7 Davie Circle PO Box 576 Chapel Hill NC 27514

COPELAND, JO, fashion designer; b. N.Y.C.; d. Samuel and Minna (Emelin) Copeland; student Parson's Sch. Design, Art Students League, N.Y.C.; m. Edward Joseph Regensburg, 1923 (div. 1944); children—Anthony S., Lois Adele (Mrs. Robert Gould); m. 2d, Mitchell Benson, May 8, 1953 (div.). Comml. artist, 1918-21; sketcher, designer Pattulo, 1921-29; dress mfr. Jo Copeland, Inc., 1931-37; with Pattulo-Jo Copeland, Inc., 1938-70, v.p. charge designing, 1938-70; now free lance cons. Writer Series on fashion for Phila. Enquirer. Adv. bd. Steven's Coll.; critic, adviser design class Parsons Sch. Design. Recipient Nieman Marcus award; Am. Silk Assn. award; citation Phila. Mus. Art; medal Ordre de la Courtoisie de France 1961; award Girls Club of N.Y., 1961. Mem. Fashion Group, Council Fashion Designers Am. (founder mem.). Home: 30 E 62d St New York City NY 10021 Office: 498 7th Av New York City NY 10018

COPELAND, JOSEPH BRYSON, physician; b. Waynesboro, Ga., Aug. 27, 1904; s. Oliver Jackson and Elma (Clinkscales) C.; B.S., U. Fla., 1926; M.D., Tulane U., 1930; m. Gladys Ware, June 8, 1935 (dec.); children—Joseph Bryson, Oliver Preston, Kay. Adminstr., Robert B. Green Hosp., San Antonio, 1933-37; pvt. practice medicine, San Antonio, 1937-63; dep. commr. Tex. Dept. Health, 1963—. Chmn., Tex. Bd. Health, 1951-63. Mem. Tex. Acad. Gen. Practice (past pres.), A.M.A. (sec.-treas., trustee), Tex. Med. Assn., Bexar County Med. Soc. (past pres.), Sigma Nu, Phi Chi, Alpha Omega Alpha. Episcopalian. Home: 5326-A Balcones Dr Austin TX 78731 Office: 1100 W 49th St Austin TX 78756

COPELAND, JOSEPH J., coll. pres.; b. Ferris, Tex., May 22, 1914; s. Henry Hillard and Cora Lemmar (Richardson) C.; B.A., Trinity U., San Antonio, Tex.; 1936, D.D., 1950; B.D., McCormick Theol. Sem., 1939; LL.D., Maryville (Tenn.) Coll., 1960; m. Glenda Lee Mullendore, May 30, 1938; children—Joseph Kirk, Karen Lee (Mrs. Meldrum Gray III). Ordained to ministry Presbyn. Ch. 1939; pastor in Okla., 1939-41, Tex., 1942-52, Tenn., 1952-61; pres. Maryville Coll., 1961—. also mem. bd. dirs. Moderator weekly TV series, sta. WBIR, Knoxville, 1956—. Mem. bd. Christian edn. United Presbyn. Ch. U.S.A., 1950-65, mem. div. radio and TV, 1957-65, moderator Synod Mid-South, 1959-60, also chmn. com. higher edn., 1945-55, chmn. Westminster Found., 1952-66; chmn. counseling com. ch. and soc. United Presbyn. Ch. U.S.A., 1961-65; mem. commn. on Delta ministry Nat. Council Chs. Christ U.S.A., 1964—. Mem. Presbyn. Coll. Union (pres. 1969), Tenn. Coll. Assn. (pres. 1970-71), Affiliated Ind. Colls. Tenn., So. Assn. Colls. and Schs. Kiwanian. Contbr. articles mags. Home: Maryville Coll Maryville TN 37801

COPELAND, KENNETH WILFORD, bishop; b. Bexar, Ark., Apr. 3, 1912; s. Rev. John Wesley and Nancy Elizabeth (Hively) C.; student Westminster Coll., Tehuacana, Tex., 1930- 32, East Tex. State Tchrs. Coll., 1933-34; B.A., So. Meth. U., 1938; student Garrett Bibl. Inst., 1947; D.D. (hon.), Southwest U., Georgetown Tex., 1951; S.T.D. (hon.), Neb. Wesleyan U., 1961; LL.D., Southern Methodist University, 1964; m. Catherine Andrews, October 5, 1933; children—Patricia Ann (Mrs. Dr. James Wilbur Ard, Jr.), Martha Sue (Mrs. Preston Hastings Dial, Jr.). Ordained to ministry Methodist Ch., 1931; pastor, Corsicana, Tex., 1931-32, Cooper, Tex., 1932-34, Dallas, 1934- 38; pres. Tex. Conf. Meth. Protestant Ch., 1938-39; pastor, Wichita Falls, Tex., 1939-40, Haskell, Tex., 1940-44, First Ch., Stillwater, Okla., 1944-49, Travis Park Ch., San Antonio, 1949-60; bishop Neb. area Meth. Ch., 1960-68, Houston area, 1968—. Alt. del. uniting conf. M.E. Ch., Meth. Protestant Ch., Meth. Episcopal Ch. South, 1939; mem. Jurisdictional confs., 1940, 48, 52, 56, 60, gen. confs., 1952, 56, 60; v.p. Gen. Bd. Missions, pres. joint commn. on edn. and cultivation, 1964-68; pres. World Div. Bd. Missions, 1968—; mem. Gen. Bd. Christian Social Concerns, 1960-68. Trustee Alaska Methodist University, Southern Methodist Univ., Neb. Wesleyan U., St. Paul Sch. Theology Methodist. Mason (K.T., Shriner), Lion. Author: A Primer of Beliefs for Methodist Laymen, 1959. Home: 2701 Westheimer Houston TX 77006 Office: 5215 S Main St Houston TX 77002

COPELAND, LAMMOT DU PONT, bus. exec.; b. Wilmington, Del., May 19, 1905; s. Charles and Louisa d'Andelot (du Pont) C.; B.S. in Indsl. Chemistry, Harvard, 1928; LL.D., U. Del., 1962, U. Pa., 1963, Am. U., 1964; D.Sc., Jefferson Med. Coll., 1963; H.H.D., Washington Coll., 1965; D.Sc. in Commerce, Drexel Inst.; D.Engring., PMC Colls., 1971; m. Pamela Cunningham, Feb. 1, 1930; children—Lammot du Pont, Louise (Mrs. James Biddle), Gerret van S. With E.I. du Pont de Nemours & Co., Inc., 1929—, dir., 1942—, mem. finance com. 1943-59, sec., 1947-54, v.p., 1954-62, chmn. finance com., 1954-59, mem. exec. com., 1959-67, pres., chmn. exec. com., 1962-67, chmn. bd., 1967-71, mem. finance com., 1962-71; dr. Dupont Co. Can., Montreal, 1949-63; v.p. Christiana Securities Co.; dir., trust com. Wilmington Trust Co. Trustee, v.p. Longwood Found.; trustee, treas. Eleutherian Mills-Hagley Found.; chmn. vis. com. sch. pub. health and univ. libraries, mem. exec. com. and com. on univ. research, mem. bd. overseers Harvard Coll; trustee, pres. Henry Francis duPont Winterthur Mus.; hon. dir., past pres. Wilmington Soc. Fine Arts; bd. mgrs., finance com. Wilmington Inst. (free library); vice chmn. bd. Del. Safety Council; trustee U. Pa., 1953-66. Decorated officer Legion of Honour (France); officer Order of Leopold (Belgium); comdr. Order Courrone de Chene (Luxembourg). Mem. Pilgrims U.S., Am. Chem. Soc., Harvard Alumni Soc. (dir. 1953-56), Mil. Order Loyal Legion, Nat. Rifle Assn., Soc. Colonial Wars Del. (gov.), Walpole Soc., Huguenot Soc. Am., Soc. Mayflower Descs. Clubs: Wilmington, Wilmington Country, Vicmead Hunt, Greenville Country (Wilmington); Harvard, University Links (N.Y.C.); Great Oak (Chestertown, Md.); Capitol Hill, City Tavern (Washington). Home: Greenville DE 19807 Office: Du Pont Bldg Wilmington DE 19898

COPELAND, LESLIE O., life ins. co. exec.; b. Clarksville, Ia., Mar. 19, 1908; s. Ira Albert and Lulu (Bolin) C.; B.A., U. Ia., 1930; m. Loretta Morrissey, July 15, 1939; children—Thomas S., Ann Louise. With N.Am. Life Ins. Co., Chgo., 1931—, actuarial dept., 1931-33, real estate and mortgage loans, 1933-43, asst. sec. bonds, stocks, real estate and mortgage loans, 1943-47, sec., home office mgmt., 1947-51, sec.-treas., dir., 1951-54, v.p., treas., 1954-58, exec. v.p., 1958-61, president, 1961-68, chairman of the board, pres., 1968—, also dir. Member Chgo. Actuarial Club, Certified Appraisers Assn., Wine and Food Soc. Chgo. Republican. Methodist. Clubs: Executives, Mid-America (Chgo.). Home: 800 Chatham Rd Glenview IL 60025 Office: 35 E Wacker Dr Chicago IL 60601

COPELAND, MORRIS ALBERT, economist; b. Rochester, N.Y., Aug. 6, 1895; s. Albert Edwards and Jenny (Morris) C.; A.B., Amherst Coll., 1917, L.H.D., 1957; Ph.D. U., Chgo., 1921; m. Mary Phelps Enders, Dec. 21, 1929; children—Helen (Mrs. R.E. Grattidge), Robert Enders. Instr. econs. Cornell U., 1921-25, asst. prof., 1925-28, prof., 1928-30, leave of absence, 1927-29; served successively with Brookings Grad. Sch. Nat. Bur. Econ. Research, U. Wis. Exptl. Coll. and Fed. Res. Bd.; prof. econs. U. Mich., 1930-36, leave of absence, 1933-35; exec. sec. Central Statis. Bd., Washington 1933-39; dir. research Bur. of Budget, Washington 1939-40; chief munitions br. WPB, 1940-44; with Nat. Bur. Econ. Research, 1944-59; prof. econs. Cornell U., 1949-65, Robert J. Thorne prof. econs., 1957-65; vis. prof. econs. U. Mo., 1966-67, State U. N.Y. at Albany, 1967-71; Fulbright lectr. Delhi (India) Sch. Econs. Fellow Am. Statis. Assn. (past v.p.); mem. Am. Econ. Assn. (past pres.), Phi Beta Kappa, Phi Delta Theta. Author: A Study of Moneyflows in the U.S., 1951; Fact and Theory in Economics, 1958; Trends in Government Financing, 1961; Our Free Enterprise Economy, 1964; Toward Full Employment, 1966. Contbr. to econ. publs. Home: Box 295 Sodus NY 14551 also 633 Alhambra Rd Venice FL 33595

COPELAND, MURRAY M., physician, educator; b. McDonough, Ga., June 23, 1902; s. Edward Meadows and Mary Elizabeth (Speer) C.; A.B., Oglethorpe U., 1923, D.Sc., 1955; M.D., Johns Hopkins, 1927; m. Jean Brown, June 20, 1931. Intern City Hosp., Balt., 1927-28; fellow Mayo Clinic, Rochester, Minn., 1929-30, Meml. Hosp., N.Y.C., 1930-33; resident surgery Union Meml. Hosp., Balt., 1933-37; instr. surgery U. Md., 1937-44, Johns Hopkins Med. Sch. and Hosp., 1937-46; chief surgery Kennedy VA Hosp., Memphis, 1946-47; prof. oncology, dir. dept. Georgetown U. Med. Center, Washington, 1947-60; asst. dir. M.D. Anderson Hosp. and Tumor Inst., 1960-62, asso. dir., 1962-67; v.p. internat. affairs U. Cancer Found., U. Tex. M.D. Anderson Hosp. and Tumor Inst., 1967—; prof. surgery U. Tex., Houston, 1963—. Clin. cons., clin. center Nat. Cancer Inst., NIH, USPHS, 1953-68, chmn. cancer control com., 1956-58, mem. nat. adv. cancer council, 1958-61, 66- 69; dir.-at-large Am. Cancer Soc., Inc., 1957-67, nat. pres., 1964-65, pres. D.C. div., 1951-53; mem. Am. Joint Com. for Cancer Staging and End Result Reporting, 1959—; adv. com. Cancer Control Program, Bur. State Services, USPHS, 1963-66. Served from maj. to col. M.C., AUS, 1942-45. Decorated Legion of Merit. Diplomate Am. Bd. Surgery. Mem. Am. Assn. Cancer Research, Am. Cancer Soc. (pres. 1964-65), Am. Med. Soc. Vienna (hon. life), Am. Radium Soc., James Ewing Soc. (past v.p., sr. mem.), N.Y. Acad. Scis., Soc. Med. Cons. to Armed Forces, So. Surgeons Club (past pres.), So. Surg. Assn., A.C.S., Am. Orthopaedic Assn. (hon.), Am. Acad. Orthopaedic Surgeons (hon.), Soc. Head and Neck Surgeons, Internat. Union Against Cancer (mem. council 1966—, v.p. for N.Am., 1970—, sec.-gen. 10th Internat. Cancer Congress 1967-70, Southeastern Surg. Congress (pres. 1969). Author: (with C.F. Geschickter) Tumors of Bone, 1931. Contbr. numerous articles, textbook chpts. on problems of cancer. Home: 1600 Holcombe Blvd Houston TX 77025 Office: 6723 Bertner Av Houston TX 77025

COPELAND, RANDALL E., business exec.; b. 1909; B.A., U. Wis., 1931; With Gimbel Bros. Co., 1931-48; gen. supt. Strawbridge & Clothier, Phila., 1948-55, v.p., 1955-58, exec. v.p., 1958-67, pres., 1967—, also dir.; dir. Germantown Savs. Bank, Girard Trust Bank, Asso. Merchandising Corp. Bd. dirs. Better Bus. Bur. Greater Phila. Greater Phila. Movement, Heart Assn. Southeastern Pa., Bryn Mawr Hosp., Eastern div. Pa. Economy League; trustee United Fund of Phila. Area. Mem. Greater Phila. C. of C. (dir.), Pa. State C. of C. (dir.), Phila. Mchts. Assn. (dir.). Office: 801 Market St Philadelphia PA 19105

COPELAND, ROBERT MILTON, librarian; b. Lincoln, Ill., Sept. 23, 1938; s. William Duncan and Evelyn (Stannard) C.; B.A., Carleton Coll., Northfield, Minn., 1960; M.A., U. Minn., 1963; m. Julia Fillmore Wallace, July 22, 1961 (div.); 1 son, Jonathan Robert; m. 2d, Nora Shirajian, Sept. 12, 1970. Asst. librarian Coll. St. Thomas, St. Paul, 1963-64; librarian Colo. Coll., Colorado Springs, Colo., 1964-68; asst. univ. librarian (readers service) Am. U. Beirut (Lebanon), 1968—. Mem. Am., Lebanese library assns., Am. Assn. U. Profs. Address: Jafet Library American Univ Beirut Beirut Lebanon

COPELAND, S. BRUCE, ins. co. exec.; b. New Castle, Pa., June 29, 1925; s. S. Bruce and Margaret (Wilson) C.; A.B. in Bus. Adminstrn., Muskingum Coll., 1947; m. Carol E. Coates, Aug. 31, 1946; children—Sue (Mrs. Thomas Meek), Thomas, Janet, Margaret. With Conn. Gen. Life Ins. Co., Hartford, 1947-63; with Fidelity Mut. Life Ins. Co., Phila., 1963—, now v.p.; sec.-treas., dir. Met. Assos. Phila. Bd. dirs., chmn. adminstrv. com. Phila. Health and Welfare Council; bd. mgrs. Am. Bapt. Home Mission Socs. Served to lt (j.g.) USNR, 1943-46. Recipient award Million Dollar Round Table, 1958, 60, Nat. Quality award, 1952-60, Lester Schriver award Oakland-E. Bay Life Underwriters Assn. 1960. C.L.U. Home: 226 Windermere Av Wayne PA 19087 Office: Fidelity Mut Life Ins Co The Pkwy and Fairmount Av Philadelphia PA 19101

COPELAND, WILLIAM GLEN, former oil co. exec.; b. Shawnee, Okla., Aug. 6, 1905; s. William Henry and Emma Gertrude (Fox) C.; B.S. in Chem Engring., Rice Inst., 1927; m. Pauline Chaddock, Sept. 18, 1936; children—Carol, William Chad. With Texaco, Inc., 1927-70, gen. mgr. refining, N.Y.C., 1957-60, v.p. refining, N.Y.C., 1960-63, Houston, 1963-70. Mem. Am. Petroleum Inst., Phi Lambda Upsilon. Methodist. Mason. Clubs: Houston, Lakeside Country. Home: 6 Woodstone Houston TX 77024

COPELAND, WILLIAM JOHN, banker; b. Uniontown, Pa., July 4, 1918; s. Thomas Alva and Jean (Hawthorne) C.; B.A., Pa. State U., 1940; J.D., U. Pitts., 1947; m. Margaret Emler, Dec. 23, 1941; children—Thomas A., Jean Clare M. (Mrs. John M. Bedwinek). With Pitts. Nat. Bank (formerly Peoples First Nat. Bank & Trust Co.), 1947—, head bus. devel. dept., trust div., 1959-64, asst. to exec. officer charge trust div., 1964-68, exec. v.p. charge trust div., 1968—; dir. Ryan Homes, Inc., United Refining Co., Rosewell Industries, Inc., Washington Oil Co. Pres. Hosp. Council Western Pa.; bd. dirs., v.p. Hosp. Planning Assn. Allegheny County; bd. dirs. Met. br.YMCA, St. Clair Meml. Hosp.; bd. dirs., chmn. finance com., treas. Western Pa. Comprehensive Health Planning Agy.; exec. v.p., mem. exec. bd. Allegheny Trails council Boy Scouts Am.; mem. adv. bd. Salvation Army of Allegheny County; trustee Robert Morris Coll. Served with USAAF, 1941-46. Clubs: Pittsburgh Athletic Assn., Duquesne, St. Clair Country (Pitts.); Catawba Island (Port Clinton, O.). Home: 22 Mission Dr Pittsburgh PA 15228 Office: 414 Wood St Pittsburgh PA 15222

COPELIN, JOHN GREGORY, ret. telecommunications mfg. exec.; b. Eng., Nov. 9, 1905; s. Arthur and Alice Katherine (Gregory) C.; ed. in Eng.; m. Esther Jeannette Knowles, Aug. 6 1930, naturalized, 1937. With Duncum, Watkins, Ford & Co., chartered accountants, Ceylon, 1926-28; comptroller's staff Internat. Tel & Tel. Corp., 1928-42, v.p., comptroller, 1959, v.p. in charge fgn. bank relations, 1960-65, v.p., dir. internat. and bus. council relations, 1965-70; v.p., comptroller, mgmt. adv. bd., ITT labs. (formerly Fed. Telecommunications), 1945-55, v.p., comptroller, gen. mgr. Litton Engring. Labs., Redwood City, Cal., 1942-45; v.p., comptroller, dir. Internat. Standard Electric Corp., 1956-58, also in charge activities West Indies, C.Am., S.Am., Australia, Can., Far East, now v.p.; v.p., dir. Internat. Tel. & Tel. Credit Corp., Kellogg Credit Corp.; v.p., treas., dir. ISE Holdings Corp., ISE Finance Holdings, Grain Drying Equipment Co., Inc., Attica, Ind. Comml. Solvents Corp. Treas., dir. Bus. Council for Internat. Understanding. Bd. dirs. Am. Portuguese Cultural Soc., Inc. Mem. Nat. Assn. Cost Accountants, English Speaking Union, Financial Execs. Inst. Clubs: Whitehall, Canadian (N.Y.C.); Madison (Conn.) Beach; Quinnipiac (New Haven). Home: Cow Hill Rd Clinton CT 06413 also 1140 Fifth Av New York City NY 10028

COPENHAVER, CHARLES LEONARD, clergyman; b. Winchester, Va., Aug. 23, 1915; s. Charles Leonard and Bernice Agnes (Swhier) C.; B.A., Ohio Wesleyan U., 1938, D.D., 1960—; M.A., Columbia, 1940; B.D., Union Theol. Sem., N.Y.C., 1941; D.D., Yankton (S.D.) College, 1958; L.H.D., Central College, Pella, Iowa, 1968; m. Marian Virginia Yinger, Aug. 27, 1941, children—Charles Leonard 3d, Janice Bernice, Martin Bancroft. Ordained to ministry Congl. Ch., 1942; minister in Spuyten Duyvil, N.Y., 1938-42, Plainfield, N.J., 1942-48, Glen Ridge, N.J., 1948-58, South Pasadena, Cal., 1958-63, Reformed Ch. of Bronxville (N.Y.), 1963—; guest preacher British Council Chs., 1958; cond. preaching mission U.S. Army, also USAF, 1950, 52, 53, radio series Art of Living, 1965—; originator radio program Let's Talk, 1961-63; asso. editor Ministers Quar., 1957. Pres. N.J. Council Chs., 1956; mem. W. coast commn. faith and order World Council Chs., 1962; mem. theologians adv. council, president's profl. assn. Am. Mgmt. Assn., 1964—. Bd. dirs. Union Theol. Sem., Prescott Coll., 1960-63, Waldensian Soc. corp. bd. Yankton Coll. Recipient Freedom Foundation award for sermon, 1969, 70. Mem. bd. edn. Reformed Ch. in Am. Mem. Ohio Soc. (v.p.), Newcomen Soc., Phi Delta Theta, Delta Sigma Rho, Theta Alpha Phi, Omicron Delta Kappa, Sigma Chi. Clubs: Field, Siwanoy (Bronxville). Home: 18 Masterton Rd Bronxville NY 10708 Office: Reformed Ch of Bronxville Bronxville NY 10708

COPENHAVER, JOHN HARRISON, Jr., educator; b. Ralston, Neb., Dec. 21, 1922; s. John Harrison and Dora (Tallman) C.; B.A., Dartmouth, 1946; M.S. (AEC fellow), U. Wis., 1949, Ph.D. (Nat. Heart Inst. fellow), 1950; m. Marion Lamson, June 30, 1946; children—John Harrison III, Margaret Ilse, Christine, Eric Charles, Lisa Carol. Asst. prof. pharmacology U. Tex., 1951-53; faculty Dartmouth, 1953—, prof. zoology, 1960-61, prof. biology, 1960—. Served with USNR, 1940-46. NSF fellow U. Cal. at Berkeley, 1960-61. Mem. Am. Chem. Soc., Am. Soc. Biol. Chemists, Phi Beta Kappa, Sigma Xi. Home: 21 Lyme Rd Hanover NH 03755

COPHER, GLOVER HANCOCK, physician, surgeon; b. Troy, Mo., October 27, 1893; s. William Harrison and Sallie Ann (Duff) C.; A.B., U. of Missouri, 1916; M.D., Washington U. School Medicine, 1918; m. Marjorie Hulsizer, Jan. 12, 1924 (died May 19, 1935); 1 dau., Marjorie Ann. Asst. resident surgeon and resident surgeon, Barnes and St. Louis Children's Hosp., 1918-22; now prof. emeritus clin. surgery Washington U. Sch. Medicine; surgeon, St. Louis City Hosp.; asst. surg. Barnes, St. Louis Children's and St. Louis Maternity hosps. Fellow Am. Coll. Surgeons. Mem. A.M.A., Mo. State Med. Assn., St. Louis Med. Soc., St. Louis Surg. Soc., Soc. of Clin. Surgery, International Society Surg., Am. Surg. Assn., Sigma Xi, Alpha Omega Alpha, Phi Beta Pi. Co-winner Leonard research prize, Am. Roentgen-Ray Soc., 1925; gold medal and certificate of merit, St. Louis Med. Soc., 1927, for aid in development of cholecystography. Author: Methods in Surgery, 1925; Diseases of the Gall Bladder and Ducts (with E. A. Graham, W.H. Cole and Sherwood Moore), 1928. Contbr. articles to jours. in field. Sponsor Copher awards. Home: 5281 Westminster Pl St Louis MO 63108 Office: Barnes Hosp St Louis MO 63110

COPI, IRVING MARMER, educator; b. Duluth, Minn., July 28, 1917; s. Samuel Bernard and Rose (Marmer) Copilowish; B.A., U. Mich., 1938, M.S., 1940, M.A. (Univ. fellow 1946-47), 1947, Ph.D., 1948; postgrad. U. Chgo., 1938-39; m. Amelia Glaser, Mar. 20, 1941; children—David Marmer, Thomas Russell, William Arthur, Margaret Ruth. Instr. philosophy U. Ill., 1947-48; faculty U. Mich., 1948-69, prof. philosophy, 1958-69, research asso., 1951-52, research asso. Engring. Research Inst., 1954-59, research logician Inst. Sci. and Tech., 1960-61; prof. philosophy U. Hawaii, Honolulu, 1969—; research asso. U. Cal. at Berkeley, 1954; vis. lectr. Air Force U., 1958-66, Georgetown U. Logic Inst., 1960; vis. prof. Princeton, 1959-60, U. Hawaii, 1967. Cons. Office Naval Research, 1952. Faculty fellow Fund Advancement Edn., 1953-54; Guggenheim fellow, 1955-56. Mem. Am. Philos. Assn., Assn. Symbolic Logic, Mich. Acad. Letters, Arts and Scis., Am. Assn. U. Profs. (chpt. pres. 1968-69), Phi Beta Kappa, Phi Kappa Phi. Democrat. Jewish religion (pres. congregation 1962-63). Author: Introduction to Logic, 3d edit., 1968; Symbolic Logic, 3d edit., 1967; Introduccion a la Logica, 1962; Introduzione alla Logica, 1965; also numerous essays. Editor: (Plato)

Theaetetus, 1949; (with J.A. Gould) Readings in Logic, 1964; (with R.W. Beard) Essays on Wittgenstein's Tractatus, 1966; (with J.A. Gould) Contemporary Readings in Logical Theory, 1967. Home: 1618 Kamole St Honolulu HI 96821

COPLAN, ROBERT CHARLES, lawyer; b. Cleve., Apr. 12, 1918; s. Morris and Camille H. (Benesch) C.; B.A., Ohio State U., 1939, J.D., 1942; m. Shirley Solomon, May 7, 1943; children—Marianne, James M., Elizabeth. Admitted to Ohio bar 1942; practiced in Cleve., 1945—; law clk. Fed. Dist. Ct., Columbus, O., 1942; mng. partner Benesch, Friedlander, Mendelson & Coplan, 1953—; v.p., dir., gen. counsel Pa. Life Ins. Co. Co-capt. Cleve. Community Fund 1963-65, Cleve. chpt. Am. Cancer Soc., 1961-65; mem. budget com. campaign cabinet Jewish Community Fedn. Cleve., 1961-65; pres. Cleve. Scholarship Programs, Inc. Mem. nat. council Ohio State U. Law Sch.; treas., trustee Bellefaire Childrens Home; mng. trustee Roy C. and Eva Markus Charitable Found.; trustee Forest City Hosp.; pres., trustee Ohio Law Opportunity Fund. Served to lt. USNR, 1942-45. Recipient Cleve. YMCA Service to Youth award, 1969. Mem. Am. Bar Assn., Am. Judicature Soc., Zeta Beta Tau, Pi Sigma Alpha. Home: 2951 Drummond Rd Shaker Heights OH 44120 Office: Citizens Bldg Cleveland OH 44114

COPLAND, AARON, composer; b. Bklyn. Nov. 14, 1900; s. Harris Morris and Sarah (Mittenthal) C.; grad. Boys High Sch. Bklyn., 1918; studied music privately; studied piano under Victor Wittgenstein and Clarence Adler, composition under Rubin Goldmark and Nadia Boulanger; H.H.D., Brandeis U., 1957, Ill. Wesleyan U., 1958; Mus. D., Princeton, 1956, Oberlin Coll., 1958, Temple U., 1959, U. Hartford, 1959, Harvard 1961, Syracuse U., U. R.I., U. Mich., 1964, Kalamazoo Coll., 1965, U. Utah, 1966. Jacksonville U., 1967, Rutgers U., 1967, Fairfield U., 1968, Ohio State U., 1970, N.Y. U., 1970, Columbia U., 1971, York U., Eng., 1971. Composer music since 1920; lectr. on music New Sch. for Social Research, N.Y.C., 1927-37; lectr. music, Harvard, spring 1935-44, composition instr., Berkshire Music Center, 1940, then asst. dir.; Charles Eliot Norton prof. poetry Harvard, 1951-52; dir. Am. Music Center; treas. Arrow Music Press. Founder (with Roger Sessions) Copland-Sessions Concerts, 1928-31; founder Am. Music Festivals at Yaddo, Saratoga Springs, N.Y., 1932. Guggenheim fellow, 1925-26. Recipient RCA Victor award $5,000), 1930; Pulitzer prize for music, 1944; N.Y. Music Critics Circle award, 1945 (for Appalachian Spring), Oscar for The Heiress film score Acad. Motion Picture Arts and Sci., 1950; gold medal for music Am. Acad. Arts and Letters, 1956; Presdl. medal of Freedom, 1964; Howland Meml. prize Yale, 1970; decorated comdr.'s Cross Order Merit (West Germany). Hon. mem. Accademia Santa Cecilia, Rome, Academia Nacional de Bellas Arts, Buenos Aires, Argentina, Royal Philharmonic Soc., London, N.Y. Philharmonic Soc., Internat. Soc. for Contemporary Music, Royal Acad. Music, London. Dir. Koussevitsky Music Found. (v.p.), Edward MacDowell Assn., Walter W. Naumberg Found. Mem. Am. Acad. Arts and Scis., League Composers (chmn. bd. dirs.) A.S.C.A.P., Nat. Inst. Arts and Letters, Am. Acad. Arts and Letters (dir.), Royal Soc. Arts London, Academie de Beaux Arts of Academie Francaise. Works: (orchestra) Orchestral Variations, 1957; First Symphony, 1928; Music for the Theatre, 1925; A Dance Symphony, 1925; Concerto for Piano and Orchestra, 1926; Symphonic Ode, 1929, 55; Short Symphony, 1933; Statements, 1935; El Salon Mexico, 1936; Music for Radio, 1937; An Outdoor Overture, 1938; Quiet City, 1940; Lincoln Portrait, 1942; (ballet) Grohg, 1925; Hear Ye, Hear Ye, 1934; Billy the Kid, 1938; Rodeo, 1942; Appalachian Spring, 1944; (opera for high schs.) The Second Hurricane, 1937; (motion pictures) The City, 1939; Of Mice and Men, 1939; Our Town, 1940; North Star, 1943; The Red Pony, 1948; The Heiress, 1949; Something Wild, 1961; (chamber music) Two Pieces for String Quartet, 1928; Vitebsk, 1929; Piano Variations, 1930; Piano Sonata, 1941; Violin Sonata, 1943; Third Symphony, 1946; In the Beginning (mixed chorus), 1947; Clarinet Concerto, 1948; Music for a Great City, 1964. Author: What to Listen for in Music, 1939, revised edit., 1957; Our New Music, rev. edit., 41, 68, Twelve Poems of Emily Dickinson, 1950; Quartet for Piano and Strings, 1950; Music and Imagination, 1952; The Tender Land (opera), 1954; Piano Fantasy, 1957; Nonet for strings, 1960; Copland on Music, 1960; Connotations for Orch., 1962; Emblems for Band, 1965; Inscape for orch., 1967; Duo for flute and piano, 1971. Contbr. to Modern Music. Address: care Boosey & Hawkes Inc 30 W 57th St New York City NY 10019

COPLAND, DOUGLAS BERRY, economist, diplomat; b. Timaru, New Zealand, Feb. 24, 1894; s. Alexander and Annie (Loudon) C.; M.A., Canterbury Coll., 1915; D.Sc., U. New Zealand, 1925; Litt.D., U. Melbourne, 1933, Queensland U., 1935, Harvard, 1936; LL.D. McGill U., 1949, Clark U., Carleton U., Univ. of B.C., 1954, U. Adelaide, 1958, U. Tasmania, 1958, Australian National Univ., 1967; D.C.L., Bishops U., 1955; m. Ruth Jones, Jan. 28, 1919; children—Joyce (Mrs. D.J. Tier), Rosemarie (Mrs. Robert MacNeil). Lectr. history, econs., dir. tutorial classes U. Tasmania, 1917, prof., 1920-24; Sidney Myer prof. commerce, dean faculty commerce U. Melbourne, 1924-44, chmn. professorial bd., 1934-37, Truby Williams prof. economics, 1944-45; prof. emeritus, 1946; chmn. State Econ. Com. of Victoria, 1938-45, commonwealth prices commr., 1939-45; commr. Victorian State Savs. Bank, 1940-45; econ. cons. to Prime Minister, 1941-45; Australian minister to China, 1946-48; first vice chancellor Australian National University, 1948-53; high commr. for Australia, Can., 1953-56; first principal for Australian Administrative Staff College, 1956-60; bd. dirs. Ansett Transport Industries. Founder Com. for Econ. Devel. Australia; pres. Nat. Council for Balanced Devel.; Beatty lectr. McGill U., 1961, Australian del. UN, 1946, 53, 54, chmn. Econ. Com. UN, 1954-55, pres. ECOSOC, 1954-55; leader of Australian Trade Mission to Canada, 1960. Decorated Companion St. Michael and St. George, Knight Comdr. Brit. Empire; recipient coronation medals. Mem. Am. Philos. Soc., Australian and New Zealand Assn. Advancement Science (pres. 1952). Club: The Melbourne (Australia). Author: Australia and the World Crisis, 1934; The Road to High Employment, 1945; The Australian Economy, 1947; Towards Total War, 1942; Back to Earth in Economics, 1948; Inflations and Expansion, 1951; The Adventure of Growth, 1960; The Changing Structure of The Western Economy (Beatty Lectures McGill U.), 1963. Editor: Giblin: the Scholar and the Man, 1960. Co-editor several books on Australian economic policy. Contbr. articles profl. pubs. Home: Darjeeling Mt Macedon Victoria Australia Office: 57 O'Shannessy St North Melbourne Victoria Australia

COPLEY, JAMES STROHN, publisher; b. St. Johnsville, N.Y., Aug. 12, 1916; s. Ira Clifton and Edith (Strohn) C.; student Phillips Acad., Andover, Mass., 1930-35; B.A., Yale, 1939; m. Helen Kinney, Aug. 16, 1965; 1 son, David Casey. Dir., mem. exec. com. The Copley Press, Inc., Aurora, Ill., 1942—, 1st v.p., 1945-52, chmn. corp., 1952—, pres., 1961-65; dir. Union-Tribune Pub. Co., San Diego, 1947-58, asst. sec., 1947-50, pres., 1950-60, pub., 1950-61, 65—, asst. treas., 1950-54, treas., 1954-58, chmn. bd., 1958—; pub. San Diego Union, Evening Tribune, 1950—; dir. So. Cal. Asso. Newspapers, Los Angeles, 1946—, v.p., 1948-53, 1st v.p., treas., 1953-57, chmn. bd., 1957—, pres., 1964; dir. San Pedro Printing & Pub. Co., 1947—, sec., 1947-53, treas., 1953-58, chmn. bd., 1958—, pres., 1964; hon. chmn., dir. Copley Internat. Corp., 1965-67; chmn., dir. (KGU) Communications, Hawaii, Inc., 1966-67. Served with USNR, 1942-46. Recipient Maria Moors Cabot, prize, 1967. Republican. Episcopalian. Elk, Moose. Clubs: Ill. Country, Union League (Aurora); Sangamo (Springfield, Ill.); Metropolitan, Nat. Press (Washington); Metropolitan, Yale (N.Y.C.); Yale, Chicago (Chgo.); Cuyamaca, The San Diego, Kona Kai (San Diego); Greater Los Angeles Press, Los Angeles Country (Los Angeles); La Jolla Country, Beach and Tennis (La Jolla, Cal.); Oahu (Hawaii) Country; La Costa Country (Carlsbad, Cal.). Home: 7007 Country Club Dr LaJolla CA 92037 Office: 7776 Ivanhoe Av La Jolla CA 92037

COPLEY, JOHN GILBERT, water mgmt. engr.; b. Lowman, N.Y., Aug. 22, 1907; s. Hovey Everitt and Eleanor (Lowman) C.; B.S. in Engring., Princeton, 1929; m. Harriet Ball, Sept. 20, 1930; children—Eleanor (Mrs. Edward W. Pattison), John Gilbert, Martha. Asst. track supr. Pa. R.R., 1929-32; with Elmira (N.Y.) Water Bd., 1932—; sec.-treas., 1937-42, gen. mgr., 1942—; v.p. Chemung Co. Indsl. Devel. Corp., 1962-65, pres., 1966-68; dir. Chemung Canal Trust Co.; chmn. bd. Mechanics Savs. Bank, Elmira; cons. mgmt. seminars ICA, 1961, AID, Brazil, 1967, Bangkok Met. Waterworks Authority, Thailand, 1968—. Mem. Am. Water Works Assn., 1942—, trustee N.Y. sect., 1952, chmn. sect., 1956-59, nat. dir., mem. exec. com., chmn. pension and retirement com., also constn. com., 1956-62, chmn. Fuller award com., 1960-61, v.p., 1962-63, nat. pres., 1963-64. Chmn. Hoffman Creek Watershed Com., 1962-63. Pres. Chemung County Community Chest, 1954-56; chmn. Chemung County United Fund drive, 1960; chmn. Chemung River Basin Water Resources Comprehensive Planning Bd. Vice pres. Arnot Ogden Hosp. Recipient Fuller award Am. Water Works Assn., 1947. Registered profl. engr., N.Y., Pa. Mem. Nat., N.Y. State (pres. Steuben area chpt. 1956-57) socs. profl. engrs., Princeton Alumni Assn. Clubs: Rotary (pres. Elmira 1953-54), Internat. Torch. Home: 744 Garden Rd Elmira NY 14905 Office: 261 Water St Elmira NY 14901

COPLIN, HASKELL ROBERT, educator, psychologist; b. Broken Bow, Okla., Jan. 9, 1922; s. Fletcher Dale and Agnes (Stoker) C.; student Okla. Baptist U., 1941-42; A.B., U. Mich., then M.A., and Ph.D. in Clin. Psychology; M.A. (hon.), Amherst Coll., 1957; m. Ann Shinaberger, June 29, 1943; children—Marilyn Sue, Robert Bruce, Joan Ellen, Stephen Kent. Teaching fellow psychology U. Mich., 1948-49, psychol. U. Mich., 1948-49, psychol. intern, Bur. Psychol. Service, Inst. Human adjustment, 1949, staff psychologist, clin. service div., 1949, staff clin. psychologist, student psychiat. services, 1949-51, instr. psychology, 1950-51; asso. prof. psychology, student counselor Amherst Coll., 1951-57, prof. psychology, student counselor, 1957—; cons. Indsl. Relations Counselors Services, Inc., N.Y.C., 1966—, Morthampton (Mass.) State Hosp., 1962—. Chmn. Area Mental Health Planning Bd., 1966-. Served as pilot USAAF, 1942-45. Mem. Am., Conn. Valley, Mass. Eastern psychol. Assns., Am. Assn. U. Profs., Am. Coll. Health Assn., Sigma Xi. Editor: Group Methods in the Training of Professional Personnel, 1967. Home: Fort Hill S East St Amherst MA 01002

COPPEDGE, ROY F., Jr., distillers and chem. exec.; b. Memphis, Oct. 25, 1915; s. Roy F. and Norma (Jones) C.; B.A., Dartmouth, 1936; LL.B., Columbia, 1939; m. Nina R. Van Vechten, Dec. 5, 1941; children—Wendy R., Roy F. III. With Breed, Abbott & Morgan, lawyers, 1939-53, partner, 1952; v.p. Nat. Distillers & Chem. Corp., 1953-57, dir., 1954-62, exec. v.p. 1957-59, pres., 1958-62, gen. counsel, 1962, now v.p., gen. counsel; dir. Manhattan Fire & Marine Ins. Co. Dir. Greater N.Y. Fund. Served as lt. col. AUS, 1941-45. Home: Rosedale Rd Princeton NJ 08540 Office: Nat Distillers Bldg New York City NY 10016

COPPEL, HARRY CHARLES, educator, entomologist; b. Galt, Ont., Can., Jan. 2, 1918; s. Archibald Aaron and Bertha (Siegal) C.; came to U.S., 1957, naturalized, 1964; B.S.A., Ont. Agrl. Coll., 1943; M.S., U. Wis., 1946; Ph.D., N.Y. State Coll. Forestry, Syracuse U., 1949; m. Joyce Lucille Vineberg, Sept. 3, 1950; children—David Brian, Ann Gail. Research scientist, div. entomology Can. Dept. Agr., Belleville, Ont., 1943-57; faculty U. Wis., 1957—, prof. entomology, 1965—. Mem. Entomol. Soc. Am. (editorial bd. 1961-66, gov. bd. 1965-67), entomol. socs. Can., Ont. (dir. 1952), Wis. Entomol. Soc., Wis. Phenological Soc., Wis. Acad. Arts, Sci. and Letters, Internat. Orgn. for Biol. Control, Wis. Entomol. Soc., Sigma Xi, Phi Sigma, Alpha Xi Sigma. Author: (with McLeod and McGugan) A Review of the Biological Control Attempts Against Insects and Weeds in Canada, 1962. Home: 4313 Bagley Pkwy Madison WI 53705

COPPENBARGER, HOWARD LEE, newspaper editor; b. Nashville, Dec. 8, 1913; s. William Lewis and Lulu (Kinnear) C.; grad. Memphis Tech. High, 1930; m. Ann Yates Thompson, May 25, 1940; children—Ann Waters, Elizabeth Calvert, Steven Lee. State editor Jackson (Miss.) Clarion-Ledger, 1932-36; copy editor Memphis Comml. Appeal, 1936-39; with Washington Daily News, 1939—, editorial page editor, 1967—; asso. professorial lectr. journalism George Washington U., Washington, 1955—. Presbyn. (deacon 1965-68). Home: 3727 Northampton St NW Washington DC 20015 Office: 1013 13th St NW Washington DC 20005

COPPER, MUNROE WALKER, Jr., architect; b. Phila., 1897; student Phila. Sch. Indsl. Art, 1918, U. Pa., 1916-20. Architect Copper, Wade Cooper & Raynes; architect Village of Gates Mills, 1945-70, Aurora, O., 1954-70, 1954-70; prin. works include Christ Episcopal Ch., Shaker Heights, O., internat. hdqrs. office bldgs. A.T.O., Inc., Willoughby, O., Bonnie Bell Cosmetic Offices and Labs, Lakewood O., Lakeridge Acad., North Ridgeville, O., St. Peters Episcopal Ch., Ashtabula, O., St. James Episcopal Ch., Boardman, O., Westlake (O.) Methodist Ch., Calvary Baptist Ch., Youngstown, O., Oglebay Mus., Wheeling, W.Va., Storer Broadcasting stas. in Cleve., Toledo and Detroit, town houses and apt. devels. Pennbury Village, Sharon, Pa., Northbury, Warren, O., Glenwood and Glendale, Youngstown, Woodlawn Village, Canton, O., Bentbrook Colony, North Canton, O., Gates Mills Community Bldg., Gates Mills; restoration of Old Keswick (a Thomas Jefferson house), Charlottsville, Va.; also residences. Served with USN, 1918-19, to lt. comdr. USNR, 1941-45. Fellow A.I.A.; mem. Soc. Archtl. Historians. Clubs: Youngstown (O.) Country; Hermit (Cleve). Home: River Rd Gates Mills OH 44040 Office: 10528 Wilbur Av Cleveland OH 44106

COPPINGER, S.J., business exec. Exec. v.p. Marshall Wells, Ltd., Winnipeg, Man., Can. Office: 1395 Ellice Av Winnipeg Manitoba Canada*

COPPLE, WILLIAM PERRY, judge; b. Holtville, Cal. Oct. 3, 1916; s. Perry and Euphie (Williams) Sonoco Products Co., 1930—, v.p., 1934-61, pres., 1961—; 14, 1936; children—Virginia (Mrs. Richard Schilke), Leonard W., Steven D. Various positions with U.S. Govt., also pvt. employers, 1936-48; admitted to Ariz. bar, 1952; practice in Yuma, Ariz., 1952-65; U.S. dist. atty. Dist. Ariz., Phoenix, 1965-66; judge U.S. Dist. Ct. Dist. Ariz., 1966—. Commnr., Ariz. Hwy. Commn., 1955-58; mem. Gov. Ariz. Com Fourteen for Colo. River, 1963-65. Chmn. Yuma County Democratic Central Com., 1953-54, 59-60. Mem. Am. Bar Assn., Am. Judicature Soc. Home: 5242 N 20th St Phoenix AZ Office: Federal Bldg Phoenix AZ 85012

COPPOC, WILLIAM JOSEPH, chemist; b. Cumberland, Ia., July 14, 1913; s. James Sunderland and Winifred (Fowler) C.; B.S., Ottawa U., 1935, D.Sc., 1955; M.A., Rice Inst., 1937, Ph.D. in Phys. and Colloid Chemistry, 1939; m. Eleanor Louise Lister, July 2, 1939; children—Teresa Anne, William Edmund. With Texaco, Inc., Beacon, N.Y., 1939—, successively chemist grease research, asst. to asst. chief chemist, Port Arthur, Tex., acting asst. supr. grease research, asst. dir. research, Beacon, N.Y., asso. dir. research, N.Y.C., 1939-53, dir. research, 1953-54, mgr. research, N.Y.C., also Beacon, 1954-57, mgr. research and devel., Beacon, 1957-60, mgr. sci. planning and information, 1960-65, gen. mgr. research and tech. dept., 1954-68, v.p. charge research and tech. dept., 1968—. Past chmn. bd. trustees Gordon Research Confs.; pres. United Fund; trustee Ottawa U. Fellow Am. Inst. Chemists; mem. Am. Chem. Soc. (past chmn. div. petroleum chemistry), Franklin Inst., Soc. Automotive Engrs., Am. Petroleum Inst., A.A.A.S., Sci. Research Soc. Am. (bd. govs., past chmn.) Assn. Research Dirs., N.Y. Acad. Scis., Dirs. of Indsl. Research, Soc. Chem. Industry (mem. exec. com. Am. sect.), Sigma Xi, Phi Lambda Upsilon. Baptist. Home: 14 Kingwood Park Poughkeepsie NY 12601 Office: PO Box 509 Beacon NY 12508

COPPOCK, JOSEPH DAVID, economist; b. Peru, Ind., Feb. 10, 1909; s. Donald Merton and Madge (Oates) C.; student Culver Mil. Acad., 1926-29; A.B., Swarthmore Coll., 1933; A.M., Columbia, 1934, Ph.D., 1940; m. Esther Elizabeth McKenzie, Aug. 1, 1940; children—David McKenzie, Jane Ann, Donald Leslie, Bruce Henry. Teacher econ., Hendrix Coll., Conway, Ark., 1934-37, Swarthmore Coll., Pa., 1937- 39, U. Cal. at Berkeley, 1939-40, Haverford Coll., Haverford, Pa., 1941. U. Ore., 1941; researcher Nat. Bur. Econ. Research, N.Y.C., 1938-39; economist U.S. Dept. Agr., 1941; spl. asst. to vice chmn. War Prodn. Bd., 1942; price exec. Chem. and Drugs br. OPA, 1943; econ. adviser, internat. trade policy, Dept. of State, 1945-53; mem. U.S. delegations to UN-ECOSOC, N.Y., Geneva, Santiago, 1946-52; civilian faculty Nat. War Coll., 1951-53; prof. econs. Earlham Coll., 1953-65, Pa. State U., 1965—; nat. research prof. Brookings Inst., 1959-60; vis. prof. econs. Ind. U., 1957-58, U. Wis., summer 1959, U. Mich., summer 1961, Am. U., Beirut, 1963-65; dir. fgn. econ. adv. staff Dept. of State, 1961-62; mem. Rockefeller Found. field staff, Bangkok, Thailand, 1969-71. Served in USN, assigned office Strategic Services, 1944-45. Ford Found. research grantee, 1957-58, 1963-64. Mem. Am. Finance Assn., Am., Midwest (pres. 1962-63) econs. assns. Phi Beta Kappa, Phi Kappa Psi. Independent. Mem. Soc. of Friends. Author: Government Agencies of Consumer Installment Credit, 1940; The Food Stamp Plan, 1947; Economics of the Business Firm, 1959, International Economic Instability, 1962; Foreign Trade of the Middle East, 1966. Home: 634 W Fairmount Av State College PA 16801 Office: Dept Econs Pa State U University Park PA 16802

COPPOCK, WILLIAM HOMER, educator; b. Lincoln, Neb., June 8, 1911; s. Homer and Carrier (Rowan) C.; B.S., Monmouth (Ill.) Coll., 1933; M.S., U. Ia. 1935, Ph.D., 1939; m. Florence Lundine, June 15, 1937; childrenTed, Kathleen (Mrs. Roland Oberg), Yvonne, Bill. Tchr. chemistry Holdrege (Neb.) High Sch., 1935- 37, Eastern Ill. State Coll., 1939-41, U. Notre Dame, 1943, Winona State Coll., 1945-46; asst. chief chemist Sangamon Ordnance Plant, 1941-42; faculty Drake U., Des Moines, 1946—, prof. chemistry head dept., 1949—. Mem. Am. Chem. Soc., Sigma Xi. Presbyn. Home: 3930 Douglas St Des Moines IA 50310

COPPS, DONALD WILLIAM, food industry co. exec.; b. Stevens Point, Wis., May 10, 1914; s. Clinton William and Jeanette (Wilson) C.; Ph.B., Carroll Coll., 1937; m. Mary Jane Krembs, Oct. 12, 1935; children—Sally (Mrs. Richard Jensen), Michael, Mary Jane, Donald, Elizabeth. Pres. Copps Corp., Stevens Point, Wis., 1946—, also Copps Distbg. Co., Copps Realty Corp., D-C Corp., Saving Stamp Corp. Mem. adv. bd. Viterbo Coll., 1970—; chmn. Citizens Youth Com., 1952-56; co-chmn. Marquette U. Civic Com., 1959-63; pres. Youth Baseball Assn., 1951-53; fund-raising drive chmn. Stevens Point Municipal Swimming Pool, 1956—. Bd. dirs. Stevens Point Area YMCA. Mem. Wis. Food and Tobacco Inst. (treas., dir. 1961-63), Super Market Inst. (dir. at large 1963-65), Ind. Grocers Alliance (dir. 1968—), President's Assn. Inc., Stevens Point C. of C. (pres. 1943), K. of C., Notre Dame of the Lake Assos. Roman Catholic. Clubs: Elks, Serra (past pres.) Kiwanis (Stevens Point). Home: 1124 Soo Marie Av Stevens Point WI 54481 Office: 2828 Wayne St Stevens Point WI 54481

COQUILLARD, GEORGE CLARK, finance co. exec.; b. South Bend, Ind., Sept. 23, 1919; s. Alexis and Mary (Clarke) C.; A.B., Harvard, 1941, M.B.A., 1943; m. Mary Theresa Voll, Jan. 21, 1950. With First Bank & Trust Co. South Bend, 1947-57, dir., 1965- -; with Assos. Investment Co., South Bend, 1957—, v.p. finance, 1965-67, v.p., sec., 1967—; dir. Sibley Machine & Foundry Corp., South Bend. Pres., dir. South Bend Art Assn., 1961—, trustee Hering House, South Bend, 1966—; treas., dir. Stanley Clark Sch., South Bend, 1963—. Served to lt. (s.g.) USNR, World War II. Club: South Bend Country. Office: 1700 Mishawaka Av South Bend IN 46624

COQUILLETTE, ROBERT MCTAVISH, chem. co. exec.; b. Ft. Wayne, Ind., Oct. 31, 1918; s. Leon and Ruby (McTavish) C.; B.S., Harvard, 1939; m. Dagmar Alvilda Bistrup, May 4, 1940; children—Daniel Robert, William Hollis. Mem. mfg. dept. Proctor and Gamble Co., 1939-44; mfg. supt. Dewey and Almy Chem. Co. div. W.R. Grace Co., 1946-50, mgr. rubber spltys. div., 1950-53, asst. to pres., 1953-55, gen. mgr. overseas chem. div., 1955-57, v.p., 1957—; pres. Ohio Rubber Co. div., also dir. Eagle-Picher Co., 1962-65, v.p. corp. adminstrn. group W.R. Grace & Co., 1965-67, corp. v.p. chem. group operations and adminstrn., 1967—. Chmn. Lexington (Mass.) Community Fund, 1954; mem. Library Bldg. Com., 1955-56; active Cub Scouts, Boy Scouts Am. Served to lt. (j.g.) USNR, 1944-46. Mem. Lexington Hist. Soc. Club: Harvard (N.Y.C.). Office: WR Grace & Co 7 Hanover Sq New York City NY 10005

CORBALLY, JOHN EDWARD, Jr., univ. pres.; b. South Bend, Wash., Oct. 14, 1924; s. John Edward and Grace (Williams) C.; B.S., U. Wash., 1947, M.A., 1950; Ph.D., U. Cal. at Berkeley, 1955; LL.D., U. Md., 1971; m. Marguerite B. Walker, Mar. 12, 1946; children—Jan Elizabeth, David William. Tchr. Clover Park High Sch., Tacoma, 1947-50; prin. Twin City High Sch., Stanwood, Wash., 1950-53; asst. prof. edn., asso. prof. Ohio State U., Columbus, 1955-60, prof., 1960-69, dir. personnel budget and exec. asst. to pres., 1960-64, v.p. adminstrn., 1964-66, provost, v.p. acad. affairs, 1966-69; chancellor, pres. Syracuse (N.Y.) U., 1969-71; pres. U. Ill., Urbana, 1971—. Dir. Marine Midland Trust Co. Central N.Y. Pres., dir. Mich.-Ohio Regional Ednl. Lab., 1966-68; mem. com. on acad. internships Am. Concil on Edn. Trustee Coll. Entrance Exam. Bd. Served to lt. (j.g.) USNR, 1943-46. Mem. Phi Beta Kappa; Phi Kappa Sigma Phi Delta Kappa. Clubs: Mid-Am. (Chgo.); University (N.Y.C.). Author: Introduction to Educational Adminstration, 4th edit., 1971; Educational Administration: The Secondary School, 2d edit., 1965; School Finance, 1962. Home: 711 W Florida Av Urbana IL 61801

CORBASCIO, ALDO NICOLA, physician, med. scientist; b. Castellana, Bari, Italy, Mar. 21, 1928; s. Vincenzo and Caterina (Zinza) C.; M.D., U. Bari, 1953; D.Sc. in Pharmacology, U. Pa., 1958; m. Anna Mallardi, Aug. 25, 1955 (div. 1963); 1 dau., Catherine; m. 2d, Elise Margareta Holgersson, Sept. 1965; children—Malcolm, Sebastian. Intern U. Bari Med. Clinic, 1952-53; resident in medicine U. Pa. Hosp., Phila., 1954-56; fellow therapeutic research U. Pa. Hosp., Phila., 1954-56; instr. pharmacology U. Pa. Med. Sch.,

1956-59; asst. research pharmacologist U. Cal. Med. Center, San Francisco, 1959-61, asso. research pharmacologist, 1961-63; asso. prof. pharmacology Coll. Phys. and Surg., U. Pacific, San Francisco, 1968-71, prof., chmn. dept. pharmacology Sch. Dentistry, San Francisco, 1963—; cons. U.S. Army Letterman Gen. Hosp.; sci. dir. Berkeley (Cal.) Biomed. Research, Inc. Mem. Ballistocardiographic Research Soc., Western Pharmacological Soc., Am. Soc. Pharmacology and Exptl. Therapeutics, A.A.A.S. Home: 6451 Florio St Oakland CA 94618 Office: U of Pacific Sch Dentistry 2155 Webster St San Francisco CA 94115

CORBATO, FERNANDO JOSE, educator; b. Oakland, Cal., July 1, 1926; s. Hermenegildo and Charlotte (Jensen) C.; student U. Cal. at Los Angeles, 1943-44; B.S. in Physics, Cal. Inst. Tech., 1950; Ph.D., Mass. Inst. Tech., 1956; m. Isabel Blandford, Nov. 24, 1962; children—Carolyn Suzanne, Nancy Patricia. With Computation Center, Mass. Inst. Tech., 1956-66, dep. dir., 1963-66; head computer systems research group of project MAC, Mass. Inst. Tech., 1963- -; mem. faculty Mass. Inst. Tech., 1962—, prof. elec. engring., 1965—. Mem. computer sci. and engring. bd. Nat. Acad. Sci., 1971—. Served with USNR, 1944-46. Mem. Assn. Computing Machinery (council 1964- 66), Am. Phys. Soc., I.E.E.E. (W.W. McDowell award 1966), A.A.A.S., Sierra Club, Sigma Xi. Co-author: The Compatible Time Sharing System, 1963; Advanced Computer Programming, 1963. Home: 88 Temple St West Newton MA 02165 Office: 545 Technology Sq Cambridge MA 02139

CORBEN, HERBERT CHARLES, univ. adminstr., physicist; b. Portland, Dorset, Eng., Apr. 18, 1914; s. Harold Frederick and Margaret (Hart) C.; B.A., U. Melbourne, 1933, B.Sc., 1934, M.A., 1936, M.Sc., 1936; Ph.D., Cambridge U., 1939; m. Beverly Balkum, Oct. 25, 1957; children—Deirdre (Mrs. John W. DeGroote), Sharon (Mrs. Allen Golden), Gregory. Came to U.S., 1946, naturalized, 1950. Lectr. math. and physics New England U. Coll., Armidale, Australia, 1941; lectr. math., physics U. Melbourne, Australia, 1942-46; acting dean Trinity Coll., Melbourne, 1942-46; asso. prof. Carnegie Inst. Tech., 1946-51, prof., 1951-56; part-time lectr. physics U. Pitts., 1947; Fulbright vis. prof. U. Genoa, Milan, and Bologna, 1951-53; part-time lectr. physics U. So. Cal., 1957-58; asso. dir. Research Lab. Ramo-Wooldrige Corp. and Space Tech. Labs, Inc., Los Angeles, 1956-58, dir. Quantum Physics Lab., 1961-68, chief scientist Phys. Research Center, 1966-68; distinguished vis. prof. physics Queens Coll., 1968; acting dean faculties Cleve. State U., 1968-69, dean faculties, 1969-70, v.p. acad. affairs, 1970—, dean Coll. Grad. Studies, prof. physics, 1968—. Commonwealth Fund fellow Us. Cal. also Princeton, 1939-41. Mem. Am. Phys. Soc., Am. Soc. Physics Tchrs., Am. Nuclear Soc., Rho Sigma Rho, Sigma Zeta, Pi Mu Epsilon. Author: Classical and Quantum Theories of Spinning Particles, 1968; Classical Mechanics, 1950, 2d edit., 1960, internat. edit., 1964; (with Philip M. Stehle) International Dictionary of Physics and Electronics, 1956. Home: 2925 Bronxton Rd Shaker Heights OH 44120 Office: Fenn Tower 907 Euclid and 24th St Cleveland OH 44115

CORBETT, ALICE, mem. Democratic Nat. Com.; b. Seattle, 1925; d. Marshall Richard and Coralyn Estelle (Bauer) Reckard; student Reed Coll.; B.S., U. Ore., 1948; postgrad. Marylhurst Coll., 1949; m. J.J. Corbett, Jan. 17, 1948. Educator, 1948-52; mem. Ore. Senate, 1959—, mem. interim com. on edn., interim com. on fed. affairs, 1965-67; pres. Corbett Investments. Nat. committeewoman Young Democrats of Ore., 1954-58; pres. Young Dems. of Multnomah County, 1954-55; vice chmn. Multnomah County Dem. Com., 1957-58; mem. Dem. Nat. Com. for Ore., 1960—. Named One of Ten Outstanding Women Grads., U. Ore. Mem. Am. Assn. U. Women. Portland Women's Forum, Urban League, Willamette Soc. (v.p. 1966—). Clubs: Jane Jefferson (pres.); Multonomah Athletic; Wome's Inv. (v.p. 1969—). Home: 2222 NE Schuyler St Portland OR 97230 also 3562 SE Harrison Salem OR 97303 Office: State Capital Salem OR 97308

CORBETT, CLETUS JOHN, shoe co. exec.; b. Columbus, O., June 18, 1907; s. Patrick J. and Mary (Byrne) C.; student Ohio State U., 1924-29; LL.B., Franklin U., 1941; J.D., Capitul U., 1966; m. Margaret P. Burns, Aug. 26, 1946. Accountant, Proctor-Gamble Co., Jackson, Miss., Memphis, 1929-33; with SCOA Industries, Inc., Columbus, 1934—, counsel, v.p., 1957-66, sec., 1966- -, dir.; admitted to Ohio bar, 1941; practiced in Columbus; dir. Canmart Shoe Co., Shoe Corp. Can. (both Toronto). Served with USAAF, 1942-45. Decorated Air medal with nine oak leaf clusters. Mem. Am., Ohio, Columbus bar assns., Am. Judicature Soc., Phi Kappa, Iota Lambda Pi. Clubs: Columbus Athletic, Scioto Country, University. Home: 4223 Clairmont Rd Columbus OH 43220 Office: 35 N 4th St Columbus OH 43215

CORBETT, ELIZABETH, author; b. Aurora, Ill., Sept. 30, 1887; d. Richard W. and Isabelle Jean (Adkins) Corbett; A.B., U. Wis., 1910. Mem. Phi Beta Kappa, Alpha Gamma Delta. Author: many books since 1916, latest of which are Immortal Helen, 1948; Eve and Christopher, 1949; The Duke's Daughter, 1950; Portrait of Isabelle, 1951; The Richer Harvest, 1952; In Miss Armstrong's Room, 1953; Our Mrs. Meigs, 1954; Family Portrait, 1955; The Head of Apollo, 1956; Professor Preston at Home, 1957; The President's Wife, 1958; Hamilton Terrace, 1960; The Wainwright Inheritance, 1960; Hidden Island, 1961; The Paige Girls, 1962; The Distant Princess, 1963; The Heart of the Village, 1963; Lisa Kennerley's Husband, 1964; Anniversary, 1964; The Continuing City, 1965; The Crossroads, 1965; The Old Callahan Place, 1966; Harry Martin's Wife, 1967; Ladies Day, 1968; The Three Lives of Sharon Spence, 1969; Hotel Belvedere, 1970; Sunday at Six, 1971. Home: 20 Commerce St New York City NY 10014 ☆

CORBETT, FRANK JOSEPH, advt. exec.; b. N.Y.C., July 5, 1917; s. Daniel and Frances (Manson) C.; Ph.G., Columbia, 1938; postgrad. U. Cal. at Los Angeles, 1947, N.Y. U., 1945-46; m. Dolores Pierce, May 23, 1959; children—Kenneth, Beverly. Dist. sales mgr., mgr. market research dept. William R. Warner Co., N.Y.C., 1944-46; dir. product devel. and market research, advt. mgr., also asst. to dir. sales Harrower Lab., Inc., Glendale, Cal. and Jersey City, 1946-51; account exec. Jordan-Sieber Advt. Agy., Chgo., 1951-55; partner, v.p. Jordan, Sieber & Corbett, advt., 1955-60; cons. pharm. field, 1960-61; founder, 1961, since pres. Frank J. Corbett, Inc., advt. Mem. Midwest Pharm. Advt. Club, Am. Pharm. Assn., Am. Med. Writers Assn. Home: 1320 N State Pkwy Chicago IL 60610 Office: 430 N Michigan Av Chicago IL 60611

CORBETT, J. RALPH, former mfg. co. exec.; b. N.Y.C., Dec. 5, 1900; s. Burnett Lewis and Pearl Corbett; LL.B., N.Y. Law Sch., 1923; D.H.L., U. Cin., 1963; m. Patricia Barry, July 23, 1930; children—Gail Barry, Thomas R. Engaged in radio broadcasting, then owner advt. agy., N.Y.C.; founder pub. co.; former chmn. bd. Nutone, Inc., Cin. Pres. Cin. Musical Festival Assn., 1971. Former chmn. bd. Cin. Symphony Orch., now trustee; mem. bd. Cin. Summer Opera Assn., Cin. Salvation Army, Conservatory of Music of U. Cin. Established Corbett Lecture Series at U. Cin. Pres. Corbett Found.; chmn. bd. Music Hall Assn. Cin. Clubs: Bohemian (N.Y.C.); Lake Shore (Chgo.); Queen City (Cin.). Author: Man Who Sells; In Spite of All. Office: 1501 Madison Rd Cincinnati OH 45206

CORBETT, JACK CROUCH, corp. exec.; b. Memphis, July 3, 1914; s. Patrick Henry and Dorothy (Crouch) C.; student Centro Estudios Historicos, 1933-34, U. Munich, 1934; B.S., Georgetown U., 1937; M.B.A., Harvard, 1939; m. Priscilla Ann Headington, Nov. 24, 1948; children—Patricia, Esme, Jacqueline Headington. With research dept. Fed. Res. Bank of New York, 1939-41; asst. econ. advisor Dept. State, 1941-43; exec. asst. War Shipping Admin., 1943-44; cons. Internat. Bank for Reconstrn. & Devel., 1946-48; 1962—. 1948-50; adv. Central Bank of Ecuador, 1940 dep. dir. Office Finance and Devel. Policy, State Dept. 1950-52, dir., 1952-57; v.p. Checchi & Co., 1957—; mem. Presdl. Mission to Bolivia, 1961. Bd. dirs. St. Stephan's Sch., Rome. Served as lt. jr. grade, U.S.N., 1944-46. Decorated by Italian Govt., 1960. Mem. Delta Phi Epsilon. Club: Washington Golf and Country; Circolo Del Golf Di Roma, Foreign Ministry, Olgiata Country, American (pres. 1960 Rome, Italy); Metropolitan (Washington). Home: 5721 Bent Branch Rd Washington DC 20016 Office: 815 Connecticut Av NW Washington DC 20006

CORBETT, JAMES DAVIDSON, investment broker; b. N.Y.C., Aug. 25, 1910; s. Theodore and Achsah (Davidson) C.; student Dartmouth, 1928-31; B.S., N.Y. U., 1942; m. Amy Seinknecht, Oct. 19, 1935; children—Suzanne (Mrs. Peter T. Cooper), Martha (Mrs. John Delong Buecking), Jane (Mrs. David G. Floyd). Security analyst Moody's Investors Service, 1934-41, Central Hanover Bank, 1941-43, Merrill, Lynch, Pierce, Fenner & Smith, 1943—, partner, 1952-58, v.p., 1959-66, sr. v.p., dir., 1966—. Mem. Delta Tau Delta. Clubs: Dartmouth; Hempstead Harbour; Wheatley Hills, Union League. Home: 40 Meritoria Dr East Williston NY 11596 Office: 70 Pine St New York City NY 10005

CORBETT, JAMES WILLIAM, physicist, educator; b. N.Y.C., Aug. 25, 1928; s. Amos Bryant and Julia (Holmes) C.; B.S., U. Mo., 1951, M.A., 1952; Ph.D., Yale, 1955; m. Joyce Winch Martin, June 21, 1953; children—Lee Alexander, Ross Gordon. Research asso. chemistry Yale, 1955; physicist Gen. Elec. Research and Development Center, 1955-68; adjunct prof. Rensselaer Poly. Inst., 1964-68; prof. physics State U. N.Y. at Albany, 1968—, chmn. dept., 1969—. Organizer Internat. Conf. Radiation Effects in Semiconductors, 1970, Internat. Conf. Radiation-Induced Voids in Metals, 1971. Committeeman Niskayuna (N.Y.) Dem. Party, 1960-63. Served to 2d lt. Signal Corps, AUS, 1946-48. O.M. Stewart fellow, 1951-52; Charles Coffin fellow, 1954-55. Fellow Am. Phys. soc.; mem. Am. Assn. Physics Tchrs., I.E.E.E., Schenectady Weavers Guild (pres. 1960-62), Am. Cryptogram Assn., Phi Beta Kappa, Sigma Xi, Pi Mu Epsilon, Sigma Pi Sigma, Sigma Phi Epsilon. Christian Scientist. Clubs: Adirondak Mountain, Mohawk Valley Hiking (Schenectady). Author: Electron Radiation Damage in Semiconductors and Metals, 1966; Radiation Effects in Semiconductors, 1971. Contbr. articles sci. jours. Home: 1047 Hickory Rd Schenectady NY 12309 Office: Physics Dept State Univ New York Albany NY 12203

CORBETT, JOHN DUDLEY, educator; b. Yakima, Wash., Mar. 23, 1926; s. Alexander Hazen and Elizabeth (Dudley) C.; B.S. cum laude, U. Wash., 1948, Ph.D. (duPont research fellow), 1952; m. Irene Lienkaemper, Aug. 7, 1948; children—John Scott, Julia Barton, James Dudley. Asst. prof., asso. chemist Ia. State U. dept. chemistry and Ames Lab. U.S. AEC, 1952-58, asso. prof., chemist, 1958-63, prof., sr. chemist, 1963—, chmn., div. chief, 1968—; chmn. molton salts Gordon Research Confs., 1963, mem. council, 1964-67; cons. E.I. duPont de Nemours & Co., 1956-63, Oak Ridge Nat. Lab., 1969—. Served with USNR, 1944-46. Mem. Am. Chem. Soc. (councilor, past chmn. Ames sect.), Am. Assn. U. Profs., Sigma Xi, Phi Lambda Upsilon, Phi Kappa Phi, Pi Mu Epsilon, Delta Tau Delta. Episcopalian. Contbr. articles profl. jours. Home: Route 4 Ames IA 50010

CORBETT, ROGER BAILEY, ret. univ. pres.; b. Morgantown, W.Va., Feb. 11, 1900; s. Lee Cleveland and Evelyn N. (Northrup) C.; B.S., Cornell U., 1922, M.S., 1923, Ph.D., 1925; Litt.D. (hon.), Coll. Artesia (N.M.); hon. degrees Universidad de Asuncion (Paraguay), 1965, Instituto Mexicano de Cultura, 1969; m. Faith L. Rogers, Nov. 25, 1927 (dec. 1939); children—Roger Lee, Ann Frances; m. 2d, Elizabeth Burn Rutter, July 22, 1963. Instr. Cornell U., 1924-25; economist R.I. State Coll., 1925-33; sr. economist U.S. Dept. Agr., 1933-35; exec. sec. New Eng. Research Council, 1935-36; dean agr. U. Conn., 1937-40; dir. Agrl. Expt. Sta., U. Md., 1940- 43; exec. sec.-treas. Am. Farm Bur. Fedn., 1943-47; asso. dean and dir. Coll. Agr., U. Md., 1947-49; agrl. counsel Nat. Assn. Food Chains, 1949-55; pres. N.M. State U., 1955-70. Past mem. El Paso br. Fed. Res. Bd.; dir. Shop Rite, Inc. Mem. nat. council Boy Scouts Am. Past pres. Am. Country Life Assn., Northeastern Dairy Conf.; past pres. Farm Film Found. Served as acting sgt. World War I. Mem. N.E.A., Phi Kappa Phi, Alpha Zeta, Kappa Delta Rho, Epsilon Sigma Phi, AGFU, Scabbard and Blade (hon.). Episcopalian. Rotarian (past pres.). Author numerous expt. sta. and extension service bulls., also articles. Home: 2900 Karen Dr Las Cruces NM 88001

CORBETT, WILLIAM CECIL, ret. telephone co. exec.; b. Ft. William, Ont., Can., July 7, 1905; s. Robert and Mary (Carson) C., B.Com., U. Toronto, 1928; m. Sara M. Hughes, Aug. 2, 1950; children—Judith Grace, Robert Hughes. With Bell Telephone Co. of Can., 1930-39, 44-70, treas., 1961-70; dir. Extremultus Transmissions, Ltd., Montreal, Can. Paying officer Brit. Purchasing Com., N.Y.C., 1939- 42; dir. establishments Brit. Ministry of Supply mission, Washington, 1942-44. Dir. met. bd. YMCA. Named hon. treas. George Williams U. Fellow Chartered Inst. Secs. Club: University. Home: Baie d'Urfe Quebec Canada

CORBETT, WILLIAM JOHN, airline exec.; b. N.Y.C., Nov. 2, 1920; s. William H. and Ida M. (Klein) C.; A.B., Cornell U., 1942; grad. Middle Mgmt. Program, Harvard, 1956; m. Lois Amy, Mar. 20, 1949; children—Karen, Michael, Susan, Peter, Amy. With Am. Airlines, Inc., N.Y.C., 1946—, asst. treas., 1955-59. asst. controller, 1959-61, treas., 1961-62, v.p. budgets, costs and standards, 1962-68, v.p. financial relations, 1968-69, v.p. facilities financing, 1970—. Trustee bd. appeals Village of Pelham Manor (N.Y.), 1971—. Clubs: Cornell (treas. 1971—) (N.Y.C.); Pelham (N.Y.) Country. Home: 461 Siwanoy Pl Pelham Manor NY 10803 Office: 633 3d Av New York City NY 10017

CORBETTA, ROGER HENRY, constrn. co. exec.; b. N.Y.C., June 9, 1896; s. Joseph and Maria (Vacca) C.; m. Thelma Weiss, Nov. 25, 1961; 1 dau., Marian (Mrs. Francis A. Vitolo). Founder, Corbetta Constrn. Co., Inc., N.Y.C., 1922, chmn. bd., 1962—; founder Corbetta Equipment Corp., N.Y.C., 1935, chmn. bd., 1962- -; pres. Roger H. Corbetta Corp., 1966—; dir. Flexicore Corp. Chmn. exec. com. Reinforced Concrete Research Council, 1962-65; pres. Concrete Industry Bd. N.Y., 1947-53, bd. dirs., 1947—; mem. N.Y. Bldg. Trades Employers Assn., 1927—, bd. govs., 1947-53, pres., 1968-71; pres. Am. Concrete Inst., 1962-63; mem. N.Y. Cement League, 1927—, pres., 1947-51; mem. N.Y. Bldg. Congress, 1922—. Chmn. zoning bd. appeals, Washington, N.Y., 1952—. Trustee Dutchess Community Coll., Poughkeepsie, N.Y., St. Francis Hosp., Poughkeepsie; bd. dirs. Astor Home for Children, Rhinebeck, N.Y., Dutchess County Agrl. Soc.; 1st v.p. N.Y. State Guernsey Breeders Co-op., Inc. Served with U.S. Army, World War I. Mem. Nat. Acad. Scis., Am. Soc. Concrete Constructors (pres. 1965-68, chmn. 1968—), Eastern Guernsey Breeders Assn. (pres. 1968), The Moles (recipient award 1970). Home: Verbank Rd Millbrook NY 12545 Office: 220 E 42d St New York City NY 10017

CORBIN, ALBERT CHARLES, shipbuilding co. exec.; b. Barbados, W.I., Apr. 11, 1913; s. Charles Alexander and Miriam Grace (King) C.; came to U.S., 1915, naturalized, 1924; B.S., Wagner Coll., S.I., 1935; postgrad. N.Y. U. Grad. Sch. Bus. Adminstrn., 1935-37; m. Helen Rowe, Jan. 21, 1939. With bur. accounts and deposits Treasury Dept., 1935-41; comptroller Todd-Bath Iron Shipbldg. Corp., New Eng. Shipbldg. Corp., 1942-46; with Todd Shipyards Corp., 1946—, treas., 1966-68, v.p. contracts and procurement, 1968-69 v.p. finance, treas., dir., 1970—. Chmn. bd. Wagner Coll., 1958-60, chmn. devel. council, 1960-63, chmn. capital fund campaign, 1963-66. Mem. Am. Soc. Naval Architects and Marine Engrs., Nat. Assn. Accountants. Clubs: Downtown Athletic (N.Y.C.); Richmond Country Yacht. Home: 1101 Todt Hill Rd Staten Island NY 10304 Office: 1 Broadway New York City NY 10004

CORBIN, CHARLES F., mining co. exec.; b. N.J., Apr. 17, 1920; s. Charles Alexander and Grace Miriam (King) C.; B.B.A., U. Miami (Fla.), 1947; C.P.A., U. State N.Y., 1952; m. Alwilda Leathe Goode, Dec. 25, 1946; 1 son, Charles Frank. Staff accountant Frank E. Dixon & Co., C.P.A.'s, N.Y.C., 1947-50; partner Hackeling, Oberkirch, Corbin & Co., C.P.A.'s, N.Y.C., 1950-54; comptroller Lummus Co., engrs. and contractors, N.Y.C., 1954-61; v.p., sec., treas. Homestake Mining Co., San Francisco, 1961—. Served to capt. AUS, 1942-46; ETO. Mem. Am. Inst. C.P.A.'s, Am. Mining Congress. Home: 872 Crestview Dr Millbrae CA 94030 Office: 650 California St San Francisco CA 94108

CORBIN, EDWIN HARTWELL, former banker; b. Oak Park, Ill., Sept. 26, 1904; s. William S. and Emma (Haecock) C.; LL.B., Southwestern U., Los Angeles, 1930; m. Adelaide Negus, June 10, 1926. With Security First Nat. Bank (name changed to Security Pacific Nat. Bank), Los Angeles, 1923—, exec. v.p., 1961- 69, now dir., chmn. gen. trust co., mem. exec. com.; dir. Earle C. Anthony, Inc. Admitted to Cal. bar, 1930. Bd. dirs. Braille Inst.; chmn. bd. trustees Claremont Mens Coll. Mem. Am. (past pres. trust div.), Cal. bankers assns., Am., Cal., Los Angeles bar assns. Clubs: California, Stock Exchange (Los Angeles). Home: 106 N Grand Av Pasadena CA 91103 Office: 561 S Spring St Los Angeles CA 90054

CORBIN, HAROLD HARLOW, Jr., former headmaster; b. Round Lake, N.Y., Nov. 16, 1914; s. Harold Harlow and Helen Hazen (Van Deusen) C.; grad. Romford Sch., Washington, Conn., 1934; A.B., Yale, 1939; summer student Columbia, 1939-42; m. Florence Bradley Smith, June 29, 1940; children—Angela Bradley (Mrs. Orville M. Deibler, Jr.), Linsey Harlow. Head dept. English, Romford Sch., 1939-42, Salisbury (Conn.) Sch., 1942-51; founder, dir. Salisbury Summer Sch. Reading and English, 1946-51; became headmaster Lake Forest (Ill.) Acad., 1951; now owner antique shop, Falls Village, Conn. Bd. dirs. Chgo. Hist. Soc.; trustee The Masters School, Dobbs Ferry, N.Y. Mem. Ind. Schs. Assn. Central States (past pres.), Independent Schs. Assn. Greater Chgo. (past pres.). Headmasters Assn., Econ. Club Chgo. Clubs: Caxton, Wayfarers, University (Chgo.); Onwentsia (Lake Forest). Address: Falls Village CT 06031

CORBIN, KENDALL BROOKS, physician, scientist; b. Oak Park, Ill., Dec. 31, 1907; s. William Sherman and Emma (Heacock) C.; A.B., Stanford, 1931, M.D., 1935; m. Eryl Portia Wallace, Jan. 2, 1932; children—Kendall Wallace, Edwin Malcolm. Instr. anatomy, Stanford, 1935-38; NRC fellow in medicine Neurology Inst., Northwestern U., 1937-38 assoc. prof. anatomy Tenn. U., then prof. and chief div. anatomy, 1938-46, in charge neurology, 1943-46; prof. neurology Mayo Found., Minn. U., and cons. in neurology Mayo Clinic, 1946—, head sect. neurology Mayo Clinic, 1956-63, sr. cons. neurology, 1963—, pres. staff, 1968; asso. dir. Mayo Found. for Med. Edn. and Research, Grad. Sch. of U. Minn., 1950-54; chmn. bd. devel. Mayo Found., 1969—. Chmn. Rochester Com. on Higher Edn. Diplomate Am. Bd. Psychiatry and Neurology. Mem. Amer. Neurol. Assn., Amer. Acad. Neurology, A.M.A., Am. Assn. Anatomists, Am. Physiol. Soc., Soc. Exptl. Biology and Medicine, Minn. Med. Assn., Central Neuropsychiat. Assn., Minn. Soc. Neurology and Psychiatry, Phi Beta Kappa, Sigma Xi. Alpha Omega Alpha. Contbr. articles on nervous system to med. jours. Home: Crocus Hill Salem Rd Rochester MN 55901 Office: Mayo Clinic Rochester MN 55901

CORBIN, SOL NEIL, lawyer; b. Bklyn., Apr. 16, 1927; s. Nathan I. and Sarah (Kaiser) C.; B.S., Columbia, 1948; LL.B. cum laude, Harvard, 1951; m. Tanya Jacobs, Aug. 6, 1963; 1 son, David J. Admitted to N.Y. bar, 1952; practiced in N.Y.C., 1952—; law clk. Judge Charles D. Breitel, 1956-58; counsel Gov. of N.Y., 1962-65; partner Corbin, Gordon & Goldman N.Y.C., 1970—. Mem. N.Y. State Banking Bd., 1969—. Chmn. N.Y. Commn. Constl. Conv., 1966- 67. Served with USNR, 1945-46. Mem. Am. N.Y.C. bar assns., Am. Arbitration Assn. (chmn. comml. law sub.-com.). Home: 1100 Park Av New York City NY 10028 Office: 866 3d Av New York City NY 10022

CORBIN, SPOTSWOOD WELLFORD, mfg. co. exec.; b. Phila., Apr. 13, 1909; s. Matthew Maury and Mary Anderson (Reinhart) C.; B.S. in Elec. Engring., Union Coll., 1930; m. Dorothy Parker, Jan. 15, 1938. With Gen. Electric Co., 1930—; v.p., 1963—; trustee Schenectady Savs. Bank; dir. Maqua Co. Mem. exec. com. Electrification Council, 1962—; bd. trustees Council Tech. Advancement-Machinery and Allied Products Inst., 1963—. Bd. dirs. Schenectady Boys Club. Mem. Am. Iron and Steel Inst. (asso.), Am. Mgmt. Assn., Am. Soc. M.E., Am. Marketing Assn., Sigma Xi, Sigma Phi, Eta Kappa Nu, Tau Beta Pi. Clubs: Mohawk, Mohawk Golf (Schenectady); Schuyler Meadows (Albany, N.Y.); Lake Placid (N.Y.); Pinnacle (N.Y.C.). Home: Maple Ave Charlton NY 11570 Office: 1 River Rd Schenectady NY 11570

CORBIN, THOMAS GOLDSBOROUGH, air force officer; b. Fremont, N.C., Jan. 14, 1917; s. Thomas Waters and Susie (Boggs) C.; B.S., Davidson Coll., 1937, U.S. Mil. Acad., 1941; grad. Royal Air Force Staff Coll., Bracknell, Eng., 1951, Nat. War College, 1957; m. Willis Potts on April 11th, 1942 (deceased on October 17th, 1963); children—Cynthia Potts, Aletha Boggs, Elizabeth Sue; m. 2d, Jean Quarles, Jan. 29, 1967. Commd. 2d lt. USAAF, 1941, advanced through grades to maj. gen. USAF; comdr. 386th Bomb Group, 1944; air insp. Hdqrs. Air Tng. Command, 1946; comdr. RAF, Schulthorpe, Brize Norton, Eng., 1951; provost marshal SAC, 1953; comdr. 4060 Refueling Wing, 1957, 818th Strategic Aerospace Div., 1958; dep. dir. Office Legislative Liaison Hdqrs. USAF, 1962; comdr. USAF Spl. Air Warfare Center, Eglin AFB, Fla. Decorated Silver Star, D.F.C. with 1 oak leaf cluster, Air medal with 6 oak leaf clusters, Commendation medal, Legion of Merit. Mem. Omicron Delta Kappa, Pi Kappa Phi.

CORBIT, ROSS, ret. distillery exec.; b. Toronto, Ont., Can., Sept. 16, 1899; s. William Joseph and Margaret Euphemia (Conley) C.; student schs. of Toronto; m. Agnes May Miller, Mar. 20, 1928 (dec. Jan. 1, 1954); m. 2d, Shirley Elizabeth Swingle; 1 son, Thomas J. Came to US 1922, naturalized, 1938. Exec. steel industry, 1929-35; with Hiram Walker-Gooderham & Worts Ltd. and or its subsidiaries, 1935- -, past v.p., dir. Hiram Walker-Gooderham & Worts Ltd., Walkerville, Ont., Can., ret.; former v.p., dir. Hiram Walker & Sons, Inc., Detroit, Hiram Walker, Inc. Detroit. Served with Canadian Army, World War I; capt. res. Clubs: Detroit Athletic, Detroit Yacht; Lost Lake, La Coquille (Palm Beach, Fla.). Home: 1700 Vernier Rd Grosse Pointe Woods MI 48236

CORBUS, WILLIAM, food store co. exec.; b. San Francisco, Oct. 5, 1911; s. Adam William and Olive Catherine (Longabaugh) C.; B.S. magna cum laude Stanford, 1933; m. Mary Louise Leistner, Oct. 5, 1934; children—William Ashley, George Barclay. With Great Atlantic & Pacific Co., 1934—, vice chmn., 1971—. Trustee Menlo Sch. and Coll., Menlo Park, Cal. Mem. Nat. Football Hall of Fame, 1957. Mem. Phi Delta Theta. Episcopalian. Clubs: University (N.Y.C.); Cypress Point Golf (Pebble Beach, Cal.); Blind Brook Golf (Port Chester, N.Y.). Office: 420 Lexington Av New York City NY 10017

CORCORAN, AMBROSE LESLIE, educator; b. Irvington, N.J., Sept. 8, 1913; s. Walter L. and Frances (Hilb) C.; B.S., Newark State Coll., 1941; M.A., Montclair (N.J.) State Coll., 1947; D.Ed., Pa. State U., 1953; m. Eileen Lynch, June 26, 1943; children—Patricia, Phyllis, Penelope. Tchr., Red Bank, N.J., 1941-43, Clifton, N.J., 1943-46; faculty State U. N.Y. Coll. at Brockport, 1946—, prof. art, 1955—, chmn. dept., 1967—; vis. prof. State U. N.Y. at New Platz, 1953-54, R.I. State Coll., 1955, U. Houston, 1964; indsl. design cons., 1942—. Sec. Silsby Hose Co., 1962-63. Recipient certificate of appreciation Brockport Kiwanis Club, 1964. Mem. Am. Soc. Aesthetics, Coll. Art Assn., Nat. Art Edn. Assn., Am. Assn. U. Profs. (local pres.), Kappa Delta Pi, Phi Delta Kappa, Delta Psi Omega, Epsilon Pi Tau. Rotarian. Research color perception. Home: 64 Centennial Av Brockport NY 14420

CORCORAN, CHARLES ALLEN, army officer; b. Laredo, Tex., Sept. 16, 1914; s. Harry and Marie (O'Laughlin) C.; grad. Arty. Sch., 1946, Armed Forces Staff Coll., 1953, Nat. War Coll., 1958; m. Anna Mae Love, Sept. 14, 1941; children—Patrick, Timothy, Dennis, Sean. Enlisted in U.S. Army, 1931, commd. 2d lt., 1939, advanced through grades to lt. gen., 1969; served in Europe, 1944-45, 46-49, 58-63, in Korea, 1953-54; chief staff MACV, 1968-69, CG II Field Force Vietnam, 1969-70; chief staff CINCPAC, 1970 —. Decorated D.S.M. with oak leaf cluster, Legion of Merit, Bronze Star, Air medal with three oak leaf clusters, Army Commendation medal; Cross Gallantry with palm, Armed Forces Honor medal 1st class, Campaign medal, Nat. Order 4th class (all Republic Vietnam); Order Nat. Security Merit 2d class, Order Merit (both Republic Korea). Home: 9 Palm Circle Ft Shafter HI 96558 Office: Chief Staff CINCPAC FPO San Francisco CA 96610

CORCORAN, CHARLES ROBERT, life ins. co. exec.; b. N.Y.C., Aug. 16, 1909; s. Peter J. and Lydia (Purcell) C.; student Fordham U., Columbia, Pratt Inst.; m. Isabel Birney, Oct. 12, 1935 (dec.); m. 2d, Ruth Joan Finnegan, Nov. 9, 1940; children—Mary (Mrs. Frank Ehmann), Jean (Mrs. Paul Schott), Charles A., Ruth Ann, Lucile. With Manhattan Life Ins. Co. of N.Y., 1928; mgr. Chgo. br. office, supt. agencies, Manhattan, 1938-43; v.p. Livermore & Knight Co., Providence, 1943-46; dir. sales promotion Equitable Life Assurance Soc. U.S., 1946-53, 2d v.p. sales promotion, sales devel., 1953-59, v.p. advt. and publs., 1959-60, v.p. advt., publs. and press relations, 1960-65, v.p. and chmn.'s staff, 1965-68, v.p. advt. and graphics and spl. assignments, 1968-70. Gov., chmn. pub. relations Human Resources Center; sec., gov. Human Resources Sch. for Handicapped Children; nat. coordinator U.S. Labor Dept. and Advt. Council. Chmn. pub. relations, chmn. spl. devel. St. Mary's Sem.; chmn. spl. devel. com. Hofstra Coll., Fordham Prep. Sch.; trustee Loretto Heights Coll., Denver. Mem. Life Advertisers Assn. (mem. exec. com. 1958-59; founder Gotham group,) Chgo. Life Underwriters Assn., Life Ins. Agy. Mgmt. Assn., Pub. Relations Soc. (chmn. pub. service com. N.Y. chpt. 1961-62, chmn. workshop com. 1962, pres. N.Y. chpt. 1968—, dir., 1963—), Inst. Life Ins., Life Office Mgmt. Assn., Ins. Inst. Am., Ins. Soc. N.Y. Club: Metropolitan. Home: 85 Southdown Rd Huntington NY 11743 also Hotel Wellington New York City NY 10019

CORCORAN, DAVID M., pres. The Sydney Ross Co.; b. Pawtucket, R.I., Aug. 28, 1903; s. Thomas P. and Mary (O'Keefe) C.; A.B., Princeton, 1925; M.B.A., Harvard, 1927; m. Joan Woltman, Aug. 22, 1942; children—Thomas, Josephine, David, Jonathan, Jennifer. Began career as mgr. Asiatic Selling Co., N.Y.C., 1927-28, Dodge & Seymour, Ltd., Osaka, Japan, 1928-30; zone mgr. Gen. Motors Japan, Ltd., Tokyo, 1930-33; with Sterling Products Internat., N.Y.C., 1933—, v.p., 1933-39, pres., 1939—; pres. The Sydney Ross Co., 1940—, Winthrop Products, 1948—; v.p., dir. Sterling Drug, Inc., 1966—; pres. Dorothy Gray Inc., 1967—, Valmont Inc., 1967—. Home: Waterville Valley NH Office: 90 Park Av New York City NY 10016

CORCORAN, HOWARD FRANCIS, U.S. judge b. Pawtucket, R.I., Jan. 25, 1906; s. Thomas Patrick and Mary Josephine (O'Keefe) C.; grad. Phillips Exeter Acad., 1924 A.B., Princeton, 1928; LL.B., Harvard, 1931; m. Esther Pierce, May 31, 1952. Admitted to N.Y. bar, 1935, D.C. bar, 1956; with Dept. Agr., 1933-34, TVA, 1934-35; legal asso. SEC, 1935-38; asst. Office U.S. Atry. for So. Dist. of N.Y., 1938-43; U.S. atty. So. Dist. N.Y., 1943; partner firm Corcoran, Kostelanetz & Gladstone, N.Y.C., 1946-54, Corcoran, Foley, Youngman & Rowe, Washington, 1954-65; U.S. dist. judge for D.C., Washington, 1965—. Served to lt. col. AUS, 1943-45. Decorated Bronze Star, Croix de Guerre with star (France). Mem. Am., Fed., N.Y. State, N.Y. County bar assns., Bar Assn. of D.C., Assn. Bar City N.Y., Phi Delta Phi. Roman Catholic. Clubs: Princeton, Harvard, Army-Navy, Congressional Country, University (Washington). Home: 9004 Congressional Ct Potomac MD 20854 Office: US Courthouse Washington DC 20001

CORCORAN, JOHN, lawyer; b. Pitts., Dec. 27, 1914; s. Sanford William and Anne (Kunes) C.; A.B., Allegheny Coll., 1935; LL.B., Harvard, 1938; m. Sara Elizabeth Young, June 19, 1939; children—John, Robert A. Admitted to Pa. bar, 1939; law clk. Supreme Ct. of Pa., 1938-39; asso. Rose & Eichenauer, Pitts., 1939-45, partner, 1945-50; asst. v.p. Pitts. Consolidation Coal Co., 1950-55, v.p., sec., gen. counsel, 1955-66, adminstrv. v.p., 1963- 65, exec. v.p., 1965-66, pres., dir., 1966—; dir. Continental Oil Co., Mellon Nat. Bank & Trust Co., St. Joseph Lead Co. Mem. Am., Allegheny County bar assns., Nat. Coal Assn. (chmn. bd. 1968), Phi Beta Kappa. Clubs: Duquesne, Shannopin (Pitts.), Laurel Valley Golf; Metropolitan (Washington), Home: 14 Wilson Dr Pittsburgh PA 15202 Office: One Oliver Plaza Pittsburgh PA 15222

CORCORAN, JOHN JOSEPH, govt. ofcl.; b. N.Y.C., Aug. 12, 1920; s. John Joseph and Ellen (Fitzgerald) C.; B.S., Georgetown U., 1948, J.D., 1951; m. Evelyn Dynan Madden, Apr. 29, 1943; children—Patricia (Mrs. David L. Holt), Joanne, John, Maureen, Mary. Admitted to D.C. bar, 1952; legal cons. Am. Legion, 1952-56; atty. adviser Nat. Security Agy., 1957; dir. Am. Legion Nat. Rehab. Commn., 1958-67; asst. to gen. counsel VA, 1968-69, gen. counsel, 1969—. Served to capt. USAAF, 1942-45. Decorated D.F.C., Air medal with three oak leaf clusters, N.Y. State Conspicuous Service Cross. Mem. Am., Fed. bar assns., Am. Legion, Phi Alpha Delta. Club: Army and Navy (Washington). Home: 9513 Cable Dr Kensington MD 20795 Office: 810 Vermont Av Washington DC 20420

CORCORAN, JOHN WILLIAM, educator, biochemist; b. Des Moines, June 12, 1927; s. Harry John and Helen (Moon) C.; B.S., Ia. State Coll., 1949; student State U. Ia., 1946-47; Ph.D., Western Res. U., 1956; m. Marianna Herrington, Aug. 7, 1948; children—John Hale, Anna Cary. Vis. fellow, then instr. Columbia Coll. Phys. and Surg., 1955-57; asst. prof., then asso. prof. biochemistry Western Res. U. Med. Sch., 1957-68; prof. biochemistry, chmn. dept. Northwestern U. Med. Sch., 1968—; acad. guest Eidg. Technische Hochschule, Zurich, Switzerland, 1964-65. Served with USNR, 1945-46. Research fellow Am. Heart Assn., 1955-58, established investigator, 1958-63; recipient Travel award Commonwealth Fund, 1964-65, Career Devel. award USPHS, 1964-68. Mem. Am. Chem. Soc., Am. Soc. Biol. Chemists, Am. Soc. Microbiology, Am. Heart Assn., A.A.A.S., Biochem. Soc. Great Britain, N.Y. Acad. Scis., Sigma Xi, Phi Lambda Upsilon. Home: 935 Oxford Lane Wilmette IL 60091 Office: 320 E Superior Av Chicago IL 60611

CORCORAN, ROBERT JAMES, lawyer; b. N.Y.C., Jan. 20, 1934; s. John J. and Sarah (Slattery) C.; B.A., Iona Coll., 1954; J.D., Fordham U., 1957; m. Joan Shields, Mar. 7, 1964; children—John D., Sarah L. Admitted to N.Y. bar, 1957, Ariz. bar, 1960, Supreme Ct. U.S., 1968; practice in N.Y.C., 1957-59, Phoenix, 1959—; mem. firm. Reid & Priest, 1958-59, Lewis & Roca, 1959-62; dep. atty. Maricopa County (Ariz.), 1962-64; mem. firm Dushoff, Sacks & Corcoran, 1964—. Bd. dirs. Planned Parenthood of Phoenix. Served with AUS, 1957-58. Mem. Maricopa County Bar Assn. (dir.). Home: 118 E Loma Lane Phoenix AZ 85020 Office: Ariz Title Bldg Phoenix AZ 85003

CORCORAN, THOMAS GARDINER, lawyer; b. Pawtucket, R.I., Dec. 29, 1900; s. Thomas Patrick and Mary Josephine (O'Keefe) C.; A.B. and A.M., Brown U., 1922; LL.B., Harvard, 1925, S.J.D., 1926; m. Margaret J. Dowd; 6 children. Sec. to Oliver Wendell Holmes, asso. justice Supreme Court of U.S., 1926-27; asso. Cotton & Franklin, lawyers, N.Y. City, 1927-32; counsel R.F.C., Washington, D.C., 1932 and 1934-41; asst. to sec. of Treasury, 1933; spl. asst. to atty. gen. of U.S., 1932-35; assisted congl. coms. in drafting Securities Act of 1933, Fed. Housing Act, 1933, Securities Exchange Act of 1934, Pub. Utility Holding Company Act of 1935, Fair Labor Standards Act of 1938; now in pvt. practice with Corcoran, Foley, Youngman and Rowe, Washington. Trustee Brown U. Democrat, 1964-69. Roman Catholic. Home: 2812 Woodland Dr NW Washington DC 20008 Office: 1511 K St NW Washington DC 20005

CORCORAN, THOMAS JOSEPH, fgn. service officer; b. N.Y.C., Sept. 6, 1920; s. John T. and Mary A. (Carroll) C.; B.S.S., St. John's U., 1940; student S.E. Asia lang. and area, Georgetown U., 1953. Mem. U.S. Fgn. Service, 1948—; vice consul, Barcelona, Spain, 1948-50, Hong Kong, 1950-51; sec. embassy, Saigon, Viet-Nam, 1951-53; charge d'affaires ad interim, Vientiane, Laos, 1951- 52, Phnom Penh, Cambodia, 1952; consul, Hanoi, N. Viet-Nam, 1954-55; officer in charge Viet-Nam affairs Dept. of State, 1956-58, Laos affairs, 1958-59; assigned Armed Forces Staff Coll., 1959-60, dep. polit. adv. to comdr. in chief Pacific, 1960-62; dep. chief mission, counselor Ouagadougou, Upper Volta, 1962-64, dir. working group, Vietnam, 1964-65; 1st sec. Saigon, 1965; consul gen. Danang, Vietnam, 1966; grad. Nat. War Coll., 1968; country dir. Laos and Cambodia, 1968- -. Served to lt. (s.g.) USNR, World War II. Home 2725 29th St NW Washington DC 20008 Office: care Dept State Washington DC 20025

CORCORAN, WILLIAM HARRISON, chem. engr.; b. Los Angeles, Mar. 11, 1920; s. William H. and Enid (Winchester) C.; B.S., Cal. Inst. Tech., 1941, M.S., 1942, Ph.D., 1948; m. Martha Nell Rogers, Nov. 7, 1942; children—Sally Kay (Mrs. Raymond K. Fisher), William Owen. Chem. engr. Cutter Lab., 1941-42; devel. engr., research supr. Cal. Inst. Tech., 1942-46, NRC predoctoral fellow, 1946-48; dir. tech. devel. Cutter Lab., 1948-52; asso. prof. chem. engring. Cal. Inst. Tech., 1952- 57, prof., 1957—, exec. officer chem. engring., 1967-69, v.p. inst. relations, 1969—; sci. dir., v.p. Don Baxter, Inc., 1957-59, sci. cons., 1959—. Mem. adv. panel Profl. Achievement in Chem. Engring. Dir. Industry Edn. Council San Gabriel Valley; vice chmn. engring. and accreditation com. Engrs. Council for Profl. Devel. Recipient Educator of Year award, chpt. 99 Am. Soc. for Tool and Mfg. Engrs., 1968; Civic Achievement award So. Cal. sect. Am. Inst. Chem. Engrs., 1970; Westinghouse Engring. Teaching Excellence award, 1970. Fellow Am. Inst. Chemists; mem. Am. Inst. Chem. Engrs. (nat. dir.), Am. Soc. Engring. Edn., Am. Chem. Soc., Am. Soc. M.E., Am. Ordnance Assn., N.Y. Acad. Scis., Am. Inst. Aeros. and Astronautics, A.A.A.S., Sigma Xi, Tau Beta Pi. Presbyn. (elder). Club: Town Hall of Cal. Author: (with J.B. Opfell and B.H. Sage) Momentum Transfer in Fluids, 1956; (with W.N. Lacey) Introduction to Chemical Engineering Problems, 1960. Contbr. articles to profl. jours. Home: 8353 Longden Av San Gabriel CA 91775

CORCOS, LUCILLE, artist; b. N.Y.C., Sept. 21, 1908; d. Joseph and Amelia (Abrams) Corcos; student Art Students League N.Y.; m. Edgar Levy, May 7, 1928; children—David Corcos, Joel Corcos. Commd. paintings include fullpage color reprodns. nat. mags. including Life, Holiday, Vogue, Fortune, etc., U.S. Gypsum Co.; series four painting Upjohn Pharm. Co., 1952; murals include Kaleidoscope, Waldorf-Astoria, 1945, 12 decorative murals in Lounge-Cafe, Waldorf-Astoria, 1940; mural N. Shore Hosp., Manhasset, L.I., 1953; one man shows: Schneider Gabriel Galleries, 1948, N.Y. and Grand Central Moderns, 1948, 1954; Rockland Found., West Nyack, New York; State Dept. Am. Embassy Show, Paris, 1954 paintings exhibited in mus. shows throughout U.S., S.Am., Gt. Britain; Met., Whitney Mus., Audubon Artists, rep. permanent collections: Whitney Mus. Am. Art, Mus. TelAviv, Israel, Shell Oil Co., Naturalizer Shoe Co., Am. Brewers Assn., CBS, R.H. Macy & Co. and in many pvt. collections. Author and illustr.: Joel Gets a Haircut, 1952; Joel Spends His Money, 1954; Joel Gets a Dog, 1958; From Ungskah to Oyaylee: A Counting Book for All Little Indians, 1965. Illustrator: A Treasury of Gilbert and Sullivan, 1941; A Treasury of Laughter, 1946; Chichikov's Journeys, 1945; Little Lame Prince, 1946; Follow the Sunset, 1952; Women Today, 1953; The Picture of Dorian Gray, 1958; Songs of the Gilded Age, 1960; Grimm's Fairy Tales, 4 vols. (for Ltd. Editions Club), 1962. Designer, illustrator multimedia library instrn. programs Libraries are for Children, 1967, Seeking and Finding, 1969. Recipient hon. mention award, 1st portrait of Am. Pepsi-Cola show 1944, Audubon Artists 5th Ann., 1946; Grumbacher purchase award 14th Ann. Audubon Artists, 1956. Mem. Artists Equity Assn. (dir. N.Y. chpt. 1964-66). Home: 167 South Mountain Rd New City NY 10956 also (summer) Robbins Rest Fire Island NY 11782

CORDASCO, FRANCESCO, sociologist, educator; b. N.Y.C., Nov. 2, 1920; s. Giovanni and Carmela Carmela (Madorma) C.; B.A., Columbia, 1942; M.A., N.Y. U., 1945. Ph.D., 1949; postdoctoral student, U. London, U. Salamanca; m. Edna Vaughn, Oct. 22, 1946; children—Michael, Carmela. Prof. English and edn. L.I.U., 1946-53; prof. edn. Fairleigh Dickinson U., then Seton Hall U., 1953-63; prof. edn. Montclair (N.J.) State Coll., 1963—; vis. prof. N.Y. U. City U. N.Y., U. London, U. P.R., State U. N.Y. at Albany; cons. migration div. Commonwealth P.R., U.S. Office Edn., also municipal, county state and fed. anti-poverty programs; cons. com. edn. and labor U.S. Ho. of Reps., com. labor and welfare U.S. Senate. Mem. bd. edn. Newark Archdiocese. Mem. exec. bd. Mt. Carmel Guild. Served with AUS, World War II. Recipient Brotherhood award Nat. Conf. Christians and Jews. Fellow Am., Brit. sociol. assns.; mem. Soc. Advancement Edn. Author: Daniel Coit Gilman and the Protean Ph.D.: The Shaping of American Graduate Education, 1960; Educational Sociology: A Subject Index of Doctoral Dissertation Literature (with Leonard Covello). 1965; The School in the Social Order: A Sociological Introduction to Educational Understanding (with others), 1969; Puerto Rican Children in Mainland Schools; A Source Book for Teachers (with Dr. Eugene Bucchioni), 1968; Research and Report Writing (with Elliott Gatner), 13th edit., 1968; The Urban Community; Crisis and Conflict in Education (with others), 1969; Jacob Riis Another Era, 1968; Junius Bibliography, 1949; Adam Smith 1950; Bohn Libraries, 1951; Minorities In The American City, 1970; also numerous articles. Editor: The Social History of Poverty: The Urban Experience, 22 vols., 1970. Home: 6606 Jackson St West New York NJ 07093 Office: Montclair State Coll Upper Montclair NJ 07043

CORDAY, ELIOT, physician; b. Prince Rupert, B.C., Can., June 29, 1913; s. David and Katie (Goldberg) C.; M.D., U. Alta., 1940; m. Marian Lipkind, Aug. 20, 1940; children—Joanne, Stephen. Came to U.S., 1946, naturalized, 1951. Intern medicine U. Atla. Hosp., 1939-41; resident cardiology Bellevue Hosp., N.Y.C., 1946, Mt. Sinai Hosp., N.Y.C., 1946-47; chief cardiology Cedars of Lebanon Hosp., Los Angeles, 1950-61, attending physician, 1947—; clin. prof. medicine U. Cal. at Los Angeles Med. Sch., 1970—; hon. prof. medicine U. Santo Tomas, Manila, Philippines, 1961—; Del Almo vis. prof. U. Barcelona and Madrid (Spain), 1957, U. Seville (Spain), 1959; hon. mem. faculty U. Chile, 1969—; mem. med. exec. com. Cedars-Sinai Med. Center, 1965—. Nat. cons. cardiology surgeon gen. USAF, 1967—. Mem. Cal. Adv. Com. Coronary Care, 1967—, Cal. Credentials Com. Crippled Children Services Program; med. adv. com. Vis. Nurse Assn. Los Angeles; mem. nat. adv. heart and lung council NIH; spl. cons. Nat. Inst. Neurol. Diseases and Blindness, 1966—; nat. adv. council Jules Stein Eye Inst., 1964—. Served to wing comdr. RCAF, 1941- 45. Fellow Am. Coll. Cardiology (pres. 1965-66), A.C.P., Am. Coll. Chest Physicians (bd. regents), Am. Soc. Nuclear Medicine, Am. Geriatric Soc., N.Y. Acad. Sci., A.A.A.S.; mem. Am. (fellow council clin. cardiology 1965, fellow council on cerebrovascular disease 1968—; bd. dirs. 1965- 66), Los Angeles County (exec. com. bd. dirs.) heart assns., Am. (chmn. sect. diseases of chest), Los Angeles Co. (gov.) med. assns. Author: The Auricular Arrhythmias, 1952; Disturbances in Heart Rate, Rhythm and Conduction, 1961; also numerous articles, monographs. Asso. and/or cons. jours. in field. Home: 810 N Roxbury Dr Beverly Hills CA 90210 Office: 436 N Roxbury Dr Beverly Hills CA 90210

CORDEAU, ROGER RAYMOND, lawyer; b. Montreal, Can., Jan. 4, 1910; s. L.B. and Albertine (Tessier) C.; B.A., Loyola Coll., 1930; postgrad. McGill U., 1931-32; LL.D., U. Montreal, 1934; m. Therese Lalonde, Sept. 13, 1955; children-Joan Cynthia, Barbara Louise, Marc Roger. Called to bar, 1934, created Queen's counsel, 1959; practice in Montreal, 1935—; mem. firm McMaster, Meighen, Minnion, Patch & Cordeau, 1964—; lectr. labour law. Mem. legal com. Liberal Party, 1935-39. Bd. govs. (life) St. Justine Hosp., Hospital Marie-Enfant, Queen Elizabeth Hosp. Served to maj. Royal Canadian Armoured Corps, 1939-45; Africa, ETO. Decorated Africa Star, 2 wound stripes. Clubs: Cercle Universitaire, St. James's, Royal Montreal Golf, Royal Canadian Automobile, Thistle Curling (Montreal); Cercle Inter-Alkies (Paris, France). Home: 4754 The Boulevard Westmount Quebec Canada Office: 129 St James St W Montreal 126 Quebec Canada

CORDELL, RICHARD ALBERT, educator, writer; b. Bloomington, Ind., July 1, 1896; s. Joseph Edward and Minnie (Bell) C.; A.B., Ind. U., 1917, A.M., 1925; student U. London (Eng.), 1930-31; m. Alice Bright, May 20, 1916. Mem. faculty Purdue U., 1919-64, prof. English, 1937-64, George Ade prof. English, 1959, now prof. emeritus, chmn. dept., 1956-57; lectr., Japan and Taiwan, 1962, France, 1963. Mem. Lambda Chi Alpha, Theta Alpha Phi. Author: Henry Arthur Jones and the Modern Drama, 1932; W. Somerset Maugham, 1937; Somerset Maugham (Ind. U. Writers award for best biography 1961), 1961; A Writer for All Seasons, 1969; Henry Arthur Jones and the Modern Drama, 1968; also numerous articles, book reviews. Editor: Representative Modern Plays, 1929; Twentieth Century Plays, 1947; Of Human Bondage, 1956; Old Broadway, 1959; Mrs. Peckham's Carouse, 1960; Husbands and Wives, 1963; The Sinners, 1964; Somerset Maugham, A Writer For All Seasons, 1969. Address: 2001 Union St Lafayette IN 47904

CORDERO-DI-MONTEZEMOLO, VITTORIO, Italian diplomat; b. Torino, Italy, July 1, 1917; s. Alberto and Maria A. (Muzi-Falconi) Cordero-di.; law degree, U. Pisa, 1939, Pol. Sci., 1940; m. Corinna Busiri-Vici, June 27, 1946; children—Alberto, Isabella, Maria Alessandra. Joined Italian Diplomatic Service, 1940; dep. counsul gen., Buenos Aires, 1949-53; consul, Mendoza, 1953-55; sec. embassy, Madrid, 1955-57 assigned Fgn. Ministry, 1957-63, with dept. econ. affairs, 1957-59; participant internat. confs. econ. coms., 1959; mem. Italian delegation internat. confs. on Common Market, Disarmament, others, 1959-63; consul gen., N.Y.C., 1963-64, minister plentipotentiary, 1964-67; ambassador of Italy to Uruguay, 1967-69, to Venezuela, 1969-71, to Israel, 1971—. Served with Italian Army, World War II. Decorated Order Merit Italian Republic. Address: Italian Embassy 24 Huberman St Tel Aviv Israel

CORDES, ALEXANDER CHARLES, lawyer; b. Buffalo, Aug. 14, 1925; s. Alexander J. and Margaret (Markens) C.; B.A., Yale, 1947; LL.B., U. Buffalo, 1950; m. Sally J. Jadwin, July 17, 1948; children—John J., Ann T., Susan A. Admitted to N.Y. bar, 1950; asso. firm Kenefick, Bass, Letchworth, Baldy & Phillips, 1950-54; asst. U.S. atty. Western Dist. N.Y., 1954-56; partner firm Phillips, Lytle, Hitchcock, Blaine & Huber, Buffalo, 1956—. Mem. Erie County Bd. Suprs., 1960-61. Served with USNR, 1943-46. Mem. Am., N.Y. State, Erie County bar assns. Home: 104 Lexington Av Buffalo NY 14222 Office: Marine Trust Bldg Buffalo NY 14203

CORDES, DONALD WESLEY, hosp. adminstr.; b. Stephenson County, Ill., Dec. 31, 1917; s. Theodore J. and Fannie (Van Osterloo) C.; A.B. cum laude, Hope Coll., Holland, Mich., 1940; M.A., U. Mich., 1941; postgrad. hosp. adminstrn., Columbia, 1945-46; m. Harriet Davies, Oct. 11, 1947; children—Beverly Ann, Karen Sue. Adminstrv. asst. St. Luke's Hosp., N.Y.C., 1944-47; adminstr. Ia. Methodist Hosp., Des Moines, 1947—. Bd. dirs. Nat. Health Council, 1969—, Ia. Mental Health Assn. Mem. Am. (trustee 1960-63), Ia. (trustee 1950-62, pres. 1952-53) hosp. assns., Upper Midwest Hosp. Conf. (trustee 1952-61, pres. 1957-58), Nat. Assn. Meth. Hosps. and Homes (pres. 1963-64), Am. Coll. of Hosp. Adminstrs. (regent 1963-64, member of the board of governors 1964-66, president

1967-68). Methodist. Clubs: Des Moines, Wakonda. Home: 5715 Woodland Rd Des Moines IA 50312 Office: Iowa Methodist Hosp Des Moines IA 50308

CORDES, EUGENE HAROLD, educator; b. York, Neb., Apr. 7, 1936; s. Elmer Henry and Ruby Mae (Hofeldt) C.; B.S., Cal. Inst. Tech., 1958; Ph.D., Brandeis U., 1962; m. Shirley Ann Morton, Nov. 9, 1957; children—Jennifer Eve, Matthew Henry James. Instr. chemistry Ind. U., Bloomington, 1962-64, asst. prof., 1964-66, asso. prof., 1966-68, prof., 1968—. NIH Career Devel. award, 1966; Alfred P. Sloan Found. fellow, 1968. Mem. Am. Chem. Soc., A.A.A.S., Am. Soc. Biol. Chemists, Am. Assn. U. Profs. Author: (with Henry Mahler), Biological Chemistry, 1966, Basic Biological Chemistry, 1969; also articles. Home: 1316 S High Bloomington IN 47401

CORDES, JOHN HENRY, rubber co. exec.; b. N.Y.C., Sept. 22, 1914; s. John Herman and Louise (Crome) C.; B.C.S., N.Y. U., 1937; m. Jessica Margaret Greenstreet, Sept. 7, 1942; 1 son, John Edmund, Sr. accountant McGrath, Doyle & Phair, N.Y.C., 1938-42, Peat, Marwick, Mitchell & Co., N.Y.C., 1943-44; asst. to controller Curtiss-Wright Corp., Buffalo, 1944-46; with Armstrong Rubber Co., West Haven, Conn., 1951—, v.p., 1966-71, treas. , 1963—, exec. v.p., 1971—, also dir.; sec.-treas. Armstrong Rubber Co. Acceptance Corp., West Haven, 1965—; v.p., dir. Direct Tire Sales, Inc., New Orleans, 1966—; dir. Arco Wheel, Inc., West Allis, Wis., Copolymer Rubber & Chem. Co., Baton Rouge. Bd. dirs. Armstrong Rubber Co. Found. C.P.A., N.Y. State. Mem. Theta Chi, Beta Gamma Sigma. Episcopalian. Clubs: Milford Yacht (commodore 1964-65, dir. 1970), Windjammers Sailing (Milford); Racebrook Country (Orange). Home: 276 Hawthorne Lane Orange CT 06477 Office: 500 Sargent Dr New Haven CT 06507

CORDES, PHILIP HERMAN, banker; b. Chgo., Aug. 23, 1910; s. Herman H. and Virginia (Foley) C.; B.S.C., Loyola U., Chgo., 1940; grad. Rutgers U. Grad. Sch. Banking, 1946; C.P.A., Ill., 1937; m. Rose Hanzel, Nov. 17, 1934; children—Philip John, Patricia Ann. Auditor, asst. v.p. Lake Shore Nat. Bank, Chgo., 1931-48; with Continental Ill. Nat. Bank and Trust Co., Chgo., 1948—, v.p., 1960-70, comptroller, sec. bd. dirs., 1967—, sr. v.p., 1970—; sec., treas. Conill Corp., 1969; sec., treas., dir. Continental Bank Internat., Continental Internat. Finance Corp. Mem. pres.'s alumni council Loyola U., Chgo.; bd. dirs. Civic Fedn. Chgo. Mem. Alpha Sigma Nu, Sigma Lambda Beta, Beta Alpha Psi, Blue Key. Home: 1406 Deerpath Lane LaGrange Park IL 60525 Office: 231 S LaSalle St Chicago IL 60690

CORDIER, ANDREW WELLINGTON, univ. dean; b. Canton, O., Mar. 3, 1901 s. Wellington J. and Ida Mae (Anstine) C.; A.B., Manchester Coll., 1922, LL.D., 1946; A.M., U. Chgo. 1923, Ph.D. (fellow), 1926; postgrad. Grad. Inst. Internat. Studies, Geneva, Switzerland, 1930-31; LL.D., Elizabethtown Coll., 1947, Albright Coll., 1953, Kent State U., 1955, MacMurray Coll., 1956, Ind. U., 1957, Oberlin Coll., 1958, N.Y. U., 1959, Fairleigh Dickinson U., 1960, Denison U., 1961, Lewis and Clark Coll., 1961, Haverford Coll., 1962, Western Mich. U., 1962, U. Pa., 1963, Brandeis U., 1966, R.I. Coll., 1967, U. Akron, 1969, Johns Hopkins, 1970, Hamilton Coll., 1970, Manhattan Coll., 1970, Jewish Theol. Sem., 1970, Rider Coll., 1971; D.P.S., Millikin U., 1961; L.H.D., Otterbein Coll., 1952; D.D., Sem., 1966; D.H.L., Susquehanna U., 1968; D.L.H., Columbia, 1970; m. Dorothy Elizabeth Butterbaugh, May 23, 1924; children-Lowell, Louise. Asso. prof. history Manchester Coll., 1923-27, chmn. dept. hist. and polit. sci., 1927-44; lectr. Social Scis. Ind. U., 1929-44; expert on internat. security Dept. of State, Washington, 1944-46; tech. expert U.S. delegation to U.N. Conf., San Francisco, 1945; chief sect. Prep. Commn. for UN, London, 1945; adviser to exec. sec. Prep. Commn.; adviser to all presidents gen. assembly UN, 1946-62; exec. asst. to sec.-gen. UN, 1946-62, held rank under-sec., coordinator U.N. activities with spl. responsibility for Gen. Assembly, spl. rep. Sec.-Gen. to Korea, 1950-52, Mount Scopus, 1958, Congo, 1960; acting pres. Columbia, 1968-69, pres., 1969-70, pres., trustee Cons. Dept. State, Ford Found. Trustee Dag Hammarskjold Found., Manchester Coll., Carnegie Endowment for Internat. Peace. Recipient Charles Evans Hughes medal, Alexander Hamilton medal, U. Chgo. Alumni medal, Ohio Gov's award, major; award N.Y.C., others. Mem. Am. Polit. Sci. Assn., Council Fgn. Relations, Fgn. Policy Assn. Clubs: University, Century Assn. (N.Y.C.). Home: 6 Merrivale Rd Great Neck NY 11201

CORDIER, HUBERT VICTOR, educator; b. North Canton, O., Apr. 27, 1917; s. Emery Andrew and Minnie (Lahr) C.; B.A., Manchester Coll. (Ind.), 1939; M.A., Mich. State U., 1942; Ph.D., U. Ill., 1955; m. Ruth Virginia Roop, Aug. 3, 1940; 1 son, Gary Michael. Tchr., coach Columbia (Ind.) City High Sch., 1939-40; teaching fellow Mich. State U., 1940-42; asst. prof. speech Allegheny Coll., Meadville, Pa., 1946-49; head dept. radio and TV, U. Ill. at Urbana, 1949-68; dir. broadcasting, prof. speech U. Ia., Iowa City, 1968—, also head. div. broadcasting and film. Bd. dirs. Nat. Ednl. Radio. Served with USAAF, 1944-46. Mem. Assn. Profl. Broadcasting Edn. (pres., bd. dirs.), Nat. Assn. Ednl. Broadcasters (chmn. publs. com.), Am. Assn. U. Profs., Speech Assn. Am., Radio and TV News Dirs. Assn. Methodist. Home: 306 Stewart Rd RR6 Iowa City IA 52240

CORDIER, RALPH WALDO, coll. dean; b. Canton, O., June 28, 1902; s. Wellington Jacob and Ida (Anstine) C.; B.A., Manchester Coll., 1925; M.A., Ohio State U., 1929, Ph.D., 1934; diploma U. London, 1951-52; m. Esta Elora Brenner, June 3, 1925; 1 son, Sherwood Stanley. Tchr. pub. schs., North Canton, O., 1925- 28; asst. Ohio State U., 1929-34; critic tchr. Eastern Ill. State Tchrs. Coll., Charleston, 1934-36; prof. history Manchester Coll., North Manchester, Ind., 1935-36; chmn. dept. social studies Clarion (Pa.) State Tchrs. Coll., 1936-46; prof. history La. State U., Baton Rouge, 1944, U. Minn., 1946; chmn. dept. social scis. Indiana U. of Pa., 1946-55, dean acad. affairs, 1955—. History adviser Brit. Jr. Ency., Chgo., 1958—; con. Coronet Hist. Films, Chgo., 1956—. Ford Found. postdoctoral fellow. Mem. Pa. Hist. Assn. (past pres.), Middle States Council Social Studies (past pres.), Nat. Council for Social Studies (pres. 1968), Pa. Council Social Studies (past pres.). Author: (with E.B. Robert) History for the Beginner, 1953; History of Young America, 1953; History of Our United States, 1958; (with S.K. Stevens) Exploring Pennsylvania, 1953; History of World Peoples, 1961. Home: 235 S 13th St Indiana PA 15701

CORDING, EDWARD ASAHEL, educator b. Osceola, Wis., Nov. 3, 1904; s. Edward James and Charlotte (Kimball) C.; diploma Moody Bible Inst., Chgo., 1928; B.S., Wheaton (Ill.) Coll., 1933; m. Ruth Margaret James, July 23, 1935; children—Edward J., Robert P., Margaret Z. Artist, Photoplating Co., Mpls., 1922-26, Meyercord Co., Chgo., 1929-33; dir. pub. relations Wheaton Coll., 1933-43; ednl. dir. Tabernacle Baptist Ch., Atlanta, 1943-45; dir. Corr. Sch., also Moody Press, Moody Bible Inst., 1945-48; dir. conservatory music, chmn. div. fine arts, also prof. ednl. adminstrn. Wheaton Coll., 1948-70. Recipient award for service in music in W. suburban Chgo. area Steinway & Sons, 1965; hon. mem. DuPage Symphony Orch., 1968. Mem. Nat. Ch. Music Fellowship (pres. 1956-57), Music Tchrs. Nat. Assn. (chmn. publicity com. nat. convs. 1957-63), Ill. State Music Tchrs. Assn. (pres. 1963-66). Republican. Home: 914 Santa Rosa Av Wheaton, IL 60187.

CORDINGLEY, WILLIAM ANDREW, newspaper pub. b. Des Moines, Aug. 24, 1917; s. William Andrew and Louise (Cookerly) C.; grad. Phillips Exeter Acad., 1936; B.S., Harvard, 1940; m. Mary Jeannette Bowles, Mar. 17, 1942; children—William Andrew, Thomas Kent, Constance Louise. With Mpls. Star and Tribune, 1940-65, nat. advt. mgr., 1949-65; pub. Great Falls (Mont.) Tribune, 1965—, dir. Great Falls Nat. Bank, 1966-70. Vice chmn. Helena br. Mpls. Res. Bank, 1970, chmn. 1971. Trustee Breck Sch., Mpls., 1962-65; bd. dirs. Great Falls Symphony, 1965-70, Russell Gallery, Great Falls, 1965—, Mpls. Curative Workshop, 1952-65; mem. council of 50, U. Mont. 1966-70. Mem. regional adv. group Mountain State Regional Med. Programs, 1967-71. Served to col. AUS, 1941-46; ETO, MTO, N. Africa. Mem. Am. Newspaper Pubs. Assn., Mpls. Sales and Marketing Execs. (v.p. 1963-65), Great Falls C. of C. (dir. 1967-70). Episcopalian. Clubs: Hazeltine Nat. (bd. govs. 1962-65) (Mpls.); Meadowlark Country (bd. dirs. 1966-69) (Great Falls); Harvard (N.Y.C.); Harvard Varsity. Home: 42 Prospect Dr Great Falls, MT 59401. Office: Great Falls Tribune Great Falls MY 59401

CORDOVA, GEORGE LUIS, Puerto Rican govt. ofcl.; b. Manati, P.R., Apr. 20, 1907; B.A., Catholic U. Am., 1928; LL.B., Harvard, 1931; m. Dora Rodriguez; children—Jorge Luis, Elvira (Mrs. Gonzalez), Irene (Mrs. Subira), Fernando. Admitted to P.R. bar, 1931; practiced in San Juan, 1931-40, 46-48; judge Superior Ct. of P.R.; asso. justice Supreme Ct. of P.R., 1940-46; resident commr., 1969—. Mem. Fed., P.R. bar assns. Mem. New Progressive Party. Roman Catholic. Office: 5519 Pollard Rd Springfield Bethesda MD 20016

CORE, EARL LEMLEY, botanist; b. Core, W.Va., Jan. 20, 1902; s. Harry Michael and Clara Edna (Lemley) C.; A.B., W.Va. U., 1926, A.M., 1928; Ph.D., Columbia, 1936; m. Freda Bess Garrison, June 8, 1925; children—Ruth (Mrs. Harry Miller), Merle, Harry, David. Instr. W.Va. U., 1928-34, asst. prof., 1934-41, asso. prof., 1941-42, prof. botany, 1942—, chmn. dept. biology, 1948-66, curator of Herbarium, 1934—; botanist Colombian Cinchona Mission, Bogotá, 1943-45; bot. exploration of Lake Erie Islands, summers, 1939-41. Mayor, City of Morgantown, W.Va., 1956-57. Mem. A.A.A.S., Bot. Soc. Am. (pres. Northeastern sect. 1950), W.Va. Acad. Sci. (pres. 1971), Assn. Southeastern Biologists, Phi Beta Kappa, Phi Epsilon Phi, Alpha Gamma Rho, Sigma Xi. Clubs: Southern Appalachian Botanical (founded club and its Jour., Castanea, 1936, pres. 1950). Kiwanis. Author: several books, 1931-48; Flora of the Erie Islands, 1948; Spring Wild Flowers, 1948; Flora of West Virginia (with P.D. Strausbaugh), Part 1, 1952, 2d edit., 1970, Part 2, 1953, 2d edit., 1971, Part 3, 1958, Part 4, 1964; Plant Taxonomy, 1955; Plant Life of West Virginia, 1960; (with others) General Biology, 1961; Vegetation of West Virginia, 1966. Editor of Wild Flower, organ Wild Flower Preservation Soc., 1946-64. Home: 460 Brockway Av Morgantown WV 26505

COREA, LUIS FELIPE, banker; b. Washington, May 23, 1910; s. Luis Felipe and India Bell (Fleming) C.; student George Washington U., 1932-36; certificate Stonier Grad. Sch. Banking, Rutgers U., 1948; m. Ann Margot Helring, Sept. 12, 1939. With Riggs Nat. Bank, Washington, 1926—, v.p., mgr. fgn. dept., 1950-63, sr. v.p., 1963—; dir. Dynalectron Corp., 1957—; mem. adv. com. Export-Import Bank U.S., 1963-64. Mem. Def. Industry Adv. Council subcom. mil. exports Def. Dept., 1963—; vice-chmn. Md. Regional Export Expansion Council, 1967—. Mem. adv. council Sch. Langs. and Linguistics, Georgetown U., 1964—; council advisers Edmund A. Walsh Sch. Fgn. Service, Georgetown U., 1965—; bd. dirs., exec. com. Internat. Student House, 1964-69; trustee, treas. Meridian House Found., 1967-69. Served to lt. comdr. USNR, 1942-45. Mem. Acad. Polit. Sci., Am. Inst. Banking, Bankers Assn. for Fgn. Trade (dir. 1958-60, 61-63, pres. 1963-64), Met. Washington Bd. Trade (World Trade award 1964), Am. Legion (comdr. post), Confrerie des Chevaliers du Tastevin (pres. Washington), English Speaking Union, U.S. C. of C., Japan Am. Soc. Washington, Washington Inst. Fgn. Affairs. Clubs: Chevy Chase (Md.); Internat. (Washington). Home: 4201 Cathedral Av NW Washington DC 20016 Office: 1503 Pennsylvania Av Washington DC 20013

CORELL, ROBERT WALDEN, educator; b. Detroit, Nov. 4, 1934; s. George W. and Grace (Hagland) C.; B.S. in Mech. Engring., Case Inst. Tech., 1956, Ph.D., 1964; M.S., Mass. Inst. Tech., 1959; m. Billie Jo Proctor, June 16, 1956; children—Robert Walden, David Richard, Beth Anne. Engr., Gen. Electric Co., Cleve., 1955, program engr., Lynn, Mass., 1956-57; instr. U. N.H., 1957-58, asst. prof., 1959-60, asso. prof., 1964-66, prof., 1966—, chmn. dept. mech. engring., 1964—; research engr. Huggins Hosp., Wolferoro, N.H., 1957-60, Highland View Hosp., Cleve., 1960-64; vis. investigator Woods Hole Oceanographic Inst., 1965. Cons., U.S. Navy Oceanographic Programs, USCG, Ford Motor Co., Corning Glass, Wood Products, Inc., Apasco Products, Huggins Hosp., Honeywell, Raytheon Co. Dist. commr. Boy Scouts Am., 1957-58. Mem. A.A.A.S., Am. Soc. Engring. Edn., I.E.E.E., Marine Tech. Soc., Sigma Xi, Tau Beta Pi, Sigma Alpha Epsilon. Contbr. articles in medicine, med. engring., ocean sci. and tech. to profl. jours. Home: Durham Point Rd Durham NH 03824

CORELLI, JOHN CHARLES, educator, physicist; b. Providence, Aug. 6, 1930; s. John and Immacolata (Caldarelli) C.; B.Sc., Providence Coll., 1952; M.S., Brown U., 1954; Ph.D., Purdue U., 1958; m. Evelyn L. Hostetter, June 20, 1959; children—Carolyn Margaret, John Joseph. Physicist, Knolls Atomic Power Lab., Gen. Electric Co., 1958-61; mem. faculty Rensselaer Poly. Inst., 1962—, prof. nuclear engring. and sci., 1962—; cons. NASA, summer 1962; NIH Fellow U. Rochester, 1971. Mem. Am. Phys. Soc., Am. Assn. U. Profs., Rensselaer Newman Found., N.A.A.C.P., Sigma Xi. Roman Catholic. Research in radiation effects in semiconductors and nucleic acid base pairs up to DNA molecules using atomic spectroscopy probes. Home: 33 Belle Av Troy NY 12180

CORENA, FERNANDO, bass; b. Geneva, Switzerland, Dec. 22, 1916; s. Dimitri and Ugolina (Albertini) C.; bacalaurea, U. Frybourg (Switzerland), 1936. Came to U.S., 1954. Operatic debut in Arena of Verona, La Scala, Milan, 1947; leading bass with Metropolitan Opera, 1954—, at Theatro Colon, Buenos Aires, 1958, Stattsoper, Berlin, 1957, Covent Garden, London, 1960, Lyric Opera, Chgo., 1956, San Francisco Opera, 1960, Vienna Staatsoper, 1963, Grand Theatre, Geneva, 1963, 64, Rome Opera, 1965; festival appearances include Salzburg, Edinburgh, Holland. Home: 15 Tatum Dr Middletown NJ 07748 Office: Metropolitan Opera House New York City NY 10023

CORETTE, JOHN E., lawyer, utilities exec.; b. Butte, Mont., Apr. 20, 1908; s. John E. and Mary Taaffe (Driscoll) C.; student U. Mont., 1926; LL.B., U. Va., 1930; LL.D., Coll. Great Falls, 1958, Carroll Coll., Helena, Mont., 1970; m. Elsie Charlotte Pauly, Jan. 2, 1932; children—Joan Elise (Mrs. Donald L. Hanley), John E., III, William Pauly, Diane (Mrs. R.F. Simperman). Admitted to Mont. bar, 1929; practiced in Missoula, 1930-34; partner Corette, Smith & Dean, Butte, 1934—; counsel Mont. Power Co., 1934-44, v.p., asst. gen. mgr., 1944-52, pres., chief exec. officer, 1952-67, chmn., chief exec. officer, 1967—, dir., 1948—; chmn., chief exec. officer, dir. Canadian-Mont. Pipe Line Co., Canadian- Mont. Gas Co., Ltd., Atlanta Exploration Co., Western Energy Co.; dir. First Bank System, Pacific Gas Transmission Co., Burlington No. Inc. U.S. del., com. electric power UN Econ. Commn. for Europe, 1957, 58; mem. utilities subcouncil Nat. Indsl. Pollution Control Council. Trustee Freedoms Found. Valley Forge, Thomas Alva Edison Found.; Initial mem. council Stanford Research Inst., bd. dirs., 1961-70; mem. pres.'s council Carroll Coll. Mem. Edison Electric Inst. (pres. 1958-59, mem. adv. com.), Nat. Assn. Electric Cos., Bus. Council, U.S., Butte chambers commerce, N.A.M., Am., Mont., Silver Bow County bar assns. Elk Clubs: Rotary (pres. 1938-39), Country (Butte); Town and Country (Helena); Chevy Chase (Md.). Home: 1245 W Platinum Butte MT 59701 Office: 40 E Broadway Butte MT 59701

COREY, CYRUS STANLEY, educator b. Blaine Me., Feb. 25, 1908; s. James H. and Bertha (Snow) C.; A.B., Colby Coll., 1928; A.M., U. Ill., 1931 Ph.D., 1933; m. Katharine Sybil Tubbs, July 12, 1934; children—Elaine, Brian. High sch. math. instr., Newport, N.H., 1928-30; high sch. prin., Mars Hill, Me., 1933-34; asso. prof. bus. and econs. Keuka Coll., 1934-35, prof., 1935- 37; asso. prof. econs. Kent (O.) State U., 1937-46, prof., 1946—, acting chmn. dept. econs., 1965-66, chmn., 1966-68, acting v.p. and provost, 1968-69; tchr. econs. U. Ill., summer 1946. Served from lt. (j.g.) to lt., USNR, 1943-46. Mem. Am. Econs. Assn., Am. Finance Assn., Nat. Tax Assn., Tax Inst. Am., Am. Assn. U. Profs., Phi Beta Kappa, Phi Sigma Kappa, Pi Gamma Mu, Kappa Phi Kappa, Delta Sigma Pi, Beta Gamma Sigma, Omicron Delta Epsilon. Mem. United Ch. of Christ. Home: 573 Vine St Kent OH 44240

COREY, EDWIN RAYMOND, educator; b. Detroit, Dec. 27, 1919; s. Joseph and Ethel (Mungeer) C.; A.B., Amherst Coll., 1941; A.M., Harvard, 1947, M.B.A., 1946, Ph.D., 1950; m. Charlotte Worrall; children—Thomas, David, Frederick, Joy, Margaret, Mary. Mem. faculty Harvard Bus. Sch., 1948—, prof. marketing, chmn. Advanced Mgmt. Program, 1963—; cons. to industry. Dir. Helmerich & Payne, Inc., Norton Co., Itek Corp. Trustee Babson Coll., Marketing Sci. Inst. Mem. Am. Marketing Assn., Am. Econ. Assn. Conglist. Club: Duxbury (Mass.) Yacht. Home: 43 Greylock Rd Wellesley MA 02181 Office: Harvard Business Sch Soldiers Field Boston MA 02163

COREY, ELIAS JAMES, chemist; b. Methuen, Mass., July 12, 1928; s. Elias and Tina (Hashem) C.; S.B., Mass. Inst. Tech., 1948, Ph.D., 1951; A.M. (hon.), Harvard, 1959; m. Claire Higham, Sept. 14, 1961; children—David, John, Susan. From instr. to asst. prof. U. Ill., 1951-55, prof., 1955-59; prof. chemistry Harvard, 1959—. Mem. bd. phys. sci. Alfred P. Sloan Found.; sci. adv. bd. Robert A. Welch Found. Recipient Swiss-Am. exchange fellowship, 1957; Guggenheim fellow 1957-58, 68-69; Alfred P. Sloan Found. fellow, 1956-59; Fritzche award Am. Chem. Soc., 1968; Intrasci. Found. award, 1968; Ernest Guenther award in chemistry of essentials oils and related products, 1968. Mem. Am. Acad. Arts and Scis., A.A.A.S., Am. (award pure chemistry 1959), Swiss, German chem soc., Nat. Acad. Sci., Sigma Xi. Author numerous sci. publs. Home: 20 Avon Hill St Cambridge MA 02140

COREY, GORDON RICHARD, utilities exec.; b. Osceola, Wis., Sept. 27, 1914; s. Ralph Watson and Bessie Mabel (Simpson) C.; B.A., U. Wis., 1936; M.B.A., Northwestern, 1940; m. Margarete Grenn, 1967; children—(by prev. marriage), Eleanor (Mrs. George Tatge), Margaret (Mrs. Ross Amundson), Ralph, Martha. Vice pres. Commonwealth Edison Co., 1953-62, exec. v.p., 1962-64, chmn. finance com., 1965—, also dir.; dir. Continental Ill. Nat. Bank & Trust Co., Chgo. Inland Steel Co., Chgo. C.P.A., Ill. Clubs: Chicago, Economic, Commercial, Wayfarers, Country Tennis. Home: 2511 Park Pl Evanston IL 60201 Office: 1 First National Plaza Chicago IL 60690

COREY, HERBERT RICE, banker b. Leominster, Mass., June 1, 1909; s. John Ruel and Carrie (Rice) C.; Asso. Sci. Accounting, Bentley Coll. Accounting and Finance, Boston, 1929; grad. Stonier Grad. Sch. Banking, Rutgers U., 1947; m. Helen Crimmins, Sept. 10, 1932; children—Andrea, Robert C. With First Nat. Bank Boston, 1929—, v.p., 1955, comptroller, 1965—; comptroller affiliate Old Colony Trust Co., 1965—; subsidiary Subsidiary Bank of Boston Internat., 1965—, dir., 1966—; trustee Melrose Savs. Bank (Mass.), 1958—, incorporator, 1963- -. Dir.-at-large Bank Adminstrn. Inst., 1970—. Chmn. Melrose Community Fund drive, 1945; mem. Melrose Planning Bd., 1953-56, Melrose Recreation Commn., 1955-57. Bd. corporators Bentley Coll. Accounting and Finance, 1964-69. Recipient Testimonial plaque Am. Bankers Assn., 1963. Mem. Am., Mass. (treas. 1966-68) bankers assns. Mason. Home: 200 Park Terrace Dr Melrose MA 02176 Office: 45 Milk St Boston MA 02106

COREY, PAUL FREDERICK, author; b. Shelby County, Ia., July 8, 1903; s. Edwin and Margaret Morgan (Brown) C.; A.B. in Journalism, U. Ia., 1925; m. Ruth Lechlitner, 1928; 1 dau., Anne Margaret. On staff The Economist, Chgo., 1925-26; with Retail Credit Co., N.Y.C., 1926; later with Ency. Brit.; with Real Estate Record and Builders Guide, N.Y.C., 1929-30; with Nat. Ency., 1930-31; ret. to a farm, Putnam County, N.Y., to write, 1931; furniture designer Cavedale Craftsman. Mem. Sci. Fiction Writers Am. Author books 1936-46: Five Acre Hill (teen-age novel), 1946; Acres of Antaeus (novel), 1946; The Little Jeep (juvenile), 1946; Shad Haul, 1947; Corn Gold Farm, 1948; Milk Flood, 1956; Homemade Homes, 1951; Home Workshop Furniture Projects, 1957; Holiday Homes: A Build-it-yourself Handbook; The Planet of the Blind (novel); also short stories. Guerrilla warfare specialist; did work on the subject in connection with First Service Command Tactical Sch., Sturbridge, Mass., 1942. Mem. Authors' Guild. Home: Sonoma CA 95476 ☆

COREY, STEPHEN MAXWELL, ret. educator; b. Rochester, N.Y., July 21, 1904; s. Stephen Jared and Edith (Webster) C.; B.S., Eureka (Ill.) Coll., 1926, LL.D., 1960; M.A., U. Ill., 1927, Ph.D., 1930; postgrad. U. Chgo., 1935; m. Martha Robb, 1929 (dec. 1952); 1 son, John Douglas; m. 2d, Elinor Karp Levie, 1953; step-children—Barbara, Tim, James. Fellow U. Ill., 1926-28; various assignments U. Ill., De Pauw U., U. Neb., U. Wis., 1928-40; prof. ednl. psychology U. Chgo., 1940-48, supt. lab. schs., 1940-44, dean of students, social sci. div., dir. Audio-visual Materials Center, 1944-48; prof. Tchrs. Coll., Columbia, 1948-65, exec. officer Horace Mann-Lincoln Inst. for Sch. Experimentation, 1948-56, head dept. Psychol. Found. and Services, 1955-57, dean, 1955-59; AID technician assigned Ministry Edn., India, 1959-62; vis. prof. U. Miami, 1962-63, prof., 1965-70, Sec., Desert Mental Health Assn., 1971—. Trustee Teaching Films Custodians, 1946-69. Fellow Am. Psychol. Assn., 1937-59; mem. Nat. Soc. for Study Edn. (dir. 1949-57, chmn. yearbook coms.), Am. Edn. Research Assn. (exec. com. 1958-60), N.E.A. (exec. com. 1953-56), Sigma Xi, Lambda Chi Alpha, Phi Delta Kappa. Author: (with others) Schools for a New World, 1947; Audio-visual Instructional Materials, 1949; Action Research to Improve School Practice, 1953; Instructional Leadership, 1954; Classroom Experimentation, 1960; Helping Other People Change, 1963. Contbr. to Ency. Ednl. Research, various profl. publs. Home: 2011 Brentwood Dr Palm Springs CA 92262

CORGAN, JOSEPH ALOYSIUS, govt. ofcl.; b. Luzerne, Pa., Feb. 2, 1907; s. John Bernard and Margaret Elizabeth (Backus) C.; student St. Thomas Coll., Scranton, Pa.; B.S. in Mining Engring., Pa. State U.,

1929; m. Katherine Elizabeth Simons, Apr. 11, 1940; children—Kathleen (Mrs. James D. Clements), Margaret (Mrs. Henry C. Kenski), Carolyn (Mrs. William F. Wells), Joseph Aloysius. Anthracite utilization activities Hudson coal Co., Scranton, Pa., 1929-35; combustion engr., D.C. Govt., 1936-37; commodity specialist Nat. Bituminous Coal Commn., 1937-40; coal economics br. U.S. Bur. Mines, 1940-45, chief anthracite and coke sect., 1945-54, chief anthracite div., 1955-68, chief, div. environment, 1968—. Mem. Am. Inst. Mining and Metall. Engrs. Author publs. U.S. Bur. Mines. Contbr. articles on coal research, coal products to trade jours. Home: 5605 Park St Chevy Chase MD 20015 Office: Dept of Interior Washington DC 20240

CORI, CARL FERDINAND, educator, biochemist; b. Prague, Czechoslovakia, Dec. 5, 1896; s. Carl I. and Maria (Lippich) C.; student Gymnasium, Trieste, Austria, 1906-14; M.D., German U. Prague, 1920; Sc.D., Yale, Western Res. U., 1947, Boston U., 1948, Cambridge U. (Eng.), U. Granada (Spain), 1966, Brandeis U., 1965; hon. degrees Monash U., Melbourne, Australia, 1966, Washington U., St. Louis, 1967, St. Louis U., 1967, Gustavus Adolphus Coll., 1963; m. Gerty Theresa Radnitz, Aug. 5, 1920 (dec. 1957); 1 son Carl Thomas; m. 2d, Anne FitzGerald Jones, Mar. 23, 1960. Came to U.S., 1922; naturalized, 1928. Asst. in pharmacology U. Graz (Austria), 1920-21; biochemist State Inst. for Study Malignant Disease, Buffalo, 1922-31; prof. pharmacology and biochemistry Washington U. Sch. Medicine, 1931-66; cons. biochemistry, vis. lectr. Mass. Gen. Hosp., Boston, 1966—. Recipient Nobel Prize in medicine and physiology, 1948; Willard Gibbs medal Am. Chem. Soc., 1948; Sugar Research Found. award, 1947, 50; Lasker award, 1946; Squibb Award 1947; St. Louis award. Mem. Nat. Acad. Scis.; hon. mem. Harvey Soc.; mem. Am. Soc. Biol. Chemists, Am. Chem. Soc. (Mid-West award 1946), A.A.A.S., Royal Soc. London, Am. Philos. Soc., Sigma Xi. Contbr. articles, chiefly on carbonhydrate metabolism and enzymes of animal tissues to Am. sci. jours. Mem. editorial bd. Jour. Biol. Chemistry, Biochimica et Biophysica Acta. Home: 1010 Memorial Dr Cambridge MA 02138

CORIDEN, GUY EDWARD, govt. ofcl.; b. Syracuse, N.Y., May 31, 1921; s. Guy Edward and Lucy (Lamb) C.; B.S., Ind. U., 1942; M.A., Marquette U., 1950, Fletcher Sch. Law and Diplomacy, 1951; m. Mary Louise Winbigler, Apr. 21, 1956. Security analyst Paul H. Davis & Co., Chgo., 1946-48; reins. underwriter AMRICO, Chgo., 1948-49; adminstrv. positions with U.S. Govt., 1951-60; staff adminstr. Pres.'s Commn. Nat. Goals, 1960-61; dir. Office European Programs, Bur. Ednl. and Cultural Affairs, State Dept., 1962—. Mem. nat. adv. com. Wayne State U. Urban Affairs Inst., 1968—; v.p. N.W. council Big Bros. Nat. Capital Area, 1971—. Served with AUS, 1942 45; ETO. Decorated Bronze Star. Mem. Urban League, Left Bank Jazz Soc., Les Cent Chevalirs du Vin. K.C. Club: Lakewood Country (Rockville, Md.). Home: 2204 Wyoming Washington DC 20008 Office: Dept of State Washington DC 20520

CORIE, JOSEPH JAMES, former aerospace co. exec.; b. N.Y.C., Dec. 19, 1916; s. Joseph and Rose (Foti) C., student Bklyn. Coll., 1936; B.C.S., Southeastern U., 1942; LL.B., Columbus U., 1947; m. Evelyn June White, Jan. 3, 1938; children—Patricia A. (Mrs. Robert Roth), Joseph R. Admitted to D.C. bar, 1946, also U.S. Supreme Ct. bar; practiced in Washington, 1947-48; asst. dir. budgets Office Sec. Def., 1948-56; staff mem. Hoover Commn., 1948, 54; asst. to exec. v.p. radioplane div. Northrop Corp., Beverly Hills, Cal., 1956, sec.-treas., 1957-59, corporate controller, 1959-65, corporate v.p. govt. procurement policies, 1965-69. Served with USNR, 1944-46. Club: Lakeside Golf (North Hollywood, Cal).

CORISH, WILLIAM S., banker. Sr. v.p. First Va. Bank. Office: 7205 Little River Turnpike Annandale VA 22003*

CORITA, SISTER MARY, artist, educator; b. Ft. Dodge, Ia., Nov. 20, 1918; d. Robert Vincent and Edith (Sanders) Kent; B.A., Immaculate Heart Coll., 1941; M.A., U. So. Cal., 1951. Entered community of Immaculate Heart Sisters, 1936; now prof. art Immaculate Heart Coll., Los Angeles. Artist specializing in serigraphy, also optical illusion art; exhibited numerous one-man shows in museums, galleries, univs. in U.S., Can. and Spain, including Cin. Art Mus., Munson Williams Proctor Inst., Brooks Meml. Art Gallery, Cal. Palace Legion of Honor, Balt. Mus., Morris Gallery, The Contemporaries, Mus. N.M., Sala Gaspar, Barcelona; rep. permanent collections Met. Mus., Mus. Modern Art, Library of Congress, Rosenwald Collection at Nat. Gallery, Cin. Mus., Cal. Palace Legion of Honor, Los Angeles County Mus., Phila. Mus., N.Y. Pub. Library, Art Inst. Chgo., Victoria and Albert Mus., London, Bibliotheque Nationale, Paris; complete collection of prints in Willis Gabriel collection; executed commns. for Internat. Graphic Arts Soc., Mus. Modern Art, Container Corp. Am., Los Angeles County Mus., Neiman-Marcus, Reynolds Aluminum. Address: 5515 Franklin Av Los Angeles CA 90028

CORK, CHARLES MADDEN, lawyer; b. Macon, Ga., Apr. 26, 1908; s. Charles D.S. and Harriet (Madden) C.; A.B., Mercer U., 1927, LL.B. cum laude, 1929; m. Josephine Hunt, May 21, 1930; children—Charles M., John Collier, Mary Jo (Mrs. D.H. Taylor, Jr.), Martha Susan (Mrs. James L. Self), Anne Maddox (Mrs. Ray Mills). Admitted to Ga. bar, 1929, since practiced in Macon; mem. firm Jones, Cork, Miller & Benton, 1938—. Dir. Ga. Loan & Trust Co., Barnes & Barnes, Inc., Hannibal Bottling Co., (Mo.). Mem. Bibb County Bd. Registrars, 1948-69. Mem. exec. bd. Appleton Ch. Home; bd. dirs., pres. Boys Club Macon, 1969-70. Mem. Am., Ga., Macon bar assns., Am. Judicature Soc., Delta Theta Phi. Episcopalian (vestryman, sr. warden), Elk (hon. life), Moose. Clubs: Men's Garden (pres. 1959), Idle Hour Country (Macon). Home: 4805 Brittany Dr Macon, GA 31204. Office: First Nat Bank Bldg Macon GA 31201

CORLE, FREDERIC WILLIAM, naval officer; b. Reno, Nev., Sept. 15, 1916; s. Frederick Burbank and Nellie (Jones) C.; B.S., U.S. Naval Acad., 1939; M.B.A., Harvard, 1953; m. Marjorie Anne Dudley, Sept. 12, 1942; 1 son, Frederic William II. Commd. ensign USN, 1939, advanced through grades to rear adm., 1966; various adminstrv. positions supply and material, Washington, 1947-51, Norfolk, Va., 1954-57; supply officer USS Franklin D. Roosevelt, Atlantic, 1953-54; mil. assistance officer U.S. European Command, Paris, France, 1957-59; supply officer U.S. Naval Shipyard, Phila., 1960-63; dir. officer personnel Bur. Supplies and Accounts, Washington, 1963-64; comdg. officer Electronics Supply Office, Great Lakes, Ill., 1964-66, Navy Ships Parts Control Center, Mechanicsburg, Pa., 1966-69; exec. dir. Def. Supply Agy., Washington, 1969—. Decorated Navy Commendation medal, Army Commendation medal, Legion of Merit. Mem. Am. Ordnance Assn. Mason. Club: Army-Navy Country (Washington). Home: 2807 Ft Scott Dr Arlington, VA 22202. Office: Def Supply Agy Washington DC 22314

CORLESS, ROBERT DOUGAN, assn. exec.; b. Longmeadow, Mass., Oct. 29, 1913; s. William Edward and Catherine Alice (Dougan) C.; grad. St. Joseph's Collegiate Inst., Buffalo, 1931; m. Adeline Ackerman, June 21, 1947; children—Susan Katherine, James Robert. Salesman indsl. supplies, 1954—; sec. Am. Philatelic Soc., 1963-64, dir., 1965-69, recorder, bd. v.p.'s 1970—. Served to 1st lt. USAAF, 1942- 46. Home: 1826 W Indianola Av Phoenix AZ 85015

CORLETT, ALLEN N., lawyer; b. Cleve., Sept. 3, 1904; s. Lynnus George and Jennie (Lindsey) C.; A.B., Western Res. U., 1926, LL.B., 1929; m. Dorothy Wilhelmy Weaver, Jan. 15, 1943; children—Mary Anne (Mrs. Robert J. Rotatori), Marsha (Mrs. Joseph C. Sarakaitis), Sister M. Jennifer, Ursuline, Allen N. Admitted to Ohio bar; practiced in Cleve.; now mem. firm Roudebush, Adrion, Brown, Corlett & Ulrich. Mem. Ohio Ho. of Reps., 1931-32; mem. Cuyahoga County Republican Exec. Com., 1946—; mem. Ohio Senate, 1947- 48; mem. Presdl. Electoral Coll., 1953. Served to capt. USNR, World War II; PTO. Mem. Am., Ohio, Cleve. (past mem. exec. com.) bar assns., Res. Officers Naval Services (past nat. v.p.), Alpha Tau Omega. Mason. Clubs: Cleveland Athletic (pres., past dir.); Shaker Heights Country. Home: 2840 Coventry Rd Shaker Heights OH 44120 Office: Williamson Bldg Cleveland OH 44114

CORLEY, EDWIN RAY, novelist, playwright; b. Bayonne, N.J., Oct. 22, 1931; s. Gordon and Lillian (Neal) C.; m. Elizabeth Zekauskas, July 5, 1953; children—Richard Patrick, Elizabeth Ann, Eugene Charles. Playwright, 5 Plays for 2 Men, Tokyo, 1951, Goodnight Sweet Prince, Tokyo, 1951, Hedda, N.Y.C., 1958, Letta Ripp, St. Louis, 1961; editor OffBroadway mag., 1954-58, films include Next Stop 28th, 1960, Up The Avenue, 1961 (Robert Flaherty award), Saturday Night on Channel 2, 1962 (Robert Flaherty award, Silver medal at Cannes); v.p. Compton Advt., 1966-68; v.p. DancerFitzgeraldSample, 1969. Served with USAF, 1947-51. Mem. Authors League Am., Nat. Assn. Broadcast Technicians. Author: Siege, 1969; The Jesus Factor, 1970; Farewell My Slightly Tarnished Hero, 1971. Address: care of Publicity Dir Dodd Mead Co 79 Madison Av New York City NY 10016

CORLEY, FRANCIS JOSEPH, clergyman, educator; b. St. Louis, Nov. 11, 1909; s. John Louis and Beulah Madeleine (Hayes) C.; student Marquette U., 1934-35; A.B., St. Louis U., 1933, M.A., 1938, S.T.L., 1941. Joined Soc. of Jesus, 1927, ordained priest Roman Catholic Ch., 1940; instr. theology and history St. Louis U., 1942-45, research asso. Inst. Social Order, 1945-58, editor Social Order, 1947-58, asst prof., 1958-61, asso. prof., 1961—, chmn. library bd., 1963—. Ford Found. grantee, Viet-Nam, S.E. Asia, 1956-57. Mem. Am. Oriental Soc., Am. Hist. Assn., Assn. for Asian Studies, Am. Friends of Vietnam (nat. com.), Royal Asiatic Soc. (Malaya), Am. Assn. U. Profs., Societe des Etudes Indochinoises (Saigon). Author: Viet-Nam Since Geneva, 1959; (with R.J. Willmes) Wings of Eagles, 1941, 67. Mem. internat. editorial adv. bd. S.E. Asia, Internat. Quar. Address: St Louis University 211 N Grand Blvd St Louis MO 63103

CORLEY, WILLIAM ANGUS, newsman; b. Bklyn., July 23, 1916; student George Washington U., 1933- 35, Inst. Film Techniques, Coll. City N.Y., 1947-50; m. Ana Luisa Aguialr, Dec. 17, 1949 (div.). With Asso. Press, N.Y.C., 1941-55; with NBC News, 1955—, formerly editor World News Roundup, N.Y.C., midwest news dir., Chgo., 1963-69, reorganized Saigon (Vietnam) News Bur., 1965-66, corr. bur. chief, Moscow, USSR, 1969—. Served with AUS. Clubs: Overseas Press (N.Y.C.). Office: NBC News Bur Moscow Union Soviet Socialist Republics

CORLISS, JOHN OZRO, educator; b. Coats, Kan., Feb. 23, 1922; s. Clark L. and Catharine (Smith) C.; B.S., U. Chgo., 1944; B.A., U. Vt., 1947; Ph.D., N.Y.U., 1951; m. Anna Jane Lea, Mar. 16, 1968; children—Susan Elizabeth, Joan Alison, Kimberley Ann, Jennifer Sara Corliss and Margaret L. Swenson. Postdoctoral fellow AEC Coll. de. France, Paris, 1951-52; instr. zoology Yale, 1952-54; asst. prof. to prof. zoology U. Ill., Urbana, 1954-64, prof. head dept. biol. scis., Chgo. Circle, 1964-69; dir. systematic zoology NSF, 1969-70; prof., head dept. zoology U. Md., College Park, 1970—; hon. research asso. zoology U. Coll., London, Eng., 1960-61; vis. prof. zoology U. Exeter, Eng., 1961-62. Mem. NSF panel systematic biology, 1966-69; mem. Nat. Com. Internat. Biol. Program, 1966-68. Served to capt. USAAF, 1943-46. Fellow A.A.A.S., Am. Inst. Biol. Scis.; mem. Soc. Protozoologists (past pres; mem. editorial bd.), Am. Micros. Soc. (editor, past pres.), Council Biology Editors (past chmn.), Am. Soc. Zoologists (pres.), Soc. Systematic Zoology (past pres.), Am. Soc. Parasitologists, Internat. Congress Systematic and Evolutionary Biology (convenor 1970—), numerous other socs., Phi Beta Kappa. Author: The Ciliate Protozoa, 1961. Contbr. numerous articles on protozoology to profl. jours. Home: 9512 E Stanhope Rd Kensington MD 20795 Office: Dept Zoology University of Md College Park MD 20742

CORMAN, JAMES CHARLES, congressman; b. Galena, Kan., Oct. 20, 1920; s. Ransford and Edna (Love) C.; B.A., U. Cal. at Los Angeles, 1942; LL.B., U. So. Cal., 1948; m. Virginia Little, 1946 (dec. May 1966); children—Mary Anne, James Charles; m. 2d, Carole Franda, 1967. Admitted to Cal. bar, 1949; practiced in Van Nuys, Cal., 1949-50, 52-57; mem. 87th-92d congresses from 22d Dist. of Cal. Mem. Los Angeles City Council, 1957-61. Served to maj. USMCR, 1942-46, 50-52. Mem. Cal., Los Angeles, San Fernado bar assns., Am. Legion, V.F.W. Democrat. Methodist. Lion. Home: 15120 Victory Blvd Van Nuys CA 91401 Office: Cannon House Office Bldg Washington DC 20515

CORMAN, ROGER WILLIAM, motion picture producer-dir.; b. Detroit, Apr. 5, 1926; A.B., Stanford, 1947; postgrad. Oxford (Eng.) U., 1950. Producer, Monster from the Ocean Floor, 1953; dir. Five Guns West, 1955; producer, dir. films, including The Wild Angels, The Trip, The Fall of the House of Usher, The Pit and the Pendulum, Masque of the Red Death, The Raven, The Saint Valentine's Day Massacre, The Intruder, The Secret Invasion, The Day the World Ended, Little Shop of Horrors, Bloody Mama, Gas-s-s; dir. Von Richthofen and Brown. Films shown at numerous film festivals. Mem. Producers Guild Am. (dir.). Office: 8831 Sunset Blvd Los Angeles CA 90069

CORN, IRA GEORGE, Jr., diversified mfg. co. exec.; b. Little Rock, Aug. 22, 1921; s. Ira George and Martha (Vickers) C.; student Little Rock Jr. Coll., 1941; A.B., U. Chgo., 1947, M.B.A., 1948; m. Louise Touchstone, Feb. 8, 1947 (div. Mar., 1961); children—Jay, John, Laura. Trainee marketing Gen. Electric Co., N.Y.C., 1947-48; asst. prof. So. Meth. U., 1948-54; corporate, financial cons. in Dallas, 1954-66; pres. Community Water Service, Dallas, 1960—, Lakeshore Apts., Indpls., 1964—; co-founder Tyler Corp., 1966, dir., 1966—, chmn. C & H Transp. Co., 1966—, co-founder Mich. Gen. Corp., 1968, chmn. exec. com., chief exec. officer, 1968— (all Dallas); chmn. bd. dirs. Aces Internat., Inc., Dallas. Speaker profl. orgns., Dallas, N.Y.C., Washington. Dir. Dallas council Boy Scouts Am., 1970—. Served from pvt. to sgt. AUS, 1942-46. Mem. Am. Mgmt. Assn., Nat. Assn. Bus. Economists, U. Chgo. Alumni Assn. (chmn. Dallas chpt. 1955—, nat. com. corporate support 1969—), Am. Contract Bridge League (bd. dirs.). Author syndicated column Aces on Bridge. Owner (with Joseph P. Driscoll) lost copy of The Declaration of Independence. Home: 4829 Forest Lane Dallas TX 75234 Office: 3108 Southland Center Dallas TX 75201

CORN, MERTON, banker; b. Bklyn., Sept. 15, 1934; s. Abraham and Rose (Stamm) C.; A.B., Bklyn. Coll., 1958; m. Hilda Bary, Mar. 26, 1959; children—Steven, Dara. With N.Y. State Banking Dept., 1958-63, Bankers Trust Co., N.Y.C., 1963- 66; with First Jersey Nat. Bank, Jersey City, 1966—, sr. v.p., 1969—; dir. Garden State Mortgage Co., Garden State Title Ins. Co., Guardian Comml. Corp. Served with USNR, 1952-55. Home: 406 Windsor Rd Englewood NJ 07631 Office: 1 Exchange Pl Jersey City NJ 07302

CORNATZER, WILLIAM EUGENE, biochemist, educator; b. Mocksville, N.C., Sept. 23, 1918; s. William Pinkston and Stella Augusta (Vogler) C.; student Mars Hill Coll., 1935- 37; B.S., Wake Forest Coll., 1939; M.S., U. N.C., 1941, Ph.D., 1944; postgrad. Oak Ridge Inst. Nuclear Studies, 1948; M.D., Bowman Gray Sch. Medicine, 1951; m. Margaret Virginia Freeman, Mar. 30, 1946; children—Nancy Freeman, William Eugene. Student asst. zoology Wake Forest Coll., 1937-38, phys. chemistry, 1938- 39; grad. and student asst. biol. and food chemistry U. N.C., 1939-41, Fels Research fellow, 1941-45; asst. prof. biochemistry Bowman Gray Sch. Medicine, 1946-51; prof., head dept. biochemistry med. sch. U. N.D., Grand Forks, 1951—, also dir. Ireland Research Lab. Mem. biochem. test com. Nat. Bd. Med. Examiners; mem. White Ho. Com. for Orgn. Conf. on Food, Nutrition and Health, 1969. Recipient Frank Billing award for original investigation; Silver medal A.M.A., 1951; Nat. Scis. Travel award to Internat. Congress Biochemistry, Paris, 1952, Tokyo, 1967; travel award Internat. Congress Cancer, London, Eng., Am. Assn. for Cancer Research, 1958; travel award to 1st Internat. Congress Pharmacology, Stockholm, 1961, Internat. Union Physiol. Sci., NSF Travel award to 7th Internat. Congress Biochemistry, Tokyo, 1967; travel award 8th Internat. Congress Nutrition, Am. Inst. Nutrition, Prague, 1969. Fellow A.C.P., N.Y. Acad. Scis., Am. Inst. Chemists; mem. Am. Assn. Oil Chemists, Am. Bd. Clin. Chemistry (dir.), Am. Assn. Clin. Chemists (nat. exec. com. 1957), Am. Assn. for Study of Liver Disease, Central Soc. for Clin. Research, Radiation Research Soc., Am. Chem. Soc., Am. Soc. Biol. Chemistry, So. Soc. for Clin. Research, Am. Fedn. for Clin. Research, Soc. Exptl. Biology and Medicine, A.A.A.S., Am. Assn. U. Profs., Am. Inst. Nutrition, Elisha Mitchell Sci. Soc., N.D. Acad. Scis. (pres. 1956), N.D. Diabetic Assn., Royal Soc. Medicine. Methodist. Author articles sci. jours. Research in properties of proteins, quinine metabolism, anti-malarial testing, phospholipide metabolism, radioactive isotopes, biol. effects of radiation. Address: University of ND Med Sch Grand Forks ND 58201

CORNBLATH, MARVIN, physician, educator; b. St. Louis, June 18, 1925; s. David and Sophia (Kornblett) C.; student Washington U., St. Louis, 1944, M.D. cum laude, 1947; m. Joan Senturia, Aug. 29, 1948; children—Nancy Alice, Polly Sarah, Ben S. Rotating intern St. Louis Jewish Hosp., 1947-48; resident pediatrics St. Louis Children's Hosp., 1948-50; asst. pediatrics Washington U. Sch. Medicine, 1948-50; instr., then asst. prof. pediatrics, Johns Hopkins Sch. Medicine, 1953-59; asst. prof., then asso. prof. Northwestern U. Med. Sch., 1959-61; asso. prof., then prof. pediatrics U. Ill. Coll. Medicine, 1961-68; prof. pediatrics, head dept. U. Md. Sch. Medicine, 1968—; research asso., adj. attending pediatrician Sinai Hosp., Balt., 1953-59; pediatrician out-patient dept. Johns Hopkins Hosp., 1956-59; asst. chmn. div. pediatrics Michael Reese Hosp., Chgo., 1959-61; attending physician, physician-in-charge neonatal service Research and Ednl. Hosps., Chgo., 1961-68; attending physician Cook County Hosp., Chgo., 1963-68; cons. in field. Served to 1st lt., M.C., AUS, 1951-53. Diplomate Am. Bd. Pediatrics. Mem. Soc. Pediatric Research, Am. Acad. Pediatrics, A.A.A.S., N.Y. Acad. Sci., Brit. Biochem. Soc., Central Soc. Clin. Research, Am. Physiol. Soc., Am. Diabetes Assn., Sigma Xi, Alpha Omega Alpha. Author numerous articles in field. Home: 3809 St Paul St Baltimore MD 21218

CORNEIL, PHILIP LESTER, banker; b. Spokane, Wash., Nov. 28, 1909; s. Christopher Philip and Ann (Bain) C.; B.S., U. Ida., 1932; m. Helen Jean Way, Sept. 18, 1944; children—Ann, Carolyn, Philip N., Virginia. Dist. mgr. Pacific Finance Corp., 1935-42; with Seattle-First Nat. Bank, 1945—, v.p., 1953-61, exec. v.p., 1961—, also dir. Mem. Seattle Area Indsl. Council, adv. bd. Seattle Salvation Army. Served to lt. comdr. USNR, 1942-46. Mem. Assn. Res. City Bankers, Blue Key, Sigma Alpha Epsilon. Episcopalian. Mason. Clubs: Rainer, Harbor, Washington Athletic (Seattle). Home: 2616 42d St Seattle WA 98199 Office: PO Box 3586 Seattle WA 98124

CORNELISON, FLOYD SHOVINGTON, Jr., educator, psychiatrist; b. San Angelo, Tex., Apr. 30, 1918; s. Floyd Shovington and Nannie Lee (Brewer) C.; B.A., Baylor U., 1939; postgrad. Northwestern U., 1939-40, Columbia, 1943-45; M.D., Cornell U., 1950; M.S., Boston U., 1958; m. Erwina Ladelle Bode, Aug. 30, 1940 (div. 1966); 1 dau., Ann Brewer; m. 2d, Ruth Reeder Williams, Sept. 17, 1966. Intern, Grasslands Hosp., Valhalla, N.Y., 1950-51; resident psychiatry Mass. Meml. Hosp., Boston U. Sch. Medicine, also Boston State Hosp., 1951-54; from asst. psychiatry to instr. Boston U. Sch. Medicine, 1951- 58; lectr. psychology Tufts Coll., 1954-56; successively asst. prof., asso. prof., cons. prof. psychiatry U. Okla. Sch. Medicine, 1958-64; prof. psychiatry, chmn. dept. Jefferson Med. Coll., Thomas Jefferson U., Phila., 1962—; past mem. staff numerous hosps., now attending psychiatrist-in-chief Jefferson Med. Coll. Hosp.; cons. area hosps., 1962—. Mem. Mental Health Film Bd., N.Y.C., 1961—. Bd. dirs. Marka T. du Pont Inst. Human Behavior, 1971—. Fellow psychiat. films Med. Audio-Visual Inst., Assn. Am. Med. Colls., 1951-53; candidate Boston Psychoanalytic Inst., 1954-58. Diplomate Am. Bd. Psychiatry and Neurology. Fellow Am. Psychiat. Assn.; mem. A.A.A.S., A.M.A., Am. Orthopsychiat. Assn., Am. Sci. Film Assn., Assn. Am. Med. Colls., Council Med. Television, N.Y. Acad. Scis., Pa. Psychiat. Soc., Pa., Phila. County med. socs., Univ. Film Producers Assn., Sigma Xi. Author articles, producer films in field. Initiated self-image experience, photographic confrontation technique in psychiat. research. Home: 244 S 9th St Philadelphia PA 19107

CORNELIUS, ADAM EDWARD, Jr., shipping co. exec.; b. Buffalo, Nov. 4, 1910; s. Adam E. and Emma (Reiser) C.; B.S., Wharton Sch., U. Pa., 1934; m. Elizabeth Becker, July 24, 1948; children—Linda Jouise, Adam E. III; children by previous marriage—Carol Anne., Bonnie Jean. Partner, Boland & Cornelius, Inc., steamship operators, Buffalo, 1934. jr. partner , 1935-39, now pres., dir.; exec. v.p. Am. Steam Ship Co., Buffalo, 1939-57, dir., 1939—, pres., 1957—, treas., 1957-63, chmn. bd., 1963-67; chmn. Amersand S.S. Co., 1953—; pres., dir. Reiss S.S. Co., 1969—; dir. Marine Trust Co. Western N.Y. Mem. adv. bd., past pres. Salvation Army Assn. Buffalo. Bd. dirs., v.p. Deaconess Hosp., Buffalo; trustee United Fund. Mem. Buffalo C. of C., Lake Carrier's Assn. (dir.). Clubs: Country, Rotary, Propeller, Buffalo. Home: 321 Depew Av Buffalo NY 14214 Office: Marine Trust Bldg Buffalo NY 14203

CORNELIUS, CHARLES EDWARD, educator; b. Huntington Park, Cal., Dec. 19, 1927; s. Samuel Paul and Alberta (Johnson) C.; B.S. in Animal Sci., U. Cal., 1949, B.S. in Vet. Sci., 1951, D.V.M., 1953, Ph.D., 1957; m. Bette Jean Watt, Sept. 2, 1948; children—Stephen, Clifford, John, Aimee. Asst. prof., then asso. prof. U. Cal. at Davis, 1957-66; chmn. dept. physiology 1965-66; prof., dean Coll. Vet. Medicine, Kan. State U., Manhattan, 1966-71; dean Coll. Vet. Medicine, U. Fla., Gainesville, 1971—. Dir. Mem. study sect. gen. medicine NIH, 1965-69, mem. nat. adv. council to health research facilities, 1969—; nat. civilian cons. for vet. medicine USAF, 1970—. Mem. Am. Physiol. Soc., Soc. Exptl. Biology and Medicine, Am. Vet. Med. Assn. Am. Gastroenterol. Assn. Author: Clinical

Biochemistry of Domestic Animals, 1963, 70. Editor (with Kaneko); Advances in Veterinary Science, 1966—. Home: 2700 SW 13th St Gainesville FL 32601

CORNELIUS, EDWARD GORDON, marketing and mgmt. specialist; b. Berea, Ky., Feb. 13, 1896; s. Frank and Nancy (Edwards) C.; A.B., Maryville (Tenn.) Coll., 1925; A.M., Vanderbilt U., 1926, Ph.D., 1936; grad. study (summers) George Peabody Coll. for Teachers, 1926, U.N.C., 1927, U. Chicago, 1928, 29, U. Cal., 1932, U. Ky., 1937, Ind. Coll. Armed Forces, 1951-52; married May Fisher, 1932. Head economics and business Southwestern Coll., Winfield, Kan., 1928, 1933; asso. prof. commerce and finance Bucknell U., 1936-46; prof. chmn. marketing and management La. Poly. Inst., 1947-51; prof. bus. adminstrn., head dept. bus. and ind. management, Tenn. Tech., Cookeville, 1951-61, prof. bus. edn., 1961-66; prof. bus. adminstrn. Belmont Coll., Nashville, 1966—. Served as non-commd. officer, U.S. Army, 1918-19. Mem. Am. Arbitration Assn., Soc. for Advancement Mgmt., Acad. Mgmt., N.E.A., Assn. Higher Edn., Sigma Iota Epsilon, Pi Gamma Mu, Kappa Alpha Order, Omicron Delta Gamma, Omicron Delta Kappa, Pi Kappa Delta, Tau Kappa Alpha. Presbyn. Author books, numerous articles and pamphlets. Home: Belmont Terrace Nashville TN 37212

CORNELIUS, FRANCIS DUPONT, artist, conservator of paintings; b. Pitts., Oct. 19, 1907; s. Henry R. and Mary (Taylor) C.; B.Arch., U. Pa., 1933; M.A., U. Pitts., 1940; m. Adele Hedges, 1951; children—Andrew Kellogg, Henry Robert, Katharine Taylor. Archtl. designer, mural painter, tchr. art and math. Colonial Sch. Pitts., 1935-40, U. Pitts., 1942-44; research fellow in conservation of paintings Met. Mus. Art, N.Y.C., 1944-52; tech. adviser Colorado Springs Fine Arts Center, 1952-55. restorer, 1955-68; conservator Cin. Art Mus., 1968-71, curator Conservation Lab., 1971—. Ind. lab. for conservation of paintings and other works of art, Colorado Springs, 1952-68, Cin., 1968—: conservator Art Gallery Mus. N.M., Santa Fe. 1955-61, U. Neb. Art Gallery, 1958—, El Paso (Tex.) Mus. Art, 1960—; lectr. on art conservation Colo. Coll., 1961-68. Fellow Internat. Inst. for Conservation Mus. Objects; mem. Am. Assn. Museums, Spanish Colonial Art Soc. (trustee 1964—). Author articles on art. Home: 8400 Blome Rd Cincinnati OH 45243 Office: Cin Art Mus Cincinnati OH 45202

CORNELIUS, JOHN CHURCH, business exec.; b. Milford, Pa., Aug. 21, 1900; s. John Church and Amy Salina (Davis) C.; A.B., U. Wis., 1924; m. Miriam A. Swartz, May 29, 1924; 1 son, John Church. Mem. advt. dept. Chgo. Tribune, 1924; mem. advt. agency Batten, Barton, Durstine & Osborn, Inc., Mpls., 1931-33, v.p. in charge Mpls. office, 1933-39, dir. 1940—, v.p. in charge western offices, 1939-43, exec. v.p. in charge western offices, 1943-55; pres. Cornelius Stamp Co.; dir. IDS Progressive Fund, Inc., Dart Industries, Inc., Investors Variable Payment Fund, Inc., Vexilar Engring. Inc., Domain Industries, Inc.; dir., also mem. exec. com. Investors Stock Fund, Inc., Investors Mut., Inc., Investors Selective Fund, Inc. Pres. Am. Heritage Found., 1955-61. Bd. dirs., pres., founder Boys Club of Mpls.; bd. dirs. Boys' Club of Am., Jr. Achievement of Mpls; dir. Trout Unlimited, 1963-67. Mem. Nat. Municipal League, Am. Assn. Advt. Agys., 1944-45, vice chmn., 1946, chmn., 1947; chmn. adv. com., 1948; dir. Advt. Council. Dir. Mpls. C. of C., Civic and Commerce Assn., Acquatennial Assn., Orchestral Assn., Inst. Fine Arts, St. Barnabas Hosp., Council Social Agys.; pres. Minn. Assn. for Crippled Children and Disabled Adults; gen. chmn. Century Celebration Community Fund drive 1942; vice chmn. five war bond drives; chmn. state U.S. Def. bonds; adv. com. Savs. Bonds div. Recipient gold medal March of Minn. radio program Advt. and Selling Assn., 1938, Good Citizenship medal Nat. Soc. S.A.R., Mpls. award Mpls. C. of C., 1955, Distinguished Citizen award Nat. Municipal League, 1958, Shape the Future award Young Man of Minn., 1959, Distinguished service award Advt. Fedn. Am., 1962, Kappa Sigma award, 1963; Gold Key award, Boys' Clubs Am., 1963; Silver Medal award Printers' Ink, 1965. Mem. Pillsbury Fellowship (U. Minn.). Republican. Episcopalian. Clubs: Minneapolis (dir.), Minikahda (dir.), Newcomen Soc. Contbr. sporting publs. Pub. Am. Boy mag. Home: 3816 W Calhoun Blvd Minneapolis MN 55410 Office: Northwestern Bank Bldg Minneapolis MN 55402 ☆

CORNELIUS, JOSEPH FRANKLIN, banker; b. Spokane, Wash., Sept. 12, 1907; s. Joseph Moran and Frida (Eike) C.; student Am. Inst. Banking, 1927-33; m. Mirth R. Hern, Oct. 2, 1931; children—Joseph Franklin, Karen Kay (Mrs. Ronald C. Crown). Asst. mgr. marketing dept. Old Nat. Bank in Spokane, 1925-30; various positions to v.p. First Nat. Bank, Spokane, 1930-52; exec. v.p. Marine Bank & Trust Co., Tampa, Fla., 1952-57, pres., 1957-60; pres. Bank of Clearwater (Fla.), 1960-69, chmn. bd., 1969—; chmn. bd. Clearwater Beach Bank, 1970—; pres. 500 Cleveland St., Clearwater, 1966—. Vice chmn. Clearwater Downtown Devel. Bd., 1971—; pres., organizer Downtown Assn. Clearwater, 1968-69; pres. Golden Triangle Civic Assn., 1963; vice chmn. Com. of 100 of Pinellas County, 1969; pres. Joseph F. Cornelius Family Found., 1964—, Hillsborough County (Fla.) Heart Assn., 1956. Bd. dirs. Fla. West Coast Ednl. Television; mem. devel. council Morton F. Plant Hosp. Assn.; bd. dirs. St. Paul's Sch., Clearwater. Mem. Am. Inst. Banking (mem. nat. exec. council 1948-52), Greater Clearwater C. of C. (treas. 1969, v.p. 1966-67), Fla. State C. of C. (past dir.), Fla. Bankers Assn. (mem. exec. council 1964). Republican. Episcopalian. Elk, Kiwanian (dir. 1969). Club: Corlouel Yacht (dir. 1970—) (Clearwater); Ye Mystic Krewe of Gasparilla (Tampa). Home: 114 Live Oak Lane Harbor Bluffs Largo FL 33540 Office: 500 Cleveland St Clearwater FL 33517

CORNELIUS, RICHARD T., mfg. co. exec.; b. 1911; married. With Cornelius Co., Anoka, Minn., 1935—, chmn. bd., 1968—, also dir. Office: 2727 N Ferry St Anoka MN 55303•

CORNELIUS, WILLIAM E., bank exec.; b. Ozark, Mo., May 29, 1899; s. Lorenz and Dorothea (Roesch) G.; A.B., Southwest State Coll., 1922; student Northwestern U., 1928; m. Everilde Louise Troendle, Jan. 12, 1927; children—Helen Louise (Mrs. John Wilder Bowden), William E. With Sunbeam Corp., Chgo., 1926-65, v.p., dir., 1946-63, exec. v.p., 1963-65, now dir.; chmn., chief exec. officer O'Hare Internat. Bank, N.A., Chgo., 1964—; dir. Ridge Motors, Inc., Orton Crane Co. Mem. Chgo. Crime Commn. Bd. dirs. Max McGraw Wildlife Found., Resurrection Hosp. Mem. Chgo. Hist. Soc., Navy League. Home: 916 N Prospect St Park Ridge IL 60068 Office: 8501 Higgins Rd Chicago IL 60631

CORNELIUS, WILLIAM EDWARD, utilities co. exec.; b. Salt Lake City, Sept. 6, 1931; s. Edward Vernon and Gladys (Bray) C.; B.S., U. Mo., 1953; m. Mary Virginia Bunker, June 13, 1953; children—Mary Jean, Linda Anne. Mgr., Price Waterhouse & Co., St. Louis, 1955-62; asst. comptroller Union Electric Co., St. Louis, 1962-64, dir. corporate planning, 1964-67, exec. v.p., 1968—, also dir. Bd. dirs. Mo. Bapt. Hosp., Mus. of Sci., Downtown St. Louis, Inc., William Woods Coll. Served to 1st lt. AUS, 1953-55. C.P.A., Mo. Mem. Financial Execs. Inst., Beta Theta Pi. Clubs: Bellerive Country, Noonday, St. Louis. Home: 55 Berrywood Dr St Louis MO 63122 Office: Memorial Dr St Louis MO 63166

CORNELL, EZRA, lawyer; b. N.Y.C., July 2, 1903; s. Henry Watson and Margaret Feek (Bouck) C.; student Colo. Coll., 1921-24; LL.B., Cornell U., 1927; m. Eleanor Anderson Branch, Jan. 22, 1931; children—Ezra IV, Nancy Branch. Admitted to N.Y. bar, 1928; with White & Case, N.Y.C., 1927—, mem. firm, 1943—. Dir. Chicago Pneumatic Tool Co., Atlantic, Gulf & Pacific Co. Bd. trustees St. Lukes Meml. Trust; mem. council Cornell U., adv. bd. Law Sch. Mem. Am., N.Y., Internat. bar assns., S.A.R., Holland Society Assn. Bar City N.Y., Cornell Law Assn. (pres.), Cornell Alumni Assn. (dir.). Clubs: Montclair Golf; Downtown Assn., Cornell of N.Y. (past pres.) (N.Y. City). Home: 550 Park St Montclair NJ 07043 Office: 14 Wall St New York City NY 10005

CORNELL, GEORGE WASHINGTON II, journalist; b. Weatherford, Okla., July 24, 1920; s. Charles H. and Gladys (Cameron) C.; A.B., U. Okla., 1943; L.H.D., Defiance Coll., 1962; m. Jo Ann Reeves, Apr. 1, 1944; children-Marion Emma, Harrison Reeves. Reporter, Daily Oklahoman, Oklahoma City, 1943-44; newsman A.P., N.Y.C., 1947-51, religion columnist, 1951—. Served to 2d lt., inf., AUS, 1944- 47. Redipient Nat. Religious Pub. Relations Council award, 1953, Religion Heritage in Am. Faith and Freedom award, 1960, Religion Newswriters Assn. Supple Meml. award, 1961. Mem. Am. Newspaper Guild, Religious Newswriters Assn. Episcopalian. Author: They Knew Jesus, 1957; The Way and its Ways, 1963; Voyage of Faith, 1964. Home: 22 Vista Way Port Washington NY 11050 Office: 50 Rockefeller Plaza New York NY 10020

CORNELL, JOSEPH, artist; b. Nyack, N.Y., Dec. 24, 1903; self-taught. One-man exhbns. include Julien Levy Galleries, N.Y.C., 1932, 33, 39, 40, Hugo Gallery, N.Y.C., 1946, Copley Gallery, Hollywood, Cal., 1948, Charles Egan Gallery, 1949, 50, Allan Frumkin Gallery, Chgo., 1953, Stable Gallery, 1957, Bennington Coll., 1959; three-man exhbn. Richard Feigen Gallery, Chgo., 1960; group exhbns. include Fantastic Art, DADA, Surrealism Mus. Modern Art, 1936, Exposition Internat. du Surrealisme, Galeries des Beaux Arts, Paris, France, 1938, Art of This Century, N.Y.C., 1942, Carnegie Inst., 1958, Art of Assemblage, Mus. Modern Art, 1961, Whitney Mus. ann., 1962; rep. permanent collections Mus. Modern Art, Whitney Mus.

CORNELL, KATHARINE, ret. actress; b. Berlin, Germany, Feb. 16, 1898 (parents Am. citizens); d. Peter Cortleyou and Alice Gardner (Plimpton) Cornell; ed. Oaksmere, Mamaroneck, N.Y.; Chancellor's Medal, U. Buffalo, 1935; Litt.D., U. Wis., 1936, Elmira Coll. for Women, 1937, Hobart Coll., 1938, U. Pa., 1938, Middlebury Coll., 1955, Kenyon Coll., 1956; L.H.D., Smith Coll., 1937, Dr. Fine Arts, Clark U., 1941, Ithaca Coll., 1947, Princeton, 1948; m. Guthrie McClintic, Sept. 8, 1921 (dec. 1961). Made debut with Wash. Square Players, N.Y.C., 1917; with Jessie Bonstelle Stock Co., 1919-20; traveled with The Man Who Came Back, 1920; appeared in Little Women, London, 1920; with Jessie Bonstelle Stock Co., 1920-21; has appeared in N.Y. prodns. of Nice People, A Bill of Divorcement, Will Shakespeare, The Enchanted Cottage, Casanova, The Way Things Happen, The Outsider, Tiger Cats, Candida, The Green Hat, The Letter, The Age of Innocence, and Dishonored Lady. Became actress-mgr. with The Barretts of Wimpole Street, 1931, Lucrece, 1932, Allen Corn, 1933, Romeo and Juliet, 1934, Flowers of the Forest, 1935, Saint Joan, 1936, The Wingless Victory and Candida, 1937, Herod and Mariamne, 1938, No Time for Comedy, 1939-40, The Doctor's Dilemma, 1941, Rose Burke, 1942, The Three Sisters, 1942-43, Lovers and Friends, 1943-44, The Barretts of Wimpole Street, overseas, 1944-45, United States, 1945, 47; Antigone, 1946; Antony and Cleopatra, 1947-48; That Lady, 1949-50; Captain Carvallo, 1950; The Constant Wife, 1951-52; The Prescott Proposals, 1953-54; The Dark is Light Enough, 1954-55; The Firstborn, 1958; Dear Liar, 1959-60; on TV in The Barretts of Wimpole Street, 1956; There Shall be no Night, 1957. Co-chmn. Plays of Living div. Family Service Assn. Am. Recipient art citation Nat. Conf. Christians and Jews, 1946; woman of Yr. award Am. Friends Hebrew U., 1959; medal for good speech on stage, Am. Acad. Arts and Letters, 1959. Clubs: Colony, Cosmopolitan (N.Y.); Garrett (Buffalo). Home: New York City NY 10001 also Vineyard Haven MA 02568

CORNELL, ROBERT WILLIAM, business exec.; b. Sherman, N.Y., Oct. 24, 1906; s. Harry S. and Mary (Miller) C.; A.B., Syracuse U., 1928; M.B.A., Harvard, 1930; m. Katharine Coe, Sept. 20, 1930; children—Robert William, Peter V.B., James J. Factory accountant Reliance Electric & Engr. Co., Cleve., 1930-40, prodn. mgr., 1934-40, works mgr., 1940-46; comptroller, treas. Parker-Hannifin Corp., Cleve., 1946-47, v.p. mfg., 1947-54, pres. Parker Aircraft Co., Los Angeles, subsidiary, 1954-58, v.p. marketing, 1958-60, exec. v.p., 1961-62, pres. parent co., 1963-69, chmn. bd., 1969—, also dir.; dir. Tremco Corp., Soc. Nat. Bank Cleve., A.G. McKee Co., Cleve., Morrison Products, Inc., Cleve., Trustee, Euclid Gen. Hosp., Cleve. Clubs: Mentor (O.) Harbor Yachting, Hermit, Union, Mayfield Country (Cleve.); Chagrin Valley Hunt (Gates Mills, O.); Bel-Air (Cal.) Country: Pepper Pike (O.). Home: Old Mill Rd Gates Mills OH 44040

CORNELL, SAMUEL DOUGLAS, former coll. pres.; b. Buffalo, N.Y., Apr. 16, 1915; s. Douglas and Gwendolyn (Fletcher) C.; A.B., Yale, 1935, Ph.D., 1938; m. Priscilla Mary Greene, Nov. 25, 1939 (dec. Mar. 1959); children—Susan Fletcher (Mrs. Thomas E. Wilkes), Deborah Greene (Mrs. Ralph J. Colwell), Samuel Douglas, Stephen Ellicott; m. 2d, Judithe Friderichsen, Sept. 27, 1969. Devel. physicist Eastman Kodak Co., Rochester, N.Y., 1938-42; dep. sec., Guided Missiles Com. of Joint Chiefs of Staff, 1946; staff of research and devel. bd. Dept. Def., Washington, 1946-52, dir. planning div., 1949-52; exec. officer Nat. Acad. Scis., NRC, 1952-65; pres. Mackinac Coll., Mackinac Island, Mich., 1965-70; sci. cons., 1970—. Served from lt. to comdr., USNR, 1942-46. Trustee Peter C. Cornell Trust. Fellow A.A.A.S.; mem. Am. Phys. Soc., Phi Beta Kappa, Sigma Xi. Clubs: Economic (Detroit); Cosmos (Washington). Address: 3526 Hamlet Pl Chevy Chase MD 20015

CORNELL, WILLIAM ASHBROOK, telephone co. exec.; b. Newark, O., Sept. 17, 1916; s. Ernest and Rose (Maynes) C.: B.S., Denison U., 1938; m. Lois Champney, Sept. 5, 1940; children—Charlene H., William Ashbrook, Jack C. With Ohio Bell Telephone Co., 1938—, gen. traffic mgr., 1959-63, v.p., gen. mgr., 1963—. Mem. exec. com. Cleve. chpt. A.R.C.; Am., Cleve. Regional Hosp. Planning Bd.; mem. Cleve. Citizens League; gen. chmn. Huron Rd. Hosp. bldg. fund. Bd. dirs. Jr. Achievement Greater Cleve., Cleve. Better Bus. Bur. Mem. econs. adv. com. Denison U. Served to capt. USAAF, 1942-46. Decorated Bronze Star with one leaf cluster. Mem. Ohio, Cleve., U.S. chambers commerce, Beta Theta Pi (trustee Denison chpt.). Presbyn. (pres. trustees). Clubs: Mayfield Country (bd. dirs.). Home: 19000 S Woodland Rd Shaker Heights OH 44120 Office: 100 Erieview Plaza Cleveland OH 44114

CORNELSEN, PAUL FREDERICK, food co. exec.; b. Wellington, Kan., Dec. 23, 1923; s. John S. and Theresa Albertine (von Klatt) C.; student U. Wichita, 1939-41, 45-46; B.S. in Mech. Engring., U. Denver, 1949; m. Floy Lila Brown, Dec. 11, 1943; 1 son, John Floyd. With Boeing Airplane Co., 1940-41, Ralston Purina Co., St. Louis, 1946—, v.p. internat. div., 1961-63, adminstrv. v.p., gen. mgr. internat. div., 1963-64, v.p., 1964—, pres. internat. group, 1964—, dir., founding mem., vice chmn. bd. Latin Am. Agribusiness Investment Corp., 1970—. Mem. industry com. on freedom from hunger FAO, hdqrs. Rome, Italy, chmn. industry coop. program UN Agys., 1969—; vice chmn. bd., mem. exec. com. Agribus. Council. Served to 1st lt. AUS, WW II, also Korean War. Decorated Silver Star. Mem. Am. Soc. M.E., St. Louis C. of C., World Trade Council St. Louis. Home: 506 Fox Ridge Rd St Louis MO 63131 Office: 901 Checkerboard Sq Plaza St Louis MO 63188

CORNELSEN, RUFUS, clergyman; b. Colony, Okla., Jan. 29, 1914; s. Isaac and Anna (Boese) C.; A.B., Southwestern State Tchrs. Coll., Weatherford, Okla., 1935; Th.B., So. Bapt. Theol. Sem., 1937; B.D., Union Theol. sem., 1939; postgrad. Columbia, 1939-40, Lutheran Theol. Sem., 1941-42, Princeton Theol. Sem., 1948-49; Litt.D., Gettysburg Coll., 1964; m. Frances Louise Deen, Aug. 4, 1946; children—Susan Kathleen, David Alan, Sara Ann. Ordained to ministry United Luth. Ch., 1942; pastor Emanuel Luth. Ch., New Brunswick, N.J., 1942-57, Luth. Student Assn., Rutgers U., 1942-57; asso. dir. social action United Luth. Ch. Am., 1957-58, dir. social action, 1958-62; Sec. for civil and econ. life Luth. Ch. in Am., 1962-65, rep. to UN, 1964-65; asso. gen. Sec. for planning and program Nat. Council of Chs. of Christ in U.S.A., 1965-68; exec. dir. Met. Christian Council of Phila., 1968—. Exec. sec. New Brunswick Council Chs., 1945-46; mem. social missions com. Luth. Synod N.Y., 1947-50; exec. bd. Luth. Synod N.J., 1950-52, mem. bd. social missions, 1950-56, pres., 1955-56; mem. commn. social responsibility United Luth. Ch., 1952-57; Luth. World Fedn. fellow study laymen's insts. in Europe, 1958; mem. bd. social ministry Luth. Ch. Am., 1966—. Bd. dirs. Union Theol. Sem., 1958—; past trustee Protestant Found. Students, Rutgers U.; mem. nat. council, nat. bd. YMCA, 1967—, mem. armed services com., 1967—; bd. govs. U.S.O. Mem. Urban League New Brunswick (dir. 1944-68, pres. 1946- 48), Nat. Council Chs. (rep. Latin Am. Conf. Ch. and Soc. 1962), World Council Chs. Contbr. articles, chpts. to religious publs. Home: 415 S Chester Rd Swarthmore PA 19081 Office: 1211 Chestnut St Philadelphia PA 19107

CORNELY, PAUL BERTAU, educator, physician; b. Guadeloupe, French W.I., Mar. 9, 1906; s. Eleodore and Adrienne (Mellon) C.; came to U.S., 1921, naturalized, 1934; A.B., U. Mich., 1928, M.D., 1931, Dr. P.H., 1934, D.Sc., 1968; m. Mae Stewart, June 23, 1934; 1 son, Paul Bertau. Intern Lincoln Hosp., Durham, N.C., 1931-32; mem. faculty Howard U. Coll. Medicine, Washington, 1934—, chief div. phys. medicine and rehab., 1959-64, prof. preventive medicine and pub. health, 1955—; med. dir. Freedmen's Hosp., Washington, 1947-58, chief div. phys. medicine and rehab., 1959-64; cons. Health and Welfare Council Nat. Capital Area, 1957—; cons. AID, 1960—; asst. to exec. med. officer United Mine Workers Welfare and Retirement Fund, Inc., 1971—. Mem. Pres.'s Commn. on Population and Am.'s Future, 1970; mem. com. of cons. on cancer Senate Com. on Labor and Pub. Welfare, 1970. Bd. dirs. Physicians Forum, 1947—, pres., 1960-61; pres. Community-Group Health Found. Recipient Sesquicentennial award U. Mich., 1967. Diplomate Am. Bd. Preventive Medicine and Pub. Health. Fellow. Am. Coll. Preventive Medicine; mem. Med. Soc. D.C. (Community Service award 1964), Am. Cancer Soc. (v.p. 1962- 63), Am. (exec. com. 1964—, pres. 1969-70, chmn. exec. bd. 1970—), D.C. (pres. 1963-65, Distinguished Service award 1971) pub. health assns. Home: 1338 Geranium St N W Washington DC 20012

CORNER, FRANK HENRY, diplomat of New Zealand; b. Napier, New Zealand, May 17, 1920; s. Charles William and Sybil (Smith) C.; M.A. in History, Victoria U., Wellington, New Zealand, 1941; m. Lynette Robinson, Dec. 29, 1943; children—Katherine, Victoria. Joined New Zealand War Cabinet Secretariat and Dept. External Affairs, 1943; 1st sec. embassy, Washington, 1948-51; sr. counsellor New Zealand High Commn., London, Eng., 1952-58; dep. sec. external affairs, 1958-62; permanent rep., A.E. and P. of New Zealand to United Nations, 1962-67, pres. trusteeship council, 1964-65; New Zealand ambassador to U.S., 1967—. Mem. New Zealand delegation to Peace Conf., Paris, France, 1946, meetings of Commonwealth Prime Ministers, 1944-58, Gen. assemblies of UN, 1948-52, 55, 60-66, Far Eastern Commn., 1948-51, Internat. Whaling Commn. 1952- 58, Geneva Conf. on Korea, 1954, Internat. Atomic Energy Agy., 1957; mem. coms. organizing Internat. Geophys. Year, 1955-57; mgmt. com. Trans- Antarctic Expdn., 1955-58; chmn. UN vis. mission to U.S. Trust Ter. Pacific Islands, 1964, New Zealand rep. UN Security Council, 1966. Home: 27 Observatory Circle NW Washington DC 20008 Office: 19 Observatory Circle NW Washington DC 20008

CORNER, GEORGE WASHINGTON, anatomist, med. historian; b. Balt., Dec. 12, 1889; s. George Washington and Florence (Evans) C.; A.B., Johns Hopkins, 1909, M.D., 1913; Dr. honoris causa, Cath. U. Chile, 1942; D.Sc., U. Rochester, 1944, Boston U., 1948, Chgo., 1958; LL.D., Tulane, 1955, Temple, 1956; M.D.S. (hon.), Women's Med. Coll., Phila., 1958; D.Sc., Oxford U., 1950, M.A., 1952; D.Litt., U. Pa., 1965; m. Betsy Lyon Copping, Dec. 28, 1915; children—George Washington, Hester Ann (dec.). Med. asst. Grenfell Labrador Mission, summers, 1912-13; asst. anatomy Johns Hopkins, 1913-14; resident house officer Johns Hopkins Hosp., 1914-15; asst. prof. anatomy, U. Cal., 1915-19; asso. prof. anatomy Johns Hopkins, 1919-23, now prof. emeritus of embryology; prof. anatomy U. Rochester, 1923-40, also curator Med. Library, 1938-40; dir. dept. of embryology Carnegie Inst. Washington, 1940-56; historian Rockefeller Inst., 1956-60, vis. prof., 1961—; exec. officer Am. Philos. Soc., 1960—; George Eastman vis. prof. Oxford U., 1952-53; Vicary lectr. Royal Coll. Surgeons, London, 1936; Vanuxem lectr. Princeton, 1942; Terry lectr. Yale, 1944; research prof. Commonwealth Fund, U. Louisville Med. School, 1946; U.S. del. Internat. Congress of Endocrinology, 1941, pres. congress, 1964; pres. Internat. Congress of Anatomists, 1960. Mng. editor, Am. Jour. Anatomy, 1939-41. Trustee Samuel Ready Sch. Received Squibb award, Soc. Study of Internal Secretions, 1940, Presdl. Certificate of Merit, 1948; Passano Found. award, 1958; Dale medal Brit. Soc. of Endocrinology, 1964. Hon. fellow Balliol College, Oxford, 1952-53. Fellow Rochester Mus. Arts and Scis., 1943. Hon. fellow Royal Soc. Edinburgh, Royal Coll. Obstetrics and Gynecology London; fellow Internat. Inst. Embriology; mem. Royal Soc. London (fgn.), Am. Assn. Anatomists (sec. 1930-38, pres. 1946-48), Soc. Exptl. Biology and Medicine, Am. Philos. Soc. (v.p. 1953-56) Nat. Acad. Scis. (v.p. 1953-57). Anat. Soc. Gt. Britain (hon.), Am. Assn. History Medicine, Phi Beta Kappa, Sigma Xi, fgn. corr. mem. numerous socs.; hon. mem. and fellow Am. and fgn. socs. Clubs: Century (N.Y.C.); Franklin Inn (Phila.). Author books, 1927—; also numerous papers in field. Address: 104 S 5th St Philadelphia PA 19106 ☆

CORNER, W. R., railroad ofcl.; b. Winnipeg, Man., Can., Jan. 3, 1922; s. Wilfred Richard and Rose Ann (McKay) C.; B.Commerce, U. Man., 1942; chartered accountant Inst. Chartered Accountants, 1949; m. Constance Irene Mahon, Jan. 18, 1951; children—Virginia, Georgie, Rosemary, Carol, Robert, Amelia, Constance. Comptroller, Man. Power Commn., 1949-55; with Canadian Nat. Rys., 1955—, co-ordinator data processing, 1959-65, comptroller, 1965-71, v.p., 1968-71, v.p. accounting and finance, 1971—; lectr. in field. Served with Royal Canadian Army, 1942-46. Fellow Inst. Chartered Accountants; Assn. Am. R.R. (2d vice chmn. accounting div.),

Financial Execs. Inst., insts. chartered accountants Man., Que. Roman Catholic. Clubs: University, Railway (Montreal); Beaconsfield (Que.) Golf. Home: 187 Hampshire Rd Beaconsfield 870 Quebec Canada Office: PO Box 8100 Montreal 101 Quebec Canada

CORNET, JOE, Jr., retail stores exec.; b. Dallas, 1921. Pres., dir. Cornet Stores, Pasadena, Cal. Home: 210 S San Rafael Av Pasadena CA 91105 Office: 411 S Arroyo Pkwy Pasadena CA 91101*

CORNET, JOE, Sr., retail stores exec. Chmn., Cornet Stores, Pasadena, Cal. Office: 411 S Arroyo Pkwy Pasadena CA 91101*

CORNETT, RICHARD ORIN, educator and cons.; b. Driftwood, Okla., Nov. 14, 1913; s. Grover Cleveland and Essie (Richardson) C.; B.S., Okla. Baptist U., 1934; M.S., U. Okla., 1937; postgrad. U. Ill., 1938-39; Ph.D., U. Tex., 1940; D.Sc., Hardin-Simmons U., 1954; Litt.D., Jacksonville, U., 1964; LL.D., Belknap Coll., 1967; m. Lorene Huston, May 26, 1943; children—Linda, Robert, Stanley. Instr. physics Okla. Bapt. U., 1935-37; asso. prof., 1940-41, prof., 1941; asst. supr. physics Pa. State Engring., Sci., Mgmt., Def. Tng. Program, 1941-42; lectr. electronics, Harvard, 1942-45; spl. research asso. OSRD 1945; asst. to pres. Okla. Baptist U., 1945-46, v.p., 1946-47, exec. v.p., 1947-51; exec. sec. Edn. Commn., So. Bapt. Conv., 1951-58, So. Assn. Baptist Colls. and Schs., 1951-58; editor So. Bapt. Educator, 1951-58; specialist for coll. and univ. orgn. and adminstrn. U.S. Office Edn., 1959, exec. asst. to dir. div. higher edn., 1959-61, acting asst. commr., dir., 1961-64, dir. div. ednl. orgn. and adminstrn., 1964-65; v.p. Gallaudet Coll., Washington, 1965—. Mem. U.S. delegation UNESCO Conf. on Devel. Higher Edn. in Africa, 1962. Democrat. Baptist. Author: (with White, Weber, Manning) Practical Physics, 1943; Algebra, A Second Course, 1945; (with others) Electron Tubes and Circuits, 1947; co-author: Cued Speech Handbook for Parents, 1971. Originator of cued speech communication method for deaf. Home: 8702 Royal Ridge Lane Laurel MD 20810 Office: Gallaudet Coll Florida Av and 7th St N E Washington DC 20002

CORNETTE, JAMES P., educator; b. Charleston, Miss., Nov. 17, 1908; s. Albieus Marvin and Winnie Jane (Johnston) C.; A.B., Ky. Wesleyan Coll., 1929; A.M., U. Va., 1930; Ph.D., George Peabody Coll. for Tchrs., Nashville, 1938; m. Mary Lawson, Feb. 26, 1930; children—Marvin Brister, James Lawson, William Richard. Tchr., athletic coach, Clark County (Ky.) High Sch., 1928-29, Mattoon (Ky.) High Sch., 1930; asso. prof. English, Western Ky. State Coll., Bowling Green, 1930-45; dean Baylor U., Waco, Tex., 1945-48; pres. West Tex. State U., Canyon, 1948—. Pres., Am. Assn. State Colls. and Univs., 1966-67. Mem. Nat. Edn. Assn., Phi Delta Kappa, Pi Kappa Delta. Democrat. Mason, Rotarian. Author: A Biography of John Henry Clagett, 1938; A History of the Western Kentucky State College, 1941; (with A. L. Crabb) Modern Language Handbooks, Grades V-VIII, 1941. Home: 4th Av Canyon TX 79015

CORNFELD, DAVE LOUIS, lawyer; b. St. Louis, Dec. 24, 1921; s. Abraham and Rebecca (David) C., A.B., Washington U., St. Louis, 1942, LL.B. (editor Law Quar. 1943), 1942; m. Martha Herrmann, May 30, 1943; children—Richard Steven, James Allen, Lawrence Joseph. Admitted to Mo. bar, 1943, since practiced in St. Louis; partner firm Husch, Eppenberger, Donohue, Elson & Cornfeld, and predecessor, 1954—; lectr. law Washington U., 1966—. Served with AUS, 1945-46. Mem. Am. (chmn. com. taxation income estates and trusts, sect. taxation 1969—), St. Louis (past chmn. taxation com) bar assns., Order of Coif. Jewish religion (trustee temple 1967—). Mason. Home: 834 Oakbrook Lane University City, MO 63132. Office: 7 N 7th St St Louis MO 63101

CORNGOLD, NOEL ROBERT DAVID, educator, physicist; b. N.Y.C., Jan. 20, 1929; s. Herman A. and Estelle (Bramson) C.; A.B., Columbia, 1949; A.M., Harvard, 1950, Ph.D., 1954; m. Cynthia Milgrom, June 29, 1952; children—Cara Eve, Jordan Lewis. Group leader theoretical reactor physics Brookhaven Nat. Lab., 1958-66; prof. applied sci. Cal. Inst. Tech., Pasadena, 1966—; cons. Los Alamos Sci. Lab., Gen. Atomic Co. Recipient certificate of merit Am. Nuclear Soc., 1966. Fellow Am. Nuclear Soc.; mem. Am. Phys. Soc., Phi Beta Kappa. Contbr. articles profl. jours. Home: 549 San Marino Av San Marino CA 91108 Office: Cal Inst Tech Pasadena CA 91109

CORNING, DUANE LEONARD, adj. gen. S.D.; b. Madison, S.D., Apr. 1, 1917; s. James Lee and Maude (Winters) C.; A.B., Sioux Falls Coll., 1939; grad. USAF Staff and Command Coll., 1949, USAF War Coll., 1954; m. Catherine Julia Schnaidt, Oct. 1, 1942; children—James, Bruce, Carol. Tchr. Sch., Sioux Falls, 1940-41; joined S.D. Army N.G., 1934, advanced through grades to maj. gen., 1964; served as officer with AC, USNR, 1941-45, USAF, 1950-52, 61-66; comdr. 114th Fighter Group, Air N.G., 1952-63; adj. gen. S.D., 1963—; dir. S.D. Civil Def., 1963—, S.D. SSS, 1963—, S.D. Emergency Planning, 1964—. Chmn., Aero. Commn. S.D., 1960—; chmn. adv. bd. Res. Forces Policy Bd., 1957-58; chmn. Gov.'s Communications Com.; mem. S.D. Crime Commn., Fed.-State Telecommunications Com. chmn. bd. All Saints Sch., Sioux Falls; mem. Black Hills council Boy Scouts Am. Decorated D.F.C., Air medal with oak leaf cluster, Navy Mem. Air Force Assn. (v.p. 1962), Sioux Falls Coll. Booster Assn. (pres. 1964), N.G. Assn., Nat. Rifle Assn., Adj. Gen.'s Assn. (exec. council), Am. Fighter Pilot Assn. (v.p.), Izaak Walton League (bd. dir.). Episcopalian (mem. bd.) Elk, Mason (Shriner). Home: 3103 Falls Dr Rapid City SD 57701 Office: Camp Rapid Rapid City SD 57701

CORNING, ERASTUS, 2d, mayor; b. Albany, N.Y., Oct. 7, 1909; s. Edwin and Louise (Maxwell) C.; A.B., Yale, 1932; m. Elizabeth N. Platt, June 23, 1932; children—Erastus III, Elizabeth (Mrs. Dudley). Pres. Albany Assos., Inc., 1932—, Ellsworth Builders Supply, 1950—, Avrora, Inc., 1955, Union River Lumber Co., 1966—; mayor Albany, 1942—. Dir. Nat. Comml. Bank. Mem. N.Y. state assembly, 1936, N.Y. state senate, 1937-41; del. N.Y. State Constl. Conv., 1967, Democratic Nat. Conv., 1968. Served with AUS, 1944-45; PTO. Mem. Am. Legion, V.F.W., Phi Beta Kappa, Chi Psi. Home: 116 S Lake Av Albany NY 12208 Office: City Hall Albany NY 12207*

CORNISH, DUDLEY TAYLOR, educator, historian; b. Carmel, N.Y., Jan. 11, 1915; s. Stanley Dyckman and Jane (Taylor) C.; A.B., U. Rochester, 1938; M.A., U. Colo., 1947, Ph.D. in History, 1949; m. Maxine Fisher, Sept. 10, 1946; 1 son, Dudley Taylor. Asst. prof., then asso. prof. Kan. State Tchrs. Coll., Pittsburg, 1949-58; prof. history Kan. State Coll., Pittsburg, 1958—, chmn. dept. social sci., 1959-61, chmn. dept. history, 1966—. Sec. Crawford County (Kan.) Democratic Central Com., 1958-60. Bd. dirs. Crawford County chpt. A.R.C., 1950-58. Served to capt. AUS, 1942-46. Mem. Kan. History Tchrs. Assn. (pres. 1957), Am., So. hist. assns., Kan. Hist. Soc. (dir. 1969—), Am. Studies Assn., Orgn. Am. Historians, Alpha Delta Phi, Omicron Delta Kappa, Phi Alpha Theta, Kappa Alpha Psi. Author: The Sable Arm: Negro Troops in the Union Army, 1861-1865, 1956. Compiler: The Negro in Civil War Books, A Critical Bibliography, 1967. Editor in chief Midwest Quar., 1959-67, asso. editor, 1967—. Office: Kan State College Pittsburg KS 66762

CORNMAN, JAMES WELTON, educator; b. Phila., Aug. 16, 1929; s. Ralph Miller and Rose (Scharfe) C.; grad. Haverford Sch., 1947; A.B., Dartmouth, 1956; M.A., Brown U., 1957, Ph.D., 1960; m. Elizabeth Marie Pedrotty, Feb. 2, 1955; children—Deborah, Julie, Diane, Elizabeth. Instr. philosophy Ohio State U., 1960-63; asst. prof. philosophy U. Rochester, 1963-65, asso. prof., 1965-67; asso. prof. philosophy U. Pa., Phila., 1967-69, prof., 1969—, chmn., 1970—. Andrew Mellon postdoctoral fellow, 1965-66; NSF grant, 1968-70, 71-73; Am. Council Learned Socs. fellow, 1970-71. Author: Metaphysics, Reference and Language, 1966; (with K. Lehrer) Philosophical Problems and Arguments, 1968; Materialism and Sensations, 1971. Home: 201 Walnut Av Wayne PA 19087 Office: Dept Philosophy U Pa Philadelphia PA 19104

CORNS, RICHARD WILLIAM, transp. co. exec.; b. Cleve., Aug. 8, 1907; s. Evan Robert and Catherine (Pascal) C.; student U. Akron, 1929; m. Doris Stroman, Nov. 5, 1932; children—Frederick Storman, Evan Robert. Trust clk., analyst Guardian Trust Co., Cleve., 1929-34; with B.F. Goodrich Co., 1934-49, gen. traffic mgr., 1947-49; with Roadway Express, Inc., 1949—, exec. v.p., 1953-61, pres., 1961-67, vice chmn. bd., 1967-70, now dir.; dir. Akron Nat. Bank & Trust Co. Trustee Children's Hosp., Akron, 1959-. Mem. Am. Soc. Traffic and Transp., Nat. Def. Transp. Assn., traffic clubs N.Y.C., Akron. Presbyn. (trustee, elder). Clubs: City, Portage Country, Akro (Akron). Home: 2490 Addyston Rd Akron OH 44313 Office: 1077 Gorge Blvd PO Box 471 Akron OH 44309

CORNUELLE, HERBERT CUMMING, bus. exec.; b. Cin., Mar. 25, 1920; s. Herbert Cumming and Gertrude (Schleitzer) C.; A.B., Occidental Coll., 1941; postgrad. U. Denver, 1942; m. Jean Bradbeer, Dec. 20, 1942; children—John, Richard, Bruce, Ann. Exec. v.p. Found. for Econ. Edn. N.Y. State, 1946-49; liaison officer Volker Fund, Burlingame, Cal., 1949-53; with Dole Corp., Honolulu, 1953-63, v.p., 1955-58, pres., dir., 1958-63; exec. v.p., dir. United Fruit Co., Boston, 1963-67, pres., 1967- 69; exec. v.p. Dillingham Corp., Honolulu, 1969-70, pres., 1970—. Chmn. bd. regents U. Hawaii, 1961-63. Served to lt. USNR, 1942-45. Mem. Govtl. Research Assn., Phi Beta Kappa. Clubs: Pacific, Oahu Country (Honolulu); Pacific Union (San Francisco). Author: Mr. Anonymous, 1951. Home: 3711 Poka Pl Honolulu HI 96816 Office: 1441 Kapiolani Blvd Honolulu HI 96814

CORNWALL, JOSEPH CLIFT, lawyer; b. Elizabeth, N.J., June 6, 1918; s. Harry Forsyth and Bess (Cover) C.; grad. Phillips Exeter Acad., 1935; A.B., Princeton, 1939; LL.B., Yale, 1942; m. Barbara Wallace, Apr. 4, 1942; children—Elizabeth S., Timothy C., John W., Joseph F., Pamela M. Admitted to N.J. bar, 1946; with firm Hood, Lafferty & Emerson, Newark, 1945-46; with Wallace & Tiernan Inc., and affiliated cos., Belleville and East Orange, N.J., 1946-69, sec., 1952-69, also dir.; Wallace Eljabar Fund, Inc., East Orange, N.J. 1969—; adv. com. Lloyd's N.Y. Trustee Kent Place Sch., Summit, N.J. House of Good Shepherd, Hackettstown, N.J., Eljabar Found., Westfield, N.J. Served with USNR, 1941-45. Republican. Episcopalian (vestryman). Clubs: University (N.Y.C.); Short Hills, Baltusrol Golf (Springfield, N.J.). Home: 45 Grosvenor Rd Short Hills, NJ 07078. Office: 50 Evergreen Pl East Orange NJ 07019

CORNWALL, RICHARD S. finance co. exec.; b. N.Y.C., Jan. 22, 1932; s. Samuel C. and Nora Adele (Fitzgerald) C.; B.A. in Econs., Wesleyan U., Middletown, Conn., 1954; grad. Rutgers U. Grad. Sch. Banking, 1964; grad. mgmt. course, Am. Mgmt. Assn. Sch., N.Y.C., 1965; student Wharton Sch. Finance, U. Pa., 1957-58; m. Nancy Lee Ness, June 30, 1956; children—S. Christopher, Richard Stephen, Bryan Robert, David, Andrew. Spl. agt., trainee Indemnity Ins. Co. N. Am., 1954-55; spl. agt. Resolute Ins. Co., 1955-56; v.p. Phila. Nat. Bank, 1956-67; exec. v.p. Bank of Commonwealth, Detroit, 1967-70; v.p., gen. operations mgr. comml. indsl. and real estate financing operations Ford Motor Credit Co., Dearborn, Mich., 1970—. Mem. Detroit Econ. Club. Clubs: Detroit Athletic; Grosse Pointe (Mich.) Yacht. Home: 1215 Three Mile Dr Grosse Pointe Park MI 48230 Office: Ford Motor Credit Co American Rd Dearborn MI 48121

CORNWELL, CHARLES DANIEL, educator, phys. chemist; b. Williamsport, Pa., Dec. 27, 1924; s. John G. and Anna (Moul) C.; A.B. with distinction, Cornell U., 1947; Ph.D. in Chem. Physics, Harvard, 1951; m. Blanche M. Haskins, Sept. 1, 1951. Research asso. State U. Ia., 1950-52; mem. faculty U. Wis., 1952—, prof. chemistry, 1960—. Served with USNR, 1944-46. Mem. Am. Phys. Soc., Am. Chem. Soc., Phi Beta Kappa, Phi Kappa Phi. Spl. research nuclear quadruple resonance, nuclear magnetic resonance, microwave spectroscopy. Home: 5421 Esther Beach Rd Madison, WI 53713.

CORNWELL, DAVID GEORGE, educator, biochemist; b. San Rafael, Cal., Oct. 8, 1927; s. John Nevius and Nora (Jonasen) C.; B.A. with honors, Coll. Wooster, 1950; M.A., Ohio State U., 1952; Ph.D., Stanford, 1955; m. Normagene Coon, Mar. 14, 1959; children—Karen Sue, David Andrew. NRC fellow Harvard, 1954-56; faculty Ohio State U., 1956—. prof. physiol. chemistry, 1963—. chmn. dept. physiol. chemistry, 1965—. Mem. nutrition study sect. NIH, 1966-70, nutrition sci. tng. rev. sect., 1970—. Served with AUS, 1945-46. Co-recipient hon. mention for research 6th Internat. Congress Hematology, 1956; named One of Ten Outstanding Men, Columbus Jr. C. of C., 1962. Mem. Am. Chem. Soc., Biophys. Soc., Am. Soc. Biol. Chemists, Am. Oil Chemists Soc., Am. Inst. Nutrition, Sigma Xi. Contbr. articles chemistry lipids and lipoproteins to profl. jours. Mem. editorial bd. Jour. Lipid Research, 1962-66, Jour. Nutrition, 1969—. Home: 2290 Middlesex Rd Columbus OH 43220

CORNWELL, DAVID JOHN MOORE, (John Le Carre), author; b. Poole, Dorset, Eng., Oct. 19, 1931; s. Ronald Thomas Archibald and Olive (Glassy) C.; student Bern (Switzerland) U., 1948-49; B.A. in Modern Langs., Oxford (Eng.) U., 1956; m. Alison Ann Sharp, Nov. 27, 1954; children—Simon, Stephen, Timothy. Tutor, Eton Coll., 1956-58; mem. Brit. Fgn. Service, 1959-64, 2d sec. embassy, Bonn, Germany, 1961-63; consul, Hamburg, Germany, 1963-64. Author: Call for the Dead, 1961; Murder of Quality, 1962; The Spy Who Came in From the Cold (Brit. Crime Novel of Year award, Somerset Maugham award, Mystery Writers Am. Annual award), 1963; The Looking-Glass War, 1965; A Small Town in Germany, 1968; The Naive and Sentimental Lover, 1971. Address: care John Farguharson Ltd 15 Red Lion Sq London WCIR 4QW England

CORNWELL, ELMER ECKERT, Jr., educator, polit. scientist; b. Holyoke, Mass., July 6, 1924; s. Elmer Eckert and Eloise (Leining) C.; A.B., Williams Coll., 1948; A.M., Harvard, 1951, Ph.D., 1953; m. Caroline Cole; children—Alison, Joan. Instr., Williams Coll., 1948-49, Princeton, 1953-55; mem. faculty Brown U., 1955—, prof. polit. sci., 1964—, chmn. dept., 1962-71. Research dir. R.I. Constl. Conv., 1965-67. Alternate delegate Democratic Nat. Conv., 1960, 64. Served with USNR, 1942-45. Mem. Am., New Eng. (pres. 1968-69), Northeast (pres. 1970-71) polit. scis. assns., Phi Beta Kappa. Author: Presidential Leadership of Public Opinion, 1965; The American Presidency: Vital Center; (with others) The American Democracy, 1969. Home: 103 Taber Av Providence RI 02906

CORNYN, WILLIAM STEWART, educator; b. Vancouver, B.C., Can., July 18, 1906; s. John and Lillian (Stewart) C.; came to U.S., 1922, naturalized, 1944; A.B. with highest honors, U. Cal. at Los Angeles, 1940; M.A., Yale, 1942, Ph.D., 1944; m. Sara Fetterman, Sept. 24, 1928; 1 son, William Stewart; m. 2d, Catherine Stockton McKee, Jan. 29, 1937; children—John McKee, Mary Elizabeth; m. 3d, Jane Robinson, Aug. 7, 1967. Mem. faculty Yale U., 1943—, prof. Slavic and S.E. Asian linguistics, 1958—, chmn. dept. Slavic langs. and lit., 1958-63, chmn. dept. linguistics, 1963-66. Served with AUS; col. Res., ret. Am. Council Learned Socs. fellow, 1942-43; Fulbright research prof. to Burma, 1949-50, 51-52, 58- 59; Guggenheim fellow, 1962-63. Mem. Linguistic Soc. Am., Am. Oriental Soc., Conn. Acad. Arts and Scis., Asia Soc., Assn. Asian Studies, Assn. Advancement Slavic Studies, Phi Beta Kappa. Clubs: Mory's, Graduates (New Haven). Author: Outline of Burmese Grammar, 1944: Spoken Burmese, 1946; Beginning Russian, 2d edit., 1960; Burmese Chrestomathy, 1956: Burmese Glossary, 1958; also articles, reviews. Address: Yale U New Haven CT 06520

CORONA, RAMON MARTIN, architect; b. Mexico City, Mexico, May 15, 1906; s. Charles Corona and Suzanne Martin; student Xaverian Coll., Oxford (Eng.) U., 1920-23; grad. Nat. Sch. Architecture U. Autonoma de Mexico, 1929; m. Amalia Lopez Negrete de Corona, Mar. 31, 1932; children—Mayita Corona de Martinez (Mrs. Luis Martinez del Rio), Ramon Corona Lopez Negrate. Pvt. practice architecture, Mexico City, 1929—. Pres. Cultural Affairs Univesidad Autonoma de Guadalajara, Mexico, 1971, mem. council, 1968-71. Gold medallist Mexican Coll. Architects. Fellow Royal Inst. British Architects, Royal Canadian Inst. Architects, Academie de France, Archtl. Inst. Jamaica, Peru, Paraguay, Brazil, Argentina, Colombia, Central Am., Am. Inst. Architects, Internat. Union Architects (pres. 1969-72), Mexican Soc. Architects, Nat. Coll. Architects (bd. honour v.p. 1961). Home: 670 Monte Libano Mexico DF 10 Mexico Office: 24 Av Veracruz Mexico DF 7 Mexico

CORPE, RAYMOND FRANCIS, physician, surgeon; b. Colfax, Ill., July 14, 1912; s. Hary W. and Fay (Comminski) C.; B.S. cum laude, Eureka (Ill.) Coll., 1934; M.D., U. Ill., 1940; m. Elizabeth Ferry, May 20, 1941; children—Carleen, Kathleen, Raymond Scott. Intern Lutheran Hosp., Ft. Wayne, Ind., 1939-40; intern Ill. Research and Edn. Hosp., Chgo., 1940-42, resident surgery, 1942-43; resident pathology Med. Coll. Va., Richmond 1941-42; commd. Officer USPHS, 1943-52; practice medicine, specializing in surgery, Rome, Ga., 1950—; chief surgery Battey State Hosp., 1952, supt., 1953—; br. dir. Tb Ga. Dept. Health. 1967—. Diplomate Am. Bd. Surgery, Am. Bd. Thoracic Surgery. Fellow A.C.S., Floyd County Med. Soc.; mem. Am. Hosp. Assn. Methodist. Address: Battey State Hosp Rome GA 30161

CORPORON, EDGAR KENNETH, utilities exec.; b. Portis, Kan., Nov. 22, 1908; s. Bert Emery and Emily (Smith) C.; student Kan. State U., 1928-31; B.A., Wichita State U., 1933; m. Mildred Lois Hadler, Sept. 9, 1934; children—Joan Kay (Mrs. R.A. Cone), Jean Carol (Mrs. Stewart A. Huff). Engr., Kan. Gas & Electric Co., Phoenix Engring. Corp., 1930-48; asst. mgr. united power pool United Light & Rys. Service Co., Davenport, Ia., 1948-50; v.p., sec. Interchange Power Services, Inc., Des Moines, 1950-57, pres., 1957-58; asst. to pres. Ia. Pub. Service Co., Sioux City, 1958-61, treas., asst. sec., 1961-71, v.p., treas., asst. sec., 1971—; treas. Energy Devel. Co.; treas. Cimmred, Inc. Bd. dirs. Ia. Taxpayers Assn., Tax Research Conf. Registered profl. engr., Kan. Mem. I.E.E.E., Ia. C. of C., Delta Tau Delta. Republican. Presbyn. (trustee). Mason (Shriner). Clubs: Sioux City Country, Hawkeye. Home: 3615 Pierce Pl Sioux City IA 51104 Office: Orpheum-Electric Bldg Sioux City IA 51102

CORR, JAMES VANIS, textile co. exec.; b. Selma, Ala., June 28, 1922; s. Mark Stroud and Julia (Dozier) C.; student Georgetown U., 1940-41, George Washington U., 1941-42; B.S., U. Ala., 1948, LL.B., 1951; m. Emily Swift Voltz, Mar. 22, 1944; children—James Vanis, William V., Emily S., Julia D. Admitted to Ala. bar, 1951, Ga. bar, 1967; partner Dent & Corr, C.P.A.'s Birmingham, Ala., 1954-61; exec. v.p. Buck Creek Industries, Inc., Atlanta, 1961-70, pres., 1970—, dir., 1961—. Speaker tax clinic U. Ala., 1954—. Mem. bd. Met. YMCA, Birmingham. Served with AC, USMCR, 1944-46. Decorated D.F.C. with 2 oak leaf clusters, Air medal with 4 oak leaf clusters. C.P.A., Ala., Ga. Mem. Ala. (past chmn. Birmingham chpt.), Ga. socs. C.P.A.'s, Am., Ala. bar assns., Am. Inst. C.P.A.'s, Ala., Ga. textile assns. Club: Exchange (Birmingham). Home: 965 Landmark Dr NE Atlanta GA 30342 Office: 3867 Roswell Rd NE Atlanta GA 30305

CORR, JOHN PATRICK, journalist; b. Phila., July 16, 1934; s. Francis Joseph and Catherine (Dougherty) C.; student pub. schs. Phila.; m. Marjorie Ann Matthews, Mar. 14, 1964; children—Helen Louise, John Douglass. With Phila. Evening Bull., 1954-59, Times Newspapers, 1959-61; reporter-columnist Camden (N.J.) Courier 1961-62; writer Harrisburg (Pa.) Patriot, 1962-63; with Phila. Inquirer, 1963—, edn. editor, 1966—. Served with USNR, 1957-59. Recipient Best Reporting award Pa. Newspaper Pubs. Assn., 1965, Best Writing award Phila. Press Assn., 1969; Carnegie Corp. grantee, 1967. Mem. Nat. Edn. Writers Assn. (sec.-treas. 1969—), Nat. Council for Advancement Edn. Writing, (dir. 1969—). Contbr. articles on edn. to mags. and jours. Home: 330 Owen Av Lansdowne PA 19050 Office: 400 N Broad St Philadelphia PA 19101

CORRA, ARTHUR BERT, educator; b. Superior, Wyo., Sept. 25, 1929; s. Fred and Francesca (Gentilini) C.; A.A., Stockton Jr. Coll., 1949; A.B., Coll. Pacific, 1951, Mus.B., 1951, Mus.M., 1958; Mus.D., Ind. U., 1968; m. Deborah Brooks, June 8, 1957; children—Denise, Margo. Tchr., Coll. of Pacific, 1952-61; asst. to dean Ind. U. Sch. Music, 1963-70; dir. U. Okla. Sch. Music, 1970-71; chmn. music dept. Ill. State U., Normal, 1971—. Mem. Evansville, Ft. Wayne philharmonic orchs.; condr. Contemporary Music Chamber Group, 1963-70. Grantee, Music Educators Nat. Conf./Comprehensive Musicianship Project, 1967-70, German Studies Inst., 1970-71. Mem. Coll. Band Dirs. Nat. Assn., Nat. Assn. Coll. Wind and Percussion Instrs., Am. Musicological Soc., Music Tchrs. Nat. Assn., Pi Kappa Lambda, Phi Kappa Phi, Phi Mu Alpha, Phi Delta Kappa. Editor: Your Musical Cue, 1963-70. Contbr. articles to profl. jours. Home: Rural Route 2 Bloomington IL 61701 Office: Music Dept Ill State U Normal IL 61761

CORRADI, PETER, constrn. and engring. co. exec.; b. Bklyn., Nov. 24, 1910; s. Manlis and Mary (Bosco) C.; B.S. in Civil Engring., N.Y.U., 1936, Sc.D., 1966; m. Helena Olive Corley, Jan. 23, 1937; children—Peter R., Patricia, Carol. Design engr. Port of N.Y. Authority, 1934-39; commd. lt. (j.g.) USN, 1940, advanced through grades to rear adm., 1961; dep. chief Bur. Yards and Docks, also dep. chief civil engr., U.S. Navy, Washington, 1958-62, chief bur., chief civil engrs., 1962-65, ret.; v.p., gen. mgr. Gibbs & Hill, Inc., cons. engrs., 1965-66, pres., chief exec. officer, 1966-69; exec. v.p., chief operating officer, dir. Raymond Internat., Inc., N.Y.C., 1969—. Am. del. Permanent Internat. Assn. Nav. Congresses, 1965. Decorated Bronze Star medal; D.S.M. Fellow Am. Soc. C.E.; mem. Nat. Soc. Profl. Engrs., Soc. Am. Mil. Engrs. (nat. pres. 1965), Moles (1st v.p., mem. exec. com.). Clubs: Engineers of N.Y.; Seaview Country (Absecon, N.J.); Atlantic City Country; Army Navy (Arlington, Va.).

Home: 2100 Wesley Av Ocean City NJ 08226 also 440 E 57th St New York City NY 10022 Office: 2 Pennsylvania Plaza New York City NY 10001

CORRADI, VAL, advt. exec.; b. Newburgh, N.Y.; s. Valentine and Helen (Farina) C.; B.S. in Journalism, Rider Coll., 1942: M.S. in Journalism, Northwestern U., 1947; m. Virginia Roberts, Jan. 28, 1950; 1 stepdau., Jo Ann (Mrs. Mitchell E. Bonnett, Jr.). With D.P. Brother & Co., Detroit, 1947-70, v.p., account exec., 1956-59, sr. v.p., 1959-70; v.p. Leo Burnett Co. Mich. Inc., 1971—. Served with USCGR, 1942-45. Clubs: Recess, Adcraft (Detroit). Home: 1631 Bracken Dr Bloomfield Hills MI 48013 Office: Gen Motors Bldg Detroit MI 48202

CORRADO, BENJAMIN WILLIAM, distillery exec.; b. Bklyn., July 16, 19ll; s. Anthony and Genevieve (La Guardia) C.; student Sch. Commerce, N.Y.U., 1930-32; m. Virginia M. McCormick, June 23, 1939. News editor, Washington editor Am. Machinist; Cleve. editor Iron Age mag.; metals and beverage specialist Poor's Pub. Co.; asst. pub. relations dir. Am. Iron and Steel Inst., 1946-48; coordinator advt., spl. asst. to pres., market research dir. Publicker Industries, Inc., 1948-50, research cons., liquor specialist, 1950-55; v.p. charge market research Nat. Distillers Products Co., 1955-64, v.p. charge industry relations, 1964—. Jr. economist, munitions br. WPB, 1943; author nat. liquor consumption estimate by states and by types, 1950-54; cons. NPA, 1951-52. Recipient indsl. marketing award of merit for best published research Am. Machinist, 1945. Mem. Am. Legion, Am. Mgmt. Assn., Nat. Assn. Bus. Econs., Ky. Distillers Assn. (v.p., dir.), Md. Distillers Assn. (v.p.), Bourbon Inst. (v.p., dir.), N.Y. Acad. Scis., Nat. Planning Assn., Am. Marketing Assn. Club: National Press (Washington). Author: Distilled Spirits Industry- Public Revenues, 1943; Liquor Marketing Handbook, 1954, 55. Contbr. articles nat. mags. Home: 6050 Boulevard E West New York NJ 07093

CORREA, GUSTAVO, educator; b. Colombia, S.Am., Sept. 20, 1914; s. Urbano and María (Forero) C.; Licenciado, Escuela Normal Superior, Bogota, 1941; Ph.D., Johns Hopkins, 1947; m. Inés Cancino, Aug. 20, 1947; children—Amanda, Albert, Patricia. Came to U.S., 1941, naturalized, 1956. Nat. dir. secondary edn., Bogota, 1948-50; vis. prof. Spanish, U. Ore., 1950-51; asso. prof. Spanish, Tulane U., 1951-54, U. Chgo., 1954-56, U. Pa., 1956- 59; prof. Spanish, Yale, 1959—. Co-editor Hispanic Rev., 1958-60, adv. editor, 1960—. Mem. Modern Lang. Assn. Am., Am. Assn. Tchrs. Spanish and Portuguese. Author: El espíritu del mal en Guatemala; ensayo de semántica cultural, 1955; La Poesía mítica de Federico García Lorca, 1957; El simbolismo religioso en las novelas de Pérez Galdós, 1962; Realidad, Ficcón y simbolo en las novelas de Pérez Galdós, 1966. Home: 163 Hepburn Rd Hamden CT 06517 Office: Dept Spanish Yale New Haven CT 06520

CORREA, HENRY A., mfg. exec.; b. N.Y.C., Mar. 9, 1917; s. Enrique A. and Maria (Helm) C.; B.S. in Bus. Adminstrn., St. Louis U., 1937; m. Elizabeth Winchester, Dec. 9, 1944. With Robertson Aircraft Corp., St. Louis, 1937-38; chief pilot, sales mgr. Atlantic Aviation Service, Wilmington, Del., 1938-41; fgn. sales mgr. Bendix Internat. div. Bendix Corp., 1945-57; v.p. fgn. operations ACF Industries, Inc., N.Y.C., 1958, v.p. marketing, 1959-63, v.p. exec. dept., 1964-65, exec. v.p., dir., 1965-66, pres., 1966—; dir. Nat. Starch & Chem. Corp., Polymer Corp. Bd. dirs. Met. Opera Guild, Inc., Met. Opera Assn.; trustee Council for Technol. Advancement; pres.'s council Mus. City N.Y. Served from 1st lt. to maj. AUS, 1943-45. Decorated Army Commendation medal; recipient hon. pilot wings Colombia Air Force, 1945. Mem. Transp. Assn. Am. (dir., gov., corp. v.p.) Ry. Progress Inst. (chmn. bd. dirs.), Machinery and Allied Products Inst., Quiet Birdmen. Clubs: Sky, Union, N.Y. Yacht, Opera, Economic (N.Y.C.); Chicago (Chgo.); Mill Reef (Antigua, B.W.I.). Office: care ACF Industries Inc 750 3d Av New York City NY 10017

CORREA, RODOLFO A., business exec.; b. Bklyn., Sept. 23, 1913; LL.B., St. Johns Law Sch. 1939. Admitted to N.Y. bar, 1940; spl. asst. to ast. atty. gen. Dept. of Justice, 1946; gen. counsel ODM, 1951-52; v.p. RCA, 1956-63; v.p. bus. devel. AMF, Inc. (formerly Am. Machine & Foundry Co.), 1963—, dir., 1964—. Home: Little Silver NJ 07739 Office: AMF Inc 261 Madison Av New York City NY 10016

CORRELL, JOHN MALCOLM, educator; b. Linton, Ind., May 3, 1914; s. John Thomas and Lista (Morgan) C.; A.B., Ind. U., 1935; Ph.D., U. Chgo., 1948; m. Ruth Armstrong, July 16, 1938; children—Elizabeth, Timothy, Mark. Developmental physicist Electric Sorting Machine Co., Grand Rapids, Mich., 1936-40; instr. phys. sci. U. Chgo., 1943-47, asst. prof., 1947- 48; prof. physics Okla. A. and M. Coll., 1948-51; Joseph Boyer prof. physics, head dept. DePauw U., 1952-61; mem. staff High Altitude Obs., Bolder, Colo., 1959-60; now prof. physics and phys. sci. Faculty Coll. Arts and Scis., U. Colo. at Boulder; vis. prof., physics cons. Mindanao State U., P.I., 1966-67. Mem. Commn. on Coll. Physics, 1960-66. Fellow A.A.A.S.; mem. Am. Assn. Physics Tchrs. (pres. 1961). Am. Phys. Soc., Am. Assn. U. Profs., Assn. for Gen. and Liberal Studies (pres. 1969), Phi Beta Kappa, Sigma Xi. Home: 320 20th St Boulder CO 80302

CORRICK, ANN MARJORIE, journalist; b. Detroit; d. John A. and Mary (Nickell) Corrick; B.J., U. Tex., 1943. Reporter Transradio Press Service, Washington, 1943-51; producer Am. Forum of the Air, also Youth Wants to Know, NBC, Washington, 1951-52; Washington corrs. and broadcaster WDSU- TV, New Orleans, 1954-58; asst. chief Washington News Bur., also reporter-broadcaster Westinghouse Broadcasting Co., Washington, 1958-66; USIA congl. liason officer Expo '67, Montreal, Can., 1967, information officer USIA Fgn. Service, Saigon, Vietnam, 1968-70; now engaged in journalism. Recipient Sylvania citation for producing and moderating TV film Dateline Washington for WDSU-TV, 1955, Theta Sigma Phi Nat. Headliner award, 1962. Mem. Radio-TV Corrs. Assn. (pres., 1961-62), Am. Women Radio and Television, Theta Sigma Phi. Club: Press of Washington (sec. 1966-67). Home and office: 2020 F St NW Washington DC 20006

CORRIGAN, DANIEL, clergyman; b. Pontiac, Mich., Oct. 25, 1900; s. Herbert James and Katherine (Burns) C.; B.D., Nashotah (Wis.) Theol. Sem., 1926, S.T.M., 1943, D.D., 1955; m. Elizabeth Waters, Sept. 21, 1926. Ordained to ministry P.E. Ch., 1924; pastor in Portage, Wis., 1925-31, Oconomowoc, Wis., 1931-43, Balt., 1944-48, St. Paul, 1948-58; chaplain St.Francis House, U. Wis., 1944; suffragan bishop Colo., 3958-60; dir. home dept. Nat. Council P.E. Ch., 1960-68; minister to coll. Amherst (Mass.) Coll., 1968-69; dean Bexley Hall, Rochester (N.Y.) Centre for theol. studies, 1969-71. Chmn. dept. Christian social relations Diocese of Minn., 1952-58; pres. Am. Ch. Inst. for Negroes, 1960—; mem. joint commn. P.E. Gen. Conv. Edn. Holy Orders, 1958—. Vice pres. Minn. Indian Commn., 1955-58; pres. St. Paul Council Human Relations, 1954-58; mem. Gov. of Minn. Commn. on Resettlement, 1955-58; Trustee Nashotah Theol. Sem. Fellow Am. Soc. Religion and Culture. Home: 930 Humboldt St Denver CO 80218

CORRIGAN, FRANCIS JOSEPH, educator; b. St. Louis, Feb. 27, 1919; s. John Francis and Catherine (Costello) C.; B.S., St. Louis U., 1941, Ph.D., 1952; M.B.A., Stanford, 1943. Auditor, Monsanto Chem. Co., St. Louis, 1943-45; investment broker Dempsey-Tegeler & Co., St. Louis, 1946-49; with St. Louis U., 1943-68, lectr. econs., 1943-49, from instr. finance to asso. prof., 1949-63, prof., 1963-68, dir. dept. mgmt., 1957-68; vis. prof. bus. adminstrn. U. Santa Clara (Cal.), 1967-68, prof. bus. adminstrn., 1968—. Financial cons. to dir. pub. welfare St. Louis, 1954-55; financial adviser Archdiocese of St. Louis, 1957-68. Mem. Am. Finance Assn., Midwest Econs. Assn., Acad. Mgmt. Republican. Roman Catholic. Author: (with Howard A. Ward) Financial Management: Policies and Practices, 1963. Home: 600 Pennsylvania Av Los Gatos CA 95030 Office: Sch of Bus U Santa Clara Santa Clara CA 95053

CORRIGAN, JOHN EDWARD, Jr., banker; b. Chgo., Sept. 26, 1922: s. John Edward and Veronica (Mulvey) C.; B.A., Harvard, 1943, LL.B., 1949; m. Eileen Williams, Nov. 4, 1950. With First Nat. Bank Chgo., 1949—, asst. v.p., 1960-61, v.p., 1961—; admitted to Ill. bar, 1950. Served with AUS, 1943-46, 51-52. Home: 135 Church Rd Winnetka IL 60093 Office: 1 First Nat Plaza Chicago IL 60670

CORRIGAN, JOHN HERBERT, lawyer; b. Red Deer, Alta., Can., Aug. 29, 1913; grad. U. Toronto, Osgoode Hall. Admitted to Ont. bar, 1938; partner firm McMillan, Binch, Toronto. Mem. Canadian Bar Assn. Office: 20 King St W Toronto 1 Ontario Canada*

CORRIGAN, LEO FRANCIS, real estate, hotel exec.; b. St. Louis, Aug. 30, 1894; s. Dennis J. and Mary (Callahan) C.; student pub. schs. St. Louis; m. Clara Catherine Redman, Dec. 6, 1917; children—Louise (Mrs. Edwin B. Jordan), Leo Francis, Real estate advt. salesman Dallas Dispatch, 1910, advt. solicitor, 1912; asst. advt. mgr. Houston Press, 1911; automotive editor St. Louis Star, 1911, also st. car advt. salesman Western Advt. Co., St. Louis; gen. real estate work, Dallas, 1912; since 1917 engaged in ownership, devel. and mgmt. real estate; controls and operates 5 hotels, some 35 shopping centers, 15 office bldgs. and 15 apt. projects; established Corrigan Ins. Agy., 1942; pres., dir. Los Angeles Biltmore Hotel Co., Dallas Hotel Co., Corrigan Properties Inc., Dallas-Corrigan-Houston, Inc., Houston; pres. Corrigan Co. of Nassau. Ltd.; joint owner C.J.C. Realty Co.; dir. Wynncor Limited, United Fidelity Life Ins. Co. Bd. dirs. Dallas Civic Opera Co. Mem. Dallas, Ft. Worth chambers commerce, Nat. Assn. Real Estate Bds., Nat. Inst. Real Estate Brokers, Dallas Real Estate Bd., Dallas Home Builders Assn., Central Bus. Dist. Association of Dallas. Clubs: Country, Book Hollow Golf, Dallas Country, Dallas, City (Dallas) Home: 4404 Versailles Dallas TX 75205 Office: 211 N Ervay Dallas TX 75201

CORRIGAN, ROBERT FOSTER, fgn. service officer; b. Cleve., Sept. 12, 1914; s. Francis Patrick and Ethel (Foster) C.; student Washington and Lee U., 1932-34; B.A., Stanford, 1937; student Central U. of Venezuela, 1939-40, Heidelberg U., Germany, 1950; m. Jane Carswell, May 15, 1952; children—Kevin, Mary Annette, Martha, Robert Foster, Susan. Dep. collector Internal Revenue, Cleve., 1937-39; corr. N.Y. Times, Venezuela, 1939-41; sec. U.S. ambassador to Venezuela, 1939-41; vice consul, attache Am. Embassy, Rio de Janeiro, 1941-45; prin. officer Am. Consulate, Natal, Brazil, 1945-46; polit. officer, Berlin and Frankfort (Germany), 1947-48; polit. adviser to comdr.-in-chief European Command, Heidelberg, 1948-52; Am. consul, Dakar, French West Africa, 1952-54; 1st sec. Am. Embassy, Chile, 1954-57; assigned Nat. War Coll., 1957-58; dep. chief protocol Dept. State, 1958-59; dep. chief of mission, counselor of embassy, consul general Am. embassy, Guatemala, 1960-65, polit. adviser to comdr.-in-chief U.S. So. Command, C.Z., with personal rank of minister, 1965-68; consul gen., Sao Paulo, Brazil, 1968—. Served as ensign with USNR, 1939-41. Mem. Found. for Religious Action Social and Civil Order (mem. standing policy com. nat. adv. council), Ohio Soc., S.A.R., Am. Fgn. Service Assn., Alpha Tau Omega. Roman Catholic. Clubs: Army and Navy, Ft. McNair Officers (Washington). Address: care Dept of State Washington DC 20521

CORRIGAN, ROBERT WILLOUGHBY, educator; b. Portage, Wis., Sept. 23, 1927; s. Daniel and Elizabeth (Waters) C.; B.A., Cornell U., 1950; M.A., Johns Hopkins, 1952; Ph.D., U. Minn., 1955; m. Mary Kathryn Kolling, Dec. 18, 1953 (div. Sept. 1960); m. 2d, Elizabeth Trevor Seneff, June 15, 1963 (div. June 1969); children—Michael Edward, Timothy Patrick; m. 3d, Jane Langley, Aug. 1, 1969. Instr. drama Johns Hopkins, 1950-52; instr. theatre, classics U. Minn., 1952-54; asst. prof., dir. drama Carleton Coll., 1954-57; asso. prof. theatre Tulane U., 1957-61, founder, editor Tulane Drama Rev. (now The Drama Rev.), 1957-62; Andrew Mellon prof., head drama dept. Carnegie Inst. Tech., 1961-64; prof. dramatic lit. N.Y. U., 1964-68, dean Sch. Arts, 1965-68; pres. Cal. Inst. of Arts, 1968—; cons. to Chandler Pub. Co., Dell Pub. Co., Houghton Mifflin. Adviser in theatre in Greece for State Dept., 1962; chmn. Internat. Council Fine Arts Deans, 1970-71. Recipient Citation of Merit, Niagara U., 1967. Mem. Am. Ednl. Theatre Assn., Nat. Theatre Conf., Nat. Council Arts Edn., Sigma Delta Chi, Sigma Phi. Episcopalian. Translator: Chekhov: Six Plays, 1962. Author or editor: New Theatre of Europe, Vol. 1, 1962, Vol. 2, 1964, Vol. 3, 1967; Theatre in the Twentieth Century, 1963; The Modern Theatre, 1964; The Art of the Theatre, 1964; The Context and Craft of Drama, 1964; Masterpieces of the Modern Theatre, 1966; The Theatre in Search of a Fix, 1970; Tragedy: Vision and Form, 1965; Comedy: Meaning and Form, 1965; Laurel Classical Drama Series, 1964-65; Laurel British Drama Series, 1965; Arthur Miller: 20th Century Views, 1969; many others. Home: 252 St Pierre Rd Los Angeles CA 90024 Office: 24700 McBean Pkwy Valencia CA 91355

CORRIGAN, WILLIAM THOMAS, news executive; b. Bridgeport, Conn., Sept. 18, 1921; s. Thomas F. and Anna M. (Callan) C.; A.A., U. Bridgeport, 1940; B.S., Am. U., 1948; m. Harriett Bell, Sept. 1, 1951; children—Kevin, Brian. Reporter, Bridgeport Herald, sports broadcaster sta. WUST, Washington, 1947; writer, producer NBC News, 1948-51; mng. editor NBC-TV, newsreel, 1951-52, assignment editor NBC-TV News, 1952-53; Washington mgr. CBS Syndication, Washington bur. chief CBS Newsfilm, 1953-59, dir. news and pub. affairs KNXT, West Coast bur. chief CBS Newsfilm, 1959-61; Am. editor Eichman Trial, Jerusalem, Israel, 1961; mgr. Washington bur. of NBC News, N.Y.C., 1962; producer Huntley Brinkley Report, Wash., 1963-65; dir. of operations. NBC, N.Y.C., 1965-68; gen. mgr. operations NBC News, N.Y.C., 1968—. Served as sgt. USAAF, World War II. Decorated D.F.C., Air medal. Mem. Radio-TV News Dirs. Assn., White House Photographers Assn., Radio-TV Corrs. Assn. (exec. bd.), Phi Sigma Kappa, Sigma Delta Chi. Clubs: Nat. Press (Washington); Los Angeles Press. Home: 76 Camp Av Darien CT 06820 Office: NBC News 30 Rockefeller Plaza New York City NY 10020

CORRIN, BROWNLEE SANDS, educator, polit. scientist; b. Bellevue, Pa., Mar. 25, 1922; s. John Grimshaw and Alice (Turkington) C.; A.B., Stanford, 1947, M.A., 1950, Ph.D., 1959; m. Mary Elizabeth Dyer, May 18, 1946; children—Adaline Elizabeth, Rebecca Sands, David Montgomery, John Brownlee. Teaching asst. Stanford, 1949-52; mem. faculty Goucher Coll., Towson, Md., 1952—, prof. polit. sci., 1965—, chmn. dept. polit. sci., 1958—, chmn. dept. internat. relations, 1958-69, dir. Field Politics Center, 1954—, chmn. faculty history and social scis., 1966-69. Elections analyst ABC, 1964—; vis. lectr. Johns Hopkins, 1962, U. Md., 1962-68; cons. Md. Constl. Conv. Common., 1965-67; dir. edn. WTOW FM-AM Balt., 1968-70. Dir. G & P. Research & Devel. Co. Chmn. working com. New Eng. Conf. Teaching Fgn. Langs., 1966; mem. Baltimore County Council Charter Revision Com., 1961-62, Md. Legislative Com. Campaign Costs, 1964; mem. bd. Library Trustees of Baltimore County, 1968—. Precinct leader, chmn. Baltimore County Republican Dist. Exec. Com., 1952-63; chmn. Md. Rep. Arts and Scis. Com., 1962; treas. for candidate to Md. Constl. Conv., 1967; mem. Rep. Nat. Arts and Scis. Com., also cons. Rep. House Conf. Com., 1963-64. Bd. dirs. UN Assn. Md., 1956-66. Served to maj. AUS, 1942-47; CBI. Mem. Am. Inst. Aero. and Astronautics, Am. Polit. Sci. Assn., Am. Soc. Internat. Law, Am. Soc. Pub. Adminstrn., Internat. Inst. Space Law, Internat. Studies Assn., Nat. Council Social Studies, D.C. Polit. Sci. Assn., Pi Sigma Alpha, Sigma Alpha Epsilon. Episcopalian. Club: Army and Navy (Washington). Contbr. articles to profl. jours. Home: 201 Dunbeath Ct Lutherville MD 21093 Office: Goucher Coll Towson MD 21204

CORRIN, EDWARD WAYNE, utilities exec.; b. Wilkinsburg, Pa., Feb. 2, 1910; s. John Bain and Laura (Robinson) C.; LL.B., U. Va., 1933; m. Maxine Law, Sept. 14, 1943; children—Judith Ann, Edward Wayne. Lease and right-of-way man Hope Natural Gas Co., Clarksburg, W.Va., 1933-41, v.p., 1951-56, pres., 1956- 65; system gas dispatcher Consol. Natural Gas Co., 1945-50, also dir.; chmn., dir. Consol. Gas Supply Corp., Clarksburg, 1965—, River Gas Co.; dir. Consol. Natural Gas Service Co., Inc., Balt. br. Fed. Res. Bank of Richmond. Pres. Harrison County United Fund, 1957. Bd. dirs. W.Va. Safety Council; mem. exec. bd. Central W.Va. council Boy Scouts Am. Served with USNR, 1942-45. Mem. Am., Pa. gas assns., Ohio Oil and Gas Assn., Am. gmt. Assn., Clarksburg C. of C. (dir.), Am. Petroleum Inst., W.Va. Oil and Natural Gas Assn. (pres.), Newcomen Soc. Club: Duquesne (Pitts.). Home: 508 E Main St Clarksburg WV 26301 Office: 445 W Main St Clarksburg WV 26301

CORRINGTON, LOUIS EARLE, Jr., banker; b. Chgo., Nov. 8, 1916; s. Louis Earle and Katrina (Oller) C.; m. Marjorie E. Hayn, Dec. 31, 1955; 1 dau., Margo Louise. Clerical positions various banks, 1934-40; asst. cashier Am. Nat. Bank & Trust Co., Chgo., 1940-54; v.p. S.E. Nat. Bank, Chgo., 1955-56; pres. Guaranty Bank & Trust Co., Chgo., 1956-62; pres., dir. Merc. Nat. Bank of Chgo., 1962-67. Served to capt. USAAF, 1942-46. Clubs: Chicago Athletic Assn., South Shore Country, Bankers, Executives, South Side Swedish (Chgo.). Home: 645 N Waukegan Rd Lake Forest IL 60045 Office: 600 N LaSalle St Chicago IL 60610

CORROON, RICHARD FRANCIS, lawyer; b. Bklyn., Aug. 5, 1913; s. James Francis and Katherine (Larkin) C.; A.B., Yale, 1935; LL.B., Harvard, 1938; m. Nancy Elms, Dec. 7, 1940; children—Nancy (dec.), Ellen (Mrs. Eric C. Petersen), Kate (dec.), Polly. Admitted to N.Y. bar, 1939, Del. bar, 1946; with firm Miller, Owen, Otis & Bailey, N.Y.C., 1938-42; partner firm Potter, Anderson & Corroon, and predecessors, Wilmington, Del., 1946—. Dir., v.p. Corroon & Black Corp.; dir. Wellington Fund, Windsor Fund, Exeter Fund, Exeter 2d Fund, Exeter 3d Fund, Gemini Fund, W.L. Morgan Growth Fund, Wellsley Fund. Mem. Del. Bd. Bar Examiners, 1951-66; vice chmn. Del. Corp. Law Revision Com., 1964-67. Mem. bd. edn., Wilmington, 1949-53; pres. Diocesan Bd. Edn., Wilmington, 1966-68; mem. Catholic Social Services Wilmington, 1960-66. Bd. dirs. Del. Curative Workshop, 1950-56, Del. Art Mus., 1969—. Served to lt. comdr. USNR, 1942-46. Decorated Purple Heart. Mem. Am., Del. bar assns., Assn. Bar City N.Y., Am. Law Inst. Home: 1105 Westover Rd Wilmington DE 19807 Office: Delaware Trust Bldg Wilmington DE 19801

CORRSIN, STANLEY, educator, fluid dynamicist; b. Phila., Apr. 3, 1920; s. Herman and Anna (Schor) C.; B.S., U. Pa., 1940; M.S., Cal. Inst. Tech., 1942, Ph.D. in Aero., 1947; m. Barbara Daggett, Sept. 25, 1945; children—Nancy Eliot, Stephen David. Research and teaching asst. aero. Cal. Inst. Tech., 1940-45, instr., 1945-47; asst. prof. aero. Johns Hopkins, 1947-51. asso. prof., 1951-55, prof. mech. engring., chmn. dept., 1955-60, prof. fluid mechanics, 1960—. Recipient distinguished alumnus citation U. Pa. Sch. Engring., 1955. Fellow Am. Phys. Soc. (chmn. div. fluid dynamics 1964), Am. Acad. Arts and Scis., Am. Soc. M.E.; mem. Am. Inst. Aeros. and Astronautics, Am. Assn. U. Profs. (pres. Johns Hopkins chpt. 1964-65), Soc. Natural Philosophy, A.A.A.S., Phi Beta Kappa, Sigma Xi, Tau Beta Pi, Pi Tau Sigma. Home: Riderwood MD 21139 Office: Johns Hopkins U Baltimore MD 21218

CORRY, ANDREW VINCENT, ret. U.S. ambassador; b. Missoula, Mont., Sept. 22, 1904; s. Arthur Vincent and Mary A.M. (Armstrong) C.; student Carroll Coll., Helena, Mont., 1922-24; A.B., Harvard, 1926, postgrad., 1926-27; B.A. (Rhodes Scholar), Oxford U., 1929, B.Sc., 1930, M.A., 1934; M.S., Mont. Sch. Mines, 1931; spl. studies Sch. Metalliferous Mining, Camborne, Cornwall, Eng. Fellow, instr., asst. prof., Mont. Sch. Mines, 1930-33; geologist, coll. instr. 1933-40; expert and cons. on minerals and metals price stabilization unit Adv. Commn. to Council of Nat. Defense, Washington, 1940-41; mem. Office of Coordinator Comml. and Cultural Relations between Am. Republics, Washington, 1940-41; cons. Div. Cultural Relations, Dept. State, 1942; prin. mem. mission Fgn. Liaison div. Lend- Lease Adminstrn., 1943; Far East Enemy br. Fgn. Econ. Adminstrn., 1943-44, Washington and abroad; spl. asst. and chief mineral advisor U.S. Fgn. Econ. Adminstrn., New Delhi (India) office, 1945; spl. cons. Dept. State, 1946; spl. asst. to dir. Office of Am. Republics, Dept. State, 1947; minerals attaché, Am. embassies India, Pakistan, Afghanistan, Ceylon and Nepal; spl. asst. to ambassador, New Delhi, 1947-54; comml. attaché, Madrid, 1955-56; dep. dir. USOM Spain, Madrid, 1956-57; consul gen., Lahore, Pakistan, 1957-61; coordinator Sr. Seminar in Fgn. Policy, Fgn. Service Inst., Dept. State, 1961-64; ambassador to Sierra Leone, 1964- 67; ambassador to Ceylon, Colombo, 1967-70, ret., 1970. Fellow Geol. Soc. London; mem. Am. Inst. Mining and Metall. Engrs., Brit. Inst. Philosophy, A.A.A.S., N.Y. Acad. Scis., Am. Catholic Hist. Assn. (former mem. exec. council), Harvard Alumni Assn., Oxford Soc.; fgn. corr. Institut Litteraire et Artistique (Paris). Democrat. Roman Catholic. Author of books and also articles in Commonwealth. Home: PO Box 1284 Alexandria VA 22313

CORSA, HELEN STORM, educator; b. Amherst, Mass., Sept. 27, 1915; d. John and Mary (Thomas) Corsa; B.A., Mt. Holyoke Coll., 1938; M.A., Bryn Mawr Coll., 1939, Ph.D., 1942. Instr. English, Hartwick Coll., Oneonta, N.Y., 1942-43; instr., asst. prof. English, Russell Sage Coll., Troy, N.Y., 1943-48; instr., asst. prof., asso. prof., prof. English, Wellesley (Mass.) Coll., 1948—. Roman Catholic. Author: Chaucer: Poet of Mirth and Morality, 1964. Home: 6 Richland Rd Wellesley, MA 02181.

CORSI, MARIO DARIO, lawyer; b. Carnegie, Pa., Jan. 31, 1926; s. Luigi and Adele (Bovara) C.; A.B., Western Res. U., 1949, LL.B., 1951, LL.M., 1965; m. Catherine Marie Toohey, Oct. 13, 1951; children—Elaine Kathleen, Ellen Marie, Emily Adele, John Matthew, Anna Maria. Admitted to Ohio bar, 1951; practice in Dover, 1952—; city solicitor, 1962—; gen. counsel Tuscarawas County U. Br. Dist.,

1966—. Chmn. Tuscarawas County Bd. Mental Retardation, 1969—. Pres. bd. trustees Dover Pub. Library. Served with USMCR, World War II. Mem. Am., Ohio, Tuscarawas County bar assns., Am. Trial Lawyers Assn., V.F.W., Beta Theta Pi, Delta Theta Phi. Roman Catholic. K.C., Lion. Home: 843 E 4th St Dover OH 44622 Office: 117 E 3d St Dover OH 44622

CORSINI, ANDREW CAMERON, jewelry co. exec.; b. Middleboro, Mass., July 29, 1935; s. Leon Henry and Margaret (Cameron) C.; B.S., Providence Coll., 1957; m. Yvonne Lorraine Grenier, Nov. 3, 1957; children—Lynn Ann, Andrew Cameron, Bryan Michael, David Eric, Stephen Paul. Audit Supr. Lybrand, Ross Bros. & Montgomery, 1967-70; v.p., sec., asst. treas. Swank, Inc., Attleboro, Mass., 1967—. Served with USNR, 1957-60. C.P.A., Mass. Mem. Am. Inst. C.P.A.'s, Mass. Soc. C.P.A.'s. Home: White Hill Lane Cumberland RI 02864 Office: 6 Hazel St Attleboro MA 02703

CORSO, GREGORY NUNZIO, poet; b. N.Y.C., Mar. 26, 1930; s. Fortunato and Michelina (Colonni) C.; m. Sally November, May 7, 1963; 1 dau., Mirandia. Manual laborer, N.Y.C., 1950-51; with Los Angeles Examiner, 1951-52; mcht. seaman Norwegian vessels, 1952-53; began appearing in poetry readings in East and Midwest, mid-1950's. Recipient Poetry Found. award. Author: (poems) The Vestal Lady on Brattle, 1955, Gasoline, 1958, Bomb, 1958, Marriage (Longview Found. award), 1959, The Happy Birthday of Death, 1960, Long Live Man, 1962, Selected Poems, 1962; (novel) The American Express, 1961; (play) This Hung-Up Age, 1955. Co-editor: Young American Poetry, 1961. Address: care New Directions Publishing Corp 333 Av of Americas New York City NY 10014*

CORSON, BOLTON L., lime co. exec.; b. Plymouth Meeting, Pa., Oct. 28, 1894; s. Walter H. and Katherine (Langdon) C.; B.S. in Mech. Engring., Haverford Coll., 1916; m. Carolyn Reeves Davis, Apr. 23, 1930; children—Walter H. II, Bolton L. With Franklin Automobile Co., 1916-17, 20-23, Hale Fire Pump Co., 1919-20; founder, pres. Mastercraft Products, Inc., 1923-24; sold co. to join G. & W. H. Corson, Inc., Plymouth Meeting, 1924, v.p., 1934-55, pres., 1955—, also dir.; dir. Corson Concrete Co., Inc., Cordol Corp., Hale Fire Pump Co., Poz-O-Pac Co. of Am.; alternate dir. Baldwin- Ehret-Hill Co. Bd. dirs. Corson Found., Friends Charity Fuel Assn.; mem. devel. com. Franklin Inst. Served to 1st lt. U.S. Army, 1917-18. Recipient Edward Longstreth Medal Franklin Inst., 1964. Mem. Am. Soc. Testing and Materials (chmn. structural lime com. 1947-65), Nat. Lime Assn. (bd. dirs., mem. exec. com.) Patentee lime hydration process, sintering machine. Home: 9427 Meadowbrook Lane Philadelphia, PA 19118. Office: G&W H Corson Inc Plymouth Meeting PA 19462

CORSON, DALE RAYMOND, univ. pres.; physicist; b. Pittsburg, Kan., Apr. 5, 1914; s. Harry Raymond and Alta (Hill) C.; A.B., Coll. Emporia, Kan., 1934; M.A., U. Kan., 1935; student Ohio State U., 1935-36; Ph.D., U. Cal., 1938; m. Nellie Elizabeth Griswold, June 17, 1938; children—David, Bruce, Richard, Janet. Instr., research fellow U. Cal., 1938-40; asst. prof. U. Mo., 1940-43, asso. prof., 1943-45; staff Radiation Lab., Mass. Inst. Tech., 1941-43; tech. adviser War Dept., 1943-45; staff Los Alamos Sci. Lab., 1945-46; asst. prof. Cornell U., 1946-47, asso. prof., 1947-52, prof., 1952—, chmn. dept. physics, 1956-59, dean Coll. Engring., 1959-63, provost, 1963-69, pres., 1969—. Recipient Presdl. Certificate of Merit, 1948. Fellow Am. Phys. Soc., Am. Acad. Arts and Scis.; mem. Phi Beta Kappa, Sigma Xi, Tau Beta Pi. Home: 144 Northview Rd Ithaca NY 14850

CORSON, FRED PIERCE, bishop; b. Millville, N.J., Apr. 11, 1896; s. Jeremiah and Mary E. (Payne) C.; A.B., Dickinson Coll., Carlisle, Pa., 1917, A.M., 1920, D.D., 1931, L.H.D., 1944; B.D., Drew U., 1920; also numerous hon. degrees; m. Frances Beaman, Mar. 22, 1922; 1 son, Hampton Payne. Ordained to ministry Methodist Episcopal Ch., 1920, consecrated bishop, 1944; pastor in Jackson Heights, N.Y., New Haven, Port Washington, N.Y., Simpson Ch., Bklyn., until 1929; supt. Bklyn. So. Dist., N.Y. East Conf., 1930-34; pres. Dickinson Coll., 1934-44, also trustee; permanent chaplain Faith of Our Fathers Chapel, Freedoms Found, 1968—; titular pastor Old St. George's Ch., 1968—. trustee Wyoming Sem., Pennington Sch. for Boys, Drew U., Westminster Theol. Sem., Lycoming Coll.; hon. pres. trustee Temple U. Pres. Council Bishops, 1952-53 (fraternal messenger to Gen. Conf. Brazil, 1950); v.p. Meth. World Council, 1956- 61, pres., 1961-66; ofcl. Meth. rep. Kirchentag Assembly, Stuttgart, Germany, 1952; mem. Bishops Commn. for Meth.-Catholic Conversations, 1968—; sr. cons. to schs. and colls. of United Meth. Ch., 1968—. Civilian dir. 32d Coll. Tng. Spl. lectr. various colls. and univs., 1945—. Del. to gen. conf., 1932, 40, 44, mem. univ. senate, mem. book com., world peace commn. Detachment (air crew), 1943-44; mem. Nat. Council Chs. of Christ, Com. on Internat. Goodwill; mem. Pa. Gov.'s CCom. for Revision State Constn.; chmn. Sec. of War's Clergy Commn. To Inspect Occupied Countries of Europe, 1948; ofcl. rep. Meth. Ch. to Centennial Celebration of Methodism in China, 1948; ofcl. Meth. rep. to Army and Navy Chaplains in Japan, 1948; del. World Council Chs., 1954; religious cons. Armed Forces in Far East Command, 1954; chaplain Republican and Democratic nat. convs., 1948, 52. Del., observer 2d Vatican Council, Rome, Italy, 1962, 63, 64, 65. Pres. Gen. Bd. Edn., Meth. Ch., 1948-60. Bd. dirs. Freedoms Found., Valley Forge, Pa. Recipient Yorktown medal Soc. of Cin.; Kappa Sigma Man of Year, 1950; St. Olav medal (Norway), 1964; Gourgas medal (Masonic decoration), 1964; Phila. Pub. Relations award, 1965; named to Football Found. Hall of Fame. Mem. Newcomen Soc., Phi Beta Kappa, Phi Beta Kappa Assos., Kappa Sigma, Omicron Delta Kappa, Tau Kappa Alpha. Mason (33, K.T.). Kiwanian. Clubs: Union League (N.Y.C., Phila.). Author: Dickinson College-A History of Function and Purpose; The Dilemma of the Liberated; The Lure of the Expected; The Obligation of the Church-Related College to the Future; Education and the Arsenal of the Democracy; A Philosophy of Education for the Postwar World; The Minister and Christian Higher Education; The Pattern of A Church; Your Church and You; Pattern for Successful Living; The Christian Imprint; How Good Is Communism; American Methodism's Magna Charta; Francis Asbury. Editor for Wesley Translation of New Testament; Bridges To Unity. Home: Cornwall Manor Cornwall PA 17016 Office: 1701 Arch St Philadelphia PA 19103

CORSON, LOUIS DAMARIN, coll. ofcl.; b. Portsmouth, O., July 30, 1915; s. Louis Damarin and Ada Russell (Moore) C.; A.B., W.Va. U., 1937, M.A., 1942; Ed.D., Stanford, 1951; m. Joan Adelaide Stifel, June 17, 1947; children—Linda Diane, Joan Adelaide. Teaching fellow dept. history W.Va. U., 1946, faculty resident men's residence halls, 1946-48; dean of men, prof. Fla. State U., 1953-55; dean of men U. Ala., 1955-57; dir. Ret. Profs. Registry, 1957-62, Warden Coll. Ch. Musicians, Washington Cathedral, 1963-67. Del. White House Conf. on Children and Youth, 1960, White House Conf. on Aging, 1961. Served as capt. USAAC, 1942-46, USAF, 1951-52; dir. air crew ground tng. night fighter tng. group. Mem. or former mem. Am. Coll. Personnel Assn., Am. Personnel and Guidance Assn., Am. Assn. U. Profs., Assn. Higher Edn., N.E.A., Nat. Assn. Student Personnel Adminstrs. (exec. com. 1955-56), Am. Acad. Polit. and Social Sci., Am. Hist. Assn., A.A.A.S., Mountain, Sphinx, Kappa Kappa Psi, Alpha Phi Omega, Alpha Epsilon Delta, Phi Kappa Psi (dir. frat. edn. 1946-48, dir. scholarship, 1958-61, dir. ednl. leadership conf. 1960-62, nat. v.p. 1960-62, pres. 1962-64), Phi Delta Kappa, Phi Eta Sigma, Phi Alpha Theta, Frat. Scholarship Assn. (v.p. 1959-60). Episcopalian. Clubs: Cosmos, University (Washington); Annapolis (Md.) Yacht; Fort Henry (Wheeling, W.Va.). Editor Frat. Scholarship Assn. Handbook for Scholarship Officers, 1960. Home: RFD 6 720 N Holly Dr Annapolis MD 21401

CORSON, PHILIP LANGDON, indsl. exec.; b. Plymouth Meeting, Pa., Oct. 31, 1898; s. Walter Harris and Katharine I. (Langdon) C.; student Haverford Coll., 1915-19; LL.D., Ursinus College, Collegeville, Pa., 1959; m. Helen Thomas Payson, Jan. 30, 1930. With G. & W. H. Corson, Inc., lime mfr., Plymouth Meeting, 1919—, plant mgr., 1923-28, v.p., mem. bd., 1928-33, pres., 1933-53; chmn. Williams & Marcus Co., Franklin Printing Co.; dir. Continental Bank. Pres. Tri-County Mental Health Clinics, Inc., Norristown. 1949-57; mem. bd. Norristown State Hosp., 1942-46, pres. bd., 1946-56. State treas. Pa. Republican party, 1967. Mem. bd. trustees Germantown Acad.; trustee, member exec. com. Ursinus Coll.; bd. dirs. Montgomery Hosp. Served as pvt. US. Army, 1918. Mem. Pa. Mfrs. Assn. (dir.). Clubs: Merion Cricket, Sunnybrook Golf, Mid-Ocean, Racquet; Pinehurst Country; Plymouth Country. Address: Plymouth Meeting PA 19462

CORSON, ROBERT WILLIAM, mfg. co. exec.; b. Chgo., Feb. 1, 1922; s. Ralph Maurice and Cora (Kohlsaat) C.; grad. Phillips Exeter Acad., 1938; A.B., Harvard, 1942, M.B.A., 1943; m. Constance Elaine Barrett, June 26, 1943; children—Marshall Ayer, Dana Barrett. With Textron, Inc., 1946-50; asst. controller Saco-Lowell Shops, 1950-58; v.p., controller Howe Scale Co., 1958-61; with Foxboro Co. (Mass.), 1961—, sec., 1964-68, treas., 1967—, also dir. Bd. dirs. Internat. Center New Eng. Trustee, treas. Milton (Mass.) Hosp. Served to lt. USNR, 1943-46. Mem. Hosps. Laundry Assn. Mass. (trustee), Machinery and Allied Products Inst. (financial council). Home: 1091 Brush Hill Rd Milton MA 02186 Office: 38 Neponset Av Foxboro MA 02035

CORT, DAVID, writer; b. Reading, Pa., July 5, 1904; s. Ambrose and Lydia Rebecca (Painter) C.; B.A., Columbia, 1924; m. Catharine Whitcomb, 1937; (div. 1942); 1 son, John Cyrus II. Editor-writer Vanity Fair mag., Vogue mag., Time mag., Life mag., UN World, The Nation. Guggenheim fellow, 1971. Author: Once More Ye Laurels, 1928; Give Us Heroes, 1932; The Great Union, 1945; The Big Picture, 1953; The Calm Man, 1954; Is There An American in the House?, 1960; The Minstrel Boy, 1961; Social Astonishments, 1963; The Glossy Rats, 1967; Revolution by Cliché 1970. Contbr. articles to nat. mags. Office: The Nation 333 6th Av New York City NY 10003

CORT, STEWART SHAW, steel co. exec.; b. Duquesne, Pa., May 9, 1911; s. Stewart Joseph and Carolyn Myrtilla (Schreiner) C.; B.A., Yale, 1934; M.B.A., Harvard, 1936; LL.D., Moravian Coll., Bethlehem, Pa., 1967, Lehigh U., 1969; m. Elizabeth Fiske Brumilier, Apr. 15, 1961. With Bethlehem Steel Corp., 1937—, asst. gen. mgr. sales, 1960-61; v.p., Pacific Coast div., 1961-63, pres., dir., 1963-71, chmn. bd., chief exec. officer, 1971—; dir. Continental Ill. Nat. Bank & Trust Co. of Chgo., Industrias Penoles, S.A., Conill Corp., Mem. exec. com. Yale Devel. Bd.; trustee Princeton Theol. Sem., Com. Econ. Devel., Blair Acad.; chmn. Radio Free Europe Fund. Decorated grand comdr. Order African Redemption (Liberia). Mem. Am. Iron and Steel Inst., Am. Inst. Steel Constrn. Steel Service Center, Institute, Advt. Council (industries adv. com.), C. of C. U.S. (nat. task force on econ. growth and opportunity), Internat. Indsl. Conf. (U.S. Council), Newcomen Soc., Pa. Soc. Club: Economic (N.Y.). Home: 1521 Prospect Av Bethlehem PA 18018 Office: 701 E 3d St Bethelhem PA 18016

CORTADA, JAMES N., fgn. trade cons.; b. N.Y.C., May 10, 1914; s. James A. and America D. (Colas) C.; B.S., Havana (Cuba) Bus. Coll., 1948; m. Shirley E. Barlow, Nov. 28, 1944; children—James William, Vera Christina, Monica Elodia. Pvt. bus., 1932-42; fgn. service officer Dept. State, 1942-70; assigned successively, Havana, Dept. Commerce, Washington, Barcelona, Spain, Dept. of State, Basra, Cairo, Egypt; dep. dir., then dir. Office Near East and South Asia Regional Affairs, Dept. State, Washington, 1960- 62; charge d'affaires, Taiz, Yemen, 1963-64; Dept. State sr. fellow U. Cal. at Los Angeles, 1964-65; dean Sch. Profl. Studies, Fgn. Service Inst., 1965-67; Am. consul gen., Barcelona, 1967-70; fgn. trade cons., 1971—. Corr. prof. fgn. trade Escuela de Administracion de Empresas, Barcelona. Orange County mem. adv. com. community relations Germanna (Va.) Community Coll. Mem. Town of Orange (Va.) Planning Commn. Mem. Middle East Inst., Royal Central Asian Soc., Am. Fgn. Service Assn., Comparative Edn. Soc. N.Am., Orange County Hist. Soc. (v.p.), Royal Acad. Belles Lettres (corr., Barcelona). Club: Woodberry Forest Golf (Orange). Home: 127 Peliso Av Orange VA 22960

CORTAZAR, JULIO, author; b. Brussels, Belgium, Aug. 26, 1914; s. Julio José and Mariá Herminia (Descotte) C.; ed. Tchrs. Coll., Buenos Aires, Argentina, 1926- 36, degree prof. lit., 1936; m. Aurora Bernárdez, Mar. 23, 1953. Author: Los Reyes, 1949; Bestiario, 1951; Final Del Suego, 1956; Las Armas Secretas, 1958; Los Premios, 1960; Historias De Cronopios y De Famas, 1962; Rayuela, 1963; Winners, 1965; Hopscotch, 1966; Blow Up and Other Stories, 1967. Address: Saignon Par Apt 9 Place du General Beuret Paris XV France

CORTE, S. CHARLES, ins. co. exec.; b. Cadore, Italy, Oct. 4, 1921; s. John and Justine (Cherubin) C.; B.S., Loyola U., Chgo., 1954; m. Amelia Camille Costalunga, July 21, 1945; children—James C., Jean L., Robert T., Susan C. Came to U.S., 1927, naturalized, 1928. Actuarial clk. VA Ins. Service, 1946-47, supr. premium accounting, 1947-49, supr. service dept., 1949-51, tng. officer, 1951-52; staff asst. premium and agy. accounting Continental Assurance Co., Chgo., 1954—, systems analyst planning dept., 1954-56, supr. planning dept., 1956-59, asst., comptroller, comptroller's dept., 1959-64, asst. v.p., asst. comptroller, 1964-65, electronics div., 1965-66, v.p., comptroller, ins. adminstrn., 1967—. Active Boy Scouts. Served with USCGR, 1942-45; ETO. Mem. Life Office Mgmt. Assn., Am. Mgmt. Assn., Ill. High Sch. Assn., Financial Execs. Inst. Clubs: Chicago Athletic, Executive's of Chicago. Home: 1323 Hillview Rd Homewood IL 60430 Office: 310 S Michigan Av Chicago IL 60604

CORTELYOU, JOHN R., univ. pres.; b. Chgo., July 21, 1914; s. B.W. and Margaret (Cuddy) C.; B.A., St. Mary's Sem., M.A., 1940; M.S., DePaul U., 1943; Ph.D., Northwestern U., 1949. Instr. dept biol. scis. DePaul U., Chgo., 1943- 46, asst. prof., 1946-50, prof., chmn. dept., 1950, now pres. univ. Mem. bd. athletics, trustee DePaul U. Mem. Am. Soc. Zoologists, A.A.A.S., N.Y. Acad. Sci., Am. Pub. Health Assn., Sigma Xi. Home: 2233 N Kenmore Av Chicago IL 60614

CORTELYOU, ROBERT VOORHEES, home furnishings co. exec.; b. Rocky Hill., N.J., Oct. 9, 1922; s. Raymond V. and Rose (Purrington) C.; B.A. in Econs., Oberlin Coll., 1947; M.B.A., U. Mich., 1951; m. June D. Watkins, Jan. 17, 1953; children—Geoffrey Hayden, Gregory Upton, Cynthia Lynn. With Chase Nat. Bank, N.Y.C., 1947-49, Dan River Mills, Inc., 1951-52, Robert Heller & Assos., Inc., Cleve., 1952-63; v.p. Mohasco Industries, Inc., Amsterdam, N.Y., 1964—, now group v.p. furniture operations; dir. Balamo S.A., Brussels, Belgium, Mohasco Industries GmbH, Hamburg, Germany. Served to 1st lt. AUS, 1943-46. Mem. Newcomen Soc. N.Am., Holland Soc. N.Y. Club: Edison (Rexford, N.Y.). Home: 108 Acorn Dr Scotia NY 12302 Office: 57 Lyon St Amsterdam NY 12010

CORTI, GINO, paleographer, historian; b. Florence, Italy, Apr. 14, 1915; s. Fortunato and Teresa (Tirinnanzi) C.; grad. econ. scis., U. Florence, 1937, in polit. scis., 1943, in arts, 1947; m. Bruna Pandolfi, Dec. 26, 1942; children—Massimo, Stefano, Monica. Tchr. Italian secondary schs., 1939-56; Ind. researcher in history, 1956—; vis. lectr. paleography U. Pa., Harvard, 1964; lectr. paleography U. Pa., Columbia, 1966-70; research asso. Center Italian Renaissance Study, 1970—. Collaborator: The Chapel of the Cardinal of Portugal. Home: 6 via C Nigra Florence Italy Office: Center Italian Renaissance Study Villa I Tatti via di Vincigliata 50135 Florence Italy

CORTISSOZ, PAUL, educator; b. N.Y.C., Nov. 9, 1924; s. Alfred and Helen (O'Brien) C.; B.A., Manhattan Coll., 1947; M.A., Columbia, 1949; Ph.D., N.Y.U., 1955; m. Geraldine Smith, Aug. 27, 1949; children—Anne, Celia Jo, Marie. Instr., Manhattan Coll., Bronx, N.Y., 1947-53, asst. prof., 1953-58, asso. prof., 1958-64, prof., 1964—, head English and world lit. dept., 1963-67, 70—. Served with USAAF, 1942-45. Recipient Founders Day award N.Y.U., 1955. Mem. Modern Lang. Assn., Am. Assn. U. Profs. Author: (with Francis Davy) Perspectives for College, 1963. Home: 35-50 85th St Jackson Heights NY 11372 Office: Manhattan Coll Pkwy Bronx NY 10471

CORTLANDT, LYN, artist; b. N.Y.C.; d. Graf Karl Gustav von Lubienski and Elinor Ernestine (Thiel) Cortlandt; student Chouinard Art Inst., Jepson Art Inst., Los Angeles, Art Students League N.Y., Art Sch. Pratt Inst., Columbia U. Sch. Painting and Sculpture, Hans Hofmann Sch. Fine Arts, China Inst. Am., N.Y.C., also pvt. instrn. Exhibited nat. shows U.S. including Pa. Acad. Fine Arts, Nat. Acad. Design, Bklyn. Mus., Art U.S.A.; exhibited Belgium, France, Greece, Holland, Italy, Japan, Portugal, Switzerland, S. Am.; works represented in permanent collections Met. Mus. Art, N.Y.C., Musée Nat. d'Art Moderne, Paris, Mus. Fine Arts, Boston, Stedelijk Mus., Amsterdam, Netherlands, Bklyn. Mus., Balt. Mus. of Art, Fogg Mus. Art, Cin. Art Mus., others, also pub. and pvt. collections. Recipient awards for oils, watercolors, graphics; medal of honor Centro Studi E Scambi Internazionali; citation humanitarian service Nephrosis Found. N.Y., N.Y. Heart Assn.; Knight of Mark Twain. Fellow Internat. Inst. Arts and Letters, Royal Soc. Art; mem. Allied Artists Am., Painters and Sculptors Soc. N.J., Phila. Water Color Club, Pen and Brush Club, Le Cercle d'Or, Internat. Platform Assn., Am. Acad. Polit. and Social Sci., N.Y. Zool. Soc., Acad. Polit. Sci., Am. Judicature Soc., Nat. Trust for Historic Preservation, UN Assn. U.S.A., Center for Study Democratic Instns., Comitato Internazionale, Centro Studi E. Internazionali, Internat. Acad. Leonardo da Vinci. Lectr. in fgn. countries. Home: 1070 Park Av New York City, NY 10028.

CORTRIGHT, EDGAR MAURICE, Jr., aero. engr.; b. Hastings, Pa., July 29, 1923; s. Edgar Maurice and Janet (Pearsall) C.; B.S. in Aero. Engring., Rensselaer Poly. Inst., 1947, M.S., 1949; m. Beverly Jane Hotaling, Mar. 24, 1945; children—Susan Joan, David Edgar. Aero. research scientist in aerodynamics Lewis Flight Propulsion Center, NACA, Cleve., 1948-58; chief advanced tech. programs NASA, Washington, 1958-60, asst. dir. lunar and planetary programs, 1960-61, dep. asso. adminstr. Office Space Scis. and Applications, 1963-67, dep. asso. adminstr. Office Manned Space Flight, 1967-68; dir. Langley Research Center, Hampton, Va., 1968—; organizer Tiros and Nimbus programs, 1958-60, Ranger, Mariner and Surveyor programs, 1960-61. Served to lt. (j.g.) USNR, 1943-46; PTO. Recipient Arthur S. Flemming award Washington Jr. C. of C., 1963; NASA medal, 1966, 67. Fellow Am. Astronaut. Soc. (Space Flight award 1971), Am. Inst. Aero. and Astronautics; mem. Sigma Xi, Tau Beta Pi, Gamma Alpha Rho, Pi Delta Epsilon, Delta Phi. Presbyn. (elder). Editor, compiler: Exploring Space With A Camera, 1968. Contbr. articles in field. Home: 1010 Wormly Creek Dr Yorktown VA 23490 Office: Langley Research Center Hampton VA 23365

CORVEY, EDWARD REGIN, mfg. co. exec.; b. St. Louis, Jan. 3, 1917; s. John Edward and Elsie (Ekey) C.; B.S. in Bus. Adminstrn., Washington U., St. Louis, 1940; m. Dorothy Doub, Sept. 3, 1951; childrenCarolyn, Patricia Ward, Dale Elisabeth, Edward Regin. Pres. Corvey Engring. Co., Washington, 1948-54; with Am. Machine & Foundry Co., 1955-, dir. marketing, 1961-63, v.p., process equipment group, 1963-67, v.p. recreational products group, 1967- 70, v.p. sports products group, 1970—; chmn. bd. AMF Voit, Inc. Served to lt. (s.g.) USNR, 1944-46. Mem. Beta Theta Pi. Beta Gamma Sigma. Republican. Presbyn. Mason (Shriner). Clubs: University (Washington); Woodway Country (Darien, Conn.); Columbia Country (Chevy Chase, Md.). Home: 683 Ponus Ridge New Canaan CT 06840 Office: 261 Madison Av New York City, NY 10016.

CORWIN, ALSOPH HENRY, chemist; b. Marietta, O., Jan. 11, 1908; s. Clifford Egbert and Elizabeth Gillet (Stimson) C.; A.B., Marietta College, 1928. D.Sc. (honorary), Marietta College, 1953; Ph.D., Harvard, 1932; m. Irene Marguerite Davis, Aug. 6, 1938. Asso. in chemistry, Johns Hopkins Univ., 1932-39, asso. prof., 1939-44, prof. since 1944, chmn. Dept. of Chemistry, 1944-47. Official Investigator Nat. Defense Research Com., 1942- 45; consultant to Army Chem. Corps., 1944, 49-59, official investigator, 1945-50; cons. metrology, Nat. Bur. Standards, 1948-52; chief investigator, Office Naval Research, 1951-53; investigator Nat. Aeros. and Space Adminstrn., 1962-65. Mem. NRC panel adv. Nat. Bur. Standards, 1960—. Mem. Am. Chem. Soc. (recipient award of merit Maryland section 1965, com. adv. to Chem. Corps), Phi Beta Kappa, Sigma Xi, Delta Upsilon. Contributor papers to scientific jour. Home: 2903 Overland Av Baltimore MD 21214 Office: Dept of Chemistry Johns Hopkins U Baltimore MD 21218

CORWIN, DAVID ROTHE, finance co. exec.; b. St. Louis, May 4, 1909; s. Louis and Rose (Yedlin) Cohen; B.C.S., St. Louis U., 1931; LL.D., Benton Coll. Law, 1936; m. Estelle Smith, June 11, 1933; children—Jacquelyne A. (Mrs. Gerald M. Kantor), Laurence A., Theodore R., Cynthia L. (Mrs. Willet F. Calvert). Sec.-treas. W.G. Shelton Co., St. Louis, 1930-42; comptroller St. Louis Jewelry Co., 1942-44; chmn. bd. ITT Aetna Corp., St. Louis, 1944—; dir. Consumer Services, Thorp Finance Co.; trustee AF Liquidating Corp., Aetna Finance Co. Profit Sharing. Pres. University City P.T.A. Council, 1962. Mem. Nat. Consumer Finance Assn. (dir.), Mo. Bar Assn. Jewish religion (pres., trustee congregation). Home: 14165 Cross Trails Dr Chesterfield MO 63017 Office: 212 S Central St Louis MO 63015

CORWIN, JAMES FAY, educator, chemist; b. Blanchester, O., Oct. 31, 1907; s. William Gayer and Edna (Betts) C.; B.A., Ohio U., 1932, M.A., 1934; Ph.D., Ohio State U., 1944; m. Gladys Wiseman Brown, Mar. 20, 1931; children—Elizabeth Gayer, James E. Metallurgist, Wheeling Steel Corp., 1928-30, 35-36; tchr. chemistry Portsmouth (O.) High Sch., 1934-35, 36-40; instr. chemistry Ohio State U., 1940-41; prof. chemistry, chmn. dept. Antioch Coll., 1941—, dir. In-Service and Summer Inst. Programs Sci. Tchrs., 1957—; asst. to pres. Varnay Labs., Yellow Springs, O., 1944—, dir., 1956—; adj. research prof. Inst. Marine Sci., U. Miami (Fla.), 1960—; cons. in field, 1961—. Chmn. Vernay Found. Award Com., 1955—; trustee Patterson Award Chem. Documentation, 1955—. Registered chem. engr., Ohio. Fellow Ohio Acad. Sci., A.A.A.S.; mem. Am. Chem. Soc. (council 1957-69), Geochem. Soc., Soc. Plastics Engrs., Am. Soc. Metals (bd. dirs. 1959-60), Sigma Alpha Epsilon. Democrat. Unitarian. Club: Engineers (Dayton, O.). Author, patentee in field. Home: 207 Fairfield Pike Yellow Springs OH 45387

CORWIN, NORMAN, writer, dir., producer; b. Boston, May 3, 1910; s. Samuel H. and Rose (Ober) C. student pub. schs., Boston, also Winthrop, Mass.; Litt.D., Columbia Coll., 1967; m. Katherine Locke, Mar. 1947; children—Anthony, Diane. Writer, producer, dir. CBS; lectr. various univs.; created radio program series, wrote, prod. individual radio broadcasts; chief spl. projects UN Radio; wrote films for RKO, MGM, 20th-Century Fox, UN; writer, dir., prod. 26 By Corwin, 1941, This is War!, 1942, An American in England, 1942, Columbia Presents Corwin, 1944-45; writer, dir. stage plays on Broadway; Rivalry, World of Carl Sandburg; The Hyphen; writer for films Lust for Life, Story of Ruth, The Blue Vell, Sandal at Scourie; creator, host TV series Norman Corwin Presnts for Westinghouse Group W, 1971. Mem. LaGuardia One World Meml. Commn. to Europe, 1948. Recipient Page One award Am. Newspaper Guild, 1944-45, Distinguished Merit award Nat. Conf. Christians and Jews, 1945; Unity award Interracial Film and Radio Guild, 1945; citation Nat. Council Tchrs. English, 1945, Assn. Tchrs. Social Studies of N.Y., 1945; award Am. Schs. and Colls. Assn., 1946; Wendell Willkie One World and (flew around world, recording speeches leaders of state, artists and scientists, June-Oct. 1946), first award Inst. for Edn. by Radio, 1946; prod. and narrated One World Flight, 1947; first place in nat. poll radio editors Billboard mag., for On a Note of Triumph, 1946; co-winner 1st prize Met. Opera awards for new Am. opera, The Warrior, produced Jan. 1947; Freedom award telecast Between Americans, 1951 hon. grant Am. Acad. Arts and Letters. Fellow Radio Hall of Fame; mem. Acad. of Motion Picture Arts and Scis. (chmn. documentary awards com., co-chmn. scholarship com.), Aspen Film Conf. (steering com.), Authors League Am., Dramatists Guild, Screen Writers Guild. Author: They Fly Through the Air With the Greatest of Ease, 1940; Thirteen by Corwin, 1942; More by Corwin, 1944; On a Note of Triumph, 1945; Untitled and Other Works, 1947; Dog in the Sky, 1952; The Plot to Overthrow Christmas, 1952; The World of Carl Sandburg, 1961; Overkill and Megalove, 1963; Prayer For the 70s, 1969. Contbr. articles to mags. Writer text of Human Rights Cantata, Yes Speak Out Yes (commd. by UN). Home: 14145 Greenleaf St Sherman Oaks CA 91403 Office: 10401 Wellworth Av Los Angeles CA 90024

CORWIN, SWIFT CHURCHILL, lawyer; b. N.Y.C., Feb. 16, 1916; s. Charles L. and Gladys (Barnes) C.; A.B., U. Mich., 1937; LL.B., Harvard, 1940; m. Elizabeth Lyon, Nov. 29, 1947; children—Joan B., Robert L., Swift Churchill. Admitted to Ohio bar, 1940, since practiced in Toledo; mem. firm Shumaker, Loop and Kendrick, 1947—. Mem. Ohio Bd. Uniform Laws, 1960—, now pres. Bd. dirs. Boys Club, Toledo, 1947—. Served to capt. AUS, 1942-46. Mem. Am., Ohio, Toledo bar assns., Am. Judicature Soc., Delta Kappa Epsilon. Republican. Episcopalian. Club: Toledo Country. Home: Route 26437 Hull Prairie Rd Perrysburg OH 43551 Office: 811 Madison Av Toledo OH 43624

CORWIN, THOMAS PARKER, mfg. co. exec.; b. Washington, Mar. 21, 1914; s. Royal Ernest and Blanche (Williams) C.; A.B., U. Md., 1935; LL.B., J.D., Georgetown U., 1942; m. Jane Collins, June 26, 1940; children—Susan Jane (Mrs. L. Dain Gary, Jr.), Nancy Williams (Mrs. C. Austin Boyd), Mary Caroline. With Riggs Nat. Bank, Washington, 1935-41; commd. 2d lt. U.S. Army Res., 1935, advanced through grades to brig. gen. USAF, 1963; active mil. service, 1941-46; admitted to D.C. bar, 1941; pvt. practice, Washington, 1946-50; recalled to active duty, 1950; dep. dir. finance Hdqrs. USAF, 1951-54; dep. comptroller USAF, Europe, 1954-57; comptroller, then chief staff Air Proving Ground Command, 1957-59; comptroller, then asst. vice comdr. Air Force Systems Command, 1959-62; vice comdr., then comdr. Air Force Accounting and Finance Center, 1962- 67, ret.; v.p., treas. C.A. Norgren Co., Littleton, Colo., 1968—; dir. Air Acad. Nat. Bank, 1968—, United Bank of Littleton, 1969—, Norgren Shipston Internat. (Eng.), 1970—. Mem. Denver Fed. Exec. Bd., 1963-67. Vice pres., trustee Tchr.'s Award Found. Colo., 1963-66; hon. v.p. Denver chpt. A.R.C., 1963-67, United Way Fund, Denver, 1963—. Decorated Legion of Merit with 1 oak leaf cluster, D.S.M., Commendation medal. Mem. Sigma Chi, Omicron Delta Kappa, Delta Theta Phi. Presbyn. Rotarian. Club: Columbine Country (Littleton); Eisenhower Golf (Colorado Springs); Plantation (Sea Pines, S.C.). Home: 7 Niblick Lane Littleton CO 80123 Office: 5400 S Delaware Littleton CO 80120

CORY, ALEC LEON, lawyer; b. Gallup, N.M., Mar. 11, 1915; s. Leon N. and Rose (Jacob) C.; B.S., U. Cal. at Berkeley, 1936, LL.B., 1939; m. Barbara S. Felker, Dec. 17, 1939; children—Linda (Mrs. Ronald R. House), Jane. Admitted to Cal. bar, 1939; pub. atty. under DeWitt C. Mitchell Trust, San Diego, 1940- 41; dep. city atty. San Diego, 1941-42; rationing atty. OPA, San Diego, 1942-43; pvt. practice, San Diego, 1946—; mem. firm Procopio, Cory, Hargreaves & Savitch, 1950—. Trustee Cal. State Colls. Served with USNR, 1943-46. Mem. San Diego County Bar Assn, (post bd. dir., pres. 1966), San Diego C. of C. Club: University Cal. Alumni San Diego County (past pres.). Home: 10355 Bonnie Lane La Mesa CA 92041 Office: First Nat Bank Bldg San Diego CA 92101

CORY, WILLIAM LEONARD, educator, mech. engr.; b. Kansas City, Mo., Aug. 25, 1907; s. Albert Wilson and Minnie Adele (Stoner) C.; B.S., U. Okla., 1928, M.E., 1951. Student engr. Westinghouse Electric & Mfg. Co., 1928-31; jr. observer Western Geophys. Co., 1934; practice of accounting, 1935-42; instrument engr. Phillips Petroleum Co., 1943; test engr. Douglas Aircraft Co., 1944-45; design engr. Calhoun Hydraulic Equipment Co., 1945-46; instr. to prof. mechanics U. Okla., 1947-61, prof., chmn. dept. theoretical and applied mechanics, prof. indsl. engring., 1966—. NSF summer inst. Notre Dame, 1963, U. Houston, 1964. Registered profl. engr., Okla. Mem. Am. Soc. M.E., Am. Soc. Engring. Edn., Sigma Tau, Tau Beta Pi. Presbyn. Lion. Home: 3210 S Chautauqua St Norman OK 73069

COSBY, BETTY WALLACE, coll. dean; b. Birmingham, Ala., Dec. 8, 1923; d. Daniel Milton and Elizabeth (Beavers) Cosby; B.S., Ala. Poly. Inst., 1944; M.A., Syracuse U., 1949. Asst. counselor women U. Miami, 1949-52; asst. dean women Ala. Poly. Inst., 1952-55; former dean Women Tex. Western Coll., El Paso. Mem. Ala. (pres. 1954-55), Tex. (chmn. coll. sect. 1956) assns. deans women, Southwest Coll. Personnel Assn., Nat. Assn. Women Deans and Counselors, Am. Assn. U. Women, C. of C., El Paso City Panhellenic Assn., Mortar Board, Kappa Delta Pi, Kappa Delta, Pi Lambda Theta, Alpha Lambda Delta. Episcopalian. Home: 2411 N Stanton St El Paso TX

COSBY, BILL, actor; b. Phila., July 12, 1937; s. William Henry and Anna Cosby; student Temple U.; m. Camille Hanks, Jan. 25, 1964; children—Erike Ranee, Erinn Charlene, Ennis William. Appeared in numerous night clubs, including The Gaslight, N.Y.C., Hungry I, San Francisco, Shoreham Hotel, Washington, Basin St. East, N.Y.C., Flamingo, Las Vegas, Nev., Harrah's Lake Tahoe; appeared on numerous TV shows; co-star TV show I Spy; star The Bill Cosby Show, 1969—; recordings include Bill Cosby Is a Very Funny Fellow-Right, I Started Out As a Child, Why Is There Air, Wonderfulness, Revenge (Grammy award Nat. Acad. Performing Arts and Scis. 1967). Pres. Rhythm and Blues Hall of Fame, 1968—. Served with USNR, 1956-60. Recipient 4 Emmy awards, 6 Grammy awards; named number 1 in comedy field Top Artists on Campus Poll (album sales), 1968. Address: care Mariette Mandell Warner Bros 4000 Warner Blvd Burbank CA 91505

COSBY, JOSEPH HATHAWAY, clergyman, school pres.; b. Hampton, Virginia, June 2, 1902; s. Joseph Hugh and Harriett Edmonds (Hathaway) C.; student Fork Union Mil. Acad., 1918-21; Th.B., So. Bapt. Theol. Sem., 1926; A.B., U. Richmond, 1929, LL.D. (hon.), 1959; M.A., U. Va., 1937; m. Helen Frances Eubank, Sept. 17, 1924; 1 dau., Jayne Hathaway. Ordained to ministry Bapt. Ch., 1928; pastor, Danville, Va., 1929-30, Irvington, 1930-35, Crozet, 1935-37, Lexington, 1937-42, Richmond, 1946-51; pres. Hargrave Mil Acad., Chatham, Va., 1951—. Moderator Augusta Bapt. Assn., 1942; recording sec., chmn. exec. com., mem. Va. Bapt. Bd. Missions and Edn., 1946-51; pres. Richmond Bapt. Ministers Conf., 1949- 50.. Chmn. A.R.C. (Lancaster and Rockbridge cos.). Mem. bd. trustees Golden Gate Bapt. Theol. Sem., Berkeley, Cal. Served as maj., combat chaplain AUS World War II. Decorated 6 battle stars. Mem. So. Assn. Colls. and Schs. (chmn. Va. com.), Nat. Study Secondary Sch. Evaluation, So. Assn. Ind. Schs. (past pres.), Newcomen Soc. N.Am., Phi Beta Kappa, Omicron Delta Kappa. Lion (charter pres. Lexington 1941). Address: Hargrave Military Academy Chatham VA 24531

COSENTINI, JOHN WALTER, educator; b. Bklyn., Feb. 2, 1909; s. Eugene L. and Vincenza (Vessichelli) C.; B.A. cum laude, St. John's Coll., 1932; M.A., N.Y.U., 1936; Ph.D., Columbia, 1951; m. Denise A. Detilleux, June 30, 1951; children—Cecilia G., Adrian G. Faculty, St. John's U., 1935—, prof. French, 1954—, chmn. dept. modern langs., 1957-61, 67-69. Mem. Am. Council Teaching Fgn. Lang., Modern Lang. Assn. Am., Am. Assn. Tchrs. French, Am. Soc. for Eighteenth Century Studies. Author: Fontenelle's Art of Dialogue, 1952; also articles in field. Home: 144-03 71st Av Flushing NY 11367 Office: St John's U Grand Central and Utopia Pkwys Jamaica NY 11432

COSER, LEWIS ALFRED, educator, sociologist; b. Berlin, Germany, Nov. 27, 1913; s. Martin and Margarete (Fehlow) C.; student Sorbonne, Paris, France, 1935-38; Ph.D. in Sociology, Columbia, 1954; m. Rose Laub, Aug. 25, 1942; children—Ellen, Steven. Came to U.S., 1941, naturalized, 1948. Instr., U. Chgo., 1948-50; mem. faculty Brandeis U., 1951-68, prof. sociology, 1960-68; distinguished prof. State U. N.Y., Stony Brook, 1969—; fellow Center for Advanced Study Behavioral Scis., Stanford, Cal., 1968-69. Vis. prof. U. Cal. at Berkeley, 1957-58. Mem. Am. Sociol. Assn., Eastern Sociol. Soc. (pres. 1964-65), Am. Civil Liberties Union, Am. Assn. U. Profs. Author: The Functions of Social Conflict, 1956; (with B. Rosenberg) Sociological Theory, 3d edit., 1969; (with Irving Howe) The American Communist Party, 2d edit., 1962; Sociology Through Literature, 1963; Men of Ideas, 1965; Georg Simmel, 1965; Political Sociology, 1967; Continuities in the Study of Social Conflict, 1967; Masters of Sociological Thought, 1970. Home: 52 Erland Rd Stony Brook NY 11790

COSGRIFF, ROBERT LIEN, educator; b. Grey Cliff, Mont., Feb. 27, 1923; s. Robert and Kaia (Lien) C.; student Mont. State Coll., 1940-43; B.S., Ohio State U., 1947, M.S., 1948, Ph.D., 1953; m. Jane Louise Ervin, Apr. 20, 1946; children—Alan Ervin, Kevin Robert, Brian Kurt. Sr. research engr. Curtiss Wright Corp., Columbus, O., 1947-50; prof. elec. engring., dir. communication and control systems labs. Ohio State U., Columbus, 1950-67; prof., chmn. dept. elec. engring. U. Ky., Lexington, 1967—. Cons. U. Denver, U.S. Dept. Commerce; sec. communication com. HRB div. Nat. Acad. Sci. Served with AUS, 1943-46. Recipient Distinguished Alumnus award Ohio State U., 1970. Mem. I.E.E.E., Am. Soc. Elec. Engrs., Eta Kappa Nu, Tau Beta Pi, Theta Tau. Republican. Methodist. Kiwanian. Author: Nonlinear Control Systems, 1958. Patentee in field. Home: 3433 Lannette Lane Lexington KY 40503

COSGRIFF, STEWART, banker; b. Salt Lake City, June 30, 1903; s. John B. and Bessie (Stewart) C.; A.B., U. Colo., 1924; m. Katharine Dawson, Dec. 19, 1927; children—Katharine (Mrs. James B. Kurtz), Peter, Susan (Mrs. Gilbert A. Mueller), Bridget (Mrs. Burt Beck Fisher, Jr.). Clk., Continental Nat. Bank, Salt Lake City, 1924-29; asst. v.p. Nat. Copper Bank, successively Security Nat. Bank, First Nat. Bank, First Security Bank of Utah. Salt Lake City, 1919-34, v.p. First Security Bank of Utah. 1934-48; v.p. Denver Nat. Bank, 1948-57, pres., 1957-63; sr. v.p. First Western Bank & Trust Co., 1961, vice chmn. bd., 1962-64, later pres. and chief exec. officer, then chmn. exec. com., dir.; dir. Colo. State Bank, Denver, Ideal Basic Industries, Inc., Am. Crystal Sugar Co. Bd. dir. Nat. Western Stock Show, Molly Mayfield Found. Mem. Robert Morris Assos., Newcomen Soc. N.Am., Town Hall. Office: Boston Bldg Denver CO 80202

COSGROVE, FRANK DENNIS, orgn. exec.; b. Paterson, N.J., Oct. 19, 1926; s. Frank J. and Elizabeth Marie (McSherry) C.; B.S. in Phys. Edn., Health and Recreation, St. Bonaventure U., 1951; m. Jean C. Drake, Dec. 28, 1948; children—Jeanne, Timothy, Dir. recreation, Clifton, N.J., 1951-56; dir. parks and recreation, Warren, Mich., 1956-64; exec. dir. Am. Youth Hostels, Inc., 1964—. U.S. del. Internat. Youth Hostel Fedn. Confs., Poland, 1965, Austria, 1966, Japan, 1968, Finland, 1970; mem. White House Confs. on Internat. Coop., 1964, Nat. Beautification, 1965, Children, 1970; mem. Pres. Johnson's Spl. Taskforce on Travel, 1968. Bd. dirs. Macomb County Assn. Retarded Children, 1959-64; trustee Macomb County Community Coll., 1964—. Served with USNR, 1944-46. Named Most Outstanding Recreation Dir. in N.J., 1955. Mem. Nat. Recreation and Parks Assn., Am. Recreation Soc., Am. Forestry Assn., Am. Soc. Assn. Execs., N.Y. Soc. Assn. Execs. Lion, Elk. Home: Cedar Grove NJ Office: 20 W 17th St New York City NY 10011

COSGROVE, FRANK PETER, univ. dean; b. Peekskill, N.Y., June 28, 1914; s. John Joseph and Mary T. (Walsh) C.; B.S., U. Notre Dame, 1938; M.A., N.Y.U., 1941; M.S., U. Colo., 1949; Ph.D., Ohio State U., 1953; m. Myrtle Lucille Bihm, June 9, 1951; children—John M., Terrance P., Susan M., Mary Anne. Prodn. supr. Burrough Welcome and Co., 1942-45; mem. faculty Southwestern State Coll., Weatherford, Okla., 1945-47, Loyola U., New Orleans, 1947-50, 55-58, U. Neb., 1953-55, U. Tex., 1958-61, 61-68; prof., dean pharmacy Ida. State U., Pocatello, 1968—. Mem. Am. Pharm. Assn., Am. Chem. Soc., Am. Soc. Hosp. Pharmacists, Sigma Xi, Rho Chi, Kappa Psi, Phi Delta Chi, Phi Kappa Phi. Contbr. articles to profl. jours. Home: 65 Fordham St Pocatello ID 83201

COSGROVE, GORDON DEAN, pipeline co. exec.; b. Oklahoma City, Mar. 2, 1934; s. Isaac H. and Gertha (Baker) C.; B.B.A., U. Okla., 1956; m. Jueretta Sue Brannon, Dec. 19, 1954; children—Kim C., Craig R., Drew R. Audit staff Price Waterhouse & Co., Tulsa, 1956-60; staff accountant Mid-Am. Pipeline Co. (name changed to MAPCO, Inc., 1968), Tulsa, 1960-64, asst. treas., 1964-67, treas., 1967—. Served to 2d lt. AUS, 1956. Mem. Am. Inst. C.P.A.'s, Okla., Tulsa socs. C.P.A.'s. Kiwanian. Home: 6260 S Hudson St Tulsa OK 74135 Office: 1437 S Boulder Av Tulsa OK 74119

COSGROVE, JOHN EDWARD, religious orgn. ofcl.; b. Keokuk, Ia., Mar. 16, 1923; s. H. Edward and Alleyne (Keefe) C.; student St. Ambrose Coll., 1940-43; J.D., U. Notre Dame, 1948; postgrad. Drake U., 1950; m. Katherine Marv Mines, Jan. 27, 1951; children—Kathleen, Patricia, Edward, Eileen, Gregg, Margaret, Ceclia, Maureen, Alice, Thomas. Admitted to Ia. bar, 1948, also U.S. Supreme Ct.; atty. office solicitor U.S. Dept. Labor, 1949-50; dir. edn. Ia. Fedn. Labor, 1951-54; asst. dir. edn. AFL-CIO, 1955; asst. dir. Office Emergency Planning Exec., Office of President 1961-67; dir. Office Regional Devel. Planning, Econ. Devel. Adminstrn., U.S. Dept. Commerce, 1967-69; dir. dept. social devel. U.S. Cath. Conf., 1969—. Lectr. Drake U., Des Moines, 1952-53, Sch. Fgn. Service, Georgetown U., 1958-60; rep. U.S. at Labor Edn. Cong. European Productivity Agy., France, 1958, to indsl. planning com., sr. civil emergency planning com. NATO, 1962. Served with A.C., AUS, 1943-46; capt. USAF, 1952. Mem. Am. Fedn. Govt. Employees. Democrat. Catholic. Contbr. assn. law jours. Home: 3953 Lantern Dr Silver Spring, MD 20902. Office: 1312 Massachusetts Av N W Washington DC 20005

COSGROVE, JOHN PATRICK, publs. co. cons.; b. Pittston, Pa., Sept. 25, 1918; s. Raymond Patrick and Alice (Gilroy) C.; ed. pub. schs., Pa.; m. Patricia Ellen O'Hara, Mar. 26, 1951. Reporter, Wilkes-Barre (Pa.) Record, 1936-37; with Assoc. Press, Washington, 1938-40; writer, research Nat. Rep. Congl. Com., Washington, 1940; exec. asst. U.S. Senator Hiram W. Johnson, 1941-42; free lance writer, 1946-48; dir. publs. Broadcasting Publs., Inc., pubs. Broadcasting Businessweekly Television monthly, Broadcasting Yearbook, Washington, 1948-68; cons. editor Acropolis Books, Ltd., 1969—; publicity dir. Honor Am. Day Celebration, 1970; exec. dir. Am. Historic and Cultural Soc., Inc., 1970—. dir. Nat. Press Bldg. Corp. Bd. dirs. Am. Irish Found. pres., 1971; Washington chpt. Nat. Multiple Sclerosis Soc., 1962—. Served with USNR, 1942. Mem. Sigma Delta Chi. Roman Cath. Clubs: Nat. Press (pres. 1961, historian 1963-65) (Washington); Nat. Headliners (Atlantic City). Editor SHRDLU-An Affectionate Chronicle, the first fifty years of the Nat. Press Club, 1959. Home: 9512 Persimmon Tree Rd Potomac MD 20854 Office: 930 Nat Press Bldg Washington DC 20004

COSGROVE, ROBERT CARVER, canning co. exec.; b. LeSueur, Minn., Apr. 18, 1919; s. Edward Bradley and Louise (Strong) C.; grad. Shattuck Mil. Sch., Faribault, Minn., 1937; student U. Va., 1941, U. Minn., 1946; m. Eleanor Dodd, Mar. 20, 1947; children—Robert Carver, Dodd Bigelow Lindsay Jeanne, William Henry. With Green Giant Co., LeSueur, 1946—, v.p. corp. planning, 1960- 62, chmn. bd., 1962-64, pres., chief exec. officer, 1964—; dir. Employees Mut., Wausau, Wis., Community Investment Enterprises, Inc., Mpls., 1st Nat. Bank of St. Paul, Minn. Mut. Ins. Co. Dir. YMCA Mpls. Trustee Com. Econ. Devel., N.Y.C., Shattuck Mil. Acad., Faribault, Minn. Served to capt. AUS, 1942-46; ETO. Decorated Silver Star, Combat Inf. badge. Mem. Grocery Mfrs. Assn., Phi Delta Theta, Alpha Chi Sigma. Mason. Clubs: Minneapolis, Woodhill (Mpls.). Home: Box 79 Route 3 Wayzata MN Office: 1100 N 4th St Le Sueur MN 56058

COSGROVE, WILLIAM BURNHAM, educator, biologist; b. N.Y.C., June 11, 1920; s. William Lindsay and Evelyn (Burnham) C.; A.B. with distinction in Zoology, Cornell U., 1941; M.S., N.Y. U., 1947, Ph.D., 1949; m. Dolores C. Mangual, Aug. 6, 1949; children—Karen L., Bruce B. Grad. asst. biology N.Y.U., 1941-42, 46-49; asso. zoology State U. Ia., 1949-51, asst. prof., 1951-56, asso. prof., 1956-57; instr. Mountain Lake Biol. Sta., U. Va., summer 1950; instr. Lake Itasca Biol. Sta., U. Minn., summer 1962; mem. faculty U. Ga., Athens, 1957—, prof. zoology, 1964-69, Alumni Found. Distinguished prof., 1969—, chmn. dept., 1964—. Served with AUS, 1942-46. Mem. A.A.A.S., Am. Soc. Cell Biology, Am. Soc. Zoologists, Soc. Protozoologists (pres. 1970-71), Assn. Southeastern Biologists, Sigma Xi, Phi Kappa Phi. Contbr. articles to profl. jours. Home: PO Box 74 Watkinsville GA 30677 Office: Dept Zoology University of Ga Athens GA 30601

COSGROVE, WILLIAM HUNH, ret. mfg. co. exec.; b. Braddock, Pa., July 30, 1892; s. Thomas and Mary (Flanagan) C.; M.E., Cornell U., 1915; m. Elizabeth Kuhn, Jan. 9, 1924; children—Thomas, John Casey, Mary Margaret, William Hugh, Mark. With Am. Sheet & Tin Plate Co., 1915-19. William Swindell & Bros., 1919-30; v.p. Swindell-Dressner Corp., Pitts., 1930-47, pres., 1947-59, chmn. bd., 1959-62, cons., 1962-67; dir. Pitts. Testing Labs., Union Nat. Bank, Pitts., Pa. Mfg. Assn. Ins. Co. Mem. Pitts. Bd. Edn., 1945-56. Trustee Duquesne U. Found.; pres. adv. bd., trustee Mercy Hosp., Pitts.; mem. adv. bd. St. Vincent Coll., Latrobe, Pa., Duquesne U. Served to 1st lt. A.C., U.S. Army, 1917-19, Mem. Pa. Mfg. Assn. (dir.), Am. Iron and Steel Inst., Assn. Iron and Steel Engrs., Engrs. Soc. Western Pa. Republican. Roman Catholic. Club: Duquesne, Longvue, Pittsburgh Field, University, Cornell of N.Y. Home: 5923 Braeburn Pl Pittsburgh PA 15232

COSGROVE, WILLIAM MICHAEL, clergyman; b. Canton, O., Nov. 26, 1916; s. William Leo and Margaret Dorothy (Leahy) C.; A.B., John Carroll U., 1938, M.A., 1959; LL.D. (hon.), Cleve.-Marshall Law Sch. Ordained priest Roman Cath. ch., 1943; aux. bishop of Cleve., 1968—. Mem. City of Cleve. Planning Commn., 1971—. Home: 18200 Harvard St Cleveland OH 44128 Office: 1027 Superior St Cleveland OH 44114

COSPER, RUSSELL A., educator; b. Lansing, Mich., May 30, 1910; s. J. D. Lincoln and Grace Alice (Bond) C.; A.B., Western Mich. U., 1933; A.M., U. Mich., 1937, Ph.D. 1947; m. Vera M. Lucas, Aug. 22, 1936; children—Ronald Lee, David Russell, Sylvia Margot. High sch. tchr., East Detroit, Mich., 1934-37; asst. prof. English, Eastern Mich. U., 1937-46; mem. faculty Purdue U., Lafayette Ind., 1946—, prof. English, 1956—, head dept., 1962-69. Served to lt. USNR, 1943-46. Mem. Am. Assn. U. Profs., Modern Lang. Assn., Nat. Council Tchrs. English. Author: This Is Your Language, 1940; Toward Better Reading Skill, 1959. Home: 1325 Sunset Lane West Lafayette IN 47906 Office: English Dept Purdue Univ Lafayette IN 46207

COSSOTTO, FLORENZA, (Mrs. Ivo Vinco), mezzo soprano; b. Crescentino, Italy, Apr. 22, 1938; d. Ettore and Marina (Ferrero) Cossotto; Diploma, Conservatorio di Musica G. Verdi, Turin, Italy, 1956; m. Ivo Vinco, June 14, 1958; 1 son, Roberto. Permanent singer LaScala, Milan, Italy, 1957—; appearances in opera houses of Milan, Rome, Naples, Florence, Venice, Vienna, London, Paris. Barcelona, also at Edinburgh Festival and in USSR. Address: Via Ezio Biondi 1 Milan Italy

COSSUTTA, ARALDO ALFRED, architect; b. Island of Krk, Yugoslavia, Jan. 11, 1925; s. Martin K. and Marija (Korosec) C.; student U. Belgrade, 1945-46, Ecole des Beaux Arts, Paris, 1946-51; M.Arch., Harvard, 1952; m. Thelma Claire Bouchet, Sept. 16, 1950; children—Louis Michel, Renée Claire. Came to U.S., 1951, naturalized, 1951. With Atelier of LeCorbusier, France, 1949; with Michael Hare & Assos., N.Y.C., 1952-55; with I. M. Pei & Partners, N.Y.C., 1955—, asso., 1959-63, partner, 1963—. Mem. A.I.A.,

Archtl. League N.Y. Important works include Denver Hilton Hotel, Hyde Park Apts., Chgo., Green Center for Earth Scis., Cambridge, Mass., L'Enfant Plaza, Washington, Christian Sci. Ch. Center, Boston. Home: 30 Beekman Pl New York City NY 10022 Office: 600 Madison Av New York City NY 10022

COST, JAMES PETER, artist; b. Phila., Mar. 3, 1923; s. Peter and Rose (Perry) C.; B.A., U. Cal. at Los Angeles, 1950; M.S., U. So. Cal., 1959; m. Betty Jo Root, Apr. 17, 1957; children—Curtis, Shelley, Janet, Nancy. Tchr. art Los Angeles City Sch. Dist., 14 yrs.; lectr. art Northwood Insts., Midland, Mich., Dallas, 1971; one-man shows Northwood Inst., Midland, 1971, R.W. Norton Gallery, Shreveport, La., 1971; exhibited in group shows at Artists Guild Gallery Am., Carmel, 1961-63, James Peter Cost Gallery, 1964—, Mus. Fine Arts, Springfield, Mass., 1965, Nat. Arts Club, N.Y.C., 1966; rep. numerous pvt. collections. Pres. Carmel Bus. Assn., 1970. Served with USCGR, 1942- 45. Republican. Christian Scientist. Office: Post Office Box 3638 Carmel CA 93921

COSTA, AUBREY M., mortgage banker, ins. exec.; b. Corsicana, Tex., July 3, 1896; s. Ralph and Minnie (Frank) C.; student Tyler (Tex.) Comml. Coll., 1914. Employee Magnolia Petroleum Co., Corsicana, later Dallas, 1914-20; supt. Ranger (Tex.) Refining & Pipe Line Co., 1920-21; pvt. oil bus., Tex. and Okla., 1921-24; organizer, chmn., dir. So. Trust & Mortgage Co., Dallas, 1924—; owner Love & Costa Real Estate Agy., Dallas; dir. Republic Ins. Co., Allied Finance Co., Indsl. Life Ins. Co., Dallas, Republic Financial Services, Inc., Republic-Vanguard Life Ins. Co. Served with USN, World War I. Recipient Distinguished Service award Mortgage Bankers Am., 1948. Mem. Mortgage Bankers Am. (pres., 1951-52), Tex. Mortgage Bankers Assn. (pres., 1939) Urban League Greater Dallas (v.p.). Mason (32, Shriner). Clubs: Dallas Athletic, Lakewood Country, Chaparral (Dallas), 21 Turtle; City. Home: 3601 Turtle Creek Blvd Dallas TX 75219 Office: First Nat Bank Bldg Dallas TX 75202

COSTA, JASPER SILVA, educator; b. Azores, Jan. 16, 1904; s. John and Christina Augusta (Silva) C.; came to U.S., 1908, naturalized, 1927; A.B., Brown U., 1927; J.D., Cornell U., 1931; LL.M., Georgetown U., 1948; S.J.D., George Washington U., 1951; m. Clarice Mapes Brown, June 10, 1930; children—Prudence Mapes, Jonathan Leeds. Admitted to N.Y. bar, 1932; practice in N.Y.C. and Boston, 1931-42; U.S. govt. lawyer, Washington, 1942-52; with U.S. Fgn. Service, 1952-68; tax adviser, Asuncion, Paraguay, 1952-54, San Jose, Costa Rica, 1954-56, Amman, Jordan, 1966-67; sr. tax financial adviser, Quito, Ecuador, 1956-57; pub. adminstrn. tax adviser, Lima, Peru, 1958-62; pub. adminstr. officer, regional tax adviser, State Dept., Latin Am., 1962-66; vis. scholar in bus. adminstrn. Knoxville (Tenn.) Coll., 1968-69; prof. Coll. Bus. Adminstrn., U. Tenn., Knoxville, 1969—. Observer, Conf. Tax Adminstrn., Buenos Aires, Argentina, 1961. Served to maj. AUS, 1942-45. Mem. Am. Bus. Law Assn., Phi Alpha Delta. Presbyn. Clubs: Holston Hills Country (Knoxville, Tenn.); Army and Navy (Washington). Author: The Law of Inventing in Employment, 1953. Home: 1400 Kenesaw Avenue S W Knoxville, TN 37919.

COSTA, JOSEPH, press photographer; b. Caltabelotta, Sicily, Italy, Jan. 3, 1904; s. Giuseppi and Francesca (Stravalli) C.; ed. pub. schs., N.Y.C.; m. Marguerite Macdonell, Oct. 18, 1930 (dec.); 1 dau., Frances Joyce; m. 2d, Margaret H. King, Nov. 22, 1967. Staff photographer N.Y. Morning World, 1920-27, N.Y. News, 1927-46; photo supr. King Features Syndicate, chief photographer Sunday Mirror Mag., 1946-63; exec. editor Nat. Press Photographer mag., N.Y.C., 1946-67, editor emeritus, 1967—; illustrations editor World Book Ency. Sci. Service, Inc., Houston, 1967-69; author weekly photo feature for newspapers, 1968-70; now head Photography for Publ., also cons. Guiding faculty, Famous Photographers Sch., Westport, Conn. Received Merit Award, Press Photographers Assn. N.Y., 1947; asso. Photographic Soc. Am., 1949, fellow, 1956; Fellowship Award and Sprague Award Nat. Press Photographers Assn., 1949; citation from Kent State U., 1949; Germain G Award, 1952; U. Mo. Honor Medal, 1954. Mem. Press Photographers Assn. N.Y., Nat. Press Photographers Assn. (founder, 1st pres., chmn. bd. dirs. 1948-64). Author: Beginner's Guide to Color Photography, 1955. Editor: Complete Book of Press Photography, 1950. Home: 25301 Outlook Dr Carmel CA 93921

COSTA, MARY, soprano; b. Knoxville, Tenn. Film voice of Sleeping Beauty by Walt Disney; appeared TV comms., 195557; debut Los Angeles Opera, 1958, in L.A Boheme, San Francisco Opera, 1959, as Violetta in La Traviata at Met. Opera, N.Y.C., 1964; appeared Glyndebourne Opera House, Royal Opera House Covent Garden, Teatro Nacional de San Carlos, Grand Theatre de Geneve; toured U.S. with Bernstein's Candide; appeared English prodn. Candide; revival Bernstein's Candide at John F. Kennedy Center for Performing Arts, 1971; tour Soviet Union, 1970; Bolshoi debut, La Traviatta, 1970; appeared internat. recitals, ochestras. Vice pres. Cal. Inst. Arts. Named Woman of Year, Los Angeles, 1959. Address: care of S Hurok 730 Fifth Av New York City NY

COSTA, NATALIE, actress and Aldonza in Man of La Mancha.*

COSTA-LOBO, ANTONIO LEAL DA, diplomat of Portugal; b. Coim ra, Portugal, May 22, 1932; s. Gumersindo Sarmento da and Maria Magdalena Teixeira (Leal) Costa-L.; law degree, U. Coimbra, 1954, complementary course hist. juridical scis., 1954-55. Atty., Coimbra, 1955-56; joined Ministry of Fgn. Affairs Portugal, 1956; chargé d'affaires, Havana, Cuba, 1961-63; sec. embassy, The Hague, Netherlands, 1963-66; consul gen. in San Francisco, 1966—. Decorated officer Order Orange-Nassau (Netherlands). Author: O Principio da Auto- Determina, cao dos Povos, 1956; also articles. Home: 3298 Washington Street San Francisco CA 94115

COSTANZA, ANGELO ANTHONY, banker; b. Rochester, N.Y., May 15, 1926; s. Nicholas and Rose (Provezzano) C.; B.A. in Econs., U. Rochester, 1951; LL.B. cum laude, Syracuse Law Sch., 1955; m. Maria Steiner, Jan. 4, 1947; children—Nicholas, Linda, Andrew, James. Admitted to N.Y. bar, 1955; partner firm Van Schaick, Woods, Strathman, Sturman and Costanza, Rochester, 1957-63; exec. v.p. Central Trust Co., Rochester, 1963-66, exec. v.p., 1966, pres., 1966-70, pres., chief exec. officer, 1970—. Exec. bd. Otetiana council Boy Scouts Am.; bd. dirs. Rochester Hosp. Service Corp., Community Chest of Rochester, A.R.C.; chmn. Rochester Rehab. and Conservation Adv. Com., 1964—; trustee Rochester Bur. Municipal Research, 1966—. Served with AUS, World War II. Decorated Combat Inf. badge. Mem. Am., N.Y. State, Monroe County bar assns., Rochester C. of C. (trustee), Rochester Assn. UN, Justian Soc., V.F.W., Order of Coif, Phi Kappa Phi, Phi Delta Phi. Clubs: Rochester, Rochester City. Home: 275 Hibiscus Drive Rochester, NY 14618. Office: 44 Exchange Street Rochester NY 14614

COSTANZO, GESUALDO, banker; b. Birmingham, Ala., Nov. 20, 1916; s. Joseph and Mary (de Falco) C.; A.B., Birmingham-So. Coll.; M.A., U. Va., 1939, Ph.D., 1941; student Brookings Instn., 1939-40; m. Lillie Gugliotta, July 4, 1940; 1 dau., Mary Valerie. Asst. prof. econs. U. Md., 1941-42; economist Dept. Commerce, 1942-43, Dept. State, 1946-48; asst. rep. to Italy, U.S. Treasury Dept., 1948-50, economist, Treasury Dept., 1950-51; U.S. mem. Greek Currency Com., Athens, Greece, 1951-55; dep. dir. Western Hemisphere dept. IMF, 1955-61; v.p. First Nat. City Bank (N.Y.), 1961-64, sr. v.p. S.Am. group, 1964-67, head overseas div., 1967, exec. v.p. overseas div., 1967—; dir. Owens-Ill. Co., Beatrice Foods Co., Nat. & Grindlays Bank Ltd.; chmn. fgn. exchange com. N.Y. Money Market; dir. Nat. Fgn. Trade Council. Trustee Birmingham-So. Coll. Served to lt. (j.g.) USNR, 1943-46. Mem. Council Fgn. Relations, Pan Am. Soc., Japan Soc. (dir. 1962-64), Council Latin Am., Phi Beta Kappa. Roman Catholic. Club: Metropolitan. Home: Toby's Lane New Canaan CT 06840 Office: 399 Park Av New York City NY 10022

COSTANZO, HENRY JOHN, govt. ofcl.; b. Edgewater, Ala., June 20, 1925; s. Joseph and Mary (De Falco) C.; student Birmingham-So. Coll., 1941-42, Georgetown U., 1942- 44; M.A., Columbia, 1949; m. Maxine Kruse, Mar. 11, 1955; children—Maria Cristina, Luisa Francesca. Economist, ECA/spl. mission to Italy, 1949- 51; asst. Treasury rep., Rome, 1952-53; Treasury rep., Seoul Korea, 1954- 55; financial adviser, chief program planning div. UN Command, Office Econ. Coordinator, Seoul, 1955-57; adviser Middle Eastern dept. Internat. Monetary Fund. 1958-61; chief S. Asia and Near East div. Office Internat. Finance, Treasury Dept., 1961-62, dir. Office Latin Am., 1962-67; dir. AID mission to Korea, 1967-71. dir./counselor econ. affairs embassy. Seoul, 1968-71; mem. bd. exec. dir. Inter-Am. Devel. Bank, Washington, 1971—. Served with AUS, 1944-46. Address: 550 N St SW Washington DC 20024

COSTEA, NICHOLAS VINCENT, hematologist; b. Bucarest, Rumania, Nov. 10, 1927; s. Nicholas and Florica (Ionescu) C.; B.A., Nat. Coll., Bucarest, 1946; student physics, chem., biology, U. Paris (France), 1949, M.D. magna cum laude, 1956. Came to U.S., 1956, naturalized, 1961. Intern St. Francis Hosp., N.Y.C., 1956-57; resident L.I. Jewish Hosp., 1957; fellow hematology Blood Research Lab., Boston, 1957-63; clin. investigator VA West Side Hosp., Chgo., 1963-66, cons. hematologist Research and Ednls. Hosps., U. Ill. Coll. Medicine, 1966—; asst., then instr. Tufts U. Coll. Medicine, 1959; mem. faculty U. Ill. Coll. Medicine, 1963—, asso. prof. medicine, 1966-70, prof. medicine, 1970—; chief hematol. U. Ill. Hosp., 1967-70; dir. hematology Cook County Hosp., Chgo., 1970—. Fellow USPHS, 1960-63; recipient Lederle Faculty award U. Ill. Coll. Medicine, 1966. Mem. Chgo. Soc. Internal Medicine, Chgo. Soc. Allergy, Central Soc. Clin. Research, Am. Soc. Immunology, A.M.A., Am. Fedn. Clin. Research, Am. Rheumatism Soc. Author: Hemolytic Anemia, 1956; Platelet Viability, 1959; Erythrocyte Antibodies, 1960; Macroglobulin Antibodies, 1964; Antibody Structure, 1968; Autoimmunization, 1970. Home: 6010 Four Lakes Av Lisle IL 60532

COSTELLO, DONALD PAUL, zoologist; b. Detroit, Sept. 27, 1909; s. Thomas William and Frances Lydia (Hering) C.; A.B., Coll. City Detroit, 1930; Ph.D., U. Pa., 1934; m. Helen Mar Miller, June 20, 1936; children—Robert Charles, George Alfred. Instr. in zoology U. Pa., 1930-34; Nat. Research fellow Hopkins Marine Sta. of Stanford U., 1934-35; Rockefeller fellow and research asso. Stanford, 1941-42; asst. prof. zoology U. N.C., 1935-40, asso. prof., 1940-43, prof. zoology, 1943-49, Kenan prof. zoology, 1949—, chmn. dept. zoology 1947-57, mem. adminstrv. bd. of grad. sch., 1948-53, mem. Univ. Research Council since 1949; mem. exec. com. (vice chmn. 1949) and adv. council N.C. Inst. of Fisheries Research, 1948-53, chmn. exec. com., 1953-57; mem. embryology course staff Marine Biol. Lab., Woods Hole, Mass., summers 1939-46, mem. exec. com., 1951-53, dir. embryology course, summers 1946-50, trustee of lab., 1946-54, trustee, 1955—, exec. com., 1955-58. Mem. morphology and genetics study sect. NIH, Bethesda, Md. 1956-58, cell biology study sect., 1958-60, 63-66, chmn. cell biology study sect. B, 1966-67. Fellow A.A.A.S., N.Y. Acad. Scis., Inst. Internat. d'Embryologie; mem. Internat., Am. socs. cell biology, Am. Soc. Zoologists, Am. Soc. Naturalists (treas. 1948-50), NSF (div. com. Biology), Sigma Xi. Editorial bd. Biol. Bull., 1947-51, mng. editor, 1951-68, editorial bd. Jour. Morphology, 1950-52, Growth, 1953-63. Author articles, reports, revs. in research of exptl. embryology and exptl. cytology. Home: 507 Monroe Street Chapel Hill, NC 27514.

COSTELLO, FRANK BARTHOLOMEW, univ. adminstr.; b. Spokane, June 12, 1921; s. Francis B. and Catherine (McDermott) C.; A.B., Gonzaga U., 1945, M.A., 1946; M.A. in Polit. Sci., Fordham U., 1949; S.T.L., Alma (Cal.) Coll., 1953; Ph.D., Georgetown U., 1959. Joined Soc. of Jesus, 1939, ordained priest Roman Cath. Ch., 1952; mem. faculty Gonzaga U., 1953-54; asst. prof. polit. sci. Seattle U., 1959-60, acad. v.p., 1960-66, exec. v.p., 1966-69; prof. Gonzaga U., Spokane, Wash., 1969—. Mem. Wash. State Ednl. TV Commn., 1965—. Mem. Cath. Assn. Internat. Peace (v.p. 1959-62), Nat. Cath. Ednl. Assn. (chmn. N.W. regional unit coll. and univ. dept. 1961—), Cath. Council on Civil Liberties (nat. adv. com. 1963), Am. Polit. Sci. Assn., Am. Acad. Polit. and Social Scis., Acad. Polit. Sci. Author: (with John P. Leary) Better a Day, 1951, I Lift My Lamp, 1955. Home: 502 E Boone Av Spokane WA 99202

COSTELLO, JOHN H., publishing exec.; b. Lowell, Mass., Apr. 28, 1914; s. Thomas F. and Mary (Harrington) C.; A.B., Dartmouth, 1937; m. Peggy E. Palmer, Oct. 1942; children—Dana, John H., Charlotte, Andrew, Alexxander, Thomas. Pres. Lowell Sun Pub. Co. (Mass.). Home: 305 Andover Street Lowell MA 01852 Office: 15 Kearney Sq Lowell MA 08152

COSTELLO, JOSEPH A., bishop; S.T.D., LL.D. Ordained priest Roman Cath. Ch., 1941; titular bishop Choma and aux. bishop Newark, 1962—. Address: 155 William Street Belleville, NJ 07109.

COSTELLO, LAWRENCE RONALD, profl. basketball coach; b. Syracuse, N.Y., July 2, 1931; s. Charles H. and Ethel M. (Greiner) C.; B.S., Niagara U., 1954; postgrad. Syracuse U.; m. Barbara C. Brown, May 4, 1963; children—Lesley Sue, Pamela Lynn, Colleen, Amy. Profl. basketball player with Phila. 76ers, Syracuse Nationals, Phila. Warriors; high sch. basketball coach; coach Milw. Bucks, 1968—. Selected for Am. Basketball Team, 1953, 54, All Pro Basketball Team; mem. Helms Athletic Found. All Star Team; recipient Niagara medal, 1954. Served with AUS, 1954-56. Home: 8873 N Mahlin Dr Milwaukee WI 53217 Office: 700 W Wisconsin Av Milwaukee WI 53233

COSTELLO, MARILYN, musician, educator; b. Cleve., July 17, 1924; d. George D. and Diana (Bevilacqua) C.; artists diploma, Curtis Inst. Music, 1947; m. L. Daniel Dannenbaum, July 12, 1958; 1 son, Daniel George. Solo harpist Phila. Orch., 1946—; instr. harp Phila. Mus. Acad., 1950-64, Temple U., 1953- , Curtis Inst. Music, 1961—; concert soloist through U.S. and abroad, 1947—; recording artist for Angel, Columbia Records; pvt. tchr. harp, 1946—. Mem. Am. Harp Soc. Author: Twentieth Century Orchestra Series- Harp, 1967. Home: 2039 Pine Street Philadelphia, PA 19103. Office: 230 S 15th St Philadelphia PA 19102

COSTELLO, MAURICE JOSEPH, dermatologist; b. N.Y.C., Feb. 23, 1901; s. Maurice Patrick and Katherine O'Connor (Hussey) C.; student Manhattan Coll., 1919-21; D.Sc., 1953; B.S., Georgetown U., 1923; M.D., 1925; m. Mary Bingham Hurlbut, Aug. 7, 1959. With dept. medicine N.Y.U., Bellevue Med. Center, 1932—. from instr. to asso. prof. clin. dermatology postgrad. div., now prof.; attending dermatologist Lenox Hill, Misericordia, St. Clare's hosps.; cons. St. Joseph's Hosp., Bergen Pines, St. Francis Benedictine Hosp., Kingston, N.Y. Polyclinic Med. Sch. and Hosp.; mem. adv. bd. Medical Specialties, Inc. Decorated knight Equestrian Order Holy Sepulchre Jerusalem, knight Order of Malta; recipient St. Vincent de Paul medal St. John U., 1960. Diplomate Am. Bd. Dermatology (sec.-treas.). Fellow A.C.P.; mem. A.M.A., Am. Dermatol. Assn., N.Y. (pres.), Manhattan dermtol. socs., N.Y. Acad. Medicine (pres., sec. dermatology sect.), Internat. Soc. Tropical Dermatology, Soc. Investigative Dermatology, Sociedad de Dermatologia y Sifilografia, Buenos Aires, Sociedad Cubana de Dermatologia y Sifilografia, Assn. Argentina de Dermatologia y Sifilogia, Sociedad Venezolana de Dermatologia Venereologia y Leprologia, Brothers of Christian Schs. (affiliate). Author numerous sci. articles, contbr. chpts. to books on dermatology. Author: The Palms and Soles in Medicine. Home: 249 E 48th St New York City NY 10017 Office: 140 E 54th St New York City NY 10022

COSTELLO, ROBERT ELLIS EDWARD, paper co. exec.; b. Montreal, Que., Can., Aug. 1, 1911; s. Robert E. and Bryde (O'Toole) C.; B.Chem. Engring., McGill U., 1935; m. Christine Castonguay, Mar. 12, 1942; children—Robert, Michael, Mary. With Can. Paper Co., Windsor Mills, Que., 1935-41, asst. paper mill supt., 1938- 41; with Brompton Pulp & Paper Co., Red Rock, Ont., 1945-46; with Abitibi Power & Paper Co., Ltd., 1946—, v.p. research and devel., 1961- 68, v.p. operations newsprint and pulp group, 1968—. Served with RCAF, 1941-45. Roman Catholic. Home: 2 Twyford Ct Islington Ontario Canada Office: Toronto Dominion Center Toronto 1 Ontario Canada

COSTELLO, ROBERT H., banker. Pres., dir. Pullman Bank & Trust Co., Chgo. Office: 400 E 111th St Chicago IL 60628*

COSTELLO, RUSSELL HILL, newspaper exec.; b. Lewiston, Me., Oct. 22, 1904; s. Louis B. and Sadie (Brackett) C.; student Bates Coll., 1924-26, Mass. Inst. Tech., 1927-30; m. Jane H. Cassidy, May 5, 1928; children—Alice Ann (Mrs. Robert E. Dillingham), James Russell, Jane Mary (Mrs. Daniel J. Wellehan, Jr.). With Lewiston Daily Sun, 1930—, treas., 1955—, pres., 1959—, also dir.; dir. First-Mfrs. Nat. Bank, Lewiston and Auburn. Mem. Gov.'s Council on Art and Culture. Mem. devel. council U. Me. Served to maj. Me. State Guard, 1943-46. Mem. Me. (past pres.), New Eng., Am. publishers assns., New Eng. Council (dir.), Lewiston C. of C. (dir., past pres.), New Eng. Mech. Assn. (past pres.). Home: 97 Bardwell Street Lewiston ME Office: 104 Park Street Lewiston ME

COSTELLO, TIMOTHY WILLIAM, city govt. ofcl.; b. Bklyn., Dec. 31, 1915; s. Thomas and Mary (Kine) C.; B.S., Fordham U., 1937, M.A., 1939, Ph.D. in Psychology, 1940; m. Genevieve Sullivan, Dec. 27, 1941; children—Genevieve (Mrs. William Cusick), Peter, Joseph, John, Mary-Kay, Barbara. Mem. faculty N.Y.U., 1941-66, prof. psychology and mgmt., 1946-66; on leave as dep. mayor- city adminstr., N.Y.C., 1966—; cons. to industry, 1950-65. Ednl. dir. Staten Island Mental Health Soc., 1950-55. Chmn. N.Y. State Liberal Party, 1962-65. Served to 1st lt. AUS, 1943-46. Mem. Am. Psychol. Assn., N.A.A.C.P. (life). Roman Cath. Author: (with W. Coville and F.L. Rouke) Abnormal Psychology, 1960; (with S. Zalkind) Psychology in Administration, 1962. Home: 75 Landis Av Staten Island NY 10305 Office: 250 Broadway New York City NY 10007

COSTELLO, WILLIAM VANIN, airlines exec.; b. Chattannooga, Aug. 27, 1921; s. William Vanin and Lela (Beall) C.; student Louisiana Coll., Pineville, 1939-41; m. Ruby Johnson, Nov. 1, 1943 (dec. 1968); 1 son, Colin V. With Delta Air Lines, Inc., 1946-64, dir. planning and research, 1963-64; v.p. regulatory affairs Eastern Air Lines, Inc., Washington, 1965—. Served as pilot USAAF, 1942-45; ETO. Decorated Air medal, D.F.C. Home: One Washington Circle Washington DC 20037 Office: 815 Connecticut Av NW Washington DC 20006

COSTELLOE, MARTIN JOSEPH, educator; b. Ames, Ia., Nov. 5, 1914; s. Martin F.P. and Mathilda (Weckbach) C.; A.B., St. Louis U., 1938, M.A., 1941, Ph.L., 1941, Th.L., 1947; grad. student Cath. U. Am., 1948-49, Gregorian U., Rome, Italy, 1950-51; Ph.D., Johns Hopkins, 1958. Joined Soc. of Jesus, 1933; ordained priest Roman Cath. Ch., 1946; tchr. Marquette High Sch., Milw., 1941-43, St. Stanislaus Sem., Florissant, Mo., 1952-56; mem. faculty Creighton U., 1957—, prof. classical langs., 1963—, chmn. dept. classical langs., 1961—; tchr. Loyola Roman Center, 1963, lectr. Classical archaeology, 1958—. Fulbright scholar, 1950. Author articles. Translator: The Roman Catacombs and Their Martyrs, 1956; Julian the Apostate, 1960; Rite and Man, 1963; St. Ambrose and His Times, 1964; Church and State in the Teaching of St. Ambrose, 1969. Address: Creighton Univ Omaha NB 68131

COSTICH, EMMETT RAND, coll. dean; b. Rochester, N.Y., July 15, 1921; s. Emmett Ray and Pearl (Thompson) C.; A.B., Colgate U., 1943; D.D.S., U. Pa., 1945; M.S., U. Rochester, 1949, Ph.D., 1954; m. Marie Zimmerman, Mar. 14, 1945; children—Emmett Rand II, Timothy D., Mary L., Peter S., Susan M., Betsy A. Instr., U. Rochester, 1947-55; asst. prof., then asso. prof. U. Mich. Sch. Dentistry, 1955-62; prof. oral surgery, chmn. dept. U. Ky. Coll. Dentistry, 1962-69, asso. dean, 1969—; cons. VA Hosps. in Lexington, Ky. and Huntington, W.Va., Nat. Inst. Mental Health Hosp., Lexington. Pres. United Cerebral Palsy Assn., 1956-58. Served with AUS, 1943-44, 51- 53. Mem. Am., Ky. dental assns., Am. Soc. Oral Surgeons, Internat. Assn. Dental Research. Rotarian. Author chpts. in books, numerous articles.

COSTIGAN, EDWARD JOHN, investment banker; b. St. Louis, 1914; grad. St. Louis U., 1935; postgrad. Stanford, 1937. Partner Edward D. Jones & Co., St. Louis; dir. Deerfield Glassine Co., Canadian Glassine Co., Ltd., Be-Mac Transport Co., Inc., Liberty Loan Corp., Infotronics Corp. Mem. Investment Bankers Am. (gov.). Home: 5565 Lindell Blvd St Louis MO 63112 Office: 101 N 4th St St Louis MO 63102

COSTIGAN, JAMES, dramatist; b. Belvedere Gardens, Cal., Mar. 31, 1926; s. Thomas Patrick Smith (né Gowan) and Joan Rose Sullivan; student Alliance Francaise, Paris, France, 1954. Author: (plays for TV) Time for the Piper, 1952, Rain No More, 1953, The Bells of Damon, 1953, A Cry of Trumpets, 1953, The World, My Cage, 1953, A Wind From the South, 1955, White Goves, 1955, Little Moon of Alban, 1958; (TV adaptations) Cradle Song, 1956, The Lark, 1957, On Borrowed Time, 1957, Wuthering Heights, 1958, The Turn of the Screw, 1959, A Doll's House, 1959; (for theatre) Little Moon of Alban, 1960; The Beast in Me, mus. revue, 1962-63; (published work) Two Plays, 1959; (for the stage) Baby Want a Kiss, 1964. Recipient Christopher award, 1956, 58, Sylvania award, 1958, Peabody award, 1958, Nat. Acad. TV Arts and Scis. award, 1958.

COSTIGAN, JOHN EDWARD, artist; b. Providence, Feb. 29, 1888; s. Jon Henry and Hanna (Cronin) C.; ed. pub. schs.; self-taught in art; m. Ida Blessin, June 1919; children—John Edward, Rosella Josephine, Elizabeth Mary, Danny M., Ida May. Awarded numerous prizes and medals for paintings and etchings since 1922, latest being Henry B. Shope Prize, Soc. Am. Etchers and Litho. Engravers Exhbn., 1948, 56; 2d prize Balt. Water Color, 1951, 52, 1st 1956; Barry Stevens award Am. Water Color Soc. Ann. Exhbn., 1953, medal, 1956; citation Am. Artist Mag., 1956. Figure and landscape artist. Represented in Art Inst. Chgo., Met. Mus. N.Y.C., Library of Congress, Washington, various other museums, pvt. collections, Smithsonian Instn. traveling exhbn., 1968-70. Murals U.S. Post Office and Agr. Bldg., Stewart, Va.; IBM collection Am. art; Rochester (N.Y.) Mus.; Wellesley Coll. collection water colors; Frye Mus., Seattle. Served as pvt. Pioneer Inf. Co., U.S.A., overseas 9 mos., World War I. N.A., 1928. Recipient Gold Medal, Nat. Art Club Exhbn., 1954; watercolor prize American Watercolor Society, 1958, 62; second popular prize Ogunquit (Maine) Art Center, 1958; Emily Lowe award, 1962; Water Color Purchase prize Butler Institute of American Art, 1962. Member Allied Artists Am., Soc. Animal Painters and Sculptors, Guild Am. Painters, Soc. Am. Etchers, Phila. Soc. Etchers, Prairie Print Makers, Am. and N.Y. water color clubs. Clubs: Salmagundi, Nat. Arts, Kit Kat, Lotus (New York). Home: Orangeburg-Hunt Rds Orangeburg NY 10962

COSTIKYAN, GRANGER, banker; b. Montclair, N.J., Mar. 29, 1907; s. Siragan S. and Mary Ransom (Kent) C.; grad. Hotchkiss Sch., 1925; B.A., Yale, 1929; student N.Y.U. Law Sch., 1932-33; m. Margaret L. Taylor, Feb. 17, 1940; children—Gail L., Joan R. (Mrs. Jarvis), Nancy H. (Mrs. Johnson), Wendy W. With N.Y. Trust Co. and successor Chem. Bank N.Y. Trust Co., Bank N.Y. Trust Co., N.Y.C., 1929-62; v.p., 1948-61, sr. v.p., 1961-62; pres., First Bank System, Mpls., 1962-69, chmn. bd., also dir., 1969; gen. partner Brown Brothers Harriman & Co., Chgo., 1969—; dir. St. Paul Cos., Inc. Mem. faculty Vt. Sch. Banking, Burlington, 1950, 53. Mem. Yale Alumni Bd., chmn. Alumni Fund, 1954-56, chmn. com. for nomination alumni fellows Yale Corp., 1960. Trustee MacAlester Coll., St. Paul. Home: 175 E Delaware Pl Chicago, IL 60611. Office: 135 S LaSalle Street Chicago IL 60603

COSTIN, FRANK, psychologist, educator; b. Louisville, Jan. 15, 1914; s. Samuel and Jennie (Ressnier) C.; A.B., U. Louisville, 1936; A.M., U. Chgo., 1941, Ph.D., 1948; m. Leala Madeline Brown, Nov. 22, 1950; children—Julia Jane, Jeanne Adeline. Tchr., Louisville Pub. Schs., 1936-42; asst. prof. to prof. psychology U. Ill., Urbana-Champaign, 1948—. Vis. prof. psychology and edn. U. Ore., 1950, 54, 56; vis. scholar U. London (Eng.), 1968; cons. Champaign (Ill.) Human Relations Commn., 1961-65. Served with USAAF, 1942-46. Fellow Am. Psychol. Assn.; mem. Am. Assn. U. Profs. Cons. editor Profl. Psychology. Contbr. articles to profl. jours. Home: 701 W Healey Street Champaign IL 61820 Office: Psychology Bldg U Ill Champaign IL 61820

COSTLEY, RICHARD JOSEPH, educator; b. St. Anthony, Ida., Mar. 13, 1912; s. Richard Grant and Priscilla (King) C.; B.S., Utah State U., 1934; M.S., U. Ill., 1936, postgrad., 1941-42; m. Virginia Peterson, Apr. 9, 1937; 1 dau., Denis Kay (Mrs. Glen O. Robinson). With Forest Service, Dept. Agr., 1936- 71, asst. regional forester No. central states, 1955-59, recreation asst. to chief Forest Service, 1959-62, asst. to chief Forest Service, 1962- 64, dir. div. recreation, 1964-71; pof. regional and resource planning U. Mass., Amherst, 1971—. Served to lt. USNR, 1943-46. Mem. Soc. Am. Foresters, Outdoor Writers Am., Orgn. Profl. Employees Dept. Agr., Izaak Walton League Am., Sigma Xi. Home: 31 Morgan Circle Amherst MA 01002

COTE, JOSEPH JULIAN JEAN-PIERRE, legislator; b. Montreal, Que., Can., Jan. 9, 1926; s. Joseph E. and Cedia (Roy) C.; ed. Longueuil (Que.) Coll. and Sch. Dental Tech.; m. Germaine Tremblay, July 31, 1949; 8 children. Owner, operator dental lab., prior to 1963; mem. Ho. of Commons for Longueuil, 1963—; postmaster gen. Can.; minister Nat. Revenue. Canadian rep. to I.L.O., Geneva, 1964. Pres. Longueuil Sch. Bd., 1961-63. Bd. dirs. Assn. Dental Technicians. Home: 228 Bienville Longueuil Quebec Canada Office: Connaught Bldg Ottawa Ontario Canada*

COTELLESSA, ROBERT FRANCIS, educator; b. Passaic, N.J., June 7, 1923, s. Joseph Cornelius and Helen (Dodds) C.; M.E., Stevens Inst. Tech., 1944, M.S., 1949; Ph.D., Columbia, 1962; m. Violette Babette Foeller, Sept. 11, 1948; children—Joseph Arthur, Anne Louise, Diane Frances. Prof. elec. engring., dir. Lab. for Electroscience Research, Sch. Engring. and Sci., N.Y.U., 1962-68; prof., chmn. elec. engring. Sch. Engring., Clarkson Coll. Tech., Potsdam, N.Y., 1968—; cons. Bridgeport (Conn.) Engring. Inst., 1962—, U.S. Naval Ship Research-Devel. Center Annapolis, 1965—. Mem. Bd. Edn., Glen Rock, N.J., 1966-68; v.p. Ridgewood-Glen Rock council Boy Scouts Am., 1967-68. Served to lt. (j.g.) USNR, 1943-46. Recipient Tau Beta Pi Faculty award Clarkson Coll. Tech., 1969. Mem. I.E.E.E., Am. Phys. Soc., Electrochemical Soc., A.A.A.S., Am. Soc. Engring. Edn., Sigma Xi, Chi Psi, Tau Beta Pi, Eta Kappa Nu, Pi Delta Epsilon. Contbr. articles profl. jours. Patentee in field. Home: RD 4 Potsdam NY 13676

COTEY, BERNARD R., bishop; b. Milw., June 15, 1921; ed. Divine Savior Sem., Lanham, Md., CUA. Ordained priest Roman Ch. in Soc. of Divine Savior, 1949; consecrated bishop of Nachingwea, Tanzania, E.Africa, 1963. Address: Salvatorian Mission Bishop's House Nachingwea Tanzania East Africa*

COTHEN, GRADY COULTER, sem. pres.; b. Poplarville, Miss., Aug. 2, 1920; s. Joseph Herbert and Mamie (Coulter) C.; B.A., Miss. Coll., 1941, D.D., 1965; D.D., Cal. Baptist Coll., 1964; M.C.T., New Orleans Bapt. Theol. Sem., 1944; LLD., William Jewel Coll., 1971; m. Martha Elizabeth Major, June 11, 1941; children—Grady Coulter, Carol Lorraine (Mrs. Don C. McChesney). Ordained to ministry Bapt. Ch., 1939; pastor in Chattanooga, 1946-48, Oklahoma City, 1948-59, Birmingham, Ala., 1959-61; exec. sec.-treas. So. Bapt. Gen. Conv. Cal., 1961-66; pres. Okla. Bapt. U., 1966-70, trustee, 1955-59; pres. New Orleans Bapt. Theol. Sem., 1970—. Mem. fgn. mission bd. So. Bapt. Conv., 1949-55, 1st v.p., 1963; exec. com. Bapt. World Alliance. Exec. com. Okla. Health Scis. Found.; mem. Okla. bd. Oklahoma City Symphony, 1966-70; chmn. edn. com. Okla. Edn. Commn., 1969-70. Trustee New Orleans Bapt. Theol. Sem. Served as chaplain USNR, 1944-46. Mem. Am. Assn. Ind. Coll. and Univ. Pres., Am. Acad. Polit. and Social Scis., Am. Assn. Higher Edn., Am. Acad. Religion, Omicron Delta Kappa, Pi Kappa Delta. Democrat. Rotarian. Author: God of the Beginnings, 1955. Home: 4111 Seminary Pl New Orleans LA 70126

COTHRAN, TILMAN CHRISTOPHER, educator; b. Hope, Ark., Nov. 17, 1917; s. Thomas C. and Willie (McClellan) C.; A.B., Ark. A., M. and N. Coll., Pine Bluff, 1939; M.A., Ind. U., 1942, Ph.D. (Gen. Edn. Bd. fellow 1945-47; Henderson award scholarship 1947), U. Chgo., 1949; m. Gladys Vivian Williams, Aug. 18, 1940; children—Brenda Faye, Tilman Christopher. Registrar, cashier Ark. A., M. and N. Coll., 1939-42, prof. sociology, chmn. dept. social sci., 1942-47, prof., chmn. div. social sci., 1949-59; prof. sociology, chmn. div. social sci. Dillard U., 1947-49; Ware prof. sociology, chmn. dept. Atlanta U., 1959-70; dir. U.S. Office Econ. Opportunity Multi-Purpose Tng. Center for Southeastern Region, 1968-70; v.p. acad. affairs Governors State U., Park Forest South, Ill., 1970—. Vis. prof. sociology, acting head dept. Tex. So. U., summer 1949; vis. prof. Western Mich. Coll. Edn., summer 1950. Research analyst Dept. Army, Japan and Korea, 1951; leader Operation Crossroads Africa for Am. students in Kenya, 1961. Chmn. Atlanta Com. Coop. Action; Ga. adv. com. U.S. Commn. Civil Rights. Bd. govs. Governors Gen. Hosp., 1970—. Fellow Am. Sociol. Soc.; mem. Nat. Council on New Careers (exec. com.), So. (exec. com.), Ga. (pres.) sociol. socs., Assn. Soc. Sci. Tchrs., Soc. Study Social Problems, Am. Assn. U. Profs., Alpha Kappa Mu, Alpha Kappa Delta, Delta Tau Kappa (hon.). Editor Phylon mag., 1959-70. Home: 2417 Athens Rd Olympia Fields IL 60461

COTHRAN, WILLIAM THOMAS, banker; b. Rome, Ga., Oct. 7, 1907; s. Walter S. and Gertrude (Jackson) C.; grad. Darlington Sch., Rome, 1924; student U. Ga., 1924-25; B.S., U. Pa., 1928; m. Margaret Ella Kidd, Mar. 16, 1935; children—Anne Sullivan (Mrs. Robert H.G. Waudby), William Thomas. With Nat. City Bank, Rome, 1925-28, First Nat. Bank, Birmingham, Ala., 1928-33; with TCI div. U.S. Steel Corp., 1933-38; treas., dir. Shannon Hosiery Mills, Inc., Columbus, Ga., 1938-46; exec. v.p. Bank for Savs. & Trusts, Birmingham, 1946-59, pres., 1959-63; with Birmingham Trust Nat. Bank, 1963—, pres., 1964-69, chmn. bd., 1969—; dir. Birmingham Centennial Corp., Avondale Mills, Sylacauga. Mem. Jefferson County Bd. Zoning Adjustment. Treas. Birmingham area Planning Commn. Trustee So. Research Inst., Birmingham Symphony Assn., Birmingham Civic Opera, Darlington Sch., Children's Hosp., Birmingham. Served to lt. comdr. USNR, 1942-45. Mem. Am. (mem. exec. com. of nat. bank div.), Ala. (past pres.) bankers assns., Stuart Cameron McLeod Soc., Sigma Alpha Epsilon, Beta Alpha Psi. Episcopalian (past sr. warden). Rotarian. Home: 3316 E Briarcliff Rd Birmingham AL 35223 Office: 112 N 20th St Birmingham AL 35202

COTLOW, LEWIS NATHANIEL, explorer; b. Bklyn., Feb. 5, 1898; s. Nathaniel and Lena (Greene) C.; student George Washington U., N.Y. U.; m. Charlotte Faith Messenheimer, Dec. 18, 1966. Ins. broker, N.Y.C.; traveling rep. U.S. Shipping Bd., vis. and reporting on important harbors in Far East, Near East and S. Am., 1919-21; extensive travels throughout world gathering lecture material, 1930-35; conducted expdn. Belgian Congo and Tanganyika, pioneering in color film of big game and primitive tribes; also lectured throughout U.S., 1937; comdr. expdn. to Upper Amazon, making pioneer color film of primitive tribes, including Yaguas (2000 miles up river) and Jivaro head-hunters (2800 miles up river), 1940; condr. 2d expdn. to Amazon, studying and filming primitive life, also filmed and produced technicolor short film Adventures in South America, 1945; co-condr. Armand Denis-Lewis Cotlow African expdn. to make authentic adventure- exploration technicolor feature picture of big game and primitive tribes of Belgian Congo, Uganda, etc., entitled Savage Splendor, produced by Armand Denis Prodns., Ind., 1946-47; condr. 3d Amazon expdn. to Ecuador, Peru, Brazil, making authentic technicolor feature film, Jungle Headhunters, collected enthnol. specimens for Am. Mus. of Natural History, 1949; condr. Lewis Cotlow 3d African expdn. to Tanganyika, Belgian Congo. producing Trucolor feature film of big game and tribes entitled Zanzabuku (Dangerous Safari), 1954-55; condr. expdn. to New Guinea, prod. color documentary film of inhabitants Primitive Paradise, 1958-59, expdn. to Ellesmere Island to make documentary film Eskimo life High Arctic, 1962; expeditions to revisit tribes of Upper Xingu River, Brazil, 1963, Pygmy tribe, Congo, 1964; fifth Amazon expdn., 1968, fifth African expdn. Served with U.S. Army, World War I; U. S. Naval Intelligence, World War II. Recipient gold medal Adventures Club, N.Y.C., 1937. Fellow of the Royal Geog. Soc. of Great Britain. Clubs: Ends of the Earth; Explorers, Adventurers (past pres.), Circumnavigators (past pres.), Dutch Treat (N.Y.C.); Adventurers (Chgo.). Author: Passport to Adventure, 1942; Amazon Head-hunters, 1953; Zanzabuku 1956; In Search of the Primitive, 1966; The Twilight of the Primitive, 1970. Lecturer. Home: 480 Park Av New York City NY 10013 Office: 540 Madison Av New York City NY 10022

COTNER, THOMAS EWING, educator, govt. ofcl.; b. Dallas, Oct. 26, 1916; s. Thomas Ewing and Nina D. (Crawford); student North Tex. Agrl. Coll., 1933-35; B.A., Baylor U., 1937; M.A., U. Tex., 1939, Ph.D. (grad. fellow 1939-40, 41-42), 1947; m. Jeanne Booth, Dec. 26, 1941; children—Thomas Ewing III, Zachary B., George R. Tchr. history Brownwood (Tex.) High Sch., 1937-39; dir. hist. div. Tex. Meml. Mus., Austin, 1939-40; instr. history U. Tex., summer 1940, Latin-Am. history Tulane U., 1940-41, polit. sci. George Washington U., 1948-52; with internat. div. U.S. Office Edn., Dept. Health, Edn. and Welfare, Washington, 1942-43, 46—, dep. asso. commr., 1962-65, dir. div. internat. exchange and tng., 1965—. Mem. U.S. del. XXIX Internat. Conf. on Pub. Edn., Geneva, Switzerland, 1966. Mem. Falls Church (Va.) Sch. Bd., 1966-69. Served to lt. USNR, 1943-46. Recipient Superior Service award, other commendation Office Edn.; Medal of Merit Belgian Govt., 1957. Mem. Am. Hist. Assn., Polit. Sci. Assn., Phi Kappa Sigma, Alpha Chi. Author: The Political and Military Career of Jose Joaquin de Herrera, 1792-1854, 1949; International Educational Exchange: A Selected Bibliography, 1961. Editor: Essays in Mexican History, 1958. Home: 228 Buxton Road Falls Church VA 22046 Office: 7th and D Streets SW Washington DC 20202

COTT, BETTY, (Mrs. Ted Cott), pub. relations exec.; b. N.Y.C., Apr. 20, 1928; d. Albert and Etta (Friedman) Cohen; student N.Y.U., 1945-49; m. Ted Cott, June 2, 1963; 1 dau., Jennifer Beth. Asst. dir. pub. relations Bond Stores, Inc., N.Y.C., 1949-53; sr. asso., v.p. Ruder & Finn, Inc., N.Y.C., 1953-70, sr. v.p., 1970—. Home: 680 W End Av New York City NY 10025 Office: 110 E 59th St New York City NY 10022

COTT, PETER, television exec.; b. N.Y.C., Apr. 4, 1924; s. Nat and Mae (Rubin) Prigozen; B.S., N.Y.U., 1946; postgrad. New Sch. for Social Research, 1949-50. Mgr., Am. Shakespeare Festival, 1955-56; pub. relations dir. Nat. Acad. Television Arts and Scis., N.Y.C., Hollywood, Cal., 1956-61, exec. dir., 1961—; founder, exec. dir. Soc. Stage Dirs. and Choreographers, 1959-61. Dir. Council on Internat. Non-Theatrical Events. Served to 1st lt. USAAF, 1943-46. Mem. Internat. Radio and Television Soc., Am. Civil Liberties Union, Citizens Union. Democrat. Office: 54 W 40th St New York City NY 10018

COTTAM, CLARENCE, biologist; b. St. George, Utah, Jan. 1, 1899; s. Thomas P. and Emmaline (Jarvis) C.; student Dixie Coll., 1919-20, U. Utah, summer 1923; B.S., Brigham Young U., 1926, M.S., 1927; student Am. U., 1931; Ph.D., George Washington U., 1936; m. Margery Brown, May 20, 1920; children—Glenna Clair (Mrs. Ivan L. Sanderson). Margery B. (Mrs. Grant Osborn), Josephine (Mrs. Douglas Day), Carolyn (Mrs. Dwayne Stevenson). Prin. consol. schs., Alamo, Nev. 1922-25; with Fish and Wildlife Service (formed in 1939 by consol of Bur. of Biol. Survey and Bur. of Fisheries) U.S. Dept. of Interior, 1939—, sr. biologist, 1939-44, in charge food habits research sect., 1939-42, in charge econ. wildlife investigations, 1942-44, asst. to dir., 1944-46, chief div. wildlife research, 1945-46, asst. dir. Fish and Wildlife Service, 1946-54; dean Coll. Biol. and Agrl. Scis., Brigham Young U., Provo, Utah, 1954-58; dir. Welder Wildlife Found., Sinton, Tex., 1955—. Recipient hon. award Utah Acad. Sci., Arts and Letters, 1948, Laval U., 1952; Conservation award, Aldo Leopold medal, Wildlife Soc., 1955; Distinguished service award in conservation and forestry Utah State U. of Agr., 1957; Nat. Audubon Conservation Distinguished Service medal, 1961, also other conservation awards, distinguished citizen award Sinton, 1958, 67; Poage Humanitarian award Soc. Animal Protection, 1962; Francis K. Hutchenson medal for conservation Garden Club of Am., 1962; Paul Bartsch award for contbn. natural history Audubon Naturalist Soc., 1962, Wisdom award of honor Wisdom Soc., 1970, Distinguished Service award Tex. chpt. Wildlife Soc., 1971, James E. Talmage Sci. Achievement award Brigham Young U., 1971. Fellow A.A.A.S., Am. Ornithol. Union, Tex. (v.p.), Utah acads. sci.; mem. Wilson, Cooper ornithol. clubs, Wildlife Soc. Am. (pres. 1949-50), Am. Wildlife Inst., Am. Fisheries Soc., Wash. Acad. Sci., Wash. Biol. Soc., Wash. Biologists Field Club, Am. Soc. Mammalogists, Ecol. Soc. Am., Internat. Platform Assn., Soil Conservation Soc. Am., Friends of Land, Nat. Audubon Soc., Tex. Ornithol. Soc. (pres. 1957), Soc. Range Mgmt., Nat. Parks Assn. (pres. or chmn. bd. 1960—), Wilderness Soc., Am. Inst. Biol. Scis., Tex. Philos. Soc., Sigma Xi. Mem. Church of Jesus Christ of Latter-day Saints. Club: Serra. Author: Food Habits of American Diving Ducks, 1939; American Insects, 1950. Co-editor: Whitewings. Contbr. chpts. to books, articles to sci. publs. Address: Welder Wildlife Found Sinton TX 78387 ☆

COTTAM, GRANT, educator; b. Sandy, Utah, Aug. 26, 1918; s. Walter Pace and Effie (Frei) C.; B.A., U. Utah, 1939; Ph.D., U. Wis., 1948; m. Diana McQuarrie, Apr. 5, 1942; children—Cynthia, Richard McQuarrie, Daniel Grant, Margaret Effie, Liatris. Tchr., Roosevelt Jr. High Sch., Salt Lake City, 1939-40; fellow U. Wis., 1946-48; asst. prof. U. Hawaii, 1948-49; mem. faculty U. Wis., 1949—, prof. botany, 1960—, chmn. dept., 1970—. Served to capt. AUS, 1941-46; PTO. Decorated Silver Star, Bronze Star; Guggenheim fellow, 1954-55. Fellow A.A.A.S.; mem. Ecol. Soc. Am., British Ecol. Soc., Wis. Acad. Sci., Arts and Letters. Contbr. profl. jours. Asso. editor Ecology, 1955-57, 63-65. Home: 2021 Kendall Av Madison WI 53705

COTTAM, HOWARD REX, UN ofcl.; b. St. George, Utah, July 27, 1910; s. Heber and Edith (Brooks) C.; A.B., Brigham Young U., 1932; Ph.B., U. Wis., 1938, Ph.D., 1941; student Nat. War Coll., 1952; m. Katherine Stokes, Aug. 30, 1934; 1 dau., Lillian Meredith. Asst. prof. Pa. State Coll., 1940-42; chief rent examiner OPA, Pitts., 1942; prin. agrl. economist U.S. Dept. Agr. and chief program appraisal War Food Adminstrn., N.E. region, N.Y.C., 1942-44; agrl. economist U.S. embassy, Paris, France, 1944-46, agrl. attache U.S. embassy, Rome, 1946-47, 1st sec. and consul, 1947-50, counselor embassy and chief food and agrl. div. E.C.A. spl. mission to Italy, 1950-52; U.S. resident liaison officer to FAO of U.N., 1951-52, N. Am. rep., 1969—; also U.S. mem. on commodity problems, com. on relations with internat. orgns., del. 6th conf.; chmn. appeals com. UN FAO; assigned to Nat. War Coll., Washington 1952-53; counselor of embassy for econ. affairs, The Hague, dep. dir. of U.S. operation missions to Netherlands, 1953-55; counselor of embassy and ICA rep. The Netherlands, 1955-56; counselor of embassy, dir. U.S. operations mission to Brazil, 1956-57, minister for econ. affairs, dir. mission, 1957-60; dep. asst. sec. Bur. Nr. Eastern and South Asian Affairs, 1960-63; Am. ambassador Kuwait, 1963-70; adviser to U.S. delegate FAO Council, Rome, 1950, 51, 52, Internat. Cotton Adv. Council, 1952; U.S. observer Internat. Fedn. Agrl. Technicians, Geneva, 1947, at Internat. Conf. Proposed David Lubin Acad., Rome, 1949. Alternate U.S. mem. permanent com. Internat. Inst. Agrl., Rome, 1947; alternate agrl. mem. U.S. Trade Agreements Com. Annecy, France, 1949; treas., bd. mem. Netherlands-U.S. Ednl. Found., 1953-56; alternate U.S. mem. Internat. Tin Study Group, The Hague, 1955-56. Hon. pres. Internat. Sch. of Kuwait, 1963-69; trustee Nr. East Found., 1969—; bd. advisers Airline Passengers Assn., 1969—; ex officio trustee Am. Freedom from Hunger Found., 1969—. Club: Cosmos (Washington). Home: 2245 46th Street Washington DC 20007 Office: 1325 C St SW Washington DC 20437

COTTEN, JOSEPH, actor; b. Petersburg, Va.; s. Joseph and Sally (Willson) C.; student Robert Nugent Hickman Dramatic Sch., Washington; m. Lenore Kip (dec.); m. 2d Patricia Medina, 1960. Actor in David Belasco prodns., Dancing Partners, Tonight or Never, 1930-31; in stock, Copley Theater, Boston, 1931-32; actor in popular stage plays, 1932-40, including The Philadelphia Story, 1939-40, Calculated Risk, 1962; writer and appeared as actor in Mercury Theatre of Air, 1938-39; radio actor America Ceiling Unlimited, Lockheed Aircraft weekly radio program, 1943-44; actor in motion pictures, 1940—, first Citizen Kane, Lydia, later films include Walk Softly Stranger, Two Flags West, 1950; September Affair, Half-Angel, 1951; Special Delivery, 1955. Stage play, Sabrina Fair, N.Y.C., 1953-54, Once More With Feeling, N.Y.C., 1958-59; Hush, Hush Sweet Charlotte, 1964; nat. road tour Seven Ways of Love, 1964. Host, narrator 20th Century-Fox TV Hour, 1955-56; narrator Hollywood and the Stars, TV show, 1963-64. Appeared in TV series On Trial, 1957-58; Angel Wore Red, 1959; Gun in Hand, 1960; other films include The Oscar, The Hellbenders, The Tramplers, The Money Trap, They Also Killed, Petulia; Dr. Phibes. Pres. Mercury Theatre, 1944. Home: Los Angeles CA Office: 6363 Wilshire Blvd Los Angeles CA 90048 ☆

COTTEN, MARION DEVEAUX, educator, pharmacologist; b. Charleston, S.C., Nov. 11, 1927; s. Marion deVeaux and Beatrice (Ferri) C.; B.S., Coll. Charleston, 1948; M.S., Med. Coll. S.C., 1951, Ph.D., 1952; m. Mary Eugenia Brown, July 1, 1961; children—Sarah Lynn, William David, Susan Elizabeth. Research asst. Med. Coll. S.C., 1948-52, asso. pharmacology, 1952-53, postdoctoral research fellow, 1953-54; asst. prof. pharmacology Tulane U., 1954-55; sr. asst. scientist Nat. Heart Inst., 1955-56, scientist, sect. head, 1956-57; asso. prof. pharmacology and physiology Emory U., 1957-61; prof., chmn. dept. pharmacology U. Okla., 1961-69, U. Neb., 1969-70; prof. pharmacology Med. Coll. Ga., 1970—. Mem. pharmacology and exptl. therapeutics study sect. Nat. Insts. Health, 1961-65, pharmacology-toxicology review group, 1966-69; cons. VA Hosp., Oklahoma City, 1963-67, W.H.O., 1964. Mem. Am. Soc. Pharmacology and Exptl. Therapeutics, N.Y. Acad. Scis., Cardiac Muscle Soc. Editor in chief of Jour. Pharmacology and Exptl. Therapeutics, 1968—, Pharm. Review, 1970—. Home: Rt 3 Box 229 Sylvania GA 30467 Office: Medical Coll Georgia Augusta GA 30902

COTTER, FRANCIS PATRICK, elec. mfg. co. exec.; b. N.Y.C., June 12, 1922; s. Patrick and Mary (Condren) C.; B.S., N.Y. U., 1943; LL.B., Cath. U. Am., 1955; children—John, Mary Alice, Catherine, Frank; m. 2d, Malinda Ann DuBose, Apr. 10, 1965; 1 son, Patrick. Spl. agt. FBI, 1947-52; profl. staff mem. Joint Com. Atomic Energy, 1952- 56, cons., 1956—; admitted to D.C. bar, 1955; exec. asst. to v.p. atomic power div. Westinghouse Electric Corp., 1956-62, v.p. atomic, def. and space group, Washington, 1963—; dep. insp. gen. fgn. assistance State Dept., 1962-63. Spl. cons. select com. astronautics and space exploration U.S. Ho. of Reps., 1958- -; cons. State Dept., 1963—, AEC; lectr. tng. classes Peace Corps, 1963; mem. nat. energy study Dept. Interior. Served to capt. USMCR , 1943-46. Mem. D.C. Bar Assn. Democrat. Roman Cath. Clubs: University, Congressional Country (Washington). Home: 3626 Quesada Street N W Washington, DC 20015. Office: 1801 K Street N W Washington DC 20006

COTTER, GEORGE EDWARD, airline co. exec.; b. Wuchang, China, May 14, 1918 (parents Am. citizens); s. Francis James Meadows and Ida Miller (Taylor) C.; grad. Hotchkiss Sch., 1937; A.B., Wesleyan U., Middletown, Conn., 1941; LL.B., Cornell U.,

1946; m. Ruth Margaret Ellen O'Hare, May 18, 1950; children—Christopher Lamont, Ellen Douglas, Carol Hollister. Admitted to Conn. bar, 1946, N.Y. bar, 1947; asso. firm Davis Polk Wardwell Sunderland & Kiendl, N.Y.C., 1946-54; with Freeport Sulphur Co., 1954-65, sec., 1964-65; sr. v.p., gen. counsel Continental Air Lines, Inc., Los Angeles, 1965—. Served to lt. USNR, World War II. Mem. Am., N.Y. State, Litchfield County (Conn.) bar assns., Am. Judicature Soc. Contbr. articles to legal jours. Home: 1033 Chantilly Rd Los Angeles CA 90024 Office: 7300 World Way West Los Angeles CA 90009

COTTER, JOSEPH FRANCIS, hotel chain controller; b. Brockton, Mass., May 18, 1927; s. Joseph and Sarah (Thornell) C.; B.S. cum laude, Boston Coll., 1949; m. Catherine Sullivan, Sept. 16, 1950; children—Robert, Michael, Richard, Mary, Kathleen, Ann, Christine, Peter. Accountant Price Waterhouse & Co., N.Y.C., 1949-67; v.p., controller Howard Johnson Co., Braintree, Mass., 1967-70; v.p., comptroller ITT Sheraton Corp. Am., Boston, 1970—. Bd. dirs. Boston Coll. C.P.A., N.Y. Mem. Am. Inst. C.P.A.'s, N.Y. Soc. C.P.A.'s, Am. Mgmt. Assn., Am. Hotel and Motel Assn., Boston Coll. Alumni Assn. (pres.). Club: Boston Serra (trustee). Home: 312 Forest Av Cohasset MA 02025 Office: 470 Atlantic Av Boston MA 02210

COTTER, PATRICK WILLIAM, lawyer; b. Merrill, Wis., Apr. 11, 1916; s. William Bernard and Clara (Ament) C.; B.A., U. Wis., 1938, LL.B., 1940, LL.M., 1946; m. Lois Katherine Schaus, July 11, 1942; children—Michael William, Patrick Sanford, Timothy John. Admitted to Wis. bar, 1940; asso. firm Loomis, Roswell & Chembers, Mauston, 1940-41; partner firm Brady, Tyrrell, Cotter & Cutler, and predecessors, Milw., 1946—. Vice pres., dir. Reinke & Schomann, Inc., Milw.; sec., bd. dirs. Sivyer Steel Casting Co., Milw.; sec.-dir. Oconomowoc Mfg. Corp. (Wis.); dir. Jewett & Sherman Co., Moraine Industries, Inc., Milw. Mem. Spl. Com. for Wis. Income Tax Simplification; vice chmn. com. on needs of handicapped children United Community Services, 1957-61, corp. mem., 1960—, exec. com. health sect., 1962—; mem. bd. Whitefish Bay Pub. Library, 1963-65; corp. mem. Children's Service Soc. Wis.; v.p., treas., dir. Caroline Draves Found., Inc., Milw.; sec., dir. Stackner Family Found., Inc., Milw.; dir. Children's Day Care Center; sec., treas., bd. dirs. Ralph Evinrude Found., Inc.; asst. sec., dir. Stern Family Found., Inc., Milw.; bd. dirs. Milw. Bar Found., Vis. Nurse Assn., Milw., U.S.O., Milw. Served from 2d lt. to maj., AUS, 1941-46. Decorated Silver Star, Bronze Star with oak leaf cluster. Mem. Am., Milw. (chmn. exec. com., pres. 1963-64), Wis. (gov. 1955-56, chmn. taxation sect. 1961-63) bar assns., Nat. Planning Assn., Ripon Coll. Assos., Benchers Soc. (charter), Am. Judicature Soc., Am. Legion (judge adv. Wis. Dept.), U. Wis. Law Alumni Assn. (pres. 1958-59, 69—), U. Wis. Found., Res. Officers Assn. (pres. Wis. dept. 1957-58). Home: 8217 N Lake Drive Milwaukee WI 53202 Office: 735 N Water Street Milwaukee WI 53202

COTTER, WILLIAM DONALD, newspaper editor; b. Hartford, Conn., June 5, 1921; s. William Joseph and Alice I. (Murphy) C.; B.A., Fordham U., 1943; postgrad. polit. Sci., St. John U., 1956-57, Syracuse U., 1958; m. Alice K. Liller, Jan. 22, 1944; children—Carol A., Mary L., Alice E., William J., James D., Donald W. Reporter, L.I. Star-Jour., Long Island City, 1947-51; night city editor Nassau Rev., Rockville Centre, N.Y., 1952-53; night editor Jersey Jour., Jersey City, 1954; mag., Sunday editor L.I. Press, Jamaica, N.Y., 1955-58; city editor Syracuse Herald-Jour./Am., 1958-66, editor, 1966—; instr. journalism Syracuse U., 1960-66. Bd. dirs. Erie Canal Mus., Association Island Corp., Boys Town of Italy; chmn. communications com. LeMoyne Coll. Served with USNR, 1943-46. Mem. Am., N.Y. State socs. newspaper editors. Roman Cath. Clubs: Syracuse Press (pres. 1964); Auburn Golf and Country (dir.). Home: RD 2 Skaneateles NY 13152 Office: Syracuse Herald-Jour/Herald American Clinton Sq Syracuse NY 13201

COTTER, WILLIAM ROSS, congressman; b. Hartford, Conn., July 18, 1926; s. William W. and Mary E. (O'Loughlin) C.; B.A., Trinity Coll., 1949. Aide to Gov. Abraham Ribicoff, 1955-58; dep. ins. commr. Conn., 1958-64, ins. commr., 1964-70; mem. 92d Congress. Active Greater Hartford Community Chest. Treas. Conn. Democratic Central Com., 1961—. Roman Catholic. K.C., Elk. Club: Wethersfield (Conn.) Country. Home: 247 Fairfield Av Hartford CT 06114 Office: Cannon House Office Bldg Washington DC 20515

COTTERELL, GEOFFREY, author; b. Southsea, Eng., Nov. 24, 1919; s. Graham and Millicent Louise (Crews) C.; ed. Bishop's Stortford Coll., Hertfordshire, Eng.; studied in Berlin and London. Served with Royal Arty., Brit. Army, 1940-46. Author: Then a Soldier, 1944; This is the Way, 1947; Randle in Springtime, 1949; Strait and Narrow, 1951; Westward the Sun, 1953; The Strange Enchantment, 1957; Errand at Shadow Creek, 1959; Tiara Tahiti, 1962; Go, Said the Bird, 1967; Bowers of Innocence, 1970. Home: 2 Fulbourne House Blackwater Rd Eastbourne Sussex England Office: care Collins Knowlton Wing Inc 60 E 56th St New York City NY 10022

COTTINGHAM, HAROLD FRED, educator; b. Charleston, Ill., Dec. 11, 1913; s. Fred Hervey and Frances (Coon) C.; B.Ed., Eastern Ill. State U., 1935, Pd.D. (hon.), 1956; M.A., U. Ia., 1940; Ed.D., Ind. U., 1947; m. Violet Costello, June 4, 1941; children—Rebecca, Sarah. Tchr., Ill. high schs., 1936-42; instr. U.S. Navy, Ind. U., 1942-44; instr. psychology, guidance dir. William Woods Coll., Fulton, Mo., 1944-45; dir. guidance and research Moline (Ill.) schs., 1945-48; asso. prof. psychology Fla. State U., Tallahassee, 1948-53, prof. edn., 1953—, head dept. guidance and counseling, 1958-68; John Mosler prof. Fordham U., N.Y.C., 1968-69; summer tchr. Ark. State Coll., N.Y.U., Colo. State Coll., U. Ia., Boston U., Northwestern La. Coll., U. So. Cal., Brigham Young U., Eastern Wash. Coll.; lectr. U. Miss., Ohio U., Butler U., U. Rochester, Mankato State Coll., U. Ala., Mich. State U., Marshall U., Ohio State U.; speaker guidance assns. in Miss., Ala., Ky., Pa., Ohio, La., Tenn. Cons. mem. subcom. counseling and testing, nat. manpower adv. com. Dept. Labor, 1963-67, 69-70, regional counseling cons., 1969-70. Mem. Nat. Vocational Guidance Assn. (pres. 1962-63), Am. Personnel and Guidance Assn. (pres. 1964-65), Am. (fellow div. counseling psychology), Fla. psychol. assns., Fla. Assn. Deans and Counselors (pres. 1954-56), Am. Coll. Personnel Assn., Assn. Counselor Edn. and Supervision, So. Assn. Counselor Edn. and Supervision (pres. 1971-72), Kappa Delta Pi, Phi Delta Kappa. Author: Guidance in Elementary Schools, 1956; (with Hopke) Guidance in the Junior High School, 1961; Counseling Guidance and Personnel Services, 1971, Editor: Guidance Bull., 1953-63. Contbr. to profl. jours., encys. Home: 1808 Westridge Drive Tallahassee FL 32304

COTTINGHAM, JOHN ELMER, educator; b. Fennimore, Wis., Aug. 5, 1938; s. Elmer John and Dorothy (Knappmiller) C.; B.S., Wis. State U. at Platteville, 1961; M.S., U. Wis., 1962, Ph.D., 1964; m. Katherine Kreul, July 10, 1960; children—Steven, David, Robert. Research, teaching U. Wis. at Platteville, 1961-64, from asst. prof. to prof., then head dept. agrl. industries, 1964—. Served with AUS. Mem. Phi Delta Kappa, Alpha Zeta. Club: Platteville Kiwanis. Home: 960 Williams St Platteville WI 53818

COTTLE, OWEN BOOTH, mfg. co. exec.; b. St. Louis, Nov. 17, 1923; s. Barnard H. and Evelyn (Davis) C.; student Pa. State U., 1941-42, Pace Coll., 1945-47; m. Florence J. Godfrey, Sept. 1, 1946 (dec. 1959); childrenDiane, Owen, Kathleen, Donald; m. 2d, Elizabeth M. Ahearn, Oct. 22, 1960; childrenChristopher, Suzanne. With Abex Corp. (formerly Am. Brake Shoe Co.), 1946-, asst. treas., 1953-64, treas., 1964-. Served with USAAF, 1943-45. Mem. Financial Execs. Inst., Theta Xi. Mason. Home: 252 Marietta Avenue Hawthorne, NY 10532. Office: 530 Fifth Avenue New York City, NY 10036.

COTTMAN, JAMES STEWART, Jr., fgn. service officer; b. Balt., Jan. 18, 1925; s. James Stewart and Edith (Russo) C.; A.B., Johns Hopkins, 1948; postgrad. Columbia, 1948-50, Am. U. Beirut (Lebanon), 1951; m. Marie-Antoinette de Fleurieu, Jan. 22, 1968. Instr., Park Sch., Balt., 1950-51; with U.S. Govt., 1951—, with exec. secretariat State Dept., 1953-56, spl. asst. to counselor, 1956- 57; dep. chief SEATO sect. Am. embassy, Bangkok, 1957-59; legislative asst. Bur. Congl. Relations, 1959-61, spl. asst. to dept. under-sec. state, 1961-62, spl. asst. Bur. Pub. Affairs, 1962-63; exec. sec. U.S. delegation to NATO, Paris, 1963-64; consul, Bordeaux, France, 1964-68; exec. asst. to dep. undersec. state for adminstrn., Washington, 1968—. Served with AUS, World War II. Decorated Bronze Star medal, Purple Heart. Mem. Johns Hopkins Alumni Assn., Alpha Delta Phi. Episcopalian. Club: Johns Hopkins Faculty (Balt.). Office: Dept of State Washington DC 20520

COTTON, AYLETT BOREL, lawyer; b. San Francisco, Apr. 10, 1913; s. Aylett Rains and Alice (Borel) C.; A.B., Stanford, 1935, LL.B., 1938; m. Martha Jane Knecht, June 29, 1940; children—Kristi (Mrs. Robert L. Spence), Gail (Mrs. Kenneth G. High, Jr.), A. Lindley. Admitted to Cal. bar, 1938; practice in San Mateo, 1939, Burlingame, 1952-59, San Francisco, 1940-42, 45-52, 59—; partner Cotton, Seligman and Ray, and predecessor firms, 1959—; adminstrv. officer, real estate div. U.S. Army C.E., San Francisco and Salt Lake City, 1942-45. Developer Borel Pl. Office Center, San Mateo, 1961—. A founder Guardsmen, San Francisco, 1947; a founder Crystal Springs Sch. for Girls, Hillsborough, Cal., 1952, pres. trustees, 1952-57, mem. bd. 1957—. Mem. Richard Nixon's personal campaign staff, 1952, 56; alternate del. Republican Nat. Conv., 1956, 60. Mem. Am., Cal., San Francisco (chmn. com. judiciary 1969), San Mateo bar assns., Soc. Cal. Pioneers, Atlantic Union, Order Hounds Tooth, Delta Kappa Epsilon, Phi Delta Phi. Conglist. Mason, Elk. Clubs: Bohemian, Pacific-Union, Commonwealth, Sierra, Guardsmen (San Francisco); Burlingame Country. Office: Alcoa Bldg 1 Maritime Plaza San Francisco CA 94111

COTTON, DANA MESERVE, univ. adminstr.; b. Wolfeboro, N.H., Oct. 17, 1905; s. Jacob Henry and Sarah Frances (Meserve) C.; A.B., U. N.H., 1928, LL.D. 1968; Ed.M., Harvard, 1943; postgrad. Columbia Tchrs. Coll., Oxford (Eng.) U.; LL.D., Am. Internat. Coll., 1953; Ed. D., Tufts U., 1955; L.H.D., New Eng. Coll., 1959; m. Geraldine Pierce, June 29, 1935; children—John Pierce, Rebecca. Dir. guidance Me. Dept. Edn., Augusta, 1940-44; faculty Harvard, 1944—, sec. faculty edn., 1957—, acting dean Grad. Sch. Edn., 1971. Rec. sec. New Eng. Sch. Devel. Council, 1950—; mem. edn. com. New Eng. Council, 1954-, New Eng. Council Econ. Devel., 1949—; exec. sec.-treas. New Eng. Assn. Colls. and Secondary Sch., 1947-70; mem. New Eng. Citizens Crime Commn., 1966—. Episcopalian. Mason. Home: 986 Memorial Drive Cambridge, MA 02138. Office: Harvard Grad Sch Education Cambridge MA 02138

COTTON, DOROTHY WHYTE, (Mrs. John M. Cotton), mag. editor; b. Auburn, N.Y., Dec. 10, 1915; d. Henry Lee and Henrietta (Harrison) Klein; B.A., U. Mich., 1934; postgrad. N.Y. Sch. Social Work, 1939; m. Donald Whyte, June 14, 1939 (div. Sept. 1946); 1 son, Michael; m. 2d, John M. Cotton, Dec. 14, 1962; stepchildren—Mary, John, Martha. Asso. editor Parents Mag., N.Y.C., 1944-47, editor-in-chief, 1965—; v.p. Parents' Mag. Enterprises, Inc., 1967—; dir. editorial bur. health and welfare Met. Life Ins. Co., N.Y.C., 1947-64. Fellow Am. Pub. Health Assn. Club: Overseas Press (N.Y.C.). Author: Teaching Your Child Right from Wrong, 1961; The Case for the Working Mother, 1965. Home: 30 E 72d St New York City NY 10021 Office: 52 Vanderbilt Av New York City NY 10017

COTTON, EMILE LOUIS, real estate broker; b. Elwood, Ind., May 15, 1899; s. Emile N. and Mary (Schach) C.; student Ind. U., 1918-19; A.B., U. Chgo., 1923; m. Mildred Galloway, Aug. 12, 1925; 1 son, Emile Louis. Tchr. jr. high sch., Elwood, 1923-24; real estate and landscaping bus., Miami, Fla., 1925-30; tchr. Dade County Sch. System, 1930-33; prin. Kendall (Fla.) Sch., 1933-37, South Miami Sch., 1937-43; real estate broker, South Miami, 1943—; pres. E.L. Cotton, Inc., 1949—, South Miami Investment Co., 1950—; dir. First Nat. Bank of South Miami, South Miami Fed. Savs. & Loan Assn. Bd. dirs. Cancer Inst. Miami, 1959-65, v.p., 1962-65; trustee U. Miami, 1959—. Served as pvt. U.S. Army, 1918. Mem. Nat. Assn. Real Estate Bds., Kendall-Perrine Realty Bd., South Miami Dist. C. of C. (dir. 1945-66), Musicians Club Am. (dir. 1960—), Alpha Sigma Phi. Methodist, Mason, Rotarian (dir. 1953-55, 64-65). Home: 11111 S W 79th Av Miami FL 33156 Office: 11505 S Dixie Hwy Miami FL 33156

COTTON, FRANK ALBERT, chemist, educator; b. Phila., Apr. 9, 1930; s. Albert and Helen (Taylor) C.; student Drexel Inst. Tech., 1947-49; A.B., Temple U., 1951; D.Sc. (hon.), 1963; Ph.D., Harvard, 1955; m. Diane Dornacher, June 13, 1959; children—Jennifer Helen, Jane Myrna. Instr. chemistry Mass. Inst. Tech., 1955-57, asst. prof., 1957-60, asso. prof., 1960-61, prof., 1961—. Cons. Am. Cyanamid, Stamford, Conn., 1958-67, Union Carbide, N.Y.C., 1964—, Polaroid Corp., 1965—. Recipient Baekland medal N.J. sect. Am. Chem. Soc., 1963. Mem. Nat Acad. Scis., A.A.A.S., Am. Crystallography Assn., Am. Chem. Soc. (award 1962), Am. Acad. Arts and Scis. Author: (with G. Wilkinson) Advanced Inorganic Chemistry, 2d edit., 1966; Chemical Applications of Group Theory, 2d edit., 1970. Editor: Progress in Inorganic Chemistry, Vols. 1-10, 1959-68; Inorganic Syntheses, Vol. 13, 1971. Home: 134 Lake Street Sherborn MA 01770 Office: Mass Inst Tech Cambridge MA 02139

COTTON, FRANK ETHRIDGE, Jr., educator; b. Corinth, Miss., Aug. 14, 1923; s. Frank Ethridge and Audie Buleah (Gray) C.; B.S. in sci., Miss. State U., 1946, B.S. in elec. engring., 1947; M.Litt., U. Pitts., 1951, Ph.D., 1962; m. Betty Gail Clark, Oct. 12, 1947; children—Pamela, Patricia, Nannette. Indsl. engr. Westinghouse Elec. Corp., East Pittsburgh, Pa., 1947-51; engr., economist Gulf Oil Corp., Pitts., 1951-58; prof., head dept. indsl. engring. Miss. State U., 1958—; cons. indsl. firms, Marshall Space Flight Center, Bur. Social Sci. Research, Inc. Served to ensign, USNR, 1943-46. Mem. Am. Inst. Indsl. Engrs. (nat. pres. 1970-71, nat. trustee), Am. Soc. Quality Control, Soc. Internat. Devel., Nat. Soc. Profl. Engrs., Am. Soc. Engring. Edn. Presbyn. Contbr. articles tech. jours. Home: 900 Howard Rd Starkville MS 39759 Office: PO Drawer U State College MS 39762

COTTON, JAMES HARRY, educator; b. Stephen, Minn., June 9, 1898; s. J. Sumner and Margaret Louella (Donaldson) C.; A.B., Coll. of Wooster, 1921, D.D., 1929; postgrad. Princeton Theol. Sem., 1921-24; Ph.D., Princeton, 1931; D.D., Wabash Coll., 1938; m. Luella Faye Goodhart, June 25, 1927; children—Margaret Jane, Luella Anne. Asst. prof. philosophy Coll. Wooster, 1926-28; pastor Broad St. Presbyn. Ch., Columbus, O., 1928-40; lectr. to univ. and mission centers in India, China, Japan under Joseph Cook Found., 1931-32; pres. McCormick Theol. Sem., Chgo., 1940-47; James Sprunt lectr. Union Theol. Sem., 1947; prof. philosophy Wabash Coll., 1947-61, 64-69; div. prof. Harvard, 1961-64; vis. prof. philosophy Purdue U., 1969-70, Kalamazoo Coll., 1970-71, Coll. Wooster (O.), 1971-72. Served with F.A., U.S. Army, 1918-19. Mem. Am. Theol. Soc., Am. Philos. Assn., Phi Beta Kappa, Delta Sigma Rho. Author: The Christian Experience of Life, 1933; Christian Knowledge of God, 1951; Royce on the Human Self, 1954; exposition of Hebrews in The Interpretor's Bible, vol. XI, 1955. Contbr. to mags. Home: 557-D Williamsburg Ct Wooster OH 44691

COTTON, JOHN, realtor; b. San Diego, Mar. 23, 1913; s. Oscar W. and Violet (Savage) C.; student San Diego State Coll., 1931, 33, Stanford, 1931, 32, 34; m. Margaret Georgia McNeil, Sept. 26, 1936; children—Lawrence M., Margaret (Mrs. John B. Harris), Joan (Mrs. Larry Cairncross). Salesman, O.W. Cotton, realtor, San Diego, 1934-46; partner O.W. Cotton Co., San Diego, 1946—; pres. Cotton Property Mgmt. Co., realtor, San Diego, 1959—; real estate broker, appraiser, counselor, property mgr.; lectr. in field. Mem. Cal. Real Estate Commn., 1968-72; chmn. San Diego Housing Adv. and Appeals Bd., 1962-69; mem. pres.'s real estate adv. com. U. Cal., 1954-56, 65-71. Mem. San Diego Realty Bd. (pres. 1951), Cal. Real Estate Assn. (pres. 1956), Nat. Assn. Real Estate Bds. (pres. 1969), Internat. Real Estate Fedn. (v.p. Am. chpt. 1971; Distinguished Service award 1968), Inst. Real Estate Mgmt. (pres. San Diego 1948), Am. Inst. Real Estate Appraisers (nat. v.p. 1966, pres. San Diego 1962), Am. Soc. Real Estate Counselors, San Diego Apt. and Rental Owners Assn. (pres. 1944-46), Cal. (pres. 1948-49), Nat. (v.p. 1953) apt. owners assns., San Diego Downtown Assn., (pres. 1961), Am. Arbitration Assn. (nat. panel arbitrators 1967-69), San Diego C. of C. (dir. 1970-72), Am. Right of Way Assn. Presbyn. (elder). Lion. Home: 2980 Nichols Street San Diego CA 92106 Office: 233 A Street San Diego CA 92101

COTTON, JOHN MELTON, psychiatrist; b. Stigler, Okla., June 9, 1908; s. Maurice Lafayette and Hattie C. (Melton) C.; B.S., Tulane U., 1930, M.D., 1932; m. Mary Marjorie Bolles, June 6, 1940 (dec. 1961); children—Mary Frances, John Maurice, Martha Melton; 3d, Elizabeth Watkins, Apr. 11, 1970. Intern Balt. City Hosps., 1932-33; resident Springfield State Hosp., Sykesville, Md., 1933-34; resident, research fellow N.Y. State Psychiat. Inst., N.Y.C., 1937-40; research asso. psychiatrist Neuro-psychiat. Inst. of Hartford (Conn.) Retreat, 1940-41; exec. officer Inst. Living, Hartford, 1946-47; asst. psychiaty Columbia Coll. Phys. and Surg., 1938-47, asso. clin. prof., 1954-65, clin. prof. psychiatry, 1965—; instr. Cornell Sch. Medicine, 1947-55; psychiatrist out- patient dept. N.Y. Hosp., 1947-54; cons. group therapy VA, 1947; expert cons. surgeon gen., 1947—; certificate psychoanalysis Psychoanalytic Clin. Tng. and Research, Columbia, 1954; dir. psychiatry, attending psychiatrist St. Luke's Hosp., N.Y.C., 1954—. Chmn. medical com. Planned Parenthood, 1964-66. Served to lt. col., M.C., AUS, 1941-46. Decorated Legion of Merit. Fellow Am. Psychiat. Assn. (pres. N.Y. County 1961), N.Y. Acad. Scis., N.Y. Acad. Medicine (chmn. com. on spl. studies 1967-71), A.A.A.S.; mem. A.M.A., N.Y. State, N.Y. County (pres. 1964-65) med. socs., Assn. Research Nervous and Mental Disease. Club: Century Assn. (N.Y.C.). Home: 560 Riverside Dr New York City NY 10027 Office: 421 W 113th St New York City NY 10025

COTTON, NORRIS, U.S. senator; b. Warren, N.H. May 11, 1900; s. Henry Lang and Elizabeth (Moses) C.; student Phillips Exeter Acad., 1916-18; Wesleyan Univ., Middletown, Conn., 1919-21, George Washington Univ. Law Sch., 1927; hon. degree U. N.H., U. Vt., New Eng. Coll., Belknap Coll.; m. Ruth Isaacs, May 11, 1927. Admitted to N.H. bar, 1928; practiced law with firm Cotton, Tesreau & Stebbins, Lebanon, N.H., until 1955; formerly pros. atty. Grafton County; justice Municipal Ct. of Lebanon, 1939-44; mem. 80th-83rd U.S. Congresses, from the second dist. N.H.; elected for term of 2 yrs. to U.S. Senate, 1954, to fill unexpired term of Senator Charles W. Tobey; re-elected for full terms ending 1963, 69, 75, mem. appropriations com., mem. commerce com. Formerly majority leader, speaker N.H. Ho. of Reps. Home: 15 Kimball Street Lebanon NH 03766 Office: Senate Office Bldg Washington DC 20510

COTTON, ROBERT HENRY, food research exec.; b. Newton, Mass., Nov. 17, 1914; s. Leonard Miller and Helen (Patenaude) C.; B.S., Bowdoin Coll., 1937; M.S., Mass. Inst. Tech., 1939; Ph.D., Pa. State Coll., 1944; m. Catherine Cobb, 1939 (div. 1947); 1 dau., Dorothy; m. 2d, Mildred Woodward Smith, Jan. 1, 1948; children—Leonard Wright, Thomas Carroll. Chemist insulation research sect. Gen. Electric Co., Pittsfield, Mass., 1939; grad. asst. plant nutrition Pa. State Coll., 1940-43, instr. human nutrition, 1943-44, asst. prof., 1944-45; dir. Plymouth Fla. div. Nat. Research Corp., 1945-47; supr. chemist, prof. U. Fla. Citrus Expt. Sta., 1947-48; dir. research Holly Sugar Corp., 1948-54, Huron Milling Co., Harbor Beach, Mich., 1954-58; with I.T.T. Continental Baking Co., Rye, N.Y., 1958—, dir. research, 1958—, v.p., 1965—. Adv. bd. mil. personnel supplies NRC. Chmn. com. on cereals and gen. products Nat. Acad. Sci.-NRC, 1969—, adviser com. on nutritional guidelines for foods, 1970; mem. vis. com. Dept. Nutrition and Food Sci., Mass. Inst. Tech., 1966-69; panel mem. White House Conf. on Food, Nutrition and Health, 1969. Fellow A.A.A.S.; mem. Assn. Research Dirs. N.Y. (pres. 1964-65), Am. Assn. Cereal Chemists (pres. 1965-66, chmn. bd. 1966-67), Am. Inst. Baking (sci. adv. bd. 1958—), Inst. Food Tech., Am. Bakers Assn. (chmn. tech. liaison com. U.S. Dept. Agr. 1959—, chmn. nutrition com.), Am. Chem. Soc. Episcopalian. Patentee, author in field food tech. and cereal chemistry. Home: 56 Intervale Pl Rye NY 10580 Office: ITT Continental Baking Co P O Box 731 Rye NY 10580

COTTON, WILLIAM DAVIS, lawyer, banker; b. Jonesville, La., Feb. 9, 1904; s. George Spencer and Lizzie (Davis) C.; student La. State U., 1922-24, J.D., 1928; m. Anna Mae Puddin Allen, Nov. 25, 1927; children—Carole, Jean Ann, Stephen Wayne. Admitted to La. bar, 1928; practice in Rayville, La., 1929—; sr. mem. firm Cotton, Bolton & Kircus, 1946—; pres., chmn. bd. First Nat. Bank Rayville, 1952—. Research fellow Southwestern Legal Found. Mem. council La. Law Inst., 1959—. Del. gen. confs. Methodist Ch., 1960, 64, 66, 68; mem. La. Commn. on Constnl. Revision, 1970—. Mem. La. Senate from 32d Dist. 1940-44; chmn. Richland Parish Democratic Exec. Com., 1961—. Trustee Glenwood Hosp., West Monroe, La., 1962—. Served to lt. col. AUS, 1941-46; ETO. Decorated Bronze Star; named Outstanding Layman, La. Miss. W. Tenn. Dist. Kiwanis, 1970, Meth. Man of Year, La., 1965. Fellow Am. Coll. of Probate Counsel, Am. Bar Found.; mem. Am., La. bd. govs. 1946-48, pres. 1965) bar assns., Am. Judicature Soc. Mason (32), Kiwanian (internat. trustee 1941-42, 46-48). Home: 219 Julia Street Rayville, LA 71269. Office: 307 Madeline Street Rayville LA 71269

COTTONE, BENEDICT PETER, lawyer; b. N.Y.C., Apr. 26, 1909; s. Pellegrino and Pina (Grisafi) C.; A.B., Cornell Univ., 1930; LL.B., Yale, 1933; m. Louise Cleverdon, Apr. 25, 1941; children—Michael Benedict, Vincent William. Admitted to N.Y. bar, 1934; pvt. practice, 1934-35; entered Fed. Govt. service, 1935, with SEC as atty. in

Protective Com. Study, 1935-36; atty. with spl. telephone investigation of FCC 1936- 37; legal staff Fed. Power Commn., 1937-38; spl. asst. to atty. gen. assigned to Temporary Nat. Econ. Com. in Congl. hearings on patent practices, 1938; sr. atty. CAA, 1938-39; chief of litigation sect., 1939, asst. gen. counsel, 1941-46, gen. counsel FCC, 1946-53; U.S. del. Anglo-Am. Telecommunications Conf., Bermuda, 1945; U.S. del. Internat. Tel. & Tel. Conf., Paris, 1949. Mem. Atty. Gen.'s Com. on Organized Crime, 1950. Mem. bars of N.Y., D.C. Mem. D.C., Am. Fed. Communications bar assns., Acad. Polit. Sci., Am. Judicature Society, Phi Beta Kappa, Phi Kappa Phi. Alpha Phi Delta. Democrat. Clubs: Yale (Washington), Cornell (N.Y.C. and Washington), Broadcasters, Broadcast Pioneers. Home: 2515 Q St NW Washington DC 20007 Office: 1730 M St NW Washington DC 20036

COTTRELL, DAVID, Jr., lawyer; b. West Point, Miss., June 7, 1908; s. David and Elma (Croom) C.; grad. N.M. Mil. Inst., 1927; LL.B., U. Miss., 1931; m. Margaret Carroll Loker, June 7, 1938; children—David III, Albert Peyton. Admitted to Miss. bar, since practiced in Gulfport; mem. firm. Eaton, Cottrell, Galloway & Lang, 1945—. Chmn. Miss. Inter- Am. Devel. Com., 1961-64; mem. Miss. Vets. Farm and Home Bd., 1946-56; mem. of export expansion council U.S. Dept. Commerce, 1962-65. Bd. trustees Insts. Higher Learning State Miss., 1953-60; pres. Miss. State Bar Found., 1966—. Served to maj., C.W.S., AUS, 1942- 45. Fellow Am. Bar Found.; mem. Am. Bar Assn. (chmn. spl. com. on relations with lawyers of other nations 1961-64), Miss. Jr. C. of C. (pres. 1936), U. Miss. Alumni Assn. (pres. 1947-48), Miss. Bar Assn. (pres. 1960-61), Phi Delta Theta, Phi Alpha Delta. Author: Lawyers, Leadership and Latin America. Home: 1518 Bert Av Gulfport MS 39501 Office: 2300 14th St Gulfport MS 39501

COTTRELL, DONALD PEERY, educator; born Columbus, O., Feb. 17, 1902; s. Harvey Van Doren and Della Stone (Miller) C.; A.B., Ohio State U., 1923; A.M., Columbia, 1927, Ph.D., 1929; m. Eleanor H. Westberg, June 15, 1928; children—Alan Peery, Dorothy Ann (Mrs. Allen E. Caswell). Engaged as tchr., adminstr. pub. schs., Harrod, O., Mentor, O., 1923-26; tutor dept. edn., Hunter Coll., 1927-29; asst. and asso. coll. adminstrn., Tchrs. Coll., Columbia, 1927-29, asst. prof. edn., 1929-31, asso. prof., 1931-41, prof. and asst. dir. div. instrn., 1941-44; acting prin. Horace Mann-Lincoln High Sch., 1943-44; prof. edn. and exec. dir. Horace Mann-Lincoln School of Tchrs. Coll., 1944-46; dean Coll. of Edn., Ohio State U., Columbus, 1946-67, prof. edn., 1967—. Condr. many surveys U.S. higher edn. since 1927; studied orgn. and function western European major univs. 1930-31, USSR, Sweden, Denmark, 1934; vis. asso. prof. edn. Stanford U., summer 1937; ednl. adviser Internat. House, N.Y.C., 1941-44; expert cons. to War Dept., advising U.S. Mil. Govt. in Germany on univ. edn., 1947. Chmn. Survey Commn. (Fgn. Missions Conf. N. Am.), on Protestant-sponsored edn. in Philippines, Japan and China, 1948; chief ednl. planning mission to Korea for U.N. Korean Reconstrn. Agy., also UNESCO, 1952-53; cons. N.Y. City Bd. Edn., 1949-50, 61-62. Bd. visitors U.S. Army Transp. Sch. Ft. Eustis, 1964- 67. Trustee Talladega Coll., Western Coll. for Women. Mem. Am. Assn. of Colls. for Tchr. Edn. (pres. 1957), N.E.A. (nat. commn. on tchr. edn. and profl. standards), Am. Assn. Sch. Adminstrs., Am. Assn. U. Profs., Soc. Advancement Edn., Soc. Profs. of Edn., Phi Delta Kappa, Kappa Delta Pi, Kappa Phi Kappa. Conglist. Author or co-author books in edn. field, including: The American High School, 1946; College Reading and Religion, 1948. Editor and co-author: Teacher Education for a Free People, 1956. Home: 6671 Olentangy River Rd Worthington OH 43085 Office: Coll Edn Ohio State U 29 W Woodruff Av Columbus OH 43210 ☆

COTTRELL, LEONARD, author; b. Wolverhampton, Eng., May 21, 1913; s. William Arthur and Beatrice Martha (Tootell) C.; ed. King Edward VI's Grammar Sch., Birmingham, Eng.; m. Doris Swain, May 1940 (div. June 1960); m. 2d, Diana Randolph, Dec. 1965. Free-lance radio writer, dir., 1936-40; staff writer, dir. radio documentaries BBC, London, 1940-55, writer, dir. BBC-TV drama documentary dept., 1955-59; war corr. RAF, 1944-45, seconded to UNESCO as radio writer and dir., Paris, 1951-53; lectr. archaeology on cruises Egypt, Middle East, Aegaean Islands; free lance contbr. TV and radio. Mem. Egypt Exploration Soc., Hellenic Soc., Roman Soc., Inst. Archaeol. Gt. Britain, Cumberland and Westmoreland Archaeol. Soc. Clubs: Savile, London, Arts Theatre (London). Author numerous books, including: The Lost Pharaohs, 1950; Madame Tussaud, 1951; The Bull of Minos, 1953; One Man's Journey, 1955; Life Under the Pharaohs, 1955; Mountains of Pharaoh, 1956; Seeing Roman Britain, 1956; Lost Cities, 1957; The Anvil of Civilization, 1958; The Great Invasion, 1958; Wonders of Antiquity, 1959; Wonders of the World, 1959; Enemy of Rome, 1960; Land of the Pharaohs, 1960; Land of Two Rivers, 1961; Tiger of Chi'in, 1962; Lost Worlds, 1962; The Lion Gate, 1963; Secrets of Tutankhamun's Tomb, 1964; Crete, Island of Mystery, 1965; Guide to Egypt, 1966; Quest for Sumer, 1966; Queens of the Pharaohs, 1966; The Warrior Pharaohs, 1968; Reading the Past, 1969; also numerous articles and book revs. for Brit. and Am. publs. Editor: Concise Ency. of Archaeology, 1960. Home: 217 Station Rd Knowle Solihull Warwickshire England Office: care Miss Ann Elmo 545 Fifth Av New York City NY 10017

COTTRELL, LEONARD S, Jr., social psychologist; b. Hampton Rds., Va., Dec. 12, 1899; s. Leonard Slater and Ruth Ella (Roane) C.; B.S., Va. Poly. Inst., 1922; M.A., Vanderbilt U., 1926; Ph.D., U. Chgo., 1933; m. Anita Rucker, Aug. 27, 1927; children—Leonard Slater III, Susan Rucker. Instr. sociology U. Chgo., 1931-35; asst. prof. sociology Cornell U., 1935-38, prof., 1938- 39, prof. sociology, chmn. dept. sociology and anthropology, 1939-48, dean, Coll. Arts & Scis., 1948-51, vis. prof., 1951-53; adj. prof. sociology N.Y.U., 1952-68; vis. prof. sociology and psychology U. N.C., Chapel Hill, 1968—; staff social psychologist Russell Sage Found., 1951-67, sec. found., 1959-67; on leave to serve as chief sociologist research br., information, edn., O.C.S., War Dept., 1942- 45; chmn. adv. group on psychol. and unconventional warfare Research and Devel. Bd., Dept. Def., 1952-53, mem. adv. panel, 1954-59; mem. sci. adv. bd. USAF, 1955-58; mem. Army Sci. Adv. Council, 1956-58; nat. adv. council Nat. Insts. Mental Health, 1955-59; adv. com. social scis. NSF, 1959-64. Mem. sci. research adv. bd. Nat. Assn. Retarded Children, 1959-65; chmn. adv. com. on behavioral research Office Emergency Planning, Nat. Acads. Sci.-NRC, 1960-63; mem. Pres.'s Panel on Mental Retardation, 1961-62; chmn. citizens adv. council to Pres.'s Com. on Juvenile Delinquency and Youth Crimes, 1961-65, also chmn. tech. review panel to com., 1961-65; chmn. bd. dirs. Telemann Soc. N.Y., 1959-64. Served with U.S. Army, 1918. Fellow A.A.A.S., Am. Sociol. Assn. (pres. 1949-50); mem. Sociol. Research Assn. (pres. 1949-50), Am. Philos. Soc., Social Sci. Research Council, Am. Psychol. Assn., Law and Soc. Assn. (trustee), Phi Beta Kappa, Sigma Xi. Club: Cosmos (Washington). Co-author 4 books to 1941; (with Sylvia Eberhart) American Opinion on World Affairs in the Atomic Age, 1948; (with S.A. Stouffer) The American Soldier, 1949; (with Nelson Foote) Identity and Interpersonal Competence, 1955; (with Stanton Wheeler) Juvenile Delinquency: Its Prevention and Control, 1966. Editor: Sociometry, 1956-60; asso. editor Psychiatry, 1950—, Social Forces, 1968—; joint editor Sociology Today; Problems and Prospects, 1959. Home: 1400 Mason Farm Road Chapel Hill NC 27514

COTTRELL, ROY HUDSON, sugar co. exec.; b. Rhinecliff, N.Y., July 17, 1892; s. Henry Mortimer and Fannie May (Dorman) C.; B.S., Colo. Agrl. Coll., 1916; m. Jane Lucile McNown, June 29, 1920 (dec. Sept. 1956); children—Dorothy G. (Mrs. Ross H. Coppock), Patricia M. (Mrs. Paul Spencer), Rosemary (Mrs. John Poskus), Frank Gordon; m. 2d Laura Danvers Sawyer, Oct. 26, 1957. Asst. gen. supt. Am. Crystal Sugar Co., Denver, 1931-33; gen. chemist Amalgamated Sugar Co., Ogden, Utah, 1927-31, gen. supt., 1933-34, 36-41, v.p. and dir. since 1941. Served as prin. economist, sugar sect., U.S. Dept. Agr., Washington, 1934-35. Mem. Am. Chem. Soc. Republican. Author: Beet-Sugar Economics (textbook). Home: 1463 28th St Ogden UT 84403 Office: First Security Bank Building Ogden UT 84401

COTTRELL, WILLIAM FREDERICK, educator; b. Idaho Falls, Ida., Aug. 19, 1903; s. William F. and Alice C. (McCubbin) S.; student Westminster Coll., Salt Lake City, 1921-24; B.A., Occidental Coll., 1925; postgrad. U. Cal., 1928; A.M., Stanford, 1929, Ph.D., 1930; m. Annice G. Lyman, Dec. 29, 1925; children—William Frederick, Robert, Lyman, Barbara Coleen. Tchr., Milford (Utah) High Sch., 1925-26, Westminster Coll., 1926-28; prof. sociology and govt. Miami U., Oxford, O., 1930—, chmn. dept. sociology and anthropology, 1956-68; Prof., Salzburg Sem. Am. Studies, 1958. Chmn., Welfare Adv. Bd. Butler County. Bd. dirs. Scripps Found. for Research Population Problems. Mem. Am. Polit. Sci. Assn., Am. Sociol.Assn. (council, exec. com.), Ohio Valley Sociol. Soc. (pres. 1949), Soc. Study Social Problems, Gerontological Soc., Population Assn. Am., Phi Beta Kappa, Pi Sigma Alpha, Alpha Kappa Delta. Author: The Railroader, 1940; Energy and Society, 1955; Technological Change and Labor in the Railroad Industry, 1970. Contbr. chpts. to books, numerous articles to profl. jours. Home: 210 N Campus St Oxford OH 45056

COTTS, ROBERT MILO, educator, physicist, b. Green Bay, Wis., Aug. 22, 1927; s. Milo Miles and Myrtle (Williams) C.; B.S. in Elec. Engring., U. Wis., 1950; Ph.D., U. Cal., Berkeley, 1954; m. Barbara Meyer, June 17, 1950; children—David, Eric, Stuart, Steven. Instr., Stanford, 1954-57; faculty Cornell U., Ithaca, N.Y., 1957—, now prof. physics lab. atomic and solid state physics; physicist Nat. Bur. Standards Lab., Washington, 1963-64; vis. prof. physics U. B.C., Vancouver, 1970-71. Chmn. advanced placement physics examining com. Coll. Entrance Exam. Bd., 1968-70. Served with USNR, 1945-46. Mem. Am. Phys. Soc., Am. Assn. Physics Tchrs., Sigma Xi, Tau Beta Pi. Unitarian. Contbr. articles profl. jours. Home: 115 Northview Rd Ithaca NY 14850

COTZIAS, GEORGE C., research physician; b. Canea, Crete, Greece, June 16, 1918; s. Constantin and Katherine (Strumpuli) C.; came to U.S. 1941, naturalized, 1952; student Nat. U., Athens, 1935-40; M.D. cum laude, Harvard, 1943; Sc.D. Med. Sci. (hon.), Catholic U. Santiago (Chile); D.Sc. (hon.), Med. Coll. Pa., St. John's U.; m. Betty Chinos, June 30, 1951; 1 son, Constantin G. Intern, then resident Peter Bent Brigham and Mass. Gen. hosps., Boston, 1943-46; asst. Rockefeller Inst., 1947-52; sr. scientist, head physiology div. Brookhaven Nat. Lab., Upton, N.Y., 1953—; prof. neurology Mt. Sinai Med. Sch.; prof. medicine U. State N.Y. at Stony Brook. Served with Royal Greek Army, 1940-41. Decorated comdr. Greek Royal Order Phoenix; recipient Albert Lasker award clin. med. research, 1969. Fellow Am. Acad. Arts and Scis.; mem. Assn. Am. Physicians, Am. Soc. Clin. Investigation, Am. Physiol. Soc. Home: 36 Brown's Lane Bellport NY 11713 Office: Brookhaven Nat Lab Upton NY 11973

COUCH, GLENN CARMER, coll. dean; b. Helena, Okla., July 25, 1909; s. Joseph Brantson and Gertrude (Carmer) C.; B.S., U. Okla., 1931, M.S., 1937; Ph.D., Ohio State U., 1941, fellow in botany, 1939-40; m. Ida Marguerite LeCrone July 30, 1933; children—Karen Carmer, Joseph Barton. Asst. botany U. Okla., 1932-35, instr., 1935-41, asst. then asso. prof., 1941- 51, prof. 1951-69, dir. student affairs, 1945-46, acting dean U. Coll., 1945-46, later dean. Dir. Okla. Nat. Bank, Norman. Fellow A.A.A.S.; mem. Bot. Soc. Am., Limnol. Soc. Am., Okla. Acad. Sci., Am. Assn. Univ. Profs., Sigma Xi, Alpha Epsilon Delta, Phi Sigma, Phi Epsilon Phi, Phi Beta Kappa, Phi Eta Sigma. Democrat. Presbyn. Home: 717 Chautauqua St Norman OK 73069

COUCH, HOUSTON BROWN, plant pathologist, educator; b. Estill Springs, Tenn., July 1, 1924; s. Charles Emmett and Grace (Watson) C.; B.S., Tenn. Technol. U., 1950; Ph.D., U. Cal., Davis, 1954; m. Billie Spencer, Oct. 3, 1945; children—Charles, Jonathan, James, Betty, Wayne. Asst. prof. plant pathology Pa. State U., 1954-60, asso. prof., 1960-65; prof. plant pathology, head dept. plant pathology and physiology Va. Poly. Inst. and State U., Blacksburg, 1965—; collaborator U.S. Dept. Agr. Regional Pasture Research Lab., State College, Pa., 1960-65; chmn. exec. com. and program com. Eastern Ecology of Root Disease Conf., 1968, mem. steering com., 1967-70; mem. research adv. com. Mid-Atlantic Food Processors Assn., Inc. Served with inf., AUS, 1942-45; ETO. Decorated Purple Heart. Mem. Am. Phytopathological Soc. (com. chmn., pres. Northeastern div.), Am. Soc. Agronomy, Soil Sci. Soc. Am., Am. Soc. Plant Physiologists, Sigma Xi. Mem. Ch. of Christ. Author: Diseases of Turfgrasses, 1962. Contbr. articles profl. jours. Home: 608 Lansdowne St Blacksburg VA 24060

COUCH, J. O. TERRELL, oil co. exec., lawyer; b. San Antonio, Mar. 3, 1920; s. Quest C. and Mattie H. (Terrell) C.; student San Antonio Jr. Coll., 1937-38; LL.B., U. Tex., 1942; grad. Advanced Mgmt. Program, Harvard, 1968; m. Willynn Miles Brooks, July 31, 1943; children—J.O. Terrell, Leland Brooks, Nancy Miles. Admitted to Tex. bar, 1942, Ohio bar, 1967; mem. firm Lattimore & Couch, Ft. Worth, 1946-49, Lattimore, Couch & Lattimore, 1949-51; asso. firm McGown, McGown, Godfrey & Logan, Ft. Worth, 1951-52; atty. Marathon Oil Co., Houston, 1952-61, div. atty., 1961-67, gen. counsel, Findlay, O., 1967—, dir., 1969—. Mem. adv. bds. Internat. and Comparative Law Center, Internat. Oil & Gas Ednl. Center Southwestern Legal Found., 1967—. Served with CIC, AUS, 1942-46; ETO, PTO. Mem. Am. (chmn. oil com. of natural resources sect. 1969-71), Houston (chmn. mineral com. 1966), Ohio, Findlay bar assns., State Bar Tex. (chmn. mineral law sect. 1961-62), Am. Petroleum Inst., Ind. Petroleum Assn. Am., Tex., Mid-Continent, Rocky Mountain, Western, N.M. (exec. com. 1965-66, adv. com. 1965-67) oil and gas assns., Alpha Tau Omega. Presbyn. Home: 910 Woodworth Dr Findlay OH 45840 Office: 539 S Main St Findlay OH 45840

COUCH, JESSE WADSWORTH, ins. co. exec.; b. Atlanta, Mar. 2, 1921; s. Jesse Newton and Laura (Day) W.; A.B., Princeton, 1947; m. Charlotte Lucretia Collins, Jan. 13, 1945; children—Robert Collins, Laura W. With 1st Nat. Bank Houston, 1947-51; devel. asso. Wray Assos., Houston, 1951-60; partner Wray, Couch & Elder, Houston, 1960-69; v.p. Marsh & McLennan of Houston, Inc., 1969—, also dir.; dir. Marsh & McLennan of Tex., Inc., Tideland Signal Corp., Houston. Mem. exec. bd. Episcopal Diocese of Tex., 1965-67, 68-71. Bd. dirs. Houston-Harris County YMCA; trustee Mus. Fine Arts, Houston. Served to capt. USAAF, 1943-46. Mem. Houston C. of C. (aviation com.). Clubs: Eagle Lake (Tex.) Rod & Gun; Houston Country, Bayou, Coronado (Houston). Home: 1814 Larchmont Rd Houston TX 77019 Office: Bank of Southwest Bldg Houston TX 77002

COUCH, JOHN NATHANIEL, botanist; b. Prince Edward County, Va., Oct. 12, 1896; s. John Henry and Sallie Love (Terry) C.; student Trinity Coll. (Duke U.). 1914-17; A.B., U. N.C., 1919, A.M., 1922, Ph.D., 1924; student U. Nancy, spring 1919, U. Wis., summer, 1923; m. Else Dorothy Ruprecht, May 28, 1927; children—John Philip, Sally Louise (Mrs. J.M. Vilas). Instr. botany U. N.C., 1917-18; sci. tchr. high sch., Chapel Hill, N.C., 1919-20, Charlotte, N.C., 1920-21; instr. botany U. N.C., Chapel Hill, 1922-25, asst. prof., 1927-28, asso. prof., 1928-32, prof., 1932-45, Kenan prof. botany, 1945-67, Kenan prof. botany emeritus, 1967—; NRC fellow in botany, Carnegie Instn., 1925-26, Mo. Bot. Garden, 1926-27; with Johns Hopkins Bot. Exploration, Jamaica, B.W.I., summer, 1926; vis. prof. Johns Hopkins, winters, 1933-35, U. Va., summer, 1933; cultural exchange specialist Dept. State, India, 1961; mem. N.C. Gov.'s Sci. Adv. Com., 1961-64; v.p. XI Internat. Bot. Congress, Seattle, 1969. Spl. adviser to chmn. OSRD, 1944. Served with U.S. Army, 1918-19. Recipient Walker grand prize Boston Soc. Natural History, 1939; Meritorious Tchrs. award Assn. Southeastern Biologists, 1954; certificate of merit Bot. Soc. Am., 1956; first N.C. award in sci., 1964. Fellow A.A.A.S. (v.p., chmn. botany sect. 1962); mem. Nat. Acad. Sci. India (hon. fgn. mem.), Bot. Soc. Am. (chmn. Southeastern section, 1951), Am. Mycol. Soc. (pres. 1943), Soc. Gen. Microbiology, Am. Mosquito Control Assn., Nat., N.C. (pres. 1946-47, Jefferson award, Poteat medal 1937) acads. sci., Internat. Assn. Plant Taxonomists, Am. Soc. Plant Taxonomists, Indian Phytopath. Soc., Elisha Mitchell Sci. Soc. (pres. 1937-38), Sigma Xi. Democrat. Baptist. Author: (with W.C. Coker) The Gasteromycetes of the Eastern United States and Canada, 1928, The Genus Septobasidium, 1938. Asso. editor Mycologia, 1937-39; editor Jour. Elisha Mitchell Sci. Soc., 1946-60. Contbr. articles on bot. subjects to profl. jours. Home: Chapel Hill NC 27514

COUCH, RICHARD BAILEY, educator; b. Portland, Ore., Apr. 7, 1911; s. Fred C. and Gertrude E. (Bailey) C.; B.S. in Naval Architecture and Marine Engring., Webb Inst. Naval Architecture and Marine Engring., 1933; Aero. Engr., N.Y.U., 1934; m. Harriet F. Gilmore, June 7, 1936; children—Richard A., John C., Frances G. Naval architect Navy Dept., 1934-57, assigned David Taylor Model Basin; chief naval architect hull design Bur. Ships, 1953-57; prof. naval architecture and marine engring. U. Mich., 1957- -. Cons. to sec. Navy, Office Sec. Def.; mem. subcom. Mohole Project NAS; standing com. Internat. Towing Tank Conf. Mem. Am. Soc Naval Architects and Marine Engrs. (chmn. Chesapeake sect. 1949-50, nat. council mem.), Tau Beta Pi, Am. Soc. Naval Engrs. Home: 75 Underdown Lane Ann Arbor MI 48103

COUCH, VIRGIL LEE, govt. ofcl.; b. Princeton, Ky., Nov. 12, 1907; s. John and Malta Ann (Duke) C.; B.S., U. Ky., 1930; m. Martha Pence Duncan, Dec. 24, 1931 (dec. Mar. 14, 1949); 1 son, John Lee; m. 2d, Violet Mae Showers, Aug. 29, 1952. Personnel officer several govtl. agys., 1935-51; dep. asst. adminstr., dir. personnel, dir. Nat. Civil Def. Coll. and Tng. Center, exec. officer for tng. and edn., dir. field exercises Atomic Test Operations, dir. warden div., dir. industry office FCDA, OCDM, also asst. dir. civil def. Office Civil Def., Dept. Def., Washington, 1951—. Chmn. Arlington County (Va.) Civil Service Commn., 1951-54; mem. Arlington County Merit System Review Bd., 1950- 51. Recipient award for greatest contbn. to nat. def.; Distinguished Alumni award U. Ky., 1961; named to Ky. Hall of Fame, 1970. Mem. Soc. Personnel Adminstrn. (nat. pres. 1949-50), Soc. Advancement Mgmt. (v.p. 1949-50), Alpha Delta Sigma, Delta Sigma Pi, Alpha Tau Omega, and others. Democrat. Methodist. Mason (32, Shriner). Clubs: University of Kentucky (Washington); Pyramid (Lexington, Ky.); Optimist. Author articles and booklets in field. Home: 4906 N 28th St Arlington VA 22207 Office: OCD-DOD Pentagon Washington DC 20310 ☆

COUCHMAN, GAYLORD M., educator; b. Popejoy, Ia., Sept. 11, 1906; s. Thomas B. and Elsie (Davidson) C.; B.A., Des Moines U., 1927; B.D., McCormick Theol. Sem., 1934; D.D., U. Dubuque, 1945; m. Esther Dunkerton, July 29, 1935; children—Barbara (Mrs. George French), Carol (Mrs. James Cramer), Mary (Mrs. John Beerling), John. Ordained to ministry Presbyn. Ch., 1934; served as pastor in Grimes, Ia., 1934-36, Lake City, Ia., 1936-39, Boone, Ia., 1939-43, Westminster Presbyn. Ch., Dubuque, Ia., 1943-53; pres. U. Dubuque, 1953-68, bd. dirs., 1946-53, also vice chmn. exec. com., dir. ch. relations Theol. Sem., U. Dubuque, 1968-71. Mem. bd. nat. mission, past chmn. council theol. edn., United Presbyn. Ch. U.S.A.; past pres. Presbyn. Coll. Union; chmn. bd. dirs. Assn. Theol. Faculties Ia., Inc. Mem. City Council, Dubuque, 1968-71, mayor, 1971. Bd. dirs. Ia. Coll. Found. Mem. Ia. Coll. Pres. Assn. (past pres.), Ia. Assn. Colls. and Univs., Am. Assn. Sch. Adminstrs., N.E.A., Ia. Assn. Pvt. Colls. and Univs. (chmn., pres. pro tem). Rotarian. Home: 274 Princeton Pl Dubuque IA 52001

COUDERT, ALEXIS CARREL, lawyer; b. N.Y.C., June 3, 1914; s. Frederic R. and Alice Tracy (Wilmerding) C.; B.A., Yale, 1935; LL.B., Columbia, 1938; m. Allison Moore, June 8, 1936 (div. 1961); children—Alexis Tracy, Allison Gottesman; m. 2d. Cora Craddock Kirby, Apr. 7, 1961. Admitted to N.Y. bar, 1938; law asst. to Justice U.S. Supreme Ct., 1938-39; mem. Coudert Bros., N.Y.C. 1942—; prof. law Columbia, 1949-56, acting dir. Parker Sch. Fgn. and Comparative Law, 1949-55; chmn. Unity Fire & Gen. Ins. Co., Gen. Security Assurance Corp.; dir. French Aerospace Corp., Pellon Corp., French-American Banking Corp., Peugeot, Inc., U.S. rep. to Internat. Com. Comparative Law, 1951-55. Pres., dir. N.Y. Eye and Ear Infirmary, 1954-62; pres. Humanities Fund, Inc., 1965—; sec., dir. Brez Found., 1940-64, pres., 1965—; bd. dirs. Alfred Jurzykowski Found., 1960—, pres., 1970—. Decorated chevalier Legion of Honor, chevalier Ordre de Sante Publique (France). Mem. Am. Assn. Comparative Study of Law, Inc. (pres. 1955-60, 65—), Assn. Bar City N.Y., Am., New York County, N.Y. State bar assns., Am. Judicature Soc., Am. Soc. Internat. Law. Clubs: Piping Rock (Locust Valley, N.Y.); Yale, Sky (N.Y.C.). Home: 12 Beekman Pl New York City NY 10021 Office: 200 Park Av New York City NY 10017

COUDERT, FERDINAND WILMERDING, lawyer; b. N.Y.C., Feb. 9, 1909; s. Frederic Rene and Alice Tracy (Wilmerding) C.; A.B. magna cum laude, Harvard, 1930, A.M., 1933; LL.B., Columbia, 1937; m. Helen F. Carey, Oct. 14, 1942. Admitted to N.Y. bar, 1938, since practiced in N.Y.C.; mem. firm Coudert Bros., 1938-64. Past pres. bd. Brez Found.; bd. dirs., past v.p. Humanities Fund; past sec., bd. dirs. C.T. Loo Chinese Ednl. Fund. Served from 1st lt. to maj., AUS, 1942-46. Mem. Am. Soc. Internat. Law, France Am. Soc. (dir.), Fedn. French Alliances (past dir.), Soc. Colonial Wars. Clubs: Paris American (past pres.); Century, University, Regency (N.Y.C.); Union Interalliee (Paris). Home: 555 Park Av New York City NY 10021 Office: Pan Am Bldg 200 Park Av New York City NY 10017

COUDERT, FREDERIC RENE, III, lawyer; b. N.Y.C., Sept. 21, 1932; s. Frederic Rene, Jr. and Paula (Murray) C.; grad. St. Paul's Sch., Concord, N.H., 1949; A.B., Princeton, 1953; LL.B., Columbia, 1956; m. Marie Eileen Moore, June 23, 1961; 1 dau., Cynthia. Admitted to N.Y. bar, 1958, D.C. bar, 1967; with U.S. Atty.'s Office, So. dist. N.Y., 1956; mem. firm Coudert Bros., N.Y.C. and Paris,

France, 1958—. Dir. Hartwell and Campbell Fund, Inc. Mem. nat. panel Am. Arbitration Assn. Sec. Brez Found., 1964—. Served with AUS, 1956-58. Mem. Assn. Bar City N.Y. Clubs: Racquet and Tennis, Princeton (N.Y.C.); Piping Rock (Locust Valley, N.Y.); Seawanhaka Corinthian Yacht (Oyster Bay). Home: Cove Neck Road Oyster Bay, NY 11771. Office: 200 Park Av New York City NY 10017

COUDERT, FREDERIC RENE, Jr., ex-congressman, lawyer; b. N.Y.C., May 7, 1898; s. Frederic René and Alice T. (Wilmerding) C.; A.B., Columbia, 1918, LL.B. (Kent scholar), 1922; m. Paula Murray, Oct. 1931. Admitted to N.Y. bar, 1923, since practiced in N.Y.C.; mem. firm Coudert Bros., 1924—; asst. U.S. atty. So. Dist. N.Y., 1924-25. Rep. candidate for dist. atty. N.Y. County, 1929; mem. N.Y. State Senate, 17th Dist., 1939-46, Ho. of Reps., 17th Dist. Manhattan, 1946; mem. 80th to 85th U.S. Congresses, 17th N.Y. Dist.; chmn. subcom. Rapp-Coudert Legislative Com. to Investigate Pub. Ednl. System; chmn. N.Y. Lawyers Committee against Jones Act, 1929; mem. temporary state commn. on govtl. operations N.Y.C., 1959-61. Served with U.S. Army, 1917-18; AEF; 1st lt. 105th U.S. Inf., 27th Div. Decorated Chevallier Legion of Honor (France); recipient U. medal for distinguished pub. service Columbia, 1941. Mem. Am., N.Y. State bar assns., Assn. Bar City N.Y., N.Y. County Lawyers Assn., Fedn. French Alliances U.S. (pres. 1965—). Clubs: Sky, Century, Pilgrims, Racquet and Tennis, Piping Rock, Seawanhaka, Corinthian Yacht, N.Y. Yacht. Home: 988 Fifth Av New York City NY 10028 also Oyster Bay NY 11771 Office: Pan Am Bldg 200 Park Av New York City NY 10017

COUELLE, JACQUES, French architect. specializing in some features of prehistoric architecture; projects include whole town of Port La Galere, France and La Castellaras, France. Address: care Robert Faherty Chez Mella 82 Av de Neuilly Neuilly (Seine) France*

COUGHANOWR, DONALD RAY, educator; b. Brazil, Ind., Mar. 11, 1928; s. Ray L. and Anna (Burdon) C.; B.S., Rose Poly. Inst., 1949; M.S., U. Pa., 1951; Ph.D. in Chem. Engring., U. Ill., 1956; m. Effie Natsis, Mar. 6, 1955; children—Corinne Ann, Christine Ann, David Donald. Process engr. Standard Oil Co. Ind., Whiting, 1951-53; prof. chem. engring. Purdue U., 1956-67; prof., head dept. chem. engring. Drexel U., 1967—; cons. Dow Chem. Co., Electronic Assos., Inc. Mem. Am. Inst. Chem. Engrs., Instrument Soc. Am., Tau Beta Pi. Author: Process Systems Analysis and Control, 1965. Home: 504 Midland Av St Davids PA 19087 Office: Drexel Inst 34th and Chestnut Sts Philadelphia PA 19104

COUGHLAN, JOHN APPLEBY, coll. adminstr.; b. Silver Spring, Md., Feb. 16, 1929; s. Paul Mackin and Frances (Appleby) C.; student U. Md., 1947-49; B.A., Villanova U., 1952; M.A., Catholic U. Am., 1958, Ph.D., 1965. Entered Order of St. Augustine, 1949, ordained priest, 1955; tchr. math. and econs., social studies dir. Archbishop Carroll High Sch., 1956-63; prof. econs., chmn. econs. dept. Villanova U., 1964-68; v.p. acad. affairs, dean of coll. Merrimack Coll., 1968—. Trustee Austin Prep. Sch., Reading, Mass. Mem. Am., Catholic econ. assns., Am. Assn. U. Profs., Am. Conf. Acad. Deans. Address: Merrimack Coll North Andover MA 01845

COUGHLAN, JOHN ROBERT, author, journalist; b. Kokomo Ind., July 7, 1914; s. William Henry and Lucile DeNevers (Ernsperger) C.; B.S., Northwestern U., 1936; m. Patricia Ann Collins, June 30, 1939; children—John Robert, Brian Christopher, Kevin Brooks, Cynthia Davis. Mem. staff Fortune mag., 1937-43, asso. editor, 1938-43; text editor Life mag., 1943-49, mem. editorial staff as writer-editor, 1943-70; now contbr. to various jours. and pubs. Recipient Benjamin Franklin award, 1953; Lasker award for med. journalism, 1954, 59; Benjamin Franklin citation, 1954; citation for excellence Overseas Press Club, 1957; Sigma Delta Chi award for Distinguished Service to Journalism, 1959, merit citation Nat. Edn. Writers Assn., 1961, award of recognition Northwestern U., 1962; Heywood Broun citation Am. Newspaper Guild, 1963; Ann. Book award Nat. Assn. Ind. Schs., 1967. Fellow Internat. Inst. Arts and Scis. Clubs: Bronxville Field; Century Assn. Author: The Wine of Genius, 1951; The Private World of William Faulkner, 1954; Tropical Africa, 1962; The World of Michelangelo, 1966; contbr. anthologies, newspapers, mags. Contbr. symposium; The Asprin Age, 1949. Address: 52 Prescott Av Bronxville NY 10708

COUGHLAN, ROBERT EDWARD, Jr., lawyer; b. Balt., Mar. 3, 1899; s. Robert Edward and Nellie Aurelia (Wheatley) C.; A.B., St. John's Coll., Annapolis, Md., 1920; LL.B., U. Md. 1924; m. Margaret Wagner, Oct. 15, 1924; children—Margaret Nourse, Robert Edward III. Admitted to Md. bar, 1928; adjuster Md. Casualty Co., 1920, corr. claim dept., 1920-25, asst. mgr. property damage claim div., 1925, mgr., 1925-28, mgr. Balt. claim div., 1929-33; trial counsel, 1933- 44; sr. partner Lord, Whip, Coughlan & Green, 1944—. Mem. bd. dirs. Legal Aid Bur., Roland Park Civic League. Served with U.S. Army, 1918. Fellow Am. Coll. Trial Lawyers; mem. Am., Md., Balt. (pres.) bar assns., Fedn. Ins. Counsel, Maritime Law Assn., Trial Table Law Club (past pres.), Barrister's Law Club (past pres.), Balt. C. of C., Am. Judicature Soc., Kappa Alpha. Democrat. Episcopalian. Mason. Clubs: Merchant's, Center. Author: Workmen's Compensation Cases. Home: 711 W University Pkwy Baltimore, MD 21210. Office: Arlington Bldg Baltimore MD 21201

COUGHLIN, DAN, journalist; b. Bremerton, Wash., Sept. 14, 1926; s. M.P. and Margaret (Fuller) C.; B.A. in Polit. Sci., U. Wash., 1950; m. Geraldine A. Testu, Aug. 29, 1959; children—Kevin, Daniel, Kerry, Kristie. With Post- Intelligencer, 1949—, formerly city editor, city govt. reporter, corr. Viet Nam, 1964, bus. and financial editor, 1964—. Sec., also treas., dir. Greater Seattle Ski Sch. Served with AUS, 1944-45; lt. col. Res. Mem. Seattle Soc. Investment Men, Sigma Delta Chi (pres. Western Wash. chpt. 1960-61), Delta Upsilon. Club: Wash. Athletic. Home: 219 N W 176th Pl Seattle WA 98177 Office: Hearst Pub Co 6th and Wall Sts Seattle WA 98121

COUGHLIN, DENNIS JOSEPH, Jr., meat co. exec.; b. Columbus, O., Feb. 24, 1928; s. Dennis J. and Margaret (Devanney) C.; B.S. in Bus. Adminstrn., Ohio State U., 1950; m. Pauline L. Morris, Sept. 16, 1950; children—Karen S., Dennis Joseph III, Timothy J., Christopher A., Mary E. With Ernst & Ernst, Columbus, 1950-51, Joyce Shoe Co., Columbus, 1953-57; asst. controller Idean Dispenser Co., Columbus, 1957-60; with Sugardale Foods, Inc., Canton, O., 1960—, controller, 1968—. Pres. North Canton Midget Football Assn., 1970. Served with AUS, 1951-53. Mem. Nat. Assn. Accountants, Canton C. of C., Beta Alpha Psi. Roman Catholic. Home: 1208 Clinton Av SE North Canton OH 44720 Office: 1600 Harmont Av Canton OH 44705

COUGHLIN, EDWARD BRYAN, investment banker; b. Chgo., Dec. 19, 1898; s. James Mace and Annie (Rafferty) C.; student Loyola U., Chgo., 1918-20; m. Helen Mary Crowley, Nov. 16, 1940; children—Edward Bryan II, Dennis Francis, John Walter. Salesman. A.C. Allyn & Co., Denver, 1928-32; with Coughlin & Co., Denver, 1933—, pres., 1966-69, chmn. bd., 1969—. Mem. Midwest Stock Exchange. Served with inf. U.S. Army, 1918. Mem. Investment Bankers Assn. Am., Nat. Assn. Security Dealers (chmn. dist. 3, 1957-58). Roman Catholic. Clubs: Serra, Bond (Denver). Home: 128 Ivy St Denver CO 80220 Office: First Nat Bank Bldg Denver CO 80202

COUGHLIN, HOWARD, union exec.; b. N.Y.C., Apr. 5, 1913; s. John and Elizabeth (Walsh) C.; student parochial schs., spl. courses. Local union pres., bus. mgr., 1937-42; organizer AFL, 1942-46; v.p. Office and Profl. Employees Internat. Union, 1951-53, pres., 1953—, gen. bd., mediation panel AFL- CIO. Mem. Pres.'s Com. Equal Employment Opportunity. Mem. Am. Arbitration Assn. (dir.). Office: 265 W 14th St New York City NY 10011

COUGHLIN, RICHARD JAMES, sociologist, educator; b. Buffalo, Dec. 12, 1917; s. Richard James and Mary (Eardley) C.; B.S., Buffalo State Coll., 1941; M.A., Yale, 1950, Ph.D., 1953; m. Margaret Morgan, Feb. 7, 1946; children—Kenneth Morgan, Elizabeth Troth. U.S. vice counsul, Saigon, 1946-48; research analyst U.S. State Dept., Washington, 1948-49; Fulbright Found. and Social Sci. Research Council grantee, Thailand, 1951-52; instr. Yale, 1953-55, asst. prof., 1955-60; rep. Asia Found., Hong Kong, 1957-59; asso. prof. York U., Toronto, 1960-63; prof. U. Va., 1963—, acting chmn. dept. sociology and anthropology, 1965-66, chmn. 1967—. Dir. Va. Council on Family Relations, 1964-67. Mem. Am., So. sociol. assns., Soc. Study Social Problems, Population Assn. Am., Assn. for Asian Studies. Author: Double Identity, The Chinese in Modern Thailand, 1960; (with Donn Hart, Phya Anuman) Southeast Asian Birth Customs, 1965. Contbr. articles profl. jours. Home: 1204 Blue Ridge Rd Charlottesville VA 22903

COUGHLIN, ROBERT LAWRENCE, Jr., congressman; b. Wilkes Barre, Pa., Apr. 11, 1929; s. Robert Lawrence and Evelyn (Wich) C.; A.B., Yale, 1950; M.B.A., Harvard, 1954; LL.B., Temple U., 1958; m. Elizabeth Poole Sellers Worrell, Sept. 6, 1958; children—Elizabeth S., Lynne W., Sara J., Robert Lawrence III. Foreman, Heintz Mfg. Co., Phila., 1954-56; asst. to mfg. v.p. Heintz div. Kelsey, Haves Co., Phila., 1956-58; admitted to Pa. bar, 1958; with firm Saul, Ewing, Remick and Saul, Phila., 1959-69, partner, 1967-69; mem. Pa. Ho. of Reps. from Montgomery County, 1965-66, mem. Senate, 1967-68; mem. 91st-92d Congresses 13th Dist. Pa. Bd. dirs. Easter Seal Soc. Rosemont-Villanova Civic Assn. Served to capt. USMCR, 1950-52. Named Outstanding Young Man, Main Line Jr. C. of C., 1965. Mem. Am., Pa., Phila. bar assns., Big Bros. Assn., Villanova U. Devel. Council, Friendly Sons St. Patrick. Republican. Episcopalian. Home: 829 Mt Moro Rd Villanova PA 19085 also 5930 Frazier Lane McLean VA Office: Cannon Office Bldg Washington DC 20515

COUGHLIN, WILLIAM JAMES, editor; b. Washington, May 29, 1922; s. Clarence William and Kathleen Leith (Ross) C.; A.B., Stanford, 1947, M.A., 1950; m. Geraldine June Tobias, Mar. 25, 1949 (div.); children—Kevin, Kerry, Kelly; m. Patricia Behling, Dec. 28, 1963. Staff Honolulu bur. United Press Assn., 1947-49, bur. mgr., San Francisco, 1950-51. Mexico City, 1951-52; Korean war corr. McGraw-Hill Publishing Co., 1952-53; West Coast editor Aviation Week mag., 1953-55; London bur. chief McGraw-Hill World News, 1956-58, Moscow bur. chief, 1958-59; West Coast bur. chief Am. Aviation Publs., Inc., 1959-60, v.p., editorial dir., 1963-67, editor Missiles and Rockets, 1961-67; chief Los Angeles Times, New Delhi bur., 1968—. Served to 2d lt. USAAF, 1942-46. Recipient Jesse H. Weal editorial award, 1966, 67, Nat. Space Club Press award, 1967. Member Aviation/Space Writers Assn. (pres. 1962-63), Am. Rocket Soc., Phi Kappa Sigma, Sigma Delta Chi. Clubs: Overseas Press (N.Y.C.); Nat. Press, Nat. Aviation, Nat. Rocket (Washington). Author: Conquered Press, 1952. Contbr. articles nat. mags. Home: 12 Raj doot Marq New Delhi, India.

COUGHRAN, TOM BRISTOL, banker; b. Visalia, Cal., Mar. 18, 1906; s. William L. and Rose (Bristol) C.; A.B., Stanford, 1927; m. Florence Montgomery, Mar. 29, 1930; 1 dau., Jane N. With Bank of Am. Nat. Trust & Savs., 1927-57, v.p. internat. banking, 1946-57; v.p. Bank of Am. (Internat.), N.Y.C., 1950- 59. exec. v.p. 1959-70, vice chmn., 1970-71; mem. export adv. com. Dept. Commerce, 1953-57; asst. sec. for internat. affairs U.S. Treasury, 1957-58; U.S. exec. dir. Internat. Bank Reconstrn. and Devel., 1957-58, Internat. Finance Corp., 1957-58; dir. U.S. Devel. Loan Fund, 1958; dir. Bank of Am., N.Y.C.; chmn. bd. World Banking Corp., Nassau, Bahamas. Mem. U.S. delegation to NATO, 1957, Colombo Conf., 1958; mem. Presdl. Fact Finding Mission to Central Am., 1958; chmn. U.S.A. bus. and industry adv. com. OECD, 1966-68. Served as lt. col. AUS, 1942-46. Mem. Council Fgn. Relations. Clubs: Internat., F Street (Washington); Pacific Union, Bohemian (San Francisco); Links, India House (N.Y.C.). Home: 923 Fifth Av New York City NY 10021 Office: 41 Broad St New York City NY 10004

COUGLIN, CHARLES L., mfg. exec.; b. 1885. With Briggs & Stratton Crop., Milw., 1910—, v.p., gen. mgr., 1923-35, pres., 1935-70, chmn. bd., chief exec. officer, 1970—. Home: 2300 E Kensington Blvd Shorewood WI 53211 Office: 2711 N 13th St Milwaukee WI 53206

COULETTE, HENRI ANTHONY, educator, author; b. Los Angeles, Nov. 11, 1927; s. Robert Roger and Genevieve (O'Reilly) C.; B.A., Los Angeles State Coll., 1952; M.F.A., U. Ia., 1954, Ph.D., 1959; m. Jacqueline Meredith, Dec. 27, 1950. Instr., Writers Workshop, U. Ia., 1957-59; mem. faculty Cal. State Coll. at Los Angeles, 1959—, now prof. English; poetry readings at univs. and museums. Served with AUS, 1945-46. Recipient Lamont Poetry award Acad. Am. Poets, 1965; James D. Phelan award for poetry 1966. Mem. Am. Fedn. Tchrs., P.E.N. Democrat. Author: The War of the Secret Agents, 1966; The Family Goldschmitt, 1971. Editor: (with Philip Levine) Character and Crisis, 1966; The Unstrung Lyre, 1971. Home: 1901 Oxley St South Pasadena CA 91030 Office: 5151 State College Dr Los Angeles CA 90032

COULLING, SIDNEY BAXTER, educator; b. Bluefield, W.Va., Feb. 13, 1924; s. Louis Roberdeau and Eva (Steger) C.; A.B., Washington and Lee U., 1948; M.A., U. N.C., 1949, Ph.D., 1957; m. Mary Price Stirling, June 23, 1958; children—Margaret Howard, Anne Baxter, Philip Price. Engaged as instr. of English, Fla. State U., 1949-52, U. Md., 1955-56; mem. faculty Washington and Lee U., 1956—, prof. English, 1965—. Served with AUS, 1943-46. Mem. Modern Lang. Assn. Am., Phi Beta Kappa. Author articles on Matthew Arnold. Home: 607 Marshall St Lexington VA 24450

COULOMBRE, ALFRED JOSEPH, embryologist; b. Boston, Aug. 15, 1922; s. Charles Alfred and Cecelia Mary (Greene) C.; B.S., Cath. U. Am., 1947, M.S., 1949; Ph.D. (Adam T. Bruce fellow 1952-53), Johns Hopkins, 1953; student, summer investigator, Jackson Lab., 1947-50, 57; m. Jane Louise Lacy, June 26, 1948. Instr. Wabash Coll., 1948; instr. anatomy Yale Sch. Medicine, 1953- 56, asst. prof., 1956-61; head sec. exptl. embryology, lab. neuro- anatomical scis. NIH, 1961-67, chief lab., 1962-67, asso. dir. intramural research Nat. Inst. Child Health and Human Devel., 1967-68; head, sect. on exptl. embryology Nat. Inst. Neurol. Diseases and Blindness, 1968-69; head sect. exptl. embryology Nat. Eye Inst., 1969-71, sr. research biologist, 1971—. Mem. adv. panel devel. biology NSF, 1958-61; mem. child health and human devel. tng. com. NIH, 1962-67; commr. Sci. Manpower Commn., 1963-69, v.p., 1966-67; mem. reprodn. tng. rev. com. Nat. Inst. Child Health and Human Devel., 1965-68. Served with AUS, World War II; PTO. Mem. Am. Assn. Anatomists, A.A.A.S., Assn. Research in Vision and Ophthalmology, Soc. Developmental Biology (treas. 1965-68), Internat. Inst. Embryology, Am. Inst. Biol. Scis. (gov. 1964- 69), Phi Beta Kappa, Sigma Xi. Club: Cosmos (Washington). Editorial bds. Devel. Biology, 1963-66, 71—, Bio-Sci., 1963-66, Jour. Exptl. Zoology, 1964-66, 70—. Home: 8315 North Brook Lane Bethesda MD 20014 Office: Nat Insts Health Bethesda MD 20014

COULSON, JOHN ELTRINGHAM, British diplomat; b. Gosforth, Eng., Sept. 13, 1909; s. Henry John and Florence (Eltringham) C.; M.A., Cambridge U., 1931; m. Mavis Ninette Beazley, Apr. 15, 1944; childrenNevil, David. Joined British Diplomatic Service, 1932; various posts at home and abroad, including minister British embassy, Washington, 1955-57; ambassador to Sweden, 1960-63; sec. gen. Europe Free Trade Assn., Geneva, Switzerland, 1965-. Created knight comdr. Order St. Michael and St. George, 1957. Home: The Old Mill Selborne, Hants, England. Office: 9-11 Rue Varembé Geneva, Switzerland.

COULSON, JOHN SELDEN, advt. exec.; b. Chgo., Aug. 14, 1915; s. Leonard Ward and Mabel (Selden) C.; B.A., U. Chgo., 1936; M.B.A., Harvard, 1938; m. Jane Eleanor Rinder, Nov. 28, 1943; children-Jane Greer, Nancy Allen, Ann Selden, Sara Rinder. With Montgomery Ward & Co., Chgo., 1938-41, 45-48; sr. asso. Joseph White & Assos., Chgo., 1948-50; research supr. Leo Burnett Co., Inc., Chgo., 1950-55, mgr. research dept., 1955-58, v.p. charge research, 1958—; lectr. U. Chgo., 1955, Northwestern U., 1960—. Mem. citizens bd. U. Chgo., 1969—. Served to lt. comdr. USNR, 1941-45. Mem. Am. Statis. Assn. (past pres. Chgo. chpt.), Am. Marketing Assn. (past pres. Chgo chpt., nat. v.p.), Am. Assn. for Pub. Opinion Research (mem. exec. council), U. Chgo. Alumni Assn. (pres.), Psi Upsilon, Alpha Kappa Psi. Club: University (Chgo.). Editor: Jour. of Marketing, 1960—. Contbr. chpts. to On Knowing the Consumer, 1966; Marketing Handbook, 1970. Home: 625 Fair Oaks Av Oak Park IL 60302 Office: Prudential Plaza Chicago IL 60601

COULSON, ROBERT, assn. exec.; b. New Rochelle, N.Y., July 24, 1924; s. Robert Earl and Abby (Stewart) C.; B.A., Yale, 1950; LL.B., Harvard, 1953; m. Cynthia Cunningham, Oct. 12, 1960; children—Cotton Richard, Dierdre, Crocker, Robert Cromwell, Christopher. Admitted to N.Y. and Mass. bars, 1954; asso. Whitnam, Ransom & Coulson, N.Y.C., 1954-61; partner Littlefield, Miller & Cleaves, N.Y.C., 1961-63; exec. v.p. Am. Arbitration Assn., N.Y.C., 1963—. Cons. N.Y. State Div. Youth, 1961-63; pres. Youth Consultation Service of N.Y., 1970. Vice pres., dir. Police Athletic League N.Y.; dir. Fedn. Prot. Welfare Agencies. Mem. Am., N.Y. State bar assns., Assn. Bar City N.Y. (sec. 1960-62). Clubs: New York Yacht; Larchmont (N.Y.) Yacht. Author: How to Stay Out of Court, 1968. Editor: Racing at Sea, 1951. Contbr. articles profl. jours. Home: 211 Central Park W New York City NY 10024 Office: 140 W 51st St New York City NY 10020

COULSON, WAYNE, lawyer; b. Wichita, Kan., Mar. 3, 1910; s. Emmett and Josephine (Armstrong) C.; A.B., U. Wichita, 1930; pvt. study law, 1931-34; m. Frances Pattison, Oct. 12, 1940. Admitted to Kan. bar, 1934, since practiced in Wichita mem. firm Fleeson, Gooing, Coulson & Kitch. Fellow Am. Coll. Trial Lawyers, Am. Bar Found. Home: 2248 N Belmont Wichita KS 67220 Office: 1600 Wichita Plaza Wichita KS 67202

COULTER, ELLIS MERTON, educator; b. nr. Hickory, N.C., July 20, 1890; s. John Ellis and Lucy Ann (Propst) C.; student Rutherford (N.C.) Coll., 1905-09; Concordia Coll., Conover, N.C., 1909-10; A.B., U. N.C., 1913; A.M., U. Wis., 1915, Ph.D., 1917; Litt.D., Marietta Coll., 1948; LL.D. (hon.), U. N.C., 1952; regents' prof., 1948; Mem. history faculty U. Wis., Marietta Coll., 1914-19; asso. prof. history U. Ga., 1919-23, prof., 1923-58, Regents prof. emeritus, 1958—. Vis. prof., lectr., numerous colls. and univs., 1923—. Trustee, Wormsloe Found., Savannah, Ga. Democrat. Lutheran. Author numerous books since 1922, those since 1950 include: Wormsloe, 1955; Lost Generation, 1956; Auraria, 1956; Confederate States of America, 1861-65; John Ellis Coulter, Small-Town Businessman of Tarheelia, 1962; Joseph Vallence Bevan, Georgia's First Official Historian, 1964; Georgia Waters, 1965; Old Petersburg and the Broad River Valley of Georgia, 1965; Their Rise and Decline, 1965; The Toombs Oak, The Tree that Owned Itself, and other Chapters of Georgia, 1966; William Montague Browne, Versatile Anglo-Irish American, 1823-1883, 1967; also hist. articles; editor several books including The Journal of Peter Gordon, 1732-1735, 1963. Mng. editor Ga. Hist. Quarterly. Home: Athens GA 30601☆

COULTER, GLENN MONROE, lawyer; b. Syracuse, N.Y., Aug. 8, 1894; s. Fred and Florence Lucretia (Mills) C.; grad. Yates Poly. Inst., Chittenango, N.Y., 1911; A.B., U. Mich., 1916, J.D., 1920, LL.D., 1958; m. Doris McDonald, Sept. 1, 1922; children—Thomas Edward and Patricia Stoddard (twins). Admitted to Mich. bar, 1920, since practiced in Detroit; counsel Hill, Lewis Adams, Goodrich & Tait. Pres. United Community Services Met. Detroit, 1950-54; trustee Detroit YMCA; bd. dirs. United Found.; chmn. exec. com. War Chest of Detroit, 1944-46. Served to maj. U.S. Army Ambulance Service, 1917-19. Fellow Am. Bar Found. (past treas.); mem. Am. Bar Assn. (past treas.; past chmn. com. on admissions and credentials, profl. ethics, scope and correlation, past state del. of Mich.); mem. Detroit Bar Assn. (pres. 1942-43, vice chmn. legal aid bur.), Am. Judicature Soc., U.S.A.A.C. Vets. Assn. (nat. comdr. 1929-30), U. Mich. Alumni Assn. (nat. pres. 1950-52), Am. Coll. Probate Counsel (regent), Mich. Hort. Soc. (1st v.p.), Phi Beta Kappa Associates, Scribes, Phi Beta Kappa, Theta Chi (past v.p. nat. bd. trustees), Phi Delta Phi. Clubs: Paul Bunyan, Prismatic (pres. 1956-57) (Detroit). Author profl. articles. Lectr., writer stained glass and mosaics. Home: 214 Merriweather Rd Grosse Pointe Farms MI 48236 Office: Penobscot Bldg Detroit MI 48226

COULTER, KIRKLEY SCHLEY, govt. ofcl.; b. Nashville, July 26, 1914; s. John L. and Phoebe E. (Frost) C.; B.A., Am. U., 1935, postgrad., 1935-37, 60-62, M.A., 1963; postgrad. U. Wis., 1936, Columbia, 1940- 41; m. Irene Maria B. Prazmowski, Aug. 16, 1945; 1 step-dau., Barbara M. Mem. staff Senator Hugh Butler, Neb., 1941-42, 46-47, adminstrv. asst., legislative asst., 1947-53; chief clk., staff dir. Senate Com. on Interior and Insular Affairs, 1953-54; asst. to undersec. interior, 1954- 55; asst. dir. Office Territories, Dept. Interior, 1955, dep. dir., 1955- 57, legislative adviser, 1957-60; chief div. internat. comml. relations U.S. Tariff Commn., Washington, 1960-62; minority economist antitrust and monopoly subcom. U.S. Senate Judiciary Committee, 1963—. Joint founder, joint co-chmn. Arlingtonians for a Better County, 1955. Chmn. Republican exec. com. Arlington County, 1954. Served 1st lt. AUS, 1942-46. Mem. Am. Econ. Assn., Omicron Delta Kappa, Pi Gamma Mu, Alpha Tau Omega. Episcopalian. Home: 6300 Lakeview Dr Falls Church VA 22041 Office: U S Senate Washington DC 20510

COULTER, LELAND EVERETT, mgmt. cons.; b. Apollo, Pa., June 2, 1913; s. George T. and Grace (Rupert) C.; B.S. in Mech. Engring., U. Mich., 1935; m. Ruth K. Jamison, Apr. 18, 1936; 1 son, Leland Everett. With Allied Products Corp., Detroit, 1936-62, v.p., 1954-58, pres., 1958-62; exec. v.p. Veeder-Root, Inc., Hartford, Conn., 1962-64; v.p. mfg. SCM Corp., mfrs. office machines, N.Y.C., 1964-66; mgmt. cons. Consol. Cons., 1966—. Served from 2d lt. to lt. col., USAAF, World War II. Decorated Bronze Star medal. Mem.

Am. Soc. Tool Engrs., Am. Ordnance Assn. Club: Detroit. Home: 153 Oenoke Lane New Canaan CT 06840 Office: 10 E Maple St New Canaan CT 06840

COULTER, LOWELL VERNON, educator; b. Marion, O., July 3, 1913; s. Emer Vernon and Nettie Florence (Ault) C. B.S., Heidelberg Coll., 1935; M.A., Colo. Coll., 1937; Ph.D., U. Cal. at Berkeley, 1940; m. Leona Newcomb, June 6, 1937; children—Michael, Andrea. Instr. chemistry Colo. Coll., 1935-37; teaching asst. chemistry U. Cal. at Berkeley, 1937-40; instr. chemistry U. Ida., 1940-42, Boston U., 1942-43; group leader Manhattan Project, Monsanto Chem. Co., Dayton, O., 1943-45; faculty Boston U., 1945—, now prof. chemistry, also chmn. Fellow A.A.A.S.; mem. Am. Chem. Soc., Am. Assn. U. Profs., Am. Phys. Soc., Unitarian Assn., Sigma Xi. Home: 244 Prince St West Newton MA 02165 Office: Boston U 675 Commonwealth Av Boston MA 02215

COULTER, NORMAN ARTHUR, Jr., educator; b. Atlanta, Jan. 9, 1920, s. Norman Arthur and Carabelle (Clark) C.; B.S., Va. Poly. Inst., 1941; M.D., Harvard, 1950; postgrad. fellow Johns Hopkins, 1950-52; m. Elizabeth Harwell Jackson, June 23, 1951; 1 son, Robert Jackson. Instr. math. dept. Va. Poly. Inst., 1946; asst. to asso. prof. physiology dept. Ohio State U., 1952-65; dir. biophysics div., physiology dept., 1962-65; asso. prof. depts. surgery and physiology U. N.C., Chapel Hill, 1965—, prof., 1967—, dir. bioengring.-biomath. tng. program, 1969—. Served to maj., A.A.A., AUS, 1941-46. Mem. Biophys. Soc., Am. Physiol. Soc., A.A.A.S., Biomed. Engring. Soc., Soc. Neurosci., I.E.E.E., Soc. Gen. Systems Research, Synergetic Soc., Assn. Computing Machinery, Sigma Xi. Contbr. articles profl. jours. Home: 1825 N Lake Shore Dr Chapel Hill NC 27514

COULTER, ROGER BROOKE, lawyer; b. Balt., July 21, 1897; s. Robert Ogilvie and Emilie Thomas (Brooke) C.; B.A., Williams Coll., 1918; LL.B., Harvard, 1922; m. Rosamond Bartlett, May 23, 1925; children—Marion Bartlett (Mrs. Philip N. Bowditch), Robert Ogilvie. Admitted to Mass. bar, 1922; also. Sawyer, Hardy, Stone & Morrison (became Parker, Coulter, Daley & White, 1948), Boston, 1922-33, partner, 1933—. Sec., dir. Brunswick Worsted Mills 1930—; dir. Pilgrim Coop. Bank. Adv. bd. town Cohasset (MA), 1938-42, chmn. bd. appeals, 1955—. Trustee Gov. Dummer Acad. Served with USMC, 1918-19, from capt. to maj., 1943-46. Fellow Am. Coll. Trial Lawyers; mem. Am., Mass. (chmn. joint com. jud. selection), Boston (council 1948-51, 57, 60, chmn. joint com. jud. selection) bar assns. Democrat. Unitarian. Home: 67 N Main St Cohassett MA 02025 Office: 50 Congress St Boston MA 02109

COULTER, SAMUEL TODD, educator; b. Weiser, Ida., Sept. 15, 1903; s. Robert O. and Annie (Jeffries) C.; B.S., Ore. State U. 1925; M.S., U. Minn., 1930, Ph.D., 1933; m. Margaret Robinson, Apr. 28, 1928; children—Nancy Ann (Mrs. Alf LeCaptain), Priscilla Jane (Mrs. Donald Witzel), Joan Elizabeth (Mrs. Chapman Stockford). Mem. faculty U. Minn., 1925-28, 30—, prof. dairy husbandry, 1945-59, prof., head dept. dairy industries, 1959-66, prof., head dept. food sci. and industries, 1966—; mgr. Minn. Expt. Sta., Albert Lea, 1928-30. Vice pres. Maple Island, Inc., Stillwater, Minn., 1954-59. Cons., 1959-65. Cons. research and devel. lab. Q.M. Corps, 1944- 48; mem. liaison and sci. adv. bd. Q.M. Food and Container for Armed Forces, 1948; mem. adv. bd. quartermaster research and devel., com. foods, Nat. Acad. Scis.-NRC, 1953-54, chmn. subcom. ad hoc study conf. whole milk powder, 1953-54; adv. FAO, 1954; del. Internat. Dairy Fedn. Seminar Handling Milk in Warm Countries, Amalfi, 1954; chmn. symposium dry milk products, com. on foods, Adv. Bd. Q.M. Research and Devel., 1955; vice chmn. sect. 3, mem. ofcl. U.S. delegation 15th Internat. Dairy Congress, London, 1959; chmn. session 18th Internat. Dairy Congress, Sydney, Australia, 1970; sec. Minn. Dairy Industry Com., 1959-71; mem. Gov. Minn. Adv. Com. Milk Industry with Relation to Iodine 131, 1962-63; mem. Gov.'s Adv. Com. Dairy Research and Marketing; speaker FAO World Conf. Dairy Edn., 1964. Fellow A.A.A.S.; mem. Am. Dairy Sci. Assn. (bd. dirs. 1960-65, v.p. 1962-63, pres. 1963-64; Borden award dairy mfg. 1951), Inst. Food Technologists (dir. Minn. sect. 1966—), Sigma Xi, Alpha Zeta, Gamma Sigma Delta. Rotarian, Elk. Author book chpt., papers, reports in field. Home: Marine on St Croix MN 55047 Office: Dept Food Sci and Industries U Minn St Paul MN 55101

COULTER, THOMAS HENRY, assn. exec.; b. Winnipeg, Can., Apr. 21, 1911; s. David and Sarah Anne (Allen) C.; B.S., Carnegie Inst. Tech., 1933; M.A., U. Chgo., 1935; m. Mary Alice Leach, Nov. 24, 1937; children—Sara, Anne, Jane, Thomas II. Investment analyst Shaw & Co., Chgo., 1935-36; sales engr. Universal Zonolite Insulation Co., Chgo., 1936-39, sales promotion mgr., 1939-40, gen. sales mgr., 1940-41, v.p., 1941-45; mgr. devel. div. Booz, Allen & Hamilton, Chgo., 1945-48, partner, 1948-50; pres. Am. Bildrok Co. 1950-54; chief exec. officer Chgo. Assn. Commerce and Industry, 1954—, pub. Commerce mag.; lectr. marketing, exec. program U. Chgo. Mem. State Dept.'s Top Mgmt. Seminar Team, Israel, 1956, Japan, 1958. Dir. Chgo. Crime Commn.; dir. Chgo. chpt. A.R.C. 1953-59; mem. City of Chgo. Com. on Criminal Justice. Mem. citizens bd., council Sch. Bus. Assn.; gov. Internat. House of U. Chgo.; mem. citizens com. U. Ill.; mem. exec. council Chgo. Civil Def. Corps; mem. Regional Export Expansion Council. Bd. dirs. Family Financial Counseling Service Greater Chgo., Better Bus. Bur. Met. Chgo.; adv. bd. Greater Chgo. Safety Council; trustee Skokie Valley Community Hosp., pres. 1955-57, 66-70; dir. Hosp. Planning Council of Met. Chgo.; mem. City Chgo. Home Rule Commn.; mem. Northwestern U. Assos.; trustee Village of Golf, Ill., 1951-55. Decorated comdr.'s Cross Order of Merit (Germany), Knight Order of Merit (Italy); recipient Silver anniversary all-Am. award Sports Illustrated, 1957, Outstanding Civilian Service medal U.S. Army, 1961, Gold Badge of Honor for Merits (Austria), 1962; Citation pub. service U. Chgo.; Alumni merit award for outstanding profl. achievement, Carnegie Inst. Tech.; Knight First Class Order Lion (Finland), 1964; Knight Royal Order Vasa (Sweden), 1965. Mem. Nat. Sales Execs., Newcomen Society in North Am., Nat. Planning Assn., Lambda Alpha. Clubs: Mid-America; Commercial, Executives (pres. 1950-51), Sales Marketing Executives (pres. 1953-54), Canadian, University, Economic (Chgo.); Glenview (Golf, Ill.). Home: 58 Overlook Drive Golf IL 60029 Office: 130 S Michigan Av Chicago IL 60603

COULTHARD, GEORGE WILLIAM, lawyer; b. Modale, Ia., May 21, 1916; s. David Lloyd and Ruth (Mintun) C.; B.S.C., Creighton U., 1937; J.D., U. Ia., 1939; m. Lena Silvagni, Aug. 8, 1942 (dec. 1955); 1 dau., Karen Jane; m. 2d, Diane Crandall, Sept. 5, 1957; children—Leslie, William, James. Admitted to Ia. bar, 1939, Nev. bar, 1945; spl. agt. FBI, 1939-45; pvt. practice, Las Vegas, 1946—. Mem. Nev. Bd. Bar Examiners, 1948-51, Legislative Counsel Bur., Nev. Legislature, 1951-54. Vice pres., dir. Las Vegas Valley Water Dist., 1950-57; active Boys Club Clark County. Mem. Nev. Legislature from Clark County, 1951-54. Mem. State Bar Nev. (pres. 1964), Am., Ia., Clark County (pres. 1952) bar assns., Las Vegas C. of C. (dir. 1965-67), Gamma Eta Gamma. Elk. Home: 601 Rancho Circle Las Vegas, CA 89107. Office: Bank of Nevada Bldg 225 E Bridger St Las Vegas NV 89101

COULTRAP, JAMES WILL, printing equipment mfg.; b. Elgin, Ill., Nov. 3, 1910; s. Harry Mansfield and Anna (Will) C.; A.B., Ohio Wesleyan U., 1932, LL.D., 1964; J.D., U. Mich., 1935; m. Virginia Lees, June 19, 1937; children—Ginna, Barbara, James. Admitted to Ill. bar, 1935; with Sidley, Austin, Burgess - Smith, Chgo., 1935-41; with Miehle Printing Press & Mfg. Co. (now MGD Graphic Systems, Inc.), Chgo., 1941-70, sec., 1943-62, asst. treas., 1943-55, v.p., 1955-59. exec. v.p., 1959-62, dir., 1959-70, pres., chief exec. officer, 1962-68, chmn., 1968-70; staff v.p. comml. products group N.Am. Rockwell Corp., Chgo., 1970—, also dir.; dir. Interlake Inc., Nalco Chem. Co., Sci. Research Assos. Trustee, Village of Hinsdale (Ill.), 1957-61, pres., 1961-65. Trustee, Ill. Inst. Tech., Com. for Econ. Devel. Mem. Am., Ill., Chgo. bar assns., Chgo. Assn. Commerce and Industry (dir.), Newcomen Soc., Order of Coif, Phi Beta Kappa, Phi Delta Theta, Phi Delta Phi, Omicron Delta Kappa. Republican. Presbyn. Clubs: Legal, Economic (pres. 1964-66, dir.), Law, Chicago, Mid-America (Chgo.); Hinsdale Golf (pres. 1969). Home: 112 N Madison St Hinsdale IL 60521

COUNCIL, S. ANTHONY, banker. Sr. v.p. Fulton Nat. Bank of Atlanta. Office: Marietta and Forsyth Sts Atlanta GA 30302*

COUNSELMAN, THEODORE BENTON, mining cons.; b. N.Y.C., Dec. 10, 1889; s. Thomas Hart Benton and Jessie D'Ella (Peebles) C.; E.M., Columbia, 1910; m. Eleanore Crabbe Eayres-Gardner, June 10, 1914; children—Theodore Benton, Edward Gardner, Revere G., Eleanor R. (Mrs. Carl Oxholm, Jr.). With Inspiration Copper Co., 1911-12, Cananea Consol. Copper Co., 1912-13, 15, Ariz. Copper Co., 1912-15, Miami Copper Co., 1915-16, Mesabi Iron Co., 1916-23; sales engr., 1924-27; with Dorr Co., 1928-55; partner, sec.-treas., v.p., dir. Behre Dolbear & Co., Inc., sr. cons., 1968—. Recipient Egleston medal Columbia, 1966, Robert H. Richards award Am. Inst. Mining Engrs., 1967. Mem. Am. Inst. Mining, Metal and Petroleum Engrs. (v.p. 1953-57, dir. 1952-57, exec. com. 1954-57), Mining and Metall. Soc. Am. (council 1960-61), Engrs. Joint Council (dir. 1955-61, exec. com. 1956-61), Columbia Alumni Fedn. (dir. 1961-62), Delta Tau Delta. Republican. Episcopalian. Mason (Shriner). Clubs: Mining (gov. 1962-64, v.p. 1963), Columbia University (N.Y.C.); Shinnecock Yacht, Quogue (N.Y.). Contbr. articles to profl. jours. Inventor various ore dressing, roasting furnaces, synthetic rubber processing machines. Home: Hotel Gramatan Bronxville NY 10708 Office: 11 Broadway New York City NY 10004

COUNTRYMAN, DAYTON WENDELL, lawyer; b. Sioux City, Ia., Mar. 31, 1918; s. Cleveland and Susie (Schaeffer) C.; B.S., Ia. State Coll., 1940; LL.B., State U. Ia., 1948, J.D., 1969; m. Ruth Hazen, Feb. 2, 1941; children—Karen, Joan, James, Kay. Admitted to Ia. bar, 1948, since practiced in Nevada; partner Hadley & Countryman, Nevada, Ia., 1949-64; county atty., Story County (Ia.), 1950- 54; atty. gen. Iowa, 1954-56. Candidate for U.S. Senate, 1956, 1960. Air Force Res. pilot, USAAF, 1941-46. Mem. V.F.W., Am. Judicature Soc., Am. Legion, Ia. State U. Alumni Assn. (pres. 1970-71), Am., Ia., Story County bar assns., Ia. 11th Jud. Dist. Assn. Methodist. Mason, Elk, Lion. Home: Route 1 Nevada IA 50201 Office: 505 J Av Nevada IA 50201

COUNTRYMAN, J. E., food processor; b. Lindenwood, Ill., Jan. 4, 1903; s. Floyd M. and Marian (Pullin) C.; student Cornell Coll., U. Ill.; m. Bernice Smith, Sept. 15, 1924; children—Jacquelyn (Mrs. Allan C. Hoganson), James. Dir., Del Monte Corp., San Francisco, Wells Fargo Co., Wells Fargo Internat., Wells Fargo Bank, Transam. Corp., Planning Research Corp., Dillingham Corp. Mem. U. Ill. Found.; mem. adv. council Sch. Bus. Adminstrn., U. Santa Clara. Trustee Cal. Council for Econ. Edn.; bd. dirs. No. Cal. Industry-Edn. Council; bd. regents U. of Pacific. Mason (Shriner). Clubs: St. Francis Yacht, San Francisco Golf; Marin Golf and Country; Bohemian; Pacific Union. Home: 1100 Sacramento St San Francisco CA 94108 Office: 215 Fremont St San Francisco CA 94119

COUNTRYMAN, VERN, educator; b. Roundup, Mont., May 13, 1917; s. Alexander and Carrie (Harriman) C.; B.A., U. Wash., 1939, LL.B., 1942; student Yale Law Sch., 1947-48; m. Vera Pound, Nov. 9, 1940; children—Kay, Debra. Admitted to Wash. State bar, 1942. Md. bar, 1955, D.C. bar, 1956. Mass. bar, 1965; law clk. to Justice William O. Douglas, 1942- 43; asst. atty. general Wash. State, 1946; instr. U. Wash. Sch. Law, 1946-47; asst., then asso. prof. law Yale Law Sch., 1948-55; practice law with firm Shea, Greenman & Gardner, Washington, 1955-59; dean U. N.M. Sch. Law, 1959-64; prof. law Harvard, 1964—. Served with USAAF, 1943-46. Mem. Am. Bar Assn., Order of Coif, Phi Beta Kappa. Home: 98 Adams St Lexington MA 02173

COUNTS, GEORGE SYLVESTER, author; b. nr. Baldwin City, Kan., Dec. 9, 1889; s. James Wilson and Mertie Florella (Gamble) C.; A.B., Baker U., Kan., 1911; Ph.D., U. Chgo., 1916; LL.D., Baker U., Kan., 1935; D.H.L., So. Ill. U., 1971; m. Lois Hazel Bailey, Sept. 24, 1913; children—Esther Mae, Martha Louise, Head dept. of edn. and dir. summer sch., Delaware Coll., Newark, 1916-18; prof. ednl. sociology, Harris Tchrs. Coll., St. Louis, Mo., 1918-19; prof. secondary edn., U. of Wash., 1919-20; asso. prof. Yale, 1920-24, prof., 1924-26; prof. of edn., U. Chgo, 1926-27; asso. dir. Internat. Inst., 1927-32; prof. of edn., Tchrs. Coll., Columbia, 1927- 56, prof. emeritus, 1956—; vis. prof. U. Pitts., 1959, Mich. State U., 1960, So. Ill. U., Carbondale, 1962—; Horace Mann lectr., 1962; dir. div. founds. edn., 1942-48. Editor of The Social Frontier, 1934-37; mem. Ednl. Policies Commn. of N.E.A., 1936-42. Pres. Am. Fedn. Tchrs., 1939-42; mem. exec. com. of Nat. Com. on Edn. and Def., 1940-42, Nat. Com. Civil Liberties Union, 1940—; mem. Commn. on Motion Pictures in Edn., 1944-48; N.Y. State chmn. Am. Labor Party, 1942-44; N.Y. chmn. Liberal Party, 1955-59. Mem. U.S. Ednl. Mission to Japan, 1946; mem. com. on Internat. Exchange of Persons, 1948-50. Recipient Annual Educator's award B'nai B'rith, 1953; Tchrs. Coll. medal for distinguished service, 1954; award for distinguished service in sch. adminstrn. Am. Assn. Sch. Adminstrs., 1968, Phi Delta Kappa award, 1967, John Dewey Soc. award, 1967. Mem. Nat. Acad. Edn., Soc. Coll. Tchrs. Edn., Nat. Edn. Assn., Am. Assn. U. Profs., P.E.N. Club: Delta Tau Delta, Phi Delta Kappa, Kappa Delta Pi Author: sixteen books, 1917-42; Education and the Promise of America (Kappa Delta Pi lecture), 1945. Co- translator of New Russia's Primer (M. Ilin), 1931; I Want to Be Like Stalin, 1947; The Country of the BlindThe Soviet System of Mind Control (with N. Lodge), 1949; American Education through the Soviet Looking Glass, 1951; Education and American Civilization, 1952; Decision-Making and American Values in School Administration, 1954; The Challenge of Soviet Education $5,000 Liberty and Justice award A.L.A., 1958), 1957; Khrushchev and the Central Committee Speak on Education, 1959; Education and the Foundations of Human Freedom, 1962; Education and American Freedom in The Age of Technology, 1958. Home: 901 Glenview Dr Carbondale IL 62901

COUNTS, JAMES CURTIS, govt. ofcl.; b. Goldfield, Colo., Aug. 2, 1915; s. James Henry and Georgine (Niesley) C.; A.B. in Polit. Sci., U. Cal. at Los Angeles, 1937; postgrad. U. So. Cal., 1937-39, Southwestern Law Sch., 1939-41; m. Virginia Lee Shugart, Oct. 10, 1940; children—Carol Lee (Mrs. Howard L. Hooper), Janis Lee (Mrs. Jon P. Swanson), Jay Curtis. With Douglas Aircraft Co., Inc., 1941-69, dir. employee relations, 1962-64, v.p. employee relations, 1964-69. Mem. Nat. Labor Mgmt. Panel, 1963-68, Pacific Coast Regional Manpower Adv. Com., 1964-68; pub. mem. Constrn. Industry Collective Bargaining Commn., 1969—; dir. Fed. Mediation and Conciliation Service, 1969—. Mem. Citizens Adv. Council on Status of Women, 1967-69. Chmn. bd. mgrs. Los Angeles YMCA, 1947—; bd. dirs. U. Cal. at Los Angeles Alumni Bd., 1962-64; bd. dirs. Santa Monica chpt. Nat. Conf. Christians and Jews, 1965—. Named one of 5 outstanding young men Cal. Jr. C. of C., 1951. Mem. Westwood (Cal.) Jr. C. of C. (pres. 1950-51), Blue Key, Zeta Psi. Presbyn. (trustee). Home: 3105 Haddington Dr Los Angeles CA 90064 Office: Fed Mediation and Conciliation Service Washington DC 20427

COUPAL, JOSEPH RICHARD, Jr., state ofcl.; b. Kingston, N.H., Feb. 28, 1923; s. Joseph R. and Esther (Langlais) C.; B.A., Harvard, 1948; M.A., U. N.H., 1950; m. Ruth E. Duston, July 10, 1943; children—Deborah Ann, Carol Beth, Jennifer Duston, Jonathan Mark. Town mgr., Bethlehem, N.H., 1949-50; asst. city mgr., Concord, N.H., 1950-51; town mgr., Ipswich, Mass., 1951-54; city mgr., Bangor, Me., 1954-66; dir. Ia. Hwy. Commn., Ames, 1966—. Vice chmn. Me. Intergovtl. Relations Commn., 1965-66. Bd. dirs. Bangor-Brewer Community Chest, 1956-58. Served to capt. USAAF, 1942-46. Mem. Internat. City Mgrs. Assn. (pres. 1965-66), Mississippi Valley Assn. State Hwy. Ofcls. (pres. 1969), Me. Municipal Assn. (pres. 1960- 61). Conglist. (bd. dirs. 1956-59, chmn. 1959, moderator, 1961, 63, bd. deacons 1961-66). Rotarian. Home: Meadow Glen Rd Ames IA 50010 Office: Ia Hwy Commn Ames IA 50010

COUPE, JOHN DONALD, educator; b. Holyoke, Mass., Aug. 29, 1931; s. Alfred and Erna (Hohenberger) C.; B.S., Worcester Poly. Inst., 1953; M.A., Clark U., 1957, Ph.D., 1960; m. V. Sylvia Kajander, Aug. 23, 1958; children—Jeffrey A., Stephen R., Cynthia E. Instr., U. Me., Orono, 1958-61, asst. prof., 1962-66, prof. econs., chmn. dept., 1966—; prof. econs. Kent State U., 1961-62; cons. Casco Bank & Trust Co., 1966-68, State Credit Research Com., 1964, 69. Chmn. Me. Manpower Adv. Com.; mem. Woodlands Taxation Study Com., 1970; mem. Me. Adv. Council on Vocational Edn. Served with U.S. Army, 1953-55. Mem. Am. Econ. Assn., Econometric Soc., Am. Assn. U. Profs., Phi Kappa Phi. Author: (with A. Raphaelson and T. Siedlik) A Study of the Vacation Industry in Maine, 1961; (with David Clark) The Bangor Area Economy: Its Present and Future, 1967. Home: 100 Forest Av Orono ME 04473

COUPER, EDGAR WILLIAMS, former banker; b. Boonville, N.Y., Feb. 14, 1899; s. Walter T. and Ruth D. (Williams) C.; A.B., Hamilton Coll., 1920, LL.D., 1953; L.H.D., Manhattan Coll., 1962; LL.D., Hofstra U., 1963, L.I.U., 1964, Hartwick Coll., 1965, Columbia, 1968; Litt.D., Elmira Coll., 1967; LL.D., Colgate U., 1969; m. Esther H. Watrous, Sept. 24, 1921; children—Richard W., Katharine (Mrs. J. B. Watrous, Jr.). Ofcl. Couper-Ackerman-Sampson, Inc., and predecessor firm, 1920-53; pres., dir. First Nat. Bank of Binghamton (N.Y.), 1954-55, pres., dir. First-City Nat. Bank of Binghamton, 1955-64, chmn. bd. dirs., 1964-70, dir. emeritus, 1970—; dir. Security Mut. Life Ins. Co., N.Y. State Electric & Gas Corp. Recipient Alfred E. Smith award N.Y. State Tchrs. Assn., 1962. Bd. regents N.Y. State Edn. Dept., 1951-68, vice chancellor, 1957-61, chancellor, 1961-68; trustee Hamilton Coll., 1957-61, 68—. Home: 186 Riverside Dr Binghamton NY 13905

COUPER, RICHARD WATROUS, library ofcl.; b. Binghamton, N.Y., Dec. 16, 1922; s. Edgar W. and Esther (Watrous) C.; A.B., Hamilton Coll., Clinton, N.Y., 1944; A.M. in Am. History, Harvard, 1948; m. Patricia Pogue, Sept. 24, 1946; children—Frederick Pogue, Barrett Williams, Thomas Hayes, Margaret Channing. With Couper-Ackerman-Sampson, Inc., and predecessor, Binghamton, 1948-62, treas., 1957-60, dir., 1957-63, v.p., 1960-63; adminstrv. v.p. Hamilton Coll., 1962-65, v.p., 1965-66, acting pres., 1966-68, v.p., provost, 1968-69, charter trustee, 1967-69; dep. commr. higher edn. N.Y. State Edn. Dept., 1969-71; pres., chief exec. officer N.Y. Pub. Library, N.Y.C., 1971—, also trustee. Dir. Security Mut. Life Ins. Co., Binghamton. Trustee, Link Found., Hamilton Coll., bd. dirs. State Communities Aid Assn., N.Y.C. Served to capt. AUS, 1942-46. Named Outstanding Young Man of Year, Binghamton Jr. C. of C., 1952. Mem. Orgn. Am. Historians, Am., N.Y. State Hist. assns., Phi Beta Kappa. Clubs: Harvard (N.Y.C.); Sadaquada Golf, Ft. Schuyler (Utica, N.Y.); Ft. Orange (Albany). Home: 110 Marcourt Dr Chappaqua NY 10514 Office: NY Pub Library 42d and Fifth Avs New York City NY 10018

COUPLAND, DON, former air force officer; b. Warsaw, Ind., July 11, 1915; s. Alfred Augustus and Abbie (Bennett) C.; B.S. in Aero. Engring., Purdue U., 1936; grad. Advanced Flying Sch., 1938, Mil. Officer Tng. Sch., 1940, USAAF Engring. Sch., 1941, USAAF Inst. Tech., 1947, Air War Coll., 1951; m. Jean Barringer, Dec. 27, 1941 (dec. Nov. 1969); children—Gail B. (Mrs. Lynn E. Wardley), Jack B., Judy B.; m. 2d, Maxine Evans. Commd. 2d lt. F.A. Res., 1936, apptd. aviation cadet, 1937, advanced through grades to maj. gen. USAF, 1957; airplane comdr., engring. officer 35th Pursuit Squadron, 1938-39; procurement and prodn. project officer USAAF Material Div., 1939-42, chief engine sect., maintenance div., 1942-44; officer-in-charge operational engring. Hdqrs. 20th Air Force, Guam, 1944-45; exec. to dep. comdr.engring Air Tech. Services Command, 1945-46; chief prodn. planning office, Directoriate Procurement and Indsl. Planning, 1947-50; asst. chief staff supply, also dep. comdr. Air Material Forces, Europe, 1951-54; asst. dir., then dir. material programs, dep. chief staff/materials Hdqrs. USAF, 1954-58; 1st dep. comdr. ballistic missiles, then dep. comdr. San Bernardino Air Material Area, Norton AFB, Cal., 1958-60; comdr. ballistic missiles center Air Material Command, Los Angeles, 1960-61; vice comdr. ballistic systems div. Air Force Systems Command, Los Angeles, 1961; comdr. Ogden Air Material Area, Air Force Logistics Command. Hill AFB, Utah, 1961-64; auditor gen. U.S. Air Force, Washington, 1964-67, ret.; pres. NGS, Inc., 1967—. Decorated Legion of Merit with four oak leaf clusters. Mem. Order Daedalians, Am. Inst. Aero. and Astronautics, Air Force Assn. (hon. life), Nat. Rifle Assn., Air Force Acad. Athletic Assn. (life charter), Nat. Def. Transp. Assn., Am. Ordnance Assn., Ogden C. of C. Clubs: Ogden Golf and Country, Weber (Ogden); AFB Golf, AFB Rod and Gun, Administrative (Hill AFB); Arrowhead Country. Home: 3705 Hemlock Dr San Bernardino CA 92404 Office: 3452 Del Rosa Av San Bernardino CA 92404

COURANT, ERNEST DAVID, educator, physicist; b. Goettingen, Germany, Mar. 26, 1920; s. Richard and Nina (Runge) C.; came to U.S., 1934, naturalized, 1940; grad. Fieldston Sch., N.Y.C., 1936; B.A., Swarthmore Coll., 1940; M.S., U. Rochester, 1942, Ph.D., 1943; M.A. (hon.), Yale, 1962; m. Sara Paul, Dec. 9, 1944; children—Paul N., Carl R. Scientist, Atomic Energy Project, Montreal, Que., Can., 1943-46; research asso. physics Cornell U., 1946-48; mem. staff Brookhaven Nat. Lab., 1947—, sr. physicist, 1960—; Brookhaven prof. physics Yale, 1962-67, vis. prof., 1961-62; prof. physics and engring. State U. N.Y. at Stony Brook, 1967—; vis. asst. prof. Princeton, 1950-51; cons. Gen. Atomic div. Gen. Dynamics Corp., 1958-59; vis. physicist Nat. Accelerator Lab., 1968-69. Fulbright research fellow Cambridge (Eng.) U., 1956. Fellow Am. Phys. Soc.; mem. A.A.A.S. Co-originator strong-focusing particle accelerators. Home: 109 Bay Av Bayport, NY 11705.

COURNAND, ANDRE F., physiologist; b. Paris, France, Sept. 24, 1895; s. Jules and Marguerite (Weber) C.; B.A., Sorbonne U., Paris, 1913, P.C.B. in Sci., 1914; M.D., U. Paris, 1930; Dr. h.c., U. Strasbourg, 1957, U. Lyon, 1958, U. Brussels, 1959, U. Pisa, 1960, Columbia U., 1965, U. Brazil, 1965, U. Nancy, 1969; D.Sc., U. Birmingham, 1961; Gustavus Adolphus Coll., 1963; m. Sibylle Blumer (dec. 1959); children—Muriel, Marie-Eve, Marie Claire; m. 2d, Ruth Fabian, 1963. Came to U.S. 1930, naturalized 1941. Prof. emeritus medicine Coll. Phys. & Surg., Columbia. Served with French Army, 1915-19. Decorated Croix de Guerre (France); recipient Laureate (silver medal), faculty medicine U. Paris; Andrea Retzius silver medal Swedish Soc. Internal Medicine; Lasker award USPHS; winner (with Dr. Dickinson W. Richards and Dr. Werner Forssman) of 1956 Nobel Prize in medicine and physiology; recipient Jiminez Diaz prize, 1970. Fellow Royal Soc. Medicine; member Nat. Academy Scis. U.S.A., de l'Academie Nationale de Medecine (France), Academie Royal de Medecine de Belgique, Am. Physiol. Soc., Assn. Am. Physicians, Brit. Cardiac Soc., Swedish Soc., Internal Medicine, Soc. Medicale Hopitaux de Paris, Academie des Sciences, Institut de France (fgn. mem.). Clubs: Century Assn., Am. Alpine. Home: 1361 Madison Av New York City NY 10028

COURREGES, ANDRE, fashion designer; b. Pau, Basses-Pyrenées, Mar. 9, 1923; s. Lucien and Celine (Coupe) C.; civil engring. and constrn. degree Ecole des Travaux Pubs. et du Btiment; m. Jacqueline Barrière, Sept. 17, 1966. Couturier with Balenciaga, 1950-60; mgr. Société André Courrèges Co., 1961- 66, pres., gen. mgr., 1966—; mgr. Courrèges-Parfums, 1966—. Club: Racing (France). Address: 40 rue Francois Paris 8 France

COURRIER, ROBERT, endocrinologist; b. Saxon-Sion, France, Oct. 6, 1895; s. Jules and Elmire (Anthoine) C.; M.D., U. Strasbourg, 1923, D.Sc., 1926; Dr. (hon.), univs. Brazil, Que., Istanbul, Louvain, Brussels, Geneva (Switzerland), Athens (Greece); m. Juliette Desmots, 1923; 2 daus. Asst. faculty medicine U. Strasbourg, 1920; profl. faculty medicine U. Algiers, 1928; prof. Coll. of France, Paris, 1938—. Fellow Royal Soc. London; mem. Acad. Sci. (perpetual sec. 1948). Author: The Endocrinology of Gestation, 1945. Home: Acad Scis 3 rue Mazarine Paris 6 France Office: College of France Paris 5 France

COURSHON, ARTHUR HOWARD, lawyer, savs. and loan exec., banker; b. Chgo., Feb. 21, 1921; s. Aaron H. and Beatrice (Pollak) C.; B.A., U. Fla., 1942; J.D., U. Miami (Fla.), 1947; m. Carol Biel, Feb. 20, 1943; children—Barbara (Mrs. Michael A. Mills), Deanne. Admitted to Fla. bar, 1947; partner firm Courshon & Courshon, Miami Beach, 1948—; organizer, chmn. bd. Washington Fed. Savs. and Loan Assn., Miami Beach, 1952—; trustee, treas., organizer First Mortgage Investors, Miami Beach, 1961—; organizer, chmn. bd., gen. counsel Jefferson Nat. Bank Miami Beach, 1964—; chmn. bd. Jefferson Nat. Bank Sunny Isles. Cons. savs. & loan system ICA, Chile, 1958—, housing finance com., 1960—; cons. housing loans to Latin Am., 1960-, Devel. Loan Fund, Inter-Am. Devel. Bank, 1961—; cons. govt. Peru, 1960—; mem. U.S. govt. task force Fed. Home Loan Bank, 1961-62, mem. Fed. Savs. and Loan Adv. Council, 1969; housing finance cons. Latin Am. Affairs Subcom., Senate Fgn. Relations Com., 1960-69; housing finance com. U.S. Operations Mission, Santiago, Chile, 1958-69, mem. housing and urban devel. adv. com. AID, 1965-68; pub. mem. Adminstrv. Conf. of U.S., 1968—; bd. dirs. S. Fla. Housing Found., 1970—. Mem. Miami Beach Planning Com., 1949-51, Met. Dade County Urban Renewal Agy., 1963-67. Fla. State chmn. Kennedy Meml. Library; mem. nat. bd. devel. Sam Rayburn Found., nat. council Eleanor Roosevelt Meml. Found. Served with USAAF, 1942-46. Recipient citation for establishment savs. and loan system in Chile, ICA, 1960; Housing and Home Finance Agy., 1961. Mem. Am., Dade County bar assns., Fla. Bar (banking liaison com.), U.S. Savs. and Loan Inst., Nat. League Insured Savs. Assns. (pres. 1969—), C. of C. of U.S., Inter-Am. Bar Assn. (sr.), U.S. Savs. and Loan League (atty.'s com.), Internat. Union Bldg. Socs. and Savs. Assn. (mem. council), Am. Legion, Miami Beach C. of C., Nu Beta Epsilon, Pi Lambda Phi. Democrat. Jewish religion. Home: 5970 N Bay Rd Miami Beach FL 33140 Office: 1701 Meridian Av Miami Beach FL 33139

COURSHON, JACK ROBERT, lawyer, banker, mortgage financier; b. Evanston, Ill., Oct. 6, 1924; s. Aaron H. and Beatrice (Pollak) C.; student U. Fla., 1941-43; J.D., U. Miami, 1948; m. Dolores Bloom, Mar. 10, 1946; children—Denise Lavan, William, Bonnie, Alison. Admitted to Fla. bar, 1948; partner firm Courshon & Courshon, 1948—; co-founder, dir. Washington Fed. Savs. & Loan Assn., Miami Beach, 1952—; organizer, mng. trustee, sec. First Mortgage Investors, Boston, 1961—; organizer, chmn. bd. First Mortgage Adv. Corp., Miami Beach, 1961—; co-founder, dir. Jefferson Nat. Bank of Miami Beach, 1963—; organizer, chmn. bd. First Realty Investment Corp., Miami Beach, 1968—; organizer, chmn. bd. trustees, mng. trustee Median Mortgage Investors, Boston, 1970—; organizer, chmn. bd. Median Mortgage Adv. Corp., Miami Beach, 1970—; co-chmn., vice chmn. bd. Jefferson Bancorp., Inc., 1970—. Bd. govs. Nat. Assn. Real Estate Investment Funds, 1962—. Trustee Greater Miami Philharmonic Soc.; bd. dirs. Miami Beach Symphony. Served from 2d lt. to 1st lt., USAAF, 1944-46; PTO. Decorated Air medal. Mem. Am., Fla., Miami Beach, Dade County bar assns. Democrat. Jewish religion. Home: 1440 W 23d St Sunset Island No 3 Miami Beach FL 33140 Office: 801 41st St Miami Beach FL 33140

COURTENAY, TOM, actor; b. Hull, Eng., Feb. 25, 1937; s. Thomas Henry and Annie Eliza (Quest) C.; student Univ. Coll., London, Royal Acad. Dramatic Arts. Stage appearances include The Seagull, Old Vic, 1960-61, Andorra, Billy Liar, Charley's Aunt, Univ. Theatre, Manchester, Eng., Cherry Orchard, Chichester Festival, Macbeth, Hamlet, She Stoops to Conquer, Peer Gynt; film appearances include The Loneliness of the Long Distance Runner, Private Potter, Billy Liar, King and County, Operation Crossbow, King Rat, Doctor Zhivago, Night of the Generals, The Day the Fish Came Out, Otley, One Day in the Life of Ivan Denisovitch. Recipient Best Actor award Venice Film Festival, also Argentine Film Festival. Club: Saville (London); The Garrick. Address: 42 Hulingham Rd London SW 6 England

COURTENAY, WALTER ROWE, clergyman; b. St. Thomas, Ont., Can., Sept. 25, 1902; s. Thomas Greer and Sarah Ann (Coote) C.; came to U.S., 1920, naturalized, 1935; A.B., Maryville (Tenn.) Coll., 1929; B.Th., Princeton, 1932; D.D., Carroll Coll., Waukesha, Wis., 1940; S.T.D., Ripon (Wis.) Coll., 1951; m. Emily Simpson, Aug. 3, 1932; children—Walter R., William James. In bus., 1918-24; candidate ministry Presbyn. Ch. U.S.A., 1924-32, ordained to ministry, 1932; pastor First Presbyn. Ch., Neenah, Wis., 1932-44, Nashville, 1944—. Moderator, Synod of Tenn., 1952. Recipient award Freedoms Found., 1951, 52, 60, 64, 65, 67, 68. Mem. Phi Delta Theta (charter mem.). Author: Where Two Paths Meet, 1936; Baptism: Service and Certification, 1947; I Believe, But-, 1950; Problems Can Be Handled, 1953; The God of Life's Corners, 1969. Twelve sermons read into Congressional Record. Home: Tyne Blvd Nashville TN 37205 Office: 4815 Franklin Rd Nashville TN 37220

COURTENAYE, RICHARD HUBERT, fgn. service officer; b. Pomona, Cal., Mar. 27, 1923; s. John and Juanita (Case) C.; student U. Cal. at Berkeley, 1940; A.B., U. Cal. at Los Angeles, 1944; postgrad. U. Mich., 1944-45; M.P.A., Harvard, 1956; m. Norma Jean Drew, July 22, 1953; children—Mary Ann, Catherine. Press, radio work War Dept., Osaka, Japan, 1946-47; joined U.S. Fgn. Service, 1947; vice consul Barcelona, Spain, 1947-48; 3d sec. embassy, Mexico City, Mexico, 1949-50; 2d sec. embassy, Quito, Ecuador, 1951-53; vice consul, Kobe-Osaka, Japan, 1953-55; 2d sec., consul embassy, Madrid, Spain, 1956-58; chief middle Am. br., Office Research and Analysis Am. Republics, State Dept., 1959-61, chief inter-Am. polit. div., 1961-62; consul gen., Que., Can., 1962-64, Windsor, Ont., Can., 1964-68, Tijuana, Baja Cal., Mexico, 1968-71, fed. regional council rep. Office Economic Opportunity, Denver, 1971—. Served to capt. AUS, 1943-46; PTO. Mem. Am. Fgn. Service Assn. Conglist. Home: 3695 Lewis St Wheat Ridge CO 80033

COURTER, ROBERT GRENFALL, automobile mfg. co. exec.; b. Saranac, Mich., Dec. 29, 1916; s. Floyd Emerson and Mathilda (Henschell) C.; B.S., Northwestern U., 1940; P.F.E., Carnegie Mellon Inst., 1961; m. Anna Lee Mitchell, June 7, 1952. Accounting clk. Chevrolet div. Gen. Motors Corp., Saginaw, Mich., 1940-41, accounting supr., 1946-49, analyst, 1949-52, asst. resident comptroller, 1952-56; resident comptroller, 1956-66, asst. div. comptroller, 1966-68, div. comptroller GMC Truck and Coach, Pontiac, Mich., 1968—. Treas. Kirk in the Hills, 1971; chmn. budget com. United Fund Flint, 1966, Mich. United Fund, 1964-66; mem. budget com. Pontiac Area United Fund, 1968—. Served with USNR, 1942-46. Mem. Phi Delta Theta. Home: 1252 Indian Mound E Birmingham MI 48010 Office: 660 South Blvd Pontiac MI 48053

COURTNEY, HOWARD PERRY, clergyman; b. Frederick, Okla., Dec. 20, 1911; s. Columbus C. and Dotty Lee (Whelchel) C.; grad. L.I.F.E. Bible Coll., 1932, D.D., 1944; m. Vaneda Harper, Mar. 21, 1932; 1 son, Howard Perry. Ordained to ministry, Internat. Ch. of the Foursquare Gospel 1933; pastor chs., Racine, Wis., 1932-34, Terre Haute, Ind., 1934, Portland, Ore., 1935-36, Riverside, Cal., 1936-39, Urbana, Ill., 1939; dist. supr., Great Lakes dist., Internat. Ch. of the Foursquare Gospel, 1940-44, gen. supr., v.p., 1950; gen. supr., dir. fgn. missions, 1944-50, v.p. and gen. supr., 1953—; co-pastor Angelus Temple, Los Angeles, 1950-53. Faculty mem. L.I.F.E. Bible Coll., 1937-39, 1944—. Chmn. adv. com. Pentecostal World Conf., 1958-61. Mem. Pentecostal Fellowship North Am. (chmn. 1953, 54, 65-66), Nat. Assn. Evangelicals (bd. mem. 1953-54, 59- 60, 66-67, 69—). Office: 1100 Glendale Blvd Los Angeles CA 90026

COURTNEY , WILLIAM FRANCIS, food and vending service co. exec.; b. Altoona, Pa., July 3, 1914; s. W. Francis and Mary Edith (Hopkins) C.; m. Mary Jane Kelley, June 5, 1946; children—Sarah Ann, William Francis, Thomas Gerard, Richard Christopher. Mgmt. staff W.T. Grant Co., 1933-37; sales mgr. Coca-Cola Co., 1937- 48; partner Automatic Refreshment Service, 1948-60; pres. Servomation, Youngstown, O., 1960—; v.p. Servomation Corp., 1963-71; pres. Serex Corp., 1971—; dir. Mahoning Nat. Bank, Youngstown. Served to capt., inf. AUS, 1945; PTO. Decorated Bronze Star. Mem. Nat., Ohio (past pres., bd. dirs.) automatic merchandising assns. Republican. Elk. Club: Youngstown. Home: 725 Blueberry Hill Canfield OH 44406 Office: 5211 Mahoning Av Youngstown OH 44515

COURTOIS, EDMOND JACQUES, lawyer, utility exec.; b. Montreal, Can., July 4, 1920; s. Edmond and Cleophee (Lefebvre) C.; A.B., Coll. de Montreal, 1940; LL.B., U. Montreal, 1943;; m. Joan Miller, Oct. 23, 1943; children-Nicole, Jacques, Marc. Called to Que. bar, 1946, created Queen's counsel, 1963; asso. firm Smith, Anglin, Laing, Weldon and Courtois, Montreal, 1946-53, partner, 1953—; chmn. bd. Gaz Met., Inc., Gaz du Que., Inc.; vice chmn., dir. Eagle Star Ins. Co. Can.; pres., dir. La Compagnie Fonciere du Man. (1967) Ltee.; chmn. exec. com., dir. Great West Internat. Equities Ltd.; dir. Bank N.S., Can. Life Assurance Co., Trizee Corp. Ltd., Great No. Gas Utilities Ltd., Can. Internat. Investment Trust Ltd., Elican Devel. Co., Ltd., Bramalea Consol. Devels. Ltd., Elwill Devel. Ltd., Bramalea Consol. Devel. Ltd., Salada Foods Ltd., Universal Savs. Equity Fund Ltd., Rolland Paper Co., Ltd., Que. Iron and Titanium Corp., No. and Central Gas Corp. Ltd., United N. Am. Holdings Ltd. Served to lt. Royal Canadian Navy, 1943-45. Mem. Canadian Bar Assn., Bar Montreal. Home: 9 Chelsea Montreal 109 Quebec Canada Office: 630 Forchester Blvd Montreal 101 Quebec Canada

COURTRIGHT, HERNANDO, hotel exec.; m. 3d, Marcelle Eva Llaca Cuillery; children—Hernando Patrick, DeVigne Francois, Carina Kelley. Propr., Beverly Wilshire Hotel; pres. Courtright Corp.; chmn. bd., chief exec. officer El Camino-Rodeo Corp.; dir. United Financial Corp. Bd. regents St. John's Hosp. Mem. Cal. Vintage Wine, So. Cal. Bordeaux Soc. (co-maitre), Beverly Hills Wine and Food Soc. (co- chmn.), Chevaliers du Tastevin Cal. (founder, grand officer), Escoffier, Chaine des Rotisseurs, L'Ordre de Grand Coteaux. Home: 919 N Crescent Dr Beverly Hills CA 90210 Office: 9500 Wilshire Blvd Beverly Hills CA 90212

COURTS, RICHARD WINN, business exec.; b. Clarksville, Tennessee, June 23d, 1896; s. Richard Winn and Mary (McPherson) C.; A.B., cum laude University of Georgia, 1918; 6 months spl. course (arranged for U.S. Army officers) Faculte de droit, U. Paris, 1918; m. Virginia Orme Campbell, Oct. 11, 1952. Mgr. trust and bond depts. Atlanta Nat. Bank, 1920-23; exec. v.p. First Trust & Savs. Corp., Atlanta, 1920-23; asst. v.p. Trust Co. Ga., 1923-25; founder and sr. partner Courts & Co., 1925-69; chmn. bd., dir. Atlantic Realty Co.; pres., dir. Atlantic Investment Co.; dir., exec. com., mem. execs. compensation com. IBM World Trade Corp.; dir., mem. finance com. Delta Air Lines, Inc.; mem. bd. dirs. Davidson Meadow Corp., So. Mills, Inc. Adv. council internat. bus. Ga. State U. Pres., trustee Courts Found., Inc.; trustee, mem. exec. com. U. Ga. Found.; trustee Episcopal Diocese Fund, Ga. YMCA; mem. adv. bd. Met. Atlanta Salvation Army; bd. dirs. Central Atlanta Progress, Inc. Served as 2d lt. U.S. Army, A.E.F., 1918-19. Fellow Met. Mus. Art N.Y.C. (life); mem. N.Y. Stock Exchange, Nat. Acad. Polit. Sci., Georgia Sportsmen's Federation, Georgia, Atlanta C.'s of C., Phi Beta Kappa, Beta Gamma Sigma, Chi Phi. Clubs: The Sphinx; Rotary, Piedmont Driving, Capital City, Commerce, Nine O'Clocks' Homosassa Fishing, Peachtree Golf, Highlands County, Fifty (Atlanta); River, Links (N.Y.C.). Home: 24 Cherokee Rd NW Atlanta GA 30305 Office: Hurt Bldg Atlanta GA 30303

COUSINEAU, LAWRENCE HENRY, mfg. co. exec.; b. Holyoke, Mass., Aug. 3, 1911; s. Adrian H. and Marie E. (Desilets) C.; grad. Bentley Coll., Boston, 1928; m. Maybelle Lane, Sept. 5, 1932; children—Richard H., Roger B., Sandra J. With Patterson, Teele & Dennis, C.P.A.'s, Boston and N.Y.C., 1942-45; with Heald Machine Co., Worcester, Mass., 1945—, chmn. bd., 1963-68, also dir.; v.p., treas., dir. Cin. Milacron Inc., 1958—; pres., dir. Cin. Milacron Comml. Corp., 1967—; dir. Cin. Internat. Finance Corp., Cin. Comienne, Lyon, France, MSO Maschinen-und Schleifmittelwerke, Offenbach. Trustee Cin. Better Bus. Bur.; Corporator Bentley Coll.; bd. dirs. Cin. Indsl. Inst. C.P.A., Mass. Mem. Am. Inst. Accountants, Financial Execs. Inst. Nat. Assn. Accountants, Am. Accounting Assn., Mass. Soc. C.P.A.'s (Gold medal finalist award 1942), Am. Ordnance Assn., Nat. Machine Tool Builders Assn., Ohio Mfrs. Assn. (trustee), Cin. C. of C. Club: Queen City (Cin.). Home: 8175 Brill Rd Cincinnati OH 45243 Office: 4701 Marburg Av Cincinnati OH 45209

COUSINEAU, MELVIN E., banker; b. Rochester, N.Y., June 24, 1923; s. Osborne and Elsie (Leisten) C.; grad. Am. Inst. Banking, U. Wis., 1965; m. Edna M. Miller, Nov. 28, 1942; children—Dolores, Elaine (Mrs. Robert Rider), Christopher. With Marine Midland Bank-Rochester, (N.Y.) 1941—, asst. auditor, 1963-64, auditor, 1964-70, v.p., 1969—. Mem. Bank Adminstrn. Inst. (pres. 1968-69), Inst. Internat. Auditors. Home: 9137 Route 5 & 20 Holcomb RD 2 NY 14469 Office: 1 Marine Midland Plaza Rochester NY 14639

COUSINS, FRANK, British govt. ofcl.; b. Bulwell, Eng., Sept. 8, 1904; ed. King Edward Sch., Doncaster; m. Annie Elizabeth Judd, 1930. Organizer road transp. sect., T.W.G.U., 1938, nat. officer sect., 1944, then nat. sec. sect., 1948, asst. gen. sec. union, 1955; mem. gen. council Trades Union Congress; former mem. Parliament; mem. Privy Council, 1964—; minister tech., 1964-66. Mem. British Joint Consultative Council, 1955-63, Minister labour Nat. Joint Adv. Council, 1956-64, 66—; exec. council Internat. Transp. Workers Fedn., 1956-64, pres., 1958-60, 62-64; mem. Colonial Labour Adv. Com., 1957-62, London Travel Com., 1958-60, Council Sci. and Indsl. Research, 1960-66; adv. council Export Credit Guarantee Dept., 1962; mem. Nat. Econ. Devel. Council, 1962—. Bd. govs. Nat. Inst. Econ. and Social Research, 1958. Mem. Inst. Transp., Polit. Economy Club. Home: 7 Pine Walk Carshalton Beeches Surrey England Office: Transport House Smith Square London SW 1 England

COUSINS, MARGARET, author, editor; b. Munday, Tex., Jan. 26, 1905; d. Walter Henry and Sue Margaret (Reeves) C.; A.B., U. Tex., 1926. Asso. editor So. Pharm. Jour., Dallas, 1927-32, editor, 1932-37; asso. editor Pictorial Rev., 1937-38; copy writer, gen. promotion dept., Hearst Mags., 1938-42; asso. editor Good Housekeeping, 1942-45, mng. editor, 1945-58; mag. editor McCall's mag., 1958-61; sr. editor Doubleday & Co., N.Y.C., 1961-70; spl. assignment Holt, Rinehart & Winston, 1970; fiction and book editor Ladies Home Jour., 1971—. Recipient Achievement medal Alpha Chi Omega, 1955; Award of Achievement Tex. Ex-Student's Assn., 1956; J.C. Penney-Mo. Sch. Journalism award for mag. writing, 1969; George Washington medal Freedoms Found. at Valley Forge, 1969. Mem. Authors League (council), Authors Guild (council), Tex. Inst. Letters, Theta Sigma Phi (Headliner award 1946), Alpha Chi Omega. Club: Cosmopolitan. Author: Uncle Edgar and the Reluctant Saint, 1948; Ben Franklin of Old Philadelphia (juvenile), 1952; Christmas Gift, 1952; We Were There at the Battle of the Alamo, 1958; collaborator (with Margaret Truman) Souvenir, 1955; Stories of Love and Marriage (anthology), 1961; Traffic with Evil (pseudonym Avery Johns), 1962; Thomas Alva Edison (juvenile), 1965. Home: 125 E 63d St New York City NY 10021 Office: 641 Lexington Av New York City NY 10022

COUSINS, NORMAN, editor; b. Union Hill, N.J., June 24, 1915; s. Samuel and Sara (Miller) C.; student Columbia, 1936; Litt.D., Am. U., 1948; L.H.D., Boston U., Colby Coll., 1953, Denison U., 1954, Colgate U., 1958; Litt.D., Elmira Coll., Ripon Coll., Wilmington Coll., 1957, U. Vt., 1957, Newark State Coll., 1958; LL.D., Washington and Jefferson Coll., 1956, Syracuse U., 1956. Albright Coll., 1957, U. R.I., 1965; Ed.D., R.I. Coll. Edn., 1958; Litt.D., Western Mich. State U., Ripon Coll., U. Bridgeport (Conn.); m. Ellen Kopf, June 23, 1939; children—Andrea, Amy Loveman, Candis Hitzig, Sara Kit. Ednl. writer N.Y. Post, 1934-35; literary editor, managing editor, Current History mag., 1935-40; exec. editor Saturday Rev., 1940-42, pres., editor, 1942—. Chmn. bd. dirs. Nat. Ednl. TV 1969-70; chmn. Nat. Programming Council for Public TV, 1970—. During war, editor U.S.A.; mem. editorial bd. Overseas bur. O.W.I., 1943-45; U.S. Govt. lectr. (Smith Mundt) in India, Pakistan, Ceylon, 1951; Japan-Am. Exchange lecturer, Japan, 1953. Chmn., Connecticut Fact Finding Commn. on Edn., 1948-52; mem. Commn. to Study Orgn. Peace; hon. pres. United World Federalists; chmn. Com. Culture and Intellectual Exchange, Internat. Cooperation Yr., 1965, Mayor's Task Force Air Pollution, N.Y.C., 1966—, Hiroshima Peace Center Assos. Trustee Charles F. Kettering Found.; bd. dirs. Samuel H. Kress Found., Ednl. Broadcasting Corp. Thomas Jefferson award for Advancement of Democracy in Journalism, 1948; Tuition Plan award for outstanding service to Am. Edn., 1951; Benjamin Franklin citation in mag. journalism, 1956; Wayne U. award for nat. service to edn., 1956; Lane Bryant citation for pub. service, 1958; John Dewey award for service to edn., 1958; N.Y. State Citizens Edn. Commn. award, 1959; Publius award N.Y. met. com. United World Federalists, 1964; Eleanor Roosevelt Peace award, 1963; Overseas Press Club award, 1965; Distinguished Citizen award Conn. Bar Assn., 1965; N.Y. Acad. Pub. Edn. award, 1966; nat. mag. award Assn. Deans Journalism Schs., 1969. Mem. World Assn. World Federalists (pres.), P.E.N., UN Assn. (dir. U.S.), Council Fgn. Relations. Clubs: Coffee House, Nat. Press, Overseas Press; Century. Author: The Good Inheritance; The Democratic Chance, 1942; Modern Man Is Obsolete, 1945; Talks with Nehru, 1951; Who Speaks for Man? 1952; In God We Trust; The Religious Beliefs of the Founding Fathers, 1958. Editor: A Treasury of Democracy, 1941; (with William Rose Benét) and Anthology of the Poetry of Freedom, 1943; Writing for Love or Money, 1949; Doctor Schweitzer of Lambarene, 1960; In Place of Folly, 1961; Present Tense, 1967. Editorial supr.; March's Dictionary-Thesaurus, 1958. Home: Silvermine Rd New Canaan CT 06840 Office: 380 Madison Av New York City NY 10017

COUSINS, RALPH WYNNE, naval officer. Vice-chief naval operations, Washington. Address: Quarters CC Potomac Annex 2300 E St Washington DC 20037

COUSINS, WILLIAM EDWARD, archbishop of Milw.; b. Chgo., Aug. 20, 1902; s. Norman B. and Theresa (Hartery) C.; student Quigley Prep. Sem., 1916-21; M.A., St. Mary of the Lake Sem., 1927; LL.D. (hon.), DePaul U. Ordained priest Roman Cath. Ch., 1927; asst. St. Bernard's Parish, 1927-32, Holy Name Cathedral, Chgo., 1932-33; superior Diocesan Mission Band, 1933-46; pastor St. Columbanus parish, 1946-52; auxiliary bishop of Chgo., 1949- 52; bishop of Peoria, Ill. 1952-59; archbishop of Milwaukee, 1959—. Address: 345 N 95th St Milwaukee WI 53226

COUSINS, WILLIAM JAMES, educator, sociologist; b. Ansonia, Conn., Jan. 25, 1924; s. William Isaac and Mary Elizabeth (Brackett) C.; B.A. in Sociology, Yale, 1944, Ph.D. (Cuyler- Foote-Hurtt, Sterling, Rosenwald fellow), 1953; postgrad. Fisk U., 1944-45; m. Gouri Bose, Dec. 29, 1954; children—Ananda Krishna, Christopher Krishna. Instr. social sci. Knoxville Coll., 1945-46; instr. sociology Wellesley Coll., 1949-52; staff mem. Friends Center, Dacca, East Pakistan, Am. Friends Service Com., 1952-53, dir. Friends Internat. Seminars in India and Pakistan, 1953-55; community devel. adviser ICA mission to India, 1955-58, ICA mission to Iran, 1959-60; chief tng. and resources br., community devel. div. ICA, 1961; Peace Corps dir. for Iran, 1962-64; dir. community work, pilot project urban community devel. Am. Friends Service Com., Baroda, India, 1964-66; asso. prof. sociology Earlham Coll., Richmond, Ind., 1966-69; asso. prof. to prof., sociology, chmn. dept., chmn. social sci. div., interim provost Fed. City Coll., Washington, 1969—. Asso., Leadership

Resources, Inc., Nat. Tng. Lab. Fellow Am. Sociol. Assn.; mem. Am. Acad. Polit. and Social Sci., Am. Acad. Arts and Scis. Home: 6120 Utah Av NW Washington DC 20015

COUSINS, WILLIAM MARTIN, Jr., mgmt. cons.; b. Lackawanna, N.Y., Aug. 4, 1924; s. William Martin and Francis Alberta (Gleason) C.; S.B. cum laude, Holy Cross Coll., 1945; M.B.A., Harvard, 1947; m. Elizabeth Ann Lawler, Oct. 13, 1945 (dec. Apr. 1960); children—John Paul, William Martin III, Mark Thomas, Charles Donaldson; m. 2d, Dorothy Dimmick, July 13, 1963 (dec. Nov. 1969); children—Barbara Francis Marie, Brian Robert. Bus. mgr. Bluefield (W.Va.) Baseball Club. 1947-48, Pawtucket (R.I.) Baseball Club, 1949; gen. mgr. Augusta (Ga.) Tigers, Inc., 1950; bus. mgr. Evansville (Ind.) Baseball Club. Inc., 1951; with Armour Research Found., Ill. Inst. Tech., 1951-63, asst. sec., treas., 1952-63, v.p., 1958-63; v.p. Nuclear- Chgo. Corp., Des Plaines, Ill., 1963-65; pres. Cousins & Preble, Inc., mgmt. cons., Chgo., 1965—; dir. Seymour of Sycamore, Inc., Tedco Marketing Services, Inc., Engring. Physics Co., Rockville, Md. Asso. trustee Coll. Holy Cross. Served to lt. (j.g.) USNR, 1944-46. Mem. Am. Mgmt. Assn., A.I.M., Econ. Club Chgo., Ill. C. of C. Execs. Club Chgo., Chicagoland Holy Cross Alumni Assn. (pres. 1954- 56), Newcomen Soc. Clubs: Harvard Business School (pres. 1956), Chicago Athletic Assn.; Skokie (Ill.). Country. Home: 590 South Av Glencoe IL 60022

COUSINS, WINDSOR FRANKLIN, former r.r. ofcl., lawyer; b. Warren, Pa., Dec. 1, 1900; s. Ralph Wayne and Anna (Christian) C.; A.B., U. Pa., 1923; LL.B., 1926; m. Edna Elise Stahl, Sept. 22, 1928; children—Windsor F., Samuel Austin, Edna Elise. Admitted to Pa. bar, 1926; asst. solicitor Pa. R.R., 1926-32, asst. gen. solicitor, 1932-42, asst. gen. counsel, 1942-46, gen. atty., 1946-58, gen. solicitor, 1958-66. Trustee U. Pa.; bd. mgrs. Wistar Inst. Anatomy, Phila. Mem. Gen. Alumni Soc. U. Pa. (dir. 1949—, pres. 1957-60), Phi Beta Kappa. Republican. Lutheran. Clubs: Rittenhouse (Phila.); Faculty (U. Pa.); Union League (Phila.). Home: 615 W Upsal St Philadelphia PA 19119

COUSTEAU, JACQUES YVES, marine explorer; b. St. André-de-Cubzac, France, June 11, 1910; s. Daniel P. and Elizabeth (Duranthon) C.; Bachelier, Stanislas Acad., Paris, 1927; midshipman Brest Naval Acad., 1930; D.Sc., U. Cal. at Berkeley, 1970, Brandeis U., 1970; m. Simone Melchior, July 11, 1937; children—Jean-Michel, Philippe. Founder Groupe d'Etudes et Recherches Sous-Marines, Toulon, France, 1946, also Office Français de Recherche Sous Marine, Marseilles, France, 1952; leader Calypso Oceanographic Expdns., 1950—; dir. Oceanographic Mus., Monaco, 1957—. Served as lt. de vaisseau, French Navy, World War II. Decorated Legion of Honor, Croix de Guerre, Merite Agricole, Merite Maritines. Recipient Motion Picture Acad. Arts and Scis. award (Oscar) for best documentary feature, The Silent World, also for The Golden Fish, 1960, The World Without Sun, 1965; author and producer eight documentary underwater films which received awards at Paris, Cannes, and Venice film festivals. Recipient Acad. Award for The Silent World, 1956. Foreign asso. Nat. Acad. of Scis. Author: The Silent World, 1952; La Plognée en Scaphandre, 1950; Captain Cousteau's Underwater Treasury, 1959; (with James Dugan) The Living Sea, 1962; World Without Sun, 1965. Co-author The Calypso, 1962. Inventor aqualung, 1943. Address: Institute Océanographique Found Albert Ier Prince de Monaco Monaco

COUTANT, VICTOR CARLISLE BARR, educator; b. East Orange, N.J., Jan. 15, 1907; s. Leslie Irving and Mary (Barr) C.; student Rutgers U., 1925-26; B.A., Columbia, 1929, M.A., 1930, Ph.D., 1936; m. Mary Hartsough, June 10, 1940; children—Leslie, William. Instr., Essex County Jr. Coll., Newark, 1933-36, Univ. Sch., Ohio State U., 1937-42, 46-47; mem. faculty Central Mich. U., Mt. Pleasant, 1947-66, prof. fgn. langs., 1954-66, chmn. dept., 1959-65; prof. fgn. langs. Western Mich. U., Kalamazoo, 1966—. Served AUS, 1943- 45; ETO. Mem. Am. Philol. Assn., History Sci. Soc., Phi Beta Kappa. Author: (with R. Meldau) A Glimpse of the U.S.A.; Theophrastus, De Igne, A Post-Aristotelian View of the Nature of Fire. Home: 1304 Trails End Kalamazoo MI 49001

COUTTOLENC, JORGE MARTIN, hotel exec.; b. Mexico, D.F., Nov. 11, 1935; s. Jose and Carmen (Elvira) C.; Dr. Economy, Escuela Hotelera de Lausanne, 1958; m. Maria Luisa Martinez, Feb. 13, 1960; children—Maria Luisa, Monica, Jorge, Alejandra. Pres., Sistema Azteca de Hoteles, 1961-64; mng. dir. Western Internat. Hotels, 1964-66, Hoteles Balsa, 1966-68, Hotel Fiesta Palace, since 1970—. Vice pres. Conv. Bur., 1968-71. Mem. C. of C., Hotel Sales Mgmt. Assn. (treas.). Kiwanian. Home: 93 Cuernavaca Mexico DF 11 Mexico Office: 80 Reforma Mexico DF 6 Mexico

COUTTS, FREDERICK, former gen. Salvation Army; b. Kirkcaldy, Scotland, Sept. 21, 1899; s. John and Mary (Jones) C.; ed. Leith Acad.; m. Bessie Lee, Nov. 14, 1925 (dec. 1967); children—Margaret (Mrs. R. Rogers), Molly (Mrs. M. West), John, Elizabeth; m. 2d, Olive Gatrall, Dec. 31, 1970. Officer, Salvation Army, 1920-70, lit. sec. to gen., 1952-53, tng. prin. William Booth Mem. Coll., 1953-57, territorial comdr., Eastern Australia, 1957-63, gen., 1963-70; chmn. Salvation Army Trust Co.; pres. Salvation Army Assurance Soc. Ltd., Reliance Bank Ltd., Salvationist Pub. & Supplies Ltd., Salvation Army Fire Ins. Corp. Ltd. Served with Royal Flying Corp, 1917-18.

COUTTS, JOHN WALLACE, chemist, educator; b. Neepawa, Man., Can., Feb. 2, 1923; s. John Wallace and Lavina (Murray) C.; B.Sc., U. Man., 1945, M.Sc., 1947; Ph.D., Purdue U., 1950; m. Blanche A. Muris, Dec. 22, 1959; 1 son, Jerry B. Ott. Came to U.S., 1946; naturalized, 1956. Asst. prof. chemistry Mt. Union Coll., Alliance, O. 1950-55; asso. prof. Lake Forest (Ill.) Coll., 1955-62, prof., chmn. dept., 1962—; vis. prof. Purdue U., summers 1955, 56, 57, Northwestern U., 1958, 60, 61, U. Cal. at Berkeley, 1967-68; Fulbright lectr. U. Peshawar (Pakistan) 1958-59. Author: (with Dwight E. Gray) Man and His Physical World, 2d edit., 1966. Home: 106 E Sheridan Rd Lake Bluff IL 60044 Office: Lake Forest College Lake Forest IL 60045

COUTU, LUCIEN LEOPOLD, educator; b. Montreal, Can., Jan. 13, 1920; s. Augustin and Marie- Louise C.; B.A., Coll. St-Jean d'Iberville, 1935; M.D., U. Montreal, 1948, Ph.D., Inst. Exptl. Medicine and Surgery, 1952; m. Denyse Lauson, July 8, 1950; children—Pierre, Monique, Jean-Yves, Marie-France. Asst. med. dept. Peter Bent Brigham Hosp., Boston, 1952-53; resident med. dept. Hotel Dieu of Montreal, 1953-54, research fellow med. dept., 1954- 55, mem. staff, 1957—, med. dir., 1960—; mem. Faculty Medicine, U. Montreal, 1955—, dean Faculty, 1962-70, prof. medicine, 1963—. Bd. govs. Coll. Phys. and Surg. Que., 1963—. Hon. fellow Coll. Internation des Chirurgiens, A.C.P. Contbr. articles profl. jours. Home: 6275 Pie IX Montreal Quebec Canada Office: 2900 Mount Royal Blvd Montreal 3 Quebec Canada

COUTURIE, JOHN DERBIGNY, aircraft co. exec.; b. New Orleans, Oct. 19, 1916; s. Reginald F. and Teresita Marie (Denis) C.; student Loyola U. of South, 1935; grad. Internat. Accountants Soc., 1936; m. Ann Haws, June 26, 1948; children—John Frederick, William Derbigny. Chief mgmt. and operations Army Exchange Service, 4th Army Area, 1945-50; v.p., asst. treas. Fred Bell Enterprises, Inc., 1950-54; with Hughes Aircraft Co., 1955—, v.p., treas., 1966—; chmn. bd. Emihus Microcomponents Ltd., Glenrothes, Scotland; pres. ESAL Co.; TelePrompter Manhattan CATV Corp.; chmn. bd. Theta Cable of Cal.; dir. Satellite Telecommunications Co., Ltd. Japan, TelePrompter Corp. Home: 6526 Sherbourne Dr Los Angeles, CA 90056. Office: Centinela & Teale Sts Culver City CA 90230

COUVE DE MURVILLE, MAURICE, French diplomat; b. Reims, France, Jan. 24, 1907; s. Edouard and Hermine (Caesar) C.; student Paris U.; m. Jacqueline Schweisguth, Nov. 10, 1932; children—Jullette, Dorothee, Beatrice. Finance insp. French Govt., 1930, asst. dir. in finance ministry, 1937, dir., 1940; sec. gen. Gen. Giraud adminstrn., 1943; mem. France Com. Nat. Liberation, 1943; mem. Adv. Council for Italy, 1944; ambassador to Rome, 1945; gen. dir. polit. affairs Fgn. Ministry, 1945; French dep. Council Fgn. Ministers, 1945- 49; ambassador in Cairo, Egypt, 1950-54; ambassador to NATO, 1954, to U.S., 1955-56, to Germany, 1956-58; fgn. minister of France, 1958-68; prime minister of France, 1968-69. Office: 3 rue Jean Jonjon Paris 8 France

COUZENS, FRANK, Jr., banker; b. Detroit, Jan. 18, 1924; s. Frank and Margaret (Lang) C.; B.S. in Finance, U. Detroit, 1948; m. Joan Ulrich, Aug. 9, 1947; children—Joan Marie, Margaret Mary, Anne Marie, Mary Carol, Frank III, William Ulrich, John Manning. With McBride Hardware Co., Birmingham, Mich., 1948- 51, with Mfrs. Nat. Bank Detroit, 1951—, sr. v.p., 1967—, sr. trust officer, 1971—; dir. Jacobson Stores, Inc., Lang Tanning Co., Ltd., Wabeek Corp. Treas., mem. exec. bd. Detroit Area council Boy Scouts Am.; v.p., treas. Inst. Econ. Edn., Detroit. Bd. dirs., treas. United Community Services Detroit; pres., trustee Oakland Housing; trustee World Med. Relief; chmn. adv. bd. Bon Secours Hosp.; bd. dirs. Greater Detroit Area Hosp. Council. Mem. Hundred Club Detroit, Econ. Club Detroit, Greater Detroit C. of C. Clubs: Detroit Athletic (bd. dirs.), Recess, Cardinal (Detroit); Grosse Pointe Yacht; Otsego (Mich.) Ski. Home: 66 Lothrop Rd Grosse Pointe Farms MI 48236 Office: 151 W Fort St Detroit MI 48226

COVALT, DONALD A., physician; b. Muncie, Ind., Nov. 11, 1906; s. Elmer F. and Maude (Fallis) C.; student DePauw U., 1924-27; B.S., Ind. U., 1932, M.D., 1933; m. Anna Mary Aloisi, Aug. 1, 1959; 1 dau., Maude Helen. Rotating intern Cleve. City Hospital, 1933-34; gen. practice, Muncie 1934-42; asst. med. dir. Med. Rehab. Service VA, 1946-47; asso. dir. Inst. Rehab. Medicine, N.Y.U. Med. Center, also prof. phys. medicine and rehab., N.Y.U. Sch. Medicine, 1947—; chief convalescent tng. div. Office Air Surgeon, Hdqrs. USAF, 1944-45, cons. phys. medicine and rehab., 1951-53; cons. phys. medicine and rehab., VA, 1950-56; mem. med. adv. com. Social Security Adminstrn., 1955-61. Past mem. N.Y. State Bd. Med. Examiners. Recipient Mark A. Light award World Com. on Employment of the Handicapped, 1961. Served Served to lt. col. M.C., USAAF, 1943-45. Diplomate Am. Bd. Phys. Medicine and Rehab. (exam. bd.). Mem. A.M.A., N.Y. County, N.Y. State med. socs., Am. Acad. Compensation Medicine (pres. 1959-60), Nat. Rehab. Assn. (W.F. Faulkes award 1954), Am. Congress Rehab. Medicine (pres. 1960-61), N.Y. Acad. Medicine. Contbr. articles profl. jours., chpts. in books. Home: 36 Narrow Rocks Rd Westport CT 06880 Office: 400 E 34th St New York City NY 10016

COVENTRY, MARK BINGHAM, physician; b. Duluth, Minn., Mar. 30, 1913; s. William Albertus and Louise (Bingham) C.; A.B., Mich., 1934, M.D., 1937; M.S. in Orthopedic Surgery, U. Minn., 1942; m. Elizabeth Ann Servis, Apr. 9, 1937; children—Anne, Jane, Martha. Intern U. Mich. Hosp., 1937-38; orthopedic surgery Mayo Clinic, Rochester, Minn., 1937—; prof., head dept. orthopedic surgery Mayo Found., U. Minn. Served to lt. comdr., M.C., USNR, 1942-46. Mem. Am. Acad. Orthoped. Surgeons, Am. Orthoped. Assn., Clin. Orthop. Soc., A.C.S., A.M.A., Internat. Soc. Orthopedics and Traumatology, 20th Century Orthop. Assn., Minn. Med. Assn., Minn., Man., Dakota Orthoped. assns. Author med. articles. Home: 1421 SW 20th St Rochester MN 55901 Office: 200 1st St SW Rochester MN 55901

COVER, EDWIN MCINTOSH, lawyer; b. Balt., May 16, 1933; s. Thomas and Olive (Brown) C.; A.B., Princeton U., 1955; LL.B., Harvard U., 1960; m. Anne Lowell Thorndike, Sept. 10, 1954; children—Carolyn Lowell, Anne McIntosh. Admitted to N.Y. bar, 1961, Tex. bar, 1964; asso. firm Kelley, Drye, Warren, Clark, Carr & Ellis, N.Y.C., 1960-63; counsel, asst. sec. Texas Industries, Inc., Dallas, 1963-67; asso. gen. counsel, asst. sec. Ling-Temco-Vought, Inc., Dallas, 1967-68; v.p., sec., gen. counsel Okonite Co., Ramsey, N.J., 1968—; pres. Ken/Tel Equipment Co., subsidiary Okonite, 1969—. Trustee Okonite Found. Served as lt. AUS, 1956-57. Mem. Assn. Bar City N.Y., Tex., Dallas, Am. bar assns., Am. Soc. Corp. Secs. Republican. Episcopalian. Clubs: Ridgewood Country; Ardsley Curling. Home: 146 E Allendale Av Saddle River NJ 07458 Office: PO Box 340 Hilltop Rd Ramsey NJ 07446

COVER, JOHN HIGSON, economist, statistician; b. Johnstown, Pa., Oct. 29, 1891; s. Charles Blair and Carrie Louise (Higson) C.; student Ohio State U., 1911- 12; B.S., Columbia, 1915, A.M., 1919, Ph.D., 1927; children by 1st marriage—Evlyn June, John Higson; m. 2d, Mary Leyman, Dec. 16, 1938. Spl. attaché Am. Embassy, Vienna, 1915-16; Journalism N.Y. and U.S. Food Adminstrn., Washington, 1917-18; instr. Columbia U., 1921-23; prof. Colo. Coll., 1923-24; prof. dir. Bur. Bus. and Social Research, U. Denver, 1924-27; prof. and dir. bur. Bus. Research, U. Pitts. 1927-30; prof. U. Chgo., 1928-40, on leave of absence and with Com. on Govt. Statistics and Information Service, Washington, 1933, U. S. Dept. of Commerce, 1939; cons. economist, 1940-41; economist and exec. officer of Lend-Lease Adminstrn., Dept. State, UNRRA, Fgn. Econ. Adminstrn., Dept. Commerce, 1942-46; also head of bus. adminstrn. dept. Army Univ. Center, Biarritz, France, 1945-46; vis. lectr. U. Rotterdam, 1945; dir. Bureau of Bus. and Econ. Research, U. Md., 1946-61; UN econ. planning expert to Govt. of Syria, 1962- 63 also Govt. Barbados, 1964-65; sabbatical leave as Fulbright lectr. research and study of India, 1952-53; on leave to U. Cal., dir. South Asia Project, 1955-56. Chmn. bd. dir. Inst. on World Orgn. Fellow emeritus A.A.A.S.; mem. Am. Econ. Assn., Nat. Assn. Am. Composers and Condrs. (v.p. Washington chpt. 1959-64), Nat. Parks Assn. (sec., trustee), Am. Statis. Assn., Econometric Soc., Am. Econ. Assn., Omicron Delta Gamma, Alpha Kappa Psi, Delta Upsilon. Author: Business and Personal Failure and Readjustment in Chicago, 1933; Retail Price Behavior, 1935; Asia is our Business, 1955; India in World Affairs, 1957. Business Research, 1941; Economic Planning and Policies in Syria, 1963; Economic Procedural and Policy Papers for Barbados, 1965; New Industries; Analytical Consideration, 1965; Location Factors and Criteria, 1965. Co- author: Some Problems of Small Business, 1941; Regulation of Economic Activities in Foreign Countries, 1941; Economy of India, 1956; Economy of Nepal, 1956; also titles under Studies in Business and Economic, 1947-61. Home: 211 Fairfield Pike Yellow Springs OH 45387 Office: Nat Parks and Conservation Assn 1701 18th St N W Washington DC 20009

COVER, MORRIS SEIFERT, veterinarian; b. Harrisburg, Pa., July 25, 1916; s. Elwood A. and Elizabeth T. (Seifert) C.; V.M.D., U. Pa., 1938; M.S., Kan. State Coll., 1942; Ph.D., U. Ill., 1952; m. June Minnich, Sept. 8, 1938 (dec.); children—Charles Elword, Wende Elizabeth; m. 2d, Janet Coblentz, May 28, 1966. Asst. poultry pathologist U.N.H., 1938-40; instr., asst. prof. anatomy and histology Kan. State Coll. Sch. Vet. Medicine, 1940-46; asst. prof. anatomy and histology, U. Ill. Vet. Med. Coll., 1946-52; asso. prof. poultry pathology U. Del. Sch. Agr., 1952-59, prof., head dept. animal poultry, 1959-67, dir. Agrl. Expt. Sta., 1962-67, asso. dean Sch. Agr., 1961-62; staff veterinarian Ralston Purina Co., 1967-68, mgr. vet. services, vet. labs., 1968—. Chmn. tech. adv. com. Nat. Poultry Research Found. Mem. Am., Del. (past sec.- treas.) vet. med. assns., Conf. Research Workers in Animal Diseases North Am., Poultry Sci. Assn., Am. Assn. Avian Pathologists (past sec.-treas.), Pub. Health Vets., New Castle County Vet. Med. Assn. (past pres.), Nat. Assn. Standard Med. Vocabulary, Sigma Xi, Phi Kappa Phi, Gamma Sigma Delta. Contbg. author: Fundamentals of Veterinary Histology, 1957. Contbg. editor: Blakiston's Med. Dictionary, Asso. editor, bus. mgr. Jour. Avian Diseases. Author numerous articles in field. Home: 131 Glen Cove Dr Chesterfield St Louis MO 63017 Office: Ralston Purina Co Checkerboard Sq St Louis MO 63102

COVER, RODNEY ADDISON, corp. exec.; b. N.Y.C., Nov. 21, 1931; s. Rodney Addison and Margaret (Stitely) C.; B.A., Williams Coll., 1954; M.B.A., N.Y. U., 1958; m. Margaret L. Gracie, Apr. 15, 1959. Asst. treas. Mfrs. Hanover-Trust Co., 1954-62; treas. Tower Capital Corp., 1962-64; v.p., treas., sec., dir. Liquidonics Industries, Inc., N.Y.C., 1964—; sec., dir. UMC Industries, Inc., St. Louis, 1969-70; dir. Greer Hydraulics Corp., N.Y. Plumbers Spltys., Inc., Filtron Co., Inc., Plainview Mfg. Corp. Served with AUS, 1955-56. Mem. Nat. Pilots Assn., Phi Sigma Kappa. Club: Williams (N.Y.C.). Home: 41 Pilgrim Path Huntington NY 11743 Office: 45 S Service Rd Plainview NY 11803

COVERT, EUGENE EDZARDS, educator, engr.; b. Rapid City, S.D., Feb. 6, 1926; s. Perry and Eda (Edzards) C.; B.S. U. Minn., 1946, M.S., 1948; Sc.D., Mass. Inst. Tech., 1958; m. Mary Solveig Rutford, Feb. 22, 1946; children—David H., Christine J., Pamela M., Steven P. Preliminary design group USNADS, Johnsville, Pa., 1948-52; mem. staff Mass. Inst. Tech. Aerophysics Lab., 1952—, asso. dir. aerophysics lab., 1963—, asso. prof. aeronautics and astronautics, 1963-68, prof., 1968—; cons. Bolt, Beranek & Newman, Inc., Hercules, Inc., Mitre Corp., Mass. Inst. Tech. Lincoln Lab., U.S. Army Research Office. Mem. panel Naval Aeroballistic Adv. Com. Served with USNR, 1943-47. Asso. fellow Am. Inst. Aero. and Astronautics; mem. A.A.A.S., Sigma Xi. Office: Mass Inst Tech 77 Massachusetts Av Cambridge MA 02139

COVERT, FRANK MANNING, lawyer, corp. exec.; b. Canning, N.S., Can., Jan. 13, 1908; s. Archibald Menzies and Minnie Alma (Clarke) C.; B.A., Dalhousie U., 1927, LL.B., 1929; m. Mary Louise Covert, Aug. 25, 1934; children—Michael, Susan, Peter, Sally. Called to N.S. bar, 1930; practice in Halifax, N.S., 1930- 40, 45—; sr. partner firm Stewart, MacKeen & Covert, 1963—; asst. gen. counsel Dept. Munitions and Supply, 1940-42. Pres. Ben's Holdings, Ltd., 1956—; pres. of Maritime Paper Products Ltd., 1959- -; dir. Royal Bank of Canada, Petrofina Canada Ltd., IAC Ltd., N.S. Light & Power Co., Maritime Steel & Foundries Ltd., Bowaters Mersey Paper Co. Ltd., Phoenix Assurance Co. Ltd., Eastern Tel. & Tel. Co., Minas Basin Pulp & Power Co. Ltd., Canadian Keyes Fibre Co. Ltd., Trizec Corp. Ltd., Nat. Sea Products Ltd., Sun Life Assurance Co. Can. Chmn. bd. Halifax Infirmary Hosp.; bd. govs. Dalhousie U. Served as navigator RCAF, 1942-45. Decorated D.F.C.; mem. Order British Empire. Home: 5885 Spring Garden Rd Halifax Nova Scotia Canada Office: Box 997 Halifax Nova Scotia Canada

COVERT, WILLIAM VANNUYS, former indsl. exec.; b. Indpls., Oct. 15, 1913; s. Paul W. and Harriet (Jeffery) C.; B.S. in Mech. Engring., Purdue U., 1934; m. Dorothy C. Jones, May 2, 1942; children—Jeffery W., Steven J., Helene L. Engr., Diamond Chain Co., Inc., Indpls., 1935-46, sr. engr., 1946-51, chief engr., 1951-58, dir., 1957; asst. v.p. AMSTED Industries Inc., Chgo., 1959-60, v.p., 1960-70. Mem. Purdue Alumni Assn. (past pres.), Phi Gamma Delta, Pi Tau Sigma. Mason. Clubs: Sunset Ridge Country (Winnetka, Ill.). Home: 2022 Burr Oak Dr Glenview IL 60025

COVEY, ALAN DALE, librarian; b. Alameda, Cal., Feb. 3, 1917; s. A.V. and Alma (Henderson) C.; A.B., U. Cal. at Berkeley, 1939, certificate in librarianship, 1946; Ed.D., Stanford, 1955; m. Alma A. Munsell, Sept. 28, 1968; children—Alan Dale, David Milton, Carlin Raymond, Patricia A. Munsell. Librarian U. Cal. at Berkeley, 1946-49; asst. head librarian San Francisco State Coll., 1949-51; coll. librarian Sacramento State Coll., 1952-62 univ. librarian Ariz. State U., Tempe, 1962-69; prof. library sci. Wis. State U., 1969—. Mem. Cal. Com. on Adult Edn., 1955-56, Cal. Adv. Com. on correctional Libraries, 1956-57. Active Boy Scouts Am. Served to 1st lt., F.A., AUS, 1942-45. Mem. A.L.A., Cal. (pres. 1959), Ariz. (pres. elect) library assns. Methodist. Editor: Ariz. Librarian, 1967-69. Office: Library Sci Dept Wis State U Oshkosh WI 54901

COVEY, CHARLES WILLIAM, editor; b. Middlesboro, Ky., Sept. 29, 1918; s. Charles G. and Bertha (Bowman) C.; B.A., in Chemistry and Physics, Lincoln Meml. U., 1940; m. Mary Ruth Gibson, Sept. 16, 1943; children—Charles C., Catherine A. Instr. army aviation course Lincoln Meml. U., 1942-43; instr. naval meteorology Auburn Poly. Inst., 1943-44; instr. instrument engr. Union Carbide Nuclear Co., Oak Ridge, 1944-49, head instrument engring. dept., Paducah, Ky., 1952-54; head customer and sales tng. Taylor Instrument Co., Rochester, N.Y., 1949-52; editor ISA Jour., Instrument Soc. Am., Pitts., 1954-62; v.p., editorial dir. Compass Publs., Inc., Arlington, Va., 1962- -. Served with USNR, 1943-44. Fellow Instrument Soc. Am. (pres. Oak Ridge 1944, Paducah 1953, nat. v.p., mem. exec. bd. 1953, chmn. nat. publs. com. 1951-52); founding mem. Marine Tech. Soc. Home: 1820 Dalmation Dr McLean, VA 22101. Office: Lynn Bldg 1117 N 19th St Arlington VA 22209

COVEY, LOIS LENSKI, see Lnski, Lois.

COVEY, MILTON H., gas transmission co. exec.; b. Tyler, Tex., Oct. 31, 1923; s. L. G. and Margaret (Matthews) C.; student Tyler Jr. Coll., 1942-43; LL.B., Baylor U., 1949; grad. Advanced Mgmt. Program, Harvard, 1965; m. Doris Martin, Dec. 6, 1947; children—Steven M., James M., Mark L. With Tenneco Inc. (formerly Tenn. Gas Transmission Co.), 1949—, asst. corp. sec., 1957- 63, corporate sec., 1963-68, v.p., sec., 1968—; corporate sec. East Tenn. Natural Gas Co., 1963—, Midwestern Gas Transmission Co., 1963—. Served with USAAF, 1943-46; PTO. Mem. Am. Soc. Corp. Secs. (nat. bd. dirs.). Baptist (deacon). Mason. Home: 14307 Carolcrest Houston TX 77024 Office: Tenn Bldg Houston TX 77002

COVEY, RICHARD BURTON, lawyer; b. Kansas City, Mo., May 12, 1929; s. Arnold B. and Eula (Henson) C.; A.B., Harvard, 1950; LL.B., Columbia, 1955; m. Jane R. Kerbeck, Sept. 9, 1955; children—Kim Elizabeth, Richard Jerome. Admitted to Mo. bar, 1955, N.Y. bar, 1958; asso. firm Stinson, Mag. Thomson, McEvers & Fizzell, Kansas City, Mo., 1955-57, Dewey, Ballantine, Bushby, Palmer & Wood, N.Y.C., 1957-63; partner firm Carter, Ledyard & Milburn, N.Y.C., 1963—; dir. Equitable Life Ins. Co. Ia.; trustee Nursing Service Inc., Ridgewood, N.J. Lectr. Practising Law Inst.,

N.Y.C., 1959—, U. Miami Inst. Estate Planning, 1967—. Spl. counsel to trust div. Am. Bankers Assn. on tax matters relating to trusts and estates. Served with USMCR, 1951-52. Mem. Am. (co-chmn. com. tax aspects decedents estates 1968-69), N.Y. bar assns. Author: The Marita Deduction and the Use of Formula Provisions, 1966. Home: 81 Lowell Rd Glen Rock NJ 07452 Office: 2 Wall St New York City NY 10005

COVI, DARIO ALESSANDRO, art historian, educator; b. Livingston, Ill., Dec. 26, 1920; s. Joe J. and Cecilia (Menghini) C.; B.Ed., Eastern Ill. U., 1943; M.A., State U. Ia., 1948; postgrad. U. London, 1949, U. Florence, 1950; Ph.D., N.Y.U., 1958; m. Anna Madeline Cundiff, Sept. 7, 1960. Instr. U. Louisville, 1956-58, asst. prof., 1958-61, asso. prof., 1961-64, prof., 1964-70, curator Art Collection, 1958-63, acting head dept. fine arts, 1960-63, chmn. dept., 1963-67; prof., chmn. dept. Duke U., Durham, N.C., 1970—. Mem. exec. com. Ky. Arts Commn., 1965-70; Ky. chmn. Com. to Rescue Italian Art, 1966-67. Bd. dirs. Art Center Assn. Louisville, 1960-68, Print Collectors Club, Louisville. Served with AUS, 1943-46. Hon. mem. Amici di Brera e dei Musei Milanesi, 1967. Fellow Am. Council Learned Socs.; mem. Coll. Art Assn. Am., Renaissance Soc. Am., Am. Assn. U. Profs. Author: Prints from the Allen R. Hite Art Institute Collection, 1963. Contbr. articles profl. jours. Home: 1010 Monmouth Av Durham NC 27701

COVILLE, CABOT, former fgn. service officer; b. Washington, Mar. 25, 1902; s. Frederick Vernon and Elizabeth Harwood (Boynton) C.; A.B., Cornell, Ithaca, N.Y., 1923; m. Lilian Waters Grosvenor, 1927; children—Gilbert Grosvenor, Cabot (dec.); m. 2d, Margaret Lapsley Post, 1949; children—Elizabeth, Brooks, Timothy. Fgn. service officer, 1926-52; assigned to U.S. embassy, Tokyo, 1927-29, 35-39; consulate, Kobe, Dairen, Tokyo and Harbin, 1930- 34; assigned to Japanese affairs Dept. State, 1939-41; polit. adviser to U.S. High Commr. Philippines, Manila and Corregidor, 1941-1942; assigned Lima and Rio de Janeiro, 1942; engaged in polit. studies in connection with post-war reconstrn. Dept. State, 1942-43; 1st sec., London, Eng., 1943-47, Stockholm, Sweden, 1944-45; asst. to sec. gen. UN Conf., San Francisco, 1945, UN Preparatory Commn. and Gen. Assembly, London, 1945-46, Tokyo Occupation Hdqrs., 1947-49; U.S. consul gen., Halifax, N.S., Can., 1950-52 . Mem. internat. conf. com. Am. Friends Service Com., 1959-68. Trustee, Sidwell Friends Sch. Mem. Washington Inst. Fgn. Affairs, Japan-Am. Soc. Washington (pres. 1963-64). Clubs: Cosmos, Chevy Chase, City Tavern, Dacor, Metropolitan (Washington); River (N.Y.C.); Chester Yacht; Somerset (Boston). Author numerous ofcl. papers, articles. Home: 3053 P St Georgetown Washington DC 20007 also Pomfret Center CT 06259

COVINGTON, CLARENCE ALLEN, Jr., lawyer; b. Chattanooga, Feb. 19, 1916; s. Clarence Allen and Mabel (Nelson) C.; A.B., Ohio U., 1938; J.D., Ohio State U., 1940; m. Mary Ellen Moore, Dec. 28, 1940; children-Constance Anne (Mrs. Drew R. Ward), Mary Katherine (Mrs. Thomas E. Lichak), Clarence Allen III, Richard M. Admitted to Ohio bar, 1940; practice in Youngstown, 1946—; sr. partner Henderson, Convington, Stein & Donchess, 1947—; counsel, sec., dir. Ajax Magnethermic Corp., Electrochems., Inc., Hynes Steel Products Co., Fox Industries, Inc., A.H. Buchrle Co., Oakwood Billets, Inc., Powell Pressed Steel Co., Renner Co., Interstate Restaurant Systems, Inc., Superior Industries, Inc., Calex Corp., Ucker Enterprises, Inc. Regional dir. OPA, 1940-43; chmn. Zoning Commn., 1948—; pres. Local Sch. Bd., 1951-59; chmn. local SSS bd., 1953—. Served to lt. USNR, 1943-46. Mem. Am., Ohio Mahoning County (past pres.), Youngstown bar assns. Home: 4123 Windsor Rd Youngstown OH 44512 Office: Wick Bldg Youngstown OH 44503

COVINGTON, GARRETT CHRISTOPHER, Jr., aircraft co. exec.; b. Pulaski, Tenn., Apr. 2, 1907; s. Garrett C. C. and Mishie (Martin) C.; B.S. in Mech. Engring., U. Ill., 1928; M.Engring. Adminstrn., Washington U., 1959; m. Patricia Rose O'Neill, Oct. 31, 1931; children—Garrett Christopher, John Patrick, Robert Neil. Jr. engr. Caterpillar Tractor Co., 1928-29; structures engr. Naval Aircraft Factory, 1929-37; aero. engr. Glenn L. Martin Co., 1937-39; asst. chief engr. McDonnell Aircraft Corp., St. Louis, 1939-43, airplane chief engr., 1943-52, v.p. airplane engring., 1952-57, v.p. gen. engring. div., 1957-71, v.p. engring., 1971—. Mem. Theta Chi, Pi Tau Sigma, Gamma Alpha Rho. Home: 7228 Henderson Rd Normandy MO 63121 Office: P O Box 516 St Louis MO 63166

COVINGTON, JOHN RALPH, lawyer, business exec.; b. Chapel Hill, Tenn., Feb. 4, 1913; s. Garrett Christopher and Mishie (Martin) C.; B.S., U. Ill., 1934; LL.B. cum laude, Harvard, 1938; m. Katherine Filson, Mar. 11, 1939; children—Christopher Hugh, Marion Elizabeth. Admitted to Ill. bar, 1938; asso. Defrees, Fiske, O'Brien & Thomson, Chgo., 1938-41; with Oliver Corp., 1941-60, asst. sec., 1942-44, sec., 1944-60, dir., 1955- 60, v.p., 1957-60; with Miami Corp., 1961-64; v.p., sec. Sargent-Welch Sci. Co., Skokie, Ill., 1965-69; mem. firm Tenney, Bentley, Howell, Ashow & Lewis, Chgo., 1969—; dir. Citizens Mut. Casualty Co., Howell, Mich., State Mut. Life Assurance Co. of Am., Worcester, Mass. Pres., Lake Co. Crime Comm., 1963- 64. Mem. Chgo. Bar Assn., Alpha Delta Phi. Clubs: Chicago; Onwentsia; Bath and Tennis. Home: 254 W Laurel Av Lake Forest IL 60045 Office: 69 W Washington St Chicago IL 60602

COVINGTON, JOSEPH ETHRIDGE, educator, lawyer; b. Nashville, Ark., Dec. 14, 1911; s. Rudolph Burton and Elizabeth (Rose) C.; A.B., U. Ark., 1932, LL.B., 1940; LL.M., Harvard, 1941, S.J.D., 1952; m. Mary Jane Hare, June 5, 1937 (div.); 1 son, John. Tchr. high sch., Blevins, Ark., 1932-33; supt. schs., Delight, Ark., 1933-35; ednl. adviser Civilian Conservation Corps, 1935-38; admitted to Ark. bar, 1941, Mo. bar, 1958; faculty U. Ark., 1941- 58, asst. prof., 1941-46, asso. prof., 1946-48, prof., 1948-58, exec. asst. to pres., 1948-51, provost, 1951-54, acting pres., 1951-52, dean Sch. Law, 1954-58; dean Sch. Law, U. Mo., Columbia, 1958-69, prof. law, 1969-70, Phil S. Gibson prof., 1970—. Cons. to ODM, 1956; chmn. Ark. Statute Revision Commn., 1954-58; adviser Mo. Com. on Legislative Research, 1959-64; mem. Mo. Emergency Planning Com., 1962-65; dir. testing Nat. Conf. Bar Examiners, 1970—. Served with USAF, 1943-46. Fellow Am. Bar Found.; mem. Am. Judicature Soc., Am., Ark., Boone County (past pres.) bar assns., Am. Law Inst., Mystical Seven, Phi Delta Kappa, Phi Alpha Theta, Kappa Alpha, Omicron Delta Kappa, Methodist. Mason; Rotarian (past pres. Columbia). Home: 326 Crown Point Columbia MO 65201

COVINGTON, WILLIAM DELTON, utility co. exec.; b. Franklinton, La., June 24, 1919; s. John I. and Mamie (Harper) C.; B.S., Centenary Coll., Shreveport, La., 1948; m. Ora Mae Thorn, Oct. 21, 1942; 1 dau., Mary Del. With Tex. Eastern Transmission Corp., 1949—, comptroller, 1968—. Served with USAAF, 1942- 45. Mem. Am. Gas Assn., Ind. Natural Gas Assn., Am. Petroleum Inst., Financial Execs. Inst. Home: 13103 Rummel Creek Dr Houston TX 77024 Office: Southern Nat Bank Bldg Houston TX 77001

COWAN, CLYDE LORRAIN, educator, physicist; b. Detroit, Dec. 6, 1919; s. Clyde Lorraine and Esther M. (Koenig) C.; B.S., Mo. U., 1940; M.S., Washington U., 1947, Ph.D., 1949; D.Sc. (hon.), U. Dallas, 1962; m. Betty Eleanor Dunham, Jan. 29, 1943; children—Elizabeth (Mrs. John A. Riordon), Michael, Marian, George. Group leader Los Alamos Sci. Lab., 1949-57; prof. physics George Washington U., 1947, Cath. U. Am., 1948—; cons. USN, USAF, A.E.C., industry. Served to capt., USAAF, 1942-46. Decorated Bronze Star; Guggenheim fellow, 1957. Fellow Am. Phys. Soc., A.A.A.S.; mem. Sigma Xi. Roman Catholic. Club: Cosmos (Washington). Author: (with Acosta and Graham) Essentials of Modern Physics, 1971; also articles. Patentee in field; discoverer with Reines of the neutrino, 1956. Home: 11108 Waycroft Way Rockville MD 20852 Office: Catholic Univ America Washington DC 20017

COWAN, DONALD ANDREW, univ. pres.; b. Ft. Worth, May 26, 1914; s. Donald A. and Verna (Hovey) C.; A.B., Tex. Christian U., 1947; Ph.D., Vanderbilt U., 1951; m. Louise Shillingburg, Apr. 6, 1939; 1 son, John Bainard. Asst. chief engr. Am. Type Founders, 1943-45; asst. prof. physics dept. Vanderbilt U., 1951-53; mgr. Nuclear Lab., Convair, Ft. Worth, 1953-55, mgr. Project AID, 1955-56, asso. prof. Tex. Christian U., 1956-59; 59; prof., chmn. physics dept. and sci. div. U. Dallas, 1959-62, pres., 1962—. Dir. S.W. Water Research Council; participant European symposium Fresh Water from the Sea, Athens, Greece, 1962; mem. Gov. Tex. Adv. Commn. on Atomic Energy; pres. Ch. Related Colls. of Tex., 1969; co-chmn. Goals for Dallas Conf., 1966-68; chmn.-elect Inter-U. Council, 1971. Recipient water desalinization research grant Tex. Bd. Water Engrs., Distinguished Alumnus award Tex. Christian U., 1968. Mem. Tex. Acad. Sci., Am. Phys. Soc., Am. Physics Tchrs. Assn., Tex. Assn. Colls. and Univs. (dir.), Assn. Grad. Edn. in Region (pres. 1969-70), Sigma Xi. Address: 9029 Broken Arrow St Dallas TX 75209

COWAN, EDWARD, journalist; b. Bklyn., Nov. 14, 1933; s. Marcy Hamilton and Jennie (Taleisnik) C.; B.A., Columbia Coll., 1954; M.A. in Econs., Johns Hopkins, 1960; m. Ann Louise Wrubel, July 1, 1962; children—Jeffrey Wrubel, Emily Martha, Rachel Jennifer. With U.P.I., 1957-62; with N.Y. Times, 1962—, Benelux corr., Brussels, Belgium, 1965-66, corr. London (Eng.) bur., 1966-67, Toronto (Can.) bur., 1967—; instr. econs. Johns Hopkins, 1956-57; cons. U.S. Bur. Budget, 1963. Served with AUS, 1954-56. Recipient Chanler Hist. Essay prize Columbia, 1954. Author: Oil and Water: The Torrey Canyon Disaster, 1968. Home: 25 Belsize Dr Toronto 295 Ontario Canada Office: NY Times 140 King St W Toronto Ontario Canada

COWAN, FAIRMAN CHAFFEE, lawyer; b. Wellesley Hills, Mass., Apr. 22, 1915; s. James Franklin and Hortense Victoria (Fairman) C.; A.B., Amherst Coll., 1937; LL.B., Harvard, 1940, grad. 44th advanced mgmt. program, Bus. Sch.; m. Martha Logan Allis, Apr. 24, 1943; children—Douglas Fairman, Frederick Allis, Leonard Chaffee. Admitted to Mass. bar, 1940; asso. Goodwin, Procter & Hoar, Boston, 1940-41, 46-52, partner, 1952-54; gen. counsel, clk., sec., v.p., dir. Norton Co., 1955—; dir. Mechanics Nat. Bank, Worcester. Bd. dirs. Worcester Legal Aid Soc.; trustee Clark U., Meml. Hosp., Worcester. Served to lt. USNR, 1942-45. Mem. Am., Mass., Worcester County, Boston bar assns., Mass. Civic League (past v.p.), citizen Plan E Assn. Worcester (past v.p.), Phi Beta Kappa, Alpha Delta Phi. Republican. Home: 48 Berwick St Worcester MA 01602 Office: 1 New Bond St Worcester MA 01606

COWAN, FRANK, photographer; b. N.Y.C., Sept. 26, 1934; s. Maurice and Susan (Romain) C.; student Coll. City N.Y.; m. Elizabeth Langley, May 18, 1968. Independent creative photographer, 1955—; photog. illustrations using real people; pres. Frank Cowan Studios, 1962—, Cowan Realty Corp., 1963—. Recipient numerous awards and gold medals. Home: Birch Hill Rd Patterson NY Office: 5 E 16th St New York City NY 10003

COWAN, FRANK, research co. exec.; b. Aberdeen, Scotland, May 23, 1906; s. Francis M. and Christina (Jenkison) C.; brought U.S., 1913, naturalized, 1918; B.S., U. Va., 1930; m. Mary Louise Shuttleworth, Nov. 27, 1956. Various adminstrv. and mgmt. positions Bell Telephone Labs., N.Y.C. and N.J., asst. treas., 1966-67, treas., 1967-71. Mem. Phi Beta Kappa. Club: Stepping Stones Yacht (N.Y.C.). Home: 105 New England Av Summit NJ 07901

COWAN, FREDERICK FLETCHER, Jr., educator; b. Washington, Jan. 17, 1933; s. Frederick Fletcher and Blanche (Davenport) C.; A.A., George Washington U., 1953, B.S. in Pharmacy, 1955; Ph.D. in Pharmacology, Georgetown U., 1959; m. Phyllis Virginia Cromwell, Nov. 26, 1960; children—Caroline Le-Compte, Kirk Cromwell. USPHS postdoctoral fellow Georgetown U. Schs. Medicine and Dentistry, 1959, instr., asst. prof. pharmacology, 1960-66; faculty U. Ore. Dental Sch., Portland, 1966—, prof. pharmacology, chmn. dept., 1968—. Recipient citation Georgetown U., 1961, Golden Apple award, 1964; Teaching award U. Ore. Dental Sch., 1967, 68, 70. Mem. A.A.A.S., Am. Assn. Dental Schs., Am. Assn. Med. Colls., Am. Assn. U. Profs., Am. Pharm. Assn., Am. Soc. Pharmacology and Exptl. Therapeutics, Assn. Pharmacology and Therapeutics Tchrs. Dentistry, Internat. Assn. Dental Research, Western Pharmacology Soc., Am. Therapeutic Soc., Sigma Xi, Rho Chi, Kappa Psi. Home: 7027 SW 8th Av Portland OR 97219

COWAN, GEORGE ARTHUR, scientist; b. Worcester, Mass., Feb. 15, 1920; s. Louis Abraham and Anna (Listic) C.; B.S. in Chemistry, Worcester Poly. Inst., 1941; Sc.D., Carnegie Inst. Tech., 1950; m. Helen Siegel Dunham, Sept. 7, 1946. Research asst. Palmer Phys. Lab., Princeton, 1941-42; with Metall. Lab., U. Chgo., 1942-45; research asso. Pupin Lab., Columbia, 1945; staff mem. Los Alamos Sci. Lab., 1945-46, staff mem., asso. div. leader, 1949-70, div. leader, 1970—; tchr. asst. Carnegie Inst. Tech., 1946-49. Dir. Los Alamos Nat. Bank, 1963—, chmn. bd. 1965—; v.p., dir. Tesuque Corp., 1962-66. Mem. subcom. radiochemistry NRC, 1959-63. Mem. Los Alamos County Adv. Bd., 1961-64; chmn. Los Alamos Utilities Bd., 1964-67; pres. Los Alamos Concert Assn., 1959-62. Bd. dirs. N.M. Opera Assn.; past bd. dirs., v.p. Los Alamos Med. Center. Recipient E.O. Lawrence Meml. award AEC, 1965. Fellow Am. Phys. Soc., A.A.A.S.; mem. Am. Chem. Soc. (chmn. div. nuclear chemistry and tech. 1970), Fedn. Atomic Scientists (chmn. Los Alamos 1955-56), Am. Nuclear Soc., Sigma Xi. Patentee in field. Home: 721 42d St Los Alamos NM 87544 Office: PO Box 1663 Los Alamos Sci Lab Los Alamos NM 87544

COWAN, HOWARD STEPHEN, utility exec.; b. Shawnee, Okla., Apr. 3, 1914; s. Stephen Granbury and Lodiska (Hall) C.; student U. Okla., 1931-32; m. Grace Lucile Shipley, Aug. 24, 1940; children—Garvin Stephen, Genevieve. Reporter, then city editor News-Star, Shawnee, 1933-40; staff writer A.P., Kansas City and Jefferson City, Mo., 1940-43, war corr. ETO, 1944- 45, corr., Toronto, Ont., Can., 1945-46; gen. mgr. Shipley Baking Co., McAlester, Okla., 1947-48, staff writer, Oklahoma City, 1949; editor McAlester News-Capital, 1949-56; dir. pub. affairs Pub. Service Co. Okla., 1956-68, v.p. pub. affairs, 1968—, also dir.; dir. Utica Sq. Nat. Bank, Tulsa. Mem. Okla. Pardon and Parole Bd., 1956-60; mem. Gov. Okla. Tourist Devel. Commn., 1964-66; adv. bd. pub. utility exec. program U. Mich. Grad. Sch. Bus. Adminstrn., 1964-69; chmn. Selective Service Bd. 76; past pres. Tulsa County Heart Assn., Okla. Heart Assn., Tulsa Safety Council, Okla. A.P. Mng. Editors Assn.; bd. dirs. Okla. Pub. Expenditure Council, Asso. Industries Okla.; past chmn. Tulsa chpt. A.R.C. Recipient award outstanding news coverage A.P. Mng. Editors Assn., 1955. Mem. Sigma Delta Chi, Phi Alpha Mu. Democrat. Baptist. Mason (33, Shriner, Jester). Clubs: Tulsa Press, Summit, Petroleum (Tulsa); Southern Hills Country. Home: 3515 S Lewis St Tulsa, OK 74105. Office: 600 S Main St Tulsa OK 74102

COWAN, IVY, textile exec.; b. N.C., Sept. 25, 1902; m. Ree Williams, Pres., treas., dir. Stonecutter Mills Corp., Spindale, N.C. Office: Stonecutter Mills Corp Spindale NC 28160

COWAN, JACK DAVID, educator, biologist; b. Leeds, Eng., Aug. 24, 1933; s. Samuel F. and Isabelle (Killen) C.; B.Sc., Edinburgh U., 1955; D.I.C., Imperial Coll., London, 1957; S.M., Mass. Inst. Tech., 1960; Ph.D., U. London, 1966; m. Jillian Abrams, July 2, 1958; children—Jeremy Simon, Sarah Jane. Came to U.S., 1967. Research engr., mathematician Ferranti, Ltd., Scotland, 1955-58; research asso. Northeastern U., summer, 1960; mem. neurophysiol. group Mass. Inst. Tech., 1960-62; acad. visitor elec. engring. Imperial Coll., London, 1962-66; guest Nat. Physics Lab., U.K., 1966-67; prof., chmn. com. math. biology U. Chgo., 1967-70, prof., chmn. dept. theoretical biology, 1970—. Mem. adv. council Lab. for Cybernetics CNR, Naples, Italy, 1968—; mem. com. epidemiology and biometry NIH, 1969-73. Mem. Biophys. Soc., Am. Math. Soc., Neuroscis. Soc., Brain Research Assn. (U.K.). Author: (with S. Winograd) Reliable Computation in the Presence of Noise, 1963. Editorial bd. Jour. Theoretacal Biology, 1968—, Acta Biotheoretica, 1968—. Office: 939 E 57th St Chicago IL 60637

COWAN, J MILTON, linguist; b. Salt Lake City, Feb. 22, 1907; s. James Brimley and Mabel Vickers (Brown) C.; A.B., U. of Utah, 1931, A.M., 1932; fellow U. of Cal. at Berkeley, 1932-33; Ph.D., U. of Iowa, 1935; student Univ. of Leipzig, Germany, 1929-30; m. Theodora Mary Ronayne, Sept. 1, 1934; children—J. Ronayne, Bruce Milton, Julia. Research asso. U. of Iowa, 1935- 1935- 38; asst. prof. German, 1938-41, asso. prof., 1942; dir. intensive language program Am. Council of Learned Socs., 1942-46, also spl. cons., War Dept., in charge of language phase of Army Specialized Training Program and other such training programs in war and state depts. and other govt. agencies; prof. linguistics and dir. div. Modern langs. Cornell U. since 1946; associated with Linguistic Inst. sponsored by Linguistic Soc. as prof. or lecturer, U. of Mich., 1938, 40, U. of N.C., 1941, U. of Wis., 1944, U. of Mich., summer 1948. Fellow Acoustical Soc. Am.; mem. Am. Council of Learned Soc. (dir. 1956-60), Linguistic Soc. of Am. (sec.-treas., bus. mgr. pubs. 1939-50, pres. 1966), Sigma Xi. Author: Pocket Guide to Arabic; English- Arabic Word List. Co-author: Spoken Arabic; Basic Arabic; Conversational Arabic. Editor: A Dictionary of Modern Written Arabic. Home: 107 Hanshaw Road Ithaca NY 14850 ☆

COWAN, JOHN COLUMBUS, Jr., former mfg. exec.; b. Rutherfordton, N.C., May 18, 1899; s. John Columbus and Viola (McDaniel) C.; A.B., U. N.C., 1921; H.H.D., N.C. State Coll.; m. Edith Jenkins, June 9, 1926; children—John Columbus III, Robert Jenkins. With Stonecutter Mills Co., Spindale, N.C., 1921- 31, Burlington Industries, Inc. (formerly Burlington Mills Corp.), Greensboro, 1931—, successively supt., v.p. charge mfg., 1938-47, dir., mem. exec. and finance coms., pres., 1947-54, vice chmn. bd., 1954-69. Chmn. bd. trustees Greensboro Coll.; trustee Meth. Children's Home; pres. Meth. Coll. Found. N.C. State dir. Payroll Savs. Bonds Div.; mem. Greensboro Bd. Edn.; bd. dirs. N.C. State Textile Found., U. N.C. Bus. Found.; exec. council Med. Found. N.C.; exec. bd. Boy Scouts Am. Recipient Silver Beaver award Boy Scouts Am. Mem. U. N.C. Alumni Assn. (dir.), Newcomen Soc. N.Am., Omicron Delta Kappa (hon.) , Phi Psi. Democrat. Methodist. Kiwanian. Home: 2011 Lafayette Av Greensboro NC 27408

COWAN, JOHN RITCHIE, agronomist, educator; b. Leamington, Ont., Can., Feb. 3, 1916; s. James C. and Gertrude (Ritchie) C.; B.S., Ont. Agrl. Coll., 1939; M.S., U. Minn., 1942, Ph.D., 1952; m. Ruth Elna Montgomery, June 29, 1947; children—Kenneth Ritchie, Mary Jane. Asst. plant breeder Dominion Exptl. Sta., Harrow, Ont., Can., 1937-42, charge cereal, forage research Exptl. Farms, N.S., Can., 1942-45; charge grass breeding Eastern Can. Central Exptl. Farm, Ottawa, Ont., 1945-46; forage breeder, tchr. agronomy Macdonald Coll. McGill U., Montreal, 1946-48; plant breeder, asst. agronomist, asst. prof. Ore. State U., Corvallis, 1948-52, asso. agronomist, asso. prof., 1952-55, prof., agronomist, 1955-59, head dept. farm crops, 1959- -. Fellow A.A.A.S., Am. Soc. Agronomy (pres.-elect 1970); mem. Am. Assn. U. Profs., Agrl. Inst. Can., Crop Sci. Soc. Am. (past pres.). Kiwanian (past pres., past lt. gov.). Contbr. articles profl. jours. Home: 1616 Dixon St Corvallis OR 97330

COWAN, JOHN STEPHEN, navy med. officer; b. Judith Gap, Nont., Nov. 26, 1913; s. Lyle A. and Louise (Starch) C.; B.S., M.B., M.D., U. Minn.; student Wayne State Grad. Sch., 1938-41, U. Pa. Grad. Sch. Medicine, 1954-55; m. Catherine Anne Ryan, Apr. 12, 1941 (dec. 1962); children—Mary Kathleen, Anne Louise, John William; m. 2d, Elizabeth J. Schilling, Jan. 17, 1970. Commd. U.S. Navy, advanced trhough grades to rear adm.; comdg. officer Naval Med. Field Research Lab., 1945-50; chief medicine Naval Hosp., Phila., 1956-60; fleet surgeon U.S. Atlantic Fleet, also dir. med. affairs SACLANT, 1960-63; exec. officer Naval Hosp., San Diego, 1963-64; comdg. officer Naval Hosp., Phila., 1964-66; Pacific Fleet med. officer, also CINCPAC, 1966—; asso. prof. medicine Hahnemann Med. Sch., 1956-60. Decorated Legion of Merit; (Order of Breast); Chinese Cloud and Banner (Order of Breast); Republic of Vietnam Army Distinguished Service medal 1st class. Fellow A.C.P.; mem. A.M.A. (chief party med. edn. project Saigon 1969-70), Internat. Soc. Internal Medicine, Assn. Mil. Surgeons U.S., Coll. Physicians Phila. Home: 28 Makalapa Dr Honolulu HI 96818. Office: CINCPAC Med Office CINCPAC Hdqrs Honolulu HI

COWAN, JOSEPH LLOYD, educator, philosopher; b. Gary, Ind., Mar. 27, 1929; s. Lloyd Hower and Gwen Alice (Boles) C.; B.A., U. Chgo., 1950, M.A., 1955, Ph.D., 1959; m. Ann Enid Bunzel, Apr. 5, 1956; children—Alan Joseph, Steven Jonas, Dena Ellen. Mem. faculty U. Ariz. at Tucson, 1958—, prof. philosophy, head dept., 1968—. Co-chmn. Ariz. New Party, 1968-69. Bd. dirs. Ariz. Civil Liberties Union, 1969—. Served with AUS, 1952-54. Le Verne Noyes scholar; Carnegie fellow. Mem. Am. Philos. Assn., Mind Assn., Am. Assn. U. Profs., A.A.A.S., Mountain Plains Philos. Assn. (bd. dirs. 1963-64), Phi Beta Kappa. Author: Pleasure and Pain, 1968; Thought and Language, 1970. Home: 2030 Calle Alta Vista Tucson AZ 85719

COWAN, KENNETH JAMES, mut. fund exec.; b. Medford, Mass., Apr. 5, 1932; s. Louis F. and Alice (O'Mara) C.; B.S., Boston Coll., 1953, M.B.A., 1966; m. Irene M. Crowe, July 10, 1954; children—John, Kenneth. Sr. accountant Peat, Marwick, Mitchell & Co., Boston, 1956-61; asst. comptroller Crompton & Knowles, Worcester, Mass., 1961-64; asst. treas. Keystone Custodian Funds, Inc., Boston, 1964-67, treas., 1967-69, sr. v.p., 1968-69, exec. v.p. operations, 1970—; dir. Investment Cos. Services Corp., Diversified Investment Services, Ltd., Keystone Apollo Fund, Keystone of Am., Ltd., Keystone Real Estate Co., Inc., Keystone of Can. Accumulation Fund, Ltd. Served to lt. (j.g.) USNR, 1953-56. C.P.A., Mass. Mem. Financial Execs. Inst., Am. Inst. C.P.A.'s. Lion. Club: Watertown Yacht. Home: 61 Flagg Rd Southborough MA 01772 Office: 50 Congress St Boston MA 02109

COWAN, LOUIS G., pub. co. exec., communications exec.; b. Chgo., Dec 12, 1909; s. Jacob J. and Hetty (Smitz) C.; Ph.B., U. Chgo., 1931; m. Pauline Spiegel, Aug. 7, 1939; children—Paul, Geoffrey, Holly, Liza. Pres., Louis G. Cowan Co., pub. relations, 1931-41, Louis G. Cowan, Inc., radio and TV prodns., 1946-55; v.p. creative services CBS, Inc., 1955-58, pres. CBS TV Network, 1958-59; dir. Morse Communication Research Center, Brandeis U., Waltham, Mass., 1961-65; dir. Spl. Programs, Grad. Sch. Journalism, Columbia, N.Y.C., 1965—; pres., editor Chilmark Press, Inc., 1962—; chmn. publs. and adv. bd. Partisan Rev.; chmn. pub. com. Columbia Journalism Rev.; dir. Franklin Book Programs, Inc. Mem. exec. com. Nat. Book Com.; chmn. Nat. Library Week. Bd. dirs. African-Am. Inst.; cons. radio sect. Bur. Public Relations, War Dept., 1941-43; dir. Voice Am., chief N.Y.C. office Overseas br. O.W.I., 1943-45. Mem. Council on Fgn. Relations, A.A.A.S., Zeta Beta Tau. Clubs: The Century Country (Purchase, N.Y.); Tavern (Chgo.); Lotos (N.Y.). Home: Westbury Hotel New York City NY 10021 Office: Grad Sch Journalism Columbia U New York City NY 10027

COWAN, OLIVER DANIEL, steel co. exec.; b. Gananoque, Ont., Can., Sept. 4, 1905; s. Freeman Britton and Mabel (McGrath) C.; ed. Trinity Coll. Sch.; grad. Roy Mil. Coll., 1926; m. Janet Matthew, Sept. 8, 1934; children—Christopher, Brian. Chmn., pres., dir. Ont. Steel Products Ltd., Toronto; dir. Falconbridge Nickel Mines Ltd., Electrovert Plastics Corp., Tycos Tool & Die Ltd. Served with Canadian Army, 1940-44. Mem. Soc. Automotive Engrs., Soc. Plastic Engrs. Anglican. Clubs: Nat.; Toronto Curling, Toronto Golf; Badminton and Racquet; Empire. Home: 14 Ancroft Pl Toronto Ontario Canada Office: 7 King St E Toronto 1 Ontario Canada*

COWAN, RICHARD SUMMER, sci. adminstr.; b. Crawfordsville, Ind., Jan. 23, 1921; s. Walter Harrison and Eura B. (Walker) C.; A.B., Wabash Coll., 1942; M.S., U. Hawaii, 1948; Ph.D., Columbia, 1952; m. Mary Frances Minnich, June 28, 1941; children—Richard A., Diedra Anne, Charles Ian. Teaching asst. U. Hawaii, 1946-48; tech. asst. N.Y. Bot. Garden, N.Y.C., 1948-52, asst. curator, 1952-57; asso. curator Smithsonian Instn., Washington, 1957-62, asst. dir. Mus. Natural History, 1962-65, dir., 1965—. Sec. nat. com. XI Internat. Bot. Congress; mem. nat. com. Internat. Biol. Program. Served with USNR, 1943-45. NSF fellow, 1952-53. Mem. Am. Inst. Biol. Scis., A.A.A.S., Am. Soc. Plant Taxonomists, Internat. Assn. Plant Taxonomy. Methodist. Contbr. articles profl. jours. Home: 4409 Tonquil Pl Beltsville, MD 20705. Office: Smithsonian Instn Washington DC 20560

COWAN, ROBERT GEORGE, banker; b. Lake Linden, Mich., Feb. 25, 1905; s. William Robert and May Agnes (Harrison) C.; student Phillips Exeter Acad., Mass. Inst. Tech.; B.S., N.Y.U., 1930; grad. Grad. Sch. Banking, Am. Bankers Assn., 1940; LL.D., Upsala Coll., 1955; m. Hazel Witherall Damon, May 29, 1930. Statistician research dept., bank examiner, chief analysis div. of bank exams. div. Fed. Res. Bank N.Y., 1927-38; cashier Nat. Newark & Essex Banking Co., Newark, 1938-40, pres., dir., 1940—; chmn. Nat. Newark & Essex Bank, 1962-70; dir. Mut. Benefit Life Ins. Co., Am. Express Co., Am. Express Internat. Banking Co., Midlantic Banks, Nat. Newark & Essex Bank, Schlumberger Co., Fireman's Fund Ins. Co., San Francisco; mgr. Howard Savs. Inst. Past pres. Greater Newark Devel. Council; trustee, treas. Newark Coll. Engring., Marcus L. Ward Home; trustee Newark Mus., Victoria Found.; bd. dirs. Morristown Meml. Hosp. Mem. N.J. C. of C. (dir.). Clubs: Essex (Newark); Somerset Hills Country. Home: Boxwood Hollow Bernardsville NJ 07924 Office: 744 Broad St Newark NJ 07103

COWAN, STUART DUBOIS, publisher, cons.; b. Tarrytown, N.Y., Apr. 30, 1917; s. Stuart DuBois and Lucy D. (Coffey) C.; B.A., Princeton, 1939; m. Pauline Horn, Nov. 2, 1940; children—Stuart A., Robert B. With Raytheon Co., Lexington, Mass., 1959-63, v.p. comml. marketing, 1960-63; pres., chief exec. officer United Research, Inc., Cambridge, Mass., 1963-69; exec. v.p. Radio Publs., Inc., 1970—, also dir.; dir. Consumer & Tech. Industries, Inc., Greenwood Union Cemetery Corp. Served with USNR, 1941-46. Mem. I.E.E.E., U.S. Naval Inst., N.A.M., Am. Marketing Assn. Clubs: Shenorock Shore, Stage Harbor Yacht; Princeton (N.Y.C.). Co-author: Vigor-How to Get in Shape for Life, 1968; Better Shortwave Reception, 1970; The Truth About Citizens Band Antennas, 1971. Home: North St Box 596 Rye NY 10580

COWAN, THOMAS ANTHONY, educator; b. Phila., Oct. 22, 1904; s. John Joseph and Sarah (Joyce) C.; B.S., Wharton Sch., U. of Pa., 1926; LL.B., U. of Pa., 1931, Ph.D., 1932; S.J.D., Harvard, 1933; m. Marianne Ordon, July 12, 1952; 1 son, John; children by previous marriageMary, Sara, Anthony, James. Instr. philosophy U. Pa., 1926-32; Research Fellow, Harvard Law Sch., 1932-34; spl. atty. U.S. Dept. Justice, 1934-36; lectr. on jurisprudence, Catholic Univ. of Am., 1934-36, C. G. Jung Inst., Zurich, 1966-68; asso. prof. law La. State U., 1936-40; asso. prof. philosophy U. of Pa., 1940-46; prof. law U. of Neb., 1946-47; prof. law Wayne U., 1947-53; prof. law Rutgers U., 1953- . Brumbaugh lectr. U. Pa., 1958; del Inst. Mgmt. Sci., 1958-; vis. prof. Case Inst. Tech.; vis. research lawyer U. Cal. at Berkeley, 1964-65, admitted Mich., D.C. Bars; cons. system Devel Corp., center for Mgmt. Sci. U. Pa., Space Scis. Lab., U. Cal. Dir. Inst. Exptl. Method; corr. Instituto Argentino de Filosofia Juridica y Social; mem. bd. govs. Philosophy of Sci. Assn.; panel mem. War Labor Bd., World War II. Mem. A.A.A.S., Am. Philos. Assn., Med.-Legal Soc. N.J. (orgn. com.), Dante Soc. Am. Soc. Polit. and Legal Philosophy, Internat. Assn. for Legal and Social Philosophy (mem. presdl. bd., chmn. Am. sect.). Author: Am. Jurisprudence Reader. Contbr. to Interpretations of Modern Legal Philosophies. Essays in Honor of Roscoe Pound, 1947; Essays in the Law of Torts, 1961; Collected Essays in Experimental Jurisprudence, 1966; contbr. to legal and philos. periodicals. Home: 117 Clark St Glen Ridge, NJ 07028.

COWAN, WALLACE EDGAR, lawyer; b. Jersey City, Jan. 28, 1924; s. Benjamin and Dorothy (Zunz) C.; LL.B. cum laude, Harvard, 1950; B.S. magna cum laude, N.Y.U., 1947; m. Ruth Daitzman, June 8, 1947; children—Laurie, Paul, Judith. Partner, Stroock, Stroock & Lavan, attys., N.Y.C., 1950—; sec. Ametek, Inc.; sec., dir. The Whitlock Corp. Mem. Teacneck (N.J.) Adv. Bd. on Parks, Playgrounds and Recreation, 1966—; pres. No. Valley Commuters Assn. Served to 1st lt. USAF, 1942-45. Decorated Air medal with Silver cluster. Mem. Beta Gamma Sigma. Home: 499 Emerson Av Teaneck NJ 07666 Office: 61 Broadway New York City NY 10006

COWAN, WALTER GREAVES, newspaper editor; b. Bond, Miss., Mar. 24, 1912; s. Decatur Douglas and Mary Hermina (Jonte) C.; grad. Gulf Coast Jr. Coll., 1932; B. Journalism, U. Mo., 1936; m. Margaret Martinez, Sept. 28, 1940; children—Walter Greaves, William Douglas. Reporter, New Orleans Item, 1936-39, asst. city editor, 1939-40; pub. relations and advt. rep. G., M. & O. R.R., 1941-45; reporter New Orleans States, 1945-46, city editor, 1946-64; mng. editor New Orleans States-Item, 1964-69, editor, 1969—. Mem. A.P. Mng. Editors Assn. (v.p. La.-Miss. 1970-71). Home: 7715 Nelson St New Orleans LA 70125 Office: New Orleans States-Item 3800 Howard Av New Orleans LA 70140

COWAN, WAYNE HARPER, editor; b. Balt., Feb. 11, 1928; s. John Eli and Mabel (Miller) C.; A.B., Western Md. Coll., 1948; student Union Theol. Sem., N.Y.C., 1951- 53; M.S., Columbia, 1958; m. Ruth Dillingham, Dec. 30, 1960; 1 son, Kristor Wayne. Short-term missionary tchr.; mem. Bd. Missions Meth. Ch., 1948-51; editorial sec. Christianity and Crisis, N.Y.C., 1954-56, mng. editor, 1956-68, editor, 1968—. Chmn. editorial com. The Intercollegian, 1961-65; bd. dirs. Asso. Ch. Press, 1966—. Cons. Nat. Conf. Christians and Jews. Mem. county com. N.Y. County Democratic party, 1960-62, Rockland County, 1968—. Bd. dirs. Rockland County Civil Liberties Union; trustee Latin Am. Found. Profl. journalism fellow Stanford U., 1969. Editor: What the Christian Hopes for in Society, 1957, editor, contbr.; Facing Protestant-Roman Catholic Tensions, 1960; Witness to a Generation, 1966, Christianity and Crisis, 1968. Home: Maple Rd Valley Cottage NY 10989 Office: 537 W 121st St New York City NY 10027

COWAN, WILLIAM EDWIN, electronics co. exec.; b. Chgo., Dec. 14, 1910; s. William and Elizabeth (Edwin) C.; student Crane Jr. Coll., Chgo., 1930-33; m. Pauline Wesse, Dec. 8, 1962; children—Penelope (Mrs. Jerry Gilbert), Pamela (Mrs. Robert Howard), Wayne Wesse, Jerry Travis. With Spiegel, Inc., 1933-54, v.p., dir., 1949-54; pres. P. Nacey Co., Chgo., 1954—, also dir.; pres., dir. Allied Radio Corp., 1964—. Active Chgo. Crusade of Mercy. Bd. dirs. Loring Sch. Girls, 1958-61. Club: Beverly Country (bd. dirs. 1951-53) (Chgo.). Home: 40 S Tower Rd Oak Brook IL Office: 833 N California Chicago IL 60622

COWAN, WILLIAM MAXWELL, educator, anatomist; b. Johannesburg, S. Africa, Sept. 27, 1931; s. Adam and Jesse (Maxwell) C.; B.Sc. with honors, U. Witwatersrand, Johannesburg, 1952; D.Phil., Oxford (Eng.) U., 1956, B.M., B.Ch., 1958, M.A., 1959; m. Margaret Sherlock, Mar. 31, 1965; children—Margaret Ruth, Stephen Maxwell, David Maxwell. Came to U.S., 1964. Deptl. demonstrator anatomy U. Oxford (Eng.), 1953-58, lectr. anatomy Pembroke Coll., 1956-60, univ. demonstrator, 1959-64, fellow, tutor anatomy Pembroke Coll., 1960- 66, lectr. anatomy Balliol Coll., 1962-66; vis. asso. prof. anatomy Washington U. Sch. Medicine, St. Louis, 1964-65, prof. anatomy, chmn. dept., 1968—; asso. prof. anatomy U. Wis. Sch. Medicine, 1966-68. Fellow Royal Micros. Soc.; mem. Anat. Soc. Gt. Britain and Ireland, Am. Assn. Anatomists. Mng. editor Jour. Comparative Neurology, 1969—. Contbr. papers in field. Home: 7001 Westmoreland Dr University City, MO 63130. Office: 660 S Euclid Av St Louis MO 63110

COWARD, NOEL PEIRCE, playwright, actor; b. London (Teddington), England, Dec. 16, 1899; s. Arthur Sabin and Violet (Vetch) C.; educated privately. Appeared first on stage 1910. Author: (plays) The Young Idea, 1920; The Rat Trap, 1921; I'll Leave It to You, 1922; Hay Fever, 1924; Fallen Angels, 1925; The Vortex, 1925; Easy Virtue, 1926; The Queen Was in the Parlor, 1926; The Marquise, 1927; This Year of Grace, Bitter Sweet, 1929; Private Lives, 1930; Cavalcade, 1931; Words and Music, 1932; Design for Living, 1933; Conversation Piece, 1934; Point Valaine, 1935; Tonight at Eight-Thirty, 1936; Operette, 1938; Nude with Violin; Present Laughter; South Sea Bubble; Look After Lulu; (musical comedy) The Girl Who Came to Supper; Waiting in the Wings, 1960; Sail Away, 1965; also Suite in Three Keys, 1966; made motion picture appearances in Our Man in Havana, Surprise Package, Bunny Lake is Missing; books include Collected Sketches and Lyrics, 1931; Present Indicative, 1937; To Step Aside, 1939; In Which We Serve (motion picture; dir., also took leading part); author Blithe Spirit (motion picture) 1942; TV appearances in This Happy Breed, Blithe Spirit. Together with Music; author: Future Indefinite, 1954; Present Indicative; Pomp & Circumstance, 1960; Pretty Polly, 1965. Frequently on radio. Address: Les Avants sur Montreux Switzerland

COWART, D.R., business exec.; b. Valdosta, Ga., 1916. Pres., dir. Morrison, Inc., Mobile, Ala.; dir. Marine Bank & Trust Co., Tampa, Fla. Home: 4525 Dale Av Tampa FL 33609 Office: PO Box 2608 Mobile AL 36601

COWART, ELTON L., banker. Vice pres., cashier Citizens & So. Nat. Bank, Savannah, Ga. Office: 300 Bull St Box 9568 Savannah GA 31402*

COWDEN, DAVID, educator; B.A., Swarthmore Coll.; M.A., Ph.D., Harvard. Prof. English Swarthmore Coll. Address: 312 Ogden Av Swarthmore PA 19081*

COWDEN, DUDLEY JOHNSTON, educator, economist; b. Grinnell, Ia., Jan. 10, 1899; s. George W. and Bertha M. (Johnson) C.; A.B., Grinnell Coll., 1919; A.M., Sch. Commerce and Adminstrn., U. Chgo., 1922; Ph.D., Columbia, 1931; m. Mercedes Seidler, Dec. 25, 1926. Instr. in econs. Lafayette Coll., 1926-29, St. John U., 1931-34, Williams Coll., 1934-35; asso. prof. econs. U. N.C., 1935, now prof. emeritus econ. statistics. Cons., U.S. Bur. Labor Statistics, Fed. Res. Bd. Hon. research asso. Univ. Coll., London, 1958. Fellow Am. Statis. Assn., A.A.A.S.; mem. Am., So. econ. assns., Phi Beta Kappa, Beta Gamma Sigma. Author 5 books on statistics. Co-author (with Mercedes S. Cowden) 2 books, (with F.E. Croxton) 5 books on statistics; also articles profl. jours. Invented flexible calendar of working days. Home: 304 Country Club Rd Chapel Hill NC 27514 ☆

COWDEN, MILES FERRELL, mfg. co. exec.; b. Polk County, Mo., June 8, 1909; s. Arthur H. and Mattie Jane (Cochran) C.; m. Lucille Yates, Feb. 1, 1930; 1 son, Donald Ray. With Farmland Industries, Kansas City, Mo., 1929—, exec. v.p. mfg. and prodn., 1967—; dir. Coop. Farm Chems. Assn., Farmers Chem. Co., Terra Resources, Inc., Nat. Coop. Refinery Assn., Nat. Petroleum Refiners Assn., CRA Internat., Inc., Terra Trinidad Tobaggo Ltd. Mem. Kansas City (Mo.) C. of C. Baptist. Home: 3400 N W Oakcrest Dr Kansas City, MO 64151. Office: 3315 N Oak Trafficway Kansas City MO 64116

COWDEN, MORTON HARRIS, educator; b. Phila., Aug. 4, 1924; s. Barney and Rebecca (Fleet) C.; B.A. with honors, U. Pa., 1949; M.A., Columbia, 1951, certificate in Russian studies, 1951, Ph.D., 1963; m. Margaret Gisondi, Sept. 8, 1953; 1 dau., Nina Lucia. Fellow govt. Coll. City N.Y., 1951-53; instr. polit. sci. Washington U., St. Louis, 1953-55; instr. pub. law and govt. Columbia U., N.Y.C., 1957-64; prof. polit. sci., dir. internat. studies Briarcliff Coll., Briarcliff Manor, N.Y., 1965-68; prof., chmn. dept. polit. sci. Western Ill. U., Macomb, 1968—. Mem. Am. Civil Liberties Union, 1963—, N.A.A.C.P., 1954—, SANE, 1960—. Served with AUS, 1943-45. Mem. Am. Polit. Sci. Assn., Am. Assn. Advancement Slavic Studies, Am. Assn. U. Profs., Am. Fedn. Tchrs., Caucus for a New Polit. Sci. Home: 821 Stadium Dr Macomb IL 61455

COWDEN, THOMAS KYLE, govt. ofcl.; b. Hickory, Pa., June 14, 1908; s. John M. and Nettie M. (Mitchel) C.; B.S., Ohio State U., 1930, M.S., 1931; Ph.D., Cornell U., 1937; LL.D., Purdue U., 1966; m. Clara Williams, Feb. 6, 1937; children—John W., Jean W. Research Pa. State Coll., 1931-36; teaching, research Purdue U., 1937-43; dir. research Am. Farm Bur. Fedn., 1943-49; head dept. agrl. econs. Mich. State U., 1949-54, dean sch. of agr., 1954-69; asst. sec. agr. USDA, 1969—. Cons. various govtl. and bus. agys. Mem. Am. Farm Econs. Assn. (past pres.), Sigma Xi, Phi Kappa Phi, Alpha Zeta, Alpha Gamma Rho. Contbr. articles on marketing and agrl. policy to periodicals. Home: 3833 N Roberts Lane Arlington VA 22207

COWDIN, ROBERT DAWES, automation co. exec.; b. Lafayette, Ind., Dec. 9, 1928; s. Thomas and Mae (Pilling) C.; student Ind. Bus. Sch. Accounting, 1946-49; m. Dorothy G. Cornett, July 9, 1922; children-Scott T., Teresa A. Buyer, Chance Vought Aircraft, Dallas, 1954-57; works mgr. Paul Omohundro Co., Los Angeles, 1957-59; exec. v.p. Consol. Am. Services, Inc., Los Angeles, 1959-61; pres. Conam Inspection, Inc., Tulsa, 1962-68; sr. v.p. Automation Industries, Inc., Century City Cal., 1968—. Served with USAF, 1950-54. Mem. Indsl. Radiographic Soc. (pres. 1969-70), Soc. Nondestructive Testing. Home: 1966 Westridge Rd Los Angeles CA 90049 Office: 1901 Av of Stars Century City CA 90067

COWDRY, EDMUND VINCENT, anatomist; b. MacLeod, Alberta, Can., July 18 1888; s. Nathaniel H. and Anna (Ingham) C.; A.B., U. Toronto, 1909; Ph.D., U. Chgo., 1913; D.Sc., Institutum Divi Thomae, Cin., 1957; m. Alice Hanford Smith, Dec. 20, 1916; children—Edmund Vincent, Alice Moira, Margaret Hanford. Came to U.S., 1909, naturalized, 1930. Asst. and asso. anatomy U. Chgo. 1909- 13, Johns Hopkins, 1913-19; prof. Peking (China) Union Med. Coll., 1917- 21; asso. mem. Rockefeller Inst., 1921-28; prof. cytology Washington U., 1928-41, anatomy, 1941-50; dir. Wernse Cancer Research Lab., 1950-60; dir. research Barnard Free Skin and Cancer Hosp., 1936-48; dir. research Sci. Assos., Inc., 1964; distinguished prof. Institutum Divi Thomae, 1959, Harvey lectr., 1923, Gross lectr., 1924, Delamar lectr., 1938, Christian Fenger lectr., 1948; vis. lectr. in oncology U. Cal., 1950. Cons. to the USPHA, 1938-46, mem. carcinogenesis panel, 1961; cons. Rand Devel. Corp., 1961-64, Cancer Inst. Miami, 1955-58, VA, 1955-58. Point 4 adviser in cancer Govt. India, also ABMAC adviser Rep. of China, Formosa, 1952. Trustee Bermuda Biol. Sta., 1927-41. Former mem. bd. dirs. Am. Cancer Soc., Nat. Cancer Found., Am. Assn. Cancer Research. Pres. Union Am. Biol. Socs., 1936-39, 4th Internat. Cancer Research Congress, 1947, 2d Internat. Gerontol. Congress, 1951, Am. Assn. Cancer Research 1951. Gerontol. Soc., 1952, Internat. Assn. Gerontology, 1951-54. Hon. pres. 1st Pan-Am. Gerontol. Congress, 1956, 1st Pan-Am. Cancer Cytology Congress, 1957. Vice pres. Am. Assn. Anatomists, Am. Soc. Naturalists, Sect. N. of A.A.A.S. Chmn. div. med. sci. NRC, 1930-31, Nat. Sci. Council, City of Hope, 1954-60, VA Adv. Com. on Aging, 1956- 57. Former mem. adv. com. Fels Inst. Child Development, Internat. Com. Study Infantile Paralysis, Yellow Fever Commn. Rockefeller Found., Cancer Prevention Com., also various med. and sci. socs. Recipient Bobst award for outstanding work in gerontology, London, 1954, award Gerontol. Research Found., St. Louis, 1956; medal ministry oi Edn., Rep. China, 1959; Bertner Foundation award, research in cancer, 1960, medal 64th meeting Japanese Assn. Anatomists, 1959, mil. decoration comdr.-in-chief Chinese Army, 1959, citation V Internat. Congress Gerontology, 1960, certificate of appreciation Am. Assn. Cancer Research, 1970. Hon. fellow Royal Micros. Soc., Soc. de Cancerologia de Guadalajara, Argentine Gerontol. Soc., Soc. Philomanthique de Paris; member Nat. Geriatrics Soc. (hon.), Academica Sinica (corr.) Author books including; Cancer Cells, 1958 (tran. into Russian); (with Finerty and Textbook of Histology, 1960; (with Emmel and others) Laboratory Technique in Biology and Medicine, 1964; (with Lansing and others) Problems of Aging, 1952; Care of Geriatric Patient, 1962 (translated into Spanish); The Etiology and Prevention of Cancer in Man, 1968. Editor, author of publications relating to field. Discover organism of heartwater, 1924, life cycle of East Coast fever parasite, 1930. Home: 4961 Laclede Ave St Louis MO 63108 Office: 660 S Kingshighway St Louis MO 63110

COWEE, JOHN WIDMER, educator; b. Wausau, Wis., Aug. 1, 1918; s. Charles Arthur and Hattie L. (Widmer) C.; B.S., U. Wis., 1947, M.B.A, 1948, Ph.D., 1951, LL.B., 1956; m. Annette Louise Oetking, Oct. 12, 1940; children—John Widmer, Jeffrey Deane. Mgr., Pantzer Lumber Co., Sheboygan, Wis., 1938-41; asst. prof. Sch. Commerce U. Wis., 1951-53; asso. prof., prof. bus. adminstrn., law U. Cal. at Berkeley, 1954-66, asso. dean, 1955-57, vice chmn., 1958- 60, dean Grad. Sch. Bus. Adminstrn., chmn. dept. bus. adminstrn., 1961-66; v.p. bus. and finance, prof. law Marquette U., Milw., 1966-68, exec. v.p., provost of univ. Sch. Medicine, 1968—, also sec. bd. trustees; dir. Marine Nat. Exchange Bank, Milw., Cutter Lab., Ind. Mem. policy owner's rev. com. Northwestern Mut. Life Ins. Co. Vice pres. Med. Center Southeastern Wis.; mem. Ins. Forum San Francisco; adviser Com. Econ. Devel. (Bay Area Assos.); adviser, cons. interim com. Cal. Legislature. Bd. dirs. Wis. Heart Assn. Served to capt., inf. AUS, 1942-46. Mem. Am. Risk and Ins. Assn., Soc. Advancement Mgmt., Comml. Club San Francisco, Purchasing Agts. Assn. San Francisco, Internat. Assn. Ins. Law, Bank Auditors and Comptrollers, Phi Alpha Delta. Editor: Risk, Insurance and Law, 1960—; editorial adviser econs. and law Ency. Brit., 1958—. Home: 4107 N Lake Dr Shorewood Milwaukee WI 53211

COWELL, CHARLES HERBERT, architect; b. Kansas City, Mo., Dec. 20, 1913; s. James Herbert and Margaret (Younkman) C.; B.S., U. Kan., 1936; m. Marjorie Walker, June 19, 1937; children—Diane L. (Mrs. John Lister), Herbert W., Judy M. (Mrs. Bob Bratton). With various archtl. firms, 1936-45; with Kenneth Franzheim, Houston, 1945-46, Pierce & Cowell, 1946-47; pvt. practice architecture, 1947; with Cowell & Neuhaus, 1948-63; pres. Koetter, Tharp & Cowell, Inc., Houston, 1963—. Mem. Tex. Bd. Archtl. Examiners, 1962-69. Dir. Vols. in Pub. Schs., Houston Ind. Sch. Dist., 1970-71. Recipient award for McAllen (Tex.) State Bank, 1962. Fellow A.I.A. (pres. Houston chpt. 1951); mem. Tex. Soc. Architects (v.p. 1964), Kappa Sigma. Episcopalian. Kiwanian. Home: 6038 Glen Cove St Houston TX 77007 Office: 1535 W Loop South Houston TX 77027

COWELL, DON RODMAN, pub. relations exec.; b. St. Paul, Dec. 13, 1914; s. William Henry and Beatrice (Ritch) C.; A.B., U. Minn., 1936; m. Doris Chandler Nov. 4, 1938; children—Bruce, Christine. Reporter Minneapolis Star, 1936-37; pub. relations dept. Ill. Bell Telephone Co., 1937-41, Chgo. Surface Lines, 1941-44, Inland Steel Co., 1944-47; pub. relations dir. Quaker Oats Co., Chgo., 1947-56; prin. Gardner, Jones & Cowell, pub. relations counsel, Chgo., retired. Chmn. pub. relations com. Chgo. Community Fund, 1956; trustee Geneva Pub. Library. Mem. Grocery Mfrs. Assn. (chmn. pub. relations com. 1956-58), Pub. Relations Soc. Am. (nat. dir., nat. v.p. 1956, pres. Chgo. chpt. 1955-56), Sigma Delta Chi. Clubs: Press, Tavern (Chgo.); Geneva (Ill.) Golf. Author sects. of books, articles in field. Home: 216 Kenston Ct Geneva IL 60134 Office: 79 W Monroe St Chicago IL 60603

COWELL, JOHN FRANKLIN, banker; b. Easton, Pa., Oct. 1, 1908; s. John and Ella (Sutter) C.; B.A., Lafayette Coll., 1930; m. Lee A. Marquez, Apr. 16, 1937; children-Lynn M. (Mrs. Garrett B. Hunter), John III. With Chase Manhattan Bank, N.Y.C., 1930-40; with Nat. Neward & Essex Bank, Newark, 1940—, sr. v.p., 1969—; dir. Supermarkets Gen. Corp., 1965—, Houdaille Const n. Materials, 1950-67. Mem. adv. bd. A.R.C., Newark, 1956—. Bd. trustees treas. Clara Maass Meml. Hosp., N.J. Symphony; trustee Greeg Found., Hartmann Found.; bd. dirs. N.J. Bus. Devel. Corp.; trustee, chmn. finance com. Upsala Coll. Recipient meritorious service award Upsala Coll., 1960, Clara Maas Hosp., 1965, A.R.C., 1959, Nat. Jewish Hosp.

Denver, 1970. Mem. Delta Kappa Epsilon. Republican. Lutheran. Home: 282 Summit Av Summit NJ 07901 Office: 744 Broad St Newark NJ 07101

COWEN, DAVID, neuropathologist; b. N.Y.C., July 29, 1907; s. David and Miriam (Goodman) C.; A.B., Columbia, 1928, M.D., 1932. Attending neuropathologist Columbia-Presbyn. Med. Center, N.Y.C., 1963—; cons. East Orange (N.J.) VA Hosp., Lenox Hill Hosp, N.Y.C.; mem. faculty Columbia, 1937—, prof. neuropathology, 1963—. Mem. Am. Assn. Neuropathologists (pres. 1962-63), Am. Neurol. Assn., Am. Acad. Neurology, Assn. Research Nervous and Mental Diseases, Am. Soc. Exptl. Pathology. Contbr. numerous articles in field. Editorial bd. jour. Neuropathology and Exptl. Neurology, 1957—. Home: 25 E 77th St New York City NY 10021 Office: 630 W 168th St New York City NY 10032

COWEN, EUGENE S., govt. ofcl.; b. N.Y.C., May 2, 1925; s. Jacob and Shirley (Sherman) C.; B.A. magna cum laude, Syracuse U., 1948, M.A., 1953; m. Phyllis Leatrice Wallach, Jan. 29, 1948; children—James Sherman, Stephanie Jane. Reporter, Syracuse (N.Y.) Herald-Jour., 1948-52; pres. sec. to Congresswoman Frances Bolton, 1953-56; information officer U.S. Govt., 1957-58; adminstrv. asst. to U.S. Senator Hugh Scott, 1959-69; spl. asst. to President Nixon, 1969—. Hon. chmn. govt. div. United Jewish Appeal. Served with USAAF, 1943-46. Decorated Air medal. Mem. Phi Beta Kappa. Republican. Jewish religion. Home: 920 Loxford Terrace Silver Spring MD 20901 Office: The White House Washington DC 20500

COWEN, MARTIN LINDSEY, univ. dean; b. Wheeling, W.Va., Aug. 26, 1920; s. Martin Lindsey and Agnes (Troll) C.; B.A., U. Va., 1942, J.D., 1947; LL.M., Harvard, 1965; m. Eleanor Boaz, Dec. 29, 1949; children—Martin Lindsey III, Velma Merrifield, William Boaz, Carolyn Troll, Eleanor Lee. Admitted to Ohio bar, 1947, Va. bar, 1955, Ga. bar, 1965; pvt. practice, Bridgeport, O., 1947-51; mem. faculty U. Va. Law Sch., 1951-64, prof. law, 1956-64, asso. dean, 1960-64; prof. law, dean U. Ga. Sch. Law, 1964—. Mem. Ga. Commn. on Unifrom State Laws. Served to lt. comdr. USNR, 1942-46. Fellow Am. Bar Found.; mem. Am. Law Inst., Order of Coif, Raven Soc., Phi Beta Kappa, Delta Tau Delta, Phi Delta Phi, Omicron Delta Kappa. Home: 525 Westview Dr Athens GA 30601

COWEN, ROBERT HENRY, lawyer; b. Williamston, N.C., Jan. 16, 1915; s. Henry Herbert and Jenette (Mobley) C.; LL.B., Wake Forest Coll., 1942; m. Sue Henderson, Aug. 6, 1953; children—Robert H., Susan Carol, Sarah Cantrell. Admitted to N.C. bar, 1942, since practiced in Williamston; atty. U.S. Dept. Labor, Richmond, 1945-46; counsel to com. on mcht. marine and fisheries U.S. Ho. of Reps.; U.S. atty. Eastern dist. N.C. 1961-69; counsel, joint com. on printing U.S. Senate, 1969—. Mayor, Williamson, 1947-57; mem. N.C. Senate, 1957-58. Bd. dirs. N.C. League Municipalities. Served to ensign USNR, World War II. Mem. Am., N.C. bar assns., Jr. C. of C., Am. Legion. Baptist. Clubs: Rotary, Roanoke Country. Home: 103 Woodlawn Dr Williamston NC 27892

COWEN, WILSON, judge; b. nr. Clifton, Tex., Dec. 20, 1905; s. John Rentz and Florence Juno (McFadden) C.; LL.B., U. Tex., 1928; m. Florence Elizabeth Walker, Apr. 18, 1930; children—W. Walker, John E. Admitted to Tex. bar, 1928; pvt. practice, Dalhart, Tex., 1928-34; judge Dallam County (Tex.), 1935-38; Tex. dir. for Farm Security Adminstrn., 1938-40, regional dir., 1940-42; commr. U.S. Ct. Claims, 1942-43, 45-59, chief commr., 1959-64, chief judge, 1964—; asst. adminstr. War Food Adminstrn., 1943-45; spl. asst. to sec. agr., 1945. Past chmn., past trustee Landon Sch. for Boys, Bethesda. Mem. State Bar Tex., Fed., Am. bar assns., Order of Coif, Delta Theta Phi. Presbyn. Mason. Clubs: Cosmos Nat. Lawyers (Washington). Home: 2500 Virginia Av NW Washington DC 20037 Office: US Court Claims Washington DC 20005

COWEN, WILSON WALKER, publisher; b. Dalhart, Tex., June 5, 1934; s. Wilson and Florence Elizabeth (Walker) C.; A.B., Harvard, 1956, Ph.D., 1965; m. Cecilia Van Strum, June 15, 1956 (dec. 1958); m. 2d, Juliette McLean Anthony, Aug. 29, 1964 (dec. 1969); m. 3d, Claudine LaHaye, Aug. 25, 1971. Advt. and promotion Little Brown & Co., 1958-59; partner Walker-deBerry Pubs., Cambridge, Mass., 1959-64; with U. Press of Va., Charlottesville, 1965—, asso. dir., 1968-69, dir., 1969—. Teaching fellow Harvard, 1959-64; lectr. English, U. Va., 1965, prof., 1971. Woodrow Wilson fellow, 1960; Timothy Dexter fellow, 1964. Mem. Am. Assn. U. Presses, Va. Hist. Soc. (council), Bibliog. Soc. U. Va. (council), Phi Beta Kappa. Democrat. Clubs: Farmington (Charlottesville); Grolier (N.Y.C.). Home: 211 Sprigg Lane Charlottesville VA 22903 Office: Box 3608 University Sta Charlottesville VA 22903

COWGER, CHARLES E., oil co. exec.; b. Danville, Ark., 1919; ed. U. Ark., 1942. Sr. v.p., mem. exec. com., dir. Murphy Oil Corp. Home: 703 Bodenhamer Dr El Dorado, AR 71730. Office: 200 Jefferson Av El Dorado AR 71730*

COWGER, WILLIAM OWEN, congressman; b. Hastings, Neb., Jan. 1, 1922; s. Rolla Henry and Catherine (Combs) C.; student Tex. A. and M. Coll., 1939-40; B.A., Carleton Coll., 1943; m. Cynthia Thompson, Mar. 19, 1945; children—Cynthia Combs, David Garvin. With Thompson & Cowger Co., Inc., real estate morgage, Louisville, 1946—, pres. 1948—; mayor City of Louisville, 1961-66; mem. 90th, 91st Congress, 3d Congl. Dist. Ky., 1966—. Chmn. for Ky., Crusade for Freedom, 1955-57; chmn. Louisville A.R.C. blood program, 1956-57. Rep. chmn. 3d Congl. Dist. Ky., 1956—; mem. Kentucky Republican Central Committee, 1956—. Bd. dirs., pres. Kentucky Municipal League; bd. dirs. Louisville Urban League, Louisville Internat. Center, Louisville chpt. A.R.C., Louisville chpt. United Cerebral Palsy Assn. Served to lt. (j.g.) USNR, World War II. Named one of 3 outstanding young men in Ky., 1955. Mem. Inter-Am. Municipal Organization (pres.), Am. Municipal Assn. (exec. com.), Mortgage Bankers Assn. Am., Louisville Mortgage Bankers Assn. (pres. 1954-55), Louisville Jr. C. of C. (pres. 1953-54), Louisville Real Estate Bd. Presbyn. (past deacon). Clubs: Louisville Country, Pendennis (Louisville). Home: 2315 Raleigh Lane Louisville KY 40206 Office: 446 S 5th St Louisville KY

COWGILL, DONALD EDGAR, investment banker; b. nr. Hillsboro, O., Nov. 13, 1917; s. Clarence O. and Carrie (Watts) C.; eve. student, U. Cin., 1937-52; m. Maud Moore, Aug. 22, 1941; children—William W., Patricia Ann, Cathe Lynn. From office boy to accountant Eagle Picher Co., 1937-47; self employed in ins. and tax service, 1947—; former financial v.p., Am. Financial Corp.; exec. v.p. Provident Bank, Cin., 1966-69. Trustee Wilmington Coll., Earlham Sch. Religion, Richmond, Ill. Served with USNR, 1942-45. Address: 5155 Stone Barn Rd Cincinnati OH 45243

COWGILL, DONALD OLEN, sociologist, educator; b. Wood River, Neb., May 10, 1911; s. Olen and Gertrude (Quisenberry) C.; A.B. with high honors in spl. field Park Coll., 1933; A.M. (Van Blarcom scholar 1934-35, U. fellow 1935-36) Washington U., 1935; Ph.D. (George Leib Harrison fellow) U. Pa., 1940; postgrad. U. Minn., summer 1941, U. Mo., 1942-43; m. Mary Catherine Strain, Sept. 1, 1935; children—Martha Jane (Mrs. Paul Burns), Donald Franklin, Catha Jean. Asst. prof. sociology Drury Coll., 1937-40, asso. prof., head dept. sociology, 1940-42, dean men, dir. counseling, 1941-42; sr. research analyst Mo. Security Commn., 1942-43; research asst. to v.p. Studebaker Corp., 1943-45; prof., head dept., sociology Drake U., 1945-46, Wichita State U., 1946- 67; prof. U. Mo., Columbia, 1967—, chmn. depts. sociology and rural sociology, 1970—; vis. prof. U. Mo., summers 1948, 66; lectr. Mindolo Ecumenical Centre, Kitwe, Northern Rhodesia, summer 1962; resident cons. Makidol U., Thailand, 1968-69; research cons. Wichita Community Planning Council, 1946-1967. Fellow Inter- Univ. Council on Aging fellow, summer 1959, Midwest Council on Aging fellow, summer 1961. Fellow Am. Sociol. Assn., Am. Assn. U. Profs.; mem. Population Assn. Am., Midwest Sociol. Soc. (pres. 1952-53). Am. Sociol. Soc., Midwest Council for Social Research on Aging (pres. 1962-64). Pi Kappa Delta. Alpha Kappa Delta. Author: Residential Mobility of An Urban Population, 1935; Mobile Homes: A Study of Trailer Life, 1941; Methodology of Planning Census Tracts, 1949; Wichita Street Index for Census Tracts, 1951; Religious Preferences of the Families of Wichita, 1958; People of Wichita, 1960; Aging and Modernization, 1971. Author articles on population, urban sociology, social gerontology Home: 819 Greenwood Ct Columbia MO 65201

COWGILL, GEORGE RAYMOND educator; b. St. Paul, Feb. 8, 1893; s. Frank Brooks and Ida Lillian (Hall) C.; student Hamlin U., 1911-13, Ph.D., 1955; B.A., Stanford U., 1916, postgrad., 1916-17; Ph.D., Yale, 1921; Sc.D. (hon.), U. So. Cal., 1947; m. Alice May Festler, Sept. 7, 1922 (dec. Dec. 1957); 1 dau., Barbara (Mrs. A. R. Perrins); m. 2d, Grace C. Deuel, Mar. 31, 1959. Research in physiology and biochemistry Yale Sch. Medicine, 1920-60, successively asst. in physiol. chemistry, instr., asst. prof., asso. prof., prof. nutrition, 1944-60, emeritus prof. nutrition, 1960-; adj. prof. biochemistry, nutrition U. So. Cal. Los Angeles, 1960—. Smith-Reed-Russell lectr. George Washington U. Sch. Medicine, 1940; De Lamar lectr. Johns Hopkins U. Sch. Hygiene and Pub. Health, 1940. Mem. civilian adv. com. to Sec. Navy, 1946; mem. food and nutrition Food bd. NRC, 1940-46; mem council on foods and nutrition A.M.A., 1938-59. Mem. Conn. Citizens Food Com., 1947-48. Served from pvt. to lt. AUS, 1917-19, AEF. Recipient Mead Johnson award For distinguished researches on Vitamin B complex, 1942; Sci. award Grocery Mfrs. of Am., 1948; Osborne and Mendel award Am. Inst. Nutrition, 1958. Fellow A.A.A.S., Am. Inst. Chemists; N.Y. Acad. Sci., Am. Inst. of Nutrition, Am. Pub. Health Assn.; mem. Am. Physiol. Soc., Am. Soc. Biol. Chemists, Soc. Exptl. Biology and Medicine (council, 1946), Am. Chem. Soc., Inst. of Food Technologists, Nat. Acad. Medicine Brazil (hon. fgn. mem.), Sociedad de Neurologia Cirugia do Rio de Janeiro (hon.), Sociedade de Neurologia, Psychiatria e Medicine Legal de Rio de Janeiro (corr.), Phi Beta Kappa, Sigma Xi, Alpha Sigma Phi, Phi Chi. Republican. Author: The Vitamin B Requirement of Man, 1934; (with W.L. Marxer) The Art of Predictive Medicine, 1966; numerous sci. papers reporting researches. Mem. editorial bd. Jour. of Nutrition, 1935-39, acting mng. editor, 1935-36, editor, 1939-59. Home: 700 Orange Grove Av South Pasadena CA 91030

COWGILL, JAMES JOSEPH, educator; b. Ronan, Mont., Mar. 20, 1914; s. James Daniel and Kathryn (Salchert) C.; B.S. in Chemistry, M.S., Gonzaga U., 1939, M.A. in Philosophy, 1940; S.T.L., Alma Coll., Los Gatos, Cal., 1946; Ph.D. in chemistry, U. Notre Dame, 1957. Ordained priest Roman Catholic Ch., 1945; mem. faculty Seattle U., 1950—, head dept. physics, 1956-67, prof. physics, 1960—, dir. NSF Summer Inst., 1963—, acting dean Grad. Sch., 1967-68, asso. dean, 1968-70, dean, 1970—, trustee, 1958-65, dir. research and instl. devel., 1968—. Bd. dirs. Jesuit Research Council Am., 1962-69. Mem. Am. Chem. Soc., Soc. Research Adminstrs., Nat. Council U. Research Adminstrs., N.W. Sci. Assn., Am. Assn. Physics Tchrs., A.A.A.S., Sigma Xi. Address: Seattle Univ Seattle WA 98122

COWHERD, RAYMOND GIBSON, historian, educator; b. Sedalia, Mo., Dec. 5, 1909; s. William S. and Margaret (Reynolds) C.; A.B., William Jewell Coll., 1933; M.A., U. Pa., 1936, Ph.D., 1940; B.D., Eastern Baptist Theol. Sem., 1936; m. Phylis L. Heller, June 26, 1968; childrenPatricia Jeannette, Patrick Riley. Asst. instr. U. Pa., 1936-37; ordained to ministry Bapt. Ch., 1936; pastor Oaklyn (N.J.) Bapt. Ch., 1940-44; asst. prof. history Kalamazoo Coll., 1944-46; asst. prof. history Lehigh U., Bethlehem, Pa., 1946-52, asso. prof., 1952-63, prof., 1963-, chmn. dept., 1966-67. Recipient research grants Am. Council Learned Socs., 1942, Am. Philol. Soc., 1958. Mem. Am. Hist. Assn., Am. Acad. Polit. and Social Sci., Conf. on Brit. Studies, Econ. Hist. Assn. Author: Politics of English Dissent, 1956; The Evangelical Humanitarians and the Ten Hour Movement in England, 1956; Humanitarian Reform of the English Poor Laws, 1962. Home 804 W Market St Bethlehem, PA 18018.

COWIE, WILLIAM ROBERTSON, ins. exec.; b. Buffalo, May 25, 1907; s. Joseph H. and Bertha M. (Emerson) C.; A.B., Columbia, 1928; m. Elinor A. Horman, Sept. 21, 1929; 1 dau., Joyce E. (Mrs. Richard S. Sherman). With Equitable Life Assurance Soc. U.S., N.Y.C., 1937—, 2d v.p., 1953-56, v.p., 1956—. Clubs: Union League (N.Y.C.); St. Andrew's Golf (Hastings-on-Hudson, N.Y.). Home: 600 W 111th St New York City NY 10025 Office: 1285 Av of Americas New York City NY 10019

COWLES, ALFRED, economist; b. Chgo., Sept. 15, 1891; s. Alfred and Elizabeth (Cheney) C.; A.B., Yale, 1913; m. Elizabeth Livingston Strong, May 10, 1924 (div. 1939); children—Richard Livingston, Ann; m. 2d, Louise Lamb Phelps, Oct. 24, 1949. Journalist, Spokesman Rev., Spokane, Wash., 1913- 15; pres. Cowles & Co., finance, Colorado Springs, 1925-38; economist, 1933—, pres. Cowles Commn. for Research in Econs., Colorado Springs, 1933-39, Chgo., 1939—. Hon. bd. dirs. Passavant Meml. Hosp.; trustee Colorado Springs Fine Arts Center (hon.); colleague Colo. Coll. Fellow Econometric Soc., A.A.A.S.; mem. Internat. Statis. Inst. Club: Commercial (Chgo.). Author: Common Stock Indexes, 1938; The True Story of Aluminum, 1958. Contbr. to Econometrica, Jour. Am. Statis. Assn. Home: 225 E Onwentsia Rd Lake Forest, IL 60045. Office: 435 N Michigan Av Chicago IL 60611

COWLES, ARTHUR WOODRUFF, advt. exec.; b. Crawfordsville, Ind., Nov. 2, 1918; s. Frank Hewitt and Mary Anne (Eby) C.; B.A., Wooster Coll., 1940; m. Luella Grassbaugh, Dec. 31, 1941; children—Kathleen, Arthur Woodruff III, Shelley Ann. With Gen. Electric Co., 1945-50, Carborundum Co., 1950-54; with Marsteller, Inc., Chgo. and Pitts., 1955-66, exec. v.p., 1960-66; v.p. exec. dept. Koppers Co., Pitts., 1966—. Served with inf. 1941-45. Vice chmn. pub. affairs council Nat. Indsl. Conf. Bd. Bd. dirs. Community Chest, Chamber Com. Clubs: Duquesne; Longue Vue Country; Laurel Valley. Home: 106 Glenhaven Lane Pittsburgh PA 15238 Office: Koppers Bldg Pittsburgh PA 15219

COWLES, FLEUR FENTON; author, artist; b. N.Y.C.; d. Matthew M. and Eleanor (Pearl) Fenton; student Columbia School Applied Art; LL.D., Elmira (N.Y.) Coll., 1955; m. Atherton Pettingell, Feb. 13, 1942; m. 2d, Gardner Cowles, Dec. 27, 1946 (div. 1955); m. 3d, Tom. Montague Meyer, Nov. 18, 1955. Newspaper columnist N.Y. World Telegram, 1935-36; exec. v.p. Dorland Internat., Pettingell & Fenton Advt. Agy., 1936-46; spl. con. Famine Emergency Com., White House, Washington, 1946; asso. editor Quick mag., 1949; became asso. editor, dir. spl. editorial depts. Look mag., 1947; editor Flair mag., 1950-51, Flair Annual, 1952; fgn. corr. Look mag., 1955-58; mem. bd. dirs. Cowles Mags., Inc. Cons. to chief of staff Hdqrs. USAF, 1950. Spl. rep. Pres. Eisenhower (with rank of spl. ambassador) at coronation of Queen Elizabeth II of Eng. Mem. Lord Mayor's Adv. Com., Mermaid Theatre Trust, London. Mem. Conn. Commn. to Study Potentials of Aging. Trustee Soc. Rehabilitation Facially Disfigured; mem. nat. adv. com. on women's participating Fed. Civil Def. Adminstrn., 1953-55; member council Am. Museum in Bath (England). Mem. bd. trustees Elmira Coll. Made Chevalier Legion of Honor (France), 1951; awarded Order of Southern Cross, Cavalier class, Brazil, 1953; Comdr. Order of Bienfasence, (Greece), 1955. Mem. Order Les Compagnons de Rabalais, Women's Nat. Press Club, Overseas Press Club. Theta Sigma Phi. Author: Bloody Precedent, 1952; The Case of Salvator Dali, 1959; The Hidden World of Hadhramoutt, 1963; Tiger Flower, 1968. Exhibited paintings, London, 1959, 63, 66, N.Y.C., 1960, 62, 64, 67, Rome, 1961, Paris, 1962, Athens, 1966, Los Angeles, 1967, Madrid, 1967, Rio de Janeiro, 1968; group shows; VIII Viennale, San Paulo, 1965, Rio de Janeiro, 1966, Hammer Galleries, 1969, Seattle Art Mus., 1970. Home: A5 Albany Picadilly London England

COWLES, GARDNER, publisher; b. Algona, Ia., Jan. 31, 1903; s. Gardner and Florence M. M. (Call) C.; grad. Phillips Exeter Academy, 1921; A.B., Harvard, 1925; LL.D., Drake U., 1942, Coe College, 1948, L.I.U., 1955, Grinnell Coll., 1957, Colls. Hobart and William Smith, 1968; L.H.D., Bard Coll., 1950, Cornell Coll., 1951, Mundelein Coll., 1968; Litt.D., Ia. Wesleyan Coll., 1955; Sc.D., Simpson Coll., 1955; Litt.D., Morningside Coll., 1958; m. Lois Thounburg, May 17, 1933 (div. 1946); children—Lois (Mrs. John Harrison), Gardner III, Kate (Mrs. Julian Strauss); m. 2d, Jan Streate Cox, May 1, 1956; 1 dau., Virginia. Virginia. City editor Des Moines Register, 1925, news editor, 1926-27; asso. mng. editor Des Moines Register and Tribune, 1927, mng. editor, 1927-31, exec. editor, 1931-39, asso. publisher, 1939-43, pres., 1943-71; chmn. bd., editor in chief Cowles Communications, Inc., N.Y.C., 1971—, pubs. Lakeland Ledger, Gainesville (Fla.) Sun newspapers, Look, Family Circle, Venture mags.; dir. Gen. Devel. Corp., R.H. Macy & Co., United Air Lines, VAL, Inc., Bankers Life Co., Lumbermens Mut. Casualty Co., Kemperco, Inc. Am. Motorists Ins. Co.; domestic dir. Office of War Information, Wash., 1942-43, resigned; with Wendell Willkie, round world flight, 1942. Trustee, U. Miami (Florida), Gardner Cowles Found., Mus. Modern Art, Drake U., Teacher Coll., Columbia U.; dir. Ia.-Wesleyan Coll.; mem. bd. of overseers Harvard. Mem. Am. Soc. Newspaper Editors (ex-mem. bd.), Des Moines C. of C. (dir. 1930-47); Greater Des Moines Com. Harvard Class of 1925 (treas.), Delta Sigma Pi, Alpha Delta Sigma. Clubs: Des Moines; Blind Brook (Purchase, N.Y.); Harvard, University, Links, River, Economic, Overseas Press, Century, (N.Y.C.); Chicago; Indian Creek Country, The Bath (Miami Beach, Fla.); Bedford (N.Y.) Golf and Tennis. Office: Cowles Communications Inc 488 Madison Av New York City NY 10022

COWLES, JOHN, newspaper pub., editor; b. Algona, Ia., Dec. 14, 1898; s. Gardner and Florence (Call) C.; grad. Phillips Exeter Acad., 1917; A.B., Harvard, 1920 as of 1921; LL.D., (hon.), Boston U., 1941, Grinnell Coll., 1955, Harvard, 1956, Macalester Coll., 1958, U. Rochester, 1959, Carleton Coll., 1961, Allegheny Coll., 1963; Litt.D., Jamestown (N.D.) Coll., 1946; L.H.D., Coe Coll., 1956; Simpson Coll., 1957, Drake U., 1958; m. Elizabeth Moreley Bates, July 1923; children—Elizabeth Morley (Mrs. Arthur A. Ballantine), Sarah Richardson (Mrs. William von Eggers Doering), John, Russell. In newspaper work since 1920; 2d v.p. Asso. Press, 1929, 1st v.p., 1930, bd. dirs., 1934-43; dir. Audit Bur. of Circulation, 1929-33; pres. Mpls. Star & Tribune Co. and predecessor corps., 1935-68, chmn., 1968—; chmn. bd. Des Moines Register and Tribune Co., 1945-70; dir. First Nat. Bank of Mpls., 1940-68. Spl. asst. to lend-lease administr., E.R. Stettinius, Jr., Washington, 1943 (received Presidential Certificate of Merit for Service); mem. Bus. Council. Mem. Hoover Commn. Com. on Nat. Def., 1948; Nat. Citizen's Com. for Pub. Schs.; mem. com. for White House Conf. on Edn., 1954-55. Trustee Am. Assembly, Columbia U., mem. bd. overseers Harvard, 1944-50, 60-66, trustee Carnegie Endowment for Internat. Peace, Phillips Exeter Acad., 1936-54, Gardner Cowles Found., Mpls. Found., Ford Found., Mpls. Soc. of Fine Arts. Served with U.S. Army, 1918. Recipient Centennial award Northwestern U., 1951; Journalism award U. Minn., 1956. Mem. Am. Legion, S.A.R., Sigma Delta Chi (past hon. nat. pres.), Alpha Kappa Psi (hon.). Mason. Clubs: Clubs: Minneapolis, Woodhill (Mpls.); The Des Moines; The Metropolitan (Washington); Mill Reef (Antigua, West Indies). Author Chapter on journalism in "America Now," 1938; also newspaper series, "Britain Under Fire," 1941; "Report on Asia," 1956. Home: 2318 Park Av Minneapolis MN 55404 Office: Star and Tribune Minneapolis MN 55440

COWLES, JOHN, Jr., newspaper exec.; b. Des Moines, May 27, 1929; s. John and Elizabeth (Bates) C.; grad. Phillips Exeter Acad., 1947; A.B., Harvard, 1951; Litt.D. (hon.), Simpson Coll., 1965; m. Jane Sage Fuller, Aug. 23, 1952; children—Tessa Sage (Mrs. Lee Coswell), John, Jane Sage, Charles Fuller. With Mpls. Star & Tribune Co., 1953—, v.p., 1957-68, pres., chief exec. officer, 1968—, editor, 1961-69, editorial chmn., 1969—; pres. Harper's Mag., Inc., 1965-68, chmn. bd., 1968—; dir. Harper & Row, Pubs., Inc., N.Y.C., 1965—, chmn., 1968—; Des Moines Register & Tribune Co., A.P., N.Y.C. Mem. adv. bd. on Pulitzer Prizes, Columbia U., 1970—. Campaign chmn. Mpls. United Fund, 1967. Bd. dirs. Guthrie Theatre Found., 1960—, pres., 1960- 63, chmn., 1964-65; bd. dirs. Walker Art Center, 1960-69; trustee Phillips Exeter Acad., 1960-65; dir. Minn. Civil Liberties Union, 1956-61, Urban Coalition Mpls., 1968—, Am. Newspaper Pubs. Assn. Found., 1969—, Mpls. Found., 1970—. Served from pvt. to 2d lt. AUS, 1951-53. Named one of ten outstanding men of year U.S. Jr. C. of C., 1964. Mem. Am. Soc. Newspaper Editors, Council on Fgn. Relations, Sigma Delta Chi. Clubs: Minneapolis, Woodhill (Mpls.); Century Assn. (N.Y.C.). Home: 1418 Mountain Curve Av Minneapolis MN 55403 Office: 425 Portland Av Minneapolis MN 55415

COWLES, JOHN EDWARD, paper co. exec.; b. Schenectady, Oct. 22, 1905; s. Henry Melville and Julia Rose (Morgan) C.; grad. Bentley Coll. Accounting and Finance, 1928; m. Marjorie Swart, Jan. 26, 1931; 1 dau., Judith Morgan (Mrs. Gary L. Schmermund). With Gen. Electric Co., Schnectady, 1928-34; with Me. Seaboard Paper Co., Bucksport, asst. treas., 1934-47, comptroller, 1944-47; with St. Regis Paper Co., 1947-56, treas., 1956—, v.p., 1962- 69, sr. v.p., 1969-70, exec. v.p., 1970—, also dir.; dir., officer subsidiary subsidiary and affiliated cos.; dir. MFB Mut. Ins. Co., Southland Paper Mills. Trustee Bentley Coll. Mem. Treasurers Club N.Y.C. Clubs: Union League, Pinnacle, Cloud (N.Y.C.); Patterson (Fairfield). Home: 2360 Bronson Rd Fairfield CT 06430 Office: 150 E 42d St New York City NY 10017

COWLES, PETER, food co. exec.; b. Chgo., May 24, 1930; s. Miles Andrew and Anne (Kales) C.; grad. Lawrenceville (N.J.) Sch.; student Princeton; B.S., Northwestern U.; J.D., Loyola U., Chgo.; m. Heidi Ruth Pfaeffli, Nov. 16, 1956 (dec.); children—Miles Andrew II, Katherine, William. Tax mgr. Price Waterhouse & Co., C.P.A.'s, 1956-57; with Beatrice Foods Co., Chgo, 1967—, controller, chief accounting officer, 1968—. Served with AUS, 1953-55, C.P.A., Ill.

Mem. Am. Inst. C.P.A.'s, Ill. Soc. C.P.A.'s, Chgo. Bar Assn. Episcopalian. Home: 2422 Lincolnwood Dr Evanston IL 60201 Office: 120 S LaSalle St Chicago IL 60603

COWLES, RUSSELL, painter; b. Algona, Ia., Oct. 7, 1887; s. Gardner and Florence (Call) C.; A.B., Dartmouth, 1909; L.H.D., 1951; D.F.A. (hon.), Grinnell Coll., 1944; m. Eleanor Stanton, 1928 (div. 1954); m. 2d, Nancy Cardozo Egleson, 1954. Exhibited in most leading nat. exhibitions; works in permanent collections Dartmouth, U. Wichita. Mpls. Inst. Art, Pa. Acad. Fine Arts, Swope Gallery, Des Moines Art Center, Blandon Gallery, Denver Art Mus., Santa Barbara Mus., Addison Gallery, Va. Mus. Ency. Brit. Collection and others, Prix de Rome, Am. Acad. in Rome, 1915-21. Club: Century Assn. of N.Y. Home: New Milford CT also 179 E 70th St New York City NY 10021 Office: Care of Kraushaar Galleries 1055 Madison Av New York City NY 10021

COWLEY, GEORGE ARTHUR, Canadian diplomat; b. Ottawa, Ont., Can., July 13, 1930; s. Arthur Thomas and Marion (Service) C.; B.A. with honors, McGill U., Montreal, Que., Can., 1951; M.A., U. Paris, 1954; m. Deborah Mason, Apr. 23, 1966; children—Christopher, Geoffrey. Rep. Owen's Comm. Directory, 1954-58; freelance corr., Africa, Asia, 1954-56; traffic cons. Canadian Pacific Airlines, Vancouver, 1958; with Canada Dept. External Affairs, 1958—; 1st sec. embassy, Havana, Cuba, 1963-68; counsellor for cultural affairs embassy, Washington, 1968—; lectr. internat. relations Carleton U., Ottawa, 1964-67. Home: 1917 23d St NW Washington DC 20008 Office: 1771 N St NW Washington DC 20036

COWLEY, LUIS M., hosp. supt., psychiatrist; b. Havana, Cuba, June 22, 1921; s. Luis M. and Guillermina (Morales) C.; M.D., Havana U., 1944; m. Yolanda M. Perez, Aug. 29, 1948; children—Ana, Margarita, Luis, Maria, Yolanda, Felipe. Came to U.S., 1960, naturalized, 1967. Student house officer Havana (Cuba) U. Hosp., 1940-44, intern, 1944-45; resident psychiatry San Juan de Dios Psychiat. Sanatorium, Havana, 1945-47, psychiatrist, vice dir., 1947-49, psychiatrist, 1949-60; psychiatrist, clin. dir. Perez Vento Psychiat. Sanatorium, Havana, 1957-60; asso. psychiatry Havana U. Hosp., 1946-50; instr., adjoined prof. clin. therapeutic Havana U. Sch. Medicine, 1946-50; clin. dir. Elizabeths Hosp., Washington, 1947; staff, physician charge intensive treatment Terrell (Tex.) State Hosp., 1961, staff physician, supr. psychiat. residency tng. and white female acute treatment program, 1961-62, clin. dir., 1963-64, supt., 1967—; psychiat. resident Parkland Meml. Hosp., Dallas, 1962-63; clin. prof. psychiatry U. Tex. Southwestern Med. Sch., 1965—. Recipient ann. award Tex. Assn. Mental Health, 1967; hon. mem. Psychology Club, East Tex. State U., 1969. Fellow Am. Psychiat. Assn.; mem. Pan Am., Am., Tex. med. assns., Kaufman County Med. Soc., Tex., Dallas neuropsychiat. assns., Guild Catholic Psychiatrists, N.Y. Acad. Scis. Address: PO Box 70 Terrell TX 75160

COWLEY, WILLIAM HAROLD, educator; b. Petersburg, Va., May 28, 1899; s. William Frederick and Elizabeth (Maddock) C.; A.B., Dartmouth Coll., 1924; Ph.D., U. Chgo., 1930; LL.D., Hamilton Coll., 1938, St. Lawrence U., 1943; L.H.D., Hobart Coll., 1939; Litt.D., Union Coll., 1940; m. Jean McCampbell, Sept. 8, 1934; children—Virginia, Ellen McCampbell. With Bell Telephone Labs., N.Y.C., 1924-25; adminstrv. staff U. Chgo., 1927-29; research asso., asst. prof. psychology Bur. Ednl. Research, Ohio State U., 1929-34, asso. prof., 1934-35, prof., 1935-38; pres. Hamilton Coll., 1938-44; prof. higher edn. Stanford, 1945-68, David Jacks prof. higher edn., 1954-68, emeritus, 1968—. George A. Miller vis. prof. U. Ill., 1959. Fulbright scholar England, 1951-52. Mem. Alpha Delta Phi, Sigma Xi, Phi Beta Kappa (hon.). Contbr. articles to mags. and jours. Address: 848 Northampton Dr Palo Alto CA 94303

COWLING, DAN CAMPBELL, Jr., architect; b. Rogers, Ark., July 21, 1928; s. Dan Campbell and Opal (Robinson) C.; student Ark. Poly. Coll., 1946-48; student U. Ark., 1948-52; m. Carrolle Hickman, May 28, 1948; children—Dan Campbell III, Dane Carroll, Lee Douglas. Asso. firm Edward F. Brueggeman, Little Rock, 1952-53, Wittenberg, Delony & Davidson, Little Rock, 1953-57; partner firm Smith & Cowling, Little Rock, 1957-61, Cowling & Roark, Little Rock, 1962-66; owner Dan Cowling & Assos. Inc., Little Rock, 1966—. Trustee Ednl. Endowment Fund Ark. chpt. A.I.A. Recipient award Am. Assn. Sch. Adminstrs., 1968. Fellow A.I.A. (mem. exec. com. Ark. chpt. 1965-66, chmn. Gulf States Regional exec. com. 1965-68, chmn. commn. on profl. soc. 1966-68, mem. nat. council commnrs. 1966-68; honor award Gulf States region 1965, 66), Greater Little Rock C. of C. Methodist. (ofcl. bd.). Home: 218 Kingsrow Little Rock AR 72207 Office: 1515 W 7th St Little Rock AR 72202

COWLING, VINCENT FREDERICK, educator, mathematician; b. St. Louis, Dec. 15, 1918; s. Ross Allen and Alice (Friedrichs) C.; B.A., Rice U., 1941, M.A., 1942, Ph.D., 1944; m. Alison Croom, Dec. 24, 1944; children—John, Margaret, Charles, Thomas, Janet. Teaching fellow Rice U., 1941-44; instr. Ohio State U., 1945-46; asst. prof. Lehigh U., 1946-49; asso. prof., then prof. U. Ky., 1949- 62; prof. Rutgers U., 1962-67; mem. Inst. Advanced Study, Princeton, 1966-67; prof. math., chmn. dept. State U. N.Y. at Albany. Samuel Fain Carter fellow Rice U., 1944; Ford Found. fellow Yale, 1955; NSF grantee, 1956-59, 61-66; recipient Alumni Meml. Research award U. Ky., 1959. Mem. Am. Math. Soc., Math. Assn. Am., Sigma Xi. Home: 113 Westchester Dr N Delmar NY 12054 Office: State U. New York, Albany NY 12203.

COWPERTHWAITE, LOWERY LEROY, educator; b. Princeton, Kan., Mar. 22, 1917; s. Lowery Isaac and Lynne Bondell (Fish) C.; B.A., Ottawa (Kan.) U., 1939; M.A., U. Ia., 1946, Ph.D., 1950; m. Margaret Elizabeth Farmer, Aug. 11, 1949; children—Thomas, Joseph. Tchr. high schs., Kan., 1939-42; instr. speech U. Ia., 1948-49; asso. prof. speech Richmond Area U. Center, 1949-54; prof. speech, dir. Sch. Speech, Kent (O.) State U., 1954—. Co-founder Va. Speech and Drama Assn., 1950, pres., 1953. Served with USAAF, World War II. Mem. Speech Communication Assn. Am. Central States Speech Assn., Ohio Speech Assn., Sigma Chi, Pi Kappa Delta, Delta Sigma Rho, Tau Kappa Alpha, Alpha Psi Omega, Omicron Delta Kappa. Episcopalian. Mason. Contbr. articles in field, also to books. Home: 615 Pioneer Av Kent OH 44240

COX, ALLAN V., geophysicist, educator; b. Santa Ana, Cal., Dec. 17, 1926; s. Vernon D. and Hilda (Schultz) C.; B.S., U. Cal., 1955, M.A., 1957, Ph.D., 1959. Geol. field asst. U.S. Geol. Survey, Alaska, 1950, 51,54, geophysicist, Menlo Park, Cal., 1959—; research asso. Stanford, 1962-67, prof. geophysics, 1967—. Mem. Nat. Acad. Sci., Geol. Soc. Am., Seismol. Soc. Am., Am. Geophys. Union, A.A.A.S., Soc. Terrestrial Magnetism and Electricity Japan, Inst. Nat. Scis. Ecuador, Sigma Xi. Office: Dept Geophysics Stanford U Stanford CA 94305

COX, ALLEN, Jr., lawyer; b. Milan, Tenn., Nov. 4, 1902; s. Allen Ennis and Lucile (Folk) C.; B.A., Vanderbilt U., 1923; LL.B., Yale, 1926; m. Hortense Beare, Feb. 10, 1931 (dec. Oct. 1954); children—Allen III, Robert Lee, Mary Reiney (Mrs. Sanford Garner, Jr.); m. 2d, Margaret Tayloe Forkin, Mar. 9, 1962. Admitted to Tenn. bar, 1925, since practiced in Memphis; partner firm Waring, Walker, Cox & Lewis, 1948—. Past pres. Travelers Aid Soc., Memphis. Fellow Am. Coll. Trial Lawyers; mem. Am., Tenn., Memphis and Shelby County bar assns., Internat Assn. Ins. Counsel, Am. Judicature Soc., Tenn. Hist. Soc., Vanderbilt U. Alumni Assn. (past pres.), Kappa Alpha, Phi Delta Phi. Baptist. Clubs: Memphis Country, Yale (past pres.), Andrew Jackson Soc., Summit (Memphis). Home: 4315 Walnut Grove Rd Memphis TN 38117 Office: 2410 Sterick Bldg Memphis TN 38103

COX, ALLYN, mural painter; b. New York, N.Y., June 5, 1896; s. Kenyon and Louise H. (King) C.; student Nat. Acad. Design, 1911-16, Art Students' League, N.Y., 1915-16; fellowship in painting, Am. Acad. in Rome, 1916-20; m. Ethel Howard Potter, Apr. 30, 1927. Mural painter 1921—. Prin. works: ceilings, W. A. Clark Jr. Library, Los Angeles, 1924-27; panels, Law Bldg., U. of Va., 1930-34; decorations, Nat. City Co., N.Y., 1928, Continental Bank, 1932, Cosmopolitan Club, New York, 1940, S.S. "America," 1940; fresco-frieze Rotunda Nat. Capitol, Washington, 1952, repaired and restored ceiling fresco, 1959; altar pieces and other decorations for the armed forces, 1942-44; murals, Guaranty Trust Co., N.Y., 1946; George Washington Masonic Memorial, Alexandria, Va., 1948-56; portrait Senate Reception Room, Nat. Capitol, 1958. Painter mem. New York City Art Commission, 1952-57; installed series of 3 Mosaics for General U.S. Grant Nat. Memorial, N.Y., 1966. Served as 1st lt. A.R.C., Italy, 1918. Trustee Abbey fund; dir. Ernest Peixotto Meml. Fund. Recipient Gold Medal of Honor, mural paintings, 1954, Archtl. League N.Y.; Triennial gold medal for achievement in the arts General Grand chapter Royal Arch Masons U.S., 1966. Mem. N.A.D.; fellow Painters, Am. Artists Profl. League, Fine Am. Acad. in Rome; mem. Nat. Soc. Mural Arts Fedn. N.Y. Club: Century Assn. (N.Y.). Address: 165 E 60th St New York City NY 10022

COX, ALVIN EARL, shipbldg. exec.; b. Norfolk, Va., May 25, 1918; s. Lucian Baum and Mabel Earl (Oliver) C.; B.S., Webb Inst. Naval Architects, 1941; postgrad. Oak Ridge Sch. Reactor Tech., 1953-54, Carnegie Inst. Tech., 1958; m. Barbara Marshall Fuller, Mar. 15, 1947; children—Susan Riedel, Catherine Baum. With Newport News Shipbldg. & Dry Dock Co. (Va.), 1941—, LHA project dir., 1966-68, DLGN 36 and 37 program mgr., 1968, sr. program mgr., 1969—; pres. White Marsh Devel. Corp. Mem. naval architecture com. Am. Bur. Shipping; mem. ship research com. Nat. Acad. Scis.-Nat. Research Council; co-chmn. subcom. Navy/Industry Adv. Com. Vice pres. Family Service-Travelers Aid, 1964, Peninsula United Fund, 1965. Served to lt. USNR, 1944-46. Certified profl. engr., Va. Mem. Soc. Naval Architects and Marine Engrs., (sect. chmn., council mem.), Am. Soc. Naval Engrs., Propeller Club Am., Port of Newport News. Clubs: Warwick Lions (v.p. 1948); James River Country (Newport News). Contbr. to Reactor Shielding Design Manual, 1956. Home: 11 Draper Lane Newport News VA 23606 Office: 4101 Washington Av Newport News VA 23607

COX, ALVIN JOSEPH, Jr., pathologist; b. Manila, P.I., Mar. 6, 1907; s. Alvin Joseph and Mary Amelia (Barnett) C.; A.B., Stanford, 1927, M.D., 1931; m. Helen Files Pollard, Feb. 2, 1947; children—Roger Allen, Barbara Anna, Carolyn Frances. Instr. pathology Stanford U., 1933-35, asst. and asso. prof. pathology, 1936-41, prof. 1941—, head dept., 1941-64, prof. pathology in dermatology, 1964—; exchange asst. Pathol. Inst., U. Freiburg (Germany), 1935-36. Mem. Am. Assn. Pathologists and Bacteriologists, Soc. for Exptl. Biology and Medicine, A.M.A., Am. Soc. Exptl. Pathology, Internat. Acad. Pathology, Am. Acad. Dermatology, Soc. Investigative Dermatology, Am. Soc. Dermatopathology, Alpha Omega Alpha, Alpha Kappa Kappa. Home: 76 Almendral Av Atherton, CA 94025. Office: 300 Pasteur Dr Stanford CA 94305

COX, ARCHIBALD, educator; b. Plainfield, N.J., May 17, 1912; s. Archibald and Frances Frances Bruen (Perkins) C.; A.B., Harvard, 1934, LL.B., 1937; LL.D., Loyola U., Chgo., 1964, U. Cin., 1967; m. Phyllis Ames, June 12, 1937; children—Sarah, Archibald, Phyllis. Admitted to Mass. bar, 1937; in gen. practice with Ropes, Gray, Best, Coolidge & Rugg, Boston, 1938-41; atty. Office of Solicitor Gen., U.S. Dept. of Justice, 1941-43; asso. solicitor Dept. Labor, 1943- 45; lectr. law Harvard, 1945-46, prof. law, 1946-61, Wilston prof. law, 1965—, solicitor 1965—, solicitor gen. U.S. Dept. Justice, 1961-65. Co-chmn. constrn. Industry Stablzn. Com., 1951- 52; chmn. Wage Stablzn. Bd., 1952. Mem. Overseers Harvard, 1962-65. Mem. Am. Bar Assn., Am. Acad. Arts and Scis. Author: (with Derek C. Bok) Cases on Labor Law, 7th on Labor Law, 7th edit., 1969; Law and the National Labor Policy, 1960; (with Mark DeWolfe Howe, J.R. Wiggins) Civil Rights, the Constitution and the Courts, 1967; The Warren Court, 1968. Home: Glezen Lane Wayland MA 01778 Office: Harvard Law Sch Cambridge MA 02138

COX, ARTHUR F., utility exec.; b. Omaha, 1909; A.B., Grinnel Coll., 1930; married. With Pioneer Natural Gas Co., Amarillo, Tex., 1933—, chief engr., 1946-51, v.p., chief engr., 1951-54, v.p. engrng. and constrn., 1954-56, v.p. gas supply, 1956-57, v.p. prodn., 1957-67, sr. v.p., 1967-69, exec. v.p., 1969—, also dir.; dir. Amarillo Oil Co., Pioneer Prodn. Corp., Amarillo Minerals Inc. Served to lt. comdr. USNR. Home: 3317 Eddy St Amarillo TX 79109 Office: PO Box 511 Amarillo TX 79105*

COX, AUSTIN BRADNER, corp. exec.; b. Bklyn., June 1, 1909; s. Charles Clinton and Ethel May (Robinson) C.; A.B., Colgate U., 1931; m. Genevieve V. Moore, July 1, 1942; children—Geoffrey, Patricia, Wendy; m. 2d, Cecilia M. Joy, July, 1962; children—Mona, Harriet, Melanie. Dir. indsl. relations Childs Co., N.Y.C., 1932-40, Penn-Dixie Cement Corp., N.Y.C., N.Y.C., 1940-42; pres. Allied Fuels Corp., Chattanooga, 1946- 47; with State Dept., 1947-48; fgn. service officer, consul U.S. Consulate Gen., Zurich, Switzerland, 1948-51, 1st sec. Am. embassy, The Hague, Netherlands, 1951; formerly dir. indsl., pub. relations, sec., dir. of indsl. relations Restaurant Assos., Inc., now v.p., dir. of indsl. relations. Bd. dirs. Nat. Conf. Christians and Jews. Jews. Mem. adv. commn. N.Y.C. Community Coll. Served to maj. AUS, 1942-46. Decorated Silver Star medal, Purple Heart, D.S.C. (U.S.); Order of Yun Hui (China). Home: 104-60 Queens Blvd Forest Hills NY 11375 Office: 1540 Broadway New York City NY 10036

COX, CALVIN KENNEDY, newspaperman; b. Greenwood, Miss., Dec. 19, 1918; s. Robert Kennedy and Katherine (Durham) C.; B.B.A., U. Ga., 1955; m. Dorothy Davis, May 3, 1940; children—Carolyn K., Eugenia, Carey. Various positions Greenwood (Miss.) Commonwealth, 1932-43; from copy editor to news editor Atlanta Constn., 1945—. Served with C.E., AUS, 1943-45. Club: Atlanta Press (pres. 1966- 67). Home: 1076 Forrest Blvd Decatur GA 30030 Office: Atlanta Constitution Atlanta GA 30302

COX, CARSON, educator, accountant; b. Greensboro, N.C., Apr. 14, 1913; s. Rufus C. and Mary C. and Mary Elnora (Coble) C.; B.S., Guilford Coll., 1934; M.S., U. N.C., 1937; postgrad. Ohio State U., 1939-41; m. Jennie Heston, Mar. 21, 1948; children—Steven H., Jennie E., Martha E. Cashier, So. Dairies, Inc., Greensboro, 1934-35; instr. Furman U., 1937-39; asst. accounting dept. Ohio State U., 1939-40, instr. accounting, 1941-42, 46, asst. prof., 1947-54, asso. prof., 1954-60, chmn. ann. inst. on accounting; personnel dir. Alexander Grant & Co., C.P.A.'s, Chgo., 1960- 67, spl. partner in charge personnel, 1961-64, gen. partner, 1964- 67; asso. prof. accounting Loyola U., Chgo., 1967—. Served to lt. USNR, 1942-46. C.P.A., Ohio, Ill. Mem. Ohio, Ill. socs. C.P.A.'s, Am. Accounting Assn. (sec.-treas. 1954- 60), Nat. Assn. Accountants (v.p. Columbus 1959-60), Am. Inst. C.P.A.'s, Beta Alpha Psi. Home: 1600 Highland Av Wilmette IL 60091 Office: 820 N Michigan Av Chicago IL 60611

COX, CHARLES CLEMMONS, lawyer; b. Louisville, Tenn., Oct. 28, 1907; s. Rufus Williams and Marie (Clemmons) C.; Ph.B. Emory U., 1929, LL.B. 1931; m. Martha Anne Logan, Mar. 22, 1947; children- Martha Anne, Logan. Admitted to Ga. bar, 1931; practice in Atlanta, 1932-35; mem. firm Candler, Cox, McLamb, Atlanta, 1935-39, Candler, Cox & Candler, 1939-47, Candler, Cox & McClain, 1947- 52, Candler, Cox, McClain & Andrews, 1952-70, Candler, Cox & Andrews, 1970—. Dir. Home Fed. Sav. & Loan Assn. Atlanta, L.R. Tucker Co., Inc., Royston, Ga.; dir., sec. Atlanta Regiscope Co., Sanitary Supply Co. Trustee Atlanta Florence Crittendon Home, 1959-65. Served to col. AUS, 1941-45; PTO. Decorated Bronze Star. Mem. Am., Ga., Atlanta bar assns., Am. Judicature Soc., Res. Officer Assn., Am. Legion, Kappa Alpha, Phi Delta Phi. Presbyn. (elder). Mason (past master). Clubs: Commerce, Peidmont Driving, Univ. Yacht, Old War Horse Lawyers, Lawyers (Atlanta). Home: 2777 Normandy Dr NW Atlanta GA 30305 Office: Atlanta Gas Light Tower Atlanta GA 30303

COX, CHARLES DONALD, microbiologist; b. Danville, Ill., Sept. 10, 1918; s. C.A. and Nina J. (Burris) C.; student Eastern Ill. State Coll., 1936-37; B.S., U. Ill., 1940, M.S., 1941, Ph.D., 1947; m. Ruth K. Swartz, Oct. 4, 1942; children—Charles, Nina M. Grad. asst. U. Ill., 1940-42, 46-47; asst. prof. Med. Coll. Va., 1947-49; asso. prof. Pa. State U., 1949-51; prof., chmn. dept. microbiology U. S.D. Sch. Med., 1951-60; head microbiology br. Office Naval Research, Washington, 1960-62; prof., head dept. microbiology U. Mass., Amherst, 1962—. Served to capt. AUS, 1942-46. Fellow Am. Acad. Microbiology, Am. Soc. Microbiology, Soc. Exptl. Biology and Medicine, N.Y. Acad. Sci., Sigma Xi. Home: 792 E Pleasant St Amherst MA 01002

COX, CHARLES J. J., airline exec.; b. Plainfield, N.J., Jan. 27, 1912; s. John Edgar Park and Bridget Filomena (Duffy) C.; student Aquinas Inst., 1925-26, St. Joseph Coll., 1926-27; m. Dorothy Virginia Moran, Nov. 22, 1941; children—Charles Robert, Margo Ann. Mgr., West Flint & Co., C.P.A.'s N.Y.C., 1929-46, B.F. Gladding & Co., South Otselic, N.Y., 1936-38; mgr. Peat, Marwick, Mitchell & Co., C.P.A.'s, Los Angeles, 1946-51; controller, asst. treas., mem. exec. staff Western Air Lines, Inc., Los Angeles, 1951-64, v.p., controller, 1964-69, v.p. finance, 1969—. Bd. mgrs. Westchester br. YMCA, Los Angeles; mem. adv. bd. Marymount Coll. Served as lt. comdr. Supply Corps, USNR, 1942-45. Mem. Financial Execs. Inst. (nat. v.p., dir., past pres. Los Angeles control), Air Transp. Assn. (pres. finance conf. 1964-65), Am. Inst. C.P.A.'s, Cal., N.Y. State socs. C.P.A.'s, Inst. Internal Auditors, Nat. Assn. Accountants, Am. Legion, Navy League. Clubs: Town Hall (Los Angeles); Palos Verdes Breakfast (pres. 1965-66). Home: 869 Rincon Lane Palos Verdes Estates CA 90274 Office: 6060 Avion Dr Los Angeles CA 90009

COX, CHARLES KENNEDY, ins. co. exec.; b. Camden, N.J., Oct. 6, 1919; s. William E. and Eleanor (Kennedy) C.; A.B. in Econs., Princeton, 1941; m. Doris Cummings, June 14, 1952; children—William Edward III, Barbara Anne, David Cummings. With Ins. Co. N.Am., 1946—, sr. v.p., 1965-67, exec. v.p., 1967-68, pres., 1968—; dir. Provident Nat. Bank, Phila. Trustee Am. Inst. Ins. Served to 1st lt. AUS, 1942-46. Decorated Order Crown Belgium. Republican. Presbyn. (trustee). Home: 5 W Walnut Av Moorestown, NJ 08057. Office: 1600 Arch St Philadelphia PA 19103

COX, CLIFTON BENJAMIN, meat co. exec.; b. Brewton, Ala., Mar. 28, 1916; s. Orren G. and Betty L. (Herrington) C.; B.S. (Sears Roebuck scholar), Auburn U., 1942, M.S., 1948; Ph.D. (Gen. Educator Bd. fellow), Purdue U., 1950; postgrad. (Econs. in Action fellow), Case Inst. Tech., 1952; m. Helen Louise Gilliland, Oct. 22, 1942; children—Stina (Mrs. John Nelson), Connie, John. Farmer, Brewton, 1934-38; with U.S. Dept. Agr., Ala., 1942-47, state adminstrv. supr. farm loans, Auburn, Ala., 1945-47; instr. Auburn U., 1948-49; researcher, instr., prof. Purdue U., 1950-60; dir. econ. div. Armour & Co., Chgo., 1960-63, v.p., 1963-65, pres. Armour Meat Products Co., 1965- 66, sr. v.p. Armour & Co., 1966, v.p., asst. to pres., 1966, gen. mgr. fresh meats div., 1967, group v.p., 1967-70, exec. v.p., 1970—, also dir. Vis. research prof. Harvard, 1957-58; vis. prof. Tex. A. and M., 1967. Mem. health rev. com. Chgo. Crusade Mercy, 1963-64; chmn. nominating com. Hinsdale (Ill.) Caucus, Library Bd., 1964; mem. Citizens' Com. for 2d High Sch., Hinsdale, 1964; pres. Sunset Ridge Subdiv., 1964. Mem. Am. Farm Econ. Assn., Am. Statis. Assn., Am. Econ. Assn., Nat. Assn. Bus. Economists, Econ. Club Chgo., Ill. C. of C. (chmn. agrl. bus. relations com. 1965—), Sigma Xi, Alpha Zeta, Gamma Sigma Delta. Presbyn. Clubs: Union League (Chgo.); Hinsdale Country. Contbr. articles profl. jours. Home: 123 N Quincy St Hinsdale IL 60521 Office: 111 E Wacker Dr Chicago IL 60601

COX, CLYDE G., hosp. adminstr. Adminstr. VA Hosp., Birmingham, Ala. Office: 700 S 19th St Birmingham AL 35233*

COX, D. MITCHELL, beverage co. exec.; b. Water Valley, Miss., Oct. 22, 1909; s. C.V. and Isabel (Whitson) C.; B.A., U. Ala., 1930; M.A., Emory U., 1936; m. Elsa McCall, July 18, 1957; stepchildren—Elsa R. Adair, F. Dodd Adair. Asso. prof. English, Ga. Inst. Tech., 1930-42; asst. to dir. sales promotion Coca-Cola Co., 1946-49; v.p. sales promotion Pepsi-Cola Co., N.Y.C., 1950-58, v.p. pub. relations, 1958—, also dir. Bd. dirs. Nat. council Boy Scouts Am., Nat. Assn. Mental Health. Served to lt. comdr. USNR, 1942-46. Home: 114 E 72d St New York City NY 10021 Office: Pepsi-Cola Co 500 Park Av New York City NY 10022

COX, EARL L., business exec.; b. 1905; grad. Rider Coll., 1926; married. With Fernald & Co., Phila., until 1956; treas., dir. Chem. Leaman Tank Lines, Inc., Downington, Pa., 1956—. Office: 520 E Lancaster Av Downington PA 19335*

COX, EDWARD HENRY, retired govt. ofcl.; b. Gloucester, N.J., July 12, 1901; s. Edward D. and Freda (Doeppen) C., LL.B. (Gold medal for scholarship 1933), Am. U., 1933; m. Florence Weale, Nov. 5, 1924. With N.Y.C. R.R., 1915-27, asst. chief clk., 1924-27; with ICC, Washington, 1927—, asst. to dir. bur. traffic, 1942-48, chmn. bd. suspension, 1948-51, asst. dir. bur. traffic, 1951-54, dir. bur., 1954-71, retired, 1971; admitted to D.C. bar, 1933. Served to lt. col. AUS, 1942- 46. Baptist. Mason. Home: 4925 Western Av NW Washington DC 20016 Office: ICC 12th and Constitution Av Washington DC 20005

COX, EDWIN, chemist; b. Richmond, Va., Sept. 20, 1902; s. Edwin Piper and Sally Bland (Clarke) C.; B.S. in chem. engring., Va. Mil. Inst., 1920, M.S. in chemistry, 1920; m. Virginia Bagby DeMott, May 19, 1927; 1 son, Edwin. With Va.-Carolina Chem. Corp., 1920-57, v.p., 1949-57; pvt. practice chem. engr., chemist, Aylett, Va., 1958—; pres. Tobacco By-Products and Chem. Corp.; partner Edwin Cox Assos., Richmond Va.; dir. Commonwealth Lab., Inc. (Richmond). Vice chmn. York River Basin Adv. Com., mem. adv. com. Va.

Bicentennial; mem. Va. Hist. Markers Com. Trustee Va. Inst. Sci. Research. Personal Aide five Va. Govs., 1926-50. Vice pres. Va. Hist. Soc. Served lt. col. Inf., AUS, 1940- 46, comdg. officer 176th inf., Joint Chiefs of Staff Secretariat, SHAEF, operational control I.G. Farben, 1945; brig. gen. Va. N.G., ret. Decorated Legion of Merit, Bronze Star medal, Army Comm. Ribbon with oak leaf cluster; recipient Distinguished Service award, Am. Chem. Soc., Va. sect., 1951; Gold medal award, Am. Inst. Chemists, 1965. Registered profl. engr., Virginia and New York. Fellow A.A.A.S., American Inst. Chemists; mem. Am. Chem. Soc., Am. Inst. Chem. Engrs., Soc. Chem. Industry, Va. Acad. Sci., Mil. Order World Wars, Va. (v.p.), Richmond hist. socs., Soc. Colonial Wars, Nat. Soc. Profl. Engrs., S.R., Jamestown Soc. (past gov.). Democrat (past chmn. 3d dist. com., past sec. Va. State Com.). Episcopalian (lay reader). Knight of Malta. Clubs: Commonwealth, Richmond (Virginia); Chemists (N.Y.C.); Cosmos (Wash.). Author articles in chem. and hist. jours. Issued 14 patents in field. Address: Holly Hill Ayeltt VA 23009

COX, EDWIN LOCHRIDGE, oil and gas exec.; b. Mena, Ark., Oct. 20, 1921; s. Edwin Berry and and Elizabeth (Lochridge) C.; student So. Meth. U., 1938-40; B.B.A., U. Tex., 1942; M.B.A., Harvard, 1943, I.A., 1946; m. Ann Rife, Jan. 5, 1944; children—Edwin Lockridge, Ann Chandler, Berry Rife. Partner oil and gas producing business, Dallas, 1947—; chmn. bd. Keebler Co., Elmhurst, Ill.; dir. First Nat. Bank in Dallas, E. Tex. Salt Water Disposal Co., Gillette Co., Boston, Southwestern Life Ins. Co., Dallas, LTV Aerospace Corp., Dallas. Mem. Dallas Citizens Council; pres. Children's Med. Center, Dallas. Bd. devel. So. Meth. U.; adv. bd. Dallas Salvation Army. Served to lt. (s.g.) USNR, 1943-46. Mem. Am. Petroleum Inst. (bd. councillors), Ind. Petroleum Assn. Am. (dir.), Tex. Mid-Continent Oil and Gas Assn. (dir.), Tex. Ind. Producers and Royalty Owners Assn. (dir.), Phi Delta Theta. Methodist. Home: 10210 Gaywood Rd Dallas TX 75229 Office: First Nat Bank Bldg Dallas TX 75202

COX, ELMUS EDWARD, govt. ofcl.; b. Attalla, Ala., Feb. 28, 1914; s. Lee A. and Dora (McClendon) C.; student Am. U., 1935, Am. Inst. Banking, 1936; m. Josephine Frick, Oct. 23, 1952; children—Barry King, Lee Sherman. With Dept. Agr., 1933, Office Comptroller of Currency, 1933-38, FHA, 1938-45; adminstrv. sec. to Congressman Albert Rains, 1945-65; spl. asst. to comptroller of currency, 1965—. Home: 6398 Lakeview Dr Falls Church VA 22041 Office: Treasury Dept 15th and Pennsylvania NW Washington DC 20220

COX, ERNEST HARLEY, Jr., lawyer; b. Fulton, Ark., Sept. 23, 1930; s. Ernest Harley and Eunice (Futrell) C.; LL.B., U. Ark., 1953; LL.M., Columbia, 1956; m. Mary Lou Thomas, Dec. 27, 1952; children—Karen Marie, Susan Elizabeth, Mary Leslie. Ark. state fire marshall, 1953; admitted to Ark. bar, 1953; practice in Pine Bluff, 1956—; atty. Coleman, Gantt, Ramsay & Cox, 1956- -. Dir. First Fed. Savs. & Loan Assn., Intermed Internat., Inc., Keymaster Corp., Midland Corp. Mem. Commn. on Coordination Higher Edn. Finance for State of Ark., 1970—; mem. Constl. Revision Study Commn., 1967; del. Ark. Constl. Conv., 1969-70. Pres., bd. dirs. Jefferson County United Fund; bd. dirs. S.E. Ark. Arts and Sci. Center, Ark. Soc. Crippled Children. Served to 1st lt., Judge Adv. Gen. Corps., USAF, 1953- 55. Mem. Am., Ark., Jefferson County bar assns., Kappa Sigma, Delta Theta Phi. Methodist. Mason (Shriner). Home: 10 Jefferson Pl Pine Bluff AR 71601 Office: Simmons Bldg Pine Bluff AR 71601

COX, EXUM MORRIS, investment mgr.; b. Santa Rosa, Cal., Feb. 5, 1903; s. Exum Morris and Mary Eleanor (Anderson) C.; A.B., U. Cal.,01924; M.B.A., Harvard, 1928; m. Elsie Margaret Storke, Sept. 6, 1934; children—Cynthia Morris (Mrs. Edward Tyler Huntting, Jr.), Susana More (Mrs. James T. Fousekis), Thomas Storke. With Dodge & Cox, 1933—, partner, 1933-59, pres., 1959—; chmn. bd. Dodge & Cox Balanced Fund, 1933—; dir. Dodge & Cox Stock Fund. Bd. dirs., v.p. community chest, San Francisco, 1946-48; bd. dirs. San Francisco Tb Assn., 1948-52; trustee San Francisco Mus. Art, pres. 1955-60, trustee Katherine Branson Sch., 1950-57; mem. citizens adv. com. to Atty. Gen. Cal. on crime prevention, 1954-58; mem. Cal. Delinquency Prevention Commn., 1963-67, San Francisco Library Commn., 1963-64; dir. Bay Area Ednl. TV Assn. Mem. Cal. Acad. Scis. (chmn., trustee, treas. 1963-67), Investment Counsel Assn. Am. (gov. 1955-58, 61-67), Sigma Chi. Clubs: Anglers (N.Y.C.); Bankers; Pacific Union; Bohemian. Home: 2361 Broadway San Francisco CA 94115 Office: 3500 Crocker Plaza San Francisco CA 94104

COX, FRANCIS ANDERSON, corp. exec.; b. N.Y.C., May 22, 1913; s. Francis Cleveland and Ingeborg V. (Anderson) C.; B.S. Magna cum laude, N.Y.U., 1935; graduate School of Business Administrn., N.Y.U.; m. Jean Prtljaga, Oct. 24, 1942; children—Carol Ann, Patricia Louise, David Michael. Accountant Haskins & Sells, C.P.A.'s, 1935-42, 46-51; chief accountant Navy Price Adjustment Bd., Washington and N.Y.C., 1942-46; asst. sec. New York Times Co., 1951- 54, treas., 1954-67, sec., 1963-67, v.p., 1967—; pres. N.Y. Times Neediest Cases Fund; dir. Spruce Falls Power & Paper Co., Interstate Broadcasting Co., Malbais Paper Co. Ltd., Quadrangle Press, Arno Press, Teaching Resources, Inc., Times Media Corp., Gaspesia Pulp and Paper Co., Ltd. Bd. dirs. West Side Assn. Commerce, also Broadway Assn. West Side Assn. Youth Found. Served as lt. comdr. Supply Corps, USNR, 1942-46. Mem. Am. Inst. Accountants, N.Y. State Soc. C.P.A.'s, Beta Gamma Sigma (dir. N.Y. alumni club). Home: 149 Cornwell Av Valley Stream NY 11580 Office: 229 W 43d St New York City NY 10036

COX, FREDERICK KINGSLEY, banker, b. Cleve., Jan. 22, 1915; s. Ernest H. and Eva Jean (Hunter) C.; A.B., Western Res. U., 1936, J.D., 1938; m. Betty Webber Pickles, Sept. 19, 1964; 1 dau., Elizabeth Aldrich. Admitted to Ohio Bar, 1938; with Cleve. Trust Co., 1938—, tax counsel, 1950—, v.p., 1962-66, mem. exec. officers com., 1964—, sr. v.p., 1966-69, exec. v.p., 1969, exec. v.p., counsel, 1970—; dir. Nat. Office Bldg. Co., Painesville, O., Gund Co., Cleve. Trustee George Gund Found., Cleve., Cleve. Mus. Natural Scis. Served to lt. USNR, 1942-46. Mem. Am., Ohio, Cleve. bar assns., Tax Club, Cleve. (pres. 1958-59), Ohio Bankers Assn. (chmn. tax com. 1952-67), Ohio C. of C., Assn. Res. City Bankers, Order of Coif, Sigma Chi, Phi Delta Phi. Presbyn. (trustee, elder). Clubs: Union, Skating (Cleve.). Home: 3254 Belvoir Blvd Beachwood, OH 44122. Office: 916 Euclid Av Cleveland OH 44101

COX, GARDNER, artist; b. Holyoke, Mass., Jan. 22, 1906; s. Allen Howard and Katherine Gilbert (Abbot) C.; student Art Student's League N.Y.C., 1924, Harvard, 1924-27, Boston Mus. Sch., 1928-30, Mass. Inst. Tech., 1929-31; m. Phyllis Moyra Byrne, Dec. 3, 1937; children—Benjamin, Katherine Gilbert Abbot, James Byrne, Phyllis Byrne. Work exhibited: Carnegie Mus., 1941, Va. Mus. Fine Arts, 1946, 1948, Art Inst. Chgo., 1948, 1949, 1951, Met. Mus. Art, 1950, U. Ill., 1950-51, Inst. Contemporary Art, Boston, one-man shows, 1953, Farnsworth Mus., Rockland, Me., 1956, Newport (R.I.) Art Assn., 1966; represented permanent collections Boston Mus. Fine Arts, Fogg Mus., Harvard, Addison Gallery, Andover, Mass., Wadsworth Atheneum, Hartford, Conn., Yale, Wellesley Coll., Wabash Coll., Mass. Inst. Tech., Mt. Holyoke Coll., Dept. State, Dept. Army, Middlebury Coll., Nat. Gallery Washington, Dept. Labor, Dept. Air Force, FAA, Nat. Portrait Gallery, Brandeis U., Princeton, others; head dept. painting Boston Mus. Fine Arts Sch., 1954-55. Exec. com. Boston Arts Festival, 1959-67; mem. Mass. Fine Arts Commn., 1965—. Trustee Am. Acad., Rome, Italy. Recipient M.V. Kohnstamm prize Am. Exhibit Water Colors, Chgo. Art Inst., 1949, Norman Walt Harris Bronze medal, 60th ann. Am. Exhibit, 1951. Mem. Am. Acad. Arts and Scis., Nat. Inst. Arts and Letters, N.A.D. (academician), Phi Beta Kappa. Clubs: Tavern, St. Botolph (Boston); Century (N.Y.C.). Home: 88 Garden St Cambridge MA 02138 Office: 30 Ipswich St Boston MA 02215

COX, GEORGE WALTER, Jr., banker; b. Tivoli, N.Y., Aug. 15, 1916; s. George Walter and Eva Marguerite (Stout) C.; B.A., Rutgers U., 1937; student Am. Inst. Banking, 1941-42; m. Mary Ellen Moore, Oct. 21, 1938; children—Susan L. (Mrs. Charles R. Salkeld), Bonnie L. (Mrs. William J. Gordon III). With Chem. Bank, N.Y.C., 1941—, sr. v.p., 1964-70, exec. v.p., 1970—; dir. Chem. Internat. Finance, Ltd., Chem. Internat. Banking Corp.; instr. Am. Inst. Banking, 1949-50, Internat. Banking Summer Sch., Stockholm, Sweden, 1950. Mem. Delta Kappa Epsilon. Club: Sleepy Hollow Country (Scarborough, N.Y.). Home: 136 Elm Rd Briarcliff Manor NY 10510 Office: 20 Pine St New York City NY 10015

COX, GILBERT EDWIN, lawyer, diversified industry exec.; b. 1917; B.B.A., U. Tex., 1938, LL.B., 1940; married. Admitted to Hawaii bar; formerly mem. firm Cades, Cox, Schutt, Fleming & Wright, Honolulu; exec. v.p., dir. Amfac Inc., 1969—; dir. Bishop Ins. Co., Honolulu, Pacific-Peru Constrn. Corp., Honolulu. Served to maj. USAF, 1940-46. Club: Silverado Country (dir.) (Napa, Cal.). Office: First Hawaiian Bank Bldg Honolulu HI 96808*

COX, GRACE DOLORES, (Mrs. Arnold J. Calle), lawyer; b. N.Y.C., Mar. 28, 1917; d. James T. and Catherine (Murphy) Cox; B.A., Hunter Coll., 1942; LL.B., N.Y. U., 1945; m. Arnold J. Calie, May 29, 1948. Admitted to N.Y. bar, 1945, since practiced in N.Y.C. Recipient Outstanding Woman Lawyer plaque, 1968, Silver plaque Girl Scouts Am., 1968. Mem. Nat. Assn. Women Lawyers (past pres.). Home: 430 E 57th St New York City NY 10022

COX, HARVEY GALLAGHER, educator; b. Phoenixville, Pa., May 19, 1929; s. Harvey Gallagher and Dorothea (Dunwoody) C.; A.B. with honors in history, U. Pa., 1951; B.D. cum laude, Yale, 1955; Ph.D., Harvard 1963; m. Nancy Nieburger, May 10, 1957; children—Rachel Llanelly, Martin Stephen, Sarah Irene. Dir. religious activities Oberlin Coll., 1955-58; program asso. Am. Baptist Home Mission Soc., 1958-62; fraternal worker Gossner Mission, East Berlin, 1962-63; asst. prof. Andover Newton Theol. Sch., 1963-65; asso. prof. church and soc. Harvard, 1965-70, Victor Thomas prof. divinity, 1970—. Cons. Third Assembly World Council Chs., New Delhi, India, 1961. Chmn. bd. Blue Hill Christian Center, 1963-66; chmn. Boston Indsl. Mission. Author: The Secular City, 1965; God's Revolution and Man's Responsibility, 1965; The Feast of Fools, 1969. Mem. editorial bd. Christianity and Crisis. Home: 65 Frost St Cambridge MA 02140 Office: 45 Francis Av Cambridge MA 02138

COX, HEADLEY MORRIS, Jr., coll. dean; b. Mt. Olive, N.C., July 25, 1916; s. Headley Morris and Frank (English) C.; A.B., Duke, 1937, A.M., 1939; postgrad. U. Colo., 1944-45; Ph.D., U. Pa., 1958; m. Irene Todd, June 26, 1940; children—John Morris, Deborah English (Mrs. Roy A. Jones), Thomas Headley. Instr., asst. prof., asso. prof., prof. English, Clemson (S.C.) U., 1939—, head dept., 1950-69, dean Coll. Liberal Arts, 1969—. Sr. Fulbright lectr. in Am. lit. Universitat Graz (Austria), 1958-59. Served with USNR, 1944-46. Mem. Modern Lang. Assn. Am., Am. Dialect Soc., Phi Beta Kappa. Methodist. Home: 213 Riggs Dr Clemson, SC 29631.

COX, HENRY BEVERLY, former fgn. service officer; b. Phila., Oct. 15, 1916; s. J. Perry and and Elizabeth (Faries) C.; grad. William Penn Charter Sch., Phila., 1934; B.A., Haverford Coll., 1938; certificate U. Heidelberg (Germany), 1936; M.A., U. Pa., 1940; postgrad. George Washington U., 1946; m. Doris Virginia Woodie, Mar. 23, 1942; children—Judith Anne, Richard Alan. Instr. fgn. langs. Bridgewater (Va.) Coll., 1939-40; spl. agt. FBI, 1941- 46; with State Dept., 1946-54, intelligence officer, 1946-49, internat. relations officer Office German Affairs, 1949-52, information specialist, 1952-54; chief exchange persons div. USIA, Am. embassy, Bonn, Germany, 1954-55, information specialist, Washington, 1955-56; fgn. service res. officer State Dept., 1956-61, spl. asst. to dep. asst. sec. asst. sec. state public affairs, 1962-63; chief polit. sec. Am. embassy, Bern, Switzerland, 1963-64, first sec., 1963-66, counselor for econ. affairs, 1964-66; chmn. European studies Fgn. Service Inst., 1966-; fgn. service officer, 1961-67, ret.; asst. exec. dir. for edn. Chgo. Council on Fgn. Relations, 1967—. Adviser U.S. U.S. delegation UN Prisoner War Commn., Geneva, Switzerland, 1952; mem. U.S. delegation Laos Conf., 1962. Mem. Delta Phi Alpha. Author articles State Dept. Bull., also articles Fgn. Service Jour. Home: 505 N Lake Shore Dr Chicago IL 60611

COX, HERALD REA, research dir.; b. Rosedale, Ind., Feb. 28, 1907; s. Leo R. and Pauline Mae (Rea) C.; A.B., Ind. State Tchrs. Coll., 1928; Sc.D., Johns Hopkins, 1931; Sc.D., U. Mont., 1942, Ind. State Coll., 1964; m. Marion A. Curry, June 19, 1932; children—Jane E., George R., Gordon L. Instr. immunology Johns Hopkins, 1931-32; asst. pathology and bacteriology Rockefeller Inst. Med. Research, 1932-36; asso. bacteriologist USPHS, 1936-40, prin. bacteriologist, 1940-42; asso. dir. viral research Lederle Labs., 1942-44, dir., 1944-67, sr. research fellow, also dir. cancer immunological research, 1967-68; dir. cancer research Roswell Park Meml. Inst., Buffalo, 1968—. Vis. lectr. microbiology Harvard Sch. Pub. Health, 1951—. Mem. adv. council U.S. Army Chem. Corps, 1952—; mem. com. influenza and polio WHO. Recipient nat. service award Jr. C. of C, 1943; Typhus Commn. medal Sec. War, 1945; Howard Taylor Ricketts award U. Chgo., 1951. Fellow Am. Pub. Health Assn., N.Y. Acad. Sci., N.Y. Acad. Medicine, Am. Soc. Tropical Medicine; mem. A.A.A.S. (Theobald Smith award 1941), Soc. Am. Bacteriologists (v.p. 1959-60), Soc. Am. Immunologists, Am. Soc. Tropical Medicine, Harvey Soc., Am. Soc. Microbiology (hon., pres. 1960- 61). Contbr. articles to sci. publs. Home: 31 E Jerge Dr Elma NY 14059 Office: Roswell Park Meml Inst Buffalo NY 14203

COX, HIDEN TOY, educator; b. Greenville, S.C., Mar. 3, 1917; s. Hiden Toy and Nora Elizabeth (Hough) C.; B.S., Furman U., 1936, A.B., 1937; M.A., U. N.C., 1939, Ph.D., 1947; m. Elizabeth Vera Rannow, Dec. 6, 1943; one dau., Elizabeth Anne. Asst. prof. biology Howard Coll., 1941-46; asso. prof. biology Agnes Scott Coll., 1946-49; asso. prof. to prof. botany Va. Poly. Inst., Blacksburg, 1949-55; on leave as dep. exec. dir. Am. Inst. Biol. Scis., Washington, 1953-54, exec. dir., 1955- 61, 62-63; coordinator research, prof. biology Cal. State Coll., Long Beach, 1963-67, dean Sch. Letters and Sci., 1967-71, prof. biology, 1971—; asst. adminstr. for public affairs NASA, 1961-62. Mem. Cal. State Curriculum Commn., 1964-66. Served from ensign to lt. USCGR, 1942- 45. Gen. Edn. Bd. fellow, 1948; fellow U. Center Ga., 1949. Recipient Communicator of Year award Chgo., Publicity Club, 1962; distinguished service citation NASA, 1962. Fellow A.A.A.S.; mem. Sigma Xi, Alpha Epsilon Delta, Chi Beta Phi. Adviser College Blue Book. Home: 461 Laurinda Av Long Beach CA 90814

COX, HOWARD TAYLOR, banker; b. El Paso, Tex., Feb. 27, 1915; s. Frank E. and Carrie (Taylor) C.; B.B.A., U. Tex., 1936; m. Tess Herlin, Dec. 10, 1936; children—Charlotte Ann (Mrs. John H. Coates), Frank Herlin. With Howard T. Cox & Co., C.P.A.'s, Austin, Tex., 1940-53; pres. Capital Nat. Bank, Austin, 1953—, now vice chmn. bd.; dir. Allright Auto Parks Co., Tex. Capital Corp., Night Hawk Restaurants, Tex. Crushed Stone Co. Past pres. Austin United Fund, Austin council Girl Scouts, Austin Symphony Orch.; treas., dir. S.W. Tex. Ednl. TV Council, 1961—, Tex. Good Roads Assn., 1955—. C.P.A., Tex. Mem. Tex. Soc. C.P.A.'s, Am. Bankers Assn., Tex. Bankers Assn. Clubs: Austin (bd. dirs.), Headliners, Austin Country, Citadel (Austin). Home; 2801 Macken St Austin TX 78703 Office: Box 550 Austin TX 78767

COX, HUGH, lawyer; b. Logan, Ia., Sept. 3, 1905; s. William Riley and Caroline (Reel) C.; A.B., U. Neb., 1926; B.A., Christ Church, Oxford (Eng.) U., 1929, B.C.L., 1930; m. Ethelyn Ayres, Oct. 24, 1934. Admitted to N.Y. bar, 1933, lawyer with Root, Clark, Buckner & Ballantine, N.Y., 1930-35; spl. asst. to atty. gen., 1935-43; counsel for Dept. of Justice before Temp. Nat. Econ. Com., 1938-39; asst. atty. gen., 1943, asst. solicitor gen., 1943-45; gen. counsel Surplus Property Adminstrn., 1945; practicing law, mem. firm Cleary, Gottlieb, Friendly & Cox, 1946, Covington & Burling, 1951. Dir. Chesapeake & Potomac Telephone Co. Mem. Phi Beta Kappa. Clubs: Cosmos, Metropolitan (Washington). Home: 210 Prince St Alexandria VA 22314 Office: 888 16th St Washington DC 20006

COX, J. D., bank exec. Sr. v.p., exec. officer Deposit Guaranty Nat. Bank, Jackson, Miss. Office: 200 E Capitol St Jackson MS 39205*

COX, JAMES CHARLES, librarian; b. Chgo., July 8, 1927; s. Ora Clay and Maude Emily (White) C.; Ph.B., Loyola U., Chgo., 1950, postgrad., 1952-53; M.A. in Library Sci., Rosary Coll., River Forest, Ill., 1956; m. Dorothy Jean Watters, Aug. 22, 1953. Mem. faculty Loyola U., Chgo., 1952—, asst. librarian univ. library at Lewis Towers, 1953-55, librarian Sch. Dentistry, 1955- 56, asst. librarian univ. Cudahy Library, 1956-58, asso. librarian univ. libraries, 1958-59, dir. libraries, 1959-71. Served with USNR, 1945-46, 50-52. Mem. Am. (mem. publs. com., pub. relations sect.), Cath. (chmn. Ill. 1962-63, program chmn. 1961-63, chmn. cataloging and classification sect. 1965-67, mem. exec. bd. 1967- -) library assns., Bibliog. Soc. Am., Bibliog. Soc. (London). Roman Catholic. Contbr. to profl. jours. Home: 1221 W Catalpa Chicago IL 60640

COX, JAMES MELVILLE, educator; b. Independence, Va., Aug. 4, 1925; s. Kyle Thomas and Elizabeth (Jordan) C.; B.A., U. Mich., 1948, M.A., 1949; Ph.D., Ind. U., 1955; m. Marguerite Naamah Hutchison, Sept. 4, 1948; children— Karen, Marian, Julia, Margaret, David, Virginia. Asst. prof., English, Emory and Henry Coll., 1950-52; instr. English, Dartmouth, 1955-57; asst. prof., then asso. prof. English, Ind. U., 1958-63; mem. faculty Dartmouth, 1963—, prof. English, 1965—. Served with U.S. Navy, 1943- 46. John H. Edwards fellow, 1954-55; fellow Am. Council Learned Socs., 1960-61. Mem. Am. Assn. U. Profs., Modern Lang. Assn. Am., Dante Soc. Am. Author: (with Alan M. Hollingsworth) The Third at Gettysburg: Pickett's Charge, 1959; Mark Twain: The Fate of Humor, 1966. Editor: Robert Frost: Twentieth Century Views, 1962. Home: Route 1 Box 72 East Thetford VT 05055 Office: Dept English Dartmouth Coll Hanover NH 03755

COX, JAMES MIDDLETON, Jr., publisher; b. Dayton, O., June 27, 1903; s. James Middleton and Mary Simpson (Harding) C.; student Culver Mil. Acad., 1917-20, Cheshire (Conn.) Acad., 1922-24; Ph.B., Yale, 1928; m. Helen Rumsey, Nov. 21, 1930. Entered newspaper work,. Dayton Daily News, 1929, gen. mgr., 1931- 38, asst. pub., 1938-39, asst. pub. and v.p., 1939-49, dir., pres., 1949- 56; pres. dir. Dayton Journal-Herald, 1948-56; vice chmn., pres. Dayton Newspapers, Inc., 1957-58, chmn., 1958—; established Radio Sta. WHIO, Dayton, 1934, WSOC, Charlotte, WSB, Atlanta, WIOD, Miami, consol. with television properties and affiliated holdings to form Cox Broadcasting Corp., chmn., 1964—; chmn. Cox Enterprises, Inc., 1968—; dir. Abitibi Paper Co., Ltd., also numerous newspapers, Ohio, Atlanta, Ga., Miami, Palm Beach. Trustee U. Miami (Fla.). Served as lt. comdr. Naval A.S., U.S.N.R., active duty, 1942-45. Episcopalian. Clubs: Augusta National, Peachtree Golf (Ga.), Indian Creek, La Gorce (Miami); Moraine Country (Dayton, O.). Home: 300 Tait Rd Dayton OH 45429

COX, JAN, painter; b. The Hague, Holland, Aug. 27, 1919; s. Hendrik and Francina Noorthoorn (van der Kruyff) C.; student painting, Higher Inst. Fine Arts, Antwerp, Belgium, 1936; student art and archeology, U. Gent (Belgium), 1937-41. Came to U.S., 1956. One man shows include Antwerp, 1942, Palais des Beaux-Arts, Brussels, Belgium, 1948, Martinet & Michiels Gallery, Amsterdam, Holland, 1950, Venice Biennale, 1956, Mus. Fine Arts Boston, 1957, Smithsonian Instn. Traveling Exhbn., 1958-59, Nova Gallery, Boston, 1959, Catherine Viviano Gallery, N.Y.C., 1960, 62, 65, Pace Gallery, Boston, 1962; group shows include Kunsthalle, Hamburg, W. Germany, Boymans Mus., Rotterdam, Holland, Mus. Contemporary Art, Skopje, Yugoslavia; nat. and internat exhbns. include Salon de Mai, Paris, 1949, 50, 65, Djakarta, Indonesia, 1951, Biennale Sao Paulo, Brazil, 1954, Curacao Mus. Fine Arts, 1954; rep. permanent collections Mus. Royale des Beaux-Arts, Brussels, Koninklijk Mus. voor Schone Kunsten, Antwerp, Mus. Fine Arts, Boston, Cin. Art Mus., Bklyn. Mus., Mus. Modern Art, Art Inst. Chgo.; founding mem. La Jeune Pienture Belge, Antwerp, 1943; scenery designer Les Mouches, 1946; mem. L'Art Contemporain, Antwerp, 1949; head painting dept. Sch. Mus. Fine Arts, Boston, 1956—. Home: 22 Evans Way Boston, MA 02115.

COX, JOHN J., hosp. adminstr.; b. Manchester, N.H., May 2, 1915; s. John J. and Katherine (Clare) C.; student St. Anselm's Coll., Manchester, 1934-36; LL.B., Columbus U., Washington, 1951; m. Anne Marie Pacioppi, Oct. 19, 1946; children—Pamela Anne, Tara Marie, Michele Katrine. With VA, 1946—, adminstr. Albany (N.Y.) VA Hosp., from 1969, now regional med. dir. So. Cal. dist., Los Angeles. Active local A.R.C. Served with AUS, World War II; PTO. Decorated Purple Heart; recipient Outstanding Performance award VA, 1967, 71. Mem. Am. Hosp. Assn., Am. Coll. Hosp. Adminstrs., Assn. Mil. Surgeons U.S., Fed. Exec. Council, Hopr. Assn. Northeastern N.Y. Address: VA Sawtelle and Wilshire Blvds Los Angeles CA 90073

COX, JOHN JACKSON, lawyer; b. Temple, Tex., Feb. 4, 1905; s. William Oscar and Etta May (Dickens) C.; B.A., U. Tex., Austin, 1925, LL.B., 1928; m. Ann Elizabeth Walker, Sept. 25, 1928 (dec. 1966); children-Ann Elizabeth (Mrs. Wendell F. Phillips), Joan Jackson (Mrs. W. Allen Keage); m. 2d, Una Chapman, Feb. 21, 1968. Admitted to Tex. bar, 1928, since practiced in San Antonio; pvt. practice, 1931-39; mem. firm Seelgson, Cox & Patterson, 1939-50, Cox, Patterson & Smith, 1950—. Dir. Pearl Brewing Co. Bd. dirs. S.W. Research Inst., Minnie Stevens Piper Found.; trustee S.W. Found. for Research and Edn., San Antonio Med. Found., U. Tex. Law Sch. Found. Fellow Tex. Bar Found.; mem. Am., San Antonio bar assns., State Bar Tex., Order of Coif, Chancellors, Phi Beta Kappa, Phi Kappa Psi, Phi Delta Phi. Episcopalian. Clubs: San Antoio Country, St.

Anthony (San Antonio); Corpus Christi Yacht. Asso. editor: Tex. Law Review, 1926-28. Home: 524 Geneseo Rd San Antonio TX 78209 Office: Nat Bank of Commerce Bldg San Antonio TX 78205

COX, JOHN PAUL, educator, astrophysicist; b. Ft. Myers, Fla., Nov. 4, 1926; s. James B. and Bess L. (Tollette) C.; A.B., Ind. U., 1949, M.S., 1950, Ph.D., 1954. Mem. faculty Cornell U., 1954-62; vis. scientist Courant Inst. Math. Scis. N.Y.U., 1962-63; vis. fellow Joint Inst. Lab. Astrophysics, Boulder, 1963; asso. prof. astrophysics U. Colo., Boulder, 1963-65, prof. physics, 1965—; cons. Smithsonian Astrophys. Obs., Cambridge, Mass., 1957, 59, 60, Los Alamos Sci. Lab., 1960—; asst. engr. Pratt & Whitney Aircraft Corp., East Hartford, Conn., 1958. Mem. Am. Phys. Soc., Am. Astron. Soc., N.Y. Acad. Scis., Internat. Astron. Union, Royal Astron. Soc., Astron. Soc. Pacific, Sigma Xi, Phi Eta Sigma. Home: 827 16th St Boulder CO 80302

COX, JOHN R., ins. co. exec.; b. 1932; B.S., N.Y.U., 1959; married. Exec. v.p. Am. Home Assurance Co., 1959—; v.p., treas. Nat. Union Fire Ins. Co. Pitts. Office: N Am Rockwell Bldg 5th Av at Wood St Pittsburgh PA 15222*

COX, JOHN ROBERT, educator; b. Denver, Colo., June 23, 1922; s. Ezra Martin and Glenn (Berry) C.; A.B. in Econs., DePauw U., 1943; M.B.A., Stanford, 1948, Ph.D., 1957; m. Jane Morris Schlosser, Feb. 19, 1945; children—Barbara Ruth, Cynthia Jane, Deborah Lynne. Sales rep. Burroughs Corp., San Francisco, 1948-49; asst. prof. Menlo Coll., Menlo Park, Cal., 1952-53; mem. faculty Sacramento State Coll., 1950-52, 53—, prof. bus. adminstrn., chmn. div., 1957-63, exec. dean coll., 1963-67, dean campus facilities, 1970—. Served as aviator USNR, 1943-46; PTO. Decorated Air medal. Mem. Acad. Mgmt., Soc. Advancement Mgmt., Am. Marketing Assn., Delta Sigma Pi, Beta Gamma Sigma. Home: 1411 Las Salinas Way Sacramento CA 95825

COX, JOHN ROGERS, artist; b. Terre Haute, Ind., Mar. 24, 1915; s. Wilson Naylor and Lassie (Gardenhire) C.; B.F.A., U. Pa., Pa. Acad. Fine Arts, 1938; m. Hermine Mayer, Dec. 29, 1929 (div. 1947); children—John Rogers, Henry, Janet (dec.); m. 2d, Ellen Theresa Hilbert, May 1, 1952 (div.); m. 3d, Donise Arlene Kibby, Oct. 1, 1963; 1 dau., Sophia Donise. With First Nat. Bank, Terre Haute, 1938-41; dir. Swope Gallery, 1941-43; instr. figure drawing, figure painting Sch. of Art Inst., Chgo., 1948-60, asst. prof., 1960-65. Exhibited Carnegie Instn., Pa. Acad. Fine Arts, Met. Mus., N.Y.C., Boston Inst. Art, Cleve. Mus., Art Inst. Chgo., John Herron Mus., Dallas Mus., Toledo Mus., others; represented permanent collections Cleve. Mus., Butler Inst., Springfield (Mass.) Mus., pvt. collections. Recipient prizes Met. Mus., 1942, Carnegie Inst., 1943, 44, others. Mem. Phi Kappa Psi. Episcopalian. Contbr. mags. Home: Route 1 Chelan WA 98816

COX, JOYCE, lawyer; b. Cameron, Tex., Sept. 16, 1904; s. Moses Gray and Mary (Joyce) C.; A.B., U. Tex., 1924, LL.B., 1927; S.J.D., Harvard, 1928; m. Gertrude Anderson, Apr. 27, 1929 (div. Jan. 1952); children—David M., Philip R., Mary Joyce (Mrs. Emery Cardell); m. 2d, Gail Wilbern Holston, May 16, 1953; children—Jim, Kathryn Gail. Admitted to Tex. bar, 1927, Ill. bar, 1936; with firm Terry, Cavin & Mills, Galveston, Tex., 1928- 36; gen. atty. A.T. & S.F. Ry. Co., Chgo., 1936-41; gen. practice, Houston, 1941; partner firm Fountain, Cox & Gaines, 1944—. Gen. counsel, dir. Kirby Lumber Corp. Fellow Am. Bar Found.; mem. Am. (rep. ho. of dels.), Houston (pres. 1959-60) bar assns., State Bar Tex. (pres. 1964-65), Houston C. of C., Chancellors, Phi Beta Kappa, Phi Delta Phi. Episcopalian. Mason (Shriner). Home: 1635 Bissonnet St Houston TX 77005 Office: Gulf Bldg Houston TX 77002

COX, JULIUS GRADY, univ. dean; b. Ayden, N.C., Dec. 6, 1926; s. George Dewey and Annie (Hurst) C.; B.S. in Chem. Engring., Auburn U., 1948, M.S. in Math., 1950; Ph.D. in Indsl. Engring., Purdue U., 1964; m. Jean Claire Ransom, Mar. 16, 1946; children—Jane Rogers (Mrs. George V. Jones), Keith Martin. With Reynolds Alloys Co., 1948, Southeastern Sand & Gravel Co., 1948-49; lab. asst., then instr. Auburn U., 1949-51; chief weapons sect. Air Proving Ground Command, Eglin AFB, Fla., 1951-52, operations anaylst, 1952-53, 55-56; asst. dir. operations analysis standby unit U.N.C., 1953-55; head math. services Vitro Corp., 1956-57; mem. faculty Auburn U., 1958—, prof. indsl. engring., 1963—, dean engring., 1969—; cons. in field. Bd. dirs. Auburn United Fund, 1967-70. Served with USNR, 1944-46. Recipient Civil Service award USAF, 1956. Registered profl. engr., Ala. Mem. Operations Research Soc. Am., Am. Soc. Engring. Edn., Am. Inst. Indsl. Engrs., Ala. Soc. Profl. Engrs., Ala. Acad. Sci., Sigma Xi, Pi Mu Epsilon, Tau Beta Pi, Phi Lambda Upsilon, Pi Tau Sigma, Omicron Delta Kappa, Alpha Phi Mu. Baptist (deacon, Sunday sch. tchr.). Author: (with J.H. Mize) Essentials of Simulation, 1968; also articles, monographs. Home: 910 Terrace Acres Auburn AL 36830

COX, KENNETH ALLEN, lawyer, communications exec.; b. Topeka, Dec. 7, 1916; s. Seth Leroy and Jean (Sears) C.; B.A., U. Wash., 1938, LL.B., 1940; LL.M., U. Mich., 1941; LL.D., Chgo. Theol. Sem., 1969; m. Nona Beth Fumerton, Jan. 1, 1943; children—Gregory Allen, Jeffrey Neal, Douglas Randall. Admitted to Wash. bar, 1941; law clk. Wash. Supreme Ct., 1941-42; asst. prof. U. Mich. Law Sch., 1946-48; with firm Little, Palmer, Scott & Slemmons, and predecessor, Seattle, 1948-61, partner, 1953-61; spl. counsel com. interstate and fgn. commerce charge TV inquiry, U.S. Senate, 1956-57; chief broadcast bur. FCC, Washington, 1961-63, commr. FCC, 1963-70; counsel to communications law firm Haley, Bader & Potts, 1970—; sr. v.p. Microwave Communications Am., Inc., 1970—. Lectr., U. Washington Law Sch., part-time 1954, 60. Vice pres. Municipal League Seattle and King County, 1960, Seattle World Affairs Council, 1960; pres. Seattle chpt. Am. Assn. UN, 1957; chmn. one of five citizen subcoms. Legislative Interim Com. Edn., 1960. Served to capt. Q.M.C., AUS, 1943-46, 51-52. Recipient Alfred I. duPont award in broadcast journalism Columbia U., 1970. Mem. Am., Fed. Communications, Wash. State bar assns., Order of Coif, Phi Beta Kappa, Phi Delta Phi. Democrat. Conglist. Home: 5836 Marbury Rd Bethesda MD 20074 Office: 1900 L St NW Washington DC 20036

COX, LAWRENCE W., banker. Sr. v.p. San Diego br. Security Pacific Nat. Bank. Office: 201 A St San Diego CA 92101*

COX, LEILYN MUNNS, ins. co. exec.; b. Ft. Bayard, N.M., Oct. 28, 1903; s. Herbert F. and Carey (Munns) C.; A.B., Coll. Emporia, 1926; children—Leilyn S., Shirley L. (Mrs. Kenneth W. Seefeld). With accounting firm, Philippines, 1926-37; with Employers Ins. Co., 1938—, dist. audit supr., N.Y.C., 1940-44, comptroller, 1944-49, v.p., comptroller, Wausau, Wis., 1949-69, now financial adminstr. C.P.A., Wis., Cal., P.I. Mem. Nat. Assn. Accountants, Financial Execs. Inst. Am. (past pres. Milw.), Adminstrv. Mgmt. Assn., Am. Inst. C.P.A.'s, Wis. Soc. C.P.A.'s, Ins. Accounting and Statis. Assn. (past pres.), Soc. Advancement Mgmt., Am. Mut. Ins. Alliance. Author: Introduction to Accounting and Partnership Accounting in the Philippines, 1935. Contbr. profl. jours. Home: 1014 McClellan St Wausau WI 55401 Office: 2000 Westwood Dr Wausau WI 54401

COX, LEWIS JOHN, heating co. exec.; b. Grinnell, Ia., Nov. 23, 1911; s. Charles F. and Stella (Mason) C.; student Behnek-Walker Bus. Coll., Portland, 1928-29, Northwestern Coll. Law, Portland, 1930-31, 46-47, Cleveland Coll., 1932- 42; m. Betty Meder, Dec. 1, 1934. With Iron Fireman Mfg. Co., Cleve., 1929—, asst. to gen. sales mgr., 1937-43, asst. to pres., 1946-51, v.p., 1951-56, v.p., gen. mgr. heating div., 1956-57, pres., 1957-62; past pres. Iron Fireman-Webster, Inc., Subsidiary of Electronic Splty. Co.; past v.p. Electronic Splty. Co. Served as lt. USNR, 1943-46. Rotarian. Home: 2111 Jefferson Davis Hwy Arlington VA 22202 Office: 815 17th St NW Washington DC 20006

COX, MERRILL, engring. and contract co. exec.; b. San Jose, Cal., June 19, 1904; s. Herbert E. and Ruth (Merrill) C.; B.S. in Chemistry, U. Cal. at Berkeley, 1929; m. Margaret Strong, Sept. 27, 1930; children—Carole (Mrs. Robert Bartol), Barbara (Mrs. John Donnelly). With U.S. Steel Corp., 1921-26; with metals div. Arthur G. McKee & Co., Cleve., starting 1930 v.p., 1953-61, exec. v.p., 1961-64, then pres., also dir., retired; dir. Union Commerce Bank of Cleve. Trustee Community Chest; bd. dirs. Greater Cleve. Growth Assn. Mem. Newcomen Soc. N.Am., Am. Iron and Steel Inst. (asso.), Blast Furnace and Coke Oven Assn. Home: 18503 Parkland Dr Shaker Heights OH 44122 Office: 2300 Chester Av Cleveland OH 44101

COX, RACHEL DUNAWAY, (Mrs. Reavis Cox), educator; b. Murray, Ky.; d. Enoch T. and Khadra (Fergeson) Dunaway; B.A., U. Tex., 1925; M.A., Columbia, 1930; Ph.D., U. Pa., 1943; m. Reavis Cox, Feb. 18, 1928; children—David J., Rosemary D. (Mrs. Masters). Editorial work, reporter N.Y. Herald Tribune, 1926-30; tchr., dir. edn. West Side YWCA, N.Y.C., 1930-35; hosp. case worker A.R.C., Walter Reed Hosp., Washington, 1944; lectr. psychology, edn. Bryn Mawr Coll., 1944-45, asst. prof., 1945-48, asso. prof., 1948-56, prof., 1956-71, dir., chmn. dept. edn. and child devel. Child Study Inst., 1944-71; pvt. practice clin. psychology, Swarthmore, Pa., 1971—. Bd. dirs. Sleighton Farm Sch. Girls, Developmental Center for Autistic Children. Fellow Soc. Projective Techniques (past sec.); mem. Am., Eastern, Pa. psychol. assns., Nat. Assn. Social Work, Am., Phila. (dir., 1950-52, past pres.) personnel and guidance assns., Phi Beta Kappa, Sigma Xi, Theta Sigma Phi. Author: Youth Into Maturity, 1970. Address: 503 Walnut Lane Swarthmore PA 19081

COX, REAVIS, economist; b. Guadalajara, Mexico, Sept. 2, 1900 (parents Am. citizens); s. Jackson Berry and Julia (Barcus) C.; A.B., U. Tex., Austin, 1921; Ph.D., Columbia, 1932; m. Rachel LaVerne Dunaway, Feb. 18, 1928; children—David Jackson, Rosemary C. Masters. In newspaper work various parts U.S., 1921-25; mem. staff Jour. of Commerce, 1926-31, market editor, 1927-31; instr. bus. adminstrn. Columbia U., 1931-35; asso. prof. U. Pa., Phila., 1935-38, prof. marketing, 1938-67, Sebastian S. Kresge prof., 1967-71, prof. emeritus, 1971, chmn. marketing dept. Wharton Sch. Finance and Commerce, 1935-41; vis. prof. marketing U. Sherbrooke, Que., Can., 1968—; vis. research prof. distributive studies Manchester Bus. Sch., 1971—; mng. editor Jour. of Marketing, 1941-42, editor in chief, 1943-44; mem. staff OPA and Civilian Supply, OPM, WPB, 1941-43; dir. research projects Retail Credit Inst. of Am., 1943-49. Served in U.S. Army, World War I. Mem. Am. Econ. Assn., Am. Marketing Assn. (pres. 1959-60), Am. Acad. Polit. and Social Sci., Am. Statis. Assn., A.A.A.S. Presbyn. Club: Cosmos (Washington). Author or co-author several books including: The Economics of Installment Buying, 1948; Theory in Marketing, 1950; Marketing in the American Economy, 1952; Theory in Marketing, 2d series, 1964; Distribution in a High-Level Economy, 1965. Home: 503 Walnut Lane Swarthmore PA 19081 ☆

COX, ROBERT DOYLE, law sch. dean; b. Vian, Okla., Sept. 22, 1926; s. Garland Granville and Callie M. (Brackett) C.; LL.B., U. Okla., 1949; LL.M., Duke, 1953; m. Mary Ann Tabor, June 25, 1955. Admitted to Okla. bar, 1949, Tenn. bar, 1953; asst. counsel Tenn. Eastman Co., Kingsport, 1953-56; pvt. practice, Wewoka, Okla., 1956-59; asst. prof. law U. Tulsa, 1959-62; dean Memphis State U. Sch. Law, 1962—. Served with 1st lt. AUS, 1945- 46. Mem. Am., Okla., Tenn., bar assns. Home: 145 N Goodlett Memphis TN 38117

COX, ROBERT G., banker; b. Newark, Dec. 27, 1919; s. John and Margaret Marie (Koch) C.; B.S., U. Ill., 1942; M.B.A., U. Pa., 1946, Ph.D., 1956; m. Amelita M. Kjellstrand, May 30, 1942; children—Robert, Janet, Stephen. Instr., U. Pa., 1945-49, asst. prof., 1949-56, asso. prof., 1956-61, vice dean Wharton Sch., 1960-64, prof., 1961-64; dean, prof. accounting Coll. Bus. Adminstrn. Syracuse (N.Y.) U., 1964-70; exec. v.p. Lincoln Nat. Bank & Trust Co., Syracuse, 1970—; dir. Farris Inst., Phila., Mass. Dental Prosthetics Co. Trustee Community Hosp. Served to capt. USAAF, 1942-45. Mem. Financial Execs. Inst., Am., Nat. accounting assns., Am. Inst. C.P.A.'s, Beta Gamma Sigma, Beta Alpha Psi, Alpha Kappa Psi, Zeta Psi. Clubs: University (Syracuse); Onondaga Golf and Country (Fayetteville). Author: (with Burley and Fisher) Drug Store Operating Costs and Profits, 1956; (with Rufus Wixon) Principles of Accounting, 1961. Contbr. to Education of the American Businessman, 1960. Home: 107 Draycott St Fayetteville NY 13066 Office: Lincoln Nat Bank & Trust Co Syracuse NY 13210

COX, ROBERT VINSANT, corp. exec.; b. Memphis, Sept. 11, 1926; s. Gordon Carruth and Daisy Wilma (Widdows) C.; student U. Miss., 1944; A.B., U. N.C., 1948, M.A., 1949; m. Catherine Cox Carlen, Dec. 20, 1947; children—Gordon Randolph, Robert Carlen, Alfred Thomas, Daniel Reams, Andrew Jennings. Asst. football coach U. N.C., 1949-51; owner Town & Campus Store, Chapel Hill, N.C., 1952-62; v.p., asst. gen. sales mgr. Pepsi-Cola Co., 1962- 66, v.p., dir. pub. relations, 1966-67; v.p. marketing Uni-Card div. Chase Manhattan Bank, 1967—. Member U.S. Jr. C. of C., 1951—, pres., 1958-59; dir.-at-large US C. of C., 1959-60. Exec. dir. Youth Fitness Commn. N.C., 1959—; mem. Pres.'s Citizens Youth Fitness Adv. Commn., 1958—. Dir. Freedoms Found., 1959-60. Served with USMCR, 1944-46. Mem. Am. Legion, Sigma Alpha Epsilon, Phi Delta Kappa, Delta Sigma Pi. Home: 232 Dover Rd Manhasset NY 11030 Office: 2000 Marcus Av New Hyde Park NY 11040

COX, RUFUS FRANCIS, educator; b. Altus, Okla., June 13, 1901; s. Robert Lafayette and Annie Elizabeth (Edwards) C.; B.S., Okla. A. and M. Coll., 1923; M.S., Ia. State Coll., 1925; Ph.D., Cornell U., 1946; m. Elsie Leona Hayes, July 17, 1926; children—Robert Eugene, Carolyn Jeanne. Instr. vocational agr. Okla., 1924-25; asst. prof. animal husbandry N.M. Agrl. Coll., 1926-30; asst. prof. Kan. State Coll., Manhattan, 1930-35, asso. prof., 1935-41, prof., 1950-71, head dept. animal husbandry, 1950-66, prof. emeritus, 1971—. Extension summer staff U. Ky., 1938-40, 43, 48; staff War Food Adminstrn., U.S. Dept. Agr., summer 1943. Fellow Am. Soc. Animal Sci. (hon.); mem. A.A.A.S., Sigma Xi, Gamma Sigma Delta, Alpha Zeta. Methodist. Mason. Contbr. articles sci. to jours. Home: 421 Edgerton Av Manhattan KS 66502

COX, WALLY, actor; b. Detroit, Dec. 6, 1924; s. George Wallace and Eleanor Frances (Atkinson) C.; student City Coll. N.Y., N.Y. U.; one child. Propr. silversmith shop, N.Y.C., 1946-48; monologue comedy Village Vanguard, 1948, Blue Angel, Manhattan, 1949-50; appeared mus. revue Dance Me A Song, Royale Theater, N.Y.C., 1940; entertainer Persian Room, N.Y. Plaza Hotel, also radio, TV shows, 1950-51; discless disc jockey radio sta. WNEW, 1951; appeared in TV prodn. The Cooper; comedy actor Mr. Peepers, NBC-TV, 1952-55; guest appearances numerous TV series; performer TV show Hollywood Squares; actor summer theater prodns. Three Men on a Horse; comedy actor Adventures Hiram Holiday NBC-TV, 1956-57; appeared in motion pictures Yellow Rolls Royce, Morituri, Fate Is the Hunter, Spencers Mountain, State Fair, The Bedford Incident, A Woman for Charlie. Served with inf. AUS, World War II. Recipient Peabody award for Mr. Peepers performances, 1953. Author plays, short stories, My Life as a Small Boy, 1961; Ralph Makes Good, 1966. Address: care Gloria Safier 667 Madison Av New York City NY 10021

COX, WARREN JACOB, architect; b. N.Y.C., Aug. 28, 1935; s. Oscar Sydney and Louise Bryson (Black) C.; grad. Hill Sch., 1953; B.A., Yale, 1957, B.Arch., 1961; m. Susan Elizabeth Shifley, Jan. 8, 1966. Partner Hartman-Cox Architects, Washington, 1965—; vis. archtl. critic Yale, 1966, Cath. U. Am., 1967; works include master plan, dormitory and chapel Mt. Vernon Coll., EURAM bldg. (Washington), Brewer residence (Chevy Chase, Md.). Mem. Georgetown Commn. Fine Arts. Recipient nat. honor awards A.I.A., 1970, 71. Mem. A.I.A. Contbr. articles profl. jours. Home: 3111 N St NW Washington DC 20007 Office: 1071 Thomas Jefferson St NW Washington DC 20007

COX, WILLIAM HAROLD, judge; b. Indianola, Miss., June 23, 1901; s. Adam Charles and Lillie Emma (Ray) C.; B.S., LL.B., U. Miss., 1924; m. Edwina Berry, June 30, 1927; children—William Harold, Joanne (Mrs. Paul Bellenger, Jr.). Admitted to Miss. bar, 1924; practiced Jackson, 1924-61; U.S. dist. judge So. dist. Miss., 1961—, now chief judge. Mem. Miss. Bd. Bar Admissions, 1932-36. Chmn. Hinds County Democratic Exec. Com., 1950-61; presdl. elector, 1952. Home: 133 Woodland Circle Jackson MS 39205 Office: US Post Office Bldg Jackson MS 39205

COX, WILLIAM PLUMMER, architect; b. Savannah, Ga., Aug. 17, 1915; s. Charles Howard and Hannah (Plummer) C.; B.Arch., U. Pa., 1937. Pvt. archtl. practice, Memphis, 1946—; mem. firm Eason, Anthony, McKinnie, Cox & Martin; lectr. U. Tenn.; works include William F. Bould Hosp., Dobbs Med. Research Inst., Le Bonheur Children's Hosp. addition, other hosps. and schs. Pres. Memphis Little Theater, 1952-53; dir. Memphis YMCA, 1955-67; mem. Memphis Youth Guidance Commn., 1955-65. Served to lt. comdr. USNR, 1941-50. Fellow A.I.A. (pres. Memphis chpt. 1951); mem. Constrn. Specifications Inst. (pres. Memphis chpt. 1961-62), Tenn. Soc. Architects (pres. 1953-54, dir. 1969-71), Am. Soc. Testing and Materials, U.S. Coast Guard Auxiliary. Clubs: Memphis Yacht (commodore 1967), Memphis Kiwanis (dir. 1965-70). Home: 1066 North Pkwy Memphis TN 38105 Office: 1391 Madison Av Memphis TN 38104

COX, WILLIAM WALTER, lawyer; b. Sidney, O., Feb. 22, 1914; s. Harry Lewis and Marguerite McKay (Goode) C.; A.B., Ohio Wesleyan U., 1935, LL.D., 1970; LL.B., Columbia, 1939; m. Nancy Heather Parratt, Mar. 7, 1946. Admitted to N.Y. bar, 1940, practice, N.Y.C., 1939-40; atty. U.S. Dept. Labor, 1940-42, Civilian Rationing Div. OPA, 1942; legal adv. UNRRA Mission to Austria, 1946-47; spl. asst. to exec. sec. Prep. Commn. for Internat. Refugee Orgn., Geneva, Switzerland, 1947-48, gen. counsel I.R.O., 1948-50; dep. dir. Div. Immunities and Treaties UN Legal Dept. 1950- 54; dep. dir. Office Legal Counsel, UN, N.Y.C., 1955-63, dep. dir. personnel, 1964-68; sec. Internat. Civil Service Adv. Bd., 1969—. Mem. UN Tech. Assistance Mission to Bolivia, 1951; legal adviser to chief staff UN Truce Supervision Orgn., Jerusalem, 1954; legal adv. comdr. UN Emergency Force, Gaza, 1957; legal adviser UN Orgn. in Congo, 1960, 61, 63. Served as lt. USNR, 1942-46. Mem. N.Y. State Bar, Am. Soc. Internat. Law, Phi Beta Kappa, Phi Gamma Delta. Editor: Columbia Law Rev., 1937-39. Home: 370 1st Av New York City NY 10010 Office: United Nations New York City NY 10017

COXE, GEORGE HARMON, author; b. Olean, N.Y., Apr. 23, 1901; s. George H. and Harriet C. (Cowens) C.; student Elmira Free Acad., 1918-19, Purdue U., 1919-20, Cornell U., 1920-21; m. Elizabeth Fowler, May 18, 1929; children—Janet, George 3d. With Santa Monica (Cal.) Outlook, 1922; successively with Los Angeles Express, Utica (N.Y.) Observer Dispatch, N.Y. Comml. and Elmira Star-Gazette to 1927; in advt. work Barta Press, Cambridge, Mass., 1927-32; writer Metro-Goldwyn-Mayer, 1936-38, 1944. Dir. Mystery Writers Am., 1946-48, 1969-70, pres., 1952. Mem. Authors Guild, Sigma Nu, Phi Zeta. Republican. Clubs: Old Lyme (Conn.) Country, Old Lyme Beach; Cornell (N.Y.C.); Plantation, Sea Pines Golf (Hilton Head, S.C.). Author: numerous mystery books since 1935, Lady Killer, 1949; Inland Passage, 1949; Eye Witness, 1950; The Frightened Fiancee, 1950; The Widow Had a Gun, 1951; The Man Who Died Twice, 1951; Never Bet Your Life, 1952; The Crimson Clue, 1953; Uninvited Guest, 1953; Focus on Murder, 1954; Death at the Isthmus, 1954; Top Assingment, 1955; Suddenly a Widow, 1956; Man on a Rope, 1956. Crime Photographer (radio), 1943-52; Murder on their Minds, 1957; One Minute Past Eight, 1957; The Impetuous Mistress, 1958; The Big Gamble, 1958; Triple Exposure, 1959; Slack Tide, 1959; One Way Out, 1960; The Last Commandment, 1960; Error of Judgement, 1961; Moment of Violence, 1961; The Man Who Died too Soon, 1962; Mission of Fear, 1962; The Hidden Key, 1963; One Hour To Kill, 1963; Deadly Image, 1964; With Intent To Kill, 1965; The Reluctant Heiress, 1965; The Ring of Truth, 1966; The Candid Imposter, 1968: An Easy Way To Go, 1969; Double Identity, 1970; Fenner, 1971; contbr. short stories, serials, novelettes to mags., 1932—; war corr., 1945. Recipient Grand Masters award, 1964. Home: Deepledge Old Lyme CT Office: care Brandt & Brandt 101 Park Av New York City NY 10017

COXE, LEWIS CROCKER, naval officer; b. Annapolis, Md., Aug. 19, 1912; s. Lewis and Lilian (Crocker) C.; B.S., U.S. Naval Acad., 1934; B.C.E., Rensselaer Poly. Inst., 1938, M.C.E., 1939; m. Nancy Lesh, June 13, 1936; 1 son, Michael Paul Morgan. Commd. ensign, U.S. Navy, 1934, advanced through grades to rear adm. C.E., 1962; assigned Phila. Navy Yd., 1939-43, Naval Air Sta., Coco Solo, C.Z., also Iceland; comdg. officer Navy Advance Base Proving Ground, Davisville, R.I., 1943-44, 81st Naval Constrn. Bn., Okinawa, 1945; design mgr. Bur. Yards and Docks, 1945-49; pub. works officer Naval Shipyard, Long Beach, Cal., 1949-50; asst. dist. pub. works officer 11th Naval Dist., San Diego, 1950-51; comdg. officer Pub. Works Center, Guam, M.I., 1951-53; dist. pub. works officer Severn River Naval Command, 1953-57; asst. chief research, planning and design Bur. Yards and Docks, 1957-60, dir. European Mid-East div., London, 1960-62, insp. gen., asst. chief adminstrn. Bur. Yards and Docks, 1963, dir. Southwest division, dep. comdr. for acquisition Naval Facilities Engring. Command, Yards and Docks Annex, Arlington, Virginia Civil and structural engr., D.C. Mem. Am. Soc. C.E. (past chmn. exec. com., rivers and harbors div.), Soc. Am. Mil. Engrs. (nat. dir.), U.S. Naval Acad. Alumni Assn., Sigma Xi, Tau Beta Pi. Clubs: Army-Navy Country, Kiwanis (San Diego). Contbr. numerous articles profl. govt. publs. Address: 1600 S Eads Arlington VA 22202

COXE, LOUIS OSBORNE, educator, poet; b. Manchester, N.H., Apr. 15, 1918; s. Charles Shearman and Helen Eyre (Osborne) C.; grad. St. Paul's Sch., Concord, N.H., 1936; B.S., Princeton, 1940; m. Edith Winsor, June 28, 1946; children—Robert Winsor, Louis Osborne, Charles Shearman, Helen Eyre. Instr., Princeton, 1946; Briggs-Copeland fellow Harvard, 1948-49; asst., then asso. prof. U. Minn., 1949-55; prof. English, Bowdoin Coll., 1955—, Pierce prof. English, 1956—. Trustee N.Y. Sch. Interior Design. Served with USNR, 1942-46. Recipient Creative Arts award Brandeis U., 1961; Sewanee Rev. fellow, 1955; Fulbright fellow, 1959- 60. Mem. P.E.N., Dramatists Guild. Author: The Sea Faring, 1947; The Second Man, 1955; The Wilderness, 1958; The Middle Passage, 1960; The Last Hero, 1965; (play with Robert Chapman) Billy Budd, 1952; Nikal Seyn and Decoration Day, 1966; Edwin Arlington Robinson: The Life of Poetry, 1969. Home: RD 2 Adams Rd Brunswick ME 04011

COX-FREEMAN, LAURENCE EDWARD, advt. exec.; b. London, Eng., Feb. 2, 1926; s. Maurice Cox and June Cox Freeman; student Seihurst School, 1938-42; m. Josephine Stogdon, May 5, 1953; children—Ivan, Alexander, Spencer. Account control J. Walter Thompson, London, 1946-50; account supr. London Press Exchange, 1950-55; mng. dir. Horniblow Cox Freeman, London, 1956—. HCF Internat., 1966—; dir. HFC Germany; HFC Italy, HFC W. Africa, HFC Trinidad, HFC Greece, HEC de Uphaugh, London. Served as flight lt. RAF, 1943-46. Fellow Inst. Practictioners Advt.; mem. Internat. Advt. Assn. (council mem. U.K.). Home: Camilla House Forest Rd East Horsley, Surrey, England. Office: Bowater House East Knightsbridge London England

COY, EDWARD W., govt. ofcl.; b. Odebolt, Ia., June 1, 1928; s. Frank H. and Ruth (O'Connell) C.; B.A., Stanford, 1950, M.B.A., 1954; m. Rossana Baglietto, May 18, 1962; children—Cathleen, Michelle, Edward. With U.S. U.S. Govt., 1954—, now dir. AID mission to Bolivia. Served with USAF, 1951- 53. Home: 42760 Wisconsin Dr Palm Desert CA 92260 Office: American Embassy La Paz Bolivia

COY, FRANCIS ANDREW, dept. store exec.; b. Cin., Mar. 9, 1914; s. John Andrew and Ellen (Holloway) C.; student U. Cin., 1934; LL.D., Wilberforce U., 1971; L.H.D., Baldwin-Wallace Coll., 1971; m. Virginia Reah Chiles, July 20, 1936; 1 son, Lawrence Andrew. With Mabley and Carew, retail store, Cin., 1936-44; v.p. mdsg. O'Neill & Co., Balt., 1943-50; divisional mdse. mgr. Higbee Co., Cleve., 1951-52; v.p. Cleland Simpson Co., Scranton, Pa., 1953-55; with May Dept. Stores Co., 1956—, pres., dir. May Co., Cleve., 1961-71, chmn., chief exec. officer, 1971—, v.p. parent co., 1956—; dir. Nat. City Bank, Cleve. Vice pres., dir. Cleve. Retail Council; dir., mem. exec. com. Ohio Retail Council. Mem. exec. com., past pres. Greater Cleve. Growth Assn.; pres. Cleve. Parade of Progress 1964; vice chmn. United Fund Campaign, 1964, Summer Pops Concert. Bd. trustees Cleve. Devel. Found., St. Luke's Hosp., Nat. Jewish Hosp. (Denver), Baldwin Wallace Coll., Cleve. YMCA; bd. dirs., past pres. Cleve. council Boy Scouts Am., also bd. dirs. region 4; mem. adv. bd. Salvation Army; chmn. exec. com. Council High Blood Pressure Research; mem. Case Inst. Devel. Council. Methodist (trustee). Clubs: Union, Cleve. Athletic, City, Pepper Pike Country, Kirtland Contry, Canterbury Golf (Cleve.); Skytop (Pa.). Home: 18975 Van Aken St Shaker Heights OH 44122 Office: The May Co Euclid Av Cleveland OH 44114

COYE, ROBERT DUDLEY, medical educator; b. Los Angeles, Dec. 17, 1924; s. Robert Dudley and Dorothy Peters (Loomis) C.; B.A., Williams Coll., 1948; M.D., U. Rochester, 1952; m. Janet Irene Loper, July 26, 1946; children—Joel, Peter, Carol. Intern, resident pathology Strong Meml. Hosp., Rochester, N.Y., 1952-55; mem. faculty U. Wis. Med. Sch., 1955—, asst. to asso. dean, 1961-70, prof. pathology, 1967—. Served with AUS, 1943-46. Decorated Combat Inf. badge. Home: 1920 Kendall Av Madison WI 53705

COYLE, ALFRED JOHNSON, investment banker; b. N.Y.C., July 30, 1921; s. Frank J. and Alice (Johnson) C.; B.A., Princeton, 1942; m. Virginia Schick, Mar. 27, 1943; children—Barbara Anne, Virginia Schick, Alfred Johnson. Asst. to partner Hemphill, Noyes & Co., N.Y.C., 1946-52; ind. mem. N.Y. Stock Exchange, 1952; gen. partner Hayden, Stone & Co., Inc., N.Y.C., 1952-60, mng. partner, 1960-61, pres., 1962-65, 69-70, chmn. bd., 1965-70, chmn. exec. com., 1970; exec. v.p. Blythe & Co., Inc., N.Y.C., 1970—; dir. Leaseway Transp. Corp., Leaseway Intercontinental Co., Am. Dual Vest Fund Inc., Societe Anonyme de Gestion et d'Investment Immobiliers. Incorporator The Stamford (Conn.) Hosp.; mem. bd. trustees of the Internat. Coll., Beirut, Lebanon. Clubs: Racquet and Tennis, Twenty-Nine, Union Recess (N.Y.C.); Wee Burn Country (Darien); Seigniory (Que., Can.). Home: 65 Pembroke Rd Darien CT 06820 Office: 14 Wall St New York City NY 10004

COYLE, DONALD WALTON, broadcasting exec.; b. London, Ont., Can., June 17, 1922; s. Lorne S. and Pearle A. (Walton) C.; came to U.S., 1924, naturalized, 1950; B.A., Amherst Coll., 1948; student Am. Inst. Banking, 1948-49; m. Patricia Robinson, June 6, 1946; children—D. Lorne, Deborah A., Sharon R. Indsl. analyst Comml. Nat. Bank & Trust Co., N.Y.C., 1947-50; with ABC, N.Y.C., 1950-70, beginning as writer, successively mgr. radio and TV network research, research mgr. and cons. radio and TV, dir. TV network research, dir. radio and TV network research, dir. TV sales devel. and research, 1950-57, v.p. TV network sales and devel. and research 1957-59; v.p. charge ABC Internat. div., Am. Broadcasting-Paramount Theaters, Inc., 1959-61; pres. A.B.C. Internat. Television, Inc., 1961- 70; founder, pres. Intercontinental Communications, Inc., N.Y.C., 1970—, also dir.; dir. Windsor Raceway, Mut. Shares Corp. Served as pilot RCAF, 1942-45. Mem. Chi Psi. Episcopalian. Club: University. Co-author: Recommended Standards for Radio and Television Program Audience Size Measurements, 1954. Home: 455 Knollwood Rd Ridgewood NJ 07450 Office: 230 Park Av New York City NY 10017

COYLE, ELIZABETH ELEANOR, educator; B.S., Coll of Wooster, 1926; M.S., Ohio State U., 1929, Ph.D., 1935. Now Danforth prof. biology Coll. of Wooster. Address: Dept Biology Coll of Wooster Wooster OH 44691*

COYLE, JAMES WILLIAM, mfg. co. exec.; b. Jersey City, N.J., Apr. 18, 1920; s. John W. and Anna (O'Neill) C.; B.S. summa cum laude Rutgers U., 1949; M.B.A., N.Y. U., 1952; m. Mildred M. Keavey, July 24, 1943; children—Patricia, Kathleen, William, Michael Ann. With Gen. Motors Corp., 1937—, mem. treas.'s staff, N.Y.C., 1937-55, dir. financial analysis, 1955-60, dir. accounting, Detroit, 1960-63, dir. cost analysis, 1963-66, dir. operations analysis, 1966, comptroller Detroit Diesel Allison div., Detroit, 1966—. Active Boy Scouts Am. Pres. bd. dirs. Guest House, Inc.; trustee Holy Name Scholarship Found. Served with AUS, World War II. Mem. Am. Ordnance Assn., Nat. Assn. Accountants (dir. 1961-66), Beta Gamma Sigma (pres. 1948-49). Home: 400 Pilgrim Birmingham MI 48009 Office: 13400 W Outer Dr Detroit MI 48228

COYLE, ROBERT ALOYSIUS, sch. supt.; b. Jersey City, Aug. 7, 1907; s. James Michael and Mary Mary (Reville) C.; student Holy Cross Coll., 1924-26; A.B., Seton Hall U., 1928, M.A., 1946; Ed.D., Rutgers U., 1956; m. Catherine A. Griffin, Aug. 13, 1938; children—Patricia (Mrs. Robert Ancipink), Barbara (Mrs. Gerhart Karg). Sect. mgr. Gimbels Dept. Store, N.Y.C., 1929-31; main floor supt. Hearns Dept. Store, N.Y.C., 1931-33; tchr. English and Latin, Jersey City schs., 1933-43, guidance counselor, athletic dir., 1943-47, vice prin. high sch., 1947-53, prin. high schs., 1953-61, supt. schs., 1961—. Treas. Jersey City br. ARC. Trustee Jersey City Library. Mem. Am. Assn. Sch. Adminstrs., N.J., Jersey City (past pres.) edn. assns., Phi Delta Kappa. K.C. Home: 225 St Paul's Av Jersey City, NJ 07306.

COYLE, ROBERT EVERET, lawyer; b. Fresno, Cal., May 6, 1930; s. Everett L. and Virginia (Chandler) C.; A.B., Fresno State Coll., 1953; LL.B., J.D., Hastings Coll. Law, 1956; m. Faye Turnbaugh, June 11, 1953; children-Robert Alan II, Richard Lee, Barbara Jean. Admitted to Cal. bar, 1956; with dist. atty.'s office, Fresno, 1956-58; partner firm McCormick, Barstow, Sheppard, Coyle & Best, Fresno, 1958—. Chmn. bd. Fresno Legal Service, Inc. Bd. dirs. Fresno Assn. Mental Retardation; trustee United Givers. Mem. Fresno County Bar Assn. (pres., bd. gov.), Delta Sigma Phi. Home: 1220 E Indianapolis St Fresno CA 93704 Office: Guarante Savs Bldg Fresno CA 93721

COYLE, VINCENT JOHN, former hotel exec.; b. Phila., Jan. 27, 1900; s. John J. and Mary A. (Donnell) C.; degree in structural engring., Pratt Inst., Bklyn., 1921; m. Honora Frawley, Feb. 12, 1928 (dec.); children—Vincent Joseph, Christina D.; m. 2d Dorothy Knoepke, May 19, 1941; stepchildren—Lois and E. Christian Stengel. Sales engr. Atlantic Terra Cotta Co., 1921-25; constrn. engr. Trinity Placer Mines, Inc., 1925-26; structural engr. Calvin Morris Constrn. Co., 1926-30; mng. dir. Carlyle Hotel, N.Y.C., 1930-38, Hampshire House, 1938-46; became v.p., mng. dir. Essex House, 1946. Mem. Am., Internat. hotel assns., Hotel Sales Mgrs. Assn., Hotel Assn. N.Y.C. (1st v.p.). Club: Baltusrol Golf (Springfield, N.J.). Home: PO Box 64 Springfield NJ 07081

COYLE, WILLIAM, educator; b. Edinboro, Pa., Nov. 8, 1917; s. William and Vere (Steadman) C.; B.S., Edinboro State Coll., 1938; M.Litt., U. Pitts., 1940, M.A., 1942; Ph.D., Western Res. U., 1948; m. Charlotte Bliley, July 27, 1940; children—Mary Jo, Daniel, Barbara. Instr. Engilsh, U. Pitts., 1939-42, 45-46, Western Res. U., 1946-48; mem. faculty Wittenberg Coll., 1948-68, prof. English, 1956-68, chmn. dept., 1964-68; prof. English, Fla. Atlantic U., Boca Raton, 1968—, chmn. dept., 1969—. Fulbright lectr., Sao Paulo, Brazil, 1962-63. Served with USMCR, 1942-45. Mem. Modern Lang. Assn., Am. Studies Assn., Nat. Council Tchrs. English, Coll. English Assn. Democrat. Lutheran. Author: Research Papers, 1959; Ohio Authors and Their Books, 1960; The Poet and the President, 1960; Paragraphs for Practice, 1960; The Frankenstein Family, 1967; Six Early American Plays, 1968; The Young Man in American Literature, 1969; also articles, revs. Home: 1098 SW 4th St Boca Raton FL 33432

COYMAN, CLIFFORD H., trust co. exec. Exec. v.p. People's Trust N.J., Hackensack. Office: 210 Main St Hackensack NJ 07601*

COYNE, ROBERT WILLIAM, trade assn. exec.; b. Bangor, Me., Feb. 26, 1904; s. Patrick Henry and Mary F. (Nichols) C.; LL.B., George Washington U., 1925; m. Rose Marie Guglberger, Apr. 14, 1934; 1 son, Robert William. Admitted to Mass. and Me. bars, 1926; spl. investigator, then asst. dist. supr. U.S. Treasury and Dept. of Justice, 1925-39; nat. field dir. War Bond program, 1940- 46; exec. dir. Am. Theatres Assn., also Theatre Owners Am., 1946-48; spl. counsel Council Motion Picture Orgns., 1950-58; pres. Distilled Spirits Inst., Washington, 1959—. Mem. Gamma Eta Gamma. Democrat. Roman Catholic. Clubs: Metropolitan (N.Y.C.); Nat. Press, Nat. Democratic, (Washington); Variety, Laurel Turf. Home: 4530 Connecticut Av NW Washington DC 20008 Office: Pennsylvania Bldg Washington DC 20004

COYULA, JUAN, bank exec. Statutory auditor Banco Nacional de Mexico S.A. Office: Avenida Isabel La Catolica 44 Mexico City 1 Mexico*

COZAD, JAMES WILLIAM, oil co. exec.; b. Huntington, Ind., Feb. 10, 1927; s. Emmett and Helen (Motz) C.; B.S., Ind. U., 1950; m. Virginia Earline Alley, Nov. 26, 1948; children—James Michael, Catherine Louise, William Scott, Jeffrey Alley, Amy Jo. With Peat, Marwick, Mitchell & Co., C.P.A.'s, Detroit, 1950-54; with Hygrade Food Products Corp., Detroit, 1954-67, v.p., treas., 1966-67; treas. Philip Morris, Inc., N.Y.C., 1967-69; financial v.p. Am. Oil Co., Chgo., 1969—. Served with USNR, 1945-46, C.P.A., Mich. Mem. Am. Inst. Accountants, Mich. Assn. C.P.A.'s, Theta Chi. Clubs: Detroit, Indiana U. Alumni (pres. 1956-57) (Detroit); Western Golf and Country (Redford Twp., Mich.); Lochmoor (Grosse Pointe, Mich.); Bankers of Am. (N.Y.C.). Office: American Oil Co 910 S Michigan Av Chicago IL 60605

COZART, REED, cons.; b. Normangee, Tex., Apr. 8, 1904; s. William H. and Anna (Reed) C.; B.A., U. Tex., 1926, J.D., 1929; postgrad. St. Mary's U., San Antonio, 1938, Coll. William and Mary, 1939; m. Ruth Mae Bourn, July 17, 17, 1931; 1 son, William Reed. Tchr., Rogers Prairie Sch., Madison County, Tex., 1921-22, Tivy High Sch., Kerrville, Tex., 1924-25; admitted to Tex. bar, 1929; with firm Morriss & Morriss, San Antonio, 1929-32; chief U.S. probation officer, San Antonio, 1932-40; asst. supr. classification Bur. Prisons, Washington, 1940; warden fed. correctional inst., Texarkana, Tex., 1941-42, Seagoville, Tex., 1945-52, LaTuna, Tex., Tex., 1956-57; asso. warden U.S. penitentiary, Leavenworth, Kan., 1942-45; dir. corrections for La., 1952-55; U.S. pardon atty., Washington, 1955-56, 58-68; cons. corrections br. U.S. Army, 1942-46, Sch. Continuing Edn., Am. U., 1966—; cons. Am. Correctional Assn., 1968—; bd. dirs., cons. Asso. Community Rehab. Enterprises, 1968-70. Chmn. Delinquency Crime Control Conf. Washington. Bd. dirs., pres., v.p. Council Council Chs. Alexandria; bd. dirs. Council Chs. Washington Met. Area, Alexandria Boys Club. Mem. Am. Correctional Assn. (bd. dirs.), Osborne Assn. (bd. dirs), Nat. Council Crime and Delinquency, Tex. Ex-students Assn., Internat. Platform Soc. Presbyn. (elder 1943—, past deacon, trustee, chmn. ch. extension com.), Tex. com.), Tex. Probation Assn. (pres.). Mason (32), Rotarian (v.p., dir.). Author articles. Home: 808 Chalfonte Dr Alexandria, VA 22305.

COZIER, J. KENNETH, lumber co. exec.; b. Aurora, Neb., Sept. 23, 1901; s. Melvin W. and Mary Catherine (Robbins) C.; B.S.C., U. Neb., 1924, L.H.D. (hon.); postgrad. N.Y. U., 1925; m. Mary Katherine Towle, Oct. 12, 1926; children—John Kenneth, Charles Towle, Nancy Cozier Whitcomb. Salesman, Chgo. Mill & Lumber Co., 1925-30; pres. Cozier Corp., Cleve., C. & B. Realty Co., Curtis Cos., Inc., Clinton, Ia. Past mem. industry adv. com. OPS, WPB. Mem. Health and Rehab. Allocation Com., Cleve.; mem. adv. com. Ohio Bur. Services for Blind; mem. nat. adv. com. Nat. Center for Deaf-Blind Youths and Adults. Past mem. Ohio Gov.'s Council on Vocational Rehab.; past mem. Commn. on Standards for Agys. Serving Blind. Past trustee Case Work Council and Health Council of Cleve. Welfare Fedn.; trustee U. Neb. Found., Am. Found for Blind, Inc., Nat. Accreditation Council for Agys. Serving the Blind, Ohio Soc. for Prevention Blindness; trustee, past pres. Cleve. Soc. for Blind. Recipient Distinguished Service award U. Neb. Alumni Assn., Cleve. Welfare Fedn., Beta Gamma Sigma. Mem. Nat. Wooden Box Assn. (pres. 1950-51, past trustee), Delta Tau Delta, Beta Gamma Sigma, Alpha Kappa Psi. Mem. Plymouth Ch. (trustee). Clubs: The Country, Union, University. Home: 2705 Dryden Rd Shaker Heights OH 44122 Office: 5031 Mayfield Rd Cleveland OH 44124

COZZA, CARMEN LOUIS, univ. football coach; b. Cleve., June 10, 1930; s. James and Carbita (DeLuca) C.; B.S. in Edn., Miami U., Oxford, O., 1952, M.S. in Edn., 1958; m. Jean Adele Annable, June 28, 1952; children—Kristen, Kathryn, Karen. Player with minor league baseball team, 1952-53; Gilmore Acad., Gates, Mills, O., 1952-54; tchr., coach Collinwood High Sch., Cleve., 1953; coach Miami U., 1956-63; asst. football coach Yale, 1963-64, head coach, 1965—. Mem. Pop Warner-Spauling adv. staff, 1965—. Mem. Delta Tau Delta, Phi Epsilon Kappa. Author articles. Home: 779 Dennis Dr Orange CT 06477 Office: Ray Thompkins House New Haven CT 06501

COZZENS, JAMES GOULD, author; b. Chgo., Aug. 19, 1903; s. Henry William and Bertha (Wood) C.; grad. Kent (Conn.) Sch., 1922; student Harvard, 1922-24; m. Bernice Baumgarten Dec. 31, 1927. Author: Confusion, 1924; Michael Scarlett, 1925; Cockpit, 1928; The Son of Perdition, 1929; S.S. San Pedro, 1931; The Last Adam, 1933; Castaway, 1934; Men and Brethren, 1936; Ask Me Tomorrow, 1940; The Just and the Unjust, 1942; Guard of Honor, 1948; By Love Possessed, 1957; Children and Others, 1964; Morning Noon and Night, 1968. Home: Shadowbrook Williamstown, MA 01267. Office: Harcourt Brace & Co 750 3d Av New York City NY 10017

CRABB, CECIL VAN METER, Jr., educator; b. Clarksdale, Miss., July 18, 1924; s. Cecil V. and Mary (Dupree) C.; A.B., Centre Coll., Danville, Ky., 1947; M.A. in Polit. Sci., Vanderbilt U., 1948, postgrad., 1950-51; Ph.D., Johns Hopkins, 1952; m. Harriet Clothilda Frierson, June 28, 1947; children—Cecil Van Meter III, Cornelia M. Asst., asso. prof. Belhaven Coll., Jackson, Miss., 1948-50; teaching fellow Vanderbilt U., 68, prof. polit. sci., 1962-68; prof., chmn. dept. polit. sci. La. State 1968—. Faculty participant Salizburg (Austria) Seminar Am. Studies, 1960; lectr. community groups, univ. and govt.; editorial cons. jours., Pubs. Served with F.A., AUS, 1943-46. Presbyn. (elder). Author: Bipartisan Foreign PolicyMyth or Reality, 1957; American Foreign Policy in the Nuclear Age, 3d edit., 1971; The Elephants and the Grass, 1965; Nations in a Multipolar World, 1968. Contbr. articles, book revs. to 5295 Timber Cove Baton Rouge, LA 70808.

CRABBE, BUSTER CLARENCE L., stock broker, former motion picture actor; b. Oakland, Cal., Feb. 7, 1908; s. Edward C.S. and Agnes (McNamara) C.; B.A., U. So. Cal., then student Lae Sch.; m. Adah Virginia Held, Apr. 13, 1933; children— —Caren Lynn, Susan Ann (Mrs. Nicholas Holt III), Cullen Held. Appeared in Flash Gordon and Buck Rogers films for Paramount Studios and Universal Studios, also as Billy the Kid for Producers Releasing Corp.; TV appearances as Captain Gallant of the Foreign Legion; exec. dir. Cascade Industries; dir. water sports Concord Hotel, Mem. Hutchinson River council Boy Scouts Am. Mem. 1st group Swimming Hall of Fame. Mem. Sigma Chi. Republican. Home: 150 Theodore Fremd Av Rye NY 10580 Office: care Ernst & Co 120 Broadway New York City NY 10005

CRABBE, JOHN CROZIER, broadcasting cons.; b. Pomona, Cal., July 3, 1914; s. Arthur and Louise A. (Wiley) C.; student Modesto (Cal.) Coll., 1931-34, Fresno (Cal.) State Coll., 1934-36; B.A., Coll. Pacific, 1937, M.A., 1940; postgrad. U. Ia., 1938, N.Y.U., 1940, Stanford, 1951, Ohio State U., 1951-52; m. Bobbin Gay Peck, June 17, 1940; children—John Crozier, William Charles, Barbara Gay. Dir. broadcasting activities Coll. of Pacific, 1937-58; lectr. radio edn. Stanford, summer 1951; asst., office radio-TV edn. Ohio State U., 1951-52; exec. sec. Delta-Sierra Ednl. TV Corp., 1953; dir. Radio and TV Nat. Music Camp, Interlochen, Mich., 1954- 55; program asso. Ednl. TV and Radio Center, Ann Arbor, Mich., 1955-56; exec. sec. Central Cal. Ednl. TV, 1955- 58; gen. mgr. sta. KVIE, 1958-69; spl. cons. radio edn., schs. Central Cal.; chmn. TV Adv. Com. State Cal., 1967-69; cons. in broadcasting (East Africa) for RTV Internat., N.Y., 1964; pres. Western Ednl. TV Network, 1967-69; mem. interim mgmt. group Corp. for Pub. Broadcasting Network Operation, 1969; cons. in pub. broadcasting, 1969—; asso. Arthur Bolton Assos.; gen. mgr. Tel-Vue Stockton, Inc. (Cal.). Served as lt. USNR, 1943-46. Mem. Assn. for Ednl. Radio-TV (pres. 1950-53), Western Radio TV Conf. (dir.), Am. Assn. U. Profs., Phi Kappa Phi, Phi Delta Kappa. Clubs: Rotary (Sacramento); Commonwealth of Cal. Contbr. articles profl. publs. Home and office: 1031 La Sierra Dr Sacramento CA 95825

CRABBE, JOHN ROTH, lawyer; b. London, Ohio, Mar. 29, 1906; s. Charles C. and Isa M. (Roth) C.; B.A., Ohio State U., 1927, M.A., J.D., 1931; LL.M., Harvard, 1932; m. Eleanor S. Hommon, Dec. 20, 1933; children—Constance (Mrs. Michael A. Dehlendorf), Benjamin R. (dec.). Admitted to Ohio bar, 1931; asst. atty. gen. Ohio, 1933-37; partner firm Crabbe & Tootle, London, O., 1937-39; dep. supt. ins. Ohio, 1939-43, supt. ins., 1943-45; asso. firm Ballard & Dresbach, Columbus, O., 1945-51; partner Crabbe, Newlon, Potts, Schmidt, Brown & Jones, and predecessor firms, Columbus, 1951—. Pres. Bexley Area Art Guild, 1967. Mem. Bexley (Ohio) City Council, 1955-72, pres., 1966- 72. Fellow Am., Ohio (trustee 1970—) bar assn. founds.; mem. Am. (chmn. sect. ins., negligence and compensation law 1962-63, chmn. standing com. unemployment and social security 1965-66), Ohio, Columbus bar assns., Internat. Assn. Ins. Law, U.S. Power Squadron, Am. Judicature Soc., Execs. Club Columbus, Assn. Life Ins. Counsel, Fedn. Ins. Counsel, Pi Kappa Alpha, Phi Delta Phi. Republican. Methodist (past chmn. ofcl. bd.). Mason. Clubs: Columbus Country, University, Crichton, Press (Columbus). Home: 225 S Stanwood Rd Columbus OH 43209 Office: 42 E Gay St Columbus OH 43215

CRABIEL, J. EDWARD, constrn. co. exec.; b. Milltown, N.J., June 20, 1916; s. Joseph M. and Helen (Glock) C.; B.C.E., Rutgers U., 1936; m. Doris Young, Dec. 29, 1939; 1 dau., Lynda (Mrs. William Cummings III). With Franklin Contracting Co., Little Falls, N.J., 1936—, v.p., 1957-67, pres., 1967—; dir. Edison Bank, South Plainfield, N.J. Mayor Borough of Milltown, N.J., 1948-51; mem. Gen. Assembly of N.J., 1954-65; mem. N.J. State Senate, 1966-71. Served with USNR, 1943-46. Office: PO Box 176 Little Falls NJ 07424

CRABILL, RALPH EDWIN, Jr., zoologist; b. Chgo., Sept. 3, 1925; s. Ralph Edwin and Josephine (Jennings) C.; A.B., Cornell U., 1949, Ph.D., 1952; m. Mary Louise Sievers; 3 children. Asst. prof. biology Ithaca Coll., 1951-54, St. Louis U., 1954-56; systematic zoologist Smithsonian Instn., Washington, 1956—. Served with USNR, World War II. Contbr. numerous articles in field. Office: Dept Entomology Smithsonian Instn Washington DC 20560

CRABTREE, EDWIN HEWARD, Jr., former found. exec.; b. Lewistown, Mont., June 16, 1904; s. Edwin Heward and Francena (Wilson) C.; E.M., Colo. Sch. Mines, 1927; m. Thelma Parthena Stukey, Oct. 24, 1930 (dec.); children—Edith Ann (Mrs. James Robert Dougherty), Mary Edwina (Mrs. Philip Jones), Edwin Heward III; m. 2d, Gerda Alice Kallberg, July 2, 1958. Asst. mill supt. Consol Lead & Zinc Co., Picher, Okla., 1927-29; mill supt. Canam Metals

Corp., Picher, 1929-31; mill supt. So. Mining Co., Poplar Bluff, Mo., 1931-32; gen. supt. Reliance Rock Asphalt Co., Nevada, Mo., 1932-35; mill supt. Eagle- Picher Co., Ruby, Ariz., 1935-40, chief metallurgist, Miami, Okla., 1943- 47, dir. milling, 1947-53; metallurgist Ariz. Bur. Mines, U. Ariz., 1940- 43; dep. mgr. AEC, Grand Junction, Colo., 1953-55; dir. Colo. Sch. Mines Research Found., Inc., Golden, 1955-70; mem. Gov.'s Oil Shale Adv. Council, 1955—; exec. reservist minerals unit Office Minerals and Solid Fuels, Dept. Interior, 1960—. Recipient Distinguished Achievement medal Colo. Sch. Mines, 1964, Robert H. Richards award Am. Inst. Mining, Metall. and Petroleum Engrs., 1966. Registered profl. engr., Colo. Mem. Am. Inst. Mining, Metall. and Petroleum Engrs., 1966. Registered profl. engr., Colo. Mem. Am. Inst. Mining, Metall. and Petroleum Engrs. (past dir., mem. exec. com.), Am. Mining Congress (past com. chmn.), Mining and Metl. Soc. Am., Colo. Mining Assn. (dir.), Colo. Sch. Mines Alumni Assn. (past pres.), Rocky Mountain Coal Mining Inst., Mining Club N.Y. and Denver, Petroleum Club Denver. Republican. Episcopalian. Mason. Clubs: Teknik, Lakewood Country, Mt. Vernon Country (Denver). Home: PO Box 465 2035 Foothills Rd Golden CO 80401 Office: PO Box 112 Golden CO 80401

CRABTREE, GEORGE WILLIAM, food co. exec.; b. St. Charles, Ill., Dec. 7, 1913; s. George L. and Edna A. (Burton) C.; student Washington U., St. Louis; m. Dorothy Y. Trowbridge, Feb. 14, 1935; childrenLois Jean, Gail K., Jim M. With Continental Can Co., Inc., 1932-52, div. mgr. mfg., Eastern div., 1949- 52; with Crown Cork & Seal Co., 1952-56, exec. v.p., dir., 1954-56; v.p. container div. Campbell Soup Co., 1957-60, operations, Camden, N.J., 1960-66, sr. v.p., 1966-69, exec. v.p., 1969—. Gov., Can Mfg. Inst.; bd. dirs. Am. Competitive Enterprise System. Presbyn. Mason. Clubs: Huntingdon Valley (Pa.) Country; Seaview Country (Ansecon, N.J.); Canadian (N.Y.C.). Home: 1881 Harte Rd Jenkintown PA 19046 Office: 375 Memorial Av Camden NJ 08103

CRABTREE, HAROLD ROY, industrialist; b. Montreal, Can., Mar. 2, 1918; s. Harold and Louisa (Stafford) C.; B.Sc., McGill U., 1938; m. Caroline Ruth Hanna, Nov. 17, 1945; children—Sandra Caroline, Harold Roy, Stafford Alexander. Trainee Howard Smith Paper Mills, Ltd., Montreal Can., Chmn. bd. Howard Smith Paper Mills, Ltd. and subsidiaries, 1957—; asst. gen. mgr. bag div. Woods Mfg. Co. Ltd., 1947-49, gen. mgr., 1949-51, 1951- 53, v.p. operations, 1951- 53, v.p., gen. mgr., 1953-56, pres., chmn. bd. Woods Mfg. Co., Ltd. and subsidiaries, 1956; pres., chmn. bd. Wabasso Ltd. and subsidiaries, 1956- -; chmn. Fraser Cos., Ltd.; dir. Bank of Montreal, United Aircraft of Canada, Dominion Glass Co., Sun Life Assurance Co., Domtar Ltd., Hinde and Dauch Paper Co., Ltd., St. Lawrence Corp. Pres. Royal Victoria Hosp.; bd. govs. Alexandra Hosp., Royal Edward Chest Hosp., Laurentian Chest Hosp.; past pres. Montreal YMCA, Boys Home of Montreal; chancellor Mt. Allison U. Served with Canadian Army, 1939-45; hon. col. Royal Canadian Hussars. Mem. Montreal Bd. Trade (pres. 1960-61), Canadian C. of C. (exec. council 1957-58), Canadian Mfrs. Assn. (chmn. Que. div. 1958-59; president 1963-64), Cotton Inst. of Canada (pres. 1954-59), Primary Textiles Inst. (pres. 1955-59), Delta Kappa Epsilon. Home: 58 Forden Crescent Westmount 217 Quebec Canada Office: 2055 Peel St Montreal 110 Quebec Canada

CRABTREE, JOHN HENRY, Jr., educator; b. Raleigh, N.C., Nov. 11, 1925; s. John Henry and Ruth (Jones) C.; B.A., U. N.C., 1950, M.A., 1951, Ph.D. (Carnegie fellow), 1957; m. Anne Brown, Aug. 28, 1948; children—John Henry III, Roy Eugene, Cynthia Anne, Ralph Newton. Asso. prof. Presbyn. Jr. Coll., Maxton, N.C., 1951-54; prof. English, Furman U., Greenville, S.C., 1957—, asso. dean acad. affairs, 1967-68, dean students, 1968—. Served with USNR, 1944-46. So. fellow U. N.C., 1959. Mem. Am. Assn. Coll. Registrars and Admissions Officers, Am. Council on Edn., Nat. Assn. Student Personnel Adminstrs., Nat. Assn. Fgn. Student Affairs, S.Atlantic Modern Lang. Assn., Southeastern Renaissance Conf., Phi Beta Kappa. Baptist. Home: Route 3 Hathaway Circle Greenville SC 29609

CRADDICK, DONALD LEE, lawyer; b. Bellingham, Wash., Mar. 21, 1932; s. Lee Donovan and Eva (Sutton) C.; student Contra Costa Jr. Coll., Pichmond, Cal., 1950-51, San Diego Jr. Coll., 1954-55; B.S., U. Cal., Berkeley, 1957, LL.B., 1960; m. Jan Patricia O'Neil, Sept. 4, 1955; children—Elaine, Steven. Admitted to Alaska Bar, 1960, since practiced in Juneau; mem. firm Faulkner, Banfield, Boochever & Doogan, 1960-70, partner, 1964-70; pub. defender for Juneau, 1970—; bar examiner Alaska Bar Assn., 1965-67, bar exam. preparation, 1969-70. Elected to Greater Juneau Charter Com., 1968; apptd. to Alaska Comprehensive Health Adv. Council, 1968. Chmn. 4th House Dist. Juneau, Republican Party of Alaska, 1970—. Bd. dirs. Salvation Army, Juneau Cancer Soc. Served with USN 1951-55. Mem. Am., Alaska, Juneau bar assns., Boalt Law Sch. U. Cal. Alumni Assn., Am. Bar Examiners Assn., Phi Alpha Delta. Episcopalian. Mason, Elk. Home: 415 Coleman Dr Juneau AK 99801 Office: Pouch AE Juneau AK 99801

CRADDOCK, CHARLES GRANVILLE, Jr., physician, educator; b. Lynchburg, Va., Mar. 19, 1921; s. Charles Granville and Katherine (Baker) C.; B.A., U. Va., 1942; m. Hilah Royster White, Sept. 14, 1944; children-Hilah (Mrs. S. William Pike), Katherine, Mary, Charles Granville III. Intern Strong Meml. Hosp., Rochester, N.Y., 1944, fellow hematology, 1946-48; asst. resident, then chief resident medicine U. Va. Hosp., Charlottesville, 1948-50; fellow psychiatry Mass. Gen. Hosp., Boston, 1950-51; Markle scholar, 1950-55; mem. faculty U. Cal. at Los Angeles Med. Sch., 1952—, prof. medicine, 1962—, head div. hematology, 1966-68, head dept. med. clinics, 1969—; head div. hematology Scripps Clinic and Research Found. 1968-69. Mem. tng. grants com. USPHS, 1966-68, hematology study sect., 1970; mem. hamatology tng. com. VA, 1968—; sciAadv. bd. USAF, 1969—. Served to lt. (j.g.), M.C., USNR, 1945-46; maj., M.C., AUS, 1955-57. Mem. A.C.P., Assn. Am. Physicians, Am. Soc. Clin. Investigation. Research mechanisms cellular immunity, kinetics prodn. and fate white blood cells in normal and disease states. Home: 1021 6th St Santa Monica CA 90403 Office: Dept Medicine Univ Cal Med Center Los Angeles CA 90024

CRADDOCK, CHARLES THOMAS, hotel exec.; b. Kansas City, Mo., Sept. 5, 1905; s. William Brownlow and Mary Lucille (Malloy) C.; grad. high sch.; m. Betty Jane Bay, Apr. 14, 1934; children—John Leigh, Thomas Joseph. Asst. to pres. Edgewater Beach Hotel, Chgo., 1937-48; sr. v.p. Schine Hotels, N.Y.C.; v.p., mng. dir. Boca Raton (Fla.) Hotel and Club, 1949-55; sr. v.p. Tisch Hotels and Motels; v.p., mng. dir. Americana Hotel, Bal Harbour, Fla., 1955-62; v.p., dir. Grand Bahama Devel. Co., N.Y.C.; exec. v.p. Hotel Operations, Freeport, Grand Bahama Island, 1962-64; sr. v.p., dir. Chase-Park Plaza Hotel, St. Louis, 1964-67; exec. v.p., chief exec. officer Ambassador Hotel Co., Los Angeles, 1967—; dir. Seaboard Internat. Investors Corp., N.Y.C. Recipient award of achievement Hotel Sales Mgmt. Assn. Internat., 1948. Mem. Am., Soc. Cal., Los Angeles hotel and motel assns., Hotel Sales Mgmt. Assn. Internat., Internat. Hotel Assn., Schloss Enzenfeld Vienna. Home: 9981 Robbins Dr Beverly Hills CA 90212 Office: 3400 Wilshire Blvd Los Angeles CA 90005

CRADDOCK, JOHN CAMPBELL, educator; b. Chgo., Apr. 3, 1930; s. John and Bernice (Campbell) C.; B.A., DePauw U., 1951; M.A., Columbia, 1953, Ph.D., 1954; m. Dorothy Dunkelberg, June 13, 1953; children—Susan Elizabeth, John Paul, Carol Jean. Geologist, Shell Oil Co., N.M., Tex., Colo., Wyo., 1954-56; asst. prof. U. Minn., Mpls., 1956-60, asso. prof., 1960-67; prof. geology U. Wis., Madison, 1967—; leader Antarctic geologic field research programs, 1959-69; cons. C.E., AUS, 1957-58, N. Star Research Inst., 1965-68; vis. scientist New Zealand Geol. Survey, 1962-63. Mem. com. on polar research NRC, 1967—, chmn. panel geology and geophysics, 1967-71; U.S. mem. working group on geology Sci. Com. on Antarctic Research, 1967—. Higgins fellow, 1951-52; NSF fellow, 1952-53, research grantee, 1957—; recipient U.S. Antarctic Service medal, 1968; Bellingshausen-Lazarev medal Soviet Acad. Scis., 1970. Fellow Geol. Soc. Am.; Mem. Internat. Union Geol. Scis. (mem. commn. on structural geology 1968—), Am. Geophys. Union, Am. Assn. Petroleum Geologists, Phi Beta Kappa, Sigma Xi. Co-editor: Geologic Maps of Antarctica, Folio 12, Antarctic Map Folio Series, Am. Geog. Soc., 1970. Contbr. articles sci. jours. Office: Dept Geology and Geophysics U Wis Madison WI 53706

CRADY, CURTIS PERRY, advt. and pub. relations exec.; b. St. Louis, Dec, 2, 1923; s. Curtis and Clara (Sullivan) C.; ed. Hadley Tech. Sch., Washington U.; m. Lera Lorene Lehde, June 21, 1944; children—Curtis Perry, Carol Lynn (Mrs. Richard Lansing). Buyer, merchandising exec. Stix, Baer & Fuller, 1946-51; with Winius-Brandon Co., St. Louis, 1952—, v.p., 1962-68, exec. v.p., 1968-70, pres., 1970—, dir., 1962—. Mem. pub. relations council St. Louis U. Bd. dirs. Boy Scouts Am.; mem. St. Louis Ambassadors; bd. dirs. Grace Hill Settlement House, 1967—, pres., 1969-70. Served with USNR, 1943-46. Mem. Advt. Club, Sales and Marketing Execs. Assn. Mem. United Ch. of Christ (deacon). Mason. Clubs: St. Louis, Missouri Athletic (St. Louis). Sculptor, poet. Home: 541 High Meadow Rd St Louis MO 63131 Office: 1015 Locust St St Louis MO 63101

CRAF, JOHN RILEY, educator; b. N.Y.C., Aug. 4, 1911; s. George Stanton and Kathryn (Riley) C.; B.S., Columbia, 1933, M.S., 1933, A.M., 1938; Ph.D., N.Y.U., 1947, M.B.A., 1952, Ph.D., 1957; m. Katherine Lovern, Aug. 29, 1960. Instr. pub. schs., N.Y.C., 1934-37; asst. to personnel dir. Chatillon Corp., 1937-40; instr. George Washington U., 1945-46; with U. Louisville, 1946—, prof. marketing, 1949—, dean Sch. Bus., 1953-64. Dir. Klarer of Ky., Inc. Pub. mem. Louisville Labor-Mgmt. Com. Served from pvt. to maj. AUS, 1941-45. Mem. A.I.M., C. of C., Sales Exec. Council Louisville. Clubs: Rotary; Harvard Business School Ky. Author: Introduction to Business Principles and Practices, 1949; Economic Development of the United States, 1952; Introduction to Business, 1957; Junior Boards of Executives, 1958. Home: 2200 Douglass Rd Louisville KY 40205

CRAFT, ALFRED THOMAS, mfg. co. exec.; b. Glouseter, O., Apr. 21, 1913; s. William Alfred and Nona (Southerton) C.; A.B., Ohio U., 1935; m. Thelma Ley, June 11, 1941; children—Susan Margaret, Deborah Ann. Asst. mgr., then owner-mgr. Press Pub. Co., Glouster, O., 1935-42; with McBee Co., 1946-56, gen. sales mgr., 1955-56; v.p. sales, data processing div. Royal McBee Corp., 1956-60; gen. mgr. bus. machines div.; then corporate v.p. Bell & Howell Co., 1961, v.p. bus. machines group, 1962-68, v.p., gen. mgr. Ditto div., 1968-71, asst. to corporate pres., 1971—. Served with USAAF, 1943-46. Mem. Ohio U. Alumni Assn. (dir. 1955- 57), Phi Delta Theta. Clubs: Columbus (O.) Athletic; Lake Forest Bath and Tennis. Home: 936 E Ringwood Lake Forest IL 60045 Office: 6800 McCormick Av Chicago IL 60645

CRAFT, EDWARD OLIVER, govt. ofcl.; b. Kingsbury, Ind., Nov. 13, 1916; s. John Allen and Olive May (Canfield) C.; A.B., Ind. U., 1938, J.D. with high distinction, 1940; m. Wilma Clare Williams, Oct. 26, 1940; children—Elizabeth, Alice, John. Admitted to Ind. bar, 1940; practice in Evansville, 1940-41; mem. legal staff Office Legislative Counsel, U.S. Ho. of Reps., 1941—, legislative counsel, 1962—. Served with AUS, 1943-45. Mem. Phi Delta Phi, Order of Coif. Student editor Ind. Law Rev., 1938-39, student chmn., 1939-40. Home: 4826 Drummond Av Chevy Chase MD 20015 Office: House Office Bldg Washington DC 20515

CRAFT, GEORGE SPRINGER, banker; b. Riverside, Ill., Nov. 13, 1909; s. Francis Marion and Edith (Springer) C.; B.S., Emory U., 1930; A.B. (Rhodes scholar), Oxford U., 1932; postgrad. Harvard, 1932-33; m. Eleanor Phinizy Spalding, June 1, 1940; children—George Springer, Hughes Spalding, Francis Marion, John S. Statistician, Trust Co. of Ga., Atlanta, 1933-37, asst. v.p., 1937-40, v.p., 1940-46, 48-57, sr. v.p., 1957-59, pres., 1959-64, chmn. bd., 1964- -; dean Sch. Bus. Adminstrn., Emory U., 1946-48; dir. Life Ins. Co. Ga., Genuine Parts Co., Trust Co. Ga., Ga. Power Co., Creomulsion Co., Retail Credit Co. Trustee Am. Assembly, Com. for Econ. Devel., Morehouse Coll.; trustee, mem. exec. com. Emory U. Mem. Atlanta Hist. Soc., Assn. Res. City Bankers, Phi Beta Kappa, Omicron Delta Kappa, Alpha Kappa Psi, Chi Phi Clubs: Piedmont Driving, Capital City, Nine O'Clocks, Homosassa Fishing; Peachtree Golf. Home: 2631 Habersham Rd NW Atlanta GA 30305 Office: PO Box 4418 Atlanta GA 30302

CRAFT, HARVEY MILTON, educator; b. Hattiesburg, Miss., Nov. 22, 1925; s. Harvey Moses and Irene (Collins) C.; B.A., U. So. Miss., 1945, M.A., 1956; M.A., U. Ala., 1948; Ph.D., Tulane U., 1964; m. Mary Beth Stoner, Aug. 28, 1946; children—Susan, Cynthia, John, Stephen. Instr. English, U. So. Miss., Hattiesburg, 1955-57, asst. prof., dir. freshman English, 1959-61; asst. prof. English, Delta State Coll., Cleve., 1957-58; faculty Tulane U., New Orleans, 1961-69, asst. dean Coll. Arts and Scis., 1966-67, head dept. English, 1967-69; dean instrn., prof. English, Miss. State Coll. for Women, Columbus, 1969—. Served to 1st lt. U.S. Army, 1951-53. Mem. Modern Lang. Assn. Episcopalian. Author: Logic, Style and Arrangement: Literature for the Composition Course, 1971. Home: 905 6th Av S Columbus MS 39701

CRAFT, LIVA MORGAN, ret. electronics co. exec.; b. Scottland, Ill., Jan. 16, 1908; s. Dan Justus and Hannah Jane (Parker) C.; B.S. in Elec. Engring., U. Ill., 1929, M.S., 1930; postgrad. Ohio State U., 1933-35; m. Mabel Mason, Nov. 27, 1930. Mem. tech. staff Bell Telephone Labs., 1930-32; with Collins Radio Co., Cedar Rapids, Ia., 1935-70, sr. v.p., 1965-70, also dir., until 1970. Fellow I.R.E.; mem. Ia. Mfrs. Assn. (past dir.), Cedar Rapids C. of C. (past dir.). Mason. Home: 295 34th St SE Cedar Rapids IA 52403

CRAFT, ROBERT, musician, writer; b. Kingston, N.Y., Oct. 20, 1923; s. Raymond and Arpha (Lawson) C.; B.A., Juilliard Sch. Music, 1946. Condr. orchestras in Europe, Am. and Japan, 1952—; made world tour, 1961-62; condr. recordings including complete recordings music Arnold Schoenberg, Alban Berg, Anton Webern, Edgar Varese; spl. seminar lectr., Dartington, Eng., 1957, Princeton, 1959. Served with AUS, 1943. Co- author: Conversations with Stravinsky, 1959; Memories and Commentaries, 1960; Expositions and Developments, 1962; Dialogues and a Diary, 1963; Themes and Episodes, 1966; Retrospections and Conclusions, 1970. Address: 1218 N Wetherly Dr Hollywood CA 90069

CRAFT, ROBERT HOMAN, industrial and r.r. exec.; b. L.I., N.Y., Feb. 9, 1906; s. George Wallace and Nellie A. (Homan) C.; B.S., U. Pa., 1929; m. Janet M. Sullivan, Feb. 5, 1938; children—Robert Homan, Carol Ann (Mrs. C. Barry Schaefer), George Sullivan. Asst. treas. Guaranty Trust Co. of N.Y., 1937-40, 2d v.p., 1940-43, v.p. treas., 1943-52; exec. vice-pres. dir. Am. Securities Corp., N.Y.C., 1953-56; pres., vice chmn. Chase Internat. Investment Corp., 1956-60; pres., chmn. exec. com. Paribas Corp., 1960- 64; chmn. bd., chmn. finance com., dir. Miss. River Corp., 1965—; chmn. finance com., dir., mem. exec. com. M.P. R.R. Co., 1965—; dir., chmn. finance com. Miss. River Transmission Corp.; trustee, exec. com. N.Y. Bank Savs.; chmn. finance com., dir. Tex. & Pacific Ry.. Co.; dir., chmn. finance com., mem. exec. com. Mo. Improvement Co., C. & E.I. R.R.; dir., chmn. finance com., mem. exec. com. Mo.-Ill. R.R. Co.; dir., mem. exec. com. Mass. Mut. Corporate Investors; adviser, mem. exec. com. Merc. Trust Co., St. Louis; mem. Lower Manhattan adv. bd. Chem. Bank N.Y. Trust Co.; dir. Mich. Chem. Corp.; dir., mem. exec. com., investment policy com. Mass. Mut. Life Ins. Co. Cons. Fed. Res. Bd., 1952. Bd. dirs. N.Y. Heart Assn., 1941-66; vice chmn. Youth Consultation Service, 1967, gen. chmn., 1968—. Mem. Investment Bankers Assn. Am. (pres. 1956-57), Newcomen Soc. Clubs: University, Bond, Economic, Wall Street (gov.); Racquet (St. Louis); Fox Meadow Tennis, Scarsdale (N.Y.) Golf; Blind Brook; Shenorock Shore, Rockefeller Center Luncheon, Chicago; Augusta Nat. Golf. Home: 2 Rectory Lane S Scarsdale NY 10583 Office: 20 Exchange Pl New York City NY 10005

CRAFTS, ALDEN SPRINGER, former educator, plant physiologist; b. Ft. Collins, Colo., June 25, 1897; s. Henry Alonzo and Elizabeth Dunscomb (Bleakley) C.; B.S., U. Cal., 1927, Ph.D., 1930; M.A., St. John's Coll. Oxford U., LL.D., U. Cal. at Davis, 1966; m. Alice E. Hardisty, June 25, 1926; children—Harold S., Helen E. (Mrs. Charles A. Hedges). NRC fellow Cornell, 1930-31; asst. botanist Cal. Agrl. Expt. Sta., Davis, 1931-36; asst. botanist, asst. prof. botany U. Cal. at Davis, 1936-39, asso. botanist, asso. prof. botany, 1939-46, botanist, prof. botany, 1946-64, prof. emeritus, 1964—, acting chmn. 1959-60, former chmn. dept. botany; vis. prof. P.R. Agrl. Expt. Sta., 1947- 48. Del. to Bot. Congress, Paris, France, 1954; chmn. Cal. Weed Control Conf., Fresno, 1951; del., vice chmn. Gordon Research Conf. on Biochemistry in Agr., 1955. Guggenheim fellow, 1938, 57; Fulbright grantee, 1957-58; Charles Reid Barnes life membership award from Am. Soc. Plant Physiologist, 1962. Fellow A.A.A.S.; mem. Am. Soc. Plant Physiology (chmn. Western sect. 1940- 41, nat. pres. 1955-56), Weed Sci. Soc. Am. (hon. mem.; pres. 1958-60), Zool.-Bot. Soc. Vienna, Botan. Soc. Am., Phi Beta Kappa, Sigma Xi, Phi Sigma, Gamma Alpha. Author: (with H. B. Currier and C. R. Stocking) Water in the Physiology of Plants, 1949; Weed Control (with W. W. Robbins and R. N. Raynor), 1942, rev. ed. 1952, rev. edit. (with W. W. Robbins), 1962; The Chemistry and Mode of Action of Herbicides, 1961; Translocation in Plants, 1961; (with S. Yamaguchi) The Autoradiography of Plant Materials; (with Carl E. Crisp) Phloem Transport in Plants, 1971. Editor Annual Review of Plant Physiology, 1956-58. Home: 626 B St Davis CA 95611

CRAFTS, EDWARD CLAYTON, conservation cons.; b. Chgo., Apr. 14, 1910; s. Harry Kent and Verna (Harris) C.; student Dartmouth, 1928-29; B.F., U. Mich., 1932, M.F., 1936, Ph.D., 1942, D.Sc. (hon.) 1968; m. Sara Sherwood, Dec. 30, 1933; children—Frederick Sherwood, Julia (Mrs. Paul G. Kaminski). Forester Intermountain Forrest and Range Expt. Sta., Ogden, Utah, 1931, Southwestern Forest and Range Expt. Sta., Tucson, 1932-40, Cal. Forest and Range Expt. Sta., Berkeley, 1940-44; chief div. fores econs., forest service U.S. Dept. Agr., 1944-50, asst. chief forest service, 1950-62; 1950-62; dir. bur. outdoor recreation Dept. Interior, 1962-69; conservation cons., cons., Washington, 1969—. U.S. del. Third World Forestry Congress, Helsinki, Finland, 1949. Mem. nat. council Boy Scouts Am. Bd. dirs. Citizens Com. on Natural Resources. Recipient Distinguished Service award USDA, 1960, Am. Inst. Park Execs., 1965, U.S. Dept. Interior, 1967; Rockefeller Pub. Service award in nat. resources, 1968. Fellow Am. Park and Recreation Soc., Am. Inst. Park Execs., Soc. Am. Foresters; mem. Am. Forestry Assn. (spl. articles editor), Nat. Park and Recreation Soc., Forest History Soc. (Dir.), Nature Conservancy, Izaak Walton League, Nat. Wildlife Fedn., Wilderness Soc., Sierra Club, Nat. Parks Assn., Sigma Xi, Phi Kappa Phi, Phi Sigma, Sigma Phi. Club: Cosmos. Author: Timber Resources for America's Future. Home: 11910 Hitching Post Lane Walnut Woods Rockville MD 20852 Office: 1346 Connecticut Av NW Washington DC 20036

CRAFTS, JAMES F., insurance exec.; b. East Orange, N.J. Former chmn. bd. Fireman's Fund Ins. Co. Home: 1945 Pacific Av San Francisco CA 94109 Office: 580 California St San Francisco CA 94119

CRAFTS, JAMES SPRAY, educator; b. Mantua, O., Feb. 2, 1913; s. James Griffin and Jessie Pearl (Spray) C.; B.A., Oberlin Coll., 1934; student Cleve. Sch. Art, summer 1935; M.A., Columbia Tchrs. Coll., 1940; M.A., Ph.D., Yale, 1957; m. Louise Anne Evenden, Oct. 27, 1944; children—Edward James, Anita Art tchr. pub. schs.; asst. prof. art chmn. dept. Tchrs. Coll. Conn., New Britain, 1946-56, asso. prof., 1956-57; prof. art Cal. State Coll., 1957—, chmn. dept., 1962-67. Exhibited one-man shows San Francisco Mus. Art, 1944, Little Gallery, Cleve., 1945, Morton Gallery, N.Y.C., 1942, YMCA, Long Beach, 1962, Joslyn Center, Torrance, Cal., 1968, Community New Britain Art Mus., Yale Art Gallery, Long Beach Art. Mus., others. Served from ensign to lt., USNR, 1942045. Mem. Conn. Acad. Fine Arts, Conn. Waterpolor Soc. (chmn. exhbn. com.), Conn. (treas., v.p., pres. 1947-57), Pacific arts assns., Nat. (regional sec. 1968-69), So. Cal. (corr. sec. 1957-62) art edn. assns., Phi Delta Kappa (chpt. pres. 1967-68). Republican. Home: 1927 Skycrest Dr Fullerton CA 92631 Office: 6101 E 7th St Long Beach CA 90801

CRAFTS, ROGER CONANT, anatomist, educator; b. Lewiston, Me., Jan. 26, 1911; s. Seldon T. and Alice (Conant) C.; B.S., Bates Coll., 1933; Ph.D., Columbia, 1941; m. Margaret Dean Findley, Aug. 10, 1938; children—Roger Conant, Susan Dean. Teaching asst. dept. biology Bates Coll., 1931-33; research asst. dept. anatomy Columbia Coll. Medicine, 1934-39, instr. anatomy, 1939-40; instr. anatomy Boston U. Sch. Medicine, 1941-43, asst. prof., 1943-49, asso. prof., 1949-50; Francis Brunning prof. anatomy, head dept. U. Cin. Coll. Medicine, 1950—, fellow Grad. Sch. U. Cin., 1961—. Cons. div. fellowships NIH, 1960-63, health facilities div., 1962-63; chmn. council faculties, Midwest-Gt. Plains region Assn. Am. Med. Colls., 1969-70. Bd. mgmt. YMCA, Cin., 1955- 57; mem. Citizens Sch. Com., 1967—, exec. com., 1967—, chmn., 1968-70. Recipient silver medallion Columbia U., 1967. Fellow A.A.A.S.; mem. Am. Inst. Biol. Scis., Am. Assn. Anatomists (chmn. nominating com. 1965-66), Midwest Anatomists Assn. (pres. 1968-69), Am. Assn. U. Profs., Assn. Am. Med. Colls., Soc. Exptl. Biology and Medicine, Acad. Medicine Cin. (asso.), Cincinnatus Assn., Phi Beta Kappa, Sigma Xi (pres. 1965-67). Episcopalian (sec. vestry 1961—). Author: A Textbook of Human Anatomy, 1966. Contbr. articles to profl. publs. Home: 3230 Daytona Av Cincinnati OH 45211

CRAGG, ERNEST ELLIOTT, ins. co. exec.; b. Franklin, Minn., Aug. 12, 1927; s. Loren E. and Inga (Hanson) C.; A.B., Carleton Coll., Northfield, Minn., 1948; C.L.U., 1956; m. Doris Laverne Anderson,

July 5, 1957; children-Lauren Carol, Jeffrey Elliott, Karyn Kristen. With Wash. Nat. Ins. Co., Evanston, Ill., 1948—, v.p., 1968—; pres. Wash. Nat. Equity Co., 1969—. Bd. dirs. U.S. Jr. C. of C., 1956-57, mem. inaugral com., 1957. Chief sgt. at arms Young Republican Nat. Conv., 1957. Served with USNR, 1944-45. Fellow Life Mgmt. Inst. Mem. Community Ch. (trustee). Club: Toastmasters Internat. Home: 1256 Asbury Av Winetka IL 60093 Office: 1630 Chicago St Evanston IL 60201

CRAGG, ERNEST THORPE, air force officer; b. Mt. Vernon, N.Y., Jan. 19, 1922; s. Edward and Jessie (Thorpe) C.; B.S., U.S. Mil. Acad., 1943; postgrad U. Mich., 1947-50; M.A., George Washington U., 1963; grad. Nat. War Coll., 1963; m. Helen Claire Petraborg, July 18, 1945; children—Edward Ernest, Peter Charles. Commd. 2d lt. USAAF, 1943, advanced through grades to maj. gen. USAF, 1970; pilot, comdr., asst. operations officer fighter bomber squadron, ETO, 1944-45; dir., chief offices various hdqrs. USAF, 1951-67; dep. chief of staff operations Hdqrs. Air Tng. Command, 1967-69; dep. dir. aerospace programs Hdqrs. USAF, Washington, 1969-71, dir., 1971—. Decorated Legion of Merit, D.F.C., Air medal, Air Force and Army Commendation medals. Mason (Shriner). Home: 2111 Jefferson Davis Hwy Arlington VA 22202 Office: The Pentagon Washington DC 20330

CRAGG, HENRY, corp. exec. With Minute Maid Co. div. Coca-Cola Co., 1946—, formerly chmn. bd., chief exec. officer, now v.p. foods div. Coca-Cola Co.; dir. Jacksonville br. Fed. Res. Bank Atlanta. Mem. Fla. Council of 100, Fla. Citrus Commn. Address: Coca-Cola Co Foods Div PO Box 2079 Houston TX 77001*

CRAGLE, RAYMOND GEORGE, educator; b. Orangeville, Pa., Feb. 28, 1926; s. Ray Ellis and Florence Mae (Decker) C.; student Del. Valley Coll., 1947-49; B.S., N.C. State U., 1951, M.S., 1954; Ph.D., U. Ill., Urbana, 1957; m. Phyllis Cornelia Russell, Aug. 5, 1950; children—Donna Lynne, Mark Robert, Matthew Bruce. Asst. prof. AEC Agrl. Research Lab. U. Tenn., Oak Ridge, 1957-60, asso. prof., 1960-68, prof. animal physiology, 1968-70; prof., head dept. dairy sci. Va. Polytech. Inst. and State U., Blacksburg, 1970—; vis. prof. Lab. Genetics U. Wis. at Madison, 1968-69; lectr. Oak Ridge Asso. Univs. Travel Lecture program, 1960-69. Explorer adviser Boy Scouts Am., 1957-61. Served as sgt. USAAF, 1944-46; as lt. AUS, 1951-52. Mem. Am. Dairy Sci. Assn., Am. Soc. Animal Sci., A.A.A.S., Am. Inst. Nutrition, Transplantation Soc., Soc. Study Reprodn., Sigma Xi, Gamma Sigma Delta, Alpha Zeta. Editorial bd. Jour. Dairy Sci., 1965-70. Contbr. articles Jour. Dairy Sci., Transplantation, Am. Jour. Physiology, Jour. Nutrition and Sci. Home: 507 Monte Vista Dr Blacksburg VA 24060

CRAGO, WILLIAM HENRY, utility exec.; b. Duluth, Minn., July 22, 1910; s. William Henry and Catharine (Cook) C.; A.B., U. Mich., J.D., 1935; m. Lori Malengo, Apr. 10, 1946; children—Victoria Ann, Elisabeth Jean. Admitted to Minn. bar, 1947; with firm Cravath, Swaine & Moore, N.Y.C., 1935-37; asst. sec. Interchem. Corp., N.Y.C., 1937-42; atty. U.S. Steel Corp., Duluth, 1946- 56; asst. to pres. Duluth, Missabe and Iron Range Ry. Co., Duluth, 1956- 63; gen. counsel, sec. Pa. Power & Light Co., 1963—, also v.p., 1971—. Bd. dirs., pres. Duluth Mental Hygiene Clinic, 1957-63. Served to capt. AUs, World War II; ETO. Mem. Am., Minn. bar assns., Phi Gamma Delta, Phi Delta Phi. Episcopalian. Home: RD 3 Bethlehem PA 18015 Office: 901 Hamilton St Allentown PA 18101

CRAGOE, ARTHUR CLEMENT, ins. co. exec.; b. Chgo., July 19, 1927; s. Claude H. and Dorothy (Heagle) C.; B.S., U. Wis., 1949; m. Louise Mattie Miller, Nov. 4, 1950; childrenDouglas, Catherine, Paul, Mary. With Equitable Life of Ia., Des Moines, 1950-60, asst. actuary, 1958-60; asso. actuary Franklin Life Ins. Co., Springfield, Ill., 1960-63, actuary, 1963-, v.p., 1967-, also dir. Served with USAAF 1945-46. Fellow Soc. Actuaries; mem. Theta Delta Chi. Republican. Presbyn. Home: 2 Linden Lane Springfield IL 62707. Office: Franklin Sq Springfield IL 62705

CRAIB, DONALD FORSYTH, Jr., ins. exec.; b. Seattle, May 4, 1925; s. Donald Forsyth and Rubye (Drysdale) C.; B.S. cum laude, U. Cal. at Los Angeles, 1949; m. Evelyn L. Poyer, Dec. 21, 1947; children-John L., Donald Forsyth, Laura L., Janet R. Regional mgr. Allstate Ins. Co., Sacramento, 1950-64, asst. sec., 1966-68, regional v.p., 1968-70, v.p. investments, 1971—; pres., chmn. bd. Met. Savs. and Loan Assn., Los Angeles, 1964-68, also dir.; dir. Allstate Savs. & Loan Assn., North Hollywood. Trustee U. Cal. at Los Angeles Found. Served with USMCR, 1943-46; PTO. Mem. Phi Kappa Sigma. Republican. Conglist. Clubs: Pauma Valley Country; Jonathan (Los Angeles). Home: Pauma Oaks Ranch P O Box 687 Pauma Valley CA 92061 Office: Allstate Plaza Northbrook IL 60062

CRAIB, RALPH GRANT, newspaperman; b. Oakland, Cal., Jan. 31, 1925; s. Alexander Leslie and Martha O.C. (Clerk) C.; B.A. with honors, San Francisco State Coll., 1950; m. Karola Maria Saekel, Dec. 4, 1962; children-Lisa Maria, Betsy Anne. Copy boy, then reporter and feature writer Oakland Tribune, 1942- 59; mem. staff San Francisco Chhronicle, 1959—, editorial writer, 1968- -; information officer, mem. staff gov. Am. Samoa, 1965-66. Bd. dirs. No. Cal. chpt. Americans Democratic Action, 1967-68. Served with AUS, World War II; ETO. Decorated Combat Inf. badge; Reid Found. fellow, 1955. Mem. San Francisco Newspaper Guild. Democrat. Club: Explorers (N.Y.C.). Home: 638 The Alameda Berkeley CA 94707 Office: San Francisco Chronicle San Francisco CA 94119

CRAIG, ALBERT MORTON, educator; b. Chgo., Dec. 9, 1927; s. Albert Morton and Adda (Clendenin) C.; B.S., Northwestern U., 1949; postgrad. Universite de Strasbourg, 1949-50, Kyoto U., 1951-53, Tokyo U., 1955-56; Ph.D., Harvard, 1959; m. Teruko Ugaya, July 10, 1953; children—John, Paul, Sarah. Instr., U. Mass., 1957-59; instr. Harvard, Cambridge, Mass., 1959-60, asst. prof., 1960-63, asso. prof., 1963-67, prof., 1967—. Served with U.S. Army, 1946-47. Mem. Assn. Asian Studies, Am. Hist. Assn., Shigakkai. Author: Choshu in the Meiji Restoration, 1961; (with others) East Asia the Modern Transformation, 1965. Co-editor: Personality in Japanese History, 1970. Home: 172 Goden St Belmont MA 02178 Office: 2 Divinity Av Cambridge MA 02138

CRAIG, ALLEN THORNTON, educator; b. Marion, Ala., Aug. 5, 1904; s. Edgar Montgomery and Vivia (Roark) C.; A.B., U. Fla., 1927, A.M., 1928; Ph.D., U. Ia., 1931. Instr. math. U. Fla., 1929-30; asso. in math. U. Ia., 1931-33, asst. prof., 1933-38, asso. prof., 1938-45, prof. math. 1945-70. Served as mem. research group M. Nat. Defense Research Com., 1942. Served as lt. (j.g.) U.S.N.R., 1942-46; released rank of lt. comdr. Mem. Am. Math Soc. and Math Assn. of Am. Fellow Inst. Math. Statistics (sec.- treas., 1935-38; v.p., 1939-41). Author (with R. V. Hogg): Introduction to Mathematical Statistics, 1959, 2d edit., 1965. Mem. editorial bd. Annals of Mathematics Statistics, 1938-50. Contbr. tech. articles in math. theory of statistics to profl. jours. Home: 1024 Woodlawn Iowa City IA 52240

CRAIG, ANDREW BILLINGS, III, banker; b. Buffalo, Mar. 20, 1931; s. Andrew Billings and Helen (House) C.; student Cornell U., 1950-54; A.B., U. Buffalo, 1955; m. Virginia Coskery Craig, Nov. 9, 1957; children—Andrea J., Laura D. With Mfrs. & Traders Co., Buffalo, 1957—, exec. v.p., 1968—; dir. Transelco, Inc., M & T Capital Corp., ANDCO, Inc. Trustee Buffalo Gen. Hosp., Buffalo Niagara Indsl. Devel. Corp.; mem. council Cornell U., bd. dirs. Western N.Y. Nuclear Research Center, Cornell Aero. Lab.; bd. regents Canisius Coll.; Mem. Phi Kappa Sigma. Republican. Presbyn. Mason. Club: Country of Buffalo, Saturn (Buffalo). Home: 59 Brandywine Dr Buffalo NY 14221 Office: 1 M & T Plaza Buffalo NY 14240

CRAIG, BEN TRUMAN, textile co. exec.; b. Gastonia, N.C., Jan. 27, 1933; s. Ben W. and Lois (Sams) C.; B.S., Davidson Coll., 1954; certificate Stonier Grad. Sch. Banking, Rutgers U., 1963-65, Exec. Program, U. N.C., 1968-69. Advanced Mgmt. Program, Harvard, 1971; m. Jane Cobb Smith, June 12, 1954; children—Cathryn, Sarah, Ben Truman. With Wachovia Bank and Trust Co., 1954-61; asst. to pres. Nat. Bank S.C., 1961-63; chief exec. officer Bank of Lancaster, 1963-65; with Springs Mills, Inc., 1965—, treas., 1968—; dir. Bank of Lancaster, Lancaster Trust Co. Bd. dirs. Lancaster County Library Bd.; bd. visitors Clemson U., 968. Served with AUS, 1955- 57. Methodist. Home: Route 4 Partridge Hill Lancaster SC 29720 Office: PO Box 70 Fort Mill SC 29715

CRAIG, BERNARD DUFFY, lawyer; b. Kansas City, Mo., Nov. 12, 1909; s. John C. and Edith M. (Duffy) C.; student Rockhurst Coll., 1929-31; J.D., U. Mo., 1936; m. Margaret Mary Conrad, June 25, 1938; children—Bernard D., JoAnne, John E., Kathleen. Admitted to Mo. bar, 1936, also U.S. Supreme Ct.; practice in Kansas City, 1936—; now mem. firm Levy and Craig; dir. Civic Plaza Nat. Bank, Civic Plaza Mortgage Investment Co., Columbian Steel Tank Co., Whitaker Cable Corp., Whitaker Cable de Mexico, S.A., Mexico City, Whitaker Inter-Am. Corp., Whitaker Cable Can. Ltd., Marcopel, S.A., Mexico City, Productos Electricas Phelps Dodge-Whitaker Venezuela. Vice chmn. gifts and bequest council Rockhurst Coll., 1960. Gen. chmn. brotherhood citation banquet Nat. Conf. Christians and Jews, 1959, nat. dir., 1966-69; adv. trustee Research Hosp., 1965-69; trustee U. Mo. at Kansas City Law Found., 1965-67; trustee Legal Aid and Defender Soc. Greater Kansas City, 1964-70, v.p., 1970; trustee Pope John XXIII Found., 1964-67. Hon. col. staff gov. Mo., 1964-72; named Knight Holy Sepulchre by Pope Paul VI, 1965. Mem. Am. (membership com. sect. corp., banking and bus. law), Mo., Kansas City bar assns., Comml. Law League Am. (pres. 1965-66). Clubs: Kansas City; Blue Hills Country. Home: 1019 W 69th St Kansas City MO 64113 Office: Walnut Street Bldg Kansas City MO 64106

CRAIG, CLAYTON BION, church dir.; b. Watertown, S.D.; s. Bion Sidney and Sarah Ann (Bigelow) C.; A.B., U. S.D., 1925; postgrad. Harvard, 1925-26; B.A., Oxford U. (Rhodes scholar), 1929, M.A., 1935; m. Mrs. Ethelbelle Alle Taylor, Dec. 17, 1931. Tchr. social scis. pvt. sch. N.Y.C., 1930-31; asst. to gen. mgr. and sales mgr. mfg. firm, Cin., 1931-36; entered pub. practice Christian Sci., 1936, authorized tchr., 1940; C.S. com. on publ. for Ohio, 1941-45; C.S. lectr., 1945-48; bd. dirs. First Ch. of Christ Scientist, Boston, 1948—. Mem. English Speaking Union, Delta Tau Delta, Delta Sigma Pi, Tau Kappa Alpha, Theta Alpha Phi. Mason (32, K.T., Shriner). Clubs: Harvard, Algonquin (Boston); Beverly Yacht (Marion, Mass.). Home: 270 Beacon St Boston, MA 02116. Office: Christian Science Center Boston MA 02115

CRAIG, CLEO FRANK, bank exec.; b. Rich Hill, Mo., Apr. 6, 1893; s. John S. and Missouri (Davis) C.; B.S. in Elec. Engring., U. Mo., 1913, LL.D., 1952; m. Laura Heck, Sept. 7, 1941 (dec.); children—John H., Laura E. (Mrs. H. Kirkwood), Robert F. Started as equipment man. St. Louis with Am. Tel & Tel. Co., 1913, became gen. mgr. long lines dept., 1933, v.p. long lines dept., 1940, v.p. several other depts., 1941-49, pres., 1951- 56, chmn. bd., 1956-57; dir. U.S. Steel Corp.; chmn. bd. Citizens First Nat. Bank and Trust Co., Ridgewood, N.J.; trustee Central Savs. Bank N.Y. Trustee Grand Central Art Galleries, Presbyn. Hosp. City N.Y., Met. Mus. Art, Voorhees Tech. Inst., Turrell Fund; chmn. Woodrow Wilson Nat. Fellowship Found. Gold Medal Award Wharton Sch. Fellow Am. Inst. E.E.; mem. Eta Kappa Nu, Tau Beta Pi. Clubs: Links (N.Y.C.); Ridgewood (N.J.) Country, Blooming Grove Fishing (Pa.); St. Maurice Hunting and Fishing (Can.). Home: 335 Mountain Av Ridgewood NJ 07450 Office: 54 E Ridgewood Av PO Box 506 Ridgewood NJ 07451

CRAIG, CONWAY C., newspaper exec.; b. Glen Cove, Tex., Aug. 31, 1901; s. James William and William and Florence Ellen (Smith) C.; B.A., Hardin-Simmons U., 1925; m. Gaynelle Porter, Mar. 21, 1926. With Abilene (Tex.) Reporter, 1926-27, Corpus Christi (Tex.) Times, 1928-29, Southwestern Engraving Co., San Antonio, 1929-30; sales rep. Mills Engraving Co., later Southwestern Engraving Co., 1929-30; with Corpus Christi Caller and Times, 1930-62, pub., 1939- 62, pres., 1945-62; pub. Express Pub. Co., San Antonio, 1962- 69, now chmn. bd. A founder United Fund Corpus Christi, 1954; pres. bd. govs. United Community Services Corpus Christi, 1961; organizer Corpus Christi Art Found., 1940, permanent v.p. charge ways and means, 1940—; and organizer Downtown Businessmen's Assn., Corpus Christi, 1954; chmn. non-Jewish div. Jewish Social Service Fedn., San Antonio, 1963; pres. Corpus Christi Symphony Soc., 1956. Bd. govs. Southwest Research Inst.; bd. dirs. San Antonio Livestock Expn., Tex. Good Roads Assn., Fiesta San Antonio Commn. Mem. San Antonio C. of C. (pres. 1964). Home: Knight Robin Dr San Antonio, TX 78209. Office: PO Box 2171 San Antonio TX 78205

CRAIG, DAVID WILLIAMSON, lawyer, educator; b. Pitts., Feb. 17, 1925; s. David and Ella (Williamson) C.; A.B., U. Pitts., 1948, LL.B., 1950; m. Ella Van Kirk, July 15, 1945; children—Linda Marie Putnam, Muriel Jean. Admitted to Pa. bar 1950; research asst. U. Pitts. Law Sch., 1950-51; law clk. Ct. Common Pleas Allegheny County, 1951-52; partner firm Moorhead & Knox, Pitts., 1952-61; city solicitor Pitts., 1961-65; dir. pub. safety Pitts., 1965-69; partner firm Baskin, Boreman, Sachs, Gondleman & Craig, 1962—. Adj. prof. Carnegie-Mellon U., 1969—. Chmn. City Planning Commn. Pitts., 1960-61; gen. counsel Pa. Housing Agy.; mem. nat. adv. council FPC, 1962-65. Served to 1st lt. USAAF, 1943-45; ETO. Decorated D.F.C. Mem. Am. Soc. Planning Ofcls. (pres. 1963-64), Am. Inst. Planners. Presbyn. (elder). Democrat. Author: Pennsylvania Building and Zoning Laws, 1951. Home: Gateway Towers Pittsburgh PA 15222 Office: Frick Bldg Pittsburgh PA 15219

CRAIG, DOUGLAS BROWARD, mining co. exec.; b. N.Y.C., Feb. 20, 1929; s. Howard Reid and Agnes (Broward) C.; A.B., Harvard, 1950, LL.B., 1953; m. Peggie-Louise Lee, Oct. 3, 1953; children—Deborah Anne, Douglas Broward, Elizabeth Jane, Robert Leslie. Admitted to N.Y. bar, 1953, Fla. bar, 1958, also U.S. Supreme Ct.; law clk. to U.S. circuit judge, 1957-58; assoc. firm Debevoise, Plimpton, Lyons & Gates, N.Y.C., 1958-64; sec. St. Joe Minerals Corp., 1964-67, v.p., sec., 1967-70, v.p. finance and devel., 1970-71, exec. v.p., 1971—, also trustee. Served with AUS, 1953-57. Mem. Am. bar Assn., Assn. Bar City N.Y., Am. Soc. Internat. Law, Am. Inst. Mining Engrs., Mining Club N.Y.C., Am. Soc. Corporate Secs., Econ. Club N.Y., Newcomen Soc. N. Am. Clubs: Harvard, Economic (N.Y.C.); Internat. Lawn Tennis U.S., Mt. Pleasant (N.Y.) Tennis; Whippoorwill. Home: Hardscrabble Rd Chappaqua NY 10514 Office: 250 Park Av New York City NY 10017

CRAIG, ELISABETH MAY, newspaper corr.; b. Coosaw, S.C.; d. Alexander and Elisabeth Anne (Essery) Adams; grad. high sch.; L.H.D. (hon.) U. Me., 1946; m. Donald Alexander Craig (dec.); children—Donald Alexander, Betty (Mrs. Albert A. Clagett). Began regular newspaper writing, 1924; has been corr. for N.Y., N.C. and Mont. newspapers; Washington corr. for Portland (Me.) Press Herald, Evening Express, Sunday Telegram, Waterville Sentinel, Kennebec Jour. (all Me.); Wash. corr. for stas. WGAN, WGAN-TV and radio stas. in Me. War corr., World War II, Korea. Contbr. feature articles to mags. and newspapers. "Meet the Press" program on radio and television. Elected to standing com. Press Galleries, Congress, 1944-46. Recipient Achievement in Journalism. Nat. Council Auxiliaries Am. Med. Center. Denver; Woman of Achievement, Fedn. Soroptimist Clubs; Outstanding Service citation Am. Legion; Distinguished Service award Nat. Fedn. Bus. and Profl. Women's Clubs. Mem. Wash. Newspaper Guild (dir.), Soc. Women Geographers, Nat. Acad. TV Arts and Scis., Theta Sigma Phi. Clubs: Women's Nat. Press (mem. bd. govs., pres. 1943) Overseas Press of Am., American Women in Radio and Television, Inc., Am. Newspaperwomen's. Home: 717 North Carolina Av SE Washington DC 20009 Office: National Press Bldg Washington DC 20004

CRAIG, EUGENE W., editorial cartoonist; b. Ft. Wayne, Ind., Sept. 5, 1916; s. James S. and Katherine (Dahl) C.; student pub. schs.; m. Joyce C. Ayers, Nov. 21, 1951; children-Sandra (Mrs. David E. Miller), Pamela, (Mrs. Stephen W. Mitchell), Mark, Steve. Artist, editorial cartoonist Ft. Wayne News- Sentinel, 1934-51; editorial cartoonist Bklyn. Eagle, 1951-55, Columbus (O.) Dispatch, 1955—. Mem. Am. Assn. Editorial Cartoonists. Creator Forever Female; Craigatures; A Round A Day. Home: 73 E Kramer St Canal Winchester OH 43110 Office: 34 S 3d St Columbus OH 43215

CRAIG, GEORGE NORTH, lawyer; b. Brazil, Ind., Aug. 6, 1909; s. Bernard Clyde and Clo (Branson) C.; student Culver Mil. Sch., summers 1923, 1924, 1925, U. Ariz., 1928-29; LL.B., Ind. U., 1932; LL.D., Ind. U., Butler U., Vincennes U. (Ind.); m. Kathryn L. Helliger, Aug. 29, 1931; children—John David, Margery Ellen. Admitted to Ind. bar, 1932, practiced in Indpls., 1932-53; gov. Ind., 1953-57. Served from 1st lt. to lt. col. AUS, 1942-46. Decorated Bronze Star medal with oak leaf cluster (U.S.); Croix de Guerre (France), French Legion of Honor. Recipient Freedom Found. award Ind. Inst. Psychiat. Research, 1950. Fellow Am. Internat. Acad.; mem. Am. Judicature Soc., Am. Legion (nat. comdr. 1949-50), Brazil C. of C., Am., Ind. bar assns., Am., Ind. (dir.) trial lawyers assns., Nat. Rifle Assn. (dir.), Delta Chi (pres.), Delta Theta Phi (pres.). Republican. Methodist. Mason. Home: 524 N Meridian St Brazil IN 47834 Office: First Bank and Trust Bldg Brazil IN 47834

CRAIG, GERALD SPELLMAN, educator; b. DeGraff, O., May 6, 1893; s. Dr. Lorain D. and Estelle Estelle (Spellman) C.; B.S., Baylor (Tex.) U., 1915; A.M., Columbia, 1917, Ph.D., 1927; student U. Pa., 1919-20; m. Prudence Bower, Dec. 27, 1915; children—Lawrence C., Alice Estelle (Mrs. Richard A. Erney). Instr. phys. sci., Ballinger (Tex.) High School, 1919-1916; Baylor U., summer 1916; instr. phys. sci., State Normal Sch., Bloomsburg, Pa., 1921-23; instr. sci. edn. Pa. State Coll., summers 1923-24; cons. in elem. sci. Horace Man Sch., Tchrs. Coll. Columbia, 1925; asso. natural scis., Tchrs. Coll. Columbia, 1927-29, asst. prof., 1929-34, asso. prof., 1934-41, prof., 1941-56, prof. emeritus natural sci., 1956—. Cons., elementary sci. pub. sch. systems, 1929- -; developed natural sci. field centers Ala., Conn., N.H., Puerto Rico, 1934-50. Served as 1st sgt. A.E.F. in France, 1917-1918. Recipient First Sci. Edn. Recognition award, 1956; citation distinguished service in sci. edn. Nat. Assn. Research Sci. Teaching, 1959; citation Council Elementary Sci. Internat., 1965, citation for distinguished service to sci. edn. Nat. Sci. Tchrs. Assn., 1969. Fellow A.A.A.S.; mem. N.Y. Acad. Scis., Elementary Sci. Syllabus Com. N.Y. State, Nat. Council of Supervisors of Elementary Sci. (pres. 1930-31), Nat. Assn. Research in Sci. Teaching (pres. 1935-36), 1935-36), Conf. on Edn. of Tchrs. in Sci. (sec. 1936-40), Sci. Edn. (pres. 1931-43), Edn. Research Assn., Philippine Sci. Tchrs. Assn. (cons. 1960). Author; Horace Mann Course of Study in Elementary Science, 1927; sections on Elementary Science in The Classroom Teacher, 1927; Pathways in Science, 1932; New Pathways in Science, 1940; Science for the Elementary School Teacher, 1940. 5th edit., 1966; Science in Childhood Education, 1944; Our World of Science, 1946; Science Today and Tomorrow sr., with others), 1954-58; What Research Says To the Teacher About Teaching Science for A.E.R.A., 1957; (with others), Science for You, 1965. Member of the 31st, 46th Yearbook Com., The Natl. Soc. for the Study of Edn., contbr. to 36th Yearbook; contbr. numerous articles for the elementary schs., tchr. edn. and field studies in sci. Studied status of sci. in European schs., 1931. Home: 8 Paseo Redondo Tucson, AZ 85705

CRAIG, GORDON, newspaper publisher; b. Detroit, Sept. 2, 1922; s. Lyman J. and Irene (Lorimer) C.; B.S., U. So. Cal., 1943; m. Barbara Booth, Mar. 10, 1945; children—David L., Warren B., Brian N. Adminstrv. trainee Ford Motor Co., 1946-47; display advt. salesman Pontiac (Mich.) Press, 1947-49; with Booth Newspapers, Inc., Detroit, 1949— pres., chmn. bd., 1968—, dir., 1960—. Trustee, Cranbrook Schs.; mem. exec. com. Cranbrook Sch. for Boys; trustee Citizens Research Council Mich. Served to ensign USNR, 1943-46. Mem. Am. Newspaper Pubs. Assn., Inland Daily Press Assn. (chmn. bd. dirs.), Internat. Newspaper Advt. Execs. Assn. Clubs: Detroit Adcraft; Detroit; Orchard Lake (Mich.) Country. Home: 1135 N Glenhurst St Birmingham MI 48009 Office: 3959 Research Park Dr Ann Arbor MI 48104

CRAIG, GORDON ALEXANDER, historian; b. Glasgow, Scotland, Nov. 26, 1913; s. Frank Mansfield and Jane Morton (Bissell) C.; A.B., Princeton, 1936, A.M., 1939, Ph.D., 1941, Litt.D., 1970; B.Litt., Oxford U. (Rhodes scholar Balliol 1936-38), 1938; m. Phyllis Halcomb, June 16, 1939; children—Susan, Deborah Gordon, Martha, Charles. Came to U.S., 1925, citizen by derivation. Instr. in history Yale, 1939-41; mem. hist. dept. Princeton, 1941-61, prof. history, 1950- 61; prof. history Stanford U., 1961—, J.E. Wallace Sterling prof. humanities, 1969—; hon. prof. Free U. Berlin, 1962—. Vis. prof. history Columbia, 1947-48, 1949-50; research asso. OSS, 1942, divisional asst. Spl. Div., Dept. State, 1943. Capt. USMCR, 1944—. Pub. mem. Fgn. Service Selection Bd., 1949. Fellow Center Advanced Study Behavioral Scis., Stanford, Cal., 1956-57; mem. Am. Hist. Assn., Am. Acad. Polit. Sci., Am. Acad. Arts and Scis., Am. Philos. Soc. Collaborating editor and contbr. to Makers of Modern Strategy: Military Thought from Machiavelli to Hitler, 1943; The Second Chance: America and the Peace, 1944; The Quest for a Principle of Authority in Europe, 1915-present, 1948. Author: The Politics of the Prussian Army, 1649-1945, 1955; From Bismarck to Adenauer: Aspects of German Statecraft, 1958; Europe Since 1815, 1961; The Battle of Königgrätz: Prussia's Victory Over Austria, 1866, 1964; War, Politics and Diplomacy: Selected Essays, 1966. Co- editor: The Diplomats, 1919-1939, 1953. Contbr. articles to profl. jours. Home: 946 Valdez Pl Stanford CA 94305 also 1000 North Point San Francisco CA 94109

CRAIG, HARALD FRANKLIN, lawyer; b. Lima O., Oct. 27, 1930; s. Harald F. and Bessie M. (Rose) C.; B.A., Bowling Green State U., 1952; J.D., Ohio State U., 1955; m. Nena A. Gray, Mar. 24, 1951;

children—Harald Franklin III, Anne Marie. Admitted to Ohio bar, 1955, since practiced in Toledo; partner firm Boxell, Bebout, Torbet & Baker, 1970—. Served with USMCR, 1955-57. Home: 2415 S Country Club Pkwy Toledo OH 43614 Office: Toledo Trust Bldg Toledo OH 43604

CRAIG, JAMES BARKLEY, editor-writer; b. W. Hebron, N.Y., Sept. 30, 1912; s. George Andrew and Gertrude (Barkley) C.; A.B. with distinction in English, Kent (O.) State U., 1936, citation for distinguished achievement in journalism, 1959; m. Marjie Hutson Reese, May 17, 1945; children—William Reese, Richard Barkley, David Livingston, Jonathan Becker, Robert Hutson, Marjorie Jennings. With Akron (O.) Times-Press, 1936-37, Athens (O.) Messenger; 1937-38, Cumberland (Md.) News, 1938-41, Cumberland Times, 1945-47; asst. editor Am. Forests, 1947-49, asso. editor, 1949-50, editor, 1950- -; mgr. N.Y.C. New Bur., Am. Forest Inst., 1950-53. Mem. steering com. Nat. Watershed Congress, 1958—; mem. who's who conservation com. Nat. Resources Council Am., 1967—. Served with AUS, 1941-46. Trustee Clara Barton Sch., 1959-68. Mem. Soc. Am. Foresters. Republican. Mem. United Ch. Christ. Club: Cosmos (Washington). Home: 7410 Arden Rd Bethesda MD 20034 Office: 1319 Eighteenth St NW Washington DC 20036

CRAIG, JAMES BAYLEY, psychiatrist; b. Augusta, Ga., Nov. 7, 1911; s. James B. and Maude (Baston) C.; M.D., U. Ga., 1937; M.S., U. Mich., 1942; m. Elizabeth Rice, Sept. 9, 1938; children—James, Patrick, Henry, Carolyn, William. Rotating intern St. Josephs Hosp., Ann Arbor, Mich., 1937-38; resident psychiatry Mercywood Sanitarium, Ann Arbor, 1938-39; staff psychiatrist Sacred Heart Sanitarium, Milw., 1939; resident psychiatry Neuro- psychiat. Inst., Ann Arbor, 1939-40, instr. psychiatry, 1940-42; practice medicine specializing in psychiatry, Savannah, Ga., 1946-52, Columbus, O., 1952-60, Milledgeville, Ga., 1960—; psychiat. cons. St. Josephs Hosp., Savannah, 1946-52, Central of Ga. Hosp., 1946-52, U.S. Marine Hosp., 1947-52; clin. dir. Columbus Receiving Hosp., 1952-60; attending physician U. Hosp. Ohio State Med. Center, neuropsychiat. cons. Columbus VA Mental Hygiene Clinic, 1952-60; psychiat. cons. VA Hosp., Dayton, 1955-60, Mt. Carmel Hosp., Columbus, 1959-60; dir. edn. Milledgeville State Hosp., 1960-61, asst. supt., 1961-66, supt., 1966—; instr. psychiatry U. Mich., 1940-42; instr. St. Josephs Hosp. Sch. Nursing, Savannah, 1946-52; asso. prof. Ohio State U., 1952-60, prof., 1955-60; clin. prof. Med. Coll. Ga., 1960—; clin. prof. psychiatry dept. psychology U. Ga., Athens 1960—. Trustee Ga. Coll., Milledgeville. Served from capt. to lt. col. AUS, 1942-46. Recipient Lay award Ga. Recreational and Park Soc. Diplomate Am. Bd. Psychiatry and Neurology. Mem. Am., Ga. psychiat. assns., Central Neuropsychiat. Assn., Guild Catholic Psychiatrists, Baldwin County Med. Soc., Med. Assn. Ga., Am. Coll. Psychiatrists, Ga. Wardens Assn., Alpha Omega Alpha. Contbr. articles to profl. jours. Address: Central State Hosp Milledgeville GA 31061

CRAIG, JOHN CYMERMAN, med. educator; b. Berlin, Germany, Jan. 23, 1920; B.Sc., U. London (Eng.), 1942, Ph.D. in Organic Chemistry, 1945; D.Sc., Sydney U. (Australia), 1961; married, 1945; 1 child. Research chemist Boots Pure Drug Co., Eng., 1945-47; lectr. organic chemistry U. London, 1947-48; lectr. Sydney U., 1948-52, sr. lectr., 1952-60; prof. pharm. chemistry U. Cal. at San Francisco, 1960—, vice chmn. dept., 1963-69, chmn. dept. pharm. chemistry Sch. Pharmacy, 1969—. Vis. scientist, NIH, 1959; mem. psychopharm. chem. panel Nat. Insts. Mental Health, 1963—. Mem. Am., Brit., Swiss chem. socs. Office: Med Scis Bldg U Cal Med Center San Francisco CA 94122*

CRAIG, JOHN MERRILL, pathologist; b. Pasadena, Cal., Oct. 14, 1913; s. Volney Howard and Elinor (Merrill) C.; A.B., U. Cal. at Berkeley. 1936, M.A., 1938; M.D. cum laude, Harvard, 1941; m. Elsa Fay Hartshorne, May 31, 1949. Intern medicine 1st div. Bellevue Hosp. N.Y.C., 1941-42, pathology Bent Brigham Hosp., Boston, 1946-47; resident pathology Children's Hosp., Boston, 1947-48, Boston Hosp. Women, 1948-49, Presbyn. Hosp., Chgo., 1949-50; from asst. pathologist to pathologist Children's Hosp. Med. Center, Boston, 1950-59, cons. pathologist, 1967—; from asso. prof. to prof. pathology Harvard Med. Sch., 1952—; dir. labs. E.S. Magee Hosp., Pitts., 1959-60; prof. pathology U. Pitts. Med. Sch., 1959-60; pathologist in chief Boston Women's Hosp., 1960—. Mem. pathology study sect. USPHS, 1959-64. Served with M.C., USNR, 1942-46. Mem. Soc. Pediatric Research (emeritus), Am. Assn. Pathologists and Bacteriologists, Internat. Acad. Pathology, Am. Pediatric Soc., Am. Soc. Exptl. Pathology, Assn. U. Pathologists (emeritus), New Eng. Soc. Pathologists (pres. 1965-66), Pediatric Pathology Club, Boston Obstet. Soc. Author numerous papers in field. Contbg. editor Jour. Pediatrics, 1956-59; asso. editor Am. Jour. Pathology, 1964—. Home: 41 Sargent Beechwood Brookline MA 02146

CRAIG, JOHN WILLIAM, elec. mfr.; b. Troy, O., Feb. 2, 1907; s. John Wesley and Julia (Conrad) C.; B.S. in Mech. Engring., U. Dayton, 1929; m. Thelma G. Stevens, Aug. 22, 1928; 1 dau., Judith Irene (Mrs. Frank E. Wilhoit). Engr. Frigidaire div. Gen. Motors Corp., 1929-37; v.p., gen. mgr. Crosley div. Avco Mfg. Corp., 1937-53; pres. Aluminum Industries, Inc., 1953-54; v.p. RCA, 1954-55; v.p., gen. mgr. Elec. Appliance div. Westinghouse Electric Corp., Mansfield, O., 1955-62, v.p., gen. mgr. spl. accounts, 1963; v.p., dir. Hupp Corp. Cleve., 1963-65; v.p. Admiral Corp., Chgo., 1965-69, exec. v.p., dir., 1969—. Recipient Navy Bur. Ordnance Devel. award. Mem. Am. Soc. Refrigerating Engrs., Hist. and Philos. Soc. Ohio, Newcomen Soc. N.A. Republican. Roman Catholic. Clubs: Queen City, Recess (Cin.). Home: 1 E Schiller St Chicago, IL 60610.

CRAIG, JUBAL EARLY, lawyer; b. San Francisco, May 31, 1874; s. William and Ruth Hairston (Thompson) C.; B.L., U. Va., 1895; m. Marie Craig, 1907 (dec. July 10, 1946); children—Lucille M. (Mrs. Malcolm C. Heffelman), Marie Ruth (Mrs. Roy M. Tait), Walter Early; m. 2d, Naomi K. Gibson, Oct. 16, 1954. Admitted to Va. and Cal. bars, 1895, Ariz., 1919; practiced law, San Francisco, 1895-1919, Phoenix, 1919—; with Fennemore, Craig, von Ammon & Udall, 1927—, sr. mem., 1948—. Fellow Am. Bar Found.; mem. Am. Bar Assn. (gen. council, ho. dels. 1935-45); State Bar Cal., State Bar Ariz. (bd. govs. 1933-34). Clubs: Arizona, Phoenix Country, Kiva (Phoenix). Home: 363 E Palm Lane Phoenix AZ 85004 Office: First Nat Bank Bldg Phoenix AZ 85004

CRAIG, LYMAN C., research chemist; b. Palmyra, Ia., June 12, 1906; s. Coy and Anna (Kitchell) C.; B.S., Ia. State Coll., 1928, Ph.D., 1931; Nat. Research fellow Johns Hopkins, 1931-33; m. Rachel Parker, Nov. 25, 1937; children—Anna, David, Mary-Elizabeth. Asst., dept. chem. pharmacology Rockefeller U., N.Y.C., 1933-37, asso., 1937-45, asso. mem., 1945-49, mem., 1949—, also prof. Recipient Lasker award for basic med. research, 1963; Fisher award analytical chemistry Am. Chem. Soc., 1966, Kolthoff medal Am. Pharm. Assn., 1971. Mem. Harvey Soc., Nat. Acad. Scis., Am. Acad. Arts and Scis., Am. Chem. Soc., Am. Assn. Biol. Chem., A.A.A.S., N.Y. Acad. Scis., Am. Inst. Chemists, Sigma Xi, Phi Lambda Upsilon. Contbr. articles to chem. jours. Home: 151 Rodney St Glen Rock NJ 07452 Office: Rockefeller U 66th St and York Av New York City NY 10021

CRAIG, MACK WAYNE, coll. dean; b. Obion, Tenn., May 13, 1925; s. Guy and Katherine (Andrews) C.; B.A., Vanderbilt U., 1946; M.A., George Peabody Coll., 1948, Ph.D., 1958; m. Dorothy Discher, Aug. 28, 1946 (dec. Nov. 1959); childrenLarry, David, Marnie. Ordained to ministry Ch. of Christ, 1942; minister in Fla. and Tenn., 1942-; instr. David Lipscomb High Sch., Nashville, 1945-49, prin., 1949-57; minister Vultee Ch. Christ, Nashville, 1968-; dean David Lipscomb Coll., 1957-, Mem. Nat., Tenn. edn. assns., Assn. Secondary Sch. Prins., Assn. Student Teaching, Assn. Deans Am. Colls., Assn. Higher Edn., Phi Beta Kappa. Author articles; editor column, Youth for Christ. Home: 1034 Woodvale Dr Nashville TN 37204

CRAIG, MARJORIE REED, (Mrs. John Thomas Crowley), author; b. Bangor, Me., Mar. 9, 1912; d. Warren Everet and Harriet (Humphrey) Craig; student Arnold Coll. (now Bridgeport U.), 1929-33; B.S. in Phys. Edn., Columbia, 1934; m. John Thomas Crowley, Sept. 9, 1935. Phys. therapist Neurol. Inst., Columbia Presbyn. Med. Center, 1934-41; supr. Richard Hudnut Success Sch. Phys. Edn., N.Y.C., 1942-52; supt. phys. edn. Elizabeth Arden Salon, N.Y.C., 1952—; pres. Crow Craig Corp. Author: Miss Craig's 21 Day Shape-Up Program, 1968; Miss Craig's Face Saving Exercises, 1970. Office: Random House 201 E 50th St New York City NY 10022

CRAIG, NANCY ELLEN, painter; b. Bronxville, N.Y., Feb. 7, 1927; d. Victor Irving and Julia (Hill) Craig; student Sweetbriar Coll. 1945-46, Bennington Coll., 1946- 48, Art Student's League, 1951, Farnsworth Sch. Art, Cape Cod, Academie Julien, Paris, 1952, Taubes Sch. Art, 1953-55; m. Preston Carter, May 10, 1963. One-man exhbn. Graham Gallery, N.Y.C., 1966, Lyford Cay Gallery, Nassau, Bahamas, 1971; represented Balt. Mus. Art, Met. Mus., N.Y.C., New Britain (Conn.) Mus. Recipient Julien F. Detmer award for best oil Hudson Valley Show, 1951; Mary E. Karasick award Nat. Assn. Women Artist, 1953, patron's prize Audubon Artists, 1955; S. Karasick prize Nat. Assn. Women Artists, 1956; Gold Medal Honor, Allied Artists, 1956; 1st Benjamin Altman prize N.A.D., 1957; Henry Ward Ranger purchase prize N.A.D., 1954. Author: Portrait Painting in Oil. Address: Box 57 Truro MA 02666

CRAIG, PAUL GENE, educator, economist; b. Middletown, O., Sept. 13, 1926; s. Raymond Butler and Ethel M. (Ledford) C.; B.A., Otterbein Coll., 1950; M.A., Ohio State U., 1951, Ph.D., 1953; m. Margaret I. Ashworth, Aug. 28, 1948; children—Laura E., Lisa Ann. Mem. faculty Ohio State U., Columbus, 1953-70, prof. econs., 1961-70, chmn. dept., 1963-68, dean Coll. Social and Behavioral Scis., 1968-70; v.p. acad. affairs Fla. State U., Tallahassee, 1970—. Vis. prof. exec. mgmt. program Pa. State U., summers 1957, 59; vis. prof. U. Hawaii, 1962-63; staff mem. Iran mgmt. program, Stanford in Teheran, summer 1962; lectr. Logistics Sch., Air Force Inst. Tech., 1957-60. Ford Found. postdoctoral fellow Inst. Basic Math. for Application to Bus., Harvard, 1959-60. Served to 2d lt., inf. AUS, 1945- 47. Mem. Am. Econ. Assn., Phi Beta Kappa, Beta Gamma Sigma. Co-author: Financing Unemployment Compensation, 1956; also articles. Home: 3111 N Middlebrooks Circle Tallahassee FL 32303

CRAIG, ROBERT CHARLES, educator; b. Sault Sainte Marie, Mich., Mar. 9, 1921; s. Frank Lyle and Sylva (Crowell) C.; B.S., Mich. State U., 1943, M.A., 1948; Ph.D., Tchrs. Coll., Columbia U., 1952; m. Rosalie Esther DeBoer, Sept. 2, 1950; children—Bruce R., Stephen F., Jeffrey A., Barbara Anne. Research asso. Columbia U. Tchrs. Coll., 1950-52; asst. prof. U. Wash., Pullman, 1952-55; research scientist Am. Insts. for Research, Pitts., 1955-58, cons. for ednl. research, 1958—; asso. prof. Marquette U., Milw., 1958-62, prof., 1962-66; prof., chmn. dept. counseling and ednl. psychology Mich. State U., East Lansing, 1966—, dir. U.S. Office Edn. Grad. research tng. program, 1966—. Lectr. psychology U. Pitts., 1956-57, dir. Project TALENT, 1957-58. Served to lt. (j.g.) USNR, 1943- 46. Fellow A.A.A.S., Am. Psychol. Assn.; mem. Am. Ednl. Research Assn., Nat. Council Measurement in Edn., Sigma Xi, Phi Delta Kappa, Phi Kappa Phi. Author: Transfer Value of Guided Learning, 1953; (with A.M. Dupuis), American Education, Origins and Issues, 1963; Psychology of Learning in the Classroom, 1966; (with H. Clarizio, William Mehrens) Contemporary Issues in Educational Psychology, 1969. Research on discovery versus reception learning. Home: 1006 Wildwood Dr East Lansing MI 48823

CRAIG, ROBERT WALLACE, design corp. exec., ednl. cons.; b. Long Beach, Cal., Sept. 16, 1924; s. Harold Fleming and Ellen Amelia (Stagg) C.; B.A. cum laude, U. Wash., 1949, B.S., 1950; M.A., Columbia, 1951; m. Carol Williams Gallun, Nov. 5, 1957; children—Kathleen Elizabeth, Jennifer Courtney, Michael Brian. Mountaineer, explorer Alaska Coast Range, 1946, Alaska Range, 1947; mem. 3d Am. Karakoram Expdn. to K2, 1953; cons. on equipment mountain and cold weather operations Dept. Army, 1951-54; exec. dir. Aspen (Colo) Inst. Humanistic Studies, 1954-64; v.p., dir. Unimark Design, Inc., 1965-71; partner, dir. Genesis Design, Inc., 1971—; prin. Robert Craig & Assos., 1966—. Trustee, v.p. Aspen Center for Physics, Indsl. Areas Found., Park City Inst. Arts and Scis.; nat. council Nature Conservancy. Served to lt. (j.g.) USNR, 1943-46. Mem. Am. Philos. Assn., A.A.A.S., Washington Inst. Fgn. Affairs. Clubs: Am. Alpine; Explorers, Cactus (Denver). Co-author: K2, The Savage Mountain, 1954. Address: PO Box 1725 Aspen CO 81611

CRAIG, SAMUEL BAUGHMAN, ret. educator; b. Stanford, Ky., Mar. 19, 1901; s. Dr. William Newton and Susan Taylor (Baughman) C.; A.B., Centre Coll., Danville, Ky., 1923, Litt.D. (hon.), 1951; A.M., Gallaudet Coll., Washington, 1925, Litt.D. (hon.) 1951; A.M., George Washington U., 1928; grad. student Am. U., U. Ky.; m. Hazel Naomi Thompson, June 12, 1930; children—William Newton, Samuel Baughman. Inst. Kentucky School for Deaf, 1923-24; prin. Kendall Sch. for the Deaf, 1925-46; instr. tchr. tng. Gallaudet Coll., 1925-46, in charge dept., 1927-46, prof. edn., 1939-46; supt. Western Pa. Sch. for Deaf, 1946-69, trustee, 1970—. Recipient Alumni Recognition award Centre Coll. Ky. Alumni Assn., 1970; Merit award Conf. Execs. Am. Schs. for Deaf, 1968; Community Service citation Pa. Acad. Opthalmology and Otobryngology, 1968. Mem. Conf. Execs. Am. Schs. for Deaf (pres. 1947-51), So. Soc. Philos. and Psychol., Conv. Am. Instrs. of Deaf, S.A.R., Pitts. Hearing Soc. (dir.), Community Hearing Council (past pres.), Am. Speech and Hearing Assn., Kappa Gamma, Phi Delta Kappa. Clubs: Cosmos (Washington), Edgewood (Pa.); University (Pitts.); Rotary (past pres.). Address: 3313 Sheffield Circle Sarasota FL 33580

CRAIG, STEPHEN WRIGHT, lawyer; b. N.Y.C., Aug. 28, 1932; s. Herbert Stanley and Dorothy (Simmons) C.; A.B., Harvard, 1954, J.D., 1959; m. Margaret M. Baker, June 10, 1958; children-Amela Audrey, Janet Elizabeth, Peter Baker. Reporter, Daily Kennebec Jour., Augusta, Me., 1956; engaged in pub. relations with Am. Savoyards, 1957; atty. Internal Revenue Service, San Francisco, 1959-61; atty.-adviser U.S. Tax Ct., 1961-63; partner firm Snell & Wilmer, Phoenix, 1963—; guest lectr. Amos Tuck Sch. Bus., Dartmouth, 1962; lectr. Ariz. and N.M. Tax Insts., 1966-67. Chmn. Jane Wayland Child Guidance Center, 1968-70 mem. Maricopa County Health Planning Council, 1969—. Mem. Ariz. Republican Com., 1967—. Bd. dirs. Combined Met. Phoenix Arts, 1968, adb. bd., 1968-69; adv. bd. Ariz. State U. Tax Insts., 1968-70; bd. dirs. Phoenix Chamber Music Soc., 1968- 69. Phoenix Community Counceil, 1970—; Served with AUS, 1954-56, Mem. Am. County bar assns., state bars Ariz., Cal. Me., Ariz. Acad., Hasty Pudding Inst., Sigma Alpha Epsilon. Home: 5387 N 46th Pl Phoenix AZ 85018 Office: Security Bldg Phoenix AZ 85004

CRAIG, SYDNEY POLLOCK, banker; b. Noblesville, Ind., Jan. 28, 1921; s. Sydney P. and Kathryn (Couden) C.; student Earlham Coll., 1939-40; B.S., Purdue U., 1947; m. Elizabeth White, Nov. 18, 1941; children—Elizabeth (Mrs. Michael Ertel), Sydney Pollock III. Co-mgr. David A. Noyes & Co., Indpls., 1961-65; vice-pres. investments Lincoln Nat. Bank & Trust Co., Ft. Wayne, Ind., 1965-68; sr. v.p., trust officer Worcester County Nat. Bank (Mass.), 1968—. Served with USAAF, World War II. Decorated Air medal. Mem. Mass. Bankers Assn. (exec. council trust div. 1970—), Worcester Estate Planning Council, Boston Security Analysts Soc., Purdue U. Alumni Assn., Earlham Coll. Alumni Assn. Mem. Soc. Friends. Clubs: Worcester Country Club, Worcester Club: Home: 5 Suburban Rd Worcester MA 01602 Office: 446 Main St Worcester MA 01608

CRAIG, WALTER, television-radio cons.; b. St. Louis, Dec. 5, 1900; s. Frank E. and May (Goodrich) C.; student Westminster Coll., Fulton, Mo., 1918; m. Margaret Guthrie Gray, Sept. 13, 1946; 1 dau., Patricia Anne. Vaudeville Actor, Keith and Orpheum Circuits, 1920-22; juvenile leads musical comedy, Broadway and road, 1923-29; dir. programs World Broadcasting System, N.Y.C. 1930-32; independent radio prodn., 1933-38; radio dir. Street & Finney, Inc., N.Y.C. 1939-40; dir. programs radio sta. WMCA, N.Y. City, 1940-42; radio dir. Benton & Bowles, Inc., 1943-45, v.p. in charge radio, 1945-47, v.p. in charge radio and television 1948-53; v.p. advt. dir. Phamaceuticals Inc., 1953-54; partner Norman, Craig & Kummel, Inc., 1955-60, TV cons., 1960—; pres. First Fla. Funding Corp., Sarasota, Fla., 1961-67; creative dir. Hansen-Rubensohn-McCann-Erickson, Sydney, Australia, 1967-69; dir. Guaranteed Weather, Inc. Mem. Sarasota C. of C. Am. Assn. of Advt. Agencies (chmn. radio and TV prodn. com., 1948-53), Assn. Nat. Advertisers, Dramatists Guild,, Author's League, Clubs: Sarasota Yacht; Athletic (N.Y.C.); Australian International (Sydney). Lectr. on TV N.Y. U., 1947-59. Home: 175 Morningside Dr Lido Shores Sarasota FL 33577 Office: Citizens Bank Bldg Sarasota FL 33578

CRAIG, WALTER EARLY, judge; b. Oakland, Cal., May 26, 1909; s. Jubal Early and Marie (Craig) C.; A.B., Stanford, 1931, LL.B., 1934; LL.D., Ariz. State U., 1963, U. San Diego, 1964; S.J.D., Suffolk U., 1964; m. Meta Elizabeth Jury, Oct. 25, 1935; children—William Early, Meta Lucille. Admitted to Cal. bar, 1934, Ariz. Bar, 1936; legal dept. regional office HOLO, 1934-36; practice of law, Fennemore, Craig, Allen & Bledsoe, Phoenix, 1936-55, Fennemore, Craig, Allen & McClennen, 1955-64; U.S. judge Ariz. dist., 1964—. Me. Ariz. Code Commn., 1951-56; appeal agt. Maricopa County Selective Service, 1945-64; mem. Ariz. Jud. Council, 1950-63. Bd. dirs. Sun Angel Found.; exec. com. planning county hosp., offices, 1952-60; bd. visitors Stanford U. Sch. Law, 1958-63; bd. dirs. Maricopa County Hosp. Devel. Assn., 1955-62; bd. dirs. Ariz. State U. Found.; chmn. bd. visitors Ariz. State U. Coll. Law. Served with USN, World War II. Decorated Order of the Southern Cross (Brazil). Fellow Am. Bar Found.; mem. Am. Law Inst., Am. (state chmn. jr. bar conf., ho. dels. 1947-61, bd. govs. 1958-61, pres. 1963-64), Ariz. (pres. 1951-52), Maricopa County (pres. 1941) bar assns., Am. Judicature Soc. (dir. 1951-61), Inter-Am. (council), Internat. (council), Canadian (hon.) bar assns., Assn. Bar of City, N.Y., El Ilustre y Nacional Colegio de Abogados de Mexico (hon.), El Colegio de Abogados de la Ciudad de Buenos Aires (hon.). Colegio de Abogados del Uruguay (hon.), W. States Bar Council (pres. 1956-57), Am. Legion, Phi Gamma Delta, Phi Delta Phi, Elk, Clubs: University Rotary, Arizona, Phoenix Country, Kiva, Stanford (past pres.), Thunderbirds (past pres.) (all Phoenix). Home: 2020 E Bethany Home Rd Phoenix AZ 85016 Office: US Court House Phoenix AZ 85003

CRAIG, WILLIAM GARROTT, lawyer; b. nr. Owingsville, Ky., June 3, 1917; s. William L. and Media (Smith) C.; A.B., U. Ky., 1939; J.D., Harvard, 1948; m. Mary Margaret Wolf Sept. 2, 1938; children-Mary Stanley, William G. Div. mgr. D.T. Davis Co., 1939-41; partner King & Craig, Henderson, Ky., 1948-56, Sandidge, Holbrook & Craig, Owensboro, Ky., 1957-60, Sandidge, Holbrook, Craig & Hager, Owensboro, 1960—. Gen. counsel Western Ky. Gas Co., 1947- -; dir., gen. counsel Wesken Corp.; pres. Griffin Contracting Co. Served to maj. AUS, 1942-46. Mem. Owensboro-Daviess County C. of C., Am., Fed. Power, Ky., Davies County bar assns., Am. Judicature Soc., Acad. Polit. Sci., Internat. Platform Assn., Am. Acad. Polit. and Social Sci., Delta Chi. Democrat. Mem. Disciples of Christ Ch. Club: Roscoe Pound Law (Harvard Law Sch.). Home: 1708 Griffith Av Owensboro KY 42301 Office: 1St Ann Bldg Owensboro KY 42301

CRAIG, WILLIAM HENRY HAYS diversified mfg. co. exec.; b. Cin., May 21, 1910; grad. Phillips Acad., Andover, Mass., 1927; B.S., Princeton, 1931; postgrad. Mass. Inst. Tech., 1931-33; m. Jean R. Holland, June 16, 1935; children--Lois A., Andrew M., James. Salesman, Brown Mfg. Co., Boston, 1932-33; jr. engr. Ball Metals Co., Carson City, Nev., 1933-36, engr., 1936-37, sr. engr., 1937-40; project engr. Kingston Engring. Co., Los Angeles, 1940-43; with dept. engring. City of Denver, 1946-50, dep. head, 1950-52; 2d v.p. Johnson Mfg. Co., Kansas City, Kansas, 1952-54, v.p. for engring., 1954-57; v.p. research Consol. Industries, Inc., South Bend, Ind., 1957-60, exec. v.p., 1960-65, pres., 1965-70, chmn. bd., chief exec. officer, 1970--, also dir.; dir. ABC Chem. Co., 2d Nat. Bank, Country Food Storage Co., Providence Indsl. Corp. Pres., Dewey High Sch., Kansas City, Mo., 1953-54; fund chmn. local div. Salvation Army, 1959-60. Mem. South Bend Republican Com., 1964-68. Bd. dirs. Ind. council Boy Scouts Am., 1969-71; trustee Lovell Found. Served to lt., Corps Engrs., AUS, 1943-45. Decorated Bronze Star medal. Member N.A.M., South Bend C. of C. (v.p. 1963-65, dir. 1965-70), Am. Mgmt. Assn., Ind. Engrs. Soc. (program com. 1961-63), Princeton Alumni Assn. Episcopalian. Home: 6823 Broad Terrace Av South Bend IN 46505

CRAIG, WILMOT RUSSELL, banker; b. Meriden, Conn., Dec. 26, 1909; s. George R. and Elsie (Cory) C.; A.B., Allegheny Coll., 1933; certificate Rutgers U. Grad. Sch. Banking, 1947; m. Jean A. Morse, Feb. 18, 1939. With trust dept. Guaranty Trust Co. of N.Y., N.Y.C., 1933-36; asst. trust officer Lincoln Rochester Trust Co. (N.Y.), 1936-51, v.p., trust officer, 1951-56, v.p. sr. trust officer, 1956, exec. v.p., 1957-61, pres., 1961-65, pres., chmn. bd., 1965-68, chmn. bd., chief exec. officer, 1968-70, chmn. bd., 1970—; dir., pres., chief exec. officer Lincoln First Banks Inc. (formerly Lincoln First Group Inc.), 1967—; dir. Rochester Gas and Electric Corp., Cin. Milacron Inc., Gannett Co., Inc., Sybron Corp., Armotek Industries, Inc., Palmyra, N.J., McCurdy & Co., Lincoln Rochester Trust Co., Widmer's Wine Cellars, Inc., Mixing Equipment Co., Inc. Dir. Rochester Credit Center, Inc.; pres. Rochester Clearing House Assn., 1966-67; trustee Found. for Full Service Banks. Bd. dirs. Rochester Community Chest, Inc., Met. Rochester Housing Found.; trustee Rochester Bus. Opportunities Corp.; dir., past pres. Rochester YMCA; trustee Otetiana council trust fund Boy Scouts Am., U. Rochester, Allegheny Coll., Meadville, Pa.; v.p., trustee Frank E. Gannett Newspaper Found.; dir. Rochester Gen. Hosp., N.Y. Higher Edn. Assistance

Corp. Mem. Rochester C. of C. (trustee 1965-67), Am. (exec. council 1965-68, co-vice chmn. com. on urban affairs), N.Y. State (pres. 1964-65) bankers assns., Assn. Registered Bank Holding Cos. (dir.), Clubs: Country of Rochester, Genesee Valley, University. Home: 15 Evergreen Lane Rochester NY 14618 Office: 183 E Main St PO Box 1939 Rochester NY 14603

CRAIGHEAD, CLAUDE C., physician; b. Shreveport, La., Aug. 30, 1914; s. Claude C. and Elizabeth (Lindley) C.; B.A., La. Tech. U., 1934; M.D., La. State U., 1939; m. Edith Dorrell; children—Mary Elizabeth, Claude C. III, Ann Dorrell. Intern, Charity Hosp., New Orleans, 1939-40, resident surgery, 1940, 46- 49, now sr. vis. surgeon; practice medicine, specializing in surgery, New Orleans; sr. in surgery Touro Infirmary; clin. prof. surgery Sch. Medicine, La. State U.; mem. active staff, chief dept. surgery Flint- Goodridge Hosp.; mem. courtesy staff Sara Mayo Hosp., New Orleans, Terrebonne Gen. Hosp., Houma, La.; mem. cons. staff VA Hosp., New Orleans; mem. adv. com. East Jefferson Gen. Hosp. Trustee Med. Group Research Fund. Served to maj. AUS, 1940-45. Recipient award for teaching New Orleans Surg. Soc., 1964. Diplomate Am. Bd. Surgery. Fellow Am. Coll. Chest Physicians, A.C.S. (past chpt. pres.), Southeastern Surg. Congress; mem. Surg. Assn. La. (program chmn., past pres., dir.), So. Surg. Assn., A.M.A., La. (past sect. chmn.), Orleans Parish (dir., v.p.) med. socs., So. Thoracic Surg. Assn., La. Thoracic Soc., New Orleans (pres., dir.), James D. Rives (pres., dir.) surg. socs., New Orleans Grad. Med. Assembly (com. chmn.). Contbr. articles profl. jours. Home: 1237 Washington Av New Orleans LA 70130 Office: 3636 St Charles Av New Orleans, LA 70115.

CRAIGHEAD, RODKEY, banker; b. Pitts., July 24, 1916; s. Ernest S. and Florence L. (Rodkey) C.; B.S., U. Pitts., 1942; postgrad. Grad. Sch. Banking, U. Wis., 1959- 61; m. Carol M. Price, June 26, 1943; children—Rodkey, Virginia, Corinne. With Mellon Nat. Bank, Pitts., 1936-41, Detroit Bank & Trust Co., 1946—, v.p., 1961-65, sr. v.p. comml. loans, 1966-69, exec. v.p., 1969—; dir. Broad Hollow Estates, Inc., Farmingdale, N.Y., Winkelman Stores, Inc., Detroit. Served to capt. AUS, 1942-46. Mem. Robert Morris Assos., Greater Detroit Bd. Commerce. Presbyn. (trustee). Clubs: Detroit Athletic, Economic (Detroit); Orchard Lake Country; Leland Country; Otsego Ski (Gaylord, Mich.). Home: 1343 Orchard Ridge Rd Bloomfield Hills MI 48013 Office: Fort at Washington Detroit MI 48321

CRAIGIE, LAURENCE C., former USAF officer; b. Concord, N.H., Jan. 26, 1902; s. John H. and Florence Marion (Carbee) C.; B.S., U.S. Mil. Acad., 1923; grad. AC Engring. Sch., 1935, Army Indsl. Coll., 1939, AC Tactical Sch., 1940; m. Henrietta Victoria Morrison, Dec. 16, 1925; children—Gale Morrison, John Harrold. Commd. 2d lt. AC, U.S. Army, 1923, advanced through grades to lt. gen., 1952; instr. Brooks and Kelly Fields Tex., 1923-28; engring. officer France Field, C.Z., 1929-31; flight comdr. Brooks and Randolph Fields, Tex., 1931-34; project officer tng. and transport aircraft Wright Field, Dayton, O., 1935-38; chief, exptl. aircraft projects sect. Wright Field, 1939-43; comdg. officer Boston Wing, I Fighter Command, 1943; comdg. gen. N.Y. Wing, I Fighter Command, Fighter Wing MTO, 1944; dep. chief engr. div., Air. Tech. Service Command, Wright Field, 1945; chief engring. div. Air Materiel Command, Wright Field, 1945; dir. research and devel. Hdqrs. USAF, 1947; comdt. USAF Inst. Tech., Wright-Patterson AFB, Dayton, 1948; vice comdr., chief of staff Far East Air Forces, Tokyo, 1950; dep. chief of staff (devel.) Dept. Air Force, 1952; comdr. Allied Air Forces, So. Europe, Naples, Italy, 1954, ret. 1955; v.p. Hydro-Aire Inc., 1956; v.p. Am. Machine & Foundry Co., 1957-64; dir. Air Force requirements Lockheed Aircraft Corp., 1964—; dir. Flying Tiger Line, Inc. Bd. dirs. Internat. Sci. Found., pres., 1971. Decorated D.S.M. with oak leaf cluster, Legion of Merit with oak leaf cluster, D.F.C., Air medal (U.S.); Legion of Honor (France); Ulchi and Gugseon medals (Republic Korea); Grand Ufficiale Al Merito Della Republica Italiana, 1957. Fellow Inst. Aero. Scis. (v.p. 1957); mem. Am. Rocket Soc., Am. Ordnance Assn. (v.p. 1970-71, pres. Los Angeles chpt. 1967), Am. Inst. Aeros. and Astronautics. Clubs: Jonathan, Lakeside Golf (Los Angeles); Burning Tree (Washington). Home: 4244 Clybourn Av Burbank CA 91505 Office: PO Box 551 Burbank CA 91503

CRAIGMYLE, RONALD M., investment banker; b. Toronto, Ont. Can., June 19, 1896; s. James M. and Jessie (Gregory) C.: A.B., Columbia, 1920, B.S. in Bus., 1921; m. Louise de Rochemont, Apr. 10, 1923; children-Ronald M., Mary Louise, Robert de Rochemont. With Minsch, Monell & Co., 1920-24; partner Burley, Peabody & Craigmyle, N.Y.C., 1924-26, Craigmyle & Co.,later Craigmyle, Pinney & Co., then Fahnestock & Co., mems. N.Y. Stock Exchange, 1926—; chmn. Giant Portland Cement Co.; dir. Consol. Rock Products Co. Vice pres. Intercollegiate Flying Assn., 1919-21. Dep. mayor Village Matinecock, N.Y. Trustee Columbia U., 1957-63. Mem. Psi Upsilon. Republican. Episcopalian. Clubs: Piping Rock, Beaver Dam; Bond, Columbia University, Metropolitan, Bankers, N.Y. Stock Exchange Luncheon, Pilgrims Society, Recess, St. Andrews Society (N.Y.C.); Creek; Seawanhaka;; Everglades; Bath and Tennis; Gulf Stream; Seminole Golf; California (Los Angeles); Meadow Brook (N.Y.). Home: Piping Rock Rd Box 321 Locust Valley NY 11560 Office: 110 Wall St New York City, NY 10005

CRAIN, BLUFORD WALTER, Jr., architect; b. Longview, Tex., Jan. 31, 1914; s. Bluford Walter and Ethel (Smith) C.; B.Arch., U. Tex., 1937; M.Arch., Harvard, 1939; m. Ann Lacy, Dec. 28, 1946; children—Lacy, Bluford Walter III, Rogers. Partner, Wilson, Morris, Crain & Anderson, Longview, 1946—; v.p. Rogers Lacy, Inc., Longview, 1947—; dir. Longview Nat. Bank. Served to lt. USNR, 1941-45. Decorated Purple Heart. Fellow A.I.A.; mem. Tex. Soc. Architects (dir. 1966), Kappa Sigma. Presbyn. (deacon 1965). Home: PO Box 2146 Longview TX 75603 Office: PO Box 352 Longview TX 75601

CRAIN, CHARLES MOODY, educator; b. Holyoke, Mass., Oct. 2, 1924; s. Orville Edward and Mae (Moody) C.; A.B. summa cum laude Bowdoin Coll., 1946; A.M., Harvard, 1948, Ph.D., 1952. Mem. faculty Norwich U., 1953—, prof. French, 1961—, chmn. dept. modern languages, 1955—. Served with AUS, 1943-46. Mem. Phi Beta Kappa, Kappa Sigma. Home: 6 Hill St Northfield VT 05663

CRAIN, G.D., Jr., pres., publisher Advertising Publs., Inc., publishers Advt. Age, Advt. Requirements, Indsl. Marketing, Market Data & Directory Number, now chmn. Address: 740 Rush St Chicago IL 60611

CRAIN, J. WENDELL, med. mfg. co. exec.; b. Roff, Okla., May 20, 1918; s. Aubrey J. and Alyce (Sharrock) C.; B.S., Northwestern U., 1941; M.B.A., Harvard, 1947; LL.B., George Washington U., 1956; m. Louise Pappas, Jan. 17, 1942; children—Carol Louise, Laura Elise. Admitted to N.J. bar, 1957; v.p. Am. Hosp. Supply Corp., Evanston, Ill., 1960-62, pres. supply div., 1962-65, group v.p., 1965-68; pres., chief exec. officer, dir. C. R. Bard Inc., Murray Hill, N.J., 1968—; dir. Summit & Elizabeth Trust Co., New Court Private Equity Corp., N.Y.C. Bd. dirs. Kessler Inst., Orange, N.J. Served to lt. col. USMCR, 1941-46. Decorated Silver Star, Purple Heart. Presbyn. Club: Baltusrol Country (Springfield, N.J.). Home: 144 Rotary Dr Summit NJ 07901 Office: 731 Central Av Murray Hill NJ 07909

CRAIN, JEANNE, actress; b. Barstow, Cal., May 25, 1925; d. George A. and Loretta (Carr) Crain; student U. Cal., Los Angeles, 1942; m. Paul Frederick Brinkman, Dec. 31, 1945; children—Paul Frederick, Michael Anthony, Timothy. Actress Twentieth Century-Fox Studios 1943—; screen debut as feature player Home in Indiana, 1944; other motion pictures include Margie, 1946, Apartment for Peggy, 1948, Letter to Three Wives, 1948, Pinky, 1949, Take Care of My Little Girl, 1951, People Will Talk, 1951, The Joker is Wild, 1957; Guns of the Timberland, 1960; The Joker, 1961, Tattered Dress, Fastest Gun Alive, Gentlemen Marry Brunettes. Roman Catholic. Home: Outpost Cove Hollywood CA 90028 Office: care Twentieth Century-Fox Studios 10201 W Pico Blvd Los Angeles CA 90064

CRAIN, JON, opera singer; b. St. Louis, Oct. 30, 1923; s. Richard Gorman and Josephine (Haley) Crowe; student Washington U., 1939-40, Oscar Seagle Music Sch., 1940-43, Juilliard Music Sch., 1946-47, Am. Theatre Wing, 1946-48; studied with Paul Althouse, Enrico Rosati and Joseph Regneas; m. Rose Mary Allegretti, June 17, 1941; children-Jon David, Michael. Operatic debut in Madam Butterfly, 1948; debut N.Y. City Opera Co., 1951, Met. Opera Co., 1953, Opera de Bellas Artes, Mexico City, 1950; recitalist, oratorio singer; leading tenor Met. Opera Co., N.Y. City Opera Co., San Francisco Opera Co.; toured with Met. Opera Co., presenting Fledermaus, 1951; appeared in N.Y. premiere Tender Land, others; in leading tenor roles, The Trail, Troilus and Cressida, School for Wives, Susannah. Dialogues of the Carmelits, other operas; European debut Tales of Hoffmann, Geneva, Switzerland, 1966; now prof. Creative Arts Center W. Va. U. Served with AUS, 1943-46, Mem. Honarium Americana, Am. Guild Musical Artists, Actors Equity Inc., Am. Guild Radio and TV Artists, Am. Assn. U. Profs. Republican. Roman Catholic. K.C. Clubs; Bohemian, Kiwanis (Oneonta, N.Y.). Home:80- 50 Baxter Av Elmhurst, NY; also 670 Westview Morgantown WV 26505 Office: care Columbia Artists, Inc. 165 W 57th St New York City, NY 10019.

CRAIN, WILBERT OSCAR, lawyer; b. Nacogdoches, Tex., Aug. 20, 1905; s. William O. and (Weeks) C.; B.A., Rice U., 1927; LL.B., U. Tex., 1931; m. Estela Groce, Nov. 30, 1940; 1 son, Wilbert Oscar. Admitted to Tex. bar, 1931; with firm Vinson, Elkins, Weems & Searls, Houston, 1931-45; atty. United Gas Corp., United Gas Pipe Line, also Union Producing Co., 1945-51, gen. counsel, 1951-67. Home: 6330 Querbes Dr Shreveport LA 71106

CRAINE, CLYDE PRATT, Jr., educator; b. Detroit, Jan. 20, 1912; s.Clyde Pratt and Mary C; A.B., U. Notre Dame, 1934; B.A. in English, Oxford U., 1938, M.A., 1940; m. Helen Ryan, June 15, 1940; children—Susan, Clyde III, Michael, Peter. Faculty, U. Detroit, 1938—, prof. English, 1958—, chmn. dept., 1961-64. Mem. library council U. Notre Dame. Mem. Modern Lang. Assn., Coll. English Assn., Nat. Council Tchrs. English, Am. Assn. U. Profs. Home: 952 Brookwood Ct Birmingham, MI 48009. Office: 4001 W McNichols St Detroit MI 48221

CRAINE, JOHN PARES, bishop; b. Cleve., June 28, 1911; s. John Lee and Hilda B. (Wright) C.; A.B., Kenyon Coll., 1932, D.D., 1952; B.D., Bexley Hall, 1935; m. Esther Judson Strong, May 31, 1940; children—Susan Lee, Elizabeth Burnaby, John Pares II. Student minister St. Mark's, Cleve., 1933-35; ordained to ministry P.E. Ch., 1935; minister-in-charge St. Philip's Ch., Cleve., 1935-36; curate Trinity Ch., Santa Barbara, Cal., 1936-38; rector Trinity Ch., Oakland, Cal., 1938-41; canon Grace Cathedral, San Francisco, 1941-44; rector Trinity Parish Ch., Seattle, 1944-50, Christ Ch., Indpls., 1950-57, also dean Christ Ch. Cathedral, Indpls., 1953-57; consecrated bishop-coadjutor Diocese of Indpls., 1957, diocesan, 1959—. Chmn. nat. standing com. on structure; mem. Ind. council Nat. Council on Crime and Deliquency. Chmn. bd. trustees Kenyon Coll.; trustee Howe Mil. Sch., Ind. U. Sch. Religion; pres. Indpls. Urban League; chmn. bd. Episcopal Radio-TV Found.; bd. dirs. Methodist Hosp., Indpls. Mem. Indpls. Hosp. Devel. Assn., Nat. Conf. Christians and Jews, J.W. Riley Meml. Assn., Loyal Legion, Newcomen Soc., Phi Beta Kappa. Clubs: Woodstock, Columbia (Indpls.). Home: 4164 Washington Blvd Indianapolis IN 46205 Office: 1100 W 42d St Indianapolis IN 46208

CRALEY, NATHANIEL NEIMAN, Jr., govt. ofcl.; b. Red Lion, Pa., Nov. 17, 1927; s. Nathaniel Neiman and Alverta (Peters) C.; grad. Taft Sch., 1946; A.B., Gettysburg Coll., 1950; m. Ruth Fortenbaugh, June 24, 1950; children—Sarah Beth, Nathaniel Neiman III, Harry E., Stacy Anne; m. 2d, Janet W. Dize, May 17, 1968; children—Cynthia Dize, Patricia Dize. Engaged in furniture mfg., Red Lion, 1950-65; instr. econs. and history York Jr. Coll., 1958-60; mem. 89th Congress from 19th Dist. of Pa.; dir. pub. affairs Trust Ty. of Pacific, 1967—. Charter mem., treas. York County Planning Comm.; mem. York Charter Study Com., mem. York Parking Authority. Chmn. York County Democratic Com. Mem. house com. York YMCA; bd. dirs., past pres. York County Heart Assn.; bd. dirs., 1st v.p. York County Council Community Services; bd. dirs. York County Council Human Relations, White Rose Motor Club (AAA). Mem. Saipan C. of C. (dir.). Lutheran (tchr. Sunday sch.). Rotarian. Home: PO Box 241 Capitol Hill Saipan Mariana Islands 96950 Office: Trust Territory of Pacific Saipan Mariana Islands 96950

CRALLEY, ELZA MONROE, agrl. adminstr.; b. Carmi, Ill., Nov. 20, 1905; s. John W. and Martha (Jones) C.; B.S., McKendree Coll., 1928; Ph.D., U. Wis., 1931; m. Cleda Ann Renner, Feb. 5, 1930; children—Barbara Ann (Mrs. Roy Shaw), Patricia Sue (Mrs. Philip E. Duncan). Asst. dept. botany U. Wis., 1928-31; successively instr., asst. prof., asso. prof. dept. plant pathology U. Ark., 1931-46, prof., 1948-52, prof., head dept., 1953-59; dir. Ark. Agrl. Expt. Sta., 1959—; pathologist U.S. Mil. Govt., Korea, 1947, Point 4 Program, Panama, 1952; cons. pathologist, Cuba, 1955, Ford Found., India, 1959. Named Ark. Man of the Year, Progressive Farmer, 1970. Mem. Alpha Zeta, Gamma Sigma Delta. Episcopalian. Rotarian. Contbr. articles in field to sci. jours. Home: 1502 Cedar St Fayetteville AR 72701

CRAM, DONALD JAMES, educator; b. Chester, Vt., April 22, 1919, s. William Moffet and Joanna (Shelley) C.; B.S., Rollins Coll., 1941; M.S., U. Neb., 1942; Ph.D. (Nat. Research fellow), Harvard, 1947; m. Jane Maxwell, Nov. 25, 1969. Research chemist Merck and Co., 1942-45; asst. prof. chemistry U. Cal. at Los Angeles, 1947-50, asso. prof., 1950-56. prof. 1956—. Chem. cons. Upjohn Co., 1952—, Union Carbide Co., 1960—; State Dept. exchange fellow to Inst. de Quimica, Nat. U. Mexico, summer 1956; guest prof. U. Heidelberg (Germany), summer 1958. Am. Chem. Soc. fellow, 1947-48, Guggenheim fellow, 1954-55; guest lectr., South Africa, 1967. Named Young Man of Year, Cal. Jr. C. of C., 1954; award for creative work in synthetic organic chemistry Am. Chem. Soc., 1965; Herbert Newby McCoy award, 1965; award for creative research organic chemistry Synthetic Organic Chemical Mfrs. Assn., 1965, Mem. Am. Chem. Soc., Nat. Acad. Scis., Am. Acad. Arts and Scis., Chem. Soc. (Eng.), Sigma Xi, Lambda Chi Alpha. Club: San Onofre Surfing. Author: (with J.B. Hendrickson and G. S. Hammond) Organic Chemistry (textbook), 1970; Fundamentals of Carbanian Chemistry, 1965; (with John H. Richards and G. S. Hammond) Elements of Organic Chemistry, 1967. Contbr. chapts. in Steric Effects in Organic Chemistry, also articles in field of sterochemistry, mold metabolites, large ring chemistry. Home: 1250 Roscomare Rd Los Angeles CA 90024

CRAM, REGINALD MAURICE, state ofcl.; b. Northfield, Vt., Apr. 29, 1914; s. Archie Rice and Beatrice (Cleveland) C.; B.S., Norwich U., 1936; postgrad. Boston U. Law Sch., 1937-38, Air Force Intelligence Sch., 1943, U.S. Army Command and Gen. Staff Coll., 1944, Nat. Art Sch., 1949, Armed Forces Staff Coll., 1951, State Dept. Fgn. Service Inst., 1961; M.A., U. Md., 1963; m. Kathryn E. Mosher, June 29, 1937; children—Robin (Mrs. Paul Lualdi), Marilyn Jane (Mrs. Vcevold Strekalovsky). With Office Adj. Gen. Vt., 1938-41; asst. U.S. property and disbursing officer State of Vt., 1946-47; commd. 2d lt. U.S. Army, 1936, advanced through grades to col. USAF, 1953; with anti-submarine campaign USAAF, 1941-42, Asiatic-Pacific Theatre with USMC, 1943-45; plans and operations officer Hdqrs. USAF, 1947-51; sec. Can./U.S. Regional Planning Group, NATO, 1951-54; dir. plans 3d USAF, Eng., 1954-55; with Supreme Hdqrs. Allied Powers, Europe, 1955-57; comdr. Orientation Group USAF, 1957-61; with Orgn. Joint Chiefs of Staff, 1961-64; ret., 1964; dep. adj. gen. Vt., 1964-66, adj. gen., 1967—. Mem. Vt. Com. on Adminstrv. Coordination, 1965—. Pres. Long Trail council Boy Scouts Am.; bd. dirs. Gen. Douglas MacArthur Awards Bd. Decorated Air medal with Gold Star medal (Navy), Joint Commendation medal, Air Force Commendation medal, Army Commendation medal. Mem. N.G. Assn. U.S. (chmn. legislative com.), Nat. Assn. Uniformed Services (dir.), Adj. Gen. Assn. U.S. (parliamentarian), N.G. Assn. Vt. (exec. council), Soc. Colonial Wars (dep. gov.-gen.), Ret. Officers Assn. (past dir.), Am. Legion (chmn. mil. affairs com. Vt.), V.F.W., Vt. Hist. Soc., Vt. Archeol. Soc., Theta Chi, Pi Sigma Alpha. Conglist. Mason, Rotarian. Home: 936 S Prospect St Burlington VT 05401 Office: Bldg #1 Camp Johnson Winooski VT 05404

CRAMBLETT, HENRY GAYLORD, pediatrician, virologist, educator; b. Scio, O., Feb. 8, 1929; s. Carl Smith and Olive (Fulton) C.; B.S., Mt. Union Coll., 1950; M.D., U. Cin., 1953; m. Donna Jean Reese, June 16, 1960; children—Deborah Kaye, Betsy Diane. Clin. research asso. Nat. Inst. Allergy and Infectious Diseases, Clin. Center, Bethesda, Md., 1955-57; faculty State U. Ia., 1957-60, asst. prof., 1958-60; faculty Bowman Gray Sch. Medicine, 1960-64, prof. pediatrics, 1963-64, dir. virology lab., 1960-64; prof. med. microbiology and pediatrics Ohio State U., Columbus, 1964—, exec. dir. Children's Hosp. Research Found., 1964—, chmn. dept. med. microbiology, 1966—. Sec. Ohio Med. Bd. Recipient Hoffheimer prize U. Cin., 1953, Eben J. Carey award in anatomy, 1950. Diplomate Am. Bd. Pediatrics, Am. Bd. Microbiology. Fellow Am. Acad. Microbiology, A.A.A.S.; mem. Infectious Diseases Soc. Am., So. Soc. for Pediatric Research (past pres.), Soc. for Pediatric Research, Am. Pediatric Soc., Am. Acad. Pediatrics, Midwest Soc. for Pediatric Research, Ohio Soc. Bacteriologists, Soc. for Exptl. Biology and Medicine, Am. Soc. for Microbiology, A.M.A., Alpha Omega Alpha. Research, publs. on etiologic assn. virus infections in illnesses of infants and children, estimation of importance of various viruses in morbidity and mortality in pediatric age group. Home: 2480 Sheringham Rd Columbus OH 43220

CRAMER, CLARENCE HENLEY, educator; b. Eureka, Kan., June 23, 1905; s. David H. and Irma E. (Henley) C.; A.B., B.S. in Edn., Ohio State U., 1927, A.M., 1928, Ph.D., 1931; m. Elizabeth A. Garman, Dec. 27, 1949. Asso. prof. history So. Ill. U., 1931-42; dir. personnel Nat. War Labor Bd., 1943-44, UNRRA Germany, 1944-47, Internat. Refugee Orgn., 1947-48; asso. and acting dean Western Res. U. Sch. Bus., 1949-54, dean Adelbert Coll., 1954-59, prof. history, 1949—, chmn. dept., 1963-67. Mem. Am. Hist. Assn., Orgn. Am. Historians, Ohio Hist. and Archeol. Assn., Phi Beta Kappa, Delta Tau Delta. Author: Royal Bob—The Life of Robert G. Ingersoll, 1952; Newton D. Baker—A Biography, 1961. Home: 11424 Cedar Rd Cleveland OH 44106

CRAMER, DALE LEWIS, educator; b. Dixon, Ill., June 25, 1924; s. Ray C. and Rebecca (Levan) C.; B.S., Bradley U., 1949, M.A., 1951; Ph.D., La. State U., 1958; m. Hula Jean Bond, Aug. 30, 1946; children—Becky (Mrs. Kenneth E. Theiss), Craig Alan, Randall Scott. Asst. prof. econs. La. State U., 1953-54, U. Tex. at El Paso, 1955-57, asso. prof., 1957-58; asso. prof. econs. U. Ala., 1958-63, prof., 1963—, head dept., 1968—. Served with AUS, 1943-46. Earhart Found. fellow, 1954-55. Mem. Am., So. econ. assns., Am. Assn. Univ. Profs., Omicron Delta Epsilon, Beta Gamma Sigma. Author: (with others) Public Finance, 1959; (with others) Economics: Principles of Income, Prices, and Growth, 1966; Workbook and Study Guide to Accompany Economics: Principles of Income, Prices and Growth, 1966; Instructor's Manual for Economics: Principles of Income, Prices and Growth, 1966. Home: 1348 Montclair Circle Tuscaloosa AL 35401 Office: Univ Alabama University AL 35486

CRAMER, EDWARD M., lawyer, performing rights licensing orgn. exec.; b. N.Y.C., May 27, 1925; s. Israel and Elsie (Neuman) C.; A.B., Columbia, 1947; LL.B. with distinction, Cornell U., Ithaca, N.Y., 1950; LL.M., N.Y. U., 1953; m. Henrietta Pantel, Sept. 7, 1947; children—Evin Joyce (Mrs. Ted Bronson), Marjorie Sue, Charles Harris. Admitted to N.Y. bar, 1950, also U.S. Supreme Ct.; teaching fellow N.Y. U. Sch. Law, 1950-51; with firm Rosenman, Colin, Kaye, Petshek, Freund & Emil, N.Y.C., 1951-60; pvt. practice law, also mem. firm Cramer & Hoffinger, N.Y.C., 1960-68; pres., chief exec. officer Broadcast Music, Inc., 1968—. Treas. Copyright Soc. U.S., 1963-68, bd. editors bull., 1953-63. Pres. Urban League N.J., 1955. Served with USNR, 1943-46. Mem. Order of Coif. Jewish religion. Home: 254 Chestnut St Englewood NJ 07631 Office: 589 Fifth Av New York City NY 10017

CRAMER, FREDERICK GAYLORD educator, biologist; b. Ames, Ia.; B.A., Ia. State U., 1936, M.A., 1937, Ph.D. with honors, 1940. Instr., Ia. State U., 1946-47; asst. prof. biology Johns Hopkins, 1947-50, asso. prof., 1950-62, prof., 1962--, chmn. dept., 1963-69; vis. lectr. Stanford, 1970-71. Active Boy Scouts Am., 4-H Club. Served with AUS, 1940-46. Mem. Am. Soc. Biologists, Md. Biologists, A.A.A.S., Am. Acad. Arts and Scis., Phi Beta Kappa. Home: 48936 W Hancock Blvd Baltimore MD 20206

CRAMER, LEONARD FREDERICK, bus. exec.; b. Alden, N.Y., Feb. 14, 1910; s. George F. and Nellie P. (Briggs) C.; grad. bus. administrn., Nichols Sch., Buffalo, 1930; student Newark Coll. Engring., 1940-41; m. Margery Claire Loewi, Jan. 19, 1935; 1 dau., Leni Claire. With Cadillac-LaSalle div. Gen. Motors Corp., Buffalo, 1930-31; mgr.-dir. North Pearl Garage, Inc., 1931-35; investigator Shell Oil Co., 1935-36; dir. sales. advt. Allen B. DuMont Labs., Inc., 1936-41, v.p. in charge sales. advt., govt. contracts, mfg. engring., 1941-45, dir., 1941-48, v.p., dir. TV broadcasting div., 1946-48, exec. v.p., dir. TV receiver div., 1948-51; asst. gen. mgr. Crosley Div. Avco Mfg. Corp., 1951-53, v.p. corp., 1952-53, v.p., gen. mgr. electronics div., 1953-55, v.p., dir. Crosley Radio & Television, Ltd., 1951-53, pres. 1953-55; v.p., dir. Avco of Can., Ltd., 1953-55; v.p., gen. mgr. TV-radio-phonograph div. The Magnavox Co., 1955-59; independent marketing and mgmt. cons., 1959-60; pres. Casco Products Corp., Bridgeport, Conn., 1960-62; exec. v.p., dir. Airtronics Internat. Corp., Fort Lauderdale, Fla.; pres. LCA, Inc.; dir. Chemair Electronics, Inc., Chgo. Hon. Trustee Pine Crest Sch., Ft. Lauderdale. Mem. Am. Arbitration Assn. (panel mem.), Newcomen Soc. Cin., Inst. Radio Engrs. Mason. (32, Shriner). Clubs: Sales Executives (N.Y.C.); Lake

Shore, Executives (Chgo.); Weimaraner of Am. (past pres., dir.). Home: 3132 NE 9th Av Ft Lauderdale FL 33304 Office: 905 N Atlantic Blvd Ft Lauderdale FL 33304

CRAMER, MAURICE BROWNING educator; b. Camden, N.J., Apr. 24, 1910; s. Alfred and Anna Browning (Doughten) C.; student William Penn Charter Sch., 1922-27; A.B., Princeton, 1931, M.A. 1934, Ph.D., 1937; m. Alice Carver, Aug. 24, 1935; children—Owen Carver, Maurice Browning. Instr. English dept. Mt. Holyoke Coll., 1934-40, asst. prof., 1940, reader entrance exam. bd., 1937, 38; asso. prof. U. Tampa, 1940-41, prof., 1941-42, chmn. English dept., 1940-42; lectr. English dept. Princeton, 1942-43; asst. prof. humanities U. Chgo., 1945-48, asso. prof., 1948-53, prof. humanities, 1953-59, chmn. humanities staff, 1951-57; Fulbright prof. Am. Life and Civilization, U. Athens (Greece), 1957-58; prof. English Pa. State U., University Park, 1959—; Thomas Shipley lectr. Haverford Coll., Pa., 1964; humanities cons., external examiner New Sch. Coll., N.Y.C., 1967-68. Recipient Quantrell award for excellence in undergraduate teaching, 1957. Mem. Modern Lang. Assn., Am. Civil Liberties Union. Am. Assn. U. Profs., Assn. Princeton Grad. Sch. Alumni (governing bd. 1964-68), Phi Beta Kappa. Author: Phoenix at East Hadley, 1941. Contbr. articles to profl. jours. Home: 445 Sierra Lane State College PA 16801 Office: Pa State U University Park PA 16802

CRAMER, MERWYN DEAN, life ins. co. exec.; b. Hardy, Neb., Oct. 19, 1909; s. Charles L. and Pearle (Scott) C.; B.S., U. Neb., 1931; m. Louise Westover, Feb. 18, 1933; childrenRobert, Richard, Jean, Larry, William, Caroly, Cathryn. With Bankers Life Ins. Co., 1925-, field v.p., 1961-63, agy. v.p., 1963- C.L.U. Mem. Life Ins. Agy. Mgmt. Assn., Agy. Officers Round Table, Am. Assn. C.L.U.'s (past pres. Los Angeles), U. Neb. Alumni Assn. (past pres. Los Angeles), Club: Des Moines, Home: 2825 Terrace Dr Des Moines, IA 50312 Office: 711 High St Des Moines IA 50307

CRAMER, MORGAN JOSEPH, Jr., internat. mgmt. exec.; b. Monessen, Pa., Oct. 6, 1906; s. Morgan J. and Cecilia (Michaels) C.; student mech. engring. Lehigh U., 1924-27; m. Miriam Fuchs, Jan. 28, 1933; 1 dau., Cynthia Jeanette, Various positions export and govt. sales operations P. Lorillard Co., 1931-46, export mgr., 1946-49, export and govt. sales mgr., 1949-54, dir. govt. operations, 1954-60, v.p., dir. internat. operations, 1960-61, dir., exec. com., pres., chief exec. officer, 1962-65; pres., chief exec. officer Royal Crown Cola Internat., Ltd., 1966-69, chmn. bd., chief exec. officer, 1969-70; v.p. internat. operations Royal Crown Cola Co., 1966-70; pres. Morgan J. Cramer Assos., Inc., N.Y.C., 1970—. Bd. dirs., exec. com. Internat. Center N.Y., Inc.; trustee N.Y. Polyclinic Hosp.; dir. Greater N.Y. Fund. Served as 1st lt. Q.M.C., AUS, 1943-46. Recipient commendation medal OQMG, 1946. Mem. Def. Supply Assn., Advt. Council, Nat. Fgn. Trade Council; Lehigh U. Alumni; Assn. (v.p.). ClubsMarco Polo, Sky, Lehigh University (N.Y.C.); Pelham (N.Y.) Country; Stanwich (Greenwich, Conn.). Home: 530 E 72d St New York City NY 10021 Office: 530 E 72d St New York City NY 10021

CRAMER, ROBERT EARL, coll. dean; b. Terre Haute, Ind., Aug. 9, 1914; s. Earl Ridgeway and Genevieve (Hayes) C.; B.S., Ind. State Tchrs. Coll., 1936; B.D., United Theol. Sem., Dayton, O., 1943; M.A., Yale, 1947, Ph.D., 1950; m. Mary Elizabeth Parker, Sept. 1, 1944; 1 dau., Deborah Lynn. Tchr. bus. Clyde (O.) High Sch., 1938-39, Charleston (Ill.) High Sch., 1940-42; chmn. dept. philosophy and psychology Ind. Central Coll., Indpls., 1947-54, dean, registrar, 1955-60, acad. dean, 1960—; chmn. dept. religion North Central Coll., Naperville, Ill., 1954-55; ordained elder United Methodist Ch., 1943. Mem. Pi Gamma Mu, Theta Phi. Mason. Club: Downtown Exchange (Indpls.). Home: 2525 Rutgers Rd Indianapolis IN 46227

CRAMER, ROBERT ELI, educator; b. Washington, June 19, 1919; s. John W. and Minnie (Smith) C.; A.B., Ohio U., 1943; S.M., U. Chgo., 1947, Ph.D., 1952; m. Margery Fay Reeser, Dec. 31, 1941; children-Judith Fay, Barbara E., Timothy R. Cartographic engr. Aero Chart and Information Center, St. Louis, 1942, 45-46, cartography cons., summer 1956; instr. geography J.S. Morton Jr. Coll., Cicero, Ill., 1947-50; asst. prof. Memphis State Coll., 1950-51; sr. indsl. research analyst Directorate of Intelligence USAF, Washington, 1951-54; prof. geography East Carolina Coll., Greenville, 1954-, chmn. dept., 1962- Mem. tech. adv. com. area devel. Gov. N.C. Spl. Adv. Com., 1960- N.C. Adv. Bd. on Peace Corps, Spl. Adv. Com. Gov. N.C., 1962. Served with USAAF, 1943-44. Mem. Assn. Am. Geographers, Nat. Council Geog. Edn. (N.C. coordinator geography, mem. exec. bd. 1962—). Author: Manufacturing Structure of the Cicero District, Metropolitan Chicago, 1952; A Work Book in Essentials of Cartography and Mapping, 1963; A Work Book in Earth and Man, 1967; Work book in Essentials of Map Reading and Interpretation, 1969. Contbr. articles profl. jours Home: 1408 Evergreen Dr Greenville, NC 27834.

CRAMER, ROBERT STANLEY, cons. co. exec.; b. Phila., Apr. 18, 1920; s. Samuel Franklin and Mildred (Katz) C.; A.B., George Washington U., 1941; m. Susan Hecht, June 10, 1957; children—Cathy Ann, Robert, Wendy. Reporter, feature writer, asst. Sunday editor Washington Post, 1937-41; editor, writer U.S. Office Coordinator Inter-Am. Affairs, 1941-45, press officer Rio de Janeiro, 1943-44, corr. U.S. South Atlantic Fleet, 1943, corr. UN Conf., San Francisco, 1945; news editor internat. press and publs. div. State Dept., 1945-47; partner Newmyer Assos., pub. relations, Washington, 1947- 58; v.p. asso. pub. Parents' mag., N.Y.C., 1958-66; sr. exec. Dudley- Anderson-Yutzy, pub. relations, N.Y.C., 1966-68; dir. corporate relations Tishman Realty & Constrn. Co., Inc., N.Y.C., 1969-71; pres. Robert S. Cramer, Inc., consultants, N.Y.C., 1971—; dir. Parents' Mag. Enterprises, Inc., N.Y.C. Vice chmn. Am. Parents Com.; mem., past chmn. bd. trustees Nat. Com. on Employment of Youth; mem., past trustee Citizens Budget Commn., Inc., N.Y.C. Mem. Pub. Relations Soc. Am., Pub. Relations Seminar. Clubs; Nat. Press (Washington); Overseas Press, Dutch Treat (N.Y.C.); Sunningdale Country (Scarsdale, N.Y.). Contbr. to newspapers, mags. Home: 337 Underhill Rd Scarsdale NY 10583 Office: 555 Madison Av New York City NY 10022

CRAMER, ROBERT VERN, coll. pres.; b. Fayetteville, Ark., Jan. 6, 1933; s. Paul and Fern (Way) C.; A.B., Monmouth (Ill.) Coll., 1954; M.A., U. Conn., 1964, Ph.D., 1965; m. M. Joan Sullivan, Sept. 6, 1953; children—Paula Jo, Melinda Kay, John Aaron. Tchr., Monmouth Jr. High Sch., 1954-56; prin. Elementary Sch., Vandalia, Ill., 1956-57; dir. publicity and publns. Monmouth Coll., 1957-59; dir. publns. and pub. information, instr. journalism Millikin U., Decatur, Ill., 1959-61; v.p. Old Sturbridge (Mass.) Village, 1961-64; asst. dean, instr. Sch. Edn., U. Conn., 1964- 65; v.p. Hanover (Ind.) Coll., 1965-68; pres. Northland Coll., Ashland, Wis., 1968-71; pres. Carroll Coll., Waukesha, Wis., 1971—. Pres. Southbridge (Mass.) Jr. C. of C., 1963-64; mem. Mayor Ashland Citizens Adv. Com. Bd. Dirs. Ashland Meml. Med. Center, 1969—. Vice pres. Wis. Found. Ind. Colls., 1969-71, pres., 1971—; mem. Wis. Coll., 1968. Bd. dirs. Waukesha Symphony. Mem. N.E.A., Am. Coll. Pub. Relations Assn. (chmn. research com. 1967- -), Nat. Assn. Watch and Clock Collectors, Phi Delta Kappa, Theta Chi. Republican. Conglist. Elk. Contbr. profl. jours. Home: 115 South East Av Waukesha WI 53186

CRAMER, SCOTT EDWARD, meat co. exec.; b. Hardy, Neb., Aug. 25, 1907; s. Charles L. and Pearle (Scott) C.; B.S. in Bus. Adminstrn., U. Neb., 1931; m. Georgina Francis, June 8, 1936; 1 dau., Jeanette. With Swift & Co., Chgo., 1931—, pres. Swift Edible Oil Co. div., 1968—. Mem. Nat. Soybean Processors Assn. (dir.), Nat. Cottonseed Products Assn. (dir.). Home: 4921 Lawn Av Western Springs IL 60558 Office: 115 W Jackson Blvd Chicago IL 60604

CRAMER, TREVOR KENT, mfg. co. exec.; b. Chgo., Sept. 7, 1908; s. Sterling B. and Lila (Wills) C.; B.S., Mass. Inst. Tech., 1930; m. Iris Rogers, Aug. 1, 1947. Chmn. bd. Ingress-Plastene, Inc.; dir. Ingress Mfg. Co. Mason (K.T.). Clubs: Sunset Ridge Country; Columbia (Indpls.). Home: 675 Sugartree Rd Crawfordsville IN 47933 Office: 1001 E College St Crawfordsville IN 47933

CRAMER, WILLIAM CATO, lawyer, former congressman; b. Denver, Aug. 4, 1922; s. Walter Bruce and Doreen Emma (Walters) C.; student St. Petersburg Jr. Coll., 1941-43; A.B., U. N.C., 1946; LL.B., Harvard, 1948; m. Alice Janet Jones, Dec. 7, 1951; children-William C., Mark, Allyn. Admitted to Fla., Mass. bars., 1948. since in practice of law; atty. Town of Pinellas Park, 1951-53; county atty. Pinellas County, Fla., 1953-55, atty. light industry council, 1953-55; mem. 84th-87th Congresses, 1st Fla. Dist., mem. 88th-91st Congresses, 12th Dist. Fla., mem. judiciary and pub. works coms. Mem. Fla. Legislature, 1950-52, minority leader, 1951; alternate del. Rep. Nat. Conv., 1952; Rep. nominee U.S. Congress, 1st Dist. Fla, 1952; chmn. Fla. Electoral Coll., 1952; hon. vice chmn. Fla. delegation Rep. Nat. Conv., 1956; Fla. nat. committeeman, 1964—; chmn. host com. Rep. Nat. Conv., 1968. Served to 1st. (j.g.) USNR, World War II. Mem. Young Rep. Nat. Fedn. (regional dir. 1951-53, nat. committeeman from Fla. 1952-55, nat. vice chmn. 1953-55), Am., Mass., Fla., St. Petersburg bar assns., V.F.W., Am. Legion, Phi Beta Kappa, Phi Alpha Phi, Ahepa, Phi Alpha Delta (hon.). Methodist. Mason (Shriner). Clubs: Moose, Grotto, Kiwanis (St. Petersburg, Fla.). Home: 1200 Monterey Blvd St Petersburg FL 33704 Office: US Federal Bldg St Petersburg FL 33701

CRAMPTON, BRUCE SIDNEY, profl. golfer; b. Sydney, Australia, Sept. 28, 1935; s. Hector Arnold and Beatrice Any (Foster) C.; certificate Canterbury (N.S.W.) Boy's High Sch., 1952; m. Joan Mary Findlay, Dec. 21, 1963; one son, Jay Arnold. Began career as amateur golfer in Australia, 1949-53; rep. Australia against New Zealand, 1953; profl. golfer, 1953—; winner Australian Open Championship, 1956, Far East Open Championship, 1959, Milw. Open Championship 1961, Motor City Open Championship, 1962, Tex. Open Championship, 1964, Bing Crosby Nat. Pro-American Tournament, 1965; Colonial National Invitational, 1965, 500 Festival Open, 1965, West End Classic, 1968, Hawaiian Open, 1969, Westchester Classic, 1970; represented Australia in Can. Cuo Matches, 1957, 63, 64. Mem. profl. golfers assns. Am., Australia, Great Britain. Home: 12 Arthur St Carlton Sydney New South Wales Australia Office: care Trust Dept Oak Cliff Bank & Trust Co PO Box 4068 Station A Dallas TX 75208

CRAMPTON, CHARLES GREGORY, educator; b. Kankakee, Ill., Mar. 22, 1911; s. Charles C. and Carrie (Beecher) C.; A.B., U. Cal. at Berkeley, 1935, M.A., 1936, Ph.D., 1941; m. Helen Mickelsen, 1958; childrenPatricia, Juanita. Teaching asst. history U. Cal. at Berkeley, 1937-40; spl. agt. FBI, 1943-45; depot historian Cal. Q.M. Depot, Oakland, 1944-45; prof. history U. Utah, 1945 -, dir. Western History Center, 1966-68. Rockefeller Found. travelling fellow Latin Am., 1941-42, 48-49; vis. prof. U. Panama, 1955. Mem. Phi Alpha Theta (pres. 1949-50). Author: Outline History of the Glen Canyon Region 1776-1922, 1959; Standing Up Country, The Canyon Lands of Utah and Arizona, 1964; also articles. Editor: The Mariposa Indian War, Diaries of Robert Eccleston; The California Gold Rush. Yosemite and the High Sierra. 1957. Home: 327 S 12th St E Salt Lake City, UT 84102.

CRAMPTON, JAMES MYLAN, educator; b. Mitchell, S.D., Nov. 26, 1923; s. Walter and Genevieve (Mylan) C.; B.S., Creighton U., 1950; M.S., Fla. U., 1951, Ph.D., 1953; m. May Lu Kelley, Aug. 19, 1950; children—JoAnn, James, Patrick, William, Mary Catherine, Elizabeth. Asso. prof. pharmacology Coll. Pharmacy, Xavier U., New Orleans, 1953-58; prof., dir. dept. biopharmacy Creighton U. Sch. Pharmacy, Omaha, 1958—, also prof. physiology and pharmacology Sch. Med., 1971—. Served with USAAF, 1943-46. Decorated Bronze Star medal. Fellow Am. Found. Pharm. Edn.; mem. Am. Pharm. Assn., Rho Chi, Alpha Sigma Nu. Home: 1512 N 75th Av Omaha NB 68114

CRANCH, EDMUND TITUS, educator, engr.,; b. Bklyn., Nov. 15, 1922; s. Clarence E. and Mary Emily (Smith) C.; student Newark Coll. Engring., 1941-43; B.S. in Mech. Engring., Cornell U., 1945, Ph.D., 1951; m. Virginia Mae Harrison, Mar. 8, 1945; children-Virginia, Edmund, Timothy. Asst. prof. Cornell U., Ithaca, N.Y., 1951-54, asso. prof., 1954-56, prof., head mechanics and 1956-64, prof. head theoretical and applied mechanics dept., 1966-68, asso. dean, 1967—. Fellow NSF, 1958-59, also 1964-65. Member of American Society of M.E., Am. Soc. Testing Materials, Am. Soc. Engring. Edn., Soc. Exptl. Stress Analysis, Sigma Xi, Tau Beta Pi, Phi Kappa Phi. Contbr. articles on applied mechanics to tech. jours. Home: 109 Harvard Pl Ithaca NY 14850

CRANDALL, ARTHUR BERT, lawyer; b. Thompson, O., Sept. 13, 1918; s. Bert G. and Lena (Pomeroy) C.; B.A., Hiram Coll., 1940; LL.B., Western Res. U., 1948; m. Mary Alice Gibbons, Oct. 3, 1947; 1 son, Douglas A. Clerk, B.G. Crandall Co., Thompson, O., 1935-40; tchr. econs., asst. coach Auburn (O.) High Sch., 1941- 42; admitted to Ohio bar, 1948, since practiced in Painesville; legal counsel, dir. Lake County Fed. Savs. & Loan Assn. Dir., clk. Lake County Bd. Elections, 1952-65; clk., mem. v.p. Painesville Twp. Bd. Edn. 1953- -. Mem. Republican Central Comm., 1964—. Vice pres., trustee Lake County Mental Health Clinic. Served with USNR, 1942-46: PTO. Mem. Am., Ohio, Lake County (past pres.) bar assns., Hiram Coll. Alumni Assn. (pres.), Painesville C. of C. (dir.). Methodist (trustee). Rotarian. (past pres.). Home: 165 Overlook Rd Painesville OH 44077 Office: 174 Main St Painesville OH 44077

CRANDALL, ARTHUR ELMER ins. co. exec.; b. Berlin, Conn., June 5, 1924; s. Arthur Edgar and Anna (Witz) C.; B.S., U. Conn., 1949; postgrad. Hartford Coll. Ins., 1953-59; m. Fay Kathleen Hoadley, Jan. 31, 1948; children—Lynn Kathleen, Deborah Ann, Gary Steven, Lori Jean, Jeane Elizabeth. With Phoenix Ins. Co., Hartford, Conn., 1949—, asst. supt., 1955-61, asst. comptroller, 1961-66, comptroller, 1966—. Treas. P.T.A., Wethersfield, Conn., 1956-58. Served with USAAF. 1943-45. Chartered Property and Casualty Underwriters. Mem. Soc. Ins. Accountants. Republican. Conglist. Home: 415 Prospect St Wethersfield CT 06109 Office: 1 Tower Sq Hartford CT 06115

CRANDALL, ARTHUR LESLIE, corp. exec.; s. George L. and Lillie (Strabel) C.; B.B.A., Northwestern U., 1950; m. Alice Dell Baker, Nov. 15, 1947; children—Stephen, Alicedel. Treasury agt. Internal Revenue Service, Chgo., 1946-52; financial analyst Renegotiation Bd., Chgo., 1952-55; tchr. Wright Jr. Coll., Chgo., 1953-55; tax mgr. McGraw-Edison Co., Elgin, Ill., 1955-67, controller, 1967—. Served with USAAF, 1943-45. C.P.A., Ill. Mem. Am. Inst. C.P.A.'s, Financial Execs. Inst., Chgo. Tax Club. Home: 2313 Kensington Av Westchester IL 60153 Office: 333 W River Rd Elgin IL 60120

CRANDALL, GORDON EDGAR, rubber products co. exec.; b. Springville, Utah, July 18, 1906; s. Myron Edgar and Evelyn (Maeser) C.; B.S., Brigham Young U., 1928; M.A., N.Y.U., 1929; m. Elene Clegg, Aug. 22, 1928; children—Virginia, Mary (Mrs. Robert D. Hales), Gordon Clegg, Dennis L., Nathan Jay. Financial analyst Standard Statistics Co., N.Y.C., 1929; security analyst Ure, Pett & Morris, security brokers, 1929-33; with Uniroyal, Inc., Los Angeles, 1938-52, N.Y.C., 1952—, now treas. Bishop, Matthews ward Ch. of Jesus Christ of Latter-day Saints, Los Angeles, 1945-52, bishop Queens ward, N.Y., 1955-59, counselor N.Y. State Presidency, 1960-67, pres. L.I. Stake, 1967-71. Home: 254-32 Walden Pl Great Neck NY 11020 Office: 1230 Av of Americas New York City NY 10020

CRANDALL, KENNETH HARTLEY, cons. geologist; b. Spencer, Ia., Feb. 10, 1904; s. Walter Gove and Gertrude (Robbins) C.; A.B., Stanford, 1924; m. Claire Wofford, Oct. 17, 1929; children—Kenneth Hartley, William Wofford. Vice pres. exploration, dir. Standard Oil Co. Cal., San Francisco, 1950-69; cons. geologist; cons. prof. Stanford, 1969—. Mem. Am. Inst. Profl. Geologists, Am. Assn. Petroleum Geologists (pres. 1969-70), Cal. Acad. Sci., Am. Geog. Soc., Geol. Soc. Am., Phi Beta Kappa. Clubs: Pacific Union, Stock Exchange (San Francisco). Home: 209 Crocker Av Piedmont CA 94610

CRANDALL, STEPHEN HARRY, educator; b. Cebu, Philippines, Dec. 2, 1920; s. William Harry and Julia Josephine (Kuenemann) C.; M.E., Stevens Inst. Tech., 1942; Ph.D., Mass. Inst. Tech., 1946; m. Patricia Estelle Stickel, Jan. 21, 1949; children—Jane S., William S. Staff mem. radiation lab. Mass. Inst. Tech., 1942-43, instr. math. 1944-46, asst. prof. mech. engring., 1947-51, asso. prof., 1951-58, prof., 1958—, head div. applied mechanics, 1957-59, 61-67, head div. mechanics and materials, 1968-71. Vis. prof., Marseille, France, 1960. Fulbright fellow, exchange prof. Imperial Coll., London, Eng., 1949; NSF sci. faculty fellow, vis. scholar U. Cal. at Berkeley, 1964-65; hon. research asso. Harvard, 1971-72. Registered profl. engr. Fellow Am. Acad. Arts and Scis., Am. Soc. M.E., Am. Acoustical Soc., A.A.A.S.; mem. soc. Indsl. and Applied Math., Am. Math. Soc., Am. Acad. Mechanics, Am. Soc. for Engring. Edn. Author: Engineering Analysis, 1956; Random Vibration in Mechanical Systems, 1963; (with others) Dynamics of Mechanical and Electromechanical Systems, 1968. Editor: Random Vibration volume 1, 1958, vol. 2, 1963; (with others) Mechanics of Solids, 1959, Contbr. papers on numerical analysis, applied mechanics, vibrations, acoustics. Home: Tabor Hill Rd Lincoln MA 01773 Office: Massachusetts Inst Technology Cambridge MA 02139

CRANDELL, CHARLES ARCHIE, hosp. adminstr., psychiatrist; b. Cleve., Oct. 5, 1900; s. Frank Foster and S. Gertrude (Coffin) C.; A.B., Coll. of Wooster, 1923; M.D., Hahnemann Med. Coll., 1927; m. Grace Stucke, July 17, 1929; children—Gertrude Margaret (Mrs. Robert E. Gordon, Jr.), Susan Evelyn (Mrs. Louis I. Flego); m. 2d, Solveig Sandvik, July 12, 1946. Intern, Shadyside Hosp., Pitts., 1927-28; pvt. practice, Wooster, O., 1928-30; resident physician N.J. State Hosp., Greystone Park, 1930-39, sr. resident physician, 1939-41, asst. clin. dir., 1941-49, asst. med. supt., 1949-50, med. supt., chief exec. officer, 1950-69. Research with Columbia Greystone Assos., human frontal lobe studies, 1947-49; cons. neuropsychiatrist to surgeon gen. USAF, 1950-; prin. investigator psychosurg. problems USPHS, 1951-54. Active local Boy Scouts Am.; mem. bd. Morristown (N.J.) chpt. A.R.C., 1935-55, Served to lt. col., MC, AUS, 1943-46; col. Res. USAF. Diplomate Am. Bd. Psychiatry and Neurology. Life fellow Am. Psychiat. Assn., A.C.P.; fellow A.A.A.S.; mem. Am. Coll. Hosp. Adminstrs. (life), Assn. Research Nervous and Mental Diseases, Aerospace Med. Assn., Assn. Mil. Surgeons U.S., Royal Soc. Health. Assn. Med. Supts. Mental Hosps. (pres. 1962), Morris County Med. Soc. (pres. 1951). Episcopalian. Mason. Club: Morristown. Address: Box 188 Greystone Park NJ 07950

CRANDELL, RICHARD BATES, food co. exec.; b. Hornell, N.Y., Mar. 5, 1911; s. Stewart and Bertha (Garlock) C.; student U. Mich., 1928-29, Kalamazoo Coll., 1929-32; m. Bertha E. Winger, Apr. 1, 1934; children—Marilyn J. (Mrs. Schleg), Marlene J. (Mrs. Thomas R. Hathaway). With Kellogg Co., 1932- -, asst. sec., 1961—, treas., 1965—, v.p., 1970—. Bd. dirs., chmn. finance com. Oakhill Cemetery Co., Battle Creek, Mich. Mem. Tax Execs. Inst., Financial Execs. Inst., Nat. Tax Assn. Kiwanian. Home: 124 Fairway Dr Battle Creek MI 49017. Office: 235 Porter St Battle Creek MI 49017

CRANDELL, WALTER BAIN, educator, surgeon; b. N.Y.C., July 26, 1911; s. Walter Solomon and Bess (Bain) C.; A.B., Dartmouth Coll., 1934; M.D., N.Y.U., 1937; m. Eloise Elizabeth Nenry, June 22, 1935; children—Anne (Mrs. Eugene Williams), Cynthia, Elizabeth (Mrs. Richard Hutchins), Eloise. Intern, Mary Hitchcock Meml. Hosp., Hanover, N.H., 1937-39; clin. asst. thoracic surgeon Hitchcock Clinic, 1939; instr. anatomy Dartmouth, 1939; resident gen. surgery Mass. Gen. Hosp., 1939-41; thoracic surgery Chest Service Bellevue Hosp., 1941-42, asst. vis. surgeon, 1946-47; instr. surgery N.Y.U., also anatomy and operative surgery, 1946-47; adj. surgeon Lenox Hill Hosp., also attending surgeon thoracic surgery VA Hosp., Bronx, 1946-47; chief surgery VA Hosp., White River Junction, Vt., 1947—; asst. clin. prof. surgery Dartmouth, 1947-61, asso. clin. prof. surgery, 1961-68, clin. prof. surgery, 1968—; surg. practice, N.Y.C., 1946-47. Served to capt. AUS, 1942-45. Decorated Bronze Arrowhead. Diplomate Am. Bd. Surgery, Am. Bd. Thoracic Surgery. Fellow A.C.S. (bd. govs.); mem. Am. Assn. for Thoracic Surgery, Am. Thoracic Soc., N.E. Surg. Soc., 2d Aux. Surg. Group, Pan Am. Surg. Assn., N.H. Med. Soc., Grafton County Med. Soc., Am. Trudeau Soc., A.A.A.S., Alpha Omega Alpha. Home: Meadow Lane Hanover NH 03755 Office: VA Hosp White River Junction VT 05001

CRANE, ALLAN CHANDLER, mfg. co. exec.; b. Bklyn., June 11, 1916; s. Allan Francis and Josephine (Chandler) C.; B.S. in Bus. Adminstrn., Lehigh U., 1938; m. Boneita Louise Henry, Dec. 25, 1938; children-Bonnie Lou (Mrs. Joseph Kulas), Laraine (Mrs. Randy Quick), Allan. Sr. analyst Carnegie Ill. Steel Corp., Pitts., 1938-43; sr. methods engr. Nat. Supply Co., 1945-46; controller Pitts. Outdoor Advt. Co., 1946-47; with A.O. Smith Corp., Milw., 1948—, v.p., controller, 1967—. Bd. dirs. N.W. Milw. YMCA, 1955—, Neighborhood House, Milw., 1960—. Served to capt. AUS, 1943-45. Mem. Nat. Assn. Accountants (nat. dir. 1960-62, 66-69, nat. v.p. 1966-67), Finance Execs. Inst. (dir. Milw. 1966—), Machinery and Allied Products Inst. (chmn. financial com. 1968-70), Stuart Cameron McLeod Soc. Club: Tripoli Golf (Milw.). Home: 505 E Henry Clay St Milwaukee WI 53217 Office: 3533 N 27th St Milwaukee WI 53201

CRANE, ARNOLD HERMAN, lawyer; b. Chgo., July 17, 1932; s. Matthew and Dorothy (Gomberg) C.; student U. Ill., 1949, Loyola U., Chgo., 1949-52; LL.B., DePaul U., 1955; m. Martha Ann Wright, Feb. 1, 1966; 1 son, David Heath. Admitted to Ill. bar, 1955; spl. asst. to appelate div. Justice Dept., 1954-55; mem. firm McKinley & Price, Chgo., 1956-58; trial atty. Judge A.W. Russell, Chgo., 1958-59; pvt. practice, Chgo., 1959-65; sr. partner firm Shapiro, Levine & Crane, Chgo., 1965—. Photo journalist for nat. mags., encys.; lectr. forensic sci.; instr. history of photography, Columbia Coll., Chgo.; photographs represented in permanent collections Art Inst. Chgo., Bibliotheque Nationale, Paris, Mus. Modern Art, N.Y.C. Mem. com. child brutality Ill. Commn. Children, 1964-65; exec. planning com. scis. div. Adult Edn. Couuncil Greater Chgo., 1962-63, 64, exec. planning bd. arts assembly, 1968-70. Served with USNR, 1955-56. Fellow Am. Acad. Forensic Scis.; mem. Brit. Acad. Forensic Scis., Chgo. Bar Assn. (sec. 1966—), Soc. Photog. Edn., MENSA, Nat., Ill. press photographers assns., Nu Beta Epsilon, Tau Delta Phi. Photog. book revs. for newspapers; contbg. author chpt. on photography and its history Compton's Ency. Home: 3240 N Lake Shore Dr Chicago IL 60657 Office: 134 N LaSalle St Chicago IL 60602

CRANE, BOB EDWARD, actor; b. Waterbury, Conn., July 13, 1928; s. Alfred T. and Rosemary (Senich) C.; grad. high sch.; m. Anne Terzian, May 20, 1949 (div. June 1970); children—Robert David, Deborah Ann, Karen Leslie; m. 2d, Patricia Olson, Oct. 16, 1970; 1 step dau., Melissa Suzanne; 1 son, Robert Scott. Broadcaster radio sta. WLEA, Hornell, N.Y., 1950, WBIS, Bristol, Conn., 1951, WICC, Bridgeport, Conn., 1951-56, KNX, Hollywood Cal., 1956-65; actor Donna Reed Show, ABC TV, 1963-65; appearing as Col. Hogan In Hogan's Heroes, CBS-TV, Hollywood, 1965-71; profl. musician, drummer with Conn. Symphony, 1944-46, various dance bands East and West coasts; appeared in motion pictures Return to Peyton Place, 1963, Mantrap, 1963, Wicked Dreams of Paula Shuutz, 1967; lead (with Helen Hayes and Lillian Gish) in TV version of Arsenic and Old Lace, 1968; sub host for Johnny Carson, Merv Griffin shows. Served with Conn. N.G., 1948-50. Emmy award nominee for role of Hogan on Hogan's Heroes, 1965, 66. Mem. Screen Actors Guild, Am. Fedn. Musicians, A.F.T.R.A., Actors Equity, Acad. Motion Picture Arts and Scis., TV Acad. Arts and Scis. Home: 218 Tilden Av Los Angeles CA 90049 Office: 780 N Gower Hollywood CA 90028

CRANE, BRUCE paper co. exec.; b. Dalton, Mass., July 27, 1909; s. Winthrop Josephine Porter (Boardman) C.; A.B., Yale, 1931; m. Winnie Davis Long, May 14, 1932; childrenWinnie and Davis (twins). With Crane & Co., Inc., Dalton, 1931—, pres., gen. mgr., 1951—; dir. Agrl. Nat. Bank. Pittsfield, Mass., Berkshire Life Ins. Co., Pittsfield. Mem. Dalton Sch. Com., 1945-51; mem. Gov.'s Council Mass., 1953-56. Rep. nat. committeeman for Mass., 1964—. Mem. Writing Paper Mfrs. Assn. (pres. 1951-52). Home: 45 Main St Dalton MA 01226 Office: Crane & Co Inc Dalton MA 01226

CRANE, CARLSON ELDRIDGE, univ. adminstr.; b. Hartford, Conn., Nov. 17, 1916; s. Frank Newton and Ingrid Marie (Carlson) C.; B.S., U. Conn., 1942; student Indsl. Adminstrn., Harvard, 1943, M.B.A., 1947; Ed. D., N.Y. U.; m. Patricia Lenore Southwick, Oct. 24, 1943; children—Sheryl Lenore, Holly Patricia, Laurie Marie, Melissa Kate. Audit clk. Travelers Ins. Co., 1934-38; sales rep. Union Hardware Co., 1947; asst. dir. div. univ. extension U. Conn., 1947-55, acting dir., 1955-58; dean div. pub. services Western Ill. U., Macomb, also prof. bus. adminstrn., 1958-70, v.p. univ. relations, 1970—. Sec. Lamoine Valley (Ill.) Assn.; mem. Prairie council Boy Scouts Am., 1948—. Served to capt. AUS, 1943-46. Recipient Silver Beaver award Boy Scouts Am., 1966. Mem. Ill. Adult Edn. Assn., Nat. Univ. Extension Assn., Assn. Higher Edn., Am. Legion, Macomb C. of C. (Past pres.), Nat. Assn. of Summer Sessions (pres. elect 1968-69), Am. Coll. Pub. Relations Assn., Am. Alumni Council, Phi Delta Kappa, Alpha Phi Omega. Home: R R 1 Macomb IL 61455

CRANE, DOUGLAS PRATT, mfg. co. exec.; b. Corning, N.Y., Nov. 24, 1928; s. Douglas L. and Eugenia P. (Vose) C.; B.A. in Econs., Goddard Coll., 1951; M.B.A., U. Chgo., 1969; m. Lois Barton Crane, Mar. 30, 1950; children—Linda Ann, Nancy, Steven, Debra. Mgmt. trainee Westinghouse Electric Co., 1951-52; mgr., prodn. control and purchasing electronic tube div. Sylvania Corp., Fullerton, Cal., 1952-56; mgr. sales and orders Sci. and Process div. Beckman, Fullerton, Cal., 1956-58; pres., gen. mgr. Coleman Instruments (became div. Perkin-Elmer Corp., Norwalk, Conn.), 1958-69; pres., gen. mgr. Perkin-Elmer de Mexico, 1964-69; v.p. spl. assignment Wickes Corp., Saginaw, Mich., 1969, group v.p. mfg. shelter and recreational vehicles, 1969-70, sr. v.p. manufactured shelter and recreational vehicles group, 1970—, dir. subsidiary cos.; dir. Townland Marketing and Devel. Corp. Trustee, chmn. Midwest Coll. Engring. Served with USAAF, 1946-48. Recipient Pres.'s award excellence in expanding exports. Mem. Am. Mgmt. Assn., Exec. Program Club, Nat. Assn. Mfrs., U. Chgo. Alumni Assn. Clubs: Saginaw Country, Saginaw. Home: 8 E Hannum Blvd Saginaw MI 48602 Office: 515 N Washington Av Saginaw MI 48607

CRANE, EDWARD MATTHEWS, Jr., publishing cons.; b. Newark, Jan. 31, 1922; s. Edward M. and Margaret (Atha) C.; A.B., Princeton, 1945; m. Mary Cordelia Thompson, Mar. 23, 1945; children—Edward Matthews III, Cordelia Houghton; m. 2d, Jean Drummond Ijams, July 20, 1966. Coll. salesman D. Van Nostrand Co., Inc., 1945- 49, asso. editor, 1949-54, mgr. coll. dept., 1954, sec., 1954-58, sec., v.p., 1958-64, pres., 1968-69; pres. Van Nostrand Reinhold Co. div. Litton Ednl. Pub., Inc., 1969-70; dir., pres. Van Nostrand Reinhold Co., Ltd.; chmn. Van Nostrand Reinhold Co., Ltd., London; cons., 1968-69; pres. Litton Internat. Pub., Inc., 1969-70, Boutwell, Crane, Moseley Assos., 1971—. Trustee, Curran Found., Wilmington, Del. Mem. Am. Polit. Sci. Assn., Am. Sociol. Soc., Am. Hist. Assn., Am. Book Pubs. Council (chmn. tech., sci. and med. book pubs. group 1967-69). Address: 53 Battle Rd Princeton NJ 08540

CRANE, FRANCES KIRKWOOD, author; 1 dau., Nancy. Mem. Phi Beta Kappa, Alpha Chi Omega, Beta Sigma Phi (hon). Author numerous books including: The Flying Red Horse, 1949; The Daffodil Blonde, 1950; The Polkadot Murder, 1951; Murder In Blue Street, 1952; 13 White Tulips, 1953; Murder in Bright Red, 1953; The Coral Princess Murders, 1954; Death in Lilac Time, 1955; Horror on the Ruby X, 1956; The Ultraviolet Widow, 1956; The Man in Gray, 1958; The Buttercup Case, 1959; 1961; The Amber Eyes, 1962; The Reluctant Sleuth, Death Wish Green, 1960; The Dock at Random Key, 1962; Three Days in Hong King, 1964; Body Beneath a Mandarin Tree, 1965; A Very Quiet Murder, 1966; Worse Than a Crime, 1968. Home: Taos NM 87571

CRANE, FRANK, state ofcl.; b. Waxhaw, N.C., Aug. 18, 1907; s. James Thomas and Emma (Lathan) C.; A.B., U. N.C., 1931, postgrad., summers 1932-34; m. Mary Browning, Cromer, Nov. 27, 1963. Tchr., coach, Welcome, N.C., 1931-34; safety dir. N.C. Indsl. Commn., 1934-39; factory safety insp. N.C. Dept. Labor, Raleigh, 1939-54; dir. N.C. Conciliation Service, Raleigh, 1941-54; commmr. labor State of N.C., Raleigh, 1954—. Mem. Soc. Safety Engrs., Vets of Safety. Democrat. Methodist. Home: 2608 Hazelwood Dr Raleigh NC 27608 Office: Labor Bldg PO Box 1151 Raleigh NC 27602

CRANE, FRANK HARRISON, editor; b. Des Moines, Feb. 8, 1912; s. Stephen A. and Minnie G. (Harrison) C.; student Drake U., 1930-32; m. Eleanor May Woods, Oct. 5, 1935; children—Carol Engledow, Stephen. Reporter, Internat. News Service, 1930-31, Des Moines Tribune, 1933-35; editor Ireton (Ia.) Ledger, 1935-37; city editor, Shippensburg (Pa.) News Chronicle, 1937- 43, mng. editor, 1946-47; copy editor Des Moines Tribune, 1943; editor Alburn Bur. Syndicate, Cleve., 1948-52; copy editor Cleve. News, 1953; mng. editor Ida. Daily Statesman, Boise, 1953-54; editorial writer Indpls. Star, 1954-61. editor editorial page, 1961-69, editor, 1969—. Pres. United Cerebral Palsy Central Ind., 1962-65, hon. v.p., 1965-67, pres., Ind., 1969-71. Recipient George Washington medal Freedoms Found., 1955, honor certificates, 1958-59. Served to 1st lt. AUS, 1943-46. Mem. Nat. Conf. Editorial Writers, Am. Soc. Newspaper Editors, Sigma Delta Chi, Methodist. Home: 8260 Windcombe Blvd Indianapolis IN 46240 Office: 307 N Pennsylvania St Indianapolis IN 46204

CRANE, GEORGE WASHINGTON, 3d, psychologist; b. Chgo., Apr. 28, 1901; s. George Washington, 2d, and Eliza Jane (Bever) C.; A.B., Northwestern U., 1922, A.M., 1923, Ph.D., 1927, M.D., 1935; student Yale, 1926-27; m. Cora Ellen Miller, Oct. 25, 1928; children—George Washington, 4th, Philip Miller, Judith Anne, Daniel Bever, David Goodrich. Instr. psychology Northwestern U., Evanston, Ill., 1922-24, George Washington U., 1924-25; research psychologist NRC and Carnegie Instn., Washington, 1924-29; lectr. applied psychology Northwestern U., 1929-38, Central Y.M.C.A. Coll., Chgo., 1930—; pres. Hopkins Syndicate, Inc.; physician, cons. psychologist. Recipient Religious Heritage award, 1969. Mem. A.M.A., Ill., Chgo. med. socs., Pan Am. Psychol. Assn., Sigma Xi, Delta Sigma Rho, Akron (O.) Dental Soc. (hon.). Republican. Methodist. Author: Psychology Applied, 1967; Radio Talks, vol. 1, 1948; How to Cash In on Your Worries, 1956. Contbr. dental mags.; daily syndicated newspaper columns The Worry Clinic (also known as Case Records of a Psychologist) and Test Your Horse Sense, daily radio program. Office: 6033 Wentworth Av Chicago IL 60621

CRANE, HORACE RICHARD, educator, physicist; b. Turlock, Cal., Nov. 4, 1907; s. Horace Stephen and Mary Alice (Roselle) C.; B.S., Cal. Inst. Tech., 1930, Ph.D., 1934; m. Florence Rohmer LeBaron, Dec. 30, 1934; children—Carol Ann, Janet (dec.), George Richard. Research fellow Cal. Inst. Tech., 1934-35; mem. faculty U. Mich., Ann Arbor, 1935—; prof. physics, 1946—, chmn. dept. physics, 1965—. Research asso. (radar) Mass. Inst. Tech., 1940-41; physicist Carnegie Inst. Washington, 1941, project dir., proximity fuze project U. Mich., 1941-43, atomic energy project, 1943-45; cons. NDRC, 1941-45; mem. standing com. on controlled thermonuclear research AEC, 1969—. Vice pres. Midwestern Univs. Research Assn., 1956-57, pres., 1957-60; mem. policy bd. Argonne Nat. Lab., 1957—. Bd. govs. Am. Inst. Physics, 1964-71, chmn., 1971—. Recipient Davisson-Genmer prize, 1967; Henry Russel lectr., 1967; Distinguished Alumni medal Cal. Inst. Tech., 1968; Distinguished Service award U. Mich., 1957. Fellow Am. Phys. Soc., A.A.A.S., Am. Acad. Arts and Scis.; mem. Nat. Acad. Scis., Am. Assn. Physics Tchrs. (pres. 1965), Sigma Xi, Clubs: Research University of Michigan (pres. 1956-57); Science Research (v.p. 1946-47, pres. 1947-48; U. Mich.). Contbr. sci. articles in profl. mags. Inventor of Race Track, a modified form of synchrotron for nuclear studies, 1946; made early discoveries in field of artificially produced radioactive atoms, 1934-39; measurements of magnetic moment of free electron, 1950—. Home: 830 Avon Rd Ann Arbor MI 48104

CRANE, HOWARD G., ins. co. exec.; b. Wethersfield, Conn., Mar. 1, 1901; student Wesleyan U., Middletown, Conn.; B.S. in Econs., U. Pa., 1923. With Nat. Council Ins. Compensation, 1924-27; with Gen. Reins. Corp., 1927—, now v.p., cons. Fellow Casualty Actuarial Soc. Home: 456 Hawthorne Pl Ridgewood NJ 07450

CRANE, JOHN EDWIN, former bus. exec.; b. Richmond, Ind., Aug. 14, 1918; s. Myran Joseph and Bess (Longstreth) C.; A.B., Harvard, 1940; M.B.A., N.Y. U., 1948; m. Phyllis Abbott Bockhoff, Dec. 24, 1941; childrenDavid Bockhoff, Deborah Sellers, Catheley Chase. Financial v.p. Home Life Ins. Co., 1957-59; v.p. First Nat. City Bank, N.Y.C., 1959-64; financial v.p. Cram & Forster, N.Y.C., 1964; dir. Am. Eagle Life Ins. Co., Nat. Automatic Tool Co. Trustee YWCA Retirement Fund. Served as pilot USAAF, 1941-45. Decorated D.F.C., Air Medal with clusters. Mem. N.Y. Soc. Security Analysts. Home: 36 Ridge Acres Rd Darien CT 06820

CRANE, JOSEPH G., lawyer; b. Charlestown, Mass., Jan. 2, 1902; A.B., Boston Coll., 1923; LL.B., Harvard, 1927. Admitted to Mass. bar, 1929; partner firm Crane, Inker & Oteri, Boston; instr. Boston Coll. Law Sch., 1932-39; prof. law, asst. dean, then dean Northeastern U. Sch. Law, 1942-56. Mem. Boston, Norfolk County, Mass. bar assns., Am. Law Inst. Author: Massachusetts Rules of Courts, Annoted, 1950, rev. edit., 1960. Office: 20 Ashburton Pl Boston MA 02108*

CRANE, NEAL DAHLBERG, mfg. co. exec.; b. Stanley, Wis., Oct. 28, 1916; s. (Dahlberg) C.; A.B., Ripon (Wis.) Coll., 1938; student U. Wis., 1938-40; m. Elizabeth Henery, 1954. Grad. asst., research asst. physics dept. U. Wis., 1938-40; staff Radiation Lab., Mass. Inst. Tech., 1941; dir. operations div. Office Tech. Services, Dept. Commerce, 1946-47; staff mem., later dir. resources div. Research and Devel. Bd., Office Asst. Sec. Def. for Research and Devel., 1947-56; cons. asst. sec. def. research and engring., 1956-62; spl. asst. to sci. dir. research labs Gen. Motors Corp., 1956-61; dir. applied devel. dept., research and devel. div. Am. Machine & Foundry Co., 1961-62, dept. dir. research and devel. div., 1962-64, v.p. research and devel. div., 1964-66; v.p., asst. group exec. process equipment group, 1966-67; pres. Ben Hogan, 1967-70, v.p., dep. group exec. sports products group AMF, Inc., 1970—. Served to lt. col., Signal Corps, AUS, 1941-46. Decorated Legion of Merit, Bronze Star medal (U.S.); Order Brit. Empire. Mem. A.A.A.S., Am. Phys. Soc., Am. Mgmt. Assn. Club: Colonial Country. Home: 3874 S Hills Circle Fort Worth TX 76109 Office: 6745 Calmont St Fort Worth TX 76116

CRANE, PAUL WILLARD, former mfg. exec.; b. Cin., Oct. 7, 1903; s. William Henry and Emilie (Esselborn) C.; M.S. and Chem.E., U. Cin., 1926; research fellow U. Munich, 1926-28; m. Verona Harman, Oct. 3, 1931; children—William Jasper, Bradford Harman, George Stephen, Robert Louis. Chem. engr. E.I. duPont de Nemours & Co., 1928-30, research supr., 1930-42, research mgr., 1942-43, tech. supt. explosives dept., 1944-45, mgr. tech. service plastics dept., 1945-48, asst. dir. sales, 1948-49, mgr. devel. polychems. dept., 1950-53; dir. indsl. product devel. Cin. Milling Machine Co., 1953-57, dir. research, 1957-59, became v.p., 1959, also dir.; dir. Carlisle Chem. Works. Mem. bd. Montclair Adult Sch., 1941-48, v.p., 1947; trustee Cin. Summer Opera, 1960, Mem. Am. Chem. Soc., Comml. Chem. Devel. Assn., Soc. Plastics Engrs., Soc. Plastics Industry, Engring. Soc. Cin., Cin. C. of C., Indsl. Research Inst. Home: Brandford Farm RD 1 Loveland OH 45140

CRANE, PHILIP MILLER, congressman; b. Chgo., Nov. 3, 1930; s. George Washington and Cora (Miller) C.; student DePauw U., 1948-50; B.A., Hillsdale Coll., 1952; postgrad. U. Mich., 1952-54, U. Vienna (Austria), 1953-56; M.A., U. Ind., 1961, Ph.D., 1963; m. Arlene Catherine Johnson, Feb. 14, 1959; children—Catherine Anne, Susanna Marie, Jennifer Elizabeth, Rebekah Caroline, George Washington V., Rachel Ellen, Sarah Emma. Advt. mgr. Hopkins Syndicate, Inc., Chgo., 1956-58; teaching asst. Ind. U., Bloomington, 1959-62; asst. prof. history Bradley U., Peoria, Ill., 1963- 67; dir. schs. Westminster Acad., Northbrook, Ill., 1967-68; mem. 91st, 92d Congresses 13th Ill. Dist. Pub. relations dir. Vigo County (Ind.) Republican Orgn., 1962; dir. research Goldwater Orgn., 1964; mem. nat. adv. bd. Young Ams. for Freedom, 1965—. Bd. dirs. Am. Conservative Union, Intercollegiate Studies Inst., Charles Edison Youth Fund; trustee Hillsdale Coll., John F. Kennedy Coll. Served with AUS, 1954-56. Recipient Distinguished Alumnus award Hillsdale Coll., 1968; William McGovern award Chgo. Soc., 1969. Mem. Am. Hist. Assn., Orgn. Am. Historians, Acad. Polit. Sci., Am. Acad. Polit. and Social Scis., Phila. Soc., A.S.C.A.P., Phi Alpha Theta, Pi Gamma Mu. Methodist. Author: Democrat's Dilemma, 1964. Office: Longworth House Office Bldg Washington DC 20515

CRANE, RADFORD RAYMOND, univ. trustee; b. Oakland, Cal., Feb. 10, 1911; s. Raymond Elmer and Ellen Elizabeth (Fearn) C.; grad. Mercersburg Acad., 1928; A.B., Washington and Jefferson Coll., 1932; m. Ruth B. Hakkila, Dec. 14, 1950; 1 child, Alpo Franssila. With Eljer Co., Ford City, Pa., 1932-53, exec. v.p., dir., 1939-53; dir. Rimersburg Coal Co., Pa. and Fla., 1940-; pres., 1953—. Trustee United Fund; mem. bd. dirs. Greater Miami YMCA, United Fund and Community Chest of Dade County, 1956-59; chmn. bd. trustees Opera Guild Greater Miami; trustee U. Miami, North Am. Wildlife Found., Washington, Raymond E. and Ellen F. Crane Found., Miami, Mem. Com. of 100. Episcopalian. Clubs: Bal Harbour, Bath, Indian Creek, La Gorce and Surf (Miami Beach); Miami; Duquesne (Pitts.); Biltmore Forest (Asheville); Rancheros Visitadores (Santa Barbara); Hendersonville (N.C.) Country. Home: 22 La Gorce Circle La Gorce Island Miami Beach FL 33139 Office: Rimersburg Coal Co Key West FL 33040

CRANE, ROBERT ELWOOD, composer, educator; b. Winchester, Mass., Dec. 24, 1919; s. Roy Elwood and Jean (Barrick) C.; Mus. B., Oberlin Coll., 1941; diploma in composition Longy Sch. Music, 1942; Mus. M., U. Rochester, 1947. Ph.D., 1950; m. Jessie Martin Starr, May 28, 1942; children—Susan, Pamela, Penelope, Peter, Andrew. Instr. music U. Wis., Madison, 1950-54, asst. prof., 1954-58, asso. prof., 1958-60, prof., 1960—. Vis. composer at festivals various univs., 1947—. Chmn., Univ. United Givers campaign, 1966-67. Served with AUS, 1942-45. Decorated Bronze Star medal. Recipient Lili Boulanger Meml. award, 1942. Mem. U. Composers Exchange (Wis. chmn.), Am. Musicological Soc., Audio Engring. Soc., Phi Mu Sinfonia (Alumni award 1952). Episcopalian. Club: University (Madison). Composer: Peter Quince at the Clavier, 1950; Sonatina for Piano, 1952; Octet for Brass, 1954; the Litany, 1960; The Golden Sequence, 1960; Passacaglia and Fugue for Band, 1961; Incantation, 1962; Chorale Fantasy on Wachtet Auf! Ruft uns der Stimme, 1963; Aleatory Suite, 1964; Fantasy on Laude Sion Salvatorem, 1964; Cantata When the Lamb Opened the Seventh Seal, 1968. Home: 1615 Adams St Madison WI 53711

CRANE, ROBERT KELLOGG, biochemist, educator; b. Palmyra, N.J., Dec. 20, 1919; s. Wilbur Fiske and Mary Elizabeth (McHale) C.; B.S., Washington Coll., Chestertown, Md., 1942; Ph.D., Harvard, 1950; m. Mildred Ellen Price, July 19, 1941 (div. Apr. 1962); children—Barbara Joan, Jonathan Townley. Chemist, Atlas Powder Co., 1942-43; instr. chemistry N.E. Mo. State Tchrs. Coll., Kirksville, 1943-44; asst. biochemist Mass. Gen. Hosp., Boston, 1949-50; mem. faculty Washington U. Med. Sch., St. Louis, 1950-62; prof. biochemistry, chmn. dept. Chgo. Med. Sch., 1963-66; prof., chmn. dept. physiology Rutgers U. Med. Sch., New Brunswick, N.J., 1966—. Mem. biochemistry test com. Nat. Bd. Med. Examiners; mem. sponsoring com. Internat. Conf. on Biol. Membranes; Sir Arthur Hurst Meml. lectr. Brit. Soc. for Gastroenterology, 1969. Fellow AEC, 1947-49. Served with USNR, 1944-46. Recipient Distinguished Achievement award Am. Gastroenterology Assn., 1969; Alumni citation Washington Coll., 1963; Community Service award St. Andrews Sch., 1963. Fellow Am. Inst. Chemists; mem. Am. Soc. Biol. Chemists, Am. Soc. Cell Biology, Corp. Marine Biol. Lab., Am. Chem. Soc., A.A.A.S., N.Y. Acad. Scis., Am. Gastroent. Assn., Biophys. Soc., Soc. Gen. Physiologists, Am. Physiol. Soc. (chmn. pub. affairs com.), Sigma Xi. Editorial com. sect. alimentary canal Handbook of Physiology; editorial bd. Gastroenterology. Biochimica et Biophysica Acta, Archives of Biochemistry and Biophysics. Contbr. numerous articles in field. Office: Rutgers Med Sch New Brunswick NJ 08903

CRANE, ROYSTON CAMPBELL, cartoonist; b. Abilene, Tex., Nov. 22, 1901; s. Royston Campbell and Mamie (Douthit) C.; student Hardin-Simmons U., 1918-19, U. Tex., 1919- 22, Chgo. Acad. Fine Arts, 1920; L.H.D. (hon.). Rollins Coll., Evelyn Hatcher, Feb. 8, 1927; childrenNancy (Mrs. Gerard Arthur), Marcia (Mrs. Charles W. Starcher III). With art dept. Fort Worth Record, 1919; reporter Austin (Tex.) Am., 1921-22; art dept. N.Y. World, 1922- 24; cartoonist-writer newspaper strip, Wash Tubbs-Captain Easy, 1924-43, Buz Sawyer, King Features Syndicate, 1943-. Recipient commendation from sec. navy as war corr., 1946; Reuben award Nat. Cartoonists Soc., 1950; Gold Medal award for distinguished pub. service U.S. Navy, 1957; Silver Lady award from Banshees as outstanding cartoonist of year, Best Story Strip award Nat. Cartoonists Soc., 1966. Mem. Nat. Cartoonists Soc., Navy League U.S., Phi Kappa Psi, Sigma Delta Chi. Club: Orlando Country. Address: 5585 Jessamine Lane, Orlando FL 32809.

CRANE, WILLIAM JOSEPH, rubber co. exec.; b. Springfield Mass., Aug. 12, 1921; s. William J. and Emily (Cyran) C.; certificate in accounting Bay Path Jr. Coll., Springfield, 1941; student accounting Am. Internat. Coll., 1941-42; m. Anna Marie Mattingly, July 19, 1947; children—Melinda Ann, William Sherwood, Debra Joan. With U.S. Rubber Co. (name now Uniroyal Inc.), 1938—, auditor, 1946-51, asst. treas., 1960, dir. Eastern mgmt. information center, 1963-65, treas., 1966-70, financial v.p., 1970—; dir. Arkwright-Boston Ins. Co., Rubicon Chems., Inc., Geismar, La., Latex Fiber Industries, Inc., Beaver Falls, N.Y.; mem. adv. bd. Chem. Bank, N.Y.C. Scoutmaster Boy Scouts Am. 1964-65. Bd. dirs. United Givers, Naugatuck, Conn., 1964-65. Served with AUS, 1941-46. Mem. Financial Execs. Inst. Home: 133 Sweet Briar Rd Stamford CT 06905 Office: 1230 6th Av New York City NY 10020

CRANE, WINTHROP MURRAY, paper mfg. exec.; b. Dalton, Mass., July 14, 1910; s. Winthrop Murray Jr. and Ethel (Eaton) C.; grad. Hotchkiss Sch., 1929; m. Katharine L.W. Pell, Jan. 29, 1946; 1 son, Brenton Pell. With Crane & Co., Dalton, Mass., 1931-39, 45—, sec., 1951—, v.p., 1960—, also dir.; dir. Byron Weston Co., Dalton, Otis Elevator Co., N.Y.C., Excelsior Printing Co., North Adams, Mass. Mass. Exec. asst. to asst. sec. state Dept. State, 1940-42; del. Am. Assembly, Arden House, 1958. Bd. dirs. Free Europe Com.; pres. bd. trustees Berkshire Mus., Pittsfield, Mass.; trustee Dalton Library, Lenox (Mass.) Library. Served with AUS, 1942-45. Mem. Paper, Stationery and Tablet Assn., Council Fgn. Relations. Republican. Conglist. Clubs: Union (N.Y.C.); Metropolitan (Washington). Home: Chilton House Dalton MA 01226 Office: Crane & Co Inc Dalton MA 01226

CRANEFIELD, PAUL FREDERIC, educator, physician; b. Madison, Wis., Apr. 28, 1925; s. Paul Frederic and Edna (Rothnick) C.; Ph.B., U. Wis., 1946, Ph.D., 1951; M.D., Albert Einstein Coll. Medicine, 1964. Fellow biophysics Johns Hopkins, 1951-53; from instr. to asso. prof. physiology State U. N.Y. Downstate Med. Center, N.Y.C., 1953-62; fellow psychiatry Albert Einstein Coll. Medicine, 1960-64; exec. sec. com. publs. and med. information, editor bull. N.Y. Acad. Medicine, 1963-67; asso. prof. pharmacology Columbia

Coll. Physicians and Surgeons, 1964—; asso. prof. Rockefeller 1966—. Chmn. bd. dirs. La Mama Exptl. Theatre Club; trustee Milton Helpern Library Legal Medicine. Mem. Am. Physiol. Soc., Biophys. Soc., Am. Assn. History Medicine. Clubs: Nat. Arts (N.Y.C.); Cosmos (Washington). Author: (with Hoffman) The Electrophysiology of the Heart, 1960; Paired Pulse Stimulation of the Heart, 1968; (with C. McC. Brooks) The Historical Development of Physiological Thought, 1959; also articles. Editor: Jour. Gen. Physiology, 1966—; cons. editor Internat. Microfilm Jour. Legal Medicine, 1969—. Home: 310 E 9th St New York City NY 10003 Office: York Av and 66th St New York City NY 10021

CRANER, JOHN LOUIS, cons.; b. Marion, O., Aug. 21, 1917; s. Levi Harvey and Daisy (Swartz) C.; student Internat. Sch. Commerce, 1938-39; m. Jane Rose Huth, June 4, 1948; children—Lee Adam and Catherine Alice (twins), Thomas David. Spl. agt. Erie R.R., Warren, O., 1940-42; prodn. mgr. Safety Grinding Wheel & Machine Co., Springfield, O., 1945-46; project accountant Austin Co., Cleve., 1946-54; asst. chief accountant Heckett Engring. Co., Butler, Pa., 1954-55; asst. to vice chancellor for Schs. of Health Professions U. Pitts., 1955-59; dir. bus. affairs Assn. Am. Med. Colls., Evanston, Ill., 1959-70; bus. mgr. Jour. Med. Edn., 1959-70; ind. cons. for methods, procedures and operations, 1970—. Served with AUS, 1942-45; ETO. Mem. Midwest Pharm. Advt. Club, Conf. Med. Soc. Execs. Greater Chgo., Profl. Conv. Mgmt. Assn., Am. Soc. Assn. Execs., Coll. and U. Personnel Assn., Evanston C. of C., Veterans of Foreign Wars. Mason (Shriner), Moose. Club: University (Evanston, Ill.). Author: (with H. Gordon) A Guide to Reproduction Processes and Costs, 1963; Personnel Policies and Handbook for Associations and Small Businesses, 1964. Home: Box 373 RR 2 Antioch IL 60002

CRANG, JAMES HAROLD, investment broker; b. Toronto, Ont., Can., Jan. 11, 1902; s. James and Lillian (McKay) C.; student Upper Can. Coll.; m. Dorothy K. Ritchie, 1933 (dec.); m. 2d, Margaret Alice Dunlap, 1961; 1 son, James Harold. Chmn. bd. J.H. Crang & Co., Ltd., Toronto, 1929—. Pres. Royal Agrl. Winter Fair, 1959-60. Vice chmn. Royal Ont. Museum. Served to maj. Canadian Arty., 1942-44. Mem. Toronto, Montreal, Canadian Arty., 1942- 44. Mem. Toronto, Montreal, Canadian stock exchanges, Winnipeg Grain Exchange, Investment Dealers Assn. Can., Atlantic Salmon Assn. (dir. 1968—). Clubs: Toronto, York, Toronto and North York Hunt, Eglinton Hunt (Toronto); Manitoba (Winnipeg); Hamilton (Can.); Mount Royal (Montreal); Racquet and Tennis (N.Y.C.); Rolling Rock (Ligonier, Pa.); Grande Romaine Salmon (Romaine, Que.); White's (London, Eng.). Home: 40 Burton Rd Toronto 10 Ontario Canada Office: 20 King St W Toronto 1 Ontario Canada

CRANKSHAW, EDWARD, corr., author; b. Jan. 3, 1909; s. Arthur and Amy Crankshaw; ed. Bishop's Stortford Coll.; m. Clare Carr, 1931. With Brit. Mil. Mission, Moscow, 1941-43; corr. Soviet affairs for The Observer, Eng., 1947—; contbr. on fgn. affairs N.Y. Times. Author: Joseph Conrad: Aspects of the Art of the Novel, 1936; Vienna: the Image of a Culture in Decline, 1938; Britain and Russia, 1945; Russia and the Russians, 1947; Russia by Daylight, 1951; The Forsaken Idea; a study of Viscount Milner, 1952; Gestapo; Instrument of Tyranny, 1956; Russia Without Stalin, 1956; Khrushchev's Russia, 1959; The Fall of the House of Hapsburg, 1963; The New Cold War: Moscow v. Pekin, 1963; Khrushchev: A Career, 1966; Maria Theresa, 1970; (novels) Nina Lessing, 1938, What Glory?, 1939, The Creedy Case, 1954. Address: Church House Sandhurst Kent England

CRANMER, H. JEROME, educator, economist; b. Morristown, N.J., June 2, 1920; s. Horace K. and Elizabeth (Fletcher) C.; A.B., Drew U., 1947; A.M. Columbia, 1949, Ph.D., 1955; m. Margaret E. Welch, June 21, 1947; children—Carol Anne, Susan Kinney, Charles Nelson, Thomas Fletcher. Mem. faculty Drew U., 1949—, prof. econs., chmn. dept., 1958—; cons. in field, 1957—. Served to capt. AUS, 1942-46. Mem. Am. Econ. Assn., Am. Finance Assn., Econ. History Assn., N.J. Council Econ. Edn. Author: New Jersey in the Automobile Age, 1964; also articles. Home: 35 Green Hill Rd Madison NJ 07940

CRANMER, RALPH R., pres. Grit. Address: 208 W 3d St Williamsport PA 17701 ‡

CRANSTON, ALAN, U.S. senator; b. Palo Alto, Cal., June 19, 1914; s. William MacGregor and Carol (Dixon) C.; student Pomona Coll., 1932-33, U. Mexico, 1935; A.B., Stanford U., 1936; m. Geneva McMath, Nov. 6, 1940; children—Robin MacGregor, Kim MacGregor. Fgn. correspondent Internat. News Service, Eng., Italy, Ethiopia, 1936-38; Washington rep. Common Council Am. Unity, Washington, 1940-41; chief fgn. lang. div. O.W.I., Washington, 1942-44; exec. sec. Council for Am.-Italian Affairs, Inc., Washington, 1945-46; partner bldg. and real estate firm Ames- Cranston Co., Palo Alto, Cal., 1947-58; controller State of Cal., 1959-67; pres. Homes for a Better America Inc., 1967-68; v.p. Carlsberg Financial Corp., Los Angeles, 1968; mem. U.S. Senate from Cal., 1969—; mem. Com. on Banking, Housing and Urban Affairs, Com. on Labor and Pub. Welfare, Com. on Vets. Affairs. Mem. exec. com. Cal. Central Com. Democratic Party, 1954-60; pres. Cal. Dem. Council, 1953-57. Served with AUS, 1944-45. Mem. United World Federalists (nat. pres. 1949-52). Club: Overseas Press Am. Author: The Big Story, 1940; The Killing of the Peace, 1945. Home: 4117 Ocean Dr Manhattan Beach CA 90266 Office: Senate Office Bldg Washington DC 20510

CRANSTORM, ALEXANDER chemist, educator; b. Chicago, 1928; B.S. in Physics, Yale, 1950; Ph.D. in Chemistry, Harvard, 1956; m. Sally Ann Jones, July 5, 1957; children--Kenneth J., Nancy A. Chemist, Acme Chem. Co., Blue Island, Ill., 1950-51; director of Research Lab., Indsl. Chemicals Corp., Cambrige, Mass., 1956-60; project coordinator environmental sect. Steinmetz Assos., Chgo., 1960-61; v.p. for research Bauer Bros. Chem. Co., Inc., Memphis, 1961-64; asst. prof. chemistry Washington U., St. Louis, 1964-66, asso. prof., 1966-70, prof., 1970--, head of chemistry dept., 1970-71. Vis. prof. So. Ill. U., summer 1967, U. of Ore., 1969. Bd. dirs. Rest Haven Home for Elderly, 1960-61; trustee of the Lutheran Hosp., 1965-71. Served from lt. to capt., AUS, 1951-53. Mem. Am. Chem. Soc., Sci. Research Soc. Am. (chpt. treas. 1967), Sigma Xi. Author: (with others) Basic Inorganic Chemistry, 1971. Home: Fairfax Apts 7291 Windermere Dr University City MO 63105 Office: Dept Chemistry Washington University St Louis MO 63130

CRANZ, F. EDWARD, educator; b. Barmen, Germany, Aug. 5, 1914 (parents Am. citizens); s. Fritz E. and Adah (Brush) C.; B.A., Syracuse U., 1935; M.A., Harvard, 1937, Ph.D., 1938; m. Eleanor Davis Southworth, June 15, 1944; children—Donald, Gretchen. Jr. fellow Soc. Fellows, Harvard, 1938-42; mem. faculty Conn. Coll., 1942—, prof. history, 1957—, Rosemary Park prof., 1963—, chmn. dept., 1957-60, 63-68. Served with AUS, 1944-45. Mem. Mediaeval Acad. Am., Medieval and Renaissance Latin Translations and Commentaries Assn. (exec. sec., editor Catalogus Translationum et Commentariorum 1969—), New Eng. Commn. on Higher Edn., Renaissance Soc. Am., Am. Hist. Assn. Author: (with G.M. Fuermann) Ninety-fifth Division History, 1918-1946, 1947; An Essay on the Development of Luther's Thought on Justice, Law and Society, 1959; also articles. Home: 7 N Ridge Rd New London CT 06320

CRAPSTER, BASIL LONG, educator; b. Taneytown, Md., July 3, 1920; s. Basil Walter and Ellen (Long) C.; grad. Mercersburg (Pa.) Acad., 1937; A.B., Princeton, 1941; A.M., Harvard, 1942, Ph.D., 1950; m. Joan Tewksbury, Nov. 27, 1953; children—Basil Tewksbury, Barbara Bruce. Mem. faculty Gettysburg (Pa.) Coll., 1949—, prof. history, 1963—, dean coll., 1966-70. Vis. instr. Coll. William and Mary, 1950, 51. Served to lt. USNR, 1942-46. Mem. Am. Hist. Assn., Phi Beta Kappa, Phi Alpha Theta. Presbyn. Contbr. articles to profl. jours. Home: 150 W Broadway Gettysburg PA 17325

CRARY, ALBERT PADDOCK, geophysicist; b. Pierrepont, N.Y., July 25, 1911; s. Frank J. and Ella (Paddock) C.; B.S. magna cum laude, St. Lawrence U., 1931; M.S., Lehigh U., 1933; m. Mildred Reade Rodgers, Feb. 16, 1968; 1 son, Frank. Oil prospector Ind. Exploration Co., Colombia, 1938-40; in Eng., Venezuela, Bahrein Island for United Geophys. Co., 1942-46; geophysicist Cambridge Research Center USAF, 1946-60; chief scientist U.S. Antarctic Research Program NSF, 1959-67, dep. dir. div. environmental scis., 1967-69, dir. div., 1969—; chief scientist IGY Program in Antarctica, 1957-59. Recipient Navy Distinguished Pub. Service award, 1959; Cullum Geog. medal Am. Geog. Soc., 1960; Distinguished Service award Dept. Def., 1959. Mem. A.A.A.S., Am. Geophys. Union, Phi Beta Kappa, Sigma Xi. Contbr. articles in field. Home: 3010 New Mexico Av NW Washington DC 20016 Office: Nat Sci Found Washington DC 20550

CRARY, ELISHA AVERY, judge; b. Grundy Center, Ia., June 24, 1905; s. Elisha Avery and Gertrude (Miner) C.; student West Point Acad., 1922-24, U. Ia., 1924-26; B.A., LL.B., U. So. Cal., 1929; m. Bertha E. Northcote, June 2, 1936 (dec. 1942); children—Elisha Avery, Oliver N.; m. 2d, Emmajane Rorer, July 4, 1946. Admitted to Cal. bar, 1930, since practiced in Los Angeles; mem. firm Meserve, Mumper & Hughes, 1936-61; apptd. to Superior Ct., State of Cal., 1961-62; U.S. dist. judge Central Dist. Cal., 1962—. Hon. consul Republic of Turkey, 1959-61. Bd. dirs. Legal Aid Found. Los Angeles, 1958-70, pres., 1963-64. Served from maj. to col. AUS, 1941-46. Decorated Legion of Merit, Bronze Star medal; Croix de Guerre (France). Fellow Am. Coll. Trial Lawyers; mem. Am., Cal., Los Angeles (trust 1952-59, pres. 1958) bar assns., Am. Judicature Soc., West Point Soc. (Los Angeles pres. 1952), Am. Law Inst., Soc. Mayflower, S.R., Phi Kappa Psi, Phi Delta Phi. Clubs: Newport Harbor Yacht (dir. 1952-57, commodore 1957), University (Los Angeles); Chancery. Home: 570 N Rossmore Av Los Angeles CA 90004 Office: 312 N Spring St Los Angeles CA 90012

CRASEMANN, BERND, educator, physicist; b. Hamburg, Germany, Jan. 23, 1922; s. Pablo Joaquin and Hildegard Carlota (Vorwerk) C.; came to U.S., 1946, naturalized, 1955; A.B., U. Cal. at Los Angeles, 1948; Ph.D., U. Cal. at Berkeley, 1953; m. Jean Millicent McEown, June 6, 1952. With Lavadora de Lanas S.A., Via del Mar, Chile, 1941-46; asst. prof. physics U. Ore., Eugene, 1953-58, asso. prof., 1958-63, prof., 1963—. Guest asso. physicist Brookhaven Nat. Lab., Upton, N.Y., 1961-62; vis. prof. U. Cal. at Berkeley, 1968-69; cons. Lawrence Radiation Lab., 1954-68, physicist, 1968-69. Mem. region XIV selection com. Woodrow Wilson Nat. Fellowship Found., 1959-61, 62-68. Recipient Ersted award for distinguished teaching U. Ore., 1959. NSF research grantee, 1954-64, U.S. AEC grantee, 1964—. Fellow Am. Phys. Soc.; mem. Am. Assn. Physics Tchrs. (pres. Ore. sect. 1956-57), Phi Beta Kappa, Sigma Xi (pres. Ore. chpt. 1958-59). Clubs: Sierra, Aclu. Author: (with J.L. Powell) Quantum Mechanics, 1961. Contbr. articles to sci. jours. Home: 2520 Woodland Dr Eugene OR 97403

CRASS, MAURICE FREDERICK, Jr., chem. engr., assn. exec.; b. Cleve., Nov. 26, 1903; s. Maurice Frederick and Emma May (Reid) C.; B.S., Case Inst. Tech., 1926, M.S., 1930; m. Mary Elizabeth Kroeger, Dec. 26, 1931; children—Mary, Maurice Frederick. Chem. engr. Goodyear Tire & Rubber Co., 1926-29; faculty mem. Case Inst. Tech., 1930-33; chief chemist Palmer Match Co., 1934-38; sec.-treas. Mfg. Chemists Assn., Inc., 1939-68, chem. cons., 1968—. U.S. employer del. to ILO, Geneva, 1955, 56, 58, 62. Mem. Am. Chem. Soc., Internat. Orgn. Chem. Employers (chmn. safety com. 1962-70), Sigma Xi, Phi Kappa Psi, Tau Beta Pi, Theta Tau. Presbyn. (elder). Clubs: Cosmos (Washington); Chemists (N.Y.C.). Author: Chemical Facts and Figures, 5 edits.; also profl. publs. on chem. statistics, econs., matches and trans. Address: 3450 Chiswick Ct Silver Spring MD 20906

CRATER, ROBERT WINFIELD, newspaperman; b. Newcomerstown, O., Jan. 8, 1912; s. Edward Irving and Hazel M. (Bramhall) C.; student pub. schs.; m. Lucille R. Salladay, Aug. 15, 1930; 1 dau., Carroll Dianne (Mrs. Steve J. Volchko). With J.G. Bair Co., Cambridge, O., 1930-36; reporter Coshocton (O.) Tribune, 1936-42; reporter Columbus (O.) Citizen, 1942-45, city editor, 1945-50; Washington corr. Cleve. Press, Cin. Post and Times Star, Columbus (O.) Citizen-Jour., 1950—. Mem. Sigma Delta Chi, Alpha Phi Gamma. Club: Nat. Press (Washington). Home: 7000 40th Av University Park MD 20742 Office: Scripps-Howard Newspapers 1013 13th St 20005

CRATHORNE, BARON, (Sir Thomas Lionel Dundale), ex-mem. Parliament; b. London, Eng., July 20, 1897; s. James Lionel and Maud (Woodroffe) d.; student Eton Coll., 1910-15, Royal Mil. Coll., Sandhurst, 1915; m. Nancy Tennant, 1936 (dec. 1969); children—Charles James, David John. Mem. Parliament representing Richmond, Yorkshire, 1929-59; parliamentary pvt. sec. to Pres. Bd. Trade, 1931, to Sec. State for Colonies, 1931-35, to Sec. State for Air, 1935, to Prime Minister, 1935- 37; Lord Commr. of Treasury, 1937-40; dep. chief govt. whip, 1941-42; Minister agr. and fisheries 1951-54, Leader U.K. delegation to Council Europe and Western European Union, 1961-65, v.p., 1963-65; United Kingdom standing com. Nato Parliamentarians Conf., 1959-65, pres. 1963. Vice chmn. Conservative Party Orgn. 1941-42, chmn. 1942-44. Served Royal Scots Greys, 1916-28, adj. Yorkshire Hussars Yeomanry, 1927. Created baronet, 1945, baron, 1959. Home: Crathorne Hall Yarmouth Yorkshire England also House of Lords Westminster London England

CRATSLEY, EDWARD KNEELAND, coll. adminstr., educator; b. Warren, O., Sept. 10, 1914; s. John Carlisle and Carolyn (Kneeland) C.; A.B., Coll. of Wooster, 1936; M.B.A., Harvard, 1938, D.C.S., 1943; m. Mary Jane Payton, Sept. 4, 1937; children—John Christopher, David Bruce. Research asst. Harvard Grad. Sch. Bus. Adminstrn., 1938-39, instr. accounting, 1939-41; comptroller, asst. prof. bus. adminstrn. St. Lawrence U., Canton, N.Y., 1941- 47, sec., 1942-43, comptroller, prof. bus. adminstrn., 1947-50; v.p., prof. econs. Swarthmore (Pa.) Coll., 1950—. Del. in edn. 9th Internat. Mgmt. Congress 1951; mem. N.Y. Milkshed Price com., 1947-49, Commn. on Higher Instns., Middle States Assn. Colls. and Secondary Schs., 1952-58, v.p., 1962, pres. 1963. Mem. Swarthmore Borough Council, 1962-69. Trustee Phila. Coll. Art, 1960—, Coll. Entrance Exam. Bd., 1966-70. Mem. Nat. Assn. Coll. and Univ. Bus. Officers (dir. 1960-65), Nat. Assn. Ednl. Buyers, Eastern Assn. Coll. and Bus. Officers (pres. 1958), Phi Beta Kappa. Republican. Presbyn. Rotarian. Home: 741 Harvard Av Swarthmore PA 19081

CRAVALHO, ELMER FRANKLIN, legislator, mayor of Maui, Hawaii; b. Paia, Maui, Hawaii, Feb. 19, 1926; s. Manuel Bartholomew and Mary (Pires) C.; student U. Hawaii, 1945-47, 48-54. Tchr. pub. schs., Maui, 1946-54; mem. Hawaii Ho. of Reps., 1954—, vice speaker, 1955, chmn. house finance com., 1957-59, speaker, 1959-67. Exec. v.p., gen. mgr., dir. M.D.G. Supply Co., Wailuku, Maui, treas., dir. Kula Community FCU, Inc., Royal Tire Motors, Inc., Maui, Factors, Inc., Molokai Services, Inc. Chmn. Community Chest drive, 1963; vice chmn. bd. regents Chaminade Coll. Chmn. Maui County Com. Democratic Party Hawaii, 1954-64; mem. Dem. Nat. Com. for Hawaii, 1964-68; mayor County of Maui, 1968—. Chmn. bd. Olinda Kula Soil and Water Conservation Dist.; pres. Hawaii Assn. Soil and Water Conservation Dist. Recipient Outstanding Young Man award Maui County Jr. C. of C., 1956; Nat. 4-H Alumni award, 1962-63. Roman Catholic. Home: Rural Route 1 Box 742 Kula Maui HI 96790 Office: Wailuku Maui HI 96793 also Iolani Palace Honolulu HI 96813

CRAVEN, AVERY ODELLE, educator; b. Warren County, Ia., Aug. 12, 1886; s. Oliver and Mary E. (Pennington) C.; A.B., Simpson Coll., 1908, LL.D., 1936; M.A., Harvard, 1914; Ph.D., U. Chgo., 1923; Litt.D., Simpson Coll., 1946, U. S.C. 1961; D.H.L., Tulane U., 1952, Wayne State U., 1957, Purdue U., 1969; M.A., Cambridge U., 1952; m. Grace Greenwood Oct. 2, 1914 (dec. 1936); 1 dau., Jean Greenwood; m. 2d, Georgia D. Watson, Sept. 26, 1938. Prof. history Coll. of Emporia (Kan.), 1920-22; asst. prof. Mich. State Coll., 1923-24; asst. prof. U. Ill., 1924-26, asso. prof., 1926-28; asso. prof. U. Chgo., 1928-29, prof. Am. history 1929—. Distinguished Fgn. prof. U. Sidney, Australia, 1947; Pitt. prof. Am. history and instns. Cambridge U., 1952- 53; lectr. Am. Seminar, Salzburg, 1953, 54; fellow Downing Coll., Cambridge, 1952-53; vis. prof. U. Cal., U. Colo., U. N.C., U. So. Cal., Northwestern U., U. Wis., Western Mich. U.; Distinguished fgn. lectr. Am. Studies Com., Japan, 1967. Cons. Library of Congress; mem. Civil War Centennial Commn., 1958—, Ill. Lincoln Sesquicentennial Commn., 1959—. Mem. So. Hist. Assn. (pres. 1952), Orgn. Am. Historians (pres. 1963-64), Am. Agrl. Soc. (past pres.), Phi Beta Kappa. Co-author; Sources of Culture in the Middle West; author several books including: The United States, Experiment in Democracy, 1947; Coming of the Civil War-The Rise of Southern Nationalism, 1953; Civil War in the Making, 1815-60, 1959; Ending of the Civil War, 1968. Contbr. articles to profl. jours. Home: 23 Circle Dr Dune Acres Chesterton IN 46304 Office: Faculty Exchange U Chicago Chicago IL

CRAVEN, CLIFFORD JOHN, univ. pres.; b. Huntington, Mass., Jan. 4, 1920; s. John and Marjorie (Perkins) C.; A.B., Syracuse U., 1942, Ed.D.,1951; M.A., Columbia, 1946; m. Marion McCarthy, Jan. 8, 1943; children—Marion (Mrs. David L. Payne), Dean, Carolyn, Nancy, Constance. Instr. polit. sci., asst. dean Syracuse U., 1946-52; dean students N.Y. State Tchrs. Coll., Oneonta, 1952-56, dean acad. affairs State U. N.Y. Coll. Oneonta, 1964-71, pres., 1971—; dean student affairs U. Okla., 1956-64. Served to capt. USAAF, 1942-45; ETO; col. Res. Mem. Am. Polit. Sci. Assn., Comparative Edn. Soc. Rotarian. Home: 19 Woodside Av Oneonta NY 13820

CRAVEN, JAMES BRAXTON, Jr., judge; b. Lenoir, N.C., Apr. 3, 1918; s. James Braxton and Katherine Simmons (Covington) C.; A.B., Duke, 1939, postgrad. Law Sch., 1946; LL.B., Harvard, 1942; m. Jean Bible, Aug. 15, 1952; children—James Braxton III, Stephen K., Elizabeth Bible. Admitted to N.C. bar, 1946; solicitor Burke County Criminal Ct., 1947; asst. U.S. atty., Charlotte-Asheville, 1948- 52; became judge Superior Ct. of N.C., 1956; U.S. judge Western dist. N.C., 1961-66; U.S. circuit judge 4th Circuit Ct. Appeals, 1966—. Vis. prof. constl. law U.N.C. Law Sch., summers 1967, 70; vis. prof. fed. cts. U. Tex. Law Sch., summer 1968. Del., Southeastern Jurisdictional Conf., Methodist Ch., 1956, 60, 64, Gen. Conf. Meth. Ch., 1964. Trustee, Duke, 1972—. Served from ensign to lt., USNR, 1942-46. Mem. Am., N.C. (v.p. 1959-60), Burke County bar assns., Am. Judicature Soc., Order of Coif, Phi Beta Kappa, Omicron Delta Kappa. Home: PO Drawer 491 Asheville NC 28802

CRAVEN, JOHN HOWARD, economist, banker; b. Eureka, Utah, Feb. 7, 1921; s. Percy H. and Anna (Mathisen) C.; A.B., Brigham Young U., 1942; M. Pub. Adminstrn., Harvard, 1946, M.A., 1947, Ph.D., 1951; m. Lucile Hess, Apr. 26, 1943; children—Michael, David, Kathryn, Christopher. Intern, Nat. Inst. Pub. Affairs, 1942-43; economist State Dept., 1945-46; asst. prof. econs. U. Wyo., 1947-50; economist program staff Dept. Interior, 1951-52; program officer Inst. Interam. Affairs, Bolivia, 1952-53; asso. economist Bank of Am., San Francisco, 1954-60, chief economist, 1960-65, v.p., 1963- 65; v.p. Fed. Res. Bank San Francisco, 1965-68, sr. v.p., 1968—. Mem. mission to Burma to study investment climate, 1961; mem. World Bank mission to Spain, 1961. Chmn. African Student Fund. Bd. dirs. No. Cal. Com. for Africa. Mem. Am., Western econ. assns., Am. Statis. Assn., World Affairs Council No. Cal. Home: 3839 Dixon Pl Palo Alto CA 94306 Office: Fed Res Bank of San Francisco Sacramento and Sansome Sts San Francisco CA 94120

CRAVEN, JOHN PINNA, univ. dean, civil engr.; b. Bklyn., Oct. 30, 1924; s. James McDougal and Mabel (Pinna) C.; B.S. in Civil Engring., Cornell U., 1946; M.S. in Civil Engring., Cal. Inst. Tech., 1947; Ph.D., U. Ia., 1951; J.D., George Washington U., 1959; m. Dorothy Drakesmith, Feb. 4, 1951; children—David John, Sarah Johanna. Hydrodynamicist, David Taylor Model Basin, 1951-59; chief scientist U.S. Navy Spl. Projects Office, 1959-71, project mgr. deep submergence systems project, 1965-67, chief scientist project, 1967-70; vis. prof. polit. sci. and naval architecture Mass. Inst. Tech., 1969-70; dean marine programs U. Hawaii, Honolulu, 1970—; marine affairs coordinator State Hawaii, 1970—. Served with USNR, 1943-46. Recipient Meritorious Civilian Service award Navy Dept., 1953, Distinguished Civilian Service award, 1960; Fleming award U.S. C. of C., 1960; William S. Parsons award Navy League, 1966; Distinguished Civilian Service award Dept. Def., 1969. Mem. Nat. Acad. Engrs. Presbyn. (trustee). Home: 4921 Waa St Honolulu HI 96821 Office: Univ of Hawaii Honolulu HI 96822

CRAVEN, WAYNE, educator; b. Pontiac, Ill., Dec. 7, 1930; s. Ernest Wayne and Vera (Cline) C.; A.B Ind. U., 1955, M.A., 1957; Ph.D., Columbia U., 1963; m. Lorna Rose Breseke, Apr. 5, 1953. Instr. art history Wheaton Coll., Norton, Mass., 1958-59; H.F. DuPont prof. art history U. Del., Newark, 1960—, coordinator Winterthur program in Early Am. Culture, 1965-70, H.F. DuPont Winterthur Mus., 1965. Chmn. bd. Del. State Arts Council, 1967-68. Trustee Soc. Preservation of Del. Antiquities. Mem. Soc. Archtl. Historians, Collectors Art Assn., Mus. Modern Art, Phi Kappa Phi. Author: Sculpture in America, 1968; American Painting, 1857-1869, 1962. Contbr. articles on Am. painting, sculpture. Organized sculpture exhibit for White House's Creative American show, 1965. Home: 300 Dove Dr Newark NJ 19711 also Route 1 Box 193 Dennis Port MA 02639

CRAVEN, WESLEY FRANK, educator; b. Conway, N.C., May 19, 1905; s. Wesley Frank and Elizabeth (Turner) C.; A.B., Duke U., 1926, M.A. 1927; Ph.D., Cornell, Ithaca, N.Y., 1928; m. Helen G.

McDaniel, May 31, 1932; childrenNancy Elizabeth, Betty Morris. Instr. history N.Y. U., 1928-30, asst. prof., 1930-37, asso. prof., 1937-40. prof., 1940-50; Edwards prof. Am. history Princeton, 1950-64, George Henry Davis '86 prof. Am. history, 1964-. Served from maj. to lt. col. AUS, AAF, 1943-46. Recipient Legion of Merit. Mem. Am., Mississippi Valley hist. assns., Colonial Soc. Mass., Mass. Hist. Soc., Am. Antiquarian Soc., Phi Beta Kappa, Delta Sigma Phi. Author: Dissolution of the Virginia Company, 1932; Introduction to History of Bermuda, 1938; The Southern Colonies in the Seventeenth Century, 1949; The Legend of the Founding Fathers, 1956; New Jersey and the English Colonization of North America, 1964. Co-editor: The Army Air Forces in World War II, vols. I-VII, 1948-58; The Colonies in Transition, 1660-1713, 1968. Contbr. learned jours. Home: 36 Scott Lane Princeton NJ 08540

CRAVENS, CARLISLE, lawyer; b. Arlington, Tex., Apr. 29, 1908; s. Milton Henderson and Mary Bird (Carlisle) C.; student Arlington State Coll., 1924-26, U. Tex., 1926-30; m. Jimmie Elizabeth Widman, Apr. 26, 1934; childrenMary Cecelia (Mrs. Walter Scott Wysong III), Ralph Thomas. Admitted to Tex. bar, 1930, since practice in Ft. Worth; asso., mem. firm. Cantey, Hanger, Gooch, Cravens & Munn and predecessors, 1930-46, mng. partner, 1962—. Incorporator, pres., chmn. bd. adv. chmn. bd. First Nat. Bank Arlington; dir. Kendavis Industries Internat., Inc., Kendavid Indsl. Supply Co., Mid-Continent Supply Co., Mid-Continent Supply Eastern Hemisphere Co., Mid-Continent Supply Western Hemisphere Co., Mid- Continent Supply Co. (Holland) N.V., Mid-Continent Supply Co. (U.K.) Ltd., Beta Devel. Co., Mid-Continent Supply Co. (Alta.) Ltd., Mid-Continent Defsco., Ltd., Great Western Drilling Co., Unit Rig & Equipment Co., Loffland Brothers de Sudamerica, C.A., Loffland Brothers Co. (Del.), Loffland Brothers Internat, Inc., Loffland Brothers Co. (Holland) N.V., Loffland Brothers Co. Can., Loffland Brothers Co. Venezuela. Loffland Brothers Co. Peru (Del.), Loffland Brothers de Venezuela, C.A., Loffland Bros. Eastern Hemisphere Inc., Cummins Sales & Service de Venezuela, C.A., MidContinent Cummins Export Eastern Hemisphere, Inc., Harrisburg, Inc., Harrisburg Sales & Service Ltd., Pionera Internacional, C.A., Diesel Internat., Inc., So. N.M. Oil Corp. Bd. dirs. Arlington Area Health Found., Ken W. Davis Found.; former vice chmn. bd. trustees Arlington Meml. Hosp. Found.; trustee Trinity Valley Sch. Served to lt. USNR, 1944-46. Mem. Am., Tex., Ft. Worth-Tarrant County (past pres.) bar assns. Clubs: Fort Worth, Shady Oaks Country (both Ft. Worth); Shady Valley Country (Arlington, Tex.). Home: 501 Fielder Rd Arlington, TX 76010. Office: First Nat. Bank Bldg. Fort Worth, TX 76102.

CRAVENS, KATHRYN, radio news commentator; b. Burkett, Tex., Oct. 27; d. John Calvin and Rose Ann (Hudson) Cochran; student Horner Inst. Fine Arts, Kansas City, Mo., Henry Kendall Coll. (now U. Tulsa), Morse Sch. Expression, St. Louis, N.Y.U.; m. Rutherford Rector Cravens, July 15, 1922 (div. 1937). Began as actress with Fox Films, Hollywood, 1919; played with Woodrow Stock Co., 1925, Mary Hart Players, 1927. Arthur Casey Co., 1929; played in Reunion in Vienna. The Barker, Lombardy, Ltd., The Masquerader, The Greeks Had a Word for It, Berkeley Square, The Cherry Orchard, Torch Bearers, A Modern Virgin; became radio actress sta. KWK. St. Louis, 1928; actress and women's hour dir. sta. KMOX, St. Louis, 1931; first woman news commentator, coast-to-coast, C.B.S., N.Y.C., 1936; became The Flying Reporter, 1937, flying over 100,000 miles a year for broadcasts and articles; programs called News Through a Woman's Eyes; began syndicated column, Thru a Woman's Eyes (articles and poems). 1938. Guest of Pres. Comacho, of Mexico Govt., while on writing assignment, 1941. Accredited to radio, World War II; covered Europe, Asia and Middle East; broadcast from Berlin following Allied victory; covered Balkan elections and early Palestine riots. Mem. N.L.A.P. (nat. radio contest chmn. 5 yrs.), Am. Theater wing, N.Y.C., League of Women Voters, Assn. Women Dirs. Nat. Assn. Broadcasters, Overseas Press Club Am. (first v.p.), Tex. Club (pres.), Bus. and Profl. Women's Club. Awarded 1st prize by Nat. League Am. Penwomen for novel, 1948; hon. mention by Women's Nat. Radio Com., 1930; 1st prize for article Helen Keller Pities the Real Unseeing, by Penwomen, 1942; voted best dressed woman in radio, and one of 10 best dressed women in the U.S., 1938-54. Mem. First Christian Ch. Author: Pursuit of Gentlemen (novel); The Lost Glove (pub. in Off the Record). Contbr. to Cosmopolitan. This Week, N.Y. Times, N.Y. Herald Tribune. Christian Sci. Monitor, etc. Home: Phantom Hill Burkett TX 76828

CRAVENS, RAYMOND LEWIS, univ. dean; b. St. Bernard, O., Dec. 5, 1930; s. R.L. and Ethel (Hammonds) C.; A.B., Western Ky. State Coll., 1952, M.A., 1955; Haggin scholar U. Ky., 1955-57, Ky. Research Found. fellow, 1957, Ph.D., 1958; m. Ann Powell, Aug. 11, 1956; childrenAndrea Lee, Alicia. Prof. govt. Western Ky. U., 1958-59, dean of coll., 1959-64, dean of faculty, 1964- 66, v.p. acad. affairs, dean faculties, 1966—. Chmn., Ky. Council of Acad. Vice Presidents; mem. adv. com. on tchr. edn. Ky. Council on Pub. Higher Edn. Served as 1st lt. USAF, 1952-54. Named one of 3 outstanding young men in state Ky. Jr. C. of C., 1964. Mem. So. Acad. Deans, So. Assn. Colls. (commn. on colls.; chmn. com. admissions to membership). Baptist. Mason. Kiwanian. Home: 43 Highland Dr Bowling Green KY 42101

CRAWFORD, ARTHUR JOHN, business devel. exec.; b. Glenn Ridge, N.J., Oct. 3, 1915; s. Arthur W. and Madeline (Ledwina) C.; undergrad. student in bus. mgmt. and engring. Sales mgr. Magnetic Engring. & Mfg. Corp., 1946-49; exec. v.p., dir. Convertoplane Corp., N.Y.C., 1949-57; mgmt. cons. N.Y.C., 1957-65; chmn. bd., pres. BARDCO, Inc. N.Y.C., 1965—; chmn. bd., pres. Crawford-Bardco Industries. Ltd. Toronto, Can. 1970—. Bd. dirs. Conger Found. Fellow A.I.M. (pres. council), Aircraft Pioneers, Audio Engring. Soc. Club: Bras Coupe Hunting and Fishing. Smithsonian Inst. accepted for permanent collection operational model demonstrating feasibility of 1st operational convertible aircraft. Home: 105 E 63d St New York City NY 10021 Office: 30 E 68th St New York City NY 10021

CRAWFORD, BRODERICK, motion picture actor; b. Phila., Dec. 9, 1911; s. Helen Broderick and Lester Crawford; m. Joan Tabor; children—Lauren, Kim, Kelly. Began on stage; screen debut, The Woman's Touch, 1937. Received Academy Award for Best Actor, 1950 for leading role in All the King's Men. Pictures include: The Real Glory, Eternally Yours, 1940; I Can't Give You Anything But Love, Baby, Slightly Honorable, When the Daltons Rode, 1942; Sin Town, Broadway, Butch Minds the Baby, 1946; The Runaround, Black Angel, 1947; Slave Girl, 1948; The Time of Your Life, 1949; All the King's Men, 1950; Born Yesterday, 1951; Night People, 1954; Not as a Stranger, 1955; Convicts 4, 1962, Fastest Gun Alive, Between Heaven and Hell, The Oscar, Gregoria and His Angels, The Texican, Hell's Bloody Devils. Head of Broderick Crawford Enterprises, 1952—. Star TV series Highway Patrol, 1958—. Address: care Columbia Pictures Corp 1438 N Gower Los Angeles CA 90028

CRAWFORD, BRUCE E., advt. agy. exec. Sr. v.p. Batten, Barton, Durstine and Osborn, Inc., N.Y.C.; pres. BBDO Internat. Office: 383 Madison Av New York City NY 10017*

CRAWFORD, BRYCE LOW, Jr., chemist, educator; b. New Orleans, Nov. 27, 1914; s. Bryce Low and Clara Hall (Crawford) C.; A.B., Stanford, 1934, M.A., 1935, Ph.D., 1937; Nat. Research fellow, Harvard, 1937-39; m. Ruth Raney, Dec. 21, 1940; children—Bryce, Craig, Sherry Ann. Instr. chemistry Yale, 1939-40; asst. prof. U. Minn., Mpls., 1940-43, asso. prof., 1943-46, prof. phys. chemistry, 1946—, chmn. dept., 1955-60, dean grad. sch., 1960-72. Mem. Grad. Record Exam. Bd., 1968-72; chmn. Council Grad Schs. in U.S., 1962-63; pres. Assn. Grad. Schs., 1970; dir. research on rocket propellants under Div. 3, Nat. Def. Research Com., 1942-45. Bd. dirs. North Star Research and Devel. Inst., 1963—. Guggenheim fellow, 1950-51, Fulbright grantee, Oxford, 1951, Tokyo, 1966; recipient Presdl. Certificate of Merit. Mem. Am. Chem. Soc. (dir. 1969-71), Optical Soc. Am., A.A.A.S., Am. Assn. U. Profs., Am. Phys. Soc., Nat. Acad. Scis., Coblentz Soc., Am. Philos. Soc., Phi Beta Kappa, Sigma Xi, Phi Lambda Upsilon, Alpha Chi Sigma. Episcopalian. Clubs: Campus, Cosmos. Editor: Jour. Phys. Chemistry, 1970—. Specialist in molecular structure and molecular spectra. Home: 1545 Branston St St Paul MN 55108 Office: U Minn Minneapolis MN 55455

CRAWFORD, BURNETT HAYDEN, lawyer; b. Tulsa, June 29, 1922; s. Burnett Hayden and Margaret Sara (Stevenson) C.; A.B., U. Mich., 1944, J.D., 1949; m. Alyn Carolyn McCann, June 5, 1946; children—Margaret Louise, Robert Hayden, William Allan; m. 2d, Virginia Baker Hastings, July 23, 1970. Admitted to Okla. bar, 1949: practiced in Tulsa, 1949-54, 61—; asst. city prosecutor, Tulsa, 1951-53; alternate municipal judge, Tulsa, 1953- 54; U.S. atty. No. dist. Okla., 1954-58; spl. asst. to dep. U.S. atty. gen., 1958-59, asst. dep. U.S. atty. gen., 1959-60. Rep. Candidate for U.S. Senate, 1960, 62, Served to lt. (j.g.) USNR, 1944-46; now Capt. Res. Mem. Am., Okla., Tulsa County bar assns., Phi Delta Theta, Phi Delta Phi. Republican. Presbyn. Home: 5206 S Harvard Av Tulsa OK 74135 Office: First Nat Bldg Tulsa OK 74103

CRAWFORD, CHARLES, assn. exec.; b. Ironton, O., July 11, 1917; s. Charles Aloysius and Beulah (Sharpe) C.; B.A., Marshall Coll., 1940; m. Anne Louise Hock, Jan. 2, 1942; 1 son, Roger S. Exec. sec. Blount County C. of C., Maryville, Tenn., 1947-49; mng. dir. Bristol (Va.-Tenn.) C. of C., 1949-54; exec. v.p. Trenton (N.J.) C. of C., 1955-57, Charlotte (N.C.) C. of C., 1957—. Mem. adv. com. Southeastern div. U.S. C. of C.; mem. faculty Southeastern Inst. Mem. adv. com. So. W.Va. for U.S. Army, 1944-45; dir. Bluefield (W.Va.) A.R.C., 1945-46. Certified chamber exec. Mem. Am., N.C. (past pres.), So. (past pres.) assns. C. of C. execs. Episcopalian. Clubs: City, Myers Park Country (Charlotte). Home: 3218 Foxcroft Rd Charlotte NC 28211 Office: 222 S Church St Charlotte NC 28202

CRAWFORD, CHARLES MCNEIL, winery exec.; b. Antioch, Cal., Sept. 23, 1918; s. Robert Elmer and Alice (Hust) C.; B.S., U. Cal. at Berkeley, 1940; M.S., Cornell U., 1941; m. Sarah Katherine Glover, Aug. 19, 1940; children—Robert McNeil, Judith Lee. Trainee, Great Western Electro-Chem. Co., Pittsburg, Cal., 1939; research asst. N.Y. State Agrl. Expt. Sta., Geneva, N.Y., 1940; winemaker-chemist Urbana Wine Co., Hammonsport, N.Y., 1941; v.p., sec. E & J Gallo Winery, Modesto, Cal., 1942—; mem. grape inspection adv. com. Cal. State Dept. Agr. Cornell U. Research fellow, 1940-41. Mem. Am. Soc. Enologists, Am. Chem. Soc., Inst. Food Technology, Wine Inst. Tech. Adv. Com., Nat. Soc. Profl. Engrs., Cal. Soc. Profl. Engrs., N.Y. Acad. Sci., Cal. Acad. Sci., A.A.A.S., Modesto Engring. Club, Alpha Zeta. Clubs: Modesto Swim and Racquet; F.W. Ski Assn.; Tahoe Yacht. Home: 1322 Edgebrook Dr Modesto CA 95351 Office: PO Box 1130 Modesto CA 95350

CRAWFORD, CHERYL, theatrical producer; b. Akron, O., Sept. 24, 1902; d. Robert K. and Luella Elizabeth (Parker) Crawford; student Buchtel Coll., 1 year; A.B. cum laude, Smith Coll., 1925, Litt.D., 1966. Produced plays while at Smith Coll.; casting dir. Theatre Guild, N.Y.C. 1926-30; one of founders and dirs. The Group Theatre, 1930-37, produced Men in White by Sidney Kingsley, Awake and Sing by Clifford Odets; produced independently Family Portrait with Judith Anderson, Gershwin's Porgy and Bess, One Touch of Venus, Shakespeare's The Tempest, Brigadoon, Love Life, Regina, The Rose Tattoo, Good as Gold, Oh, Men! Oh, Women!, 1954, Comes a Day, Camino Real, Shadow of a Gunman, Rivalry, Sweet Bird of Youth, Period of Adjustment, 1960, Andorra, Jennie, Brecht on Courage, 1962, Mother Courage and Her Children, 1963, Double Talk, 1964, Celebration, 1969, Colette, 1970. Named Woman of Year 1959; recipient Achievement medal Brandeis U., 1964. Home: 400 E 52d St New York City NY 10022 Office: 301 W 45th St New York City NY 10036

CRAWFORD, CHESTER S., former business exec.; b. Tarentum, Pa., 1904; s. Thomas W. and Anna (Fox) C.; A.B., Pa. State U., 1926; m. Jeanne Davison, June 20, 1931; children—Natalie, Peter. Dir., Whitehall Cement Mfg. Co., Westmoreland Coal Co., Gen. Coal Co. Trustee, Lankenau Hosp. Republican. Presbyn. Clubs: Merion Cricket; Midday, Racquet, Philadelphia Country (Phila.). Home: 1120 Spring Mill Rd Villanova PA 19085

CRAWFORD, CLARENCE CLAY, steel exec.; b. Longmont, Colo., June 5, 1918; s. Clarence Clay and Helen (Brown) C.; Met.E., Colo. Sch. Mines, 1940; m. Jo Evelyn Moore, Mar. 28, 1969; children by previous marriage—Crete St. Clair, Wilson Clay, James Paul. With CF & I Steel Corp., 1946—, works mgr., Pueblo, Colo., 1961-65, v.p. operations, Denver, 1965-70, pres., dir., Pueblo, 1970—; dir. First Nat. Bank Pueblo. Served to maj., C.E., AUS, 1940-46; PTO. Recipient distinguished achievement medal, Colo. Sch. Mines, 1967. Mem. Am. Iron and Steel Inst. (dir.), Am. Petroleum Inst., Am. Soc. Metals, Assn. Iron and Steel Engrs., Beta Theta Pi. Presbyn. Home: 2922 7th Av Pueblo CO 81003 Office: CF & I Steel Corp Canel and Abriendo Sts Pueblo CO 81004

CRAWFORD, CLARENCE LEONARD, educator; b. Nicholls County, Neb., Dec. 13, 1902; s. Arthur Benjamin and Nora (Hoge) C.; A.B.,Cotner Coll., Neb. 1925; M.A., U. Neb., 1928; postgrad. Harvard, summer 1931; Ph.D. (John Henry and Helene Moehlman Fellow), U. Mich., 1936; m. Lillian Schlentz, May 24, 1926; children—Rosalee Josephine (Mrs. Sperlich), Richard Almer. High sch. tchr., Edison, Neb., 1924-25; high sch. prin. Trumbull (Neb.) Consol. Schs., 1925-26, supt. schs., 1926- 28; supt. schs., Wood River, Neb., 1928-29, Wagner, S.D., 1929-33; dir. research Mich. Dept. Edn., Lansing, 1935-37; asst. supt. schs. charge bus. affairs, Muskegon, Mich., 1937-40; tchr. summer sessions U. Neb., 1939-40, U. Omaha, 1945; supt. schs., Council Bluffs, Ia., 1940-46; pres. Mankato (Minn.) State Coll., 1946-65; Distinguished prof. edn. Fla.-Atlantic U., Boca Raton, 1965—. Mem. Commn. Higher Edn., 1947-49, Tchr. Edn. and Profl. Standards Commn., Minn. Edn. Assn., 1958-65; mem. N. Central Assn. Commn. on Colls. and Univs., 1957-60, subcom. on tchr. edn. in multipurpose instns., 1960- 65; mem. bd. Minn. Council on Econ. Edn., 1961-65; mem. Nat. Commn. on Accrediting, 1964-65. Pres., Mankato United Fund, 1957-58; past pres. Mankato City Planning Commn. Recipient war fund citation for service as war fund chmn. A.R.C., 1944; Mankato Exchange Club Book of Golden Deeds award, 1961. Mem. Mich. (life), Minn. (adv. com. tchr. edn., 1947-49, past pres. div. higher edn.) edn. assns., Commn. Colls. and Univs., Am. Assn. Colls. for Tchr. Edn. (state liaison officer 1955-58), Nat. Aviation Council (teaching edn. com. 1956-58), Am. Assn. Sch. Adminstrs. Rotarians. Club: Iowa Schoolmasters. Author: Variations in Purchasing Power of the Dollar (ednl.), 1936. Mem. ednl. adv. bd. The Nation's Schs. Mag., 1942-69. Contbr. articles to various ednl. pubs. Home: 1156 SW 14th St Boca Raton FL 33432

CRAWFORD, DAVID MACKAY, sulphur co. exec.; b. Phila., Jan. 5, 1916; s. Thomas Frew and Margaret (Mackay) C.; A.B., Cornell U., 1938; LL.B., Yale, 1941; m. Elizabeth MacDonald, Mar. 15, 1947; children Thomas MacDonald, David Mackay, Barbara Ann, Elizabeth Margaret. Admitted to N.Y. bar, 1941, Ill. bar, 1962; atty. firm Lord, Day & Lord, N.Y.C., 1946-48; asso. prof. maritime law Yale Law Sch., 1946-48; with Office Gen. Counsel; ECA, 1948-51; with office gen. counsel, also mgr. dept. intergovtl. affairs Socony Mobil Oil Co., 1951-61; sec., gen. counsel Abbott Labs., 1961-63; sec., mgr. pub. and govtl. relations Tex. Gulf Sulphur Co., 1964-. Trustee Peck Sch., Morristown, N.J., 1958-61; adv. bd. Internat. and Comparative Law Center, S.W. Legal Found., 1961—. Served to lt. comdr. USNR, 1941- 45. Mem. Am. Bar Assn., Am. Soc. Internat. Law, N.A.M. (chmn. com. protection pvt. investment 1964-), U.S. C. of C., Phi Delta Phi, Sigma Phi. Clubs: Sky, Yale (N.Y.C.); Morristown Field; Essex Hunt (Peapack, N.J.); Somerset Hills Country. Home: James St New Vernon, NJ 07976. Office: 200 Park Av New York City NY 10017

CRAWFORD, DWAIN A., mfg. co. exec.; b. Carroll County, O., 1903; A.B., Hiram Coll., 1931; LL.B., McKinley Law Sch., 1930; married. Admitted to Ohio bar, 1932; practiced law, 1932-43; asst. sec. Diebold, Inc., Canton, O., 1947-56, asst. treas., 1951—, sec., 1956—, also dir. Mem. Ohio Bar Assn. Home: 3405 Blackburn St NW Canton OH 44718 Office: 818 Mulberry Rd SE Canton OH 44702*

CRAWFORD, EARL BOYD, former govt. ofcl.; b. Washington, Apr. 13, 1906; s. James Albert and Olla Lola (Nigh) C.; student Strayer Bus. Coll., 1924; grad. Mt. Pleasant Sch. for Secs., 1929; m. Gertrude Galloway, June 15, 1927; 1 son, Christopher Paul. Sec. to mem. of Congress, 1932-36; sec., chief staff to dir. gen. U.S. Constn. Sesquicentennial Commn., 1936-39; staff adminstr., clk. Com. Fgn. Affairs Ho. of Reps., 1939-70; mem. U.S. delegation UN Conf. Internat. Orgn., San Francisco, 1945; mem. U.S. delegation UN Gen. Assembly, London, 1946, N.Y., 1946, 49, 50, 53, Paris, 1951; sec. U.N. com. U.N.R.R.A., 1946, mem. U.S. delegation Fourth Council Meeting, 1946; staff mem. US delegation Consultative Assembly Europe, Strasbourg, France, 1965, 66. Mem. adv. com. inst. position U.S. world affairs Am. U., lectr. U.S. fgn. policy, 1949, 50; served with spl. Congl. study mission, Alaska, 1947, Europe, 1951, Far East, South Asia, Middle East, 1954, Mediterranean, 1956. Guatemala, Mexico, 1957, Japan, Vietnam, Thailand, 1965, Colombia, 1968; congl. del. 6th-8th NATO Parliamentarian's Conf., Paris; mem. del. Brit.-Am. Parliamentary Conf., Bermuda, 1961, 63, 64, 66, 68, staff mem., 1966, 68; U.S. del. Commonwealth Parliamentary Conf., Wellington, New Zealand, 1965, Consultative Assembly Council Europe, 1968. Mem. Am. Polit. Sci. Assn., Am. Acad. Polit. and Social Sci., Am. Soc. Internat. Law. Author ofcl. report U.S. Constn. Sesquicentennial Commn. contained in History of the Formation of the Union Under the Constitution, 1941. Home: 7401 Idylwood Rd Falls Church VA 22043

CRAWFORD, EARL RUSSELL, naval officer; b. Peru, Ind., May 2, 1913; s. Anderson and Julia (Lowe) C.; B.S., U.S. Naval Acad., 1936; grad. Naval War Coll., 1955; m. Dorothea Jo Knauer, June 4, 1938; 1 son, Joseph. Commd. ensign U.S. Navy, 1936, advanced through grades to rear adm., 1964; comdr. submarines S-46 and Roncador, World War II, submarine Blueback after World War II; exec. officer U.S.S. Northampton, 1953; comdr. U.S.S. Tulare, 1957, Amphibious Squadron 1, 1962; assigned Joint Staff, Joint Chiefs Staff, 1963; comdr. Amphibious Tng. Command, Atlantic Fleet, 1964, Amphibious Group 2, 1965, U.S. Naval Base, Guantanamo Bay, Cuba, 1966-68; comdr. tng. command Atlantic Fleet, 1968-69, with office of CNO Navy Dept., Washington, 1969—. Decorated Legion of Merit, Joint Service Commendation medal. Episcopalian. Address: Office of CNO Navy Dept Washington DC 20350

CRAWFORD, ERNEST STANLEY, physician; b. Evergreen Ala., May 12, 1922; s. J. Lloyd and Myrtle (Godwin) C.; B.A., U. Ala., 1943; M.D., Harvard, 1946; m. Carolyn Easter; children—Clay Easter, John Lloyd, Bruce Godwin, Carolyn. Mem. faculty Baylor U. Coll. Medicine, now prof. surgery. Served to lt. (j.g.) USNR, 1947-49. Home: 3028 Ella Lee Lane Houston TX 77019.

CRAWFORD, EUGENE BENSON, Jr., health adminstr.; b. Tuskegee, Ala., Apr. 18, 1925; s. Eugene B. and Madge (Abercrombie) C.; B.S., U. N.C., 1948, grad. exec. program, 1966; certificate N.C. Bapt. Hosp., 1949; m. Elizabeth Virginia Wilson, Oct. 2, 1948; children—Elizabeth Kenyon, Madge Lane, Virginia Wilson. Adminstrv. resident N.C. Bapt. Hosp., Winston-Salem, 1948-49; asst. adminstr. Moore Meml. Hosp., Pinehurst, N.C., 1949-51; asso. dir. to dir., asst. prof. N.C. Meml. Hosp. of U. N.C., 1951-66; v.p. adminstrn. Wilmington (Del.) Med. Center, 1966—. Mem. med. adv. com. Wilmington Vets. Hosp., 1968—; cons. Dept. HEW. Served with USNR, 1942-46. Fellow Am. Coll. Hosp. Adminstrs.; mem. Assn. Del. Hosps. (pres. 1970), Am. Hosp. Assn., Am. Assn. Med. Colls. Club: Rotary (Wilmington). Home: 2603 Deepwood Dr Chalfonte Wilmington DE 19810 Office: PO Box 1668 Wilmington DE 19899

CRAWFORD, FRANK STEVENS, educator; b. Scranton, Pa., Oct. 25, 1923; s. Frank Stevens and Louise (Kindl) C.; Ph.D., U. Cal., Berkeley, 1953; m. Bevalyn D. Bunker, June 2, 1962; children—Sarah T., Matthew B. Research asso. Lawrence Radiation Lab., 1953-58; asst. prof. physics U. Cal., Berkeley, 1958-60, asso. prof., 1960-65, prof., 1965—. Served with USAAF, 1943-45. Mem. Am. Phys. Soc., Am. Assn. Physics Tchrs. Author: Waves, 1968. Home: 2826 Garber St Berkeley CA 94705

CRAWFORD, FREDERICK COOLIDGE, former mfg. corp. exec.; b. Watertown, Mass., Mar. 19, 1891; s. Fred E. and Mattie (Coolidge) C.; A.B., Harvard, 1913, M.C.E., 1914; Dr. Eng., Case Sch. Applied Science, 1942; LL.D., Bowling Green (O.) State U., 1944; So.D., Clarkson Coll. Tech., 1947; LL.D., Western Res. U., 1957; LL.D., Temple U., 1958; L.H.D., Lake Erie Coll., 1958; Dr. Space Sci., Fla. Inst. Tech., 1967; m. Audrey Bowles, Oct. 17, 1932. With Thompson Products. Inc. (changed to Thompson Ramo Wooldridge, Inc., 1958), 1916-66, beginning as millwright helper, dir., 1926-66, pres., 1933, chmn. 1953-58; chmn. exec. com. TRW, Inc. (formerly Thompson Ramo Wooldridge, Inc.), 1958-67, hon. mem. bd. dirs., 1967—; pres. Bluecoats, Inc., Cleve.; dir. Cleve. & Pitts. R.R. Co., Armstrong Cork Co. Trustee, pres. Am. Sch. Classical Studies Athens, Euclid- Gen. Hosp. Assn., St. Luke's Hosp., Found. Econ. Edn., Inc., Mus. Art Assn.; trustee Corporate 1% Program for Higher Edn., Cleve., Vocational Guidance and Rehab. Services, Cleve; trustee, chmn. bd. Cleve. Zool. Soc.; hon. trustee, hon. chmn. bd. trustees Case Western Res. U.; bd. overseers Hoover Inst. War, Revolution and Peace. Recipient Cleve. Medal for Pub. Service, 1941; Franklin Inst. Vermilye Medal, 1958; Wright Bros. Meml. trophy, 1960. Mem. Nat. Assn. Mfrs. (pres. 1943, dir.), Greater Cleve. Growth Assn. (pres. 1939, life mem.) Cleve. Engring. Soc., Soc. Automotive Engrs.,

Harvard Engring. Soc., Western Res. Hist. Soc. (pres., trustee), Newcomen, S.A.R., Phi Beta Kappa. Clubs: Harvard (N.Y.C.); Harvard, Union, Country, Pepper Pike, Skating (Cleve.); Bohemian (San Francisco); Wianno (Mass.); Explorers (N.Y.C.); Oyster Harbors (Osterville. Mass.); Cat Cay Ltd. (Bahamas). Home: 1 Bratenahl Pl Cleveland OH 44108 Office: PO Box 3036 Cleveland OH 44117

CRAWFORD, HOMER, paper co. exec., lawyer; b. St. Louis, Nov. 28, 1916; s. Raymond S. and Mary (Homer) C.; A.B., Amherst Coll., 1938; LL.B., U. Va., 1941; m. Esther Wilkinson, Oct. 4, 1944 (div. 1949); 1 dau., Candace C.; m. 2d, Sara E. Twigg, May 3, 1952; childrenGeorgianna, William Twigg. Admitted to N.Y. State bar, 1942; with firm LeBoeuf, Lamb & Leiby, 1942-54, partner, 1954-56; sec. St. Regis Paper Co., 1956—. v.p., 1970—, also dir.; dir. Northwestern Pulp & Power Ltd., St. Regis Paper Co. (Can.) Ltd., Bates do Brazil, S.A., Cia. Argentina de Productos de Papel Strylease Corp. Mem. Am., N.Y. State bar assns., Am. Soc. Corporate Secs. (dir.), N.Y. State C. of C., Theta Delta Chi. Republican. Presbyn. Home: 1170 Fifth Av New York City, NY 10029. Office: St Regis Paper Co 150 E 42d St New York City, NY 10017.

CRAWFORD, JAMES CHARLES, oilwell drilling and exploration co. exec.; b. Brandon, Man., Can., Sept. 20, 1934; s. Charles and Lyda Mary (Maher) C.; B.S., U. Man., 1958, LL.B., 1964; postgrad. U. Sask., 1958-59; m. Karen R. Morrison, May 10, 1958; 1 son, Charles Sean. Geologist, Dome Petroleum, Ltd., 1956-58, Stekall Petroleum Corp., 1958-60; called to bar, Alta., 1965; pvt. practice law, Calgary, 1965-70; sec., gen. counsel Westburne Internat. Industries, Ltd., Calgary, 1970—; dir. Commonwealth Petroleum Services, Ltd. Pres. Young Progressive Conservative Assn., 1962-63; candidate for Provincial Legislature Alta., 1967. Mem. Law Soc. Man., Law Soc. Alta., Canadian Petroleum Tax Soc. (v.p.), Calgary Petroleum Club. Mason. Editor Man. Law Sch. Jour., 1963. Home: 2748 Wolfe St SW Calgary Alberta Canada Office: 535 7th Av SW Calgary 2 Alberta Canada

CRAWFORD, JOAN, drink co. exec., actress; b. San Antonio, Mar. 23, 1908; ed. schs. Kansas City; student Stephens Coll., Columbia, Mo.; m. Douglas Fairbanks, Jr., June 3, 1929 (div.); m. 2d, Franchot Tone, Oct. 11, 1935 (div.); m. 3d, Phillip Terry, July 21, 1942 (div.); m. 4th, Alfred Nu Steele, May 10, 1955 (dec. Apr. 1959); children—(adopted) Christina, Christopher, Cynthia, Cathy. Appeared as dancer on stage as Lucille le Sueur; entered movies in 1926; starred in following films: Dancing Daughters; Blushing Brides; Untamed; Modern Maidens; Paid; Laughing Sinners; Possessed; Grand Hotel; Rain; Dancing Lady; The Gorgeous Hussy; The Bride Wore Red; Mannequin; Forsaking All Others; No More Ladies; The Last of Mrs. Cheyney; Ice Follies of 1939; The Shining Hour; The Women; A Woman's Face; They All Kissed the Bride; Above Suspicion; Reunion in France; Hollywood Canteen; Mildred Pierce; Humoresque; Daisy Kenyon; Flamingo Road; The Damned Don't Cry; Harriet Craig; Goodbye, My Fancy; This Woman Is Dangerous; Sudden Fear; Torch Song; Johnny Guitar; Female on the Beach; Queen Bee; Autumn Leaves; The Story of Esther Costello; The Best of Everything; What Ever Happened to Baby Jane; The Caretakers; Strait Jacket; I Saw What You Did; Berserk; Trog. Dir., Pepsi-Cola Co., Purchase, N.Y. Recipient Acad. award for role in Mildred Pierce, 1946. Hon. fellow Brandeis U. Author: (with Jane Kesner Ardmore) A Portrait of Joan, 1962. Home: 8008 W Norton Av Los Angeles CA 90046

CRAWFORD, JOHN, Jr., utility co. exec.; b. Spring Canyon, Utah, May 27, 1925; s. John and Alice (Ruff) C.; B.A., U. Utah, 1947, J.D., 1949; m. Marilyn Jeanne Reiser, Aug. 24, 1949; childrenKathryn, Thomas John, Mary Lou, Robert Bruce. Admitted to Utah bar, 1949; clk. to dist. judge, Salt Lake City, 1950-51; gen. practice law, Salt Lake City, 1951-52; asst. supt. claims U.S. Fidelity and Guaranty Co., Salt Lake City, 1952-56; with Mountain Fuel Supply Co., 1957-, sec., gen. counsel, 1968-. Mem. Utah State BAr, Am., Salt Lake County bar assns., Pacific Coast, Am. gas assns., Rocky Mountain Mineral Law Found. Rocky Mountain Gas and Oil Assn., Salt Lake City C. of C., Am. Judicature Soc., Ind. Petroleum Assn. Am., Pi Kappa Alpha, Phi Delta Phi. Home: 1585 S 2200 East Salt Lake City, UT 84108. Office: 180 E First South Salt Lake City UT 84111

CRAWFORD, JOHN CALVIN, Jr., lawyer; b. Maryville, Tenn., July 24, 1906; s. John Calvin and Mary Maud (Farnham) C.; A.B., Maryville Coll., 1927; LL.B., Harvard, 1931; m. America Arey Moore, Jan. 1, 1933; children—Carolyn (Mrs. J. Calvin Chesnutt). John Calvin, Duncan Venable. Admitted to Tenn. bar, 1931; pvt. practice, Maryville, 1931-53, 61—; U.S. dist. atty. Eastern Dist. Tenn., 1953-61. Mem. adv. commn. rules practice and proc. Supreme Ct. Tenn., 1966—. State senator, Tenn., 1941-45; mayor of Maryville, 1947-53, mem. utilities bd. 1963-. Presdl. elector, 1964. Mem. Am, Tenn., Maryville bar assns. Republican (del. nat. conv. 1952). Presbyn. (ruling elder). Mason (33). Club: Lions. Home: Duncan Dr Maryville TN 37801 Office: Maryville TN 37801

CRAWFORD, JOHN EDWARD, marine scientist; b. Richmond, Va., June 6 1924 s. James Henry and Loretta Ellen (Bankerd) C.; B.A., Johns Hopkins, 1947; m. Mary Elizabeth Ayres, May 15, 1948; children—Michelle Lorraine, Caprice Lizette. Geologist uranium exploration program U.S. Geol. Survey, 1948-51; nat. stockpile materials specialist Munitions Bd., Office Sec. Def., 1951-53; prodn. engr. uranium in Tenn. and Fla., AEC, 1953-54; specialist on source, feed, fissionable materials Bur. Mines, 1954-57, nuclear tech. adviser to dir. Bur. Mines, 1957-60, chief nuclear engr. for atomic research programs, 1960-64, dir. Marine Mineral Tech. Center, Tibourn, Cal., 1963-65; pres., founder Crawford Marine Specialists, Inc., San Francisco, 1966—. Served with AUS, 1943-46. Mem. Am. Soc. Oceanography, Marine Tech. Soc. (past chmn. marine resources com.), Delta Upsilon. Author: Facts Concerning Uranium Exploration and Production, 1956. Contbr articles to profl. jours. Home: 716 Birchwood Ct Terra Linda San Rafael CA 94903 Office: Piers 38-40 The Embaracadero San Francisco CA 94107

CRAWFORD, JOSEPH PAUL, Jr., bank and trust co. exec.; b. Phila., June 27, 1904; s. J.P. and Florence (Felton) C.; B.S., U. Pa., 1926; m. Ruth Newcombe Pressinger, June 2, 1934; children—Joseph Paul III, Jean N. Stephen, Richard D. With Guaranty Co. N.Y., 1926-30; asst. cashier Phila. Nat. Bank, 1931-40, v.p., 1941-43; v.p. First Nat. Bank of Phila. 1944-46; exec v.p., dir Slater System, Phila., 1947-48; v.p. Chem. Bank (merger Chem. Corn Exchange Bank and N.Y. Trust Co.), N.Y.C., 1949-61, regional v.p., 1962-63, sr. v.p., 1964-69, mem. adv. bd., 1969—; pres., dir. Internat. Utilities Investment Corp., Iu Overseas Investment Corp.; v.p. dir. Internat. Utilities Overseas Capital Corp.; dir. Princeton Bank & Trust Co. (N.J.), Goodall Rubber Co. Clubs: University, Brook (N.Y.C.); Pine Valley (N.J.) Golf; Bedens Brook (Princeton); Racquet (Phila.). Home: Old Green Farm Pennington NJ 08534 Office: 1500 Walnut St Philadelphia PA 19102

CRAWFORD, KENNETH GALE, journalist; b. Sparta, Wis., May 27, 1902; s. Robert Levy and Madge (Gale) C.; B.A., Beloit Coll., 1924, Litt.D., 1954; LL.D., Olivet Coll.; m. Elisabeth Bartholomew, July 21, 1928; children— William, Gale. Reporter and bur. mgr. UPI, St. Paul, St. Louis, Cleve., Lansing and Indpls., 1924-27, Washington corr., 1927-29; columnist Buffalo (N.Y.) Times, 1929-32; Washington corr. N.Y. Post, 1932-40; Washington corr. and bur. mgr. PM (newspaper), 1940-43; war corr. Newsweek, N. Africa, Italy, Middle East, Eng., France, 1943-44, Washington corr., polit. columnist, 1944-70; now syndicated newspaper columnist. Decorated Navy Commendation (U.S.); French Liberation medal. Pres., Am. Newspaper Guild, 1939-40. Clubs: Nat. Press, Overseas Writers, Cosmos (Washington); Players (N.Y.C.). Author: The Pressure Boys, 1939; Report on North Africa, 1943. Home: 1412 30th St NW Washington DC 20007 Office: 1750 Pennsylvania Av Washington DC 20006

CRAWFORD, MEREDITH PULLEN, psychologist, profl. orgn. exec.; b. Sweetbriar, Va., Oct. 13, 1910; s. Leonidas Wakefield and Helen May (Meredith) C.; A.B., Vanderbilt U., 1931; A.M., Columbia, 1932, Ph.D., 1935; m. Helen Cartwright Grizzard, Aug. 20, 1936; children—Meredith P., Ann C., Susan B. Univ. fellow in psychology Columbia, 1933-34; research asst. Lab. Primate Biology, Yale, 1934-39; Instr. psychology Barnard Coll., Columbia, 1939-40; asst. prof., then prof. psychology Vanderbilt U., Nashville, 1940-51, dean instrn. Coll. Arts and Sci., 1949-51; dir. George Washington U. Human Resources Research Office, 1951-69; pres. Human Resources Research Orgn., 1969—. Served as officer USAAF aviation psychology program, 1942-45. Recipient Distinguished Civilian Service award Sec. Army, 1961. Fellow A.A.A.S., Am. Psychol. Assn. (treas. 1958-67); mem. Am. Ednl. Research Assn. (financial adviser 1970-72), Phi Beta Kappa, Sigma Xi, Delta Kappa Epsilon. Methodist. Club: Cosmos. Home: 5605 Montgomery St Chevy Chase MD 20015 Office: 300 N Washington St Alexandria VA 22314

CRAWFORD MICHAEL PATRICK actor; b. Salisbury, Eng., Jan. 19 1942; s. Arthur Dumbell-Smith and Doris (Pike) C.; student St. Michael's Coll., 1950, Oakfield Coll., 1953; m. Gabrielle Lewis, Dec. 19, 1965; childrenEmma Jane, Lucy Mary. Singer with English Opera Group, 1956-57; numerous stage, radio and TV appearances in Eng., 1957-; motion pictures include The Knack, 1966, A Funny Thing Happened on the Way to the Forum, 1965, The Jokers, 1967, How I Won the War, 1967, Hello Dolly; Broadway appearance in Black Comedy, 1967, The Games, 1969; profl. photographer, 1966—. Recipient award as most promising newcomer Variety Club Gt. Britain, 1966; Whitebread for Black Comedy, 1967. Home: 50 Marryat Rd Wimbledon London S.W. England. Office: care William Morris Agy Melrose House 4 Saville Row London W1 England

CRAWFORD, MORRIS DECAMP, Jr., banker, b. Nyack, N.Y., Sept. 11 1915; s. Morris DeCamp and Grace (Blauvelt) C.; S.B. magna cum laude, Harvard, 1937, LL.B., 1940; m. Dorothy Duncan Babcock, May 2, 1942; children—Duncan, Gordon, Linda. Admitted to N.Y. bar, 1940: with firm Cadwalader, Wickersham, Taft, N.Y.C., 1940-53; with Bowery Savs. Bank, N.Y.C., 1953—, exec. v.p., 1959-62; pres. 1962-66, chmn. bd., Chief exec. officer, 1966—; trustee Tchrs. Ins. & Annuity Assn. dir. Savs. Banks Trust Co.; mem. Grand Central adv. bd. Chem. Bank. Cons. com. Internat. Savs. Banks Inst.; mem. Pres. Nixon's Commn. on Financial Structure and Regulation. Chmn., Regional Plan Assn.; chmn. bus. adv. council N.Y. State Urban Devel. Corp.; campaign chmn. U.S.O., N.Y.C. Mem. bd. N.Y. Urban Coalition; bd dirs. Nat. Corp. for Housing Partnerships; trustee Grant Found.; mem. N.Y.C. adv. board Salvation Army; trustee Russell Sage Found; bd. councilors Urban Center, U. So. Cal, Served to maj. AUS, 1942-46; PTO. Mem. Nat. Assn. Mut. Savs. Banks (dir., pres. 1964-65). Mem. P.E. Ch. Clubs: Union League, Sky, Harvard (N.Y.C.); Greenwich (Conn.) Country. Home: 71 Gilliam Lane Riverside CT 06878 Office: 110 E 42d St New York City NY 10017

CRAWFORD, RALPH J., Jr., banker; b. 1921; A.B., U. Cal. at Berkeley, 1943; grad. Pacific Coast Banking Sch., 1955, U. Cal. Grad. Sch. Bus. Adminstrn., 1959; married. Clk., Bank of Hawaii, 1946-47; with Well Fargo Bank, N.A., 1947—, exec. v.p., 1968—. Served with AUS, 1943-46. Address: 464 California St San Francisco CA 94120*

CRAWFORD, RALSTON, artist; b. St. Catharines, Ont., Can. Sept. 25 1906; s.George Burson and Lucy (Colvin) C.; brought to U.S., 1910, naturalized citizen; student Otis Art Inst., Los Angeles, 1927. Pa. Acad. Fine Arts, Phila., 1927-30. Barnes Found., 1928-30, Breckenridge Sch., Columbia, others; m. Margaret Stone, Oct. 17, 1932; children—James Ralston, Robert Frederick; m. 2d, Margaret Elizabeth Frank, Feb. 5, 1942; children—Neelon Frank, John Colvin. Began career with Walt Disney, 1927; painter, lithographer, etcher, photographer, illustrator; tchr. drawing, painting Cinn. Art. Acad., Buffalo Sch. Fine Arts, Art Sch. of Bklyn. Mus., U. Minn., La State U., U. Colo., New Sch. Social Research, N.Y.C., Honolulu Acad. Art; asso. prof. dept. art Hofstra Coll., Long Island, 1960-62; photographic research cons. New Orleans Jazz Archives, Tulane U., Photog. studies Indian cave temples, 1945; art observer Bikini atom bomb test, 1946; exhibited nationally and internationally in group shows; one man shows include Md. Inst. Art. Balt., Flint (Mich.) Inst. Arts, Seattle, Portland art museums, Howard U., Honolulu Acad. Arts, Santa Barbara Mus., Milw. Art Inst., St. George's Gallery, London, U. Minn., San Francisco Mus., U. Neb., Wesleyan U., Creighton U., Omaha, Century Assn., N.Y.C., and others; represented in permanent colls. U. Ga., Ala. Poly. Inst., Butler Mus Am. Art, Whitney Mus. Am. Art, Duke U., N.Y. Pub. Library, Vassar Coll., Walker Art Center, Library Congress, Met. Mus. Art. Mus. Modern Art. N.Y.C., Cin. Art Mus., Toledo Art Mus., others; Ford Found. vis. artist U. Neb., 1965; vis. artist U. Ill., 1966; commd. spl. art program U.S. Dept. Interior, 1969. Articles, Illustrations, numerous mags. and jours.; work featured in Richard B. Freeman's The Lithographs of Ralston Crawford, 1962. Home: 60 Gramercy Park New York City NY 10010 Studio: 10 E 23d St New York City NY 10010

CRAWFORD, ROBERT PERRY, ins. co. exec.; b. Glens Falls, N.Y., June 22, 1914; s. George Perry and Helene (Davidson) C.; grad. Worcester (Mass.) Acad., 1933; A.B., Dartmouth, 1937; m. Madeline Hanford, Feb. 8, 1941; children—Robert Perry, Bruce Hanford, Lynn Fitch. With Glens Falls Ins. Co., 1937-66, pres., 1961-66; v.p. adminstrn. Am. Fgn. Ins. Assn., N.Y.C., 1966-70, exec. v.p., 1970—. Chmn. Warren-Washington Counties chpt. A.R.C., 1954-57, mem. Eastern area adv. council, 1958-60. Served with U.S. Mcht. Marine, World War II. Mem. Delta Kappa Epsilon. Home: 855 Norgate Rd Ridgewood NJ 07450 Office: 110 William St New York City NY 10038

CRAWFORD, ROBERT PLATT, educator, author; b. Council Bluffs, Ia., Dec. 7, 1893; s. Nelson Antrim and Fanny (Vandercook) C.; A.B., U. Neb., 1917; A.M., Columbia 1926; unmarried. Reporter Neb. State Jour., Lincoln, 1914-16; agrl. editor U. Neb., 1917-18; asst. editor U.S. Dept. Agr., Washington, 1918; asso. editor Neb. Farmer, Lincoln, 1919-21; hist. research for U. Neb., 1922, asst. prof. journalism, 1923, asso. prof., 1924, prof., 1926-59, now emeritus, asst. to chancellor, 1928-38; sec. U. Neb. Found., 1937-39, est. course in creative thinking, 1931. Vis. prof. journalism U. Tex., 1940-41; sr. field rep. OWI, 1944; specialist on bus. and finance, Washington, Overseas Br. OWI, 1945; journalism faculty U.S. War Dept. U., Florence, Italy, 1945; sr. publs. analyst (in charge mag. analysis), Civil Information and Ed., SCAP, Tokyo, Japan, 1946-47; chief neutral property Civil Property Custodian, 1947, hist. banking and finance (both SCAP, Tokyo), 1948. Fellow Royal Econ. Soc.; mem. Am. Econ. Assn., Midland Authors (v.p.), Asso. Club: London Authors. Author: These Fifty Years, 1925; The Magazine Article, 1931; Think for Yourself, 1937; How to Get Ideas, 1948; The Techniques of Creative Thinking, 1954 (also in German, Swedish and Japanese under different titles); Direct Creativity with Attribute Listing, 1964. Orginated nat. syndicated daily feature Dollars and Sense, 1922; spl. writing for Barron's, 1924-26, Country Gentleman, 1926-31; econ. investigations for Barron's 1942-44; Financial World (Realty series), 1952-60. Extensive travel in Europe, Siberia, Manchuria, Japan, Australia, New Zealand. Address: PO Drawer 1231 Lincoln NB 68501

CRAWFORD, THOMAS JAMES, educator; b. Pitts., Dec. 14, 1916; s. James and Margaret (Millar) C.; B.S., U. Pitts., 1938, M.A., 1940, Ph.D., 1956; postgrad. Columbia, 1948- 49, Harvard, 1943-46; m. Marilyn Rose Hayes, Aug. 1, 1961; children—Mary Jane, Nancy Jeanne. Tchr. bus. courses Washington (Pa.) High Sch., 1938-39; head dept. bus. edn. Johnstown Jr. Coll., 1939-40; instr. U. Pitts., summer sessions, 1941, 51, 52; instr. Womans Coll., U. N.C., 1940-42; faculty Greensboro (N.C.) Sr. High Sch., 1940-42; instr. USN Supply Corps Sch., Bayonne, N.J., 1946; asst. prof. Ind. U., 1947-53, asso. prof., 1953-64, prof., 1964—, chmn. dept. bus. edn. and office mgmt., 1967—; vis. prof. Fresno State Coll., summers 1953, 57, 63; vis. prof. San Francisco State Coll., summer 1955; lectr. U. P.R., 1958; established Center for Tng. in Office Adminstrn., Lembaga Administrasi Negara, sponsored by Govt. Indonesia, Ford Found. and Ind. U., 1963-65; cons. Peace Corps on Office Tng. Programs, 1965, Ednl. Testing Service, Princeton, N.J., 1966, U. P.R., 1969, So. Assn. Colls. and Schs., Atlanta, 1969. Dir. Ann. Conf. on Bus. Edn., Bloomington, Ind., 1958—; mem. Gov. Ind.'s Com. on Vocational Edn., 1962- 63; mem. Ind. Adv. Com. for Bus. Edn., 1964-66; mem. Ind. Com. on Tchr. Licensing, 1970. Charter mem. Internat. Commn. on Bus. Edn., 1965. Served to lt. USNR, 1943-46. Recipient Delta Pi Epsilon research awards, 1942, 56, Thoroughbred award Central Ky. Bus. Edn. Assn., 1967, Gold Book award Southwestern Pub. Co., 1964; named Distinguished lectr. in bus. edn. Okla. State U., 1968; Ky. col. Mem. Internat. Bus. Edn. Assn., Nat. Bus. Edn. Assn. (mem. exec. bd.), Nat. Assn. for Bus. Tchr. Edn. (pres., mem. com. standards for accreditation), Adminstrv. Mgmt. Soc., Eastern Bus. Tchrs., Assn., Nat. Soc. for Study Edn., Ind. Bus. Edn. Assn. (mem. exec. bd., past pres.), Catholic Bus. Edn. Assn. (mem. exec. bd.), Assn. for Higher Edn., Ind. Bus. Educators Club (past pres.), Beta Gamma Sigma, Phi Delta Kappa, Pi Omega Pi (hon.), Delta Pi Epsilon, Omicron Delta Lambda, Delta Delta Lambda. Author: (with D.D. Lessenberry) 20th Century Typewriting, 1947, TV Typing, 1958; Production Typewriting, 1960; (with Lessenberry and Erickson) Methods and Materials for Teaching Typewriting, 1962; (with others) Practices and Preferences in Teaching Typewriting, 1967. Contbr. articles profl. jours. Home: Audubon Dr Route 1 Bloomington IN 47401

CRAWFORD, VERNON D'ORSAY, ednl. adminstr.; b. Amherst. N.S., Can., Feb. 13, 1919; s. Roy David and Lydia (Edgett) C.; B.A., Mt. Allison U., Sackville, N.B., 1939; M.S., Dalhousie U., Halifax, N.S., 1943; Ph.D., U. Va., 1949; m. Helen Dell Avison, May 15, 1943; children—Lynn Kathleen (Mrs. David Hood), Dell Marie (Mrs. Ronald Byrd). Came to U.S., 1947, naturalized, 1953. Physicist, Naval Research Establishment of Can., Halifax, 1943-45; lectr. Dalhousie U., 1944-47; asso. prof. physics Ga. Inst. Tech., Atlanta, 1949-55, prof., 1955-64, dir. Sch. Physics, 1964-68. prof. physics, dean Gen. Coll., 1968, acting pres., 1969, v.p. acad. affairs, 1969—. Bd. dirs. Atlanta chpt. Leukemia Soc. Am. Mem. Sigma Xi, Phi Kappa Phi, Sigma Pi Sigma, Omicron Delta Kappa, Phi Kappa Sigma. Home: 1526 Walthall Ct NW Atlanta GA 30318

CRAWFORD, WALTER HAMILTON, community developer; b. Hattiesburg, Miss.; Aug. 16, 1906; s. Walter and Ada (Richardson) C.; student Gulf Coast Mil. Acad., 1922-23, U. Ala., 1924-26; m. Lillian Marie Williams, July 22, 1927; children—Carolyn, Catherine. Bus. mgr., supt. South Miss. Infirmary, Hattiesburg, 1926-33; founder Crawford Corp., New Orleans, 1934, pres., 1934—; pres. Crofton Corp. (Md.), Mem. Regional Vol. Credit Ext. Com., 1954-59, community builders council Urban Land Inst., 1949-51; mem. Nat. Housing Center Bd. 1955-57, chmn., 1955. Pres., United Givers Fund, 1958. Recipient citation for overseas housing U.S. Army Engrs., 1940; ann. award for excellence in merchandising Practical Builder mag., 1951, 53. Mem. Nat. Assn. Home Builders, Home Mfrs. Assn., Miss. Hosp. Assn. (organizer 1931), New Orleans, Jackson, Baton Rouge chambers commerce, Sigma Chi. Baptist. Mason (32), Shriner). Clubs: Union League (Chgo.); New Orleans Athletic; Baton Rouge Country, City (pres. 1959). Home: 1855 Country Club Dr Baton Rouge LA 70808 Office: Crofton Corp Crofton MD 21113 also Crawford Corp Baton Rouge LA 70806

CRAWFORD, WILLIAM AVERY, ret. U.S. ambassador; b. N.Y.C., Jan. 14, 1915; s. John Raymond and Pauline Marguerite (Avery) C.; A.B., Haverford Coll., 1936, student U. Madrid, summer 1936; diploma Ecole Libre des Sciences Politiques, 1938; postgrad. Harvard, 1944- 45, Russian Inst., Columbia, 1949-50; m. Barbara Gardner, Oct. 19, 1940; children—Barbara, Pauline, William, John, Elizabeth. Apptd. fgn. service officer, vice consul of career, sec. diplomatic service, 1941; 3d sec., vice consul, Havana, Cuba, 1941-44; mem. U.S. delegation Allied Commn. on Reparations, Moscow, 1945; 3d sec., vice consul, Moscow, 1945-47, 2d sec., 1947; USSR desk officer Dept. State, 1947; polit. adviser U.S. delegation UN Gen. Assembly, 1949; 2d sec., consul, Paris, 1950-52, 1st sec., 1952-54; dep. dir. Office Eastern European Affairs, Dept. of State, 1954-56, assigned to Nat. War Coll., 1956-57; counselor, dep. chief of mission, Prague, 1957- 59, dir. Office Research and Analysis for Sino-Soviet Bloc, Dept. State, 1959-61; E.E. and M.P. to Rumania, 1961-64, A.E. and P., Rumania, 1964-65; spl. asst. internat. affairs to Supreme Allied Comdr. Europe, Paris, 1965-67; sr. fgn. service insp., 1967-70. Clubs: Metropolitan, Chevy Chase (Washington). Home: 6218 Perthshire Ct Bethesda MD 20034

CRAWFORD, WILLIAM DONHAM, utilities exec.: b. Little Rock, June 22, 1923; s. Sidney Robert and Blanche (Donham) C.; grad. Columbia Mil. Acad., 1940; student U. Ark., 1941-43; B.S., U.S. Naval Acad., 1947; M.S., Cal. Inst. Tech., 1948; m. Colene King, June 6, 1947; children—Carol, Bruce Donham, Philip King. Chief, Office Sci. and Tech., Pan Am. Union, Washington, 1949-50; staff AEC, 1951-54; with Middle South Utilities, Inc., N.Y.C., 1955-63, asst. sec., asst. treas., 1956-59, v.p., 1959-63; v.p. Consol. Edison Co., N.Y., 1963-69, adminstrv. v.p., 1966-69; mng. dir. Edison Electric Inst., N.Y.C., 1969-70, pres., 1971—. Mem. Nat. Air Quality Council. Trustee Thomas A. Edison Found. Served as ensign, Supply Corps, U.S. Navy, 1947- 49. Mem. Christ Ch. Clubs: Baltusrol Golf (Springfield, N.J.); Union League (N.Y.C.). Home: 58 Portland Rd Summit NJ 07901 Office: 90 Park Av New York City NY 10003

CRAWFORD, WILLIAM F., corp. exec.; b. Chgo., Apr. 11, 1911; s. William Wilberforce and Mona (Richards) C.; student Northwestern Mil. and Naval Acad., 1925-29, U. Chgo., 1929-31; m. Ruth M. Fellinger, May 4, 1935; children—Judith (Mrs.Stephen W. Smith), Susan (dec.), Constance (Mrs. Paul R. Dry), Barbara (Mrs. William P. Boger), William Edwin. Sec., Edward Valves, Inc. (formerly Edward Valve & Mfg. Co., Inc.). East Chicago, Ind. 1931-37, v.p., 1937-41, pres., dir., 1941-63; pres, dir. Republic Flow Meters Co.,

Chgo., 1957-61, Valve Products, Inc., Knox, Ind., 1950-63, W. E. Bowler Co., Phila., 1954-63, Maters Co., Chgo., 1957-61, Valve Products, Inc., Knox, Ind., 1950-63; v.p., dir. Rockwell Mfg. Co., Pitts., 1945—, chmn. finance com., 1963—; v.p., dir., chmn. exec. com. Mfrs. Capital Corp., Chgo.; v.p., dir. Chgo. Fittings Corp.; dir. Muter Co., Chgo., Washington Steel Corp. (Pa.), First Nat. Bank of East Chicago, Circle Z Ranch, Patagonia, Ariz. Chmn. Council of Assns. Representing Mfrs. of Components for Piping and Fluid Power Systems. Bd. trustees Crawford Found., Chgo., Ill. Inst. Tech. Research Inst., Ill. Inst. Tech. Mem. valve industry adv. com. WPB, 1941-45, 50-52. Mem. Valve Mfrs. Assn. (pres. 1958-65), Am. Soc. M.E., Am. Petroleum Inst., Army Ordnance Assn., Newcomen Soc., Pa. Soc., Art Inst. Chgo., Delta Upsilon. Republican. Conglist. Clubs: Union League, South Shore Country, Economic, Tavern (Chgo.), Engineers (N.Y.C.); Duquesne (Pitts.). Home: 4950 Chicago Beach Dr Chicago IL 60615 Office: 185 Wabash Av Chicago IL 60601 also 400 N Lexington Av Pittsburgh PA 15208

CRAWFORD, WILLIAM HULFISH, cartoonist; b. Hammond, Ind., Mar. 18, 1913; s. William Hulfish and Katharine (McCulland) C.; B.A., Ohio State U., 1935; m. Claire Olita Trillo, Feb. 11, 1950; childrenKatharine, Dale. Cartoonist, Washington Post and Washington Daily News, 1936-38; editorial page cartoonist Newark News, 1938-62; chief editorial page cartoonist Newspaper Enterprise Assn., N.Y.C., 1962-; illustrator of 19 books; profl. sculptor and lectr. Mem. Nat. Cartoonists Soc. (pres. 1960-61, named Best Editorial Cartoonist in Country 1957, 58, 59, 66). Club: Dutch Treat (N.Y.C.). Home: Prospect Rd Atlantic Highlands NJ 07716 Office: 230 Park Av New York City NY 10017

CRAWFORD, WILLIAM J., savs. and loan exec.; b. Columbus, O., 1920; grad. Ohio State U., 1948. Pres. Gt. Western Savs. & Loan Assn. So. Cal., Long Beach. Pres., dir. Curtis Ins. Co., C.M.C. Realty, Inc. Elk, K.C. Home: 11662 Newbury Rd Los Alamitos CA 90720 Office: 5000 E 2d St Long Beach CA 90803*

CRAWFORD, WILLIAM RAY, dir. univ. publ.; b. Oklahoma City, Dec. 24, 1930; s. William Hudson and Mary Lamb (Ray) C.; B.A., Baylor U., 1952; M.A., U. Mich., 1953; Ph.D., Yale, 1958; m. Barbara Colby Deshon, Sept. 5, 1953; children—Geoffrey, Dudley, Margaret, Elizabeth, David, Kathryn. Instr. English, Colby Coll., 1957-59; asst. prof. English, Dartmouth, 1959-66; asst. prof. English, Boston U., 1966-69; exec. editor Press of Case Western Res. U., Cleve., 1969-70, dir., 1970—. Fulbright fellow, 1954-55; Dartmouth Faculty fellow, 1963-64. Mem. Modern Lang. Assn., Mediaeval Acad. Am. Author: Bibliography of Chaucer, 1954-1963, 1967; contbr. to Chaucer Rev. Home: 3226 Chadbourne Rd Shaker Heights OH 44120

CRAWLEY, PETER LINTON, mathematician, educator; b. Pasadena, Cal., Jan. 29, 1936; s. Emerson Linton and Helene (Ottinger) C.; B.S., Cal. Inst. Tech., 1957, M.S., 1958, Ph.D., 1961; m. Donna Louise Foss, Sept. 5, 1960; children—Gay Louise, John Linton, Anne Helene, Carolyn Elizabeth, Matthew Foss. Office Naval Research postdoctoral research asso. U. Wash., 1960-61; asst. prof. math. U. Minn., 1961-63; vis. asst. prof. math. U. Cal., Berkeley, 1962-63; asst. prof. math. Cal. Inst. Tech., Pasadena, 1963- 65, asso. prof., 1965-68, prof., 1968—. Bd. dirs. San Gabriel Valley council Boy Scouts Am. Mem. Am. Math. Soc., Utah, Mo. hist. socs. Republican. Mem. Ch. of Jesus Christ of Latter-day Saints. Contbr. articles profl. jours. Home: 3570 Landfair Rd Pasadena CA 91107

CREAMER, ANDREW GATES, banker; b. Detroit, May 15, 1929; s. Francis B. and Margaret (Gates) C.; B.A., U. Va., 1950; postgrad. U. Detroit Law Sch., 1954-56; grad. Stonier Grad. Sch. Banking, Brunswick, N.J., 1964; m. Laura M. Murphy, Sept. 16, 1950; children—Andrew Gates, Charles M., Mark B., Warren M. III. Group underwriter Aetna Life Ins. Co., Hartford, Conn., 1950-51; trainee to asst. br. mgr. Detroit Bank, 1953-56; with Hartford Nat. Bank & Trust Co., 1956-71, cashier, 1960-63, v.p., cashier, 1963-67, sr. v.p., 1967-71; pres. Bank of Lansing (Mich.), 1971—; instr. econs., money and banking and bank investments for Hartford and New Britain chpts. Am. Inst. Banking. Treas., bd. dirs. Urban League Greater Hartford, St. Francis Hosp. Assn.; treas., trustee Westledge Sch., Inc.; trustee Big Bros., Inc., Hartford Assn. for Retarded Children, Hartford Rehab. Center; corporator Hartford and St. Francis Hosps. Served to 2d lt., arty. U.S. Army, 1951-53. Clubs: Hartford Tennis, Hartford Golf. Home: 4 Locust Lane Lansing MI 48910 Office: PO Box 1170 Lansing MI 48904

CREAMER, GERARD J., banker; b. Mt. Vernon, N.Y., June 22, 1916; s. Joseph J. and Marie (Watts) C.; B.S., U. Pa., 1939; grad. Harvard Advanced Mgmt. Program, 1962; m. Mary Louise Hays, Apr. 14, 1943; children—Susanne (Mrs. William Harrigan), Christopher, Louise, Ann, John. With Mfrs. Hanover Trust Co., N.Y.C., 1939—, v.p., 1958-69, sr. v.p., 1969—. Active Scarsdale Community Fund; mem. Scarsdale Recreation Commn., 1965-69. Served with USAAF, 1941-45. Decorated D.F.C., Air medal. Mem. Alpha Sigma Phi. Club: Scarsdale Golf (treas., gov.). Home: 28 Rodney Rd Scarsdale NY 10583 Office: 350 Park Av New York City NY 10022

CREAMER, THOMAS FISHBACK, banker; b. Bklyn., Sept. 29, 1917; s. William G. and Blanche (Fishback) C.; S.B., Mass. Inst. Tech., 1940; m. Phoebe Johnson, Feb. 1, 1955; children—Elizabeth, Thomas C., George, Jane, Deane. Asst. to pres. Mass. Inst. Tech., Cambridge, 1940-42; exec. asst. to Dr. Karl T. Compton, head Office Field Service OSRD, 1942-46; with First Nat. City Bank of N.Y., N.Y.C., 1946—, asst. v.p., 1950-56, v.p., 1956-66, sr. v.p., 1966-69, exec. v.p., 1969—; dir. Cerro Corp. Chmn. budget com. Scarsdale Community Fund, 1964. Presbyn. (trustee 1961-68). Clubs: University, Massachusetts Institute Technology (N.Y.C.); Golf, Fox Meadow Tennis (Scarsdale, N.Y.); Mid-Ocean (Bermuda); Ausable (Keene Valley, N.Y.); Pine Valley Golf (N.J.). Home: 80 Greenacres Av Scarsdale NY 10583 Office: 399 Park Av New York City NY 10022

CREAN, JOHN GALE, hat mfr.; b. Toronto, Ont., Can., Nov. 4, 1910; s. Adam G. C. and Lauda (Gale) C.; B.Commerce, U. Toronto, 1932; m. Margaret Dobbie, Dec. 2, 1939; children—John F.M., Jennie S., Susan M., Patricia L. With Robert Crean & Co., Ltd., hat mfrs., Toronto, 1932—, pres., 1947—; pres. Adam Hats Can., Ltd., 1955-70; dir. Kelsey Wheel Co. Ltd., Scythes & Co. Ltd., D.V. Group Ltd, Chmn. Ont. regional com. Canadian C. of C., 1952- 53, vice chmn. exec. council, 1952-53, mem. Can.-U.S. com., 1950-53, 61-65, chmn., 1961-62, immigration com., 1949, pres., 1955-56; dir. Canadian council Internat. C. of C., 1962—, pres. Canadian council, 1970—, v.p. Internat. C. of C., 1970—. Chmn. council Bishop Strachan Sch., 1954-65; v.p. Canadian bus. and industry adv. com. OECD; v.p., bd. govs. Hillcrest Convalescent Hosp.; chmn. bd. Ont. Sci. Centre, 1964-69; exec. com. Trinity Coll., U. Toronto, 1968—. Mem. Canadian Inst. Internat. Affairs (exec. com. 1963), Canadian Centenary Council (dir. 1964-69). Kappa Sigma. Club: University, Badminton and Racquet (Toronto); St. James's (Montreal); Royal Canadian Yacht. Home: 161 Forest Hill Rd Toronto 7 Ontario Canada Office: 161 Forest Hill Rd Toronto 7 Ontario Canada

CREAN, ROBERT playwright; m. Kate Crean; 9 children. Author: (plays) A Time To Laugh, 1962; My Father and My Mother, 1968. Address: Larchmont NY 10538*

CREANZA, JOSEPH, ret. educator; b. N.Y.C., Mar. 1, 1905; s. Peter and Maria (Pappalardi) C.; B.S., Lewis Inst., 1932; A.M., U. Chgo., 1935; m. LaVerne Engeson, June 12, 1943; children—Carol Marie (Mrs. Michael Freeman), Kathleen (Mrs. Richard Hastings II), Adrienne, Philip. Instr. French, Lewis Inst. Chicago, 1932-28; prof., chmn. modern lang. dept. Central YMCA Coll., 1938-44; prof. mod. langs. and chmn. dept. Roosevelt U., 1944- 45, dir. sch. of music, 1945-70, trustee univ., dean of its Chgo. Musical Coll., 1954-70. Founder and dir. Chgo. Folk Festival, 1940-46. Trustee Hinsdale (Ill.) Hosp. and Sanitarium. Mem. N.E.A., Modern Lang. Assn., French Teachers Nat. Assn., Nat. Assn. Schs. Music, Music Teachers Nat. Assn., Music Educators Nat. Conf. Contbr. to profl. mags. Home: 1 N 157 Main St Glen Ellyn IL 60137

CREASEY, JOHN, author; b. Surrey, Eng., Sept. 17, 1908; s. Joseph and Ruth (Creasey) C.; ed. elementary and secondary schs., London; m. Margaret Cooke, 1935 (div. 1939); m. 2d. Evelyn Jean Fudge, Feb. 16, 1941 (div. 1970); children—Colin, Martin John, Richard John; m. 3d, Jeanne Williams, 1970. Author novels, 1932—, total now being 552 pub. in Eng., 250 pub. in U.S.; author Gideon series under pseudonymn J. J. Marric, 1955—, West Toff series, also series under pseudonymns Anthony Morton, Jeremy York, Gordon Ashe, others; also author motion picture scripts, travel books. Chmn. fund raising coms. for famine relief and refugee orgns. Liberal Party candidate for Bournemouth Constituency, 1950; mem. Brit. Liberal Party Council, 1945-50; founder All Party Alliance Movement Gt. Britain, 1966. Decorated mem. Order Brit. Empire; recipient Best Crime Novel award Mystery Writers Am., 1961. Mem. Crime Writers Assn. (chmn. 1953-56). Mystery Writers Am. (pres. 1966-67). Clubs: Paternosters (chmn. 1960) Nat. Liberal, Royal Automobile (London); Westeners (Tucson). Home: New Hall Bodenham Salisbury England also 4330 Osage Dr Tucson AZ 85702 Office: care Harold Ober Assoc 40 E 49th St New York City NY 10017

CREASMAN, RALPH DEDRICK, investment counselor; b. Etowah, Tenn., Aug. 10, 1921; s. Jess W. and Ollie (Womac) C.; student Carson-Newman Coll., 1944-45; B.S., U. Ill., 1947; m. Doris L. Davis, July 6, 1947; children—Janet Lyn, Kenneth Robert. Bond analyst No. Trust Co., Chgo., 1947-48; analyst Security 1st Nat. Bank, Los Angeles, 1948-50; analyst Lionel D. Edie & Co., Los Angeles, 1950-53, counselor, 1953-54, mgr., 1954-59, dir., 1959—, pres., 1964—, chmn. bd., 1970—; pres. Edie Fund Sales, Inc., N.Y.C., Edie Mgmt. Services, Inc.; chmn. bd. Edie Internat. Ltd.; v.p., dir. Merrill Lynch, Pierce, Fenner & Smith, Inc., 1969—. Trustee U. Redlands. Served with USNR, 1941-45. Clubs: Lincoln (Los Angeles); Sky (N.Y.C.); Wee Burn Country (Darien, Conn.). Home: 36 Ox Ridge Lane Darien CT 06820 Office: 530 Fifth Av New York City NY 10036

CREASY, WILLIAM NEVILLE, business exec.; b. Bournemouth, Eng., Mar. 8, 1908; s. Frederick Kenwood and Alice Mary (Palethorp) C.; Pharm. B., U. Toronto, 1929; m. Edith Margaret Shore, Aug. 1939; children—William Neville, Robert K. with Burroughs Wellcome & Co. (U.S.A.), Inc., 1938—, pres., gen. mgr., 1945-68, chmn., 1948-68; mgr. Burroughs Wellcome & Co., Can., 1942- 45; pres. Burroughs Wellcome Fund, 1955—. Bd. dirs. U. Toronto Assos.; trustee Nat. Kidney Found.; bd. dirs., treas. Royal Soc. Medicine Found.; mem. bd. grants Am. Found. Pharm. Edn.; bd. dirs. Am. Allergy Found. Fellow Royal Soc. Medicine (hon.). Clubs: Saint Andrew's Golf; Canadian (N.Y.C.); Seigniory, Mahopac Curling. Home: 8 Oak Bend Bronxville NY 10708

CREDE, ROBERT HENRY, educator, physician; b. Chgo., Aug. 11, 1915; s. William H. and Ethel (Starke) C.; A.B., U. Cal. at Berkeley, 1937, M.D., at San Francisco, 1941; m. Marjorie L. Lorain, Aug. 29, 1947; children—William, Victoria, Christina. Commonwealth fellow, instr. medicine U. Cin. Coll. Medicine, 1947-49; intern San Francisco City and County Hosp., 1941-42; asst. resident medicine U. Cal. Hosp., San Francisco, 1945-46, chief resident medicine, 1946-47, U. Cal. Hosp.; mem. faculty U. Cal. Sch. Medicine, San Francisco, 1949—, prof. medicine, 1960—, vice chmn. dept., 1965—, asso. dean, 1960—, dir. Gen. Med. Clinic, 1965—, chmn. div. ambulatory and community medicine, 1965—. Served to capt., M.C., AUS, 1942-46. Recipient Guy K. Woodward prize internal medicine U. Cal. Sch. Medicine, 1941, Gold Headed Cane award, 1941. Diplomate Am. Bd. Internal Medicine. Mem. Am. Fedn. Clin. Research, Am. Pub. Health Assn., Am. Psychosomatic Soc., N. Cal. Psychosomatic Soc., Am., Cal. med. assns., San Francisco Med. Soc., Soc. Tchrs. Preventive Medicine. Author articles in field. Office: Univ Cal Med Center San Francisco CA 94122

CREE, ALBERT ALEXANDER, pub. utilities exec.; b. Spruce Creek, Pa., June 15, 1898; s. Harry C. and Minnie Louella (Irvin) C.; B.A., Columbia Coll., New York, 1919; m. Marie Louise Coizet on July 3, 1920 (dec. May 1952); children—Anne Marie (Mrs. Earl C. McGuire), Albert Alexander. With Lee, Higginson & Co., N.Y.C., 1919-32; asst. treas. Lee Higginson Corp., 1932- 34; with N.E. Pub. Service Co., Augusta, Me., 1934-35, dir., 1943-53; v.p. Central Vt. Pub. Service Corp., also Twin State Gas & Electric Co., Rutland, Vt., 1935-36; pres., dir. Twin State Gas & Electric Co., 1936- 43; co. merged into Central Vt. Public Corp., dir. 1936—, pres., 1936- 61, chmn., 1961—, chief exec. officer, 1961-68; pres., dir. Conn. Valley Electric Co., Inc., N.H., 1949-68, Vt. Yankee Nuclear Power Corp., 1966—, Vt. Electric Power Company, Inc., 1957—; dir. Gen. Telephone Corp. of Vt., 1948-66, Am. Woolen Co., 1954-55, Textron-Am., Inc., 1955, Yankee Atomic Electric Co., 1954-68. Chmn., Electric Coordinating Council of N.E., 1952-53, pres., 1959—. Dir. Civil Def., Vt., 1941-45. Trustee Green Mountain Coll. Served as aviator pilot, U.S. A.S., 1917-19. Mem. Nat. Assn. Electric Cos. (dir. 1955—), Am. Legion (comdr. Vt., Nat. vice comdr., 1947-48), Vt. C. of C. (pres 1938-41), Vt. Elec. Assn. (pres. 1938), V.F.W., Phi Kappa Sigma. Mason, Elk. Home: 9 Mansfield Pl Rutland VT 05701 Office 77 Grove St Rutland VT 05701

CREECH, DANTON DAYLE, coll. pres.; b. Seiling, Okla., Aug. 1, 1917; s. Jesse Blaine and Frankie (Jacobs) C.; student John Brown U., 1933-35; B.S., Southwestern State Coll., 1938; M.S., Okla. State U. 1949; Ed.D., U. Okla., 1966; m. Dorothy Aline Buss, June 5, 1947; children—Cynthia Jan, James Robert, Danton Dayle. Tchr., Royal (Okla.) High Sch., 1938-40, Mutual (Okla.) High Sch., 1940-42; principal Sharon (Okla.) High Sch., 1946-47; supt. Fargo (Okla.) Pub. Schs., 1947-50, Arnett (Okla.) Pub. Schs., 1950-57. Velma-Alma Pub. Schs., Velma, Okla., 1957- 60. Pryor (Okla.) Pub. Schs., 1960-68; state supt. pub. instrn., Oklahoma City; 1968-70; pres. Northeastern Okla. A and M Coll., Miami, 1970—. Served with USNR, 1942-46. Mem. Am., Okla. assns. sch. adminstrs., N.E.A., Okla. Edn. Assn., Frontiers of Sci., Am. Legion. Republican. Methodist. Mason. Office: Northeastern Okla A and M Coll Miami OK 74354

CREECH, FULTON HUNTER, shipbldg. exec.; b. Washington, July 8, 1929; s. Fulton Hunter and Pauline MacKay (Bryan) C.; B.A., U. Va., 1951, LL.B., 1957; m. Betty Frost Baldwin, Dec. 3, 1967; children—Kathryn, Leslie, Nancy, Rone, Carol, Clark, Hunter III. Admitted to Va. bar, 1957; atty. Navy Dept., 1957-61; contract adminstr. Kaman Aircraft, Bloomfield, Conn., 1961-62; atty. Ingalls Shipbldg., 1962-64; asst. to gen. counsel Newport News Shipbldg. and Dry Dock Co. (Va.), 1964-66, asst. personnel mgr., 1966, asst. gen. counsel, 1966-67, asst. sec., asst. gen. counsel, 1967-70, sec., gen. counsel, 1970—. Bd. dirs. Peninsula Family Service and Travelers Aid, Inc., Peninsula Symphony Orch., Peninsula United Fund. Served to lt. (j.g.) USN, 1951-54. Mem. Va., Fed. bar assns., Sigma Nu. Presbyn. (elder). Mason. Clubs: Nat. Lawyers (Washington); Propeller; James River (Va.). Home: 117 Yorkville Rd Yorktown VA 23490 Office: 4101 Washington Av Newport News VA 23607

CREECH, HUGH JOHN, chemist; b. Exeter, Ont., Can., June 27 1910; s. Richard Newton and Edith (Sanders) C.; B.A., U. Western Ont., 1933, M.A., 1935; Ph.D., U. Toronto (research fellow), 1938; postgrad. Harvard, 1938-41; m. E. Marie Hearne, July 10, 1937; children—Richard Hearns, Joan Marie. Came to U.S., 1938, naturalized, 1945. Asst. prof. U. Md., 1941-43, asso. prof., 1943-45; lectr. Bryn Mawr (Pa.) Coll., 1945-47; immunochemist Inst. for Cancer Research and Lankenau Hosp. Research Inst. Phila., 1945-47, head dept. chemotherapy, 1947-57, chmn. div. chemotherapy, 1957—, chmn. adminstrv. com. Inst. Cancer Research, 1947-54. Mem. U.S. nat. com. Internat. Union Against Cancer, 1957-60; antimalarial research U. Md. with OSRD, Washington, 1943-45; expert cons. to Surgeon Gen. U.S. Army, 1947-49. Recipient numerous awards for research NIH, Am. Cancer Soc. Mem. Am. Assn. Cancer Research (sec-treas.), Am. Chem. Soc., Sigma Xi. Club: Philadelphia. Organic Chemists. Home: 702 Preston Rd Erdenheim Philadelphia PA 19118 Office: Inst for Cancer Research Fox Chase Philadelphia PA 19111

CREEGAN, ROBERT FRANCIS, educator; b. Battle Creek, Mich., Mar. 27, 1915; s. Charles Cole and Harriet (Stephenson) C.; student Oberlin Coll., 1932-34; A.B. Marietta Coll., 1936; M.A., Duke 1939, Ph.D., 1939; m. Doris Ryan, Dec. 27, 1940; 1 son, Charles Louis. Asst. at the Coll. of William and Mary 1939-40; asst. prof. Bucknell U., 1944-45, Whitman Coll., 1945-47, Carleton Coll., 1947-48, Ohio U., 1948-52; prof. philosophy dept. State U. N.Y. at Albany, 1952—; vis. prof. U. Ariz., summer 1970; cons. in philosophy Aerial Phenomena Research Orgn., 1970—; lectr. Bd. dirs. Albany Planned Parenthood Assn.; nat. sponsor Univs. Com. on Problems of War and Peace. Mem. Internat. Platform Assn., Am. Acad. Polit. and Social Sci., A.A.A.S., Am. Philos. Assn., Am. Psychol. Assn., Am. Assn. U. Profs., Internat. Phenomenological Soc., Soc. Advancement Edn., Albany Sci. and Profl. Group for Pub. Information, N.Y. Acad. Scis. Presbyn. Abstractor, Psychol. Abstracts. Author: The Shock of Existence, 1954; also articles profl. jours., ednl. reports. Home: 28 Wellington Rd Delmar NY 12054 Office: State U NY at Albany Albany NY 12203

CREEGER, GEORGE RAYMOND, univ. dean; b. Attleboro, Mass., Sept. 1, 1925; s. Marion James and Florence (Rader) C.; student Middlebury (Vt.) Summer Sch. German, 1943; B.A., DePauw U., 1945; M.A., Yale, 1948, Ph.D., 1953; m. Elva Parkhurst Stearns, June 16, 1951; children—Catherine Elizabeth, Carl Philip, Christopher James. Instr. English and German, DePauw U., 1947-48; mem. faculty Wesleyan U., Middletown, Conn., 1951—, prof. English, 1963—, dean coll., 1971—; Fulbright guest prof. Julius- Maximilians-Universität, Würzburg, Germany, 1959-60, J.F. Kennedy Inst. for Am. Studies, Free U. Berlin (Germany), 1968-69. Served with USAAF, 1946-47. Mem. Modern Lang. Assn. Am., Am. Assn. U. Profs., Melville Soc., Phi Beta Kappa. Spl. research 19th century Am. and English lit. Home: Apple Garth Middle Haddam CT 06456 Office: 130 Wesleyan Sta Middletown CT 06457

CREEL, DANA SHANNON, found. exec.; b. College Park, Ga., May 24, 1912; s. Dana Anderson and Mary Virginia (Shannon) C.; LL.B., Emory U., 1934; M.B.A., Harvard, 1936; LL.D., Cornell Coll., 1962; m. Jane Rebecca Haislip, June 11, 1955. With Irving Trust Co., 1936-39, Prentice Hall Co., 1939-40; asso. philanthropy John D. Rockefeller, Jr., 1940-42, 46-60; sec. Rockefeller Bros. Fund, 1947-51, dir., 1951-68, pres., trustee, 1968—; sec. Sealantic Fund, 1947-51, dir., trustee, 1951—; pres., trustee Sleepy Hollow Restorations, 1951—. Admitted to Ga. Bar, 1934, N.Y. bar, 1939. Trustee Seamen's Bank for Savs.; dir. Morningside Heights, Inc. Mem. sr. execs. adv. council Conf. Bd., 1969—; mem. N.Y. Urban Coalition, 1967—. Trustee African- Am. Inst., 1957—, chmn. bd., 1964—; trustee, v.p. Interchurch Center, 1958—; trustee Inst. Coll. and U. Adminstrs., 1960- 67, Am. Conservation Assn., 1963—; pres., trustee Martha Baird Rockefeller Fund for Music, 1962—; dir. Rockefeller Family Fund, 1967—. Served with AUS, 1942-46. Mem. Council Fgn. Relations, African Affairs Soc. Am. Ltd. (dir. 1966-67). Club: Century Assn. Home: 15 W 55th St New York City NY 10019 Office: 30 Rockefeller Plaza New York City NY 10020

CREEL, HERRLEE GLESSNER, sinologist, educator; b. Chgo., Jan. 19, 1905; s. Herr Lee Glessner and Lena Adel (Peterson) C.; student U. Okla., 1923-24, Creighton U., 1924; Ph.B., U. Chgo., 1926, A.M., 1927, Ph.D., 1929; research fellow Harvard, 1930-32; m. Wilhelmine Schaefer, Oct. 13, 1925 (div. 1937); m. 2d, Lorraine Johnson, Aug. 28, 1937. Asst. prof. psychology Lombard Coll., 1929-30; research fellow Am. Council Learned Socs., 1930- 31, 32-33, Harvard-Yenching Inst., 1931-32, 33-35, China, 1932-35, 39-40; instr. Chinese history and lang. U. Chgo., 1936-37, asst. prof. early Chinese lit. and instns., 1937-40, asso. prof., 1940-49, prof., 1949—, Martin A. Ryerson Distinguished Service prof. Chinese history, 1964—, chmn. com. on Far Eastern civilizations, 1951- 57, chmn. dept. Oriental langs. and civilizations, 1954-62; research fellow Rockefeller Found., 1936, 45-46. Mem. joint com. on research on Asia, Am. Council Learned Socs.-Social Sci. Research Council, 1964-68. Served from maj. to lt. col. AUS, 1943-45; research analyst, M.I. Service, War Dept., 1942-43. Mem. Am. Oriental Soc. (pres. 1955-56), Far Eastern Assn. Author books, latest: Confucius, the Man and the Myth, 1950; Chinese Thought, from Confucius to Mao Tse-tung, 1953; The Origins of Statecraft in China, Vol. I: The Western Chou Empire, 1970; What Is Taoism?, 1970. Home: Palos Park IL 60464

CREEL, JOE, lawyer; b. Guntersville Alta., Oct. 23, 1912; s. Elisha O. and Florence A. (Bynum) C.; A.B., U. Ala., 1932, LL.B., 1934; m. Nellie Joe Morton, Sept. 21, 1935; children—Sallie R. (Mrs. Warren Quillian), Joe Morton. Admitted to Ala. bar 1934, Fla. bar, 1945; spl. asst. U.S. atty. No. Dist. Ala., 1943-44; regional litigation atty. OPA, Southeastern Area, 1944, chief enforcement officer, Miami, dist., 1945; city atty., Guntersville, Ala., 1941-43; pvt. practice, Miami 1945—; pres. Russell Aluminum Corp., 1955-56, sec.-treas., dir., 1956-70; dir. Sheffield Steel Products, Inc., Miami Window Corp. Panama. Mem. Dade County (pres. 1958-59), Marshall County (Ala.) bar assns., Phi Beta Kappa, Phi Delta Phi, Omicron Delta Kappa, Tau Kappa Alpha. Home: 1246 Algardi Av Coral Gables FL 33146 Office: DuPont Bldg Miami FL 33131

CREELEY, ROBERT WHITE, author; b. Arlington, Mass., May 21, 1926; s. Oscar Slade and Genevieve (Jules) C.; student Harvard, 1943-46; B.A., Black Mountain Coll., 1954; M.A., U. N.M., 1960; m. Bobbie Louise Hall, Jan. 27, 1957; children— Kirsten, Sarah, Katherine. Instr. Black Mountain Coll., 1954-55; vis. lectr. U. N.M., Albuquerque, 1961-62, lectr. English, 1963-66; vis. prof. State Univ.

N.Y. at Buffalo, 1966-67, prof. English, 1967—; lectr. U. B.C., Vancouver, 1962-63; vis. prof. English, U.N.M., 1968-69; vis. prof. creative writing San Francisco State Coll., 1970-71. Served with Am. Field Service, 1944-45; CBI. Recipient Levinson prize, Poetry mag., 1960, Blumenthal-Leviton award, 1965; D.H. Lawrence fellow, 1960, Guggenheim fellow, 1964, 71; Rockefeller grantee, 1965; Union League Civic and Arts Found. prize Poetry mag., 1967. Author: Le Fou, 1952; The Immoral Proposition, 1953; The Kind of Act of, 1953; The Gold Diggers, 1954; rev. 1965; All That is Lovely in Men. 1955; If You, 1956; The Whip 1957; A Form of Women, 1959; For Love, Peoms, 1950-60, 1962; The Island 1963; Poems 1950-65, 1966; Words, 1967; The Finger, 1968; The Charm, 1968; Numbers, 1968; Pieces, 1969; A Quick Graph, 1970; 1234567890, 1971; St. Martin's, 1971. Editor: (with Donald M. Allen) New American Story, 1965, The New Writing in the U.S.A., 1967; Black Mountain Rev., 1954-57; Selected Writings of Charles Olson, 1967. Home: Box 344 Bolinas CA 94924 Office: Annex B State U NY at Buffalo Buffalo NY 14214

CREER, PHILIP DOUGLAS, architect, educator; b. Phila., Aug. 31, 1903; s. Robert C. and Ada L. (Skinner) C.; B.Arch., U. Pa., 1927; m. Esther B. Allen, Dec. 1, 1933; children—Philip Douglas, Robert Craine; m. 2d, Cleon Adair Kerr, Oct. 25, 1951. Instr. architecture U. Pa., 1928-31; head dept. architecture Wanamaker Inst., 1927-32, R.I. Sch. Design, Providence, 1933- 56; dir. Sch. Architecture U. Tex., Austin, 1956-67; practice of architecture, Austin, 1935—; sr. partner Creer, Kent, Cruise & Aldrich, Providence, 1946-61; partner Creer & Roessner, Austin, 1958-63, P.D. Creer, Austin, 1963—. Mem. architects adv. com. Providence Bldg. Code, 1952-54; mem. Mayor Providence adv. com. to write minimum housing standards code, 1953-56, mem. exec. com., chmn. subcom. screening, 1953-56; sec-treas. Tex. Archtl. Found., 1957-63; architects adv. com. Tex. Bldg. Commn., 1958- 60; mem. Austin Parks and Recreation Bd., 1966-70. chmn., 1969. Past pres. R.I. Soc. Crippled Children and Adults. Recipient award for Hartford Park Pub. Housing Project, Providence, 1951; selected one of 10 best in U.S. by architects adv. com. Pub. Housing Authority, 1951—. Fellow A.I.A. (past pres. R.I.; pres, N.E. regional council 1952-55; nat. dir. nat. judiciary com., 1952-55, chmn. 1954-55, 58-59, centennial subcom. Commemorative stamp 1956; pres. Central Tex. chpt., 1960, recipient Edward C. Kemper award 1960, chmn. honor awards com. 1966-67); mem. Tex. Soc. Architects (chmn. fellowship nominating com., mem. profl. devel. com.), R.I. Hist. Soc., Soc. Colonial Wars, Shakespear's Head Assn., Phi Sigma Kappa. Clubs: Art (past gov.), University (Providence); Headliners, Citadel (Austin). Publ. bd. Tex. Architect. Archtl. works include schs., hosps., pub. housing, overseas army bases, comml., indsl. and instl. bldgs. R.I. dist. officer Historic Am. Bldgs. Survey, 1935-41; Home: 1605 Gaston Av Austin TX 78703

CREER, WILLIAM EDWARD, ret. air force officer; b. Spanish Fork, Utah, June 26, 1912; s. William Robert and Annie (Youd) C.; B.S. in Chemistry, Brigham Young U., 1934; grad. Air Corps Flying Sch., 19360 M.A. in Internat. Relations, Stanford, 1949; grad. Nat. War Coll., 1955; m. Vivienne Taylor, Oct. 29, 1937; children—Carolyne, Elizabeth. Commd. 2d lt. USAAF, 1936, advanced through grades to maj. gen. USAF, 1965; various assignments U.S. and Panama, 1937-43; squadron comdr.; dir. operations 94th Bombardment Group, Eng., 1944; comdr. 34th Bomb Group, Eng., 1944-45; staff officer, orgn. and tng. div. War & Dept. Gen. Staff, 1945-47; staff officer chief plans br., directorate plans, Hdqrs. SAC, 1949-52, dir. operations air. divs., 1952-53; dept. comdr. 305th Bombardment Wing, 1953-54; chief operational plans br. SHAPE, Paris, France, 1955-57; dep. comdr.16th Air Force, Madrid, Spain, 1957-58; div. comdr. 801st Air Group, Lockbourne AFB, O., 1958-60; comdr. 72d Bombardment Wing, Ramey AFB, P.R., 1960-62, 45th Air Div., Loring AFB, Me., 1962-64, 823d Air Div., Homestead AFB, Fla., 1964-67; dept. comdt. Nat. War Coll, Ft. McNair, 1967-68, ret., 1968. Decorated Distinguished Service medal, also Legion of Merit, D.F.C. with 2 oak leaf clusters, Air medal with 3 oak leaf clusters, Commendation medal (Army and Air Force); Distinguished Flying Cross (U.K.); Croix de Guerre with aplm (France). Mem. Air Force Assn., Mil. Order World Wars, Ret. Officers Assn., Pi Sigma Alpha. Republican. Mem. Ch. of Jesus Christ of Latter Day Saints. Address: Fairway House 3500 Townsend Blvd Jacksonville FL 32211

CREIGH, THOMAS, Jr., utility exec.; b. Evanston, Ill., Jan. 3, 1912, s. Thomas and Frances (Connor) C.; grad. Mercersburg (Pa.) Acad., 1929; A.B., Wabash Coll., 1933; m. Dorothy Claire Weyer, July 17, 1948; children—Mary Elizabeth, Thomas III, John, James. With No. Natural Gas Co., 1933-36; with Kan.- Neb. Natural Gas Co., Inc., 1936—, v.p., 1951-61, pres., 1961—, also dir.; v.p., dir. Excelsior Oil Corp., 1955-68, pres., 1968—; pres., dir. Western Gas Corp., 1967—; v.p., dir. Melium, Inc., 1960—; sec., dir. Western Plastics Corp., 1953-69; dir. Dunne Gardner Drilling Co., City Nat. Bank, Hastings, Western Alfalfa Corp., Williams Pressure Service Corp. Cape Constrn. Co. Trustee Hastings Coll. Mem. Am. (dir. 1969—), Midwest (dir. 1965-68) gas assns., Ind. Natural Gas Assn. (dir. 1967—), Neb. Assn. Commerce and Industry (past pres.), Neb. Council Econ. (chmn. 1967-70), Presbyn. (trustee). Home: 1650 N Elm St Hastings NB 68901 Office: Kan-Neb Natural Gas Co Hastings NB 68901

CREIGHTON, HARRIET BALDWIN, educator, assn. exec.; b. Delavan, Ill., June 27, 1909; s. Cyrus Murray and Bertha (Baldwin) Creighton; B.A., Wellesley Coll., 1929; Ph.D., Cornell U., 1933. Lab. asst. botany Cornell U., 1929-33 instr., 1933-34; instr. botany Conn. Coll., 1934-39, asst. prof., 1939-40; asso. prof. botany Wellesley Coll., 1940-52, prof., 1952—; Fulbright lectr. genetics Australia 1952-53, Peru, 1959-60. Nat. Sci. Found. genetics cons., India, 1968, 69. Served lt. comdr. USNR, 1943-46. Fellow A.A.A.S. (v.p. sect. G. 1964); mem. Bot. Soc. Am., Inc. (pres. 1956), Society Am. Naturalists, Genetics Soc. Am., Soc. Developmental Biology, Am. Genetic Assn., Am. Soc. Plant Physiologists, Am. Soc. Cell Biologists, Phi Beta Kappa, Sigma Xi, Phi Kappa Phi. Contbr. articles profl. jours. Office: Wellesley Coll Wellesley MA 02181

CREIGHTON, HENRY JERMAIN MAUDE, chemist; b. Dartmouth, N.S., Mar. 2, 1886; s. Henry Dolby and Helen James (Robson) C.; B.A., Dalhousie U., 1906, M.A., 1907, LL.D., 1948; M. Sc., U. Birmingham (Eng.), 1909; student U. Heidelberg (Germany), 1909-10; D.Sc., Fed. Polytech, Zurich, Switzerland, 1913; Sc.D., Swathmore Coll., 1957; m. Jean Hamilton Walker, June 21, 1916; children— Robert, Rosamond (Mrs. Seymour J. Ettman). Came to U.S., 1912. Lectr. on chemistry Dalhousie U., 1911; instr. in chemistry Swarthmore Coll., 1912- 13, asst. prof., 1913-24, asso. prof., 1924-27, prof. 1927-52, now emeritus prof., head chemistry dept., 1927-49; cons. on electrochemistry; on leave of absence with Manhattan Project at Columbia U., 1943-46. Columbia U. War Research Medallion, 1946. Recipient Longstreth medal, 1918, Potts Gold medal, 1939, Modern Pioneer award, 1940. Acheson Gold Medal and Prize, 1946. Rep., Electrochem. Soc. on Research Com. Am. Electroplaters' Soc. 1948- 51. Mem. A.A.A.S., Am. Chem. Soc. (chmn. Phila. sect. 1940- 41), Electrochem. Soc. (v.p. 1936-38, pres. 1939-40), Chem. Soc. (London), Soc. Chem. Industry, Faraday Soc., Franklin Inst. (chmn. com. on sci. and arts, 1918; mem. Franklin medal com., 1922-52, chmn. 1933), Nova Scotian Inst. Sci., N.Y. Acad. Sci., Chem. Inst. Can., Phi Beta Kappa (hon.), Sigma Xi (chmn. nat. lectureship com. 1938-43). Clubs: Chemists Men's Faculty of Columbia U. (N.Y.); University (Montreal); Halifax Royal Nova Scotia Yacht Squadron; English-Speaking Union, Royal Commonwealth Soc., Over-Seas League (London, Eng.). Author: Principles of Electrochemistry, 4th edit., 1943. Home: Glen Margaret Nova Scotia Canada

CREIGHTON, JOHN DOUGLAS, newspaper exec.; b. Toronto, Ont., Can., Nov. 27, 1929; s. Stanley Dixon and Ethel Grace (Armstrong) C.; grad. Humberside Collegiate (Can.), 1948; m. Marilyn June Chamberlain, June 20, 1953; children—Scott, Bruce, Donald. With Toronto Stock Exchange, 1948; reporter Toronto Telegram, 1948-62, asst. city editor, 1962-65, sports editor, 1965-67, city editor, 1967-69, mng. editor, 1969—. Active Big Bros. of Can., 1969—. Mem. Toronto Men's Press Club (pres. 1959). Anglican. Club: Boulevard (Toronto). Contbg. editor Almanac of Can., 1968-69. Home: 220 Riverside Dr Toronto 159 Ontario Canada Office: 440 Front St W Toronto 2B Ontario Canada

CREIGHTON, THOMAS E., air lines exec.; b. 1913; B.A., St. John's U., 1935; m. With Eastern Air Lines Inc., 1937—; v.p. corp. sec., 1963—. 10 Rockefeller Plaza New York City, NY . 10020.*

CREIGHTON, THOMAS HAWK, architect; b. Phila., May 19, 1904; s. Frank W. and Maude (Hawk) C.; A.B., Harvard, 1926; grad. Beaux Arts Inst. Design, 1929; m. Gwen Lux, 1959; children by previous marriage—Thomas Hawk, Anne Genung. Archtl. designer Shultze & Weaver, Charles B. Meyers, N.Y.C., Freeman, French, Freeman, Burlington, Vt., 1926-38; sr. architect, dept. hosps. N.Y.C. 1938-40; asso. Alfred Hopkins & Assos., 1940-46; editor Progressive Architecture, 1946-63, editorial dir., 1963-64; partner, v.p. John Carl Warnecke & Assos., architects, San Francisco, 1963- 66; architect and planner, Honolulu, 1966. Adj. prof. architecture Columbia, 1962-63; vis. lectr. U. Hawaii, 1968-69, univ. architect, 1970; spl. columnist Honolulu Advertiser, 1968—. Mem. Honolulu Planning Commn., 1971—. Fellow A.I.A.; mem. Constrn. Specifications Inst. (hon.). Author: Planning To Build, 1945; Houses, 1947; Building for Modern Man, 1949; The American House Today, 1951; Quality Budget Houses, 1954; Designs for Living, 1955; (with Katherine Morrow Ford) Contemporary Houses, 1961; The Architecture of Monuments, 1962; American Architecture, 1964. Home and office: 5112 Maunalani Circle Honolulu HI 96816 Office: 850 Richards St Honolulu HI 96813

CREIGHTON , WILBUR F., Jr., business exec. Pres., Foster & Creighton Co., Nashville. Office: 633 Thompson Lane Nashville TN 37204*

CREIGHTON, WILLIAM FORMAN, bishop; b. Phila., July 23, 1909; s. Frank Whittington and Maud R. (Hawk) C.; B.A., U. Pa., 1931, S.T.B., Phila. Div. Sch., 1934, D.D., 1957, Va. Theol. Sem., 1959; L.H.D., Rikkyo U., Tokyo, Japan, 1964; m. Marie-Louise Forrest, June 2, 1934; children—William Wendel, Michael Whittington, Maxwell Forrest. Ordained deacon Episcopal Ch., priest, 1934; vicar St. Mark's, Oakes, N.D., 1934-37; rector St. Clements Ch., St. Paul, 1937-43, St. Johns Ch., Bethesda, Md., 1946-59; bishop co-adjutor Diocese of Washington, 1959-62, bishop of Washington, 1962—. Trustee Phila. Div. Sch., 1961—, Va. Theol. Sem., 1962—; chmn. bd. Church Pension Fund. Served as chaplain USNR, 1943-46. Home: 5233 Partridge Lane NW Washington DC 20016 Office: Episcopal Church House Mount Saint Alban Washington DC 20016

CRELIN, EDMUND SLOCUM, educator, anatomist; b. Red Bank, N.J., Apr. 26, 1923; s. Edmund Slocum and Agatha (Bublin) C.; B.A. cum laude, Central Coll. (Ia.), 1947, D.Sc., 1969; Ph.D., Yale, 1951; m. Marjorie Joyce McCain, Sept. 11, 1948; children—Sheryl, Edmund Slocum III, Robert, Carole. USPHS fellow Yale, 1949-51, instr. anatomy, 1951-55, asst. prof., 1955-61, asso. prof., 1961-68, prof., 1968—; asso. editor Anatomical Record; cons. CIBA Pharm. Co., Summit, N.J. Recipient Yale U. Sch. Medicine F.G. Blake award, 1961. Mem. A.M.A., Am. Assn. Anatomists, A.A.A.S. Author: Anatomy of the Newborn, 1969; In the Twilight of Christendom: Hegel vs. Kierkegaard on Faith and History, 1972. Editor AAR Studies in Religion, 1971—. Contbr. articles profl. jours. Home: 124 Sunset Hill Dr Branford CT 06405 Office: Sterling Hall Medicine 333 Cedar St New Haven CT 06510

CRELLIN, JOHN C., journalist; b. Port Huron, Mich., Feb. 29, 1916; s. Charles and Kathleen Crellen; grad. high sch.; m. Grace Reuther, Apr. 11, 1936; children-James, John, Michael, Thomas, Kathleen, Christopher, Jeffrey. Reporter, Detroit Times, 1935-60; bus. writer, asst. city editor, city editor Detroit News, 1968-69, nat. labor editor, 1969—. Served with USNR, 1944-45. Mem. Detroit Press Club (past dir.). Home: 34590 Jefferson St Mount Clemens MI 48043 Office: 615 W Lafayette St Detroit MI 48226

CREMER, JACOB THEODOR, tobacco co. ofcl.; b. Haarlem, Holland, Apr. 1, 1902; s. Herbert and Adriane Willemine (van Marken) C.; student U. Amsterdam, Holland, 1920- 23; m. Jonkvrouwe Johanna Alexandra Pauw van Wieldrecht, July 18, 1928; children—Elisabeth Dagmar (Mrs. G.H. Shaw), Herbert Henry, Thelma Theodora (Mrs. R.C. Sherrer). Came to U.S., 1940, naturalized, 1950. Partner tobacco brokerage G. Harkema, Amsterdam, Holland, 1927-37; mng. dir. Deli Maatschappij, N.V., Amsterdam, 1938—; pres. N.V. Deli Maatschappij, Amsterdam, 1958—; former chmn. Imperial Agrl. Corp., Hartford, Conn., Imperial Commodoties Corp., N.Y.C., Am. Sumatra Tobacco Corp., N.Y.C., also dir., Imperial Prodn. Corp., San Antonio. Trustee Cremer Found., N.Y.C. Served as lt. col. Netherlands Indies Army, World War II, mem. rubber study group U.S., United Kingdom, Netherlands. Decorated as Officer in the Order of Orange Nassau (Netherlands), 1942, Clubs: Racquet and Tennis, Downtown Assn. (N.Y.C.); Fishers Island (N.Y.), Bedford Golf and Country (Bedford Hills, N.Y.). Home: McLain St Mount Kisco NY 10549 Office: 110 Wall St New York City NY 10005

CREMERS, BERT, bus. cons.; b. St. Cloud, Minn., Aug. 13, 1903; s. Anthony and Elizabeth (Lehner) C.; student Northwestern Coll. Law, Mpls., also pvt. tutors; m. Catherine Wilson, Sept. 9, 1928; children—Barbara Ann, Norbert Wilson, Margaret Mary; m. 2d, Margaret Martin, Nov. 6, 1948. Clk., gen. store, S.D.; apprentice printer Craddick Advt. Agy., Mpls., 1918, mgr. multigraphing dept., 1920; service mgr. Multicolor Sales Co., Mpls., 1920-24; traveling salesman; real estate agt. in Fla., 1924-27; sales rep. John T. Stanley Co., 1927; sales rep. Mchts. Chem. Co., N.Y.C., 1927, sales mgr., 1932; mgr. distbn. sales div. Mich. Alkali Co., 1938, sales mgr., 1939, dir. sales, 1941, v.p. indsl. chems. group Wyandotte Chems. Corp. (Mich.). 1955-66, sr. v.p., 1966- 68; chmn. bd. Nat. Tape Corp., Mamaroneck, N.Y., 1968—; gen. bus. cons., 1968—; dir. Saginaw Products Co. (Mich.). Travel. Homes (Mich.), Brooks & Perkins (Mich.), Howe Martz Mich., Castleton Industries, Inc., Fla., Multi-Systems & Products. Clubs: Detroit Athletic, Country of Detroit; Chemists (N.Y.C.); Grosse Pointe (Mich.); Old (Mich.) Address: 1715 Shore Club Dr N St Clair MI 48080

CREMIN, CORNELIUS CHRISTOPHER, Irish diplomat; b. Ireland. Dec. 6, 1908; B.A. with 1st class honours Ancient Classics, Commerce, U. Coll., Cork, Ireland, 1929, B.Commerce, 1930, M.A., 1931; travelling studentship in ancient classics, Nat. U. Ireland, 1931, LL.D. honoris causa, 1965; student in Athens, Rome, Munich and Oxford, 1932-34; diploma in Classical Archaeology with distinction, Oxford U., 1934; m. Patricia O'Mahony, Apr. 24, 1935. Joined Irish Fgn. Service, 1935; 3d sec. Dept. External Affairs, 1935-37; 1st sec., Paris, France, 1937-43; charge d'affaires ad interim, Berlin, Germany, 1943-45, Lisbon, Portugal, 1945- 46; counsellor Dept. External Affairs, 1946-48, asst. sec., 1948-50; E.E. and M.P., later A.E. and P., Paris, also head permanent delegation to OEEC, 1950-54; A.E. and P. to Holy See, 1954-56, to London, 1956-58; sec. Dept. External Affairs, 1958-63; A.E. and P. to London, 1963-64; permanent rep. of Ireland to UN, 1964-. Decorated knight grand cross Order Pius (Holy See); grand officer Legion of Honor (France); Grand Cross Merit (Fed. Republic Germany). Home: 1 East End Ave New York City NY 10021. Office: 866 UN Plaza New York City NY 10017

CREMIN, LAWRENCE ARTHUR, educator; b. N.Y.C., Oct. 31, 1925; s. Arthur T. and Theresa (Borowick) C.; B.S. in Social Scis., Coll. City N.Y., 1946; A.M., Columbia, 1947, Ph.D., 1949; m. Charlotte Raup, Sept. 19, 1956; children—Joanne Laura, David Lawrence. Mem. faculty Columbia Tchrs. Coll., N.Y.C., 1948—, Frederick A.P. Barnard prof. edn., 1961—, dir. div. philosophy, social scis., edn., 1965—. Guggenheim fellow, 1957-58; fellow Center for Advanced Study in Behavioral Scis., 1964-65, 71-72. Trustee, Dalton Schs., Children's TV Workshop. Served with USAAF, 1944-45. Recipient Bancroft prize Am. history for The Transformation of the School, 1962; research award Am. Ednl. Research Assn., 1969. Mem. Hist. Edn. Soc. (pres. 1959-60), Nat. Acad. Edn. (pres. 1969—), Nat. Soc. Coll. Tchrs. Edn. (pres. 1961-62), Nat. Acad. Edn. (pres. 1969—). Author: The American Common School, 1951; (with R. Freeman Butts) A History of Education in American Culture, 1953; (with D.A. Shannon, M.E. Townsend) A History of Teachers College, Columbia University, 1954; The Republic and the School, 1957; The Transformation of the School, 1961; The Genius of American Education, 1965; The Wonderful World of Ellwood Patterson Cubberley, 1965; American Education: The Colonial Experience, 1970. Gen. editor Classics in Education, 1957—. Office: Teachers Coll Columbia New York City NY 10027

CRENNA, RICHARD, actor; b. Los Angeles; ed. U. So. Cal. Actor radio programs including Boy Scout Jamboree, A Date with Judy, The Great Gildersleeve, Johnny Dollar, Our Miss Brooks; TV programs Our Miss Brooks, The Real McCoys. Slattery's People; films Pride of St. Louise, It Grows on Trees, Red Skies Over Montana, John Goldfarb, Please Come Home, Wait Until Dark, Star, 1968, The Sand Pebbles, The Deserter. Owner Penick Enterprises, 1966—. care of William Morris Agy 151 El Camino Beverly Hills CA 90212*

CRENSHAW, CRAIG MOFFETT, physicist; b. Chinkyiang, China, Sept. 24, 1916 (parents Am. citizens); s. John Crawford and May (Moffett) C.; student Marshall Coll., Huntington, V.Va., 1933-35; B.S. with honors, Southwestern U. at Memphis, 1937; Ph.D., N.Y.U., 1942; m. Florence Fannon Wade, Aug. 12, 1942; children—Craig Moffett, Florence Elizabeth, David Sherer, William Crawford. Grad. asst. physics N.Y.U., 1937-41, asst., 1941-42; physicist U.S. Army Signal Research and Devel. Lab., Ft. Monmouth, N.J., 1942-56, dir. phys. scis. div., 1956-57, chief scientist research and devel. Office Chief Signal Officer, Washington, 1957-62, chief scientist U.S. Army Materiel Command, 1962—. Project leader operations Crossroads, Sandstone and Greenhouse. atmosphere on sound ranging accuracies, measuring upper air meterol. Bd. dirs. Boys Club Washington. Recipient Exceptional Civilian Service award Dept. Army, 1958, Meritorious Civilian Service award, 1959. Mem. Am. Phys. Soc., A.A.A.S., N.Y. Acad. Sci., Armed Forces Communications Electronics Assn., I.E.E.E., Assn. U.S. Army. Spl. research limiting effects atmosphere on sound ranging accuracies, measuring upper air meterol. parameters using sound grenades on rockets. 1424 Waggaman Circle McLean VA 22101 Office: US Army Material Command Washington DC 20315

CRENSHAW, GORDON LEE, tobacco co. exec.; b. Richmond, Va., Jan. 19, 1922; s. Walter and Hattie (Ready) C.; B.A., in Econ., U. Va., 1943; m. Deubne Anne Roper, May 12, 1945; children—Clarke Hutchins, Gordon Lee. With Universal Leaf Tobacco Co., 1946—, v.p., 1958-65, pres., 1965—, chief exec. officer, 1966—, also dir.; dir. Life Ins. Co. Va., Va. Indsl. Devel. Corp., United Van/State Planters Bank. Bd. dirs. Richmond Boys Club Am., Salvation Army, Richmond, Nat. Tobacco Festival; pres. bd. govs. Richmond Home for Boys; trustee Richmond Meml. Hosp. Served to lt. USNR, 1943-46. Mem. Tobacco Assn. U.S. (gov., past pres.), Richmond C. of C. (dir.). Episcopalian. Club: Commonwealth (dir.). Home: 111 Windsor Way Richmond VA 23221 Office: Hamilton & Broad Sts Richmond VA 23219

CRENSHAW, JACK, lawyer; b. Hendersonville, N.C., Aug. 9, 1905; s. H. Files and Pauline (Smith) C.; A.B., U. Ala., 1923, student Law Sch., 1923-24; LL.B., Harvard, 1926; m. Catherine Westcott, July 11, 1928; children-Mary Ann, Jack Westcott. Admitted to Ala. bar, 1926, since practiced in Montgomery; mem. firm Crenshaw & Waller, 1965—; spl. asst. atty. gen. Ala., 1938-39; Ala. atty. OPA, 1942-45; spl. asst. justice Supreme Ct. Ala., 1951. Sec., dir. Brown Printing Co., Montgomery. Trustee Presbyn. Childrens Home; bd. dirs. Ala. Tb Assn. Mem. Am., Ala.., Montgomery County (pres. 1944) bar assns., Am. Judicature Soc., Gideons Internat. (Ala. sec. 1968-70), Am. Trial Lawyers Assn. Phi Phi Beta Kappa, Phi Delta Theta, Phi Delta Phi. Republican. Presbyn. (elder). Mason (Shriner). Author articles. Home: 3155 Gilmer Av Montgomery AL 36105 Office: Washington Bldg Montgomery AL 36104

CRENSHAW, KIRBY E., petroleum co. exec.; b. Elberton, Ga., Apr. 6, 1908; s. George W. and Sarah M. (Sims) C.; B.S. in Civil Engring., N.C. State U., 1930; grad. Advanced Mgmt. Program, Harvard; LL.D., Okla. Christian Coll., 1970; m. Mary F. Lemmond, 1934; children—Millicent, George. Jr. engr. Cities Service Oil Co., Bartlesville, Okla., 1930-31; compressor sta. oiler, meter insp., prodn. engr., asst. supt. Cities Service Gas Co., Bartlesville, also Pampa, Tex., 1931-38, tax engr., Bartlesville, 1939-40, exec. v.p., dir., Oklahoma City, 1956-58, pres., dir., 1958-68; engr., v.p. Gas Advisers, Inc., N.Y.C., 1940-54; asst. mgr. natural gas Cities Service Petroleum, Inc., N.Y.C., 1954-56; pres., dir. Cities Service Oil Co., 1968—; dir. Nat. Bank Tulsa. Exec. com. Frontiers Sci. Found. of Okla., Inc.; trustee Okla. Safety Council, U. Tulsa; sponsor Corporate Leadership Com. Meetings; bd. dirs. Okla. Petroleum Council, Gilcrease Inst. Am. History and Art, Internat. Petroleum Exhbn.; mem. finance and devel. com., nominating and screening com. of bd. govs. Am. Citizenship Center, Oklahoma City; Tulsa YMCA; adv. bd. KANCHI, Tulsa, Salvation Army, Tulsa. Registered profl. engr., Okla. Mem. Kan., Tulsa (leadership sounding bd.) chambers commerce, Mid-Continent Oil and Gas Assn. (exec. com. Kan.-Okla. div.), Gen., Tex. mid-continent oil and gas assns., Am. Petroleum Inst. (natural gas com.). Presbyn. Clubs: Bankers (N.Y.C.); Twenty-Five Year of Chicago; Southern Hills Country, Tulsa, Summit (Tulsa); Cherokee Yacht. Home: 3868 S Atlanta Pl Tulsa OK 74105 Office: Cities Service Bldg Tulsa OK 74102

CREPIN, JEAN ALBERT, army officer; b. Bernaville, France, Sept. 1, 1908; s. Albert E. and Jeanne (Petit) C.; grad. Ecole Poly., 1930; m. Simone Michele Granday, Apr. 1, 1948; children—Francoise (Mrs. J. Van Der Plaetsen), Bernadette (Mrs. G. Menahem). Commd. 2d lt. French Army, 1930, advanced through grades to gen. d'Armee, 1960; served with colonial arty. in China, then Cameroons, also campaigns of Fezzan and Tripoli, 1943-44; arty. comdr. 2d Free French Div., 1943-45; dept. to comdr. troops in N. Indochina and 9th Div. Inf. Coloniale, 1945-46; commnr. ad interim for Tonkin and N. Annam, 1946-47; assigned Inst. Higher Studies Nat. Def., 1947-48; asst. dir. colonial troops, 1949-54; head spl. gen. staff Ministry Nat. Def., 1954; dep. sec. gen. nat. def., 1954-55; insp. gen. mfr. and armed forces program, 1955-59; comdr. 13th Inf. Div., also S. Algerian Zone, 1959-60; comdr. army corps, Algeria, 1960, comdr.-in-chief, 1960-61; comdr.-in-chief French Forces in Germany, 1961-63, in Central-European sector, 1963-66; mem. Higher Council War, 1960. Chmn. Nord- Aviation, Societe Nationale de Constructions Aéronautiques, 1967—. Decorated grand officer of the Legion of Honor, Fellow of Liberation, War cross 1939-45, Theatre d'Operation Exterieurs, Distinguished Service Order, Silver Star, Bronze Star, Legion of Merit (France). Home: 51 rue de l'Assomption Paris 16e France. Office: Nord- Aviation 2-18 rue Béranger 92 Chatillon-sous-Bagneaux France

CRESCI, ROBERT J., educator; b. N.Y.C., Oct. 9, 1932; s. Louis and Mary (Lusardi) C.; B. Aero. Engring. cum laude, Bklyn. Poly Inst., 1953, M. Aero Engring., 1957, Ph.D., 1960; m. Marion Jane McBride, Aug. 13, 1955; children Sharon, Daniel, Roger. Aero. engr. N. Am. Aviation Co., 1953-55; mem. faculty Bklyn. Poly. Inst., 1955-, prof. aerospace engring, 1966-, asst. dir. gas dynamics lab., 1967-; cons. to industry, 1960-. Mem. Am. Inst. Aero and Astronautics, Am. Assn. U. Profs., Sigma Xi, Tau Beta Pi. Research on supersonic and hypersonic aerodynamics, aerodynamic heat transfer problems, hypersonic wind tunnel research, supersonic compressors, boundary layer theory. Home: 115 The Helm East Islip, NY 11730. Office: Route 110 Farmingdale NY 11735

CRESKOFF, JACOB JOSHUA, cons. engr.; b. Belz, Russia, Mar. 30, 1900; s. Louis and Tillie (Lerner) C.; brought to U.S., 1905; student South Phila. High Sch., 1914- 18; grad. Gratz Coll., Phila., 1919; B.S. in C.E., Towne Sci. Sch. (U. Pa.), 1922; m. Mildred Blumenthal, Mar. 16, 1935; children—Stephen, Ruth. Made investigation of Washington Monument for spalling and aseismic qualities; cons. to depts. of U.S. Govt. on design of earthquake-proof bldgs., and on recording and analysis of structural vibrations, including aeronautical structures; devised first practical dynamic system of aseismic design; method of distbn. of wind and earthquake forces to walls and columns; method of using site vibrations as check on geol. findings; method of using periods of vibration of structures as guide to end fixities and to detect invisible damage; v.p. Vacuum Concrete Corp., 1938-42, 46-50; resident v.p. McCloskey & Co., 1942-46; pres. Thermo-Fluid Corp., 1950-59, Vacuum Concrete Corp. of Am., 1959-69; chmn. bd. Aerovac Corp., 1969—; guest prof. Grad. Sch. Engring., Villanova U. since 1962. Served in Engrs. S.A.T.C., U.S. Army, 3 months, 1918; lt. comdr. Civil Engr. Corps, USNR, 1938—. Citation, Distinguished Engineer, U. Pa., 1955. Mem. Am. Concrete Inst. Jewish religion. Author: Dynamics of Earthquake Resistant Structures, 1934. Contbr. on engring. subjects. Home: Thomas Wynne Apts Wynnewood PA 19096 Office: 6111 Lancaster Av Philadelphia PA 19151

CRESON, LARRY BARKLEY, justice; b. Memphis, Jan. 17, 1906; s. Robert Franklin and Etta (Thomas) C.; student Memphis U. Sch., grad. Vanderbilt U., 1928. LL.B., 1929; m. Gertrude Jean Hooper, Aug. 29, 1934; childrenJean Edrington (Mrs. Allen Cooper Dell), Larry Barkley. Admitted to Tenn. bar, 1929; practiced in Memphis, 1930-65; past mem. firm Laughlin, Watson, Creson, Garthbright & Halle; associate justice Supreme Court of Tennessee, judge Chancery Court of Shelby County, Tenn., 1947-54. Past member board trust Vanderbilt U. Served as lt. comdr., air combat intelligence, USNR, World War II. Mem. Vanderbilt Alumni Assn. (dir., past pres., Memphis), Am., Tenn., Memphis and Shelby County, (pres. 1960-61) bar assns., Sigma Alpha Epsilon, Phi Delta Phi. Home: 1529 Vance Ave Memphis TN 38104. Office: State Office Bldg 170 N Main St Memphis TN 38103

CRESPIN, REGINE, (Mrs. Lou Bruder), soprano; b. Marseilles, France; d. Henri and Margherite (DiMeirone) Crespin; student Lycee Francais, Conservatoire de Paris; m. Lou Bruder, Apr. 16, 1960. Appeared in numerous operas including Lohengrin, Mulhouse, France, 1950, Paris, 1951, N.Y.C., 1964, Tosca, Il Trovatore, Otello, Die Walkuere, Oberon, Fidelio, Der Rosenkavalier, Marseilles, Le Nozze di Figaro, Paris, 1956, Dialogues of the Carmelites, 1957, Parsifal, 1958, Ballo in Maschera, 1958, Fedra, Milan, Italy, 1959, Die Walkuere, Vienna, 1959, Der Rosenkavalier, Berlin, 1960, as the Marshallin, London, 1961, Les Troyens, Paris, 1961, Penelope, Buenos Aires, 1961, Otello, Ballo in Maschera, Die Walkuere, Der Rosenkavalier, Vienna, also Rosenkavalier, N.Y.C., 1962, Flying Dutchman, N.Y.C., 1962, Ballo in Maschera, N.Y.C., 1962, La Vestale, N.Y.C., 1962, Herodiade, N.Y.C., 1963, Fidelio, Ballo in Maschera, Tannhauser, Fidelio, Chgo., 1963; soloist N.Y. Philharmonic, 1964-65; appeared in recital Hunter Coll., 1965. Office: Columbia Artists Mgmt Inc 165 W 57th St New York City NY 10019

CRESSEY, DONALD RAY, educator, sociologist; b. Fergus Falls, Minn., Apr. 27, 1919; s. Raymond Wilbert and Myrtle Athelma (Prentiss) C.; B.S., Ia. State U., 1943; Ph.D., Ind. U., 1950; m. Elaine Smythe, Dec. 16, 1943; children—Martha, Ann, Mary. Sociologist, Ill. State Penitentiary, Joliet, 1949; lectr. sociology U. Cal. at Los Angeles, 1949, instr., 1950, asst. prof., 1951-56, asso. prof., 1956-59; vice chmn. dept. anthropology and sociology, 1957-58, chmn. dept., 1958-61, prof. sociology, 1959-62, dean div. social sci., 1960-61; vis. prof. criminology U. Cambridge, 1961-62, U. Oslo, 1965, U. Washington, summer, 1968, U. Minn., summer 1969, Hebrew U., 1970, Churchill Coll., Cambridge U., 1971; dean Coll. Letters and Sci., U. Cal. at Santa Barbara, 1962-67, prof. sociology, 1962—. Mem. mental health tng. com. Nat. Inst. Mental Health, 1963-67, chmn. 1966-67, policy and planning bd., tng. and manpower resources br., 1964-67; cons. Pres.'s Commn. on Law Enforcement and Adminstrn. Justice, 1965-66, Nat. Commn. Causes and Prevention Violence, 1968, Nat. Inst. Law Enforcement and Criminal Justice, 1969-70. Russell Sage Found. research grantee 1955-56; travel grantee Am. Council Learned Socs., 1960; research grantee Ford Found., 1960. Served with USAAF, 1943-46. Recipient Research citation Ill. Acad. Criminology, 1964. Research citation Am. Soc. Criminology, 1967. Fellow Am. Sociol. Assn. (council 1961-63, vis. scientist 1963-65, chmn. criminology sect. 1966-67); mem. Law and Soc. Assn., Internat. Soc. Criminology, Pacific Sociol. Assn. (pres. 1959-60), Am. Rocket Soc., Am. Correctional Assn. Club: Earl of Derby (pres. 1962-63) (Cambridge, Eng.). Author: Other People's Money, a Study in the Social Psychology of Embezzlement, 1953; (with Edwin H. Sutherland) Principles of Criminology, 5th edit., 1955, 8th edit. 1970; (with Richard A. Cloward, others) Theoretical Studies in Social Organization of the Prison, 1960; Delinquency, Crime and Differential Association, 1964; Functions and Structure of Confederated Crime, 1967; Theft of the Nation, 1969; (with David A. Ward) Delinquency, Crime and Social Process, 1969. Editor: The Prison, Studies in Institutional Social Organization and Change, 1961; Crime and Criminal Justice, 1971; asso. editor Am. Sociol. Rev., 1953-56, Am. Jour. Sociology, 1958-61, Transaction: Soc. Sci. and the Community, 1963-69; Harper and Row Social Problems Series, 1965—. Contbr. articles to profl. jours. Home: Hope Ranch 4310 Via Esperanza Santa Barbara CA 93105

CRESSMAN, GEORGE PARMLEY, meteorologist; b. West Chester, Pa., Oct. 7, 1919; s. George R. and Martha S. (Parmley) C.; B.Sc., Pa. State Coll., 1941; M.Sc., N.Y.U., 1942; Ph.D., U. Chgo., 1949; m. Nelia M. Hazard, Feb. 28, 1942; children—Ruth, George, Catherine, Florence. Engaged in research, teaching U. Chgo., 1946-49; cons. USAF Weather Service, 1949-54; dir. joint weather bur. Navy-Air Force Numerical Weather Prediction Unit, Silver Spring, Md., 1954—, Nat. Meteorol. Center, 1958-64, dir. Nat. Meteorol. Service, 1964- 65, dir. U.S. Weather Bur., Silver Spring, 1965-70, Nat. Weather Service, 1970—. Served to capt. AUS, 1942-45, Recipient Exceptional Civilian Service award USAF, 1956, Exceptional Service award Dept. Commerce, 1961. Mem. Am. Meteorol. Soc. (councilor 1956-59, asso. editor jour. 1954-65), Wash. Acad. Scis. Home: 9 Old Stage Ct Rockville MD 20852 Office: National Weather Service 8060 13th St Silver Spring MD 20910

CRESSMAN, RALPH DWIGHT, educator, surgeon; b. Oglesby, Ill., Jan. 17, 1909; s. Ralph Gates and Emily (Blackmore) C.; A.B., U. Cal. at Berkeley, 1929, M.A., 1931, M.D., 1934; m. Bernice Moore Klein, Aug. 16, 1935; children—Russell R., Ann (Mrs. Rodney Baker). Intern Alameda County Hosp., Oakland, Cal., 1935; postgrad. surg. tng. U. Cal., Vanderbilt U. and San Francisco Gen. hosps., 1935-41; practice surgery, Palo Alto (Cal.) Med. Clinic, 1946—, head sect. gen. surgery, 1960—; prof. surgery Stanford Med. Sch., 1970—. Served with M.C. AUS, 1942-45. Mem. A.C.S. (gov. 1962- 68, sec. bd. govs. 1967-68), San Francisco Surg. Soc., Pacific Coast Surg. Assn. (sec.-treas. 1964-68). Author articles in field. Home: 360 Everett Av Palo Alto CA 94301 Office: 300 Homer Av Palo Alto CA 94301

CRESSON, MARGARET FRENCH, sculptor; b. Concord, Mass., Aug. 3, 1889; d. Daniel Chester and Mary Adams French; ed. Clarke Pvt. School and Brearley School (both N.Y.C.); m. William Penn Cresson, Jan. 10, 1921 (dec. May 1932). Studied under Daniel Chester French, Abastenia St. Leger Eberle and George Demetrios. Works include bronze busts, bronze reliefs, portrait heads. and meml. plaques. Exhibited Paris Salon, N.Y. World's Fair. Mem. N.A.D. Founder Chesterwood Studio Mus., trustee Daniel Chester French Found.; bd. trustees Chesterwood Studio, Stockbridge, Mass., St. Gaudens Meml. Cornish, N.H.; Berkshire Mus. Pittsfield, Mass. Nat. Academician. Fellow Nat. Sculpture Soc. (sec. 1940-41); mem. Architectural League N.Y. (2d v.p. 1944-46), N.A.D., Allied Artists Am., Audubon Artists, Grand Central Art Galleries of N.Y., Winner Shaw Meml. prize N.A.D., 1927; hon. mention Jr. League Exhbn., N.Y.C., 1928; Soc. Washington Artists. Corcoran Gallery of Art. 1929; Crowninshield Sculpture prize and Popular prize, Stockbridge Art Exhbn., 1929; bronze medal Soc. Washington Artists, 1937; hon. mention. Stockbridge Art Exhbn., 1938; Popular prize Dublin Hill Art Show, 1939; Popular prize Contemporary Am. Masters, 1944; Grand Nat. Gold medal Am. Artist Profl. League, 1959. Author: Journey Into Fame, 1947; Daniel Chester French, 1949; Laurel Hill, 1953. Contbr. articles on art and artists to Reader's Digest, Am. Heritage, N.Y. Times Sunday mag. Home and Studio Chesterwood Stockbridge MA 01262

CRESSWELL, DONALDSON, lawyer, orgn. exec.; b. Phila., 1902; ed. Princeton, 1924, U. Pa., 1927 Chmn. bd., dir. Blue Cross of Phila.; trustee Phila. Savs. Fund Soc. Chmn., dir. Corp. for Relief of Widows of Episcopal Clergymen in Pa. Home: 409 Hillbrook Rd Bryn Mawr PA 19010 Office: care Blue Cross Widener Bldg 1333 Chestnut St Philadelphia PA 19107

CRESTON, PAUL, composer; b. N.Y.C., Oct. 10, 1906; s. Gaspare and Carmela (Collura) Guttoveggio; student pub. schs., N.Y.C.; m. Louise Gotto, July 1, 1927; children—Joel Anthony, Timothy William. Organist St. Malachy's Ch., N.Y.C., 1934-67; faculty N.Y. Coll. Music, 1964-68; distinguished vis. prof. Central Wash. State Coll., Ellensburg, 1967, composer-in- residence, prof. music, 1968—; made concert tour as pianist and accompanist, 1936; mus. dir. The Hour of Faith Program, ABC, 1944-50. Guggenheim fellow in composition, 1938, 39. Recipient citation of merit Nat. Assn. Am. Composers and Condrs., 1941, 43; music award Am. Acad. Arts and Letters, 1943; N.Y. Music Critics award for Symphony No. 1, 1943; Alice M. Ditson award for Poem for Harp and Orch., 1945; Fedn. Music Clubs award for Symphony No. 2, 1947; Music Library Assn. award for Two Choric Dances, 1948; 1st prize for Symphony No. 1, Paris Referendum Concert, 1952; State Dept. grant as Am. specialist for Israel and Turkey, 1960; gold medal Nat. Arts Club, 1963, Composer award Lancaster Symphony, 1970. Life fellow Internat. Inst. Arts and Letters; mem. Nat. Assn. Am. Composers and Condrs. (pres. 1956-60, life mem.), A.S.C.A.P. (dir. 1960-68), Bohemians (gov. 1950-68), Nat. Music Council (exec. com. 1950-68). Author: Principles of Rhythm. Home: PO Box 794 Ellensburg WA 98926

CREUTZ, EDWARD CHESTER, physicist; b. Beaver Dam, Wis., Jan. 23, 1913; s. Lester Raymond and Grace (Smith) C.; B.S., U. Wis., 1936, Ph.D., 1939; m. Lela Rollefson, Sept. 13, 1937; children—Michael John, Carl Eugene, Ann Jo Carmel. Research asso. Princeton, 1939-40, instr. physics, 1940-41; physicist NDRC, 1941-42, metall. lab. U. Chgo., 1942-44, Manhattan Project, Los Alamos, 1944-46; asso. prof. Carnegie Inst. Tech., 1946-49, prof. chmn. dept. physics, dir. Nuclear Research Center, 1949-55; dir. John Jay Hopkins Lab. for Pure and Applied Sci., 1955-59; dir. research Gen. Atomic Div., Gen. Dynamics Corp., 1955- 59, v.p. research devel., 1959-67; v.p. research and devel. Gulf Gen. Atomic, 1967-70; asst. dir. for research NSF, Washington, 1970—. Mem. Adv. council Water Resources Center, U. Cal., 1958-65, mem. sea water conversion comm., 1958-68; mem. adv. com. Office Sci. Personnel, NRC, 1960-63; council exec. bd. Argonne Nat. Lab., 1946- 51; cons. NSF, 1950-68; scientist-at-large project Sherwood div. research AEC, 1955-56; cons. Oak Ridge Nat. Lab., 1946-58; adv. panel gen. scis. Dept. Def., 1959-63; research adv. com. electrophysics NASA, 1964. Vice Pres., bd. dirs. San Diego Hall Sci. and Planetarium; v.p., past dir. San Diego Industry-Edn. Council, 1956-65; exec. council community edn. resources Dept. Edn. San Diego County. Fellow Am. Phys. Soc. (rep. to NRC 1956-57), Am. Nuclear Soc., San Diego Soc. Natural History (pres. fellows 1965-66, dir. 1966-70); mem. Physics Soc. Pitts. (pres. 1949), Am. Soc. Engring. Edn., I.R.E., San Diego Industry Edn. Council (v.p., dir.), Am. Soc. M.E., Am. Assn. Physics Tchrs., Am. Assn. U. Profs., I.E.E.E., Am. Inst. Physics (steering com. vis. scientists program 1958-66, dir.-at-large, bd. govs. 1965- 68, standing com. controlld nuclear br. AEC 1971—), Pa., N.Y., Cal. acad. scis. Co-editor: Handbuch der Physik, vols. 14, 15; mem. editorial bd. Ann. Rev. Nuclear Sci., 1961-66. Handbook of Chemistry and Physics, 1961—; editorial adv. com. Nuclear Sci. and Engring., 1959—. Home: 6624 River Rd Bethesda MD 20034 Office: 1800 G St NW Washington DC 20550

CREWE, ALBERT VICTOR, physicist, research adminstr.; b. Bradford, Yorkshire, Eng., Feb. 18, 1927; s. Wilfred and Edith Fish (Lawrence) C.; B.S. in Physics, U. Liverpool (Eng.) 1947, Ph.D., 1951; m. Doreen Blunsdon, Apr. 9, 1949; children—Jennifer, Sarah, Elizabeth, David. Came to U.S., 1955, naturalized, 1961. Asst. lectr. U. Liverpool (Eng.), 1950-52, lectr., 1952-55; research asso. U. Chgo., 1955-56, asst. prof., 1956-58, asso. prof., 1958-63, prof. dept. physics and Enrico Fermi Inst., 1963-71, dean phys. scis. div., 1971—; dir. particle accelerator div. Argonne Nat. Lab., 1958-61, dir. Argonne Nat. Lab., 1961-66. Chmn. Chgo. Area Research and Devel. Council. Recipient Outstanding Local Citizen in Field of Sci. award Chgo. Jr. Assn. Commerce and Industry, 1961; Outstanding New Citizen of Year award Citizenship Council Chgo., 1962; award for outstanding achievement in field of sci. Immigrant's Service League, 1962; Man of Year in Research award Indsl. Research, Inc., 1970. Fellow Am. Phys. Soc., Am. Nuclear Soc.; mem. Sci. Research Soc. Am., Electron Microscopy Soc. Am. Nuclear physics research using particle accelerators; devel. particle accelerator, external beams from cyclotrons and synchrotron design, devel. electron microscopes. Home: 63 Old Creek Rd Palos Park IL 60464

CREWS, ROBERT NELSON, constrn. co. exec.; b. Texline, Tex., Feb. 28, 1924; s. John S. and Ellizabeth (Shankle) C.; B.Engring., Tulane U., 1948; m. Joy V. Kleck, Aug. 17, 1946; children—Robert Nelson, Elizabeth Ann, Mary Lesley. With J. Ray McDermott & Co., Inc., New Orleans, 1946—, exec. v.p., 1967—; also dir. Served with USNR, World War II. Home: 533 Woodvine Av Metairie LA 70005 Office: Saratoga Bldg New Orleans LA 70160

CRIBARI, SAMUEL LEWIS, cement mfg. co. exec.; b. Keezer, Colo., June 27, 1905; s. Angelo and Josephine (Leo) C.; student DePaul U., 1931; m. Angela Marie Guizzetti, June 19, 1928; 1 son, Samuel Lewis. With Marquette Cement Mfg. Co., Chgo., 1920- -, beginning as office boy, successively So. credit mgr., gen. credit mgr., asst. treas., asst. to pres., 1920-50, v.p., dir. marketing, 1950- -. Mem. Chgo. Bldg. Congress (dir. 1967—). Chgo. Sales Execs. Club. Clubs: Executives, Builders, Svithiod, Tower (Chgo.); Evanston (Ill.) Country. Home: 8601 Skokie Blvd Skokie IL 60076 Office: 20 N Wacker Dr Chicago IL 60606

CRIBBET, JOHN EDWARD, univ. dean; b. Findlay, Ill., Feb. 20, 1918; s. Howard H. and Ruth (Wright) C.; B.A., Ill. Wesleyan U., 1940, LL.D., 1971; J.D., U. Ill., 1947; m. Betty Jane Smith, Dec. 24, 1941; children—Carol Ann, Pamela Lee. Admitted to Ill. bar, 1947; practiced in Bloomington, 1947; prof. law U. Ill. at Urbana, 1947—, dean Coll. Law, 1967. Chmn. com. on jud. ethics Ill. Supreme Ct. Pres. United Fund, Champaign County (Ill.), 1962-63, Trustee Ill. Wesleyan U. Served to maj. AUS, 1941-45. Decorated Bronze Star medal, Croix de Guerre. Mem. Am., Ill., Champaign County bar assns., Order of Coif. Rotarian. Author: Cases and Materials on Judicial Remedies, 1954; Cases on Property, 2d edit., 1966; Principles of the Law of Property, 1962. Editor: U. Ill. Law Forum, 1947-55. Contbr. articles to law revs. Home: 1412 Waverly Dr Champaign IL 61822

CRICHLEY, EDWIN HENRY, mfg. co. exec.; b. Pitts., July 31, 1916; s. Charles H. and Alice (McGrath) C.; diplomat Robert Morris Coll., 1940; m. Jean Marie Mowers, May 16, 1942; childrenBonnie Jean, Donna Sue, Cynthia Louise, Sandra Lee. Chief account officer Hood Chem. Co., Pitts., 1946-49; asst. comptroller Aero Supply Mfg. Co., Corry, Pa., 1954-56; corp. comptroller Parker-Hannifin Corp., Cleve., 1956-. Served with AUS, 1942-45. C.P.A., Pa. Mem. Cleve. C. of C., Financial Execs. Inst., Machinery and Allied Products Inst., Am. Legion. Baptist. Club: Acacia Country (Lyndhurst,O.). Home: 4392 W. Anderson Rd South Euclid, OH 44121. Office: 17325 Euclid Av Cleveland OH 44112

CRICHLEY, WILLIAM ALLEN, chem. co. exec.; b. Pitts., Apr. 1, 1908; s. Thomas Henry and Mary Emma (Hindmarch) C.; student Carnegie Inst. Tech.; student Robert Morris Sch. Accounting; m. Alice Wetter, Oct. 12, 1935; children—Judith Ann (Mrs. James C. Blue), Joyce Alice (Mrs. David C. Hunter). Employed with Crichley Lumber Co., 1926-33, Gulf Oil Co., 1933-35, Price, Waterhouse & Co., C.P.A.'s 1935-43; with Diamond Alkali Co., Cleve., 1943—, controller, 1945-60, treas., 1960—; dir. Kendale Industries, Mangill Chem. Co. Trustee Florence Crittenton Home: treas., trustee Huron Rd. Hosp. C.P.A., Ohio, Pa. Mem. Am. Inst. C.P.A.'s Ohio, Pa. socs. C.P.A.'s. Republican. Presbyn. Mason. Home: 3240 Rumson Rd Cleveland, OH 44118. Office: Union Commerce Bldg Cleveland, OH 44115.

CRICHTON, JOHN HENDERSON, assn. exec.; b. Padroni, Colo., Mar. 4, 1919; s. John Henderson and Lyda (McClain) C.; B. Journalism, U. Mo., 1940; m. Zula Miller, Nov. 24, 1939; children—John Michael, Kimberly, Douglas Christopher, Catherine. With newspapers, Colo., Mont., 1940-41; with Advt. Age Mag., Chgo., 1941- 42, N.Y.C., 1946-62, editor, 1958-62; pres. Am. Assn. Advt. Agencies, Inc., N.Y.C., 1962—. Mem. adv. com. U.S. council Internat. C. of C.; mem. commerce information adv. com. Dept. Commerce; sec., dir. Advt. Council; dir. Traffic Audit Bur. Mem. nat. adv. council Hampshire Coll. Bd. dirs. Advt. Research Found., Nat. Center for Voluntary Action Served to lt. (j.g.) USNR, 1944-46. Mem. U.S. C. of C., Am. Marketing Assn. Clubs: Lake (New Canaan); Union League, Sky, Economic, Metropolitan (N.Y.C.); Nat. Press (Washington); Norwalk Yacht. Author: (with W. H. Mullen) The New Competition, 1956. Home: 98 Thayer Pond Rd New Canaan CT 06840 Office: 200 Park Av New York City NY 10017

CRICHTON, JOHN MICHAEL, author; b. Chgo., Oct. 23, 1942; s. John Henderson and Zula (Miller) C.; A.B. summa cum laude, Harvard, 1964, M.D., 1969. Postdoctoral fellow Salk Inst., LaJolla, Cal., 1969-70. Recipient Edgar award Mystery Writers Am., 1968; named med. writer of year Assn. Am. Med. Writers, 1970. Mem. Authors Guild, Writers Guild Am. West, Phi Beta Kappa. Club: Aesculaepian (Boston). Author: The Andromeda Strain, 1969; Five Patients, 1970. Office: care IFA 1301 Av Americas New York City NY 10019

CRICK, FRANCIS HARRY COMPTON, molecular biologist; b. Northampton, Eng., June 8, 1916; s. Harry and Annie E. (Wilkins) C.; B.Sc. in Physics, Univ. Coll., London, 1937; Ph.D., Cambridge U., 1954; m. Ruth Doreen Dodd, 1940 (div. 1947); 1 son, Michael F.C.; m. 2d, Odile Speed, 1949; children—Gabrielle A., Jacqueline M.T. Med. Research Council student Strangeways Lab., Cambridge, 1947-49; mem. staff Med. Research Council Lab. Molecular Biology, Cambridge, 1949—; mem. protein structure project Bklyn. Poly. Inst., 1953- 54; vis. prof. chemistry Harvard, spring, 1959, vis. prof. biophysics, Mar. 1962; fellow Churchill Coll., Cambridge U., 1960-61, fellow Univ. Coll., London, 1962. Warren Triennial prize lectr. (with J.D. Watson) Mass. Gen. Hosp., 1959; Korkes Meml. lectr. Duke, 1960; Franklin I. Harris lectr., Mt. Zion, 1962—; non-resident fellow Salk Inst. Biol. Studies, San Diego, 1962; recipient (with J.D. Watson and M.H.F. Wilkins) Lasker award, 1960, prix Charles Leopold Mayer, French Acad. Scis., 1961, Research Corp. award (with J.D. Watson), 1961, Gardiner Found. award, Toronto, 1962, Nobel prize for medicine (with J.D. Watson and M.H.F. Wilkins), 1962. Fellow Royal Soc.; fgn. hon. mem. Am. Acad. Arts and Scis. fgn. asso. U.S.

Acad. Scis.; mem. German Acad. Sci., Leopoldina. Author papers structure DNA, polynucleotides, polypeptides, proteins, viruses. Home: 19 Portugal Pl Cambridge England Office: Medical Research Council Lab Molecular Biology Hills Rd Cambridge England

CRIDER, BLAKE, psychologist; b. Personville, Tex., Aug. 7, 1902; s. Allen Blake and Delia (Newsome) C.; B.A., U. No., 1924; M.A., U. Chgo., 1928; Ph.D., Western Res. U., 1933; m. Doris Towne, June 15, 1932; children—Andrew Blake, Harlan Towne. Tchr. Orange (Tex.) High Sch., 1924-26; instr. psychology Albion (Mich.) Coll., 1926-29; psychologist Shaker Heights (O.) Schs., 1929-31; staff psychologist psychiat. pediatric clinics St. Luke's Hosp., Mt. Sinai Mental Hygiene Clinic, Cleve. State Hosp., Windsor Sanitarium, Behavior Day Nursery Assn., Cleve., 1933-50; prof. psychology Cleve. State U., 1934-70, emeritus, 1970—; pvt. practice psychotherapy. Certified psychologist N.Y., Ohio, Diplomate Am. Bd. Examiners in Psychology, Ohio Psychology Assn., Am. Bd. Examiners in Clin. Hypnosis. Fellow Am. Psychol. Assn.; mem. Internat. Soc. Comprehensive Medicine, Soc. for Sci. Study Sex, Internat. Soc. Clin. and Exptl. Hypnosis, Cleve. Inst. for Gestalt Therapy, Am. Acad. Psychotherapists, Nat. Assn. Standard Med. Vocabulary, Asociacion de Charros de Ajijic (Jalisco, Mexico), Inter-Am. Psychol. Assn., Soc. Clin. and Exptl. Hypnosis, Phi Delta Kappa, Alpha Tau Omega. Contbr. sci. articles to profl. jours. Address: 1900 E 30th St Cleveland OH 44114

CRIDLAND, CHARLES, pub. co. exec.; b. Phila., Mar. 5, 1915; s. George Shober and Estelle (Heyland) C.; B.A., U. Pa., 1936; M.B.A., Drexel Inst. Tech., 1949; m. Margery McKay, Nov. 23, 1939; children—Jean (Mrs. John O'Connor), Ruth (Mrs. William A. Brunnell), George. With Matheison, Aitken, C.P.A.'s, Phila., 1936-46; instr. Drexel Inst. Grad. Sch., 1940-61; treas. David McKay Co., 1946- 49, pres., 1950; treas. Thomas Nelson, Inc., Camden, N.J., 1950-62, pres., 1962- 67, chmn. bd., treas., 1967-70, financial cons., 1970—; pres., dir. Thomas Nelson & Sons, Toronto, Ont., Can., 1965-68, chmn. bd., 1968-69. Treas. Community Nursing Service of Delaware County, Pa., 1952-62. Served to lt. (s.g.) USNR, 1942-45. C.P.A., Pa. Home: Taunton Lakes Marlton PO NJ 08053 Office: Thomas Nelson Copewood and Davis Sts Camden NJ 08103

CRIHFIELD, BREVARD EWING, assn. exec.; b. Bloomington, Ill., Feb. 10, 1916; s. Roy Horace and Helen Louise (Stevenson) C.; student Ill. Wesleyan U., 1933-35; A.B., U. Chgo., 1937; M.S., Syracuse U., 1942; m. Mary Elizabeth Owens, Feb. 12, 1949; children—Mary Elizabeth, John Brevard, Owen Stevenson. Office asst. to chmn. bd. Marshall Field & Co., 1937, credit man. 1938-39; loan officer Indsl. Nat. Bank, Chgo., 1939-41; mng. dir. Schenectady Bur. Municipal Research, 1942-44; Washington rep. Council State Govts., 1944- 46, research asso., 1947, Eastern regional rep., 1948-58, exec. dir., 1958-; sec. Nat. Governors' Conf., 1958-. Mem. President's Citizen Adv. Com. Fitness of Am. Youth, 1958, President's Com. on Employment Physically Handicapped, 1959; mem. nat. adv. com. White House Conf. on Aging, 1959; mem. Census Adv. Com. on State and Local Government Statistics, 1963-; mem. program adv. com. Office Emergency Planning, Exec. Office: Pres., 1963-; mem. Nat. Def. Exec. Res., 1963-. Bd. directors Nat. Safety Council, 1961-64; chmn. bd. trustees Pub. Administrn. Service, 1963-. Mem. Conn. Prison Assn. (v.p. 1957-58), Sigma Chi. Author articles on govt. Home: 5 Oak Dr Dune Acres Chesterton IN 46304 Office: 1313 E 60th St Chicago, IL 60637.

CRIKELAIR, GEORGE FRANCIS, educator, surgeon; b. Green Bay, Wis., July 15, 1920; s. Frank L. and Alma (Stenger) C.; student St. Norbert Coll., 1941; B.A., U. Wis., 1942, M.D., 1944; m. Eleanor P. Hossli, July 29, 1944; children—John, David, Thomas, Amy, Carol, Paul, Mary. Rotating intern U.S. Naval Hosp., San Diego, 1944-45; resident, preceptor gen. surgery, Stevens Point, Wis., 1946-47; resident gen. surgery City Detroit Receiving Hosp.-Wayne State U., VA Hosp., Dearborn, Mich., 1947-50; resident plastic surgery Presbyn. Hosp., N.Y.C., 1950-52; asst. instr. surgery Wayne State U., 1949-50; instr. surgery Columbia Coll. Phys. and Surg., 1952-58, asst. prof. clin. surgery, 1958-59, asso. prof., 1959-60, prof., 1960—; dir. plastic surgery service Columbia Presbyn. Med. Center, N.Y.C., 1959—; cons. Harlem Hosp., N.Y.C., 1964—, U.S. Naval Hosp., St. Albans, N.Y., 1968—. Mem. health and safety com. Boy Scouts Am. Served with USNR, 1944-45, USMCR, 1945-46. Recipient Silver Beaver award Boy Scouts Am. Diplomate Am. Bd. Plastic Surgery (chmn. 1970-71). Mem. N.Y. county, N.Y. State, Bergen County med. socs., N.Y. Acad. Medicine, A.M.A., A.C.S., Am. Cleft Palate Assn., Am. Soc. Plastic and Reconstructive Surgeons (pres. 1971-72), Am. Assn. Plastic Surgeons, N.Y. Regional Soc. Plastic and Reconstructive Surgery (pres. 1966-67), Clin. Soc. U. Plastic Surgeons, Soc. Alumni Presbyn. Hosp., Internat. Soc. Burn Injuries, Royal Coll. Surgeons, Am. Burn Assn. Contbr. articles to med. jours. K.C. Home: 210 Heights Rd Ridgewood NJ 07450 Office: 161 Fort Washington Av New York City NY 10032

CRIKELAIR, ROBERT JOHN, paper co. exec.; b. Green Bay, Wis., Nov. 27, 1916; s. Frank L. and Alma (Stenger) C.; student St. Norbert Coll., DePere, Wis., 1934-36; B.A., U. Wis., 1938; grad. exec. devel. program U. Ill., 1960; m. Adeline Seidel, Jan. 30, 1943; children—Martha (Mrs. George Wohlford III), Frank, Robert, Linda, Daniel, Lisa. With Haskins & Sells, C.P.A.'s, N.Y.C. and Chgo., 1938-46; with Kimberly-Clark Corp., Neenah, Wis., 1946- -. asst. comptroller, 1961-63, comptroller, 1963-70, v.p. adminstrv. services, 1970—. Campaign chmn. Neenah-Menasha Community Chest, 1954, bd. dirs., 1955-60. Served to maj. USAAF, 1941-45; ETO. C.P.A., Ill., Wis. Mem. Financial Execs. Inst. (dir. Milw. chpt.), Am. Paper Inst. (past chmn. financial mgmt. com.), Sigma Nu, Beta Alpha Psi. C.C. (past grand knight Neenah-Menasha). Home: 721 Congress Pl Neenah WI 54956 Office: Kimberly-Clark Corp N Lake St Neenah WI 54956

CRILE, GEORGE, Jr., surgeon; b. Cleve., Nov. 3, 1907; s. George and Grace (McBride) C.; Ph.B., Yale, 1929; M.D., Harvard, 1933; m. Jane Halle, Dec. 5, 1935 (dec.); children—Ann, Joan, Susan, George; m. 2d, Helga Sandburg, Nov. 9, 1963. Intern, Barnes Hosp., 1933-34; resident surgeon Cleve. Clinic, 1934-37, mem. surg. staff, 1937—, head dept. gen. surgery, 1956-69, sr. cons. dept. surgery, 1969—. Hon. civilian cons. to surgeon gen. USN. 1951-55. Served from 1st lt. to comdr. USNR, 1942-45. Fellow A.C.S.; mem. Am., Central, So. surg. assns., Am. Thyroid Assn. Author: (with Frank Shively) Hospital Care of the Surgical Patient, 1943; Practical Aspects of Thyroid Disease, 1949; Cancer and Common Sense, 1955; (with Jane Crille), Treasure Diving Holidays, 1954; More than Booty, 1966; A Biological Consideration of the Treatment of Breast Cancer, 1967; A Naturalistic View of Man, 1969; To Act as a Unit (The Story of Cleveland Clinic with A.T. Bunts), 1970; (with H. Sandburg) Above and Below, 1970. 2060 Kent Rd Cleveland OH 44106 Office: Cleveland Clinic Cleveland OH 44106

CRILL, CHESTER CLEOPHAS, educator; s. Albert G. and Anna (Stockburger) C.; A.B., Greenville Coll., 1935; M. Mus. U. Okla., 1941; D.Mus., Pasadena Coll., 1966; m. Alice E. Fairbanks, Aug. 12, 1937; children—C. Charles, Carole (Mrs. John Cochran), Virginia (Mrs. Christopher Embree). Choral and vocal tchr. Roberts Wesleyan Coll., 1935-38; chmn. div. fine arts Bethany Nazarene Coll., 1938-47, Pasadena Coll., 1947—. Mem. adv. com. revision of church hymnal Church of the Nazarene. Mem. Nat. Assn. Tchrs. of Singing. Home: 784 Eaton Dr Pasadena CA 91107

CRILLY, JOSEPH, catering co. exec.; b. Glasgow, Scotland, July 12, 1932; s. James and Agnes (McErlain) C.; accounting degree, Glasgow U., 1957; m. June Fraser, Oct. 7, 1967; children—Allyson, Beverly Ann, Caroline Elizabeth. Came to U.S., 1959. Pub. accountant, Scotland, 1949-59; sr. qualified asst. Thomson McLintock, Glasgow, 1958-59; sr. assistant Price Waterhouse, Los Angeles, 1959-60; sr. auditor Am. Airlines, N.Y.C., 1960-64; with Sky Chefs, N.Y.C., 1964—, dir. accounting, 1965-66, treas., controller, 1966—. Mem. Scottish Inst. Chartered Accountants, Am. Inst. C.P.A.'s, N.Y. State, Cal. socs. C.P.A.'s, Am. Mgmt. Assn. Home: 57-55 81st St Elmhurst Queens NY 11373 Office: Sky Chefs Inc 605 3d Av New York City NY 10016

CRILLY, WILLIAM MICHAEL, paper co. exec.; b. Chgo., Aug. 12, 1924; s. William Michael and Frances (Tuteur) C.; B.S., Notre Dame U., 1946; M.B.A., Stanford, 1950; m. Virginia Cozad, Mar. 19, 1949; children—Jo Ann, Thomas Michael. Market analyst preliminary design Douglas Aircraft Co., Santa Monica, Cal., 1946-48, exec. asst., 1950-52; dir. marketing, transp. research Planning Research Corp., Los Angeles, 1954-57; asst. to pres. Hawaiian Airlines, Honolulu, 1957-58, v.p. planning and devel., 1959-61, v.p. maintenance and engring., 1961-63; v.p. Eastern Airlines, 1964-66, sr. v.p., 1966-69; v.p., gen. mgr. forest products and real estate div. Riegel Paper Corp., Greenwich, Conn., 1969—; dir. Techbuilt, Inc., Community Concepts Corp. Served to lt. USNR, 1943-46. Clubs: Tamarack Country (Greenwich); Union League (N.Y.C.). Home: 261 Saw Mill Rd Stamford CT 06903 Office: 51 Weaver St Greenwich CT 06830

CRIMI, JAMES ERNEST, coll. pres.; b. Toledo, Aug. 27, 1916; s. Ernest and Bertha (Kraft) C.; B.A., Aurora (Ill.) Coll., 1938; M.A., U. So. Cal., 1941; Ph.D., U. Chgo., 1959; m. Pauline Crouse, Apr. 14, 1943; childrenAnn, Martha, Stephen. Mem. faculty Aurora (Ill.) Coll., 1941—, successively instr., prof. sociology, registrar, 1946-55, dean of coll., 1955-62, pres., 1962—. Bd. dirs. United Community Services, Mental Health and Retardation Services, Inc. Served to capt. AUS, World War II. Mem. Asso. Colls. Ill. (past chmn.), Aurora C. of C. (past dir.), Am. Sociol. Soc., Adult Edn. Assn., N.E.A. Author: Adult Education in the Liberal Arts Coll. (pamphlet), 1957. Home: 1307 Marseillaise Pl Aurora IL 60506

CRIMMINS, ALFRED STEPHEN, Jr., mfg. co. exec.; b. Bayonne, N.J., Dec. 6, 1934; s. Alfred Stephen and Agnes Veronica (Corcoran) C.; B.B.A. cum laude, City Coll. N.Y., 1960; m. Catherine Lechner, June 11, 1960; children—Karen, Douglas, Jennifer, Michael. With Price Waterhouse & Co., C.P.A.'s, 1960-65; mgr. profit analysis Trans World Airlines, Inc., 1965-68; controller Keene Corp., N.Y.C., 1968—. Served with USNR, 1955-56. C.P.A., N.Y. Mem. Financial Execs. Inst., Am. Inst. C.P.A.'s, N.Y. State Soc. C.P.A.'s, Beta Gamma Sigma, Beta Alpha Psi. Home: 404 Beveridge Rd Ridgewood NJ 07450 Office: 345 Park Av New York City NY 10022

CRIMMINS, JOHN HUGH, fgn. service officer; b. Mass., Nov. 26, 1919; A.B. Harvard, 1941; student Nat. War Coll., 1956-57; m. Marguerite Virginia Carlson, 1946; childrenDeborah, John Hugh. Intelligence officer, spl. projects staff Dept. State, Washington, 1946, asst. polit. intelligence officer, 1946, intelligence officer, 1946-51, chief Am. Republics sect. spl. projects staff, 1951-54, intelligence research officer, 1954-57; became first sec. Am. Embassy, Rio de Janiero, Brazil, 1957; dir. Office Caribbean and Mexican Affairs Dept. State, 1961-63, coordinator Cuban affairs, 1963-66; counselor embassy, Santo Domingo, 1966, charge d'affaires, 1966, ambassador, 1966-69; dep. asst. sec. state for inter-Am. affairs, 1969-. Served as lt. col. AUS., 1941-46. Address: care State Dept Washington DC 20520

CRIMMINS, JOHN MICHAEL, lawyer; b. Chattanooga, Aug. 31, 1910; s. Patrick Joseph and Mary (Costello) C.; student Columbus Coll., Dubuque, Ia., 1926-28; A.B., St. Gregory's Sem., Cin., 1930; J.D., Notre Dame U., 1933; m. Catherine Lucile O'Malley, Aug. 26, 1939; childrenPatrick, Michael, Timothy, Sean, Constance, Martin, Thomas, Kevin, Terrance. Admitted to Ind. bar, 1932, Ill. bar, 1936, Pa. bar, 1944; counsel RFC, 1935-40, Def. Plant Corp., Washington, 1941-42; with Koppers Co., Pitts., 1942-66, asst. chief counsel, 1950-60, v.p., gen. counsel, 1960-66; pvt. practice law, Pitts., 1966—. Mem. Am., Pa., Allegheny County bar assns. Home: 5519 Darlington Rd Pittsburgh PA 15217 Office: Frick Bldg Pittsburgh PA 15219

CRIMMINS, JOSEPH BRENDAN, ins. co. exec.; b. N.Y.C., Mar. 19, 1909; s. Cornelius and Rose Anne (Maguire) C.; m. Margaret M. Walsh, June 15, 1940; childrenRose Anne, Margaret, Brendan, Joseph, Kathleen. With Met. Life Ins. Co., N.Y.C., 1926—, exec. v.p., 1970—. Fellow Soc. Actuaries. Home: 7 Peter Cooper Rd New York City NY 10010 Office: 1 Madison Ave New York City NY 10010

CRING, MARQUIS RITCHEY, ret. railroad exec.; b. Logan County, O., Dec. 14, 1900; s. Marquis Daniel and Harriet B. (Ritchey) C.; ed. high sch., bus. coll. m. Irene Charlotte Ellerbeck, Feb. 1, 1929; 1 dau., Susan Irene (Mrs. Edward H. Blaine). With the M.-K.-T. R.R., St. Louis, 1925-71, successively clk.-stenographer exec. dept., sec. to pres., exec. asst. to pres., dir. publicity and advt., asst. to pres. pub. relations, 1925- 61, v.p. pub. relations, 1961-70. Bd. dirs. Jr. Achievement Miss. Valley Inc. Mem. Assn. Am. Railroads (emeritus, adv. council pub. relations), R.R. Pub. Relations Assn. (emeritus), Pub. Relations Soc. Am. (emeritus, past nat. dir., past pres. St. Louis), Advt. Club St. Louis. Clubs: Mo. Athletic, Press (St. Louis). Home: 20 Stratford Lane Brentwood MO 63144

CRIPE, NICHOLAS MCKINNEY, educator; b. Goshen, Ind., Jan. 25, 1913; s. Nicholas M. and Eva Letitia (McKinney) C.; A.B., Goshen Coll., 1949; M.A., Northwestern U., 1949, Ph.D., 1953; m. Dorothy Mae Dunivan, Jan. 19, 1945. With Goshen Rubber Co., 1935-42; instr. speech U. Vt., 1949-50; grad. asst. Northwestern U., 1950-52; lectr. speech Grinnell Coll., 1952-53; head dept. speech Butler U., Indpls., 1953—, prof. speech, 1954—; pub. speaker, 1946—. Candidate for state rep. Ind., 1956; chmn. Marion County (Ind.) Citizens for Kennedy, 1960. Served with inf. AUS, 1942-46. Recipient Baxter award for outstanding teaching Butler U., 1954, Outstanding Prof. award, 1962. Mem. Am. (pres. 1961-63), Midwest (Ind. pres. 1969-71) forensic assns., Central States Speech Assn., Speech Assn. Am. (legislative assembly 1965-66), Ind. Speech Assn. (pres. 1970-72), Tau Kappa Alpha, Delta Sigma Rho (nat. council 1970—, nat. sec. 1966-69). Phi Kappa Phi. Contbr. articles profl. jours. Home: 142 E 48th St Indianapolis IN 46205

CRIPPEN, CURTISS EDMUND, r.r. exec.; b. Austin, Minn., Dec. 20, 1907; s. John Edmund and Cora Mable (Fairbank) C.; B.S. in C.E., U. Minn., 1930; grad. Advanced Mgmt. Program. Harvard, 1953; m. Mary McKnight Pierce, June 8, 1932; children—Mary Barbara (Mrs. John I. Marshall), Richard Pierce. With C., M., St. P & P. R.R. Co., 1930, successively instrument man, asst. engr., div. engr., trainmaster, asst. supt., chmn. pres.'s com., supt., gen. supt., 1930-53, gen. mgr. lines West, 1953-55, asst. to v.p. operations, 1955-58, asst. to pres., 1958-61, v.p. finance and accounting, 1961-66, pres., dir., 1966—; dir. Merc. Nat. Bank. Served as lt. col. Transp. Corps., AUS. World War II. Decorated Bronze Star medal. Mem. Nat. Def. Transp. Assn., Nat. Def. Exec. Res., U.S., Ill. (dir.) chambers commerce, Chgo. Assn. Commerce and Industry, Navy League of U.S., Delta Upsilon, Theta Tau, Phi Sigma Phi. Conglist. Clubs: Union League, Executives, Chicago, Economics, Mid America (Chgo.); Sunset Ridge Country. Home: 1500 Sheridan Rd Wilmette IL 60091 Office: 516 W Jackson Blvd Chicago IL 60606

CRIQUI, WILLIAM EDMUND, machinery mfg. co. exec.; b. Irvington, N.J., June 25, 1922; s. William Valentine and Josephine Anna (Dotterwiech) C.; B.S. in Accounting, Rutgers U., 1955; certificate machine accounting N.Y. U., 1958; M.B.A., Seton Hall U., 1966; m. Margaret Elizabeth Burke, Apr. 22, 1950; children—William John, Robert Joseph. Sr. auditor Worthington Corp., Harrison, N.J., 1958-62, dir. internal auditing, 1962-67, asst. treas., 1967-69; asst. treas. Studebaker-Worthington, Inc., also treas. Worthington Corp., N.Y.C., 1969—; v.p., treas. Worthington Pump Internat., 1971—. Treas., Nutley (N.J.) County Com., 1969-71; 1st v.p. Nutley Republican Club, 1971; committeeman Essex County, 1968-71. Bd. dirs. Nutley Family Service Bur. Served with AUS, 1942-46. Decorated Purple Heart, Bronze Star, Combat Inf. badge. Mem. Inst. Internal Auditors (pres. 1962-63, bd. govs. 1964—), Holy Name Soc. Elk (mem. crippled childrens com. 1969—). Home: 30 Hickory Rd Nutley NJ 07110 Office: 270 Sheffield St Mountainside NJ 07092

CRISCUOLA, LOUIS, actor; b. N.Y.C., Jan. 23, 1934; s. Neil and Jenny (Madonna) C.; m. Elisa De Marko, Nov. 27, 1965; children—Gregory, Neil, Maria (by previous marriage). TV appearances include Naked City, Route 66, East Side, West Side, Combat, Untouchables, Defenders; appeared on stage in Fiorello, My Fair Lady, Oliver, Man of La Mancha. Life mem. Boys Club N.Y. Mem. Actor's Equity (com. to review constn. and bylaws).

CRISER, MARSHALL, lawyer; b. Rumson, N.J., Sept. 4, 1928; s. Marshall and Louise (Johnson) C.; B.S. in Bus. Adminstrn., U. Fla., 1951, LL.B., 1951, (replaced by J.D., 1967); m. Paula Porcher, Apr. 27, 1957; children—Marshall III, Edward, Mary, Glenn, Kimberly, Mark. Admitted to Fla. bar, 1951; practiced in Palm Beach, 1953—; partner firm Gunster, Yoakley, Criser, Stewart & Hersey, 1955—; attny. Palm Beach County Sch. Bd., 1958-64. Dir. Home Fed. Savs. & Loan Assn. Palm Beach; v.p. 1st Nat. Bank in Palm Beach. Chmn. Installment Land Sales Bd., 1963-64. Mem. Fla. Bd. Regents, 1965, 71—. Served with AUS, 1951-53. Fellow Am. Bar Found.; mem. Am. Bar Assn. (ho. dels. 1968—), Fla. Bar (gov. 1960—, pres. 1968-69), Fla. Blue Key, Phi Delta Phi, Sigma Nu. Home: 115 Royal Palm Way Palm Beach FL 33480 Office: First Nat Bank Bldg Palm Beach FL 33480

CRISLER, HERBERT FRITZ ORIN, dir. univ. athletics; b. Earlville, Ill., Jan. 12, 1899; s. Albert B. and Katherine (Thompson) C.; A.B., U. Chgo.; m. Dorothy Adams, Apr. 12, 1923; 1 son, Prescott A. Baseball coach, asst. football coach U. Chgo., 1922-30; dir. athletics, football coach U. Minn., 1930-31; football coach Princeton, 1932-37; football coach U. Mich., Ann Arbor, 1938-48, dir. athletics, 1941—. Dir. Adrian Steel Corp. (Mich.). Served with inf. U.S. Army, World War I; to maj. AUS, World War II. Recipient Nat. Football Hall of Fame award; Helms Found. Hall of Fame award; Mich. Hall of Fame award. Mem. Am. Football Coaches Assn. (past pres.), Nat. Collegiate Athletic Assn. (football rules com., past chmn; life mem.). Author: Practical Football, 1933; Modern Football, 1949. Home: 2999 Overridge Dr Ann Arbor, MI 48104.

CRISLER, ROBERT MORRIS, educator; b. Columbia, Mo., Jan. 5, 1921; s. Otto Smith and Ruby (Buckman) C.; A.B., U. Mo., 1941; M.S., Northwestern U., 1947, Ph.D., 1949; m. Shirley Spohn, Aug. 18, 1943; childrenCharles Robert, John Allen. Asst. prof. geography Washington U., St. Louis, 1948-54; mem. faculty U. Southwestern La., Lafayette, 1954-, prof. geography, 1957-, head dept. social studies, 1956-. Pres. U. Southwestern La. Credit Union, 1961; mem. La. Council Govtl. Reorgn., 1966—. Served with AUS, 1942-46, 50-52. Mem. Assn. Am. Georgraphers (chmn. Southwestern div. 1970-72), Auto License Plate Collectors' Assn. (3d v.p. 1970-71), Nat. Council Geog. . Edn., Southwestern Social Sci. Assn., Hist. Soc. Mo., La. Hist. Assn. (bd. dirs. 1960-63), La. Tchrs. Assn. (pres. U. Southwestern La. 1960-61), Sigma Xi, Phi Kappa Phi, Phi Alpha Theta, Sigma Gamma Upsilon, Delta Upsilon. Democrat. Presbyn. Rotarian (bd. dirs. Pinhook 1960, 64). Author: (with L.F. Thomas) A Manual of the Economic Geography of the United States, 1953; co-author: The Rivers and Bayous of Louisiana, 1968. Home: 154 Ronald Blvd Lafayette LA 70501

CRISLEY, FRANCIS DANIEL, microbiologist; b. Braddock, Pa., Aug. 19, 1926; s. Frank and Julia (Andrascik) C.; B.S., U. Pitts., 1950, M.S., 1952, Ph.D., 1959; m. Margaretta Schmitt, May 28, 1960; children—Faith, John, Kathleen. Instr., Miami U., Oxford, O., 1952-54, U. Pitts., 1954-58, NSF sci. faculty fellow, 1958-59, research asso., 1959-61; research microbiologist USPHS, 1961-67; prof., chmn. dept. biology Northeastern U., Boston, 1967—. Served with AUS, 1944-46. Mem. A.A.A.S., Am. Soc. Microbiology, Soc. Gen. Microbiology, Human Ecology Soc., Sigma Xi, Phi Sigma. Author. Contbr. articles to profl. jours. Home: 26 Grosvenor Rd Needham MA 02192 Office: Northeastern University 360 Huntington Av Boston MA 02115

CRISMON, JEFFERSON MARTINEAU, physician, educator; b. Phila., Feb. 4, 1908; s. Kenneth Allen and Alley Preston (Martineau) C.; A.B., Stanford, 1931, M.D., 1938; m. Cathrine Alice Stanton, June 12, 1937; children—Patricia Shanna, Daniel Stanton. Teaching asst. physiology Stanford, 1932-33, 35-36, acting instr., summers 1936, 37, research asst. pharmacology, 1936-37, instr. physiology, 1937-38, asst. prof., 1938-47, asso. prof., 1947-51, acting exec. dept. physiology, 1949-51, exec., 1951-63, prof., 1951—. Cons. Aeromed. Lab., Material Command, USAAF, Wright Field, O., 1944; cons. pharmacology div. Dept. Agr., 1948; cons. cold injury Office Naval Research, 1952-53; mem. adv. com. environmental medicine Office Surgeon Gen., Dept. Army, 1952-71. Hon. fellow research Pediatrics Yale, 1940-41; Guggenheim fellow, 1957-58. Fellow A.A.A.S.; mem. Am. Heart Assn. (research com., council on basic sci.), Am. Physiol. Soc., Western Soc. for Clin. Research, Sigma Xi. Contbr. articles to profl. jours. Assoc. editor Ann. Rev. Physiology, 1946-52; editorial bd. Circulation Research, 1952-57, Circulation, 1958-67. Home: 1805 Guinda St Palo Alto CA 94303 Office: Dept Physiology Stanford U Stanford CA 94303

CRISONA, JAMES JOSEPH, judge; b. N.Y.C., Aug. 30, 1907; s. Frank and Rachel (Fantino) C.; B.C.S., N.Y.U., 1928, LL.B., 1931; m. Claire Peysson, July 8, 1934; children—Claire Mary, Cynthia. Sr. partner Crisona Bros., N.Y.C., 1945-57; gen. counsel, dir. Hudson & Manhattan R.R., 1948-54; v.p., gen. counsel, dir. Phoenix-Campbell Corp., 1951- 57; pres. Boro of Queens, N.Y.C., 1957-59; supreme ct. justice State N.Y., 1959—. Former assemblyman and state senator N.Y. Mem. Am, Queens County bar assns., N.Y. County Lawyers Assn., N.Y. Law Inst. K.C., Elk; mem. Ind. Order Foresters. Club: Deepdale Golf. Home: 201 E 62d St New York City NY 10021 also Neponsit NY Office: Supreme Court of State of NY New York City NY 10021

CRISP, PORTER LEE, newspaper editor; b. Asheville, N.C., Nov. 29, 1927. Reporter The Asheville Times, 1949-57; with Greensboro (N.C.) Record, 1957—, mng. editor, 1964-68, exec. news editor Greensboro Daily News and Record, 1968—. Mem. Am. Soc. Newspaper Editors. Recipient Freedoms Found. award, also Honor medal, both 1950. Office: 200 N Davie St Greensboro NC 27420

CRISPE, A. LUKE, lawyer; b. N.Y.C., Oct. 17, 1911; s. Peter and Theresa (Carillo) C.; LL.B., Ind. U., 1933; m. Miriam B. Hughes, June 27, 1945; childrenLawrin Peter, Elizabeth Susan, Helen Therese, Diane Hughes. Admitted to N.H. and Vt. bars, 1934; practice in Brattleboro, Vt., 1934- -; dep. states atty., 1939-40; legal counsellor-atty. to gov. Vt., 1949- 51. Dir., v.p. Mt. Ascutney Ski Area, Windsor, Vt.; dir., clk. Stratton Mt. Ski Area, Londonderry, Vt.; chief cons. Haystack Mountain Ski Area, Wilmington, Vermont, 1964- ; v.p., dir Dutch Hill Ski Area, Heartwellville, Vt.; pres. Hillwinds Area, Brattleboro, Vermont; dir. Ludlow Savs. Bank. Mem. Com. to Study Proposals to Vt. Constn., 1950. Moderator, Town of Newfane, Vt., 1956—; del. Republican Nat. Conv., 1956; candidate for gov. Vt., 1960; chmn. Vt. Independent Party, 1962-65. Vice Pres., trustee Leland & Gray Sem., Townshend, Vt.; bd. trustees Windham Coll., Putney, Vt., Grace Cottage Hosp., Townshend. Served with AUS, 1941-45. Recipient Freedom Found. award, 1951. Fellow Am. Coll. Trial Lawyers; mem. Am., Vt. (pres. 1960-61) bar assns., Am. Legion (comdr. Vt. 1949, chmn. Nat Americanism Commn., 1950, chmn. subcom. edn. 1955-67), vice chmn. Nat. Americanism Commn. 1967—), Army, Navy and Air Force Vets in Can. (U.S. unit)(life). Author: Ski Suits, 1964, Home: Newfane VT 05345 Office: 114 Main Street Brattleboro VT 05301

CRISPELL, KENNETH RAYMOND, physician, univ. ofcl.; b. Ithaca, N.Y., Oct. 30, 1916; s. Leslie and Pauline (Wichell) C.; B.S., Phila. Coll. Pharmacy, 1938; postgrad. Cornell U., 1938-39; M.D., U. Mich., 1943; m. Marjorie Risk, Apr. 11, 1942; children—Ann (Mrs. Robert Ross), Kathleen (Mrs. Charles Blackmer), Barbara (Mrs. Richard Johnson), Marjorie, Constance, John (dec.). Intern, Robert Packer Hosp., Sayre, Pa., 1943-44, resident internal medicine, 1944; resident Ochsner Clinic, New Orleans, 1947-48; fellow biophysics Tulane U., New Orleans, 1948-49; pvt. practice, Ithaca, N.Y., 1946-47; Commonwealth fellow, instr. medicine U. Va., Charlottesville, 1949-51, mem. faculty, 1951-58, 60—. prof. medicine, 1960—, dean Sch. Medicine, 1964-71, v.p. health services, 1971—; prof. medicine, chmn. dept. N.Y. Med. Coll., 1958-60. Fellow A.C.P.; mem. Am. Soc. Clin. Investigation, Am. Fedn. Clin. Research, So. Soc. Clin. Research (pres. 1963), Am. Goiter Assn., Endocrine Soc., N.Y. Acad. Scis., A.A.A.S., A.M.A., Med. Soc. Va., Assn. Am. Physicians, Sigma Xi, Alpha Omega Alpha. Author numerous articles, monograph in field. Home: Pavilion I West Lawn Charlottesville VA 22901

CRISPIN, JAMES HEWES, engring, constrn.co. exec.; b. Rochester, Minn., July 23, 1915; s. Egerton Lafayette and Angela (Shipman) C.; A.B. in Mech. Engring., Stanford, 1938; M.B.A., Harvard, 1941; grad. Army Command and Gen. Staff School, 1943; m. Marjorie Holmes, Aug. 5, 1966. Engaged in mfg., engring., comptrolling C.F. Braun & Co., Alhambra, Cal., 1946-62; treas. Bechtel Corp., San Francisco, 1962—, v.p., sec., mem. finance com., 1967—. Served to lt. col. Ordnance Corps. AUS., 1941- 46. Registered profl. mech. engr., Cal. Mem. Mil. Order World Wars, Soc. Sons Revolution, Soc. Colonial Wars Cal., Baronial Order Magna Carta, Mil Order Crusades, Am. Ordnance., Assn., Financial Execs. World Affairs Council of No. Cal., Beta Theta Pi. Clubs: California, Chaparral (Los Angeles): Annandale Golf (Pasadena); Pauma Valley Golf; Commonwealth of N. Cal., Bankers, St. Francis Yacht, The Family, Olympic, San Francisco Golf, World Trade (San Francisco); Harvard (N.Y.) Home: 3737 Washington St San Francisco CA 94118 Office: 5O Beale St San Francisco, CA 94119

CRISS, MABEL LEONE, ins. exec.; b. Ia.; d. John W. and Jessie B. (Flanders) Chambers; m. Dr. C.C. Criss (dec.). Founder (with Dr. C.C. Criss) Mut. Benefit Health & Accident Assn., 1909; now dir. personnel and planning; co- founder United Benefit Life Ins. Co., Omaha, 1926, dir. personnel and planning, 1st v.p., 1948—, also dir. Mem. planning com. City of Omaha. Bd. dirs. Children's Meml. Hosp., Clarkson Meml. Hosp. First woman recipient award for outstanding mgmt. Nat. Office Mgmt. Assn., 1951. Home: 216 Fairacres Rd Omaha NB 68132 Office: United Benefit Life Insurance Co 33d at Farnum St Omaha NB 68114

CRISSEY, WALTER HOWARD, securities cons.; b. Bayonne, N.J., Aug 26, 1903; s. Walter Howard and Mary Louise Clara (Pouch) C.; m. Anna Petrisko, Jan. 20, 1923; children— William Francis, Walter Howard 3d. With Whitehouse & Co., N.Y.C., 1917-42, Haskin & Sells, C.P.A.'s, N.Y.C., 1942-48; with N.Y. Stock Exchange, 1948-68, v.p., 1958-68; v.p. subsidiary Stock Clearing Corp., 1958-68; mgmt. cons, 1968—; created Central Certificate Service, 1957. Mem. exec. com. purchases and sales, tabulating div. Assn. Stock Exchange Mem. Stock Transfer Assn., Data Processing Mgmt. Assn. Designed accounting procs. for using data processing machines to verify audits phys. securities; devel. accounting procedures, operating methods to expedite mergers, dissolutions large securities brokerage firms. Address: 909 Lake Shore Dr Lake Park FL 33403

CRISSMAN, FRANCIS H., utility exec.; b. Vincennes, Ind., June 4, 1908; s. John Adam and Frances (Bultman) C.; m. Angeline Lanz, Aug. 16, 1933; 1 son, Robert. Sr. v.p., dir., chief financial officer Columbia Gas System, Inc., N.Y.C.; dir. Columbia Gas System Service Corp., Columbia Hydrocarbon Corp., Columbia Gulf Transmission Co. Home: 13 Woodland Av North Caldwell NJ 07006 Office: 20 Montchanin Rd Wilmington DE 19807

CRIST, FREDERIC EUGENE, security co. exec., b. Dayton, O., Dec. 1, 1916; s. William H. and Devone (Double) C.; A.B., Miami Coll., Dayton, 1935; LL.B., N.Y.U., 1950; m. Leta Clark, Apr. 8, 1939; children—Barbara, Beverly. Indsl. administr. Am. Machine & Foundry Co., 1950-53; sec., dir., mem. exec. com. Sun Chem. Corp., 1953-57; exec. v.p., mem. exec. com. Asso. Spring Corp., 1957-66, dir., 1958—; pres., dir., mem. exec. com. Electronics Splty. Co., Los Angeles, 1966-68; exec. v.p., mem. exec. com., dir. Burns Internat. Security Services Inc., Briarcliff Manor, N.Y., 1968-70, pres., 1970—. Admitted to N.Y. bar, 1951, U.S. Supreme Ct. bar, 1951. Bd. dirs. Conn. Mfg. Assn., 1964-66. Mem. bd. finance, Bristol, Conn., 1963-66. Bd. dirs. Bristol A.R.C., 1960-62, Bristol United Fund, 1960-63; corporator Bristol Hosp., 1957-66. Mem. N.Y. Bar Assn. Mason (Shriner); mem. Order Eastern Star. Home: 32 Cowdin Circle Chappaqua NY 10514 Office: 320 Old Briarcliff Rd Briarcliff Manor NY 10510

CRIST, JUDITH, (Klein), film, drama critic; b. N.Y.C., May 22, 1922; d. Solomon and Helen (Schoenberg) Klein; A.B., Hunter Coll., 1941; teaching fellow State Coll. Wash., 1942-43; M. Sc. in Journalism, Columbia, 1945; m. William B. Crist, July 3, 1947; 1 son, Steven Gordon. Civilian instr. 3081st AAFBU, 1943-44; reporter N.Y. Herald Tribune, 1945-60, editor arts, 1960- 63, film, theater critic, 1963-66; film, theater critic NBC-TV Today Show, 1963—; film critic World Jour. Tribune, 1966-67; critic-at- large Ladies Home Jour. 1966-67; film critic TV Guide, 1965—, N.Y. mag., 1968—, The Washingtonian, 1970—; Instr. Journalism Hunter Coll., 1947, Sarah Lawrence Coll., 1958-59; asso. journalism Columbia Grad. Sch. Journalism, 1959- 62, lectr. journalism, 1962-64, adj. prof., 1966—. Recipient Page One award N.Y. Newspaper Guild, 1955; George Polk award 1951, N.Y. Newspaper Women's Club award, 1955, 59, 63, 65, 67, Edn. Writers Assn. award, 1952, Columbia Grad. Sch. Journalism Alumni award, 1961, named to 50th Anniversary Honors List, 1963; Centennial Pres.'s medal Hunter Coll., 1970. Mem. Columbia Journalism Alumni (pres. 1967-70). Sigma Tau Delta. Author: The Private Eye, The Cowboy and the Very Naked Girl, 1968. Contbr. articles to nat. mags. Office: 180 Riverside Dr New York City NY 10024

CRISTOL, STANLEY JEROME, educator; b. Chgo., June 14, 1916; s. Myer J. and Lillian (Young) C.; B.S., Northwestern U., 1937; M.A., U. Cal. at Los Angeles, 1939, Ph.D., 1943; m. Barbara Wright Swingle, June 1957; children—Marjorie Jo, Jeffrey Tod. Research chemist Standard Oil Co. Cal., 1938-41; research fellow U. Ill., 1943-44; research chemist USDA, 1944-46; asst. prof., then asso. prof. U. Colo., 1946-55, prof., 1955—, chmn. dept. chemistry, 1960-62. Vis. prof. Stanford, summer 1961; with OSRD, 1944-46; adv. panels NSF, 1957-63, 69—, NIH, 1969—; cons. E.I. duPont de Nemours & Co., Inc. Guggenheim fellow, 1955-56. Fellow A.A.A.S., Chem. Soc. London; mem. Am. Chem. Soc. (chmn. organic chemistry div. 1961-62, adv. bd. petroleum research fund 1963-66, council policy com. 1968—), Am. Assn. U. Profs., Colo.-Wyo. Acad. Sci., Phi Beta Kappa, Sigma Xi, Phi Lambda Upsilon. Author: (with L.O. Smith, Jr.) Organic Chemistry, 1966. Editorial bd. Chem. Revs., 1957-59, Jour. Organic Chemistry, 1964-68. Contbr. research articles to sci. jours. Home: 2918 3d St Boulder CO 80302

CRISWELL, W.A., clergyman; b. Eldorado, Okla., Dec. 19, 1909; s. Wallie Amos and Anna (Currie) C.; A.B., Baylor U., 1931, D.D., 1945; Th.M., So. Bapt. Theol. Sem., Louisville, 1934, Ph.D., 1937; m. Betty Harris, Feb. 14, 1935; 1 dau., Mabel Ann. Ordained to ministry First Bapt. Ch., Amarillo, Tex., 1937; pastor First Bapt. Ch., Chickasha, Okla., 1937-41, Muskogee, Okla., 1941-44, Dallas, 1944—. Dir. Relief and Annuity Bd. So. Bapt. Conv.; pres. So. Bapt. Conv., 1968-70; mem. exec. bd. Tex. Bapt. Conv. Trustee So. Bapt. Theol. Sem., Louisville; trustee Baylor U. Author: The Gospel According to Moses, 1950; These Issues We Must Face, 1953; Did Man Just Happen?, 1956; Five Great Questions of The Bible, 1958; (with others) Passport to the World, 1951; Five Great Affirmations of the Bible, 1959: Expository Notes on Gospel of Matthew, 1961; Expository Sermons on the Revelations, 1962; The Bible in Today's World, 1965; The Holy Spirit in Today's World, 1966; In Defense of the Faith, 1967; Preaching at the Palace, 1968; Expository Sermons on Daniel, 1968; Why I Preach that the Bible is Literally True, 1969; Look Up Brother, 1970; The Scarlet Thread Through the Bible, 1971. Home: 5901 Swiss Av Dallas TX 75214 Office: First Bapt. Ch Dallas, TX 75201.

CRITCHFIELD, CHARLES LOUIS, physicist; b. Shreve, O., June 7, 1910; s. Roy and Clara Mae (Prince) C.; B.S., George Washington U., 1934, M.A., 1936, Ph.D., 1939; m. Jean LaZelle Anderson, Aug. 31, 1935; children—Lewis, Robert, Barbara, Douglas. Instr., U. Rochester, 1939-40; Nat. Research fellow, Princeton, 1940-41; instr. Harvard, 1941-42, physicist Geophys. Lab., 1942-43; group leader, Los Alamos, 1943-46; asso. prof. George Washington U., 1946; prin. physicist Monsanto Chem. Co., Oak Ridge, Tenn., 1946-47; asso. prof. U. Minn., 1947-49, prof. physics, 1949-55; dir. sci. research sci. research dept. Convair div. Gen. Dynamics Corp., San Diego, 1955-60; v.p. research Telecomputing Corp., San Diego, 1960-61; asso. div. leader Theoretical Physics Div., Los Alamos Sci. Lab., 1961—. Mem. planetology subcom. NASA, 1964-69. Recipient George Washington U. Gen. Alumni Assn. Achievement award, 1963. Fellow Am. Phys. Soc.; mem. Am. Assn. Physics Tchrs., Am. Rocket Soc., Sigma Xi. Author: (With G. Gamow) Theory of Atomic Nucleus and Nuclear Energy Sources, 1949. Asso. editor: Physical Rev., 1951-54. Jour. of Franklin Inst.; mem. editorial com. Ann. Revs. of Nuclear Scis., 1957-61. Address: 391 El Conejo Los Alamos NM 87544

CRITCHFIELD, JACK B., coll. pres.; b. Middlecreek Twp., Pa., May 23, 1933; s. Charles Robert and Dorothy (Barron) C.; B.S., Slippery Rock State Coll., 1955; M.A., U. Pitts., 1955, Ed.D., 1968; m. Nancy Jordan Wilson, Dec. 12, 1959; children—Mark Wilson, Lisa Anne. High sch. history tchr., Rockwood, Pa., 195759; asst. dir. admissions U. Pitts., 1959-61; dir. admissions and placement Westminster (Pa.) Coll., 1961-62; dir. student aid U. Pitts., 1962-64, dean admissions and student aid, 1964-67, dean students, 1967- 68, asst. chancellor, 1968-69; pres. Rollins (Fla.) Coll., 1969—, also trustee. Cons. Coll. Entrance Exam. Bd., also mem. bd. govs. Coll. Scholarship Service; cons. U.S. Office Edn., N.C. Bd. Higher Edn.; 1st exec. dir. Pa. Higher Edn. Assistance Agy.; mem. spl. com. to recommend to Pres. long-range planning on greater access to higher edn. Dept. Health, Edn. and Welfare. Bd. dirs. Ind. Colls. and Univs. of Fla., Fla. Ind. Colls. Found. Served with AUS, 1955-57. Mem. Assn. Coll. Admissions Counselors, Omicron Delta Kappa, Kappa Delta Pi. Home: 482 Lakewood Dr Winter Park, FL 32789.

CRITCHFIELD, RICHARD PATRICK, journalist; b. Mpls., Mar. 23, 1931; s. Ralph James and Ann (Williams) C.; B.A., U. Wash., 1953; M.S., Columbia, 1957; student Leopold Fraenzens U., Innsbruck, Austria, 1958, U. Vienna (Austria), 1958-59, Northwestern U., 1960. Reporter, Cedar Valley Daily Times, Vinton, Ia., 1955-56; Washington corr. Salt Lake City Deseret News, also other papers Munroe News Bur., Washington, 1957-58; acting asst. prof. U. Nagpur (India), 1960-62; Asian corr. Washington Star, 1963-68, nat. corr., Washington, 1968—. Vice pres. Internat. Relations Club, Nagpur, 1961-62. Served with AUS, 1953-55; Korea. Recipient Alicia Patterson Fund award for travel and research abroad, 1970-71. Mem. Phi Kappa Psi. Clubs: Overseas Press (award best daily reporting Viet Nam 1965) (N.Y.C.); Nat. Press (Washington) Author: The Indian Reporter's Guide, 1962; The Long Charade: Political Subversion in the Vietnam War, 1968; also articles. Editor, illustrator; Lore and Legend of Nepal, 1962. Home: Bannockburn Farm Blake La Oakton VA 22124 Office: Evening Star 2d and Virginia Sts Washington DC 20003

CRITES, LOWRY HYER, former food mfg. co. exec.; b. Lawton, Okla., July 21, 1906; s. Cloyd Clayton and Jewell (Hyer) C.; student Midwestern U., Wichita Falls, Tex., 1926, U. Okla., 1929; m. Mary Jane Nelson, May 23, 1931; 1 dau., Jane Ann (Mrs. John W. Ellicott, Jr.). With Gen. Mills, Inc., 1939-71, gen. mgr. grocery products div., 1961-71, v.p., 1958-71, administrator consumer food activities, 1964-71, dir., 1965-71. Dir. Cereal Inst. Mem. Kappa Alpha (So.). Club: Minneapolis Golf. Home: 2639 Irving Av S Minneapolis MN 55408

CRITES, RAYMOND DAVID, architect; b. Danville, Ill., Dec. 6, 1925; s. William Guy and Bertha Marie (Howie) C.; B.Arch., Ia. State U., 1953; Dr. Fine Arts (hon.), Coe Coll., 1961; m. Virginia Lee Bolenbaugh, Feb. 2, 1947; children—Laura Ellen, David Alan, Melissa Ann. Instr., Sch. Architecture, Ia. State U., 1955-56; partner Crites & McConnell, Cedar Rapids, Ia., 1957—. Served with USNR, 1943-46. Mem. A.I.A. (Design Honor awards 1965, 67). Important works include Ia. State U. Cultural Center including C.Y. Stephens Theatre and Hilton Coliseum. Home: 4626 Bever Av SE Cedar Rapids IA 52403 Office: 316 17th St SE Cedar Rapids IA 52403

CRITES, STEPHEN DECATUR, philosopher religion, educator; b. Elida, O., July 27, 1931; s. Beryl Anderson and Ruth (Hook) C.; B.A., Ohio Wesleyan U., 1953; B.D., Yale, 1956, M.A., 1959, Ph.D., 1961; Fulbright fellow, Rockefeller fellow, U. Heidelberg, 1959-60; m. Gertrude Elizabeth Bremer, Sept. 11, 1955; children—Dorothea Elizabeth, Stephanie Ruth, Lilian Alison, Hannah Louise. Ordained to ministry Methodist Ch., 1956; pastor Grace Meth. Ch., Southington, Conn., 1956-58; faculty Colgate U., Hamilton, N.Y., 1960-61; faculty Wesleyan U., Middletown, Conn., 1961—, now prof. religion; vis. prof. U. Cal., Berkeley, 1965, U. Cal., San Diego, 1969. Lilly postdoctoral fellow, 1966. Mng. editor: The Christian Scholar, 1963-65. Translator: (Kierkegaard) Crisis in the Life Of An Actress and Other Essays on Drama, 1967. Contbr. articles profl. jours. Home: 89 Bretton Rd Middletown CT 06457

CRITTENDEN, GAZAWAY LAMAR, banker; b. Flushing, N.Y., Apr. 15, 1918; s. Jerome Parker and Paulina (Jones) C.; grad. Phillips Exeter Acad., 1937; A.B., Princeton, 1941; m. Gertrude Bramwell Shaw, Jan. 23, 1943; childrenGazaway Lamar, Penelope Shaw (Mrs. William B. Bacon, Jr.), Jane Mason. With First Nat. Bank Boston, 1945—, sr. v.p. charge investment div., 1967—. Chmn. Finance Adv. Bd. Mass., 1968—. Trustee, chmn. finance com., treas. Mass. Gen. Hosp., 1968- -. Served to lt. comdr. USNR, 1941-45. Mem. Investment Bankers Assn. (govtl. securities com.). Clubs: Dedham (Mass.) Country and Polo; The Country (Brookline, Mass.). Home: Strawberry Hill St Dover, MA 02030. Office: 67 Milk St Boston MA 02106

CRITTENDEN, WILLIAM, bishop; b. New Boston, Pa., June 28, 1908; s. Ernest H. and Sue (Cook) C.; B.S., Lafayette Coll., 1929, D.D., 1954; student Harvard, 1935-36; B.D., Epis. Theol. Sch., Cambridge, Mass., 1936; LL.D., Gannon Coll., 1963; m. Eleanor Setchel, Dec. 26, 1931; children—William S., Joan M. With Bell Telephone Co., 1929-31, 33; curate St. Paul's Ch., Brookline, Mass., 1934-35; vicar Grace Ch., Dalton, Mass. St. Luke's Ch., Lanesboro, 1936-39; rector St. John's Ch., North Adams, Mass., 1939-42; student pastor, asst. prof. religion, asst. to pres. Lafayette Coll., 1942-45; exec. sec., div. youth Nat. Council P.E. Ch., 1945-49; arch deacon Diocese So. Ohio, 1949-52; consecrated bishop Episcopal Diocese of Erie, 1952; pres. Province of Washington, Episcopal Ch., 1963-65; lectr., preacher colls. in U.S., abroad. Lectr., chaplain Chautauqua Inst., 1943-69, now trustee; Bible study leader 2d World Conf. Youth, Oslo, Norway, 1947; sr. del. youth sect. First Assembly World Council Chs., Amsterdam, Holland, 1948; mem. bd. Ecumenical Inst., Geneva, Switzerland, 1948-52; mem. gen. bd. Nat. Council Chs. of Christ, 1960—, v.p., 1963-66, Trustee Western Coll., Oxford, O.; pres. bd. trustees Bishop Crittenden Sch., Erie. Recipient Currick award for Jewish-Christian relations Nat. Council Chs. of Christ. Mem. Newcomen Soc. Eng. and Am., Theta Delta Chi. Clubs: Kahkwa University (Erie). Contbr. articles to ch. publs. Home: 4521 Upland Dr Erie PA 16509 Office: 145 W 6th St Erie PA 16501

CRITZ, HARRY HERNDON, banker; b. Teague, Tex., Feb. 26, 1912; s. Ivan Chancelumm and Suzie (Herndon) C.; student Tex. A. and M. Coll., 1929-31; B.S., U.S. Mil. Acad., 1935; m. Sarah Alice Gregor, Feb. 26, 1938; children—Terry (Mrs. Russell A. Mericle, Jr.), Harry Kimbrough, James Richard. Commd. 2d lt., arty. U.S. Army, 1935, advanced through grades to lt. gen.; assigned 1st Inf. Div., Africa and Europe, 1941-46; sec. Arty. Sch., 1948-50; assigned Army War Coll., 1950-51, Hdqrs. 6th Army, San Francisco, 1951-52, I Corps and 8th Army, Korea, 1953-54, Office Asst. Sec. Def. for Internat. Affairs, 1954-57; chief staff 101st Airborne Div., Ft. Campbell, Ky., 1957-60; sec. staff SHAPE, Paris, France, 1960- 63; comdg. gen. 101st Airborne Div., Ft. Campbell, 1963-64; comdg. gen. U.S. Army Arty. and Missile Center, also comdt. U.S. Army Arty. and Missile Sch., Ft. Sill, Okla., 1964-67; comdg. gen. I Corps Korea, 1967- 68, Fourth U.S. Army, Ft. Sam Houston, Tex., 1968-71, ret., 1971; exec. v.p. Ft. Sill Nat. Bank (Okla.), 1971—. Decorated D.S.M., Silver Star, Legion of Merit with two oak leaf clusters, Bronze Star medal with oak leaf cluster, also fgn. decorations. Office: Fort Sill National Bank Fort Sill OK 73503

CRITZER, WILLIAM ERNEST, transp. co. exec.; b. Cleve., Aug. 11, 1934; s. Ernest H. and Gertrude (Bell) C.; B.B.A. cum laude, U. Miami (Fla.), 1960; m. Patricia Suzanne Hawk, Aug. 16, 1957; childrenStephen, David. Asst. to gen. auditor W.P. R.R., 1960-63; with Consol. Freightways, Inc., San Francisco, 1963—, treas., 1967-. Served with USAF, 1954-58. Home: 2173 Sierra Ventura Dr Los Altos, CA 94022. Office: 601 California St San Francisco CA 94108

CRNOBRNJA, BOGDAN, diplomat of Yugoslavia; b. Vrgin Most, Yugoslavia, Dec. 16, 1916; s. Mihajlo and Saveta (Cumura) C.; m. Angelina Grabric, Sept. 13, 1944; children—Misa, Stanko. Tchr., 1940- 41; mem. Parliament, 1945-53; dep. minister fgn. trade, 1946-51; dep. minister fgn. affairs, 1951-54, 58-61; ambassador to India, 1954-58; sec. gen. to pres. Yugoslavia, 1961-67; ambassador to U.S., 1967—. Mem. Central Com. League Communists; mem. Central Com. Socialist Alliance. Contbr. articles profl. jours. Home: 2221 R St NW Washington DC 20008 Office: 2410 California St NW Washington DC 20008

CROAKE, THOMAS F., U.S. judge; b. Saranac Lake, N.Y.; s. Thomas F. and Margaret W. (Starr) C.; student Union U.; LL.B., Albany (N.Y.) Law Sch.; m. Marian Elizabeth Peck, July 23, 1930; children—Margaret (Mrs. Rudolph Cherico), Mary Anne (Mrs. J. David Ryan), Michael F. Admitted to N.Y. bar; former Clinton County judge; former corporation counsel City of Plattsburgh; U.S. Judge So. District N.Y., 1961—. Mem. 9th Jud. Dist. Com. on Character and Fitness, 1949-61. Mem. bd. tax appeals, White Plains, N.Y. Hon. mem. lay bd. St. Agnes Hosp., White Plains. Recipient Brotherhood award White Plains. Mem. Am. Coll. Trial Lawyers, N.Y. State (past v.p.), Westchester County (past pres.) bar assns. Democrat. Roman Catholic. K.C., Elk (hon. life, past exalted ruler). Club: University (pres. White Plains 1946-47). Home: Cameo Manor 2 Old Mamaroneck Rd White Plains NY 10605 Office: US Courthouse Foley Sq New York City NY 10007

CROASDALE, HANNAH THOMPSON, botanist, educator; b. Daylesford, Pa., Nov. 18, 1905; d. John Pusey and Mary (Okie) C.; B.S., U. Pa., 1928, M.S., 1931, Ph.D., 1935. Mem. staff Biol. Abstracts, Phila., 1928-32; research asst. Dartmouth, 1935-46, research asso., 1946-59, asst. prof., 1959-64, asso. prof., 1964-68, prof. botany, 1968-71, prof. emeritus, 1971—. Mem. Soc. Sci. Fennica (hon.), Phi Beta Kappa, Sigma Xi. Translator sci. Latin. Illustrator textbooks. Contbr. articles to sci. jours. Home: McKenna Rd Norwich VT 05055 Office: Dept Biol Science Dartmouth Coll Hanover NH 03755

CROASMUN, HOMER O., govt. ofcl.; b. 1915. With U.S. Govt., 1936—; with Internal Revenue Service, 1952—, now Western regional commr. Address: 870 Market St San Francisco CA 94102

CROCCO, LUIGI, phyicist; b. Palermo, Italy, Feb. 2, 1909; s. Gaetano Arturo and Bice (Patti) C.; M.E., Rome U., 1931, Ph.D., 1936; m. Simone Delettre, Jan. 18, 1939. Came to U.S., 1949. Asst. prof. U. Rome, 1937, prof., 1939; theoretical and exptl. research in high speed aerodynamics and jet propulsion done in connection with Univ. of Rome, Italian Air Ministry, indsl. firms and French War Ministry, 1928-49; dir. Guggenheim Jet Propulsion Center, Princeton 1949—, also prof. aero. engring.; now Robert H. Goddard prof. aerospace propulsion. Recipient G. Edward Pendray award Am. Rocket Soc., 1960. Contbr. sci. jours. Home: 168 Fitz Randolph Rd Princeton NJ 08540

CROCE, ALEXANDER LOUIS, packing co. exec.; b. San Francisco, June 27, 1908; s. Ettore and Clelia (Tamietti) C.; B.S., U. Cal., 1929; m. Raymonda Wilson, Oct. 16, 1933; children—Sandra H., Barrie L. With Del Monte Corp., San Francisco, 1929—, sec., asst. treas., 1950-66, v.p., sec., 1966—. Mem. Cal. C. of C., Am. Soc. Corporate Secs., Scabbard and Blade, Pi Kappa Phi. Mason, DeMolay Legion of Honor, Clubs: St. Francis Yacht, Stock (San francisco). Home: 333 Santa Clara Av San Francisco CA 94127 Office: 215 Fremont St San Francisco 94119

CROCKER, JOHN HOLBROOK, banker; b. Maroa, Ill., Nov. 6, 1897; s. John and Arabella (Baird) C.; student Millikin U., 1915-16, Northwestern U., 1918-20; m. Mariam Flint, Aug. 23, 1923; children—Jane (Mrs. John F. Patterson), John. With Crocker & Co., bankers, Maroa, Ill, 1920-36; asst. cashier Citizens Nat. Bank of Decatur, 1936-41, v.p., dir., 1941-50, pres., 1950-61, chmn. chief exec. officer, 1961-; dir. Fed. Res. Bank Chgo. Mem. Comptrollers Nat. Bank Adv. Com., 1965—. Served as ensign, aviation, U.S. Navy, World War I; officer, World War II. Named hon. Ky. Col. Mem. Am. (exec. council 1944-47, 53-56, 59—, treas. 1963—), Ill. (past treas.) bankers assns., Ill. C. of C. (past v.p., dir.), Decatur Assn. Commerce (past dir., v.p.). Clubs: Union League; (Chgo.); Decatur, Country of Decatur (Ill.). Home: 7 Forest Knolls Decatur IL 62521 Office: Citizens Nat. Bank Decatur, Illinois. 62525.

CROCKER, LESTER GILBERT, educator; b. N.Y.C., Apr. 23, 1912; B.A., N.Y.U., 1932, M.A., 1934; certificat de littérature française, U. Paris, 1933; Ph.D., U. Cal., 1936; m. Billie Lyman Danziger, Feb. 16, 1934; childrenRoger, Leslie Joyce. Asst. prof. romance langs. Wittenberg Coll., 1937-39, Queens Coll., 1939-44; dir. prodn. Eastern Sound Studios, 1944-48; asso. prof. Sweet Briar Coll., 1948-50; prof., chmn. dept. modern langs. Goucher Coll., 1950-60; distinguished prof., chmn. dept. romance langs. Case Western Res. U., Cleve., 1960-67, dean humanities, 1967-71, also dean Grad. Sch., 1963-67; prof. French, chmn. French and gen. linguistics U. Va., 1971—; Guggenheim fellow, Fulbright research scholar U. Paris, 1954-55; mem. Inst. Advanced Study, Princeton, 1958-59; vis. lectr. U. London, spring 1963. Decorated chevalier dans l'ordre des Palmes academiques, Chevalier de la Légion d'honneur. Fellow Royal Soc. Arts; mem. Internat. Soc. for Study of 18th Century (v.p. 1968-71), Am. Soc. for 18th Century Studies (pres. 1969-71), Modern Lang. Assn., Am. Assn. Tchrs. French, Am. Assn. U. Profs., Société d''Histoire Littéraire (hon. mem., corr.), Phi Beta Kappa. Club: Union Interalliée (Paris). Author: La Correspondance de Diderot, 1939; Two Diderot Studies, 1952; The Embattled Philosopher, 1954, rev. edit. 1966; An Age of Crisis: Man and World in Eighteenth Century French Thought 1959; Nature and Culture, Ethical Thought in the French Enlightenment, 1963; Jean-Jacques Rousseau, The Quest (1712-1758), 1968; Rousseau's Social Contract, an Interpretive Essay, 1968. Editor: Confessions of Rousseau; Don Quixote, Montaigne's Essays, Candide; Diderot's Selected Writings, 1966; The Age of Enlightenment, 1969; and others. Cons. editor, Larousse-Pocket Book French Dictionary, 1955. Contbr. profl. jours. Office: University Virginia Charlottesville VA 22903

CROCKER, LIONEL GEORGE, prof. of speech; b. Ann Arbor, Mich., Jan. 17, 1897; s. George and Jennie (Musson) C.; A.B., U. of Mich., 1918, A.M., 1921, Ph.D., 1933; D.Pd. (hon.), Otterbein College, 1967; Dr. of Humanities (hon.), Drury Coll., 1967; m. Geraldine Hamilton, Aug. 15, 1925; children—Joan Elizabeth, Laurence Gordon, Thomas Hamilton (deceased). Tchr. of speech, U. of Minn., 1919, U. of Mich., 1920-21, Waseda U., Tokyo, Japan, 1921-22, U. of Mich., 1922-26, U. of Colo., summer 1924, Floating Univ. 1926-27, U. of Mich., 1927-28; head dept. of speech, Denison U., Granville, O., 1928-67, sr. prof. 1954-67; tchr. of speech, various summers, 1929—, at Mich. State Teachers Coll., U. of Mich., Mich. State Coll., Ind. State Teachers Coll., U. Me., Stanford, Coll. of Pacific, Ind. State U., U. Redlands; prof. in pub. utilities execs. program U. Mich., Upward Bound program Redlands Univ., 1968, 69, 70. Mem. staff The Ministers Research Found., Inc. Served with M.C. U.S. Army 1918-19. Mem. Nat. (v.p. 1934; exec. council 1946), Ohio (pres. 1938) assns. of coll. tchrs. of speech, Speech Assn. Am. (1st v.p. 1951, pres. 1952), Am. Assn. U. Profs. (sec. local chpt.), Phi Beta Kappa (pres. Denison chpt.), Tau Kappa Alpha (editor The Speaker 1938-48; sec. 1940-48, historian), Delta Sigma Rho (historian), Theta Chi, Omicron Delta Kappa, Pi Delta Epsilon. Republican. Baptist. Rotarian (pres.). Asso. editor, Quar. Jour. of Speech, 1937-44. Author several books, including: Augmentation & Debate, 1944, 3d edit. 1955; Oral Reading, 1947, 56; Effective Speaking, 1948, rev. edit. 1959; Business and Professional Speech, 1951; Introduction to Interpretative Speech, 1952; Advice to Freshmen by Freshmen, 1952; Public Speaking for College Students, 1954, rev. edit. 1965; Effective Speaking, 1959; Effective Debating, 1961; (with Paul Carmack) Readings in Rhetoric; Rhetorical Analysis of Speeches, 1967; An Analysis of Lincoln and Douglas as Speakers and Debaters, 1968; Harry Emerson Fosdick on Preaching, 1971. Editor Central States Speech Jour., 1948-50; asso. editor Jour. of Communication, 1962-63. Home: 423 E College St Granville OH 43023

CROCKETT, CAMPBELL, univ. dean; b. Nicholasville, Ky., Apr. 25, 1918; s. O.B. and Catherine (Campbell) C.; A.B., U. Cin., 1940. A.M., 1941, Ph.D., 1949; m. Genevieve Kuntz, Oct. 22, 1942 (div.); children—Peter Campbell, Catherine Kuntz. From instr. to prof. U. Cin., 1949-60, dean, fellow Grad. Sch., 1959-67, dir. Inst. Research, Tng. Higher Edn., 1967-71, acting dean Coll. Arts and Scis., 1970-71, dean, 1971—; lectr. Conservatory Music, 1949-54, Art Acad. Cin., 1958-60; Ford faculty fellow U. Mich. and Harvard, 1951-52; Fulbright research scholar U. Oslo, 1953-54. Fellow Nat. Tng. Labs. Bd. dirs. Cin. Playhouse in the Park; adv. bd. Inquiry. Served with USAAF, 1942-46. Mem. Am. Soc. Aesthetics, Am. Philos. Assn, Am. Civil Liberties Union, Am. Assn. U. Profs., Am. Assn. Humanistic Psychology. Contbr. articles to profl. publs. Home: Fleming House 1110 Springfield Pike Cincinnati OH 45215

CROCKETT, CLYLL WEBB, lawyer; b. Preston, Ida., Feb. 16, 1934; s. Frank Lee and Alta (Webb) C.; B.S., Brigham Young U., 1958; M.B.A., Northwestern U., 1959; LL.B., U. Ariz., 1962; m. Nan Marie Mattice, June 27, 1958; children—Jeffrey Webb, Nicole, Karen. Admitted to Ariz. bar, 1962; clk. Ariz. Supreme Ct., 1962- 63; partner firm Fennemore, Craig, von Ammon & Udall, Phoenix 1968—. Instr. eve. div. Mesa (Ariz.) Community Coll. Mem. charter rev. com., Scottsdale, Ariz., 1966-67, bd. adjustment, Scottsdale, 1968—. Mem. Am., Maricopa County bar assns., State Bar Ariz., Phoenix C. of C., Ariz. Acad. Republican. Mem. Ch. of Jesus Christ of Latter Day Saints. Kiwanian. Mem. editorial bd. Ariz. Law Rev., 1961. Home: 2302 N 81st Way Scottsdale AZ 85257 Office: 411 N Central Av Phoenix AZ 85004

CROCKETT, GIBSON M., editorial cartoonist; b. Washington, Sept. 18, 1912; s. Hal Gibson and Gertrude Virginia (Lentz) C.; grad. Dobyns Bennett High Sch., Kingsport, Tenn., 1929; m. Florence E. Abbott, July 4, 1937; childrenGary A. (dec.), Sandra Lea. Mem. staff Washington Evening Star, 1933-, editorial cartoonist, 1947—, sport cartoonist, 1940-46; art dir. Am. Pub. Co., Washington, 1945—; free lance illustrator (mag), 1943—; exhibited landscape paintings in local and nat. exhbns. Mem. Editorial Cartoonists Assn. Presbyn. Club: Manor Country (Norbeck, Md.). Home: 4713 Great Oak Rd Rockville MD 20853 Office: 225 Virginia Av SE Washington DC 20003.

CROCKETT, J. ALLAN, judge; b. Smithfield, Utah, Jan. 19, 1906; s. John Allan and Rachel M. (Homer) C.; A.B., U. Utah, LL.B., 1931; m. Eulalia Smith, Feb. 3, 1934; 1 son, Calvin John. Admitted to Utah bar, 1931; asst. atty. Salt Lake County, 1933-38; exec. sec., counsel Pub. Service Commn. Utah, 1938- 40; dist. judge, 3d Dist., 1941-51; justice Utah Supreme Ct., 1951, chief justice, 1959-61, 67-71, formerly asso. justice. Mem. exec. council Nat. Conf. Chief Justices, 1959—; chmn. Utah Jud. Conf., 1963-65. Chmn. Family Service Soc., 1954-55; mem. bd. dirs. Nat. Legal Aid, 1955-65; pres. Utah Council on Family Relations, 1967-68. Bd. dirs. Utah State Inst. Fine Arts 1941-51 (chmn. 1949-51), Utah Symphony Orch. (dir. 1942-64, pres. 1951-52). Utah Legal Aid Soc., 1940—; chmn. Utah Social Hygiene Assn. Member Order of Coif, Phi Alpha Delta. Mem. Ch. of Jesus Christ of Latter Day Saints. Lion. Author: Jury Instructions for Utah; also prose articles and poetry. Home: 536 13th Av Salt Lake City UT 84103 Office: State Capitol Salt Lake City UT 84110

CROCKETT, KENNEDY MCCAMPBELL, ret. fgn. service officer; b. Kingsville, Tex., Jan. 18, 1920; s. Frank Harrison and Alice Rachel (Kennedy) C.; student N. Tex. Agrl. Coll., 1937-39, U. Tex., 1939-40, 41-42; m. Mary Corinne Campbell, Sept. 8, 1943; children—Laura Susan, John Kennedy, Judith Ann, Mary Melinda, Teresa Alice. Clk., Nuevo Laredo, Mexico, 1943, vice consul. 1944-45; vice consul. Tegucigalpa, Puerto Cortez, also La Cieba, Honduras. 1946- 48, Mexico City, Mexico, 1948-51; consul in charge, Tampico, Mexico, 1951-55; spl. asst. for consular affairs, officer in charge Mexico affairs Dept. of State, 1955-57; 1st sec. Am. embassy, Guatemala, 1958- 60; Am. consul gen., Tijuana, Mexico, 1960-62; dep. dur. Office of Caribbean and Mexican Affairs. Dept. of State, 1962-63, dir. Office Caribbean Affairs, 1965-65; counselor embassy, dep. chief mission San Jose, Costa Rica, 1965-67; ambassador to Nicaragua, 1967-70. Recipient Superior Honor award U.S. Dept. State, 1966. Mem. Am. Fgn. Service Assn. Home: 1602 Washington St PO Box 278 Laredo TX 78040 1

CROCKETT, RICHARD CALLWELL, former implement dealer, ins. co. exec., farmer; b. Langdon, N.D., Aug. 30, 1919; s. Nathaniel J. and Lillian M. Crockett; B.S., N.D. State U., 1942; postgrad. Harvard Sch. Bus., 1942; m. Janice Adair Nelson, Dec. 28, 1942; children—Richard Boyd, Douglas David. Extension agt. State N.D., 1946-48; ty. mgr. Agrl. Supply Co., Grand Forks, N.D., 1948-49; owner, mgr. Langdon Farm Supply, 1949-64; owner, operator farm, nr. Fargo, N.D., 1947-; owner Crockett Ins. Agy., Langdon, 1958-64; dir. Sundeen Grain Co. Precinct committeeman, county chmn. Cavalier County Rep. party, 1960-64, mem. State platform com., 1958-60. Mem. Langdon Park Bd., 1957-64. Served with USAAF, 1943-45. Mem. U.S. Durum Growers Assn. (pres. 1958-62, bd. dirs., chmn. durum wheat industry adv. com. 1962-64), Am. Soc. Farm Mgrs. and Rural Appraisers, Am. Legion, Airplane Owners and Pilots Assn., N.D. C. of C. (exec. v.p. 1964- -), Central Livestock Assn. (dir.). Presbyn. (trustee). Mason (Shriner), Elk. Home: 1519 Elm St Fargo ND 58102. Office: 303 N 5th St Fargo ND 58102

CROCKETT, WILLIAM JAMES, adminstrv. co. exec.; b. Cimarron, Kan., July 22, 1914; s. James Blaine and Ilda May (Furse) C.; B.S., U. Neb., 1946; m. Verla R. Koelling, June 10, 1936; 1 son, Robert James. Asst. cashier City Nat. Bank, Hastings, Neb., 1933-41, asst. v.p., 1948-51; asst. to dir. adminstrn. U.S. Maritime Commn., Naples. 1946-47; owner, mgr. Hi-Way Signs Co., Denver, 1947-48; with Dept. State, 1951-67; exec. officer, Beirut, Lebanon, 1951-52; attache, Karachi, 1952-54, Rome, Italy, 1954- 58; assigned Dept. State, Washington, 1958-67, dep. asst. sec. for budget and finance, 1960-61, asst. sec. for adminstrn., 1961-63, dep. under sec. for adminstrn., 1963-67, ret., 1967; v.p. for human relations Saga Adminstrv. Corp., Menlo Park, Cal., 1967—. Served as capt. AUS, 1942-46, 51. Mason (Shriner). Home: 2430 Sharon Oaks Dr Menlo Park CA 94025 Office: Saga Adminstrv Corp 1 Sage Lane Menlo Park CA 94025

CROFT, A.C., publisher; b. Cleve., May 26, 1890; s. John Henry and Lucetta (Shirk) C.; ed. pub. schs. Cleve., m. Christine Marquis, Sept. 9, 1920; 1 son Noyes. With A.W. Shaw Co. Inc., pubs., Chgo., 1912-28, McGraw-Hill Pub. Co., Inc., N.Y.C., 1928-36, dir. circulation, 1937—; chmn. bd., Nat. Foremen's Inst., New London, Conn., 1937—; dir. Am. Arbitration Assn., 1950—; pres. Housing Found., Motivation, Inc., A.C. Croft, Inc., Aim Co., Inc.; pub. The Hosp. Execs. Letter, Personnel Jour, Republican. Home: 1742 Reedsvale Lane Los Angeles CA 90049 Office: 100 Park Av Swarthmore PA 19081 also 1832 Franklin St Santa Monica CA 90404

CROFT, HERBERT STANLEY, former banker; b. Rutherford, N.J., Nov. 25, 1905; s. Arthur S. and Laura (Brice) C.; B.S., N.Y. U., 1935; LL.B., John Marshall Law Sch., 1939; diploma Rutgers U. Grad. Sch. Banking, 1942; J.D., N.Y. Law Sch., 1956; m. Beatrice Wright, Aug. 30, 1930; children—Barbara Marakle, Audrey (Mrs. James Watson). Mgr. corporate trust dept. Comml. Nat. Bank Bank & Trust Co. (merged with Bankers Trust Co.), N.Y.C., 1929-35; trust officer First Nat. Bank, Jersey City, 1935-49, v.p., trust officer, 1954-64; v.p., trust officer Alamo Nat. Bank, San Antonio, 1949-54; sr. v.p., gen. trust officer First Union Nat. Bank of N.C., Charlotte, 1964-71; lectr. trust bus. Am. Inst. Banking, Hudson County, N.J., 1939-40; lectr. banking and finance Rutgers U., 1944-46, thesis panel examiner Grad. Sch. Banking, 1959-61; faculty mem. Nat. Assn. Bank Auditors and Controllers Sch., U. Wis., 1954-63; admitted to Tex. bar, 1957, N.Y. bar, 1961, also U.S. Supreme Ct. Mem. Twp. Com., Lake Mohawk, Sparta, judge Municipal Ct., Lake Mohawk, 1948-49 Mem. trust adv. com. Campbell Coll., Buie's Creek, N.C., 1968—. Served with N.J. N.G., 1921-22. Mem. Am., N.C., N.Y. State, Tex., San Antonio bar assns., N.Y. County Lawyers Assn., Am. Judicature Soc., Lawyers Club N.Y.C., Am., N.C. bankers assns., Charlotte C. of C., Phi Delta Phi. Episcopalian. Mason. Clubs: San Antonio Country; Myers Park Country (Charlotte). Contbr. articles profl. jours. Home: 1333 Queens Rd Charlotte NC 28207

CROFT, RICHARD GRAHAM, ret. business exec.; b. Pitts., Jan. 18, 1901; s. Harry William and Mary Augusta (Graham) C.; grad. Pomfret Sch.; A.B., Princeton, 1924; m. Jean Brooke Riley, Sept. 25, 1926; children—Joan Struthers (Mrs. William J. Huffer), Richard Graham. With Hayden, Stone & Co., investment bankers and brokers, N.Y.C., 1924-36, mgr. stock dept., 1933-35, mgr. investment dept., 1936; exec. sec. John Hay Whitney, N.Y.C., 1937-41; partner J.H. Whitney & Co., 1946- 58; chmn. bd. Gt. No. Paper Co., 1950-66; dir. Gen. Signal Corp., Hartford Courant Co. Trustee Am. Mus. Natural History, Pomfret Sch., Manhattan Sch. Music. Served with AUS, 1941-45, Office of Undersec. of War, Washington, 1941-42, Civil Affairs and Mil. Govt., ETO, 1942-45. Presbyn. Clubs: Union, Brook (N.Y.C.). Home: 1021 Park Av New York City NY 10028 Office: 522 Fifth Av New York City NY 10036

CROFT, THOMAS GRIMERSON, banker; b. Fort Worth, Sept. 19, 1922; s. William John and Peggy (Patterson) C.; LL.B., U. Tex., 1949; m. Neita Beaupre, Oct. 23, 1943; 1 son, Thomas Grimerson III. Admitted to Tex. bar, 1949; gen. practice, Fort Worth, 1949-55; indsl. relations specialist Gen. Dynamics Corp., 1950-67; sr. v.p. Republic Nat. Bank of Dallas, 1967—. Served to capt. USAAF, 1943-46. Mem. Dallas, Fort Worth bar assns., Tex. State Bar Assn. Home: 2525 Turtle Creek Blvd Dallas TX 75219 Office: P O Box 5961 Dallas TX 75222 Hope Coll., 1967. Mem. A.A.A.S., Soc. Protozoologists, Am. Soc. Parasitologists, Am. Soc. for Microbiology, Nat. Assn. Biology Tchrs. Home: RD 2 Brookview Dr Hamilton NY 13346

CROFT, VICTOR ALLEN, electronics co. exec.; b. Chgo., Jan. 23, 1926; s. Hyman and Lena (Walovitch) C.; B.S., U. Cal. at Los Angeles, 1950; m. Edna Citron, Feb. 7, 1948; children—Gene Sandra, Steven Martin, Daniel Richard, Mary Sara. Sales trainee Leo J. Myberg Co., Los Angeles, 1950-54; sales mgr. radio- hono dept., then sales mgr. TV, RCA, 1954-64; gen. mgr. Admiral Corp., 1964-66, exec. v.p., 1966-71. Active Chgo. Crusade of Mercy, 1967. Served with AUS, 1943-46. Decorated Combat Inf. badge. Mem. Electric Assn. (bd. dirs.). Home: 3936 Enfield St Skokie IL 60076

CROFT, WILLIAM CROSSWELL, corp. exec.; b. Greenville, S.C., Jan. 8, 1918; s. Edward S. and Mary (Crosswell) C.; student The Citadel, 1935-36; B.S., U.S. Naval Acad., 1940; m. Helen Barbara Engh, Mar. 7, 1942; children—William Crosswell, Mary Barbara, Douglas E., Helen W., Jean Ann. Tech. supr. Anaconda Wire & Cable Co., Orange, Cal., 1946-48; gen. mgr. William J. Moran Co., Alhambra, Cal., 1948-50; works mgr. Pyle-Nat. Co., Chgo., 1950-52, v.p., 1953-54, exec. v.p., 1955, pres., dir., 1955-70, pres. Pyle-Nat. div. Harvey Hubbell, Inc., Bridgeport, Conn., 1970—, also dir. parent co.; dir. Cherry-Burrell Corp., Cedar Rapids, Uarco, Inc., Chgo. Belden Corp., Chgo., First Nat. Bank & Trust Co. Evanston (Ill.). Mem. Gov's Adv. Com. Trustee Converse Coll., Spartanburg, NC. Served from ensign to lt. comdr. USN, 1940-46. Mem. Execs. Club Chgo., Econ. Club Chgo., Chgo. President's Orgn., Ill. Mfrs. Assn. (past pres. dir.). U.S. Naval Acad. Alumni Assn. Clubs: Union League, Chicago, Glen View Mid-America, Chicago Commonwealth. Executives' (Chgo.). Home: 1100 Romona Rd Wilmette IL 60091 Office: 1334 N Kostner Av Chicago IL 60651

CROFTCHIK, VICTOR PAUL, educator; b. Martin, Pa., June 27, 1917; s. Nickolas and Mary (Dorash) C.; B.S., Central Mich. U., 1938; M.A., U. Mich., 1947; Ed.D., Mich. State U., 1959; m. Lela L. Miller, June 8, 1940; 1 son, Gregory Jan. Pub. sch. tchr., Mich. 1938-41, 46-48; tchr. art Central Mich. U., 1948- , chmn. art dept., 1958-; engr. Curtis-Wright Corp., 1941-46. Mem. Nat., Mich. art edn. assns., Western Arts Assn., Mich. Edn. Assn., Nat. Com. Art Edn., Internat. Soc. Edn. Through Art. Republican. Presbyn. (deacon, elder). Home: 1010 Glen Ave Mt Pleasant MI 48858

CROGHAN, HAROLD HEENAN, corp. exec., lawyer; b. Sioux City, Ia., May 28, 1924; s. Edmund Harold and Marie Agnes (Heenan) C.; A.B. cum laude, Lawrence U., 1947; Dexter Perkins fellow U. Rochester, 1947-48; LL.B., Cornell U., 1953; m. Gertrude Anna Murphy, Feb. 4, 1948; children—Catherine, John, Loretto, Margaret. Admitted to Mo. bar, 1953, Ohio bar, 1967; with firm Stinson, Mag, Thomson, McEvers & Fizzell, Kansas City, Mo., 1953-54, Margolin & Kirwin, Kansas City, Mo., 1954-56; atty. Kansas City Gas Service Co., 1956-66; house counsel Philips Industries, Inc., Dayton, O., 1966-67, asst. sec.-corporate counsel, 1967, v.p., sec., corporate counsel, 1968—; dir. Dexter Axle Co., Elkhart, Ind., Winbro, Inc., Michigan City, Ind., Malta Mfg. Co., Gahanna, O. Served to capt. USMC, 1943-46, 50-52. Mem. Phi Beta Kappa, Phi Delta Theta, Phi Delta Phi. Republican. Roman Catholic. Clubs: Chancery, Vanguard, Rockhill, Hollinger Tennis (Dayton). Home: 204 Lookout Dr Dayton OH 45419 Office: 4801 Springfield St Dayton OH 45401

CROHN, MAX HENRY, Jr., mfg. co. exec.; b. Asheville, N.C., Feb. 4, 1934; s. Max Henry and Edith Pearl (Hoffman) C.; B.A. in Polit. Sci., U. N.C., 1955; LL.B., Georgetown U., 1961; m. Barbara Jean Morris, Jan. 28, 1960; children—David Michael, Edith Ann, Randall Morris. Admitted to D.C. bar, 1961; since practiced in D.C., 1961-68; trial atty. Bur. Restraint of Trade, 1963-65; atty. adv. to chmn. FTC, 1965-66; asso. mem. firm Arnold & Porter, Washington, 1966-68; asso. counsel R.J. Reynolds Industries, Inc., Winston-Salem, N.C., 1968—, sec. R.J. Reynolds Tobacco Co., 1971—. Bd. dirs. Forsyth County Econ. Devel. Corp. Vice-chmn. edn. com. Greater Winston-Salem C. of C. Served to lt. (j.g.) USNR, 1955-58. Mem. Am. Bar Assn. Kiwanian. Home: 440 Archer Rd Winston-Salem NC 27106 Office: 4th and Main Winston-Salem NC 27102

CROKER, RICHARD JAMES, utility co. exec.; b. Kansas City, Kan., July 18, 1929; s. Patrick Walter and Margaret (Kennedy) C.; B.S., Central Mo. State Coll., 1956; LL.B., U. Kan., 1958, J.D., 1959; m. Mary Sue Glanville, Aug. 25, 1956; children—Richard James III, Daniel Shane, Joseph Patrick. Admitted to Kan. bar, 1958; with firm Boddington & Boddington, Kansas City, Kan., 1958-66; sec., asst. treas. United Utilities, Inc., 1965-68, v.p., sec., 1968-71; v.p. Washington Counsel, 1971—; dir. United Computing Systems, Inc., Quivira, Inc. Active local Boy Scouts Am. Served with USMCR, 1953-55. Mem. Phi Delta Theta, Phi Delta Phi (pres. 1958). Catholic (lector). Home: 725 Clear Spring Rd Herndon VA 22070 Office: 1700 K St NW Washington DC 20006

CROMBIE, DAVID JOSEPH, airline exec.; b. Hartford, Conn., May 5, 1915; s. David H. and Ida (Vannie) C.; A.B., Fordham U., 1938, M.A., 1940; m. Frances O'Brien, Aug. 31, 1940; childrenDavid A., Michael F., Timothy J., Alison E., Nicholas E., Pamela A., Jean F. Instr. Fordham U., 1938-41; with Underwood Corp., N.Y.C., 1941-59, beginning as engr., successively factory mgr., v.p. mfg., v.p. indsl. relations, v.p. adminstrn.; v.p. indsl. relations Trans World Airlines, N.Y.C., 1960-. Mem. Fordham U. Alumni Assn. Home: 31 Gurley Rd Stamford CT 06902 Office: 605 3d Ave New York City NY 10016

CROMER, EARL OF, (George Rowland Stanley Baring), banker; b. Hitchin, Eng. July 28, 1918; s. Rowland, 2d Earl of Cromer and Lady Ruby Elliot; ed. Trinity Coll., Cambridge U.; LL.D. (hon.) N.Y. U., 1966; m. to Esme Harmsworth, Jan. 10, 1942; 2 sons, 1 dau. With Baring Bros. & Co. Ltd., 1946-47, mng. dir., 1947-59; student banking with J. P. Morgan & Co., Inc. and Kidder Peabody & Co., N.Y.C., 1947-48; head U.K. treasury and supply delegation, also econ. minister British embassy, Washington, and exec. dir. Internat. Bank Reconstrn. and Devel. Internat. Monetary Fund, Internat. Finance Corp. and Internat. Devel. Assn., 1959-61; gov. Bank of Eng. 1961-66; mng. dir. Baring Bros. & Co., Ltd., 1967-70; ambassador to U. S.A. 1971—; hon. chmn. Harris & Partners Ltd., Toronto. Served to lt. col.

Brit. Army, 1939-46. Succeeded father as Earl of Cromer, 1953. Clubs: Brooks's (London); Metropolitan (Washington); Brook (N.Y.C.). Home: 8 Bishopsgate London E C 2 England

CROMER, VOIGT RHODES, clergyman, coll. cons.; b. Rhodhiss, N.C., July 31, 1906; s. Joseph Lee and Lillie Mae (Rhodes) C.; A.B., Lenoir Rhyne Coll., 1925, D.D., 1947, L.H.D., 1967; A.M., U. S.C., 1927; B.D., Lutheran Theol. So. Sem., Columbia, S.C., 1928; S.T.M., Hartford Sem. Found., 1929; postgrad. Union Theol. Sem. N.Y.C. 1939; LL.D. Gettysburg Coll., 1956; m. Sara Elizabeth Dreher, Aug. 17, 1932; children—Elizabeth Rhodes (Mrs. Robert Carswell), Rebecca Ruth (Mrs. Richard Campbell). Ordained to ministry Luth. Ch. 1928, served pastorates in Summerville, S.C. (St. Lukes), 1929-30, Lincolnton, N.C. (Emmanuel), 1930-36, Concord, N.C. (St. James), 1936-41, Hickory, N.C. (Holy Trinity), 1941-47; pres. United Evang. Luth. Synod of N.C., 1947-49; pres. Lenoir Rhyne Coll., 1949-67, pres. emeritus cons. 1967—, trustee, 1936-47); v.p. Howell Mfg. Co., Cherryville, N.C., 1950—. Mem. bd. social missions. United Luth. Ch. Am., 1948-60, mem. bd. Am. missions, 1960-62; mem. exec. council Luth. Ch. in Am., 1962-70; commr. United Luth. Ch. in Am. to Joint Commn. on Luth. Unity, to Nat. Luth. Council, 1948-54; pres. Conf. Ch.-Related Colls. So., 1954-55; pres. Luth. Ednl. Conf. Am. 1955; chmn. Catawba County chpt. A.R.C., 1942-45. Recipient Lenoir Rhyne Distinguished Alumnus award, 1966; Nat. Luth. Brotherhood award, 1967. Mem. N.E.A., Assn. Sch. Adminstrs. Clubs: Hickory Rotary (dir., past pres. Lincolnton club), Catawba Valley Executives (pres. 1970-71). Contbr. to synod publs. Home: 222 7th Ave NE Hickory NC 28601

CROMER, WILLIAM ELLSWORTH, assn. exec.; b. Findlay, O., July 1, 1916; s. H. Fred and Alpha (Radebaugh) C.; B.S., Miami U. (O.), 1938; m. Betty Anne Schiewetz, Dec. 28, 1940; children—William Ellsworth, Carol Anne (Mrs. Anson), Kenneth Richard. With Gen. Electric Co., 1938-60, mgr. product cost accounting jet engine dept., Cin., 1951-59, mgr. bus. planning, 1959-60; asst. v.p., comptroller Kaman Corp., Bloomfield, Conn., 1960-61; controller East Ohio Gas Co., Cleve., 1961-69; comptroller Boy Scouts Am., North Brunswick, N.J., 1969—. Mem. Financial Execs. Inst., Raritan Valley Regional C. of C. (dir. 1971—), Miami U. Alumni Assn. (pres. 1968-69), Phi Kappa Tau, Omicron Delta Kappa, Beta Alpha Psi, Delta Sigma Pi, Phi Eta Sigma. Republican. Presbyn. Mason. Home: 231 Bertrand Dr Princeton NJ 08540 Office: Boy Scouts of America North Brunswick NJ 08902

CROMIE, ROBERT ALLEN, author; b. Detroit, Feb. 28, 1909; s. Robert and Annie Gertrude (Crosby) C.; A.B., Oberlin Coll., 1930, postgrad., 1931-33; m. Alice Hamilton, May 22, 1937, children—Michael, Richard, Barbara, James. Reporter Pontiac (Mich.) Daily Press, 1934-35; reporter Chgo. Tribune, 1936-42, war corr., 1942-46, news reporter, 1946-48, sportswriter, 1948- 60, book editor, 1960-69, daily columnist, 1969—; host Book Beat (syndicated Nat. Ednl. TV), 1964—, Cromie Circle, WGN-TV, Chgo., 1969—. Recipient Peabody award for Book Beat, 1969; Irita Van Doren award Am. Booksellers Assn., 1968. Mem. Chgo. Hist. Soc., Soc. Midland Authors, Authors Guild, A.F.T.R.A., Friends of Lit. Club: Press (Chgo.). Author: The Great Chicago Fire, 1958; New Angles on Putting and Chip Shots, 1960; Dillinger, A Short and Violent Life (with Joe Pinkston), 1962; Par for the Course (anthology), 1964; Golf for Boys and Girls, 1965; Where Steel Winds Blow (poetry anthology), 1968; Chicago in Color (with Archie Lieberman), 1969; The Great Fire: Chicago 1871 (with Herman Kogan), 1971. Contbr. Readers Digest, Sat. Eve. Post, Golf, Am. Legion, Esquire, other mags. Home: RD 1 Box 42 Grayslake IL 60030 Office: 435 N Michigan Av Chicago IL 60611

CROMIER, CLAYTON PAUL, oil co. exec.; b. Bay City, Mich., Oct. 9, 1932; s. Clayton E. and Thelma (Curtis) C.; student U. Notre Dame, 1950-51; B.B.A., U. Mich., 1954, M.B.A., 1957; program for sr. execs. Mass. Inst. Tech. Alfred P. Sloan Sch. Mgmt., 1968; m. Gretchen Schoehof, May 9, 1959; children— Clayton Paul, Karen Claudia, Jane Candace. Financial analyst Standard Oil Co. (N.J.), N.Y.C., 1957-61; sr. fgn. finance analyst Esso Internat., Inc., 1961-62; formerly with Creole Petroleum Corp., Caracas, Venezuela, asst. treas., 1962-65, formerly treas.; dir. Creole Investment Corp., Lago Investment Co., Central Hipotecaria, Sociedad Financiera. Treas. Creole Found. Served with AUS, 1954-56. Mem. Am. C. of C. Venezuela, Sigma Phi, Beta Gamma Sigma, Roman Catholic, Clubs: Caracas Country; Sands Point (N.Y.) Bath and Tennis; Club Doscientos (Caracas). Home: Quinta Bretta Calle Caroni Colinas de Bello Monte Caracas Venezuela

CROMILLER, HAROLD LEE, banker; b. New Orleans, Nov. 3, 1920; s. Harold William and Nell (Lee) C.; student Tulane U., 1944; grad. Am. Inst. Banking, 1956; m. Ellen Patricia Sutton, Oct. 3, 1953; children—Suzanne Marie, Cynthia Ann, Diane Patricia, Pamela Paige, Renee Magdelaine. With Hibernia Nat. Bank, New Orleans, 1938—, v.p., comptroller, 1966—; treas., dir. Hibernia Bldg. Corp., 1966—. Mem. Am. Inst. Banking (pres. New Orleans 1961), Bank Adminstrn. Inst. (pres. New Orleans 1962), Am. Soc. Ins. Mgmt., Internat. House, Financial Execs. Inst., Assn. Internal Auditors. Clubs: Metairie (La.) Country; Paul Morphy Chess, Plimsoll. Home: 5016 Purdue Dr Metairie LA 70003 Office: 313 Carondelet St New Orleans LA 70130

CROMLEY, ALLAN WRAY journalist; b. Topeka, Apr. 11, 1922; s. Frank George and Elsie May (Leedom) C.; B.S. in Journalism (Summerfield scholar 1940-43, 46), U. Kan., 1948; m. Marian Minor, Jan. 30, 1949; children—Kathleen, Janet, Carter. Reporter, Kansas City Kansan 1948-49, Oklahoma City Times, 1949-53; Washington corr. Daily Oklahoman and Oklahoma City Times, 1953—. Dir., Nat. Pres. Bldg. Corp. Sec. standing com. corr. House and Senate Press Galleries, 1961. Bd. visitors U. Okla., 1970—. Served to 1st lt. AUS, 1943-45; ETO. Mem. Sigma Delta Chi (treas. Washington chpt. 1965), Omicron Delta Kappa. Clubs: Nat. Press (gov. 1964-68, vice chmn. bd. 1966, v.p. 1967, pres. 1968), Nat. Gridiron (Washington). Home: 3320 Stoneybrae Dr Falls Church VA 22044 Office: Nat Press Bldg Washington DC 20004

CROMLEY, RAYMOND AVOLON, syndicated columnist; b. Tulare, Cal., Aug. 23, 1910; s. William James and Grace Violet (Bailey) C.; B.S., Cal. Inst. Tech., 1933; student Japanese Lang. Inst., Tokyo, 1936-39, Strategic Intelligence Sch., Washington, 1954; m. Masuyo Marjorie Suto (dec. Apr. 1946); m. 2d, Helen Sue Holcomb (dec. July 1967); children—Donald Stowe, Helen Sue (Mrs. David Bowles), Jessica Lynn, Linda Grace, William Holcomb, Mary Ann, John Austin. Reporter, Pasadena (Cal.) Post, 1928-34, Honolulu Advertiser, 1934-35, Flintridge Sch., Pasadena, 1935-36; reporter, then financial editor Japan Advertiser, Tokyo, 1936-40; editor Trans Pacific, econ. and financial weekly, 1938-40; with Wall St. Jour., 1938-55, imprisoned by Japanese, 1941-42, far Eastern corr., 1938-47, Washington corr., 1947- 55; sci. editor radio program Monitor, 1955-56; econ. and financial commentator NBC radio, 1956-57; asst. producer CBS Radio, 1957-58; mil. analyst Newspaper Enterprise Assn., 1958-64, syndicated columnist, 1964—. Asst. logic, freshman English, Cal. Inst. Tech., 1928-30; lectr. Air War Coll., 1952, 54, Dept. State Fgn. Service Inst., 1955, 65-67; cons. guerilla war, Asian politics, 1952—. Chmn. dist. bds. charter rev. Boy Scouts Am., 1956-60; sec. bishop's com. pastoral benefits Va. Conf. Meth. Ch., 1967-68; organizer com. establishment Martha Washington Library, Mt. Vernon, Va., 1954; chmn. Inter-ch. Council Teen Activities and Teen Clubs, Mt. Vernon, 1955-57; chmn. World Council Youth, 1932-35. Served to col. AUS, 1943-46. Decorated Legion of Merit, Bronze Star medal. Mem. Nat. Trust for Historic Preservation, Asiatic Soc. Japan, State Depts. Corrs. Assn. (pres. 1954-55), White House Corrs. Assn., Ret. Officers Assn., Smithsonian Assos., Assn. Corcoran Gallery Art, Sigma Delta Chi, Pi Kappa Delta. Republican. Methodist (lay speaker, Sunday sch. tchr.). Clubs: Tokyo Correspondents (exec. com. 1947); Overseas Writers (Washington). Author: Veterans Benefits, 1966-70; Educational Benefits, 1968. Home: 1912 Martha's Rd Hollin Hills Alexandria VA 22307 Office: 1013 13th St NW Washington DC 20005

CROMPTON, ALFRED W., museum dir., educator; b. Durban, S. Africa, Feb. 21, 1927; s. William Lister and Grace (Bishenden) C.; B.Sc., U. Stellenbosch, S. Africa, 1947, M.Sc., 1949, D.Sc., 1951; Ph.D., U. Cambridge (Eng.), 1953; m. Mary Anne Oosthuisen, Feb. 20, 1954 (dec.); children—Peter, Mary Jane, John; m. 2d, Ann Martin, May 30, 1968. Came to the U.S., 1964. Curator paleontol. collections Nat. Mus., Bloemfontein, S. Africa, 1954-56; dir. S. African Mus., Capetown, 1956-64; prof. geology and biology Yale, also dir. Peabody Mus. Natural History, 1964-70; prof. biology Harvard, dir. Mus. Comparative Zoology, 1970—, also chmn. com. profs. in organismic and evolutionary biology, 1970—. Chmn. S. African Parliamentary and Sci. Soc., 1959; vice chmn. S. African Assn. Advancement Sci., 1958-59. Fellow Zool. Soc., London, Am. Acad. Arts and Scis. Contbr. articles in field. Home: 9 Farrar St Cambridge MA 02138

CROMPTON, LOUIS WILLIAM, educator; b. Port Colborne, Ont., Can., Apr. 5, 1925; s. Clarence Lee and Mabel Elsie (Weber) C.; B.A., U. Toronto, 1947, M.A., 1948; A.M., U. Chgo., 1950, Ph.D., 1954. Came to U.S., 1955, naturalized, 1961. Lectr. math. U. B.C., 1948-49; lectr. English, U. Toronto, 1953-55; asst. prof. U. Neb., 1955-60, asso. prof., 1960-64, prof. English, 1964—; vis. asst. prof. U. Chgo., 1959, U. Cal., Berkeley, 1961. Recipient Christian Gauss award in lit. criticism Phi Beta Kappa, 1969. Mem. editorial bd. Shaw Rev., 1970—; editor (with J.H. Raleigh) Shaw Series in Bobbs-Merrill Library of Lit., Shaw the Dramatist, 1969; editor Great Expectations (Dickens), 1964, Arms and the Man (Shaw), 1969, The Road to Equality (Shaw), 1971. Home: 1806 D St Lincoln NB 68502

CROMWELL, EDWIN BOYKIN, architect; b. Manila, P.I., Nov. 13, 1909; s. James Ellis and Ada (Henley) C.; grad. Mercersburg Acad., 1927; A.B., Princeton, 1931, postgrad., 1931-32; m. Henrietta Thompson, May 22, 1937; children—Gertrude (Mrs. Eugene P. Levy), Mildred (Mrs. Harper Cooper), Patricia Ellis. Instr. mathematics West Point (Miss.) Pub. Schs., 1933-35; archtl. planner Resettlement Adminstrn., Washington and Ark., 1935-56; archtl. designer for ednl., housing and health projects, Little Rock, 1936-41; partner Cromwell, Neyland, Truemper, Millett & Gatchell, Little Rock, 1941—; dir. Urban Planning & Devel. Corp., Prospect Terrace, Inc., Univ. Terraces, Inc.; archtl. cons. Dept. Health, Edn. and Welfare cons. Harrison (Ark.) Arts and Crafts Center; works include U. Ark. at Little Rock, Ark. Arts Center, Little Rock, Ark. Children's Colony, Winrock Farms (Morrilton, Ark.), restoration of residential bldgs. Quapaw Quarter (Little Rock). Dir. 50 for Future, 1964-69; mem. Ark. Sesquicentennial Commn., 1967-70; dir. Lighthouse for Blind, 1966—; dir. YMCA, 1964-68; trustee U. of South, Princeton Alumni Council, Ark. Arts Center, Ark. Territorial Restoration Commn., Fellow A.I.A. Episcopalian. Home: 1720 Beechwood Rd Little Rock AR 72207 Office: 416 Center St Little Rock AR 72201

CROMWELL, HARVEY, coll. dean, author; b. Wanette, Okla., Aug. 16, 1907; s. Sheldon Winfield and Martha Jane (Hibbard) C.; B.S., Okla. East Central Coll., 1930; M.A., U. Okla., 1940; Ph.D., Purdue U., 1949; m. Mattie Lou Patterson, June 10, 1931; children—Harvey, Betty Jane (Mrs. Henry D. Lawrence). High sch. instr. speech and mathematics, Okla., 1929-33; agt. Met. Life Ins. Co., Oklahoma City, 1933-37; instr. speech, El Reno (Okla.) High Sch. and Jr. Coll., 1938-40; head dept. speech McMurry Coll., 1940-42; coordinator instr. tng. USAF, Sheppard Field and Amarillo, Tex., 1942-44; instr., debate coach Purdue U., 1944-49; prof. speech Miss. State Coll. for Women, 1949—, head dept., 1949-66, dir. program for superior students, 1961-64, dean Grad. Sch., 1966—, dean instrn., 1967-69, dir. research, 1969—; vis. prof. speech No. Mich. U., 1950, 53, U. Miss., 1951, 54, U. Southwestern La., 1955-59, N.M. Highlands U., 1960, Stamford U., 1962, Miami-Dade Coll., 1969. Cons. spl. edn., chmn. regional screening com. Miss. Dept. Edn., 1954-69; mem. coordinating coms. neurol. and sensory div. project Miss. Bd. Health, 1964-65. Pres.'s Com. Employment of Handicapped, 1966—; mem. Miss. Vocational Rehab. Planning Com., 1967-69. Mem. Nat. Forensic League, Miss. (pres. 1952, exec. council 1951-64), So. (exec. council 1951-52, 67-69) speech assns., Speech Assn. Am. (legislative assembly 1958-61), Assn. So. Deans, Pi Kappa Delta (nat. pres. 1959-61), Tau Kappa Alpha, Phi Kappa Phi. Democrat. Baptist. Author: An Oral Approach to Phonetics (with C.R. Van Dusen), 1969; A Compact Guide to Parliamentary Procedure, 1966; Working for More Effective Speech, 1955; Suggestions for the Beginning Course in Speech, 1956; Student Guide and Instructor's Guide for Speech I and II, 1957; (with A.H. Monroe and L.S. Winch) Interview Problems, 1946. Contbr. articles profl. jours. Home: 310 N 12th St Columbus MS 39701

CROMWELL, JAMES HENRY ROBERTS, corp. exec.; b. N.Y.C., June 4, 1898; s. Oliver Eaton and Lucretia (Roberts) C.; prep. edn. Lawrenceville Sch.; student Wharton Sch. Finance and Commerce, U. Pa., 2 years; hon. LL.D., John Marshall Coll., Jersey City, N.J., 1939, Bethany Coll, 1940; m. Delphine Dodge, June 20, 1920 (div. 1928); 1 dau., Christine; m. 2d, Doris Duke, Feb. 13, 1935 (div. 1948); m. 3d, Maxine MacFetridge, Apr. 1948; 1 dau., Maxine Hope. Began with Drexel & Co., Phila., then pres. Cromwell, Dodge Corp., automobile finance; pres. Am. Brit. Improvement Corp., then v.p. Peerless Motor Car Corp.; partner Cromwell's Co., indsl. cons.; pres., dir. Bonnyville Oil & Refining Co., Ltd. (Can.), 1955-57; pres. Kardar Canadian Oils, Ltd., 1957-69. U.S. envoy to Can., Jan.-May 1940; Am. adviser Pres. Syngman Rhee, Korea, 1941-45. Mem. N.J. Tax Law Revision Commn., 1938- 39; Democratic candidate for U.S. senator from N.J., 1940. Served with USN, USMC, World War I; capt. USMC Res. to 1924. Mem. Marine Corps League, Mil. Order Fgn. Wars. Clubs: Metropolitan, St. Nicholas Soc. (N.Y.C.). Author: Voice Young America, 1933; In Defense of Capitalism, 1937; Pax Americana, 1941. Home: 2913 Southwood Rd Birmingham AL 35223

CROMWELL, JARVIS, ret. corp. exec.; b. N.Y.C., Nov. 5, 1896; s. Lincoln and Mabel Wheeler (Smith) C.; student Allen-Stevenson Sch., N.Y., 1906-10, St. Mark's Sch., Southborough, Mass., 1910-14; A.B., Princeton, 1919; m. Barbara Mildred Kissel, June 21, 1924; children—David Everett, Patricia Mary (Mrs. Lindley G. Miller), Roger James Kissel; m. 2d, Edith Ely Kirk, Apr. 9, 1969. Dir. Iselin-Jefferson Financial Co., Inc., Mut. Benefit Life Ins. Co.; dir. emeritus mfrs. Hanover Trust Co., Dan River, Inc. Chmn. Greater N.Y. Red Cross War Fund, 1945-46. Trustee N.Y. Hist. Soc., Boys Club of N.Y., St. Luke's Hosp.; bd. dirs. John and Mary R. Markle Found. Served as 1st lt. U.S. Army, 1917-18; maj., 17th regt. N.Y. Guard, 1940-45. Republican. Episcopalian (vestryman). Clubs: Racquet and Tennis, Princeton, Century. Home: 580 Park Av New York City NY 10021 Office: 111 W 40th St New York City NY 10018

CROMWELL, LESLIE, educator, elec. engr.; b. Manchester, Eng., Apr. 2, 1924; s. Bernard and Lily (Robinson) C.; B.Sc. Tech. in Elec. Engring., U. Manchester, 1943, M.Sc. Tech., 1961; M.S., U. Cal. at Los Angeles, 1951, Ph.D., 1967; m. Pamela Goddard, 1944 (div. 1956); children—Russell Norman, Martin Frank, Carol Anne; m. 2d, Irina Malkin, June 2, 1956. Came to U.S., 1948, naturalized, 1954. Research engr. Salford Elec. Instruments, Heywood, Eng., 1943-44; aircraft elec. design engr. English Electric Co., Bradford, Eng., 1944-46; elec. engr., mgr. B. Cromwell & Co., Ltd., Manchester, 1946-48; lectr. engring. U. Cal. at Los Angeles, 1948-53, cons. Engring. Ednl. Devel. Program, 1961—; asst. prof. engring. Los Angeles State Coll., 1953-56, acting head engring. dept., asso. prof., 1956-57, head engring. dept., 1957-64, prof., 1957—, chmn. inter-disciplinary engring. dept., 1968—; cons. Gray & Huleguard, Inc., Los Angeles, 1954-57, Naval Civil Engring. Research and Evaluation Lab., Port Hueneme, Cal., 1957-58, Pacific Telephone, 1959, 61—; research asso. Cedars-Sinai Med. Research Inst. Mem. engring. liaison com. State Cal., 1959-63. NSF Sci. Faculty fellow, 1965-66. Recipient Distinguished Service award U.S. Jr. C. of C.; Eminent engineer, Tau Beta Pi, 1968; Distinguished Prof. award Cal. State Coll., 1968. Registered profl. elec. engr., Cal. Mem. I.E.E.E. (sr., vice chmn. Pacific S.W. sect. 1959-60, chmn. Los Angeles group, engring. in medicine and biology 1968-69), A.A.A.S., Blue Key, Phi Kappa Phi, Eta Kappa Nu. Clubs: Optimist (pres. 1955-56, v.p. 1959-60, pres. 1965-66, zone lt. gov. 1966-67, dist. leadership tng. chmn. 1968-69). Author: (textbook) Basic Electric Circuits, 1957. Home: 2219 Hillhurst Av Los Angeles CA 90027

CROMWELL, NORMAN HENRY, coll. dean, chemist; b. Terre Haute, Ind., Nov. 22, 1913; s. Henry and Ethel Lee (Harkelroad) C.; B.S. with honors (Rea scholar 1932-35), Rose Poly. Inst., 1935; Ph.D., U. Minn., 1939; m. Grace N. Newell, Jan. 20, 1955; children—Christopher Newell, Richard Earl. Teaching asst. U. Minn., 1935-39; instr. organic chemistry U. Neb., 1939-42, asst. prof., 1942-45, asso. prof., 1945-48, prof., 1948—, Howard S. Wilson regents prof., 1960-70, chmn. dept. chemistry, 1964-70, exec. dean for grad. studies and research, 1970—; guest dept. chemistry Mass. Inst. Tech., 1967; hon. research asso. Univ. Coll., London, 1950- 51, 58-59, Cal. Inst. Tech., 1958; Am. Chem. Soc. tour lectr., 1952-70, frontiers of chemistry lectr. Wayne State U., 1958, research lectr. U. Coll., Dublin, Ireland, 1958; vis. prof. U. Cal. Med. Center, 1961; Gordon Research Conf. lectr., 1961, conf. discussion leader, 1970; Hungarian Chem. Soc. lectr., 1962; Sigma Xi nat. lectr., 1964; Keynote speaker Nat. Com. Adminstrn. Research Conf., 1970; cons. Parke Davis & Co., 1943-46, Smith, Kline & French Labs., 1946-51, Am. Cancer Soc., 1956-58, Philip Morris, Inc., 1964—; cons. USPHS, 1952—, chmn. medicinal chem. study sect., 1960-64; Nat. Cancer Inst., 1964—; pres. 2d Internat. Congress Heterocyclic Chemistry, Montpellier, France, 1969; dir. coop. coll. tchr. devel. program for Neb., NSF, 1960-63. Mem. bd. Lincoln Bryan Hosp. Fulbright advanced research scholar, 1950-51; Guggenheim Meml. fellow, 1950, 58. Mem. Am. Chem. Soc., Chem. Soc. London, Am. Assn. U. Profs., Neb. Art Assn. (trustee 1958—, v.p. 1971—), Sigma Xi, Phi Lambda Upsilon, Sigma Tau, Gamma Alpha, Tau Nu Tau, Alpha Chi Sigma, Alpha Tau Omega. Asst. editor Jour. Heterocyclic Chemistry, 1967—. Contbr. articles research publs. Home: 6600 Shamrock Rd Lincoln NB 68506

CROMWELL, RICHARD P., ins. co. exec.; b. Medford, Mass., Dec. 12, 1903; s. Harry P. and Edith (Graves) C.; student Harvard, 1925; m. Margaret Elizabeth Miller, Oct. 12, 1933; children—Virginia, Robert, John. Pres. Cromwell & Co., 1931-50; now sr. v.p. Am. Mut. Liability Ins. Co., Boston, and v.p. Allied Am. Mut. Fire Ins. Co. and Am. Policyholders Ins. Co.; pres. Lexington Savs. Bank. Mem. planning bd., sch. com., Lexington. Home: 29 Curry Lane Osterville MA 02655 Office: 142 Berkeley St Boston MA 02116

CRONBACH, LEE JOSEPH, educator, psychologist; b. Fresno, Cal., Apr. 22, 1916; s. Emil George and Cora Mae (Wise) C.; A.B., Fresno State Coll., 1934; M.A., U. Cal. at Berkeley, 1937; Ph.D., U. Chgo., 1940; m. Helen Claresta Bower, Dec. 31, 1938; children—Richard, Barbara, Robert, Joyce, Janet. Tchr. high sch., Fresno, 1936-38; from instr. to asso. prof. State Coll. Wash., 1940- 46; asso. psychologist U. Cal. Div. War Research, 1944-45; asst. prof. U. Chgo., 1946-48; asso. prof., then prof. edn., psychology U. Ill., 1948-64; prof. edn. Stanford U., 1964-66, Vida Jacks prof. edn., 1966—; mem. Inst. for Advanced Study, Princeton, 1960-61; sci. liaison officer Office Naval Research, London, 1955-56; fellow Center for Advanced Study in Behavioral Scis., Stanford, Cal., 1963-64; Fulbright lectr. U. Tokyo, 1967-68. Trustee Am. Psychol. Found., 1956-63, pres., 1961-63. Guggenheim fellow, 1970-71. Fellow Am. Psychol. Assn. (pres. 1956-57), Am. Statis. Assn., A.A.A.S.; mem. Am. Ednl. Research Assn. (pres. 1964-65), Social Sci. Research Council (chmn. com. learning and edn. process 1962-66, dir. 1964—), Psychometric Soc. (pres. 1953-54), Am. Philos. Soc., Am. Acad. Arts and Scis., Nat. Acad. Edn., Sigma Xi, Phi Delta Kappa, Pi Kappa Phi. Author: Essentials of Psychological Testing, 1949, 3d edit., 1970; Educational Psychology, 1954, 2d edit., 1963; (with Goldine C. Gleser) Psychological Tests and Personnel Decisions, 1965; (with Patrick C. Suppes) Research for Tomorrow's Schools, 1969. Home: 16 Laburnum Atherton CA 94025 Office: Stanford U Stanford CA 94305

CRONBACH, ROBERT M., sculptor; b. St. Louis, Feb. 10, 1908; s. Lee and Ruby (Lowenhaupt) C.; student St. Louis Sch. Fine Arts, 1925-26, Pa. Acad. Fine Arts, 1927-30; European travel, Cresson scholarship, 1929-30; m. Maxine Judd Silver, Oct. 12, 1934; childrenPaula, Michael Theodore, Lee. Asso. prof. at Adelphi Coll.; exhibited sculpture Mus. Modern Art, N.Y. C., Nat. Inst. Arts and Letters, Bertha Schaefer Gallery, Whitney Mus., Phila. and St. Louis art mus., other mus., galleries; one man shows Bertha Schaefer Galleries, N.Y., 1956, 67, 70; exhbn. group show Hemisfair, San Antonio, 1968; sculptor decorations lime stone St. Louis Municipal Auditorium, 1932; tamped concrete decorations Willerts Park Housing Project, Buffalo, 1939; sculptor two bronze statues Social Security Bldg., Washington, 1940; 120 foot bronze screen Dorr-Oliver Bldg., Stamford, and bronze wall sculpture for UN Gen. Assembly Bldg., 1960; Reynolds Metal Corp. Ann. Award Trophy, 1961; Fifteen-foot fountain St. Louis Fed. Bldg., 1963; fountain for plaza Charleston (W.Va.) Pub. Library, 1967; decorations pub. and pvt. bldgs., fountains. Mem. Nat. Council on Arts and Govt. Bd. govs. Skowhegan Sch. Painting and Sculpture. Served with Mcht. Marine, World War II. Mem. Sculptors Guild, Inc., Municipal Art Soc., Fedn. Modern Painters and Sculptors, Archtl. League N.Y., Century Assn. Address: 170 Henry St Westbury NY 11590

CRONE, REGINALD, transp. co. exec.; b. Moose Jaw, Sask., Can., July 12, 1935; s. Harry and Lilian (Gilbert) C.; B. Comm., U. Sask., 1959; m. Georgina Elizabeth Woodall, Nov. 11, 1956; children—Leslie, Loren, Jeffrey, James. Partner R.L. Bamford & Co., Moose Jaw, 1959; v.p. Trimac Transp. Ltd., Calgary, Alta., 1960-68; exec. v.p. Westburne Internat. Industries Ltd., Calgary, 1970; pres. Trimac Ltd., Calgary, 1971—; dir. Adby Transport Ltd., Columbia Bulk Carriers, J. Kearns Transport (Alta.) Ltd., J. Kearns Transport

Ltd., Mercury Tanklines Ltd., Municipal Tank Lines Ltd., Trimac Leasing Ltd., H.M. Trimble & Sons Ltd., Trimac Investments Ltd., Trimac Marine Terminals Ltd. Clubs: Petroleum; Earl Grey Golf and Country, Ranchmen's (Calgary). Home: 6819 Lowell Ct SW Calgary 10 Alberta Canada Office: 535 7th Av SW Calgary 2 Alberta Canada

CRONE, RICHARD IRVING, army officer, physician; b. Salt Lake City, June 6, 1909; s. Maurice B. and Mildred (Rheinstrom) C.; student U. Cal. at Los Angeles, 1927-30; A.B., U. Cal. at San Francisco, 1931, M.D., 1935; m. Alla M. Ernst, Mar. 26, 1946;; children—Richard A., William E. Rotating intern Alameda County Hosp., Oakland, Cal., 1934-35; med. resident U. Cal. Hosp., San Francisco, 1935-36, surg. resident, 1937-38; practice medicine specializing in internal medicine, San Francisco, 1936-37; clin. instr. medicine U. Cal. Med. Sch., 1936-37; commd. 1st lt. M.C., U.S. Army, advanced through grades to brig. gen., 1965; contract surgeon Letterman Gen. Hosp., San Francisco, 1939; resident internal medicine Madigan Gen. Hosp., Tacoma, 1947-48, asst. chief med. service, 1948-49, chief dept. medicine, 1961-63, chief dept. medicine, dir. med. edn., 1962-63, comdg. gen., 1965-69; chief med. service 130th Sta. Hosp., Heidelberg, Germany, 1949-51, 51-52, comdg. officer, 1951; med. cons. Hdqrs. U.S. Army in Europe, Heidelberg, 1952-53, 58-61; asst. chief dept. medicine, asst. dir. med. edn. Letterman Gen. Hosp., San Francisco, 1953- 56, chief dept. medicine, asst. dir. med. edn., 1956-57; chief med. service, chief profl. services, dir. med. edn. 2d Gen. Hosp., Landstuhl, Germany, 1957-58; chief dept. medicine, cons. to surgeon gen. on internal medicine Walter Reed Gen. Hosp., Washington, 1963-65, ret., 1969; dir. edn. Group Health Coop. Puget Sound, 1969—. Decorated D.S.M., Legion of Merit with oak leaf cluster, Bronze Star medal, Air medal; Order Yun Hui (Nationalist China). Diplomate Am. Bd. Internal Medicine. Fellow A.C.P.; mem. A.M.A., Pierce County (Wash.) Med. Soc., Am., Wash. socs. internal medicine, Tacoma Acad. Internal Medicine (hon.), Phi Beta Pi. Home: 8637 NE 20th St Bellevue WA 98004 Office: 200 15th Av E Seattle WA 98102

CRONHEIM, CHARLES A., retail merchandising exec.; b. Newark, Apr. 20, 1916; s. Albert S. and Ethel (Hartt) C.; student U. Newark; m. Elizabeth Tripp, Aug. 20, 1938; childrenCharles F. William J. With Fed. Trust Co., Newark, 1933-40, Industrial Bank of Commerce, N.Y.C., 1940-42; with Bambergers N.J., Newark, 1942-59, sr. v.p., 1959; exec. R. H. Macy & Co., Inc., N.Y.C., -, formerly v.p. planning and development, now sr. v.p., 1967- , also dir.; dir. Garden State Plaza Corp., Paramus, N.J. Served from pvt. to 2d lt., AUS, 1944-46. Member International Council Shopping Centers. Club: Union League; Rockaway River Country (trustee, past pres.). Home: 1 East Shore Rd Mountain Lakes NJ 07046 Office: 151 W 34th St New York City NY 10001

CRONIN, ARCHIBALD JOSEPH, author; b. Cardross, Scotland, July 19, 1896; s. Patrick and Jessie (Montgomerie) C.; M.B., B. Chir. and M.D., Glasgow; D.Litt., Bowdoin U., Lafayette Coll.; m. Agnes Mary Gibson, 1921; children—Vincent Archibald, Patrick, Robert Francis Patrick, Andrew James. Began as doctor of medicine, in South Wales, 1919, later practiced in London, 1930; became med. insp. mines for Great Britain, 1924; author, 1930—. Life gov. Sussex Gen. Hosp.; mem. Fischer Com.; mem. of Council of Authors Soc. Author: Hatters Castle, 1931; Three Loves, 1932; Grand Canary, 1933; The Stars Look Down, 1935; The Citadel, 1937; Jupiter Laughs (3-act play), 1940; The Keys of the Kingdom, 1941, The Green Years, 1944; Shannon's Way, 1948; The Spanish Gardener, 1950; Adventures in Two Worlds, 1952; Beyond this Place, 1953; A Thing of Beauty, 1956; The Northern Light, 1958; The Judas Tree, 1961; A Song of Sixpence, 1964; A Pocketful of Rye, published in 1969. Clubs: Links, University (N.Y.C.). Home: Champ-Riond 1815 Baugy sur Clarens VD Switzerland Office: Little Brown & Co 34 Beacon St Boston MA 02108

CRONIN, GROVER JEREMIAH, Jr., educator; b. Waltham, Mass., June 23, 1914; s. Grover Jeremiah and Helen (Conolly) C.; grad. Boston Latin Sch., 1931; B.A., Boston Coll., 1935; B.A., Hertford Coll., Oxford U., 1937; Ph.D., U. Wis., 1940; m. Jane Williams Ganey, Sept. 13, 1946; children—Grover Jeremiah III, Jane G., Helen C., Mathew W., Hannah S. Instr. English dept. Fordham Coll. and Grad. Sch., 1939-42; asst. prof., 1946-52, asso. prof., 1952-60, prof., 1960—, chairman dept., 1950-65; editorial staff Yale edit. Horace Walpole's Corr., 1946-55. Dir. Grover Cronin, Inc., Grover Cronin Realty Corp. Mem. Modern Lang. Assn., Medieval Acad. Home: 162 Nyac Av Pelham NY 10803

CRONIN, DANIEL ANTHONY, bishop; b. Newton, Mass., Nov. 14, 1927; s. Daniel George and Emily Frances (Joyce) C.; S.T.L., Gregorian U., 1953, S.T.D. summa cum laude, 1956; LL.D., Suffolk U., Boston, 1969. Ordained priest Roman Catholic Ch., 1952; attache Apostolic Internunicature, Addis Ababa, Ethiopia, 1957-61; attache Secretariat of State, Vatican City, 1961-68; named Monsignor by His Holiness Pope John XXIII, 1962; named titular bishop of Egnatia and aux. bishop of Boston, 1968; Episcopal ordination from Richard Cardinal Cushing, archbishop of Boston, 1968; pastor St. Raphael Ch., Medford, Mass., 1968-70; bishop of Fall River, Mass., 1970—. Trustee Cath. U. Am. K.C. (4). Address: 362 Highland Av Fall River MA 02722

CRONIN, JAMES WATSON, educator, physicist; b. Chgo., Sept. 29, 1931; s. James Farley and Dorothy (Watson) C.; A.B., So. Methodist U., 1951; Ph.D., U. Chgo., m. Annette Martin, Sept. 11, 1954; children—Cathryn, Emily, Daniel. asso. Brookhaven Nat. Lab., 1955-58; mem. faculty Princeton, 1958-, prof. physics, 1965-. Recipient Research Corp. Am. award, 1967; Sloan fellow, 1964-66; Guggenheim fellow, 1970-71. Mem. Am. Acad. Arts and spark chambers; co-discover CP-violation, 1964. Home: 248 Hartley Av Princeton, NJ 08540.

CRONIN, JOHN WILLIAM, librarian; b. Lewiston, Me., Feb. 10, 1905; s. Daniel James and Ellen (Connors) C.; A.B., Bowdoin Coll., 1925; LL.B., Georgetown U., 1929; m. Esther Johnson, Sept. 24, 1938. Asst., card div. Library of Congress 1928-32, asst. chief card div. 1932-38, acting chief, 1938-40, chief, 1940-44, asst. dir. processing dept., 1944-52, dir., 1952-68, library cons., 1968—. Recipient Melvil Dewey award, 1964. Mem. Am. Library Assn. (recipient Margaret Mann citation in cataloging and classification, 1961), Am. Documentation Inst., Bibliog. Soc. Am., Cath. Library Assn. Roman Cath. Home: 2129 32d Pl S E Washington, DC 20020. Office: Library of Congress Washington DC 20540

CRONIN, JOSEPH, baseball exec.; b. San Francisco, Oct. 12, 1906; s. Jeremiah and Mary (Carolin) C.; grad. high sch.; m. Mildred June Robertson, Sept. 1934; 3 sons, 1 dau. Profl. baseball player in Am. League, 1928; mgr. Washington Senators, 1932-34; mgr. Boston Red Sox, 1935-45, gen. mgr. of club, 1945-58; pres. Am. League Profl. Baseball Clubs, 1958—, also sec., treas. Co-founder, dir. Mass. Com. Catholics, Protestants and Jews. Winner Am. League pennant, 1933; named to Baseball Hall Fame, 1956. Knight of Malta. Club: Variety (recipient Great Heart award for work in Jimmy Fund, Boston). Office: Am League Office 520 Boylston St Boston MA 02116

CRONIN, THOMAS DILLON, physician; b. Houston, Apr. 8, 1906 s. Phillip H. and Julia K. (Dillon) C.; student Rice Inst., 1924-28; M.D., U. Tex., 1932; m. Anne C. Heyck, Nov. 6, 1935; children—Thomas Dillon, Robert Hillsman, Anne Frances. Intern Kansas City (Mo.) Gen. Hosp., 1932-33; resident surgery St. Joseph's Hosp., Houston, 1933-34; fellow plastic and oral surgery Mayo Found., Rochester, Minn., 1937-39; now clin. prof. plastic surgery Baylor U., also asso. prof. plastic surgery U. Tex. Postgrad. Sch. Medicine; chief plastic surgery St. Josephs Hosp., 1941-63, dir. plastic surgery residency tng. program, 1970—; chief plastic surgery Herman Hosp., 1941-69, St. Lukes Episcopal Hosp., 1954—, Tex. Children's Hosp., 1954—. Served from maj. to lt. col., M.C., AUS, 1943-46. Diplomate Am. Bd. Plastic Surgery (mem. bd. 1961-67). Mem. Am. Assn. Plastic Surgeons (pres. 1963-64), Am. Soc. Plastic and Reconstructive Surgeons, A.C.S., Am. Assn. Physicians and Surgeons, A.M.A., Southwestern Surg. Congress, Tex. (v.p. 1960), Houston (pres. 1971-72) surg. socs. Clubs: Country, Yacht, Doctors (Houston). Contbr. numerous papers in field plastic surgery. Home: 2121 Brentwood Dr Houston TX 77019 Office: 5419 Caroline St Houston TX 77004

CRONIN, TIMOTHY X., electronics co. exec. Pres., treas. Cramer Electronics, Inc., Newton, Mass. Office: 320 Needham St Newton MA 02161*

CRONK, EDWIN M., fgn. service officer; b. Mpls., May 20, 1918; s. William Frederick and Edith (Hanson) C.; student Deep Springs Coll., 1936-39; A.B., Cornell, 1941; student George Washington U.; m. Dorothy Montgomery, Jan. 9, 1943; children—Mary Ed, James Montgomery, Nancy Lee. Adminstrv. asst. Surplus Marketing Adminstrn., Dept. Agr., 1941-42, 46-47; economist hdqrs. Supreme Comdr. Allied Powers, Tokyo, Japan, 1947-49; economist Dept. Army, Washington, 1949-51, Dept. State, Washington, 1951-55; U.S. fgn. service officer, 1954—; 1st sec., consul Am. embassy, Seoul, Korea, 1956-59, counselor embassy for econ. affairs, 1959-60; fellow Center for Internat. Affairs, Harvard, 1960-61; minister for econ. affairs Am. embassy, Bonn, Germany, 1961-65; dep. chief mission Am. embassy, Canberra, Australia, 1965-69; dep. asst. sec. state for internat. trade policy Bur. Econ. Affairs, Dept. State, Washington, 1969—. Served to 1st lt. USAAF, 1942-46. Home: Washington DC Office: Dept of State Bureau of Economic Affairs Washington DC 20025

CRONKHITE, LEONARD WOOLSEY, Jr., physician; b. Newton, Mass., May 4, 1919; s. Leonard Woolsey and Orpah Glencor (Brewster) C.; B.S., Bowdoin Coll., 1941; M.B., Harvard, 1950; LL.D., Northeastern U., 1970; m. Joan Patricia Dunn, July 2, 1955; children—Judith, Marcia, Janice, Wendy. Intern Mass. Gen. Hosp., 1950-51, asst. resident, 1951-52, resident, 1952-53, USPHS fellow, 1953-54; gen. dir. Children's Hosp. Med. Center, Boston, 1962-71, exec. v.p., 1971—; lectr. preventive medicine Harvard Med. Sch., 1952—; pvt. practice medicine, Boston, 1955—. Pres. Baytron Inc., 1962—; v.p. Cloutman Inc., 1961—; pres. Health Inc., 1970—; Bd. dirs. New Eng. Grenfell Mission, Day Found; trustee Bowdoin Coll. Served with AUS, 1940-46; maj. gen. Res. Decorated Legion of Merit, Army Commendation medal. Mem. Soc. Med. Adminstrs. (pres. 1971). Home: 12 Hathaway Rd Marblehead MA 01945 Office: 300 Longwood Av Boston MA 02115

CRONKITE, WALTER, radio-TV news correspondent; b. St. Joseph, Mo., Nov. 4, 1916; s. Walter Leland and Helen Lena C.; student U. Tex., 1933-35; LL.D., Rollins Coll., 1966, Bucknell U., Syracuse U.; L.H.D., Ohio State U.; hon. degree Am. Internat. Coll.; m. Mary Elizabeth Maxwell, Mar. 30, 1940; children—Nancy, Mary, Walter Leland III. News writer, editor Scripps-Howard, also United Press, Houston, Kansas City, Dallas, Austin, El Paso, N.Y.C.; United Press war corr., 1942-45; fgn. corr., reopening bureaus in Amsterdam, Brussels, chief corr. Nuremberg war crimes trials, bur. mgr., Moscow, 1946-48; lectr., mag. contbr., 1948-49; CBS-TV correspondent, 1950—; mng. editor CBS Evening News with Walter Cronkite. Recipient Peabody award 1962; William A. White award for journalistic merit, 1969; Emmy award Acad. Television Arts and Scis., 1970; George Polk Journalism award, 1971. Mem. Acad. TV Arts and Scis. (pres. nat. acad. N.Y. chpt. 1959), Assn. Radio News Analysts, Chi Phi. Clubs: Nat. Press, Overseas, Writers, N.Y. Yacht, Players, Indian Harbor Yacht. Office: CBS News 524 W 57th St New York City NY 10019

CRONON, EDMUND DAVID, Jr., educator, historian; b. Mpls., Mar. 11, 1924; s. Edmund David and Florence Ann (Meyer) C.; student Macalester Coll., 1942-43; A.B., Oberlin Coll., 1948; A.M., U. Wis., 1949, Ph.D., 1953; postgrad. Manchester (Eng.) U., 1950-51; m. Mary Jean Hotmar, May 13, 1950; children—William John, Robert David. Instr., then asst. prof. history Yale, 1953-59; asso. prof., then prof. history U. Neb., 1959-62; prof. history U. Wis., Madison, 1962—, chmn. dept., 1966-69, dir. Inst. for Research in Humanities, 1969—; lectr. for State Dept., Europe and Near East, 1966. Served to 1st lt., inf. AUS, 1943-46. Fulbright fellow, 1950-51; Stimson fellow, 1958-59. Mem. Am. Hist. Assn., Orgn. Am. Historians (exec. bd.), Wis. (bd. curators, pres.). Neb. hist. socs., So. Hist. Assn. (bd. editors), Am. Assn. U. Profs., Phi Beta Kappa. Unitarian. Author: Black Moses: The Story of Marcus Garvey and the Universal Negro Improvement Association, 1955; Josephus Daniels in Mexico, 1960; Government and the Economy: Some Nineteenth Century Views, 1960; Contemporary Labor-Management Relations, 1960; The Cabinet Diaries of Josephus Daniels, 1913-1921, 1963; Labor and the New Deal, 1963; Twentieth Century America; Selected Readings, 2 vols., 1965-66; The Political Thought of Woodrow Wilson, 1965. Home: 5601 Varsity Hill Madison WI 53705

CRONQUIST, ARTHUR JOHN (Franklin Arthur Beers), botanist; b. San Jose, Cal., Mar. 19, 1919; s. Frank and Edith Marguerite (Cronquist) Beers; student U. Ida., 1934-36; B.S., Utah State Coll., 1938, M.S., 1940; Ph.D., U. Minn., 1944; m. Mabel Allred, Dec. 25, 1940; children—John August, Elizabeth Lynne. Mem. staff N.Y. Bot. Garden, 1943-46, 52—, dir. botany, 1971—; asst. prof. U. Ga., 1946-48; asst. prof. State Coll. Wash., 1948-51, research asso., 1953—; tech. adviser Belgian Govt., 1951-52. Mem. Internat. Assn. Plant Taxonomists, Bot. Soc. Am., Am. Soc. Plant Taxonomists (pres. 1962), Torrey, New Eng. bot. clubs, A.A.A.S., Am. Inst. Biol. Scis., Ecol. Soc. Am., Cal. Bot. Soc. Author: Introductory Botany, 1961, 2d edit., 1971; The Evolution and Classification of Flowering Plants, 1968; also numerous articles. Co-author: Manual of the Vascular Plants of Northeastern U.S. and Adjacent Canada, 1963; Vascular Plants of the Pacific Northwest, 5 vols., 1955- 69; Natural Geography of Plants, 1964. Home: 29 Dunderave Rd White Plains NY 10603 Office: NY Botanical Garden Bronx NY 10458

CRONVICH, JAMES ANTHONY, educator; b. New Orleans, Oct. 26, 1914; s. James A. and Louise (Lester) C.; B.E. in Mech. and Elec. Engring., Tulane U., 1935, M.S. in Elec. Engring., 1937; S.M. in Elec. Engring., Mass. Inst. Tech., 1938; m. Mary Silberberg, June 16, 1951; children—James Thomas, Mary Claire, Paul Gerard, George Vincent, Stephen Joseph. Mem. faculty elec. engring. Tulane U., 1938-41, 42—, prof. elec. engring. charge instrn. electronics and communications, also prof. bio-engring. dept. medicine, 1949—, head dept. elec. engring., 1956—; asst., then asso. elec. engring., spl. engring. div., 3d locks projects, Panama Canal, 1941-42. Fellow I.E.E.E. (chmn. New Orleans 1959-60); mem. Am. Soc. for Engring. Edn., Sigma Xi, Tau Beta Pi. Co-author: Spatial Vectorcardiography. Editorial bd. Am. Heart Jour. Home: 101 Colonial Club Dr New Orleans LA 70123

CRONYN, HUME, actor, writer, dir.; b. London, Ont., Can., July 18, 1911; s. Hume Blake and Frances Amelia (Labatt) C.; grad., Ridley Coll., 1930; student McGill U., 1930-31; grad., Am. Acad. Dramatic Art, 1934; m. Jessica Tandy, Sept. 27, 1942; children—Susan (Mrs. John Tettemer), Christopher, Tandy. Came to U.S., 1932. First profl. theatre appearance Nat. Theatre Stock Co., Washington, 1931; appeared in Hippers Holiday, 1st appearance N.Y.C., 1934; various plays, N.Y.C., including: High Tor, Room Service, The Three Sisters, The Weak Link, Retreat to Pleasure, The Survivors (star); motion pictures include: Shadow Of A Doubt, 1943; Life Boat, 1944; The Seventh Cross, 1944; The Postman Always Rings Twice, 1946; The Green Years, 1946; A Letter for Evie (star), 1945; Brute Force (star), 1947; Top O' The Morning (star) 1949; People Will Talk, 1951; starred in ANTA touring prodn. of Hamlet, 1949; co- starred with Jessica Tandy in The Little Blue Light, Brattle Theatre, Cambridge, Mass., 1950, The Fourposter, 1951-53; Madame Will You Walk, 1953-54; The Honeys; A Day by the Sea, 1955, The Man in the Dog Suit, 1958; dir. Portrait Of A Madonna, Los Angeles, 1946, Now I Lay Me Down To Sleep, 1949-50, Hilda Crane, 1950, The Egghead, 1957 (all N.Y.C.); appears major network dramatic shows TV, including Show of the Week; appeared in film Sunrise at Campobello, 1960, film Cleopatra, 1963, Gaily Gaily, 1968, The Arrangement, 1968, There Was a Crooked Man, 1969; appeared in the comedy prodn. Big Fish, Little Fish, 1961; with Tyrone Guthrie Prodns., Mpls., 1963; played Polonius, Hamlet, N.Y.C., 1964, Newton in the Physicists, 1964; producer Slow Dance on the Killing Ground, 1964; produced and starred (with Jessica Tandy) The Marriage (a dramatic series), 1954, Triple Play, 1958, 59; appeared title role Richard III, 1965; appeared in Cherry Orchard, 1965, as Harpagon in The Miser, Minneapolis, 1965; as Tobias in A Delicate Balance, 1966, 67, revival The Miser, Mark Taper Forum, Los Angeles, 1968; as Friar William Rolfe in Hadrian VII, Stratford Nat. Theatre Co. Can., 1969, tour, 1969-70; as Capt. Queeg in Caine Mutiny Court Martial, Los Angeles, 1971-72; lectr. drama Am. Acad. Dramatic Arts, N.Y.C., 1938-39, Actors' Lab., Los Angeles, 1945-46. Recipient Barter Theatre award for outstanding contbn. to theatre, 1961; Delia Austria medal N.Y. Drama League for Big Fish, Little Fish, 1961; Antoinette Perry (Tony) award, also Variety N.Y. Drama critics poll of performance as Polonius, 1964; 9th ann. award Am. Acad. Dramatic Art, 1964. Mem. A.F.T.R.A, Screen Actors Guild, Screen Writers Guild, Actors Equity Assn., Soc. Stage Dirs. and Choreographers. Author: Rope (screen version), 1947; Under Capricorn (screen version), 1948; also various short stories and mag. articles. Home: Box 85A Round Ridge NY 10576

CRONYN, JOHN BRUCE, brewery exec.; b. London, Ont., Can., Dec. 3, 1920; s. Verschoyle Philip and Dorothy Vivian (Bruce) C.; student Ridley Coll.; B.A.Sc., U. Toronto, 1947; m. Barbara Jean Duff, June 22, 1946; children—Hume Duff, Marilyn Ruth, Martha Ann. Apprentice brewer John Labatt, Ltd., 1947-49, prodn. mgr., 1950-52, dir. prodn., 1952-56, v.p. prodn., 1956-62, exec. v.p., 1962-66, sr. exec. v.p., 1966-68, exec. v.p. corporate affairs, 1968-71, sr. v.p., 1971—, also dir.; dir. London Life Ins. Co., Lucky Breweries, Inc., Manning's Internat. Ltd., Laura Secord Candy Shops Ltd., Jon lab Investments Ltd., Talisman Ski Resort Ltd., Triarch Corp. Ltd. Ogilvie Flour Mills, Co. Ltd., Schwarz Services Internat. Ltd., The Parkdale Wines, Ltd., Delmar Chemicals, Ltd., Kemp Products Ltd., Ellis-Don Ltd. Adv. bd. engring. sci. course U. Western Ont.; chmn. Ont. govt. com. on govt. productivity. Bd. dirs. Shaw Festival. Served lt. Royal Canadian Engrs., 1942-46. Mem. Engring. Inst. Can., Assn. Profl. Engrs. Ont., Ont. C of C. (dir.), Kappa Alpha. Mem. Anglican Ch. (people's warden 1958-59). Clubs: London, London Hunt and Country. Home: 21 Doncaster Av Office: 150 Simcoe St London Ontario Canada

CROOK, DOROTHY, (Mrs. C. Sprague Hazard), exec. economist; b. N.Y.C., June 21, 1911; d. Samuel and Mary (Beekman) Crook; B.A., Barnard Coll., 1933; M.A., Columbia, 1938; m. C. Sprague Hazard, Jan. 22, 1947; children—Jonathan Sprague, Neil Livingstone. Editorial asst. div. press intelligence, White House, 1933- 35; jr. economist Treasury Dept., 1935-37; asst. to economist Chase Nat. Bank, N.Y.C., 1937-39; cons. war savs. staff Treasury Dept., 1943-42; dir. pub. affairs and legislation Nat. Fedn. Bus. and Profl. Women, 1939-42; pub. affairs officer OWI, London, Eng., 1942-47; econ. analyst Voice of Am., Washington, 1947-52, chief talks and features br., 1952-54, econs. editor, 1963—. press and pub. affairs officer U.S. Mission to UN, 1954-60; exec. dir. U.S. Com. for UN, 1960-63. Mem. Am. Econs. Assn., UN Assn. U.S.A., Phi Beta Kappa. Club: Women's National Press. Home: 4710 Langdrum Lane Chevy Chase MD 20015 Office: HEW Bldg Washington DC 20204

CROOK, PHILIP GEORGE, educator; b. Washington, Oct. 21, 1925; s. Philip Harry and Marion (Lilly) C.; B.S., U. Md., 1949; M.S., U. N.M., 1951; Ph.D., Pa. State U., 1955. Prof. Hope Coll., Holland, Mich., 1955-68, chmn. biology dept., 1962-66; Charles A. Dana prof., chmn. biology dept. Colgate U., Hamilton, N.Y., 1968—; vis. prof. Silliman U., Dumaquete City Philippines, 1967. Served with USNR, 1944-46. Named Outstanding Tchr., Hope Coll., 1967. Mem. A.A.A.S., Soc. Protozoologists, Am. Soc. Parasitologists, Am. Soc. for Microbiology, Nat. Assn. Biology Tchrs. Home: RD 2 Brookview Dr Hamilton NY 13346

CROOK, WILLIAM GRANT, physician; b. Jackson, Tenn., Sept. 13, 1917; s. Jere Lawrence and Millian Cooke (Green) C.; B.A., U. of the South, 1937; M.D., U. Va., 1942; m. Betsy Buckner Noe, Jan. 16, 1943; children—Elizabeth (Mrs. Morton B. Howell III), Nancy (Mrs. Edward G. Harness), Cynthia. Intern Pa. Hosp., Phila., 1942-43; pediatric intern, asst. resident Vanderbilt U. Hosp., Nashville, 1946-48; chief resident Sydenham Hosp., Johns Hopkins U., Balt., 1948; practice pediatrics Jackson, Tenn., 1949—; mem. staff Jackson Madison County Gen. Hosp., chief staff, 1967; sr. partner Children's Clinic, Jackson, 1952—; pres. Child Health Center Am., Inc., Jackson, 1969—. Author syndicated column Child Care, Los Angeles Times Syndicate, 1965—; cons. Med. Communications, Inc., 1968—. Served to maj., M.C., AUS, 1943-46. Diplomate Am. Bd. Pediatrics. Fellow Am. Coll. Allergists (asso.); mem. Am. Acad. Pediatrics, Tenn. Pediatric Soc. (past pres.), Phi Alpha Theta, Pi Gamma Mu, Omicron Delta Kappa. Republican. Episcopalian. Club: Jackson Golf and Country. Author: Answering Parents' Questions, 1963. Cons. editor Clin. Pediatrics, 1971. Contbr. profl. jours. Home: 109 Oakslea Pl Jackson TN 38301 Office: PO Box 3116 Jackson TN 38301

CROOK, WILLIAM HERBERT, former U.S. ambassador; b. Momence, Ill., Apr. 18, 1925; s. William George and Violet (Devine) C.; A.B., Baylor U., 1949; grad. student U. Edinburg, 1949-50; student Southwestern Sem., Ft. Worth, 1954; m. Eleanor Butt, Jan. 2, 1954; children—William Herbert, Mary Beth, Noel Eileen. Pres. San Marcos (Tex.) Acad., 1960-65; regional dir. Office Econ. Opportunity, 1965-67; asst. dir. Office Econ. Opportunity, also Exec. Office of Pres., nat. dir. Vols. Service to Am., 1967-68; U.S. ambassador to Australia, 1968-69. Mem. Task Force Returning

Vietnam Vets., 1967-68; U.S. commr. U.S.-Mexico Border Devel. Commn., 1967-68; U.S. sr. del. World Conf. Nat. Voluntarism, New Delhi, India, 1967; U.S. observer Nat. Voluntarism, Israel, 1967, Can., 1967-68; White House cons. Office Econ. Opportunity, 1965; mem. White House Conf. Civil Rights, 1964; White House observer Middle Lever Manpower Conf., P.R. 1962; observer Internat. Refugee Centers, Western Europe, 1958. Dir. Tex. Student Adv. Coms., 1964; mem. Tex. City Planning Commns. and Indsl. Bds., 1965. Bd. dirs., trustee Colls. in S.W., 1965. Served with USAAF, World War II. Author: (with Ross Thomas) Warriors for the Poor, 1969; Seven Who Fought, 1969; also articles. Address: 227 N Mitchell St San Marcos CA 92069

CROOKER, JOHN H., Jr., lawyer; b. Houston, Oct. 26, 1914; s. John H. and Marguerite (Malsch) C.; B.A. with distinction, Rice U., 1935; LL.B. with highest honors, 1937; m. Kay Berry, children—Carolyn (Mrs. W.E. Schwing), John H. III, Linda, Tara, Allison. Admitted to Tex. bar, 1937, D.C. bar, 1953; practice law Houston and Washington, 1937-67, 70—; chmn. CAB, 1968-69. Dir. Houston Citizens Bank & Trust Co. Bd. regents State Sr. Colls. Tex. Served to lt. comdr. USNR, 1941-45. Decorated Bronze Star. Mem. State Bar. Tex. (past chmn. corp. sect.), Am. Bar Assn., Am. Law Inst. Office: Bank of Southwest Bldg Houston TX 77002

CROOKER, JOHN HENRY, lawyer; b. Mobile, July 15, 1884; s. Norman W. and Margaret J. (Kelton) C.; m. Marguerite Malsch, Dec. 31, 1913; children—John Henry, Robert W. Admitted to Tex. Bar, 1911; judge inferior ct., Houston, 1911-14; dist. atty., Houston, 1914-17; mem. firm Fulbright & Crooker, Houston, and successor firm, Fulbright, Crooker, Freeman, Bates & Jaworski, Houston, 1919—, now of counsel. Dir. First City Nat. Bank, Houston. Served as maj., div. judge adv., 16th Div., U.S. Army, 1918-19. Episcopalian (past sr. warden, vestryman). Mason (grand master Tex. 1934-35). Home: Inwood Manor 3711 San Felipe Houston TX 77027 Office: Bank of Southwest Bldg Houston TX 77002

CROOKS, ALEXANDER RICHARD, tenor; b. Trenton; s. Alexander Struthers and Elizabeth (Gore) C.; ed. high sch., Trenton; Mus.D., Temple U., Lafayette Coll.; m. Mildred Wallace Pine, July 23, 1921; children—Patricia, Richard. Began as boy soprano soloist in ch.; made debut as boy soprano with Mme. Schumann-Heink, Asbury Park, N.J., 1910; debut as tenor with N.Y. Symphony Orch., Walter Damrosch, condr., 1922; European concert tour, 1925; operatic debut in Tosca, Hamburg (Germany) Opera, 1927; debut Met. Opera, N.Y.C., 1933; concert tour of Australia, New Zealand and Tazmania, 1936. Served as cadet flying officer, Air Service, U.S. Army, World War I. Episcopalian. Home: 557 Cresta Vista Lane Portola Valley CA 94025

CROOKS, EDWIN WILLIAM, educator; b. Parkersburg, W.Va., July 29, 1919; s. Edwin William and Rebecca (Dils) C.; B.S., W.Va. U., 1941, M.A., 1942; M.B.A., Harvard, 1947; D.B.A., Ind. U., 1959; m. Joan Schleuniger, Sept. 13, 1952; children—Edwin William III, Ann, Alice. Mdse. controller Halle Bros. Co., Cleve., 1947-54; prof. marketing, asst. dean W.Va. U., 1954-56, 58- 66; chancellor, prof. bus. adminstrn. Ind. U. S.E., Jeffersonville, 1966- -. Dir. Dils Bros. & Co., Parkersburg. Bd. dirs. So. Ind. Symphony Orch., Inc., United Fund, Steamboat Cabin Theater, Nat. Steamboat Mus. Served to lt. comdr. USNR, 1942-46. Ford Found. fellow, 1956-58. Mem. Am. Marketing Assn., Jeffersonville C. of C., Phi Beta Kappa, Beta Theta Pi, Beta Gamma Sigma. Methodist. Rotarian. Club: Executive. Author: Buying Practices of Independent Retailers in W.Va., 1963; Retail Credit Policies in W.Va., 1965. Contbr. articles profl. jours. Home: 1807 Utica Pike Jeffersonville IN 47130

CROOKS, RICHARD M., corp. exec.; b. Seabright, N.J., 1905. Vice pres., dir. Thompson & McKinnon, Auchincloss, Inc., N.Y.C. Trustee N.Y. Stock Exchange Gratuity Fund. Home: 12 Westminster Rd Summit NJ 07901 Office: 11 Wall St New York City NY 10005

CROOKS, WILLIAMS RAMSDEN, educator; b. Modesto, Cal., Sept. 3, 1912; s. William Henry and Priscilla Urania (Ramsden) C.; B.A., U. Cal. at Berkeley, 1937; M.A., U. Conn., 1939; Ph.D., U. Minn., 1952; m. Betty Lightsey, July 1, 1942; children—William Henry, Sarah Jane, Jeffry Graham. Teaching asst. U. Conn., 1937-39; instr. Suffolk U., 1939-40, asst. prof., 1940-41; staff asst. Life Office Mgmt. Assn. N.Y.C., 1941; personnel technician WPB, 1942; asso. Edwin Shields Hewitt and Assos., Chg., 1946-47; faculty Ore. State U., 1947-49, 50—, prof. psychology, 1957—, chmn. dept., 1956—; teaching asst. U. Minn., 1949-50. Served to comdr. USNR, 1942-46. Mem. Am., Ore. psychol. assns., Phil Delta Kappa. Author articles. Home: 1609 Lester Av NW Corvallis OR 97330

CROOKSTON, J. IAN, investment banker; b. Ayr, Scotland, 1910. Pres., Nesbitt Thomson & Co. Ltd., Toronto, Ont., Can.; dir. Canadian Indsl. Gas & Oil Newconex Holdings Ltd., Am. Zinc Co., Preston Mines Ltd., Rio Algom Mines Ltd., Noctin Investment Corp. Ltd. Mem. Investment Bankers Assn. Am. Home: 70 Ardwold Gate Toronto Ontario Canada Office: PO Box 35 Toronto 1 Ontario Canada

CROOP, ARTHUR VERNON, editor; b. San Jose, Cal., Feb. 24, 1904; s. Arthur M. and Kate May (Wright) C.; A.B., U. Rochester, 1926; m. Florence Margaret Smith, Mar. 21, 1931; children—George, Marilyn (Mrs. Ross Schillaci), David. Reporter Rochester (N.Y.) Times-Union, 1925-32, copy editor, 1932-36, state editor, 1936-38, city editor, 1938-41, mng. editor, 1950-66; news editor, acting mng. editor Rochester Democrat and Chronicle, 1941-48; chief Washington bur. Gannett Newspapers, 1948- 50; gen. exec. Gannett Co., Inc., Rochester, 1966-69, cons., 1969—. Mem. Asso. Press Mng. Editors (dir. 1959-62, 64-67), N.Y. State Soc. Editors, Rochester C. of C., Sigma Delta Chi, Sigma Chi. Presbyn. Club: Oak Hill Country. Home: 78 Maywood Av Rochester NY 14618 Office: care Gannett Co Inc Rochester NY 14614

CROPP, FREDERICK WILLIAM, III, geologist, coll. adminstr.; b. Wheeling, W.Va., Dec. 9, 1932; s. Frederick William, Jr. and Ruth (Perkins) C.; B.A., Coll. of Wooster, 1954; M.A., U. Ill., 1956, Ph.D., 1958; m. Helen Cameron Townsend, June 15, 1955; children—Frederick William IV, Julia Anne, Carol Ruth, Thomas Wilson. Grad. asst. geology U. Ill., Champaign-Urbana, 1954-58, instr., 1958-59, asst. prof., 1959-64, asst. dean Coll. Liberal Arts and Scis., 1961-64, vis. lectr., 1966, 67; vis. lectr. Syracuse U., summer 1960; vis. scientist Am. Geol. Inst., 1961, 62; Ellis L. Phillips Found. intern acad. adminstrn. U. Cal. at Riverside, 1962-63; asso. dean, asso. prof. geology Coll. of Wooster, 1964-67, acting dean, 1967-68, dean, v.p. for acad. affairs, prof. geology, 1968—. Fellow Geol. Soc. Am., A.A.A.S.; mem. Am. Assn. Petroleum Geologists, Soc. Econ. Paleontologists and Mineralogists, Am. Assn. Higher Edn., Ohio Acad. Sci., No. Ohio Geol. Soc., Sigma Xi, Phi Kappa Phi. Presbyn. (deacon 1966-68, elder 1969—). Rotarian (dir. 1970). Contbr. articles profl. jours. Home: 1042 Ashwood Dr Wooster OH 44691

CROSBIE, STANLEY BLANDFORD, physician, hosp. adminstr.; b. Mpls., May 12, 1906; s. William and Eva (Blandford) C.; student Carleton Coll., 1924-26; B.A., U. Minn., 1936, M.D., 1941; m. Helen Blair, Dec. 20, 1937; 1 dau., Joan. Intern Jersey City Med. Center, 1941-42; resident psychiatry Hudson River State Hosp., Poughkeepsie, N.Y., 1942-43; resident medicine VA Hosp., Mpls., 1946-47; practice medicine, specializing in gastroenterology, Alburquerque, 1947- 49, Grand Junction, Colo., 1949-59, Mpls., 1959-62, Dearborn, Mich., 1962-65; chief gastro-intestinal service VA Hosp., Albuquerque, 1947-49; chief med. service VA Hosp., Grand Junction, 1949-59; dir. profl. services VA Hosp., Mpls., 1959-62; dir. VA Hosp., Dearborn, 1962-65, Denver, 1965-70, Phoenix, 1970—; asst. prof. medicine U. Minn., 1959-62, asst. dean Med. Sch., 1959-62; asso. prof. Wayne State U., 1963-65; asso. prof. medicine U. Colo., 1966-70. Served to maj. M.C., AUS, 1943-46. Fellow A.C.P.; mem. Am. Hosp. Assn., A.M.A., Chi Psi. Home: 1919 E Claremont St Phoenix AZ 85016

CROSBY, BING, (Harry Lillis), actor; b. Tacoma, Wash., May 2, 1904; s. Harry Lowe and Catherine C.; student Gonzaga U., Spokane, Washington, 1914-24, Ph.D. (hon.), 1937; m. Wilma W. Wyatt, Sept. 29, 1930 (dec. 1952); children—Gary Evan, Dennis Michael, Philip Lang, Howard Lindsay; married 2d, Olive Grandstaff (Kathryn Grant), Oct. 24, 1957; children—Harry Lillis III, Mary Frances and Nathaniel Patrick. Began career as a singer with dance bands, 1925-30; broadcasting with Columbia System, 1931-35, NBC 1936-57; with A.B.C. 1947-49; Columbia since 1950; screen actor with Paramount Prodn., Inc., since 1931; among picture titles: Here Is My Heart, Pennies From Heaven, The Road To Singapore, Road to Zanzibar, Birth of the Blues, Holiday Inn, Road to Morocco, Star Spangled Rhythm, Going My Way, Bells of St. Mary's, Welcome Stranger, Blue Skies, Road to Rio, The Emperor Waltz, Mr. Music, Here Comes the Groom, Little Boy Lost, White Christmas, Country Girl, Anything Goes, Stage Coach. Pres. Bing Crosby Ltd. Roman Catholic. Clubs: Lakeside Golf, Bel-Air Country, Friars (N.Y.C.). Office: 780 N Gower St Los Angeles CA 90038

CROSBY, EDWIN L., assn. exec.; b. Rochester, N.Y., Aug. 18, 1908; s. Edwin Lorenzo and Alice H. (Hammond) C.; A.B., Union Coll., 1929; M.D., Albany Med. Coll., 1933; M.P.H., Johns Hopkins, 1936. D.P.H., 1937; D.Sc. (hon.) Union Coll., N.Y., 1955; m. Harriett O. O'Neil, May 20, 1930; children—Ruth, Ann, Sue. With N.Y. State Dept. of Health, Albany, 1935- 39; Johns Hopkins U., 1937-52, asst. prof. biostatistics and preventive medicine adj. prof. pub. health adminstrn., Johns Hopkins Hosp., dir., 1946-52; dir. Joint Commn. on Accreditation of Hosps., 1952-54; pres. Nat. Intern Matching Plan; pres. Adv. Bd. for Med. Spltys. 1960-63; exec. pres. Am. Hosp. Assn., Chgo. Mem. adv. bd. Salvation Army. Diplomate Am. Bd. of Preventive Medicine and Pub. Health. Fellow Am. Pub. Health Assn., Am. Coll. Hosp. Adminstrs., A.M.A.; mem. Am. Hosp. Assn. (pres. 1952-53), Internat. Hosp. Fedn. (pres. 1953-67), Nat. Health Council (pres. 1964). Contbr. to hosp. and med. jours. Home: Box 10 Winnetka IL 60093 Office: Am Hosp Assn 840 N Lake Shore Dr Chicago IL 60611

CROSBY, EVERETT NATHANIEL, personal bus. mgr.; b. Roslyn, Wash., Apr. 5, 1900; s. Harry L. and Catherine C. (Harrigan) C.; student Gonzaga U.; m. Florence George Guthrie, May 9, 1939; 1 dau., Mary Sue (Mrs. Charles D. Shannon, Jr.). Mgr., Bing Crosby, 1929—; pres. Bing Crosby Enterprises, Everett Crosby Prodns.; v.p. Northwest Leasing Corp.; dir. Astor Pictures, N.Y.C., Sprayfoil Corp., Mpls.; sec. Crosby Investment Co. Served with AEF, World War I. Address: care Bing Crosby Prodns 5451 Marathon Los Angeles CA 90062

CROSBY, HAROLD BRYAN, univ. pres.; b. Jacksonville, Fla., Sept. 21, 1918; s. Arthur Francis and Marie (Long) C.; student Northwestern U., 1934-35, 36-37; J.D., U. Fla., 1948; m. Margaret Frances Dutton, Apr. 18, 1939; children—Susan Frances, Anne Bryan. With Atlantic Coast R.R. Co., 1937-41; res. prof. law U. Fla. Coll. Law, 1948; admitted to Fla. bar, 1948; pvt. practice, Kissimmee and Pensacola, 1948-55; circuit judge 1st Jud. Circuit Fla., 1955-60; prof. law U. Fla., 1960-64, asst. dean Coll. Law, 1961-62, dean univ. relations and devel., 1962-64; pres. U. W. Fla., Pensacola, 1964- -. Dir. Fla. Trial Judges Seminar, 1960-61, 64; Southeastern dir. Joint Com. Effective Adminstrn. Justice, 1961-62; dir. Southeast Seminar State Trial Judges, 1962; mem. Nat. Conf. Commrs. Uniform State Laws, 1962- 64; cons. Fla. Constl. Adv. Commn., 1956-57; Fla. commr. to promote uniformity legislation, 1962-64; mem. com. standard jury instructions Supreme Ct. Fla., 1962-64; Mem. exec. com. Fla. Assn. Colls. and Univs. 1970; mem. commn. on colls. So. Assn. Colls. and Schs., 1969—; chmn. Assn. Upper Level Colls. and Univs., 1970. Chmn., 1969—. W. Fla. Natural Resources Council, 1969—. Trustee U. Fla. Law Rev., 1961, U. Fla. Law Center Assn., 1961; bd. dirs. U. Fla. Center, 1962-64. Served to maj. USAAF, 1942-45, USAF, 1951-53. Mem. Fla. Bar (bd. govs. 1950-52, pres. jr. bar sect. 1951-52), Am. Bar Assn. (Fla. chmn. jud. bar sect. 1951), Order of Coif, Fla. Blue Key, Theta Xi, Phi Alpha Delta, Phi Kappa Phi. Methodist (trustee, past mem. ofcl. bd.). Contbr. articles legal jours. Home: 30 Rockwood Rd River Gardens Pensacola FL 32504

CROSBY, HARRY HERBERT, educator; b. New England, N.D., Apr. 18, 1919; s. Guy L. and Eva (McClellan) C.; B.A., U. Ia., 1941, M.A., 1947; Ph.D., Stanford, 1953; m. Jean E. Boehner, Apr. 11, 1943; children—Stephen, April, Jeffrey, Rebecca. Instr., U. Ia., 1946-47, 50-51; asst. instr. Stanford, 1947-50; instr. San Jose State Coll., 1950; asst. prof. U. Ia., 1951-58, writing supr., 1956-58; asso. prof. Boston U., 1958-59, prof. rhetoric, 1959—, chmn. div. communications Coll. Basic Studies, 1958-65, chmn. div. rhetoric, 1966—; dir. studies Pakistan Air Force Acad., Risalpur, West Pakistan, 1960-62. Cons. U.S. Air Force Acad., 1953-60. Mem. bd. aldermen, Newton, Mass., 1970—. Served to lt. col. USAAF, 1942-45. Decorated Air medal (Army), D.F.C. with 2 oak leaf clusters, Bronze Star medal (U.S.), Croix de Guerre (France). Mem. Modern Lang. Assn., Nat. Council Tchrs. English, Phi Eta Sigma (hon.). Co-author: The McLuhan Explosion, 1968; College Writing, 1968; Just Rhetoric, 1971. Home: 48 Ruthven Rd Newton MA 02158 Office: Boston U Coll Basic Studies Boston MA 02215

CROSBY, JOHN CAMPBELL, columnist; b. Milw., May 18, 1912; s. Fred G. and Edna (Campbell) C.; grad. Phillips Exeter Acad., student Yale, 1931-33; m. Mary B. Wolferth, Dec. 7, 1946 (div.); children—Michael Wolferth, Margaret; m. 2d, Katharine J. B. Wood, Dec. 1, 1964; one son, Alexander. Began career as reporter Milw. (Wis.) Sentinel, 1933; reporter N.Y. Herald Tribune, 1935-41; syndicated columnist 1946-65; columnist The Observer, London, Eng., 1965—. Served with AUS, 1941-46. George Foster Peabody Award, George K. Polk Meml. Award. Author: Out of the Blue, 1952; With Love and Loathing, 1963; Sappho In Absence, 1969. Home: Woodbourne Cottage Hempstead Norris Newbury Berkshire England

CROSBY, JOHN O'HEA, conductor, opera mgr.; b. N.Y.C., July 12, 1926; s. Laurence Alden and Aileen Mary (O'Hea) C.; grad. Hotchkiss Sch., 1944; B.A., Yale, 1950; Litt.D., U. N.M., Mus. D., Coll. of Santa Fe (N.M.), 1968. Accompanist, opera coach, conductor, N.Y.C., 1951-56; gen. dir., mem. conducting staff Santa Fe Opera, 1957—; conductor U.S. stage premiere Daphne, 1964, world premiere Wuthering Heights, 1958. Served with inf. AUS, 1945-46; ETO. Roman Catholic. Clubs: Metropolitan Opera, University (N.Y.C.). Home: PO Box 333 Santa Fe NM 87501 Office: PO Box 2408 Santa Fe NM 87501

CROSBY, JOSEPH WILLIAM, chem. co. exec.; b. Toronto, Can., 1896; ed. U. Toronto; married. Lab. asst., asst. mgr. planning dept., mgr. devel. dept. Gutta Percha & Rubber Ltd., Toronto, 1919-36; with Thickol Chem. Corp., Bristol, Pa., 1936—, pres., 1944-64, chmn. bd., chief exec. officer, 1964-70, chmn. exec. com., dir., 1970—; dir. Nat. Beryllia Corp. Home: Effingham Rd Morrisville PA 19067 Office: Thiokol Chem Corp Box 27 Bristol PA 19007*

CROSBY, KATHRYN GRANT, actress; m. Bing Crosby, Oct. 24, 1957; children—Harry Lillis III, Mary Frances, Nathaniel Patrick. Numerous appearances on stage and with stock companies. Address: 170 N Robertson Blvd Beverly Hills CA 90211*

CROSBY, LAURENCE ALDEN, sugar corp. exec., atty.; b. Bangor, Me., Dec. 20, 1892; s. James and Emily (Alden) C.; B.A., Bowdoin Coll., 1913; B.A., Oxford (Eng.) U., 1915; B.C.L., 1916, M.A., 1919; LL.B., Columbia, 1917; m. Aileen Mary O'Hea, Sept. 5, 1923; children—James O'Hea, John O'Hea. Admitted to N.Y. bar, 1917; enlisted in U.S. Army, 1917, 1st lt., 1919; engaged in practice of law, N.Y.C., 1919-46; mem. law firm Sullivan & Cromwell, 1927-46; pres. Central Violeta Sugar Co., 1936-58, Cuban Atlantic Sugar Co., 1937-59, vice chmn. Atlantic del. Golfo Sugar Co., 1959—. Chmn. U.S. Cuban Sugar Council, 1954-60. Decorated comdr. Cuban Order Carlos Manuel de Cespedes; Grand Cross Cuban Order Agrl. Ind. Merit. Mem. N.Y.C. Bar Assn., Am. C. of C. of Cuba (pres. 1949-53). Roman Catholic. Clubs: Down Town Assn. (N.Y.C.); Havana Yacht, Havana Country. Author: (with Frank Aydelotte) Oxford of Today, 1922 (2d edit. with Frank Aydelotte and Alan Valentine), 1927. Home: Box 333 Santa Fe NM 87501

CROSBY, LUCIUS OSMOND, Jr., corp. exec.; b. Bogue Chitto, Miss., Oct. 6, 1907; s. Lucius Olen and Margaret Henrietta (Reed) C.; grad. Jefferson Mil. Coll., Washington, Miss., 1926; B.S. in Commerce, U. Miss., 1931; m. Dorothy Frances Hagert, Oct. 6, 1935; children—Dorothy Lynn (Mrs. Lynn Crosby Gammill), Lucius Osmond III. Employee relief adminstr. and farm mgr. Goodyear Yellow Pine Co., Picayune, Miss., 1931-33, personnel and farm mgr., 1934-35; v.p. in charge sales and mfg. Crosby Lumber & Mfg. Co., 1936-41, v.p., dir., 1936-66; pres., gen. mgr. Crosby Forest Products Co., Picayune, 1941—. also dir.; chmn., dir. Pearl River Valley R.R. Co. Pres. Pine Burr Area council Boy Scouts, 1955-57, exec. bd. nat. council, regional chmn., 1958-62, chmn. nat. com. on exploring, 1963-69; past dir. state, local YMCA; past dir. So. States Indsl. Council. Chmn. 6th Congl. Dist., Miss. Citizens for Eisenhower Commn., 1957; mayor, City Picayune, 1957-61. Past trustee New Orleans Bapt. Theol. Sem. Recipient citizen of year award, Picayune, 1948; Man of the Year in Tung award, 1960; Silver Beaver, Silver Antelope, Silver Buffalo awards Boy Scouts Am. Mem. N.A.M. (past dir.), Am. Tung Oil Assn., Tung Oil Research and Devel. League (dir.), Miss. Forestry Assn. (v.p. 1950-58), Nat. Tung Oil Marketing Coop. (dir.), Pan-Am, Tung Research and Devel. League (pres. 1964-67), Sigma Chi. Baptist. Mason. Home: 1630 3d Av Picayune MS 39466 Office: 200 S Crosby St Picayune MS 39466

CROSBY, RALPH WILLIS, mining co. exec.; b. Waverley, N.S., Can., Nov. 8, 1902; s. Harold L. and Lillian L. (Auld) C.; B.Sc. in Mining Engring., Tex. Sch. Mines, 1924; m. Flora E. Colbath, Oct. 1, 1929; 1 son, James C. Engr., Benguer Consol. Mining Co., Antamok, Philippines, 1925-27; gen. supt. Balatoc Mining Co. (Philippines), 1927-30; mines supt. Itogon Mining Co., Sangilo, Philippines, 1930-33; gen. supt. Suyoc Consol. Mining Co. (Philippines), 1933-36; gen. mgr. No. div. Marsman & Co., Inc., Baguio- Manila, Philippines, 1936-41, supr. engr. 1945-48; with Benguet Consol., Inc., Baguio, Philippines, 1948—, pres., 1962—, also chmn. Interned Santo Tomas U., Manila, 1942-45. Mem. Am. Inst. Mining, and Metall. Engrs., Philippine Soc. Mining, Metall. and Geol. Engrs. Address: P O Box 817 Myers Bldg Portaera Manila Philippines

CROSBY, SUMNER MCKNIGHT, educator; b. Mpls., July 29, 1909; s. Franklin Muzzy and Harriet (McKnight) C.; student Blake Sch., Hopkins, Minn., 1916-26; student Phillips Acad., Andover, Mass., 1926-28; A.B., Yale, 1932, Ph.D., 1937; student Ecole des Chartes, Paris, France, 1934-35; A.F.D. (hon.), Mpls. Sch. Art, 1965; m. Sarah Rathbone Townsend, Oct. 19, 1935; children—Sumner McKnight, William F., Frederick T., Gerrit L. Instr. Yale, 1936-40, asst. prof. history of art, 1940-43, 1945-47, asso. prof., 1947-52, prof., 1952—, chmn. dept. history art, 1947-53, 62-65, excavated in Abbey Ch. St. Denis, north of Paris, summers 1938, 39, 46, 47, 48, 67, 68, 69; curator Art Gallery, 1946—; fellow Berkeley Coll., Yale, 1939—. Dir. The Crosby Co. Vis. com. fine arts Harvard, 1959-65; member visiting com. dept. art and archaeology Princeton, 1962-68. Dir. Internat. Center Romanesque Art, 1956—, pres., 1965-68; mem. internat. com. history art, 1950—. Trustee Am. Fedn. Arts, 1940-45, 49-50. Mem. Coll. Art Assn. (dir. 1939-45 and 1947-52, pres. 1940-44); exec. sec. Am. Council of Learned Socs. Com. on Preservation of Cultural Materials in War Areas, 1943-44; spl. adviser Am. Commn. for the Protection and Salvage of Artistic and Historic Monuments in War Areas, 1944-46; spl. adv. on Restitution of Cultural Materials, Dept. State, 1945. Recipient Guggenheim F. Decorated Chevalier Legion d'Honor. Mem. Medieval Acad. Am., Archaeol. Inst. Am. (trustee 1966-69), Société d'Archéologie Francaise, Soc. Nat. des Antiquaires de France, Alpha Delta Phi. Republican. Presbyn. Clubs: Century Assn., Yale (N.Y. City); Walton Fishing (Cornwall Bridge, Conn.); Elizabethan, Wolf's Head of Yale. Author: Abbey of St. Denis I, 1942; L'Abbaye Royale de Saint- Denis, 1952; The Apostle Bas-Relief at Saint-Denis, 1972. Mem. bd. Speculum, 1946-54. Editor: Art Through the Ages, 1959; Religious Art in France Thirteenth Century; Corpus Vitreanum Medii Aevi. Mem. editorial bd. Art Bull. Home: Fairgrounds Rd Woodbridge CT 06525 Office: Yale Art Gallery New Haven CT 06707

CROSBY, THOMAS M., financier; b. Mpls., Oct. 29, 1914; s. F.M. and Harriet (McKnight) C; grad. Phillips Acad., 1933; A.B., Yale, 1937; m. Ella Pillsbury, July 31, 1937; children—Thomas M., David P., Eleanor L., Mary E., Lucy S., Robert F. With Gen. Mills, 1939-60, dir., 1960—; now pres. Northwest Growth Fund; v.p. Crosby Co., 1960—, also dir.; dir. Northwest Bancorp., Northwestern Nat. Life Ins. Co. Chmn., Community Chest Drive, 1960. Trustee Blake Sch., Dunwoody Indsl. Mpls. Found. Served as 1st lt. USMC, 1942-45. Decorated Bronze Star. Presbyn. (trustee). Clubs: Minneapolis; Woodhill Country (Wayzata, Minn.). Home: 745 Spring Hill Rd Wayzata MN 55391 Office: Northwestern Bank Bldg Minneapolis MN 55402

CROSBY, WILLIAM HOLMES, Jr., medical educator; b. Wheeling, W.Va., Dec. 1, 1914; s. William Holmes and Frances Irene (Forrester) C.; A.B., U. Pa., 1936, M.D., 1940; m. Naomi Ruth Benjamin, Feb. 8, 1959; children—Holmes, John, Mary (Mrs. Douglas Blankinship), Seth, David, Susanna, Jonathan. Intern Walter Reed Hosp., Washington, 1940, chief hematology, 1951-65; med. specialist Queen Alexandra Mil. Hosp., London, Eng., 1950; prof. medicine, chief hematology Tufts-New Eng. Med. Center, 1965—; cons. in field. Bd. dirs. Blood Research Found., Nat. Hemophilia Found., Internat. Com. Standardization in Hematology. Served with U.S. Army, 1940-65. Decorated Legion of Merit, Bronze Star, Combat Med. Badge. Decorated Order Carlos J. Finlay (Cuba); recipient Stitt award, 1964, McCollum award, 1970. Mem. A.C.P.,

A.A.A.S., Am. Fedn. Clin. Research, A.M.A., Am. Soc. Hematology, Am. Soc. Clin. Investigation, Assn. Mil. Surgeons, Assn. Am. Physicians, Internat. Soc. Hematology, Soc. Exptl. Biology and Medicine. Editorial bd. Archives of Internal Medicine, 1965—, Transfusion, 1960—. Contbr. articles profl. jours. Patentee gastroenterologic instruments. Home: 4 Woodcliff Rd Wellesley MA 02181 Office: 171 Harrison Av Boston MA 02111

CROSEN, ROBERT GLENN, ret. educator; b. Maitland, Mo., Mar. 12, 1900; s. John Ulysses and Sarah Elizabeth (Mitchell) C.; B.S., Tarkio Coll. (Mo.), 1923; M.A., U. S.D., 1925, Ph.D., Columbia, 1933; m. Alice Gwendolyn Stevenson, Aug. 29, 1925; children—Mary Alice (Mrs. Keith V. Michael), Robert Glenn, Sarah E. (Mrs. Richard Bonello). Asst. in chemistry U. S.D., 1923-25, instr. chemistry, 1925-28; instr. chemistry Columbia Extension Div., 1930-31; instr. chemistry Lafayette Coll., 1931-34, asst. prof. chemistry, 1934-38, asso. prof. 1938-57, acting dean, 1941-43, dean, 1943-46, dean of faculty, 1946-57; head dept. chemistry Abadam (Iran) Inst. Tech., 1957-62, acting pres., 1961-62; prof. chemistry Sterling (Kan.) Coll., 1962-70, also chmn. dept., prof. emeritus, 1970—. Past chmn. dirs. Easton Family Service Assn.; past pres. trustees Easton Community Chest. J. Packard Laird fellow for cancer research Columbia, 1929-30. Mem. Kan. Acad. Sci., Am. Chem. Soc., Sigma Xi, Alpha Phi Omega, Phi Lambda Upsilon, Kappa Delta Rho (nat. pres. 1953-55). Republican. Presbyn. Mason, Rotarian. Contbr. articles to sci. jours. Home: 718 N 6th St RD 2 Sterling KS 67579

CROSLAND, CHARLES ANTHONY RAVEN, Brit. govt. ofcl.; b. St. Leonards-on-Sea, Sussex, Eng., Aug. 29, 1918; s. Joseph Beardsell and Jessie (Raven) C.; M.A. with First Class Honours in Modern Greats, Trinity Coll., Oxford U., 1946; m. Hilary Anne Sarson, 1952 (marriage dissolved 1957); m. 2d, Mrs. Susan Catling, 1964. Fellow, lectr. econs., also jr. dean Trinity Coll., 1947-50; mem. Parliament for S. Gloucestershire, 1950-55, for Grimsby, 1959—; sec. Ind. Commn. Inquiry into Coop. Movement, 1956-58; minister of state for econ. affairs, 1964-65; sec. of state for sci. and edn., 1965-67; pres. Bd. of Trade, 1967-69; sec. state for local govt. and regional planning, 1969—. Mem. exec. com. Fabian Soc., 1947-53, chmn., 1961-62; mem. council Consumers Assn., 1952—. Served with British Army, 1939-45. Mem. Labour Party. Author: Britain's Economic Problem, 1953; The Future of Socialism, 1956; The Conservative Enemy, 1962. Contbr. various publs. Home: 37 Lansdowne Rd London W 11 England Office: House of Commons London England

CROSLAND, DOROTHY MURRAY (Mrs. James Henley Crosland), librarian; b. Stone Mountain, Ga., Sept. 13, 1903; d. Robert and Lena (Jones) Murray; certificate library sci., Emory U., 1923; m. James Henley Crosland, Aug. 18, 1928; 1 dau., Dorothy Evelyn. In catalog dept. Carnegie Library of Atlanta, 1923-25; asst. Ga. Inst. Tech. library, 1925-27, librarian, 1927-52, dir. libraries, 1953—. Chief investigator NSF grant for study-feasibility tng. sci. information specialists, 1961-62. Trustee Atlanta Art Assn., 1956-62. Mem. A.I.M. Nat. Assn. Cost Accountants, Am. Documentation Inst., Ga. Edn. Assn., A.L.A., Assn. Coll. and Research Libraries, S.E. (pres. 1952-54), and Ga. (pres. 1949-51) library assns., Emory U. Library Grads. Assn. (pres. 1929), Spl. Libraries Assn., Am. Assn. Textile Chemists and Colorists, Am. Chem. Soc., Am. Foundrymens Assn., Am. Soc. Engring. Edn., Internat. Assn. Tech. Univ. Libraries (U.S. rep.), Hwy. Research Bd., NRC. Named Atlanta's Woman of Year in Edn., 1945. Democrat. Presbyn. Club: Library (pres. 1937-38) (Atlanta). Contbr. articles profl. jours. 125 Lakeview Av N E Atlanta, GA 30305. Office: Georgia Inst of Technology Atlanta GA 30332

CROSLAND, EDWARD BURTON, telephone co. exec.; b. Montgomery, Ala., Jan. 6, 1912; s. David Woolley and Virginia (Burton) C.; student U. of South, 1930-32; J.D., U. Ala., 1935; m. Helen Burns, Oct. 21, 1939; children—Edward Burton, Lucien Burns. Admitted to Ala. bar, 1935, practiced in Montgomery, 1935-38; asst. atty. gen., chief div. local finance State of Ala., 1938-42; atty. So. Bell Tel. & Tel. Co., Atlanta, 1946, gen. atty., 1949; asst. v.p., atty. Am. Tel. & Tel. Co., Washington, 1952-55, asst. to pres., N.Y.C., 1955-58, v.p., 1958—; dir., former chmn. bd. Fed. Home Loan Bank of N.Y.; dir. Chesapeake & Potomac Telephone Co. Va., South Central Bell Telephone Co. Former trustee Overlook Hosp., Summit, N.J. Served as lt. col. Judge Adv. Gen. Dept., AUS, 1942-46. Decorated Legion of Merit. Mem. Am., Ala., Ga. bar assns., Mil. Order World Wars, Res. Officers Assn. U.S., Armed Forces Communications Assn., N.Y. So. Soc., Kappa Sigma, Phi Delta Phi, Omicron Delta Kappa. Clubs: Army-Navy Country, Burning Tree, Metropolitan, Carlton (Washington); Baltusrol Golf (Springfield, N.J.); Short Hills (N.J.); Chevy Chase (Md.). Home: 9012 Belmart Rd Potomac MD 20854 Office: 195 Broadway New York City NY 10007

CROSON, J.M., savs. and loan assn. exec. Pres., First Fed. Savs. and Loan Assn., Orlando, Fla. Office: 145 Magnolia Av Orlando FL 32802*

CROSS, BERT S., mfg. co. exec.; b. Superior, Wis., Oct. 16, 1905; s. Herbert Mills and Grace (Smith) C.; student U. Minn., 1924-29; m. Bernice Fischer, Aug. 20, 1927. Exec. v.p., dir. Minn. Mining & Mfg. Co., 1957-63, pres., chief exec. officer, 1963-66, chmn. bd., chief exec. officer, 1966-70, chmn. finance com., 1970—, also dir.; dir. First Nat. Bank, St. Paul Ins. Cos., Northwestern Bell Tel. Co., Standard Oil Co., N.J., Dow Jones; mem. internat. adv. council Morgan Guaranty Trust Co. N.Y. Mem. Business Council. Trustee Mayo Found. Presbyn. Mason (K.T., Shriner), Clubs: White Bear Yacht, St. Paul Athletic, Minnesota (St. Paul); Tucson Nat. Golf. Home: Pine Tree Hills Dellwood MN 55115 Office: 3 M Co 3 M Center St Paul MN 55101

CROSS, CHARLES TENNEY, ambassador to Singapore; b. Peiping, China, May 4, 1922; s. Rowland McLean and Adelie Louise (Tenney) C.; B.A. cum laude, Carleton Coll., 1947; student Advanced Internat. Studies, Washington, summer 1947; M.A. in Far Eastern Studies and Internat. Relations, Yale, 1949; m. Shirley Annette Foss, Jan. 12, 1946; children—Ann C., Kathleen A., Richard T. Joined U.S. Fgn. Service, 1949; asst. pub. affairs officer, Hong Kong, 1952-54; consul, Kuala Lumpur, Malaya, 1955-57, Alexandria, Egypt, 1957-59; officer-in-charge Burma affairs State Dept., 1959-61, Laos affairs, 1961-63; counselor of embassy, Nicosia, Cyprus, 1964-66; polit. officer Am. embassy, London, 1966-67; dep. to comdg. gen. III Marine Amphibious force for Pacification Programs Vietnam, 1967-69; U.S. ambassador to Singapore, 1969—. Mem. U.S. delegation Laos Conf., 1961-62. Served to 1st lt. USMCR, 1942-46. Decorated Bronze Star. Address: care American Embassy Singapore Malaysia

CROSS, CLAUDE B., lawyer; b. Enterprise, Miss., Oct. 22, 1893; s. John Clifton and Mary Elizabeth (Killam) C.; A.B., U. Mo., 1914; A.M., Harvard, 1915, LL.B., 1920, J.D., 1969; Dr. Juridical Sci., Suffolk U., 1970; m. Jeannette MacDonald, Apr. 9, 1921. Asst., Office of Pres. N.Y. Central Lines, 1920-21; admitted to Mass. bar, 1922; trial work with Sherman L. Whipple, Boston, 1921-30; sr. partner Withington, Cross, Proctor & Park, and successor firms, now Withington, Cross, Park & Groden, Boston, 1931—. Chmn. Mass. chpt. Multiple Sclerosis, 1954-56, now hon. chmn. Trustee Newton Theol. Sch., New Eng. Baptist Hosp.; adminstrv. com. Andover-Newton Theol. Sch. Served from 2d lt. to capt., 7th F.A., 1st Div., U.S. Army, 1917-19. Fellow Am. Bar Found., Am. Coll. Trial Lawyers; mem. Am. Law Inst., Am., Mass., Boston (pres. assns. Baptist (deacon). Club: Country (Brookline). Home: 255 Dudley St Brookline MA 02146 Office: 73 Tremont St Boston MA 02108

CROSS, EASON, Jr., architect; b. Bisbee, Ariz., Nov. 14, 1925; s. Eason and Olive (Hardwick) C.; B.A., Harvard, 1949, M.Arch., 1951; m. Diana Johnson, June 17, 1950; children—Ben, Becca, Amy, Susan. With Prentiss Huddleston & Assos., Tallahassee, Fla., 1950-51, W.D. Compton, Cambridge, Mass., 1951-52, Deigert & Yerkes, Washington, 1952; asso. Charles M. Goodman, Washington, 1952-59, Keyes, Lethbridge & Condon, 1959-61; partner Cross & Adreon, Washington, 1961—; spl. instr. George Washington U., 1964-65. Dir. Hollin Hills Community Assn.; v.p. Hollin Hills Recreation Assn.; mem. Hollin Hills Archtl. Review Bd. Served with USNR, World War II. Recipient Ware prize, 1950, Washington Bd. Trade design award, 1965, Bethesda-Chevy Chase C. of C. design awards, 1966, 67; house and home awards A.I.A., 1965-66, Mid-Atlantic design awards, 1967, 69, nat. honor award, 1968; nat. honor award Am. Inst. Steel Constrn., 1967, 4 H.U.D. awards Washington Center Urban Studies furniture competition, 1971. Mem. A.I.A., Washington Bd. Trade, Fairfax County C. of C. Democrat. Unitarian. Clubs: Harvard, Sierra, Fox; Hasty Pudding, Institute of 1770 (Harvard). Patentee fastenings and furniture. Home: 2309 Glasgow Rd Alexandria VA 22307 Office: 901 27th St NW Washington DC 20037

CROSS, EDWARD BROWN, univ. med. center ofcl.; b. Forrest City, Ark., Feb. 11, 1922; s. John H. and Margia A. (Brown) C.; B.A., Philander C. Smith Coll., 1943; student Columbia, 1946-47; B.S., Howard U., 1948, M.D., 1952; m. Abbye E. Riley, Dec. 21, 1947; children—Zina C., Analisa, Rona M. Intern USPHS, 1952-53, resident, 1953-58, health services officer, 1958-62; med. dir. Peace Corps, Ethiopia, 1962-64; health service officer USPHS, 1964-68; dir. Office of Health and Med. Care, Dept. Health, Edn. and Welfare, 1968-70; retired from USPHS as asst. surgeon gen., 1970; vice provost for health scis. U. Mo. at Kansas City, 1970—; med. adv. Ethiopian Imperial Ct. Physician, 1962-64; asso. prof. medicine Howard U. Med. Sch., 1966—. Pres. South West Tri-Sch. Dist. PTA 1969-70; mem. Southwest Neighborhood Assembly, Washington, 1966-70; mem. President's Com. Employment Handicapped, 1968-70; mem. gov. council D.C. Pub. Health Assn., 1969-70. Bd. dirs. Health Resources Inst. Kansas City, Mo.; exec. com. Kansas City Gen. Hosp. Served with AUS, 1942-45. Diplomate Am. Bd. Internal Medicine. Fellow Am. Coll. Cardiology; mem. Omega Psi Phi. Methodist (trustee 1965-70). Home: 2608 W 67th St Shawnee Mission KS 66208

CROSS, FRANK MOORE, Jr., educator; b. Ross, Cal., July 13, 1921; s. Frank Moore and Mary (Ellison) C.; A.B. Maryville Coll., 1942, Litt.D., 1968; B.D. McCormick Theol. Sem., 1946; Ph.D., Johns Hopkins 1950; M.A. (hon.), Harvard, 1957; m. Elizabeth A. Showalter, June 20, 1947; children—Susan E., Ellen M., Priscilla Rachel. Nettie McCormick fellow Johns Hopkins, 1946-48; Rayner fellow in semitics, jr. instr. Johns Hopkins, 1949-50; vis. instr. McCormick Theol. Sem., 1948-49; Kent fellow Nat. Council Religion in Higher Edn. Johns Hopkins, 1949-50; instr. bibl. history Wellesley Coll., 1950-51; instr. McCormick Theol. Sem., 1951-53, asst. prof., 1954-55, asso. prof., 1955-57; asso. prof. of O. T., Harvard Div. Sch., 1957-58, Hancock prof. Hebrew and other oriental langs. Coll. Arts and Scis., Harvard, 1957—, also curator Semitic Mus., 1958-61, chmn. dept. neareastern langs., 1958-65; ann. prof. Am. Sch. Oriental Research, Jerusalem, 1953-54; Haskell lectr. Oberlin Grad. Sch. Theology, 1957; Jeffrey lectr. Goucher Coll., Balt., 1958; vis. scholar Univ. Center, Ga., 1957, Richmond (Va.) U. Center; Alumni lectr. Eden Theol. Sem.; Rushton lectr. Samford U., 1967. Mem. Internat. staff for editing Dead Sea Scrolls, 1953—; co-dir. archaeol. expdn. to Judaean Buqeiah, 1955; archaeol. dir. Hebrew Union Coll., Jerusalem, 1963-64; v.p. Albright Inst. Archaeol. Research, 1970—. Fellow Am. Acad. Arts and Scis.; mem. Am. Philos. Soc., Am. Oriental Soc., Soc. Bibl. Lit., Bibl. Colloquium, Phi Beta Kappa. Author: (with David N. Freedman) Early Hebrew Orthography, 1952; The Ancient Library of Qumran, 1958; Studies in Ancient Yahwistic Poetry, 1964. Editor: Scrolls from the Wilderness of the Dead Sea, 1965; co-editor: The Biblical Archaeologist, 1952-59. mem. editorial bd., 1959—; asso. editor Harvard Theol. Rev., 1963—, Bull. of Am. Schs. Oriental Research, 1969—. Contbr. articles for profl. jours. Home: 31 Woodland Rd Lexington MA 12173 Office: 6 Divinity Av Cambridge MA 02138

CROSS, GEORGE LYNN, former univ. pres.; b. Woonsocket, S.D., May 12, 1905; s. George Jemima (Dawson) C.; B.S., S.D. State Coll., 1926, M.S., 1927, D.Sc., 1960; Ph.D., U. Chgo., 1929; LL.D., Oberlin Coll., 1960; m. Cleo Sikkink, Oct. 28, 1926; children—Mary Lynn, George W., Braden Rieh. Instr. botany U. S.D., 1930-34; prof. botany U. Okla., 1934-38, head dept. botany, 1939-42, acting dean Grad. Coll., 1942-44, acting dir. Research Inst., 1942-44, pres. univ., 1944-68, emeritus, 1968—; pres. Okla. Health Scis. Found., 1968—. Chmn. Fed. Home Loan Bank Topeka, 1960-68; chmn. bd. Am. Exchange Bank, Norman, Okla.; dir. Friendly Nat. Bank, Oklahoma City. Public panel mem. 8th Dist. War Labor Bd., 1942. Mem. bd. of univ. presidents William Rockhill Nelson Trust, Kansas City, Mo.; exec. council U. Okla. Research Inst., research com. Okla. Med. Research Found.; dir. Midwest Research Inst. Elector N.Y.U. A.A.A.S.; mem. Fed. Home Loan Bank Bd. (mem. fed. savs. and loan adv. council, 1959), Nat. Assn. State Univs. (pres. 1959-60), Assn. Sci. U. Profs., Nat. Farm Chemurgic Council, Torrey Bot. Club, Bot. Soc. Am., N.E.A., Okla. Acad. Sci., Nat. Geog. Soc., Am. Soc. Naturalists, Okla. Hist. Soc., Norman C. of C., Newcomen Soc., Phi Beta Kappa, Phi Sigma, Alpha Phi Omega. Presbyn. Home: 812 Mockingbird Lane Norman, OK 73069.

CROSS, GEORGE R., ins. co. exec.; b. N.Y.C., May 9, 1923; s. George W. and Mae E. (Fish) C.; A.B., Syracuse U., 1947; J.D., Bklyn. Law Sch., 1951; C.P.C.U., 1960; m. Shirley Jean Williams, June 24, 1950; children—Stephen, Pamela, Jeffrey, Mark. Admitted to N.Y. bar, 1952, U.S. Supreme Ct., 1958; with Atlantic Mut. Ins. Co., 1947-49, adjuster, 1949-52; asst. gen. counsel Nat. Assn. Ins. Agts., 1952-59; with Gt. Am. Ins. Co., N.Y.C., 1959-70, gen. atty., 1963-68, v.p., 1967-70, gen. counsel, 1968-70, sec., 1963-67, 68-70; v.p., asso. gen. counsel Crum & Forster Ins. Cos., N.Y.C., 1970—, also dir., sec. Served to 1st lt. USAAF, 1943-45: ETO. Mem. Am. Arbitration Assn., N.Y. Bar Assn., New York County Lawyers Assn. Home: 23 Terrace Av Nanuet NY 10954 Office: 110 William St New York City NY 10038

CROSS, GORDON BISMARCK, coll. pres.; b. Beaver Harbor, N.B., Can., Jan. 30, 1911; s. John Franklin and Myra Brooks (Barteau) C.; brought to U.S., 1911, naturalized, 1929; B.S., Bates Coll., 1931; M.B.A., U. Miami, 1951; Ph.D., N.Y. U., 1956; m. Mary Louise Martin, July 10, 1935 (div. 1950); 1 son, John Douglas; m. 2d, Helen Stark, Sept. 3, 1954 (div. 1965); 1 dau., Melissa Betsy; m. 3d, Evelyn Mae Bradbury, June 24, 1966. Asst. prin. Brigham Acad., Bakersfield, Vt., 1931-32; mgmt. tng. S.S. Kresge Co. 1935-41; div. merchandiser Montgomery Ward & Co., 1941-42; with Vets. Canteen Service, Va, 1946-47; merchandising div. May Dept. Stores, 1947-49; instr. U. Miami, 1949-51; store mgr. Winn-Dixie, Inc., 1951-52; from instr. to asso. prof. N.Y.U., 1952-59; dean Sch. Bus. Adminstrn., U. Hartford (Conn.), 1959-66, acting provost, 1964-65; pres. Nichols Coll., Dudley, Mass., 1966—; retailing cons., 1952—. Overseer Old Sturbridge Village, 1971—. Served from lt. (j.g.) to comdr. USNR, 1942-46; comdr. Res. ret. Recipient Founders award N.Y. U., 1956. Mem. Eta Mu Pi, Delta Mu Delta. Asst. contbg. editor Jour. Retailing, 1952-59. Home: Dudley Hill Dudley MA 01570

CROSS, HENRY ALLEN, Jr., educator, exptl. psychologist; b. Oklahoma City, Mar. 11, 1927; s. Henry Allen and Corlis (Scott) C.; B.A., Bethany (Okla.) Nazarene Coll., 1949; M.S., U. Okla., 1951; Ph.D., Ohio State U., 1959; m. Elizabeth Wynne Hale, Jan. 1, 1948; children—Connie Lee, Terri Beth, Thomas Henry. Research asso. Primate Lab., U. Wis., 1959-60, vis. scientist, summers 1962-65; asst. prof. No. Ill. U., 1960-61; asso. prof. Okla. State U., 1961-64, Tex. Tech. Coll., 1964-66; prof. psychology, chmn. dept. Wittenberg U., Springfield, O., 1966-69, univ. coordinator, 1967-67; prof. psychology Colo. State U., Ft. Collins, 1969—. Served with USNR, 1945-46. Grantee Okla. State Research Found., 1961-64, Nat. Inst. Mental Health, 1963-64, NSF, 1966-67, 67. Wittenberg Faculty Fund, 1966-67. Mem. Am., Midwestern, Southwestern psychol. assns., Psychonomics Soc., A.A.A.S., Internat. Primatological Soc., Am. Assn. U. Profs., Sigma Xi. Contbr. profl. jours. Home: 1406 Peterson Fort Collins CO 80521

CROSS, HERSHNER, Mfg. co. exec.; b. Aiken, S.C., Jan. 20, 1916, s. Ernest S. and Abby Maye (Hershner) C.; A.B., Johns Hopkins, 1937; M.B.A., Harvard, 1939; m. Daphne Joensson, Aug. 26, 1939; children—Linda L. (Mrs. Grant G. Nugent), Marjorie M. (Mrs. Duncan McDougall), Nancy N. With Gen. Electric Co., 1946—, gen. mgr. Trumbull components dept., Plainville, Conn., 1953-54, gen. mgr. distbn. assemblies dept., 1954-56, with marketing services div., N.Y.C., 1956-59, gen. mgr.radio and TV div., DeWitt, N.Y., 1959-62, v.p., gen. mgr. div., N.Y.C., 1962-63, v.p., group exec. indsl. group, 1963-70, sr. v.p., 1970—; dir. Gen. Electric Broadcasting Corp., Gen. Electric Cablevision Corp.; chmn. Gen. Electric Pension Trust. Mem. bus. and industry adv. com. OECD. Mem. Episcopal Bd. Theol. Edn. Served to lt. col. AUS, 1940-46. Mem. N.A.M. (dir., chmn. marketing com.), Harvard Bus. Sch. Assn. (mem. exec. council, awards com.), Omicron Delta Kappa, Pi Delta Epsilon. Clubs: Randolph (N.H.) Mountain; Marco Polo (N.Y.C.). Home: 175 E 62d St New York NY 10021 Office: General Electric Co 570 Lexington Av New York NY 10022

CROSS, JAMES ADAM, clergyman, former coll. pres.; b. Crawfordsville, Fla., Dec. 12, 1911; s. William H. and Elizabeth A. (Walker) C.; grad. Ch. of God Bible Tng. Sch., 1932; A.A., Tenn. Temple Coll., 1948, U. Chattanooga, 1949; B.A., Lee Coll., 1948, D.D., 1967; m. Nellie McClure, Sept. 24, 1934; children—Marvin H., Allen H., Norman J. Licensed evangelist, 1933; ordained to ministry Ch. of God, 1936; pastor, Sanford, Fla., 1934-35, Lemmons, S.D., 1936, Lake Worth, Fla., 1938-40, Manatee, Fla., 1940-43, Tampa, Fla., 1943-44, Chattanooga, 1945-50; overseer, Neb., 1937-38, Pa., 1951-52, S.C., 1953-54; asst. gen. overseer Ch. of God, 1954-58, gen. overseer, 1958-62, also chmn. state overseer appointing bd., supreme council and ministers pension plan, 1958-62; state overseer Chs. of God in State of Fla., 1962-66, in Ala., 1970—; pres. Lee Coll., Cleveland, Tenn., 1966-70; treas. Pathway Mut. Ins. Co., Tampa, Fla., 1963-67. Adv. bd. World Pentecostal Fellowship, 1961-64, mem. supreme council; mem. commn. evangelism and ch. extension Nat. Assn. Evangelicals, 1957-67, mem. bd. adminstrn., 1954-57; mem. exec. council Ch. of God, 1968—, chmn. world missions bd., 1970—; overseer Chs. God Ala., 1971—. Chmn. bd. dirs. Ch. of God Orphanage, 1947-50, Lee Coll., 1952-54; bd. dirs. Appalachian Studies. Mem. Phi Delta Kappa, Phi Delta Omicron. Author: Glorious Gospel, 1956; Healing in the Church, 1962. Contbr. articles religious jours. Home: 5426 Bessemer Hwy Birmingham AL 35228

CROSS, JAMES ELIOT, corp. exec., educator; b. N.Y.C., Oct. 8, 1921; s. Eliot and Martha (McCook) C.; grad. Groton Sch., 1940; certificate Yale, 1943; LL.B., U. Va., 1948; m. Mary Eleanor Goelet, June 25, 1949; children—Sarah Willard, Eliot Goelet; m. 2d, Meredith Abell Morgan, Nov. 28, 1958; children—Rosalind Morgan, Daniel Carroll. With CIA, 1948-51; reseach asst. Inst. Advanced Study, Princeton, N.J., 1951-52; research asso. Center Internat. Studies, Mass. Inst. Tech., 1952-57; staff U.S. delegation Manila Conf., 1954; staff Nat. Security Resources Panel (Gaither Com.), 1957; spl. asst. to Sec. Navy, also to Asst. Sec. Research and Devel., 1957-61; mem. Inst. Def. Analyses, 1961-64, sec., 1964—; vis. professorial lectr. Sch. Internat. Service, Am. U., 1963-69. Member board of trustees Washington Hospital Center, 1967—. Served with OSS. 1943-45; ETO Decorated Medal of Freedom (U.S.), 1946, U.S. Navy Distinguished Civilian Service award, 1961; King Christian X Medal (Denmark), 1947. Mem. Council Fgn. Relations N.Y., Washington Inst. Fgn. Affairs. Clubs: Metropolitan (Washington); Knickerbocker, Racquet and Tennis (N.Y.C.). Author: Conflict in the Shadows; The Nature and Politics of Guerrilla War, 1964. Contbr. articles periodicals. Home: 2950 University Terrace NW Washington DC 20016 Office: 400 Army-Navy Dr Arlington VA 22202

CROSS, JAMES U., state ofcl.; b. Andalusia, Ala., Apr. 25, 1925; s. James Kension and Susie (Wells) C.; student U. Nev., 1943, Augurn U., 1946-49, U. Md., 1959-61; m. Marie Campbell, July 6, 1945; children—June Marie (Mrs. Randall Lee McCann), Brenda Jean, Carolyn Joan, John Kevin. Commd. 2d lt., U.S. Army Air Corps, 1944, advanced through grades to brig. gen.; airplane comdr. transport aircraft CBI Theater, World War II; transport pilot Philippines, 1948-51; transp. pilot, operations staff officer, Greenville, S.C., 1951-55; operations staff officer, Goose Bay, Labrador, 1956; comdr., operations officer Mil. Air Transport Service, North Atlantic, 1957-58; airplane comdr. Spl. Air Missions fleet Mil. Air Transport Service, Washington, 1958-65; Armed Forces aide to Pres. Johnson and pilot Pres.'s aircraft, 1965-68; air combat, Vietnam, 1968; air comdr. Bergstrom AFB, Tex., 1969-71, ret., 1971; exec. dir. Tex. Parks and Wildlife Dept., Austin, 1971—. Decorated Air Force Outstanding Unit award with cluster, Presdl. Service badge, D.F.C., Legion of Merit, Air medal. Mem. Auburn Alumni Assn., Air Force Assn. Home: 501 Pearson St Austin TX 78743 Office: Parks and Wildlife Dept State Capitol Austin TX

CROSS, JOHN HENRY AARON, advt. exec.; b. Monticello, Ia., Jan. 22, 1920; s. Henry A. and Pearl (Heisey) C.; B.A., U. Cal. at Berkeley, 1941; m. Alice Sheehan, Apr. 7, 1951; children—H. Andrew, David McN. With Compton Advt., 1950-69, exec. v.p., 1967-69, also dir.; partner, dir. Jack Tinker & Partners, 1969-70; N.Y.C., 1969-70; sr. v.p. Lennen & Newell, N.Y.C., 1970—. Served with AUS, 1942-48. Club: Sleepy Hollow Country (Scarborough). Home: Linden Circle Scarborough NY 10510 Office: 380 Madison Av New York City NY 10017

CROSS, JOHN JOSEPH, Jr., banker; b. Oak Park, Ill., Apr. 5, 1931; s. John Joseph and Bernice (Corcoran) C.; B.S., U. Ky., 1953; m. Mimms Stevenson, Sept. 6, 1952; children—John Thomas, Mildred, William. Sales rep. IBM Corp., Louisville, 1956-61; asst. v.p. Citizens Fidelity Bank & Trust Co., Louisville, 1961-64, v.p., 1964-69, sr. v.p., head operations div., 1969- -; faculty U. Wis. Sch. Banking, Bank Adminstrn. Inst. Treas., Jefferson County Crime Commn. and Regional Crime Council Jefferson County; bd. dirs., mem. exec. com. Falls Region Health Council. Served to 1st lt., inf., U.S. Army,

1953-55. Mem. Am. Bankers Assn. (exec. council, chmn. operations/automation com.). Republican. Roman Catholic. Clubs: Pendennis (Louisville); Harmony Landing Country (Goshen, Ky.). Home: 609 Fatima Lane Louisville KY 40207 Office: 437 W Jefferson St Louisville KY 40201

CROSS, JOHN MILTON, educator; b. Little Falls, N.J., Jan. 2, 1915; s. Robert and Mabel (Savidge) C.; B.S., Rutgers U., 1936; M.S., U. Md. 1939, Ph.D., 1943; m. Patricia M. Rogers, June 28, 1945; childrenJohn Milton, James Best, Merrill, Philip. Asst. pharmacy U. Md., 1936-41, asst. chemistry, 1941- 42; research chemist Merck&Co., Inc., Rahway, N.J., 1942-46; asst. prof. pharmacy Rutgers U., 1946-49, asso. prof. chemistry, 1949-52, prof. pharm. chemistry, chmn. dept., 1953-. Mem. Am. Pharm. Assn., Am. Chem. Soc., Am. Assn. Colls. Pharmacy (rep. to A.A.A.S.), A.A.A.S., Sigma Xi Rho Chi. Contbr. articles to profl. jours. Home: 960 Cedar Brook Rd Plainfield NJ 07060 Office: 1 Lincoln Av Newark NJ 07104

CROSS, JOHN STORRS, cons.; b. Birmingham, Ala., Sept. 18, 1904; s. Thomas C. and Elise Fairfax (Troy) C.; student McCallie Sch. for Boys, Chattanooga, Marion Mil. Inst., Ala.; B.S. in Elec. Engring., Ala. Poly. Inst., 1923; m. Ruth Fuller, Dec. 23, 1932; childrenJohn Fuller, Claude Christopher. Exptl. engring. lab. Studebaker Corp., Detroit, 1923-24; staff Realty Trust Co., U.S. Mortgage Bond Co., Detroit, 1924-26; constrn. supt. S.S. Kresge Co., 1926-27; asst. resident engr. S.C. Hwy. Dept., 1927; survey chief Mich. Hwy. Dept., 1928-30; staff Dept. Interior Nat. Park Service, 1931-41, successively design engr. water systems San Francisco office, field engr. in charge constrn. Hot Springs Nat. Park, then chief survey design and road div., asst. chief engring. Washington office; asst. chief telecommunications div. Dept. State, 1946-58; commr. FCC, 1958-63; pres. Cross Communication Cons., 1963—. Chmn. U.S. delegation Internat. Meeting on Marine Radio Aids to Nav., N.Y.C., New London, Conn. 1947, Internat. Radio Consultative Com., Warsaw, Poland, 1956, Maritime VHF Radio Telephone Conf., The Hague, Netherlands, 1957. Served from lt. comdr. to cap. USN, 1942-46. Decorated Legion of Merit. Clubs: Manor Country (Norbeck, Md.); Congressional Country (Potomac, Md.). Home: Audubon Rd Bethesda MD 20014 Office: 5416 Audubon Rd Bethesda MD 20014

CROSS, JOHN WALKER, lawyer; b. Sheldon, Mo., Aug. 29, 1902; s. John William and Sarah Juliza (Warnick) C.; B.S., Kan. State Tchrs. Coll., 1924; LL.B., George Washington U., 1931; m. 2d, Agnes Hoerner, Sept. 24, 1963; children by previous marriage—Carol, John Earle. Sec. C. of C., Dodge City, Kan., 1924-27; sec. Hon. Clifford Hope, mem. Congress, 1928-31; admitted to D.C. bar, 1930; partner Denning & Cross, Washington, 1931-47, Cummings, Stanley, Truit & Cross, 1947-55, Cross, Murphy & Smith, 1955—; gen. counsel Govt. Services, Inc., Washington, 1934—; counsel Air Transit Services, Inc., Washington; dir., Washington counsel Nat. Airlines, Inc. of Miami, Fla., 1938—; Washington counsel Boyce-Harvey Machinery Co., Baton Rouge. Trustee Kan. State Tchrs. Coll. Endowment Fund. Mem. Am., D.C. bar assns., Kappa Delta Pi, Delta Tau Delta, Delta Theta Phi, Pi Kappa Delta. Republican. Presbyn. Clubs: Metropolitan, Congressional Country, Nat. Aviation, Capitol Hill, International (Washington). Home: 6600 Bradley Blvd Bethesda MD 20034 Office: 729 15th St Washington DC 20005

CROSS, LESLIE FRANK, journalist; b. Milw., May 12, 1909; s. James L. and Zoe S. (Windfelder) C.; student Beloit Coll., 1927-28; m. Helene Catherine O'Keeffe, Mar. 9, 1929; children—Dion Leslie, James O'Keeffe. Reporter, copy editor Milw. Leader, 1929-38; copy editor New Milw. Leader, 1938-39; copy editor, news editor, asst. to editor, columnist Milw. Post, 1939-41; sec. Wis. Guardian Pub. Co., 1940-41; reporter, copy editor Milw. Jour., 1941-46, exchange editor, writer, 1946-51, columnist, book editor, 1951—. Recipient 1st Bookfellow of Year award Bookfellows of Milw., 1966; decennial award Wis. Com. Nat. Library Week, 1967; Distinguished Service award Soc. Midland Authors, 1969. Mem. Soc. Midland Authors (recipient distinguished service award 1969), Council Wis. Writers, Sigma Delta Chi. Club: Milw. Press. Contbr. articles mags. Home: 400 E Belle Av Milwaukee WI 53217 Office: Milw Jour Jour Sq Milwaukee WI 53201

CROSS, LOUIS JOHN, investment banker; b. Chgo., Sept. 10, 1897; s. John Robert and Mary Ann (Barry) C.; student Cathedral Coll., Chgo., 1912-16, Kenrich Sem., St. Louis, 1916-19; m. Gladys B. Boyce, Dec. 31, 1921 (dec. June 1963); children—Louis Robert, Margery (Mrs. William Brice Buckingham); m. 2d, Frances S. Kluck, June 27, 1964. Served as salesman H.T. Holtz & Co., investment bankers, Chgo., 1920-25, sales mgr., 1925-29; Paul H. Davis & Co., 1929-39, partner, mgr. investment dept., 1939; gen. partner Hornblower & Weeks-Hemphill, Noyes, 1953—; director and mem. exec. com. Jessop Steel Co., River Forest State Bank; dir., financial cons. Longines-Wittnauer Watch Co., Inc., Vacheron- Constantin Watch Co.; dir. Green River Steel Co., Jessop Steel Ltd., Steel Warehousing div. Jessop Steel Co., House of Vision, Inc., Jessop Steel of Cal., South Shore Oil and Devel. Co. Mem. Chgo. Regional Port Dist. Bd. Citizens bd. Loyola U. Bd. dirs. Cath. Charities, Chgo. Mem. Nat. Assn. Securities Dealers (1st chmn. 8th dist.), Ill. C. of C., Chgo. Hist. Soc. (life), Art Inst. Chgo. (life), Newcomen Soc. of N.A. Republican. Roman Catholic. Clubs: Attic, Economic, The Arts, Bond, Chicago, Chicago Golf, Germania, Yacht, Saddle and Cycle, The Tavern (Chicago, Illinois); Country, Stock Exchange (Los Angeles); The Eldorado Country (Palm Desert, Cal.); Tennis (Palm Springs). Home: 1550 N State Pkwy Chicago IL 60610 also 76-370 Shoshone Dr Palm Desert CA 92260 Office: 72 W Adams St Chicago IL 60603

CROSS, MILTON, radio announcer; b. N.Y.C., Apr. 16th, 1897; LL.D. (Hon.), Ithaca (N.Y.) Coll., 1969; m. Lillian Ellegood, 1925; one daughter, Lillian (dec.). Announcer for the Metropolitan Opera broadcasts, 1931-, other programs including Information Please, Radio City Music Hall, Town Hall. Recipient gold medal for good diction on radio Am. Acad. Arts and Letters, 1929; George Frederic Handel medallion, City of N.Y., 1969. Hon. life mem. Liederkranz Soc. Home: 52 Riverside Dr Office: ABC 7 W 66th St New York City NY 10023

CROSS, NEAL MILLER, educator; b. Greeley, Colo., Oct. 16, 1910; s. Ethan Allen and Mae (Miller) C.; A.B., Colo. State Coll., 1933, A.M., 1933; Ed.D., Stanford, 1943; m. Mabel Ponder, May 1, 1937 (dec. 1957); m. 2d, Arline M. Goyette, Oct. 25, 1957. Tchr. English, Burris Sch. of Ball State Tchrs. Coll., Muncie, Ind., 1934-36; instr. English, Menlo Sch. and Coll., Menlo Park, Cal., 1936-40; research specialist com. reading Am. Council Edn., 1938-39; mem. faculty U. No. Colo., Greeley, 1941—, prof. English 1945—, chmn. humanities div., 1962-66, chmn. dept. English, 1966-69; lectr. European div. U. Md., 1964-65; acting instr. English, Stanford, summer 1940; instr. Columbia Tchrs. Coll., summer 1941; vis. prof. N.Y.U., 1948, Ariz. State Alpha Sigma Phi, Phi Delta Kappa. Conglist. Author: (with E.A. Cross) Types of Literature, 1944; (with E.A. Cross) Heritage of World Literature, 1944; (with L.D. Lindou) The Search for Personal Freedom. rev. edit., 1960, 3d edit. (with Lindou, R.C. Lamm); also articles. Home: 2128 18 St Rd Greeley CO 80631

CROSS, PAUL CLIFFORD, chemist, educator, research adminstr.; b. Bruin, Pa., July 19, 1907; s. Henry Anderson McLean and Catherine P. (Smith) C.; B.S., Geneva Coll., 1928, Sc.D., 1963; M.S., U. Wis., 1930, Ph.D., 1932; M.S. ad eundum, Brown U., 1942; Sc.D., Waynesburg Coll., 1963; m. Sara Agnes Groves, June 18, 1932; children—Carroll Edward, Robert Henry, Beverly Jane, Elizabeth Ann. Alumni research fellow U. Wis., 1932-33; nat. research fellow Cal. Inst. Tech., 1933-35; Carnegie Found. fellow Stanford, 1935-36, asst. prof., 1936-38; asso. prof. Brown U., 1938-42, prof., 1942-49, dir. Metcalf Research Lab., 1946-49, chmn. chemistry dept., 1947-49; prof., exec. officer dept. chemistry U. Wash., 1949-61; pres., chief exec. officer, trustee Mellon Inst., Pitts., 1961-67, v.p. for research Carnegie-Mellon U., 1967-71, cons. to pres., 1971-72, bd. dirs. Mellon Inst., 1967-71, trustee Carnegie-Mellon U.; adj. prof. chemistry U. Pitts., 1962—. Lectr. summers Harvard, 1941,46, U. Wis., 1951; cons. weapons systems evaluation group Dept. Def., summer 1953; cons. Wright Air Devel. Center, summers 1954, 55; cons. various govt. agys.; research dir. Underwater Research Lab., USN Woods Hole Oceanographic Inst., 1943-44, research dir., 1944-46. Bd. dirs. Duquesne U.; trustee Geneva Coll., Garnegie-Mellon U. Recipient Life G Alumni award Geneva Coll., 1958. Fellow Am. Phys. Soc., Am. Acad. Arts and Sci., A.A.A.S., Am. Chem. Soc. (dir.-at-large 1967-71); mem. Spectroscopy Soc. Pitts., Pa. Soc., Western Pa. Conservancy, Phi Beta Kappa, Sigma Xi, Alpha Chi Sigma, Gamma Alpha, Phi Lambda Upsilon. Clubs: University, Chemists, Rolling Rock (Pitts.). Author: (with E.B. Wilson, Jr., J.C. Decius) Molecular Vibrations, 1955; (with H.C. Allen, Jr.) Molecular Vib-Rotors, 1963. Contbr. numerous articles to profl. publs. Home: 1067 Blackridge Rd Pittsburgh PA 15235 Office: Mellon Inst 4400 5th Av Pittsburgh PA 15213

CROSS, RALPH EMERSON, mech. engr.; b. Detroit, June 3, 1910; s. Milton Osgood and Helen (Heim) C.; student Mass. Inst. Tech., 1933; m. Eloise Florence Fountain, June 18, 1932; children—Ralph Emerson, Carol (Mrs. Peter G. Wodtke), Dennis W. Vice pres. Cross Co., Fraser, Mich., 1932-67, pres., gen. mgr., 1967—; pres. Cross Internat. A.G., Fribourg, Switzerland, Cross Europa Werk, GmbH, West Germany. Asst. adminstr. Bus., Def. Services Adminstrn. U.S. Dept. Commerce, 1954; spl. cons. to asst. sec. Air Force for Material, 1955-59. Recipient Engring. citation Am. Soc. Tool Engrs., 1956. Mem. Nat. Acad. Engring., Soc. Automotive Engrs., Am. Soc. Mfg. and Tool Engrs., Engring. Soc. Detroit. Club: Detroit Athletic. Home: 50 N Deeplands Rd Grosse Pointe Shores MI 48236 Office: 17801 Fourteen Mile Rd Fraser MI 48026

CROSS, RICHARD CLAYTON, savs. and loan assn. exec.; b. Mpls., Nov. 21, 1924; s. Clayton C. and Ruth (Bronsdon) C.; B.S.L., U. Minn., 1948, J.D., 1950; m. Virginia M. Mooers, June 15, 1949; childrenWilliam C., James R., Barbara J., Nancy A. Admitted to Minn. bar, 1950; pvt. practice, Mpls., 1950-61; exec. v.p. Home Fed. Savs. and Loan Assn. Mpls., and predecessors, 1961-62, pres., 1962— also dir.; dir. Fed. Home Loan Bank Des Moines. Served Marine, 1942-45. Mem. U.S., Minn. (bd. dirs.)savs. and loan leagues, Delta Upsilon. Mason (Shriner). Clubs: Minneapolis Athletic; Interlachen Home: 5804 View Lane Edina MN 55436 Office: 730 Hennepin Av MN 55403

CROSS, RICHARD EUGENE, lawyer; b. Madison, Wis., Sept. 20, 1910; s. Frank L. and Josephine Anne (Loranger) C.; A.B., U. Mich., 1935, LL.B., 1938; L.H.D., Lawrence Inst. Tech.; m. Mary Caroline Stirling, Aug. 5, 1939; children—Caroline, Virginia, Richard, Martha. Admitted to Mich. bar, 1938; legal counsel Cross, Wrock, Miller & Vieson. Dir. Am. Motors Corp., chmn. 1962-66; dir. Mfrs. Life Ins. Co. Toronto, Mountain States Pipe & Supply Co., Packer Corp., Hiram Walker-Gooderham & Worts, Ltd. Chmn. Mich. exec. com. United Negro Coll. Fund. Bd. dirs. Detroit Round Table of Nat. Conf. Christians and Jews, Detroit Ednl. TV, Roseland Park, Woodlawn assns.; trustee Detroit Symphony Orch. Assn., Gen. Real Estate Shares, Inc., Detroit. Fellow Am. Bar Found.; mem. Inter-Am., Am., Detroit bar assns., State Bar Mich., Am. Judicature Soc., Aircraft Pilots Assn., Chamber Music Soc., Phi Kappa Phi. Clubs: Hundred (chmn., sec.), Detroit Golf, Recess, Economic (dir.), Detroit, Detroit Athletic; Raven Class Yachting Assn. Home: 20008 Lichfield Rd Detroit MI 48221 Office: Penobscot Bldg Detroit MI 48226

CROSS, RICHARD JAMES, physician educator; b. N.Y.C., Mar. 31, 1915; s. W. Redmond and Julia A. (Newbold) C.; grad. Groton Sch., 1933; B.A., Yale, 1937; M.D., Columbia, 1941, Med. Sc.D., 1949; m. Margaret W. Lee, June 28, 1939; children—Richard James, Margaret Lee, Alan Whittemore, Anne Redmond, Jane Randolph. Intern Presbyn. Hosp., N.Y.C., 1941-42, asst. resident, 1946-48; instr. medicine Columbia, 1947-49, asso. medicine, 1951-57, asst. prof. 1957-59, asst. dean, 1957-59; asso. dean, asst. prof. medicine U. Pitts. Sch. Medicine, 1959-63; dean faculty medicine U. Ghana, West Africa, 1963; asso. prof. medicine Temple U., 1963-64; asst. to exec. dir. Assn. Am. Med. Colls., 1964-65; lectr. Northwestern U. Sch. Medicine, 1965; prof. medicine, asso. dean Rutgers Med. Sch., Coll. Medicine and Dentistry of N.J., 1965-70, prof., acting chmn. community medicine dept., 1970—. NRC fellow Pub. Health Research Inst. N.Y.C., 1949-51. Mem. Fair Lawn (N.J.) Bd. Edn., 1951-54. Served to capt., M.C., AUS, 1942-46. Decorated Bronze Star, Purple Heart. Mem. A.M.A., Assn. Am. Med. Colls., A.A.A.S., Am. Pub. Health Assn., Nat. Med. Soc. Home: 210 Elm Rd Princeton NJ 08540

CROSS, RICHARD JOHN, banker; b. Denver, May 22, 1929; s. Arthur Chester and Gertrude Eva (Ryan) C.; B.S., U. Colo., 1950; M.B.A, Wharton Sch. Finance U. Pa., 1955; m. Mildred Louise Mouton, Jan. 19, 1957; children—John Charles, Carolyn Louise, Paul Arthur. Asst. v.p. First Nat. Bank, Boulder, Colo., 1955-60; exec. v.p. Arapahoe Nat. Bank, Boulder, 1960-62; with First Western Bank & Trust Co., 1962—, br. mgr., Castro Valley, Cal., 1962-64, regional loan supr., Oakland, Cal., 1964-65, regional v.p., Sacramento, 1965-67, regional v.p., Fresno, Cal., 1967-68, regional v.p., Los Angeles, 1968-70, sr. v.p., 1970—, head trust div., 1971—. Mem. real estate adv. bd. Chabot Coll., San Leandro, Cal., 1963. Councilman, Boulder, 1959-62. Served with USN, 1950-53. Mem. Cal. Bankers Assn., So. Cal. Trust Officers Assn., Boulder Hist. Soc., Delta Tau Delta, Phi Epsilon Phi. Democrat. Roman Catholic. Rotarian. Clubs: Sutter (Sacramento); Jonathan (Los Angeles); Oakmont Country (Glendale, Cal.). Home: 1430 Greenbriar Rd Glendale CA 91207 Office: 548 S Spring St Los Angeles CA 90013

CROSS, ROBERT BRANDT, educator; b. Stockton, Cal., Dec. 9, 1914; s. LaRue Ackley and Theresa (Brandt) C.; A.B. in Greek, U. Cal. at Los Angeles, 1937; M.A., U. Cal. at Berkeley, 1939; Ph.D. in Greek-Latin, U. So. Cal., 1948. Asst. prof. classical langs. U. So. Cal., Los Angeles, 1948-57; prof. classics U. Ark., Fayetteville, 1957—. Served with USAAF, 1942-45. Mem. Classical Assn. Middle West, South (v.p. for Ark. 1957—), Egyptian Exploration Soc. Democrat. Episcopalian. Translator: Le Voudoo Haitien, Milo Rigaud, 1970. Home: Box 663 Fayetteville AR 72701

CROSS, ROBERT DOUGHERTY, coll. pres.; b. Grinnell, Ia., Jan. 21, 1924; s. Edward Weeks and Bessie (Dougherty) C.; A.B., Harvard, 1947, A.M., 1951, Ph.D., 1955; m. Barbara Edna Myers, June 16, 1951 (dec. June 1967); children—Frederick Rowland, Pamela E.; m. Ruth Cunningham Brown, Oct. 12, 1968. Teaching fellow Harvard, 1949-52; instr., then asst. prof. history Swarthmore Coll., 1952-59; mem. faculty Columbia, 1959-66, prof. history, chmn. dept., 1964-67; pres. Hunter Coll., N.Y.C., 1967-69; pres. Swarthmore (Pa.) Coll., 1969—. Chief reader Advanced Placement Program Am. History, 1964- 67; dir. Am. Immigration and Citizenship Conf., 1965—, v.p., 1967—. Bd. dirs. Lenox Hill Neighborhood House Assn.; trustee Professional Children's School. Served as pilot USAAF, 1943-46. Decorated Air medal. Mem. Am. Hist. Assn., Orgn. Am. Historians, Am. Studies Assn., Phi Beta Kappa. Author: The Emergence of Liberal Catholicism in America, 1958. Editor: Critical Periods in History, 1960; The Churches and the City, 1966. Home: 324 Cedar Lane Swarthmore PA 19081

CROSS, ROSAMOND, sch. adminstr.; b. Lunenburg, Mass., Apr. 20, 1907; s. Frederick Cushing and Dorothea (Farquhar) Cross; A.B., Bryn Mawr Coll., 1929; A.M., 1934; L.H.D., Mt. Holyoke Coll.; Ed.D., Brown U.; LL.D., Swarthmore Coll., 1967. Tchr. history Concord (Mass.) Acad., 1929-32; reader dept. history, asst. in dept. econs. Bryn Mawr (Pa.) Coll., 1932-34; tchr. history Lincoln Sch., Providence, 1934-37; dir. Upper Sch. and tchr. history Baldwin Sch., Bryn Mawr, 1937-41, head of sch., 1941-70, vice chmn. bd. Mt. Holyoke Coll.; bd. visitors Women's Coll. Duke U.; mem. adv. com. to dean of women U. Pa. Club: Cosmopolitan (Phila.). Address: The Baldwin School Bryn Mawr, PA . 19010.

CROSS, SAMUEL, meat packing co. exec. Chmn., Cross Bros. Meat Packers, Inc. Office: 3600 N Front St Philadelphia PA 19140*

CROSS, STANLEY D., business exec.; b. Arlington, N.J., May 4, 1906; s. Charles V. and Grace (Zellers) C.; B.S.C., N.Y. U., 1929; m. Barbara M. Stover, Aug. 20, 1934; children—Gary S., Gail N. With J.J. Newberry Co., 1935-66, dist. supt., 1932-40, div. mgr., 1940-57, v.p., div. mgr. charge New Eng. and N.Y. State, 1957-66; pres. Reading Devel. Co. Mem. corp. New Eng. Baptist Hosp., Boston. 17 Longview Rd Reading MA 01867

CROSS, THEODORE LAMONT, corp. exec., lawyer; b. Newton, Mass., Feb. 12, 1924; s. Gorham Lamont and Margaret Moore (Warren) C.; grad. Deerfield Acad., 1942; A.B., Amherst Coll., 1946; LL.B. (editor law rev. 1948-50), Harvard, 1950; m. Sheilah Burr Ross, Sept. 16, 1950; childrenAmanda Burr, Lisa Warren. Admitted to Mass. bar, 1950, N.Y. bar, 1953; with firm Hale and Dorr, Boston, 1950-52; treas., sec., v.p. legal affairs, mem. finance com. bd. dirs. Sheraton Corp. Am., 1963-; dir. Sheraton Internat., Inc., Warren, Gorham & Lamont, Inc., Mgmt. Reports, Inc., Record Pub. editor-in-chief Bankers mag., 1962-. Founder Banking Law Inst., 1965, chmn., 1965—; dir. Bank Tax Inst., 1964—. Served to ensign USNR, 1945- 47, Author: Black Capitalism: Strategy for Business in the Ghetto Atomic Energy Law Jours., 1959-. Home: 2 E 88th St New York City, NY . 10028. Office: 870 7th Av New York City NY 10019 also 89 Beach St Boston MA 02111 and 470 Atlantic Av Boston MA 02210

CROSS, TOM GYNN, gas co. exec.; b. Sweetwater, Tex., June 11, 1910; s. Ewing S. and Eula (Paul) C.; student Sul Ross State Coll., 1926-28; LL.B., So. Methodist U., 1949; m. E. Lois Dugger, June 9, 1932; children—Tommie Jean, Mary Ellen, John F. Cashier Comml. Finance Co., El Paso, Tex., 1929-30; with Lone Star Gas Co., Dallas, 1930—, tax agt., 1946-53, mgr. tax dept., 1954-59, asst. sec., 1962-63, sec., 1963-69, v.p. ad valorem and spl. taxes, since 1969—. Mem. Am. Gas Assn., Ind. Petroleum Assn. Am., Nat. Assn. Gas Pipeline Tax Mgrs., Mid-Continent Oil and Gas Assn. Home: 5115 S Regatta Dr Dallas TX 75232 Office: 301 S Harwood St Dallas TX 75201

CROSS, WILLIAM REDMOND, Jr., banker; b. N.Y.C., Apr. 26, 1917; s. William Redmond and Julia (Newbold) C.; grad. Groton (Mass.) Sch., 1937; B.A., Yale, 1941; m. Sally Curtiss Smith, June 14, 1958; children—William Redmond III, Pauline Curtiss, Frederic Newbold. With Hanover Bank, N.Y.C., 1941-43, N.Y. Trust Co., 1946-59, v.p., 1951-59; v.p. Safe Deposit Co. N.Y. Trust Co., 1952-59; v.p. Morgan Guaranty Trust Co., N.Y.C., 1959-64, head Midtown offices, 1962-65, adminstrv. head met. group, 1965—, sr. v.p., 1964-, head met. div. gen. banking dept., 1967-71, sr. credit officer gen. banking div., 1971—; dir. Crompton Co., Inc. Bd. dirs. Valeria Home, Oscawana, N.Y., 1955—; trustee Childrens Aid Soc., 1962—, Chapin Sch., 1969—. Served to lt. (j.g.) USNR, 1943-46. Clubs: Yale (dir., past treas.), Racquet and Tennis, Sky (N.Y.C.); Bedford (N.Y.) Golf and Tennis. Home: 10 E 80th St New York City NY 10021 R D 2 Box 299 South Bedford Rd Mt Kisco NY 10549 Office: 23 Wall St New York City NY 10015

CROSSE, HOWARD DILLISTIN, banker; b. Paterson, N.J., July 19, 1910; s. Franklin and Lina (Dillistin) C.; B.A., Dartmouth, 1931; M.B.A., N.Y. U., 1935; m. Dorothy J. Bowman, Sept. 30, 1933; children—Judith Mary (Mrs. Robert D. Fouchaux), Anne Elizabeth (Mrs. Robert A. Jones), Dorothy Linda (Mrs. Rogelio Garcia). With Fed. Res. Bank N.Y., 1932-65, v.p. bank supervision, 1960-65; vice chmn. bd., dir. Franklin Nat. Bank, N.Y.C., 1965—; adj. prof. finance N.Y.U. Grad. Sch. Bus., 1963—; dir. Humanic Designs Corp. Author: Management Policies for Commercial Banks, 1962. Home: 18 Central Av Glen Rock NJ 07452 Office: 130 Pearl St New York City NY 10015

CROSSE, VICTORIA MARY, physician; b. Rye, Sussex, Eng., May 17, 1900; d. Arthur John William and Mary Charlotte (Sisson) Crosse; M.B., B.S., London Sch. Medicine Women and Royal Free Hosp., 1926, M.D., 1930, D.P.H., 1930. Various resident hosp. appointments in London, Windsor, Birmingham, 1926-30; med. officer charge maternity and child welfare hosps. Birmingham City Health Dept., 1931-48; cons. pediatrician Birmingham Regional Hosp. Bd., 1948-61; lectr. pediatrics and child health U. Birmingham, 1948-61; vis. prof. Haceteppe Childrens Hosp., Ankara, Turkey, 1961; lectr. Australia and New Zealand, 1962, South Africa, Kenya, Rhodesia, Uganda, Japan, Formosa, Hong Kong, Manila and U.S., 1963, India, 1964; cons. N.Y.C. Health Dept., 1961, Govt. Kuwait, 1962, Adelaide, Australia, Auckland, New Zealand, 1963. Mem. spl. com. prematurity WHO, 1950, mem. expert adv. panel maternal and child health, 1950-70, short term cons. Philippines, 1953, Israel, 1954, Egypt, 1955, Yugoslavia, 1956, adviser Internat. Definition Prematurity, 1957, 60, 63, mem. Expert Maternal and Child Health Com. on Low Birth Weight, 1960; mem. Birmingham Hosp. Mgmt. Com., 1948-60; v.p. Nat. Baby Welfare Council, 1961. Decorated Order Brit. Empire; hon. fellow Am. Pub. Health Assn. Mem. Brit. Med. Assn. (pres. Birmingham 1952-53), Med. Women's Fedn. (pres. Birmingham 1955-56, mem. council 1955-58, nat. pres. 1964-65), Med. Women's Internat. Assn. (treas. 1968—), Soc. Med. Officers Health (exec. com. maternity and child welfare group 1946-50), Pediatric Soc. Paris (corr.). Author: The Premature Baby, 6th edit., 1966; A Surgeon in the Early Nineteenth Century: The Life and Times of John Green Crosse, 1968; also articles, chpts. in books. Address: 1 Pitmaston Ct Goodby Rd Birmingham 13 8 RJ England

CROSSEN, JOHN E., food co. exec.; b. 1919; A.B., Wayne State U., 1941; married. With Harry Ferguson. Inc., 1941-47; with accounting dept. Ford Motor Co., 1947-51; with Gen. Foods Corp., 1951-68, v.p.

business devel., 1967-68; sr. v.p. Latin Am. and Pacific H.J. Heinz Co., 1968—, also dir. Address: 1062 Progress St Pittsburgh PA 15230*

CROSSER, ROBERT MAURICE, banker, b. Evansville, Ind., Feb. 17, 1928; s. Maurice and Rona (Little) C.; B.A., Ind. U., 1951; LL.B., U. Mich., 1954; m. Norma J. Raper, Aug. 31, 1951; children—Kevin W., Karen L. Admitted to Mich. bar, 1956; pvt. practice in Grand Rapids, 1956-59; trust rep. Genesee Mchts. Bank & Trust Co., 1959-60; v.p. charge Lansing trust div. Mich. Nat. Bank, 1960- -. Treas. Mich. Capitol council Girl Scouts Am., 1963-69. Served with USNR, 1946, U.S Army, 1954-56. Mem. Mich., Ingham County bar assns. Kiwanian. Club: City (Lansing). Home: 3888 Raleigh Dr Okemos MI 48864 Office: PO Box 1320 Lansing MI 48904

CROSSETT, DONALD SIDNEY, advt. exec.; b. Rochester, N.Y., Dec. 2, 1933; s. Sidney M. and Thelma (Case) C.; A.B., Harvard, 1956; M.B.A., Wharton Sch. of U. Pa., 1961; m. Norma Jean Loekle, May 29, 1965. Project adminstr. electronics products div. RCA, 1963-65; with J. Walter Thompson, 1965—, controller, 1968—. Served to lt. (j.g.) USNR, 1956-59. Mem. Am. Mgmt. Assn., Harvard Alumni Club, Wharton Alumni Club. Club: N.Y. Athletic (N.Y.C.). Home: 301 E 64th St New York City NY 10021 Office: 420 Lexington Av New York City NY 10017

CROSSETTE, GEORGE, research geographer; b. Chgo., July 12, 1910; s. Louis Faulkner and Marie (Pearce) C.; B.A., Geroge Washington U., 1935; Sc.D., Nat. Inst. Urbiculture, 1960; m. Elizabeth Uhle Ferg, July 1, 1933; 1 dau., Anne. Supr. wanted criminals sect. FBI, 1934-38; chief geog. research div. Nat. Geog. Soc., 1939—. Vice pres. Montogomery County Workshop, 1951-54. Mayor, Chevy Chase View, Md., 1942-43; dep. sheriff Hamilton County, N.Y. Recipient Meritorious Wartime award Nat. Rifle Assn., 1944. Mem. Defenders of Wildlife (bd. dirs. 1967), D.C. Wildlife Fedn. (sec. treas. 1954-64), U.S. Flag Library Assn. (1st v.p. 1963), Lake George (N.Y.) Hist. Soc. (trustee), Md., Wash. acads. sci., A.A.A.S., U.S. Mil. Engrs. Am. Assn. Geographers. Clubs: Cosmos (chmn. admissions com. 1967-69, history com. 1968—), Nat. Press (Washington); Cliff Dwellers (Chgo); Explorers (N.Y.C.) Author: Founders of the Cosmos Club of Washington, 1966; John Wesley Powell, 1969; The Oceans, 1969; Herbert Wendell Gleason; also articles. Home: 4217 Glenrose St Kensington MD 20795 Office: Nat Geographic Society 17th and M Sts Washington DC 20036

CROSSFIELD, ALBERT SCOTT, airline co. exec., pilot; b. Berkeley, Cal., Oct. 2, 1921; s. Albert Scott and Lucia (Dwyer) C.; B.S. in Aero. Engring., U. Wash., 1949, M.S. in Aero. Sci., 1950; m. Alice Virginia Knoph, Apr. 21, 1943; children—Becky Lee, Thomas Scott, Paul Stanley, Anthony Scott, Sally Virginia, Robert Scott. Mem. U. Wash. staff charge wind tunnel operation, 1946-50; wind tunnel test analyst, project engr., also pilot research airplanes X-1, X-4, X-5, D-558-I and II, X-F-92, F-102, F-100, F-86, NASA, 1950-55; participation proposal, design, 1st pilot X-15 research aircraft, design specialist, also chief engring. test pilot 61, div. dir., test and quality assurance, space and information systems div., 1961-66, test dir. test and operations, research and engring., space and information systems div., 1966—; N.Am. Aviation, Inc., v.p. flight research and devel. div. Eastern Air Lines, Miami, Fla., to 1971, staff v.p. transp. systems devel., Washington, 1971—; spl. work on the WS-131b Apollo, Saturn S-II, Paraglider programs. Mem. adv. council Sci. Explorer Scout Post, Downey, Cal., 1963—; mem. exec. bd. YMCA, Westchester, Los Angeles County, 1961—. Served to lt., fighter pilot, USNR, 1942-46. Recipient Lawrence Sperry award Inst. Aero. Scis., 1954, Octave Chanute award, 1957; Achievement award Am. Astron. Soc., 1959; Cal. wing Air Force Assn., 1959, David C. Shilling award, 1961; Astronautics award Am. Rocket Soc., 1960; Ivan C. Kincheloe award Soc. Exptl. Test Pilots, 1960; Godfrey Cabot award Aero Club New Eng., 1961; Internat. Harmon trophy, 1961; Collier trophy, 1962; hon. mayor, Westchester, 1960-62; John J. Montgomery award Nat. Soc. Aerospace Profls., 1962, Kittyhawk award Los Angeles C. of C., 1969. Fellow Soc. Exptl. Pilots (co-founder), Am. Inst. Aero. and Astronautics (chmn. flight test tech. com. 1963-64), Aerospace Med. Assn. (hon); mem. Am. Soc. Quality Control (sect. chmn. Los Angeles 1964- 66), Flying Physician Assn., Exptl. Aircraft Assn., Sigma Xi, Tau Beta Pi. Republican. Episcopalian. Author: Always Another Dawn, 1960; also articles. Home: 12100 Thoroughbred Rd Hedron VA 22070 Office: Eastern Air Lines 1030 15th St NW Washington DC 20005

CROSSLAND, SAMUEL HESS, heavy constrn. co. exec.; b. Tulsa, Aug. 30, 1929; s. Samuel Hess and Louise (Weaver) C.; student U. Tulsa, 1947-48, 52-53: B.A., U. Okla., 1955, LL.B., 1957; m. Yolonda Phillips, Sept. 18, 1958; 1 dau., Julia Allison. Admitted to Okla. and D.C. bars, prosecuting atty., Tulsa County, Okla., 1957-59; chief legal counsel to gov. of Okla., 1959-62; partner firm Stuart, Symington, Hollings & Crossland, Washington, 1962- 64; atty. Morrison-Knudsen Co., Inc., 1964—, corporate sec., counsel, 1968—, sec., gen. counsel, 1969—. Served with USNR, 1948-52. Mem. Am., Okla., D.C. bar assns., Phi Alpha Delta. Club: Hillcrest Country (Boise). Home: 3531 Hillcrest Dr Boise ID 83705

CROSSLAN D, STANLEY THEODORE, oil co. exec.; b. Blue Island, Ill., Apr., 1907; s. Nicholas H. and Elizabeth (Witt) C.; student U. Ill., 1926-27; m. Fay Kohlhase, June 4, 1932. Spl. asst. to bd. dirs., RFC, Washington, 1940-45; exec. v.p. Rubber Res. Co., 1940-45; v.p. War Damage Corp., 1941-45; v.p., treas., dir. Ethyl Corp., N.Y., 1945-54; v.p. Texaco, Inc., N.Y.C., 1955—. Clubs: Cloud (N.Y.C.); Apawamis (Rye, N.Y.); Blind Brook (Port Chester, N.Y.). Home: Osborn Rd Harrison NY 10528 Office: 135 E 42d St New York City NY 10017

CROSSLEY, ARTHUR WEBSTER, engr., bus. exec.; b. Somerset, Colo., Dec. 16, 1908; s. George Lewis and Sarah Elizabeth (Jowett) C.; B.S., Franklin Inst., 1928; LL.B., Southeastern U., 1939; LL.M., M. P.L., 1940, B.C.S., 1941; m. Margaret M. Neu, Oct. 15, 1932; children—Anne Jowett, Jane Elizabeth, Susan Margaret. Engr. Dennison Mfg. Co., 1928-30, Washington Gas Light Co., 1930-33, H.J. Saunders (cons. engr.), Washington, 1933-34, Pub. Utilities Commn., D.C., 1935-38; asst. dir., chief engr. Pub. Works, D.C., 1938-40, dir., 1940-41; asst. gen. mgr. Potomac Electric Co., 1941-48; treas. Diamond Alkali Co., 1948-55; dir. finance Theo. Hamm Brewing Co., St. Paul, Minn., 1956-60, v.p. finance, 1960-68, sec., dir., 1965-68; chmn. bd. Marquette Corp., 1969—. Served as col. chemical corps AUS, 1942-45. Decorated Legion of Merit with oak leaf cluster, Commendation medal with 2 clusters. : em. Am. Inst. Management. Club: Army-Navy (Washington). Iome: 91 Birnamwood St Burnsville MN 55378 Office: 3800 N Dunlap St St Paul MN 55112

CROSSLEY, JAMES GARDNER, ret. newspaper editor; b. Honesdale, Pa., Jan. 6, 1905; s. Thomas A. and E. Blanche (Sumner) C.; student Northwestern U., 1922-25; m. Mary E. Beaird, July 12, 1935; 1 son, James. Mem. staff Indpls. Star, later Wayne County Citizen, Honesdale, Buffalo News and Times, Newark Star Eagle; with Scripps-Howard newspapers, 1929-71; mng. editor Akron (O.) Times-Press, 1932-38, Columbus (O.) Citizen, 1943-54; news editor Cin. Post, 1938-43; mng. editor for NEA Service, Inc., 1954-71. Mem. Sigma Alpha Epsilon, Sigma Delta Chi. Home: 27023 Normandy Rd Bay Village OH 44140

CROSSLEY, RANDOLPH ALLIN, corp. exec.; b. Cupertino, Cal., July 10, 1904; s. John P. and Elizabeth (Hall) C.; student A. to Zed Coll. Prep. Sch., 1921-23. U. Cal., 1923-25; m. Florence Pepperdine, July 23, 1928; 1 dau., Meredith (Mrs. Jack E. Young). Founder Crossley Advt., Honolulu, 1929; pres. Hawaiian Tuna Packers, Ltd., Honolulu, 1930-34, Hawaiian Fruit Packers, Ltd., 1936-54, Aloha Stamp Co., Ltd., 1954-64, Nonou Devel. Co., Ltd., Honolulu; pres., exec. officer Crossley Contracting Co., 1954-63, Crossco, Ltd., 1964—; pres., chief exec. officer Am. Pacific Group, Inc., 1967-69, chmn., chief exec. officer, 1969—; pres. Am. Pacific Life Ins. Co. Ltd., 1967—; chmn. Hawaii Corp., 1968-69, pres., chief exec. officer, 1969—; pres., dir. Pacific Savs. and Loan Assn., 1962-65; chmn. Medi-Fund Corp., San Francisco; dir. Master Oil & Gas Fund, Inc., Los Angeles, Falcon Capital Corp., Encino, Cal., Amelco Engrs. Pty. Ltd., Sydney, Australia. Mem. Pub. Utilities Commn., 1945-47. Mem. Hawaii Ho. of Reps., 1943-45, Constl. Conv., 1950, Hawaii Senate, 1959-64; chmn. Rep. party Hawaii, 1950-52: Rep. candidate for gov., 1966; Rep. nat. committeeman from Hawaii, 1967-69. Mem. N.A.M. (dir. 1970—), C. of C. Hawaii (dir. 1954-59, 70—), Newcomen Soc., N. Am. (trustee), Rancheros Visitadores (Cal.). Past trustee, treas. Kawaiahao Ch. Clubs: Oahu Country, Outrigger Canoe, Pacific (Honolulu); Metropolitan (N.Y.C.); Bohemian (San Francisco). Home: 3073 Noela Dr Honolulu HI 96815 Office: Alexander Young Bldg Honolulu HI 96813

CROSSLEY, ROBERT PIERCE, retired mag. editor; b. nr. Council Bluffs, Ia., Jan. 1, 1914; s. Bruce William and Mary Mitchell (Wilson) C.; grad. in printing Los Angeles Trade-Tech. Jr. Coll., 1931; B.S., Ia. State U., 1939; m. Mary Elizabeth Hansen, Sept. 5, 1937; children—Sheila Mary (Mrs. Thomas Hanks). Margaret Jane (Mrs. Timothy Titus). Editor, pub. Denison (Ia.) Rev., 1939-45; family life dept. Better Home and Gardens, 1946-51; lectr. mag. journalism Ia. State U., 1948-51; editor Household, 1951-57; editorial dir. Capper's Farmer, 1952-55; Better Living editor McCall's mag., 1957-58, exec. editor, 1958-60; exec. editor Woman's Day, 1960; editor Popular Sci., 1962-64; dir. Popular Sci. Pub. Co., 1963-64; mag. cons., free-lance writer, 1965: editor Popular Mechanics mag., 1966-71, retired, 1971. Served as lt. (j.g.) USNR, 1944-46, signal officer U.S.S. Concord. Mem. Am. Agrl. Editors Assn., Am. Soc. Mag. Cardinal Key, Sigma Delta Chi, Alpha Zeta, Gamma Sigma Delta, Phi Kappa Phi. Home: 43 Glendale Rd Stamford CT 06906

CROSSMAN, JEROME KENNETH, lawyer, corp. exec.; b. Gainesville, Tex., Sept. 14, 1896; s. Bernard and Sarah (Goodman) C.; LL.B., U. Tex., 1918; m. Pauline Gans, Sept. 8, 1920; children—Betty, Stanley. Admitted to Tex. bar, 1917; with firm Scurlock, Crossman & Dale, Wichita Falls, Tex., 1918-19; pvt. practice of law, Dallas, 1919—. Dir. Lomas & Nettleton Financial Corp., Inc., Gt. Am. Res. Ins. Co. Pres. Dallas Citizens Interracial Assn. Bd. govs. Menninger Foundation; trustee Tex. Research Found., Southwestern Legal Found.; dir. Nat. Conf. Christians and Jews, Dallas Theatre Center, Inc., Greater Dallas Planning Council, Ednl. Television Found., Tex. Psychiat. Found., Children's Devel. Center, Dallas Council World Affairs; adv. council W.A.I.F.; mem. adv. council Girl Scouts Am., Citizens Charter Assn.; chmn. bd. Dallas Heart Assn., 1950-54. Dir. Children's Hosp. of Tex.; Trustee, v.p. Nat. Jewish Hosp., Denver. Mem. Tex. State adv. com. Civil Rights Commn. Recipient Linz award for outstanding civic work in Dallas, 1954. Headliner of year award Press Club Dallas 1954. Mem. Am., Dallas bar assns., State Bar Tex., Dallas C. of C. (pres. 1954-55 dir.), Jewish religion (temple trustee). Home: 3601 Turtle Creek Dallas TX 75219 Office: Republic Nat Bank Tower Dallas TX 75201

CROSSON, FREDERICK JAMES, univ. dean; b. Belmar, N.J., Apr. 27, 1926; s. George Leon and Emily (Bennett) C.; B.A., Cath. U. Am., 1949, M.A., 1950; postgrad. U. Paris (France), 1951-52; Ph.D., U. Notre Dame, 1956; m. Mary Patricia Burns, Sept. 5, 1953; children—Jessica, Christopher, Veronica, Benedict. Instr. U. Notre Dame, 1953-56; asst. prof., 1956-62, asso. prof., 1962-66, prof., 1966—, dean Coll. Arts and Letters, 1968—. Served with USNR, 1943-46. Mem. Am. Assn. U. Profs., Am. Philos. Assn., Phi Beta Kappa. Author: The Modeling of Mind, 1963; Philosophy and Cybernetics, 1967; Science and Contemporary Society, 1967. Home: 1307 E Jefferson Blvd South Bend IN 46617 Office: Coll Arts and Letters Notre Dame IN 46556

CROSSON, WILLIAM T., glass mfg. co. exec. Sr. v.p. Glass Container Corp., Fullerton Cal. Office: 535 N Gilbert Av Fullerton CA 92633*

CROSTEN, WILLIAM LORAN, musicologist, pianist, educator; b. Des Moines, Sept. 7, 1909; s. William Taber and Sidney Frances (Graber) C.; Mus.B., Drake U., 1930; A.M., State U. Ia., 1936; Ph.D., Columbia, 1946; m. Mary Perry, Aug. 26, 1936; children—Stephen Perry, Lesley Ann. Faculty mem. State U. Ia., 1935-37, Columbia, 1939-42; asso. prof. music Stanford, 1946-51, prof., 1951—, exec. head dept. music, 1946—. Served to lt. comdr. USNR, Guggenheim fellow, European travel, 1954. Recipient Distinguished Alumnus award Drake U.; Steinway award for service to music. Mem. Am. Musicol. Assn., Coll. Music Soc. (pres. 1965-67), Am. Assn. U. Profs., Music Library Assn., Royal Musical Assn. Author: French Grand Opera: An Art and A Business, 1948. Contbr. profl. publs. Office: Dept of Music Stanford U Stanford CA 94305

CROTEAU, JOHN TOUGAS, economist, educator; b. Holbrook, Mass., Mar. 10, 1910; s. Narcisse Leon and Mary (Tougas C.; A.B., Holy Cross Coll., 1931; M.A., Clark U., 1932, Ph.D., 1935; LL.D., St. Joseph's U. Can., 1956; m. Gertrude D. Gallant, June 2, 1936 (dec. Mar. 1961); m. 2d, Jeanne R. Miller, Aug. 20, 1969. Carnegie chair econs. and sociology Prince Wales Coll., St. Dunstan's Coll., Charlottetown, P.E.I., Can., 1933-45; dir. program adult edn., rural rehab., P.E.I., 1936-45; mng. dir. P.E.I. Credit Union League, also mng. dir. Coop. Union P.E.I., and exec. sec. Adult Edn. League, 1936-45; asso. prof. econs. Xavier U., 1946-47; asso. prof. econs. Catholic U. Am., 1947-53; asso. prof. econs. U. Notre Dame, 1953-56, prof., 1956—; cons. Bur. Fed. Credit Unions. Project dir. credit union use by low income groups Social Security Adminstrn. Fellow Royal Econ. Soc.; mem. Am. Econ. Assn., Am. Finance Assn., Agrl. History Soc., Am. Assn. U. Profs., Canadian Polit. Sci. Assn. (past dir.), Credit Union Nat. Assn. (past dir.). Author: A Regional Library and Its Readers, 1940; Cradled in the Waves: The Story of a People's Cooperative Achievement in Economic Betterment on Prince Edward Island, 1951; The Federal Credit Union: Policy and Practice, 1956; The Economics of the Credit Union, 1963. Contbr. articles to profl. jours. Home: 124 N Eddy St South Bend IN 46617

CROTHERS, DONALD HAWK, judge; b. Spokane, Wash., Mar. 4, 1923; s. Leslie John and Della J. (Hawk) C.; student N.D. State U., 1941-43, Loyola U., Chgo., 1946-48; J.D., U. N.D., 1951; m. Marion Krause, Jan. 21, 1955; children-David Judson, Daniel John. Admitted to N.D. bar, 1951; practice in Fargo, 1951- 70; editor N.D. Taxpayer Mag., 1954-64; exec. dir. Asso. Industries of Fargo-Moorhead, 1956-59; asso. Lanier & Knox, 1965-70; municipal judge, West Fargo, 1966-70; chief justice High Ct of Am. Samoa, Pago Pago, 1970- -; spl. asst. atty. gen. N.D., 1955-57; mem. Am. Samoa Territorial Criminal Justice Planning Agy., 1970. Mem. Cass County Housing Authority, 1963; mem., chmn. West Fargo Urban Renewal Agy., 1965-68; pres. Ducks Unlimited N.D., 1962-64. Vice pres. Nat. Young Republican Orgn., 1950-52; mem. N.D. Ho. of Reps., 1953-55. Served to ensign USNR, 1943-46; PTO. Mem. Am., Am. Samoa, Fed., N.D., Cass County bar assns., Am. Judicature Soc., N.Am. Judges Assn., V.F.W., Am. Legion, Lawyer- Pilots Assn., Phi Delta Phi. Lion, Elk, Rotarian. Home: 127 S Utulei Pago Pago American Samoa 96920 Office: High Ct of Am Samo Pago Pago American Samoa 96920

CROTTY, HAROLD CLIFFORD, labor union exec.; b. Oregon, Wis., Sept. 17, 1911; s. John and Alma Katherine (Christensen) C.; grade trade union program, Harvard Bus. Sch., 1948; m. Josephine Helen Cavanaugh, Sept. 24, 1938. With C. & N.-W. Ry. Co., 1930-45; mem. Brotherhood of Maintenance Way Employees, 1930—, dep. grand lodge pres., 1948-49, asst. to pres., 1949-58, internat. pres., 1958—; dir., mem. exec. bd. Union Labor Life Ins. Co. Chmn. bd. Labor Coop. Ednl. and Pub. Soc.; mem. Com. on Mich.'s Econ. Future; chmn. Maintenance of Way Polit. League; vice chmn. Congress Ry. Unions, also chmn. exec. com. Mem. transp. dept. com. of nat. bd. YMCA. Mem. Ry. Labor Execs. Assn. Editor Brotherhood of Maintenance of Way Employees Ry. Jour. Office: Home: 20113 Fairway Dr Grosse Pointe Woods MI 48236

CROTTY, HOMER DANIEL, lawyer; b. Oakland, Cal., Mar. 15, 1899; s. Daniel and Mary Frances (O'Connor) C.; A.B., U. Cal., 1920, J.D., 1922; LL.M., Harvard, 1923; LL.D., Trinity Coll., U. Dublin (Ireland); L.H.D., Cal. Western U., 1964; m. Ida Hull Lloyd, May 12, 1934; children—Daniel Lloyd, Mary Elizabeth, Anne Lloyd, Peter Lloyd. Asst. to dir. Chabot Obs., Oakland, Cal., 1917-22; with Gibson, Dunn & Crutcher, L.A., 1923—, mem. firm, 1930—; spl. asst. to U.S. Atty Gen., 1953-55; lectr. on legal profession Law Sch. U. So. Cal., 1952-63; dir. Lloyd Corp. Ltd., Parkview Apts. Trustee emeritus Claremont U. Center; dir. I.N. and Susannah H. Van Nuys Found., 1943—, pres., 1945-70; dir. and Southwest Mus.; mem. council fellows Pierpont Morgan Library, 1959- 62; chmn. bd. trustees Henry E. Huntington Library and Art Gallery, 1957- -. Dir. emeritus Los Angeles World Affairs Council. Fellow Am. Bar Found.; mem. Internat., Inter-Am., Am. (chmn. sect. on legal edn. 1959-60), Los Angeles County bar assns., State Bar Cal. (pres. 1950- 51), A.A.A.S., Am. Law Inst. (com. legal edn. 1948-51, mem. council, 1956—). Am. Soc. Internat. Law, Am. Judicature Soc. (dir., v.p. 1953-59), Assn. Ind. Cal. Colls. and Univs. (trustee 1955- 63), Assn. Bar City N.Y., Inst. Jud. Adminstrn., Inc., Council Fgn. Relations, Los Angeles Com. Fgn. Relations, Am. Acad. Social Sci., Honnold Library Soc. (dir.), Astron. Soc. Pacific, Selden Soc. (council mem.) (London), Stair Soc. (Edinburgh), Cal., So. Cal. hist. socs., Order of Coif, Tau Kappa Epsilon. Republican. Clubs: California, Chancery, Sunset (pres. 1956) Stock Exchange, Town Hall, Zamarano, Jonathan; Harvard (So. Cal.; N.Y.); Grolier, (N.Y.C.); Commonwealth (San Francisco); Valley Hunt, Athenaeum (Pasadena). Author: Glimpses of Don Quixote and La Mancha, 1963. Home: 1155 Shenandoah Rd San Marino CA 91108 Office: 634 S Spring St Los Angeles CA 90014

CROUCH, ALLIN BLAND, ret. banker; b. Detroit, Sept. 27, 1904; s. James H. and Ella A.B., U. Mich., 1926; m. Norma E. Guilbault, Aug. 16, 1952; children—Ellen Crouch Lehmann, Allin Bland. Bus. trainee Gen. Electric Co., Schenectady, 1926-33, auditor corporate accounts, 1933-42, asst. comptroller, 1942-50; v.p., comptroller Iving Trust Co., N.Y.C., 1950- 1961, sr. v.p., comptroller, 1961-65, exec. v.p., 1965-69. Mem. Financial Execs. Inst., Sigma Alpha Epsilon. Club: Baltusrol Golf (Springfield N.J.). Home: 55 Forest Dr Springfield NJ 07081

CROUCH, COURTNEY CHET, lawyer; b. Collins, Mo., June 23, 1912; s. William Edward and Lura V. (Heare) C.; LL.B., U. Mo. at Kansas City, 1933; m. Marie E. Loftis, May 24, 1936; childrenCourtney Chet, Michael E., James E. Admitted to Ark. bar, 1933; practice in Springdale, 1933-38, 47-; with Braun and Co., mgmt. cons., Los Angeles, 1938-47. Mem. Ark. Bd. Law Examiners. 1955-58. Mayor Springdale, 1936-38. Trustee U. of Ark. Law Sch. Found., 1965-, trustee Southwestern Legal Found. Dallas, 1968—, mem. exec. com. Lawyers, Am. Bar Found.; mem. Am., Ark. (exec. com. 1961-67, pres. 1965- 66) bar assns., Am. Judicature Soc. Home: 19008 Pin Oak Dr Office: 111 Holcomb St Springdale AR 72764

CROUCH, FORDYCE WILLIAM, lawyer; b. Curlew, Ia., Feb. 12, 1914; s. Alfred William and Ida Mae (Nicholson) C.; student Ft. Dodge Jr. Coll., 1931-33; B.S., U. Minn., 1935, LL.B. 1937; m. Alice Welch, July 2, 1938; children—Ford William, John Steven, Thomas Nicholson. Admitted to Ia. bar, 1937, Minn. bar, 1938; practice of law, Mpls., 1938—; with M., St. P. & S.S. Ry., Mpls., 1938—, gen. counsel, 1957—; v.p., gen. counsel Soo Line R.R. Co. Mem. Am., Minn. bar assns. Republican. Conglist. Club: Minneapolis Athletic. Home: 4937 Fremont Av Minneapolis MN 55409 Office: Soo Line Railroad Co Minneapolis MN 55440

CROUCH, HUBERT BRANCH, univ. dean; b. Jacksonville, Tex., Dec. 1, 1906; s. George Washington and Cornelia (Ragsdale) C.; B.A., Tex. Coll., 1927; M.S., Ia. State U. 1930, Ph.D., 1936; m. Mildred Shipp, Mar. 14, 1930; childrenMarinelle (Mrs. William M. Moses), Hubert Branch. Prof. biology, chmn. dept. Ky. State Coll., Frankfort, 1931-44; prof. biology, head dept., sci. dir. Tenn. A. and I. State U., Nashville, 1944-51, dean Grad. Sch., 2516 Shreeve Lane Nashville TN 37207

CROUCH, JAMES ENSIGN, educator, Zoologist; b. Urbana, Ill., Jan. 28, 1908; s. Harry Ensign and Mary Jane (Pierce) C.; B.S., Cornell U., 1930, M.S., 1931; Ph.D., U. So. Cal., 1939; m. Mary Vrooman Page, Nov. 28, 1931; childrenJeanette Elnor (Mrs. Alex Rigopoulos), James Page. Mem. faculty San Diego State Coll., 1932—. prof. zoology, 1940—. chmn. div. life scis., 1962—. Fellow San Diego Zool. Soc., San Diego Mus. Natural History; mem. Nat. Audubon Soc. Sigma Xi, Phi Kappa Phi, Phi Sigma. Democrat. Unitarian. Author: Introduction to Human Anatomy, 1958; Introduction to Human Anatomy, 1958; Functional Human Anatomy, 1965; Atlas of Cat Anatomy, 1969. Home: 10430 Russel Rd La Mesa CA 92041 Office: San Diego State Coll San Diego CA 92115

CROUCH, JORDAN JONES, banker; b. Johnson City, Tenn., July 10, 1909; s. Adam Bowman and Agnes (Jones) C.; A.B., Milligan Coll., 1931; LL.D., 1970; postgrad. Northwestern 1931-32; Vanderbilt U., 1933; m. Elizabeth Wright, June 22, 1933; 1 son, William Wright. Mgr., Chapman Park Hotel, Los Angeles, 1934-40; asst. to works mgr., mfg. div. Lockheed Aircraft Co., 1940-45; credit analyst Bank of Am., Los Angeles hdgrs., 1945-49; v.p. First Nat. Bank of Nev., Reno, 1949-63, sr. v.p., 1963-70, exec. v.p., 1971—. Active treas. U.S.O., Reno; past pres. Reno-Sparks United Fund; exec. com. Lake Tahoe Area Council; exec. bd. Nev. Area council Boy Scouts of Am.; mem. Nev. 4-H Adv. Council; adv. bd. Milligan Coll.; treas. Nev. Blue Shield. State chmn. Found. for Comml. Banks: bd. dirs. Nev. Jr. Achievement. Recipient Silver medal Printers' Ink mag., 1967; Nev. award Christians and Jews Assn., 1965. Mem. Am. (past mem. exec. council, v.p.), Nev. (chmn. pub. relations) bankers assns.,

Bank Pub. Relations Assn. (past pres.). Reno C. of C. (dir.), Nev. Press Assn., Nev. Mining Assn., Colo. River Water Users Assn., Beta Gamma, Kappa Sigma. Clubs: Rotary (past pres.), Executive (past pres.) (Reno); Prospectors. Home: 140 Crestview Pl Reno NV 89502 Office: 1 E 1st St Reno NV 80504

CROUCH, MARSHALL FOX, educator, physicist; b. St. Louis, Nov. 22, 1920; s. Marshall Choate and Edna (Fox) C.; B.S., U. Mich., 1941; student Harvard, 1947-48; Ph.D., Washington U., St. Louis, 1950; m. Katherine Francis Carmickle, Jan. 30, 1949; children—Thomas, Michael, Kenneth, Katherine. Staff mem. Radiation Lab., Mass. Inst. Tech., 1941-43, Los Alamos Sci. Lab., 1943; mem. faculty Case Western Res. U., 1950—, prof. physics, 1966—; vis. prof. U. Tokyo (Japan), 1956-57; dep. sci. attache Am. embassy, Tokyo, 1959-61; participation research Case Wits Deep Underground Lab., Johannesburg, S. Africa, 1964—. Served to 1st lt. AUS, 1943-46; PTO. Spl. research cosmic rays, neutron physics, neutrino physics. Home: 35800 Chardon Rd Willoughby Hills OH 44094 Office: 10900 Euclid Av Cleveland OH 44106

CROUCH, THOMAS HENRY, air force med. officer; b. Douglas, Ariz., Aug. 26, 1915; s. Aziel Guy and Jewell (Coggin) C.; student U. Ariz., 1933-34; M.D., Tulane U., 1939; m. Alfreda Kemp King, June 14, 1939; children—Thomas Jeffrey, James Alfred, Mary Lynn (Mrs. William E. Spangler). Intern City County Hosp., El Paso, Tex., 1939-40; commd. 1st lt. M.C., U.S. Army, 1940, advanced through grades to maj. gen. M.C., USAF, 1969; assigned PTO, World War II; orthopaedic surg. tng. Fitzsimons Gen. Hosp., Denver, 1947-50; chief surg. service Clark AFB, Philippines, 1950-52; hosp. comdr. Westover AFB, Mass., 1952-55, Wiesbaden, Germany, 1955-59, Carswell AFB, Ft. Worth, 1959-61; surgon 2d Air Force, Barksdale AFB, La., 1961-62; dep. dir. then dir. med. staff and edn. Hdqrs. USAF, 1962-65; comdr. Wilford Hall USAF Hosp., Lackland AFB, Tex., 1965-69; dir. profl. services Office Surgeon Gen., 1969-70, dep. surgeon gen., 1970—; cons. orthopaedics surgeon gen. USAF, 1955-. Decorated Legion of Merit with oak leaf cluster, Air Force Commendation medal with oak leaf cluster, various unit and area ribbons. Diplomate Am. Bd. Orthopaedic Surgeons, Am. Bd. Preventive Medicine. Fellow A.C.S. (bd. govs.), Am. Acad. Orthopaedic Surgeons, Am. Coll. Preventive Medicine, Aerospace Med. Assn.; mem. Soc. Air Force Clin. Surgeons (pres. 1963), Inst. Fed. Hosp. Adminstrs. (pres. 1964), Am., Tex. med. assns., Air Force Assn., San Antonio Surg. Soc., Soc. USAF Flight Surgeons, Loyal Order Boar, Sophos, Kappa Sigma, Alpha Kappa Kappa. Episcopalian. Mason (32), Rotarian. Contbr. profl. jours. Home: 5001 River Hill Washington DC 20016 Office: Hdqrs USAF (AF/SG) Washington DC 20314

CROUCH, WINSTON WINFORD, educator; b. Vandalia, Ill., July 4, 1907; s. James Wilson and Daisy Edith (Zimmerman) C.; A.B., Pomona Coll., 1929; M.A., Claremont Coll., 1930; Ph.D., U. Cal., 1933; m. Elizabeth Lois Kimbrough, July 14, 1937; 1 dau., Marilyn Arlene. Teaching fellow U. Cal., 1930-32; instr. polit. sci. U. Cal. at Los Angeles, 1936-40, asst. prof., 1940-43, asso. prof., 1946-52, dir. bur. govtl. research, 1948-62, prof. polit. sci., 1952—, chmn. dept. polit. sci., 1956-59; welfare adminstr. Cal. State Relief Adminstrn., 1933-35; instr. Pomona Coll., 1935; lectr. Occidental Coll., 1941; vis. prof. Boston U., 1947. Ednl. adviser Nat. Inst. Pub. Affairs, 1947-48; commr. Los Angeles County Civil Service Commn., 1948-61, pres., 1959-60; mem. personnel commn. Los Angeles Jr. Coll. Dist., 1969—. Fulbright Research Scholar in India, 1954-55. Bd. dirs. Western Govtl. Research Assn., Joint Coll.-Fed. Service Council So. Cal. Mem. citizens' legislative adv. commn. Cal. Legislature. Trustee John Randolph Haynes and Dora Haynes Found. Served as lt. comdr. USNR, ETO, 1943-46; comdr. USNR. Mem. Pacific S.W. Acad. Polit. and Social Sci. (pres. 1947- 48, Town Hall (chmn. municipal and county govt. sect. 1942-43), Am. Polit. Sci. Assn., Am. Soc. Pub. Adminstrn., Nat. Municipal League (council), Pi Sigma Alpha, Delta Sigma Rho, Phi Gamma Mu, Kappa Theta Epsilon. Presbyn. Mason (K.T.); mem. Eastern Star. Author: State Aid to Local Govt. in Cal., 1938; The Initiative and Referendum in California (with V.O. Key), 1938; California Government: Politics and Administration (with D. E. McHenry; rev. edit.), 1949; California State and Local Government (with McHenry, Bollens, Scott), 1952, 60; Intergovernmental Relations, 1954; Southern California Metropolis (with B. Dinerman), 1963; Employer-Employee Relations in Council-Manager Cities, 1969; others. Home: 1035 Anoka Pl Pacific Palisades CA 90272

CROUNSE, ROBERT MABIE, lawyer; b. Mpls., Feb. 18, 1893; s. Avery and Hannah (Seabury) C.; B.A., U. Minn., 1904, LL.B., 1916; m. Lura Mai Harper, Jan. 17, 1933. Admitted to Minn. bar, 1916, since practiced in Mpls., specializing in real estate and probate law; mem. firm Mackall, Crounse, Moore, Helmey & Holmes, 1922—. Dir. Pub. Markets, Inc. Past mem. adv. bd. Mpls. Salvation Army. Served with U.S. Army, 1918. Mem. Am. Legion (past comdr. Lufbery post). Republican. Methodist. Kiwanian. Clubs: Minneapolis, Minneapolis Athletic, Six O'Clock (past pres.) (Mpls.). Home: 200 N Mississippi River Blvd St Paul MN 55104 Office: First Nat Bank Bldg Minneapolis MN 55402

CROUT, PRESCOTT DURAND, mathematician, educator; b. Columbus, O., July 28, 1907; s. Ray Durand and Mary (Sharp) C.; S.B., Mass. Inst. Tech., 1929, S.M., 1929, Ph.D., 1930; m. Charlotte Louise Zander, Jan. 2, 1933; children—Charlotte Louise, Barbara Anne, Prescott Durand, Robert Ray. Elec. and mech. engring. Gen. Electric Co., 1930-32, Raytheon Mfg. Co., 1932-34; tchr. applied math. and research Mass. Inst. Tech., 1934—, in theoretical group Radiation Lab., 1941-45, now prof. math.; cons. U.S. Naval Weapons Center, 1955—. Mem. Nat. Rifle Assn., Am. Math. Soc., Soc. for Indsl. and Applied Math., I.E.E.E. (sr.), Sigma Xi. Author papers based on research in applied math., numerous tech. reports. Patentee elec. and mech. devices. Home: 5 Pinewood St Lexington MA 02173 Office: Mass Inst Tech Dept Math Cambridge MA 02139

CROW, DUWARD LOWERY, air force officer; b. Ft. Payne, Ala., June 26, 1919; s. James Oscar and Cora (Lowery) C.; B.S., U.S. Mil. Acad., 1941; M.B.A., Harvard, 1948; grad. Air War Coll., 1958; m. Eleanor Stribling Dance, Dec. 15, 1945; children—Eleanor (Mrs. Riedel), Cheney Gaylord, Elizabeth Rainey. Commd. 2d lt. U.S. Army, 1941, advanced through grades to lt. gen. USAF, 1969; comdr. Air Depot Group, CBI, World War II; mem. staff Munitions Bd., 1948-52; chief programs div. Air Material Command, 1952-53; comptroller 5th Air Force, Korea, 1954, Central Air Def. Force, 1955-58; dep. dir. budget Hdqrs. USAF, 1961-63, dir. budget, 1964-69, comptroller Air Force Systems Command, 1963-64, comptroller of air force, Washington, 1969—. Decorated D.S.M., Legion of Merit, Bronze Star, Army Commendation ribbon. Mem. Am. Soc. Mil. Comptrollers. Club: Harvard Business School (Washington). Home: 69 Westover Av Bolling AFB Washington DC 20332 Office: Hdqrs USAF (AF/AC) Washington DC 20330

CROW, EDMUND BURWELL, banker; b. Raleigh N.C., Nov. 11, 1904; s. Edmund Burwell and Mary (Dinwiddie) C.; student Davidson Coll., 1921-23; B.S. Commerce, U. N.C., 1926; m. Margaret Elizabeth Wright, Feb. 16, 1929; children—Margaret (Mrs. Charles D. Barham, Jr.), Mary (Mrs. Dale R. Rheineck), Susan (Mrs. Eugene E. Record, Jr.), Elizabeth Burwell. Accountant, A.M. Pullen & Co., Richmond, Va., 1926-30; with Branch Banking & Trust Co., Wilson, N.C., 1931—, sr. v.p., 1956—, sr. trust officer, 1958-71, also dir. Mem. sch. bd., Wilson. C.P.A., N.C. Mem. N.C. Assn. C.P.A.'s Elk. Clubs: Sphinx (Raleigh); Wilson Country. Home: 309 Sunset Dr Wilson NC 27893 Office: 223 W Nash St PO Box 1847 Wilson NC 27893

CROW, FRANCIS LUTHER, see Luther, Frank, singer, song writer.

CROW, JAMES FRANKLIN, educator; b. Phoenixville, Pa., Jan. 18, 1916; s. H. Ernest and Lena (Whitaker) C.; A.B., Friends U., 1937; Ph.D., U. Tex., 1941; m. Ann Crockett, Aug. 9, 1941; children—Franklin, Laura, Catherine. Instr., then asst. prof. zoology Dartmouth, 1941-48; faculty U. Wis., 1948—, prof. genetics, 1954—, chmn. dept. med. genetics, 1958-63, 65-71, acting dean sch. medicine, 1963-65. Chmn. genetics study sect. NIH, 1965-68. Mem. Nat. Acad. Scis. (chmn. com. genetic effects atomic radiation 1960-63), Genetics Soc. Am. (pres. 1960), Am. Soc. Human Genetics (pres. 1963). Author: Genetics Notes, 5th edit., 1965; Introduction to Population Genetics Theory, 1970; also articles. Home: 24 Glenway Madison WI 53705

CROW, JAMES SYLVESTER, banker, ry. exec.; b. Mobile, June 23, 1915; s. James S. and (Jackson) C.; student U. Ala., 1946-48; grad. Rutgers Sch. Banking, 1959; m. Helene De Blanc, Apr. 20, 1945; childrenMichele Marie, Denise Anne, Marcia Lynn, Deborah Jane. Clk., First Nat. Bank Mobile, 1932-41, 45-48, mgr. bond dept., 1949-50, asst. cashier, 1951, asst. v.p., 1952; sales mgr. Hendrix & Mayes Investment Bankers, Birmingham, Ala., asst. cashier First Nat. Bank Birmingham, 1954-55, asst. v.p., 1955-56, v.p., 1957-60, sr. v.p., 1961-66, exec. v.p., 1966-67; v.p. finance So. Ry. Co., Washingto, 1967-70; exec. v.p. First Nat. Bank Mobile, 1970—, 67; dir. several railroads Ala. chmn. Am. Cancer Soc., 1971. Mem. Ala. Security Dealers Assn. 1955), Ala. Bankers Assn. (v.p. 1966-67), Newcomen Soc. N. Am. Episcopalian. Clubs: Country, Downtown, (Birmingham); Athelstan, Country, Lakewood, (Mobile). Home: 217 Berwyn Dr Mobile AL 36608 Office: PO Box 1467 Mobile AL 36601

CROW, JANE HANES, educator; b. Monroe, N.C., Oct. 16, 1916; d. Edward Wilson and Mary (Hanes) Crow; B.S., Salem Coll., 1937; M.S., U. Md., 1938; Ph.D., Cornell U., 1961; summer student Columbia Tchrs. Coll., U. Va. Instr. home econs. Salem Coll., 1938-44; mem. faculty U. Md., 1944-60, asso. prof. home econs., head dept. home and instl. mgmt., 1956-60; research asst. Cornell U., 1960-61; prof. home econs., dir. Sch. Home Econs., U. Me., 1961-65; prof. home econs., dir. mgmt. and housing area U. N.C., Greensboro, 1965—; spl. home demonstration agt. N.C. Coop. Extension Service, 1943; instr. U. Va., summers 1955, 56. Mem. adv. com. consumer credit counseling service Family Service-Travelers Aid Assn. Bd. dirs., mem. edn. com. N.C. Consumer Council. Recipient citation U. Md. Home Econs. Alumnae Assn., 1957; citation Me. Home Econs. Assn., 1965. Mem. Am., Md. (chmn. membership 1949-51, councilor 1952-54, pres. 1956-58), N.C. (chmn. family econ. com., sec. 1959—) home econs. assns., Bus. and Profl. Womens Club, N.C. Dietetic Assn. (v.p., publicity chmn. 1942; pres. 1943) , A.A.A.S., Am. Assn. U. Women, Am. Assn. Housing Educators (v.p. 1970), Illuminating Engring. Soc., Omicron Nu, Phi Kappa Phi, Pi Lambda Theta. Address: U N C Greensboro NC 27412

CROW, JOHN ARMSTRONG, college prof., writer; b. Wilmington, N.C., Dec. 18, 1906; s. George Davis and Olive Lois (Armstrong) C.; A.B., U. of N.C., 1927; M.A., Columbia, 1930; Ph. D., Litt.D., U. of Madrid, Spain, 1933; m. Josephine Gorden, 1956; children—Diane O., John Armstrong. Instr. U. N.C. 1926-27, Davidson Coll., N.C., 1927-28, N.Y.U., 1928-37, U. Calif., Los Angeles, since 1937; chmn. Spanish dept., 1949-54. Helped organize Internat. Inst. of Ibero-Am. Literature (Mexico City 1938), sec., 1938-40; co-editor Jour. Revista Iberoamericana, pub. Mexico City, 1940-42; chmn. Sect. of Cultural Exchange, since 1940; editor Latin Am. entries and revisions to Ency. Americana, 1942. Mem. Soc. Mayflower, Authors League Am., Desc. Knights of Garter, Phi Beta Kappa. Author books, latest: Panorama de las Americas, 1949; Epic of Latin America, 1952; California As a Place to Live, 1953; Mexico Today, 1957; Spanish American Life, 1963; Spain—The Root and the Flower, 1963; Italy: a Journey Through Time, 1965; Greece: the Magic Spring, 1970. Contbr. articles on lit., history, art, dancing to leading mags. U.S. and Latin Am. also encys. Home: 218 N Bundy Dr Los Angeles CA 90049 ☆

CROW, JOHN ORIEN, govt. ofcl.; b. Salem, Mo. Sept. 7, 1912; s. Charles Drake and Lucy (Murray) C.; grad. Haskell Inst., Lawrence, Kan., 1933; m. Juanita James, July 21, 1934 (div. 1956); 1 dau., Emily (Mrs. James G. Gilbert); m. 2d, Bernese Bonga, Nov. 23, 1957. With Bur. Indian Affairs, Dept. Interior, successively supt. Truxton Canon Agy., Ariz., Mescalero Agy., N.M., Ft. Apache Agy., Ariz., Uintah and Ouray Agy., Utah, 1942-57, dep. asst. commr., 1957-59, chief br. of realty, 1959-60, acting commr., 1961, dep. commr., 1961-66, 71—, assoc. dir. Bur. Land Mgmt., 1966-71. Recipient Outstanding Fed. Career Service award Nat. Civil Service League, 1964; Distinguished Service medal Dept. Interior, 1968. Mason (32). Home: 2386 N Edgewood Arlington VA 22207 Office: Bur Indian Affairs Dept Interior Washington DC 20242

CROW, WILLIAM LANGSTAFF, bldg. co. exec .; b. N.Y.C., Mar. 15, 1910; s. Ralph L. and Ella (McClenahan) C.; grad. Hotchkiss Sch., 1929; A.B., Princeton, 1933; m. Barbara Baker, Sept. 14, 1936; children—William Langstaff III, Margo B. (Mrs. Randall S. Reis), Sandra B. (Mrs. Edward Luneburg) Barbara, Ella McClenahan. With Wm. L. Crow Constrn. Co., N.Y.C. 1934—, pres., dir., 1935—; pres., dir. William L. Crow Constrn. Co. (Bahamas) Ltd., 1960—. Fair Sky Inc., 1963—, Crow-Hettinger Corp., San Juan, P.R., 1965—; dir. J.A. Jones Constrn. Co.; trustee U.S. Trust Company N.Y. 1951—. Union Sq. Savs. Bank, United Mutual Saving Bank, N.Y.C., 1957—; dir. Webster Apts., N.Y.C., 1952—. Chmn. Rye (N.Y.) Housing Authority, 1964; chmn. bldg. trades div., N.Y.C. com. Am. Cancer Soc., 1962-63. Trustee United Hosp., Port Chester, N.Y., 1947-59, exec. com., 1947-59 chmn. bldg. and grounds com., 1947-58, mem. joint exec. com. bd. trustees and mgrs., 1947-59, asst. sec., 1948-50, v.p., 1957-59, hon. trustee, 1959- -; trustee Rye United Fund, 1956-57; mem. Princeton Grad. Council, 1950- -; trustee St. Luke's Hosp., N.Y.C.; bd. govs. Hundred Yr. Assn. N.Y., Inc.; mem. adv. council Sch. of Architecture, Princeton U., 1966—. Served to maj., C.E., AUS, 1942-45; ETO. Decorated Bronze Star. Mem. N.Y. Bldg. Congress (bd. govs. 1941-42, 50-54, 62-66, v.p. 1946- 50), Princeton Engring. Assn. (pres. 1962-63, exec. com. 1956—), Princeton Alumni Council (exec. com, 1960—), Princeton Alumni Assn. Westchester County (pres., 1949-51). Republican. Episcopalian. Clubs: Princeton (bd. govs. 1957-66), (N.Y.C.); Am. Yacht (commodore 1951-52), (Rye); Cruising Am.; Cap and Gown, Nassau (Princeton); Porcupine (Nassau, Bahamas). Home: Pine Island Lane Rye NY 10580 Office: 250 Park Av New York City NY 10017

CROWDER, WALTER, FREDERICK, educator; b. Bethany, Ill., Nov. 25, 1903; s. Thomas Hickland and Grace (Hudson) C.; B.S. in Commerce, U. Ill., 1926, M.S., 1929; Ph.D., U. Ia., 1932; m. Frances Elizabeth Saywell, Mar. 3, 1945. Tchr., U. Ia., 1929- 36; govt. research Bur. Fgn. and Domestic Commerce, 1936-45; editor and publisher Indsl. Distbn. mag., 1945-65; prof. marketing, chmn. dept. Pace Coll., 1965-71; cons. in field, 1960—. Mem. Order Artus, Scabbard and Blade, Delta Sigma Pi, Pi Sigma Epsilon, Club: Whispering Pines (N.C.) Country. Author: Methods of Statistical Analysis, 1933; also monograph. Home: Pine Ridge Dr Whispering Pines NC 28389

CROWDUS, WILLIAM W., lawyer; b. St. Louis, May 22, 1899; s. James Caldwell and Elizabeth Grice (Elliott) C.; LL.B., Washington U., 1922; m. Virginia Deane Garrett, Feb. 12, 1927; childrenSusan Deane (Mrs. Forrest E. Heacock), William Warren 11. Admitted to Mo. bar, 1922; pvt. practice William W. Crowdus, St. Louis; instr. med. jurisprudence Washington U. Sch. Medicine, 1937-62; interim U.S. atty. Eastern Dist. Mo., 1953. Vice pres. Mo. Inst. Adminstrn. justice; pres. Jefferson Nat. Expansion Meml. Assn., 1949-59, 66-68, chmn. bd., 1968-; mem. U.S. Terr. Expansion Meml. Commn. Pres. The Lighthouse for the Blind. Mem. Am. Bar Assn. (ho. dels. 1946-48), Am. Judicature Soc., St. Louis (pres. 1942-43), Mo. (gov. 1944-47) bar assns., Phi Delta Phi. Clubs: Noonday, University (St. Louis). Contbr. profl. jours. Home: 7316 Pershing Av St Louis MO 63130 Office: 506 Olive St St Louis MO 63101

CROWE, BETTINA LUM, author; b. Mpls., Apr. 27, 1911; d. Burt Francis and Bertha (Bull) Lum; ed. privately; m. Colin Crowe, May 21, 1938. Mem. Soc. Women Geographers. Author: (under name Peter Lum) Stars in Our Heaven, 1948; Fabulous Beasts, 1953; Peking, 1950-53, 1958; The Purple Barrier, 1960; The Story of the Great Wall of China, 1960; Italian Fairy Tales, 1963; Fairy Tales From the Barbary Coast, 1967; The Holiday Moon, 1963; Fairy Tales of China, 1959; The Growth of Civilization in East Asia, 1969. Address: Pigeon House Bibury Cirencester Gloucester England

CROWE, BRIAN LEE, British diplomat; b. London, Eng., Jan. 5, 1938; s. Eric Eyre and Virginia Rolling (Teusler) C.; 1st class honors in Philosophy, Politics and Econs., Magdalen Coll., Oxford U., 1961; m. Virginia Willis, Jan. 16, 1969. Joined Fgn. Service U.K., 1961; 3d sec., Moscow, 1962-64; assigned London, 1965-67; 2d sec. Brit. High Commn. Aden, 1967-68; 1st sec., Washington, 1968—. Served with Brit. Army, 1957: Malaya. Home: 3752 Jocelyn St Washington DC 20015 Office: 3100 Massachusetts Av NW Washington DC 20015

CROWE, CHARLES MONROE, clergyman; b. San Antonio, Feb. 6, 1902; s. John Henry and Elizabeth (Schreiner) C.; A.B., So. Meth. U., 1924; B.D., Union Theol. Sem., N.Y.C., 1928; D.D., DePauw U., 1955, McKendree Coll., 1955; m. Lucy-Avis McElvaney, Apr. 25, 1931. Ordained to ministry Methodist Ch., 1930; pastor in Bartless, Tex., 1928-29, Waco, Tex., 1929-30, Waxahachie, Tex., 1933-36, Shreveport, 1937-38, St. Louis, 1938-46, Wilmette (Ill) Parish, 1946-66; lectr., TV and radio speaker. Pres. Ch. Fedn. Greater Chgo., 1961-62. Mem. Phi Beta Kappa, Tau Kappa Alpha, Theta Phi. Clubs: Union League Rotary (Chgo.). Author: Sermons for Special Days, 1951; On Living with Yourself, 1952; Sermons On the Parables of Jesus, 1953; Sermons From the Mount, 1954; The Years of Our Lord, 1955; Getting Help from the Bible, 1957; Getting Ready for Tomorrow, 1959; Stewardship Sermons, 1960; The Best of the Sanctuary, 1963; In This Free Land, 1964; also annual Lenten Booklet, Sanctuary, 1949-67. Home: PO Box 2743 Pompano Beach FL 33062

CROWE, SIR COLIN, Brit. govt. ofcl.; b. Yokohama, Japan, Sept. 7, 1913; s. Sir Edward Thomas Frederick and Eleanor (Lay) C.; M.A., Oriel Coll. (Eng.), 1935; grad. Imperial Def. Coll., 1957; m. Bettina Lum, May 21, 1938. Vice-consul Brit. embassy, Peking, China, 1936-38, Shanghai, 1938-40; 2d and 3d sec. Brit. embassy, Washington, 1940-45; mem. staff Fgn. Office, 1945-48; 1st sec. permanent U.K. del. Orgn. European Econ. Coop., 1948-49; 1st sec. Brit. legation, Tel Aviv, 1949-50; 1st sec., Peking, 1950-53; head Far Eastern Dept., Fgn. Office, 1953-56; minister, head Brit. Property Commn., Cairo, 1959; charge d'affaires Brit. Diplomatic Mission, Cairo, 1959-61; dep. permanent rep. to UN, N.Y.C., 1961-63, ambassador to Jedda, 1963-64; chief adminstrn. Diplomatic Service, 1965-68; Brit. high commnr., Ottawa, 1968-70; permanent rep. U.K. to UN, N.Y.C., 1970—. Supernumery fellow St. Anthony's Coll., Oxford U., 1964-65. Club: Traveller's (London). Home: Pigeon House Bibury Glos England Office: UK Mission to UN 845 3d Av New York City NY 10022

CROWE, EUGENE BERTRAND, mgmt. cons.; b. Wadley, Ala., Nov. 2, 1916; s. Will Mack and Eudoxie (Bonner) C.; B.S. in Pub. Adminstrn., Am. U., 1945; children—Ray, Robert, Harold, Julie. With SEC, 1938-40, VA, 1946-48; mgmt. and budget analyst CAA, 1948-50; analyst State Dept., 1950-51; budget examiner Exec. Office Pres., 1951-54; asst. controller Bur. Ordnance, 1954- 58; prof. polit. sci. Bir Zeit (Jordan) Coll., 1960-61; pub. adminstrn. adviser to King Hussein of Jordan, 1959-61; dep. asst. postmaster gen., controller Post Office Dept., 1963-66, exec. asst. to dep. postmaster gen., 1967-68; private mgmt. cons., Tallahassee, 1968—. Served to maj. USAAF, 1942-46. Cited by King Hussein, 1961. Mem. Am. Soc. Pub. Adminstrn., Soc. Internat. Devel., Fed. Govt. Accountants Assn., Pi Kappa Alpha. Episcopalian. Author: (with Sir Eric Franklin) Economic Development in Jordan, 1961. Home: 2125 Jackson Bluff Rd Tallahassee FL 32304 Office: PO Box 1832 Tallahassee FL 32302

CROWE, GUTHRIE FERGUSON, dist. judge; b. La Grange, Ky., July 24, 1910; s. Robert Thomas Florence (Eastes) C.; student Ky. Mil. Inst., 1926-27, U. Ky., 1928-29, U. Louisville, 1930-32; LL.B., Cumberland U., 1933; m. Sue Eliza Vance, Jan. 18, 1939; 1 dau., Betty Gwyn. Admitted to Ky. bar, 1933; practiced law, La Grange, 1933-42, 46-52; judge La Grange, 1938-42; U.S. dist. judge Canal Zone, 1952—. Elected state rep. 53d Dist. Ky., 1942; commr. Ky. State Police, 1948-52. Bd. dirs., chmn. bd. mgmt. Balboa (C.Z.) YMCA, Boy Scouts; chmn. C.Z. chpt. A.R.C. Served as lt. comdr. USN, 1942-45. Decorated Bronze Star, Navy and Marine Corps Medal, Sec. Navy Citation. Pres. Ky Assn. Theater Owners. 1945-52. Mem. Am. Legion (dept. comdr. Ky. 1948- 49), V.F.W., Fed. Bar Assn., (pres. C.Z. chpt. 1964), Phi Delta Theta, Sigma Delta Kappa, Democrat. Methodist. Home: 207 Gorgas Rd Balboa Heights CZ Office: Box 2006 Balboa Heights CZ

CROWE, JAMES ROGER, rice planter; b. Lanes Ferry, Tenn. Apr. 11, 1895; s. Bennett and Emma (Kirkpatrick) C.; student Highland Park Coll.; m. Hazel Price Davis, Jan. 10, 1917; 1 dau., Patricia (Mrs. Lewis M. Gravis). Pres. Ark. Irrigation, 1940—. Roger Crowe Farms, Inc.; dir. First Nat. Bank, Ark. La. Gas Co.; rice planter, 1918—. Chmn. Ark. Game and Fish Commn.; mem. Stuttgard (Ark.) City Council, 1928-30, Sch. Bd., 1930- 36, Ark. Bd. Finance, 1936-40. Trustee Ducks Unlimited, Inc. of Am., 1948—; chmn. bldg. com. Stuttgart Meml. Hosp. Mem. Stuttgart C. of C. Mason (Shriner, K T.). Clubs: Little Rock Country, Little Rock; Stuttgart Country. Home: 1000 S Grand Av Stuttgart AR 72160

CROWE, JOHN WILLIAM, chem. co. exec.; b. Rossburn, Man., Can., Mar. 31, 1918; s. William Johnson and Georgina (Gammon) C.; C.A., Canadian Inst. Chartered Accountants, 1942; B.A., U. Man., 1947; m. Edith Margaret Dawnay, Nov. 1, 1947; children—Carolyn, Leighan. Various positions with Canadian Industries, Ltd., 1947-68, controller, 1969-71; v.p. I.C.I. Am., Inc., Stamford, Conn., 1971—. Served with Canadian Army, 1943-46; ETO. Mem. Canadian Inst. Chartered Accountants, Soc. for Advancement Mgmt. (past pres.

Montreal chpt., v.p. Canadian region). Unitarian Contbr. articles profl. jours. Home: 38 Dulan Dr Stamford CT 06904 Office: ICI Am Inc PO Box 1274 Stamford CT 06904

CROWE, KENNETH MORSE, educator; b. Boston, Oct. 6, 1926; B.S., Brown U., 1948, Ph.D. in Physics, 1953; married; 4 children. Research asso. High-Energy Physics Lab., Stanford, 1951-56; physicist Radiation Lab. U. Cal. at Berkeley, 1949-51, 56—, asst. prof. physics, 1958-60, asso. prof., 1960-68, prof., 1968—. Served with USNR, 1944-46. Mem. Am. Phys. Soc. Office: LeConte Hall U Cal Berkeley CA 94720*

CROWE, PHILIP KINGSLAND, conservationist, ambassador; b. N.Y.C., Jan. 7, 1908; s. Earl and Kathleen McClellan (Higgins) C.; grad. U. Va., 1932; m. Irene Pettus, June 21, 1937; children—Phillippa, Irene, Mary. Reporter, N.Y. Evening Post, 1933; chief customers dept. Milmine Bodman, broker, N.Y.C. 1934-35; explorer, hunter big game, French Indo-China, 1935-37; dir. travel advt. Life mag., 1937-38; advt. staff Fortune mag., 1938-41, 44-48; spl. rep. ECA, China, 1948-49; ambassador to Ceylon, 1953-56; U.S. del. ECAFE Conf. UN, 1954; spl. asst. to sec. state, 1957-59; U.S. ambassador to Union of South Africa, 1959-61, Norway, Oslo, 1969—. Leader, Wildlife Mission to Near East, 1963, S.Am., 1964, Far East, 1965, Middle East, 1966, Central Am., 1967, South Africa, 1968. Mem. bd. adv. Sch. Advanced Internat. Studies, Johns Hopkins. Trustee Fgn. Service Ednl. Found.; Bd. dirs. World Wildlife Fund, African Wildlife Leadership Found. Served lt. col. USAAF, 1941-44, chief intelligence OSS, CBI. Decorated Bronze Star (U.S.); Order of Yun-Hui (Republic of China); officer French Legion Honor; grand ofcl. Mil. Order Christ; Portugal, 1963. Fellow Royal Asiatic Soc., Royal Geog. Soc.; mem. Council Fgn. Relations, Soc. Colonial Wars, Huguenot Soc., St. Nicholas Soc., Soc. Cin., Ex-mems. Assn. Squadron A (N.Y. N.G.) Am. Com. for Internat. Wildlife Protection, Tobique Salmon Club, Atlantic Salmon Assn., Clubs: Racquet and Tennis, Explorers, Brook, Anglers, Century Assn., Bonne and Crocket (N.Y.C.); Lokota; Round Table, Country (Woodstock, Vt.); Harvard Travellers (Boston); Hill (Ceylon); Dacor House, Metropolitan (Washington); Boodles, Flyfishers (London); Rand (Johannesburg) South Africa; Chesapeake Bay Yacht (Easton, Md.); Norske Selscab, Royal Norwegian Yacht (Oslo). Author: Sport is Where you Find it, 1953; Diversions of a Diplomate in Ceylon, 1957; Sporting Journeys, 1966; The Empty Ark, 1967; World Wildlife-the Last Stand, 1970; Out of the Mainstream, 1970. Address: Am Embassy Oslo Norway

CROWE, ROBERT MICHAEL, educator; b. Providence, July 21, 1935; s. Harvey R. and Anna L. (Morrill) C.; B.S. in Bus. Adminstrn., Boston Coll., 1957; M.A. in Econs., U. Pa., 1960, Ph.D., 1963; m. Patricia M. Solan, June 13, 1959; children—Robert Michael, Elaine M., Russell D. Asst. prof. finance and ins. Northeastern U., Boston, 1959-61; dir. exams. Am. Coll. Life Underwriters, Bryn Mawr, Pa., 1961-64; asso. prof. ins., asst. v.p. for research adminstrn. U. S.C., 1964-68; dean Coll. Bus. Adminstrn., prof. econs. U. Tulsa, 1968—. Cons. to pvt. bus., govt. agys., ednl. instns.; mem. Nat. Def. Execs. Res., 1967—. Fellow S.S. Huebner Found. C.L.U., C.P.C.U. Mem. Am. Soc. C.L.U.'s, Soc. C.P.C.U.'s, Am. Risk and Ins. Assn., Beta Gamma Sigma, Delta Sigma Pi. Editor (with Robert D. Eilers) Group Insurance Handbook, 1965. Home: 4109 E 72d Pl Tulsa OK 74136

CROWE, ROBERT WILLIAM, lawyer; b. Chgo., Aug. 20, 1924; s. Harry James and Miriam (McCune) C.; A.B., U. Chgo., 1948, J.D., 1949; m. Virginia C. Kelley, Mar. 25, 1955; children—Robert Kelley, William Park. Admitted to Ill. bar, 1949; practice in Chgo., 1949-57; with R.R. Donnelley & Sons Co., Chgo., 1957—, sec., 1965—, v.p., 1970—; sec., dir. Lakeside Bank, Chgo. Bd. dirs., v.p. Chgo. Child Care Soc., 1963—; bd. dirs. Civic Fedn. Chgo., 1966—; chmn. bd. trustees Christian Century Found., 1966—. Served to 1st lt. USAAF, 1943-45. Decorated Air medal with 5 oak leaf clusters. Mem. Am., Ill., Chgo. bar assns. Republican. Conglist. Clubs: Law, Legal, Economic, University (Chgo.). Home: 311 Rosewood Av Winnetka IL 60093 Office: 2223 King Dr Chicago IL 60616

CROWE, VINCIL PENNY, lawyer; b. Braymer, Mo., July 7, 1897; s. Thomas William and Laura Belle (Penny) C.; A.B., Central Coll., Fayette, Mo., 1918; LL.B., U. Mo., 1921; m. Katherine Frances Latimer, Nov. 19, 1925. Admitted to Mo. bar, 1920, Okla. bar, 1921, since practiced law, Oklahoma City; mem. firm Crowe, Dunleavy, Thweatt, Swinford, Johnson & Burdick; co. attys., Garfield Co., 1923-24, asst. Atty. Gen. Okla., 1925-29. Dir. Liberty Nat. Bank & Trust Co. Oklahoma City, Chmn. Okla. Co. Ration Bd., 1942-46. Pres. Sunbeam Home of Okla. City, 1948-49. Mem. bd. dirs. Family and Children's Service of Okla. City, 1949-51. Fellow Am. Coll. of Trial Lawyers; mem. Am. (del.). Okla. (pres. 1960), Okla. Co. bar assns., Okla. City C. of C., Phi Alpha Delta, Delta Sigma Rho. Democrat (nominee for Congress, 8th Okla. Dist., 1924). Methodist. Clubs: Oklahoma City Golf and Country, Men's Dinner. Home: 2229 NW 57th St Oklahoma City OK 73118 Office: 100 Park Av Bldg Oklahoma City OK 73102

CROWELL, ALBERT DARY, physicist, educator; b. Dover, N.H., Feb. 12, 1925; s. Milton Frederick and Esther Ann (Dary) C.; B.S. in Engring. summa cum laude, Brown U., 1946, Ph.D. in Physics, 1950; M.S. in Applied Physics, Harvard, 1947; m. Janet Louise Wright, June 21, 1947; children—Judith Ann, Susan Wright, Cynthia Dary. Instr., then asst. prof. Amherst Coll., 1950-55; mem. faculty U. Vt., Burlington, 1955—, prof.,physics, chmn. dept., 1961—; spl. research adsorption gases on solids. Regional counselor physics State of Vt., 1963-67; vis. prof. phys. chemistry U. Bristol (Eng.), 1968—. Served with USNR, 1943-46. Mem. A.A.A.S. Am. Phys. Soc., Am. Assn Physics Tchrs., Sigma Xi. Author: (with D.M. Young) Physical Adsorption of Gases, 1962. Home: 30 Warner Av Essex Junction VT 05452 Office: U Vt Burlington VT 05401

CROWELL, ALFRED AUGUSTUS, educator; b. Coweta, Okla., Apr. 28, 1907; s. Robert Augustus and Amelia King (Crumpton) C.; A.B., U. Okla., 1929, A.M., 1934; M.S.J., Northwestern U. 1940; m. Florence Wyman, Mar. 4, 1939; children—Robert, Richard (dec.). Publicity rep., employee pub. editor Am. Airlines, Inc., LaGuardia Field, N.Y.C., 1940- 41; photographer, reporter, telegraph editor Columbus (Ga.) Ledger, 1942; mng. editor Columbus Inquirer, 1943, Middletown (O.) Jour. 1944; asso. prof., univ. editor Kent State U., 1944-49, originator and dir. annual Indsl. Editors Inst., 1948, 49, dir. and reinstated annual Photo Short Course, 1946, 47; prof., head dept. journalism and pub. relations U. Md., 1950-67, prof., 1967—. Mem. Am. Soc. Journalism Sch. Adminstrs. (pres. 1957), Internat. Council Indsl. Editors, Assn. Edn. in Journalism, Md. Press Assn. (edn. com.; chmn. better newspaper contest com.). Author: Creative News Editing, 1969; booklets on contempt of ct., press law. Co-author: Industrial Editing, 1962. Home: 6921 Carleton Terrace College Park MD 20740

CROWELL, CHARLES MONROE, lawyer; b. Lancaster, Pa., Apr. 23, 1910; s. Charles M. and Mabelle (Hagans) C.; A.B., Yale 1933, LL.B., 1936; m. Peggy Johnson, June 26, 1937; children—Betsy, Susan. Admitted to Wyo. bar, 1936, since practiced in Casper; mem. firm Crowell & Chapin; 1955—; municipal judge, Casper, 1945-47; faculty law Casper Coll., 1945-60. Pres. Wyo. Bd. Bar Examiners, 1958-62; mem. Commn. Uniform State Laws, 1955-57; pres. Wyo. Game and Fish Commn., 1969-71, mem., 1967—; chmn. legislative-exec. commn. on reorgn. of Wyo. Govt., 1969-71. Mem. Casper Civil Service Commn., 1948-51; mem. distbn. com. Casper Found., 1948-51; drive chmn. Casper Community Chest. Mem. Wyo. Ho. of Reps., 1945-49; mem. Wyo Republican Com., 1951-57; chmn. Wyo. Rep. Conv., 1956. Trustee Casper Meml. Hosp. 1952-57, pres., 1956-57. Mem. Am., Wyo. (pres. 1959-60), Natrona County (pres. 1945-46) bar assns., Alpha Sigma Phi. Episcopalian (sr. warden 1947). Elk, Kiwanian (lt. gov. 1951), Mason. Home: 1133 S Wolcott Casper WY 82601 Office: First Nat Bank Bldg Casper WY 82601

CROWELL, EDWARD PRINCE, assn. exec.; b. Chillicothe, O., Sept. 17, 1926; s. Harrison P. and Jeannette (Sturtevant) C.; student U. Me., 1946-48; D.O., Kirksville (Mo.) Coll. Osteopathy and Surgery, 1952; m. Elaine Sophie Kittelberger, Apr. 14, 1956. Intern Waterville (Me.) Osteopathic Hosp., 1952-53; chief resident physician hosps. Phila. Coll. Osteopathic Medicine, 1953-56; sr. attending internist Waterville Osteopathic Hosp., 1956-63, chmn. dept. medicine, med. dir., 1958-63; asst. exec. dir. Am. Osteopathic Assn., Chgo., 1964-66, asso. exec. dir. 1966-68, exec. dir., 1968—, bur. convs., 1968-, chmn. dept. bus. affairs, 1968-. Mem. adv. council Me. Hosp. Constrn. Com., 1959-64. Served with USNR, 1944-46. Diplomate Am. Osteopathic Bd. Internal Medicine. Fellow Am. Coll. Osteopathic Internists. Home: 3245 Prestwick Lane Northbrook IL 60062 Office: 212 E Ohio St Chicago IL 60611

CROWELL, GEORGE KENNETH, ret. paper co. exec., lawyer; b. Almond, Wis., Jan. 6, 1908; s. Orestes A. and Anna Belle (MacGregor) C.; A.B., U. Wis., 1929; LL.B., Harvard, 1932; m. Helen J. Metcalf, Apr. 21, 1934. Admitted to Wis. bar, 1932, Ill. bar, 1940; practicing atty., Milw., 1932-38; dep. dir. Wis. Dept. Securities, Madison, 1938-40; practicing atty., Chgo., 1940-42; mem. firm Carney, Crowell & Leibman, also Crowell & Leibman, Chgo., 1945-62; v.p., dir., exec. com., Kimberly-Clark Corp., Neenah, Wisc., 1955-59, exec v.p., dir. exec. com., 1959-67; counsel to firm Leibman, Williams, Bennett, Baird & Minow, 1968—; dir. Menasha Wooden Ware Co., Soo Line R.R. Vice chmn. Coordinating Com. Higher Edn. Wis., 1965-68. Served to lt. col. CIC, AUS, 1942-45. Decorated Bronze Star medal (U.S.); Croix de Guerre (France). Mem. Am., Wis., Chgo. bar assns., Artus, Phi Beta Kappa, Phi Kappa Phi, Sigma Alpha Epsilon. Clubs: Chicago, Racquet (Chgo.); Country of Fla., Ocean (Delray Beach); Biltmore (N.C.) Forest Country; Crystal Downs Country (Frankfort, Mich.). Home: 130 Crystal Downs Frankfort MI 49635 also Country Club of Florida Delray Beach FL 33444 Office: 1 First National Plaza Chi cago IL 60670

CROWELL, JOHN CHAMBERS, educator, geologist; b. State College, Pa., May 12, 1917; s. James W. and Helen H. (Chambers) C.; B.S. in Geology, U. Tex., 1939; M.A. in Meteorology, U. Cal. at Los Angeles, 1946, Ph.D. in Geology, 1947; D.Sc. h.c., U. Louvain (Belgium), 1966; m. Betty Marie Bruner, Nov. 22, 1946; 1 dau., Martha Lynn. Jr. geologist Shell Oil Co., Inc., 1941- 42; mem. faculty U. Cal. at Los Angeles, 1947-67, prof. geology, 1960- 67, chmn. dept., 1957-60, 63-66; prof. geology U. Cal. at Santa Barbara, 1967—; spl. research structural geology, tectonics, interpretation sedimentary rocks, studies San Andreas fault system, tectonics Cal., ancient glaciation, continental drift. Served to capt. USAAF, 1942-46. Fellow Geol. Soc. Am.; mem. Am. Assn. Petroleum Geologists, Am. Geophys. Union, A.A.A.S., Am. Inst. Profl. Geologists. Home: 4604 Via Gennita Santa Barbara CA 93111

CROWELL, PRINCE SEARS, Jr., biologist; b. Natick, Mass., May 2, 1909; s. Prince Sears and Ethel Iona (Moody) C.; A.B., Bowdoin Coll., 1930; M.A., Harvard, 1931, Ph.D., 1935; m. Villa Elizabeth Bailey, July 2, 1938; childrenPersis Ann (Mrs. James A. Gessaman), Polly Foster (Mrs. Fred C. Feitler), Prince Sears III. Instr., Bklyn. Coll., 1935-36; instr., then asso. prof. Miami U., Oxford, O., 1936-48; mem. faculty Ind. U., 1948-, prof. zoology, 1962- ; instr. invertebrate zoology Marine Biol. Lab., Woods Hole, Mass., 1936-41, 53, 64, trustee, 1958-66, 67—, exec. com., 1962-65, 67-70; Ind. Sci. Talent Search, 1962, 63. Fellow A.A.A.S.; mem. Am. Soc. Zoologists (program officer 1957-59), Am. Inst. Biol. Scis., Am. Ornithol. Union, Soc. for Development Biology, Internat. Inst. Embryology, Sigma Xi. Mng. editor jour. Am. Home: 1717 Ruby Lane Bloomington IN 47401

CROWELL, RICHARD HENRY, mathematician, educator; b. Northeast, Pa., Apr. 6, 1928; s. Milton Frederick and Esther (Dary) C.; A.B., Harvard, 1949; postgrad. U. Amsterdam, (Netherlands), 1950-51; M.A., Princeton, 1953, Ph. D., 1955; Dartmouth, 1968; m. Marilyn Nelson, Apr. 2, 1955; childrenPhilip Nelson, Peter Dary. Research asst. Princeton, 1955-56; lectr. Mass. Inst. Tech., 1956-58; asst. prof. Dartmouth, 1958-63, asso. prof., 1963- 67, prof., 1967-. Mem. Am. Math. Soc., Math Assn. Am., Phi Beta Kappa. Mem. United Ch. of Christ. Author: (with R.H. Fox) Introduction to Knot Theory, 1963; (with R.E. Williamson and H.F. Trotter) Calculus of Vector Functions, 1968; (with W.E. Slesnick) Calculus with Analytic Geometry, 1968 Home: 16 Rayton Rd Hanover NH 03755

CROWELL, ROBERT LELAND, publishing co. exec.; b. Montclair, N.J., May 11, 1909; s. Thomas Irving and Minnie Helen (Leland) C.; student Phillips Acad.. Andover, Mass., 1923- 27; A.B., Yale, 1931; m. Ruth Brown Shurtleff, Dec. 23, 1938 (div.); children—John Leland, Timothy Adams, Benjamin Shurtleff; m. Muriel B. Hutchinson, Dec. 19, 1967. With Thomas Y. Crowell Co., N.Y.C. 1931—, became pres., 1937, treas., 1937-60, chmn. bd., 1960-68, pres., prin. exec. officer, 1968—, also dir.; dir. Franklin Pubs., Inc., 1952-63, treas., 1958-63. U.S. Dept. State, 1951-63; adv. com. on books abroad Dept. State USIA, 1952-63. Bd. gov. Yale U. Press, 1952-67; trustee Archaeol. Inst. Am., Am. Schs. Oriental Research. Dept. State grantee, lectr., India, 1957. Mem. Alpha Sigma Phi. Mem. Soc. of Friends. Clubs: Players, Century Assn. (N.Y.C.). Office: 201 Park Av New York City NY 10003

CROWELL, RUSSELL ROLAND, labor union exec.; b. Walthil, Neb., Apr. 23, 1919; s. Charles and Susan (Bloof) C.; ed. U. Cal. at Berkeley, 1946; m. Marian Raisner, Dec. 24, 1940; children—Steven Russell, William Frank, Wanda Ann. Sec. Cal. Council Cleaners Unions, 1952-58; pres., mem. exec. bd. Central Labor Council, Alameda County, Cal., 1958—; pres. Laundry and Dry Cleaning Internat. Union, AFL-CIO, 1960—, mem. exec. bd. maritime trades dept., 1960—; tchr. Laney Trade Sch., Oakland, Cal., 1948-52. Served with AUS, 1944-46; PTO. Office: 610 16th St Oakland CA 94612

CROWELL, THOMAS IRVING, educator; b. Glen Ridge, N.J., July 9, 1921; s. Thomas Irving and Pauline Patten (Whittlesey) C.; B.S., Harvard, 1943; A.M., Columbia, 1947, Ph.D., 1948; m. Mary Miller Wheat, Sept. 16, 1950; children—Leslie Adams, Mary Allison. Research asst. Manhattan Project, 1943-45; instr. math. Bard Coll., 1946-47; mem. faculty U. Va., Charlottesville, 1948—, prof. chemistry, chrm. dept., 1957-62; research chemist E.I. du Pont de Nemours & Co., Inc., summer 1951. Bd. dirs. Camp Robin Hood, Sargentville, Me. Mem. Am. Chem. Soc., Va. Acad. Sci., N.A.A.C.P., Sigma Xi. Home: 1884 Field Rd Charlotteville VA 22903

CROWELL, WARREN H., investment banker; b. Los Angeles, 1905; ed. U. Cal. at Los Angeles, 1927. Partner Crowell, Weedon & Co., Los Angeles; dir. Pomona Tile Mfg. Co., Seaboard Finance Co., New Idria Mining & Chem. Co., Waste King Home: 801 Bel Air Rd Los Angeles CA 90024 Office: 1 Wilshire Blvd Los Angeles CA 90017*

CROWELL, WILLIAM J., lawyer; b. Tucson, Aug. 30, 1913; s. William J. and Juanita (Saralegui) C.; A.B., U. Nev., 1934; LL.B., U. Cal., 1937; m. M. Harriet C. Lamson, June 26, 1940; childrenWilliam J., Robert L. Admitted to Nev. bar, 1937, since practiced in Carson City; dist. atty., Nye County, Nev., 1947-54; gen. counsel Nev. Indsl. Commn., 1960-64. Mem. State Bar Nev. (gov. 1949-55, pres. 1956-57), Am. Bar Assn. Democrat (Nev. chmn. 1951-53). Presbyn. Mason, Rotarian (past pres.) Home: 930 W Robinson Office: 402 N Carson St Carson City NV 89701

CROWL, GEORGE HENRY, geologist, educator; b Wooster, O., Apr. 10, 1910; s. Henry F. and Jesse (Wilson) C.; A.B., Wooster Coll., 1932; A.M., Harvard, 1934; Ph.D., Princeton, 1950; m. Virginia Anderson, Oct. 19, 1935; children—George H., Judith L., Roland W. With Gulf Oil Corp., Arabia and Venezuela, 1935- 37; with Shell Oil Co., 1938-39; instr. geology Rutgers U., 1939-42; instr. Vanderbilt U., 1942043; asst. prof. Hamilton Coll., Clinton, N.Y., 1943-44; geologist Carter Oil Co., 1944-46; asst. prof. Pa. State U., 1946-47; asst. prof., asso. prof. geology Ohio Wesleyan U., 1947- 55, prof. geology, 1955-; vis. prof. geology Rangoon U. Burma, 1952-54; tech. officer Geol. Survey Can., summers 1955-64; mem. U.S. Edn. Mission to India, 1966. Fellow Geol. Soc. Am.; mem. Am. Assn. Petroleum Geologists. Home: 248 W Lincoln Av Delaware OH 43015

CROWL, PHILIP AXTELL, educator, historian; b. Dayton, O., Dec. 17, 1914; s. Frank Denton and Clementine (Axtell) C.; A.B., Swarthmore Coll., 1936; postgrad. Yale Law Sch., 1936-37; M.A., U. Ia., 1939; Ph.D., Johns Hopkins, 1942; m. Mary Ellen Wood, Sept. 9, 1943; children—Ellen Wood (Mrs. Frank A. O'Neil), Catherine Pauline, Margaret Axtell. Instr., Princeton, 1941-42, asst. prof. history, 1945-49, research asso., 1964; historian Dept. Army, 1949-55; intelligence officer State Dept., 1957-67; dir., cons. John Foster Dulles Oral History Project, Princeton, 1964-66; prof., chmn. dept. history U. Neb., 1967—. Pres. adv. bd. archival affairs Nat. Archives region 6, Kansas City, Mo.; bd. dirs. Harry S. Truman Library Inst.; mem. hist. adv. bd. to comdt. USMC, 1969—. Served to lt. comr. USNR, 1942- 45. Decorated Silver Star medal. Mem. Am. Hist. Soc., Orgn. Am. Historians, Am. Assn. U. Profs., Am. Mil. Inst., U.S. Naval Inst., Phi Beta Kappa, Delta Upsilon. Clubs: Cosmos (Washington); Nassau (Princeton, N.J.); University (Lincoln, Neb.). Presbyn. Author: Maryland During and After the American Revolution, 1943; (with J.A. Isely) The U.S. Marines and Amphibious Warfare, 1951; Seminare of the Gilberts and Marshalls, 1955; (with E.G. Love) Seizure of the Gilberts and Marshalls, 1955; Campaign in the Mariannas, 1960. Editor (with J. Smith) Prince George's County Maryland Court Records, 1696-1699, 1964. Editorial bd. Mil. Affairs. Home: 2108 S 24th St Lincoln NB 68502

CROWL, RICHARD BERNARD, metal co. exec.; b. New Brunswick, N.J., Aug. 10, 1931; s. R. Bernard and Ella (Hermann) C.; student U. Notre Dame, 1950-51, Am. U., 1953; B.S. in Bus. Adminstrn., Rutgers U., 1955; m. Lydia M. Canonico, Aug. 15, 1952; children—Joan Barbara, Robert Bern. With Am. Metal Co. Ltd., and predecessor, 1955—, treas. 1967—, v.p., 1970—. Served with USAF, 1951-53. Address: 1270 Av of Americas New York City NY 10020

CROWLEY, ARCHIE HENRY, bishop; b. Lynn, Mass., Jan. 17, 1907; s. Benjamin and Matilda (Cumberland) C.; A.B., Dartmouth, 1929; B.D., Episcopal Theol. Sem., Cambridge, Mass., 1934; D.D., Kenyon Coll., 1960; m. Jean Durgin Higbie; childrenLawrence Higbie, Daniel Fenwick. Ordained to ministry Episcopal Ch., 1934; asst. St. Paul's Cathedral, Boston, 1934-35; curate Grace Ch., Lawrence, Mass., 1935-37, rector, 1937-49; rector St. James' Ch., Grosse Isle, Mich., 1949-54; suffragan bishop Episcopal Diocese Mich., 1954-. Pres. Mich. Council Chs., 1965-66; pres. Met. Detroit Council of Chs., 1968-69. Chmn. Gov. Mich. Commn. Fair Campaaign Practices, 1964- ; dir. Mich. Commn. Human Resources, 1966-; mem. Mayor Detroit Com. Hosp. Needs for City, 1966-67. Chmn. bd. dirs. Lynn Hosp., Lincoln Park, bd. dirs. Camp O-At-Ka, East Sebago, Me.; pres. Am. Indian Found. 1954-. Recipient citation for services Mich. Council Chs., 1967. Home: 1986 Fairway Dr Birmingham MI 48009 Office: 4800 Woodward Av Detroit MI 48201

CROWLEY, CALE J., lawyer; b. Butte, Mont., Oct. 30, 1912; B.A., U. Mont., 1936, LL.B., 1936. Admitted to Mont. bar, 1936; now mem. firm Crowley, Kilbourne, Haughey, Hanson & Gallagher, Billings, Mont. Fellow Am. Coll. Trial Lawyers; mem. Am., Mont. (pres. 1965-66), Yellowstone County bar assns., Internat. Soc. Barristers, Internat. Assn. Ins. Counsel, Am. Law Inst. Office: Electric Bldg Billings MT 59101*

CROWLEY, DANIEL FRANCIS, pub. co. exec.; b. Yonkers, N.Y., Nov. 23, 1915; s. Cornelius Daniel and Elizabeth M. (Treacey) C.; A.B., Columbia, 1936, M.S., 1937; m. Margaret M. Murphy, June 8, 1946; children—Margaret Mary, Daniel Francis. Mem. staff Haskings & Sells, C.P.A.'s, N.Y.C., 1937-42, 46-47; with McGraw-Hill, Inc., 1947—, corporate controller, v.p., controller publs. div., 1961-63, corporate v.p., controller, 1963-68, sr. v.p., finance, data processing, 1968, exec. v.p. finance and adminstrn., 1970—, Adv. com. athletics Columbia, 1966—; mem. Columbia-Presbyn. Hosp. Joint-Adminstrv. Bd., 1970—; treas. Columbia-Presbyn. Med. Center Fund, Inc., 1971—. Alumni trustee Columbia. Served to comdr. USNR, World War 11. Mem. Financial Execs. Inst. (pres. N.Y.C. chpt. 1967-68, Eastern area v.p. 1971—), Am. Inst. C.P.A.'s, Alumni Assn. Columbia Grad. Sch. Bus. (past pres.), Columbia Alumni Fedn. (past sec.-treas.), Am. Legion, Friendly Sons St. Patrick. Clubs: Columbia (N.Y.C.); St. Andrews Golf (Hastings-on-Hudson, N.Y.); Columbia Varsity C (past pres.). Knight of Malta. Home: 41 Euclid Av Hastings-on-Hudson NY 10706 Office: 330 W 42nd St New York City NY 10036

CROWLEY, EDWARD JOSEPH hotel exec.; b. Los Angeles, Aug. 14, 1905; s. Edward Joseph and Orpha (Soule) C.; student U. Ore., 1925-27; A.B., Leland Stanford Jr. Coll., 1929; 1 son, Robert Edward. Asst. mgr. Hollywood Roosevelt and Miramar hotels, 1932-41; also publicity and promotion Arrowhead Springs Hotel, Hollywood; asst. mgr. Hilton Hotels Corp., Los Angeles, 1941-47, gen. mgr. 1947-60; v.p., gen. mgr. Sheraton West Hotel, Los Angeles, 1960-68; dir. West Coast devel. Sheraton Corp., 1968—. Apptd. mem. Recreation and Parks Commn., City of Los Angeles, 1971—, Los Angeles Coliseum Commn., 1971—; former treas. community Redevelopment Agy. Trustee Bob Hope Desert Classic Golf Tourney. Chief 11th Naval USCG Res., 1942-45. Mem. Am. (gov.), So. Cal. (dir.), Cal. (dir. hotel assns., Del Mar Race Track (dir.) Wilshire C. of C. (dir.), Phi Gamma Delta, Alpha Kappa Psi. Clubs: Country (Wilshire, Cal.); La Quinta (Cal.) Country; Desert Inn Golf (Las Vegas, Nev.); De Caza Y Pesca Las Cruces (Baja, Cal.); La Costa Country; Kenya Safari. Address: 2961 Wilshire Blvd Los Angeles CA 90005

CROWLEY, FRANCIS EDWARD, dairy products co. exec.; b. Arlington, N.Y., Mar. 22, 1912; s. James K. and Catherine (Schier) C.; B.S. in Bus. Adminstrn., Syracuse U., 1936; m. Ann F. Bove, Jan.

3, 1944; children—Mary Ann, Jane Catherine. Pres. Francis Edwards Ice Cream Co., Inc., Yonkers, N.Y., 1938-43; v.p. Crowley's Milk Co., Inc., Binghamton, N.Y., 1948-53, pres., 1953—; dir. First City Nat. Bank, Binghamton. Chmn. Indsl. Council Broome County, N.Y., 1960-61. Mem. adv. council Inst. Food Sci., Cornell U., 1971—. Bd. dirs. Susquehanna Valley Children's Home, 1954-60, Gen. Hosp. Found. Binghamton, 1962—, Nat. Assn. Boys Clubs Am., 1959-71; bd. regents LaMoyne Coll., Syracuse, N.Y., 1963—; adv. bd. Lourdes Hosp., Binghamton, 1963-70. Served with AUS, 1942-46. Mem. Pres. Profl. Assn., Assn. Industries N.Y. State (bd. dirs.). Republican. Roman Catholic. Home: 247 Riverside Dr Binghamton NY 13905 Office: 145 Conklin Av Binghamton NY 13903

CROWLEY, FRANCIS JOSEPH, educator, b. New Haven, July 13, 1902; s. Patrick and Mary (Kelleher) C.; B.A., Yale, 1924; M.A., Princeton, 1927, Ph. D., 1931. Inst. French, Iowa State College, 1924-25; inst. French and Spanish, St. John's Coll. (Md.), 1925-27; research asso. Spanish, Princeton, 1931; instr. French, U. Cal., Los Angeles, 1931-32, asst. prof., 1932- 40, asso. prof., 1940-48, prof., 1948-; mem. corr. Institut Voltaire de Belgique. Served to lt. comdr. USNR, 1942-46. Decorated Grande medaille de l'Alliance Francaise. Mem. French History Soc., Modern Lang. Assn. Am. (past mem. editorial bd. publs.), Philol. Assn. Pacific Coast. Club: Princeton (N.Y.C). Author: Voltaire-Poeme sur la Loi naturelle, 1938. Contbr. articles profl. jours. Home: 12239 Shetland Lane Los Angeles CA 90049 Office: 405 Hilgard Av Los Angeles CA 90024

CROWLEY, GEORGE CHARLES, mfg. co. exec.; b. Keansburg, N.J., Dec. 7, 1919; s. George Reginald and Florence (Jackson) C.; B.S. in Elec. Engring., U. Notre Dame, 1942; m. Virginia Helen Kozlowicz, Aug. 17, 1942; children—Virginia D. (Mrs. David Scott), Susan M. (Mrs. James H. Brewster III), Karen T. Elizabeth A. Engaged as mgr.-engr. Gen. Electric Co., 1952-59; Elec. Ltd., London, Eng., 1959-62; v.p. engring. Norge div. Borge-Warner Corp., Chgo., 1962-64; v.p. engring. Philco-Ford, Corp., Phila., engring. No. Electric Co., Chgo., 1969—. Registered engr., Conn., N.C. Home: 231 Forest St Winnetka IL 60093

CROWLEY, JAMES WORTHINGTON, lawyer; b. Cookville, Tenn., Feb. 18, 1930; s. Worth and Jessie (Officer) C.; B.A., George Washington U., 1950, LL.B., 1953; m. Laura June Bauserman, Jan. 27, 1951; children—James Kenneth, Laura Cynthia; m. 2d, Joyce A. Goode, Jan. 15, 1966; children—John Worthington, Noelle Virginia. Admitted to D.C. bar, 1954; underwriter, spl. agt. Am. Surety Co. of N.Y., Washington, 1953-56; adminstrv. asst., contract adminstr. Atlantic Research Corp., Alexandria, Va., 1956-59, mgr. legal dept., asst. sec., counsel, 1959-65, sec., legal mgr., counsel, 1965-67; sec., legal mgr., counsel Susquehanna Corp. (merger with Atlantic Research Corp.), 1967-70; pres., dir. Gen. Communication Co., Boston, 1962-70; v.p., gen. counsel LTV Electrosystems, Inc., 1970—; dir. Cemco, Inc., Continental Electronic Systems, Inc. Mem. Nat. Security Indsl. Assn., Omicron Delta Kappa, Alpha Chi Sigma, Phi Sigma Kappa. Democrat. Methodist. Home: 15755 Daleport Circle Dallas TX 75240 Office: PO Box 6030 Dallas TX 75222

CROWLEY, JEROME JOSEPH, paint co. exec.; b. Chgo., Nov. 17, 1909; s. Jerome J. and Henrietta (O'Brien) C.; Ph.B., U. Notre Dame, 1931; m. Rosaleen A. Giblin, Nov. 4, 1938; children—Jerome Joseph, Maureen (Mrs. Thomas Cahir), Joseph, Alice, Sheila, Thomas, Paul, Barbara, John, Anne. With O'Brien Corp., South Bend, Ind., 1931—, pres., 1948—; chmn. bd. Dixie-O'Brien Corp., 1966- -; pres. Fuller O'Brien Corp., 1967—; dir. Nat Bank & Trust Co., South Bend. Trustee U. Notre Dame; asso. trustee St. Mary's Coll. Roman Catholic. Home: 1516 E Washington Av South Bend IN 46617

CROWLEY, JOHN JOSEPH, Jr., fgn. service officer; b. Albuquerque, Feb. 10, 1928; s. John Joseph and Myrtis (Duffield) C.; A.B., W. Va. U., 1949; M.A., Columbia, 1950; grad. Nat. War Coll., 1970; m. Ileana Rivera Cintron, June 12, 1953; children—Gail Marie, Ileana Marie. Instr. U.P.R., 1950-52; joined U.S. Foreign Service, 1952; vice-consul, Maracaibo, 1952-55; vice-consul, 3d sec., Lima, Peru, 1955-59; 1st sec. Am. embassy, Brussels, Belgium, 1960- 64; officer charge Venezuelan affairs Dept. of State, 1964-66; counselor, dep. chief of mission, Quito, Ecuador, 1966-69, charge d'affairs, 1967-68; counselor, dep. chief of mission, Santo Domingo, Dominican Republic, 1970—. Served with AUS, 1946-48. Decorated Order of Merit Ecuador Govt., 1969. Mem. Am. Fgn. Service Assn., Wilderness Soc. Roman Catholic. Home: 6013 Roosevelt St Bethesda MD 20034 Office: Santo Domingo Dept of State Washington DC 20521

CROWLEY, JOSEPH B., lawyer; b. Chgo., July 15, 1905; ed. Crane Jr. Coll., Northwestern U.; J.D., Chgo.-Kent Coll. Law, 1926. Admitted to Ill. bar, 1926; now mem. firm Boodell, Sears, Sugrue & Crowley, Chgo. Mem. Chgo. Bar Assn. Office: Boodell Sears Sugrue & Crowley 33 N LaSalle St Chicago IL 60602*

CROWLEY, JOSEPH R., coll. pres.; b. Butte, Mont., Mar. 31, 1914; s. Daniel H. and Margaret (Combo) C.; B.A., U. Wash., 1937; M.A., Mont. State U., 1951, Ed.D., 1963; m. Dorothy Pat O'Brien, Feb. 12, 1941; children—Jo Pat, Peggy. Sec.-treas. Mineral Hill Mining Co., 1937-43; dir. counseling Butte pub. schs., 1950-58; asst. prof. psychology No. Mont. Coll., Havre, 1959-61, pres., 1963—; head counselor edn. Ida. State U., 1962-63. Mem. Gov. of Mont. Com. Higher Edn., 1958. Chmn. Hill County (Mont.) City-County Planning Bd., 1963-64, Hill County chpt. A.R.C. fund raising drive, 1964. Bd. dirs. Assn. Mentally Retarded, 1961. Mil. service, 1943-45. Mem. Am. Personnel and Guidance Assn., Assn. Counselor Edn. and Supervision, Am. Coll. Personnel Assn., Nat. Vocational Guidance Assn., Am. Ednl. Research Assn., Rocky Mountain Psychol. Assn., Phi Delta Kappa, Chi Psi. Elk. Club: Montana. Home: 916 3d Av Havre MT 59501

CROWLEY, LAWRENCE G., surgeon, med. educator; b. Newark, 1919; M.D., Yale, 1944. Surg. intern New Haven Hosp., 1944-45, resident in surgery, 1947-53; fellow vascular research Emory U. Hosp., 1949; practice medicine, specializing in surgery, 1949—; attending surgeon Kaiser Found. Hosp., Los Angeles, 1953-59, cons., 1959-64; attending tumor surgeon Los Angeles County Hosp., 1954-64; mem. surg. staff Pomona Valley Community Hosp.; attending surgeon Palo Alto-Stanford Hosp.; chief surgeon Palo Alto VA Hosp., 1964—; from instr. in surgery to asst. clin. prof. U. So. Cal., 1951-64; asso. prof. surgery Stanford, 1964-69, prof., 1969—. Served to capt. M.C., AUS, 1945-47. Diplomate Am. Bd. Surgery. Fellow A.C.S.; mem. A.M.A., Pacific Coast Surg. Assn. Office: VA Hosp 3801 Miranda St Palo Alto CA 94304*

CROWLEY, LEO T., corp. ofcl.; b. Milton Junction, Wis.; s. Thomas Franklin and Catherine Elizabeth (Ryan) C.; student pub. schs., Madison. Wis. Pres. Gen. Paper & Supply Co., 1917—; chmn. bd. Standard Gas & Electric Co., 1939-47, Phila. Co., 1942-48, Wis. Pub. Service Corp., 1948—; chmn. FDIC, 1934- 45; served as Alien Property Custodian, mem. Pres. Roosevelt's cabinet, 1942-43; head Office Econ. Warfare, 1943. Fgn. Econ. Adminstrn., 1943- 45; chmn. C.M., St. P. & P. Ry., 1945-63, 66-70, former chmn. finance com., now dir. Mem. Phi Beta Kappa. Democrat. Roman Catholic. Clubs: Chicago, Duquesne. Home: 1110 Edgewood Av Madison WI 53711 Office: Union State Bldg Chicago IL 60606

CROWLEY, MART, author Boys in the Band. Address: care Farrar Straus and Giroux Inc 19 Union Sq W New York City NY 10003*

CROWLEY, MICHAEL THOMAS, savs. and loan assn. exec.; b. Milw., May 14, 1913; s. Michael A. and Frances (Hogan) C.; student U. Wis., 1929-31; B.S., Marquette U., 1933; m. Alice T. Doherty, Sept. 16, 1941; childrenMichael Thomas, Margaret M. With Mut. Fed. Savs. & Loan Assn., Milw., 1933—, pres., 1965—. 2107 E Kensington Blvd Milwaukee WI 53211 Office: 510 E Wisconsin Av Milwaukee WI 53202

CROWLEY, PATRICK F., lawyer; b. Chgo., Sept. 23, 1911; s. Jerome J. and Henrietta Louise (O'Brien) C.; A.B., U. Notre Dame, 1933; J.D., Loyola U., Chgo., 1938; m. Patricia Caron, Oct. 16, 1938; children—Patricia Ann, JoAnn (dec.), Mary Anne, Catherine, Patrick, Theresa. With trust dept. Chgo. Title & Trust Co., 1933-38; admitted to Ill. bar; mem. firm Barry & Crowley, Chgo., 1938-43; gen. atty. Office Alien Property Custodian, 1943-44; mem. firm Crowley, Sprecher, Barrett & Karaba, and predecessors, Chgo., 1944—; sec., gen. counsel, dir. Caron Spinning Co., Hartland Plastics, KAR Products; v.p., treas., gen. counsel O'Brien Corp. Pres., Internat. Confedn. Christian Family Movements; sec. Little Brothers of Poor. Trustee Calvert Found.; bd. dirs. Marillac House, Fund for Republic, Cath. Scholarships for Negroes, Gt. Books Found., Webster Coll., Immaculate Heart Coll., Bus. Opportunities for Blind; adv. council Notre Dame Law Sch. Recipient Pro Ecclesia medal Pope Pius XII; recipient Laetare medal, 1966. Mem. Am., Chgo., Ill. bar assns. Home: 175 E Delaware Pl Chicago IL 60611 Office: 111 W Monroe St Chicago IL 60603

CROWLEY, WILLIAM JAMES, pub. utility exec.; b. Joliet, Ill., Oct. 7, 1905; s. William James and Hildegarde (Thompson) C.; B.S.C. cum laude, Northwestern U., 1936, M.B.A., 1946; J.D., DePaul U., 1957; LL.M., John Marshall Law Sch., 1963; C.P.A., Ill., 1937; m. Claire Frances Gierman, Aug. 30, 1930; children—William Janes, Susan Claire (Mrs. Jack Crosby), Rowe Ellen Maryin Moore). With Pub. Service of No. Ill., 1926-53, Commonwealth Edison Co., 1953-54; comptroller No. Ill. Gas Co., 1954-56, v.p., comptroller, 1956-63, v.p. finance, comptroller, 1963-64, exec. v.p. finance, 1964-68, exec. v.p. finance and corporate services, 1968-70. also dir.; chmn. Postal Rate Commn., 1970—; dir. Aurora Nat. Bank; dir., chmn. South Suburban Fed. Savs. & Loan Assn., Harvey, Ill.; lectr. Northwestern U., 1936-51. Admitted to Ill. bar, 1957. Mem. Revenue Study Com. State Ill.; dir. Ill. Com. Constl. Conv., Hosp. Planning Council Met. Chgo.; trustee Ill. Council Econ. Edn., Ingalls Meml. Hosp., Harvey. Mem. Am., Chgo. bar assns., Ill. C. of C. (pres., dir.), Financial Execs. Inst. Tax Inst. Am., Taxpayers Fedn. Ill., Civic Fedn. Clubs: Mid-Day, Commercial, Economic (Chgo.); Country. Home: 18456 Perth Av Homewood IL 60430 Office: PO Box 190 Aurora IL 60507

CROWN, EDWARD A., phys. and surg., corp. exec.; b. Mar. 10, 1905; s. Arie and Ida (Gordon) C.; A.S., Crane Coll., 1926; B.S., Loyola U., 1928, M.D., 1929. Intern St. Catherine''s Hosp., 1928; staff Oak Park Hosp., 1929; resident in charge Bridewell Hosp., 1929, Edgewater Hosp., 1930; faculty Chicago Med. Sch., 1932-42; resident obstetrics Cook County Hosp., 1932-33; cons. gynecology State of Ill. Women's Prisons, 1942-45; charge obstetrics clinics Bd. Health, City of Chgo., 1952-54; dir. med. dept. Material Service Corp., 1933-. staff Cloumbus Hosp., Am. Hosp., Cuneo Hosp.; cons. obstetrics Am. Hosp. Pres., Stearns Lime & Stone Co., 1932; 50; v.p., dir. Material Service Corp., 1934-; chmn., pres. RiteWay Products Co., 1947-53, G & D Mfg. Co., 1950-57; v.p., dir. Garden City Sand & Fuel Co., 1950—; pres., dir. Framont Corp., 1953—; v.p., dir. Trimco Corp.; dir. in charge farm operations material service div. Gen. Dynamics Corp.; me. dir. Freeman Coal Co. v.p., dir. Arie and Ida Crown Memorial, Mt. Sinai Med. Research Found. Founding fellow Am. Coll. Obstetricians and Gynecologists; fellow Internat. Coll. Surgeons; mem. A.M.A., Ill., Chgo. med. socs. Office: 1150 N State St Chicago IL 60610

CROWN, HENRY, business exec.; b. Chgo., June 13, 1896; s. Arie and Ida (Gordon) C.; student pub. schs., Chgo.; m. Rebecca Kranz, Aug. 12, 1920 (dec. Oct. 1943); children—Robert (dec. July 1969), Lester, John Jacob; m. 2d, Gladys Kay, Mar. 1946. Clk., Chgo. Fire Brick Co., 1910-12; traffic mgr. Union Drop Forge Co., 1912-16; partner S.R. Crown & Co., 1916-19; treas. Material Service Corp., bldg. materials, 1919-21, pres., 1921-41, chmn. bd., 1941- 59; chmn. Material Service div. Gen. Dynamics Corp., also chmn. exec. com., dir. Gen. Dynamics Corp., 1959-66, chmn. exec. com., dir. of Corp., 1970—; chmn. bd. Henry Crown & Co., 1967—; dir. Waldorf Astoria Corp.; v.p., dir. 208 S LaSalle St. Bldg. Corp.; dir., chmn. finance com., mem. exec. com. C., R.I. & P. Ry. Mem. Chgo. Civil Def. Corps. Bd. dirs. Chgo. Boys Clubs; trustee U. Chgo. Cancer Research Found., DePaul U.; mem. U. Ill. Citizens Com., Loyola U. Citizens Bd.; mem. Northwestern U. Assos.; fellow St. Joseph's Coll., Rensselaer, Ind.; asso., fellow Brandeis U.; mem. nat. council Boy Scouts Am. Served as col. C.E., AUS, World War II. Decorated Legion of Merit (U.S.); chevalier Legion d'Honneur (France); Gold Cross Royal Order Phoenix (Greece); Order Ruben Dario (Nicaragua); recipient Horatio Alger award Am. Schs. and Colls. Assn., Damen award Loyola U., Chgo. Mem. Mil. Order World Wars Mason (Shriner, 33). Clubs: Executives, Mid-Day, Standard, Tavern (Chgo.). Home: 900 Edgemere Ct Evanston IL 60202 Office: 300 W Washington St Chicago IL 60606

CROWN, JOHN, journalist. Editorial writer Atlanta Jour. Office: Atlanta Newspaper Inc 10 Forsyth St Atlanta GA 30302*

CROWN, LESTER, corp. exec.; b. Chgo., June 7, 1925; s. Henry and Rebecca (Kranz) C.; B.S. in Chem. Engring, Northwestern U., 1947; M.B.A., Harvard, 1949; m. Renee Schine, Dec. 28, 1950; children—Arie, James, Patricia, Daniel, Susan, Sara, Janet. Instr. math. Northwestern U., 1946-47; v.p., dir., chem. engr. Marblehead Lime Co., 1950-56, pres., 1956-66; v.p., dir. Material Service Corp. div. Gen. Dynamics Corp., Chgo., 1953-66, pres., 1970—; v.p. Gen. Dyanamics Corp., 1960-66; exec. v.p. Henry Crown & Co., Chgo., 1966-69, pres., 1969—; dir. Urban Investment & Devel. Co., Continental Ill. Nat. Bank & Trust Co., Trans World Airlines, Inc., Swift & Co., St. Louis Blues Hockey Team. Trustee Northwestern U., Michael Reese Hosp. and Med. Center Boca Raton (Fla.) Community Hosp.; bd. dirs. John Crerar Library, Cradle Soc., Meml. Hosp. Mem. Harvard Bus. Sch. Alumni Assn., Tau Beta Pi, Pi Mu Epsilon, Phi Eta Sigma. Clubs: Lake Shore Country, Northmoor Country, Standard, Mid-America (Chgo.); John Evans (Northwestern U.). Home: 1155 Mohawk Rd Wilmette IL 60091 Office: 300 W Washington St Chicago IL 60606

CROWNOVER, DAVID, archaeologist, Exec. sec. U. Pa. Mus., mem. U. Pa. Museum-British joint expdn. to uncover Tell al-Rimah in N. Iraq. Home: 1714 Panama St Philadelphia PA 19103 Office: 112 Museum U Pa Philadelphia PA*

CROWSON, DELMAR LESTER, govt. ofcl., b. Belleville, Ill., Feb. 28, 1917; s. Lester Davis and Anna (Vivjoda) C.; B.A., U. Cal. at Los Angeles, 1940; M.S., Inst. Tech., 1941; m. Betty Parker, Mar. 2, 1946; childrenStanley, Margaret Anne (Mrs. H. Joseph Brooks) Louise, Andrew. Commd. 2d lt. USAAF, to brig. gen. USAF, 1963; dep. chief Air Research and Devel. Command, Balt., 1951-54; asst. to asst. sec. def. for atomic energy, 1955-60; dep. chief staff Research and Devel., Field Command, Albuquerque, 1960- 62; dep. dir. mil. applications AEC, 1962-64, became dir., 1964, now ret.; now dir. office safeguards and materials mgmt. A.E. C. Decorated Legion of Merit with oak leaf cluster, Commendation ribbon with 2 oak leaf clusters, D.S.M.; recipient Service medal AEC. Methodist. Author articles high altitude photography (rockets) for meteorol. forcasting purposes, also nuclear materials RFD 3 Box 32 Frederick MD 21701

CROWTHER, BOSLEY, ret. journalist; b. Lutherville, Md., July 13, 1905 s. F. Bosley (Leisenring) C.; student Woodberry Forest Sch.; B.A., Princeton, 1928; m. Florence Marks, Jan. 20, 1933; childrenBosley, John M., Jefferson H. Joined news staff N.Y. Times, 1928, as gen. reporter, rewrite man, served as asst. drama editor, 1932-37, asst. screen editor, 1937-40, screen critic and editor, 1940-68, critic emeritus, 1968; cons. Mem. N.Y. Film Critics (past chmn.). Contbr articles on motion pictures to mags. Recipient Screen Dir. Award, 1953. Club: Century (N.Y.C.). Author: The Lions Share, 1957; HOllywood Rajah, 1960; The Great Films, 1967. Home: White Plains NY 10602 Office: 711 Fifth Ave New York City NY 10022

CROWTHER, GWYNN KENNETH, banker; b. Lutherville, Md., Feb. 6, 1908; s. Gwynn and Mabel L. (Cox) C.; grad. Marston U. Sch., Ruxton, Md., 1926; LL.B., U. Va., 1932; m. Mary M. Jenkins, Jan. 12, 1935. Vice pres. Morgan Guaranty Trust Co. of N.Y. Mem. Robert Morris Assos. (pres. N.Y. chpt. 1951-52, nat. pres. 1960-61), Delta Chi, Phi Delta Phi. Author articles on bank credit. Home: 16 Sutton Pl New York City NY 10022 Office: 23 Wall St New York City NY 10015

CROWTHER, HAROLD ELLSWORTH, ret. govt. ofcl.; b. Laurel, Md., Sept. 16, 1910; s. William Aloha and Catherine (Hare) C.; B.A., U. Md., 1933, M.S., 1935; m. Gertrude Bradford Harwood, June 15, 1946; 1 dau., Nancy Bradford. Research indsl. preservatives and deodorants Aquacide Co., Washington, 1935-43; dir. research Atlantic Coast Fisheries Co., Boston, 1946-49, 53-55, exec. v.p., 1955-56; chief tech. and exploratory fishing sects. U.S. Fish and Wildlife Service, Dept. Interior, 1949-53, with Bur. Comml. Fisheries, 1956-69. dep. dir., 1963-67, dir., 1967-69; dep. commr. U.S. Fish and Wildlife Service, 1969-71. Halibut Commn., 1961-71. Served to capt. USMCR, 1943-45. Mem. Am. Fisheries Soc. Inst. Food Technologists, A.A.A.S. Home: 7105 Claymore Av West Hyattsville MD 20782

CROWTHER, JACK PAGE, supt. schs.; b. Salt Lake City, Oct. 9, 1909; s. Samuel Walter and Lavinia L. (Page) C.; B.A., U. Utah, 1932; M.S., U. So. Cal., 1955; m. Violet C. Strom, Nov. 17, 1933; children—Jack Page, Richard, Russell, Kevin. Mem. staff and faculty Los Angeles City pub. schs., 1934—; prin., 1948-56, asst. supt., legislative adviser, asso. supt. budget, 1956-62, supt. schs., 1962-70. Served with USAAF, 1941-45, with USAF, 1954-55. Decorated Legion of Merit. Mem. Educare, Gamma Rho Tau. Home: 1643 N Queens Rd Los Angeles CA 90069 Office: Box 3307 Terminal Annex Los Angeles CA 90054

CROWTHER, LORD, (Geoffrey Crowther), bus. exec.; b. Leeds, Eng., May 13, 1907; s. Charles and Hilda Louise (Reed) C.; M.A., Clare Coll., Cambridge U., 1929; postgrad. (Commonwealth Fund fellow), Yale, 1929-30, Columbia 1930-31; LL.D., Nottingham, 1951, Swarthmore Coll., 1957, Dartmouth, 1957; D.Sc., London, 1954; LL.D., U. Mich., 1960, Liverpool U., 1961; Litt.D., Leeds U., 1970; m. Margaret Worth, Feb. 9, 1932; children—Judith V. (dec. 1955), Anne H. (Mrs. Jonathan Sofer), Charles W., David R.G., Felicity M., Nicola M. Investment banking, N.Y.C., London, 1931-32; joined staff Economist, London, 1932, editor, 1938-56, chmn., 1963—; mem. adv. bd. internat. bus. Chem. Bank N.Y. Trust Co.; dir. Comml. Union Assurances Co., Trust Houses Forte Ltd.; Royal Bank Can., Internat. Utilities Corp., Ency. Brit., Inc. Chmn., Central Adv. Council for Edn. (Eng.), 1956-60; served with Ministries of Supply, Information and Prodn., London; with Combined Prodn. and Resources Bd., Washington, World War II; chmn. Commn. on Constn. (U.K.), 1969—. Chancellor, Open Univ.; mem. governing bd. London Sch. Econs. Created life peer, 1968. Clubs: Brooks (London); Yale, Links (N.Y.C.). Home: 51 Hyde Park Gate London SW 7 England Office: 25 St James St London SW 1 England

CROXTON, FREDERICK EMORY, ret. statistician, educator; b. Washington, May 23, 1899; s. Fred C. and Mattie M. (Stocks) C.; A.B., Ohio State U. 1920, M.A., 1921; Ph.D., Columbia, 1926; m. Rosetta Ruth Harpster, Sept. 14, 1921; children—Frederick Emory, Rosetta Harpster (Mrs. William Clark). Asst. in econs. Ohio State U. 1919-21, instr. econs. 1921-26 (on leave 1924-26); univ. fellow in econs. Columbia , 1924-26; lectr. statistics Ohio Wesleyan U., 1920-21, U. Chgo., summer 1926, U. Colo., summer 1948; lectr. statistics Columbia, N.Y.C., 1926-27, asst. prof., 1927-37, asso. prof. 1937-44, prof. statistics, 1944-64, prof. emeritus, 1964—; spl. asst. to v.p. and provost, 1951-53; interim dir. univ. admissions, 1951-53; asso. with U.S. Personnel Classification Bd., 1928, mem. research staff Nat. Bur. Econ. Research, 1929-30; lectr. statistics N.Y. Sch. Social Work, 1930-32, 44; dir. div. statistics N.Y. State TERA, 1933-34. Served in U.S. Army, 1918-19. Fellow A.A.A.S., Am. Statis. Assn.; mem. Phi Beta Kappa, Phi Delta Kappa, Beta Gamma Sigma. Author, or joint author numerous books in field: Applied General Statistics, 3d edit., 1967; Workbook in Applied General Statistics, 5th edit., 1967; Elementary Statistics with Application in Medical and Biologiical Sciences, 1959; Practical Business Statistics, 4th Edit., 1969; also pamphlets and articles.

CRUDUP, ARTHUR, (Big Boy), blues singer, guitarist and composer; recording artist for Delmark Records. Address: care Delmark Records 7 W Grand Chicago IL 60611*

CRUDUP, JOSIAH, ret. coll. pres.; b. Hot Springs, N.C., March 27, 1901; s. Josiah Corelli (Renfrey) C.; B.A., Mercer U., 1923, LL.D., 1958; M.A., Peabody Coll., 1929; Ph. D., U. Chgo., 1939; m. Beulah Elizabeth Caylor, Aug. 16, 1924; childrenJosiah, John Newton. Instr. physics Mercer U., 1923; sci. tchr. athletic coach Ala. Agr. Sch., 1924-25; prof. physics, Ga. State Woman's Coll., 1925; prof. physics, Bessie Tift Coll., 1926; head physics dept. Mercer U., 1927-33, 37-45; physics, Peabody Coll., summers, 1925-31; Gen. Edn. Bd. fellow U. Chgo., 1934-37; pres. Brenau Coll., 1945-70. Pres. Ga. Found. Ind. Colls., 1960—. Trustee Macon YMCA; pres. Macon Community and War Chest; mem. Gainesville (Ga.) C. of C. Received Man of Year award Rotary of Gainesville. Mem. So. Assn. Colls. for Women (pres. 1946), Am. Phys. Soc., Ga. Acad. Sci., Ga. Assn. Colls. and Univs. (pres.), Am. Assn. Colls. (arts com.). Phi Delta Kappa, Kappa Phi Kappa, Kappa Alpha. Democrat. Baptist. Club: Kiwanian (pres. Macon; lt. gov. Ga.). Author: (articles) The Science Teacher and World Peace; Shower Producing Cosmic Rays; Thirty Years of Progress. Public lectures on sci. gen. culture and religion. Address: 835 Holly Dr NW Gainesville GA 30501

CRUICKSHANK, ALEXANDER MIDDLETON, educator; b. Marlborough, N.H., Dec. 13, 1919; s. George and Edith (Coutts) C.; B.S., R.I. State Coll., 1943, M.S., 1945; Ph.D., U. Mass., 1954; m. Irene Bromley, Jan. 13, 1945; children—Elaine, Gary Alexander. Instr., U. Mass., 1948-52; asst. prof. U. R.I., Kingston, 1953-59, asso. prof., 1959-69, prof. chemistry, 1969—; asst. dir. Gordon Research Confs., 1947-68, dir., 1968—; cons. chemist. Pres., Town Council, South Kingston, 1961-65; mem. Selective Service Bd., 1969—. Mem. Am. Chem. Soc., Am. Inst. Chemists, A.A.A.S., Am. Assn. Textile Chemists and Colorists. Lion. Home: 1235 Kingstown Rd Kingston RI 02881

CRUICKSHANK, WILLIAM MELLON, educator; b. Detroit, Mar. 25, 1915; s. Ward and Alice (Shanor) C.; A.B., Eastern Mich. U., 1936, Sc.D., 1962; M.A., U. Chgo., 1938; Ph.D., U. Mich., 1945; Sc.D., Eastern Mich. U., 1962; m. Dorothy Jane Wager, Dec. 26, 1940; children—Alice Ann (Mrs. Roger Johanson), Dorothy Patricia (Mrs. David Crosson), Carol Jean. Margaret O. Slocum distinguished prof. edn., psychology, dir. div. spl. edn. and rehab. Syracuse U., 1946-66, dean summer sessions, 1953-66; dir. Inst. for Study Mental Retardation and Related Disabilities, prof. psychology, prof. edn. U. Mich., Ann Arbor, 1966—. Fulbright lectr., 1968, asso. dir. Inst. San Gabriel Arcangel, Peru, 1962-63; author, lectr.; former cons. N.Y. State Assn. Crippled Children; mem. profl. adv. com. Nat. Soc. Crippled Children and Adults, Nat. Soc. for Prevention Blindness; cons. Teaching Resources Corp. 1966—, also health and ednl. instns., Japan, Eng., France, Denmark, Sweden, Germany, India, 1962—; mem. Canadian-U.S. Study Group on Mental Retardation, 1968—; mem. bd. consultants Center for Research on Exceptional Children. U. N.C., 1969- -; mem. adv. com. dept. edn. Govt. Am. Samoa, 1969—; mem. profl. adv. bd. Pathway Sch., Norristown, Pa., 1966-70; adviser Ednl. Policies Commn.; mem. N.Y. State Regents' Council Physically Handicapped; adv. com. tchr. edn. Am. Found. for Blind; ednl. adv. com. Fed. Epilepsy League, United Cerebral Palsy Assn. Trustee Cove Schs., Racine, Wis. Served to 1st lt. adj. gen. dept., AUS, 1942-45. Recipient Catedratico Honorario Universidad Nacional Mayor de San Marcos, Lima, Peru, 1962; J.E. Wallace Wallin award Nat. Council for Exceptional Children, 1965, Outstanding Profl. award Assn. for Learning Disabilities, 1970. Fellow of Am. Psychol. Assn. (pres. Div. 22, psychol. aspects phys. disability 1969-70), Am. Assn. Mental Deficiency, Am. Acad. Mental Retardation; mem. Am. Acad. Cerebral Palsy. Internat. Council Exceptional Children (pres. 1952-53), N.Y. State Psychol. Assn., Nat., Mich., Washtenaw County assns. for retarded children. Author, editor, co-editor books on cerebral palsy, exceptional children. Editorial cons. Syracuse U. Press, 1966—; editorial adviser Prentice-Hall, Inc. Home: 2855 Whipoorwill Lane Ann Arbor MI 48103

CRUIKSHANK, NELSON HALE, labor economist; b. Bradner, O., June 21, 1902; s. Jesse Lincoln and Jessie Margaret (Wright) C.; student Oberlin Coll., 1920-21; A.B., Ohio Wesleyan Coll., 1925; B.S., Union Theol. Sem. N.Y.C., 1929; m. Florence Crane, Aug. 30, 1928 (dec.) 1 dau., Alice-Marie (Mrs. Howard S. Hoffman). Dir. Social Service dept. Bklyn. Fedn. Chs., 1931-33; labor edn. services, govt. adviser, 1933-42; exec. asst. to labor mem. Nat.; Mgmt.-Labor Policy Com., War Manpower Commn. and dep. vice chmn. in charge of labor relations, War Manpower Commn., 1943-44; dir. European Labor div., ECA, 1950-52; mem. A.F. of L. advisers to President's Council of Econ. Advisers, 1948-50; mem. adv. com. on safety in industry, Bur. Labor Standards, Dept. Labor, 1947-50; mem. U.S. delegation to First Gen. Assembly WHO, Geneva, 1948; rep. A.F. of L. at Econ. and Social Council of UN, Geneva, 1948; mem. nat. hosp. adv. council USPHS, 1946-50; dir. Social ins. activities AFL, 1953-55; dir. dept. social security, AFL-CIO, 1955-65; mem. Fed. Adv. Council, Dept. Labor, 1953-60, 62-65; mem. stautory adv. council Social Security Financing, 1957-58; mem. Health Ins. Benefits Adv. Council, 1965—; vis. prof. Sch. Labor and Indsl. Relations, Mich. State U., 1966; lectr. Sch. Social Work U. Mich., 1967; vis. prof. social sci. Pa., State U., 1969. Mem. U.S. Nat. Commn. for UNESCO (exec. com.), 1946-50, Nat. Planning Assn. (labor com.). Mem com. on experts on social security ILO, 1962—; pres. Nat. Council Sr. Citizens 1969- -; Mem. U.S. Del. to 1st gen. conf. UNESCO, Paris, 1946; mem. cons. group to Sec. Dept. Health, Edn., Welfare; active in Nat. Council Chs. of Christ in U.S., 1952—. Bd. visitors Div. Sch., Duke Recipient Merit award Group Health Assn. Am., 1965. Fellow Am. Coll. Hosp. Adminstrs. (hon.); mem. Seafarer's Internat. Union Democrat. Methodist. Contbr. to labor and religious periodicals. Home: 3001 Veazey Terrace NW Washington DC 20008 Office: 1627 K St NW Washington DC 20006

CRULL, ELGIN ENGLISH, banker; b. Louisville, July 17 1908 s. Harley R. and Anna M. (English) C.; student Purdue U., 1926, U. Mo., 1927-30; m. Katherine Virginia Galbraith, Mar. 23, 1935. Newspaper reporter, Louisville, Dallas, 1930-39; asst. to city mgr. Dallas, 1939-42, 45-51, asst. city mgr., 1951-52, city mgr., 1952-66; v.p. Republic Nat. Bank of Dallas, 1966—. Served as maj. USAAF, 1942-46. Mem. Internat. City Mgrs. Assn. Rotarian. Home: 9424 Hobart St Dallas TX 75218 Office: PO Box 5961 Dallas TX 75221

CRULL, HARRY EDWARD, educator; b. Chgo., Feb. 7, 1909 s. Roy and Janette (Ostrom) C.; A.B., U. Ill., 1930; A.M., 1931, Ph.D., 1933; m. Edna Hale, Sept. 3, 1932; childrenJanet Lee, Royale, Harry. Lectr. Adler Planetarium, Chgo., 1933-34; prof. math. and head dept. Park Coll., Parkville, Mo., 1934-47, dean, 1946-47; head math. dept., prof. math. and astronomy Butler U., 1947-65, also dir. Univ. Coll., 1948-54, J.L. Holcomb Obs., 1954-65; prof. astronomy State U. N.Y., Albany, 1965—, dir. Henry Hudson Planetarium, 1965—. Served with USNR, 1942-46. Mem. Math. Assn. Am., Am. Astron. Soc., Ind. Acad. Sci., Phi Beta Kappa, Sigma Xi. Home: 102 Heritage Rd Guilderland NY 12084 Office: State U NY Albany NY 12203

CRUM, HAROLD WEBSTER, mgmt. cons.; b. Columbus, O., Nov. 26, 1903. s. Harry C. and Edith (Mix) C.; B.S. in Civil Engring., Ohio State U., 1927; m. Lucille Waldon, July 17, 1928; children—H. Webster, Carolyn Lou. Constrn. engr. Ohio, 1927-28; design engr. Goodyear Zeppelin Corp., 1929-37; chief engr. Wingfoot Lake (Akron) Airship Base, 1937-42, coordinator Navy blimp bldg. program, 1942, mgr. new projects dept., 1946; sales mgr. Goodyear Aircraft Corp., 1946-54; v.p., gen. sales mgr. Lycoming div. Avro Mfg. Corp., 1954; v.p. Avco Corp. charge all def. and indsl. sales, 1954-68; pres. H. Webster Crum & Assos., consultants, 1968—. Chmn. Gen. Aviation Council, 1963. Served as tech. sgt. USAAFR, 1925-28. Mem. Quiet Birdmen, Aviation Distbrs. and Mfrs. Assn. (pres. 1963, dir.). Episcopalian. Mason, (32). Home: 3701 E Orange Dr Phoenix AZ 85018

CRUM, JAMES MERRILL, lawyer; b. Virginia, Ill., Oct. 14, 1912, s. Elton M. and Anna C. (Freitag) C.; A.B. with honors, Ind. U. 1937, J.D. with distinction, 1939; m. Thelma Mae Williams, June 28, 1941; children—Suzanne, Deborah, James Frederick. Admitted to Ind. bar, 1939, Fla. bar, 1947; practiced in Evansville, 1939-40, Indpls., 1941-47, Ft. Lauderdale, Fla., 1947—; asso. firm Kahn & Dees, 1939-40; law clk. U.S. Dist. Ct., Indpls., 1941, 46; agt., acting agt. charge U.S. Secret Service, 1941- 45; partner firm McCune, Hiaasen, Crum, Ferris & Gardner, 1947—; city atty., Hallandale, Fla., 1949-53, 57-63, Plantation, Fla., 1953-59, Miramar, Fla., 1955-59. Supr. Old Plantation Water Control Dist., 1952—; mem. Broward County Law Library Com., 1955-65. Mem. City Council, Miramar, 1955-59. Mem. Fedn. Ins. Counsel, Am., Fla., Broward County bar assns., Order of Colf. Club: One Hundred of Broward County (Ft. Lauderdale). Home: 441 Holly Lane Plantation FL 33313 Office: Broward Nat Bank Bldg Fort Lauderdale FL 33302

CRUM, JOHN WESLEY, educator; b. Kempton, Ill., Jan. 29, 1913; 1913; s. John Wesley Charlotte Elizabeth (Heavisides) C.; student Greenville Coll., 1930-31, Los Angeles Pacific Coll., 1932-34; B.S., Seattle Pacific Coll., 1936; M.S., U. Wash., 1938, Ph. D., 1950; postdoctoral trg. Harvard, 1959; m. Jennie Enid Wren, Aug. 7, 1938; children—David Michael, Meri Linda. Rural sch. tchr., 1931-32; chemistry teaching fellow U. Wash., 1937-38; high sch. tchr. Foster Consol. Sch. Dist. 144, King County, Wash., 1938-42, dir. audio-visual edn., 1940-42; supt. South Central Pub. Schs., King County, 1942-45, Chehalis, Wash., 1945- 49; vis. instr. edn. Central Wash. State Coll., summer 1949; asso. prof. acting dir. office visual edn., 1949-50, prof. edn., 1950—, dean of instrn., 1953-66, dean edn., 1966-68, dir. summer term, Tokyo, Wash. Wing, Civil Air Patrol, 1963—, chmn. nat. aerospace edn. adv. com., 1968-69. Mem. Wash. Edn. Assn. (past pres.) Wash. State Tchrs. Retirement System (past dir.) N.E.A., Am. Assn. Sch. Administrs., Nat. Aerospace Edn. Council (past pres.), Am. Assn. U. Profs., Sigma Xi, Phi Kappa, Kappa Delta Pi, Phi Lambda Upsilon. Methodist, Kiwanian. Contbr. ednl. publs. Home: 20 Skyline Dr Ellensburg WA 98926

CRUMB, GEORGE HENRY, composer, educator; b. Charleston, W.Va., Oct. 24, 1929; s. George Henry and Vivian (Reed) C.; B.Mus., Mason Coll., 1950; M.Mus., U. Ill., 1952; Fulbright fellow Hochschule fuer Musik, Berlin, Germany, 1955-56; postgrad. Berkshire Music Center, Tanglewood, Mass., summer 1955; D.Mus. Arts, U. Mich., 1959; m. Elizabeth May Brown, May 21, 1949; children—Elizabeth Ann, David Reed, Peter Stanley. Instr. theory Hollins Coll. (Va.) 1958-59; asst. prof. composition and piano U. Colo., 1959- 64; creative asso. composition State U. N.Y. at Buffalo, 1964-65; asst. prof. composition U. Pa., Phila., 1965-66; asso. prof., 1966-71. prof., 1971—. Guggenheim fellow, 1967. Recipient Broadcast Music Inc. Composition prize, 1957, Koussevitzky Internat. Rec. award, 1971, Rockefeller Found. grantee 1964. Koussevitzky Found. Comm., 1964, Bowdoin Coll., 1965, U. Chgo., 1966. Mem. Am. Soc. U. Composers, A.S.C.A.P., Pi Kappa Lambda, Phi Mu Alpha, Composer: String Quartet, 1954; Sonata for Solo Violincello, 1955; Variazioni (for large orch.) 1959; Five Pieces (for piano), 1962; Night Music I (for soprano, Keyboard and percussion), 1963; Four Nocturnes Night Music II (for violin and piano) 1964; Madrigals, Books I and II, 1965, (for solo voice and instruments); Eleven Echoes of Autumn, 1965 (for violin, alto flute, clarinet and piano), 1966; Echoes of Time and the River (Pulitzer prize 1968), 1967; Songs, Drones and Refrains of Death for baritone and electric instruments (U. Ia. commn.), 1968; Madrigals, Books III and IV for soprano and instruments, 1969; Night of the Four Moons for alto and instruments, 1969; Black Angels (Thirteen Images from the Dark Land) for electric string quarter (U. Mich. commn.), 1970; Ancient Voices of Children for soprano and instruments (Coolidge Found. Commn.), 1970; Vox Balaenae for electric flute, electric cello and electric piano, 1971. Home: 240 Kirk Lane Media PA 19063 Office: Music Bldg U Pa Philadelphia PA 19104

CRUME, BEN W., railroad ofcl.; b. 1916; A.B., U. Louisville, 1938; M.B.A. U. Chgo., 1941; married. Tax accountant Container Corp. Am., 1945-47; chief accountant Franklin Forwarding Co., Chgo., 1947-49; treas., controller Remco Inc., Chgo., 1949-57; with C., R.I. & P. R.R., 1957—, treas, 1967—. Served to capt. AUS, 1941-45. Address: 139 W Van Buren St Chicago IL 60605*

CRUMM, WILLIAM JOSEPH, air force officer; b. N.Y.C., Mar. 20, 1919; s. Charles Anthony and Frances Ruth (Seidel) C.; student U. Va., 1938-41; grad. Air Command Flying Sch., 1942, Air Command and Staff Sch. 1948; m. Ella Jane Tenney, Apr. 25, 1943; children—William Joseph II, Barbara (Mrs. Richard L. White), Deborah, Pamela, Ronald Charles, Michael Weston. Commd. 2d lt. USAF, 1942, advanced through grades to maj. gen., 1964; B-17 pilot in Eng., 1942-43; personnel officer 2d Air Force, 1943-44; comdr. 61st Bomb Quadron, 20th Air Force, Pacific, 1944-45; chief strategic div. Dept. Chief of Staff for Operations, Hdqrs. USAF, 1958-60; chief atomic operations div. Joint Chiefs of Staff, 1960; sr. Air Force rep. Joint Strategic Target Planning Staff, 1960-62; chief operational plans div. Joint Strategic Target Planning Staff, 1962-65; became comdr. 3d Air Div., Guam, 1965. Decorated Legion of Merit with oak leaf cluster, D.F.C., D.S.M., Air Medal with 5 oak leaf clusters; 1st class Vietnamese Air Force Distinguished Service Order. Mem. Sigma Alpha Epsilon. Office: HQ 3d Air Division APO San Francisco CA 96334

CRUMMER, M. THOMAS, ins. co. exec.; m.; 5 children. Financial v.p. treas. United Benefit Life Ins. Co. Home: United Benefit Life Ins Co 3301 Dodge St Omaha NB 68131

CRUMP, NORRIS ROY, ry. exec.; b. Revelstoke, B.C., Can. July 30, 1904; s. Thomas Huntley and Eleanor Jane (Edwards) C.; B.S., Purdue U., 1929; M.E., 1936, Dr. Engring. (hon.) 1951; LL.D. honoris causa, Queen's U., Kingston, Ont., 1950; D.Sc., U. Laval, 1956; LL.D., U. Montreal, 1958; others; m. Stella Elvin, Aug. 23, 1930; children—Ann Louise, Janice Elvin. With Canadian Pacific Ry., Revelstoke, B.C., 1920, promoted through various divs. and jobs to gen. mgr. Eastern lines, 1946, v.p. and gen. mgr., 1947, v.p. Eastern Region, 1947- 48, v.p. all lines, Montreal, 1948-55, dir., 1949—, v.p. co., exec. com., 1949-55, pres., 1955-61, chmn. pres., 1961-64, chmn., chief exec. officer, 1964-69, chmn., 1969—; chmn., dir. several subsidiaries and affiliated cos.; dir. Cominco Ltd. MacMillan Bloedel Ltd., Canadian Fund, Inc., Bank of Montreal (Que.), Canadian Investment Fund, Ltd., Internat. Nickel Co. Can. Ltd. Mem. Montreal and Toronto Bds. of Trade, Engring. Inst. Can., Canadian Assn. R.R. Supts., Profl. Engrs. Que., Newcomen Soc., Internat. (dir. Can. council), Canadian chambers commerce, Canadian Exporters Assn. Mem. United Ch. Clubs: Canadian, Canadian Railway, St. James's; Mt. Stephen, St. Denis, Mount Royal (Montreal); Rideau (Ottawa); York (Toronto). Home: Montreal Quebec Canada Office: c/o G Windsor Station Montreal 101 Quebec Canada ☆

CRUMPACKER, JOHN WEBBER, ret. naval officer; b. LaPorte, Ind., July 13, 1908; s. Harry Blanche (Bosserman) C.; B.S., U.S. Naval Acad., 1931; grad. Indsl. Coll. Armed Forces, 1953; grad. Advanced Mgmt. Program, Harvard; m. Gwendolyn M. Binsted, June 5, 1931 (dec. May 1968); children—Joanne (Mrs. John Fisher), Harry Lewis II, J. Peter; m. 2d, Vera M. Buehm Mauger, 1968. Commd. ensign USN, 1931, advanced through grades to rear adm., 1956; assigned in U.S.S. Saratoga, and other naval ships, 1931-38, U.S.S. Princeton, 1945-46; held 5 major commands, including Aviation Supply Office, Phila., 1956-59; staff Chief Naval Operations, 1959-61; chief Bur. Supplies and Accounts, Dept. Navy, 1961-65; ret., 1965; adminstrv. dir. Navy Marine Coast Guard Residence Foundation, 1965-68; financial transp., logistics cons., 1968—; exec. dir. Easter Seal Treatment Center, Rockville, Md., 1969—. Mem. Nat. Def. Transp. Assn. (hon. pres.). Clubs: Army and Navy (Washington); N.Y. Yacht. Contbg. author: Transportation Century; Transporation Progress. Home: 3717 Nelson St Arlington VA 22207

CRUMPACKER, SHEPARD J., Jr., ex-congressman; b. South Bend, Ind., Feb. 13, 1917; s. Shepard J. and Grace (Dauchy) C., Sr.; B.S., Northwestern U., 1938; J.D., U. Mich., 1941; m. Marjorie Patton, Feb. 18, 1950; one son, Richard Owen, Admitted to the Ind. State bar, 1941, practiced in South Bend, 1946-50, 1956—; partner firm Crumpacker, May, Levy and Searer; city atty. South Bend, Ind., 1969—. U.S. del. NATO Parliamentary Conf., Paris, 1955. Mem. 82-84th Congresses, 3d Ind. Dist.; mem. U.S. delegation Internat. Copyright Conv., 1952. Entered U.S. Army, 1941; disch. to Res. as 1st lt., 1946; maj. U.S. Air Force Ret. Res. Mem. Air Force Assn. (local past comdr., past chmn. No. Ind. chpt.), Isaak Walton League Am. (past pres. St. Joseph County chpt.) Republican. Mason, Elk, Rotarian. Home: 237 Timber Lane South Bend IN 46615 Office: 244 W Jefferson Blvd South Bend IN 46601

CRUMPLER, THOMAS BIGELOW, educator; b. Louisa, Ky., July 20, 1909; s. Thomas R. and Sarah E. (Jones) C.; B.S., Va. Poly. Inst., 1931, M.S., 1932; Ph. D., U. Va. 1936, postdoctoral fellow, 1936-37; m. Margaret L. Ballard, Aug. 5, 1935, (div. 1949); childrenMargaret (Mrs. Peter M. Campbell), Mary (Mrs. Theodore Weiss); m. 2d, Nancy B. Morris, Dec. 15, 1951; stepchildren—William, Thomas, Lucie (Mrs. Charles Levine), Catharine (Mrs. Edward Wood). Mem. Faculty chemistry Tulane U. New Orleans, 1937—, prof. 1943—, chmn. dept., 1943-62, vis. instr. U. Va., summers 1937, 39, 40; vis. prof. Adams Coll., summer 1947, U. Ore., summers 1948, 50. Trustee St. Martin's Episcopal Sch. Ford Found. fellow, 1951-52. Fellow Am. Inst. Chemists; mem. Am. Chem. Soc. (past pres. La.), Am. Assn. for UN (past pres. New Orleans), Sigma Xi, Alpha Chi Sigma, Phi Delta Epsilon. Democrat. Episcopalian (vestry). Club: Pickwick. Author: (with John H. Yoe) Chemical Computations and Errors, 1940; also articles. Contbr. chpt. Cane Sugar Handbook, 9th edit, 1963. Home: 515 Audubon St New Orleans LA 70118

CRUMRINE, CARIL T., former exec. v.p., dir. pres. and chief operating officer Berman Leasing Co.; now v.p., gen. mgr. T/M Leasing, Trailmobile div. Pullman Inc., Chicago. Home: Route 2 Box 351 Long Grove Rd Long Grove IL 60047 Office: 200 S Michigan Av Chicago IL 60604

CRUSE, HAROLD, author. Vis. prof. U. Mich., Ann Arbor. Mem. Phi Kappa Phi. Author: The Crisis of the Negro Intellectual, 1967; Rebellion or Revolution (essay collection); 1968. Home: 827 Arch Ann Arbor MI 48104 Office: Haven Hall U Mich Ann Arbor MI 84104

CRUSE, WILLIAM THOMAS, business exec.; b. Helena, Mont., Dec. 29, 1903; s. William Joseph and Carolyn (Benninghoff) C; B.S. in Econs., U. Pa., 1927; m. Marjorie Wright, Oct. 21, 1939. Sales dir. Celluloid Corp., N.Y.C., 1936- 40; editor Modern Plastics Industry mag., N.Y.C. 1940-41; exec. v.p. soc. Plastics Industry, Inc., N.Y.C., 1941-68; pres. William T. Cruse Co., Hoboken, N.J., 1968—. Sec. Bachner award. Mem. U.S. plastics delegation to USSR, 1958. Club: University. Office: 77 River St Hoboken NJ 07030

CRUTCHFIELD, DOUG WILLIAM, dancer, actor, educator; b. Cin., Apr. 30, 1938; s. Howard, Sr., and Jean (Grant) C.; ed. Walter Eyer Drama Sch., Syvilla Fort Sch. Dance. Dancer, actor appearing Cin. Playhouse, 1958-59, Syvilla Fort Workshop, 1961, 63; works include Volpone, Caligula, Caesar and Cleopatra, Scheherazade, Boys in the Band, television plays; operator pvt. dance sch. for handicapped, Copenhagen, Denmark; film Dancing Prophet. Served with USMC, 1958-59. Home: Ellehoj 14 Hellerup Copenhagen 2900 Denmark

CRUTCHFIELD, EUGENE BENJAMIN, utility co. exec.; b. Roanoke Rapids, N.C., Oct. 17, 1911; s. Benjamin Arnold and Callie (Mitchell) C.; B.S. in M.E., N.C. State U., 1933; m. Eugenia Johnson, Oct. 20, 1934 (dec. July 1967); children—Eugene Benjamin, Carole; m. 2d, Margaret Edwards Hutcheson, July 26, 1969. With Va. Electric and Power Co., Richmond, 1933—, v.p. power, 1963-67, sr. v.p. engring., operation and constrn., 1967—; exec. v.p., dir. Laurel Run Mining Co., 1971—; v.p., dir. Carolinas-Va. Nuclear Power Assos. Mem. adv. panel Northeast power failure FPC, 1965-67, adv. com. on reliability of bulk power supply, 1966—, Southeast regional adv. com., 1967; mem. adv. com. Nat. Electric Reliability Council, 1968—; exec. bd. Southeastern Electric Reliability Council, 1970—; mem. water and air com. Va. Mfrs. Assn., 1968—. Bd. dirs. Roanoke River Basin Assn. Served to lt. col. AUS, 1942-46, 51-52; PTO, Korea. Decorated Bronze Star. Mem. Va. State, Richmond chambers commerce, Newcomen Soc. N. Am., Tau Beta Pi. Club: Willow Oaks Country (Richmond). Home: PO Box 197 Manakin-Sabot VA 23103 Office: PO Box 26666 Richmond VA 23261

CRUTCHFIELD, ROBERT RENNOLDS, naval officer; b. Norfolk, Va., Nov. 26, 1918; s. Lee Gary and Nannie (Parker) C.; B.S., Randolph Macon Coll., 1939; M.B.A., Harvard, 1953; grad. Naval War Coll., 1958; m. Kathryn Smillie Gillelan, July 26, 1944; children—Pamela (Mrs. Edward A. Ruckner, Jr.), Wanda (Mrs. Stuart F. White), Robert Renolds. Athletic coach, tchr., Rockingham County, Va., 1939-40; commd. ensign U.S. Navy, 1940, advanced through grades to rear adm., 1967; various assignments to ships, 1940-46; project officer SURANTISUBDEVDET, Key West, Fla., 1946-48; asst. anti-submarine warfare and shipping control, staff CINCLANTFLT, 1948-51; comdg. officer in U.S.S. New, 1953-55; surface anti-submarine warfare, staff COMOPTEVFOR, 1955- 57; ensign assignment office Bur. Naval. Personnel, 1958-59, adminstrv. to chief naval personnel, 1959-60; comdr. DESDIV 282, 1960-61; comdg. officer dir. Anti-submarine Warfare Tactics Sch., 1961-63; comdg. officer U.S.S. Dale, 1963-64; comdr. DESRON 15, also DESDIV 151, 1964, DESRON 26, 1965; chief staff and aide CRUDESLANT, 1965-67; asst. chief naval personnel for plans and programs Bur. Naval Personnel, 1967-70; comdr. Cruiser Destroyer Flotilla Six, 1970-71; comdr. U.S. Naval Base, Newport, R.I., 1971—. Decorated Legion of Merit with combat V and gold star. Mem. Phi Beta Kappa, Omicron Delta Kappa, Sigma Phi Epsilon. Home: Quarters A US Naval Base Newport RI 02840 Office: Comdr Naval Base Newport RI 02840

CRUTCHFIELD, WILLIAM GAYLE, surgeon; b. Henry County, Ky., Sept. 28, 1900; s. Pinkney H. and Amanda (Malin) C.; A.B., U. Ky., 1923; M.D., Johns Hopkins, 1927; m. Theresa Salzsieder, Nov. 2, 1929; children—Emma Lou, Jean Hartford, William Gayle, Intern, Woman's Hosp., Balt., 1927-28; surg. house officer Peter Bent Brigham Hosp., Boston, 1928-29; resident neurol. surgery Med. Coll. of Va., Richmond, 1930-33, asst. prof. neurol. surgery, 1935-41; prof. neurol. surgery U. Va., Charlottesville, 1941—, also chmn. dept. neurol. surgery, 1941-69; neurol. cons. U.S. Naval Med. Center, NIH, Bethesda, Md., VA Hosp., Richmond, Mem. Am., So. med. assns., So. Surg. Assn. (v.p. 1951), So. Neurosurg. Soc. (pres. 1956), Harvey Cushing Soc. (v.p. 1956), Va. Neuropsy. Soc. (pres. 1935), Soc. Neurol. Surgeons, Kappa Alpha, Nu Sigma Nu, Alpha Omega Alpha. Clubs: Farmington Country, Farmington Hunt (Charlottesville, Va.). Author articles in med. jours. Introduced Skeletal Traction for treatment of neck injuries 1933. Home: Blue Ridge Rd Charlottesville VA 22204 Office: University of Va Hosp Charlottesville VA 22202

CRUZ, JOSE BEJAR, educator; b. Bacolod City, P.I., Sept. 17, 1932; s. Jose P. and Felicidad (Bejar) C.; B.S. in Elec. Engring., U. Philippines, 1953; M.S., Mass. Inst. Tech., 1956; Ph.D., U. Ill., 1959; m. Patria Cunanan, June 23, 1953; children—Fe E., Ricardo A., Rene L., Sylvia C., Loretta C. Came to U.S., 1954, naturalized, 1969. Instr. elec. engring. U. Philippines, Quezon City, 1953-54; research asst. Mass. Inst. Tech., 1954-56; instr. U. Ill., 1956-59, asst. prof., 1959-61, asso. prof., 1961-65, prof. elec. engring., 1965—, research prof. coordinated sci. lab., 1965—, asso. mem. Center Advanced Studies, 1967-68; vis. asso. prof. U. Cal. at Berkeley, 1964-65. Mem. theory com. Am. Automatic Control Council, 1967—. Fellow I.E.E.E. (chmn. linear systems com., group on automatic control 1966-68, asso. editor Trans. on Circuit Theory 1962-64, adminstrv. com. Control Systems Soc. 1966—); mem. Soc. Indsl. and Applied Math., Am. Assn. U. Profs., A.A.A.S., Sigma Xi, Phi Kappa Phi, Eta Kappa Nu. Author: (with M.E. Van Valkenburg) Introductory Signals and Circuits, 1967; (with W.R. Perkins) Engineering of Dynamic Systems, 1969; Feedback Systems, 1972. Editor Trans. on Automatic Controls, 1971—. Contbr. articles fields network theory, automatic control systems, system theory, sensitivity theory of dynamical systems to sci., tech. jours. Home: 2014 Silver Ct W Urbana IL 61801

CRUZ, RAMON ERNESTO, pres. Honduras; b. Oct. 18, 1930; ed. Princeton, Harvard. Pres. Honduras, 1971—. Address: Presidential Palace Tegcigalpa Honduras*

CRUZE, GIFFORD, ret. accountant, govt. ofcl.; b. Maryville, Tenn., Nov. 5, 1909; s. Alvin Ellis and Myrtle May (Oglesby) C.; student Maryville Coll., 1928-29; B.S., U. Tenn., 1933; m. Kathryn Belle McNutt, May 18, 1935; children—Alvin McNutt, Carolyn. With Aluminum Co. of Am.; accounting work TVA, 1934-45, asst. comptroller, 1945-51, comptroller, 1951-71. C.P.A., Tenn. mem. Am. Accounting Assn., Am. Inst. C.P.A.'s Tenn. Soc. C.P. A.'s. Presbyn. (deacon). Club: Green Meadow Country (Maryville). Home: 1109 Young Av Maryville TN 37801

CRYSLER, FREDERICK SAFFORD, packaging services co. exec.; N.Y., June 23, 1909; s. Arthur Garfield and Pearl (LaShier) C.; B.S., N.Y. State Coll. Forestry and Syracuse U., 1932; m. Emma Lou Bailey, Oct. 8, 1938; children—Frederick S., Richard B. With Container Corp. Am., Wabash, Ind., 1933—. successively chemist, supt., gen. mgr., Phila., v.p., 1954, exec. v.p. for paper mills and forest lands, 1961—; dir. Container Corp. Am., Marcor, Inc. Chmn. Solid Waste Council of Paper Producing and Consuming Industries. Mem. exec. Com. Brown U. Devel. Council. Bd. dirs., mem. exec. com., past pres. Syracuse Pulp and Paper Found.; past dir. U. Me. Pulp and Paper Found. Recipient Man of Year award PIMA, 1966; Centennial medal Syracuse U., 1970. Mem. Nat. Paperboard Assn. (past pres.), Boxboard Research and Devel. Assn. (past pres.) Am. Paper Inst. (exec. com., dir. 1968—; past chmn. paperboard group, chmn. solid waste council paper producing and consuming industries), Kappa Sigma, Alpha Xi Sigma, Alpha Chi Sigma, Conglist. Rotarian. Clubs: Ithaca (N.Y.) Yacht; Mid-Day, University (Chgo.). Home: 256 Meadowbrook Dr Northbrook IL 60062 Office: Container Corp Am First National Plaza Chicago IL 60670

CRYSLER, RALPH WILLIAM, mfg. co. exec.; b. Mpls., May 16, 1908; s. John Pliny and Inez Ethel (Brigan) C.; student U. Minn., 1926-27; m. Frances Marie Sundstrom, June 18, 1938; 1 son, Dean William. Engaged in oil burner mfg., installation and service, 1927-33; with Honeywell, Inc., and predecessor, 1933—, nat. sales mgr. comml. div., 1957-, v.p., 1964-. Mem. Am. Soc. Heating, Refrigeration and Air Conditioning Engrs. Conglist. Mason. Home: 2724 Raleigh Av S St Louis Park MN 55416 Office: 2737 4th Av S Minneapolis MN 55408

CSATORDAY, KAROLY, Hungarian diplomat; married; 4 children. Served in Holland, 1949-51, China, 1951-55, Vietnam, 1955; chief of protocol Ministry Fgn. Affairs, Budapest, 1956-60; ambassador to Japan, 1960-62; head permanent mission of Hungarian People's Republic to UN, 1962-71, chmn. polit. and security com., 1965, v.p. Gen. Assembly, 1966-71, mem. Security Council, 1968-69, pres., 1969, dep. fgn. minister, 1971—. Address: Foreign Affairs Ministry Budapest Hungary

CSOKA, STEPHEN, painter, etcher; b. Gardony, Hungary, Jan. 2, 1897; s. Istvan and Julianna (Nagy) C.; student Royal Acad. Art, Budapest, 1922-27; m. Margaret Muller, Mar. 18, 1934; children—Clara Eve, Frank Stephen. Came to U.S., 1934; naturalized, 1941. Work shown at internat. exhbns., also Corcoran Gallery, Washington, 1945, 47. One man shows: Contemporary Arts, N.Y.C., 1940, 43, 45, 56, Phila. Art Alliance, 1943, Minn. State Fair, 1943, Merrill Gallery, N.Y.C., 1963. Represented in several museums, including Library of Congress. Recipient numerous awards and prizes, the later of which are: La Tausca Pearl Co. award, 1945; $1,000 purchase prize-etching nat. Print Competition, Assn. Am. Artists, 1947; $1,000 Grant-Am. Acad. of Arts and Letters, 1948; First in oil Bklyn. Artists, 1949; John Taylor Arms Prize, etching, Soc. Am. Etchers, 1952; several hon. mentions. Art instr. Coll. City N.Y., Fashion Inst. Tech., N.A.D. Sch. Fine Art. Mem. Soc. Am. Etchers, N.A.D., Audubon Soc. Author: Pastel Painting, 1962. Home: 85-80 87th St Woodhaven NY 10021

CSONKA, LARRY RICHARD, profl. football player; b. Akron, O., Dec. 25, 1946; s. Joseph Adam and Mildred Anita (Heath) C.; student Syracuse U., 1968; m. Pamela Faye Conley, Jan. 29, 1966; children—Douglas Steven, Paul Scott. With Miami Dolphins, Ltd., Miami, Fla., 1968—, fullback through 1970 season. Home: 887 Allamanda Ct Plantation FL 33313 Office: 330 Biscayne Blvd Miami FL 33132

CUA, ANTONIO S., educator; b. Manila, Philippines, July 23, 1932; s. Oh and Chio (So) C.; B.A., Far Eastern U., Manila, 1952; M.A., U. Cal. at Berkeley, 1954, Ph.D., 1958; m. Shoke-Hwee Khaw, June 11, 1956; 1 dau., Athene K. Came to U.S., 1953; naturalized, 1971. Instr., asst. prof. Ohio U., 1958-62; prof., chmn. dept. philosophy State U. N.Y., Coll. at Oswego, 1962-69; prof. philosophy Catholic U. Am., Washington, 1969—. Mem. Am., Am. Cath. philos. assns., Metaphysical Soc. Am., Soc. for Asian and Comparative Philosophy. Author: Reason and Virtue: A Study in the Ethics of Richard Price, 1966. Contbr. articles profl. jours. Home: 7525 Cayuga Av Bethesda MD 20034 Office: Sch Philosophy Cath U Am Washington DC 20017

CUARON, ALFREDO, educator, scientist; b. Mexico City, Mexico, June 29, 1933; s. Jose M. and Elisa (Santisteban) C.; M.D., U. Nacional Autonoma de Mexico, Mexico, 1957; postgrad. London U. Med. Sch., 1959-61, U. Leyden (Holland), 1962; m. Cristina Orozco de Cuaron, Sept. 11, 1959; children—Alfredo David, Alfonso, Christina, Carlos. Head dept. nuclear medicine Hosp. Gen., Centro Medico Nacional. of Inst. Mexicano del Seguro Social, 1963—; lectr. nuclear medicine Sch. Medicine, U. Nacional Autonoma de Mexico, 1963—, prof. nuclear medicine, 1969—, Recipient Squibb award Mexico, 1957. Fellow A.C.P., Royal Soc. Medicine; mem. Soc. Nuclear Medicine. Latin Am. Assn. Nuclear Medicine. Author numerous articles in field. Home: 21 Tepeji Mexico DF Mexico

CUBBAGE, RICHARD TAYLOR, r.r. exec.; b. Des Moines, June 21, 1913; s. Roy Edwin and Carrie (Taylor) C.; A.B. cum laude, Drake U., 1934, LL.B. summa cum laude, 1937; m. Yvonne Phillips, Sept. 14, 1964; children—Richard Taylor, Jean (Mrs. Laurence Sternal), James Cox. Admitted to Ill. bar, 1938; atty. C., B. & Q. R.R., Chgo., 1937-41, contract atty., 1941-45, asst. to gen. counsel, 1945-52, corp. counsel, 1952-54, asst. gen. counsel, 1954-69, gen. counsel, 1969-70; asst. v.p., gen. counsel Burlington No. R.R., Chgo., 1970—; pres. Burlington Equipment Co., 1961-70. Mem. Am., Chgo. bar assns., Order of Coif, Sigma Alpha Epsilon, Phi Alpha Delta. Home: 9418 Central Park Evanston IL 60203 Office: 547 W Jackson Blvd Chicago IL 60606

CUBBAGE, THOMAS LEON, ret. petroleum co. exec.; b. Okarche, Okla., Aug. 27, 1907; s. Guy S. and Mary Catherine (Shearn) C.; B.S. in Mech. Engring., U. Okla., 1937; m. Mildred Hart, Jan. 2, 1937; children—Thomas Leon II, Nancy (Mrs. Thomas L. Oakley). With Phillips Petroleum Co., 1926-71, v.p. subsidiary Phillips Chem. Co., 1951-63, v.p. chem. dept. parent co. 1963-71, also dir.; v.p., dir. H.P. Smith Paper Co., Sealright Co., Inc., Phillips Products Co., Inc., Phillips Films Co., Inc., Phillips Fibres Corp., Revonah Spinning Mills, Wall Tube & Metal Products Co.; v.p., gen. mgr. Phillips Pacific Chem. Co.; dir. Can. Western Cordage Co. Ltd., Applied Automation, Inc. Bd. dirs. Sulphur Inst. Mem. Mfg. Chemists Assn., Am. Mgmt. Assn., Internat. Inst. Synthetic Rubber Producers (dir.), Bartlesville C. of C., Sigma Chi, Sigma Tau, Tau Beta Pi. K.C. Home: 2325 Windsor Way Bartleville OK 74003

CUBER, JOHN FRANK, sociologist, educator; b. Chgo., Aug. 31, 1911; s. John Charles and Lillian (Vomacka) C.; A.B., Western Mich. Coll. Edn., 1932; Ph.D., U. Mich., 1937; m. Armine Gulesserian, Dec. 10, 1949 (div.); 1 dau., Armine Anne; m. 2d, Peggy Buckwalter Harroff, Dec. 15, 1964. Fellow sociology U. Mich., 1932-35; chmn. dept. econs. and sociology Sioux Falls Coll., 1935-36; asst. prof. Marietta Coll., 1936- 39, Kent State U., 1937-39, asso. prof., 1939-41, prof. sociology, 1941-44; asso. prof. Ohio State U., Columbus, 1944-46, prof. sociology, 1946—; prof. summer sessions U. Chgo.-U. Mich.-Kellogg Found., 1941-42, U. Cal., 1949. Bd. dirs. Nat. Council Family Relations, 1948-53. Mem. Ohio Valley (sec.-treas. 1940-41), Am. sociol. socs., Am. Assn. U. Profs., Soc. for Study Social Problems, Phi Beta Kappa. Author: Sociology: A Synopsis of Principles, 1947, rev. edit., 1968: (with R.A. Harper) Problems of American Society, 1948, rev. edit., 1951, 64: Marriage Counseling Practice, 1948; Social Stratification in the U.S. (with William Kenkel), 1954; with Peggy B. Harroff) Readings in Sociology: Sources and Comment, 1962, The Significant Americans: A Study of Sexual Behavior Among the Affluent, 1965. Editor: Ohio Valley Sociologist, 1946-48, Appleton Century Crofts Sociology Series, 1948—. Home: RFD 1 Cardington OH 43315

CUBETA, PAUL MARSDEN, educator; b. Middletown, Conn., Mar. 12, 1925; s. Salvatore T. and Marion (Bacon) C.; B.A., Williams Coll., 1947; Ph.D., Yale, 1954; m. Elizabeth Bransfield Brown, Aug. 25, 1948; children—Philip, David, James. Instr. English, Williams Coll., 1947-49; Carnegie fellow gen. edn. Harvard, 1956-57; mem. faculty Middlebury (Vt.) Coll., 1952—, prof. English, 1964—, chmn. div. humanities, 1963-67, dean faculty, 1967-70, acad. v.p., 1970—. Asst. dir. Bread Loaf Writers Conf., 1955-64; dir. Bread Loaf Scn. English, 1964—; mem. advanced placement com. English, Coll. Entrance Exam. Bd., 1964-68. Served to lt. (j.g.) USNR, 1943-46. Mem. New Eng. Coll. English Assn. (dir. 1959-62). Am. Assn. U. Profs., Modern Lang. Assn., Phi Beta Kappa. Editor: Modern Drama for Analysis, 3d. edit., 1962. Home: 39 Seminary St Middlebury VT 05753

CUCULLU, LIONEL JOSEPH, former utility exec.; b. New Orleans, Mar. 25, 1906; s. Theophile Joseph and Rita (Bienvenu) C.; B.S. in Sugar Engring., La. State U., 1927; m. Eugenie Cavani, July 3, 1929; children—Lynn J., Alan C., Anita M. (Mrs. Louis A. Frey), Carl R., Lionel G. With New Orleans Pub. Service Inc., 1930-71, pres., chief exec. officer, 1968-71, also dir.; former dir. La. Power & Light Co., Middle South Services, Inc., Middle South Utilities, Inc. Home: 4630 Arts St New Orleans LA 70122

CUDAHY, EDWARD A. III, former meat packing co. exec.; b. Chgo., June 5, 1923; s. Edward A., Jr. and Margaret (Carry) C.; student Princeton; m. Nancy Cochran, Nov. 30th, 1945. With Cudahy Packing Co., Omaha, 1945-55, pres., chmn. bd., Phoenix, 1963-66, chmn. bd., 1966-67; self-employed, 1955-63; now engaged in cattle raising, cattle feeding, investments; dir. Mut. Omaha Ins. Co., United Benefit Life Ins. Co. Omaha. Trustee Cate Sch., Santa Barbara, Cal. Served with U.S. Maritime Service and USNR, 1942-45. Office: 100 W Clarendon Phoenix AZ 85013

CUDAHY, RICHARD DICKSON, corp. exec.; b. Milw., Feb. 2, 1926; s. Michael F. and Alice (Dickson) C.; grad. Canterbury Sch., New Milford, Conn., 1943; B.S., U.S. Mil. Acad., 1948; LL.B., Yale, 1955; m. Ann Featherston, July 14, 1956; children—Richard Dickson, Norma Kathleen, Theresa Ellen, Daniel Michael, Michaela Alice. Commd. 2d lt. U.S. Army, 1948, advanced through grades to 1st lt., 1959; resigned, 1952; law clk, to U.S. Ct. Appeals Judge Charles E. Clark, 1955-56; asst. to legal adviser State Dept., 1956-57; asso. firm Isham, Lincoln & Beale, Chicago, 1957-61, pres. Patrick Cudahy, Inc. (Wis.), 1961—, Patrick Cudahy Family Co., 1969—; lectr. Law Marquette U. Law Sch., 1961-66; vis. prof. law Univ. Wis., 1966-67. Pres. Milw. Urban League, 1965-66; commnr. Milw. Harbor, 1964-66; pres. Gambrinus Soc., 1969; chmn. Wis. Regional Export Expansion Council, 1962-64; bd. dirs. Nat. Inst. Polit. Communication, 1969—; bd. dirs. bus. adv. council Office Econ. Opportunity, 1966—. Chmn. Wis. Democratic Party, 1967-68; Dem. candidate for Wis. atty. gen., 1968. Bd. dirs. United Community Services, Milw., 1965-66. Mem. Am., Wis., Milw., Chicago bar assns., Am. Meat Inst. (bd. dirs., 1969) Roman Cath. Author articles. Home: 4217 N Lake Dr Milwaukee WI 53211 Office: 411 E Mason St Milwaukee WI 53202

CUDD, HERSCHEL HERBERT, corp. exec.; b. Memphis, Tex., July 29, 1912; s. Joseph Nathan and Lou (Tatum) C.; B.A., Tex. Coll. Arts and Industries, 1933; M.A., U. Tex., 1936, Ph.D., 1941; m. Maxine Agan, Aug. 7, 1933; children—Joy C. Greene, Herschel Herbert. Research chemist rayon tech. div. E.I. duPont de Nemours, 1941-42; supr. inorganic chemistry Internat. Mineral and Chem. Corp., 1942-46; dir. Lantuck div. West Point Mfg. Co., 1946- 50; dir. engring. expt. sta. Ga. Inst. Tech., 1950-54; v.p. in charge research Am. Viscose Corp., 1954-50; pres. Avisun Corp., 1960-63; v.p. dir. 1963—; pres., dir. Amoco Chems. Corp., Chgo., 1963—. Mem. Am. Chem. Soc . (chmn. Ga. sect. 1947, councilor 1948-49), Am. Inst. Chem. Engrs., Sigma Xi. Episcopalian. Clubs: Chemist's (N.Y.C.); Chicago, Mid-America (Chgo.); Glen View. Home: 209 Dickens Rd Northfield IL 60093 Office: Amoco Chemicals Corp 130 E Randolph Dr Chicago IL

CUDDY, DANIEL HON, banker; b. Valdez, Alaska, Feb. 8, 1921; s. Warren N. and Nancy B.A., Stanford, 1946; m. Betty Puckett, Oct. 6, 1947; children—Roxanna, David, Gretchen, Jane, Lucy, Laurel. Admitted to Alaska bar, 1948; practice in Anchorage, 1948-53; pres. First Nat. Bank Anchorage, 1951-. Mem. nat. adv. bd. Sport Fisheries and Wildlife, U.S. Dept. Interior. Home: Anchorage AK 99501 Office: First Nat Bank 4th Av and G St Anchorage AK 99501

CUDLIP, WILLIAM BYRNES, lawyer; b. Iron Mountain, Mich., Mar. 4, 1904; s. William John and Luella (Byrnes) C.; student Swarthmore Coll., ex- 1925; LL.B., U. Mich., 1926; m. Lynwood Rockwell Bope, Jan. 5, 1929; children—Mary Luella (Mrs. John S. Jenkins), William John II, David Rockwell, Lynwood Jean (Mrs. John P. Ryan), Charles Thomas. Admitted to Mich. bar, 1926, since practiced in Detroit; partner firm Dickinson, Wright, McKean & Gudlip, 1933—. Dir. McLouth Steel Corp. Mem. commn. recodification Mich. laws on financial instns., 1936-37, Commn. for Compilation Mich. Statutes, 1948; mem. Mich. Constl. Conv., 1961-62; mem. nat. adv. council Small Bus. Adminstrn., 1959. Bd. regents U. Mich.; trustee Inst. Econ. Edn., Detroit. Fellow Am. Bar. Found.; mem. Am., Detroit bar assns., Mich. State Bar, Phi Kappa Psi, Phi Delta Phi. Republican. Roman Catholic. Clubs: Country of Detroit, Detroit; Little Harbor (Harbor Springs, Mich.). Home: 900 Lake Shore Rd Grosse Pointe Shores MI 48236 Office: 1st Nat Bldg Detroit MI 48236

CUDLIPP, HUGH, Brit. newspaper exec.; b. Aug. 28, 1913; s. William Cudlipp; ed. Howard Gardens Sch., Cardiff, Wales; m. 2d, Eileen Ascroft, 1945 (dec. 1962); m. 3d, Jodi Hyland, 1963. With provincial newspapers in Cardiff and Manchester, Eng., 1927-32; feature editor Sunday Chronicle. 1932-35; feature editor Daily Mirror, London, 1935-37, editorial dir., 1952-63; editor Sunday Pictorial (now Sunday Mirror), 1937-40, 4649, editorial dir., 1952-63; mng. editor Sunday Express, 1950-52; joint mng. dir. Daily Mirror Newspapers Ltd., Sunday Pictorial Newspapers Ltd., 1950-63; chmn. Daily Newspapers Ltd., 1963—, Oldhams Press Ltd., 1961-63. Daily Herald Ltd., 1961-64; editorial dir. Internat. Pub. Corp., Ltd., London, 1963—, dep. chmn., 1964-68, chmn., 1968—; dir. Asso. TV Ltd. Served with Brit. Army 1940-46. Decorated officer Order Brit. Empire. Author: Publish and Be Damned, 1955; At Your Peril, 1962. Daily Mirror Newspapers Ltd Holborn Circus London EC i England *

CUELLAR, MIGUEL ANGEL, (Mike), pitcher with Baltimore Orioles Profl. Baseball Team; b. Santa Clara, Cuba, May 8, 1937; m. Emma A. Jimenez Reyes, Nov. 18, 1957. Address: care Memorial Stadium Baltimore MD 21218*

CUETO, MANUEL RICHARD, ins. co. exec.; b. Bklyn., May 27, 1906; s. Maximo and Emilia (Garcia) C.; student New Utrecht Sch., Bklyn., 1920-24; m. Cathleen Annabelle Pennell, May 9, 1936; childrenJohn Manuel, Anthony Richard. With New York Life Ins. Co., N.Y.C., 1924—, successively actuarial supr., asst. actuary, asso. actuary, actuary, 2d v.p. and actuary, 1944-62, v.p. charge electronic planning and devel., 1962-65, v.p. charge electronic operations and planning, 1965-. Chmn. Industry Adv. Com. Automation. Mem. com. United Fund of Manhasset. Fellow Soc. Actuaries; mem. Assn. Computing Machinery, Actuaries Club N.Y., Internat. Congress Actuaries. Contbr. articles in field. Home: 211 Dover Rd Manhasset NY 11030 Office: 51 Madison Av New York City NY 10010

CUEVAS, CANCINO FRANCISCO, Mexican diplomat; b. Mexico, D.F., May 7, 1921; s. Jose Luis Cuevas and Sofia Cancino; Law degree Free Faculty Law, Mexico City, 1943; M.C.L., McGill U., 1946; m. Ana Hiditch, Sept. 19, 1946 (dec.) children—Pablo, Ana Manuela, Jose Luis; m. 2d. Esmeralda Arboleda, Nov. 30, 1968. Joined Mexican Fgn. Service, 1946; sec. ambassy, London, England, 1946-49; mem. UN Secretariat, 1950, 52-54; adviser to sec. Ministry Fgn. Affairs, 1955- 58; jud. counsellor Mexican Mission to UN, 1959-60; alternate rep. Mexico to the U.N., 1962-65, permanent rep., 1965-70. Guggenheim fellow, 1951. Rockefeller fellow, 1961; recipient Simon Bolivar prize Bolivarian Soc. Venezuela, 1947, Suárez prize Royal Acad. Moral and Polit. Scis., Madrid, Spain, 1951, 2d prize Venezuelan Government, X Inter American Conf., 1954. Club: Knickerbocker, (N.Y.C.). Author: La Nullite des actes juridiques, 1950; Bolivar, El ideal panamericano del Libertador, 1951; La doctina de Suárez sobre el derecho natural. 1952; Roosevelt y la Buena Vecindad, 1954; Del Congreso de Panamá a la Conferencia de Caracas. 2 vols. 1955; Tratado sobre la organizacion internacional, 1962; also numerous articles. Home: 450 E 63d St New York City NY 10021 Office: 8 E 41st St New York City NY 10017

CUGAT, XAVIER, violinist, condr.; b. Barcelona, Spain, Jan. 1, 1900, s. Juan and Mingall (de Bru) C; student Jesuit Sch. and Coll. Spain: m. Carmen Castillo, Oct. 17, 1929; m. 2d, Lorraine Allen, 1947; m. 3d, Abbe Lane (div.); m. 4th, Charro, 1966. First appearance as guest artist Cuban Symphony at age of 6; toured World with Enrico Caruso as assisting artist and accompanist at age of 16; gave concerts in Europe and U.S.; formed his own dance orch. and has played in all the prominent hotels and night clubs: has conducted many radio programs; does caricatures of prominent artists as a hobby, also paints murals and theater curtains. Mem. A.S.C.A.P.

CUKOR, GEORGE DEWEY, motion picture dir.; b. N.Y.C., July 7, 1899, s. Victor F. and Helen (Gross) C. Began as asst. stage mgr. in N.Y. Prodns. directed many N.Y. prodns. starring such players as Ethel Barrymore, Jeanne Eagels, Laurette Taylor, etc.; stage dir. Empire Theatre, N.Y.C., for Frohman Co., 1926-29; dir. and mgr. Lyceum Theatre, Rochester, N.Y., 1921-28; entered motion picture field, 1929; became dir. for Metro-Goldwyn-Mayer Corp., 1933; directed Dinner at Eight, 20 Little Women, 1933, David Copperfield, 1934, Romeo and Juliet, Camille, 1936, Holiday, 1937, Zaza, 1938, The Women, 1939, Susan and God, 1939, Philadelphia Story, 1940, A Woman's Face, The Twins, Keeper of the Flame, 1942, Gaslight, 1943, Winged Victory, 1943, Double Life, 1947, Edward My Son, 1948, Adam's Rib, 1949, A Life Her Own, Born Yesterday, 1950, Kitty and the Marriage Broker, 1951, The Marrying Kind, 1951, Pat and Mike, 1952, The Actress, 1953, It Should Happen To You, 1954, A Star is Born, 1954, Bhowani Junction, 1955, Les Girls, 1957, Wild is the Wind, 1957, Heller in Pink Tights, 1958, Let's Make Love, 1959, The Chapman Report, 1961, My Fair Lady, 1964, Justine, 1968. Hon. discharge U.S. Army. Home: 9166 Cordell Dr Los Angeles CA 90069

CULBERG, JACK JEROME, former mfg. co. exec.; b. Chgo., July 28, 1914; s. Samuel and Rose (Rabin) C.; student DePaul U., 1931-32; m. Eve Katz, Mar. 14, 1935; children—Joseph, Paul. Salesman, Snider-Catsup, Chicago, 1933-36; various positions wholesale grocery house, mail order co., asbestos pipe covering co. and punchcard bus., 1936-46; with Ekco Products, Chgo., 1947-61, successively sales staff, dist. sales mgr., Chgo., specialty sales mgr. div. sales mgr. and gen. sales mgr. for housewares operation, 1947-53, v.p., 1954-57, dir. Ekco products and sr. v.p. marketing 1958- 61; sr. v.p. sales, then sr. v.p. market devel. Revlon, Inc., N.Y.C., 1961-63; pres., chief exec. officer Schick Electric, Inc. (formerly Schick, Inc.) Lancaster, Pa., 1963-66; pres. CPS Industries, Inc., Chgo., 1966-71. Active fund-raising campaigns Brandeis and Roosevelt univs. Recipient Man of Year in Housewares Industry, 1961. Mem. Am. Mgmt. Assn. Clubs: Arts (Chgo.); Briarwood Country (Deerfield, Ill.) Home: 1300 N Lake Shore Dr Chicago IL 60610

CULBERSON, GEORGE WILLIAM, former govt. ofcl.; b. Hartsford City, Inc., Jan. 17, 1905; s. Lewis B. and Lura Belle (Spangler) C.; A.B., Ball State U., 1927; Ed.M., U. Pitts., 1940; m. Luella I. Duell, Dec. 24, 1927; children—Janet I. (Mrs. Stewart Dolg), George William, Amy L. (Mrs. Preston Wier), Wayne B., John C. Tchr., vocational counsellor, vice prin. and elementary sch. prin. Pitts. Pub. Schs., 1928-46; exec. dir. 110th St. Community Center, N.Y.C., 1947-50; bus. mgr. Meth. Bd. Missions, N.Y.C., 1950-53; exec. dir. Commn. Human Relations, Pitts., 1953-62; sr. specialist USAF Equal Employment Opportunity Program, 1962-65; asso. dir. community relations service Dept. Justice, 1965-66, dep. dir., 1966-70, ret. 1970. Bd. govs. Wesley Theol. Sem., Washington, 1944—. Mem. Nat. Assn. Intergroup Relations Ofcls. (pres. 1960-61). Home: 5504 22d Av Hillcrest Heights MD 20031

CULBERT, TAYLOR, coll. dean; b. Bklyn., Sept. 15, 1917; s. Isaac Taylor and Fannie (Blauvelt) C.; A.B., Yale, 1939; M.A., U. Mich., 1947, Ph.D., 1957; m. Anne Clark, Aug. 25, 1949; children—Jane Lindsay, John Taylor, Robert Alan. Mem. faculty Ohio U., 1953—, prof. English, 1965—, dean Grad. Coll., 1965-70, v.p., dean faculties, 1969—; pres. Ohio Univ. Press, 1964—. Served to maj. AUS, 1940-46. Home: Strouds Run Rd Athens OH 45701

CULBERT, WILLIAM EVES, fgn. service officer; b. Camden, N.J., Oct. 24, 1925; s. William Eves and Irene Dorothy (Gilbert) C.; B.S. in Econs., Wharton Sch. of U. Pa., 1948; M.A., Sch. Advanced Internat. Studies, Washington, 1949; m. Elizabeth Louise Anderson, June 16, 1950; children—Linda, Patricia, Jay, Timothy, John, Geoffrey. Internat. economist State Dept., 1950-52; assigned U.S. mission to NATO, European Regional Orgn., Paris, France, 1952-56; joined U.S. Fgn. Service, 1955; with Office European Regional Affairs, State Dept., 1957-60, officer-in-charge OEEC affairs, 1959-60; with embassy, Tokyo, Japan, 1961-64, 1st sec. econ. affairs, 1963-64; officer-in-charge gen. comml. policy div. Office Internat. Trade, State Dept., 1964-66, asst. chief, gen. comml. policy div., 1966-68, chief comml. policy div., 1968—, acting dir. Office Internat. Trade, 1968—. Mem. sr. seminar fgn. policy Fgn. Service Inst., 1968-69; counselor econ. affairs U.S. Mission Geneva, 1969—. Served with USAAF, 1943-45. Recipient Superior Honor award Dept. State, 1967. Home: 4908 Kingston Dr Annandale VA 22003 Office: Dept State Washington DC 20520

CULBERTSON, DAVID J., mfg. co. exec.; b. Paterson, N.J., Nov. 17, 1926; s. Edward and Elizabeth (McKewen) C.; B.A. in Econs., Cornell U., 1950, M.B.A., 1951; m. Helen Marie Eaton, Dec. 27, 1948; children—Amy Elizabeth, John Edward. Dir. exec. devel., adminstrv. asst. to treas. IBM World Trade Corp., 1951-68; with Xerox Corp., Stamford, Conn., 1968—, v.p., controller, 1970—. Active local United Fund. Served with AUS, 1945-46. Mem. Financial Exec. Inst., Soc. Advancement Mgmt., U.S. Jr. C. of C., U.S. C. of C. of Netherlands, Sigma Chi. Kiwanian. Home: Dew Lane Darien CT 06820 Office: Xerox Corp Stamford CT 06904

CULBERTSON, HORACE COE, ins. co. exec.; b. Los Angeles, Apr. 24, 1924; s. Henry Coe and Irene A. (Blood) C.; A.B., Occidental Coll.; 1949; student U. So. Cal., 1948; m. Janet Ann Fadley, Dec. 27, 1949; children—Timothy Coe, Gary Dan, William Craig. With Fidelity and Deposit Co. Md., 1949—, exec. v.p., 1966—, also dir., mem. exec. com.; dir., mem. exec. com. Union Trust Co. Md., 1968—; dir. Am. Gen. Ins. Co. Houston. Instr. U. Cal. at Los Angeles, 1953-54. Trustee, mem. exec. com. Community Chest Balt., 1968—; group chmn. Balt. United Appeal, 1967-68; bd. dirs. Balt. Area Council Alcoholism, 1969—; solicitor Balt. Symphony, 1968-69; dir. A.R.C. Balt., 1970—. Served with USNR, 1943-46. Mem. Surety Assn. Am. (rep. exec. com. 1969—), Am. Ins. Assn. Am. (rep. exec. com. 1968), Surety Underwriters Assn. So. Cal. (pres. 1964), Ins. Information Inst. (alternate dir. 1970-71), Beavers Heavy Engring. Contractors Assn. (dir.), Met. Balt. C. of C. (dir. 1970—), Am. Legion, Alpha Tau Omega. Republican. Presbyn. Clubs: Center (Balt.), Towson Golf and Country. Home: 512 Wyngate Rd Timonium MD 21093 Office: Fidelity Bldg Baltimore MD 21201

CULBERTSON, JOHN MATHEW, educator, economist; b. Detroit, Aug. 25, 1921; s. Glen A. and Lydia (Hawley) G.; B.A., U. Mich., 1946, M.A., 1947, Ph.D., 1956; m. Frances Mitchell, Aug. 27, 1947; children—John, Joanne, Lyndall, Amy. Economist to bd. govs. Fed. Res. System, 1950-57; mem. faculty U. Wis., Madison, 1957—, prof. econs., 1962—. Vis. prof. U. Cal. at Berkeley, 1962-63, 66-67, dir. Financial and Fiscal Research Center, Social Systems Research Inst., U. Wis., 1963-64, 67-68. Served with USAAF, 1943-46. Decorated Air medal. Mem. Am. Econ. Assn., Am. Finance Assn., Econometric Soc., Am. Statis. Assn. Author: Full Employment or Stagnation, 1964; Macroeconomic Theory and Stabilization Policy, 1968; Economic Development: An Ecological Approach, 1971; also articles. Asso. editor Jour. Finance, 1964-67. Home: 5305 Burnett Dr Madison WI 53705

CULBERTSON, ROBERT ELMORE, govt. ofcl.; b. Los Angeles, Aug. 6, 1916; s. George William and (DeArmond) C.; B.S., U. So. Cal. 1938; M.S., 1942; m. Frances Ogilvie, Sept. 15, 1938; childrenMary Frances, Roberta Anne, Robert Elmore. Instr. pub. adminstr. U. So. Cal., 1938-40; personnel methods cons. Social Security Adminstrn., 1939-43; regional personnel rep. Fed. Security Agy., 1946-48; asst. adminstr. social ins. system, Govt. Greece, 1948-50; chief personnel standards, state merit systems service Fed. Security Agy., 1950-51; dir. div. industry, mgmt. and tech. services Inst. Inter-Am. Affairs, State Dept., 1951-53; dept. Near East rep. Ford Found., 1953-56; v.p. Am. U. at Cairo (Egypt), 1956-58; rep. in Pakistan, Ford Found., 1958-60, program asso. charge S. Asia Affairs, 1960-61; dir. Agy. for Internat. Devel. in Peru, 1961-66; asso. dir. Agy. Internat. Devel., Viet Nam, 1966-68; dep. asst. sec. State, 1968-70; dir. AID in Guatemala, also econ. counsellor Am. U.S. and Cal. Employment Services, 1946-48. Served to lt. (j.g.) USNR, 1943-46. Mem. Soc. Pub. Adminstrn., Am. Polit. Sci. Assn., Soc. Internat. Devel., Asia Soc. (sec. Pakistan com.), Phi Beta Kappa. Home: USAID Guatemala APO New York City, NY 09891. Office: Dept of State Washington DC 20525

CULBERTSON SAMUEL ALEXANDER II bus. exec.; b. Louisville, June 2, 1915; s. Alexander Craig and Florence (McFatrich) C.; student U. Va., 1934-37, Law Sch., U. Va., 1937- 40; m. Beatrice Kunhardt, June 16, 1938; (div.); children—Samuel, William; m. 2d Nancy Madlener, June 18, 1957; childrenCatherine, Edward. With Murine Co., Inc., Chgo., 1940—, gen. mgr., sec., 1948, v.p., sec., 1952-61, chmn., exec. com., sec., 1961—; dir., mem. exec. Mem. Ill. Bldg. Authority; mem. bd. dirs. Joint Youth Devel. Com.; pres. John Howard Assn., 1950-57; chmn. exec. com. Seeing Eye Inc., Chgo., 1952-57; chmn. North Av. Larabee YMCA, 1954- 57. Bd. dirs. Civic Fedn., Greater N. Mich. Av. Assn., Grant Hosp. Infant Welfare, Chgo. Youth Assn. Republican. Episcopalian. Mason (32 Shriner). Clubs: Racquet. Tavern, Saddle and Cycle (Chicago); Glenview (Ill.) Golf; Lake Geneva (Wis.) Country; Augusta National. Shagbark 717 Walden Rd Winnetka, IL 60093. Office: 660 N Wabash Av Chicago IL 60611

CULBERTSON, WALTER LEROY, petroleum co. exec.; b. Dederick, Mo., July 29, 1918; s. Alfred Eli and Ethel Ida (Belong) C.; B.S. in Mech. Engring., magna cum laude, Kan. State U., 1939; m. Wanda Marian Atkins, Sept. 29, 1940; children—Philip LeRoy, Robert Alan. With Phillips Petroleum Co., 1939—, dept. mgr., Bartlesville, Okla., 1956-64, v.p. gas and gas liquids dept., 1964—; v.p., dir. subsidiaries Phillips Natural Gas Co., 1964—, Alamo Chem. Co., 1964—. Mem. engr. adv. council Kan. State U., 1971—. Mem. Dist. Sch. Bd., 1953-62. Recipient Engring. Service award Kan. State U., 1970; named Engr. of Year in Okla., Okla. Soc. Profl. Engrs., 1970. Registered profl. engr., Okla. Mem. Natural Gas Processors Assn. (v.p. 1971—), Ind. Natural Gas Assn. Am. (dir. 1965-70), Am. Soc. M.E., Am. Inst. Chem. Engrs., Nat. Soc. Profl. Engrs., Contbr. numerous articles to tech. jours. Mem. Christian Ch. (life elder, ofcl. bd. 1944—). Home: 1801 McKinley Rd Bartlesville OK 74003 Office: Phillips Bldg Bartlesville OK 74004

CULBERTSON, WILLIAM, clergyman; b. Phila., Nov. 18, 1905; s. William Jr. and Lydia Barnes (Roper) C.; S.B., Temple U., 1939; B.D., Ref. Episcopal Theol. Sem., Phila., 1939, D.D., 1939; LL.D., Bob Jones U., 1948; m. Catharine Havilla Gantz, Mar. 16, 1929; children—Joy Anne, William Robert, Paul Gantz, Ruth Catharine. Ordained deacon Ref. Episcopal Ch., 1927, presbyter, 1928; consecrated bishop, 1937; rector Grace Ch., Collingdale, Pa., 1927-30, St. John's- by-the-Sea, Ventnor, N.J., 1930-33, Atonement, Germantown, Phila., 1933- 1933-42, episcopacy N.Y. and Phila. Synod Ref. Episcopal Ch., 1937-42; lect. Ref. Episcopal Theol. Sem., 1929-42; dean Moody Bible Inst., Chgo., 1942-47, acting pres. and dean of edn., 1947-48, pres., 1948-71, chancellor, 1971—. Trustee Ref. Episcopal Theol. Sem., 1930—. Mem. N.Am. council Overseas Missionary Fellowship, 1940—. Asst. editor Episcopal Recorder, 1932-37, asso. editor, 1937—; editor Moody Monthly, 1947-71. Mem. Evang. Theol. Soc. Home: 1360 N Sandburg Terrace Chicago IL 60610 Office: 820 N LaSalle St Chicago IL 60614

CULBREATH, HUGH LEE, Jr., electric utility exec.; b. Tampa, Fla., May 11, 1921; s. Hugh Lee and Daphne (Jackson) C.; B.S., U.S. Naval Acad., 1944; m. Betty King, June 8, 1944; children—Betty Kay, Hugh Lee III. Commd. ensign USN, 1944, advanced through grades to lt., 1954; resigned, 1954; mem. adminstrv. sales staff Raybro Electric & Supplies Inc., 1954-57; with Tampa Electric Co., 1958—, v.p. finance, sec. treas., 1966-71, exec. v.p., sec., treas., 1971, pres., 1971—; dir. First Fed. Savs. & Loan Assn. Tampa, Exchange Nat. Bank Tampa, Exchange Bancorp. Mem. Tampa Civil Service Bd., 1964—; counselor U. Tampa, 1965-70, bd. fellows, 1970—. Bd. dirs. St. Joseph Hosp. Found.; trustee U.S. Naval Acad. Found., Berkeley Prep. Sch. Mem. Greater Tampa C. of C. (gov., exec. com., treas.) Sigma Alpha Epsilon. Episcopalian (vestryman 1963- 65, 67-69, treas. 1967). Clubs: Tampa Yacht and Country (commodore 1963), University, Exchange (pres. 1961), Palma Ceia Golf and Country, Ye Mystic Krewe of Gasparilla (Tampa). Home: 5019 Shore Crest Circle Tampa FL 33609 Office: PO Box 111 Tampa FL 33601

CULHANE, FRANK JAMES, carpet mfg. exec.; b. Chgo., Feb. 25, 1923; s. Frank O. and Lillian (Kearney) C.; B.S., U. Notre Dame, 1948, LL.B., 1950; m. Mary Seng, Aug. 16, 1947; children—James, Michael, Cathy, Ann, Patricia. Admitted to Ill. bar, 1950; tax accountant, auditor Arthur Andersen & Co., Chgo., 1950-55; asst. treas. Formfit Co., Chgo., 1955-57, treas., 1957-63; pres. Formintern div. Genesco, Inc., Chgo., 1963-64, group v.p. Genesco, Inc., Nashville, 1964-67, mem. bd. gov., corp. dir. Genesco of Can., Conf. San RemoTreviso. Italy; v.p., treas. Hart, Schaffner & Marx, Chgo., 1967-71; sr. v.p. finance and adminstrn. Ozite Corp., Libertyville, Ill., 1971—, also dir.; dir. Formfit Founds., Ltd., London, Eng., Formfit-France, S.A. (Paris), Formfit Pty. Ltd. Sydney, Australia. Treas., Village Park Forest Ill. 1954-57. Served as lt. (j.g.) USNR, 1944-46, to lt., 1951-52. Recipient Superior Achievement Recognition award Genesco, Inc., 1963. Mem. Chgo. Bar Assn., Internat. Trade Club Chgo. (sec. 1969, v.p. 1970). Clubs: Caymanas Golf (Jamaica, W.I.); Chicago Athletic Assn.; Michigan Shores (Wilmette, Ill.). Home: 64 Indian Hill Rd Winnetka IL 60093 Office: 1755 Butterfield Rd Libertyville IL 60048

CULLEN, ABBEY BOYD, Jr., educator; b. Oxford, Miss., Dec. 25, 1915; s. Abbey Boyd and Vivian (Palmer) C.; B.A., U. Miss., 1937, M.A., 1942; Ph.D., U. Va., 1947; m. Mari Christine Kizman, Oct. 8, 1943; 1 son, Malcolm Charles. Research electronic devices applied to physiology U. Miss. Sch. Medicine, 1937- 40; engr.-physicist Naval Research Lab., 1942-45; faculty dept. physics and astronomy U. Miss., Oxford, 1947—, prof., 1954—, chmn. dept., 1957—. Mem. Am. Phys. Soc., Sigma Xi. Home: 812 Lincoln Av Oxford MS 38655

CULLEN, BILL, (William Lawrence Cullen), radio and TV entertainer; b. Pitts., Feb. 18, 1920; student U. Pitts., m. Ann Macomber. Announcer radio Sta. WWSW, Pitts., 1939, later master ceremonies, until 1944; staff announcer CBS, 1944-46, became master ceremonies Winner Take All, 1946; TV Debut I've Got a Secret, 1952; other appearances coast-to-coast TV programs, also network radio shows; master ceremonies Place the Face, Quick as a Flash, Hit the Jackpot, Give and Take, Down You Go, Price is Right, Eye Guess, 1966—, Three on a Match, NBC-TV, 1971—, Emphasis, NBC radio, 1971—, Monitor, 1971—. Patrol pilot Civilian Air Def. Home: 530 Fifth Av New York City NY 10022

CULLEN, GEORGE, editor; b. Jersey City, June 6, 1901; s. John Joseph and Ella Catherine (Mallon) C.; student pub. schs., Jersey City; m. Mabel Bell, Mar. 10, 1923. With United Press, New York City, 1918-21; editor Flushing Jour., 1921-22; editorial staff Democrat and Chronicle, Rochester, N.Y., 1922- 36; editor A.P., Albany, N.Y.C., then Washington, 1936-43; bd. editors Bur. Nat. Affairs, Inc., Washington, 1943-; dir. Nat. Press Bldg. Corp. Washington. Mem. Periodical Press Galleries of Congress (chmn. exec. com. 1953-63), Sigma Delta Chi. Club: National Press (bd. govs., pres. 1962) (Washington). Home: 4545 Connecticut Av NW Washington, DC 20008. Office 1231 25th St NW Washington DC 20037

CULLEN, JAMES ALOYSIUS, super market exec.; b. Syracuse, N.Y., July 27, 1912; s. Michael Joseph and Nan (Danaher) C.; ed. pub. schs.; m. Florence Hanrahan, Sept. 3, 1935; children—Michelle (Mrs. John Del Ponti), Mary Ann (Mrs. Walter Miller), Patricia (Mrs. William Groom), Carolyn, James Aloysius, Kathleen, Michael, Thomas, Brian. With King Kullen Grocery Co., 1930—, gen. mgr., 1936-60, pres., 1960—, chmn. bd. 1964—. Mem. Am. Fedn. Musicians, Republican. Catholic. Club: Wheatly Hills Golf (E. Williston, L.I.). Home: 16 Point Rd Bellport NY 11713 Office: 1194 Prospect Av Westbury NY 11590

CULLEN, JAMES DANIEL, lawyer; b. St. Louis, May 18, 1925; s. James Daniel and Frances C. (Parnell) C.; LL.B., St. Louis U., 1948; m. Joyce M. Jackson, Aug. 9, 1950; children—Mary Lynn, James D., Michael Parnell, Carol Ann. Admitted to Mo. bar, 1948; pvt. practice law, 1948-49; partner Cullen & Godfrey, 1949-51; sr. partner Thomas, Busse, Cullen, Clooney & Weil, St. Louis, 1951—. Dir. Mound City Trust Co., Mo. Arena Corp. Hon. mem. Harry S. Truman Library Inst. Served to 1st lt., USAAF, 1943-45. Mem. Am., Mo., St. Louis bar assns., Newcomen Soc. N.A. Club: Missouri Athletic (St. Louis). Home: 16 Berkshire St Richmond Heights MO 63117 Office: 418 Olive St St Louis MO 63102

CULLEN, JOHN KNOX, physician, former air force officer; b. Pitts., Dec. 18, 1907; s. John Berton and Mary Etta (Buchanan) C.; B.S., U. Pitts., 1930. M.D., 1932; m. Rachel Louise Bryson, Aug. 17, 1957; children—John Knox, Robert Prather, Mary Suzanne. Intern, Western Pa. Hosp., Pitts., 1932-33; commd. 1st lt. M.C., U.S. Army, 1933, advanced through grades to maj. gen. USAF, 1960; dir. pub. health and welfare U.S. Mil. Govt., Korea, 1946; dep. dir. plans and hosps. Office Surg. Gen., USAF, 1950-54, 56, dir., 1957-59; dep. surg. gen. USAF, 1959-61; surgeon U.S. Air Forces in Europe, 1961-65, ret., 1965; med. dir. Pan Am. World Airways, Jamaica, N.Y., 1965—. Diplomate Am. Bd. Preventive Medicine in aviation medicine. Fellow Am. Coll. Preventive Medicine; mem. Alpha Omega Alpha. Home: 49 Willow St Garden City NY 11530 Office: JFK Internat Airport Jamaica NY 11430

CULLEN, MICHAEL J., union ofcl. Pres., Nat. Assn. Spl. Delivery Messengers AFL-CIO. Office: 20 East St NW Washington DC 20001*

CULLEN, PATRICIA, (Mrs. Edward Hurshell), soprano; b. Seattle, June 25, 1936; d. Charles Campbell and Ruth Margaret (Kahler) Cullen; student New Eng. Conservatory Music, Berlin Music Conservatory, Vienna Music Conservatory; m. Edmond Hurshell, Dec. 4, 1954; children—Jennifer Lynn, Michael Charles. Made European debut as Margiana in Barber of Baghdad, Barcelona, Spain, 1965, Austrian debut as Lucia in Lucia di Lammermoor, Salzburg, 1965, German debut as Salome in Salome, Cologne, 1965. Am. debut as Lulu in Lulu, Indpls., 1967, N.Y.C., Chgo. debuts, 1967; with Cologne Opera, 1966—; roles include Donna Anna in Don Giovanni, Konstanze in Il Seraglio, Jenny in Mines of Sulphor; made guest appearances as Adina in Elixir d'Amore, Queen of the Night in Zauberflote, Violetta in La Traviata, Gilda in Rigoletto, Adele in Die Fledermaus. Address: Schmidt Opern-Agentur Leopoldstrasse 44/VI 8000 Munich Germany 23*

CULLEN, ROBERT GERARD, Irish diplomat; b. Dublin, Ireland, May 20, 1929; s. Daniel and Mary (Taylor) C.; certificate Blackrock Coll., 1947; B.Vet. Medicine, University College Dublin, 1953; diploma animal health London U., 1968. Gen. vet. practice, County Leitrim, Ireland, 1954; joined Ministry Agr., London, 1955, vet. insp., Herefordshire, Eng., 1955-60; vet. insp. Irish Dept. Agr., Dublin, 1960-70; agrl. counselor, Washington, 1970—. Mem. Irish Vet. Assn. (exec. bd.), Royal Dublin Soc., Bloodstock Breeder's Assn., Royal Coll. Vet. Surgeons. Mem. editorial bd. Brit. Vet. Jour., 1969—, Irish Vet. Jour., 1966-70. Home: 4201 Cathedral Av NW Washington DC 20016 Office: 2234 Massachusetts Av NW Washington DC 20008

CULLEN, STUART CHESTER, physician; b. Milton Junction, Wis., Jan. 31, 1909; s. Archibald H. and Myrtle E. (Killam) C.; A.B., U. Wis., 1931; M.D., 1933; m. Caroline Swannel, June 25, 1932; children—Carol Lynn, Bruce Frederick. Intern Mulnomah County Hosp, 1933-34; resident Bellevue Hosp., 1936-38; chmn. div. anesthesiology, prof. surgery State U. Ia., 1938-58, mem. bd. control athletics 1946-58; prof. anesthesia U. Cal. Med. Center at San Francisco, 1958—; chmn. dept. anesthesia, 1958-66, asso. dean Sch. Medicine, 1963-66, dean, 1966-70. Mem. med. mission to Austria sponsored by WHO and Unitarian Service Com., 1947, India, 1953; sr. instr., organizer internat, course anesthesiology, Copenhagen, WHO, 1950-52, 54, 58, 62; cons. WHO, Middle East, 1962. Recipient Distinguished Service award Am. Soc. Anesthesiologists. Diplomate Am. Bd. Anesthesiology. Mem. A.M.A., San Francisco Med. Soc., Am. Soc. Anesthesiologists, Am. Soc. Pharmacology and Exptl. Therapeutics, Soc. Exptl. Biology and Medicine, N.Y. Acad. Medicine, Central Surg. Assn., Osterreichische Gesellschaft fur Anesthesiologie, Nordisk Anestesiologisk Foresning, Alpha Omega Alpha. Author. Anesthesia in General Practice, 1946; Medical Emergencies (with E.G. Gross), 1949. Editor; Year Book of Anesthesia, 1961-69. Home: 73 Westshore Belvedere CA 94920 Office: U Cal Med Center San Francisco CA 94122

CULLENBINE, CLAIR STEPHENS, lawyer; b. Beardstown, Ill., Nov. 29, 1905; s. Robin James and Victoria (Stephens) C.; LL.B., Washington U., St. Louis, 1928; m. Jean Williams, Aug. 23, 1930; children—Carol Ann (Mrs. Neal B. Wineman), Robert Stephens. Admitted to Mo. bar, 1928; practice law, St. Louis, 1928-33; local counsel Md. Casualty Co., 1933-35; spl. counsel Asso. Industries of Mo., 1935-36; dir. research, dir. indsl. relations, 1937-43; dir.; indsl. relations mgr. Gaylord Container Corp., 1943-48, counsel, 1948-56; dir. Crown Zellerbach Corp. Industry mem. regional, nat. War Labor Bds., World War II. Mem. Cal. Mfrs. Assn. (dir.), Am. Arbitration Assn. (dir.) Club: Burlingame Country. Home: 2110 Redington Rd Hillsborough CA 94010 Office: 1 Bush St San Francisco CA 94119

CULLER, ARTHUR DWIGHT, educator; b. McPherson, Kan., July 25, 1917; s. Arthur Jerome and Susanna (Stover) C.; B.A., Oberlin Coll., 1938; Ph.D., Yale, 1941; m. Helen Lucile Simpson, Sept. 14, 1941; childrenJonathan Dwight, Helen Elizabeth. Instr. English, Cornell U., 1941-42; instr., then asst. Yale, 1946-55 prof. English, 1958—; asso. prof. English, U. Ill., Fulbright fellow in Eng., 1950-51; Guggenheim fellow, 1961-62. Mem. Modern Lang. Assn., Phi Beta Kappa. Author: The Imperial Intellect; A Study of Newman's Educational Idea, 1955. Editor: (J.H. Newman) Apologia pro Vita Sua, 1956; (with G.P. Clark) Student and Society, 1959; Poetry and Criticism of Matthew Arnold, 1961; Imaginative Reason: The Poetry of Matthew Arnold, 1966. Home: 80 Tokeneke Dr North Haven CT 06518 Office: Dept English Yale U New Haven CT 06520

CULLER, FLOYD LEROY, Jr., chem. engr.; b. Washington, Jan. 5, 1923; s. Floyd LeRoy Culler; B.Chem. Engring. cum laude, Johns Hopkins, 1943; m. Della Hopper, 1946; 1 son, Floyd LeRoy III. With Eastman Kodak and Tenn. Eastman at Y-12, Oak Ridge, 1943-47; design engr. Oak Ridge Nat. Lab., 1947-53, dir. chem. tech. div., 1953-64, asst. lab. dir., 1965-70, dep. dir., 1970—; research design chem. engring. applied to atomic energy program, chem. processing nuclear reactor plants. Chmn. 1st Municipal Planning and Zoning Commn. Oak Ridge. Chmn. bd. trustees Coll. of Oak Ridge. Recipient Ernest Orlando Lawrence award, 1964; Atoms for Peace award, 1969. Fellow Am. Nuclear Soc., Am. Inst. Chemists, A.A.A.S., Inst. Chem. Engrs.; mem. Am. Chem. Soc. Home: 109 Oneida Lane Oak Ridge TN 37830 Office: Oak Ridge Nat Lab Oak Ridge TN 37830

CULLER, GEORGE D., pres. art coll.; b. McPherson, Kan., Feb. 27, 1915; s. Arthur Jerome and Mary (Stover) C.; grad. Cleve. Inst. Art, 1936; B.S. in Edn., Western Res. U., 1936, M.A. in Aesthetics and Art History, 1939; m. Margaret Kate Johnson, Aug. 1, 1939; children—John Hubbard, Stephanie Margaret. Instr., then asst. prof. art Kan. State Tchrs. Coll., Emporia, 1939-42; head illustrator dept. prodn. illustrations Boeing Airplane Co., 1942- 45; instr. painting Cleve. Inst. Art, 1946; supr., then asst. curator edn. Cleve. Mus. Art, 1946-49; dir. Akron (O.) Art Inst., 1949-55; dir. mus. edn. Art Inst. Chgo., 1955-58; asso. dir. San Francisco Mus. Art., 1958-61, dir., 1961-65; pres. Phila. Coll. of Art, 1965—. Lectr. Stanford. Mem. exec. com. Internat. Design Conf., Aspen, Colo., 1954-61, chmn., 1958, program chmn., 1960; mus. dirs. adv. com. Century 21 Exposition, Seattle, 1962; art adv. com. Gold Gateway Redevel., San Francisco, 1962-65; dir. Nat. Assn. Schs. of Art, 1965—, sec., 1969—; mem. exec. com. inst. for Study Art in Edn., 1966—; chmn. art commn. Phila. Redevel. Authority, 1971—. Bd. dirs. Union Ind. Colls. Art, 1966-69, pres., 1969—. Painter, print-maker, 1936—; exhbns. include Kansas City, May Shows in Cleve., New Years Exhbns. Butler Inst. Am. Art. Home: 620 Spruce St Philadelphia PA 19206 Office: Phila Coll Art Broad and Pine Sts Philadelphia PA 19102

CULLEY, PERRY HAGER, fgn. service officer; b. Los Angeles, Dec. 19, 1918; s. Perry Mohler and Anne Marie (Hager) C.; student Pasadena Jr. Coll., 1935-37, George Washington U., 1938-39, 49, Georgetown U., 1940-41; advanced mgmt. program Harvard, 1955; m. Harriet Winston Pullen, Sept. 8, 1945. News editor OWI, 1941-42; radio news editor United Press Bur., Washington, 1942; Washington corr. March of Time and Time Views the News, 1942- 45; news editor ABC Radio Network, sta. WMAL, 1945; with fgn. service 1945—, successively information officer Am. embassy, Paris, information specialist Dept. of State, spl. asst. to ambassador Am. embassy, Montevideo, asst. to dir. exec. secretariat, 1954; counselor Am. embassy, Quito, Ecuador; detailed to 1959-60, session U.S. Naval War Coll.; then sr. fgn. service insp.; later consul gen. Am. embassy, Paris, France; dep. insp. gen. U.S. Fgn. Service; now minister-counselor, dep. chief mission Am. embassy, Paris. Served as ambulance driver Am. Field Service, Brit. 8th Army, 1943-44; NATOUSA. Decorated Bronze Cross of Merit with crossed swords (Poland). Mem. Am. Fgn. Service Assn., Am. Field Service Assn., Georgetown U. Alumni Assn. Episcopalian. Clubs: Harvard, Travellers (Paris). Contbr. articles in mags. Home: 10 Av Emile Deschanel Paris France Office: American Embassy Paris France

CULLIGAN, GLENDY, book reviewer; b. Chgo., Oct. 26, 1915; d. Albert Francis and Marie (Sage) Culligan; B.A., Newcomb Coll., 1936; M.A., Am. U., 1959; m. Frank R. Dawedeit, Feb. 1, 1950 (div. 1953); 1 dau., Nora Sage; m. 2d, William R. Pabst, Jr., Aug. 1, 1964. Reporter, editor New Orleans Item, 1937-49; asst. woman's editor feature editor Washington Post, 1949-56, book editor, 1956-65; free-lance writer, 1965—; instr. Montgomery Coll., 1969-71. Mem. awards adv. com. Nat. Books Awards, 1961-65. Home: 3420 Quebec St NW Washington DC 20016

CULLIGAN, MATTHEW JOSEPH, communications exec.; b. N.Y.C., June 25, 1918; s. Matthew and Sarah Jane (Hogan) C.; student Columbia; m. Doris Dernberger, May 1946; children—Kerry William, Susan Laureen, Caroline, Eileen. With Royal Typewriter Co., 1938-39; lectr. N.Y. World's Fair, Am. Standard Corp., 1939-40; successively space salesman to mgr. home bldg. dept. Hearst Mags., 1945-50; advt. dir. Ziff-Davis Publs., 1951-52; sales mgr. NBC TV shows, 1952-53, nat. sales mgr. TV network, 1954-55, v.p., dir. sales TV network, 1955-56, exec. v.p. NBC Radio Network, 1956-62; gen. corporate exec., dir. McCann- Erickson, Inc.; dir. McCann-Erickson Internat., M-E Prodns., Communications Affiliates, Inc.; former chmn. bd., pres., chief exec. officer Curtis Pub. Co.; pres., chief exec. officer MBS, 1966-68; founder and pres. Culligan Communications Corp., 1968—; founder Pilgrim Prodns., 1968—; v.p. Diebold Group; dir. Mut. Broadcasting Corp., Bantam Books. Former pres. Internat. Radio and TV Soc. Trustee Am. Child Guidance Found. Served as 1st lt. AUS, World War II. Clubs: Apawamis Country; Pine Valley Golf, Sky, Key Largo Anglers. Author: The Curtis-Culligan Story: How to Defend Yourself Against the Menaces of the Seventies. Home: Polly Park Rd Rye NY 10580

CULLINAN, ELIZABETH, writer; b. N.Y.C., June 7, 1933; d. Cornelius G. and Irene (O'Connell) Cullinan; B.A., Marymount Coll., N.Y.C., 1954. Author 11 short stories pub. New Yorker mag., 1960—. Houghton Mifflin literary fellow, 1970; recipient new writers award, Great Lakes Colls. Assn., 1970. Author: House of Gold, 1970; The Time of Adam, 1971.

CULLINAN, JOHN J., vicar gen. Archdiocese St. Paul. Home: 226 Summit Av St Paul MN 55102*

CULLINAN, TERRENCE, recreation exec.; b. San Francisco, June 15, 1940; s. Vincent and Elizabeth (Erlin) C.; student Pomona Coll., 1957-58; B.A., Stanford U., 1961, M.B.A., 1964; Fulbright scholar, U. Florence and Freiburg U., 1961-62; m. Leola Pauline Barnes, Mar. 21, 1964; children—Tracey Cormac, Cory Patrick. Cons. Mitsui & Co., Tokyo, 1963, Industria Papelera, S.A., Guatemala City, 1965; economist, project mgr. Stanford Research Inst., Menlo Park, Cal., 1966-68; corporate sec. U.S. Natural Resources, Inc., Menlo Park, 1969—; dir. operations Lassen Nat. Park Co.; cons. tourism and econ. devel.; pres., dir. Terrybukk, Inc. Head task force on policy-minority community relations Urban Coalition, 1969-71. Sec.-treas. Am. Friends of Wilton Park, Inc.; pres., dir. Terrybukk Found., Ltd. Served to capt. AUS, 1964-66. Recipient award Advt. Assn. West, 1968. Mem. Nat. Service Secretariat (adv. bd.). Contbr. articles periodicals. Home: 333 Linfield Pl Menlo Park CA 94025 Office: 3000 Sand Hill Rd Menlo Park CA 94025

CULLITON EDWARD MILTON Canadian judge; b. Grand Forks, Minn., Apr. 9, 1906 (parents citizens) s. John Joseph and Katherine M. (Kelly) C.; B.A., U. Sask., 1926, LL.B., 1928, D.C.L., 1962; m. Katherine M. Hector, Sept. 9, 1939. Admitted ot Sask. bar. 1930; practice in Gravelbourg, 1930-51; mem. Sask. Legislature, 1935-44, 48-51; provincial sec. Patterson Govt., 1938-41; minister without portfolio, 1941-44; judge Ct. Appeal Sask., 1951-62; chief justice Sask., Regina, 1962—. Chancellor, U. Sask. Served with Canadian Army, 1941-46. Home: 3140 Albert St Regina Office: Court House Regina Saskatchewan Canada

CULLITON, JAMES WILLIAM, educator; b. Buffalo, Aug. 20, 1911; s. William Clement and Katherine Mary (Airey) C.; A.B., Canisius Coll., 1932; M.B.A., Harvard, 1934, D.C.S., 1941; m. Jane Kathryn Hogan, July 7, 1937; children—William Stephen, Edward Francis, Stephen James, Richard Eugene. Indsl. accountant, 1934-37, research asst., 1937-41; prof., chmn. dept. mgmt. Boston Coll., 1941-42; exec. dir. postwar planning com. Commonwealth Mass., 1942-44; asso. prof. Harvard Grad. Sch. Bus. Adminstrn., 1944-51, vis. prof., team leader Harvard adv. group, Manila, Philippines, 1968-71; pres. Asian Inst. Mgmt., Makati, Rizal, Philippines, 1971—; prof. U. Notre Dame Coll. Bus. Adminstrn., 1951-62, dean, 1955-62; commr. U.S. Tariff Commn., Washington, 1962-68; Mem. Harvard Bus. Sch. Assn. Roman Catholic. Contbr. articles to bus. publs. Home: 22 Mercedes Bel Air Makati Philippines Office: Asian Inst of Management MCC Box 898 Makati Rizal D-708 Philippines

CULLITY, BERNARD DENNIS, educator; b. Havre, Mont., Nov. 9, 1917; s. Eugene Dennis and Elizabeth (Dougherty) C.; B.Engring., McGill U., 1940; M.S., U. Minn., 1942; Sc.D., Mass. Inst. Tech., 1947; m. Elizabeth Kercheval, Jan. 31, 1953. Instr. metallurgy Mont. Sch. Mines, 1940-42, U. Minn., 1942-43; group leader Manhattan Project, Mass. Inst. Tech., 1943-45; postdoctoral fellow Ecole des Mines, Paris, France, 1947-48; sci. liasion officer Office Naval Research, Am. Embassy, London, England, 1948-49; mem. faculty U. Notre Dame, 1950—, prof. metallurgy, 1959—, mem. Grad. Council, 1957-60. Mem. Am. Inst. Mining, Metall. and Petroleum Engrs., Am. Soc. Metals, Inst. Metals, Am. Crystallographic Assn., Sigma Xi. Author: Elements of X-Ray Diffraction, 1956. Home: Box E Notre Dame IN 46556

CULLMAN, ALAN A., ret. utility exec.; b. Jersey City, 1905; s. Jacob and Louise (Smith) C.; m. Florence FitzGerald, Oct. 26, 1927 (dec. Jan. 1963); children—Constance L., Diane M., Alan A. (dec.); m. 2d, Karin Lindelof, July 14, 1968. Former treas. Columbia Gas System, Inc.; former v.p., dir. Columbia Gas System Service Corp.; dir. Columbia Hydrocarbon Corp., Inland Gas Co. WOC dir. gas planning div. Petroleum Adminstrn. for Def., 1952-53; con. to Pres. Eisenhower's Cabinet Com. on Energy Supplies and Resources, 1954. First pres. Kinnelon (N.J.) Free Pub. Library, 1963-66; vol. Internat. Exec. Service Corps, 1969—. Mem. Am. Gas Assn. (chmn. accounting sect. 1950-51). Mason. Home: RD 1 Ringoes NJ 08551

CULLMAN, EDGAR MEYER, tobacco co. exec.; b. N.Y.C., Jan. 7, 1918; s. Joseph F., Jr. and Frances Nathan (Wolff) C.; student Hotchkiss Sch., Lakeville, Conn., 1932-36; B.A., Yale 1940; m. Louise Bloomingdale, August 28, 1938; children—Lucy B. (now Mrs. Frederick M. Danziger), Edgar Meyer, and Susan R. With Underwriters Trust Co., New York City, 1940-42; with Office Alien Property Custodian, Washington and N.Y.C., 1942-44; partner Culliman Bros., mems. N.Y. Stock Exchange, N.Y.C., 1946-65; sr. v.p. Culliman Bros., Inc., tobacco and investments, 1944-62, now dir.; v.p., dir. B. Bros. Realty Corp., Lyman G. Realty Corp.; pres., chmn. exec. com., dir. Gen. Cigar Co., Inc.; pres., dir. T & A Corp.; dir. Companion Life Ins. Co., U.S. Rubber Reclaiming Co., Inc., Mut. of Omaha. Vice chmn. Yale Devel. Bd. Bd. dirs. Mt. Sinai Hosp. Sch. Nursing; trustee Mt. Sinai Hosp. Mem. Cigar Inst. Am. (gov.), Cigar Mfrs. Assn. Am. (dir.). Clubs: India House, Century Country, Yale, (N.Y.C.); Turf and Field; Steeplechase and Hunt Assn., Tumble Brook Country, Lotos, Raffles, Pinnacle. Home: 885 Park Av New York City NY 10021 Office: 605 3d Av New York City NY 10016

CULLMAN HOWARD STIX civic leader; b. N.Y.C., Sept. 23, 1891; s. Joseph F. and Zillah (Stix) C.; grad. Phillips Exeter (N.H.) Acad., 1909; A.B., Yale U., 1913; LL.D. Syracuse U., 1947, N.Y.U., 1952, Columbia, 1954; LL.D., Rutgers U., 1959, Hamilton Coll., 1963, Philippine Womens' U., 1967; m. Elsie Gottheil, Mar. 9, 1915 (dec.); children—Hugh, Paul Thomas; m. 2d, Marguerite Magner; children—Marguerite, Brian. Commr. of Port of N.Y. Authority, 1927—, chmn., 1945-55, hon. chmn., 1955—. Pres., Cullman Bros., Inc., N.Y.C.; chmn. bd. Chanin Bldg.; dir. several corps., including adv. bd. Philip Morris Inc., dir. Nat. Distillers and Chem. Corp. Commr. gen. Brussels Internat. Exhbn., 1958. Hon. trustee Fordham Univ. Pres. Tobacco Mchts. Assn.; chmn. bd. Beekman Downtown Hosp.; trustee Nat. Fund for Med. Edn. Decorated grand officer L'Ordre de Leopold (Belgium); comdr. Order of St. Sylvestre (Pope John XXIII); Presdl. Medal of Merit (P.I.); recipient silver medal for distinguished service U.S. Dept. State, 1967. Club: Lotos (past pres.) Home: 480 Park Av New York City NY 10022 Office: 425 Park Av New York City NY 10022 ☆

CULLMAN, HUGH, tobacco co. exec.; b. N.Y.C., Jan. 27, 1923; s. Howard S. and Elsie (Gottheil) C.; B.S., U.S. Naval Acad., 1945; m. Nan Alva Ogburn, May 12, 1951; children—Katherine Victoria, Hugh, Alexandra Miriam. With Benson & Hedges, 1948-54, mgr. research, 1952-54; with Philip Morris Inc., 1954—, treas., 1959-60, v.p., asst. chief operations, 1960-64, exec. v.p. operations, 1966—, also dir.; exec. v.p. Philip Morris Internat., 1964-66, pres., 1967—, also dir.; dir. Cullman Bros., Inc., United Va. Bank State Planters, Richmond. Served from ensign to lt. USN, 1945-52; PTO, Germany. Mem. Fgn. Policy Assn. (dir.). Clubs: Players, Marco Polo (N.Y.C.); Westchester Country (Rye, N.Y.). Home: North Manursing Island Rye NY 10580 Office: 100 Park Av New York City NY 10017

CULLMAN, JOSEPH FREDERICK, III, cigarette mfr.; b. N.Y.C., Apr. 9, 1912; s. Joseph F., Jr., and Frances Nathan (Wolff) C.; grad. Hotchkiss Sch., 1931; A.B., Yale, 1935; m. Susan Lehman, Aug. 2, 1935; 1 dau., Dorothy Marshall (Mrs. Norman Treisman). Started career as Eastern sales mgr. Webster Tobacco Co., N.Y.C., 1936-41; v.p. Benson & Hedges, N.Y.C., 1946-53; exec. v.p., 1953, pres. 1955—; v.p. Philip Morris Inc., 1954, exec. v.p., 1955-57, pres., chief exec. officer, 1957-66, chmn. bd., chief exec. officer, 1967—, also dir.; dir. IBM World Trade Corp., Bankers Trust Co., Ford Motor Co., Levi Straus, Inc., Braniff Airlines, others. Mem. Yale Devel. Com. Trustee Montefiore Hosp. Clubs: Yale, Century, Sleepy Hollow. Home: 715 Sleepy Hollow Rd Briarcliff Manor NY 10510 Office: 100 Park Av New York City NY 10017

CULMER, MARJORIE MEHNE, orgn. exec.; b. Duluth, Minn., Mar. 4, 1912; d. John H. and Nettie (Morey) Mehne; B.A., Lawrence Coll., 1933; J.D., Northwestern U., 1947; LL.D., Elmhurst Coll., 1962; m. Charles U. Culmer, Sept. 4, 1936. Mem. profl. staff Girl Scouts of U.S.A., 1934-40, mem. nat. staff, 1943-44, field com. nat. orgn., 1948-56, vice chmn. orgn. and mgmt. com., 1954-57, chmn. Blue Book (policies) com., 1955-57, bd. dirs., 1955—, exec. com., 1956-63, pres. nat. orgn., 1957-63, 1st v.p.; chmn. field com. Chgo. orgn., 1953-55, mem. bd., 1952-59, 61—, pres., 1955-57, del. 16th World conf. Brazil, 1957; del. World Conf. Girl Guides and Girl Scouts, Greece, 1960, vice chmn., mem. planning com., Denmark, 1963, del., Japan, 1966, Finland, 1969; tech. cons. Ill. Activities for 1970 White House Conf. for Children and Youth, 1968-70. Trustee, mem. Nat. Assembly for Social Policy and Devel., 1967—, Com. Internat. Social Devel., 1969—. Specialist with Bur. of Edn. and Cultural Affairs, Dept. State, India, 1964. Mem. com. pub. welfare. Welfare Council Met. Chgo., 1964-69; mem. com., Camp Algonquin, 1951—; bd. dirs. United Charities Chgo., 1953—, Family Service com., 1960-63; mem. Legal Aid Com., 1956-64; forum leader White House Conf. Children and Youth, 1960, mem. nat. com., 1958-60; trustee Lawrence U. Recipient Distinguished Service award Lawrence Coll., 1959; Merit award Norhtwestern U., 1960. Mem. Am., Ill., Chgo. bar assns., Women's Bar Assn. Ill., World Assn. Girl Guides and Girl Scouts (world com. 1963—, vice chmn. 1966-69, chmn. 1969—), Order of Coif, Mortar Bd., Phi Beta Kappa. Home: 900 W Lake St Libertyville IL 60048

CULMSEE, CARLTON FORDIS, former educator; b. St. Ansgar, Ia., Sept. 18, 1904; s. Ludwig Alfred and Clara Belia (Hansen) C.; B.S., Brigham Young U., 1932; M.A., 1937; postgrad. U. So. Cal., 1933; Ph.D., State U. Ia., 1940; m. Edna Mae Ball, June 5, 1932; 1 son, Ralph McPherson (dec.) Sch. tchr., Utah, 1922-23, 27- 29; free-lance writer, rancher, 1923-29; sec. extension div., instr. journalism Brigham Young U., 1932-37, asst. prof., 1937-39, asso. prof. journalism, dir. extension div., 1939-40, prof., dir. extension div., 1940-42; dean univ. coll., prof. journalism Utah State Agrl. U., 1945-59; dean Coll. Humanities and Arts, prof. Am. civilization Utah State U., Logan, 1956-70, prof. emeritus, 1970—. Vis. prof. Nat. Chengchi U., Formosa, 1955-56. Served with AC, USNR, 1942-45; lt. comdr. Res. Mem. Utah Acad. Sci., Arts and Letters (pres. 1961-62), Utah Writers (pres., 1942, 54, 55), C. of C., Phi Kappa Phi. Editor: State Verse Anthology, Utah Sings, vol. II, 1942. Free lance writer, verse writer. Home: 1642 Saddle Hill Dr Logan UT 84321

CULP DELOS POE univ. pres.; b. Clanton, Ala., July 26, 1911; s. Joseph Daniel and Lela (Popwell) C.; student Jacksonville State Coll., 1932-34; B.S., Auburn U., 1937, M.S., 1940; Ed.D., Columbia, 1949; m. Martha Edwardine Street, Dec. 23, 1934; children—Martha (Mrs. W. M. Flanigan), James, John. Tchr., prin. Chilton, Butler counties, Ala., 1935-42; supt. Chilton County Schs., 1942-46; supr. pub. sch. transp., asst. dir. div. adminstrn. and finance Ala. Dept. Edn., Montgomery, 1946-51; prof. edn. Ala. Poly. Inst. 1951-54; pres. Livingston State Coll., 1954-63, Ala. Coll., 1963-68, E. Tenn. State U., Johnson City, 1968—. Dir. 1st Bank. Mem. spl. study commn. Ala. Dept. Edn., 1967-68; mem. of the survey team Philippine Sch. Bur. Survey, 1959-60; mem. Nat. Commn. Safety Edn.; Gov. Ala. Commn. Status Women. Mem. bd. advisers Meth. Children's Home. Selma, Ala.; exec. dir. Ala. Edn. Commn., 1957- 59. Mem. Am. Assn. U. Profs., Am. Assn. Sch. Adminstrs., Ala. Hist. Assn., Nat., Ala. edn. assns., Kappa Delta Pi, Phi Kappa Phi, Kappa Phi Kappa. Democrat. Methodist. Rotarian. Home: Univ Pres's Home Johnson City TN 37601 Office: E Tenn State U Johnson City TN 37601

CULP, ORMOND SKINNER, urologist; b. Toronto, Ont., Nov. 18, 1910; s. Frank and Dora (Skinner) C.; A.B., Ohio Wesleyan U., 1931, D.Sc. (hon.), 1963; M.D., Johns Hopkins, 1935; m. Helen M. Ericson, Aug. 19, 1938; 1 dau., Pamela. Intern Johns Hopkins Hosp., 1935-36, asst. resident urology, 1938-40, resident urology, 1941-42; instr. pathology McGill U., 1936-37; resident physician St. Mary's Hosp., Pierre, S.D., 1937-38; instr. urology Johns Hopkins, 1938-42; resident urology Ancker Hosp., St. Paul, 1940-41; asso. surgeon-in-charge Henry Ford Hosp., Detroit, 1942-50; urologic cons. VA, 1946-52; cons. urology Mayo Clinic, Rochester, Minn., 1950-62, head urologic sect., 1962—; asso. prof. urology Mayo Found., U. Minn., 1951-62, prof., 1962—. Served from capt. to lt. col., M.C., AUS, 1942-46. Diplomate Am. Bd. Urology. Fellow A.M.A., A.C.S.; mem. Am. Urol. Assn. (pres. N. Central sect. 1965), Pan Pacific Surg. Assn., Pan Am. Med. Assn. (hon.), Am. Assn. Genito-Urinary Surgeons, Internat. Soc. Urology, Forum Clin. Investigation; hon. mem. Mexican, N.W. urologic socs., St. Paul, Bay surg. socs., Venezuela Urologic Soc. Home: 1032 Plummer Circle Rochester MN 55901 Office: Mayo Clinic Rochester MN 55901

CULP, PERRY, Jr., advt. agy. exec. Vice pres., exec. asst. to pres. Cole & Weber, Inc., Seattle. Office: 3100 S 176th St Seattle WA 98188*

CULP, VANN, lawyer; b. Crockett, Tex., Nov. 4, 1929; s. Maynard Vann and Gracie (Rawls) C.; B.S., U. Tex., 1951; LL.B., St. Mary's U., San Antonio, 1955; m. Marilyn McBrine, Apr. 2, 1953; children-Catherine Signe, Ginger Lynn, Patrick Vann. Tchr., Alamo Heights Sch. Dist., San Antonio, 1952- 56; admitted to Tex. bar, 1956; practice in San Antonio, 1956-60, Odessa, 1961-62, Midland, 1962—; mem. firm Lynch, Chappell, Allday & Culp, 1962—. Sec.-treas. Scholars, Inc. County chmn. Midland County Democratic Exec. Com., 1969—. Named Outstanding Jaycee City of San Antonio, 1958. Mem. Am. Bar Assn., State Bar Tex., Midland Scotish Rite Assn. (pres.), Phi Delta Phi. Home: 2905 Sentinel St Midland TX 79701 Office: 201 Wall Towers East Midland TX 79701

CULP, WILLIAM WHITFIELD, art inst. exec.; b. Chester, S.C., June 24, 1909; s. Charles Howard and Mildred (Kirkpatrick) C.; B.S., U.S. Mil. Acad., 1932; D.Sc., Webber Coll., 1963; grad. Advanced Mgmt. Program, Harvard, 1959, also numerous service and instl. schs., including Army War Coll., Armed Forces Staff Coll.; m. Winifred Louise Stilwell, Dec. 6, 1946; children—William S., Mildred L., Edmund H. Commd. 2d lt. U.S. Army, 1932, advanced through grades to col., 1944; troop and staff assignments 7th Cav., 4th Cav., 13th Cav. Mechanized, 5th and 13th Armored Divs., 1st Cav. Div., 1932-43; served in PTO, World War II; mem. faculty Army Transp. Sch., 1947-49; comdg. officer Replacement Tng. Center and Camp Tortuguero, P.R., 1950-52; dir. dept. V, U.S. Army Command and Gen. Staff Coll., 1953-55, dean instrn., 1955-56; dep. post comdr. Ft. Leavenworth, Kan., 1956-58; comdt. Army Mgmt. Sch., 1958-62; ret., 1962; pres. Ohio Coll. Applied Sci. and Ohio Mechanics Inst. (merged with U. Cin. 1969), Cin., 1962-69; dean, 1969-71, dean emeritus, 1971—; dir. planning Cin. Inst. Fine Arts, 1971—. Mem. Creative Leadership Council, Creative Edn. Found., Buffalo, 1961—; mem. tech. edn. adv. Ohio Bd. Regents. Decorated Legion of Merit with oak leaf cluster; recipient Cross Mil. Service (World War II, also Korean conflict), U.D.C. Mem. Am. Soc. Engring. Edn., Assn. Grads. U.S. Mil. Acad., Am. Ordnance Assn. (dir. Cin.), U.S.C. Alumni Assn., Engring. Soc. Cin., Cin. C. of C., Mil. Order World Wars, Mexican Nat. Acad. Mil. Studies (hon.), Ky. Cols. (hon.), Iota Lambda Sigma (hon.). Clubs: Cincinnati, Faculty, Harvard Business School (Cin.), St. Nicholas. Home: 2 Beech Crest Lane Cincinnati OH 45206

CULPEPPER, JAMES HENRY, paint and building supplies co. exec.; b. Norfolk, Va., Mar. 15, 1914; s. James Henry and Otey (Minor) C.; B.S. in Elec. Engring., Va. Mil. Instr., 1936; m. Frances Baldwin, Apr. 22, 1939; children—Robert Stuart, James Henry. With Chesapeake & Potomac Telephone Co., 1936-38; with Smith-Douglass Co., Inc. (now Smith-Douglas div. Borden Chem. Co.) Norfolk, 1938-66, v.p. farm fertilizer and specialty fertilizer div., 1957-62, exec. v.p., 1962-66, also dir,; pres. C.A. Nash & Son, Inc., Norfolk, Va., 1968—; dir. Seabord Citizens Nat. Bank, Finance com. Tidewater div. Girl Scouts U.S.A., trustee Norfolk Acad., Bonney Home for Girls, Norfolk; bd. dirs. Va. Found. Ind. Colls., Norfolk Gen. Hosp., United Communities Fund; dir. Navy YMCA, Norfolk; alumni sec. Va. Mil. Inst., 1937-38; chmn. bd. Research Found. of Old Dominion Coll. Served to maj. AUS, 1943-46; mem. Norfolk C. of C., Va. Mfrs. Assn. (dir.) Va. Mil. Inst. Alumi Assn. Clubs: Norfolk Yacht and Country, Virginia, Harbor, Norfolk (Va.) German; Princess Anne Country (Virginia Beach, Va.) Home: 1315 N Brandon Av Norfolk VA 23507 Office: 730 Granby St Norfolk VA 23517

CULPEPPER, STERLING G. Jr., lawyer; b. Montgomery, Ala., May 25, 1936; s. Sterling G. and Lula W. (Williams) C.; B.S., Auburn U., 1959; LL.B., U. Ala., 1961; m. Katherine Kelly, Mar. 2, 1963; 1 son, Sterling G. III. Admitted to Ala. bar, asst. U.S. atty. Middle Dist. Ala., 1961-62; partner law firm Smith, Bowman, Thagard, Crook & Culpepper Montgomery, 1967—. Served with USAF, 1962- 67. Mem. Am., Ala., Fed. (sec.-treas.) bar assns., Phi Delta Theta, Phi Delta Phi. Episcopalian. Home: 2764 S Colonial Dr Montgomery AL 36111 Office: Bell Bldg Montgomery AL 36104

CULVAHOUSE, JACK WAYNE, physicist; b. Mt. Park, Okla., Sept. 15, 1929; s. Victor Hugo and Sybil (Nichols) C.; B.S., U. Okla., 1951; M.A., Harvard U., 1954, Ph.D., 1958; m. Ruth Ann Roberts, June 8, 1952; children—John Thomas, Jeffry Scot, Alison. Physicist Gen. Elec. Co., Richland, Wash., 1951-53; asst. prof. physics U. Okla., 1957-58; asst. prof. physics U. Kan., 1958-62, asso. prof., 1962-64, prof., 1964—; vis. prof. U. Wis., 1964; vis. fellow Oxford U., 1968-69. Guggenheim fellow, 1968-69. Fellow Am. Phys. Soc.; mem. A.A.A.S. Home: 2651 Arkansas St Lawrence KS 66044

CULVER, DAVID M., aluminum co. exec.; b. Winnipeg, Man., Can., Dec. 5, 1924; s. Albert Ferguson and Fern Elizabeth (Smith) C.; B.Sc., McGill U., 1947; M.B.A., Harvard, 1949; certificate Centre d'Etudes Industrielles, Geneva, Switzerland, 1950; m. Mary Cecile Powell, Sept. 20, 1949; children—Michael, Andrew, Mark, Diane. With

Alcan Group, 1949—, v.p., dir. Alcan Internat. Ltd., 1956-62, pres., 1962—; chief sales officer Alcan Aluminum Ltd., 1962-68, exec. v.p. fabricating and sales, dir., 1968—; dir. Aluminum Co. Can., Ltd., Alcan (U.K.) Ltd., Alcan Aluminum Corp., Saquenay Shipping Ltd., Alcan R & D, Ltd., other Alcan group cos. Served with Canadian Inf. Corps, World War II. Mem. Alpha Delta Phi. Home: 3511 Redpath St Montreal 109 Quebec Canada Office: 1 Pl Ville Marie Montreal Quebec Canada

CULVER, DWIGHT WENDELL, educator; b. New Haven, Feb. 15, 1921; s. Mearl Peter and Louisa (Collier) C.; B.A., Carleton Coll., 1941; B.D., Yale, 1944, Ph.D., 1948; m. Margaret Louise Augustine, June 7, 1943; children—Enid Louise, Timothy Dwight, Jane Christine, Laura Bernice. Asst. prof. sociology Purdue U., 1947-52, asso. prof., 1952-61; asso. dir. Lilly Endowment Study of Pre-Sem. Edn., Mpls., 1961-63; prof. sociology, dept. chmn. St. Olaf Coll., 1963-68; acad. dean Coll. St. Catherine, 1968-71, prof. sociology, 1971—; examiner-cons. North Central Assn. Colls. and Secondary Schs., 1970—. Mem. City Planning Commn., Northfield, Minn., 1966-68; Del. Republican convs. Ind., 1954—, Minn., 1964-65, 68. Bd. dirs. Religious Research Assn. Mem. Am., Midwest sociol. socs., Soc. Sci. Study Religion, Am. Soc. Christian Ethics, Religious Edn. Assn., Phi Beta Kappa. Methodist. Author: Negro Segregation in the Methodist Church, 1953; We Can and We Will, 1961; (with Keith Bridston) The Making of Ministers, 1964, Pre-Seminary Education: Report of the Lilly Endowment Study, 1965. Home: 1831 Bayard Av St Paul MN 55116

CULVER, EDWARD HOLLAND, advt. agy. exec.; b. Mount Vernon, N.Y., Jan. 14, 1918; s. Ralph Farnsworth and Elizabeth (McMillin) C.; B.S. in Indsl. Adminstrn., Sheffield Sci. Sch. Yale, 1940; m. Mary Lee Oliver, July 15, 1942; children—Lee F. (Mrs. William L. Renfro), Edward Holland, Anne A. Exec. v.p. Cory Snow, Inc., advt. agy., Boston, 1946-50; co-owner, v.p., treas. Meissner & Culver, Inc., Boston, 1950-56; founder, pres., treas. Culver Advt., Inc., Boston, 1956—; chmn. Culver Mgmt. Services, Inc., Boston, 1969—, Culver Internat., Inc., Boston, Tokyo, Japan, Seoul, Korea, 1970—, Graham & Gillies & Culver, Ltd., London, Eng., 1971—. Mem. N. Woods Camp com. Boston YMCA, chmn. 1965-67. Trustee Children's Mus. Boston. Served to maj. F.A., AUS, 1941-46. Decorated Bronze Star medal. Mem. Assn. Indsl. Advertisers, Am. Assn. Advt. Agys. (gov. Eastern region 1962-63, 68-70, chmn. New Eng. council 1962-63, nat. dir. 1968-69), Internat. Advt. Assn., Advt. Club Boston, Yale Engring. Assn. Episcopalian. Clubs: Algonquin, University of Boston, Yale (Boston); Yale of New York City; Dedham (Mass.) Country and Polo. Home: 3 Wampatuck Rd Dedham MA 02026 Office: 535 Boylston St Boston MA 02116

CULVER, JOHN C., congressman; b. Rochester, Minn., Aug. 8, 1932; A.B. cum laude, Harvard, 1954, LL.B., 1962; postgrad. (Lionel de Jersey Harvard scholar), Emmanuel Coll., Cambridge U.; m. Ann Cooper; children—Christina, Rebecca, Catherine, Chester John. Dean men Harvard Summer Sch., 1960; legislative asst. to Sen. Edward Kennedy, 1962-63; mem. 89th to 92d Congresses from 2d Dist. Ia. Served to capt. USMCR. Mem. Ia., County bar assns. Democrat. Presbyn. Home: Marion IA 52302 Office: House Office Bldg Washington DC 20515

CULVER, ROBERT DE WITT, ins. co. exec.; b. Albany, N.Y., July 17, 1909; s. De Witt Clinton and Alice (Wright) C.; student Bryant Bus. Coll.; m. Mary Eleanor Goodwin, Oct. 17, 1932; children—Roberta Lee (Mrs. Donald R. Johnson), Judith Marilyn (Mrs. James S. White), Robert De Witt, Jr. With Indsl. Mut. Ins. Co., Boston, 1929-61, v.p., 1945-54, pres., 1954-60, chmn., 1960-61; chmn. bd. dirs. Arkwright Mut. Ins. Co., Boston, 1961-67; vice-chmn. Arkwright Boston Mut. Ins. Co., Waltham, Mass., 1968—; vice-chmn. Mut. Boiler & Machinery Ins. Co., Waltham, Mass., 1968—; trustee, bd. investment Melrose Savs. Bank (Mass.); dir. F. M. Ins. Co. Ltd., London, Eng. Chmn. Greater Boston adv. bd. Salvation Army, 1969—. Trustee, mem. exec. com. Melrose-Wakefield Hosp. Club: Algonquin (Boston). Home: 29 Sheffield Rd Melrose MA 02176 Office: 225 Wyman St Waltham MA 02154

CULVER, VIRGINIA, journalist. Religion editor Denver Post. Office: 650 15th St Denver CO 80202*

CUMING, GEORGE SCOTT, lawyer, gas co. ofcl.; b. Lakewood, O., Apr. 10, 1915; s. George Scott and Josephine (MacInnes) C.; A.B., cum laude, Western Res. U., 1937; postgrad. Harvard Law Sch., 1941-42, 45-46; J.D., Northwestern U., 1948; m. Dorothy Jane Herbst, May 12, 1943; children—Holiday (Mrs. Jason Baker Tuttle), Noelle (Mrs. John David Brock), George Scott, IV. Reid MacInnes. Employed as auditor, Gen. Electric Co., Cleve., 1937- 41; admitted Ill. bar, 1948, Mich. bar, 1950; asst. sec., asst. gen. atty. Mich-Wis. Pipeline Co., Detroit, 1948-52, Pacific N.W. Pipeline Corp., Salt Lake City, 1955-59; tax accountant Arthur Andersen & Co., Chgo., 1952-55; asst. sec. El Paso Natural Gas Co. (Tex.), 1960-65, Rocky Mountain Regional counsel, 1960-64, Washington counsel, 1964-65, gen. counsel, 1965—, v.p., 1969—. Served to lt. USNR, 1942-45. Mem. Am., Ill. bar assns., State Bar Mich., Delta Phi Alpha, Delta Sigma Rho, Sigma Delta Psi, Phi Delta Phi. Episcopalian. Clubs: Congressional Country, Metropolitan (Washington); University (Salt Lake City); El Paso, Coronado (El Paso). Home: 433 Borealis Lane El Paso TX 79912 Office: El Paso Natural Gas Bldg El Paso TX 79999

CUMLEY, RUSSELL WALTERS editor, publisher; b. Anson, Tex., Apr. 15, 1910; s. James Thomas and Dedie (Jones) C.; B.A., U. Tex., 1931, M.A., 1931, Ph.D., 1938; m. Delores Burkel, 1947; childrenJoseph Dunham, Rosemary Cay. Draftsman, Bur. Econ. Geology, Austin, Tex., 1929-31; geologist, Wichita Falls, Tex., 1931-33; tutor bacteriology U. Tex., Austin, 1933, instr. zoology, 1935-38; instr. Tex. Wesleyan Coll. Acad., 1933-34; sci instr. Univ. Sch., Austin, 1934-35; research asso. immunological genetics U. Wis., 1938-43; editor What's New, house organ Abbott Research Lab., North Chicago, Ill., 1946-47; head dept. publs. U. Tex. M.D. Anderson Hosp. Tumor Inst. Houston, 1947—; dir. gen. mgr. Med. Arts Pub. Found., Houston, 1949-, exec. editor Cancer Bull., 1948-, Psychiat. Bull., 1950-60, Heart Bull., 1952—; sci. editor Elsevier Press. Inc., 1954-56; co-editor Yearbook of Cancer, 1956—; owner Profl. Publ. Producers, Houston, 1956—. Served to capt. San. Corps, AUS, World War II. Mem. A.A.A.S., Pub. Health Cancer Assn., Sigma Xi. Author: Sportsman Guide to Birds of Texas and New Mexico, 1959; Sportsman's Guide to Game Mammals of Texas and New Mexico, 1960. Editor: (with R. Lee Clark) The Book of Health, 1952. Contbr. numerous articles to jours., mags. Home: 835 Country Lane Houston, TX 77024. Office: 1603 Oakdale St Houston TX 77004

CUMMING, ALISON ARCHIBALD, chem. mfg. co. exec.; b. Truro, N.S., Canada, Aug. 17, 1907; s. Melville and Mary (Archibald) C.; B.Sc. in Chemistry, Dalhousie U., 1930; m. Anne Berry, Jan. 20, 1932; children—William A., Thomas A., Robert A. Joined Nat. Carbon, Ltd. and Assos., U.S. and Can., 1934, became pres. Nat. Carbon, Ltd., Toronto, 1953, pres., dir. Union Carbide of Can., Ltd., Toronto, 1956-65, chmn. bd., 1965-67; dir. Toronto-Dominion Bank, Guarantee Co. N.Am., Am. Growth Fund. Served with USAAF, 1942-45. Mem. Assn. Profl. Engrs. Ontario, Canadian Mfg. Assn. (pres. 1964-65) Home: 5 Bayview Wood Toronto 12 Ontario Canada Office: 123 Eglinton Av Toronto 12 Ontario Canada

CUMMING, GORDON ROBERTSON, hosp. adminstr.; b. Carmangay, Alta. Can., July 31, 1911; s. William R. and Ivy (Parkinson) C.; came to U.S., 1925, naturalized, 1932; A.B., U. Cal. at Berkeley, 1933, M.A., 1935; m. Helen Stanford, Dec. 24, 1935; children—Douglas Stanford, Janice Dorothy. Student investigator, bur. efficiency County Los Angeles, 1934-35; adminstrv. asst., then asst. dir. Los Angeles County Hosp., 1935-48; chief bur. hosps. Cal. Dept. Pub. Health, 1948-63; adminstr. Sacramento Med. Center 1963—. Dir., pres. Cal. Health Data Corp.; trustee Blue Cross, 1969—, chmn. bd., 1970—. Mem. joint com. areawide planning hosps. and related health facilities Am. Hosp., Assn.-USPHS, 1961, joint com. planning facilities long-term treatment and care, 1962; mem. hosp. research study sect. NIH, 1955-59, mem. council on regional medical programs, 1964-65, mem. Cal. Health Rev. and Program Council, 1966-70; mem. Commn. for Adminstrv. Services in Hosps., 1969-71. Mem. Am. Assn. Hosp. Planning (past pres.), Am. (chmn. council on legislation 1970, spl. com. on provision health services 1970-71), Cal. (pres., 1967—, trustee 1965—, award of merit 1955, award of valor 1971) hosp. assns. Served to maj. AUS, 1942-46. Home: 6416 Fordham Way Sacramento CA 95831 Office: 2315 Stockton Blvd Sacramento CA 95817

CUMMING, HUGH EVERSHED, food co. exec.; b. Rochester, N.Y., Sept. 12, 1921; s. Howard T. and Margaret (Myers) C.; B.S., Yale, 1942; M.B.A., Harvard, 1947, Advanced Mgmt. Program, 1968; m. Sally A. Forsyth, July 27, 1947; children—Kate A., Thomas E. Accountant, Taylor Instruments Cos., Rochester, 1947-49; from engring. trainee to v.p. prodn. Curtice Bros. Co., Rochester, 1949-61; exec. v.p. Curtice-Burns, Inc., Rochester, 1968—, also dir. Mem. adv. council N.Y. State Coll. Agr., 1970—. Served to comdr. USNR, 1944-46. Mem. Asso. N.Y. State Food Processors, Inc. (past pres.), Nat. Canners Assn. (dir.), Am. Frozen Food Inst. (dir.), Tau Beta Pi. Rotarian. Club: Country (Rochester). Home: 209 Whitewood Lane Rochester NY 14618 Office: 315 Alexander St Rochester NY 14604

CUMMING, HUGH SMITH, Jr., ret. govt. ofcl. b. Richmond, Va., Mar. 10, 1900; s. Hugh Smith and Lucy A. (Booth) C.; student Va. Mil Inst., 1917-20, U. Va., 1920-24; m. Winifred Burney West, Sept. 21, 1935. Mem. Va. Bar; banker, London, Bombay, Singapore, Peking, 1924-27; tech. advisor State Dept., 1928; asst. to U.S. delegation Internat. Econ. Conf., London, and 7th Pan-Am. Conf., Montevideo, 1933; exec. asst. to sec. of state 1934; detailed to U.S. consulate, Geneva, in connection Italo-Ethiopian affairs, 1935-36; spl. mission to Scandinavia and Netherlands, 1939; mem. exec. com. U.S. Antartic Service, 1939-41; spl. mission Greenland, 1941; mem. Econ. Warfare Mission, also U.S. del. Internat. Whaling Conf., London, 1943; spl. mission to Sweden, 1943; rep. State Dept. on Anglo-Swedish-Am. Commn., and chief div. No. European Affairs, 1944; polit. liaison officer U.S. delegation UN Conf. on Internat. Orgn., San Francisco, 1945; spl. mission Iceland, 1946; counselor Am. embassy Stockholm 1947-50; counselor Am. embassy with personal rank of minister, Moscow, 1950-52; dep. sec. gen. for polit. affairs NATO, Paris, 1952-53; ambassador to Indonesia, 1953-57; spl. asst. to sec. of state, dir. intelligence Dept. State, 1957-61, spl. asst. to sec. of state, 1961; cons. Dept. State, 1961-64. Chmn. John Foster Dulles oral history project Princeton. Past mem. bd. dirs. Columbia Hosp. for Women, Washington; trustee Meridian House Found. Family and Child Services Washington, Washington Inst. Fgn. Affairs, Washington Cathedral; pres. Bath County Community Hosp., Hot Springs, Va.; dir. Historic Georgetown, Inc.; pres. Nat. Cathedral Assn. Served as 2d lt. U.S. Army, 1918. Mem. U. Va. Law Sch. Assn., Mil. Order World Wars, S.A.R., Raven Soc., Diplomatic and Consular Officers Ret. (past pres.), Zeta Psi. Episcopalian. Clubs: Metropolitan (past pres.), Cosmos, Alibi (Washington); Chevy Chase (Md.); Royal Swedish Yacht, Sallskapet (Stockholm). Home: 2811 O St NW Washington DC 20007 also Overlook Hot Springs VA 24445

CUMMING, JOSEPH BRYAN, lawyer; b. Augusta, Ga., Aug. 10, 1893; s. Bryan and Mary Gairdner (Smith) C.; Litt.B., Princeton U., 1915; student Harvard Law Sch., 1915- 17; m. Virginia Neville Burum, Nov. 15, 1922; children—Neville Cumming Riley, Joseph Bryan, Nancy C. Connolly. Admitted to Ga. bar, 1920, since practiced in Augusta; mem. firm Cumming & Harper, now Cumming, Nixon, Yow, Waller & Capers, Augusta. Dir. Georgia R.R. Bank & Trust Co., Ga. R.R. & Banking Co., Augusta. Mem. Gen. Assembly of Ga., 1923-24; mem. Pres.'s Adv. Council Hist. Preservation. Chmn. bd. trustees Summerville Cemetery; vice chmn. Acad. of Richmond County, Tubman Home; trustee Clinton Anderson Hosp., Augusta Mus., Herbert Meml. Inst. Art; pres. trustees Young Men's Library Assn. Fund; chmn. Ga. Hon. Ambassador of the Cherokee Nation. Fellow Am. Bar Found., Am. Coll. of Trial Lawyers; mem. Augusta (pres. 1935-36), Ga. (pres. 1938-39), Am. bar assns. Democrat. Episcopalian. Home: 2231 Cumming Rd Augusta GA 30904 Office: Georgia Railroad Bank Bldg Augusta GA 30902

CUMMING, ROBERT A., mfg. co. exec.; b. Peoria, Ill.; grad. mech. engring. Purdue U.; m.; 1 dau., Andrea. Formerly with engine div. Caterpillar Tractor Co., Peoria; then dir. engine sales, constrn. and indsl. equipment Cummins Engine Co. Inc., Columbus, Ind.; later pres. Perkins Engines, Inc., N.Am. operations, Wixom, Mich.; dir. marketing White Motor Corp., pres. subsidiary Mpls.-Moline, Inc., Hopkins and Mpls., Minn., 1967-. Served with USNR, World War II; PTO. Office: 130 9th Av S Hopkins MN 55343

CUMMING ROBERT DENOON educator; b. Sydney, Can., Oct. 27, 1916; s. Charles Gordon and Minnie Lenore (Smith) C.; came to U.S., 1917, naturalized, 1935; B.A. in Classics magna cum laude, Harvard, 1938; Rhodes scholar, New Coll., Oxford (Eng.) U., 1938-40; Ph.D., U. Chicago, 1950; student Sorbonne, Paris, France, 1945-46, Fulbright fellow, 1959; m. Jeanne Anne Hannan, June 11, 1948; childrenCharles, Ann. Faculty Columbia, 1948-, prof. philosophy, 1960-, chmn. dept., 1959-64. Served with French Army, World War II. Decorated Purple Heart, Legion of Merit; Croix de Guerre with étoile (France). Author: The Philosophy of Jean-Paul Sartre, 1965. Editor: Euthyphro, Apology, Crito, 1956; Jour. Philosophy, 1958-64. Home: 29 Claremont Av New York City, NY 10027.

CUMMINGS, BARTON A., advt. exec.; b. Rockford, Ill., Feb. 4, 1914; s. Earl M. and Myrle (Smith) C.; B.S., U. Ill.; m. Regina Haven Pugh. Feb. 24, 1940; children—Ann, Peter, Susan. Chmn. exec. com. Compton Advt., N.Y.C.; chmn. bd. Dai-Ichi Compton, Inc., Tokyo, Compton Advt. Australia Pty. Ltd.; vice chmn. Compton Partners Ltd., London; dir. Anti-Pollution Systems, Inc. Chmn. creative support group Drug Abuse Information Advt. Campaign. Chmn. exec. com. James Webb Young Fund; chmn. advt. div. N.Y. Heart Assn. Fund; dir. Better Bus. Bur. of Met. N.Y. Inc. Mem. Am. Assn. Advt. Agys. (adv. council), Phi Delta Theta, Pi Alpha Mu. Clubs: Adirondack League; Queen City (Cin.); Sky, Economic (N.Y.C.); President's (U. Ill.). Home: 200 E 64th St New York City NY 10021 Office: 625 Madison Av New York City NY 10022

CUMMINGS, BOB, motion picture, stage, TV performer; b. Joplin, Mo., June 9, 1910; s. Charles C. and Ruth A. (Kraft) C.; student Carnegie Inst. Tech., Drury Coll., Am. Acad. Dramatic Arts; m. Regina Young; children—Robert Richard, Mary Melinda, Sharon Patricia, Laurel, Anthony, Charles Clarence. Actor in starring roles motion pictures, 1936—, including Kings Row, Princess O'Rourke, You Came Along, Dial M for Murder, The Carpetbaggers, What a Way to Go, others; star, dir. television series The Bob Cummings Show. Dir. advt. and promotion Holiday Magic Inc., also dir.; dir. advt. and promotion Spectrum Air Inc., Novato, Cal. Comml. airplane pilot. Founding mem. Ecology Found. U.S., Washington. Recipient Emmy award as best actor, 12 Angry Men, 1954, award as best actor in comedy Billboard, 1955, best comedy series award for Bob Cummings Show, Billboard, 1955; nominated for Emmy award as dir. and actor, 1955-59. Author: Stay Young and Vital, 1960. Office: PO Box 5347 Beverly Hills CA 90210

CUMMINGS, EDWARD MCLEAN, banker; b. Chgo., Sept. 10, 1921; s. Walter J. and Lillian (Garvy) student Chgo. Latin Sch., 1930-36, Hotchkiss Sch., 1936-38; A.B., Yale, 1942; m. Hèléne de Marcellus, Feb. 26, 1949; childrenHenry de Marcellus, Amory, Lawrence Bacon, Lillian, Ogden, Rose, Alexander, McLean. Asst. v.p. Chem. Bank & Trust Co., N.Y.C., 1946-48; 2d v.p. Continental Ill. Nat. Bank & Trust Co. of Chgo., 1948-51, v.p., 1951-69, sr. v.p., 1969—; dir. E.J. Brach & Sons, Am. Gen. Ins. Co., Maremont Corp., Kellwood Co., Victor Comptometer Corp., Md. Casualty Co. Served from ensign to lt. USNR, 1942-46. Trustee DePaul U., U. Chgo. Cancer Research Found. Treasurer Ill. Soc. Prevention Blindness (dir.). Mem. Alliance Francaise Chicago (dir.). Roman Catholic. Kinght of Malta. Clubs: Chicago; Onwentsia (Lake Forest, Ill.); Casino; Racquet. Home: 2430 Lake View Av Chicago, IL 60614. Office: 231 S LaSalle St Chicago IL 60604

CUMMINGS, EVERETT A., bank exec. Sr. v.p. Citizens Comml. & Savs. Bank, Flint, Mich. Office: 328 S Saginaw St Flint MI 48502*

CUMMINGS, FRANK CURTIS, clergyman; b. Minter, Ala., Apr. 4, 1929; s. Edmond and Annie (Moultrie) C.; B.A., Seattle Pacific Coll., 1952; D.D., Shorter Coll., 1970; m. Martha Coleen Colly, Mar. 5, 1954; 1 dau., Paschell Coleen. Ordained to ministry African Methodist Episcopal Ch., 1948; pastor African Methodist Episcopal Ch., Alridge, Ala., 1948-49, Bremerton, Wash., 1952-53, Santa Barbara, Cal., 1954-60, St. Louis, 1961-68; sec.-treas., dept. ch. extension African Methodist Episcopal Ch., St. Louis, 1968—; pres. A.M.E. Mgmt. Agy. Inc. Vice-chmn. Civil Service Commn. St. Louis, 1965-71. Pres. bd. dirs. West End Hosp. Assn. Served with USAF, 1949-51. Mem. Alpha Phi Alpha. Home: 4919 Maffitt Pl St Louis MO 63113 Office: 3526 Dodier St St Louis MO 63107

CUMMINGS, HERBERT KELLERT, business exec.; b. Montreal, Que., Can., May 20, 1924; s. Nathan and Ruth (Kellert) C.; came to U.S., 1939, naturalized, 1943; grad. bus. adminstrn., Babson Inst., 1946, advanced mgmt. course, Stanford, 1962; m. Irene Lenore Harris, Jan. 4, 1947; children—James Kellert, Richard Alan, Patricia Ruth. With Monarch Foods Co., Chgo., 1947-51; with U.S. Products Corp., San Jose, Cal., 1952-55, regional sales mgr., 1953-55; with Rosenberg Bros., San Francisco, 1955-58, exec. v.p., 1957-58; pres. internat. div. Consol. Foods Corp., San Francisco, 1958-62, v.p., asst. to pres. parent co., 1962-66; pres. Jimpatrick, Inc., Herbert K. Cummings, Inc., 1965—; dir. Pelorex Corp., Buffalo, TAW Data Systems, Internat. Leasing, N.Y.C., Asso. Products, New York. Bd. dirs. San Jose YMCA, 1953-55, Santa Clara Heart Assn., 1953-55, San Jose Jewish Community Council, 1953-55; trustee, fellow, chmn. of fellows, mem. pres.' council Brandeis U. Served with AUS, 1943-45; ETO. Mem. N.A.A.C.P., Young Pres.'s Orgn., Pi Tau Pi. Jewish religion (past pres., dir. temple). Mason. Clubs: Optimist (Life), Standard, Brandeis U. (pres. 1969-70) (Chgo.). Home: 825 Glenoak Dr Winnetka IL 60093 Office: 1603 Orrington Av Evanston IL 60201

CUMMINGS, JOHN JOSEPH, Jr., banker; b. Providence, May 28, 1923; s. John Joseph and Helen Ann (Curran) C.; student Holy Cross Coll., 1940-42; A.B., St. Mary's U., 1944; m. Alice Frances Nash, Feb. 3, 1951; children—John Joseph III, Joseph Ward, James Nash. With Union Trust Co., Providence, 1947-53, auditor, 1950-53; comptroller Providence Union Nat. Bank, 1953-55; v.p. Indsl. Nat. Bank Providence, 1955-63, exec. v.p. dir., 1963-68, pres. 1968—; pres. Indsl. Nat. Corp., 1968—; mem. stockholders adv. bd. Fed. Res. Bank Boston, 1964-69; dir. AT Cross Co. Pres., Providence Off-St. Parking, 1963-65; trustee Realty Income Trust. Trustee, R.I. Pub. Expenditure Council, 1959—; chmn. R.I. Spl. Com. Study Govtl. Orgns. and Operations, 1961-62, Providence Civic Center Authority, 1969—; chmn. exec. com. Bus. Devel. Co. R.I.; former mem. Providence Redevel. Agy., Providence City Plan Commn. Chmn., Catholic Fund Appeal, Diocese Providence, 1964; chmn. exec. com. Urban Housing Corp. Trustee R.I. Charities Trust, St. Joseph's Hosp., Diocese of Providence Pension Plan; trustee at large Found. for Full Service Banks. Decorated knight comdr. with star. Knights St. Gregory. Mem. Am. Bankers Assn. (pres. nat. bank div. 1968-69, adminstrv. com.). Clubs: R.I. Country (Barrington); Turks Head, University (Providence); Dunes (Narraganset, R.I.); Union League (N.Y.C.). Home: 40 Roslyn Av Providence RI 02908 Office: 111 Westminster St Providence RI 02901

CUMMINGS, MARTIN MARC, physician, sci. adminstr.; b. Camden, N.J., Sept. 7, 1920; s. Samuel and Cecelia (Silverman) C.; B.S., Bucknell U., 1941; M.D., Duke, 1944; D.Sc. (hon.), Bucknell U., 1968, U. Neb., Emory U.; L.H.D. (hon.), Georgetown U., 1971; m. Arlene Sally Avrutine, Sept. 27, 1942; children—Marc Steven, Lee Bernard, Stuart Lewis. Intern, resident Boston Marine Hosp., 1944-46; resident Tb Grasslands Hosp., Valhalla, N.Y., 1946-47; dir. Tb evaluation lab. Communicable Disease Center, USPHS, Atlanta, 1947-49; instr. medicine Emory U. Sch. Medicine, 1948- 50, asso. medicine, 1950-52, asst. prof., 1953; chief Tb sect., also dir. Tb research lab. VA Hosp., Atlanta, 1949-53; dir. research service VA Central Office, Washington, 1953-59; spl. lectr. microbiology George Washington U. Sch. Medicine, 1953-59; prof. microbiology, chmn. dept. Okla. U. Sch. Medicine, 1959-61; chief Office Internat. Research, NIH, USPHS, 1961-63, director Nat. Library of Medicine, 1964—. Chmn. com. med. research Nat. Tb Assn., 1958-59; chmn. panel Sarcoidosis NRC-Nat. Acad. Scis., 1958-60. Served with AUS, 1943-44. Recipient Exceptional Service award VA, 1959; Distinguished Service award Dept. Health, Edn. and Welfare, 1968. Diplomate Am. Bd. Microbiology. Sr. mem. Am. Soc. Clin. Investigation, Am. Fedn. Clin. Research; mem. Assn. Am. Med. Colls., Am. Clin. and Climatol. Assn. Club: Cosmos. Author: (with Dr. H.S. Willis) Diagnostic and Experimental Methods in Tuberculosis, 1952. Contbr. chpt. on Tubercle Bacilli, Diagnostic Procedures and Reagents, 1950. Home: 11317 Rolling House Rd Rockville MD 20852 Office: Nat Library Medicine Bethesda MD 20014

CUMMINGS, MELBOURNE WESLEY, pub. co. exec.; b. Beverly, Mass., Aug. 15, 1906; s. Edgar Raymond and Alberta Maud (Rines) C.; student engring. U. N.H., 1929, LL.D., 1962; m. Barbara Lamson, June 2, 1934; 1 dau., Diane (Mrs. H. David Bonner). Sales mgr. Record Press, Rochester, N.H., 1929-30; salesman Spaulding-Moss Co., Boston, 1930-35; sales mgr. Lew A. Cummings Co., Manchester,

N.H., 1935-46; founder Addison-Wesley Pub. Co., Inc., Reading, Mass., 1962—, pres., 1947-69, chmn. bd., 1947—, chief exec. officer, 1969—; chmn. bd. Addison-Wesley Can., Ltd., Don Mills, Ont., 1966—, Cummings Pub. Co., Inc., Menlo Park, Cal., 1968—, W.A. Benjamin, Inc., Menlo Park, 1970—, Fondo Educativo Interamericano S.A., Panama, 1967—. Mem. Book Builders Boston, New Eng. Council, U. N.H. 100 Club, Lambda Chi Alpha. Home: Melrose MA 02176 also 1 Olde Penzance Rd Rockport MA 01966 Office: Jacob Way Reading MA 01867

CUMMINGS, MILTON K., engring. co. exec.; owner Milton K. Cummings Cotton Co., 1937-52; pres. Brown Engring. div. Teledyne Co., Huntsville, Ala.; chmn. bd. Brown Engring. Div. Teledyne Co.; dir. 1st Nat. Bank Huntsville, 1959—. Cons. cotton OPA, Washington, 1951-52. Chmn. conf. Am. Youth U.S. Probation Office No. Ala., 1947; chmn. Huntsville Bd. Edn., 1948-54; chmn. Madison County (Ala.) Surplus Food Distbn., 1956-57; chmn. advance gifts div. Huntsville United Givers Fund, 1959; chmn. Gov. Ala. Com. Employment Phys. Handicapped, 1960; mem. med. adv. com. U. Ala., 1955-64, chmn. research com., 1961; chmn. HuntsvilleMadison County Community Action Com., 1965—; adv. Madison County Literacy Project, 1960; bus. adv. War on Povety Office Econ. Opportunity, Washington, 1964; anti-poverty program investigator, Huntsville, 1964; past mem. Huntsville Housing Authority, Madison County Bd. Pub. Welfare, Huntsville-Madison County Ad Hoc Citizens Com. for Comprehensive Community Mental Heath Center: currently mem. Huntsville Indsl. Expansion Com., Pres.'s Com. Employment Phys. Handicapped, Small Bus. Adv. Council Ala., Nat. Citizens Com. Community Relations, adv. com. 3d Army, Redstone Arsenal. Ala., internat. sponsors com. Robert Hutchings Goddard Library Prog. Mem. Huntsville City Council, 1946-47. Founder Christmas Charities Services, 1949, bd. dirs., 1949-63; chmn. Human Resources Found, 1958-59; bd. lay govs. St. Bernard (Ala.) Coll.; trustee Huntsville Civic Symphony; hon. trustee Huntsville Youth Band; dir. Huntsville Catholic Charities. Named Distinguished Citizen HuntsvilleMadison County C. of C., 1964, Employer of Year, Gov. Ala. Com. Employment Handicapped, 1966; recipient Brotherhood award Ala. Nat. Conf. Christians and Jews, 1965, Medal of Merit V.F.W., 1965. Asso. fellow Am. Inst. Aero. and Astronautics; hon. mem. Com. of 40 Sacred Heart Coll., Cullman, Ala.; life mem. Rocket City Astron. Assn.; founding mem. Assn. Huntsville Area Cos. (pres. 1963-64, exec. com. 1964—); adv. mem. Madison County Jr. Engring. Tech. Soc.; mem. Nat. Urban League (trustee 1967—), Soc. Personnel Adminstrn., Nat. (bd. dirs. 1955-57). Ala. (bd. dirs. 1954-57) assns. metal health. Presbyn. (deacon). Home: 421 Echols Av SE Huntsville AL Office: Brown Engring Research Park Huntsville AL 35807

CUMMINGS, NATHAN, industrialist; b. St. John, N.B., Canada, Oct. 14, 1896; s. David and Esther (Saxe) C.; ed. grade sch. and Economist Tng. Sch. N.Y.C.; m. Ruth Lillian Kellert, Dec. 30, 1919; (dec. Mar. 1952) children—Beatrice Violet Mayer, Herbert Kellert, Alan Harris; m. 2d., Joanne Ruth Toor, Aug. 9, 1959. Shoe bus., 1914-17, wholesale shoe business, 1917-24, shoe mfg., 1924-30, importing gen. merchandise, 1930- 34, mfg. buscuits and candy (all in Can.), 1934-38; pres. C.D. Kenny Co., Baltimore, Me., 1939—, acquired Sprague Warner & Co., Chgo., 1942; acquired Western Grocer Co. and Marshall Canning Co. of Marshalltown, Ia., 1944; acquired Reid, Murdoch & Co., Chicago, 1945; chm. bd. Consol. Grocers Corp., Chicago, 1947-68, name changed to Consol. Foods Corp. 1954, since which time some 30 food cos. have been acquired, now hon. chmn. and chmn. exec. com.; chmn. bd. Asso. Products.; dir. Rothschild Enterprises, Gen. Dynamics Corp. Governing life mem. Art Inst. Chgo.; hon. trustee Met. Mus. Fine Arts; patron Montreal Mus. Fine Arts; patron, governing mem. Mpls. Soc. Fine Arts; mem. Bus. Com. for Arts; citizens bd. U. Chgo.; religious com. City Chgo.; life gov. Jewish Gen. Hosp., Montreal; patron Lincoln Center Performing Arts. Decorated chevalier French Legion of Honor, commendatore Order of Merit (Italy), comandador Order of Merit (Peru). Mem. N.Y.C. C. of C. Jewish Religion. Clubs: Mid-Day, Standard, Executives, Mid-America (Chgo.); Montefiore (Montreal); Economic, Canadian, Marco Polo, Fifth Avenue, Sky, Governor's, Escholiers (N.Y.C.). Home: Waldorf Towers 100 E 50th St New York City NY Office: 375 Park Av New York City NY 10022

CUMMINGS, NAURICE GRANT, former bus. exec.; b. Beeville, Tex., Oct. 25, 1901; s. Grant Barnett and Alma (Morrow) C.; student U. of South, 1919-20, Southwestern U., 1918-19; m. Katy Lynch Davidson, Nov. 19, 1924; 1 dau., Katherine. Ret. v.p., Nat. Supply div. Armco Steel Corp.; dir. First City Nat. Bank of Houston, TransOcean Oil, Inc. Mason (Shriner). Clubs: Bayou, Ramada, Country (Houston). Home: 1619 North Blvd Houston TX 77006

CUMMINGS, PARKE, writer; b. West Medford, Mass., Oct. 8, 1902; s. Henry Irving and (DeVoo) P.; grad. Mercersburg Acad.; B.S., Harvard, 1925; m. Mary Virginia Obear, Apr. 6, 1935; childrenJohn Obear, Patricia Ann. Free- lance writer humor, sports articles, 1925-. Author: The Whimsey Report, 1948; The Dictionary of Sports, 1949; The Dictionary of Baseball, 1950; I'm Telling You Kids for the Last Time, 1951; American Tennis, 1957; Baseball Stories, 1959; The Fly in the Martini, 1961. Contbr. articles, verse to popular mags. Home: Compo Rd Westport CT 06880

CUMMINGS, RALPH WALDO, agronomist; b. Reidsville, N.C., Dec. 13, 1911; s. William Cummings and Sarah Elizabeth (Huffines) C.; B.S. Agr., N.C. State Coll., 1929-33; Ph.D., Ohio State U., 1938; D.Sc., Nehru Agrl. U., 1967, N.C. State U., 1968, Punjab Agrl. U., 1970; m. Mary Catherine Parrish, June 22, 1936; children—Ralph Waldo, Walter Bradley, William Kenneth, Mary Ann. Asst. in soil survey Ohio Agrl. Exptl. Sta., 1934-35; tech. asst. pomology Cornell U., 1936; asso. soil chemist N.C. Agrl. Exptl. Sta., 1937; asst. prof. soil tech. Cornell U., 1937-39, asso. prof. and soil technologist, Agrl. Expt. sta., 1940-42; head dept. agronomy N.C. State Coll., 1942-44, head dept. agronomy and asst. dir. Agrl. Expt. Sta., 1944-47, asso. dir., 1948-50, dir. research, 1950-54; chief N.C. U. Agrl. Research Mission in Peru, 1955-56; field dir. Indian Agrl. Program Rockefeller Found., 1957-66, asso. dir. for agr. scis., 1963-68; adminstrv. dean research N.C. State U., Raleigh, 1968-71; program adviser in agr. Ford Found., 1971—. Bd. dirs. Ohio State U. Research Found., 1969—; asso. dir. Agrl. Scis., Rockefeller Found., 1963-68; acting dean postgrad. Sch. Indian Agrl. Research Inst., 1959-60; chmn. com. on agrl. univs. govt. India, 1960-64; trustee Internat. Rice Research Inst., Philippines, 1966-68; pres. bd. govs. Am. Internat. Sch., New Delhi, 1962-63; collaborator Nat. Soil and Fertilizer Lab. Bd. dirs.; treas. U.S. Edn. Found. India; mem. N.C. Bd. Sci. and Technology, 1969-71. Recipient Internat. Agronomy award Am. Soc. Agronomy, 1970; Centennial award Ohio State U., 1970 Fellow Am. Soc. Agronomy; mem. Indian Soc. Genetics and Plant Breeding, Indian Phytopath. Soc., Madras Acad. Agrl. Scis. (pres. 1961), Am. Soc. Agronomy, Am. Chem. Soc., Soil Sci. Soc. Am., Raleigh (N.C.) C. of C., Sigma Xi, Gamma Alpha, Phi Kappa Phi, Alpha Zeta. Bantist. Rotarian. Home: 812 Rosemont Av Raleigh NC 27607 Office: Ford Found 320 E 43d St New York City NY 10017

CUMMINGS, RICHARD HOWE, banker; b. Springfield, Mass., Nov. 20, 1921; s. Charles H. and Gladys (Howe) C.; B.A. cum laude, Amherst Coll., 1943; M.B.A. with high distinction, Harvard, 1948; m. Cynthia Holt, May 31, 1947; 1 son, Roger Holt. With Nat. Bank Detroit, 1948—, sr. v.p., 1968—; pres., dir. Internat. Bank Detroit, 1969—; dir. Braun Engring. Co., Handleman Co., Macoid Industries, Union Investment Co., (all Detroit); Energy Conversion Devices, Troy, Mich. Served to capt. USAAF, 1942-46. Clubs: Detroit, Detroit Athletic; Bloomfield Hills (Mich.) Country; Birmingham (Mich.) Country. Home: 646 N Glengarry Rd Birmingham MI 48010 Office: Nat Bank Detroit Detroit MI 48232

CUMMINGS, SAMUEL BILLINGS, Jr., educator, psychologist; b. Irwin, Pa., Oct. 28, 1904; s. Samuel and Margaret (Guffey) C.; A.B., Amherst Coll., 1926; M.A., Columbia, 1928; Ph.D., Princeton, 1938. Instr. Dartmouth, 1928-30, Syracuse U., 1930-32; resident clin. psychologist N.J. Dept. Instns. and Agencies, 1936-38; mem. faculty Kenyon Coll., 1938-, prof. psychology, 1945-, chmn. dept., 1945-65; vis. scientist NSF, 1964-68. Served to lt. comdr. USNR, 1942-45. Simpson fellow, The Sorbonne, Paris, France, 1927; Walker fellow Princeton, 1935. Fellow A.A.A.S.; mem. Am. Psychol. Assn., Phi Beta Kappa, Delta Kappa Epsilon. Episcopalian. Contbr. articles in Home: Box 246 Gambier OH 43022.

CUMMINGS, TILDEN, banker; b. Chicago, Sept. 18, 1907; s. William Charles and Frances May (Stevens) C.; B.S., Princeton, 1930; M.B.A., Grad. Sch. of Bus. Adminstrn., Harvard, 1932; m. Hester Harton Browne, Mar. 29, 1933; children—Hester Hollyday (Mrs. Karl Jensen), Richard, Tilden, Douglas. With Continental Ill. Nat. Bank and Trust Co., Chicago 1932—, now pres.; dir. No. Natural Gas. Co. Omaha, Abex Corp., Consol. Foods Corp., Consolidation Coal Co., C., M., St.P. & P. R.R. Treas., dir. Chgo. Cubs Baseball for Boys; v.p. bd. trustees Northwestern U.; bd. govs. Hosp. Research and Ednl. Trust; vice chmn. Chgo. chpt. A.R.C., 1961-62, dir. Member Am. Hosp. Assn. (hon.), Delta Kappa Epsilon. Republican. Episcopalian. Clubs: Old Elm, Commercial, University, Economic, Commonwealth, LaSalle Street, Chicago (Chgo.); Princeton; Bankers; Glenview; Bohemian (San Francisco); Augusta (Ga.) National Golf. Home: 1025 Hill Rd Winnetka IL Office: 231 S LaSalle St Chicago IL 60690

CUMMINGS, WALTER J., U.S. circuit judge; b. Chgo., Sept. 29, 1916; s. Walter J. and Lillian (Garvy) C.; student St. Alban's Sch., 1933- 34; A.B., Yale, 1937; LL.B., Harvard, 1940; m. Therese Farrell Murray, May 18, 1946 (dec. Nov. 1968); children—Walter J., Keith M., Mark F. Admitted to Ill. bar, 1940; mem. staff U.S. solicitor gen., Washington, 1940-46; spl. asst. to U.S. atty. gen., 1944-46; partner firm Sidley, Austin, Burgess & Smith, Chgo., 1946-66; solicitor gen. U.S., 1952-53; judge 7th circuit U.S. Ct. Appeals, Chgo., 1966—. Former mem. Joint Coms. Jud. Articles and Uniform Comml. Code; former greivance commr. Ill. Supreme Ct. Bd. visitors Stanford Law Sch.; mem. vis. com. U. Chgo. Law Sch.; past nat. bd. dirs., vice chmn. Ill. div. Am. Cancer Soc.; adv. bd. St. Vincent's Infant Hosp., Chgo.; bd. dirs. Madonna Center Found.; trustee Loyola U., Chgo.; bd. govs. Citizens Greater Chgo. Named knight of Malta, knight of Holy Sepulchre. Mem. Am. (past chmn. spl. com. fed. rules procedure, past chmn. com. jud. center, Ross essay contest), Ill. (past chmn. internat. law sect., antitrust sect., comml. and bankruptcy law com., com. jud. ethics), Chgo. (past chmn. com. constl. revision, grievance com. div. III A, bd. mgrs., past chmn. com. founds.) bar assns., Bar Assn. 7th Fed. Circuit (past pres.), Am. Law Inst., Am., Chgo. bar founds., Harvard Soc. Ill. (dir.). Roman Catholoc. Clubs: Law, Legal, Racquet, Saddle and Cycle, Shoreacres (Chgo.); Metropolitan (Washington); Yale (N.Y.C.). Home: 1420 Lake Shore Dr Chicago IL 60610 Office: 219 S Dearborn St Chicago IL 60604

CUMMINGS, WILLIAM C., banker. Hon. chmn. bd., dir. Drovers Nat. Bank. Office: 1542 W 47th St Chicago IL 60609*

CUMMINS, ALFRED BYRON, engr., educator; b. Ute, Ia., Mar. 19, 1905; s. Daniel Byron and Myrtle (Chase) C.; B.S. cum laude, State U. Ia., 1931, J.D. cum laude, 1936, M.S., 1938; postgrad. Mass. Inst. Tech., 1931-32, U. Minn., 1938- 41, U. Pa., 1941-42; m. Maxine Ellen Price, Dec. 23, 1934; children—Mary Alice (Mrs. Wilson), Judith Maxine (Mrs. Morrison). Prodn. civilian specialist Armed Services, Phila., 1942- 46; chief indsl. engr. Wilkening Mfg. Co., Phila., 1943-46; cons. mgmt. engr., 1946—; prodn. cons. Armed Services, War Labor Bd., WPB, Engring. Sci. Mgmt. War Tng. Program, U. Pa., 1941-45; prof. mgmt. dept. Case Western Res. U. Sch. Mgmt., 1947—; organizer, dir. Hough Mfg. Co.; chmn. L-C-L, Inc., Cleve. Cons. OEEC-EPA, Paris; mgmt. cons. VA hosps.; dir. research pub. health mgmt. systems; mem. nat. panel arbitrators Fed. Mediation and Conciliation Service. Registered profl. mgmt. engr. Mem. Ia. Bar Assn., Soc. for Advancement Mgmt. (past pres. Phila.), Am. Arbitration Assn. (nat. panel arbitrators), Sigma Xi, Tau Beta Pi, Beta Gamma Sigma, Delta Sigma Pi. Patentee office equipment, athletic tng. equipment. Contbr. tech. articles to profl. jours. Home: N Miles Rd Chagrin Falls OH 44022 Office: Case Western Reserve U Cleveland OH 44106 ☆

CUMMINS, BOBBY DEAN, tobacco co. exec.; b. English, Ind., Sept. 29, 1926; s. Densil Highfill and Rue (Nash) C.; B.S., Ind. U., 1949; grad. advanced mgmt. program Harvard, 1963; m. Gladys Gonzalez, June 24, 1950; children—John Raymond, Dean Robert. Controller Shirley Corp., Indpls., 1948-53; audit supr. Ernst & Ernst, Indpls., 1953-59; v.p., controller Huffman Mfg. Co., 1959-66; controller Brown & Williamson Tobacco Corp., Louisville, 1966—. C.P.A., Ind. Mem. Financial Execs. Inst. (dir. Louisville chpt. 1969), Am. Inst. C.P.A.'s, Ind. Soc. C.P.A.'s, Indpls. Jr. C. of C. (1st v.p. 1958). Home: 3309 Springcrest Dr Louisville KY 40222 Office: 1600 W Hill St Louisville KY 40201

CUMMINS, CARL CLINTON, coll. dean; b. San Diego, Mar. 23, 1919; s. Carl Clinton and Fern (Fay) C.; A.B., U. Cal. at Santa Barbara, 1948; M.S., U. So. Cal., 1952; Ph.D., U. Cal. at Los Angeles, 1957; m. Rhea Joyce Dick, Nov. 23, 1949; childrenSteven Carl, Michael Richard. Design engr. Rohr Aircraft Corp., San Diego, 1946-49; instr. San Diego city schs. and jr. coll., 1949-53; prof. indsl. arts San Diego State Coll., 1953-58; prof., head dept. tech. arts Cal. State Polytech. Coll., San Luis Obispo, 1958-61, dean human devel. and edn., 1961—. Mem. adv. bd. Cal. Dept. Corrections; campaigns Community Chest, YMCA, Boy Scouts Am. Mem. N.E.A., Cal. Tchrs. Assn., Am. Vocational Assn., Cal. Indsl. Edn. Assn., Phi Delta Kappa. Episcopalian (vestry). Home: 172 Highland Dr San Luis Obispo CA 93401

CUMMINS, KENNETH BURDETTE, educator; b. New Washington, O., July 27, 1911; s. Royal Clinton and Pearl (Rittenour) C.; A.B., Ohio Wesleyan U., 1933; M.A., Bowling Green State U., 1939; Ph.D., Ohio State U., 1958. Tchr. sci. and math. Sulphur Springs (O.) High Sch., 1933-40, New Washington High Sch., 1941-57; asst. prof. math. Kent State U., 1957-59, asso. prof., 1959-64, prof., 1964—, chmn. dept., 1964-65. Dir. Math. Inst., NSF. Recipient alumni award for distinguished teaching, Kent State U., 1968. Mem. Math. Assn. Am., Nat. Council Tchrs. Mathematics, Central Assn. Sci. and Math. Tchrs., Ohio Acad. Sci., Phi Beta Kappa, Sigma Pi Sigma, Pi Mu Epsilon, Kappa Delta Pi. Author: Teaching of Mathematics, 1970. Contbr. articles profl. jours. Home: 421 Center St New Washington OH 44854 Office: Kent State University Kent OH 44242

CUMMISKEY, CHARLES JOSEPH, educator, univ. dean; b. St. Louis, Feb. 12, 1924; s. Charles Joseph and Sarah (Hickey) C.; B.S., U. Dayton, 1943; M.S., Northwestern U., 1952; Ph.D., U. Notre Dame, 1956. Joined Soc. of Mary, 1941; tchr. math. and sci. secondary schs., 1943-52; mem. staff dept. chemistry St. Mary's U., San Antonio, 1955—, prof. 1965—, chmn. dept., 1957-66, v.p., dean faculties, 1966—; research asso. A.E.C. radiation project U. Notre Dame, 1953-55. Vis. scientist secondary schs. Am. Chem. Soc., 1962-65; dir. NSF undergrad. research participation program, 1959-60. Grantee Robert A. Welch Found., 1962—. Mem. Am. Chem. Soc. (past pres. San Antonio sect.), Albertus Magnus Guild, Tex. Acad. Sci., Sigma Xi. Research on properties of complex anionic species. Address: 2700 Cincinnati Av San Antonio TX 78284

CUMMISKEY, JOHN WILLIAM, lawyer; b. Detroit, Apr. 19, 1917; s. James Peter and Edna (Common) C.; LL.B., U. Mich., 1938, J.D., 1941; m. Elenore Fink, Feb. 23, 1946; children—Susan Ann, John William, Paul Michael, Karen Christine. Admitted to Mich. bar, 1941; with firm Dickinson, Wrights, Davis, McKean & Cudlip, Detroit, 1941, 46; asso., then partner firm McCobb, Heaney & Dunn, Grand Rapids, 1946-59; partner firm Miller, Johnson, Snell & Cummiskey, Grand Rapids, 1959—. Gen. counsel Employers Assn. Grand Rapids, Furniture Mfrs. Assn. Grand Rapids, Mut. Ins. Co. Grand Rapids. Bd. dirs. Labor Policy Assn., Wash.; adv. council U Mich. Wayne State U. Inst. Indsl. Relations. Served to maj. AUS, 1941-45. Decorated Army Commendation ribbon; recipient Henry M. Campbell award U. Mich. Law Sch., 1941. Mem. Am. (ho. dels. 1958—, bd. govs. 1968-71), Grand Rapids bar assns., State Bar Mich. (chmn. jr. bar sect. 1947-48, pres. bar 1956-57), Am. Judicature Soc., Nat. Legal Aid and Defender Assn. (v.p., dir.), Phi Alpha Delta (Outstanding Service award Campbell chpt. 1957). Home: 2121 Shiawassee SE Grand Rapids MI 49506 Office: Old Kent Bldg One Vandenberg Center Grand Rapids MI 49502

CUNDEY, PAUL EDWARD, refining co. exec.; b. Phila., June 14, 1909; s. Clarence E. and Mabel (Owen) C.; B.S., Franklin and Marshall Coll., 1932; m. Ann E. Morris, Sept. 18, 1935; children—Paul, Ann (Mrs. Richard Deasy), David, Linda (Mrs. P. Terence Kohler) With Atlantic Refining Co. (co. name changed to Atlantic Richfield Co.), Phila. 1941—, asst. treas., 1955-66, sec., 1961-65, treas., 1966—; treas. and/or dir. numerous subsidiaries and firms, including: W.G. Sterner & Sons Inc., Atreco Investment Co., J.P. Frank Chem. & Plastic Corp., Jung, Atlantic Refining GmbH, O'Brien Oil Corp., Atlantic Petroleum Ltd., Bellox Corp., Hanford House Corp., Hondo Oil & Gas Co., Nuclear Materials & Equipment Corp., San Marino Tankers Inc., Tri-City Equities Corp. Home: Wyncote House Wyncote PA 19095 Office: 717 Fifth Av New York City NY 10022

CUNDIFF, EDWARD WILLIAM, educator; b. Long Beach, Cal., Sept. 28, 1919; s. Harry Thomas and Martha Magdalene (Koltes) C.; B.A., Stanford, 1940, M.B.A., 1942, Ed.D., 1952; Ford fellow, Harvard Sch. Bus. Adminstrn., 1956; m. Margaret Wallace Stroud, Sept. 8, 1956; children—Richard Wallace, Gregory Edward, Geoffrey William. Retailing exec., 1946-48; instr. marketing San Jose State Coll., 1949-52; asst. prof., later asso. prof. marketing Syracuse U., 1952-58, asst. dean, 1954-58; prof. marketing, chmn. dept. marketing adminstrn., U. Tex., 1958—; vis. prof. marketing, Fontainebleau, France, Palmermo, Sicily, 1960-61. Served to lt. (s.g.) USNR, World War II. Mem. Am., So. (pres. 1967-68) marketing assns., Nat. Sales Execs. Club, Beta Gamma Sigma, Delta Sigma Pi, Theta Chi. Author: (with R.R. Still) Sales Management: Decisions, Policies and Cases, 1958, rev. edit., 1969; (with R.R. Still) Basic Marketing: Concepts, Environment, and Decisions, 1964, rev. edit., 1970; Essentials of Marketing, 1966. Home: 5400 Ridge Oak Dr Austin TX 78731

CUNDIFF, PAUL ARTHUR, educator; b. Ferguson, Ky., Nov. 14, 1909; s. William Gilbert and Cynthia Isbelle (Haney) C.; A.B., Georgetown (Ky.) Coll., 1933; A.M., U. of Ky., 1935; Ph.D., Cornell, 1940; m. Mary Christine Fritsche, Aug. 7, 1948. English instr. U. of Ky., 1934-36, Cornell, 1937-40; English tchr. Wright Jr. Coll., Chgo., 1940-42; English instr. Northwestern U., 1945-46; chmn. English dept. Sampson Coll., N.Y., 1946- 47; prof. and head English Dept., Butler U., 1947-53, prof. English, 1947-61, dean coll. liberal arts and scis., 1953-59; chmn. dept. English, U. Del., 1961-66, H. Rodney Sharp prof. English, 1966—. Served to lt. AUS, 1942-45; ETO; historian 8th Corps, writing history of Battle of the Bulge for Corps. Decorated Bronze star. Mem. Am. Assn. Academic Deans (sec.), Modern Lang. Assn. of Am., Am. Assn. Univ. Profs., Coll. English Assn., Phi Kappa Phi, Sigma Tau Delta, Pi Kappa Delta, Lambda Chi. Club: Literary (Indpls.). Contbr. articles to profl. jours. Home: 400 Stamford Dr Newark DE 19803

CUNEO, ERNEST, lawyer,publisher; b. Carlstadt, N.J., May 27, 1905; s. John J. and Louise (Tosi) C.; A.B., Columbia, 1927; LL.B., St. Johns U., 1931; LL.D., Fla. So. Coll., 1960; m. Margaret Watson, Oct. 29, 1946; childrenSandra, Jonathan. Admitted to N.Y. bar, 1932, D.C., 1945; law sec. Fiorello H. La Guardia, 1931-32; practice of law 1932—; asso. counsel Dem. Nat. Com., 1936-40; chmn. bd. N. Am. Newspaper Alliance, Inc., 1950-63. White House liaison officer OSS, 1942-45. Decorated by Italy and Britain. Mem. Bar Assn. City N.Y., D.C., Am. bar Assns. Clubs: Varsity, National Press, Overseas Press, Columbia University. Author: Life with Fiorello; Science and History; Dynamics of World History. Home: 2911 33d Pl Washington DC 20005 Office: 1511 K St NW Washington DC 20005

CUNEO, GILBERT ANTHONY, lawyer b. St. Marys, Pa., June 29, 1913; s. George L. and Cunigunda (Jaeger) C.; A.B., St. Vincent Coll., Latrobe, Pa., 1934; LL.B., Harvard, 1937; m. Mary Rita Garrigan, Nov. 18, 1944; 1 dau., Mary Kathleen. Admitted to N.Y. bar, 1938, D.C. bar, 1953, U.S. Supreme Ct. bar, 1947; practiced in N.Y.C., 1937-42, 46; mem. Armed Services Bd. Contract Appeals, Washington, 1946-58; mem. firm Sellers, Conner & Cuneo, Washington, 1958—. Served with AUS, 1942-46. Mem. Am. (chmn. pub. contracts div. adminstrv. law sect. 1962-64, chmn. sect. public contract law 1968-69), D.C., Fed. bar assns., N.Y. County Lawyers Assn., Am. Judicature Soc. Roman Catholic. K.C. Clubs: Cosmos, Columbia Country, Metropolitan, Nat. Lawyers, University (Washington). Author: Government Contracts Handbook 1962. Contbr. articles to profl. jours.; lectr. on govt. contracts. Home: 5000 Rockmere Ct Sumner MD 20016 Office: 1625 K St NW Washington DC 20006

CUNEO, JOHN F., printer and binder; b. Chicago, Dec. 24, 1885; s. Frank and Amelia (Gondolfo) C.; ed. Chicago Latin Sch.; grad. Univ. Sch., Chgo.; student Yale, 1904-06; m. Julia Reed Shepherd, June 24, 1930; children—John F., Jr., Consuela. Became pres. of John F. Cuneo Co., 1907; pres. The Cuneo Press, Inc., of Chicago, New York, Kokomo, Phila., Milw., Boston, 1919—; former chmn. exec. com. Nat. Tea Co.; former dir. Continental Ill. Nat. Bank, Chgo. Served as asso. chief Poster Div., Information and Ednl. Service, Dept. Labor, Washington, World War I; mem. Nat. War Labor Bd., World War II. Decorated Knight Equestrian Order Holy Sepulchre Jerusalem, Knight St. Sylvester of Gt. Cross with Grand Cross, Knight of Malta. Roman Catholic. Clubs: The Cloud Club, Yale Club, Recess Club, Bankers (New York); Chicago Athletic Assn., Chicago Golf,

The Tavern, Racquet (Chicago); Knollwood (Lake Forest). Home: Hawthorn Farms Libertyville IL 60048 Office: 2242 S Grove St Chicago IL 60616

CUNHA, TONY JOSEPH, educator; b. Los Banos, Cal., Aug. 22, 1916; s. Anthony August and Maria (Silvera) C.; student Cal. Poly Coll., 1936-39; B.S., Utah State U., 1940, M.S., 1941; Ph.D., U. Wis., 1944; m. Gwen Smith, Sept. 1, 1941; childrenBecky Jane, Sharon Marie, Susan Ann. Instr. Wash. State U., 1944, asst. prof., 1945, asso. prof. dept. animal sci. U. Fla., 1948-50, prof., head dept., 1950-. Named Alumnus of the Year, Cal. Poly. Coll., 1956; Sr. Faculty award Fla. chpt. Gamma Sigma Delta, 1959; Man of Yr. award in Fla. agr., Progressive Farmer mag., 1966; Morrison award for $2000 for distinguished research, Am. Soc. Animal Sci., 1968. Fellow A.A.A.S.; mem. Am. Soc. Animal Sci. (v.p. 1961, pres. 1962), Am. Inst. Nutrition, Am. Assn. U. Profs., Newcomen Soc. Am., Fla. Acad. Sci., Soc. Exptl. Biology and Medicine. Sigma Xi, Gamma Sigma Delta (Fla. pres. 1958), Alpha Zeta, Gamma Alpha, Phi Sigma Alpha, Gamma Rho. Roman Catholic. Rotarian. Author: Swine Feeding and Nutrition 1957. Co-editor: Crossbreeding Beef Cattle, 1963; Factors Affecting Calf Crop. 1967. Contbr. articles to profl. publs. Home: 1641 NW 10th Av Gainesville FL 32601

CUNINGGIM, AUGUSTUS MERRIMON (KUN'INGGIM) found. exec.; b. Nashville, May 12, 1911; s. Jesse Lee and Maud Lillian (Merrimon) C.; A.B., Vanderbilt U., 1931; A.M., Duke, 1933, LL.D., 1963; B.A. (Rhodes scholar), Oxford U., England, 1935; B.D., Yale, 1939, Ph.D., 1941; Litt.D., Central Coll., Fayette, Mo., 1952, Pomona (Cal.) Coll., 1961; m. Annie Whitty Daniel, June 10, 1939; childrenJessica (Mrs. John Neff), Penelope (Mrs. Ira Horowitz), Margaret Merrimon. Dir. of religious activities Duke, 1936-38; prof. of religion Emory and Henry Coll., Emory, Va., 1941-42; prof. of religion Dension U., Granville, O., 1942-44; prof. of relgion Pomona Coll., Claremont, Calif., 1946-51; chaplain Asso. Colls. of Claremont (Calif.) 1948-50; dean Perkins Sch. Theology, So. Meth. U., 1951-60; exec. dir. Danforth Found., St. Louis, 1960-66, pres., 1966—. Trustee Vanderbilt U., Duke U., St. Louis Symphony, Arts Mem. Soc. for Religion in Higher Edn., Phi Beta Kappa, Omicron Delta Clubs: Rotary; University (New York); Cosmos (Washington). Author: The College Seeks Religion, 1947; Freedom's Holy Light, 1955; Christianity and Communism, 1958; Protestant Stake in Higher Education, 1961. Home: 9 Wydown Terrace St Louis, MO 63105.

CUNINGGIM, MARGARET LOUISE, univ. dean; b. Nashville, Oct. 15, 1914; d. Jesse Lee and Maud (Merrimon) Cuninggim; B.A., Duke, 1936; M.A., Columbia, 1937; Ed.D. (resident counselor fellow 1942-43, 55-56, tuition scholar 1955-56), Northwestern U., 1958. Instr. art Ala. Coll., Montevallo, 1937-42; dean women Ripon (Wis.) Coll., 1943-46; asst. prof. art, head of residence Hockaday Jr. Coll., Dallas, 1946-49; dean of women Tenn. Poly. Inst., Cookeville, 1949-54, U. Tenn., 1957-66, Vanderbilt U., Nashville, 1966—. Mem. Nat. Assn. Women Deans and Counselors, Tenn. Assn. Women Deans (pres. 1958-60), Am. Assn. U. Women, Kappa Pi, Theta Alpha Phi, Pi Lambda Theta, Alpha Lambda Delta, Mortar Bd., Kappa Alpha Theta. Methodist. Home: Wellington Arms Apt Nashville TN 37205

CUNNINGHAM, ARTHUR FRANCIS, apparel co. exec.; b. Bklyn., Mar. 23, 1922; s. John Michael and Alice (Heggerty) C.; student Am. U., 1946-47; B.S., L.I. U., 1950; LL.B., Bklyn. Law Sch., 1953; postgrad. N.Y.U. Grad. Sch., 1954-56; M.B.A., U. Detroit, 1958; m. Maureen Reidy, Feb. 13, 1970; 1 dau. by previous marriage, Linda June. With Fairbanks, Co., N.Y.C., 1950-51, Lever Bros. Co., N.Y.C., 1951-55; admitted to N.Y. bar, 1954; sr. financial analyst Ford Motor Co., 1955-56; gen. sales mgr. DWG Cigar Corp., Detroit, 1956-60; asst. to pres. Nalley's, Inc., Tacoma, 1960-61, exec. v.p., dir., 1961-62; exec. v.p. Seeman Bros., Inc. Carlstadt, N.J., 1962- 65, dir.; v.p., gen. mgr. food div. Leslie Salt Co., San Francisco, 1965- 67; pres., dir. Koratron Co., Inc., San Francisco, 1967—; pres., dir. Koratec, Inc.; v.p., dir. Koracorp Industries, Inc.; dir. Koratec Communications, Inc., San Francisco, Prodesco, Inc. Perkasie, Pa.; Richen, Inc., Greenville, N.C., Incopa Ind., Inc., Bristol, Tenn. Food chmn. United Good Neighbors Campaign, Tacoma, 1962. Served with USAAF, 1942-45. Mem. Newcomen Soc. Clubs: Commonwealth (San Francisco); N.Y. Athletic. Home: 2001 Broadway San Francisco CA 94115 Office: 617 Mission St San Francisco CA 94105

CUNNINGHAM, CARL ROBERT, music critic, educator; b. Los Angeles, Oct. 21, 1931; s. William Clement and Ruth (George) C.; Mus.B., U. Notre Dame, 1952; M.A., U. So. Cal., 1965, Instr. piano and theory Punabou Sch., Honolulu, 1960-63; lectr. music theory U. Hawaii, 1962-63; choir dir. Sacred Heart Cath. Ch., Honolulu, 1959-63; music critic San Francisco Chronicle, 1965-66; music editor Houston Post, 1966—; spl. lectr. music U. St. Thomas, Houston, 1968-70, chmn. dept., 1970—. Served with USNR, 1952- 56. Rockefeller Found. fellow, 1964-66. Address: 4747 Southwest Freeway Houston TX 77027

CUNNINGHAM, CHARLES CREHORE, dir. Art Inst. Chgo.; b. Mamaroneck, N.Y., Mar. 7, 1910; s. Stanley and Esther Lowell (Burnett) C.; A.B., Harvard, 1932; B.A. diploma, London (Eng.) U., 1933; Arts D. (hon.), U. Hartford, 1959; L.H.D. (hon.), DePaul U., 1970; m. Eleanor Lamont, June 27, 1932 (dec. May 1961); children—Charles Crehore, Priscilla, Thomas Lamont, James Stanley; m. 2d, Elinor Gregory, June 19, 1962. Asst. curator paintings Mus. Fine Arts, Boston, 1934-41; dir. Wadsworth Atheneum, Hartford, Conn., 1946-66, Art Inst. Chgo., 1966—. Mem. Chgo. Commn. on Hist. and Archtl. Landmarks. Vis. com. Smith Coll., Harvard U.; trustee Internat. Exhbns. Found., Ravinia Festival Assn. Served as lt. comdr. USNR, World War II. Decorated Bronze Star medal, Commendation Ribbon for combat duty aboard aircraft carriers; Order of Merit, Republic of Italy. Recipient Benjamin Franklin fellow Royal Soc. Arts, London. Mem. Assn. Arts Mus. Dirs. (pres. 1958), Internat. Council Museums (chmn. U.S. nat. com.), A.I.A. (hon.), Am. Inst. Interior Designers (hon.), Archeol. Inst. Am., Am. Fedn. Arts (mem. bd. trustees), Coll. Art Assn., Internat. Inst. Conservation of Works of Art, Am. Assn. Museums (council). Republican. Episcopalian. Clubs: Century Assn. (N.Y.C.); Harvard (Chgo. and N.Y.C.); Shoreacres (Lake Bluff); Tavern, Chicago, Arts (Chgo.). Author: Modern French Painting and Drawing in Art Institute of Chicago, Japanese edit., 1970; co-author: Rembrandt After 300 Years, 1969. Editorial bd. Art in Am. Editor: Art in New England, 1939. Contbr. Art in Am., Art News, Art Quar. Home: 513 Sheridan Rd Kenilworth IL 60043 Office: 125 E Monroe St Chicago IL 60603

CUNNINGHAM, CREIGHTON PARNELL, ins. co. exec.; b. Yankton, S.D., Aug. 4, 1907; s. James M. and Vivan (Peterson) C.; student Morningside Coll., Sioux City, Ia., 1925-26, U. Chgo., 1926-28; m. Letha E. Cummings, July 1, 1929; children—James C., Robert C., Michael C. Casualty ins. underwriter Continental Casualty Co., Chgo., 1934-37; casualty ins. underwriter Zurich Ins. Co., head office, also br. office, Pitts., 1937-50, asst. U.S. mgr. charge eastern operations, N.Y.C., 1950-56; pres., dir. Am. Home Assurance Co., also affiliate Insurance Co. State of Pa., 1956-62; pres., dir. N.Y. Fire & Marine Underwriters, Inc. (name changed to N.Y. Guaranty Corp.), 1962-. Mem. Phi Gamma Delta. Clubs: Drug and Chemical (N.Y.C.); Baltusrol Golf (Springfield, N.J.). Home: 14 Forest Dr Springfield NJ 07081 Office: 501 Fifth Av New York City NY 10017

CUNNINGHAM, DAVID, metals co. exec.; b. Ligonier, Ind., Sept. 2, 1909; s. Joseph Rush and Sarah Jane (Rose) C.; student Ft. Wayne Bus. Coll., 1927-28, Ind. U., 1930-32, Purdue U., 1933-35; m. Madge E. Carmichael, Aug. 7, 1932; children—David Douglas, John Daniel, William Rush. With Tokheim Corp., Ft. Wayne, Ind., 1928—, dir., 1962—, exec. v.p., 1964-66, pres., chief exec. officer, 1966—; dir. Peoples Trust Bank. Met. chmn. Nat. Alliance of Businessmen, 1971-72; gen. chmn. United Fund of Allen County, 1955-56. Pres. YMCA; bd. dirs. Varied Industry Plan, Lincoln Nat. Balanced Fund, Lincoln Nat. Capital Fund, Parkview Meml. Hosp.; bd. mgrs. Lincoln Nat. Variable Annuity Fund A and Fund B; trustee Ind. Inst. Tech. Mem. N.A.M. (dir.), Ind., Ft. Wayne (pres.) chambers commerce, Asso. Employers of Ind., Ind. Mfrs. Assn. (past dir.). Republican. Methodist (trustee). Mason, Elk. Clubs: Fort Wayne Country, Fort Wayne Quest, Indiana Soc. of Chgo. Home: 9713 Covington Rd Fort Wayne IN 46804 Office: 1602 Wabash Av Fort Wayne IN 46801

CUNNINGHAM, DAVID F., bishop; b. Walkerville, Mont., Dec. 3, 1900; ed. St. Michael's Coll., Toronto, Ont., Can., St. Bernard's Sem., Rochester, N.Y., also Cath. U. Am. Ordained priest Roman Cath. Ch., 1926; titular bishop Lampsacus and auxiliary of Syracuse, 1950-70, bishop of Syracuse, 1970—. Address: 307 Bradford Pkwy Syracuse NY 13224

CUNNINGHAM, DON RICHARD, advt. exec.; b. Gary, Ind., Jan. 30, 1925; s. A. Lester and Floy (Tidrick) C.; student Hamilton Coll., 1943-44; B.S. in journalism, Northwestern U., 1948; m. Dorothy A. Radosevich, Feb. 26, 1949; children—Michael P., Kristie L. Brand asst. advt. dept. Procter & Gamble, Cin., 1948-50; account supr. Stockton, West, Burkhart, Cin., 1950-55, Earle Ludgin, Chgo., 1955-56; with Foote, Cone & Belding, 1956—, sr. v.p. gen. mgr., Los Angeles, 1968—, dir., 1970—. Western region chmn. Am. Advt. Fedn., 1971; bd. dirs. Los Angeles Advt. Club, 1970. Active John Tracy Clinic, 1969, Opera Assos., 1970—. Served with USAAF, 1943-46. Mem. Sigma Delta Chi, Alpha Delta Sigma, Pi Kappa Alpha. Episcopalian. Clubs: Jonathan; Wilshire Country. Home: 5210 La Canada Blvd La Canada CA 91011 Office: 2727 W 6th St Los Angeles CA 90057

CUNNINGHAM, FREDERIC, educator; b. Cooperstown, N.Y., Sept. 6, 1921; B.S., Harvard, 1943, M.A., 1947, Ph.D. in Mathematics, 1953; married, 1947; three children. Teaching fellow math. Harvard, 1947-50; instr., N.H., 1951-53, asst. prof., 1953-56; lectr. Bryn Mawr Coll., 1956-57, became asso. prof., 1959, now prof. math.; asst. prof. Wesleyan U., 1957-59. Served to 1st lt. AUS, 1943-46. Mem. A.A.A.S., Math. Soc., Math. Assn., Math. Soc. France. Office: Math Dept Bryn Mawr Coll Bryn Mawr PA 19010*

CUNNINGHAM, GLENN CLARENCE, govt. ofcl.; b. Omaha, Sept. 10, 1912; s. George Warner and Emma (Seefus) C.; A.B., U. of Omaha, 1935; m. Janis Thelen, July 25, 1941; children—Glenn Clarence, Judith, Mary, James Robert, David George, Ann Melissa. Salesman Aetna Life Ins. Co., Omaha, 1935-37; mgr. Jr. Chamber of Commerce, Omaha, 1937-40, pres., 1945-46; mgr. Convention Bur., Omaha C. of C., 1941; mgr. Omaha Safety Council, 1941-47; mem. 85th-91st Congresses, 2d Neb. dist.; asst. to dir. Bur. Outdoor Recreation, Dept. Interior, Washington, 1971—. Fire commr., also mem. bd. edn., City of Omaha, 1947-48. Mayor, Omaha, 1948-54; del. Republican Nat. Conv., 1948, 52. Bd. dirs. Neb., U.S. Savs. Bond div. U.S. Treas., 1954-56. Named Omaha's Outstanding Young Man, 1945, Neb. Outstanding Young Man, 1945. Decorated Legion of Honor, Order of De Molay. Mem. U. Omaha Alumni Assn., Theta Phi Delta, Pi Kappa Alpha. Republican. Episcopalian. Eagle. Home: 6421 Glenwood Rd Omaha NB 68132

CUNNINGHAM, HARRY BLAIR, corp. exec.; b. Home Camp, Pa., July 23, 1907; s. Ezra James and Jane (Farley) C.; student Miami U., Oxford, O., 1925-27; D.B.A., Hillsdale (Mich.) College, 1963; LL.D., Tri-State Coll., 1967; LL.D., Miami U., 1969; m. Margaret Diefendorf, Aug. 28, 1935; children—Jane (Mrs. William Herrington), Sally (Mrs. Gary Downey), Ann (Mrs. James A. Glime). Began as reporter Harrisburg (Pa.) Patriot, 1927-28; with S.S. Kresge Co., Lynchburg, Va., 1928-29, Washington, 1930, Bklyn., 1931-32, Detroit, 1933-35, Wheeling, W. Va., 1936, Lafayette, Ind., 1936-38, Munice, Ind., 1939-40, Grosse Pointe, Mich., 1940-41, Highland Park, Mich., 1942-46, supt. stores, 1947-50, asst. sales dir., 1951-52, sales dir., 1953-57, gen. v.p. S.S. Kresge Co., 1957-59, former pres., chmn., chief exec. officer, 1967—; pres., dir. S.S. Kresge Co. Ltd. (Can.); chmn. K mart Australia Ltd.; dir. Warner-Lambert Corp., Burroughs Corp., Bendix Corp., Nat. Bank Detroit. Bd. dirs. Detroit Symphony, Jr. Achievement, Met. Fund, Detroit United Found.; trustee Grace Hosp., Detroit, Citizens' Research Council, Oakland U. Found.; adv. council Mich. State U. Grad. Sch. Bus. Adminstrn. Mem. Delta Upsilon. Presbyn. Clubs: Orchard Lake Country (Birmingham, Mich.); Detroit, Detroit Athletic; Economic (dir.); Bloomfield Hills (Mich.) Country. Home: 210 Lowell Ct Bloomfield Hills MI 48013 Office: 2727 2d Av Detroit MI 48232

CUNNINGHAM, JACQUES, electric utility exec.; b. Oklahoma City, June 22, 1920; s. Morrison B. and Lucy (Weaver) C.; B.S. in Bus. Adminstrn., Okla. State U., 1942; m. Theda Mae Harrell, July 21, 1942; children—Jacqueline, Jacques H. Personnel supr. Am. Airlines, Inc., Tulsa, 1946-48; indsl. mgr. Tulsa C. of C., 1948-54; v.p. Pub. Service Co. Okla., 1954-. Chmn. City of Tulsa- Rogers County Port Authority, 1963-65, Port of Catoosa Facilities Authority, 1969—; pres. Downtown Tulsa, Unltd., 1971; mem. City of Tulsa Econ. Devel. Commn., 1970—, Okla. Gov.'s Com. on River Planning, 1970; sec. Ark. Basin Devel. Assn., 1971; v.p. Tulsa YMCA, 1966; mem. exec. bd. Indian Nations council Boy Scouts Am., 1955—. Bd. dirs. Water Resources Congress, 1971. Served to capt. USAAF, 1942-45, USAF, 1951-52. Recipient Gold Knight award Nat. Mgmt. Assn., 1969. Mem. Tulsa C. of C. (dir.), Retail Mchts. Assn., Tulsa Safety Council, Am. Legion, Sigma Alpha Epsilon. Democrat. Methodist (steward). Mason (Shriner). Clubs: Rotary, Propeller (nat. v.p. 1971), Petroleum, Tulsa Country (Tulsa). Author: Analysis of Industrial Foundations, 1949; Machine Tool Inventory—Tulsa Industry, 1950; (with Jack Story Jr.) Inland Waterways Port Analysis, 1962. Home: 6725 S Gary St Tulsa OK 74105 Office: 600 S Main St Tulsa OK 74102

CUNNINGHAM, JAMES EVERETT, constrn. co. exec.; b. Cresco, Ia., Apr. 14, 1923; s. Franklin and Julia (Conners) C.; B.S. in Chem. Engring., U. Ala., 1946; m. Delores Foytik, Jan. 31, 1959; children—Sharon Lee, Sandra Dee, Matthew Joseph, Susan Elizabeth, Michael James. Also. with the Flour Corp., Houston, Tex., 1947-54; self-employed in oil bus., 1955-58; with J. Ray McDermott & Co., Inc., New Orleans, 1958—, treas., 1964—, also exec. v. p., dir. Served with USNR, World War II. Home: 16 Tennyson Pl New Orleans LA 70114 Office: Bank New Orleans Bldg 1010 Common St New Orleans LA 70112

CUNNINGHAM, JAMES VINCENT, poet; b. Cumberland, Md., Aug. 23, 1911; s. James Joseph and Anna Mattingly (Finan) C.; student St. Mary's (Kan.) Coll., 1928; A.B., Stanford, 1934, Ph.D., 1945; m. Barbara Francesca Gibbs, June 18, 1937 (div. 1942); 1 dau., Marjorie Ann (Mrs. George Lupien); m. 2d, Dolora Gallagher, Mar. 26, 1945 (div. 1949); m. 3d, Jessie MacGregor Campbell, June 3, 1950. Instr., Stanford, 1937-45; asst. prof. U. Hawaii, 1945-46, U. Chgo., 1946-52, U. Va., 1952-53; asso. prof. then prof. English, Brandeis U., Waltham, Mass., 1953—, chmn. dept., 1953-59, 61-62, 68-69, chmn. Sch. Humanities 1960-61, 70-71. Vis. prof. Harvard, 1952, U. Wash., 1956, Ind. U., 1961, U. Cal. at Santa Barbara, 1963. Guggenheim fellow, 1959-60, 67; Nat. Endowment for Arts grantee, 1966-67. Mem. Malone Soc., Bibliog. Soc. of U. Va. Author: The Helmsman, 1942; The Judge is Fury, 1947; Doctor Drink, 1950; The Quest of the Opal, 1950; Woe or Wonder; The Emotional Effect of Shakespearean Tragedy, 1951; The Exclusions of a Rhyme: Poems and Epigrams, 1960; Tradition and Poetic Structure, 1960; The Journal of John Cardan, 1964; To What Strangers, What Welcome, 1964; The Renaissance in England, 1967; The Collected Poems and Epigrams, 1971. Home: 17 Singletary Lane Sudbury MA 01776 Office: Dept English Brandeis Univ Waltham MA 02154

CUNNINGHAM, JOHN CHARLES, physician; b. Boston, Mar. 5, 1910; s. John Joseph and Rose Millicent (Murphy) C.; student Holy Cross Coll., 1927-29; A.B., U. Vt., 1931, M.D. cum laude, 1935; m. Sarah Evalyn Odell, June 20, 1942; children—John Charles, James Michale, Elizabeth Ann, William Lawther, Barbara Rose. Rotating intern St. Francis Hosp., Hartford, Conn., 1936-37; eye resident Eye Inst., Columbia-Presbyn. Hosp., N.Y.C., 1937-40; instr. ophthalmology N.Y. U., 1940-41; clin. practice, Dubuque, Ia., 1941-42; prof. ophthalmology U. Vt., 1946-, chmn. dept. eye, nose and throat, 1956—; attending surgeon ophthalmology Mary Fletcher Hosp., pres. staff, 1951; attending surgeon Bishop DeGoesbriand Hosp., Burlington; ophthal. cons. Heaton, Plattsburgh, Ticonderoga, Vt. State hosps.; instr. postgrad. courses Am. Acad. Ophthalmology, Chgo.; ophthal. rep. Vt. State Med. Soc. to Pub. Health Com. Served as 1st lt. M.C., U.S. Army, 1935-36, capt. M.C. USAAF, 1942-46; chief ophthalmology AAF Regional Hosp., Wright-Patterson Field, Dayton, O., 1943-46. Recipient Distinguished award for contbns. to several alumni groups Vt. Med. Soc.; Distinguished Service award U. Vt. Med. Alumni Assn. Diplomate Nat. Bd. Med. Examiners, Am. Bd. Ophthalmology. Fellow Am. Coll. of Surgeons; mem. Am. Acad. of Ophthalmology, N.E. Ophthal. Soc., Pan-Am. Ophthal. Assn., Assn. Research Ophthalmology, C. of C. (past dir.), Am. Assn. Ophthalmology (trustee), Assn. Univ. Profs. Ophthalmology, Vt. Ophthalmol. Soc. (pres.), Coll. Medicine (exec. com.), U. Vt. Med. Alumni Assn. (pres.), Nu Sigma Nu, Sigma Nu. Roman Catholic. Home: 74 Bilodeau Ct Burlington VT 05401 Office: 49 S Winooski Av Burlington VT 05401

CUNNINGHAM, JOSEPH AUSTIN, air force officer; b. Weston, W.Va., Dec. 21, 1915; s. John Emory and Flossie (Powell) C.; B.A., W.Va. U., 1938; grad. Command and Gen. Staff Coll., 1947, Armed Forces Staff Coll., 1951, Nat. War Coll., 1958; m. Mary Henry, June 16, 1939; children—Jo Ann (Mrs. Erick Carlgren), Catherine, Patricia. Commd. 2d lt. USAAF, 1939, advanced through grades to maj. gen. USAF, 1963; various assignments, U.S., 1939-43; asst. chief staff 12th Fighter Command, N. Africa, 1943-44; dep. comdr., adj. 330th AAFBU, Greenville, S.C., 1944-45; comdr. 119th AAF, Morris Field, N.C., 1945; dep. comdr. 56th Tng. Wing, Greenville, 1945; comdr. 140th AAFBU, Moody Field, Ga., 1945, 2225th AAFBU, Moody Field, 1945-46; asst. dep. chief staff, A-3, 11th Air Force, Harrisburg, Pa., 1947-48; asst. dir. air def. Directorate of Operations, Hdqrs. ADC, Mitchel AFB, N.Y., 1948- 49; chief operations div. Eastern Air Def. Force, Mitchel AFB, 1949, dir. combat operations, 1948-50; staff plans officer, war plans div. Hdqrs. USAF, 1951-52, chief Western hemisphere div., 1952-54; comdr. 317th Troop Carrier Wing, Germany, 1954-56, 7101st Support Group, Germany, 1956-57; spl. asst. to comdr., later vice comdr. Hdqrs. Air Rescue Service, MATS, Orlando AFB, Fla., 1958-59, comdr., 1959-63; dep. chief staff operations Hdqrs. MAC, Scott AFB, Ill., 1963-66; comdr. 22d Air Force, MAC, Travis AFB, Cal., 1966-68; dep. dir. directorate for civil disturbance plans and operations, Office Chief Staff, Dept. Army, Washington, 1968-69; commander Alaskan Air Command, Elmendorf, Alaska, 1969—. Decorated D.S.M. (Air Force), D.S.M. (Army), Legion of Merit with oak leaf cluster, Air medal with one oak leaf cluster, Army Commendation medal, numerous campaign and area ribbons; recipient W.Va. Distinguished Service medal. Mem. Order of Daedalions, Delta Tau Delta. Rotarian (hon.). Home: 5-500 G St Elmendorf AFB AK 99506 Office: Hdqrs Alaskan Air Command APO Seattle WA 98742

CUNNINGHAM, JOSEPH PATRICK, wire co. exec.; b. Chgo., Mar. 19, 1914; s. Patrick Joseph and Anne (Reilly) C.; B.S., DePaul U., 1933; m. Carlie Copeland, June 21, 1947. Sr. auditor, systems specialist Chesnutt, Murphy & Poole, C.P.A.'s, Chgo., 1942-45; auditor, controller Essex Wire Corp., Ft. Wayne, Ind., 1945—; adviser div. tech. studies U. Ind. Mem. Accounting Careers Council Northeastern Ind. Sponsor, adviser Nations United Club, 1967—. Mem. Nat. Assn. Accountants, Financial Execs. Inst., Inst. Internal Auditors (past chpt. pres.). Home: 4243 Old Mill Rd Ft Wayne IN 46807 Office: 1601 Wall St Ft Wayne IN 46804

CUNNINGHAM, JULIA WOOLFOLK, author; b. Spokane, Oct. 4, 1916; d. John George and Sue (Larabie) Cunningham; grad. St. Anne's Sch., Charlottesville, Va., 1933. Children's book buyer and book-seller Tecolote Book Shop, Santa Barbara, Cal., 1959—. Mem. Internat. P.E.N., Authors Guild. Author: (juveniles) The Vision of Francois the Fox, 1960, Dear Rat, 1961, Macaroon, 1962, Candle Tales, 1964, Dorp Dead (Children's Spring Book Festival award), 1965, Violet, 1966, Onion Journey, 1967, Burnish Me Bright, 1970; Wings of the Morning, 1971. Home: 1812 Anacapa St Santa Barbara CA 93101 Office: Tecolote Book Shop Santa Barbara CA 93102

CUNNINGHAM, LEON WILLIAM, univ. dean; b. Columbus, Ga., June 9, 1927; s. Leon W. and Annie (Bussey) C.; B.S., Auburn U., 1947; M.S., U. Ill., 1949, Ph.D., 1951; m. Jean Swingle, Aug. 21, 1948; children—Hugh, Pamela, Sue Ellen. Research fellow protein chemistry Wash. U., Seattle, 1951-53; asst. prof. biochemistry Sch. Medicine, Vanderbilt U., Nashville, 1953-60, asso. prof., 1960-65, prof., 1965—, asso. dean Sch. Medicine, 1967—. Served with USNR, 1945-46. USPHS spl. fellow Netherlands Nat. Def. Orgn., 1961-62. Mem. A.A.A.S., N.Y. Acad. Sci., Chem. Soc., Soc. Biol. Chemistry. Home: 4619 Shys Hill Rd Nashville TN 37215

CUNNINGHAM, LUVERN LEE, educator; b. Kennard, Neb., June 28, 1925; s. William Myron and Matilda (Carlsen) C.; A.B., Midland Coll., Neb., 1949; M.S., U. Omaha, 1952; Ed.D., U. Ore., 1958; m. Georgean Alice Hunteman, June 11, 1946; children—Richard Lee, Steven Lee. Prin., tchr., Shelby (Neb.) High Sch., 1948-49; supt. schs. Snyder (Neb.) Pub. Sch., 1949-52; admissions counselor Midland Coll., 1952-53; supt. Battle Creek (Neb.) Pub. Schs., 1953-56; research asso., teaching fellow U. Ore., 1956-58; asst. prof., asst. dir. Midwest Adminstrn. Center, U. Chgo., 1958-62, prof. edn., dir. center, 1964-67; dean Ohio State U. Coll. Edn., Columbus, 1967—; prof. edn. U. Minn., 1962-64. Vice pres. bd. trustees univs. council ednl. adminstrn., 1966—; trustee Met. Sch. Columbus; bd. dirs. Midland Luth. Coll., Nat. Acad. for Sch. Execs.; mem. exec. com. Urban Coalition, Columbus, 1968-71. Served with inf. AUS, 1944-46. Decorated Purple Heart with oak leaf cluster. Center for Advanced

Study in Behavioral Scis. fellow, 1969-70. Mem. Am. Ednl. Research Assn., Nat. Conf. Profs. Ednl. Adminstrn. (past chmn.), Am. Assn. Sch. Adminstrs., Nat. Soc. for Study Edn., Phi Delta Kappa (Named Young Man of Year in Ore. 1958). Author: (with others) The Organization and Control of American Schools, 1965, 70; (with others) The Blue Island Study of Equal Educational Opportunity, 1966; (with others) The Merger Issue, 1966; (with others) A Report to the Columbus Board of Education, 1968; (with others) New Forms of Citizen Participation, 1969; (with others) Priorities for the Seventies, 1971; Governing Schools-New Approaches to Old Issues, 1971; Home: 2576 McCoy Rd Columbus OH 43220 Office: 1945 N High Columbus OH 43210

CUNNINGHAM, MARCUS EDDY, engring. exec.; b. Lynn, Mass., Jan. 16, 1907; s. Daniel and Susie (Goad) C.; B.S., Yale, 1928; postgrad. Boston U., 1929; m. Mary Eloise Baird, Feb. 14, 1931 (dec. Nov. 1964); children—Susan Mary (Mrs. G. Bretnell Williams), Charles Baird, Marcus Eddy; m. 2d, Marilyn A. Eneix, Oct. 1, 1966. Gen. supt. Daniel Cunningham Constrn. Co., Boston, 1928-32, Austin Co., Cleve., 1932-40; pres., treas., dir. Brady Hill Co., Detroit, 1940—; chmn. bd., chief exec. officer, treas., dir. Cunningham-Limp Co., Detroit, 1948—, Cunningham-Limp, Ltd., Toronto, Ont., Can., 1959—; dir. Cunningham-Limp de las Americas, S.A., Cunningham-Limp Internat. S.A., Cunningham-Limp de Espaa, Cunningham-Limp (France) S.A.R.L., Cunningham-Limp Deutschland Gmb H. Dir. Gulfstream Park Racing Assn., Hallandale, Fla., 1963—. Bd. dirs. Detroit, Nat. councils Boy Scouts Am. Mem. Engring. Soc. Detroit, A.I.M. (pres.' council). Clubs: Yale (N.Y.C. and Detroit); Bloomfield Hills (Mich.) Country; Oakland Hills Country (Birmingham, Mich.); Indian Creek Country (Miami Beach, Fla.); Recess (Detroit). Home: 104 Brady Lane Bloomfield Hills MI 48013 (winter) Golden Beach FL 33160 Office: 1400 N Woodward Av Birmingham MI 48011

CUNNINGHAM, MAURICE PATRICK, educator; b. Nicholson, Pa., Aug. 27, 1913; s. James Joseph and Anna (Finan) C.; A.B., U. Cal. at Berkeley, 1938, Ph.D., 1941; m. Regina Marie Conley, June 17, 1941; children—Ann Margaret, Patrick Myles. Instr. classics Stanford, 1945-46, Smith Coll., 1946-47, Yale, 1947-49; mem. faculty Lawrence U., Appleton, Wis., 1949—, prof., 1960—, Hiram A. Jones prof. classics, 1960—. Vis. prof. U. Mich., 1959-60, 67, Trinity Coll., Hartford, Conn., summers 1963, 64. Am. rep. Thesaurus Linguae Latinae, Munich, Germany, 1967-72. Mem. Am. Philol. Assn., Am. Inst. Archeology, Classical Assn. Middle West and South, Classical Assn., Phi Beta Kappa. Mem. editorial bd. Classical Philology, 1970—. Contbr. articles to profl. jours. Home: 1630 S Connell St Appleton WI 54911

CUNNINGHAM, MERCE, dancer; b. Centralia, Wash.; student Bennington (Vt.) Summer Sch. Dance, 1940. Soloist, Martha Graham co., 1940-45; 1st solo concert, 1944; own dance co., 1952—; several tours U.S., also Europe, 1949, 58, 60, world tour, 1964; tchr. Sch. Am. Ballet, 1947; propr. own dance sch., N.Y.C., 1959—; prin. works choreographed include: The Seasons, 1947, Les Noces, 1952, Sixteen Dances for Soloist and Company of Three, 1951, Septet, 1953, Minutiae, 1954, Suite for Five, 1956, Nocturnes, 1956, Antic Meet, 1958, Summerspace, 1958, Rune, 1959, Crises, 1960, Aeon, 1960, Story, 1963, Winterbranch, 1964, Variations V, 1965, How to Pass, Kick, Fall, and Run, 1965, Place, 1966, Scramble, 1967, Rain Forest, 1968, Walkaround Time, 1968, Canfield, 1969. Mem. N.Y.C. Cultural Council. Guggenheim fellow, 1954, 59; recipient medal Soc. Advancement Dance in Sweden, 1964. Office: 463 West St New York City NY 10014

CUNNINGHAM, MORRIS, newspaperman; b. McMinnville, Tenn., July 27, 1917; s. Oscar Lafayette and Jessie Lee (Crawford) C.; m. Helen Henry Morris, Oct. 25, 1947; children—Diane, Morris Frank. Corr., state news editor, state capitol reporter Nashville Tennessean, 1935-43; reporter, news editor A.P., Nashville and N.Y.C., 1943-45; corr. Time, Life, Fortune mags., Nashville, 1945-53; Nashville corr. Memphis Comml. Appeal, 1945-53, Washington corr., 1953—. Adv. com. tchrs. deaf Office Edn., 1962- 64. Mem. White House Corrs. Assn., Overseas Writers, A.G. Bell Assn. for Deaf, Sigma Delta Chi. Methodist. Clubs: Kenwood Golf and Country; National Press (Washington). Home: 6002 Woodacres Dr Wood Acres Washington DC 20016 Office: 1013 13th St NW Washington DC 20005

CUNNINGHAM, MORTON C., former coll. pres.; b. Fulton, Mo., Feb. 29, 1904; s. John Thomas Scott (Vivion) C.; A.B., Westminster Coll., 1926; Ed.M., U. Mo., 1937, Ed.D., 1944; postgrad. U. Minn., 1948; m. Lottie Emory Dover, Dec. 28, 1929; childrenMorton Christy II, Marianne. Tchr., King City, Mo., 1926-28; prin. Silkeston (Mo.) High Sch., 1928-31; supt. schs., Desloge, Mo., 1931-39; dir. financial accounting Mo. State Dept. Edn., 1939-41; dir. Horace Mann Lab. Sch., Maryville, Mo., 1941-47; chmn. edn. dept. N.W. Mo. State Tchrs. Coll., 1944-47, dean faculty, 1945-49; pres. Fort Hays Kan. State Coll., 1949-69. State Dept. rep. ednl. tour Pakistan, 1964. Pres., Coronado council Boy Scouts Am., 1964-65. Mem. Kan. Tchrs. Assn., N.E.A., Am. Assn. Sch. Adminstrs., Nat. Assn. Intercollegiate Athletics (pres. 1967-68, mem. exec. com.), Kan. Educators Club., C. of C., Pi Gamma Mu, Pi Delta Kappa, Phi Delta Kappa, Phi Kappa Phi. Club: Lion. Home: S St Vrain Lyons CO 80540

CUNNINGHAM, MRS. MONA, banker; b. Ashland, Kan., d. Elmer R. and Myrtle (Hankins) Wallingford; grad. Wichita Bus. Coll.; m. Deane Cunningham, Mar. 5, 1954 (dec. May 1955). With Union Nat. Bank of Wichita, 1934-, asst. v.p., 1952-63, v.p., 1963-; pres. Nat. Assn. Bank-Women, Inc., N.Y.C., 1966- 67. Bd. dirs Wichita YMCA, Midway-Kan. chpt. A.R.C. Mem. Am. Soc. Personnel Adminstrn., Wichita Personnel Mgmt. Assn. Club: Pilot (past pres., dist. finance chmn. Wichita). Home: 625 S Quentin Wichita KS 61218 Office: 150 N Main St Wichita KS 67202

CUNNINGHAM, PAUL MILLARD, writer-editor; b. Stigler, Okla., Oct. 25, 1915; s. Marcus and Nora (Modlin) C.; B.A., U. Ark., 1937; m. Marian Frances Wimmers, Feb. 11, 1961; children—Barry, Gary; stepchildren—John, Daniel, David Schardine. Reporter, Ft. Smith (Ark.) Times-Record and S.W. Am., 1937; report-writer Cin. Post (now Post and Times-Star), 1937-68, chief editorial writer, editor editorial page, 1968—; instr. U. Cin. Eve. Coll., 1945-55. Home: 6523 Parkland Av Cincinnati OH 45233 Office: 800 Broadway Cincinnati OH 45202

CUNNINGHAM, R. JOHN, stock exchange exec.; b. 1926; grad. U. Notre Dame, 1950; M.B.A., N.Y.U.; married, seven children. Formerly mgmt. cons. Arthur Young and Co.; past pres. Midwest Stock Exchange Clearing Corp., Midwest Stock Exchange Service Corp.; then sr. v.p. Midwest Stock Exchange until 1967; exec. v.p. N.Y. Stock Exchange, 1967—. . Address: NY Stock Exchange 11 Wall St New York City NY 10005*

CUNNINGHAM, R. WALTER, astronaut; b. Creston, Ia., Mar. 16, 1932; s. Walter Wilfred and Gladys (Backen) C.; B.S. in Physics, U. Cal. at Los Angeles, 1960, M.A., 1961; m. Lo Ella Irby, July 12, 1956; children—Brian Keith, Kimberly Anne. Research asst. Planning Research Corp., Westwood, Cal., 1960-61; physicist RAND Corp., Santa Monica, Cal., 1961-64; astronaut NASA, 1964- crew member of first manned Apollo spacecraft; Apollo 7; v.p. operations Century Devel. Corp. Founder, Earth Awareness Found. Served with USNR, 1951-52; as fighter pilot USMCR, 1952-56; col. Res. Recipient NASA Exceptional Service award, also Haley Astronautics award, Profl. Achievement award U. Cal. at Los Angeles Alumni, 1969, Spl. Trustee award Nat. Acad. Television Arts and Scis., 1969. Mem. Soc. Exptl. Test Pilots, Am. Inst. Aeros. and Astronautics, Am. Geophys. Union, Sigma Pi Sigma. Office: 1 Greenway Plaza E Houston TX 77046

CUNNINGHAM, RICHARD GREENLAW, educator; b. Olney, Ill., Sept. 23, 1921; s. Rexford John and Florence (Greenlaw) C.; B.S. in Mech. Engring., Northwestern U., 1943, M.S., 1947, Ph.D., 1950; m. Suzanne Kimberly Barrett, Feb. 19, 1944; children—Stephen Barrett, Kimberly Ann, Elizabeth Ann. Research engr. research and devel. lab. Pure Oil Co., Crystal Lake, Ill., 1950-51; research engr. research lab. Shell Oil Co., Wood River, Ill., N.Y.C., 1954-55, research group leader, 1955-60, sr. research engr., 1960-61; project engr., asso. prof. engring. research Pa. State U. at University Park, 1951-54, prof. mech. engring., 1961—, head dept., 1962—. Trustee Centre Community Hosp. (co-chmn. charity ball 1969). Served with USNR, 1943-46. Mem. Am. Inst. Aeros. and Astronautics, Am. Soc. M.E. (policy bd. edn.), Am. Soc. E.E., Engrs. Council Profl. Devel. (dir.; bd. visitors engring. curricula accredition), Sigma Xi (pres. 1966-67), Tau Beta Pi, Pi Tau Sigma, Phi Eta Sigma. Methodist. Contbr. articles profl. jours. Home: 900 Outer Dr State College PA 16801

CUNNINGHAM, ROBERT LOUIS, educator; b. Birmingham, Mar. 22, 1926; s. Louis John and Marie Virginia (Schillinger) C.; B.A., St. Gregory Sem., 1947; Ph.D., Laval U., 1951; m. Margery Ann Winters, Aug. 20, 1949; children—Christine, Michael, Sheila, Mark, Gregory, Virginia, Roberta, Lisa. Asst. prof. philosophy Xavier U., Cin., 1951-53; asst. prof. philosophy San Francisco Coll. for Women, 1953-56, asso. prof., 1956-58; asso. prof. philosophy U. San Francisco, 1958-63, prof., 1963—; vis. prof. Rockford Coll., 1966, Queens Coll., summer 1967; research asso. in philosophy U. Cal. at Berkeley, 1967-68. Mem. council of advisers Inst. Humane Studies, Palo Alto, Cal., 1965—. Relm Found. grantee, 1965-66, Inst. for Interdisciplinary Research grantee, 1967-68, Carnegie fellow Inst. Legal and Polit. Philosophy, U. Cal. at Irvine, summer 1969. Mem. Am. Philos. Assn., Am. Cath. Philos. Assn., Mont Pelerin Soc. Author: Situationism and the New Morality, 1970; also articles. Home: 2227 19th Av San Francisco CA 94116

CUNNINGHAM, ROBERT MARIS, Jr., editor; b. Chgo., May 28, 1909; s. Robert Maris and Beda (Dickson) C.; Ph.B., U. Chgo., 1931; m. Deborah Libby, Nov. 24, 1934; childrenDennis, Damon, Margaret, Robert Maris. Asst. to pres. Armour (now Ill.) Inst. Technology, Chgo., 1932-34, sales and sales promotion Shell Petroleum Corp., 1934-37; dir. pub. relations Chgo. Blue Cross hospitalization plan, 1938-41; asso. editor Hygeia (published by A.M.A.), 1941-45; mng. editor The Modern Hosp. mag., 1945-51, editor, 1951-63, 67—, pub., 1963-67; editorial dir. The Nations Schools, pub., 1963-67, Coll. and Univ. Bus., 1967—, pub., 1963-67; The Hosp. Purchasing File, 1967—, pub., 1963-67; editor Modern Nursing Home, 1964—, pub., 1964-67; cons. A.C.S., 1955-59; v.p., dir. F.W. Dodge Crop., 1959-63. Dir. Health Industries Assn., 1966-69, pres., (hon.); mem. Psi Upsilon. Author: Hospitals, Doctors and Dollars, 1961; The Third World of Medicine, 1968; also articles on hosp. and med. subjects. Home: 1900 N Lincoln Av Chicago IL 60614 Office: 230 W Monroe St Chicago IL 60606

CUNNINGHAM, ROBERT MORTON, communications co. exec.; b. Ardmore, Pa., Nov. 27, 1907; s. Andrew and Mary (Neely) C.; B.S., Haverford Coll., 1929; m. Emily Thomas, June 23, 1934; children—Carol (Mrs. H.R. Reynolds), Robert A. With Bell Telephone Co., Pa., 1929-42, sr. staff engr., 1942; instr. elec. engring. Drexel Inst. Tech., evenings 1929-42; with Am. Tel. & Tel. Co., 1942-55, exec. asst., 1955; with Pacific Tel. & Tel. Co., 1955—, asst. v.p., 1958-60, v.p. bus. research, 1960-66, v.p., sec., treas., 1966—, also dir.; asso. dir. Security Pacific Nat. Bank; dir. Bell Telephone Co. Nev. Mem. borough council Franklin Lakes, N.J., 1950-53. Mem. Cal. Taxpayers Assn. (pres., dir.), I.E.E.E., Episcopalian (vestryman). Clubs: Olympic, Transportation, Commonwealth, Stock Exchange, Villa Taverna, Bankers (San Francisco); California (Los Angeles). Home: 440 Davis Ct San Francisco CA 94111 Office: 140 New Montgomery St San Francisco CA 94105

CUNNINGHAM, ROSS LEE, editor; b. St. Paul, Apr. 13, 1906; s. Ralph Lee and Agnes Mary (Tyrrell) C.; student U. Wash., 1934-35; m. Charlotte Helen Logan, Mar. 7, 1931; children—Alan Tyrrell, Gayle Lee. With Seattle Star, 1923-28; v.p. Alaska Washington Airways, 1928-31; staff Seattle Star-Seattle Post Intelligencer, 1931-38; staff Seattle Times, 1938-41, asso. editor, 1944- 56, asso. editor, editorial page editor, 1956-68, editorial dir., 1968—; asst. to gov. Wash., 1941-44. Chmn. freedom of information com. Wash. Asso. Press Unit, 1953-56. Recipient Distinguished Service to Journalism award Wash. State Press Club, 1953. Mem. Seattle C. of C., Community Devel. Assn. Seattle, Am. Soc. Newspaper Editors, Philippine-Am. Soc. (bd. govs.), Internat. Press Inst. Clubs: Washington Athletic, Seattle Golf, China (v.p., trustee) (Seattle); Queen City Yacht. Home: 962 NW Elford Dr Seattle WA 98177 Office: Seattle Times Fairview Av and John St Seattle WA 98111

CUNNINGHAM, THOMAS JAMES, lawyer, univ. adminstr.; b. Los Angeles, Sept. 24, 1905; s. John William and Pearl Mae (Best) C.; A.B., U. Cal. at Los Angeles, 1928; J.D., U. So. Cal., 1931; LL.D., Chapman Coll., 1960; m. Ruth Overton Taylor, May 7, 1932; children—Ruth Eleanor (Mrs. Jacques Hunter), Thomas James, Richard Best. Lectr. edn. U. Cal. at Los Angeles, 1931-32, asst. prof. mil. sci. and tactics, 1941-43, ex-officio regent U. Cal., 1953-55, gen. counsel of regents, 1955—, v.p. univ., 1960-66. Admitted to Cal. bar, 1932; asso. law firm Fredericks, Hanna & Morton, now Hanna & Morton, 1932-39; with Thomas J. Cunningham, Los Angeles, 1939-47; judge Superior Ct. of Los Angeles, 1947-55, presiding judge domestic relations dept., 1949, criminal dept., 1951. Mem. Citizens Legislative Adv. Commn. Cal. Mem. Cal. Legislature, 1935, 37. Dir. Cal. Inst. Cancer Research. Served from capt. to col., inf., AUS, World War II. Decorated Legion of Merit; recipient Alumnus of Year award U. Cal. at Los Angeles, 1961. Mem. Nat. Assn. Coll. and Univ. Attys. (dir. 1963-68, pres. 1965), U. So. Cal. Alumni Assn., U. Cal. Los Angeles Alumni Assn. (pres. 1955-57), Am. Judicature Soc., Am., Alameda County bar assns., State Bar of Cal., Am. Acad. Polit. and Social Sci., Am. Legion, Assn. Former Cal. Legislators, Phi Beta Kappa, Phi Delta Phi, Delta Tau Delta, Pi Sigma Alpha, Pi Kappa Delta. Baptist. Mason (32); mem. Legion of Honor of Order of De Molay. Clubs: Athenian-Nile (Alameda, Cal.); Guardians, Lincoln (Los Angeles); Commonwealth of California (San Francisco). Contbr. articles legal, ednl. jours. Home: 1095 Arlington Av El Cerrito CA 94530 Office: 2200 University Av Berkeley CA 94720

CUNNINGHAM, THOMAS WILLIAM, clergyman, educator; b. Jersey City, June 7, 1911; s. Joseph A. and Mary A. (Snell) C.; student St. Peter's Prep. Sch., 1923-27; A.B., Seton Hall U., 1931; student Immaculate Conception Theol. Sem., 1931-35; M.A., Fordham U., 1943, Ph.D., 1950. Ordained priest Roman Cath. Ch., 1935; asst. pastor St. John's Ch., Orange, N.J., 1935-40; instr., later asst. prof. English lit. Seton Hall U., 1940-46, prof. English lit., head dept. English, 1946-53, dean coll. arts and scis., co-ordinating dean all schs., 1951-53, v.p. charge instrn., 1953-63; pastor Immaculate Conception Ch., Montclair, N.J., 1963—; apptd. domestic prelate, 1964. Lectr. Cath. Forum Newark Critic's Circle N.Y. Chmn. Newark Archdiocese Ecumenical Commn.; mem. Priest's Senate, Newark, 1971—. Recipient James Roosevelt Bayley award Seton Hall U., 1964; Coronat award St. Edward's U., 1964; For God and Country award, Cath. War Vets., 1968. Mem. Modern Lang. Assn. Mediaeval Acad. Am., Am. Cath. Hist. Assn., Nat. Cath. Ednl. Assn., St. Paul's Guild N.Y. K.C. Clubs: Serra Vocation; Mercier. Author: Saints Off Pedestals, 1953; also articles, book revs. Appointed Papal Chamberlain, 1958. Home: 30 N Fullerton Av Montclair NJ 07042

CUNNINGHAM, VINCENT ANTHONY, mfg. co. exec.; b. N.Y.C., Oct. 18, 1923; s. John P. and Nora (McDermott) C.; A.B. in Econs., U. Notre Dame, 1950, LL.B., 1952; m. Helen M. Cregan, Feb. 12, 1953; childrenIsabel, Helen, John, Anne, Mary, Noreen, Eileen. Admitted to N.Y. bar, 1953; asso. counsel firm Smith and Perrell, N.Y.C., 1952-54; staff counsel Grand Union Co., E. Paterson, N.J., 1954-59; sec., counsel S. H. Kress and Co., N.Y.C., 1959- ; asso. corp. counsel Genesco, Inc., N.Y.C., 1963-. Served with USAAF, 1942-45. Mem. N.Y. State Bar Assn., N.Y. County Lawyers Assn., U. Notre Dame Law Assn. Home: 21 Ruble St Midland Park NJ 07432 Office: 730 Fifth Av New York City NY 10019

CUNNINGHAM, WALTER JACK, educator, elec. engr.; b. Comanche, Tex., Aug. 21, 1917; s. Walter Jack and Percy Adele (Moore) C.; A.B., U. Tex., 1937, A.M., 1938; Ph.D., Harvard, 1947; m. Barbara Virginia Lynch, Feb. 26, 1944; childrenLawrence Bradford, John Hartwell. Instr. physics and communication engring. Harvard, 1939-46; part-time research OSRD, in acoustics and electric circuits, 1939-46; asst. prof. elec. engring. Yale, 1946-50, asso. prof., 1950-56, prof. engring. and applied science, 1956—; asso. chmn. dept. engring. and applied sci., Mem. Acoustical Soc. Am., I.E.E.E., Am. Soc. Engring. Edn., Sigma Xi. Author: Introduction to Nonlinear Analysis, 1958; tech. papers. Bd. editors Am. Scientist, 1955-, Jour. Franklin Inst., 1962-. Home: 200 Dessa Dr Hamden, CT , 06517. Office: Dunham Lab Yale U New Haven CT 06520

CUNNINGHAM, WILLIAM ALEXANDER, III, army officer; b. Athens, Ga., May 10, 1911; s. William Alexander II and Elizabeth (Ritter) C.; B.S., U.S. Mil. Acad., 1934; m. Madera Maddux, June 16, 1937; children—William Alexander IV, Susan Madera. Commd. 2d lt. U.S. Army, 1934, advanced through grades to maj. gen., 1961; bn. comdr. N. African invasion, 1943; prin. staff officer Okinawan invasion, 1945; assigned Army Gen. Staff, 1948-50, Army War Coll., 1952; plans and policy officer CINCPAC Joint Staff, 1952-55; regtl. comdr. 1st Inf. Div., 1955-57, chief staff, 1957-58; G-3, 8th U.S. Army, 1958-59; asst. div. comdr. 1st Cav. Div., 1959-60; asst. comdt. Command and Gen. Staff Coll., 1960-61; dep. chief staff personnel and adminstrn. Hdqrs. U.S. Army, Europe, 1961-63; comdg. gen. 24th Inf. Div., 1963-65; comdg. gen. Hdqrs. IV U.S. Army Corps., 1965-66; transp. programs coordinator, N.Y.C., 1966-68; asst. gen. mgr. Pacific Architects & Engrs., Saigon, Vietnam, 1968-69; exec. dir. Lake Lanier Devel. Authority, Atlanta, 1969—. Chief U.S. delegation Council Internat. Mil. Sports, 1962—, hon. mem., 1963—. Decorated Silver Star, Legion of Merit, Bronze Star with 2 oak leaf clusters, Commendation ribbon with 1 oak leaf cluster, Purple Heart, Combat Inf. badge, Presdl. citation, D.S.M., Korean Order of Ulchi. Club: Army and Navy. Home: 746 Green St NE Gainesville GA 30501 Office: PO Box 126 Buford GA 30518

CUNNINGHAM, WILLIAM PILPEL, univ. dean; b. Boston, Oct. 11, 1922; s. William Hayes and Mildred G. (Pilpel) C.; grad. Phillips Exeter Acad., 1940; A.B., Harvard, 1944, LL.B., 1948; m. Dorothy A. Havey, Dec. 9, 1950; children—Steven, Janet. Admitted to Mass. bar, 1948, Md. bar, 1954; asso. firm Brown, Field & McCarthy, Boston, 1948-50, Haussermann, Davison and Shattuck, Boston, 1951-53; teaching fellow Harvard Law Sch., 1953-54; mem. faculty U. Md. Sch. Law, Balt., 1954—, prof. law, 1960—, dean, 1962—. Mem. Md. Bd. Commrs. on Uniform Laws, 1965—; mem. Com. To Revise Md. Code, 1970—; chmn. Board of Ethics, Balt. City, 1967—. Served with USAAF, 1943-45. Mem. Am., Md. (exec. dir., dir. continuing legal edn. 1960-62), Balt. City bar assns. Home: 1802 Pot Spring Rd Lutherville MD 21093 Office: Univ Maryland Law Sch Baltimore MD 21201

CUPP, PAUL J., corp. exec.; b. Johnstown, Pa.; grad. Wharton Sch. Commerce, U. Pa., 1924; LL.D., Bloomfield Coll., Eastern Bapt. Coll. Now chmn., former chief exec. officer Acme Markets; dir. Phila. Nat. Bank, Provident Mut. Life Ins. Co., John Wanamaker Phila., Alan Wood Steel Co., Chem. Leaman Tank Lines, Inc., Western Sav. Fund Soc. Bd. dirs. Greater Phila. Movement; trustee U. Pa. Mem. Phila. C. of C. Club: Union League (Phila.). Home: 933 Muirfield Rd Bryn Mawr PA 19010 Office: 124 N 15th St Philadelphia PA 19102

CURATOLO, ALPHONSE FRANK, architect; b. Chgo., Sept. 20, 1936; s. Joseph and Pearl (Loizzo) C.; B.A., U. Ill., 1961. Architect Masonite Corp., Chgo., 1963-66, Playboy Clubs Internat., Chgo., 1966—; exec. v.p., head architect Internat. Design Studios, Inc. Recipient award for Lake Geneva Playboy resort A.I.A., 1969, Earl prize for outstanding archtl. design, 1961, instns. award for outstanding design, Lake Geneva, 1969, trophy for outstanding entertainer of the year, Universal Artists, Chgo., 1968. Served with AUS, 1961. Mem. A.I.A., Assn. Registered Architects, Nat. Council Archl. Registration Bds. Republican. Roman Catholic. Home: 1446 W Lexington St Chicago IL 60607 Office: 919 N Michigan Av Chicago IL 60611

CURCIO, LOUIS LEROY, educator; b. Walla Walla, Wash., May 1, 1911; s. Sam and Rose (Venneri) C.; B.A., Whitman Coll., 1932, M.A., 1933; Ph.D., Columbia, 1951; m. Mary Stine, Apr. 9, 1949; children—Robert, Paul. Dir. Cultural Center, USIA, Rosario, Argentina, 1949-51, San Jose, Costa Rica, 1952-54; Am. specialist, Haiti and Ecuador, summer 1959; chmn. fgn. lang. dept. Bradley U., 1954-60; chmn. modern lang. dept. Bradley U. dept. Hollins (Va.) Coll., 1960-62; prof. French Ind. State U., 1962—. Mem. Modern Lang. Assn., Am. Assn. Tchrs. French, Am. Assn. U. Profs., Dramatist Guild. Co-author: The Bridge (Rosamond Gilder award), 1961; Ponce de Leon, 1961; De Soto, 1961; The Goncourts, Historians, 1951; Coronado, 1966; Los Capalleros de la Cruz, 1966; Neighbors, 1968. Home: R R 31 Box 182 Terre Haute IN 47803

CURE, CHARLES WILLIAM, neurol. surgeon; b. Martinsville, Ind., June 1, 1920; s. Jesse William and Hester (Hensley) C.; A.B., Ind. U., 1942, M.D., 1944; M.Sc., McGill U., 1958; fellow Montreal Neurol. Inst., 1946-47; Ph.D., U. Chgo., 1950; m. Eloise Maria Greer, Aug. 19, 1946; childrenKaren Elizabeth, Eric Greer. Intern Mpls. Gen. Hosp., 1945; resident, also instr. U. Chgo. Clinics, 1948-50; practice neurol. surgery, Indpls., 1950-; attending physician Community, St. Vincents, St. Francis hosps.; chmn. neurol. surgery Methodist Hosp.; asst. prof. neurol. surgery Ind. U., 1959-. Served to capt., M.C., AUS, 1953-55. Diplomate Am. Bd. Neurol. Surgery. Fellow A.C.S.; mem. Am., Ind. med. assns., Marion County Med. Soc.

(sec. 1966), Congress Neurol. Surgeons, Harvey Cushing Soc., Phi Chi. Home: 414 Kessler Blvd W Indianapolis, IN 46208. Office: 1815 N Capital Av Indianapolis IN 46202

CURETON, EDWARD EUGENE, educator; b. San Jose, Cal., Jan. 16, 1902; s. Edward and Elva (Sawyer) C.; A.B., San Jose State Coll., 1925; M.A., Stanford, 1927; Ph.D., Columbia Tchrs. Coll., 1931; m. Ruth Duncan, Aug. 8, 1931; children—Mary, Ann; m. 2d, Louise R. Witmer, Aug. 28, 1948. Asso. prof. edn. Ala. Poly. Inst., 1931-37, prof., 1937- 41; asst. chief research and statistics sect. U.S. Office Edn., 1941-42; chief test unit Hdqrs. ASF, 1942-43; chief civilian personnel research War Dept. Adj. Gen. Office, 1943-45, chief tech. operations and control, 1946-47; staff Richardson, Bellows, Henry & Co., psychol. cons., 1945- 46, 1947-48; prof. psychology U. Tenn., 1948—, head dept. philosophy and psychology, 1950-59, head dept. psychology, 1959-63; asso. editor Jour. Exptl. Edn., 1936-44, 66-71; bd. editors Psychometrika, 1936- -; bd. dirs. Psychometric Corp., 1951-53. Fellow A.A.A.S., Am. Psychol. Assn. (pres. div. evaluation and measurement 1953-54); mem. Psychometric Soc. (pres. 1946, treas. 1947-50), Am. Statis. Assn., Inst. Math. Statistics, Southeastern (pres. 1956- 57), Tenn. (pres. 1953) psychol. assns., Sigma Xi, Phi Kappa Phi, Phi Delta Kappa, Kappa Delta Pi. Home: 2008 Velmetta Circle Knoxville TN 37920

CURFMAN, LAWRENCE EVERETT, lawyer; b. Champaign, Ill., Apr. 13, 1909; s. Lawrence Everett and Winifred (Williams) C.; A.B., U. Mich., 1930, J.D., 1932; m. Maygaret Sylvia Baldwin, May 1, 1937; children-Lawrence Everett III, Elizabeth Ann (Mrs. Peter Koch), John Edward. Admitted to Kan. bar, 1932, since practiced in Wichita; partner firm Weigand, Curfman, Brainerd, Harris and Kaufman, 1940—; atty. Wichita Employees Retirement Bd., 1948—. Dir. Internat. Cold Storage Co., Inc., Southwest Paper Co., Inc., Mid- West Surg. Supply. Co. Pres. Wichita Pub. Library Bd., 1954, 57, 58. Trustee E.A. Watkins Found. Mem. Am. (chmn. sect. local govt. law 1970- 71), Wichita (pres. 1956) bar assns., City Attys. Assn. Kan. (pres. 1953). Club: University (pres. 1965-66) (Wichita). Author articles. Home: 122 N Pershing St Wichita KS 67208 Office: First Nat Bank Bldg Wichita KS 67202

CURIE, EVE, author, lecturer; b. Paris, France, Dec. 6, 1904; d. Pierre (Nobel prize winner for work in radium, 1903) and Marie (Sklodowska) (Nobel prize winner in radio-active substances, 1903, in chemistry 1911) Curie; B.S. and Ph.B., Sevigne Coll.; L.H.D. (hon.), Mills Coll., 1939, Russell Sage Coll., 1941; Litt.D. (hon.), U. Rochester, 1941; m. Henry Richardson Labouisse, Nov. 19, 1954. Took up study of music and gave her first concert as pianist, Paris, 1925; later gave concerts in France and Belgium; musical critic for Candide (weekly jour.) for several years; also wrote articles on motion pictures and the theater; made first visit to U.S. with her mother, 1921; on 2d visit lectured in 10 U.S. cities (she speaks English, French and Polish), 1939; witnessed the fall of France, 1940, and went to London to work for the cause of Free France; came to U.S., Jan. 1941, and lectured on the war in France and England; because of her pro-ally activities she was deprived of her French citizenship by the Vichy Govt., Apr. 1941. Served in Europe with Fighting French as officer in Women's div. of army; one of pubs. of Paris Presse (daily), resigned to return to ind. writing, 1949. Spl. adviser to Sec. Gen., NATO, 1952-54. Decorated Chevalier Legion of Honor (France), 1939; Polonia Restituta (Poland), 1939; Croix de Guerre (France), 1944. Author: Madame Curie, 1937selection of Lit. Guild, Jr. Guild, Book-of-the-Month Club, Sci. Book of the month, Nat. book award for non-fiction, 1937; Journey Among Warriors (Literary Guild Selection), 1943. Home: 1 Sutton Pl S New York City NY 10022

CURL, ROBERT FLOYD, clergyman, educator; b. Winfield, Ala., July 3, 1897; s. Levi Slaten and Daniel Catherine (Logan) C.; A.B., So. Meth. U., 1931; A.M., Perkins Sch. Theology, 1932; D.D., Southwestern U., 1949; m. Lessie Waldene Merritt, June 8, 1922; childrenMary Gessner (Mrs. Norris A. Kurio), Robert Floyd. Ordained to ministry Meth. Ch., 1922; pastor in Alice, Bastrop, Brady, Del Rio, Kinsville, Mesquite, Harlandale, San Antonio (all Tex.), 1922-41; dist. supt., McAllen, Austin and San Antonio dists., 1941-47, 53-57; exec. sec. S.W. Tex. Conf., 1947-53; prof. ch. adminstrn., dir. field work Perkins Sch. Theology, Dallas, 1957- 63, emeritus, 1963—; supt. McAllen dist., 1963-65; supt. San Antonio district, 1965-67; pastor 1st Meth. Ch., Ozona, Tex., 1967- 69; pastor Hunt (Tex.) United Meth. Ch., 1969—. Mem. Uniting Conf. of Methodism, 1939; mem. Gen. Conf. Meth. Ch., 1940, 44, 48, 52, 56; mem. Council on World Service and Finance, 1944-56, jud. council, 1956-64; mem. gen. bd. Nat. Council Chs. Christ in Am., 1963-; pres. Tex. Meth. Planning Commn., 1948-51, Tex. Met. Student Movement, 1950-57; del. World Meth. Council, Oslo, Norway, 1961. Mem. Tex. Council Chs. (pres. 1953-56), Alpha Theta Phi, Eta Sigma Pi. Democrat. Mason, Rotarian. Author: Southwest Texas Methodism, 1952. Home: 517 East Lane Kerrville, TX 78028. Office: Methodist Church Hunt TX 78024

CURL, ROBERT FLOYD, Jr., educator; b. Alice, Tex., Aug. 23, 1933; s. Robert Floyd and Lessie (Merritt) C.; B.A., Rice U., 1954; Ph.D. (NSF fellow), U. Cal. at Berkeley, 1957; m. Jonel Whipple, Dec. 21, 1955; children—Michael, David. Research fellow Harvard, 1957-58; asst. prof. chemistry Rice U., Houston, 1958-63, asso. prof., 1963-67, prof., 1967—, master Lovett Coll., 1968—. Alfred P. Sloan fellow, 1961-63; NATO postdoctoral fellow, 1964; recipient Clayton prize Instn. Mech. Engrs., London, 1958. Mem. Am. Chem. Soc., Phi Beta Kappa, Sigma Xi. Methodist. Contbr. articles profl. jours. Home: Lovett House Rice Univ Houston TX 77001

CURLE, CHARLES THOMAS WILLIAM ADAM, educator; b. Ile Adam, France, July 4, 1916; s. Richard Henry Parnell and Cordelia (Fisher) C.; B.A., B.S., M.A., Oxford U., 1947, Ph.D., 1950; A.M. (hon.), Harvard, 1965; L.H.D. (hon.), Sioux Empire Coll., 1966; m. Pamela N. Hobson, Oct. 13, 1939, (div. Jan. 1958); children—Christina (Mrs. Peter E. Goldfine), Anna (Mrs. Philip Pollard); m. 2d, Anne Grace Edie, May 27, 1958; 1 dau., Deborah Grace. Staff mem. Tavistock Inst. Human Relations, 1947-50; lectr. social psychology Oxford U., 1947-50; prof. edn., psychology Exeter U., 1952-56; adv. social affairs Govt. Pakistan, 1956-59; prof. edn. U. Ghana, 1959-61; vis. prof. edn. Harvard, 1961-62, lectr. edn., 1962-65, dir. Center Studies in Edn. and Devel., 1962-67, prof. edn., 1965—. Mem. council U. Exeter, 1955-56, U. Ghana, 1960-61; cons. World Bank, Ford Found., UN spl. agys., fgn. nat. govts. Mem. coll. cons. Internat. Inst. Ednl. Planning, 1964-66. Bd. dirs. Franklin Books Program; trustee Human Devel. Found., Moses Brown Sch., Cambridge Friends Sch.; hon. trustee Sioux Empire Coll. Served to maj. Brit. Army, 1940-46. Fellow Am. Acad. Arts and Scis.; mem. Phi Delta Kappa. Mem. Soc. of Friends. Author: The Role of Education in Development, 1962; Educational Strategy for Developing Societies, 1963; Planning for Education in Pakistan, 1966; The Role of the Advisor in Educational Planning, 1967; Educational Problems of Developing Societies, 1969; The Identity of the Educational Planner, 1969; Making Peace, 1971; Mystics and Militants, 1971. Asso. editor Jour. Ednl. Sociology, 1967—. Home: 27 Robinson St Cambridge MA 02138

CURLETT, JOHN NEWTON, mfg. exec.; b. Balt., Nov. 28, 1905; s. Lewis R. and Florence (Balke) C.; A.B., Ohio Wesleyan U., Delaware, Ohio, 1928, LL.D., 1966; m. Sarah Neilson, June 18, 1932; children—Sarah Louise (Mrs. J. H. MacLeod), John Newton, Mary Carolyn (Mrs. David S. Cooper), Charles Neilson. With McCormick & Co., Inc., Balt., 1930—, beginning as mgmt. trainee, successively mem. jr. bd. execs., mgr. flavoring extract and insecticide depts. sr. bd. dirs., 1935—, v.p., 1936, exec. v.p., 1950-55, pres., 1955-69, chmn. bd., chief exec. officer, 1969-70; chmn. bd., 1970—; dir. McCormick Foods (U.K.) Ltd.; mem. adv. bd. Md. Nat. Bank; dir. Md. Properties, Inc., U.S. Fidelity & Guaranty Co., Balt., Balt. Ice Sports, Inc., Indsl. Corp., Provident Savs. Bank of Balt., Noxell Corp., Balt., McCormick de Mexico, S.A., Mexico D.F., Mexico. Former chmn. Commn. for Expansion of Pub. Higher Edn. in Md.; chmn. Govs.'s Com. for Exec. Reorgn.; formerly chmn. Commn. for Modernization of Exec. Br. of Md. Govt. Former exec. dir. Food Ind. War Com., World War II; former asst. chief, food br. WPB. Past pres. bd. sch. commrs. Dept. Edn., Balt. Trustee Greater Balt. Med. Center, Food and Drug Law Inst., Inc.; bd. dirs. Nutrition Found.; gov. Acad. Food Marketing, St. Joseph's Coll., Phila. Adv. com. Church Home and Hosp., Balt. Hon. mem. Red Shield Boys Club, Baltimore. Mem. Chem. Specialities Mfrs. Assn. (past pres. and gov.), Grocery Manufacturers of Am. (dir.), N.A.M. (past dir.), C. of C. Met. Balt., Inc. (dir., v.p.), Phi Gamma Delta, Omicron Delta Kappa. Mason (32, K.T., Shriner). Clubs: Baltimore Country, Maryland, Merchants (Balt.); Seaview Country (Absecon, N.J.). Home: 5313 Springlake Way Baltimore MD 21212 Office: 11350 McCormich Rd Cockeysville MD 21030

CURLEY, JOHN MARTIN, Jr., steel co. exec.; b. Boston, Dec. 13, 1933; s. John Martin and Marietta (Cullen) C.; grad. Thayer Acad., Braintree, Mass., 1951; m. Jane Marie Walker, Apr. 30, 1955; children—John Martin III, Robert Edward, Jane Marie, Janet Marietta. Vice pres. Easco Corp. (formerly Eastern Stainless Steel Corp.), Balt., 1960-63, pres., 1963-69, chmn., chief exec. officer, 1969—; dep. chmn., dir. R.M.B. Alloys (Pty.) Ltd., South Africa; dep. chmn. Middleburg Steel & Alloys (Pty) Ltd. South Africa; dir. Md. Nat. Bank, U.S. Fidelity & Guaranty Co. (both Balt.), The A. Finkl & Sons Co., Chgo. Regional bd. Nat. Conf. Christians and Jews; exec. bd. Balt. area council Boy Scouts Am.; bd. dirs. Am. Diabetes Assn.; pres. bd. Loyola Coll., Balt.; trustee Ch. Home and Hosp., Balt. Home: 115 Churchwardens Rd Baltimore MD 21212 Office: Arlington Bldg 201 N Charles St Baltimore MD 21201

CURLEY, ROBERT ARNOLD, photocopy co. exec., lawyer; b. Chgo., July 13, 1931; s. Stanley J. and Rose (Spry) C.; B.S., U. Ill., 1953; J.D., DePaul U., 1957; m. Betty Jean Morris, Apr. 21, 1957; children—Robert A., Leslie Elizabeth, Catherine Ann. Sr. atty. Brunswick Corp., Chgo., 1957-62; sec., gen. atty. Simonize Co., Chgo., 1962-66; sec., gen. counsel Am. Photocopy Equipment Co., Evanston, Ill., 1966—, v.p., 1968—. Bd. dirs. St. Mary's Sch., Riverside, Ill. Served to 1st lt. U.S. Army, 1953-55. Mem. Am., Ill., Chgo. bar assns., Ill., Evanston chambers commerce. Home: 403 Audubon Rd Riverside IL 60545 Office: 2100 W Dempster St Evanston IL 60202

CURME, GEORGE OLIVER, Jr. indsl. research chemist; b. Mount Vernon, Ia., Dec. 24, 1888; s. George Oliver and Caroline Chenoweth (Smith) C.; B.S., Northwestern U., 1909, D.Sc. (hon.), 1933; postgrad. Harvard, 1909-10; Ph.D., U. Chgo., 1913, D.Sc. (hon.), 1954; student U. Berlin, 1913-14; m. Lillian Hale, June 29, 1916; childrenKatharine Hale (Mrs. Randolph C. Neely), George Oliver III, Mary Ellen (Mrs. Charles P. Cooper, Jr.), Florence Louise (Mrs. Richard C. Horton), John Henry. Indsl. research chemist Mellon Inst., 1914, conducting research on organic synthesis based on natural hydrocarbons, on behalf of cos. which later became units of Union Carbide and Carbon Corp.; became chief chemist, Carbide and Carbon Chemicals Corp., Inc. to commercialize results of preceding research, with plants near Charleston, W. Va., 1920, v.p. and dir. of research, 1929-44, v.p., 1944-51; v.p. Union Carbide and Carbon Research Lab., Inc., 1938-52, chmn. bd., 1952-54; v.p., dir. Carbide and Carbon Chemicals Ltd., 1944-55; v.p. research Union Carbide Corp. (formerly Union Carbide & Carbon Corp.), 1951-55, dir., 1952-61. Chandler medalist, 1933, Perkin medalist, 1935, Elliott Cresson medalist, 1936, Willard Gibbs medalist, 1944; recipient Nat. Modern Pioneer Award, 1940. Mem. Am. Chem. Soc., Am. Inst. Chem. Engrs., Soc. Chem. Industry, A.A.A.S., Nat., N.Y. acads. sci., Phi Beta Kappa, Sigma Xi, Sigma Alpha Epsilon, Phi Lambda Upsilon. Clubs: Chemists, University (New York). Home: 9 Ednam Village Route 3 Charlottesville, VA 22901. Office: 270 Park Av New York City NY 10017

CURNEN, EDWARD CHARLES, Jr., physician; b. Yonkers, N.Y., Jan. 5, 1909; s. Edward Charles and Florence (Mayer) C.; grad. Hill Sch., 1927; A.B., Yale, 1931; M.D., Harvard, 1935; m. Marion Clement, Apr. 18, 1942 (dec. May 1967); children—Sheila, Edward C. III, Constance Avery; m. 2d, Dr. Mary Godenne McCrea, Oct. 12, 1968; stepchildrenAndrew, Pierre, Claire, John. Successively res. bacteriologist, med. intern, med. res. Infants, Childrens Hosp., Boston, 1935-39; Harvard research fellow Thorndike Meml. Lab., Boston City Hosp., 1938; asst. pediatrics Harvard Med. Sch., 1938-39; asst. Rockefeller Inst. Med. Research, 1939-46, asst. resident physicians hosp. of Inst., 1939-46; asst. prof. preventive medicine Yale Sch. Medicine, 1946-48, mem. Poliomyelitis study unit, 1946-52, asso. prof. pediatrics and preventive medicine, 1948-52, fellow Berkeley Coll., Yale, 1947-52; successively asso. physician, asso. pediatrician and head bacteriology labs., Grace-New Haven Community Hosp., 1946-52; prof. pediatrics, chmn. dept. U. N.C. Sch. Medicine, 1952-60; chief pediatrics service N.C. Meml. Hosp., 1952-60, chief staff, 1959-60, also cons. pediatrician N.C. State Bd. Health, Watts Hosp., Durham and Womack Army Hosp., Ft. Bragg; Carpentier prof. pediatrics, 1960—, chmn. dept. Columbia Coll. Phys. and Surg., 1960-70; dir. pediatrics service Presbyn., Babies hosps., 1960-70, attending pediatrician, 1960—; cons. St. Alban's Hosp., St. Luke's Hosp. Asso. commn. influenza Armed Forces Epidemiological Bd., 1947-69; planning com. studies cardiovascular effects influenza NIH, 1957, bd. sci. counselors div. biologics standards, 1959-63; infectious diseases and tropical medicine tng. grant com. Nat. Inst. Allergy and Infectious Diseases, 1960-63. Chmn. allergy and infectious diseases panel Health Research Council City of New York, 1962-68, mem. exec. com., 1969—. Trustee of Assos. Yale Medical Library, 1962-66, Nightingale-Bamford School, 1966—. Served to comdr., M.C., USNR, 1942-46. Recipient Presdl. award Internat. Poliomyelitis Congress. Fellow Am. Acad. Microbiology, A.A.A.S., Am. Pub. Health Assn., N.Y. Acad. Sci.; mem. Am. Acad. Pediatrics (chmn. com. control infectious diseases 1957-59, cons. 1959- 60), Am. Assn. History Medicine, Am. Assn. Immunologists, Am. Assn. U. Profs., Am. Fedn. Clin. Research, A.M.A., Am. Pediatric Soc. (council 1956-61, chmn. 1960-61, v.p. 1968-69), Am. Soc. Clin. Investigation, Assn. Am. Med. Colls., Beaumont Med. Club, Boylestion, Yale (pres. 1951-52) med. socs., Harvey Soc., Interurban Clin. Club, Soc. Exptl. Biology and Medicine, Soc. Pediatric Research, Am. Soc. Microbiology, Aesculanian Club, N.Y. Clin. Soc., Practitioners Soc. New York, Infectious Diseases Soc. (founding council 1961-64), Sigma Xi, Alpha Omega Alpha. Contbr. articles profl. jours. and books. Editorial bd. Medicine, 1955—. Home: 103 Paulin Blvd Leonia NJ 07605

CURRAN, ALICE TURLEY, pub. exec., ret. fgn. service officer; b. Washington, July 17, 1914; d. John and Amelia Mary D.T. (Park) Turley; ed. pub. schs., also Stravers Coll. Accountancy; LL.D., Temple U., 1962; m. William H. Curran, August 9, 1938 (dec. Jan. 1964); 1 dau., Johanne Marie. With U.S. Govt., 1933-68, Dept. Agr., 1933-38, NLRB, 1938-41, Office Facts and Figures, 1941-42, OWI, 1942-45, with Dept. State, 1945-68, consul gen., Manchester, Eng., 1959-63, Birmingham, Eng., 1963-65; faculty Fgn. Service Inst., Dept. State, 1966-68, coordinator consular tng., 1966-68; dir. office Washington affairs Ency. Brit. Cos., Washington, 1968—. Mem. Am. Fgn. Service Assn., Diplomatic and Consular Officers Ret. Episcopalian. Clubs: Am. Newspaper Women's (pres. 1958-60), Washington Press (Washington). Home: 1413 27th St NW Washington DC 20007 Office: 1510 H St NW Washington DC 20005

CURRAN, EDWARD MATTHEW, judge; b. Bangor, Me., May 10, 1903; s. Michael Joseph and Mary Anges (Callinan) C.; A.B., U. Me., 1928; LL.B., Catholic U., 1927; student for S.J.D., Georgetown U., 6 mos.; m. Katherine Cecilia Hand, June 6, 1934; children—Eileen, Mary Catherine Anne Elizabeth, Edward Matthew. Began practice law, 1929; in practice with Milton W. King, Washington, 1929- 34; asst. corp. counsel for D.C., 1934-36; judge Police Court, D.C., 1936-40; became U.S. atty. for D.C., 1940; asso. justice Dist. Court of U.S. for D.C., now chief judge; mem. law faculty, Catholic U., 1930-35; instr. debate Trinity Coll., D.C., 1930; instr. law. Columbus U., D.C., 1935. Mem. Am., D.C., Jr. bar assns., Washington Bd. Trade, Gamma Eta Gamma, Phi Kappa. Democrat. Roman Catholic, Writer of several legal articles. Home: 6607 Western Av NW washington DC 20015 Office: US Dist Court 4th and Indiana Av NW Washington DC 20004

CURRAN, FRANK EARL, mayor; b. Cleve., Dec. 19, 1913; s. William E. and Anna (Haver) C.; student San Diego Jr. Coll., Balboa Law Sch., San Diego State Coll., U. Cal. extension; m. Florence McKenney, Apr. 15, 1936. Dep. county assessor San Diego County, 1935-41; city storekeeper, Oceanside, Cal., 1937-38; supr. procurement critical materials Navy Dept., 1940-49; sec.- mgr. Fraternal Order Eagles, San Diego, 1949-60; with Shoreline Ins. Co., San Diego, 1960-63; councilman, San Diego, 1955-63, vice mayor, 1957, 58, 61, 62, mayor, 1963—. Gen. chmn. Inter-Am. Municipal Orgn. Congress, San Diego, 1960, presiding officer, Punta del Este, Uruguay, 1962—, mem. nat. bd. dirs., 1962—; bd. dirs. League Cal. Cities, 1964- -, dir.-at-large exec. com., 1964—, mem. resolutions coms., 1964—. city rep. to league com. on internat. municipal coop., 1961—; mem. policy com. San Diego-Border Area Program, 1963—; bd. dirs. Palm City Sanitation Dist., 1964—; mem. Gov. Cal. Adv. Com. Aviation, 1963—; spl. rep. gov. Cal. to Commn. Californias, 1964—; mem. community relations com. U.S. Conf. Mayors, 1965—; chmn. com. internat. municipal coop. Nat. League Cities, 1965—, v.p., 1969, pres., 1970, bd. dirs., 1971; chmn. Coop. Area Manpower Planning System, 1970; mem. Govt. Task Force on Coastline Preservation, 1970. Bd. dirs. Nat. Center Voluntary Action, 1970. Democrat. Home: 4901 Westover Pl San Diego CA 92102 Office: Adminstrn Bldg Community Concourse San Diego CA 92101

CURRAN, GEORGE LALLY, med. educator; b. N. Adams, Mass., July 31, 1920; s. George Lally and Claire (Russell) C.; A.B., Harvard, 1941; M.D., Columbia, 1944; m. Caro Paget Shugg, Dec. 29, 1945; childrenGeorge Lally, Richard Russell, Stephen Paget. Intern, asst. resident medicine Presbyn. Hosp., N.Y.C., 1944-45, 47-48; from asst. to asso. medicine Columbia, 1950-54; from asst. prof. to prof. medicine U. Kan. Sch. Medicine, 1954-64; prof. medicine Columbia, 1964—; chief of med. service Francis Delafield Hosp., 1968-. Mem. metabolism study sect. USPHS, 1961-65. Served to capt., M.C., AUS, 1945-47. Episcopalian. Author articles cholesterol biosynthesis, lipid metabolism, trace elements. Mem. editorial com. Jour. Clin. Investigation, 1957-61. Home: 445 E 80th St New York City, NY . 10021.

CURRAN, HUGH C., mayor; b. Bridgeport, Conn., Jan. 20, 1924; s. Hugh A. and Mary (Ennis) C.; ed. Coll. Holy Cross, Boston Coll. Law Sch.; m. Eleanor Reagan, June 28, 1952; children—Maura, John E., Hugh, Mary Pat, Mary Kate, Mary Ellen. Mem. Conn. Ho. of Reps., 1955-57; city atty., Bridgeport, 1958-65, mayor, 1965—; commr. Conn. Dept. Aeros.; pres. Conn. Conf. Mayors; mem. Conn. Dept. Community Affairs; mem. Gov.'s Traffic Commn. Com. Standardization Traffic Control Devices; mem. Bridgeport Democratic Town Com.; mem. Conn. Dem. Central Com., currently. Served to 1st lt. USAAF; ETO. Decorated D.F.C., Air medal with 12 oak leaf clusters, Presidential citation with 2 oak leaf clusters. Mem. Am. Legion (past post comdr.), Bridgeport C. of C., East Bridgeport Trade and Civic Assn., St. Charles Holy Name Soc. K.C., Elk, Moose. Clubs: Harding Fathers (exec. bd.), Varsity H, YMCA Business Mens. Address: 133 Hickory St Bridgeport CT 06610*

CURRAN, JOSEPH EDWIN, seaman, labor leader; b. N.Y.C., Mar. 1, 1906; s. Eugene and Ida (Cohan) C.; student parochial sch., Westfield, N.J.; m. Retta Toble, Oct. 19, 1939 (dec. Nov. 1963); m. 2d, Florence B. Stetler, 1965. Factory worker, Garwood, N.J., 1919; shipped to sea, 1922, and has since been seaman; nat. pres. Nat. Maritime Union (AFL-CIO), 1937-; became v.p. AFL-CIO, 1955, now mem. exec. council, chmn. maritime com., mem. ethical practices com.; v.p. United Seamens Service; co-chmn. Labor Mgmt. Maritime Com. Mem. adv. com. N.Y. Area, War Manpower Commn. Am. Labor Party. Roman Catholic. Author column and articles in orgn. paper, Pilot, and other publs. Office: 36 7th Av New York City NY 10011

CURRAN, PETER FERGUSON, educator, biophysicist; b. Waukesha, Wis., Nov. 5, 1931; s. Peter Hugh and Norma (Ferguson) C.; A.B., Harvard, 1953, Ph.D., 1958; M.S. (hon.), Yale, 1969; m. Barbara Jean Werra, July 7, 1956; 1 dau., Maura Elizabeth. NSF post-doctoral fellow U. Copenhagen (Denmark), 1958-60; asso. biophysics Harvard Med. Sch., 1960-63, asst. prof. biophysics, 1963-67; mem. faculty Yale Sch. Medicine, 1967—, prof. physiology, 1969—. Mem. molecular biology panel NSF, 1968-71; biophys. sci. tng. com. NIH 1968-70, physiology study sect. 1971—. Recipient Research Career Devel. award NIH, 1962-67. Mem. Biophys. Soc. (council 1970-73), Am. Physiol. Soc. (Bowditch lectr. 1967, chmn. publs. com. 1971-73), Soc. Gen. Physiologists (council 1968-70, pres. 1972). Author: (with A. Katchalsky) Nonequilibrium Thermodynamics in Biophysics, 1965; also numerous articles. Mem. editorial bd. Biophys. Jour., 1967-70, Jour. Gen. Physiology, 1972—; editorial bd. Am. Jour. Physiology, 1964-68, sect. editor, 1968—. Home: 205 Bayard Av North Haven CT 06473 Office: 333 Cedar St New Haven CT 06510

CURRAN, THOMAS RAPHAEL, newspaperman; b. Lincoln, Neb., Dec. 27, 1901; s. John and Margaret (Michie) C.; student U. Neb., 1920-24; m. Emma Tyndale Westermann, June 11, 1925 (dec. Mar. 1969); children—Jamie Gilbert and Constance Margaret (twins), Sheila Louise; m. 2d, Elizabeth Ellis Graves, Oct. 8, 1970. Telegrapher-corr. United Press, A.P. and Internat. News Service while attending high sch. U. Neb., Lincoln, 1917- 22; corr. Internat. News Service, Lincoln, 1923-25; city editor Klamath Falls (Ore.) News, 1925; Hollywood bur. mgr., Internat. News Service, Los Angeles, 1926-27; bus. rep. United Press Coast Div., hdqrs. at San Francisco and Los Angeles, 1927-33, So. Div. mgr., Atlanta, 1933-35,

Central Div. mgr., Chgo., 1935-43, gen. S.Am. mgr., Buenos Aires, Argentina, Feb. 1943-Jan. 1946, v.p. and S.Am. mgr., 1946- 56, formerly v.p., gen. European mgr., in charge operations in Europe, Middle East and Africa, v.p., asst. gen. mgr., 1965-66, now gen. cons. Mem. Sigma Delta Chi. Clubs: Overseas Press; American, Buenos Aires Lawn Tennis, Jockey (Buenos Aires); Lansdowne, Annabel's, Curzon House (London); University (Lincoln); Los Angeles Press. Home: 48 Berkeley Square London W 1 X5DB England Office: 8 Bouverie St London EC 4 England

CURRENT, RICHARD NELSON, educator, historian; b. Colorado City, Colo., Oct. 5, 1912; s. Park Curry and Anna (Christiansen) C.; A.B., Oberlin Coll., 1934; M.A., Fletcher Sch. Law and Diplomacy, 1935; Ph.D., U. Wis., 1939; m. Rose Metcalf Bonar, Dec. 20, 1937; children—Annabelle, Dana Bonar. Instr. social sci. Md. State Tchrs. Coll., 1938-42; asst. prof. history and polit. sci. Rutgers U., 1942-43; asst. prof. History Hamilton Coll., 1943-44; prof. history No. Mich. Coll., 1944-45; asso. prof. history Lawrence Coll., 1945-47; May Treat Morrison prof. Am. history Mills Coll., 1947-50; asso. prof. U. Ill., 1950-53, prof., 1953-55; prof., head dept. history and polit. sci. Woman's Coll., U. N.C., 1955-60; prof. history U. Wis., Madison, 1960-66, William F. Allen prof., 1964- 66; Distinguished prof. Am. history U. of N.C., 1966—; lectr. Doshisha Univ. Kyoto, Japan, summer 1958; State Dept. lectr., India, 1959; Fulbright lectr. U. Munich, Germany, May-July, 1959, U. Chile, 1968; Harmsworth prof. Oxford U. (Eng.), 1962-63. Mem. Am. Hist. Assns., Orgn. Am. Historians (mem. exec. com. 1966-69), Wis. Hist. Soc., Phi Beta Kappa. Author: Old Thad Stevens, 1942; Pine Logs and Politics, 1950; Secretary Stimson, 1954; The Typewriter and the Men Who Made It, 1954; Daniel Webster and the Rise of National Conservatism, 1955; (with J.G. Randall) Lincoln the President; Last Full Measure 1955 (Bancroft prize 1956); The Lincoln Nobody Knows, 1958; (with T. H. Williams, F. Freidel) A History of the U.S., 1959; Lincoln and the First Shot, 1963; John C. Calhoun, 1963; Three Carpetbag Governors, 1967. Bd. editors Am. Hist. Review, 1960-65. Home: 1805 Brookcliff Dr Greensboro NC 27408

CURRENT, WAYNE GAST, newspaper exec.; b. Redkey, Ind., Mar. 14, 1912; s. Robert Emory and Josephine (Gast) C.; m. Clarice Arwilda Hardin, July 10, 1937; children—Carol Ann (Mrs. David Searfoss), Michael Wayne. With Lima Locomotive Works (O.), 1930-32, Lima News, 1932-57; gen. mgr. Lima Citizen, 1957-64; asst. to pub. Toledo Blade, Toledo Times, 1964-66, gen. mgr., 1966—; dir. Toledo Blade Co., 1966—, also v.p.; pres., dir. Buckeye Cablevision; sec., dir. Red Bank Register; pres., dir. Vistula Printing Co.; sec., dir. Monterey Peninsula Herald Co.; trustee, asst. treas. Clear Water, Inc. Home: 418 River Rd Maumee OH 43537 Office: 541 Superior St Toledo OH 43604

CURRENT-GARCIA, EUGENE, educator; b. New Orleans, July 8, 1908; s. Joseph and Bertha (Ehrhardt) C.-G.; A.B., Tulane U., 1930, M.A., 1932; A.M., Harvard, 1942, Ph.D., 1947; m. Alva Adele Garrett, June 18, 1935; children—William J., Alison Eugenia (Mrs. Raymond F. Heyd), Adele (Mrs. Lewis F. Mayson). Teaching fellow Tulane U., 1930-33; instr. English, U. Neb., 1936-39; tutor Harvard, 1942-43; instr. La. State U., 1944-47; from asst. prof. to prof. Auburn U., 1947-64, Hargis prof. Am. lit., 1964—. Ford Found. fellow, 1953; Fulbright lectr., Greece, 1956-58. Mem. Southeastern Modern Lang. Assn. (exec. com. 1967-70), So. Humanities Conf. (v.p., sec.-treas. 1960-64), Phi Beta Kappa, Phi Kappa Phi, Omicron Delta Kappa, Delta Upsilon. Author: O. Henry, 1965; (with W.R. Patrick), American Short Stories, rev. edit., 1964; What Is the Short Story, 1961; Short Stories of the Western World, 1969; Realism and Romanticism in Fiction, 1962. Co-editor So. Humanities Rev., 1967—. Home: 510 E Samford Av Auburn AL 36830

CURRERI, ANTHONY RUDOLPH, surgeon; b. N.Y.C., Sept. 18, 1909; s. Peter and Marie (Chiucara) C.; B.A., U. Wis., 1930, M.A., 1931, M.D., 1933; m. Dorothy Christiana Huebsch, Oct. 12, 1935; children—Peter William, Cynthia Marie (Mrs. George J. Maisel, Jr.), Joanne Dorothy (Mrs. David Falcon). From instr. to asso. prof. surgery U. Wis., Madison, 1939-53, prof., 1953—, chmn. dept. surgery, 1968—, also dir. div. clin. oncology; mem. Nat. Adv. Cancer Council, USPHS, 1962-64; cons. to Surg. Gen., U.S. Army; also chmn. central clin. drug evaluation program; sci. adv. bd. consultants Armed Forces Inst. Pathology; mem. Def. Sci. Bd., 1965—, Nat. Adv. Council Regional Med. Program, 1968-70, Nat. Adv. Council Gen. Med. Scis., 1970—. Decorated Legion of Merit; recipient bronze medal Am. Cancer Soc., 1950, Distinguished Service award U. Wis., 1968. Diplomate Am. Bd. Surgery, Am. Bd. Thoracic Surgery. Fellow A.C.S.; mem. Am. Central, Western surg. assns., Am. Assn. Thoracic Surgery, Am. Assn. Cancer Research, Internat. Surg. Soc., Soc. Med. Cons. to Armed Forces, Sigma Xi, Phi Beta Pi. Republican. Conglist. Mason (Shriner). Clubs: Army and Navy, Nat. Press, (Capitol Hill Washington); Madison, University (Madison); Kenwood Country (Bethesda, Md.). Contbr. articles to surg. jours. Home: 3636 Lake Mendota Dr Madison WI 53705

CURRIE, ALBERT S., banker. Sr. v.p., trust officer First Nat. Bank Passaic County. Office: 515 Union Blvd Borough Totowa NJ 07511*

CURRIE, ALLAN BALDWIN, constrn. co. exec.; b. Atlanta, May 26, 1937; s. Clifford George and Lulu (Baldwin) C.; B.A., Mich. State U., 1961; m. Sandra Jean Shintock, Aug. 27, 1960; children—Kimberly Jean, Julie Anne, Lynn Robin. Audit supr. Lybrand, Ross Bros. & Montgomery, Detroit, 1961-68; sec.-treas. Utley-James, Inc., Pontiac, Mich., 1968—. C.P.A., Mich. Mem. Am. Inst. C.P.A.'s, Mich. Assn. C.P.A.'s Southfield Jr. C. of C. (sec. 1965-66). Home: 4528 Valleyview Dr Orchard Lake MI 48033 Office: 1100 Opdyke Rd Pontiac MI 48056

CURRIE, GEORGE ROBERT, former justice; b. Princeton, Wis., Jan. 16, 1900; s. William F. and Cora (Clark) C.; student Wis. State Tchrs. Coll., 1917-19; LL.B., U. Wis., 1925; LL.D., Carthage Coll., 1966, St. Norbert Coll., 1966; m. Gladys Bremer, July 10, 1926; children—Ann, Janet. Admitted to Wis. bar, 1925, practiced in Sheboygan, 1925-51; justice Wis. Supreme Ct., 1951-68, chief justice, 1964-68; vis. prof. law U. Wis., 1968-70. Pres. Sheboygan Pub. Library Bd., 1935-51; dir. Wis. Welfare Council, 1952-57; chmn. Gov.'s Conf. on Aging, 1958. Mem. Am. Legion, Inst. for Jud. Adminstrn., Inc., Order of Coif, Gamma Eta Gamma. Mason (33). Clubs: Kiwanis, Literary (Madison); Town and Gown, Civil War Round Table. Home: 122 Marinette Trail Madison WI 53705

CURRIE, JAMES SLOAN, utilities exec.; b. Clarkton, N.C., Mar. 17, 1919; s. George Hendon and Marie (Sloan) C.; student Davidson Coll., 1935-36; B.S., U. N.C., 1939, J.D., 1948, M.S., 1949; m. Virginia Layton Spruill, Sept. 3, 1946; children—Marie Sloan, Mary Virginia Spruill. Securities analyst Jefferson Standard Life Ins. Co., 1940-41; underwriting aide FHA, 1941- 42; admitted to N.C. bar, 1948; practiced in Chapel Hill, 1948-50; dir. N.C. Dept. Tax Research, mem. State Bd. Assessments and Tax Rev. Bd., 1950-57; N.C. commr. revenue, chmn. State Bd. Assessments, mem. Tax Rev. Bd., 1957-61; asst. treas. Carolina Power & Light Co., Raleigh, N.C., 1961-67, treas., 1967—; dir. Wachovia Bank & Trust Co. Exec. sec. N.C. Tax Study Commn., 1955-57, chmn., 1967-69. Chmn. bd. Wake County chpt. A.R.C., 1960-61; pres. Wake County Opportunities, Inc., 1965-66; mem. Raleigh adv. bd. Salvation Army, 1967. Served to maj., Transp. Corps, AUS, 1942-46; PTO. Decorated Bronze Star, Cross Mil. Service. Mem. Raleigh C. of C., N.C., Wake County bar assns., Nat. Tax Assn., Southeastern Assn. Tax Adminstrs. (past pres.), Edison Electric Inst., Adminstrv. Mgmt. Soc. (past chpt. pres.), Raleigh Execs. Club (past pres.), Pi Kappa Alpha, Phi Alpha Delta. Presbyn. Rotarian. Home: 631 Marlowe Rd Raleigh NC 27609

CURRIE, JOHN CECIL, educator, mathematician; b. Oxford, Miss., Nov. 20, 1913; s. John William and Ruth (McLeod) C.; B.S., U. So. Miss., 1933; M.A., U. Miss., 1936; Ph.D., La. State U., 1948; m. Pauline Estella Smith, Dec. 24, 1938; children—Jean Sylvia (Mrs. Robert MacArthur Beard), Catherine McLeod; m. 2d, Caroline H. B. Snyder, Mar. 20, 1971; 1 stepdau., Sharon. Faculty, N.E. La. State Coll., Monroe, 1938-46, La. State U., Baton Rouge, 1946-47, Auburn (Ala.) U., 1948-49; faculty Ga. Inst. Tech., Atlanta, 1949—, now prof. math.; with Lockheed Aircraft Corp., Marietta, Ga., summers and part-time, 1951-55. Mem. Am. Math. Soc., Math. Assn. Am., Sigma Xi. Democrat. Presbyn. Home: 603 Clairmont Av Decatur GA 30030 Office: 225 North Av Atlanta GA 30332

CURRIE, LAUCHLIN MACLAURIN, cons. engr.; b. Chapel Hill, N.C., August 13, 1898; s. Daniel and Stella Alston (Hogan) C.; B.A., Davidson Coll., 1918, D.Sc., 1951; Ph.D., Cornell U., 1925; D.Sc., Clarkson Inst., 1950; m. Ethel Snyder Jopp, Aug. 11, 1921; childrenHelen Catherine, Christian MacLaurin. With Union Carbide Corp., 1925-58, successively research chemist, plant supt., dir. vinylite div., 1925-40, plant supt. Bakelite Co., 1940-42, v.p., dir. research Nat. Carbon Co., 1945-55, v.p. Union Carbide Nuclear Co., 1955-58; v.p. Babcox & Wilson Co., N.Y.C., 1958-62, also dir.; dir. devel. Research Triangle N.C., 1962-64; cons. U.S. AEC, Phila. Fund, SFAIR, Paris. Chairman adv. com. isotopes and radiation AEC. Asso. dir. div. war research Manhattan Engring. Dist., 1943-45; observer Bikini Bomb Tests, 1946; del. OEEC, Nancy, France, 1954, Geneva Conf. UN, 1955, 58, Calder Hall, London, 1956; chmn. N.Y. State adv. bd. atomic energy, 1957-58; chmn. nuclear energy commn. N.A.M., 1957-62, also dir. commn. Served from 1st lt. to maj. AUS, Chem. Industry, Am. Nuclear Soc., Newcomen Soc., Sigma Xi, Phi Gamma Delta. Republican. Presbyn. Clubs: Chemists (N.Y.C.); Monterey Peninsula Country; Rotary (Monterey, Cal.). Home: 57 del Mesa Carmel Carmel, CA 93921.

CURRIE, LEONARD JAMES, architect, educator; b. Stavely, Alta., Can., July 28, 1913; s. Andrew and Florence (McIntyre) C.; B.Arch., U. Minn., 1936; M.Arch., Harvard, 1938, Wheelwright traveling fellow, 1940-41; m. Virginia M. Herz, Feb. 8, 1937; children—Barbara E., Robert G., Elizabeth A. Worked for Walter Gropius, Marcel Breuer, Cambridge, Mass., 1938-40; archeologist div. hist. research Carnegie Instn. Expdn. to Copan, Honduras, 1941; airport constrn. Pan Am. Airways, U.S. Govt., Guatemala and Nicaragua, 1941-42; asst. prof. architecture Harvard, 1946-51; architect Architects Collaborative, Cambridge, Mass., 1946-51; chief tech. aid mission on housing U.S. Govt., Costa Rica, 1951; organized, directed Inter-Am. Housing Center, Bogota, Colombia, 1951-56; prof., head dept. architecture Va. Poly. Inst., 1956-62; dean Coll. Architecture and Art, U. Ill., Chgo. Circle 1962—; also partner firm Atkins, Currie and Payne, architects, engrs. and planners; prin. works include schs. and residences New Eng., chs., Wesley Found. bldgs., residences in Va., plan for resort in W. Va., regional plan Sagamoso Valley, Colombia, (with others) Six Moon Hill, coop. community, Lexington, Mass., Grad. Center, Harvard; cons. Rockefeller Found. phys. facilities planning, Colombia, 1967; campus planning cons. Nat. U. Nicaragua, 1969-70. AID campus planning cons. Central Am. univs. 1964. Mem. City of Chgo. Cultural Com., 1963-66, Va. Com. on Sch. Bldg. Research, 1956-62; chmn. subcom. on comprehensive community planning, mem. exec. com. Community Improvement Adv. Com. of City of Chgo. Bd. mem. Chgo. Sch. Architecture Found. Served as officer AUS, 1942-45, ret. lt. col. Res. Decorated Medalla de Merito (Colombia), 1956. Fellow Internat. Inst. Arts and Letters, A.I.A. (1st honor award 1963); mem. Sociedad Colombiana de Arquitectos (hon.), Soc. Archtl. Historians, Internat. Council Fine Arts Deans, Met. Housing and Planning Council, American Inst. Planners, Inter-Am. Planning Soc., Assn. Collegiate Schs. Architecture. Author: (with Rafaela Espino) Housing in Costa Rica, 1951; Planning of Central American Campuses, 1964. Contbr. articles to profl. publs. Home: 1246 W Lexington Chicago IL 60607

CURRIE, MALCOLM RODERICK, scientist; b. Spokane, Wash., Mar. 13, 1927; s. Erwin Casper and Genevieve (Hauenstein) C.; A.B., U. Cal. at Berkeley, 1949, M.S., 1951, Ph.D., 1954; m. Sunya Lofsky, June 24th, 1951; children—Deborah, David, Diana. Research engr. Microwave Lab., U. Cal. at Berkeley, 1949-52, elec. engring. faculty, 1953-54; lectr. U. Cal. at Los Angeles, 1955-57; research engr. Hughes Aircraft Co., 1954-57, v.p., 1965-66, v.p., dir. research labs., 1963-65, v.p., div. mgr., research and devel. div., 1965-69, head electron dynamics dept. Hughes Research Labs., Culver City, Cal., 1957-60, dir. physics lab., Malibu, Cal., 1960-61, asso. dir. Hughes Research Labs., 1961-63; v.p. research and devel. Beckman Instruments, Inc., 1969—. Served with USNR, 1944-47. Named nation's outstanding young elec. engr. Eta Kappa Nu, 1958; named one of 5 outstanding young men of Cal., Cal. Jr. C. of C., 1960. Fellow I.E.E.E.; mem. Nat. Acad. Engring., Am. Phys. Soc., Am. Rocket Soc., Phi Beta Kappa, Sigma Xi, Lambda Chi Alpha. Author articles. Patentee in field. Home: 1022 Maroney Lane Pacific Palisades CA 90272 Office: Beckman Instruments Fullerton CA 92634

CURRIE, OVERTON ANDERSON, lawyer; b. Hattiesburg, Miss., Nov. 28, 1926; s. Edward Alexander and Terry (Anderson) C.; Asso. Sci., Marion Inst., 1944; B.B.A., U. Miss., 1948, LL.B., 1949; B.D., Emory U., 1958; LL.M., Yale, 1958; m. Lavona Stringer, Dec. 31, 1949; children—Iva Terry, Overton Anderson, Martha Lavona, Lucy Flora, Judy Stringer. Admitted to Miss. Bar, 1949, Ga. bar, 1959; practice in Hattiesburg, Miss., 1949-55, Atlanta, 1959—; county prosecuting atty., 1952-55; spl. asst. atty. gen. Miss., 1954-55; faculty Yale Law Sch., 1958-59; partner Smith, Currie & Hancock, 1959—; faculty Emory U. Law Sch., 1966-71; lectr. Asso. Gen. Contractors Chpt. Seminars on Constrn. Law, Ga., 1967, S.Fla., 1967-68, 71, Carolinas, 1968-71, Okla., 1968, Ind., 1969, 71, Pa., 1969, N.Y., 1969-70. Bd. dirs. Ga. Assn. Pastoral Care; mem. profl. adv. com. Pastoral Counseling Service. Served with U.S. Mcht. Marine Corps, USNR, 1944-46. Mem. Am. Bar Assn. (nat. chmn. sect. on pub. contract law 1971—, mem. council), Am. Trial lawyers. (past nat. v.p.), Am. Arbitration Assn., State Bar Ga., Lawyers Club Atlanta, Phi Delta Theta, Phi Delta Phi, Omicron Delta Kappa, Phi Kappa Phi (nat. pres.), Beta Gamma Sigma, Phi Sigma Alpha. Club: Commerce (Atlanta). Author: Preparing Construction Claims for Settlement, 1968; Subcontracts and Labor Problems, 1969. Home: 1055 Nawench Dr NW Atlanta GA 30327 Office: 1405 Fulton Nat Bank Atlanta GA 30303

CURRIER, ALBERT ELDRED, educator; b. Bklyn., Feb. 8, 1905; s. William Gideon and Gertrude (Hastings) C.; B.S., Harvard Coll., 1927, M.A., 1928, Ph.D., 1930; student U. Munich (Germany) 1930-31; m. Erna Schildberger, May 20, 1931, (dec. Dec. 1945); 1 son, Albert William; m. Lynor K. Olson, Dec. 21, 1947. Instr. math. Harvard, 1931-35; instr. math. U.S. Naval Acad., 1935-39, asst. prof., 1939-46, asso. prof. 1946-54, prof., 1954—. Mem. Am. Math. Assn. Presbyn. Clubs: Harvard (pres. 1937-40), Yacht (Annapolis). Author: Analytic Mechanics, 1950. Home: 1925 Harwood Rd Annapolis MD 21401

CURRIER, NORMA STUDLEY, co. exec.; b. Rochester, N.H., Apr. 4, 1899; d. Joel Wilber and Minnie E. (Norris) McCrillis; B.S., Simmons Coll., 1920; D.C., Ph.C., Palmer Sch. Chiropractic, 1924; m. Joshua Studley, June 27, 1925 (dec. June 1952); m. 2d, Ray Bertrand Currier, Sept. 15, 1956 (dec. Jan. 1970); 1 step-dau., Corinne (Mrs. Walter Greeley). Tchr. Essex County Agrl. Sch., Danvers, Mass., 1921-22; pvt. practice as chiropractor, 1924-30; pres., treas. Studley Flower Gardens, Inc., 1952-71. Mem. N.H. Ho. of Reps., 1949-59, mem. jud. com., 1951-59; asst. chmn. N.H. Rep. State Com., 1954-58, 64-65, nat. committeewoman for N.H., 1956-64, chmn. women's div. 1954-58, 64-65; pres. Rochester Women's Rep. Club, 1969; presdl. electro, 1968. Vice chmn. N.H. Council on Problems of Aging, 1957-61; del. White House Conf. Aging, 1961; mem. Assay Commn., 1960. Mem. N.H. Fedn. Bus. and Profl. Women's Clubs (pres. 1936-38), D.A.R. (past regent, vice regent N.H. Soc. 1971—). Mem. United Ch. of Christ (trustee N.H. conf.). Mem. Order Eastern Star (worthy matron of James Farrington chpt. 1932-33, worthy grand matron, 1940-41, worthy grand chaplin Gen. Grand chpt. 1947-49). Clubs: Rochester Business and Professional Women's (pres. 1930-31); Rochester Woman's, N.H. Simmons. Home: 84 Wakefield St Rochester NH 03867

CURRIER, STEPHEN R., pres. Urban America, Inc. Address: 1717 Massachusetts Av Washington, DC 20036.*

CURRIGAN, THOMAS GUIDA, air line co. exec.; b. Denver, July 8, 1920; s. Thomas G. and Mary Fredericka (Wheaton) C.; B.A. cum laude, U. Notre Dame, 1941; m. Gertrude Curtis, Aug. 11, 1942; children—Colleen, Thomas Guida. Adminstrv. asst. to Mayor of Denver, 1951-53; clk., recorder City and County of Denver, 1953-55, auditor, 1955-63, mayor, 1963-69; staff v.p. civic and community affairs, Continental Air Lines, Los Angeles, 1969—. Mem. solicitations com. Mile High United Fund, 1953-. Served to capt. USAAF, 1942-46. Mem. Am. Municipal Assn. (exec. com.), Am. Legion, Am. Soc. Pub. Adminstrn. Home: 15719 Varden St Encino CA 91316 Office: Continental Air Lines International Airport Los Angeles CA 90009

CURRY, ABRAM STAUFFER, clergyman; b. Hershey, Pa., Apr. 6, 1913; s. Amos K. and Annie S. (Stauffer) C.; B.S., Elizabethtown Coll., 1935; S.T.B., Wesley Theol. Sem., Washington, 1939; A.M., Cath. U. Am., 1945; Ph.D., N.Y. U., 1948; m. Eleanor Marguerite Neff, 1950; children—Jeanne Eleanor, Robert Stauffer. Tchr. sci. Lebanon (Pa.) Jr.-Sr. High Sch., 1935-36; ordained to ministry Ch. of the Brethren, 1935; pastor Westminster (Md.) Ch. of the Brethren, 1936-40; Southeastern regional sec. Ch. of the Brethren, Bridgewater, Va., 1940-45; dir., sec. field program service com. Ch. of the Brethren Gen. Offices, Elgin, Ill., 1946-49, editor ch. sch. publs., 1955-60, dir. Family Edn. and Men's Fellowship, 1960-67; dir. interfaith activities Fellowship of Reconciliation, Nyack, N.Y., 1967-70; program analyst spl. asst. in drug abuse edn. dept. psychiatry Beth Isreal Med. Center, N.Y.C., 1970—; pres., adult adviser Eastern Md. Youth Cabinet, 1937-40; tchr. Bridgewater (Va.) Coll., 1943-45; exec. sec. Nat. Service Bd., Washington, 1949-55; informal rep. for Ch. of the Brethren, Washington, 1949-55; reader, sec., asso. moderator Ch. of the Brethren Annual Conf., 1953-54, 59-64, moderator, 1954-55, 64-65. Chmn. citizens adv. council Elgin Pub. Schs. Trustee Bethany Brethren Hosp., Chgo.; v.p. Fellowship of Reconciliation. Mem. Am. Psychol. Assn., Kappa Delta Pi. Kiwanian, Rotarian. Author: Current Status of Brethren Curriculum, 1960. Contbr. articles profl. jours. Home: 614 Cortlandt Av Mamaroneck NY 10543 Office: Dept Psychiatry Beth Israel Med Center Morris J Bernstein Inst 307 2d Av New York City NY 10003

CURRY, ANDREW GIBSON, ret. investment banker; b. Windsor, N.S., Can., Apr. 6, 1901; s. Rufus and Cornelia (Faulkner) C.; student Kings Coll. Sch., Windsor, N.S., St. Andrew Coll., Toronto; B.A., U. Toronto, 1922; m. Dorothy Dawson Page, Jan. 14, 1938; children—John Page, Cornelia (Mrs. Alfred M. Christiansen). Came to U.S., 1930, naturalized, 1949. With A.E. Ames & Co., 1922-66, partner, 1955-65; pres. A.E. Ames & Co., Inc., 1951-65, chmn., 1965-68, ret.; dir. A.E. Ames & Co., Ltd., 1951- 65. Mem. Canadian Soc. N.Y., Phi Gamma Delta. Republican. Clubs: Bankers Club Am., Bond Club N.Y., Canadian (N.Y.C.); Fox Meadow Tennis (Scarsdale, N.Y.), Scarsdale Golf; Chester (N.S.) Yacht. Home: Brook Lane Hartsdale NY 10530

CURRY, B.W., Jr., constrn. co. exec Vice pres., treas. Turner Constrn. Co., N.Y.C. Office: 150 E 42d St New York City NY 10017*

CURRY, C.W., banker. Pres., Columbus Bank & Trust Co. (Ga.). Office: 1148 Broadway Columbus GA 31902*

CURRY, EDWARD THOMAS, lawyer; b. Homestead, N.J., July 7, 1890; s. Thomas Edward and Annie (Ryan) C.; LL.B., U. Pa., 1913; m. Ethel Vincent Reeve, Apr. 8, 1916; children—Ethel Emma (Mrs. James E. Sturgis), Edward Thomas. Admitted to N.J. bar, 1913; asso. firm Grey & Archer, later Norman Grey, Camden, N.J., 1913-24; partner firm Curry, Purnell & Greene; now counsel Brown, Connery, Kulp, Wille, Purnell & Greene, Camden, N.J.; spl. asst. to atty. gen. of U.S., 1950-58, hearing officer, 1958—. Served to 2d lt. U.S. Army, 1917-19. Fellow Am. Bar Found.; mem. Am., N.J. (pres. 1953-54, gen. council 1954—), Camden County (pres. 1940) bar assns., Am. Judicature Soc., Am. Legion, Sigma Phi Sigma. Presbyn. Mason. Club: Tavistock Country (dir.). Home: 422 Washington Av Haddonfield NJ 08033 Office: Parkade Bldg 518 Market St Camden NJ 08102

CURRY, GENE GILBERT, lawyer, exec.; b. Chgo., May 5, 1908; s. Robert R. and Marguerite (Wren) C.; A.B., U. So. Cal., 1929, LL.B., 1931; m. Cornelia Verplank, June 13, 1936; children—Robert R., Barbara J. (Mrs. George E. Wood), Judith C. (Mrs. Laurence Mansbach), Joseph J. Admitted to Cal. bar, 1931, N.Y. bar, 1962; practiced in Los Angeles, 1931-59; asst. counsel Pacific Finance Corp., 1933-43; mem. firm Williamson, Hoge & Curry, and predecessors, 1943-54; sec., gen. counsel Blue Diamond Corp., Los Angeles, 1956-59; sec., legal counsel Flintkote Co., N.Y.C., 1959-68, v.p., gen. counsel, sec., 1968—; sec., dir. Ariz. Quarry & Stone Co., Campanella Corp., Flintkote Communications Co., Flintkote Internat. Corp., Flintkote Internat. Licensing Co., Kosmos Portland Cement Co., Flintkote Co. Can., Ltd., Flintkote Mines, Ltd., King Paving & Materials Ltd., Stradwick Industries, Ltd. Mem. Am., N.Y., Cal. bar assns., Am. Soc. Corporate Secs., Delta Chi, Phi Alpha Delta. Club: Santa Monica (Cal.) Yacht, Old Greenwich (Conn.) Yacht; Innis Arden Golf. Home: 49 Willowmere Circle Riverside CT 06878 Office: 400 Westchester Av White Plains NY 10604

CURRY, GEORGE MILBURN, clergyman, publisher; b. Hillsboro, W.Va., July 20, 1905; s. George Ryder and Nancy (Cobb) C.; student Asbury Coll., 1923-25; A.B., W.Va. Inst. Tech., 1939; B.D., Chandler Sch. Theology, Atlanta, 1942; D.D. (hon.), W.Va. Wesleyan Coll., 1952; m. Amanda Cook, July 16, 1927; 1 dau., Virginia Nan (Mrs. Charles T. Lytle). With ARMCO, 1927-30; ordained deacon Methodist Ch., 1933, elder, 1935; pastor in Wheelwright, Ky.,

1931-35, Gauley Bridge, W.Va., 1935-39, Kimball, W.Va., 1941-43, Ronceverte, W.Va., 1943-47, Hinton, W.Va., 1947-49; supt. Parkersburg Dist., 1949-55; pastor in Logan, W.Va., 1955-58; asso. pub. Meth. Pub. House, Nashville, 1958-. Mem. gen. and jurisdictional confs. Meth. Ch., 1952, 56; mem. W.Va. Conf. Bd. Edn., 1942-48; v.p. W.Va. Bd. Missions, dirs. Camden-Clark Hosp., Parkersburg, 1953-56, W.Va. Mental Health Assn., 1956-58. Mason, Rotarian. Home: 3525 Pleasant Valley Rd Nashville TN 37204 Office: 201 8th Av South Nashville TN 37203

CURRY, HASKELL BROOKS, educator, mathematician; b. Mills, Mass., Sept. 12, 1900; s. Samuel S. and Anna (Baright) C.; A.B., Harvard, 1920, A.M., 1924; postgrad. Mass. Inst. Tech., 1920-22; Ph.D., U. Göttingen (Germany), 1930; NRC fellow U. Chgo., 1931-32; m. Mary Virginia Wheatley, July 3, 1928; children—Anne Wright (Mrs. Richard Shaner Piper), Robert Wheatley. Instr. Harvard, 1926-27, Princeton, 1928-29; asst. prof. Pa. State U., 1929-33, asso. prof., 1933-41, prof., 1941-60, Evan Puch research prof., 1960-66, emeritus, 1966—; prof., dir. Inst. Foundational Research, U. Amsterdam, 1966-70, emeritus, 1970—; vis. Andrew Mellon prof. U. Pitts., 1971-72. Mem. Inst. Advanced Study, Princeton, 1938-39; Fulbright research scholar, vis. prof. U. Louvain, Belgium, 1950-51, recipient medal, 1951, hon. vis. prof., 1951—. Mathematician Frankford Arsenal 1942-44, Johns Hopkins Applied Physics Lab., 1944-45, Aberdeen Proving Ground, 1945-46; mem. Conf. Bd. Math. Scis., 1958-63; U.S. nat. com. Internat. Union History and Philosophy of Sci., 1959-63. Trustee Curry Coll., 1940-51. Mem. Assn. Computing Machinery, Assn. Symbolic Logic (pres. 1938-40), A.A.A.S. (council 1937), Am. Math. Soc. (council 1945-47), Am. Assn. U. Profs., Am. Philos. Assn., Math. Assn. Am., Am. Ornithologists Union, Nat. Geog. Soc., Academie Internationale de Philosophie des Sciences (assessaur 1961-65, v.p. 1965—), Nederlandse Ornithologische Unie, Wiskundig Gerootschap to Amsterdam, Sigma Xi, Pi Mu Epsilon, Sigma Pi Sigma. Author: Outlines of a Formalist Philosophy of Mathematics (Amsterdam), A Theory of Formal Deducibility, rev. edit., 1957; (with Robert Feys) Combinatory Logic (Amsterdam), 1958; Foundations of Mathematical Logic, 1963. Home: 220 E Prospect Av State College PA 16801

CURRY, HOWARD MILLARD, educator; b. Haverhill, Mass., Mar. 8, 1924; s. Howard Henry and Blanche Alberta (Millard) C.; B.S., Northeastern U., 1945; A.M., Boston U., 1947, Ph.D., 1950; m. Phyllis Ann Nida, July 12, 1947; children—Rebecca, Glen. Instr. Bates Coll., 1949-50; asso. prof. Drury Coll., 1950-51; prof. Wittenberg U., Springfield, 1951—, cons. organic chemistry Charles F. Kettering Found., Yellow Springs, O., 1957-61. Chmn. Undergraduate Scholarship Com.; active Central Ohio Heart Assn. Mem. Am. Chem. Soc., Univ. Profs. Acad. Order. Republican. Presbyn. Club: Clark County Stamp. Contbr. articles profl. jours. Home: 1328 N Lowry Av Springfield OH 45504

CURRY, HUGH ARTHUR, banker; b. Point Pleasant, W.Va., Dec. 13, 1909; s. William D. and Mabel (Smith) C.; student Duke, 1929-30; B.S.C., Drake U., 1934; grad. Grad. Sch. Credit and Financial Mgmt., Tuck Sch., Dartmouth, 1961; m. Elizabeth Jane Burnside, Dec. 19, 1936; children—Harold D., Michael B., Philip. With Kanawha Valley Bank, Charleston, W.Va., 1946—, exec. v.p., 1966-67, pres., 1967—. Mem. Kanawha County Parks and Recreation Commn., 1968—; treas. Episcopal Diocese W.Va., 1958—. Trustee Morris Harvey Coll. Mem. Am., W.Va. bankers assns., Charleston Area C. of C. (pres.). Democrat. Clubs: Berry Hills Country, Edgewood Country (Charleston). Home: 1553 Bridge St Charleston WV 25314 Office: PO Box 1793 Charleston WV 25326

CURRY, JOHN ARTHUR, retail co. exec.; b. St. Cloud, Minn., June 13, 1920; s. Arthur James and Alice Emma (Cater) C.; B.B.A., U. Minn., 1942; m. Harriett Orlady, Apr. 14, 1950; children—Steven, Lewis, Charlotte. Asst. to gen. auditor Gen. Mills, Inc., 1946-52; internal auditor Dayton Hudson Corp., 1952, office mgr., 1952-54; asst. controller, 1954-58, controller, 1958-61, v.p., controller, 1961-67, v.p., corporate controller, 1967-70; sr. v.p. planning and control, dir. J.L. Hudson, Detroit, 1970—. Served to lt. USNR, 1942-46. Mem. Financial Exec. Inst. (dir. Twin Cities chpt. 1956—), Detroit Econ. Club. Clubs: Lochmoor Country (Grosse Pointe); Detroit Athletic. Home: 71 Stephens Rd Grosse Pointe Farms MI 48236 Office: 1206 Woodward Av Detroit MI 48226

CURRY, JOHN FOSTER, educator; b. Bloomington, Ind., Dec. 14, 1921; s. Robert W. and Elva (McMillan) C.; B.S., Ind. U., 1947, M.S., 1948, Ed.D., 1955; m. Eunice Davis, June 14, 1947; children—Elaine, Eileen. Tchr., Delphi (Ind.) High Sch., 1947- 48, Kodiak (Alaska) Naval Base, 1948-51; grad. asst. Ind. U., 1951-52; prin. pub. sch., Cadiz, Ind., 1952-54; tchr. Westan Hills High Sch., Cin., 1954-56; Mem. faculty North Tex. State U., 1956—, prof. edn., 1964—, chmn. div. inter- profl. studies, 1969—. Served with AUS, 1943-45. Decorated Bronze Star, Silver Star, Purple Heart with 3 oak leaf clusters. Presbyn. (elder 1969—). Author: Writing of a Proposal for a Thesis or Dissertation, 1969. Home: 617 Mimosa St Denton TX 76201

CURRY, JOHN FRANCIS, ret. air force officer; b. N.Y.C., Apr. 1886; s. James Francis and Mary (McKinnon) C.; student Coll. City N.Y., 1901-04; B.S., U.S. Mil. Acad., 1908; grad. Signal Corps Aviation Sch., 1915, Air Corps Engring. Sch., 1924, Air Corps Tactical Sch., 1928, Command and Gen. Staff Sch., 1929, Army War Coll., 1936; m. Eleanor Montgomery, Jan. 4, 1921; children—Sheila, (Mrs. Duane Dekalb), Joan. Commissioned 2d lieutenant of infantry, U.S. Army, 1908, promoted through grades to maj. gen., 1940; jr. mil. aviator, 1916; mem. 1st Aero Squadron, Pershing Expdn. into Mexico, 1916; with aviation sect. Signal Corps, 1916-17; chief staff A.S., 2d Army, 1918; with A.C., 1920-40, chief air service, engring. div., Dayton, O., 1924-27, comdt. A.C. Tactical Sch., 1931-35; mem. Gen. Staff, War Dept., 1936-38; comdg. gen. N.W. Air Dist. and 2d Air Force, 1940-41; head Civil Air Patrol, Washington, Dec. 1941-Mar. 42; comdg. gen. 4th dist. Tech. Tng. Command and Western Tech. Tng. Command, 1942-44; pres. A.A.F.-M.T.O. Evaluation Bd., 1944-45, dir. aeronautics, Colo., 1946; dir. aviation, Denver, 1947. Cons. to The Ramo-Wooldridge Corp., 1956-61. Chmn. Red Rocks Music Festival with Denver Symphony Orch., 1947-49. Vice pres. Denver Council Boy Scouts Am. 5 yrs. Decorated Officer de L'Etoile Noir, Officer Legion of Honor (France); D.S.M., Legion of Merit (U.S.); recipient dist. service citation CAP, 1951, citizenship medal V.F.W., 1954; spl. citation for contbns. to devel. aviation, City Denver, 1964; Early Birds of Aviation plaque, 1965; Aerospace plaque Pioneer of Hawaiian Aviation, 1965. Officially credited destruction one German balloon, 1918. Mem. Denver C. of C., Daedalians, Am. Legion, Alliance Francaise, English-Speaking Union (v.p. Denver branch), Aero Club Am. (expert aviator 1916), Early Birds of Aviation (board of trustees 1963—, 2d v.p.), Am. Meteorological Soc., Alpha Delta Phi. Roman Catholic. Knight of the Golden Circle. Clubs: Army-Navy (Washington); Denver, Mile High (Denver). Army aero ratings J.M.A., M.A. pilot, command pilot, combat observer. First nat. comdr. Civil Air Patrol. Home: 520 Elm St Denver CO 80220

CURRY, LAVERNE LEON, educator; b. Stony Creek, Mich., Apr. 17, 1914; s. Leon and Nellie (Rockwood) C.; A.B., Eastern Mich. U., 1938; M.A., U. Mich., 1948; Ph.D., Mich. State U., 1952; m. M. Catherine Palmer, July 29, 1939; children—Leon, Kenneth, Karl, Matthew, Catherine, Jane. Tchr. pub. schs., Mich., 1938-46; mem. faculty Central Mich. U., Mt. Pleasant, 1946—, prof. biology, 1956—, chmn. dept., 1960—. Research radioactive uptake studies AEC, 1954-62; prof. biology NIH, 1957-62; mem. health physics com. Central Mich. Community Hosp., 1960-67; pres. Mich. Bd. Examiners in Basic Sciences, 1970—; cons. Gt. Lakes-Ill. River Basins Project, 1962- 66. Pres. Saginaw Valley Multiple Sclerosis Soc., 1967-69, Mich. chpt. Nat. Multiple Sclerosis Soc., 1968-69. Chmn. bd. dirs. Wesley Found., 1959-66, Wesley Founds. Mich., 1961-62; trustee Three Lakes Assn., 1965-69, Mich. Soc. Multiple Sclerosis, 1967-71. Mem. Mich. Entomol. Soc., Internat. Assn. Gt. Lakes Research. Midwest Benthological Soc. (pres. 1955-56), Mich. (citation 1961). Wis. acads. sci., arts and letters, Am. Assn. U. Profs., Am. Soc. Limnology and Oceanography, Mich. Edn. Assn. Mason. Author articles to profl. jours. Home: 619 S University St Mount Pleasant MI 48858

CURRY, M. J., bakery exec.; b. 1906; grad. U.S. Mil. Acad.; m. 1928. Credit mgr. Gen. Motors Corp., 1929-33; asst. code adminstr., examiner NRA, also NLRB, 1934-38; with S.H. Kress Co., 1938-42, 45-47; cons. labor relations, 1947-50; sr. v.p. Am. Bakeries Co. Served with USAAF, 1945-47. Office: 10 S Riverside Plaza Chicago IL 60606*

CURRY, MILTON KING, Jr., coll. pres.; b. Magnolia, Ark., Nov. 5, 1910; s. Milton and Lena (Easter) C.; A.B., Morehouse Coll., 1932; M.A., Atlanta U., 1933; D.D., Okla. Sch. Religion, 1952; m. Marjorie Stewart, Oct. 21, 1937; 1 dau., Jeanette. Instr., Edward Waters Coll., Jacksonville, Fla., 1933-34, Pattern High Sch., Amarillo, Tex., 1934-37; instr. Butler Coll., Tyler, Tex., 1935-37, pres., 1945-48; instr. Booker T. Washington High Sch., Wichita Falls, Tex., 1937-45, asst. prin., 1938-45; ordained to ministry Baptist Ch., 1938; pastor Antioch Bapt. Ch., Wichita Falls, Tex., 1940- -; asst. sec. Nat. Bapt. Convention U.S.A., Inc., 1946—, corr. sec., 1954—, sec. Tex. Bapt. Conv., 1950-52; pres. Bishop Coll., 1952—. Mem. Am. Bapt. Edn. Assn. (pres. 1959-60), Religious Edn. Assn., Scientific Soc., Beta Kappa Chi, Alpha Kappa Mu, Omega Psi Phi. Democrat. Mason, K.P.

CURRY, OSCAR H., food co. exec.; b. Camden, N.J., Jan. 2, 1909; s. John S. and Rachel (Kay) C.; student U. Pa.; m. Helen Lafferty, Feb. 21, 1932. With Campbell Soup Co., Camden, N.J., 1927—, v.p. corporate planning, 1957-65, sr. v.p., 1965—; dir. Pepperidge Farm, Inc. Mem. Am. Mgmt. Assn. Clubs: Tavistock Country; Seaview Country. Home: 1 Eve's Lane Haddonfield NJ 08033 Office: 375 Memorial Av Camden NJ 08101

CURRY, OTHEL JACKSON, coll. dean; b. Santa Anna, Tex., Oct. 25, 1904; s. Charlie Lee and Fannie (Jackson) C.; B.B.A., U. Tex., 1930, M.B.A., 1932; Ph.D., U. Mich., 1940; m. Mary Leonora Kelso, May 28, 1928; children—Betty Jeannette, Jack Kelso. High sch. athletic coach, Melvin, Tex., 1925-27; with Amerada Petroleum Corp., 1928; prin. Eldorado High Sch., 1928-30; faculty Austin High Sch., 1930-35; instr. econs. U. Mich., 1936-38; asso. prof. finance U. Ark., 1938-40; asso. prof. accounting U. Pa., 1941-44; faculty North Tex. State U. 1945—, prof., former dean sch. bus. Asst. sec.-treas. Petroleum Industry War Council, 1943-44. Mem. Am. Accounting Assn., Nat. Assn. Cost Accts. Soc. Advancement Mgmt., Co. of C., Southwestern Social Sci. Assn. (pres. 1956-57). Presbyn. (elder). Club: Kiwanis. Home: 1209 Highland Park Rd Denton TX 76201

CURRY, PETER DUNCAN, investment dealer; b. Copenhagen, Denmark, July 12, 1912; s. Duncan Steele and Bertha (Laxdal) C.; ed. Ridley Coll., St. Catherines, Ont., also Bishop's U., Lennoxville, Que.; LL.D. (hon.), U. Man., 1963; m. Constance Noreen Murphy, Dec. 27, 1937; children—Duncan Steele, Gerald Mark, Constance Kathleen, Patrick Murphy. Chmn. bd., dir. Investors Group, Investors Syndicate Ltd., Investors Securities Mgmt. Ltd., Great-West Life Assurance Co., Greater Winnipeg Gas Co., Cablecasting Ltd., vice chmn., dir. Canadian Indemnity Co.,; pres. Peter D. Curry & Co. Ltd., Dromore Investment Co. Ltd., Greater Winnipeg Cablevision Ltd,; v.p., dir. United Canadian Shares Ltd.; dir. Ford Motor Co. Can., Ltd., Investors Growth Fund Can. Ltd., Investors Internat. Mut. Fund Ltd., Investors Mut. Can. Ltd., Investors Group Trust Co. Ltd., Molson Industries Ltd., No. and Central Gas Corp. Ltd., Provident Mut. Fund Ltd., Provident Stock Fund Ltd., Shawinigan Industries Ltd., Internat. Nickel Co. Can., Ltd., Power Corp. Can., Ltd., Investors Japanese Growth Fund Ltd., CAE Industries Ltd. Mem. Canadian Econ. Policy Com. Chancellor U. Man.; trustee Winnipeg Gen. Hosp., N. Am. Wildlife Found. Mem. Anglican Ch. Clubs: St. Charles Country; Manitoba; Toronto; Mount Royal (Montreal, Que.). Home: 729 Wellington Crescent Winnipeg 9 Manitoba Canada Office: 280 Broadway Winnipeg 1 Manitoba Canada

CURRY, RICHARD A., mfr.; b. Hoizington, Kan., Mar. 15, 1926; s. Joseph A. and Mary (Meuli) C.; student Pittsburg (Kan.) State Coll., 1945; B.A. Wichita State U., 1949, M.B.A. cum laude, 1968; m. Dolores Steinkirchner, May 31, 1948; children—Mary Elizabeth, Roberta Anne, Theresa Catherine, Patricia Sue, Joseph Richard. With The Coleman Co., Inc., Wichita, Kan., 1948—, treas., 1966—. Dir. YMCA, 1967—. Served with USNR, 1944-46. Mem. Financial Execs. Inst., Nat. Assn. Accountants (past pres., past nat. dir.), Wichita C. of C. K.C. Home: 1733 N Meridian St Wichita KS 67203 Office: 250 N St Francis Av Wichita KS 67201

CURRY, RICHARD EARL, journalist; b. Waxahachie, Tex., Sept. 21, 1933; s. Otwell Travern and Mabel (Walters) C.; B. Journalism, U. Tex., 1954; m. Para Lee Cain, Oct. 6, 1956; children—David Lee, Richard Tillman, Charles Frederick, Rebecca Louise. Mem. staff Dallas Times Herald, 1956—, financial editor, 1964—. Mem. regional export expansion council Dept. Commerce. Served with AUS, 1954-56. Recipient award Headliner's Club of Austin, 1962, 68, 69, 70; A.P. and U.P.I. writing awards. Mem. Dallas C. of C., Sigma Delta Chi. Author: Wall Street's Language, 1969. Home: 1934 Dancliff St Dallas TX 75224 Office: Dallas Times Herald Dallas TX 75202

CURRY, ROBERT LEE, lawyer; b. Lamont, Wis., May 10, 1923; s. Irving Gregg and Emma (Zimmerman) C.; B.S., Lawrence U., 1948; LL.B., U. Wis., 1953; m. Muriel Clapp, July 29, 1950; children—Robert Lee J., Laura Lynne, Melinda Ann. Admitted to Wis. bar, 1953; asso. firm Boardman, Suhr, Curry & Field, Madison, Wis., 1953-56, sr. partner, 1956-70; v.p., gen. counsel CUNA Mut. Ins. Soc., Madison, 1964-70; dir. CUNA Credit Union, 1965-70, pres., 1968-69. Served with USAAF, 1942-46. Mem. Am. Law Inst., U. Wis. Law Alumni Assn. (dir. 1967-70, pres. 1969-70), Order of Coif. Home: 4805 Fond du Lac Trail Madison WI 53705 Office: 110 E Main St Madison WI 53705

CURRY, STOWERS LEIGH, Jr., govt. ofcl.; b. Bklyn., Sept. 19, 1924; s. Stowers Leigh and Frances (Upton) C.; A.B., George Washington U., 1948, LL.B., 1950; m. Jacqueline F. Marois, Aug. 21, 1954. Admitted to D.C. bar, 1950; also U.S. Supreme Ct. bar, 1968; atty.-adviser HHFA, 1950-54, asst. regional counsel San Francisco office, 1954-56, chief counsel Urban Renewal Adminstrn., 1956-66; chief counsel Renewal Assistance Adminstrn., Dept. Housing and Urban Devel., 1966-68; asso. gen. counsel Dept. Housing and Urban Devel., 1968—. Served with AUS, 1943-46; PTO. Mem. Am., Fed. bar assns. Home: 6236 Lakeview Dr Falls Church, VA 22041. Office: 451 7th St SW Washington DC 20410

CURRY, THOMAS HARVEY, govt. ofcl.; b. Sullivan County, Ind., Oct. 7, 1921; s. John Porter and Myrtle (Barnett) C.; B.S. in Chem. Engring., Purdue U., 1942; Ph.D. in Chemistry, Ohio State U., 1953; m. Eleanor Neel, June 6, 1945; children—John, Emily, Neel. At Holston Ordnance Works, 1942-45; part-time instr. Antioch Coll., 1950-52; asst. prof. chemistry Ohio U., 1953- 57, asso. prof. chem. engring., chmn. dept., 1957-61; asso. dean Coll. Tech., U. Me., 1961-62, dean, 1962-67; dir. resident research associateships Office Sci. Personnel, Nat. Acad. Scis.-NRC, Washington, 1967-69, dir. associateships, 1969—. C.F. Kettering Found. fellow, 1947-53; NSF Sci. Faculty fellow, 1957-59. Mem. Am. Chem. Soc., Am. Assn. U. Profs., Am. Soc. Engring. Edn., Am. Inst. Chem. Engrs., Sigma Xi, Phi Lambda Upsilon, Tau Beta Pi. Office: 2101 Constitution Av Washington DC 20418

CURRY, WILLIAM HIRST, Jr., geologist; b. Kansas City, Mo., July 9, 1904; s. William Hirst and Ida F. (Carr) C.; student U. Wash., 1922-23; A.B., Johns Hopkins, 1926; m. Ruth B. Skeen, May 22, 1928; children—William Hirst III, John S. With Shell Oil Co., 1927-36; chief geologist Wellington Oil Co., San Antonio, 1936-42; research, dist. geologist Atlantic Refining Co., 1942-49; Rocky Mountain mgr. Far West Oil Co., Casper, Wyo., 1949-54; ind. cons. geologist, Casper, 1955—; dir. First Nat. Bank Casper, 1955—. Chmn. indsl. devl. com. Wyo. Natural Resource Bd. 1963-69. Mem. Geol. Soc. Am., Am. Assn. Petroleum Geologists (pres. 1970-71), Rocky Mountain Oil and Gas Assn. (pres. 1957-57), U.S. C. of C. Home: 544 E 11th St Casper WY 82601 Office: PO Box 572 Casper WY 82601

CURSON, THEODORE, musician; b. Phila., June 3, 1935; s. Leroy and Reava (Paige) C.; student Granoff Music Conservatory, Phila., 1952-53; m. Marjorie N. Goltry, Apr. 1, 1967; children—Charlene, Theodore II. Mem. Charles Mingus' Jazz Workshop, 1959-60; trumpeter with Max Roach, Philly Joe Jones, Cecil Taylor, Eric Dolphy, 1960-63; appeared radio, TV, clubs, also jazz festivals, including Antibes, Lugano, Bologna, Prague, Bled, Warsaw, Molde, 1964-71; appeared U.S. festivals Birdland, Newport Rebels Festival, Univ. concerts, including Columbia, N.Y.U., Grinnell Coll., U. Cal. at Santa Monica; guest instr. U. Vt. Festival of Contemporary Music, 1968; instr. music Warsaw U.; guest soloist Norddeutscher Rundfunk TV; pres. Nosruc Pub. Co., Jersey City, 1961—. Named New Star Monterey Jazz Festival, 1962; winner Trumpet sect. Down Beat Internat. Critics Poll, 1966; names New Jazz Artist Jazz Podium, Germany; recipient L.I. Musicians Soc. award, 1970. Mem. Am. Fedn. Musicians. Composer Nosruc Waltz, 1960; Flatted Fifth, 1960; Straight Ice, 1965; Typical Ted, 1970; The Leopard, 1964. Recording artist: Plenty of Horn, 1961; Fire Down Below, 1963; Tears for Dolphy, 1964; New Thing and Blue Thing, 1965; Urge, 1966; Ode to Booker Ervin, 1970. Music for films include Teorema, 1968; Notes for a Film on Jazz, 1968. Address: 130 Arlington Av Jersey City NJ 07305

CURTI, MERLE EUGENE, historian; b. Papillion, Neb., Sept. 15, 1897; s. John and Alice (Hunt) C.; A.B. summa cum laude, Harvard, 1920, A.M., 1921, Ph.D., 1927; student Sorbonne, 1924-25; L.H.D., Northwestern U., 1950, U. Pa., 1962, Western Reserve U., 1962, U. Mich., 1964, Adelphi Univ., 1965, U. Neb., Drake U., 1967, U. Wis. at Milw., 1969; Litt.D., Rider Coll., 1970; m. Margaret Wooster, June 16, 1925 (dec. Sept. 1961); children—Nancy Alice Holub, Martha Margaret Wohlforth; m. 2d, Francis Bennett Becker, Mar. 9, 1968. Vis. prof., Clark U., U. Chgo., U. Cal., U. Vt.; instr. history Reloit Coll., 1921-22; asst. prof. Smith Coll., 1925-27, asso. prof., 1927- 29, prof. 1929-35, Dwight Morrow prof., 1936-37; prof. history Tchrs. Coll., Columbia, 1937-42; prof. history U. Wis., 1942-68, Frederick Jackson Turner prof., 1947-68, now emeritus; Guggenheim fellow, 1929-30; vis. prof. Watumull Found. to univs. India, 1946-47; vis. prof. history U. Tokyo, 1959-60, U. Melbourne, 1964. Fulbright Conf. Am. Studies, Cambridge, 1952, Hyderabad, 1964. Bd. dirs. Harry S. Truman Library, 1958-61. Fellow Center Advanced Study in Behavioral Scis., 1956. Recipient award for dist. scholarship Am. Council Learned Soc., 1960. Hon. fellow Wis. Acad. Sci., Arts and Letters; mem. Am. Assn. U. Profs., Am. Hist. Assn. (pres. 1953-54), Miss. Valley Hist. Assn. (bd. editors 1936- 40; pres. 1951-52), Wis. Hist. Soc. (bd. of curators), Soc. Sci. Research Council, Am. Council Learned Socs. (vice chmn. bd. dirs. 1958-59), Am. Phil. Soc., Am. Acad. Arts and Scis., Nat. Council for Social Studies Phi Beta Kappa (senator 1947-52, pres. Wis. 1957-58), Phi Alpha Theta. Clubs: University; Harvard (N.Y.). Author: Austria and the U.S. 1848- 1852, 1947; Am. Peace Crusade, 1929; Bryan and World Peace, 1931; Social Ideas of Am. Educators, 1935; The Learned Blacksmith; Letters and Jours. of Elihu Burritt, 1937; Growth of Am. Thought (Pulitzer Award), 1943; Introduction to Am., 1944; Roots of Am. Loyalty, 1946; (with Vernon Carstensen) U. of Wis., a history, 1949; (with L. P. Todd) Am.'s Hist. 1950; (with W. Thorp and C. Baker) American Issues, 1950; (with R.H. Shryock, T.C. Cochran and F.H. Harrington) An American History, 1950; (with others) American Scholarship in the Twentieth Century, 1953; (with Kendall Birr) Prelude to Point Four, 1954; Probing Our Past, 1955; The American Paradox, 1956; The Making of an American Community, 1959; (with Paul Todd) Rise of the American Nation, 1960; American Philanthropy Abroad: A History, 1963; (with Roderick Nash) Philanthropy in the Shaping of American Higher Education, 1965; Rise of the American Nation, 1966; Human Nature in American Historial Thought, 1969, also articles. Contbr. to scholarly periodicals. Home: 2015 Van Hise Av Madison WI 53705 also Lyme Center NH 03769

CURTIN, DAVID YARROW, educator, chemist; b. Phila., Aug. 22, 1920; s. Ellsworth Ferris and Margeretta (Cope) C.; A.B., Swarthmore Coll., 1943; Ph.D., U. Ill., 1945; m. Constance O'Hara, July 1, 1950; children—Susan McLean, Kathy Gardner, David Ferris, Jane Yarrow. Pvt. asst. Harvard, 1945-46; instr., then asst. prof. chemistry Columbia, 1946-51; mem. faculty U. Ill., Urbana, 1951—, prof. chemistry, 1954—, head div. organic chemistry, 1963-65. Vis. lectr. Inst. de Quimica (Mexico), summer 1955, U. Tex., 1959; Reilly lectr. U. Notre Dame, 1960. Mem. Am., Brit., Swiss chem. socs., Nat. Acad. Sci., Am. Crystallographic Assn. Mem. editorial bd. Organic Reactions, 1954- 64, adv. bd., 1965—; mem. bd. editors Jour. Organic Chemistry, 1962-66. Spl. research organic reaction mechanisms, stereochemistry, exploratory organic chemistry, reactions in solid state. Home: 3 Montclair Rd Urbana IL 61801

CURTIN, FRANK DANIEL, educator; b. Crafton, Pa., Nov. 10, 1905; s. Daniel Francis and Clara (Schlessman) C.; B.A., U. Pitts., 1927, M.A., 1929; Ph.D., U. Chgo., 1939; m. Mary McKenna, Sept. 16, 1941; children—Daniel, Jeremy, Hugh, Elizabeth. Instr. English, U. Pitts., 1929-38; instr. English, Cornell U., 1938-42; asst. prof. English, St. Lawrence U., Canton, N.Y., 1942-45, asso. prof., 1945-47, prof., 1948-71, prof. emeritus, 1971—, chmn. dept., 1948-71; asso. prof. English, Washington and Jefferson Coll., 1947-48. Ford fellow, 1953-54; Ford Humanities grantee, 1970. Mem. Am. Assn. U. Profs., Modern Lang. Assn., Omicron Delta Kappa. Contbr. books, articles profl. jours. Home: 52 E Main St Canton NY 13617

CURTIN, JOHN T., judge; b. 1921; B.S., Canisius Coll., Buffalo; LL.B., U. Buffalo. Admitted to bar, 1949; formerly U.S. atty. Western Dist. N.Y.; U.S. dist. judge Western Dist. N.Y., 1967-.

CURTIN, JOHN WILLIAM, plastic surgeon; b. Pjtts., Mar. 1, 1922; s. Patrick John and Nelle (Joyce) C.; B.S., U. Pitts., 1943, M.D., 1947; m. Jean Ellen Stewart, Dec. 29, 1951; childrenJohn William, Shawn Ellen. Intern Mercy Hosp., Pitts., 1947-48; surg. resident Pitts. Hosp., 1948-50, U.S. Naval Hosp., 1950-51; resident plastic surgery U. Ill. Research and Ednl. Hosp., 1953- 55; mem. faculty U. Ill. Coll. Medicine, 1953-, clin. prof. surgery, head div. plastic surgery, 1964-; attending plastic surgeon U. Ill. Hosp., 1953—, W. Side VA Hosp., 1954—, Cleft Palate Center, U. Ill. Coll. Medicine, 1955-, Presbyn.-St. Luke's Hosp., 1953- ; cons. plastic surgery C., R. I. & P. R.R., Chgo. Municipal Tb Sanitarium, Chgo. Tb Sanitarium, Great Lakes Naval Hosp. Served with USNR, 1950-52; Korea. Diplomate Am. Bd. Plastic Surgery. Mem. A.M.A., Ill., Chgo., Pa. med. socs., Chgo., Central surg. assns., A.C.S., Am. Soc. Plastic and Reconstructive Surgeons, Inst. Medicine Chgo., Midwest Surg. Assn., Am. Assn. Plastic Surgeons, Soc. Internat. de Chirurgie, Am. Cleft Palate Assn., Clin. Soc. U. Surgeons, Pan-Am., Pan-Pacific med. assns., Am. Assn. Surgery Trauma. Contbr. med. jours. Home: 1180 Hill Rd Winnetka, IL 60093. Office: 310 S Michigan Av Chicago IL 60604

CURTIN, PHILIP DE ARMOND, educator, historian; b. Phila., May 22, 1922; s. Ellsworth F. and Margaretta (Cope) C.; B.A., Swarthmore Coll., 1948; M.A., Harvard, 1949, Ph.D., 1953; m. Phyllis Smith, Aug. 24, 1946 (div. 1956); m. 2d, Anne Gilbert, Sept. 14, 1957; children—Steven D., Charles G., Christopher C. Instr. then asst. prof. Swarthmore Coll., 1953-56; mem. faculty U. Wis., Madison, 1956—, prof. history, 1961—, M.J. Herskovits prof. history and African studies, 1970—, chmn. program comparative tropical history, 1959-, chmn. African studies program, 1961-64, acting chmn. dept. African langs. and lit., 1963-64. Mem. joint com. Africa Social Sci. Research Council-Am. Council Learned Socs., 1963—. Served with U.S. Merchant Marine, 1943-46. Ford fellow, 1958-59; Guggenheim fellow, 1966. Mem. African Studies Assn. (pres. 1971, past dir.), Am. Hist. Assn. (council 1967-70), Social Sci. Research Council (council 1967—), Conf. Brit. Studies, Phi Beta Kappa. Author: Two Jamaicas, 1955; The Image of Africa, 1964; (with Michael B. Petrovich) The Human Achievement, 1967; Africa Remembered, 1967; The Atlantic Slave Trade: A Census, 1969; (with Paul Bohannan) Africa and Africans, 1971. Contbg. editor Current History, 1955-59; editorial bd. Jour. African History, 1960—. Home: 3964 Plymouth Circle Madison WI 53705

CURTIN, PHYLLIS, singer; b. Clarksburg, W.Va.; d. E. Vernon and Betty R. (Robinson) Smith; student Monticello Coll., 1939-41; B.A., Wellesley College, 1943; m. Eugene Cook, May 6, 1956; 1 dau., Claudia Madeleine. Made recital debut, Town Hall, N.Y.C., 1950, 53, 57; opera debut N.Y.C. Opera in U.S. premiere of The Trial, 1953; recitals throughout U.S. and fgn. countries; soprano soloist, leading symphony orchestras; performer, tchr. Aspen Mus. Festival, 1953-57; appeared as Cressida in Troilus and Cressida in N.Y. premiere, 1955; title role in Susannah, world premiere, Tallahassee, 1955; title role in Medea, U.S. premiere, Brandeis U., 1955; world premiere opera Wuthering Heights, 1958; leading soprano Vienna Staatsoper, 1960, 61; debut Met. Opera Co. as Fiordiligi in Cosi Fan Tutte, 1961; debut La Scala Opera, Milan, 1962; guest soloist Stuttgart, Frankfurt opera cos., 1961-62; world premiere opera Passion of Jonathan Wade, N.Y.C. Opera, 1962; world premier of Darius Milhaud's opera La Mère Coupable, Geneva, Switzerland, 1966. Home: 110 Riverside Dr New York City NY 10024 Office: 113 W 57th St New York City NY 10019

CURTIN, RICHARD DANIEL, retired air force officer, corp. exec.; b. Taunton, Mass., Apr. 2, 1915; s. Patrick Henry and Della (Hart) C.; student Brown U., 1933-35; B.Sc., U.S. Mil. Acad., 1939; M.Sc., U. Mich., 1950. Commd. 2d lt. U.S. Army, 1939, advanced through grades to maj. gen. USAF, 1963; various assignments U.S., Panama, Eng., France, Germany, 1939-46; instr. Air U., Maxwell AFB, Ala., 1946-48; plans officer, war plans div. Hdqrs. USAF, Washington, 1950-54; dir. plans, later chief staff Hdqrs. 17th AF, North Africa, 1954-56; exec. weapons systems Hdqrs. ARDC, Balt., 1956-58; asst. dep. comdr. tech. operations, dep. comdr. space programs AF Ballistic Missile Div., Inglewood, Cal., 1958-60; dir. systems devel., DCS/D, Hdqrs. USAF, Washington, 1960; dir. Office Space Programs, Office Sec. Air Force, Washington, 1960-62; dir. devel. plans DCS/R&D, Hdqrs. USAF, Washington, 1962-65; dep. def. advisor USRO, NATO, Paris, France, 1965-67, ret., 1967; v.p., dir. Southwestern Research & Gen. Investment Corp., Phoenix, 1967—; dir. mgmt. engring. Bell Aerosystems Co., Buffalo. Decorated Legion of Merit with 2 clusters, Bronze Star with cluster; Distinguished Service Citation (Dept. Air Force); Croix de Guerre, etoile Vermeille. Fellow Am. Inst. Aeros. and Astronautics; mem. Air Force Assn., Am. Ordnance Assn. Roman Catholic. Club: Army-Navy. Office: 31 E Boca Raton Rd Phoenix AZ 85022

CURTIN, ROBERT HARRIMAN, government ofcl.; b. Winchendon, Mass., July 27, 1916; s. James Francis and Anne (Harriman) C.; student Rensselaer Poly. Inst., 1934-35; B.S., U.S. Mil. Acad., 1939; M.S., Harvard, 1948; grad. Air War Coll., 1954, Indsl. Coll. Armed Forces, 1957-58; m. Jane Helen Quinn, June 24, 1939; children—Robert Harriman, Jane Harriman. Commd. 2d lt., C.E., U.S. Army, 1939, advanced through grades to maj. gen. USAF, 1947; assigned C.Z., 1939-43, Fla., 1943-44, ETO, 1944-47; with Directorate Installations, Hdqrs. USAF, 1948-53; dep. chief staff installations, Hdqrs. 3d Air Force, U.K., 1954-57; with Directorate Civil Engring., Hdqrs. USAF, Washington, 1957-, dir. civil engring., 1963-68, ret., 1968; dir. facilities NASA, 1968—. Decorated Legion of Merit, Bronze Star with oak leaf cluster, Air Force Commendation medal; Croix de Guerre with palm, Order Leopold with palm (Belgium). Registered profl. engr., D.C. Mem. Nat. Soc. Profl. Engrs., Am. Inst. Plant Engrs., Am. Soc. C.E., Soc. Am. Mil. Engrs. (pres. 1964-65). Club: Army Navy Country (chmn. bd. govs. 1962-65, pres. 1964-66) (Arlington, Va.). Home: 3604 Orlando Pl Alexandria VA 22305 Office: NASA Washington DC 20546

CURTIN, TERRENCE MICHAEL, vet. physiologist, educator; b. Spencer, S.D., June 9, 1926; s. Leo J. and Margaret (Carlon) C.; student S.D. State U., 1946-50; B.S., U. Minn., 1953, D.V.M., 1954; M.S., Purdue U., 1963, Ph.D., 1964; m. Betty A. Duetsch, Dec. 26, 1952; children—Melissa, Joseph, Laura, James. Pvt. practice vet. medicine, Emery, S.D., 1954-58; postdoctoral fellow, asst. prof. Purdue U., 1958-66; prof., chmn. dept. vet. physiology and pharmacology U. Mo. at Columbia, 1966—. Served with AUS, 1943-46. Mem. Am., Mo. vet. med. assns., Am. Phys. Soc., N.Y. Acad. Sci., A.A.A.S., Am. Soc. Animal Science Research Workers Animal Diseases, Sigma Xi, Phi Zeta. Home: 208 Rothwell Dr Columbia MO 65201

CURTIS, ANTHONY, (Tony), actor; b. N.Y.C., June 3, 1925; s. Manuel and Helen (Klein) Schwartz; student drama New Sch. Social Research; m. Janet Leigh, June 4, 1951 (div.); children—Kelly, Jamie; m. second, Christine Kaufmann, February 8, 1963; children—Alexandra, Allegra; m. third, Leslie Allen, April 20, 1968. Motion picture actor under contract to Universal Pictures, 1948—; movie roles include Houdini, Black Shield of Falworth, Six Bridges to Cross, So This is Paris; Trapeze; Mister Cory; The Eyes of Father Tomasino; Sweet Smell of Success; Midnight Story; The Vikings; Defiant Ones; Some Like It Hot; Perfect Furlough; Spartacus; The Great Imposter; Pepe; The Outsider; Taras Bulba; Forty Pounds off Trouble; Paris When it Sizzles; The List of Adrian Messenger; Captain Newman; Wild and Wonderful; Sex and the Single Girl; Goodbye Charlie; The Great Race; Boeing, Boeing; Arriverderci, Baby; Not with My Wife, You Don't; Don't Make Waves; Boston Strangler; others. Club: Friars (Los Angeles). Office: care Joseph Warren Curtis Enterprises 6901 Wilshire Blvd Beverly Hills CA 90211

CURTIS, CARL THOMAS, U.S. senator; b. Minden, Neb., Mar. 15, 1905; s. Frank O. and Alberta Mae (Smith) C.; attended Neb. Wesleyan U., LL.D., 1958; m. Lois Wylie-Atwater, June 6, 1931 (dec. Sept. 1970); children—Clara Mae (Mrs. James A. Hopkins) (dec.), Carl Thomas. Tchr. Minden Schs.; admitted to Neb. bar, 1930, practiced in Minden, county atty., 1931-34; mem. 76th to 83d congresses, from 1st dist. Neb.; U.S. senator, 1955—. Mem. Neb. Bar Assn., Theta Chi. Republican. Presbyn. Mason, Odd Fellow, Elk, Rotarian. Home: Minden NB 68959 Office: Senate Office Bldg Washington DC 20510

CURTIS, CHARLOTTE MURRAY, editor; b. Chgo.; d. George Morris and Lucile (Atcherson) Curtis; B.A. in Am. History, Vassar Coll., 1950. Reporter, society editor Columbus (O.) Citizen, 1950-61; reporter N.Y. Times, 1961—, women's news editor, 1965—. Freelance writer, 1950—; tchr. narrative and short story writing Columbus (O.) YWCA, 1952-54; radio commentator sta. WMNI, Columbus, 1959-60, sta. WQXR, N.Y.C. Founder, pres. Young Assos. Columbus Symphony Orch.; chmn. edn. Columbus Jr. League, 1958-60; mem. N.Y. Jr. League, 1964—. Recipient various awards for reporting, writing N.Y. Newspaper Women's Club, Ohio Newspaper Women's Assn., Am. Newspaper Women's Club. Mem. N.Y. Newspaper Women's Club, N.Y. Reporters Assn., Am. Newspaper Guild (v.p. Columbus local 13, 1956 60). Author: First Lady, 1963. Home: 40 E 10th St New York City NY 10003 Office: 229 W 43d St New York City NY 10036

CURTIS, DORIS S. MALKIN, geologist; b. Bklyn., Jan. 12, 1914; d. Meyer and Mary (Berkowitz) Malkin; B.A., Bklyn. Coll., 1933; M.A., Columbia, 1934, Ph.D., 1949. Paleontologist, stratigrapher, geologist Shell Oil, 1942-50, stratigrapher, 1959-61, sr. geologist, 1961-66, staff geologist, 1966- -; asst., then asso. prof. geology U. Houston, 1950-52; research geologist Scripps Instn. Oceanography, 1952-54; asst. prof. geology, asso. prof. U. Okla., 1955-59. Fellow A.A.A.S., Geol. Soc. of Am.; mem. League Women Voters (dir. La.), Am. Assn. Petroleum Geologists, Internat. Assn. Sedimentologists, Soc. Econ. Paleontologists and Mineralogists, Fedn. Am. Scientists, Sigma Xi. Home: 996 Germain St New Orleans LA 70124 Office: PO Box 60775 New Orleans LA 70160

CURTIS, DOUGLAS ARCHIBALD, mfg. exec.; b. Lima, O., Apr. 1, 1932; B.S., U. San Francisco, 1954; M.S., Stanford University, 1956; m. Rosemarie Lois Brown, May 15, 1955; 1 son, Anthony Robinson. Sales rep. Ames-Brockton Fabricated Products, Akron, O., 1956-58, sales mgr. Coshocton, Ohio, 1959-61, gen. manager plant, 1961-68, v.p. sales, 1968--. Instr. bus. Coshocton Jr. College, 1968-69. Mem. Coshocton C. of C. (vice president 1967-68, pres. 1969-70), English Speaking Union, Coshocton Sertoma Club, Nat. Assn. Mfrs., Sales Executives Institute, Phi Beta Kappa, Sigma Chi, Phi Mu. Democrat. Mem. Christian Ch. (lay reader). Mason (32, Shriner). Clubs: Coshocton Country, Coshocton City, Running Deer Country. Home: 2d Av Coshocton OH Office: 3d Av Coshocton OH

CURTIS, EDWARD PECK, banker; b. Rochester, N.Y., Jan. 14, 1897; s. Guerney T. and Alice (Peck) C.; student Williams Coll., 1914-16, M.A. (hon.), 1941; LL.D., Hobart Coll., 1949, U. Rochester, 1949; D.Sc. (hon.), Stevens Inst. Tech., 1957; m. Agness Bartlett, Oct. 25, 1924; children—Diane (Mrs. Sherwood Francis), Ruth (Mrs. C.F. Hoffman), Edward Peck. Joined Eastman Kodak Co., Rochester, 1921, sales mgr. motion picture film dept., 1929, v.p. in charge motion picture film bus. supr. gen. bus. Europe, 1945, also dir.; chmn. exec. com. Security Trust Co., Rochester; dir. Mohawk Airlines. Dir. Nat. Fgn. Trade Council; apptd. spl. asst. to Pres. Eisenhower for aviation facilities planning, 1956. Bd. dirs. Rochester Community Chest; bd. govs. A.R.C.; bd. visitors Air Force Acad. Served with Am. Field Service, 1916-17; combat pilot 95th Aero Squadron, AAF; mem. Gen. W. Mitchell's staff; sec. U.S. commr. Baltic Provinces of Russia, 1917-19, disch. as maj.; asst. exec. to Gen. Spaatz, chief staff strategic Air Force, Europe, advancing from maj. to maj. gen., World War II Decorated D.S.C., D.S.M., Legion of Merit, Silver Star, Bronze Star medal; companion of Bath (Gt. Britain); Russian Order of St Anne; Legion of Honor, Croix de Guerre' (France); recipient Collier Trophy Nat. Aero. Assn., 1958. Mem. Rochester C. of C. (trustee), Rochester Assn. of UN (dir.), Air Force Assn. (dir.). Clubs: Country, Genesee Valley (Rochester); University, Wings (N.Y.C.); Bucks (London, Eng.); Travellers (Paris, France); Metropolitan (Washington). Home: 3541 Elmwood Av Rochester NY 14610 Office: 1 East Av Rochester NY 14604

CURTIS, ELLWOOD F., business exec.; b. Mishawka, Ind., May 14, 1914; s. Warren H. and Marian (Robbins) C.; A.B., Dartmouth, 1935; m. Helen Yeomans, Apr. 12, 1936; children—Count, Don, Barron. Accountant Haskins & Sells, 1935-39; accountant Deere & Co., 1939-44, became comptroller, 1944, dir., 1951—, pres., 1964—. Mason. Club: Union League, Chicago (Chgo.). Home: 4005 7th Av Moline IL 61265 Office: Deere & Co John Deere Rd Moline IL 61265

CURTIS, GARNISS HEARFIELD, educator; b. San Rafael, Cal., Man 27, 1919; s. Chester A. and Garniss (Hearfield) C.; B.S., U. Cal. at Berkely, 1942, Ph.D., 1951; m. Dorette Davis, May 15, 1942; children—Penelope (Dudley Yasuda), Ann, Robin. Mining engr. Christmas Copper Corp. (Ariz.), 1942-45; geologist Shell Oil Co., 1945-46; mem. faculty U. Cal. at Berkeley, 1949—, prof. geology, 1964—; mem. U.S. Geol. Survey, 1954-69. Recipient Newcomb Cleveland award A.A.A.S., 1962. Fellow Cal. Acad. Sci.; mem. Geol. Soc. Am., Am. Geophys. Union. Home: 10 St James Ct Orinda CA 94563 Office: Dept Geology and Geophysics Univ Cal Berkeley CA 94720

CURTIS, GEORGE MARTIN, II, former bus. exec.; b. Clinton, Ia., Aug. 8, 1905; s. George L. and (Wilcox) C.; student Hotchkiss Sch., 1920-23; A.B., Yale, 1927; LL.D., Parsons Coll.; m. Louise Scully, Oct. 3, 1931 (dec. 1956—. Instr. municipal corps, Denver Law Sch., 1937-41. Served to lt. dept. Curtis Cos., Inc., Clinton, 1928-34, traveling sales rep., 1935-40, sec., 1938-47, v.p., sec., 1947-50, exec. v.p., 1950-51, pres., 1951-61, chmn. bd., pres., 1959-61, chmn. bd., 1961-70, ret., Mem. staff lumber code authority NRA, Washington, 1934. Mem. Nat. Office: First Nt Bank Bldg Denver CO 80202 pres., past treas.), Ponderosa Pine Woodwork Assn. (past pres.), N.A.M. (past dir.), U.S. C. of C. (past nat. counselor). Presbyn. Mason Clubs: Clinton (Ia.) Country; Tavern (Chgo.) Home: 1115 2d Av Rd Clinton IA 52732 Office: 114 12th Av S Clinton, IA

CURTIS, GILBERT LEWIS, air force officer; b. Bridgeport, Conn., Aug. 29, 1917; s. John Burr and Hester (Lewis) C.; student Lehigh U., 1938; student Air Comd. and Staff Coll. 1950, Indsl. Coll. Armed Forces, 1960; m. Lorraine Johnson, Feb. 12, 1942; children—Gilber Lewis II, John Elliott, Charles Lloyd, Robert William, James Murray. Commd. 2d lt. USAAF, 1940, advanced through grades to maj. gen., USAF, 1954; with Hdqrs. USAF, also Mil. Airlift Command, Scott AFB, Ill., 1971—. Bd. dirs. N.Y. USO. Mem. Air Force Assn., Order Daedalians. Home: 153 W 8th St Scott AFB IL 62225 Office: Hdqrs MAC Scott AFB IL 62225

CURTIS, HENRY BALDWIN, lawyer; b. New Orleans, Dec. 7, 1895; s. Edward Burnham and Hallette Sarsvield (Baldwin) C.; A.B., Loyola U., New Orleans, 1914; LL.B., 1917; student U. Paris (France), 1919; m. Marquerite B. Grant, Dec. 5, 1923. Admitted to La. bar, 1917; practice in New Orleans, 1919—; asst. city atty., New Orleans, 1925-40, 46-49, city attorney, 1949-57; mem. firm Curtis, Foster, Hyde & Mooney, predecessors, 1921—. Pres., dir. La. So. Ry. Co., 1938-40; div. counsel So. Ry. Co., 1953—. sec.-treas. New Orleans Cultural Centre Commn. Mem. New Orleans Council, 1957—. Bd. curators Cabildo, 1953-56. Served with La. N.G. on Mexican Border, 1916; as 2d lt., F.A., U.S. Army, 1917-18; AEF in France; served to col., F.A., AUS, 1941-46; ETO. Decorated Bronze Star medal. Mem. Am. (chmn. municipal law sect. 1960-61), La., New Orleans bar assns., Nat. Inst. Municipal Law Officers (pres. 1954-55). Roman Catholic. Home: 8142 Panola St New Orleans LA 70118 Office: 707 Nat Bank Commerce Bldg New Orleans LA 70112

CURTIS, HOWARD JAMES, physiologist; b. Lansing, Mich., Dec. 11, 1906; s. Harvey Lincoln and Anna (Puffer) C.; B.S., U. Mich., 1928; A.M., Swarthmore Coll., 1929; Redlands , 1970—; instr. summer Ph.D., Yale, 1932; Rockefeller fellow Johns Hopkins Sch. Medicine, com. Inst. Internat. Edn.; 1938-40; m. Dorothy Albert, Aug. 27, 1932; children—Brian Albert, Richard Harvey, Barbara Ann. Biophysicist, The Biol. Lab., Cold Springs Harbor, N.Y., 1932-35; asso. in physiology Coll. Physicians and Surgeons, Columbia, 1935-38, asst. prof. physiology, 1941-43, asso. prof., 1946-47; prof. of physiology and head physiology dept. Vanderbilt Redlands Racquet. Author articles in U.S. U. Med. Sch., 1947-50. Med. cons. to AEC, 1946—; cons. in radiobiol. to USPHS, 1946—, chmn. radiation study sect., 1955—; mem. Nat. Com. on Radiation Protection; mem. sci. council of Am. Cancer Soc., 1956; cons. in radioisotopes to VA, 1948—. Del. Atoms for Peace Conf., Geneva, 1958. Active in adv. capacity in formulating nat. legislation of atomic energy and on NSF; mem. Nat. Council Radiation Protection, 1962—. Mem. NRC (mem. space sci. bd. 1959—, mem. com. on growth; chmn. com. on radiobiology); v.p. Radiation Research Soc., 1956; chmn. biology dept. Brookhaven Nat. Lab., 1950—. Mayor of Village of Shoreham, N.Y. Mem. bd. of sci. councilors Nat. Inst. Neurol. Diseases and Blindness, 1958—. Mem. L.I. Biol. Assn. (dir.), Am. Phys. Soc., Am. Physiol. Soc., Harvey Soc., A.A.A.S., N.Y. Acad. Sci. Author: (with J.H. Lawrence) Advances in Medical Physics, Vol.II, 1949; (with F.M. Liver) Biophysical Research Methods, 1949; (with Philip Bard) Medical Physiology; Biological Mechanisms of Aging. Editor: Physiological Reviews, 1951. Contbr. research articles to sci. publs. Home: Shoreham LI NY 11786 Office: Brookhaven Nat Labs Upton LI NY 11973 ☆

CURTIS, HUGH EVERETT, Jr., educator; b. Rock Island, Ill., June 19, 1907; s. Hugh Everett and Mary Augusta (Dart) C.; B.A., Grinnell Coll., 1931; m. Martha Page Hippee, Sept. 26, 1934; children—Hugh Everett III, Sara Easton. Asst. circulation mgr. Better Homes and Gardens mag., 1931-34; editorial asst. Successful Farming mag., 1934-35, asso. editor charge farm structures and housing, 1935-43, mng. editor charge structures and electricity, 1943-50; mng. editor Better Homes and Gardens mag., 1950-52; editor, 1952-60; editorial cons., dir. services div. Webb Pub. Co., St. Paul, 1960-62; prof., dean Sch. Journalism, Drake U., Des Moines, 1962-69, prof. mag. journalism, 1969—. Names Hon. Ia. Farmer, Future Farmers of Am., 1937. Mem. Indsl. Editors, Future Famrers Am., Phi Beta Kappa, Kappa Tau Alpha, Sigma Delta Chi, Omicron Delta Kappa. Episcopalian. Clubs: Embassy, Pow Wow, Advertising (Des Moines). Home: 7799 SW 52d Av Des Moines IA 50321

CURTIS, IVOL I., Protestant Episcopal bishop Diocese Olympia. Address: 1551 10th Av E Seattle WA 98102*

CURTIS, JEROME NATHANIEL, lawyer; b. Cleve., July 13, 1902; s. Nathan and Leah (Goldsmith) C.; A.B., Western Res. U., 1924, LL.B., 1926; m. Iris Goldberg, June 12, 1938; 1 son, Robert M. Admitted to Ohio bar, 1926, also U.S. Supreme Ct.; practiced in Cleve., 1926—; mem. Ulmer, Berne, Laronge, Glickman & Curtis; asst. U.S. atty., 1936-41; chief asst. U.S. atty., 1942-43; spl. asst. to atty. gen. U.S. for hearing of conscientious objector cases, 1948-55. Mem. Ohio Bd. Bar Examiners, 1938-43. Mem. Ohio Ho. of Reps., 1933-34. Past pres. Cleve. Jewish Childrens Bur.; past v.p., bd. dirs. Cleve. Jewish Community Fedn.; past bd. dirs. Cleve. Community Fund, Cleve. Welfare Fedn., Cleve. Law Library Assn., Bellefaire, Nat. Council Jewish Welfare Fedns. and Welfare Funds, Jewish Family Service Assn., Mt. Sinai Hosp. Cleve. Mem. Am., Fed., Ohio, Cuyahoga County, Cleve. bar assns., Am. Judicature Soc., Order of Coif, Phi Beta Kappa, Delta Sigma Rho. Home: 17607 Fernway Rd Shaker Heights OH 44120 Office: Keith Bldg Cleveland OH 44115

CURTIS, JESSE WILLIAM, Jr., U.S. dist. judge; b. San Bernardino, Cal., Dec. 26, 1905; s. Jesse William and Ida L. (Seymour) C.; A.B., U. Redlands, 1928; J.D., Harvard, 1931; m. Mildred F. Mort, Aug. 24, 1930; children—Suzanne, Jesse W., Clyde Hamliton, Christopher Cowles. Admitted to Cal. bar, 1931; pvt. practice, 1931-35; mem. firms Guthrie & Curtis, San Bernardino, 1935-40, Curtis & Curtis, 1946-50, Curtis, Knauf, Henry & Farrell, 1950-53; judge Superior Ct. of Cal., 1953-62; U.S. judge Central Dist. of Cal., 1962—. Chmn. San Bernardino Sch. Bd., 1942-46, mem. 1946-49; mem. Del Rosa Bd. Edn., 1950-53. Chmn. San Bernardino County Heart Fund; dir., past pres. YMCA; dir. Good Will Industries, Crippled Children's Soc., Arrowhead United Fund; adv. bd. Community Hosp. Mem. Am., Los Angeles County bar assns., Cal. State Bar, Am. Judicature Soc., Am. Law Inst., Los Angeles World Affairs Council, Town Hall, Phi Delta Phi. Democrat. Conglist. Club: Balboa Yacht. Home: 305 Evening Star Lane Newport Beach CA 92660 Office: US Court House Los Angeles CA 90012

CURTIS, JOHN KIMBERLY, physician; b. Redlands, Cal., Mar. 14, 1905; s. Clinton James and Lucy (Kimberly) C.; B.A., Yale, 1928; M.D., Columbia, 1932; m. Margaret McAllister, Oct. 5, 1936; children—Kimberly J., James McAllister, Catherine. Intern, Presbyn. Hosp., N.Y.C., 1932-34, asst. attending physician, 1935-42; resident 1st div. Bellevue Hosp., N.Y.C., 1934-35; asso. prof. U. Wis., Madison, 1951-53, prof. internal medicine, 1953—; chief medicine VA Hosp., Madison, 1951-68. Served with M.C., USNR, 1942- 46; ETO. Mem. A.M.A., Wis. Heart Assn. (pres. 1956-57), Dane County Med. Soc. (pres. 1952-53). Research pulmonary physiology. Home: 3301 Topping Rd Madison WI 53705

CURTIS, JOSEPH, coll. dean; B.S., LL.B., LL.M., N.Y.U. Prof. law Coll. William and Mary, 1948-69, dean Marshall Wythe Sch. Law, 1962-69; Balt., 1969—. Address: Univ of Baltimore 1420 N Charles St Baltimore MD 21201

CURTIS, KENNETH MERWIN, gov. of Maine; b. Curtis Corner, Me., Feb. 8, 1931; s. Archie M. and Harriet (Turner) C.; B.S., Me. Maritime Acad., 1952; LL.B., Portland (Me.) U., 1959; LL.D., U. Me., 1967; m. Pauline Brown, Nov. 17, 1956; children—Susan (dec.), Angela. Admitted to Me. bar, 1959, also U.S. Supreme Ct., asst. to U.S. Congressman James C. Oliver, 1959-61; legislative research service, also legal research Library of Congress, 1961; coordinator Por Me., Area Redevel. Adminstrn., 1961-64; sec. of state Me., 1965-67; gov. of Me., 1967—. Chmn., New Eng. Govs. Conf.; co-chmn. New Eng. Regional Commn. Pres. So. Maine chpt. Nat. Cystic Fibrosis Research Found., 1962-63; dir. Me. March of Dimes, 1966-67, 68-69. Served with USNR, 1953-55. Mem. Am. Legion. Home: Blaine House State St Augusta ME 04330 Office: State House Augusta ME 04330

CURTIS, LEWIS PERRY, historian, educator; b. Southport, Conn., Nov. 3, 1900; s. Roderick Perry and Louisa (Wells) C.; B.A., Yale, 1923, Ph.D., 1926; m. Jeanet Ellinwood Sullivan, Dec. 26, 1929; children—Lewis Perry, Nancy Ellinwood (Mrs. Michael D. Padnos). Mem. faculty Yale, 1927-69, Colgate prof. history, 1967—. Traveling fellow Am. Council Learned Soc., 1931-32; Guggenheim fellow, 1941-42. Mem. Am. Hist. Assn. Editor: Letters of Laurence Sterne, 1935, 1965; Gibbon's Paradise Lost in the Age of Johnson, 1949; Chichester Towers, 1966; Anglican Moods of the Eighteenth Century, 1966. Home: 479 Whalley Av New Haven CT 06511

CURTIS, MARK HUBERT, coll. pres.; b. Medford, Minn., July 7, 1920; s. James Hubert and Lydia (Krueger) C.; B.A. Yale, 1942, M.A., 1947, Ph.D., 1953; m. Maria Isabel Bird y Zalduondo, Nov. 7, 1945; children—Mary Katherine, Thomas Mark. Instr. history Williams Coll., 1950-53; mem. faculty U. Cal. at Los Angeles, 1953-64, asso. prof. history, 1959-64, asso. dean grad. div., 1962-64; pres. Scripps Coll., Claremont, Cal., 1964—; lectr. Danforth Summer Seminar, Pacific Sch. Religion, Berkeley, Cal., 1957; fellow Folger Shakespeare Library, 1962, research prof., cons., summer 1964. Mem. Am. Council Edn. Commn. Acad. Affairs, Assn. Am. Colls. Commn. Liberal Learning; exec. com. Anglo.-Am. Assos., Yale Grad. Sch. Alumni Assn. Trustee Claremont Area Pastoral Counselling Center, Westridge Sch., Pasadena, Hawaii Loa Coll., Honolulu, Loyola U., Los Angeles, Conf. Brit. Studies. Served to lt. comdr. USNR, 1942-46. Social Sci. Research Council fellow, 1948-49; Guggenheim fellow, 1959-60. Fellow Soc. Religion in Higher Edn., Royal Hist. Soc.; mem. Am. Hist. Assn. (Robert Livingston Schuyler prize, 1961), Renaissance Soc. Am., Renaissance Conf. of So. Cal. (treas. 1956-59, pres. 1963-64), Western Coll. Assn. (pres.). Presbyn. Author: Oxford and Cambridge in Transition, 1558-1642, 1959; also articles. Home: President's House Scripps Coll Claremont CA 91711

CURTIS, MONTGOMERY JAMES, chemist, educator; b. Chicago, 1928; B.S. in Physics, Yale, 1950; Ph.D. in Chemistry, Harvard, 1956; m. Sally Ann Jones, July 5, 1957; children--Kenneth J., Nancy A. Chemist, Acme Chem. Co., Blue Island, Ill., 1950-51; director of Reseach Lab., Indsl. Chemicals Corp., Cambridge, Mass., 1956-60; project coordinator environmental sect. Steinmetz Assos., Chgo., 1960-61; v.p. for reseach Bauer Bros. Chem. Co., Inc., Memphis, 1961-64; asst. prof. chemistry Washington U., St. Louis, 1964-66, asso. prof., 1966-70, prof., 1970--, head of chemistry dept., 1970-71. Vis. prof. So. Ill. U., summer 1967, U. of Ore., 1969. Scoutmaster, Boy Scouts America, University City, Mo., 1968-70. Bd. dirs. Rest Haven Home for Elderly, 1960-61; trustee of the Lutheran Hosp., 1965-71. Served from lt. to capt., AUS, 1951-53. Mem. Am. Chem. Soc., Sci. Research Soc. Am. (chpt. treas. 1967), Sigma Xi. Author: (with others) Basic Inorganic Chemistry, 1971. Contbr. articles to profl. jours., encys., also chpts. to books. Home: Fairfax Apts 7291 Windermere Dr University City MO 63105 Office: Dept Chemistry Washington University St Louis MO 63130

CURTIS, MORTIMER WILLIAMS, educator, biologist; b. Ames, Ia.; B.A., Ia. State U., 1936, M.A., 1937, Ph.D. with honors, 1940. Instr., Ia. State U., 1946-47; asst. prof. biology Johns Hopkins, 1947-50, asso. prof., 1950-62, prof., 1962--, chmn. dept., 1963-69; vis. lectr. Stanford, 1970-71. Active Boy Scouts Am., 4-H Club. Served with AUS, 1940-46. Mem. Am. Soc. Biologists, Md. Soc. Cell Biológists, Am. Soc. Exptl. Biology, Internat. Union Biologists, A.A.A.S., Am. Acad. Arts and Scis., Phi Beta Kappa. Home: 48936 W Hancock Blvd Baltimore MD 20206

CURTIS, PHILIP C., artist; b. Jackson, Mich., May 26, 1907; A.B., Albion Coll., 1930; postgrad. law U. Mich.; certificate Yale Sch. Fine Arts, 1935; hon. degree Albion Coll., 1971. Exhibited one-man shows San Francisco Mus. Art, 1949, Ariz. State Coll., Tempe, 1957, Phoenix Art Mus., 1960, 63, Knoedler's, N.Y.C., 1964, Cal. Palace Legion of Honor, 1966, Feingarten Gallery, Los Angeles, 1966, Betty Thomen's Gallery, Basel, Switzerland, 1967, Galerie Krugier et Cie, Geneva, 1967, Ariz. State U., Tempe, 1970, U. Ariz., Tucson, 1970, Amon Carter Mus. Western Art, Ft. Worth, 1970, Okla. Art Center, Oklahoma City, 1970, Coe Kerr Gallery, N.Y.C., 1970, Palm Springs (Cal.) Desert Mus., 1971; group show Weyhe Gallery, N.Y.C., 1950. Supr. mural painting WPA Art Project, N.Y.C., 1935. Established Phoenix Art Center (now Phoenix Art Mus.), 1936. Fellow Royal Soc. Arts. Address: 109 Cattle Track Scottsdale AZ 85251*

CURTIS, PHILIP CHADSEY, Jr., educator; b. Providence, Mar. 6, 1928; s. Philip C. and Marion (Brown) C.; A.B., Brown U., 1950; M.A., Yale, 1952, Ph.D., 1955; m. Dorothy K. Smith, July 15, 1950; children—Philip C. III, Anne, Peter, Marion, Alan. Fulbright fellow, 1950-51; asst. prof. mathematics U. Cal. at Los Angeles, 1957-61, asso. prof., 1961-67, prof., 1967—, vice chmn. dept., 1967-71, chmn. dept., 1971—; vis. prof. U. Aarhus (Denmark), 1969-70; cons. T.R.W., 1956-69. Served with AUS, 1946-47. Mem. Am. Math. Assn., Math. Assn. Am., Phi Beta Kappa, Sigma Xi. Home: 3441 Grandview Blvd Los Angeles CA 90066

CURTIS, RALPH, educator; b. Cuba City, Wis., Oct. 20, 1936; s. Thomas J. and Wilda (Sampson) C.; B.S., Wis. State U. at Platteville, 1958; Ph.D., Ia. State U., 1962; m. Rita Vaassen, July 16, 1957; children—Michael, Catherine, Kelly. Postdoctoral asso. Ia. State U., 1962-63; asst. prof. to prof. chemistry Wis. State U. at Platteville, 1963-69, head chemistry dept., 1969—. U.S. Steel fellow, 1959-61. Mem. Am. Chem. Soc., Am. Soc. Metals. Home: 885 Hathaway St Platteville WI 53818

CURTIS, RICHARD KENNETH, educator; b. Worcester, Mass., Jan. 22, 1924; s. Albert Wyman and Vena (Masters) C.; Th.B., No. Bapt. Theol. Sem., 1950; M.S., Purdue U., 1951, Ph.D., 1954; m. M. Elizabeth Fisher, July 7, 1945; children—Stephen Dana, David Alan, Laurel Elizabeth. Ordained to ministry Bapt. Ch., 1951; pastor Russiaville (Ind.) Bapt. Ch., 1947-52; chmn. speech-English dept. Barrington (R.I.) Coll., 1952-56; chmn. speech dept. Bethel Coll., St. Paul, 1956-62; sr. minister Immanuel Bapt. Ch., Kansas City, Kan., 1962-67; chmn. speech dept. Muskingum Coll., New Concord, O., 1967-69; prof., chmn. dept. communication Ind. U.-Purdue U. at Indpls., 1969—. Gen. chmn. Community Coll. Expansion Council, Kansas City, Kan., 1966-67. Served to 1st lt. USAAF, 1943-46. Decorated D.F.C. Mem. Speech Communication Assn. (chmn. research com. Religious Interest Group 1957-62), Am. Assn. U. Profs. Author: They Called Him Mister Moody, 1962. Home: 4525 Berkshire Av Indianapolis IN 46226

CURTIS, RICHARD LEIGH, banker; b. Howe, Okla., Nov. 19, 1923; s. James Konrad and Laura (Knowlton) C.; student S.D. State Coll., 1941-42, Macalester Coll., St. Paul, 1945-46, Rutgers U., 1958-61; m. June E. Swanson, Apr. 4, 1953; children-Christopher, Laurel. Asst. mgr. Brookings br. N.W. Nat. Bank of Sioux Falls, S.D., 1940-42; nat. bank examiner 9th Fed. Res. Dist., Mpls., 1947-59; v.p. First Nat. Bank, St. Paul, 1959-63; pres. Michigan Av. Nat. Bank, Chgo., 1963—; dir. Michigan Av. Financial Group, Inc., First Drovers Corp. Treas. United Cerebral Palsy Greater Chgo., 1968-71; commr. Chgo. Area council Boy Scouts Am., 1969-71. Trustee Ill. Masonic Hosp., Chgo. Foundlings Home. Served with USAAF, 1943-45. Home: 20 Brighton Lane Oak Brook IL 60521 Office: 30 N Michigan Av Chicago IL 60602

CURTIS, ROBERT BOSWELL, govt. ofcl.; b. Nevada, Mo., Sept. 4, 1909; s. Ross Blair and Emily Adeline (Gilbreath) C.; student U. Cal., 1946-47; m. Evelyn Gabrielle Fillmore, Feb. 14, 1942. Purchasing mgr. Buzza-Cardozo, Los Angeles, 1935-42; with various C.P.A. firms, 1946-48; auditor U.S. Army Audit Agy., 1948-51; with Fgn. Aid Missions, State Dept., 1951—, controller in P.I., Yugoslavia, Pakistan, Korea, India, Brazil, 1951-70, area auditor gen. for Latin Am. S., including Argentina, Bolivia, Brazil, Chile, Paraguay, Uruguay, 1970—. Served with AUS, 1942-45. C.P.A., Cal. Episcopalian. Clubs: Yacht, Itanhanga Golf (Rio de Janeiro). Home: 3902-15 Vista Campana N Oceanside CA 92054 Office: AID Rio de Janeiro AAG APO New York City NY 09676

CURTIS, ROGER WILLIAM, artist, art instr.; b. Gloucester, Mass., Dec. 20, 1910; s. William Howard and Etta Elinda (Elwell) C.; grad. Burdett Coll., 1931; student Boston U., 1938-39, also pvt. art studies; m. Winifred Joan Fountain, Sept. 30, 1939; children—Hannah Joan, Alan Howard, William Arthur, David Philip. Art instr. specializing marines; painting demonstrations on technique of seascapes; exhbns., Boston, N.Y.C., Sheldon Swope Mus., Terre Haute, Ind., Chgo., Detroit, Fresno, Cal.; treas. Cape Ann Festival of Arts, 1951-59; dir. Burlington Art Gallery, 1954-59, Boston Gallery, 1957-62; dir. Mass., Nat. Art Week, 1958; cons. exhbns. for circulation; works in permanent exhbns. hosps., schs., art galleries, also pvt. collections; founder New Eng. Artists Group, 1961—; art dir. Legendsea Gallery of A. T. Hibbard; art dir. Downtown Gallery, Boston, 1966—. Treas. Patterson Co. Inc., Boston, 1935-55. Treas., Com. for Fair Representation in Art Exhbns. Inc. Recipient Waters of World award marine painting, 1968. Mem. Am. Artists Profl. League (v.p. Boston chpt. 1962), Copley Soc. (bd. govs. 1957-60), North Shore Arts Assn. (pres. 1955-59, dir. 1960-63, treas. 1966—), Burlington Art Assn. (pres. 1958- 62), New Eng. Guild Fine Arts (treas.), Concord Art Assn. (dir.), Guild Boston Artists (bd. mgrs. 1969, treas. 1970—). Mason. Home and office: 30 Riverview Rd Gloucester MA 01930

CURTIS, ROY, paper co. exec.; b. Oldham, Eng., Jan. 30, 1921; s. Alfred and Ethel (Eckersley) C.; C.A., Queens U., 1945; m. Marion Edith Steele, Aug. 14, 1943; 1 son, Michael Roy. Sr. auditor P.S. Ross & Sons, chartered accountants, Toronto, Ont., 1940- 45; treas. Canadian Breweries, Ltd., Toronto, 1945-55; comptroller Abitibi Paper Co., Ltd., Toronto, 1956—, also mem. mgmt. com. Served with Royal Canadian Ordnance Corps, 1943. Mem. Canadian Ont. insts. chartered accountants. Home: 8 Douglas Crescent Toronto Ontario Canada Office: Toronto Dominion Centre Toronto Ontario Canada

CURTIS, SAMUEL RALSTON, Jr., iron ore co. exec.; b. Cleve., Dec. 3, 1919; s. Samuel Ralston and Mary Elizabeth (Steinen) C.; B.A., Kenyon Coll., 1941; J.D., Cleve. Marshall Law Sch., 1953; m. Betty Ethel Hillier, Feb. 12, 1944; children—Deborah (Mrs. David P. Puffer), Gary Ralston. With Cleve.-Cliffs Iron Co., Cleve., 1941—, asst. sec., 1961-70, sec., 1970—. Served as capt., USAAF, 1941-45. Mem. Am., Ohio, Cleve. bar assns., Am. Soc. Corporate Secs., Delta Kappa Epsilon. Office: Union Commerce Bldg Cleveland OH 44115

CURTIS, STATON RUSSELL, univ. dean; b. Portland, Me., Mar. 19, 1921; s. Clarence Leroy and Eva May (Rand) C.; B.S., Gorham (Me.) State Coll., 1942; M.Ed., Springfield (Mass.) Coll., 1947; m. Ruth Alden, Oct. 17, 1943; children—Sharon Leigh, Martha Gail. Tchr.-coach pub. schs., Barre, Vt., 1946; faculty chmn. student activities, instr. phys. edn., athletic coach, Brunswick campus U. Me., 1947-49; dir. Hyde Meml. Rehab. Center and Pine Tree Camp, Bath, Me., 1949-50; dir. municipal recreation, Brunswick, Me., 1950-56; dir. Meml. Union, U. N.H., 1956-60; dean of men, dir. Univ. Union, Boston U., 1960-63, dean of students, 1963-69, dean student affairs, 1969—. Served with USNR, 1943-45; lt. comdr. Res. Mem. Nat. Assn. Student Personnel Adminstrs., Eastern Assn. Coll. Deans and Advisers to Students, Lambda Chi Alpha. Home: 19 Winsor Lane Topsfield MA 01983 Office: Boston Univ 775 Commonwealth Av Boston MA 02215

CURTIS, THOMAS BRADFORD, publishing co. exec.; b. St. Louis, May 14, 1911; s. Edward Glion and Isabel (Wallace) C.; A.B., Dartmouth, 1932, M.A., 1951; LL.B., Washington U., St. Louis, 1935; LL.D., Westminster Coll., 1962; m. Susan R. Chivvis, June 28, 1941; children—Elizabeth, Leland, Allan, Charles, Jonathan. Admitted to Mo. bar, 1934, and practiced in St. Louis; partner firm Biggs, Hensley, Curtis & Biggs; mem. 82d Congress 12th Dist. Mo., 83d-90th Congresses 2d Dist.; now v.p., gen. counsel Ency. Britannica. Mem. Mo. Bd. Law Examiners, 1949-50. Mem. President Nixon's Task Force Internat. Devel., President Nixon's Commn. on All-Vol. Armed Forces, Nat. Commn. Foundations and Pvt. Philanthropy; chmn. task force financing Congl. campaigns 20th Century Fund; chmn. spl. adv. panel fgn. trade policy U.S. C. of C.; trustee Nat. Planning Assn.; mem. Com. Econ. Devel., Com. Improvement Mgmt. in Govt. Mem. bd. election commnrs. St. Louis County, 1940. Trustee Dartmouth, William Woods Coll. Served with U.S. Navy, 1942-45. Recipient Congl. Distinguished Service award Am. Polit. Sci. Assn., 1963-64, Perry award Nat. Fedn. Blind, 1961, Silver Beaver award Boy Scouts Am., 1964. Mem. Am. Law Inst., Am. Polit. Sci. Assn., Phi Delta Phi, Phi Sigma Kappa. Republican. Unitarian. Author: 87 Million Jobs: A Dynamic Solution for Unemployment. Home: 505 N Michigan Av Chicago IL 60611

CURTIS, THORNTON ALLEN lawyer, corp. exec.; b. Kent, O., 1922. Home: 23 Beacon St Boston MA 02107

CURTIS, VERN ORVEL, restaurant co. exec.; b. Idaho Falls, Ida., May 23, 1934; s. Orvel W. and Louise Ann (Kunz) C.; student Utah State U., 1952-54; B.S. in Accounting, U. Utah, 1957; m. Phyllis K. Olson, Aug. 23, 1961; children—Alison, Cathryn, Kristen. Audit mgr. Arthur Young & Co., Los Angeles, 1960-66; controller, treas. Data Dynamics, Inc., Los Angeles, 1966-68; treas., chief financial officer Denny's Restaurants, Inc., La Mirada, Cal., 1968—. Served with AUS, 1959-60. C.P.A., Cal. Mem. Nat. Assn. Accountants. Home: 4201 Branford Dr Huntington Beach CA 92647 Office: Denny's Restaurants Inc 14256 E Firestone Blvd La Mirada CA 90638

CURTIS, WALTER LOUIS, Jr., naval officer; b. Ahoskie, N.C., July 25, 1915; s. Walter Louis and Ruth (Dowell) C.; student U. N.C., 1932-33; B.S., Wake Forest Coll., 1936; postgrad. Gen. Line Sch., 1946-47, Indsl. Coll. Armed Forces, 1957-58; m. Janet Hartz Gallagher, Dec. 7, 1956; stepchildren—Janet Gallagher (Mrs. Charles Linnan), Linda Gallagher. Commd. ensign USNR, 1937, trans. to U.S. Navy, 1946, advanced through grades to rear adm., 1965; pilot, landing signal officer U.S.S. Hornet, 1941-42, U.S.C. Princeton, 1942-44; air officer in new U.S.S. Princeton, 1945-47; chief staff officer to comdr. Atlantic Res. Fleet, 1948-50; comdg. officer Scouting Squadron 31, 1950-52; 0 staff officer Office Chief Naval Operations, Navy Dept., Washington, 1952-54; exec. officer U.S.S. Randolph, 1954; asst. operations officer Staff Comdr. Sixth Fleet, Mediterranean, 1955-57; assigned European Command Div., 1958, Joint Staff Office, Joint Chiefs staff, 1959, Office Chmn., Joint Chiefs Staff, 1960; comdr. U.S.S. Thetis Bay, 1961-62, U.S.S. Kitty Hawk, 1962-63; chief staff, aide to comdr. First Fleet, 1963-64; asst. chief naval personnel for personnel control Bur. Naval personnel, Navy Dept., Washington, 1964-66; comdr. Carrier Div. Nine, now vice adm. Decorated Bronze Star. Address: care of Bur Personnel Dept Navy Washington DC 20025

CURTIS, WILLIAM EDGAR, composer, conductor, educator; b. Aberdeen, Scotland, Mar. 11, 1914; s. William Alexander and Florence (Malseed) C.; B.Mus. magna cum laude, Edinburgh U., 1935, M.A. magna cum laude, 1936; Bucherand Frazer travel scholar in Europe, 1936-40; postgrad. Curtis Inst. and Berkshire Music Center, 1940-41, Cleve. Orch. Condrs. Workshop, 1956; m. Doris Gray Schauffler, June 20, 1942; children—Michael Gray, Julie Malseed (Mrs. Robert J. Reed), Anne Harvey. Came to U.S., 1940, naturalized, 1944. Founder Curtis String Orch., Boston, 1942, condr., 1942-44; condr. Albany Symphony, 1948-66; founder Northeastern N.Y. Philharmonia, 1966, conductor, 1966—: guest conductor Boston Symphony, B.B.C. Radio Zürich, Oslo Philharmonic, Brabant Orkest, Rheinisches Kammerorchester; prof. music Union Coll., Schenectady, 1956—, chmn. dept. arts, 1967—; founder Northeastern N.Y. Student Orch., 1965, condr., 1965—. Adviser, N.Y. State Council Arts, 1962—. Served with USNR, 1944-46. Recipient Am. Fedn. Musicians award, 1952. Mem. Am. Fedn. Musicians, Am. Assn. U. Profs., St. Andrews Soc. Composer: Suite For Contralto, Viola and Orch., 1966; Concerto for Organ, 1967; Three Piano Pieces, 1968; Suite for Solo Flute, 1969; Double Exposure for String Quartet and Prerecorded Tape, 1969. Home: RD 1 Petersburg NY 12138 Office: Dept Arts Union Coll Schenectady NY 12308

CURTIS, WILLIAM HALL, lawyer; b. Arkansas City, Kan., Oct. 9, 1915; s. John Warner and Addie (Thompson) C.; A.B., U. Neb., 1937; LL.B., Harvard, 1940; m. Vivian Swearingen, Apr. 2, 1947; children—Gregory, Ann, John, Carolyn. Admitted to Mo. bar, 1940, since practiced in Kansas City; partner firm Morrison, Hecker, Cozad, Morrison & Curtis, 1950—. Dir. New Ear Milling Co., Arkansas City, Atlas Mut. Ins. Co., Kansas City. Mem. bench and bar com. Jackson County (Mo.) Circuit Ct.; mem. Kansas City region Met. Planning Commn. Hon. trustee Kansas City (Mo.) Research Hosp. Served to maj. AUS, 1941-46. Mem. Am., Kansas City bar assns., Lawyers Assn. Kansas City (pres. 1965-66), Assn. Life Ins. Counsel, Am. Life Conv., Assn. R.R. Trial Counsel. Clubs: Kansas City Blue Hills Country (pres. 1960), Kansas City. Home: 5736 Wyandotte St Kansas City, MO 64113. Office: Bryant Bldg Kansas City MO 64106

CURTIS, WILLIAM RODOLPH, govt. ofcl.; b. Franklinville, N.C., Oct. 27, 1908; s. Rodolph Clinton and Ora Alma (Bray) C.; A.B., U. N.C., 1930, M.A., 1931; Ph.D., U. Ill., 1935; m. Luceil May Hamilton, June 22, 1935; children—Margaret Lucille, Aletha Estelle, William Edward. Tchr. econs. U. Ill., 1931-35, U. Ala., 1935-36; economist WPA, Washington, 1936-37; chief research, dir., acting chmn. Unemployment Compensation Commn. of N.C., 1937-45; chief adminstrn. standards div. Bur. Employment Security, Social Security Bd., 1945-48; exec. sec. Interstate Conf. Employment Security Agys., 1948-58; dep. adminstr. bur. employment security U.S. Dept. Labor, Washington, 1958-69, regional manpower adminstr., Phila., 1969-70, dep. asso. manpower adminstr., Silver Spring, Md., 1970—. Mem. Social Security tech. staff ways and means com. Ho. of Reps., 1945-46; U.S. del. 3d session adv. com. Salaried Employees and Profl. Workers ILO, Geneva, 1954; alternate mem. study com. on unemployment compensation and employment service Commn. on Inter-Governmental Relations, 1954-55. Mem. Am. Econ. Assn., Internat. Assn. Personnel in Employment Security, Phi Beta Kappa, Phi Kappa Phi, Phi Eta, Delta Sigma Pi. Baptist. Mason. Author articles on labor subjects. Home: 725 Hillsboro Dr Silver Spring MD 20902 Office: 7923 Eastern Av Silver Spring MD 20910

CURTISS, CHARLES FRANCIS, educator, chemist; b. Chgo., Apr. 4, 1921; s. Ralph Charles and Camille (Guthormsen) C.; B.S., U. Wis., 1942, Ph.D., 1948; m. Lois Pauline Hruska, Mar. 23, 1946; children—Larry A., Glenn D., Ned S. Faculty U. Wis., 1949—, prof. chemistry, 1960—. Fellow Am. Phys. Soc., A.A.A.S.; mem. Am. Chem. Soc. Author: (with others) Molecular Theory of Gases and Liquids, 1954; also research papers. Home: 5760 Forsythia Pl Madison WI 53705

CURTISS, JOHN HAMILTON, mathematician; b. Evanston, Ill., Dec. 23, 1909; s. David Raymond and Sigrid Sofia (Eckman) C.; A.B., Northwestern U., 1930; S.M., State U. Ia., 1931; Ph.d. Harvard, 1935. Instr. John Hopkins, 1935-36; instr. Cornell U., 1936-39, asst. prof., 1939-43; asasst. to dir. Nat. Bur. Standards, 1946-47, chief Applied Math. Labs., 1947-53; vis. lectr. Harvard, 1953; sr. scientist, adj. prof. math. Inst. Math Sci., N.Y.C., 1953-54; exec. dir. Am. Math. Soc., 1954-59; prof. math. U. Miami (Fla.), 1959, chmn. dept., 1959-61. Served to lt. comdr. USNR, 1943-46. Recipient medal of award Dep. Commerce. Fellow A.A.A.S., Inst. Math. Statistics, Am. Statis. Assn.; mem. Am. Math. Soc., Math. Assn. Am., Econometric Soc., Soc. Indsl. and applied Math., Phi Beta Kappa, Sigma Xi, founder; editor Nat. Bur. Standards Applied Math. Series, 1946-53; editor various Nat. Bur. Standards Am. Math. Soc. symposia vols. Author numerous tech. papers. Office: Dept Mathematics Miami Coral Gables FL 33124

CURTISS, JOHN SHELTON, educator; b. Buffalo, July 15, 1899; s. Harlow Clarke and Ethel (Mann) C.; A.B., Princeton, 1921; M.A., Columbia, 1929, Ph.D., 1940; m. Edna Sutter, Sept. 21, 1925; children—John Sutter, Anne (Mrs. Merwin Fong). Engaged in bus., Buffalo, 1921-25, in farming, Ariz., 1925-28; tchr. history, Buffalo, 1930-31, 32-33; instr. history Columbia, 1934-36, Coll. City N.Y., 1935-36, Bklyn. Coll., 1936-41; jr. archivist Franklin D. Roosevelt Library, Hyde Park, N.Y., 1941-42; research analyst OSS, 1942-45; faculty Duke, 1945-69, James B. Duke prof. history, prof. emeritus, 1969—; exchange prof. with Inst. of History, Acad. of Scis., Moscow, USSR, 1964. Sr. fellow Russian Inst., N.Y.C., 1946-48; Guggenheim fellow, 1954-55; Am. Council Learned Socs. sr. fellow, 1963-64. Mem. Am. (Herbert Baxter Adams prize 1940), So. hist. assns., Am. Assn. Advancement Slavic Studies. Author: Church and State in Russia, 1940; An Appraisal of the Protocols of Zion, 1941; The Russian Church and Soviet State, 1953 (German edit. 1957); The Russian Revolutions of 1917, 1957; The Russian Army Under Nicholas I, 1825-1855, 1965. Editor: Essays in Russian and Soviet History, 1963. Home: 4418 Guess Rd Durham NC 27705

CURTISS, PAUL HERBERT, Jr., medical educator; b. Kokomo, Ind., June 2, 1920; s. Paul Herbert and Georgia Ella (Tanner) C.; B.A., U. Wis., 1941, M.D., 1945; m. Maria Elizabeth Moreton, June 29, 1945; children—Jonathan, Stacey. Intern Med. Sch. Hosp. and Clinic, U. Ore., 1944-45; gen. surg. resident Beckman Downtown Hosp., N.Y.C., 1947-48; mem. staff N.J. Orthopaedic Hosp., Trenton, Hosp. for Spl. Surgery, N.Y.C., Kingsbridge VA Hosp., Bronx, N.Y., 1948-52; asso. prof. orthopaedic surgery Western Res. U. Med. Sch., 1952-65; prof., dir. orthopaedics Coll. Med., Ohio State U., 1965—; chmn. dept. orthopaedics Children's Hosp., Columbus, 1965; cons. staff Riverside Methodist Hosp., Columbus. Served to capt. AUS, 1945-47. Recipient Kappa Delta award for research, 1963; Traveling fellow to Great Britian, Am. Orthopaedic Assn., 1957. Diplomate Am. Bd. Orthopaedic Surgery (treas. 1968). Mem. Am. Orthopaedic Assn., A.C.S., Orthopaedic Research Soc., A.M.A., Franklin County, Columbus acads. medicine, Ohio Orthopaedic Soc., Russell E. Hibbs Soc., Am. Assn. Surgery Trauma, LeRoy G. Abbott Orthopaedic Soc., Orthopaedic Travel Club, Am.-Brit. Canadian Club. Editorial bd. Jour. Bone and Joint Surgery, 1962-68, Arthritis and Rheumatism, 1969. Contbr. research publications. Home: 86 N Cassady Columbus OH 43209 Office: 410 W 10th Av Columbus OH 43210

CURTISS, RICHARD HOLDEN, fgn. service officer; b. Grand Rapids, Mich., June 13, 1927; s. Fred Adelbert and Alma Clement (Holden) C.; B.A. in Journalism, U. So. Cal., 1949; m. Donna Jean Bourne, June 18, 1950; children—Diana Ruth, Delinda Louise, Andrew Bourne, Raymond Holden. Reporter, Whittier (Cal.) Reporter, 1949-50; newswriter U.P., Los Angeles, 1950-51; publs. officer USIS, Djakarta, Indonesia, 1951-53, information-editorial specialist, Bonn, Germany, 1953-54, information officer, Stuttgart, Germany, 1954-56; press attache Am. Embassy, Ankara, Turkey, 1957-59; newswriter USIA, Washington, 1959-61; Arabic lang. trainee, Beirut, Lebanon, 1962-63; press attache Am. Embassy, Baghdad, Iraq, 1963-66; pub. affairs officer Am. Embassy, Damascus, Syria, 1966-67; program coordinator for Nr. East and South Asia, USIA, Washington, 1967-69; dir. Voice of Am. Program Center, Rhodes, Greece, 1969—. Served with AUS, 1945-47. Mem. Am. Fgn. Service Assn., Archaeol Inst-Am., Sigma Delta Chi. Unitarian. Home: 7601 Dumosa Av Yucca Valley CA 92284 Office: Am Embassy (VOAR) APO New York City NY 09253

CURTISS, WILLIS DAVID, lawyer, educator; b. Sodus, N.Y., May 31, 1916; s. Willis David and Louise Anna (Shoecraft) C.; A.B., Cornell U., 1938, LL.B., 1940; m. Mary Melissa Fowler, June 29, 1951; children—David Fowler, Melissa Anne. Admitted to N.Y. bar, 1940; gen. practice, Sodus, 1940-42; dist. atty. Wayne County, N.Y., 1941; asst. prof. law U. Buffalo, 1946-47; asst. prof. law Cornell U. Law Sch., Ithaca, N.Y., 1947-51, asso. prof., 1951-56, prof., 1956—, asso. dean, 1958-62. Vis. prof. U. Mich. Law Sch., summer 1950; spl. atty. Dept. Justice, 1954. Research cons. N.Y. State Law Revision Commn., 1952-56, exec. sec., 1956-60; mem. N.Y. Temporary Commn. on State Ct. System, 1970—. Faculty trustee Cornell U., 1966-71. Served to lt. comdr. USNR, 1942-46. Mem. Am., N.Y. State, Tompkins County bar assns., Am. Law Inst., Order of Coif, Phi Beta Kappa, Phi Kappa Phi, Delta Sigma Rho, Phi Delta Phi, Sigma Nu. Democrat. Presbyn. Home: 108 Hampton Rd Ithaca NY 14850

CURTIS-VERNA, MARY, opera and concert singer, soprano; b. Salem, Mass.; d. Charles Leverett and Josephine (Nason) Curtis; student Abbott Acad., Andover, Mass.; A.B., Hollins Coll.; m. Ettore Verna, Aug. 3, 1954 (dec. 1962). Debut in Otello, Milano, Italy, 1949; appeared La Scala, Milano, San Carlo, Naples, Opera Rome, Massino of Palermo, Opera Lyon, France, Gaity of Dublin, others; Am. debut Phila. Civic Opera Co.; 1951, also San Francisco Opera Assn., Monterey, Mexico and Lima, Peru; N.Y. debut City Center Opera Co., 1954; debut Metropolitan Opera, N.Y.C., 1957; appearing soprano roles Met. Opera, 1957—; appearing concerts N. Am., Opera Lyon France, Phila. Grand Opera, Miami Opera, Festival Opatija Yugoslavia. Professor music U. Wash., Seattle, 1969—. Mem. Sigma Alpha Iota (hon.). Home: 308 E 79th St New York City NY 10021 Office: care Ludwig Lustig Management 111 W 57th St New York City NY 10019

CURTIUS, KLAUS, German diplomat; b. Duisburg, Germany, May 18, 1906; s. Julius and Adda (Carp) C.; student law, univs. Heidelberg, Munich and Berlin; student Columbia, 1931-32; m. Hertha Schneider, 1935; 1 dau., Constanze (Mrs. Gotthard Scholz). With German Fgn. Office, 1934-35; chief econ. dept. German embassy, Stockholm, 1952-55; foreign office chief Western and No. desk econ. division, 1955-58; consul general, Calcutta, 1958-61; charge recruitment, selection and tng., 1961-64; consul gen., N.Y.C., 1964—; counsellor at law, Berlin Dist. Law Ct., 1935-45, Heidelberg- Mannheim Law Ct., 1945-52. Decorated comdrs. cross Order of Merit, Fed. Republic of Germany; knight comdr. Order of Christ (Portugal); comdr.'s cross Order of Vasa (Sweden); comdrs. cross Order of Falcon (Iceland); officers' cross Order of Merit (Fed. Republic of Austria). Clubs: Rotary, Heidelberg, (N.Y.C.). Author: (with Mrs. Curtius) Rechtslexikon, rev. edit., 1961. Home: 740 Park Av New York City NY 10021 Office: 460 Park Av New York City NY 10022

CURVIN, JONATHAN WADHAMS, educator; b. Brockport, N.Y., July 14, 1911; s. Francis Gilbert and Mabel (Wadhams) C.; B.A., Cornell U., 1932, M.A., 1934, Ph.D., 1941; m. Helen Elizabeth Champlain, Aug. 24, 1935; childrenSusan (Mrs. Jeffrey Leonard), Jonathan. Chmn. dept. speech and theatre Hobart and William Smith Colls. 1934-41, Vanderbilt U., 1941-43; prof. speech and theatre U. Wis., 1956-; Fulbright research scholar, Helsinki, Finland, 1957-58. U.S. del. Internat. Theatre Congress, 1959. Served with USNR, 1943-46. Mem. Am. Ednl. Theatre Assn. (editor jour, 1962-65), Speech Assn. Am. Home: 2125 Chadbourne Av Madison, WI 53705

CURZON, CLIFFORD concert pianist; b. London, Eng., May 18, 1907; s. Michael and Constance (Young) C.; student Royal Acad. of Music, London, 1920; studied later under Katherine Goodson; also studied under Schnabel, Berlin, 1928; under Landowska and Boulanger, Paris, 1930; D.Mus. (hon.), Leeds U., 1970; m. Lucille Wallace, July 16, 1931. Toured Europe for Brit. Council, 1936 and 1937; recent tours throughout world; coast to coast tours in U.S.A. Decorated comdr. Order Brit. Empire. Fellow Royal Acad. Music, London. Home: The White House Millfield Pl London N 6 England

CUSHING, CHARLES COOK, educator, composer; b. Oakland, Cal., Dec. 8, 1905; s. Henry Dexter and Edna (Cook) C.; A.B., U. Cal. at Berkeley, 1928, M.A., 1929; student of Nadia Boulanger, also at Paris, France, Ecole Normale de Musique, 1929- 31; m. Charlotte Crosby Cerf, Aug. 11, 1935; children—Jennifer (Mrs. Alan Curtis), Elizabeth (Mrs. Richard John Lamb III), Jonathan Caleb. Mem. faculty U. Cal. at Berkeley, 1931—, prof. music, 1949-68, conductor univ. Concert Band, 1934-52. Recipient George Ladd Prix de Paris, 1929-31; chevalier Legion of Honor (France), 1952; commn. Ford Found., 1959. Composer; 2d Sonata for Violin and Piano, 1932; Thesmaphoriazusae (incidental music), 1933; Carmen Saeculare, 1935; String Quartet No. 2 in A, 1936; Three Eclogues for 2 Clarinets and Bassoon, 1938; Psalm XCVII for Chorus and Band, 1939; Phrygian Toccata (piano), 1941; Wine from China (men's chorus and piano 4 hands), 1945; Lyric Set (flute, soprano, viola), 1946; Saint Ursula and The Radishes (men's chorus, contralto solo, 4 winds), 1946; Divertimento (4 movements for string orch.), 1947; Fantasy (flute, clarinet, bassoon), 1949; Angel Camp (variations for concert band), 1952; What are Years? (mixed chorus), 1954; Sonata for Clarinet and Piano, 1957; Poem for Baritone and Orch., 1958; Laudate Pueri (suite for 2 clarinets), 1959; Cereus (poem for orch.), 1960; Ondine (incidental music), 1961; The Tempest (incidental music), 1964; also many songs to texts Am. poets. Home: 2239 Summer St Berkeley CA 94709

CUSHING, FREDERIC SANFORD, pub. co. exec.; b. Providence, June 13, 1920; s. Frederic Charles and Julia M. (Sanford) C.; B.A., Colgate U., 1942; postgrad. Brown U., 1947, Carnegie Inst. Tech., 1949; m. Jean Marie Byers, Dec. 18, 1947; 1 son, James Byers. With Rinehart & Co., Inc., 1947-59, asst. dir. coll. dept., nat. sales mgr., 1954-59; v.p., gen. mgr. coll. div. Holt, Rinehart & Winston, 1959-65, v.p. corp. marketing, 1965-66; dir. Holt, Rinehart & Winston, Ltd., London, Can., 1965-66; pres. Glenoce Press., 1966—; v.p. Macmillan Co., 1966—; spl. cons. CIA, 1953-54. Chmn. coll. sect. Am. Textbook Pubs. Inst., 1959-60, bd. dirs., 1965-66. Served to capt. USMCR, 1942-46; PTO. Mem. Beta Theta Pi. Democrat. Episcopalian. Contbr. articles profl. jours. Home: 3010 Lake Glencoe Dr Beverly Hills CA 90210

CUSHING, HARRY COOKE IV, investment banker; b. N.Y.C., Apr. 2; s. Harry Cooke and Cathleen (Vanderbilt) C.; student Cornell U., 1945; m. Ruth Swift Dunbar, Jan. 14, 1961 (div.); 1 son, Harry Cooke V. Adviser for European operations to chmn. bd. Ventures Ltd., 1955-59; pvt. adviser individuals and corps. for limited partner Hallgarten & Co., N.Y.C., 1966—. Chmn. polo com. People-to-People Sports Com., 1962—. Served with AUS, 1942-46. Mem. S.R. Clubs: Turf, White's (London, Eng.); Travellers, Polo (Paris, France); Polo, Golf (Rome, Italy); Hurlingham (Buenos Aires, Argentina); Racquet and Tennis, Brook, River (N.Y.C.); Corviglia (St. Moritz, Switzerland). Home: care Racquet and Tennis Club Via Sardegna 29 Rome Italy

CUSHING, RICHARD GOLLE, govt. ofcl.; b. N.Y.C., Apr. 30, 1917; s. Melvin Abbott and Ida Blanche (Goll) C.; student U. Cal. at Berkeley, 1935-38; B.A., San Francisco State Coll., 1947; m. Nancy Virginia Heizer, Mar. 24, 1940; children—Jeffrey, Martha, Lincoln Marshall. Reporter, editor A.P., San Francisco, 1935-44, war corr., Pacific Theater, 1945, fgn. corr., China, 1945-46, editor A.P., 1947-49; press attache Am. embassy, Santiago, Chile, 1950-52; pub. affairs officer Am. embassy, Havana, Cuba, 1952-57; dir. Office Pub. Information, USIA, 1958-60; dep. pub. affairs officer, attache Am. embassy, Mexico City, 1960- 62; counsellor for pub. affairs Am. embassy, Caracas, Venezuela, 1962-67; dep. dir. Voice of Am., 1967-69, acting asst. dir., 1969-70; pub. affairs officer Am. embassy, Nairobi; Kenya, 1970—. Dir. pub. relations Am. Nat. Exhbn. in Moscow, 1959. Mem. Pub. Relations Soc., Alpha Mu Gamma. Clubs: Overseas Writers, National Press (Washington). Office: care USIA Washington DC 20547

CUSHING, VINCENT JEROME, research sci.; b. Evanston, Ill., Apr. 17, 1924; s. John F. and Harriet (Weber) C.; B.S. in Physics, U. Notre Dame, 1945, M.S. in Mathematics, 1946; Ph.D. in Physics, Ill. Inst. Tech.; m. Marie Donnelly, June 16, 1945; children—Joan, Vincent Jerome, Nancy, David, Brian, Michael and Daniel. Employed as an engr. engaged in Ohio waterway dredging operation, 1948-49; with Eugene Mittleman, devel. induction flow meter; asso. engr., supr. compressible flow and missiles sect. Armour Research Found., Chgo., 1950-54, asst. mgr. propulsion and fluids research dept., 1954-55, mgr., 1955-59; contbd. to theory of nonstationary model for formula applicable to predicted-fire weapons, anti-aircraft missiles, semi-guided missiles; assisted devel. extreme altitude head radiation measuring device for rockets; tactical systems mgr., missiles and space div., United Aircraft Corp., East Hartford, Conn., 1959-60; pres. Engrng.-Physics Co., 1960—. Mem. Am. Phys. Soc., Am. Rocket Soc., Am. Ordnance Assn., Sigma Xi. Home: 9804 Hillridge Dr Kensington MD 20795 Office: 12721 Twinbrook Pkwy Rockville MD 20852

CUSHMAN, EDWARD L., univ. adminstr.; b. Boston, Apr. 6, 1914; s. Robert and Sarah Cushman; A.B., U. Mich., 1937; m. Katherine Jean Moore, Nov. 18, 1938; children—Robert Moore, Elizabeth Ann. Successively economist, civil service dir., asst. to employment service dir. Mich. Unemployment Compensation Commn., 1937-42; dep. dir. for Mich., War Manpower Commn., 1942-43, dir., 1943-46; spl. asst. to sec. of labor, 1946; prof. pub. adminstrn. Wayne U., 1946-54; v.p. indsl. relations Am. Motors Corp., 1954-59, v.p., 1959-66, now dir.; exec. v.p. Wayne State U., Detroit, 1966—. Mem. Nat. Acad. Arbitrators, Indsl. Relations Research Assn. Office: David Mackenzie Hall Wayne State U Detroit MI 48202

CUSHMAN, JEROME, librarian; b. Chgo., June 1, 1914; s. Maxwell and Lottie (Rositsky) C.; A.B. in English lit., Park Coll., Parkville, Mo., 1940; B.S. in L.S., La. State U., 1941; m. Hanna Trilinsky, Nov. 1, 1936 (dec. 1966); children—Keith, Debora, Sarah; m. 2d, 1969; stepson, Evan. Mgr. traveling libraries, reference librarian Mo. State Library, 1941-43; librarian Salina (Kan.) Pub. Library, 1946-61, New Orleans Pub. Library, 1961-65; prof. summer library schs. U. Denver, U. Minn., Kan. Wesleyan U., Drexel Inst. Tech.; sr. lectr. children's lit. Sch. Library Service, also dept. of English, Univ. Cal. at Los Angeles, 1965—; cons. Mo. State Library Spring Inst., 1965. Com. drop-outs New Orleans Social Welfare Planning Council, 1963—; mem. com. cultural and recreational needs older people Guste Housing, 1963—; mem. com. study Jewish adolescent in New Orleans. Bd. dirs. Anti-Defamation League New Orleans, So. Cal. Council Lit. Children and Young Adults; panel mem. community programs Nat. Endowment for the Humanities, 1970. Served with AUS, 1943-45; ETO. Mem. A.L.A. (exec. bd. 1962-66, council 1960-64), La. Libraries Assn. (parliamentarian, dir.), La. Adult Edn. Assn. (mem. bd.), Fgn. Relations Assn. New Orleans (bd. 1963-64), Cal. Library Assn. (mem. council 1970-71). Jewish religion. Mason; mem. B'nai B'rith. Author: (juvenile) Marvella's Hobby, 1962; Tom B. and the Joyful Noise, 1970; also articles, chpts. in books. Contbr. to the Library and the City, 1965. Home: 7447 Sausalito Av Canoga Park CA 91304 Office: Dept English U Cal Los Angeles CA 90024

CUSHMAN, LEWIS ARTHUR, Jr., bakery co. exec.; b. N.Y.C., July 28, 1929; s. Lewis Arthur and Martha- Bryan (Allen) C.; student St. Marks Sch., 1943-47, Harvard, 1947-49, Babson Inst., 1949-50; m. Cornelia Lee Collins, Nov. 11, 1959 (div. Aug. 1960). Dir. Am. Bakeries Co., Chgo., 1963—, chmn. bd., 1969, chmn., pres., 1970—. Served with USAF, 1950-54. Mem. Nat. Assn. Flight Instrs. (dir.), Newcomen Soc. N.Am., Mayflower Soc. Clubs: Union League (Chgo.), Racquet and Tennis (N.Y.C.). Home: Lake Point Tower 505 N Lake Shore Dr Chicago IL 60611 also Red Shutters Farm Patterson NY 12563 Office: 10 S Riverside Plaza Chicago IL 60606

CUSHMAN, MARTELLE LOREEN, educator; b. Kalamazoo, Mar. 9, 1908; s. Clifton L. and Stella M. (Doty) C.; A.B., Western Mich. U., 1932; M.A., U. Mich., 1937; Ph.D., Cornell U., 1943; m. Florence S. Haas, June 20, 1933; children—Cedric A., Clifton E., Marnita L., Marlene L. Prin. High Sch., Ellsworth, Mich., 1928-31; coach, tchr. W.K. Kellogg Sch., Augusta, Mich., 1932-35; supt. schs., Cedarville, Mich., 1935-38, Richmond, Mich., 1938-41; prof. edn. Ia. State U., 1945-54; dean Coll. Edn., U. N.D., Grand Forks, 1954—, prof. edn., 1954—. Pres. Internat. High Sch. Music Camp, Inc., 1956—. Lt. col. Civil Air Patrol, N.D. Wing, Dept. Edn., 1958. Mem. N.E.A. (pres. rural dept. 1953-54), Am. Assn. Coll. Tchrs. Edn. (chmn. studies com. 1961), Nat. Assn. State Univs. and Land Grant Colls. (mem. exec. com. assn. deans edn. 1968-71), Phi Delta Kappa (pres. 1955-57). Home: 536 Oxford St Grand Forks ND 58201

CUSHMAN, ROBERT, abrasives mfg. co. exec.; b. Winchester, Mass., Apr. 29, 1916; s. Norman Locke and Madeline (Porter) C.; grad. Phillips Acad., Andover, Mass., 1935; B.A., Dartmouth, 1939; m. Mary Shorey, July 26, 1940; children—Mary Allerton (Mrs. Mary C. Higgins), Louise Gibbs. Salesman; Gulf Oil Corp., 1939-44; with Norton Co., Worcester, Mass., 1944—, v.p., gen. mgr. abrasive div., 1961-67, exec. v.p., 1967-71, pres., chief exec. officer, 1971—, also dir.; trustee State Mut. Investors, Inc., Worcester County Instn. for Savs.; dir. Mechanics Nat. Bank Worcester; bd. mgrs. Paul Revere Variable Annuity Ins. Co. Corporator Worcester Boys Club, Worcester Natural History Soc.; mem. Community Services, Inc.; fund chmn. Worcester chpt. Am. Cancer Soc., 1970. dir. Mass. div.; hon. bd. dirs. Worcester Children's Theatre. Trustee, past pres. bd. bd. trustees Shepherd Knapp Sch., Boylston, Mass.; past trustee Worcester Rehab. Center; trustee Worcester Found. Exptl. Biology, Leicester Jr. Coll., New Eng. Aquarium, Boston. Mem. Mass. Soc. Mayflower Desos., Research Inst. Am., Internat. Sales and Marketing Execs., Theta Delta Chi. Unitarian. Clubs: Dartmouth (past pres. Worcester County); Tatnuck Country, Worcester, Laurel Brook, Black Brook Salmon, Midas. Home: 14 Westwood Dr Worcester MA 01609 Office: 1 New Bond St Worcester MA 01606

CUSHMAN, ROBERT EARL, divinity sch. dean; b. Fall River, Mass., Dec. 26, 1913; s. Ralph Spaulding and Maud (Hammond) C.; student Denver U., 1932-34; A.B., Wesleyan U., Middletown, Conn., 1936; B.D., Yale, 1940, Ph.D., 1942; L.H.D., Belmont (N.C.) Abbey, 1966; m. to Barbara Priscilla Edgecomb, Sept. 12, 1936; children—Robert Earl, Thomas Spaulding, Elizabeth Jane. Ordained to ministry Methodist Ch., 1940; pastor in Meriden, Conn., 1936-40, Hamilton, N.Y., 1941; instr. theology Yale Div. Sch., 1942-43; prof. religion U. Ore., 1943-45; asso. prof. theology Duke Div. Sch., 1945-48, prof., 1948-58, dean, 1958-71, research prof., 1971—. Ofcl. Meth. del. World Conf. Faith and Order, Lund, Sweden, 1952; mem. commn. ecumenical consultation Meth. Ch., 1958-64, mem. commn. ecumenical affairs United Meth. Ch., 1964—, v.p., 1971—; mem. N.A. commn. worship World Council Chs., 1956-63; ofcl. Meth. del. 4th World Conf. Faith and Order, Montreal, 1963; Meth. observer 2d Vatican Council, Rome, 1963-65; mem. N.C. conf. Wesley Soc., 1955—; mem. commn. on ecumenical affairs Nat. Council Chs., 1965-70; mem. World Meth. Council, 1970—; chmn. bd. dirs. Oxford Edit. Wesley Works Project, 1959-71, gen. editor, 1971—; fellow Ecumenical Inst. for Advanced Theol. Studies, Jerusalem, 1971-72; del. Gan. Conf., Meth. Church, 1966, 68, 70, 72. Tchr.-Scholar award Wesleyan U., 1967. Mem. Assn. United Meth. Theol. Schs. (pres. 1964-66; mem. exec. com.), Doudecim Theol. Group, Am. Theol. Soc., Phi Beta Kappa. Author: Therapeia; Plato's Conception of Philosophy, 1958; The Heritage of Christian Thought, 1966. Contbr. Jour. Religion, Ch. History, Theology Today, Holbein Rev., Religion in Life. Home: 2719 Spencer St Durham NC 27705

CUSHMAN, ROBERT EVERTON, Jr., govt. ofcl.; b. St. Paul, Dec. 24, 1914; s. Robert E. and Jennie Lind (Cumley) C.; B.S., U.S. Naval Acad., 1935; m. Audrey Boyce, Jan. 17, 1940; children—Roberta, Robert Everton III. Commd. 2d lt. USMC, 1935, advanced through grades to lt. gen. 1967; asst. to v.p. for nat. security affairs, 1957-61; asst. chief staff USMC, 1962-64; comdg. gen. USMC Base, Camp Pendleton, Cal., 1964-67, comdr. 3d Marine Amphibious Force, Vietnam, 1967-69; dep. dir. CIA, 1969—, Mem. bd. control U.S. Naval Inst. Proc., 1957-61. Decorated Navy Cross, D.S.M. (2), Legion of Merit, Bronze Star. Office: care Central Intelligence Agency Washington DC 20505

CUSHMORE, CHARLES LAURENCE, Jr., lawyer; b. Phila., Mar. 29, 1907; s. Charles Laurence and Anna (Magee) C.; J.D., Temple U., 1930; m. Edna Alice Tracey, June 27, 1931; children—Tracey Ann (Mrs. J. Hankinson Carter, Jr.), Joyce Barbara (Mrs. Martin Bradley), Charles Laurence 3d. Admitted to Pa. bar, 1928; messenger, stenographer, asso. firm White, Parry & Maris, Phila., 1925-37; partner successor firm White & Williams, Phila., 1937—; solicitor Southampton Water Authority, 1946-58. Dir., Globe Dye Works. Dist. chmn. Phila. Boy Scouts, 1960, dist. commr., 1961, neighborhood commr., 1962-70. Pres. Southampton Playground and Youth Center, 1945-46; treas., dir. Friends Meeting House Fund, Inc., 1959—; dir. Friends of Chamounix Mansion Phila. Internat. Youth Hostel, Inc., 1966—, chmn., 1968-70; trustee Newtown Friends Monthly Meeting, 1952-58, Phila. Friends Yearly Meeting, 1955—, New Sch. of Music, 1962—, Berean Inst., 1961—. Mem. Am., Pa., Phila. bar assns., Am. Friends Service Com., Spring Garden Civic Assn. (pres. 1961- 67, v.p. 1967-68). Mem. Soc. of Friends. Clubs: Union League, Undine Barge, Stagecrafters (dir. 1971—) (Phila.). Author: Pennsylvania Community Property Law, Annotated, 1948. Home: 2341 Pennsylvania Av Philadelphia PA 19130 Office: Land Title Bldg Philadelphia PA 19110

CUSHWA, CHARLES B., metal products mfg. exec.; b. Youngstown, O., Apr. 30, 1909; s. Charles B. and Mary (Coll) C.; A.B., U. Notre Dame, 1931; m. Margaret Hall, Oct. 15, 1932; children—Charles, William W., Mary Ellen. Chmn., pres. Comml. Shearing and Stamping Co., Youngstown, O.; dir. Union Nat. Bank; v.p., dir. Watson Terminal & Warehouse Co.; dir. Home Savs. & Loan Co., Youngstown Bldg. Material and Fuel Co. Mem. sci. and engring. bd. U. Notre Dame; pres. adv. bd. St. Elizabeth Hosp., also chmn. bd. trustees; trustee, treas. Youngstown Ednl. Mem. C. of C. (dir.). Home: 250 Tod Lane Youngstown OH 44504 Office: 1775 Logan Av Youngstown OH 44501

CUSIC, WAYNE NORRED, coll. pres. emeritus; b. Griggsville, Ill., Apr. 19, 1905; s. Henry Foster and Lily (Norred) C.; A.B., Ill. Coll., 1928, LL.D., 1959; M.S., La. State U., 1941; hon. doctorate Ill. Coll., 1959; m. Lucille Kenon, Aug. 9, 1930; 1 son, Wayne Kennon. Tchr., coach Minden (La.) High Sch., 1928-29, Lynch (Ky.) High Sch., 1929-30, 37-40; prin., coach Stanford (Ky.) High Sch., 1930-36; coach Pikeville (Ky.) Jr. Coll., 1936-37; faculty McNeese State U., Lake Charles, La., 1940—, prof. edn., dean of men, 1950-55, pres., 1955-70, now emeritus. Dir. Calcasieu Savs. & Loan Co. Mem. Greater Lake Charles Water Bd. Bd. dirs. Nat. Conf. Christians and Jews. Mem. N.E.A., Brotherhood Jews, Caths. and Protestants, Blue Key, Pi Kappa Delta (hon.). Episcopalian. Mason. Home: 1508 W Sale Rd Lake Charles LA 70601

CUSSON, ANNETTE FOREST, state ofcl.; b. Providence, Mar. 12, 1907; d. Aurele J. and Anna (Trottier) Forest; grad. St. Xavier's Acad., 1924; m. Horace A. Cusson, May 4, 1940; 1 son, Paul Ernest. Active Dem. Party, 1937—; mem. Young Dems. R.I., 1938—, R.I. Dem. Womens Club, 1938—; mem. R.I. Dem. Platform Com., 1958, R.I. Dem. Speakers Program, 1956; chmn. Kennedy's Golden Girls of R.I., 1960; mem. Dem. Nat. Com. from R.I., 1960-69, mem. nationalities div. Subcom.; mem. platform com. Dem. Nat. Conv., 1964, sec. com. on permanent orgn., 1968; program coordinator R.I.

State Council on Arts, 1969—. Founding mem. R.I. Assn. Retarded Children; mem. R.I. Adv. Commn. on Women. Bd. dirs. Internat. Inst. of Providence; hon. mem. Rhodes Island Opera Guild. Mem. Fedn. Francaise du R.I., Alliance Francaise. Home: 151 Althea St Providence RI 02907 Office: RI State Council on Arts 47 The Arcade Providence RI 02903

CUSTER, RAYMOND THOMAS, wholesale elec. supply co. exec.; b. Lowell, Mass., Oct. 6, 1913; s. James J. and Della A. (Connerton) C.; B.A., St. Anselm's Coll., Manchester, N.H., 1937; student U. Ill., 1942, Harvard, 1945, Dartmouth, 1953-55; m. Eleanor Fitzgerald, Nov. 28, 1940; children—Raymond Thomas, Rosemary. With Graybar Electric Co., 1937—, sec., comptroller, 1968-, also dir., mem. exec. com.; summer faculty and staff mem. Grad. Sch. Credit and Financial Mgmt., Tuck Sch., Dartmouth, 1959-60. Trustee St. Anselm's Coll. Served with USNR, 1942-46. Mem. Nat. Assn. Credit and Financial Mgmt. Interchange Bur. (chmn. bd. govs.), New Eng. Assn. Credit Execs. (pres.), New Eng. Elec. Inst. (treas.). Author articles. Home: 7 Tanglewood Trail Darien, CT 06830 Office: 420 Lexington Av New York City NY 10017

CUSTIN, MILDRED, dept. store exec.; b. Manchester, N.H., 1906; grad. Simmons Coll., 1927; L.H.D., Temple U., 1966, Russell Sage Coll., 1968. With controller's office R.H. Macy Co., 1928; buyer gifts, china, glassware R.H. White & Co., Boston, 1933-35; buyer gifts John Wanamaker, Phila., 1935, then mdse. mgr. fashion div., v.p. and mdse. mgr. ready to wear and fashion accessories depts., 1951-58; pres. Bonwit Teller, Phila., 1958-65; pres. Bonwit Teller N.Y. (subsidiary of Genesco) and 12 brs., 1965-69, chmn. bd., chief exec. officer, 1969-70; pres. Mildred Custin Ltd., 1970—, also exec. cons. to Genesco, 1970—. Active civic, philanthropic endeavors. Decorated La Croix de la Chevalier del ' Ordre du Merite (France). Recipient Distinguished Alumnae award Simmons Coll., 1964; Tobe award for distinguished contbn. to retailing, 1969. Home: 480 Park Av New York City NY 10022 Office: 767 Fifth Av New York City NY 10022

CUSUMANO, STEFANO, painter; b. Tampa, Fla., Feb. 5, 1912; s. Ignazio and Rosa (Albano) C.; student Cooper Union, 1928-29, Met. Art Sch., 1930-32; m. Antoinette Ferrari, Aug. 16, 1939; children—Noelle (Mrs. Louis Marak), Peter Anthony. Tchr. painting Cooper Union, 1954—, N.Y.U., 1951—; one-man shows include Montross Gallery, N.Y.C., 1942, George Binet Gallery, N.Y.C., 1946, 47, 48, 50, Passedoit Gallery, N.Y.C., 1953, 56, 57, 59, Mari Gallery, Woodstock, N.Y., 1962, Gallery 63, N.Y.C., 1963, 64, Phila Art Alliance, 1948, Woodmere Art Gallery, Phila., 1950, Tampa Art Inst., 1949, Ore. State Coll., 1951, Wash. State U., 1951, Gallery 63, Rome, Italy, 1964, T. Dintenfass Gallery, N.Y.C., 1967; Tweed Mus. Art, Duluth, Minn., 1971; nat. exhbns. include Mus. Modern Art, Whitney Mus., U. Ill., Pa. Acad., Corcoran Gallery, Carnegie Inst., Am. Inst. Arts and Letters, numerous others; represented in permanent collections Nat. Gallery, Met. Mus. Art, Whitney Mus., Bklyn. Mus., Phila. Mus., Newark Art Mus., Pensacola (Fla.) Art Mus., U. Ill., Wesleyan U. Ill., Johns Hopkins, Joslyn Art Mus., Omaha, Tweed Mus. Art. Recipient Ford Found. Purchase prize, 1962; Childe Hassam award Am. Inst. Arts and Letters, 1968; Dillard Purchase award, Weatherspoon Mus., 1969. Address: 170 W 73d St New York City NY 10023

CUTCHINS, CLIFFORD ARMSTRONG, III, banker; b. Southampton County, Va., July 12, 1923; s. Clifford Armstrong Jr. and Sarah (Vaughan) C.; B.S. in Bus. Adminstrn., Va. Poly. Inst., 1947; grad. Stonier Grad. Sch. Banking, 1953; m. Ann Woods, June 21, 1947; children—Clifford Armstrong IV, William Witherspoon, Cecil Vaughan. From asst. cashier to pres. Vaughan & Co., bankers, Franklin, Va., 1950-62; pres., cashier dir. Tidewater Bank & Trust Co., Franklin, 1962-63; bank merged with Va. Nat. Bank, Norfolk, 1963, exec. v.p., 1965- 69, pres., 1969—, also dir.; pres., dir. Southampton Supply Co.; dir. Franklin Equipment Co., Franklin Concrete Products Corp., Unimin Corp. Bd. visitors Va. Poly. Inst., 1965—; bd. dirs. Camp Found., Franklin, 1962—; trustee Am. Century Mortgage Investors. Served to 2d lt. AUS, World War II; PTO. Baptist. Clubs: Commonwealth (Richmond); Norfold Yacht and Country, Virginia, Harbor (Norfolk); Princess Anne Country (Virginia Beach, Va.); Cypress Cove Country (Franklin, Va.). Home: 7320 Glenroie Av Norfolk VA 23505 Office: One Commercial Pl Norfolk VA

CUTHBERT, KENNETH NEIL, coll. dean; b. Barron, Wis., Dec. 25, 1917; s. Frederick Bruce and Bertha (Gilbertson) C.; Mus.B., U. Wis., 1939, Mus.M., 1942; M.A., Columbia, 1946, Ed.D., 1947; m. Evelyn Alice Zipse, June 1, 1941; children—Carolyn Frances, Frederick Neil. Asst. to dir. bands U. Wis., 1939-40; dir. music Sun Prairie, Mt. Horeb Merrill, Wis., high schs., 1940-43; personal affairs and information edn. officer USAAF, 1943-45; instr. music edn. Columbia Tchrs. Coll., 1945-47; dir. grad. studies, prof. music Ill. Wesleyan U., 1947-48, dean Sch. Music, condr. Bloomington Normal Symphony, Ill. Wesleyan U., 1948-51; dir. dept. music, condr. East Carolina Symphony, mus. dir. Greenville Passion Play, East Carolina Coll., 1951-58; dean Sch. Music, North Tex. State U., Denton, 1958—. Chmn. coll. and univ. sect. N.C. Music Edn. Nat. Conf., 1949-51, nat. co- chmn. music in the church com., 1952-54. Bd. dirs. Dallas Symphony Orch. Mem. Nat. Assn. Schs. Music (regional v.p. 1956-58, chmn. S. W. region, 1965-66, chmn. music educators nat. conf.; liaison com. 1960-64, chmn. com. improvement of teaching 1965—), Tex. Assn. Music Schs. (pres. 1965-66), Am. Symphony Orch. League (v.p. 1950-52) Tex. Assn. Schs. Music (dir.), Phi Mu Alpha (province gov. 1948-58). Kiwanian (dir. Denton). Home: 1919 Mistywood Lane Denton TX 76201

CUTHBERT, MARVIN PEARE, physician; b. Kingman, Ind., Sept. 15, 1910; s. Frederick Sheets and Caroline (Peare) C.; B.S., Ind. U., 1936, M.D., 1937; postgrad. U. Pa. Grad. Sch. Medicine, 1939; m. Marjorie Faye Bell, Apr. 18, 1936; children—Frederic Sheets II, Stephen James. Resident in ophthalmology Hosp. of U. Pa., Phila., 1939-40, N.Y. Eye and Ear Infirmary, N.Y.C., 1940-42, Cornell U. Coll. Medicine, N.Y.C., 1942-44; practice medicine specializing in ophthalmology, Indpls., 1947—; now asso. prof. ophthalmology Ind. U. Med. Center, Indpls. Served to maj. Med. Corps, AUS, 1944-47. Diplomate Am. Bd. Ophthalmology. Mem. A.M.A., Assn. for Prevention Blindness, Assn. for Glaucoma Research, Pan Am. Assn. Ophthalmology, Am. Legion, Culver Legion, Phi Kappa Psi. Clubs: Sports Car of Am.; Traders Point Hunt; Varsity, Alumni (U. Ind.); University (Indpls.). Home: Route 2 Box 386 Carmel IN 46032 Office: 3266 N Meridian St Indianapolis TN 46208

CUTHBERT, VIRGINIA (Mrs. Philip C. Elliott), artist; b. West Newton, Pa., Aug. 27, 1908; d. Richard Bruce and Frances Irene (Cartwright) Cuthbert; B.F.A. (Augusta Hazard fellow), Syracuse U., 1930; postgrad. Academie de la Grande Chaumiere, Academie Colarossi, Paris, 1930, Chelsea Poly. Inst., London, 1931, George Luks, N.Y.C., 1932, U. Pitts., 1933-34, Carnegie Inst. Tech., 1934-35; m. Philip Clarkson Elliott, June 8, 1935. Instr. painting Albright Art Sch., Buffalo, 1943-54, U. Buffalo, 1954—, State U. N.Y. at Buffalo, 1962-65; exhibited one-man shows Carnegie Inst., 1938, Butler Art Inst., 1938, Syracuse Mus. Fine Arts, 1939, Syracuse U., 1945, Contemporary Arts, N.Y.C., 1945, 49, 53, Rehn Gallery, N.Y.C., 1958-66, N.Y. State Coll. Tchrs. Albany, 1959, Chautauqua (N.Y.) Art Assn., 1959, Albright-Knox Art Gallery, 1963, many others throughout U.S.; exhbns. include: Met. Mus. Art, Whitney Mus. Am. Art, Art Inst. Chgo., Pa. Acad. Fine Arts, Carnegie Internats., Ft. Worth Art Center, Butler Inst. Am. Art, Albright-Knox Art Gallery, others; represented in collections Albright-Knox Art Gallery, Hundred Friends of Pitts. Art, Syracuse U., Princeton Mus. Art, Phila. Mus. Art, others, pvt. collections. Recipient prizes Asso. Artists Pitts. Ann., 1934, 36-40, Butler Art Inst., 1940, Western N.Y. Exhbn., 1944, 46, 50, 52, 55, 58, 65, 66, Pepsi-Cola Ann., 1946-47, Nat. Inst. Arts and Letters, 1954; Chataugua prize, 1955; prize Sisti Exhbn., Buffalo, 1956, 57, Albright Art Gallery, 1958, Cover of Fortune, 1951. Mem. Patteran Artists, Kappa Alpha Theta. Methodist. Home: 147 Bryant St Buffalo NY 14222

CUTHBERTSON, GEORGE RAYMOND, mgmt. cons., educator; b. Liberty, Mo., June 23, 1910; s. William Nancy R. (Shephard) C.; B.A., William Jewell Coll., 1931, LL.D. (hon., 1964; M.A., Harvard, 1933, Ph.D., 1935; m. Mary Louise Archer, Sept. 3, 1931; children—Nancy (Mrs. Frank H. Halley), George Raymond, David Archer. Teaching fellow Harvard, 1931-35, research asst., 1935-36; research chemist U.S. Rubber Co., 1936-50, asst. dir. devel. Tire Div., 1951, factory mgr. Los Angeles tire plant, 1952-1953, prodn. mgr. all tire plants, 1953-1955, asst. gen. mgr., 1955- 1956, became v.p., gen. mgr. Tire div., 1956, then v.p. research and devel. U.S. Rubber Tire Co. div. until 1963, tech. dir. textile div., 1963-70; mgmt. cons., 1970—; asso. prof. engring. mgmt. dept. U. Mo., devel. synthetic rubber tires, 1941-45. Mem. Am. Mgmt. Assn., Soc., Kappa Alpha, Theta Chi Delta, Sigma Pi Sigma, Alpha Chi Sigma. Baptist. Club: Oak Meadow (Rolla). Patentee in field. Home: 1106 Sycamore Dr Rolla MO 65401 Office: 301 Harris Hall U Mo Rolla MO 65401

CUTHBERTSON, KENNETH MCLEAN, univ. adminstr.; b. San Francisco, Apr. 8, 1919; s. Frank Goodwin and Evleyn (McLean) C.; A.B., Stanford, 1940, M.B.A., 1947; student Harvard Grad. Sch. Bus. 1940-41; m. Coline Nancy Upshaw, Sept. 13, 1941; children—Janet, Thomas Upshaw, James Goodwin, Nancy. Asso., McKinsey & Co., mgmt. cons., San Francisco, 1947-50; partner Levison Bros., ins., San Francisco, 1950-54; asst. to pres. Stanford (Cal.), 1954-59, v.p. finance, 1959-71, v.p. devel., 1971—. Trustee The Inst. Ednl. Mgmt., Boston. Served to lt. comdr. USNR, 1941-47. Presbyn. (elder). Clubs: Palo Alto (Cal.); Los Angeles. Home: 399 Stevick Dr Atherton CA 94025 Office: Stanford Univ Stanford CA 94305

CUTHELL, DAVID CAMERON, fgn. service officer; b. N.Y.C., Apr. 22, 1921; s. Chester W. and Dorothy (Banta) C.; grad. Phillips Acad., 1939; B.A., Yale, 1942, M.A., 1947; m. Dawn Hagman, Nov. 20, 1950; children—David Cameron, Charles Erik. Joined U.S. Fgn. Service, 1947; assigned Canberra, Australia, 1947- 49, Athens, Greece, 1949-51, Manila, Cebu, Philippines, 1951-53, Washington, 1953-58; became polit. officer consulate gen., Istanbul, Turkey, 1958; deputy dir. Office Southwest Pacific Affairs Dept. State until 1964, dir., 1964-66, assigned sr. seminar, 1966-67; dir. Fgn. Affairs Tng. Program, 1967-68; detailed to White House, 1968; polit. counselor Am. embassy, Ankara, Turkey, now dep. chief mission. Served to 1st lt., 11th Airborne Div. AUS, 1943-46. Home: 6616 Barnaby St NW Washington DC 20015 Office: Am Embassy APO New York City NY 09254

CUTINI, GARY SANTO, ins. co. exec.; b. Niagara Falls, N.Y., May 22, 1913; s. Marian D. and Donna (D'Addezzio) C.; student U. Ga., 1947-49; m. Caeleste F. Stokes, June 6, 1936; 1 dau., Diana Edna (Mrs. Millard H. Simmons III). Agt., Met. Life Ins. Co., 1937; asst. ins. officer VA, 1946-48; with Life Ins. Co. Ga., Atlanta, 1948—, dir. agys., 1955-67, officer 1967—. Vice chmn. DeKalb County Bd. Health, Met. Atlanta Comprehensive Health Planning Council. C.L.U. Mem. Sales and Marketing Execs. Internat. (pres. 1967, 1968), Atlanta C. of C., Atlanta Sales and Marketing Execs. Club (past pres.), Nat. Sales and Marketing Execs. (dir.), C.L.U. Soc. (past pres. local chpt.), Alpha Kappa Psi, Pi Sigma Epsilon, Pi Kappa Delta. Mason (Shriner,32). Club: Atlanta Civitan. Home: 2147 Council Bluff Ct NE Atlanta GA 30329 Office: 600 W Peachtree St Atlanta GA 30308

CUTKOSKY, RICHARD EDWIN, educator, physicist; b. Mpls., July 29, 1928; s. Oscar F. and Edna (Nelson) C.; B.S., M.S. in Physics, Carnegie Inst. Tech., 1950, Ph.D., 1953; m. Patricia Ann Klepfer, Aug. 28, 1952; children—Mark, Carol, Martha. Mem. faculty Carnegie-Mellon Univ., 1953—, prof. physics, 1961- -, Buhl prof. theoretical physics, 1963—; NSF fellow Niels Bohr Inst., Copenhagen, Denmark, 1954-55, NORDITA, Copenhagen, 1961-62. Alfred P. Sloan Found. fellow, 1957-61; Overseas fellow Churchill Coll., Eng., 1968-69. Mem. Am. Phys. Soc., A.A.A.S. Home: 1209 Wightman St Pittsburgh PA 15217

CUTLER, BERNARD JOSEPH, newspaperman; b. N.Y.C., May 26, 1924; s. Joseph Louis and Sophie (Appel) C.; B.S. in Mech. Engring., Pa. State Coll., 1945; m. Carol Ann Rataic, Mar. 6, 1948. Reporter, Pitts. Press, 1945-51; reporter N.Y. Herald Tribune, 1951-56, Moscow corr., 1956-58, chief Paris bur., 1958-60, mng. editor European edit., Paris, 1960, editor European edit. 1961-66; European corr. Scripps-Howard Newspapers, 1966—. Bd. dirs. Am. Center Students and Artists, Paris. Mem. Anglo-Am. Press Assn. Club: American (Paris). Author: Reactionary! Sgt. Lloyd W. Pate's Story, 1956. Home: 4 Rue de la Renaissance Paris 8e France

CUTLER, BURTON, business exec.; b. Los Angeles, May 25, 1926; s. Joseph and Naomi (Tucker) C.; student Stanford 1943-44, M.S. in Elec. Engring., 1949; student Tex. A. and M. Coll., 1945; m. Diana Patricia Tucker, Dec. 19, 1947; children—Carol Joan, Jay Alan, Corey. Design engr. Glifillan Bros., Inc., Los Angeles, 1949-53, supr., program mgr., 1953-63. dir. engring. v.p., 1963-67, pres., 1967-69; pres. Inst. for Career Devel., Los Angeles, 1969—; pres. chmn. Teaching Aids Inst. div. Cutler-Ball, Inc., Los Angeles, 1961-69; chmn. CutlerBall, Inc.; dir. New Cal Tech., Inc. Served with AUS, 1943-45. Democrat. Pantentee Concepts for automatic control of aircraft during final approach to airports. Office: 3870 S Crenshaw Blvd Los Angeles CA 90008

CUTLER, EDWARD I., lawyer; b. Phila., Sept. 21, 1913; s. Samuel and Elizabeth (Esterman) C.; A.B., U. Pa., 1934, LL.B., J.D., 1937; m. Roseline Adams, Aug. 12, 1938; children—Janet, Edward, Robin. Research asst., asst. law librarian U. Pa., 1937-39; law sec. to chief justice to Pa., 1937-39; admitted to Pa. bar, 1938, Fla. bar, 1948; practiced in Phila., 1938-44; exec. asst. Hooker's Point Shipyard, Tampa, Fla., 1944- 46; engaged as real estate broker, Tampa, 1947; practiced in Tampa, 1948—; partner firm Carlton, Fields, Ward, Emmanuel, Smith & Cutler, Tampa, Orlando, Fla., 1961—, treas., 1969—. Sec., C.W.A.G. Found., 1950-70, Indsl. Supply Corp., 1950—. Asst. procedural and equity rules coms. Supreme Ct. Pa., 1940-44; Am. Bar Assn. co-chmn. to Nat. Conf. Lawyers and Collection Agys., 1970—. Co-chmn. West Coast Fla. chpt. Nat. Conf. Christians and Jews, 1964-67. Mem. exec. com. U.S. Fla. Found., 1962—. Mem. Am. (standing com. unauthorized practice law 1970—), Phila., Tampa, Hillsborough County bar assns., Fla. Bar (chmn. unauthorized practice law com. 1964- 68; lectr. continuing legal edn. on secured creditor's rights 1964—), Am. Judicature Soc., Comml. Law League Am., Am. Law Inst., Order of Coif, Phi Beta Kappa. Mason (Shriner); mem. B'nai B'rith. Note editor U. Pa. Law Rev., 1936-37; Fla. contbr. Compendium, Nat. Comml. Finance Conf. Club: University (Tampa). Home: 192 Ceylon Av Tampa FL 33606 Office: Exchange Nat Bank Bldg PO Box 3239 Tampa FL 33601

CUTLER, ELLIOTT CARR, Jr., army officer; b. Boston, June 15, 1920; s. Elliott Carr and Caroline Pollard (Parker) C.; B.S., U.S. Mil. Acad., 1942; M.S. in Elec. Engring., Ga. Inst. Tech., 1954, Ph.D., 1960; grad. Command and Gen. Staff Coll., 1955; m. Genevieve Sparks Spalding, June 5, 1946; children—Elliott Carr III, Genevieve Spalding. Commd. 2d lt. U.S. Army, 1942, advanced through grades to col. 1961; served in ETO, 1944-45; instr. U.S. Mil. Acad., West Point, N.Y., 1945-48; with 24th Div., Korea, 1950-51; mem. faculty U.S. Mil. Acad., 1955—, prof. electricity, 1958—, head dept., 1961—. Decorated Bronze Star with oak leaf cluster, Purple Heart, Legion of Merit. Mem. Assn. U.S. Army, I.E.E.E., Am. Assn. Physics Tchrs., Armed Forces Communications and Electronics Assn. Home: Quarters 108 West Point NY 10996

CUTLER, HOWARD ARMSTRONG, educator; b. Webster City, Ia., Apr. 27, 1918; s. Harry O. and Myrtle (Armstrong) C.; A.B., State U. Ia., 1940, M.A., 1941; grad. certificate Harvard, 1943; Ph.D., Columbia, 1952; m. Enid Ellison, Jan. 2, 1943; children—Cheryl Varian, Kristen Ellison, Sherwood Thor. Instr. econs. State U. Ia., 1946; asst. to economist Irving Trust Co., N.Y.C., 1946- 47; instr. econs. U. Ill., Urbana, 1948-50, asst. prof., 1950, asst. to dean Coll. Commerce, 1949-51; asst. prof. econs. Pa. State U., 1951-53, asso. prof., 1953-56, prof., 1956-62, head dept., 1953-58, dir. gen. edn., 1957-62, asst. to v.p. acad. affairs, 1958-61, asst. to pres., 1961-62; acad. v.p., prof. econs. U. Alaska, 1962-66; exec. v.p. Inst. Internat. Edn., N.Y.C., 1966—; vis. prof. U. Chgo., 1955-56. Mem. Martin Luther King, Jr. Fellowship Selection Com., 1968—; mem. pub.-at-large Commn. on Fgn. Med. Grads., 1970—; mem. chancellor's panel on univ. purposes State U. N.Y., 1970—; mem. Nat. Liaison Com. Fgn. Student Admissions, 1968—; mem. adv. com. Carl Duisberg Soc., 1968—. Bd. dirs. Internat. Schs. Services, 1971—; pres. bd. dirs. Axe-Houghton Found., 1970—. Served from ensign to lt., USNR, 1942-46, Mem. Am. Econ. Assn., Am. Statis. Assn., A.A.A.S., Phi Beta Kappa, Beta Gamma Sigma, Pi Gamma Mu, Omicron Delta Epsilon. Bd. editors, Jour. Gen. Edn., 1960—. Home: 88 Old Colony Rd Hartsdale NY 10530 Office: Inst Internat Edn 809 UN Plaza New York City NY 10017

CUTLER, HUGH CARSON, educator, botanist; b. Milw., Sept. 8, 1912; s. Manuel and Mary A.B., U. Wis., 1935, A.M., 1936; Ph.D., Washington U., 1939; m. Marian W. Cornell, Aug. 26, 1940; 1 son, William Cornell. Research asso. Washington U., 1939-40, Bot. Mus., Harvard, 1941-47; field technician Rubber Devel. Corp., Brazil, 1943-45; curator econ. botany Chgo. Natural History Mus., 1947-52; asso. prof. botany Washington U., St. Louis, 1953—, asso. dir. Mo. Bot. Garden, 1954- 56, acting dir., 1957-58, exec. dir., 1958-64, curator useful plants, 1964—. Cons. asso. Paleo-Indian Inst., Eastern N.M. U.; research asso. Mus. No. Ariz. Guggenheim fellow, 1942-43, 46-47. Mem. Sigma Xi. Contbr. articles to tech. jours. Home: 5 Shaw Pl Saint Louis, MO 63110

CUTLER, IVAN BURTON, educator; b. Salt Lake City, Jan. 11, 1924; s. Ralph and Virginia (Burton) C.; B.S., U. Utah, 1947, Ph.D., 1951; m. Beth Ashton, June 6, 1945; children—Coy (Mrs. Dennis Hogan), Claudia (Mrs. Louis Van Orden), Christopher A., Raymond A., Bonita, Connie, Ralph A., Willard A., Louise. Instr. ceramic engring. U. Utah, Salt Lake City, 1951-52, asst. prof., 1952-56, asso. prof., head dept. ceramic engring., 1956—, prof., 1959-67, prof. mech. engring., 1965—; vis. prof. ceramic engring. U. Ill., 1967-68. Chmn. Gordon Research Conf., 1965. Served to ensign USNR, 1944-46. Fellow Am. Ceramic Soc., mem. Brit. Ceramic Soc., Sigma Xi, Phi Kappa Phi, Tau Beta Pi. Home: 4036 Golden Circle Salt Lake City UT 84117

CUTLER, JOHN CHARLES, physician; b. Cleve., June 29, 1915; s. Glenn Allen and Grace Amanda (Allen) C.; B.A., Western Res. U., 1937, M.D., 1941; M.P.H., Sch. Hygiene and Pub. Health, Johns Hopkins U., 1951; m. Eliese Helene Strahl, Nov. 21, 1942. Commd. asst. surgeon (lt. j.g.), USPHS, 1941, advanced through grades to asst. surgeon gen. (rear adm.), 1958; intern USPHS Hosp., S.I., N.Y., 1941; med. officer USCG Nourmshal, 1942; venereal disease investigations Pub. Health Service Venereal Disease Research, Lab., Stapleton, N.Y., 1943-46; venereal research and demonstration, Guatemala, 1946-48; assigned WHO, 1949-50; with Venereal Disease div., USPHS, 1951-54; program office Bur. State Services, 1954-57; asst. dir., Nat. Inst. Allergy and Infectious Diseases, 1958; asst. surgeon gen. for program, 1958-59; health officer Central dist. Allegheny County Health Dept., 1959-61; adj. asso. prof. pub. health practice Grad. Sch. Pub. Health, U. Pitts., 1959-60; dep. Pan Am. San. Bur., regional office for Americas WHO, 1961-68; prof. internat. health, dir. population div., 1968—; acting head dept. pub. practice, acting dean, Grad. Sch. Pub. Health, U. Pitts., 1968-70. Chmn. population and devel. to secretariat of the OAS. Diplomate Am. Bd. Preventive Medicine and Pub. Health. Fellow Am. Pub. Health Assn.; mem. Internat. Union Against Venereal Diseases and Treponematoses (tech. councelor), Phi Beta Kappa. Contbr. med. articles profl. publs. Home 210 S Dallas Av Pittsburgh, PA 15208 Office: Grad Sch Pub Health U Pitts Pittsburgh PA 15213

CUTLER, JOHN LEWIS, psychiatrist; b. Campbell, Neb., May 9, 1912; s. Morgan George and Ellen (Organ) C.; B.S. in Medicine, U. Ill., 1936, B.M., 1936, M.D., 1937; m. Jeanne Bump, May 17, 1938; children—Robert Lewis, Richard Morgan, Bruce Harold; m. 2d, Sonya Bour, June 28, 1969. Intern, Latter-day Saints Hosp., Salt Lake City, 1936-38; resident Ill. Dept. Welfare Facilities, 1950-57; practice indsl. medicine, surgery Kemmerer Coal Co. (Wyo.), 1938-43; practice indsl. surgery Utah Copper Co., U.S. Smelting, Refining & Mining Co., Am. Smelting Refining Co., 1943-47; pvt. practice medicine, Scottsbluff, Neb., 1947-50; with Ill. Dept. Pub. Welfare, 1950—, Elgin State Hosp. in resident tng. program psychiatry, supervision acute hosp., supr. vets. service; staff Tinley Park State Hosp., 1957—, acting supt., 1957-58, supt., 1958-66; sr. psychiatrist Chgo. Archdiocesan Mental Health Clinic, 1968—; cons. Chgo. Archdiocesan Marriage Tribunal, 1971—; mem. staff Little Co. of Mary, Mercy hosps. Psychiat. cons. Bremen Twp. Com. on Youth; cons. Oak Lawn Family Counseling Service, South Suburban Cook Country Commn. on Alcoholism; mem. Ill. Gov.'s Adv. Council, 1969—, Ill. Mental Health Commn., 1970—. Mem. A.M.A., Ill., Chgo. med. socs. Am., Ill. psychiat. assns., Am. Acad. Med. Adminstrs., Assn. Med. Supts. Mental Hosps., Am. Geriatrics Soc., U. Ill. and Med. Coll. Alumni Assn., Holy Name Soc. Roman Catholic. K.C. Club: Illini (Chgo.). Office: 2400 W 95th St Chicago IL 60642

CUTLER, LAUREL, advt. exec.; b. N.Y.C., Dec. 8, 1926; d. A. Smith and Dorothy (Glaser) Cutler; B.A., Wellesley Coll, 1946; m. Stanley D. Bernstein, July 3, 1952; children—Jonathan Cutler, Amy, Seth Perry. Vice pres. Fletcher, Richards, Calkins & Holden, N.Y.C., 1956-63; sr. v.p., mng. dir., creative dir. McCann- Erickson, Inc., N.Y.C., 1963—, dir., 1970—. Mem. Fashion Group. Author articles. Home: 378 West End Rd South Orange NJ 07079 Office: 485 Lexington Av New York City NY 10017

CUTLER, LAWRENCE MARK, physician, univ. trustee; b. Old Town, Me., Oct. 22, 1906; s. Edwin and Rachel (Rawinski) C.; B.A., U. Me., 1928; M.D., Tufts U., 1932; m. Catherine Epstein, Oct. 14, 1939; children—Eliot, Joshua, Joel. Intern Me. Gen. Hosp., Portland, 1932-33; house officer Boston City Hosp., 1933-34; pvt. practice, Bangor, Me., 1934-41, 46—; chief med. service Eastern Me. Gen. Hosp., Bangor, 1950-68; cons. staff Eastern Me. Med. Centre, 1968—. Mem. Arthritis and metabolic diseases adv. council NIH, 1951-55. Mem. Bangor Sch. Bd., 1945-55, chmn., 1948-52; del. White House Conf. Edn., 1955; chmn. Gov. Me. Adv. Com. Edn., 1957-58; mem. Com. Coordination High Edn. of Maine; adviser to the State Legislature, 1967-68; mem. Nat. Com. Support Pub. Schs., 1963—. Bd. trustees U. Me., 1956—, v.p., 1962-63, pres., 1963- -; bd. dirs. Eastern Me. Guidance Center, Bangor, 1960-64. Served to lt. col., M.C., AUS, 1941-46; PTO. Decorated Bronze Star. Mem. Am., Me., Penobscot med. assns., Newcomen Soc., Am. Jewish Hist. Soc. (exec. council 1965-67), Bangor Mechanics Assn. Home: 33 Grove St Bangor ME 04401 Office: 31 Grove St Bangor ME 04401

CUTLER, LLOYD NORTON, lawyer; b. N.Y.C., Nov. 10, 1917; s. Aaron Smith and Dorothy (Glaser) C.; A.B. cum laude, Yale, 1936, LL.B. magna cum laude, 1939; m. Louise W. Howe, Feb. 15, 1941; children—Deborah Norton, Beverly Winslow, Lloyd Norton, Louisiana Winslow. Admitted to N.Y. bar, 1940, D.C. bar, 1946; practiced in N.Y.C., 1940-42, Washington, 1946—; partner Cox, Langford, Stoddard & Cutler, 1946-62; partner Wilmer, Cutler & Pickering, 1962—. Dir. Kaiser Industries Corp., Alza Corp., N. & W. Ry. Co. Lend-Lease mem. N. African Econ. Bd., 1942; asst. fgn. liquidation commr. for Latin Am. Dept. State, 1945-46; sec. Lawyers Com. Civil Rights Under Law, 1963-65; vice chmn. Bus. Leadership Adv. Council, Office Econ. Opportunity, 1965; chmn. D.C. Com. on Adminstrn. Justice under Emergency Conditions, 1968; exec. dir. Nat. Commn. on the Causes and Prevention of Violence, 1968-69. Vis. com. econs. div. Brookings Instn.; bd. dirs. Nat. Symphony Orch.; mem. Yale U. Council, 1966-71; bd. visitors Econs. Div. Brookings Instn., Sch. for Advanced Internat. Studies. Served to 1st lt. AUS, 1942-45. Mem. Am. Soc. Internat. Law, Am. Law Inst., Am. Bar Assn. (chmn. sect. ind. rights and responsibilities 1968, mem. ho. dels. 1969), Fgn. Policy Assn. (dir.), Yale Law Sch. Assn. (past pres., chmn exec. com.). Clubs: Federal City, Metropolitan, Internat., Kenwood Country (Washington); Yale (N.Y.C.). Home: 5215 Chamberlin Av Chevy Chase MD 20015 Office: 900 17th St NW Washington DC 20006

CUTLER, MAX, surgeon; b. Jitomir, Russia, May 9, 1899; s. Sam and Esther (Tchudnowsky) C.; brought to U.S. in 1907, naturalized, 1914; B.S., U. of Ga., 1918; M.D., Johns Hopkins, 1922; postgrad. Curie Inst., Paris and Radiumhemmet, Stockholm; m. Bertie Burger, Apr. 12, 1946; children—Nina, Nancy, Susie. Surg. intern Johns Hopkins Hosp., 1922-23; cons. in cancer, dir. cancer research, Edward Hines VA Hosp. and U.S. VA, 1931-46; asso. in surg. Northwestern U. Med. Sch., 1935—; vis. prof. surgery Peking (China) Union Med. Coll., 1936-37; now mem. surg. staff Cedars of Lebanon Hosp., Los Angeles; founder, also dir. Chgo. Tumor Inst. First pres. Am. Assn. Study Neoplastic Diseases, 1933-34. Mem. Nat. Adv. Cancer Council, 1939-42. Served in U.S. Army, World War I. Mem. N.Y. Acad. Medicine, Chgo. Inst. Medicine, Am. Radium Soc., Am. Assn. Cancer Research, A.M.A., Chgo. Med. Soc., Internat. Coll. Surgeons; hon. mem. Cuban Radiol. Soc., Radiol. Soc. Chile, Phi Epsilon Pi, Phi Delta Epsilon, Phi Beta Kappa, Alpha Omega Alpha. Jewish religion. Mason. Clubs: Tamarisk, Racquet, Garden Aire. Author: (with Sir George Lenthal Cheatle) Tumors of the Breast, 1931; Cancer, Its Diagnosis and Treatment, 1938; Tumors of the Breast: Their Pathology, Symptoms, Diagnosis and Treatment, 1961. Contbr. articles to profl. jours. Home: 38550 Florence St Beaumont CA 92223 Office: 436 N Roxbury Dr Beverly Hills CA 90210

CUTLER, PAUL W., lawyer; b. Valparaiso, Ind., Sept. 11, 1906; ed. Dartmouth; LL.B., Northwestern U. Admitted to Ill. bar, 1932; now mem. firm Chapman & Cutler, Chgo. Office: 111 W Monroe St Chicago IL 60603*

CUTLER, RICHARD MORTIMER, investment co. exec.; b. Dover, Mass., Sept. 24, 1920; s. Donald F. and Margaret (Lionberger) C.; grad. Phillips-Andover Acad., 1939; student Harvard, 1939-41; m. Mary Randolph Cecil, Dec. 4, 1948; children—Richard Mortimer, Charles C., Nicholas B., John R. S. Loan officer First Nat. Bank Boston, 1946-54; v.p. Parker Corp., Boston, 1954-64; sr. v.p. finance, treas., sec., dir. Putnam Mgmt. Co., Boton, 1964—; v.p., treas., dir. Putnam Investors Fund, Boston, 1964—; v.p., treas. Putnam Income Fund, 1964—; v.p., treas., clk. George Putnam Fund of Boston, Putnam Growth Fund, Putnam Equities Fund, Inc., Putnam Vista Fund, Inc., Putnam Voyager Fund, Inc., Putnam Duofund, Inc.; dir. 18th St. Bldg. Co., St. Louis. Trustee Austen Riggs Center, Stockbridge, Mass., 1960—, chmn., 1964—; trustee Brookwood Sch., Manchester, Mass.; mem. corp. Peter Bent Brigham Hosp.; bd. dirs. Mass. Audubon Soc. Served to capt. USMCR, 1942-46. Home: Preston Pl Beverly MA 01920 Office: 265 Franklin St Boston MA 02110

CUTLER, RICHARD WOOLSEY, lawyer; b. New Rochelle, N.Y., Mar. 9, 1917; s. Charles Evelyn and Amelia (MacDonald) Co.; B.A., Yale, 1938, LL.B., 1941; m. Elizabeth Fitzgerald, Oct. 18, 1947; children—Marguerite Blackburn, Alexander MacDonald, Judith Elizabeth. Admitted to Conn. bar, 1941, N.Y. bar, 1942, Wis. bar, 1950; practiced in N.Y.C., 1941-49, Milw., 1949—; asso. firm Donovan, Leisure, Newton & Lumbard, 1941-42; atty. Legal Aid Soc., 1946- 47, RCA Communications, Inc., 1947-49; partner firm Wood, Warner, Tyrrell & Bruce, 1954-57, Milw., Brady, Tyrrell & Bruce, 1958-66, Brady, Tyrrell, Cotter & Cutler, 1967—. Dir. White Constrn. Co., Steinman Lumber Co., Kelch Corp. Chmn. Milw. br. Fgn. Policy Assn., 1951-53. Pres. Childrens Service Soc. Wis., 1961-63; pres. Neighborhood House; sec. Southeastern Wis. Regional Planning Commn.; bd. dirs. Wis. Dept. Resource Devel., 1967-68; Met. Milw. Study Commn. 1957-61. Served to capt. USAAF, 1943-46. Mem. Am., Wis., Milw. bar assns., Phi Beta Kappa. Republican. Conglist. Clubs: Milwaukee Country, Milwaukee, University, Town, River Tennis (Milw.). Author: Zoning Law and Practice in Wisconsin, 1967. Home: 230 E MacArthur Rd Milwaukee WI 53217 Office: 735 N Water St Milwaukee WI 53202

CUTLER, ROBERT, former banking exec.; b. Brookline, Mass., June 12, 1895; s. George Chalmers and Mary Franklin (Wilson) C.; A.B. cum laude, Harvard, 1916, LL.B. cum laude, 1922; LL.B., Trinity Coll., 1943, Norwich Coll., 1948, Northeastern U., 1949, Colby Coll., 1951, Clark U., 1955, Springfield Coll., 1955, Wesleyan U., 1956; L.H.D., Boston U., 1952, Tufts U. 1953, U. N.H., 1963; D.Sc., Lowell Technol. Inst. 1956. Instr. Harvard, 1916-17; editor Harvard Law Rev., chmn. bd. advisers Harvard Law Sch., 1919-22; admitted to Mass. bar, 1922, practiced in Boston, 1922-42, asso. firm Herrick, Smith, Donald & Farley, 1922-28, partner, 1928-40; corp. counsel City of Boston, 1940-42; pres., dir. Old Colony Trust Co., 1946-53, chmn., 1953, 55-57, 58-60; U.S. exec. dir. Inter-Am. Devel. Bank, 1960-62; spl. asst. to secy. of treasury, 1960-62; spl. asst. to Pres. U.S. for nat. security affairs, 1953-55, 57-58; mem. operations coordinating bd., mem. council on fgn. econ. policy, chmn. Nat. Security Council Planning Bd., 1953-55, 57-58, trustee Boston Five Cent Savs. Bank; now ret. Served to 1st lt. inf., A.E.F., U.S. Army, 1917-19; with A.E.F., France, 1918; adj. 3d Army Mil. Police, Germany, 1919; commd. col., U.S. N.A., 1942 and advanced through grades to brig. gen., 1945; asst. dep. dir. Army Specialist Corps, 1942; chief procurement div. Officer Procurement Service, 1942-43; with gen. staff corps office of Sec. of War, 1943-45; coordinator for soldier voting for army, 1944-45; exec. officer U.S. War Ballot Commn., 1944-45. Awarded D.S.M., Legion of Merit, Medal of Freedom. Gen. chmn. Greater Boston 1937 Community Fund Campaign and div. chmn., 1936, 1939 and 1940 campaigns; chmn. adv. bd. Pub. Welfare Dept. of Mass., 1940-42; trustee and officer Peter Bent Brigham Hosp., 1936—; bd. overseers Boston Symphony Orch.; bd. advisers Nat. Fund for Med. edn.; chmn. Citizens Com. to Survey Health, Social and Welfare Agys. of Greater Boston, 1957-59; nat. treas. Nat. Security Com. Trustee Brookline (Mass.) Public Library, 1932- 38; pres., dir. Community Chests and Councils, Inc., 1939-42, Nat. Commn. Financing Hosp. Care, 1951-52. Fellow Am. Acad. Arts and Scis., Am. Coll. Hosp. Adminstrs. (hon.), A.C.S. (hon.); mem. Greater Boston C. of C. (v.p.), Phi Beta Kappa. Episcopalian. Clubs: Somerset, Tavern, Harvard (Boston); Harvard (N.Y.C.). Author: Louisburg Square, 1917; The Speckled Bird, 1922; No time for Rest, 1966. Home: 41 Beacon St Boston MA 02108

CUTLER, ROBERT H., transp. exec.; b. Portland, Ore., July 13, 1917; s. Frank W. and Hilma (West) C.; student U. Ore., 1940; m. Ellouise Gunn, July 19, 1941; children—Virginia Lee, Cathryn Louise. Asst. to pres. Consol. Freightways Inc., Portland, 1940-50; exec. v.p. Bekins Van Lines, Salt Lake City, 1950-52; pres. Tex. Ariz. Motor Freight Inc., El Paso, Tex., 1952-62; chmn. bd. Ill. Cal. Express Inc., El Paso, Tex., 1962—; chmn. bd., dir. Ben Miller Boot Co., IDC Real Estate Co. (both in El Paso); dir. Mid-Am. Nat. Bank, Chgo., Orchid Isle Ford Auto Center, Hilo, Hawaii, Cummins Engine Sales Hawaii, Honolulu, Bank of El Paso, Trans. Indemnity Co., Los Angeles, Stevens Steel Warehouse, Salem, Ore., El Paso Terminal Warehouse. Bd. dirs. El Paso Devel. Corp., 1963—; sec.-treas. Trucking Employers, Inc., Washington. Chmn. finance com., bd. dirs. Rio Grande council Girl Scout U.S. Served to capt. AUS, 1942-45. Mem. Am. Trucking Assn. (pres. 1966-67), El Paso C. of C. (dir.). Clubs: Internat. Colony (pres., dir. Lahaina, Maui, Hawaii); El Paso Country (past dir.). Home: 520 Linda Av El Paso, TX 79922. Office: 400 Raynolds Blvd El Paso TX 79987

CUTLER, ROBERT WARD, architect; b. Ridgway, Pa., June 27, 1905; s. Robert W. and Olga (Holmberg) C.; B.Arch., Syracuse U., 1928; m. Doris Saxton, June 29, 1929; children—Denise (Mrs. Kent Gordon Kimball), Robert Ward; m. 2d, Morene Parten, Apr. 27, 1954. Employed in various archtl. offices, N.Y.C., 1928-37; asso. Skidmore and Owings, N.Y.C., 1937-45; partner Skidmore, Owings & Merrill, N.Y.C., 1949—. Mem. art commn. N.Y.C., 1958-66; mem. adv. council N.Y. Pub. Library. Trustee Community Service Soc. N.Y.; pres. dir. Fifth Avenue Assn. N.Y.; dir., past pres. Bldg. Research Inst.; life mem., past pres. N.Y. Bldg. Congress; cons. N.Y. Civic Center; trustee Syracuse U. Recipient George Arents Pioneer medal Syracuse U., 1968. Fellow A.I.A. (past pres. N.Y. chapter); mem. Royal Architectural Inst. Canada, Architectural league (past pres.), Am. Hosp. Assn., Sigma Chi. Epilcopalian. Clubs: Century Assn., N.Y. Athletic. Metropolitan (N.Y.C.). Home: 17 W 54th St New York City NY 10019 Office: 400 Park Av New York City NY 10022

CUTLER, THEODORE HAROLD, psychologist, educator; b. Des Moines, Aug. 4, 1907; s. Jonas Parcus and Etta (Coglasier) C.; B.A., Drake U., 1929; student Harvard, 1929-30, 32- 33; Ph.D., U. Colo., 1948; m. Norma Curtis, Nov. 30, 1933; children—Ted, Norma Joan. Indsl. psychologist Ralston Purina Co., St. Louis, 1930-31; asst. mgr. Colo. Employment Service, 1933-35; instr. U. Denver, 1934-39, asst. mgr. Colo. Employment Service, 1933-35; instr. U. Denver, 1934-39; asst. prof. psychology, 1939-46, prof. psychology, adminstrn., 1946—, chmn. div. prodn. mgmt., 1950-55, dean Coll. Bus. Adminstrn., 1955-66; vis. prof. mgmt. Fresno State Coll., 1969-70; regional personnel adviser Resettlement Adminstrn., San Francisco, 1935-37; chief examiner Colo. Civil Service Commn., 1941-42; regional personnel officer OPA, Denver, 1942-43; labor relations officer Mare Island Naval Shipyard, 1943-46; spl. examiner U.S. Civil Service Commn., 1950; cons. Time, Inc., Chgo., 1950-55, United Air Lines, Denver, 1951- 55. Diplomate Am. Bd. Profl. Psychology. Fellow Am. Psychol. Assn.; mem. Am. Legion, Am. Assn. Collegiate Schs. Bus. (exec. com. 1962- 65), Sigma Xi, Psi Chi, Alpha Tau Omega. Presbyn. Club: University. Home: 4301 S Holly St Englewood, CO 80110. Office: University Park Denver CO 80210

CUTLIP, MAURICE IRVIN, corp. exec.; b. Wakefield, O., July 4, 1925; s. Walter Ferman and Louise (Brand) C.; student Miami Jacobs Coll., 1948-50; m. Ella Mae Freeland, Feb. 21, 1947; children—Jeffrey, David. Agt., Internal Revenue Service, 1951-61; gen. auditor E.F. MacDonald Stamp Co., 1961-63; treas. E.F. MacDonald Co., Dayton, O., 1963-66, financial v.p., 1966-67, exec. v.p., 1967—, also dir. co. and subsidiaries. Bd. Dirs. Dayton United Fund, 1963—, Dayton Better Bus. Bur., 1963—. Served with USAAF, 1943-46. Office: 129 S Ludlow St Dayton OH 45402

CUTLIP, RANDALL BROWER, coll. pres.; b. Clarksburg, W.Va., Oct. 1, 1916; s. M.N. and Mildred (Brower) C.; A.B., Bethany Coll., 1940; M.A., E. Tex. U., 1949; Ed.D., U. Houston, 1953; LL.D., Bethany Coll., 1965; m. Virginia White, Apr. 21, 1951. Tchr., adminstrs. Tex. pub. chs., 1947- 50; dir. tchr. placement U. Houston, 1950-51, supr. counselling, 1951- 53; dean student Atlantic Christian Coll., Wilson, N.C., 1953-56, dean coll., 1956-58; dean personnel, dir. grad. div. Chapman Coll., Orange, Cal., 1958-60; pres. William Woods Coll., Fulton, Mo., 1960—. Chmn. bd. visitors Mo. Mil. Acad., 1968—. Served with AUS, 1943-45. Mem. Am. Personnel and Guidance Assn., Alpha Sigma Phi, Phi Delta Kappa, Kappa Delta Pi, Alpha Chi. Address: President's Home William Woods Coll Fulton MO 65251

CUTLIP, SCOTT MUNSON, educator; b. Buckhannon, W.Va., July 15, 1915; s. Okey Scott and Janet (Munson) C.; student W.Va. Wesleyan Coll., 1932-34; A.B., Syracuse U., 1939; Ph.M., U. Wis., 1941; Litt.D., W.Va. Wesleyan Coll., 1971; m. Erna Katherine Flader, May 21, 1947; 1 son, George Carper. Reporter, editor various newspapers, W.Va., 1932-36; dir. pub. relations W.Va. Rd. Commn., 1941-42; asst. prof. U. Wis. at Madison, 1946-47, asst. to pres., 1947-49, asso. prof., 1949-58, prof., 1958—; vis. prof. Cornell U., 1955-56, U. Ida., 1954-58, Utah State U., 1967. Mem. pub. affairs adv. com. U.S. Air Force Acad. Served to maj. USAAF, 1942-46. Mem. Hist. Soc. Wis. (bd. curators, past pres.). Am. Assn. U. Profs., Assn. for Edn. in Journalism, Internat. Pub. Relations Assn. Club: Madison Literary. Author: (with Allen Center) Effective Public Relations, 1952, 4th edit., 1971; Fund Raising in the United States: Its Role in America's Philanthropy, 1965. Compiler: A Public Relations Bibliography, 2d edit., 1965. Home: 142 Larkin St Madison WI 53705

CUTRELL, BENJAMIN ELWOOD, publisher; b. Scottdale, Pa., Mar. 28, 1923; s. George W. and Frances H. (Nissley) C.; student Eastern Mennonite Coll., 1941-42; B.S., Carnegie-Mellon U., 1944; m. Dorothy Lucille Stutzman, Dec. 2, 1944; children—Kathleen (Mrs. Wayne Royer), David B. Gen. mgr., partner LeBlanc Printers, Denver, 1945-55; bus. mgr. Mennonite Pub. House, Scottdale, 1955-61, pub., 1961—. Mem. Mennonite Ch. (chmn. congregation 1962-66, elder 1966-70). Home: Route 1 Box 244-A Scottdale PA 15683 Office: 616 Walnut Av Scottdale PA 15683

CUTRER, LEWIS W., lawyer; b. Osyka, Miss., Nov. 5, 1904; s. Richard Wiltz and Elizabeth (Lewis) C.; B.A., U. Miss., 1925, LL.B., 1926; m. Cathrine H. Hopson, Oct. 11, 1927; children—Lewis W., Mallory (Mrs. David D. Allen), Richard H. Admitted to Tex. bar, 1929, since practiced in Houston; partner in firm Cutrer & Jefferson; city atty., Houston, 1941-46; gen. counsel Houston Ind. Sch. Dist., 1954-56. Dir. Fannin Bank, Houston, 1954-57, 64—. Pres. Am. Municipal Assn., 1962-63, Tex. Municipal League. 1963, Tex. City Attys. Assn., 1946; trustee, dir. U.S. Conf. Mayors, 1960-63. Mayor of Houston, 1958-63. Active local YMCA, Boy Scouts Am., United Fund, Salvation Army, also Houston Symphony, Houston Grand Opera, Houston Art Mus. Mem. Am., Houston (pres. 1954) bar assns., State Bar Tex., Houston, Houston Jr. (pres. 1934) C.'s of C. Democrat. Methodist. Elk, Kiwanian, Mason (32, Shriner). Clubs: Houston Country, Houston, Champions Country, President's Health (Houston). Home: 3636 Ella Lee Lane Houston TX 77027 Office: Fannin Bank Bldg Houston TX 77025

CUTSHALL, ALDEN, educator; b. Olney, Ill., Apr. 12, 1911; s. George Oliver and Ethel (Slichenmyer) C.; B.Edn., E. Ill. State U., 1932; M.A., U. Ill., 1935; postgrad. Northwestern U., 1935-36; Ph.D., Ohio State U., 1940; m. Freda Elizabeth Dolton, Mar. 29, 1933; children—Arlene, Alden. Tchr., Ill. pub. schs., 1932-34, 37-39; mem. faculty U. Ill., 1940—, prof. geography, head dept. at Chgo. Circle Campus, 1964-69. Asso. mem. Center Advanced Study, U. Ill., 1962-63; prin. research analyst OSS and State Dept., 1944-46; with U.S. Soil Conservation Service, summer 1937, Ball State Tchrs. Coll., summer 1941, Army Map Service, summer 1942, George Peabody Coll. Tchrs., summer 1943, UNESCO, Manila, P.I., summer 1951. Fulbright grantee, Philippines, 1950-51, 57-58. Mem. A.A.A.S., Assn. Am. Geographers, Nat. Council Geog. Edn., Philippine, Ill. (pres. 1963-64), Chgo. geog. socs., Ill. Acad. Sci., Sigma Xi. Author: The Philippines: A Nation of Islands, 1964; asso. author: World Political Geography, rev. edit., 1957. Home: 667 N Elizabeth St Lombard IL 60148 Office: U Ill Chicago Circle Chicago IL 60680

CUTTER, CHARLES RICHARD III, educator; b. Woodward, Okla., Feb. 8, 1924; s. Charles Richard and Mary (Lowry) C.; B.A., Baylor U.; B.D., Th.D., Southwestern Baptist Theol. Sem.; m. Phyllis Marie Fletcher, Nov. 15, 1942; children—Cynthia Marie (Mrs. Robert Wheeler Jr.), Marcia Ellen. Ordained to ministry Bapt. Ch.; pastor Kopperl (Tex.) Bapt. Ch., 1957—; prof. Classics Baylor U., 1958; propr. Cutter Food Market, Gruver, Tex., 1946-51. Served as navigator USAAF, 1942-45. Decorated Air medal with five clusters. Mem. Am. Philol. Assn., Soc. Bib. Lit. Home: 2425 Charboneau St Waco TX 76710

CUTTER, GEORGE OLIN, mfg. co. exec.; b. Boston, Dec. 18, 1915; s. George O. and Violet F. (Creber) C.; student Dartmouth, 1936-39; m. Anita Marie Engen, July 9, 1938; children—Joan V., Gail O., Ann M., Beth C. Mgr., W. Bowman Cutter, Inc., retail hardware, Roxbury, Mass., 1939-42, pres., treas., 1946-48; with ordnance dept. War Dept., 1942-45, quality control chief, insp. with Gillette Safety Razor Co., 1948-64, v.p. safety razor div., 1960- 64; v.p. mfg. and devel. new products Gillette Co., 1964-66, v.p., gen. mgr. Western Hemisphere div., 1966-67, group v.p., gen. mgr. internat. operations, 1968-69, sr. v.p. co. planning and tech. operations, 1969—, vice chmn. bd. dirs., 1970—. Mem. Nat. Metal Traders Assn. (dir. Boston), Am. Soc. Quality Control (past pres. Boston). Mason (Shriner), K.P. Home: 26 Sherman Rd Melrose MA 02176 Office: Gillette Co Prudential Tower Bldg Boston MA 02199

CUTTER, MARGOT ELIZABETH, fgn. service officer; b. Augusta, Ga.; d. William Dick and Margaret (Moir) Cutter; B.A., Northwestern U., 1934; M.A., Inst. Fine Arts, N.Y.C., 1940; postgrad. Inst. Art and Archeology, Paris, France, 1937. Editorial asst. Inst. Advanced Study, Princeton, 1937-43; with A.R.C., Italy, 1943-45; fine arts editor, Princeton U. Press, 1945-52; mng. editor Art Bull., 1948-52; cultural affairs officer USIA, Bologna, Milan, Italy, 1952-54, fgn. affairs officer, Washington, 1954-58, research officer, Paris, 1959-61, regional book officer, 1961-65, dep. chief, publs. Information Center Service, Washington, 1966, agy. planning officer Office Policy and Research, 1966-69, cultural attache Am. embassy, Rabat, Morocco, 1969—. Mem. Phi Beta Kappa. Author: Caravaggio in the Seventeenth Century (Marsyas I), 1941. Home: PO Box 1611 Winter Park FL 32789 Office: Am Embassy Rabat Morocco

CUTTER, RICHARD AMMI, judge; b. Salem, Mass., May 11, 1902; s. Louis Fayerweather and Perkins (Osgood) C.; A.B., Harvard, 1922; LL.B., 1925; D Sc. Jur (hon.), Suffolk U., 1960; m. Ruth Dexter Grew, June 10, 1925; childrenLouis Ammi, Henry Sturgis Grew and Helen (Mrs. Robert A.R. Maclennan). Admitted to Mass. bar, 1926; asso. firm Goodwin, Proctor, Field and Hoar, 1926-27; asst. atty. gen., Mass., 1927-30; adviser to gov. P.R., 1930-31; partner Storey, Thorndike, Palmer & Dodge, and successor firm Palmer, Dodge, Gardner & Bradford, Boston, 1931-42, 1946- 56; asso. justice Supreme Jud. Ct., Boston, 1956-. Cons. to sec. air force, 1951, to dir. off-shore procurement, 1954, to dir. Internat. Coop. Adminstrn., 1956. Mem. bd. of overseers Harvard, 1966—. Served from maj. to col., Gen. Staff Corps, AUS, 1942-46. Decorated Legion of Merit with cluster. Mem. Am., Mass., Boston bar assns., Am. Law Inst. (1st v.p.; council), Harvard Law Sch. Scis., Colonial Soc. Mass. Episcopalian. Clubs: Harvard (N.Y.C.); Randolph (N.H.) Mountain; Country (Brookline, Mass.); Union, Curtis, Tavern (Boston); Metropolitan (Washington); Appalachian Mountain. Home: 62 Sparks St Cambridge, MA 02138. Office: Supreme Judicial Court Court House Boston MA 02108

CUTTER, ROBERT KENNEDY, pharm. mfr.; b. Fresno, Cal., May 23, 1898; s. Edward A. and Margaret (Kennedy) C.; B.A., M.A., U. Cal.; M.D. cum laude, Yale, 1923; grad. study allergy Cornell div. N.Y. Hosp.; m. Virginia White, Sept. 9, 1922 (dec. July 1969); children—Robert Kennedy, Richard White, David Lee; m. 2d, Alice Knapp, June 10, 1971. Intern San Francisco Hosp., 1923-24; practice of medicine specializing in allergy, Oakland, Cal., 1924-26; asst. med. dir. Cutter Labs., Berkeley, Cal., 1924-28, asst. to pres., 1928-30, chief exec. officer, 1930-45, pres., 1945-62, chmn. bd., 1963—. Bd. dirs. Trustees for Conservation. Mem. Am. Pharm. Mfrs. Assn. (pres. 1956-57), Cal. Mfrs. Assn. (pres. 1952-53), Delta Sigma Phi, Nu Sigma Nu. Patentee disposable syringes, intravenous injection equipment, snake bite kits. Home: 107 Southampton Av Berkeley CA 94707 Office: Cutter Laboratories 4th and Parker Sts Berkeley CA 94710

CUTTING, HEYWARD, designer, planner, mus. ofcl.; b. N.Y.C., Dec. 3, 1921; s. Heyward and Constance (Roberson) C.; grad. Eton, 1939; student Harvard, 1939-41; B.Sc., Ill. Inst. Tech. 1953; m. Jeremy Hohenstein, Jan. 17, 1948; children—Heyward, Francis Brockholst, William Bayard. Partner Chermayeff & Cutting, architects and indsl. designers, 1954-56; pvt. practice architecture, Cambridge, 1957; v.p., sec., dir. Geometrics, Inc., architects, engrs. and cons. specialized structures, Cambridge, 1958-68; asst. dir. Mus. Fine Arts, Boston 1968—, trustee, 1961-68. Former trustee Mt.

Auburn Hosp., Cambridge; past mem. vis. com. dept. archaeology and dept. fine arts Harvard. Served to maj. KRRC, 60th Rifles, Brit. Army, 1941-45; Egypt, Italy. Mentioned in Dispatches. Clubs: Somerset, Tavern (Boston); The Brook (N.Y.C.). Home: 1715 Cambridge St Cambridge MA 02138 Office: 465 Huntington Av Boston MA 02115

CUTTING, RALPH HENRY, fibre co. exec.; b. South Paris, Me., July 17, 1906; s. George A. and Iva (Haggett) C.; grad. high sch.; m. Amelia C. D'Archangelo, July 27, 1929, 1 dau., Nancy (Mrs. Richard M. Coveney). Bookkeeper, Fairfield Mfg. Co., Portland, Me., 1925-28; with Keyes Fibre Co., Waterville, Me., 1928—, beginning as clk. successively purchasing agt., asst. treas. and office mgr., asst. gen. mgr. treas., v.p., gen. mgr., 1928-57, pres., 1957-65, vice chmn., 1965—, also dir.; v.p., dir. Poland Spring Bottling Corp.; dir. Kennebec River Pulp and Paper Co., Inc., Fed. Trust Co., Canadian Keyes Fibre Co., Ltd., Union Mut. Life Ins. Co. Dir., Me. Council Econ. Edn.; mem. New Eng. Interstate Water Pollution Control Commn., 1955-58. Dir. Asso. Industries Me. (pres. 1966-67). Bd. dirs. Me. Children's Home for Little Wanderers (pres. 1955-67); sec. U. Me. Pulp and Paper Found. (dir. 1958-66); trustee Thayer Hosp. Assos. (pres. 1962-67), U. Me. Mem. Me. C. of C., Am. Paper Inst., N.A.M. (past dir.). Baptist. Mason. Clubs: Rotary, Waterville Country (Waterville). Home: 4 Greylock Rd Waterville ME 04901 Office: Keyes Fibre Co Waterville ME 04901

CUTTING, WINDSOR COOPER, physician; b. Campbell, Cal., July 30, 1907; s. Theodore A. and Mary Elizabeth (Cooper) C.; A.B., Stanford, 1928, M.D., 1932; m. Mary E. Weaver, May 3, 1935; children—Cecil Cooper, John Weaver, David Windsor, Ann Ely, April Bourne, Susan Mary Atwood. Intern, sch. medicine Stanford, 1931-32, asst. resident medicine, 1932-34, resident, 1934-35, asst. prof. therapeutics, 1938-41, asso. prof., 1941-46, prof. therapeutics, 1946-50, exec. prof. pharmacology and therapeutics, 1950- 54, prof. pharmacology, 1954-58, prof. exptl. therapeutics, 1958-64, dean, 1953-57; dir. Pacific Biomed. Research Center, U. Hawaii, 1964-66, dean Sch. Med., 1966-71. NRC fellow in medicine Courtauld Inst. Biochem., London, Eng., 1935-36; fellow med. and pharmacology Johns Hopkins, 1936-38. Mem. Am. Soc. Pharmacology and Exptl. Therapeutics, Soc. Exptl. Biology and Med., Am. Soc. Cancer Research, Cal. Acad. Med. Author: Manual of Clinical Therapeutics, 1943, rev. edit., 1948; Actions and Uses of Drugs, 1946; Handbook of Pharmacology, 1962, rev. edit., 1969. Exec. com. U.S. Pharmacopeia, 1950-60, bd. dirs. 1960-70, Annual Revs., inc., 1959-70. Editor Annual Review Pharmacology, 1959-70. Contbr. profl. jours. Home: 769 Sunset Av Honolulu HI 96816 Office: Leahi Hosp Honolulu HI 96816

CUTTINO, JOHN TINDAL, educator, pathologist; b. Sumter County, S.C., Aug. 15, 1912; s. Harry Wells and Lydia Beulah (Tindal) C.; B.S., Coll. of Charleston, 1934, LL.D. (hon.), 1961; M.D., Medical Coll. of S.C., 1936; m. Nell Parrott Seabrook, June 11, 1938; children—Harriette Wells, John Tindal. Rotating intern Roper Hosp., Charleston, S.C., 1936-37; asst. physician S.C. State Hosp., 1937-40; vol. fellow St. Elizabeth's Hosp., Washington, 1940; instr., sch. medicine Duke, 1946-47, asso. in pathology, 1957-50, asst. prof. pathology, 1950; acting dean med. coll. Med. Coll. S.C., 1950-51, dean, 1951-60, asso. prof. pathology, 1950-52, prof. 1952—, acting pres., 1960-62; dir. labs. Charlotte Meml. Hosp., 1965-70, dir. Sch. Med. Tech., 1970—. Served to lt. col. M.C., AUS, 1941-45. Diplomate pathologic anatomy Am. Bd. Pathology, 1947, clin. pathology, 1949. Fellow Coll. of Am. Pathologists, Am. Assn. Clin. Pathologists; N.E.A., Huguenot Soc., Am., Soc., N.C. med. assns., Am. Assn. Pathologists and Bacteriologists, A.A.A.S., Pi Kappa Phi, Phi Chi, Alpha Omega Alpha. Ind. Democrat. Presbyn. (elder). Rotarian. Contbr. articles med. jours. Home: 101 Highland Forest Dr Matthews NC 28105 Office: Charlotte Meml Hosp Charlotte NC 28101

CUTTLE, TRACY DONALD, physician, former naval med. officer; b. Mont., Aug. 23, 1908; s. (Tracy) C.; A.B., U. Cal. at Berkeley, 1931; M.D., U. Pa., 1935; m. Hanna Lore Remmers, Dec. 22, 1960; children by previouss marriage—Alexa (Mrs. Edward Cottingham), Lynn (Mrs. Wayen C. Wirth), Cynthia (Mrs. Roy Jackson). Intern, Pa. Hosp., 1935-37, research fellow, 1939-41; exchange fellow medicine St. Bartholomew's Hosp., London, Eng., 1937-39; asso. medicine Jefferson Med. Coll., Phila., 1939-41; research fellow, attending physician Pa. Hosp., 1939- 41; commd. lt. (j.g.) M.C., USN, 1938, advanced through grades to capt., 1955; med. officer LST Flotilla 5, 1943-44, U.S.S. Bennington, 1944, 6th Marine Div., 1944-45; chief medicine U.S. Naval Hosp., Treasure Island, San Francisco, 1946; med. officer U.S. Naval Hosp., Oakland, Cal.,1946-51; chief medicine U.S. Naval Hosp., Chelsea, Mass., 1951-53, U.S. Naval Hosp., Yokosuka, Japan, 1953-55; asst. chief medicine Naval Hosp., Oakland, 1955-58; force med. officer CRU DES PAC, 1958-60; depot med. officer MCRD, San Diego, 1960-62; sr. med. officer U.S. Naval Shipyard, Portsmouth, N.H., 1962-64; comdg. officer Naval Hosp., Portsmouth, 1964-66, Chelsea, 1966-69; ret., 1969; practice internal medicine, San Francisco, 1969—. Physicians; mem. Am. Fedn. Clin. Research, Am., Indsl. med. assns. Contbr. articles to profl. jours., sects. to books. Home: 198 450 Sutter St San Francisco CA 94108

CUTTS, CHARLES EUGENE, engring. educator; b. Sioux Falls, S.D., May 15, 1914; s. Charles Clifford and Ethel May (Gardner) C.; B.C.E., U. Minn., 1936, M.S. in Civil Engring., 1939, Ph.D., 1949; m. Jane Bebensee, Mar. 16, 1946; children—George Gardner, Elizabeth Ann. Instrumentman Milw. R.R., 1936- 38; teaching asst. dept. civil engring. U. Minn., 1938-39, instr., asst. prof., 1946-50; engr. C. F. Haglin & Sons, summer 1939; asst. prof. dept. civil engring. Robert Coll., Istanbul, Turkey, 1939-42; engr. Braithwaite Co., Ltd., Iskenderun, Turkey, summer 1942, 43; asso. prof., asso. research engr. U. Fla., 1950-53; engr. Engring. Scis. Program, NSF, Washington, 1953-56; profl. lectr. civil engring. George Washington U., 1955-56; prof., chmn. dept. civil engring. Mich. State U., 1956-69, prof., 1969—. Served to maj., C.E., AUS, 1943-46; lt. col. Res. ret. Registered profl. engr., Minn., Fla., Mich. Mem. Nat. Acad. Scis. (fellowship com. 1961-63), Am. Soc. C.E. (chmn. com. on mech. properties of materials 1965, pres. Mich. sect, 1967, chmn. com. on engring. edn. 1969-70), Am. Concrete Inst., Am. Soc. Engring. Edn. (chmn. civil engr. div. 1965-66, v.p. 1970—), Engrs. Council Profl. Devel. (vice chmn. region 6, 1969—), Nat. Soc. Profl. Engr., Column Research Council, Tau Beta Pi, Chi Epsilon. Author: Structural Design in Reinforced Concrete, 1954; other tech. publs. Home: 4599 Ottawa Dr Okemos MI 48864 Office: Michigan State University East Lansing MI 48823

CUYKENDALL, TREVOR RHYS, physicist; b. Denver, Nov. 30, 1905; s. Frank and Maud (Rhys) C.; B.S., U. of Denver, 1926, M.S., 1927; Ph.D., Cornell U., 1935; m. Muriel Fetterly, Aug. 1931; children—Mary Jean, Robert Rhys. Instr. U. of Denver, 1927-29; instr., Cornell U., 1930-36, asst. prof., 1937-41, asso. prof., 1945-48, prof. of engring. physics, 1948—, asst. dir. engring. physics dept., 1951-57, dir. 1957-62, asso. dir. dept. engring. physics and materials sci., 1962-65, Spencer T. Olin prof. engring., 1966—, dir. Sch. Engring. Physics, 1967-71, chmn. fellowship bd. Cornell Grad. Sch.; physicist, Naval Ordnance Lab., Washington, 1941-43; scientist, Los Alamos (N.M.) Sci. Lab., 1943-45, Oak Ridge Nat. Lab., 1950-51, Brookhaven Nat. Lab., 1958. Mem. AEC-NSE Fellowship Bd., Oak Ridge, 1963-70, chmn., 1965; cons. div. nuclear edn. and tng. AEC. In charge of Am. Iron and Steel Inst. sponsored studies at Cornell on behavior of thin structural shapes, 1938- 41. Recipient U.S. Naval Ordnance Development award, 1946; distinguished Engring. Alumnus award U. Denver, 1962. Fellow Am. Phys. Soc.; mem. Am. Soc. Engring. Edn. (chmn. physics div. 1961-62, chmn. com. AEC relations 1962-67). Am. Nuclear Soc., Am. Assn. U. Profs., Sigma Xi, Tau Beta Pi, Phi Kappa Phi. Contbr. articles in profl. jours. Author of method for measurement of soil moisture by neutron scattering (with H. S. Sack), 1950. Home: 207 Kline Woods Rd Ithaca NY 14850

CYERT, RICHARD MICHAEL, educator, economist; b. Winona, Minn., July 22, 1921; s. Walter Michael and Anne Fostine (Brown) C.; B.S. in Econs., U. Minn., 1943; Ph.D., Columbia, 1951; m. Margaret Shadick, Sept. 8, 1946; children—Lynn Anne, Lucinda Carol, Martha Sue. Instr., U. Minn., 1946, 48, Coll. City N.Y., 1948; asst. prof. econs. and indsl. adminstrn. Carnegie Inst. Tech. (now Carnegie-Mellon U.), Pitts., 1949-55, asso. prof. econs. and indsl. adminstr., head indsl. mgmt. dept., 1955-60, prof. econs. and indsl. adminstrn., 1960-62, dean Grad. Sch. Indsl. Adminstrn., 1962—. Dir. Gemini Systems, Inc.; dir. Pitts. br. Fed. Res. Bank Cleve. Chmn. research adv. com. Nat. Planning Assn.; mem. research adv. com. Brookings Instn.; cons. Office Higher Edn. and Research, Ford. Found. Served USNR, 1943-46. Ford fellow, 1959-60; Guggenheim fellow, 1967-68. Mem. Am. Econ. Assn., Am. Statis. Assn., Econometric Soc., Inst. Mgmt. Scis. (pres.), Am. Assn. U. Profs., Am. Inst. C.P.A.'s (mem. accounting objectives group), Phi Beta Kappa, Beta Gamma Sigma. Author: (with R.M. Trueblood) Sampling Techniques in Accounting, 1957; (with H.J. Davidson) Sampling for Accounting Information, 1962; (with J.G. March) A Behavioral Theory of the Firm, 1963; (with K.J. Cohen) Theory of the Firm: Resource Allocation in a Market Economy, 1965. Contbr. articles to profl. jours. Bd. editors Behavioral Sci., Adminstrv. Sci. Quar. Home: 35 Chapel Ridge Rd Pittsburgh PA 15238

CYNKAR, STANLEY JOHN, savs. and loan exec.; b. Mosinee, Wis., Dec. 25, 1915; s. Joseph and Aniela (Rymar) C.; student Northwestern U., 1933-37; m. Grace B. Grzemski, Sept. 30, 1939; 1 son, Robert J. Credit mgr. Formfit, Chgo., 1933-39; asst. sec. to pres. Northwestern Savs. & Loan Assn., Chgo., 1939-59; dir., organizer Bank for Savs. and Loans. Served with AUS, World War II; ETO. Mem. Execs. Club Chgo., Polish-Am. Savs. and Loan League (sec.), Cook County Council Insured Assns. (pres. 1966-67). Club: Polish American of Chicago (sec.). Home: 6751 Edgebrook Terrace Chicago IL 60646 Office: 2300 N Western Av Chicago IL 60647

CYR, FRANK W., educator; b. Franklin, Neb., July 17, 1900; s. Howard V. and Nellie (Phoenix) C.; B.S., U. of Neb., 1923; Ph.D., Columbia, 1933; two children (by former marriage)—Katherine, William. Supt. Deuel Co. High Sch., Chappell, Neb., 1923-30; asso. in rural edn., Teachers Coll., Columbia, 1930-34, asst. prof. edn., 1934- 38, asso. Supplementary Ednl. Center. Dir. survey on pupil transp., Columbia, 1937-39; chmn. conf. 48 state reps. on sch. bus. standards, 1939, 45; chmn. com. on program and policy, rural dept. N.E.A., pres. dept., 1940; asso. dir. Nat. Citizenship Edn. Program, Washington, D.C., 1941-42; chmn. conf. state and fed. officials which formulated wartime sch. transportation policy, 1942; mem. White House Conf. on Rural Edn., 1946-47; cons. on rural edn. to Am. Inst. of Cooperation, 1945-51; dir. Study Dist. Superintendency N.Y. and County Superintendency Pa. American del. Internat. Country Life Conf., Brussels, Belgium, 1926, Nat. Commn. on Safety Edn., 1944-48; mem. Nat. Conf. Rural Edn., 1954; commn. on relation Christian ethics to econ. life of Nat. Council Chs.; nat. council Boy Scouts Am. Mem. N.E.A., Am. Assn. School Adminstrs., N.Y. State Tchrs. Assn., Phi Delta Kappa, Kappa Delta Pi, Alpha Zeta. Republican. Methodist. Author: Responsibility for Rural School Administration, 1933; The Small School in Wartime, 1942; Rural Education in the United States (transl. into Spanish and Portuguese), 1943. Co-author: The Small High School at Work, 1936; An Introduction to Modern Education, 1937; Paying for Our Public Schools, 1938; Schools in Small Communities, 1939 (yearbook of Am. Assn. Shc. Adminstrs.); A Policy for Rural Education in United States, 1940; Planning the Rural Community School Building, 1949. Contbr. to ednl. jours. Exec. sec. Catskill Area Project Small Sch. Design, 1957-61. Address: Stamford NY 12167

CYR, GEORGE WILLIAM, broadcasting co. exec.; b. Amesbury, Mass., Feb. 10, 1920; s. George Frederick and Elizabeth Mary (Burke) C.; grad. Twin Cities Television Labs., 1949; student Columbia Coll., Chgo., 1946-47, U. Minn., 1947-48; m. Josephine Catherine Perme, Apr. 30, 1955; children—Darcie, Melody, George, Johnna, Christopher. Dir., program mgr. WNBK, Cleve., 1949-56; program mgr. WRCV, Phila., 1956-59, WGR, Buffalo, 1959-61, WDAU, Scranton, Pa., 1961-62, WNAC-TV, Boston, 1962-69; gen. mgr. WHCT-TV, Hartford, Conn., 1969—. Pub. relations chmn. Lions Gallery for Sightless, Hartford, 1970—. Bd. dirs. Hartford Better Bus. Bur. Served to capt. USAAF, 1942-46. Decorated D.F.C., Air medal with 3 oak leaf clusters; recipient numerous awards for programs produced. Mem. Nat. Assn. Broadcasters, Advt. Club Hartford, Conn. Broadcasters Assn. (dir.). Lion (dir.; Lion of tr. award 1971). Home: Hatchet Hill Rd East Granby CT 06026 Office: 555 Asylum St Hartford CT 06105

CYR, LEO GEORGE, fgn. service officer; b. Limestone, Me., July 28, 1909; s. Louis Alfred and Laura (Franck) C.; A.B., Holy Cross Coll., 1930; M.S. in Fgn. Service, Georgetown U., 1933, LL.B., 1939; grad. Nat. War Coll., 1949; m. Katherine Powell McCormick, Apr. 30, 1941; children—Leo Marshall, Katherine Ann (Mrs. Richard Godlewski), Nancy Louise. Aide to N.R.A. dep. adminstr. for P R., 1933-36; asso. legal adviser Nat. Archives, 1937-41; admitted to D.C. bar, 1939; with U.S. State Dept., 1941—, trade intelligence, 1941-45, surplus property work, 1946, asst. chief aviation div., 1947-48; with Office African Affairs, 1949—, dep. dir., 1952-55, dir., 1955-57; consul gen. Tangier, Morocco, 1957-60; counselor Am. embassy, Yaounde, Cameroon, 1960-61, Tunis, Tunisia, 1961-65; diplomat-in-residence Ohio U., Athens, 1965-66; ambassador to Rwanda, 1966—. Lion. Home: 5205 Hampden Lane Bethesda MD 20014 Office: B P 28 Am Embassy Kigali Rwanda

CYRANKIEWICZ, JOSEF, Polish govt. ofcl.; b. 1911. Sec. Socialist Party in Cracow, 1935, sec.- gen., 1945-47; imprisoned by Germans, 1939, escaped and organized resistance Province of Cracow, arrested and sent to Oswiecim concentration camp, 1941, liberated by Allies, 1945; prime minister, 1947-52, dep. prime minister, 1952-54, prime minister, 1954-70; chmn. Council of State, 1970—. Sec. central com. United Polish Workers Party, mem. polit. com., 1948. Office: Council State Warsaw Poland

CZARNIK, MARVIN RAY, aero engr.; b. St. Louis, Sept. 19, 1932; s. Stanley Bernard and Laura (Kramer) C.; student Valparaiso U., 1950-51; B.S. in Elec. Engring., Washington U., St. Louis, 1954; extension student, U. Mo., 1964; m. Mary Ann Miller, Nov. 26, 1955; children—Kristy Kay, Carol Lee. With McDonnell-Douglas Corp., St. Louis, 1955—, sr. group engr., guidance and control 1964-68, skylab program devel., 1968—; developed guidance system Gemini space rendevous. Mem. Am. Inst. Aeros. and Astronautics. Home: 7507 English Coach Lane Hazelwood MO 63042 Office: PO Box 516 St Louis MO 63166

DAANE, ADRIAN HILL, educator, chemist; b. Stillwater, Okla., June 18, 1919; s. Adrian and Bessie (Hill) D.; B.S., U. Fla., 1941; Ph.D., Ia. State U., 1950; m. Jean Plunkett, June 22, 1944; children—Susan, Peter, Ann. Research asso., group leader Manhattan Project, Ia. State U., 1942-45, from grad. teaching asst. to prof. chemistry, 1946-63, grad. research asst., then sr. chemist Ames Lab., 1948-50, 58-63; prof. chemistry, head dept. Kan. State U., Manhattan, 1963—. Mem. materials adv. bd. Nat. Acad. Sci., 1958—. Mem. bd. edn. Am. Baptist Conv., 1958-63. Fellow Am. Inst. Chemists; mem. Am. Chem. Soc., Am. Soc. Mining, Metall. and Petroleum Engrs., Am. Vacuum Soc., Am. Assn. U. Profs., A.A.A.S., Kan. Acad. Sci. Home: 741 Canfield Dr Manhattan, KS 66502.

DAANE, JAMES DEWEY, govt. ofcl.; b. Grand Rapids, Mich., July 6, 1918; s. Gilbert L. and Mamie (Blocksma) D.; A.B. magna cum laude, Duke, 1939; M.P.A., Harvard, 1946, D.P.A.(Littauer fellow), 1949; m. Blanche M. Tichenor, Apr. 28, 1941 (div. 1952); 1 dau., Elizabeth Marie (Mrs. Ronald Mallek); m. 2d, Onnie B. Selby, Jan. 23, 1953 (dec. Dec. 1961); m. 3d, Barbara W. McMann, Feb. 16, 1963; children—Elizabeth Whitney, Olivia Quartel. With Fed. Res. Bank, Richmond, Va., 1939-60, asst. v.p., 1953-57, v.p., 1957-60, also cons. to pres. bank; asso. economist Fed. Open Market Com., 1955-56, 58-59; chief IMF Fiscal Mission to Paraguay, 1950-51; adviser to pres. Fed. Res. Bank, Mpls., 1960; asst. to sec. treasury, 1960-61; dep. undersec. treasury for monetary affairs, 1961-63; bd. govs. Fed. Res. System, 1963—. Mem. Am. Econ. Assn., Am. Finance Assn., Asso. Harvard Alumni (dir.), Harvard Grad. Soc. for Advanced Study and Research. Home: 1137 N Ivanhoe St Arlington, VA 22205. Office: Fed Res Bldg Washington DC 20551

DAANE, RUSSELL MELVILLE, banker; b. Grand Rapids, Mich., Oct. 10, 1905; s. Hubert and Mary (Witters) D.; A.B., Mich. State U., 1928; grad. comml. bank mgmt. course, Columbia, 1959; m. Hildreth Van Haitsma, Dec. 27, 1929 (dec.); children—Roderick K., Ellen (Mrs. Laurence A. Chrouch II), Arthur R.; m. 2d, Elizabeth M. Littlejohn, Nov. 30, 1968. Bank examiner Mich. Banking Dept., 1928-32; chief examiner, asst. mgr. Detroit office RFC, 1932-35; exec. v.p. Plymouth United Savs. Bank (Mich.), 1936-43; with Daisy Mfg. Co., Plymouth, 1946-58, v.p., 1957-58; with Ft. Wayne Nat. Bank (Ind.), 1958—, exec. v.p., 1961-63, pres., 1963-68, chmn. bd., pres., chief exec. officer, 1968-71, vice chmn., dir., 1971—. Served to lt. comdr. USNR, 1943-46. Recipient Distinguished Alumnus award Mich. State U., 1967. Mem. Am. Inst. Banking, Ind. Bankers Assn. (pres. 1967-68), Ind. C. of C., Sigma Chi. Presbyn. (elder). Rotarian (pres. Plymouth 1940-41). Clubs: Ft. Wayne Country (dir., treas. 1964-65), Press, Quest (pres. 1963-64) (Ft. Wayne); Columbia (Indpls.). Home: 1711 Dell Cove Dr Fort Wayne IN 46804 Office: 110 W Berry St Fort Wayne IN 46802

DABBS, HENRY ERVEN, TV art dir.-producer; b. Clover, Va., Oct. 15, 1932; s. Charles E. and Gertrude (Hudson) D.; B.F.A., Pratt Inst., 1955; m. Loretta D. Young, Jan. 9, 1957. Book designer Berton Wink, Inc., N.Y.C., 1958- 62; art dir.-producer Dancer, Fitzgerald Sample, N.Y.C., 1963—; original paintings depicting famous Afro-Americans in Am. history in permanent collection Frederick Douglass Mus., Washington. Served with AUS, 1955-58. Mem. N.A.A.C.P. Creator Afro-American History Fact Pack, 1968. Author: Afro-Englishtown History Highlights, 1968. Home: 24 Whittier Dr Englishtown NJ 07726 Office: 347 Madison Av New York City NY 10018

DABBS, JACK AUTREY, educator; b. Mercury, Tex., Jan. 31, 1914; s. John Franklin and Florence Susan (Boyd) D.; B.A., U. Tex., Austin, 1935, M.A., 1936, Ph.D., 1950; m. Anna Viola Johnson, May 24, 1940; 1 dau., Danielle Elizabeth. Tchr., Tex. Wesleyan Acad., Austin, 1935-36; tchr. Lockhart (Tex.) High Sch., 1937-38; instr. St. Edward's U., Austin, 1938-40, 48-50; asst. prof., asso. prof., prof. Tex. A. and M. U., College Station, 1950—, head dept. modern langs., 1964—; dir. Am. Lang. Inst., Baghdad, Iraq, 1957- 58. Served with inf., U.S. Army, 1940-48. Mem. Am. Name Soc. (past pres.), Linquistic Soc. Am., Modern Lang. Assn., Societe Linguistique de Paris. Author: A Short Bengali-English, English-Bengali Dictionary, 1962; History of the Discovery and Exploration of Chinese Turkestan, 1963; The French Army in Mexico 1861-1867, 1963; The Mariano Riva Palacio Archives, 1967-68. Home: 1011 Edgewood St Bryan TX 77801 Office: Dept Modern Langs Tex A and M U College Station TX 77843

DABNEY, FRANCIS LEWIS, mgmt. cons.; b. Seattle, Dec. 13, 1907; s. John Pomeroy and Beatrice Mildred (Gunter) D.; B.S. in Mech. Engring. and Bus. Adminstrn. cum laude, Harvard, 1931; m. Helen Wheeler Baldwin, Sept. 9, 1933; children—John Baldwin, Sally (Mrs. Everett H. Parker), Stephen Francis. With Great Atlantic & Pacific Tea Co., Boston, 1931-34; with Charles F. Rittenhouse & Co., Boston, 1934-37; with Landers, Frary & Clark, New Britain, Conn., 1937-51, controller, 1941-42, sec.-treas., 1942-51; financial v.p. Fairmont Foods Co., Omaha, Neb., 1951-53; with Bullard Co., Bridgeport, Conn., 1953-68, sec.-treas., 1955-58, v.p., 1958-59, exec. v.p., 1959-68, also dir.; mgmt. cons., 1968—. Mem. Nat. Machine Tool Builders' Assn. (1st v.p. 1966-67, pres. 1967-68, dir.), Financial Execs. Inst. Club: Harvard (N.Y.C.). Home: 4909 Congress St Fairfield CT 06430

DABNEY, HOVEY SLAYTON, banker; b. Charlottesville, Va., Sept. 18, 1923; s. Wythe O. and Mabel (Williams) D.; B.A., U. Va., 1946, LL.B., 1949; grad. exec. program U. N.C., 1962; m. Patricia Schmidt, Feb. 14, 1948; children—Hovey Slayton, Ann Williams, Jill Godsell. With Nat. Bank & Trust Co., Charlottesville, 1949—, v.p., 1956-62, exec. v.p., 1962-64, pres., 1964—, also dir.; chmn. bd., dir. St. Anne-Belfield, Inc.; pres., dir. NB Corp., NB Service Corp., NB Mortgage Corp., Ridge Electronics Corp., Inland Service Corp., Charlottesville Parking Center, Inc.; dir. Inland Service Corp., Ridge Electronics Corp. Vice chmn. Charlottesville Sch. Bd., 1967. Bd. dirs. Martha Jefferson House; bd. dir. Charlottesville chpt., also nat. bd. Student Aid Found.; mem. bd. Blue Cross Va.; chmn. bd. govs. St. Anne's-Belfield, Inc. Served with USAAF, World War II. Decorated Air medal with oak leaf cluster, Purple Heart. Mem. Am. Inst. Banking, Va. Bankers Assn. (chmn. regional adv. com. banking policies and practices; pres., dir.), Am. Bankers Assn. (edn. com.), U.S. C. of C., Newcomen Soc., Theta Chi (v.p.), Sigma Nu Phi. Presbyn. (deacon). Clubs: Farmington Country (v.p.), Redland (dir.). Boar's Head (Charlottesville). Home: 2117 Morris Rd Charlottesville VA 22903 Office: 123 E Main St Charlottesville VA 22902

DABNEY, VIRGINIUS, author; b. University, Va., Feb. 8, 1901; s. Richard Heath and Lily Heth (Davis) D.; A.B., U. Va., 1920, A.M., 1921; D.Litt. (hon.), U. Richmond, 1940; LL.D., Lynchburg Coll., Coll. William and Mary, 1944; m. Douglas Harrison Chelf, Oct. 10, 1923; children—Douglas Gibson (Mrs. James S. Watkinson), Lucy Davis (Mrs. Alexander P. Leverty), Richard Heath II. Tchr. French, Episcopaal High Sch., 1921-22; reporter Richmond News Leader, 1922-28; editorial staff Richmond Times-Dispatch, 1928-34, chief editorial writer, 1934-36, editor, 1936-69; contbr. to N.Y. Times, Dictionary Am. Biography, London Economist. Spent six months in

Central Europe in 1934 under grant from Oberlaender Trust. Lectr. on "New South," Princeton session 1939-40; lectr. Fulbright Conf. Am. Studies, Cambridge U., 1954. Bd. dirs. U. Va. Press, 1966-70; chmn. Gov.'s Statewide Conf. on Edn., 1966; 1st rector Va. Commonwealth U., 1968-69; trustee, 1969—. Guggenheim fellow. Recipient Lee Editorial award Va. Press Assn., and Lee Sch. Journalism, Washington and Lee Univ. for "distinguished editorial writing during the year 1937," Pulitzer Prize for editorial writing, 1947; Nat. Editorial award Sigma Delta Chi, 1948, 52. Mem. Am. Soc. Newspaper Editors (dir. 1946-59. pres. 1957-58), Va. Hist. Soc. (pres. 1969-71), Raven, Omicron Delta Kappa, Delta Kappa Epsilon, Phi Beta Kappa, Sigma Delta Chi. Episcopalian. Clubs: Country of Virginia. Author: Liberalism in the South, 1932; Below the Potomac, 1942; Dry Messiah: The Life of Bishop Cannon, 1949; Virginia: The New Dominion, 1971. Contbr. national mags. Home: 14 Tapoan Rd Richmond VA 23226

DABNEY, WALTER H., ednl. adminstr.; B.S. in Civil Engring., Howard U.; M.S. in Hwys., Ia. State U. Dean Sch. Engring., prof. civil engring. Tenn. State U., Nashville. Office: Tenn State U Nashville TN 37203*

DABNEY, WATSON BARR, investment banker; b. Louisville, Dec. 24, 1923; s. William Cecil and Florence (Joyes) D.; student Phillips Exeter Acad., 1939-42, Princeton, 1942-43; m. Lucy Campbell Mercer, July 23, 1953. With J.J.B. Hilliard, W.L. Lyons & Co., Louisville, 1951—, partner, 1954—. Pres., trustee Am. Printing House for Blind; bd. dirs. Ky. Indsl. Devel. Financing Authority, Louisville Indsl. Found. Served with AUS, 1942- 45. Mem. Nat. Assn. Securities Dealers (bd. govs.). Home: Mockingbird Valley KY 40207 Office: 545 S 3d St Louisville KY 40202

DABNEY, WILLIAM KROEHLE, mfg. co. exec.; b. Cleve., June 22, 1933; s. John Carpenter and Mary (Kroehle) D.; A.B., Harvard, 1955; M.B.A., Columbia, 1960; m. Valerie Daniels, Aug. 10, 1962; children—Monica Kroehle, Joseph Daniels, Fiona MacFarlane. With Ford Motor Co., 1960-67; dir. financial planning and analysis Polaroid Corp., 1967-69; treas. Dictaphone Corp., Rye, N.Y., 1969—. Served to capt. USAF, 1956-58. Home: 64 West Hill Circle Stamford CT 06902 Office: 120 Old Post Rd Rye NY 10580

DA CAL, ERNESTO GUERRA, educator; b. Ferrol, Spain, Dec. 19, 1911; s. Roman Perez and Laura (Guerra) Da Cal; B.S., Inst. General y Tecrico de San Isidro, Madrid, 1928; M.A., U. Central, Madrid, 1936; Ph.D., Columbia, 1950; Dr. honoris causa, U. da Bahia, Salvador, Brazil, 1959; m. Elsie Allen, 1966; son, Enrique. Instr. Bklyn. Coll., 1939- 41; instr. to asso. prof. N.Y.U., 1941-56, prof., 1956-64, chmn. dept. Spanish and Portuguese, 1955-60; prof. Romance langs. Queens Coll., City U.N.Y., 1964—. exec. officer doctoral program in Portuguese lang. and Luso-Brazilian lit. City U. N.Y., 1965-70. vis. lectr. Princeton, 1942-43; lectr., asst. to dir. ASTP, Coll. City N.Y., 1943-44; lectr. Columbia, summer 1939-45; featured writer, broadcaster Western European div. Voice of Am. USIA. Decorated Ordem Nacional do Cruzeiro do Sul; Great Cross Order of St. James of Sword (Portugal); recipient Rosalia Castro prize for poetry, Portugal, 1960; named hon. citizen Rio de Janeiro, 1960; knight-comdr. Order Prince Henry The Navigator, Portugal, 1968. Mem. Internat. Acad. Portuguese Culture, Am. Assn. Tchrs. Spanish and Portuguese (pres. N.Y. chpt.), Modern Lang. Assn. Am. (chmn. Portuguese bibliography), N.Y. Acad. Scis., Hispanic Inst. U.S., Hispanic Soc. Am. (trustee N.Y.) Spanish Inst. N.Y., Phi Beta Kappa, Phi Lambda Beta (charter mem. exec. council 1966), Sigma Delta Pi, Trigonom. Author: Lengua y Estilo de Eca de Queiroz, 1954; Lua de Alen-Mar, 1959; Rio de Sonho e Tempo, 1963. Contbr. articles to profl. publs. 47 South Bay Av Amityville NY 11701 Office: Queens Coll Flushing, NY 11367.

DACEY, JOHN ELMER, corp. exec., ret. naval officer; b. Biloxi, Miss., Sept. 14, 1916; s. John Albert and Iris (Elmer) D.; B.S. in Elec. Engring., U.S. Naval Acad., 1938; student ordnance engring. U.S. Naval Postgrad. Sch., 1946-47; M.S. in Nuclear Physics, Mass. Inst. Tech., 1949; grad. Nat. War Coll., 1958; m. Constance deFuniak, Mar. 28, 1947; 1 dau., Dale. Commd. ensign U.S. Navy, 1938, advanced through grades to rear adm., 1965; served in battleships and cruisers, World War II; engaged in research and devel., 1949-51; assigned Bur. Naval Weapons, 1959-62; comdg. officer U.S.S. Dyess, 1952-54; comdr. Destroyer Div. 212, 1958-59, Destroyer Devel. Group 2, 1962-63; comdg. officer U.S.S. Chicago, 1963-65; sr. navy mem. Weapons Systems Evaluation Group, 1965-66; comdr. Cruiser Destroyer Flotilla 12, 1967-68; with Office of Chief of Naval Operations, 1968-70, ret., 1970; asst. to pres. Gibbs Mfg & Research Corp., 1970-71. Decorated Legion of Merit; recipient Gardner L. Caskey meml. prize U.S. Naval Acad., 1938. Mem. Am. Phys. Soc., Sigma Xi. Home: 4420 Exeter Dr Longboat Key Sarasota FL 33577

DACEY, TIMOTHY JOHN, Jr., air force officer; b. Marshfield, Mass., Aug. 12, 1917; s. Timothy John and Esther (Coleman) D.; B.A., Boston Coll., 1939; m. Sara Rogers, Aug. 19, 1915; children—Timothy John III, Michael R., Mary P., Sara Ruth, Kathleen. Commd. 2d lt. USAAF, 1940, advanced through grades to maj. gen., 1968; base comdr., wing comdr., personnel officer SAC, 1966-68; chief of staff SAC, Offutt AFB, Neb., 1968—. Decorated Legion of Merit with oak leaf cluster. Home: Quarters #10 Offutt AFB NB 68113 Office: Hdqrs SAC Offutt AFB NB 68113

DACHE, LILLY, hat designer; b. Beigles, France; student pub. schs. of France; m. Jean Despres, 1931. Came to U.S., 1924. Apprentice in millinery Reboux's, Paris; millinery salesgirl R. H. Macy, N.Y.C.; now designer hats Daché's, N.Y.C.; mfg. activities also include dresses, accessories, jewelry; pres. Lilly Daché. Recipient American Design award for creation of half-hat Lord & Taylor, 1941; design award for creation Neiman Marcus; many award from major firms. Author: Lilly Daché's Glamour Book: Talking Thru My Hat. Home: Bedford Village NY 10506 Office: 303 E 57th St New York City NY 10022

DACK, GAIL MONROE, physician, educator; b. Belvidere, Ill., Mar. 4, 1901; s. John Henry and Cora May (McAllister) D.; B.S., U. Ill., 1922; Ph.D., U. Chgo., 1927, M.D., 1933; m. Martha Pierson Bowsfield, Dec. 25, 1926; children—John Colvin, Carol Jean. Instr. hygiene, bacteriology U. Chgo., 1925-29, asst. prof., 1929-37, asso. prof. bacteriology, 1937-46, prof., 1946-66, prof. emeritus microbiology, 1966—, dir. Food Research Inst., 1946-66; prof. Food Research Inst. U. Wis., 1966-71. Cons., FDA, USPHS, Army. Chmn. Nat. Research Council Com. Foods, 1951-54; chmn. com. on microbiology Nat. Acad. Sci., NRC, 1958—; mem. cons. panel Robert A. Taft San. Engring. Center, 1956—; adv. bd. Lobund Inst., 1956-64. Served as medical cons., chief safety div. Camp Dietrick, Md., 1943-46. Recipient Ricketts' prize U. Chgo., 1925; Exceptional Performance of Duty citation Sec. War, 1946; Babcock-Hart award Inst. Food Technologists, 1956; Pasteur award Soc. Ill. Bacteriologists, 1957. Mem. Q.M. Food and Container Inst., Soc. Exptl. Biol. and Med., Soc. Am. Bacteriologists (pres. 1953, chmn. adv. com. to chief chem. corps 1955—), Central Society Clin. Research, A.A.A.S., Am. Pub. Health Assn., Food Technologists, Soc. Ill. Bacteriologists, WHO (expert adv. panel environmental sanitation), Research and Devel. Assos. (chmn. bd.), Am. Acad. Microbiology, Sigma Xi, Gamma Alpha, Alpha Omega Alpha. Author: Food Poisoning, 1949, 3d edit., 1956. Home: 494 Wing Park Blvd Elgin IL 60120

DACK, SIMON, physician; b. N.Y.C., Apr. 19, 1908; s. Isidore and Rebecca (Beitch) D.; B.S., Coll. City N.Y., 1928; M.D., N.Y. Med. Coll., 1932; m. Jacqueline Rosett, Jan. 23, 1949; children—Jerilyn Beth, Leonard. Intern Mt. Sinai Hosp., N.Y.C., 1932-33, research fellow cardiology, 1934-38, clin. staff cardiology, 1938—, adj. physician cardiology, chief cardiac clinic, 1945-58, attending physician Mt. Sinai Hosp., 1966—; lectr. cardiology Columbia; asso. prof. medicine N.Y. Med. Coll., 1959—; asso. clin. prof. medicine Mt. Sinai Sch. Medicine, 1966-70, clin. prof. medicine, 1970— ; chief cardiac clinics Met. Hosp., N.Y.C., 1955-62, attending vis. physician, 1962—; asso. physician in cardiology Mount Sinai Hosp., N.Y.C., 1958-70, attending physician cardiology, 1970—; attending physician Flower Fifth Av. Hosp., 1966—. Served as maj. M.C., AUS, 1942-45. Distinguished Fellow award Am. Coll. Cardiology, 1969. Fellow A.C.P., Am. Med. Writers Assn., Am. Coll. Cardiology (trustee 1952—, pres. 1956-57); mem. N.Y. Acad. Scis., A.M.A., Am. Heart Assn. (council on clinical cardiology 1962—), Am. Fedn. Clin. Research, Am. Coll. Chest Physicians, Alpha Omega Alpha. Contbr. articles profl. jours. Editor: Am. Jour. Cardiology. Home: 85 East End Av New York City NY 10028 Office: 1111 Park Av New York City NY 10028

DACKAWICH, S. JOHN, educator; b. Loch Gelley, W.Va., Jan 31, 1926; s. Samuel and Estelle (Jablonski) D.; B.A., U. Md., 1955; Ph.D., U. Colo., 1958; m. Shirley Jean McVay, May 20, 1950; children—Robert John, Nancy Joan. Instr. U. Colo., 1955- 57; instr. Colo. State U., 1957-59; prof., chmn. sociology Cal. State Coll., 1959-70; prof., chmn. sociology Fresno State Coll., 1970—; pvt. practice survey research, 1962-68. Mem. Cal. Democratic State Central Com., 1960-62; co-dir. Long Beach Central Area Study, 1962-64. Served with USMCR, 1943-46, AUS, 1950-53. Mem. Am., Pcific sociol. assns. Home: 1439 W Paul Av Fresno CA 93703

DACOSTA, EDWARD HOBAN, plastics and fibre mfr.; b. Phila., Sept. 19, 1918; s. 1968);, 1 son, and Edna (Hoban) DaC.; student Villanova U., 1936-38, Wharton Sch. of U. Pa., 1946-47; m. Joyce Jehl, Oct. 7, 1944 (dec. Nov. 1946); 1 son, Stephen Edward; m. 2d, Elizabeth Brendlinger, Feb. 26, 1949; 1 son, David Hoban; m. 3d, Sarah McDonnell Kratz, Dec. 28, 1968; 2 step daus., Carolyn Ann, Beverly Randolph. With Taylor Corp. (formerly Taylor Fibre Co. Valley Forge, Pennsylvania, 1938-, gen. mgr. Western division, LaVerne, Cal., 1953-56, v.p. marketing, 1956-61, pres., dir. 1961-69; Synthane Corp., 1968-69; chmn., chief exec. officer Synthane-Taylor Corp., 1969—; pres. Alcosta Corp., 1969—; mng. dir., dir., Alco Standard Corp., 1969—. Past gen. chmn., Elec. Insulation Conf., N.Y., pres. Pa. United Fund, Harrisburg, 1964-67; past pres. Pathway Sch., Norristown, Phila. United Fund; pres. bd. trustees Norristown State Hosp. 1963—; dir; trustee Community Services of Pa., Harrisburg; past pres. Central Montgomery County United Fund. Served to maj., pilot, USAAF, 1942-46. Mem. Montgomery County Mfg. Assn. (v.p.), (chmn. vulcanized fibre sect. 1958-61. dir. 1959-61, mem. bd. govs., Clubs: Union League (Phila.); St. Davids Golf (Radnor, Pa.); 1633 Monk Rd Gladwyne, PA Office Synthane-Taylor Corp Valley Forge PA 19481

DACSO, MICHAEL MIHALY, physician, educator; b. Tovaros, Hungary, June 25, 1909 (parents Am. citizens); s. Laszlo and Hedvig (Bauer) D.; M.D., Royal Hungarian U. of Budapest, 1934; m. Magda Rona, June 6, 1936; 1 son, Clifford. Research asso. Municipal Research Inst. for Rheumatic Diseases, Budapest, 1934- 40; intern, resident Goldwater Meml. Hosp., N.Y. U. Med. Div., 1941-44, asso. vis. physician in medicine, 1945-52, dir. Rehab. Medicine Service, 1949-68, cons., 1968—, pres. med. bd., 1967-68; cons. Manhattan State Hosp., Wards Island, N.Y., 1964-67; vis. physician Bellevue Hosp., N.Y. U. div., 1947-68; attending physician Univ. Hosp., N.Y. U. Med. Center, 1945-68, staff physician Inst. Rehab. Medicine, 1948-68; cons. Mary Manning Walsh Home, 1951—; mem. med. adv. bd. Peabody Home, 1962—; attending physiatrist Mt. Sinai Hosp., 1968—; clin. asst. in medicine N.Y. U. Sch. Medicine, 1944-47, asst. prof. clin. rehab. medicine, 1948-54, asso. prof., 1954-58, asso. prof. rehab. medicine, 1958-63, prof., 1963-68; prof. health scis. Hunter Coll., City U. N.Y., 1968—, dean Inst. Health Scis., 1968—; prof. rehab. medicine Mt. Sinai Sch. Medicine, City U. N.Y., 1968—, prof. community medicine, 1969—. Chmn. sub-com. on med. care Mayors Adv. Com. for Aged, N.Y.C., 1955-58; mem. Nat. Adv. Com. on Chronic Disease and Health of Aged, 1957-59; cons. gerontology br. Dept. Health, Edn. and Welfare, 1963-64, cons. rehab. medicine div. direct health services, 1967-68, chmn. med. research study sect. Social and Rehab. Service, 1969—; mem. adv. com. on health careers City U. N.Y., 1966—; cons. City U. N.Y. Feasibility Study on Proposed Inst. Health Scis. in cooperation with Hunter Coll. and Mt. Sinai Sch. Medicine, 1967-68; mem. Health Resources Commn. Task Force, N.Y. Dept. Health, Albany, 1968—. Mem. med. adv. com. N.Y. County chpt. Nat. Multiple Sclerosis Soc.; mem. tech. adv. com. Community Service Soc., 1955; mem. adv. com. Pub. Health Nursing Project, 1959; co-chmn. health exec. com. on aging Community Council Greater N.Y., 1960; mem. tech. adv. com. Found. for Med. Tech., 1962; mem. project adv. bd. Goodwill Industries Greater N.Y., 1968—. Vice pres., bd. dirs. Nat. Council on Aging; trustee Sirovich Day Center; bd. govs. Human Resources Center, Albertson, N.Y. Recipient AFLCIO Dist. 65 award for services to aged, 1959, Japan Rehab. Assn. scroll for contbn. to process in rehab. medicine in Japan, 1966, Meritorious Services diploma City of N.Y. Dept. Hosps., 1969. Diplomate Hungarian Bd. Phys. Medicine, Am. Bd. Phys. Medicine and Rehab. Fellow Medicine (com. chmn.), Am. Heart Assn., A.C.P., Am. Pub. Health Assn., Health Assn., Am. Acad. Compensation Medicine; mem. Am. Congress Rehab. Medicine, Am. Acad. Phys. Medicine and Rehab. (past pres.), A.M.A., N.Y. State and County Med. Soc., Assn. Am. Med. Colls., Am. Hungarian Med. Assn., Pub. Health Assn. N.Y.C. (dir.), Mexican Soc. Phys. Medicine and Rehab., Internat. Soc. Electromyographic Kinesiology, Norwegian Asso. editor Am. Lecture Series. Mem. editorial bd. Jour. Chronic Chronic Diseases, 1954. Contbr. articles profl. jours. Home: 56 Middle Neck Rd Roslyn NY 11576 Office: 108 E 91st St New York City NY 10028

DADDARIO, EMILIO QUINCY, lawyer, ex-congressman; b. Newton Centre, Mass., Sept. 24, 1918; s. Attilio Dante and Giovanna (Ciovacco) D.; grad. Tilton Acad., 1934, Newton Country Day Sch., 1935; B.A., Wesleyan U. (Conn.), 1939; student Boston U. Law Sch., 1939-41; LL.B., Conn. U., 1942; D.Sc. (hon.), Wesleyan U.; LL.D., Rensselaer Poytech. Inst.; m. Berenice Carbo, 1940; children—A. Edward, Stephen, Richard. Admitted to Conn., Mass. bars, 1942; practice of law, Middletown, Conn., 1942—, partner Daddario, Slitt, Jacobs and Sullivan, Hartford, Conn. Mem. 86th to 91st Congresses, First Congl. Dist. of Conn. Mayor, Middletown, 1945-48; judge of Middletown Municipal Ct., 1948-50. Trustee Wesleyan U.; bd. regents U. Hartford; adv. com. Harvard U. Program Tech. and Soc. Served from pvt. to capt. U.S. Army, 1943-45; with OSS, MTO; served as major with Far East Liaison Group, Korea and Japan, 1950-52. Decorated Legion of Merit (U.S.); Medaglia d'Argento (Italy). Fellow Am. Acad. Arts and Scis.; mem. U. Conn. Law Sch. Alumni Assn. Theta Nu Epsilon, Phi Nu Theta. Democrat. K.C., Elk. Home: 1462 Asylum Av Hartford CT 06105 Office: 242 Trumbull St Hartford CT 06103

DADO, MIOGRAZ DJURIC, artist; b. Centinje, Yugoslavia, 1933. One-man exhbns. include Galerie Daniel Cordier, Paris, 1958-64, Galerie Arnre Francois Petit, Paris, 1967, Daniel Cordier Gallery, N.Y.C., 1962-65, also internat. exhbn. Carnegie Inst., 1967. Address: care Galerie Andre Francois Petit, 122 Bad Haussmann Paris 8e, France.*

DAESCHNER, CHARLES WILLIAM, Jr., physician, educator; b. Houston, Dec. 24, 1920; s. Charles William and Maxie Virginia (Hulsey) D.; B.A., Rice Inst., 1942; M.D., U. Tex., 1945; m. Norma Sederholm, Nov. 14, 1948; children—Charles William III, Mary Lynn, Martha Ann. Rotating intern Hermann Hosp., Houston, 1945-46; resident St. Louis Children's Hosp., 1948-50; Children's Med. Center, Boston, 1950-51; instr., then asso. prof. Baylor U. Med. Coll., 1951-60; prof. pediatrics, chmn. dept. U. Tex. Med. Br., Galveston, 1960—; cons. in field. Mem. taskforce med. aspects mental retardadtion Gov. Tex. Com. Combat Mental Retardarion, 1965-66; med. adv. com. Tex. Bd. Mental Health and Mental Retardation, 1967—; maternity and newborn adv. com. Children's Bur., Dept. Health, Edn. and Welfare, 1964-66; program cons. Nat. Found., 1966—, now mem. exec. com. Galveston County chpt.; mem. Med. Adv. Bd. Ednl. Film Prodn., 1966—; mem. part III Nat. Bd. Med. Examiners, 1970—; med. adv. bd. Houston chpt. Nat. Kidney Found., 1964-67. Mem. Galveston Planning Commn. Trustee Moody Retirement Home, William Temple Community Center Found. Served to capt., M.C., USAF, 1946-48. Diplomate Am. Bd. Pediatrics (bd. dirs., ofcl. examiner). Mem. Am. Acad. Pediatrics (chmn. com. med. edn. 1965-70), Soc. Pediatric Research (v.p. 1965-66), Am. Pediatric Soc., So. Soc. Clin. Research, So. Soc. Pediatric Research, A.M.A., Galveston Research Club, Tex. Pediatric Soc. (chmn. mental health com. 1965-66), Galveston County Med. Soc., Assn. Med. Sch. Pediatric Dept. Chmn. (pres. 1970—), Sigma Xi. Club: Bayou (past pres.) (Galveston). Author numerous articles in field. Home: 1102 Harbor View Dr Galveston TX 77550

DAFF, ALFRED EDWARD, motion pictures exec.; b. Melbourne, Australia, Aug. 18, 1902; s. Alfred Ernest and Ruth (Shearer) D.; student MacDonald's Pvt. Sch., Kings Ch.; m. Opal Petrausch; 1 dau., Heather Ruth; m. 2d Joan MacDonald, July 14, 1948 (div. 1955); m. 3d, Annalisa Soderblom. Aug. 15, 1956. Came to U.S., 1939, naturalized, 1945. Office boy Progressive Films, Melbourne, 3 mos., 1919; booker, asst. projectionist Coop. Films, 6 months, 1919; successively booker, salesman, asst. mgr., mgr. Universal Pictures, Melbourne, 1920-36, mng. dir. for Japan, controlling Japan, Manchuko and Formosa, 1936-38, Far Eastern supr., 1938, Far East and Eastern supr., 1939-42, Far East, Middle East and African supr., 1942, Eastern Hemisphere rep., 1943; v.p. Universal Internat. Films, also fgn. sales supr., 1944-50, pres. since 1950; v.p. Universal Pictures Co., Inc., 1950-52, exec. v.p., 1952-58, cons., 1958-; dir. World Sales, 1951-. Mem. Acad. Motion Picture Arts and Scis., Am. Australian Assn. Club: Green Room (Melbourne, Australia); American National, Australian Golf (Sydney, Australia). Home: Quirang 6 Trelawney St Woollahra 2025 New South Wales Australia

DAFFIN, IRL ALONZO, industrialist; b. Denton, Md., May 28, 1902; s. Alonzo S. and Arkansas Virginia (Dorsey) D.; ed. Md. pub. schs.; m. Hildegarde Snow, Oct. 23, 1943; children—David K., Damaris Rebecca. Sales mgr. Dellinger Mfg. Co., Lancaster. Pa., 1932-40; pres. New Holland Machine Co., 1940-47, New Holland Mfg. Co., Mountville, Pa., 1945-47; exec. v.p. New Holland Metals Co., 1947; sec. Lancaster Engring. Corp. (Pa.), 1946-47, pres., 1947—; pres. Atlas Corp., 1948-49, Hertzler & Zook, Belleville, Pa., 1942-46, Daffin Mfg. Co., Lancaster, 1949-60, Narvon Mines, Ltd., 1962—, Irl. Daffin Assos., Inc., 1962—, Warwick Corp., 1970—; chmn. Daffin Corp., Hopkins, Minn., 1960-62, Eastern Corp., 1970—. Bd. dirs. Lancaster Gen. Hosp.; trustee Lancaster Country Day Sch. Mem. Newcomen Soc. Eng. C. of C. (dir.). Republican. Presbyn. Mason (Shriner), Elk. Clubs: National Press; Lake Shore, Lancaster County Riding, Hamilton, Lancaster County, Rotary, University, Radnor Hunt, Beaufort Hunt, Great Oak Lodge and Yacht, Lyford Cay, Porcupine; Rose Tree Hunt. Home: Warwick Rd Lititz PA 17543 Office: Lancaster PA 17604

DAFOE, CARMIE R., Jr., lawyer; b. Portland, Ore., June 22, 1920; B.A., Reed Coll., 1946; LL.B. cum laude, Harvard, 1949. Admitted to Ore. bar, 1949; now mem. firm Lindsay, Nahstoll, Hart, Duncan, Dafoe & Krause, Portland. Mem. Am., Multnomah County bar assns., Ore. State Bar, Phi Beta Kappa. Office: Loyalty Bldg 317 SW Alder St Portland OR 97204*

DAFOE, DONALD MALCOLM, edn. adminstr.; b. Sheyenne, N.D., Jan. 15, 1915; s. Dennis Wilson and Avis Beauvais (Carlton) D.; B.A., State Tchrs. Coll., Valley City, N.D., 1937; M.S., U. Ida., 1947; Ed.D., Stanford, 1961; m. Lois Smith, May 20, 1938; 1 dau., Judith Olive. High sch. tchr., coach, Bliss, Ida., 1937 39, supt. schs., 1939-43; high sch. print. Rupert, Ida., 1943-44, supt. schs., 1944-51; asst. supt. schs., Anchorage, Alaska, 1951-53; commr. edn. Ty. Alaska, 1953-59; with U.S. Office Edn., State Sch. Adminstrn. br., 1959-61; supt. schs. Anchorage, Alaska, 1961-66; provost univ., prof. edn. U. Alaska, 1966-69, v.p. pub. service, 1971—; exec. sec. Council Chief State Sch. Officers, 1969-71. Mem. Alaska White House Conf. Com. Mem. Am. Assn. Sch. Adminstrs., Alaska, Ida. (pres. 1948-49) edn. assns., N.E.A. (hon. v.p. 1953-54). Mason. Clubs: Rotary (pres. 1965), Toastmasters (pres.). Address: 104 Bunnell Bldg U Alaska College AK

DAGGETT, ALBERT FREDERICK, educator; b. Concord, N.H., Oct. 23, 1906; s. Albert Henry and Eva (Hancock) D.; B.S., U. N.H., 1928, M.S., 1930; Ph.D., Columbia, 1934; m. Marion Avis Phelps, Aug. 15, 1931; children—Sandra (Mrs. John Beggs McManus), Frederick Phelps. Mem. faculty U. N.H., 1928-31, 35—, prof. chemistry, 1946—, dean Grad. Sch., 1949-52; instr. Hunter Coll., N.Y.C., 1934-35; cons. AID at U. San Marcos, Lima, Peru, 1956-66. Treas. Durham chpt. Nat. A.R.C., 1968—. Named Catedratico Honorario of the Faculty of Chemistry, Nat. U. San Marcos, 1958. Mem. N.Y. Acad. Scis., Am. Assn. U. Profs., Am., Peruvian chem. socs., Sigma Xi, Phi Kappa Phi, Phi Lambda Upsilon. Author: (with W.B. Meldrum) Qualitative Analysis, 1946, Quantitative Analysis, 1955. Contbr. articles profl. jours. Home: 95 Madbury Rd Durham NH 03824

DAGGETT, ATHERN PARK, educator; b. Springfield, Mo., Jan. 10, 1904; s. William Athern and Evelina (Park) D.; A.B., Bowdoin Coll., 1925; A.M. Harvard, 1928, Ph.D., 1931; m. Catherine Jordan Travis, Sept. 4, 1936; children—William, Ellen (Mrs. Glatter). Instr. Eng. Lafayette Coll., 1925-27; summer faculty U. Maine, 1930; instr. gov. Bowdoin Coll., 1930-31, 32-34, asst. prof., 1934-40, asso. prof., 1940-46, prof. 1946—, William Nelson Cromwell prof. constl., internat. law and govt. since 1951, acting pres. of coll., 1967-68; instr. polit. sci. Dartmouth Coll., 1931-32; adj. prof. polit. sci. Randolph-Macon Woman's Coll., 1932; vis. prof. polit. sci. Brown U., 1948-49; summer faculty Columbia, 1953. Trustee Bangor Theol. Sem. Mem. Am. Soc. Internat. Law (exec. council 1940-43), Am.,

N.E. (exec. com. 1953-54, pres. 1956-57) polit. sci. assns., Congl. Christian Conf. Maine (pres. 1946-47), Phi Beta Kappa. Conglist. Home: 6 Longfellow Av Brunswick ME 04011

DAGGETT, ELEANOR NINA, author; b. Chama, N.M., May 21, 1919; d. Arthur George and Mattie Clare (Taylor) D.; grad. Spanish-Am. Normal Sch., El Rito, N.M., 1935; student corr. schs. U.N.M., 1966—; m. Oswell A. Washburn, Oct. 22, 1938; 1 dau., Rochelle (Mrs. Joseph D. Genre). Corr. New Mexican, 1967—; free lance naturalist, author. Mem. North Central N.M. Comprehensive Health Planning Council. Bd. dirs. N.M. Wildlife Fedn. Mem. N.M. Ornithol. Assn., Nat. Wildlife Fedn. Presbyn. Mem. Order Eastern Star. Author: Nature Trek column, 1968—. Contbr. articles profl. jours. Home: Chama NM 87520 Office: Box 275 Los Alamos NM 87544

DAGGETT, MALCOLM DANIEL, educator; b. Pasadena, Cal., Dec. 13, 1907; s. Fred Eugene and Katherine Arlington (Knight) D.; A.B., Bowdoin Coll., 1929; A.M., Harvard, 1932, Ph.D., 1939; m. Frances Hutchinson Lintner, Aug. 25, 1937; 1 son, David Malcolm. Instr. in French, Bowdoin Coll., 1929-30, Harvard, 1930-32, U. Rochester, 1932-36; instr. in Romance langs. and tutor Harvard, 1936-43; research analyst OSS, Washington, 1943-45; prof. of Romance langs. U. Vt., 1945—, chmn. dept., 1945-67, dir. grad. study, 1949-52. Decorated Chevalier de l'Ordre des Palmes Academiques. Mem. Modern Lang. Assn., Am. Assn. Tchrs. French, Phi Beta Kappa, Alpha Tau Omega, Delta Psi. Episcopalian. Home: 88 Robinson Pkwy Burlington VT 05401

DAGNINO, EDMOND FREDERICK, savs. and loan exec.; b. Boston, May 19, 1903; s. John Romolo and Emily (Currotti) D.; student Dean Acad., 1920, Bates Coll., 1921, U. N.H., 1923; m. Gertrude M. Bean, June 16, 1934; 1 son, David R. Wholesale grocer, 1926-28; clk. Boston Fed. Savs. and Loan Assn., 1928-32, treas., 1937-41, v.p., 1941-52, pres., 1952-68, chmn. bd., 1952—; trustee First Mortgage Investers, Mass. Title Ins. Co. Mem. planning bd., Stoneham, Mass., 1939-46, bd. appeal, Tuftonboro, N.H., 1971. Served with USCGR, 1944-46. Mem. Alpha Tau Omega. Mason (Shriner), Rotarian. Clubs: Bald Peak Colony (Melvin Village, N.H.); Kingswood Golf (Wolfeboro, N.H.); Madison Square Garden (Boston). Home: Mirror Lake PO NH 03853 Office: 30 Federal St Boston MA 02110

DAHI, JAWDAT, banker. Dep. gen. mgr. Comml. Bank Syria, Damascus. Office: PO Box 933 Moawia St Damascus Syria*

DAHINDEN, BLANCHE HARRIET, assn. exec.; b. Seattle, Mar. 31, 1910; d. John Benjamin and Blanche (Bacon) Dahinden; A.B., Milw.-Downer Coll., 1931. Membership sec. Civil Service Assembly, U.S. and Can., Chgo., 1942-47; sec. to asst. mgr. Washington Athletic Club, Seattle, 1947-49; legal sec. Bendinger, Hayes & Kluwin, Milw., 1949-55; exec. sec. Internat. Assn. Ins. Counsel, Milw., 1955—. Mem. Milw.-Downer Coll. Alumnae Assn., Nat. Wildlife Fedn., Wis. Humane Soc., Milw. County Zool. Soc. Home: 4130 W Martin Dr Milwaukee WI 53202 Office: 229 E Wisconsin Av Milwaukee Wi 53202

DAHL, ARLENE, actress, columnist, fashion designer; b. Mpls., Aug. 11; d. Rudolph and Idelle (Swan) Dahl; student (1st, 2d, 3d prizes for fashion designs) U. Minn., Minn. Inst. Art, Minn. Coll. Music, Minn. Bus. Coll.; m. Rounsevelle Schaum; 1 son, Rounsevelle Adreas. Broadway appearances include Mr. Strauss Goes to Boston, Questionable Ladies, Cyrano de Bergerac; played Chgo. in One Touch of Venus, The Camel Bell, Blithe Spirit; toured in Liliom, The King and I, Roman Candle, I Married an Angel, Bell, Book and Candle; night club act Flamingo Hotel, Las Vegas, Latin Quarter, N.Y.C.; motion pictures include debut in My Wild Irish Rose, 1947, Three Little Words, Desert Legion, Sangaree, Kisses for My President, Woman's World, Journey to the Center of the Earth, Les Poneyettes, The Landgrabbers, The Way to Kathmandu; syndicated beauty columnist, 1950—; designer sleepwear for A.N. Saab & Co.; TV appearances include Lux Video Theatre, 1952, 53, Pepsi-Cola Theatre, 1954, Opening Night series, 1958, Arlene Dahl's Beauty Spot, 1966, also guest appearances; pres. Woman's World div. Kenyon & Eckhart, 1967—, also v.p. Kenyon & Eckhart; nat. beauty adviser Sears Roebuck, 1969—. Hon. life mem. Father Flannagan's Boys Town; bd. dirs. Hollywood Museum. Author: Always Ask a Man, 1965; 12 Beautyscope books, 1968. Address: PO Box 911 Beverly Hills CA 90213

DAHL, ARNDT E., banker; b. Taylor, Wis., Apr. 25, 1897; s. Anton A. and Lena (Elstad) D.; grad. in law Internat. Corr. Schs., 19—; m. Agnes Foster, Jan. 25, 1947; 1 dau., Verley (Mrs. Harris Torgerson). Admitted to S.D. bar, 1927; with First Nat. Bank Toronto (S.D.), 1917-26, Citizens State Bank Castlewood (S.D), 1927-51; S.D. bank examiner, 1931-32; receiver Pennington County Bank, Rapid City, S.D., 1932-34; pres. Rapid City Nat. Bank, 1934-52, chmn., 1952-70; chmn. bd. Nat. Bank S.D. (merger Rapid City Nat. Bank and Nat. Bank S.D.), 1968—. Bd. regents Augusta Coll., Sioux Fall, S.D. Served with USNR, World War I. Mem. State Bar S.D. Lutheran. Elk, Rotarian. Home: 824 Columbus St Rapid City SD 57701 Office: P O Box 2008 Rapid City SD 57701

DAHL, CHARLES RAYMOND, paper co. exec.; b. Bklyn., July 13, 1921; s. Oswald and Alice (Christoffersen) D.; B.M.E., Cooper Union, 1943; M.B.A., Stanford, 1947; m. Clara Joyce Glendon, Dec. 31, 1949; children—Kathleen Merle, Eric Allen, Connie Loraine. With Westinghouse Electric Co., 1947-50; with Crown Zellerbach Corp., 1950—, exec. v.p., 1969-70, pres., 1970—, also dir. Mason, Elk. Clubs: California Golf, Commonwealth (San Francisco). Home: 498 Seacliff Av San Francisco CA 94121. Office: 1 Bush St San Francisco CA 94119

DAHL, ERNO JOYCE, univ. ofcl.; b. Waco, Tex., Nov. 11, 1928; s. Hans Bernhard and Sylvia (Nelson) D.; B.A., Luther Coll., Decorah, Ia., 1952; B.Th., Luther Theol. Sem., St. Paul, 1955; Ph.D., Durham (Eng.) U., 1957; m. Suzanne Louise Preus, July 24, 1953; children—Jeremy Eliot Preus, Jeffrey Erno. Prof. theology Tex. Luth. Coll., Seguin, 1957-68, acad. dean, 1964-68; dean coll. Wittenberg U., Springfield, O., 1968-70, v.p. acad. affairs, 1970—; ordained to ministry Luth. Ch., 1960. Chmn. Luth. Faculty Conf. S.W., 1964-68; mem. commn. pub. relations Tex. Council Ch. Related Colls., 1964-68; mem. commn. standards and classification Assn. Tex. Colls. and Univs., 1967- 68. Served with USMCR, 1946-48. Mem. Am. Assn. Higher Edn., Am. Assn. Colls. Tchrs. Edn., Am. Acad. Religion, Soc. Sci. Study Religion, Luth. Soc. Music, Worship and Fine Arts. Home: 1101 Redbud Lane Springfield OH 45504

DAHL, FRANCIS W., cartoonist; b. Wollaston, Mass., Oct. 21, 1907; s. J. Frank and Mildred (Boyd) D.; m. Louise C. Bartlett, June 4, 1933; children—Jane, Francis W., Jr. (dec.), Linda. Daily cartoons, Boston Herald Traveler, 1930—. Author: (books) Left Handed Compliments, 1941; Dahl's Cartoons, 1943; What! More Dahl? 1944; Dahl's Boston, 1946; Dahl's Brave New World, 1947; Birds, Beasts and Bostonians, 1954. Address: The Boston Herald Traveler Boston MA 02118

DAHL, GEORGE LEIGHTON, architect; b. Mpls., May 11, 1894; s. Olaf G. and Laura (Olson) D.; B.Arch., U. Minn., 1921; m.Arch., Harvard, 1922; student Am. Acad. in Rome, 1923; Nelson Robinson traveling fellow, Africa and Europe, 1922-24; m. Lillie E. Olsen, Sept. 24, 1921 (dec. Apr. 1957); 1 dau., Gloria Lille (Mrs. Ted M. Akin). Designer, Myron Hunt & H. C. Chambers, Los Angeles, 1925; designer, mem. firm Herbert M. Greene, Dallas, 1926-28; mem. firm Herbert M. Greene, LaRoche & Dahl, Dallas, 1928-33, LaRoche & Dahl, Dallas, 1933-35; propr. firm George L. Dahl, architects and engrs., Dallas, 1935-; tech dir. Tex. Centennial Exposition, 1935-37; architect, engr. Dallas Meml. Auditorium, 1956. Mem. Tex. Bd. Archtl. Examiners, 1951-63, chmn., 1955-; mem. Dallas City Planning Adv. Com., 1943-45, Greater Dallas Planning Council, 1948-56. Mem. Tex. Bd. Corrections, 1950-60; bd. dirs. Dallas Better Bus. Bur. Past chmn. exec. com. Dallas Nat. Conf. Christians and Jews, Dallas Community Chest, Dallas council Boy Scouts Am., Dallas chpt. A.R.C., Dallas Salvation Army, Tex. Soc. Crippled Children, Dallas City-County Boy's Industrial Home, Dallas Civic Opera; bd. dirs. Dallas YMCA. Served to 1st lt. U.S. Army, World War I. Fellow A.I.A. (past pres. Dallas); mem. Texas Soc. Architects (past pres.), Soc. Am. Mil. Engrs. (past v.p. Dallas, nat. dir.), Dallas C. of C., Dallas Symphony Assn., Harvard Archtl. Soc., Dallas Art Assn., Harvard Found. Advanced Study, Nat. Council Archtl. Registration Bds. Mason (Shriner). Clubs: Rotary (past pres.), Town and Gown, Dallas Athletic, Dallas Country, Downtown, Engineers, Knife and Fork, Dallas, City, Harvard (Dallas); Brookhollow. Author: (monograph) Portals, Doorways and Windows, Home: 3601 Turtle Creek Blvd Dallas TX 75219. Office: 2101 N St Paul St Dallas TX 75201

DAHL, JOHN ANTON, educator; b. Ft. Dodge, Ia., Feb. 14, 1922; s. Harry Arthur and Margaret (Schumacher) D.; B.A., San Jose (Cal.) State Coll., 1944; M.A., Stanford, 1950,0Ed.D., 1952; m. May-Margaret Johnson, Sept. 8, 1964; children by previous marriageJohn B., Kenneth M.; stepchildren Douglas Wright, Kimberley Wright. Tchr., counselor, adminstr. Cal. pub. high schs., 1946-50; sec. coordinator and cons. guidance Tulare County (Cal.) schs., 1952-55; mem. faculty Cal. State Coll., Los Angeles, 1955-, prof. edn., 1960—; dean Sch. Edn., 1966-68, acting v.p. for bus. affairs 1970—; vis. lectr. Claremont Grad. Sch., 1960-62, Occidental Coll., 1962-63, Fresno State Coll., 1953-54; cons. in field, 1956-. Served with USAAF, 1944-45. Mem. San Joaquin Valley Guidance Assn. (pres. 1954-55), Cal. Assn. Secondary Sch. Curriculum Coordinator, (pres. 1960-61), Cal. Assn. Secondary Sch. Adminstrs. (dist. officer, state rep.), Am. Assn. Colls. Tchrs. Edn. (state liaison rep.), Am. Assn. U. Profs., Nat. Soc. Study Edn., Am. Personnel and Guidance Assn., Phi Delta Kappa. Author: (with others) Student, School and Society, 1964; also articles. Home: 509 E Baseline Rd Claremont, CA 91711. Office: 5151 State College Dr Los Angeles CA 90032.

DAHL, LEO PETER, former air force officer; b. Ely, Minn., May 6, 1909; s. Edward Michael and Emelia Matilda (Narva) D.; student Ely Jr. Coll., 1928; B.S., U.S. Mil. Acad., 1932; student Advanced Flying Sch., 1933; M.S., Cal. Inst. Tech., 1939; grad. Air War Coll., 1947, Advanced Mgmt. Program, Harvard, 1958; m. Nancy Virginia Denning, Nov. 17, 1936; children—Nancy Page, Leo Peter, Edward Denning. Commd. 2d lt., A.C., U.S. Army, 1932, advanced through grades to maj. gen. USAF, 1954; various squadron and group duties, 1933- 41; chief operations, directorate of meteorology Hdqrs. USAAF, Washington, 1941-42, dep. chief operations Northwest African Allied Air Force, 1942; chief operations 12th Air Force, Italy and So. France, 1943- 45; dir. combat operations Air Force Sch. Applied Tactics, Orlando, Fla., 1945; chief program monitoring Hdqrs. Air Force, Washington, then exec. officer, comptroller, 1945-46; asst. chief staff personnel Hdqrs. Air Tng. Command, Barksdale AFB, La., 1947-48; chief materiel sect., supply div., then dep. chief supply div. Hdqrs. Air Materiel Command, 1948-50, chief mutual def. materiel div., 1950-53; comdr. 3090th Depot Flight, Wright-Patterson AFB, O., also Madrid, Spain, 1953-54; comdr. Spain Air Materiel Area, Madrid, 1954-56; comptroller Hdqrs. Air Materiel Command, Wright-Patterson AFB, 1956-60; comdt. Command and Staff Coll., Maxwell AFB, Ala., 1960, War Coll., USAF, 1960-62, ret. 1962. Bd. dirs., Montgomery chpt. A.R.C. Decorated Legion of Merit with cluster, Bronze Star medal, Air medal with cluster, D.S.M.; Croix de Guerre with palm (France); Medal of Merit for Aero. (Spain). Mem. Armed Forces Mgmt. Assn., Comptroller Inst., Air Force Assn., U.S. Mil. Acad. Alumni Assn., Cal. Inst. Tech. Alumni Assn., Harvard Alumni Assn., Montgomery Ret. Officers Assn., English-Speaking Union (dir. Montgomery). Address: 1376 Wedgewood Dr Montgomery AL 36111

DAHL, MILFORD WILLITS, lawyer; b. Pasadena, Cal., Apr. 18, 1919; s. Edward W. and Anita (Willits) D.; A.A., Santa Ana Coll., 1938; J.D., U. Cal. at Hastings, 1941; m. Barbara W. Foye, July 4, 1939; children—Milford W., Theo Louise (Mrs. Lynn Cortner). Escrow officer Security Title Co., Santa Ana, Cal., 1941-43; materiel liason Douglas Aircraft Co., Long Beach, Cal., 1943- 45; admitted to Cal. bar, 1942; practiced in Santa Ana, 1945—; partner firm Rutan & Tucker, 1955—. Vice pres. Rossmoor Water Co., Laguna Hills, Cal., 1962, Rossmoor Sanitation Co., Laguna Hills, 1962. City councilman, Santa Ana, 1951-57, mayor, 1956-57; mem. Charter Com. of City of Santa Ana, 1961, 65-66. Mem. exec. bd. Orange Empire council Boy Scouts Am., 1960—, pres., 1967-68. Bd. dirs. Goodwill Industries, 1961—. Mem. Am., Orange County bar assns., State Bar of Cal. (pres. 1956), Am. Arbitration Assn. (bd. arbitrators 1970—), Photographic Soc. Am., Santa Ana Jr. C. of C. (pres. 1947), Phi Alpha Delta. Mason, Kiwanian, Elk. Presbyn. (elder). Home: 916 River Lane Santa Anna CA 92706 Office: 401 Civic Center Dr West Santa Ana CA 92702

DAHL, NORMAN CHRISTIAN, found. ofcl.; b. Seattle, May 21, 1918; s. Gjermunn Helgeson and Anna (Carlson) D.; B.Sc., U. Wash., 1941; Sc.D., Mass. Inst. Tech., 1952; D.Sc., Indian Inst. Tech., Kanpur, 1968; m. Dorothy Sabra Sweet, Nov. 23, 1943; children—Christian, Sabra. Project engr. Webster-Brinkley Co., Seattle, 1941-42; engr. NRC, Princeton, N.J., London, Eng., 1942-44; sci. cons. Office Field Service, Hawaii and Guam, 1944-45; operations analyst USAAF, 1945-46; faculty Mass. Inst. Tech., 1948- 68, prof. mech. engring., 1959-68; dep. rep. Ford Found. in India, 1968- 71, program adviser Internat. div., N.Y.C., 1971—; Fulbright lectr. Cambridge (Eng.) U., 1950-51. Program leader Kanpur (India) Indo-Am. Program, Indian Inst. Tech., 1962-64; mem. study team on sci. and engring. in USSR, U.S. Office Edn., 1965; cons. Govt. Saudi Arabia, 1966; U.S. rep. UNESCO planning meeting for 1969 Internat. Congress Engring. Edn., 1967. NRC postdoctoral fellow, 1946-48; recipient Army-Navy certificate appreciation, 1948. Mem. Am. Acad. Arts and Sci., A.A.A.S., Am. Soc. M.E., Am. Civil Liberties Union, Sigma Xi, Tau Beta Pi, Pi Tau Sigma. Author: (with S.H. Crandall, others) An Introduction to the Mechanics of Solids, 1959. Contbr. articles to profl. jours. Patentee in field. Home: 78 Irving Pl New York City NY Office: Ford Found 320 E 43d St New York City NY 10017

DAHL, RICHARD A., meter mfg. co. exec. Sec., Am. Meter Co., Phila. Office: 13500 Philmont Av Philadelphia PA 19116*

DAHL, ROALD, writer; b. Llandaff, South Wales, Sept. 13, 1916; s. Magdalene (Hesselberg) D.; student Repton (Eng.) Sch., 1930-34; m. Patricia Neal, July 2, 1953; childrenOlivia (dec.), Tessa, Theo. Ophelia, Lucy. Served to wing comdr. RAF, 1939-45. Recipient Edgar Allen Poe award Mystery Writers Am. Soc., 1954, 59, Author: (juveniles) The Gremlins, 1943, James and the Giant Peach, 1962, Charlie and the Chocolate Factory, 1964; The Magic Finger, 1965; Boggis and Bunce and Bean, published 1970; (short stories) Over to You, 1945, Someone Like You, 1953, Kiss Kiss, 1960; (fable) Sometime Never, 1948; (play) The Honeys, 1953. Address: Gipsy House Great Missenden Bucks, England.

DAHL, ROBERT ALAN, educator; b. Inwood, Ia., Dec. 17, 1915; s. Peter Ivor and Vera (Lewis) D.; A.B., U. Wash., 1936; Ph.D., Yale, 1940; m. Mary Louise Bartlett, June 20, 1940 (dec. 1970); children—Ellen Kirsten, Peter Bartlett, Eric Lewis, Christopher Robert. Mgmt. analyst Dept. Agr., 1940; economist OPM, WPB, 1941-42; faculty Yale, 1946—, Eugene Meyer prof. polit. sci., 1955-64, Sterling prof. polit. sci. 1964—, Ford research prof., 1957-58; fellow Center Adv. Study Behavioral Scis., 1955-56, 67; Walgreen lectr. U. Chgo., 1955. Mem. U.S. Group Control Council, Germany, 1945; cons. State Govt. Reorgn. Commn. Served from pvt. to 1st lt., AUS, 1943-45. Decorated Bronze Star medal with cluster; Guggenheim fellow, 1950. Mem. Am. (pres. 1966-67), So., New Eng. (pres. 1951) polit. sci. assns., Am. Philos. Soc., Am. Acad. Arts and Sci., Am. Civil Liberties Union, Phi Beta Kappa. Author: Congress and Foreign Policy, 1950; Politics, Economics and Welfare (with C. E. Lindblom), 1953; A Preface to Democratic Theory, 1956; Who Governs?, 1961; Modern Political Analysis, 1963; Political Oppositions in Western Democracies, 1966; After the Revolution?, 1970; Dabyarchy: Participation and Opposition, 1971. Home: 17 Cooper Rd North Haven CT 06473 Office: Dept Polit Sci Yale U New Haven CT 06473

DAHL, ROBERT EMMETT, lawyer; b. Grafton, N.D., May 4, 1919; s. Thorvald Iver and Ethel Mary (Haffey) D.; B.S. in Commerce, U. N.D., 1941, J.D., 1948; m. Jean E. Midgarden, Apr. 12, 1947; children—Kristen, David, Barbara, Margaret, Jon. Admitted to N.D. bar, 1948, since practiced in Grafton; atty. for City Grafton, 1954-58, City of St. Thomas, 1957-68; pres. Dahl, Dahl & Greenagel, Ltd., 1970—; instr. English dept. U.N.D., 1946-48. Dir. Brodeur Construction, Inc., KGPC, Inc. Chmn. Four-Star district Boy Scouts of Am., 1967-70; chmn. Walsh County chpt. A.R.C., 1956-70; dir. Service to Mil. Families, 1960—. Pres. U. N.D. Law Sch. Found., 1964-65. Served to capt. USAAF, 1942-45; ETO; lt. col. N.D. N.G. ret. Decorated Bronze Star medal. Mem. Am. (mem. standing com. profl. grievances 1966—), 2d Jud. Dist. (past pres.) bar assns., State Bar Assn. N.D. (chmn. grievance com. 1, 1967—, pres., 1965-66; exec. com. 1960-62, 64-67), Grafton C. of C. (dir. 1970—), Am. Judicature Soc., Nat. Conference of Bar Presidents, Am. Legion, Phi Eta Sigma, Beta Gamma Sigma, Theta Chi, Phi Alpha Delta, Blue Key. Democrat. Roman Catholic. K.C., Eagle, Elk. Clubs: Grafton Curling (pres. 1966-67); Fair Oaks Golf (dir. 1970—). Home: 1144 McHugh Av Grafton ND 58237 Office: 710 Hill Av Grafton ND 58237

DAHL, SAM, coll. dean; b. Omaha, July 6, 1911; s. Kjell Gustav William and Lillian Marie (Hurd) D.; student Augustana Coll., 1929; B.Sc., Neb. State Tchrs. Coll., 1936; M.A., U. Nev., 1946, Ph. D., 1952; m. Ione Freeland, May 28, 1935; childrenVirginia Gwen, Nancy Ruth, Susan Marie, David William. Tchr. rural elementary sch., 1933-35, secondary schs., 1936-38; supt. schs., Upland, Neb., 1938-42, Dorchester, Neb., 1942-47; supr. secondary edn. Neb. Dept. Pub. Instrn., 1947-52; prof. edn., chmn. dept. Neb. Wesleyan U., Lincoln, 1952-54, dean Coll., 1954—, actin g pres., summer 1957. Coordinator liberal arts study North Central Assn. Secondary Schs. and Colls.; mem., former chmn. bd. Christian higher edn. Augustana Luth. Ch. Mem. Lincoln Centennial Planning Commn., 1958-59; scholarship com. Lincoln Community Council; chmn. Lincoln Council Chs. Trustee Bethpage Mission, Midland Luth. Coll. Mem. Grange, Phi Delta Kappa, Kappa Delta Pi, Theta Chi. Republican. Lutheran. Odd Fellow Rotarian. Club: Nebraska Schoolmasters. Home: 1240 N 33d St Lincoln NB 68503

DAHLBERG, BRUCE THEODORE, educator; b. Buffalo, N.Y., Dec. 19, 1924; s. Edwin Theodore and Emilie (Loeffler) D.; B.A. Syracuse U., 1948; B.D., Union Theol. Sem., 1952; Ph.D., Columbia U., 1963; m. Janet Edwards Robbins, Aug. 2, 1952; children—Seth James, Judith, Andrew. Ordained minister Baptist Ch.; pastor Lefferts Park Baptist Ch., Bklyn. 1951-54; mem. faculty Smith Coll., 1956—, prof. religion 1970—; Henry Thayer fellow Am. Schs. Oriental Research, Jerusalem, Jordan, 1964-65. Served with AUS, 1943-45. Mem. Soc. Bibl. Lit., Am. Acad. Religion, Am. Assn. U. Profs. Contbg. author: The Interpreter's Dictionary of the Bible, 1962, The Interpreter's One-Volume Commentary on the Bible, 1971. Home: 33 Harlow Av Northampton MA 01060

DAHLBERG, EDWARD, author; b. Boston, July 22, 1900; s. Saul Gottdank and Elizabeth Dahlberg; student U. Cal., 1922-23; B.S. in Philosophy, Columbia; m. Winifred Donlea, Mar. 4, 1942; children-Geoffrey, Joel; m. 2d Julia Lawlo r, June 13, 1967. Began writing novels in Monte Carlo, 1926; lived and wrote in London and Paris, 1926- 28. Prof., Columbia, 1968. Author: (novels) Bottom Dogs, 1930 (trans. into Spanish and pub. in Chile, 1940) From Flushing to Calvary, 1932; Kentucky Blue Grass, 1932; Those Who Perish, 1934; (literary criticism) Do These Bones Live, 1941, Sing O Barren (foreward by Herbert Read), 1947; Flea of Sodom, 1950; The Sorrows of Priapus (illustrated by Ben Shahn), 1957; Can These Bones Live (illus. by James Kearns), 1960; (with Sir Herbert Read) Truth Is More Sacred, 1961; Because I Was Flesh (autobiography), 1964; Alms for Oblivion; The Anxious Years; Moby DickAn Hamitic Dream; Reasons of the Heart, 1965; Cipang's Hinder Door, 1965; Edward Dahlberg Reader, 1967; Epitaphs of our Times, The Letters of Edward Dahlberg, 1967; The Leafless American, 1967; The Carnal Myth, published 1968. Contributor Fortnightly Rev., Poetry, New Republic, The Nation, also Holiday Mag., New Directions Annual, N.Y. Times, Tomorrow, several others. Carolyn Benton Cockefair prof. U. Mo. at Kansas City, 1964-65, prof. lang. and lit., 1966—; prof. Columbia, 1968. Nat. Inst. Arts and Letters, for 1961 Letters. Home: Soller novel, Longview Found. award; award Nat. Found. on Arts and Humanities. Rjockefeller grantee, 1965, 66; Ariadne Found grant. Mem. Inst. Arts and Letters. Home: Soller de Mallorca Espana. Office: care George Braziller Pub 1 Park New York City NY 10016.

DAHLBERG, LEROY WALDO, lawyer; b. Boone, Ia., Aug. 14, 1904; s. Oscar Frederick and Vendla Sophia (Johnson) D.; student Wayne State U., 1920-22; A.B., U. Mich., 1925; J.D., U. Chgo., 1930; m. Julia France, Mar. 10, 1945; children—Christine, Lyle. Admitted to Ill. bar, 1930, Mich. bar, 1931; partner firm Dahlberg, Mallender & Gawne, Detroit, 1931—. Dir. Mfrs. Nat. Bank Detroit. Trustee Wayne State U. Fund, Cranbrook Inst. Sci., chmn. 1968—; trustee Childrens Aid Soc. Detroit, Detroit Swedish Council. Fellow Am. Bar Found.; mem. Newcomen Soc. Episcopalian. Clubs: Detroit Athletic, Detroit; Otsego Ski (Gaylord, Mich.); Bloomfield Hills (Mich.) Country. Home: 185 Lone Pine Rd Bloomfield Hills MI 48013 Office: 1400 N Woodward Av Birmingham MI 48013 also Ford Bldg Detroit MI 48226

DAHLEM, MAURICE JACOB, accountant;b. Rialto, Cal., Dec. 23, 1912; s. Rudolph Jacob and Lonie (Beckley) D.; A.B. in Econs., U. Cal. at Los Angeles, 1934; m. Harriet Janet Ruth, Dec. 20, 1938; children—Susan Marie (Mrs. Craig K. Harris), John Stephen, Gregory Stewart, With Price Waterhouse & Co., C.P.A.'s, Los Angeles, 1934—, partner, 1952—, also mem. exec. com. Past pres., mem. bd. govs., Town Hall, Los Angeles; mem. exec. bd. Crescent Bay area council Boy Scouts Am., 1957—, commnr., 1957-62. Pres. Republican Assos., Los Angeles. Treas. U. Cal. at Los Angeles Found.; bd. dirs. Cal. Mus. Sci. and Industry. C.P.A., Cal., other states. Mem. Am. Inst. C.P.A.'s (mem. council 1962—, exec. com. 1964-68), Cal. Soc. C.P.A.'s (pres. 1962-63), Nat. Assn. Accountants (nat. dir. 1955-57), U. Cal. at Los Angeles Alumni Assn. (bd. dirs. 1962-65, Treas. 1963-65), Los Angeles Area C. of C. (dir., chmn. law and order com.). Episcopalian. Rotarian. Clubs: Los Angeles Country, California, University (Los Angeles). Home: 2141 La Mesa Dr Santa Monica CA 90402 Office: 606 S Olive St Los Angeles CA 90014

DAHLEN, CHESTER ARTHUR, army officer; b. Detroit Lakes, Minn., Sept. 4, 1910; s. Henry S. and Lydia (Elvesetter) D.; B.S., U.S. Mil. Acad., 1933; grad. Inf. Sch., 1937, Command and Gen. Staff Coll., 1947, Air War Coll., 1950, Army War Coll., 1952; m. Ursula Mae Erickson, Dec. 23, 1935; childrenSydney (Mrs. Elstran), Karen (Mrs. Fisher, Jr.). Commd. 2d lt., infantry, U.S. Army, 1933, advanced through grades to maj. gen., 1960; various assignments, U.S., 1933-41; regt. comdr. 24th Inf. Div., S.W. Pacific, 1941-45; instr. Inf. Sch., 1946-47; mem. faculty Command and Gen. Staff Coll., 1947-49; mem. research and devel. bd. Office Sec. Def., 1950-51; asst. G-3, Hdqrs. 4th U.S. Army, Ft. Sam Houston, 1952-53; comdg. officer 23d Inf. Regt., 2d Inf. Div., Korea, 1953; sr. adviser I ROK Corps, Korea, 1953-54; dep. chief staff Hdqrs. 4th U.S. Army, Fort Sam Houston, Texas, 1954-56; deputy chief of the Military Advisory Assistance Group, Madrid, Spain, 1956-58; asst. div. comdr. 2d Inf. Div., Ft. Benning, Ga., 1958-59: asst. comdt. Inf. Sch., Ft. Benning, 1959-60; chief Mil. Adv. Assistance Group, Taiwan, 1960-62; comdg. gen. 7th Inf. Div., Korea, 1962-63, XIV U.S. Army Corps, Mpls., 1963-64; chief staff Allied Forces So. Europe, Naples Italy, 1964-66; dept. comdg. gen. 4th U.S. Army, Ft. Sam Houston, Tex., comdg. gen. hdqrs. Ft. Sam Houston, 1966-. Commnr. Mediterranean dist. Trans-Atlantic council Boy Scouts Am., 1964-66. Decorated Silver Star with oak leaf cluster, Legion of Merit with two oak leaf clusters, Bronze Star with oak leaf cluster, Purple Heart; chevalier Legion of Honor, Croix de Guerre with bronze star (France); Mil. Order of Merit Ulchi (Republic Korea); Great Cross of Mil. Merit Spain; Armed Forces Expeditionary medal; Order Service Merit, 3d class, Republic Korea. Lutheran. Club: Army and Navy Country (Arlington, Va.). Home: Quarters 10 Staff Post Fort Sam Houston, TX 78234.

DAHLER, JOHN SPILLERS, chemist; b. Wichita, Kan., May 7, 1930; s. Raymond Edward and Agnes (Spillers) D.; B.S., U. Wichita, 1951, M.S., 1952; Ph.D., U. Wis., 1955; m. Lanaya Dorothy Williams, June 30, 1954; children—Kurt Williams, Gwendolyn Kay. NSF postdoctoral fellow, Amsterdam, 1955-56; prof. chemistry and chem. engring. U. Minn., 1959—; NSF sr. postdoctoral fellow U. Cal. at Berkeley, 1965. Del. Dem. State Conv., 1968; mem. Minn. Dem. Central Com., 1968-70. Served to 1st lt. USAF, 1956-58. Mem. Am. Phys. Soc., Soc. Natural Phil. Asst. editor Physics of Fluids, 1964-67. Asso. editor Chem. Engring. Sci. 1968, Jour. Statis. Physics, 1969—. Mem. editorial bd. on chem. engring. Prentice-Hall, 1966. Contbr. articles profl. jours. Home: 91 Crocus Pl Saint Paul MN 55102 Office: U Minn Dept Chemistry and Chem Engring Minneapolis MN 55455

DAHLGREN, GEORGE, educator, chemist; b. Chgo., Apr. 12, 1929; s. George Axel and Helen (Galloway) D.; B.S., Ill. Wesleyan U., 1951; M.S., U. Wyo., 1956, Ph.D., 1958; m. Mary Basler, Sept. 1, 1951; children—Sarah Jane, Kirsten Anderson, Andrew Basler. Postdoctoral fellow Cornell U., 1957-59; faculty U. Alaska, 1959-66, asso. prof. chemistry, 1962-66, head dept. chemistry, 1964-66; prof. chemistry U. Cin., 1966—, head dept., 1971—. Fellow A.A.A.S. (exec. sec. Alaska div. 1960-65); mem. Am. Chem. Soc., Am. Assn. U. Profs., Sigma Xi. Contbr. articles on periodate oxidations, hydrogen bonding, analysis to sci. jours. Editor Sci. in Alaska, Proc. of Alaskan Sci. Confs., vols. 11-15, 1961-65. Home: 3767 Middleton Av Cincinnati OH 45220

DAHLGREN, LAWRENCE JUNGBLOM, lawyer; b. Chgo., Aug. 21, 1906; s. A. Godfrey and Amanda W. (Jungblom) D.; J.D., John Marshall Law Sch., Chgo., 1926; m. Lorna Rasmussen, Jan. 1, 1945; children—Beverly (Mrs. James White), Phyllis (Mrs. Vincent Funovits). With Chgo. Title & Trust Co., Chgo., 1922-28; admitted to Ill. bar, 1928, since practiced in Chgo.; pvt. practice, 1922-68; partner Bergstrom, Rohde, Dahlgren & Olson, 1968—; v.p., sec., dir. Melin Tool Co., Inc., Cleve.; dir. Allied Arts Corp. Opera House, Chgo.; pres., bd. dirs. Layman Tithing Found., Chgo.; past pres., trustee Arlington Heights Park Dist.; treas., trustee, gen. counsel Luth. Gen. Hosp., Deaconess Hosp., Park Ridge, Ill. Served to lt. comdr. USNR, 1942-45. Mem. Am., Chgo. bar assns., Nordic Law Club, Am. Srs. Golf Assn., Delta Theta Phi. Lutheran (v.p. local ch.). Clubs: Swedish (Chgo.), Oak Park (Ill.) Country. Home: 1440 N Lake Shore Dr Chicago IL 60610 Office: 39 S LaSalle St Chicago IL 60603

DAHLIN, DAVID CARL, physician, educator; b. Beresford, S.D., Sept. 3, 1917; s. David Carl and Rose (Hult) D.; B.S., U.S.D., 1938; M.D., Rush Sch. Medicine, 1940. Intern Ancker Hosp., St. Paul, 1940-41, resident, 1941-42; postgrad. Sch. Mayo Found., 1945-48; now prof. pathology Mayo Found., U. Minn. Grad. Sch. Medicine; cons. surg. pathology Mayo Clinic. Home: 618 SW 14th Av Rochester MN 55901 Office: Mayo Found Rochester MN 55901

DAHLMAN, DONALD LEE, broadcasting co. exec.; b. Cin., July 24, 1918; s. Benjamin B. and Gertrude M. (Miller) D.; B.B.A., U. Cin., 1941; m. Phyllis O'Connor, Mar. 27, 1944; children—Teresa (Mrs. Edward Ruch), Patricia, Martin. Sales rep. Div. United Artists TV, Inc., Cin., 1955-63; sales mgr. WLWD-TV, Dayton, O., 1963-65, v.p., gen. mgr., 1965—. Mem. lay adv. bd. Good Samaritan Hosp., Dayton, 1969—; bd. dirs. Dayton Opera Assn., Miami Valley council Boy Scouts Am.; bd. trustees Dayton-Miami Valley Consortium. Served with AUS, 1941-46. Mem. Dayton Area C. of C. (dir. 1967-70). Home: 3520 Echo Springs Kettering OH 45429 Office: 4590 Avco Dr Dayton OH 45401

DAHLMANN, BERNARD CLEMENT, ins. co. exec.; b. Chgo., Sept. 5, 1910; s. B. J. and Rose (Isele) D.; grad. DePaul Acad., 1928; grad. Sch. of Commerce, Northwestern U., 1934; m. Eleanora Bihler, 1934; children—Dennis Alan, Neil Owen. Mgr., Can. Kemper Ins. Co., Toronto, Ont., 1936-52; exec. v.p., sr. officer, sec., dir. Fed. Mut. Ins. Co. div. Kemper Ins., Decatur, Ill., 1952-63; exec. v.p. Am. Motorists Ins. Co., Lumbermens Mut. Casualty Co., Am. Mfrs. Mut. Ins. Co., 1963—; pres., dir. Fed. Mut. Ins. Co., 1963—, Sequoia Ins., Kemper Security Sales Co.; chmn., dir. Fed. Kemper Life Assurance Co.; Ia. Kemper Mut. Ins. Co., Economy Fire & Casualty Co., Fidelity Life Assn.; v.p., dir. Kemperco, Inc., Kemper Security Ins. Co.; dir. Empire State Mut. Life Ins. Co., Bank of Chgo. Chmn. Toronto Jr. Bd. Trade, 1942-43; mem. council Toronto Bd. Trade, 1944-45. Pres. adv. bd. St. Mary's Hosp., Decatur, 1963-64. Mem. Ill. C. of C. (dir.), Decatur Assn. Commerce (pres. 1958-59). Club: Tower (Chgo.); Seven Lake Country (Palm Springs, Cal.). Home: 711 Bluff Rd Lake Bluff IL 60044 Office: 4750 Sheridan Chicago IL 60640

DAHLQUIST, LLOYD WILLIAM, clergyman; b. Wheaton, Minn., Apr. 6, 1906; s. Charles Eric and Christine (Sundin) D.; Th.B., Bethel Theol. Sem., 1928; B.A., Macalester Coll., 1930; m. Ruth Ellen Ostrom, Aug. 27, 1930; 1 dau., Merilyn Ruth. Ordained to ministry Bapt. Ch., 1928; pastor in Minn., N.J. and Ill., 1928-59, Evanston, Ill., 1970—. Gen. sec. Bapt. Gen. Conf., 1959-69; mem. Gen. Commn. Chaplains, 1957-69; mem. Keswick council Mid Am. Keswick Conv., 1960-62; mem. Council Reference Am. Messianic Fellowship, 1957—. Served as chaplain USAAF, 1942-46. ETO. Author: Concerning Church Membership, 2d edit., 1964. Home: 2311 Ruth St Park Ridge IL 60068

DAHLSTROM, DONALD ALBERT, equipment mfg. co. exec.; b. Mpls., Jan. 16, 1920; s. Raymond Estin and Dora Adina (Bloomgren) D.; student Macalester Coll., 1937-39; B.S. in Chem. Engring., U. Minn., 1942; Ph.D., Northwestern U., 1949; m. Betty Cordelia Robertson, Dec. 4, 1942; children—Mary Elizabeth, Donald Raymond, Christine Dora, Stephanie Lou, Michael Jeffrey. Petroleum engr. Internat. Petroleum Co., Ltd., Negritos, Peru, 1942-45; from instr. to asso. prof. chem. engring. Northwestern U., 1946-56; with Eimco Corp., Palatine, Ill., 1952—, v.p., dir. research and devel., 1960—, also dir.; dir. Process Engrs., Inc. Am. mem. internat. sci. com. 6th Internat. Mineral Processing Congress, 1963; mem. adviser council on engring. NSF. Mem. sch. bd. dist. 110, Deerfield, Ill., 1959-61; pres. Riverwoods Residents Assn., 1962-63; chmn. bd. Northwestern YMCA, 1950-52; trustee Village of Riverwoods, 1966-69, Served with USNR, 1945-46. Recipient Merit award Northwestern U., 1965. Mem. Am. Inst. Chem. Engrs. (bd. dirs. 1960-62, v.p. 1963, pres. 1964-65, chmn. environmental div. 1971) Am. Inst. Mining, Metall. and Petroleum Engrs. (chmn. minerals benefication div. 1963-64, bd. dirs. soc. mining engrs. 1965—, Rossiter W. Raymond award 1952), Am. Chem. Soc., Water Pollution Control Fedn., Canadian Inst. Mining and Metallurgy, The Filtration Soc. (London), Sigma Xi (Holgate award Northwestern U. chpt. 1949), Phi Lambda Upsilon, Tau Beta Pi (nat. pres. 1958-62). Club: Chemists (N.Y.C.). Presbyn. Contbr. to handbook. Home: 5340 Cottonwood Lane Salt Lake City UT 87117 Office: The Eimco Corp Box 300 Salt Lake City UT 84117

DAICHES, DAVID, author, educator; b. Sunderland, Eng., Sept. 2, 1912; s. Rev. Salis and Flora (Levin) D.; student George Watson's Coll., Edinburgh, Scotland, 1919-30; (M.A. with 1st class honors), U. of Edinburgh, 1930-34; (M.A., D. Phil.); Balliol Coll., Oxford U., 1934-37; L.H.D., Brown U., 1964; m. Isobel Janet Mackay, July 28, 1937; children—Alan Harry, Jennifer (Mrs. Angus Calder), Elizabeth Mackay (Mrs. Derek Austin). Asst. In English, U. of Edinburgh, 1935-36; Andrew Bradley fellow Balliol Coll., 1936-37; asst. prof. English, U. Chgo., 1937-43; prof. English, Cornell U., 1946-51; joined staff British Information Services, 1943; second sec. Brit. Embassy, Washington, 1944-46; U. lectr. in English, Cambridge U. 1951-61; prof. English, U. Sussex, dean sch. English studies, 1961-68; vis. prof. criticism Ind. U., 1956-57; Elliston lectr. U. Cin., 1960; fellow Jesus Coll. Cambridge, 1957-62; Whidden lectr. McMaster U., 1964; Hill Found. vis prof. U. Minn., 1966; Ewing lectr. U. Cal. at Los Angeles, 1967. Fellow Royal Soc. Lit. Author: The Novel and the Modern World, 1939; Virginia Woolf, 1942; A Study of Literature, 1948; Robert Burns, 1951; Two Worlds; Critical Approaches to Literature; Literary Essays, 1956; Milton, 1957; The Present Age, 1958; A Critical History of English Literature, 1960; The Paradox of Scottish Culture, 1965; More Literary Essays, 1968; Some Late Victorian Attitudes, 1969; Scotch Whisky, 1969; Walter Scott and His World, 1971. Contbr. poetry, articles essays various periodicals. Home: Downsview Welhouse Lane Burgess Hill Sussex England

DAIGH, RALPH FOSTER, editorial dir., writer; b. Springfield, Ill., Oct. 12, 1907; s. Everett Lee and Mabel Ellen (Foster) D.; student Huron Coll. and Columbia U. A.B., B.J., U. of Mo., 1930; m. Kate Cordelia Reynolds, April 7, 1934; childrenPolly Lee, Sally Jane. Correspondent Kansas City Star, 1928-30. Globe-Democrat, St. Louis, 1928-30; sports editor Mason City (Iowa) Globe-Gazette, 1930; editor Fawcett Publishers, Minneapolis, Minn., 1930-31; editor Dell Pub. Co., N.Y. City, 1931-32; mng. editor Popular Publs., Chicago, Ill., 1932-33; mem. staff World- Telegram, N.Y. City, 1933; free lance writer, 1933-34; v.p. and editorial dir. Fawcett Publications, N.Y.C., 1935-69, pres. 1969—. Mem. Artists and Writers, Sigma Delta Chi, Pi Kappa Delta. Clubs: Lambs, Sports Car, Pelham Country. Contbr. short stories and serials to popular mags. Home: 1405 Park Lane Pelham NY 10803 Office: 67 W 55th St New York City NY 10036

DAIGNAULT, ALEXANDER TROUP, corp. exec.; b. Woonsocket, R.I., Mar. 12, 1916; s. Raphael P. and Elsie (Troup) D.; B.A., Yale, 1937; M.B.A., Harvard, 1939; m. Elizabeth B. Kendrick, June 3, 1944; children—Anne, Alexander Troup. Indsl. engr. U.S. Rubber Co., Naugatuck, Conn., 1939-41; indsl. specialist research and devel. br. Office Q.M. Gen., Washington, 1941-46; asst. to pres. Dewey & Almy Chem. Co., Cambridge, Mass., 1946-48, treas., 1948- 53; v.p. charge finance Westinghouse Air Brake Co., Pitts., 1953-55; exec. v.p. W. R. Grace & Co., 1956—, also dir.; dir. Cordis Corp., Miami, Fla., Nat. Life Ins. Co., Montpelier, Vt. Treasurer, trustee Marine Biological Lab., Woods Hole, Mass. Mem. Financial Execs. Inst. Clubs: Harvard Business School (N.Y.C.); Allegheny (Pa.) Country; Woods Hole Golf (Mass.); Quissett Yacht (Mass.); India House (N.Y.C.); Economic (N.Y.). Home: 200 E 66th St New York City NY 10021 Office: 7 Hanover Sq New York City NY 10005

DAILEY, BENJAMIN PETER, educator; b. San Marcos, Tex., Sept. 1, 1919; B.A., Southwest Tex. State Tchrs. Coll., 1938; M.A., U. Tex., 1940. Ph.D. in Chemistry, 1942; married, 1945; three children. Research asso. Explosives Research Lab., Pa., 1942-45; fellow Harvard, 1946-47; mem. faculty chemistry Columbia, 1947—, prof., 1956—, chmn. dept., 1968-70. Sr. fellow NSF., 1963-64; Guggenheim fellow, 1971-72. Fellow Am. Phys. Soc.; mem. Am. Chem. Soc., Am. Acad. Arts and Scis. Research thermodynamic properties, molecular structure, microwave spectra, nuclear magnetic resonance. Address: 440 Riverside Dr New York City NY 10027*

DAILEY, DONALD EARL, indsl. design cons.; b. Mpls., July 25, 1914; s. William Earl and Carrye Elizabeth (Fluhart) D.; student U. Toledo, Toledo Museum Sch. Design, 1934-37; m. Elizabeth Meall, Oct. 25, 1941; children—Deanne Carol, William Bruce. Design dir. Phila. office Harold Van Doran & Assos., 1940-46; propr. Donald Dailey Designers, Phila., 1946-50; v.p. Products Planning Servel, Inc., 1950-55; propr. Don Dailey & Assos., product design cons. to industry, Evansville, Ind., 1955—. Chmn. city beautification Ohio Jr. C. of C., 1939; v.p., dir. Evansville Mus. Art and Sci., 1951-55, also chmn. bldg. com.; cons. city center devel. com. Evansville Future, Inc., 1964—; lectr. U. Lehigh, Syracuse U., U. Mich., McGill U., others; exhibited painting and sculpture museums throughout Midwest. Recipient Bronze Medal award Indsl. Designers Inst., 1953, Master Design award Product Engring. mag., 1959, 64. Fellow Indsl. Soc. Am. (founder jour.; v.p. 1965-66); mem. Mystic Marine Hist. Soc., Internat. Oceanographic Found., Am. Soc. Indsl. Designers (pres. 1964-65). Clubs: Coral Reef Yacht; Petroleum, Evansville Country. Patentee in field. Address: 9307 Petersburg Rd Evansville IN 47711

DAILEY, HENRY LAMAR, former banker; b. Kenedy, Tex., Feb. 5, 1918; s. Henry Walter and Nancy Joan (Eaton) D.; student Harvard Bus. Sch., 1942, Ariz. State U., 1957-59, U. Ala., 1962-63; m. Dorothy Jean Riley; 1 dau., Jeanne Alaire (Mrs. Fred E. Ingerson, Jr.). Bookkeeper, Firs-Nichols Nat. Bank, Kenedy, Tex., 1935-38, Capital Nat. Bank, Austin, Tex., 1938-41; sales rep. IBM Corp., 1946-48; commd. 2d lt. USAAF, advanced through grades to lt. col. USAF; grad. Air War Coll., 1963; ret., 1969; controller Valley Nat. Bank, Phoenix, 1969-71; v.p. Phoenix Clearing House Assn., 1971—. Pres. P.T.A., London, Eng., 1953-54. Decorated Army Commendation medal with oak leaf cluster, USAF Commendation medal. Mem. Am. Soc. Mil. Controllers, Am. Inst. Banking (v.p. Austin 1940-41), Bank Adminstrn. Inst., Protestant Men of The Pentagon (v.p. 1968-69), Nat. Office Mgmt. Assn. (v.p. local chpt. 1947-48), Randolph AFB (pres. 1956), Luke AFB (pres. 1958-59) res. officers assns. Lutheran (financial sec.). Home: 3329 E Oregon Av Phoenix AZ 85018

DAILEY, PETER HEATH, advt. exec.; b. New Orleans, May 1, 1930; s. John William and Abigail (Heath) D.; B.S., U. Cal. at Los Angeles, 1954; m. Jacqueline Ann Biggerstaff, 1953; children—Michael, Ann, Sydney Jean, Peter Heath, Elizabeth Mary, Partricia Lynn. Various positions to v.p. Erwin Wasey, Ruthrauff & Ryan, Inc., Los Angeles, 1956-63; v.p. Foote, Cone & Belding, 1963-64; sr. v.p., dir. Western and Far Eastern regions Campbell-Ewald Co., Los Angeles, 1964-67; pres. Dailey & Assos., Los Angeles, 1968—. Bd. dirs. Big Bros. of Am., Los Angeles, Arthritis Found., So. Cal. Choral Music Assn., Los Angeles Orthopaedic Found. and Hosp.; founding trustee U. Cal. at Los Angeles Found. Served to lt. USNR, 1954-56. Named Chi Psi of Year, 1952. Mem. Los Angeles C. of C., U. Cal. at Los Angeles Alumni Assn. (v.p., dir. devel., bd. dirs. 1966-70), San Francisco, Los Angeles advt. clubs, Chi Psi. Clubs: Family (San Francisco); Sportsmen of the South, California, Saddle and Sirloin, Bruin Football Alumni (Los Angeles); Rancheros Vistadores (Santa Barbara, Cal.); Lakeside Golf. Home: 10311 Valley Spring Lane North Hollywood CA 91602 Office: 3807 Wilshire Blvd Los Angeles CA 90005

DAILEY, ROBERT WINSTON, advt. exec.; b. Olney, Ill., Oct. 15, 1912; s. William E. and Carrye (Fluhart) D.; student U. Toledo, 1930-34; m. Virginia C. Jackman, Aug. 8, 1937; children—Donna, Christine, Robert J. Reporter, Toledo Blade, 1934-37; news editor NBC, 1937, mgr. news and spl. events, also newscaster and sports announcer NBC sta. WTAM, Cleve., 1937-44; successively copywriter, radio mgr., account exec., radio-TV mgr., account supr. McCann-Erickson, Inc., Cleve., 1944-52, v.p., gen. mgr., 1952-57, v.p. bus. devel., mem. plans bd., Chgo. office, 1958; v.p. Cunningham & Walsh, N.Y.C., 1959, exec. v.p. Western region, gen. mgr. San Francisco office, 1959-62; pres., chmn. bd. Venturi, Inc., 1963—; pres. Krypto Corp., 1963-67. Mem. bd., exec. com. San Mateo County Better Bus. Bur. Mem. San Francisco Advt. Club, San Francisco Sales Execs. Club. Republican. Conglist. Clubs: California Golf, Rotary, World Trade (San Francisco). Home: 1200 Frontera Way Millbrae CA Office: Venturi Inc 1610 Rollins Rd Burlingame CA 94010

DAILY, JAMES WALLACE, educator, engr.; b. Columbia, Mo., Mar. 19, 1913; s. Wallace Edgar and Marjory Isabel (McGrath) D.; A.B., Stanford, 1935; M.S., Cal. Inst. Tech., 1937, Ph.D., 1945; m. Sarah Vanderlip Atwood, Sept. 10, 1938; children—John Wallace, Sarah Anne Vanderlip. Test engr. Byron Jackson Co., Berkeley, Cal., 1935; research asst. hydraulics Cal. Inst. Tech., 1936-37, research fellow, mgr. hydraulic machinery lab., 1937-40, instr. mech. engring., 1940-46; hydraulic engr. OSRD, Navy Research Projects, 1941-46; asst. prof. hydraulics Mass. Inst. Tech., 1946-49. asso. prof., 1949-55, prof., 1955-64; prof. engring. mechancis, chmn. dept., U. Mich., 1964—; vis. prof. Tech. U. of Delft (Netherlands), 1971; vis. scientist France Centre de Recherches et d'Essais, Paris, 1971; cons. various firms. Mem. sch. com. Town of Arlington, Mass., 1959-65. Recipient Naval Ordnance Devel. award, 1945. Registered profl. engr. Mem. Internat. Assn. Hydraulic Research (pres. 1967-71), Am. Soc. C.E., Boston Soc. Civil Engrs., Am. Soc. M.E., Sigma Xi, Tau Beta Pi, Chi Epsilon. Conglist. Club: Cosmos (Washington). Author: (with D.R.F. Harleman) Fluid Dynamics; (with R.T. Knapp and F.G. Hammitt) Cavitation. Contbr. tech. articles Am., fgn. jours. Home: 375 Rock Creek Dr Ann Arbor MI 48104

DAINOW, JOSEPH, educator; b. Montreal, Can., July 5, 1906; s. Aaron and Pearl (Sourkes) D.; B.A., McGill U., Montreal, 1926, B.C.L., 1929; Docteur en Droit, U. Dijon (France), 1931; S.J.D., Northwestern U., 1938; LL.D., U. Ghent (Belgium), 1964; m. Frieda Fineman, Aug. 23, 1933; children—Jariel David, Keren Judith. Lectr. in Roman law McGill U., 1931-32; gen. law practice, Montreal, Can., 1932-33; research asso. Northwestern U., 1933-35; prof. law Loyola U., New Orleans, 1935-38; asst. prof. law La. State U., 1938-42, asso. prof., 1942-47, prof. law, 1947—, dir. Inst. of Civil Law Studies, 1967—. Vis. prof. law U. P.R., 1950, Northwestern U., 1956, U. Tex., 1957, U. Mich., 1958, N.Y. U., 1959. Fulbright lectr. U. Paris, U. Lyon (France), 1954, U. Ghent (Belgium), 1962-63. Mem. U.S. nat. commn. UNESCO, 1957-59. Served to lt. col., Judge Adv. Gen. Dept., AUS, 1942-46; chief of research branch Washington office, in charge all research facilities and publns. including Mil. Laws U.S. and monthly bull. of Judge Adv. Gen. of Army; prepared research materials for use in connection with Nurenberg trial, June-Aug. 1945; mem. legal staff of Am. prosecution in Nurenberg, Aug.- Dec. 1945. Guggenheim fellow. Mem. Internat. Acad. Comparative Law, Am. Soc. Internat. Law (exec. council 1959-62), La. Bar Assn. (bd. govs. 1949-50, 55-56), Am. Bar Assn., Am. Assn. U. Profs., Am. Fgn. Law Assn., La. State Law Inst. (mem. council), Am. Assn. Comparative Study Law (dir.), Order of Coif, Omicron Delta Kappa, Phi Kappa Phi, Gamma Eta Gamma. Jewish religion. Reporter. Compiled Edit. of Civil Codes of Louisiana (La. State Law Inst.), Vol. 1, 1940, Vol. 2, 1942. Editor: Civil Code of Louisiana, 1947, 61; Essays on the Civil Law of Obligations, 1969. Mem. bd. editors Am. Jour. Comparative Law. Contbr. articles to law revs. in U.S., Can., France. Home: 1956 Glendale Av Baton Rouge LA 70808

DAINS, ORTH IRVEN, retired banker; b. Monmouth, Ill., Aug. 24, 1904; s. Irven F. and Mary R. (Orth) D.; student Monmouth Coll., 1924-25; m. Marguerite L. Gehlman, Aug. 15, 1931; children—Roger O., Gretchen M., Stephen I. Asst. nat. bank examiner 7th Fed. Res. Dist., 1926-33; bank examiner Ill., 1933-36; auditor Marion Nat. Bank (Ind.), 1936-37; examiner First Wis. Bankshares Corp., Wis., 1937-40, chief examiner, 1940-52, sec.-treas., 1952-56, sec.-treas., v.p., 1956-69, retired, 1969; dir. 1st Wis. Nat. Bank, Eau Claire, Nat. Presto Industries, Inc., Eau Claire. Mason (Shriner). Club: Milwaukee Athletic. Home: 1620 Drummond St Eau Claire WI

DAINTON, FREDERICK SYDNEY, educator; b. Sheffield, Eng., Nov. 11, 1914; s. George Whalley and Mary Jane (Botterill) D.; M.A. (Casberd scholar and prizeman), St. John's Coll., Oxford U., 1937, B.Sc., 1940; Ph.D., Sidney Sussex Coll., Cambridge U., 1940, Sc.D., 1951; m. Barbara Hazlitt, Aug. 27, 1942; childrenJohn Bourke, Mary Crawford, Rosalind Hazlitt. Fellow, praelector St. Catharine's Coll., Cambridge U., 1944-50; H. O. Jones lectr. phys. chemistry U.

Cambridge, 1946-50; chmn., prof. phys. chemistry Sch. Chemistry, U. Leeds, 1953-65; vice chancellor U. Nottingham (Eng.), 1965-70; Dr. Lee's prof. Oxford U. 1970—; Arthur D. Little vis. prof. chemistry Mass. Inst. Tech., 1958-59; Tilden lectr. Chem. Soc. of London; Baker lectr. Cornell U. 1961; Boomer lectr. U. Alta., 1962. Mem. council for Sci. Policy, 1965-, Central Adv. Council on Sci. and Tech., 1967-; chmn of Adv. Com. on Sci. and Tech. Information, 1966-; chmn. Nat. Libraries Com., 1967-69. Recipient Sylvanus Thompson medal Radiological and Roentgen. Socs. Fellow Royal Soc. (Davey medal 1969); mem. Faraday Soc. (pres. 1965-66), Assn. Radiation Research (chmn. 1964-66). Author: Chain Reactions, 1956. Contbr. sci. papers jours. of learned socs. Home: Fieldside Water Eaton Lane Kidlinston Oxford England

DAITCH, HERBERT BRAHAM, supermarket chain exec.; b. N.Y.C., Jan. 28, 1914; s. Louis and Sarah (Dubin) D.; B.S., N.Y.U., 1935; student agr. Cornell U., 1935; m. Hilda Feinberg, Dec. 15, 1935; children—Sandra, Lawrence. Shipping clk. L. Daitch & Co., 1935; country plants mgr. Delaware County Dairies, Roxbury, N.Y., 1942-45, now pres., dir. Delaware County Dairies, Inc.; v.p., dir. L. Daitch & Co., 1945-49, pres., 1949-52; pres. Daitch Crystal Dairies, N.Y.C., 1952-55, chmn., treas., 1955—; mem. Bronx and Upper Manhattan adv. com. Chase Manhattan Bank N.Am.; trustee Bronx Savs. Bank. Mem. Chgo. Merc. Exchange. Trustee Union Welfare Fund, Union Pension Fund. Mem. Marketmen's Assn. Greater N.Y. (dir. 1951-52), N.Y. Merc. Exchange (dir. 1949-51), Young Pres. Orgn., Kappa Nu. Jewish religion. Mason. Club: New York Univ. Home: Justin Rd Harrison NY 10528 Office: 400 Walnut Av New York City NY 10454

D'AIUTO, LEONARD N., lawyer; b. Dover, Ohio, Feb. 19, 1932; s. Nick L. and Theresa (Minadeo) D'A; student Kent State U., 1950-52; LL.B. with honors, U. Fla., 1960, J.D. with honors, 1960; m. Rose Marie Preisel, Dec. 26, 1953. Admitted to Fla. bar, 1960; labor adminstr. Eastern Airlines, Miami, Fla., 1960- 61; with firm Langbein and Burdick, West Palm Beach, Fla., 1961-62; mem. firm Howell, Kirby, Montgomery and Sands, Jacksonville, 1962-64; mng. partner firm Howell, Kirby, Montgomery and D'Aiuto, Cocoa, 1964-68; pres. profl. assos. Howell, Kirby, Montgomery and D'Aiuto (name now Howell), Kirby, Montgomery, D'Aiuto & Hallowes, P.A.), Jacksonville, Daytona Beach, Cocoa, Ft. Lauderdale and West Palm Beach, 1968—. Served as aviator USNR, 1952-56; comdr. Res. Rotarian (pres. Cocoa 1968-69). Home: 1024 Fairlawn Dr Rockledge FL 32955 Office: 200 E Robinson Av Orlando FL 32801

DAKAN, NORMAN EUGENE, librarian; b. Beaver City, Neb., Sept. 16, 1926; s. Everett Sylvester and Avis Belle (Fowler) D.; B.A., U. Cal., Berkeley, 1953, B.L.S., 1954; m. Miyoko Muranaka, Jan. 24, 1957; 1 dau., Margot Toshiko. Asst. reference and order librarian Cal. State Polytech. Coll. Library, San Luis Obispo, 1954-56; base librarian Ashiya AFB, Japan, 1956-57; chief librarian Itazuke AFB, Japan, 1957-60; base librarian Hickam AFB, Hawaii, 1960-62; chief librarian Fuchu Air Sta., Japan, 1962-66, Kadena AFB, Okinawa, 1966-68; base librarian Hickam AFB, Hawaii, 1968-70; chief librarian Yokota AFB, Japan, 1970-71; 6100th Air Base Wing supervisory librarian Yokota AFB, Japan, 1971—. Served with USNR, 1944-46. Compiler, Pacific Air Forces basic bibliographies: Intelligence, Black Literature. Home: PSC Box 1161 6100th Air Base Wing APO San Francisco CA 96328 Office: Base Library FL5209 6100th Air Base Wing APO San Francisco CA 96328

DAKE, MARCIA ALLENE, nurse educator; b. Bemus Point, N.Y., May 22, 1923; d. Earl B. and Bernice DeLeo (Haskin) D.; student Crouse Irving Hosp. Sch. Nursing, Syracuse, N.Y., 1944; B.S., Syracuse U., 1951; M.A., Tchrs. Coll., Columbia, 1955, Ed. D., 1958. Sch. nurse, tchr., Greenwood and Jasper Central Schs., N.Y. State, 1946-48, Falconer Central Sch., 1948-50, Ogdensburg Pub. Schs., 1951-52; chmn. health dept. State U. N.Y., State Tchrs. Coll., Oneonta, 1952-56; dean Coll. of Nursing, U. of Ky., 1958- -. Mem. Ky. Bd. Nursing Edn. Nurse Registration, 1969-70, pres., 1970—. Nurse officer Civil Def., Otsego County, N.Y., 1953-56; mem. Def. Dept. Adv. Com. on Women in Services, 1963-65; mem. Kentucky Comprehensive Health Planning Council, 1968-71. Served as 2d lt., Army Nurse Corps, 1945-46. Fellow Nat. League Nursing; mem. League Women Voters, Am., Ky. (mem. com. on edn. 1968—; chmn. ednl. admistrs., cons. and tchrs. sect. 1970-71) nurses assns., Ky. Assn. Registered Nurses (chmn. program com. 1959), N.Y. State Nurses Assn. (1st v.p., legis. chmn. 1954-56), Ky. League for Nursing (dir. 1959-61, pres. 1961-65), N.E.A., Bus. and Profl. Women, Ky. Pub. Health Assn., Kappa Delta Pi, Pi Lambda Theta. Club: Zonta (Lexington). Home: 580 Albany Rd Lexington KY 40502

DAKIN, ALLIN WINSTON, ednl. adminstr.; b. Mason City, Ia., June 2, 1905; s. Channing Ellery and Norra (Allin) D.; A.B., State U. Ia., 1926, A.M., 1927; M.B.A., Harvard, 1931; LL.D., Westmar Coll., 1961. Instr. in commerce State U. Ia., 1926-29; with J. & W. Seligman &. Co. and Tri-Continental Corp., N.Y.C., 1931-34; bursar and with commerce dept. Robert Coll., Istanbul, Turkey, also bursar Am. Coll. for Girls, Istanbul, 1934-39; controller Pomona Coll., Scripps Coll. and Claremont (Cal.) Colls., 1940-44; administrv. dean State U. Ia., Iowa City, 1944—. Mem. regional exec. com. nat. council Boy Scouts Am. Trustee Sch. Religion, State U. Ia., Meth-Wick Manor; pres. Ia. div. UN Assn., 1962-70. Served as lt., O.R.C., 1926-36. R.T. Swaine fellow Harvard, 1929. Fellow Am. Geog. Soc., Archaeol. Inst. Am.; mem. Institucion Internat. de Ideales Americanistas (Mexican sect.), Order of Artus, Scabbard and Blade, Alpha Phi Omega, Sigma Nu, Delta Sigma Rho, Pi Gamma Mu, Omicron Delta Kappa. Mem. Unitarian Ch. Mason (Shriner), Elk. Clubs: Harvard (N.Y.C.); Rotary (dist. gov., dir. 1955-57, 3d v.p. 1956-57, chmn. found. fellowships com., chmn. 1960 conv.; chmn. finance com. 1964-65, chmn. program com. 1965- 66; pub. relations com. 1966-67, chmn. youth activities 1968-69, chmn. community service 1970-71), Triangle (Iowa City). Home: 329 Ellis Av Iowa City IA 52240

DALAI LAMA (born Tanchu Tsiring), ruler of Tibet; b. Kokonor region, Tsinghai, Mongolia, China, June 6, 1935; s. Chog-chu and Dhakya Tsiring; believed to be reincarnation of 13th Lama, so was taken to Lbasa and enthroned as 14th Lama, Feb. 22, 1940; rights exercised by regency, then assumed power, 1950; now known as Ling-ehr Lamatanchu; Communists advanced a rival Lama, 1948, and their military success in Tibet caused Ling-ehr Lamatanchu to flee to Yatung, nr. India, Jan. 1951; Communists gained control of Tibet, but by terms of agreement to end hostilities they agreed to maintain present position of Dalai Lama; supreme head Buddhists sects, Tibet. Author: My Land and People, 1962; Losar Migje, 1963. Address: The Kchen Choling Dharmsala Cantt Kangra Punjab India

DALBECK, ROBERT ELLIS, oil co. exec.; b. Los Angeles, Jan. 12, 1913; s. G. E. and Anna (Holcomb) D.; extension student U. So. Cal., Tex. A. and M. U., U. Houston; m. Mary Virginia Gibson, Oct. 31, 1941; children—Nancy Jean (Mrs. George James Kenagy), Robert Gibson, Richard Warren. Comptroller Union Oil Co. Cal. Mem. Am. Petroleum Inst. Republican. Baptist. Clubs: Jonathan (Los Angeles); Oakmont Country. Home: 3351 Country Club Dr Glendale CA 91208 Office: 461 S Boylston St Los Angeles CA 90017

DALBY, MAX FOREMAN, music educator; b. Driggs, Ida., Aug. 22, 1920; s. Cleon Ezra and Ethelwynne (Griggs) D.; B.A. with high honors, Brigham Young U., 1942; M.A., San Diego State Coll., 1950; student U. Utah, 1951-52; Ed.D., Utah State U., 1961; student U. Colo., summer 1960; m. Betty Marler, Dec. 18, 1941; children—Diana Edvalson (Mrs. Melvin Edvalson), Kim Christian, Jonathan Marler, Christopher Max, Rebecca, Bruce Foreman, Victoria, Cynthia, Mariann. Dir. instrumental music San Diego parochial schs., 1946-50, Cyprus High Sch., Granite Dist., Salt Lake County, 1950-51; dir. Inst. Music, Ogden (Utah) High Sch., 1951-55, Weber State Coll., Ogden, 1955-57; dir. bands Utah State U., 1957-71, head music dept., 1965—; music cons. Intermountain Sch., 1967-68; solo clarinetist Salt Lake City Municipal Band, also Utah Symphony Orch., 1940-42; concert dir. Universal Acad. for Music European Tours. Served with AUS, 1942-45. Recipient Robins Service award Utah State U., 1960. Mem. Utah Music Educators Assn. (pres. 1955-59), Music Educators Nat. Conf. (organizer Western div. all conf. band, orch. and chorus 1959, exec. com. 1962-64, pres. Western div. Bakersfield conv. 1961-63). Conductor, clinician and adjudicator, 22 states and Can. Home: 193 East 6th North Logan UT 84321

DALCHER, LAURENCE P., govt. ofcl.; b. Quincy, Mass., Nov. 7, 1917; S. John T. and Amy (Foster) D.; student N.Y.U., 1939; student Mass. Inst. Tech., 1956, Nat. War Coll., 1962-63; m. Janet Southwell, Sept. 5, 1953; childrenSara Hughes, Bruce peter. Engaged as editor and book pub., 1935-41; adviser to Gen. Clay in Berlin, Germany, 1947-49; joined U.S. Fgn. Service, 1949; pub. Wiener Kurier, Vienna, Austria, 1952-56; dir. radio sta. RIAS, Berlin, 1956-59; chief information officer embassy, New Delhi, India, 1963-69; senior field rep., in Saigon, Vietnam, 1969-. Served to maj. AUS, 1942- 46; ETO. Conglist. Author: Confuse and Control, 1951. Editor: Report After Action, 1945; Our Foreign Policy, 1952; John F. Kennedy Speaks, 1964. Home: 4513 Davenport St N W Washington DC 20016. Office: Saigon, Vietnam.

DALDIN, HERMAN JACK, hotel exec.; b. Piney Fork, O., Jan. 22, 1912; s. John and Mary (Sarena) D.; student Kent (Ohio) State U., 1931-32; children—Herman, John, Tommy, Larry, Vicki. With Milner Hotel System, 1932—, mgr., 1932- 37, supr., 1937-38, real estate officer, 1939-41, pres. Millner Hotels Mgmt. Co., 1941—; v.p., also gen. mgr. real estate and property mgmt.; owner, mgr., dir. Milner Corps., 1947—; pres., dir. Star Hotel Co. Mem. Mich. Real Estate Bd., Greater Detroit Bd. of Commerce, Hotel Sales Mgmt. Assn., Detroit Area Council World Affairs, Internat. Platform Assn. (pres. Mich. chpt). Roman Catholic. Clubs: Economic (chmn. coll. com.), Adcraft, Detroit Athletic (Detroit); Admirals; Circumnavigators. Home: 2751 Silverhill Silverlake Pontiac MI 48055 Office: Penobscot Bldg Detroit MI 48226

DALE, BRUCE ALBERT, photographer; b. Tiffin, O., Oct. 10, 1938; s. Clyde Enoth and Helen (Snanigan) D.; student journalism seminars, U. Mo., Syracuse U., U. Miami (Fla.), Mich. State U.; m. Joyce Ann Peterson, June 11, 1960; childrenGregory, Jeffrey, Christopher. Photographer, Chesshire Studios, Cleve., 1953-56, Cleve. Clinic, 1956-57, Toledo Blade, 1957-64, Nat. Geog. mag., 1964—. Recipient award Ohio Press photographers Assn., 1959, 61, 62, 63. Mem. Nat. Press Photographers Assn. (award 1958, 59, 63, 64, 65, 66; 3d place mag. photographer of year 1966; magazine photographer of year award 1967), White House News Photographers Assn. (award 1966). HOme: 1546 N Ivanhoe St Arlington, VA 22205. Office: Nat Geographic Soc 17th and M Sts Washington DC 20036.

DALE, EDGAR, univ. prof.; b. Benson, Minn., Apr. 27, 1900; s. Eric and Mary Dorothy (Romfo) D.; A.B., U. N.D., 1921. A.M., 1924, H.H.D., 1958; Ph.D., U. Chgo., 1929; m. Elizabeth Kirchner, Aug. 7, 1926; children—Dorothy Elizabeth, Richard. Rural sch. tchr., 1918-19; supt. schs., Webster, N.D., 1921-24; tchr. Jr. High Sch., Winnetka, Ill., 1924-26; editorial dept. Eastman Teaching Films, Rochester, N.Y., 1928-29; research asso. and asst. prof. of edn. Bur. Ednl. Research and Service, Ohio State U., Columbus, 1929-34, research asso. and asso. prof. 1934-39, research asso. and prof., 1939-70, prof. emeritus, 1970—; civilian cons. to Army Air Forces, 1943. Trustee World Edn., Inc. Head coordination div., Bur. Motion Pictures, OWI Washington, D.C., 1942—. Served in inf. U.S. Army, 1918. Mem. Ednl. Policies Commn., 1956—; mem. exec. com., dept. of visual instrn. N.E.A., pres. of dept. of visual instrn., 1937- 38; chmn. of motion pictures and visual edn. Nat. Congress of Parents and Teachers; del. to child welfare com. League of Nations, Geneva, 1936; mem. U. S. Nat. Commn. for UNESCO, 1947-51, chmn. com. vol. internat. assistance. Recipient Eastman Kodak Gold Medal award Soc. Motion Picture and TV Eng., 1968. Mem. Nat. Soc. Study Edn. (dir.), Nat. Assn. for Better Radio and TV (dir.). Mem. Community Church, Columbus. Club: Faculty. Author several books on edn. since 1935; Audio-visual Methods in Teaching, 1946, 3d ed., 1969: Stories for Today, 1954: Stories Worth Knowing, 1954; Can You Give The Public What It Wants?, 1967. Compiler: Motion Pictures In Education (with others). 1937. Co-editor News Letter. Mem. editorial adv. bd. Field Enterprises Ednl. Corp., Inc., World Book Ency.; editorial bd. Education. Contbr. to jours. Home: 2614 Tremont Rd Columbus OH 43221

DALE, EDWARD EVERETT, research prof. history; b. Keller, Tex., Feb. 8, 1879; s. John Franklin and Mattie Counts (Colley) D.; grad. Central State Tchrs. Coll., Edmond, Okla., 1909; A.B., U. of Okla., 1911; A.M., Harvard, 1914, Ph.D., 1922; m. Rosalie Gilkey. July 18, 1919; 1 son, Edward Everett. Cowboy and ranchman, 1896-1901; tchr. country sch., 1902-06; supt. schs., Headrick, 1906-07, Roosevelt, 1910, Blair, Okla., 1912-13; instr. in history. U. of Okla., 1914-24, prof. history and head dept., 1924 42; graduate prof. history, 1942-43; dir. Frank Phillips collection, 1927-52; research prof. history, 1943-, now research prof. history, emeritus; Fulbright lectr. in history U. Melbourne. Australia, 1953; vis. prof. history U. Houston, 1954-55, M. D. Anderson prof. history, 1958-59. Collaborator in hist. research, U.S. Dept. Agr. 1925; mem. Indian Survey Commn., U.S. Inst. for Govt. Research. 1926-27. Trustee Frank Phillips Fund of U. of Okla., Mary E. Laing Scholarship Fund. Mem. Agrl. Hist. Soc. (pres. 1925-27), Am. Miss. Valley (pres. 1936 -37), So. Okla. hist. assns., Okla. State Folk Lore Assn. (ex-pres.), Ark, Ill. State Ind. hist. socs., Tex. Inst. of Letters Phi Beta Kappa, Acacia. Democrat. Mason. Clubs: Authors' Twentieth Century (Boston); Zamorano (Cal.). Author: Territorial Acquisitions of the UsS., 1912; Tales of the Teepee, 1919; (with J.S. Buchanan) A History of Oklahoma, 1924; The Prairie Schooner and Other Poems, 1929; The Range Cattle Industry, 1930; Cow Country, 1942. Compiler: Letters of Lafayette, 1926; Readings in Oklahoma History (with J. L. Rader), 1930; Frontier Trails, 1930; A Rider of the Cherokee Strip, 1936; Cherokee Cavaliers (with Gaston Litton), 1939; History of U.S. (with D. L. Dumond and E. B. Wesley), 1948; History of Oklahoma (with M. L. Wardell), 1948; Oklahoma, The Story of a State, 1949; The Indians of the Southwest, 1949; (with J. D. Morrison) Pioneer Judge, 1958; Frontier Ways, 1960; The Cross Timbers: Memories of A North Texas Boyhood, 1966. Home: 920 Elm St Norman OK 73069

DALE, ERWIN RANDOLPH, lawyer, author; b. Herrin, Ill., July 30, 1915; s. Henry and Lena Bell (Campbell) D.; B.A., Tex. Western U., 1937; J.D., U. Tex., 1943; m. Charline Vincent, Aug. 27, 1955; children—Allyson Ann, Kristan Charline. Admitted to Tex. bar, 1943, D.C. bar, 1953, Mich. bar, 1956, N.Y. bar, 1960; atty. Internal Revenue Service, 1943-56, chief reorgn. and dividend br., 1954-56; legal staff Gen. Motors Corp., 1956-57; partner firm Chapman, Walsh & O'Connell, N.Y.C. and Washington, 1957-59, 59-64 Hawkins, Delafield & Wood, N.Y.C., 1959—; lectr. tax matters. Dir. Md. Electronics Mfg. Corp., 1948-58; dir., treas. The Renaissance Corp., 1968—; dir., asst. treas. Shancom Reconstrn. Corp., 1968—, Newhaven Corp., 1968—. Mem. Am. (chmn. com. consol. returns sect. taxation 1959-60), Tex., Mich., N.Y. State (chmn. corp. tax com. tax sect. 1967, 68; mem. exec. com. 1968-70) bar assns., Tax Inst. of Am. (dir. 1967-69, treas. 1966), Assn. of Bar of the City N.Y., Nat. Tax Assn., Ex-Students Assn. U. Tex. Mason. Clubs: Nat. Lawyers, Nat. Press (Washington); Bronxville Field, Siwanoy Country (Bronxville, New York). Author numerous articles fed. tax matters. Bd. editors Tex. Law Rev., 1941-42, 42-43. Home: 4 Crampton Rd Bronxville NY 10708 Office: 67 Wall St New York City NY 10005

DALE, FRANCIS LYKINS, pub., lawyer; b. Urbana, Ill., July 13, 1921; s. Charles Sherman and Sarah (Lykins) D.; A.B., Duke, 1943; LL.B., U. Va., 1948; LL.D., Eastern Ky. U., U. Cin., Ohio Wesleyan U., Salmon P. Chase Coll. of Law; m. Kathleen Hamlin Watkins, Mar. 20, 1947; children—Mitchell Watkins, Myron Lykins, Kathleen Hamlin, Holly Moore. Admitted to Ohio bar, 1948; asso. Frost & Jacobs, Cin., 1948-53, partner, 1953—. Asst. sec. Cin. Enquirer, Inc., 1952—, pres., pub., 1965—; pres. The Cin. Reds, Inc., Videotronics; dir. 1st Nat. Bank Cin. Mem. Hamilton County Rep. Finance Com. Active United Appeal; dir. Goodwill Industries, v.p., 1968; dir. mem. exec. com. Cin. area chap. A.R.C.; bd. dirs. Boys Clubs of Am.; chmn. Bethesda Home; bd. dirs. Bethesda Hosp., Boys Club Cin. Dir. Cin. Bengals. Served with USNR, World War II. Named Outstanding Young Man of Year, Cin., 1951; recipient Gov.'s award for adding prestige Ohio, 1968. Fellow Am. Bar Assn.; mem. Ohio (pres. 1966-67), Cin. (pres. 1961-62) bar assns., Council Chs. Greater Cin. (pres. 1959-61), Order of Coif, Omicron Delta Kappa. Methodist (dist. lay leader 1958-64). Clubs: University, Queen City, Rotary (Cin.). Home: 1421 Herschel Av Cincinnati OH 45208 Office: 617 Vine St Cincinnati OH 45202

DALE, HOMER LEE, Jr., constrn. co. exec.; b. El Paso, Tex., Nov. 16, 1923; s. Homer Lee and Anne Beatrice (Waldo) D.; student Yale, 1943-44; B.B.A., U. Tex., 1948; m. Florence Mae Ohswaldt, Oct. 28, 1944; children—Merri Jean (Mrs. Donald Lee Jones), Stephen Francis, Jeffrey Todd. Chief accountant Robert E. McKee, Inc., El Paso, 1948-60, comptroller, 1960-70, treas., 1970—, also dir.; dir., treas. Zia Co., Los Alamos. Bd. dirs. El Paso Boys Club, 1966-69, El Paso United Fund, 1970, Jr. Achievement, 1970-71. Served with USNR, 1942-45. Episcopalian (sr. warden). Home: 5708 Burning Tree El Paso TX 79912 Office: PO Box 20562 El Paso TX 79998

DALE, JOHN DENNY, economist; b. N.Y.C., May 16, 1916; s. Francis Colgate and Imogen (James) D.; A.B., Hamilton Coll., 1936; M.B.A., N.Y.U., 1954, Ph.D., 1962; m. Louise Boyd Lichtenstein, Oct. 22, 1938 (dec.); children—Anne, John Denny; m. 2d, Madeline Houston McWhinney, June 23, 1961; 1 son, Thomas Denny. Div. mgr. Am. Steel Export Co., 1936-40; asst. to pres. Charles Hardy, Inc., N.Y.C., 1940, v.p., dir., 1941-45, pres., chmn., 1945-55, chmn., 1955-63; sec., dir. Hardy Metall. Co., 1940-46; tech. dir. Charles Hardy, Ltd., London, 1946-63; chmn. Mfrs. Marketing Co., 1949-50; pres. Dale, Elliott & Co., Inc., 1955-65, 1971—; financial economist Litton Industries, Inc., 1965-68, Am. Export Industries, Inc., 1968-70; v.p. Litton Industries Leasing Corp., 1966-68; dir. Premium Iron Ores, Ltd., Sea-Pool Fisheries, Ltd., Steep Rock Iron Mines, Ltd. Adviser to WPB, 1941, to Gov. N.Y., 1948-51, to Chief Ordnance U.S. Army, 1952-55, Gov. Monmouth Med. Center, 1954-71. Trustee Mannes Coll. Music, 1957-60; pres. N.Y.U. Alumni Council; alumni council Hamilton Coll., 1948-52. Served from pvt. to maj. AUS, 1942-45, Korean War, 1951-52. Mem. Am. Ordnance Assn. (dir.), Hudson River Conservation Soc. bd. dirs., Am. Inst. Mining and Metall. Engrs., Metal Powder Assn., Am. Soc., Metals, U.S. Naval Inst., Am. Soc. Tool Engrs., Nat. Assn. Accountants, Am. Mgmt. Assn., Order St. John, Knights Malta, Soc. Mayflower Descs., Soc. Colonial Wars, Soc. War of 1812, Huguenot Soc., Mil. Order Fgn. Wars, Vet. Corps Arty., Soc. Am. Wars, S.R., St. Nicholas Soc., Res. Officers Assn., Psi Upsilon. Mason. Clubs: University Glee, Racquet and Tennis, N.Y. Athletic (N.Y.C.); Rumson (N.J.) Country; Navesink Country. Author: Mangerial Accounting in the Small Company, 1961. Home: 24 Blossom Cove Rd Red Bank NJ 07701 Office: 30 E 62d St New York City NY 10004

DALE, THOMAS RANDALL, educator; b. Toronto, Ont., Can., July 27, 1916; s. Ernest Abel and Mary (Bulloch) D.; B.A., Univ. Coll., Toronto, 1938; M.A., U. Toronto, 1939; tchr. certificate, Ont. Coll. Edn., 1940; Ph.D., U. Chgo., 1951; m. Isobel Grace Hampton, Aug. 29, 1942; children—Ian Randall Hampton, Gillian Mary, Susan Isobel. Came to U.S., 1949. High sch. tchr., 1940- 41; mem. faculty St. John's Coll., Winnipeg, Man., Can., 1941-42, U. Western Ont., 1946-49; asst. prof. Monmouth (Ill.) Coll., 1950-53, No. Ill. State Coll., 1953-55; asso. prof. English, then prof., chmn. dept. Milw. Downer Coll., 1955-64; Miller-Wheelock prof. English Lawrence U. 1964—, chmn. Sir Walter Scott Bicentenary celebration, 1971. Served to lt. comdr. Royal Canadian Navy, 1942-46. Mem. Nat. (Wis. chmn. Achievement awards 1966-69), Wis. (chmn. articulation com. 1962-64) councils tchrs. English. Episcopalian. Author articles. Home: 518 N Mary St Appleton WI 54911

DALE, WESLEY JOHN, univ. dean; b. Milw., Aug. 8, 1921; s. Colin B. and Irma P. (Pohl) D.; B.S. in Chemistry with highest honors, U. Ill., 1943; Ph.D., U. Minn., 1949; m. Pattie Surine, Aug. 20, 1949; 1 dau., Claudia. Teaching asst. U. Minn., 1943; research chemist Govt. Synthetic Rubber Research Program, 1943-46; mem. faculty U. Mo. at Columbia, 1949-66, prof. chemistry, 1958-66, chmn. dept., 1961-64, asst. to dean Coll. Arts and Scis., 1954-55; staff asso. sci. facilities evaluation group, div. instl. programs NSF, 1964, sr. staff asso. sci. devel. evaluation group, div. instl. programs, 1964-66; dean Sch. Grad. Studies, prof. chemistry U. Mo. at Kansas City, 1966—, univ. research adminstr., 1969—, acting provost and dean faculties, 1971—; cons. long range acad. planning. Chmn. Midwest Conf. Grad. Study and Research, 1970-71. Bd. dirs. Sci. Pioneers, Kansas City, Mo., 1967—, Inst. Community Studies, Kansas City, Mo., 1970—. Mem. A.A.A.S., Am. Chem. Soc., Sigma Xi, Phi Kappa Phi, Phi Eta Sigma, Phi Lambda Upsilon, Pi Mu Epsilon, Gamma Alpha, Alpha Chi Sigma. Contbr. articles profl. jours. Home: 5600 State Line Shawnee Mission KS 66208 Office: 5100 Rockhill Rd Kansas City MO 64110

DALE, WILLIAM BROWN, govt. ofcl.; b. Detroit, Mar. 24, 1924; s. William H. and Grace M. (Brown) D.; B.A. in History, U. Mich., 1944; M.A., Fletcher Sch. Law and Diplomacy, 1947; m. Deborah Jane Parry, July 27, 1946; childrenWilliam P., Susan D. Christopher A., Judith A., Katherine S. With Treasury Dept., 1948-55, rep. Middle East, 1953-55; program mgr. internat. research Stanford Research Inst., 1956-61; dir. Bur. Internat. Programs, Dept. Commerce, 1961-62, dep. asst. sec. internat. affairs, 1962; exec. dir. for U.S., Internat. Monetary Fund, 1962-; special assistant to the secretary of treasury. Served with USNR, 1943-46. Mem. Soc. Internat. Devel. Unitarian. Home: 6008 Landon Lane Bethesda MD20014 Office: Internat Monetary Fund Washington DC 20431

DALE, WILLIAM NORRIS, fgn. service officer; b. Washington, Feb. 7, 1919; s. Nelson Clark and Marion Ethel (Norris) D.; B.A., Harvard, 1940. M.A., 1942; m. Jane Elizabeth Capen, Oct. 25, 1942; children—William Norris, Bernard Capen, Nelson Clark III. Charge advt. Savage Arms Corp., Utica, N.Y., 1940-41; mem. U.S. Fgn. Service, 1946—, beginning as vice consul, 3d sec., Copenhagen, Denmark, successively 2d sec., Ottawa. Can., Canadian affairs specialist Dept. State, on loan to dir. mut. security for Nat. Security Council Affairs, 1952-53; 1st sec. U.S. Embassy, London. 1954- 56, officer Charge U.K. affairs Dept. State, 1957-58, dep. dir. Brit. Commonwealth and No. European affairs, 1958-60; counselor of embassy for mut. security affairs Am. Embassy, Ankara, Turkey, 1960-64; then counsel gen. Am. Consulate General, Tel Aviv, Israel; now dep. adminstr. security consular affairs Dept. of State, Washington. Served lt. USNR, 1942-45. Mem. U.S. Fgn. Service Assn., Phi Beta Kappa. Episcopalian. Home: 8051 Parkside Lane Washington DC 20012 Office: State Dept Washington DC 20525

DALEHITE, THOMAS HIRAM, govt. ofcl.; b. Memphis, Sept. 14, 1918; s. Samuel Curtis and Bessie (Knight) D.; B.S. in Aero. Engring., Miss. State U., 1939; m. Catherine Florence Green, Aug. 6, 1942; children—Deborah Anne, Thomas Hiram II, Richard Green. Instr., Miss. State U., 1939-41; chief methods and procedures div. USAAF, Brookley AFB, Ala., 1946-47; tech. dir., adviser Air Proving Ground Command, Eglin AFB, Fla., 1949, 49-58, tech. dir. devel. and test on Pl-313, 1958-60; dir. plans and programs on PL-313, Supreme Hdqrs. Allied Powers, Air Def. Tech. Center, The Hague, Netherlands, 1960-62; sci. adviser, PL-313, dep. chief staff/fgn. tech. Air Force Systems Command, Andrews AFB, Md., 1962-63; dep. for engring. Office Sec. Air Force, 1963-66; chief scientist Armament Devel. and Test Center, Eglin AFB, Fla. 1966—. Dir. Valparaiso Bank and Trust Co. Active local Boy Scouts Am. Served to lt. comdr. USNR, 1941-45. Recipient Exceptional Service award USAF, 1962, 65, 70. Mem. Am. Ordnance Assn., Am. Inst. Aeros. and Astronautics, Kappa Alpha. Mason. Clubs: Lake Lorraine Country; Eglin Officers. Author numerous tech. reports. Home: 47 Longwood Dr Shalimar, FL Office: Armament Development and Test Center Air Force Systems Command Eglin AFB FL 32542

DALES, RICHARD CLARK, educator; b. Akron, O., Apr. 17, 1926; s. Gerald Lee and Lucile (Miller) D.; A.B., U. Rochester, 1949; M.A., U. Colo., 1952, Ph.D., 1955; m. Nancy Gene Vogeler, July 7, 1950; children—Susan Zoe, David Richard. Instr. history N.D. State Coll., 1954-55; from instr. to asso. prof. Lewis and Clark Coll., Portland, Ore., 1955-62; vis. asso. prof. U. Cal. at Santa Barbara, 1963-64; from asso. prof. to prof. U. So. Cal, 1964—, chmn. dept. history, 1969—; mem. Inst. Advanced Study, 1966-67. Served with C.E., AUS, 1946-47. Am. Council Learned Socs. fellow, 1960-61. Author: Robert Grosseteste's Scientific Works, 1961; Anonymi De Elementis, 1965. Editor: Roberti Grosseteste Commentarius in VIII Libros Physicorum Aristolelis, 1963. Home: 3631 Monterosa Dr Altadena CA 91001

D'ALESANDRO, THOMAS, Jr., former govt. ofcl.; b. Balt., August 1, 1903; s. Thomas and Mary Anne (Foppiano) D'A.; student Calvert Bus. Coll., Balt.; m. Annuciata M. Lombardi, Sept. 30, 1928; children—Thomas III, Nicholas, Franklin D. Roosevelt, Nicholas J., Hector, Joseph, Annunciata. Owner pres. D'Alesandro Jr. & Sons Balt.; mem. Md. Ho. of Dels., 1926-33; gen. dep. collector internal revenue, 1933- 34; mem. Balt. City Council, 1935-38; mem. 76th to 80th congresses from 3d Md. Dist; mayor Balt., 1947-59. Democratic nat. committeeman Md. 1952-56; del. nat. convs. Mem. Renegotiation Bd., 1961-69. Mem. U.S. Conf. of Mayors (chmn. standing com. on legislation), Advt. Club Md., Md. Hist. Soc., Vincent dePaul Soc. Holy Name Soc. St. Leo's Confrat. Roman Catholic. K.C. (40), Elk (life), Eagle, Moose. Club: Hickory. Home: 245 Albemarle St Baltimore MD 21202

D'ALESANDRO, THOMAS J. III, mayor of Baltimore. Address: 2803 Bartol Av Baltimore MD 21209

D'ALESSANDRO, FRANK S., food processing co. exec.; b. Bklyn., Dec. 24, 1909; s. Jerome Charles and Mary (Esposito) D'A.; evening student N.Y.U., 1928-33; m. May Warren, May 5, 1937 (dec. May 1970). Treas. Milbank Mgmt. Corp., Chgo., 1936-39; chief accountant Elec. Household Utilities Corp., Cicero, Ill., 1939-42, Stewart-Warner Corp., 1942-45; with Standard Brands, Inc., N.Y.C., 1945—, mfg. div. controller, 1948-51, asst. comptroller, 1951-61, comptroller, 1961-68, v.p. and comptroller, 1968-70, v.p., dir., 1970—; dir. Curtiss Candy Co., Fleischmann Distilling Corp., Standard Brands Ltd. (Can.), Melville Confections, Inc., Dr. Ballard's Animal Foods Ltd., Planters Nut & Chocolate Co. Ltd., ICC Foods Ltd., Mem. Financial Execs. Inst., Am. Mgmt. Assn. Home: 26 Linwood Rd New Rochelle NY 10804 Office: 625 Madison Av New York City NY 10022

DALEY, ARTHUR JAMES, newspaper editor; b. St. Paul, Aug. 15, 1916; s. John and Mary (Mayer) D.; student pub. schs., Fond duLac, Wis.; m. Lorayne Mary Mongan, June 7, 1941; children—Michael, Kay. Advt. salesman Fond du Lac (Wis.) Commonwealth Reporter, 1936, sports editor, 1937-40; sports writer Green Bay (Wis.) Press-Gazette, 1941-43, sports editor, 1946-68, telegraph editor, 1968—; co-pub. Green Bay Packer Yearbook, 1960—. Mem. Wis. Hall of Fame Com.; mem. bd. of selectors Nat. Profl. Football Hall of Fame, Canton, O. Served with AUS, 1943-46; ETO. Mem. A.P. Sports Writer Assn., Holy Name Soc. Roman Catholic. Elk. Clubs: Oneida Golf and Riding; Optimist. Home: 1146 High View Lane Green Bay WI 54305 Office: 435 E Walnut St Green Bay WI 54305

DALEY, ARTHUR JOHN, sports writer; b. N.Y.C., July 31, 1904; s. Daniel M. and Mary (Greene) D.; B.A., Fordham U., 1926; grad. spl. courses Columbia, N.Y.U.; m. Betty Blake, Nov. 28, 1928; children—Robert, Kevin, Patricia, Katharine. Sports writer N.Y. Times, 1926—, writer column Sports of the Times, 1942—. Recipient Pulitzer prize, 1956; Grantland Rice award, 1961; Sportswriter of the Year award, 1963; Pro Football Writers' Distinguished Writing award, 1970. Roman Catholic. Author: Times at Bat, 1950; Sports of the Times, 1959; Knute Rockne, Football Wizard of Notre Dame, 1960; Kings of the Home Run, 1962; Pro Football's Hall of Fame, 1963; (with John Kieran) Story of the Olympic Games, 1969. Home: 120 Stonehedge Dr N Greenwich, CT 06830. Office: 229 W 43d St New York City NY 10036

DALEY, ARTHUR STUART, educator; b. Osceola, N.Y., Sept. 16, 1908; s. Keron A. and Mary (Adams) D.; A.B., Syracuse U., 1932; postgrad. Harvard, 1932-33; Ph. D., Yale, 1942; m. Jean Abendroth, Aug. 29, 1942; 1 son, Arthur Stuart. Instr. English, Syracuse U., 1935-37, Ind. U., 1946-47, U. Cal. at Los Angeles, 1947-49; asst. prof. English, U. Nev., 1949-54; prof. English, chmn. dept. Coe Coll., 1954-59; prof. English, Drake U., Des Moines 1959—, chmn. dept., 1959-65, coordinator humanities div., 1967—. Served to Lieutenant col. AUS, 1941-46, 51-53; lt. col. Res. Decorated Bronze Star medal. Mem. Renaissance Soc. Am., Malone Soc., Oxford Bibling Soc., Modern Lang. Assn. Am., Assn. U.S. Army, Theta Alpha Phi, Sigma Nu. Co-author: Private Charity in England, 1747-1757, 1938. Contbr. articles, revs. to profl. jours. Home: 5831 Waterbury Circle Des Moines IA 50312

DALEY, DANIEL HAYES, air force officer; b. Elmira, N.Y., Mar. 9, 1920; s. Charles Augustine and Irene (Hayes) D.; B.S. in Mech. Engring., Purdue U., 1942; S.M. in Aero. Engring., Mass. Inst. Tech., 1946; m. Roberta Jean Buechele, Oct. 27, 1945; children—Martha Jean (Mrs. Bruce Ferguson), Daniel Charles, David Keith, James Christopher. Commd. 2d lt. USAAF, 1942, advanced through grades to col. USAF, 1965; rated command pilot, 1958; assigned U.S., 1942-44; asst. prof. aero. engring. Air Force Inst. Tech., 1946-49, asso. prof., acting head dept. mech. engring., 1949-55; pilot 4093d Test Support Group, Eniwetok Atoll, Pacific, 1955-56; wing flying safety officer 483d Troop Carrier Wing, Ashyia, Japan, 1956-58; chief aerodynamics sect. B-70 Weapon System Project Office, 1958-61; asso. prof. USAF Acad., 1961-64, prof., head dept. aero. engring., 1965, 67—; prof., head dept. aerospace engring. Pakistan Air Force Coll. Aero. Engring., Karachi, 1965-67. Dir. Pakistan Am. Cultural Center, Karachi. Registered profl. engr., Ohio. Mem. Am. Inst. Aeros. and Astronautics, Japan Soc. Aerospace Scis., Pakistan Inst. Engrs. (life), Sigma Xi, Tau Beta Pi, Pi Tau Sigma. Home: Quarters 4138 USAF Acad CO 80840 Office: Dept of Aeronautics USAF Academy CO 80840

DALEY, DANIEL JOSEPH, med. dir.; b. Luzerne, Pa., Dec. 24, 1909; s. John Patrick and Margaret M. (Millnamow) D.; B.S., Villanova (Pa.) Coll., 1932; M.D., Georgetown U., 1937; M.P.H., Johns Hopkins U., 1953; m. Margaret M.P. McCormick, Sept. 14, 1939; children—Daniel, Patricia, John. Intern, Wilkes-Barre (Pa.) Gen. Hosp., 1937-38; ward surgeon U.S. Marine Hosp., Ellis Island, N.Y., 1938-39, U.S. Marine Hosp., San Francisco, 1942; exec. officer U.S. Penitentiary Hosp., Leavenworth, Kan., 1940-41; chief med. officer U.S. Maritime Service Tng. Sta., Avalon, Cal., 1942-45; chief med. officer Pattern Hosp., U.S. Mcht. Marine Acad., Kings Point, N.Y., 1945-47; med. dir. U.S. Maritime Commn., Washington, 1948-49; chief div. fed. employee health USPHS, 1949-50, asst. chief div. hosp. facilities, 1950—, med. dir., 1949—, chief div. hosp. and med. facilities USPHS, 1949-53; med. officer in charge USPHS Hosp., Balt., 1958-61, USPHS Hosp., S.I., 1961-63; med. dir. Grad. Hosp., Phila., 1964—. Mem. Am. Legion, A.M.A., Am. Hosp. Assn., Assn. Indsl. Physicians and Surgeons, Fed. Safety Council (mem. tech. com.), Alumni Assn. of Villanova Coll. Clubs: Rotary, Kenwood Country. Home: 819 Wickfield Rd Wynnewood PA 19096 Office: Grad Hosp Philadelphia PA 19146

DALEY, JAMES AUGUSTUS, banker; b. Yonkers, N.Y., July 29, 1927; s. James Joseph and Regina (Rode) D.; B.S., Mass. Inst. Tech., 1950; m. Alice L. Stokes, Oct. 7, 1950; children-James Joseph II, Mark Thomas, Elizabeth Alice, Joseph Christian. Dir. ins. systems Prudential Ins. Co., 1950-68; exec. v.p. Hartford Nat. Bank & Trust Co. (Conn.), 1968—; pres. Hartford Gen. Services Corp., 1970—, HNC Securities Clearance Corp., 1970—. Pres. Chatam Township (N.J.) Sch. Bd., 1966-67. Served with USNR, 1945-46. Mem. Conn. Bankers Assn. (chmn. payment systems subcom.), Am. Mgmt. Assn., Am. Inst. Banking, Bank Adminstrn. Inst. Methodist (trustee). Home: 1221 Woodhaven Dr Avon CT 06001 Office: 777 Main St Hartford CT 06115

DALEY, JOSEPH T., bishop; D.D. Ordained priest Roman Cath. Ch., 1941; titular bishop Barca and aux. bishop Harrisburg, 1963-. Address: Sylvan Heights Home Summit and Chestnut Sts Harrisburg, PA 17104.*

DALEY, LEROY MACKENZIE, electronics co. exec.; b. St. Catharines, Ont., Can., Nov. 6, 1923; s. Ollie Leroy and Elsie B. (Mackenzie) D.; ed. St. Catherine's Collegiate Inst.; m. Doris E. Gretton, June 15, 1946; children—Richard J., Robert M., Deas M. With Gen. Motors Corp., 1939, Exide Battery Co., 1946, John Inglis Co., 1946; with Canadian Marconi Co., 1947—, exec. v.p. operations, 1965-67, pres., 1967—, now chief exec. officer, also dir. Served to flying officer RAF, 1941-45. Mem. Electronic Industries Assn. Can. (bd. dirs.) Clubs: Mt. Stephen; Royal St. Lawrence Yacht; St. James's. Home: 11 E Gables Ct Beaconsfield Quebec Canada Office: 2442 Trenton Av Montreal 16 Quebec Canada

DALEY, PAUL HUBERT, steel co. exec.; b. Pawtucket, R. I., July 23, 1919; s. Joseph H. and Rosella (Coyle) D.; B.S., U. Paris (France), 1940; M.A., Fordham U., 1941; m. Mary D. Kosowicz, Nov. 21, 1942; children—mary Ellen, Paul Coyle, Steven Joseph. Mgmt. engr. Thompson & Lightner Co., Boston, 1944- 46; with Heppenstall Co., Pitts., 1946-, v.p. sales., 1960-62, exec. v.p., 1962-, also dir.; exec. v.p., dir. Midvale-Heppenstall Co., Phila., 1962-; pres. Heppenstall-Midvale A.G., Zug, Switzerland, 1961- ; dir. Terni-Heppenstall Co., Rome, Italy, Acieries & Forges d'Anor, Nord, France, Nat. Finance Corp., Lonsdale, R.I. Served to 2d lt. AUS, 1942-43. Mem. Am. Soc. M.E., Am. Ordnance Assn., Am. Mgmt. Assn. Home: 714 Cascade Rd Pittsburgh PA 15221. Office: 4620 Hatfield St Pittsburgh PA 15201.

DALEY, RICHARD J., mayor Chgo.; b. Chgo., 1902; s. Michael and Lillian (Dunne).; LL.B., DePaul U., 1933; m. Eleanor Guilfoyle, June 23, 1936; childrenPatricia, Mary Carol, Eleanor, Richard, Michael, John, William. Admitted to Ill. bar, 1933. Democratic mem. Ill. Ho. of Reps., 1936-38; Ill. Senate 1939-46; dir. Revenue for State Ill., 1948-50; clk. Cook County, 1950-55; mayor Chgo., 1955—. Chmn. Democratic Party Cook County. Bd. Dirs. Valentine Boys Club, St. Joseph Home of Friendless, Fellowship House Chmn., Bridgeport Area Boy Scouts Am. Mem. Am., Ill., Chgo. bar assns., U.S. Conf. Mayors (pres. 1959); K. C., Moose, Elk. Home: 3536 Lowe Ave Chicago IL 60609 Office: Office of Mayor City Hall Chicago IL 60602

DALEY, ROBERT BLAKE, author; b. N.Y.C., May 10, 1930; s. Arthur John and Betty (Blake) D.; B.A., Fordham U., 1951; m. Peggy Ernest, May 31, 1954; children—Theresa, Suzanne, Leslie Anne. Publicity dir. N.Y. Football Giants, 1953-58; fgn. and war corr. N.Y. Times, Europe, N.Africa, 1959-64. Photographer, journalist, novelist. Apptd. dep. commr. N.Y. Police Dept., 1971—. Served with USAF, 1951-52. Exhibited photographs Balt. Mus., Art Inst. Chgo., N.Y. Gallery Modern Art, 1968-69. Mem. Author's Guild. Author: The World Beneath the City, 1959; Cars at Speed, 1961; The Bizarre World of European Sports, 1963; The Cruel Sport, 1963; The Swords of Spain, 1965; The Whole Truth, 1967; Only A Game, 1967; A Priest and a Girl, 1969; A Star in the Family, 1971; articles, fiction, photos appearing in mags., including Life, Vogue, Playboy. Address: 5 Spring St Riverside CT 06878

DALEY, ROGER A., newspaper exec. Pres., bus. mgr. News Sentinel, Knoxville, Tenn. Office: 204 W Church Av Knoxville TN 38901*

DALEY, WILLIAM RAYMOND, investment banker; b. Ashtabula, O., Sept. 26, 1892; s. Flory and Margaret (Coade) D.; A.B., Adelbert Coll., Western Res. U., 1915; LL.B., Western Res. U., 1917; m. Florence Catherine Doran, Nov. 20, 1920; children—Kathleen, Jane. Admitted to Ohio bar, 1917; asso. with Bulkley, Hauxhurst, Inglis & Saeger, Cleveland, 1917-28, partner, 1925-28; with Otis & Co., investments, 1928—, pres., dir., 1931—; ltd. partner Milw. Brewers Baseball Co.; chmn. Reading Co.; trustee U.S. Realty Investments; dir. Murray Ohio Mfg. Co., also various corps. Trustee Cath. Charities Corp.; chmn. Cleve. Opera Assn. Mem. bd. lay trustees U. Notre Dame. Served as sgt. Machine Gun Co., 331st Inf., later lt. 27th F.A. 1917-18; mem. Troop A, 107th Cav., 1919-23. Mem. Investment Bankers Assn. (gov. 1937-39), Cleve. Bar Assn., Pi Kappa Alpha, Delta Theta Phi, Order of Coif. Roman Catholic. Clubs: Seminole Golf (Palm Beach, Fla.); Union, Mayfield Country, Pepper Pike Country (Cleve.); Pinnacle, Marco Polo (N.Y.C.). Home: 24449 Cedar Rd Cleveland OH 44124 Office: Terminal Tower Cleveland OH 44113

D'ALFONSO, JOSEPH, educator; B.A., Boston U., 1928, S.T.B., 1931, Ph.D., 1942; m. Erma Marie Dimlich, June 30, 1942; children—Raymond Joseph, Donald Roderick (dec.). Ordained to ministry Methodist Ch., 1931; minister, Jefferson N.H., 1931-34, Warren, N.H., 1934-38, Methuen, Mass., 1938-42, Woodland, Me., 1942-44; prof. philosophy Bates Coll., Me., 1944—. Chmn. adult edn. com. Me. Council Chs., 1944-46. Mem. Am. Philos. Assn., Mind Assn., Metaphys. Soc. Am., Am. Assn. U. Profs., Me. Philos. Inst. Home: 71 Googin St Lewiston ME 04240

DALGARNO, ALEXANDER, educator; b. London, Eng., Jan. 5, 1928; s. William and Margaret (Murray) D.; B.Sc., U. London, 1947, Ph.D., 1951; M.A. (hon.), Harvard, 1967; m. Barbara W.F. Kane, Oct. 31, 1957, children—Penelope, Rebecca, Piers, Fergus. Lectr., Queen's U., Belfast, No. Ireland, 1951-56, reader, 1956-61, prof. math. physics, 1961-67, dir. computation lab., 1961-66; prof. astronomy Harvard, 1967—; chmn. dept., 1972—, acting dir. Harvard Coll. Obs., 1971-72; research scientist Smithsonian Astrophys. Obs., Cambridge, Mass., 1967—. Mem. Phys. Soc. (London), Am. Geophys. Union, Am. Acad. Arts and Scis., Am. Astron. Soc. Contbr. articles to profl. jours. Home: 602 Huron Av Cambridge MA 02138

DALGLIESH, WILBERT HAROLD, educator, historian; b. London, Ont., Can., Mar. 13, 1902; s. William James and Margaret Louise (McCallum) D.; B.A., U. Western Ont., 1922, M.A., 1923; Ont. Govt. scholar, U. Paris (France), 1924-25; Ph.D. (Harrison scholar 1923-24, Harrison fellow 1926-27), U. Pa., 1931; m. Elizabeth J. Rhodes, June 10, 1929; children—Margaret Elizabeth (Mrs. Leroy Broun IV), William John Marshall. Came to U.S., 1923, naturalized, 1940. Asst. history U. Pa., 1923-24; instr. Lafayette Coll., 1927-33; mem. faculty U. Utah, 1933—, prof. history, 1948-70, prof. emeritus, 1970—, head dept., 1960-63; vis. prof. San Diego State Coll., summer 1964; research asso. Council Fgn. Relations, N.Y.C., 1945-46; archival research Paris and Lorient, France, also London, Eng. Sec. Salt Lake Com. Fgn. Relations, 1942-45, 46-48, chmn., 1954-56. Mem. Am. Hist. Assn., Orgn. Am. Historians, Soc. for French Hist. Studies, Western History Assn. (charter mem.), Societe d' Histoire Moderne, Utah Acad. Scis., Arts and Letters, Am. Assn. U. Profs. (pres. U. Utah chpt. 1951-52). Episcopalian (sr. warden 1959-60). Author: Company of Indies, 1933; Britain and the Commonwealth, 1954; Syllabus: World War II and Ensuing East-West Controversy, 1969. Compiler: Community Education in Foreign Affairs, 1946. Home: 1108 E South Temple Salt Lake City UT 84102

DALGLISH, KEITH GORDON, corp. exec.; b. Toronto, Can., Feb. 20, 1930; s. Thomas Gordon and Kathleen (Pearson) D.; B.A., U. Toronto; m. Gail Elizabeth Bagwell, Sept. 27, 1958; children—Todd, Ian, Tracy, Allison. With Price Waterhouse, Toronto, 1953-60; sec.-treas. Internat. Computers & Tabulators Can., Toronto, 1960-62; parnter Thonre, Gunne, Helliwell & Christenson, Toronto, 1962-67; v.p., mng. dir. George Weston Ltd., Toronto, 1967-68, formerly pres., mng. dir. Mem. Bd. Trade Met. Toronto Retived sub lt. Royal Canadian Navy (R), 1952. Chartered accountant. Mem. Canadian Inst. Chartered Accountants. Home: 65 Douglas Dr Toronto 5 Ontario Canada Office: 25 King St W Toronto 1 Ontario Canada*

DALHOUSE, WARNER NORRIS, banker; b. Roanoke, Va., June 4, 1934; s. Jerfferson William and Gay-Nell (Henley) D.; B.S. in Commerce, U. Va., 1956; grad. Va.-Md. Sch. Bank Mgmt., 1960, Stonier Grad. Sch. Banking, Rutgers U., 1966; m. Carol Bewley, June 16, 1956; children—Ann Lauren, Julia Lea. With First Nat. Exchange Bank, Roanoke, 1956—, sr. v.p., 1969—; mem. marketing adv. com. Nat. BankAmericard Inc.; mem. faculty Stonier Grad. Sch. Banking, Sch. Consumer Banking of U. Va. Vice pres. Miss Virginia Pageant. Bd. dirs. Sch. for Neurologically Impaired Children. Me. Am., Va. (pres. young bankers sect.) bankers assns., Roanoke Valley C. of C. (pres. 1971). Clubs: Shenandoah, Hunting Hills Country, Squires (Roanoke). Home: 1201 Persinger Rd SW Roanoke VA 24015 Office: 201 S Jefferson St Roanoke VA 24010

DALI, SALVADOR, Surrealist artist; b. Figueras, nr. Barcelona, Spain, May 11, 1904; s. Salvador and Felipa (Domeneck) D.; student pub. sch. and pvt. acad. conducted by Bros. of the Marist Order, Figueras, Sch. of Fine Arts, Madrid, 1921-26; m. Gala Dali, Sept. 1935. Completed two paintings, portrait of Helen of Troy, Joseph Greeting His Brethren, before he was 10; influenced by Italian Futurists, 1923-25; became a Surrealist, Paris, France, 1929; designed jewelry, furniture, and art nouveau decorations, 1929-31; symbolic interpretations of legend of William Tell and Millet's The Angelus, 1934; made first visit to U.S., 1934; series of beach scenes at Rosas, Spain, literal pictures of his dreams, 1934-36; decorated residence of Edward James, London, 1936; made 3 visits in Italy, 1937-39; designed Dali's Dream House, N.Y. World's Fair, 1939; made 2d visit to U.S., 1940. Ballets: Bacchanale, Metropolitan Opera House, 1939, music: Richard Wagner; scenery and costumes by Dali); Labyrinth book, costumes, scenery by Dali; music: Schubert), 1941; Cafe de Chiuita, Spanish Festival, Met. Opera, 1942. Exhbns. include One-Man shows Julien Levy Gallery, N.Y., 1933; Arts Club, Chgo. 1941; Dalzell Hatfield Galleries, Los Angeles, Calif.; Museum of Modern Art, N.Y. (exhibit loaned to many cities U.S.); Knoedler Gallery, N.Y.; many in Paris, London, Barcelona, and N.Y.C. Recipient $5000 Huntington Hartford Found. award, 1957. Author: Secret Life of Salvador Dali (autobiography), 1942; Diary of a Genius, 1965. Address: Hotel St Regis New York City NY 10022

DALIS, IRENE, mezzo-soprano; b. San Jose, Cal., d. Peter N. and Mamir (Boitano), Dalis; A.B., San Jose State Coll., 1946, M.S. (hon.), 1957; M.A., Columbia Tchrs. Coll., 1947; studied voice with Edyth Walker, N.Y.C., 1947-50, Pauls Althouse, 1950-51, Dr. Otto Mueller, Milano, Italy, 1952-; m. George Loinaz, July 16, 1957; 1 dau., Alida Mercedes. Operatic debut as dramtic mezzo-soprano Berlin Staedtische Opera, 1956; debut Met. Opera, N.Y.C., 1957, now leading mezzo-soprano. 1st Am.- born singer Kundry Bayreuth Festival, 1961; opened Bayreuth Festival in Parsifal, 1963 Commemorative Wagner 150th Birth Anniversary; opened 1963 Met. Opera Season in Aida. Recipient Fulbright award for study in Italy, 1951. Home: 845 West End Av New York City NY 10025 Office: 111 W 57th St New York City NY 10019

DALITZ, RICHARD HENRY, educator, physicist; b. Dimboola, Australia, Feb. 28, 1925; s. Frederick William and Hazel (Drummond) D.; B.A., Melbourne (Australia) U., 1945, B.Sc., 1946; Ph.D., Cambridge (Eng.) U., 1950; m. Valda Suiter, Aug. 10, 1946; childrenRodric, Katrine, Heather, Ellyn. Came to U.S., 1957. Lectr. math. physics Birmingham Eng.) U., 1949-55, reader math. physics, 1955-56; on leave for research Cornell U., Inst. Advanced Study, Princeton, also Brookhaven Nat. Lab., 1953-55; prof. Enrico Fermi Inst. Nuclear Studies, U. Chgo., 1956-66; Royal Soc. research prof. Oxford (Eng.)U., 1963—; cons. in field, 1958—. Fellow Phys. Soc.,

Royal Soc., Am. Phys. Soc., Sigma Xi. Author: Strange Particles and Strong Interactions, 1962; Nuclear Interactions of the Hyperons, 1965. Home: 28 Jack Straws Lane Oxford, England.

DALLAPICCOLA, LUIGI composer; b. Pisino, Istria, Italy, Feb. 3, 1904; s. Pio and Domitilla (Alberti) A.; Masters deg. in Piano, Conservatory of Florence, Italy, 1924, Masters degree in Composition, 1931; Doctor honoris causa, U. Mich., 1967; m. Laura Coen Luzzatto, Apr. 30, 1938; 1 dau., Annalibera. Tchr. Conservatory of Florence, 1934-67; composition tchr. Berkshire Music Center, Tanglewood, Mass., summers 1951, 52; vis. prof. Queens Coll., 1956-57, 59-60, U. Cal. at Berkeley, 1962-63. Hon. mem. acads. of Munich, Rome, Berlin, Stockholm, N.Y., Buenos Aires, Graz; mem. Am. Acad. of Arts and Letters, Institut de France, Royal Acad. Music (London), Nat. Inst. Arts and Letters. Composer: (chorus) Sei Cori di Michelangelo Buonarroti il Giovane, 1933-36; (operas) Volo di Notte, 1937-39; The Prisoner, 1944-48; (ballet) Marsyas, 1942-43; (sacred) Job, 1950; (choruses) Songs from Captivity, 1938-41, Songs from Liberation, 1952-55, and also Requiescant, 1957-1958; (voice and chamber orch.) Three Laudi, 1936-37, Greek Poems, 1942-45, Goether-Lieder, 1953; Cinque Canti, Concerto per la Notte di Natale, 1956; (orchestrations) Two Pieces for Orchestra Variations; chamber music Dialoghi (cello and orchestra), 1960; Prayers (baritone and chamber orchestra), 1962; Parole di San Paolo, 1964; Sicut umbra, 1970; (opera) Ulysses, 1960-68, Appunti, Incontri, Meditazioni, 1970. Address: 34 Via Romana Florence Italy

DALLAS, SHERMAN FORBES, coll. dean; b. Buffalo, May 22, 1919; s. Sherman L. and Mabel (Forbes) D.; B.A., Ohio No. U., 1949; M.A., Ind. U., 1951, Ph.D., 1955; m. Betty Lou Sears, May 11, 1945; children—Barbara (Mrs. T. Allan Wilson), George Sherman. Asst. prof. Ga. Inst. Tech., 1952-54; lectr. Ind. U., 1954-55; asso. prof. Ind. State Coll., 1955-58; commr. Fed. Mediation and Conciliation Service, 1958-59; asso. prof. Ga. Inst. Tech., 1959-61, prof., 1961—, dean Coll. Indsl. Mgmt., 1969—; cons. Center Disease Control, George C. Marshall Space Flight Center, Kennedy Space Flight Center, Jacksonville Naval Air Sta. Dir. internat. dept. Citizens & So. Nat. Bank; dir. Ellijay Telephone Co. (Ga.); permanent arbitrator Canton Mills, textile workers, Atlanta Housing Authority. Served from pvt. to 2d lt., AUS, 1942-46. Mem. Am. Econ. Assn., Indsl. Relations Research Assn., Phi Kappa Phi, Beta Gamma Sigma, Omicron Delta Kappa, Pi Gamma Mu, Alpha Kappa Psi. Home: 3325 Valley Rd NW Atlanta GA 30305

DALLDORF, GILBERT, pathologist; b. Davenport, Ia., Mar. 12, 1900; s. Julius and Hulda (Leisner) D.; B.S., State U. Ia., 1921; M.D., N.Y.U., 1924; D.Sc., Bowdoin Coll., 1953; D., U. Freiburg (Germany), 1957; m. Frances Elizabeth Barnhart, Apr. 6, 1926; children—Elizabeth (Mrs. Robert Martin), Frederic. Rotating intern Norwegian Hosp., Bklyn., 1924-25; fellow pathology Pathologisches Inst., Freiburg, 1925-26; pathologist N.Y. Hosp., N.Y.C., 1926-29; instr. pathologic anatomy Cornell Med. Coll., 1926-32; pathologist Grasslands Hosp., Valhalla, N.Y., 1929-43; dir. labs. and research Westchester County, 1943-45; dir. div. labs. and research N.Y. Dept. Health, Albany, 1945-57; dir. research Nat. Found., 1958-59; mem. Sloan-Kettering Inst., Walker Lab., 1959-68; prof. pathology Sloan Kettering div. Cornell U. Med. Coll., 1960-68; chmn. Brown Hazen Fund Research Corp., N.Y.C. Commn. on Plasma Blood Research Inst. Recipient Fisher Meml. award, 1955; Distinguished Service award Coll. Medicine, N.Y. U., 1956; Lasker Award, 1959; medal N.Y. Acad. Medicine, 1964. Diplomate Am. Bd. Pathology Mem. A.A.A.S., Am. Assn. Immunologists, A.M.A., Am. Soc. Exptl. Pathology, Assn. Am. Physicians, Nat. Acad. Sci., N.Y. Acad. Medicine, N.Y. Assn. Pub. Health Labs., N.Y. Med. Soc., Soc. Exptl. Biology and Medicine, Am. Epidemiological Soc. Address: Oxford MD 21654

D'ALLELIO, GAETANO FRANCIS, educator, chemist, inventor; b. Charlestown, Mass., Dec. 26, 1909; s. Severino and Francesca (Polcari) D'A.; A.B., Boston Coll., 1931; Ph.D., Johns Hopkins, 1935; m. Josephine Marie McCarthy, Sept. 5, 1932; children—Denny, Ellen, Jane, William. Asso. chemistry Boston Coll. Grad. Sch., 1935-36; dir. plastic research Gen. Electric Co., Pittsfield, Mass., 1936-39, dir. research devel. and control labs., 1939-41, mem. mgrs. staff, 1941-43; dir. research Pro-phy-lac-tic Brush Co., Florence, Mass., 1943-44, v.p., 1944-46; mgr. high polymer research Indsl. Rayon Corp., Cleve., 1946-47; asst. dir. research Koppers Co., Inc., Pitts., 1947-49, v.p., mgr. research, 1949-54; head dept. chemistry U. Notre Dame, 1955-60, research prof., 1960—; indsl. cons., 1955—; dir. Dal-Mon, Inc., Cleve., 1959—. Cons. to referee bd. chmn. branch office prodn. research and devel.. WPB, 1942; mem. adv. panel to com. Q.M. problems NRC, 1943; cons. war research Manhattan project Columbia, 1944, Naval Bur. Ordnance, 1944; dir., coordinator Gen. Electric lab. research on plastic rocket launchers; cons. U.S. Army Chem. Corps Engring. Command, 1959-61; mem. Research adv. com. on materials NASA, 1961-62, apptd. polymer expert cons. to NASA, 1963-66; mem. labs. com. Franklin Inst., Phila., 1963-71; mem. vertically integrated coupling program USAF, Wright-Patterson AFB, O., 1966-69. Bd dirs. Aeolian Choral Soc., South Bend. Fellow Am. Inst. Chemists, A.A.A.S., N.Y. Acad. Scis.; mem. Nat. Acad. Scis. (com. radiation preservation of food 1965—), Am. Chem Soc., Textile Inst., Am. Assn. U. Profs., Ind. Acad. Sci., Chem. Soc. London, Am. Inst. Chem. Engrs., Assn. U.S. Army, Armed Forces Chemical Assos., Hist. Sci. Soc., Acad. Applied Scis., Phi Beta Kappa, Sigma Xi, Phi Lambda Upsilon. Republican. Roman Catholic. Clubs: University (South Bend, Ind.); Kiwanis (dir. 1946), Duquesne (Pitts.). Author: (with R. L. Guile) Laboratory Manual of Synthetic Plastics and Resinous Materials, 1942; A Laboratory Manual of Plastics and Synthetic Resins, 1943; Experimental Plastics and Synthetic Resins, 1946; Fundamentals of Polymerization, 1952. Contbr. profl. publs. Patentee in field; inventor secret radar insulation and sulfonated styrene-type ion exchange resins. Editorial bd., asso. editor Jour. Macromolecular Sci.-Chemistry, 1968—. Home: 2011 E Cedar St South Bend IN 46617 Office: Univ of Notre Dame Notre Dame IN 46556

DALLIN, ALEXANDER, educator; b. Berlin, Germany, May 21, 1924; s. David J. and Eugenia (Bein) D.; came to U.S., 1940, naturalized, 1943; B.S., Coll. City N.Y., 1947; M.A., Columbia, 1948, Ph.D., 1953; m. Florence R. Cherry, June 26, 1953; children—Linda, Natasha, Andrew. Asso. dir. research program on USSR, N.Y.C., 1951-54; dir. research War Documentation Project, Washington, 1954-56; faculty Columbia, 1956—, prof. internat. relations, 1961-65, Adlai Stevenson prof. internat. relations, 1965-71, former dir. Russian Inst.; vis. prof. polit. sci. U. Cal at Berkley; prof. history and polit. sci. Stanford U., 1971—. Albert Shaw lectr. Johns Hopkins, 1964; James Biddle Duke lectr. Duke U., 1970. Cons. U.S. Govt., 1962-70. Served with AUS, 1943-46. Fellow Social Sci. Research Council, 1950-51; Guggenheim fellow, 1961-62; Fulbright Hays fellow, 1965-66. Mem. Am. Assn. Advancement Slavic Studies, Am. Polit. Sci. Assn., Council Fgn. Relations, Am. Civil Liberties Union, Phi Beta Kappa. Author: German Rule in Russia, 1941-1945, 1957; The Soviet Union at the United Nations, 1962; (with others) The Soviet Union and Disarmament, 1965; Political Terror in Communist Systems, 1970; also articles, chpts. in books. Editor: Soviet Conduct in World Affairs, 1960; Diversity in International Communism, 1963; Politics in the Soviet Union: Seven Cases, 1966; Soviet Politics Since Khrushchev, 1968. Home: 607 Cabrillo Av Stanford CA 94305

DALLY, JAMES WILLIAM, educator; b. Sardis, O., Aug. 2, 1929; s. William Hiram and Martha (Siebert) D.; B.S., Carnegie Inst. Tech., 1951, M.S., 1953; Ph.D., Ill. Inst. Tech., 1958; m. Anne E. Tziritas, Dec. 22, 1955; children—Lisa K., William J., Michelle M. Sr. research engr. Armour Research Inst., 1953- 58; asst. prof. Cornell U., 1958-61; asst. dir. IIT Research Inst., 1961- 64; prof. mechanics, Ill. Inst. Tech., 1964-71; head mech. engring. U. Md., College Park, 1971—; cons. in field, 1958—. Mem. Am. Soc. M.E., Soc. Exptl. Stress Analysis (v. p. 1968-70, pres. 1970-71), Sigma Xi. Mason. Author: (with W.F. Riley) Experimental Stress Analysis, 1965; also tech. papers. Patentee in field. Home: Silver Spring MD Office: U Md Coll Engring College Park MD 20742

DALMAN, GISLI CONRAD, educator; b. Winninpeg, man., Can., Apr. 7, 1917 (parents Am. citizens); Fs. Conrad Fred and Valgedur (Thorsteinsdottir) D.; B.E.E., Coll. City N.Y., 1940; M.E.E., Poly. Inst. Bklyn., 1947, D.E.E., 1949; m. Catherine Stewart, Dec. 24, 1941; childrenDiana (Mrs. Bruce Dotson), Kristine, Karen, Conrad. Mfg. engr. RCA, 1940-45; mem. tech. staff Bell Telephone Labs., 1945-47; engring. sect. head Sperry Gyroscope Co., Great Neck, N.Y., 1949-56; faculty Cornell U., Ithaca, N.Y., 1956—, prof. elec. engr ing., 1956—, Adj. prof. Poly. Inst. Bklyn., 1954-56; chmn. bd. Cayuga Assos., Cornell Research Park, Ithaca, 1967; cons. to industry, 1956—. Project mgr. UN Spl. Fund China Project, Chiao Tung U., Hisnchu, Taiwan, 1962-63. Fellow I.E.E.E.; mem. Am. Phys. Soc., A.A.A.S., Sigma Xi, Tau Beta Pi, Eta Kappa Nu. Contbr. papers to profl. lit. Home: 506 Hanshaw Rd Ithaca, NY 14850.

DALMAU, EDWARD MARTINEZ, bishop; b. Havana, Cuba, June 29, 1893; s. Cecil Martinez and Sophie Dalmau; ed. philosophy and theology, Rome, Italy, 1908-16. Ordained priest Roman Cath. Ch.; prof. history and canon law, Rome, 1917-26; bishop of Cienfuegos, Cuba, 1933-61; titular bishop, Euzi, W. Palm Beach, Fla., 1961—. Decorated officer Legion of Honor; great cross Carolos M. Cespeo (Cuba). Address: 208 Evernia St West Palm Beach FL 33401

DALRYMPLE, CHARLES, Jr., librarian; b. Topeka, June 29, 1915; s. Charles E. and Bessie (Jones) D.; A.B., U. Kan., 1939; B.L.S., U. Ill., 1942; m. Peggy Clayton, June 5, 1938 (div.); children—Charles McVey, Robert George, Jonathan; m. 2d, Martha Walsh; m. 3d, Barbara Mae Dalrymple. Biology librarian U. Kan. Watson Library, 1939-40; asst. librarian, circulation dept. U. Ill. Library, 1941-42; librarian Manhattan (Kan.) Pub. Library, 1946-49; dir. Lincoln (Neb.) City Libraries, 1949—. Field asst. oil field sect., div. sanitation Kan. Bd. Health, hdqrs. Lawrence, 1942-46; co-ordinator S.E. Multi-Regional Library Network. Mem. exec. bd., sec. Lincoln City Library Found. Mem. A.L.A., Kan., Neb., Mountain Plains (v.p., pres.-elect 1965, pres. 1967) library assns., Lincoln C. of C., Midwest Canoe Assn. (commodore 1969). Home: 5901 Garfield Lincoln NB 68506 Office: Bennett Martin Pub Library Lincoln City Libraries 136 S 14th St Lincoln NB 68508

DALRYMPLE, JEAN, theatrical producer, publicist; b. Morristown, N.J., Sept. 2, 1910; d. George Hull and Elizabeth Van Kirk (Collins) Dalrymple, ed. pvt. tutors; D.F.A. (hon.), Wheaton Coll., 1959; m. Ward Morehouse, Mar. 31, 1932 (div. 1937); m. 2d, Philip De Witt Ginder, Nov. 1, 1951. Actress, writer, 1926-29; publicist for John Golden, 1929-33; publicist, mgr. for artists including Jose Iturbi, Grace Moore, Lily Pons, Bidu Sayoa, Glinka Milanov, Nathan Milstein, Leopold Stokowski, 1933-44; perm. dir. N.Y.C. Center Theatre Co.; theatre publicist: Tallulah Bankhead, Mary Martin, Margaret Sullivan; (plays) One Touch of Venus; Voice of the Turtle; Anna Lucasta; Ballet Russe de Monte Carlo, N.Y.C. Center, Lewisohn Stadium concerts; producer: Hope For The Best, 1944; Brighten the Corner, 1945; Burlesque, 1946-48; Red Gloves, 1948-49; prod., dir. summer circuit: The Second Man, Harvey, Voice of the Turtle, Petrified Forest, 1950-53; producer 4 plays for City Center with Jose Ferrer, 1953-54, Winter Play Festival of 1954-55, The Feathered Fauna, 1955, others including South Pacific, Pajama Game, Carousel, Annie Get Your Gun, Wonderful Town, Oklahoma, Finian's Rainbow, The King and I, Say Darling, Most Happy Fella, Lute Song, The Country Girl, The Rose Tattoo, Elizabeth The Queen, Carousel (spl. Christmas Show); dir. numerous others. Coordinator U.S. Performing Arts Program, Brussels World's Fair, 1958. Dir. N.Y.C. Center Music and Drama, Soldiers, Sailors and Airmens Club. Profl. Children's Sch. (all N.Y.C.). Bd. dirs. N.Y. World's Fair 1964-65; cons. Performing Arts Program, N.Y. World's Fair; dir. U.S. Performing Arts Program, Fed. Pavilion, N.Y. World's Fair. Mem. adv. bd. Nat. Arts Council, N.C. Sch. Arts. Decorated knight Order Crown for Brussels World's Fair work (Belgium); recipient 2 citations for City Center Work from mayor N.Y.C. Mem. Am. Nat. Theatre and Acad. (bd. dirs., treas., exec. dir.). Author: September Child, 1963; Careers and Opportunities in the Theatre, 1969; Jean Dalrymple's Pinafore Farm Cookbook, 1971; also articles, sketches, plays, Pioneered in prodn. operas, dramas for Pay-TV. Home: 150 W 55th St New York City NY 10019

DALRYMPLE, JOHN CLIFTON, army officer; b. Brazil, Ind., Feb. 10, 1912; s. Ezra Mahlon and Mary P. (Siegelin) D.; B.S. in Elec. Engring., Rose Poly. Inst., 1933; M.S. in Civil Engring., Ia. State Coll., 1948; grad. Nat. War Coll., 1960, Armed Forces Staff Coll., 1954, Command Mgmt. Sch., 1955, Command and Gen. Staff Coll., 1947; m. Dorotha Bell Smith, Jan. 13, 1934. Commd. 2d lt., C.E., U.S. Army, 1933, advanced through grades to maj. gen., 1968; chief plans br., later plans div. Army Research and Devel., 1955-58; asst. exec. officer, exec. officer sec. army, 1958-59; sr. engr. adviser Republic of Korea Army, 1960-61; dist. engr. U.S. Army Corps Engrs., Little Rock, 1961-62; div. engr. N. Atlantic div. U.S. Army Corps Engrs., N.Y.C., 1962-65; dir. mil. constrn. Office Chief Engrs., 1965-66; dir. installations Dept. Army, 1966-70. Decorated D.S.M., Silver Star, Legion of Merit with oak leaf cluster, Bronze Star medal for valor with oak leaf clusters, Army Commendation medal. Registered profl. engr., Ark., D.C. Mem. Soc. Am. Mil. Engrs. (N.E. regional dir. 1963-65), Engr. Joint Council (bd. dirs. 1963-65), Assn. U.S. Army, Tau Nu Tau, Theta Xi. Home: 306 Lee Circle Alexandria VA 22305 Office: Dept Army care Adjutant General Washington DC 20310

DALRYMPLE, RUTH, coll. dean; b. Phila., Feb. 16, 1916; d. John Hart and Edith (Wyckoff) Dalrymple; B.S., Muskingum Coll., 1937; M. Nursing, Western Res. U., 1940, M.S. in Nursing Edn., 1952; M.P.H., U. Pitts., 1962, D.P.H., 1966 Staff nurse Univ. Hosps., Cleve., 1940-41; instr. nursing Med. Coll. Va., 1941-46; instr. nursing Woman's Coll., U. N.C., 1946-49, asst. prof., coordinator pre-nursing program, 1950-51; asso. prof., 1951-55, prof., 1955-60, asst. dean, 1962-67; dean Coll. Nursing and Health, U. Cin., 1968-. Chmn. N.C. Com. Patient Care, 1966-67. Mem. Am., Ohio nurses assns., Nat. League Nursing, Am. Pub. Health Assn., Sigma Theta Tau. Home: 5720 Winton Rd Cincinnati OH 45232.

DALRYMPLE, THOMAS LAWRENCE, lawyer; b. Wellsburg, W. Va., May 20, 1921; s. Lawrence Chester and Ethel May (Taylor) D.; A.B., U. Mich., 1943, J.D., 1947; m. Marjorie May Keeler; children-Bruce Lawrence, Dale Brian. Admitted to Ohio bar, 1947 also Supreme Ct.; practiced in Toledo, 1947—; asso. Williams, Eversman & Morgan and successor firms, 1947-50; asso. Welles, Kelsey, Fuller, Harrington & Seney and successor firms, 1950-52; partner Fuller, Seney, Henry & Hodge and predecessor firms, 1953—. Mem. Trout Unlimited, Toledo Mus. Art. Served to Capt., Inf., Aus, 1943-46. Decorated Combat Inf. badge, Silver Star medal, Purple Heart. Fellow Am. Coll. Trial Lawyers; mem. Internat. Assns. Ins. Counsel, Am., Ohio, Toledo bar assns., Order of Coif, Phi Beta Kappa. Home: 4307 Stannard Dr Toledo OH 43613 Office: 405 Madison Av Toledo OH 43604

DALSEMER, LEONARD, paper mfg. exec.; b. Halt., Sept. 28, 1906; B.A., Johns Hopkins, 1928; m. Emily DeWitt; childrenRichard, Leonard, John, Rhodena, Susan, David. Joined Lord Baltimore Press, Inc. (now div. Internat. Paper Co.), 1928, exec. v.p., 1957, pres. 1958-61, chmn., 1961-66; v.p. Internat. Paper Co., 1958-62 exec. v.p. 1962—, also dir.; chmn. bd. subsidiary Davol Corp., 1968—; dir. Northeast Airlines. Mem. adv. bd. Sch. Advanced Internat. Studies, Johns Hopkins. Home: 680 Madison Av New York City NY 10017 Office:220 E 42d St New York City NY 10017

DALSIMER, PHILIP T., lawyer; b. Far Rockaway, N.Y., June 18, 1913; s. Philip T. and Florence (Furth) D.; B.S., U. Mich., 1934; LL.B., Columbia, 1936; m. Dorothy Williams, May 30, 1935; children—William Robert, Nan (Mrs. Glen A. Corliss). Admitted to N.Y. bar, 1937; asso. Edwards, Bower & Poole, 1936-37, Duell & Kane, 1937-45; partner Kane, Dalsimer, Kane, Sullivan & Kurucz, N.Y.C., 1945—; dir. N. European Oil Co. Mem. Am., N.Y. patent law assns., Am. Bar Assn., U.S. Trademark Assn. Clubs: U. Mich. of N.Y.; Columbia U. Home: 860 United Nations Plaza New York City NY 10017 Office: 420 Lexington Avenue New York City NY 10017

DALTON, FRANCIS EDWARD, former electric mfg. co. exec.; b. Monson, Mass., Aug. 27, 1904; s. Michaael E. Michael E. and Mary (Fitzgerald) D.; grad. Advanced Mgmt. Program, Harvard; m. Josephine Dalton, Nov. 1934. With Westinghouse Electric Corp., 1923-70, controller, 1957-64, v.p., 1964-67, sr. v.p., 1967-70, ret., 1970; bd. dirs. Westinghouse Credit Corp. Mem. Financial Execs. Inst., Harvard Bus. Sch. Assn. Democrat. Roman Cath. Club: Pitts. Athletic Assn. Home: 226 Academy Av Pittsburgh PA 15228 Office: 3 Gateway Center Pittsburgh PA

DALTON, HARRY LEE, business exec.; b. Winston-Salem, N.C., June 13, 1895; s. Rufus I and Cora (McCanless) D.; A.B., LL.D. (hon.), Duke; post grad. work N.Y. Univ. Coll. Tech., Manchester, Eng.; m. Mary Keesler, April 28, 1928; childrenDavid McRae, Mary Elizabeth. Chmn. bd. Microtron Corp., Shaw Mfg. Co., Falco Corp.; pres. Kartex Oil Co.; v.p. Minerals Research & Devel. Corp.; dir. Carlton Yarn Mills, Wachovia Bank & Trust Co., Nationwide Securities, Melodaire, AVC Corp., Nationwide Investment, YMIT; Chmn. finance com. Shaw Securities; dir. mem. exec. com. Pyramid Life Ins. Co.; adv. bd. 45th St. Br. Chase Nat. Bank; chmn. exec. com. Am. Credit Corp.; mem. exec. com. Thermoplastics Corp.; con. Viscose div. F.M.C. Corp. Dir. Chief silk and nylon sect. WPB, Washington, 1941-44; cons. Nat. Distbn. Council, U.S. Dept. Commerce. Dir. Mint Mus.; dir. and mem. adv. council So. Research Inst.; mem. nat. panel arbitrators Am. Arbitration Assn., Charlotte Memorial Hosp. trustee The Pennsylvania Hosp. trustee Queens Coll. Textile Research Inst., Princeton, Phila. Textile Inst. Crozer Theol. Sem.; mem. library com. Duke U.; dir. Ludington Library; chmn. bd. visitors Davidson Coll.; mem. finance com. Presbyn. Found.; mem. finance com., chmn. patrons Queens Coll.; mem.' bd. Charlotte Country Day, N.C. Arts Soc.; chmn. patrons Montreat; bd. visitors St. Andrews Presbyn. Coll.; adv. bd. Wingate Coll.; mem. N.C. Arts Council; mem. bd. N.C. Mus. of Art. Presbyn. Clubs: Augusta Nat.; Links, University (N.Y.C.); Charlotte Country, Executives, Good Fellows (dir.), Metropolitan (Washington): Pine Valley Country, Rittenhouse, Merion Cricket, Acorn. Philadelphia Country Orpheus (Phila.); Old Town (Winston-Salem, N.C.), Country of N.C. (Pineburst); Biltmore Forest Country (N.C.): Quail Hollow Country Formerly editor So. Textile Bull Home: 322 Eastover Rd Charlotte NC 28207 Office: Wachovia Bank Bldg Charlotte NC 28202

DALTON, HOWARD CLARK, biologist, educator; b. Bklyn., Aug. 7, 1915; s. Howard Augustus and Elizabeth (Clark) D.; B.A., Wesleyan U., Middletown, Conn., 1936, M.A., 1937; Ph.D., Stanford, 1940; m. Eleanora Alice Keene, June 19, 1948. Instr., U. Rochester, 1940-41, Brown U., 1946-47; asst. prof. Bates Coll., 1946-47; mem. faculty N.Y.U., 1950-67, prof. biology, chmn. dept Univ. Coll., 1961-67; prof. biology Pa. State U., University Park, 1967- -. Pres. Westchester (N.Y.) Ethical Soc., 1956-57. Served to capt. AUS, 1941-46; PTO, Fellow N.Y. Acad. Sci.; mem. Am. Assn. Anatomists, Am. Soc. Naturalists, Am. Soc. Zoologists, Soc. Developmental Biology, Sigma Xi. Home: 316 Hubler Rd State College PA 16801 Office: Life Sci Bldg Pa State U University Park PA 16802

DALTON, JACK, librarian; b. Holland, Va., Mar. 21, 1908; s. John Preston and Selma Hatcher (Butler) D.; student Va. Poly. Inst., 1924-27; B.S., U. Va., 1930, M.S., 1935; student U. Mich., 1935-36; m. Mary Armistead Gochnauer, Sept. 6, 1933; 1 son, John Preston, III. Instr. in English, Va. Poly Inst., 1930-34; reference librarian, U. Va., 1936-42, asso. librarian, 1942-50, librarian 1950-56; dir. internat. relations office, A.L.A., 1956-59; dean Sch. Library Service Columbia U., 1959-70, Library dir. Library Devel. Center, 1970—. Mem. A.L.A., Bibliog. Soc. Am., Bibliog. Soc. (London). Home: 445 Riverside Dr New York City NY 10027

DALTON, JOHN MONTGOMERY, lawyer; b. Vernon County, Mo., Nov. 9, 1900; s. Fred A. and Ida Jane (Poage) D.; LL.B., U. Mo., 1923; LL.D., Drury Coll. U. Mo., Westminster Coll., William Jewell Coll.; m. Geraldine Hall, Nov. 22, 1925; children—John Hall, Julia Hall. Admitted to Mo. bar, 1923, practiced, Kennett, Mo., 1923-52; city counselor, Kennett, 1944-53; legislative counsel Mo. Rural Electrification Coop. Assn., 1951-52; atty. gen. Mo., 1952-60; gov. Mo., 1961-65; practice law, Jefferson City, Mo., 1965—. Chmn., Fed. Home Loan Bank, Des Moines, Ia. Mem. bd. visitors U. Mo., 1949-53; trustee Westminister Coll., The School of the Ozarks; mem. bd. curators Stephens Coll. Mem. Nat. Assn. Attys. General (past pres.), Phi Delta Phi, Phi Gamma Delta. Dem. Presbyn. Mason, Lion (gov. Mo. 1931-32). Home: 1207 Moreau Dr Jefferson City MO 65101 Office: 425 Madison St Jefferson City MO 65101

DALTON, MARTHA BERNICE MAYFIELD (Mrs. George Francis Dalton III), harpist, coll. trustee; b. Hutchinson, Kan., Feb. 25, 1919; d. Lionel M. and Bernice (Townsend) Mayfield; B.Mus., Oberlin Coll., 1941; m. George Francis Dalton III, June 22, 1943; childrenAnne Rawlings, Douglas Mayfield, Deborah Whitmore. Instr. fine arts U. Tex., 1941-43; 2d harpist Cleve. Orch., 1945-; solo and ensemble performances Cleve. and area, 1945-. Pres. Laurel Sch. chpt. Am. Field Service, 1962-64; mem. music therapy com. Cleve. State Hosp., 1964-; exec. com., trustee Oberlin Coll., 1963. Mem. Pi kappa Lambda, Mu Phi Epsilon. Home: 55 S Lane Chagrin Falls, OH 44022. Office: Severance Hall Euclid Av Cleveland OH 44114

DALTON, PARKS H., Jr., securities co. exec.; b. Charlotte, N.C., 1929; grad. Davidson Coll., 1952. Exec. v.p. Interstate Securities Corp., Charlotte. Home: 3842 Abingdon Rd Charlotte NC 28211 Office: 221 S Tryon St Charlotte NC 28202

DALTON, PETER, sculptor; b. Buffalo, N.Y., Dec. 26, 1894; s. Peter P. and Ellen (O'Sullivan) D.; ed. Art Sch. Albright Art Gallery, Buffalo; Art Students' League (New York), 1915-18; Nat. Acad. Sch., 1919; one year in Europe, 1920-21; m. Dorothea Chace, June 21, 1924. Taught sculpture at Albright Art Gallery School, 1916-17; worked in N.Y. City, since 1922. Received grant from Am. Acad. Arts and Letters, 1945. Awarded Gold medal for sculpture, Allied Artists of Am. 1935; 2d prize for sculpture "Dance International," 1937; Elizabeth M. Watrous gold medal Nat. Acad. prize for sculpture, 1947, S.F.B. Morse gold medal, 1951. Mem. N.A.D. Nat. Sculpture Soc., Nat. Inst. Arts and Letters, Century Assn. Home: 114 River Rd Grand View Nyack NY 10960

DALTON, PHILIP BENJAMIN, chem. co. exec.; b. Bklyn., July 21, 1923; s. Abraham and Bertha (Nagin) D.; B.A., U. Ill., 1944; M.A., Columbia, 1947; m. Elaine Kaufman, Feb. 26, 1944; children—Linda, Barbara. Research chemist Sun Chem. Co., 1946, 47-49; tchg. asst. Columbia, 1947; with Colgate Palmolive Co., 1949-54, research chemist, 1951-54; with GAF Corp., 1954—, dir. comml. devel. chem. div., 1963-64, v.p., gen. mgr. comml. devel., 1964-67, v.p. photo and reprodn. div., 1967, exec. vice pres., 1967—, also dir. Served to lt. USNR, 1943-46. Fellow A.A.A.S., Am. Inst. Chemists; mem. of Comml. Chem. Devel. Assn., Am. Chem. Soc., N.Y. Acad. Sci., Soc. Chem. Industry (dir.). Clubs: Hemisphere, Economic (N.Y.C.). Author, patentee in field. Home: 7 Victorian Lane Brookville NY 11545 Office: 140 W 51st St New York City NY 10020

DALTON, PHYLLIS, costume designer; b. London, Eng. Mem. wardrobe dept. London studios Metro-Goldwyn-Mayer; created costumes for motion pictures Lawrence of Arabia, Anastasia, Our Man in Havana, Lord Jim, Dr. Zhivago (Ocar award 1966). Address: 3 Golden Sq W1 London, England.*

DALTON, ROBERT HATCHER, educator; b. Holland, Va., Jan. 30, 1912; s. John Preston and Selma Hatcher (Butler) B.; A.B., Duke, 1934; B.D., Hartford (Conn.) Theol. Sem., 1937; M.A., Trinity Coll., Hartford, 1938; Ph.D., Harvard, 1949; m. Alice Elizabeth Pond, June 4, 1937; children—Alice, Anne, Robin, Peter. Chaplain U.S. Penitentiary, Lewisburg, Pa., 1938-40; ednl. dir. N.J. State Hosp., Greystone Park, 1940-42; staff Harvard Psychol. Clinic, Cambridge, Mass., 1942-43; faculty psychology dept. U. N.C., Woman's Coll., Greensboro, N.C., 1943-44; prof. child devel. family relationships and psychology Cornell U., 1944—, head dept. child devel. and family relationships, 1944-53, mem. exec. com., gov. social sci. research center; cons. behavior problems of adolescents George Jr. Republic, Freeville, N.Y., 1955—; dir. research in child devel. St. Thomas (V.I.) Bur. Mental Health, 1962—; lectr. med. psychology U. Cal., 1950-51; lectr. cons. state ednl. orgns. Mem. senate State U. N.Y. Diplomate clin. psychology Am. Bd. Examiners Profl. Psychology. Licensed Psychologist, N.Y. State. Mem. Am., N.Y. State psychol. assns., Am. Assn. U. Profs., Nat. Council Religion in Higher Edn. Author: Personality and Social Interaction, 1961; Mothers and Children, 1967; Behavior Problems in Social Perspective, 1969. Contbr. articles to profl. jours. Home: St Thomas VI 00801

DALTON, ROBERT MICHAEL, hosp. supt.; b. Detroit, July 21, 1908; s. Robert M. and Helen (Siebert) D.; student Georgetown U., U. Detroit, Wayne State U., Detroit Inst. Tech.; m. Josephine Pakos (div.); children—Jean Elizabeth (Mrs. William Kroger), Patricia (Mrs. Donald Dauphin), Lawrence, Kathleen; m. 2d, Marion Hewnes; children—Naureen, Michael. With Detroit Dept. Parks and Recreation, 1928-33; prin. investigator Detroit Dept. Welfare, 1933-43; exec. sec. to mayor Detroit, 1943-47; supt. Herman Kiefer Hosp., Detroit, 1947—. Mem. Wayne County Civic League. Mem. Am. Coll. Hosp. Adminstrs., Internat. Assn. Laryngecomes (charter; past pres.). Clubs: Press, Anamilo (bd.), Fifth Wheel, Crisis (bd.). (Detroit). Home: 4669 Courville St Detroit MI 48224 Office: Herman Kiefer Hosp 1151 Taylor Av Detroit MI 48202

DALTON, TED, dist. judge; b. Caroll County, Va., July 3, 1901; s. Curell and Lodoska Vernon (Martin) D.; A.B., Coll. of William and Mary, 1924, LL.B., 1926; LL.D. (hon.), Milligan Coll., 1966; m. Mary Turner, Jan. 4, 1932; 1 son, John N. Admitted to Va. bar, 1923; commonwealth's atty., Radford, Va., 1928-36. Mem. State Senate of Va., 1944-59; mem. for Va., Rep. Nat. Com., 1952-59; U.S. dist. judge Western Dist. Va., 1959—, chief U.S. dist. judge, 1960. Rep. candidate for gov. Va., 1953, 57. Mem. Commn. on Va. Constn. Revision, 1969. Recipient Distinguished Service award Va. Trial Lawyers Assn., 1971. Mem. Va. (v.p. 1944), Montgomery-Radford-Floyd (pres. 1948-49) bar assns., Order Coif, Phi Beta Kappa, Alpha Kappa Psi. Omicron Delta Kappa, Sigma Nu, Phi Delta Phi. Club: Flat Hat. Address: Radford VA 24141

DALTON, VAN BROADUS, oral surgeon; b. Burkesville, Ky., July 25, 1885; s. Lafayette and Elmira (Norris) D.; student Bethel Coll., Russelville, Ky., 1901-02. Auburn Ky.) Mil. Acad., Auburn, 1902-03; D.D.S., Ohio Coll. Dental Surgery, Cin., 1907; m. Anna Stone, Dec. 16, 1914 (dec. 1950); children—Dorothy Fay (Mrs. J. H. Platz), William (dec.), Van Broadus (dec 1931). Began career as demonstrator in operative clinics. Ohio Coll. of Dental Surgery, 1907, prof. orthodontia, exodontia and anaesthetics, 1908-20; asst. dir. dental dept., Cin. Gen. Hosp., 1920-21; mem. med. staff, Children's Hosp., Cin. 1917-19; engaged in pvt. practice, 1916—; hon. staff Bethesda Hosp.: sr. staff Christ Hsop.; cons. staff Good Samaritan Hosp. Mem. mouth hygiene council Cin. Pub. Health Fedn.; Cin. and Hamilton Co. exec. council Am. Cancer Soc. Diplomate Am. Bd. Oral Surgery. Fellow Am. Coll. Dentists; mem. Am. Dental Assn., Am. (past pres.), Gt. Lakes, Cin. (past pres.) socs. oral surgeons Am. Acad. History Dentistry (past pres.) Am. Assn. History of Medicine, Ohio Acad. History Medicine, Ohio State (past pres.), Cin. (past pres.) dental socs., Ohio State Archaeol. and Hist. Soc., State Hist. Soc. Mo., Acad. Medicine Cin. (asso.), Fedn. Dentaire Internationale (asso.), T.I. Way Dental Forum (hon.), Psi Omego (hon). Clubs: Kenwood Country (life mem.), Cuvier Press, Automobile, The Cincinnati (Cin.). Author: Essentials of Orthodontia, 1914; The Genesis of Dental Education in the United States, 1946; also sci. and clin. articles for profl. publs. Address: Cinti Club 30 W 8th St Cincinnati, OH 45202.

DALVIT, LEWIS DAVID, Jr., symphony condr.; b. Denver, Dec. 11, 1925; s. Lewis David and Anita (Lyreman) D.; B.A., Beloit Coll., 1950; M.S., Vandercook Coll., 1956; m. Patricia Dougan, Aug. 28, 1949; children—Jacqueline, Stephanie. Joined music faculty, 1960, in residence Beloit (Wis.) Coll., 1964, acting chmn. music dept., 1965-66; condr. Beloit Symphony Orch., 1953-63, 64—; asst. condr. Honolulu Symphony, 1963-64; mem. music faculty Milton Coll., 1952-63; now condr. Jackson (Miss.) Symphony. Guest condr. U.S., 1964, Mexico, 1964, 65, Germany, 1965. Served with USAF, 1944-46. Address: P O Box 4584 Fondren Sta Jackson MS 39216

DALY, BRIAN LOTT, life ins. co. exec.; b. Phila., May 26, 1920; s. Christopher and Marion (Lott) D.; A.B., U. Pa., 1941; m. Isabel R. Benkert, Aug. 18, 1945; children—Barbara (Mrs. Thomas R. Metcalf), Florence (Mrs. David Battis), William L., Ruth, Susan. With Penn Mutual Ins. Co., 1941—, v.p., actuary, 1961-71, sr. v.p., 1971—. Bd. dirs. Phila. Housing Assn. Fellow Soc. Actuaries. Home: 208 E Gowen Av Philadelphia PA 19119 Office: 530 Walnut St Philadelphia PA 19105

DALY, CHARLES ULICK, univ. adminstr.; b. Dublin, Ireland, May 29, 1927; s. Ulick de Burgh and Violet (Sealy-King) D.; came to U.S., 1934, naturalized, 1940; B.A. in Internat. Relations, Yale, 1949; M.S. in Journalism, Columbia, 1959; m. Mary Larmonth, June 11, 1949; children-Michael, Douglas. v.p. Mexican subsidiary Pacific Molasses Co., 1949-50, 52-58; Am. Polit. Sci. Assn. Congl. fellow, 1959-60; editor Stanford, 1961; staff asst. to Presidents Kennedy and Johnson, 1962-64; v.p. pub. affairs U Chgo., 1964-67, v.p. for devel. and public affairs, 1967—; free- lance writer, 1958-. Participant Am. Assembly, 1965, White House Conf. Edn., 1965; cons. Small Bus. Adminstrn., Post Office Dept., Peace Corps. Served with USNR, 1945-46, with USMCR, 1950-52. Decorated Silver Star, Purple Heart. Mem. Am. Polit. Sci. Assn. Democrat. Episcopalian. Clubs: Federal City (Wash.); Tavern, Yale, (Chicago). Home: 1222 E 56th St Chicago, IL 60637.

DALY, E.A., publisher; b. Tuscaloosa, Ala., Nov. 16, 1891; s. Ralph F. and Lillie L. (Floyd) D.; student Talladega Coll., 1911-13, Morris Brown Coll., 1914-18; m. Lillian Madora Hilton, June 3, 1919. Editor, pub., owner Cal. Voice, Oakland, 1926—. Active Little League Baseball, Y.M.C.A.; hon. life mem. N.A.A.C.P. No. Cal. chmn. Jess Unruh for Gov., also Sen. Allen Cranston campaign, 1965-70. Served with U.S. Army, 1918-19. Licensed real estate broker. Mem. A.M.E. Ch. Mason (Shriner), K.P. Home: 1106 Trestle Glen Rd Oakland CA 94610 Office: 814 27th St Oakland CA 94607

DALY, GEORGE J., consumer product. co. exec.; b. Phila., Jan. 26, 1919; s. George J. and Frances Hehl (Denzler) D.; grad. with honors in finance Wharton Sch., U. Pa., 1942; m. Marjorie Colleen Bishop, June 7, 1946; 1 dau., Colleen Bishop. Sr. analyst Provident Tradesmens Nat. Bank, Phila., 1937-48; dir., controller Dorville Corp., Phila., 1948-52; spl. cons. to U.S. Sec. of Army, Washington, 1952-54; various positions to chief exec. officer, dir. Elgin Nat. Watch Co. (Ill.), 1954-60; spl. asst. to pres. Champion Papers, Hamilton, O., 1961; v.p., dir. Dart Industries, Inc., Los Angeles, 1961-68, exec. v.p., treas., 1969—. Served to capt. USAAF, 1942-46, to capt., 1952. Decorated Air medal with two oak leaf clusters, D.S.C. Mem. Financial Execs. Assn., Sigma Kappa Phi. Clubs: Eldorado Country (Palm Springs, Cal.); Bel Air Country (Los Angeles); Cal. Yacht.; Royal Danish Yacht (Denmark). Home: 10649 Capello Way Los Angeles CA 90024 Office: 8480 Beverly Blvd Los Angeles CA 90054

DALY, HUGH COLLINS, (DAILY), utilities exec.; b. Hamilton, Ont., Can., July 16, 1917; s. Hugh Leo and Blanche (Porter) D.; Ph.B. U. Detroit, 1939; m. Margaret Mary Meurer, July 9, 1943; childrenHugh C., Patricia A., Margaret M. News reporter, re-write man, Detroit Times, 1936-42, Washington corr., 1946-50; now exec. v.p., dir. Mich. Consol. Gas Co.; dir. Am. Natural Gas Co., Gt. Lakes Gas Transmission Company, Michigan Wisconsin Pipeline Co. Served with inf., U.S. Army, 1942-46. Roman Catholic. Clubs: Detroit Athletic, Detroit Country Detroit. Home: 820 Edgemont Park Grosse Pointe MI 48236 Office: 1 Woodward Ave Detroit MI 48226

DALY, JAMES, actor; b. Wisconsin Rapids, Wis., Oct. 23, 1918; s. Percifer Charles and Dorothy Hogan (Mullen) D.; student U. Wis., 1933, State U. Ia., 1935-36, Carroll Coll., 1937-38; B.A., Cornell Coll., 1941, D.F.A., 1956; m. Hope Newell, Feb. 21, 1942; childrenPegeen, Tyne, Glynn, Timothy. Broadway debut in Born Yesterday, 1946; other theatrical appearances include Virginia Reel, 1947, Man and Superman (tour), 1948-49, The Cenci, 1950, The Devil's Disciple, 1950, Major Barbara, 1950-51, Billy Budd, 1951, Mary Rose, 1951-52, St. Joan, 1951, Miss Julie, 1956, Glass Menagerie, 1956, Back to Methuselah, 1957, This is Goggle, 1958, Handful of Fire, 1958, J B, 1959-60, Period of Adjustment, 1960-61, The Advocate, 1963, The White House, 1964; summer stock roles with Port Players, Oconomowoc, Wis., 1948-50, Lakewood Theater, Skowhegan, Me., 1951, Bucks County Playhouse, New Hope, Pa., 1954, 62-63; with State Dept. tour to Germany to open Congress Hall in Berlin, 1957; films include The Court Martial of Billy Mitchell, 1955, The Young Stranger, 1957, I Aim at the Stars, 1960; major TV appearances, 1947-, including roles in series Foreign Intrigue, 1953-54, Hallmark Hall of Fame show in Give Us Barabbas, Ominbus role in Henry Adams, and Armstrong Circle Theatre role in Cross and the Dragon. Served as ensign USNR, World War II. Recipient Daniel Blum Theatre World award, 1951; Emmy award as outstanding actor in supporting role in Eagle in a Cage, Hallmark Hall of Fame, 1966. Mem. A.F.T.R.A., Screen Actors Guild, Authors Guild, Actors Equity Assn. Home: 360 E 55th St New York City NY 10022 Office: care Stephen Draper Agy 37 W 57th St New York City NY 10019

DALY, JAMES JOSEPH, newspaper exec.; b. Jersey City, June 11, 1916; s. Bernard B. and Anna (Leiner) D.; student St. Peters Coll.; m. Catherine Mary Adams, June 26, 1937; children-Ann, Catherine. Classified advt. mgr. N.Y. Sun, 1946-49, World Telegram Sun, 1950-55; with Washington Post, 1955—, v.p., gen. mgr., 1965—. Dir. Washington Post Co., Postrib Corp.; exec. com. Newspaper I. Mem. exec. com. Washington Conv. and Visitors Bur.; chmn. v.p. Tenafly (N.J.) Community Chest, 1955; budget com. Washington Health and Welfare Council, 1961-64. Bd. dirs. United Givers Fund. Served with AUS, 1943-45. Mem. Washington Advt. Club, Washington Bd. Trade, John Carroll Soc., Silurians. Rotarian. Clubs: Nat. Press, Columbia Country (Washington). Home: 6340 Falmouth Rd. Spring Hill Washington DC 20016 Office: 1515 L St NW Washington DC 20005

DALY, JEROME G., banker; b. N.Y.C., 1923; grad. Pace Coll., 1949. Vice pres., comptroller N.J. Bank, Clifton. Home: 117 Stony Ridge Dr Hillsdale NJ 07642 Office: 1184 Main Av Clifton NJ 07011*

DALY, JOHN CHARLES, Jr., radio and TV news corr. and Analyst; b. Johannesburg, South Africa on Feb. 20, 1914 (father Am. Citizen) s. John Charles and Helene Grant (Tennant) D.; student Marist Brothers Coll., Johannesburg, 1920-23; grad. Tilton (N.H.) Sch., 1930; student Boston Coll., 1930-33; D.Litt., St. Bonaventure U., 1959; D.H.L., Am. Internat. Coll., 1963; LL.D., Norwich U., 1964; m. Margaret Criswell Neal, Jan. 7, 1937 (dec.) children—John Neal, John Charles, Helene Grant; m. 2d, Virginia Warren, Dec. 22, 1960; childrenJohn Warren, John Earl Jameson, Nina. Came to U.S., 1923. Schedule engr. Capital Transit Co., Washington, 1935-37; corr. and news analyst, CBS, 1937-49; spl. events reporter and Whit House corr., 1937-41, asst. producer-dir. and narrator Spirit of 41, Washington, 1941, N.Y.C. 1941-42, Middle East-Italy, 1943-44), service in U.S.A., Europe and South Am., for C.B.S., 1945-49; corr.-analyst, ABC moderator programs on all networks (programs include: We Take Your Word, What's My Line, March of Time Thru the Years, News of the Week, etc.), N.Y. c., 1949-53; v.p. ABC in charge of news, spl. events and pub. affairs, 1953-60; dir. Voice of Am. 1967-68; lectr. Mem. Water Pollution Control Adv. Bd., 1960-62. Pres. bd. trustees Tilton (N. H. Sch., trustee Norwich U. Mem. Artists and Writers Assn., Radio TV Execs. Soc. (past pres.), Assn. Radio News Analysts, Radio Corr. Assn., Sigma Delta Chi. Episcopalian. Clubs: Burning Tree Country, Columbia Country, National Press (Washington); Overseas Press of America (past pres.), Metropolitan (N.Y.C.); The Family (San Francisco). Contbr. articles in nat. mags. Address: 225 E 57th St New York City, NY 10022.

DALY, JOHN F., otolaryngologist; b. Jersey City, June 10, 1912; s. Peter J. and Kathryn (Madigan) K.; B.A., Fordham U., 1933; M.D., L.I. Coll. of Medicine, 1937; m. Annette R. O'Mealia, July 1, 1941; 1 dau., Sharon Ann. Splty. tng. Manhattan Eye, Ear and Throat Hosp., N.Y.C., 1939-41; dir. otolaryngology Bellevue Hosp., N.Y.C., 1948 Univ. Hosp. 1949—; prof. oto., chmn. dept. N.Y. U. Sch. Medicine, 1949—; cons. aural surgeon N.Y. Eye and Ear Infirmary; cons. otorhinolarynogology Hackensack, VA St. Albans Naval Brookhaven hosp.; dir. Hearing and Speech Center, Bellevue Hosp.; prof. adv. com. N.Y. State Assn. Crippled Children, N.Y. Acad. Scis. med. cons. Mary Manning Washington Home. Chmn. tech. adv. com. on hearing and speech N.Y. C. Dept. Health hon. police surgeon N.Y.C., cons. otolaryngology Phelps Meml., Bergen Pines County, St. Joseph's, Stamford hosps., Stamford, Conn., Holy Name Hosp., Teaneck, N.J., Greenwich Nyack Elizabeth A. Horton Meml. Middletown, N.Y. Columbus Hosp. speech Rehab. Inst., N.Y.C. Bd. Edn., Man Manhattan Eye Ear Nose and Throat Hosp). Served as Maj. USAAF, 1942-46. Recipient Encaenia award Fordham U., 1958. Diplomate Am. Bd. Otoloaryngology. Fellow Am. Coll. Chest Physicians, Am. Laryngol. Assn., A.C.S., Am. Otol. Society, N.Y. Acad. Medicine, Am. Laryngol. Rhinol. and Otol. Soc., Am. Acad. Ophthalmology and Otolaryngology 1st v.p. 1968), Am. Soc. Head and Neck Surgery (pres. 1965-67), Soc. U. Otolaryngologists (pres. 1965-67), Am. Assn. U. Profs., Am. Cancer Soc., Med. Soc. N.Y.; mem. A.A.A.S., N.Y. Acad. Scis., N.Y. Laryngol. Soc., N.Y. Otol. Soc., N.Y. Cancer Soc., Internat., Am. broncho-esophagological assns., Am. Laryngol. Assn. (1st v.p. 1967-68), James Ewing Soc., Alpha Omega Alpha. Clubs: Century, University. Home: 16 N Brae Court Tenafly, NJ Office: 506 First Av New York City 16, NY

DALY, JOHN FRANCIS, ball bearing co. exec.; b. N.Y.C., Dec. 13, 1922; s. John F. and Caroline (Pohl) D.; B.S., Rensselaer Poly. Inst., 1943; m. Casilda Boyd, July 16, 1953; children—Jo-Ann, Avis, Carol, Peter, Alexia. Vice pres. Inernat. Steel Co., Evansville, Ind., 1956-59; exec. v.p. Universal Wire Spring Co., Bedford, O., 1959-60; v.p. Hoover Ball & Bearing Co., Ann Arbor, Mich., 1960-66, exec. v.p., 1966-68, pres., 1968—, also dir.; dir. Comml. Savs. Bank, Adrian, Mich., Aluminum Extrusion Co., Cadiz R.R. Bd. dirs. Siena Heights Coll., Adrian, Mich. Served to capt. USAAF, 1943-46. Mem. Theta Xi. Home: 905 Berkshire Rd Ann Arbor MI 48104 Office: PO Box 1003 Ann Arbor MI 48106

DALY, JOHN JOSEPH, banker; b. N.Y.C., Nov. 22, 1922; s. John and Ellen (O'Brien) D.; B.B.A., St. John's U., 1947; M.B.A., N.Y. U., 1950; M.S., Columbia, 1952; m. Dolores Agnes Cooper, Oct. 26, 1963; children—Deirdre Ann, Dolores Jacqueline. Accountant, Price Waterhouse & Co., N.Y.C., 1947-54; sec.- treas. Monti Marine Corp., Bklyn., 1954-56; asst. to mng. partner White, Weld & Co., N.Y.C., 1956-62; asst. v.p. Harlem Savs. Bank, N.Y.C., 1962-68, v.p., auditor, 1968—. Mem. Am. Inst. C.P.A.'s, N.Y. State Soc. C.P.A.'s, N.Y. Savs. Bank Officers Forum, Alpha Kappa Psi, Delta Mu Delta, Republican. Roman Catholic. Home: 417 Crescent Pkwy Sea Girt NJ 08750 Office: Harlem Savs Bank 205 E 42d St Box 390 New York City NY 10017

DALY, JOHN JOSEPH Jr., newspaper editor; b. Waterbury, Conn., June 19, 1931; s. John Joseph and Helen (Fisk) D.; B.A., Catholic U. Am., 1953; B.S. in Journalism, Marquette U., 1954; m. Mary Neitzey, June 11, 1955; children—John M., Thomas A., Patrick J., Mary E. Staff writer, news service U.S. Cath. Conf., Washington, 1954-66; news editor Cath. Transcript, Hartford, Conn., 1966- -. Mem. Sigma Delta Chi. Democrat. Roman Catholic. Author articles, columns. Home: 400 Cornwall St Hartford CT 06112 Office: 785 Asylum Av Hartford CT 06105

DALY, JOSEPH MICHAEL, biologist; b. Hoboken, N.J., Apr. 9, 1922; s. Michael and Julia (Yarwood) D.; B.S., U. R.I., 1944; M.S., U. Minn., 1947, Ph.D., 1952; m. Cecilia Rieger, Sept. 1, 1951; children—Katherine, Stephen, Timothy, Martha, Cecilia, Anne, Constance, Melissa. Instr. U. Minn., 1949; asst. prof. biology U. Notre Dame, 1952-55; faculty U. Neb., Lincoln, 1955—, prof., 1958—, regent's prof., 1966-68, C. Petrus Peterson prof. biochemistry and nutrition, 1968—. Mem. Am. Soc. Plant Physiologists, Am. Phytopath. Soc., A.A.A.S. Studies, publs. on biochemistry and physiology of plant diseases designed to understand nature of disease, disease resistance with expectation for improved control of disease either through natural resistance or applied chems. Home: 8230 Henry St Lincoln NB 68520

DALY, JOSEPH RAYMOND, advt. exec.; b. N.Y.C., May 14, 1918; s. William C. and Mary (Hendrick) D.; A.B. Fordham U., 1940; m. Elizabeth R. Schulte, Apr. 19, 1947; children—Dorothy E., Suzanne J., Peter J., Timothy J., Mark, Andrew, Jennifer. With John A. Cairns, advt., 1946-49; with Doyle Dane Bernbach, N.Y.C., 1949—, sr. vice president, management superintendent, 1959-69, president, 1968—. Served to lt. comdr., Air Corps, USNR, 1940-46; PTO. Decorated Navy Cross, Purple Heart, Air medal. Clubs: Turf and Field (N.Y.C.); Huntington Yacht. Home: 150 Bay Av Huntington NY 11743 Office: 20 W 43d St New York City NY 10036

DALY, KAY FRANCES, (Mrs. Warren Leslie), advt. exec.; b. County Tyrone, Ireland, Jan. 8, 1919; d. Joseph and Margaret (Kelly) Daly; brought to U.S., 1922; B.A., Rosary Coll., River Forest, Ill., 1939; m. Richard Patterson Bradford, Apr. 6, 1953 (div. Dec. 1960); children—Kelly, Peter, Richard Patterson; m. 2d, Warren Leslie. Started career as copywriter Gimbels, Milw., 1940-43; fashion and beauty editor Chgo. Herald American, 1943-47; account exec. Foote, Cone & Belding, advt. agy., 1947-49; v.p. Norman Craig & Kummel, Inc., N.Y.C., 1949-61; v.p. creative services Revlon, Inc., N.Y.C., 1961—. Mem. Fashion Group, Inc. Home: 220 Central Park S New York City NY 10019 Office: 767 Fifth Av New York City NY 10022

DALY, LEO ANTHONY, architect; b. Omaha, July 29, 1917; s. Leo Anthony and Madeline (Peterson) D.; student Creighton U., 1935-36; B.S. in Architecture, Cath. U. Am., 1939; m. Rosemary Gaughan, May 31, 1941; children—Leo Anthony III, John Gaughan. With Leo A. Daly Co., Omaha, 1939-, v.p., 1948-52, pres., 1952—; dir. U.S. Nat. Bank, Omaha, Central Nat. Ins. Co., Omaha, Northwestern Bell Telephone Co. Mem. U.S. delegation 10th Pan Am. Hwy. Congress, Montevideo, Uruguay, 1967; pres. Omaha Devel. Council, 1961-69; trustee Omaha Indsl. Found.; mem. nat. adv. council Small Bus. Administrn., 1966-69; envoy Neb. Diplomats; mem. citizens cons. com. SAC. Gen. chmn. United Community Services, 1959-60, bd. dirs., 1967-69; gen. chmn. Omaha All Am. City Recognition Com. and Banquet, 1958; nat. trustee Nat. Conf. Christians and Jews, 1966-69; gen. chmn. Mid-Am. council recognition dinner Boy Scouts Am., 1968. Bd. govs. Knights Ak-Sar-Ben, 1961-62; bd. dirs. Nat. Sch. Facilities Council, 1964-69, Omaha Boys Clubs, Omaha Jr. Achievement; trustee Cath. U. Am., Josyln Soc. Liberal Arts, Neb. Ind. Coll. Found., Fontenelle Forest Assn.; adv. bd. Archbishop Bergan Mercy Hosp.; bd. dirs. Creighton U., Father Flanagan's Boys Home; pres. trustees Girls Town. Recipient 1st TV award for most outstanding service to pub. sta. KMTV, Omaha, 1958; Americanism citation Henry Monsky Lodge, B'nai B'rith, 1959; Boss of Year award Ak-Sar-Benchptat. Secs. Assn., 1960; Nat. Brotherhood citation Nat. Conf. Christians and Jews, 1966; Air Force Exceptional Service medal, 1963; Alumni award for distinguished achievement in Architecture and engring. Cath. U. Am., 1962, Alumni award Creighton Prep., 1970; created knight St. Gregory, 1964; co. has also received numerous archtl. awards. Registered architect. Mem. Nat. Council Archtl. Registration Bds., A.I.A. (mem. human resources council exec. com.), Neb. Assn. Architects (v.p. 1952, bd. dirs. 1951, chmn. pub. relations council 1951), Profl. Engrs. Neb., Soc. Am. Mil. Engrs., London Inst. Practicing Design, Miss. Valley Assn., Nat. Housing Conf., Am. Hosp. Assn., Omaha (bd. dirs.), San Francisco chambers commerce, Air Force Assn., Assn. U.S. Army, Nat. Aero. Assn., Navy League U.S., Am. Mgmt. Assn., Ad Sell League, Cath. U. Am. Alumni Assn. (pres. 1966-67). Roman Catholic. Clubs: Press, Omaha, Omaha Country, Plaza (Omaha); Marco- Polo (N.Y.C.). Home: Rosemont 9600 W Dodge Rd Omaha NB 68114 Office: 8600 Indian Hills Dr Omaha NB 68114

DALY, LLOYD WILLIAM, educator; b. Plano, Ill., Oct. 6, 1910; s. William H. and Jessie H. (Fidlar) D.; A.B., Knox Coll., 1932, Litt.D., 1955; M.A., U. Ill., 1933, Ph.D., 1936; m. Alice Bernadine Abell, Aug. 22, 1935; children—Caryl Abell (Mrs. Horton A. Johnson), Sara Sue (Mrs. Jay A. Rothenberger). Research asst. in classics U. Ill., 1936; acting prof. Greek, Kenyon Coll., 1937; mem. Am. Sch. Classical Studies in Athens, 1937-38, mem. mng. com., 1953—; mem. 4th campaign Johns Hopkins Archeol. Expdn. to Olynthus, Greece, 1938; from instr. to asso. prof. classical langs. and lit. U. Okla., 1938-47; asso. prof. classical studies U. Pa., 1947-54, prof., 1954—, Allen Meml. prof. Greek, 1958—, chmn. dept. of classical studies, 1960-67, vice dean Grad. Sch. Art and Scis., 1951-52, acting dean, 1966, dean of coll., 1952-59. Guggenheim fellow, 1959-60. Mem. Mediaeval Acad. Am., Am. Philol. Assn., Archaeol. Inst. Am., Classical Assn. Atlantic States, Pa. State Assn. Classical Tchrs., Am. Assn. U. Profs., Phi Beta Kappa, Phi Kappa Phi, Eta Sigma Phi. Author: The Altercatio Hadriani Augusti et Epicteti Philosphi (with W. Suchier), 1939; Aesop Without Morals, 1961; History of Alphabetization, 1967; Brito Metricus, 1968. Editor and author in part of Graeco-Roman articles in Thesaurus of Book Digests, 1949; asso. editor Classical Philology, 1953-55. Contbr. Realenzyklopadie der Altertumswissenschaft, Lexicon der altern Welt, Am. Illustrated Mediaeval Dictionary. Author articles learned jours. Home: 310 Morton Av Ridley Park PA 19078 Office: College Hall U Pa Philadelphia PA 19104

DALY, MAGGIE DOROTHEA (Mrs. Arthur Bazlen), columnist, lectr.; b. Castle Caufield, County Tyrone, Ireland, July 2, 1917; d. Joseph and Margaret (Kelly) Daly; student pub. schs.; m. Arthur Bazlen, Aug. 31, 1939 (dec. Dec. 1957); 1 dau., Brigid. Profl. model, Milw. and Chgo., 1945-52; fashion coordinator Chez Paree Show on radio, 1952-54; feature writer Ladies Home Jour., 1954; appeared on Home Show, TV, 1954; now lectr. on fashions to women's and men's groups; now also columnist Chgo. Today. Dir. Chgo. U.S.O.; hon. chmn. Chgo. Mental Health Assn. Mem. Adult Edn. Assn., Fashion Group of Chgo. Author: Guide to Charm, 1955; Kate Brennan, 1957. Office: Chicago Today 441 N Michigan Av Chicago IL 60611

DALY, NORMAN DAVID, painter, sculptor; b. Pitts., Aug. 9, 1911; s. James Ambrose and Rose (Owens) D.; B.F.A., U. Colo., 1937; M.F.A., Ohio State U., 1940; grad. student Inst. Fine Arts, N.Y. U., 1941; m. Helen Ogden Gebbie, Aug. 31, 1942; children—David, Nicholas. Exhbns. include Whitney Mus., Met. Mus. Art, Carnegie Inst., Phila. Acad. Art, Chgo. Art Inst., U. Ill. Annual, others; rep. permanent collections Oberlin Coll., Walker Art Mus., St. Paul, White Art Mus., Cornell U., Proctor-Munson-William Inst., Utica, Rochester Meml. Art Gallery, N.Y. State U. at Cortland, Ithaca Coll., Arnot Art Gallery, Elmira, N.Y., U. Wash., Everson Art Mus., Syracuse, N.Y., works in sound, writing, painting, sculpture and crafts; prof. art Cornell U., 1952—. Home: 110 N Quarry St Ithaca NY 14850

DALY, OWEN II, banker; b. Denver, Sept. 4, 1924; s. O. Gordon and Dorotita (O'Donnell) D.; A.B., Princeton, 1948; grad. Rutgers U. Grad. Sch. Banking, 1955; m. Marian Riggs Bailliere, Nov. 17, 1950; children—Owen III, Gordon Bailliere, Clinton Riggs, Thomas O'Donnell. With Merc. Safe Deposit & Trust Co., and predecessor, Balt., 1948-65, asst. v.p., 1954-58, v.p., 1958-63, sr. v.p., 1963-65; exec. v.p., dir. Equitable Trust Co., Balt., 1965-67, pres., dir., 1967—. Trustee Goucher Coll., Gilman Sch., Balt.; bd. dirs. Balt. A.R.C. Served to lt. USNR, 1943-46, 50-52. Mem. Balt. Met. C. of C. (treas., dir.). Clubs: Maryland, Center, Elkridge (Balt.). Home: 12 Overhill Rd Baltimore MD 21210 Office: Equitable Trust Co Calvert and Fayette Sts Baltimore MD 21203

DALY, RAYMOND E., banker. Chmn. bd. Bank Ind., N.A., Gary. Office: 575 Broadway Gary IN 46401*

DALY, RICHARD L., life ins. co. exec.; b. O'Neill, Neb., Oct. 26, 1914; s. Charles M. and Cecelia (Brenn) D.; student Creighton U., m. Dorothea Kunkel, June 10, 1939; children—Mary Kay (Mrs. John J. Graham), Donna. With No. Natural Gas Co., Omaha, 1932-34, Wachob-Bender Corp., Omaha, 1934-42, Kansas City Life Ins. Co. (Mo.), 1942-49; with United Benefit Life Ins. Co., Omaha, 1949—, v.p., treas., 1956-60, financial v.p., 1960-65, exec. v.p. finance, 1965—, also dir. Home: 9456 Jackson St Omaha NB 68114 Office: United Benefit Life Insurance Co 33d at Farnham St Omaha NB 68131

DALY, ROBERT FREDERIC, physician; b. Middletown, Ind., Apr. 11, 1908; s. James Garrett and Laura (Brakeman) D.; B.A., Wabash Coll., 1929; M.D., Ohio State U., 1937; m. Margaret Dunn, Aug. 1, 1932; children—David F., Sally (Mrs. Stephen N. CaJacob). Tchr., Alexandria (Ind.) High Sch., 1931-33; intern, resident obstetrics and gynecology Ohio State U. Hosps., Columbus, 1937-41; gen. practice medicine, Newcomerstown, O., 1941-43; practice medicine, specializing in obstetrics and gynecology, Columbus, 1943—; mem. staff Ohio State Coll. Medicine, 1943—; clin. prof. obstetrics and gynecology Ohio State U. Coll. Medicine, 1965—; chmn. obstetrics-gynecology dept. Mt. Carmel Hosp., Columbus, 1945-62. Diplomate Am. Bd. Obstetrics and Gynecology. Fellow A.C.S., Am. Coll. Obstetrics and Gynecology (a founder); mem. A.M.A., Columbus Acad. Medicine, Central Assn. Obstetrics and Gynecology, Delta Tau Delta, Nu Sigma Nu. Presbyn. Mason (Shriner, K.T.). Home: 1000 Urlin Av Columbus OH 43212

DALY, WILLIAM THOMAS, ret. air force officer; b. Eureka, Cal., Mar. 23, 1916; s. Patrick M. and Marie (Bandel) D.; student U. San Francisco, 1934-36; B.S., Humboldt State Coll., Arcata, Cal., 1936-38; M.S. in Edn., U. So. Cal., 1950; grad. Air War Coll., 1954; m. Marguerite Legarra, May 30, 1942. Flying cadet USAAF, 1941; commd. 2d lt. USAAF, 1941, advanced through grades to maj. gen. USAF, 1961; air officer Caribbean Command, 1946-48; assigned Air U., 1948-51; comdr. 316th Air Div., Rabat, Morocco, 1956; chief staff USAF Europe, 1957-60; comdr. 464th Troop Carrier Wing, also 838th Air Div., 1961-64; dep. for operations Hdqrs. 9th Air Force, 1964- 66; chief U.S. Mil. Mission to India, New Delhi, 1966-67; chief operations and intelligence Hdqrs. Allied Forces Central Europe, 1967-70. Decorated D.S.M., Legion of Merit, Air Force Commendation medal. Home: 4400 Hacienda del Sol Tucson AZ 85718

DALZELL, FRED BRIGGS, corp. exec.; b. Bklyn., Sept. 23, 1922; s. Fred Briggs and Claire (Baxter) D.; grad. Lawrenceville Sch., 1940, Amherst Coll., 1944; m. Marie Conroy, Sept. 18, 1943; children—Victoria Ann, Fred Briggs. Pres. Dalzell Towing Co. div. McAllister Bros., Inc.; dir. George W. Rogers Constrn. Corp., Carnegie-Hill 91st Street Corp.; trustee Dollar Savs. Bank N.Y. Chmn. bd. mgrs. Seamen's House, YMCA of N.Y.; sec., trustee South St. Seaport Mus.; trustee Am. Seamen's Friend Soc.; chmn. Internat. Seamen's Recreation Council. Served with USAAF, 1943-45. Mem. N.Y. Maritime Assn., St. Andrew's Soc., Pilgrims U.S. Clubs: India House, Yacht, Racquet & Tennis (N.Y.C.); Creek (Locust Valley); Nat. Golf Links (Southampton, N.Y.). Home: 15 E 91st St New York City NY 10028 Office: 17 Battery Pl New York City NY 10004

DAM, CARL PETER HENRIK, biochemist; b. Copenhagen, Denmark, Feb. 21, 1895; s. Emil and Emilie (Peterson) D.; M.S. in Chem., Poly. Inst., 1920; D.Sc. in Biochemistry. U. of Copenhagen, 1934; D.Sc. (hon.), St. Louis U., 1965; m. Inger Olsen, July 15, 1924. Came to U.S., 1940. Instr. in chemistry Sch. Agr. and Vet. Medicine, Copenhagen, 1920- 23; instr. in biochemistry U. Copenhagen, 1923, asst. prof., 1928, asso. prof., 1929-41; prof. biochemistry Poly. Inst., Copenhagen, 1941 (appointment in absentia), emeritus prof. biochemistry, 1965—; sr. research asso. in biochemistry U. Rochester (N.Y.), 1942-45; asso. mem. Rockefeller Inst., 1945-48; head biol. div. Danish Fat Research Inst., 1956-62. Recipient Christian Bohr award in physiology for discovery of vitamin K, 1939; Nobel prize in physiology and medicine (joint award), 1943: Honorary fellow Royal Society (Edinburgh); fellow Am. Inst. Nutrition; mem. Soc. Exptl. Biology and Medicine, Am. Soc. Biol. Chemistry, Danish Nutrition Soc., (pres. 1967-70), Internat. Union Nutritional Scis. (hon. pres.), Chem. Soc. and Biological Soc. (Copenhagen), Swiss Chem. Soc., Royal Danish Acad. Scis. and Letter, Danish Acad. Tech. Scis. Lectr. U.S. and Can., under auspices of Am.-Scandinavian Found., 1940-41, 49; in Copenhagen, 1946—. Contbr. many papers relating to vitamins, lipids, nutrition, blood coagulation, formation of gallstones to sci. jours. of U.S. and Europe. Address: Danmarks Tekniske Hojskole Afdeling for Biokemi og Ernaering Ostervoldgade 10 L Copenhagen Denmark 1350

DAMAZ, PAUL F., architect; b. Portugal, Nov. 8, 1917; s. Pierre L. and Maria A. (Leite) D.; B.A. architecture, Ecole Speciale d'Architecture, 1941; M. Town Planning, U. Paris, Sorbonne, 1946; m. Annie Beckard, Nov. 30, 1958. Came to U.S., 1947, naturalized, 1953. Archtl. designer UN Hdqrs., N.Y.C., 1948-51, Harrison & Abramowitz, N.Y.C., 1951-53; chief designer Cajetan Baumann, N.Y.C., 1953-61; partner Damaz & Weigel, N.Y.C., 1962—; design critic Columbia, 1953; writer, critic, lectr. maj. univs. and television. Mem. Citizens Housing and Planning Council, nat. panel arbitrators Am. Arbitration Assn. Served as capt., French Army, 1941-45. Mem. A.I.A., French Ordre des Architectes, Archtl. League N.Y. (past v.p.; Arnold W. Brunner award 1958), Municipal Arts Soc., French-Am. Soc. Author: Art in European Architecture, 1956, Art in Latin American Architecture, 1962. Home: 302 E 88th St New York City NY 10028 Office: 1010 3d Av New York City NY 10022

D'AMBOISE, JACQUES JOSEPH, dancer, choreographer; b. Dedham, Mass., July 28, 1934; s. Andrew Ahearn and Georgette d'Amboise; m. Carolyn George, Jan. 1, 1956; children—George Jacques, Christopher R.; Charlotte Lorraine and Catherine Liza (twins). Mem. N.Y. City Ballet Co., 1949—; motion pictures include Seven Brides for Seven Brothers, Carousel, The Best Things in Life are Free; Broadway prodn. Shinbone Alley. Office: care N Y City Ballet 131 W 55th St New York City NY 10019

DAME, LAWRENCE, author, art critic; b. Portland, Me., July 2, 1898; s. Edward Lawrence and Katherine (Gunn) D.; ed. Harvard, Ecole des Hautes Etudes Sociales (Paris), Univ. of Grenoble, Univ. of Toulouse (France), Instituto de Burgos (Spain), Boston U.; m. Rachel Wells, Sept. 25, 1958. Editorial staffs, 1919-39; explored Yucatan and Quintana Roo, 1940-41; relief worker Unitarian Service Com., Portugal, 1941; art editor and special writer Boston Herald-Traveler, 1940-48; staff critic Art Digest, (London), 1950-53; with Turkish Times, Istanbul, il Mattino d'Italia Centrale, Florence, and Rome Daily Am., 1952-53; asso. editor Nantucket (Mass.) Inquirer and Mirror, 1953-54; art, books and theatre editor Sarasota (Fla.) Herald-Tribune, 1954-61; with Social Pictorial, Palm Beach, Fla., 1961—; dir. Harvard U. News Office, 1943-45, 46-47. Served arty., France, 1917-18. Decorated by French and Portuguese govts. for war work, 1941. Mem. S.A.R., Soc. Colonial Wars, Wine and Food Soc. of Boston (gov.), Wine and Food Soc. of Palm Beach (pres.), Harvard Musical Assn., Sarasota Literary Forum (pres.). Clubs: Vet. Motor Car of Am., Rolls-Royce Owners, Overseas Press (New York), Harvard (Palm Beach); Pacific, Wharf Rat (Nantucket Island, Mass.). Author: New England Comes Back, 1940, Yucatan, 1941; Maya Mission, 1967; Backabush Jamaica; co-author: Boston Murders, 1948. Contbr. articles to mags. Cycling and Wine authority. Home: Horse Guards Plantation Maidstone PO Jamaica West Indies Office: PO Box 2392 Palm Beach FL 33480 ☆

DAMES, CHARLOTTE ANN, educator, chemist; b. St. Louis, May 4, 1916; d. Alphonse Ferdinand and Charlotte Ann (Lynch) Dames; B.A., Duchense Coll., Omaha, 1940; M.S., Cath. U. Am., 1949; Ph.D., Stanford, 1954. Joined Order of Religious of Sacred Heart, 1935; tchr. elementary and secondary schs., 1938-45; instr. chemistry San Francisco Coll. Women, 1945-47; mem. faculty Barat Coll., Lake Forest, Ill., 1952—, prof. chemistry, 1957—, chmn. dept., 1960—; tchr. Digby Stuart Coll., London, Eng., 1969-70. Chem. Soc., Am. Phys. Soc., A.A.A.S., Am. Assn. U. Profs., Sigma Xi, Iota Sigma Pi. Address: Barat Coll Lake Forest IL 60045

DAMIAN, HORIA, artist; b. Bucharest, 1922. Worked in studio of Andre Lhote, then Fernanna Leger; abstract style, 1949, but returned to symbolists; one- man exhbns. Galerie Arnaud and Galerie Stadler (both Paris). Address: 8 Rue Pierre Curie Paris 5e, Frânce.*

DAMIANTO, ROBERTO, Jr. mfg. exec.; b. Lima, O., Apr. 1, 1932; B.S., U. San Francisco, 1954; M.S., Stanford University, 1956; m. Rosemarie Lois Brown, May 15, 1955; 1 son, Anthony Robinson. Sales rep. Ames-Brockton Fabricated Products, Akron, O., 1956-58, sales mgr. Coshocton, Ohio, 1959-61, gen. manager plant, 1961-68, v.p. sales, 1968--. Instr. bus. Coshocton Jr. College, 1968-69. Secretary Coshocton YMCA, 1960-61; active Boy Scouts of America. Named Man of Year, Coshocton Junior Chamber of Commerce, 1968. Mem. Coshocton C. of C. (vice president 1967-68, pres. 1969-70), English Speaking Union, Coshocton Sertoma Club, Nat. Assn. Mfrs., Sales Executives Institute, Phi Beta Kappa, Sigma Chi, Phi Mu. Democrat. Mem. Christian Ch. (lay leader). Mason (32, Shriner). Clubs: Coshocton Country, Coshocton City, Running Deer Country. Home: 2d Av Coshocton OH Office: 3d Av Coshocton OH

DAMKROGER, STANLEY FRANCIS, communications co. exec.; b. Sacramento, Feb. 22, 1907; s. John Wesley and Elizabeth (Mangner) D.; student St. Mary's Coll., Cal., 1923-26; m. Irene F. Marschk, Oct. 6, 1934. Salesman Pacific Tel. & Tel. Co., San Francisco, 1928- 30, sales mgr., Bakersfield, Cal., 1930-35, Stockton, Cal., 1935-38, div. sales mgr., 1938-46, gen. sales mgr., San Francisco, 1946-53, gen. comml. mgr., Seattle, 1953-57; asst. v.p. comml. Am. Tel. & Tel. Co., N.Y.C., 1957-59, asst. v.p. marketing, 1959-61, dir. sales operations, 1961—. Served to lt., USNR, 1942-45. Mem. Sales and Marketing Execs. Internat. (pres.). Home: 201 E 62d St New York City NY 10021 Office: 195 Broadway New York City NY 10007

DAMMANN, RICHARD WEIL, lawyer; b. N.Y.C., Oct. 23, 1911; s. Milton and Reta (Weil) D.; A.B., Princeton, 1932; LL.B., Harvard, 1935; m. Marjorie Spiegel, Aug. 22, 1935; children—Deborah, Pamela, Penelope. Admitted to N.Y. bar, 1935, since practiced in N.Y.C.; partner law firm Dammann & Heming, 1935—. Chmn. bd. U.S. Rubber Reclaiming Co., Inc. Vicksburg; dir. Philip Morris Co., N.Y.C. Home: Kirby Lane Rye NY 10580 Office: 380 Madison Av New York City NY 10017

DAMMIN, GUSTAVE JOHN, med. educator; b. N.Y.C., Sept. 17, 1911; s. Gustave Frank and Anna Barbara (Anselm) D.; A.B., Cornell U., 1934, M.D., 1938; certificate in trop. medicine, U. Havana, 1937; M.A. (hon.), Harvard, 1953; m. Anita Coffin, July 19, 1941; childrenSusan, Tristram, Abigail. House staff mem. Johns Hopkins Hosp., 1939-40; house staff Peter Bent Brigham Hosp., Boston, 1940-41, pathologist in chief, 1952—; adv. med. bd. Leonard Wood Meml., 1969—, instr. Columbia Coll. Phys. and Surg., 1941; prof. pathology, chmn. dept. Wash. U. Med. Sch. 1946-52; prof. pathology, med. sch. Harvard, 1952-62, Elsie T. Friedman prof. pathology, 1962—; Niles lectr. Cornell Med. Coll., 1953; Phi Delta Epsilon lectr. Yale Sch. Medicine, 1956, I.W. Held lectr. Beth Israel Hosp., N.Y.C., 1963; Wadsworth lectr. N.Y. Lab Soc., Syracuse, 1970; cons. to surgeon gen. Dept. of Army, USPHS; nat. cons. global preventive medicine and epidemiology to surgeon gen. USAF: lab. cons. OCDM, 1950-60; pres. Armed Forces Epidemiol. Bd., 1960—; sci. adv. bd. Armed Forces Inst. Pathology, 1961-; WHO expert adv. panel on enteric diseases, chmn. com., 1963—; bd. dirs. Gorgas Meml. Inst., 1967—; nat. cons. to surgeon gen. USAF, 1968. Mem. Cholera adv. com. NIH, 1965—. Served from 1st lt. to lt. col. M.C., AUS, 1941-46; dir. labs. div. Office Surgeon Gen., 1945-46; now col. Res. Decorated Legion of Merit. Diplomate Am. Bd. Pathology, Nat. Bd. Med. Examiners. Mem. N.Y. Acad. Scis., Am. Soc. Clin. Investigation, Am. Assn. Pathologists and Bacteriologists. Internat. Acad. Pathology (exec. council), A.M.A. (vice chmn. sect. pathology and physiology), Transplantation Soc., Am. Soc. Tropical Medicine and Hygiene, Am. Soc. Exptl. Pathology, Assn. Am. Physicians, NIH (tropical medicine and parasitology study sect.), Soc. Med. Cons. to the Armed Forces (pres. 1963), Central Soc. Clin. Research, Res. Officers Assn., Assn. U.S. Army, Japanese-Am. Soc. Pathologists, Assn. Mexican Pathologists, Korean Med. Assn., 38th Parallel Med. Soc. Korea, Infectious Diseases Soc. Am. Sigma Xi, Alpha Omega Alpha. Editorial com. Ann. Rev. Medicine, 1957-60. Editorial bd. Circulation Research, Jour. Infectious Diseases, editorial com. Human Pathology, 1969—. Home: 721 Huntington Av Boston MA 02115

DAMON, EDWARD KENT, office equipment co. exec.; b. Ft. Dodge, Ia., Dec. 5, 1918; s. Edward Orne and Georgia (Mason) D.; B.A., Amherst Coll., 1940; M.B.A., Harvard, 1942; m. Evelyn Wilcox Waddell, Oct. 4, 1940; children—Edward Kent, Bradley Mason, Kathleen Elizabeth, Sally Georgia. Chief accountant Tobin Packing Co., Fort Dodge, 1946-49; asst. to controller Xerox Corp., Rochester, N.Y., 1949-52, asst. treas., 1952-53, treas., sec., 1953-60, v.p., treas., sec., 1960—; dir. Marine Midland Trust Co., Bausch & Lomb, Inc.; chmn. bd. Schlegel Mfg. Co.; trustees Community Savs. Bank. Bd. dirs. Rochester Hosp. Service, Convalescent Hosp. For Children; trustee Monroe Community Coll., Rochester Center for Govtl. and Community Relations, Inc., Rochester Inst. Tech.; mem. corp. Community Chest. Served to lt. USNR, 1942-46. Republican. Episcopalian. Clubs: Rochester Country; Genesee Valley; Monroe Golf. Home: 65 Country Club Dr Rochester NY 14618 Office: Xerox Sq Rochester NY 14603

DAMON, MASON ORNE, lawyer; b. Ft. Dodge, Ia., Sept. 7, 1905; s. Edward Orne and Georgia Anna (Mason) D.; A.B., Amherst Coll., 1926; J.D. Harvard, 1929; m. Harriet Louise Provost, June 16, 1930; childrenMason Orne (dec.), Laura Provost (Mrs. G. Thomas Martin). Admitted to N.Y. bar, 1930, since practiced in Buffalo; partner firm Ohlin, Damon, Morey, Sawyer & Moot, and predecessor, 1940—; with procurement legal div. Navy Dept., 1943- 46, gen. counsel Bur. Ships, 1945-46; part-time prof. U. Buffalo Law Sch., 1942-43. Sec. Bell Aircraft Corp., 1957-60, Bell Aerospace Corp., 1960-70; dir. Bank of N.Y. C., Inc., Niagara Frontier Bank N.Y. Pres. bd. dirs. Buffalo Pub. Library, 1949-54; trustee Buffalo and Erie County Pub. Library, 1954—, vice chmn., 1954-55, chmn. 1956- 57, 66-67; trustee Park Sch., Buffalo, 1947-, v.p., 1948-55, pres., 1955-57; bd. dirs. Internat. Inst. Buffalo, 1962—, pres., 1969-70. Served to lt. comdr. USNR, 1943-45. Mem. Phi Beta Kappa, Delta Sigma Rho, Beta Theta Phi. Clubs: Buffalo Midday (pres. 1954) (Buffalo); Cherry Hill (Ridgeway, Ont., Can.). Home: 127 Chapin Pkwy Buffalo NY 14209 Office: Liberty Bank Bldg Buffalo, NY 14202.

DAMON, PAUL EDWARD, educator; b. Brooklawn, N.J., Mar. 12, 1921; s. Lester Rowley and Ellen (Keigan) D.; B.S., Bucknell U., 1943; M.S., U. Mo., 1949; Ph.D., Columbia, 1957; m. Mary Janet Winter, Mar. 29, 1947; children—Timothy Winter, John Edward. Research asso. U. Ark., 1949, asst. prof. geology, 1950-54; research asso. Columbia, 1954-57; asso. prof. U. Ariz., 1957-62, prof., 1962—; cons. Isotopes, Inc., Westwood, N.J., 1957; chief scientist lab. isotope geochemistry, U. Ariz., 1958—. Mem. N.A.A.C.P., 1950—, Am. Civil Liberties Union, 1957—, UN Assn., 1960—, Sierra Club, 1970—. Chmn. Ariz. New Party, 1970. Served to lt. USNR, 1943-46. Recipient Research Corp. Unrestricted Venture grant, 1960. Fellow A.A.A.S., Geol. Soc. Am., Ariz. Acad. Sci.; mem. Am. Assn. U. Profs., Am. Geol. Union, Geochemical Soc., Ariz. Geol. Soc., N.M. Geol. Soc., Sigma Xi. Mem. Soc. Friends. Contbr. profl. jours. Home: 2321 E Hawthorne St Tucson AZ 85719

DAMON, ROBERT JOHN CUNNINGHAM, mfg. pumps and meters; b. Chgo., June 20, 1930; s. Robert Hosken and Margarite (Cunningham) D.; B.A., Dartmouth, 1951; LL.B., U. Wis., 1954; m. Virginia Lee Myers, July 14, 1951; children—Debra, Jamie, Heidi, Robert. Admitted to Ill. bar, 1954, and practiced in Chgo. until 1957; pres. Johnson Fare Box Co., Chgo., 1958-60, dir., 1960; exec. v.p. Bowser, Inc., Chicago, Ill., 1960-61, former pres., chief exec. officer; dir. Bowser Internat., Inc., S. F. Bowser Co., Ltd., Briggs Filtration Co., Gudeman Co., Nat. Sci. Labs., Inc. Mem. Young Pres. Orgn., Phi Delta Theta, Phi Delta Phi. Club: Tavern (Chgo.). Home: 2323 Pebble Fork Lane Northfield IL 60093

DAMON, ROGER CONANT, banker; b. Fitchburg, Mass., Aug. 4, 1906; s. Isaac Newton and Marion (Conant) D.; A.B., Yale, 1929; postgrad. Stonier Grad. Sch. Banking Rutgers U., 1942; LL.D., Northeastern U., 1971; m. Ruth T. Hawley, Aug. 15, 1931; 1 dau. Martha Hawley (Mrs. Andrew H. Ward, Jr.). Asst. cashier First Nat. Bank Boston, 1936-41, asst. v.p., 1941-43, v.p., 1943-52, sr. v.p., 1952-59, pres., chmn. exec. com., 1959-66, chmn. bd., chief exec.

officer, 1966—, also dir.; dir. incorporator Firstbank Financial Corp.; chmn. First Capital Corp. Boston; dir. Bank Boston Trust Co. (Bahamas) Ltd., Liberty Mut. Ins. Co., Boston Overseas Financial Corp., Bank of Boston Internat., Raytheon Co., The Mitre Corp., Boston Edison Co., New Eng. Mut. Life Ins. Co., Eastern Air Lines, Inc., Mem. Nat. Adv. Com. on Banking Policies and Practices. Bd. dirs. Mass. Bay United Fund; trustee Fessenden Sch., trustee Childrens Hosp. Med. Center, Boston; mem. corp. Northeastern U., Mus. Sci. Mem. Am. Inst. Banking. Clubs: Commercial, Yale (pres. 1951-52), Union (Boston); Country (Brookline); Acoaxet (Westport Harbor, Mass.); Algonquin. Home: 172 Beacon St Boston MA 02116 Office: 67 Milk St Boston MA 02110

DAMONE, VIC, (Vito Farinola), singer, actor; b. Bklyn., June 12, 1928; m. Pier Angeli, 1954; l son, Perry Rocco Luigi; m. second, Judy Rawlins, Nov. 1963; one dau. Appeared as singer Godfrey Talent Scout show, 1945; night club debut La Martinique, N.Y.C.; motion pictures include Rich, Young and Pretty, 1951; Athena, 1954; Hit the Deck, 1955; Kismet, 1955; Hell to Eternity; star TV show Vic Damone Show, 1958, Lively Ones, 1962. Address: 9966 St Ives Dr Hollywood CA 90069*

DAMORA, ROBERT MATTHEW, architect; b. N.Y.C., Mar. 2, 1912; s. Matthew Robert and Giacinta (Volonnino) d'Amora; student dept. architecture N.Y. U., evenings, 1932- 41; B.Arch., Yale, 1953; m. Sirkka Heikkinen, Feb. 27, 1950; children—Jesa Sirkka, Matthew Robert. Archtl. journalist-photographer, designer, 1935—; practice architecture, 1955—; dir. Seeds for Architecture program Universal Atlas Cements div. U.S. Steel Corp., 1956- 58; asso. prof. architecture, design critic Columbia U., 1963-64. Served to lt. (j.g.), spl. devices div. Bur. Research and Invention, USNR, 1943- 46. Recipient 1st prize Portland Cement Assn. Horizon Homes, 1962; Record House of Year, Archtl. Record, 1962; Merit award A.I.A./House & Home, 1962; 1st prize A.I.A. Conv. Products Exhibit, 1963, 64; Gold medal archtl. photography, A.I.A., 1965, Honor award in architecture, 1965. Guggenheim fellow in archtl. research, 1966-67. Registered architect N.Y., Conn., Mass., Vt., Fla. Mem. A.I.A. (nat. and local coms.), Archtl. Photographers Assn. (pres. 1947-49). Prin. works include prefabricated interchangeable concrete components system for tract housing, Cape Cod, Mass., 1962; prefabricated custom house constructed 3 reduplicated concrete components, Ft. Lauderdale, Fla., 1967; Low-cost minimal housing Community Nassau, Bahamas, 1968; exhibited in Visionary Architecture show Mus. Modern Art, 1960. Work featured on various TV programs, in numerous profl. jours. and newspapers. Home: Pound Ridge Rd Bedford NY 10506

D'AMOUR, ROBERT ARTHUR, mfg. co. exec.; b. Escanaba, Mich., Aug. 15, 1923; s. Elder Arthur and Marian (Lillie) D'A.; B.S. in Mech. Engring., Mich. Tech. U., 1948; m. Ruby Kolich, Sept. 4, 1948; children—Michael, Marc, John, Mary, Joan, Martin, Suzan, Catherine. With Cummins Engine Co., 1948-52; with Waukesha Motor Co. (Wis.), 1952—, sr. v.p. marketing, 1969-70, pres., 1970—. Served with USNR, 1942-46. Mem. Soc. Automotive Engrs., Am. Gas Assn. (Hall of Fame citation 1964), Engine Mfrs. Assn., Materials Handling Inst., Gas Appliance Mfrs. Assn. Clubs: University (Milw.); Merrill Hills Country (Waukesha). Home: Beggs Mainland Dr Oconomowoc WI 53066 Office: 1000 W St Paul Av Waukesha WI 53186

DAMOUR, WILLIAM H., distilling co. exec.; b. Clinton, Ia., 1906; ed. Harvard Sch. Bus. Adminstrn., 1929. Treas., dir. Am. Distilling Co. Home: 169 Oak Cliff Ct Peoria IL 61614 Office: 245 Park Av New York City NY 10003*

DAMPEER, JOHN LYELL, lawyer; b. Cleve., June 3, 1916; s. James W. and Felicia (Gressitt) D.; S.B., Harvard, 1938, LL.B., 1942; student New Coll., Oxford (Eng.) U., 1938-39; m. Lucie Augustin Kennerdell, June 30, 1950; children—Lyell B., David K., G. Geoffrey. Admitted to Ohio bar, 1946, since practiced in Cleve.; partner firm Thompson, Hine and Flory, 1955—. Sec., dir. Fisher Foods, Inc., Van Dorn Co.; dir. J.M. Smucker Co. Trustee Family Assn. Cleve., 1951-70. Henry fellow, 1938-39. Mem. Am., Ohio (chmn. corp. law com. 1959-62), Cleve. (exec. com. 1958-61) bar assns. Republican. Baptist. Clubs: Union, Kirtland Country (Cleve.). Home: 2465 Marlboro Rd Cleveland Heights OH 44118 Office: Nat City Bank Bldg Cleveland OH 44114

DAMPIER, JOSEPH HENRY, clergyman, educator; b. Guelph, Ont. Can., Mar. 7, 1908; s. Robert Alexander and Elizabeth (Hindely) D.; came to U.S., 1925, naturalized, 1940; A.B., Cin. Bible Sem, 1931; Ed.M., U. Pitts., 1941; D.D., Atlanta Christian Coll., 1952; LL. D., Johnson Bible Coll., 1957; m. Ione Margaret Chandler, 1928 (dec. 1960); 1 dau., Phyllis (Mrs. Harry E. Fontaine); m. 2d, Mildred Feagans, 1963. Pastor, Christian Church, Alfordsville, Ind. and Antioch, Ind., 1927-28, Lawrenceburg, Ind., 1929-34, First Christian Ch., McKeesport, Pa., 1934- 41, First Ch., Johnson City, Tenn., 1941-58; provost Milligan Coll. (Tenn.), 1958-65, dean Emmanuel Sch. of Religion, 1965-69, prof. Christian ministries, 1969—, Pres. North Am. Christian Conv., 1950-51; mem. Commn. of Restudy, Disciples of Christ; trustee East Tenn. Christian Home, Milligan Coll., Atlanta Christian Coll. Mem. Am. Acad. Religion, Soc. Bibl. Lit. Mason (32, K.T.), Kiwanian (past pres.). Author: Workbook on Christian Doctrine, 1943, Mem. publs. com. Standard Pub. Contbr. to religious mags. Address: Box 12 Milligan College TN 37682

DANA, RICHARD HENRY, univ. ofcl.; b. N.Y.C., Mar. 5, 1912; s. Richard Henry and Ethel Nathalie (Smith) D.; grad. cum laude, Phillips Exeter Acad., 1930; A.B. cum laude, Harvard, 1934; m. Nina Katharine Montgomery, Nov. 20, 1948; children—Richard Henry, Cornelia Marshall, Nathalie Pepperell. Engaged in promotion, also as acting sales mgr. Alfred A. Knopf, 1935-39; founder, pres. Music Press, Inc., 1939-49; promotion mgr. J.B. Lippincott Co., Phila., 1950-52, Ballantine Books, 1952-54; asst. to David Rockefeller in personal and philanthropic activities, 1955-69; bus. mgr. publs. Asso. Council of the Arts, N.Y.C., 1970; spl. asst. to sec. Rockefeller U., N.Y.C., 1970—. Pres. Diller Quaile Sch. Music, N.Y.C., 1966—. Bd. mgrs. Seamen's Ch. Inst., 1961—; bd. dirs. Contemporary Music Soc., 1960—. Served to 1st lt. AUS, 1942-45: ETO. Club: Century (N.Y.C.). Home: 180 E 95th St New York City NY 10028 Office: Rockefeller Univ New York City NY 10021

DANAHER, JOHN ANTHONY, judge; b. Meriden, Conn., Jan. 9, 1899; s. Cornelius J. and Ellen (Ryan) D.; A.B., Yale, 1920; postgrad. Yale Law Sch., 1922; m. Dorothy King, Feb. 3, 1921; children—John A., Robert Cornelius, Jeanne. Law clk. White & Case, N.Y.C., 1921-22; admitted to Conn. bar, 1922, practiced Hartford, Conn., and Washington, 1922-53; asst. U.S. atty., 1922- 34; sec. State Conn., 1933-35; U.S. senator, 1938-45; counsel Rep. Senatorial Com., 1946-53; U.S. circuit judge U.S. Court of Appeals, Washington, 1953-69; sr. U.S. circuit judge, Hartford, Conn., 1969—. Del. Rep. Nat. Conv., 1944, Congl. aide, Rep. Nat. Com., 1945-46; exec. dir. U.S. Senatorial Campaign, 1948. Mem. Pres.'s Commn. Internal Security and Individual Rights, 1951; mem. Pres.'s Conf. Adminstrv. Procedure, 1953-54; dir. div. spl. activities Eisenhower campaign, 1952. Served as 2d lt. F.A., U.S. Army, 1918. Mem. D.C., Conn., Hartford County bar assns., Beta Theta Pi, Elihu. Republican. Roman Catholic. Clubs: Hartford (Conn.); Metropolitan (Washington). Home: 31 Wyndwood Rd West Hartford CT 06107 Office: Fed Bldg Hartford CT 06103

DANBY, JOHN BLENCH, editor; b. North Riding, Yorkshire, Eng., June 3, 1905; s. John and Edith A. (Smith) D.; student pub. schs., Eng., also Del., Pa.; m. Helen Agens Boyce, June 14, 1941; children—David Boyce, Deborah Boyce. News editor Wilmington (Del.) Jour. Every Evening, 1934-42; asst. telegraph news editor N.Y. Herald Tribune, 1942-45; successively asst. articles editor, asso. editor, editor Liberty mag., N.Y.C., 1945-50; exec. editor Redbook mag., N.Y.C., 1950-60; managing editor Good Housekeeping magazine, N.Y.C., from 1960, now exec. editor. Mem. President's Committee on Employment of the Handicapped. Mem. ACLU Clubs: National Press (Washington); Overseas Press (N.Y.C.). Home: 11-15 12th Fair Lawn NJ 07410 Office: 959 8th Av New York City NY 10019

DANCE, FRANCIS ESBURN XAVIER, educator; b. Bklyn., Nov. 9, 1929; s. Clifton Louis and Catherine (Tester) D.; B.S., Fordham U., 1951; M.A., Northwestern U., 1953, Ph.D., 1959; m. Nora Alice Rush, May 1, 1954; children-Clifton Louis III, Charles Daniel, Alison Catherine, Andrea Frances, Frances Sue, Brandan Rush. Instr. speech Bklyn. Adult Labor Schs., 1951; instr. humanities, coordinator radio and TV, U. Ill.-Chgo., 1953-54; instr. Univ. Coll., U. Chgo., 1958; asst. prof. St. Joseph's (Ind.) Coll., 1958-60; asst. prof., then asso. prof. U. Kan., 1960-63; mem. faculty U. Wis.-Milw., 1963—, prof. communication, 1970—, dir. Speech Center, 1963-70; partner Helix Press, Shorewood, Wis., 1970—; cons. in field. Bd. dirs. Milw. Mental Health Assn., 1966-67. Served to 2d lt. AUS, 1954-56. Knapp Univ. scholar in communication, 1967-68; recipient Outstanding Prof. award Standard Oil Found., 1967. Mem. Internat. Communication Assn. (pres. 1967), Psi Upsilon. Author: The Citizen Speaks, 1962; (with Harold P. Zelko) Business and Professional Speech Communication, 1965; Human Communication Theory, 1967; (with Carl E. Larson) Perspectives on Communication, 1970; also articles. Editor Jour. Communication, 1962-64, Speech Tchr., 1970-72; adv. bd. Jour. Black Studies; editorial bd. Jour. Psycholinguistic Research. Home: 2619 E Wood Pl Shorwood WI 53211 Office: Dept Communication Univ Wis Milwaukee WI 53201

DANCE, MAURICE EUGENE, coll. v.p.; b. Bismarck, N.D., Jan. 14, 1923; s. Alvin Cecil and Jennie (Brown) D.; B.A., U. Wash., 1947; M.S., U. Wis., 1949. Ph.D., 1953; children—Muriel, Maurice C., Marcia, Mark, Michelle, Michael, Myles, Jennifer; m. 2d, Anita Ruth Bell, Apr. 10, 1965. Asst. prof. econs. Los Angeles State Coll., 1950-56; with San Fernando Valley State Coll., Northridge, Cal., 1956-69, prof. econs., 1956-69, chmn. dept. 1956-64, asst. to v.p. for acad. affairs, 1964-65, dean Sch. of Letters and Scis., 1965-69; v.p. acad. affairs Cal. State Coll., Hayward, 1969—. Econs. cons. Mem. Am. Econs. Assn., Indsl. Relations Research Assn., Am. Assn. U. Profs. Home: 5341 Greenridge Rd Castro Valley CA 94546

DANCE, WALTER DAVID, mfg. co. exec.; b. Amherst, N.S., Can., May 13, 1917; s. Walter H. and Gertrude I. (Jones) D.; came to U.S., 1923, naturalized, 1942; A.B., Dartmouth, 1940; m. Jane P. Clune, Mar. 31, 1942; children—Susan P., Peter D., Robert A., Richard M. With Gen. Electric Co., 1948—, gen. mgr. Hotpoint div., 1962-64, v.p., 1964—, gen. mgr. maj. appliance and Hotpoint div., exec. appliance and TV group, 1968, exec. TV group, 1970, sr. v.p. corporate exec. staff, 1970—; dir. Gen. Electric Co. Served with AUS, 1941-45. Mem. Assn. Home Appliance Mfrs. (dir.), Ky. (dir.), Louisville (dir.) chambers commerce. Home: 940 Forest Av Rye NY 10580 Office: 570 Lexington Av New York City NY 10022

DANCO, SUZANNE, soprano; b. Brussels, Belgium, Jan. 22, 1911; studied Brussels Conservatory. Appeared in Paris, London, other European cities; Am. debut, 1950. Address: care London Records Inc 51 W 25th St New York City NY 10001*

D'ANDREA, ALBERT PHILIP, artist, educator; b. Benevento, Italy, Oct. 27, 1897; s. Gregory and Emilia (Mainella) d'A.; brought to U.S., 1901, naturalized, 1911; A.B., Coll. City N.Y., 1918; postgrad. U. Rome, 1922; m. Rose Castaldo, July 5, 1924; children—Gilbert, Philip. Instr. art Townsend Harris High Sch., 1918-35; asst. prof. Coll. City N.Y., 1935-40, asso. prof., 1940-48, prof., chmn. dept. art, 1948-68, prof. emeritus Coll. City N.Y., 1968, dir. planning and design of coll., 1945-67. Portraiture includes Bernard M. Baruch, 1954 (bronze bas-reliefs), Dr. W. B. Guthrie, 1939, Dean E. R. Mosher, 1946 (oil paintings); exhibited N.A.D., 1944, Nat. Sculpture Soc. Ann., 1951—, Audubon Artists Annual, 1953- -; represented collections Library of Congress, Mus. City N.Y., N.Y. Hist. Soc., Smithsonian Instn., Hyde Park Meml. Library, Bibliotheque Nationale, Bibiloteca Apostolica Vaticana, Jewish Mus., N.Y.C., Nat. Portrait Gallery, Washington. Designer medals, including Bernard M. Baruch medal, 1954, Jones E. Salk medal, 1955, George William Eggers medal, 1959, Edison award, 1959, Buell G. Gallagher Medallion, 1961, Dr. Robert Hofstadter medal, 1962, James K. Hackett medal, 1964, Grover Cleveland medal, Andreas Vesalius, 1967, Gen. Douglas MacArthur medal, Martin Luther King medal, 1968, Phi Beta Kappa Centennial medal, 1967, Jane Addams Commemorative medal, 1969, David B. Steinman medal Coll. City N.Y. Coll. Engring., Phillis Wheatley medal Am. Negro Commemorative Soc., 1970, others. Recipient Alumni Service medal Coll. City N.Y., 1933, also Townsend Harris medal Engrs. of France, 1954; hon. academician Academia di Belle Arti, Perugia, 1952. Benjamin Franklin fellow Royal Soc. Arts (London); mem. Am. Artists Profl. League, Soc. Archtl. Historians, Audubon Artists, Am. Assn. U. Profs., Nat. Sculpture Soc. (Lindsey Morris prize 1963), Phi Beta Kappa (chpt. pres. 1965). Roman Catholic. Inventor transichrome process. Home and studio: 2121 Bay Av Brooklyn NY 11210

DANDRIDGE, FRANK, photographer; b. Bklyn., Jan. 31, 1938; s. Franklin and Mercedes (Shinmery) D.; student City Coll. N.Y.; m. Gloria St. Clair Hayes, Aug. 25, 1964; children—Donna Young, Bernard Edward Young, Tamara Paulette Richardson. Staff photographer Citizen Call, Harlem, N.Y.C., 1961-62; magazine assignments for pageant, 1962, Good Housekeeping, 1962, Life, 1963; essay for Look mag. Two Faces of Harlem (Art Dirs. award), 1964; photographer Sat. Eve. Post, 1964—; assignments for nat. mags., German and Canadian mags., also syndicates, 1964—; spl. photographer for Paramount, Warner Bros. pictures. Served with USMCR, 1952-55. Mem. Am. Soc. Mag. Photographers. Office: care Lubell 103 Park Av New York City NY 10003 also 7 E 14th St New York City NY 10003

DANDURAND, JAMES L., banker. Pres., dir. Bank Ind., N.A. Office: 575 Broadway Gary IN 46401*

DANDY, JOHN PERCY, bus. exec.; b. Morrisburg, Ont., May 19, 1902; s. William Percy and Anna Bethune (Parker) D.; student Harbord Collegiate, 1913-19; B.A., U. Toronto, 1923; Fellow Acturarial Soc., Am. Inst. Actuaries, 1927; m. Dorothy Camilla Davidson, July 30, 1925; children—William Bethune, Thomas Gordon. Came to U.S., 1942, naturalized, 1948. Asst. actuary Confederation Life Assn., Toronto, Can., 1930-35; asso. actuary Nat. Life Assurance Co. Can., 1935-37, actuary, 1937-42; asst. actuary Occidental Life Ins. Co. Cal., 1942-45, asso. actuary, 1945-46, actuary, 1946-48, v.p., 1948-66, sr. v.p., 1966-67; cons. actuary, 1967—. Fellow Soc. Actuaries. Club: Oakmont Country. Home and office: 844 Chehalem Rd La Canada CA 91011

DANE, BARBARA, singer, guitarist; b. Detroit, May, 12, 1927; classical voice tng., 1940- 45; student piano, self taught of guitar; m. Byron Menendez; three children. Singer folk songs on radio in San Francisco own series, 1st TV folk music show, Folksville USA; night club debut with Turk Murphy, 1956; appeared Newport Jazz Festival, other festivals, 1958-59; with Jack Teagarden combo Detroit Jazz Festival, 1959. Timex TV Jazz Spectacular, 1959, also with Louis Armstrong; recording artist for Dot, Barbary Coast records. Address: 2144 Rockledge Rd Hollywood CA 90028*

DANE, EDWARD, business exec.; b. Brookline, Mass.,; grad. Harvard, 1929; hon. chmn., dir. dir. Brookline Trust Co.; dir. John Hancock Mut. Life Ins. Co., Boston. Trustee New Eng. Deaconess Hosp., Belknap Coll., Centre Harbor, N.H. Home: Hearthstone Center Harbor NH 03226

DANE, MAXWELL, former advt. exec.; b. Cin., June 7, 1906; s. Abraham and Sophie (Sall) D.; m. Belle Sloan, Apr. 4, 1933; 1 son, Henry James. Advt. dept. Stern Bros., N.Y.C., 1928-32; retail promotion mgr. N.Y. Jour., 1933-36; account exec. Dorland Internat., 1937-39; advt. promotion mgr. Look mag., 1939-41; sales promotion mgr., radio sta. WMCA, 1941-44; pres. Maxwell Dane, Inc., advt., N.Y.C. 1944-49; exec. v.p., sec.-treas., dir. Doyle Dane Bernbach, Inc., N.Y.C., 1949-71, chmn. exec. com., 1969-71. Mem. publ. com. Commentary mag.; chmn. advt. and pub. div. United Jewish Appeal. Trustee Citizens' Budget Commn., N.Y.C.; trustee Haverford Coll., 1967—. Mem. N.Y. Civil Liberties Union (vice chmn. 1960-66, dir., treas. 1966—), Anti-Defamation League (chmn. nat. program com. 1969—), Fedn. Jewish Philanthropies (trustee). Jewish religion. Clubs: Harmonie, City Athletic, City (N.Y.C.); Old Oaks Country (Purchase, N.Y.). Home: 650 Park Av New York City NY 10021 Office: 20 W 43d St New York City NY 10036

DANE, NATHAN, II, educator; b. Lexington, Mass., May 24, 1916; s. Francis Smith and Annie (Edmands) D.; A.B., Bowdoin Coll., 1937; M.A., U. Ill., 1939, Ph.D., 1941; m. Caroline Maxine Anderson, Apr. 2, 1942; children—Nathan III, Caroline Anderson, Joseph Anderson. Instr. Latin, Oberlin Coll., 1941- 42; mem. faculty Bowdoin Coll., 1946—, prof. classics, 1954, Winkley prof. Latin, 1963—. Served with AUS, 1942-46. Mem. Am. Philol. Assn., New Eng. Classical Assn. (pres. 1963-64), Phi Beta Kappa, Psi Upsilon. Author: Introduction to Languages and Literatures of Greece and Rome, 1952. Tide Mill Cove Rd South Harpswell ME 04079 Office: Bowdoin Coll Brunswick ME 04011

DANENBARGER, WILLIAM FOWLER, radio sta. exec., univ. regent; b. Concordia, Kan., Apr. 7, 1910; s. William Henry and Lola (Fowler) D.; A.B., U. Kan., 1933; m. Winifred Wright, Mar. 30, 1934; children—William Wright, John K. Pres., gen. mgr. radio sta. KNCK, Concordia, 1954—. 0011970—; bd. regents Washburn U., 1961-65; mem. 1970—; Concordia Library Bd., 1949-61, pres., 1960-61; trustee Kan. Council Econ. Edn. Address: 1250 Willow St Concordia KS 66901

DANENBERG, LEIGH, former newspaper pub.; b. N.Y.C., Sept. 23, 1893; s. Ury and Bertha (Filer) D.; student Townsend Harris Hall, 1906-09; A.B., N.Y. U., 1913; postgrad. Columbia Sch. Journalism, 1914; m. Nina Sutherland Purdy, 1920; m. 2d, Elsie Nicholas, June 23, 1928 (div.); children—Shirley, Dale, Leigh, Elsa Ann, Darryl Ann; m. 3d, Anne Bridge, May 22, 1965. Reporter, N.Y.C., Washington, San Francisco newspapers, 1914-17; free lance corr. in Germany, 1921-23; editor Norwalk Sentinel, 1923-29; pres., treas. Bridgeport Herald Corp., 1930-69; pub., editor Bridgeport (Conn.) Sunday Herald, 1930-65. Served as staff sgt. M.C., AUS, 1917-18. Clubs: Nat. Press, Overseas Press. Home: 5 Burritt's Landing N Westport CT 06880

DANES, GIBSON A., univ. dean; b. Starbuck, Wash., Dec. 13, 1910; s. B.A. and Ruth F. (Davison) D.; student U. Ore., 1930-32; B.F.A., Sch. Art Inst., Chgo., 1932-36; student U. Chgo., 1935-36; B.S. (univ. fellow), Northwestern U., 1937, M.A., 1938; Carnegie scholar Institut d'Art et a'Archeologie, U. Paris, summer 1938; Ph.D. in Art History (univ. fellow 1946, grant-in- aid Coll. Art Assn. 1946, Rockefeller post-war fellow 1947-48), Yale, 1948; D.F.A., Lake Erie Coll. 1962; m. Claire Tomowske, Mar. 9, 1939 (dec. Sept. 1953); 1 son, Christopher; m. 2d, Joan P. Dewan, Dec. 26, 1954 (dec. Jan. 1964); 1 son, Mark; m. 3d, Ilse Getz, July, 1964. Tchr. dept. edn. Art Inst. Chgo., 1936-38, Stephens Coll., 1938-40, Northwestern U., 1939- 40; asst. prof. U. Tex., 1940-43, asso. prof., 1946; instr. Yale, 1947; asso. prof. Ohio State U., 1948-52; prof., chmn. dept. art U. Cal. at Los Angeles, 1952-58, acting dean Coll. Applied Arts, 1955; dean Sch. Art and Architecture, Yale, 1958-68; dean visual arts State U. N.Y. at Purchase, 1968—. Served at lt., naval air intelligence USNR, 1943-46. Recipient meml. prize for pictorials composition Art Inst. Chgo., 1934; study aid grant Am. Council Learned Socs., 1948; Ford fellow, 1951-52. Mem. Coll. Art Assn. Am. Soc. Archtl. Historians, Am. Fedn. Art, A.I.A. (hon.), Nat. Assn. for Arts in Edn. (bd. dir.). Author, editor; Looking at Modern Painting. Contbr. articles to mags., revs.; author exhbn. catalogs; book reviewer. Home: Sawmill Rd Newtown CT 06470 Office: State Univ of NY Purchase NY 10577

DANFORD, EDWARD COYLE, life ins. co. exec.; b. Caldwell, O., Sept. 2, 1912; s. James and Elpha (McLaughlin) D.; B.S. in Bus. Adminstrn., Ohio State U., 1934; C.L.U., 1940; grad. Advanced Mgmt. Program, Harvard, 1961; m. Ann M. Collins, Feb. 18, 1939; children—Ellen C., Philip C. With Mut. Life Ins. Co. (co. name changed to Mut. of N.Y. 1960), N.Y.C., 1935—, v.p. field mgmt., now v.p. sales manpower. Mem. com. mgmt. NY edn. Am. Coll. Life Underwriters. Sec. 40th class Advanced Mgmt. Program. Harvard; v.p., dir. Harvard Advanced Mgmt. Assn.; bd. govs. Internat. Ins. Seminars. Trustee Charles W. Griffith Meml. Found. Ins. Edn. Home: 72 Winthrop Dr Riverside CT 06878 Office: 1740 Broadway New York City NY 10019

DANFORTH, ARTHUR EDWARDS, banker; b. Cleve., Jan. 23, 1925; s. Arthur Edwards and Jane (Hillyard) D.; B.A., Yale, 1949; m. Elizabeth Wagley, Mar. 17, 1956; children—Hillyard Raible, Nicholas Edwards, Jonathan Ingersoll, Elizabeth Wagley, Michael Stowe. With Hayden Miller Co., Cleve., 1949- 54, First Nat. City Bank, N.Y.C., 1954-63, asst. mgr. Buenos Aires office, 1959-61; treas. Bunge Corp., N.Y.C., 1963-65; sr. v.p., treas. Colonial Bank & Trust Co., Waterbury, Conn., 1965-70; chmn., chief exec. officer Farmers Bank of Del., Wilmington, 1970—. Vice chmn. group I, United Council and Fund of Greater Waterbury, 1969-70; bd. dirs. United Fund of Del.; pres. Wilmington Clearing House Assn. Served as ensign USNR, 1945-46. Mem. Waterbury C. of C. (fgn. affairs com. 1969-70), Audubon Soc. Conn. (dir.). Clubs: Pequot Yacht (Southport, Conn.); Nantucket (Mass.) Yacht; Yale (N.Y.C.); Rehoboth Beach (Del.) Country. Home: Twaddell Mill Rd and Route 100 Centerville DE 19807 Office: Farmers Bank 10th and Market Sts Wilmington DE 19801

DANFORTH, DAVID NEWTON, physician, educator; b. Evanston, Ill., Aug. 25, 1912; s. William Clark and Gertrude (MacLean) D.; B.S., Northwestern U., 1934, M.S., 1936, Ph.D., 1938, M.D., 1939; m. Gladys Blaine, 1938; 1 son, David Newton. Intern, N.Y. Postgrad. Hosp., N.Y.C., 1938-39; resident Sloane Hosp. for Women, Columbia, 1939-44; clin. asst. obstetrics and gynecology Northwestern U. Med. Sch., 1946-47, asst. prof. obstetrics and gynecology, 1947-52, asso. prof., 1952-59, prof., 1959—, chmn., 1965—; asst. attending obstetrician and gynecologist Wesley Meml. Hosp., Chgo., 1946-47, chmn. dept. obstetrics and gynecology, 1965—; chief dept. obstetrics and gynecology Evanston Hosp., 1947-65. Served to lt. (s.g.), M.C., USNR, 1944-46. Diplomate Am. Bd. Obstetrics and Gynecology (dir. 1966—, v.p. 1970-71). Mem. Am. Fertility Soc. (pres. 1963), A.C.S., Soc. Gynecol. Investigation, Am. (council 1962-64), Chgo. (pres. 1961) gynecol. socs., Am. Coll. Obstetricians and Gynecologists (1st v. p. 1969), Inst. Medicine Chgo., Soc. Exptl. Biology and Medicine, A.A.A.S., A.M.A., Central Assn. Obstretricians and Gynecologists. Editor, contbr. Textbook of Obstetrics and Gynecology, 1966. Contbr. articles profl. jours. Home: 300 Warwick Av Kenilworth IL Office: 251 E Chicago Av Chicago IL 60611

DANFORTH, DONALD, JR., feed mfg. exec.; b. St. Louis, Mar. 26, 1932; s. Donald and Dorothy (Claggett) D.; student Princeton, 1954; B.A., Washington U., St. Louis, 1955; m. Carolyn Borders, July 6, 1957; childrenCarol, Kathy, Laura. With Ralston Purina Co., 1957-, mgr. Richmond (Va.) plant, 1960-61, asst. to exec. v.p. gen. office, St. Louis, 1961-63, dir., 1961-, v.p. in-charge-of Chow div., 1963, now exec. v.p. Trustee St. Louis Country Day Sch., Am. Youth Found., St. Louis, St. Louis Children's Hosp.; bd. dirs. United Service Orgns. St. Louis. Served to 1st lt. AUS, 1955-57; ETO. Mem. Phi Delta Theta. Clubs: Stack, University, Noonday, St. Louis Country. Home: 31 Upper Ladue Rd Ladue, MO 63124. Office: 835 S 8th St St Louis MO 63102

DANFORTH, DOUGLAS DEWITT, mfg. co. exec.; b. Syracuse, N.Y., Sept. 25, 1922; s. Dewitt Ward and Ruth Cordellia (Ward) D.; student Fenn Coll., Cleve., 1940-41; B.S. in Mech. Engring., Syracuse U., 1947; m. Janet Mae Piron, May 15, 1943; children—Barbara Lee, Susan Jean, Debra Lynn and Douglas Dewitt (twins). Supt. planning Easy Washer Machine Co., Syracuse, N.Y., 1942-46; v.p., gen. mgr. in Mexico, Internat. Gen. Electric Co., 1947-53; plant mgr. Gen. Electric Co., Balt., 1953-55; exec. v.p., gen. mgr. Industria Electrica De Mexico, 1956-61, dir., 1958—; v.p. Westinghouse Electric Corp., Pitts., 1962-65, group v.p., 1965-69, exec. v.p., 1969—. Mason. Home: 917 Old Hickory Rd Pittsburgh PA 15243 Office: 3 Gateway Center PO Box 2278 Pittsburgh PA 15230

DANFORTH, GEORGE EDSON, educator, architect; b. Laharpe, Kan.; B.A., Armour Inst. Tech., 1940; grad. study architecture with Mies van der Rohe, 1940-43. Instr. dept. architecture Ill. Inst. Tech., 1941-48, adminstrv. asst. dept., asst. prof., 1948-53, prof., chmn. dept., 1959—, dir. Sch. Architecture and Planning, 1968—; chmn. dept. architecture Western Res. U., 1953-59. Architect with Mies Van Der Rohe architect, 1939-44; archtl. cons. U.S. Steel Corp., 1957-66, Internat. Nickel Co., 1961-65. Licensed architect, Ohio, Ill., Ia., Ky. Fellow A.I.A.; mem. Am. Soc. Engring. Edn., Am. Assn. U. Profs., Am. Soc. Aesthetics (sec.- treas. 1955-59), Scarab. Home: 211 W St Paul St Chicago, IL 60614. Office: 3340 S State St Chicago IL 60616

DANFORTH, JOHN CLAGGETT, atty. gen. Mo., lawyer; b. St. Louis, Sept. 5, 1936; s. Donald and Dorothy (Claggett) D.; A.B., Princeton, 1958; B.D., Yale, 1963, LL.B., 1963; L.H.D., Lindenwood Coll., 1970; LL.D., Drury Coll., 1970; m. Sally B. Dobson, Sept. 7, 1957; children—Eleanor, Mary Dorothy, Johanna. Admitted to N.Y. bar, 1964, Mo. bar, 1966; with firm David Polk Wardwell Sunderland & Kiendl, N.Y.C., 1964-66, Bryan, Cave, McPheeters and McRoberts, St. Louis, 1966-68; atty. gen. Mo., 1968—; ordained deacon Episcopal Ch., 1963, priest, 1964; asst. rector, N.Y.C., 1963-66; asso. rector, Clayton, Mo., 1966-68, Grove Ch., Jefferson City, 1969—. Republican nominee U.S. Senate, 1970. Recipient Distinguished Service award St. Louis Jr. C. of C., 1969; named Outstanding Young Man, Mo. Jr. C. of C., 1968. Republican. Clubs: St. Louis Country, Noonday (St. Louis); Jefferson City Country. Home: 340 Fox Creek Rd Jefferson City MO 65101 Office: Supreme Ct Bldg Jefferson City MO 65101

DANFORTH, JOSEPH D., educator, chemist; b. Danville, Ill., Mar. 7, 1912; s. James and Bertha Ann (Garrard) D.; B.A., Wabash Coll., 1934; Ph.D., Purdue U., 1938; m. Geraldine Hoffman, July 6, 1940; children—James Davis, Cheryl, David Edward, Patricia Ann. Research chemist Universal Oil Products Co., 1938- 47; mem. faculty Grinnell Coll., 1947—, prof. chemistry, 1953—, Roberts Honor prof., 1962-63, chmn. dept. chemistry, 1961-64, Dack prof. chemistry, 1964—; vis. scientist chemistry for colls., Am. Chem. Soc., 1959—, mem. vis. scientist com., dir. high sch. program chemistry, 1961- 64; cons. in field. Hon. cons. sci. teaching sect. UNESCO, 1964. Recipient Coll. Chemistry Tchr. award Mfg. Chemists Assn., 1963. Mem. Midwest Assn. Chemistry Tchrs. (pres. 1962), Am. Chem. Soc. (treas. div. chem. edn. 1967), A.A.A.S., Ia. Acad. Sci., Phi Beta Kappa. Mason, Elk. Author, pantentee in field. Home: 1332 Broad St Grinnell, IA 50112.

DANFORTH, LOUIS FREMONT, banker; b. Los Angeles, Nov. 15, 1913; s. Louis F. and Louise (Bauerle) D.; grad. Columbia, 1954; postgrad. N.Y. U., 1952; m. Leota V. Schwulst, Sept. 9, 1944; children—David Louis, Victoria Leota. With investment dept. Guaranty Trust Co., N.Y.C., 1946-55; charge investment dept. Liberty Nat. Bank & Trust Co., Oklahoma City, 1955—, also chmn. investment com., cost and pricing com., mgmt. com.; dir. Investors Trust Co., Duncan, Okla.; vis. prof. econs. Oklahoma City U.; faculty Southwestern Grad. Sch. Banking, So. Meth. U. Chmn. econ. resources sub- com. Health and Hosp. Planning Com., 1960—. Pres., bd. dirs., mem. exec. com. Better Bus. Bur.; past pres. Central Okla. Council for Children with Learning Disabilities; bd. dirs., mem. exec. com., past pres. Sunbeam Home and Family Service; bd. dirs. Asso. Industries Okla., Okla. Council on Econ. Edn., Okla. State U.; treas., bd. dirs., mem. exec. com. Deaconess Hosp.; trustee, chmn. budget com. United Appeal Greater Oklahoma City Area; mem. adv. council Oklahoma City U. Bus. Research Center. Served to capt., inf. AUS, 1941-46. Decorated Bronze Star medal with oak leaf cluster, Purple Heart with oak leaf cluster, Combat Inf. badge. Mem. Econ. Club Okla. (pres.), Okla. Soc. Financial Analysts (past pres.), Okla. Financial Fedn. (past regional v.p.), Nat. Assn. Bus. Economists. Republican. Episcopalian. Clubs: Mens Dinner, Quail Creek Golf and Country, Petroleum, Press (Okalhoma City). Home: 12912 Twisted Oak Rd Oklahoma City OK 73120 Office: PO Box 25848 Oklahoma City OK 73125

DANFORTH, PAUL L., banker. Sr. v.p. People's Nat. Bank Wash. Office: 1414 4th Av Seattle WA 98111*

DANFORTH, WILLIAM HENRY, physician; b. St. Louis, Apr. 10, 1926; s. Donald and Dorothy (Claggett) D.; A.B., Princeton, 1947; M.D., Harvard, 1951; m. Elizabeth Anne Grey, Sept. 1, 1950; children—Cynthia, David, Ann, Elizabeth. Intern Barnes Hosp., St. Louis, 1951-52, resident, 1954-57, now mem. staff; asst. prof. medicine Washington U., St. Louis, 1960-65, asso. prof., 1965-67, prof., 1967—, vice chancellor for med. affairs, 1965-71, chancellor, 1971—; pres. Washington U. Med. Sch. and Asso. Hosps., 1965-71; program coordinator Bi- State Regional Med. Program, 1967-69. Mem. nat. adv. heart and lung council Nat. Heart and Lung Inst. Trustee, chmn. bd. Danforth Found.; trustee Am. Youth Found., Princeton U. Served with USN, 1952-54. Mem. Am., Central socs. for clin. research. Home: 10 Glenview Rd St Louis MO Office: Washington U St Louis MO 63130

DANGEL, ROBERT FREDERICK, pipe line co. exec.; b. New Castle, Pa., June 29, 1926; s. Fredrick M. and Sara (Artz) D.; B.S., U. Pitts., 1950; m. Colleen H. Bottorf, Nov. 1, 1947; children—Robert R., Richard F., Matthew P. With Mich. Wis. Pipe Line Co., Detroit, 1950—, treas., 1969—. Served with AUS, 1944-46. Mem. Am. Gas Assn., Ind. Natural Gas Assn. Home: 1609 Grant St Lincoln Park MI 48146 Office: 1 Woodward Av Detroit MI 48226

D'ANGELO, GIANNA, soprano; b. Hartford, Conn.; d. Stephen Howard and Dorothy (Holt) Angelovich; studetn Mt. Ida Jr. Coll., 1947-48, then Juilliard Conservatory; pupil of Hazel Porter Snow, Giuseppe de Luca, Tuti dal Monte. Debut, Baths of Caracalla, 1954; appearances major opera houses Europe and U.S., 1954—; debut Met. Opera, 1961. Recipient Gold medal Barcellona, Spain, 1958, Gold medal Luxemburg, 1959. Address: Via Stresa 15 Milan Italy

DANGERFIELD, GEORGE, author; b. Newbury, Berkshire, Eng., Oct. 28, 1904; s. George and Ethel Margaret (Tyrer) D.; student Forest Sch., Walthamstow, Essex, Eng., 1916- 22; B.A. Hertford Coll. Oxford U., 1927, M.A. Oxford U., 1968; m. Helen Mary Deey Spedding, June 28, 1928; m. 2d, Mary Lou Schott, June 29, 1941; children—Mary Jo, Hilary, Anthony. Came to U.S., 1930; naturalized, 1943. Asst. editor Brewer, Warren & Putnam, N.Y.C., 1930-32; lit. editor Vanity Fair mag., 1933-35; writer, lectr., 1935—; Benjamin D. Shreve fellow Princeton, 1957-58; Guggenheim fellow, 1970. Lectr. history U. Cal. at Santa Barbara, 1968—. Served 102d inf. div., AUS 1942-45. Recipient Bancroft prize in Am. history, Columbia, 1953, Pulitzer prize in Am. history, 1953. Mem. Ams. for Dem. Action, Civil Liberties Union, Friends Santa Barbara Pub. Library. Author: Bengal Mutiny, 1933; The Strange Death of Liberal England, 1935; Victoria's Heir, 1941; The Era of Good Feelings, 1952; Chancellor Robert R. Livingston of New York, 1960; The Awakening of American Nationalism, 1815-1828, 1965; Defiance to the Old World, 1970; (with Otey M. Scruggs) Henry Adams' History of the United States, 1963. Home: 883 Toro Canyon Rd Santa Barbara CA 93103

D'ANGIO, GIULIO JOHN, educator, radiologist; b. N.Y.C., May 2, 1922; s. Carlo and Rose (Calderazzo) D'A.; A.B., Columbia, 1943; M.D., Harvard, 1945; m. Jean Chittenden Terhune, Aug. 27, 1955; children—Carl Terhune, Peter David. Intern Children's Hosp., Boston, 1945-46, asst. radiology, 1956-59, asso. radiologist, 1959-62, radiotherapist, 1963-64; fellow pathology Babies Hosp., N.Y.C., 1948; resident pathology VA Hosp., W. Roxbury, Mass., 1948-49; resident radiology Boston City Hosp., 1949-53, asst. radiology, 1953-55, assting physician for radiology, 1955- 64; research asso. radiology Children's Cancer Research Found., 1956-59, radiotherapist, 1959-64; asst. radiologist Mass. Gen. Hosp., 1961-62, cons., 1962-63; mem. faculty Harvard Med. Sch., 1953-64, clin. asso. radiology, 1962-64; asso. research radiologist Donner Lab., U. Cal. at Berkeley, 1962-63, cons., 1964—;prof. radiology, dir. div. radiation therapy U. Minn. Hosps., 1964-68; cons. radiation therapy Hennepin County Gen. Hosp., Mpls., 1966-68; chmn. dept. radiation therapy Meml. Hosp., N.Y.C., 1968—; prof. radiology Cornell U. Med. Coll., 1968—; chief div. radiation therapy research Sloan-Kettering Inst. Cancer Research, 1968—; prof. biophysics Sloan-Kettering div. Grad. Sch. Med. Sci., Cornell U. Med. Coll., 1968—; attending radiologists N.Y. Hosp., 1968—. Chmn. Nat. Wilms' Tumor Study Com. Served with AUS, 1946-48. Decorated Commendation medal. Affiliate fellow Am. Acad. Pediatrics; mem. Royal Soc. Medicine, Phi Beta Kappa, Sigma Xi. Contbr. numerous articles med. jours., books. Home: 40 Mohegan Rd Larchmont NY 10538 Office: 444 E 68th St New York City NY 10021

DANHOF JOHN JAMES, lawyer; b. Grand Haven, Mich., July 15, 1884; s. John John and Anna (Medema) D.; A.B., U. Mich., 1907, J.D., 1912; J.D. (hon.), Detroit Coll. Law, 1948; m. Erma Mueller, Feb. 14, 1914; childrenRosemary (Mrs. George I. Hammerschmidt), John James, Annabel (Mrs. Samuel A. Hess). High sch. prin., 1907-11; admitted to Mich. bar, 1912; atty. in office of Campbell, Bulkley & Ledyard, Detroit, 1912-13; atty. M.C. R.R. solicitor U. S. R.R. Adminstrn., 1919-20; atty., 1913-19, asst. gen. atty. M.C. R.R. Co., 1920-30; gen. atty. N.Y.C. R.R. Co., jurisdiction over M.C. R.R., 1930-31; gen. counsel N.Y.C. R.R. Co., jurisdiction over M.C. R.R., M.C. R.R. Co., 1931-51, Detroit Terminal R.R. Co. 1932-51, ret. 1951; counsel Mich. Railroads Assn., chmn. exec. com., retired, 1952. Mem. exec. com. Detroit Tomorrow Com. Pres., trustee Detroit Coll. Law. Mem. Am. Bar Assn. (chmn. coms. on cooperation, 1938-40), State Bar of Mich. (chmn. com. Legal Edn. and Admission to Bar, 1938-39), Detroit Bar Assn. (chmn. Integration Bar com., 1934-35, Legislative com., 1937-38), Assn. Interstate Commerce Commn. Practitioners (past v.p.; chmn. Mich. Regional com. on admission to practice 1941-53), U. Mich. Alumni Assn. (past v.p., past dir.), Am. Judicature Soc., Newcomen Soc., Phi Alpha Delta, Delta Sigma Phi., Order of Coif. Republican. Conglist. Mason (K.T., Shriner). Clubs: Detroit, (past pres.) Prismatic, Detroit Golf, Economic (dir.), Spring Lake Country; University (Washington); Lawyers (Ann Arbor, Mich.). Home: 19381 Stratford Rd Detroit MI 48221 Office: 130 E Elizabeth St Detroit MI 48201

DANHOF, RALPH JOHN, clergyman; b. Chgo., July 28, 1900; s. John and Marie (Hoekstra) D.; A.B., Calvin Coll., 1922, Th.B., 1925; Th.D., Free U. Amsterdam, Netherlands, 1929; m. Margaret Van Dellen, Sept. 22, 1926; children—John William, Helene (Mrs. Richard DeHoek), Calvin, Roger. Ordained to minstry Christian Ref. Ch., 1929; pastor, Pella, Ia., 1929-34, Holland, Mich., 1934-45, Neland Av. Ch., Grand Rapids, Mich., 1945-56; stated clk. Christian Ref. Ch., 1945—, also exec. sec., 1956—. Del. to Assembly of Chs., South Africa, 1949. Home: 3041 Burton St SE Grand Rapids MI 49506 Office: 2850 Kalamazoo Av SE Grand Rapids MI 49508

DANIEL, EDWIN CLYDE, journalist; b. Hannibal, Mo., Apr. 15, 1941; s. Cecil Earl and Lorna (Howell) D.; B.A., U. Mo.-Kansas City, 1967; m. Sandra Kay Skinner, Dec. 2, 1961; children—Brian Mark, Aaron Dean. With Kansas City Star, 1963-70, editorial writer, 1968-70; editorial writer Urban Renewal Agy., Kansas City, Kans., 1970—. Mem. poetry com. Am. Poet Series in Kansas City. Mem. C. of C. Greater Kansas City. Democrat. Mem. Christian Ch. Home: 1866 S 32d St Kansas City KS 66106 Office: 755 Minnesota Av Kansas City KS 66101

DANIEL, ELBERT CLIFTON, Jr., newspaperman; b. Zebulon, N.C., Sept. 19, 1912; s. Elbert Clifton and Elvah (Jones) D.; A.B., U. N.C., 1933. D.Litt., 1970; m. Margaret Truman (d. Harry S. Truman, former-Pres. U.S.), Apr. 21, 1956; children—Clifton Truman, William Wallace, Harrison Gates, Thomas Washington. Asso. editor Daily Bulletin, Dunn, N.C., 1933-34; reporter News and Observer, Raleigh, N.C., 1933-37; with Asso. Pres. in N.Y.C., Washington, Bern, London, 1937-43; with N.Y. Times, 1944—, stationed in London, with SHAEF Hdqrs. in Paris, in Middle East, in Germany, U.S.S.R., 1954-55, N.Y.C., 1955—, asst. to mng. editor, 1957-59, asst. mng. editor, 1959-64, mng. editor, 1964—, asso. editor, 1969—. Recipient Overseas Press Club award for best reporting abroad, 1955. Mem. Phi Delta Theta. Clubs: Nat. Press (Washington); Century (N.Y.). Office: 229 W 43d St New York City NY 10036

DANIEL, GERALD RUSSELL, educator; b. Murphysboro, Ill., June 28, 1916; s. William John and Emogene (Hudson) D.; student So. Ill. U., 1934-36; B.M., Ill. Wesleyan U., 1938, M.M., 1941; Ph.D., U. Ia., 1949; m. Irene Gianedakis, Aug. 15, 1949; 1 son, William Costas. Tchr. music Anua-Jonesboro Community High Sch., Anna, Ill., 1938-42, Long Beach (Cal.) Poly. High Sch., 1950-53; mem. faculty Long Beach City Coll., 1953-68, adminstrv. dean 1956-58, dean instrn., 1958-68; prof. music, chmn. dept. Cal. State Coll., 1968—; mus. dir. Long Beach Civic Light Opera, 1959-61. Bd. dirs. Long Beach Museum Assn. Served with USAAF, 1942-46. Home: 1850 Carfax Av Long Beach CA 90815

DANIEL, HARBEN WINFIELD, broadcasting co. exec.; b. Nashville, Aug. 6, 1906; s. John and Grace Olive (Knight) D.; student Vanderbilt U., 1924-26, Watkins Inst., 1927-28; m. Catherine Murrey, Sept. 25, 1934; children—Catherine (Mrs. Robert Long), Mary (Mrs. Eugene Cay III); m. 2d, Caroline Noble Jones Wright, Dec. 30, 1970. From account exec. to comml. mgr. radio sta. WSM, Nashville, 1930-39; pres. WSAV, Inc., Savannah, Ga., 1939—. Chmn. 3d Army Civilian Adv. Com., 1949-53; pres. Porter G. Pierpont Ednl. Fund, 1950-51; area chmn. Vanderbilt U. Alumni Endowment Devel., 1963—; mem. adv. council to edn. Chatham County Pub. Schs., 1969-70. Mem. Savannah Airport Commn., 1968—. Bd. dirs. United Community Appeal. Mem. Savannah C. of C. (dir.), Sigma Delta Chi, Sigma Chi. Rotarian (pres.) Clubs: Savannah Yacht and Country, Oglethorpe, Chatham (Savannah). Contbr. profl. publs. Home: 310 E 45th St Savannah GA 31405 Office: PO Box 2429 Savannah GA 31402

DANIEL, HAWTHORNE, author; b. Norfolk, Neb. Jan. 10 1890; s. Dr. David Rush and Nancy Ann (Kyner) D.; student U.S. Naval Acad., 1908, Ia. State Coll., 1909- 10, N.Y.U., 1914-15, Columbia, 1914-15; m. Nelle M. Ryan, 1922; 1 dau., Nancy Nelle. Reporter Omaha Bee, 1915; editorial staff World's Work, 1916-23; mng. editor Boys' Life, 1923-25; editor Natural History Mag., 1927-35; curator, printing and pub., Am. Museum Natural History 1927-35; mng. editor, The Commentator, 1936-39. Ensign USNR, 1917; officer U.S.S. Harvard, duty in Bay of Biscay and English Channel; lt. U.S. Tank Corps, 1918-19, 303d and 306th Batt., In U.S., England and France as reconnaissance officer. Visited the Arctic Coast of Can., 1921. War Corrs., World War II, with Army and Navy in Pacific, Asiatic, Mediterranean, and European areas; visited islands of Pacific and East Indies, Australia, India, China, etc. Awarded U.S. Navy commendation. Clubs: Columbia University, Explorers (N.Y.C.). Author numerous books including: End of Track, 1936 (medal of Ore. Trail Meml. Assn.); For Want of a Nail (The Influence of Logistics on War), 1948; Judge Medina: A Biography, 1952; The Inexhaustible Sea (with Frances Minot), 1954; The Captain Leaves His Ship (with Jan Cwiklinski), 1955; The Happy Warrior, a biography of Alfred E. Smith (with Emily Smith Warner), 1956; The Ordeal of the Captive Nations, 1958 (citation from Assembly of Captive European Nations 1960); The Hartford of Hartford, 1960; Public Libraries For Everyone, 1961; Ferdinand Magellan (biography), 1964; A Different Kind of War (with Vice Adm. Milton E. Miler), 1967; also articles and short stories in mags. Lectr. Home: 37 Standish Av Tuckahoe, NY 10710.☆33

DANIEL, JAMES, writer, editor; b. Davidson County, N.C., June 6, 1916; s. James Manly and Bert (Fletcher) D.; A.B., U. N.C., 1937; Nieman fellow, Harvard, 1942-43; m. Ramona Teijeiro, Apr. 15, 1939; children—Jane Clare (Mrs. John S. Nagy), Ramona Nina. Reporter, Raleigh (N.C.) News & Observer, 1937-40, Washington Daily News, 1941, city editor, 1946-47; with OWI in CBI, 1943-45; Washington corr. Scripps-Howard Papers, 1948-56; contbg. editor Time mag., 1957-60; roving editor Reader's Digest, 1961—. First selectman, Weston, Conn., 1967-69. Clubs: National Press (Washington); Harvard (N.Y.C.). Author: (with J. G. Hubbell) Strike in the West, The Complete Story of the Cuban Crisis, 1963. Editor: Private Investment, The Key to International Development, 1958. Home: 183 Good Hill Rd Weston CT 06880 Office: care Reader's Digest Pleasantville NY 10570

DANIEL, JAMES MARTIN, hosp, adminstr.; b. Greenville, N.C., Sept. 4, 1915; s. James M. and Ellen L, (Garrett) D.; A.B., Duke U., 1936, course in hosp. adminstrn., 1938; m. Virginia Elizabeth Skinner, Nov. 9, 1940; children—James Martin III, Elizabeth S. Asst. sec.-treas. Hosp. Care Assn., Durham, N.C., 1938-40; asst. supt. James Walker Meml. Hosp., Wilmington, N.C., 1940-43; adminstr. Rockingham Meml. Hosp., Harrisonburg, Va., 1943-46; supt. Columbia Hosp. of Richland County, Columbia, S.C., 1946—. Dir. S.C. Hosp. Service Plan, Columbia, Graphic Communications, Milw. Chmn. Richland County area council Boy Scouts Am.; bd. dirs. A.R.C., Harrisonburg, Va., Richland County Crippled Children's Assn.; mem. hosp. adv. council S.C. Bd. Health, 1947—, chmn., 1965—, chmn. licensing com. hosp. adv. council, 1947-65. Bd. dirs., pres. Hosp. Data Center S.C., Inc. Fellow Am. Coll. Hosp. Adminstrs.; mem. Am. (ho. dels. 1950-60, bd. trustees 1960-62; delegate at large ho. of delegates 1968—), S.C. (pres. 1948, bd. trustees, treas.) hosp. assns. Episcopalian. Clubs: Rotary, Civitan (past v.p.), Lions (past pres.); Forest Lake Country. Home: 213 Pinebrook Rd Columbia SC 29206 Office: 2020 Hampton Columbia SC 29204

DANIEL, JAQUELIN JAMES, lawyer, corp. exec.; b. Jacksonville, Fla., Sept. 22, 1916; s. Richard Potts and Mary Goff (Palmer) D.; A.B., Princeton, 1939; LL.B., U. Fla., 1942; LL.D. (hon.), Fla. State U., 1965; m. Anne Page Coachman, Oct. 18, 1947; children—Eleanor Page (Mrs. Richard Barkell), Jaquelin Palmer. Admitted to Fla. bar, 1942; mem. firm Daniel & Daniel, Jacksonville, 1942-60; pres. Stockton, Whatley, Davin & Co., Jacksonville, 1960—; pres. State Investment Co., Ponte Vedra Co.; chmn. bd. State Bank Jacksonville; dir. Seaboard Coast Line R.R. Co., Alico Land Devel. Co., Gen. Am. Oil Co., Fla. Pub. Co. Fund campaign chmn. A.R.C., 1947; chmn. Duval County Bd. Visitors, 1947-50; vice chmn. Dist. Welfare Bd., 1948-50; chmn. budget com. Community Chest, 1948-50; chmn. citizens com. to organize United Fund Appeal, 1954; pres. Community Chest-United Fund of Duval County, 1955, 62; vice chmn. Fla. Ednl. TV Commn., 1957-59; mem. bd. control Fla. Instns. Higher Learning, 1957-61, chmn., 1959-61; chmn. Duval County Local Govt. Study Commn. Del. Democratic Nat. Conv., 1956. Chmn. bd. visitors Davidson Coll., 1965; trustee Daniel Meml. Home for Children; chmn. bd. trustees George Peabody Coll., 1967-70; trustee Children's Museum of Jacksonville, 1954-58, Evergreen Cemetery Assn., 1956. Served from ensign to lt. comdr., USNR, 1942-45. Decorated Bronze Star medal; recipient Distinguished Service award U.S. Jr. C. of C., 1950; Distinguished Citizen award Nat. Municipal League, 1968; Brotherhood award Nat. Conf. Christians and Jews, 1970. Mem. Am., Jacksonville bar assns., Fla. Bar (chmn. com. unauthorized practice of law 1950), English Speaking Union (pres. Jacksonville br. 1957), Community Chest and

Councils Am. (mem. nat. budget com. 1955-58), Kappa Alpha. Democrat. Episcopalian. Clubs: Florida Yacht (commodore 1956), River (past pres.), Timuquana Country, Ponte Vedra (Jacksonville). Home: 4985 Morven Rd Jacksonville FL 32210 Office: 100 W Bay St Jacksonville FL 32233

DANIEL, JOE H., lawyer; b. Daniel's Landing, Tenn., Oct. 17, 1917; B.A., U. Miss., J.D., 1940. Admitted to Miss. bar, 1940; now partner firm Daniel, Coker, Horton & Bell, Jackson, Miss. Fellow Am. Coll. Trial Lawyers; mem. Am., Hinds County (pres. 1958-59) bar assns., Miss. State Bar, Miss. Def. Lawyers Assn., Internat. Assn. Ins. Counsel, Phi Delta Phi. Contbr. articles to profl. jours. Office: 405 Tombigbee St at S Congress St Jackson MS 39201*

DANIEL, JOHN, church ofcl.; b. Mystic, Conn., Nov. 8, 1912; s. John S. and Anna (Galdun) D.; A.B., Concordia Coll., 1932; B.D., Concordia Sem., 1936, D.D., 1962; M.A., Lehigh U., 1947; m. Elizabeth Lisy, Apr. 15, 1937; children—John Lisy III, David Paul, Richard Joel. Ordained to ministry Lutheran Ch., 1936; pastor St. John Luth. Ch., Bethlehem, Pa., 1936—; pres. Evang. Luth. Synodical Conf. of N. Am., 1960—; lectr., tchr. Lehigh U., Muhlenberg Coll., children—Robert Coll., Pa. State U., 1947-56. Active Bethlehem chpt. A.R.C.; mem. Bethlehem Redevel. Authority, 1959- 62, Bethlehem Authority, 1960—, Bethlehem Vocational Tech. Sch. Bd. Authority, 1968—; mem. Bethlehem Citizens Sch. Com. Mem. Am. Hist. Assn., Ch. History Soc., Phi Alpha Theta. Author: Labor, Industry and the Church, 1957. Contbr. to religious publs. Home: 1240 E 4th St Bethlehem, PA 18015.

DANIEL, KENNETH RULE, iron and steel mfg. co. exec.; b. Milford, Conn., Oct. 13, 1913; s. Cullen Coleman and Margaret Estelle (Elliott) D.; B.S., U. Ala., 1936, Profl. Degree in Mech. Engring., 1957; m. Virginia Moody Simpson, June 11, 1938; children—Kenneth Rule, Cullen Coleman, Robert Tennent Simpson, William Francis McKemie. With Am. Cast Iron Pipe Co., Birmingham, Ala., 1936—, chief engr., 1948-55. v.p. engring., 1955-59, v.p. engring and purchases, 1959-61, exec. v.p., 1961-63, pres., 1963—, also dir., dir. various subsidiaries; dir. Seaboard Coast Line R.R., Exchange Security Bank. Mem. Ala. Bd. of Registration for Profl. Engrs. and Land Surveyors, 1967—; mem. regional adv. council Conf. Bd. 1967— , Ala. Export Council, 1966-69; dir. Community Chest, Jr. Achievement, Birmingham Urban League, 1968-70, Birmingham Centennial Corp., Warrior Tombigbee Devel. Assn.; gen. co-chmn. United Appeal, 1964, chmn. indsl. div., 1958; chmn. Radio Free Europe, Birmingham, 1966; mem. Jefferson County Judicial Commn., 1967—; chmn. adv. bd., mem. adv. council home and hosp. Salvation Army. Trustee Foundry Ednl. Found. (pres. 1964-65); trustee, mem. exec. com. So. Research Inst.; trustee, v.p. Birmingham Symphony Assn.; dir. Carraway Meth. Hosp. Served to lt. col. AUS, 1941-46; ETO. Decorated Bronze Star, Legion of Merit; Croix de Guerre (France); recipient Gold Knight of Mgmt. award Nat. Mgmt. Assn., 1965, William Booth award Salvation Army, 1967; named Engr. of Year, Birmingham Engring. Council, 1967. Registered profl. engr. Ala. Fellow Am. Soc. M.E. (chmn. Birmingham sect. 1950-51); mem. N.A.M. (bd. dirs. 1967-70), Asso. Industries Ala. (bd. dirs.), Birmingham Area C. of C. (pres. 1969), Assn. Iron and Steel Engrs. (chmn. Birmingham Sect. 1954, nat. dir. 1955), Am. Ordnance Assn. (pres. Birmingham post 1964), Am. Foundrymen's Soc., Am. Soc. for Engring. Edn., Engring. Soc. Birmingham, Newcomen Soc. N. Am., Sigma Alpha Epsilon, Theta Tau, Tau Beta Pi. Methodist (past chmn. bd. stewards). Kiwanian. Clubs: Birmingham Country, The Club, Mountain Brook. The Downtown, The Relay House, Vestavia Country (Birmingham); Indian Hills Country (Tuscaloosa, Ala.). Home: 3212 Brookwood Rd Birmingham AL 35223 Office: PO Box 2727 Birmingham AL 35202

DANIEL, LAWRENCE RICHARD, JR., engring. educator; b. Shreveport, Aug. 2, 1922; s. Lawrence Richard and Mable (Tassin) D.; B.S. in Mech. Engring., La. State U., 1943; M.Automotive Engring., Chrysler Inst. Engring., 1948; B.S. in Civil Engring., La. Poly. Inst., 1954; Ph.D., Mich. State U., 1959; m. Mary Alive Danos, Apr. 24, 1954; childrenLawrence Richard III, Colleen, Pamela. Engr., Chrysler Corp., 1946-48; mem. faculty La. Poly. Inst., 1948-61, prof. mech. engring., 1957-61; faculty La. State U., 1961-, prof., head mech. and aerospace engring. dept., 1964-67, prof., head mech., aerospace and indsl. engring., 1967—; cons. Manned Spacecraft Center, NASA, Houston, 1962-. Served with USNR, 1944-46; lt. comdr. Res. Registered profl. engr., La. Mem. Nat. Soc. Profl. Engrs., Am. Soc. M.E., Am. Soc. Engring. Edn., Soc. Automotive Engring., La. Engring. Soc, La. Tchrs. Assn., Sigma Xi, Omicron Delta Kappa, Tau Beta Pi, Pi Mu Epsilon, Pi Tau Sigma. Home: 1084 Magnolia Woods Baton Rouge, LA 70808.

DANIEL, LOIS H., librarian; b. Columbia, Tenn., May 12, 1911; d. David and Mahalah (Lloyd) Daniel; B.S., Tenn. Agrl. and Indsl. State U., 1933; B.S. in L.S., Hampton Inst., 1937; A.M., U. Chgo., 1945. Tchr. math., history Central High Sch., Alamo, Tenn., 1933-34; asst. librarian Tenn. Agrl. and Indsl. State U., 1934-36, head cataloging dept., instr. library sci., 1937-44, head librarian Martha M. Brown Meml. Library, also head library service dept., 1945—, dir. library, also prof. of library science. Mem. advisory com. Hadley Park bd. Nashville Pub. Library. Mem. A.L.A., Am. Assn. Sch. Librarians, Assn. Coll. Reference Librarians, Alpha Kappa Mu, Alpha Kappa Alpha (regional dir.). Club: Library of Nashville (vice chmn.). Office: Library Service Tennessee Agricultural and Industrial State U Nashville TN 37203

DANIEL, OLIVER, musicologist; b. De Pere, Wis. Nov. 24, 1911; s. Charles and Ange (Beaver) D. student St. Norbert Coll., West De Pere, Wis., 1925-29; student piano, Amersterdam, Berlin and Boston. Tchr., Boston Conservatory, 1936-38, Marot Coll., Thomson, Conn., 1939-42; music dir. ednl. div. CBS, 1942-44, producer mus. documentary and dramatic programs, 1947-54; supr. serious music ABC, 1944-46; v.p. concert music adminstrn. Broadcast Music, Inc., 1954—; a founder Composers Recordings, Inc., 1954, dir., 1954—; co-founder Contemporary Music Soc., 1952, pres. bd. dirs., 1966—; bd. dirs. Am. Music Center, 1966—, Am. Symphony Orch., 1962—, Composers Forum and Nat. Music Council, 1957- -, Soc. Asian Music, 1967-69, Thorne Music Fund, 1970—, Mem. Pres's music com. People-to- People Program, 1958-62; rep. U.S., Internat. Music Council, UNESCO, 1958, 61, 64, 67, individual mem., 1969—; rep. Nat. Music Council on U.S. Nat. Commn. for UNESCO, 1966—; mem. music adv. panel USIA, 1967-69; chmn. UNESCO com., congress adminstrn., Sixth Internat. Music Conf., 1968. Recipient Laurel Leaf award Am. Composers Alliance, 1956. Mem. Internat. Music Council, Phi Mu Alpha (hon. life). Editor: The Harmony of Maine, 1949; Down East Spirituals, 1949; The Music of Williams Billings, 1943-67. Home: Box 658 Scarsdale NY 10583 Office: 589 Fifth Av New York City NY 10017

DANIEL, PRICE, judge; past gov. of Texas; b. Dayton, Tex., Oct. 10, 1910; s. Marion Price and Nannie (Partlow) D.; A.B., Baylor U., 1931, LL.B., 1932; LL.D., Baylor U., 1951, Hardin-Simmons U., 1956; m. Jean Houston Baldwin, June 28, 1940; children—Price, Jean, Houston, John. Reporter, Ft. Worth Star Telegram, 1926-27, Waco News Tribune, 1929-31; admitted to Tex. bar, 1932, and practiced law, Liberty, Tex., 1932-43; speaker Tex. Ho. of Reps., 1943; atty. gen. of Tex., 1946-53; U.S. senator from Tex., 1953-56; gov. State of Tex., 1956-63; practice law, Austin, Tex., 1963-67; dir. Office of Emergency Preparedness, asst. to Pres. for fed.-state relations, mem. Nat. Security Council, 1967-69; judge Tex. Supreme Ct., 1971—. Co-pub. Liberty Vindicator and Anahuac Progress since 1939. Vice chmn. Adv. Commn. Intergovtl. Relations, 1967-69. Served with AUS, 1943-46; with Security Intelligence Corps., 1 yr.; served in Pacific area and Japan; disch. with rank of capt. Mem. State Dem. Exec. Com., 1939-41; mem. speakers' bur. Dem. nat. campaigns, 1932, 36, 40. Member Sigma Delta Chi, Am. Soc. Internat. Law, Internat. Law Assn., Pi Kappa Delta, Am., Tex. bar assns., Liberty C. of C. (pres. 1939-41). Democrat. Mason (Shriner), Elk, Woodman, Rotarian. Author treatises on Tex. Ownership of Submerged Lands and The Annexation Agreement between Texas and the U.S. Home: Holly Ridge Ranch Liberty TX 77575 Office: Supreme Ct Bldg Austin TX

DANIEL, ROBERT EDWIN, church ofcl. b. Joplin, Mo., Aug. 19, 1906; s. Robert Brown and Lilian (Boswell) D.; A.B. magna cum laude, Ottawa U., 1927; LL.D., Whitworth Coll., 1971; m. Margaret Moir, July 16, 1932; children—Robert William, Phillip Merrill, Linda Jane. With Blyth & Co., 1928-31, Pacific Northwest Co., Seattle, 1931-41, 46-66, pres., 1959-66; v.p. United Pacific Corp. Chmn. regional bus. conduct com. Nat. Assn. Securities Dealers, 1959-60. Trustee, treas. Wash.-Alaska Synod United Presbyn. Ch., now dir. finance. Served to maj. AUS, 1941-45. Mem. Seattle C. of C. Republican. Presbyn. (elder). Clubs: Rainier, Bond (Seattle). Home: 3214 8th St W Seattle WA 98119 Office: 720 Seneca St Seattle WA 98101

DANIEL, ROBERT HOWISON, investment co. exec.; b. Chunju, Korea, July 11, 1912; s. Thomas H. and Sarah (Dunnington) D.; B.S., U. Va., 1933, M.S., 1934; diploma Grad. Sch. Banking, Rutgers U., 1948; m. Elizabeth L. A0derson, Mar. 11, 1946; childrenSarah Frances, Robert Howison. With Bank of N.Y., 1935-41; v.p. First Nat. Exchange Bank, Roanoke, Va., 1941-59; exec. v.p. Investors Mgmt. Co., Inc., Elizabeth, N.Y., 1959-65, pres., 1965-, also dir.; v.p. Anchor Corp., 1965—, also pres. of Investment Management div.; dir. Longview Corp.; mem. faculty Grad. Sch. Banking, Rutgers U., 1950-59. Pres. Roanoke chpt. A.R.C., 1954. Served to comdr. USNR, 1942- 46; PTO. Decorated Bronze Star. Mem. Pi Kappa Alpha, Alpha Kappa Psi. Kiwanian (bd. dirs. Roanoke 1957-59). Clubs: Farmington Country (Charlottesville, Va.); Echo Lake Country (Westfield); Harbor View, University (N.Y.C.). Home: 821 Bradford Av Westfield, NJ 07090. Office: 40 Parker Rd Elizabeth NJ 07207

DANIEL, ROBERT HUGH, constrn. co. exec.; b. Anderson, S.C., Sept. 1, 1906; s. James Fleming and Mildred Leila (Adams) D.; B.A., The Citadel, 1929, D.Sc., 1957; m. Martha Stone Cobb, Dec. 14, 1936; children—Robert Hugh, Charles William. With Daniel Constrn. Co., Birmingham, Ala., 1935—, v.p., 1935-54, pres., 1954-64, chmn., treas., 1964—, also dir.; dir. Ala. Gas Co., Central Bank & Trust Co., Fla. Nat. Banks of Fla., Jacksonville, Birmingham, So. Bank & Trust Co., Greenville, S.C., Jim Walter Corp., Tampa, Fla. Chmn. fund drive Jefferson County United Appeal, 1954; dir. Jefferson County Community Chest, 1961-63. Bd. dirs. Birmingham Mus. Art. Served to lt. (sg.) USNR, 1943-45. Home: 3316 Dell Rd Birmingham AL 35223 Office: Daniel Bldg Birmingham AL 35201

DANIEL, ROBERT WOODHAM, educator; b. Memphis, Apr. 13, 1915; s. Robert Woodham and Nannie (Gailor) D.; A.B., U. of South, 1935; Ph.D., Yale, 1939; m. Mary Dabney Ware, Aug. 21, 1940; children—Elizabeth, Thomas. Instr., Yale, 1939-44, Harvard, 1944; asst. prof. U. Okla., 1944-47; asst. prof., then asso. prof. U. Tenn., 1947-60; mem. faculty Kenyon Coll., 1960—, prof. English, 1961—, chmn. dept., 1964—; Fulbright prof. Am. lit. U. Athens (Greece), 1954-55. Mem. Modern Lang. Assn., Am. Assn. U. Profs., Nat. Council Tchrs. English, Phi Delta Theta. Democrat. Episcopalian. Author: A Contemporary Rhetoric, 1967; also articles. Editor: (with others) Theme and Form, An Introduction to Literature, 2d. rev. edit. 1969; (with Glenn Leggett) The Written Word, 1960. Home: Box 247 Gambier, OH 43022.

DANIEL, ROLLIN AUGUSTUS, Jr., surgeon; b. Union Point, Ga., June 14, 1908; s. Rollin Augustus and Mary (Frazer) D.; B.A., Vanderbilt U., 1930, M.D., 1933; m. Ann Kelley, Jan. 5, 1939; children—Ann, Rollin Augustus III. Intern Vanderbilt U. Hosp., Nashville, 1933-34, resident, 1934-38; asst. resident surgeon Barnes Hosp., St. Louis, 1934-35; asst. prof. surgery Vanderbilt U. Sch. Medicine, 1941-47, asso. prof. surgery, 1947-51, prof. surgery, 1951-54, prof. clin. surgery, 1954—; chief surg. service St. Thomas Hosp., 1962- 66, 70—; cons. thoracic surgery VA Hosp., Nashville, 1946—. Diplomate Am. Bd. Surgery, Am. Bd. Thoracic Surgery (chmn. 1966-67, sec.-treas. 1968—). Fellow A.C.S.; mem. Middle Tenn. Heart Assn. (past pres.), Vanderbilt U. Alumni Assn. (bd. dirs), Am., So. surg. assns., Soc. Clin. Surgery, Am. Assn. Thoracic Surgery, Am., So., Tenn. med. assns., Nashville Surg. Soc., Nashville Acad. Medicine. Baptist. Club: Belle Meade Country (Nashville). Home: 618 Lynwood Blvd Nashville TN 37203 Office: St Thomas Hosp 2000 Hayes St Nashville TN 37203

DANIEL, RUBY KATHRYN, eye physician and surgeon; d. Dr. Robert Harry and Beulah May (Fite) Daniel; M.D., Baylor U., 1928; M.S., U. Minn., 1938. Intern at Lane-Stanford Teaching Hosp., San Francisco, 1928-29; Intern in ophthalmology, U. Chgo. clinics, 1932-33, asst. resident in ophthalmology, 1933-34; fellowship in ophthalmology, Mayo Clinic Found., Rochester, Minn., 1934-36; mem. teaching staff and asso. in ophthalmology, Pieping, (China) Union Med. Coll. (Rockefeller Found.), 1936-37; vis. prof. opthalmology, Women's Med. Coll. of Vellore (South India), 1937; 1st asst. ophthalmology, Mayo Clinic, 1938- 39; asst. clin. prof. ophthalmology, Southwestern Med. Found., Dallas, 1943—; in pvt. practice, Dallas, 1939—; chief med. cons. Lighthouse for the Blind. Diplomate Am. Bd. Ophthalmology. fellow A.C.S., Internat. Coll. Surgeons; mem. A.M.A., A.A.A.S., Am. Acad. Ophthalmology and Otolaryngology, So. Clin. Soc., Dallas County Med. Soc., Dallas Acad. Ophthalmology and Otolaryngology (past pres.), Alumni Assn. Mayo Found, Mortar Bd. Methodist. Clubs: Brook Hollow Golf, Knife and Fork, Coll. Women's Writers (Dallas). Has Initiated and incorporated 2 philanthropic organizations for salvaging eyes and rehab. after eye difficulties (pres. both orgns.). Contbr. articles: Allergy and Cataracts, Jour. A.M.A., 1935; Exophthalmos Associated with Hyperthyroidism, staff meetings of Mayo Clinic, Oct., 1938; Healing of the Iris in Rabbits Following Experimental Iridectomy. Archives of ophthalmology, April 1944. Home: 6710 Robin Rd Dallas TX 75209 Office: Med. Arts Bldg Dallas, TX 75201.

DANIEL, VICTOR JAMES, Jr., utility exec.; b. Meridian, Miss., Dec. 7, 1916; s. Victor James and Nell (Henry) D.; student U.S. Naval Acad., 1936-38; B.E.E., Miss. State U., 1940; m. Marjorie Mary Bailey, July 18, 1942; children—Elizabeth Ann (Mrs. Kyser Cowart Ptomey), Amy Lynn. With Miss. Power Co., 1945—, comml. sales engr., Gulfport, Miss., 1945-48, sales supr., Laurel, Miss., 1948-51, new industries rep., Gulfport, 1951-53, asst. comml. mgr., 1953-55, comml. mgr., 1955-62, v.p., 1962-69, exec. v.p., 1969—, dir., 1964—. Mem. engring. adv. com. Miss. State U., 1965-69; div. chmn. Am. Heart Assn., 1961; group chmn. United Fund, 1970. Served with USAF, 1941-45. Mem. Am. Soc. Profl. Engrs., Miss. Soc. Profl. Engrs., Capital City Petroleum Club, Newcomen Soc., Sigma Alpha Epsilon. Presbyn. Clubs: Broadwater Country (pres. 1965); Downtown. Home: 1109 2d St Gulfport MS 39501 Office: 2992 W Beach St Gulfport MS 39501

DANIEL, WALTER CLARENCE, univ. pres.; b. Macon, Ga., May 12, 1920; s. Walter E. and Annie (Jones) D.; B.A., Johnson C. Smith U., 1941; M.A., S.D. State U., 1959; M.A., Western Res. U., 1949; Ph.D., Bowling Green State U., 1962; m. Launa Harris, May 13, 1968. Tchr. pub. schs., Los Angeles, 1946-58; prof. English, St. Augustine's Coll., 1961-62; prof. English, N.C. Coll., Durham, 1962-63; chmn. div. humanities N.C. A. and T. State U., Greensboro, 1965-67, dir. 13 Colls. Program, 1967-68; pres. Lincoln U., Jefferson City, Mo., 1968-; cons. U.S. Office Edn. Served with USAAF, 1941-44. Mem. Modern Lang. Assn., Coll. Lang. Assn., Am. Assn. U. Profs., Greensboro C. of C. Contbr. articles profl. jours. Home: 601 Jackson St Jefferson City MO 65101

DANIEL, WILBUR CLARENCE, congressman; b. Chatham, Va., May 12, 1914; s. Reuben Earl and Georgia Lee (Grant) D.; student Averett College, Danville, Va., 1954- 56; m. Ruby Gordon McGregor, Sept. 30, 1939; 1 son, Jimmie Foxx. With Dan River Mills, Inc., Danville, Va., 1939—, successively laborer, clk., foreman, supr., interviewer, employment mgr., 1939-54, personnel exec., 1954-57, asst. to pres., 1957-68; mem. 91st-92d Congresses 5th Dist. Va. Member Virginia House of Delegates, 1959-68. Active worker A.R.C., Salvation Army, Boy Scouts Am., Nat. Soc. Crippled Children; nat. chmn. Points for Polio, 1957; mem. Gov's. Hosp. Com., 1952-57, Gov.'s Com. for Employment Physically Handicapped, 1957; mem. Va. Commn. on Constl. Govt., adv. com. to Fed. Civil Rights Commn. Civilian adviser 2d Army. Decorated Star of Solidarity (Italy). Mem. of Va. State (v.p.) and Danville (pres.) Tb assns., Am. Legion (dept. comdr. 1951, nat. vice comdr., 1952, comdr. 1956-57). Mason. Elk, Kiwanian. Author articles on Americanism, Socialism and child welfare. Home: 130 Beverly Rd Grove Park Danville VA 24541 Office: House Office Bldg Washington DC 20515

DANIEL, WILLIAM P., lawyer, rancher; b. Liberty County, Tex., Nov. 20, 1915; s. Price and Nannie (Partlow) D.; LL.B., Baylor U., 1938; m. Vara Faye Martin, Dec. 28, 1939; children—Will, Ann, Susan, Dani. Admitted to Tex. bar, 1938; gen. practice, Liberty, 1938—; county atty., 1943-44; gov. Guam, 1961- 63; cons. to Dept. Interior. Pres. Daniel Land Co., Inc., 1938—; owner, restorer, historic Plantation Ranch; coordinator and actor in motion picture, Alamo, 1960; producer Big Thicket Charity Trek, 1955-61, Liberty Bi-centennial, 1956; roped rhinoceros and other African big game alive, helped produce movie Kwaheri, 1960; dir.-gen. U. Tex. Rodeo, 1956- 61; judge Tex. Prison Rodeo, 1957-60. Del. Nat. Conv. Boy Scouts Am., 1954-55; host ann. Crippled Children's Party at Plantation Ranch, for under privileged children from Tex. and La., ann. Easter egg hunt for gen. public, Tex. and La.; leader Santa Claus caravan horses and carriages, to distribute Christmas candy and fruit to children in several towns. Sec. Democratic Exec. Com. Tex., 1939-41; mem. Tex. Legislature, 1949-54. Atty., trustee Kersting Meml. Hosp., Liberty, Tex., Meth. Hosp., Houston Meth. Orphans Home, Waco, Tex.; trustee Meth. Conf. Bd. Edn.; atty. and mgr. Daniel- Baylor U. Trust. Served with AUS, World War II. Named Titled Texan, Houston Post, 1956; named Man of Year, Nat. Intercollegiate Rodeo Assn., 1957-58; Texas ranger, 1959—; Tex. ambassador-at-large, 1957-61; recipient Silver Merit award Nat. Vets. Fgn. Wars, 1961; Tex. Heritage Found. Distinguished Service medal. Mem. Am., Tex., Guam, Alaskan, Trust Territory of the Pacific Islands, Liberty County bar assns., Am. Judicature Soc., Liberty C. of C. (dir.), Sons Republic Tex., S.A.R., Am. Legion, Hollywood Screen Actors Guild. Methodist (trustee, steward; pres. Beaumont Dist. Bd. Missions 1939-44; del. to gen. and juris. conf. Mason (32, Shriner), Lion, Rotarian (Liberty and Guam), Woodman. Address: PO Box 87 Liberty TX 77575

DANIELEY, JAMES EARL, coll. pres.; b. Burlington, N.C., July 28, 1924; s. Henry Hubbard and Grace Elizabeth (Mansfield) D.; A.B., Elon Coll., 1946; M.A., U. N.C., 1949, Ph.D. in Organic Chemistry, 1954; postdoctoral research Johns Hopkins, 1956-57; m. Verona Annie Daniels, Sept. 1, 1948; children—Ned Daniels, Mark Samuel, Jane Elizabeth. Instr. Elon Coll., 1946-47, asst. prof., 1947-48, asso. prof., 1948-50, prof. chemistry, 1952—, dean coll., 1953-56, pres., 1957—. Lectr. chemistry U. N.C., 1952; vis. prof. chemistry, summers 1953, 54, 56. Pres., So. Nat. Com. Churchmen's Fellowship and chmn. council for lay life and work bd. dirs. So. Conf. United Ch. of Christ. Pres. N. C. Found. of Church-Related Colls., 1968; pres. Piedmont U. Center, 1968. Named Young Man of Year, Burlington (N.C.). Jr. C. of C., 1957, North Carolina Young Man of Yr., N.C. Jr. C. of C., 1958, Alamance County Citizen of Year, Burlington Kiwanis Club, 1961, Distinguished Citizenship award N.C. Dist. Civitan Internat., 1961-62. Mem. Nat. Assn. Parliamentarians, Am. Chem. Soc., N.C. Acad. Sci., Sigma Xi, Phi Delta Kappa, Delta Psi Omega. Mem. United Ch. of Christ (deacon). Rotarian. Home: Box 245 Elon College NC 27708

DANIELIAN, LEON, ballet dancer, choregrapher; b. N.Y.C., Oct. 31, 1920; s. Frank and Varsik (Coolidganian) D.; student Mikhail Mordkin Ballet Arts and Am. Ballet Sch. alternately for 5 yrs. With Ballet Russe de Monte Carlo since 1943; dir. American Ballet Theatre Schs., 1967—; repertoire includes Les Sylphides, Swan Lake, Blue Bird, The Nutcracker, Pas de Deau Classique, Madronos, Cirque de Deux, Nijinsky's ballet L'Apres Midi d'Une Faun, and Fokine's Spectre de la Rose; character roles in Gaite Parisienne and Frankie and Johnny; guest artist Ballet des Champs Elyseés, Paris and North Africa, winter season 1951-52; world tour as guest star with San Francisco Ballet; ballet master Ballet Russe Sch. Recipient Best Performing Male Dancer of Year award East Coast critics, 1949; Dance Masters of Am. Ann. award, 1971. Address: 33 W 67th St New York City NY

DANIELIAN, NOOBAR RETHESOS, economist, b. Constantinople, Turkey, Sept. 12, 1906; s. Réthésos and Anne (Papazian) D.; A.B., Harvard, 1928, M.A., 1929, Ph.D., 1932; m. Grace A. Apelian, Aug. 28, 1936; children—Sandra Elizabeth, Ronald Lawrence. Came to U.S., 1923, naturalized, 1928. Instr. dept. econs. Harvard, 1929-35; financial, utility expert FCC, 1935-38; dir. St. Lawrence survey U.S. Dept. Commerce, 1939-43; dir. program staff Fgn. Econ. Adminstrn., 1943-44; cons. Office Sec. Commerce, Office Undersec. State, 1944-45; v.p. Gt. Lakes-St. Lawrence Assn., 1949-52, pres., 1952- 65; mem. adv. bd. U.S. St. Lawrence Seaway Devel. Corp. 1961-66; editor, pub. The Heartland, 1953-56, Port Cons., Detroit, 1955-56; econ. adviser Lorain, O. 1955-59. Recipient Certificate of Merit, Amvets, 1955. Mem. Internat. Econ. Policy Assn. (pres. 1957—), Am. Econ. Assn., Am. Acad. Polit. Sci., Nat. Assn. Bus. Economists, Phi Beta Kappa. Episcopalian. Clubs: Congressional Country (Bethesda, Md.); Detroit: Harvard (N.Y.C.); Harvard, National Press, Metropolitan and International (Washington). Author: The St. Lawrence Survey (7 vols.), 1941. Editor: U.S. Balance of Payments, an Appraisal of U.S. Economic Strategy, 1966; U.S. Balance of Payments, A Reappraisal, 1968. Contbr. profl. publs., mags. Home: 4701 Willard Av Chevy Chase MD 20015 Office: Cafritz Bldg Washington DC 20006

DANIELLI, JAMES FREDERIC, biologist, educator; b. Wembley, Eng., Nov. 13, 1911; s. James Frederic and Helena (Hollins) D.; Ph.D., London (Eng.) U., 1933, Cambridge (Eng.) U., 1942; D.Sc., London U., 1938, Gent (Belgium) U., 1956, Med. Coll. Pa., 1970; m. Mary Guy, Jan. 4, 1937; children—Richard, Corinne. Fellow, Princeton, 1933- 35, St. John's Coll., Cambridge U., 1942-45; physiologist Marine Biol. Assn., 1946; reader cell physiology Royal Cancer Hosp., 1946-49; prof. zoology, chmn. dept. King's Coll., London, 1949-61; prof. medicinal chemistry and biochem. pharmacology State U. N.Y. at Buffalo, 1962-65, chmn. dept. biochem. pharma- cology, 1962-64, prof. theoretical biology, dir. Center for Theoretical Biology, 1965—, provost faculty sci. and math., 1967-69, asst. to pres., 1969—; cons. various indsl. firms, pubs., govt. orgns. Fellow Royal Soc.; mem. Inst. Biology, Biochem. Soc., Physiol. Soc., Soc. for Biology, Am. Soc. Exptl. Biology and Medicine, Am. Inst. Biol. Scis. Author: Permeability of Natural Membranes, 1942; Cell Physiology and Pharmacology, 1952; Cytochemistry, 1953. Editor: Symposia Soc. for Exptl. Biology, 1946-56, Internat. Soc. for Cell Biology, 1950-60, Internat. Rev. Cytology, 1951—, Jour. Theoretical Biology, 1960—, Gen. Cytochem. Methods, 1958-65, Progress in Surface Sci., 1962—, Molecular Pharmacology, 1964—. Contbr. articles profl. jours. Office: Center for Theoretical Biology 4248 Ridge Lea Rd Amherst NY 14226

DANIELS, ALFRED HARVEY, merchandising exec.; b. Pitts., Mar. 12, 1912; s. Harry and Irene Daniels; B.A., Harvard, 1933, M.B.A., 1935; m. Ada M. Schoenberg, Oct. 1935; children—James, Molly; m. 2d, Stella Goldstein, 1959. Divisional mdse. mgr. Abraham & Straus, 1940-48, mdse. v.p., 1948-55; v.p. Federated Dept. Stores, Inc., Cin., 1956—, also cons., group pres., dir. Federated Dept. Stores, 1969—; cons. Hudson's Bay Co. Canda; chmn. bd., chief exec. officer Burdine's, 1961-68; bd. dirs. Asso. Merchandising Corp.; sr. research asso. Columbia U. Sch. Bus. Bd. dirs. Oper Guild; bd. trustees United Fund, U. Miami; mem. Orange Bowl Com., 1963-68. Mem. Fla. Retail Fedn. (dir.), Nat. Retail Mchts. Assn. (exec. com.). Clubs: Lotos, Harvard (N.Y.C.); Miami; Bankers, Concordia (San Francisco). Contbr. articles trade reviews. Home: 1000 Mason St San Francisco CA 94108

DANIELS, ARTHUR NOYES, mfg. exec.; b. Los Angeles, Oct. 1, 1908; s. Ralph Chandler and Myra (Winn) Daniels; B.S. cum laude, U.S. Naval Acad., 1931; M.S. Harvard, 1936: m. Dolores Dedons de Pierrefeu, June 18, 1931; children—Leonora, Delia, Theodore. Ensign USN, 1931-35; asst. prof. engring. Dartmouth, 1937-41; founding partner MPB, Inc., Keene, N.H., 1939-46; founder, chmn. New Hampshire Ball Bearings, Inc., Peterboro, N.H., 1946—; dir. Micro Ball Co., Monadnock Nat. Bank. Chmn. indsl. adv. com. Gov.'s Commn. Vocational Rehab., 1968. Trustee Hancock Ednl. Assn., 1946-55; trustee, dir. Cathedral of the Pines; dir. MacDowell Colony Assn. Served to comdr. USNR, 1941-46: PTO. Mem. Am. Soc. M.E., Am. Ordnance Assn., Newcomen Soc., Anti Friction Bearing Mfrs. Assn. Clubs: Harvard, New Bedford Yacht. Home: RD 1 Hancock NH 03449 Office: New Hampshire Ball Bearings Inc Jaffrey Rd Peterboro NH 03458

DANIELS, CONRAD L., mfg. co. exec.; b. N.Y.C., July 21, 1915; s. Carl S. and Mollie (Eitelberg) D.; B.S. Coll. City N.Y., 1945; M.B.A., N.Y.U., 1956; m. Ruth Cuttler, June 25, 1939 (dec. 1966); childrenLawrence S., Frederick M., Robin M.; m. 2d Betty V.; children—Russell, Candra, Douglas. Started career as br. mgr. Universal Camera Corp., 1937- 41; plant mgr. Mergenthaler Linotype Co., 1943-59; gen. mgr. J.I. Case Co., 1959-62; v.p. operations Olin Mathieson Chem. Corp. 1962- 65; v.p. operations Pratt & Whitney div. of Colt Industries, 1965—; pres. Hydreco div. Gen. Signal Corp., Kalamazoo. Mem. bd. edn. Sch. Dist. 20, N.Y. State, 1958-59; mem. Nassau County council Boy Scouts Am., 1958-. Mem. Am. Soc. Quality Control, Am. Mgmt. Assn., Alumni Assn. N.Y.U., Am. Ordnance Assn., Phi Gamma Kappa. Home: Route 1 Hickory Corners MI 49060. Office: Hydreco Division General Signal Corp Kalamazoo MI 49203

DANIELS, DERICK JANUARY, newspaper editor; b. Washington, Dec. 6, 1928; s. Worth Bagley and Josephine Poe (January) D.; grad. St. Albans Sch., Washington, 1946; A.B. in Journalism, U. N.C., 1950; m. Elizabeth Long Blalock, Aug. 10, 1950; children—Leigh Churchill, Scott Daniels. Reporter, Durham (N.C.) Herald, 1950, St. Petersburg (Fla.) Times, 1950-51, Atlanta Constn., 1951-55; sub- editor, then city editor Miami (Fla.) Herald, 1955-61; with Detroit Free Press, 1961—, exec. editor, 1967—; dir. News and Observer Pub. Co., Raleigh, N.C. Mem. devel. com. Am. Press Inst., Columbia, 1970. Bd. dirs. Detroit Area Council World Affairs, United Found. Detroit; mem. founders soc. Detroit Inst. Arts. Mem. Am. Soc. Newspaper Editors (chmn. editorial bd. bull.), Econ. Club Detroit, Alpha Tau Omega. Episcopalian. Clubs: Detroit, Adcraft (Detroit). Home: 1048 Harvard Rd Grosse Pointe MI 48230 Office: 321 Lafayette Blvd Detroit MI 48231

DANIELS, DOMINICK VINCENT, congressman; b. Jersey City, Oct. 18, 1908; s. John and Carmela (De Stefano) D.; student Fordham U.; LL.B., Rutgers U., 1929; m. Camille Curcio, Sept. 15, 1935; children—Dolores, Barbara. Admitted to N.J. bar, 1930, since practiced in Jersey City; magistrate Jersey City Municipal Ct., 1952-58; mem. 86th-92d Congresses, 14th Dist. N.J. City chmn. Po Valley Flood Relief Com.; vice chmn. Jersey City Civil Rights Com., 1952-55. Mem. N.J., Hudson County bar assns. Democrat. Elk, K.C. (4). Club: University of Hudson County. Home: Jersey City NJ 07306 Office: House Office Bldg Washington DC 20515

DANIELS, DRAPER, advt. exec.; b. Morris, N.Y., Aug. 12, 1913; s. John Albert and Fanny Martha (Draper) D.; B.S., Syracuse U., 1934; m. Louise Parker Lux Cort, Oct. 9, 1937 (div. 1967); children—John, Bruce, Marie, Curtis; m. 2d, Myra Janco, Aug. 18, 1967. Sales, advt. depts. Vick Chem. Co., N.Y.C., 1935-40; copywriter Young & Rubicam, N.Y.C., 1940-44, 46-47, copy chief, Chgo., 1947, v.p., 1948, chmn. plans bd., 1949-54; copy supr. McCann- Erickson, Kenyon & Eckhardt, N.Y.C., 1944-46; copy supr. Leo Burnett Co., Inc., Chgo., 1954, v.p., 1954-56, v.p. in charge copy, mem. plans bd., 1956-57, dir., v.p. charge creative depts., 1957-58, exec. v.p. creative services, exec. com., 1958-61, chmn. exec. com., dir., 1961-62; nat. export expansion coordinator U.S. Govt., 1962-63; exec. v.p. McCann-Erickson, Inc., 1963-64, Compton Advt. Inc., 1964-65, chmn. bd., chief exec. officer Draper Daniels, Inc., Chgo., 1965—. Member adv. bd. Sch. Journalism, Syracuse U.; adv. bd. Coll. Bus. Adminstrn. Roosevelt U., also fellow. Mem. Mfg. Export Adv. Com., Ill., 1967, 70. Chmn. Dem. Central Com., Lake County, Ill., 1954-56; del. Dem. Nat. Conv., 1956. Club: University (Chgo.). Home: 910 Lake Shore Dr Chicago IL 60611 Office: 520 N Michigan Av Chicago IL 60611

DANIELS, EDWARD BERNARD, librarian; b. Marblehead, Mass., Feb. 19, 1921; s. Earl Goddle and Mary (Savoy) D.; A.B., Boston U., 1948; M.S., Simmons Coll., 1950; m. Edith Dorothy Wilson, Mar. 23, 1942; childrenDonna Ingrid, Deborah Ann. Tchr. English, Endicott Jr. Coll., 1948-49; library asst. Enoch Pratt Free Pub. Library, Balt., 1950-52, young peoples librarian, 1952-54, br. librarian, 1954-55; dir. adult services Worcester (Mass.) Free Library, 1955-56; chief librarian Dearborn (Mich.) Pub. Library, 1956-62; librarian Columbus, (O.) Pub. Library, 1962—, Bus. mgr. Md. Librarian, 1953-55. Served with USN, 1939-46. Mem. Am., Mich. (vice chmn., chmn. 1958- 59) Ohio (pres. 1969) library assns. Rotarian. Home: 4200 Rudy Rd Columbus OH 43214. Office: 96 S Grant Av Columbus, OH 43215.

DANIELS, EDWIN ADAMS, ret. bus. exec.; b. Dayton, O., Nov. 8, 1899; s. Charles and Susie W. (Ayers) D.; student N.Y. U. Sch. Commerce, 1919-20; m. Frances F. Aull, June 20, 1923; children—Nancy (Mrs. Arthur L.S. Waxter), Edwin Adams. Joined Lowe Bros. Co., Dayton, 1920, asst. gen. sales mgr., 1933-37, gen. sales mgr., 1937-45, exec. v.p., 1945-54, became pres., 1954, also dir., now ret.; dir. Gem City Savs. Assn. Bank and Trust Co., Dayton, O. Mem. Dayton Area C. of C. Clubs: Miami Valley Hunt and Polo (past pres.), Ye Buz Fuz (Dayton). Home: 508 Elderwood Rd Kettering OH 45429 Office: 424 E 3d St Dayton OH 45402

DANIELS, ELLIOT BERNARD, accountant; b. N.Y.C., Jan. 21, 1919; s. Morris and Mildred (Lewis) D.; B.S. in Accounting, N.Y.U., 1941; m. Sheila Goldberg, Dec. 28, 1947; children—Sharon, Scott. Engaged in pub. accounting, 1946—; partner Sa- ders & Daniels Co., C.P.A.'s, N.Y.C., 1958—; dir., mem. exec. com. U.S. Smelting & Refining Corp.; dir. Cudahy Co., Phoenix, Fed. Pacific Electric Corp., Newark, Phoenix Steel Corp., Phoenxville, Pa. Formerly auditor Roosevelt (N.Y.) Civic Assn. Past co-chmn. fund raising com. United Jewish Appeal, Roosevelt. C.P.A., N.Y. Mem. N.Y. State Soc. C.P.A.'s, N.Y. Credit Men's Assn. Jewish religion (pres., trustee temple). Club: New York University Alumni (N.Y.C.). Home: 209 Putnam Av Freeport NY 11520 Office: 475 Fifth Av New York City NY 10017

DANIELS, ELMER HARLAND, sculptor, indsl. designer; b. Owosso, Mich., Oct. 23, 1905; s. H. J. and Blanche (Tuthill) D.; student Grand Rapids (Mich.) Coll., 1924-25, John Herron Art Inst., Indpls., 1925-27, Beaux Arts Inst. Design, N.Y.C., 1927-29; study in Europe, Eng., France and Italy (sculpture), 1931; student Columbia, summer 1930; m. Madge Kuhn, 1933; children—Stephen, Carol, Richard, Julia. Tchr., Art Center Sch., Indpls., 1935-38; conducted pvt. studio classes, Indpls, 1938-40; indsl. designer, Hollywood and Oakland (Cal.), 1942—; organized Daniels Assos. archtl. firm, 1943-50, Daniels and Zermack Assos., Ann Arbor, 1950-72; designer Domore Furniture Co.; designed bank buildings, Mich., Ohio, Ind., Ill; important works include Lincoln Meml. Lincoln City, Ind. (commissioned by State of Ind.), 1941, Heroic Head of Lincoln in Ala. marble, State Capitol Bldg., Indpls., 1939; Three Heroic Stone Figures, St. Joseph Ch., Jasper, Ind., 1941; six stone panels for Arts Bldg., Ball State Teachers Coll., Mincie, Ind., 1933; Brotherhood of Maintenance of Way meml., Detroit; Bay County War Meml., Bay City, Mich., Family Group, Detroit & No. Savs. & Loan, Flint, Mich., 5 terra figures, Loma Linda Restaurant, Ann Arbor, Mich., mural in oil, Union Bank, Steubenville, O. Portraits include: Paul V. McNutt (bronze), Col. Richard Lieber, Evans Wollen, William Fortune, Joseph Coured, Bobbs Merrial Pub. Co., Ernest Hemmingway (bronze), Albert Switzer (bronze), Albert Einstein (bronze). Indsl. designer for Kaiser Industries, Heywood Wakefield Co., Plomb Tool Co., Steelcase, Inc., Stow- Davis Furniture Co., Bear Archery Co., etc. Recipient Harry Johnson award, 1931; Ind. Artists Sculpture prize, 1938; C. V. Hickox prize, 1942. Mem. Am. Soc. Indsl. Designers, Nat. Sculpture Soc., Archtl. League N.Y., Ind. Artists, Painters and Sculptors of N.J., Ind. Lincoln Union, Lincoln Fellowship of So. Cal. (hon. mem., 1944), Mich. Acad Sci., Arts and Letters, Pasadena, Palm Beach, Ann Arbor art assns., Washtenaw, Mich. hist. socs., Ann Arbor, Mich., Pompano Beach, Fla. chambers of commerce. Clubs: University of Pasadena, Pasadena Maestros; Miscowabik (life) Calumet, Mich.); Ann Arbor (Mich.) Town. Contbr. articles on sculpture and art in gen., to Stone and Quarry, Pacific Plastics, Western Automotives, Mich. Investor, Mich. Tradesman. Sculpture work exhibited in Life, Look, Sat. Eve. Post. Home: 200 NW 29th Pl Pompano Beach FL Office: 2080 S State St Ann Arbor MI 48104

DANIELS, FARRINGTON, educator; b. Mnpls. Mar. 8, 1889; s. Franc Burchard and Florence Louise (Farrington) D.; B.S., U. of Minn., 1910, M.S., 1911; Ph. D., Harvard, 1914; D.Sc., U. R.I., U. Minn., U. Dakar, U. Louisville, U. Wis.; m. Olive M. Bell, Sept. 15, 1917; children—Farrington, Florence Mary (Drury), Miriam (Ludwig), Dorin. Instr. chemistry, Worcester (Mass.) Poly. Inst., 1914-17, asst. prof., 1917-18; electrochem. U.S. Nitrogen Research Lab., Washington, 1919-20; asst. prof. chemistry U. of Wis., 1920-24, asso. prof., 1924-28, prof., 1928-59, now prof. emeritus, chmn. dept. chemistry 1952- 59, research Solar Energy Lab., Engring. Expt. Sta.; prof. chemistry Stanford, summer 1930; George Fisher Baker non-res. lectr. chemistry, Cornell U., Feb-June 1935; vis. scholar Cranbrook Inst. Sci., 1968. Dir. metall. lab., U. Chgo., 1945-46; chmn. bd. govs., Argonne Nat. Lab., 1946-48. Served as 1st lt., U.S. Chem. Warfare Service, 1918. Guggenheim fellow, 1952. Fellow A.A.A.S. (chmn. chem. sect. 1937, 1947); mem. Am. Chem. Soc. (pres. 1953; Willard Gibbs medal; Priestley medal), Nat. Acad. Scis. (v.p. 1957-61), Am. Acad. Arts and Scis., Geochem. Soc. (pres. 1958), Am. Philos. Soc., Solar Energy Society (pres. 1964-66), Sigma Xi (pres. 1965-66), Phi Beta Kappa, Alpha Delta Phi, Alpha Chi Sigma. Conglist. Author: Mathematical Preparation for Physical Chemistry; Chemical Kinetics; Direct Use of the Suns Energy. Co-author: Physical Chemistry; Experimental Physical Chemistry; Challenge of Our Times; Solar Energy Research. Research chem. kinetics, nitrogen oxides, thermoluminescence of crystals, atomic energy and solar energy. Home: 1129 Waban Hill Madison WI 53711

DANIELS, FARRINGTON, Jr., educator, physician; b. Worcester, Mass., Sept. 29, 1918; s. Farrington and Olive (Bell) D.; A.B., U. Wis., 1940, M.A., 1942; M.D., Harvard, 1943, M.P.H., 1952; m. Alice Mae Monroe, June 9, 1951; children—Elizabeth, George, Christopher. Intern N.Y. Hosp., N.Y.C., 1944, resident and research fellow, 1947-49; head stress physiology br. U.S. Army Research and Devel. Command, Lawrence, Natick, Mass., 1950-55; asst. prof. dermatology U. Ore., Portland, 1955-61; asso. prof. U. Ill., 1961-62; asso. prof. medicine, head dermatology div. N.Y. Hosp. Cornell Med. Center, N.Y.C., 1962-70, prof. medicine, 1970—; cons. Meml., James Ewing hosps. Mem. photobiology com. Nat. Acad. Scis. Served to capt., M.C., AUS, 1944-47. Fellow A.A.A.S.; mem. Soc. Investigative Dermatology, Am. Acad. Dermatology, Am. Dermatol. Assn., N.Y. Dermatol. Soc., N.Y. Acad. Medicine, N.Y. Acad. Sci., Human Factors Soc., Internat. Soc. Biometerology, Am. Assn. Phys. Anthropology. Contbr. articles profl. jours. Home: 58 Harmon Av Pelham NY 10803 Office: 1300 York Av New York City NY 10021

DANIELS, FRANK ARTHUR, newspaper exec.; b. Raleigh, N.C., June 8, 1904; s. Josephus and Addie Worth (Bagley) D.; A.B., U. N.C., 1927; m. Ruth Aunspaugh, Nov. 20, 1929; children—Frank Arthur, Patricia Woronoff. With mechanical circulation, advt. depts. News and Observer. Raleigh, 1927-32, treas., 1932-56, gen. mgr., 1942-. pres., 1956-, pub., 1966-; chmn. Raleigh bd. N.C. Nat Bank; dir. A.P. 1964-67, Atlantic & East Carolina Ry. Company. Chmn. N.C. Bd. Pub. Welfare, 1949- 56; mem. N.C. Tax Study Commn., 1955-56. Dir. Research Triangle Inst.; chmn. bd. trustees Rex Hosp., Raleigh, 1960-68. Mem. Am. (dir. 1956-64), So. (pres. 1951-52) newspaper pubs. assns. Presbyn. Clubs: Carolina Country, Sphinx (Raleigh). Home: 1515 Glenwood Ave Raleigh NC 27608 Office: News and Observer-Raleigh Times 215 S McDowell St Raleigh NC 27601

DANIELS, FREEMAN J., lawyer; b. Beverly, W.Va., Apr. 6, 1902; s. O. C. and Lovett (Schoonover) D.; A.B., Davis and Elkins Coll., 1922, LL.D., 1963; A.M., U. Va., 1926, LL.B., 1929; m. Mary Edmondson, Aug. 22, 1935; 1 dau., Mary (Mrs. John Lowry, Jr.). Admitted to N.Y. bar, 1932, since practiced in N.Y.C.; sr. partner Perkins, Daniels, McCormack. Dir. Helme Products, Inc., John Lowry, Inc., Trust Bd. of First Nat. City Bank Co., Golightly & Co., Internat., Inc., Gulf Port Shipping Co. (Can.), George Hall Corp., Hall Corp. of Can. Trustee U. Va. Grad. Sch. Bus., Mary Duke Biddle Found., Marjorie Merriweather Post Found., Lyndhurst council Nat. Trust Hist. Preservation; dir. Am. Symphony Orch. Mem. Am., N.Y. bar assns., Am. Judicature Soc., Phi Beta Kappa Assos. Presbyn. Clubs: University, Bronxville Field, American Yacht, Long Island Country; Farmington Country, Siwanoy Country, Boar's Head, Rockefeller Center Luncheon. Home: 274 Pondfield Rd Bronxville, NY 10708. Office: 30 Rockefeller Plaza, New York City NY 10020.

DANIELS, GEORGE GOETZ, journalist; b. Bklyn., Aug. 17, 1925; s. George Bryant and Katherine June (Goetz) D.; grad. Lawrenceville Sch., 1943; B.A. cum laude, Harvard, 1949; m. Doris Alden Billings, Dec. 19, 1965; 1 dau., Katherine Billings; children by previous marriage—Peter, Michael, Robert, Geoffrey. Corr., Time mag., Detroit, 1949-50, contbg. editor, 1950-56, asso. editor, 1956-60, sr. editor, 1960-71; editorial chief. Time-Life Records, 1971—. Dir. Main-Pearl Corp., Buffalo. Served to 1st lt. USAAF, 1943-46. Mem. Am. Ornithologists Union. Clubs: Harvard; Explorers; Bermuda Anglers. Home: Taconic Rd Greenwich CT 06830 Office: Time and Life Bldg Rockefeller Center New York City NY 10020

DANIELS, JOE E., lawyer: b. Ulysses, Pa., Nov. 30, 1899; s. George W. and Flora M. (Borst) D.; A.B., U. of Kansas, 1920; LL.B., Columbia U., 1922; m. Martha Mackle. Aug. 25, 1926; childrenMartha J. (Mrs. E. Richard Hurst), Susan F. (Mrs. John Cannon, Jr.). Admitted to N.Y. Bar, 1923; pvt. practice in N.Y., 1923-37; asst. to gen. counsel. R.C.A. Manufacturing Co., Inc., Camden, N.J., 1937-42; asst. commr. of patents, 1947-50; engaged in practice of law, N.Y.C., 1950—. Served with Inf. U.S. Army, 1918; Signal Corps, AUS, 1942-46. Mem. Am. Bar Assn., N.Y. Patent Law Assn., Sigma Nu. Republican. Mason. Home: 88 Ridge Rd Rumson NJ 07760 Office: 253 Broadway New York City NY 10007

DANIELS, JOHN HANCOCK, corp. exec.; b. St. Paul, Oct. 28, 1921; s. Thomas L. and Frances (Hancock) D.; student St. Paul Acad., 1932-37; grad. Phillips Exeter Acad., 1939; B.A., Yale, 1943; grad. Advanced Mgmt. Program, Harvard, 1957; m. Martha H. Williams, Dec. 23, 1942; children—Martha M. (Mrs. Willard C. Shull III), John Hancock, Jane P., Christopher W. With Archer-Daniels-Midland Co., Mpls. 1946—, successively mem. staff linseed oil div., prodn. mgr. alfalfa div., mgr. feed div., v.p., dir., 1946-53, pres., dir., 1958-67, chmn., 1967—; dir. Nat. City Bank Mpls., Soo Line R.R. Co., Warwick Electronics Inc. Bd. dirs. Decatur Meml. Hosp.; Bus. Council; trustee Com. Econ. Devel. Served from 2d lt. to capt., F.A., AUS, 1943-46. Decorated Bronze Star medal. Republican. Episcopalian. Clubs: Links (N.Y.C.); Chicago; Minneapolis, Sprindale Hall (Camden, S.C.). Home: Route 1 Box 112 Moweaqua IL Office: Box 1470 Decatur IL 62525

DANIELS, JONATHAN WORTH, editor, author; b. Raleigh, N.C., Apr. 26, 1902; s. Josephus and Addie Worth (Bagley) D.; A.B., U. N.C., 1921, M.A., 1922; postgrad. Columbia U. Law Sch., 1922-23; m. Elizabeth Bridgers, Sept. 5, 1923 (dec. Dec. 1929); 1 dau., Elizabeth Bridgers (Mrs. C. B. Squire); m. 2d, Lucy Billing Cathcart, Apr. 30, 1932; children—Lucy (Mrs. Thomas P. Inman), Adelaide (Mrs. B. J. Key), Cleves (Mrs. Cleves Daniels Rich). Reporter Louisville (Ky.) Times; then reporter Raleigh (N.C.) News and Observer, Washington corr., 1925-28, asso. editor, 1932- 33, editor, 1933-42, exec. editor, 1947, editor, 1948-70, editor emeritus , 1970—; asst. dir. Office Civilian Def., 1942; adminstrv. asst. to Pres., 1943-45; press sec. to Pres., 1945; U.S. mem. UN sub- com. on Prevention of Discrimination and Protection of Minorities, 1947- 53; mem. pub. adminstrv. bd. ECA and Mut. Security Agy., 1948-53; Dem. Nat. Committeeman from N.C., 1949-52; Mut. Security Agy., 1948-53; Dem. Nat. Committeeman from N.C., 1949-52; mem. Fed. Hosp. Council, 1949-53; on editorial staff, Fortune mag., N.Y.C., 1930, 31-32; contbr. weekly page, "A Native at Large," to Nation, 1941-42. Trustee Vassar Coll., 1942-48; Guggenheim fellow, 1930-31. Mem. Delta Kappa Epsilon. Democrat. Episcopalian. Club: National Press (Washington). Author: Clash of Angels (novel), 1930; A Southerner Discovers the South, 1938; A Southerner Discovers New England, 1940; Tar Heels: A Portrait of North Carolina, 1941; Frontier on the Potomac, 1946; The Man of Independence, 1950; The End of Innocence, 1954; The Forest is the Future, 1957; Prince of Carpetbeggars, 1958; Mosby, Gray Ghost of the Confederacy, 1959; Stonewall Jackson, 1959; Robert E. Lee, 1960; The Devil's Backbone; The Story of the Natchez Trace, 1962; They Will Be Heard, 1965; The Time Between The Wars, 1966; Washington Quadrille, 1968; Ordeal of Ambition-Jefferson, Hamilton, Burr, 1970. Contbr. articles and revs. to mags. Office: News and Observer Raleigh NC 27602

DANIELS, JOSEPH J., lawyer; b. Indpls. Apr. 13, 1890; s. Edward and Virginia (Johnston) D.; A.B., Wabash Coll., 1911; LL.B. cum laude, Harvard, 1914; m. Katharine A. Holliday, June 20, 1918 (dec. Apr. 1935); 1 dau., Katharine (Mrs. L.I. Kane); m. 2d, Robertine B. Fairbanks Apr. 2, 1945; 1 stepson, Michael B. Fairbanks (dec.). Practice of law, Indpls., 1914-67, ret., 1967; counsel firm Baker & Daniels; dir. Electric Steel Castings Co.; hon. dir. Nat. Starch & Chem. Corp. Hon. gov. Riley Hosp.; bd. corps. Crown Hill Cemetery, Indpls. Served from 1st lt. to capt. U.S. Army, 1917-1919. Mem. Phi Beta Kappa, Phi Beta Kappa Assos., Beta Theta Pi. Clubs: Indianapolis Literary, University (Indpls.). Home: 7034 Washington Blvd Indianapolis IN 46220 Office: Fletcher Trust Bldg Indianapolis IN 46204

DANIELS, MELVIN JOE, athlete; b. North Brook Twp., N.C., July 20, 1944; s. Maceo and Bernice (Clemmons) D.; student Burlington (Ia.) Jr. Coll., 1963-64; student U. N.M., 1964—; m. Cecilia Josephine Martinez, Oct. 2, 1967. Forward position Minn. Muskies, Mpls.-St. Paul, 1967-68; center position Ind. Pacers, Indpls., 1968—. Named to All League Team, 1968, 69, 70, 71, rebound leader, 1967-68, 68-69, 70-71; 1st team center All Star Game, 1968-71; Most Valuable Player, All Star Game, 1971; Rookie of the Year, 1968; Most Valuable Player, Am. Basketball Assn., 1968, 71. Mem. Omega Psi Phi. Home: 6404 Sunset Lane Indianapolis IN 46260 Office: Ind Pacers 638 E 38th St Indianapolis IN 46205

DANIELS, MYRA JANCO (Mrs. Draper Daniels), advt. exec.; b. Gary, Ind., June 25, 1925; d. Elias and Cecelia (Remstein) Janco; B.S., Ind. State Tchrs. Coll., 1948, M.A., 1954; postgrad. Ind. U., 1955-57; m. Draper Daniels, Aug. 19, 1967. Advt. dir. Meis Bros. Co., Terre Haute, Ind., 1944-50; v.p., account exec. Gregory & House Advt., Cleve., 1951-53; pres. Wabash Advt. Agy., Terre Haute, Ind., 1950-54; account supr. Kuttner & Kuttner, Chgo., 1954-62; v.p. Roche, Rickerd & Cleary (name later changed to Roche, Rickerd, Henri & Hurst, then to Roche, Rickerd, Henri, Hurst, Inc.), Chgo., 1962-63, exec. v.p., 1963-65; pres. Draper Daniels, Inc., Chgo., 1965—; mem. faculty Ind. U., 1957—, asso. prof. advt.,1958-61; advt., sales cons. Named Nat. Advt. Woman of Year, 1965; recipient

Distinguished Alumni award Ind. State U., 1966. Mem. Am. Humane Assn., Sales Execs. Club, Am. Marketing Assn., Am. Assn. U. Profs., Gamma Alpha Chi, Kappa Delta Pi, Pi Omega Pi, Pi Lambda Theta, Delta Pi Epsilon, Tau Kappa Alpha, Theta Sigma Phi. Club: Altrusa. Contbr. articles to profl. jours. Home: 910 Lake Shore Dr Chicago IL 60611 Office: Draper Daniels Inc 520 N Michigan Av Chicago IL 60611

DANIELS, PAUL CLEMENT, former U.S. ambassador; b. Buffalo, Oct. 26, 1903; s. John H. and Flora (Pike) D.; grad. cum laude Phillips Acad., Andover, Mass., 1920; B.A., Yale, 1924; postgrad. Univs. of Dijon and Grenoble (France), 1924, U. Toulouse (France), 1924-25; spl. studies for Am. fgn. service, 1926- 27; m. Theodora Olivier, Aug. 28, 1937; children—Jean Montague, Dorothy (dec.), John Alden (dec.). Tchr. French, Riverdale Country Sch., 1925-26; entered Am. fgn. service holding consular and diplomatic posts, 1928-43; chmn. Inter-Am. Coffee Bd., 1941-43; tech. adviser U. S. dels. conf. food and agr., Hot Springs, Va., 1943; counselor embassy, Bogotá, Columbia, 1943-45; Rio de Janeiro, Brazil, 1945-47; ambassador to Honduras, 1947; U.S. rep. Inter-Am. Econ. and Social Council, 1947-48; dir. Am. Rep. Affairs, State Dept., 1947-49; U.S. del. 9th Internat. Conf. Am. States, Bogota, 1948; ambassador to Council of Orgn. Am. States, 1948-50; U.S. ambassador to Ecuador, 1951-53. Spl. adviser on Antarctica, Dept. State, 1957-59. Mem. Antarctican Soc. (hon. pres.), Beta Theta Pi, Phi Beta Kappa. Home: Lakeville CT 06039 ☆

DANIELS, RALPH HEREFORD, Jr., broadcasting co. exec.; b. California, Dec. 22, 1927; s. Ralph Herford and Marian G. (Rogers) D.; B.A. in Econs., Pomona Coll.; student U. Cal.; m. Rosemary J. Sheedy, Oct. 18, 1963; children—Katherine, Elizabeth, Margaret. Account exec. radio sta. KNXT, Los Angeles, then radio sta. CBS, N.Y.C.; nat. sales mgr. radio sta. KNXT, Los Angeles then gen. sales mgr.; v.p., gen. mgr. WCBS-TV; pres. CBS TV Stas. div. Pres. World Youth Forum. Bd. mgrs. YMCA; bd. regents, mem. media adv. com. U. State N.Y. Recipient Dist. Service award Am. Cancer Soc. Served with USNR, 1951-55. Mem. Assn. Study Negro Life and History, Internat. Radio and TV Soc., Nat. Acad. TV Arts and Scis., Regional Planning Assn. Home: 14 Grove Av Larchmont NY 10538 Office: CBS Inc 51 W 52d St New York City NY 10019

DANIELS, RAYMOND HARRIS, art gallery ofcl.; b. Manchester, N.H., Feb. 22, 1901; s. Charles Addison and Annie (Sheldon) D.; Ph.B., Yale, 1924; m. Doris W. Talmage, Apr. 28, 1928; children—Ann (Mrs. Byron T. Hacker, Jr.), Deborah (Mrs. Roland W. Lovejoy). With S.A. Felton & Son Co., 1924-65, v.p., gen. mgr., 1953-55, pres., 1955-65; dir. Amoskeag Nat. Bank; trustee Amoskeag Trust Co. Pres., Currier Gallery of Art, 1969—, Spaulding Youth Center, 1967-69. Trustee Elliott Hosp.; bd. dirs. United Community Services. Mem. exec. com. Yale Alumni Bd.; pres. Manchester YMCA. Club: Yale of New Hampshire (sec.-treas.). Home: 2544 Elm St Manchester NH 03104

DANIELS, ROBERT SANFORD, educator, psychiatrist; b. Indpls., Aug. 12, 1927; s. Harry H. and Mary (Bassett) D.; B.S., U. Cin., 1948, M.D., 1951; m. June Gibson, July 1, 1950; children—Stephen, Allen, Lynn, Judith. Intern Cin. Gen. Hosp., 1951; resident U. Cin. Hosp., 1954-57; faculty U. Chgo., 1957—, dir. psychiat. cons. service, 1961-63, asso. prof. psychiatry, acting chmn. dept., 1963-66, clin. dir., 1966-68, asso. dean community and social medicine, 1968—, prof. psychiatry and social medicine, 1970-71, dir. Center Health Adminstrn. Studies, Grad. Sch. Bus., 1970-71, dir. div. psychiatry U. Cin., 1971—. Cons., Cook County Hosp., Ill. State Psychiat. Inst.; spl. research community and group psychiatry, health planning, community health, 1967-69. Chmn., Ill. Mental Health Planning Bd.; mem. pub. adv. bd. Ill. Hosp. Assn.; vice chmn. Mid South Health Planning Orgn. Bd. dirs. Pritaker Hosp. Served with AUS, 1946-47, USAF, 1952-54. Recipient Stella Feis Hoffheimer award U. Cin., 1951. Mem. A.M.A., Am. Psychiat. Assn., Am. Group Psychotherapy Assn., Ill. Group Psychotherapy Soc. (pres. 1965-66); Ill. Psychiat. Soc. (pres. 1967), Am. Pub. Health Assn., Phi Beta Kappa, Alpha Omega Alpha. Home: 6742 Constance Av Chicago IL 60649

DANIELS, ROBERTSON BALFOUR, educator; b. Princeton, N.J., Aug. 6, 1900; s. Winthrop More and Joan (Robertson) D.; A.B., Princeton, 1922; LL.B., Yale, 1925, M.A., 1932, Ph.D., 1934, J.D., 1971; m. Lola Burran, June 3, 1936; children—Penelope (Mrs. F.J. Pearson, Jr.), David Winthrop. Admitted to N.Y. bar, 1926; gen. law practice in N.Y.C., 1926-29, asso. Hornblower, Miller & Garrison, 1925-26, Larkin, Rathbone & Perry, 1927-29; instr. English, U. Tenn., 1935; chmn. English dept. Edinburg Coll., 1935-37; asso. prof. English, Kan. State Tchrs. Coll., Pittsburg, 1937-39; asst. prof. U. Houston, 1939-46, asso. prof., 1946-47, prof. 1947-70, asso. dean coll. arts and sci., 1950-51, dean 1951-58, dean grad. sch., 1958-69. Served as pvt. S.A.T.C., 1918; from 1st lt. to major USAAF, 1942-46, to lt. col. USAFR, 1955. Mem. Am. Legion, Mil. Order World Wars (comdr. Houston chpt. 1950-51, state comdr. Tex., 1952-53), Modern Lang. Assn., S. -Dentral Modern Lang. Assn. (editor S. Central Bull. 1966-68), Am. Name Soc. Retired Officers Assn., Conf. Coll. Tchrs. English, Phi Eta Sigma, Phi Delta Phi, Phi Kappa Phi (pres. U. Houston chpt. 1950-51). Presbyn. (elder). Clubs: Briar, Torch (Houston); Princeton (N.Y.C.); Nassau (N.J.); Princeton Tower (N.J.); Cosmos (Washington). Author: Some Seventeenth Century Worthies, 1940, 2d edit., 1971; To the Dark Covert, 1947. Contbr. articles profl. publs. Home: 20 N Wynden Dr Houston TX 77027

DANIELS, STANLEY LEE, architect; b. Washington, Apr. 28, 1937; s. Morris Joseph and Rose (Bomel) D.; student Emory U., 1954-56; B.S., B. Arch., Ga. Inst. Tech., 1960; certificate with honors Ecoles d'Art Americaines, Fontainebleau, France, 1961. Designer, draftsman various archtl. firms; v.p.-treas. Jova/Daniels/Busby, architects, Atlanta, 1966—. Chmn. architects and engrs. div. United Appeal, 1970. Recipient certificate of service A.I.A. 1964; award of Honor for design excellence A.I.A., 1966, 70. Mem. A.I.A. (chmn. regional conv. com., 1966- 67, 68, v.p. 1969, human resources council 1971), Atlanta Arts Assn., Constrn. Specifications Inst. Greater Atlanta Arts Council (dir. 1965—, pres.), Ga. Inst. Tech., Emory U., Fontainebleau alumni assns., Ga. Archtl. and Engring. Soc., Atlanta, Atlanta Jr. C. of C., Tau Epsilon Phi. Mem. B'nai B'rith. Clubs: Commerce, Atlanta Press (Hon.). Home: 843 Mentelle Dr NE Atlanta GA 30308 Office: 175 Peachtree St NE Atlanta GA 30309

DANIELS, WILLIAM BURTON, educator; b. Buffalo, Dec. 21, 1930; s. William C. and Sophia (Penner) D.; B.S. in Physics, U. Buffalo, 1952; M.S., Case Inst. Tech., 1955, Ph.D., 1957; m. Adriana A. Braahman, Sept. 2, 1958; children—Charlotte, William Fredrik, Donald Christopher. Instr. to asst. prof. Case Inst. Tech., 1957-59; research scientist Union Carbide Corp., 1959-61; mem. faculty Princeton, 1961—, prof. solid state scis., 1967—. Research collaborator Brookhaven Nat. Lab.; cons. U.S. Army Research Lab. Mem. Am. Phys. Soc., A.A.A.S. Research, publs. properties materials at high pressure, equation of state of solids, experimentation on solidified rare gases, instrumentation high pressure research. Home: 257 Cordova Rd Pricneton NJ 08540

DANIELS, WILLIAM DAVID, actor; b. Bklyn., Mar. 31, 1927; s. David Dryden and Irene (Bolger) D.; B.S., Northwestern U., 1951; m. Bonnie Bartlett, June 30, 1951; children—Michael, Robert. Broadway appearances incclude The Zoo Story, 1960, A Thousand Clowns, 1964. On a Clear Day, 1966, Daphne in Cottage D. 1968, 1776, 1969; film appearances include The Graduate, Two for the Road, President's Analyst. A Thousand Clowns. Address: 180 Riverside Dr New York City NY 10024

DANIELS, WORTH BAGLEY, physician; b. Raleigh, N.C., Apr. 8, 1899; s. Josephus and Addie Worth (Bagley) D.; grad. St. Albans Sch., 1916; A.B., U. N.C., 1920; M.D., Johns Hopkins, 1924; D. Sci., Georgetown U., 1962; m. Josephine Poe January, Sept. 3, 1923; children—Worth Bagley, Derick. Intern Bellevue Hosp., N.Y.C., 1925-26, house physician, 1926-27; pvt. practice medicine, Washington, 1927-42, 1946—; instr. phys. diagnosis George Washington Med. Sch., 1927-30; instr. medicine Georgetown Med. Sch., 1927-33, clin. prof. medicine, 1933-64, emeritus clinical prof. medicine, 1964—; jr. attending physician Emergency Hosp., Washington, 1928-30, sr. attending physician 1930-58; sr. attending physician Washington Hosp. Center, 1958-61, sr. adv. physician 1961—, trustee; med. cons. Walter Reed Gen. Hosp., 1946-47; sr. cons. in medicine Mt. Alto VA Hosp., 1947-53; sr. cons. internal medicine to surgeon gen. U.S. Army, 1950—. Trustee Johns Hopkins, 1954-57; regent Nat. Library Medicine, chmn., 1957-58, 61-62. Served from maj. to col. AUS, 1942-46. Diplomate Am. Bd. Internal Medicine, Fellow A.C.P.; me. Assn. Am. Physicians, Am. Clin. and Climatol. Assn. (past pres.), Am., D.C. med. assns., Soc. Med. Coxn. to Armed Forces (past pres.), Alpha Omega Alpha. Democrat. Episcopalian. Clubs: Alfalfa, Alibi, Metropolitan. Home: 1516 28th St Washington DC 20007 Office: 2001 Eye St NW Washington DC 20006

DANIELSEN, ALBERT VICTOR, univ. trustee; b. St. Thomas, Danish West Indies, Jan. 19, 1893; s. Ernest and Mary (Sorensen) D.; brought to U.S., 1900, naturalized, 1917; grad. McDonogh Sch., Md.; student philosophy Harvard, 1930-31; L.H.D., Boston U.; D.D. (hon.), Franklin Pierce Coll.; m. Jessie Muir Boyd, June 24, 1939. Investor, real estate sales; organizer real estate firms; dir. Congress St. Safe Deposit Vaults, Inc., Warwick Co., Inc., Regent Co., Inc., Albob Co., Inc., N. Beacon St. Co., Inc., 250 Beacon St. Co., Inc., Gould Farm Assos., Gt. Barrington, Mass.; trustee Littleton Park Trust, Foster St. Trust, Olympia Indsl. Park Trust, Barrington Court Trust, Graphic Arts Bldg. Trust, Md. Bldg. Trust, Nordan Trust, Pelham Hall Trust. Established Albert V. Danielsen Sch. Philosophy, Ethics and Religious Thought, Brandeis U., also chmn., prin. donor Albert V. Canielsen Fund for Harlan Chapel and Protestant activities, also donor chair of Christian thought Bandeis U. Past treas. Mass. Civil Liberties Com. Pres. and donor Danielsen Fund, Inc., Wellesley Hills, Mass.; dir. Mass. Cancer Prevention and Detection Clinic, Morgan Meml., Inc. (Goodwill Industries), Salvation Army; mem. corp., hon. trustee, asso. founder Boston U.; trustee Wellesley Scholarship Fund; fellow Brandeis U.; mem. pres.'s council Franklin Pierce Coll.; founder Albert V. Danielson Gallery and Fine Arts Sch., trustee Bethune-Cookman Coll. Recipient citations Boston U. Sch. Theology, 1956, Wellesley Human Relations Service, 1963, YMCA, 1959, Wellesley council Girl Scouts U.S.A., 1963; Official commendation from Govt. Denmark, 1965. Served with ordnance dept. U.S. Army, World War I. Mem. Mass., Boston (dir.) councils chs. Mason (32). Speaker before groups, author articles on religious subjects. Donor Danielsen Counseling Center, also Albert V. Danielsen chair of psychology and pastoral care Sch. Theology, Boston U. Home: 10 Saunders Terrace Wellesley Hills MA 02181

DANIELSON, FRANK D., mgmt. cons.; b. Chgo., Dec. 10, 1894; s. Eskil and Amanda (Holmberg) D.; B.S., Northwestern, 1918, M.A., C.E., 1920; m. Dorothy Reay Killey, Dec. 28, 1921; children—Dorothy Ann (Mrs. Bernard Reid Smith, Jr.), Richard Killey. Various mgmt.; devel., operations positions pub. service cos., 1920-27; asst. to v.p and gen. mgr., v.p. Utilities Power & Light Corp., Chgo., 1928-38; exec. v.p., dir. Interstate Power Co., Dubuque, Ia., 1938-49; v.p. operations, dir. Pub. Service Co. of Ind., Inc., Plainfield, 1949-54; asst. to pres. Ill. Power Co., Decatur, 1954- 60; cons. mgmt. engr. Trustee King Bruwaert House, Hinsdale, Ill. Registered Profl. engr., Ill. Mem. Western Soc. Engrs., U.S.C. of C. Club: Union League (Chgo.). Home: 310 Vanderbilt Rd Asheville NC 28803

DANIELSON, GEORGE ELMORE, congressman; b. Wausa, Neb., Feb. 20, 1915; s. August and Ida (Youngner) D.; student Wayne State Coll., 1933-35; B.A., U. Neb., 1937, LL.B., 1939; m. Gladys C. Ohanian, June 20, 1953. Spl. agt. FBI, throughout U.S., 1939-44; adminstrv. asst. to v.p. in charge Spl. Products div. Borden Co., Waterloo, Ia., N.Y.C., 1946-48; admitted to Cal. bar, 1949; asst. U.S. atty., Los Angeles, 1949-51; pvt. practice, Los Angeles, 1951—; assemblyman Cal. Legislature, 1963-66, chmn. Democratic caucus; mem. Cal. Senate, 1967-71, chmn. com. pub. utilities and corps.; mem. 92d Congress 29th Dist. Cal.; asst. majority whip, mem. jud. and vets. affairs coms. Del. Democratic Nat. Conv., 1968. Served to lt. USNR, 1944-46; PTO. Named Senator of Year, Cal. Trial Lawyers Assn., 1970. Mem. Soc. Former Spl. Agts. FBI, Phi Alpha Delta. Elk.‡

DANIELSON, GORDON CHARLES, educator, physicist; b. Dover, Ida., Oct. 28, 1912; s. Gust and Olga (Olson) D.; B.A., U. B.C., 1933, M.A., 1935; Ph.D., Purdue U., 1940; m. Dorothy Edna Thompson, June 24, children—Ellen Kathleen (Mrs. Karl Richard Fox), Lee Robert, Keith Gordon, Neil David. Research physicist U.S. Rubber Co., Detroit, 1940-41; asst. prof. physics U. Ida., 1941-42; asso. group leader Beacons Radiation Lab., Mass. Inst. Tech., 1942-46; mem tech. staff Bell Telephone Labs., Murray Hill, N.J., 1946-48; asso. prof. physics Ia. State U., Ames, 1948-53, prof. physics, sr. physicist Inst. for Atomic Research, 1953—, chmn. physics grad. adv. com., 1951-53, mem. metallurgy curriculum com., 1949-54, chmn. physics colloquium com., 1959-60, distinguished prof. scis. and humanities, 1964—. Mem. metallurgy and solid state rev. com. Argonne Nat. Lab., 1960-63, chmn., 1962-63; mem. solid state panel Nat. Acad. Scis.-NRC, 1962-71; cons. NSF, 1963-66; civilian cons. USAF, Eng., 1944-45; chmn. com. on thermoelectric conversion Office Naval Research, 1958. Recipient Army-Navy certificate appreciation, 1948. Guggenheim fellow U. Cambridge (Eng.), 1958-59. Fellow Am. Phys. Soc. (exec. com. div. solid state physics 1963-66), Ia. Acad. Sci.; mem. Am. Inst. Physics (vis. scientist 1960-71), UN Assn. (pres. Ames chpt. 1964-66), Sigma Xi (pres. Ia. State U. chpt. 1967-68). Unitarian (past pres., treas. Ames fellowship). Contbr. articles prof. jours., books. Research on practical Fourier analysis, domain orientation in barium titanate, counting diamonds, thermal diffusivity, tungsten bronzes, semi-conducting compounds. Home: 2007 Country Club Blvd Ames IA 50010

DANIELSON, JOHN OSWALD, coll. v.p.; b. Park Rapids, Minn., July 2, 1913; s. John Otto and Mary (Quinlivan) D.; B.S., Wis. State Coll., Superior, 1940; M.A., U. Wis., 1942, postgrad., 1947, 50-51, 52; m. Phyllis G. Strong, Sept. 19, 1942; 1 dau., Rosannah Mary. Grad. asst. U. Wis., 1940-42; civil service USN, 1942-43; prof. math. Wis. State U., Superior, 1946-55, chmn. dept. math., 1955-57, dean instrn. 1957-62, now exec. v.p. Bd. dirs. WDSE-TV. Chmn. Wis. Engring. Edn. Improvement Com., 1967; pres. Wis. Adv. Com. Extension Programs; vice chmn. Wis. Planning Com. Edn. Beyond High Sch.; mem. Wis. Higher Edn. Com. on Inter-instnl. Cooperation. Pres. Superior Assn. Commerce, 1963-64. Pres. Holy Family Hosp., Superior. Served from ensign to lt. (s.g.), USNR, 1943-46. Mem. Soc. Instrnl. and Applied Math., Wis. Acad. Arts and Scis., Math. Assn. Am., A.A.A.S., Wis. Edn. Assn., Lake Superior Ednl. Assn., Superior Hist. Soc. (v.p.), Pi Mu Epsilon, Phi Delta Kappa, Fex Frat., Sigma Pi Sigma. Club: Optimists (dir. Superior 1957-59, past pres.; dist. lt. gov., 1961—). Home: 1510 N 19th St Superior WI 54301

DANIELSON, LEE ERLE, educator; b. Youngstown, O., Dec. 20, 1920; s. LeRoy E. and Mary (Crowley) D.; B.S. in Edn., Antioch Coll., 1947; M.A., U. Mich., 1949, Ph.D. in Indsl. Psychology, 1956; m. Mildred Ruth Mack, Mar. 18, 1950; childrenMichael Lee, Lisa Kaye, Chris Charles. Research psychologist U.S. Civil Service, Wright Air Devel. Center, Dayton, O., 1949-50; mem. faculty Grad. Sch. Bus. Adminstrn., U. Mich., 1953-, prof., 1963-; mgmt. cons., 1956-. Served to capt. USMCR, 1950-52. Mem. Am. Psychol. Assn., Acad. Mgmt., A.A.A.S., Indsl. Relations Research Assn., Sigma Xi. Author: Characteristics of Engineers and Scientists, 1960; also articles. Home: 1000 Vesper Rd Ann Arbor, MI 48103.

DANIELSON, MICHAEL NILS, educator; b. N.Y.C., Apr. 8, 1934; s. Vergil Andrew and Dorothy (DeLucas) D.; A.B., Rutgers U., 1955, M.A., 1956; Ph.D., Princeton, 1962; m. Ruth Patricia Schevon, Sept. 3, 1955; children—Jessica Aidan, Jeffrey Andrew. Instr. U. Omaha, 1957-59, Rutgers U., 1961; research asso. Inst. Pub. Adminstrn., N.Y.C., 1961-63; asst. prof. to prof. polit. sci. Princeton, 1963—; cons. Gov. N.J., N.J. Dept. Transp., N.J. Dept. Community Affairs, U.S. Dept. Housing and Urban Devel. Commr. Tri-state Transp. Commn., 1966—. Trustee Glassboro State Coll., 1967—. Served to lt., USAF, 1956-59. Mem. Am. Polit. Sci. Assn., Am. Assn. U. Profs., Nat. Model R.R. Assn. Democrat. Author: Federal-Metropolitan Politics and the Commuter Crisis, 1965; Metropolitan Politics, 1966; Modern American Democracy, 1969; American Democracy, 1971. Home: 283 Hartley Av Princeton NJ 08540

DANIELSON, PAUL JOSEPH, educator; B.S., U. Wis., 1941, M.S., 1942, Ph.D., 1951. Prof., head dept. counseling and guidance U. Ariz., Tucson. Office: Coll Edn U Ariz Tucson AZ 85721*

DANIELSON, WAYNE ALLEN, univ. dean; b. Burlington, Ia., Dec. 6, 1929; s. Arthur Leroy and Bessie Ann (Bonar) D.; B.A., State U. Ia., 1952; M.A., Stanford, 1953, Ph.D., 1957; m. Beverly Grace Kinsell, Mar. 19, 1955; children—Matthew Henry, Benjamin Wayne, Grace Frances, Paul Arthur. Reporter, research mgr. San Jose (Cal.) Mercury-News, 1953-54; acting asst. prof. Stanford, 1956-57; asst. prof. journalism U. Wis., 1957-59; mem. faculty U. N.C., 1959-69, prof. journalism, 1963-69. research prof. Inst. Research Social Sci., 1963-69, dean Sch. Journalism, 1964-69; dean Sch. Communication, U. Tex., Austin, 1969—. Mem. steering com. News Research Center, Am. Newspaper Pubs. Assn., 1964—, research com. A.P. Mng. Editors Assn., 1963—. Mem. pub. relations com. N.C. Heart Assn., 1963-67. Mem. Assn. Edn. Journalism (chmn. publs. com. 1968—, pres. 1970-71), Am. Assn. Schools and Depts. Journalism (v.p. 1966-67, pres. 1967-68), Am. Assn. Pub. Opinion Research, Am. Sociol. Assn., So. Sociol. Soc., Phi Beta Kappa, Sigma Delta Chi, Kappa Tau Alpha. Author (with G. C. Wilhoit, Jr.) A Computerized Bibliography of Mass Communication Research, 1944-64; (with Blanche Prejeah) Programed Newspaper Style, 1971. Contbr. articles profl. jours. Editor Journalism Abstracts, 1963—; editorial bd. Journalism Quar., 1964—. Office: School of Communications Univ of Texas Austin TX 78712

DANILEK, JOSEPH ARTHUR, toiletries co. exec.; b. N.Y.C., Mar. 16, 1905; s. Nicholas and Mary (Fill) D.; B.A., Coll. City N.Y., 1929; m. Mary Dedina, July 19, 1931; 1 son, Donald J. Controller, Helena Rubinstein, 1928-38; controller, gen. mgr. Elizabeth Arden, 1938-42; asst. to pres. Dorothy Gray, gen. sales mgr. Tussy, 1942-46; controller, asst. pres. Revlon, 1946-48; pres., gen. mgr., dir. Mary Chess, Inc., N.Y.C., 1948-; dir., mem. exec. com. Lake Placid Company; dir. Parfums Schiaparelli, Parfums Lucien Lelong, Marie Earle Corp., Seaforth Corp. Chmn. exec. com. Fragrance Found. Named knight of Malta, knight of Holy Sepulchre. Mem. Toilet Goods Assn. (pres.). Clubs: Lake Placid (v.p., gov.); Old Guard Society (Palm Beach, Fla.); N.Y. Athletic, Touchdown (N.Y.C.); Pinehurst (N.C.), Cherry Valley (Garden City, L.I.); West Side Tennis (Forrest Hills, N.Y.); Garden City Country. Home: 187 Euston Rd Garden City, L.I., NY Office: 597 Fifth Av New York City NY 10017

DANILOV, VICTOR JOSEPH, editor, pub.; b. Farrell, Pa., Dec. 30, 1924; s. Joseph M. and Ella (Tominovich) D.; B.A. in Journalism, Pa. State U., 1945; M.S. in Journalism, Northwestern U., 1946; Ed.D. in Higher Edn., U. Colo., 1963; m. Carolyne A. Klockner, July 1, 1950; children—Duane P., Denise S., David K. With Sharon (Pa.) Herald, 1942, Youngstown Vindicator, 1945, Pitts. Sun-Telegraph, 1946-47, Chgo. Daily News, 1947-50, Kansas City Star, 1953; instr. journalism U. Colo., 1950-51; asst. prof. journalism U. Kan., 1951-53; mgr. pub. relations Ill. Inst. Tech. and IIT Research Inst., 1953-57; dir. univ. relations and pub. information U. Colo., 1957-60; pres. Profile Co., Boulder, Colo., 1960-62; exec. editor, exec. v.p. Indsl. Research Inc., Beverly Shores, Ind., 1962-69, pub., exec. v.p., 1969—. Mem. rural industrialization adv. group Dept. Agr., 1967; panel internat. transfer tech. Dept. Commerce, 1968; sci. information council NSF, 1969. Mem. Am. Bus. Press Inc., Am. Coll. Pub. Relations Assn. (pres. Rocky Mountain dist. 1959-60). Assn. Edn. Journalism, Edn. Writers Assn., Internat. Sci. Writers Assn., Nat. Assn. Sci. Writers, Nat. Conf. Indsl. Research (conf. 1966-70), Nat. Indsl. Research Week (chmn. observance 1967-70), Pub. Relations Soc. Am. (v.p. Colo. 1960, chmn. seminar 1960), Soc. Bus. Mag. Editors, Soc. Tech. Writers and Pubs., Kappa Delta Pi, Phi Delta Kappa. Sigma Delta Chi (pres. Colo. 1959, chmn. nat. historic sites com. 1958). Author: Public Affairs Reporting, 1955; also articles. Author, editor: Crucial Issues in Public Relations, 1960; Corporate Research and Profitability, 1966; Innovation and Profitability, 1967; Research Decision-Making in New Product Development, 1968; New Products—and Profits, 1969; Applying Emerging Technologies, 1970; Nuclear Power in the South, 1970. Editor profl. proc. Home: 2734 Floral Trail Michigan City IN 46360 Office: Indsl Research Bldg Beverly Shores IN 46301

DANILOVA, ALEXANDRA, ballet dancer; b. Peterhof, Russia; d. Dionis and Claudia (Gotovtzeva) Danilov; ed. Theatrical Sch., Petrograd, curriculum comprising gen. and coll. edn. Came to the U.S., 1934. Mem. Russian State Ballet. Maryinsky Theatre, 1922-24; soloist. Diaghileff Ballet, 1925, Ballerina, 1929; Ballerina Monte Carlo Opera House. 1930-31; star Sir Oswald Stoll's production Waltzes from Vienna. Alhambra Theatre. London, 1932, Ballerine, Col. de Basil's Ballet Russe, 1933-38; prima ballerina, Ballet Russe de Monte Carlo, 1938-58; currently head own co. touring various countries; guest star several ballets; star Broadway musical Oh Captain, 1958; guest choreographer Metropolitan Opera Co., Washington Ballet, 1962-64. Recipient Capezio Dance Award, 1958. Mem. Greek Orthodox Ch. Address: RFD 2 Church Rd Lakewood NJ

DANINOS, PIERRE, author; b. Paris, France, May 26, 1913; student Lyceé Janson de Sailly, Paris, 1922-30. Journalist, 1931-40; liaison agt. British Army, Flanders, 1940. Author: Le Carnet du Bon Dieu, 1947; Sonia, les autres et moi, 1952; Les Carnets du Major Thompson, 1954; Un certain Monsieur Blot, 1960; Le Jacassin, 1962;

Snobissimo, 1964; Le 36éme desls lious, 1966; LeMajor Tricolore, 1968; Le Plus que Parfait, 1970. Home: 81 rue de Grenelle Paris 7éme France

DANIS, PETER GODFREY, physician; b. Ottawa, Ont., Can., Apr. 12, 1909; s. Peter Godfrey and Helene (Burns) D.; student Gonzaga Coll., Spokane; B.S., St. Louis U., 1929, M.D., 1931, M.S., 1935; m. Katherine Kramer, Apr. 6, 1931; children—Peter Godfrey, Richard, Joanne, Mary Katherine, James, Laura, David, Timothy and Thomas (twins), Deborah. Intern St. Louis U. Group Hosps., 1931-32, fellow pediatrics, 1932-34; chmn. dept. pediatrics St. Louis U., 1947-57, asso. prof. pediatrics, 1948-51, prof. clin. pediatircs, 1951—; chief staff Cardinal Glennon Meml. Hosp. St. Mary's Hosp., 1969—. Chief pediatric cons., dir. health services St. Mary's Hosp., 1969—. Spl. Edn. St. Louis County. Bd. dirs. health and hosp. div. Social Planning Council, 1946-49; exec. bd. Cath. Charities, St. Louis, also med. dir. children's dept. Recipient Alumni Honor award St. Louis U., 1968. Diplomate Am. Bd. Pediatrics. Mem. Am. Acad. Pediatrics (state chmn. 1949-53, chmn. nat. com. hosps. and dispensaries 1950-52), St. Louis Med. Soc., St. Louis Pediatric Soc., A.M.A., Am. Acad. Cerebral Palsy, Am. Acad. Neurology (asso.). Home: 16 Villa Coublay Frontenac St Louis MO 63131 Office: 2821 N Ballas Rd Town and Country St Louis MO 63131

DANISH, ROY BERTRAM, broadcasting exec.; b. N.Y.C., Mar. 2, 1919; s. Max D. and Anne (Rich) D.; A.B., Columbia, 1940; M.B.A., Harvard, 1942; m. Jane Byington Millar, Apr. 12, 1953; children—Elisabeth Jane, Caroline Anne. Asst. dir. research Mut. Broadcasting System, N.Y.C., 1946-47, sta. relations mgr., 1948-51, dir. sta. relations, 1952, dir. comml. operations, 1952- 53, asst. to pres., 1953-54, v.p., 1954-55; v.p. McCann-Erickson, Inc., 1956-59; partner Smith/Greenland Advt., N.Y.C., 1959-60; asst. dir. TV information office Nat. Assn. Broadcasters, N.Y.C., 1960-62, dir., 1962—. Mem. Men's Com. for Lighthouse, 1965—. Vice pres. Internat. Radio and TV Found. Served to lt. USNR, 1942-46. Mem. Nat. Acad. TV Arts and Scis. (nat. trustee, gov. N.Y. chpt. 1964- 68), Internat. Radio and TV Soc. (bd. dirs.), Broadcast Pioneers (pres. 1969-70), Columbia Coll. Alumni Assn., Beta Sigma Rho. Club: Harvard Business School. Home: 5 Riverside Dr New York City NY 10023 Office: 745 Fifth Av New York City NY 10022

DANKIN, ROGER, editor; b. Gloucester, Mass., May 27, 1905; s. John Arthur and Gertrude (Brinnick) D.; student pvt. schs.; m. Helen Craig Smith, Sept. 6, 1929 (dec. June, 1953); m. 2d, Alexandra Lewandowska, Sept. 9, 1954. Rewrite man New York Telegram, 1929-33; rewrite, asst. city editor N.Y. Daily News, 1933-40; asst. mng. editor P M, 1940-43; asso. editor Woman's Home Companion, 1943-52, editor Collier's. 1952-55; editorial mgr. Gen. Foods, 1956-62, asso. dir. pub. relations, 1962-64, mgr. editorial and publs., 1964-70. Home: 10 Estabrook Circle West Lebanon NH 03784

DANKMEYER, THEODORE ROGNALD, lawyer; b. Balt., Feb. 19, 1903; s. Charles and Caroline Antonia Genevieve (Ohle) D.; LL.B., U. Md., 1924; m. Anne Virginia Burrier, July 31, 1928; childrenAnne Elizabeth (Mrs. Samuel Hopkins), Gretchen (Mrs. Richard Henry Stock), Theodore Rognald. Admitted to Md. bar, 1924; mem. firm Niles, Barton & Wilmer, specializing admiralty and shipping law, Balt., 1938-. Editor, pres. Am. Maritime Cases, Inc., 1952-; director Balt. Life Ins. Co., Schenuit Industries, Inc. Mem. com. to revise admiralty rules to conform to amendment to Fed. Rules of Civil Procedure. Mem. bd. dirs. Lutheran Hosp. of Md., Inc.; mem. bd. Sch. of the Chimes (handicapped children). Mem. Am. Judicature Soc., Am., Md., Balt. bar assns., Maritime Law Assn. U.S., Inter-Am. Bar Assn., Navy League U.S., Md. Hist. Soc., Md. Bar Found. (charter), Delta Theta Phi. Democrat. Lutheran. Mason. Clubs: Propeller of U.S.; University, (sec. Baltimore City); Merchants, 14 W. Hamilton St. (Balt.). Home: 9 Wendover Rd Baltimore MD 21218 Office: 929 N Howard St Baltimore MD 21201

DANLY, JAMES C., mfg. co. exec.; b. Chgo., 1916; ed. Yale, 1939; m. Ann; children- Mrs. David Brevier, James C., Linda, Anne, Michael, Maria, Lisa, Laura. Formerly v.p. engring., now pres., chmn. dir. Danly Machine Corp., Inc., chmn., chief exec. officer Onsrud Machine Works; dir. Cicero State Bank. Mem. Nat. Machine Tool Builders Assn. (dir.), Ill. Mfrs. Assn. (dir.). Home: 1418 Clinton Pl River Forest IL 60305 Office: 2100 S Laramie Av Chicago IL 60650

DANN, MATTHEW EDWARD, headmaster; b. N.Y. City, Sept. 27, 1902; s. Edward Grant and Mary (Fahy) D.; student Trinity Coll., 1922-23, L.H.D., 1947; A.B., Columbia U., 1926, M.A., 1927; in brokerage business with J.H. Oliphant & Co., 1920-22; master Trinity Sch., N.Y. City, 1927-36, asst. headmaster 1936- 38, headmaster, 1938-55, also headmaster Trinity-Pawling (N.Y.), Sch., 1946—; headmaster St. Agatha Sch. for Girls, N.Y. City, 1940-41. Chmn. Selective Service Bd., N.Y.C., 1940-44, appt. to Appeal Bd., 1944; mem. N.Y. State Comm. on Physical Fitness; mem. Commn. Secondary Schs. Middle States Assn. Colls. and Secondary Schs. Mem. Headmasters Assn. Mem. Delta Phi. Episcopalian. Republican. Clubs: University, St. Andrews Golf (Hastings, N.Y.); Quaker Hill. Home: Pawling Pawling NY 12564

DANN, MICHAEL HAROLD, TV exec.; b. Detroit, Sept. 11, 1921; s. Moe and Dorothy (Bobrof) D.; B.A., U. Mich., 1943; m. Joanne Himmell, Dec. 2, 1949; children—Jonathan, Patricia, Priscilla. Comedy writer, 1946-47; pub. relations staff New Haven R.R., 1947-48; trade editor press dept. NBC, 1948-49, coordinator program package sales, 1949-50, supr. spl. telecasts, 1950-52, mgr. TV program dept., 1952-54, dir. program sales, 1954-56, v.p. TV program sales, 1956-58; v.p. network programing N.Y., CBS-TV, 1958-63, v.p. programs CBS-TV, 1963-66; sr. v.p. CBS, 1966-70, v.p., asst. to pres. Children's TV Workshop, 1970—. Home: 111 Paulding Dr Chappaqua NY 10514 Office: Children's TV Workshop 1 Lincoln Plaza New York City NY

DANN, ROBERT ROY, lawyer; b. N.Y.C., Mar. 27, 1918; B.S., N.Y.U., 1937; LL.B., Yale, 1940. Admitted to N.Y. bar, 1941, U.S. Supreme Ct. bar, 1946; atty. Dept. of Justice, 1941-42; asst. U.S. atty. So. Dist. N.Y., 1942-43; spl. asst. U.S. Atty. Gen., 1943-47; chief War Frauds Prosecution, Dept. of Justice, N.Y., 1943-45; now mem. firm Aranow, Brodsky, Bohlinger, Einhorn & Dann, N.Y.C. Decorated knight 1st class Order of Lion (Finland). Mem. Fed. Bar Assn. (counsel chpt. 1945—), Assn. Bar City N.Y. (com. on state crs. of superior jurisdiction 1968—), Consular Law Soc., Am. Arbitration Assn., Phi Beta Kappa, Tau Kappa Alpha. Office: 122 E 42d St New York City NY 10017*

DANNAN, ROBERT HOWARD, drug co. exec.; b. Homer, N.Y., Sept. 30, 1919; s. R. Emmet and Emma (Steger) D.; B.C.S. cum laude, So. Western U., 1948; postgrad. U. Cal., Los Angeles, 1949; m. Renee Gronchi Lispi, July 22, 1943; childrenMichael Robert, Patrick Anthony, Anthony Sheldon. With McClaren Goode, C.P.A.'s, Los Angeles, 1949-51; treas. Brunswig Drug Co., Los Angeles, 1951-; v.p. Brunswig-Mont. Drug Co.; dir. Hibbard-Med. & Surg. Co., San Francisco, Treas., bd. dirs. Whittier Community Theatre. Served with AUS, 1942-45. Mem. Vernon (dir.), Los Angeles Jr. C.'s of C. V.F.W. Republican. Roman Catholic. K.C., Rotarian, Home: 13958 Mar Vista Whittier, CA 90602. Office: Box 231A Los Angeles, CA 90054.

DANNAY, FREDERIC writer (co-writer with Manfred B. Lee under pseud. Ellery Queen); m. Hilda Wiesenthal; children—Douglas, Richard. Co-author: Roman Hat Mystery, 1929; French Powder Mystery, 1930; Dutch Shoe Mystery, 1931; Tragedy of X, 1932; Greek Coffin Mystery, 1932; Tragedy of Y, 1932; Egyptian Cross Mystery, 1932; American Gun Mystery, 1933; Tragedy of Z, 1933; Siamese Twin Mystery, 1933; Drury Lane's Last Case, 1933; Chinese Orange Mystery, 1934; Adventures of Ellery Queen, 1934; Spanish Cape Mystery, 1935; Halfway House, 1936; Door Between, 1937; Challenge to the Reader, 1938; Devil To Pay, 1938; Four of Hearts, 1938; Dragon's Teeth, 1939; New Adventures of Ellery Queen, 1940; 101 Years' Entertainment, 1941; Calamity Town, 1942; Detective Short Story (bibliography), 1942; Sporting Blood, 1942; There Was an Old Woman, 1943; Female of the Species, 1943; Misadventures of Sherlock Holmes, 1944; Best Short Stories from Ellery Queen's Mystery Magazine, 1944; Casebook of Ellery Queen, 1945; Murderer Is A Fox, 1945; Roques' Gallery, 1945; To the Queen's Taste, 1946; The Queen's Awards, 1946-53; Murder by Experts, 1947; 20th Century Detective Stories, 1948; Ten Days' Wonder, 1948; Cat of Many Tails, 1949; Double Double, 1950; Literature of Crime, 1950; Origin of Evil, 1951; Queen's Quorum, 1951; Calendar of Crime, 1952; King is Dead, 1952; Scarlet Letters, 1953, The Golden Summer, 1953; (under pseudonym Daniel Nathan), Glass Village, 1954; Ellery Queen's Awards, 1954-57; Q.B.I., 1955; Inspector Queen's Own Case, 1956; In The Queens' Parlor, 1957; Finishing Stroke, 1958; Ellery Queen's Mystery Anns., 1958-61; Ellery Queen's Anthologies, 1960—; Quintessence of Queen, 1962; To Be Read Before Midnight, 1962; Mystery Mix, 1963; Player on the Other Side, 1963; and on the Eighth Day, 1964; Double Dozen, 1964; Queens Full, 1965; Fourth Side of the Triangle, 1965; 20th Anniversary Annual, 1965; Study in Terror, 1966; Crime Carousel, 1966; Face to Face, 1967; All-Star Lineup, 1967; Poetic Justice, 1967; House of Brass, 1968; Mystery Parade, 1968; Q.E.D., 1968; Cop Out, 1969; Murder Menu, 1969; Minimysteries, 1969; Last Woman in His Life, 1970; Grand Slam, 1970; Golden 13, 1971; Fine and Private Place, 1971; Headliners, 1971, Ellery Queen's Mystery Mag., 1941—. Vis. prof. U. Tex., Austin, 1958-59. Co- recipient Edgar Allan Poe awards (Edgars), 1945, 47, 49, 51, 60 (Grand Master). Address: 29 Byron Lane Larchmont NY 10538

DANNENFELDT, KARL HENRY, univ. ofcl.; b. Humboldt, Neb., June 13, 1916; s. Paul Louis and Emilie (Koehler) D.; A.B., Valparaiso U., 1939; M.A., Ind. U., 1940; Ph.D., U. Chgo., 1948; m. Ida Maria Brune, June 15, 1947; children—Karla Gretchen, Paula Maria. Instr., Concordia Jr. Coll., Ft. Wayne, Ind., 1940-41; lectr. Roosevelt U., Chgo., 1947-48; from asst. prof. to prof., head div. social scis. Elmira (N.Y.) Coll., 1948-56; mem. faculty Ariz. State U., 1956—, prof. history, head dept. social studies, 1956-57, head div. behavioral and social scis., 1957-62, dean Coll. Liberal Arts, 1963-67, acad. v.p., 1967—. Cons. examiner N. Central Assn. Colls. and Secondary Schs., 1960—; Am. editor Archiv fuer Reformationsgeschichte, 1962-67. Served to maj., inf., AUS, 1941-46: ETO. Decorated Bronze Star medal. Mem. Renaissance Soc. Am., Am. Hist. Assn., Am. Soc. Ch. History, Am. Soc. Reformation Research (sec. treas. 1957-62, v.p. 1965, pres. 1966), Am. Assn. U. Profs., Phi Kappa Phi, Phi Alpha Theta. Lutheran. Author: Leonhard Rauwold, 1968. Contbr. profl. jours. Home: 236 E Concorda Dr Tempe AZ 85282

DANNER, HARRY E., banker; b. 1907; student Wharton Eve. Sch.; grad. Stonier Grad. Sch. Banking, Rutgers U., also Am. Inst. Banking; married. Vice pres., dir. Upper Darby Nat. Bank, until 1956; with Fidelity Bank, Phila., 1963—, exec. v.p. personal banking dept., 1966—. Address: Fidelity Bank Broad and Walnut Sts Philadelphia PA 19109

DANNETT, EMANUEL, lawyer; b. N.Y.C., Feb. 24, 1905; s. Elias and Sali D.; B.S., Coll. City N.Y., 1925; LL.B., Columbia (Kent scholar), 1927; m. Sylvia G. Liebovitz, June 29, 1933; children—Kenneth Samuel, Wendy Elizabeth. Admitted to N.Y. bar, 1928; mem. Lauterstein, Spiller, Bergerman & Dannett, 1935-46; exec. v.p. Publix Shirt Corp., 1946-47; corporate counsel indsl. relations R.H. Macy & Co., Inc., 1948; mem. firm Graubard, Moskovitz, McGoldrick, Dannett & Horowitz and predecessor firm; adj. prof. labor law N.Y. U. Law Sch. Bd. govs. Am. Jewish Com., chmn. personnel com., mem. Domestic Affairs Council, mem. Mgmt. Council, mem. retirement, budget and evaluation coms.; chmn. labor com. Fedn. Jewish Philanthropies. Mem. Am., N.Y. State bar assns., Assn. Bar City N.Y. (chmn. com. labor and social security legislation), N.Y. County Lawyers Assn. Home: 9 Reimer Rd Scarsdale NY 10583 Office: 345 Park Av New York City NY 10022

DANO, ROYAL EDWARD, actor; b. N.Y.C., Nov. 16, 1922; s. Caleb Edward and Mary Josephine (O'Connor) D.; m. Peggy Lambert Nevin; children—Royal Edward, Richard Arthur. Broadway debut in Finians Rainbow, 1941, also 4 X 12 48, Mrs. Gibbons Boys, Metropole, Three Wishes For Jamie; television debut on Americana, 1947, followed by Suspense, Web, Colgate Theatre, Pulitzer Prize Theatre, Studio One, Climax, Camera Three, Fireside Theatre, Wagon Train, Virginian, Rawhide, Big Valley, James Agee's Abraham Lincoln, Hitchcock Presents, Hawaii 5 O, Gunsmoke; appeared in numerous motion pictures, 1950—, including Under The Gun, 1950, Red Badge of Courage, Bend of the River, Johnny Guitar, Trouble With Harry, Moby Dick, Saddle the Wind, Trooper Hook, Man of the West, Undercover Girl, Hound Dog Man, Crime of Passion, King of Kings, 7 Faces of Dr. Lao, Huckleberry Finn, Face of Fire, Evil Gun, Santiago, The Day They Gave Babies Away, Undefeated, Great Northfield Minnesota Raid, 1971, Skin Game, 1971. Served with AUS, 1943-46; CBI. Mem. Acad. Motion Picture Arts and Sci., Nat. Acad. Television Arts and Scis., ANTA, Screen Actors Guild, Actors Equity, A.F.T.R.A. Home: Santa Monica CA 90402 Office: William Morris 151 El Camino Beverly Hills CA 90212

DANOWSKI, THADDEUS STANLEY, physician; b. Wallington, N.J., Sept. 6, 1914; s. Anton and Theresa (Kosciuh) D.; B.A., Yale, 1936, M.D. magna cum laude, 1940; m. Phyllis Little, June 22, 1949; 1 son, Stanley T. Intern in medicine, New Haven Hosp., 1940-41; prof. medicine, sch. medicine U. Pitts. 1947—; physician in charge Renziehausen Meml. Ward and Clinic, 1948-56; sr. staff physician, Presbyn. Woman's and Children's Hosps. of Pitts., 1947—, Elizabeth Steel Magee Hosp., 1949—. Mem. Med. Mission to Japan, 1950; mem. NRC panel, Com. on Growth, 1951; pres. Pa. div. Am. Cancer Soc., 1961-62. Fellow Berkeley Coll., Yale U., 1943-47. Named Jr. C. of C. Med. Man of the Year, Pitts., 1948; Guggenheim fellow, 1953-54; recipient Jurzykowski award 1969. Diplomate Nat. Bd. Med. Examiners, 1941, Am. Bd. of Internal Medicine, 1947. Fellow A.C.P., A.M.A., A.A.A.S., Am. Diabetes Assn. (pres. 1965); mem. Am. Soc. Clin. Investigation, Am. Physiol. Soc., Fedn. of the Am. Investigation, Am. Physiol. Soc., Fedn. Am. Socs. for Exptl. Biology, Thyroid Assn., N.Y. Acad. Scis., Allegheny County Med. Assn., Pa. State Med. Soc., Clinic Soc. of the Pitts. Diabetes Assn. (pres., 1950-51), Phi Beta Kappa, Sigma Xi, Alpha Omega Alpha. Club: Interurban Clinical. Author articles. Home: 5415 Howe St Pittsburgh PA 15232 Office: Magee Women's Hosp Pittsburgh PA 15213 ☆

DANSON, EDWARD BRIDGE, anthropologist; b. Glendale, O., Mar. 22, 1915; s. Edward Bridge and Ann (Allen) D.; B.A., U. Ariz., 1940; M.A., Harvard, 1948, Ph.D., 1952; m. Jessica Harriet MacMaster, Nov. 7, 1942; children—Jessica Ann, Edward Bridge III. Asst. prof. anthropology U. Colo., 1949-50, U. Ariz., 1950- 56; asst. dir. Mus. No. Ariz., 1956-58, dir., 1958—. Mem. bd. Nat. Park Service, 1958-64, mem. adv. council, 1964—; mem. Ariz. Hist. Adv. Com., 1966—; mem. adv. com. on multiple-use mgmt. Coconino Nat. Forest, 1964—; chmn. Colo. Plateau Environmental Adv. Council, 1970—. Served from ensign to lt. comdr., USNR, 1942-45. Trustee Southwestern Parks and Monuments Assn., 1958—; bd. dirs. Flagstaff Symphony Assn., 1962, chmn., 1967-69. Fellow Am. Anthrop. Assn., A.A.A.S., Ariz. Acad. Sci. (pres. 1958-59); mem. Soc. Am. Archaeology, No. Ariz. Soc. Sci. and Art (mem. bd. 1954-56), Ariz. Hist. Assn., Sigma Xi. Episcopalian. Home: PO Box 674 Flagstaff AZ 86001 Office: Box 1389 Flagstaff AZ 86001

DANTO, ARTHUR COLEMAN, educator; b. Ann Arbor, Mich., Jan. 1, 1924; s. Samuel Budd and Sylvia (Gittleman) D.; B.A., Wayne State U., 1948; M.A., Columbia, 1949, Ph.D., 1952; postgrad. U. Paris, 1949-50; m. Shirley Rovetch, Aug. 9, 1946; children—Elizabeth, Jane. Instr., U. Colo., 1950-51; mem. faculty Columbia, 1952—, now prof. philosophy. Served with AUS, 1942- 45. Fulbright fellow, 1949; Guggenheim fellow 1969; Am. Council Learned Socs. fellow, 1961, 70. Mem. Am. Philos. Assn. (v.p. 1969). Author: Analytical Philosophy of Knowledge, 1968; What Philosophy Is, 1968; Analytical Philosophy of History, 1965; Nietzsche as Philosopher, 1965. Editor Jour. of Philosophy, 1965—; Harper Essays in Philosophy, 1970. Home: 420 Riverside Dr New York City NY 10025

DANTON, JOSEPH PERIAM, librarian, educator; b. Palo Alto, Cal., July 5, 1908; s. George Henry and Annina (Periam) D.; ed. U. Leipzig (Germany), 1925-26; A.B. magna cum laude, Oberlin Coll., 1928; B.S., Columbia, 1929; A.M., Williams Coll., 1930; Ph.D., U. Chgo., 1935 (Carnegie fellow, 1933-35); m. Lois King, Dec. 25, 1948; children—Jennifer, Joseph Periam. With N.Y. Pub. Library, 1928-29; reference asst. Williams Coll. Library, 1929-30; with A.L.A., 1930-33; librarian, asso. prof. bibliography Colby Coll., Waterville, Me., 1935-36, Temple U., Phila., 1936-46; dean Sch. Librarianship, U. Cal., 1946-61, asso. prof., 1946-47, prof., 1947—. Nat. library cons. U.S. Works Progress Adminstrn., 1937; vis. prof. Grad. Library Sch., U. Chgo., 1942, Columbia, 1946; vis. lectr. U. Toronto, 1963, Hebrew U., Jerusalem, Univs. of Belgrade, Ljubljana, Novi Sad, Zagreb, 1965, U. Brit. Columbia, 1968, McGill U., 1969, U. P.R., 1970; Fulbright research scholar, Germany, 1960-61, Austria, 1964-65; surveyor and cons. numerous libraries, including, Haile Selassie I Univ.; UNESCO Library Cons., Jamaica 1968. Del. Internat. Fedn. Library Assns. meeting, The Hague, 1939, 66, Rome, 1964, Toronto, 1967, Frankfurt, 68, Copenhagen, 1969, Moscow, 1970; dir. Dept. State-A.L.A. Multi-Area Group Librarian Program, 1963-64. Ford Found. cons. on libraries in S.E. Asia (with R. C. Swank), 1963. Mem. exec. bd. Phila. Bibliog. Center, chmn. com. on microphotography, 1940-46. Served as lt. USNR, 1942-44; PTO. lt., USNR, Recipient Coll. and Research Libraries grant, 1960-61; Council on Library Resources grant, 1967-69; Guggenheim fellow, 1971. Mem. A.L.A. (various coms. since 1934), Assn. Coll. and Ref. Libraries (treas. 1938-40), Cal. Library Assn., Assn. Am. Library Schs. (pres. 1949-50), Bibliog. Soc., Sigma Alpha Epsilon. Democrat. Club: Faculty (Berkeley, Cal.). Compiler (with others): Library Literature 1921-32, 1934; (with M.F. Tauber) Theses and Dissertations, 1942; Union List of Microfilms, 1942- 46; translator of sects. on German libraries in Popular Libraries of the World, 1932. Author: Education for Librarianship, 1946; Education for Librarianship, Paris, 1950; United States Influence on Norwegian Librarianship, 1890-1940, 1957; Book Selection and Collections: A Comparison of German and American University Libraries, 1963; Index to Festschriften in Lebrarianship, 1970; Between M.Ss. and Ph.D., 1970. Editor: The and Climate of Book Selection; Social Influences on Sch. and Pub. Libraries, 1959. Contbr. ednl. and book reviews jours. Mem. editorial bd. Coll. and Research Libraries Monograph Series. 1966-69, Library Quar., 1968—, Internat. Library Rev., 1968—. Home: 700 Grizzly Peak Blvd Berkeley CA 94708 Office: Sch Librarianship U Cal Berkeley CA 94720

D'ANTONI, JOSEPH STEVEN, physician, corp. exec.; b. New Orleans, Sept. 3, 1907; s. Salvador and Mary (Vaccaro) D'A.; M.D., Tulane, 1932; m. Helen Skelly, Oct. 19, 1933 (dec.); children—Maura Ann, Joseph Steven, Patrick Skelly. Intern Charity Hosp., New Orleans, 1932-33, asst. vis. physician, 1934-38, vis. physician, 1938-47, sr. vis. physician, 1947-54; instr. lab. clin. medicine, Tulane U., 1933-35, instr. dept. medicine, 1933-40, instr. dept. tropical medicine, 1935-40, asst. prof., 1940-43, asso. prof., 1943-46, prof. clin. tropical medicine, 1946-56, lectr. dept. tropical medicine and hygiene, 1957—; head, div. tropical medicine, Lakeshore Hosp., New Orleans, 1946-49; vis. physician Baptist Hosp. New Orleans, 1950—; dir. Standard Fruit & S.S. Co., 1950—, med. dir. 1951- 53, pres., 1953-64, chmn. bd., 1954-70, hon. chmn. bd., 1971—; chmn. bd. Structural Systems Corp., New Orleans; pres. Harbor Banana Distrbrs., Long Beach, Cal.; dir. La. & So. Life Ins. Co. Dir. Internat. Trade Mart, New Orleans; mem. bd. commrs. Port of New Orleans, 1967—, pres., 1970. Fellow A.C.P., A.A.A.S., Am. Soc. Tropical Medicine (pres. 1947-48); mem. A.M.A., Am. Soc. Parasitologists, Am. Acad. Tropical Medicine, La. State, Orleans Parish med. socs., Nat. Malaria Soc., So. Med. Assn. Home: 2100 St Charles Av New Orleans LA 70140 Office: Standard Fruit and SS Co 2 Canal St PO Box 50830 New Orleans LA 70150

D'ANTONIO, NICHOLAS, bishop; b. Rochester, N.Y., July 10, 1916; s. Pasquale and Josephine (Salza) D'A.; student St. Francis Seraphic Sem., Andover, Mass., 1931, St. Anthony Friary, Catskill, N.Y., 1939. Ordained priest Roman Catholic Ch., 1942; pastor, Trail, B.C., Can., 1943-45; provincial del. of U.S.A. Friars working in Guatemala, Honduras and El Salvador, 1953-63; named prelate of Olancho, Honduras, 1963, bishop Diocese Olancho, 1966—. Mem. Order of Friars Minor. Home: Casa Episcopal Juticalpa Olancho Honduras

D'ANTONIO, WILLIAM V., educator, B. New Haven, Feb. 7, 1926; s. Albert and Marie (Nuzzo) D'A.; B.A., Yale, 1949; M.A., U. Wis., 1953; Ph.D., Mich. State U., 1958; m. A. Lorraine Giorgio, June 15, 1950; children—JoAnne, Albert, Nancy, Carla, Raissa, Laura. Tchr. Spanish, wrestling coach Loomis Sch., Windsor, Conn., 1949-54; instr. sociology Mich. State U., 1957-59; prof. sociology U. Notre Dame, 1959-71, chmn. dept. sociology and anthropology, 1966-71; chmn. dept. sociology U. Conn., Storrs, 1971—. Pres. Ohio Valley Sociol. Soc., 1968-69; chmn. Cath. Com. Population and Govt. Policy. Mem. Mayor S. Bend Adv. Com. Community Devel. Bd. dirs. Urban League, Family Planning St. Joseph County. Served with USNR, 1944-46. Mem. Am. Sociol. Assn., Am. Assn. U. Profs., Midwest Council Assn. Latin Am. Studies. Author: (with W.H. Form) Influentials in Two Border Cities: A Study of Community Decision Making, 1965. Co- editor: Power and Democracy in America, 1961; Religion, Revolution and Reform; New Forces for Change in Latin America, 1964; (with DeFleuer) Sociology: Man in Society. Home: Metcalf Rd Tolland CT 06084

D'ANTUONO, ELEANOR (Mrs. Alexander Horvath), ballerina; b. Cambridge, Mass., Oct. 13, 1939; d. Louis and Marie (D'Autuono) Jacobs; student Am. Corr. Schs.; m. Alexander Horvath, Aug. 27,

1964. Appeared with Ballet Russe De Monte Carlo, 1954-60, soloist, 1956-60; appeared with Robert Joffrey Ballet, 1960-61; soloist Am. Ballet Theatre. N.Y.C., 1961-63. prin. dancer, ballerina, 1963-. Home: 77 7th Av New York City NY 10011 Office: care Am Ballet Theatre 1790 Broadway New York City NY 10019

DANTZIG, GEORGE BERNARD, educator; b. Portland, Ore., Nov. 8, 1914; s. Tobias and Anna (Ourisson) D.; A.B. in Math., U. Md., 1936; M.A. in Math. (Horace Rackham scholar) U. Mich., 1937; Ph.D. in Math. (teaching fellow), U. Cal. at Berkeley, 1946; m. Anne Shmuner, Aug. 23, 1936; children—David Franklin, Jessica Rose, Paul Michael. Chief combat analysis br., statis. Control Hdqrs., USAAF, 1941-46, math. adviser, 1946-52; research mathematician, Rand Corp., Santa Monica, Cal., 1952-60; prof. chmn. Operations Research Center, U. Cal. at Berkeley, 1960-66; prof. operations research and computer sci. Stanford, 1966—. Cons. to industry 1947—; adviser environmental hazards Cal. Dept. Health, 1967- 70; com. computer diagnosis of disease Kaiser Found., 1963—; mem. com. applied math. Nat. Acad. Sci., 1967-70. Recipient Exceptional Meritorious Service medal War Dept., 1944. Fellow Econometrica Soc., Operations Research Soc. Am., Inst. Math. Statistics, A.A.A.S.; Mem. Am. Math Soc. (selected hour speaker Reno, 1964), Nat. Acad. Scis., Inst. Mgmt. Sci. (pres. 1966), Phi Kappa Phi, Sigma Chi, Pi Mu Epsilon, Author: Linear Programming and Extensions 1963; also articles. Asso. editor Algebra and its Applications, Jour. Combinatorial Theory, Computers and Biomed. Research Jour. Home: 821 Tolman Dr Stanford CA 94305 Office: Stanford Univ Stanford CA 94305

DANY, GEORGE BERNARD, air force officer; b. Philippine Islands, Feb. 17, 1910 (parents U.S. citizens); s. George and Emily (Avery) D.; B.S., U.S. Mil. Acad., 1934; grad. Air War Coll., 1950. Nat. War Coll., 1954; m. Kathleen Hennessey, June 22, 1935; children—Diane (Mrs. Jack Brooks), Kathleen (Mrs. Peter Russo). George Bernard, Michael Peter, Patrick John, Jeanne Marie, Mary Coleen. Commd. 2d lt. U.S. Army, 1934, advanced through grades to maj. gen. USAF, 1962; comdr. navigation sch. bases Hondo Field, Tex., also Selman Field, La., 1941-44; chief staff 8th Air Force, 1945; comdg. officer Naha AFB, 1946; dep. dir. tng., Hdqrs. USAF, 1950-53; comdr. 1611th Air Transp. Wing, McGuire AFB, 1954-56; airlift task comdr. Hungarian Airlift, 1956-57; comdg. officer U.S. Forces, Azores, 1958-61; dep. chief staff operations Mil. Air Transp. Service, 1961-63; comdr. Western Transp. Air Force, Travis AFB, Cal., 1963-66; former chief staff U.S. So. Command, Quarry Heights, C.Z. Active Panama Council of Boy Scouts Am. Decorated Legion of Merit with 2 oak leaf clusters, Army Commendation ribbon with 1 oak leaf cluster. Mem. Nat. Def. Transp. Assn., Order Daedalians. Club: Army Navy Country. Home: Quarters 2 Quarry Heights CZ

DANZIG, AARON LEON, lawyer; b. Newark, Sept. 9, 1913; s. Saul and Sarah (Goldenberg) D.; A.B., Columbia, 1933, LL.B., 1935; LL.M. in Taxation, N.Y.U., 1952; m. Elinor Moskowitz, Aug. 16, 1940 (dec. Mar. 1954); childrenRichard, Jill; m. 2d. Gwen Seinfeld, June 9, 1957. Admitted to N.Y. bar, 1936; practice in N.Y.C., 1937-44; partner firm Nemeroff, Jelline, Danzig, Paley & Kaufman, and predecessor, 1944—; lectr. taxation N.Y.U. Inst. Fed. Taxation, also Ia. Tax Inst.; lectr. on UN, 1955-; lecture series John L. Elliot Inst. Human Relations, 1966, lectr. U.R.I. Law of Sea Inst. Pres. U.S. Financial Co., Inc., N.Y.C., 1960-; dir. Paragon Industries, Inc., Mineola, N.Y.; sec. Vikoa Inc., 1968—, dir., 1969—. Gen. counsel Nat. Amputation Found., 1950—; mem. Pres. Com. Employment Handicapped, 1950—, Gov. N.Y. Com. Employment Physically Handicapped, 1953-; mem. nat. adv. com. to med. service VA, 1944-; charter mem. World Peace Through Law Center, now also chmn, UN charter com.; mem. Commn. to Study Orgn. Peace, 1968—. Bd. dirs. Fedn. Handicapped, 1948-69. treas., 1951- 69. Mem. Am. Assn. UN (chmn. bd. dirs. Manhattan chpt. 1958-59); Am. (sec. on taxation), Internat. bar assns., Bar Assn. City N.Y. Author: Handbook for One-Handers, 1957; also articles. Home: 1361 Madison Av New York City NY 10028. Office: 350 Fifth Av New York City NY 10001.

DANZIG, CHARLES, lawyer, city ofcl.; b. Walkawishkas, Russia, Jan. 15, 1905; s. Harry and Rebecca (Friedland) D.; S.B., Harvard, 1929, LL.B., 1932; m. Sydney J. Baskin, Dec. 1, 1935. Admitted to N.J. bar, 1934, since practiced in Newark, mem. firm Riker, Danzig, Scherer & Brown, 1939—. Water Commr., East Orange, N.J., 1954—. Fellow Am. Coll. Trial Lawyers; mem. Am., N.J., Essex County bar assns., Harvard Law Sch. Assn. N.J. (pres. 1956), Phi Beta Kappa. Home: 252 Conway Ct South Orange NJ 07079 Office: 744 Broad St Newark NJ 07102

DANZIG, JEROME ALAN, broadcasting exec.; b. N.Y.C., Feb. 7, 1913; s. Jerome J. and Helen Madeline (Wolf) D.; grad. Horace Mann Sch. for Boys, 1930; B.A., Dartmouth, 1934; m. Sarah Palfrey, Apr. 27, 1951; stepchildren—Jerome Palfrey, Diana. Staff reporter N.Y. Jour. 1934-35; spl. events dept., comml. program mgr., publicity dir. sta. WOR, N.Y.C., 1935-42; program dir. sta. WINS, N.Y.C., Crosley Broadcasting Co., 1946-48; asso. dir. network programs, supr. color broadcasting, producer CBS-TV, 1948-55; dir. program planning and devel. NBC owned stas. and spot sales, 1955- 56; v.p. charge radio network programs NBC, 1956-59, v.p. participating programs NBC-TV, 1959-61; TV-radio cons. N.Y. Republican City Com., 1961; spl. asst. to Gov. N.Y. for radio-TV, 1962-69, spl. asst. to the dir. Communications Gov.'s staff, 1969—. Former pub. relations com. Alumni Council, Dartmouth; former trustee Jewish Bd. Guardians, N.Y.C.; trustee Jewish Home and Hosp. for Aged, N.Y.C. Served as officer USNR, 1942-46. Mem. Acad. TV Arts and Scis., Internat. Radio and TV Soc., Alpha Delta Phi. Club: Quaker Hill (Pawling, N.Y.); Dartmouth. Home: 993 Park Av New York City NY 10028 Office: 22 W 55th St New York City NY 10019

DANZIGER, FREDERICK SIMON, lawyer; b. N.Y.C., Apr. 15, 1911; s. Ernst and Martha (Bachmann) D.; B.A., Harvard, 1930; LL.B., Yale, 1936; m. Louise Paskus, June 24, 1935; children-Richard Martin, Frederick Michael. Admitted to N.Y. bar, 1936, since practiced in N.Y.C.; mem. firm Oppheimer, Haiblum & Kupfer, 1936-40; partner Kupfer, Silberfeld, Nathan & Danziger, 1940—. Dir. Amerace Corp., Superior Mfg. & Instrument Corp. Pres., chmn., trustee Altro Rehab. Services, Inc. Served to maj. USAAF, 1942-45. Decorated Air medal. Mem. Assn. Bar City N.Y., Am. Bar Assn., N.Y. County Lawyers Assn. Home: 1 Buckhout Rd White Plains NY 10604 Office: 405 Lexington Av New York NY 10017

DA PARMA, EDWARD ULYSSES, mech. engr.; b. N.Y.C., Sept. 20, 1915; s. Edward E. and Edith (Scelzi) Da P.; B.S., N.Y.U., 1936; m. Constance Gregas, Aug. 12, 1950; children—Catherine, Mark. With Sperry Gyroscope Co., Great Neck, 1936-70, successively asst. works mgr., works mgr., v.p., v.p. mfg., 1952-58; exec. v.p. Sperry Gyroscope Co. div. Sperry Rand Corp., 1958-65, pres. Remington Rand div., 1965-70; v.p. Sperry Rand Corp., 1967-70; v.p. Saxon Industries, N.Y.C., 1970—; sr. v.p., mgr. Standard Packaging Corp., N.Y.C., 1970-71; dir. Human Resources, Inc.; chmn. bd. Abilities Inc. 1968. Chmn. Human Resources Center, 1969. Mem. Am. Soc. M.E., Army Ordnance Assn., Nat. Aero. Assn., Am. Arbitration Assn. (panel 1961—), Navy League. Clubs: Hemisphere, Squadron A, Naval Officers (N.Y.C.); Huntington (N.Y.) Crescent; Pine Valley (N.J.) Country; North Hills Country (Manhasset, L.I.). Home: Dogwood Av Roslyn NY 1157 Office: 450 7th Av New York City NY

DAPHNIS, HELEN AVLON, artist, educator; b. N.Y.C., June 18, 1932; d. Telemakos and Evangeline (Baromis) Avlonitis; B.F.A., Hunter Coll., 1953, M.A., 1957; student N.Y.U., Bklyn. Coll., Colorado Springs Fine Arts Center, Bklyn. Mus. Art Sch.; m. Nassos Daphnis, Mar. 24, 1955; children—Artemis, Demetrios. One man-show at United Fedn. Tchrs. Art Gallery, N.Y.C., 1969; 2-man show at Brata Gallery, N.Y.C., 1969. Exhbns. include Waddell Core Exhbn., 1965-67, Gallery East, 1964, 66, 67, Bertha Schaeffer Gallery, 1965, PVI, 1965, Provincetown Art Assn., 1959-67, St. Mary's Ch., 1967, Phoenix Gallery, N.Y.C., 1962- 64, also Balt. Art Mus., Chrysler Mus., Rochester Mus., Ill. Art Center, Riverside Mus. 1968, Gallery East, 1968; U.F.T. Art Gallery, 1968- 69, Shakespeare Theatre Peace Exhbn., Happenings Palm Gardens, 1968, Chrysler Mus., Riverside Mus., Provincetown (Mass.) Art Assn., also many others; original mem., dir. New Gallery, 1956; dir. dance and stage design Afro Unltd., N.Y.C., 1969; tchr. for N.Y.C. Bd. Edn., Bklyn Coll., Bklyn Mus.; designer, artistic cons. Edith Stephen Dance Co., Bklyn. Acad., 1970—. Mem. Chelsea Park Redesign Com. Mem. Mus. Modern Art, Provincetown Art Assn., P.A.L.A., United Fedn. Tchrs. Art and Peace, Provincetown Taxpayers Assn., A.F.T., U.F.T. Mem. Greek Am. Ch. Club: Arts (pres. 1950-53). Address: 400 W 23d St New York City NY 10011 also 463 West St New York City NY

DAPHNIS, NASSOS, artist; b. Krokeai, Greece, July 23, 1914, (parents U.S. citizens); s. Panagiotes A. and Stamatico (Georgoulis) D.; student Art Students League, N.Y.C., 1946-49, Academie Frochot, Paris, 1950-51, Instituto Statale D'Arte, Florence, Italy, 1951-52; m. Helen Avlonitis, Mar. 24, 1956; children—Artemis, Demetrios. Exhibited one man shows at Contemporary Arts Gallery, N.Y.C., 1938-49, Gallerie Collette Allendy, Paris, France, 1950, Leo Castelli Gallery, N.Y.C., 1959-61, 63, 65, 68, Galerie Iris Clert, Paris, 1962, Toninelli, Milan, 1961, Franklin Siden Gallery, Detroit, 1967, retrospective Albright-Knox Art Gallery, 1969, Everson Mus. Art, Syracuse, N.Y., 1969; exhibited in group shows at Pitts. Internat., 1958-61, 70, Whitney Ann., N.Y.C., 1959, 61, 62, 64, 65, 67, 69, Corcoran Gallery, Washington, 1959, 63, 69, Contemporary Am. Painting, Columbus, O., 1960, Guggenheim Mus., N.Y.C., 1961, Walker Art Center, Mpls., 1962, Washington Gallery Modern Art, 1963, de Cordova Mus., Lincoln, Mass., 1965; represented permanent collections at Mus. Modern Art, Whitney Mus., Albright-Knox Gallery, Utica (N.Y.) Art Mus., Balt. Mus. Art, Providence Sch. Design, Chrysler Art Mus., Provincetown, Mass., Tel Aviv Mus., Israel, Norfolk (Va.) Mus., U. Mich. Mus. Art, Mus. Art Carnegie Inst., Pitts. award, 1962, Nat. Found. Arts and Humanities award, 1966. Home: 400 W 23d St New York City NY 10011.

DAPPLES, EDWARD CHARLES, geologist, educator; b. Chgo., Dec. 13, 1906; s. Edward C. and Victoria (Gazzolo) D.; B.S., Northwestern U., 1928, M.S., 1934; M.A., Harvard, 1935; Ph.D., U. Wis., 1938; m. Marion Virginia Sprague, Sept. 2, 1931; children—Marianne Helena, Charles Christian. Geologist, Ziegler Coal Co., 1928, Truax-Traer Coal Co., 1928-32, mine supt., 1932; instr. Northwestern U., 1936-41, asst. prof., 1941, asso. prof., 1942-50, prof. geol. scis., 1950—; geologist Ill. Geol. Survey, 1939, Sinclair Oil Co., 1945-50, Pure Oil Co., 1950; dir. Evanston Exploration Corp,; sr. vis. scientist U. Lausanne, Switzerland, 1960-61; vis. prof. U. Geneva, 1970. Fellow Geol. Soc. Am., Soc. Econ. Geologist, A.A.A.S.: mem. Am. Inst. Mining Engrs., Assn. Petroleum Geologists, Internat. Assn. Sedimentologists, Soc. Econ. Paleontologists and Mineralogists (pres. 1970), Geochem. Soc., Geophys. Union. Author: Basic Geology for Science and Engineering, 1959; Atlas of Lithofacies Maps, 1960. Home: 9446 Hamlin Av Evanston IL 60203

DARACK, ARTHUR J., newspaperman; b. Royal Oak, Mich., Jan. 1, 1918; s. Edward Charles and Sonia (Resnikov) D.; Mus.M., Cin. Conservatory, 1949; Ph.D., Ind. U., 1951; m. Jean Claire Puttmyer, May 28, 1942; children—Glenn Arthur, Brenda Lee. Music editor Cin. Enquirer, 1951-61, feature writer, columnist, 1961-62, book and art editor, 1962—; editor Dimension; Cin., monthly mag., Chgo., 1963-65; asso. editor Ency. Brittanica, 1967-70; sr. editor Actual Specifying Engr. monthly mag., 1970—. Program annotator Cin. Symphony Orch., 1952-61; adj. asso. prof. music Coll. Music, U. Cin. Served with AUS, 1941-45. Mem. Pi Kappa Lambda. Home: 9018 Sleeping Bear Rd Skokie IL 60076. Office: 1801 Prairie Chicago IL

DARBO, HOWARD HELSETH, lawyer; b. Milw., Dec. 9, 1909; s. John and Mathilda (Heinrich) D.; B.S. in Chem. Engring., U. Wis., 1932; J.D., U. Mich., 1935; m. Elizabeth Jane Kidder, July 31, 1933; children—Ann Christine (Mrs. Andrew B. Cvercko), John Howardson. Admitted to Ill. bar, 1936, since practiced in Chgo. and Arlington Heights; staff patent atty. C.F. Burgess Labs., Inc., 1936-38; partner Darbo, Robertson & Vandenburgh and predecessor firms, 1938—. Pres., dir. Geneva Sales Co., St. Charles, Ill. Chmn. Zoning Commn., 1951-59; city commr., city councilman, 1959-63; mem. Pollution Control Commn., Comml. Blight Com., Wheaton, Ill., 1969—. Pres. Whitewater (Wis.) Lake Property Owners Assn.; pres., bd. dirs. Triangle Frat. Edn. Found. Mem. Am., Chgo. patent law assns., Am., N.W. Suburban, Dupage, Chgo. bar assns., Triangle Frat. (past nat. pres.). Club: Chicago Engineers. Home: 1110 N Wheaton Av Wheaton IL 60187 Office: 15 N Arlington Heights Rd Arlington Heights IL 60006

D'ARBOUSSIER, GABRIEL, diplomat; b. Djenne, Mali, Jan. 14, 1908; s. Henri and Aminata Ali (Koita) d'A.; grad. Faculte de Droit, Toulouse, Paris, France, 1935; M.A. in Law, Ecole Coloniale, Paris, 1938; m. Antoinette Neves, June 27, 1946; children—Mireille, Henri, Jeanne, Claire, Comdr., Territory Yako, 1941-43; dir. polit bur. Ivory Coast, 1943-44; dir. polit. bur. of gov.- gen. French Equatorial Africa, 1944-45; parliamentarian in Europe and Africa, 1945—; participant drafting French Constn., 1945, 58, Fed. Constn. Mali, 1959, Constn. Republic Senegal, 1962; mem. Nat. Assembly Senegal, 1959—; minister of justice of Senegal, 1960-62; practice law in Dakar and Paris, 1953-60; head Senegal delegation to UN, 1960; rep. Senegal at Common Market negotiations, 1961; ambassador to France, 1963- 64, also permanent del. UNESCO; under-sec. UN, also exec. dir. UN Inst. Tng. and Research, 1965-68; ambassador of Senegal to Federal Republic of Germany, Austria and Switzerland, Bonn, 1968—. Director weekly Reveil, publ. of Rassemblement Democratique Africain, 1941-50; chmn. bd. monthly rev. La Vie Africain, 1961—; Internat. lectr., 1949—. Mem. Council U. Dakar, 1957-64; trustee Inst. Ecom. and Social Devel. Studies of U. Paris, 1958-. Decorated grand croix de l'Ordre national (Senegal); commendeur Legion of Honor, comdr. Palmes Academiques (France); grand croix du Merite allemand (Germany); grand croix de l'Ordre national du Cedre du Liban (Lebanon); comdr. du Million d'Elephants et du Parasol blanc (Laos); comdr. de l'Ordre du Merite Francais d'Outre-Mer, medaille d'Honneur pour Belles Actions (France). Author: L'Afrique vers l'Unite, 1958; also numerous articles. Address: 121a Adenaueralle 53 Bonn Federal Republic Germany

DARBY, EDWIN WHEELER, financial editor; b. Oakland, Md., Jan. 7, 1922; s. John Dade and Nell (Bosley) D.; B.S. in Journalism, Ohio U.; children—Ann Wheeler, John Dade; m. 2d, Susan E. Kroening, Mar. 14, 1970. White House corr. Time mag., 1948-55; medwest corr. Time and Fortune mags., 1956-58; financial editor Chgo. Sun-Times, 1958—. Clubs: Tavern, Attic (Chgo.). Home: 1834 N Orleans St Chicago IL 60614 Office: Chicago Sun-Times Chicago IL 60611

DARBY, HARRY, former U.S. senator, mfg. exec.; b. Kansas City, Kans., Jan. 23, 1895; s. Harry and Florence Isabelle (Smith) D.; B.S. in Mech. Engring., U. Ill., 1917, M.E., 1929; LL.D., St. Benedict's Coll., Atchison, Kan., Westminster Coll., Fulton, Mo., Kan. State U., Manhattan and Washburn U., Topeka, Kan.; m. Edith Marie Cubbison, Dec. 17, 1917; children—Harriet (Mrs. Thomas H. Gibson, Jr.), Joan (Mrs. Roy A. Edwards, Jr.), Edith Marie (Mrs. Ray Evans), Marjorie (Mrs. Eugene D. Alford). With Mo. Boiler Works Co., Kansas City, 1911-19; with Darby Corp., 1920—, now chmn. bd., owner; founder, chmn. Leavenworth Steel, Inc., Darby Ry. Cars, Inc.; dir. numerous corps. U.S. senator from Kan., 1949-50; mem. Republican Nat. Com. for Kan., 1940-64. Active in work of 4-H Club, Boy Scouts Am., Trustee various cultural instns., assns; trustee, chmn. Eisenhower Found., Abilene, Kan.; chmn. Eisenhower Presdl. Library Commn., Abilene; mem. Gov.'s Com. Kan. State Fair; mem. exec. com. Agrl. Hall of Fame; trustee Nat. Cowboy Hall of Fame. Recipient awards for civic activities. Served from 2d lt. to capt., F.A., U.S. Army, 1917-19; with AEF. Former chmn. Am. Royal Livestock and Horse Show; mem. exec. com. Kan. Livestock Assn.; dir. U. Kan. Research Found., Kan. Heart Assn., Palomino Horse Exhibitors of Kan. Fellow Am. Soc. M.E.; Mem. Navy League of U.S., Kansas City Crime Commn., Kan. Registration Bd. Profl. Engrs., U. Ill. Found., Am. Soc. C.E., Nat., Kan. soc. profl. engrs., Am. Hereford Assn., Am. Nat. Livestock Assn., Society of Am. Mil. Engrs., Am. Soc. Agrl. Engrs., V.F.W., Am. Legion, 40 and 8, Mil. Order World Wars. Episcopalian. Mason (32, Shriner, Jester). Clubs: Kansas City, Automobile of Missouri, Saddle and Sirloin, Rotary, River, Terrace, Man of the Month (Kansas City, Kan.); Chicago; Chevy Chase, Capitol Hill (Washington); Cherry Hills (Denver); Burning Tree (Bethesda, Md.). Home: 1220 Hoel Pkwy Kansas City KS 66102 Office: 1st St and Walker Av Kansas City KS 66110

DARBY, SAMUEL NORMAN, architect; b. Rockford, Ill., July 9, 1934; s. John Earnest and Alice (Johnson) D.; B.Arch., U. Ill., 1962; m. Carol Sue Anderson, Apr. 2, 1955; children—Christian Jay, Paul Evan, Ann Carol. Project architect C. Edward, 1962-64; v.p. Larson & Darby, Inc., Rockford, 1964—. Co-chmn. Rockford City Planning Commn.; chmn. Civic Beautification Com. Served with AUS, 1957-59. Recipient top ten plant award for Sundstrand Aviation Co., McGraw-Hill Co., 1968, award of merit for Rockford Clinic, A.M.A. and A.I.A., 1969, design award for Riverlane Sch., Ill. Assn. Sch. Bds., 1970. Mem. A.I.A. Presbyn. Clubs: Rockford Country, University (Rockford). Home: 213 N Highland Av Rockford IL 61107 Office: 1330 E State St Rockford IL 61108

DARBY, WILLIAM JEFFERSON, Jr., educator; b. Galloway, Ark., Nov. 6, 1913; s. William J. and Ruth (Douglass) D.; B.S., U. Ark., 1936, M.D., 1937; M.S., U. Mich. (Univ.- Sigma Xi fellow, 1939-40, Horace H. Rackham fellow 1940-41), 1941, Ph.D., 1942, D.Sc. (hon.), 1966; m. Elva Louise Mayo, June 12, 1935; children—William J., James Richard, Thomas Douglass. Instr. in phys. chemistry, U. Ark. Sch. Medicine, 1937-39; asst. prof. biochemistry, also asst. prof. medicine, Sch. Medicine, Vanderbilt U., 1944-46, asso. prof. biochemistry, 1946-48, prof. biochemistry, chmn. dept., dir. div. nutrition, 1949—, prof. nutrition, 1964—, prof. medicine in nutrition, 1965—. Mem. study sect. biochemistry and nutrition, div. research grants and fellowships of U.S.P.H.S., 1948-53, chmn. study sect. on metabolism and nutrition, 1948-53, chmn. study sect. on gen. medicine, 1956-59, mem. com. on selection sr. research fellowships, 1956-59, chmn. study sect. nutrition 1959-61; mem. food and nutrition bd. Nat. Research Council, 1949-71, mem. food protection com., 1950-71, chmn., 1954-71, mem. advisory bd. Inst. Nutrition Central Am. and Panama, 1950-64; mem. WHO Expert Adv. Panel on nutrition, 1950—; mem. FAO and WHO Joint Expert Com. on Nutrition, 1954, 57, 61, 66; sci. adv. com. Samuel R. Noble Found., 1953-63, chmn.; 1955, 58, 61; chmn. Joint FAO-WHO Expert Com. on Food Additives, 1956; cons. Interdeptl. Com. on Nutrition for Nat. Def. 1955-66; co-ordinator WHO Protein advisory group, 1956-60; mem. FAO/WHO/UNICEF Protein Adv. Group, 1960-62; mem. scientific advisory com. Nutrition Found., 1958-65, 67—, Sci. Adv. Com. Nat. Vitamin Found., 1950-64; Kempner lectr. U. Tex. Med. Br., Galveston, 1961; chmn. adv. com. United Health Found., 1962-70; tech. adv. com. Inst. Nutrition Scis., Columbia, 1966-70; vis. com. dept. nutrition and food sci. Mass. Inst. Tech., 1963-68; nat. cons. USAF Surgeon Gen., 1967—; mem. council on foods and nutrition A.M.A., 1948-62, 65—, chmn., 1967-70; mem. commn. on pesticides Sec. Health, Edn. and Welfare, 1969—; mem. long range planning com. FASEB, 1969-70; mem. Tenn. Gov.'s Adv. Commn. on Consumer Protection, 1969-70; mem. adv. com. on nutrition AID, 1968—; vis. prof. U. Cal. Davis, 1967; adv. com. on pers. for research Am. Cancer Soc., 1962-65; pub. trustee Food Law Inst., 1962—; mem. bd. basic sci. examiners state of Tenn., 1961—, pres., 1962—. Recipient Mead-Johnson B-Complex award, 1947; Joseph Goldberger Award, A.M.A., 1964; Thomas Jefferson award Vanderbilt U., 1969; Charles Franklin Craig lecturer, Am. Soc., Tropical Med., 1950; decorated Order Rodolfo Robles (Guatemala); Star of Jordan, 1963; Roberts Meml. lectr. U. P.R., 1966; Phi Beta Kappa scholar, 1966-67. Fellow A.C.P., A.A.A.S.; mem. Am. Chem. Soc., Am. Inst. Nutrition (pres. 1958); Osborne-Mendel award 1962, Am. Public Health Assn., Am. Medical Assn., (chmn. council foods and nutrition 1960-62, 67- 70), Am. Soc. Biol. Chemists, Soc. Exptl. Biology and Medicine, Nutrition Soc. (British), So. Soc. for Clin. Research (v.p., 1948), Am. Fedn. for Clin. Research, Am. Soc. Clin. Investigation, Assn. Am. Physicians, Austrian Pub. Health Assn. (hon.), Nat. Med. Assn. Panama, Serlian Acad. Sci. (hon.), Philippine Dietetic Assn. (hon.). Co-author: Nutrition and Diet in Health and Disease. Asso. editor Nutrition Revs., 1944-50, Jour. Clin. Investigation 1950-54, Co-discoverer Vitamin M and of activity of pteroyglutamic acid in sprue. Home: Route 2 Box 165 Thompson Station TN 37179 Office: Vanderbilt U Nashville TN 37203

DARBY, WILLIAM LEONARD, corp. exec.; b. Eng., 1919; s. Frederick and Mary (Simpson) D.; came to U.S., 1921, naturalized, 1928; B.A., Wayne U., 1942, M.A., 1955; m. Dorothy Ruth Hyman, Mar. 14, 1941; 1 son, William Duane. Cost accountant Fisher Body div. Gen. Motors Corp., 1941-42, 46-47; with Allen Industries, 1948—, v.p., controller, 1965—; v.p. Colonial Rubber Works, Inc., Star Textile & Research Co., Nat. Dyeing & Finishing Corp.; v.p., treas. Frisch Corp., Gordon Chapman Co., Allen Industries Can., Ltd. Served to capt. AUS, 1942-46, 51-52. Lutheran (v.p.). Home: 589 Anita St Grosse Pointe MI 48236 Office: 17515 W 9 Mile Rd Southfield MI 48075

D'ARCAMBAL, THOMAS RADFORD, diversified industry exec.; b. Hartford, Conn., Apr. 7, 1931; s. A.H. and Helen (Hathaway) d'A.; B.B.A., U. Mich., 1956, M.B.A., 1957;; m. Joan Hooper, Aug. 9, 1958; children—Michelle, Melissa. Auditor, Price Waterhouse & Co., C.P.A.'s, Los Angeles, 1957-59; controller Trousdale Constrn. Co.,

Los Angeles, 1959-60; treas. Trousdale Enterprises, Honolulu, 1960-65; financial v.p. Amfac Properties, Honolulu, 1965-68; controller Amfac Inc., Honolulu, 1968—, v.p., 1969—. Served with AUS, 1951-53. C.P.A., Cal. Mem. Am. Inst. C.P.A.'s, Hawaii Soc. C.P.A.'s, Alpha Delta Phi. Clubs: Outrigger Canoe, Oahu Country, Pacific (Honolulu). Home: 919 Maunawili Rd Kailua HI 96734 Office: 700 Bishop St Honolulu HI 96801

D'ARCANGELO, ALLAN MATTHEW, artist; b. Buffalo, June 16, 1930; s. Bartholemew and Anna (Petrella) D'A.; B.S., U. Buffalo, 1952; postgrad. Coll. City N.Y., 1955-56, Mexico City Coll., 1957-59; m. Sylvia Rachel Resnick, Feb. 7, 1954; children—Christopher David, Gabrielle Anna, Gideon Bartholomew. Exhbt. one man shows at Galerie Genova, Mexico City, 1958, L.I. U., 1961, Fischbach Gallery, 1963, 64, 65, 67, Ileana Sonnabend Gallery, Paris, 1965, Rudolf Zwirner Gallery, Cologne, Germany, 1965. Hans Neuendorf Gallery, Hamburg, Germany, 1965, Gallery Muller, Stuttgart, Germany, 1965. Dwan Gallery, Los Angeles, 1966. Wurttembergischer Kunstverein, Stuttgart, Germany, 1967, Galerie Ricke, Kassel, Germany, 1967, Minami Gallery, Tokyo, Japan, 1967; exhbt. numerous group shows, including Gemeent Mus., The Hague, 1964, Mus. Modern Art, 1966, Stedelijk Mus., Amsterdam, 1966, Am. Pavillion Expo 7, Montreal, 1967, IX Bienal de Sao Paulo, Brazil, 1967; represented in permanent collections at Mus. Modern Art, N.Y.C., Gemeent Mus., Aldrich Mus., Ridgefield, Conn.; executed mural for Transp. and Travel Pavillion N.Y. World's Fair, 1963; artist in residence Aspen (Colo.) Inst. Humanistic Studies, 1965, 67; vis. artist Cornell U., 1968, Yale, 1969. Served with Signal Corps, U.S. Army, 1954-55. Recipient First Purchase award Nat. Small Painting Show U. Omaha, 1966, List Art Poster Program Commn. award, 1967, First prize Hofstra U., 1967. Home and studio: 76 W 69th St New York City NY 10023

DARCY, DAVID KEENE, banker; b. Bklyn., July 21, 1922; s. David Keene and Lillian (Webb) D.; B.S., Lehigh U., 1946; grad. Advanced Mgmt. Program, Harvard, 1967; m. Betty Marie McDow, Sept. 5, 1947; children—Donna Marie, Linda Carol, Maureen Teresa. With Irving Trust Co., N.Y.C., 1946—, asst. sec., 1951-54, asst. v.p., 1954-58, v.p., 1959-68, sr. v.p., 1968—. Served with USAAF, 1942-45. Mem. Phi Kappa Theta. Roman Catholic. Club: Garden City (N.Y.) Country. Home: 123 Wickham Rd Garden City NY 11530 Office: One Wall St New York City NY 10015

DARCY, GEORGE ROBERT, communications co. exec.; b. Rochester, N.Y., Aug. 23, 1920; s. George N. and Agnes (Hogan) D.; A.B., U. Rochester, 1942; m. Martha Louise Harbrecht, Apr. 5, 1950; children—George H., Patricia A., Kevin B., Michael J., Elizabeth A. Coll. rep. McGraw-Hill Book Co., N.Y.C., 1947-48; editor indsl. and bus. books McGraw-Hill Book Co., 1949-52; mgr. book div. F.W. Dodge Corp., N.Y.C., 1952- 54; sr. v.p. adminstrn. Rumrill Co., Inc., Rochester, 1954-59; pres. Darcy Communications, Inc., Rochester, 1959—; chmn. bd., chief exec. officer Hutchins/Darcy Inc. dir. Smith, Legge & Darcy, Inc. Pub. information chmn. U.S. Golf Assn. Open Championship, 1968; mem. Monroe County Human Relations Commn., 1970—. Chmn. Independents for Rockefeller, Monroe County, 1970. Trustee Penfield (N.Y.) Bd. Edn., 1959-60, Meml. Art Gallery, U. Rochester, 1968—. Served to lt. (s.g.), USNR, 1942-46. Mem. Pub. Relations Soc. Am. (del. nat. assembly 1964-67), Rochester C. of C. (trustee), U. Rochester Assos. (vice chmn.). Home: 1110 Allen Creek Rd Rochester NY 14618 Office: Security Tower Rochester NY 14604

D'ARCY, JOHN, Jr., industrialist b. St. Louis, June 7, 1916; s. John and Julia (Barclay) D'A.; A.B., U. Mich., 1939; student U. Akron, U. Ind.; m. Marian Smith, Apr. 19, 1941 (dec.); children—John Barclay, Marian, David Arlington; m. Marguerite Helmantoler, Nov. 12, 1955; 1 son, Thomas George. With Quaker Oats Co., Chgo., 1939—, now sr. vice president for operations and adminstrn., also director; dir. Chicago, R.I. and Pacific Railroad Co., Sears Bank & Trust Co., Gen. Color Graphics, Inc. Bd. dirs. United Charities Chgo., Community Fund Chgo., Chgo. unit Am. Cancer Soc.; v.p. Episcopal Charities; v.p. bd. trustees Community Hosp., Geneva, Ill.; bd. dirs. United Negro Coll. Fund, mem. Chgo. com. Episcopalian. Club: Chicago Sunday Evening (trustee). Home: Foxford Lane Geneva IL 60134 Office: 345 Merchandise Mart Plaza Chicago IL 60654

D'ARCY, MARTIN CYRIL, clergyman, writer; b. Bath, Eng., June 15, 1888; s. Martin Valentine and Madoline (Keegan) D'A.; M.A. (Locke scholar 1917, Green Moral Philosophy prize 1922), Oxford U., 1916; D.D., Gregorian U., Rome, Italy, 1923; D.Litt. (hon.), Georgetown U., 1935, Fordham U., 1940, Marquette U., 1950, Nat. U. of Ireland, 1955. Entered Soc. of Jesus, 1906, ordained priest Roman Cath. Ch., 1921; lectr. philosophy Oxford U., 1926-45, master of Campion Hall, Oxford, 1932-45; provincial of English Province, Soc. of Jesus, 1945-50; lectr. at Fordham U., Notre Dame U., Georgetown U., 1939-40, 41-42, 50, 54-56, 58-59; Danforth lectr. Cornell U., 1959; Roman Cath. rep. on BBC 1936-45; lectr. for Brit. Council on Humanities in Italy, Spain, Portugal, Malta; conventual chaplain Knights of Malta. Mem. Royal Coll. Lit.; hon. mem. Am. Acad. Arts and Scis. Clubs: Athenaeum (London). Author: The Mass and the Redemption, 1926; Thomas Aquinas, 1932; The Nature of Belief, 1933; Death and Life, 1942; The Problem of Pain, 1943; The Mind and Heart of Love, 1945; Communism and Christianity, 1957; The Meeting of Love and Knowledge, 1958; The Meaning and Matter of History, 1959; No Absent God, 1962; Of God and Man, 1964; Dialogue with Myself, 1966; Facing The People, 1967; Humanism and Christianity, 1969; Facing the Truth, 1969. Address: 114 Mount St London W 1 England

D'ARCY, ROBERT H., journalist. Editorial writer Detroit News. Office: Evening News Assn 615 Lafayette Blvd Detroit MI 48231*

DARCY, TOM FRANCIS, polit. cartoonist; b. Bklyn., Dec. 19, 1932; s. Clinton F. and Iva (Cress) D.; student Terry Art Inst., Coral Gables, Fla., 1953-54, Sch. Visual Arts, N.Y.C., 1954-56; m. Audrey K. Stolzenberger, Nov. 2, 1957; children—Kelly Lynn, Regan Thomas, Thomas Jason, Bradley William. Polit. cartoonist Newsday, N.Y.C., 1958-59, Phoenix Gazette, 1959-60, Houston Post, 1965-67, Phila. Bull., 1967-68, Newsday, 1968—; syndicated cartoonist through Newsday Spls., 1968—. Served with USNR, 1951-53. Recipient Pulitzer prize in journalism, editorial cartooning, 1970; Overseas Press Club Am. citation for excellence, 1970; award Internat. Salon Cartoons, 1966. Mem. Nat. Editorial Cartoonists Soc., Nat. Cartoonists Coc. Author: The' Good Life, 1970. Home: 1177 Albert Rd North Bellmore NY 11710. Office: 550 Stewart Av Garden City NY 11530

DARDEN, COLGATE WHITEHEAD, Jr., ret. pres. U. Va.; b. Southampton Co., Va., Feb. 11, 1897; A.B., U. Va; M.A. and LL.B., Columbia; Carnegie fellowship, Oxford U. In practice of law in Va.; mem. Va. Gen. Assembly, 1930-33; mem. 73d Congress Va. at large, 74th, 76th and 77th Congresses 2d Dist. Va.; Gov. of Va., for term expiring Jan. 1946; apptd. vice chmn. Navy's Civilian Adv. Com., 1947; pres. U. Va., 1947-59, ret. Mem. Bd. Cons. to Pres. on Mut. Security, Fgn. Intelligence. U.S. del. 10th Session of Gen. Assembly of UN. Mem. bd. of visitors U.S. Navel Acad., 1936, 39. Served with U.S. Marine Corps, also French Army, World War I. Democrat. Address: 1536 Va National Bank Bldg Norfolk VA 23510

DARDEN, SEVERN TEACKLE, actor; b. New Orleans; s. Severn T. and Geraldine (Rubenstein) D.; ed. Mexico City Coll., U. Mexico, U. Chgo., Bard Coll.; m. Ann Barodel Grant, 1958 (div.); m. 2d, Cynthia Jane Williams, 1968. Appeared in Improvisational theater at Barter Theatre, 1953—56, then Compass Theatre, Chgo., St. Louis, N.Y.C., 1955-58 , Second City, Chgo., Los Angeles, N.Y.C., London, Dublin, 1959-64; played in Am. Shakespeare Festival, Stratford, 1957-59, in A Murderer Among Us, 1964; asso. as actor, and/or producer, writer with films Goldstein, 1963, Double Barreled Detective Story, 1964, Fearless Frank, 1965, The Virgin Pres., 1965, Dead Heat on A Merry-Go-Round, 1966, Luv, 1966, P.J., 1967; The President's Analyst, 1967, The Mad Room, 1968; The Model Shop, 1968; broadway; Leda Had a Little Swan, 1968; films: The Shoot Horses Don't They, 1969; Pussycat, Pussycat I Love You, 1969; Spanish Portrait, 1969, The Last Movie, 1970, The Hired Hand, 1970, Vanishing Point, 1970. Address: 3220 Laurel Canyon Blvd North Hollywood CA 91604

DARDEN, SPERRY EUGENE, educator, physicist; b. Chgo., Aug. 16, 1928; s. Sperry E. and Catherine (Mahoney) D.; B.S., Ia. State U., 1950; M.S., U. Wis., 1951, Ph.D., 1955; m. Marcia Brienen, June 26, 1954; children—Timothy, Kristin, Ruth, Stephen. Research asst. U. Basel, Switzerland, 1955-56, guest asso. prof., 1965-66; faculty U. Wis., 1956-57, 61-62; mem. faculty U. Notre Dame, 1957-61, 62-65, 66—, prof. physics, 1965—. Fellow Am. Phys. Soc. Research, publs. on interactions of neutrons with nuclei, spin polarization phenomena in nuclear interactions of neutrons and deuterons. Home: 1929 Beverly Pl South Bend IN 46616 Office: Physics Dept U Notre Dame Notre Dame IN 46556

DARDEN, WILLIAM HORACE, judge; b. Union Point, Ga., May 16, 1923; s. William Washington and Sara (Newsom) D.; B.B.A., U. Ga., 1946, LL.B., 1948; m. Mary Parrish Viccellio, Dec. 31, 1949; children—Sara, Martha, William Horace, Dan. Admitted to Ga. bar, 1948; sec. to Senator Richard B. Russell, 1948-51; chief clk. U.S. Senate Com. Armed Forces, 1951-53, profl. staff mem., later chief staff, 1954-68; judge U.S. Ct. Mil. Appeals, 1968—. Served to lt. (j.g.) USNR, 1943-46. Home: 7517 June St Springfield VA 22150 Office: 450 E St NW Washington DC 20442

DARE, GROVER E., banker. Vice pres., auditor Nat. Savs. & Trust Co., Washington. Office: New York Av at 15th St NW Washington DC 20005*

DARE, JAMES ASHTON, naval officer; b. Seattle, Dec. 5, 1915; s. Lewis Ashton and Muriel (Rucker) D.; student U. Wash., 1933-35; B.S. in Elec. Engring., U.S. Naval Acad., 1939; M.S., Mass. Inst. Tech.; grad. Nat. War Coll., 1962; m. Jeanne Muriel Howie, Aug. 6, 1941; childrenAlexa Jeanne, James Ashton, Commd. ensign U.S. Navy, 1939, advanced through grades to rear adm., 1967; assigned U.S.S. Arizona, 1939-41, U.S.S. Maryland, 1941-44, U.S. Postgrad. Sch., 1944-46, Los Alamos Lab., 1947-51; comdr. U.S.S. Douglas H. Fox, 1951-53; assigned Naval Ordnance Lab., 1953-56; comdr. U.S.S. Compass Island, 1956-58; mem. faculty Mass. Inst. Tech., 1958-59; mem. staff Office Chief Naval Operations, 1959-61, comdr. in chief Pacific, 1962-64; comdr. Amphibious Squadron 10, 1964-65, Naval Ordnance Lab., 1965-66; dep. dir. Def. Atomic Support Agy., 1966-68; comdr. S. Atlantic Force, Atlantic Fleet, 1968-70; comdr. Mine Forces, Atlantic Fleet, 1970—. Chief Joint Atomic Information Exchange Group, 1966-68. Decorated Legion of Merit, Bronze Star. Mem. Am. Orchid Soc., Sigma Xi, Phi Kappa Sigma. Home: Quarters Z US Naval Sta San Juan PR 00932 Office: Commander Mine Forces US Atlantic Fleet Charleston SC 29408

DAREFF, HAL, author, editor; b. Bklyn., May 8, 1920; s. Barnett and Bessie (Littman) D.; attended New Sch. for Social Research, N.Y.C.: m. to Gladys Wilkowitz, Sept. 12, 1944; children—Scott, Brooks. Free-lance writer and editor, 1946-52; editor children's Digest of Parents' Inst. and Better Reading Found., 1952-67; gen. editor Dell Seal Books of Dell Pub. Co., 1963-65, also editorial cons. pub. co.; contbg. editor Parents' magazine, 1965-66; editor-in-chief juvenile and young adult books Grosset and Dunlap, Inc., N.Y.C., 1967-69; v.p., pub. Greenwood Press, Inc., also affiliate Negro Univs. Press, Westport, Conn., 1969-70; pub. cons. New Am. Library, Inc., 1970—. Served with Army of U.S., 1941-45. Mem. Authors Guild, Authors League of Am. Author: The First Microscope (one of books of year Child Study Assn. 1962), 1962; Man in Oribit, 1962; Jacqueline Kennedy: A Portrait in Courage, 1965: Fun with ABC and 1-2-3, 1965; The Story of Vietnam (a Book of the Yr., Child Study Assn. Am.; chosen 1 of 75 best books of Yr. N.Y. Times, 1966) 1966; From Vietnam to Cambodia, 1971. Home: 3 Colony Rd Weston CT 06880

D'AREZZO, JOSEPH PAUL, business exec.; b. Providence, July 18, 1917; s. Louis and Erminia (Perillo) D'A.; B.S., U.S. Naval Acad., 1940; M.S., Johns Hopkins, 1949; m. Helen Iwinski, Dec. 11, 1943; children—Carol, Vivian, Paul William, Mark Louis. Served with USN, 1934-40; commd. officer U.S. Army, 1940, advanced through grades to lt. col., Arty. Corps; mem. Army Gen. Staff, 1953-55; divisional v.p. Am. Machine & Foundry Co., Alexandria, Va., 1955-57, divisional v.p., dir. planning, spl. asst. to pres., 1957-60, v.p., 1960—, group exec., elec. products group, 1961—. Recipient Legion of Merit. Mem. Am. Ordnance Assn. Club: Army and Navy (Arlington, Va.). Home: 3412 Sterling Av Alexandria VA 22304 Office: 110 N Royal St Alexandria VA 22314

DARFLER, WALTER LEROY, former stock broker; b. Yorkville, Ill., Sept. 10, 1900; s. Jacob C. and Mary Louise (Swan) D.; m. Lucille Miller, July 30, 1921 (dec. Mar. 1963); children—Donald Lawrence, Charles Jay, Gene Edward, Jeanne Marilyn. With Halsey, Stuart & Co., Inc. 1920-69, sec.-treas. 1941-66, v.p., 1944-66, pres., 1966-68, chmn. bd. 1968-69, also dir., ret., 1969. Served with USMC, 1918-19. Republican. Conglist. Mason, Elk, Clubs: Union League, Bond, Attic (Chgo.). Home: Route 1 Sandwich IL 60548 Office: 123 S LaSalle St Chicago IL 60690

DARGIE, R. NORMAN, aviation exec.; b. Malden, Mass., Nov. 17, 1918; s. Percival Charles and Edith Edna (Chute) D.; B.S., St. Louis U., 1948; m. Dorothy Walker, Feb. 11, 1949. Various mgmt. and exec. positions Trans World Airlines, 1948-61; dir. tech. services Ethiopian Airlines, 1961-64; exec. v.p. World Air Center, Inc., div. World Airways, 1964—; corporate dir. World Airways, Inc., Worldamerica Investors Corp. Dist. chmn. Boy Scouts Am. Served with USAAF, 1940-45. Mem. N.A.A.C.P., St. Louis U. Alumni, Newcomen Soc. Home: 321 Laguna Vista Alameda CA 94501 Office: Oakland International Airport Oakland CA 94614

DARGUSCH, CARLTON SPENCER, lawyer; b. Batavia, N.Y., Aug. 19, 1900; s. Julius Herman and Etta (Burnham) D.; student Ind. U., 1921-22, Ohio State U., 1922- 25; m. Genevieve Johnston, Nov. 6, 1923; children Carlton Spencer, Evelyn Byrd (Mrs. CHarles A. Lanphere). Legislative draftsman, Ohio Gen. Assembly, 1925; atty., Tax Commn. of Ohio, 1925-33; tax commr. of Ohio, 1933-37, resigned Jan. 1937; engaged in pvt. practice of law, specializing in taxation, Columbus, O., 1937-65; dir. Clark Grave Vault Co.; cons. Engring. Manpower Commn. Mem. com. specialized personnel, asst. dir. manpower ODM. 1955-57. Trustee Mt. Carmel Hosp.; trustee Ohio State U., 1938-59, 63-65, chmn. bd. trustees, 1944-45, 51-52, 58-59, dir. Ohio State U. Research Found., 1951-62. Active duty lt. col., Judge Adv. General's Dept., U.S. Army, 1940-47; dep. dir. nat. hdqrs. SSS; promoted colonel, 1942; brig. gen., 1946. Awarded D.S.M., 1946. Helped draft plans for SSS, World War II and present; also plans for Universal Mil. Tng. Mem. Omicron Kappa Upsilon (hon.), Kappa Sigma, Phi Delta Phi, Mil. Order World Wars. Mason. Clubs: Chevy Chase, (Md.); Army and Navy (Washington); Columbus Country, Columbus, Ohio State Faculty (Columbus, O.); Engineers, The Players (N.Y.C.); Union (Cleveland); Queen City (Cincinnati). Author: Estate and Inheritance Taxation (with John R. Cassidy), 1930, rev. 1956 (with Jack H. Bertsch); The Operation of Selective Service in World War II, 1956. Home: 271 N Columbia Av Columbus OH 43209 Office: 218 E State St Columbus OH 43215

DARGUSCH, CARLTON SPENCER, Jr., lawyer; b. Columbus, O., May 24, 1925; s. Carlton Spencer and Genevieve (Johnston) D.; B.S., Ohio State U., 1948, LL.B., 1951; m. Joyce B. Baltzell, June 7, 1947; children—Carlton Spencer III, William D., Timothy B., Jonathan D. Admitted to Ohio bar, 1951; now partner law firm Dargusch & Day, Columbus. Exec. v.p., treas. Ohio Assn. Broadcasters, Columbus; gen. counsel Ohio Dental Assn., Columbus counsel Armco Steel Corp.; v.p., sec., gen. counsel, dir. Copeland Refrigeration Corp., Sidney, O. Served with USNR, 1943-46; col. Ohio N.G., 1947—. Mem. Phi Delta Phi, Beta Theta Pi. Republican. Rotarian. Clubs: The Columbus, Golf, Columbus Country, Columbus Athletic; Ft. Henry (Wheeling, W.Va.); Lyford Cay (Nassau, Bahamas). Home: 2655 Brentwood Rd Columbus OH 43209 Office: 218 E State St Columbus OH 43215

DARIN, BOBBY, singer, songwriter; b. Bronx, N.Y., June 14, 1936; student Hunter Coll. Appeared Dorsey Bros. TV Show, Mar. 1956; first recording Rock Island Line, Dealer in Dreams, 1957; numerous recordings Decca Records; compositions include Splish, Splash, 1958; Dream Lover; That's All; Multiplication; If a Man Answers; others; wrote score film The Lively Set; appeared numerous nightclubs and TV shows. Pres. T.M. Music, Inc. Address: 745 5th Av New York City NY*

DARION, JOE, librettist, lyricist; b. N.Y.C., Jan. 30, 1917; s. Isak and Rose (Nadelle) D.; student journalism, Coll. City N.Y.; m. Hellen Solomon, June 8, 1940. Lyricist of popular songs, including Ricochet, Changing Partners, Midnight Train, 1954-58; librettist operas, cantatas, song cycles, including Archy and Mehitabel (jazz opera), New Orleans Cantata, 1956-60; playwright, lyricist for Broadway prodns. Shinbone Alley, 1957; lyricist Broadway prodns. Man of La Mancha, 1965, Illya Darling, 1967; librettist for oratorio Galileo, 1967; writer English sect. bilingual musical The Megilla, 1968; screenplay, lyrics Archy and Mehitabel, 1969; librettist for cantata ' And David Wept ' , 1970. Served with USNR, World War II; PTO. Recipient Antoinette Perry award, 1965, 66, Drama Critics Circle award, 1965-66, Outer-Critics Circle award, 1965, 66, Internat. Broadcasting award, 1964, also Gold Records award. Mem. A.S.C.A.P., Am. Guild Authors and Composers, Dramatists Guild, Nat. Acad. Recording Arts and Scis. Jewish religion. Address: 110 Riverside Dr New York City NY 10024

D'ARISTA, ROBERT AUGUSTUS, artist; b. N.Y.C., July 2, 1929; s. Umberto and Caroline (Maruzzella) D'A.; student N.Y.U., 1948-50, Columbia, 1950-52; m. Jane Webb, Oct. 30, 1954; children—Carla, Peter, Thomas, Antonia. Self employed as artist, 1954-61; art instr. Wash. Bd. Edn., 1961; mem. teaching staff Am. U., 1961—; one man shows N.Y.C., 1955, 56, 59, 62, 64, 67, 68, Washington, 1957, 62; group shows include Carnegie Internats., Whitney Anns., Pa. Acad., Art Inst. Chgo., Guggenheim Mus., Ill. Biennial, Bogota Biennial, Detroit Mus., Bklyn. Mus., others; rep. perm. colls. Toledo Mus., Yale, Hirshorn, Neuberger. Fulbright grantee to Italy, 1955; recipient Richard and Hinda Rosenthal Found. award Nat. Inst. Arts and Letters, 1967. Home: 3125 Quebec Pl NW Washington DC 20008

DARITY, WILLIAM ALEXANDER, educator; b. Flat Rock, N.C., Jan. 15, 1924; s. Aden Randall and Elizabeth (Smith) D.; B.S., Shaw U., 1948; M.S.P.H., N.C. Central U., 1949; Ph.D., U. N.C., 1964; m. Evangeline Royall, Dec. 23, 1950; children—William A., Janki Evangelia. Community health educator, Charlotte and Danville, Va., 1949-52; prof. pub. health Am. U. Beirut (Lebanon), 1956-58, U. Alexandria (Egypt), 1959-60; dir. program devel. N.C. Fund, 1964-65; asso. prof. pub. health U. Mass., Amherst, 1965-68, prof., 1968—, head dept., 1969—. Mem. pub. health rev. com. NIH. Bd. dirs. Sex Information and Edn. Council U.S., 1970, Planned Parenthood Fedn. Am., Western Mass. Health Plan Council. Served to 1st lt. AUS, 1943-48. Fellow Am. Pub. Health Assn.; mem. Hampshire (pres.), Hampshire Area (pres.) health assns., Am. Sch. Health Assn., Nat. Council on Family Life. Soc. Pub. Health, Am. Nat. Council Health Edn. Pub., Sigma Xi, Delta Omega, Phi Kappa Phi. Home: 105 Heatherstone Rd Amherst MA 01002

DARK, PHILIP JOHN CROSSKEY, educator, anthropologist; b. London, Eng., May 15, 1918; s. John Noel and Annie (Crosskey) D.; student Bradfield Coll., Berkshire, Eng., 1935; diploma in art, Slade Sch. Fine Art, London, 1948; M.A., Yale, 1950, Ph.D. in Anthropology (spl. fellow social sci. 1950-51), 1954; m. Mavis Helena Boam, Mar. 7, 1942; children—Gail Susan, Victoria Eve. Adminstrv. sec., asst. registrar W. African Inst. Social and Econ. Research, U. Ibadan (Nigeria), 1954-56; sr. research fellow U. Ibadan, 1957-60; prof. anthropology So. Ill. U., 1960—, chmn. dept., 1963-66; research asso. African ethnology Field Mus. Natural History, 1963—. Served to lt. Royal Naval Vol. Res., 1940-46. Leverhulme Research fellow Univ. Coll., London, 1956-57; Sigma Xi-Kaplan Research award for anthropol. research in New Guinea, 1968. Fellow Am. Anthrop. Assn., Royal Anthrop. Inst.; mem. Internat. African Inst., Soc. des Oceanistes, Am. Assn. U. Profs., R.N.V.R. Officers Assn., Central States Anthrop. Soc., Am. Ethnol. Soc., Hakluyt Soc., Nigerian Hist. Soc., Papua and New Guinea Soc. Author: Bush Negro Art, 1954; Mixtec Ethnohistory: A Method of Analysis of the Codical Art, 1958; (with W. and B. Forman) Benin Art, 1960; The Art of Benin, A Catalogue of the A.W.F. Fuller and Chicago Natural History Museum Collections of Antiquities from Benin, Nigeria, 1962. Home: 912 Taylor Dr Carbondale IL 62901

DARKEN, ARTHUR H., univ. dean; B.A., Bates Coll.; B.D., Union Coll.; Ph.D., Columbia. Dean Sch. Letters and Sci., Wis. State U., Oshkosh. Office: Sch Letters and Sci Wis State U Oshkosh WI 54901*

DARKEN, LAWRENCE STAMPER, phys. chemist; b. Bklyn., Sept. 18, 1909; s. William Henry and Gertrude Ann (Stamper) D.; A.B., Hamilton Coll., 1930; Ph.D., Yale, 1933; m. Margaret Elizabeth FitzGerald, Sept. 6, 1939; children—Joanne Savage, Mary Cummins, Lawrence Stamper, William Henry II, Marjorie Beth, Edward Reynolds. With U.S. Steel Corp., 1935—, dir. fundamental research, 1962- -; instr., adj. prof. Poly. Inst. Bklyn., 1942-53. Recipient Francis J. Clamer award Franklin Inst., 1966. Fellow N.Y. Acad. Scis., A.A.A.S., Metall. Soc., Am. Soc. Metals (Gold medal 1971); mem. Nat. Acad. Scis., Am. Inst. Mining, Metall. and Petroleum Engrs. (recipient Robert W. Hunt Silver medal 1967), Am. Chem. Soc., Faraday So., Am. Iron and Steel Inst., Phi Beta Kappa, Sigma Xi, Lambda Chi Alpha. Author: (with R. W. Gurry) Physical Chemistry of Metals, 1953; also numerous articles. Home: 101 RR 7 Irwin PA 15642 Office: US Steel Corp Research Center Monroeville PA 15146

DARLAND, RAYMOND WINSTON, univ. provost; b. Codell, Kan., Mar. 22, 1911; s. Herbert Otis and Alice Dora (Frazier) D.; B.S., Kan. State Coll., Ft. Hays, 1933, M.S., 1936; Ph.D., U. Neb., 1947; m. Jewell Royse, Nov. 29, 1933; children—Jeanette, Richard Royse. Instr. sci., asst. coach Sheridan Co. Community High Sch., Hoxie, Kan., 1933-35, prin., instr. biology, 1935-41; instr. field zoology Kan. State Coll., Ft. Hays, summers 1939-41; instr. plant ecology U. Neb., 1941-43, asst. prof. biology, 1946-48; asso. prof. of biology U. Minn., Duluth, 1948-49, head biology dept., 1949-52, prof. biology, 1951-53, acad. dean, 1952-53, provost, 1953—. Cons. Tribhuvan U., Nepal, 1970. Mem. bd., v.p., exec. dir. Alworth Scholarships. Served as lt. USNR, 1944-46. Decorated comdr. Order of Lion (Finland); recipient meritorious service citation USAF, 1964. Mem. Ecol. Soc. Am., Minn. Acad. Sci. (pres. 1953), C. of C., Kitchi Gammi Club, S.A.R., Sigma Xi, Phi Delta Kappa. Methodist. Rotarian (pres. Duluth 1966-67). Home: 2531 E 7th St Duluth MN 55812

DARLEY, JOHN GORDON, psychologist; b. Pitts., Feb. 20, 1910; s. William Watson and Edith (Gordon) D.; A.B., Wesleyan U., Middletown, Conn., 1931; A.M., U. Minn., 1932, Ph.D., 1937; m. Kathleen B. McConnon, Aug. 15, 1936; children—John, Janet. Research asst. and psychol. examiner U. Minn. Employment Stblzn. Research Inst., 1931-35; asst. prof. and research counselor, gen. coll., U. Minn., 1935-38, dir. and asst. prof. psychology, student counseling bur., 1938-43, dir. and prof. psychology, 1946-47, asso. dean and prof. psychology grad. sch., 1947- 59, exec. sec. social sci. research center and lab. for research in social relations, 1948-59; exec. officer Am. Psychol. Assn., 1959-62; prof. psychology U. Minn., 1962, chmn. dept. psychology, 1963—. Research asso. Nat. Def. Research Com., Camp Murphy, Fla., 1943-44; mem. sci. adv. bd. U.S. Air Force, 1966—; bd. dirs. Psychol. Corp., 1964—; adv. com. Office Sci. Personnel, NRC, 1966—. Served as lt., U.S.N.R., Bur. Medicine and Surgery, Navy Dept., 1944-46. Mem. adv. panel on human relations Office Naval Research 1946-52; sec.-treas. Am. Bd. Examiners in Profl. Psychology, 1947-51; mem. panel on selection and tng., com. on human resources, Research and Devel. Bd., 1947-49. Democrat. Clubs: Cosmos, Campus. Mem. editorial bd. Jour of Ednl. and Psychol. Measurement, 1941-54, Ann. Revs. in Psychology, 1948-54; editor Jour. of Applied Psychology, 1955-60, Am. Psychologist, 1959-62. Home: 1550 E River Terrace Minneapolis MN 55414 ☆

DARLEY, WARD, physician, educator; b. Denver, Oct. 30, 1903; s. Ward and Mary (Bolles) D.; A.B., U. Colo., 1926, M.D., 1929, LL.D., 1958; D.Sc., Colo. Coll., 1954, U. Neb., 1956, N.Y. Med. Coll., 1965, U. Ill., 1965, Brown U., 1966; LL.D., Loyola U., 1965, Northwestern U., 1965, U. N.M., 1966; m. Pauline Braiden, Apr. 29, 1930; children—Donna Jean, Ward Braiden. Intern and resident U. Colo. Sch. Medicine and Hosp., 1929-31; pvt. practice of medicine, Denver, 1931-44; asso. prof. medicine, U. Colo. Sch. Medicine, 1944-46, prof., 1946-56, dean, 1945-48, v.p. univ., dean dept. medicine, 1949-53, pres., 1953-56, visiting prof. medicine, 1965—. Mem. bd. cons., div. medicine and public health Rockefeller Found., 1952-53; Western Interstate Commn. Higher Edn., exec. commr. Colo., 1951-56; med., ednl. sci. adv. council Nat. Fund Med. Edn., 1953-55; bd. visitors Air U., USAF, 1955-58, chmn., 1955-56; trustee Nat. Merit Scholarship Corp., 1955-63; mem. Med. Sch. Grants adv. com. Ford Found., 1956; adv. com. on personnel for research Am. Cancer Soc., 1956-59, chmn., 1956-58; mem. USPHS Surgeon Gen.'s Cons. Group on Med. Edn., 1959; exec. v.p. at. Intern Matching Program, 1967-68; bd. dirs. Interuniv. Communications Council. Recipient Abraham Flexner award Assn. Am. Med. Colls., 1965; John M. Russel award for outstanding contbns. to acad. medicine (Markle Scholars), 1965. Diplomate Nat. Bd. Med. Examiners, 1931, Am. Bd. Internal Medicine, 1938. Fellow A.C.P., Am. Coll. Hosp. Adminstrs. (hon.); mem. Asso. Am. Med. Colls. (exec. council 1945-51, pres. 1952-53, exec. dir. 1956-64, cons. 1965-68), Acemed. Assn., Phi Beta Kappa, Alpha Omega Alpha, Sigma Xi, Delta Sigma Rho, Phi Kappa Tau. Presbyn. Contbr. articles profl. publs. Home: 955 Endora St Denver CO 80220 Office: 4200 E 9th Av Denver CO 80220

DARLING, EDWARD, editor, author; b. Roxbury, Mass., June 19, 1907; s. Charles B. and Effie (MacNaughton) D.; A.B., Dartmouth, 1929; postgrad. Harvard, 1930-31; m. Dorothea Dane Parker, July 11, 1932; 1 dau., Nancy Joan (Mrs. Carl Hard, Jr.). Head English dept. Yarmouth High Sch., Bass River, Mass., 1934-39; head social scis. dept. Belmont (Mass.) Jr. High Sch., 1940-45; sales mgr. Beacon Press, Boston, 1945-58, dir., 1958-62; dir. dept. publs. Unitarian Universalist Assn., Boston, 1958-69; gen. editor Am. Unitarian Assn., 1969—. Author: Three Oldtimers, 1936; (documentary novel) How We Fought for Our Schools, 1954; Old Quotes at Home, 1966; (with Ashley Montagu), The Prevalence of Nonsense, 1967; They Cast Long Shadows, 1969; When Sparks Fly Upward, 1970; (with Ashley Montagu) The Ignorance of Certainty, 1970. Club: St. Botolph (Boston). Home: Box 333 Dennis MA 02638 Office: 25 Beacon St Boston MA 02108

DARLING, FRANK CLAYTON, educator; b. Chgo., May 8, 1925; s. Frank D. and Nora (Pomeroy) D.; B.A., Principia Coll., Elsah, Ill., 1951; M.A., U. Chgo., 1957; Ph.D., Am. U., 1960; m. Ann Bardwell, June 10, 1952; children—Diane Christine, Heather Ann, Elizabeth Carolyn. Lectr., Chulalongkorn U., Thailand, 1953-56; prof. U. Colo., 1960-67; prof. polit. sci., head dept. DePauw U., 1967—. Served with USNR, 1943-46. Mem. Am. Polit. Sci. Assn., Assn. Asian Studies. Author: Thailand and The United States, 1965. Home: 714 Dogwood Lane Greencastle IN 46135

DARLING, GEORGE BAPST, Jr., b. Boston, Mass., Dec. 30, 1905; s. George Bapst and Alice Emma (Smith) D.; ed. Phillips Acad., Andover Mass.; S.B., Mass. Inst. of Tech., Cambridge, 1927; Dr. P.H., U. of Michigan, 1931; M.A. (hon.) Yale, 1947; m. Ann F. Shaw, June 25, 1931, Research asso, asst. epidemiologist, Dept. Health, Detroit, 1927-32; with W. K. Kellogg Found., Battle Creek, Mich., 1932-43, beginning as asso. dir., mem. bd. trustees and asso. sec.-treas., 1934-37; comptroller, 1937, pres. and comptroller, 1940-43; dir. Atlas Properties, Inc., 1934- 43; pres. 1940-43; dir. Kellogg Co., 1941-43; exec. sec. coms. on mil. med., Nat. Research Council, 1943-45; vice chmn. div. med. sciences, 1944-45, 1947-48; exec. sec. Nat. Acad. Sci. and Nat. Research Council, 1946; dir. med. affairs, Yale U., 1946-52, prof. human ecology, 1952—; dir. Atomic Bomb Casualty Commn., Hiroshima and Nagasaki, Japan, 1957—; vis. lectr. Hiroshima Sch. Medicine, Hiroshima Sch. Nursing. Dir. Grace New Haven Community Hosp., 1946-59 (exec. com. 1946-53), dir. Conn. Health League, Civilian observer Joint Task Force 1, Bikini Atom Bomb test, 1946. Fellow Am. Pub. Health Assn. (mem. com. on administrative practice); mem. Washington Acad. Medicine, Conn. Med. Soc. (Asso.), Radiation Research Soc. of Japan, Japan Pub. Health Assn., Hiroshima Medical Soc. (hon.) Am. C. of C. of Japan, Delta Omega (past pres.), Pi Delta Epsilon, Theta Chi, Mortar and Ball, Ursa Major. Clubs: Hiroshima Tonan (Japan) Rotary, Yale (N.Y.) Faculty (New Haven); Cosmos (Washington). Unitarian. Contbr. articles on pub. health and edn. to jours. Home: 11 Burns St New Haven CT 06511

DARLING, HUGH, lawyer; b. Tacoma, Sept. 4, 1901; s. Oscar E. and Maude (Taylor) D.; student U. Cal., 1919-22; LL.B., U. So. Cal., 1928; m. Hazel Smith, June 10, 1937. Admitted to Cal. bar, 1928, since practiced in Los Angeles; partner Darling, Hall Rae & Gute; director Western Air Lines, Inc. Mem. City Council, Beverly Hills, 1957-64, mayor, 1960-61. Mem. Am., Los Angeles County (past pres.), Beverly Hills bar assns., State Bar Cal. (bd. govs. 1965-68), Phi Delta Phi, Order of Coif. Clubs: Thunderbird Country (Palm Springs, Cal.); California, Los Angeles Country (Los Angeles). Home: 629 Hillcrest Rd Beverly Hills CA 90210 Office: 523 W 6th St Los Angeles CA 90014

DARLING, LOIS MACINTYRE (Mrs. Lois Darling), illustrator-author; b. N.Y.C., Aug. 15, 1917; d. Malcolm and Grace (Hamilton) MacIntyre; student Grand Central Sch. Art, pvt. study, 1935- 40; student zoology Columbia, 1947-51; m. Louis Darling, June 3, 1946. Staff artist dept. paleontology Am. Museum Natural History, N.Y.C..1952- 54; author, illustrator, 1948-. Served with WAVES, 1943-45. Nat. Women's Sailing Champion, 1941. Mem. Conn. Conservationists, Inc. (dir., treas. 1955-56), Nat., Westport (conservation chmn, 1955-61), Audubon socs., Nature Conservancy, Am. Inst. Biol. Scis., Catboat Assn. Ecol. Soc. Am., A.A.A.S., Animal Behavior Soc., Thames Sci. Center. Author illustrator (with Louis Darling); Before and After Dinosaurs, 1959; Sixty Million Years of Horses, 1960; Turtles, 1962; The Science of Life, 1961; Bird, 1962; Coral Reefs, 1963; The Sea Serpents Around Us, 1965; (with Louis Darling) A Place in the Sun, 1968. Illustrator: Sou'West and by West of Cape Cod, 1948; The Middle Road, 1961; Evolution of the Vertebrates, 1955, 1969; Where the Sea Breaks Its Back, 1966; others; (with Louis Darling) Silent Spring, 1962; The Birds, 1963; Animal Behavior, 1965; The Appalachians, 1965; others. Address: RFD 2 Old Lyme, CT 06371.

DARLING, NELSON JARVIE, Jr., investment banker; b. Erie, Pa., Dec. 27, 1920; s. Nelson J. and Jeannette C. (Devine) D.; B.S., Harvard, 1942, LL.B., 1948; m. Ruth W. LaCroix, June 11, 1948; children—William H., Esther, Sarah, Morris F., Thomas W., Jeanette C. Admitted to Mass. bar, 1948; with Ropes & Gray, Boston, 1948-50; with Paine, Webber, Jackson & Curtis, Inc., 1950—, chmn. bd., 1970—; dir. Big Sandy Co., Copper Range Co., Gen. Telephone and Electronics Corp. Club: Bond (Boston). Home: 74 Beach Bluff Av Swampscott MA 01907 Office: 24 Federal St Boston MA 02110

DARLING, PAUL GIFFORD, economist, educator; b. Pleasantville, N.Y., June 28, 1916; s. Samuel Boyd and Edith (Van Ingen) D.; B.A., Yale, 1937; M.A., N.Y.U., 1947; Ph.D., Columbia, 1954; m. Frances J. Koss, Jan. 9, 1945 (dec. Aug. 1967); children—Gail Candace (Mrs. Steven Delibert), Douglas Van Ingen (dec. Apr. 1967); m. 2d, Elizabeth B. Johnsen, June 29, 1968. Jr. accountant W.S. Whittlesey, C.P.A., N.Y.C., 1937-38; mem. auditing staff, asst. to comptroller Title Guarantee & Trust Co., N.Y.C., 1938- 41; with stockholder relations dept. Am. Tel. & Tel. Co., N.Y.C., 1941- 42; instr. econs. Rutgers U., 1945-49; asst. prof. econs. Carnegie Inst. Tech., 1949-56; asso. prof. econs. Bowdoin Coll., Brunswick, Me., 1956- 60, prof., 1960—, chmn. dept., 1965-67. Econ. cons. Joint Econ. Com. U.S. Congress, 1961-62; research team Social Sci. Research Council, 1961-62; research prof. Brookings Instn., 1960-61. Chmn. finance com. Town Brunswick, 1959-61, mem. superintending sch. com., 1962-66. Bd. corporators Brunswick Savs. Inst. Served to 1st lt., Med. Adminstrv. Corps, AUS, 1942-45: ETO. Mem. Am. Econ. Assn., Am. Finance Assn., Am. Assn. U. Profs. (past pres. Bowdoin Coll. chpt.). Contbr. articles profl. jours. Home: 4 Sparwell Lane Brunswick ME 04011

DARLING, RICHARD LEWIS, librarian, univ. dean; b. Great Falls, Mont., Jan. 19, 1925; s. Harry and Faye (Willey) D.; B.A., U. Mont., 1948, M.A., 1950; M.L.S., U. Mich., 1954, Ph.D., 1960; m. Persis Ann Williams, Dec. 11, 1947; children—Richard Lewis, Jere Andrew, Katherine Elizabeth. Tchr., Choteau (Mont.) Pub. Schs., 1950-51; librarian U. Mich. High Sch., 1951-56; asst. prof. U. Mont., 1956-59; coordinator sch. libraries Livonia (Mich.) Pub. Schs., 1959-62; sch. library specialist U.S. Office Edn., 1962-64; supr. libraries Montgomery County Pub. Schs. (Md.), 1964-65, asst. dir. dept. edn. media and tech., 1965-66, dir., 1966-70; dean Sch. Library Service, Columbia, N.Y.C., 1970—. Served with AUS, 1943-46. Recipient Dutton-MacRae award Am. Library Assn., 1959. Mem. N.E.A., Nat. Assn. Ednl. Broadcasters, Am. Assn. Sch. Librarians (past pres.), Am. Library Assn. (2d v.p., chmn. bldgs. and equipment sect.). Author: Survey of School Library Standards, 1964; The Rise of Children's Book Reviewing in America, 1865-1881, 1968. Home: 560 Riverside Dr New York City NY 10027

DARLING, ROBERT CROLY, physician, educator; b. Syracuse, N.Y., Mar. 17, 1908; s. Clarence W. and Elizabeth (Croly) D.; A.B., Harvard, 1929, M.D., 1934; m. Esther Hill, June 17, 1938; children—Nancy Elizabeth, Thomas Robert, Intern, resident Presbyn. Hosp., N.Y. City, 1935-38; research resident Columbia Service, Goldwater Meml. Hosp., 1938-40; with Fatigue Lab., bus. sch., Harvard, 1940-46, asst. prof. indsl. physiology, asst. dir., 1944-46; asos. prof. medicine coll. physicians and surgeons, Columbia and Presbyn. Hosp., 1946-52, coordinator phys. medicine and rehabilitation, 1949-52, prof., exec. officer phys. medicine and rehabilitation, 1952- 60. Baruch prof. phys. medicine and rehab., 1960—; cons. Inst. Crippled and Disabled, 1947-52, chmn. med. bd., 1952. Cons. Q.M. Gen. Office, 1943-46. Diplomate Nat. Bd. Med. Examiners, Am. Bd. Internal Medicine, Am. Bd. Phys. Medicine and Rehabilitation, Fellow N.Y. Acad Medicine; mem. Am. Acad. Phys. Medicine and Rehab. (past pres.), Am. Medical Assn., Am. Physiol. Soc., Am. So. Clin. Investigation, Am. Congress Phys. Medicine. Harvey Soc., Phi Beta Kappa, Nu Sigma Nu, Alpha Omega Alpha, Delta Upsilon. Author articles med. jours. Home: 157 Glenwood Av Leonia NJ 07605 Office: 630 W 168th St New York City NY 10032

DARLING, STEPHEN FOSTER, educator; b. Desmet, S.D., May 1, 1901; s. Andrew Delos and Harriet Elizabeth (Sturgeon) D.; B.S., U. Minn., 1922, M.S., 1924; A.M., Harvard, 1926, Ph.D., 1928; postgrad. U. Vienna, 1928-29; m. Delphine Deziel, Aug. 20, 1930; children—Stephen Deziel, Charlotte Elizabeth, Anne Marie, Andrew Delos. Instr., Harvard, 1926-28; Sheldon traveling fellow, 1928-29; asso. prof. Lawrence Coll., Appleton, Wis., 1929-37, Robert McMillan prof., head dept. chemistry, 1937-66, prof. emeritus, 1966—; research asso. Inst. Paper Chemistry, Appleton, 1930-70. Pres. Outagamie Equity Coop., dist. 9 Midland Coops. Inc.; sec. Valley Coop. Services. Served as 1st lt., C.W.S. Res., 1926-36. Fellow Am. Inst. Chemists; mem. Wis. Acad. Arts, Scis. and Letters (pres. 1956), Am. Chem. Soc., Photog. Soc. Am., Am. Philatelic Soc., Soc. Philatelic Ams., Sigma Xi, Alpha Chi Sigma, Gamma Alpha, Phi Lambda Upsilon. Home: 617 E Alice St Appleton WI 54911

DARLING, WILLIAM MYRON, Jr., aviation co. exec.; b. Washington, Oct. 22, 1919; s. William Myron and Louise (Anderson) D.; B.S. in Engring., U. Md., 1941; m. Patricia Ruth Stedman, Sept. 15, 1943; children—William Myron III, John P., Douglas R. Civilian aero. engr. USAAF, 1941-42; With N.Am. Rockwell Corp. (formerly N. Am. Aviation Co.), 1946—, project engr. Navaho missile, 1948-50, asst. chief preliminary design, then chief proposals, 1950-56, asst. to sr. v.p. engring. and planning, 1956-60, v.p., 1960—. Served to capt. USAAF, 1942-46. Registered profl. engr., Ohio. Mem. Am. Soc. M.E. Home: 960 Granvia Altamira Palos Verdes Estates CA 90274

DARLINGTON, CHARLES FRANCIS, govt. ofcl.; b. N.Y.C., Sept. 13, 1904; s. Charles Francis and Letitia Craig (O'Neill) D.; grad. St. Mark's Sch., Southborough, Mass., 1922; A.B., Harvard, 1926; postgrad. New Coll., Oxford (Eng.) U., 1926-27, U. Geneva (Switzerland), 1928-29; m. Alice Nelson Benning, Nov. 3, 1931; children—Charles Francis III, Alice Letitia, Christopher Nelson. Mem. financial sect. League Nations Secretariat, Geneva, 1929-31; mem. central banking dept. Bank Internat. Settlements, Basle, Switzerland, 1931-34; asst. chief trade agreements div. State Dept., Washington, 1935- 39; fgn. exchanges mgr. overseas operations Gen. Motors Corp., N.Y.C., 1940-41; sec. exec. steering, coordination and jurists coms. San Francisco Conf. on UN, 1945; with Socony Vacuum Oil Co., Inc., 1946-61; chmn. Standard Fuel Oil Co., 1949-53; dir. Iraq Petroleum Co., and asso. cos., 1949-53; v.p., dir. Socony Vacuum Overseas Supply Co., 1952- 56; v.p., then pres. Near East Devel. Corp., 1953-58; alternate dir. Iranian Consortium, 1955-56; A.E. and E.P. to Rep. Gabon, 1961- 65; personal rep. of Pres. Kennedy to independence ceremonies Kingdom Burundi, 1962. Bd. dirs. Boys Club, Mt. Kisco, N.Y., 1942-61; trustee Bedford-Rippowam Sch., Bedford, N.Y., 1946-49, treas., 1948-49. Served with USNR, 1943-44. Mem. St. Nicholas Soc. N.Y., Huguenot Soc. Am. (hon.), Council Fgn. Relations. Democrat. Clubs: Brook's (London Eng.); Cosmos (Washington); Leander (Henley-on-Thames, Eng.). Author: (with wife) African Betrayal, 1968; also articles. Home: Charles Rd Mount Kisco NY 10549

DARLINGTON, CYRIL DEAN, biologist; b. Chorley, Eng., 1903. Keeper Oxford Bot. Garden; Sherardian prof. botany Oxford, 1953. Dir. John Innes Hort. Instn., Hertford. Fellow Royal Soc. London, Author: The Facts of Life, 1953; Evolution of Genetic Systems, 1958; Darwin's Place in History, 1959; Chromosome Botany and the Origins of Cultivated Plants, 1963; Genetics and Man, 1964; Cytology, 1965; The Evolution of Man and Society, 1968; (with others) The Chromosome Atlas, 1956; The Handling of Chromosomes, 1969; The Elements of Geoetics, 1969. Address: Oxford U Botany Sch Oxford, England.

DARLINGTON, OSCAR GILPLN, historian, educator; b. Downingtown, Pa., Feb. 21, 1909; s. Oscar Gilpin and Emily Jane (Bareford) D.; B.A., Pa. State Coll., 1932, M.A., 1933; Ph.D., U. Pa., 1938; student Harvard, summer 1931, Temple U., summer 1932; m. Miriam Howe Wilson, Dec. 31, 1938; children—Helen Spear, Dawn, Mahlon Spear, Phoebe, Lynette, Gerbert, Eunice, Emily-Jane, Bernice. Asst. in ancient, mediaeval history U. Pa., 1934-38; instr. history Hofstra Coll., N.Y.U., 1938, asst. rof., 1939, asso. prof., 1940, prof., 1941-50, chmn. dept. history, 1942-50, dir. summer session, 1949; prof. history, polit. sci., head dept., dir. area social scis. Champlain Coll., State U. N.Y., 1950-53; acad. dean InterAm. U. Puerto Rico, 1953-55; dean Coll. Liberal Arts, Ohio Northern U., 1955-66, dean European-Am. Study Center, Basel, Switzerland, 1967-68, prof. European history, 1968—, dir. summer session, 1956-59; faculty adv. Student Christian Assn., Champlain Coll. Bd. dirs. Regional Council for Internat. Edn., 1964—. Mem. L.I. Hist. Soc., N.E.A., Mediaeval Acad. Am., Am. Hist. Assn., Am. Soc. Ch. History, Am. Acad. Social and Polit. Sci., Phi Alpha Theta. Pi Gamma Mu, Phi Kappa Psi, Sigma Delta Pi. Republican. Methodist (lay preacher Chazy, West Chazy Meth. chs., 1952-53). Rotarian. Club: Torch (pres. 1961) (Lima). Author: The Travels of Odo Rigaud, Archbishop of Rouen (1248-1275), 1940; Contemporary Europe: A Symposium, 1941 (with others); Causes and Consequences of World War II, 1948 (with others); Glimpses of Nassau Co. History, 1949; newspaper column History Back of the News, 1942-45; articles (Gerbert [Pope Sylvester II] and 10th C. France), revs. hist. jours. Editor, trustee Nassau Co. Hist. Jour., 1944-50. Home: 602 S Johnson St Ada OH 45810

DARLINGTON, PHILIP JACKSON, Jr., educator, biologist; b. Phila., Nov. 14, 1904; s. Philip Jackson and Rebecca Taylor (Mattson) D.; grad. Phillips Exeter Acad., 1922; B.A., Harvard, 1926, M.S., 1927, Ph.D., 1931; m. Elizabeth Koch, May 28, 1942; 1 son, Philip Frederick. Entomologist, Colombia div. United Fruit Co., 1928-29; asst. curator insects Mus. Comparative Zoology, Harvard, 1932- 52, curator insects, 1952-64, Agassiz prof. zoology, 1964—, mem. Harvard Australian Expdn., 1931-32, other field work in W. Indies, Australia, S. Am. Served to maj. San. Corps., AUS, 1942-46: PTO. Mem. Nat. Acad. Scis. Author: Zoogeography, 1957; Biogeography of the Southern End of the World, 1965. Home: 71 Juniper Rd Belmont MA 02178 Office: Museum Comparative Zoology Harvard Univ Cambridge MA 02138

DARMAN, MORTON H., business exec.; b. Woonsocket, R.I., 1916; grad. Brown U., 1937. Pres. dir. Top Co., Boston; pres., dir. Top Fibers Corp.; dir. Ivy Enterprises, Inc., Johhnson Products, Inc. Home: 139 Abbot Rd Wellesley Hills MA 02181 Office: 470 Atlantic Av Boston MA 02210

D'ARMS, EDWARD FRANCIS, found. exec.; b. Buffalo, Jan. 14, 1904; s. John Martin George and Charlotte (vonTacky) D'A.; A.B., Princeton, 1925, Ph.D., 1936; B.A., Oriel Coll., Oxford (Eng.) U., 1928, M.A. (Rhodes scholar), 1931; m. Cristina Coney, June 24, 1930; children—John H., Edward Francis, Philip W. Instr. classics Princeton, 1928-30; asst. prof. Latin, Vassar Coll., 1932-35; asst. prof. Greek U. Minn., 1935-37; prof. classics, head dept. U. Colo., 1937-47, dir. honors, 1940-43, dean, 1943; chief edn. and religious policy civil affairs div., War Dept., 1946-47; asst. dir. humanities Rockefeller Found., 1947-50, asso. dir., 1950-57; program asso. humanities and arts program Ford Found., 1957-60, asso. dir., 1960-66, program officer, 1966-69, cons., 1969-70, vis. prof. U. Mich., 1972. Served to maj. AUS, 1943-45. Mem. Am. Philol. Assn., Archaeol. Inst., Assn. Princeton Grad. Alumni (pres. 1954-55), Phi Beta Kappa. Clubs: Century (N.Y.C.); Savile (London, Eng.). Home: 551 Riverside Dr Princeton NJ 08540 Office: 320 E 43d St New York City NY 10017

DARNEILLE, GEORGE JOSEPH, indsl. devel. exec.; b. Needles, Cal., May 29, 1916; s. Benjamin Johnson and Elanora Cecile (Johnson) D.; student Occidental Coll., 1933-36; m. Roberta Shepherd Higgins, Feb. 17, 1942; children—Catherine Addison (dec.), Sarah Ann, Wallace Lambert, Digges Armistead (dec.), George Joseph. Vice pres. Revelation Films, London, Eng., 1937-39; cons. mgmt. engring., Los Angeles, N.Y.C., 1939-42; various exec. positions with asso. cos. Brown & Root, Inc., Houston, 1945—; v.p. Highland Resources, Inc., Houston, 1965—; pres. Beaumont Devel. Co., Houston, 1960—, also dir.; chmn. bd. dirs. Texstar Corp., Grand Prairie, Tex., 1970—; pres. Metals Devel. Co., Houston, 1950—, also dir.; pvt. rancher, E. Camden, Ark., 1965—; engaged in ind. oil and gas prodn.; dir. Shumaker Pub. Service Corp. Mem. Ark. Adv. Commn. Vocational Tng., 1968—. Bd. dirs. Panamanian Edn. Found.; bd. dirs., chmn. Camden (Ark.) United Fund. Served from pvt. to capt., USAAF, 1942-45. Recipient numerous citations Arkansas and Camden civic bodies. Mem. Kappa Alpha Pi, Kappa Sigma. Episcopalian. Clubs: Forest (Houston); Camden Country; Toastmasters Internat. (hon. life) (Los Angeles). Home: PO Box 3108 East Camden AR 71701 Office: San Jacinto Bldg Houston TX 77002

DARNELL, CARL, Jr., ret. army officer; b. New Orleans, May 14, 1910; s. Carl and Edith (Gardner) D.; B.S., U.S. Mil. Acad., 1933; grad. Command and Gen. Staff Coll., 1946. Armed Forces Staff Coll.,

1947, Army War Coll., 1953; m. Louise Nielsen, Apr. 27, 1946; children—Edith, Carl III, Cynthia. Command. 2d lt. U.S. Army, 1933, advanced through grades to maj. gen., 1962; various assignments U.S. and abroad, 1933-52; chief field tng. team 3d Turkist Army, 1953-54; dep. dir. Office Spl. Weapons Devel., 1954-60; comdg. gen. 1st Cav. Div. Arty, Korea, 1960-61; dep. asst. to chief of staff for res. components Dept. Army, 1961, chief Office Res. Components, 1962-63; comdg. gen. U.S. Army, Hawaii, 1963-66; comdg. gen. 5th region Army Air Def. Command, 1966-68; dep. comdg. gen. 6th U.S. Army Presidio San Francisco, 1968-69; ret., 1969. Decorated Bronze Star medal, D.S.M., Legion Merit with oak leaf cluster, Army Commendation ribbon. Home: 500 University Av Honolulu HI 96814

DAROFF, JOSEPH ALFRED, men's clothing mfg. co. exec.; b. Phila., Dec. 18, 1898; s. Harry and Ethel (Stavitsky) D.; student U. Pa. Evening Sch.; m. Sylvia Gaber, June 7, 1921, 1 dau., Lynn (Mrs. Burton Lane). Vice pres. H. Daroff & Sons, Inc., Phila., 1935-64, pres., 1964—; v.p., dir. Botany Industries. Treas. Middle Atlantic sect. Jewish Welfare Bd., 1942—; chmn. Phila. Fellowship Commn. Membership Enrollment, 1954-55. V.p., bd. dirs. Lucien Moss Home; v.p. YMHA. Recipient Community Service award Jewish Theol. Sem., 1961, nat. award, 1962; nat. award Nat. Jewish Hosp., 1964. Mem. Am. Jewish Congress (past chmn. exec. com., pres., v.p.). Jewish religion (chmn. bd. trustees congregation, pres.). Mason. Clubs: Golden Slipper Square; Locust; Philmont Country. Home: 220 W Rittenhouse Sq Philadelphia PA 19103 Office: 2320 Walnut St Philadelphia PA 19103

DAROFF, MICHAEL, clothing mfg. co. exec.; b. Phila., Dec. 11, 1903; s. Harry and Ethel (Stavitsky) D.; D. Textiles (hon.), Phila. Coll. Textiles and Sci; m. Esther Fruchbom, May 1924; children—Mitchell Norman, Deborah (Mrs. Frank Yannessa). Pres., H. Daroff & Sons, Inc., mfr. mens clothes, Phila., 1946-64, chmn., 1964—; chmn., pres. Botany Industries, Inc.; dir. Brand Names Found. Trustee Perkiomen Sch., Pennsburg, Pa.; adv. bd. lay trustees Villanova U. Recipient Man of Year award Phila. Men's Apparel Assn., 1946, Albert J. Ettelson Humanitarian award, 1960. Humanitarian award Nat. Conf. Christians and Jews, 1961. Mem. Clothing Mfrs. Assn. Am. (dir.), Am. Inst. Men's and Boys Wear (dir.)., Phila. Textile Inst. (dir.). Clubs: Locust-Midcity (Phila.); Philmont Country (dir.) (Huntingdon Valley, Pa.). Home: Rittenhouse Plaza Apts 1901 Walnut St Philadelphia PA 19103 Office: 2320 Walnut St Philadelphia PA 19103

DARR, JOHN WALKER, educator, mgmt. cons.; b. Terre Haute, Ind., Sept. 24, 1916; s. Barney and Hazle (Cooprider) D.; B.S., Ind. U., 1949, M.B.A., 1950; Ph.D., U. Ala., 1957; m. Marian Burnett, Dec. 28, 1968; 1 son, John Geoffrey. Lectr., Ind. U., 1950; asst. prof. U. Ga., 1950-53, Bowling Green State U., 1953-56; lectr. U. Ala., 1956-57; prof., chmn. dept. mgmt. Miss. State U., 1953-56; dir. mgmt. devel. program and dir. internship program School Bus., prof. bus. adminstrn. Bowling Green (O.) State U., 1965-67; prof. mgmt., dir. mgmt. devel. porgram U. Mo., 1967-69; prof. mgmt. U. Dayton (O.), 1969—. Cons. numerous cos.; lectr., speaker. Mem. Am., So. econs. assns., Am. Tng. Dirs. Assn., Personnel Dirs. Assn., Acad. Mgmt., Soc. Advancement Mgmt., So. Mgmt. Assn. (dir., chmn. membership com.), Beta Gamma Sigma, Chi Gamma Iota, Alpha Kappa Psi, Sigma Chi, Omicron Delta Kappa, Author publs. in field. Home: Bowling Green OH 43402 Office: Dept Mgmt Univ Dayton Dayton OH 45409

DARR, MILTON FREEMAN, Jr., banker; b. Oak Park, Ill., Oct. 30, 1921; s. Milton Freeman and Frances Anna (Kaiser) D.; B.S., U. Ill., 1942; m. Margaret Claire Phipps, Jan. 27, 1945; children—Alan Phipps, Bruce Milton. With LaSalle Nat. Bank, Chgo., 1946—, asst. cashier, 1950-53, asst. v.p., 1953, v.p., 1954-62, exec. v.p., dir., 1962-64, pres., 1964-68, chmn. bd., chief exec. officer, 1968—. Mem. Bd. Edn. Dist. 88 Community High Sch., 1963-68. Chmn. commerce and industry com., treas. Chgo. Com. for Project Hope; state crusade chmn. Ill. div. Am. Cancer Soc., 1967, 68; chmn. bd. mgrs. YMCA Met. Chgo. Served to maj. USAAF, 1942-46. Mem. Am. Inst. Banking (pres. Chgo. chpt. 1955-56, mem. exec. council 1956-59, nat. v.p. 1959-60, nat. pres. 1960-61), Am. Bankers Assn. (adminstrv. com., exec. council 1960-61), Assn. Res. City Bankers (treas. 1969-72), Robert Morris Assos. (pres. Chgo. chpt.), Theta Chi. Presbyn. Rotarian. Clubs: Chicago, Bankers, Economic, Executives, Union League (pres. 1968-69), Commerical, Attic (Chgo.); Glen Oak Country. Home: 1 S 316 Forest Trail Elmhurst IL 60126 Office: 135 S LaSalle St Chicago IL 60603

DARRAH, LOUIS JAMES, JR., lawyer; b. Hattiesburg, Miss., July 17, 1906; s. Louis James and Callie Blanche (Clower) D.; student U. Miss., 1924-26; LL.B., Loyola U., New Orleans, 1932; m. Patti Catherine Trim, May 15, 1936 (dec. Feb. 1963); 1 dau., Frances (Mrs. Everett G. Schaefer, Jr.). Admitted to La. bar, 1932, since practiced in New Orleans; exec. counsel New Orleans Pub. Service Inc., 1934-51; sr. partner firm Jones, Walker, Waechter, Poitevent, Carrere & Denegre, 1951-. Mem. Am., La., New Orleans bar assns., Am. Judicature Soc., C. of C. New Orleans Area. Presbyn. Clubs: Internat. House, Pickwick (New Orleans). Home: 4007 St Charles Av New Orleans LA 70115 Office: 225 Baronne St New Orleans LA 70112.

DARRE, JEANNE-MARIE, concert pianist; b. Givet, France, July 30, 1905; d. Jean and Jeanne (Libert) Darre; grad. (premier prix piano 1919, Jere Medaille 1916), Conservatory Nat. M.J. Philipp, Paris, France, 1919. Debut at Salle Erard, Paris, 1920; Am. debut with Boston Symphony Orch., 1962; performances maj. orchs. U.S., 1962—; tours of Europe, Africa, U.S., 1921—; prof. piano Nat. Conservatory, Paris, 1958—; recording artist for Vanguard and Pathe Marconi. Decorated officer Legion of Honor, chevalier Arts and Letters. Address: 25 rue Rennequin Paris 17e France

DARREL, PETER, dancer, choreographer, dir.; b. Richmond, Surrey, Eng., 1929; student Royal Ballet Sch. An orignal mem. Sadler's Wells Theatre Ballet; later mem. London's Festival Ballet; co-founder, artistic dir. Western Theatre Ballet, 1957-59, later prin. choreographer, now dir. Choreographer: Harlequinade, Le-Chimères, Tell-Tale Heart, The Gift, Prisoners, Non- Stop, Impasse, Chlarosouro, Ode, Bal de la Victoire, Mods and Rockers. Address: 1 Montaque St London W C 1 England*

DARREL, ROBERT DONALDSON, writer; b. Newton, Mass., Dec. 13, 1903; s.Ernest Willis and Elizabeth (Donaldson) D.; student Harvard, 1922, New Eng. Conservatory Music, 1923-26; m. Emma Cartwright Bourne, Sept. 30, 1930 (div. 1936). Staff writer, record reviewer Phonograph Monthly Rev., Boston and Cambridge Mass., 1926-30, editor, pub., 1930-1931; free lance writer, 1932-34; asso. editor, reviewer Music Lovers' Guide, N.Y.C., 1932-34; record researcher Gramophone Shop, N.Y.C., 1934-39, editor Gramophone Shop Supplement, 1937-39; editor Steinway Rev. Permanent Music, later syndicated Rev. Recorded Music, N.Y.C., 1939-43; sr. writer, later supervising editor instrn. book dept. Hazeltine Electronics Corp., Little Neck, N.Y., 1943-46; editor Rev. Recorded Music, 1947-50; record revs. Down Beat, 1952; audio columnist Saturday Rev., 1953-55; columnist High Fidelity mag., 1955—, contributing editor, 1956—; also contributing editor Audiocraft magazine, 1955-58. Discographic cons. music div. N.Y.C. Pub. Library, 1952. Guggenheim fellow, 1939. Mem. Audio Engring. Soc., Acoustical Soc. Am., Ulster County Hist. Soc., Assn. Recorded Sound Collections. Democrat. Club: Radio of America. Author: The Highroad to Musical Enjoyment, 1943; Good Listening, 1953. Compiler: Gramophone Shop Encyclopedia of Recorded Music, 1936; Schirmer's Guide to Books on Music and Musicians, 1951; Tapes in Review, 1963. Contbr. profl. publs. Home: Balmoral The Vly Stone Ridge NY 12484

DARRELL, NORRIS, lawyer; b. St. Kitts, B.W.I., Jan. 30, 1899; s. Norris de Mouilpied and Maria Arabella MacDonald (Pandt) D.; brought to U.S., 1900, naturalized, 1910; LL.B., U. Minn., 1923; m. Doris Clare Williams, June 24, 1925 (dec. 1943); children—Norris Williams, Richard Wheeler; m. 2d, Mary Hand Churchill; June 28, 1945; 1 stepson, Jonathan Churchill. Admitted to Minn. bar, 1923, N.Y. bar, 1927; legal sec. Hon. Pierce Butler, asso. justice U.S. Supreme Ct., 1923-25; asso. law firm Sullivan & Cromwell, N.Y.C., 1925—, Paris and Berlin rep., 1928-30, mem. firm, 1934—. Tech. advisor Fiscal Com. Econ. Devel., 1947-65; dir. Schroders Ltd. (London), 1959-70, Schroders, Inc., J. Henry Schroder Banking Corp., Schroder Trust Co., Harper & Row, Pubs., Inc., A. Johnson & Co., Inc. Chmn. joint com. continuing legal edn. Am. Law Inst.-Am. Bar Assn., 1966—; pres. Am. Law Inst., 1961—, mem. council, 1947— mem. Lawyers' Com. for Civil Rights Under Law. Bd. dirs. Goodwill Industries of Greater N.Y., Inc.; trustee Practising Law Inst., Tax Found. Inc. Adv. bd. Internat. Bur. Fiscal Documentation; past. mem. various tax adv. coms., N.Y. State and U.S. govtl. bodies. Served in inf., U.S. Army, 1917-19. Recipient Merit award U. Minn. Law Alumni Assn., 1962; Outstanding Achievement award, U. Minn., 1965; Marshall-Wythe medallion award Coll. William and Mary Marshall-Wythe Sch. Law, 1965. Fellow Am. Bar Found.; mem. Nat. Legal Aid and Defender Assn., Internat. Legal Aid Assn., Pilgrims U.S., Newcomen Soc. N. Am., Tax Inst., Am. Soc. Internat. Law, Internat., Am. (ho. of dels. 1965—), N.Y. State, N.Y. County bar assns., Nat. Inst. Social Sci., Assn. Bar City N.Y. (v.p. 1956-58), Nat. Tax Assn., Inst. Jud. Adminstrn., Inc., Am. Judicature Soc., Council Fgn. Relations, Scribes, Grey Friars, Order of Coif, Alpha Tau Omega, Phi Delta Phi. Methodist (trustee 1968—). Clubs: Century, River (bd. govs.), University, Down Town (N.Y.C.); Bedford Golf and Tennis (N.Y.); Nat. Lawyers, Metropolitan (Washington). Contbr. articles legal jours. Home: 1107 Fifth Av New York City NY 10028 also Long Ridge Rd Bedford NY 10506 Office: 48 Wall St New York City NY 10005

DARRIGAN, THOMAS OWEN, mag. pub. co. exec.; b. N.Y.C., May 14, 1912; s. Andrew T. and Anna (Baumann) D.; B.A., St. John's U., 1936; B.B.A., Pace coll., 1939; m. Adele O'Brien, June 11, 1934; children—Thomas M., Maureen (Mrs. R. E. Murphy), Diane (Mrs. K. P. Walsh), Judith (Mrs. K. Murphy), Gerard O. Asst. to treas. John J. Casale, Inc., N.Y.C., 1937-42; cost accountant Callowhur Chem. Corp., N.Y.C., 1942-45; with Newsweek, Inc., N.Y.C., 1945—, asst. treas., 1958-61, treas., 1961—, sec., dir., 1961—, v.p., 1962-71, exec. v.p., 1971—; asst. sec. Washington Post Co. Club: New York Athletic. Home: 640 N Merrick Av Merrick NY 11566 Office: 444 Madison Av New York City NY 10022

DARRIN, HOWARD ADDISON, automobile designer, builder; b. Cranford, N.J., May 16, 1897; s. David David Herbert and Beatrice (Townsend) D.; ed. high sch.; m. Eleanor B. Bacot, June 30, 1919; children—Dorothy C. (Mrs. Bryon Anderson), Howard A., Jacqueline (Mrs. Troy Horton); m. 2d, Pattie L. Shofstall, Apr. 23, 1944; children—Patrick Frazer, Camille. Engring. trainee D. H. Darrin & Co., Corp., N.Y.; v.p. Aero Ltd., 1919; agt. LeBaron Co., Paris sales engr. Westinghouse Co., Paris, France; with Hibbard & Darrin, motor car and coach builders, Paris, 1922-32, Fernandez & Darrin, Paris, 1932-37; Fernandez & Darrin, Paris, 1932-37; cons. engr. Wilys Motors Co., Rolls-Royce, Gen. Motors Corp., Dodge, Mercedes, Studebaker, Moon Motors, St. Louis, Armstrong--Siddeley, Minerva, Stutz, Renault, Citroën, Bugatti Molsheim, France; propr. Darrin of Paris , Hollywood, Cal. 1937—; design cons. Kaiser jeep, 1949-50; with Kaiser-Darrin, Willow Run, Mich., 1945-58, builder contractor, fiberglass prodn. sports car, 1953; designer D. K. W. Darrin product of Auto Union Germany. Served as lt. 302d Engrs., U.S. Army, 1917, observer French and Am. air forces; recruiting officer Canadian Aviation Bur., Los Angeles, 1941; capt. Cavalry, Cal. N.G., 1942; field comdr. UN Mil. Flight Acad., Los Vegas, 1943-44. Recipient Grand Prix Concour de Elegance, Paris, 1928- 37, Cannes, France, 1960; Blenheim Rolls Royce trophy (twice) for most beautiful Rolls Royce Town car, 1964-67; various Am. awards for automotive design, 1938-59. Contbr. articles to Automobile Quarterly, Classic Car, Motor Trend. Patentee in field. Address: 130 Ocean Way Santa Monica CA 90402

DARRONE, DONALD WILLIAM, tool corp. exec.; b. Syracuse, N.Y., Feb. 20, 1916; s. Leon Oliver and Ethel (Halladay) D.; B.S., N.Y. State Coll. Forestry, Syracuse U., 1937; m. Doris Julia Allen, Sept. 10, 1938; children—Richard W., Allen E., Dorothy A., David A. With Allen Tool Corp., Syracuse, 1937—, pres., 1954—, also dir.; dir. Kenneth A. Taylor, Inc. Past v.p. Onondaga council Boy Scouts Am.; mem., past dir Urban League; past pres. Syracuse U. Parents Assn. Alfred U. Parents Assn. Past pres. bd. trustees Rescue Mission Alliance; dir. Syracuse YMCA. Mem. Nat. (past pres., trustee), Syracuse tool, die and precision machining assns., Am. Ordnance Assn., Met. Devel. Assn. , Citizens' Found., Mfrs. Assn. Syracuse (dirs.), Syracuse C. of C. (past dir.), Syracuse Govt. Research Bur. (past dir.), Am. Welding Soc., Am. Soc. Metals, Soc. Mfg. Engrs. (past dir.), Syracuse U. Alumni Assn., Syracuse Tech. Club. Republican. Methodist (trustee). Clubs: Kiwanis; University (Syracuse). Home: 113 Bradford Lane Syracuse NY 13224 Office: 308 Maltbie St PO Box 1382 Syracuse NY 13201

DARROW, DON ORVILLE, former air force officer; b. Tacoma, June 5, 1908; s. Osmon Vincent and Nellie Rosetta (Peltz) D.; student Coll. Puget Sound, 1926-28; B.S. in Elec. Engring., Ore. State Coll., 1932; grad. Army Air Corps Flying Sch., 1933, Army Air corps Tactical Sch., 1940, Command and Gen. Staff Sch., 1941, Nat. War Coll., 1950; m. Martha Paxton Bell, Nov. 21, 1936; children—Donna (Mrs. Charles White), Mary (Mrs. Kenneth Griffin). Commd. 2d lt. USAC Res., 1933, advanced through grades to maj. gen. USAF, 1958, permanent commn. Regular Army, 1936; various assignments fighter, attack and reconnaissance-type aircraft, 1933-40; aircraft comdr. mass flight B-17's from U.S. to Hawaii, 1941; asst. operations officer 4th Air Force, Hamilton AFB, 1941-43; dir. operations 4th Air Force, San Francisco, 1943-44; dep. dir. Air Evaluation Bd., S.W. Pacific area, 1944-45; mem. Joint War Plans Com., Joint Chiefs of Staff, Washington, 1946; staff war plans div. Hdqrs. USAF, Washington, 1947-49, plans div. Far East Air Forces Hdqrs., Tokyo, 1950; sr. staff officer, adviser Air Force del., UN Armistice Delegation for Korean armistice negotiations, 1951-53; dep. chief staff for materiel Mil. Air Transport Service, Andrews AFB, 1953-57; dep. comdr. Pacific div. Mil. Air Transport Service, Travis AFB, 1957-58; dep. chief staff for operations Hdqrs. Allied Air Forces, Central Europe, Fontainebleau, France, 1958-61; dep. for plans, Hdqrs. Tactical Air Command, Langley AFB, Va., 1961-64; comdr. 19th Air Force, Seymour Johnson AFB, N.C., 1964-66; comdr. 9th Air Force (TAC), Shaw AFB, S.C., 1966-67; with Hdqrs. USMACV, Saigon, S. Vietnam, 1967-68; chief staff Tactical Air Command, Langley AFB, Va., 1968-69, ret., 1969. Decorated Legion of Merit with 5 clusters, D.F.C., Air medal, D.S.M. Home: 5714 Canterbury Lane Myrtle Beach SC 29577

DARROW, RICHARD WILLIAM, pub. relations cons.; b. Champaign County, O., Sept. 24 1915; s. Ben H. and Frances (Carter) D.; B.A. cum laude, Ohio Wesleyan U., 1936; m. Nelda Darling, Sept. 17, 1938; children—William Richard, John Harrison. Reporter, circulation promotion Daily Citizen, Urbana, O., 1933-34; reporter Internat. News Service, Washington, 1935; reporter, aviation editor, asst. city editor Columbus (O.) Citizen, 1936-41; mgr. pub. relations Curtiss-Wright Corp., Columbus, 1941-43, asst. dir. pub. relations, Buffalo, 1943-44, N.Y.C., 1944-45; asst. to pres. Am. Meat Inst., Chgo., 1945-46; dir. pub. relations Glenn L. Martin Co., Balt., 1946-52; v.p. Hill & Knowlton, Inc., N.Y.C., 1952-55, exec. v.p., 1955- 66, pres., 1966—. Mem. Scarsdale Recreation Council, 1956-63, vice chmn. 1958-62; chmn. Scarsdale Youth Relations Com., 1966-67; mem. Com. for Second Regional Plan Met. N.Y., 1966-68. Mem. nat. exec. bd. Boy Scouts Am., 1962—, nat. chmn. pub. relations, 1962-68, chmn. communications com., 1968-71, chmn. pub. relations Greater N.Y. councils, 1959-66, chmn. camping com., 1966-71, v.p., 1970—, mem. exec. com. Nat. council, 1966—; chmn. camp devel. com., 1971—. Recipient Silver Beaver award, 1963, Silver Buffalo award, 1966, Distinguished Eagle award, 1969. Mem. village bd. trustees, police commr., Scarsdale, N.Y., 1967—. Hon. dir. White Plains Hosp.; trustee Ohio Wesleyan U., 1957-67, chmn., 1968—; bd. dirs. Regional Plan Assn., 1968, also mem. exec. com., 1968—. Chmn. civilian vol., pub. relations adv. comm., U.S. Mil. Acad., 1960—. Named Outstanding Young Man Balt., 1950; recipient TWA aviation writing awards, 1940, 41; Latin Am. pub. relations award, 1947. Mem. Ohio Wesleyan U. Alumni Assn. (pres. N.Y. 1957-58, mem. nat. exec. com., 1958, v.p. counselors sect. 1962-63), Aviation Writers Assn., Assn. Petroleum Writers, Am. Petroleum Inst., Ohio Soc. N.Y. (trustee 1954-57, 62-65, v.p. 1957-59), Phi Beta Kappa, Phi Gamma Delta (sect. chief 1958-61), Omicron Delta Kappa, Pi Delta Epsilon, Pi Sigma Alpha. Conglist. Clubs: Union League, Overseas Press, Cloud (N.Y.C.); Nat. Press (Washington); Scarsdale (N.Y.) Golf, Town (bd. govs. 1960-67, pres. 1964-65). Co-author: Dartnell Public Relations Handbook, 1965. Home: 50 Barry Rd Scarsdale NY 10583 Office: 150 E 42d St New York City NY 10017

DARROW, WHITNEY Jr., cartoonist; b. Princeton, N.J., Aug. 22, 1909; s. Whitney and May Temperance (Barton) D.; A.B., Princeton, 1931; m. Mildred Lois Adkins, Oct. 23, 1942; children—Whitney Barton, Linda Ann. Began as cartoonist, 1934, in various nat. mags. and New Yorker mag., regularly 1934; also cartoons for nat. advertisers, mag. articles, books. Clubs: Coffee House, Dutch Treat (N.Y.C.). Author: You're Sitting on My Eyelashes (book of collected cartoons), 1943; Please Pass the Hostess, 1949; Stop, Miss, 1958; Give Up (new collected cartoons), 1966; Illustrator: Whitney Darrow, Jr.'s Unidentified Flying Elephant (by R. Kraus), 1968; Sex and the Single Child (by Sam Levenson), 1969; Penny Candy (by Jean Kerr), 1970, others. Home: 331 Newtown Turnpike Wilton CT 06897

DARSIE, PAUL H., physician, educator; b. Lexington, Ky., 1916; M.D., U. Rochester, 1942. Intern, Strong Meml. Hosp., Rochester, N.Y., 1942-43; resident in internal medicine U. Cal. Hosp., San Francisco, 1943-44, Presbyn. Hosp., N.Y.C., 1944-45; asst. in internal medicine Mary Imogene Bassett Hosp., Cooperstown, N.Y., 1945-46; attending physician Cornell Clinic and Infirmary, Ithaca, N.Y.; now prof. clin. medicine Cornell U. Office: 135 Northview Rd Ithaca NY 14850*

DART, EDWARD DUPAQUIER, architect; b. New Orleans, La., May 28, 1922; s. Henry Plauche and Suzanne (Dupaquier) D.; student U. Va., 1940-42; B.Arch., Yale U., 1949; m. Wilma Cornelia Plansoen, Jan. 19, 1946; children—Elaine Dupaquier, Philip Edward. Pres. Edward D. Dart & Assos., Chgo., 1950-65; v.p. Loebl Schlossman Bennett & Dart, Chgo., 1965-69, pres., 1969—; asso. prof. arch. U. Ill., 1963-64. Served to capt. USNR, 1942-45. Fellow A.I.A. Home: 66 Dundee Lane Barrington IL 60010 Office: 333 N Michigan Av Chicago IL 60601

DART, HENRY P., Jr., lawyer; b. New Orleans, La., July 22, 1883; s. Henry P. and Mary L. (Kernan) D.; A.B., Tulane U., 1903, LL.B., 1905; m. Suzanne Dupaquier, June 9, 1915; children—Henry P., III, Eugenie L., Suzanne Micheline (Mrs. John T. McCutcheon, Jr.), Edward D. admitted to La. bar, 1905, and since practiced in New Orleans; sr. mem. Dart & Dart. Member La. (pres. 1949), Am. (mem. Ho. Dels as state del. from La., 1936-40), New Orleans bar assns., Am., La. law insts., Am. Judicature Soc., Order of Coif, Comml. Law League Am., C. of C. New Orleans, Sigma Alpha Epsilon. Methodist. Clubs: Boston, Rotary, Round Table of New Orleans (pres. 1942-43). Home: 936 Webster St New Orleans LA 70118 Office: Nat Bank of Commerce Bldg New Orleans LA 70112

DART, JUSTIN WHITLOCK, drug co. exec.; b. Evanston, Ill., Aug. 17, 1907; s. Guy Justin and Laura (Whitlock) D.; student Mercersburg (Pa.) Acad., 1924-25; A.B., Northwestern U., 1929; m. Ruth Walgreen, Oct. 9, 1929 (div. 1939); children—Justin Whitlock, Peter Walgreen; m. 2d, Jane O'Brien, Dec. 13, 1939; children—Guy Michael, Jane, Stephen. With Walgreen Co., drug store chain, Chgo., 1929-41, in supervision dept., 1930-32, gen. charge of store operations, 1932-39, gen. mgr., 1939-41, dir., 1934-41; resigned Oct., 1941; Joined Rexall Drug Co., Nov. 1941, dir., v.p., 1942; pres. Rexall Drug, Inc., April 1943—; pres. Liggett Drug Co., 1942-46; pres. Rexall Drug & Chem. Co. (name changed to Dart Industries Inc.), 1946—; dir. United Air Lines. Chmn. bd. trustees U. So. Cal. Mem. Beta Theta Pi. Republican. Clubs: Racquet and Tennis (N.Y.C.); Rancheros, Vistadores (Santa Barbara, Cal.); Bohemian (San Francisco); Bel Air Country; California; Chicago Athletic. Office: 8480 Beverly Blvd Los Angeles CA 90048

DART, RAYMOND OSBORNE, ret. army officer; b. Kansas City, Kan., July 5, 1890; s. Ernest Clinton and Jenny (Osborne) D.; A.B., U. of Kan., 1914; M.D., Rush Med. Coll., 1916; Sternberg medalist and hon. grad. Army Med. Sch., 1921, grad. basic course Med. Field Service Sch., Carlisle Barracks, Pa., 1921; m. Mary Eleanor Thomas, Sept. 8, 1917; children—Raymond Thomas, Robert Clinton, William Carleton. Interne, Presbyterian Hosp., Chicago, 1916- 17, resident in gen. surgery Wichita (Kan.) Hosp., 1917 (7 mos.); commd. 1st lt., M.C., U.S. Army, 1917, and advanced through grades to brig. gen., 1948; asst. bn. surgeon, 814 Pioneer Engr. Bn., Rimacourt and Dijon, sanitary officer Dijon dist., asst. dist. surgeon, 1918-19; san. officer, Brest, France, 1919; ward surgeon and mess officer, sta. hosp., Coblenz, Germany, 1919-21; pathologist 3d Army Area, Camp Meade, Md., 1922; pathologist Army Med. Mus., instr. Army Med. Sch., 1923-27, 1932- 36, curator, 1935-36; asst. chief preventive medicine div., Office Surgeon Gen., 1924-26; pathologist bd. health lab., Ancon Canal Zone, 1928-32; chief of lab. service Letterman Gen. Hosp., 1936-42; comdg. officer, 105th Gen. Hosp. Unit, S.W. Pacific Area, 1942-43, surgeon Base Sect. 3, Feb.-Sept. 1943, Advanced and Intermediate sect., Services of Supply, New Guinea, Sept. 1943-Mar. 1944, dept. chief surgeon, Apr. 1944- Oct. 1945; dir. Army Inst. of Pathology, Wash., 1946-50; cons. in pathology to surgeon gen., Dept. of Army, 1946-50; dir. Washington Regional Blood Center, A.R.C.,

Washington, 1954-65, ret.; cons. Armed Forces Inst. Pathology, Washington. Decorated Bronze Star Medal, Legion of Merit (U.S.), Medal of Epidemics for work on influenza (France). Fellow A.M.A., Am. Soc. Clin. Pathologists. A.A.A.S., Am. Coll., Physicians, Coll. Am. Pathologists; asso. Am. Urol. Assn.; mem. Internat. Acad. Pathology, Am. Assn. Pathologists and Bacteriologists, Medical Society of District of Columbia, Am. Acad. Oral Pathology (hon.), Assn. Mil. Surgeons, Am. Acad. Ophthalmology and Otolaryngology (hon.), Mil. Order of Carabao, Academy of Medicine of Washington, Washington Soc. Pathologists (charter mem.), Nu Sigma Nu. Mason. Home: 210 E Fairfax St Falls Church VA 22046

DARWENT, BASIL DE BASKERVILLE, chemist, educator; b. Trinidad, W.I., May 20, 1913; s. Edgar Nicholas and Mary (Henderson) D.; B.S., McGill U., 1941, Ph.D., 1943; m. Jocelyn Margaret Taitt, Apr. 20, 1938; 1 son, John Nicholas de Baskerville. Postdoctoral research McGill U., 1943-44, Oxford U., 1948-49; with NRC, Ottawa, Ont., Can., 1944-48, asso. research scientist, 1949-52; mgr. phys. chemistry research Olin Mathieson Chem. Corp., New Haven, 1952-55; research prof. chemistry Cath. U. Am., Washington, 1955-57, prof., 1957- -, head dept. chemistry, 1961-67. Fellow Royal Soc. Can.; mem. Am. Chem. Soc., Chem. Soc. (London), Faraday Soc., Washington Acad. Sci. Research, publs. on factors controlling rates of chem. reactions, elementary reactions of atoms and free radicals, photochemistry. Home: 1736 Q St NW Washington DC 20009

DASHEFF, WILLIAM, advt. exec.; b. N.Y.C., July 23, 1903; s. Nathan and Jane (Fertman) D.; student N.Y.U., Parson's Sch. Fine Arts; m. Patricia Carbery, Mar. 16, 1949; children—William Nathan, Elizabeth Carbery. Exec. v.p., dir. Buchanan & Co., Inc.; sr. v.p., mgmt. supr. Lennen & Newell Co., N.Y.C.; dir. 860 Fifth Av. Corp., Sevird Corp. (both N.Y.C.), Home: 860 Fifth Av New York City NY Office: 380 Madison Av New York City NY 10017

DASHEFSKY, EDWARD LEO, electronics co. exec.; b. Malden, Mass., Nov. 4, 1914; s. Barnett and Rebecca (Bernstein) D.; B.S. in Aero. Engring., Mass. Inst. Tech., 1936; m. Rose Zelermyer, Dec. 25, 1938; children—Gloria, Barry. Aerodynamics and structural design engr. Sikorsky Aircraft Co., 1937, Curtiss-Wright Airplane Co., 1938-45; chief structures, project engr. Lark missile, guided missile div. Fairchild Engine and Airplane Co., 1946-51; with Raytheon Co., 1951—, mgr. Sparrow III missile prodn., Lowell (Mass.) plant, 1951-60, mgr. microwave and power tube div., 1961-69, v.p., 1962-69, sr. v.p., 1969—; dir. The Machlett Labs., Inc., Springdale, Conn., Machlett Can., Ltd., Downsview, Ontario, Can., Abergas, Ltd., Caerpilly, U.K., HTM Europe, Brussels, Belgium, New Japan Radio Co., Ltd., Tokyo. Bd. dirs. Newton (Mass.) Junior Coll. Mem. Am. Inst. Aeros. and Astronautics (past pres. Boston), Air Force Hist. Found., Def. Supply Assn., Armed Forces Communications and Electronics Assn., Assn. U.S. Army. Mason. Home: 15 Great Meadow Rd Newton Centre MA 02159 Office: Raytheon Co 190 Willow St Waltham MA 02154

DASHER, BENJAMIN JOSEPH, educator; b. Macon, Ga., Dec. 27, 1912; s. Benjamin Joseph and Odille (King) D.; B.S., Ga. Inst. Tech., 1935, M.S., 1945; Sc.D., Mass. Inst. Tech., 1952; m. Anne Moore Brooks, June 7, 1941; childrenBenjamin Joseph III, Anne B., Preston B., Elizabeth S., David, Carole. Instr., asst. prof. elec. engring. Ga. Inst. Tech., 1940-46, asso. prof., 1952, prof. elec. engring., 1953—, dir. Sch. Elec. Engring., 1954-69, asso. dean engring., 1969—. Fellow I.E.E.E.; mem. Am. Soc. Engring. Edn., Nat. Soc. Profl. Engrs., Sigma Xi, Eta Kappa Nu. Home: 1560 Cave Rd NW Atlanta GA 30327

DASHIELL, JOHN FREDERICK, educator; b. Indpls., Apr. 30, 1888; s. John William and Fannie Sophia (Myers) D.; B.S., Evansville (Ind.) Coll., 1908, B.Litt., 1909, Sc.D., 1961; A.M., Columbia, 1910, Ph.D., 1913; m. Clara Sylvia Knowles, Sept. 17, 1912 (dec. May 1948); children—Frederick Knowles, Dorothy Ann (Mrs. Adrian Waddell Smith); m. 2d, Thelma Hill Smith, Sept. 5, 1950 (dec. Nov. 1970). Instr. history Evansville Coll., 1908-09; asst. philosophy Columbia, 1910-13; prof. philosophy and biology Waynesburg Coll., 1913-14; instr. philosophy Princeton, 1914-15; instr. philosophy U. Minn., 1915-16, instr. psychology, 1916-17; asst. prof. psychology Oberlin Coll., 1917-19; mem. faculty U. N.C., 1919—, Kenan prof. psychology, 1935-58, emeritus, 1958—; prof. psychology Wake Forest Coll., 1958-61; vis. prof. Syracuse U., summer 1925, Clark U., summer 1926, U. Tex., summer 1927, Columbia, summer 1928, U. So. Cal., summers 1930-32, U. Ore., summers 1939-40, U. Wis., summer, 1945, Duke, summer 1946, U. Wyo., summer 1947, U. Cal. at Los Angeles, fall 1949-50, U. Fla., spring 1950, U. Rochester, summer 1961, Fla. State U., 1961-62, U. Del., summer 1962, Emory U., 1962-63, Fla. Presbyn. Coll., 1964-65. Mem. fellowship com. NRC, 1937-38. Mem. So. Soc. Philosophy and Psychology (pres. 1924), Soc. Exptl. Psychologists (pres. 1937), A.A.A.S. (v.p. sect. I, 1939), Am. (pres. 1937, past chmn. com. sci. and profl. ethics), N.C. (pres. 1959), Southeastern (pres. 1961) psychol. assns., N.C. Acad. Sci. (pres. 1960). Author: Fundamentals of Objective Psychology, 1928; An Experimental Manual in Psychology, 1931; Fundamentals of General Psychology, 2d edit., 1949. Cons. editor McGraw-Hill, 1931-50; contbg. editor Ency. Americana, 1957—. Home: 507 Dogwood Dr Chapel Hill NC 27514

DASHINE, PAUL, mfg. co. exec.; b. Bklyn., Jan. 1, 1924; ed. Newark Coll. Engring., U. Cal. at Los Angeles. With Republic Steel Corp., 1946-47, Fairbanks Morese and Co., 1947-49, Westocer Engrs., 1949-51; chief engr. Nat. Seal Co., 1951-54; pres., gen. mgr. Calumet div. Calumet and Hecla, Inc., 1954-61, also pres., gen. mgr. uranium div. Calumet and Hecla, Inc., v.p., gen. mgr. Lake Chem. Soc. and v.p., gen. mgr. Calumet de Mexico; pres. No. Nev. R.R. Co., also mgr. tech. services Kennecott Copper Corp., 1961-66; chmn. bd., pres., chief exec. officer Okonite Co., 1966—; dir. N.J. Bank and Trust Co. Bd. dirs. Passaic (N.J.) Gen. Hosp., Passaic Boys Club. Served as pilot USAAF, 1943-46. Mem. Am. Mgmt. Assn., Am. Inst. Mining Engrs., Mining and Metall. Soc. Am., Mining Club, Assn. Am. Railroads, Internat. Assn. Elec. Inspectors, Pacific Coast Elec. Assn., Elec. Mfrs. Club. Club: Pennington (bd. dirs.) (Passaic). Home: 1 Washington Dr Ramsey NJ 07446 Office: PO Box 340 Ramsey NJ 07446

DASHNER, LEE ALBERT, govt. ofcl.; b. Renault, Ill., Aug. 18, 1913; s. Albert Lee and Elizabeth Esther (Franklin) D.; B.S.C., St. Louis U., 1935; M.C.S., Benjamin Franklin U., 1938; m. Zelma Gale Kelley, Sept. 1, 1938; 1 son, Richard Lee. With Dept. Labor, 1935-36, Social Security Bd., 1936-38, FCA, 1938- 44, Bur. of Budget, 1944-54; with Dept. Agr., 1954-62; dir. Office of Budget, Dept. State, 1963-64; dir. mgmt. services div. Fgn. Agrl. Service, Dept. Agr., 1964—. Home: 6501 Persimmon Tree Rd Bethesda MD 20034 Office: Dept of Agr Washington DC 20250

DA SILVA, HOWARD, actor; b. Cleve., May 4, 1909; student Carnegie Inst. Tech. Formerly with Civic Repertory Theatre, Theatre Union Group, also Mercury Theatre; plays include Master Builder, Alice in Wonderland, Three Sisters, Alison's House, Liliom, Doll's House, Sailors of Cattaro, Waiting for Lefty, Golden Boy, Cradle Will Rock, Abe Lincoln in Illinois; films include I'm Still Alive, Abe Lincoln in Illinois, Sea Wolf, Nine Lives Are Not Enough, Big Shot, Omaha Trail, Tonight We Raid Calais, Lost Weekend, Duffy's Tavern, Unconquered, Blaze of Noon, They Live by Night, Underworld Story, Three Husbands, Wyoming Mail, Fourteen Hours, M, David and Lisa, The Zula and the Zayda, Topkapi; dir. N.Y. prodn. Cradle Will Rock, 1965. Address: care Theatre Four 424 W 55th St New York City NY 10019*

DASILVA, MARIE-HELENE VIEIRA, artist; b. Lisbon, Portugal, 1908; student studios of Bourdelle and Despiau, Paris, engraving, with Hayter; m. Szenes, 1930. Exhbns. include Galerie Jeanne Bucher, 1933—, Galerie Pierre, 1949—; regular contbr. to Salon de Maj; rep. French and Fgn. museum collecions, Recipient grand prize Biennale Sao Paulo, also Grand Nat. Prize in Art, 1966. Address: care Galerie Pierre Domec, 33 Rue St PlaEide Paris 6e, France.*

DASMANN, RAYMOND FREDRIC, ecologist; b. San Francisco, May 27, 1919; s. William H. and Mary (McDonnell) D.; A.B., U. Cal. at Berkeley, 1948, M.A., 1951, Ph.D., 1954; m. Elizabeth Sheldon, May 30, 1944; children—Sandra, Marlene, Lauren. Faculty, Humboldt State Coll., 1954-59, 62-66; research biologist Nat. Museums Rhodesia, 1959-61; lectr. zoology U. Cal. at Berkeley, 1961-62; ecologist Conservation Found., Washington, 1966-70; sr. ecologist Internat. Union Conservation Nature, Morges, Switzerland, 1970—. Mem. Ecol. Soc. Am., Am. Soc. Mammalogists, Wildlife Soc. (pres.), Cal. Acad. Scis., Assn. Tropical Biology, Faunal Preservation Soc. Author: Pacific Coastal Wildlife, 1957; Environmental Conservation, 1959; African Game Ranching, 1963; Last Horizon, 1963; Wildlife Biology, 1964; Destruction of California, 1965; A Different Kind of Country, 1968; No Further Retreat, 1971. Contbr. articles profl. jours. Home: Chemin des Mouettes 1028 Preverenges Switzerland Office: IUCN 1110 Morges Switzerland

DASPIT, ALEXANDER BARROW, fgn. service officer; b. Baton Rouge, Jan. 14, 1909; s. Justin Charles and Lise (Barrow) D.; B.A., La. State U., 1929; M.A., U. Mo., 1930; B.A., Oxford (Eng.) U., 1934; student Harvard, 1937-39; m. Natalie Norton, Aug. 22, 1935. Instr. govt. Harvard, 1937-39; asso. prof. govt. La. State U., 1940-42; U.S. del. Inter-Allied Reparations Agy., Brussels, Belgium, 1948-50; politico-mil. adviser Dept. State, 1951-54; 1st sec. Am. embassy, Karachi, 1954-56, Athens, Greece, 1957-59; regional aid coordinator Dept. State, 1960-61; dir. AID Mission, Guatemala, 1962-63; dep. U.S. rep. Devel. Assistance Com., Paris, France, 1963-67; spl. asst. to asst. adminstr. AID, 1967-69, staff dir., 1969—. Home: 3633 Fulton St NW Washington, DC 20007. Office: Agency for International Development Dept State Washington DC 20523

DASSIN, JULES, motion picture dir.; b. Middletown, Conn., Dec. 18, 1911; s.Samuel and Berthe (Vogel) D.; m. Beatrice Launer, 1933 (div. 1962); children—Joseph, Richelle, Julie; m. 2d Melina Mercouri, 1966. Dir. motion pictures: Brute Force, 1946; Naked City, 1947; Thieves Highway, 1948; Night and The City, 1949; Du Rififi chez les Hommes, 1955; He Who Must Die, 1956; The Law, 1958; Never on Sunday, 1960; Phaedra, 1962; Topkapi, 1964; 10:30 P.M. Summer, 1966; Uptight, 1968; Promise At Dawn, 1969. Home: Lausanne Palace Lausanne, Switzerland. Office: 18-20 Place de la Madeleine Paris, France.

DAU, FREDERICK JENSEN, ret. air force officer, mfg. co. exec.; b. Fresno, Cal., Mar. 18, 1907; s. Christian Jensen and Mary (Jensen) D.; B.S., U.S. Mil. Acad., 1928; B.S. in Civil Engring., U. Cal., 1932; student Army Engring. Sch., 1932- 33, Army-Navy Staff Coll., 1945; m. Susan Childress King, July 5, 1929 (dec.); 1 dau., Susan Thorne (Mrs. Thomas Julian Fannon); m. 2d, Helen Singer, Oct. 24, 1969. Commd. 2d lt., C.E., U.S. Army, 1928, advanced through grades to maj. gen. USAF; with 14th Engrs., P.I., 1928-31; asst. prof. mil. sci. and sci. and tactics Mich. Coll. Mining and Tech., 1934-37; research and devel., Wright Field, O., 1937-41, Ft. Belvoir, Va., 1941-43; intelligence duty Chief Engrs., also gen. staff War Dept., 1943-45, hdqrs. China Theater, 1945-46; asst. mil. attache, China, 1946-48; dir. program standards and cost control, hdqrs. USAF, Washington, 1949-52; asst. for materiel coordination Air Materiel Command, 1952-54, dir. supply and services, 1954-59; ret. 1959; with Champion Papers, Inc., Hamilton, O., 1959-67, v.p., until 1964, exec. v.p., 1964-67; sr. v.p., dir. U.S. Plywood-Champion Papers, Inc., 1967- 68, exec. v.p., 1968—; dir. Sargent Industries, Inc., Huntington Park, Cal. Trustee Logistics Mgmt. Inst., Washington, 1961—. Decorated Legion of Merit with 2 oak leaf clusters (Army), D.S.M.; Order of Yun Hui (China), others. Home: 400 E 56th St New York City, NY 10022. Office: 777 3d Av New York City NY 10017

DAUBEN, WILLIAM GARFIELD, educator; b. Columbus, O., Nov. 6, 1919; s. Hyp J. and Leilah (Stump) D.; A.B., Ohio State U., 1941; A.M., Harvard, 1942, Ph.D., 1944; m. Carol Hyatt, Aug. 8, 1947; children—Barbara, Ann. Edward Austin fellow Harvard, 1941-42, teaching fellow, 1942-43, research asst., 1943-45; instr. U. Cal. at Berkeley, 1945-47, asst. prof. chemistry, 1947-52, asso. prof., 1952-57, prof., 1957—; lectr. Am.-Swiss Found., 1962. Mem. med. chem. study sect. USPHS, 1959-64; mem. chemistry panel NSF, 1964-67. Recipient award Cal. sect. Am. Chem. Soc., 1959. Guggenheim fellow, 1951, 66, sr. fellow NSF, 1957-58. Fellow London, Swiss chem. socs.; mem. Am. Chem. Soc. (chmn. div. organic chemistry 1962-63, councilor organic div. 1964—, mem. council publ. com. 1965-70), Nat. Acad. Sci., Phi Beta Kappa, Sigma Xi, Phi Lambda Upsilon, Phi Eta Sigma, Sigma Chi. Mem. bd. editors Jour. of Organic Chemistry, 1957-62, Organic Syntheses, 1959-67; editor-in-chief Organic Reactions, 1967. Contbr. articles profl. jours. Home: 20 Eagle Hill Berkeley CA 94707

DAUBER, CLARENCE ANDREW, mech. engr.; b. Cleve., Feb. 17, 1904; s. Henry John and Hannah (Behnke) D.; B.S., Case Inst. Tech., 1926; postgrad. U. Mich. Grad. Sch. Bus. Adminstrn., Columbia Grad. Sch. Bus. Adminstrn.; m. Catherine Mary Yeagle, July 15, 1933; children—Judith Ann (Mrs. Grady Guye), Debora Claire (Mrs. John D. Mosher), James Henry. Participated design major pipeline for transporting coal; with Cleve. Electric Illuminating Co., 1928-61, dir. civil and mech. engring., 1953-61; with Charles T. Main, Inc., Boston, 1961—, now corporate v.p., v.p. charge thermal power and utility engring.; now partner Uhl, Hall & Rich; past dir. Atomic Power Devel. Assos.; past trustee High Temperature Reactor Devel. Assos. Past mem. bd. govs. Cleve. Engring. and Sci. Center; past v.p. prime movers com. Edison Electric Inst. Registered profl. engr., Mass., Ohio, N.Y., Va., Pa., Mich., Wis., Md., N.H., Conn., Vt., W.Va., N.C., Fla., Colo. Fellow Am. Soc. M.E.; mem. I.E.E.E. (sr.), Am. Inst. Cons. Engrs., Engring. Soc. New Eng., Engrs. Club N.Y., Sigma Xi, Tau Beta Pi, Zeta Psi. Conglist. (deacon). Club: University (Boston). Home: 780 Boyleston St Boston MA 02199 Office: Southeast Tower Prudential Center Boston MA 02199

D'AUDNEY, WALLACE NOEL, telephone co. exec.; b. Auckland, New Zealand, Dec. 28, 1919; s. Wallace E. and Sarah Elsie (Laurie) D'A.; grad. U. New Zealand; asso. chartered accountant, New Zealand, 1947; m. Weslee Wootten, July 1, 1945; children—John, David, Laurie, Carol, Bruce. Came to U.S., 1947, naturalized, 1950. With Pacific Tel. & Tel. Co., San Francisco, 1947-54, 55-59; mem. comptrollers dept. Am. Tel. & Tel. Co., 1954-55, gen. accountant, 1960-63; v.p., comptroller Northwestern Bell Telephone Co., Omaha, 1963—. Served as pilot Royal New Zealand Air Force, 1940-45; ETO. Mem. New Zealand Soc. Accountants, Financial Execs. Inst., Omaha C. of C. Clubs: Omaha, Oak Hills Country. Home: 3014 Paddock Rd Omaha NB 68124 Office: 100 S 19th St Omaha NB 68102

DAUER, MANNING JULLAN, Jr. univ. prof.; b. Wilmington, N.C., Aug. 12, 1909; s. Manning J. and Martha Eddins (Fitts) D.; A.B., U. of Fla., 1930, A.M., 1931; Ph.D., U. of Ill., 1933; unmarried. Instr. dept. history and polit. science, U. of Fla., 1933-34, asst. prof. 1934-41, asso. prof. 1941-46, prof. 1946—, head dept., 1950—, also dir. of div. of social scis.; managing editor of the Journal of Politics, 1939-41, 1946—; cons. govt. orgn. and adminstrn.; visiting prof. polit. sci., U. Ala. summer 1952; vis. prof. N.Y.U., 1957. Cons. Fla. Adv. Constl. Com., 1956. Atty. gen. Fla.; cons. So. Regional Edn. Bd. Served as 2d lt., A.U.S. Air Forces, 1942, 1st lt., 1943, 1944, maj. 1945-46; service with 5th Air Force 1944-45. Australia, New Guinea, Netherlands, East Indies, Philippines, Okinawa, and Japan (6 battle stars); lt. col. USAF Res., 1953—. Mem. Am. Hist. Assn., Am. (mem. council 1953-55, v.p. 1965-66), Southern (pres. 1954-55) political sci. assns. Fla. Historical Soc., Am. Assn. U. Profs. (pres. Fla. chapter 1939-41), Phi Beta Kappa (sec. Fla. chap. 1938-41, pres. 1947-48), Phi Kappa Phi, Pi Gamma Mu, Kappa Delta Pi, Florida Blue Key. Author: The Basis of the Support of John Adams in the Federalist Party, 1933; The Adams Federalists, 1953; author articles and pamphlets in field; contbr. publs. Home: 2255 NW 5th Pl Gainesville FL 32601

DAUER, WILLIAM EUGENE, chamber of commerce exec.; b. Lincoln, Neb., July 26, 1925; s. William Michael and Elsie Elizabeth (Halek) D.; B.S., Neb. Wesleyan U., 1950; m. Edna Maria Pearson, Oct. 1, 1948; children—Lori Kay, Brad Alan. Asst. mgr. Grand Island (Neb.) C. of C., 1950-52, mgr., 1954-56; mgr. Lexington (Neb.) C. of C., 1953; gen. mgr. Springfield (Mo.) C. of C., 1956-59; exec. v.p. Kansas City (Mo.) C. of C., 1959-64; exec vice pres. San Francisco C. of C., 1964—; pres. Am. C. of C. Execs., 1963; v.p. Cal. C. of C. Execs. Spl. rep. Small Bus. Adminstrn., 1957—; No. Cal. chmn. Internat. Exec. Service Corps; mem. Export Expansion Council; treas. Cal. League Handicapped; dir. St. Anthony's Dining Room. Served with USMCR, 1943-45. Recipient Distinguished Service award Springfield Jr. C. of C., 1956, Internat. award Rotary Club, 1959. Mason (Shriner). Home: 1455 Tartan Trail Hillsborough CA 94010 Office: 400 Montgomery San Francisco CA 94104

DAUGHADAY, WILLIAM HAMILTON, physician; b. Chgo., Feb. 12, 1918; s. C. Colton and Marian (Sharpe) D.; A.B., Harvard, 1940, M.D., 1943; m. Hazel Judkins, Jan. 22, 1945; children—Elizabeth Colton (Mrs. Bruce Axelrod), John Freer. Intern, Boston City Hosp., 1944; asst. resident Barnes Hosp., St. Louis, 1946-47, cons. clin. chemistry, mem. staff, 1950—; mem. faculty Washington U. Sch. Medicine, St. Louis, 1949—, Nat. Insts. Health fellow biol. chemistry, 1949-50, instr., then asst. prof. medicine, 1950-56, asso. prof., 1956-63, prof., 1963—. Mem. endocrine study sect. Nat. Insts. of Health; mem. adv. bd. Nat. Pituitary Agy. Served as capt., M.C., AUS, 1944-46. Diplomate Am. Bd. Internal Medicine. Mem. Central Soc. Clin. Research, Am. Soc. Clin. Investigation, Endocrine Soc., Assn. Am. Physicians. Editor Jour. of Lab. and Clin. Medicine, 1960-66. Author sci. papers on metabolism, endocrinology. Home: 1414 W Adams Kirkwood MO 63122 Office: 660 S Euclid St Louis MO 63110

DAUGHERTY, ALFRED CLARK, mfg. co. exec.; b. Wilkinsburg, Pa., July 12, 1923; s. Horace William and Helen Claney (Bradley) D.; B.A., Pa. State U., 1946; m. Janet Elliott, Dec. 14, 1946; 1 dau., Christine Lynn. With Rockwell Mfg. Co., Pitts., 1946-, asst. to pres., 1954-57, exec. asst. to pres. subsidiary, 1957- 61, div..v.p., 1961-63, v.p. adminstrn., 1963-64, pres., 1964-, also dir.; dir. Kennametal, Inc., Latrobe, Pa., Hanklson Corp., Canonsburg, Pa. Trustee, mem. exec. com. Inst. Gas Tech., Chgo. Mem. Machinery and Allied Products Inst. (exec. com.). Clubs: Laurel Valley Golf, Rolling Rock (Ligonier, Pa.); Duquesne, Longue Vue, Fox Chapel Golf (Pitts.) Home: 3 Indian Hill Rd Pittsburgh PA 15238 Office: 400 N Lexington Av Pittsburgh, PA 15208.

DAUGHERTY, CARROLL ROOP, economist, labor arbitrator; b. Annville, Pa., Dec. 3, 1900; s. Benjamin Franklin and Della Frances (Roop) D.; A.B., Lebanon Valley Coll., 1921; A.M., U. Pa., 1924, Ph.D., 1927; m. Miriam Craiglow, 1928; children—James Carroll, David Henry; m. 2d, Marion Roberts, 1940; 1 dau., Frances Marion. Instr., Mercersburg (Pa.) Acad., 1921-23, Wharton Sch., U. Pa., 1925-28; prof. econs. U. Ala., 1928-31, U. Pitts., 1931-40; prof. econs., chmn. dept. Hunter Coll., 1940-46; prof. labor relations Northwestern U., 1946-68, chmn. dept., 1948-58; prin. economist for labor productivity studies, U.S. Bur. Labor Statistics, 1936; chief economist, Wage and Hour div., U.S. Dept. Labor, 1938-40; mem. Com. on Postwar Price Problems, Nat. Bur. Econ. Research 1944-46; wage stblzn. dir. Nat. War Labor Bd., 1942-45; lend lease dir. in New Zealand for State Dept., 1945-46; chmn. Pres.'s steel-labor fact-finding bd., 1949, Pres.'s r.r. labor emergency bds., 1951-52; referee Nat. R.R. Adjustment Bd., 1952—; pvt. arbitrator, labor relations cons.; tchr. mgmt. devel. U.S. and abroad. Mem. Am. Econ. Assn., Indsl. Relations Research Assn. (exec. bd. 1954-56), Am. Assn. U. Profs., Am. Arbitration Assn., Nat. Acad. Arbitrators, Alpha Sigma Phi, Delta Sigma Pi, Beta Gamma Sigma. Club: Executives (Chgo.). Author: Labor Problems in American Industry 1933, 34, 38, 41, 48; Labor Under NRA, 1934; co-author books including: Economics of Iron and Steel Industry, 1939; Principles of Political Economy, 1950; Labor Problems of American Society, 1952; Conflict and Cooperation, 1968. Home: 1013 Judson Av Evanston IL 60202 ☆

DAUGHERTY, FREDERICK ALVIN, U.S. judge; b. Oklahoma City, Aug. 18, 1914; s. Charles Lemuel and Felicia (Mitchell) D.; LL.B., Cumberland U., 1934; postgrad. Oklahoma City U., 1934-35, Okla. U., 1936-37; m. Marjorie E. Green, Mar. 15, 1947 (dec. 1964); m. 2d, Betsy F. Amis, Dec. 15, 1965. Admitted to Okla. bar. 1937; gen. practice, Oklahoma City, 1937-40; mem. firm Ames, Ames & Daugherty, Oklahoma City, 1946-50, firm Ames, Daugherty, Bynum & Black, Oklahoma City, 1952-55; judge 7th Jud. Dist. Ct. Okla., 1955-61; U.S. dist. judge Western, Eastern and No. Dists. Okla., 1961—. Active local A.R.C., 1956—, nat. bd. govs., 1963-69, 3d vice chmn., 1968-69; active United Fund Greater Oklahoma City, 1957—, pres., 1961, trustee, 1963—; mem. profl. adv. com. Oklahoma County Assn. Mental Health, 1963—; adv. bd. Okla. Sci. and Arts Found., 1964—; pres. Community Council Oklahoma City and County, 1967-69; mem. exec. com. Oklahoma City Council Alcoholism, 1964-; exec. com. Okla. Med. Research Found. 1966-69. Served as officer with AUS, 1940-45, 50-52. Decorated Legion of Merit with 2 oak leaf clusters, Bronze Star with oak leaf cluster; recipient award to mankind Oklahoma City Sertoma Club, 1962, Outstanding Citizen award Oklahoma City Jr. C. of C., 1965. Mem. Am., Fed., Okla., Oklahoma County bar assns., Am. Bar Found., Sigma Alpha Epsilon, Phi Delta Phi. Episcopalian (sr. warden 1957). Kiwanian (lt. gov. 1959), Elk, Mason (32, Shriner, Jester). Club: Men's Dinner Oklahoma City (pres. 1966-69).). Home: 1800 Coventry Lane Oklahoma City, OK 73120. Office: US Courthouse Oklahoma City OK 73102

DAUGHERTY, JAMES HENRY artist; b. Ashville, N.C., June 1, 1889; s. Charles M. and Susan Peyton Peyton (Telfair) D.; prep. edn., Central High Sch., Washington, D.C.; student Corcoran Sch. Art,

Washington, Pa., Acad. Fine Arts, Phila. pupil Frank Brangwyn, London, Eng.; m. Sonia Medwedeff, 1913; 1 son, Charles M. Represented at Yale Mus. Art, Mus. Modern Art, N.Y.C., Whitney Mus. Am. Art, N.Y.C., Mus. Legion of Honor, San Francisco, Spencer collection N.Y. Pub. Library, Smithsonian Inst., Washington, Montclair (N.J.) Mus.; executed mural paintings, Lowes State Theatre, Cleve., Sesquicentennial Exposition, Phila., Stamford High Sch., Ship camoufleur, designer war posters for U.S. Navy and Shipping Bd., World War I. Recipient Newberry medal for most distinguished contribution to Am. literature for children, 1939. Mem. Authors Guild, Silvermine Guild Artists, P.E.N. Illustrator numerous books. Author and illustrator: Of Courage Undaunted, 1951; A. Lincoln; Daniel Boone; Poor Richard; Andy and the Lion; The Magna Charta; The Picnic, 1958; William Blake, 1961; Walt Whitman's America, 1964; others. Home: Westport CT 06880 ☆

DAUGHERTY, PAUL JOHN, chamber of commerce exec.; b. Sharon, Pa., Nov. 6, 1910; s. Joseph McBurney and Alice Gertrude (Taylor) D.; B.A., Wesleyan U., 1933; postgrad. Ohio State U., 1935-37; m. Eleanor Agnes Greene, Apr. 14, 1934; children—Susan (Mrs. Philip Shafer), Judith (Mrs. Robert Butler), Priscilla (Mrs. John Mead, Jr.), Sarah Jane (Mrs. Michael Sussman). With Ohio C. of C., 1937—. exec. v.p., 1966—. Treas. Council State Chambers of Commerce; pres. Ohio Trade Assn. Execs., 1957. Mem. legislative com. Ohio Sesquicentennial. 1953; pres. Upper Arlington P.T.A., 1955. Bd. dirs. Upper Arlington Civic Assn., 1958-59. Recipient Distinguished Service Mgmt. award C. of C. Execs. Ohio, 1956; Service award Ohio Wesleyan U. Alumni Assn. Mem. Phi Beta Kappa, Omicron Delta Kappa, Sigma Chi. Republican. Mem. Community Ch. Rotarian, Mason (hon. 33#55). Clubs: Columbus University; Ohio Wesleyan University Odevene. Home: 2257 Abington Rd Columbus OH 43221 Office: 17 S High St Columbus OH 43215

DAUGHERTY, RICHARD DEO, educator, anthropologist; b. Aberdeen, Wash., Mar. 31, 1922; s. Charles D. and Audrey (Ross) D.; B.A., U. Wash., 1946, Ph.D., 1954; m. Phyllis J. McCullough, Mar. 2, 1944; children—Melinda, Carol, Richard Deo. Faculty, Wash. State U., Pullman, 1950—, prof. anthropology, 1963—, chmn. dept. anthropology, 1969—; mem. Pres.'s Adv. Council on Historic Preservation, 1967-69; adv. bd. Nat. Trust. Named Distinguished Citizen State Wash., 1969. Mem. Am. Anthrop. Assn., Soc. for Am. Archaeology, N.W. Anthrop. Conf. (past chmn.), A.A.A.S., Gt. Basin Archaeol. Conf. (past chmn.), Am. Assn. U. Profs. (past chpt. pres.), Western Canadian Archaeol. Council, Sigma Xi, Alpha Kappa Delta, Gamma Theta Upsilon, Phi Kappa Phi. Contbr. articles profl. jours. Home: 309 Spring St Pullman WA 99163

DAUGHERTY, WILLIS VANCE, former mgg. exec.; b. Wichita, Kan., June 10, 1897; s. James and Louella (Leeper) D.; A.B., Harvard, 1920, spl. student bus. school, 1931; LL.D., Hamilton Coll., 1967; m. Helen Sawyer, Feb. 3, 1933; children—Barbara, Willis Vance. Plant mgr. Nash Motors Co., Milw., 1920- 31; pres. Thomas Devlin Mfg. Co., Burlington, N.J., 1933-40; exec. v.p. Utica Drop Forge & Tool Corp. (N.Y.). 1940-49, pres., 1949-56; corp. v.p. gen. mgr. Utica Drop Forge div. Kelsey Hayes Co., 1956-58; pres. Hamilton Research Assos., Inc., 1959-62, chmn. bd., 1962-68; chmn. bd. Am. Emblem Co., Utica, 1960-62; bus. mgr. Hamilton Coll., 1959-62, now trustee; exec. dir. N.Y. Job Devel. Authority, 1962-63; dir. Spl. Metals, Inc., Divine Bros. Co., Oneida Nat. Bank & Trust Co., Mohawk Airlines, Inc., Dale Engring. Co. Past Chmn. bd. trustees Mohawk Valley Community Coll. Former mem. Gov.'s Bus. Adv. Council; dir. YMCA. Served as ensign USN, 1917- 19. Mem. Utica Indsl. Assn. (dir.). Home: Bristol Rd Clinton NY 13323

DAUGHTON, DONALD FREDERICK, lawyer; b. Grand River, Ia., Mar. 11, 1932; s. Frederick Joseph and Ethel (Edwards) D.; B.S.C., State U. Ia., 1953, J.D., 1956; m. Helen Mathilde Rollow, Mar. 15, 1958; children-Erin Ellen, Thomas Frederick, Andrew Michael, James Patrick. Admitted to Ia. bar, 1956, Ariz. bar, 1958; asst. atty. Polk County, Ia., 1958-59; practice in Phoenix, 1959- 65; judge Superior Ct. Ariz., 1965-67; partner firm Browder, Gillenwater & Daughton, Phoenix, 1967—. Bd. dirs. Maricopa County Legal Aid Soc., Maricopa County March Dimes, Jane Wayland Child Guidance Center, Creative Living Found. Served to 1st lt. USAF, 1956-58. Mem. Am., Ia. Marisopa County bar assns., State Bar Ariz., Ariz. Acad., Sigma Alpha Epsilon, Phi Delta Phi. Democrat. Home: 4545 N 5th St Phoenix AZ 85108 Office: First Fed Savs Bldg Phoenix AZ 85012

DAUM, OSCAR ROBERT, Jr., printing co. exec.; b. Chgo., Mar. 28, 1921; s. Oscar Robert and Ellen (Connelley) D.; B.S., Purdue U., 1942; M.B.A., Harvard, 1946; m. Betty Joyce Hoover, Nov. 14, 1943; childrenJanet, Nancy, Barbara, Ruth. With R.R. Donnelly & Sons Co., Chgo., 1946—., v.p., div. dir. Willard Mfg. div., 1962-64, v.p. adminstrv. div., 1964-65, sr. v.p., 1965-; dir. Lakeside Bank, Chgo. Trustee Willard (O.) Community Fund; Willard Meml. Hosp. Served to capt. Q. M.C., AUS, World War II. Home: 4136 Clausen Av Western Springs, IL 60558. Office: 2223 South Park Way Chicago IL 60616

DAUNER, WOLFGANG, pianist, composer, trumpetist, valve trombonist; b. Stuttgart, Germany, Dec. 30, 1935; student of profl. tchr., 1941; student trumpet and composition Stuttgart Coll. Music, 1958. Tour with comml. band, 1957; participant German jazz festivals, 1962, 64; played in Stuttgart with Leo Wright, Benny Bailey, Attila Zoller: composer music for comml. film; also arrangements for German TV show, 1965; with own trio, then with John Freund; recording artist with CBS Records. Address: 7 Stuttgart Münster Elbestr 131 Federal Republic of Germany*

DAUNORAS, RICHARD A., chem. co. exec.; b. Chgo., 1926; B.S. in Accounting, Walton Coll., 1950; married. Treas., controller Advanced Transformer Co., 1955-63, now dir.; v.p., treas. Thompson-Hayward Chem. Co., 1963-65; v.p., controller N.Am. Philips Corp., N.Y.C., 1965—; controller PEPI, Inc., 1967—; dir. Philips Roxane, Inc., Anchor Serum Co., Chgo. Magnet Wire Corp., Advance Transformer Co., Ltd., Alliance Mfg. Co., Plastic Ware, Inc., Anchor Bruch Co. C.P.A., N.Y. Home: 2 Lake View Av North Tarrytown NY Office: 100 E 42d St New York City NY 10017*

DAUPHIN, CLAUDE LE GRAND MARIA EUGENE, actor, writer; b. Corbell, France; Aug. 19, 1903; s. Franc Nohan and Madeleine Dauphin; ed. Sorbonne and Inst. des Beaux Arts, Paris, France; m. Norma Eberhardt, May 21, 1955. Set designer for Comedy Française, Paris, 1923-31; dir. Claude Dauphin Theatre Co., Paris, 1945-50; Broadway appearances include No Exit, 1947, The Happy Time, 1950, Janus, 1956, Clerambard, 1958, Deadly Game, 1959, Giants Sons of Giants, 1962, The Full Treatment, 1962; appearances plays in France include: Une Femme Libre, 1932, Adam, 1938, La Soif, 1949, Adorable Julia, 1962; Hedda Gabler, 1963; also all plays by Henry Bernstien, 1933-39; appeared in Death of a Salesman, 1967, Battle of Ink, 1967, Voyage for Two, 1967, Barbarella, 1968: The English Lover of Marguerite Duras, 1969; motion pictures include 16 American, 5 British and 70 French. Served to lt. French Army, World War II; mem. Free French Army. Decorated Legion of Honor, War Cross, Medal of de Gaulle. Address: Peter Pan Farm Oakhurst NJ 07755 also care of Filmco 6 rue Lincoln Paris 8e France

DAUPHINAIS, GEORGE ARTHUR, engring. exec.; b. Waterbury, Conn., Apr. 11, 1918; s. Arthur J. and Nell (Phillips) D.; B.S. in Mech. Engring., La. State U., 1942; m. Sarah McConnell, Dec. 27, 1942; children—Carol Joe, George William, Sarah Marie. Advanced engring program Gen. Electric Co., Schenectady, 1942, engr., 1942-47; with H.K. Porter Co., Inc., Phila., 1947-59, successively plant engr., works mgr., 1947-52, v.p., gen. mgr., 1952-59; v.p. Electric Autolite Co., Toledo, 1960—, pres. Prestolite Internat. Co. div. Eltra Corp., 1964—; group v.p. Sangamo Electric Co., Springfield, Ill., 1965—. Mem. Am. Soc. M.E., Soc. Automotive Engrs., Tau Beta Pi, Sigma Alpha Epsilon. Home: Willemoore St Springfield IL 62704 Office: Sangamo Electric Co Springfield IL 62701

DAUTEN, CARL ANTON, educator; b. St. Louis, June 2, 1913; s. Paul Martin and Louise (Heyer) D.; A.B., Washington U., 1936, A.M., 1939, Ph.D., 1944; m. Dorothea Hoeman, July 18, 1942; children—Thomas, Jane, Mary. Prodn. control chemist Nat. Lead Co., St. Louis, 1937-38; prof. bus. adminstrn. Shurtleff Coll., Alton, Ill., 1940-44; sr. adminstrv. asst. U.S. Civil Service Commn., Detroit, 1942; prof. econs., acting treas., bus. mgr. Mo. Valley Coll., Marshall, 1944-45; asst. prof. bus. adminstrn. U. Ark., 1945; mem. faculty Washington U., St. Louis, 1945—, prof. finance, banking, 1952—, dir. doctoral program Grad. Sch. Bus. and Pub. Adminstrn., 1960-63, asso. provost, 1962-64, vice chancellor adminstrn., 1964-67, vice chancellor, asso. provost, 1967-69, exec. vice chancellor, 1969—; mem. exec. develop. program, mgmt. study program. Dir. Concordia Pub. House, 1965—, chmn. bd., 1971. Mem. Citizens Adv. Com. Jr. Coll. Dist., St. Louis, 1964-65; chmn. edn. commn. Council Lutheran Chs. Greater St. Louis, 1961-65, bd. dirs., 1961-65. Mem. adv. bd. Concordia Sem. Research Center. Mem. Phi Beta Kappa, Beta Gamma Sigma, Omicron Delta Kappa. Author: Business Finance, 1948; Business Cycles and Forecasting, 1955; Financing the American Consumer, 1956; Principles of Finance, 1958; Consumer Finance Companies in a Dynamic Economy, 1959; The Role of the Mississippi-Missouri River Systems in the Development of the St. Louis Region, 1961. Asso. editor Jour. Finance, 1956-59. Home: 720 Cranbrook St St Louis MO 63122

DAVANT, JAMES WARING, investment banker; b. McComb, Miss., Dec. 1, 1917; s. Guy Hamilton and Em Reid (Waring) D.; student U. Va., 1939; m. Mary Ellis Westlake, Apr. 4, 1942; children—Mary Diane, John Hamilton, Patricia Jean. With Paine, Webber, Jackson & Curtis, 1945—, gen partner, 1956—, chmn. br. office com., 1963—, mem. policy com., 1963—, mng. partner, 1964—. pres., chief exec. officer, 1970—; dir. Essex Internat., Inc., Ft. Wayne, Ind., Green Giant Co., Mpls. Chmn. Assn. Stock Exchange Firms, 1966-68, mem. bd. govs. Bond Club N.Y.C., 1965—, v.p., 1971—; mem. Bankers Club Am., 1966—. Chmn. financial dinnerama Boy Scouts Am., 1967; chmn. Nat. Conf. Christians and Jews dinner, 1970; commerce and industry com. Nat Cystic Fibrosis Research Found. Served to lt. comdr. USNR, 1940-45. Episcopalian. Clubs: Economic, Pilgrims of U.S. (N.Y.C.); Minneapolis (Mpls.). Home: 200 E 66th St New York City NY 10021 also 9 Maplewood Rd Wayzata MN 55391 also Horseshoe Rd Mill Neck NY 11765 Office: 140 Broadway New York City NY 10005

DAVENNY, WARD MCCONNELL, educator, musician; b. Ashtabula, O., July 28, 1916; s. Frank E. and Ellen (McClanning) D.; Mus. B., Cleve. Inst. Music, 1934; Mus. B., Yale, 1936, Mus. M., 1937; student Accademia di Santa Cecilia, Rome, 1938-39; m. Ena Nelson, July 8, 1940; childrenSusan (Mrs. Yehudi Wyner), Ellen Katherine, Ward Leslie. Mem. faculty Yale Sch. Music, 1940-43,60—, prof. music, 1963—, dir. Hartford (Conn.) Sch. Music, 1946-54, Cleve. Inst. Music, 1954-60; also Summer Sch. Music and Art, Norfolk, Conn.; concert pianist, 1931-; chamber music performer, 1935—; pianist Albeneri Trio, 1956-60. Served with AUS, 1943-46. Home: 821 Oakwood Rd Orange, CT 06477. Office: Yale Sch Music New Haven, CT 06520.

DAVENPORT, DEMOREST, educator, biologist; b. Utica, N.Y., Sept. 26, 1911; s. William Rufus and Alice (Demorest) D.; grad. St. George's Sch., 1929; A.B., Harvard, 1933, Ph.D., 1937; M.A., Colo. Coll., 1934; m. Winnifred Bailey, June 10, 1941; childrenMary Stuart, Evelyn Curtis. Instr. biology Reed Coll., 1937-40, asst. prof., 1941-42; asst. prof. U. Cal. at Santa Barbara, 1946-52, asso. prof., 1952-60, prof., 1960-, chmn. dept. biol. scis., 1962-66; vis. asso. prof. Kerckhoff Marine Lab. of Cal. Inst. Tech., 1954, 56; vis. prof. oceanographic labs. U. Wash., Friday Harbor, 1959- 60; staff Marine Biol. Labs., Woods Hole, Mass., 1958; research asso. Harvard, 1965. Served from 2d lt. to capt., USAAF, 1942-45. Guggenheim fellow, 1951-52, 61-62. Fellow A.A.A.S.; mem. Am. Soc. Zoologists, Ecol. Soc., Brit. Soc. Study Animal Behaviour, Marine Biol. Assn. U.K., Western Soc. Naturalists, Sigma Xi. Contbr. articles profl. jours. Home: 1045 Winther Way Santa Barbara, CA 93105.

DAVENPORT, FRED MARSHALL, physician, educator; b. Scranton, Pa., Nov. 30, 1914; s. Fred Marshall and Laura May (Church) D.; B.A., Columbia, 1936, M.D., 1940, Sci. Med.D., 1945; m. Clara J. Dommerich, June 14, 1941; children—Laura May, Steven Marshall, Clara Josephine. Asst prof. dept. epidemiology U. Mich. Sch. Pub. Health, Ann Arbor, 1951-52, asso. prof., 1953-58, prof., 1958—, chmn., 1969—; asst. prof. dept. internal medicine Univ. Hosp., Ann Arbor, 1951- 52, asso. prof., 1953-58, prof., 1958—. Dir. Commn. on influenza Armed Forces Epidemiological Bd., Office of Surgeon Gen., 1955—; chmn. U.S. Viral Disease Panel, U.S. Japan Coop. Med. Sci. Program, NIAID, 1969—; adv. panel on virus diseases WHO, 1958—. Served to capt., M.C., AUS, 1942-46. Mem. Am. Epidemiological Soc., Fedn. Socs. Exptl. Biology, Am. Soc. Bacteriologists, Am. Acad. Microbiology, Am. Pub. Health Assn., Central Soc. for Clin. Research, Am. Assn. Immunologist, Harvey Soc., Robert Koch Inst. (hon.), N.Y. Acad. Scis., Assn. Am. Physicians, Am. Soc. Clin. Investigation, Soc. Exptl. Biology and Medicine, Assn. Tchrs. Preventive Medicine, Alpha Omega Alpha, Delta Omega. Home: 1038 Martin Pl Ann Arbor MI 48104

DAVENPORT, GWEN, (Mrs. John Davenport), author; b. Colon, C.Z., Oct. 3, 1910 d. James Farquharson and Gwen (Wigley) Leys; A.B. Vassar Coll., 1931; m. John Davenport, Feb. 5, 1937; childrenChristopher, John Farquharson, Juliet Rathbone. Author: A Stranger and Afriad, 1943; Return Engagement, 1945; Belvedere (motion picture prodn. Sitting Pretty), 1947; Family Fortunes, 1949; Candy for Breakfast, 1950; The Backelor's Baby, 1957; The Wax Foundation, 1961; Great Loves in Legend and Life, 1964. Contbr. short stories to nat. mags. Home: 6 Rio Vista Dr Louisville KY 40207

DAVENPORT, HORACE ELSTUN, coal co. exec.; b. Buffalo, Jan. 26, 1907; s. William Ashley and Pauline Jameson (Tilley) D.; A.B., Columbia, 1929; m. Elizabeth Christine Rohrs, Dec. 14, 1932; children—Susan Wyatt (Mrs. John W. Peirce), Peter MacLaren, Michael Elstun. Sales staff Delaware, Lackawanna & Western Coal Co., 1930; pres. Prew Coal Co., Holyoke, Mass., 1931; asst. pres. Sunrise Coal Co., Bklyn.; pres. Hudson River Yards, Tarrytown, N.Y., 1933; pres. George W. Pickering Co., Salem, Mass., 1934-53, chmn., 1954; pres. Burns Bros., N.Y.C., 1953; v.p. Pocahontas Fuel Co., pres. Pocahontas Steamship Co., 1954-57; v.p. Consol. Coal Co., Pitts., 1957- 69, dir., 1959-69, pres. New Eng. div. Consol. Coal Co., 1957-69; chmn. bd. Northeast Petroleum Industries, Inc., Boston, 1969—; trustee Salem Savs. Bank. Past dir., fund chmn. Salem-Danvers-Marblehead Community Fund; dir. Salem YMCA, Lynn (Mass.) Boys Club. Chairman bd. Nat. Rowing Foundation; trustee Proctor Acad., Fryeburg (me.) Acad.; life trustee Salem Hosp. Mason. Home: 1 Salem St Swampscott MA 01907 Office: 295 Eastern Av Chelsea MA 02150

DAVENPORT, HORACE WILLARD, physiologist; b. Phila., Oct. 20, 1912; s. Horace Willard and Elizabeth (Langendorf) D.; B.S., Cal. Inst. Tech. 1935, Ph.D., 1939; B.A., U. Oxford, Eng. (Rhodes scholar 1935-38), 1937, B.Sc., 1938, D.Sc., 1961; m. Virginia Dickerson, Feb. 1, 1945 (dec. Mar. 1968); two sons; m.2d, Ingeborg V Epstein, Aug. 15, 1969. Instr. physiology U. Pa. Med. Sch., Phila., 1941-1943; instr. physiology Harvard Med. Sch., 1943- 45; prof., head dept. physiology U. Utah Med. Sch., 1945-56; prof., chmn. dept. physiology U. Mich., 1956—. Vis. prof. Mayo Found., 1962-63. Mem. Am. Physiol. Soc. (pres. 1961-62). Contbr. to profl. jours. Home: 3063 Overridge Ann Arbor MI 48104

DAVENPORT, JAMES FRANKLIN, former utility exec.; b. Fall River, Mass., Dec. 20, 1903; s. James F. and Jessie A. (Gage) D.; B.S., Harvard, 1926; m. Margaret Goodhue Ives, May 27, 1937; children—Elinor Ives (Mrs. Robert B. Travers), James Franklin. With So. Cal. Edison Co., Los Angeles, 1926-68, successively draftsman, engr., supt., asst. mgr., asst. v.p., v.p., gen mgr., 1954-56, exec. v.p., 1956-68, dir., 1955-68; v.p. Edison Securities Co., 1951-57, pres., 1957-59; dir. Edison Electric Inst., 1956-60; cons. engr., 1969—. Dir. Atomic Indsl. Forum, 1966-68. U.S. rep. UN Electric Power Com., Geneva, 1956. Trustee Harvey Mudd Coll., Claremont, Cal. Dep. adminstrn., adminstr. Def. Electric Power Adminstrn., 1952-53. Served from capt. to col. USAAF, 1941-46. Decorated Legion of Merit; Commendation medal with 2 oak leaf clusters; recipient Distinguished Service Award, Dept. of Interior. Registered profl. elec. engineer, Cal. Mem. Los Angeles C. of C. (dir. 1956-60, v.p. 1958), I.E.E.E., Mchts. and Mfrs. Assn. (dir. 1960-68), Pacific Coast Elec. Assn. (pres. 1965-66). Republican. Episcopalian. Clubs: California, Valley Hunt, Twilight; Harvard (N.Y.C.). Home: 611 Westover Pl Pasadena CA 91105 Office: 601 W 5th St Los Angeles CA 90017

DAVENPORT, JOHN ALFRED, former editor; b. Phila., Sept. 11, 1904; s. Russell Wheeler and Cornelia W. (Farnum) D.; A.B., Yale, 1926; work in philosophy, econs. Yale, 1935-36; m. Marie Hayes, Oct. 11, 1941; children—Ann, Glorianna, Susan, Amy, John, Sharon, Caroline. Reporter, N.Y. World, 1927-30; mem. staff Fortune mag. (Time Inc.), N.Y.C., 1937-49, mem. bd. editors, 1941-49, 55- 68, asst. mng. editor, 1958-65; editor Barron's Weekly, 1949-54. Recipient Freedom Found. award, 1949, 50; award Am. Bar Assn., 1971. Clubs: Century Assn. (N.Y.C.); Metropolitan (Washington). Author: (with Charles J. V. Murphy) Lives of Winston Churchill; The U.S. Economy, 1964. Home: 302 E 65th St New York City NY 10021

DAVENPORT, JOHN SIDNEY III, lawyer; b. Richmond, Va., Mar. 14, 1905; s. John Sidney and Marguerite (Warwick) D.; B.A., Yale, 1927, LL.B., 1930; m. Edna Wylie McAdams, June 23, 1932 (dec. Nov. 1966): 1 dau., Marguerite Warwick (Mrs. J. Stephen Lord); m. 2d, Eliza Tabb Mason, May 4, 1968. Admitted to Va. bar. 1930, since practiced in Richmond; sr. partner Denny, Valentine & Davenport, 1939-66; sr. partner Mays, Valentine Davenport & Moore, 1967-; with Office Gen Counsel WPB, 1942-44, OSS, 1944-45. Dir., mem. trust com. First & Mchts. Nat. Bank; dir. Richmond Fed. Savs. & Loan Assn. Mem. Richmond City Council, 1948-52; vice mayor, Richmond, 1948-50. Bd. dirs., past pres. Sheltering Arms Hosp.; trustee Funds of Diocese Episcopal Ch. Recipient Good Govt. award Richmond First Club, 1962, Spl. award for outstanding community service Jr. C. of C., 1962. Fellow Am. Coll. Trial Lawyers, Am. Bar Found.; mem. Am., Va. (pres.-elect), Richmond (past pres.) bar assns., Richmond C. of C. (past pres.), Corbey Ct., Alpha Delta Phi, Phi Delta Phi. Episcopalian. Home: 23 Chatham Sq Richmond VA 23226 Office: Ross Bldg Richmond VA 23219

DAVENPORT, LEE LOSEE, electronics co. exec.; b. Schenectady, Dec. 31, 1915; s. Harry Lee and Faith (Losee) D.; B.S., Union Coll., 1937; M.S., U. Pitts., 1940, Ph.D., 1946; m. Anne Stephenson, Jan. 27, 1944; children—Jeanne Lee, Carol Lee. Mem. staff Mass. Inst. Tech. Radiation Lab., 1941- 46, Harvard Nuclear Lab., 1946-50; exec. v.p. Perkin-Elmer Corp., 1950- 57; pres. Sylvania-Corning Nuclear Corp., 1957-60; v.p. planning Sylvania Electric Products, Inc., 1960-62; pres. Gen. Telephone & Electronics Labs., Inc., 1962—; dir. GTE Internat. System Corp. Trustee, Union Coll., Schenectady. Recipient of citation for OSRD activities Def. Dept., 1947. Fellow Am. Phys. Soc.; mem. Am. Nat. Standards Inst. (dir.), Am. Inst. Physics, A.A.A.S., Sci. Research Soc. Am., Sigma Xi, Sigma Pi Sigma. Clubs: Cosmos, Harvard. Home: Winding Lane Greenwich CT 06830 Office: GTE Labs Inc 730 3d Av New York City NY 10017

DAVENPORT, MANUEL MANSON, educator; b. Colorado Springs, Colo., June 14, 1929; s. Ernest Alfred and Anna (Brauer) D.; A.B., Bethany Nazarene Coll., 1950; M.A., Colo. Coll., 1953; Ph.D., U. Ill., 1956; m. Maxine Mildred Neely, May 26, 1951; children—Marian, Mark, Mitchel. Instr., Colo. Coll., 1956-57; asst., asso. prof. Colo. State U., 1957-67; prof., head dept. philosophy Tex. A. and M. U., College Station, 1967—; elementary sch. tchr., 1950-52. First v.p. Brazos Civil Liberties Union, 1968-71; campus liaison Peace Corps, 1968—. Bd. dirs. Fine Arts Council. Served with U.S. Army, 1952. Recipient Faculty Achievement awards, 1959, 60, 69, Rockefeller Found. grant, 1962-63, 1st prize Albert Schweitzer Edn. Found. Essay Contest, 1960. Danforth Assn. Mem. Am. Assn. U. Profs. (past chpt. pres.), Southwestern Philos. Soc.. (past mem. exec. com.), Am., Mountain-Plains (past chmn.) philos. assns., Phi Kappa Phi, Omicron Delta Kappa. Home: 3715 Stillmeadow St Bryan TX 77801 Office: Academic Bldg College Station TX 77843

DAVENPORT, MARCIA, author; b. N.Y.C., June 9, 1903; d. Alma Gluck (Efrem Zimbalist, step- father); student Friends Sch., Phila., Shipley Sch., Bryn Mawr. Pa., Wellesley Coll., m. Russell Wheeler Davenport, 1929 (dec. 1954). Editorial staff New Yorker, 1928-31; engaged in writing, 1932-34; music critic Stage mag., 1934-39; commentator Met. Opera broadcasts. Mem. nat. bd. Nat. Book Com. Mem. of P.E.N., Authors Guild, Club: Cosmopolitan. Author: Mozart (biography), 1932, bicentennial edit., 1956; of Lena Geyer (novel), 1936; Valley of Decision, 1942; East Side, West Side, 1947; My Brother's Keeper, 1954; Garibaldi (juvenile), 1957; The Constant Image, 1960; Too Strong for Fantasy, 1967. Contributor to the Sat. Eve. Post, McCall's, Reader's Digest, New Yorker, Fortune, others. Home: 1 East End Av New York City NY 10021

DAVENPORT, RAYMOND RIPLEY, life ins. co. exec.; b. Bellevue. Tex., Feb. 26, 1904; s. Green W. and Josephine (Russell) D.; B.A., So. Meth. U., 1931; m. Rosa Mae Wilson, Sept. 28, 1925; childrenFrancha, Diane, Raymond Ripley. Sch. supt. to 1933; with Southwestern Life Ins. Co., Dallas, 1933-, successively agt., sales dir., asst. agy. dir., v.p., agy. dir., 1933-62, exec. v.p., vice chmn. bd.,

1962-69, now mem. exec. com., dir. chmn. agy. sect. Am. Life Conv. 1963-64. C.L.U., 1941. Mem. Life Ins. Agy. Mgmt. Assn. (pres. 1954-55). Home: 4001 Normandy St Dallas, TX 75205. Office: Southwestern Life Bldg Dallas, TX 75221.

DAVENPORT, WILBUR BAYLEY, Jr., educator; b. Phila., July 27, 1920; s. Wilbur Bayley and Cora (Reifsnyder) D.; B. Elec. Engring., Ala. Poly. Inst., 1941; M.S. in Elec. Engring., Mass. Inst. Tech., 1943, D.Sc., 1950; m. Joan Purington, Nov. 3, 1945; children—Mark Wilbur, Sally Davenport. Mem. faculty Mass. Inst. Tech., 1946—, prof. elec. engring., 1960—, asso. head dept. elec. engring., asst. dir. Lincoln Lab., 1963-65, asso. dir. research lab. electronics, 1961-63; cons. to govt. and industry, 1961—. Served to lt. (j.g.) USNR, 1943-46. Recipient certification of commendation, Navy Dept., 1960. Fellow I.E.E.E., A.A.A.S.; mem. Sigma Xi, Tau Beta Pi, Phi Kappa Phi, Eta Kappa Nu, Spiked Shoe. Author: (with William L. Root) An Introduction to the Theory of Random Signals and Noise, 1958; Probability and Random Processes, An Introduction for Applied Scientists and Engineers, 1970. Home: Garfield Rd Concord MA 01742 Office: 77 Massachusetts Av Cambridge MA 02139

DAVENPORT, WILLIAM A., lawyer; b. Butte, Mont., July 6, 1911; grad. U. Minn.; J.D., Georgetown U., 1935. Admitted to Mont. bar, 1936, Wash. bar, 1946; partner firm Witherspoon, Kelley, Davenport & Toole, Spokane, Wash. Mem. Am., Wash. State, Spokane County bar assn. Office: 1114 Old National Bank Bldg Spokane WA 99201*

DAVENPORT, WILLIAM HENRY, educator, editor; b. Bridgeport, Conn., March 26, 1908; s. William Enright and Evelyn Agnes (Hills) D.; A.B., Dartmouth Coll., 1929; A.M., Tufts Coll., 1931; Ph.D., Yale, 1938; summer sch. Grenoble, 1928, Harvard 1930, Munich, 1936; m. Frances Isobel Shriner, Oct. 21, 1938; childrenLinda Reiver, Marcia Hills. Teaching fellow English, Tufts Coll., 1929-31; instr. Carnegie Inst. Tech., 1931-35. Smith Coll., 1938; asst. prof. English, U. of So. Cal., 1938-42, assoc. prof., 1942-49, acting head of dept., 1948-49, prof., 1949-55, head dept., 1955-57; prof. English, Harvey Mudd Coll., Claremont, Cal., 1957— chmn. dept. humanities, 1957-68; vis. prof. U. Cal. at Los Angeles, 1946, N.Y. U., 1952; vis. Lectr. Cal. Inst. of Tech. 1944-47, editor U.S. Navy Rocket publs., 1944-45; research asso. Harvard Univ., 1968-69. Member Nat. Council Tchrs. of English, Am. Soc. Engring. Edn., Modern Lang. Assn., Philol. Assn. of Pacific Coast, Phi Beta Kappa, Kappa Sigma. Presbyn. Editor: Dominant Types in British and Am. Literature (with L. Wimberly and H. Shaw), 1949; Nine Modern American Plays, 1951; Voices in Court, 1958. The Good Physician, 1962; Engineering: Role in Society (with D. Rosenthal), 1967; (with B. Siegel) Biography Past and Present, 1965; The One Culture, 1970; others. Address: Harvey Mudd Coll Claremont CA 91711

DAVERN, JEANNE MARGUERITE, editorial cons.; b. Plattsburgh, N.Y.; d. Jeremiah William and Marguerite (Beaucaire) Davern; B.A., Wellesley Coll., 1944. Reporter, Plattsburgh Press Republican, 1944-48; staff Archtl. Record, 1948-69, mng. editor, 1963- 69. Mem. Archtl. League N.Y., Soc. Archtl. Historians, Nat. Trust for Historic Preservation, Municipal Art Soc., Nat. Council on Arts in Govt. Address: 80 Park Av New York City NY 10016 Office: 330 W 42d St New York City NY 10036

DAVES, DELMER LAWRENCE, motion picture dir., writer, producer; b. San Francisco; s. Arthur Lawrence and Nan (Funge) D.; grad. Los Angeles Polytechnic, 1922; Stanford U., 1927; m. Mary Lou Lender, July 11, 1938; children—Michael Lawrence, Deborah Lou, Donna Lee. Started as property-boy, 1927; actor and writer, 1928; dir.-writer Warner Bros., 1943-58, dir. producer, writer, 1959-67; dir., writer Twentieth Century-Fox, 1949, producer, 1954; pres. Diamond D Prodns. Mem. Producers Guild of Am., Dirs. Guild of Am. (nat. bd.), Stanford Assos., Am. Fedn. of Art, Mus. of Modern Art, Museum of Natural History, Mineral. Society of Am., Writers Guild of Am., Motion Picture Acad. Arts and Scis. (gov.), Sigma Alpha Epsilon, Phi Delta Phi. Republican. Episcopalian. Author numerous screen plays; dir., writer, producer; Destination Tokyo, The Red House, Dark Passage, Task Force, Bird of Paradise, Drum Beart, Jubal, The Last Wagon, A Summer Place, Parrish, Susan Slade, Rome Adventure, Spencer's Mountain, Youngblood Hawke; dir. Pride of the Marines, Broken Arrow, 3:10 to Yuma, Cowboy, Kings Go Forth, The Hanging Tree, Demetrius & The Gladiators, Screen plays include following: Flirtation Walk, Shipmates Forever, Love Affair, Stage Door Canteen, An Affair to Remember. Home: 107 N Bentley Av Los Angeles CA 90049 also 1730 Valdez Dr La Jolla CA 92039 ☆

DAVES, JESSICA ret. editor; b. Cartersville, Ga.; d. Walter and Annie (Hopkins) Daves: m. Robert Allerton Parker, Dec. 20, 1930. Fashion mdse. editor Vogue (Conde Nast Publs., Inc.), 1933-36, mng. editor, 1936-46, editor in chief, 1946-63. Decorated Italian Star of Solidarity; French Legion of Honor. Mem. Fashion Group Am. (pres.), MacDowell Assn. (bd. dir.). Clubs: Cosmopolitan (N.Y.C.); Nat. Press (Washington). Author: Vogue Book of Menus; Ready-Made Miracle. Co- author: The World in Vogue. Home: 1040 Park Av New York City, NY 10028.

DAVEY, ANTHONY JOHN, ins. co. exec.; b. Bridgeport, Conn., May 31, 1925; s. Peter Martin and Janet (Otley) D.; B. Social Studies cum laude, Holy Cross Coll., 1947; LL.B. (Root Tilden scholar), N.Y. U., 1955; m. Judith Crawford, Sept. 19, 1961. Admitted to N.Y. State bar, 1956; asso. firm Wilkie, Farr, Gallagher, Walton & FitzGibbon, N.Y.C., 1955-64; head legal dept., sec. Diamond Internat. Corp., N.Y.C., 1964-67, gen. counsel, 1967-69; v.p.-counsel USLIFE Corp., N.Y.C., 1969—. Served to lt. USNR, 1943-46, 50-52: MTO. Mem. Am., N.Y. State bar assns., Bar Assn. City N.Y., Phi Delta Phi, Delta Epsilon Sigma. Home: 420 E 23d St New York City NY 10010 Office: 125 Maiden Lane New York City NY 10038

DAVEY, CHARLES BINGHAM, educator; b. Bklyn., Apr. 7, 1928; s. Francis Joseph and Mary Elizabeth (Bingham) D.; B.S., Syracuse U., 1950; M.S., U. Wis., 1952, Ph.D., 1955; m. Elizabeth Anne Thompson, July 11, 1952; children—Douglas Alan, Barbara Lynn, Andrew Martin. Soil scientist Research Service, Dept. Agr., Beltsville, Md., 1957-62; asso. prof. N.C. State U., Raleigh, 1962-65, prof., 1965—, head dept., 1970—. Served with AUS, 1955-57. Fellow A.A.A.S., Am. Soc. Agronomy; mem. Soc. Am. Foresters, Soil Sci. Soc. Am., Internat. Soil Sci. Soc., Sigma Xi (Research award), Phi Kappa Phi, Gamma Sigma Delta. Editor: Tree Growth and Forest Soils, 1970; asso. editor Soil Sci. Soc. Am. proc., 1967—; patentee, publs. in field. Home: 3704 Avent Ferry Rd Raleigh NC 27606

DAVEY, CLARK WILLIAM, journalist; b. Chatham, Ont., Can., Mar. 3, 1928; s. William and Marguerite (Clark) D.; B.A. in Journalism, U. Western Ont., 1948; m. Joyce Gordon, Sept. 13, 1952; children—Richard Gordon, Kevin William, Clark Michael. With Chatham Daily News, 1948-51; mng. editor No. Daily News, Kirkland Lake, Can., 1951; hydro. seaway corr. Globe and Mail. 1951- 55; mem. Parliamentary Press Gallery, Ottawa, 1956-60; fgn. editor Globe and Mail 1960-63, mgr. editor, 1963—. Home: 2180 Portway Av Port Credit Ontario Canada Office: 140 King St W Toronto Ontario Canada

DAVEY, GEOFFREY, ins. co. exec.; b. Melksham, Eng., Mar. 6, 1913; s. Sidney Dyer and Eleanor (Major) D.; B.S., London U., 1935; M.S., So. Meth. U., 1948; J.D., U. Mich., 1952; LL.M., N.Y.U., 1955; m. Muriel L. Rowan, Feb. 6, 1970. Came to U.S., 1946, naturalized, 1950. Admitted to N.Y. bar, 1953; practice in N.Y.C., 1953-55; asso. Watters & Donovan, 1952- 55; asst. to controller Continental Ins. Cos., N.Y.C., 1956-57, asst. treas., 1957-58, sec., 1958—, v.p., 1959; v.p., sec. Continental Corp., N.Y.C., 1968—; dir. Bankers & Shippers Ins. Co., N.Y., Jersey Ins. Co. N.Y., Tower Underwriters Ltd., London, Eng., Royal Gen. Ins. Co. Can., Am. Title Ins. Co., Miami; tchr. So. Meth. U., U. Mich. Sec., Continental Research Inst., also 80 Maiden Lane Found. Served to flight lt. R.A.F., 1940-46. Mem. Am. Soc. Corp. Secs., Am., N.Y. State bar assns., N.Y. County Lawyers Assn., Nat. Planning Assn. Clubs: University (N.Y.C.); Stanwich (Greenwich). Home: 499 N Broadway White Plains NY 10603 Office: 80 Maiden Lane New York City NY 10038

DAVEY, WINTHROP NEWBURY, physician, educator; b. Jackson, Mich., May 19, 1918; s. Samuel James and Katharine (Ingraham) D.; student Jackson Jr. Coll., 1935-37; A.B., U. Mich., 1939, M.D., 1942; m. Loretta Georgette Maton, Feb. 5, 1949; children—Melissa Anne, Michele Marie, Mark Douglas. Intern, asst. resident, then resident internal medicine U. Mich. Med. Center, Ann Arbor, 1944-47, instr. to asso. prof., 1947-60, prof., 1960—; dir. med. Tb unit U. Mich. Hosp., 1947—. Pres. Tb Sanatorium Commn. 1956-60; mem. adv. council Tb Hosps., 1960-65; mem. Mayor's Task Force on Tb, N.Y.C., cons. Tb program Nat. Communicable Disease Center, 1960—. Fellow A.C.P., Am. Coll. Chest Physicians; mem. A.A.A.S., Mich. Tb and Respiratory Disease Assn. (pres. 1968-70), Am. Thoracic Soc. (past pres.), A.C.P., A.M.A., Mich. County Med. Soc., Mich. Trudeau Soc. (past pres.). Editor U. Mich. Med. Bull., 1958-63. Home: 495 Hillspur Rd Ann Arbor MI 48105 Office: 1405 E Ann St Ann Arbor MI 48104

DAVID, BERT ALISON, army officer; b. Lehighton, Pa., July 4, 1924; s. Bert B. and Florence (Fritch) D.; student Pa. State U., 1942-43; B.S., U.S. Mil. Acad., 1946; grad. Command and Gen. Staff Coll., 1956, Armed Forces Staff Coll., 1961, Indsl. Coll. of Armed Forces, 1965; M.S., George Washington U., 1965; m. Shirley Fagan, June 8, 1946; children—Bert Alison, Scott C., Jon R., Lance B. Commd. 2d lt. U.S. Army, 1946, advanced through grades to brig. gen., 1969; platoon leader, co. comdr. 24th Inf. Regt., Japan, 1947-49; mem. regtl. and div. staff during Korean conflict; instr. Air Command and Staff Coll., Maxwell AFB, Ala., 1956-57; personnel staff officer Dept. Army, 1957-60; dep. comdr. 1st bn. 7th Inf., 1961-62; dep. G3 Hdqrs. VII Corps, Germany, 1963-64; dep. dir. Joint Actions Office Dept. Chief of Staff, Logistics, Washington, 1966-67; comdg. officer 2d Brigade, 9th Inf. Div., Vietnam, 1967-68; asst. dep. chief of staff for logistics Hdqrs. U.S. Army, Europe, 1968-69; asst. div. comdr. 3d Inf. Div., Germany, 1969-70; comdg. gen. 1st ROK Army Detachment, KMAG, sr. adviser 1st ROK Army, Korea, 1970-71, chief army sect. Joint U.S. MAG, 1971—. Decorated Silver Star, Legion of Merit with 2 oak leaf clusters, Bronze Star, Air medal with 7 oak leaf clusters, Army Commendation medal, Gallantry Cross with palm, Combat Inf. badge. Mem. Am. Legion, World War II, Korean and Vietnam last man clubs, Assn. U.S. Army, West Point Alumni Assn., ICAF Alumni Assn., Army Athletic Assn. Mason, Elk. Home: 131 N 7th St Lehighton PA 18235 Office: Army Sect JUSMAG-K APO San Francisco CA 96302

DAVID, DONALD KIRK, ret. found. exec.; b. Moscow, Ida., Feb. 15, 1896; s. Frank Alva and Ella (Jameson) D.; A.B., U. Ida., 1916, LL.D., 1941; M.B.A., Harvard, 1919, LL.D., 1948; LL.D., St. Lawrence U., 1947, Washington & Lee U., 1949, Northeastern U., 1951, Carleton Coll., 1952, Colgate U., 1954, U. Cal. at Los Angeles, 1964; Litt.D., U. Western Ont., 1951, Ohio U., 1962; m. Elizabeth Soulen, Aug. 30, 1917; children—Helen Jameson, Philip Kirk. Instr. grad. sch. bus. adminstrn., Harvard, 1919- 21, asst. dean, 1920-27, asst. prof. marketing, 1921-26, asso. prof., 1926-27, asso. dean, 1942, dean, 1942-55; exec. v.p. Royal Baking Powder Co., 1927-29, pres., 1929-30; v.p. Standard Brands, Inc., 1929-30, Gt. Island Corp., 1930-41; pres. American Maize Products Co., 1932- 41; vice chmn. bd. The Ford Found., 1955-66; dir. R. H. Macy & Co., Pan Am. World Airways, Inc., Alean Aluminium, Ltd., Gt. Atlantic & Pacific Tea Co. Mem. Bus. Council; chmn. bd. Com. Econ. Devel., 1957-62. Bd. trustees Rockefeller U., N.Y.C. Served with USN, World War I. Decorated Order of Orange-Nassau. Mem. Phi Beta Kappa, Phi Delta Theta. Republican. Conglist. Order of St. Olaf. Clubs: University, Links (N.Y.C.); Mill Reef; Wianno. Author: Retail Store Management Problems, 1922; Problems in Retailing (with Malcolm P. McNair), 1926. Home: Osterville MA 02655 also 200 E 66th St New York City NY 10021

DAVID, EDWARD EMIL, Jr., govt. ofcl.; b. Wilmington, N.C., Jan. 25, 1925; s. Edward Emil and Beatrice (Liebman) D.; B.S., Ga. Inst. Tech., 1945; M.S., Mass. Inst. Tech., 1947, Sc.D., 1950; D.Engring. (hon.), Stevens Inst. Tech., 1971, Poly. Inst. Bklyn., 1971; m. Ann Hirshberg, Dec. 23, 1950; 1 dau., Nancy. Exec. dir. research Bell Telephone Labs., Murray Hill, N.J., 1950-70; sci. adviser to Pres. Nixon, dir. Office Sci. and Tech., Washington, 1970. prof. elec. engring. Stevens Inst. Tech. Dir. Summit (N.J.) Speech Sch., 1967-70. Served with USNR, 1943-46. Recipient George W. McCarty award Ga. Inst. Tech., 1958, award Summit Jr. C. of C., 1959. Fellow I.E.E.E., Acoustical Soc. Am., Am. Acad. Arts and Scis., A.A.A.S., Audio Engring. Soc.; mem. Nat. Acad. Sci., Assn. Computing Machinery, Engring. Soc. Detroit, Nat. Acad. Engring. Author: (with Dr. J.R. Pierce) Man's World of Sound, 1958; (with Dr. J.R. Pierce and W.A. van Bergeikj) Waves and the Ear, 1960; (with Dr. J.G. Truxal) Man-Made World, 1969. Contbr. articles profl. jours. Patentee in field. Office: Executive Office Bldg Washington DC 20506

DAVID, HAL, lyricist with Burt Bacharach. Songs include: Walk On By, Trains and Boats and Planes, Anyone Who Had a Heart, What the World Needs Now is Love, What's New Pussycat, Alfie, Raindrops Keep Fallin' on My Head, (Acad. award); Broadway show Promises, Promises. Address: Elm Dr East Hills Roslyn NY 11576

DAVID, HENRY, social scientist adminstr., b. N.Y.C., Dec. 5, 1907; s. George and Esther (Silver) D.; B.A., Coll. City of N.Y., 1929; M.A., Columbia, 1930, Ph.D., 1936; M.A., Cambridge, 1969; m. Bryna Ball, Nov. 20, 1959; 1 son (by previous marriage), Paul Allan. Instr. hist. dept. Coll. City of N.Y., 1930-38; lectr. New Sch. for Social Research, 1936-37; prof. hist dept. Queens Coll., 1938-54; prof. grad. sch. bus. Columbia U., 1954-59; dean grad. faculty polit. and social sci. New Sch. for Social Research, prof. econs., dean of grad. faculty, 1959-61, pres. sch., 1961- 63; dir. research BBC, 1942-45, adviser on Am. affairs, 1945-47; cons. Rand Corp., 1948-55, 63-64; exec. dir. Nat. Manpower Council, 1951- 61, mem., 1961-66; head, officer sci. resources planning, NSF, 1964-66; exec. sec. div. behavioral scis. Nat. Acad. Scis.-NRC, 1966—; Pitt prof. U. Cambridge, Eng.; cons. editor labor Random House. Benjamin Franklin fellow Royal Soc. of Arts; mem. Am. Hist. Assn., Soc. Am. Historians, Indls. Relations Research Assn., Acad. Polit. Sci., A.A.A.S., Phi Beta Kappa. Author: History of the Haymarket Affair, 1936, 58; Manpower Policies for a Democratic Society, 1963; (with others) History of Western Civilization, 1935; Labor Problems in America, 1940; House of Labor, 1951; America in Crisis, 1952; 11 publs. Nat. Manpower Council, 1952-65; Common Frontiers of the Social Sciences, 1957; Public Education in America, 1958, contbr. articles and reviews to periodicals. Co-editor: The Economic History of the United States Series, 1945-. Contbg. editor Labor and Nation, 1946- 52. Home: 2206 Wyoming Av NW Washington, DC 20008. Office: 2101 Constitution Av NW Washington, DC 20418.

DAVID, MICHAEL D., corp. exec.; b. Cleve., 1916; B.A., Ohio State U., 1942; LL.B., Stanford, 1947. Vice pres. Cerro Corp.; v.p., dir. Cerro de Pasco Corp., Cerro Fund, Inc.; pres., dir. Cerro Mining Co. Can. Ltd.; v.p., sec., dir. Compania Industrial del Centro, S.A.; dir. Cerro de Pasco Petroleum Corp., Cerro Exploration Co., Inc., Big Mike Corp., Cerro Gas & Oil Corp. Home: 327 Pleasant St Haworth NJ 07641 Office: 300 Park Av New York City NY 10022

DAVID, PAUL THEODORE, educator, polit. scientist; b. Brockton, Mass., Aug. 12, 1906; s. Ira E. and Bernice Grace (Harrison) D.; student Ga. Sch. Tech., 1924-26; A.B., Antioch Coll., 1928; A.M., Brown U., 1930, Ph.D., 1933; m. Opal Mary Davis, May 31, 1935. Instr. econs. Brown U., 1930-31; research fellow Brookings Inst., 1931-32; adminstrv. asst., economist T.V.A., 1933-36; staff mem. Pres. com. Adminstrv. Management, 1936; sec., asst. dir. U.S. Adv. Com. on Edn., 1936-39; asso. dir., chief economist Am. youth commn. Am. Council on Edn., 1939-42; mem. econ. staff, fiscal div. Bur. Budget, Washington, 1942-46; alternate U.S. rep. council Internat. Civil Aviation Orgn., Montreal, 1946-50, sr. staff mem. Brookings Instn., 1950-60; prof. govt. and fgn. affairs U. Va., 1960—; fellowship Center for Advanced Study in Behavioral Sciences, Stanford, Cal., 1959-60; vis. lectr. Salzburg Seminar in Am. Studies, summer 1963. Cons. commn. rules Democratic Nat. Com, 1969—. Recipient Ford Found. faculty award, 1968-69. Mem. Am. Econ. Assn., Am. Polit. Sci. Assn., Am. Soc. Pub. Adminstrn., Nat. Planning Assn., Phi Beta Kappa. Clubs: Nat. Capital Democratic, Nat. Press, Cosmos (Washington); Colonnade (Charlottesville Va.). Author: Economics of Air Mail Transportation, 1934; The Politics of National Party Conventions (with R. M. Goldman and R. C. Bain), 1960; (with Ralph Eisenberg) Devaluation of the Urban and Suburban Vote, Vols. I and II, 1962. Sr. author Vol. I of Presidential Nominating Politics in 1952, sr. editor other 4 vols., 1954. Home: Route 5 Box 335-B Charlottesville, VA 22901.

DAVID, ROBERT THOMAS, mfg. co. exec.; b. Logansport, Ind., June 18, 1938; s. Robert R. and Janet (Johnston) D.; B.A., Harvard, 1960, M.B.A., 1965; m. Linda Phillips, June 11, 1960; children—Eric J., Katherine L. With Gen. Signal Corp., N.Y.C., 1965—, v.p., treas., 1969—. Served to lt. USNR., 1960- 63. Clubs: Harvard (N.Y.C.); Stanwich (Greenwich). Home: 19 Stanwich Lane Greenwich CT 06830 Office: 280 Park Av New York City NY 10017

DAVID, VACLAV, Czechoslovak diplomat; b. Studeny, Sept. 23, 1910; ed. Commercial Coll. Worked for CKD, Liben 1929-32; mem. illegal Central Com., Communist Party of Czechoslovakia, 1944-45; mem. Nat. Assembly, 1945-69; minister fgn. affairs Czechoslovak Socialist Republic, 1953-68; ambassador to Bulgaria, 1969—. Mem. Central Com., Communist Party of Czechoslovakia, 1945—; dep. to House People Fed. Assembly, 1969—; dep. chmn. Central Com. Czechoslovak-Soviet Friendship Union, 1969—. Address: Czechoslovak Embassy Sofia Bulgaria

DAVIDOFF, FOSTER, coll. pres.; b. Boston, Sept. 28, 1917; s. Samuel David and Elizabeth (Struhl) D.; A.B., Fresno State Coll., 1953, M.A., 1955; postgrad. student U. So. Cal., 1958, U. Cal. at Los Angeles, 1961. Mem. faculty Compton (Cal.) Coll., 1955-71, dean adminstrn., instrn. and of coll., 1957-62, pres., 1962-68, prof., 1968-71; pres. Crafton Hills Coll., 1971—. Bd. dirs. Southeast Area Welfare Planning Council; mem. adv. council, leadership program U. Cal. Kellogg Found. Served to capt. USAAF, 1940-51. Decorated D.F.C. with 2 clusters, Air medal with 3 clusters; Order Flying Cloud (China). Mem. Cal. Jr. Coll. Assn., Cal. Tchrs. Assn. Contbr. profl. jours. Home: 475 E Cypress Av Redlands CA 92373 Office: Crafton Hills Coll Yucaipa CA 92399

DAVIDON, WILLIAM COOPER, educator; b. Fla., Mar. 18, 1927; s. Jack and Ruth (Simon) D.; student Purdue U., 1943-44; B.S., M.S., Ph.D., U. Chgo.; m. Ann Morrissett; children—Alan (by previous marriage), Ruth and Sarah. Engaged as research dir. of the Nuclear Chgo. Co., 1948-54; research asso. Fermi Inst., U. Chgo., 1954-56; asso. physicist Argonne Nat. Lab., 1956- 61; asso. prof. physics, Haverford Coll., 1961-69, prof. physics, 1969- -, chmn. physics dept., 1969-70; vis. asso. prof. U. Wash., 1958; Fulbright research scholar, 1966-67. Participant 3d, 10th 17th Pugwash Confs. Scientists, 1958, 62, 67. Mem. Nat. Steering Com. of Resist; mem. nat. bd. Citizens's Orgn. for Sane World, 1968-. Named One of Ten Outstanding Young Men of Chgo., Chgo. Jr. C. of C., 1960. Mem. Soc. for Social Responsibility in Sci. (pres. 1965-67), Fedn. Am. Scientists (vice chmn. 1960-61), Am. Assn. Physics Tchrs. Home: 7 College Lane Haverford, PA 19041.

DAVIDOVSKY, MARIO, composer; b. Medanos, Buenos Aires, Argentina, Mar. 4, 1934; s. Natalio and Perla (Bulanska) D.; m. Elaine Balustein, Oct. 19, 1961; children—Matias Gabriel, Adriana. Came to U.S., 1960. Asso. dir. Electronic Music Center, Princeton and Columbia univs., 1964—. Vis. lectr. Sch. Music, U. Mich., 1964; guest prof. Inst. di Tella, Buenos Aires, 1965; recordings on Columbia, Sonnova, C.I.R. Records. Guggenheim fellow, 1961-62, 62-63; Rockefeller fellow, 1965; recipient award Koussevitzky Found., 1964, Library of Congress, 1964, Nat. Inst. Arts and Letters, 1965, Am. Acad. Arts and Letters, 1965; creative arts award Brandeis U., 1965; Aaron Copland award, Tanglewood, 1966; Pulitzer prize in music, 1971. Composer chamber music, orchestral works, also works for electronic music. Home: 490 West End Av New York City NY 10024

DAVIDOW, LEONARD S., publisher; b. N.Y.C., May 30, 1900; s. Morris J. and Lillian (Stone) D.; extension courses City Coll. of N.Y., Columbia, Wharton Sch. U. Pa.; m. Claire Sondheim, Nov. 12, 1931; children—Ann H. (Mrs. Leo A. Goodman), William H. Chmn., Consol. Book Pubs., John A. Dickson Pub. Co., A.J. Cox Co., N.Am. Ednl. Guild, Ltd., Libros Basicos, S.A., Bibl. Press; pres. Family Weekly Mag., Inc.; v.p. Processing & Books, Inc., Republic Capitol Corp. Home: 46 Lakeview Terrace Highland Park IL 60035 Office: 1727 S Indiana Av Chicago IL 60616

DAVIDS, ANTHONY, psychologist; b. Providence, Aug. 28, 1923; s. William J. and Louise (Nahigan) D.; A.B. magna cum laude, Brown U., 1949; A.M., Harvard, 1951, Ph.D., 1954; m. Martha J. St. Germain, Sept. 17, 1949. Research asso., lectr. Harvard, 1953-55; mem. faculty Brown U., Providence, 1955—, prof. psychology, 1964—; chief psychologist Emma Pendleton Bradley Hosp., Riverside, R.I., 1955-64, dir. psychology, 1965—. USPHS spl. research fellow Inst. Personality Assessment and Research, U. Cal. at Berkeley, 1963-64. Fellow Am. Psychol. Assn., A.A.A.S., Am. Orthopsychiat. Assn., Soc. for Projective Techniques; mem. Soc. for Research in Child Devel., Psychonomic Soc., Phi Beta Kappa, Sigma Xi. Adv. editor Jour. Cons. and Clin. Psychology, 1964- -, Contemporary Psychology, 1968-. Research and publs. on personality assessment of normal and abnormal children and adults, intellectual and personality factors related to acad. achievement, psychol. factors in pregnancy, childbirth and early mother-child relations, cognitive functioning in emotionally disturbed children in residential treatment and normal children in pub. schs. Home: 218 Burgess Av East Providence RI 02914 Office: Psychology Dept Brown U Providence RI 02912

DAVIDS, LEWIS EDMUND, educator, economist, author; b. N.Y.C., Apr. 21, 1917; s. William T. and Janet (Reid) D.; B.S., N.Y.U., 1941, M.B.A., 1942, Ph.D., 1949; student Wake Forest Coll., 1943, U. Paris (France), 1945; postdoctoral student Southwestern Grad. Sch. Banking, So. Methodist U., 1958, Grad. Sch. Banking, U. of Wis., 1966; m. Anna Ruth Dornbush, May 29, 1941; childrenJanet Ruth (Mrs. Ralph Shaw), Judith Ann, Lewis Edmund. Clk., Chase Nat. Bank, N.Y.C., 1935-39; accountant Williamsburgh Savs. Bank, N.Y.C., 1939-47; research asso. Inst. Internat. Finance, N.Y.C., 1947-48; economist Bankers Trust Co., N.Y.C., 1948; asst. prof. finance Drake U., 1949-51; prof. bus. adminstrn. Tex. A. and M. U., 1951-59; prof. econs. and finance U. Ga., 1959-61; Hill prof. bank mgmt. U. Mo. at Columbia, 1961-; vis. prof. case method Harvard, 1963; prof. finance and control, Santiago, Chile, 1959; faculty fellow Sch. of Mortgage Banking Northwestern U., 1967; vis. prof. Southwestern Grad. Sch. Banking So. Meth. U., Sch. Banking South-Louisiana State U., 1967-; faculty mem., counselor Assemblies for Bank Dirs. of So. Meth. U. Chmn. bd. Director Publications, Inc., 1968—. Chief econ. analyst Ia. dist. of the Econ. Stabilization Agy., OPS, 1951; cons. Mo. Bankers Assn., 1961-; economist Nat. Com. Monetary Policy, 1956-. Counselor Assemblies For Bank Dirs., 1968—. Served with USAAF, 1943-45. Recipient certificate Council Internat. Progress Mgmt., 1960, Inst. Chileno de Adminstrn. Racional de Empresas, 1959. Mem. Am. (chmn. So. dist. 1960), So. (pres. 1961) finance assns., Mo. Bankers Assn. (chairholder banking 1961—), Midwest Case Research Assn. (pres. 1964-66), Am., Midwest, So. econ. assns., Midwest Bus. Adminstrn. Assn. (dir.), Lakeshore Estates Assn. (pres. 1966-67), Alpha Kappa Psi. Author: Problems of Small Business Financing, 1958; Dictionary of Insurance, 3d edit., 1970; Small Business Founders, 1963; Money and Banking Casebook, 1965; Money and Banking, 1969, 3d edit., 1970; Banking in Mid-America 1969; Instant Business Dictionary, 1970. Columnist Mid-Continent Banker, Midwestern Banker, 1961-. Editor: The Bank Board. Home: 2401 Topaz Dr Columbia, MO 65201.

DAVIDS, MARK, investment banker; b. Los Angeles, Apr. 4, 1896; s. Mark A. and Elizabeth (Pickering) D.; A.B., Stanford, 1917; m. Helen L. Mosher, Sept. 15, 1923 (dec. 1946); children—Mark M., Suzanne; m. 2d, Ann Robinson, Oct. 29, 1949. Pacific coast dist. mgr. Reading Iron Co., 1923-25; sales mgr. Banks Huntley & Co., Los Angeles, 1925-30; Chgo. resident partner B.B. Robinson & Co., 1930-39; exec. v.p. Lester & Co., investment bankers, Los Angeles, 1940-51; gen. partner successor co. Lester, Ryons & Co., 1951-59; ltd. partner Hornblower, Weeks, Hemphill Noyes, 1959—. Trustee Boys Republic, 1959—. Served as 1st lt. U.S. Army, World War I; AEF in France. Mem. Investment Bankers Assn. (gov. 1959-61, v.p. 1964). Mason. Clubs: Bond (pres. 1959), California (Los Angeles); El Dorado Country. Home: 424 S Windsor Blvd Los Angeles CA 90005 Office: 623 S Hope St Los Angeles CA 90017

DAVIDSOHN, ISRAEL, physician; b. Tarnopol, Poland, Apr. 20, 1895; s. Jacob and Rachel (Halpern) D.; M.D., U. Vienna, 1921; postgrad. U. Berlin, 1921-23; D.Sc., Chgo. Med. Sch., 1964; m. Clara Freud, Oct. 10, 1923; children—Ellen Doris, Samuel James. Came to U.S., 1923, naturalized, 1930. Pathologist, dir. labs. Mt. Sinai Hosp. Phila., 1925-30; dir. dept. pathology Mt. Sinai Hosp., Chgo., 1930-65, dir. dept. exptl. pathology, 1965—; prof. dept. pathology Chgo. Med. Sch., 1947—. Cons., Armed Forces Inst. of Pathology, Washington. Pres. Am. Bd. of Pathology, 1964-65. Recipient Morris H. Parker award Chgo. Med. Sch., 1956; John Elliott award Am. Assn. Blood Banks, 1958; joint award for distinguished services to socs. and to Am. pathology Am. Soc. Clin. Pathologists and Coll. Am. Pathologists, 1966. Mem. A.M.A., Chgo. Inst. Medicine, Am. Soc. Clin. Pathologists (pres. 1951-52, Ward Burdick award 1954), Ill. (pres. 1951). Am. (pres. 1952-53) assns. blood banks, Coll. Am. Pathologists (gov. 1956-58), Chgo. Pathol. Soc. (hon. mem.). Jewish religion. Author and co-author med. books. Asso. editor Am. Jour. of Clin. Pathology. Home: 3100 N Sheridan Rd Chicago IL 60657 Office: 2755 W 15th St Chicago IL 60608

DAVIDSON, ALFRED E., lawyer; b. New York, N.Y., Nov. 11, 1911; s. Maurice Philip and Blanche (Reinheimer) D.; B.A., Harvard, 1933; LL.B., Columbia, 1936; m. Claire Dreyfuss, June 28, 1934; children—Thomas, Kenneth. Admitted to N.Y. bar. 1936; asst. to gen. counsel, wage and hour div., U.S. Dept. Labor, Washington, 1938-40, with review section, office of solicitor, 1940-41; legislative counsel Office of Emergency Mgmt. in Exec. Office of Pres., 1941-43; asst. gen. counsel Lend-Lease Adminstrn., which later, with other agencies became Fgn. Economic Adminstrn., 1943-45, gen. counsel since Jan., 1945; general counsel U.N.R.R.A., Nov., 1945;. counsel Prep. Commn. for Internat. Refugee Orgn., 1947; dir. European hdqrs. UNICEF, 1947-51; advisor Office of Sec. Gen. U.N., 1951-52; gen. counsel UN Korean Reconstrn. Agy., 1952-54; exec. asst. to chmn. bd. Rio Tinto of Can., 1955-58; v.p., gen. counsel Tech. Studies, 1957—; gen. counsel, dir. Constrn. Capital Co. Dir., Channel Tunnel Study Group; lectr. internat. relations Am. Coll. in Paris, 1965-67. Chmn. Democratic Party Com. of France; chmn. Bi-Partisan Com. on Absentee Voting. Mem. Am., Internat. polit. sci. assns., Acad. Polit and Social Sci., Assn. Bar of City of New York, Council Fgn. Relations, Am. C. of C. in Paris, American Acad. Polit. and Social Sci. Clubs: Harvard, Standard Athletic, American Paris. Home: 4 Rue Octave Feuillet Paris 16 France Office: 12 Rue de la Paix Paris 2 France ☆

DAVIDSON, ARTHUR OLE, coll. pres.; b. Hancock, Minn., Sept. 27, 1910 s. Andrew and Rosella (Flom) D.; A.B., Luther Coll., Decorah, Ia., 1931; M.A., U. Minn., 1938; Ed.D., Harvard 1952; LL.D., Hartwick College, 1965; m. H. Corinne Hellie, Dec. 29, 1948: children—Karen Flom, Daphne Loe. Elementary, jr. and high sch. prin., Ia., 1931-38; high sch., prin.- supt. schs., Sleepy Eye, Minn., 1938-40; supt. schs., Springfield, Minn., 1940-41; chmn. edn. dept. Luther Coll., 1941-48, v.p., 1954-61; chmn. dept. edn. Dartmouth, 1948-54; lectr. Grad. Sch. U. Minn., summers 1951-56; pres. Wagner Coll., S.I., 1961—. Dir. Empire State Found. of Ind. Liberal Arts Coll., Inc., Dir., New Brighton Savs. & Loan Assn., S.I., Luth. Brotherhood Ins. Co., Mpls.; mem. S.I. adv. com. Chase Manhattan Bank. Active Luth. Laymens Movement. Served to comdr. USNR, 1942-46; PTO. Mem. Am. Assn. U. Profs., Am. Assn. Sch. Adminstrs., Am.-Scandinavian Found., Nordmanns Forbundet, S.I. Hist. Soc., Norwegian-Am. Hist. Assn., Navy League, Kappa Phi Kappa, Omicron Delta Kappa, Phi Delta Kappa, Phi Mu Alpha, Sinfonia. Lutheran. Rotarian. Clubs: Minneapolis; Richmond Country (S.I.); Harvard, Liederkranz (N.Y.C.). Home: 41 Sunrise Terrace Staten Island NY 10304

DAVIDSON, BASIL, writer; b. Bristol, Eng., Nov. 9, 1914; s. Thomas and Jessie (Craig) D.; m. Marion Ruth Young, July 7, 1943; children—Nicholas, Keir, James. Mem. editorial staff The Economist, London, Eng., 1938-39, The Times, London, 1945-49; vis. prof. U. Cal. at Los Angeles, 1965, 71. Served to lt. col. Brit. Army, 1940-45. Decorated Mil. Cross; Bronze Star medal (U.S.); named hon. citizen Genoa, Italy, 1945; recipient Haile Selassie prize for African research, 1970. Author: (novels) Highway Forty, 1949; Golden Horn, 1952; The Rapids, 1955; Ode to a Young Love, 1959; The Andrassy Affair, 1966; (non- fiction) Partisan Picture, Yugoslavia, 1943-44, 1946; Germany, What Now?; From Potsdam to Partition, 1950; Report on Southern Africa, 1952; (with A. Ademola) The New West Africa, 1953; Daybreak in China, 1953; The African Awakening, 1955; Turkestan Alive, New Travels in Chinese Central Asia, 1957; The Lost Cities of Africa (Anisfield-Wolf award 1960), 1959; Black Mother, 1961; The African Past, 1964; Which Way Africa?, 1964; History of West Africa to 19th Century, 1966; History of East Africa to 19th Century, 1967; Africa in History: Themes and Outlines, 1969; The Liberation of Guinea, 1969; The African Genius 1970; Discovering Our African Heritage, 1971. Contbr. numerous jours. Address: care Barclays Bank Ltd 19 Fleet St London EC 4 England

DAVIDSON, BRUCE, journalist. Business editor Boston Globe. Office: 135 Morrissey Blvd Boston MA 02107*

DAVIDSON, BRUCE MERRILL, educator; b. Ironwood, Mich., Mar. 16, 1924; s. Harold Osborn and Alma (Knoepp) D.; B.S. in Civil Engring., U. Mich., 1949; M.S., U. Wis., 1951, Ph.D., 1956; m. Mary Catherine Wank, Jan. 29, 1949; children—Mark C., Diane M., Mary Ann. Adminstrv. asst. geog. sect. Allied Translation and Interpretation Sect., Tokyo, Japan, 1946-47; teaching asst. U. Mich., 1947-49; mem. faculty U. Wis., 1949-51, 53-55, 56-66, asso. dean Coll. Engring., 1962-66, prof. civil engring., 1964- 66; traffic engr. Wis. Hwy. Commn., 1955-56, chmn. dept. civil engring. Wash. State U., Pullman, 1966-71; acad. dean U.S. Naval Acad., Annapolis, Md., 1971—. Mem. joint com. edn. Am. Soc. Engring. Edn.-Am. Gen. Contractors; NSF teaching cons. Roorkee (India) U., 1969. Mem. Madison Traffic Commn., 1960-64; U. Wis. chmn. Madison United Givers, 1964—. Alderman, Madison, 1956-64; del. Wis. Republican Conv., 1956—. Bd. dirs. Madison Library, 1956-64, pres., 1960. Served with AUS, 1943- 46, 51-53. Mem. Am. Soc. C.E., Am. Soc. Engring. Edn., Am. Ry. Engring. Assn., Triangle, Sigma Xi, Tau Beta Pi, Chi Epsilon, Psi Kappa Phi. Presbyn. Rotarian. Research and publs. in field. Home: 1602 Wheatland Dr Pullman WA 99163

DAVIDSON, BRYANT, ret educator; b. Conway, Ark., Nov. 30, 1903; s. George Granville and Zora Mae (Bryant) D.; A.B., Hendrix Coll., 1925, LL.D., 1960; M.A., Columbia U., 1928, postgrad., 1932-33; m. Elizabeth Reynolds, June 8, 1929. Tchr. pub. schs., Ark., 1926, instr. Centenary Coll., Shreveport, La., 1928, asso. prof., 1932, prof., head dept. history 1936-70, chmn. social sci. div., 1946, prof. emeritus, 1970—; Carnegie grant for spl. study philosophy of Communism, 1948; lectr. and radio commentator; chmn. Radio Forum series; adviser to bd. dirs. Pioneer Bank & Trust Co., Shreveport. Recipient Alumni Outstanding Tchr. award, 1969. Mem. La. State Adv. Council. Mem. Am. Assn. U. Profs., Pi Kappa Delta, Kappa Alpha, Omicron Delta Kappa. Methodist (mem. bd. world peace). Kiwanian. Home: 4016 Independence St Shreveport LA 71109

DAVIDSON, CHALMERS GASTON, historian; b. Chester, S.C., June 6, 1907; s. Zeb V. and Kate (Gaston) D.; A.B., Davidson Coll., 1928; A.M., Harvard, 1930, Ph.D., 1942; A.M., U. Chgo., 1936; m. Alice G. Gage, Mar. 20, 1937; children—Robert Gage, Alice Graham, Mary Gage. Instr. Chamberlain Hunt Mil. Acad., Point Gibson, Miss., 1928-29, Blue Ridge Sch. for Boys, Hendersonville, N.C., 1933-34, The Citadel, Charleston, S.C., 1934-35; prof. history, dir. library Davidson Coll., 1936—. Reynolda House lectr. (N.C.), 1967-68. Chmn. parent's adv. council Converse Coll., 1968-69. Mem. Carolina Charter Tercentenary Comm., 1963—; trustee Hezekiah Alexander Found., 1969—. Served as armed guard comdr. Pacific area USNR, 1944-46. Recipient Charles A. Cannon award for contbn. to N.C. history, 1951, U.D.C. Mil. Cross, 1970. Mem. N.C. Lit. and Hist. Assn. (pres. 1961-62), Hist. Soc. N.C. (pres. 1966-67), Meckleburg Hist. Assn. (pres. 1956-57), N.C. Writers Conf. (chmn. 1960-61), Soc. Cincinnati, Phi Beta Kappa, Omicron Delta Kappa, Sigma Upsilon, Beta Theta Pi (dist. chief 1952- 57). Presbyn. Club: Charlotte Country, Blowing Rock Country. Author: Rural Hill, 1943; Cloud over Catawba, 1949; Friend of the People, 1950; Mecklenburg Declaration of Independence Verse (editor), 1951; Piedmont Partisan, 1951, rev. edit., 1968; Mid-Point for '28, 1953; Gaston of Chester, 1956; Plantation World Around Davidson, 1969. Contbr. hist. jours., Dictionary of Am. Biography. Ency. Americana. Home: Hurricane Hill Davidson NC 28036

DAVIDSON, CHARLES EDWARD, educator; b. Walton, N.Y., Mar. 21, 1922; s. Frank Clyde and Edith (Sloan) D.; A.B., Princeton, 1946; M.A., Yale, 1949, Ph.D., 1953; m. Eleanor McMichael, Sept. 10, 1954; childrenEllen Jean, Kristin Joan, Anne Carol. Mem. faculty Coll. William and Mary, 1949-, prof. English, 1964- ; cons. Combat Operations Research Group, Tech. Operations, Inc., Ft. Monroe, Va., 1961-62. Served with AUS, 1943-45; ETO Mem. Modern Lang. Assn., Mediaeval Acad. Am. Democrat. Presbyn. Home: 215 Kingswood Dr Williamsburg, VA 23185.

DAVIDSON, CHARLES SPRECHER, physician; b. Berkeley, Cal., Dec. 7, 1910; s. Charles Sprecher and Mary (Blossom) D.; A.B., U. Cal. at Berkeley, 1934; M.D., C.M., McGill U., 1939; M.A. (hon.), Harvard, 1953. Intern, house officer medicine San Francisco Hosp., 1939-41; research fellow medicine Harvard Med. Sch. and asst. resident physician Thorndike Meml. Lab., Boston City Hosp., 1941-42; various appointments, 1942-44; asso. dir. of II and IV Harvard Med. Services, Boston City Hosp. and asso. physician Thorndike Meml. Lab., 1948-63, asso. dir., 1964-70, acting dir., 1970—, vis. physician Boston City Hosp., 1965-70, acting head dept. medicine, 1970—; asso. prof. medicine Harvard med. Sch., 1953-68, prof., medicine Harvard Med. Sch., 1953-68, prof., 1969- -; cons. VA Hosp., Boston, Lemuel Shattuck Hosp., Boston, Cambridge City Hosp.; cons. nutrition program Nat. Center for Chronic Disease Control, 1969—; mem. cholera adv. com. Dept. Health, Edn. and Welfare, USPHS, Bethesda, Md.; mem. com. metabolism, subcom. on liver Office Surgeon Gen., U.S. Army; sci. adv. com. United Health Founds., Inc. Fellow A.C.P.; mem. Am. Gastroenterological Soc., Am. Acad. Arts and Scis., Assn. Am. Physicians. Mem. editorial bd. Contbr. profl. jours. Home: 100 Memorial Dr Cambridge MA 02142 Office: Thorndike Meml Lab Boston City Hosp Boston MA 02118

DAVIDSON, CHARLES WILLIAM, hosp. adminstr.; b. Tuxedo, N.Y., Aug. 12, 1915; s. Charles and Elizabeth (Bentley) D.; B.Accounting, Rider Coll., 1934; m. Mildred H. Woolley, Apr. 9, 1938; children—Carol Ann, Patricia Lee. Bookkeeper, Comml. Credit Corp., Asbury Park, N.J., 1934-35; accountant Greenman MacNicol & Co., N.Y.C., 1935-38; comptroller, asst. dir. Monmouth Meml. Hosp., Long Branch, N.J., 1938-41; supr. dept. record and information United Hosp. Fund N.Y., 1941-46; comptroller St. Luke's Hosp., N.Y.C., 1946-49, asst. dir., 1949-62, exec. dir., 1962—. Bd. dirs. Morningside Heights, Inc.; v.p., Hosp. Credit Exchange, 1970; treas. Hosp. Assn. N.Y. State, 1970; pres. Greater N.Y. Hosp. Assn. 1970-71. C.P.A., N.Y. Fellow Am. Colls. Hosp. Adminstrs. Episcopalian. Home: 32 Laurel Av Tenafly, NJ 70670. Office: St Luke's Hosp Center Amsterdam Av and 114th St New York City, NY 10025.

DAVIDSON, CROW GIRARD, lawyer, former Dem. nat. committeeman; b. Lafayette, La., July 28, 1910; s. James Joseph and Lilla May (Kennedy) D.; A.B., Southwestern La. Inst., 1930; LL.B., Tulane U., 1933; Sterling fellow, Yale, 1933-34, J.S.D., 1936; m. Mercedes Hester, Ja. 21, 1939 (div. Jan. 1952); children—Michael Cobb, Joan Hester; m. 2d, Joan F. Kaplan, Dec. 20, 1953 (div. Mar. 1967); children—John Matthew, Girard, Alice Elizabeth, Peter, Sylvia; m. 3d, Sylvia Nemer, Oct. 4, 1967. Admitted to La. bar, 1933; cons. atty. Bonneville Power Adminstrn., Portland, Ore., 1940-42, gen. counsel, 1943-46; cons. OPM, Washington, 1941-42; asst. gen counsel WPB, 1944-45; asst. sec. of the interior, 1946-50; now mem. law firm Davidson, Sharkey & Cummings. Pres. Alaska Pacific Lumber Co.; cons. city N.Y., 1967-68. Alternate del. from Ore., Democratic Nat. Conv., 1952; nat. Dem. elector, 1952; mem. Dem. Nat. Com. from Ore., 1956-63; chmn. nat. Dem. Com. on Natural Resources; chmn. Western States Dem. Conf., 1960-63. Mem. Am., La., Ore., Alaska bar assns., Order of Coif, Beta Theta Pi, Phi Alpha Delta, Omicron Delta Kappa. Democrat. Methodist. Club: Portland City. Contbr. legal, other periodicals. Home: 1054 SW Douglas Pl Portland OR 97205 Office: Commonwealth Bldg Portland OR 97204 also Commerce Bldg 1700 K St NW Washington DC 20006 also Nat Bank of Alaska Bldg Juneau AK 99801 ☆

DAVIDSON, DANIEL I., lawyer; b. Bklyn., Sept. 19, 1936; s. Mitchell and Minnie (Needleman) D.; A.B., Columbia Coll., 1957; LL.B., Columbia, 1959; m. Susan Bettina Juliet Thomas, Mar. 13, 1966. Asso. firm Cravath, Swaine & Moore, N.Y.C., 1961-65; spl. asst. to asst. sec. state East Asia and Pacific Affairs, 1965-67; spl. asst. to ambassador U.S. Dept. State, 1967-68; U.S. del. to Paris Peace Talks on Vietnam, 1968-69; mem. staff Nat. Security Council, Washington, 1969; asso. firm Wilmer, Cutler & Pickering, Washington, 1969—. Mem. Phi Beta Kappa. Jewish religion. Home: 2900 Brandywine St NW Washington DC 20008 Office: 900 17th St NW Washington DC 20006

DAVIDSON, DAVRE JACOB, corp. exec.; b. Portland, Ore., July 6, 1911; s. Abraham and Celia (Levy) D.; student Long Beach (Cal.) Jr. Coll., 1930; L.H.D., Lincoln (Ill.) Coll., 1967; m. Charlotte Sheffer, May 28, 1939; children—Harold Alan, Celia Ann (Mrs. Robert Farkas). Propr., Davidson Co., Los Angeles, 1936-39, partner, 1939-46, pres., 1946-59; pres. ARA Services, Inc. (formerly Automatic Retailers of Am., Inc.), Los Angeles, 1959-64, chmn. bd., chief exec. officer, 1959—; dir. The TI Corp. (of Cal.). Cons. prof. bus. adminstrn. U. So. Cal. Vice pres. Crescent Bay area council Boy Scouts Am., 1964—. Bd. councilors Grad. Sch. Bus., U. So. Cal., 1966—; bd. fellows Claremont (Cal.) U. Center; bd. dirs. Found. Jr. Blind, 1961—, pres., 1970; bd. dirs. Vista Del Mar Child Care, 1963—; pres. Automatic Retailers Am. Ednl. Found., 1961—. Recipient Horatio Alger award Am. Assn. Sch. and Colls., 1967. Mem. Alpha Kappa Psi, Beta Gamma Sigma (hon.). Home: 1007 N Hillcrest Rd Beverly Hills CA 90210 Office: 10889 Wilshire Blvd Los Angeles CA 90024

DAVIDSON, DONALD CURTIS, librarian, historian; b. Vancouver, B.C., Can., Dec. 11, 1911; s. James Grant and Alice M. (Curtis) D.; came to U.S., 1933, naturalized, 1941; B.A., U. B.C., 1933; M.A., U. Cal. at Berkeley, 1934, Ph.D., 1937, library certificate, 1941; m. June Aileene Reynolds, Aug. 15, 1936; children—Gale E. (Mrs. Ronald E. Busch), Jean G. Research asso. Carnegie Endowment for Internat. Peace, 1934-35; reader, teaching asst., head teaching asst. history U. Cal. at Berkeley, 1934-37; ednl. adviser Huntington Library, San Marino, Cal., 1937-41; librarian, asst. prof. history U. Redlands (Cal.), 1941-43, asso. prof., 1943-46, prof. 1946-47; univ. librarian, lectr. history U. Cal. at Santa Barbara, 1947—, acting dean applied arts, 1956-57, acting dean letters, scis. 1957-59. Fulbright sr. vis. research fellow U. Sheffield (Eng.), 1966-67; library cons. Cal. Acad. Sci., San Francisco, U. Alaska, U.S. Navy Postgrad. Sch., Monterey, Boise (Ida.) State Coll., Fund for Advancement Edn. Served with AUS, 1943-46; PTO. Decorated Bronze Star medal. Mem. Santa Barbara Hist. Soc. (bd. dirs. 1949-56), Am. (councillor-at-large, chmn. coll., library bldg. sects., coms.), Cal. (councillor-at- large, pres. Los Padres dist.) library assns., Am. Assn. U. Profs. Contbr. articles library, hist. jours. Home: 7332 Aviano Av Goleta CA 93107 Office: Library Univ California Santa Barbara CA 93106

DAVIDSON, DONALD HERBERT, educator; b. Springfield, Mass., Mar. 6, 1917 s. Clarence Herbert and Grace (Anthony) D.; B.A., Harvard, 1939, M.A., 1941, Ph.D., 1949; m. Virginia Baldwin, Dec. 31, 1942; 1 dau., Elizabeth Ann. Instr. philosophy Queen's Coll., 1947-50; from asst. prof. to prof. philosophy Stanford, 1951-67; prof. philosophy Princeton, 1967-70, chmn. dept. philosophy, 1968-70, lectr. with rank of prof., 1970—; prof. philosophy Rockefeller U., 1970—; vis. prof. Tokyo (Japan) U., 1955; gave Gavin David Young lectures U. Adelaide, 1968, gave John Locke lectures Oxford U., 1970; vis. prof. U. of Sydney, 1968. Cons. NSF, 1966-68. Served to lt. (s.g.) USNR, 1942-45; MTO. Teschemacher fellow in classics and philosophy, 1939-41; Rockefeller fellowship in humanities, 1945-46; Rockefeller fellowship for research, 1948; Ford Faculty fellowship, 1953-54; Am. Council Learned Socs. fellowship, 1958-59; NSF research grants, 1964-65, 68; fellow Center Advanced Study Behavioral Scis., 1969-70. Mem. Council Philos. Studies, Am. Philos Assn. (sec. Pacific Coast div. 1956-59, v.p. 1961), Am. Assn. U. Profs., Assn. Symbolic Logic. Author: (with Patrick Suppes) Decision Making: An Experimental Approach, 1957; also articles. Co-editor: Words and Objections, 1969; Semantics for Natural Language, 1970; mem. editorial bd. Synthese, 1966—, Cognitive Psychology, 1970—, Philosophia, 1970—. Office: Philosophy Dept Rockefeller U New York City NY 10021

DAVIDSON, EUGENE ARTHUR, editor; b. N.Y.C., Sept. 22, 1902; s. William and Bertha (Passarge) D.; A.B., Yale, 1927, postgrad. 1927-28; m. Louise Keil, Apr. 6, 1928 (div.); children—Eugene Passarge, Lisa; m. 2d, Suzette Morton Zurcher, Nov. 1968. Mem. editorial dept. Yale Univ. Press, 1929-59, editor, 1931-59, a dir., 1938-59, chmn. com. publs.; editor of Modern Age, 1960-70; pres. Found. Fgn. Affairs, Washington, 1957-70. Chmn. Conf. European Problems. Clubs: P.E.N. (N.Y.C.); Arts (Chgo.); Elizabethan (New Haven). Author: The Death and Life of Germany, 1959; The Trial of the Germans, 1967. Contbr. book reviews, articles and poetry to mags. including The Freeman, Am. Mercury, Yale Rev., Sat. Rev. Lit., The Progressive. Address: 1301 N Astor St Chicago IL 60610

DAVIDSON, FLOYD FRANCIS, educator; b. Ferris, Tex., Aug. 23, 1906; s. Burlington James and Minnie (McKee) D.; B.A., Baylor U., 1932, M.A., 1933; Ph.D. (fellow 1939-41), U. Tex., 1941; m. Lorene Taylor, Jan. 29, 1943. Asst. biology Baylor U., 1930-33; prin. Grandview (Tex.) High Sch., 1937-39; instr. biology U. Tex., 1939-41; prof. biology Stephen F. Austin State Coll., Nacogdoches, Tex., 1941-42; mem. faculty Baylor U., 1946—, prof. biology, 1948—, chmn. dept., 1966-. Active local Boy Scouts Am., United Fund; mem. Fort House Museum, 1946—, Cameron Park Residential Area Orgn., 1946—; mem. Kninard House Com., 1946-. Served to capt., Med. Adminstrv. Corps, AUS, 1942-46. Fellow Ulric Dahlgren Meml. Fund, Mt. Desert Island Biol. Sta., summer 1949; grantee NIH, 1954-70. Mem. Tex. Acad. Sci. (past pres.), N. Tex. Biol. Socs. (past pres.), Am. Assn. U. Profs. (past pres. Baylor U. chpt.), Am. Bot. Soc.,

Am. Soc. Plant Physiologists, Tex. Ornithol. Soc. (chmn. nominating com. 1954-56), Am. Inst. Biol. Scis., Am. Physiol. Soc., Baylor Alumni Assn., Sigma Xi (past pres. Baylor U. chpt.), Beta Beta Beta (sponsor, charter mem.), Alpha Epsilon Delta. Mason. Home: 516 Edgewood St Waco TX 76708

DAVIDSON, GARRISON H., ret. army officer, real estate exec.; b. N.Y., Apr. 24, 1904; B.S., U.S. Mil. Acad., 1927; LL.D., U. Akron, 1958, Williams Coll., 1959; L.H.D. Hobart Coll., 1965; m. Verone M. Gruenther, June 21, 1934; children Garrison Holt, Thomas, Alan, Linda Lee, Bonny, Gail. Commd. 2d lt. C.E., 1927, trans. to inf., 1949, advanced to lt. gen.; comdt. Command and Gen. Staff Coll., 1954-56; supt. U.S. Mil. Acad., 1956-60; comdg. gen. 7th Army, West Germany, 1960-62; chmn. U.S. delegation UN Mil. Staff Commn., also comdg. gen. 1st U.S. Army, 1962- 64, ret.; asst. v.p. adminstrn. U. Cal., 1964-66; now resident exec. Embarcadero Center, San Francisco. Decorated D.S.M. with 2 oak leaf clusters, Legion of Merit, Silver Star, Bronze Star medal (U.S.); Legion of Honor, Croix de Guerre (France); comdr. Order Brit. Empire; Mil. Order Merit, Taeguk (Korea); Gt. Star Mil. Merit (Chile); knight comdr. Order Merit (Fed. Republic Germany); others. Mem. Mil. Order World Wars, Pilgrims of U.S. Clubs: N.Y. Athletic, Claremont Country. Home: 5730 Margarido Dr Oakland, CA 94618. Office: 1 Embarcadero Center San Francisco CA 94111

DAVIDSON, GEORGE, painter; b. near Warsaw, Poland, May 10, 1889; s. Benjamin and Fannie D.; student Nat. Acad. Design, 1909-12; fellow Am. Acad. in Rome, 1913-16; m. Elsie M. Regan; 1 son, Alan. Came to U.S., 1897. Teacher of mural painting, Cooper Union, N.Y., 1925-32; tchr. landscape painting Yale Sch. Fine Arts, 1938. Prin. works: mural paintings and ceiling decorations, portraits in pub. bldgs. Pictures in perm. colls. of Neb. Art Assn., Lincoln, Neb., Addison GAllery, Andover Coll. and Mattatuck Hist. Soc., Waterbury, Conn. Served as 1st lt. Am. Red Cross in Italy, World War I. Recipient Elliott Bronze medal N.A.D., 1910; medal of honor, Architectural League of N.Y., 1926. N.A., 1942. Mem. Mural Painters Soc., Archtl. League N.Y. Home: 156 Soundview Av Shelton CT 06484

DAVIDSON, GEORGE FORRESTER, broadcasting corp. exec.; b. Bass River, N.S., Can., Apr. 18, 1909; s. Oliver Wendell and Emma (Sullivan) D.; A.B., U. of B.C., 1928; A.M., Harvard, 1930, Ph.D., 1932; LL.D., U.B.C., 1955, U. Victoria, 1968; D.H.L., Brandeis U., 1961; m. Elizabeth Ruth Henderson, July 9, 1935; childrenRoger Reynolds, Craig Sullivan, Barbara Louise, Supt. Welfare and Neglected Children, Provincial Govt. of B.C., 1934-35; exec. dir. welfare Fedn. and Council of Social Agys., Vancouver, B.C., 1935-39; dir. Social Welfare, Provincial Govt., B.C., 1939-42; exec. dir. Canadian Welfare Council at Ottawa, 1942-44; dep. minister Nat. Welfare, 1944-60; dep. minister Citizenship and Immigration, 1960-63; dir. Bur. of Govt. Orgn., 1963-64; sec. Treasury Bd., 1964-68; pres. Canadian Broadcasting Corp., 1968—. Canadian rep. Social Commn. of UN, 1947-52; mem. Canadian delegation to Econ. and Social Council, 1946-58 (pres. 1958); chmn. social, humanitarian and cultural com., 1953; 2d v.p. Nat. (U.S.) Conf. of Social Work, 1951; pres. Can. Inst. Pub. Adminstrn., 1950-51. Mem. Canadian (pres. 1952-54), Internat. (pres. 1956-60) confs. social work, Internat. Broadcast Inst. Mem. United Ch. of Can. Home: 2900 Carling Ottawa Ontario Canada Office: 1500 Bronson Av Ottawa Ontario Canada

DAVIDSON, GWYNNE WELDON, ins. co. exec., publisher; b. Gracemont, Okla., Apr. 11, 1920; s. Altus W. and Gladys (McAdams) D.; student U. Okla., 1938-40, 49-50; LL.B., Oklahoma City U., 1956; D.D., Defenders Theol. Sem., Rio Piedras, P.R., 1960; m. Evelyn Cole, June 16, 1942; children—David Cole, Jack Weldon, Diane Kay, Kent Alan. Owner-mgr. Davidson Flying Service, Shawnee, Okla., 1946-49; owner automobile dealership, Chickasha and Enid, Okla., 1949-55; pres. and chmn. bd. Nat. Savs. Ins. Co., Ardmore, Okla., 1956- -; owner Royal Crown Cola Co., Ardmore, 1964-65; pres. Land-Davidson Mfg. Corp., Ardmore, 1966—; chmn. bd. Am. Mercury mag., 1960-62; pres. Defenders of the Christian Faith, Inc., 1959-63. Served with AUS and USAAF, 1942-46. Decorated Air medal. Mem. Delta Theta 229 229 Woods Lane Ardmore OK 73401 Office: Nat Savs Bldg Ardmore OK 73401

DAVIDSON, HAROLD PRESCOTT, educator; b. N.Y.C., July 19, 1908; s. Harold Sidney and Christine (Bruce) D.; B.A., Pomona Coll., 1929; M.A., Claremont Coll., 1932; postgrad. U. So. Cal.; m. Rosalie Evelyn Cleek, Aug. 30, 1929; children—Douglass Sidney, Malcolm Bruce. Head music dept. Emerson Jr. High Sch., Pomona, Cal., 1929-36; dir. All-City P.T.A. Chorus, Pomona, 1932-36; master tng. tchr. Claremont Coll., 1931-36; head music dept. Cal. State Poly. Coll., 1936—, also dir. coll. glee clubs, vocal ensembles, bands; adjudicator, guest condr. San Luis Obispo County Choral Festival, 1957. Active fund raising drives Boy Scouts Am., Salvation Army, A.R.C. Mem. of A.S.C.A.P., Coll. Music Soc., also mem. of Phi Delta Kappa, Alpha Gamma Sigma. Republican. Presbyn. Rotarian (past pres. San Luis Obispo). Composer: (choral works for men's glee club) Pardon for Puns, 1950, Collections of Ballads, 3 sets, 1955, arrangement Mussorgsky's Hopak, 1959, Derby Ram, 1955; (coll. songs) Ride High You Mustangs, 1947, All Hail Green and Gold, 1936, Poly Memories, 1960; Love's Delights, 1964; Miserere Meus, Dei (for women's voices), 1965; others. Home: 1706 Conejo Dr San Luis Obispo CA 93401

DAVIDSON, HARVEY JUSTIN, univ. dean; b. Gentryville, Ind., Nov. 15, 1930; s. Harvey Harrison and Dorothy (Eberhardt) D.; B.S. in Indsl. Mgmt., Carnegie-Mellon U., 1952, M.S. in Math. Econs., 1955; C.P.A.; m. Shirlee Jean Ploeger, Sept. 4, 1954; children—Charles Justin, John Clinton, James Christopher, Mary Jennifer. Staff asst. Operations Evaluation Group, U.S. Navy-Mass. Inst. Tech., 1955-56; economist Arabian-Am. Oil. Co., 1956-58; mgmt. cons. Touche Ross & Co., 1957-64;; partner, 1964-69; dean Grad. Sch. Bus. and Pub. Adminstrn., Cornell U., 1969—. Dir. Gen. Magnetics, Ltd. Served to 1st lt., C.E., AUS, 1952-54. Decorated Bronze Star. Mem. Am., Pa. insts. C.P.A.'s Ill. Soc. C.P.A.'s, Mich. Assn. C.P.A.'s Inst. Mgmt. Sci., Am. Statis. Assn. Unitarian. Co-author: Statistical Sampling for Accounting Information, 1961; The Future of Accounting Education, 1961. Home: 208 Kline Rd Ithaca NY 14850

DAVIDSON, HENRY ALEXANDER, physician, author; b. Newark, May 27, 1905; s. Louis L. and May (Tannenbaum) D.; B.S., Columbia, 1925; M.D., Jefferson Med. Coll., 1928; M.S., U. Pa., 1931; m. Adelaide Frances Heyman, Oct. 20, 1936; children—Laurence John, Ellen May. Intern Beth Isreal Hosp., Newark, 1928-29; resident Orthopedic Hosp. and Infirmary Nervous Diseases, Phila., 1929-31; practice medicine, Newark, 1931-41; chief program devel., psychiat. service VA, Washington, 1947-54; clin. dir. Essex County Overbrook Hosp., Cedar Grove, N.J., 1954-57, supt. 1957-69; individual practice psychiatry, East Orange, 1969—. Served to maj. M.C., AUS, 1941-47. Diplomate Am. Bd. Psychiatry and Neurology. Fellow Am. Psychiat. Assn. (parliamentarian); mem. Med. Soc. N.J. Author: Short History of Chess, 1948; Forensic Psychiatry, 1952; Handbook of Parliamentary Procedure, 1955; Guide to Medical Writing, 1957; Opportunities in a Psychiatric Career, 1964. Editor N.J. State Med. Jour., 1941—. Home and office: 270 Prospect St East Orange NJ 07017

DAVIDSON, HUGH MACCULLOUGH, educator; b. Lanett, Ala., Jan. 21, 1918; s. Robert Calvin and Anne Della (Stripling) D.; A.B., U. Chgo., 1938, Ph.D., 1946; m. Loretta Miller, June 15, 1951; 1 dau., Anne Stripling. Instr. French, U. Chgo., 1946-48, asst. prof., 1948-53, asst. dean of Coll., 1949-52, chmn. Coll. French staff, 1951-53; asst. prof. romance langs. Dartmouth, 1953-56, prof. romance langs., 1956-62, chmn. dept., 1957-59; prof. French, Ohio State U., Columbus, 1962—. Fulbright research fellow France, 1959-60; sr. fellow Nat. Found. Arts and Humanities, 1967-68. Served as capt. USAAF, 1942-46. Mem. Modern Lang. Assn., Am. Assn. Tchrs. French, Am. Soc. 18th Century Studies, Assn. internationale des etudes francaises, Phi Beta Kappa. Episcopalian. Gen. editor: The Idea and Practice of General Education, 1950. Author: Audience, Words and Art: Studies in 17th Century French Rhetoric, 1965; also articles on French lit., fgn. lang. teaching. Home: 3838 Chiselhurst Pl Columbus OH 43220

DAVIDSON, IAN DOUGLAS, banker, co. dir.; b. Isle of Man, U.K., Oct. 27, 1901; s. John and Elizabeth (Whyte) D.; grad. King Williams Coll., 1920; m. Eugenia Bermejillo, Aug. 6, 1938; children—Claire (Mrs. Hugh Peppiatt), Monica. With Royal Dutch Shell Group, 1921-61; pres. Mexican Eagle Oil Co., 1935-48, Cia Shell de Venezuela, 1953-57, Canadian Shell Ltd., 1957-61; dir. Cerro Corp., Shell Investments Ltd., Canadian Imperial Bank Commerce, Western Assurance Co., Debhold, Ltd., Anglo Am. Corp. of Can., Schering Corp. Ltd., Mem. bd. govs. U. Toronto; trustee Toronto Gen. Hosp., Ont. Mental Health Found., 1964—. Decorated comdr. Order Brit. Empire, Orden del Libertador (Venezuela): Order St. Mark (Lebanon). Presbyn. Home: 115 River View Dr Toronto 12 Ontario Canada

DAVIDSON, IRWIN DELMORE, former congressman, judge; b. N.Y.C., Jan. 3, 1906; s. Lafay and Tillie (Bechstein) D.; B.S., Washington Sq. Coll., 1927; LL.B., N.Y. U., 1928; m. Berenice Feltenstein, June 4, 1936; children—James Sylvan, Mark Lewis; m. 2d, Marion Doniger, May 31, 1965. Admitted to N.Y. bar, 1929, since practiced in N.Y.C.; counsel N.Y. State Bill Drafting Commn., 1935-36; sec. Senator Wagner, 1938. Mem. N.Y. State Assembly, 1936-49, ranking Dem. mem. judiciary com., 1944-48, sec. legislative investigating com., 1945-46; justice Ct. Spl. Sessions, City of N.Y., 1949-55; mem. 84th Congress from 20th N.Y. Dist.; judge of Ct. of Gen. Sessions N.Y. County, 1957-62; justice Supreme Ct. State of N.Y., 1962—. Dir. Men's League in Aid of Crippled Children; trustee Fedn. for Support Jewish Charities, United Jewish Appeal. Mem. Am., N.Y. State bar assns., Assn. Bar City N.Y. N.Y. County Lawyers Assn. Jewish religion. Author: The Jury is Still Out. Home: 785 Fifth Av New York City NY 10022 Office: 100 Centre St New York City NY 10013

DAVIDSON, J. LYONS, banker. Chmn. bd. Fidelity Nat. Bank, Lynchburg, Va. Office: 901 Main St Lynchburg VA 24505*

DAVIDSON, JAMES FREDERIC, coll. dean; b. Newton, Kan., Oct. 4, 1924; s. Scoville E. and Margaret (Gates) D.; B.A., Yale, 1945, postgrad., 1946-47; postgrad. Nat. Inst. Pub. Affairs, Washington, 1947-48; M.A., George Washington U., 1951; Ph.D., U. Chgo., 1954; postgrad. Center for Study Higher Edn., U. Mich., 1962-63; m. Mary Elizabeth Harnden, July 16, 1949; children—James Harnden, Margaret Foard, Mary Priscilla, John Ellsworth. Com. sec. Far Eastern Commn., Washington, 1948-50; adminstrv. asst. ECA, Washington, 1950-51; staff Pub. Adminstrn. Clearing House, Chgo., 1952-54; faculty U. Tenn., 1954-64, prof. polit. sci., 1962-64, asst. dean Coll. Liberal Arts, 1959-61, asso. dean, 1963-64; dean faculty Concord Coll., Athens, W.Va., 1964-69; dean, prof. polit. sci. Newcomb Coll., Tulane U., New Orleans, 1969—. Served with USNR, 1943-46. Mem. Am. Polit. Sci. Assn., Am. Assn. U. profs., Conf. on Brit. Studies, Am. Conf. Acad. Deans. Unitarian (mem. Commn. on Edn. for Profl. Religious Leadership 1969-71). Contbr. articles profl. jours. Home: 43 Newcomb Pl New Orleans LA 70118

DAVIDSON, JAMES JOSEPH, Jr., lawyer; b. Lafayette, La., June 24, 1904; s. James Joseph and Lilla May (Kennedy) D.; student Southwestern La. Inst., 1919-22; A.B., Tulane U., 1925, J.D., 1927; m. Virginia L. Dunham, Aug. 6, 1930; 1 son, James Joseph III. Admitted to La. bar, 1927; practiced in New Orleans, 1927- 29, Lafayette, 1929—; mem. firm Davidson, Meaux, Onebane & Donohoe, 1952—. Mem. La. Supreme Ct. Bar Examining Com., 1936-50, Dir. 1st Nat. Bank Lafayette. Bd. govs. La. Civil Service League; mem. exec. com. Evangeline Area Council Boy Scouts Am.; mem. La. Commn. on Human Relations Rights and Responsibilities; bd. dirs. Council for a Better Louisiana. Fellow Am. Bar Found., Southwestern Legal Found.; mem. La. Judiciary Commn., La. Civil Service League, Nat. Municipal League (mem. council), Internat. Assn. Ins. Counsel, Am. (mem. house of delegates 1964-68), La. (pres. 1958), Lafayette, 15th Jud. Dist. bar assna., Am. Law Inst., Louisiana Law Institute (vice pres. of council), Am. Counsel Assn., American Judicature Soc., Am. Coll. Trial Lawyers, American College of Probate Counsel, Assn. of Bar City N.Y., Lafayette C. of C. (past pres.), Lafayette Library Assn. (past pres.), Lafayette Community Concert Assn. (past pres.), Order of Coif, Phi Alpha Delta, Phi Kappa Phi. Methodist. Mason. Clubs: Internat. House, Pickwick (New Orleans); Rotary (past pres. Lafayette); Boston (New Orleans). Home: 537 Girard Park Dr Lafayette LA Office: 201 W Main St Lafayette LA

DAVIDSON, JOHN, utilities exec.; b. N.Y.C., Oct. 8, 1916; s. John and Elizabeth (Kelly) D.; B.S., N.Y. U., 1944; m. Charlotte J. Duffy, Apr. 22, 1950; (dec.) children—Jane K., Sara G., Kirsten M.; m. 2d, Inge Riebeth, May 23, 1970. With Consol. Natural Gas Company, Inc., N.Y.C., 1943—, tax dept., 1943, asst. mgr. tax dept., 1953-58, mgr., 1958-61, asst. treas., 1961-63, asst. v.p. adminstrn., 1963-70, sec., 1967-70, v.p. adminstrn., 1970—. Mem. Employees Real Estate Adv. Com. Am. Gas Assn. Home: 6 Bradford Ct Tenafly NJ 07670 Office: 30 Rockefeller Plaza New York City NY 10020

DAVIDSON, JOHN, singer, actor; grad. Denison U.; actor film The One and Only Genuine, Original Family Band; 1967; also TV performer. Address: care Walt Disney Prodns 500 S Buena Vista St Burbank CA 91505*

DAVIDSON, JOHN LEFLER, Jr., lawyer; b. Oak Park, Ill., Nov. 26, 1915; s. John Lefler and Lulu (Walters) D.; student Harvard, 1933-34, 35-37, U. Chgo., 1934-35; B.S.L., Northwestern U., 1938, LL.B., 1940; m. Sara Jane Woodyard, May 14, 1942; children—John Woodyard, Mary Oliver, Fred Woodyard. Reporter Chicago American, 1934-35, Boston American, 1935; free-lance reporter, 1936-40; admitted to Ill. bar, 1940, Mo. bar, 1956, D.C. bar, 1964; atty. C.&N.-W. Ry., 1947, gen. atty., 1948-52; 1st asst. atty. gen. of Ill., 1953-56; gen. counsel Wabash R.R. (merged into Norfolk & Western Ry. Co. 1964), 1956-59, v.p. gen. counsel, 1959-64; v.p. Norfolk & Western Ry. Co., 1964-65; served as gen. counsel to several R.R.'s; counsel to law firm Lewis, Rice, Tucker, Allen & Chubb, St. Louis, Mo., 1964-68; partner Greenfield, Davidson & Mandelstamm, 1969—; lectr. Coll. Law, U. Ill., 1955. Legal counsel to trustees Barnes Hosp. Served to lt. comdr., USNR, 1940-45. Fellow Am. Coll. Trial Lawyers; mem. Bar Assn. St. Louis, Am. (chmn. standing com. pub. utilities sect. 1963-64), Ill., Chgo. bar assns., Mo. Bar Integrated, Soc. Trial Lawyers of Chgo., Soc. Hosp. Attys., Nat. Def. Transp. Association (life), Navy League, St. Louis Merc. Library Assn. (dir., pres. 1970—), Newcomen Soc. N. Am. Republican Episcopalian. Mason (32, Shriner). Clubs: Noonday, Harvard (St. Louis); Nat. Lawyers (Washington); Law (Chgo.): Harvard, (N.Y.C.). Contbr. articles legal publs. Home: 1363 Greentree Lane Glendale MO 63122 Office: 721 Olive St St Louis MO 63101

DAVIDSON, JOSEPH QUENTIN, lawyer; b. Ft. Valley, Ga., Oct. 11, 1905; s. Joseph Elijah and Belle (Aultman) D.; B.A. magna cum laude, U. Ga., 1926; LL.B. summa cum laude, Mercer U., 1929; m. Maude Ray Adams, Sept. 28, 1929; children—Barbara Lynette (Mrs. Lee H. Henkel, Jr.), Joan Elaine (Mrs. George W. Mize), Joseph Quentin. Admitted to Ga. bar, 1929; asso. Slade & Swift, Columbus, Ga., 1929-31; partner Swift, Pease, Davidson & Chapman, and predecessor, 1931—. Dir. United Oil Corp., Columbus, Ga. Bd. edn., Muscogee County, Ga.; mem. bd. publs. Methodist Ch., mem. bd. pensions, bd. hospital and homes South Ga. Conf. Meth. Ch. Past pres. United Givers; bd. dirs. Columbus YMCA, local chpt. A.R.C.; local adv. council Salvation Army; chmn. bd. mgrs. City Hosp.; v.p., trustee South Ga. Meth. Home for Aging, Americus, Ga.; trustee Mercer U., Columbus Coll. Found., Inc. Recipient Algernon Sidney Sullivan bronze medallion and certificate Mercer U., Walter F. George Sch. Law faculty medal. Fellow Am. Coll. Probate Counsel; mem Columbus C. of C. (chmn. edn. com.), Phi Beta Kappa, Phi Kappa Phi, Sigma Upsilon, Phi Alpha Delta, Delta Tau Delta. Methodist (mem. ofcl. bd.). Elk. Clubs: Rotary (past pres.), Columbus Executives, Country (v.p., mem. governing bd.) (Columbus). Home: 1916 Leonard St Columbus 31906 Office: 1043 3d Av Columbus GA 31901

DAVIDSON, JOSEPH LEROY, educator; b. Cambridge, Mass., Mar. 16, 1908; s. Edward A. and Mary (Susser) D.; A.B., Harvard, 1930, M.A., Inst. Fine Arts, N.Y.U., 1936; Ph.D., Yale, 1951; m. Martha Aginsky, Aug. 38, 1932; 1 son, Gergory Edward. Asst. dir., curator Walker Art Center, Mpls., 1939-43; research analyst War Dept., Washington, 1943-45; visual art specialist Dept. of State, Washington, 1945-47; asst. prof. Yale, 1947-55; prof. U. Ga., 1955-56; prof. art history, Claremont Grad. Sch., 1956-61; prof. art history, dir. Art Council, U. Cal. at Los Angeles, 1961—, now also chmn. dept. art. Participant archeol. expdn. India, 1963-64. Fulbright fellow, 1952-53. Author: Lotus Sutra in Chinese Art, 1954. Contbr. articles profl. jours. Home: 140 Acari Dr Los Angeles CA 90049

DAVIDSON, LAWRENCE, opera and concert singer; b. Chgo., Oct. 4, 1917; s. Harry and Victoria (Kavitz) D.; grad. Wilson Jr. Coll., 1937; student Chgo. Conservatory of Music, 1930-43, MacBurney Studios, 1935-43, Am. Theatre Wing, 1946; m. Theresa Zimmerman, July 2, 1939; children—Jonathan Davidson, Stephen Davidson. Made opera debut as Crespel, Tales of Hoffman, Chicago Opera Co., 1942; sang numerous roles as oratorio specialist; appeared on Broadway in Carousel, 1946; with Am. Lyric Theatre, White Plains, N.Y., Central City Festival Colo., New Orleans Opera Co.; with Metropolitan Opera Co., 1947—; debut in Tosca; baritone soloist Temple Isaiah Israel, Chgo., 1941-43, Free Synagogue, N.Y.C., 1946; dir. music Riverdale Temple, 1947—; cantor Congregation Shaaray Tefila, N.Y.C., 1959—. Artist in residence Newark State Coll. Mem. Nat. Assn. Tchrs. Singing, Am. Fed. TV and Radio Artists, Am. Guild Musical Artists (treas. 1959—), Equity, N.Y. Singing Tchrs. Assn. (trustee), Jewish Music Liturgical Soc. (gov.), Met. Opera Assn. (retirement plan com.), Served as cpl. AUS, 1943-45. Home: 35 Berkshire Rd Great Neck NY 11023 Office: 160 W 73d St New York City NY 10023

DAVIDSON, LLOYD JOHNSTON, educator; b. Louisville, Ky., May 26, 1911; s. Harry A. and Virginia (Gaggs) D.; student Harvard, 1928-29; Ph.B., U. Chgo., 1932, M.A., 1934, Ph.D., 1947; m. Ellen Peirce Chubb, Sept. 11, 1937. Instr. English, State Coll. Wash., 1934-35, U. Neb., 1935-36, U. Chgo., 1936-42; asst. prof. English, Johns Hopkins, 1948-51; vis. lectr. U. Wash., 1951-52; chmn. dept. English, Wells Coll., Aurora, N.Y., 1952-55; prof. English, Va. Mil. Inst., 1955—, dean of faculty, 1955-65. Served as capt. with USAAF, 1942-46; hist. officer with the Fourth Air Force, also chief editorial sect. Air Force Hist. Office; maj. USAF Res., 1946-53; brig. gen. Va. Militia, 1955-65. Adv. panel on ROTC to sec. of Air Force; 1960-63. Fellow Am. Council Learned Soc.; mem. Am. Assn. U. Profs., Modern Lang. Assn. Am., Phi Beta Kappa. Episcopalian. Home: 204 Johnstone St Lexington VA 24450

DAVIDSON, LORIMER ARTHUR, ins. co. exec.; b. Granby, Que., Can., Nov. 7, 1902; s. Thomas Ferguson and Gertrude (Short) D.; student Stanstead (Can.) Wesleyan Coll., 1920- 21; m. Gael Valentine, Oct. 15, 1927; 1 son, Thomas Ferguson II. Came to U.S., 1924, naturalized, 1950. Bond salesman Herbert Turrell & Co., N.Y.C., 1924-30; partner Steers & Davidson, 1931-37; bond salesman Frenkel, Kovac & Co., 1937-40, E. R. Jones & Co., Balt., 1946-48; asst. to pres. Govt. Employees Ins. Co., Washington, 1948-50, pres., 1958-64, chmn., 1964-70, chmn. emeritus, chmn. exec. coms., 1970—; chmn. bd. Govt. Employees Life Ins. Co., Govt. Employees Corp., Govt. Employees Finance and Ind. Loan Corp., Govt. Employees Variable Annuity Life Ins. Co., Internat. Ins. Underwriters, Inc., Govt. Employees Financial Corp., Criterion Ins. Co.; dir. Riggs Nat. Bank of Washington. Served from lt. to maj., Royal Canadian Army Arty., 1940-46. Mem. Washington Soc. Security Analysts. Republican. Episcopalian. Home: Grosvenor Park 10401 Grosvenor Pl Rockville MD 20852 Office: Government Employees Insurance Operations Bldg 5260 Western Av Washington DC 20015

DAVIDSON, MARSHALL BOWMAN, editor, author; b. N.Y.C., Apr. 26, 1907; s. Henry F. and Frances Aubrey (Holt) D.; B.S., Princeton, 1928; m. Ruth H. Bradbury, Aug. 20, 1935. Asso. curator Am. wing Met. Mus. Art, N.Y. City, 1935-47, editor publs., 1947-61; mng. editor Horizon Books, 1961-63; editor Horizon mag., 1964-66, sr. editor, 1966—. Author: Life in America, 1951; The American HeritageHistory of Colonial Antiques, 1967; The American Heritage—History of American Antiques, 1784-1860, 1968; The American Heritage—History of Antiques, USA, 1865-1917, 1969; The American Heritage— History of Notable American Houses, 1971; also articles in Am. decorative art jours., others. Adv. editor Am. Heritage mag. Editor: The Original Water-color Paintings of John S. Audubon, 1966. Home: 140 E 83d St New York City NY 10028 Office: Am Heritage Pub Co 551 Fifth Av New York City NY 10017

DAVIDSON, NORMAN JOHN, aero. exec.; b. Phila., Dec. 17, 1913; s. David and Ann (Spirt) D.; B.S., Temple U., 1937; m. Elaine Roma, Jan. 11, 1942; children—June Beth (Mrs. Harvey Dale Paley), Lynn Rae, Ian Richard. Pres. of Wright Corp., 1956—, now v.p.; chmn. bd. Ecol. Sci. Corp. Served from flying cadet to lt. col., USAAF, 1941-46. Mem. Air Force Res., Am. Ordnance Assn. Home: 12600 Biscayne Bay Dr Keystone Island North Miami FL 33161 Office: US 441 at NW 202d St Miami FL 33169

DAVIDSON, NORMAN RALPH, educator; b. Chgo., Apr. 5, 1916; s. Bernard Ralph and Rose (Lefstein) D.; B.S., U. Chgo., 1937, Ph.D., 1941; B.Sc. (Rhodes scholar), U. Oxford (Eng.), 1938; m. Annemarie Behrendt, July 11, 1942; children—Terence Mark, Laureen, Jeffrey Norman, Brian Lee. Research asso. plutonium project U. Chgo., 1942-45; research engr. RCA Labs., 1945-46; faculty Cal. Inst. Tech., 1946—, prof. chemistry, 1957—, exec. officer for chemistry, 1967—. Mem. National Acad. Scis., Am. Chem. Soc. (Cal. sect. award 1954). Am. Phys. Soc., Biophys. Soc. Author: Statistical Mechanics, 1961. Home: 318 E Laurel Av Sierra Madre CA 91024 Office: Cal Inst Tech 121 E California Blvd Pasadena CA 91109

DAVIDSON, OLIVER WESLEY, educator; b. Phila., Aug. 14, 1903; s. John Wesley and Ann Eliza (Moss) D.; B.S., Rutgers U., 1928, M.S., 1930, Ph.D., 1933; m. Eunice Bell DeClark, July 8, 1939; children—Devon Lindsay, Donald DeClark. Asst. research pomology Rutgers U., 1933-36, instr. pomology, 1936-39, asst. prof., 1939-45, asso. prof. ornamental horticulture, 1945-48, prof., research specialist floriculture, since 1948; research on orchid culture, development liquid fertilizers; cons. editor Soil Science. Bd. dirs. N.Y. Internat. Flower Show, Inc., Am. Orchid Soc. Fund for Edn. and Research, Inc. Fellow A.A.A.S., Am. Soc. Hort. Sci.; mem. Am. Soc. Plant Physiology, Am. Orchid Soc. (sec. since 1950), N.J. Florists Assn., Am. Carnation Soc., N.J. Plant and Flower Growers Association, New York Florists Club (pres. 1970), Sigma Xi, Alpha Zeta, Pi Alpha Xi (nat. pres. 1949-50). Republican. Contbr. chpts. to Hunger Signs in Corps, 1941; Grounds for Living, 1946. Home: 1156 Kearney Dr Colonial Gardens North Brunswick NJ 08902

DAVIDSON, PHILIP GRANT, Jr., ednl. adminstr.; b. Omaha, Neb., May 28, 1902; s. Philip Grant and Jessie (Hartwell) D.; B.S., U. of Miss., 1922; A.M., University of Chicago, 1925, Ph.D., 1929; Litt.D. (hon.), U. South, 1954; LL.D., U. Akron, 1960, University of Kentucky, 1965; L.H.D. (hon.), Bellamine College, in 1967; m. to Jane Campbell Foot, August 10, 1922; children—AdaPage (Mrs. Everett M. Clayton, Jr.), Philip Grant. High school principal, Indianola, Mississippi, 1922-23; prin. Avon, Miss., 1923-24, Swifttown, Miss., 1924-24; prof. of history, Agnes Scott Coll. (Ga.), 1928-42; exec. sec., Adv. Faculty Council, The Unvi. Center in Ga., 1938-42; dean sr. coll. and grad. sch. Vanderbilt U., 1942-48, provost univ. and dean grad. shc., 1948-51; pres. U. Louisville, 1951-68; program adviser higher edn. S.E. Asia, Ford Found., 1968—. Pres. Assn. Urban Univs., 1957-58. Pres., Conf. of Deans of S-. Grad. Schs., 1949-50; bd. Woodrow Wilson Nat. Fellowship Found.; chmn. board of appeals of National Council for Accreditation of Teacher Education; member of Phi Beta Kappa lectureship panel. Decorated officer Order of British Empire. Mem. American Hist. Assn., So. Hist. Assn., Newcomen Soc., Phi Beta Kappa, Omicron Delta Kappa. Episcopalian. Clubs: Century, Unviersity (N.Y.C.); Rotary; Royal Bangkok (Thailand) Sports. Author: Propaganda and the American Revolution, 1941. Address: Ford Foundation PO Box 436 Bangkok Thailand

DAVIDSON, PHILLIP BUFORD, Jr., army officer; b. Hachita, N.M., Nov. 26, 1915; s. Phillip Buford and Jennie (Matthews) D.; B.S., U.S. Mil. Acad., 1939; grad. Army War Coll., 1954, Nat. War Coll., 1962; m. Jeanne Eleanor Considine, Nov. 23, 1940; children—Phillip Buford III, John Considine, Thomas Matthews. Commd. 2d lt. U.S. Army, 1939, advanced through grades to maj. gen., 1968; comdr. Armored Bn., exec. officer Armored Regt., World War II; instr. Command and Staff Coll., 1946-48; G-2 sec. Far East Command, 1948-52; instr. U.S. Mil. Acad., 1953; chief of staff, combat comdr. 1st Armored Div., Hdqrs. U.S. European Command, 1958-61, OSD, 1963; J-2 mil. asst. comdr. Saigon, 1967-69; comdg. gen., Ft. Ord, Cal., 1969-71; asst. chief of staff for intelligence Hdqrs. DA, 1971—. Decorated D.S.M., Silver Star medal, Legion of Merit with three oak leaf clusters, Bronze Star medal, Purple Heart, French Croix de Guerre. Author: (with Maj. Gen. Robert R. Glass) Intelligence is for Commanders, 1948. Home: Qtrs 27-B Fort Myers VA 22211 Office: OACI Washington DC 20310

DAVIDSON, RALPH KIRBY, economist, found. exec.; b. Webster, S.D., May 13, 1921; s. Alfred and Grace (Christensen) D.; student Mont. State U., Missoula, 1946-48; B.A. (Rhodes scholar 1948-51), Keble Coll., Oxford (Eng.) U. 1950, M.A., 1954; M.A., Johns Hopkins, 1953, Ph.D. with distinction, 1954; m. Laura Agnes Devine, Dec. 28, 1940; children—Karen Ruth (Mrs. Charles E. Tate), Laura Gay (Mrs. Bhiraj Tanna). Printer, newspaper reporter and Farmer, Webster, 1936-41, printer, 1946; editor McPherson County Herald, Leola, S.D., 1942; part-time linotype operator Univ. Press, The Leader, also The Missoulian, Missoula, 1946-48; instr. McCoy Coll., Balt., 1952-53; linotype operator Balt. News Post, 1951-54; mem. faculty Purdue U., 1954-62, asst. prof., 1954-57, asso. prof., 1957-60, prof. econs., 1960-62, crew coach, 1955- 61, asst. dean Grad. Sch., 1959-62; cons. Rockefeller Found., also vis. prof. econs. Makerere, Kampala, Uganda, 1962-63; asso. dir. for humanities and social scis. Rockefeller Found., 1962-64, dep. dir., 1964- 70, dep. dir. social scis., 1971—. Vice pres. W. Lafayette (Ind.) Jr. High Sch. Bldg. Corp., 1961. Served with AUS, 1943-46; PTO. Social Sci. Research Council fellow, 1953- 54. Mem. Am., Royal econ. assns., Am. Assn. Rhodes Scholars, Regional Sci. Assn., A.A.A.S., Econometrics Soc., Council Fgn. Relations, Phi Beta Kappa. Episcopalian. Club: Church of New York. Author: Price Discrimination in Selling Gas and Electricity, 1955; (with V. L. Smith and J. W. Wiley) Economics; An Analytical Approach, rev. edit., 1962; also articles, book revs. Home: 2 Washington Sq Village New York City NY 10012 Office: 111 W 50th St New York City NY 10020

DAVIDSON, RAY, editor; b. Callahan County, Tex., Nov. 14, 1918; s. Benjamin A. and Winnie (Williams) D.; B.A., Hardin-Simmons U., 1939; m. Evelyn Talyor, Nov. 18, 1939; 1 dau., Lynn. Reporter, copyreader for various newspapers, 1937-42; with Houston Shipbldg. Corp., 1942-44; copyreader Houston Chronicle, 1946; rep. Am. Newspaper Guild, 1946-48; editor, publicity dir. Oil, Chem. and Atomic Workers Internat. Union, 1948—. Vice pres. Internat. Labor Press Assn., 1959-65, pres., 1966-67; cons. ICA, Japan, 1958. Mem. exec. bd., treas. Colo. br. Am. Civil Liberties Union. Capt., Denver Dem. Party, 1967—. Served with AUS, 1944-46. Mem. Am. Newspaper Guild. Author: Peril on the Job, 1970. Home: 1840 S Niagara Way Denver CO 80222 Office: 1840 California St Denver CO 80202

DAVIDSON, ROBERT FRANKLIN, ret. coll. dean; b. Chester, S.C., Apr. 27, 1902; s. Zeb Vance and Kate (Gaston) D.; A.B., Davidson Coll., 1923; M.A. (Rhodes scholar from S.C., 1926), Oxford, 1933; Ph.D., Yale, 1937; Litt.D., 1971; m. Eve Carlton, July 13, 1928; children—Robert Franklin, Willaim Lee, Terrell C. Asso. prof. religion and philosophy Southwestern, Memphis, 1931-33; prof. philosophy and Christian ethics Hiram (O) Coll., 1933-43; with div. of philosophy and religion Stephens Coll., 1943-46; chmn. humanities, U. Coll., U. of Fla., 1946-62; dean St. Andrews Presbyn. Coll., Laurinburg, N.C., 1962- 71; chmn. humanities com. coll. entrance examination bd., 1949-50; fellow, coop. study in gen. edn. U. Chgo., 1941, Ohio Commn. on Christian Edn., 1937-42. Ednl. cons., USAAF, 1942-43, cons. in philosophy U.S. Armed Forces Inst., 1943-45. Sec. Fla., Rhodes Scholarship Com., 1950-60. Mem. Am. Philos. Assn., Assn. of Am. Rhodes Scholars, Phi Beta Kappa, Omicron Delta Kappa, Beta Theta Pi. Presbyn. Author: Rudolf Otto's Interpretation of Religion, 1947; Philosophies Men Live By, 1952. Editor: The Humanities in Contemporary Life, 1955, rev., 1960; The Search for Meaning in Life, 1962; The Humanistic Tradition, 1964. Home: 3110 SW 4th Ct Gainesville FL

DAVIDSON, ROBERT H., mfg. co. exec.; b. Springfield, Mass., Jan. 15, 1919; s. Ellis Webb and Mildred Florence (Burgess) D.; B.A. cum laude, Amherst Coll., 1940; m. Anne Breeding, Aug. 30, 1947; 1 dau., Anne Stowell. Various sales and mgmt. positions Gen. Foods Corp., 1947-59, adminstrv. v.p., marketing dir. Econs. Lab., Inc., 1960-63; group v.p. marketing, dir. A.E. Staley Mfg. Co., 1963-67; pres. Anderson, Clayton Foods, 1967-70; pres., chief exec. officer Fanny Former Candy Shops, Inc., 1970—, dir. Adv. Council S.W. Center Advanced Studies. Trustee Nutrition Found., Am. Fund Dental Edn., Adv. Council Edn. and Research Fund. Served from pvt. to col., USMCR, 1940-46. Decorated Silver Star medal, Bronze Star medal, Presdl. citation, Purple Heart. Mem. Am. Mgmt. Assn., Am. Marketing Assn., Newcomen Soc., Decatur Assn. Commerce (dir.), Delta Upsilon. Clubs: Manursing Island, Apawamis (Rye, N.Y.); Country, Decatur City (Decatur); Chaparral, City (Dallas). Home: 73 Court St Dedham MA 02026 Office: Preston Ct Bedford MA

DAVIDSON, ROBERT LAURENSON DASHIELL, coll. pres.; b. Dover, Del., Jan. 11, 1909; s. John Milton and Miriam P. (Sheppard) D.; A.B., Dickinson Coll., 1931, LL.D., 1956; A.M., Temple University, 1937, D.Ed., 1946; student N.Y.U., 1937- 41, Northwestern U., 1942, U. Pa., 1954; L.H.D., Rider Coll., 1969; LL.D., Lindenwood Coll., 1969; m. Lois Buckingham, June 18, 1938; children—Roberta Ann (Mrs. Ronald E. Wallen), Francis Gaylord. Tchr. Clayton (N. J.) High Sch., 1931-37, prin., 1937-41; prin. Lambertville (N.J.) High Sch., 1941-42; faculty dept. history Temple U., 1945-48, dir. placement, 1946-48, asso. dean community coll. and tech. inst., 1948-55, asso. prof. social sci., 1948-55; pres. Westminster Coll., Fulton, Mo., 1955—; dean Nat. Philatelic Museum Inst., 1948-55. Chmn. the Fulton City Planning Commn., 1961-68. Del. to the World Alliance Ref. Chs., Frankfurt, Germany, 1964. Exec. com. Phila. council Boy Scouts Am., 1954- 55; state chmn. U.S.O., 1962. Served as lt. comdr. USNR, 1942-45. Mem. commn. on grad. and profl. studies Assn. Am. Colls., 1963-67; chmn. spl. com. on state scholarships Mo. Assn. Colls. and Univs., 1965; chmn. Mid- Mo. Asso. Colls., 1965-68. Mem. N.E.A., Am. Assn. Sch. Adminstrs., Hist. Soc. Pa., Mo. Hist. Soc., State Hist. Soc. Mo., Am. Arbitration Assn. (panel arbitrators), Am. Philatelic Congress (pres. 1964-69), Ind. Coll. and Univ. Mo. (pres. 1966), S.R., Mo. Colls. Fund (pres. 1970), Phi Beta Kappa, Phi Delta Kappa (award for research 1946), Phi Alpha Theta, Sigma Chi, Omicron Delta Kappa. Presbyn. Kiwanian. Clubs: University (St. Louis); Mo. Athletic. Author: War Comes to Quaker Pennsylvania, 1957. Home: 229 St Francis Fulton MO 65251

DAVIDSON, ROBERT WILLIAM, sculptor; b. Indpls., May 13, 1904; s. Oscar L. and Julia Louise (Souder) D.; student John Herron Art Inst., Indpls., 1920- 24, Sch. of Am. Sculpture, N.Y.C., 1926, Bavarian State Fine Arts, Munich; m. Maryetta Mauck, Apr. 4, 1928; children—Anthony (dec.), Julia (Mrs. Claude Seward). Represented permanent collections John Herron Art Inst., various pub. bldgs. and instns.; sculpture, portraits in many exhbns. including Nat. Acad., N.Y.C., 1933; John Herron Art Inst., 1925, 1935; N.Y. World's Fair, 1939; Albright show, Artists of Western Hemisphere; Bronze in permanent collection Munson-Williams-Proctor Inst., Utica, N.Y., 1953. Awarded prize of the John Herron Art Inst., 1925 and 1928; sculpture prize, Hoosier Salon, Chgo., 1927, 33, 36. Completed series of war sculptures. Prof. art, resident sculptor, Skidmore Coll.; currently engaged in print making. creative work in metal and ceramics. Author: A Sculptor's Handbook. Home: Highlands Rock City Falls NY 12863 ☆

DAVIDSON, SIDNEY, educator; b. Chgo., May 29, 1919; s. Mendel and Eva (Slosberg) D.; A.B., U. Mich., 1941, M.B.A., 1941, Ph.D., 1950; m. Freda Joy Sendler, June 23, 1946; children—Jonathan, Victoria Ann. Instr. econs. accounting U. Mich., 1947-49; asst. prof. accounting Johns Hopkins, 1949- 52, asso. prof., 1952-56, prof. accounting, 1956-58; prof. accounting Sch. Bus. U. Chgo., 1958-62; Arthur Young Prof. of accounting Grad. Sch. Bus. U. Chgo., 1962—, dir. Inst. Profl. Accounting, 1962-69, dean Grad. Sch., 1962—. Vis. prof. U. Cal. at Berkeley, summer 1950, London Sch. Econs., 1956-57, U. Hawaii, summer 1962, Stanford, summer 1964, Hebrew U., Jerusalem, 1965. Cons. Md. Commn. on Pub. Service Law Revision, 1952-53, operations research office U.S. Army, 1955-62; cons. to Treasury Dept., 1961-68. Served from ensign to lt., USNR, 1942-46. Guggenheim fellow, 1956-57. C.P.A., Md. Mem. Am. Accounting Assn. (dir. research 1955-56, pres. 1968-69), Am. Inst. C.P.A.'s (accounting principles bd. 1965-70), Am. Econ. Assn., Operations Research Soc. Am., Nat. Assn. Accountants, Phi Beta Kappa, Phi Kappa Phi, Beta Gamma Sigma. Author: The Plant Accounting Regulations of the Federal Power Commission, 1952; Fundamentals of Accounting, 1959; (with W. Baxter) Studies in Accounting Theory, 1962. Editor: Handbook of Modern Accounting, 1970. Contbr. to profl. publs. Home: 5719 Kenwood Av Chicago IL 60637

DAVIDSON, SIDNEY WETMORE, lawyer; b. Augusta, Ga., Dec. 30, 1894; s. William Treat and Carolin Amelia (Wetmore) D.; grad. Lawrenceville Sch., 1912; B.A., Yale, 1916, LL.B., 1918; LL.D., Tufts Coll., 1952, Pratt Inst., 1965; L.H.D., Bates Coll., 1960; m. Mary Alice Hooker, June 24, 1916; children—Jean Hooker (Mrs. Horace A. Fay), Sidney Wetmore, Katharine Douglas (Mrs. John S. Walker), Robert Treat Hooker, Alice Hooker (Mrs. John O. Outwater), Louise Treat (Mrs. Davidson Ross). Admitted to N.Y. bar, 1920; asso. with firm Carter, Ledyard & Milburn, N.Y.C., 1920-45, mem. firm, 1929-45; mem. firm Gasser, Hayes & Davidson, 1945-49, Davidson, Dawson & Clark since 1949; partner Brown & Ives, Providence; trustee emeritus Bklyn. Savs. Bank; dir. Globe Newspaper Co., Boston; mem. adv. bd. Chem. Bank N.Y. Trust Co. Mem. fed. alien enemy hearing bd., eastern dist., N.Y., 1942-45. Trustee Lawrenceville Sch., Bingham Asso. Fund (for advancement of medicine), Bethel, Me., N.E. Med. Center Hosp., Boston, (hon. chmn.), Bklyn. Inst. of Arts and Sci., Gould Acad., Bethel, Me., Pratt Inst. (emeritus); former chmn. Bklyn. Mus.; hon. chmn. exec. com. Yale Law Sch. Assn.; former trustee, Packer Collegiate Inst. (Bklyn.). Served with USNR, 1918-19. Mem. Am., N.Y. State bar assns., Bar Assn. City of N.Y., Zeta Psi, Phi Delta Phi, Corbey Court. Unitarian. Clubs: Century Assn., Downtown Assn., University, Yale (N.Y.C.); Rembrandt (Bklyn.); Elihu, Graduates (New Haven); Saratoga (N.Y.) Reading Room. Home: 1 Pierrepont St Brooklyn Heights Brooklyn NY 11201 summer Graylane Camp Sebec Lake ME 04482 Office: 345 Park Av New York City NY 10022

DAVIDSON, WALTER H., former utility exec., cons.; b. Ft. Worth, Aug. 14, 1902; s. Wiliam H. and Mary Belle (Cox) D.; B.S. in Civil Engring., Tex. A. and M. Coll., 1924; m. Gladys Roberts, Aug. 12, 1928; 1 dau., Mrs. Anton de Kanter, Jr. Engr., constrn. engr. Cities Service Co., 1924-30; constrn. engr. Continental Constrn. Co., 1930-31; dist. pipe line supt., sta. supt. gen. compressor Natural Gas Pipe Line, 1931-47, gen. compressor, 1931-47; gen. constrn. supt. Fish Constructors, 1947-49; with Transcontinental Gas Pipe Line, Houston, 1950-68, v.p., gen. supt., 1954- 56, v.p. operations, 1956-57, sr. v.p., 1967-68, ret., 1968; now cons. Mem. Am. Gas Assn. (past chmn. operation sect.). Episcopalian. Club: Memorial Drive Country. Home: 3212 Merrick St Houston TX 70025 Office: 3100 Travis St Houston TX 77001

DAVIDSON, WILLIAM, clergyman; b. Miles City, Mont., July 20, 1919; s. Thomas and Catherine (Gold) D.; B.S., Mont. State U., 1940; S.T.B., Berkeley Div. Sch., 1946, D.D., 1966; m. Mary Ernestine Shoemaker, June 3, 1942; children—Carol (Mrs. Ronald Carpenter), Thomas, George, Robert. Tchr. agr. Sidney (Mont.) High Sch., 1940-43; ordained to ministry Episcopalian Ch., 1947; minister, then rector various chs. in Mont., 1946-56; asso. sec. nat. council div. town and country, home dept. Episcopal Ch., 1956-62; rector Grace Ch., Jamestown, N.D., 1962-65; bishop of Western Kan., 1966—. Chmn. trustees St. John's Mil. Sch., Salina, Kan., 1966—, St. Francis' Boys' Homes, Salina, 1966—. Named Young Man of Year, Lewistown (Mont.) Jr. C. of C., 1954. Mem. Salina C. of C. Rotarian. Home: 1004 Manor Rd Salina KS 67401 Office: PO Box 1383 Salina KS 67401

DAVIDSON, WILLIAM BIRD, banker; b. Penrith, Cumberland, Eng., May 18, 1912; s. John Noble and Martha (Scott) D.; grad. grammar sch.; m. Christina M. Ireton, Oct. 31, 1941; children—John S., Edward S. With Nat. Provincial Bank, Eng., 1929-68, chief gen. mgr., 1967-68, dir., 1968; dir., joint chief exec. Nat. Westminster Bank, London, 1968-69, dir., chief exec., 1969—; dir. Ulster Bank Ltd., Belfast, Westminster Fgn. Bank Ltd., London. Served to capt. Brit. Army, 1939-45. Fellow Inst. Bankers. Home: Rose Cottage 9 Starrock Rd Coulsdon Surrey England Office: 41 Lothbury St London EC 2 England

DAVIDSON, WILLIAM MAURICE, telephone cons.; b. Winchester, Mass., Oct. 11, 1904; s. William Andrew and Eugenie (McDonald) D.; B.S., Mass. Inst. Tech., 1926, M.S., 1927; m. Sarah Harrison Frye, Jan. 5, 1929; children—Jean Louise (Mrs. Donald Cox), Richard Maurice, Robert Michael. With Bell Telephone Co. Pa., 1927-52, 54-69, v.p. engring., 1962-65, v.p. planning, 1965-69; regional plant extension engr. Am. Tel. & Tel. Co., 1952-54; v.p. engring. Diamond State Telephone Co., 1962-65; cons. to Republic of China, Taiwan, 1970—. Mem. adv. bd. Mgmt. Sci. Center, U. Pa. Mem. I.E.E.E., A.A.A.S., Franklin Inst., Phila., U.S. chambers commerce, Armed Forces Communications and Electronics Assn., Tau Beta Pi. Clubs: Urban (Phila.); Overbrook Country (Bryn Mawr, Pa.); Mass. Inst. Tech. (pres. Alumni Assn. Western Pa. 1950-52, hon. sec. 1940—). Home: 522 Conshohocken State Rd Gladwyne PA 19035

DAVIDSON, WILLIAM ROBERT, educator, author, cons.; b. Gove County, Kan., July 19, 1919; s. William Bryan and Clara (Wecker) D.; A.B., Coll. Emporia, 1940; M.B.A., Washington U., 1947; Ph.D., Ohio State U., 1951; m. Anne Elizabeth Anderson, Oct. 16, 1945; children—Joyce West, Judith Anne. With F.W. Woolworth Co., 1940-41; mem. faculty Coll. Adminstrv. Scis., Ohio State U., Columbus, 1947—, dir. exec. devel. program, 1955-58, prof. marketing, 1958—, chmn. marketing faculty group, 1968-70; vis. prof. Grad. Sch. Bus. Stanford, 1958-59; cons. asso. Mgmt. and Bus. Stanford, 1958-59. Chmn., Mgmt. Horizons, Inc.; dir. Mgmt. Horizons Data Systems, Inc., Computer Horizons Can., Ltd.; dir., mem. exec. com. Gilbert Shoe Stores, Inc. Trustee Columbus Sch. for Girls, 1960-67. Served to lt. (s.g.) USNR, 1941-45. Decorated D.F.C. Elected to the Hall of Fame in Distbn., 1964. Mem. Am. Marketing Assn. (pres. 1963-64), Council for Profl. Edn. for Bus. (exec. com. 1964-67), Am. Acad. Polit. and Social Sci. Episcopalian. Author: The Wholesale Wine Trade, 1955; (with T. N. Beckman and James L. Engel) Marketing, 8th edit., 1967; (with Alton F. Doody) Retailing Management, 3d edit., 1966; (with James R. Lowry) Leased Departments in Discount Merchandising, 1968. Contbr. articles to trade, profl. jours. Home: 247 Preston Rd Columbus OH 43209

DAVID-WEILL, PIERRE SYLVALN DESIRE GERARD, banker; b. Paris, France, Mar. 8, 1900; s. David and Flora (Raphael) David-Weill; Ph.B., Paris Academie, 1916; m. Berthe Haardt, Feb. 17, 1932; children-Michael Alexandre, Elaine Francoise Louise. Entered banking bus. with Lazard Freres & Cie., Paris, 1924; partner since 1927; partner Lazard Freres & Co., N. Y. C. 1944; dir. Lazard Bros. & Co., Ltd.; London, Banque de l'Indo-Chine, Banque de Paris et des Pays Bas, Rhone Fowlene S.A. President Conseil Artistique de la Rēunion des Musées Nationaux de France. Lieutenant 4 Rt. d'Auto-Mitrailleuses, French Army, 1940. Awarded Croix de Guerre, 1939-40, 2 citations; decorated Officer Legion of Honor. Mem. de l'Institut de France, Club: Travellers (Paris). Home: 16 Rue St Guillaume Paris France Office: 5 Rue Pillet-Will Paris, France.

DAVIE, DONALD ALFRED, educator, author; b. Barnsley, Eng., July 17, 1922; s. George Clarke and Alice (Sugden) D.; B.A., St. Catharine's Coll., Cambridge, Eng., 1947, M.A., 1948, Ph.D., 1951; m. Doreen John, Jan. 13, 1945; children—Richard Mark, Diana Margaret, Patrick George. Lectr., Dublin (Ireland) U., 1950-54; fellow Trinity Coll., Dublin, 1954-57; vis. prof. U. Cal. at Santa Barbara, 1957- 58; lectr. English, U. Cambridge, 1958-64, fellow Gonville and Caius Coll., 1959-64; prof. lit. U. Essex, Colchester, Eng., 1965-68, dean comparative studies, 1964, pro-vice-chancellor, 1965; vis. prof. Grinnell Coll., 1965; Leo S. Bing prof. English and Am. lit. U. So. Cal., 1968-69; prof. English, Stanford, 1969—. Mem. London Library. Author: Purity of Diction in English Verse, 1952; Articulate Energy, 1957; Ezra Pound; Poet as Sculptor, 1964; (poetry) Brides of Reason, 1955; A Winter Talent, 1957; The Forests of Lithuania, 1960; New and Selected Poems, 1961; Events and Wisdoms, 1965; Essex Poems, 1969; Six Epistles to Eva Hesse, 1970; (verse-translations) The Poems of Doctor Zhivago, 1965. Home: 989 Cottrell Way Stanford CA 94305

DAVIE, EUGENIE MARY (Mrs. Preston Davie), civic and polit. leader; b. N.Y.C., d. Adolph and Emily (Stevens) Ladenburg; ed. Westover Sch., pvt. tutors; m. Preston Davie, May 31, 1930. Finance chmn. N.Y. Rep. State Com., 1933-34; del. Rep. Nat. Conv., 1936; chmn. Landon Vols., Eastern Seaboard States, women's div. Rep. Nat. Com.; chmn. women's auxiliary N.Y. Rep. County Com., 1946-61, 1st v.p., 1958-64; mem. Rep. Nat. Finance Com., 1962-; alternate del. Rep. Nat. Conv., 1960; asst. treas. Robert A. Taft Nat. Finance Com., 1952. Mem. bd. regents Nat. Library Medicine, 1958-60; trustee, mem. exec. com. Taft Meml. Found., 1955-64; chmn. Robert A. Taft Inst. of Govt., 1961-, also trustee, mem. exec. com.; former trustee L.I.U.; chmn. hospitality com. N.Y. state Pavilion World's Fair, mem. N.Y. State Comm. of the Fair, 1962-63. Chmn. civilian operating com. Army Emergency Relief, 2d Service Command, 1942-44; dir. vols. Army Personnel Affairs Div., Mil. Dist. No. l, 1944. Decorated Gold Cross of Merit (Poland), cross in grade of dame Order of St. Dennis of Zante (Greece). Mem. D.A.R., Daus, of Cincinnati, Am. (bd. v.p. 1955-57), N.Y. (hon. chmn. bd. dirs 1966—) heart assns. Episcopalian. Clubs: Women's Nat. Rep. (past bd. dir.). Colony. Contbr. articles on politics to newspapers, other publs. Home: 71 E 71st St New York City NY 10021 Office: 420 Lexington Av New York City NY 10017

DAVIES, ALED PIERCE, trade assn. exec.; b. Penrhyndeudraeth, North Wales, Gt. Britain, Nov. 8. 1910; s. Enoch and Janet (Hughes) D.; student Skerry's Coll., Liverpool , Eng., 1927-28, Madryn Agr. Coll., Wales, 1928, Columbus Law Sch., Washington, 1934-36; D.Sc.,

Clemson Agrl. Coll., 1955; m. Mildred Tatum, Oct 8, 1937; children☆Richard Gwyn, John Hughes. Came to U.S., 1929, naturalized, 1943. Office boy Davies Bros., slate mchts., Portmadoc, Wales, 1929; factory worker S.M. Jones Co., Toledo, 1930; clk. Commerce Guardian Bank, Toledo, 1930-31; salesman Brunswick-Balke- Collender Co., Chgo., N.Y.C., 1931-33; clk. Bank of Montreal, N.Y.C., 1933; pub. relations staff Jones-Walter Agy., Washington, 1934- 36; asst. to dir. Republican Nat. Com., 1936; Washington rep. Nat. Com. to Uphold Constn., 1937-38; Washington corr. Gannett Newspapers, 1938-40; asst. to v.p. Am. Meat Inst., Chgo., 1940-53, dir. dept. livestock, 1953-60, v.p., 1960-; cons. dir. food rationing OPA, Wahsington, 1943-44; cons. to pres. Commodity Credit Corp., 1954-56; dir. meat div. U.S. exhibit Brit. Food Fair, London, 1956. Exec. com. Food for Peace Council, 1961- -; U.S. del. 5th Internat. Food Congress, N.Y.C., 1962, FAO, Rome, 1963. Amsterdam Internat. Trade Fair, 1963, chmn. 2d World Food Congress, La Hague, Holland, 1969; mem. Presdl. Market Devel. Mission to Western Europe, 1964. First v.p. Am. Freedom from Hunger Found., 1970—. Del. Ind. Rep. Conv .,1948, 52. Clubs: National Press, Capitol Hill, International (Washington); Michigan City (Ind.) Yacht; Reform (London, Eng.), Home: Bryn Awelon Farm Valparaiso, IN 46383. Office: 59 E Van Buren St Chicago IL 60605.

DAVIES, ALFRED INGRAM, chain store exec.; b. Fort Worth, Sept. 22, 1912; s. Alfred Ingram and Jessie Lou (Johnson) D.; B.S. in Econs., Tex. A. and M. Coll., 1935, M.S. in Marketing Finance, 1935; m. Mildred Musslewhite, Oct. 5, 1936; childrenNancy Carolyn (Mrs. Malcolm C. McGee), Donna Sue (Mrs. Eugene Y. Stratton), Alfred Ingram, Deborah Ann. Ednl. adviser Civilian Conservation Corps, 1935-37; with Sears, Roebuck & Co., 1937-, gen. mgr., Memphis, 1951-60, v.p. operating, Chgo., 1960-66, v.p. Southwestern terr., 1966—, also dir.; dir. Allstate Ins. Cos., Homart Devel. Co., Republic Nat. Bank of Dallas, Lone Star Gas Co. Dallas, Mem. adv. bd. Salvation Army, Dallas, exec. com. Trinity Improvement Assn., Dallas; planning com. Goals for Dallas; adv. council S.W. Center Advanced Studies; chmn. Citizens Coordinating Com. for Road Planning. Trustee Tex. Research Found., Renner, Southwestern Med. Found., Dallas, Presbyn. Hosp. Dallas, Callier Hearing and Speech Center, Dallas SCOPE, Tex. 4-H Youth Devel. Found.; bd. dirs. Dallas Citizens Council, Dallas County United Fund (pres. 1971), Greater Dallas Planning Council , Dallas Summer Musicals, State Fair Tex.,(v.p. 1971), Cotton Bowl Athletic Assn., So. Meth. Found. Bus. and Econs., Tex. Research League, Tex. Retail Fedn. bd. devel. Dallas Baptist Coll., Bishop Coll., Dallas. Served to Lt. Col. AUS, 1942-46. Recipient Outstanding Citizen award Memphis Civitan Club, 1959. Mem. Dallas C. of C. (dir.). Methodist (mem. ofcl. bd.) Mason. Clubs: Northwood, Dallas, City (Dallas) . Home: 5209 Tanbark Rd Dallas TX 75229 Office: 1409 S Lamar St Dallas TX 75202.

DAVIES, MRS. CHARLES P., see Banning, Elizabeth.

DAVIES, DANIEL R., educator; b. Plymouth, Pa., Feb. 21, 1911; s. John R. and Minnie (Kocher) D.; A.B., Harvard, 1933; A.M., Bucknell U., 1943; Ph.D., Columbia, 1946; m. Winifred Evans, June 14, 1941; children—Cathie, Wendy. Tchr. Forty Fort (Pa.) High Sch., 1934-44, head dept. English, 1940-44; asst. supt. schs., Briarcliff Manor, N.Y., 1944-45; asst., dept. edn. adminstrn. Columbia, 1945-46, asst. prof. edn., exec. officer div. adminstrn. and guidance, 1946-49, asso. prof., exec. officer Tchrs. Coll., 1949-50, prof. edn., dir. coop. program in ednl. adminstrn., Middle Atlantic region, 1950-59; del. Coop. Center for Ednl. Adminstrn., 1955-59; asso. dir. Indsl. Mgmt. Work Conf., Columbia U. Sch. Engring., and Indsl. Research Conf., 1955-60; exec. dir. U. Council for Edn. Adminstrn., 1958-59; editorial cons. A.C. Croft Publs., New London, Conn., 1958-60, dir. research and devel. Croft Ednl. Services, 1960—, v.p. research, devel. and dir. Croft Cons. Services, Tucson, 1966—. Lectr., U. Ariz., 1962-64; vis. prof. San Diego State, summer 1957, U. N.M., summer 1960, Okla. A. and M., summer 1963, Tex. A. and M., U. Scranton, summer 1964, U. Neb, summer 1971, mem. Nat. Com. Advancement Ednl. Adminstrn., 1955-57. Ford Found. grantee, Europe, 1966. Fellow A.A.A.S.; mem. Soc. Applied Anthropology, N.E.A., Am. Assn. U. Profs., Nat. Soc. Study Edn. (contbr. Yearbook 1954), Am. Assn. Sch. Adminstrs., Nat. Study Status Adminstrv. Tng. (dir. 1949-50), Nat. Conf. Profs. Ednl. Adminstrn. (exec. com., sec.-treas. 1948-58), Am. Edn. Research Assn., Phi Delta Kappa. Clubs: Skyline Country, Old Pueblo (Tucson); Westmoreland (Wilkes-Barre, Pa.). Author numerous books including Dynamics of Group Action, 8 vols., 1954; Patterns of Educational Leadership (with V. Anderson), 1956; (with H.M. Brickell) Davies-Brickell System for School Board Policy Making, 1957, Board Policy Letter, 1958; You and Management (with R.T. Livingston), 1958, (translated into Japanese, published 1968); (with Margaret Handlong) Teaching of Art, 1962; The Administrative Internship, 1962; (with D.E. Griffiths) Executive Action, 1962; (with W.S. Elsbree, Louise H. Nelson) Educational Sec., 1962; Catholic Schools Adaptation of the Davies-Brickell System, 1968: (with Father James R. Dineen) New Patterns for Catholic Education, 1968. Spl. cons. on installing Davies-Brickell System in schs., U.S.A., Can., also Am. Schs., France, Holland, Greece, Italy. Home: 4100 Avenida Del Cazador Tuscon AZ 85718 also 45 Yaeger Av Forty Fort PA 18704 Office: Tucson Fed Tower Tucson AZ 85702 ☆

DAVIES, DAVID ARTHUR, meteorologist; b. Barry, Wales, Nov. 11, 1913; s. Garfield Brynmor and Mary Jane (Michael) D.; B.Sc., U. Wales, 1933, 1st class honors math., 1934, physics, 1935, M.Sc., 1940; Dr. Honoris Causa, U. Bucharest, 1970; m. Mary Shapland, Mar. 5, 1938; children—Michael Shapland, Rosalind Shapland, Margaret Shapland. Tech. officer Meteorol. Office, London, Eng., 1936-39, prin. sci. officer, 1947-49; dir. East African Meteorol. Dept., Nairobi, Kenya, 1949-55; sec.-gen. World Meteorol. Orgn., Geneva, 1955—. Meteorol. officer RAF 1939-47. Fellow Inst. Physics London, Royal Meteorol. Soc. (London), Royal Inst. Pub. Adminstrn., Am. Meteorol. Soc. (hon.), Contbr. profl. jours. Home: Chemin des Rojalets 1296 Coppet VD Switzerlannd Office: Av Guiseppe Motta Geneva Switzerland

DAVIES, DAVID GEORGE, lawyer; b. Waukesha, Wis., July 19, 1928; s. David Evan and Ella Hilda (Degler) D.; B.S., U. Wis., 1950, J.D., 1953; m. Elaine Kowalchik, May 12, 1962; children—Thea Kay, Bryn Ann, Degler Evan. Trust rep. First Nat. Bank of Ariz., Phoenix, 1957-58, asst. trust officer, 1958-62, trust officer, head bus. devel. in trust dept., 1962-66, v.p., trust officer, 1966; admitted to Wis. bar, 1953, Ariz. bar, 1959; practice in Phoenix, 1967—; asso. Wales & Collins, 1967-68; partner Wales, Collins & Davies, 1968—. Instr. bus. law local chpt. C.L.U.'s, 1965; instr. estate planning Phoenix Coll., 1968—. Pres. Central Ariz. Estate Planning Council; pres., bd. dirs. Vis. Nurse Service, United Fund Agy.; bd. dirs. Phoenix chpt. Nat. Hemophilia Found. Served from 1st lt. to capt., judge Adv. Gen. Corps. A.U.S., 1953-57. Mem. Central Assn. Life Underwriters (asso.), Am., Wis. bar assns., State Bar Ariz. Conglist. (chmn. bd. trustees, asso. moderator). Home: 4730 E Exeter Blvd Phoenix AZ 85018 Office: 14 W Adams St Phoenix AZ 85003

DAVIES, DAVID LLOYD, lawyer; b. Falls City, Neb., Oct. 17, 1903; s. David Morris and Alice (Griffiths) D.; A.B., Stanford, 1925, J.D., 1927; m. Barbara Coit Elliott, Sept. 10, 1930; children—Barbara Ann (Mrs. Davies Thorsen), David Coit. Admitted to Ore. bar, 1927, since practiced in Portland; mem. firm Davies, Biggs, Strayer, Stoel & Boley, and predecessors, 1937- -. Dir. U.S. Nat. Bank, Portland. Dir., treas. Ore. State Motor Assn.; trustee Med. Research Found. of Ore. Chmn. financial adv. com. Fruit and Flower Day Nursery, Portland; past pres. Portland Art Assn.; dir., past pres. Ore. Hist. Soc.; past pres. Portland Community Chest; dir., treas. Library Assn. Portland; overseer Whitman Coll., trustee E. Henry Wemme Endowment Fund. Mem. Am., Ore., Multnomah County bar assns., Am. Law Inst. Republican. Presbyn. Clubs: Arlington, Waverley, University (Portland); Century (N.Y.C.). Home: 01400 SW Military Rd Portland OR 97219 Office: 900 SW 5th Av Portland OR 97204

DAVIES, DAVID WILLIAM, librarian; b. Winnipeg, Can., May 23, 1908; s. Owen H. and Catherine C. (McCaffrey) D.; A.B., U. Cal. at Los Angeles, 1932, A.M., 1940; Ph.D., U. Chgo., 1947; m. Thelma E. Stengel, Nov. 10, 1936. Staff mem. Henry E. Huntington Library, San Marino, Cal., 1927-28; research asst. to Herbert I. Priestley, dir. Bancroft Library, U. Cal., 1933-36, in charge rare books and manuscripts, 1938-41; asst. dept. rare books Henry E. Huntington Library, 1936-38; asst. prof. edn., librarian Utah State Coll., 1941-43; dir. libraries U. Vt., 1946-47; librarian Pomona, Claremont and Claremont Men's colls., 1947-52, Pomona Coll., 1947-67; now lectr. Cal. State Coll., Fullerton; prof. library sci. Immaculate Heart Coll.; vis. sr. lectr. Coll. Librarianship, Wales, 1967-68; lectr. history of books and printing. Immaculate Heart Coll. Lectr. on Am. libraries in Netherlands under auspices Internat. Univ. Found., 1950; Guggenheim fellow, 1963-64. Served as 1st sgt., AUS, 1943-46. Mem. Am. Library Assn., Renaissance Soc., Conf. on Brit. Studies, Utrecht Historisch Genootschap. Democrat. Clubs: Grolier (N.Y.C.); University (Los Angeles). Author: The World of The Elseviers, 1580-1712, 1954; A Primer of Dutch 17th Century Overseas Trade, 1961; Elizabethans Errant, the Strange Fortunes of Sir Thomas Sherley and His Three Sons, 1967; An Enquiry into the Reading of the Lower Classes, 1970. Editor: Sir Roger Williams' The Actions of the Low Countries, 1963. Contbr. mags. and jours. Home: 524 W 10th St Claremont CA 91711 Office: Immaculate Heart Coll 2021 N Western Av Los Angeles CA 90027

DAVIES, ELAM, clergyman; b. Grovesend, Swansea, Wales, June 15, 1916; s. Thomas Gwynfa and Sarah Ann (Williams) D.; B.A. with honors, U. Wales 1941; B.A. with honors in theol. tripos, Cambridge (Eng.) U., 1943, M.A., 1947; D.D. (hon.), Temple U., 1956, Lebanon Valley Coll., 1962; m. Grace Elleanor Mary Owen, July 8, 1944; 1 dau., Judith Ann. Came to U.S., 1952, naturalized, 1961. Ordained to ministry Presbyn. Ch., 1944; minister in Wales, 1944-52, Bethlehem, Pa., 1952-61; prof. philos. theology and Christian ethics Temple U., 1953-55; minister 4th Presbyn. Ch., Chgo., 1961-. Bd. mgrs. central dept. Evangelism, Nat. Council Chs., 1956-66; v.p. Ch. Fedn. Greater Chgo., 1962-64; moderator North Wales Coast Presbytery, 1951-52, Lehigh (Pa.) Presbytery, 1960-61; mem. com. long range strategy Chgo. Presbytary, 1962-66, mem. dept. urban ch., 1963- 69. Trustee McCormick Theol. Sem. Chgo., 1964-70; bd. dirs. Presbyn. Home, Evanston, Ill., 1961-67; mem. bd. Christian edn. United Presbyn. Ch. U.S.A., 1968-; mem. exec. com . Fifty Million Fund United Presbyn. Ch. of U.S.A., 1964-68. Mem. Chgo. Cleric. Club: Lake Shore. Author: This Side of Eden, 1964. Home: 866 N Michigan Av Chicago IL 60611 Office: 126 E Chestnut St Chicago IL 60611

DAVIES, G.C., business exec. Chmn., Theo. H. Davies and Co., Ltd., Honolulu. Office: 841 Bishop St Honolulu HI 96813*

DAVIES, GEORGE OWEN, business exec.; b. Jamestown, N.Y., 1908; s. Thomas E. and May E.D.; B.S. in econs., U. Pa., 1934; m. Jean Galbraith; 1 son, Thomas Galbraith. With P. Lorillard Co., N.Y.C., 1950—, treas., 1951-67, v.p., 1957-64, exec. v.p., 1964—, also dir.; v.p., dir. Fed. Tin & Paper Products, Inc., P. Lorillard Pan-Am., Inc.; treas. Reed Candy Co., Usen Canning Co. Home: 17 Bennett Pl Westfield NJ 07090 Office: 119 W 40th St New York City NY 10018

DAVIES, HORTON MARLAIS, educator, clergyman; b. Cwmavon, South Wales, Mar. 10, 1916; s. D. Marlais and Martha Reid (Davies) D.; M.A. with honors, U. Edinburgh 1937, B.D. with honors, 1940; Ph.D., Oxford U., 1943, D. Litt., 1970; D.D., U. South Africa, 1950; D.Litt. (hon.), LaSalle Coll., 1966; m. Brenda Mary Deakin, Sept. 8, 1942; children—Christine Mary, Hugh Marlais, Philip Marlais. Ordained to ministry Congl. Ch., 1942; minister Wallington Ch., South London, 1942-45; religious adviser, dir. edn. YMCA, operating with Brit. Army, 1945-46; prof., head dept. div. Rhodes U., Grahamstown, S. Africa, 1946-53, dean faculty, 1951-53; travelling fellow U.S., Carnegie Corp. of N.Y., also Old St. Andrew's Meml. lectr. Emmanuel Coll., U. Toronto, 1952; head joint dept. ch. history Mansfield and Regents Park colls. Oxford U., 1953-56; prof. religion Princeton, 1956- 59, Henry W. Putman prof., 1959—. Guggenheim Found. fellow, 1959-60, 64- 65; vis. prof. ch. history Union Theol. Seminary, N.Y.C., 1959, 1966; cons. on missionary research com. Joint Internat. Missionary Council and World Council Chs., 1954—; Select preacher, vis. lectr. Cambridge U., Eng., 1960; Mullins lectr, So. Bapt. Theol. Sem., Louisville, 1961; sr. F. Council Humanities, Princeton U., 1961-62; vis. lectr. Princeton Theol. Sem., 1962, 65, 69, Pacific Sch. Religion, Berkeley, 1962, Eden Theol. Seminary, Webster Groves, Mo., 1965; Zabriskie lectr. P.E. Sem., Alexandria, Va., 1963; vis. lectr. ecclesiastical art Union Theol. Sem., Richmond Va.; vis. lectr. Mansfield Coll., Oxford, 1969; vis. prof. Drew U., 1969; research grantee Huntington Library, San Marino, 1967-68, Founding trustee Inst. Ecumenical and Cultural Research, St. John's Abbey and U., Collegeville, Minn., 1967—. Mem. Am. Soc. Ch. History, Am. Theol. Soc. Author: Christian Worship: Its Making and Meaning, 1946; The Worship of the English Puritans, 1948; The English Free Churches, 1952; Christian Deviations, 1954; A Mirror or the Ministry in Modern Novels, 1959; Worship and Theology in England, vols. I, 3-5, 1961-70; Varieties of English Preaching, 1900-1960, 1963. Editor: (with R.H.W. Shepherd) An Anthology of South African Missions, 1953. Asso. editor Worship, 1967—. Contbg. editor Studia Liturgica (Rotterdam). Contbr. periodicals. Home: 101 Laurel Rd Princeton NJ 08540 summer 3 Hawk Mountain Pittsfield VT 05762

DAVIES, HUNTER, author, journalist; b. Renfrew, Scotland, Jan. 7, 1936; s. John Hunter and Marion (Brechin) D.; B.A., Univ. Coll., Durham, Eng., 1957; m. Margaret Forster, June 11, 1960; children—Caltlin, Jake. Reporter, Manchester Eve. Chronicle, 1958, Sunday Times, London, 1960, writer Atticus column, 1961—. Author: Here We Go Round the Mulberry Bush, 1966; The Other Half, 1966; The New London Spy, 1966; The Beatles (the ofcl. biography), 1968; The Rise and Fall of Jake Sullivan, 1969; I Knew Daisy Smuten, 1970; A Very Loving Couple, 1971. Home: 11 Boscastle Rd London NW 5 England

DAVIES, JACK, educator; b. Yorkshire, Eng., Aug. 24, 1919; s. William and Mary Ann (Boyce) D.; B.Sc., Leeds U., 1941, M.B. Ch.B. (Rochefeller Found. student fellow 1941-43), 1943, M.D., 1946; M.D., State U. Ia., 1943; M.A. (hon.), Cambridge (Eng.) U., 1946; m. Elizabeth Ann Conroy, Feb. 11, 1946; children—Patricia Ann, John Edwar Came to U.S., 1951. naturalized, 1954. Demonstrator anatomy Leeds U. Med. Sch., 1941-42; demonstrator, lectr. anatomy Cambridge U., 1942-51, fellow St. John's Coll., 1947-5l; asst. prof. anatomy State U. Ia., 1951-55; asso. prof., then prof. anatomy Washington U. Med. Sch., St. Louis, 1955-63; prof. anatomy, chmn. dept. Vanderbilt U. Sch. Medicine, 1963-. Cons. USPHS, 1957-. Markle scholar medicine, 1952-55. Mem. Am. Assn. Anatomists. Episcopalian. Author: Survey of Research in Gestation, 1960; Human Developmental Anatomy, 1963. Home: 6632 Elsemere Rd Nashville TN 37205.

DAVIES, JAMES CHOWNING, educator; b. Wauwatosa, Wis., May 6, 1918; s. Howell David and Julia (Merrell) D.; A.B., Oberlin Coll., 1939; postgrad. in law U. Chgo., 1939- 40, U. Tex., 1945-46; Ph.D., U. Cal. at Berkeley, 1952; m. Eleanor Johnstone Getze, Jan. 10, 1943; 1 dau., Sarah Louise. Supr. prodn. scheduling Consol. Vultee Aircraft Corp. (now Gen. Dynamics), San Diego, also Ft. Worth, 1942-45; research tng. fellow Social Sci. Research Council, 1950-51; Carnegie fellow polit. sci. U. Mich. Survey Research Center, 1951-53; asst. prof. to prof. polit. sci. Cal. Inst. Tech., Pasadena, 1953-63, faculty research fellow Social Sci. Research Council, 1961-62; prof. U. Ore., Eugene, 1963—, head dept. polit. sci., 1964-67; vis. asst. prof. U. Cal. at Los Angeles, summer 1956; vis. asso. prof. U. Cal. at Berkeley, 1959-60. Served with AUS, 1946-47. Rockefeller Found. fellow, 1962-63, sr. research fellow U. Pa. Fgn. Policy Research Inst., 1969. Mem. Am. Polit. Sci. Assn. (council 1965-67), Western Polit. Sci. Assn. (pres. 1969-70), A.A.A.S., Phi Beta Kappa. Author: Human Nature in Politics, 1963. Editor: When Men Revolt And Why, 1971. Home: 1560 Prospect Dr Eugene OR 97403

DAVIES, JAMES H., air force officer; b. Piedmont, Cal., October 25, 1903; s. Hugh and Anne (Davis) D.; A.B., U. of Cal., 1928; grad. Air Corps Primary Flying Sch., 1929, Advance Flying Sch., bombardment course, 1930, Tactical Sch., 1939; grad. Air War Coll., 1947, Nat. War Coll., 1949; m. Ethel Warner MacGregor. Commd. 2d lt., Air Corps, U.S. Army, 1930, advanced through the grades to maj. gen.; served as group comdr. 27th Bombardment Group, Phillippines Islands, 1941; comd. 27th Bombardment Gorup and 3d Bombardment Group, South Pacific area, later becoming chief of staff, then comdg. gen. 5th Bomber Command; comdg. gen. 313th Bombardment Wing (serving in Pacific area), 1945; operations officer 4th Air Force Hdqrs, Hamilton Field, Cal., 1945-46; comdr. A.T.S., Air Transport, Command Washington, 1947-48, chief of staff ATRC, Scott Air Force Base, Ill., 1949-51; comdg. gen. 3510th Flying Tng. Wing-Randolph Air Force Base, Tex.; comdg. gen. Alaskan Air Command. Dir., El Dorado Bank, Napa. Decorated D.S.C. Silver Star (with oak leaf cluster). ribbons Pacific and European theaters. Mem. Kappa Sigma. Clubs: St. Francis Yacht (San Francisco); Silverado Country (Napa). Home: 1547 Silver Trail Napa CA 94558 Office: 1420 2d St Napa, CA

DAVIES, JOHN LODWICK, Jr., lawyer; b. Columbus, O., May 30, 1909; s. John Lodwick and Pearl (Slemmons) D.; B.A., Ohio State U., 1930; LL.B., 1932; m. Anne Turner, Nov. 36, 1949; childrenKristen, Lisa, Megan. Admitted to Ohio bar, 1932, since practiced in Columbus; first v.p. David Davies, Inc., Columbus, 1956-. Trustee, sec. Columbus Gallery of Fine Arts. Served with AUS, 1942-46. Mem. Am., Ohio, Columbus (pres. 1959-60) bar assns. Presbyn. (trustee). Club: Athletic (pres. 1965). Home: 2741 Leeds Rd Columbus OH 43221 Office: 88 E Broad St Columbus OH 43215

DAVIES, JOHN SHERRARD, govt. ofcl.; b. Delphos, O., Apr. 4, 1917; s. Homer M. and Elizabeth (Sherrard) S.; B.A., Ohio Wesleyan U., 1939; m. Marie Evelyn Donat, July 8, 1940; children—John Morgan, Anne Donat (Mrs. Melvin Hunter). With Bell Telephone System, 1941-69; spl. asst. to Pres. Nixon, also head Office White House Visitors, 1969—. mem. Nat. Visitor Facilities Adv. Commn., 1969—. Bd. dirs. Los Angeles County chpt. Am. Cancer Soc., 1968-69. Served with USAAF, 1942-46. Decorated Bronze Star; officer Order Brit. Empire. Mem. Sigma Chi, Omicron Delta Kappa. Office: The White House Washington DC 20500

DAVIES, JULIEN TOWNSEND, lawyer; b. N.Y.C., Aug. 13, 1895; s. Julien Townsend and Marie Rose (de Garmendia) D.; Ph.B. cum laude, Yale, 1917, LL.B. cum laude, 1922; m. Faith de Moss Robinson, June 26, 1920 (div. 1933); children—Julien Townsend, Faith Robinson (Mrs. George R. Le Sauvage, Jr.), John Robinson (dec.); m. 2d, Marie O'Connor Quinn, July 7, 1933 (div. 1960); m. 3d, Ida Pasquali, May 20, 1960. Admitted to N.Y. bar, 1924, since practiced N.Y.C.; partner Davies, Hardy, Loeb, Ives & Lawther and predecessor firms, 1928-71. Trustee, Village Flower Hill, Nassau County, N.Y., 1937-40, mayor, 1940-44. Served as ensign , chief gunner's mate, U.S. Navy, 1917-19. Mem. Order of Coif, Sigma Xi, Delta Psi. Club: St. Anthony. Home: 200 E 66th St New York City NY 10021 Office: 2 Broadway New York City NY 10004

DAVIES, MARTIN, museum ofcl.; b. London, Eng., Mar. 22, 1908; s. Ernest and Eleanor (Taylor) D.; grad. Rugby, 1926; B.A., King's Coll., Cambridge (Eng.) U., 1930; D.Litt. (hon.), Exeter (Eng.) U., 1966. Mem. staff Nat. Gallery, London 1932—, dir., 1968—. Decorated comdr. British Empire. Fellow Brit. Acad., Soc. Antiquaries London. Home: 16 Rupert House Nevern Sq London SW 5 England Office: National Gallery Trafalgar Sq London WC 2 England

DAVIES, MEREDITH, orch. conductor; b. Birkenhead, Eng., July 30, 1922; jr. exhibitioner, part-time scholar piano, Royal Coll. Music, London, Eng., then scholar organ; advanced course conducting, St. Cecilia Acad., Rome, Italy, 1952, 55. Chief organist Hereford (Eng.) Cathedral; cond. Three Choirs Festival; cond. major orchs. in France, Sweden, Italy, Argentina and Eng., also broadcasts with orchs. on BBC; cond. opera Covent Garden. also Sadler's Wells; guest conductor Vancouver (B.C., Can.) Symphony Orch., 1961, now mus. dir., condr.; mus. dir. Bach Choir, Vancouver; condr. world premiere Benjamin' Britten's War Requiem, 1962, opera Billy Budd at Covent Garden, 1965; prin. condr. B.B.C. Tng. Orch., 1969—. Mem. jury Liverpool (Eng.) Internat. Conductors Competition, 1966. Recipient prize Internat. Competition Rome, 1955. Home: 59 Fishpool St Saint Albans ertshire England Office: 601 Cambie St Vancouver 3 British Columbia Canada

DAVIES, PAUL EWING, clergyman, educator; b. Fort Wayne, Ind., Sept 14, 1898; s. George Ewing and Mabel Augusta (Currie) D.; ed. Westminster Jr. Coll.; A.B., Princeton, 1920; B.D., McCormick Theol. Sem., 1923; Ph.D., U. Edinburgh, 1928; Dr. Divinity, Tusculum Coll., 1950; m. Marjorie Olive Billings, Aug. 21, 1924; children—Majorie Anne, Katharine Billings, Paul Ewing. Ordained to ministry Presbyn. Ch., 1923; N.T. fellow McCormick Theol. Sem., Chgo., 1923-25, asst. prof., 1931-35, prof. N. T., Greek and Exegesis, 1935-68; dir. McCormick Summer Conf. for Ministers, 1956-62; pastor Oakland Presbyn. Ch., Springfield, O., 1925-30, Merriam Park Presbyn. Ch., St. Paul, Minn., 1930-31; vis. prof. Lane Sem., Cin. 1931-32; Editor: McCormick Speaking, 1947-60, McCormick Quar., 1960-68, Bibl. Research Bd. dirs. Chgo. Commons Assn. Mem. Chgo. Soc. Biblical Research, Soc. Biblical Lit. and Exegesis, Am. Acad. Religion. Presbyn. Clubs: Stylites, Tower (Princeton, N.J.). Contbr. jour. of Bible and Religion. Jour. of Biblical Lit., Interpretation. Home: 81 Salem Lane Evanston IL 60203 Office: 800 W Belden Av Chicago IL 60614

DAVIES, PAUL LEWIS, banker; b. Cozad, Neb., July 27, 1899; s. Robert and Emma Estella (Bennison) D.; student U. Cal. at Berkeley, 1917-21, Harvard Sch. of Bus., 1921-22; m. Faith Crummey, Oct. 2, 1926; children—Paul Lewis, Nancy (dec.), Judith. Clk., Nat. Bank of

Commerce, 1922; asst. cashier, asst. v.p., and v.p. Am. Trust Co., 1922- 28; v.p., v.p. and treas., pres. Food Machinery & Chem. Corp. (now FMC Corp.), 1928-56, chmn. bd., chief exec. officer, 1956-66, dir., chmn. exec. com., 1966-67, sr. dir. and dir., 1967—; sr. partner Lehman Bros., N.Y.C., 1966—; dir. Lehman Corp., So. Pacific Co., IBM, Caterpillar Tractor Co. Mem. Bus. Council; hon. trustee Com. Econ. Devel. Bd. dirs. Stanford Research Inst.; adv. bd. U. Cal. Sch. Bus. Adminstrn. Served U.S. Army, 1918. Mem. Smithsonian Inst. Assos. (dir.), Alpha Sigma Phi. Methodist. Mason. Clubs: Blind Brood (Portchester, N.Y.); Sainte Claire (San Jose, Cal.); Pacific Union, Bohemian (San Francisco); Links, Pinnacle, Recess (N.Y.C.); Cypress Point (Pebble Beach, Cal.); Cotton Bay (Eleuthera Island, Bahamas). Home: 1598 University Av San Jose CA 95126 Office: 1105 Coleman Av San Jose CA 92110 Office: 1 William St New York City NY 10004

DAVIES, PETER MAXWELL, composer; b. Manchester, Eng., Sept. 8, 1934; s. Thomas and Hilda (Howard) D.; student Royal Manchester Coll. Music, also Manchester U., 1952-56; Italian Govt. scholar Petrassi-Rome, 1957-58; Harkness fellow, Princeton, 1962-64, Dir. music Cirencester (Eng. Grammar Sch., 1959-62; asso. with Pierrot Players, Eng., 1967—. Composer: Prolation for Orchestra, 1959; O Magnum Mysterium for Choir, Instrumentalists and Organ, 1960; Frammenti di Leopardi for Soprano, Contralto and Instruments, 1962; Veni Sancte Spiritus for Soprano, Contralto and Bass Soli, Chorus and Orchestra, 1963; Second Fantasia for Orchestra, 1964; Revelation and Fall for Soprano and Instruments, 1965; L'Homme Armé for Chamber Ensemble, 1968; Eight Songs for a Mad King, for Baritone and Instrument, 1969; St. Thomas Wake, Foxtrot for Orchestra, 1969; (opera) Taverner, 1970; (film score) The Devils', 1971. Address: 26 Fitzroy Sq London W1 England

DAVIES, RALPH KENNETH, bus. exec.; b. Cherrdale, Va., Sept. 9, 1897; s. Percival and Nellie (Waldron) D.; student Fresno High Sch., 1909-12; spl. studies, U. of Calif. Ext., Berkeley and San Francisco; m. Louise Stivers, Aug. 29, 1927; children—Mrs. Maryon Davies Lewis, Ellen (Mrs. R. Stockton Rush, Jr.), Alice. With Standard Oil Co. of Cal., 1912-46, dir., 1930-42, sr. v.p., 1935-46; with Anglo Oil Eng., 1928-29; organizer and exec. v.p. Internat. Bitumen Emulsions Co., 1929, pres., 1938-41; exec. v.p. Standard Stations, Inc., 1930-38, pres., 1938-40; pres. Trunkline Gas Supply Co., 1947-49, dir., 1947-52; pres., dir. Am. Ind. Oil Co., 1947-58, Am. Ind. Oil de Mexico, S.A. de C.V., 1949-58, Am. Independent Oil Co. of Iran, 1955-58; dir., chmn. bd. Am. Ind. Oil Co., 1958-62; chmn. bd. dirs. Independent Tankships, Inc., 1948-57; dir., chmn. exec. com. Golden State Co., Ltd., 1948-54; mem. bd. dirs. Am. Pres. Lines, 1948—, chmn. bd. 1952—; pres. dir. APL Assos. Inc., 1952-56; chmn. bd., dir. Natomas Co., 1956—, Natomas Co. of Peru, 1961—, St. Mary's Sq., Inc., 1961; dir. Bank of Cal., 1956- -; cons. prof. marketing, Stanford U. Grad. Sch. of Bus., 1937-61. Trustee Franklin Hosp., San Francisco, pres. bd. trustees, 1967—. Chmn. FTC Code Committee, 1936; pres. Fair Practices Assn. (Petroleum Products), 1937-39. Deputy petroleum administrator Petroleum Adminstrn. for War, 1942-46; mem. President's Mission to London to negotiate Anglo-Am. oil treaty; special cons. to sec. of the interior, 1946-47. Awarded Presidential Medal for Merit in recognition of distinguished war service, 1945. Organized and served as 1st dir. Oil and Gas Div. Interior Dept., 1946; mem. Nat. Petroleum Council, 1950, Mem. Cal. C. of C. (dir. 1935-41). Clubs: Pacific Union. Menlo County (San Francisco); Sulgrave (Washington). Home: Woodside CA 94062 Office: 601 California St San Francisco CA 94108 ☆

DAVIES, RHYS, author; b. Rhondda, Wales, Nov. 9, 1903; s. Thomas Rhys and Sarah (Lewis) D.; ed. Porth Grammar Sch., Wales. Decorated Order Brit. Empire. Author: The Withered Root, 1927; A Pig in a Poke, 1931; Count Your Blessings, 1932; The Red Hills, 1932; Love Provoked, 1933; Honey and Bread, 1935; The Things Men Do, 1936; A Time to Laugh, 1937; Jubilee Blues, 1938; Under the Rose, 1940; Tomorrow to Fresh Woods, 1941; The Black Venus, 1944; The Trip to London, 1946; The Dark Daughters, 1947; Boy With a Trumpet, 1949; Marianne, 1951; The Painted King, 1954; Collected Stories, 1955; The Perishable Quality, 1957; The Darling of Her Heart, 1958; Girl Waiting in the Shade, 1960; The Chosen One, 1967; Print of A Hare's Foot, 1969; Nobody Answered The Bell, 1971; also articles. Home: 15 Russell Ct Woburn Place London WC 1 England Office: care Curtis Brown Ltd 13 King St London WC2, England

DAVIES, RICHARD TOWNSEND, fgn. service officer; b. Bklyn., May 28, 1920; s. John W.A. and Laura (Townsend) D.; A.B., Columbia, 1942; m. Jean Stevens, Dec. 5, 1949; children—John Stevens, Michael Hardie, Glyn Townsend, Stephen Arthur. Instr. German, Poly. Inst. Bklyn., 1946-47; 3d sec. Am. embassy, Warsaw, Poland, 1947-49, 2d sec., Moscow, 1962-63, Kabul, Afghanistan, 1955-58; polit. officer internat. staff NATO, Paris, France, 1953-55; pub. affairs adviser Office Soviet Union Affairs, Dept. State, Washington, 1958-61, dep. exec. sec., 1964; asst. dir. (Soviet Union and Eastern Europe) USIA, Washington, 1965-68; U.S. consul gen., Calcutta, India, 1968-69; mem. planning and coordination staff Dept. State 1969-70; dep. asst. sec. state for European affairs, 1970—. Served with AUS, 1942- 45. Recipient Honor award USIA, 1968. Home: 3511 Leland St Chevy Chase MD 20015 Office: Dept of State Washington DC 20520

DAVIES, ROBERT ERNEST, educator, biochemist; b. Barton-upon-Irwell, Eng., Aug. 17, 1919; s. William Owen and C. Stella (Spencer) D.; B.Sc., U. Manchester, 1941, M.Sc., 1942, D.Sc., 1952; Ph.D., U. Sheffield, 1949; M.A., Oxford U., 1956; m. Helen Jean Rogoff, Sept. 8, 1961; childrenDaniel J., Richard D. British citizen. Mem. faculty U. Manchester, 1941-42, U. Sheffield, 1942-54, U. Heidelberg (Germany), 1954, Oxford U., 1954-59; mem. faculty U. Pa., 1955—, prof. biochemistry, 1955-70, Benjamin Franklin prof. molecular biology, 1970—; chmn. grad. group molecular biology, 1962—, chmn. dept. animal biology, 1962—. Mem. British Home Guard, 1940-45, British Nat. Fire Service, 1940-45. Fellow Royal Soc.; mem. Am. Chem. Soc., Am. Soc. Biol. Chemists, Am. Physiol. Soc., Sigma Xi, Phi Zeta. Mem. editorial bd. Biochem. Jour., 1951-56. Spl. research biochemistry muscle contraction, function of kidney medulla, mechanism hydrochloric acid secretion in stomach. Home: 7053 McCallum St Philadelphia PA 19119.

DAVIES, ROBERT HOLBORN, mfg. exec.; b. Galesburg, Ill., Sept. 19, 1919; s. Gomer and Ethel Mae (Holborn) D.; student U. Minn., 1936-39, Santa Ana Coll., 1939; m. Eleanor Belle Cogan, May 12, 1940; children—Michael Joseph, Stephen Dewi. Cons. engr. Lincoln Electric Co., Cleve., 1943-49; v.p. Baker Raulang Co., Cleve., 1949-51; v.p. Clark Equipment Co., Buckanan, Mich., 1951-59; pres. Electric Autolite Co., Toledo, 1958-63; chmn. bd. Eltra Corp., Toledo, 1963-64; pres. Sangamo Electric Co., 1964—; dir. Dana Corp. Mem. N.A.M. (dir.), Am. Ordnance Assn., Soc. Automotive Engrs., Aircraft Owners and Pilots Assn., Nat. Pilots Assn., Nat. Aero. Assn., Newcomen Soc. N.A., Material Handling Inst. (past pres.). Clubs: Toledo, Belmont Country, Toledo Country (Toledo, O.); Detroit Athletic; N.Y. Yacht, Cloud, Sky (N.Y.C.); Union League, Chicago (Chgo.); Belmont Country (Toledo). Office: Sangamo Electric Co Springfield FL 62705

DAVIES, ROBERT MORTON, ednl. adminstr.; b. Carmi, Ill., Sept. 22, 1920; s. John Morton and Helen Wallace) D.; B.A., Wheaton (Ill.) Coll., 1941; M.A., U. Pa., 1945, Ph.D., 1954; postgrad. N.Y. U., 195556; m. Elizabeth Bell, July 2, 1955; children—Henry H., Robert W., J. Wallace. Asso. prof. The King's Coll., Briarcliff Manor, NY., 1943-50; dean men Perkiomen Sch., Pennsburg, Pa., 1951-52; asst. prof. English, adminstrv. asst. Valley Forge Jr. Coll., Wayne, 1952-55; 195255; instr. N.Y. (C.) Maritime Coll., 195558; prof., chmn. English dept. and div. humanities Thiel Coll., Greenville, Pa., 195864; dean Ithaca (N.Y.) Coll., 1964 66, provost, 1966—. Asst. instr. English, U. Pa., Phila., parttime 1946; asst. prof. English, Rutgers U., New Brunswick, N.J., parttime, 1955-58. Mem. Am. Conf. Acad. Deans, Am. Mgmt. Assn., Modern Lang. Assn., Alpha Psi Omega, Pi Delta Epsilon, Delta Mu Delta. Author: The Humanism of Paul Elmer More. 1958. Contbr. articles, book revs., essays to profl. jours. Home: 202 South Hill Terrace Ithaca NY 14850 Office: Ithaca Coll Ithaca NY 14850

DAVIES, RODGER PAUL, fgn. service officer; b. Berkeley, Cal., May 7, 1921; s. John Leslie and Catherine Paul (Rodgers) D.; B.A., U. Cal. at Berkeley, 1942; student U.S. Army War Coll., 1958-59; m. Sarah Ann Burgess, Sept. 29, 1948; children—Ann Dana, John Burgess. Joined U.S. diplomatic service, 1946; 3d sec. and vice consul, Jidda, 1946-48; assigned Fgn. Service Inst. for Arabic tng., 1948-49, 2d sec. and consul, Damascus, 1949-5l; 2d sec. and consul, Beirut and Amman, 1950-5l, also consul, Jerusalem, 1950-51; dep. chief Near East, South Asia and Africa div., Internat. Broadcasting Service, 1951-54; prin. officer Am. Embassy, Benghazi, Libya, 1954-56; counselor of embassy and dep. chief of mission Am. Embassy, Tripolli, Libya, 1956-58; with U.S. Army War Coll., 1958; became counselor Embassy and dep. chief Mission at Baghdad, Iraq, 1959; dir. Office Near Eastern Affairs, Dept. of State, 1962-65; dep. asst. sec. state for Near Eastern and South Asian affairs, 1965—, career minister, 1969. Epsilon. Home: 35 Hillcrest Rd Berkeley CA 94705 Office: Dept of State Washington DC 20525

DAVIES, RONALD N., judge; b. Crookston, Minn., Dec. 11, 1904; s. Norwood S. and Minnie M. (Quigley) D.; A.B., U. N.D., 1927, LL.D., 1961; LL.B., Georgetown U., 1930; m. Mildred M. Doran, Oct. 10, 1933; children—Timothy Q., Mary Jo, Thomas A., Catharine A., Jean M. Practice of law, Grand Forks, N.D., 1930-32; judge Municipal Ct., Grand Forks, 1932-40; lectr. U. N.D. Sch. Law, 1952-55; U.S. dist judge, Dist. of N.D., Fargo, 1955—. Mem. N.D. Bd. Pardons, 1933, N.D. Athletic Commn., 1935. Served from 1st lt. to lt. col., AUS, 1942-46. Recipient Outstanding Alumnus award Georgetown U. Law Center, 1958. Fellow Am. Bar Found.; mem. N.D. Bar Assn., N.D. (exec. dir. 1947-55), Grand Forks C. of C. (pres. 1953), Am. Legion, Am. Bar Assn., 40 and 8, Order of Coif, Sigma Nu, Phi Alpha Delta. Roman Catholic. Elk, K.C. Home: 1449 S 10th St Fargo ND 58102 Office: US Courthouse Fargo ND 58102

DAVIES, THOMAS DANIEL, naval officer; b. Cleve., Nov. 3, 1914; s. David A. and Katherine (Smith) D.; student Case Inst. Tech., 1931-33; B.S., U.S. Naval Acad., 1937; grad. Nat. War Coll., 1962; M.S. in Internat. Affairs, George Washington U., 1966; m. Eloise English, Apr. 27, 1945; childrenThomas Daniel, Douglas, Ronald, Meredith. Commd. ensign U.S. Navy, 1937, advanced through grades to rear adm., 1965; assigned cruisers U.S.S. Portland and U.S.S. Witchita. 1937-41; designated naval aviator, 1942; exec. officer Bombing Squadron 192, 1942-44; assigned offices and burs. in Washington, also mem. staff comdr. Fleet Air Mediterranean, 1952-54; comdr. Task Group 68.7, 1948; comdg. officer Naval Air Engring. Facility, Phila., 1954-58, U.S.S. Caliente, 1960-61; comdr. Fleet Air Wing 3, 1962-63; comdg., officer U.S. Naval Air Sta., Norfolk, Va., 1963- 64; dir. Office Program Appraisal, Navy Dept., 1965-67; comdr. Carrier Div. 20, 1967-69; dep. chief naval material (devel.) Navy Dept., Washington, 1969-. Exec. sec. Mac Short Found., 1951-. Decorated Legion of Merit, D.F.C. with gold star, numerous unit and area ribbons; Brazilian Order So. Cross. Mem. Inst. Navigation. Home: 1102 S Stanmore Dr Potomac MD 20854 Office: Deputy Chief Naval Material (Devel) Navy Dept Washington DC 20360

DAVIES, THOMAS HARRISON, chemist; b. Balt., Feb. 21, 1912; s. Seabury and Arabella Knight (Harrison) D.; A.B., Johns Hopkins, 1935, Ph.D., 1938; m. Esther S. Farney, June 30, 1940; children—Arabelle, Jennifer, Seabury. NRC fellow medicine Cal. Inst. Tech., 1938-40; research chemist Lederle Labs., 1940-43; asso. sect. chief Manhattan Project, Oak Ridge, Tenn., 1943-46; asso. prof. U. Chgo., 1946-52; adminstrv. fellow Mellon Inst., Pitts., 1952-57, dir. research, 1957-67; prof. chemistry Carnegie-Mellon U., 1967—. Mem. Am. Chem. Soc., Fedn. Am. Scientists. United World Federalists (Pitts. bd. 1957—). Asso. editor: Bull. Atomic Scientists, 1948-52. Home: Evergreen Hamlet Pittsburgh PA 15209 Office: Mellon Inst Pittsburgh PA 15213

DAVIES, WALTER HENRY, Jr., merchandising exec.; b. Chgo., May 26, 1916; s. Walter Henry and Flora (Allenger) D.; Ph.B., Northwestern U., 1947; M.B.A., U. Chgo., 1959; m. Besselou Hunter, Jan. 1, 1937; children—Ronald, Geoffrey, Walter Henry III, Leslie, Melissa. Asst. treas. Comml. Credit Corp., 1937-43; v.p. Exchange Nat. Bank, Chgo., 1943-55; asst. treas. Sears, Roebuck & Co., 1955-62; v.p., treas., dir. Gamble-Skogmo, Inc., 1962-68, exec. v.p., treas., 1968-69, vice chmn., treas., 1969—, also dir.; chmn., dir. Gambles Continental Bank; dir. Aldens, Inc., Bd. dirs. Met. Med. Center, Mpls. Episcopalian. Clubs: University (Chgo); Lafeyette, Minneapolis, Rotary, Minnetonka Country, Minikahda (Mpls.). Home: Woodside Rd Route 1 Excelsior MN 55331 Office: 5100 Gamble Dr Minneapolis MN 55440

DAVIES, WILBUR HUGH, book pub.; b. Boston, Feb. 2, 1903; s. Hugh and Lillie (Giggy) D.; student Boston U., 1922-25; m. Vera Gillis, Oct. 10, 1927; children—Norma Joy (Mrs. Marden L. Perry), Carol Gay, Linda Love (Mrs. Richard Pounds). Employed with The Pilgrim Press Book Store, Boston, 1922-30, head mail order dept., 1927-30; sec. publ. dept. Nat. council YMCA, 1930-42; with Fleming H. Revell Co., Westwood, N.J., 1942-69, exec. v.p., 1961-62, pres., 1962-68, chmn. exec. com., 1968-69; also dir.; dir. Booster St. Realty Corp., Stackpole Co., Harrisburg, Pa. Mem. Assn. Press com. Nat. bd. YMCAs, 1950-70; chmn. religious pubs. group Am. Book Pubs. council, 1952; mem. Laymen's Nat. Bible Com. Chmn. corner stone div. Pascask Valley (N.J.) Hosp. campaign. Mem. pres. bd. Pepperdine Coll., Los Angeles, Mem. Am. Booksellers Assn. (past dir.) Mason. Rotarian (pres. Westwood 1962). Author articles. 348 Main St Emerson NJ

DAVIES, WILLIAM DAVID, clergyman and educator; b. Carmarthenshire, England, Dec. 9, 1911; s. David and Rachel (Powell) D.; M.A., Cambridge U., 1942; D. D., U. Wales, 1948; hon. degree, St. Andrews, 1968; m. Eurwen Llewelyn, Jan. 1942; 1 dau., Rachel Mary. Came to U.S., 1950. Ordained to ministry Congl. Ch., 1942; minister, Cambridgeshire, Eng., 1942-46; asst. tutor Cheshunt Coll., Cambridge, 1942; prof. N.T. studies Yorkshire United Coll., 1946-50; prof. bibl. theology Duke U. Div. Sch., 1950-55; prof. religion Princeton, 1955-59; Edward Robinson prof. Union Theol. Sem., and adjunct prof. religion Columbia, 1959-66; George Washington Ivey prof. advanced studies and research in Christian origins Duke, 1966—. Exec. com. New Brit. Translation of the Bible, 1948-50; corr. fellow N.T., Seminar, Uppasala, Guggenheim fellow, 1960, 1966-67; Burkitt Medal British Acad., 1964. Corresponding fellow British Academy; mem. Soc. for Bibl. Lit. and Exegesis, Studiorim Novi Testamenti Societas, Am. Schs. Oriental Research, Soc. O.T. Studies of Eng. Author: Paul and Rabbinic Judaism, 1948; Torah in the Messianic Age and/or The Age to Come, 1952. Editor: (with D. Daube) The Background of the New Testament and its Eschatology (Studies in Honor of C.H. Dodd), 1956; Christian Origins and Judaism, 1962; The Setting of the Sermon on the Mount, 1963; Introduction to Pharisaism, 1965; An Invitation to the New Testament, 1965; The Sermon on The Mount, 1966. Contbr. profl. publs. Home: 228 Monticello Av Durham NC 27705

D'AVIGDOR-GOLDSMID, HENRY JOSEPH, banker; b. June 10, 1909; s. Sir Osmond Eilm d'Avigdor-Goldsmid; M.A., Balliol Coll., Oxford (Eng.) U., 1938; m. Rosemary Margaret Horlick, 1940; one dau. Alderman of Kent, 1951, justice of peace, 1949; high sheriff, 1953; mem. Parliament for Walsall South, 1955—; Parliamentary pvt. sec. to minister housing and local govt., 1955-56; chmn. Anglo Isreal Bank Ltd., 1961—. Mem. Conservative Party. Clubs: White's, Carlton (London). Address: Somerhill Tonbridge Kent England*

DAVILA, CARLOS V., justice; b. Bayamon, P.R., May 2, 1914; s. Sebastian and Luisa Dávila; B.A., B.L.L., U. P.R., 1938; m. Adaljisa Vélez, Nov. 28, 1959; children—Mariá, Adaljisa, Carlos Sebastián. Asso. justice Supreme Ct. of P.R. Address: Tribunal Supreme de P R Apartado 2392 San Juan PR 00903

D'AVINO, CARMEN, motion picture co., exec.; b. Waterbury, Conn., Oct. 31, 1918; s. Anthony and Florence (Denze) D'A.; student Art Student's League, N.Y.C., 1938- 41, Colorado Springs (Colo.) Fine Arts Center, 1941, Ecoles des Beaux Arts, Paris, France, 1946-47, Acad. de la Grande Chaumiere, Paris, 1947- 48, 50-51, Ecole Technique de Photographie et Cinematographic, Paris, 1949-50; m. Helena Elfving, Nov. 17, 1951; 1 son by previous marriage, Anthony. Created all animation sequences for 12-12-42 (Grand prize Oberhausen Film Festival), 1966, Adventure in Color (Nat. Visual Presentation Assn. award, also Chris award), Market in Motion (Golden Eagle award, also Bronze medal, Atlantic Film Festival), E.S.S. Touch of Tomorrow (Golden Eagle award); other prodns. include Theme and Internat. Film and TV Festival), 1966; other prodns. include Theme and Transition (Creative Film Found. award), 1956; The Big O (Creative Film Found. award, Montevideo Internat. Film Festival award), 1958; The Room (Creative Film Found. award, Uruguaian award), 1959; A Trip (Creative Film Found. award), 1960; Stone Sonata (spl. jury prize Arnecy Internat. Film Festival), 1963; Pianissimo (Blue ribbon award Ednl. Film Library Assn.), 1963; A Finnish Fable, 1965; Tarantella, 1966; Like a Bird (spl. award Expo 67), 1967; Minestrone with Music, 1967; one man exhbns. paintings New Delhi and Bombay, India, 1948-49. Tiffany Found. fellow painting, 1949; Ford Found. grantee, 1964. Served with inf. AUS, 1941- 45. Decorated Bronze Star. Address: 220 E 14th St New York City NY 10003.

DAVIS, A. M., lawyer; b. N.Y.C., 1883; A.B., Columbia, 1904, LL.B., 1906. Admitted to N.Y. bar, 1906; mem. firm Davis, Gilbert, Levine and Schwartz, N.Y.C. Mem. Assn. Bar City N.Y., Am., N.Y. State bar assns., N.Y. County Lawyers Assn., Phi Beta Kappa. Office: 500 Fifth Av New York City NY 10036*

DAVIS, A. ABRAHAM L., Jr., lawyer, corp. exec.; b. Kent, O., 1922; B.A., Yale, 1943, LL.B., 1944; m. Mae Reed, May 2, 1949; 1 son. Admitted to Massachusetts bar, 1944; practiced in Boston, 1947--; gen. counsel Acme Mfg. Co., Boston, 1966--; dir. 1st Nat. Bank. Home: 23 Beacon St Boston MA 02107

DAVIS, A. ARTHUR, lawyer; b. Sioux City, Ia., Oct. 12, 1928; s. Edward R. and Isabel (Baron) D.; B.S., Northwestern U., 1950, LL.B., 1952; m. Joan Benham Below, Aug. 6, 1955; (div. May 1970); children-Pamela Benham, Mark Baron. Admitted to Ia. bar, 1952; practice in Des Moines, 1955—; asso. Brody, Parker, Roberts, Thomas & Harriss, 1955-59; partner Thoma, Schoenthal, Davis, Hockenberg & Wine and Predecessor firm, 1959—; lectr. pub. speaking Drake U., 1955-60. Dir. Economy Forms Corp., Midwest Packaging Corp., Constrn. Products, Inc., C.M.C., Inc., Weitz Co., Inc., Metal Products Mfg. Co., Triple F, Inc. Mem. Des Moines Commn. on Human Rights, 1960-63; mem. Bd. Edn. Des Moines Ind. Community Sch. Dist., 1963-69, pres., 1967-68. Pres., bd. dirs. Des Moines Child Guidance Center; bd. dirs. Knalba Found., Polk County chpt. A.R.C. Served to 1st lt. U.S. Army, 1953-55. Recipient Nat. award People to People Program, 1961. Mem. Order of Coif, Delta Sigma Rho, Phi Delta Phi, Phi Elsilon Pi. Democrat. Jewish religion. Club: Des Moines. Author articles. Home: 1400 Woodland Des Moines IA 50309 Office: Empire Bldg Des Moines IA 50309

DAVIS, ALLAN CONRADT, engr., tobacco co. exec.; b. Balt., Feb. 14, 1896; s. E. Asbury and Jennie (Conradt) D.; student Friends Sch., Balt., 1905-13; A. B., Johns Hopkins, 1917; m. Dorothy Lewis Hamilton, Oct. 20, 1927. Entered U.S. Naval Res. as machinist's mate, 2d class, 1917; entered U.S. Naval Acad., Annapolis, 1918, commd. ensign. U.S.N., 1918, resigned as lt. (j.g.), 1919; now chmn. F.A. Davis and Sons, Inc., Balt.; dir. Nat., Central Bank, Balt. Trustee Johns Hopkins, Balt. YMCA: bd. dirs. Balt Goodwill Industries, Balt. Eye, Ear and Throat Hosp. Mem. Nat. Assn. Tobacco Distbrs. (dir.), Md. Acad. Scis. (pres.), Delta Upsilon, Omicron Delta Kappa. Clubs: Engineers, Baltimore Country, Ice (Balt.); Md. Yacht. Home: 100 W Cold Spring Lane Baltimore MD 21210 Office:119 S Howard St Baltimore MD 10101

DAVIS, ALLEN, profl. football coach and exec.; b. Brockton, Mass., July 4, 1929; s. Louis and Rose (Kirschenbaum) D.; student Wittenberg Coll., 1947; A.B., Syracuse U., 1950; m. Carol Segall, July 11, 1954; 1 son, Mark. Asst. football coach Adelphi Coll., 1950-51; head football coach, Ft. Belvoir, Va., 1952-53; player-personnel scout Baltimore Colts, 1954; line coach The Citadel, 1955-56, U. So. Cal., 1957-59; asst. coach San Diego Chargers, 1960-62; gen. mgr., head coach Oakland Raiders, 1963-66, now managing gen. partner and general partner; commissioner American Football League, 1966. Served with AUS, 1952-53. Named Profl. Coach of Year, A.P., U.P.I., Sproting News, Pro-Football Illustrated, 1963; Young Man of Yr., Oakland, 1963. Mem. Am. Football Coaches Assn. Home: 6094 Fairlane Dr Oakland CA Office: 7811 Oakport St Oakland CA 94621

DAVIS, ALLEN REED, educator; b. Franklin, W.Va., Apr. 16, 1910; s. William Lloyd and Annie (Brill) D.; student U. N.M., 1929-30, Hampden Sydney Coll., 1931-32; B.S., Marshall U., Huntington, W. Va., 1934; M.A., Colo. State Coll., 1938, Ed.D., 1954; m. Mary Richardson, Aug. 17, 1935; children—Samuel, Steven. Head commerce dept. Marlinton (W.Va.) High Sch., 1935-48; chmn. div. bus. adminstrn. and econs. W.Va. Inst. Tech., Montgomery, 1948-57, 59- 61, dean coll., 1961—; prof. bus. adminstrn. N.S. Summer Sch., Halifax, Can., 1956, Coll. of Guam, Agana, 1957-59. Served with AUS, 1943-45. Mem. Nat., So. (pres. 1961) bus. edn. assns., N.E.A., W.Va. Assn. Acad. Deans (pres. 1968-69), Phi Delta Kappa, Delta Pi

Epsilon, Sigma Chi. Democrat. Methodist. Mason, Rotarian. Author field studies, chpts. in books, editorials. Home: Upper Tech Campus Unit 14 Montgomery WV 25136

DAVIS, ALVA LEROY, educator; b. Bicknell, Ind., May 15, 1915; s. Reese and Grace (Murphy) D.; A.B., Ind. State U., 1938; M.A., U. Mich., 1940, Ph.D., 1948; m. Marjorie Koch, Dec. 24, 1939. Asst. prof. Western Res. U., 1948; asso. prof., dir. Am. Lang. Center, Am. U., 1952-54; dir. overseas tng. English Lang. Services, Washington, 1959-60; dir. Turkish Lang. Sch., Izmir, 1960-61; dir. humanities Delta Coll., Saginaw, Mich., 1961-63; prof. English and linguistics Ill. Inst. Tech., dir. Center Am. English, Chgo., 1963—; vis. prof. U. Mich., 1959, U. Chgo., 1963, 65; cons. U.S. Office Edn., 1963-66. Served with AUS, 1943-46. Postgrad. fellow Ohio State U., 1950; Smith-Mundt lectr., Lebanon, 1957; research grantee Am. Council Learned Socs., 1970. Mem. Am. Dialect Soc., Linguistic Soc. Am., Nat. Assn. Fgn. Student Advisers (v.p. 1956-58), Am. Assn. U. Profs. Author articles in field. Home: Box 407 Ogden Dunes Portage IN 46368

DAVIS, ALVIN, editor, writer; b. N.Y.C., May 10, 1925; s. Morris and Ethel (Levowitz) D.; student Coll. City N.Y., 1941-42, U. Paris (France), 1947; B.S., Columbia, 1951; Nieman fellow Harvard, 1943-54; m. Marie-Antoinette Ozil, Jan. 23, 1948; children—Marc (dec.), Anita, Frank. Reporter, N.Y. Post, 1942; sports editor So. German edit. Stars and Stripes, 1946; staff N.Y. Post, 1946-65, night city editor, 1955-56, night mng. editor, 1957-60, mng. editor, 1960-64, columnist, 1965; editorial dir. Tuesday Publs., Inc., N.Y.C., 1965—; producer TV Canadian Broadcasting Corp., 1966-67; dir. programming RCA Spl. Devel. Projects, 1967-68; reporter, producer NBC News, 1970—. Adj. prof. journalism Coll. City N.Y., 1950-65. Served with AUS, 1943-46; ETO. Home: 22 Willow Pl Brooklyn NY 11201 Office: 1250 6th Av New York City NY 10020

DAVIS, AMOS HERBERT, utility exec.; b. Murphysboro, Ill., July 28, 1923; s. Amos Herbert and Lillian Mattie (Quigley) D.; B.S. in Mech. Engring., Bradley U., 1948; m. Frances Edith Engelbrecht, Nov. 8, 1945; children—Ann Carolyn, John Richard. With Central Ill. Light Co., Peoria, 1948—, supt. elec. prodn. and transp., 1961-67, v.p. operations, 1967-70, pres., 1970—, also dir.; dir. Comml. Nat. Bank Peoria, Bituminous Coal Research, Inc., Monroeville, Pa.; trustee High Temperature Reactor Devel. Assos., Inc., San Diego. Commr. Peoria Pub. Bldg. Commn., 1967—. Bd. dirs. Peoria City Beautiful, Peoria County Civic Center Authority, Tri-County Comprehensive Health Planning Agy., Proctor Community Hosp. Peoria. Served with AUS, 1942-45, 50-52. Decorated Purple Heart, Bronze Star medal with clusters, Silver Star. Mem. Am. Soc. M.E. Methodist. Clubs: Creve Coeur, Willow Knolls (Peoria). Home: 406 W Wolf Rd Peoria IL 61614 Office: 300 Liberty Peoria IL 61602

DAVIS, ARCHIBALD KIMBROUGH, bank exec.; b. Winston-Salem, N.C., Jan. 22, 1911; s. Thomas W. and Frances (Conrad) D.; A.B., U. N.C., 1932; student Grad. Sch. Banking, Rutgers U., 1940; m. Mary L. Haywood, May 12, 1938; children—Archibald Hilliard, Louise Bahnson, John Haywood, Thomas Whitmell III. With Wachovia Bank and Trust Co. N.A., 1932—, asst. cashier 1938-40, asst. v.p., 1940-42, v.p., 1942-46, sr. v.p. in charge Winston-Salem office, 1946- 56, dir., chmn. bd. 1956—; dir. Royal Cotton Mills, So. Ry. Co., Sellers Mfg. Co., Sellers Dyeing Co., Jordan Spinning Co., Chatham Mfg. Co., Am. Tel. & Tel. Company; dir. Charlotte br. Fed. Res. Bank of Richmond, 1950-56. Mem. State Legislative Bldg. Commn. Founder, 1st pres., chmn. Northwest N.C. Devel. Assn.; pres. dir. Research Triangle Found. of N.C. Trustee Salem Acad. and Coll., U. N.C., Converse Coll. State senator, Forsyth County, 1959, 61. Trustee Com. Econ. Devel., Joint Council Econ. Edn. Mem. U.S. C. of C. (dir., v.p. 1958-61, pres. 1971, chmn. finance com. 1958-64), Am. Bankers Assn. (pres. state bank div. 1957; pres. 1965-66), Robert Morris Assos. (former dir., mem. exec. com.), Old Salem, Inc. (pres. 1961-63, dir.), Phi Beta Kappa, Delta Kappa Epsilon. Democrat. Mem. Moravian Ch. Clubs: Grail, Golden Fleece, Forsyth Country, Rotary (pres. 1958-59). Home: 2828 Forest Dr Winston-Salem NC 27101 Office: Wachovia Bank & Trust Co NA Winston-Salem NC 27101

DAVIS, ARLEIGH, lawyer; b. Marion County, Ark., Aug. 22, 1896; s. Oscar and Minnie (Corbin) D.; student Southwestern U., 1913-14, Sam Houston State Tchrs. Coll., 1914-15; LL.B., U. Tex., 1921; m. Blannie McLarty, Dec. 24, 1925; 1 dau., Gloria (Mrs. P. C. Waldo, Jr.). Admitted to Okla. bar. 1921, Ill. bar, 1942; practiced in Wilson, also Ardmore, Okla., 1921-36; atty. Bur. Internal Revenue, Springfield, also Peoria, Ill., 1936-42; gen. practice law, Peoria, 1942—, sr. partner Davis, Morgan & Witherell, 1957—, sr. partner Davis, Morgan & Witherell, 1957—. Dir. Jefferson Trust & Savs. Bank of Peoria, Sturm Freightways Inc., Kiefer Elec. Supply Co., Sutton & Moore Inc., Logan Printing Co. Mayor, Wilson, Okla., 1925-32; mem. Okla. Legislature, 1931-35. Bd. Meth. Hosp. of Central Ill., pres., 1953-56. Mem. Am., Ill., Okla., Peoria bar assns., Delta Tau Delta. Methodist (trustee). Clubs: Rotary (pres. 1930) (Wilson, Okla.); Kiwanis (pres. 1949), Country, Creve Coeur, University (Peoria). Home: 5856 Prospect Rd Peoria IL 61612 Office: First Nat Bank Bldg Peoria IL 61602

DAVIS, ARLENE (Mrs. Max T. Davis), aviatrix, assn. exec.; b. Cleve., Mar. 2; d. Philip and Anna (Hepp) Palsgraff; student Central Radio Sch., Kansas City, Mo., Sundorph Aero. Sch., Cleve., Western Res. U.; student Baldwin-Wallace Coll., 1951—; m. Max T. Davis, Feb. 4, 1928. Received pvt. pilot license, 1931, multi- rating land and sea instrument rating to fly blind, 1937; winner first all-women's air race, 1934; instr. instrument flying army trainees, 1943; nat. chmn. adv. com. Wing Scouts of Girl Scouts Am., 1946-49; former dir., sec. Nat. Aero. Assn.; U.S. del. Fedn. Aeronatique Internationale, 1954—. Vice pres., treas. Peerless Packing Co., Cleve. Chmn. Operation Skywatch for Ohio, Va., Pa.; mem. bd. Ohio Aviation Planning Co., 1949—; chmn. vols. Ground Observer Corps of Cuyahoga County, O.; exec. com., mem. bd. Ohio Safety Council; vice chmn. Nat. Model Plane Contest. Ohio aviation chmn. Citizens for Eisenhower Com. First v.p. Cleve. Boys Sch., Hudson, O., 1956—; mem. bd. Friendly Inn for Underprivileged Children, Cleve.; mem. bd. sr. advisers Nat. Intercollegiate Air Meet. Recipient Paul Tissandiar diploma Monaco, internat. citation, 1961; named woman of yr. aviation Women's Nat. Aero. Assn.; hon. angel U.S. Air Force R.O.T.C.; mem. Mach Buster's Club (exceeding speed of sound USAF F-100 F Super Sabre). Mem. Cleve. Fedn. Women's Clubs (dir. aviation 1954—), Nat. Aero. Assn. (hon. life), Assoc. Women Engrs. (life), Profl. Race Pilots Assn., Soaring Club Am., Am. Helicopter Soc., Acad. Model Aero. (adminstrv. leader, ofcl. contest dir.), Ninety-Nines (internat. v.p. 1951-52), Zonta Internat., Delta Zeta (Woman of Year award 1960), Alpha Eta Rho. Compiler Wing Scout Manual, 1949. Home: 12506 Edgewater Dr Cleveland OH 44107 Office: 3290 W 65th St Cleveland OH 44102

DAVIS, ARMSTEAD RALPH, clergyman; b. Memphis, Apr. 22, 1902; s. Charles Wesley and Sarah (Elkins) D.; A.B., Shaw U., 1926; student U. Minn. Law Extension Sch., 1929; m. Esther A. Hunter, Dec. 20, 1936. Ordained to ministry Christian Methodist Episcopal Ch., 1933; pastor, St. James, 1934, Wheeler Chapel, 1934-39, 40-43, New Hope, 1939-40, Carter Met., 1943-54, Cleaves Temple, 1954-59, Lena A. Hamlett, 1965-69, St. Mark, 1969—; pres. Ministers and Laymen's Council Christian M.E. Ch., 1955- 63, sec. Gen. Conf., 1958-70, presiding elder Chgo. dist., 1959-65, sec. Gen. Bd., 1959-70. Mem. Nat. (pres. minister sect.), Detroit (v.p. ministers sect.), Omaha (v.p. ministers sect.) councils chs. Mason. Home: 6432 S Green St Chicago IL 60621

DAVIS, ARTEMUS DARIUS, grocery exec.; b. Henderson, Ark., Nov. 22, 1905; s. William Milton and Ethel (Chase) D.; B.S., U. Ida., 1929; m. Mary J. Richardson (dec. Oct. 1969); children (by previous marriage)—Robert D., Lee W.; m. Pauline McCormick. Mgr. Table Supply Store, Little River, Fla., 1925-29; v.p. Table Supply Store, Little River, Fla., 1925-29; v.p. Table Supply Stores, Inc., Tampa, Fla., 1929- 34, pres., 1934-39; pres., dir. Winn-Dixie Stores, Inc. (formerly Winn & Lovett Grocery Co., Inc.), Jacksonville, Fla., 1939-65, chmn. exec. com., 1965-71, vice chmn. bd., 1965—; dir. Northeast Airlines, So. Bell Tel. & Tel. Co., Fla. State Fair. Chmn. Fla. Council Industry and Commerce, 1951-53. Home: 700 Old Grove Manor Jacksonville FL 33217 Office: 5050 Edgewood Court Jacksonville FL 33205

DAVIS, ARTHUR KYLE, Jr., educator; b. Petersburg, Va., Sept.20, 1897; s. Arthur Kyle and Lucy Pryor (McIlwaine) D.; B.A., U. Va., 1917, M.A., 1919, Ph.D., 1924; Rhodes scholar from Va., Balliol Coll., Oxford U., 1920-23, diploma in econs. and polit. sci., 1921, and B. Litt. (Oxon), 1923, Head Latin and Greek dept. Episcopal High Sch. of Va., Alexandria, 1917-18; instr. English, U. Va., 1923-24; asst. prof. English, 1924-27, assos. prof., 1927-40, prof. English, 1940-68, professor of English emeritus, 1968—; lecturer Harvard Univ., summer 1926; vis. prof. Sweet Briar (Va.) Coll., 1926-27; sterling research fellow, Yale, 1928-29; Am. Council Learned Socs. grant for study Va. folk songs, 1932. Sec.-treas. bd. trustees Southern Coll. Served as 2d lt. inf., U.S. Army, 1918; from lt. to lt. comdr. USNR, 1943-45. Recipient Chgo. Folklore award, 1961; mem. Hororable Order Ky. Cols.- 1963. Mem. Va. Folklore Soc. (archivist 1924- 68, pres. and archivist 1968—), Am. Folklore Soc. (mem. adv. bd. 1962- -), Modern Lang. Assn. Am. (chmn. comparative lit. group II 1936-38), Am. Folksong Soc. (trustee), S.E. Folklore Soc. U.S. (pres. 1940-41), Coll. English Assn. (v.p. 1948-50), Am. Assn. U. Profs., Oxford Society, Phi Beta Kappa (president University fo Virginia chapter 1948-50), Kappa Alpha, Sigma Upsilon, Raven Soc., Skull and Keys. Democrat. Episcopalian. Clubs: Colonnade (University, Va.); Torch (Charlottesville- Albemarle); Farmington (Charlottesville, Virginia). Author: Traditional Ballads of Virginia, 1929; Folksongs of Virginia, 1949; More Traditional Ballads of Virginia, 1960; Matthew Arnold's Letters: A Descriptive Checklist, 1968. Editor-in-chief College Verse, 1936-37; advisory editor Southern Folklore Quarterly; Virginia representative Dictionary of Am. Popular Beliefs and Superstitions, 1962—. Presently engaged in compilation correspondence of Matthew Arnold, also collecting, publishing folklore of Va. Home: 11 Faculty Apts 203 Rugby Rd Charlottesville VA 22903

DAVIS, ARTHUR QUENTIN, architect; b. New Orleans, Mar. 30, 1920; B.S. in Architecture, Tulane U., 1940, B.Arch., 1941; M.Arch., Harvard, 1946; m. Mary H. Wineman, Aug. 30, 1942; children—Arthur Quentin, Pamela Henriette, James Matthew. Partner Curtis & Davis & Asso., architects, New Orleans, 1946- -; prin. works include Thomy Lafon Sch., New Orleans, 1957, La. State Penitentiary, Angola, 1957, New Orleans Pub. Library, 1958, George Washington Carver Sch. and Helen Sylvania Edward Elementary Sch., New Orleans, 1958, Tulane U. Student Center, 1959, El Miramar Hotel, San Juan, P.R., 1960, Berlin Med. Center, Berlin, West Germany, Am. Embassy, Saigon, Vietnam, IBM Office Bldg., Pitts., 1964, Fed. Office Bldg., Washington, 1965; faculty Tulane U. Sch. Architecture, 1948-49; faculty mem. Pratt Inst. Design, Bklyn., 1966; vis. archtl. critic Va. Polytech. Inst., 1953, Yale, 1957, Harvard, 1960; mem. jury design awards program Progressive Architecture mag., 1957, hon. awards program Tex. Soc. Architects, 1959; design seminar U. Fla., 1959. Pres. Orleans Gallery Contemporary Art; bd. mgrs. Touro Infirmary; trustee Metairie Park Country Day Sch., Isaac Delgado Mus. Art Assn., United Fund Greater New Orleans, 1959-61. Served to lt. USNR, 1943-45. Recipient 1st honor award Thomy Lafton Sch., A.I.A., 1954, 1st hon. award for Sako Clinic for Children, Gulf States region A.I.A., 1954, for La. State Penitentiary, 1956; 1st hon. award edn. for Carver Sch., Progressive Architecture mag., 1957; 1st hon. award design competition House and Home, 1959; 1st award for Immaculate Conception Ch., Cath. Edn. Assn., others. Fellow A.I.A.; mem. La. Architects Assn., New Orleans C. of C., Tulane U. Alumni Assn., Young Men's Bus. Club Greater New Orleans. Club: Harvard of La. Home: 5 Bamboo Rd New Orleans LA 70124 Office: 2475 Canal St PO Box 53406 New Orleans LA 70119 also 126 E 38th St New York City NY 10016

DAVIS, BARNEY MCCOY, utility exec.; b. Sommerville, Tex., Aug. 22, 1913; s. Robert L. and Lela (Woods) D.; B.S., Sam Houston State U., 1937; m. Pamelia A. Smith, Aug. 8, 1943; 1 son, Barney McCoy. Elementary sch. prin., 1933-38; with Central Power & Light Co. Tex., 1938—, pres., chief exec. officer, 1969- -, also dir.; dir. Central and South West Corp. Bd. dirs. Tex. Atomic Energy Research Found.; bd. regents Pan Am. Coll. Served to 1st lt. AUS, World War II. Mem. Corpus Christi C. of C., Nat. Assn. Elec. Companies (b d. dirs.), S. Tex. C. of C. (exec. com.). Methodist. Mason. Clubs: Corpus Christi Country, Mustang, Town (Corpus Christi). Home: 715 Upper S Broadway Corpus Christi TX 78401 Office: 120 N Chapparral Corpus Christi TX 78401

DAVIS, BENJAMIN BERNARD lawyer; b. Lithuania, 1902 (parents U.S. Citizens); s. Max and Dora (Flaxman) D.; student U. Colo., 1918-19; Ph.B., J.D., U. Chgo., 1923; m. Janice Muller, Dec. 23, 1931; 1 son, Muller Davis. Law clk. Charles E. Erbstein, Chgo., 1921-23, asso., 1923-27; admitted to Ill. bar, 1923; partner Socrates & Davis, 1927-33, mem. firm. Socrates, Davis & Cohen, 1933-37; pvt. practice of law, 1937-46; associated in practice with William C. Boyden, Chgo., 1946—, now partner law firm Davis, Jones & Baer. Mem. Am., Ill., Chgo. bar assns. Jewish religion. Clubs: Tavern, Standard, Lakeshore Country. Home: 1335 Astor St Chicago IL 60610 Office: 120 S La Salle St Chicago IL 60603

DAVIS, BENJAMIN OLIVER, Jr., ret. air force officer, govt. ofcl.; b. Washington, Dec. 18, 1912; s. Benjamin Oliver and Sadie (Overton) D.; student Western Res. U., 1929, U. Chgo., 1930-32; B.S., U.S. Mil. Acad., 1936; grad. Air War Coll., Maxwell AFB, Ala., 1950; m. Agatha Scott, June 20, 1936. Commd. 2d lt. inf. U.S. army, 1936, advanced through grades to lt. gen., 1965; comdr. Co. F., 24th Inf., 1936-37; R.O.T.C. isntr. Tuskegee Inst., Ala., 1938-41, flight tng. Tuskegee Air Field, 1941-42, troop exec. 1942, squadron comdr. 99th Fighter Squadron, Tuskegee, 1942-43; group comdr. 332d Fighter Group. Balkans, Germany, France, 1943-45; comdr. Godman Field, Ky., 1945-46; wing comdr. 332d Fighter Wing. Lockbourne AFB, O., 1947-49; chief fighter br. Dep. for Operations, Hdqrs, USAF, 1950-53; jet pilot tng. Nellis AFB, Nev., 1953; wing comdr. 51st Fighter Interceptor Wing, 5th Air Force, 1953-54; dir. operations and tng. Hdqrs. Far East Air Forces Tokyo, 1954-55; comdr. Air Task Force 13 Provisional, 1955-57; chief of staff 12th Air Force, 1957-59; dep. chief staff operations Hdqrs. USAFE, 1957-61; dir. manpower and organization U.S. Air Force, 1961-65; chief of staff U.S. Forces, Korea, and chief of staff United Nations Command, 1965-67; command pilot; former safety dir. Cleve.; now head Office Civil Aviation Security. Decorated Legion of Merit, Silver Star, Distinguished Flying Cross, Air Medal with clusters D.S.M., (U.S.); Croix de Guerre with palm (France); Star of Africa. Home: London House 1001 Wilson Blvd Arlington VA 22206 Office: Office Civil Aviation Security Dept Transp 400 7th Av SW Washington DC 20590

DAVIS, BEN REEVES, newspaper editor; b. Huntington, Ark., Apr. 1, 1927; s. Lester Belton and Jessie (Reeves) D.; B.A. in Journalism, U. Ala., 1949; m. Margaret Lee Rogers, Nov 26, 1950; 1 son, Ben Reeves. Reporter, Selma (Ala.) Times-Jour., 1949-50; mng. editor Jasper (Ala.) Mountain Eagle, 1950-52; sports writer, copy editor Birmingham (Ala.) News, 1952-56; mng. editor Tuscaloosa (Ala.) News, 1956-64; exec. mng. editor Montgomery Advertiser and Ala. Jour., 1964—. Bd. dirs. Montgomery United Appeal. Served with USNR, 1945-46. Mem. A.P. Mng. Editors Assn., Ala. A.P. Assn. (pres. 1964- 65), Sigma Delta Chi, Pi Kappa Phi. Methodist. Home: 1411 Bancroft Av Montgomery AL 36111 Office: 107 S Lawrence St Montgomery AL 36102

DAVIS, BERNARD DAVID, med. scientist; b. Franklin, Mass., Jan. 7, 1916; s. Harry and Tillie (Shain) D.; A.B., Harvard, 1936, M.D., 1940; m. Elizabeth Menzel, June 19, 1955; children—Franklin A., Jonathan H., Katherine J. Intern, fellow Johns Hopkins Hosp., 1940-41; commd. officer USPHS, 1942-54, successively assigned NIH, Columbia, Pub. Health Research Inst. of N.Y., Rockefeller Inst., and charge USPHS Tb Research Lab. at Cornell U., 1947-54; prof. pharmacology, chmn. dept. N.Y.U., 1954-57; prof. bacteriology, chmn. dept., Harvard, 1957-68, Adele Lehman prof. bacteriology and immunology, 1963-68, Adele Lehman prof. bacteriological physiology, dir. bacteriology physiol. unit, 1968—; div. com. for biology, medicine NSF, 1954-57; mem. med. adv. bd. Hebrew U., 1956-70. Recipient Waksman medal Soc. Am. Bacteriologists, 1952. Mem A.A.A.S., Am. Soc. Biol. Chemists, Nat. Acad. of Scis., Am. Acad. of Arts and Sciences, Am. Soc. Microbiology, Am. Soc. Cell Biology, Soc. Gen. Physiology (pres. 1964-65), Harvey Soc., Phi Beta Kappa, Sigma Xi, Alpha Omega Alpha. Home: 23 Clairemont Rd Belmont MA 02178

DAVIS, BERNARD GEORGE, pub., educator; b. Pitts., Dec. 11, 1906; s. Charles and Sarah (Harris) D.; student U. of Pa., 1923-24; Columbia, summer 1926; B.S. U. of Pitts., 1927; m. Sylvia Friedman, Nov. 20, 1930; children—Joel, Carol. Editor of Pitt Panther, U. of Pitts., 1926; sec.-treas. Assn. of College Comics of the East, 1926-27; v.p. and dir. Ziff-Davis Publishing Co., 1936-46, pres., 1946-57; pres. Davis Publs., Inc., 1957-67, chmn., 1967—. Mag. pub. rep. Am. Council Edn. Journalism, 1960-66; dir. internat. programs U. Palm Beach, Fla., 1969—. U.S. del. Civil Air Patrol. Internat. Cadet Exchange Program Conf., Lisbon, 1955, Lima, 1956. Mem. Mag. Pub. Assn. (mem. bd. dirs. 1955-68, treas., 1959-67), Sigma Delta Chi. Club: Ocean Beach. Home: 2180 Ibis Isle Rd Palm Beach FL 33480 Office: 229 Park Av S New York City NY 10003

DAVIS, BERTRAM HYLTON, educator, assn. exec.; b. Ozone Park, N.Y., Nov. 30, 1918; s. Hubert Edwin and Gladys (Greenidge) D.; grad. Phillips Acad., Andover, Mass., 1933-37; student Hamilton Coll., Clinton, N.Y., 1937-39; A.B., Columbia, 1941, M.A., 1948, Ph.D., 1956; m. Ruth Austin Benedict, Jan. 11, 1946; children—Ralph Paul, Kathryn Austin, Richard Austin. Lectr. English, Hunter Coll., 1947-48; instr., then asst. prof. English, Dickinson Coll., 1948-57; staff asso. Am. Assn U. Profs., 1957-63, dep. gen. sec., 1963-67, gen. sec., 1967—. Served to capt. AUS, 1941-46. Mem. Modern Lang. Assn., Johnsonians, Catch Soc. Am. (exec. bd.), Am. Civil Liberties Union. Author: Johnson Before Boswell, 1960. Editor (Sir John Hawkins) Life of Samuel Johnson LL.D., 1961. Editor bull. Am. Assn. U. Profs., 1960-65. Home: 3009 Daniel Lane NW Washington DC 20015 Office: 1 DuPont Circle Washington DC 20036

DAVIS, BETTE RUTH ELIZABETH, actress; b. Lowell, Mass., Apr. 5, 1908; d. Harlow Morrell and Ruth (Favor) Davis; ed. Cushing Acad., Ashburnham, Mass.; m. Harmon Oscar Nelson, Jr., Aug. 18, 1932 (div.); m. 2d, Arthur Farnsworth, Dec. 1940 (dec. Aug. 25, 1943); m. 3d, William Grant Sherry, Nov. 30, 1945; 1 dau., Barbara Davis; m. 4th, Gary Merrill, Aug. 1950 (div.); 2 adopted children—Margot, Michael. Began as moving picture actress, 1931; leading pictures are: Of Human Bondage, Bordertown, Dangerous, The Petrified Forest, Jezebel, Dark Victory, Juarez. The Old Maid, The Private Lives of Elizabeth and Essex, The Great Lie, The Bride Came C.O.D.: All Above Eve, 1950; Payment on Demand, 1951; Phone Call from a Stranger, 1952; The Star, 1953; The Virgin Queen. 1955; Storm Center, The Catered Affair, 1956; John Paul Jones, 1959; The Scapegoat, 1959; What Ever Happened to Baby Jane; (play) The Night of the Iguana; films Dead Ringer, Painted Canvas, 1963, Where Love Has Gone, Hush, Hush, Sweet Charlotte, 1964, The Nanny, 1965; The Anniversary, 1967, Connecting Rooms, 1969, Bunny O'Hare, 1970. Recipient award of the Motion Picture Academy of Arts and Sciences as the best woman actress of the year, 1935 (in picture Dangerous), 1938 (in picture Jezebel). Author: The Lonely Life, 1962. Home: Westport CT 06880 Office: care Gottlieb Schiff Fabricant and Sternrlar 555 Fifth Av New York City NY 10017

DAVIS, BRUCE DEYLEN, chem. co. exec.; b. Bklyn., Jan. 22, 1928; s. Rowland Fenner and Sophie Marie (Deylen) D.; B.Chem. Engring., Cornell U., 1950, M.B.A., 1952; LL.B., St. John's U., 1960; m. Bernadette Rose Hearty, May 29, 1955; children—Bruce Deylen, Neil, Dwight, Sean. Various mfg. positions and tech. service positions to group mfg. mgr. Procter & Gamble, S.I., N.Y., 1951-64, Cin., 1964-66, Kansas City, 1966-68; dir. mfg. services, v.p. mfg., sr. v.p. Inmont Corp., N.Y.C., 1968—; dir. Porvair, Ltd., Tennants Textile Colors, Ltd. (U.K.). Bd. dirs. Am. Found. Religion and Psychiatry. Served with U.S. Army, 1954-56. Address: 1133 Av Americas New York City NY 10036

DAVIS, BRUCE GREGORY, civil engr.; b. Kansas City, Mo., Nov. 24, 1908; s. Herbert Rowan and May (Merritt) D.; B.S., Antioch Coll., 1932; grad. Indsl. Coll. Armed Forces, 1954; m. Ruth Penfield Hollenbeck, June 14, 1934; children—Susan (Mrs. David Pearce Snyder), Margaret, Engr. constrn. Boulder Canyon Project, Nev., 1934-40; area engr. Gatum Third Locks, Panama, C.Z., 1941-45; constrn. contract adminstrn. Bur. Reclamation, Denver, 1945-49, chief schedules br., Washington, 1950-57, chief div. program coordination and finance, 1958-67; irrigtation engr. Internat. Bank Reconstrn. and Devel., 1968—. Registered profl. engr., D.C. Mem. Am. Soc. C.E. Home: 9924 Carter Rd Bethesda MD 20433 Office: 1818 H St NW Washington DC 20433

DAVIS, BURKE, writer; b. Durham, N.C., July 24, 1913; s. Walter Burke and Harriet (Jackson) D.; student Duke, Guilford Coll.; B.A. in Journalism, U. N.C., 1937; m. Evangeline McLennan, Aug. 11, 1940; children—Angela M., Burke III. Staff, Charlotte (N.C.) News, 1937-47, Balt. Evening Sun, 1947-51, Greensboro (N.C.) News, 1951-60, Colonial, Williamsburg, Va., 1960—. Author: Whisper My Name; The Ragged Ones; Yorktown; They Called Him Stonewall; Gray Fox; (juvenile) Roberta E. Lee; Jeb Stuart; To Appomattox; Our Incredible Civil War; Marine: The Life of Gen. L. B. (Chesty) Puller, USMC; The Cowpens-Guilford Courthouse Campaign; (juvenile)

America's First Army; The Summer Land; The Billy Mitchell Affair; (with Evangeline Davis) Rebel Raider, a Biography of Adm. Raphael Semmes, C.S.N.; A. Williamsburg Galaxy; (with Roy King) The World of Currier and Ives; Get Yamamoto; The Campaign That Won America: The Story of Yorktown; (juveniles) Heroes of the American Revolution, Jamestown, Thomas Jefferson's Virginia, The Billy Mitchell Story, Amelia Earhart, The Biography of a Leaf. Home: 2 Prince Charles St Williamsburg VA 23185 Office: Box 502 Williamsburg VA 23185

DAVIS, CHAMPION MCDOWELL, ret. ry. ofcl.; b. nr. Hickory, N.C., July 1, 1879; s. Robert Burns and Cornelia (Nixon) D.; ed. pub. schs.; ScD., The Citadel, 1952. Beginning as messenger Wilmington & Weldon R.R. (now S.C.L.R.R.), 1893, became successively clk., stenographer freight rate clk., chief rate clk., to 1902, chief clk. traffic dept., 1902-06. asst. gen. freight agt., 1906-11, gen. freight agt. lines south of Charleston, S.C., 1911-16, gen. freight agt. entire system, 1916-18; mem. so. freight traffic com. U.S. R.R. Adminstrn., 1918-20, so. freight rate com., representing so. rail and water carriers, 1920; asst. freight traffic mgr. A.C.L. R.R., 1921-25, freight traffic mgr., 1925- 28, v.p. traffic, 1928-39, v.p. all depts., 1939, exec. v.p., 1940-42, pres., 1942-57, ret., 1957; former dir. Jefferson Standard Life Ins. Co. Dir. U.S. C. of C., 1949-52, former mem. governing bd. Nations Business. Mem. nat. council P.E. Ch., 1946-52; trustee Cape Fear Tech. Inst., Wilmington, N.C.; former trustee Episcopal Radio-TV Found., P.E. Theol. Sem. Va., N.C. Ednl. Radio and Television Commn.; chmn. bd. trustees Cape Fear Meml. Hosp., Inc., Wilmington, N.C.; dir. emeritus Episcopal Ch. Found.; founder and prin. donor Champion McDowell Davis Charitable Found., 1963, Cornelia Nixon Davis Nursing Home, Porters Neck Plantation. Served as pvt. and cpl., 2d Regiment, N.C. Inf., Spanish-Am. War, 1898, later with 2d N.C. State Guard; resigned as capt., 1901. Mem. United Spanish War Vets. (vice comdr.), N.C. Soc. Cin., N.Y. So. Soc., Am. Soc. Traffic and Transp. (charter mem.), Am. Ry. Engring. Assn., Am. Assn. Passenger Traffic Officers (hon.) Transp. Assn. Am., Newcomen Soc. Episcopalian. Clubs: Cape Fear, Cape Fear Country (Wilmington, N. C.); Surf (Wrightsville Beach, N.C.); Wilmington Press. Home: Porter's Neck Plantation Route 1 Box 621 Wilmington NC 28401

DAVIS, CHARLES CARROLL, aquatic biologist, educator; b. Azusa, Cal., Nov. 24, 1911; s. William Allen and Maude (Snyder) D.; A.B., Oberlin Coll., 1933; M.S., U. Wash., 1935, Ph.D., 1940; m. Sally May Jacobsen, June 11, 1936; children—Peter Thomas, Betsy Ann. Biologist II, State of Md., 1942-43; instr. sci. Jacksonville Jr. Coll., 1944-46; asst. prof. zoology U. Miami, Coral Gables, Fla., 1946-48; asst. prof. biology Western Res. U., Cleve., 1948- 52, asso. prof., 1953-63, prof., 1964-68; prof. biology Meml. Univ. of Newfoundland, 1968—. Cons. for zoology terms New World Dictionary, 1965-69. Fellow A.A.A.S., Ohio Acad. Sci.; mem. Ecol. Soc. Am., Am. Soc. Limnology and Oceanography, Phycological Soc. Am., Assn. for Tropical Biology, Am. Micros Soc., Plankton Soc. Japan, Internat. Soc. Limnology. Author: The Pelagic Copepoda of the Northeastern Pacific Ocean, 1949; The Marine and Fresh-water Plankton, 1955. Contbr. numerous articles on plankton, eutrophication of Lake Erie, hatching mechanisms of invertebrate eggs, biol. prodn. to prof. jours. Home: Site 3 Box 15 Rural Route 1 Donovans Newfoundland Canada Office: Dept of Biology Memorial Univ of Newfoundland Saint John's Newfoundland Canada

DAVIS, CHARLES FRANCIS, Jr., architect; b. Montgomery, Ala., Dec. 13, 1908; s. Charles Francis and Catherine (West) D.; B.Arch., Auburn U., 1931, B.Archl. Engring., 1932; m. Helen Sellers, Nov. 1, 1935; children—Charles Francis III, Helen West, Neil Edward. Draftsman Miller, Martin & Lewis, 1935-38; designer E.B. Van Keuren, 1938-46, partner, 1946-49; partner Van Keuren, Davis & Co., 1949-47; partner Davis, Speake & Thrasher, Birmingham, Ala., 1957-63, Davis, Speake & Assos., Birmingham, 1963—; works include all bldgs. Samford U., Bapt. Med. Center, Library, Haley Center and plant scis. bldgs. Auburn U., dormitory complex Birmingham-So. Coll. Chmn. bd. mgmt. Five Points YMCA, 1963. Adv. bd. Salvation Army; dir. Birmingham Boys Club; trustee Montreat-Anderson Coll. Recipient 1st Honor award Ala. chpt. A.I.A., 1952, award of merit, 1952, 66. Fellow A.I.A. (dir. Birmingham chpt.); mem. Phi Kappa Phi, Omicron Delta Kappa, Lambda Chi Alpha. Presbyn. (elder). Clubs: Birmingham Exchange, Birmingham Country. Home: 20 Pine Crest Rd Birmingham AL 35223 Office: 3004 7th Av S Birmingham AL 35233

DAVIS, CHARLES HUBBARD, state supreme ct. justice; b. Fairfield, Ill., Jan. 7, 1906; s. Horace Hubbard and Helen M. (Decker) D.; A.B., U. Ill., 1928; J.D., U. Chgo., 1931; m. Ruth Peugh, Oct. 19, 1935; children—Jean, Joan, Martha (Mrs. Russell Dearing), Mary (Mrs. John Dadday), Ruth (Mrs. Thomas Hazen), John Jay, and Thomas C. Admitted to the Ill. state bar, 1931, practiced in Rockford, 1931- 55, mem. firm of Thomas & Davis, 1945-55; justice Ill. Supreme Ct., 1955- 60, 70—, chief justice, 1957-58; mem. firm Thomas, Davis and Kostantacos, 1960-65; justice 2d Dist. Ill. Appellate Ct., 1965-70. Past pres., dir. Winnebago Farm Sch. for Boys. Mem. Am., Ill., Winnebago Co. bar assns., Am. Coll. Trial Lawyers, Phi Delta Phi. Republican. Conglist. Mason (Shriner). Home: 6 Clayshire Lane Rockford IL 61107 Office: Talcott Bldg 321 W State St Rockford IL 61101

DAVIS, CHARLES MALCOLM, banker; b. Roslyn, N.Y., July 24, 1918; s. Charles Palmer and Jane (Hopkins) D.; B.S., N.Y.U., 1941; m. Ann Kes, Nov. 14, 1942; children—Susan K., Craig M., Bruce, Grant. With Fed. Res. Bank of N.Y., 1935-41; asso. First Nat. City Bank (formerly First Nat. Bank City of N.Y.), 1946-55, asst. cashier, 1948-50, asst. v.p., 1950-52, v.p., 1953- 55; v.p. Fidelity Union Trust Co., Newark, 1955-58, sr. v.p., 1958-60, pres., 1960-69, chmn., chief exec. officer, 1969—, also dir.; dir. Allied Bank Internat. Pennwalt Corp., Thomas & Betts Corp., Bamberger's Pub. Service Electric & Gas Co., Newark, Prudential Ins. Co. Am. Served to capt. AUS, 1942-46. Mem. Beta Gamma Sigma. Episcopalian. Clubs: Essex, Down Town, Somerset Hills Country, Baltursrol Golf. Address: Old Farm Rd R D 1 Basking Ridge NJ 07920

DAVIS, CHARLES MOLER, ret. geographer, educator; b. Denver, Dec. 11, 1900; s. Charles Moler and Margaret Bigger (Porter) D.; A.B., U. Mich., 1925, A.M., 1926, Ph.D., 1935; m. Margaret Beal, Oct. 31, 1931. Instr. in geography, U. Mich., 1931-38, asst. prof., 1938-42, asso. prof., 1945-49, prof., 1949-71, prof. emeritus, 1971—, chmn. dept. geography, 1956-66. Vis. prof. U. Cal. at Los Angeles, summer 1947, U. Tex., summer 1951, also U. Wash., summer 1963; Fulbright research scholar, Australia, 1952; geographer, Inst. for Fisheries Research, 1931-32; asst. land negotiator, U.S. Biol. Survey, 1935; Carnegie vis. prof. U. Hawaii, 1962; sect. organizer 10th Pacific Science Congress, Honolulu, 1961; geographer U.S. Geol. Survey, 1966-67, mem. NRC Com. on Remote Sensing Adv., 1966—; dir. Inst. on Remote Sensing for Geographers. Served from lt. comdr. to capt., USNR, 1942-60; plans officer, Spl. Air Task Force, U.S. Fleet, 1943-44; mem. acad. library adv. bd. USAF Acad., 1958. Chmn. com. on geog. field techniques NRC, 1949-53; mem. com. adv. to geog. br. Office of Naval Research, 1949-51. Recipient Carnegie Corp. grant-in-aid, 1939-40. Mem. Assn. of Am. Geographers (del. to Nat. Acad. Science-NRC 1959-62), Mich. Acad. of Sci., Phi Kappa Phi, Phi Sigma, Chi Gamma Phi, Delta Tau Delta. Club: University (Ann Arbor). Contbr. articles on geog. subjects to profl. mags. Home: 2965 Hickory Lane Ann Arbor MI 48104

DAVIS, CHARLES SHEPARD, coll. pres.; b. Mobile, Ala., Aug. 13, 1910; s. Mattew and Ruth (Shepard) D.; B.S., Ala. Poly. Inst., 1931, M.S., 1932; Ph.D., Duke U., 1938; m. Mary G. Merritt, June 6, 1936; children—Mary (Mrs. Charles Atherton), Catherine (Mrs. Antoine Vinel), Charlotte (Mrs. F. Strait Fairey, Jr.). Asso. prof. history, Ala. Poly. Inst., 1941; mem. faculty, Fla. State U., since 1947, asst. dean, coll. arts and scis., 1949, asso. dean 1950, acting dean 1951, dean 1952, prof. history 1949-59, dean faculties, 1958-59; pres. Winthrop Coll., S.C. College for Women, 1959—. Chmn. bd. dirs. Home Fed. Savs. & Loan Assn., Rock Hill. Pres. S.C. Assn. Colls., 1964-65. Trustee Voorhees Coll.; bd. dirs. Regional Learning Lab. Carolinas & Va. Served as maj. C.E., AUS, 1942-45; colonel USAF Res. Decorated Bronze Star Medal. Mem. Rock Hill C. of C. (pres. 1964, dir.), So. Assn. Colls. and Secondary Schs., N.E.A., Newcomen Soc. Eng., So., Hist. Assn., Council Pres.'s State Colls. and Univs. (chmn. S.C. 1962-64), Phi Beta Kappa, Phi Kappa Phi (nat. pres. 1957-62), Omicron Delta Kappa, Scabbard and Blade, Pi Kappa Alpha, Blue Key, Democrat. Episcopalian. Author: The Cotton Kingdom of Alabama, 1939. Editor: Report of Operations of the U.S. Seventh Army, 1945; Colin J. McRae: Confederate Financial Agent, 1961. Contbr. articles. Home: 601 Oakland Av Rock Hill SC

DAVIS, CHESTER R. Jr., lawyer; b. Chgo., Aug. 30, 1930; s. Chester R. and Mead (Scoville) D.; grad. Phillips Exeter Acad., 1947; A.B., Princeton, 1951; LL.B., Harvard, 1958; m. Anne Meserve, Mar. 3, 1962; children—John Chester, Julia Snow, Elizabeth Meserve. Admitted to Ill. bar, 1958; mem. firm Bell, Boyd, Lloyd, Haddad & Burns, partner, 1968—. Mem. nat. panel arbitrators Am. Arbitrators Assn. Asso. Presbyn.- St. Lukes Hosp., Chgo., 1964—, Adlai Stevenson Inst. Internat. Affairs, 1968—. Sec., bd. dirs. Vascular Disease Research Found.; mem. alumni council Phillips Exeter Acad. Served to lt. (j.g.) USNR, 1952-56. Mem. Am., Ill., Chgo. (com. chmn.) bar assns., Am. Soc. Internat. Law, Am. Arbitration Assn., Harvard Law Soc. Ill. (past pres.), Harvard Law Sch. Assn. (v.p. 1970—). Episcopalian. Clubs: University, Economic, Legal (Chgo.); Princeton (N.Y.C.). Home: 636 Walden Rd Winnetka IL 60093 Office: 135 S LaSalle St Chicago IL 60603

DAVIS, CLARENCE ALBA, lawyer; b. Beaver City, Neb.; s. Thomas Milburn and Nannie (Gelvin) D.; A.B., Nev. Wesleyan U., 1913; student U. Neb., 1911-13, LL.D.; LL.B., Harvard, 1916; LL.D., Lincoln Meml. U.; L.H.D., Neb. Wesleyan U.; m. Florence Wells, Aug. 2, 1916; 1 son, Thomas Milburn. In practice at Omaha, Neb., 1916-17; moved to Holdrege, Neb., 1917; atty. gen. of Neb., 1919-13; solicitor Dept. Interior, 1953-54, undersec. Dept. of Interior, 1954-57; now in law practice, Washington, Lincoln, Neb.; mem. firm Davis, Thone, Bailey. Pols. Counsel to Neb. interstate water litigation, and in preparation Neb.-Colo. Compact reference South Platte River, 1923; counsel to Mo. Valley Devel. Assn., 1945-46. Lectr. on adminstrv. law, U. Neb., 1943. Mem. commn. compiling Neb. statutes, 1922. Del. Rep. Nat. Conv., 1928, 32. Trustee Neb. Wesleyan U., 1923-27. Mem. Am. (ho. dels. 1951-58; gov. 1965—), Fed. (pres. 1955-56), Neb. (pres. 1950-51), Lincoln bar assns., Nat. Conf. Bar Assn. Presidents (council 1951-53), Inst. Jud. Administrn., Am. Law Inst., Neb. Hist. Soc. (gov.), Am. Judicature Soc., Order of Coif (hon.), Pi Kappa Delta. Republican. Episcopalian. Mason (33, Shriner). Mem. adv. bd. editors Am. Bar Assn. Jour., 1948-52. Clubs: University, National Lawyers, Cosmos, Metropolitan (Washington); Lawyers (N.Y.C.); University (Lincoln). Tennis champion of Neb., 1912- 16. Contbr. law reviews. Home: 1633 Dakota Circle Lincoln NB 68502 Office: Commonwealth Bldg Washington DC also Stuart Bldg Lincoln NB

DAVIS, CLARENCE DANIEL, physician, educator; b. Pittsford, N.Y., Nov. 20, 1912; s. Arthur Everett and Gertrude (Benrose) D.; B.S., Mass. Inst. Tech., 1935; M.D., Johns Hopkins, 1939; M.S., Yale, 1964; m. Beatrice Ann McKellar, Aug. 5, 1939; children—Susan, Daniel, Peter. Rotating intern Robert Packer Hosp., Sayre, Pa., 1939-40, Genesee Hosp. Rochester, N.Y., 1940-41; intern obstetrics and gynerology Univ. Hosp., Mpls., 1941-42; asst. resident endocrinology dept. obstetrics and gynecology Duke Hosp., Durham, N.C., 1942, resident, 1942-43, instr. endocrinology, 1943-46; practice medicine specializing in obstetrics and gynecology, Seattle, 1946-49, Durham, 1950-53, Columbia, Mo. 1954-57, New Haven, 1957—; clin. asso. physiology U. Wash. Med. Sch., Seattle, 1946-50, clin. asso. obstetrics and gynecology, 1948-50; asso. div. med. gynecology Mason Clinic, Seattle, 1946-50; asso. in obstetrics and gynecology Duke Hosp., 1950- 52, asst. prof., 1952-54; prof., chmn. dept. obstetrics and gynecology U. Mo. Sch. Medicine, 1954-57; asso. prof. obstetrics and gynecology Yale Sch. Medicine, 1957-64, prof., 1964—; cons. maternal and child health sect. Conn. Dept. Health, St. Raphaels Hosp., New Haven, Stamford (Conn.) Hosp., Griffin Hosp., Derby, Conn.; regional admissions rep. Duke. Pres. Conn. League for Abortion Law Repeal; mem. exec. bd. New Haven chpt. Nat. Found.-March of Dimes. Diplomate Am. Bd. Obstetrics and Gynecology. Fellow Am. Coll. Obstetricians and Gynecologists (com. chmn.), A.M.A., New Haven Obstet. Soc. Club: Nick Carter Travel (Durham, N.C.). Home: 76 Swarthmore St Hamden CT 06517 Office: 333 Cedar St New Haven CT 06510

DAVIS, CLAYTON MERLE, lawyer; b. Iola, Kan., Nov. 18, 1905; student Kan. State U., 1923-24; J.D., Washburn U., 1929. Admitted to Kan. bar, 1929; practice in Topeka, 1932—; partner firm Davis & Bennett, 1970—; asst. atty. Shawnee County, 1937-38. Chmn. Kan. Supreme Ct. Nominating Commn., 1970—. Bd. regents Washburn U., 1943-56. Fellow Am. Coll. Trial Lawyers; mem. Am., Kan. (exec. council, past pres.), Topeka (past pres.) bar assns. Home: 3642 S E Tomahawk Dr Topeka KS Office: Capitol Fed Bldg Topeka KS 66603

DAVIS, CLIFFORD V., educator; b. Judith Gap, Mont., July 23, 1914; s. Phillip D. and Esther (Miller) D.; B.S., Mont. State U., 1937; M.S., U. Mich., 1945; Ph.D., Ore. State U., 1961; m. Maude Phillips, Aug. 1, 1937; children—Nancy Lee (Mrs. Gary Davies), Allan Vernon, Clifford Sewall. Tchr. sci. Gallatin County High Sch., Bozeman, Mont., 1938-46; instr. Mont. State U. at Bozeman, 1946-48, asst. prof., 1948-54, asso. prof., 1954-61, prof. zoology, 1961—, asst. dean letters and scis., 1961-69, dean gen. studies, 1969—. Mem. Mont. Acad. Scis. (editor Proceedings, 1955-59; pres., 1967), Wilson, Cooper ornithol. socs., Am. Ornithologists Union, Phi Kappa Phi, Phi Delta Kappa. Club: Sacajawea Audubon (pres. Bozeman 1967-69). Research in life study of the distbn. of birds of Mont. Home: 1620 S 3rd St Bozeman MT 59715

DAVIS, COLIN REX, orch. condr.; b. Weybridge, Eng., Sept. 25, 1927; s. Reginald George and Lilian (Colbran) D.; student Royal Coll. Music, London, 1944-49; m. April Cantelo, 1949; children—Suzanne, Christopher; m. 2d, Ashraf Naini, 1964; children—Kurosh, Kavus. Household Cav. for Nat. Service, 1946-48; asst. condr. BBC, Scottish Orch., 1957-59; mus. dir. Sadler's Wells Opera Co., London, Eng., 1961-65; chief condr. BBC Symphony Orch., 1967-71; dir. Royal Opera House, Covent Garden, London, 1971—. Decorated comdr. Brit. Empire. Address: care Pears-Phipps Mgmt 8 Halliford St London N1 3HE England

DAVIS, CURTIS WOODWARD, glass mfr.; b. Charleston, W.Va., Jan. 4, 1901; s. Henry and Lizzie (Brazeal) D.; student pub. schs., Charleston; m. Mary Emory Londeree, Jan. 8, 1922; children—Curtis Woodward, David E. With Libbey-Owens-Ford Co., Toledo, 1923—, successively clk. stores dept., Charleston, supr. stores, established new stores system, Rossford, O., office mgr. Charleston plant, in charge control dept., indsl. engring. div. at Toledo, asst. mgr. Rossford plant, mgr., gen. factories mgr., Toledo, v.p., 1949-55, exec. v.p. prodn., 1955-59, exec. v.p., 1959-63, pres., 1963-64, pres., chief exec. officer, 1964-67, now mem. exec. com.; v.p. of Londere Music Co., Charleston; co-owner Colonial Mdse. Co., Toledo; dir. Herrison Marina, Toledo, Ohio Citizens Trust Co. Mem. bd. trustees Toledo YMCA, Toledo Hosp., Toledo Mus. Art. Mem. C. of C. Baptist. Mason. Clubs: Sylvania Country, Toledo, Belmont Country (Toledo). Home: 2443 Meadowwood Dr Toledo OH 43606 Office: 1st Nat Bank Bldg Toledo OH 43624

DAVIS, DARREY ADKINS, lawyer; b. Lawtey, Fla., Mar. 14, 1910; s. Darrey Deoma and Ora Lee (Adkins) D.; LL.B., U. Fla., 1934; m. Mary Sue Weakley, Nov. 23, 1940; children—John Weakley, Susan Davis Logan. Admitted to Fla. bar, 1934; mem firm Meyer, Davis & Weiss, 1934-45, Cleveland, Sibley & Davis, 1946- 48, Sibley & Davis, 1948-57; county atty. for Dade County, Fla., 1957—, 64; mem. firm Hector, Faircloth & Davis, 1964-66, Mc-Carthy, Steel, Hector and Davis, Miami, Fla., 1966—. Vice chmn. long term capital improvement com. City of Miami, 1948-50; mem. circuit ct. commn. 11th Jud. Dist. Fla., 1946-50. Trustee, 1st v.p. Greater Miami Coalition. Mem. bd. trustees United Fund Dade County, Dade County Law Library. Chmn. bd. of trustees Miami Beach Law Library, 1947-48. Served as lt. USNR, 1943- 45. Recipient Distinguished Service award Stetson U., 1956. Fellow Am. Bar Found., 1955—; Am. Coll. Trial Lawyers; mem. Am. Judicature Soc. (dir.), Fla. C. of C. (dir. 1954-55), Am. (ho. dels. 1951-60), Fla. (bd. govs. 1949-55, exec. com. 1952-53, pres. 1954-55), Dade County (dir. 1942, 46-49, sec. 1946-47; pres. 1948-49), Miami Beach (dir. 1946-58), v.p. 1946-47) bar assns. Clubs: Riviera Country (Coral Gables, Fla.); Miami. Home: 1226 Algardi Av Coral Gables FL 33134 Office: 1st Nat Bank Bldg Miami FL 33131

DAVIS, DAVID IV, lawyer; b. Bloomington, Ill., July 29, 1906; s. David and Edith (Melluish) D.; A.B., Williams Coll., 1928; J.D., U. S.D., 1931; m. Nancy Sandstrom, Aug. 16, 1941; children—Alice D. (Mrs. Royce E. Cates), David V, Elizabeth G. Admitted to Ill. bar, 1931; practice in Bloomington, 1932—. Chmn. bd. Nat. Bank of Bloomington. Coordinator McLean County (Ill.) civilian pilot tng. program, 1940-41; lt. Civil Air Patrol, 1941-46; pres. bd. Community Chest, 1942-43, McLean County War Chest, 1943-46; vice chmn. Ill. Sch. Problems Commn., 1954-64; chmn. senate edn. com. Ill. Higher Edn. Commn., 1957-67; bd. dirs. Aero. Advisers, 1957-63; chmn. Commn. on Intergovtl. Coop., 1957-67; bd. mgrs. Council State Govts., 1957-67; organizer, chmn. com. on Midwestern agrl. problems Midwestern Conf. Council State Govts., 1959-62, v.p., chmn. bd. mgrs. Council State Govts., 1963, chmn. Midwestern Conf., 1965; mem. steering com. Constn. Study Commn., 1965-67, Constn. Adv. Commn., 1967-69; del. 6th Ill. Constl. Conv., 1969-70. Mem. Ill. Senate, 1953-67. Recipient Jr. C. of C. Community Service award, 1941, good govt. award, 1971. Mem. Am., Ill., McLean County (past pres.) bar assns., Am. Judicature Soc. Presbyn. (trustee). Home: 1114 E Monroe St Bloomington IL 61701 Office: 207 E Jefferson St Bloomington IL 61701

DAVIS, DAVID BRION, educator, historian; b. Denver, Feb. 16, 1927; s. Clyde Brion and Martha (Wirt) D.; A.B summa cum laude, Dartmouth, 1950; A.M., Harvard, 1953, Ph.D., 1956; m. Frances Warner, Oct. 22, 1948; children—Jeremiah Jonathan, Martha Elizabeth, Sarah Brion. Scheduler, Cessna Aircraft Co., Wichita, Kan., 1950-51; instr. history Dartmouth, 1953-54; mem. faculty Cornell U., 1955-69, prof. history, 1963-69, Ernest I. White prof. history, 1964-69; prof. history Yale, 1969—. Fulbright lectr. Hyderabad, India, 1967; Walter Lynwood Fleming lectr. So. history La. State U., 1969; Harmsworth prof., Oxford, O., 1969-70. Served with AUS, 1945-46. Recipient Anisfield Wolf award in race relations, 1967, Pulitzer prize for nonfiction, 1967, Mass Media award Nat. Conf. of Christians and Jews, 1967; Guggenheim fellowship, 1958-59. Mem. Am. Hist. Assn., Am. Studies Assn., Orgn. Am. Historians. Author: Homicide in American Fiction, 1790-1860; A Study in Social Values, 1957; The Problem of Slavery in Western Culture, 1966. Home: 33 Ridge Court E West Haven CT 06516 Office: Dept of History Yale New Haven CT

DAVIS, DAVID E., Jr., advt. agy. Sr. v.p., asso. dir. Campbell-Ewald Co., Detroit. Office: 3044 W Grand Blvd Detroit MI 48202*

DAVIS, DAVID EDWARD, educator, ecologist; b. Chgo., July 18, 1918; s. David John and Almira (Jones) D.; B.S., Swarthmore Coll., 1935; M.S., Harvard, 1936, Ph.D., 1939; m. Emily Rodgers, Oct. 8, 1942; children—Susan, Alice, Jean. Postdoctoral fellow U. Chgo., 1940; zoologist Rockefeller Found., Rio de Janeiro, Brazil, 1941-43; scientist USPHS, San Antonio, 1943-45; faculty John Hopkins Sch. Pub. Health, 1945-59; prof. zoology Pa. State U., University Park, 1959-67; prof., head dept. zoology N.C. State U., Raleigh, 1967—; cons. USPHS, 1956—. Mem. Ecol. Soc., Am. Ornithol. Union, Am. Soc. Mammalogists, Am. Inst. Biol. Scis. (pres. 1971), Animal Behavior Soc., Wildlife Disease Assn. (pres. 1962-64). Author: Principles in Mammalogy (with Frank Golley), 1963; Integral Animal Behavior, 1966. Research and publs. on regulation animal populations, social behavior birds, role hormones in behavior. Home: 2911 Fairview Rd Raleigh NC 27608

DAVIS, DEANE CHANDLER, governor of Vermont, and lawyer; b. East Barre, Vt., Nov. 7, 1900; s. Earl Russell and Lois (Hillary) D.; LL.B., Boston U., 1922, LL.D., 1969; LL.D., U. Vt., 1957, Middlebury Coll., 1964; Litt.D. (hon.), Norwich U., 1963; m. Corinne Eastman, June 14, 1924, (dec. Mar. 9, 1951); children—Deane (dec.), Marian (Mrs. Frank R. Calcagni), Thomas C.; m. 2d Marjorie Smith Conzelman, July 5, 1952. Admitted to Vt. bar, 1922; practiced law, Barre, Vt., 1922-31 and 1936- 40; city atty., Barre, 1924-26 and 1928-30; states atty., Washington County, Vt., 1926-28; superior judge State of Vt., 1931-36; mem. law firm, Wilson, Carver, Davis & Keyser, Barre, Vt., and Chelsea, Vt., 1936- 40; gen. counsel, Nat. Life Ins. Co., 1940-50, v.p., 1943-50, pres., 1950-66, chmn. bd., chief exec. officer, 1966-67, chmn. bd., 1967-68, dir., 1950-68; dir. People's Nat. Bank, Barre, Vermont, Union Mut. Fire Ins. Co. Governor of Vermont, 1969—. Mem. city council, Barre, 1923-24. Pres. Vt. State C. of C., 1942-43; mem. Dairy Income Study Com.; mem. Vt. Trails Bd., State Recreation Dept.; sponsor Com. for Effective Use Internat. Ct.; mem. adv. council Champlain Coll., Boston U. Law Sch. Del. to Republican Conv., 1948, mem. resolutions committee. Trustee Vt. Coll., Montpeller; asso. trustee Rehab. Center of DeGoesbriand unit Med. Center Hosp. Vt.; pres. Calvin Coolidge Meml. Found. Dir. Life Ins. Med. Research Fund, 1955-57, Mary Fletcher Hosp., 1955-59. Mem. Am. (gov. 1945-48, chmn. Vt. com. representing council on legal edn. and admissions to bar), Vt. (pres. 1942) bar assns., Life Ins. Assn. America (dir. 1953-63, pres. 1959-60), Am. Life Conv. (v.p.), Inst. Life Ins. (dir. 1961-64, chmn. bd. 1963), Am. Judicature Soc., Vt. Morgan Horse Assn. (pres.), Green Mountain Horse Assn. (v.p.),

Morgan Horse Club (pres.), Delta Theta Phi. Methodist. Mason; K.P. Home: 5 Dyer Av RD 1 Montpelier VT 05602 Office: National Life Dr Montpelier VT 05602

DAVIS, DONALD, actor; b. Canada. Founder, with brother of Straw Hat Players, Ontario, Can.; appearances in Eng. with Britol Old Vic, Glasgow Citizens Theatre, also Wilson Barrett Co., 1950-53; founder, with brother of Crest Theatre, Toronto, 1953; mem. Stratford (Ont.) Shakespeare Festival Co., 1954-56; appearance in London with Crest Theatre in The Glass Cage, 1957, in N.Y.C. in Krapp's Last Tape (Obie award), 1959; mem. Am. Shakespeare Festival Co., Stratford, Conn., also rep. company spl. White House performance, 1961; other Broadway prodns. include Outstick, Roar Like a Dove, The Creditors, Photo Finish, Who's Afraid of Virginia Wolff; TV appearances include The Defenders, The Nurses, Play of the Week; appearance in Chgo. in Becket; motion picture Joy in the Morning, 1965.*

DAVIS, DONALD CHISHOLM, retail lumber co. exec.; b. Middletown, Conn., Jan. 11, 1917; s. Frank Twichell and Miriam Modell (Chisholm) D.; B.A., Wesleyan U., Middletown, 1939; m. Jeanne Fitzpatrick, July 10, 1941 (dec.); children—Rosemary, Miriam Chisholm, Lewis Olcott III; m. 2d, Joan Smith Nobert, Oct. 4, 1969. With Am. Fore Ins. Group, N.Y.C., 1939-42, Wilcox-Crittenden & Co., Inc., Middletown, 1942-45; with L.O. & E.S. Davis, Inc., Middletown, 1945—, pres., 1948—; dir., chmn. mortgage and loan com. Middletown Savs. Bank; dir. Middlesex Mut. Assurance Co.; mem. Middletown area com. Hartford Electric Light Co. Pres. No. Middlesex YMCA, 1950-52, bd. dirs., 1947-69, trustee, 1969—, mem. New Eng. area bd., 1959-61; mem. Conn. YMCA Camp Hazen Com., 1948-69, chmn., 1959-61, exec. com., 1959-69; pres. Middletown United Fund, 1959, campaign chmn., 1954; exec. council Middlesex County council Boy Scouts Am., 1946; mem. City Middletown Redevel. Agy., 1954-66. Chmn. bd. Middlesex Meml. Hosp.; trustee Wesleyan U., 1963-66. Recipient Gold medal award Middletown United Fund, 1960. Mem. Conn. Retail Lumber Dealers Assn. (past pres., dir.), Northeastern Retail Lumbermen's Assn. (past dir.), Middletown C. of C. (past dir.), Eastern Conn. Yacht Racing Assn. (vice commodore). Home: Cherry Hill Rd Rockfall CT 06481 Office: 1 DeKoven Dr Middletown CT 06458

DAVIS, DONALD GOODWIN, Jr., educator; b. Stoneham, Mass., Aug. 23, 1932; s. Donald Goodwin and Elizabeth (Fowler) D.; B.A., Wesleyan U., Middletown, Conn., 1954; Ph.D., Harvard, 1957; m. Janet M. Alford, June 26, 1954; children—Donna Lee, Barbara Elizabeth, Scott Jeffrey. Mem. faculty Ga. Inst. Tech., Atlanta, 1957-59; asso. prof. chemistry La. State U., New Orleans, 1959-63, prof., 1963—, chmn. dept., 1960-64, dean Grad. Sch., 1965-69. Sci. adviser FDA, 1965—. Vice pres. New Orleans Sci. Fair, 1967—. Mem. Am. Chem. Soc., Electrochem. Soc., A.A.A.S., N.Y. Acad. Sci., Phi Beta Kappa, Sigma Xi. Contbr. articles in field to profl. jours., reference books. Home: 1739 Filmore Av New Orleans LA 70122

DAVIS, DONALD WALTER, steel co. exec.; b. Springfield, Mass., June 10, 1921; s. Donald Walter and Laura Helen (Mansfield) D.; A.B., Pa. State U., 1942; M.B.A., Harvard, 1948; m. Mary Virginia Cooper, Aug. 2, 1947; children—Randall C., Deborah M., Donald Walter III, Palmer R., Jennifer D., Ruth A. With Stanley Works, New Britain, Conn., 1948—, asst. gen. mgr. steel strapping div., 1960-61, v.p., gen. mgr. div., 1961-62, exec. v.p., 1962-66, pres., 1966—, also chief exec. officer; bd. dir. Internat. Stanley Co., Omaha, Prentice Mfg. Co., New Britain, New Britain Nat. Bank. Mem. New Britain Bd. Edn., 1958—, chmn., 1960-61. Mem. Paper Industry Mgmt. Assn., Am. Mgmt. Assn., Phi Delta Theta. Home: 514 Shuttle Meadow Av New Britain CT 06052 Office: Stanley Works New Britain CT 06050

DAVIS, DORLAND JONES, USPHS officer; b. Chgo., July 2, 1911; s. David John and Myra Helen (Jones) D.; student Internat. Sch., Geneva, Switzerland, 1927-28; B.S., U. Ill., 1933; M.D., Johns Hopkins, 1937, Dr.P.H., 1940; m. Caroline Gertrude Baker, July 15, 1938; children—David Howard, Constance Elaine. Commd. asst. surgeon, USPHS, 1939, advanced through grades to asst. surg. gen.; investigations infectious diseases, including poliomyelitis, trypanosomiasis, psittacosis, hepatitis, conjunctivitis, influenza; assigned State Dept. for duty North Africa, 1943-44; with NIH, 1939-43, 44—, chief lab. infectious diseases Nat. Mircrobiol. Inst., 1954-56; asso. dir. Nat. Inst. Allergy and Infectious Dis., 1956-64, dir., 1964—. Recipient Edward Rhodes Stitt award, 1955; USPHS Meritorious Service medal, 1967. Fellow Am. Acad. Microbiology, A.A.A.S., Am. Pub. Health Assn., Am. Coll. of Preventive Med.; mem. Soc. Am. Bacteriologists, Soc. Exptl. Biology and Medicine, A.M.A., Am. Assn. Mil. Surgeons, Am. Epidemiological Soc., Am. Assn. Immunologists, Phi Beta Kappa, Beta Theta Pi, Delta Omega, Sigma Xi. Club: Cosmos (Washington). Home: 6 West Dr Bethesda MD 20014 Office: Nat Insts Health Bethesda MD 20014

DAVIS, DOROTHY SALISBURY, author; b. Chgo., Apr. 26, 1916; d. Alfred Joseph and Margaret Jane (Greer) Salisbury; A.B., Barat Coll., Lake Forest, Ill., 1938; m. Harry Davis, Apr. 25, 1946. Mystery and hist. novelist; short story writer. Mem. Authors League, Mystery Writers of Am. (pres.), Writers Guild of Am. Author: A Gentle Murderer, 1951; A Town of Masks, 1952; Men of No Property, 1956; Death of an Old Sinner, 1957; A Gentleman Called, 1958; The Evening of the Good Samaritan, 1961; Black Sheep, White Lamb, 1963; The Pale Betrayer, 1965; Enemy and Brother, 1967; (with Jerome Ross) God Speed The Night, 1968; Where the Dark Streets Go, 1969. Home: Sneden's Landing Palisades NY 10964

DAVIS, DWIGHT M., supt. schs.; b. Lynnville, Ia., Mar. 12, 1920; s. Orland G. and Gertrude (McClung) D.; B.A., Ia. State Tchrs. Coll., 1941; M.A., State U. Ia., 1947, Ph.D., 1953; m. Alice Fredrickson, Aug. 20, 1941; children—Gilbert Kenneth, Trevor Dwight. Tchr. math, Williamsburg, Ia., 1941-42, Iowa Falls, Ia., 1942-43; prin. high sch., dean jr. coll., Bloomfield, Ia., 1947-48; prin. high sch., Hampton, Ia., 1948-50, U. High Sch. of State U. Ia., Iowa City, 1950-53; dean Moline (Ill.) Community Coll., 1953-55; supt. schs. Moline, 1955-65, Des Moines, 1965—. Pres. Girls-Home Sch.; active Community Chest, Boy Scouts Am.; mem. Gov.'s Task Force on Edn.; life mem. P.T.A. Served with C.E., AUS, 1943-46. Mem. N.E.A., Am., Ia. assns. sch. adminstrs., Phi Delta Kappa, Phi Mu Epsilon. Kiwanian, Rotarian. Home: 505 Glenview Dr Des Moines IA 50312*

DAVIS, E. K., savs. and loan assn. exec. Pres., Pasadena Fed. Savs. and Loan Assn. Office: 199 N Lake Av Pasadena CA 91109*

DAVIS, EARL LEWELLYN, Jr., lawyer, corp. exec.; b. Kent, O., 1922. Home: 23 Beacon St Boston MA 02107

DAVIS, EARLE ROSCO, educator; b. Coin, Ia., Jan. 3, 1905; s. David Milton and Mary Isabel (Watterson) D.; A.B., B.Mus., Monmouth Coll., 1927; M.A., U. Ill., 1928; Ph.D., Princeton, 1935; m. Kathrine K. Laurie. Aug. 4, 1938; children—Nina Virginia, Joseph Scott L., Earle Rosco, Sallie K., Charles W. Instr. English, Monmouth Coll., 1928-33; prof., chmn. dept. English, U. Wichita, 1935-49; prof. English, Kan. State U., 1949-50, head dept., 1950—. Fulbright lectr. U. Adelaide, Australia, 1963, U. Coll., Cork, Ireland, 1969-70. Mem. Modern Lang. Assn. Episcopalian. Author: Flint And The Flame, 1964; Vision Fugitive, 1968; also books of poetry, textbooks, articles and poems in mags. Home: 1711 Fairchild St Manhattan KS 66502

DAVIS, EDWIN ADAMS, educator; b. Alba, Mo., May 10, 1904; s. Frank Byrd and Willie Belle (Greever) D.; B.S., Kan. State Tchrs. Coll., 1925; M.A., U. Ia., 1931; Ph.D., La. State U., 1936; m. La Verna Mae Rowe, May 8, 1925; 1 son, Edwin Adams. High sch. tchr., asst. prin., Mo., Kan., Ia., 1922-23, 25-31; asso. prof., acting head dept. history Drury Coll., Springfield, Mo., 1931-32; asst. history La. State U., 1932-34, instr., 1934-36. asst. prof., 1936-43, asso. prof., 1943-50, prof., 1950—, head dept., 1952-63, spl. asst. to the pres. univ., 1962-67; was editorial asst. Jour. So. History, 1935-36; founder, head dept. archives La. State U., 1935-46; vis. prof. U. Tex., summer 1937; state sponsor, editorial cons. publs. La. Hist. Records Survey, Works Project Adminstrn. La., 1937-43; spl. archival cons. various state depts. La. archives, govt. agencies. 1937—; historian Acadian Bicentennial Celebration Assn., 1954-56; chief cons. La. Archives Survey, 1955-56, chief cons. State Archives and Records Commn., 1956—. State chmn. com. conservation cultural resources Nat. Resources Planning Bd., World War II. Mem. com. on history source materials Am. Council Learned Soc., 1942-45. Mem. Am. (com. on hist. source materials 1942-45), So. (founding mem., exec. council 1947-50), Miss. Valley (exec. council tchrs. sect. 1952-55) La. (pres. 1958) hist. assns., Soc. of Am. Archivists (com. archival terminology 1937-39, com. on tng. archivists 1941-45), Soc. Am. Historians, La., Miss. hist. socs., Phi Kappa Delta, Kappa Delta Pi, Sigma Mu Delta. Episcoplian. Author: Plantation Life in the Florida Parishes of Louisiana, 1943; Of the Night Wind's Telling, Legends from the Valley of Mexico, 1946; William Johnson's Natchez: the Ante-Bellum Diary of a Free Negro (with W. R. Hogan), 1951; The Barber of Natchez (with W. R. Hogan), 1954; Louisiana, The Pelican State, 1959; The Story of Louisiana, 1960; Louisiana, A Narrative History, 1961; Fallen Guidon, 1962; Heroic Years, Louisiana and the War for Southern Independence, 1964; Heritage of Valor: The Picture Story of Louisiana in the Confederacy, 1964. Editor: (with M. H. Hall) A Campaign from Santa Fe to the Mississippi, 1961; Louisiana History 1960-63, 69—; The Rivers and Bayous of Louisiana, 1968. Contbr. articles profl. gen. publs. Home: 506 Stanford Av Baton Rouge LA 70808

DAVIS, ELLABELLE, singer; sang Aida with Opera Nacional of Mexico City. Address: care Opera Nacional Mexico City Mexico*

DAVIS, ELLSWORTH INGALLS, ret. army officer; b. Vancouver, Wash., Sept. 28, 1910; s. Arthur J. and Muriel (Ingalls) D.; B.S., U.S. Mil. Acad., 1932; M.S. in Civil Engring., Mass. Inst. Tech., 1937; grad. Army War Coll., 1953; m. Lily Dengre McCall, May 4, 1936 (dec. Aug. 1970); children—Harriet (Mrs. Duncan de P. Parham), Joan Frances (Mrs. C. W. Butler III), Ellsworth Ingalls (dec.). Commd. 2d lt. C.E., U.S. Army, 1932, advanced through grades to maj. gen., 1962, ret., 1966; instr. U.S. Mil. Acad., 1938-41; comdg. engr. combat groups, World War II and Korea; charge constrn. Pacific area for U.S. Army and USAF, 1957-60; chief engr. U.S. Army, Europe, 1960-62; pres. Miss. River Commn., Vicksburg, 1962-66, ret., 1966; exec. v.p. Met. Area Com., New Orleans 1966-68. Mem. Bd. Engrs. for Rivers and Harbors, 1963-66; chmn. Red River Compact Commn., 1963-66. Decorated D.S.M., Legion of Merit with oak leaf cluster, Army Commendation medal. Fellow Am. Soc. C.E.; mem. Soc. Am. Mil. Engrs., N.Y. Soc. Mil. and Naval Officers World Wars, Sigma Xi. Author: Vicksburg-Mississippi River City with a Historic Past and a Promising Future, 1964. Home: 3435 Camp St New Orleans LA 70115

DAVIS, ELWOOD M., mfg. co. exec.; b. Phila., May 13, 1906; student N.Y. Mil. Acad.; grad. Advanced Mgmt. Program; m. Mary Madenford; children—Elwood M., Natalie D. With Pitney-Bowes, Inc., 1929—, v.p. sales, service and marketing, 1957—, exec. v.p. marketing, 1963-69, exec. v.p., 1969—, also dir.; dir. Malco Plastics, Inc., Monarch Marking Systems, Thomas Collator, Inc., Pitney-Bowes of Canada, Ltd. Bd. dirs. Davis and Elkins Coll., Distributive Edn. Found. Conn., Inc. Mem. Am. Mgmt. Assn., Bus. Equipment Mfrs. Assn., Sales Execs. Club N.Y., Sales and Marketing Execs. Internat. (dir.). Clubs: Scarsdale Golf. Home: 16 Stonehouse Rd Scarsdale NY 10583 Office: Pitney-Bowes Inc Walnut & Pacific Sts Stamford CT 06904

DAVIS, ERNEST B., state ofcl.; b. Danielsville, Ga., Sept. 12, 1919; s. James Wyle and Lora (Burroughs) D.; B.C.S., Ga. State Coll., 1947; m. Mary Louise Walton, Jan. 10, 1946; children—Lane Nannette, Lauren Patricia. Sec.-treas. bd. health State of Ga., 1951-61, budget officer, 1962-65, state auditor, 1965—. Home: 1679 Timberland Rd Atlanta GA 30345 Office: State Capitol Bldg Atlanta GA 30334

DAVIS, EVELYN NORRIS, brewery exec.; b. Saskatoon, Sask., Can., Nov. 30, 1916; s. Louis J. and Eleanore (Fuerst) D.; student Dalhousie U., 1936-37; LL.B., U. Sask., 1938; m. Isla Winnifred Brandon, July 22, 1940; children—Barbara Ann (Mrs. David Tarr), Thomas B., John L., Mary Eleanore. Personnel mgr. Campbell Soup Co. Ltd., New Toronto, Ont., 1947-52; chmn. labour relations bd. Ont. Govt., 1952-53; dir. personnel services Campbell Soup Co. Ltd., 1953-59; with Canadian Breweries, Ltd., Toronto, 1959—, exec. v.p., 1969—; v.p. adminstrn. Carling Breweries, Ltd., 1965-66, Employer rep. Regional War Labour Bd., 1942-45; mem. Ont. Labour Relations Bd., 1948-52; dir. Tech. Services Council, 1964—. Mem. Toronto Bd. Trade. Mem. Conservative Party. Presbyn. Clubs: Vancouver (B.C., Can.); Chinguacousy (Brampton, Ont.); Albany (Toronto). Home: 1536 Truscott Dr Clarkson Ontario Canada Office: 79th St Clair Av E Toronto Ontario Canada

DAVIS, EVELYN Y., editor, author; b. The Netherlands, Aug. 16, 1929 (parents Am. citizens); d. Herman H. and Marian (Witteboom) DeJong; student Western Md. Coll., George Washington U., N.Y. Inst. Finance; m. William Henry Davis, 1957 (dec. 1958); m. 2d, Marvin Knudsen, 1969 (div. 1970). UN corr. newspaper Philippine-Am., 1962-63; editor, pub. Highlights and Lowlights of Annual Meetings, 1964—; lectr. on stockholder relations. Contbr. articles on bus. and travel to various publs. Office: 871 7th Av New York City NY 10019

DAVIS, FINIS E., orgn. exec., educator; b. Lead Hill, Ark., Aug. 29, 1911; s. John Preston and Mary Elizabeth (Cagle) D.; student Ark. Polytech. Coll., 1932; B.S. in Edn., U. Ark., 1938; m. Ethlyn Watkins, July 15, 1933; children—Marybel (Mrs. Robert Black), Juliann (Mrs. R. B. McBride), Linda Sue (Mrs. Bruce Henry Broecker). Engaged as tchr. Ark. Sch. for the Blind, Little Rock, 1933-39, supt., 1939-47; v.p., gen. mgr. Am. Printing House for Blind, Louisville, 1947—. Sponsoring com. Internat. Conf. Educators of Blind Youth, 1951-52, U.S. del. to conf., Bussum, Holland, 1952, mem. exec. council, 1952—, chmn. U.S. delegation to conf., Oslo, Norway, 1957. Mem. Lions Internat., 1941—, pres. Little Rock club, 1946-47, dist. gov. 7-B Ark., 1947, pres. Louisville club, 1950-51, dist. gov., 1953-54, internat. bd. dirs., 1954-56, 1st v.p., 1959-60, pres., 1960-61. Mem. bd. Quapaw area council Boy Scouts Am., dist. commnr., also chmn. leadership tng., 1941-46. Mem. bd. trustees Pikeville (Ky.) Coll., Louisville Presbyn. Sem. Recipient Key award Lions Internat., 1944, Extension award, 1952, 100 Percent Dist. Gov. award, 1953, Merit award, 1956, Ambassador of Goodwill award, 1957. Internat. Pres. award, 1956, Humanitarian award, 1968; hon. mem. Order Arrow, Boy Scouts Am.; named Ark. Traveler, 1950, Ky. col., 1954, hon. citizen N.C., 1954, hon. citizen Del., 1957. Mem. Am. Assn. Instrs. Blind (dir. 1950-55, pres. 1950-52), Am. Found. for Blind (dir. 1950-52), Am. Assn. Workers for Blind, English-Speaking Union, Presbyn. (elder). Mason (Shriner). Club: Pendennis (Louisville). Home: 6106 Rodes Dr Louisville KY 40222 Office: 1839 Frankfort Av Louisville KY 40206

DAVIS, FLORENCE NIGHTINGALE, educator; b. Hereford, Eng., Aug. 23, 1909; d. William Richard and Florence (James) David; B.S., U. London, 1931, Ph.D., 1937, D.Sc., 1951. Research asst. to Karl Pearson, 1933-35; mem. faculty Univ. Coll., U. London, 1935-39, 45-67; sr. statistician Home Office, also Ministry Home Security, 1939-45; prof. statistics, head dept. U. Cal. at Riverside, 1967—; vis. prof. U. Cal. at Berkeley, 1961-62; cons. Pacific S.W. Range and Expt. Sta., Dept. Agr., Pacific State Hosp. Fellow Inst. Math. Statistics, Am. Statis. Assn., Royal Statis. Soc.; mem. Internat. Statis. Inst., Biometric Soc. Author: Tables of the Correlation Coefficient, 1938; Probability Theory for Statistical Methods, 2d edit., 1961; Elementary Statistical Exercises, 2d edit., 1962; A Statisical Primir, 1953; Combinatorial Chance (with D.E. Narton), 1961; Games, Gods and Gambling, 1962; Symmetric Functions and Allied Tables (with M.G. Kendall and D.E. Barton), 1967; also articles. Editor: Festschrift for J. Neyman, 1966. Home: 156 Highland Blvd Berkeley CA 94708 Office: Life Scis Bldg Univ Cal Riverside CA 92502

DAVIS, FRANCIS KAYE, meteorologist; b. Scranton, Pa., May 4, 1918; s. Francis and Anna Jane (Wooten) D.; B.S., West Chester State Coll., 1939; M.S., Mass. Inst. Tech., 1944; Ph.D., N.Y.U., 1957; m. Ida Mae Lamplugh, Sept. 25, 1941; children-Richard Kaye, Frances Kay. Chemist Sun Oil Co., Marcus Hook, Pa., 1939-42; instr. physics Drexel U., 1946-48, asst. prof., 1948-55, asso. prof., 1955-59, prof., 1959-63, head physics dept., 1963-70, dean Coll. Sci., 1970—; meteorologist stas. WFIL and WFIL-TV, Phila., 1947- -; dir. Sonex, Inc., 1960—; cons. in field. Police commr., Lower Chichester Twp., 1946-48; active various community drives. Served to capt. USAAF, 1942-46. Recipient distinguished alumni award West Chester State Coll., 1968, other certificates achievement. Mem. Am. Inst. Med. Climatology, Am. Meteorol. Soc., Am. Phys. Soc., Am. Assn. Physics Tchrs., Air Polution Control Assn., Am. Geophys. Union, A.A.A.S., Franklin Inst., Sigma Xi, Phi Kappa Phi, Sigma Pi Sigma. Presbyn (sch. supt.). Contbr. articles profl. jours. Home: 103 Avonbrook Rd Wallingford PA 19086 Office: Dean Coll Sci Drexel U Philadelphia PA 19104

DAVIS, FRANK BELL, educator; b. Alba, Mo., Jan. 3, 1913; s. Frank B. and Willie (Greever) D.; B.A., Hendrix Coll., 1935; M.A., U. Ia., 1936; Ph.D., La. State U., 1949; m. Elizabeth Young, Aug. 30, 1941; children—Sue Carol, Kim Elaine, John Roy. Instr. to asso. prof. Colo. State U., 1937-47; prof. Auburn U., 1948—, head dept. speech, 1956—. Dir. Englewood Press, Inc., Twin City Concrete Co. Chmn. Community Chest, 1952-53. Trustee Columbia Theol. Sem., 1967—, chmn., 1971—. Served to capt. USCGR, 1942-46. Mem. Speech Assn. Am. (legislative assembly), So. Speech Assn. (past pres.), Blue Key, Phi Kappa Phi. Presbyn. (elder). Club: Auburn Rotary (past pres.). Home: 330 Cary Dr Auburn AL 36830

DAVIS, FRANK EDGAR, pub. exec.; b. Bound Brook, N.J., Mar. 23, 1917; s. Cecil and Marie Louise (Conover) D.; A.B., Dartmouth, 1937; m. Dorothy R. Campbell, Mar. 27, 1942; children—Frank Edgar, Geoffrey Campbell. With Nat. Export Advt. Agy., 1938-41; advt. sales Newsweek mag., 1946-47, mgr. internat. edits., 1947-49, asst. to publisher, 1949-52, circulation mgr., 1952-55, circulation dir., 1955-57, v.p., circulation dir., 1957-60, v.p., gen. mgr., 1961—. Dir. Audit Bur. Circulations. Trustee Wardlaw Country Day Sch., 1959-66; bd. govs. Muhlenberg Hosp. Served to lt. comdr. USNR, 1941-45. Mem. Phi Kappa Psi. Clubs: Plainfield (N.J.) Country; Log Cabin Gun. Home: 1080 Rahway Rd Plainfield NJ 07060 Office: 444 Madison Av New York City NY 10022

DAVIS, FRANK ELWOOD, lawyer; b. Washington, Dec. 15, 1915; s. Leonard Henry and Anne Mae (MacCarthy) D.; LL.B., George Washington U., 1942; grad. Grad. Sch. Banking, Rutgers U., 1950; m. Eleanor Louise Grunwell, Sept. 19, 1942; children—Robert Elwood, Anne Louise, Lynne Lockwood. With Riggs Nat. Bank, 1934-50, now mem. adv. bd.; admitted to D.C. bar. 1946; partner firm Reasoner Davis & Vinson and predecessor firm, Washington, 1950—. Gen. counsel D.C. Soc. Crippled Children, George Washington U., Peoples Drug Stores, Inc., Equitable Life Ins. Co.; past pres. Washington Bd. Trade, 1965-66; dir. Equitable Life Ins. Co., Nat. Engring. Products, Inc., Security Storage Co., Capital Film Labs., Jefferson Fed. Savs. & Loan Assn., Parsons Paper Co. Bd. dirs. Boys Club of Washington. Chmn. Citizens Joint com. on Nat. Representation for D.C. Served to lt. USNR, 1942-46. Recipient Washingtonian award Jr. C. of C., 1954, Civic award Alpha Kappa Psi, 1960, Distinguished Service award Cosmopolitan Club, 1961. Mem. Soc. Friendly Sons of St. Patrick, Omicron Delta Kappa. Clubs: Metropolitan Army and Navy, Chevy Chase Country, Columbia Country, Burning Tree, Kiwanis (Washington). Author: History of Trust Business for District of Columbia, 1950. Home: 2301 California St NW Washington DC 20008 Office: 800 17th St NW Washington DC 20006

DAVIS, FRANK FAVILLE, aviation corp. exec.; b. N.Y.C., Nov. 16, 1918; s. Frank Faville and Florence (Custer) D.; B.S. in Mech. Engring., Princeton, 1940; m. Dorothy Arrasmith, Dec. 1957 (div. May 1968); 1 dau., Susan June; m. 2d, Rosalind Wong, Aug. 1971. With United Air Lines, 1940-42, 45-54, asst. to v.p. engring. and maintenance, 1951-54; with Lockheed Aircraft Corp., 1954-61, dir. comml. sales Cal. div., 1960-61; v.p. Kaiser engr. div. Kaiser Industries Corp., 1961-70; sr. v.p. Pan Am. World Airways, 1970-71, group v.p., 1971—, also dir.; dir. Mysore Cements Ltd., Bangalore, India, 1961-70, N.Y. Airways, 1970—. Served to lt. comdr. USNR, 1942-45. Mem. Am. Inst. Aero. and Astronautics, Am. Ordnance Assn. Clubs: Sky, Wings (N.Y.C.). Home: 67 Park Av New York City NY 10016 Office: 200 Park Av New York City NY 10017

DAVIS, FRANKLIN MILTON, Jr., army officer; b. Malden, Mass., July 19, 1918; s. Franklin M. and Florence (Cummings) D.; B.A., U. Mass., 1940; M.A., George Washington U., 1963; m. Erma Stuart Alvord, July 18, 1942; children—Stephen W. (Dec.), Nathaniel A. Commd. 2d lt. U.S. Army, 1940, advanced through grades to maj. gen., 1969; with 18th Airborne Corps and 3d Armored Div., Europe, World War II; mem. faculty U.S. Army War Coll., 1960-62; mem. Army Gen. Staff, 1968-71; comdg. gen. 199th Light Inf. Brigade, Vietnam, 1968; dir. mil. personnel policies Hdqrs. Dept. Army, Washington, 1969-71; comdt. Army War Coll., 1971—. Decorated D.S.M., Legion of Merit, D.F.C., Bronze Star, Purple Heart (U.S.); Order Merit 5th Class (Vietnam). Mem. Nat. Muzzle Loading Rifle Assn., Internat. Brotherhood Magicians, Theta Chi. Author: Come as a Conqueror, 1967. Home: Quarters 1 Carlisle Barracks PA 17013

DAVIS, FRED, educator; b. Norris, Miss., July 25, 1922; s. James Houston and Sue (Roland) D.; B.S., Miss. State U., 1949, M.S., 1950; Ph.D., U. Ala., 1967; m. Irma Grace Holley, Sept. 24, 1954; children—Nancy Mozelle, James William, Robert Hugh. Head

Applied Math. div. Air Proving Grounds Comd. Eglin AFB, Fla., 1951-58; dir. Computing Center Miss. State U., State Coll. Miss., 1958—; head computer sci. dept. Miss. State U., 1967—, prof. applied math., 1962-67, prof. math., computer sci., 1967—. Mem. Math. Assn. Am., Am. Math. Soc., Assn. for Computing Machinery, Soc. for Indsl. and Applied Math. Rotarian. Home: 110 Cedar Lane Starkville MS 39759 Office: Drawer CC State College MS 39762

DAVIS, FREDERICK BARTON, psychologist; b. Boston, Mass., Aug. 27, 1909; s. Ernest Lewis Frederick and Dorothy (Barton) D.; B.S., Boston U., 1931; Ed.M., Harvard, 1933, Ed.D., 1941; m. Charlotte W. Croon, Oct., 1940; 1 dau., Dorothy Barton (Mrs. James Franklin Truitt, Jr.). Psychologist Avon (Conn.) Old Farms Sch., 1936-39; editor, Co-operative Test Service, N.Y.C., 1939-42; prof. psychology and head dept. psychology George Peabody Coll. Tchrs., Nashville, 1947-49; prof. edn. Hunter Coll., 1949-64; prof. edn., dir. bur. ednl. research and service, U. Pa., 1964—; lectr. Wellesley College, 1936-37, Univ. Cal., 1947, 56, 57, Harvard 1948, Tchrs. Coll. Columbia U., 1953-54, 60-62, 67-68; dir. Test Research Service U. Amsterdam, 1947—, Fulbright lectr., 1957-58; vis. research prof. Rutgers U., 1970-71. Cons. Am. Council on Edn., 1947; spl. cons. Sec. of War. 1941-42, Sec. of Air Force, 1947-51; research cons. Philippine Center Lang. Study, Manila, 1959-68, Edn. Records Bur., 1966, Ford Found., 1967, Getulio Vargas Found., Rio de Janeiro, 1968—; mem. Coll. Entrance Exam. Bd., 1970-71. Served as aviation psychologist, USAAF, 1942-46; discharged as maj. Awarded Legion of Merit. Diplomate Am. Psychol. Assn. Fellow Psychometric Soc. Unitarian. Author: The AAF Qualifying Examination, 1947; Utilizing Human Talent, 1947; Itam Analysis Data, 1946; Davis Reading Tests, 1958, 62; Educational Measurements and Their Interpretation, 1964; Item Analyse (Dutch), 1964; Analyse des Items (French), 1966; The Philippine Language-Teaching Experiments, 1967; Comprehension Skills of Mature Readers, 1967. Editor: Am. Edn. Research Jour.; psychometric Monographs. Home: 10 Kent Rd Bronxville NY 10708 Office: Grad Sch Edn U Pa Philadelphia PA 19104

DAVIS, FREDERICK CARR, shipbldg. co. exec.; b. Seven Springs, N.C., Jan. 6, 1907; s. Herbery William and Harriette (Isler) D.; B.S., N.C. State Coll., 1928; grad. mgmt. problems for execs., U. Pitts., 1954; m. Mary Annette Parker, Apr. 18, 1931; children—Frederick Carr, George Parker. Formerly with Newport News Shipbldg. and Dry Dock Co., from 1928, gen. mgr., 1964-65, v.p., gen. mgr., from 1965; v.p. Peninsula Savs. and Loan Assn.; dir. Employees Credit Union. Treas. Newport News Democratic Exec. Com. Mem. Soc. Naval Architects and Marine Engrs. (asso.), Am. Soc. Naval Engrs., Welding Research Council, Phi Kappa Phi, Theta Tau, Golden China, Blue Key. Clubs: Rotary (past pres.), Propeller (past pres.), James River Country (Newport News). Home: 43 Rivermont Dr Newport News VA 23601

DAVIS, GALE ELWOOD, ins. co. exec.; b. Omaha, July 18, 1909; s. Stanley A. and Frances Mary (Evans) D.; LL.B., U. Neb., 1931; m. Margaret Nell Lavelle, Nov. 30, 1933; children—Stanley L., Sally K., Molly F. Admitted to Neb. bar, 1931; with Mut. Omaha Ins. Co., 1932-65, v.p., 1950-59, exec. v.p., 1959-65; pres. United Benefit Life Ins. Co., 1965—, also dir. Trustee Clarkson Hosp., Childrens Therapy Center Omaha, Omaha Home for Boys, U. Neb. Found.; trustee, chmn. profl. div. United Community Service Omaha. Mem. Omaha C. of C. (dir.), Am., Neb. bar assns., Delta Upsilon, Phi Delta Phi. Mason (Shriner, Jester). Clubs: Omaha, Omaha Country; Nat. Lawyers (Washington); Plaza. Home: 6620 Underwood Av Omaha NB 68132 Office: 3301 Dodge St Omaha NB 68131

DAVIS, GARY, blues singer. Address: care Prestige Records 203 S Washington Av Bergenfield NJ 07621*

DAVIS, GAYLORD, lawyer; b. Lincoln, Neb., Sept. 16, 1897; s. Walter Clyde and Minerva (Caldwell) D.; A.B., U. Neb., 1920; LL.B., Columbia, 1925, M.S., 1925; m. Susan Scott, July 4, 1925; 1 dau., Susanne Davis Newberry. Instr. accounting U. Neb., 1920-21, Sch. Bus. Columbia, 1921-25; admitted to N.Y. bar, 1926, practiced in N.Y. C., 1925-46; with Root, Clark, Buckner & Ballantine, 1925-28; with Cadwalader, Wickersham & Taft, 1928-46, mem. firm, 1942-46; gen. counsel, treas., sec. Am. Enka Corp. (N.C.), 1946-50, gen. counsel, treas., v.p., 1950-54, financial v.p., gen. counsel, 1954-62. Mem. bd. dirs. Asheville Symphony Soc.; gen. agt. in U.S.A. Algemene Kunstzijde Unie N.V. of Arnhem Holland, 1947-67. Mem. bd. Wachovia Bank and Trust Co., Asheville, N.C., 1952-67; Pres., director Asheville Community Concert Assn., Inc. Trustee N.C. Symphony Soc. Inc.; dir. Bus. Found. N.C., Inc., 1959-64. Mem. C. of C., Am., N.C. bar assns., Soc. Mayflower Descendants, Newcomen Soc. of Eng., Phi Beta Kappa, Beta Gamma Sigma, Phi Kappa Psi, Sigma Delta Chi, Alpha Kappa Psi, Sr. Hon. Soc. Innocents (U. Neb.). Republican. Mason (32). Clubs: University (N.Y.C.); Biltmore Forest Country, Mountain City (Asheville, N.C.). Home: 12 Fairway Pl Biltmore Forest Asheville NC 28803 Office: Parkway Office Bldg Asheville NC 28801

DAVIS, GENE BERNARD, artist; b. Washington, Aug. 22, 1920; s. Arthur G. and Edna Mae (Stout) D.; student U. Md., 1938-39, Wilson Tchrs. Coll., Washington, 1939-41; m. Florence Elizabeth Coulson, Nov. 24, 1960. One man shows Corcoran Gallery Art, 1964, 68, 70, Mass. Inst. Tech., 1966, Hofstra Univ., 1966, San Franciso Mus. Art, 1968, Washington Gallery Modern Art, 1968, Jewish Mus., 1968; rep. shows Chgo. Art Inst., Los Angeles County Mus., Detroit Mus. Fine Arts, Brandeis U. Mus., Mus. Modern Art, Buenos Aires, Mus. Modern Art, Rio de Janeiro, Art Gallery of Toronto, Can., Munson-William-Proctor Inst., Utica, N.Y., Corcoran Gallery of Art, Washington, Walker Art Center, Mpls., Isaac Delgado Mus., New Orleans, Atlanta Art Assn.; group shows Mus. Modern Art, 1966, San Francisco Mus. Art, U.S. Embassies Art Program, White House Art Program, Los Angeles Country Mus., 1964, Whitney Mus., 1967, 69, 71; instr. Corcoran Gallery Art Sch. Painting, Washington; instr. painting and drawing Am. U., 1968- 69. Recipient Bronze medal Corcoran Gallery Biennial Am. Painting, 1965; grant for contbn. to Am. art Nat. Council on Arts, 1967. Address: 4120 Harrison St NW Washington DC 20015

DAVIS GENE CARLTON, lawyer; b. Chgo., June 15, 1917; s. Carl DeWitt and Alta (Hoff) D.; A.B., U. Chgo., 1938; LL.B., Chgo. Kent Coll. Law, 1941; m. Roberta Wilson, Mar. 14, 1942; children—Bruce Carlton, Barbara Jean. Admitted to Ill. bar, 1942, since practiced in Chgo.; with firm Isham, Lincoln & Beale, 1943—, partner, 1953—. Dir. So. Nev. Telephone Co., 1956-60, Parker Aleshire & Co., 1962—. Trustee Orchestral Assn. Chgo. Served with AUS, 1942-43. Fellow American College of Probate Counsel; mem. Am., Ill., Chgo. (chmn. admissions com. 1955, entertainment com. 1952, probate com. 1962) bar assns. Presbyn. Clubs: Law, Legal (pres. 1965), Saddle and Cycle, Mid-Day (Chgo.); Racquet. Author: Estate Planning A Client's Handbook, 1967. Home: 1358 N State St Chicago IL 60610 Office: 1 First Nat Plaza Chicago IL 60670

DAVIS, GEORGE ALFRED, food co. exec.; b. Montclair, N.J., Feb. 26, 1928; s. Robert Greener and Ruth (Conroy) D.; A.B. cum laude, Dartmouth, 1952, M.B.A. with distinction, Amos Tuck Sch., 1953; m. Maria Nekos, June 30, 1956; children—Stephen Greener, Carol Elizabeth, Leslie Ann. Accountant, Arthur Andersen & Co., N.Y.C., 1953-59; with Thomas J. Lipton, Inc., 1960—, controller, 1965—; controller Good Humor Corp., Continenal Foods, Inc., Good Humor Food Service, Inc. Mem. corps. com. Fairleigh Dickinson U. Trustee, v.p. Tenafly Community Chest, 1969-71. Served with AUS, 1946-48. C.P.A., N.J. Mem. Am. Inst. C.P.A.'s, Financial Execs. Inst., Nat. Assn. Accountants, N.J. Soc. C.P.A.'s. Episcopalian (vestryman, treas. 1966-68). Clubs: Knickerbocker Country (Tenafly); Dartmouth of Bergen County (trustee, treas. 1965-68). Home: 144 Highland Av Tenafly NJ 07670 Office: 800 Sylvan Av Englewood Cliffs NJ 07632

DAVIS, GEORGE ARTHUR, army ofcr., ret.; b. Lynn, Mass., Dec. 19, 1902; s. Arthur and Jennie Florence (Holmes) D.; grad. Inf. Sch., 1925, Command and Gen. Staff Sch., 1933, Army War Coll., 1936, Army Indsl. Coll., 1937; B.S. in Foreign Service, Georgetown U., Washington, D.C., 1937; m. Mary Josephine Whittaker, Aug. 7, 1920 (div.); children—George (killed in action Korea); m. 2d Alice Aug. 18, 1947. Private and corpl., 1st Inf., Schofield Barracks, Hawaii, 1912-15; commd. 2d lt., Aug. 15, 1917, and advanced through the grades to brig. gen., Mar. 17, 1943; participated in operations, Chateau Thierry and Aisne-Marne Offensive, with 2d Div.; with U.S. troops in China, 1929-31; chief of staff 10th Corps, 1942-43; chief staff 3d Army, Feb. 1943-Apr. 1944; asst. div. comdr. 28th Inf. Div., Normandy, Northern France, Germany, Ardennes, Colmar; now brig. gen., U.S. Army, ret. Asst. prof. mil. science Boston U., 1920-24; prof. mil. sci. Ripon Coll., Wis., 1933-35; instr. and asst. dir. training, Inf. School, 1937-41. Decorated Legion of Merit with oak leaf cluster, Silver Star with oak leaf cluster, Bronze Star with 2 oak leaf clusters, Legion of Honor, Croix de Guerre with Palm, Croix de Guerre with two citations (France), Chateau-Thierry Medal, Heroes de la Cte 204 (Willa de Chateau-Thierry, 1918), Citoyen d'Honneur Essmes-Sur-Marne, Citoyen d'Honneur de la Commune Libre de Centreville, Villa de Chateau-Thierry (France); recipient Minute Man award S.A.R., 1963. Mem. S.A.R. (past pres. Me.; nat. trustee 1959-64, v.p. gen. New Eng. dist. 1961-63), Soc. Colonial Wars (dep. gov. gen. 1962-67), Founders and Patriots Am., New England Hist. and General. Soc., Baronial Order Magna Charta, Mil. Order Crusades, Soc. Descs. Colonial Clergy, Order Crown Charlemagne U.S.A., also mem. Auguatan Society. Author, pub.; Davis and Fifty Allied Colonial Families of New England; 1956; Some Royal, Noble, and Colonial Ancestors, 1959; Descent From a Hundred Kings, 1964, 2d edit., 1965. Home: Twin Coves Southport ME 04569

DAVIS, GEORGE BROWN, librarian; b. Hobart, N.Y., Dec. 26, 1924; s. Andrew Ferris and Frances (Brown) D.; B.A., Union Coll., Schenectady, 1945; M.A., Oberlin Coll., 1946; certificate U. Sorbonne, Paris, France, 1947; Ph.D. in French, Brown U., 1956; M.A., U. Chgo. Grad. Library Sch., 1960; m. Marcia Jean Thompson, Aug. 18, 1956. Teaching asst. French, U. Mich., summer 1946; teaching fellow French, Brown U., 1947-49, mem. staff John Hay Library, 1952-56; instr. fgn. langs. U. Bridgeport (Conn.), 1949-51; asst. to publisher Guideposts mag., 1951- 52; asst. prof. French, head librarian Centenary Coll., Shreveport, La., 1956-59; librarian Bennett Coll., Millbrook, N.Y., 1960-65; librarian, asso. prof. modern langs. Va. Mil. Inst., Lexington, Ky., 1965—. Mem. Am., Va. library assns., Modern Lang. Assn. Home: 502 Pickett St Lexington KY 24450

DAVIS, GEORGE CUNDALL, lawyer; b. Waupun, Wis., Apr. 28, 1899; s. Burr William and Lillian K. (Hooker) D.; A.B., U. Wis., 1922, J.D., 1925; m. Hope Watson, Aug. 30, 1934; children—Audrey Hope (Mrs. Edward R. Trowbridge III), Patricia Watson (Mrs. Richard A. Cooper). Admitted to R.I. bar, 1926, since practiced in Providence; partner firm Tillinghast, Collins & Graham, 1936—. Commnr. Uniform State Laws, 1959-61; mem. Commn. Revision Corp. Laws, 1949-50. Pres., dir. Hosp. Service Corp. R.I. (Blue Cross), 1939- -; dir. mem. exec. com. R.I. Health Services, Inc. Past sec., trustee R.I. Hosp.; bd. dirs. Heritage Found. R.I.; bd. dirs., past pres. R.I. Hist. Soc., Providence Boys' Clubs; bd. dirs. U. R.I. Found. Served with USNRF, 1918-19. Fellow Am. Bar Found.; mem. Nat. Conf. Pres., Am., R.I. (pres., exec. com. 1962-66, ho. dels. 1970—) bar assns., Am. Law Inst., Am. Judicature Soc., Soc. Colonial Wars (past gov. dep. gov. gen.), Providence C. of C., World Peace through Law Center, Alpha Tau Omega, Phi Delta Phi. Republican. Episcopalian. Rotarian. Clubs: Hope, Art (Providence); Dunes, Point Judith Yacht (Narrangansett, R.I.). Home: 168 Post Rd Wakefield RI 02879 also 52 Lloyd Av Providence 02906 Office: Hospital Trust Bldg Providence RI 02903

DAVIS, GEORGE ILSLEY, ins. co. exec.; b. Needham, Mass., Feb. 1, 1906; s. J. Irving and Edith (Ilsley) D.; B.S., Dartmouth, 1928; m. Marion F. Brown, Jan. 24, 1931; children—Steven I., Beth C. with Glens Falls Ins. Co. (N.Y.), 1928—, successively clk., treas., 1928-40, sec., 1940—, v.p., 1950—, chmn. exec. and finance com., 1957—, chmn. bd., 1962-71, also dir.; ret., 1971; dir. Kansas City Fire & Marine Ins. Co. of Kansas City, Mo., Glens Falls Nat. Bank & Trust Co., Marine office Appleton & Cox Corp., Capital Finance Corp., Economy Savs. & Loan Co., Nat. Reins. Corp., Capital Finance Corp., INSCO, Nat. Life Assurance Co. of Canada, Continental Ins. Co., Continental Corp. Trustee, treas. Skidmore Coll.; trustee Albany Med. Coll.; bd. mgrs. Hudson-Mohawk Assn. Colls. and Univs. Served as lt. col. AUS, 1942-46, staff hdqrs. ASF and War Dept. Gen. Staff. Decorated Legion of Merit. Club: University (N.Y.C.). Home: 29 Garrison Rd Glens Falls NY 12801 Office: 291 Glen St Glens Falls NY 12801

DAVIS, GEORGE KELSO, educator, nutrition biochemist; b. Pitts., July 2, 1910; s. Ross Irwin and Jennie (Kelso) D.; B.S., Pa. State U., 1932; Ph.D., Cornell U., 1937; m. Ruthanna Wood, Jan. 25, 1936; children—Dorothy Jeanne (Mrs. Arthur C. Aikin, Jr.), Mary Ellen (Mrs. W. Edgar Benedict), Ruthanna Marie (Mrs. Donald W. Davidson), Virginia Kay (Mrs. John M. Fedison), Robert Wyatt, George William. Research asst. Cornell U., 1932-37; research asst. prof. chemistry Mich. State U., 1937-42; prof. nutrition U. Fla., 1942—, animal nutritionist, 1942—, dir. nuclear scis., 1960-65, dir. biol. scis., 1965-70, dir. research, 1970—. Mem. Fla. Nuclear Commn.; chmn. Internat. Biol. Program Sect. Use and Mgmt. Biol. Resources; chmn. U. Fla. Council Oak Ridge Asso. Univs.; cons. minister agr., Costa Rica, univs. Costa Rica, Buenos Aires, San Marco (Peru), U. Agraria (Peru), Sao Paulo (Brazil), FAO, Dept. Agr., OEA-INTA (Argentina), Dept. Health, Edn. and Welfare Nutrition Found., Fla. Dept. Agr.; mem. food and nutrition bd., com. animal nutrition. internat. biol. program com. Nat. Acad. Sci.-NRC; rev. bds. NSF, Nat. Acad. Scis., NIH. Recipient Faculty award Fla. Blue Key, 1958, Distinguished Faculty award U. Fla., 1960; U. Fla. Faculty lectr., 1960; hon. prof. U. Chile, 1961—. Mem. Am. Inst. Biol. Scis. (chmn. S.E. regional council biol. satellite programs 1965—), Am. Inst. Nutrition (chmn. com. nutrition and trace elements 1961—, nat. exec. com. 1961; Borden award 1964), Am. Chem. Soc. (sec.-treas. Fla. 1955, chmn. 1958; Fla. award 1956). Am. Soc. Animal Sci. (nat. v.p. 1961-62, sec. So. sect. 1962-63), A.A.A.S., Am. Soc. Biol. Chemists, Soc. Exptl. Biology and Medicine, Am. Dairy Assn., Am. Nuclear Soc., Sigma Xi (pres. Fla. 1956-57), Alpha Zeta, Phi Lambda Upsilon, Gamma Sigma Delta, Phi Eta Sigma, Phi Sigma, Gamma Sigma Epsilon. Blue Key; hon. mem. Sao Paulo Vet. Soc., Peruvian Vet. Assn. Mem. editorial bd. Jour. Nutrition, Jour. Animal Sci. Contbr. profl. jours., chpts. books. Home: 2903 SW 2d Ct Gainesville FL 32601

DAVIS, GEORGE MONROE, naval med. officer; b. Bixby, Okla., June 6, 1916; s. George Monroe and Letty (Buchanan) D.; student Northeastern State Tchrs. Coll. Okla., 1933- 34; B.S. in Medicine, U. Okla., 1936, M.D., 1939; m. Helen Maria Hendershot, Apr. 15, 1938; 1 dau., Carol Jean (Mrs. James E. Grise). Commd. lt. (j.g.), M.C., U.S. Navy, 1939, advanced through grades to vice adm., 1969; intern U.S. Naval Hosp., San Diego, 1939-40; assigned 2d Marine Brigade, San Diego, 1940, 2d Def. Battalion. San Diego, 1940- 41, U.S. Marine Def. Force, Dutch Harbor, Alaska, 1941, Naval Air Sta., Dutch Harbor, 1941-42, Naval Air Sta., Norman, Okla., 1942-43, Hdgrs. and Service Co, 4th Med. Battalion, 4th Marine Div., Fleet Marine Force, PCA, 1943-45, Navy Dispensary, Washington, 1945-46; postgrad. tng. internal medicine Northwestern U. Sch. Medicine, 1946-47; chief med. service Naval Hosp., Annapolis, Md., 1947-50; assigned U.S. Naval Hosp., San Diego, 1950-52, 54-56; chief medicine naval hosp. ship U.S.S. Haven, 1952-54; chief med. service Naval Hosp., Great Lakes, Ill., 1956- 58; chief medicine Naval Hosp., Oakland, Cal., 1958-60, exec. officer, 1960-62; comdr. Naval Hosp., Yokosuka, Japan, 1962-65; comdg. officer Naval Hosp., Bethesda, Md., 1965-66, Nat. Naval Med. Center, Bethesda, 1966-68; dep. surgeon USN, 1968-69; surgeon gen. USN, 1969-. Decorated Naval Commendation medal. Diplomate Am. Bd. Internal Medicine. Fellow A.C.P. (USN gov.), Am. Coll. Chest Physicians, Am. Coll. Cardiology. Home: Quarters A Nat Naval Center Bethesda MD 20014 Office: Office Bureau of Medicine and Surgery Dept of Navy Washington DC 20390.

DAVIS, GEORGE PHILIP, lawyer; b. Waltham, Mass., Mar. 19, 1892; s. John F. and Carrie G. (Smith) D.; A.B., Harvard, 1914, LL.B., 1917; m. Edith F. Totten, June 12, 1917; children—Priscilla (Mrs. Robert G. Hoye), Lydia (Mrs. H. J. Scarborough). Admitted to Mass. bar, 1917; asso. Nutter, McClennen & Fish and predecessor firm, Boston, 1919-29, partner, 1929—. Vice pres. Waltham S. Bank, 1948-65, hon. trustee, 1965—; bd. dirs. Conrad & Chandler, Inc. Trustee of Hiram Francis Mills Fund, Frank Huntington Beebe Trust, pres. Leland Home, Waltham, 1934-54, chmn., 1954-; chmn. Mass. Council for Aging, 1954-60; life mem. Nat. Council on Aging, panel mem. Fed. Council on Aging, 1956, White House Conf. on aging, 1961; mem. Mass. Conglist. Fund, 1952-69; pres. Sr. Living, Nat. Fedn. for Elderly. Founder, trustee Assn. Mass. Homes for Aging; pres. Waltham Tng. Sch. for Nurses. Served as lt. (j.g.) USN, 1917-19; retired as lt. comdr., USNR, 1942. Mem. Am., Mass., Boston bar assns., Phi Beta Kappa. Republican. Conglist. Mason. Clubs: Weston Golf, Union (Boston). Author: Massachusetts Conveyancers' Handbook, 1956, 2d edit., 1966; also legal articles. Home: 85 Robin Rd Weston MA 02193 Office: 75 Federal St Boston MA 02110

DAVIS, GEORGE W., motion picture art dir.; b. Kokomo, Ind., Apr. 17, 1914; s. Harry Allen and Buella Bernice (Booher) D.; student of architecture, U. So. Cal., 1932-36; m. Barbara Louise Davies, June 21, 1938; childrenKaren Louise, George Christopher. Sketch artist Universal Internat. Studios, 1937- 38; asst. art. dir. Warner Bros. Studios, 1938-41; art dir. 20th Century- Fox Film Corp., 1941-56. supervising art dir. R.K.O. Studios, now MGM; dir. among others of All About Eve, 1950, David and Bathsheba, 1951, The Robe (Academy Award for color art direction), 1953, The Egyption, 1954; recently Funny Face, also Diary of Anne Frank. Served from capt. to maj., USMC, 1943-46. Mem. Acad. of Motion Picture Arts and Sciences. Soc. Motion Picture Art Dirs. (pres. 1956-57, dir.), Phi Kappa Psi. Club: Rivera Country (Los Angeles). Home: 939 San Vincente Blvd Santa Monica CA 90402 Office: 780 N Lower St Hollywood CA 90038

DAVIS, GEORGE WILLIAM, investment exec.; b. Alder Springs, Cal., 1894; s. Charles W. and Minnie J. (Mercer) C.; student U. Ore., U. Cal.; m. Ruth Robinson, 1920; children—Donald W., Richard M., Nancy R. Bond Salesman Los Angeles office Anglo Cal. Trust Co. San Francisco, 1927—; Founder, partner Davis, Skages & Co., San Francisco, 1927—, now hon. chmn. Gov., San Francisco div. Pacific Coast Stock Exchange, 1957-58, chmn. bd., 1959; mem. N.Y. Stock Exchange Mem. Investment Bankers Assn. Am. (gov. 1948-51, v.p. 1051-52, pres. 1955-56), Compiler tng. booklet: Manual on Securities Salesmanship. Home: 80 Santa Clara Av San Francisco CA 94104 Office: 160 Sansome St San Francisco CA 94104

DAVIS, GIFFORD, educator; b. Portland, Me., June 11, 1906; s. Marshall and Marguerite (Gifford) D.; A.B., Bowdoin Coll., 1927; A.M., Harvard, 1928, Ph.D., 1933; m. Helen Adams Peabody, Aug. 9, 1930; children—Elizabeth Hale (Mrs. Charles Usher, Jr.), Anne Webster. Instr., Romance langs., tutor Harvard, 1929-30; faculty Duke, 1930-, prof. Romance langs., 1953- , chmn. dept., 1957-64, dir. summer sch. Spanish studies, 1950-56, dir. undergrad. studies in Spanish, 1964—. Mem. Am. Assn. Tchrs. Spanish and Portuguese (past pres. N.C.), S. Atlantic Modern Lang. Assn., Am. Assn. U. Profs. Presbyn. (elder). Contbr. articles on 19th century novel and medieval period in Spanish lit. to profl. lit. Home: 2248 Cranford Rd Durham, NC 27706.

DAVIS, GINIA, singer; b. Phila., Mar. 10, 1923; d. Meyer and Hilda (Emery) Davis; student drama Carnegie Inst. Tech., 1939-41; vocal pupil Frances Lewando, Doris Monteux, 1939-50; coached with Povla Frijsh, Pierre Monteux, Queena Mario, Pablo Casals; Madeleine Grey; m. Morris M. Wexler, Oct. 1968. Performed as Polly Peachum in The Beggar's Opera, 1941, Bar Harbor (Me.) Stock Co., Chautauqua, N.Y. Bucks County Playhouse; leading roles Student Prince, Roberta, Sally, Firefly, New Moon, Toledo Light Opera Co., 1945; appeared on Broadway in Susan and God, 1942, Call Me Mister, 1946; made operatic debut as Gretel in Hansel and Gretel with Pitts. Opera Soc., 1943; ann. recital, N.Y.C., 1948-65; toured U.S.A., 1947—, Europe, 1949, 50; appeared at Holland Festival, 1950, in 1st U.S. performances of Flaminio of Pergolesi, 1953; with Royal Opera of Brussels, 1955; broadcasts U.S., Europe; appeared with symphony orch. U.S., Europe, Middle-East, 1955—; voice tchr. Mich. State U., East Lansing, 1962; stage dir. Domaine Opera Sch., Hancock, Me., summer 1961; dir. Hancock County Chamber Music Soc., Sorrento, Me. (now Hancock County Friends of Arts, East Sullivan, Me.), 1962—; made six months world tour, Africa, Asia, 1966; guitar concerts, 1965. Recs. songs Music Library Records, Inc., folk music div. Library of Congress; appearances Am. Folksong Festival; adviser folk music Nat Arts Found.; authority on folksongs; collecter, transcriber, interpreter folklore Ky. mountains (with Jean Thomas (the Traipsin' Woman), 1950—, also other nations Canada, Cuba, Czechoslavakia, France, Germany, Holland, Ireland, Mexico, Developer unique recital program Portraits in Song, 1947; entertainer Armed Forces, U.S., Europe. Recipient grand prize Internat. contest interpretation French song, 1958. Home: 1801 Kennedy Blvd Philadelphia PA 19124 also East Sullivan ME 04632

DAVIS, GLENN ROBERT, congressman; b. Vernon, Wis., Oct. 28, 1914; s. Charles W. and Jennie (Wachendorf) D.; B. Edn., U. Wis., 1934, LL. B., 1940; m. Kathryn J. McFarlane, Nov. 29, 1942; children—Kathleen, Margaret, James, Janet, Elizabeth. Admitted to Wis. bar, 1940, since practiced in Waukesha; mem. firm Love, Davis & McGraw, 1957-64; mem. Wis. Assembly from Waukesha County, 1941-42; mem. 80th- 84th Congresses 2d Dist. Wis., 89th-92d Congresses 9th Dist. Wis. Pres., dir. New Berlin State Bank, 1959-65. Served with USNR, 1942-45. Named one of ten outstanding young men, U.S. Jr. C. of C., 1947. Mem. United Ch. of Christ. Mason (Shriner), Kiwanian. Home: 3790 S Center Rd Waukesha WI 53186 Office: House Office Bldg Washington DC 20515

DAVIS, GRAHAM POWELL, investment banker; b. Norfolk, Va., Aug. 23, 1927; s. Hugh W. and Florence (Brookes) D.; grad. Woodberry Forest Sch., 1943; B.S. in Elec. Engring., Va. Mil. Inst.; m. Eve Rogers Mapp, Nov. 7, 1960; children—Hugh Wheelwright, Holland Powell. With Scott, Horner & Mason, Lynchburg, Va., 194952, Willis, Kenny & Avres, Richmond, Va., 195255; with Investment Corp. Va., Norfolk, 1956—, pres., 1968—. Past pres. Bond Club Va. Served with AUS, 194648. Home: 1013 S Bay Shore Dr Virginia Beach VA 23451 Office: 5 Main Plaza East Norfolk VA 23510

DAVIS, H. BRAITH, chem. co. exec.; b. Balt., 1907; grad. U. Pa., 1931. Chmn. exec. com., dir. ConChemCo, Inc., Kansas City, Mo.; pres. John W. Masury & Son, Inc.; dir. University Laundry, Burns & Russell Co., Anchor Post Products Co. Home: 100 W Cold Spring Lane Baltimore MD 21210 Office: 18th and Garfield Sts Kansas City MO 64127*

DAVIS, H. RICHARD, textile co. exec.; b. N.Y.C., July 10, 1919; s. Rubin R. and Dora (David) D.; student Baruch Sch. Bus., City Coll. N.Y., evenings 1936-41; m. Estelle Randell, Aug. 16, 1941; childrenRichard M., Lynne B. With S.D. Leidesdorf & Co., C.P.A.'s, N.Y.C., 1941-46; with United Merchants & Mfrs. Inc., N.Y.C., 1946-, corp. controller, 1967-. Served with USNR, 1942-45. C.P.A., N.Y. Mem. Am. Inst. C.P.A.'s, N.Y. Inst. Internal Auditors. Home: 183-41 Grand Central Pkwy Jamaica Estates NY 11432 Office: 1407 Broadway New York City NY 10018.

DAVIS, H. WEIR, lawyer; b. Montreal, Que., Can., Dec. 3, 1906; B.A., McGill U., 1938, B.C.L., 1931. Admitted to Que. bar, 1931; partner firm Laing, Weldon, Courtois, Clarkson, Parsons, Gonthier & Tetrault, Montreal. Mem. Canadian Bar Assn. Office: 630 Dorchester Blvd W Montreal 101 Quebec Canada*

DAVIS, HAL CHARLES, labor union exec.; b. Pitts., Feb. 27, 1914; s. Harry J., Sr., and Tillie (Reitzel) D.; student Duquesne U., 1931-32, 50; m. Marion Gray, Feb. 16, 1963; children—Joyce (Mrs. Raymond Smith), Ruth (Mrs. George Ayres). Profl. musician, percussionist, 1943-48; staff musician radio sta. KDKA., Pitts., 1943-48; pres. Pitts. local Am. Fedn. Musicians, 1948—, internat pres., N.Y.C., 1970—. Exec. dir. Pitts. Central Labor Union Com. Polit. Edn., 1956-65; mem. exec. bd. Allegheny County Labor Council, 1952-65; v.p. Pa. AFL-CIO, 1952-71. Mem. bd. Allegheny County Port Authority, 1958-70. Mem. bd. St. John's Hosp., Pitts., 1951-70; mem. Pa. Council on Arts, 1956-70. Served with USMC, World War II. Home: 642 Rankin Rd Brielle NJ 08730 Office: 641 Lexington Av New York City NY 10022

DAVIS, HAMILTON SEYMOUR, anesthesiologist; b. Pitts., Oct. 28, 1920; s. Karl Eugene and Vassie Sophia (Miller) D.; A.B. cum laude, Colgate U., 1942; M.D., Western Res. U., 1945; m. Marjorie Jean Wright, July 5, 1946; children—Eric Templeton, Scott Harold, Kim Elizabeth, Christopher Quay. Intern Grassland Hosp., Valhalla, N.Y., 1945-46, resident anesthesiology, 1948- 50; asso. anesthesiologist VA Hosp., also temporary chmn. dept. anesthesiology St. Mary's Hosp., Grand Junction, Colo., 1950-51; mem. faculty Western Res. U. Sch. Medicine, 1952-66, prof. anesthesiology, 1961-66; dir. dept. anesthesia Lakeside Hosp., 1953-66; attending anesthesiologist Met. Gen. Hosp., 1953-66; formerly cons. Cleve. VA Hosp., Lake County Meml. Hosp.; team physician Kenston Sch. Dist., 1957- 66; mem. jet injection immunization programs, Cleve. 1955-66; prof. anesthesiology, chmn. dept U. Cal. at Davis Scholl Medicine, 1966—; dir. dept. anesthesia U. Cal. at Davis- Sacramento Med. Center, 1966—. Camp physician Golden Empire council Boy Scouts Am., 1967-69. Pres. bd. dirs. Chagrin Falls Park Community Center, 1960-66; v.p. Geauga County Econ. Opportunities Council, 1966; bd. dirs. Chagrin Falls Park Well-Baby Clinic, 1959-66. Served to capt. M.C., AUS, 1946- 48. Diplomate Am. Bd. Anesthesiology. Mem. Am., Ohio, Cuyahoga County med. assns., Cleve. Acad. Medicine (pres. sect. anesthesiology 1957), Am. Standards Assn. (chmn. com z-79, 1956-63, vice chmn. 1963-66), Am. (chmn. com. standardization and equipment 1956-63), Ohio, Cleve. (pres. 1956) socs. anesthesiologists, Internat. Anesthesia Research Soc., Am. Coll. Anesthesiologists (bd. govs.), Assn. Univ. Anesthetists, Soc. Acad. Anesthesia Chairmen, Royal Soc. Medicine, Cal. Med. Soc. (sec. 1967, vice chmn. 1968, chmn. 1969 anesthesiology sect.), Yolo County Med. Assn., Cal Soc. Anesthesiologists. Editor: Jour. Anesthesiology, 1965—. Contbr. numerous articles in field to profl. jours. Home: 1221 Fordham Dr Davis CA 95616

DAVIS, HARMER ELMER, educator; b. Rochester, N.Y., July 11, 1905; s. Elmer and Charlotte A. (Harmer) D.; B.S., U. Cal., 1928, M.S., 1930; m. Clare Housel Melbin. Research asst. U. Cal., 1928-30, research engr. engring. materials lab., 1930-48, dir. inst. transp. and traffic engring., 1948—, instr. civil engring, 1930-36, asst. prof., 1936-39, asso. prof., 1939- 48, prof., 1948—, chmn. div. transp., 1949-54, chmn. dept. civil engring., 1954-59. Chmn. exec. com. Hwy. Research Bd. Recipient Roy Crum Distinguished Service award Hwy. Research Bd., 1959; James Laurie prize Am. Soc. C.E., 1967. Registered engr., Cal. Fellow Am. Soc. C.E. (chmn. exec. com. hwy. div. 1956-57, pres. San Francisco sect. 1959, nat. dir. 1960-63); mem. NRC (mem. Div. Engring. and Indsl. Research 1960—, mem. div. exec. com. 1961-64), Am. Soc. Testing and Materials, Nat. Acad. Engring., Am. Concrete Inst., Am. (dir. 1964—), Cal (dir. 1956—) automobile assns., Am. Pub. Works Assn. (hon. 1961), Phi Beta Kappa, Sigma Xi, Tau Beta Pi, Chi Epsilon. Clubs: Cosmos, Washington; Faculty (U. Cal. at Berkeley); Commonwealth, Bohemian (San Francisco). Author: Making and Testing of Plain Concrete, 1938; Testing and Inspection of Engineering Materials, 1941, 64; Composition and Properties of Concrete (with G.E. Troxell), 1956, 2d edit. (with G. E. Troxell, J. W. Kelly), 1968. Cons. editor of McGraw-Hill Book Co., 1955—. Contbr. articles tech. publs. Home: 200 Yale Berkeley CA 94708

DAVIS, HAROLD E., historian, educator; b. Girard, O., Dec. 3, 1902; s. Henry E. and Katherine (Zeller) D.; A.B., Hiram (O.) Coll., 1924; A.M., U. Chgo., 1927; Ph.D., Western Res. U., 1933; m. Audrey Hennen, Aug. 31, 1929; 1 dau., Barbara Lee. Prof. history, polit. sci. Hiram Coll., 1927-47, dean adminstrn., 1944-47; dir. div. edn. and tchr. aids Office Inter- Am. Affairs, 1943-45; instr. Latin-Am. history Am.-Army U., Biarritz, France, 1945-46; organizer Washington Semester program with cooperating colls. and univs., 1947; prof. history and govt., chmn. div. social studies, Am. U., Washington, 1947-59, prof. Latin Am. history, govt., 1959-63, Univ. prof. Latin Am. Studies, 1963—., dean Coll. Arts and Scis., 1952-57. Lectr., Washington Internat. Center: cons. Cin. Council on World Affairs Faculty Enrichment Program Latin Am. with cooperating colls., 1969-71; cons. U.S. Armed Forces Inst.; Fulbright lectr. U. Chile, 1958-59; vis. prof. U. Mexico, 1962, India Sch. Internat. Studies, New Delhi, 1965-66; lectr. Inter-Am. Def. Coll., Nat. War Coll., Army War Coll., Fgn. Service Inst. Mem. Internat. team observers Dominican Republic elections, 1962; mem. Gov.'s Commn. on history Ohio, World War II. Decorated Order of Colón, Dominican Republic. Mem. Instituto Indigenista Interamericano, Am. Hist. Assn., Latin Am. Studies Assn., Am. Polit. Sci. Assn., Instituto de Historia del Derecho Ricardo Levene (Argentina), Instituto Histórico y Geográfico del Uruguay (corr.), Omicron Delta Kappa. Phi Kappa Phi, Phi Sigma Alpha, Phi Alpha Theta. Mem. Disciples Christ Ch. Club: Cosmos (Washington). Author: Makers of Democracy in Latin America, 1945, 68; Origins and Consequences of World War II (with others), 1948; Latin American Leaders, 1949, 68; Social Science Trends in Latin America, 1950; The Americas in History, 1953; (others) Contemporary Social Science, 1953; (with others) Development of Historiography, 1954; Development of Social Thought in Latin America, 1956; Government and Politics in Latin America, 1958; Material and Spititual Factors in American History, 1958; Latin American Social Thought, 1961, 63, 66; The United States in History, 1968; (with Harold Durfee) The Study of Philosophy in the United States, 1964, Os Estados Unidos na Historia, 1966; Los Estados Unidos en la historia, 1967; History of Latin America, 1968; Points of Focus-Latin America, 1970; Hinsdale of Hiram, 1971. Editor: Inter-American Conferences, 1826-1954 (S.G. Inman), 1965. Contbr. to World Book, Colliers, Americana, Brit. encys., yearbooks, profl. jours. Cons., New Jefferson Ency. Chmn. bd. editors World Affairs. Home: 4842 Langdrum Lane Chevy Chase MD 20015 Office: Am U Washington Washington DC 20016

DAVIS, HAROLD FENIMORE, pub. relations exec.; b. N.Y.C., May 17, 1916; s. Eddie and Anna (Tannenbaum) D.; grad. high sch.; m. Evelyn R. Leach, Apr. 6, 1941; children—Kenneth Edwin, Richard Paul, Marcy Ellen. News and publ. mgr. CBS, 1935-39; publ. and promotion mgr. Columbia Records, 1940-41; partner Davis-Lieber, 1941-42; v.p., promotion dir., dir. Kenyon & Eckhardt, Inc., 1945-56; v.p., asst. to pres., asst. to chmn., mgmt. supr. Grey Advt., Inc., 1956-68; pres. Grey & Davis, N.Y.C., 1968—; creator, producer How to Form a Rock Group, 1968; lectr. N.Y. U. New Sch.; producer London Records. Bd. dirs. Symphony for a New World; gov. Strathmore Village Civic Assn. Served with USNR, 1942-45. Fellow Brandeis U. Mem. Nat. Acad. TV. Home: 171 Village Rd Manhasset NY 11030 Office: Grey & Davis Inc 777 3d Av New York City NY 10016

DAVIS, HAROLD L., editor; b. Phila.; B.S. in Physics, Carnegie-Mellon U., 1949; Ph.D. in Exptl. Physics. Cornell U., 1954; m. Eleanor Morin; two children. Formerly analytical physicist Pratt and Whitney Aircraft Co., then adj. asst. prof. Rensselaer Poly. Inst. Hartford (Conn.) Grad. Center; asso. editor Nucleonics mag. 1957-64, mag. editor, 1964-66; now sr. editor Scientific Research; formerly adj. asso. prof. Bklyn. campus L.I.U.; editor Physics Today, 1969—. Bd. dirs. Joint Coun. Mental Services. Served with AUS. World War II. Mem. Nat. Psychol. Assn. Psychoanalysis (chmn. legislative com.), Am. Phys. Soc., N.Y. Acad. Scis., Am. Soc. Cybernetics, Sigma Xi, Gamma Alpha. Address: care Scientific Research McGraw-Hill Inc 330 W 42d St New York City NY*

DAVIS, HAROLD THAYER, educator; b. Beatrice, Neb., Oct. 5, 1892; s. Harry Watson and Hellen Thayer (Moulton) D.; A.B., Colo. Coll., 1915; A.M., Harvard, 1919; Ph. D., U. Wis., 1926; LL.D., Colo. Coll. 1949; m. Agnes Marie Holm, Sept. 3, 1921; children—Hellen Dagmar (Mrs. Leon Little), Donald Holm, Harold Moulton. Instr. math. U. Wis., 1920-23; asst. prof. math. Ind. U., 1923-29, asso. prof., 1929-34, prof., 1934-37; acting prof. econometrics Colo. Coll., 1936-37; prof. math. Northwestern U., 1937-60, chmn. ddept., 1942-55; prof. math. Trinity U., San Antonio, 1962—, chmn. dept., 1963-65, asso. Southwest Found., 1960-; dir. Mind Sci. Found., San Antonio, 1960-62. Asso., Cowles Commn. for Research in Econs. Mem. Math. Assn. Am. (sec.-treas. Ind. sect. 1924- 33), Econometric Soc., Phi Beta Kappa, Sigma Xi, Delta Epsilon, Tau Kappa Alpha. Republican. Club: University (Evanston, Ill.). Author sci. publs. including: Political Statistics, 1948; Essays in the History of Mathematics, 1948; The Differential Equations of Mathematical Physics, 1949; (with Vera Fisher) Index and Bibliography of Mathematical Tables, 1949; Quantitative Aspects of the Action of Carcinogenic Substances, 1951; Quantitative Aspects of tre Carcinogenic Radiations, 1952; Philosophy and Modern Science, 1953; The Fine Art of Punning, 1954; Alexandria, The Golden City, 1956; Studies in Differential Equations, 1956; Nonlinear Differential and integral Equations, 1961; (with M.G. McCown) General Mathematics, 1962; Summation of Series, 1962; vol. 3, Mathematical Function (with Vera Fisher), 1962; Adventures of an Ultra-Crepidarian, 1962. Contbr. to sci., math. assns. jours. Translator: (with J.J. Buchanan) Zosimus' Historia Nova, 1967. Home: 131 Park Hill Dr San Antonio TX ☆

DAVIS, HAROLD TRUSCOTT, lawyer; b. Worcester, Mass., June 15, 1895; s. Charles Francis and Eva Leolen (Truscott) D.; A.B. magna cum laude, Harvard, 1918, LL.B., 1921; m. Ruth M. Lent, Oct. 26, 1956; 1 dau. by previous marriage, Eleanor (Mrs. Chester E. Claff). Admitted to Mass. bar, 1921, since practiced in Boston; partner Nutter, McClennen & Fish, 1929—; dir. Davis & Furber Machine Co., Beckler Press, Inc., Carter's Ink Co., Hollingsworth & Vose Co., Rapid Service Press, Inc., Rapid Service Realty Corp., Tremblay Trade Bindery, Inc.; sec., dir. Carter's Realty Corp.; corporator Hingham Instn. Savs. New Eng. Bapt. Hosp. Propr., treas. Social Law Library, Boston; trustee Hingham Pub. Library, south Shore Hosp., High St . Cemetery, Olive Higgins Prouty Found., Eliot A. Carter Found. Mem. Am. Judicature Soc., Am., Mass., Boston bar assns., Phi Beta Kappa, Alpha Sigma Phi. Republican. Conglist. Club: Union (Boston). Home: Bare Cove Lane Hingham MA 02043 Office: 75 Federal St Boston MA 02110

DAVIS, HARRY, govt. ofcl.; b. N.Y.C., Dec. 2, 1909; s. Joseph and Annie (Goldner) D.; B.S., Coll. City N.Y., 1931, E.E., 1933; M.E.E., Poly. Inst. Bklyn., 1948; m. Fay Oxhorn, 1931. Project engr. design and devel. meteorol. direction finders Signal Corps, sect. chief in charge devel. nav. systems, 1940-45; in charge devel. nav. equipment Air Force Watson Lab., 1945-50; chief Naval Lab., 1949-51; tech. and sci. dir. Rome Air Devel. Center, 1951-60; dep. for research asst. sec. Air Force, Washington, 1960-66, dep. asst. sec. research and devel., 1966-68, dep. under sec. systems rev. Office Under Sec. Air Force, 1968—. Lectr., U. Cal. at Los Angeles, 1966—; faculty elec. engring. staff Columbia, 1956—; mem. sci. adv. com. Harry Diamond Labs., US Army; mem., chmn. panels Def. Dept. Recipient Harry Diamond Meml. award I.E.E.E., 1968; George W. Goddard award Soc. Photog. Instrumentation Engrs., 1969; citation of honor Air Force Assn., 1969, named Man of Year award Hap Arnold chpt., 1970. Fellow I.E.E.E.; mem. Am. Ordnance Assn., Am. Phys. Soc., A.A.A.S., Sigma Xi. Holder patents in communications and missile guidance, radar for def. against ballistic missiles. Home: 3536 Pinetree Terrace Falls Church VA 22041 Office: SAFUS Pentagon Washington DC 20330

DAVIS, HARRY WILLARD, chemist, univ. ofcl.; b. Pelzer, S.C., Nov. 7, 1915; s. Eugene Montville and Mary (Fennel) D.; B.S., U. S.C., 1937; M.S., U. Cin., 1939, Ph.D. 1941; m. Mary Watson, Aug. 28, 1937; children—Anne Lenhardt, Harry Willard, James Henry. Grad. asst. U. Cin., 1937- 40, Laws fellow, 1940-41; adj. prof. chemistry U. S.C., Columbia, 1941-44, asso. prof. 1944-49, prof., head dept. chemistry, 1949-60, dean Coll. Arts and Sci., 1960-66, v.p. acad. affairs, 1966-68, v.p. advanced study and research, dean grad. sch., 1968—. Prin. scientist Oak Ridge Asso. Univs., 1959-60, rep. univ. to council, 1950-67, bd. dirs., 1967—, pres., 1970—; exec. sec. So. Regional Edn. Bd. adv. commn. on chemistry and chem. engring. Mem. Am. Chem. Soc. (chmn. S.C. sect. 1953), S.C. Acad. Sci., Blue Key, Phi Beta Kappa, Phi Lambda Upsilon, Alpha Chi Sigma, Sigma Xi. Rotarian. Club: Cosmos. Home: 715 Abelia Rd Columbia SC 29205

DAVIS, HARTWELL, lawyer; b. Auburn, Ala., Dec. 18, 1906; s. Christopher Hartwell and Elizabeth Myrick (Dowdell) D.; student U. Fla., 1923-24; B.S., Auburn U., 1928; Woodrow Wilson Meml. Scholar, U. Va. Law Sch., 1929-30; LL.B., Emory U., 1931; m. Elizabeth Mardre, Feb. 24, 1933; childrenHartwell, Letitia Dowdell. Clk. Bradenton Bank & Trust Co. (Fla.), 1924-25; admitted to Ga., Ala. and Fla. bars, 1931. and since practiced at Opelika and Montgomery, Ala; asst. U.S. Atty. Middle Dist. of Ala., 1932-51, U.S. atty., 1953-62; city atty., Montgomery, 1951-53; spl. asst. atty. gen. Ala., 1964-. Del. S.E. jurisdictional confs. Meth. Ch., 1948, 52, 56; mem. Meth. Gen. Bd. Evangelism, 1952-56; sec.-treas. Meth. Ala. Conf. Bd. Lay Activities, 1945-60. Pres. Montgomery YMCA, 1939-40, dir., 1935-57; chmn. Ct. of Honor, Tuckabatchee area Boy Scouts Am., 1951-52, chmn. merit badge com., 1953. Trustee George Wheeler Meml. Scholarship Fund; dir. Ala. Meth. Children's Home. Mem. Am., Ala., Fed., Montgomery bar assns., Am. Trial Lawyers Assn., Am. Judicature Soc., Ala. Hist. Assn., C. of C., Sigma Nu, Phi Alpha Delta, Theta Alpha Phi. Republican. Clubs: Kiwanis (pres. 1938), Montgomery Gun. Home: 2216 Allendale Pl Montgomery AL 36111. Office: First Nat Bank Bldg Montgomery, AL 36104.

DAVIS, HARTWELL, assn. exec.; b. Keokuk, Ia., Mar. 12, 1921; s. Albion and Constance Langdon (Hall) D.; B.A., Grinnell (Ia.) Coll., 1947; m. Nancy Caroline Richards, June 28, 1944; children—William Hartwell, Margaret Lynn. Richard Hall, Roger Langdon, James Palmer. Personnel officer Omaha Nat. Bank, 1947-52; asst. sec. Am. Inst. Banking sect. Am. Bankers Assn., N.Y.C., 1952-58, asso. sec., 1958-63, nat. sec., 1963-70, adminstrv. dir., Washington, 1970—, editor Bull. Am. Inst. Banking, 1956—. Dist. chmn. orgn. and extension Boy Scouts Am., 1958-60. Served to capt. USAAF, World War II. Decorated Air medal with clusters. Mem. Am. Soc. Assn. Execs. Methodist (trustee). Mason. Home: 10907 Thanlet Lane Restou VA 22070 Office: 1120 Connecticut Av NW Washington DC 20036

DAVIS, HENRY CLYDE, dept. store exec.; b. Ferris, Tex., Oct. 2, 1907; s. William A. and Kalie (Brown) D.; m. Shirley Corbin, Sept. 29, 1934; children—Alan, Tom. With C.R. Anthony Co., Oklahoma City, 1936—, exec. v.p., 1962—. Past chmn. Dan Beard Dist. Boy Scouts Am. Rotarian (dir local club). Home: 6602 Hillcrest St Oklahoma City OK 73116 Office: 701 N Broadway Oklahoma City OK 73101

DAVIS, HERBERT HAYWOOD, Jr., investment banker; b. Omaha, Mar. 23, 1924; s. Herbert Haywood and Olga (Metz) D.; grad. Choate Sch., 1942; B.C.E., Cornell U., Ithaca, N.Y., 1948; m. Nell Merideth Evans, Feb. 17, 1945; children—Herbert Haywood 3d, Deborah Lynn (Mrs. David Horacek). With Kirkpatrick, Pettis, Smith, Polian, Inc., Omaha, 1948—, pres., 1967—; chmn. bd. Davis Golf Courses; dir. Lozier Corp., Art's Way Mfg. Co. Mem. Omaha Indsl. Found. Mem. exec. com., bd. dirs. Jr. Achievement Omaha; mem. Pres.'s Council Creighton U.; trustee Kirkpatrick, Pettis, Smith, Polian Found. Served to 2d lt. USAAF, 1943-45. Mem. Investment Bankers Assn. Am. (bd. govs.), Omaha C. of C. (dir., chmn. indsl. com.), Chi Psi. Episcopalian (sr. warden). Clubs: Omaha, Omaha Country, Press, Plaza (Omaha); Little (Chgo.). Home: 1118 S 118th St Omaha NB 68144 Office: Omaha Bldg Omaha NB 68102

DAVIS, HERMAN, advt. agy. exec. Sr. v.p., creative div. supr. Compton Advt., Inc., N.Y.C. Office: 625 Madison Av New York City NY 10022*

DAVIS, HERMON S., Jr., govt. ofcl.; b. Evanston, Ill., Jan. 3, 1928; s. Hermon S. and Owena (Hunter) D.; B.S., Hampton Inst., 1947; M.S., U. Ill., 1951; student U. Wis., 1951, U. Paris, 1951-52; m. Kari Randi Woldstad, July 5, 1952; children—Hermon S. III, Sven-Eric, Claude Marc. Chief planning and design, Chatearoux, France, 1942-54; project engr., Bordeaux, France, 1954-57; dep. chief design operations, Paris, 1957-60; dep. engr. Seine Area Command, 1960-62; chief housing adv. US AID Mission, Mali, 1962-64, asst. dir., Costa Rica, 1965-67, dep. dir., Tunisia, 1968-70, dir., Congo, 1970—. Home: American Embassy APO New York City NY 09662 Office: Dir AID Am Embassy Kinshasa Congo

DAVIS, HORANCE GIBBES, Jr., educator, journalist; b. Manchester, Ga., July 14, 1924; s. Horance Gibbs and Florence Gray (Beavers) D.; B.A. in Journalism with high honors, U. Fla., 1948, M.A., 1952; m. Marjorie Lucile Davis, June 23, 1948; children—Gregory Rawson, Jennifer Diane. Reporter, Fla. Times-Union, Jacksonville, 1949, state capitol corr., 1950-54; faculty U. Fla., Gainesville, 1954—, prof., 1965—. Editorial cons. Gainesville Daily Sun, 1962—. Served to 1st lt. USAAC, 1943-46; PTO. Decorated Air medal; recipient Pulitzer prize for editorial writing, 1971; Sidney Hillman award, 1963. Mem. Assn. for Edn. in Journalism, Sigma Delta Chi (award for distinguished service in journalism, 1963, nat. v.p. 1969-72), Omicron Delta Kappa, Phi Kappa Phi, Kappa Tau Alpha, Delta Tau Delta. Episcopalian (layreader 1956—). Home: 3290 NW 37th St Gainesville FL 32601

DAVIS, HOWARD, lawyer; b. Otoe, Neb., Feb. 5, 1907; s. Howard Orlando and Lydia Louise (Paap) D.; student Oklahoma City U., 1923-24; B.A., Okla. U., 1927, LL.B., 1931; m. Dorothy Kennedy, Nov. 4, 1937 (div. Oct. 1940); 1 dau., Lucy E. (Mrs. Charles A. Rey); m. 2d, Ruth Caldwell, June 27, 1944; 1 son, Howard Caldwell. Admitted to Okla. bar, 1931; with firm Shirk, Danner & Phelps, Oklahoma City, 1931-32; pvt. practice, Oklahoma City, 1932-36; mem. legal HOLC, 1936-37, Continental Oil Co., 1937-48; with firm Bulla and Bynum, Oklahoma City, 1948-50; partner Kerr, Davis, Irvine & Burbage, predecessor firms, Oklahoma City, 1950-. Mem. Am., Okla. (chmn. real property com.) Oklahoma County bar assns., Mineral Lawyers Soc. Oklahoma City (pres. 1955-56), Title Lawyers Group, Oklahoma City C. of C., Alpha Sigma Phi. Club: Twin Hills Golf & Country. Methodist. Home: 1231 Wilshire St Oklahoma City OK 73116. Office: Kermac Bldg Oklahoma City OK 73102.

DAVIS, HOWARD A., utility exec.; b. 1913; married. With Washington Gas Light Co., 1931—, chief accountant, 1953-64, asst. comptroller, 1964-67, comptroller, 1967—. Office: 1100 H St NW Washington DC 20005*

DAVIS, HOWARD ALLAN, air force officer; b. Cochocton, O., Nov. 30, 1915; s. Lee Verde and Myrta (Power) D.; B.A., Miami U., Oxford, O., 1939; M.B.A., Harvard, 1949; m. Mary Elise Davis, Nov. 14, 1944; children—Victoria Lee (Mrs. Ersin Bacinoglu), Catherine Elise, Howard Allan. Commd. 2d lt. USAAF, 1942, advanced through grades to maj. gen. USAF, 1965; assigned N. Africa and Italy, World War II; comdr. B-47; Bombardment Wing, SAC, 1958- 59, Heavy Bombardment Wing, 1959-63, air div. comdr., 1963-64, dep. dir.

plans, 1964-65; asst. chief staff studies and analysis Hdqrs. USAF, from 1965; now vice comdr. 8th Air Force, Westover AFB, Mass. Co-dir. Aksarben, Omaha, 1963, dir. drive, 1964. Decorated Distinguished Service Medal, Silver Star with oak leaf cluster, Legion of Merit, D. F.C. with oak leaf cluster, Air medal with 17 oak leaf clusters. Home: 218 5th Av Westover AFB MA 01022 Office: Westover AFB MA 01022

DAVIS, HOWARD HALSEY, supermarket co. exec.; b. Brockton, Mass., Mar. 21, 1902; s. Maynard Alton and Emma Smith (Walker) D.; B.S., Mass. Agrl. Coll., 1924; M.B.A., Harvard, 1926; m. Phyllis Caroline Smith, Oct. 19, 1926; 1 son, Howard Graham. With Brockton Pub. Market (Mass.), 1926-28, 29—, v.p., 1941—; with Ken Caryl Ranch Co., 1928-29; v.p. George C. Shaw Co., Portland, Me., 1936- 41, pres., 1941—; pres. Me. Savs. Bank, Portland, 1953-69, also trustee; dir. New Eng. Tel. & Tel. Co., Nat. Life Ins. Co., H.P. Hood & Co. Trustee Me. Med. Center, Westbrook Jr. Coll. Home: 178 Woodville Rd Falmouth ME 04105 Office: 585 Congress St Portland ME 04101

DAVIS, HOWARD JUNE, steel co. exec.; b. Kansas City, Mo., June 13, 1910; s. Millard Littleton and Anna Beth (Luchsinger) D.; m. Marion Francis Embree, Apr. 4, 1931. Sales engr. constrn. materials, 1932-40; sales engr., sales mgr., mgr. product devel., asst. to pres., fed. govt. liaison Colo. Fuel & Iron Corp., 1940-55; v.p. Borg-Warner Corp., Chgo., 1955—, now group v.p. steel. Mem. Am. Iron and Steel Inst., Chicago Heights Mfrs. Assn. (past mem. pres.'s adv. com.). Mason (32, Shriner). Home: 613 Bruce St Flossmoor IL 60422 Office: 200 S Michigan Av Chicago IL 60604

DAVIS, HUBERT EUGENE, librarian; b. Topeka, Feb. 2, 1926; s. Harold E. and Emma G. (Dickey) D.; A.A., Ft. Scott Jr. Coll., 1946; B.A., Holy Cross Coll., 1948; M.A., St. Thomas Theol. Sem., 1953; M.A. in L.S., Rosary Coll., 1955; student U. Chgo, 1955-57, 1962-63, 1968-69; m. Hermia Meeds, Aug. 19, (div. Dec. 1967). Librarian St. Thomas Coll., 1951-53; bus. mgr., editorial adviser Scepter Pub. Co., Chgo., 1953-55; prin. reference asst. Chgo. Pub. Library, 1955-57; librarian Tex. So. U., 1957- 66, Southwest Coll., Chgo., 1966—. Cons., media specialist Columbia Coll ., Chgo. Mem. Am., Ill. library assns., Am. Philos. Assn., Cath. Renascence Soc., Am. Assn. U. Profs. Author: Learning Resources Centers—Concepts of Design, 1969. Home: 7346 S Shore Dr Chicago IL 60649 Office: 7500 S Pulaski St Chicago IL 60652

DAVIS, I. G., oil co. exec.; b. Cistern, Tex., 1908; m. Grace M. Davis, 2 children. Exec. v.p. Gulf Oil Corp., Pitts., Mene Grande Oil Co.; dir. Cities Service Co. Home: 601 Berkshire Dr Pittsburgh PA 15215 Office: PO Box 1166 Pittsburgh PA 15230

DAVIS, ILUS WINFIELD, lawyer; b. Kansas City, Mo., Apr. 22, 1917; s. Dean and Emma Josephine (Severs) D.; A.B., U. Kan., 1937; LL.B., U. Mo., 1939; m. Beatrice Buecking, Nov. 8, 1946; children—Christopher Dean, Caroline Dalton. Admitted to Mo. bar, 1939; with Dietrich, Davis, Burrell, Discus & Rowlanands and predecessor firms, Kansas City, 1939—; mayor City of Kansas City, Mo., 1963-71. Chmn. bd. Balt. Bank; dir. North Hills Bank, Blue Ridge Bank. Councilman, Kansas City, Mo., 1948-55, chmn. mayor's com. on municipal finances, 1955-57. Trustee U. Mo., Kansas City; bd. dirs. Kansas City Philharmonic Assn. Served from 1st lt. to maj., inf. AUS. 1942- 46. Fellow Am. Bar Assn.; mem. Mo. Bar Assn., (sec.), Mo. Bar (bd. govs. 1956-61, pres. 1960), Mo. (pres. 1969), Nat. (exec. com.) Municipal leagues, Lawyers Assn. Kansas City. Mem. Disciples Ch. Ch. Home: 1001 W 59th Terrace Kansas City MO 64113 Office: Dwight Bldg Kansas City MO 64105

DAVIS, J. F., banker. chmn. bd. First Nat. Bank of Omaha. Chmn. bd. Aksarben-Clarkson Hosp., Creighton U. Indsl. Found., Joslyn Art Mus. Home: 425 N 62d St Omaha NB 68132 Office: First Nat Bank of Omaha 16th and Farnam Sts Omaha NB 68102

DAVIS, J. LUTHER, utility exec.; b. Memphis, May 8, 1924; s. Luther and Sarah (Carter) D.; B.S. in Bus. Adminstrn., U. Ariz., 1946, LL.B., 1949; m. Natalie Young, Jan. 26, 1947; children—James Luther, Fred C., Peggy E. Admitted to Ariz. bar, 1949; pvt. practice Tucson, 1949-52; asst. city atty. Tucson, 1952-53, city mgr., 1953-55; with Tucson Gas & Electric Co., 1955—, exec. v.p., 1958-59, pres., 1959—, chmn. bd., 1967—. Bd. dirs. Tucson Airport Authority, 1959-62, 1964-70, pres. 1965; bd. dirs. Tucson Med. Center, 1955-65, Tucson Indsl. Devel. Bd., 1959-62, Ariz. Acad., v.p. 1965—; bd. dirs. Ariz. Traffic Safety Found., 1960-65, Health Planning Council Tucson, 1964—; bd. dirs. Green Fields Sch., 1964-69, chmn. mem. bd., 1964-66; mem. Ariz Hosp. Adv. and Survey Coastrn. Council, 1970—; bd. dirs. Tucson Regional Plan, 1966—; mem. U. Ariz. Found. Mem. Am., Tex., Ariz. bar assns., N.A.M., Pacific Coast Gas Assn., Tucson C. of C., Blue Key, Phi Gamma Delta, Alpha Kappa Psi, Phi Delta Phi. Clubs: Tucson Country, Old Pueblo, Tucson National. Home: 1815 N Norton Av Tucson AZ 85719 Office: 220 W 6th St Tucson AZ 85702

DAVIS, JACOB ERASTUS, business exec.; b. Beaver, O., Oct. 31, 1905; s. George O. and Kathryn (Leist) D.; A.B., Ohio State U., 1927; LL.B., Harvard, 1930; m. Minnie Eleanor Middleton, Sept. 18, 1929; children—Jacob Erastus, Eleanor Middleton. Admitted to Ohio bar, 1930, practiced, Waverly, 1930-37; pros. atty. Pike Co., O., 1931-35; elected rep. Ohio Gen. Assembly, 1935- 37, speaker pro tem, majority floor leader, 1936-37; judge Ct. Common Pleas, Pike Co., O., 1937-40; mem. Ho. Reps. 77th Congress, 6th dist. Ohio, 1941-43; spl. asst. Sec. Navy, asst. gen. counsel Navy Dept., 1943-44; v.p. Kroger Co., Cin., 1945—, dir., 1949—, exec. v.p., 1961, president, 1962-70, chmn. bd., 1969-70. Pres. trustee Ohio Council Retail Mchts.; mem. exec. com., dir. Nat. Assn. Food Chains. Trustee Ohio State U. Clubs. Cincinnati, Queen City, Cincinnati Country. Home: 1122 Rookwood Dr Cincinnati OH 45208 Office: 1014 Vine St Cincinnati OH 45202

DAVIS, JAMES, (Othello), physician, educator; b. Tahlequah, Okla., July 12, 1916; s. Zemry and Villa (Hunter) D.; M.A. in Zoology, U. Mo., 1939, Ph.D., 1942, B.S. in Medicine, 1943; M.D., Washington U., 1945; m. Florrilla Louise Sides, Dec. 27, 1941; children—Janet Ruth, James Lawrence. Intern Barnes Hosp., St. Louis, 1945-46; investigator Lab. Kidney and Electrolyte Metabolism, Nat. Heart Inst., Bethesda, Md., 1949-57, chief sect. on exptl. cardiovascular disease, 1957-66; asso. prof. physiology Temple U. Sch. Medicine, Phila., 1955-56; vis. asso. prof. physiology Johns Hopkins Sch. Medicine, 1961-64; vis. prof. physiology U. Va. Sch. Medicine, 1964; prof. chmn. dept. physiology U. Mo. Sch. Medicine, Columbia, 1966- -. Served with AUS, 1943-45, USPHS, 1946-66. Recipient A.M.A. Golden Apple award for teaching U. Mo., 1968; Sigma Xi Research award U. Mo., 1971. Mem. Am. Heart Assn. (mem. med. adv. council, vice chmn. council for high blood pressure research 1970- 72), Am. Physiology Soc., Endocrine Soc., Soc. Exptl. Biology and Medicine, Nat. Inst. Health Extramural Program, Sigma Xi, Alpha Omega Alpha. Mem. editorial bd. Am. Jour. Physiology, 1961-63, 66-69; Endocrinology, 1962-65; Circulation Research, 1962-66. Home: 612 Maplewood Dr Columbia MO 65201

DAVIS, JAMES ALLAN, educator, sociologist; b. Chgo., Nov. 2, 1929; s. Robert G. and Mary (McMurray) D.; B.S., Northwestern U., 1950; M.S., U. Wis., 1952; Ph.D., Harvard, 1955; m. Martha Hocking Davis, Jan. 28, 1950; childrenMary James. Andrew, Martha, Research asso. Harvard Sch. Pub. Health, 1954-56; asst. prof. Yale, 1956-57; from asst. prof. to asso. prof., also sr. study dir. Nat. Opinion Research Center, Chgo., 1957-67; prof. sociology Dartmouth, 1967-. Author: Great Books and Small Groups; Education For Positive Mental Health; Stipends and Spouses; Undergraduate Career Decisions; Great Aspirations: The Graduate School Plans of America's College Seniors, Elementary Survey Analysis, also articles. Home: Elm Rd Etna NH 03750 Office: Dept Sociology Dartmouth Coll Hanover NH 03755

DAVIS, JAMES BASSEL, lawyer; b. San Francisco, Nov. 2, 1929; s. Joe Ray and Mary Lou (Bassel) D.; B.S., U. Cal. at Berkeley, 1952; J.D., Boalt Hall, 1956; m. Mary Jane Hudson, Sept. 17, 1961; children-Alison Lynn, Janet Straughan. Admitted to Cal. bar, 1957; dep. atty. gen. State of Cal., 1956-61; mem. firm Weinmann, Rede, Burnhill & Moffit, Alameda, Cal., 1961-65; partner Davis, Craig & Bartalini, Alameda, 1965—. Chmn. bd. Alameda Fed. Savs. & Loan Assn., 1969—, Alfed Service Corp., Alameda, since 19—. Vice pres. Alameda Boys Club, 1968-69, bd. dirs., 1964—; trustee Reclamation Dist. Served with AUS, 1948-49, to 2d lt., 1952-53. Mem. Alameda C. of C. (v.p. 1968, dir. 1964—), Alameda County Bar Assn., State Bar Cal. Rotarian. Home: 2722 Bayview Dr Alameda CA 94501 Office: 1516 Oak St Alameda CA 94501

DAVIS, JAMES BURNAM, fgn. service officer; b. Lilly, Ill., July 22, 1909; s. Charles William and Etta Eliza (Rutherford) D.; student Eastern Ky. State Tchrs. Coll., 1927-29, U. Ky., 1927-28, 33-34; A.B., Berea Coll., 1933; Social Sci. Research Council, Brookings Instn., 1934-36. Am. U., 1936, 39- 40, 51; Conservation fellow Harvard, 1950-51, M.A., 1966; m. Delpha Lee Payne, Mar. 24, 1931; childrenCarol Anne, Patricia Louise; m. 2d, Mary Martha Banks, Jan. 28, 1949. High sch. tchr., Maysville, Ky., 1929; tchr., basketball coach, Washington, Ky., 1929-30; economist Brookings Instn., 1934; economist, adminstrv. officer, agriculturist Dept. Agr., 1935-43; prin. agriculturist, chief program operations East Central Region A.A.A., 1943; chief marketing div. East Central Region, Prodn. and Marketing Adminstrn., 1946-47, agriculturist Prodn. and Marketing Adminstrn., 1947-51, chief program devel. and operating methods, 1951, acting chief Pakistan br. TCA, 1951-52. Sr. fgn. affairs officer specializing South Asia, TCA, ICA, 1952-56, dep. chief agriculturist U.S. Tech. Coop. Mission to India, 1956-58, staff ICA, Washington, 1958- 60; chief food and agr. officer, AID, Lagos, Nigeria, 1961. Iran, 1965, Afghanistan, 1966, dep. asso. dir., Vietnam, 1968, asso. dir., 1969—. Served from lt. (j.g.) to lt. USNR, 1943-46. Methodist. Home: Saigon Vietnam Office: AID/ADDP APO San Francisco CA 96243.

DAVIS, JAMES CURRAN, lawyer, ex-congressman; b. Franklin, Ga., May 17, 1895; s. Thomas Benjamin and Lura Viola (Mooty) D.; student Reinhardt Coll., 1909-10, Emory Coll., 1910-12; m. Mary Lou Martin, Dec. 26, 1932; 1 dau., Mary Martin (Mrs. Edward G. Bowen). Admitted to Ga. bar, 1919; gen. law practice, Atlanta, 1919-34; DeKalb County rep. Ga. State Gen. Assembly, 1924- 28; atty. Ga. Dept. Indsl. Relations, Atlanta, 1928-31; atty. DeKalb County, 1931-34; judge superior cts. Stone Mountain Jud. Circuit, 1934- 47; mem. 80th-87th U.S. Congresses, 5th Dist. Ga.; chmn. exec. com., dir DeKalb County Fed. Savs. & Loan Assn. Del. Dem. Nat. Conv., 1952; mem. Ga. Dem. Exec. Com. Served in USMC, 1917-19. Mem. Sigma Alpha Epsilon. Methodist. Mason. Clubs: Atlanta Lions, Lawyers of Atlanta (past pres.), Ga. Motor (bd. dir.). Address: 6000 Winterthur Ridge NW Atlanta GA 30328

DAVIS, JAMES ELSWORTH, food exec.; b. Henderson, Ark., July 31, 1907; s. William M. and Ethel (Chase) D.; student U. Ida., 1925-27; H.H.D., Stetson U., 1960; LL.D., Bethune-Cookman Coll., 1964; m. Florence Novinger, Jan. 27, 1932; children—Dorothy Jean (Mrs. Brice R. Smith, Jr.), Andrew Dano. Pres., Economy Wholesale Grocery Co., 1939-42, v.p., dir., 1925-65; exec. v.p. Winn & Lovett Grocery Co., 1946-50; v.p., dir. Economy Wholesale Foods, Inc.; chmn. bd. Winn-Dixie Stores, Inc.; v.p. Economy Wholesale Distbrs., Inc.; chmn. bd., dir. Am. Heritage Life Ins. Co.; chmn. bd., v.p. Crackin' Good Bakers Inc.; pres., dir. Danov Corp.; pres. Estuary Corp., D.D.I., Inc.; v.p., dir. Deep South Products; v.p. Astor Products, Inc.; dir. Barnett Nat. Bank (Jacksonville), Monterey Canning Co. Trustee Bethune-Cookman Coll., bd. dirs. Bolles Sch.; v.p. Winn-Dixie Stores Found.; pres. J. Elsworth Davis Found.; dir. St. Luke's Hosp. Assn., Jacksonville, Fla. Served from capt. to lt. col. AUS, 1943-45; officer charge Q.M.C. Market Center, N.Y.C., 1944-45; perishable foods. ETOUSA, MTOUSA, NATOUSA. Decorated Legion of Merit. Mem. Nat. Assn. Food Chains, Alpha Kappa Psi. Sigma Chi. Mem. Christian Ch. Clubs: Florida Yacht, Ponte Verdra, The River. Home: 3960 Ortega Blvd Jacksonville FL 32210 Office: Box B Jacksonville FL 32203

DAVIS, JAMES F., lawyer; b. Muskogee, Okla., Mar. 7, 1933; B.B.A., U. Okla., 1955, LL.B., 1957. Admitted to Okla. bar, 1957; now partner firm Andrews, Mosburg, Davis, Elam, Legg & Kornfeld, Oklahoma City. Mem. Am., Okla., Oklahoma City bar assns., Phi Alpha Delta. Mng. editor Okla. Law Review, 1956-57. Office: United Founders Tower 5900 Mosteller Dr Oklahoma City OK 73112*

DAVIS, JAMES FRANKLIN, govt. ofcl.; b. Fort Wayne, Ind., Aug. 11, 1934; s. John Forrest and Lucrece (Shoemaker) D.; B.S. with honors in Chem. Engring.; U. Ill., 1957; J.D., Georgetown U., 1963; m. Mary Karen Biddle, Dec. 29, 1957; children—John Montgomery, Mary Melinda. Jennifer Susan. Admitted to Ill., D.C. bars, 1964; examiner U.S. Patent Office, 1961-62; patent atty. firm Wenderoth, Lind & Ponack, Washington, 1962-63, Bair, Freeman & Molinare, Chgo., 1964-66; law clk. to judge U.S. Ct. Customs and Patent Appeals, 1963-64; commnr. U.S. Ct. of Claims, Washington 1966—; instr. chemistry U.S. Naval Acad., 1959-61; adj. prof. law Georgetown U. Law Sch., 1966-68. Served with USNR, 1957-59. Mem. Am. Bar Assn., Am. Patent Law Assn., Phi Lambda Upsilon. Theta Chi. Home: 8000 Hampden Lane Bethesda MD 20014 Office: 717 Madison Pl Washington DC 20005

DAVIS, JAMES H., former gov. La.; b. Quitman, La.; student Louisiana Coll. Pub. service commr. 3d Dist. La.; commr. pub. safety, Shreveport, 1938-42; gov. La., 1944-48. 60-64. Singer. composer. Democrat. Office: State Capitol Baton Rouge LA 70804

DAVIS, JAMES MCCOY, coll. pres.; b. Columbus, O., Oct. 19, 1914; s. James McCoy and Laura V. (Smith) D.; B.S., Ohio State U., 1937; B.D., Oberlin Coll., 1942; M.A., Columbia, 1947, Ed.D., 1953; m. Phyllis Ruth Rowe, Jan. 24, 1948; children—Perine Marie, Linda Victoria. Carol Corrine, Paul James, Jamie Elizabeth. Ordained to ministry Congl. Ch., 1941; minister First Congl. Ch., Riavenna, O., 1939-42; field exec. war services Inst. Congl. Chs., 1942-43; counselor internat. service U. Wash., 1948-54; dir. Internat. Center U. Mich., 1954-64, asst. prof. edn., 1954-59, asso. prof. higher edn., 1959-64, v.p. fgn. student programs Inst. Internat. Edn., 1964-66, v.p. student exchange programs, 1966-67; provost U.S. Internat. U., San Diego, 1967-69; pres. Northwestern Mich. Coll., Traverse City, 1970—. Lectr., Columbia Tchrs. Coll., 1965-67; cons. Ford Found., AID, other orgns. Exec. dir. Found. Internat. Understanding Through Students, 1948-54; mem. Traverse City Indsl. Fund; chmn. Pres. Kennedy's Task Force on Internat. Ednl. Exchange, 1959- 60; field reader Office Edn., 1966—; mem. San Diego Mayor's Internat. Affairs Bd., 1968-70; mem. bd. visitors Internat. Career Tng. Program experiment in internat. living, 1967—. Served as chaplain AUS, 1943-46: CBI. Decorated Bronze Star medal with oak leaf cluster; Rockefeller Found. grantee trip around world, 1951. Mem. Nat. Assn. Fgn. Student Advisers (pres. 1960-61), Nat. Council on Community Services to Internat. Visitors (exec. com. 1959-64, 1959-61. treas. 1961-62), Mich. Community Coll. Assn. (trustee), Phi Delta Kappa (commn. on internat. relations in edn. 1960-68, chmn. 1962- 64), Kappa Delta Pi, Phi Gamma Delta. Mason, Rotarian. Author: IIE Survey of the African Student. 1961. Contbr. to profl. jours. Home: 1140 Peninsula Dr Traverse MI 49684

DAVIS, JAMES OSCAR, Jr., lawyer; b. Opelika, Ala., Dec. 27, 1923; s. James Oscar and Sarah O. (Messick) D.; student Auburn U., 1941-43, U. So. Cal., 1945; LL.B., U. Ala., 1949; m. Cody Fowler, Nov. 2, 1956; childrenJames Oscar III, Cody Fowler. Admitted to Ala. bar, 1949, Fla. bar, 1955; judge Ct. Common Pleas, Lee County, Ala., 1949-54; mem. firm Fowler, White, Gillen, Humkey & Trenam, Tampa, Fla., 1955-65, McClain, Turbiville and Davis, Tampa, 1965-68, Glos and Davis, Tampa, 1968-. Chmn. port devel. committee Tampa C. of C., 1962-. Bd. dir. Hillsborough County chpt. Am. Cancer Soc. Capt., USAF Res. Mem. Fedn. Ins. Counsel, Internat. Assn. Ins. Counsel, Def. Research Inst., Maritime Law Assn., Atlanta Claims Assn., Am. (chmn. standing com. admiralty and maritime law 1962-63, 67- 68), Fla., Ala. bar assns., Phi Alpha Delta, Kappa Sigma. Democrat . Episcopalian. Mason. Clubs: Propeller, Gasparilla Krewe, Tampa Yacht and Country, University (Tampa); India House (N.Y.C.). Home: 96 Adelia Av Tampa FL 33606 Office: First Federal Bldg Tampa FL 33602

DAVIS, JAMES PAXTON, educator, novelist; b. Winston-Salem, N.C., May 7, 1925; s. James Paxton and Emily (McDowell) D.; student Va. Mil. Inst., 1942-43; A.B., Johns Hopkins, 1949; m. Wylma Elizabeth Pooser, June 6, 1951; children—Elizabeth Keith, Anne Beckley, James Paxton III. Reporter, Winston-Salem Jour., 1949-51, Richmond (Va.) Times-Dispatch, 1951-52, Twin City Sentinel, Winston-Salem, 1952-53; faculty Washington and Lee U., 1953—, prof. journalism, 1963—, chmn. dept., 1968—; book editor Roanoke (Va.) Times, 1961—. Served with AUS, 1943-46; CBI. Mem. Phi Beta Kappa, Omicron Delta Kappa. Author: Two Soldiers, 1956: The Battle of New Market, 1963; One of The Dark Places, 1965; The Seasons of Heroes, 1967. Home: Fincastle VA 24090

DAVIS, JAMES PETER, archbishop; b. Houghton, Mich., June 9, 1904; s. John F. and Elisabeth (Didier) D.; A.M., St. Patrick's Coll., Menlo Park, Calif., D.D., 1943. Sec. to bishop of Tucson, Ariz., 1929; sec.-chancellor, Diocese of Tucson, 1930-32; pastor, parishes at Tempe, Douglas, Tucson, Bisbee (all Ariz.), 1932-43; official of Diocese of Tucson, 1937; consecrated bishop of San Juan, Puerto Rico, Oct. 6, 1943, installed, San Juan, Nov. 25, 1943, apptd. archbishop, 1960; archbishop of Santa Fe, 1964—. Mem. Canon Law Soc. Am. K.C. Address: 202 Morningside Dr Albuquerque NM 87108

DAVIS, JAMES WILLIS, educator; b. Valley City, N.D., Aug. 1, 1920; s. Rufus R. and Catherine (Hennessy) D.; B.A., Valley City State Coll., 1941; M.A., U. Minn., 1949, Ph.D., 1961; m. Nanette J. Trexler, Sept. 6, 1952; children—Katherine, Susan, Elizabeth, Timothy, Michael, Patricia. Instr., U. Minn., 1948-51; administry. officer Dept. Army, 1952-59; asso. prof. St. Cloud (Minn.) State Coll., 1959-66; prof., chmn. dept. polit. sci. Central Mich. U., 1966—. Del. Democratic Nat. Conv., 1964; chmn. Minn. Dem. Platform Com., 1962. Recipient Danforth Found. award, 1962; Louis and Maud Hill Found. award, 1961, Mem. Am., Midwest polit. sci. assns., African Studies Assn. Author: Springboard to the White House, 1967. Home: 520 Sunset Dr Mt Pleasant MI 48858

DAVIS, JAY, Jr., pub. utility exec.; b. Uvalde, Tex., July 27, 1913; s. Jay and Maddie (Wootton) D.; student Fresno State Coll., 1935-37, U. So. Cal., 1937-38; m. June C. McDowell, Aug. 24, 1940 (dec. Aug. 1969); children—Jay Michael, Scott Murray; m. 2d, Sylvia M. Peat, May 3, 1970. With So. Countries Gas Co. Cal. (merged with So. Cal. Gas Co. 1970), Los Angeles, 1938—, asst. v.p. 1948- 54, v.p., dir., 1954-70, v.p. adminstrv. services, dir., 1970—. Mem. Gen. Gen. Services Pub. Adv. Council, 1969—. Trustee Queen of Angels Clinic and Research Found. Mem. Am. (mng. com.), Pacific Coast (exec. com.) gas assns., Theta Chi. Republican. Presbyn. Home: 1007 Oakforest Lane Pasadena CA 91107 Office: 810 S Flower St Los Angeles CA 90017

DAVIS, JEFFERSON, lawyer, utilities exec.; b. Indianola, Miss., July 3, 1909; s. Sidney F. and Florence L. (Heard) D.; A.B., Southwestern U., 1931; J.D., Cumberland U., 1932; m. M. Jerdone Kimbrough, Apr. 28, 1934; children—Jefferson, A. Kimbrough, M. Jerdone. Admitted to Miss. bar, 1932, Ga. bar, 1947; gen. practice law, Indianola, Miss., 1932-41; asst. att. gen. Miss., 1941-46; exec. asst., legal adviser to gov. Miss., 1946-47; atty. So. Bell Tel. & Tel. Co., Atlanta, 1947-49, gen. atty., 1949-52, gen. solicitor. 1952-56, gen. counsel, 1956—, v.p., 1961- -; dir. Nat. Bank Ga. Bd. dirs., trustee YMCA Met. Atlanta, pres., 1964-68, v.p. So. Area council, 1966-68; bd. dirs. Nat. council, 1967-71; trustee Southwestern U., Memphis. Mem. adv. bd. Cumberland Sch. Law Sanford U. Served with USNR, World War II. Mem. Am., Miss., Ga., Atlanta bar assns. Am. Law Inst., Alpha Tau Omega, Omicron Delta Kappa. Presbyn. (elder). Democrat. Mason (32, K.T.). Clubs: Lawyers, Commerce. Capital City (Atlanta). Home: 3651 Rembrandt Rd NW Atlanta GA 30327 Office: Hurt Bldg Atlanta GA 30303

DAVIS, JEROME, educator, sociologist; b. Kioto, Japan, Dec. 2, 1891 (parents Am. citizens); s. Jerome Dean and Frances (Hooper) D.; A.B., Oberlin Coll., 1913, D.D., 1933; grad. Union Theol. Sem., 1920; M.A., Columbia, 1919, Ph.D., 1922; LL.D., Hillsdale, 1933; D.Litt., Fla. So. U., 1947; m. Mildred Rood, July 20, 1920; children—Frances Elizabeth (dec.), Helen Patricia, Wilfred Grenfell. Tchr. evening extension courses, Mpls., sec. civic work Mpls. Civic and Commerce Assn., 1913; lectr. extension courses, N.Y.C., 1914; sec. to Dr. Wilfred Grenfell, Labrador, 1915; Russian war work, 1916-18 (acting in charge 1917-18); surveyed Russian in Am. for Inter-Ch. World Movement, 1919-20; lectr. Am. Soc. for Extension Univ., Gilder fellow Columbia, 1920-21; asst. prof. sociology Dartmouth, 1921-24; Gilbert L. Stark chair practical philanthropy Yale Div. Sch., 1924-37; dir. work in Prisoner-of-War Camps for all Can. representing world's com. YMCA 1940-43; war corr., lectr., 1943- -. Vis. prof. Hiram Coll., 1947-48, U. Colo., 1950, Fisk U., 1954. Pres., Am. Fedn. Tchrs., 1936-39; head Peace Mission to Europe, 1949; spl. investigation co-ops., Scandinavia, 1950; spl. mission to Soviet Union, 1943; spl. investigations Europe, 1947, 49; head Am-European Seminar touring maj. countries Europe, 1960-62, 64, 66, 68, group profs. around world, 1967, Peace Seminar of 50 profs., tchrs., Europe, 1969, 70, 71, Internat. Peace Mission 30 profs., Europe, summer 1966; dir. Peace Mission to Europe, summer 1959; Investigator conditions coal fields W.Va., 1923, conditions in Russia, summer 1926, 27, 32; exec. dir. Promoting Enduring Peace; Paine Found. lectr. theol. sems., 1952; vis. prof. Internat. Christian U.,

Japan, 1965. Del. Democratic Nat. Conv., 1940. Chmn., Conn. State Legislative Commn. on Jails, 1931-39; pres. Eastern Sociol. Conf., 1936-37; v.p. speakers research com. UN; trustee Oberlin Coll.; mem. Nat. Social Service Commn. Congl. Chs. (exec. com.), Social Service Commn. Fed. Council of Chs. Mem. Am. Social Soc. (com. on internat. relations, 1922-24), Am. Econ. Assn., Nat. Conf. Social Work. Am. Assn. U. Profs., Loyal Legion, Alpha Chi Rho. Conglist. Club: Cosmos (Washington). Author books including: Introduction to Sociology, 1927; Readings in Sociology, 1927; Contemporary Social Movements, 1930; Character Assassination, 1950; Peace, War and You, 1952; Religion In Action, 1956; On the Brink, 1959; Citizens of One World, 1961; World Leaders I Have Known, 1963; DisarmamentA World View, 1964; A Life Adventure for Peace, 1967; Peace of World War III, 1969. Contbr. to periodicals. Home: Friends House C-25 Sandy Spring MD 20860 ☆

DAVIS, JESS HARRISON, coll. pres.; b. Columbus, O., July 29, 1906; s. Willard Ellsworth and Winifred (Jones) D.; B.S., Ohio State U., 1928. M.S., 1933, D.Sc., 1956, St. Lawrence U., 1949; D.Eng., Clarkson Coll. Tech., 1951, Newark Coll. Engring., 1963; LL.D., Rutgers, 1954; m. Dorothy Carrigan, 1928 (dec. 1969); 1 dau., Sarah Louise (Mrs. Edward S. Boslow, Jr.); m. 2d, Mary Grattan Roper, July 1970. Student engr., asst. to maintenance supt. Ohio Bell Telephone Co., Columbus, 1928-29; mech engr. Atmospheric Nitrogen Corp., Hopewell, Va., 1929; instr. mech. engring. Clarkson Coll., Potsdam, N.Y., 1929-31, asst. prof., 1931-36, asso. prof., 1936-40, prof. heat power and exptl. engring., 1947, pres. 1948; pres. Stevens Inst. Tech., Hoboken, N.J., 1951—; prof., chmn. dept. mech. engring Speed. Sci. Sch., U. Louisville, 1944-46; mech. engr. Ala. Power Co., 1936, Am. Locomotive Co., 1937, Central N.Y. Power Co., 1940, Foster Wheeler Corp., 1941; cons. engr. Hydraulic Controls, Inc., 1942, N.Y. Air Brake Co., 1943-45, D.M. McBean, 1945-47, DeWolfe Furnace Corp., 1945-47; dir. Philip Morris, Inc., Pub. Service Electric & Gas Co., Nat. Biscuit Co., Prudential Ins. Co. Am., 1st Jersey Nat. Bank, Carrier Corp., Bethlehem Steel Corp., Pennwalt Corp. Commr., Port of N.Y. Authority, 1952-59. Registered Profl. engr., N.J., N.Y., Ky. Mem. Engrs. Council Profl. Devel., Am. Soc. M.E.s (bd. tech. 1954, Richards award 1952), Am. Soc. for Engring Edn., Am. Soc. Testing and Materials, Ky. Soc. Profl. Engrs., Louisville Adv. Com. on Smoke Abatement (chmn. 1944-45), Sigma Xi, Tau Beta Pi, Pi Mu Epsilon. Clubs: University, Engineers (N.Y.C.); Saucon Valley Country (Bethlehem, Pa.). Home: Hoxie House Castle Point Hoboken NJ 07030

DAVIS, JOE HUDGINS, banker; b. Arlington, Tenn., Aug. 28, 1910; s. Charles A. and Ella (Vesey) D.; student Northwestern U., Sch. Financial Pub. Relations, 1955; m. Ruth Hipps, July 23, 1932; children-Carolyn (Mrs. William T. Whitley, Jr.), Margaret Ellen (Mrs. Dewey C. Whitenton), Joe Hudgins. With First Nat. Bank Memphis, 1928—, exec. v.p., 1969—; pres. N. Ala. Computer Service Center, Inc., 1967-70, N.E. Miss. Computer Service Center, Inc., 1968-70, S.E. Mo. Computer Service Center, Inc., 1969-70, W. Tenn. Computer Service Center, Inc., 1970. Lectr. Sch. Banking, La. State U., 1958-62, Consumer Banking Sch., U. Va., 1961-63. Vice chmn. Shelby United Neighbors, 1954; pres. Memphis Goodwill Industries, 1957- 58, Greater Memphis State U., 1962-64; v.p. Mid-South Fair assn., 1959- 61; pres. nat. bd. finance Cumberland Presbyn. Ch., 1948-56, 57-66. Mem. Am. Bankers Assn. (pres. marketing-savs. div. 1969, exec. council 1966- 69), Bank Marketing Assn. (bd. dirs. 1958-60), Assn. Res. City Bankers, Memphis Marketing and Sales Club (pres. 1958-59), Pi Sigma Epsilon. (life). Home: 235 Green Glade Rd Memphis Tn 38117 Office: 165 Madison Av Memphis TN 38101

DAVIS, JOEL, publisher; b. Chgo., Apr. 5, 1934; s. Bernard George and Sylvia (Friedman) D.; student Columbia, summer 1953; B.A., Brown U., 1957; m. Carol Sue Barnett, Aug. 3, 1958; children—Charles Michael, Andrew Barnett, Jonathon William. With Davis Publs., Inc., N.Y.C., 1957—, exec. v.p. 1959-68, pres., pub., 1969—, co. pubs. Ellery Queen's Mystery mag., Income Opportunities, Camping Jour., Sci. and Mechanics, 29 Spl. interest publs. Mem. exec. com. gen. devel. council Brown U., 1962- 67, nat. chmn. univ. fund, 1965-68, regional dir. Asso. Alumni 1965-67, trustee, mem. corp., 1968—; vice chmn. Brown Devel. Council, 1968-69. Mem. Am. Arbitration Assn. (nat. panel), Young Presidents' Orgn., Mag. Pubs. Assn. (dir.) Pi Lambda Phi. Clubs: Brown (gov. N.Y.C. 1963-70, treas. 1967-68); Players. Home: 15 Crooked Mile Rd Westport CT 06880 Office: 229 Park Av S New York City NY 10003

DAVIS, JOE LEE, educator; b. Lexington, Ky., Feb. 22, 1906; s. Robert Lee and Jo (Greene) D.; A.B., U. Ky., 1926, A.M., 1927; Ph. D., U. Mich., 1934; m. Lorene Elizabeth Burke, June 10, 1929; 1 dau., Shirley Jo. Instr. in English, U. Ky., 1927-30; mem. faculty, U. Mich., 1930—, prof. English, 1948—, acting chmn. dept., summers, 1958, 69, chmn. program in American culture, 1952-69; vis. prof. English, U. Minn., summer 1949, No. Mich. Coll., summers 1945, 53, 61. Mem. Mich. Acad., Modern Lang. Assn. of Am., Cabell Soc. (pres. 1968-69), Phi Beta Kappa. Author: Boyhood Dreams (poems), 1917; The Sons of Ben: Jonsonian Comedy in Caroline England, 1967. Editor: Am. Lit.; An Anthology and Critical Survey, 2 vols. (with John T. Frederick and Frank Luther Mott), 1948-49; Charlotte Bronte's Jane Eyre in Rinehart edits., 1950; James Branch Cabell in Twayne U.S. Author Series, 1962. Adv. coll. ed., Charles Scribner's Sons, 1949-59. Home: 2216 Independence Blvd Ann Arbor MI 48104

DAVIS, JOE WILLIAM, city ofcl.; b. New Market, Ala., Oct. 22, 1918; s. Samuel Clifton and Sophie (Walker) D.; B.S in Social Sci., E.Tenn. State Coll., 1941; M.A. in Edn. Adminstrn., Peabody Coll., 1953; m. Dorothy Allen, Dec. 21, 1951; children—Joe William, Jeffrey Clifton, Julia Evelyn. Tchr., prin. Huntsville (Ala.) schs., 1946-55; personnel mgr. U.S. Indsl. Chem. Corp., Tuscola, Ill., 1955-59, asst. mgr. indsl. relations and safety, also security adminstr., 1959-63; adminstrv. asst. to mayor Huntsville, 1964-68, mayor, 1968—. Served with USNR, 1943-46. Mem. V.F.W., Am. Legion. Elk, Mason (Shriner), Lion, Moose, Eagle. Office: Home: 1412 Big Cove Rd Huntsville AL 35801

DAVIS, JOHN, industrialist; b. London, Eng., Nov. 10, 1906; s. Sydney Myering and Emily (Harris) D.; ed. City of London Sch.; m. Marion Gaved, 1947; children—Janet, Susan; m. 2d, Dinah Sheridan. Mar. 3, 1954; stepchildren—Jeremy, Jennifer Hanley. With Brit. Thomson Houston Group, 1931-38; with Rank Orgn. and predecessor firm, 1938—, mng. dir., 1948-62, chmn., chief exec. officer, 1962—. Mem. the Cinematograph Films Council of Gt. Britain. Bd. govs. Brit. Film Inst. Decorated knight Order St. John Jerusalem, 1962; knight Gt. Brit. Fellow Chartered Inst. Secs. Home: Crowhurst Pl Lingfield RH7 6Ly Surrey England Office: 38 South St London W1A 4 QU England

DAVIS, JOHN ANDERSON, educator; b. Springfield, Ill., June 8, 1924; s. Emerson and Mae (Denney) D.; student Trinity U., San Antonio, 1942-43; B.A., So. Meth. U., 1949, M.A., 1950; Ph.D., U. Ala., 1957; m. Lois Colvin, Sept. 16, 1947; 1 son, Stephen Colvin. Asst. state mgr. Inter-Ocean Ins. Co., Tex., 1945-50; asst. prof. econs. Lincoln Meml. U., Harrogate, Tenn., 1950-51; instr. social scis. Memphis State U., 1951-54; research asso. Ala. Bus. Research Council, U. Ala., 1955-56, univ. instr. econs., 1956-57; asso. prof. econs. Miss. State U., 1957-59, prof., head dept., 1959—. Sec.-treas. Dallas Assn. Accident and Health Underwriters, 1945-50; mem. Ala. Bus. Research Council, 1955-56, Com. Miss. Economy, 1957-58; chmn. bd. advisers YMCA Miss. State U., 1963-64; chmn. Miss. Council on Econ. Edn., 1968. Mem. Miss. (sec. 1964-65), So. econ. assns., Miss. Mfrs. Assn., Am. Econ. Assn., Am. Assn. U. Profs., Southwestern Social Sci. Assn., Acad. Miss. Economists (editor annals, pres. 1966-67), Beta Gamma Sigma, Alpha Kappa Psi, Delta Sigma Phi. Editor Miss. Quar., Jour. So. Culture, 1965—. 103 Briarwood Dr Starkville MS 39759 Office: Dept Econs Miss State U State College MS 39762

DAVIS, JOHN BRADFORD, Jr., supt. schs.; b. Haverhill, Mass., Sept. 14, 1921; s. John Bradford and Edna (Maxfield) D.; B.A., U. N.H., 1944; m. Barbara W. Burns, Feb. 20, 1943; children—Nancy (Mrs. Stephen Lasar), Martha (Mrs. Jeffrey Pattee), John Bradford III, Deborah, Susan, Lincoln, Rebecca, Sarah. Tchr., Laconia (N.H.) High Sch., 1944-45; asst. to pres. U. N.H., 1945-47, asst. dean men; 1949, acting dean men, 1949-50; field agt. Mass. Assn. Adequate State Financing Pub. Edn., 1948-49; exec. sec. New Eng. Sch. Devel. Council, 1950-59; lectr. Harvard Grad. Sch. Edn., 1955-56, asso., 1970—; host TV program Dimensions, Boston, 1955-57; supt. schs., Lincoln, Mass., 1959-63, Worcester, Mass., 1963-66, Mpls., 1967—. Trustee Farmers & Mechanics Savs. Bank Mpls., Ednl. Testing Service, 1971—. Del., White House Conf. Edn., 1955; mem. adv. bd. Field Enterprises Ednl. Corp.; mem. adminstrv. bd. sch. univ. program research and devel. Harvard Grad. Sch. Edn., 1956-59. moderator Advanced Adminstrv. Inst. Sch. Adminstrs., Harvard, summer 1958; mem. adv. com. Mass. Council Pub. Schs., 1950—; mem. Universalist-Unitarian Commn. Edn. and Liberal Religion, 1962; mem. Mass. Commn. Edn. Study, 1962-65; mem. spl. task force Pres.'s Sci. Adv. Com.; mem. Pres.'s commn. on sch. finance, 1970—; mem. Citizens Com. Pub. Edn.; mem. nat. adv. council Hampshire Coll., Amherst, Mass. Mem. St. Paul- Mpls. Com. on Fgn. Relations; bd. dirs. Asso. Harvard Alumni, 1965—, YMCA of Met. Mpls., Am. Council on German Studies, Nat. Humanities Faculty; trustee Mpls. Soc. Fine Arts, KTCA, Channel 2 TV; incorporator Met. Nature Center; mem. selection com. Alfred North Whitehead Fellows (Harvard Grad. Sch. Edn.). Served with AUS, 1943-44. Mem. N.E.A., Am. Assn. Sch. Adminstrs., Harvard Grad. Sch. Edn. Alumni Assn. (pres. 1963-65), Phi Delta Kappa, Tau Kappa Alpha. Rotarian. Contbr. articles to profl. jours. Home: 2407 Irving Av Minneapolis MN 55405

DAVIS, JOHN C. III, business exec. Pres., Davis Bros., Inc., Denver. Office: 501 W 44th Av Denver CO 80216*

DAVIS, JOHN CORDON, economist; b. South Olive, O., July 2, 1904; s. Willard D. and Mary Valinda (Rennard) D.; A.M., Ohio State U., 1931; postgrad. Columbia, 1939; spl. study London Sch. Econs., 1938; m. Dorothy Louise Roberts, Dec. 31, 1931; children—Richard, Rennard, Robert, Beatrice, John Willard. Instr., Mich. State U., East Lansing, 1931-34, asst. prof. econs., 1935-43, asso. prof., 1943-44, charge indsl. relations courses, 1936-44; vice chmn. Shipbldg. Commn., Washington, 1945; dir. constrn. labor div. Nat. Housing Agency, 1946; top economist (Labor) Council Econ. Advisers, Exec. Office Pres., 1947-53; former dir. mblzn. program devel. and evaluation Office Sec. U.S. Dept. Labor, Washington; now cons. economist; lectr. Mem. com. on apprentice tng. State Mich., 1935- 36, mem. state adv. council to Mich. Unemployment Compensation Commn., 1936-37; mem. tech. adv. com. on econ. statistics for 17th Decennial Census of Population. Mem. Indsl. Relations Assn., Am. Econ. Assn. Contbr. articles to profl. Jours. Home: 266 Floramar Terrace New Port Richey FL 33552

DAVIS, JOHN EDWARD, govt. ofcl.; b. Mpls., Apr. 18, 1913; s. James Ellsworth and Helen (Wilson) D.; B.S., U. N.D., 1935; m. Pauline Huntley, June 4, 1938; children—John Edward II, Richard James, Kathleen Anne (dec.). Dir. Civil Defense, Office of Sec. Army, Washington, 1969—. Pres. First Nat. Bank McClusky, N.D., 1959—. Mayor, McCluskey, 1946-52; gov. N.D., 1956-60; chmn. Republican Nat. Com. N.D., 1961. Served with AUS, 1941-45. Decorated Silver Star, Bronze Star, Purple Heart. Mem. Am. Legion (nat. comdr. 1966-67), V.F.W., Beta Theta Pi. Mason (33, Shriner). Lutheran. Home: 2000 S Eads St Arlington VA 22202 Office: Dir Civil Defense OSA Pentagon Washington DC 20510

DAVIS, JOHN EISELE, rehab. specialist; b. New Britain, Pa., Aug. 16, 1895; s. Thomas Sculi and Annie (Eisele) D.; student law Richmond U., 1913-14; A.B., Washington Coll., Chestertown, Md., 1918, A.M., 1920, D.Sc., 1945; m. Lillian Hicks, June 18, 1920; 1 son, John Eisele. Active 25 years in study recreational therapy for mentally ill, developer pioneering techniques; as chief athletics assisted in orgn. athletic activities for VA; chief corrective phys. rehab. VA, 1946—, sr. phys. dir. VA Hosp., Perry Point, Md., 1923—; cons. to state hosps., rehab. services; founder Assn. for Phys. and Mental Rehab., pres. assn., 1957-58, exec. dir., 1959—; organizer (with aid Karl Menninger) sch. for therapists VA Hosp., Topeka. Fulbright lectr. U. Oslo, Norway; Exec. dir. Nat. Rehab. Tng. Inst., 1969—; nat. cons. Dept. Health, Edn. and Welfare, 1969—; cons. in rehab. to Dept. Health, Edn. and Welfare, VA, U.S. Govt.; project dir. Research Grant on Voluntarism Dept. Health, Edn. and Welfare, 1971. Mem. Pres.'s Com. on Employment Handicapped; mem. bd. visitors and govs. Washington Coll. Recipient award as founder Assn. for Phys. and Mental Rehab., Chgo., 1947. Fellow A.A.H.P.E.R.; mem. Am. Congress Phys. Medicine (asso.), Am. Occupational Therapy Assn., Research Council on Problems of Alcohol, Assn. Mil. Surgeons U.S., N.P. Anonymous (chmn. com. pub. edn.), Am. Legion, V.F.W., D.A.V., Assn. Phys. and Mental Retardation (chmn. com. mental retardation), Sigma Phi Epsilion. Baptist. Mason. Author: Play and Mental Health; Principles and Practice of Rehabilitation, rev. edit., 1947; Recreational Therapy; Clinical Applications of Recreational Therapy, 1952; Recovery From Schizophrenia, the Roland Method, 1957; also articles. Home: 105 St Lawrence St Rehoboth Beach DE 19971 Office: VA Central Office Washington DC 20420

DAVIS, JOHN H., Jr., educator; b. Cumberland County, Va., July 16, 1901; s. John Henry and Susan Beverly (Morton) D.; B.S., M.A., Davidson Coll., 1924; Ph. D., U. Chgo., 1929; m. Emma Caroline Adcock, June 2, 1933; children—Emma Virginia, Susan Morton. Asso. prof. biology Davidson Coll., 1925-27, 28- 30; prof. biology Presbyn. Coll., 1930-33, Southwestern Coll., Memphis, 1935-41; research asso. Carnegie Instn., Washington, summers 1936-40, Fla. Geol. Survey, 1941-48; vis. prof. botany U. Va. Mountain Lake Lab., 1941, 43, 45, 47; prof. botany U. Fla., 1946-69, emeritus, 1969—; ecology cons., 1969—; vis. prof. Auckland U. Coll., New Zealand, 1950, U. Mandalay, Burma, 1958-60, Nat. Taiwan U., Taipei, 1964-65. Mem. Ecol. Soc. Am., Assn. Southeastern Biologists, Fla. Acad. Sci., Phi. Beta Kappa, Sigma Xi, Phi Sigma, Gamma Sigma Epsilon, Sigma Upsilon. Democrat. Presbyn. Author: Natural Features of Southern Florida; Forests of Burma; Influences of Man upon Coast Lines, The Role of Mangroves, others; also survey reports, bulls. Home: 1729 NW 8th Av Gainesville FL 32601

DAVIS, JOHN J., corp. exec.; b. Gloucester, Mass., 1915; ed. Boston U., 1937. Exec. v.p. Ryder System, Inc.; pres., dir. Ryder Computer Systems, Inc., Ryder Temporary Per., Ryder Schs., Inc.; v.p., dir. Ryder Realty, Inc., Ryder Truck Rental, Inc., Ryder Truck Rental (Can.) Ltd., Morrison Plan, Inc., RDR, Inc., Ryder Service Centers, Inc., Greer Tech. Inst., Inc., Radio TV Tech. Sch., Inc., numerous others; v.p. numerous cos. Home: 200 Arvida Pkwy Coral Gables FL 33156 Office: 2701 S Bayshore Dr Miami FL 33133

DAVIS, JOHN JOSEPH, former army officer; b. Leavenworth, Kan., Mar. 19, 1909; s. Robert E. and Julia (Fahay) D.; B.S., U.S. Mil. Acad., 1931; Grad. Command and Gen. Staff Coll., 1946, Armed Forces Staff Coll., 1949, Strategic Intelligence Sch. 1949, Army War Coll., 1953; m. Wilma Zimmerman, Nov. 9, 1957; children—Robert Anthony, Lucile Lellani (Mrs. Leonard F. Schenkel), John Joseph. Commd. 2d lt. U.S. Army, 1931, advanced through grades to lt. gen.; assigned arty. units, 1942-45; asst. corps arty. comdr. XII Corps, 1945; asst. dir., then dir. communications Arty. Sch., 1946-48; mil. research asst. Middle East sect., mil. br., intelligence dept. Gen. Staff U.S. Army, 1949; army attache Union of S. Africa, 1949-52; chief plans and policy div. Nat. Security Agy., 1953- 55; comdg. officer arty. 4th Armored Div., Fort Hood, Tex., 1955-56, 24th Inf. Div., Army Forces, Far East, 1956-57; dir. fgn. intelligence Office, asst. chief Staff Intelligence, 1957-61, 63-66; asst. dir. prodn. Nat. Security Agy., 1961-63; asst. dir. (WEC) U.S. Arms Control and Disarmament Agy., Washington, 1966-70. Decorated Legion of Merit, Bronze Star medal with oak leaf cluster, Air medal with oak leaf cluster, D.S.M., Joint Service Commendation medal. Home: 2346 S Meade St Arlington VA 22202

DAVIS, JOHN KENNERLY, utilities exec.; b. Bristol, Tenn., Oct. 5, 1906; s. John Fletcher and Caroline Frances (Bosang) D.; B.S. in Elec. Engring., Va. Mil. Inst., 1929; grad. Command and Gen. Staff Sch., 1943; m. Ruth Addington Powers, July 11, 1931; children—John Kennerly, Dorothy Gordon. Jr. engr. Pub. Sevice Co. Colo., Denver, 1929-30; engr. E. Tenn. Light & Power Co., Bristol, 1930-36, supt., Greenville, Tenn., 1936-41, mgr., Erwin, Tenn., 1941-42; personnel dir. Toledo Edison Co., 1946-49, v.p., dir., 1949-55, mem. exec. com., 1950- -, v.p., asst. gen. mgr., 1953-57, exec. v.p., asst. gen. mgr., 1957-59, pres., gen. mgr., 1959—; exec. v.p., dir. Atomic Power Devel. Assos.; dir. Ohio Valley Electric Corp., Ohio Citizen's Trust Co.; mem. exec. bd. E. Central Area Coordinating group, Central Area Coordinating gp.; trustee Power Reactor Devel. Co. Trustee Boys' Club Toledo, Masonic Toledo Trust, Community Improvement Corp. Toledo. Mem. finance com. Greater Toledo Community Chest; trustee Toledo Hosp., Toledo Mus. Art, Toledo Soc. Crippled Children. Served as lt. col. AUS, 1942-46. Decorated Bronze Star medal, Registered profl. engr., Ohio. Mem. I.E.E.E., Assn. Electric Illuminating Cos., Am. Mgmt. Assn., A.I.M., Toledo Zool. Soc., Ohio C. of C., Engring. Soc. Toledo, Nat., Ohio socs. profl. engrs., Am. Legion, Edison Electric Inst., Newcomen Soc. N.Am. Methodist. Rotarian. Clubs: Toledo, Inverness, Belmont Country, Belmont Gun. Home: 3804 Sulphur Spring Rd Toledo OH 43606 Office: Toledo Edison Co Edison Bldg Toledo OH 43601

DAVIS, JOHN LOWELL, former coll. pres.; b. Morehead, Ky., Sept. 4, 1904; s. Clifton Dean and Lillian Leah (Brown) D.; A.B., Eureka (Ill.) Coll., 1927, LL.D., 1931; postgrad. Chgo. Theol. Sem., 1927-28. U. Chgo., 1929-30; A.M., U. Cin., 1931, Ph. D. (Taft fellow), 1933; D.D., Pacific Sch. Religion, 1963; m. Hazel Huffman, June 11, 1927; children—Robert L., Judith A. Ordained to ministry Disciples of Christ Ch., 1925; pastor Christian Ch., Deland, Ill., 1925-27; asst. pastor First Congl. Ch., Maywood, Ill., 1927-28; pastor Christian Ch., Silver Grove, Ky., 1928-29; asst. dir. recreation St. Chrysostom's Community Center, Chgo., 1929-30, grad. asst. U. Cin., 1930-31; prof. English, chmn div. lang. and lit. Lynchburg (Va.) Coll., 1933-42, dean, 1936-42; exec. sec. Bd. Higher Edn., Disciples of Christ, 1942-46; prof. English, Hiram Coll., 1946-57, dean, 1947-50, 1953-57; pres. Chapman Coll., Orange, Cal., 1957-71, pres. emeritus, cons. public relations, 1971—. Mem. adv. com. on sch. and coll. teaching, chmn. subcom. on student teaching Va. State Bd. Edn., 1940-42; pres. Lynchburg Council on Adult Edn., 1938-42, Campbell Inst., 1938- 39; mem. Nat. Commn. on Christian Higher Edn. of Assn. Am. Colls., 1941- 47; mem. Commn. World Order, Disciples of Christ, 1943-50, vice chmn. Commn. Edn., 1946-47; coordinator com. on liberal arts edn. N. Central Assn. Colls., 1949-55, co-dir. N. Central Workshop, U. Chgo., 1951. Trustee, Disciples Sem. Found., chmn. bldg. com., 1963. Corporate mem. Am. Inst. Family Relations; chmn. Disneyland Awards Com., 1970. Mem. Modern Lang. Assn., Assn. Ind. Cal. Colls. and Univs. (sec. 1963-65, exec. com. 1969—), Tau Kappa Alpha, Sigma Tau Delta, Psi Alpha Lambda. Democrat. Clubs: Fortnightly Forum (pres. 1938). Author: The Church and the New World Mind: A Study Guide. Contbr. to Christian mag. Editor: Values, 1942-46, The Scroll, 1946-47; contng. editor World Call, 1942-46. Home: 1908 N Greenleaf St Santa Ana CA 92706 Office: 833 N Glassell St Orange CA 92666

DAVIS, JOHN MACDOUGALL, lawyer; b. Seattle, Feb. 20, 1914; s. David Lyle and Georgina (MacDougall) D.; B.A., U. Wash., 1936; childrenJean, John, Bruce, Ann, Margaret, Elizabeth. Admitted to Wash. bar, 1940, since practiced in Seattle; partner firm Davis, Wright, Todd, Riese & Jones. Dir. Seattle- First Nat. Bank, No. Life Ins. Co. Dir. Mercer Island Sch. Dist., 1956-65; pres. King County Sch. Dirs. Assn., 1958-59. Trustee Va. Mason Hosp. Assn., Seattle, 1950—, pres., 1970—. Mem. Am., Wash. State, Seattle-King County (pres. 1960-61) bar assns., Order of Coif, Phi Delta Phi, Alpha Delta Phi. Clubs: Rainier, Golf (Seattle); Mountaineers (pres. 1968-69). Home: 7662 SE 22d St Mercer Island WA 98040 Office: Seattle-First Nat Bank Bldg Seattle 98104.

DAVIS, JOHN MOORE KELSO, printing corp. exec.; b. Hartford, Conn., Aug. 18, 1908; s. John Henry Kelso and Edith Hollister (Brainard) D.; grad. Kent Sch. 1925; B.A., Yale, 1929; m. Mignon Estabrook Foerderer, May 20, 1939; 1 dau., Ethel Foerderer (Mrs. Nolen S. Pendergrast). Chmn. bd., dir. Conn. Printers, Inc., Hartford 1952—; dir. Taylor & Fenn Co., Hartford Nat. Bank & Trust Co., Smyth Mfg. Co. Past dir., v.p. Council on Founds.; mem. distbn. com. Hartford Found. Pub. Giving, 1954- -; mem. State Conn. Bldg. Commn., 1953-67. Trustee, v.p. Colt Bequest; trustee P.E. and E.B. Foerderer Found., Phila. Mem. C. of C. (past dir., chmn.), Printing Industry Am., Mfrs. Assn. Hartford County (bd. dirs.), Conn. Hist. Soc. Episcopalian (past vestryman, sr. warden). Home: Avon CT Office: 55 Granby St Bloomfield CT 06002 also PO Box 538 Hartford CT 06101

DAVIS, JOHN ROWLAND, educator; b. Mpls., Dec. 19, 1927; s. Roland Owen and Dorothy (Norman) D.; student Ia. State U., 1947-48; B.S., U. Minn., 1949, M.S., 1951; postgrad. Purdue U., 1955-57; Ph.D., Mich. State U., 1959; m. Lois Marie Falk, Sept. 4, 1946; children—Joel C., Jacque L., Michele M., Robin E. Hydraulic engr. U.S. Geol. Survey, Lincoln, Neb., 1950-51; instr. Mich. State U., 1951-55; asst. prof. Purdue U., 1955-57; lectr. U. Cal. at Davis, 1957-62; hydraulic engr. Stanford Research Inst., South Pasadena, Cal., 1962-64; prof. U. Neb., Lincoln, 1964-65, dean Coll. Engring. and Architecture, 1965-71; prof. head dept. agrl. engring. Ore. U., Corvallis, 1971—. Cons. Stanford Research Inst., Dept. Agr.; dir. Engrs. Council Profl. Devel. Served with USNR, 1945-46, Recipient citation for meritorious service State Ind., 1957. Registered profl. engr., Neb., Cal. Mem. Am. Soc. for Engring. Edn., Am. Soc. Agrl.

Engrs. (dir.), Am. Soc. C.E., A.A.A.S., Neb. Reclamation Assn. (bd. dirs.), Nat. Soc. Profl. Engrs., Sigma Xi. Contbr. articles to profl. jours. Address: Dept Agrl Engring Ore State U Corvallis OR 97331

DAVIS, JOHN STAIGE, physician; b. Charlottesville, Va., Sept. 13. 1900; s. John Staige and Volunnia (Staples) D.; B.A., U. Va., 1921, M.D., 1925; student London Sch. Tropical Medicine; m. Camile Ruth Cole, 1930 (div. 1937); children—John Staige IV, Camille Ruth; m. 2d Florence Roome, 1940 (dec. 1943); m. 3d, Margaret Diggins, Nov. 1943 (div. 1952); children—Paul Staige, Roslyn, Elaine; m. 4th, Mary Benzell, Jan. 19, 1954. Intern St. Luke's Hosp., N.Y.C., 1925-27, attending physician, 1931-, chief arthritis clinic, 1932-; asst. resident Rockefeller Inst., N.Y.C., 1927-28; practice internal medicine, N.Y.C., 1929-; asso. attending physician Bellevue Hosp., 1947- -; cons. physician Southampton-Midtown hosps. Chmn. bd. Dathol Corp. Chmn. med. sect., dir. N.Y. Bd. Trade; chmn. health and safety council Manhattan chpt. Boy Scouts Am. Served to Col., M.C., AUS, 1942-45; col. Res. Fellow A.C.P., N.Y. Acad. Medicine; mem. Harvey Soc., Assn. Mil. Surgeons U.S., Am. Rheumatism Assn., Mil. Order Fgn. Wars, St. Hubert Soc. Am. (pres.), Raven Soc., Navy League (v.p. Montauk), Med. Strollers N.Y., Mil. Order World Wars, Sons of Confederate Vets., Phi Beta Kappa, Sigma Xi, Alpha Omega Alpha, Delta Kappa Epsilon, Phi Rho Sigma. Clubs: University, Touchdown, Adventurers; (pres.), Club Limited, Camp Fire Club Am., Assn. Am. Sportsmen, Deep Sea (fleet surgeon, v.p.), Boone and Crockett, Governors Island Officers Open Mess. Home: 54 Riverside Dr New York City NY 10024. Office: 135 E 64th St New York City NY 10021

DAVIS, JOHN WARREN, educator; b. Milledgeville, Ga., Feb. 11, 1888; s. Robert Marion and Katie (Mann) D.; student U. Chgo., 1911-18; A.B., Morehouse Coll., Atlanta, 1911, A.M., 1920; D. Litt., State College, Orangeburg, S.C., 1931; LL.D., Wilberforce U., 1939, Howard U., 1940, Va. State Coll., Morgan State Coll., 1952, Harvard, 1953; D.C. L., U. Liberia (West Africa), 1956, H.H.D., 1960; H.H.D., W.Va. State Coll., 1956; LL.D., Central State Coll. (O.), 1965, Morehouse Coll., 1965, Shaw U., 1967; m. Bessie Rucker, Aug. 24, 1916 (dec.); children—Constance Rucker (dec.), Dorothy Long; m. 2d, Ethel McGhee, Sept. 2, 1932; 1 dau., Caroline Florence. Tchr. Morehouse Coll., Atlanta, 1911-15, registrar, 1914-17; exec. sec. 12th Street branch, YMCA, Washington, 1917-19; pres. W.Va. State Coll., 1919-53, pres. emeritus since 1953. U.S. dir. Tech. Coop. Adminstrn., Monrovia, Liberia, 1953-54; mem. U.S. Nat., Commn. for UNESCO, 1960-62; mem. U.S. 1962 Fgn. Service Selection Bd.; spl. dir. dept. tchr. information and security N.A.A.C.P. Legal Def. and Ednl. Fund, Inc., 1953—; dir. talent study Phelps-Stokes Fund, 1956; spl. dir. Herbert Lehman Edn. Fund, 1964. Bd. trustees Shaw U., Bergen County (N.J.) Community Coll., African-Am. Inst. Mem. Hoover's Orgn. on Unemployment Relief, Nat. Adv. Com. on Edn. of Negroes; mem. Nat. Land Grant Coll. Survey Staff, 1928, Nat. Adv. Com. on Edn., 1929; mem. Commn. on Instns. of Higher Edn. of North Central Assn. of Coll., 1936-48; mem. exec. com. North Central Assn. Colls. and Secondary sch., 1947; mem. N.E.A. Com. for Def. of Democracy Through Edn., 1945-52, chmn. , 1950-52; mem. North Central Assn. Com. on Evaluation of Accrediting Procedures, 1948; mem. Nat. Sci. Bd., NSF, 1950-56; mem. U.S. Office of Edn., Wartime Commn. Decorated Grand Officer Order Nat. Honor of Merit Haiti, 1948; Grand Comdr. Star Africa, 1936; recipient James Weldon Johnson award, 1963. Granted Harmon Award in Edn., 1926. Mem. N.Y. State Colonization Soc., Am. Soc. African Culture, N.E.A., Assn. Tchrs. in Colored Schs. (pres. 1928), Nat. Freedom Day Assn. (v.p. since 1948), Phi Beta Kappa, Sigma Pi Phi. Republican. Baptist. Mason (33, Shriner). Home: 112 Reade St Englewood NJ 07631 Office: 10 Columbus Circle New York City NY 10019

DAVIS, JOHN WILLIAM, congressman; b. Rome, Ga., Sept. 12, 1916; s. John Camp and Era (DeLay) D.; A.B., U. Ga., 1937, LL.B., 1939; m. Vivian Hawkins, Feb. 6, 1944 (dec. Feb. 1969); children—Katherine DeLay, John William, Mary Ellen. Admitted to Ga. bar, 1939; practice in Rome, 1939-42, Summerville, 1945-55; solicitor gen. Rome Circuit, 1950-53; judge Lookout Mountain Jud. Circuit, 1955-60; mem. 87th-92d Congresses 7th Dist. Ga. Served with AUS, World War II. Democrat. Mason, Lion. Home: 100 Espy St Summerville GA 30747 Office: House Office Bldg Washington DC 20515

DAVIS, JONATHAN, farmer; b. Sterling, Mass., Oct. 7, 1905; s. John A. and Maude (Shattuck) D.; B.S. in Bus. Adminstrn., Dartmouth, 1927; m. Elisabeth Maddison, Nov. 15, 1933; children—John M., Robert S. Pres., dir. Agway Inc., Syracuse, N.Y., 1964—; pres. Davis Farms Trust, Sterling Junction, Mass; dir., chmn. bd. Agway Ins. Agy.; dir. Internat. Life Ins. Co., dir. Worcester County National Bank, Bd. dirs. Charles H. Hood Dairy Found.; life trustee Mass. Hort. Research Center. Mem. Alpha Zeta. Home: Sterling Junction MA 01565 Office: 300 S Geddes St Syracuse NY 13201

DAVIS, JONATHAN FARR, advt. exec.; b. Auburn Twp., Pa., Aug. 15, 1893; s. Clarke and Minnie (Farr) D.; B.S. in Agr., U. Del., 1918; m. Mae L. Clark, Jan. 22, 1923; children—Jean A. (Mrs. Lang, dec.), Nancy M. (Mrs. William F. Nyhan). Extension specialist agrl. econs. U. Del., 1919-20; country agrl. agt. U. Md., 1920-21; agrl. marketing N.W. Ayer & Son, Phila., 1922-24; with Griswold Eshleman Co., Cleve., 1924-69, chmn., treas., 1957-69, now dir.; propr. Jofad Land Co. Chmn. bd. Euclid- Glenville Hosp., 1950-53, life trustee 1953—. Mem. Cleve. Advt. Club, Phi Kappa Phi, Kappa Alpha. Republican. Kiwanian. Clubs: Midday (Cleve.); Rockwell Springs; Mentor Harbor Yachting. Home: 22150 Hadden Rd Euclid OH 44117 Office: 55 Public Sq Cleveland OH 44113

DAVIS, JUDITH BLAKE KINCADE, (Mrs. Kingsley Davis), educator; b. N.Y.C., May 3, 1926; d. Forrest James and Sylvia (Blake) Kincade; B.S., Columbia, 1950, Ph.D., 1961; m. Kingsley Davis, Nov. 4, 1954; 1 dau., Laura Isabelle; 1 step-son, Jefferson Kingsley. Research asso. Conservation Found., N.Y.C., 1954-57; lectr. Sch. Nursing, U. Cal. at San Francisco, 1957-59, asst. prof. demography at Berkeley, 1962-65, chmn. group in demography, 1965-67, asso. prof., 1966-69, prof., 1969—, chmn. dept. demography, 1967—. Fellow Am. Sociol. Assn., Am. Pub. Health Assn.; mem. Population Assn. Am. (dir.), Am. Assn. Pub. Opinion Research, Internat. Union Sci. Study Population, Sociol. Research Assn. Author: Family Structure in Jamaica, 1961; Western European Censuses, 1960; An English Language Guide, 1971. Contbr. articles profl. jours. Home: 7 Selborne Dr Piedmont CA 94611

DAVIS, JULIUS E., lawyer; b. Mpls., Apr. 21, 1912; s. Isadore and Molly (Edelman) D.; student Lawrence U., 1929-30; B.S., U. Minn., 1933, J.D., 1936; m. Lillian Stacia Kropman, May 26, 1940; children—Stephen J., Lawrence A. Admitted to Minn. bar, 1936, since practiced in Mpls.; pvt. practice, 1936-38; mem. firm Robins & Davis, 1938-43; sr. partner Robins, Davis & Lyons, Mpls., 1946—. Pres., dir. Sugar Lakes, Inc.; pres. Tam Sixty Corp., Miami, Fla.; v.p., dir. Albert Enterprises, Inc., Win-San Bldg. Corp. (both Bal Harbour, Fla.); chmn. bd. Kodlak, Inc.; dir. Polar Ice, Inc., Bal Harbour Towers, Inc. (Fla.), Lawndale Industries, Inc. Aurora, Ill., Equity Capital Co., EQC Co., Inc., Viking Realty Co., Brown-Mpls. Tank & Fabricating Co., Atlantic Coast Properties, Inc., Fla., Northland Mobile Homes Inc., Duluth, Minn., Jennie-O Foods, Inc., Willmar, Minn. Vice pres. Robins, Davis & Lyons Found.; trustee U. Minn. Found., Merrill Cohen Meml. Fund, Sch. Bus. Adminstrn. U. Minn., Jewish Community Center Greater Mpls., Radio Free Europe; bd. govs. Mount Sinai Hosp., Mpls., Served with AUS, 1943-45. Mem. Am., Minn., Hennepin County bar assns., Am. Judicature Soc., Am. Arbitration Assn., Nat. Lawyers Club, U. Minn. Law Sch. Alumni Assn. (bd. dirs.). Club: Drug and Chemical (N.Y.C.). Home: 1650 Dupont Av Minneapolis MN 55403 Office: 33 S 5th St Minneapolis MN 55402

DAVIS, KATHRYN WATERMAN, author and corp. exec.; b. Phila., Feb. 25, 1907; d. Joseph and Edith (Stix) Wasserman; grad. Miss Madeira's, Washington; B.A., Wellesley Coll., 1928; M.A., Columbia, 1931; Ph.D., U. Geneva (Switzerland), 1934; m. Shelby Cullon Davis, Jan. 4, 1932; children—Shelby Moore Cullom, Diana Cullom, Priscilla Alden (dec.). Partner Shelby Cullom Davis & Co., 1947—. Pres. Shelby Cullom Davis Found. Asst. in preparation of yearly vol. U.S. in World Affairs, Council Fgn. Relations; pres. Nat. Council Household Employment, 1940- 44; chmn. Westchester Children's Assn. Mem. com. for suggested improvements Social Security laws Pa., 1937; chmn. speakers bur. Westchester Country chpt. A.R.C., 1942-44; radio chmn. Mental Hygiene Assn. Westchester County, 1950-51. Mem. Briarcliff League Women Voters (pres. 1942-43), Westchester League Women Voters (chmn. fgn. policy 1943), Scarborough Presbyn. Guild (pres. 1944-45). Clubs: National Republican (chmn. fgn. policy discussion group), York (v.p.) (N.Y.C.); Wellesley in Westchester (pres. 1952-53); Bar Harbor (Me.). Author: The Soviets at Geneva, 1934; also articles various mags. including The American, Reader's Digest. Lectr. fgn. affairs, India, Russia. Address: US Embassy Bern Switzerland

DAVIS, KEITH E., distillery exec.; b. Mahomet, Ill., 1920; Ed.B., Ill. State U., 1943; M.A. in Bus. and Econs., State U. Ia., 1947; postgrad. U. Mo., 1963; married. Sr. accountant Ernst & Ernst, Chgo., 1947-51; v.p., treas. Black Sivalls & Bryson, 1951-55; v.p., treas. Glenmore Distilleries Co., Louisville, 1965-68, 1st v.p., treas., dir., 1968—. Served to lt. USNR, 1943-46. Mem. Ky. C. of C. (dir.). Home: 5 Arden Rd Glenview KY 40025 Office: 660 S 4th St Louisville KY 40202*

DAVIS, KENNETH CULP, educator; b. Leeton, Mo., Dec. 19, 1908; s. Samuel Houston and Charlotte (Culp) D.; A.B., Whitman Coll., 1931; LL.B., Harvard, 1934; m. Carol Seeds, June 20, 1934; children—Malcolm Fletcher, Margaret Lynn; m. 2d, Inger Pedersen, June 14, 1962. Admitted to Ohio bar, 1935; practiced in Cleve., 1934-35; asst. prof., asso. prof. W.Va. U., 1935-39; with Dept. Justice, 1939-40; prof. law U. Tex., 1940-48, U. Minn., 1950-61; John P. Wilson prof. law U. Chgo., 1961—. Vis. prof. law Harvard, 1948-50; staff mem. Bd. Investigation and Research, 1942. Mem. Phi Beta Kappa, Delta Sigma Rho, Phi Delta Theta. Author: Administrative Law, 1951; Cases on Administrative Law, 1951; Adminstrative Law Treaties. 4 Vols., 1958; Supplement, 1971; Administrative Law Cases, 1959; Administrative Law Cases-Text Problems, 1960, 2d edit., 1965; Administrative Law and Government, 1960; Discretionary Justice, 1969. Home: 5830 Stony Island Chicago IL 60637

DAVIS, KENNETH NEWTON, Jr., electronic equipment co. exec.; b. Greenfield, Mass., Mar. 26, 1926; s. Kenneth Newton and Barbara (Lufkin) D.; grad. Phillips Acad., Andover, Mass., 1943; B.S. in Mech. Engring., Mass. Inst. Tech., 1946; M.B.A., Stanford, 1949; m. Corinne Terry Burge, May 27, 1950; children—Cynthia Learned, Barbara Beth, Robin Terry. With IBM Corp., 1949-69, corp. controller, 1961-63, treas., 1963-66, v.p., 1966-69; asst. sec. commerce for domestic and internat. bus., 1969-70; cons. internat. trade and finance, 1970-71; exec. v.p., dir. Gen. Instrument Corp., N.Y.C., 1971—; dir. MPB Corp., Keene, N.H.; mem. adv. bd. Mgmt. and Finance, S.A., Geneva, Switzerland. Served to lt. (j.g.) USNR, World War II. Club: Waccabuc (N.Y.) Country. Home: Stone Hill Rd Pound Ridge NY 10576 Office: 1775 Broadway New York City NY 10019

DAVIS, KENNETH PICKETT, educator, forester; b. Denver, Sept. 2, 1906; s. Gilbert Louis and Charlotte (Pickett) D.; B.S.F., Mont. State U., 1928; M.F., U. Mich., 1932, Ph.D., 1940; m. Mary Eliza Shope, Sept. 10, 1929; children—Lawrence Spalding, Lenore, Charlotte, Richard Shope. Forest ranger U.S. Forest Service, 1928-31, silvicultural research No. Rocky Mountain Forest and Range Expt. Sta., 1933-39, asst. chief div. forest mgmt. research, Washington, 1940-43, chief div., 1944-45; dean Mont. State U. Sch. Forestry, 1945-49; prof. forest mgt. U. Mich. Sch. Natural Resources, 1949-67, chmn. dept. forestry, 1950-67, acting chmn., 1965-66; prof. forest land use Yale Sch. Forestry, 1967—. Forestry cons. to pub. agys. and industry. Fulbright lectr. forestry, Finland, 1963. Mem. Soc. Am. Foresters (chmn. Washington sect. 1943, No. Rocky Mountain sect. 1948, Wis.-Mich. sect. 1961-62, mem. council 1958-61, v.p. 1966- 69, pres. 1970-71, Mont. Conservation Council (pres. 1948-49, 70—), Am. Forestry Assn., Sigma Xi, Theta Chi. Episcopalian. Author: American Forest Management, 1954; Forest Fire; Control and Use, 1959; Forest Management; Regulation and Valuation, 1966. Forestry cons. McGraw-Hill Ency. Scis. and Tech., 1961—. Home: 52 Westerly Dr Mt Carmel CT 06518 Office: School of Forestry New Haven CT 06502

DAVIS, KENNETH REXTON, educator; b. Glendive, Mont., Aug. 15, 1921; s. Robert T. and Edith M. (Root) D.; Ph.B., U. Wis., 1946, M.B.A., 1947; Ph.D., U. Chgo., 1955; m. Mary Elizabeth Gunn, Dec. 29, 1945; children—Jane Claire, John Gunn. Instr., U. Wis., 1947-49; asst. prof. U. N.C., 1949-53; asst. prof. Amos Tuck Sch. Bus. Adminstrn., Dartmouth, Hanover, N.H., 1953-57, prof., 1957—. Mgmt. cons.; vis. prof. Inst. pour l'etude des méthodes de direction de l'enterprise, Lausanne, Switzerland. Served from pvt. to capt. USAAF, 1943-45. Mem. Am. Marketing Assn., Am. Assn. U. Profs., Delta Upsilon, Beta Gamma Sigma. Author: Furniture Marketing, 1957; (with Albert W. Frey) The Advertising Industry, 1958; Marketing Management, 1961; 2d edit., 1966; (with F.E. Webster Jr.) Sales Force Management, 1968; Readings in Sales Force Management, 1968. Home: 10 Kingsford Rd Hanover NH 03755

DAVIS, KIEFFER D., physician; b. Holliday, Mo., Jan. 14, 1913; s. Paul C. and Gertrude M. (Dixon) D.; A.B., Westminster Coll., 1934; B.S., Mo. U., 1936; M.D., Louisville Sch. Medicine, 1938; m. Keitha Lee McCoy, Dec. 20, 1937; children—Paul, Peter, Candice, Thomas. Intern, St. Louis City Hosp., 1938-39; pvt. practice medicine, Nowata, Okla., 1939-45, Bartlesville, Okla., 1945-47; med. dir. Phillips Petroleum Co., Bartlesville, Okla., 1947—; med. mem. corp. Jane G. Phillips Meml. Hosp., 1949—; mem. vis. faculty Okla. U. Med. Sch. Mem. Pres.'s, Gov.'s commns. for employment handicapped. Diplomatic Am. Bd. Occupational Medicine. Fellow Indsl. Med. Assn., (past pres.); mem. Am. Med. Assn. (council on occupational health), Am. Petroleum Inst., So., Okla. State Med. Socs., Kappa Alpha, Phi Beta Pi. Home: 1915 Hillcrest Dr Bartlesville OK 74003 Office: Adams Bldg Bartlesville OK 74003

DAVIS, KINGSLEY, sociologist; b. Tuxedo, Tex., Aug. 20, 1908; s. Joseph Dier and Winifred (Kinsley) D.; A.B. cum laude, U. Tex., 1930, M.A. (Oldright fellow in philosophy), 1932; M.A. (Henry Bloomfield Rogers Meml. fellow), Harvard, 1933, Ph.D., 1936; m. Judith Blake, Nov. 4, 1954; 1 dau., Laura Isabelle; children by previous marriageJo Ann, Jefferson Kingsley. Faculty Smith Coll., 1934-36, Clark U., 1936-37; asso. prof., Pa. State U., 1937-42, prof., 1942-44, head div. sociology, 1937-44; vis. research asso. Office Population Research, Princeton, 1942-44; asst. prof. Princeton, 1944-48; asso. prof. sociology grad. faculty polit. sci., Columbia, 1948-52, prof., 1952-55, asso. dir. bur. applied social research, 1948-49, dir., 1949-52; prof. sociology U. Cal. at Berkeley, 1955—. chmn dept., 1961-63, dir. Internat. Pop. and Urban Research, 1957—; Guy Stanton Ford lectr. U. Minn. 1960; Messenger lectr. Cornell U., 1963. Dir. contract research studies of Human Resources Research Inst., Maxwell AFB, 1950-53; dir. research project on population trends and demographic behavior in Jamacia, 1952- 54; cons. population studies Conservation Found., 1953-54; trustee Population Reference Bur., Inc., 1955-; U.S. rep. populations commn. UN, 1955-61; mem. behavioral scis. division NRC, 1963-, chmn. designate, 1964-66, chmn., 1966-68. Fellow Center Advanced Study in Behavioral Scis., 1956-57, NSF, 1963-64. Fellow Am. Statis. Assn., A.A.A.S. (chmn. Sect. K 1963, v.p.); mem. National Acad. Scis., Population Assn. Am. (pres. 1962-63), Am. Sociol. Soc. (pres. 1959). Regional Sci. Assn., Am. Eugenies Soc., Internat Union Sci. Study Population, Am. Assn. U. Profs. (council 1962-64), Internat. Statis. Inst., Sociol. Research Assn. (pres. 1960), Am. Philos. Soc.,Am. Acad. Arts and Scis. Author (with Bredemeier and Levy) Modern American Society, 1949; Human Society, 1949; The Population of India and Pakistan, 1951; (with others) World's Metropolitan Areas, 1959. Editor: World Population in Transition, vol. 237, 1945; Current Sociology, 1953- 63. Mem. editorial bd. Economic Development and Cultural Change, 1958-, Population Review, 1957—. Internat. Jour. Comparative Sociology, 1960—. Mem. sr. editorial council New Ency. of Social Scis. Contbr. articles profl. jours., encys. Home: 199 Hillcrest Rd Berkeley CA 94705

DAVIS, LAMBERT, editor; b. Lynchburg, Va., June 1, 1905; s. Horatio Minor and Lottie Suydam (Lambert) D.; student Ga. Sch. of Tech., 1921-22; A.B., U. of Va., 1925, A.M., 1926; m. Isabella Winston Symmers, June 24, 1933; childrenCharlotte Lambert (Mrs. Montgomery Furth), Martha Winston (Mrs. Basil King), William Minor. Mem. editorial staff, Street and Smith and Doubleday, Doran and Co., 1926-28; mng. editor Va. Quarterly Review, 1928-33, editor, 1933-38; N.Y. editor Bobbs-Merrill Co., 1938-40; editor Harcourt, Brace and Co., 1940-48; dir. U. N.C. Press, 1948-70; acting dir. East-West Center Press, 1971. Mem. exec. com. Assn. Am. U. Presses, 1954-58, pres., 1955-57; mem. exec. com. N.C. Tercentenary Commn., 1959-61. Mem. Raven, Phi Beta Kappa, Phi Kappa Sigma. Democrat. Episcopalian. Club: Colonnade. Home: Greenwood Rd Chapel Hill NC 27514

DAVIS, LAURENCE LAIRD, financial cons.; b. Cin., June 6, 1915; s. Thomas Jefferson and Jane (Brown) D.; grad St. Mark's Sch., 1934; A.B., Harvard, 1938; postgrad. London (Eng.) Sch. Econs., 1939; m. Charlotte Rowe Nichols, Oct. 12, 1940; childrenSally Laird (Mrs. Arthur D. Pratt), Laurence Laird, Thomas Jefferson II. With First Nat. Bank Cin., 1939-42, 46-70, v.p., 1949-64, vice chmn. bd., 1964-70, also dir.; vice consul, econ. analyst State Dept., 1943-45; financial cons., 1970—; dir. Burning Springs Collieries, Logan and Kanawha Coal Co., Millers Creek Mineral Devel. Co., Roberta Coal Co., Elkay Mining and Buffalo Mining, Burning Springs Land Co. Chmn., English Speaking Union 1965-, Cin. Symphony Orch., 1965-68. Bd. dirs. Christ Hosp. Mem. Greater Cin. C. of C. (pres. 1967-69). Clubs: Commonwealth, Camargo, Queen City (Cin.). Home: 6910 Given Rd Cincinnati, OH 45243. Office: Carew Tower Cincinnati OH 45201

DAVIS, LAWRENCE ARNETTE, coll. pres.; b. McCrory, Ark., July 4, 1914; s. Virgil and Pawnee (Willimas) D.; A.B., Agrl., mech. and Normal Coll., Pine Bluff, Ark., 1937; A.M., U. Kan., 1941; grad. study, N.Y. U.; Ph. D., U. Ark., LL.D., Lane Coll. 1948, Morehouse Coll., 1950; m. 1936; childrenLawrence Arnette, Larnell Wilkerson, Ronald Laval; m. 2d, Rachel Lorraine Johnson, October 4, 1946; childrenSharon, Michael, Gail and Janice. Registrar and ass. to pres. of Mechanical Coll. now Agrl. Tech. and Normal Coll. Pine Bluff, Ark., 1939-42, dean administr., 1941-43, acting pres., 1942-43, pres., 1943—. Mem. Com. on Action to Improve Conditions of Farm Laborers, etc., U. Chicago, 1946. Certificate of Merit from Chgo. Defender. Mem. Negro Land Grant Coll. Presidents Assn. (exec. com.), N.E.A., Am., Ark tchrs. assns., Nat. Council Tchrs., English Am. Assn. Sch. Adminstrs., Omega Psi Phi, Alpha Kappa Mu, Omega Psi Phi. Mason (33). Address: Agricultural and Mechanical College Pine Bluff AR 71601

DAVIS, LELAND, chain food store exec.; b. Huntington, W.Va., Apr. 27, 1923; s. Leland Elmer and Vivian Elaine (Chapman) D.; B.A., U. Cin., 1949, M.A., 1950; m. Patricia Haase, Aug. 26, 1950; childrenMelissa Lee, Shelley, Christian, Timothy. With Kroger Co., 1951-55, N.W. Ayer & Son, advt., 1955-60, Young & Rublicam, Inc., advt., 1960-62; v.p. advt. Kroger Co., Cin., 1962-. Served with USAAF, 1942-45. Mem. Phi Beta Kappa, Omicron Delta Kappa, Phi Delta Theta. Presbyn. Clubs: Queen City, Coldstream Country (Cin.). Home: 6440 Honeysuckle Dr Cincinnati, OH 45230. Office: 1014 Vine St Cincinnati, OH 45201.

DAVIS, LEONARD MCCUTCHAN, educator; b. Duffy, W.Va., July 14, 1919; s. Arch Goff and Ressie (McCutchan) D.; A.B., W.Va. U., 1948, M.A., 1950; Ph.D., Northwestern U., 1958; m. Mary Abrilla Bateman, Aug. 28, 1948; children—Leonard McCutchen, Anne Edmondson, James Mansfield. Dir. forensics Ala. Coll., 1950-53; grad. teaching asst. Northwestern U., 1953-54, instr. Nat. High Sch. Speech Inst., 1954; prof. W.Va. U., Morgantown, 1954-, chmn. dept. speech, 1966—. Vis. prof. speech U. Cal., Santa Barbara, 1965-66, 67-68, U. Ariz., summer 1966; faculty Va.-Md. Banking Schs.; lectr. bus. and profl. communications U. Cal., Los Angles. Served with AUS, 1941-45. Named Speech Tchr. of Year, W.Va., U., 1964, 65. Mem. Am. Assn. U. Profs., Am., Western, So., Eastern States speech assns., Beta Theta Pi, Delta Sigma Rho. Methodist. Mason, Rotarian. Club: Toastmasters (Clarksburg, W.Va.). Author: Mr. Lincoln Goes to Gettysburg, 1960; Night of Assassins (Death and Funeral of Abraham Lincoln), 1959; (with Mrs. Donald Portnoy) General Nathan Goff, Orator and Statesman, 1951; (with J.H. Henning) Communications in High-Risk Occupations, 1970. Home: 401 Rotary St Morgantown, WV 26505.

DAVIS, LESTER FRANK, Jr., chain store exec.; b. Scranton, Pa., Mar. 25, 1910; s. Lester Frank and Gwenette E. (Phillips) D.; m. Margaret M. McGinty, June 16, 1945; 1 son, Lester Frank III. With F.W. Woolworth Co., N.Y.C., 1931—, gen. mgr. Woolco Dept. Stores div., 1961—, v.p. co., 1964—, dir. mem. exec. com. co., 1966—; dir. Richman Bros. Co. Served to maj. USAAF, 1942-46. Home: 20 Glendale Rd Summit NJ 07901 Office: Woolworth Bldg New York City NY 10007

DAVIS, LEVERETT, Jr., educator; b. Elgin, Ill., Mar. 3, 1914; s. Leverett and Susan (Gulick) D.; student U. Wash., 1930-32; B.S., Ore. State Coll., 1936; M.S., Cal. Inst. Tech., 1938, Ph.D., 1941; m. Victoria Merrill Stocker, June 19, 1943; 1 son, Jeffrey Leverett. Fellow faculty Cal. Inst. Tech., Pasadena, 1941—. prof. physics, 1956—. Recipient Exceptional Achievement award NASA, 1970.

Mem. Am. Phys. Soc., Am. Astron. Soc., Internat. Astron. Union, Am. Geophys. Union. Home: 1772 N Grand Oaks Av Altadena CA 91001 Office: Dept Physics California Inst Tech Pasadena CA 91109

DAVIS, LEWIS BERKLEY, electric co. exec.; b. Lewisport, Ky., Oct. 27, 1911; s. Scarlet Berkley and Elora (Taylor) D.; student U. Ky., 1934; m. Elizabeth Miller, Aug. 6, 1942; children—Lewis Berkely, Cynthia Lawton. Engr., Ken-Rad Tube & Lamp Corp., Owensboro, Ky., 1934-38, charge tube prodn. engring., 1938- 41, chief engr. Ken-Rad Transmitting Tube Corp. (acquired by Gen. Electric Co. 1945), 1941-43, plant mgr. Owensboro operations, 1943-45, 45-49; co. gen. mgr. receiving tube operations Gen. Electric Co., 1949-56, gen. mgr. electronic components div., 1956-60, v.p., 1960-66, gen. mgr. Def. Programs Div., Washington, 1966-71, with corporate office; dir. Spindletop Research, Inc. Bd. dirs. Jr. Achievement; chmn. bd. Owensboro Daviess County Indsl. Found., 1958-63; mem. Owensboro Bd. Edn., 1930-34; city commnr. Owensboro, 1954-57. Fellow I.E.E.E.; mem. Owensboro C. of C. (past pres.), Asso. Industries Ky. (past pres.), Electronics Industries Assn. (past pres.), U. Ky. Alumni Assn. (past pres.). Mem. Christian Ch. Clubs: University, Georgetown (Washington); Congressional Country (Bethesda). Home: 2500 Virginia Av NW Washington DC 20037 Office: 777 14th St NW Washington DC 20005

DAVIS, LLOYD HOWELL, govt. ofcl.; b. Dyersburg, Tenn., Dec. 11, 1919; s. Joseph and Melvina (Minor) D.; B.S., Cornell U., 1942, M.S., 1947, Ph. D., 1951; m. Hazel McIntyre, Apr. 7, 1944; childrenDianne, Linda, Donald, Allan. Asst. county agrl. agt., Wyoming County, N.Y., 1946; asst. prof. extension teaching and information Cornell U., 1947-49, asso. prof. agrl. econs., 1951-56; chief fruit and vegetable br., div. agrl. econs. Fed. Extension Services, Dept. Agr., 1956-59, field rep. administr.'s office, 1962, dep. adminstr., 1962-63, adminstr., 1963-70, dir. sci. and edn. staff Dept. Agr., 1970—; asso. dir. extension U. Mass., 1959-62. Mem. Am. Farm Econs. Assn. Home: 2119 Carhill Rd Vienna VA 22180 Office: Dept Agr Washington DC 20250

DAVIS, LOUIS FREEMAN, petroleum co. exec.; b. Longview, Tex., May 5, 1914; s. Edward William and Bertha (Lee) D.; B.S. in Mech. Engring., U. Tex., 1934; postgrad. Tex. A. and M. Coll., 1935; m. Duskianne Few, Aug. 2, 1936; children—Fred Edward, Louis Freeman. With Atlantic Refining Co., 1935- 66, v.p. gen. mgr. N.Am. producing dept., 1965-66; sr. v.p. N.Am. producing div. Atlantic Richfield Co., Dallas, 1966-68, exec. v.p., dir., 1968—; dir. Calumet Creek Oils, Ltd., pres., dir. Hondo Oil & Gas Co.; chmn bd. Atlantic Richfield Can. Ltd. Mem. petroleum engring. adv. bd. U. Tex. Mem. Am. Petroleum Inst., Soc. Petroleum Engrs., Mid-Continent Oil and Gas Assn., Dallas C. of C., Tex. Research League. Methodist. Clubs: Petroleum, Brook Hollow (Dallas). Home: 7027 Desco Dr Dallas TX 75225 Office: PO Box 2819 Dallas TX 75221

DAVIS, LOYAL, neurol. surgeon; b. Galesburg, Ill., Jan. 17, 1896; s. Albert and Laura (Hensler) D.; student Knox Coll., 1912-14, D. Sc., 1933; M.D., Northwestern U., 1918, M.S., 1921, Ph.D., 1923; D.Sc., Temple U., 1961; m. Edith Luckett, May 21, 1929; children—Richard, Nancy. Intern Cook County Hosp., 1918-19; surg. asst. to Dr. A.B. Kanavel, Chgo., 1920-23; fellow NRC 1922-24; vol. asst. to Dr. Harvey Cushing, 1923-24; asso. prof. surgery Northwestern U., 1925-32, prof., chmn. dept. surgery, 1932-63, emeritus prof., 1964—; cons. neurol. surgery VA, 1927-63; attending surgeon Passavant Meml. Hosp., 1929—. Editor Surgery, Gynecology and Obstetrics 1938—. Served as lt. M.C., World War I; col. AUS, 1942-43; ETO. Hon. fellow Royal Coll. Surgeons Eng., Royal Coll. Surgeons Edinburgh; fellow A.C.S. (chmn. bd. regents 1960-62; pres. 1963); mem. A.M.A., Am. Neurol. Soc., Soc. Neurol. Surgeons, Am. (pres. 1957), So., Western surg. assns., Soc. Clin. Surgery, James IV Assn. Surgery (pres. 1970—), Beta Theta Pi. Clubs: Casino, Commercial. Office: 55 E Erie St Chicago IL ☆

DAVIS, M. AUSTIN, retail grocer; b. Gamaliel, Ark., Jan. 8, 1911; s. William M. and Ethel (Chase) D.; student U. Ida., 1931; m. Alice Katherine Freedlund, May 21, 1933; childrenCarole Ann, A. Kay, Sanra Jean. Sr. v.p., dir. Winn-Dixie Stores, Inc.; dir. United Nat. Bank, Miami, Coral Gables First Nat. Bank. Mem. Sigma Chi. Home: 3845 Alhambra Ct Coral Gables FL 33134 Office: PO Box 352 Biscayne Annex Miami FL 33152

DAVIS, M. EDWARD, physician, educator; b. Cheyenne, Wyo., Oct. 27, 1899; s. Max and Dora (Flaxman) D.; student U. Colo., 1916-19; B.S., U. Chgo., 1920; M.D., Rush Med. Coll., 1922; postgrad. Berlin, Vienna, 1927- 28; fellow Carnegie Instn. of Embryo, 1933-34; m. Jeannette Sanger, July 12, 1927; children—Barbara Adele, M. Edward. Intern, Los Angeles Gen. Hosp., 1922-23; resident obstetrician Chgo. Lying-in Hosp., 1925- 27; staff Chgo. Lying-In Hosp., U. Chgo Clinics; Instr. obstetrics Northwestern, 1929-30; asst. prof.. obstetrics and gynecology U. Chgo., 1930-34, asso. prof., 1934-42, prof., 1942-66, prof. emeritus, 1966—, Joseph Bollvar DeLee prof. obstetrics and gynecology, 1947-66, chief of service Chgo.-Lying-in Hosps., chmn dept. obstetrics and gynecology, 1954-66; cons. Chgo. Bd. Health, 1966-67; cons., asst. dir. Am. Coll. Obstetrics and Gynecology, 1967-68. Recipient Rubin award Am. Soc. for Study Sterility, 1960. 1st Gold Medal award Barren Found., 1961. Diplomate Am. Bd. Obstetrics and Gynecology. Hon fellow History Medicine Soc Tulane; fellow A.C.S., Am. Fertility Soc. (v.p. 1965-66), Chgo. Gynecol. Soc., Am. Coll. Obstetricians and Gynecologists, Am. Fertility Soc., Inst. Medicine Chgo. (acad.); hon. mem. Sociedade de Obstetrcia e Ginecologla de Brasil, Sociedad Cubana de Obstet. y Ginecol., Sociedad de Obstet. y Ginecol. de Veneguela, A.F.A. King Obstet. Soc. of George Washington U., Honolulu. Obstet. and Gynecol. Soc.; corr. mem. Sociedad Latino Americana para el Estudio de la Esterilidad; mem. Am. Gynecol. Soc. (v.p. 1965-66), Am. Assn. Parenthood Physicians (pres. 1965-66), Soc. Gynecologic Investigation, Endocrine Soc., A.M.A. (Gold medal for work on ergot 1935), Soc. Exptl. Biology and Medicine, Am. Soc. Pharm. and Exptl. Therapeutics, Central Soc. Clin. Research, Internat. Corrs. Soc. Obstetricians and Gynecologists. Author: DeLee's Obstetrics for Nurses, 1944, 47, 51, 57, 62, 66; Have Your Baby Keep Your Figure, 1963. Editor: Cancer of the Uterus (English editor), 1963, Jour. Fertility and Sterility 1957-70; editorial bd. Geriatrics, Aoga Cytologica, Psychosomatics, Exerpta Medica, Current Therapy, Ob-Gyn News, 1967-, Jour. Reproductive Medicine, Lying-in. Contbr. articles to profl. jours. Home: 5760 Blackstone Av Chicago, IL 60637. Office: 5841 Maryland Av Chicago, IL 60637.

DAVIS, MACK PARKER, univ. dean; b. Knoxville, Tenn., Oct. 20, 1911; s. Wallace Freeman and Minnie Rose (McCarrell) D.; A.B., Carson-Newman Coll., 1934; M.Ed., U. Tenn., 1942, D.Ed., 1954; m. Mildred Alice Fleming, Aug. 25, 1936; childrenParker Fleming, Sarah Margarette. Tchr., prin. Knox County (Tenn.) Schs., 1934-42, supr. instrn., 1942-47; faculty E. Tenn. State U., Johnson City, 1947—, dir. Sch. Edn., 1955-58, dean univ. 1958—. Mem. Joint Com. Tenn. Colls. and Univs., 1956—. Tenn. Pub. Sch. Survey and Survey Higher Edn. Tenn., 1956; mem. exec. bd. Tenn. Coll. Assn., 1968-69. Served with USNR, 1943-45. Mem. Knox County Tchrs. Assn. (pres. 1938), So. Council Tchrs. Edn. (bd. 1960-), Tenn., E. Tenn. (exec. sec. 1948-) edn. assns., Am. Assn. Sch. Adminstrs., Acad. Deans So. States, Phi Delta Kappa, Delta Kappa Pi, Phi Kappa Phi, Pi Gamma Mu. Baptist. Rotarian. Club: Beta (Tenn. bd.). Home: 105 W 12th Av Johnson City TN 37601

DAVIS, MALCOLM MCTEAR, editor; b. St. Louis, Sept. 2, 1921; s. Dr. Arthur Jobe and Elizabeth Crawford (McTear) D.; student U. Ga., 1939-40, N.Y.U., 1947-48. Various positions Atlanta Constitution, 1940-41; travel writer Am. Express, N.Y.C., 1946-48, spl. corr., 1948; contbr., researcher Information Please Almanac, 1947, 50, compiler, arranger world travel sect. 1947 edit.; editor co. mag. Going Places, 1947-48; roving corr. Brit. Travel Assn., 1948; asso. editor Am. Soc. Travel Agts. News, 1948-49; editor Let's Go, 1949-50, Travel, 1950—. Served as yeoman USNR, 1942-45. Recipient spl. Lafayette medal, France, 1957; named hon. Tar Heel by Gov. N.C., 1968. Mem. Soc. Am. Travel Writers, Drama Desk, N.Y. Travel Writers Assn. (pres. 1963-66), Am. Soc. Mag. Editors. Contbr. to Our Navy, 1944, The Smart Traveler, ann. yearbooks Am. Peoples Ency., 1953-58, World Book Ency., 1934-64, Readers Digest, travel publs., gen. mags. Home: 226 E 70th St New York City NY 10021 Office: Travel Bldg Floral Park NY 11002

DAVIS, MARGUERITE, news editor; b. Huntington, W.Va.; d. Eugene and Marguerite (Saunders) Davis; student Lausanne Sch. for Girls, Memphis, Gulf Park Coll., Gulfport, Miss., Sophie Newcomb Coll., New Orleans. Joined U.P.I., Madison, Wis., 1943, mgr. Lincoln (Neb.) bur., 1945, Chgo. radio bur. mgr., 1951, mgr. combined Chgo. radio and news depts., 1955-59, corr., Washington, 1959-. Mem. Kappa Kappa Gamma. Club: Women's Nat. Press (Washington). Home: 2475 Virginia Av NW Washington, DC 20037. Office: Nat Press Bldg Washington, DC 20004.

DAVIS, MARTIN DAVID, educator; b. N.Y.C., N.Y., Mar. 8, 1928; s. Harry and Helen (Gotlieb) D.; B.S., Coll. City N.Y., 1948; M.A., Princeton, 1949, Ph.D., 1950; m. Virginia Whiteford Palmer, Sept. 21, 1951; children—Harold, Nathan. Research instr. U. Ill., 1950-52; mem. Inst. Advanced Study, 1952-54; asst. prof. U. Cal. at Davis, 1954-55, Ohio State U., 1955-56; asst. prof., then asso. prof. Rensselaer Polytech. Inst., 1956-59; mem. faculty N.Y.U., 1959-60, 65—, prof. Grad. Sch. Arts and Scis., 1969—; prof. Belfer Grad. Sch. Sci., Yeshiva U., 1962—; vis. prof. Westfield Coll., U. London, 1968-69; cons. Bell Telephone Labs., IBM. Mem. Am. Math. Soc., Assn. Symbolic Logic, Assn. Computing Machinery. Author: Computability and Unsolvability, 1958. Home: 326 W 85th St New York City NY 10024

DAVIS, MARTIN SANDFORD, motion picture co. exec.; b. N.Y.C.; s. Carl and Pauline (Surasky) D.; student N.Y. U., Coll. City N.Y.; m. Delores Farhat; children—Martin Sandford, Philip Thomas. Eastern dir. advt., publicity Samuel Goldwyn Prodns., N.Y.C., 1945-55, Allied Artists Pictures Corp., N.Y.C., 1955- 58; dir. advt., publicity Paramount Pictures Corp., N.Y.C., 1958—, v.p. advt. and corporate pub. relations, 1958-66, exec. v.p., chief operating officer, mem. exec. com., 1966-71, dir., 1966—; sr. v.p., chmn. corporate devel. com., dir. Gulf & Western Industries, Inc.; dir. Famous Players Canadian Corp., Ltd., Paramount Pictures Corp. Served with AUS, 1943-46. Mem. Overseas Press Club, Grand St. Boys Assn., Big Bros. of Am., Am. Film Inst. (trustee). Office: 1 Gulf and Western Plaza New York City NY 10023

DAVIS, MATTHEW DINSDALE, physician, ophthalmologist; b. Madison, Wis., Oct. 25, 1926; s. Frederick Allison and Edith (Swenson) D.; B.A., U. Wis., 1947; M.D., U. Pa., 1950; m. Barbara Ann Archer, Sept. 8, 1951; childrenMatthew G., AnnD., Peter A., Amelia S., Lisa M. Intern U. Wis. Hosp., 1950-51, resident ophthalmology, 1951-55; fellow retina service Mass. Eye and Ear Infirmary, 1956; prof. chmn. dept. (Opthalmology) U. Wis. Med. Sch., 1970—. Served with USNR, 1953-55. Mem. A.M.A., Am. Acad. Opthalmology and Otolaryngology, Assn. Research Ophthalmology, Retina Soc. Research natural history diabetic retinopathy. Home: 6026 S Highlands Av Madison, WI 53705.

DAVIS, MATTIE BELLE EDWARDS, county judge; b. Ellabell, Ga., Feb. 28, 1910; d. Frank Pierce and Eddie (Morgan) Edwards; student law in law office; m. Troy Carson Daivs, June 6, 1937 (dec. Aug. 1948); stepchildren—Jane (Mrs. Cordie L. Pearson, Jr.), Betsy (Mrs. James W. Clark, Jr.). Legal sec., 192736; admitted to Fla. bar, 1936, U.S. Supreme Ct. bar, 1950; practice with husband in Miami, 1936-48; pvt. practice, Miami, 1948-59; judge Met. Ct. Dade County Fla., 1959—. Mem. exec. com. Women's Conf. Nat. Safety Council. 1960—, chmn., 1968-70; mem. bd. dirs. Nat. Safety Council, 1965—; mem. Nat. Hwy. Safety Adv. Com., 1967—; mem. registrants adv. bd. SSS World War II; pres. Dade County Tb Assn., 1960-62; exec. com. Fla. Tb and Respiratory Disease Assn., 1960-66; pres. Haven Sch. Mentally Retarded, 1958-60, sec., 1960-69. Trustee Andrew Coll., Cuthbert, Ga. Mem. Nat. (treas. 1961-62, corr. sec. 1962-63, v.p. 1963-64, pres. 1965-66). Fla. (pres. 1957-58) assns. women lawyers, Am. (ho. of dels. 1967—). Dade County bar assns., Fla. Bar, Internat. Fedn. Women Lawyers. Miami Bus. and Prof; Women's Club (pres. 1952-54), Nat. Fedn. Bus. and Profl. Women's Clubs (dir. dist. Fla. 1956-57). Kappa Beta Pi. Democrat. Methodist (supt. Sunday sch. 1948-54. chmn. ofcl. bd. 1957-60, trustee 1952-67, ofcl. bd. 1968—). Club: Zonta Internat. Home: 402 Como Av Coral Gables FL 33146 Office: 1351 N W 12th St Miami FL 33125

DAVIS, MAXINE, (Mrs. James Marshall McHugh), writer; b. Terre Haute, Ind.; d. Maxwell and Rose Davis; m. James Marshall McHugh, Apr. 3, 1943. Newspaper reporter for N.Y. World, United Press Assn., Detroit Free Press, 1924-28; proprietor syndicate, Capital News, 1926-30; free lance writer 1932—. Author: The Lost Generation, 1936; They Shall Not Want, 1937; Woman's Medical Problems, 1945; Through the Stratosphere, 1946; Facts About Menopause, 1951; The Sexual Repsonsibility of Woman. 1956; Sex and the Adolescent, 1958; How to Get the Most Out of Your Best Years, 1960; Every Woman's Book of Health, 1961; Sexual Responsibility in Marriage, 1963; Hope for the Childless Couple, 1963. Contbr. to nat. mags. Home: 3403 Ordway St NW Washington DC 20016

DAVIS, MELTON S., author; b. N.Y.C., Dec. 27, 1910; s. Charles Samillow, and Jean (Zicklin) D.; student U. Ala., 1928-30, U. Cal., 1936-37, Am. U., 1944, Centre Cultural Internat. de Royaumont, Asnieres, France, 1947-48; m. Ferda Firat, Nov. 27, 1968. Pub. relations officer Office Fgn. Liquidation Commr., State Dept., Paris, 1946-47; editor UNESCO, Paris, 1948-50; dir. radio Marshall Plan for Europe, Africa and Middle East, 1950-52; Mediterranean editor World mag., also polit. columnist N.Y. Post, 1954—; chief bur. Italy, MBS, 1962—. Served with AUS, World War II. Mem. Soc. Mag. Writers. Author: All Rome Trembled, 1957; The Voluptuaries, 1964. Address: 11 Via Scip one Gaetano 00197 Rome Italy

DAVIS, MENDELL MCLILLIAN, assn. exec.; b. Wiggins, Miss., Oct. 20, 1915; s. Thomas David and Lillian (Matheson) D.; B.S., Millsap Coll., 1937; postgrad. Am. U., 1937; m. Lois Taylor, Apr. 9, 1948. Staff mem. Jackson C. of C., 1940- 52, gen. mgr., 1952-60, exec. v.p., 1960—. Trustee Southeastern Ins. for C. of C. Execs., 1951-57, pres., 1955-56; mem. exec. operating council Inst. Orgn. Execs. at U. N.C., 1957-59. Served to lt. USNR, 1942-45. Mem. Am. C. of C. Execs. (sec.-treas., pres.), So., Miss. (pres. 1952) assns. chamber commerce execs., U.S. C. of C. (chmn. local com. 1959-60, mem. transp. and communications com. 1967- 68), Newcomen Soc. N.Am. (Miss. com. 1963—). Contbr. textbook in field. Home: 4106 Comanche Dr Jackson MS 39211 Office: Lamar Life Bldg Jackson MS 39201

DAVIS, MEYER, musician; b. Ellicott City, Md., Jan. 10, 1899; s. Sol and Rose (Benjamin) D.; student George Washington U., 1914-16; m. Hilda Emery, June 17, 1917; childrenVirginia, Garry, Emery, Marjorie. Head Meyer Davis' Music, soc. dance orchs., 1915—; pres. Meyer Davis' Music, Inc. Clubs: Nat. Press, Woodmont Country (Washington); Lotos, Lambs, Friars (N.Y.C.) Home: 101 Central Park W New York City NY 10023 Office: 119 W 57th St New York City NY 10019

DAVIS, MILES DEWEY, trumpet player, composer; b. Alton, Ill., May 25, 1926; studied music Juilliard Sch., 1945. Played in high school band; with Eddie Randall, St. Louis, 1941-43; with Parker, Coleman Hawkins, then on tour with Eckstine's Band, 1945-48; leader bands Royal Roost; appeared Paris Jazz Festival, 1949, N.Y.C., 1950, 51; on tour with Jazz Inc., 1952; appeared Cafe Bohemia, N.Y.C., 1957; background music for Elevator to the Gallows, French motion picture, Paris, 1958. Recordings include Modern Idiom, Trumpet Stylists, Cool and Quintet, Miles Ahead, Miles Davis Plus 19, Relaxing', Walkin', Cookin', Bags' Groove, Collector's Items, Birth of the Cool, Round About Midnight. Recipient JAY award poll for #4 jazz album Miles Smiles, 1967; named #1Trumpeteer, #2Jazz Man of Yr., #1Small Group, #2Jazz album for Miles Smiles, by 3d Ann. Readers poll, 1968; named #1Combo, #1Trumpet, #2record of yr. for Sorcerer, 16th Internat. Jazz Critics Poll, 1968.*

DAVIS, MORGAN JONES, geologist; b. Anson, Tex., Nov. 19, 1898; s. John Wesley and Gabrella (Jones) D.; student Tex. Christian U., 1916-18; B.A. in Geology, U. of Tex., 1925; student Harvard Grad. Sch. of Bus. Adminstrn., 1947; D.Eng. (hon.), Colo. Sch. Mines, 1964; m. Veta Clare Moore, Aug. 8, 1926; childrenMorgan J., Jr., James H. Worked on Tex. cattle ranch, 1915-16; engr., later asst. supt., Tulsa Spavinaw Water Project, Tulsa, Okls., 1921-24; became geologist Humble Oil & Refining Co., 1925; with Nederlandsche Kolonidale Petroleum Maatschappij, geologist in Java, resident geologist producing fields, Sumatra, Indonesia, 1929-34; with Humble Oil & Refining Co., 1934, chief geologist, 1941, mgr. exploration dept., 1946, dir. in charge exploration, 1948, v.p., 1951-56, exec. v.p., 1956-57, pres., 1957-61, chmn. board, chief exec. officer, 1961- 63; dep. chmn. bd. dirs. Fed. Res. Bank of Dallas, 1961-63; dir. First City Nat. Bank, Houston; petroleum cons. Bd. trustees Kinkaid Sch., Houston; mem. vis. com. Grad. Sch. Bus. Adminstrn., Harvard, 1963-68; chmn. adv. council Geology Found., U. Tex. Bd. dirs., past pres. Nat. Space Hall of Fame. Recipient Distinguished Service award, Tex. Mid-Continent Oil and Gas Assn., 1960. Mem. Philos. Soc. Tex., Houston Geol. Soc. (life), Tex. Hist. Assn., Am. Assn. Petroleum Geologists (pres. 1952-53), Am. Inst. Profl. Geologists, Am. Petroleum Inst. (dir.), Mid-Continent Oil and Gas Assn., Am. Geog. Soc., Am. Inst. Mining, Metall. and Petroleum Engrs. Tex. Acad. Sci., Am. Geophys. Union, Geol. Soc. Am., Sigma Iota Epsilon, Delta Kappa Epsilon, Sigma Gamma Epsilon. Mason. Clubs: Harvard Business School, Houston Country, Ramada, River Oaks, Petroleum, Bayou (Houston); Boston (New Orleans); Mill Reef (Antigua, W.I.); St. Charles Bay Hunting (Rockport, Tex.); Twenty-Five Years of Petroleum Industry (pres. 1963); Harvard (Boston); Marco Polo (N.Y.C.). Home: 3207 Inwood Dr Houston, TX 77019. Office: Capital Nat Bank Bldg Houston, TX 77002.

DAVIS, NATHANAEL VINING, mfr.; b. Pitts., June 26, 1915; s. Edward Kirk and Rhea Ada (Reineman) D.; grad. Harvard, 1938; m. Lois Howard Thompson, 1941; children—James Howard Dow, Katharine Vining. With Alcan Aluminium Ltd. (formerly Aluminium Ltd.), 1939—, pres., dir., 1947—; dir. Alcan Aluminum Corp., Cleve., other Alcan group subsidiaries, Can. Life Assurance Co., Toronto, Bank of Montreal. Home: 3050 Trafalgar Av Montreal 218 Quebec Canada Office: 1 Place Ville Marie Montreal Quebec Canada

DAVIS, NATHANIEL, govt. ofcl.; b. Boston, Apr. 12, 1925; s. Harvey Nathaniel and Alice Marian (Rohde) D.; grad. Phillips Exeter Acad., 1942; A.B., Brown, 1944, LL.D., 1970; M.A., Fletcher Sch. Law and Diplomacy, 1947, Ph.D., 1960; postgrad. Russian lang. and area, Columbia, Cornell U., Middlebury Coll., 1953-54; U. Central de Venezuela, 1961-62; m. Elizabeth Kirkbride Creese, Nov. 24, 1956; children—Margaret Morton, Helen Miller, James Creese, Thomas Rohde. Asst. history Tufts Coll., 1947; joined U.S. Fgn. Service, 1947; 3d sec., Prague, Czechoslovakia, 1947-49; vice consul, Florence, Italy, 1949-52; 2d sec., Rome, Italy, 1952-53, Moscow, USSR, 1954-56; Soviet desk officer State Dept., 1956-60; 1st sec., Caracas, Venezuela, 1960-62; spl. asst. to dir. Peace Corps, 1962-63, dept. asso. dir., 1963-65; U.S. minister to Bulgaria, 1965-66; sr. staff Nat. Security Council, 1966-68; U.S. ambassador, Guatemala, 1968—. Lectr., U.S. history Centro Venezolano-Americano, 1961; lectr. Russian, Soviet history Howard U., 1962-65, 66-68. Bd. dirs., chmn. Inner City Childrens and Youth Program, Nat. Capital area Council Chs., 1958-59. Served to lt. (j.g.) USNR, 1944-46. Recipient Cinco Aguilas Blancas Alpinism award Venezuelan Andean Club, 1962. Mem. Am. Fgn. Service Assn. (bd. dirs., vice chmn 1964), Council on Fgn. Relations, Am. Hist. Assn., Phi Beta Kappa. Mem. United Ch. Christ. Club: Cosmos. Home: care Fife 613 Hudson St Hoboken, NJ 07030

DAVIS, NELSON VINCENT, educator; b. Pitts., June 12, 1921; s. Harry H. and Marie (Miller) D.; student Eastman Sch. Music, 1939-41; A.B., Franklin and Marshall Coll., 1943; M.A., Princeton, 1946, Ph.D., 1957; m. Barbara Williams, Apr. 30, 1947; children—Molly, Matthew. Instr. English, Princeton, 1945-46; asst. prof. Marietta Coll., 1947-56; faculty Ripon (Wis.) Coll., 1956—, now prof. English, chmn. dept. Served with AUS, 1946-47. Fulbright fellow, Italy, 1950-51. Recipient Severy award, 1959, Uhrig award, 1967. Mem. Phi Beta Kappa. Home: 223 Thorne St Ripon, WI 54971.

DAVIS, NOAH KNOWLES, pub. utility cons.; b. Atlanta, Feb. 20, 1904; s. Archibald H. and Susan (Topliff) D.; B.S. in Elec. Engring., Ga. Inst. Tech., 1925; E.E., Cornell U., 1926; m. Jean Nutting, June 21, 1932; 1 dau., Jean (Mrs. Daniel F. Flowers). Transmission engr. Ga. Power Co., 1926-32; chief engr. Ga. Pub. Service Commn., 1933-41; chief power allocation WPB, 1942- 44; dir. utilities div. Ga. Pub. Service Commn., 1945-55; dir. rates Tenn. Gas. Transmission Co., 1956-58, v.p., 1959-67, sr. v.p., asst. to pres., 1967-69, cons., 1969—. Guest lectr. Ia. State U., 1963, Practicing Law Inst., N.Y.C., 1954, Am. Law Inst., 1967, AGA Financial Sem., 1968, guest speaker, cons. in field; admitted to Ga. bar, 1952. Chmn. toll rate subcom. Nat. Assn. R.R. and Utilities Commrs., 1951. Registered profl. engr., Ga., Tex. Mem. Nat., Tex. secs. profl. engrs., Ga. Engring. Soc., Am., Ga., Fed. Power bar assns., Am. Judicature Soc., Houston C. of C., Houston Engring. and Sci. Soc. Democrat. Presbyn. Rotarian. Clubs: Piedmont Driving (Atlanta); National Lawyers (Washington); Petroleum (Houston). Home; 3420 Overbrook Lane Houston TX 77027 Office: P O Box 2511 Houston TX 77001

DAVIS, O. C., natural gas pipeline co. exec.; b. Roseclare, Ill., May 7, 1920; s. Luther and Elizabeth (St. John) D.; B.S. in Mech. Engring., A. and M. Coll. Tex.; m. Thelma Sheery, Nov. 14, 1942; children—Henry T., Jon F. with Natural Gas Pipeline Co. Am., 1947—, v.p. charge storage, 1963- 66; exec. v.p., now pres., also dir. Served to capt. USAAF, World War II. Mem. Am., Soc. gas assns., Ind. Natural Gas Assn. Am., Am. Inst. Mining and Metall. Engrs. Club: University (Chgo.). Home: Rural Rt 1 Box 636 Pheasant Trail Frankfort IL 60423 Office: 122 S Michigan Av Chicago IL 60603

DAVIS, OSCAR ESKO, army officer; b. Tucson, July 18, 1918; s. Oscar W. and Leta Katherine (Hoffman) D.; B.S., U. Ariz., 1941; m. Patty Ferguson, Nov. 8, 1941; children—Worthen A., Candace J. (Mrs. Charles A. Barnes), Norman O., Rodney E. Commd. 2d lt. U.S. Army, 1941, advanced through grades to brig. gen., 1967; battalion comdr., Korea, 1952; dir. airborne dept. Inf. Sch., Ft. Benning, Ga., 1953; chief air delivery br. Office Research and Devel., Dept. Army, 1961-64; comdg. officer Support Command, 101st Airborne Div., 1964-66; asst. div. comdr. 1st Cav. Div., Vietnam, 1967-68; comdr. Army Tng. Center, Ft. Benning, 1968-69; chief staff XVIII Airborne Corps, Ft. Bragg, N.C., 1970—. Decorated D.S.M., D.F.C., Silver Star with oak leaf cluster, Legion of Merit with oak leaf cluster, Bronze Star with 2 oak leaf clusters, Air medal with 33 oak leaf clusters, Army Commendation medal with oak leaf cluster. Episcopalian (lay leader 1954—). Home: 5 Hoyle Plaza Fort Bragg NC 28307 Office: Chief Staff XVIII Airborne Corps Fort Bragg NC 28307

DAVIS, OSCAR HIRSH, U.S. judge; b. N.Y.C., Feb. 27, 1914; s. Jacob and Minnie (Robison) D.; A.B., Harvard, 1934; LL.B., Columbia, 1937. Admitted to N.Y. bar, 1938; pvt. practice, N.Y.C., 1937-39; with Dept. Justice, 1939-42, 46-62, first asst. to solicitor gen., 1954-62; assoc. judge U.S. Ct. Claims, 1962-. Served to capt. USAAF, 1942-46. Mem. Am., Fed. bar assns., Am. Law Inst., N.Y. County Lawyers Assn., N.Y. State Bar Assn. Home: 1101 3d St SW Washington, DC 20024. Office: US Ct Claims Washington, DC 20005.

DAVIS, OSSIE, author, actor; b. Cogdell, Ga., Dec. 18, 1917; s. Kince Charles and Laura (Cooper) D.; student Howard U., 1935-38; m. Ruby Ann Wallace, Dec. 9, 1948; childrenNora, guy, LaVerne. Appeared on Broadway as Jeb Turner in Jeb, 1946, Jacques in Wisteria Trees, 1950, Cicero in Jamaica, 1957, Walter Lee Younger in A Raisin in the Sun, 1959, Purlie Victorious Judson in Purlie Victorious (also author), 1962; in motion picture The Cardinal as Father Gillis, 1963; in the Zula and the Zayda, 1965. Mem. Actors Equity Assn., N.A.A.C.P. Home: 44 Cortland Av New Rochelle NY 10801

DAVIS, PAUL HERBERT, college cons.; b. Sutherland, Ia., June 2, 1897; s. Dr. Warren Bartlett and Nettie (Adams) D.; B.S., Stanford University, 1922, E.E., 1923; m. Helen Brack, June 16, 1928; children—Herbert Paul, Brack, Forster Adams. General mgr. Bd. of Athletic Control, Stanford U., 1922- 25; mgr. Empresas Electricas Brasileiras, Reeife, Maceio and Natal, Brazil, 1928-33; mgr. Emergency Relief Adminstrn., San Francisco, 1934- 35; gen. sec. Stanford U., 1936-46, v.p. devel., 1946-50; coll. cons. Readers' Digest, 1956—. Bd. dirs. San Francisco Community Chest, 1925-28; bd. dirs. Stanford Fund and Stanford Assos., 1936-47. Served as 2d lt., aviation pilot, U.S. Army, 1917-20. Republican. Mem. Soc. of Friends. Club: California (Los Angeles). Home: Barrington Plaza 11740 Wilshire Blvd Los Angeles CA 90025

DAVIS, PAUL P., motor freight co. exec.; b. Goldsboro, N.C., Aug. 21, 1915; s. John Samuel and Mary (Porter) D.; B.S., U. N.C., 1935; m. Margaret Mebane, June 12, 1937; childrenPaul Michael and Allen Mebane (twins), John Kent. With McLean Trucking Co., Winston-Salem, N.C., 1943-, v.p. sales, dir., 1948-55, pres., dir., 1955-61, pres., chmn. exec. com., dir., 1961- 70, chmn. bd., chief exec. officer, dir., 1970—; mem. exec. com., dir. Transport mgmt. Co., Dallas. Transport Ins. Co., Dallas; dir. N.C. Nat. Bank. Winston-Salem. Pres., So. Motor Carriers Rate Conf.' Mem. Am. Trucking Assn. (v.p. at large), Am. Soc. Traffic and Transp., Trucking Employers (bd.dir.), Traffic Club Winston-Salem. Elk. Clubs: Twin City, Oldtown Country (Winston-Salem). Home: 1055 Kent Rd Winston-Salem, NC 27104. Office: P O Box 213 Winston-Salem, NC 27102.

DAVIS, PEARCE, economist, educator, arbitrator; b. Washington, Mar. 3, 1908; s. Harold and Ida Adele (Pearce) D.; B.S., U. Pa., 1928; A.M., George Washington U., 1931; Ph.D., Harvard, 1938; m. Lucia Banks, Bates, June 20, 1929; childrenLucia Lee Newcomb, Michael Davis, Instr., tutor econs. Harvard, 1934-38, head instr., tutor, 1938-41; instr. Radcliffe Coll., 1939-41; asst. prof. econs. Hunter Coll., 1941-43; dir. dept. indsl. engring. Ill. Inst. Tech., 1947-53, prof. econs., chmn. dept. bus. and econs., 1946-; vis. lectr. Clark U., 1940-41. Prin. economist War Labor Bd., Region 2, N.Y., 1943, br. chief, asst. dir. nat. wage stblzn. div., 1943- 44, pub. mem. wage adjustment bd. constrn. industry, 1944-45, chmn., pub. mem. Nat. Telephone Commn., 1945, Regional Wage Stblzn. Bd., Region 1, Boston, 1946; pub. mem. acting chmn. Nat. Meat Packing Commn., Chgo., 1946-47; mem. presdl. bd. inquiry labor dispute in meat packing industry, 1947; mem. Meat Packing Panel, 1950; cons. Nat. WSB, 1951; mem. nat. labor panel Am. Arbitration Assn., 1947-; arbitrator Fed. Mediation and Conciliation Service, 1947-. Mem. Am. Econ. Assn., Am. Soc. Engring. Edn., Nat. Acad. Arbitrators (chmn. ann. meeting program 1958, gov. 1958-), Indsl. Relations Research Assn., Pi Gamma Mu, Sigma Iota Epsilon. Author: (with H. J. Meyer) Report on Wage Stabilization Policy in the Operating Telephone Industry, 1945, The Development of the American Glass Industry, 1949; (with Gerald J. Matchett) Modern Labor Economics; an Analysis of Labor-Management Relations, 1954. Editor: (with H. J. Meyer) Labor Dispute Settlements in the Telephone Industry, 1942-45, 1946. Contbr. chpts.; Fiscal Policy for Total War (W. L. Crum and others), 1942; (with H. J. Meyer) Terminal Report to the President, National War Labor Board, 1948, Arbitration Today, 1955. Home: 216 S Stone Av LaGrange IL 60525 Office: Technology Center Chicago L 60616

DAVIS, PETER FRANK, television writer and producer; b. Los Angeles, Jan. 2, 1937; s. Frank and Tess (Slesinger) D.; A.B magna cum laude, Harvard, 1957; m. Johanna Mankiewicz, Sept. 13, 1959; children—Timothy, Nicholas. Editorial asst. N.Y. Times, 1958-59; free-lance writer TV and mags., 1959-61; writer Sextant Film Prodns., 1961-64; asso. producer television documentaries NBC News, 1964; writer, producer television documentaries CBS News, N.Y.C., 1965—. Served with AUS, 1959-60. Recipient awards for television documentary Saturday Rev., 1970, 71, award Nat. Acad. TV Arts and Scis., 1971, George Foster Peabody award, 1971. Television documentaries include The Heritage of Slavery, 1968, Hunger in America, 1968, The Battle of East St. Louis, 1969, The Selling of the Pentagon, 1971. Home: 63 Charles St New York City NY 10014 Office: 524 W 57th St New York City NY 10019

DAVIS, PHIL, educator, physician; b. Mt. Vernon, Tex., Feb. 2, 1924; s. Roger Franklin and Anne (Barrett) D.; student Tex. A. and M. U., 1940-43, Stanford, 1943; M.D., Baylor U., 1947; m. Joyce Elaine Stripling, Mar. 27, 1946; children—Roger, Diane, Mark Owen, Philip Scott. intern, St. Louis City Hosp., 1947-48, Parkland Hosp., Dallas, 1948-49; resident Jefferson Davis Hosp., Houston, 1949-50, 53-55; pvt. practice medicine, specializing in internal medicine, Mt. Vernon, 1950-51; instr. to prof. medicine Baylor U. Coll. Medicine, Houston, 1955—. Served with AUS, 1943-46; to 1st lt., M.C., U.S. Army, 1951-53. Diplomate Am. Bd. Internal Medicine. Fellow A.C.P.; mem. Alpha Omega Alpha. Home: 4314 Cheena St Houston TX 77035 Office: 1200 Moursund St Houston TX 77025

DAVIS, RALPH LANIER, educator; b. Kennedy, Ala., Sept. 10, 1921; s. Oran and Ethel (Richardson) D.; B.S., Auburn U., 1943; M.S., Purdue U., 1948, Ph.D., 1950; m. Betty Simpson, Aug. 20, 1943. Asst. prof. Prudue U., 1950-53, asso. prof., 1953-57, prof. dept. agronomy, 1957—, asst. dean Grad. Sch., 1965—, asso. dir. div. sponsored program, 1966—. Vis. prof. Ore. State U., 1959-60. Chmn., Nat. Alfalfa Improvement Conf., 1963-64. Served to lt. (j.g.) USNR, 1943-46. Fellow Am. Soc. Agronomy, A.A.A.S.; mem. Crop Sci. Soc. Am. (pres.-elect, gen. program chmn. 1962, pres. 1963), Sigma Xi (local v.p.), Alpha Zeta, Omicron Delta Kappa, Gamma Sigma Delta, Phi Kappa Phi. Editor: Crop Sci. 1964-67. Home: 906 Essex St West Lafayette IN 47906

DAVIS, RALPH M., utility exec.; b. Douthat, Okla., Aug. 4, 1919; s. Carl and Edna (Crystal) D.; student Linfield Coll., McMinnville, Ore., 1937-40; B.S., U. Wash., 1946, LL.B., 1948; m. Evelyn S. Steahely, Feb. 11, 1944; children—Robert Ralph, William Allan, John Michael. Admitted to Wash. bar, 1948; pvt. practice, Belingham, 1948-49; law reporter Supreme Ct. Wash., 1949-52; asst. atty. gen., legislative counsel to Gov. Wash., 1952-55; chmn. Wash. Pub. Service Commn., 1955-57; with Puget Sound Power & Light Co., 1957—, v.p., sec., 1961-62, pres., 1962—, chief exec., also dir.; pres., dir. Puget Properties, Inc.; dir. Tally Corp., Puget Western Inc., Diamond Ice & Storage Co. Chmn. Gov.'s Adv. Com. Dept. Commerce and Econ. Devel.; dir. Edison Electric Inst. and other trade assns.; trustee Internat. Trade Fair, Seattle Symphony Orch.; mem. citizens adv. com. North Cascades Nat. Park, Bonneville Power Adminstrn.; trustee Seattle C.of C. Mem. Am., Wash., Seattle-King County bar assns., Nat. Council Nat. Planning Assn., Seattle Community Devel. Round Table. Republican. Clubs: Rainier (pres.), Wash. Athletic. Home: 2727 104th St SE Bellevue WA 98004 Office: Puget Power Bldg Bellevue WA 98004

DAVIS, RAYMOND GILBERT, marine corps officer; b. Fitzgerald, Ga., Jan. 13, 1915; s. Raymond Roy and Zelma (Tribby) D.; B.S. with honors, Ga. Inst. Tech., 1938; grad. Jr. Amphibious Sch., 1947, Sr. Amphibious Sch., 1954, Nat. War Coll., 1960; m. Willa Knox Heafner, Apr. 25, 1942; children—Raymond Gilbert, Gordon Miles, Willa Kay. Commd. 2d lt. USMC, 1938, advanced through grades to lt. gen., 1970; various assignments on ships and shore, 1939- 42; participated in Guadalcanal Tulagi landings, capture and def. of Guadalcanal, Eastern New Guinea and Cape Gloucester campaigns and Peleliu operations, World War II; tactical insp. Quantico Marine Corps Schs., 1944-45, chief inf. sect., 1945-47; assigned 1st Provisional Marine Brigade, Guam, 1947-49; insp.-instr. 9th Marine Corps Res. Inf. Bn., Chgo., 1946-50; comdr. 1st Bn., 7th marines, Korea, 1950; exec. officer 7th Marines, 1950-51; asst. G-3 Hdgrs. Marine Corps, 1951-53; asst. dir., later dir. Sr. Course Marine Corps Schs., 1955-57; asst. G-2 Hdqrs. Marine Corps, 1957-59; chief analyses br. J-2, staff, comdr. in chief Europe, 1960-63; asst. div. comdr. 3d Marine Div., FMF, Okinawa, 1963-64; comdg. gen. SEATO Expeditionary Brigade, EXLIGTAS, P.I., 1964, 9th Marine Expeditionary Brigade, China Sea Contingency Operations, 1964; asst. chief staff, G-1, Hdqrs. Marine Corps, 1964-68; dep. comdg. gen. Provisional Corps, Vietnam, 1968; comdg. gen. 3d Marine Div., Vietnam, 1968-70; comdg. gen. Marine Corps. Devel. and Edn., Quantico, Va., 1970-71; now asst. comdt. U.S. Marine Corps. Active local Boy Scouts Am., Little League, Babe Ruth League. Bd. dirs. U.S. Marine Youth Found. Decorated Medal of Honor, Navy Cross, D.S.M., Silver Star with gold star, Legion of Merit with Combat V and gold star, Bronze Star with Combat V, Purple Heart. Mem. 1st Marine Div. Assn. (pres. 1968,) Marine Corps Assn. (dir.). Methodist. Contbr. to Marine Corps Gazette. Home: care JT Davis Milner GA 30257

DAVIS, REGINALD STUART, govt. ofcl.; b. Saskatoon, Sask., Can., Sept. 21, 1915; s. Edward John and Agnes Clara (Bowerman) D.; A.B., San Diego State Coll., 1939; postgrad. U. Cal. at Los Angeles, 1939-40; m. Barbara Lawrence Russell, Nov. 22, 1941; 1 son, Christopher Stuart. Civil radio engr. Army Signal Corps, P.I., 1947-48; radio engr., Middle East, 1949-52; electronic specialist Dept. Def., 1952-54; police adviser communications, Indonesia, 1955-59; pub. safety adviser, 1960—; asst. pub. safety officer AID, Vietnam, 1960-71. Served with USAAF, 1941-47. Decorated Bronze Star; Govt. Vietnam honor. Mem. Am. Orchid Soc. Author: Philippine Orchids, 1952. Home: 4209 46th St San Diego CA 92115 Office: CORDS PSD APO San Francisco CA 96243

DAVIS, RENNIE, orgn. ofcl.; b. Lansing, Mich., May 23, 1940; s. John Cordon and Dorothy (Roberts) D.; B.A., Oberlin Coll., 1962; student U. Ill., 1962-63, U. Mich., 1963-65, U. Chgo., 1965. Nat. dir. econ. research and action project Students for Demoratic Soc., 1964-68; community organizer JOIN Community Union, 1965-67; dir. Center Radical Research, Chgo., 1967; travel to N. Vietnam, 1967; nat. coordinator Summer of Support. 1968. Nat. Mblzn. Com. to End War in Vietnam, 1968—; dir. anti-war demonstration projects, 1968—; parttime tchr. labor edn. Roosevelt U. Address: 28 E Jackson St Chicago IL 60604

DAVIS, RICHARD BEALE, educator; b. Accomack, Va., June 3, 1907; s. Henry Woodhouse and Margaret Josephine (Wills) D.; A.B., Randolph-Macon Coll., 1927, Litt. D., 1955; A.M., U. Va., 1933, Ph. D., 1936; m. Lois Camp Bullard, Aug. 25, 1936. Instr. English, McGuire U. Sch., Richmond, Va., 1927-30, Randolph-Macon Acad., 1930-32; instr., teaching fellow U. Va., 1933-36; asso. prof. Mary Washington Coll. U. Va., 1936- 40; asso. prof. U. S.C., 1940-46, prof. English, 1946-47; prof. English, in charge Am. lit. U. Tenn. 1947-62, prof. Am. lit., 1962—. Vis. prof. Am. lit. U. Va., summers, 1938-42, U. Tex., 1949; research grantee, Huntington Library, 1947, 50, Am. Philos. Soc., 1951-52, 58, 62, Folger Library, 1955, Am. Council Learned Socs., 1966; Fulbright vis. prof. U. Oslo, Norway, 1953-54; U.S. State Dept. lectr. to Indian univs., 1957; Guggenheim fellow, 1947, 60-61; vis. prof. Claremont Grad. Sch., 1957, Duke, 1965; chmn. So. Humanities Conf., 1960—. Served USNR, 1943-46. Named Col. Williamsburg. Mem. S. Atlantic Modern Lang. Assn. (pres. 1964-65), Modern Lang. Assn., Bibliog. Soc. Am., Am. Assn. U. Profs., Raven Soc., Internat. Assn. Profs. English, Blue Key, Phi Beta Kappa, Phi Kappa Phi, Lambda Chi Alpha, Sigma Upsilon. Episcopalian. Club: Colonnade. Author: Francis Walker Gilmer: Life and Learning in Jefferson's Virginia, 1939; (with Fredson Bowers) George Sandys: A Bibliographical Catalogue of Printed Editions in England to 1700, 1950; George Sandys. Poet-Adventurer, 1955; The Abbe Correa in American, 1955; William Fitzhugh and His Chesapeake World, 1676-1701, 1963; Intellectual Life in Jefferson's Virginia, 1790-1830 (Am. Assn. State and Local History award 1963), 1964; American Literature through Bryant, 1969. Contbr. articles to profl. jours. Editor: Jeffersonian America; Tenn. Studies in Lit., 1956- -; Correspondence of Thomas Jefferson and Francis Walker Gilmer; Chivers' Life of Poe, 1952; The Colonial Virginia Satirist, 1967; Collected Poems of Samuel Davis, 1723-1761, 1968; The Wept of Wish-ton- Wish (Cooper), 1970; The Letters of the British Spy (William Wirt), 1970; (with C.H. Holman, L. Rubin, Jr.) Southern Writing, 1970. Co-editor: American Cultural History, 1607-1829, 1961. Address: 543 Noelton Dr Knoxville TN 37919

DAVIS, RICHARD HARDING, banker; b. Aurora, Mo., Apr. 5, 1916; s. Frank A. and Nell M. (Duroni) D.; student U. Mo., 1934-38; m. Aurelia Costea, July 16, 1964; children by previous marriageBarbara (Mrs. F. Bruce Correll), Carolyn M., Patricia F., Janet E., Richard Harding. Examiner, FHLB, Cin., 1941; with Hall, Kistler & Co., C.P.A.'s, Canton, O., 1945-65, partner, 1956-65; exec. v.p. Harter Bank & Trust Co., Canton, O., 1965-, also dir.; dir. Gibbs Mfg. Co., Capital Plastics Co., Helfrich Die Casting Co. Trustee Canton Art Inst. Served to capt. AUS, 1941- 45. C.P.A., Ohio. Mem. Am. Inst. C.P.A.'s, Ohio Soc. C.P.A.'s, Ohio Bankers Assn., Greater Canton C. of C. (treas.), Am. Legion. Clubs: Canton; Congress Lake (Hartville, O.). Home: 8821 N Market Av North Canton OH 44721 Office: 126 Central Plaza N Canton, OH 44702.

DAVIS, RICHARD JOSEF, aerospace co. exec.; b. N.Y.C., Feb. 9, 1917; s. Emanuel S. and Betty (Alexander) D.; B.A., U. Wis., 1939; m. Helyne E. Weber, Dec. 16, 1942; childrenRichard Josef, Linda Anne. Corr., Washington bur. Newsweek mag., 1940-58; with Douglas Aircraft Co., 1958-, dir. pub. relations, 1960-, v.p., 1963-67, v.p. for external relations McDonnell Douglas Corp., St. Louis, 1967-. Served to lt. USNR, 1942-45. Mem. Pub. Relations Soc. Am., Sigma Delta Chi. Clubs: National Press (Washington) : St. Louis Press. Home: 9 Ladue Crest Lane St Louis, MO 63124. Office: Lambert Field St Louis, MO 63166.

DAVIS, RICHARD MARDEN, lawyer; b. West Somerville, Mass., May 26, 1912; s. Henry C. Jr. and Dell (Marden) D.; grad. Phillips Acad. 1929; B.A., Yale, 1933, U. Cambridge Eng., 1935; postgrad Harvard Law Sch., 1935-36; m. Nancy Newton, July 10, 1935; childrenPamela, Richard Marden. Admitted to Mass bar, 1936, Colo. bar, 1937; partner Davis, Graham & Stubbs, predecessor firms, Denver, 1937—. Dir. Am. Crystal Sugar Co., United Bank of Denver, Van Schaack & Co. Pres. Colo. Expenditure Council, 1957-62; civilian aide to sec. army, 1950-52; mem. Adminstrv. Conf. of U.S. 1960-62. Trustee Denver Art Mus., Denver Mus. Natural History, Denver Country Day Sch. Served from 2d, lt. to lt. col., Air Transport Command, USAAF, 1942- 45. Decorated Bronze Star medal. Mem. Am., Colo. (bd. gov.), Denver (pres. 1959-60) bar assns., Colo. C. of C. Am. Inst. Research. Rotarian (pres. Denver 1969-70). Home: 860 Gaylord St Denver CO 80206 Office: 818 17 St Denver CO 80202

DAVIS, RICHARD SMITH, metallurgist, educator; b. Winnipeg, Man., Can., Mar. 1, 1926; s. Richard E. and Suesane (Smith) D.; B.A. Sc., U. Toronto (Ont., Can.), 1951, M.A. Sc., 1952, Ph.D., 1954; m. Helena R. Nelson, May 10, 1952; children—Richard Robert, William Paul. Came to U.S., 1954, naturalized 1960. Research fellow Harvard, 1954-56, asst. prof. metallurgy, 1956-59; mem. sr. staff Arthur D. Little, Inc., Cambridge, Mass., 1959-62, v.p., 1962-68; prof., dean Coll. Tech. U.N.H., 1968—. Dir. Greenfield Components, Inc., Kinimatics Inc., Materials Devel. Corp. Served with Royal Canadian Army, 1944-46. Contbr. articles profl. jours. Home: Riverview Rd Durham NH 03824

DAVIS, ROBERT FISHER, lawyer; b. Indpls., Nov. 14, 1905; s. Samuel Newsom and Bertha (Baldwin) D.; LL.B., Ind. U., 1927; A.B., George Washington U., 1930, M.P.L., 1930, J.D., 1930; M.A., Am. U., 1932; m. Margaret Louise Warren, Jan. 14, 1943; children—Robert Warren, Steven Lamont. Admitted to Ind. bar, 1927, N.Y. bar, D.C. bars, 1932, also U.S. Supreme Ct.; founder, partner firm Stevens, Davis, Miller & Mosher, and predecessor, Washington, 1933—. Mem. Fairfax County Sch. Bd., 1952-60, chmn. 1964. County and state rep. Democratic Conv., 1952; alternate del. Va. Dem. Conv., 1952. Served as aviator USNR, World War II. Mem. Am. Bar Assn., Am. Patent Law Assn., Am. Chem. Soc., Chemists Club. Mason. Author: Flight Through Instruments, 1943. Contbr. articles to profl. jours. Home: 1299 S Ocean Blvd Boca Raton FL 33432 Office: 1911 Jefferson Davis Hwy Crystal Mall I Arlington VA 22202

DAVIS, ROBERT GUY, utility exec.; b. Dallas, Sept. 22, 1935; s. Robert Enos and Marge (Stuart) D.; B.A., LL.B., St. Mary's U., 1959; m. Helen Machock, Feb. 7, 1959; children—Guy, Gregory, Melanie, Stephanie. Admitted to Tex. bar, 1959; with Lone Star Gas Co., 1961—, corp. sec., asst. gen. counsel, 1969—. Named Outstanding Young Leader, Nat. Council Cath. Youth, 1956. Mem. State Bar Tex., Dallas Bar Assn., Am. Soc. Corp. Secretaries. Clubs: Cadence Dance (pres. 1969); Toastmasters Internat. (pres. Dallas 1962; Outstanding area gov. 1964; dist. gov. 1966). Roman Catholic (chmn. adv. council). K.C. Home: 1122 Dumont St Richardson TX 75080 Office: 301 S Harwood St Dallas, TX 75201.

DAVIS, ROBERT PAUL, physician, educator; b. Malden, Mass., July 3, 1926; s. Samuel and Sarah (Lemberg) D.; A.B. cum laude, Harvard, 1947, M.D. magna cum laude, 1951, A.M., 1955; A.M. (ad eundem), Brown U., 1967; m. Ruby Black, Sept. 5, 1953; children—Edward L., John R., Elizabeth A. Intern Peter Bent Brigham Hosp., Boston, 1951-52, asst. medicine, 1952-55, sr. asst. resident physician, 1955-56, chief resident physician, 1956-57; jr. fellow Soc. of Fellows of Harvard, 1952-55; asst. medicine Harvard Med. Sch., 1956-57; asst. prof. medicine U. N.C., 1957-59; asst. prof. medicine Albert Einstein Coll. Medicine, 1959-66, asso. prof., 1967; career scientist Health Research Council, N.Y.C., 1962-67; asst. vis. physician Bronx Municipal Hosp. Center, 1959-65, asso. vis. physician, 1966-67; physician in chief Miriam Hosp., Providence, 1967—; prof. med. sci. Brown U., 1967—, leader sect. in medicine div. biol. and med. scis., 1971—. Traveling fellow Commonwealth Fund, 1965-66; Willard O. Thompson Meml. Traveling Scholar, A.C.P., 1965; vis. scientist Inst. Biol. Chemistry of U. Copenhagen, 1965-66; mem. corp. Butler Hosp., Jewish Family and Children's Service; trustee Interhosp. Organ Bank (Boston), 1969, treas., 1970. Served as ensign, USNR, 1944-46, as lt. (j.g.) M.C., 1951. Fellow A.A.A.S., A.C.P.; mem. Am. Fedn. Clin. Research, Harvey Soc., Biophys. Soc., N.Y. Acad. Medicine, Am. Heart Assn., N.Y. Acad. Sci., Am. Soc. Cell Biology, Soc. Gen. Physiologists, Am. Physiol. Soc., Am. Soc. Artificial Internal Organs, Internat. Soc. Nephrology, Clin. Diabetes Assn. R.I. (pres. 1970-71), Providence, R.I. med. socs., Am. Soc. Nephrology, Phi Beta Kappa, Sigma Xi. Asso. editor R.I. Med. Jour., 1971—. Contbr. articles profl. jours. Research on ion transport and cell metabolism. Home: 75 Prospect St Providence RI 02906 Office: Miriam Hospital Providence RI 02906

DAVIS, ROBERT S., ins. co. exec.; b. Stillwater, Minn., Aug. 5, 1914; s. Jed H. and Margarita (Culver) D.; B.B.A. cum laude, U. Minn., 1934; m. Lorrain Lembke, June 15, 1938; children—Gretchen (Mrs. Thomas H. Underwood), Barbara (Mrs. John W. Sample). Security analyst Minn. Mut. Life Ins. Co., 1935-36, First Bank Stock Corp., 1936-40; rep. St. Paul office John Nuveen & Co., municipal bonds, 1940-45; with St. Paul Fire & Marine Ins. Co., 1945—, v.p., investment officer, 1962-69, now dir.; financial v.p. St. Paul Cos., Inc., 1969—; dir. St. Paul Mercury Ins. Co., Western Life Ins. Co., Otter

Tail Power Co., Webb Pub. Co. Bd. dirs. Tozer Found. Home: 1029 3d Av South Stillwater MN 55082 Office: 385 Washington St St Paul MN 55102

DAVIS, ROBERT TYRRELL, educator; b. N.Y.C., Aug. 24, 1920; s. William Pitt and Cora (Allen) D.; B.A., Harvard, 1942, M.B.A., 1946, D.C.S., 1954; m. Hazel Harriet deHaas, Sept. 28, 1946; children—Stephen Hunt, Peter Allen, John Andrew. Asst. prof. St. Lawrence U., 1946-68, Dartmouth, 1948-52, Harard Bus. Sch., 1957-58; prof. Inst. pour L'Etude des Methodes Chefs D'Enterprises, Lausanne, Switzerland, 1957-58; prof. marketing Stanford Bus. Sch., 1958—, dir. Sloan Program, 1958—. Vice pres. marketing Varian, 1964-66; dir. Omark Industries, Computing & Software, Inc., Blitz Weinhard Co., Granite Rock Co., Northrop Tech. Devel. Inc. Served with AUS, 1943-46. Recipient Salgo-Noren Distinguished Tchr. award, 1968. Mem. Am. Marketing Assn. Author articles in field. Home: 14410 Miranda Rd Los Altos Hills CA 94022 Office: Stanford Univ Grad Sch Bus Stanford CA 94305

DAVIS, ROBERT WILSON, educator, veterinarian; b. Crinnell, Ia., Oct. 20, 1910; s. Phillip Franklin and Bertha Belle (Wilson) D.; student Bakersfield Jr. Coll., 1928-30; D.V.M., Colo. A. and M. Coll., 1935, M.S. in Animal Pathology, 1952; graduate study Med. Sch. Colo, University, 1938-39; research m. Donna Bailey, Aug. 20, 1938; childrenEmily Ann. Phillip, Lee Edward, Jeffrey. Field vet. U.S. Bur. Animal Industry, 1935-37; also gen. vet. practice, Great Falls, Mont.; mem. teaching staff dept. medicine and anatomy Colo. State U., Ft. Collins, 1937-42, asso. prof. anatomy, 1946- 48, head dept., anatomy, 1948—; research tropical deseases Vet. Research Inst., India, Burma, 1943-44. Served from 1st lt. to capt. Vet. Corps, AUS, 1942-46, now maj. Outstanding profl. ednl. exhibit Nat. Am. Vet. Med. Assn. Conv., Detroit, 1949; recipient Harris T. Guard Distinguished Faculty award, 1960; Top Prof.'s award Colo. State U., 1962, named Centennial Prof., 1970. Fellow N.Y. 1952; postgrad Med. Sch. Colo. U., 1938-39; Am. Inst. Biol. Scis., Am., Colo. vet. med. assns., World, Am. (pres. 1954) assns. vet. anatomists, Wildlife Disease Assn., Internat. Platform Assn., Sigma Xi, Phi Kappa Phi, Alpha Psi, Phi Kappa Tau. Mem. Christian Ch. Kiwanian. Contbr. articles to profl. jours. Home: 1728 W Vine Dr Ft Collins CO 80521

DAVIS, ROGER EDWIN, lawyer; b. Lakewood, O., Dec. 29, 1928; s. Russell G. and Irma (Aboline) D.; A.B., Harvard, 1950; LL.B., U. Mich., 1953; m. Eva Grace Keeler, July 25, 1953; children—Susan Lee, Lisa Ann, Steven Russell. Admitted to Mich. bar, 1953; practice in Detroit, 1955—; asso. Langs, Molyneaux & Armstrong, 1955-60; counsel Avis Enterprises, 1961-62; with legal dept. S.S. Kresge Co., 1963-70, v.p., gen. counsel, sec., 1970—. Served with U.S. Army, 1953-55. Mem. State Bar Mich., Fla. Bar, Am., Detroit bar assns., Am. Soc. Corporate Secs. Home: 4700 Heather Lane Birmingham MI 48010 Office: 2727 2d Av Detroit MI 48232

DAVIS, ROSS DANE, govt. ofcl.; b. Bklyn., Mar. 21, 1919; s. Abraham N. and Gertrude (Ross) D.; B.A., Brown U., 1941; LL.B., Columbia, 1947; m. Margaret Gould Roos, May 30, 1958. Admitted N.Y. bar, 1948, D.C. bar, 1968, also U.S. Supreme Ct.; asso. firm Davis & Heffner, N.Y.C., 1947-51; with U.S. Govt., 1951-69; dir. Center for Program Implementation, Nat. League cities-U.S. Conf. Mayors, Washington, 1969—. Exec. adminstr., acting adminstr. Small Bus. Adminstrn., 1965-66; adminstr. Econ. Devel. Adminstrn., 1966; asst. sec. econ. devel. U.S. Dept. Commerce 1966-69., Mem. Nat. Capitol Democratic Club. served to capt. AUS, 1942-46; PTO. Mem. Am., Fed. bar assons. Clubs: Nat. Lawyers, City Tavern Assn. (Washington). Contbr. articles in field to profl. jours. Home: 3421 N St NW Washington, DC 20007. Office: 1612 K St NW Washington DC 20006

DAVIS, ROY TASCO, ret. diplomatist, ambassador, educator; b. Ewing, Mo., June 24, 1889; s. John A. and Bessie (White) D.; A.B., LaGrange (Mo.) Coll., 1908; Ph.B., Brown U., 1910; m. Loyce Enice, Aug. 16, 1913; children—Roy T., Mercedes. Statistician Mo. Bur. Census and Labor, 1911; clk. to commn. that built Mo. State Capitol, 1912, 13; sec., also bus. mgr. Stephens Coll., Columbia, Mo., 1914-21, asst. to pres., also dir. pub. relations, 1933-37; of Guatemala, 1921-22, Republic of Costa Rica, 1922-29, Republic of Panama, 1930-33; chmn. Honduran- Guatemalan Boundary Commn., 1928; del. of U.S. govt. to North Am. Radio Conf., Mexico City, 1933; apptd. mem. Inter-Am. Commn. of Inquiry, 1938; pres. Nat. Park Coll. (formerly Nat. Park Sem.), Forest Glen, Md., 1937-42, when coll. was taken over by Govt. for a hosp. under war emergency act; spl. field rep. in Latin Am. for Reconstrn. Finance Commn., 1942-43; dir. Inter-Am. Schs. Service of the Am. Council on Edn., 1943; chmn. commn. making ednl. survey of Bolivia, 1943; elected state senator, Nov. 5, 1946, mem. Md. State Sch. and Finance Commn.; U.S. ambassador, Haiti, 1953-57, ret. Dir. Latin-Am. Orientation Program, Dept. State, 1959; lectr. Fgn. Service Inst. Dept. State, 1961- -. Mem. Adv. Council for Higher Edn., State Md., 1964. Decorated Order Vasco Nuez de Balboa (Panama), National Red Cross (Costa Rica). Clubs: Union (Panama); Cosmos (Washington). Address: 3802 Thornapple St Chevy Chase, MD 20015.

DAVIS, ROY TASCO, Jr., ret. fgn. service officer; b. Columbia, Mo., Sept. 9, 1915; s. Roy T. and Loyce (Enloe) D.; A.B., U. Mo., 1937; student George Washington U. Law Sch., 1947; grad. Nat. War Coll., 1958; m. Helen Elizabeth Winkler, Oct. 6, 1945; childrenRoy Tasco III, John Albert, Susan Michael. Page, U.S. Senate, 1927; asst. to pres. Nat. Park Coll., 1937-41; admitted to D.C. bar, 1947; fgn. service officer, 1947-68; 2d sec., vice consul, Rio de Janeiro, Brazil, 1947-48; asst. cultural attache, Buenos Aires, Argentina, 1948-51, 2d sec., consul, 1952; 2d sec., consul, then 1st sec., Panama, 1952-55; staff asst., div. internat. orgns., Dept. of State, 1955-57; became consul, Naples, Italy, 1958, then consul gen. Rio de Janeiro; supr. consular services U.S. Consulate Gen., Hong Kong, 1967-68; fgn. affairs cons., 1968—; mem. bd. Fgn. Service Research, Inc. Served ensign to lt. comdr. USNR, 1941-46. Mem. Am. Soc. Internat. Law, Fgn. Service Assn., Phi Beta Kappa, Beta Theta Pi, Phi Alpha Delta, Sigma Delta Pi, Delta Sigma Pi. Home: 7222 Leonardo Da Vinci Tucson AZ 85704

DAVIS, ROY WRIGHT, metals co. exec.; b. Richmond, Va., Nov. 20, 1914; s. George Henry and Elizabeth Belle (Chappell) D.; certificate bus. adminstrn. Va. Mechanics Inst., 1936; student FBI Acad., 1942; m. Dorothy May Kenyon, June 21, 1945; children—Roy W., Christopher K., Linda Gaye. Accounting clk. Standard Oil Co. N.J., 1932-36; staff accountant Ernst & Ernst, C.P.A.'s Richmond, 1936-42; spl. agt. FBI, 1942-48; with Reynolds Metals Co., Richmond, 1948—, asst. treas., 1953-61, treas., 1961—; also officer, dir. subsidiaries; dir. Home Capital Funds, Inc., Small Bus. Investment Co. N.Y., Inc. Vice pres., bd., dirs. Richmond Area Tb Assn.; bd. dirs., treas. Richmond Symphony. C.P.A., Va. Mem. Am. Inst. C.P.A.'s, Va. Soc. C.P.A.'s Am. Accounting Assn., Newcomen Soc. N.Am. Methodist (ofcl. bd.). Mason (Shriner). Home: 207 Wexleigh Dr Dorset Woods Richmond VA 23229 Office: Reynolds Metals Bldg Richmond VA 23261

DAVIS, RUSSELL C., city ofcl.; b. Rockville, Md., Aug. 31, 1922; married. Mem. Miss. Ho. of Reps., 1960-69; mayor of Jackson, Miss., 1969—. Bd. dirs. Hinds-Rankin Red Cross, Pearl River Valley Devel. Dist. Mem. S.C.V., C. of C., Am. Legion, Miss. Municipal Assn. (exec. com.), Nat. League of Cities (municipal com.), Sertoma. Democrat. Methodist. Office: City Hall Jackson MS*

DAVIS, RUSSELL GERARD, educator; b. Hopkinton, Mass., Oct. 29, 1922; s. Edward William and Hazel May (McLellan) D.; A.B. cum laude, Holy Cross/Dartmouth, 1943; M.Ed., Harvard, 1953, Ed.D., 1955; m. Mary Elizabeth Carroll, Apr. 24, 1946; children—Cynthia (Mrs. Robert Sbaschnig), Christopher, Geoffrey, Marcia, Timothy, Russell, Lisa. Tchr., Cranwell Sch., Lenox, Mass., 1946-51; instr. Harvard, 1952-54, lectr., research asso. prof., 1969, Latin Am. adv. panel, 1967-70, prof. edn. and devel., 1969—. Specialist, U.S. Govt., Far East, 1953; ednl. adviser AID, Ethiopia, 1955-57; research dir. Boston Coll., 1957-60; adviser ednl. planning Latin Am., 1960-62; chmn. U.S. Mexican Ednl. Com., 1965-68. Dir. Asia Region Peace Corps, 1969-70; cons. State Dept., Ford Found., Venezuela Govt.; mem. Norberg Espey Mission, Uruguay, 1963; mem. adv. panel State Dept., 1967-69; mem. Gardner Mission to Vietnam, 1968. Trustee Human Devel. Found. Served with USMCR, 1942-46. Recipient various lit. awards and citations. Eliot scholar, Harvard, 1963-64. Fellow A.A.A.S.; mem. Internat. Devel. Soc., Latin Am. Specialist Assn., Linguistic Soc., Acad. Polit. Sci., N.E.A. Author: Lion's Whiskers, 1959; Choctaw Code, 1961; Chief Joseph, 1962; Marine War, 1962; Land in the Sun, 1964; Planning Human Resource Development, 1966; Build A Mill, Build A City, Build a School, 1969. Home: 15 Rogers St Newton Highlands MA 02161 Office: Roy Edward Larsen Hall 5 Harvard Cambridge MA 02138

DAVIS, RUSSELL LEONARD, librarian; b. Blackfoot, Ida., Oct. 25, 1924; s. John Leonard and Mary Verna (Robertson) D.; student Weber Jr. Coll., 1948-50; B.S., Utah State U., 1952; A.M. in Library Sci., U. Mich., 1952-53; m. Emma Lou Barnes, June 10, 1949; childrenDan, Kathleen, Kirk, Susan, Eileen, Alan, Julie. Teaching asst. U. Mich. Lib. Sch., 1952-53; engring. librarian Utah State U., 1953-54, circulation librarian, 1954-57, instr. library sci., 1953-57, extension librarian, 1955-57; dir. Utah State Library Commn., 1957-. Mem. A.L.A., Utah (pres. 1960-61), Mountain Plains (pres. 1964- 65) library assns. Mem. Ch. of Jesus Christ of Latter-day Saints (bishop). Home: 575 E 1350 North Bountiful UT 84010 Office: 2150 S 2d W Salt Lake City UT 84104

DAVIS, SAMMY, Jr., entertainer; b. N.Y.C., Dec. 8, 1925; s. Sammy and Elvira (Sanchez) D.; student Calvert Corr. Sch.; m. Loray White, 1958 (div. 1959); m. 2d, May Britt, Nov. 13, 1961 (div.); children—Tracey, Mark, Jeff; m. 3d, Altovise Gore, May 11, 1970. Began profl. career, 1928; appeared in film Rufus Jones for Pres., 1930, also Season's Greeting; vaudeville appearances with Will Mastin Trio, 1930-48, singer, dancer, impressions in hotel, night club shows; recorded songs Decca Records; now rec. Motown-Ecology Records; role Broadway show Mr. Wonderful, 1956-57, Anna Lucasta, Porgy and Bess, 1959, Golden Boy; film Ocean's 11, Pepe, 1960; recent films Sergeants Three, Convicts Four, Johnny Cool, Robin and the Seven Hoods, Sweet Charity, A Man Called Adam, Salt and Pepper, One More Time, The Pigeons; TV appearances Mod Squad, Name of the Game, Laugh-In, Lucy Show, others; producer TV show The Trackers. Served with AUS, 1943-45. Mem. Am. Soc. Mag. Photographers. Club: Friars (N.Y.C.). Author: Yes I Can (autobiography), 1965. Address: 9000 Sunset Blvd Los Angeles CA 90069

DAVIS, SAMUEL ALPHONSO, Jr., holding co. exec.; b. Mobile, Ala., July 3, 1913; s. Samuel Alphonso and Mamie (Roycroft) D.; student U. Ala., 1946-48; m. Helen Luenberg Holloman, Apr. 27, 1937; children—Linda Ann (Mrs. John Chason Gray), Samuel Alphonso III. Adminstr., U.S. C.E., Mobile, 1939-43; with So. Industries Corp., Mobile, 1947—, now v.p., sec. Bd. dirs. Mobile Assn. for Blind. Served with C.E., AUS, 1943-46; ETO. Mem. Mobile C. of C., Mardi Gras Mystic Socs. Methodist. Clubs: Internat. Trade (Mobile); Lakewood Golf (Pointclear, Ala.); Isle Dauphine Country (Dauphin Island, Ala.) Home: 3925 Pembrocke Av Mobile AL 36608 Office: E A Roberts Bldg Mobile AL 36601

DAVIS, SAMUEL HENRY, Jr., educator; b. Houston, Dec. 19, 1930; s. Samuel Henry and Irene (Lohman) D.; B.A., Rice Inst., 1952, B.S., 1953; Sc.D., Mass. Inst. Tech., 1957; m. Deirdre Lane Donoho, Sept. 2, 1967; children—Merrill Leigh, Allison Ashley. Engr., Gen. Electric KAPL, Schenectady, 1956-57; asst. prof. Rice U. Houston, 1957-61, asso. prof., 1961-65, prof., 1969—, dir. continuing studies, 1969—; cons. NASA-MSC, Houston, 1965—, Thermonetics, Houston, 1969—; vis. prof. Delft U., Netherlands, 1964. Guggenheim fellow, 1964-65. Mem. Am. Inst. Chem. Engrs. Home: 6106 Piping Rock Houston TX 77027

DAVIS, SAVILLE ROGERS, journalist; b. Watertown, Mass., Apr. 5, 1909; s. Francis Woodward and Esther (Saville) D.; A.B., Williams Coll., 1930; M.B.A., Harvard, 1932; m. Anita Pawolleck de Varon, Aug. 12, 1935; 1 dau., Julie Fee. Reporter, Christian Sci. Monitor, Boston, N.Y.C., 1932-39, radio news writer, broadcaster, 1934-36, State Dept. corr., Washington, 1939, Mediterranean corr., Rome, Italy and Madrid, Spain, 1939-41, asst. to editor, 1941-45, chief London (Eng.) news bur., roving corr. European internat. confs., 1945-47, Am. news editor, 1947-57, mng. editor, 1957-61, chief editorial writer, 1961-64, chief Washington news bur., 1965-71, spl. corr., 1971—. Intermittent lectr., radio news analyst; free lance journalist, 1971—. Trustee Wheelock Coll., chmn, 1963-65. Mem. Harvard Bus. Sch. Alumni Assn. (pres. 1960-61), Am. Acad. Arts and Scis., Internat. Inst. for Girls in Spain (pres. 1949-69), Phi Beta Kappa. Christian Scientist. Clubs: National Press, Federal City (Washington); Harvard (Boston). Address: Winter St Lincoln MA 01773

DAVIS, SCOTT, stockbroker; b. Geneva, Ill., Feb. 22, 1925; s. Ralph W. and Geraldine (Scott) D.; grad. cum laude, Fountain Valley Sch., Colorado Springs, Colo., 1942; student Amherst Coll., 1942; investment banking course, Northwestern U., 1946-47; m. Nancy Fox, 1943; m. 2d, Solveig Grennard-Hjelm, 1951; childrenJ. James, Jeffrey G., Elizabeth, Porter. Investment sales Hornblower & Weeks, Chgo., 1946-47; mem. Chgo. Stock Exchange, 1947-50, Midwest Stock Exchange, 1950-71; gen. partner Paul H. Davis & Co., Chgo., 1951-53, Ralph W. Davis & Co., investments, Chgo., 1953-70; chmn. Ralph W. Davis & Co., Inc., 1970—. Gov. Midwest Stock Exchange, 1956-62, 64-66, chmn. bd. govs., 1966-68; dir. Midwest Stock Exchange Service Corp., 1961-71; mem. N.Y. Stock Exchange, 1960-70; chmn. Chgo. Assn. Stock Exchange Firms, 1964-66. Mem. nat. council Boy Scouts Am., 1964-65, mem. exec. bd. Chief Shabbona council, 1958-65. Served as sgt. Signal Corps, AUS, 1943-45. Mem. S.A.R., Chi Psi. Episcopalian. Clubs: Economic, The Street (past pres.), Chicago, Mid-Day, (Chgo.); Hinsdale (Ill.) Golf. Home: 856 Cleveland Rd Hinsdale IL 60521 Office; 120 S La Salle St Chicago, IL 60603.

DAVIS, SHELBY CULLOM, ambassador; b. Peoria, Ill., Apr. 1, 1909; s. George Henry and Julia Mabel (Cullom) D.; student Lawrenceville (N.J.) Sch., 1924-26; A.B., Princeton, 1930; A.M., Columbia, 1931; D. Polit. Sci., U. Geneva (Switzerland), 1934; m. Kathryn Edith Waterman, Jan. 4, 1932; children—Shelby Moore Cullom, Diana Cullom, Priscilla Alden (dec.). Spl. corr., also asso. with Columbia Broacasting Co., Geneva, 1932-34; economist Investment Corp. Phila., 1934-37; treas. Delaware Fund, Inc., 1937-39; econ. adviser Thomas E. Dewey, 1940, presdl. campaigns; mem. N.Y. Stock Exchange, 1941—; chief fgn. requirements sect. WPB, Washington, 1942, chief div. statistics and research, N.Y., No. N.J., 1943; 1st dep. supt. ins. N.Y. State, 1944-47; mng. partner Shelby Cullom Davis & Co., investment bankers, N.Y.C., 1947-69; U.S. ambassador to Switzerland, Bern, 1969—. Chmn., History Adv. Council, Princeton Trustee Coll. Retirement Equities Fund, Jackson Lab., Plimoth Plantation. Mem. Financial Analysis Assn. (past pres.), Gen. Soc. S.R., Soc. Colonial Wars (lt. gov.), Mayflower Soc. Republican. Clubs: Knickerbocker, University, Sleepy Hollow Country, Princeton, Players (N.Y.C.,); Hartford; Bar Harbor (Me.); Down Town Assn., Charter (Princeton); Everglades (Palm Beach, Fla.), Author: Your Career In Defense, 1942, others. Former bus. editor Current History and Forum mags. Contbr. articles to several jours. Home: Broad Oak Tarrytown NY 10591 also 14 Taubenstr Bern Switzerland Office: 93 Jubilianstr Bern Switzerland ☆

DAVIS, SID, news corr.; b. Youngstown, O., Nov. 13, 1927; s. Morris and Hilda (Friedman) D.; B.S., Ohio U., 1952; m. Barbara J. Flint, July 21, 1960; children—Lawrence Jay, Morse Robert. News reporter sta. WJEH, Gallipolis, O., 1950-51; news dir. Sta. WKBN, Youngstown, 1952-59; White House corr. Westinghouse Broadcasting Co., Washington, 1959-68, chief of Washington news bur., 1968—; producer Dialogue on Dallas, eyewitness account Kennedy assassination, 1963. Served with USNR, 1946-48; duty in U.S.S. Toledo, U.S.S. Astoria. Named Sigma Delta Chi Outstanding Journalism Grad., Ohio U., 1952. Mem. White House Corrs. Assn. Radio, TV News Dirs. Assn., Sigma Delta Chi, Omicron Delta Kappa, Tau Kappa Alpha. Clubs: National Press, Federal City (Washington). Covered Khrushchev's tour U.S., 1959, U.S. space launchings, 1960-63, Kennedy tours abroad as pres., Johnson's travels as pres. One of three reporters to witness swearing in of Pres. Johnson in Dallas, polit. reporting of major nominating convs., campaigns and elections beginning in 1960, including extensive travel with all Presdl. candidates. Home: 7103 Annan Pl Bethesda MD 20034 Office: 1625 K St NW Washington DC 20006

DAVIS, SMITH BURCHFIELD, utility exec.; b. Lincoln, Neb., July 5, 1916; s. Oak E. and Adelia (Smith) D.; A.B., U. Neb., 1946, M.A., 1947; m. Mary Bullock, June 10, 1942 (div. 1951); 1 dau., Ann Davis (Mrs. James Kuhlman); m. 2d, Jean Eversden, Oct. 29, 1953. With comptrollers dept. Douglas Aircraft Co., 1940-45; grad. asst. U. Neb., 1947; asst. dir. sales promotion Tension Envelope Corp., Kansas City, Mo., 1947-48; with So. Cal. Edison Co., Los Angeles, 1948—, comptroller, 1962—, v.p., 1963- 64, financial v.p., 1964—; dir. Electric Systems Co., Asso. So. Investment Co., Energy Services, Inc., Mono Power Co. Bd. dirs., v.p. Cal. Taxpayers Assn.; former chmn. investor relations com. Edison Electric Inst. Adviser U. Cal. at Los Angeles Grad. Sch. Bus. Bd. dirs. United Way, Los Angeles; investment bd. Children's Hosp., Los Angeles. Mem. Pacific Coast Elect. Assn. (treas.), Financial Execs. Inst., Nat. Fedn. Financial Analysts, Los Angeles Soc. Security Analysts, Los Angeles Town Hall, Los Angeles C. of C., S.A.R. (past pres., dir. Los Angeles), Delta Upsilon, Sigma Upsilon. Clubs: Downtown Investment (pres.), Los Angeles, University (Los Angeles); Pacific Coast (Long Beach, Cal.). Home: 501 N Rossmore Av Los Angeles CA 90004 Office: PO Box 351 Los Angeles CA 90053

DAVIS, STANLEY NELSON, educator; b. Rio de Janeiro, Brazil, Aug. 6, 1924 (parents Am. citizens) s. Nelson Caryl and Mary Faye (Caulkins) D.; B.S. in Geology, U. Nev., 1949; M.S. U. Kan., 1951; Ph.D., Yale, 1955; m. Barbara Jean Wickham, Apr. 14, 1949; childrenGerald Nelson, Ruth Ann, Darlene Grace, Randall Wayne, Betty Jean, Nancy Faye. Geologist, U.S. Bur. Reclamation, 1949, Mo. Geol. Survey, 1952, 53, 55; instr. U. Rochester, 1953-54; mem. faculty Stanford, 1954-67, prof. geology, 1965-67; prof. geology U. Mo., 1967—; chmn. dept., 1969—; vis. prof. U. Chile, Santiago, 1960-61; tchr. Bowling Green U., summer 1963, Princeton, summer 1965, U. Hawaii, fall 1966; instr. U. Oriente in Venezuela, summer 1967-68; lectr. Am. Geol. Inst., mem. East Greenland Expdn., Arctic Inst. N. Am., summer 1959; cons. to govt. and industry, 1955-. Served with AUS, 1943-46; PTO. Fellow Geol. Soc. Am.; mem. Am. Geophys. Union, Assn. Engring. Geologists, A.A.A.S., Soc. Econ. Paleontolgists and Mineralogists, Nat. Water Resources Assn., Sigma Xi. Author: Hidrogeologia, 1961; (with R. M. DeWiest) Hydrogeology, 1966; also articles. Home: 2607 Luan Ct Columbia, MO 65201.

DAVIS, STEPHEN SMITH, educator; b. Phila., Oct. 24, 1910; s. Stephen Smith and Rosa Elizabeth (Norris) D.; B.S. in Mech. Engring., Howard U., 1936; M.S. in Mech. Engring., Harvard, 1947; m. Aileen Priscilla Harris, June 25, 1938; 1 son, Stephen Harris. Mem. faculty Howard U., 1938-, prof. mech. engring., 1938—, head dept., 1962, dean Sch. Engring. and Architecture, 1964- 70; mech. engr. Nat. Bur. Standards, 1943-45; cons. Naval Ordnance Lab., 1953-63. Mem. Am. Soc. M.E., Am. Soc. Engring. Edn., A.A.A.S., Washington Acad. Sci., Nat., D.C. socs. profl. engrs., Tau Beta Pi. Inventor holding patent flexible wing-tunnel nozzle. Home: 2847 University Terrace NW Washington, DC 20016.

DAVIS, STUART, savs. and loan assn. exec.; b. Santa Monica, Cal., Mar. 29, 1916; s. William Arthur and Ida Mae (Honson) D.; B.S., St. Mary's (Cal.) Coll., 1938; m. Eleanor Vander Slice; children—Elenor Lynn (Mrs. Arthur Alarcow), Richard Edward. With First Savs. & Loan Assn., San Francisco, 1938—, chmn. bd., 1961—; chmn. bd. Gt. Western Financial Corp., Los Angeles, Gt. Western Savs. & Loan Assn., San Francisco. Bd. dirs. Action, Inc. Mem. U.S. (mem. exec. com. 1956-59), Cal. (pres. 1956) savs and loans league, Savs. & Loan Found., U.S. C. of C. (dir.). Office: Gt Western Savs & Loan 401 California St San Francisco CA 94104

DAVIS, THOMAS CECIL, paper co. exec.; b. Montreal, Que., Can., Apr. 24, 1913; s. George Finlay and Georgina Mary (Eddy) D.; Chartered Accountant, McGill U., 1935; m. Elizabeth Furness MacLeod, Mar. 23, 1940; children—Susan M.L. (Mrs. W. Jerome Holstein), Thomas R.M., Christopher E.F. Comptroller, St. Regis Paper Co. (Can.) Ltd., Montreal, 1948- 59, pres., 1971—; resident mgr. Kraft div. Kraft Center, Pensacola, Fla., 1960-63; asst. treas. St. Regis Paper Co., N.Y.C., 1960, 63-65, treas., 1965-71; dir., treas. N. Western Pulp & Power Ltd., St. Regis Properties Ltd. (all Hinton, Alta., Can.); treas. St. Regis Pulp & Paper Corp.; treas., dir. Bates do Brazil, S.A., Compania Argentina de Productos de Pagel, S.A., Creamery Package Mfg. Co. Can. Ltd., Toronto, Ont., Mech. Contractors Ltd., Montreal. Pres., Montreal United Services Inst., 1950; mem. exec. council, chmn. finance com. Gulf Coast council Boy Scouts Am., 1960-63. Trustee Financial Execs. Research Found., 1955-60, 65-69. Served to group capt. RCAF, 1939-45. Mem. Air Force Vets Assn. (past pres.). Clubs: Canadian of N.Y. (gov.), Cloud (N.Y.C.); Sharon (Conn.) Country; Royal Montreal Golf, United Services (past pres.) (Montreal). Home: Northrup Rd Sharon CT 06069 also Apt 1501 3470 Stanley St Montreal Quebec Canada Office: 1245 Sherbrooke St W Montreal Quebec Canada

DAVIS, THOMAS HENRY, airline exec.; b. Winston-Salem, N.C., Mar. 15, 1918; s. Egbert L. and Annie (Shore) D.; student U. Ariz., 1935-39; m. Nancy Caroline Teague, Oct. 28, 1944;

children—Thomas Henry, Winifred (Mrs. Alfredo Torres Bond), George Franklin, Nancy Caroline, Juliana. Aircraft salesman Piedmont Aviation, Inc., Winston-Salem, 1940, v.p., treas., 1941-43, pres. , treas., 1943—; dir., mem. exec. com. Wachovia Corp. Mem. Urban Redevelopment Commn., 1955—. Trustee Wake Forest U. Recipient Winston-Salem and N.C. Jr. C. of C. Distinguished Service award, 1954, Frank Davison trophy for outstanding service to aviation in N.C., 1949. Mem. Air Transport Assn. (dir.), Nat. Aviation Club. Soaring Soc. Am., Newcomen Soc., Winston Salem C. of C. (past pres.). Pi Kappa Alpha. Democrat. Baptist. Rotarian. Clubs: Forsyth Country. Old Town (Winston-Salem, N.C.); Wings (N.Y.C.). Home: 1190 Arbor Rd Winston-Salem NC 27104 Office: Smith Reynolds Airport Winston-Salem NC 27102

DAVIS, THOMAS KENNEDY, natural gas co. exec.; b. Kenton, O., Oct. 3, 1917; s. Frank K. and Mary (Dickinson) D.; B.B.A., U. Houston, 1953; grad. Advanced Mgmt. Program, Harvard, 1960; m. Geraldine Cooper, Dec. 13, 1941; children—Thomas Kennedy, Frank Kennedy II. With No. Natural Gas Co., 1937-42; with Tenn. Gas Transmission Co., 1946-61, v.p., 1958-61; pres. E. Tenn. Natural Gas Co., 1961—. Mem. Tenn. Indsl. and Agr. Devel. Com., 1964—. Served with USNR, 1942-45. Mem. So. Gas Assn. Home: 8601 Hempstead Dr Knoxville TN 37919 Office: PO Box 10245 Knoxville TN 37919

DAVIS, THOMAS WILDERS, chemist; b. Upper Nyack, N.Y., Aug. 1, 1905; s. George Francis Whitfield and Elisabeth (Guenther) D.; B.S., N.Y. U., 1925, M.S., 1926, Ph.D., 1928; m. Ruth Emily George Jahn, June 2, 1942; children—George P. Jahn (stepson), William F. W., James J. D. Research chemist Combustion Utilities Corp., Linden, N.J., 1928-29; instr. N.Y.U., 1929-38, asst. prof., 1938-48, asso. prof., 1948-51, prof., 1951—, chmn. chemistry dept., 1955-64. Vis. prof., mem. senate U. Leeds (Eng.), 1964-65; instr. Rand Sch., 1932; research chemist metall. labs. U. Chgo., 1942; research chemist Clinton Nat. Lab., 1946-47; research chemist Brookhaven Nat. Lab., 1948, 1950, cons., 1948-49; research chemist U.S. Naval Ordnance Test Sta., Inyokern, 1952, Oak Ridge Nat. Lab., 1954; resident research asso. Argonne Nat. Lab. (Ill), 1955—. Mem. Am. Chem. Soc., Am. Inst. Chemists, Fedn. Am. Scientists, Radiation Research Soc., Phi Beta Kappa, Sigma Xi, Phi Lambda Upsilon. Club: New York University. Asso. editor Ency. of Chem. Reactions, 1946-59. Home: 42 Le Furgy Av Dobbs Ferry NY 10522 Office: NYU University Heights New York City NY 10452

DAVIS, THURSTON N., clergyman; Phila., Oct. 12, 1913; s. Nobel Thurston and Rose Mary (Carey) D.; A.B., Georgetown Coll., 1937; S.T.L., Woodstock Coll., 1943; A.M., Harvard, 1946, Ph. D., 1947; Litt.D., LaSalle Coll., 1959, Loyola Coll., Balt., 1964. Joined Soc. of Jesus, 1931, ordained priest Roman Cath. Ch., 1942; tchr. Regis High Sch., N.Y.C., 1938-39; instr. grad. sch. arts and scis. Fordham U., 1947-49, dean Coll. Arts and Scis., 1949-53; contbg. editor Am., 1953-54, asso. editor, 1954-55, editor-in-chief, 1955-68, also Cath. Mind, 1955-68; dir. John LaFarge Inst., John Courtney Murray Forum, 1967-70; with communications dept. U.S. Cath. Cont., N.Y.C., 1970—. Vice pres. Appeal of Conscience Found., 1965—; lectr. Inst. Religious and Social Studies. Bd. dirs. Georgetown U. Mem. Middle States Assn. Colls. and Secondary Schs., Religious Edn. Assn. Club: Harvard (N.Y.C.). Editor: A John LaFarge Reader, 1956; Between Two Cities, 1962. Home: 352 Riverside Dr New York City NY 10025

DAVIS, TINE WAYNE, grocery exec.; b. Gamaliel, Ark., Jan. 8, 1914; s. William Milton and Ethel (Chase) D.; student U. Fla., 1933-34, U. Ida., 1934-35; m. Eunice Chandler, Dec. 5, 1936; children—Dianne, Tionna, Tine Wayne. Sr. v.p., dir. Winn-Dixie Stores, Inc.; dir. Peoples Bank & Trust, Montgomery, Ala., Am. Heritage Life Ins. Co., Jacksonville, Exchange Security Bank, Birmingham, Ala., Peoples Nat. Bank, Huntsville, Ala., North Ala. Broadcasters, Huntsville, Ryder System, Inc., Miami. Home: 2036 Allendale Rd Montgomery AL Office: P O Box 2029 Montgomery AL

DAVIS, TOM EDWARD, educator; b. Akron, O., June 11, 1929; s. David Edward and Edith (Larson) D.; A.B. magna cum laude, Tufts Coll., 1950; M.A., Johns Hopkins, 1952, Ph.D., 1956; m. Patricia Ann Elwin, June 13, 1953; children—Derek, Heather. Fulbright fellow, Social Sci. Research Council fellow London (Eng.) Sch. Econs., 1953-55; 69-70; research asso. econs. Johns Hopkins, 1955-56; asst. prof. U. Chgo., 1956-58; with Econ. Research Center, Cath. U. Chile, 1957-61; asso. prof. U. Chgo., 1958-62; faculty Cornell U., 1962—, prof. econs., 1967—, chmn. dept., 1967-70, asso. dir. Latin Am. program, 1964-65, dir., 1965-67, 71—, dir. Nat. Bur. Econ. Research, 1969—. Chmn., Latin Am. Research Rev. Bd., 1965-67; dir. Center for Devel. and Social Change, Cambridge, Mass., 1968—, v.p., 1969-70; cons. in field, 1961—. Ford fellow, 1965- 66; Fulbright fellow, 1970-71. Mem. Am. Econ. Assn., Latin Am. Studies Assn. Contbr. articles to jours., contbns. to books. Home: 211 N Triphammer Rd Ithaca NY 14850

DAVIS, TRUE, business exec.; b. St. Joseph, Mo., Dec. 23, 1919; s. William True and Helen (Marstella) D.; student Cornell, 1937-40; L.H.D., Tarkio U., 1963; m. Virginia Bruce Motter, Jan. 24, 1948 (dec. Sept. 1969); children—William True, Bruce Motter, Lance Barrow. Salesman Anchor Serum Co., St. Joseph, Mo., 1940-42, v.p., sales mgr., 1945-50, pres., 1950-60; pres., dir. Research Labs., Inc., 1952-60, Pet's Best Co., 1954-60, World Health Inst., Ltd., 1958-60, Peters Serum Co., Kansas City, 1956-60, Wilke Labs., Inc., West Plains, Mo., Wilke Labs. of Tenn., Memphis, 1956-60, Peerless Serum Co., 1956-60, Med. Industries, Inc., 1957-60, Gothic Advt., Inc., 1956-60, Certified Labs., Inc., 1956-60; True Davis Found., Inc., 1954—, Davis Estate, Inc., 1958—, (all St. Joseph, Mo.), Carolina Vet. Supply, Inc., Charlotte, N.C., 1956-60, Anchor Serum Co. of Ind., Indpls., Inc., 1959-60, Anchor Serum Co. N.J., Camden, 1959-60, Anchor Serum Co. Minn., So. St. Paul, 1960; chmn., dir. Chemico Labs., Inc., Miami, Fla., 1960-63, chmn. Thompson Hayward Chem. Co., Kansas City, Mo., 1961-63; pres., dir. Philips Roxane, Inc., N.Y.C., 1959-63; v.p., dir. Philips Electronics and Pharm. Industries Corp., 1959-63; U.S. exec. dir. Inter-Am. Devel. Bank, 1966- 68; dir. St. Joseph Light & Power Co.; ambassador to Switzerland, 1963- 65; now pres., chmn. bd. dirs. Nat. Bank of Washington. Chmn. U.S. Port Security Com., 1965-68, N.Y. Pier Com., 1966-68, Pub. Adv. Com. Customs Adminstrn., 1966-68; mem. Fgn. Trade Zones Bd., 1965-68; U.S. del. Internat. Maritime Coordinating Orgn., London, 1966, GATT Conf. Anti-Dumping Laws, Geneva, 1966; adviser U.S. delegation to World Bank and IMF. Mem. bd. trustees Missouri Pub. Expenditure Survey, 1962-63; member Dept. Commerce Export Expansion Council, 1962-63. Pres. Animal Health Inst., 1954-56; dir., 1946-59; mem. Nat. Serum Control Agy., 1947-58, chmn., 1954-55. Dir. Nat. Asso. Boys Clubs Am., 1952-64; dir. Little League, 1958-60; police commr., St. Joseph, 1949; exec. com. United Fund, 1960; bd. govs. Am. Royal, K.C., Mo., 1960—; mem. Cornell U. Council, 1962-68. Served it. USNR, 1943-45; chief test pilot Naval Air Sta., Pearl Harbor. Col., staff gov. of Mo., 1949-54, 58-68, Ky., 1953-54. Recipient Vets. Fgn. Wars Outstanding Citizen award, St. Joseph, 1960, St. Joseph Jr. C. of C. Boss Year award, 1960; Nat. VFW Gold Medal award for Americanism, 1967. Mem. N.Y. Acad. Scis. (life), Thoroughbred Breeders Assn., Nat. Live Stock San. Assns., Newcomen Soc., Am. Legion, Vets. Fgn. Wars (mem. nat. Americanization com. 1961-63, chmn. Americanization com. State of Mo. 1960-63), Mo. Acad. Squires, Phi Gamma Delta. Democrat. Elk. Clubs: Marco Polo, New York Athletic, Cornell, Brook (N.Y.C.); River (Kansas City, Mo.); Minnesouri Angling (Alexandria, Minn.); F Street, Georgetown, Metropolitan (Washington). Contbr. articles to trade, farm publs. Home: 3000 Ashland Av St Joseph MO 64506 also 2860 Woodland Dr NW Washington DC 20008 Office: 619 14th St NW Washington DC 20005

DAVIS, W. REX, banker; b. Rutland, O., Oct. 19, 1909; s. Roy Allen and Blanche E. (Nelson) D.; ed. Ohio State U., 1934, Am. Inst. Banking, 1933, Stonier Grad. Sch. Banking, Rutgers U., 1944; m. Alice Louise Powell, June 14, 1935; children—Dianne L. (Mrs. Gerald L. Annis,) Sharon Kay. With Huntington Nat. Bank, Columbus, O., 1927-63, exec. v.p., 1963; pres., dir. Central Nat. Bank, Cleve., 1963-69, vice chmn., dir., 1969-70; pres., dir. Continental Bank, Cleve., 1971—; dir. Cleve. Indians Baseball Co., Arnold Wholesale Corp., Cleve. Mem. Am., Ohio bankers assns., Newcomen Soc. N. Am. Mason (33). Clubs: 50, Union (Cleve.); Scioto Country (Columbus). Home: 19913 Shelburne Rd Shaker Heights OH 44118 Office: 1255 Euclid Av Cleveland OH 44115

DAVIS, WALTER R., petroleum corp. exec.; b. 1920; married. With Rumbly Gas Co., Fresno, Cal., 1948-52; with Perminan Corp. (acquired by Occidental Petroleum Corp.) 1952—, sr. exec. v.p., dir. Occidental Petroleum Corp., 1966— . Address: 10889 Wilshire Blvd Los Angeles, CA 90024.*

DAVIS, WALTER STRETHER, coll. pres.; b. Canton, Miss., Aug. 9, 1905; s. Walter M. and Annie Belle (Anderson) D.; B.S., Tenn. Agrl. and Indsl. State Coll., 1931; M.S., Cornell U., 1933, Ph.D., 1941; m. Ivanetta Hughes, December 24, 1936; one son, Ivan Rizzie. Engaged as football coach, Tenn. Agrl. and Indsl. State Coll., 1933-36, dir. and prof. agr., state teacher trainer of agrl. edn. in Tenn., 1933-43, pres., 1943-68, pres. emeritus 1968-. Mem. bd. Central Midwestern Regional Ednl. Lab., Inc.; mem. Tenn. Commn. on Youth Guidance; trustee Meharry Med. Coll. Mem. Metropolitan Transtitional Bd. Edn., 1962-64. State dir. Tenn. Bus. Inst.; state chmn., Victory Bond Drive, Negro Div. Mem. New Farmers of Am., (nat. exec. sec., 1941-43), Am. Vocational Assn., N.E.A., Am. Teachers Assn., Tenn. Edn. Congress, Alpha Kappa Mu, Omega Psi Phi, Sigma Pi Phi, Chi Boule. Baptist Elk, Mason (33). Clubs: Nashville Sportsman, Agora Assembly (Nashville.) Address: 1006 35th Av N Nashville TN 37209

DAVIS, WAYMOND AUSTIN, aerospace co. exec.; b. Wood County, Tex., June 25, 1914; s. Nathaniel Casworth and Della (Moore) D.; B.S. in Mech. Engring., Tex. Tech. Coll., Lubbock, 1936; grad. Advanced Mgmt. Program, Harvard, 1949; grad. Indsl. Coll. Armed Forces, 1954; m. Josephine Newman, Oct. 26, 1939; childrenAustin N. Richard E. Commd. 2d lt., Air Corps, U.S. Army, 1937, advanced through grades to lt. gen. USAF, 1964; assigned various tactical groups, 1936-41, Wright Field, 1941; pioneer high performance reconnaisance aircraft; comdr. 5th Photo Reconnaisance Group, MTO, World War II; engaged in air force procurement and prodn., 1945-67; comdr. aero. systems div. Air Force Systems Command, Andrews AFB, Washington, 1961-62; comdr. ballistic systems div. Air Force Systems Command, Norton AFB, Cal., 1962-64; vice comdr. Air Force Systems Command, Andres AFB, Washington, 1964-67; v.p. aircraft group N.Am. Aviation, Inc., El Segundo, Cal., 1967—. Decorated Distinguished Service medal, Legion of Merit, Air medal, numerous campaign and area ribbons. Home: 645 Paseo de la Playa Redondo Beach CA 90277 Office: 1700 E Imperial Hwy EL Segundo CA 90245

DAVIS, WAYNE HEARTLEY, food wholesale co. exec.; b. Wood River, Ill., July 29, 1930; s. Arthur G. and Alice (Heartley) D.; student So. Ill. U., 1948-52; B.S. in Bus. Adminstrn., Washington U., St. Louis, 1957; postgrad. St. Louis U., 1957- 58; m. Betty L. Allen. Dec. 21, 1958; childrenStacey, Tommy. Internal auditor, mem. adminstrn. staff Pet Milk Co., St. Louis, 1954-62; asst. to treas. Hardy Salt Co., St. Louis, 1963; corp. controller Wetterau Foods, Inc., Hazelwood, Mo., 1963-69, v.p., controller, 1969—. Served with AUS, 1952-54. Mem. Theta Xi. Home: 7492 Wagon Wheel Lane Hazelwood MO 63042 Office: 8400 Pershall Rd Hazelwood MO 63042

DAVIS, WILLARD JOHN, agrl. co. exec.; b. Benson, Minn., Mar. 30, 1911; s. John I. and May (Clapp) D.; B.A., Macalester Coll., 1932; LL.B., St. Paul Coll. Law, 1941; m. Sybil M. Dunlap, Oct. 14, 1933; children—Susan (Mrs. Robert Jakubic), Jacqueline (Mrs. David Wilson), John W., William C. Asst. dir. Minn. Income Tax Dept., 1937-42; formerly with Archer-Daniels-Midland Co., Mpls., asst. treas., 1958-59, treas., v.p.; now asst. controller Gen. Mills, Inc., Mpls.; dir. Valley Nat. Bank. Mem. Minn. Bar Assn. Home: 6616 Cornelia Dr Minneapolis MN 55435 Office: 9200 Wayzata Blvd Minneapolis MN 55402

DAVIS, WILLARD KENNETH, exec. engr.; b. Seattle, July 26, 1918; s. Elbert Willard and Alice Marie (Kingman) D.; student U. Cal. at Berkeley, 1936-38; B.S. in Chem. Engring., Mass. Inst. Tech., 1940, M.S. in Chem. Engring., 1942; m. Margaret Ellen Bean, June 14, 1941; children—Kerry Suzanne, Warren Kenneth, Gail Marie. Asst. dir. Buffalo sta. Mass. Inst. Tech. Sch. Chem. Engring. Practice, 1941-42; sr. research engr. Cal. Research Corp., 1942-47; sr. engr. Ford, Bacon & Davis, Inc., 1947-49; asso. prof. engring. U. Cal. at Los Angeles, 1949-53, prof. engring., 1953, Regents' lectr., 1961; chief devel. engr. Cal. Research & Devel. Co., 1951-52, mgr. research, 1952-54; asst. dir. reactor devel. div. AEC, 1954, dep. dir., 1954, dir., 1955-58; v.p. Bechtel Corp., San Francisco, 1958—, v.p. internat. power div., 1967- 71, v.p. power and indsl. div., 1971—; v.p. Bechtel Nuclear Corp., 1958—. Mem. adv. bd. Naval Ordnance Test Sta., Invoken, Cal., 1955-60; dir. Atomic Indsl. Forum, 1960-67, v.p., 1962-64, pres., 1964-67, hon. dir., 1967—. Mem. U.S. Nat. Com. World Energy Conf. Exec. v.p. Point Reyes Nat. Seashore Found. Recipient Fleming award, 1956; Profl. Progress award Am. Inst. Chem. Engrs., 1958, Robert E. Wilson award, 1969. Fellow Am. Nuclear Soc. (dir. 1957-60); mem. Am. Inst. Chem. Engring. (chmn. nuclear engring. div. 1958), Am. Chem. Soc., Am. Soc. M.E., Nat. Acad. Engring., A.A.A.S., Am. Soc. Engring. Edn., Brit. Nuclear Soc., (com. radioactive waste mgmt. 1968—), Sigma Xi, Chi Phi. Presbyn. Clubs: World Trade; Engineers, Commonwealth (San Francisco); Sierra, Cosmos (Washington). Home: 209 Fairhills Dr San Rafael CA 94901 also PO Box 1033 3280 Edgewater Dr Dollar Point Tahoe City CA 95730 Office: PO Box 3965 50 Beale St San Francisco CA 94119

DAVIS, WILLIAM POTTER, III, banker; b. Phila., Dec. 29, 1909; s. William Potter, Jr. and Alice (Mowbray) D.; grad. William Penn Charter Sch., 1927; A.B., Princeton, 1931; m. Phoebe Harding, Dec. 5, 1940; 1 son, Henry A. With First Pa. Banking & Trust Co., and predecessor, Phila., 1931—, sr. v.p., 1958-63, exec. v.p., 1963-65, vice chmn., dir. 1965—. Served to col. AUS, 1941-45. Decorated Legion of Merit with oak leaf cluster. Order British Empire. Home: 111 Ringwood Rd Rosemont PA 19010 Office: First Pa Banking & Trust Co 15th and Chestnut Sts Philadelphia PA 19101

DAVIS, WILLIAM COLUMBUS, educator; b. Birmingham, Ala., Aug. 28, 1910; s. William Columbus and Maude (Gray) D.; A.B., U. Ala., 1931, M.A., 1932; M.A., Harvard, 1943, Ph.D., 1948; m. Mildred J. Dorman, July 24, 1948. Adminstrv. positions U.S. Senate, 1933-46; asst. prof. history U. Ga., 1948-51; faculty George Washington U., 1951-66, prof. Latin-Am. history and govt., 1960-66, dir. Latin-Am. studies, 1952-66; prof. internat. affairs, dir. lecture program Nat. War Coll., Washington, 1963—. Dir., participant numerous radio, programs in field. Mem. Phi Beta Kappa, Pi Kappa Phi. Author: The Last Conquistadores, 1950; The Columns of Athens, 1951. Co-author: Soviet Bloc Latin American Activities and Their Implications for United States Foreign Policy, 1960. Editor: Index to the Writings on American History, 1902-1940, 1956; Am. Hist. Assn's Guide to Historical Literature, 1960. Home: 1323 Darnall Dr McLean, VA 22101. Office: Nat War Coll Washington, DC 20315.

DAVIS, WILLIAM EUGENE, univ. pres.; b. Wamego, Kan., Feb. 15, 1929; s. Eugene Kenneth and Willa (Dickinson) D.; B.S., U. Colo., 1951; M.A., Colo. State Coll., 1958; Ed.D., U. Colo., 1963; m. Pollyanne Peterson, Mar. 17, 1951; children—Deborah, Rebecca, Douglas, Brooke, Bonnie. Asst. to dean men U. Col., 1951; tchr. English, coach Loveland (Colo.) High Sch., 1954-55, Rapid City (S.D.) High Sch., 1955-59, Greeley (Colo.) High Sch., 1959; alumni dir., head football coach, dean men U. Colo., 1960-63; exec. asst. to pres. U. Wyo., 1963-65; pres. Ida. State U., Pocatello, 1965—. Ida. commnr. Western Interstate Compact for Higher Edn., 1965-; mem. Ida. exec. com. Mountain State Regional Med. Program, 1966—, Served with USMCR, 1951-54. Mem. A.I.M., Assn. Rocky Mountain Univs. (dir.), Alpha Tau Omega, Phi Delta Kappa, Omicron Delta Kappa. Methodist. Elk, Rotarian. Author: Glory ColoradoA History of the University of Colorado, 1965. Home: 341 S 7th St Pocatello, ID 83201.

DAVIS, WILLIAM GORDON, Jr., cotton oil co. exec.; b. Temple, Tex., Aug. 15, 1913; s. William Gordon and Nora (Davis) D.; student Tex. A. and M. Coll., 1934; m. Anna Belle Mitchell, Sept. 2, 1938 (div.); children—Brack M. (dec.), Wendy L.; m. 2d, Mary Harris, Apr. 3, 1969; 1 dau., Michel. S.W. dist. mgr. Carver Cotton Gin Co., Dallas, 1939-47; gen. supt. oil mills West Coast div. Anderson Clayton & Co., Los Angeles, 1947-52; gen. mgr. Kingsburg Cotton Oil Co. of Cal. (formerly Kingsburg Cotton Oil Co.), 1952-60, sec.-treas., exec. v.p., 1957-60, v.p., gen. mgr., treas., dir., 1960—; pres., dir. Kingsburg Carolina Gin Co., Welcome Growers Gin Co., Kern Cottonseed Acid Delinting Co., 1956-60. Bd. dirs., v.p. Nat. Inst. Oil Seed Products; bd. dirs. Nat. Cotton Council. Mem. Internat. Oil Mill Supts. Assn. (past pres.), Nat. Cottonseed Products Assn. (dir., v.p.). Mason (Shriner). Home: 10721 Tollhouse Rd Clovis CA 93612 Office: PO Box 277 Kingsburg CA 93631

DAVIS, WILLIAM J., Jr., steel co. exec.; b. Pitts.; ed. U. Pitts. Treas., Copperweld Steel Corp. Home: 1550 Redfern Dr Pittsburgh PA 15241 Office: Frick Bldg Pittsburgh PA 15219*

DAVIS, WILLIAM LIPSCOMB, furniture mfr.; b. Nashville, July 15, 1900; s. G. A. and Mamie (Lipscomb) D.; student Vanderbilt U., 1921; m. Annee Haley, Oct. 25, 1922; childrenMartha (Mrs. Houston Sarratt), William Lipscomb; m. 2d Adelaide Shull, Oct. 31, 1942; 1 son, Harrison Shull. Chmn., dir. Davis Cabinet Co., Nashville; dir. 3d Nat. Bank of Nashville, N.C. & St. Louis R.R. Co., Magic Chief, Inc., Kingsbury Homes, Inc. Mem. WLB, 1943-44. Trustee Vanderbilt U., MeLarry Med. Coll.; bd. dirs. Davidson County chpt. A.R.C. Served with SATC, World War I. Mem. Tenn. Mfg. Assn. (dir.), Nashville C. of C. (dir.). Mem. Ch. of Christ. Home: 929 Tyne Blvd Nashville TN 37220 Office: Davis Cabinet Co 5th and Crutcher Sts Nashville TN 37213

DAVIS, WILLIAM LUCE, Jr., elec. mfg. co. exec.; b. Grand Rapids, Mich., Jan. 27, 1918; s. William Luce and Alice (Tripp) D.; student Carleton Coll., 1935-39, Curtiss- Wright Tech. Inst., 1939-40, Mass. Inst. Tech., 1945; m. Audrey Bryngleson, Dec. 7, 1940 (dec.); children—William Luce III, Raymond Scott, Jeffery Bryng, Susan, Beth, m. 2d, Margaret R. Frazier, Jan. 3, 1969, With Curtiss-Wright Corp., 1940-42; with Emerson Electric Co., St. Louis, 1942—, pres., 1965-69, vice chmn., chief adminstrv. officer, 1969—; also dir.; dir. Merc. Trust Bd. dirs. St. Louis Area council Boy Scouts Am., Girl Scouts U.S.A., United Fund Greater St. Louis, Jr. Achievement Mississippi Valley, Mo. Pub. Expenditure Survey, St. Louis Met. UMCA, St. Louis Arta and Edn. Council, St. Louis Conv. and Tourist Bd.; trustee Washington U., KETC Channel 9 Ednl. TV Mem. Am. Ordnance Assn., Mo. C.of C., Assn. U.S. Army, Engrs. club St. Louis, Air Force Assn., Newcomen Soc. N.Am. Home: 13 Clermont Lane St Louis MO 63124 Office: 8100 Florissant Av St Louis MO 63136

DAVIS, WILLIAM POTTER, Jr., educator; b. Cleve., Aug. 27, 1924; s. William Potter and Vesper (Wood) D.; A.B., Oberlin Coll., 1948; M.S., U. Mich., 1949, Ph.D., 1954; M.A. (hon.), Dartmouth, 1967; m. Barbara Noel Day, Aug. 30, 1947; children—Glynis Wood, Jennifer Lanning, Christopher Lewis, Bethany Grinnel, Timothy Lord. Faculty, Dartmouth, Hanover, N.H., 1955—, instr. to prof. physics, asso. provost, 1967-70, acting dean Thayer Sch. Engring., 1969-70, budget officer, 1970—. Asso. program dir., pre-coll. edn. sci. div. NSF, 1965-66. Served with USNR, 1943-46. Mem. Dartmouth Sci. Assn., Am. Assn. Physics Tchrs., No. New Eng. Acad. Sci., A.A.A.S., Am. Mus. Nat. History, Sigma Xi, Phi Kappa Phi. Democrat. Conglist. Contbr. articles to profl. jours. Home: 7 Church St Norwich VT 05055 Office: Parkhurst Hall Dartmouth Coll Hanover NH 03755

DAVIS, WILLIAM ROBERT, banker; b. Clearfield, Pa., Sept. 24, 1916; s. E. Clair and Gertrude M. (Slcik) D.; grad. Peirce Sch. Bus., 1937, Stonier Grad. Sch. Banking Rutgers U.; m. Nan I. Pratt, June 15, 1940; 1 dau., Marilyn Ann. With Central-Penn Nat. Bank, Phila., 1937- 57; v.p. Camden Trust Co. (name changed to Bank of N.J.), 1957-58, pres., dir. 1958—; dir. Camden Fire Ins. Assn., Pub. Service Electric & Gas Co., Potomac Ins. Co., Pa. Gen. Ins. Co., mem. adv. com. Gen. Accident Group Ins. Cos.; mem. N.J. Banking Adv. Bd. Vice pres., trustee West Jersey Hosp.; trustee Greater Camden Movement, Camden County YMCA, Inst. for Med. Research, United Fund Camden County, Hosp. Survey Com., Pierce Jr. Coll. Mem. N.J. Bankers Assn. (pres. 1967-68), N.J. Soc. Pa., Camden County C. of C. (dir.). Clubs: Union League (Phila.), Tavistock Country (Haddonfield, N.J.); Seaview Country (Absecon, N.J.); Pine Valley Golf. Home: 301 Bellevue Av Haddonfield NJ 08033 Office: Bank of NJ Broadway at Market St Camden NJ

DAVIS, WILLIAM THOMAS, lawyer, corp. exec.; b. Salt Lake City, Apr. 1, 1908; s. Moses Cozzens and Maybelle (Thurman) D.; B.A., U. Cal., at Los Angeles, 1931, LL.B., at Berkeley, 1934; m. Elizabeth Lloyd, Oct. 18, 1938; children—William Lloyd, Elizabeth Lou. Admitted to Cal. bar, 1934; practice in Los Angeles, 1934-41; pres. Aircraft, Inc., Aircraft Parts Co., Lorraine, Inc., Santa Monica, Cal., 1941-48, Nat. Screw & Mfg. Co. of Cal., Los Angeles, 1948-50, Western Fruit Growers Sales Co., Fullerton, Cal., 1957- -, Blue Goose Growers, Inc., Fullerton, 1959—; former mem. firm Davis & Davis, Beverly Hills, Cal.; dir. The Lloyd Corp., Ltd., Beverly Hills. Mem. State Bar Cal., Los Angeles Bar Assn., U. Cal. at Los Angeles Alumni

Assn. (pres.), Alpha Delta Sigma, Delta Tau Delta. Home: 934 N Foothill Rd Beverly Hills CA 90210 Office: 9944 Santa Monica Blvd Beverly Hills CA

DAVIS, WILLIAM VIRGINIUS, orgn. exec.; b. Savannah, Ga., Jan. 28, 1902; s. William Virginius and Winifred (Bonney) D.; B.S., U.S. Naval Acad., 1924; m. Margaret Cary, Oct. 1, 1927; children—Judith Cary, Mary Winifred, William Virginius, Margaret Wright. Commd. ensigh USN, 1924, advanced through grades to vice adm., 1956; comdg. officer Torpedo Squadron 5, USS Yorktown, 1940-41; officer in charge aircraft armament unit Air Sta., Norfolk, Va., 1941-43; staff, comdr. aircraft Central Pacific Force, Pacific Fleet, 1943-44, dep. chief staff for operations, 1944, comdr. shore- based air force forward area Central Pacific, 1944, chief staff hdqrs. strategic air force Pacific Ocean Areas, 1944-45; comdr. USS Tulagi, 1945-46; project coordinator operational devel. force Atlantic Fleet, Norfolk, 1946-47; dir. flight tests Air Test Center, Patuxent River, Md., 1947-50, comdg. officer, 1951; comdg. officer USS Franklin D. Roosevelt, 1950-51; dep. comdr. field command Armed Forces Spl. Weapons Project, Sandia Base, 1952-55; comdr. carrier div. 5, Pacific Fleet, 1955-56; dep. chief Naval Operations (Air), 1956-58; dep. comdr.-in-chief U.S. Atlantic Fleet, 1958-60; sr. mil. adviser Lockheed Aircraft Corp., 1960-64; exec. dir. USS Alabama Battleship Commn., 1964—. Mem. Nat. Adv. Com. Aeros., 1956- 58. Decorated D.F.C., Legion of Merit Recipient Nat. Air Council ann. award for helicopter devels., high altitude jet flight, 1949. Home: 375 Franchilla Circle Fairhope AL 36532 Office: USS Battleship Commn PO Box 65 Mobile AL 36601

DAVISON, BILL WILLIAM, cornet player; b. Defiance, O., Jan. 5, 1906. Played banjo, mellophone, in high sch. band; record debut with Chubb Steinberg orch., 1924; played with theatre bands, Chgo., 1927-33; formed own group, Milw., 1933-40; leader of group, then with combo in Katherine Dunham Show, N.Y.C., 1940; performed with Art Hodes, Village Vanguard, then Condon's Club, 1946-57; ann. tour Europe, 1957—, with Dixieland bands in Germany, Switzerland, Austria; leader own quartet, U.S. Served with AUS, 1943-45. Address: 22 Central Park S New York City NY 10019*

DAVISON, CHARLES MARSHALL, Jr., educator; b. Richmond, Va., June 19, 1914; s. Charles Marshall and Katharine (Janney) Stonestreet D.; B.A., U. Va., 1935, J.D., 1937; m. Alida Wilson, Sept. 10, 1938; 1 dau., Katherine Stonestreet. Admitted to Va. bar, 1937, D.C. bar, 1941, W.Va., 1941; gen. practice law, Richmond, 1937-38, Clarksburg, W.Va., 1941-42, Washington, 1942-44, 46-47; with U. S. Treasury Dept., 1938-41; gen. tax atty. So. Ry. System, 1947- 51, gen. solicitor, 1951-54, comptroller, 1954-56, v.p. finance and taxation, Washington, 1956-63; prof. law U. Va., Charlottesville, 1963—; reporter Supreme Ct. Appeals of Va., 1967—. Served as 1st lt. USMCR, 1944- 46. Mem. Raven Soc., Order of Coif, Omicron Delta Kappa. Democrat. Episcopalian. Clubs: Metropolitan (Washington); Chevy Chase (Md.), Farmington (Charlottesville, W.Va.). Home: 1856 Edgewood Lane Charlottesville VA 22903

DAVISON, DANIEL POMEROY, banker; b. N.Y.C., Jan. 30, 1925; s. Frederick Trubee and Dorothy (Peabody) D.; grad. Groton (Mass.) Sch., 1943; B.A., Yale, 1949; LL.B., Harvard, 1952; m. Catherine Cheremeteff, June 27, 1953; children—Daniel Pomeroy, George Peabody, Henry Pomeroy. Admitted to N.Y. bar, 1952; asso. firm White & Case, N.Y.C., 1952-55; asst. sec., then sec. J.P. Morgan & Co., Inc., N.Y.C., 1955-59; with Morgan Guaranty Trust Co., N.Y.C., 1959—, v.p., 1961—, now v.p., gen. mgr., London, Eng.; dir. Northwestern State Portland Cement Co., Scovill Mfg. Co. Trustee Met. Mus. Art, Ch. Pension Fund, N.Y.C. Served with USAAF, 1943-45. Home: 85 Chester Sq London SW 1 England Office: 33 Lombard St London EC 3 England

DAVISON, DENVER N., justice Okla. Supreme Ct.; b. Rich Hill, Mo., Oct. 9, 1891; s. Benjamin P. and Lottie (Jones) D.; LL.B., U. Okla., 1915; m. Barbara Wilhelm, July 29, 1917; 1 son, Denver B. (dec.). Practiced law, Coalgate, Okla., 1915-27, Ada, Okla., 1927-37; mem. Supreme Ct. Okla., Oklahoma City, 1937—, chief justice on two occasions. Mem. original Will Rogers Commn. Served with U.S. Army, World War I. Mem. Alpha Tau Omega, Phi Delta Phi. Elk, Mason, K.P. Home: 1806 Huntington St Oklahoma City OK 73116 Office: State Capitol Bldg Oklahoma City OK 73102

DAVISON, ENDICOTT PEABODY, univ. ofcl., lawyer; b. N.Y.C., June 15, 1923; s. F. Trubee and Dorothy (Peabody) D.; grad. Groton Sch., 1941; B.A., Yale, 1948; LL.B., U. Va., 1951; m. Jane Ingalls, July 3, 1948; children—F. Trubee II (dec.), Endicott Peabody, Jane, David I., Malcolm. Admitted to N.Y. bar, 1951; practiced in N.Y.C., 1951-71; partner Winthrop, Stimson, Putnam & Roberts, 1959-71; corp. officer for instnl. devel. and capital support Yale U., 1971—. Bd. dirs. Union Theol. Sem.; trustee Groton (Mass.) Sch. Served with USAAF, World War II. Mem. Am. Bar Assn., Assn. Bar City N.Y., Nat. Recreation and Park Assn. (past chmn. bd.). Home: 221 Benedict Hill Rd New Canaan CT 06840 Office: 40 Wall St New York City NY 10005

DAVISON, FRANCIS WELLS, physician; b. Easton, Pa., June 20, 1902; s. Alvin and Kate (Wells) D.; B.S., Lafayette Coll., 1924; M.D., U. Pa., 1928; m. Margaret Vaughan Smith, June 9, 1928; childrenJoan Dudley (dec.), Richard Alvin. Intern Geisinger Hosp., Danville, Pa., 1928-29, resident otolaryngology, 1929- 31; asso. dept. otolaryngology and bronchoesophagology, 1931-36; dir. dep. otolaryngology and bronchoesophagology Geisinger Med. Center, Danville, 1936-64, senior cons., 1965-. Fellow American Laryngolog. Assn. (pres. 1968-69); mem. Am. Otological Soc. Am. Laryngolog., Rhinol. and Otol. Soc. (pres. 1965), Am. Broncho- Esophagological Assn. (pres. 1959). Home: Box 135 Danville, PA 17821. Office: Geisinger Med Center Danville, PA 17821.

DAVISON, FREDERIC ELLIS, army officer; b. Washington, Sept. 28, 1917; s. Albert Charles and Sue (Bright) D.; B.S. cum laude, Howard U., 1938, M.S., 1940; M.A., George Washington U., 1963; postgrad. Army War Coll., 1962-63; m. Jean Elizabeth Brown, Apr. 6, 1941; children—Jean Marie, Andrea Susan, Dayle Antoinette, Carla Molis. Commd. 2d lt. U.S. Army, 1939, advanced through grades to maj. gen., 1971; co. comdr., bn. operations officer, 1942-45; asst. prof. mil. sci. and tactics A. and M. Coll. S.C., 1947-50; exec. to dep. under sec. army, 1962-63; comdg. gen. 199th Light Inf. Brigade, 1968-69; dir. enlisted personnel Dept. Army, Washington, 1969—. Bd. dirs. Pentagon Fed. Credit Union. Decorated D.S.M., Legion of Merit, D.F.C., Bronze Star, Army Commendation medal. Mem. Kappa Alpha Psi. Roman Catholic. Home: 4205 18th St NW Washington DC 20011 Office: Pentagon Washington DC 20310

DAVISON, FREDERICK CORBET, univ. pres.; b. Atlanta, Sept. 3, 1929; s. Frederick Collins and Gladys (Carsley) D.; D.V.M., U. Ga., 1952; Ph.D., Ia. State U., 1963; m. Dianne Castle, Sept. 3, 1952; childrenFrederick Corbet, William Castle, Anne Harper. Pvt. practice vet. medicine, Marietta, Ga., 1952-58; research asst. Ia. State U., 1958-60, asst. prof., 1960-63, asso. Inst. Atomic Research, 1960-63; asst. dir. dept. sci. activities Am. Vet. Med. Assn., 1963-64; dean U. Ga. Sch. Vet. Medicine, Athens, 1964-66, vice chancellor univ. system, 1966-67, pres. univ., 1967—. Dir. Clarke Fed. Savs. & Loan Assn.; mem. Inst. Animal Resources, Nat. Acad. Sci.-NRC, 1965— Pres., N.E. Ga. commn. Boy Scouts Am. Trustee Rabun Gap-Nacoochee Sch. Mem. Am., Ga. vet. med. assns., Council Biol. and Therapeutic Agts., Sigma Xi, Phi Kappa Phi, Sigma Alpha Epsilon, Omega Tau Sigma, Alpha Zeta, Phi Zeta, Gamma Sigma Delta. Rotarian. Contbr. articles to profl. jours. Home: 570 Prince Av Athens, GA 30601.

DAVISON, JEAN MARGARET, educator. Prs. classical langs. and history U. Vt., Burlington. Office: Dept Classics U Vt Burlington VT 05401*

DAVISON, MICHAEL SHANNON, army officer; b. San Francisco, Mar. 21, 1917; s. Paul Root and Gladys Marie (Hamm) D.; B.S., U.S. Mil. Acad., 1939; M.P.A., Harvard, 1951; m. Jean Helen Miller, June 22, 1940; children—Michael Shannon, Mary Jean, Donald Angus. Commd. 2d lt. U.S. Army, 1939, advanced through grades to lt. gen., 1968; comdg. officer bn., 45th Inf., Div., 1944; with G-3 VI Corps, 1945; mem. Office Chief Staff, U.S. Army, 1951-54; assigned Nat. War Coll., 1957-58; staff Office Chief Research and Devel., U.S. Army, 1958-61; comdg. officer combat command A, 3d Armored Div., 1961; chief staff V Corps, 1962; comdt. cadets U.S. Mil. Acad., 1962-65; mem. staff Pentagon, Washington, 1965-66; comdt. Command and Gen. Staff Coll., Ft. Leavenworth, Kan., 1966-68; dep. comdr. U.S. Army Pacific, Ft. Saafter, 1968—. Decorated Silver Star, Legion of Merit, Bronze Star, Army Commendation medal, D.S.M.; Croix de Guerre (France). Home: 9 Palm Circle Dr Ft Shafter HI 36558 Office: care of Office Adj Gen Dept Army Washington DC 20310

DAVISON, PETER HUBERT, editor, writer; b. N.Y.C., June 27, 1928; s. Edward and Natalie (Weiner) D.; A.B. magna cum laude, Harvard, 1949; Fulbright scholar, St. John's Coll., Cambridge (Eng.) U., 1949-50; m. Jane Auchincloss Truslow, Mar. 7, 1959; children—Edward Angus, Lesley Truslow. Page, U.S. Senate, 1944; asst. editor Harcourt, Brace & Co., 1950-51, 53-55; asst. to dir. Harvard U. Press, 1955-56; asso. editor Atlantic Monthly Press, 1956-59, exec. editor, 1959- 64, dir. 1964—, dir. Atlantic Monthly Co. Mem. adv. bd. Nat. Transl. Center, 1965-68. Trustee Fountain Valley Sch. Served with AUS, 1951-53. Winner competition Yale Series Younger Poets, 1963. Mem. Phi Beta Kappa. Democrat. Clubs: Examiner, St Botolph Boston, Editor's Lunch, Harvard, Century (N.Y.C.), Signet Soc. (Cambridge, Mass.). Author: (poems) The Breaking of the Day, 1964, The City and the Island, 1966; Pretending to Be Asleep, 1970. Contbr. poems, articles to numerous mags., anthologies. Home: 11 Mellen St Cambridge MA 02138 Office: 8 Arlington St Boston MA 02116

DAVISON, ROBERT HOWELL, lawyer; b. Boston, May 30, 1896; s. Frank Gilman and Virginia (Hackett) D.; A.B., Harvard, 1917, LL.B., 1921; m. Elisabeth Ten Broeck Jackson, Sept. 1, 1923; children—Robert Ten Broeck, Judith S. (Mrs. Langdon Hockmeyer), Nicholas S. Admitted to Mass. bar, 1921; partner firm Haussermann, Davison & Stattuck, Boston, 1921—. Treas. Elizabeth Carleton House, Boston, 1959-69, trustee, 1947—. Served to lt. (j.g.) USN, 1917-22. Republican. Clubs: Country (Brookline, Mass.); Harvard (Boston and N.Y.C.). Home: 285 Warren St Brookline MA 02146 Office: 15 State St Boston MA 02109

DAVISON, ROBERT WILLIAM, mfg. co. exec.; b. Kansas City, Mo., Jan. 13, 1917; s. John E. and Willa (McCoy) D.; student U. Mo., 1935-39; m. Margaret L. Barnard, July 10, 1942; children—Robert William, Margaret Eleanor. Salesman, product mgr., asst. area mgr., area mgr., dir. sales planning, asst. exec. v.p. Armco Steel Corp., Middletown, O., 1940-62; div. gen. mgr., div. v.p., gen. mgr., exec. v.p. H.K. Porter Co., Inc., Pitts., 1962—. Home: 202 Buckingham Rd Pittsburgh PA 15215 Office: HK Porter Co 6th and Grant Sts Pittsburgh PA 15215

DAVISON, RODERIC HOLLETT, educator, historian; b. Buffalo, Apr. 27, 1916; s. Walter Seaman and Eloise (Hollett) D.; A.B., Princeton, 1937; A.M., Harvard, 1938, Ph.D. (fellow Social Sci. Research Council, Kent fellow Nat. Council Religion in Higher Edn.) 1942; m. Louise Atherton Dickey, June 18, 1949; childrenR. John, Richard H. Instr. history Princeton, 1940-42, 46- 47; faculty history George Washington U., 1947-, prof., 1954-, chmn. dept., 1960-64, 69-70. Lectr. diplomatic history Johns Hopkins Sch. Advanced Internat. Studies, 1951-52, 55-58; vis. lectr. Harvard, 1960. Served with Am. Friends Service Com., 1942-44; Civilian Pub. Service Camp, 1944- 46. Faculty fellow Fund for Advancement Edn., 1953-54; Guggenheim fellow, 1970-71. Mem. Am. Hist. Assn., Am. Assn. U. Profs., Nat. Council Religion in Higher Edn., Phi Beta Kappa, Author: The Near and Middle East: An Introduction to History and Bibliography, 1959; Reform in the Ottoman Empire, 1856-1876, 1963; Turkey, 1968. Contbg. author: The Diplomats 1919-1939, 1953; Guide to Hist. Lit., 1961. Adv. bd. editors Middle East Jour., 1954—. Contbr. articles to profl. jours. Home: 3506 Lowell St NW Washington, DC 20016.

DAVISON, VERNON GILL, educator; b. Pineland, Tex., Dec. 11, 1907; s. Dan D. and Esther Lee (Gill) D.; A.B., Howard Payne Coll., 1932; Ph.D., So. Bapt. Theol. Sem., 1939, Th.M., 1934; m. Marjorie F. Winebrenner, Aug. 13, 1933; 1 dau., Oran Francis (Mrs. Charles Creel). Ordained to ministry Bapt. Ch., 1932; faculty Samford U., Birmingham, Ala., 1939—, prof. religion and phiosophy, 1939—, chmn. div., 1957—. Served as chaplain USNR, 1943- 46. Mem. So. Bapt. Assn. Tchrs. Religion, Soc. Bibl. Lit. and Exegesis, Nat. Assn. Bibl. Instrs., Am. Acad. Religion, Soc. for Sci. Study Religion, Omicron Delta Kappa, Kappa Phi Kappa. Research cultural background India in Calcutta, 1962, Chinese community, 1963. Home: 550 Lakeshore Dr Birmingham AL 35209

DAVISON, WILBURT CORNELL, pediatrician; b. Grand Rapids, Mich., Apr. 28, 1892; s. William L. (D.D.) and Mattie E. (Cornell) D.; A.B., Princeton, 1913; Sr. Demy (Rhodes scholar 1913-16), Magdalen Coll., Oxford, Eng., 1915-17; B.A., Oxford U., 1915, B.Sc., 1916, M.A., 1919; M.D., Johns Hopkins, 1917; D.Sc., Wake Forest Coll., 1932; LL.D., U. N.C., 1944, Duke, 1961; m. Atala Thayer Scudder, June 2, 1917; children—William Townsend, Atala Jane Scudder Levinthal, Alexander Thayer. Instr., asso. prof., acting head dept. pediatrics, asst. dean, Johns Hopkins Med. Sch., 1919-27; asso. pediatrician, acting pediatrician in charge, editor Bull. Johns Hopkins Hosp., 1919-27; dean, James B. Duke prof. pediatrics Duke Sch. Medicine, 1927-61; cons. Womack Army Hosp; mem. medico adv. bd. CARE; trustee Duke Endowment; v.p. bd. dirs. Doris Duke Found. Mem. div. med. scis. NRC, vice chmn. 1942-43; cons. office Surgeon Gen., U.S. Army; adv. group Armed Forces Med. Library; mem. com. on vets. med. problems; mem. com. atomic casualties NRC; mem. med. adv. com. N.C. Bd. Mental Health; mem. med. adv. panel Oak Ridge Inst. Nuclear Studies; mem. council chief cons. VA; mem. dean's com. Durham VA Hosp.; mem. N.C. gov's working com. Research Triangle Devel. Council, N.C. Nuclear Energy Adv. Com; dir. Playtex Park Research Inst.; med. adv. com. Research Found.; nat. adv. com. Chronic Disease and Health of Aged; trustee Ednl. Council Fgn. Med. Grad.; mem. Civilian Health and Med. Adv. Council; chmn. OSD Hosp. Planning Group. Served with AEC, 1914-15. France, Serbia; capt. M.C., U.S. Army AEF, 1917-19; served to col. AUS. Recipient Alvaranga prize, 1917. Master A.C.P.; mem. Am. Acad. Pediatrics, Am. Coll. Clin. Adminstrn. (hon.), Am. Pediatric Soc., Soc. for Pediatric Research, Am. Soc. Clin. Investigation, N.C. Pediatric Soc., Am. Acad. Gen. Practice (hon.), Assn. Pediatricians de Guatemala (hon.), Phi Beta Kappa, Sigma Xi, Omicron Delta Kappa, Alpha Omega Alpha (pres.). Democrat. Methodist. Clubs: Cosmos (Washington). Hope Valley Country, Roaring Gap Yacht. Author: Pediatric Notes, 1925; (with S.A. Waksman) Enzymes; 1926; The Compleat Pediatrician, 1934, 38, 40, 44, 46, 49, 57, 61. Contbr. articles to profl. jours. Home: Roaring Gap NC 28668

DAVIT, ALEXANDER JOSEPH, govt. ofcl.; b. Phila., Dec. 22, 1917; s. Joseph and Cecile Marie (Janavel) D.; student Girard Coll., 1935-36; B.S., W.Chester State Tchrs. Coll., 1939; postgrad. Temple U., eves. 1940-41, Grad. Sch., Princeton, 1956-57, Indsl. Coll. Armed Forces, 1964-65; m. Margaret Collier, Feb. 7, 1942; children—Alexander Joseph, M. Cecile. Exec. sec. Fire Assn., Phila., 1939; adminstr. asst. Camden Storage and Warehousing Co., 1940; 3d sec., vice consul Am. embassy, Damascus, 1946; vice consul, Port Elizabeth, 1949; 2d sec., consul, Tangier, 1950; assigned Liberian desk State Dept., 1952; 1st sec., consul, Kuala Lumpur, 1957; comml. attache, Paris, 1960; coordinator jr. officer tng. State Dept., 1965, chmn., 1971—, comml. counselor, Paris, 1967; mem. bd. examiners, 1971; vis. lectr. Princeton, 1956. Served to capt. AUS, 1942-45. Decorated Bronze Star, Purple Heart with cluster. Mem. Girard, West Chester Coll. alumni assns. Club: Lions (Kuala Lumpur). Contbr. Ency. Britannica. Home: 500 23d St NW Washington DC 20037

DAVITT, THOMAS EDWARD, educator; b. Adrian, Mich., May 6, 1904; s. Thomas James and Anna (Howley) D.; A.B., U. Detroit, 1932; M.A., St. Louis U., 1936, Ph.D., 1950. Asst. prof. jurisprudence St. Louis U., 1947-53, asso. prof., 1953-54; asso. prof. Marquette U., 1954-60, prof. philosophy, 1960—; adv. editor Am. Jour. Jurisprudence, 1955—. Guggenheim fellow for research in European Legal Centers, 1956-57; Am. Philos. Soc. grantee, 1960-61, 61-62. Mem. Am. Arbitration Assn. (mem. nat. panel arbitrators). Author: The Nature of Law, 1951; The Elements of Law, 1959; The Basic Values on Law-A Study of the Ethico-Legal Implications Psychology and Anthropology, 1968; Ethics in the Situation, 1970. Home: 1131 W Wisconsin Av Milwaukee WI 53233 Office: 1103 W Wisconsin Av Milwaukee WI 53233

DAVRATH, NETANIA, singer; student music in Israel, with Jennie Tourel in U.S. Leading roles with Israel Opera, also with Israel Philharmonic, London Philharmonic, Utah Symphony, others; debut Town Hall, N.Y.C., 1962; rec. artist Vanguard. Address: care Vanguard Rec Soc 154 W 14th St New York City NY 10011

DAVY, GLORIA, soprano; b. Bklyn., Mar. 29, 1931; d. George and Lucy (Crick) Davy; B.S., Juilliard Sch. Music, 1953; m. Hermann Penningsfeld, Jr., Nov. 17, 1959; one son, Jean-Marc Penningsfeld. Made debut with Little Orchestra Soc., Town Hall, 1954, Vienna State Opera, 1959, Convent Garden Opera, 1960; opera debut Am., Met. Opera Co., Inc., N.Y.C., 1958, now mem. co. guest performances La Scala in Milan, San Carlo, Naples, Teatro Communale, Bologna, Teatro Massimo, Palermo, Teatro Reggio, Parma; others; guest contract, Deutsche Oper Berlin, 1962-64; yearly concert tours Italy, Germany, France, Switzerland, U.S. Recipient Marian Anderson award, 1951, Marian Anderson spl. award, 1952; award Music Edn. League, N.Y.C., 1953. Home: 30 rue du Nant Geneva Switzerland Office: care Maurice Feldman 745 Fifth Av New York City NY 10022

DAVY, LEE GEORGE, mfg. exec.; b. Boulder, Colo., Nov. 16, 1908; s. George W. and Hettie (Shaub) D.; A.B., Cornell U., 1931, Ph.D., 1934; D.Sc., King Coll., 1962; m. Helen L. Pratt, June 9, 1931; children—L.Nevil, George P., Susan J. With Tenn. Eastman Co., Kingsport, 1934—, research chemist, chief chemist RDX devel. work Holston ordnance works, asst. div. supt., div. supt., gen. supt., dir. new product devel., exec. v.p., 1934-63, exec. v.p., 1963—. Pres., Kingsport Symphony Orch. Assn. Trustee King Coll. Mem. Am. Chem. Soc., A.A.A.S., Am. Inst. Chem. Engrs., Sigma Xi, Phi Kappa Phi. Rotarian (past pres.). Home: 1532 Belmeade Dr Kingsport TN 37664 Office: Tenn Eastman Co Eastman Rd Kingsport TN 37662

DAWALT, KENNETH FRANCIS, aerospace co. exec.; b. Salem, Ind., Aug. 18, 1911; s. Dan and Nelle (Whitson) D.; student DePauw U., 1929-32; B.S., U.S. Mil. Acad., 1936; grad. Command and Gen. Staff Coll., 1943, Army War Coll., 1954; m. Kathryn Marie King, June 9, 1940; children—Karen King (Mrs. Ernest Baynard III), Karie Whitson. Commd. 2d lt. U.S. Army, 1936, advanced through grades to brig. gen., 1961; instr., then asst. prof. physicis U.S. Mil. Acad., 1941-45; assigned 442d Arty. Group, 1945; comdr. 999th F.A. Battalion, also 1st Republic Korea Div. Arty., 1950-51; assigned research and devel. Dept. Army, 1951-53; mem. faculty Command and Gen. Staff Coll., 1954-57; U.S. del. to NATO, 1957-60; comdr. 2d U.S. Army Missile Command, 1960-61, 30th Arty. Brigade, 1961-63; dep. dir. Def. Atomic Support Agy., 1963-66; dep. dir. army research and devel. (internat. programs), 1966-70; mem. mil. liaison com. AEC, 1966-70, NATO Army Armanents Group, Brussels, Belgium, 1966-70; exec. v.p. French Aerospace Corp., N.Y.C., 1970—. Dir. Investors Equity Benefit Assn., Norfolk, Va., 1966—. Decorated Silver Star, Legion of Merit with one oak leaf cluster, Army Commendation ribbon with 1 oak leaf cluster, Distinguished Service Medal. Mem. Assn. U.S. Army, Assn. Grads. U.S. Mil. Acad., Beta Theta Pi. Methodist. Mason. Club: Army-Navy Country (bd. govs.) (Arlington, Va.). Home: 6316 Golf Course Square Alexandria VA 22307 Office: French Aerospace Corp 1145 19th St NW Washington DC 20036

DAWBER, BRYAN ASTON, life ins. co. physician; b. Eng., Apr. 30, 1909; s. Mark Aston and Mary (Hope) D.; came to U.S., 1911, naturazlied, 1923; B.S., Hahnemann Coll. Sci., Phila., 1937; M.D., Hahnemann Med. Coll., 1937; m. Ethel Marie Neveling, July 1, 1938 (dec. 1965); 1 son, Mark Aston II; m. 2d, Gloria C. Bruno, Apr. 30, 1966. Intern, Chestnut Hill Hosp., Phila., 1937- 38; pvt. practice, Seaford, Del., 1938-39; with USPHS, 1939-48, med. officer U.S.S. Nourmahal, 1942, sr. med. officer, base surgeon USCG Tng. Sta., Groton, Conn., 1942; resigned, 1948; mem. med. staff Penn Mut. Life Ins. Co., 1948—, med. dir., 1959—. Med. dir. U.S. Pub. Health Service Res. Diplomate Bd. Life Ins. Medicine. Fellow Phila. Coll. Physicians; mem. Am., Pa., Philadelphia County med. assns., Life Ins. Med. Dirs. Assn., Life Ins. Mgmt. Assn. Home: 2501 Pine St Philadelphia PA 19103 Office: 530 Walnut St Philadelphia PA 19105

DAWES, GEOFFREY SHARMAN, med. researcher; b. Derbyshire, Eng., Jan. 21, 1918; s. William and Olive (White) D.; B.A., Oxford (Eng.) U., 1939, B.Sc., 1940, B.M., B.Ch., 1943, D.M., M.A., 1947; m. Margaret Joan Monk, Apr. 15, 1941; children—Caroline Harriet, Alison Jennifer, Nicholas William, Martin Geoffrey. Fellow, Worcester Coll., Oxford (Eng.) U., 1947; dir. Nuffield Inst. Med. Research, Oxford U., 1948—. Vis. prof. U. Cal. at San Francisco, 1966; Rockefeller fellow Harvard, 1946; recipient Max Weinstein award United Cerebral Palsy Assn., 1963; Gairdner Foun. annual award, 1966; James Spence medal Brit. Pediatric Assn., 1969. Gov., Sir John Port's Charity, Repton Sch., 1959—, chmn., 1971—. Fellow Royal Coll. Obstetricians and Gynecologists, Royal Soc.; mem.

Neonatal Soc. (pres. 1965-69). Author: Foetal and Neonatal Physiology, 1967. Home: 8 Belbroughton Rd Oxford England Office: Nuffield Inst Med Research Osler Rd Headington Oxford England

DAWES, IRVING HEMPHILL, petroleum exec.; b. Stoughton, Wis., Nov. 19, 1907; s. Julius and Estella (Wilkinson) D.; LL.B., U. Wis., 1931; m. Ruth Lindall, June 19, 1933; children—Elizabeth, Constance. Admitted to Wis. bar, 1932; pvt. practice corporate law, Milw., 1931-43. Chmn. exec. com. Clark Oil & Refining Corp. Chmn. Wis. Petroleum Council. Mem. Am., Wis. bar assn. Mason. Home: 13330 Blue Mound Rd Milwaukee WI 53226 Office: 8350 W National Av Milwaukee WI 53227

DAWES, RICHARD IRVING, metals co. exec.; b. Arlington, Mass., Nov. 24, 1919; s. Irving Desmond and Corinne Lee (Thies) D.; A.B., Harvard, 1940, M.B.A., 1942; m. Elisabeth Hewitt Coffin, Apr. 2, 1949; children—Alan Stuart, Carol Winfield, Beverly Gail. Adminstrv. asst. inventory control dept. Reynolds Metals Co., Richmond, Va., 1946-48, scheduling mgr. printing div., 1948-53, staff asst. to gen. prodn. control mgr., 1953-57, asst. corporate sec., 1957-70, corporate sec., 1970—; sec., asst. sec., dir. various subsidiaries and affiliates Reynolds Metals Co. Chmn. March of Dimes drive, 1953, chmn. Richmond-Henrich chpt., 1954. Bd. dirs. West End Community Center, Richmond, 1959—, treas., 1959—. Served to lt. USNR, 1942-46. Mem. Am. Soc. Corporate Secs., Richmond C. of C., Va. Mfrs. Assn., Asso. Harvard Alumni (Middle Atlantic area v.p. 1961-64), Collegiate Schs. Patrons Assn. (v.p., pres. elect 1971—). Presbyn. (asst treas. 1963—, deacon, 1971—). Clubs: Harvard of Virginia (past pres.), Country of Virginia, Richmond Gentry (dir., sec.) (Richmond). Home: 8900 Watlington Rd Richmond VA 23229 Office: 6601 Broad St Rd PO Box 29003 Richmond VA 23261

DAWKINS, BEN C., Jr., judge; b. Monroe, La., Aug. 6, 1911; s. Ben C. and Alice (McLeod) D.; A.B., Tulane U., 1932; J.D., La. State U., 1934; m. Harriet White, Jan. 1, 1936; children Cynthia, Ben C., Franklin White. Admitted to La. bar, 1934, practiced in Monroe, 1934-35, Shreveport, 1935-53; mem. firm Blanchard, Goldstein, Walker & O'Quin, 1935-53; U.S. dist. judge Western Dist. La. 1953—. Pres., Shreveport Recreation Council, 1941; dir. Children's Service Bur., 1947-51, Child Guidance Clinic, 1952; mem. sch. bd. Caddo Parish Sch., 1949-53, pres., 1950-52. Served as lt. comdr., air navigator USNR, 1942-45. Research fellow Southwestern Legal Found. Mem. Am., La. (bd. govs. 1950-52), Shreveport (v.p. 1941- 42, sec.-treas. 1947-48, pres. 1949-50) bar assns., Shreveport C. of C., Jr. C. of C., Am. Legion, V.F.W. (post comdr. 1946-47, judge adv. La. dept. 1947-48), Delta Kappa Epsilon, Phi Delta Phi, Omicron Delta Kappa. Episcopalian (vestryman). Rotarian. Home: 054 Baltimore St Shreveport LA 71106 Office: Federal Bldg Shreveport LA 71101

DAWLEY, MELVIN EMERSON, retail store exec.; b. Grand Rapids, Mich., Feb. 9, 1905; s. Albert Emerson and Mary (Vandenberg) D.; B.S., Northwestern U., 1927; m. Dorothy Tisch, June 26, 1931; children—Donna Gayle, David Albert. Supr. stores Marks Stores, Inc, Grand Rapids, Mich., 1927-33; asst. to sales v.p. Montgomery Ward & Co. Chgo., 1933-35, display dir., 1935-36; buyer, mdse. mgr. Lord & Taylor, N.Y.C., 1936-46, v.p., 1946-59, dir., 1947—, pres., chief exec. officer, 1959-68, chmn. chief exec. officer, 1968—. Pres., Fifth Av. Assn., 1966-68, chmn., 1968—; v.p., dir. Asso. Dry Goods Corp. Trustee Citizens Budget Commn. N.Y.; hon. chmn. bd. dirs. Ednl. Found. Apparel Industry; bd. dirs. Better Bus. Bur. Hon. life fellow Met. Mus. Art; Mem. Met. N.Y. Retail Mchts. Assn. (dir.), Delta Tau Delta, Alpha Kappa Psi. Mem. Protestant Ref. Ch. Clubs: Field, Siwanoy Country (Bronxville); University (N.Y.C.); National Golf Links Am. Home: 17 Elm Lane Bronxville NY 10708 Office: 424 Fifth Av New York City NY 10018

DAWLEY, POWEL MILLS, educator, clergyman; b. Newport, R.I., Mar. 1, 1907; s. William James and Mabel Cleveland (Wilson) D.; Ph. B., Brown U., 1929, A.M., 1931, D.D., 1965; B.D. (Phillips Brook fellow), Episcopal Theol. Sch., 1936, D.D., 1961; Ph.D., U. Cambridge (Eng.) Corpus Christi Coll., 1938; S.T.D. Gen. Theol. Sem. 1955; m. Dorothy Wainwright Knapp, Dec. 1, 1941; children—Victoria Wainwright, Pamela Wilson, Dorothy Maris. Ordained dean P.E. Ch., 1935, priest, 1936; asso. rector St. David's Ch., Balt., 1938-42; dean St. Luke's Cathedral, Portland, Me., 1942-45; prof ecclesiastical history Gen. Theol. Sem., N.Y.C., 1945-71, sub-dean, prof. emeritus, 1971—. Mem. Am. Soc. Ch. History, Lambda Sigma Nu. Mason (32), Author: The Religion of The Prayer Book, 1943; Chapters in Church History, 1950; The Words of Life, 1950; John Whitgift and the English Reformation, 1954; The Episcopal Church and its Work, 1955; Our Christian Heritage, 1959; The Story of the General Theological Seminary, 1969; The Story of the General Theological Seminary, 1969. Home: 6 Sparwell Lane Brunswick ME 04011

DAWN, CLARENCE ERNEST, educator; b. Chattanooga, Dec. 6, 1918; s. Fred Hartman and Hettie Lou (Gibson) D.; B.A., U. Chattanooga, 1941; M.A., Princeton, 1947, Ph.D., 1948; m. Pansie Mozelle Dooley, July 8, 1944; children—Julia Anne, Carolyn Louise. Instr. dept. history U. Ill., Urbana, 1949-52, asst. prof., 1952-55, asso. prof., 1955-60, prof., 1960—. Social Sci. Research Council World Area fellow, 1948-49; fellow joint com. on Near and Middle East, Social Sci. Research Council and Am. Council Learned Socs., 1966-67; Fulbright-Hays fellow,, 1966-67. Served with AUS, 1942-46, U.S. Army, 1951-52. Mem. Am. Hist. Assn., Middle East Studies Assn., Middle East Inst. Home: 1504 S Grove St Urbana IL 61801

DAWSON, CHARLES R., educator; b. Peterboro, N.H., Apr. 9, 1911; s. John C. and Eva B. (Trueman) D.; B.S., U. N.H., 1933, M.S., 1935, D.Sc. (hon.) 1953; fellow, Columbia, 1937-38, Ph. D., 1938; Cutting traveling fellow Cambridge (Eng.) U., 1938-39; m. Dorothea A. Lockard, Aug. 21, 1937; childrenPatricia Louise, Sarah Mae, John Harold. Instr. chemistry U. N.H., 1933-35; asst. organic chemistry Columbia, 1935-37, instr., 1939- 42, asst. prof., 1942-46, asso. prof. organic chemistry, 1946-52, now prof. chemistry; asst. to dean Columbia Coll., 1944-55; research cons. fields enzyme chemistry and natural products, poison ivy, cashew nutshell oil, copper proteins. Bd. dirs. N.Y. Bot. Gardens, 1962—; pres. Bd. Edn. Leonia, N.J., 1958-60, chmn. Recreation Commn., Leonia, 1965-68. Fellow Am. Inst. Chemists; mem. Am. Chem. Soc. (chmn. N.Y. sect. 1967-68), A.A.A.S., N.Y. Acad. Sci., Am. Soc. Biol. Chemists, Sigma Xi, Phi Lambda Upsilon, Phi Kappa Phi, Alpha Chi Sigma. Republican. Contbr. articles profl. jours. Home: 177 Lakeview Av Leonia NJ 07605 Office: Columbia U New York City NY 10027

DAWSON, CHRISTOPHER MOUNSEY, educator; b. Sunderland, Eng., Apr. 20, 1908; s. Christopher Mowbray and Eugenie Mary Anne (Mounsey) D.; B.A., Emmanuel Coll. Cambridge, 1929, diploma classical archaeology, 1930; Ph. D., Yale, 1941; m. Marjorie Elliott Morse, June 29, 1933; 1 dau., Julia Anne. Came to U.S., 1938, naturalized, 1945. Asst. prof. classics Acadia (N.S.) U., 1930-38; faculty Yale, 1940—, prof. Greek, 1950-52, Talcott prof. Greek, 1952—. Recipient Medaglia di benemerenza in connection with bicentenary of Pompeii's discovery, 1948, Guggenheim fellow, 1957. Mem. Am. Philol. Assn., New Eng. Classical Assn. Author: Romano— Campanian Mythological Landscape Painting, 1944; The Iambi of Callimachus, 1950.. Translater with notes Letters of Alexandro Malaspina (1790-1791), 1944; transl. with commentary Aeschylus, The Seven Against Thebes, 1970. Contbr. articles to profl. jours. Home: 121 Old Farm Rd Hamden, CT 06517. Office: Silliman Coll Yale U New Haven CT 06520

DAWSON, CLAYTON LEROY, educator, author; b. Seattle, Mar. 25, 1921; s. Charles Brady II and Lillie (Stenmoe) D.; B.A., U. Wash., 1949; M.A., Harvard, 1951, Ph.D., 1954; m. Elizabeth Grace Abbott, Mar. 31, 1951; childrenRobert Freeland, Margaret Ferne. Asst. prof., asst. dir. E. European lang. program Syracuse U., 1953-57; lang. adviser Air Force Inst. Tech., 1957- 59; prof., chmn. dept. Slavic langs. and lits. Syracuse U., 1959-66; prof., head dept. Slavic langs. and lits. U. Ill., Urbana, 1966—. Cons. in field, 1961—. Mem. subcom. grants Russian and Soviet studies Am. Council learned Socs., 1966—; Mem. inaugural selection com. Center for 20th Century Studies, U. Wis. Milw., 1969—. Served with AUS, 1942-45. Mem. Linguistic Soc. Am., Modern Lang. Assn., Am. Assn. Tchrs. Slavic and E. European Langs. (sec.-treas. Ill. 1968-69, pres. 1969-70. Author: Intensive Russian, 5 vols., 1954-57; (with A. Humesky, C. Bidwell) Modern Russian I, 1964; (with A. Humesky) Modern Russian II, 1965. Home: 1106 Silver St Urbana, IL 61801.

DAWSON, CLYDE CHALKLEY, lawyer; b. Canon City, Colo., Aug. 20, 1905; s. Clyde C. and Kathryn (Russell) D.; Ph.B., Yale, 1927; LL.B., Denver Law Sch., 1930; m. Mary Henry, Jan. 4, 1936; 1 dau., Caroline. Admitted to Colo. bar, 1930, since practiced in Denver; asso. Pershing, Bosworth, Dick & Dawson, 1928- 34, partner, 1934-56; sr. mem. firm Dawson, Nagel, Sherman & Howard, 1956—. Instr. municipal corps, Denver Law Sch., 1937-41. Served to lt. comdr. USNR, 1943-45. Mem. Am., Colo., Denver bar assns. Clubs: Denver Country, University, Mile High (Denver); Garden of the Gods (Colorado Springs). Home: 1250 Humboldt St Denver CO 80210 Office: First Nt Bank Bldg Denver CO 80202

DAWSON, DAVID HAIGH, chemist; b. Phila., Sept. 3, 1908; s. Josiah and Anne (Haigh) D.; B.S., in Chem. Engring., Drexel Inst. Tech., 1930, M.S., 1931, Ph.D., 1933, D. Eng. (hon.), 1947; m. Ann Fox, Aug. 25, 1933; children—Ann Elizabeth, David Bruce, Thomas Michael. Teaching asst. Ohio State U., 1930-33; research chemist Krebs Pigment & Color Corp., Balt., 1933-35; research supr. pigments dept., E. I. du Pont de Nemours & Co., Wilmington, Del., 1935-44, asst. dir. research, 1944-46, dir. sales, 1946-48, asst. gen. mgr., 1948-51, asst. gen. mgr. fabrics and finishes dept., 1951-53, asst. gen. mg. textile fibers dept., 1953-55, v.p., dir., mem. exec. com., 1955—. Fellow A.A.A.S.; mem. Am. Chem. Society, Mfg. Chemists' Assn. Home: RFD 1 Chadds Ford PA 19317 Office: Dupont Bldg Wilmington DE 19801

DAWSON, E.P., savs. and loan assn. exec. Exec. v.p. First Fed. Savs. and Loan of Broward County (Fla.). Office: 301 E Las Olas Blvd Fort Lauderdale FL 33302*

DAWSON, EUGENE ELLSWORTH, coll. pres.; b. Kansas City, Kan., Jan. 23, 1917; s. Harold L. and Bessie (Ross) D.; A.B., Kan. State Tchrs. Coll., 1940; S.T.B. (Williams scholar), Harvard, 1944; Ph.D., Boston U., 1949; postgrad. U. Chgo., 1953; L.H.D., Regis Coll., U. Colo.; Litt.D., Keuka Coll.; m. Arlene Clark, June 6, 1935; children—Eugene Ellsworth, LoLita, Edward, Brent, Deborah. Asst. prof. psychology, dir. religious activities Kan. State Tchrs. Coll., 1946-49, prof. psychology, dean adminstrn. and students, 1949-57; nat. coordinator tchr. edn. religion project Am. Assn. Colls. Tchr. Edn., 1954-56; pres. Temple Buell Coll., 1957-70; pres. U. Redlands (Cal.), 1970—. Instr. summer sessions U. Chgo., Kent State U., U. Houston, Ore. Coll. edn.; mem. adv. com. Inst. Internat. Edn. Bd. dirs. Redlands YMCA, Boy Scouts Am. Mem. N.E.A., Colo. Schoolmasters, (hon. mem.), Central Assn. Colls. and Secondary Schs. (mem. com. colls. and univs.), Psi Chi, Pi Kappa Delta. Baptist. Clubs: Rotary, (pres. Denver 1964-65, dist. gov. 1967-68), Univerity (Los Angeles); Redlands Country, Redlands Swim and Tennis, Redlands Racquet; California. Contbr. articles in U.S. and fgn. ednl., religious jours. Home: 325 Grove St Redlands CA 92373

DAWSON, FRANK MATTHEWS, oil co. exec.; b. Houston, 1908; s. Frank and Mary J. (Matthews) D.; B.S. in Chem. Engring., Rice Inst., 1928; m. Bessie M. Griffith, June 10, 1929; children—Frank G., George. With Texaco, Inc., 1928—, refinery supt., 1942-54, mgr. purchasing dept., 1954-55, v.p., 1955-62; former pres. Texaco Can. Ltd. Mem. Phi Lambda Upsilon. Clubs: Cloud (N.Y.C.); Mt. Royal (Montreal). Home: 1460 McGregor St Montreal 25 Quebec Canada

DAWSON, GEORGE GLENN, editor; b. Shelter Island, N.Y., Aug. 16, 1925; s. Harry and Frances (Menafee) D.; B.S. summa cum laude, N.Y.U., 1956, M.A., 1957, Ph.D. (Danforth fellow), 1959; m. Shirley Catherine Meader, Jan. 18, 1947. Instr. edn. N.Y.U., 1957-59, asst. prof. social studies edn., 1959-62, asso. prof., 1962-65, prof., head social studies div., 1965-70, chmn. dept. social studies edn. Sch. Edn., 1965-70, dir. Peace Corps Somalia project, 1962-64, dir. Center Econ. Edn., 1965-70; dir. research and publns. Joint Council Econ. Edn., 1970—; mng. editor Jour. Econ. Edn., 1970—, Econ. Topics Series, 1970—; cons. econ. edn. to bus., labor unions, bds. edn. Bd. dirs. N.Y.C. Council on Econ. Edn. Served with USNR, 1942-46, 50-51. Recipient Founders Day award N.Y.U., 1956, 1st Place in Kazanjian awards program, 1967. Mem. Am. Econ. Assn., Am. Acad. Polit. and Social Sci., African Studies Assn., Council on Consumer Information, Indsl. Relations Research Assn., Am. Assn. U. Profs., Nat. Council for Social Studies, Phi Delta Kappa (adviser), Kappa Delta Pi. Author: Guide to Economics, 1963; Collegiate Guide to Economics, 2 vols., 1965; Our Nations Wealth, 1968; Foundations of Our Economy, 1969; co-author: The American Economy: Analysis and Policy, 1969. Editor: Communism: Menace to Freedom, 1962; Freedom: America's Choice, 1962; Econ. Edn. Experiences Enterprising Tchrs. Contbr. articles profl. jours. Home: 2292 Arby Ct Bellmore NY 11710

DAWSON, GILES EDWIN, educator; b. Columbus, O., Mar. 4, 1903; s. William Leon and Frances (Ackerman) D.; A.B., Oberlin Coll., 1925; A.M., Cornell, Ithaca, N.Y., 1926, Ph.D., 1931; m. Margaret Williams, 1926 (dec. 1957); children—Pamela Mary (Mrs. Jay P. Moffat), Giles Nicholas; m. 2d, Margaret White, 1959; children—Victoria T., Geoffrey O.S. , Seth Q.A. Instr. English, U. N.D., 1926-27, Western Res. U., 1927-32; reference librarian Folger Shakespeare Library, Washington, 1932-46, curator books and manuscripts, 1946-68; lectr. English, grad. sch. Cath. U. Am., 1935-67, prof. English, 1967—. Served as lt. comdr. USNR, 1942-45. Mem. Malone Soc. Episcopalian. Club: Cosmos (Washington). Author: The Seven Champions of Christendom, 1929; Plays and Players in Kent, 1450-1642, 1965; Elizabethan Handwriting: A Manual, 1966; also articles and revs. Editor: July and Julian, 1955. Editorial bd. Shakespeare Quar., Washington. Home: 3025 Macomb St Washington DC 20008 (summer) Creighton Farm Warren ME 04264 Office: Catholic Univ of America Washington DC 20017

DAWSON, HORACE, lawyer; b. Knoxville, Tenn., Nov. 18, 1897; s. William Robert and Elizabeth (Elmore) D.; student Maryville (Tenn.) Coll. Prep. Sch., until 1914; A.B., Maryville Coll., 1918; studied Chemistry U. Chgo. Grad. Sch., 1919-21; J.D., U. Chgo., 1923; m. Frances Ledile, June 26, 1929; children Jeannette Elizabeth, Margaret Lydia. Admitted to Ill. bar, 1923, and since practiced in Chgo., specializes in patent, trademark and copyright law; mem. firm of Dawson, Tilton, Fallon, & Lungmus; lectr. U. Chgo. Law Sch., 1933-38. Pres. Evanston School World Affairs, 1952. Served as comdr. USNR, World Warr II. Mem. Am., Ill., Chgo. bar assns., Patent Law Assn., Phi Alpha Delta. Republican. Presbyn. Clubs: Law, Chemists, Literary, Westmoreland Country: Highland Park Florida (Lake Wales, Fla.). Home: 2609 Lincoln St Evanston IL 60201 Office: 209 LaSalle St Chicago, IL 60604.

DAWSON, HOWARD ATHALONE, Jr., U.S. judge; b. Okolona, Ark., Oct. 23, 1922; s. Howard Athalone and Mamie (Watson) D.; B.S. in Commerce, U. N.C., 1946; J.D., George Washington U., 1949; m. Marianne Atherholt, Feb. 2, 1946; childrenAmy, Suzanne. Admitted to D.C. bar, 1949, Ga. bar, 1958; pvt. practice, Washington, 1949- 50; atty. civil div. Office Chief Counsel, Internal Revenue Service, 1950-53, asst. regional counsel Atlanta region, 1953-56, regional counsel, 1957, asst. chief counsel adminstrn., Washington, 1958-62; judge U.S. Tax Ct., Washington, 1962—. Served with AUS, 1943-45; ETO; capt. Res. Mem. Am., Fed. bar assns., Chi Psi, Delta Theta Phi. Club: National Lawyers (Washington). Home: 7408 Nevis Rd Bethesda MD 20034 Office: US Tax Ct Washington DC 20044

DAWSON, JAMES ROBERTSON, educator, pathologist; b. Birmingham, Ala., Jan. 19, 1908; s. James Rpbertson and Theresa (Mushat) D.; A.B., Vanderbilt U., 1928, M.D., 1931; m. Margaret Geny; children—Ernest G., John H., Kate Geny, Ann Geny, James Mushat, Thomas Christopher. Asst., instr. pathology Vanderbilt U., 1931-34, asst. prof., asso. prof., prof., 1938-49; asst. Rockefeller Inst., 1934-35; instr. Cornell U., Ithaca, N.Y., 1935-38; prof., head dept. pathology U. Minn., 1949-70. prof. pathology U. Miss. Sch. Medicine, Jackson, 1970—. Home: 2216 Southwood Rd Jackson MS 39211

DAWSON, JOHN ALBERT, investment dealer, religious ofcl.; b. Chgo., Sept. 3, 1904; s. John Henry and Ida Louise (Hellman) D.; student Northwestern U., 1925-27; LL.D. (hon.), Alderson-Broaddus Coll.; m. Annie Joe Howel, Mar. 24, 1934; children—Ann (Mrs. Myron Stanton), Mary (Mrs. Kirk L. MacKinnon), John H. Gen. partner John A. Dawson & Co., Chgo., 1931—; mem. Midwest Stock Exchange, Chgo., 1950—. Past world chmn. men's dept., mem. exec. com. Bapt. World Alliance; past pres. Chgo. Bapt. assn., Am. Bapt. Conv., Am. Bapt. Assembly, Green Lake, Wis., Mem. Chgo. Crime Commn. Trustee Central Bapt. Children's Home, Bapt. Home and Hosp., Maywood, Ill., Bapt. Theol. Union (U. Chgo.), No. Bapt. Theol. Sem., Oakbrook, Ill; chmn. trustees Judson Coll., Elgin, Ill. Mem. Nat. (trustee), Ill. (past pres.) socs. S.A.R., Soc. Mayflower Descs. in Ill. (gov. 1960-63), Phi Kappa Sigma. Republican. Home: 141 Sheridan Rd Winnetka IL 60093 ; (summer) Green Lake WI 54941 Office: 1 N LaSalle St Chicago IL 60602

DAWSON, JOHN FREDERICK, architect; b. Stambaugh, Mich., Sept. 4, 1930; s. Frederick John and Myrtle (Olson) D.; B.Arch., U. Mich., 1953; m. Ruth Jennette Opland, May 8, 1954; children—Craig Frederick, Cindy Paulette. Instr. U. Mich., 1956-60, asst. prof. architecture, 1960-63; dir. govtl. affairs The Am. Inst. Architects, Washington, 1963-65; v.p. Louis G. Kingscott & Assos. Inc., Washington also Kalamazoo, Mich., 1965-70; pres. Development Services, Inc., Kalamazoo, Mich., 1970—. Bd. dirs. Pretty Lake Vacation Camp for Underprivileged Children. Served with AUS, 1953-55. Registered profl. architect Mich., Washington, D.C., Ia., Ind., Wis. Mem. A.I.A. Mich. Soc. Architects. Home: 2221 Winchell St Kalamazoo MI 49001 Office: 4611 W Main St Kalamazoo MI 49007

DAWSON, JOHN HARPER, coll. pres.; b. Erie, Pa., Sept. 10, 1914; s. John Adolphus and Julia Ada (Peters) D.; A.B., Adrian Coll., 1938; S.T.B., Westminster Theol. Sem., 1941; M.Ed., U. Pitts., 1946, Ph.D., 1954; D.D., Albion Coll., 1960; m. Virginia Evelyn Bates, Oct. 11, 1941; children—John Robert, Marsha Elizabeth. Chaplain, Kiskiminetas Springs Prep. Sch., Saltsburg, Pa., 1942-43; lectr. sociology U. Pitts., 1946- 48; ordained to ministry Meth. Ch., 1942; minister, Clymer, Wilmerding and Pitts., 1941-55; pres. Adrian (Mich.) Coll., 1955—. Mem. Pitts. (bd. ministerial tng.), Detroit confs. Meth. Ch., Am. Assn. Commons Clubs. Rotarian. Home: 155 S Madison St Adrian MI 49221

DAWSON, JOHN MINTO, librarian; b. Alva, Scotland, July 4, 1917; s. William and Margaret Mackenzie (Minto) D.; came to U.S., 1926, naturalized, 1952; B.A., Tulane U., 1940; B.S. in Library Sci., La. State U., 1941; Ph.D., U. Chgo., 1956; m. Margaret Marcene Madden, Mar. 15, 1942; 1 son, Robert Minto. Bus. mgr. U. Ala. Library, 1941-42; asst. dir. Tulane U. Library, 1945- 47, U. Chgo. Library, 1948-58; dir. libraries U. Del., Newark, 1958—. Library cons., 1956—; mem. adv. com. PL 480, Library of Congress, 1959-64, co- chmn. Joint Com. Del. Libraries, 1961-63; com. certification State Library, 1963-66. Bd. dirs. Newark Pub. Library, 1964-70, State Library Council, 1969—, pres., 1969-70. Served to 1st. lt. AUS, 1942-45. Council on Library Resources fellow, 1969-70. Mem. Am. (council chmn. personnel sect., mem. exec. bd. 1965—, pub. bd. 1967-69, chmn univ. libraries sect. 1966-67), Del. (pres. 1964-65) library assns., Assn. Coll. and Research Libraries, Phi Beta Kappa, Beta Phi Mu. Club: Philobiblon. Contbr. articles to profl. jours. Home: 390 Briar Lane Newark DE 19711

DAWSON, JOHN PHILIP, educator, lawyer; b. Detroit, July 24, 1902; s. John Philip and Cecil (Frumveller) D.; A.B., U. Mich., 1922, J.D., 1924; D.Phil., Oxford U., Eng., 1930; LL.D., U. Mich., 1968; m. Emma Van Nostrand McDonald, Aug. 20, 1927; children—John Philip, David Michael, Peter McDonald. Admitted to Mich. bar, 1924; asst. prof. law U. Mich., 1927-30, asso. prof., 1930-36, prof., 1936-57; vis. prof. law U. Chgo., 1955; prof. Harvard Law Sch., 1956—. Chief counsel rent sect. OPA, 1942-43; chief Middle East div. Fgn. Econ. Adminstrn., 1943-45, spl. rep. Middle East area, 1945-46; dir. Fgn. Trade Adminstrn., Greek Govt. 1947-48. Democratic cnadidate for Congress, 2d Dist. Mich., 1950, 52. Sec.- treas. Assn. Am. Law Schs., 1947. Mem. Phi Delta Phi, Order of Goif (pres. 1956-58). Club: Century Assn. Author: Unjust Enrichment, A Comparative Analysis, 1951; A History of Lay Judges, 1960; (with George E. Palmer) Cases on Restitution, 1958, 69; (with William B. Harvey) Cases on Contracts, 1958, 69; The Oracles of the Law, 1968. Contbr. articles to law rev. Home: 17 Arlington St Cambridge MA 02140

DAWSON, JOHN SYDNEY, lawyer; b. Waterbury, Conn., Dec. 21, 1909; s. Sydney T. and Agnes E. (Behan) D.; A.B., Holy Cross Coll., 1930; M.B.A., Harvard, 1932; LL.B., 1937; m. Penelope G. Young, Aug. 1940; 1 son, Jonathan. Admitted to Mass. bar, 1937, Conn. bar, 1948; practice law Hurlburt, Jones, Hall & Bickford, Boston, 1937-42; instr. Northeastern U., 1937-42; gen. counsel Bridgeport Brass Co. (Conn.), 1942-62, asst. sec., 1945-47, sec., 1947- 62, v.p., 1953-62; chmn. The Thames Hotel Corp.; pres. The Trading Cove Land Co.; chmn., director of White Supply Company; spl. counsel Marsh, Day & Calhoun, Bridgeport, Conn., counsel Hedrick and Lane, Washington. Clubs: Harvard (Boston); Union League (N.Y.C.); Country (Fairfield, Conn.); Pequot Yacht; University (Bridgeport).

Author: Cases on Torts and Crimes in Business, 1940. Home: Hoydens Hill Rd Fairfield CT 06430 Office: 955 Main St Bridgeport CT 06603

DAWSON, KECK RUSSELL, coal co. exec.; b. Springfield, Ill., Feb. 10, 1922; s. Leonard and Werra (Keck) D.; B.S. in Accounting, U. Ill., 1948; m. Fey Jane Rendleman, Apr. 29, 1961. Accountant, Arthur Andersen & Co., C.P.A.'s, Chgo., 1948- 53; with Peabody Coal Co., St. Louis, 1954-71, asst. treas., 1964-65, treas., 1965-69, v.p.-finance, 1969-71; investor, 1971—. Served to 1st lt. USAAF, 1942-46. Decorated Air medal. C.P.A., Ill. Home: 425 Fourwynd Dr St Louis MO 63141

DAWSON, LAWRENCE RUSSELL, Jr., educator; b. Kalamazoo, Apr. 6, 1921; s. Lawrence Russell and Elaine Gertrude (Anderson) D.; B.A., Western Mich. U., 1943; M.A., U. Mich., 1948; Ph.D., 1959; m. Eleanor Mae Polk, Aug. 14, 1942; 1 son, Jeffrey Lawrence. Tchr. English high schs., Davison and Warren, Mich., 1946-47; teaching fellow U. Mich., 1947-51; instr. English, Colo. State U., 1951-56, asst. prof., 1956-62, asso. prof., 1962-68, prof., 1968; prof., chmn. dept. English, Central Mich. U., 1968—. Mem. civic and state arts councils, Ft. Collins, Colo., 1966-68. Precinct chmn. Democratic Party, Ft. Collins, 1964. Served with USAAF, 1944-46. Mem. Modern Lang. Assn., Modern Humanities Research Assn., Assn. Depts. English. Episcopalian. Contbr. articles profl. jours. Home: 1140 Eastwood Dr Mount Pleasant MI 48858

DAWSON, LYLE RAMSAY, educator; b. Long Point, Ill., Apr. 21, 1904; s. Marcus and Jessie (Ramsay) D.; Ed.B., Ill. State Normal U., 1928; M.S., U. Ill., 1932; Ph.D., U. Ia., 1935; D.Sc., U. Ky., 1971; m. Lucile Sanders, Aug. 11, 1926; 1 dau., Venita Lu. Science tchr. high schs., Ill., 1929-34; acting head dept. chemistry State Tchrs. Coll., Eau Claire, Wis., 1935-36; asst. prof. chemistry U. Omaha, 1936-37; research chemist Universal Atlas Cement Co., 1937-39; asst. prof., asso. prof., prof. chemistry La. Poly. Inst., 1939-43; research chemist and group leader Metall. Lab., U. Chgo., 1943-45; prof. phys. chemistry U. Ky., 1945-70, dist. prof., 1956—, head dept. chemistry, 1945-65, acting dean grad. sch., 1954-56, 60-61. Mem. Oak Ridge Council, 1950-58. Fellow A.A.A.S., Am. Inst. Chemist; mem. Am. Chem. Soc., Electro-chem. Soc., Ky. Acad. Sci., Am. Assn. U. Profs., Sigma Xi, Phi Lambda Upsilon, Kappa Delta Pi, Kappa Mu Epsilon, Alpha Chi Sigma, Omicron Delta Kappa Democrat. Presbyn. Mason, Kiwanian. Clubs: Informal, Torch. Contbr. profl. publs. Home: 129 Barberry Lane Lexington KY 40503

DAWSON, MARTHA EATON, (Mrs. James Melvin Dawson), educator; b. Richmond, Va., Jan. 21, 1922; d. John John J. and Sarah (Cousins) Eaton; B.S., Va. State Coll., 1943; M.S., Ind. U., 1954, Ed.D., 1956; m. James Melvin Dawson, Sept. 12, 1942; children—Greer (Mrs. Samuel B. Wilson Jr.), James Melvin, Martina. Tchr. elementary schs., Richmond, 1943-56; grad. asst. Sch. Edn. Ind. U., 1953- 55, vis. prof., summer 1967; cons. tchr. Richmond Pub. Schs., 1955-58; asso. prof. Hampton (Va.) Inst. 1956-64, chmn. dept. elementary edn., 1958—, prof., 1964—; initiated Ann. Undergraduate Workshop in Elementary Edn., 1960, 1961, organized Hampton Inst. researcher Exploratory Study Elementary Sch. Practices and Materials from grant by Lilly Endowment Corp., 1964-65; cons. Dept. Health, Edn. and Welfare, 1964—, evaluator inst. proposals, 1965-66, dir. Inst. on Nongraded Approach to Curriculum for Adminstrs. and Tchrs. of Disadvantaged, 1966; dir. Summer Inst. on Nongraded Sch. Programs by grant from So. Edn. Found., 1964-66; mem. nongraded adv. com. Brevard County Pub. Schs., Melbourne, Fla., 1966—; mem. working proposal com. Mid-South Regional Lab., Durham, N.C., 1966-67; sci. research asso. cons. for nongraded insts., 1966—; vis. cons. Hartford Intensive City U. Tchr. Tng. Project U. Hartford, summer 1967. Recipient certificate for outstanding scholarship Ind. U., 1967, Christian R. and Mary F. Lindback Dist. Teaching award, 1966-67. Mem. Assn. For Student Teaching, Nat. Council Tchrs. English, Catholic Daughters Am., N.E.A., Internat. Reading Assn., Am. Assn. of Univ. Women (1st v.p. Hampton br. 1968-70), Zeta Phi Beta, Kappa Delta Pi, Phi Lambda Theta. Author: (with Helen A. Holston) Hampton Inst. Nongraded Laboratory School Handbook, 1966. Author, sci. research asso. Nongraded Newsletter, Dawson Letters, 1967-68, Nuts and Bolts of Elementary Education newsletter series, 1968-69. Home: 1113 Aberdeen Rd Hampton VA 23366

DAWSON, RAY FIELDS, educator, cons.; b. Muncie, Ind., Feb. 13, 1911; s. Emmett Hamilton and Elsie (Fields) D.; A.B. (Rector scholar), DePauw U., 1935; Ph.D. (Hooker fellow), Yale, 1938; m. Helen Dunham, Aug. 11, 1942. NRC fellow Columbia, 1938-39, asst. prof. Princeton, 1942-45; asst., asso. prof. Columbia, 1945-52, prof. plant biochemistry, 1952-59, Torrey prof. botany Grad. Faculty Pure Sci., 1959-66, adj. prof., 1966-68; prof. plant biology, dir. Internat. programs Coll. Agr., Rutgers U., New Brunswick, N.J., 1966—; instr. DePauw U., 1939-40; asst. prof. U. Mo., 1940-42. Research collaborator Brookhaven Nat. Lab., 1952-65; sci. adviser Benson & Hedges, 1953-54; cons. tobacco and agrl. chem. industries, 1952- -; sci. adviser to pres. Gen. Cigar Co., 1957-58; chief cons. Julian Labs., 1957-60; mem. bd., treas. Lancaster Labs., Inc., Lancaster Products, Inc. Mem. Tobacco Sci. Council; co-pres. 3d World Tobacco Sci. Congress, South Rhodesia, 1963. Recipient Stephen Hales award Am. Soc. Plant Physiologists, 1945; 2d Ann. Research award Cigar Mfrs. Am. and Cigar Inst. Am., 1952; DePauw U. Alumni citation, 1953. Sigma Xi nat. lectr., 1959-60. Mem. Am. Chem. Soc., Am. Soc. Plant Physiologists, Assn. for Tropical Biology, Phi Beta Kappa, Sigma Xi. Club: Nassau (Princeton). Contbr. articles to sci. jours. Home: 152 Westcott Rd Princeton, NJ 08540. Office: New Brunswick, NJ 08903.

DAWSON, RAYMOND HOWARD, coll. adminstr.; b. Camden, Ark., Oct. 12, 1927; s. Hilary Herbert and Mildred Mae (Pye) D.; A.B. summa cum laude, Coll. of Ozarks, 1949; M.A., Vanderbilt U., 1951; Ph.D., U. N.C., 1958; m. Alice Jo McKeehen, May 26, 1949; children—Alice Catherine, Carolyn Marie. Asso. prof. Presbyn. Jr. Coll., Maxton, N.C., 1951-55; teaching fellow U. N.C., Chapel Hill, 1955-56, instr., 1958-59, asst. prof., 1960-63, asso. prof., 1963-68, prof., 1968, dean Coll. Arts and Scis., also Gen. Coll., 1968—; Mershon postdoctoral fellow Ohio State U., Columbus, 1959-60. Fulbright lectr. Kings Coll., U. London (Eng.), 1964-65; vis. asso. prof. Inst. War and Peace Studies, Columbia, 1967-68. Served with AUS 1945-47. Recipient Tanner award for excellence in undergrad. teaching U. N.C., 1962; E. Harris Harbison prize for distinguished teaching Danforth Found., 1968. Mem. Am., So. polit. sci. assns., Inst. Strategic Studies. Democrat. Author: The Decision to Aid Russia, 1941; Foreign Policy and Domestic Politics, 1959. Home: 304 Glendale Dr Chapel Hill NC 27514

DAWSON, SAMUEL COOPER, Jr., motel co. exec.; b. Alexandria, Va., Sept. 21, 1909; s. Samuel Cooper and Edna French (Horner) D.; grad. Episcopal High Sch., Alexandria, 1928; B.A. in Commerce, U. Va., 1932; m. Frances Margaret Boatwright, Mar. 24, 1945; childrenSamuel Cooper III, Marion Boatwright. Tchr. sci. St. Christopher's Sch., Richmond, Va., 1932-36; underwriter Md. Casualty Co., Balt., 1936-39; mgr. Penn-Daw Motor Hotel, Alexandria, 1939-; pres. Penn-Daw Hotels Corp., Alexandria, 1960-, Penn-Daw Shopping Center, Alexandria, 1958—; former dir. Washington- Lee Savs. & Loan Assn. Past pres. Va. Travel Council. Pres. Camp Alleghany for Girls, Lewisburg, W.Va. bus. mgr. Episcopal High Sch. Served with USNR, 1942-46; capt. Res.; group comdr. 47 reserve units Washington area. Recipient Hall fame award Hospitality magazine, 1961; Distinguished Servece award Am. Motor Hotel Assn., 1964. Mem. Am. Automobile Assn. (chmn. No. Va. adv. bd.), Va. Hotel Assn. (dir.), Va. Motel Assn. (past pres.), Alexandria Jr. C. of C. (past pres.; Outstanding Young Man award 1942), Washington Restaurant Assn. (past pres.), Am. Motor Hotel Assn. (past pres.; chmn. legislative affairs com.), Washington Civil War Round Table, S.A.R.(past pres. George Washington chpt.), Nat. Restaurant Assn. (bd. dirs.). Episcopalian. Club: Army Navy Country (Arlington, Va.). Home: 206 N Quaker Lane Alexandria VA 22304 Office: P O Box 56 Alexandria VA 22313

DAWSON, THOMAS HARRINGTON, broadcasting exec.; b. Appleton, Minn., Feb. 19, 1914; s. Thomas Henry and Marjorie (Dawson) D.; student U. Minn., 1932-36; m. Marjorie Kastberg, 1958; children—David, Thomas, Deborah Anne. With Pillsbury Flour Mills, 1936-37; staff mem. Stat. WCCO, Mpls., 1938-41; stat. rep. for Petry, 1950-51; spot sales CBS-TV, 1951-53, network sales, 1953-57, v.p. network sales, 1957-63, v.p. sales, 1963-66, pres., 1966-69; pres. CBS-TV Network, 1969-70; dir. radio-TV for major league baseball Office of Commr., 1970—. Served to lt. comdr. (aviator) USNR, 1942-45. Home: 22 Orchard Dr Greenwich CT 06830 Office: 51 W 52d St New York City NY 10019

DAWSON, WILLIAM J., restaurant exec. Sec., Chicken Delight, Inc., Des Plaines, Ill. Office: 1505 S Mt Prospect Rd Des Plaines IL 60018*

DAWSON, WILLIAM LEVI, composer, condr.; b. Anniston, Ala., Sept. 26, 1899; s. George W. and Eliza M. (Starkey) D.; student composition, orchestration Washburn Coll.; Mus. B. Horner Inst. Fine Arts, Kansas City, Mo., 1925; M. Composition, Am. Conservatory Music, Chgo., 1927; Mus. D., Tuskegee Inst.; 1955; postgrad. Eastman Sch. Music; m. Cornella D. Lampton, May 25, 1927 (dec. Aug. 1928); m. 2d, Cecile D. Nicholson, Sept. 21, 1935. Dir. music, Topeka, Kansas City, 1921-25, then 1st trombonist Chgo. Civic Symphony Orch.; dir. Tuskegee Inst. Sch. Music, Tuskegee Choir; led Tuskegee Choir at opening Radio City Music Hall, 1932-33, on many tours, in concert series NBC, CBS, ABC; guest condr. numerous state choral festivals, choral groups in Spain under auspices U.S. State Dept., 1956, Kansas City Philharmonic Orch., 1966, Nashville Symphony Orch., 1966, Talladega Choir and Mobile Symphony Orch., 1968. Winner Rodman Wanamaker contest for composition, 1930, 31; Chgo. Daily News contest for band condrs., 1929; recipient award and citation U. Pa. Glee Club, 1967; Alumni Achievement award U. Mo. at Kansas City, 1963. Composer: numerous arrangements Negro folk songs for voices, Break, Break (with orch.); Out in the Fields; Scherzo for Orch.; Negro Work Song for Orch.; Trio in A (violin, cello, piano), Sonata in A (violin and piano); Negro Folk Symphony. Address: P O Box 1052 Tuskegee Institute AL 36088

DAY, ARTHUR GROVE, educator, author; b. Phila., Apr. 29, 1904; s. Arthur Sinclair and Clara T. (Hogeland) D.; A.B. in English, Stanford, 1926, M.A., 1942, Ph.D., 1944; m. Virginia Teresa Molina, July 2, 1928. Tchrs. Coll., 1926-27, Stanford, 1932-36, asst. dir. engring., sci. and mgmt. war tng., 1943-44; mem. faculty U. Hawaii, 1944- 69, sr. prof. English, 1961-69, prof. emeritus, 1969—, chmn. dept., 1948-53; propr. White Knight Press, Honolulu, 1946—. Chmn. pub. com. 10th Pacific Sci. Congress, 1961; Fulbright sr. research fellow, Australia, 1955; Smith-Mundt vis. prof. Am. studies U. Barcelona (Spain), 1957-58; Fulbright vis. prof. Am. studies U. Madrid (Spain), 1961-62. Mem. Modern Lang. Assn., Honolulu Acad. Arts, Bernice P. Bishop Mus. Elk. Club: Adventurers' (Honolulu). Author: (with F.J. Buenzle) Bluejacket, 1936; Coronado's Quest: The Discovery of the Southwestern States, 1940; The Sky Clears: Poetry of the American Indians, 1951; (with James A. Mitchener) Rascals in Paradise, 1957; Hawaii and Its People, 3d ed., 1968; Hawaii, Fiftieth Star, 1960, 69; The Story of Australia, 1960; (with R.S. Kuykendall) Hawaii, A History, 2d edit., 1961; They Peopled the Pacific, 1964; James A. Michener, 1964; Louis Becke, 1966; Explorers of the Pacific, 1967; Coronado and the Discovery of the Southwest, 1967; Pirate of the Pacific, 1967; Adventurers of the Pacific, 1969; Jack London in the South Seas, 1971. Editor: (in Spanish) Despatches from Mexico by Fernando Cortez, 1935; (with Carl Stroven) The Spell of the Pacific: An Anthology of Its Literature, 1949; (with W.F. Bauer) The Greatest American Short Stories, 1953; (with Carl Stroven) A Hawaiian Reader, 1959; (with Carl Stroven) Best South Sea Stories, 1964; Stories of Hawaii (by Jack London), 1965; Mark Twain's Letters from Hawaii, 1966; (with Carl Stroven) True Tales of the South Seas, 1966; (with Virginia M. Day) The Spanish in Sydney, 1793, 1967; South Sea Supercargo (by Louis Becke), 1967; (with Carl Stroven) The Spell of Hawaii, 1968; Melville's South Seas, 1970; The Art of Narration: The Short Story, 1971; The Art of Narration; The Novella, 1971. Editor-in-chief Pacific Science, 1947-49. Home: 1434 Punahou St Honolulu HI 96822

DAY, BENJAMIN MULFORD, lawyer; b. North Plainfield, N.J., Jan 24, 1886; s. Benjamin M. and Martha E. (Hanna) D.; grad. Hamilton Inst., N.Y., 1905; LL.B., N.Y. U., 1907, LL.M., 1908. Admitted to N.Y. bar, and began practice in N.Y.C. Sec. com. on indsl. Interests and relations of Constl. Conv., State of N.Y., 1915; sec. Mayor's Com. on Nat. Def., 1917; chief dep. collector internal revenue, N.Y., 1921-25; apptd. commr. of immigration, Ellis Island, 1926, re-apptd. 1930, resigned, 1931; apptd. mem. N.Y.C. Alcoholic Beverage Control Bd., 1933. Pres. N.Y. Young Republican Club and sec. Nat. Republican Club. Capt. Mil. Intelligence Div., U.S. Army, 1917-19. Sec. judicial sect. of Am. Bar Assn., 1934; pres. N.Y. Soc. for Prevention of Crime, 1940, 41, 42. Mem. English-Speaking Union of U.S., Pilgrims of U.S., St. Nicholas Soc. of N.Y., Colonial Soc. of Pa., Phi Delta Phi. Baptist. Clubs: National Republican, City, University. Home: 320 E 42d St New York City NY 10017

DAY, BOYSIE EUGENE, educator; b. Halle, La., Sept. 9, 1917; s. John Henry and Martha (Beasley) D.; B.S., U. Ariz., 1939, M.S., 1940; Ph.D., U. Cal. at Berkeley-Davis, 1950; m. Constance E. Everett, Jan. 1, 1941; children—Martha E., Everett E., Kathryn Ann. Faculty, U. Cal. at Riverside, 1950—, prof. hort. scis. 1950—, chmn. dept., 1966—, dir. expt. sta., 1968—. Chmn. subcom. weeds Nat. Acad. Sci.-NRC, 1965-69. Mem. Riverside Airport Commn., 1956-59. Served to lt. col., inf. AUS, 1940-46: PTO. Mem. A.A.A.S., Bot. Soc. Am., Am. Soc. Plant Physiologists, Am. Inst. Biol. Scis., Weed Sci. Soc. Am. (pres. 1968- 69), Sigma Xi. Home: 43 Western Dr Richmond CA 94801

DAY, CARL ALBERT, optical instruments mfg. co. exec.; b. Bigtimber, Mont., Aug. 9, 1907; s. Harry Edward and Edith (Nogle) D.; B.S., U.S. Naval Acad., 1931; m. Janet Makely, Nov. 28, 1934; children—Marcia (Mrs. Glenn Jackson), Carolyn (Mrs. Fred Sharer). Corr., instrument sales Bausch & Lomb Optical Co. (now Bausch & Lomb, Inc.), Rochester, N.Y., 1931-42, mil. products coordinator, 1942-45, works mgr., 1945-53, v.p., 1953-65, exec. v.p., dir., gen. mgr. Sci. Instrument div.; chmn. bd. Herron Optical Co., Internat. Glass Corp., Diecraft Corp.; pres. Pioneer Sci. Corp., Rochester, 1958—. Mem. Am. Mgmt. Assn., Optical Soc. Am., Am. Soc. M.E., C. of C. Clubs: Rochester; Monroe Golf (bd. govs. 1951—). Home: 2505 East Av Rochester NY 14610 Office: 635 Saint Paul St Rochester NY 14605

DAY, CECIL LEROY, educator; b. Dexter, Mo., Oct. 4, 1922; s. Cecil Lawrence and Katherine (Kleffer) D.; B.S. in Agrl. Engring., U. Mo., 1945, M.S., 1948; Ph.D., Ia. State U., 1957; m. Peggy Eunice Thrower, Aug. 29, 1948; children—Stanley K., Thomas L. Mem. faculty U. Mo. at Columbia, 1945—, prof. agrl. engring., 1962—, chmn. dept., 1969—. Pres. Penreico, Inc., 1968—. Chmn. elec. appeals bd., Columbia, 1966—. Mem. Am. Soc. Agrl. Engrs., Am. Soc. Engring. Edn., Mo. Soc. Profl. Engrs. Mem. Ch. of Christ (elder). Author articles, bulls. Home: 504 Crestland Av Columbia MO 65201

DAY, DANIEL EDGAR, govt. ofcl.; b. Montgomery, Ala., Dec. 10, 1913; s. Thomas and Gertrude (Ford) D.; student Crane Jr. Coll., Chgo., 1932-33; student Am. U., 1946, 62, 64, U. Chgo., 1958; m. Sanone Nickerson, Jan. 18, 1942; children—Sandra Ann (Mrs. Robert Burney), Gregory Alan. With Robert S. Abbott Pub. Co., Chgo., 1929-40, asst. city editor, 1936-40; enlisted as sgt. U.S. Army, 1941, advanced through ranks to lt. col., 1952; ret. 1961; asst. chief, then chief Negro interest sect. Bur. Pub. Relations, War Dept., Washington, 194346; stationed Hdqrs. 8th Army, Japan, 194649; prof. mil. sci. Fla. A. and M. U., Tallahassee, 1955-61; Washington corr. Nat. Newspaper Pubs. Assn., 1961-66; adminstrv. officer USDA, Washington, 1966; information specialist Dept. Housing and Urban Devel., Washington, 1966-68, dep. dir. pub. information div., 1968-70, pub. information officer, 1970—. Mem. Nat. Press Club (membership com. 1962—), Capital Press Club, Investors 12 Club. Clubs: 14 Gents, Pigskin (Washington). Home: 8212 Eastern Av N W Washington DC 20012 Office: Dept Housing and Urban Devel Washington DC 20410

DAY, DAVID ALLEN, educator; b. Ann Arbor, Mich., Nov. 22, 1924; s. Edmund Ezra and Emily Sophia (Emerson) D.; grad. Deerfield (Mass.) Acad., 1942; B.C.E., Cornell U., Ithaca, N.Y., 1945; M.S., U. Ill., 1951; m. Mary Warrick Squires, Sept. 8, 1945; children—Marilyn, Barbara Emily, Suzanne. Frederick, Caroline. Constrn. engr. Raymond Concrete Pile Co., 1946-47, Gen. Paving Co., 1947-48, Peter Kiewit Sons Co., 1950; cons. constrn. engring, 1952—; tchr. civil engring. U. Ill., 1948-58; prof. civil engring. U. Denver, 1958—, dean engring., 1960-68. Cons. Danforth Asso. program Danforth Found. Served to lt. USNR, 1945-46. Recipient Epstein award U. Ill., 1957. Registered profl. engr., Ill., Colo. Mem. Am. Soc. C.E.s (Cornell sr. award Ithaca sect. 1945, exec. bd. constrn. div. 1967—), Am. Soc. Engring. Edn. (chmn. RWI div. 1969), Nat. Soc. Profl. Engrs., Cornell Soc. Engrs., Profl. Engrs. Colo. (pres. 1971), Theta Delta Chi, Chi Epsilon, Tau Beta Pi, Phi Kappa Phi. Episcopalian. Author: Survey of Construction Education, 1961; Associated General Contractors' Directory of Construction Education, 1968. Contbr. articles to profl. jours. Home: 3756 S Forest Way Denver CO 80237

DAY, DONALD SHELDON, lawyer; b. Boston, Nov. 3, 1924; s. Israel and Frances (Goldberg) D.; B.A., Bates Coll., 1946; LL.B., Cornell U., 1948; m. Edythe Greenberg, July 8, 1945; children—Clifford L., Richard J., Halee Beth. Admitted to N.Y. bar, 1948, since practiced in Buffalo; sr. partner firm Saperston, Wiltse, Day & Wilson, and predecessor firm, 1962—. Pres., Dir. various corps. Pres. Bur. Jewish Edn. Served with AUS, 1942-45. Mem. Am., N.Y. State, Erie County bar assns., Order of Coif, Phi Kappa Phi. Jewish religion (pres. temple). Mason; mem. B'nai B'rith. Home: 56 Devonshire Ct Kenmore NY 14223 Office: Liberty Bank Bldg Buffalo NY 14202

DAY, DONALD SNOW, steel co. exec.; b. Cleve., Dec. 24, 1914; s. J. Hudson and Edna M. (Davison) D.; A.B., Western Res. U., 1936; m. Alma B. Balbach, Apr. 9, 1938; children—Donald H., Thomas R., Robert K. With Erie R.R., 1936-54, successively office boy, clk., Cleve., stenographer, Marion, also Jamestown, N.Y., chief clk., Columbus, O., comml. agt., Phila., traffic asst. research dept., Cleve., gen. agt., Boston, div. freight agt., Jamestown, 1947-51, asst. gen. freight agt., Youngstown, O. 1951-54; asst. gen. traffic mgr. Youngstown Sheet & Tube Co. (O.), 1955, gen. traffic mgr., 1956-58, v.p., 1959—; pres., dir. Chicago Short Line R.R., 1958—; pres. Dearborn Leasing Co., 1965—, Transoceanic Terminal Co., 1966—; dir. The Youngstown Steel Door Co. Mem. Nat. Def. Transportation Assn., Am. Soc. Traffic and Transportation, Nat. Freight Traffic Assn., traffic clubs Chgo., Pitts. Presbyn. Mason (Shriner). Clubs: Youngstown, Youngstown Country; Chicago; Duquesne. Home: 7825 Spring Lake Lane Canfield OH 44406 Office: 7655 Market St Youngstown OH 44512

DAY, DORIS, singer; b. Cin., Apr. 3, 1924; d. Frederick Wilhelm and Alma Sophia von Kappelhoff; student pub. schs., Cin; m. Al Jorden, Mar. 1941 (div. 1943); 1 son, Terry; m. 2d, George Weilder, 1946 (div. 1949); m. 3d, Marty Melcher, Apr. 3, 1951. Made profl. dancing appearances Doherty & Kappelhoff, Glendale, Cal.; was singer Karlin's Karnival, radio sta. WCPO; singer with bands, Barney Rapp, Bob Crosby, Fred Waring, Les Brown; singer, leading lady Bob Hope NBC radio show, 1948-50, Doris Day CBS show, 1952-53; singer Columbia Records, 1950—; star Warner Brothers Studio motion pictures include Romance on the High Seas, 1948, My Dream is Yours, 1949, Young Man With a Horn, Tea For Two, West Point Story, 1950, Lullaby of Broadway, On Moonlight Bay, I'll See You in My Dreams, 1951, April in Paris, 1952, By the Light of the Silvery Moon, 1953, Lucky Me, Yankee Doodle Girl, 1954, Love Me or Leave Me (selected as 1 of 10 best films by N.Y. Heärald Tribune), 1955, Pajama Game, 1957, Teacher's Pet, Tunnel of Love, 1958, It Happened to Jane, 1959; Pillow Talk, 1959, Midnight Lace, 1960; Jumbo, 1962; That Touch of Mink, 1962; The Thrill of It All, 1963; Please Don't Eat the Daisies; Lover Come Back; Send Me No Flowers: Do Not Disturb, 1965; The Glass Bottom Boat, 1966; Caprice; The Ballad of Josie; Where Were You When The Lights Went Out; With Six You Get Eggrolls; star TV series The Doris Day Show. Winner 1st prize (with Jerry Doherty) as best dance team in Cin.; Laurel award as leading new female personality in motion picture industry, 1950; top audience attractor, 1962. Christian Scientist. Office: care Warner Brothers Studios Burbank CA 91503

DAY, EDWARD CHARLES, judge; b. Denver, Dec. 21, 1908; s. Edward Charles and Mary Ellen (Sampson) D.; A.B., Regis Coll., 1930; postgrad. U. Denver Law Sch., 1930-31; LL.B., Westminister Law Sch.,, 1933; m. Lillian Margaret Famular, June 18, 1931; children Edward Charles, Mary Diane. Admitted to Colo. bar, 1934; pvt. practive, 1934-48; atty., supr. state examining and licensing bds. State Colo., 1935-42, dep. rent dir., 1942-43, state rent dir., 1946-47; judge Denver Municipal Ct., 1947-48, Dist. Ct., 1949-57; asso. justice Supreme Ct. Colo., Denver, 1957—, chief justice, 1962-63. Solicitation chmn. pub. div. Denver Community Chest, United Fund, 1954; dir. Denver Cath. Charities. Served from lt. (j.g.) to lt. USNR, 1943-46. Mem. Colo., Denver bar assns., Am. Legion, V.F.W., Am. Judicature Soc., Phi Alpha Delta. Democrat. Roman Catholic. K.C., Moose. Club: International Footprinters (Denver). Home: 615 S Alton Way Denver, CO 80231. Office: State Capitol Bldg Denver CO 80203

DAY, EDWARD W., judge; b. Cranston, R.I., May 24, 1901; Ph.B., Brown U., 1922; LL.B., Harvard, 1925. Admitted to R.I. bar, 1925; practiced in Providence; mem. Gardner, Day & Sawyer; clk. 8th Dist. Ct., 1929-30; 1st asst. atty. gen. of R.I., 1930-33; city solicitor Cranston, 1935-43; chmn. R.I. Civil Service Commn., 1939-41; judge U.S. Dist Ct. R.I., Providence, 1953—. chief judge, 1966-71, judge, 1971—. Mem. Am., R.I. bar assns. Address: U S Court House Providence RI 02903

DAY, EDWIN MINOR, ret. air force officer, aerial survey co. exec.; b. Greensburg, Pa., Dec. 20, 1903; s. Lawrence Minor and Elizabeth (Hatcher) D.; student Johns Jopkins, 1924-26, Nat. War Coll., Washington, 1948; m. Diane Pockrus, Aug. 3, 1O34. Commd. 2d lt., USAC, 1929, advanced through graded to brig. gen., USAF, 1950, ret., 1958; various jr. grade assignments, 1928-41; chief staff Fly Tng. Commd, 1943-44; comdr. 6th Bomber Command, 1942-43; staff Tng. Command, 1945-47; comdg. gen. Saudi Arabian Theatre, 1947-49, SAC-1G, 1949-52; comdr. APCS, 1952-58. Pres. Fairchild Aerial Survey, Los Angeles, 1958-. Decorated Legion of Merit with cluster. Mem. Air Force Assn. Clubs: Los Angeles Athletic; Nat. Aviation (Washington). Home: 224 E 11th St Los Angeles CA 90015

DAY, EMERSON, physician; b. Hanover, N.H., May 2, 1913; s. Edmund Ezra and Emily Sophia (Emerson) D.; B.S., Dartmouth, 1934; M.D., Harvard, 1938; m. Ruth Fairfield, Aug. 7, 1937; children—Edmund Perry, Robert Fairfield, Nancy, Martha, Sheryl. Intern Presbyn. Hosp., N.Y.C., 1938- 40; fellow cardiology Johns Hopkins, 1940-42; asst. resident medicine N.Y. Hosp., 1942; med. dir. internat. div. Trans World Airline, N.Y. C., 1945-47; asst. prof. preventive medicine and pub. health Cornell U. Med. Coll., 1947-50, asso. prof. clin. preventive medicine and pub. health, 1950-54, prof. preventive medicine Sloan Kettering div., 1954- 64; chmn. dept. preventive medicine Meml. Hosp., N.Y.C., 1954-63, dir. Strang Cancer Prevention Clinic, 1950-63; mem., chief div. preventive medicine Sloan-Kettering Inst., N.Y.C., 1954-64; cons. in geriatrics Cold Spring Inst., Cold Spring-on-Hudson, N.Y., 1952- 57; dir. N.Y.C. Dept. Health Cancer Detection Center, 1947-50; dir. Strang Clinic, Inc., 1963-66, PMI-Strang Clinic, 1966-69; pres. Preventive Medicine Inst., 1966-69, hon. pres., 1969—; v.p., med. dir. Medequip Corp., 1969—; attending physician, mem. med. bd. James Ewing Hosp., Meml. Hosp., N.Y.C., 1950-64; sr. mem. PMX Med. Group, N.Y.C., 1956—70; adj. prof. biology N.Y. U., 1965—. Mem. cancer detection com. Internat. Union Against Cancer, 1954-70; pres. N.Y.C. div. Am. Cancer Soc., 1963-64. Served as flight surgeon USAAF, A.T.C., 1942- 45. Recipient Bronze medal, Am. Cancer Soc., 1956. Fellow A.C.P., N.Y. Acad. Medicine, N.Y. Acad. Scis. (pres. 1965), Am. Pub. Health Assn., Indsl. Med. Assn., Am. Geriatrics Soc.; mem. Am. Soc. Cytology (founding mem., pres. 1958), Internat. Acad. Cytology (hon. fellow), Ewing Soc., Harvey Soc., Ill., Cook County med. socs., A.M.A., Am. Assn. Cancer Research, N.Y. Cancer Soc., Phi Beta Kappa, Alpha Omega Alpha, Zeta Psi. Contbr. articles profl. jours. Home: 320 Pebblebrook Dr Northbrook IL 60062 Office: 205 Touhy Av Park Ridge IL 60068

DAY, FRANK R., banker. Sr. v.p., exec. officer First Nat. Bank, Jackson, Miss. Office: 248 E Capitol St Jackson MS 39025*

DAY, GARDINER MUMFORD, clergyman; b. S.I., N.Y., Feb. 22, 1900; s. Nathaniel Briggs and Mary (Copelin) D.; A.B., Yale, 1922, M.A. (hon.), 1952; M.A., Columbia, 1925; B.D., Episcopal Theol. Sch., 1926; D.D. (hon., Va. Theol. Sem., 1959, Calvin Coolidge Coll., 1960; m. Katharine Pierson Bennett, Apr. 2, 1932; childrenJonathan Atwater, Russell Bennett. Ordained to ministry Episcopal ch., 1925; minister- in-charge Ch. of Good Shepherd, Boston, 1925-26; asst. minister Trinity Ch., Boston, 1926-29; chaplain Mass. Ho. Reps., 1928-29; asso. minister St. John's Ch., Williamstown, Mass., 1929-30, rector, 1930-36; rector St. Stephen's Ch., Wilkes Barre, Pa., 1936-41; bd. dirs., council Diocese of Bethlehem, 1936-41; rector Christ Ch., Cambridge 1941-66; hon. asso. Grace Ch., Manchester, N.H., 1967-. Fellow Yale U. Corp., 1952-68; bd. dirs. Union Theol. Sem., 1953-59. Episcopal del. Nat. Council Chs., 1950-66; V.P. Mass. Council Chs., 1954-56, mem. gen. bd., 1957-66, dir., 1948-50; chmn. social action N.H. Council Chs.; mem. standing Com., Docese Mass., gen. chmn. com. for Episcopalian Gen. Conv., 1952; bd. dirs. Children's Service Center, 1936-41. Mem. Mass. Soc. Prevention Cruelty to Children (dir. 1930-36), Episcopal Evang. Fellowship (pres. 1940-46), Wyo. Valley Family Soc. (dir. 1936-41), Wyo. Valley Ministerial Assn., Civil Liberties Union of Mass. (chmn. 1959—), N.H. Civil Liberties Union (chmn. 1970—), S.R., Zeta Psi. Rotarian. Author: Old Wine in New Bottles, 1949; The Biography of a Church, 1952; The Lord's Prayer, 1954; Christ Speaks From The Cross; The Apostles Creed, 1963. Home: Amherst, NH 03031.

DAY, HARRY GILBERT, biochemist, educator; b. Monroe County, Ia., Oct. 8, 1906; s. John Freeman and Minta Emma (Spencer) D.; A.B., Cornell Coll., 1930, D.Sc., 1967; Sc.D., Johns Hopkins, 1933; m. W. Marie Miller, July 10, 1933 (dec. 1968); children—Margaret Louise, Barbara Jean, Robert Miller; m. 2d, Gertrude Parr Bruce, Aug. 14, 1969. Asso. biochemistry Johns Hopkins, 1936-40; asst. prof. chemistry Ind. U., Bloomington, 1940- 45, asso. prof., 1945-50, prof., 1950—, chmn. dept. chemistry, 1952-62, asso. dean for research and advanced studies, 1967—. Mem. Bloomington (Ind.) City Council. NRC fellow Johns Hopkins, 1933-34; Gen. Edn. Bd. fellow Yale, 1934-36. Fellow Am. Inst. Chemists; mem. Am. Chem. Soc., Am. Soc. Biol. Chemists, Am. Inst. Nutrition (pres. elect 1970), Soc. Exptl. Biology and Medicine, Sigma Xi, Phi Beta Kappa, Phi Lambda Upsilon, Alpha Chi Sigma. Methodist. Kiwanian. Contbr. articles to profl. jours. Home: 916 E University St Bloomington IN 47401

DAY, HARRY M., corp. exec.; B.S. in Metall. Engring., Yale, 1934, Ph.D. in Phys. Metallurgy, 1937; m. M. Powell; children—Harry Dale, Jerrold Kim. Vice pres. Ekco Products Co., 1946-51, Thomas Industries, 1951-56, Universal Am. Corp. N.Y., 1956-61; pres. Norma-Hoffamnn Bearings Corp., Stamford, Conn., 1956-60, chmn. bd., 1960-65; pres. Amron Corp., Waukeska, Wis., 1956-65, chmn. bd., 1965-69; chmn. bd. Amron Orlando Corp. (Fla.), 1971—, Norma FAG Bearings Corp., Stamford, 1969—, also dir.; dir. Shattuck Denn Mining Corp., Barnes Engring. Co., State Nat. Bank Conn. (both Stamford). Served to comdr. USNR, 1941-46. Trustee Stamford Hosp.; bd. dirs. Silvermine Guild. Recipient citation Sec. Navy. Mem. Mfs. Assn. Conn. (dir., past pres.), Conn. Bus. and Industry Assn. (dir.), Mgmt. Council Southwestern Conn. (past pres.), Sigma Xi. Club: Woodway Country (gov., past pres.) (Darlen, Conn.). Mem. Mfrs. Assn. Conn. (v.p.). Clubs: Woodway Lane; Bay Hill (Orlando, Fla.); Citrus Club; Woodway Country. Home: 46 Cedar Lane New Canaan CT 06840 Office: Norma FAG Bearings Corp Stamford CT 06902

DAY, HENRY LAWRENCE, mine co. exec.; b. Spokane, Wash., Oct. 4, 1902; s. Harry Loren and Helen (Dwyer) D.; B.S. in Mining Engring., U. Cal., 1923; postgrad. Harvard, 1924-25; LL.D., Gonzaga U., 1969, U. Ida., 1969; m. Lois Eckis Floher, July 28, 1937 (dec. June 1940); 1 dau., Barbara (Mrs. Whitesel). Mining engr. 1923—; chmn. bd., dir. Day Mines, Inc., producing silver, lead, gold and zinc concentrates. Mem. Am. Inst. Mining Engrs. Elk, Rotarian, K.C. Home: 114 Cedar St Wallace ID 83873 Office: Day Bldg Wallace ID 83873

DAY, HUNTINGTON TOWNSEND, lawyer; b. St. Louis, Apr. 21, 1901; s. Dwight Huntington and Molly (Townsend) D.; grad. Phillips Acad., Andover, Mass., 1915-19; B.A., Yale, 1923, LL.B., 1928; m. Cornelia Addis Campbell, May 3, 1924; children—Molly Townsend (Mrs. M. Day Scott), Cornelia H. Huntington (Mrs. William E. Bloomer), Anne Campbell (Mrs. Abraham P. Schalet). With Deepwater Coal & Iron Corp., Jasper, Ala., 1923-25; admitted to Conn. bar, 1928, since practiced in New Haven; partner Wiggin & Dana, 1934—. Dir. Union Trust Co., New Haven Savs. Bank, United Illuminating Co. Bd. dirs. Gaylord Farm Assn., Wallingford, Conn. Mem. Am., Conn., New Haven County bar assns., Am. Judicature Soc., Am. Bar Found., Yale Law Sch. Assn., Order of Coif. Republican. Presbyn. Clubs: Lawn, Graduate, Quinnipiack, Yale (New Haven); Yale (N.Y.C.). Home: 100 Reservoir St New Haven CT 06511 Office: 205 Church St New Haven CT 06508

DAY, JAMES EDWARD, lawyer; b. Jacksonville, Ill., Oct. 11, 1914; s. James Allmond and Frances (Wilmot) D.; A.B., U. Chgo., 1935; LL.B. cum laude, Harvard, 1938; LL.D., Ill. Coll., U. Nev., m. Mary Louise, Burgess, July 2, 1941; children—Geraldine (Mrs. James Zurn), Mary Louise, James Edward Day. Editor Harvard Law Rev., 1936-37; admitted to Ill. bar, 1938; with Sidley, Austin, Burgess & Harper, 1939- 41, 45-49; legal and legislative asst. to Gov. Adlai Stevenson, Springfield, Ill., 1949-50; mem., sec. Ill. Commn. Intergovtl. Coop., 1949-53; commr. ins. Ill., 1950-53; asso. gen. solicitor Prudential Ins. Co. Am., 1953-56, asso. gen. counsel, 1956, sr v.p. charge Western operations, Los Angeles, 1957-61; postmaster gen. U. S., 1961-63; now partner in charge Washington office Chgo. law firm Sidley and Austin. Dir., mem. exec. com. 6 cos. in Zurich Ins. Group, dir., mem. exec. com. Peoples Life Insurance Co., Washington. Spl. counsel consumer electronics group Electronic Industries Assn. Vice chmn. Gov.s' Commn. Met. Area Problems, Cal., 1959-61; mem. adv. bd. U.S. Customs Bur., 1966-68; mem. Gov. Cal. Bus. Adv. Council, 1959-61; v.p. Nat. Capital Council Boy Scouts Am.; gen campaign chmn. 1959 Los Angeles YMCA. Chmn. Democratic Asso., Los Angeles County, 1958-61; del. Dem. Nat. Conv., 1960. Trustee of Meridian House Found.; mem. bd. fellows Claremont Coll., Cal., 1958-65; chmn. nat. devel. com. Georgetown U.; bd. mem. Citizens Research Found. Served from ensign to lt., USNR, 1940-45. Mem. Nat. Civil Service League (pres. 1964-66), Citizens Conf. State Legislatures (chmn. 1965-70), Nat. Assn. Ins. Commrs. (chmn. Midwestern zone 1950- 53), Am., Fed., Chgo, bar assns. Bar Assn. D.C., Md. Farm Bur., Am. Devon Cattle Assn., Phi Kappa Psi. Democrat. Methodist. Clubs: Federal City, Nat. Press, Internat., Nat. Lawyers (Washington); Legal (Chgo.). Author: Bartholf Street; Descendants of Christopher Day of Bucks County Pennsylvania; My Appointed Round—, 929 Days as Postmaster General; Humor in Public Speaking, 1965. Contbr. to legal and ins. publs. Home: 5804 Brookside Dr Chevy Chase MD 20015 Office: 1625 I St NW Washington DC 20006

DAY, JAMES FREDERICK, educator; b. Cobleskill, N.Y., Dec. 10, 1920; s. Emmons and Alice (McCustey) D.; B.A., Colgate U., 1942; B.D., Yale, 1949, Ph.D., 1958; m. Janet A. Stewart, Aug. 23, 1947; children—Stewart, Jonathan, Christopher, Stephen. Reader in philosophy Yale, 1949-50; asst. prof. philosophy, dir. religious activities St. Lawrence U., Canton, N.Y., 1951-55; mem. faculty Allegheny Coll., Meadeville, Pa., 1955—, prof. philosophy and religion, 1968—, dir. Summer Sch. and grad. studies, 1968—. Served as pilot, USAAF, 1943-45. Decorated D.F.C., Air medal with 5 oak leaf clusters. Mem. Am. Philos. Assn., Am. Assn. U. Profs., Am. Acad. Religion, Metaphys. Soc. Am. Methodist (elder). Editor: (with C.B. Ketcham) Essays in Faith and Freedom, 1969. Home: 544 E College St Meadville PA 16335

DAY, JAMES VINCENT, govt. ofcl.; b. S. Brewer, Me., Nov. 27, 1914; s. Thomas Patrick and Mary Ellen (Ryan) D.; edn. certificate Wash. State Tchrs. Coll., 1934; m. Deima Irene McCormick, July 11, 1946; children—Teresa (Mrs. John P. Lynch), Daniel, James Vincent, Thomas, Timothy, Mary. Sales Supr. H.J. Heinz Co., 1936-41; pres. Spillers, Inc., Kennebunk, Me., 1951-55; nat. dir. pub. relations Am. Legion, 1956-61; vice chmn. Fed. Maritime Commn., 1961-. Mem. exec. com. Am. Legion P.T.A., 1961—; bd. advisers Blinded Vets. Assn., 1964—. Republican candidate for Congress from Me., 1956. Served to 1st lt. AUS, World War II. Named col., mil. staff Gov. Me., 1955; recipient Pres.'s award Am. Legion Press Assn., 1961, ann. Golden Record award best services in nat. def., 1960, Big M award State of Me. Soc., 1965. Mem. Am. Legion (nat. vice comdr. 1956—), Me. Soc. Washington (pres. 1963), Pub. Relations Soc. Am., Kappa Delta Phi. Home: 5524 Westbard Av Bethesda MD 20016. Office: Fed Maritime Commn Washington DC 20537

DAY, JAMES WARREN, pub. acct.; b. Brownwood, Tex., Dec. 10, 1903; s. William Riley and Martha Jane (Warren) D.; A.B., Tex., Christian U., 1928, M.A., 1929; m. Tommie Hazel Diestelhorst, Mar. 22, 1934; 1 dau., Diane Shepherd. Sr. partner Day, Benton & Covey, 1949; partner Day, Benton & Frazier, C.P.A.'s 1949-69; now asso. Brantley, Spillar & Frazier, C.P.A.'s; prof. eve. coll. Tex. Christian U., 1936-62; sec. dir. William N. Edwards & Co., investment bankers, 1944-66, Hopkins Co. Broadcasting Co., Sulphur Springs, Tex., 1948—; dir. of Union Bank of Fort Worth. Former mem. of the citizens council Scott and White Meml. Hosp., Scott, Sherwood and Brindley Found.; past v.p., dir. Met. Dinner Club Greater Ft. Worth. Bd. dirs. Nat. Council Alcoholism. Mem. lay adv. bd. St. Joseph Hosp.; adv. council S.W. Bapt. Theol. Sem. Received Distinguished Service award U.S. Jr. C. of C., Ft. Worth, 1933; Distinguished Alumnus award Tex. Christian U., 1966. Mem Am. Accounting Assn., Municipal Finance Officers Assn. of U.S. and Can., Nat. Assn. Cost Accts. (pres. Ft. Worth chpt. 1950-51), Am. Inst. of Accountants, Tex. Soc. of C.P.A.'s, Joint Civilian Orientation Conf. No. 19, Def. Orientation Conf. Assn. Ind. Democrat. Baptist. Mason, Elk (past exalted ruler). Clubs: Optimist (pres. Ft. Worth 1939-40, dist. gov. 1945-46, internat. pres. 1952-53, chmn. boys work council 1959-60), Ridotto, Knife and Fork, Fort Worth (Ft. Worth). Home: 3711 Westcliff Rd N Fort Worth TX 76109 Office: 3000 Continental Nat Bank Bldg Fort Worth TX 76102

DAY, JULIUS GILBERT, Jr., lawyer; b. Shelton, Conn., July 23, 1906 s. Julius Gilbert and Grace (Wanning) D.; grad. Taft Sch., 1923; A.B., Yale, 1927; LL.B., 1930; m. Alice R. Hotchkiss, Dec. 9, 1937; childrenCynthia H., John Gilbert. Admitted to Conn. bar, 1930, since practiced in Hartford; partner firm Day, Berry & Howard, 1935-; asst. counsel, acting gen. counsel A.R.C., Washington, 1942-45. Corporator Inst. for Living, Hartford. Sec., chmn. exec. com. Yale Class of 1927. Republican. Home: Bushnell Towers 1Gold St Hartford CT 06103 Office: One Constitution Plaza Hartford, CT 06103.

DAY, KARL S., airline exec.; b. Ripley County, Ind., May 30, 1896; s. Franklin Groves and Edith (Schmolsmire) D.; B.A., Ohio State U., 1917; m. Margaret Raine, Oct. 16, 1925; children—John Franklin, Nancy (Mrs. Howard M. Trowern, Jr.). Served from 2d lt. to lt. gen., USMC and USMC Res., 1917- 57; operations mgr. Curtiss-Wright Flying Service, 1929-32; with Am. Airlines, Inc., 1932-62, successively instrument instr., pilot, check pilot, asst. flight supt., flight supt., 1932-46, dir. flight dispatch, 1946-62. Marine Corps mem. Res. Forces Policy Bd., 1954-57; pres. Marine Corps Res. Officers Assn., 1953-56, chmn. bd. dirs., 1961-68, chmn. emeritus, 1968—. Recipient Navy Cross, Bronze Star Mem. Delta Tau Delta. Mason (32). Clubs: Caterpillar, University (Washington). Author: Instrument and Radio Flying, 1938. Pioneered instrument flying and aerial navigation by radio. Home: 25 Summit Av East Williston NY 11596

DAY, LEE MONROE, educator; b. Thayer, Ia., Feb. 25, 1923; s. Samuel Gordon and Helen McCleary (Swindler) D.; B.S., Ia. State U., 1947, M.A., 1948; Ph.D., U. Minn., 1953; m. Joan Meredith, Sept. 8, 1948; children—Michael Gordon, Meredith Lee. Asst. prof. agrl. econs. U. Wis., 1950-55; agrl. economist U.S. Dept. Agr., 1955-67; prof. agrl. econs. Pa. State U., 1967—, head dept. agrl. econs. and rural sociology, 1969—. Served with USNR, 1943-46. Mem. Am. (bd. dirs. 1971), N.E. agrl. econs. assns., Alpha Zeta, Phi Delta Kappa, Gamma Sigma Delta, Phi Kappa Phi. Democrat. Chmn. editorial adv. bd. Am. Bibliography Agrl. Econs., 1970—. Home: 649 Wiltshire Rd State College PA 16801

DAY, LEROY EDWARD, govt. ofcl.; b. Doswell, Va., Jan. 2, 1925; s. Ira Eugene and Sallie (Lester) D.; B. Aero. Engring., Ga. Inst. Tech., 1946; M.S. in Engring., U. Cal. at Los Angeles, 1955; M.S. in Indsl. Mgmt., Mass. Inst. Tech., 1960; m. Mary Elizabeth Hornbuckle, May 18, 1947; children—David, Jean, Michael. Dep. head missile program dept. U.S. Naval Missile Center, 1946- 62; with NASA, 1962—, dep. dir. space shuttle, 1969—; lectr. U. Cal. at Los Angeles, 1958-59. Local troop chmn. Boy Scouts Am., 1962. Served with USN, 1943-48. Sloan fellow, 1959; recipient Superior Achievement award NASA, 1967, Exceptional Service medal, 1969. Mem. Research Soc. Am., Tau Beta Pi, Phi Kappa Phi. Republican. Episcopalian. Contbr. papers profl. leit. Home: 11709 Magruder Lane Rockville MD 20852 Office: 600 Independence Av Washington DC 20003

DAY, LEWIS I., business exec.; b. Bellaire, O., 1912; grad. Ohio State U., 1935. Vice pres. finance, sec.-treas., dir. Buckeye Internat., Inc., Columbus. Mason. Home: 2049 Wyandotte Rd Columbus OH 43212 Office: 2211 Parsons Av Columbus OH 43207*

DAY, MABEL SIPE, assn. exec.; b. Staunton, Va., Feb. 22, 1912; d. James Walter and Grace (Weaver) Sipe; grad. Templeton Bus. Coll., Staunton, Va., 1928; m. John Louis Day, Oct. 28, 1939 (dec.); 1 dau., Donna Anne (Mrs. Sorrell). Sec. Md. Casualty Co., Staunton, 1928-35; sec. to Sen. Warren Barbour, Washington, 1935-36; sec. Moyle & Wilkinson, Washington, 1936-37; sec. to exec. dir. A.I.A., Washington, 1937-69; exec. adminstr. A.I.A. Found., Inc., Washington, 1970—. Mem. A.I.A. (hon.). Home: 2700 Virginia Av NW Washington DC 20037 Office: 1799 New York Av NW Washington DC 20006

DAY, MAHLON MARSH, mathematician; b. Rockford, Ill., Nov. 24, 1913; s. Mahlon Harlow and Mary Ellis (Marsh) D.; student U. Ore., 1930-32; B.S., Ore. State Coll., 1935; Sc.M., Brown U., 1937, Ph.D., 1939; Corinna Borden Keen research fellow Brown U. at Inst. Advanced Study, 1939-40; m. Elizabeth Coone, July 15, 1939 (dec. 1951); childrenMahlon Michael, Susan, George; m. 2d, Frances Morfoot Mautner, July 21, 1952; childrenJean Mautner (foster dau.), Donald, Dorothy. Instr. U. Ill., 1940-45, asst. prof., 1945-47, asso. prof., 1947-49, prof., 1949-, head dept., 1958-65; mem. Applied Math. Group, Brown U., 1944-46, Inst. Advanced Study, 1948-49; sr. postdoctoral fellow NSF, 1956-57. Fellow A.A.A.S.; mem. Am. Math. Soc., Math. Assn. Am. Author: Normed Linear Spaces, 1958. Home: 713 W Oregon St Urbana IL 61801

DAY, MAURICE JEROME, industrialist; b. Saginaw, Mich., Jan. 3, 1913; s. Thomas and Margaret (Cavanaugh) D.; B.S., Mich. State Coll., 1934, M.S., 1935, Ph.D., 1937; m. Mary Fitzgerald, Aug. 12, 1944; children—Mary Joann, Jeanne Ellen, Paul Maurice, Barbara Claire. Metallurgist, Carnegie- Ill. Steel Corp., Gary, Ind., 1937-38, tech.; trade rep., Chgo., 1941-45, mgr. alloy div., 1945-47; phys. chemist U.S. Steel Research Lab., Kearny, N.J., 1938-41; metall. engr. U.S. Steel Corp., Pitts., 1947-52; mgr. materials and processes div. Armour Research Found., Chgo., 1952-53, asst. dir., 1953-54; v.p. research and devel. Crucible Steel Co. Am., Pitts., 1955-57, v.p. tech., 1957-59, v.p. comml., 1959-63, sr. v.p., 1963-65; indsl. cons., 1965-68; pres., dir. Hawley Mfg. Co., San Francisco, Cal., 1966—; pres. Ameritee, Inc., Pitts., 1966—; dir., chmn. bd. Argus, Inc, 1969—, pres., 1970—; dir. Brown Co. N.Y.C., Crucible Steel Co. Can., Oxford Electric Corp., Argus, Inc., Crucible Steel Internat., S.A., Trent Tube Co. Chmn. manganese panel, minerals and metals adv. bd., mem. panel guided missiles Nat. Acad. Scis. Trustee Packaging Found., chmn. bd., 1963-65. Mem. Am. Ordnance Assn., Am. Navy League U.S., Am. Soc. Metals, Def. Orientation Conf. Assn., A.I.S.I., Pa. Soc. Club: Duquesne (Pitts.). Home: 830 Larchmont Rd Pittsburgh PA 15243 Office: Oliver Bldg Mellon Sq Pittsburgh PA 15222

DAY, MILTON HOWARD, corp. exec.; b. Cimarron, Kan., Jan. 23, 1913; s. Samuel M. and Luelva (Crow) D.; A.B., Friends U., Wichita, 1935; postgrad. U. Cal. at Los Angeles, 1955; m. Dora de Hoyos, Jan. 25, 1942; children—Steven, Mary, Jeanette, Samuel. Accountant, Wichita (Kan.) Beacon, 1936-40; with Times- Mirror Co., Los Angeles, 1940—, controller, 1956-65, treas., controller, 1965-68, v.p. and controller, now v.p., treas. Served to 1st lt., anti-aircraft, AUS, 1942-45. Mem. Inst. Newspaper Controllers and Finance, Financial Execs. Inst. Methodist. Home: 9427 Tierra Blanca Whittier CA 90603 Office: Times-Mirror Sq 202 W 1st St Los Angeles CA 90603

DAY, NANCY JANE, ret. librarian; b. Pendleton, S.C., May 1, 1905; d. Robert Bolt and Kate (Eskew) Day; B.A., Furman U., 1925; B.S., Columbia, 1933; M.A. in L.S., U. Mich., 1943. Tchr. pub. schs., Winston-Salem, N.C., 1925-30; asst. librarian Woman's Coll. Furman U., 1933-34; asst. librarian Greenville (S.C.) Pub. Library, 1934-35. Furman U., 1935, Fla. State Coll. Women, 1935-39; instr. library sci. Winthrop Coll., 1939- 43, dir. workshop, 1947; asst. prof. Emory U., 1943-46; supr. library service S.C. Dept. Edn., 1946-71; dir. workshop Madison Coll., 1950; instr. summer session U. N.C., 1950, post session U. So. Cal., 1952; Fulbright lectr. Chulalongkorn U., Thailand, 1953-54. Mem. exec. com. Tenn. Valley Library Council for Southeastern States Coop. Survey, 1946- 49. Mem. Am. (council 1949-53, bd. edn. for librarianship 1952-58), S.C. (sec. 1947), Southeastern (pres. 1954-56) library assns., Am. Assn. Sch. Librarians (pres. 1954-55), N.E.A., Am. Assn. U. Women, League Women Voters, Delta Kappa Gamma. Baptist. Home: 3210 Duncan St Columbia SC 29205

DAY, PATRICIA JEAN, publishing co. exec.; b. Villisca, Ia., Nov. 5, 1926; d. Russell Wayne and Brenice Leona (King) D.; B.A., Barnard Coll., 1948; M.A., State U. Ia., 1950; postgrad. U. Paris, 1951-52, Columbia, 1958-60; m. Sol Stein, Mar. 31, 1962; children—Robert Bruce, David Day, Elizabeth Day. Vice pres. Mid-Century Book Soc., N.Y.C., 1959-62; v.p., sec.-treas. Stein and Day, Inc., N.Y.C., 1962—. Trustee Scarborough (N.Y.) Sch. Home: Linden Circle Scarborough NY 10150 Office: 7 E 48th St New York City NY 10017

DAY, POMEROY, banker; b. Hartford, Conn., June 21, 1906; s. Arthur Pomeroy and Lucy (Bunce) D.; A.B., Yale, 1928; LL.B., 1931; LL.D., Trinity Coll., 1969; m. Katherine Flateau Long, Feb. 11, 1938 (dec. Sept. 1966); children—Pamela (Mrs. Robert H. Pelletreau, Jr.), Elizabeth (Mrs. Thomas C. Bolton). Roger P., George C.; m. 2d, Ella M. Stover, May 1969. Admitted to Conn. bar, 1931; practice in

Hartford, 1931-58; mem. firm Robinson, Robinson & Cole, 1936-58; pres. Conn. Bank & Trust Co., 1961-66, chmn., 1966-70, chmn. exec. com., 1970—; dir. Hartford Fire Ins. Co., Internat. Tel. & Tel. Corp., Arrow-Hart, Inc., Spencer Turbine Co., Conn. Natural Gas Co., Conn. Bank & Trust Co.; co-trustee Conn. Gen. Mortgage & Realty Investments. Mem. Conn. Revenue Task Force, 1969-71. Bd. dirs. Hartford Hosp.; trustee Wadsworth Atheneum (pres. 1970—). Served to lt. col. M.I., AUS, 1942-45. Decorated Bronze Star Republican, Episcopalian. Clubs: Hartford (pres. 1955-56), Hartford Golf; Woods Hole Golf; York River Fishing. Home: 1076 Prospect Av Hartford CT 06105 Office: 1 Constitution Plaza Hartford CT 06115

DAY, PRICE, newspaper editor; b. Plainview, Tex., Nov. 4, 1907; s. John Walter and Zillah (Price) D.; A.B., Princeton, 1929; m. Alice Alexander, Dec. 28, 1931; childrenAnthony, Joseph, Thomas, James. Cartoonist and occasional writer free lance, N.Y. and Fla., 1929-35; writer mag. fiction Sat. Eve. Post, Colliers, and others, 1935-41; city editor Fort Lauderdale (Fla.) Times, 1942; war corr. Balt. Sun, Mediterranean-ETO, 1943-45, fgn. and field corr., 1945-60; editor-in-chief Balt. Sunpapers, 1960-. Recipient Pulitzer prize for internat. reporting (articles on independence in India), 1949. Democrat. Home: W Lake Av Baltimore MD 21210 Office: The Sun Baltimore MD 21203

DAY, RICHARD WARD, educator; b. Boston, Aug. 14, 1916; s. Hilbert Francis and Elizabeth (Richards) D.; grad. Belmont (Mass.) Hill Sch., 1934; A.B., Yale, 1938; M.A., Harvard, 1940, Ph.D., 1950; m. Katharine MacAusland, Nov. 30, 1943; children—Richard Ward, Andrew MacAusland, Lydia Melville. Tchr. history, athletic coach Choate Sch., Wallingford, Conn., 1941-42; tchr. algebra and history, head dormitory, coach athletics St. Paul's Sch., Concord, N.H., 1938-39, 48-52; headmaster Germantown Academy, 1952-56, Hawken Sch., Cleve., 1956-64; prin. Phillips Exeter Acad., 1964—. Mem. vis. com. lang. and lit. Western Res. U., 1959-64; chmn. N.H. Commn. Human Rights, 1965-68; Served to maj., inf., AUS, 1942-46. Mem. Am. Hist. Soc., Headmasters Assn., Country Day Sch. Headmasters Assn. Clubs: Tavern (Cleve.); Duxbury (Mass.) Yacht; Tavern (Boston). Author: A New England Schoolmaster, a Biography of Henry Franklin Cutler, 1950. Home: 46 Front St Exeter NH 03833

DAY, ROBERT EDGAR, educator, artist; b. Clinton Falls, Minn., Dec. 27, 1919; s. Judson LeRoy and Blanche Leone (Finch) D.; student U. Minn., 1937-39; B.A., St. Olaf Coll., 1943; M.A., State U. Ia., 1946, Ph.D., 1958; m. Helen Marie Hanson, Aug. 13, 1944 (dec.); children—Marion Eve, Cynthia, Brian Louis; m. 2d, Kathryn Jean Waitz, June 7, 1969. Instr. art and English, also art supr., public schools of Owatonna, Minn., 1943-45; art supr. public schools, Winona, Minnesota, 1946-49; instr., asst. prof. art edn. and appreciation Kent State U., 1949-56; asso. prof. art history and sculpture No. Ill. U., 1958-60; prof., chmn. dept. fine arts La. State U., 1960-65; prof. U. of Colorado, Boulder, 1965- -, chmn. dept. of fine arts, 1965-68, chmn. adv. com. Anglo-Am. Art Mus., 1961-63. Discussant panel Place of History of Art in Pub. Schs., conv. Nat. Art Edn. Assn., N.Y.C., 1959; exhibited the Harvester, Regional Sculpture Invitational, Beaumont (Tex.) Art Mus., 1963. Recipient Danforth Found. tchr. grant, 1957; purchase award Ohio Printmakers Assn., Dayton (O.) Mus., 1951. Mem. Coll. Art Assn. Am. Presbyn. Home: 838 Spruce St Boulder CO 80302

DAY, ROBERT JAMES, magazine cartoonist; b. San Bernardino, Cal., Sept. 25, 1900; s. James Anderson and Estelle Strowbridge (Brooks) D.; student Otis Art Inst., 1919-27; m. Ethel H. Fabian, Aug. 29, 1904; children—Estelle E. (Mrs. Robert L. Parker), James Anderson II. Mem. art dept. Los Angeles Times, 1919-27, Los Angeles Examiner, 1927-29, N.Y. Herald Tribune, 1930; contbr. New Yorker, Look, Saturday Evening Post, Sports Illus., This Week, Sat. Rev., Punch, other nat. mags.; advt. campaigns nat. corps.; cartoons exhbt. throughout U.S. and Europe. Author: All Out for the Sack Race, 1945. Illustrator: We Shook the Family Tree, 1946; Fun Fare, 1949; Lower Prices Are Coming, 1950; (Arthur Godfrey) Stories I Like to Tell, 1952; Little Willie, 1953; Any Old Place With You, 1957; Seen Any Good Movies Lately, 1958; The Mad World of Bridge, 1960; Over the Fence is Out, 1961; What Every Bachelor Knows, 1961; I've Only Got Two Hands and I'm Busy Wringing Them, 1966; Rome Wasn't Burned in a Day, 1971. Address: 11 Cornwell St Rockville Centre NY 11570

DAY, THOMAS JOSEPH, lawyer; b. Guelph, Ont., Can., July 11, 1901; ed. Loyola Coll., Montreal, Que., Can., Osgoode Hall, Toronto. Admitted to Ont. bar, 1925; partner firm Day, Wilson & Campbell, Toronto. Mem. Canadian Bar Assn. Office: 600 Bank Canada Bldg Toronto 110 Ontario Canada*

DAY, TIMOTHY TOWNLEY, food co. exec.; b. Bklyn., May 9, 1937; s. David M. and Janice F. (Fowler) D.; B.A., Wesleyan U., Middletown, Conn., 1959; M.B.A., Harvard, 1964; m. Janet L. Vaill, June 5, 1959; children—Leslie, Timothy, Bryan. Controller for Eastern region sales and services Trans World Airlines, 1964-68; v.p., treas. Gen. Host Corp., N.Y.C., 1968—. Served to capt. USMCR, 1959-61. Mem. Chi Psi. Co-author: Mangement of Racial Integration in Business, 1964. Home: 21 Deer Run Trail Weston CT 06880 Office: 245 Park Av New York City NY 10017

DAY, VIRGIL BALDWIN, mfg. co. exec.; b. Montgomery, Ala., Oct. 18, 1915; s. Virgil Baldwin and Florence (Fairfield) D.; A.B. with honors, Northwestern U., 1936, J.D., 1939; grad. Advanced Mgmt. Program, Harvard, 1951; m. Eugenia Brunson, Aug. 9, 1947; children—John Baldwin, Baldwin, Peter Fairfield. Admitted to N.Y. bar, 1939; atty. Met. Life Ins. Co., 1939- 41; with firm Wickes, Riddell, Bloomer, Jacobi & McGuire, N.Y.C., 1941- 47; with Gen. Electric Co., 1947—, mgr. union relations, 1953-59, mgr. pub. affairs service, 1959-61, v.p. mgmt. devel. and employee relations service, 1961-66, v.p. personnel and indsl. relations services, 1966-68, v.p. indsl. relations, 1968-70, v.p. bus. environment, 1970—. Employer del. ILO, 1956, 62. Bd. dirs. Internat. Exec. Service Corps. Mem. Am. Bar Assn., Am. Mgmt. Assn., Commerce and Industry Assn. N.Y., N.A.M., Pub. Relations Soc. Am., C. of C. U.S., Order of Coif. Theta Xi, Phi Delta Phi, Delta Sigma Rho. Clubs: University (N.Y.C.); Mt. Kisco (N.Y.) Country (bd. govs.). Editor: Northwestern U. Law Rev. Home: 45 Cowdin Lane Chappagua NY 10514 Office: 570 Lexington Av New York City NY 10022

DAY, WILLIAM EDWIN, commnr. U.S. Ct. Claims; b. Washington, July 17, 1912; s. Ralph Edwin and Mary Agnes (Smith) D.; LL.B., Nat. U., 1935, LL.M., M.P.L., 1937; m. Mary Redmond, May 28, 1938. Admitted to D.C. bar, 1936; with Govt. Printing Office, 1931-37; instr. printing Coll. Engring., Carnegie Inst. Tech., 1937-40; pvt. practice law, Washington, 1940-41; spl. atty. antitrust div. Dept. Justice, 1941-42, spl. asst. to atty. gen. antitrust div., 1945-49; commr. U.S. Ct. Claims, 1949—. Served to lt. comdr. USCGR, 1942-45. Mem. Am., D.C. bar assns. Clubs: Army-Navy Country (Arlington); Culpeper (Va.) Country. Home: 3601 N Roberts Lane Arlington VA 22207 Office: US Court Claims 717 Madison Pl NW Washington DC 20005

DAY, WILLIAM L., banker; b. Jenkintown, Pa., Dec. 5, 1907; s. Charles and Margaret (Dunning) D.; B.S., U. Pa., 1931; m. Marcella Morgan, Oct. 25, 1935; children—Charles, Louise M. (Mrs. Leon R. Cook), Margaret D. (Mrs. Hugh F. Jones), Patricia L. (Mrs. Finley H. Perry, Jr.), Susan C. Engr., Day & Zimmerman, Inc., Phila., 1931-36; statistician Morgan Stanley & Co., N.Y.C., 1936-41; partner Drexel & Co., 1941-48; exec. v.p., dir. First Pa. Banking & Trust Co., Phila., 1948-52, pres., dir., 1952-55, chmn., 1955—; chmn. Old Phila. Devel. Corp.; dir. John Wanamaker Stores, Mut. Assurance Co., Rorer-Amchem Inc., Peoples Gas System, Inc.; bd. mgrs. Phila. Savs. Fund Soc. Co-chmn. Greater Phila. Movement. Chmn. bd. trustees U. Pa. Clubs: Philadelphia, Racquet, Mid Day (Phila.). Home: Beaumont Rd Devon PA 19333 Office: 15th and Chestnut Sts Philadelphia PA 19101

DAY, WILLIAM M., communications exec.; b. Pitts., Aug. 8, 1905; s. F.B. and Florence (Utley) D.; A.B., Yale, 1927; m. Elizabeth Hartman, Sept. 14, 1929. Successively rep., asst. mgr. and mgr. comml. dept., asst. engr., office mgr., customers relations supr. N.Y. Telephone Co., 1928- 39; pub. relations asst. and supr. Am. Tel. & Tel. Co., 1939-41, asst. v.p., 1945-48; v.p. pub. relations Mich. Bell Telephone Co., Detroit, 1948-50, v.p., gen. mgr., 1950-56, dir., 1950—, pres., 1956- 68, chmn. bd., chief exec. officer, 1968—; dir. Nat. Bank Detroit, Burroughs Corp. Spl. asst. to Donald Nelson, WPB, 1941-43. Trustee U. Detroit, Childrens Hosp.; bd. dirs. Greater Detroit Area Hosp. Council, Detroit Symphony Orch., Greater Detroit Bd. Commerce, United Found., Greater Mich. Found. Served to lt. col., Service Forces, AUS, 1943-45; chief facilities br., 1943, supervision controlled materials plan, 1944. Decorated Legion of Merit. Mem. Yale Alumni Assn., Telephone Pioneers Am., Newcomen Soc. Clubs: Detroit, Economic, Detroit Athletic Country (Detroit); Grosse Pointe Country; University (N.Y.C.). Home: 24 Winthrop Pl Grosse Pointe Farms MI 48236 Office: 1365 Cass Av Detroit MI 48226

DAY, WORDEN, sculptor, printmaker; b. Columbus, O.; d. Daniel E. and Amelia (Worden) Day; M.A., N.Y. U.; student Maurice Sterne, Vytlacil, Hoffman, Hayter. Tchr., Stephens Coll., U. Louisville, U. Wyo., State U. Ia., Pratt Inst., New Sch., Art Students League N.Y.; exhibited one man shows Perls Gallery, Bertha Schaefer Gallery, Krasner Gallery, Grand Central Moderns, Smithsonian Instn., U. Minn., Cin., Norfolk and Balt. museums art, Va. Mus. Fine Arts, Phila. Art Alliance; represented permanent collections Mus. Modern Art, N.Y.C., Whitney Mus., Bklyn. Mus., Library of Congress, Phila. Mus. Art, Met. Mus. Art, many others. Guggenheim- Rosenwald fellow, 1951-53, 61-62. Mem. Fedn. Modern Painters and Sculptors. Home: 285 Claremont Av Montclair NJ 07042

DAYAN, MOSHE, Israeli army officer; b. May 20, 1915; ed. agrl. high sch., Nahalal, Staff Coll., Camberley; LL.B., Tel-Aviv U., 1959; m. Ruth Schwartz; children—Yael, Ehui, Assaf. Trained Haganah (Jewish militia), 1929, becoming 2d in command to Capt. Orde Wingate, 1937; imprisoned by British when Haganah declared illegal, 1939, released for tng. as intelligence scout, Syria, 1941; apptd. gen., 1950, lt. gen., 1953; leader in war with Arabs, 1948-49; chief of staff, 1953-58; mem. Knesset, 1959—; minister of agrl., 1959-64; now def. minister of Israel. Author: Diary of the Sinai Campaign, 1966. Address: Knesset Jerusalem Israel*

DAYDE, LIANE, dancer; b. Paris, France, Feb. 27, 1934; d. Raoul and Marie (Roullot) Dayde; student Lycee Lamartine, also Paris Opera Sch.; m. Claude Giraud, Feb. 9, 1961; 1 son, Alain. Premiere danseuse Etoile de l'opera de Paris, 1951-, Danscuse Etoile Grand Ballet Classique de France, 1965; appearances opera houses throughout world, also internat. ballet cos. Roman Catholic. Home: 26 Rue Beriloz Paris France Office: 252 Faubourg Saint Honore Paris, France

DAY-LEWIS, CECIL, writer, educator; b. Ballintubber, Ireland, Apr. 27, 1904; s. Rev. F. C. and Kathleen Blake (Squires) Day-L.; student Sherborne Sch., Wadham Coll., Oxford; D. Litt. (hon.), Exeter U., D.Litt., U. Hull, 1969, Trinity Coll., Dublin, 1968; m. Constance Mary King, 1928 (div. 1951); children—Sean Francis, Nicholas Charles; m. 2d, Jill Angela Henriette Balcon, 1951; children—Lydia Tamasin, D. Daniel Michael. Asst. master at Summer Fields, Oxford, 1927-28, Larchfield, Helensburgh 1928-30, Cheltenham Coll., 1930-35; editor books and pamphlets Ministry of Information, 1941-46; Clark lectr. Trinity Coll., Cambridge, 1946-51; prof. poetry Oxford U., 1951-56; Charles Eliot-Norton prof. poetry Harvard 1964-65; also writer detective novels under pseudonym Nicholas Blake. Dir. Chatto & Windus, pubs.; v.p. London Library. Decorated comdr. Order Brit. Empire; companion of lit. Royal Soc. of Lit.; hon. fellow Wadham Coll., Oxford, 1968; poet-laureate of Eng., 1967—. Fellow Royal Soc. Lit. (v.p.); mem. Am. Acad. Arts and Letters (hon.), Irish Acad. Letters. Author: Collected Poems, 1954; A Hope for Poetry; Poetry for You; The Poetic Image; Pegasus; The Gate; The Buried Day; The Room; The Whispering Roots; various others. Translator of books, including the Georgics of Virgil; The Aeneid of Virgil; The Eclogues of Virgil. Home: 6 Crooms Hill Greenwich London SE 10 England Office: care Chatto & Windus 40 William IV St London WC 2 England also care Acad Am Poets 1030 Fifth Av New York City NY 10028

DAYTON, BRUCE BLISS, merchant; b. Mpls., Aug. 16, 1918; s. G. N. and Grace (Bliss) D.; B.A., Yale, 1940; m. Gwendolen Brandt, June 21, 1944. With Dayton's, Mpls., 1940—, beginning as trainee, successively treas., 1946-50, exec. v.p., dir., 1950-65, pres., 1965—; now chmn., chief exec. officer Dayton-Hudson Corp.; dir. First Nat. Bank of Mpls., Northwestern Nat. Life Ins. Co. of Mpls., 1st Bank Stock Corp. Trustee Mpls. Soc. Fine Arts. Home: 900 Old Long Lake Rd Wayzata MN 55391 Office: 700 Nicollet Av Minneapolis MN 55402

DAYTON, DAVID DRAPER, food service exec.; b. Mpls., Oct. 19, 1919; s. David Draper and Louise (Winchell) D.; B.A., Princeton, 1941; M.B.A., Harvard, 1943; m. Adriance Caroline Letts, Dec. 28, 1940; children—David Draper III, Peter Delano, Nelson Tenny, Adriance Chadwick. Treas., Smoky Mountain Canteen Co., Knoxville, Tenn., 1946-54; treas. Tenn. Service Co., Knoxville, 1950-54, pres., 1955-60; v.p. ARA Services, Inc., Phila., 1960—, dir., 1961-63. Vice pres., bd. dirs. Knoxville Boys Club; v.p. Knoxville Symphony. Served from ensign to lt., USNR, 1943-45. Mem. Nat. Automatic Merchandising Assn. (past dir.). Presbyn. (deacon). Club: Knoxville Civitan (past pres.). Home: 1332 Monk Rd Gladwyne PA 19035 Office: ARA Service Inc Independence Sq W Philadelphia PA 19106

DAYTON, DONALD CHADWICK, financial exec.; b. Mpls., Aug. 13, 1914; s. George Nelson and Grace (Bliss) D.; A.B., Yale, 1937; m. Lucy Jackson, Aug. 5, 1937; childrenEdward Nelson, Robert Jackson, John Webster. With Dayton Corp., Mpls., 1937-68, pres., 1950-65, chmn. bd., 1965- 68, gen. mgr., 1947-60, now dir.; dir. Burlington-Northern, Inc., St. Paul, Minnesota, Northwestern Nat. Bank, Mpls., Northwest Bancorp., Mpls., Northwestern Bell Telephone Co., Omaha. Voted outstanding young man, Mpls., 1947. Clubs: Minneapolis, Woodhill Country (Wayzata, Minn.); Minikahda (Mpls.). Home: Orono Wayzata MN 55391 Office: Roanoke Bldg Minneapolis, MN 55402.

DAYTON, GEORGE DRAPER II, dept. store exec.; b. Mpls., Sept. 21, 1907; s. David Draper and Louise (Winchell) D.; B.A., Princeton, 1928; m. Marion Harriet McDonald, June 26, 1928; children—George Draper III, Harriett McDonald (Mrs. Benjamin S. Jaffray), Margaret (Mrs. DeWalt H. Ankeny, Jr.). With The Dayton Co., Mpls., 1928-68, sec., 1936-37, treas., 1937-47, exec. mdse. mgr., 1954- 58, exec. v.p., 1947-68, with Dayton Hudson Corp., Mpls., 1968-71; trustee Farmers & Mechanics Savs. Bank. Mpls., 1940—; dir. Twin City Lines, 1958-65. Mem. Capital Long Range Improvements Com. Mpls., 1958-71, Citizens Auditorium Finance Com, 1961-65; mem. exec. com. Citizens Adv. Com. Community Improvement Program Mpls., 1962-65. Trustee Macalester Coll., 1940—, chmn. bd., 1963-67; trustee Twin City Area Ednl. TV Corp., 1955—, pres., 1962-66; trustee United Hosp. Fund Mpls. and Hennepin County, 1956—, gen. campaign chmn., 1956-59; bd. dirs., mem. exec. com. Planning Agy. Hosps., Met. Mpls., 1964-69; bd. dirs. Jr. Achievement Mpls., 1960—; bd. dirs. McCormick Theol. Sem., Chgo., 1939- 46, v.p., 1942-46; trustee United Theol. Sem., New Brighton, Minn., 1970—. Recipient Community Service citation Minn. chpt. Pub. Relations Soc. Am., 1958; Distinguished Service award Community Chest and Council Hennepin County, 1959; Dr. Francis E. Harrington award U.S. Jr. C. of C., 1960; named hereditary knight comdr. justice Sovereign Order St. John Jerusalem, Knights of Malta, 1961; hon. consul Republic of Korea, 1969—. Mem. Minn. Hist. Soc. (exec. council 1953-59), U.S. (bd. dirs. 1960-66, chmn. mfr.-domestic distbn. com. 1965-66), Mpls. (bd. dirs. 1958-66, v.p. 1959-61) chambers commerce, Nat. Retail Mchts. Assn. (bd. dirs. 1955-60). Republican. Presbyn. (deacon 1929-34, elder 1934—). Clubs: Minneapolis; Woodhill Country (Wayzata). Home: Cedarhurst Wayzata MN 55391 Office: First Nat Bank Bldg Minneapolis MN 55402

DAYTON, KENNETH NELSON, retail mdse. co. exec.; b. Mpls., July 20, 1922; s. G. Nelson and Grace (Bliss) D.; B.A., Yale, 1944; m. Julia Davis Winton, June 12, 1953; children—Judson McDonald, Duncan Nelson. With Dayton's, Mpls, 1946-65, gen. mdse. mgr., 1950-54, v.p., gen. mdse. mgr., 1954-65; exec. v.p., gen. mgr. Dayton Corp., Mpls., 1965-67, exec. v.p., 1967-69, pres. Dayton Hudson Corp., Mpls., 1969-, also dir.; dir. Gen. Mills, Inc., Northwestern Nat. Bank Mpls. Mem. Rockefeller Bros. Fund Panel for Performing Arts, 1964-65, Bus. Com. for Arts, 1968—, Nat. Council on Arts, 1970—. Bd. dirs. Minn. Orchestral Assn. Served with AUS, 1943-46. Home: 392 S Ferndale Rd Wayzata, MN 55391. Office: 700 Nicollet Mall Minneapolis, MN 55402.

DAYTON, SAMUEL GREY, Jr., investment banker; b. Media, Pa., Feb. 3, 1921; s. Samuel Grey and Mary S. (Wurts) D.; A.B., Princeton, 1943; m. Frances Imbrie, June 17, 1943; children—Alice S., Samuel Grey 3d, Andrew I. Partner, Elkins, Morris, Stroud & Co., investment bankers, Phila. Mem. Midwest Stock Exchange; allied mem. Am. Stock Exchange; gov., past pres. Phila.-Balt-Washington Stock Exchange; allied mem. N.Y. Stock Exchange. Served as lt. AUS, World War II. Mem. Financial Analysts Phila., Phila. Securities Assn., Municipal Forum N.Y.C. Club: Bond (Phila.). Home: Cedar Hill Farm Media PA 19063 Office: Stock Exchange Bldg Philadelphia PA 19403

DEACON, JOHN CAMPBELL, lawyer; b. Newport, Ark., Sept. 26, 1920; s. John Campbell and Marie (Brennan) D.; B.A., U. Ark., 1941, J.D., 1948; m. Dorine Barrett, Sept. 4, 1947; children-Marie, Barry, John Campbell, Rush. Admitted to Ark. bar, 1948; with firm Rose, Meek, House, Barron & Nash, Little Rock, 1949- 51; partner firm Barrett, Wheatley, Smith & Deacon, Jonesboro, 1952—. Dir. Citizens Bank of Jonesboro. Chmn. Ark. Commn. Uniform State Laws, 1969—; mem. Ark. Commn. Interstate Coop., 1969—. Pres. adv. bd. St. Bernards Hosp., 1955—; trustee Craighead Countty Library, 1956—, United Fund Jonesboro, 1954—. Served to maj. AUS, World War II, Korea. Named Outstanding Young Man of Jonesboro, 1955. Mem. Am. (ho. of dels. 1967—), Ark. (pres. 1970-71), Craighead County (pres. 1968-69), N.E. Ark. (pres. 1966-68) bar assns., Ark. Conf. Local Bar Assns. (pres. 1961- 63). Home: 1004 E Nettleton Av Jonesboro AR 72401 Office: Citizens Bank Bldg Jonesboro AR 72401

DEACON, PAUL SEPTIMUS, editor and pub.; b. Toronto, Can., June 9, 1922; s. Frederick Herbert and Ethel Record (Emmerson) D.; B.A., U. Toronto, 1943, M.Com., 1947; m. Charlotte Adelle Smith, Feb. 25, 1950; children—Anne, Wendy, James, Andrew, Jennifer. With The Financial Post, Toronto, 1947—, Eastern editor, Montreal, 1949-52, investment editor, Toronto, 1952-64, editor, 1964—, pub., 1968—. Dir. Ont. div. Canadian Cancer Soc., John Howard Soc. Ont., Nat. Ballet Guild of Can. Served as pilot, R.C.A.F., 1942-45. Mem. Toronto Soc. Financial Analysts (pres. 1961-62). Mem. United Ch. of Can. Clubs: University, Rosedale Golf, Canadian (Toronto). Home: 41 Nanton Av Toronto 287 Ontario Canada Office: 481 University Av Toronto 101 Ontario Canada

DEACY, THOMAS EDWARD, Jr., lawyer; b. Kansas City, Mo., Oct. 14, 1918; s. Thomas Edward and Grace (Scales) D.; J.D., U. Mo., 1940; M.B.A., U. Chgo., 1949; m. Jean Freeman, July 10, 1943; children—Bennette Kay (Mrs. Kramer), Carolyn G., Margaret, Thomas, Ann. Admitted to Mo. bar, 1940, Ill. bar 1946; practice law, Kansas City, 1940-42; partner firm Taylor, Miller, Busch & Magner, Chgo., 1946-55, Deacy & Deacy, Kansas City, 1955-; lectr. Northwestern U., 1949-55, U. Chgo., 1950-55. Dir. St. L.-S.F. Ry., 1962-. Mem. Juvenile Protective Assn. Chgo., 1947-55, pres., dir., 1950-53; mem. exec. bd. Chgo. council Boy Scouts Am., 1952-55; pres. Kansas City Philharmonic Orch. 1961-63, chmn. bd. trustees, 1963-65. Trustee U. Kansas City, Kansas City Conservatory Music, Sunset Hill Sch. Served to capt., AUS, 1942-46. Fellow Am. Coll. Trial Lawyers (regent 1968—); mem. Am., Ill., Chgo., Mo., Kansas City bar assns., Lawyer's Assn. Kansas City, Beta Gamma Sigma. Clubs: Legal, Chicago (Chgo.); University, Kansas City, Mission Hills Country (dir., sec. 1968—) (Kansas City, Mo.). Home: 2722 Verona Circle Shawnee Mission KS 66208 Office: Bryant Bldg Kansas City MO 64106

DEADERICK, LUCILE, librarian; b. Knoxville, Tenn., June 22, 1914; d. Paul Stuart and Josephine Lee (Galyon) Deaderick; B.A., U. Tenn., 1934; B.S. in L.S., U. Ill., 1937. With Lawson McGhee Library, Knoxville, 1934-41; librarian A.L.A., Chgo., 1941-47, Ft. Loudoun Regional Library, Lenoir City, Tenn., 1947-51, Knox County schs., Knoxville, 1951-68; asso. prof. library service U. Tenn., 1968-69; dir. Knoxville-Knox County Pub. Library, 1970—. Mem. Am., Southeastern, Tenn. library assns., Assn. Preservation Tenn. Antiquities, E. Tenn. Hist. Soc. (bd. dirs.), Tenn. Farm Bur. Democrat. Roman Cath. Home: Route 17 Knoxville TN 37921 Office: 500 W Church Av Knoxville TN 37902

DEAHL, WARREN ANTHONY, lawyer; b. South Bend, Ind., Sept. 18, 1918; s. Floyd Anthony and Sarah (Rosenbury) D.; A.B. cum laude, U. Notre Dame, 1941, J.D., 1944; m. Marjorie Katherine Sears, Nov. 29, 1941; children—Floyd Richards, John Orlo. Admitted to Ind. bar, 1944; practiced in South Bend, 1946—; sr. partner Thornburg, McGill, Deahl, Harman, Carey & Murray. Instr. bus. law

Ind. U., 1947-49, ins. law and tax Ind. U. Extension, 1947-50, law U. Notre Dame, 1948, 69; counsel South Bend Community Sch. Corp.; dir. Drewrys, Ltd. U.S.A., Inc.; mem. Estate Planning Council, South Bend. Sec., bd. dirs. Central Blood Bank, Inc.; asst. treas. Episcopal Diocese No. Ind.; past trustee YMCA; atty., mem. adv. bd. Vis. Nurse Assn. South Bend. Served with inf., AUS, 1943-44, CIC, 1944-46. Decorated Bronze Star medal. Fellow Am. Coll. Probate Counsel; mem. Am., Ind., St. Joseph County (past bd. govs.) bar assns., Am. Judicature Soc., South Bend- Mishawaka Area C. of C. (dir., past pres.). Club: Indiana (past pres., dir.) (South Bend). Asso. Editor: Notre Dame Lawyer, 1943. Home: 60300 Abshire Dr South Bend IN 46614 Office: First Bank Bldg South Bend IN 46601

DEAKIN, JAMES, newspaperman; b. St. Louis, Dec. 3, 1929; s. Rogers and Dorothy (Jeffrey) D.; A.B., Washington U., St. Louis, 1951; m. Doris Marie Kanter, Apr. 14, 1956; 1 son, David Andrew. Mem. staff St. Louis Post- Dispatch, 1951—, Washington corr., 1954—, White House corr., 1965—. Mem. White House Corrs. Assn. (mem. exec. com.), Author: the Lobbyists, 1966; Lyndon Johnson's Credibility Gap, 1968; also numerous articles. Home: 4432 Windom Pl NW Washington, DC 20016. Office: 1701 Pennsylvania Av NW Washington DC 20006

DEAL, GEORGE LAWRENCE, mfg. exec.; b. Canton, O., Sept. 5, 1914; s. Alva L. and Luella (Richards) D.; A.B., Oberlin Coll., 1936; M.B.A., Harvard, 1939; LL.B., William McKinley Sch. Law, 1949. Admitted to Ohio bar, 1949; treas. Timken Ordnance Co., 1942-44; asst. treas. Timken Roller Bearing Co., Canton, 1947-53, treas., 1953-55, sec.-treas., 1955-64, v.p. finance, 1964—, also dir. Trustee Philomatheon Soc. Trust, 1953-. Mem. Canton C. of C. (dir.). Home: 2974 Midvale (Avondale) Canton, OH 44718. Office: 1835 Dueber Av SW Canton, OH 44706.

DEALE, HENRY VAIL, Jr., librarian; b. Balt., May 14, 1915; s. Henry V. and Sarah Lippincott (Sisson) D.; student Dickinson Coll., 1931-33; B.A., DePauw U., 1936; M. Library Sci., U. Ill., 1937; M.A., Drake U., 1947-50; m. Jane Niehaus, June 7, 1944; 1 dau., Sarah Sisson. Circulation asst., stack supt. Northwestern U. Library, 1937-39; circulation asst., pub. relations dir. Bloomington (Ill.) Pub. Library, 1939-41; civilian pub. service, 1941-45; asst. librarian Ripon (Wis.) Coll., 1946; reference librarian Drake U. Library, 1946-48, humanities librarian, 1948-51; librarian Ill. Wesleyan U., 1951-53; dir. libraries Beloit Coll., 1953—, also chmn. dept. library sci. Fulbright scholar Pahlavi U., Shiraz, Iran, 1965-66; Fulbright lectr. faculty U. Tehran, Iran, 1970-71. Mem. Am., Ill., Ia., Wis. (pres. 1959-60) library assns., Am. Assn. U. Profs., Midwest Acad. Librarians (chmn. 1957-59), Assn. Coll. and Reference Libraries (pres. coll. sect. 1964-65, chmn. grants com. 1967—). Editor: Library Trends, 1969. Contbr. articles to profl. jours. Home: 1427 Chapin St Beloit WI 53511

DEALEY, JAMES QUAYLE, Jr., ret. educator; b. Providence, Sept. 21, 1899; s. James Quayle and Clara (Learned D.; A.B., Brown U., 1920; B.A. (Rhodes Scholar 1921-23), Oxford (Eng.) U., 1923, M.A., 1928; Ph.D., Harvard, 1928; m. Esther Poole Reed, June 24, 1932; 1 son, William Reed. With personnel dept. Lycoming Rubber Co., 1920; trust dept. R.I. Hosp. Trust Co., 1924-25; instr. govt. Harvard, 1925-28; asst. prof. polit. sci. Western Res. U., 1928-31; asst., then asso. prof. Hamilton Coll., 1931-46; with hist. sect. War Dept., 1946-47; prof. polit. sci. U. Toledo, 1947-70, prof. emeritus, 1970—, chmn. dept., 1954-65. Pres. Toledo Council World Affairs, 1961-63. Mem. Oneida County (N.H.) Pub. Welfare Com., 1937-43. Served with inf., U.S. Army, 1918, from capt. to lt. col. AUS, 1943-46. Mem. Am., Canadian Polit. sci. assns., Phi Beta Kappa, Phi Kappa Phi, Delta Upsilon. Home: 2534 Goddard Rd Toledo OH 43606

DEALEY, JOSEPH MACDONALD, newspaper exec.; b. Dallas, July 18, 1919; s. Edward Musgrove and Clara (MacDonald) D.; A.B., U. Tex., 1941; m. Doris Carolyn Russell, Jan. 18, 1947; children—Joseph MacDonald, Russell Edward, Pamela Carolyn, Frances Patricia. Reporter, Dallas Morning News, 1942-50, asst. sec., 1950-55, dir., 1952—, sec., 1955-60, pres., 1960—. Pres., County chpt. A.R.C., 1961-63; bd. govs. Am. Nat. Red Cross; mem. exec. com. Community Council Greater Dallas, 1960—, pres., 1965-66; bd. dirs. Dallas Citizens Council, 1960—, pres., 1964-65; bd. dirs. Childrens' Med. Center, 1950—, pres., 1964-67; bd. dirs. Dallas Council Social Agys., 1958—; trustee Dallas Theater Center; bd. dirs. Dallas County United Fund, 1961—, mem. exec. com., 1962—, v.p., 1963-65, pres., 1967, campaign chmn., 1966-67; bd. dirs. United Community Funds and Councils Am.; bd. dirs. State Fair Tex.; mem. U. Tex. Devel. Bd. and Chancellor's Council, chmn., 1967-68. Served to lt. USAAF, 1942-46. Mem. Dallas C. of C. (dir.), Am. (dir.), So. (dir., pres. 1969) newspaper pubs. assns., Tex. Daily Newspaper Assn. (mem. exec. com., pres. 1969), Press Club Dallas, Sigma Delta Chi, Phi Delta Theta. Clubs: Dallas Country, Koon Kreek, Las Colinas Country. Home: 4332 Arcady St Dallas TX 75205 Office: Dallas Morning News Dallas TX 75222

DE ALMEIDA, ANTONIO, condr.; b. Paris, 1928; B.Mus., Yale; studied with A. Ginastera, Buenos Aires, Serge Koussevitsky, Paul Hindemith; m. Lynn Erdman; 2 sons, 1 dau. Condr., Portuguese Radio, 1957-60; music dir. Stuttgart Philharmonic, 1962-64, Paris Opera; now condr. Houston Symphony; guest condr. Berlin Philharmonic, Phila. Orch., Orch. National, Suisse Romande, Leningrad Philharmonic, others. Author: Thematic Catalogue Works by Offenbach. Editor: Offrande Musicale Orchestral Series (Heugel). Office: 612 Louisiana Houston TX 77002*

DE ALVAREZ, RUSSELL RAMON obstetrician, gynecologist; b. N.Y.C.; s. John and Isidora (Torres y Sanchez) de A.; B.S., U. Mich., 1931, M.D., 1935, M.S., 1940; m. Betty Jane Casey, Sept. 11, 1943; children—Ann, Russell Ramon. Intern U. Mich. Hosp., 1935-36, asso. attending gynecologist U. Ore. Hosps., 1946-48; lst prof. and head dept. obstetrics and gynecology U. Wash. Med. Sch., 1948-64; prof., chmn. dept. obstetrics and gynecology, Temple U., Phila., 1964—; obstetrician and gynecologist in chief King County Hosp., 1948-64; cons. Phila. Gen. Hosp., VA Hosp.; cons. in obstetrics- gynecology to surgeon gen. U.S. Army. Served as lt. comdr. USNR, 1944- 46. Diplomate Am. Bd. Obstetrics and Gynecology (asso. examiner). Fellow A.C.S., Am. Coll. Obstetricians and Gynecologists (asst. sec. 1958-59), Soc. Gynecologic Investigation (pres. 1959); mem. A.M.A., Am. Assn. Obstetricians and Gynecologists, Am. Fedn. Clin. Research, Central Assn. Obstetrics and Gynecology, Wash. (hon.), Ore. socs. obstetrics and gynecology, Seattle Gynecol. Soc. (hon. life, pres. 1961-62), Western Soc. Clin. Research, Obstet. Soc. Phila. (council 1968- 71, 1st v.p. 1970-71, pres. elect 1971-72), Pacific Northwest Soc. Obstetricians and Gynecologists (pres. 1962- 63), Am. Gynecol. Soc., Am. Coll. Obstetrics and Gynecology, Research Soc. U. Wash., Norman F. Miller Gynecologic Soc. (Pres. 1962-63), Pa., Phila. County med. socs., Am. Soc. Human Genetics, Soc. Obstetrics and Gynecology Can., Washington Obstet. Soc., Reno Surg. Soc., Assn. Profs. Gynecology and Obstetrics, Am. Nephrology Soc., Soc. Reprodn., Am. Assn. U. Profs., N.J. (hon.), Pacific Coast, S.W., Los Angeles, Pacific Northwest (hon. life), Honolulu obstet. and gynecol. socs., A.A.A.S., Hollywood (Cal.) Acad. Medicine, Pacific N.W. Obstet. and Gynecol. Assn. (pres. 1962), U. Mich. Med. Alumni Soc. (bd. govs.), Am. Legion, Venezuelan Obstet. and Gynecol. Soc. (hon.), Sigma Xi, Alpha Omega Alpha, Nu Sigma Nu. Clubs: University, College, Seattle Golf (Seattle): Union League, Doctors Golf, Wayfair, Phila. Country (Phila.). Editorial bd. Western Jour. Surgery, Obstetrics and Gynecology, Am. Jour. Obstetrics and Gynecology; editor- in-chief Quar. Rev. Obstetrics and Gynecology. Editor: Clinical Obstetrics and Gynecology. Contbr. med. publs. Home: 810 Waverly Rd Bryn Mawr PA 19010 Office: 3401 Broad St Philadelphia PA 19140

DE ALWIS, WATUTANTIRIGE SUSANTA LESLIE, diplomat of Ceylon; b. Colombo, Ceylon, Aug. 17, 1932; s. W. Leslie and Emily (Soysa) de A.; LL.B., Y. Ceylon, 1952; B.Litt., Oxford U., 1961; m. Achala Pandita Gunewardena, July 31, 1959; children—Chamini, Darshini, Ruvan. Barrister-at-lw, Grays Inn, London, 1960; advocate Supreme Ct. Ceylon, 1957; journalist, editorial staff Ceylon Daily News, Colombo, 1952-57; with Ceylon Fgn. Service, 1957—; asst. sec. Ministry Def. and External Affairs, 1957-62; asst. high commr. for Ceylon in Madras, India, 1962-66; chargé d'affaires ad interim for Ceylon, Indonesia, 1966-67; asst. sec. fgn. relations Ministry Def. and External Affairs, 1968-70; 1st sec. Ceylon embassy, Washington, 1970, chargé d'affaires ad interim, 1970—. Mem. Ceylon delegation Afro-Asian Legal Consultative Com., 1959-64, UN Conf. Jud. Remedies and Adminstrv. Law, 1959, UN Law Sea Conf., Geneva, 1960, Indo-Ceylon Talks, New Delhi, 1964, 24th session UN Gen. Assembly, 1969, Asian Non-aligned Conf., 1970, others. Home: 10308 Julep Av Silver Spring MD 20902 Office: 2148 Wyoming Av Washington DC 20008

DEALY, JOHN FRANCIS, lawyer, aerospace co. exec.; b. Bklyn., May 4, 1939; s. John Edward and Marie (Jones) D.; B.S., Fordham Coll., 1961; LL.B., N.Y.U., 1964; m. Nana Louise May, Oct. 7, 1967; children—Anne Louise, Marian Jones. Admitted to N.Y. bar, 1964; atty.-adviser to Sec. Air Force, 1964-67; gen. counsel Fairchild Ind., Germantown, Md., 1967-68, v.p., gen. counsel, 1968—; pres. Fairchild-Germantown Devel. Co., Inc.; dir. Fairchild Aviation (Holland) N.V. Served at capt. USAF, 1965-68. Named Outstanding Young Man of Am., 1971. Mem. N.Y.U. Law Sch. Alumni Assn. (pres. Washington chpt.), Washington Met. Area Ice Hockey Assn. (pres. 1965-66). Notes editor N.Y.U. Law Rev., 1963-64. Home: 11504 Westhill Dr Rockville MD 20852 Office: Sherman Fairchild Tech Center Germantown MD 20767

DEAM, EDWARD LEE, architect, educator; b. Chgo., Nov. 10, 1928, s. Arthur Francis and Thyra (Soderberg) D.; B.A.,U. Pa., 1951, M.A., 1955; m. Doris Margaret Prohl, Nov. 18, 1951; children—Karin Jane, Norman Andrew and Nancy Alicia (twins), Judy Marie. Asst. prof. U. Ill. at Urbana, 1958-62, asso. prof. at Chgo., 1962-64, prof., 1965—, chmn. com. grad. program in urban planning and policy, 1970-71, acting asso. dean Coll. Architecture and Art, 1968-69, asso. dean, 1970—; pvt. archtl. practice and cons. architecture, 1958- -; architect Ganster & Henninghausen, 1955-58, 64-65, Richardson, Severns, Scheeler & Assos., Champaign, Ill., 1961-62, O'Donnell, Wicklund & Pigozzi, Evanston, Ill., 1965, Loebl, Schlossman, Bennett & Dart, Inc., Chgo., 1966-67; achtl. cons. McFaozean & Everly, Winnetka, 1968—. Bd. dirs. Summer Sch. Painting, Saugatuck, Mich., 1965—; curriculum cons. Milw. Sch. Engring., 1966. Served to lt. comdr. USNR, 1951-54. Recipient Paul Philippe Crete prize, 1951, Thorton Oakley award, 1951, Albert Kahn Meml. scholarship in architecture, 1951-52, Miles Day prize, 1958, Phila. Print Club award, 1951. Mem. Assn. Collegiate Schs. Architecture Club: Cliff Dwellers (bd. dirs. 1970-72) (Chgo.). Presbyn. (ruling elder 1969—). Important works include William Brunkow Residence, Condit Twp. Home: 1585 Ridge Rd Highland Park IL 60035 Office: Dept Architecture Box 4348 Chicago IL 60680

DEAN, ABNER, artist; b. New York, N.Y., Mar. 18, 1910; s. Louis and Deana (Grozcky) Epstein; A.B., Dartmouth, 1931; student Nat. Acad. of Design. Free lance artist; has done drawings for advertising, illustrations and cartoons for magazines, 1931—. Member of Society of Illustrators. Author: It's a Long Way to Heaven (satirical drawings), 1945; What Am I Doing Here?, 1947; And on the Eighth Day, 1949; Come As You Are, 1952; Cave Drawings for the Future, 1954; Wake Me when Its Over (verse and cartoons), 1955; Not Far From the Jungle, 1956; Abner Dean's Naked People, 1963. Patent on multilevel folding table. Address: 166 E 61st St New York City NY 10022

DEAN, ALAN LOREN, govt. ofcl.; b. Portland, Ore., July 27, 1918; s. Claude Lorenzo and Alfhild (Jacobson) D.; B.A. in Polit. Sci., Reed Coll., 1941; M.A. in Pub. Adminstrn., Am. U., 1955; m. Vera Alta Sisson, Jan. 9, 1944; children—Claudia, Diana, Laura. Dir. civilian personnel U Umatilla Ordnance Depot, Dept. War, 1941-43, insp. civilian personnel programs Office Sec. War, 1943-45, dir. Dept. War Sch. Civilian Personnel Adminstrn., 1946-47; sr. analyst govt. orgn. Bur. Budget, 1947-59; asst. adminstr. mgmt. services FAA, 1959-61, dep. adminstr. for adminstrn., 1961-63, asso. adminstr. for adminstrn., 1963-67; asst. sec. adminstrn. Dept. Transp., 1967—. Mem. bd. gen. adminstrn. Dept. Agr. Grad. Sch., 1961-70; mem. Interagy. Adv. Com. on Mgmt. Improvement, 1960-66. Mem. bd. suprs. Arlington County, 1952, planning commn., 1958- 60, commn. on incorp., 1958-59; pres. Fairlington Civic Assn., 1950-51; vice chmn. Arlingtonians for a Better County, 1962-63; pres. Donaldson Run Civic Assn., 1955-56. Trustee Reed Coll., Portland, Ore. Recipient award for meritorious civilian service Dept. War, 1945, Career Service award Nat. Civil Service League, 1965; Exceptional Service award FAA, 1965; Outstanding Service award Dept. Transp., 1969. Mem. Am. Polit. Sci. Assn., Am. Soc. Pub. Adminstrn. (pres. D.C. chpt. 1961-62, nat. council 1962-66), Fed. Exec. Officers Group (chmn. 1959-66), Conf. Pub. Service, Nat. Acad. Pub. Adminstrn. Conglist. Club: Nat. Aviation. Home: 3037 N Stafford St Arlington VA 22207 Office: 400 7th St SW Washington DC 20590

DEAN, ARTHUR HOBSON, lawyer; b. Ithaca, N.Y., Oct. 16, 1898; s. William Cameron and Maud J.J.D.; A.B., Cornell U., 1921, LL.B., 1923; LL.D., Hamilton Coll., Allegheny Coll., 1954, Rutgers-The State U., 1958, Washington U., 1958; Brown U., Dartmouth, Bowdoin Coll., 1962, C.W. Post Coll., 1963; LL.D., Adelphi U., 1964, Otterbein Coll., 1964; D.C.L., Hofstra Coll., 1961; L.H.D., Washington Coll., 1963; D. of Litt. Lafayette Coll., 1968; m. Mary Marden, June 25, 1932; children—Nicholas B. Marden, Patricia Cambell (Mrs. Leonidas Manoils. Admitted to N.Y. bar, 1923, since practiced in N.Y.C. with firm Sullivan & Cromwell, partner, 1929—; gen. counsel various corps.; dir., mem. exec. com., gen. counsel Am. Metal Climax, Inc.; dir., mem. exec.com. Am. Bank Note Co.; dir. Bank of N.Y., Bank of N.Y. Co., Inc., Bank N.Y. Internat. Corp., Nat. Union Electric Corp., El Paso Natural Gas Co., Crown Zellerback Corp., Adela Investment Co. S.A., N.W. Prodn. Corp. Dickinson lectr. Harvard, 1950. Rep., chmn. dels. of U.S. to UN Confs. on Law of Sea, Geneva, 1958, 60; represented U.S. and 16 nations contbg. troops in negotiations at Panmunjom; spl. U.S. ambassador to Korea, 1953-54; exdep. to sec. of state for polit. conf. envisaged by Korean Armistice; del. 16th, 17th Gen. Assemblys of UN; chmn. U.S. delegation Conf. on Discontinuance of Nuclear Weapons Tests, Geneva, 1961-62; chmn. U.S. delegation 18-Nation Disarmament Conf., Geneva, 1962; mem. exec. com. Lawyers' Com. Civil Rights Under Law. Mem. joint adminstrv. bd. N.Y. Hosp.-Cornell Med. Center; mem. co-ordinating bd. Sloan- Kettering div. Cornell Med. Coll.; v.p., dir. N.Y. Hosp.-Cornell Med. Center Found., Inc.; trustee Cornell U.; chmn. Com. for Corp. Support of Am. Univs.; trustee Hochschild Found., Planting Fields Assn., Asia Found.; bd. dirs. Netherlands-Am. Found., Teagle Found., Spanish Inst. Chubb fellow Yale, 1955. Decorated officer French Legion of Honor; recipient Gold medal, N.Y. State Bar Assn., 1962; Theodore Roosevelt Assn. Distinguished Service medal, 1962. Fellow Am. Coll. Trial Lawyers; mem. Acad. Polit. Sci., Am. Acad. Polit. and Social Sci., Am., N.Y. State bar assns., Asia Soc., Internat. C. of C. (dir. U.S. council), Am. Judicature Soc., Am. Soc. Internat. Law (pres. 1961-62), Fellows Am. Bar Found., Am. N.Y. law insts., Assn. Bar N.Y.C. (v.p.), Cornell Law Assn., Council Fgn. Relations (dir.), Fgn. Policy Assn., Internat. Law Assn., Japan Soc., Inc. (hon.). Am. Econ. Assn., Assn. for Aid Crippled Children (mem. finance com.), N.Y. County Lawyers Assn., Pilgrims U.S., UN Assn. (dir.), France-Am. Soc., Nantucket Ornithol. Assn. (trustee). Clubs: Pacific Union (San Francisco); Cold Spring Harbor Beach (L.I.); Century Assn., Lunch, University, Links, Recess; Metropolitan (Washington); Piping Rock (Locust Valley, N.Y.). Writer and lectr. on financial subjects, reorgn., internat. law, nuclear test ban and disarmament. Home: Mill River Rd Oyster Bay Long Island, NY 11771 ; also 10 Gracie Sq New York City, NY 10028. Office: 48 Wall St New York City, NY 10005.

DEAN, BEALE, lawyer; b. Ft. Worth, Feb. 26, 1922; s. Ben J. and Helen (Beale) D.; B.A., U. Tex., Austin, 1943, LL.B., 1947; m. Margaret Ann Webster, Sept. 3, 1948; children—Webster Beale, Giselle Liseanne. Admitted to Tex. bar, 1946; asst. dist. atty., Dallas, 1947-48; asso. Martin, Moore & Brewster, Ft. Worth, 1948-50; mem. firm Martin, Moore, Brewster & Dean, 1950-51, Pannell, Dean, Pannell & Kerry and predecessor firms, 1951-65; partner firm Brown, Herman, Scott, Young & Dean, Ft. Worth, 1965—. Dir. Security State Bank River Oaks. Served with AUS, 1942-45; ETO. Mem. Am., Ft. Worth, Tarrant County (past v.p., dir., pres. elect 1970-71) bar assns., Am. Coll. Trial Lawyers, State Bar Tex., Tex. Bar Found (charter). Presbyn. Clubs: Ft. Worth Boat, Ridglea Country, Fort Worth. Home: 3709 Cresthaven Terrace Fort Worth TX 76107 Office: Ft Worth Club Bldg Fort Worth TX 76102

DEAN, BURTON VICTOR, educator; b. Chgo., June 3, 1924; s. Samuel and Dorothy (Eisner) D.; B.S., Northwestern U., 1947; M.S., Columbia, 1948; Ph.D., U. Ill., 1952; m. Barbara Louise Arnoff, Nov. 26, 1958; children—Howard David, Paul Evan, Heather Diana, Theodore Samuel. Instr. math. Columbia, 1947-49, Hunter Coll., 1949-50; research fellow math. U. Ill., 1950-52; mathematician Nat. Security Agy., 1952-55; research mathematician Operations Research, Inc., 1955-57; asso. prof. operations research Western Res. U., Cleve., 1957-65, prof. organizational scis, chmn. operations research group, 1965-67, prof., chmn. dept. operations research, 1967—; on leave as vis. prof. indsl. and mgmt. engring. Technion-Israel Inst. Tech., 1962-63; cons. U.S. industry and govt., 1957—, TAHAL Water Planning for Israel, 1962-64. Pres. Univ. Assos., Inc.; dir. Computer Mgmt., Inc., Cleve., Met. Savs. Assn. Bd. dirs. Cleve. Active Council Human Relations, Cleve. Inst. Music, Friends of Cleve. Orch., Cleve. Art Mus., Cleve. Philharmonic Orch. Fellow A.A.A.S. (v.p. chmn. indsl. sci. sect.), Operations Research Soc. (chmn. tech. sect. council), Inst. Mgmt. Scis. (chmn. coll. research and devel. 1969—, council 1966-67, past chmn. No. Ohio chpt.), Am. Math. Soc., Assn. for Computing Machinery. Author: Operations Research in Research and Development, 1963; (with Sasienj and Gupta) Mathematics of Modern Management, 1963; Evaluation, Selection and Control of R & D Projects, 1968; also articles. Editor of Mgmt. Sci., 1962—; asso. editor OPSEARCH, 1968—; editor I.E.E.E. Trans. on Engring Mgmt., 1968—; (Gordon and Breech) Studies in Operations Research. Home: 2920 Broton Rd Cleveland OH 44120

DEAN, CHARLES THOMAS, educator; b. Humboldt, Neb., Feb. 11, 1918; s. Asa Franklin and Carrie Myrtle (Mort) D.; B.A. (fellow chemistry 1941-42), Peru (Neb.) State Tchrs. Coll., 1942; M.S., Ia. State U., 1948, Ph.D., 1951; m. Marjorie Ellen Kennedy, Apr. 11, 1941; children—Carolyn Kay, Thomas Alan, Nancy Ann. Tchr. sci. and indsl. arts Indianola (Ia.) High Sch., 1946-47; asst. prof. indsl. edn. Ia. State U., 1947-51; prof. indsl. arts Cal. State Coll., Long Beach, 1952—, chmn. div. applied arts and scis., 1962- -, dir. Aerospace Program, 1956—, Cambodian Contract, 1963-68, dean Sch. Applied Arts and Scis., 1967—. Mem. tech. adv. coms. Compton (Cal.) Coll., Harbor Jr. Coll., Los Angeles, Orange Coast Coll., Costa Mesa, Cal., El Camino (Cal.) Coll.; mem. Cal. Curriculum Com. Indsl. Arts Edn.; membership com. Am. Council Indsl. Arts Tchr. Educators, 1957- 63; cons. tech. edn., Cambodia, 1962-69; dir. research project NASA, 1962- 64, 66; cons. tech. and vocational edn. U.S. Office Edn. Mem. Long Beach council United Way, 1969. Served to lt. (j.g.) USNR, 1943-45, 51-53; capt. Res. Recipient Louise Mears geog. award Peru State Tchrs. Coll., 1941; Air Power award 1st Res. Squadron, Air Force Assn., 1960, named Outstanding Aviation Educator for Cal., 1961; recipient Aero. Space citation Cal. Aero. Commn., 1962, Merit award citation aviation edn. FAA, 1958, 64, 69, Aerospace Edn. Leadership award Civil Air Patrol 1966, 69, many others. Mem. Am. Indsl. Arts Assn. (co-chmn. nat. conv. 1959, Cal. Indsl. Edn. Assn. (pres. So. sect. 1958, co-chmn. conv. 1958, pres. 1965-66), Cal. Aviation Edn. Assn. (v.p. 1960), Am. Vocational Assn., Nat. Assn. Indsl. and Tech. Tchr. Educators (hon. mem.), Internat. Platform Assn., Blue Key, Epsilon Pi Tau (laureate mem.), Sigma Alpha Epsilon, Beta Beta Beta, Phi Delta Kappa, Psi Chi, Phi Kappa Phi (lectr. of year 1970), Kappa Delta Pi, Gamma Sigma Delta. Presbyn. (elder, trustee). Mason. Co-author: Principles of Electricity, 1950. Editor: Wade Reynolds, The Man and His Art, 1968. Contbr. chpts. yearbooks. Home: 4602 Hazelbrook Av Long Beach CA 90808

DEAN, DEWEY HOBSON, Jr., banker; b. Donalds, S.C., Jan. 3, 1920; s. Dewey Hobson and Mary Elizabeth (Smith) D.; student So. Methodist U., 1937-39; m. Sara Burney Chapman, Apr. 4, 1941; children—Patricia Dean Ray, Jeanette Dean Watts, Mark Wayne. With Republic Nat. Bank, Dallas, 1936—, asst. cashier, 1951- 54, asst. v.p., 1954-55, v.p., 1955-68, sr. v.p., 1968—. Trustee Caruth Meml. Rehab. Center, Met. Dallas chpt. Nat. Found. Served to 1st lt. USAAF, 1943-45, USAF, 1951-52. Mem. Kappa Sigma. Mem. Christian Ch. (deacon). Club: Lakewood Country (Dallas). Home: 6532 Westlake Dallas TX 75214 Office: Republic Nat Bank Pacific at Ervay St Dallas TX 75222

DEAN, DONALD STEWART, educator; b. Lakewood, O., Nov. 21, 1916; s. Harris Jerome and Edith Luella (Knight) D.; B.S., Baldwin-Wallace Coll., 1938; M.S., U. Mich., 1949, Ph.D., 1953; m. Dora Elizabeth Wood, Aug. 22, 1944; children—Nancy (Mrs. Robert Rosselli), Kathleen (Mrs. Frank L. Moore II), Sally (Mrs. Richard Swegan). Tchr., Cleve. pub. schs., 1938-42, 45-47; mem. faculty Baldwin-Wallace Coll., 1947—, head dept. biology, 1971—, prof., 1959—; staff biologist Commn. Undergrad. Edn. in Biol. Scis., 1969-70. Served to lt., USNR, 1942-45; PTO. Recipient Strosacker award, Baldwin-Wallace Coll., 1966. Fellow Ohio Acad. Sci. (chmn. sect. genetics, chmn. sect. botany); mem. Ohio Coll. Biology Tchrs. (pres. 1967), A.A.A.S., Am. Assn. Univ. Profs., Am. Inst. Biol. Scis., Bot. Soc. Am., Am. Genetics Assn., Nat. Assn. Biology Tchrs., Phi Beta Kappa, Sigma Xi. Methodist. Author: Preservice Preparation of College Biology Teachers, 1970; (with D Peter Snustad) Genetics Experiments with Viruses, 1971. Home: 80 Kraft St Berea OH 44017

DEAN, FRED MURRAY, air force officer; b. E. St. Louis, Ill., Dec. 19, 1916; s. Fred Murray and Ada (Carter) D.; B.S., U.S. Mil. acad., 1938; grad. Air Corps Flying Sch., 1939, Nat. War Coll., 1953; m. Rosemary Weathered, June 8, 1957; 1 dau., Anne Murray; 1 stepdau., Pamela Jane Dailey. Commd. 2d lt. U.S. Army, 1938, advanced through grades to lt. gen. USAF; fighter pilot, 1939-43; exec. officer, chief adv. council to Gen. H.H. Arnold, 1943-46; mem. Joint Brazilian-U.S. Mil. Commn., Rio de Janeiro, 1946-48; mem. war plans div. Hdqrs. USAF, 1948-50; comdr. Jet Flying Sch., Big Spring, Tex., 1953-54; vice comdr. Flying Tgn. Air Force, Waco, Tex., 1954-57; comdr. Air Task Force 13, chief air force sect. MAAG, Taipei, Taiwan, 1957-60; dir. operations, joint staff Joint Chiefs Staff, Washington, 1960-63; comdr. Hdqrs. 12th Air Force, Waco, 1963-64; asst. dir. US Arms Control and Disarmament Agy., Washington, 1964-66; dep. comdr. in chief U.S. Strike Command, MacDill AFB, Fla., 1966-68; comdr. Allied Air Forces So. Europe, 1968—. Decorated D.S.M., Silver Star, Legion of Merit, D.F.C. with one oak leaf cluster, Air medal with 9 oak leaf clusters; Brit D.F.C.; Aero. medal of merit (Brazil); Cloud and Banner, Precious Tripod (China). Mem. Air Force Aid Soc., Hist. Air Soc., Daedalians. Clubs: Army-Navy Country (Arlington, Va.); Georgetown (Washington). Home: Naples Italy Office: COMAIR South Box 101 FPO NY 09524

DEAN, GEORGE G., trust co. exec. Sr. v.p., regional adminstr. L.I. Trust Co., Garden City, N.Y. Office: 1401 Franklin Av Garden City NY 11530*

DEAN, GRAHAM M., newspaper pub.; b. Lake View, Ia., Aug. 10, 1904; s. William M. and Ellen C. Dean; A.B. in Journalism, U. Ia., 1929; m. Ruthe S. Wheeler, Apr. 16, 1928; 1 dau., Elizabeth W. Mng. editor Iowa City Press-Citizen, 1925-35, bus. mgr., 1935-36; pub. Saliness (Cal.) Index-Jour. and Morning Post, 1936-39, Reno Evening Gazette, Nev. State Jour., 1939- 51, Western Horseman, 1943-46; owner, pub. Ashland (Ore.) Daily Tidings, 1951-60, Siskiyou Daily News, Yreka, Cal., 1951-70; pres. So. N.M. Newspapers, Inc., pub. Artesia (N.M.) Daily Press, 1957-70, Porterville (Cal.) Evening Recorder, 1960—. Doming (N.M.) Newspapers, 1966-70. Mem. Am. Soc. Newspaper Editors. Author 32 books for boys and girls. Office: 115 E Oak Av Porterville CA 93257

DEAN, HAROLD LESTER, educator; b. Springfield, Vt., June 5, 1908; s. Lyman E. and Flora (Lawrence) D.; Ph.B., Brown U., 1934, A.M., 1936, Ph.D., 1943; m. Lenora M. Owen, June 27, 1938; 1 son, Lawrence E. Instr., English, Brown U., 1944-46; mem. faculty Marietta (O.) Coll., 1946—, prof. English, 1958—, head dept., 1963—. Mem. Modern Lang. Assn., Am Studies Assn., Phi Beta Kappa. Home: 216 Beaver St Marietta OH 45750

DEAN, HARRIS WILLIAM, univ. adminstr.; b. Moores Hill, Ind., Mar. 4, 1909; s. William P. and Ethel (Bruce) D.; B.E., Ill. State U., 1929; M.A., State U. Ia., 1936; M.E. U., 1946, Ed.D., 1947; m. Helene Irene Tuschhoff, May 31, 1936; children—Ronald L., Martha Jane. Tchr., Alvin (Ill.) High Sch., 1929-33, Lexington (Ill.) High Sch., 1933-36, Heyworth (Ill.) High Sch., 1936-39; supt. pub. schs., Lexington, 1939-42; instr. U. Ill., 1946-47; asso. prof. Ball State U., 1947-48; prof., head dept. Fla. State U., 1948-60; prof. edn. U. South Fla., 1961-64, dean acad. affairs, 1964-67, v.p. for acad. affairs, 1967-70, acting pres., 1970—. Served to lt. comdr. USNR, 1942-46. Mem. So. Assn. Colls. and Schs. (chmn. commn. secondary edn. 1955-56, chmn. commn. on research and service 1959-62, pres. 1964-65, trustee 1968—), N.E.A., Fla. Edn. Assn., Am. Assn. Sch. Adminstrs., Am. Ednl. Research Assn., Nat. Assn. Secondary Sch. Prins., Nat. Conf. Profs. Ednl. Adminstrn., Assn. Supervision and Curriculum Devel., Assn. Higher Edn., Phi Delta Kappa, Kappa Delta Pi, Pi Kappa Delta, Theta Alpha Phi. Editor: Handbook for Florida's School Principals, 1954; (with others) The Junior High School Program, 1958. Home: 434 Pinehurst Av Temple Terrace FL 33617 Office: 4202 Fowler Av Tampa FL 33620

DEAN, HOWARD BRUSH, stock broker; b. N.Y.C., Feb. 18, 1921; s. Howard B. and Maria (Cook) D.; grad. Pomfret Sch., 1938; student Yale, 1938-40; m. Andree Maitland, Sept. 26, 1947; children—Howard Brush III, Charles Maitland, James Howell, William Gardiner. With Pan Am. Airways-Africa Ltd., 1941-43, China Nat. Aviation Corp., 1943-46; with Harris, Upham & Co., N.Y.C., 1946-69, partner, 1952-65, 1st v.p., dir. Harris Upham & Co., Inc., 1965-69; gen. partner Reynolds & Co, 1969—. Bd. govs. Assn. Stock Exchange Firms, 1959-65, exec. com., 1961-65, v.p., 1961-62; bd. govs. Am. Stock Exchange, 1961-64. Trustee Browning Sch., N.Y.C. Mem. Investment Bankers Assn. Am. (gov. 1965-69). Episcopalian (vestry 1959-65, sr. warden 1966—). Home: 1035 Park Av New York City NY 10028 Office: 120 Broadway New York City NY 10005

DEAN, HOWARD FREDERICK, life ins. co. exec.; b. Alden, N.Y., Sept. 8, 1910; s. John Rudd and Charlotte (Funke) D.; B.S.C., Northwestern U., 1932; m. Esther Louis Osness, Oct. 8, 1938; children—Jane Elizabeth (Mrs. Thomas R. Duncan), William Howard, Kathryn Louise (Mrs. Thomas J. Flynn). With Bankers Life Co., Des Moines, 1934- -, v.p. securities, 1958-61, v.p., treas., 1961-71, sr. v.p., 1971—. Mem. Beta Gamma Sigma. Presbyn. Home: 1616 68th St Des Moines IA 50322 Office: 711 High St Des Moines IA 50307

DEAN, J. SIMPSON, corp. exec.; b. Rome, Ga., Sept. 24, 1898; s. J. E. and Eva (Simpson) D.; grad. Lawrenceville (N.J.) Sch., 1917; A.B., Princeton, 1921; m. Paulina du Pont, Oct. 6, 1923; children—Paulina (Mrs. Albert G.S. Stewart), J. Simpson, Lisa (Mrs. J.F. MacGuigan). Bd. dirs., exec. com. Wilmington Trust Co. (Del.), 1933—; dir. Uniroyal Inc., 1960—; pres. Nemours Corp., 1924—. Home: Montohanin DE 19710 Office: du Pont Bldg Wilmington DE 19801

DEAN, JAMES WILLIAM, univ. dean; b. McKeesport, Pa., Sept. 17, 1920; s. John William and Nannie B. (Bruner) D.; B.A., Grove City Coll., 1949; M.A. (Grad. fellow), Bucknell U., 1950; Ph.D., Pa. State U., 1956; postgrad. U. Pitts., 1956-57; m. Betty Jane Yanik, Nov. 23, 1949; 1 dau., Courtney Ellen. Asst. prin. Midland (Pa.) High Sch., 1949-52; asst. dean men Pa. State U., 1952-55; dean students Coe Coll. (Ia.), 1955-56; asst. mgr., supr. ednl. programs Westinghouse Electric Corp., Pitts., 1956-58; dean students Va. Poly. Inst., Blacksburg, 1958—, now v.p. student affairs. Pres., Blacksburg Community Assn., Montgomery County Easter Seal Assn. Bd. dirs. Va. Crippled Childrens Assn. Served to maj. USAAF, 1941-45, USAF, 1952; CBI. Decorated Silver Star medal, D.F.C., Air medal, Purple Heart. Mem. Va. Deans Assn. (pres.), Alpha Phi Omega (nat. exec. bd. dirs.), Phi Delta Kappa, Omicron Delta Kappa. Presbyn. (elder). Home: 1002 Draper Rd Blacksburg, VA 24060.

DEAN, JOEL, educator, mgmt. cons.; b. Vershire, Vt., Oct. 5, 1906; s. Benjamin Angus and Eloise (Partridge) D.; A.B., Pomona Coll., 1927; M.B.A., Harvard, 1929; Ph.D., U. Chgo., 1936; hon. degrees U. Torino (Italy), 1966, Pace Coll., 1964; m. Phyllis van Dyk, June 24, 1939 (dec. Mar. 1 1963); children—Joel, Gretchen, Gillian, Jurrien. Dir., Inst. of Statistics and asst. prof. U. Chgo., 1939- 45; price exec. OPA, Washington, 1941-42, dir. fuel rationing div., 1942-44; prof. bus. econs. Columbia U., 1945-69, prof. emeritus, 1969—; pres. Joel Dean Assos. Fellow Nat. Assn. Bus. Economists; mem. Am. Econ. Assn., Financial Execs. Inst. Am. Mgmt. Assn. (planning council), Am. Marketing Assn. (dir.) (recipient Nat. Award), Beta Gamma Sigma. Clubs: Century Association (N.Y.C.); Columbia, Faculty. Author: Statistical Determination of Cost, 1936; Cost Behavior and Price Policy (with others), 1942; Managerial Economics., 1951; Capital Budgeting, 1951; (with others) Handbook of Industrial Engineering and Management; (with others) The Corporate Merger, 1966; (with others) Measuring the Investment Performance of Pension Funds, 1969; (with others) Handbook of Modern Marketing, 1970; (with others) Conglomerate Mergers, 1970. Editor: Social Control of Business (with E. Hoover), 1943. Bd. editors: Jour. Indsl. Econs. Home: 25 Claremont Av New York City NY 10027

DEAN, JOHN CLEMENT, sales financing co. exec.; b. Lawrence, Mass., Feb. 2, 1923; s. Clement Edwin and Julia (Donahue) D.; B.S., Boston U., 1948; m. Monica A. Webb, Aug. 21, 1943; children—Karen (Mrs. John Stutz), Jeryl Ann, John Clement, Maryann, Mark, Michael, James. Supervisory and managerial positions Ford div. Ford Motor Co., 1953-59, mgr. in finance staff, 1959-61, asst. controller, Dearborn, Mich., 1961-68; exec. v.p. Ford Motor Credit Co., Dearborn, 1968-69, pres., 1969—. Chmn. bd. dirs. United Community Services Met. Detroit, 1971—; mem. priorities subcom. spl. studies com. Detroit United Found., 1969—. Served to 1st lt. USAAF, 1942-46. Mem. Mich. Assn. C.P.A.'s, Boston U. Gen. Alumni Assn. (regional v.p.). Club: Serra (Dearborn). Home: 4357 Barchester Dr Bloomfield Hills MI 48013 Office: The American Rd Dearborn MI 48121

DEAN, JOHN LADD, lawyer; b. Rollersville, O., Mar. 26, 1905; s. George Cook and Lone (Ladd) D.; A.B., Ohio Wesleyan U., 1926; LL.B., Case Western Res. U., 1930; m. Margaret Blakely, Aug. 16, 1930; children—J. Thomas, Dorothy Lone (Mrs. Ronald G. Floridis). Admitted to Ohio State bar, 1930, Fed. bar, 1931, practiced in Cleve., 1930—; partner firm Hahn, Loeser, Freedheim, Dean & Wellman, 1940—. Mem. exec. com., dir. Carling Brewing Co.; dir. Midland Enterprises, Inc., Canadian Breweries, Ltd.; dir., sec. Nat. Telephone Supply Co.; v.p., gen. counsel, mem. exec. com., mem. bd. dirs. of Ohio River Co; trustee, mem. exec. com. Eastern Gas & Fuel Assos. Mem. Citizens League Cleve. Mem. exec. com., trustee Christian Residences Found.; exec. com. St. Luke's Hosp.; chmn. Assos. Ohio Wesleyan U. Mem. Am., Ohio (council dels. 1950-53), Cleve. (pres. 1970-71) bar assns., Chi Pi, Phi Delta Phi, Delta Sigma Rho. Republican. Methodist (trustee). Mason. Clubs: Union, Midday, Rowfant, City (Cleve.); Shaker Heights Country (O.) Home: 2035 Chestnut Hills Dr Cleveland Heights OH 44106 Office: Nat City E 6th Bldg Cleveland OH 44114

DEAN, JOHN WILSON, Jr., retired army officer, mcht.; b. Evanston, Wyo., Mar. 8, 1918; s. John Wilson and Reta (Murdock) D.; student Brigham Young U., 1935-37, 39-41; grad. Armed Forces Staff Coll., 1954, Nat. War Coll., 1959; m. Lucille Lorraine Forster, July 3, 1942; children—Patricia Ann (Mrs. William J. Staffa), John Wilson III. Commd. 2d lt. F.A., U.S. Army, 1941, advanced through grades to brig. gen., 1967; retired, 1971; pres. Colo. Clothiers, Ltd., Hibbs Clothing Co. Utah. Decorated D.S.M., Legion of Merit with 2 oak leaf clusters, Bronze Star with oak leaf cluster, Army Commendation medal with 4 oak leaf clusters; also decorated by France, Belgium, Italy, Netherlands. Mem. Assn. U.S. Army, Mil. Order World Wars. Home: 1921 Academy Blvd Colorado Springs CO 80909 Office: 21 S Tejon St Colorado Springs CO 80912 also 210 S Main St Salt Lake City UT 84101

DEAN, JOSEPH EDWARD, Jr., lawyer, brewing co. exec.; b. Milw., Sept. 2, 1913; s. Joseph Edward and Hazel Mary (Tracy) D.; A.B., Marquette U., 1935, LL.B., 1937; m. Gracemary Billings, May 30, 1942; children—Joseph Edward III, John Patrick, David Billings, Thomas Jude, Timothy Peter James, Mary Margaret. Admitted to Wis. bar, 1937; with firm Timlin, Dean & Klug, Milw., 1937-41; spl. agt. FBI, 1941-47; mem. legal staff Allis-Chalmers Mfg. Co., Milw., 1947-51; with McGraw-Edison Co., Milw., 1951-67, gen. counsel, 1958-67; v.p., sec., gen. counsel Jos. Schlitz Brewing Co., Milw., 1967—. Chmn. lay bd. St. Vincent's Home, Milw. Home: 6020 N Berkeley Blvd Whitefish Bay WI 53217 Office: 235 W Galena St Milwaukee WI 53201

DEAN, LEONARD FELLOWS, educator; b. Three Rivers, Mich., Dec. 24, 1909; s. Ray E. and Kate (Fellows) D.; A.B., Harvard, 1931; M.A., U. Mich., 1933, Ph.D., 1940; m. Dorothy G. Thomas, 1932; children—Nancy Ann, Elizabeth Jane (Mrs. John R. Murphy). Began his career as teacher English Mt. Clements (Mich.) High Sch., 1935-37; teaching fellow English, U. Mich., 1937-39; instr., later prof., head dept. English, Tulane U., 1939-48; prof., head dept. English, U. of Conn., Storrs, 1948-65, U. Illinois, Urbana, 1965-67; prof. English, N.Y. U., N.Y. City, 1967—. Mem. Modern Lang. Assn. of Am., Am. Assn. U. Profs. Author articles profl. jours. Editor: Nine Great Plays, 1950; College Omnibus, 1951; English Masterpieces, 1950 (with Mack and Frost); Perspectives, 1953; Shakespeare: Modern Essays in Criticism, 1957, rev., 1967; Essays on Language and Usage, 1959 (with K. G. Wilson); Conrad's Heart of Darkness: Backgrounds and Criticisms, 1960; A Case Book on Othello, 1961; (with J.A.S. McPeek) Shakespeare's Twelfth Night, 1965; Twelve Great Plays, 1970; (with W. Gibson and K. G. Wilson) The Play of Language, 1971. Home: 100 Bleecker St New York City NY 10012

DEAN, PAUL REGIS, legal educator; b. Leetonia, O., July 12, 1918; s. Edward Joseph Catherine (Sheets) D.; student DeSales Coll., Toledo, 1936-38; B.A., Youngstown U., 1940; LL.B., Georgetown U., 1946, LL.M., 1952, LL.D., 1969; m. Delores M. Fitch, July 14, 1945; children—Mary E., Lawrence E., Patricia, John, Paul, William, Delores, Teresa, Brian. Admitted to D.C. bar, 1946, Va. bar, 1954; law clk. to Andrew M. Hood, D.C. Ct. of Appeals, 1946-47; prof. law Georgetown U., 1947-54, 69—, dean U. Law Center, 1954-69. Legal adviser to Pres.'s Com. Govt. Contract Compliance, 1952-53. Served to lt. USNR, 1942-46. Mem. Am., Va., D.C. bar assns., Am. Arbitration Assn., Am. Law Inst., Delta Theta Phi. Home: 3313 Garland Dr Falls Church VA 22041 Office: 506 E St Washington DC 20001

DEAN, RICHARD ALBERT, educator; b. Columbus, O., Oct. 9, 1924; s. Lindley Richard and Belle (Bream) D.; A.B., Denison U., 1947; B.S., Cal. Inst. Tech., 1945; M.S., Ohio State U., 1948, Ph.D., 1953; m. Dorothy Jean Green, Sept. 5, 1948; 1 son, Jason Richard. Instr., Middlebury Coll., 1947; mathematician U.S. Dept. Def., Washington, 1954; research fellow Cal. Inst. Tech., Pasadena, 1954, asst. prof. 1955-59, asso.prof., 1959-66, prof. math., 1966—. Cons. Cal. Curriculum Commn., 1960-67; mem. Sch. Math. Study Group, 1955, 66. Served with USNR, 1943-46, to lt., 1952-54. Mem. Am. Math. Soc., Math. Assn. Am., Omicron Delta Kappa, Phi Beta Kappa, Sigma Xi. Author: Elements of Abstract Algebra, 1966. Home: 2186 Lambert Dr Pasadena CA 91107

DEAN, ROBERT CHARLES, architect; b. Memphis, Dec. 5, 1903; s. Charles and Martha (Little) D.; B.S., Mass. Inst. Tech., 1926, M.Arch., 1927; traveling fellow, 1928, Fontainebleau Sch. of Fine Arts, 1925; LL.D., Furman U., 1971; m. Ruth Andrew, Sept. 10, 1927; children—Robert C., Ruth Cameron, Nancy Elizabeth, Andrew John. Asst. prof. Ga. Sch. Tech., 1927-28; instr. Mass. Inst. Tech., 1930-41; designer Perry, Dean & Hepburn, and predecessor firm, Boston, 1930-40, partner, 1940—; architect Phila. Sheraton Hotel, Am. Mil. Cemetery, Cambridge, Eng., Furman U., Greenville, S.C., Bentley Coll., Waltham, Mass., Fine Arts and Sci. Center, Macalester Coll., St. Paul, Greenville (S.C.) County Library. Mem. Mass. N.G., 1930-41. Served to col. AUS, 1941-45; brig. gen. ret. AUS. Decorated Bronze Star, Army Commendation medal (U.S.); Croix de Guerre, Etoile Vermeil (France); Croix de Guerre with palm (Belgium); officer Order of Orange Nassau (Netherlands). Fellow A.I.A.; mem. Boston Soc. Architects (past pres.), Mass. Assn. Architects, Am. Legion, Sigma Chi. Republican. Episcopalian. Clubs: Union (Boston); Army Navy (Washington); Poinsette (Greenville, S.C.). Home: 29 Hundreds Rd Wellesley Hills MA 02181 Office: Park Sq Bldg Boston MA 02116

DEAN, ROBERT CHARLES, Jr., educator, corp. exec.; b. Atlanta, Apr. 13, 1928; s. Robert C. and Ruth C. (Andrew) D.; B.S., M.S., Mass. Inst. Tech., 1949, Sc.D., 1954; m. E. Nancy Hayes, Sept. 22, 1951; children—Margaret S., James C., Elizabeth S., Martha A., Charles E. Project engr. Ultrasonic Corp., 1949-51, cons., 1960-64; head advanced engring. dept. Ingersoll-Rand Co., 1956- 60; dir. research Thermal Dynamics Corp., 1960-61; dir. Ecol. Sci. Corp., 1968-70; pres. Creare Inc., 1961—; pres. Ecol. Research Corp., 1968-70; asst. prof. mech. engring. Mass. Inst. Tech., 1951-56; prof. engring. Thayer Sch. Engring., Dartmouth, 1960—. Mem. turbine and compressor subcom. NACA, 1954-55. Recipient Gold medal Pi Tau Sigma, 1953; Master Designer award Product Engring. mag., 1967. Mem. Am. Soc. M.E. (chmn. hydraulics div. 1962-63, dir. turbomachinery course 1968—), Am. Inst. Aero. and Astronautics, Tau Beta Pi. Author numerous articles in field. Home: Main St Norwich VT 05055 Office: PO Box 71 Hanover NH 03755

DEAN, ROBERT HAL, food co. exec.; b. Mitchell, S.D., June 27, 1916; s. Bernie Bonney and Edna May (Halladay) D.; B.A., Grinnell Coll., 1938; m. Doris Reger, Sept. 28, 1940; children—Donna (Mrs. T.W. Doan), David. Mgr., Checkerboard Elevator Co., Buffalo, 1941-43; mgr. Ralston Purina Co., Circleville, O., 1943-45, grain div., St. Louis, 1945-58, pres. internat. div., St. Louis, 1958—, v.p. co., asst. to pres., 1958-61, exec. v.p., dir., 1961-63, pres., chief operating officer, 1964-68, chmn. bd., 1968—, chief exec. officer, 1969—, also dir. Home: 4 Devon Rd Glendale MO 63122 Office: 835 S 8th St St Louis MO 63102

DEAN, ROBERT WILLIAM, fgn. service officer; b. Hinsdale, Ill., May 25, 1920; s. James William and Mary Elizabeth (Peterson) D.; U. Chgo. exchange student U. Sao Paulo (Brazil), 1941; M.A. in Internat. Relations, U. Chgo., 1952; m. Doris May Wilkins, Dec. 16, 1948; children—James William, Karen Anna, Shelley Elizabeth, Virginia Lee. Joined U.S. Fgn. Service, 1942; econ. analyst consulate gen., Sao Paulo, 1942-45; regional cons. Inst. Internat. Edn., N.Y.C., 1948-49; resident officer U.S. High Commn. for Germany, Kitzingen am Main, Bavaria, 1949-52; vice consul, Belem, Brazil, 1952-54; consul, polit. officer, Rio de Janeiro, Brazil, 1954- 57; chief A.A.M. br. Office Research and Analysis for Am. Republics, State Dept., 1957-58, chief inter-Am. polit. Intelligence div., 1958-61; State Dept. exchange officer assigned Dept. Army, 1961-62; student Nat. War Coll., 1962- 63; polit. counselor, officer charge, Brasilia, Brazil, 1963-65; dep. chief mission, Chile, 1965-69; country dir. Brazilian affairs Dept. State, 1969—. Served with USNR, 1945-46, PTO. Mem. Fgn. Service Assn., Alpha Delta Phi. Home: 369 Marion St Elmhurst IL 60126 Office: Brazilian Affairs Dept State Washington DC

DEAN, RUTH JOSEPHINE, educator; b. N.Y.C., Mar. 10, 1902; d. Amos C. and Louisa (Mallory) Dean; B.A., Wellesley Coll., 1922; B.A. (honours), Oxford (Eng.) U.; 1924, M.A., 1928, D.Phil., 1938. Mem. faculty Mt. Holyoke Coll., 1934-67, prof. French, 1950-67, prof. French emerita, 1967—, chmn. dept. French lang. and lit., 1951-54, Mary Lyon prof., 1966-67, Mary Lyon prof. emerita, 1967—; medieval bibliographer U. Pa. Library, lectr. depts. English and Romance langs. U. Pa., Phila., 1969—. Mem. Inst. Advanced Study, Princeton, 1943- 44, 50-51. Workman fellow, 1937-38; Palmer fellow, 1943-44; Guggenheim fellow, 1948-49; Nat. Endowment for Humanities sr. fellow, 1967-68. Decorated chevalier Ordre des Palmes Academiques, 1949, officer, 1963. Fellow Mediaeval Acad. Am.; mem. Modern Lang. Assn. Am., Modern Humanities Research Assn., Am. Assn. Tchrs. French, Am. Assn. U. Profs., Phi Beta Kappa. Home: 1810 Rittenhouse Sq Philadelphia PA 19103

DEAN, SANFORD JAMES, educator; b. Mpls., Dec. 20, 1921; s. William James and Mary (Armstrong) D.; B.A., Hamline U., 1948; M.A., Ohio State U., 1951, Ph.D., 1953; m. Betty Louise Click, Dec. 24, 1943; children—Carol Jo, Michael Bruce, Laura Beth. Asst. prof. psychology Stanford, 1953-56; asst. prof. Syracuse U., 1956-60, asso. prof., 1960-65, prof. psychology, 1965-69, dir. clin. tng. program, 1965-69; vis. prof. U. Conn., Storrs, 1968-69; prof., chmn. dept. psychology No. Ill. U., DeKalb, 1969—. Mem. Bd. Edn., Baldwinsville, N.Y., pres., 1963-68. Served from pvt. to capt. AUS, 1942- 46; ETO; AUS, 1950-51. Mem. Am., Eastern, Midwest psychol. assn., Psychonomic Assn., Sigma Xi. Author: (with others) The Investigation of Psychotherapy, 1966. Contbr. articles to profl. jours. Home: 835 Edgebrook DeKalb IL 60115

DEAN, SIDNEY WALTER, Jr., bus. and marketing exec.; b. Boston, May 20, 1905; s. Sidney W. and Marian (Perry) D.; A.B., Yale, 1926; m. Eugenia Serios, Nov. 2, 1963. With J. Walter Thompson Co., 1927-42, mgr. Trade & Indsl. Dept., dir. of media. v.p., 1937-42; exec. v.p., dir. Telecoin Corp., 1945-47; cons. marketing and mgmt., 1947-50; v.p. McCann-Erickson, Inc., 1950-61; pres. Ventures Devel. Corp., 1961—; dir. Knickerbocker Fed. Savs. & Loan Assn., Zip-A-Lope Corp., Marketmath, Inc., Fluted Paper Products Co., Inc. Trustee Met. Ednl. TV Assn., 1954-59; dir. of Audit Bureau of Circulations, 1957-61. Mem. bd. dirs. Ams. Democratic Action; vice chmn. Nat. Businessmen's Council; bd. dirs. Greenwich Village Planning Bd. Served as capt. USAF, with OSS, Lend-Lease Adminstrn., 1943-45. Decorated Bronze Star medal. Mem. Nat. Planning Assn., Am. Mgmt. Assn., Am. Econs. Assn. Democrat. Clubs: Yale, City (trustee) (N.Y.C.). Author: Mass Communications in Modern Society, 1948; Planning for Integrated Marketing, 1949; Cable Television in New York, 1970. Home: 27 Washington Sq N New York City NY 10011

DEAN, VERA MICHELES, editor, author, lectr.; b. St. Petersburg, Russia, Mar. 29, 1903; d. Alexander and Nadine Micheles; A.B., Radcliffe Coll., 1925; A.M., Yale, 1926, Ph.D., 1928; LL.D., Wilson Coll., 1940; D.H.L., U. Rochester, 1943; hon. degrees Smith, Rockford, Cedar Crest, Colby, Skidmore Monmouth colls., N.H. Coll. Women; m. William J. Dean, Aug. 9, 1929 (dec. 1936); children—Elinor (Mrs. Charles W. Wilder), William Johnson. Came to U.S., 1919, naturalized, 1928. Research asso. Foreign Policy Assn., also editor research publs., 1931-38, research dir., editor, 1938-61; vis. prof. Smith Coll., 1952-54; vis. prof. govt. U. Rochester, also dir. non-Western civilizations program, 1954-61; prof. internat. devel. Grad. Sch. Pub. Adminstrn., N.Y.U., 1962-71, mem. Center Internat. Studies, 1971—. Recipient Jane Addams medal, 1954; French Legion of Honor. Episcopalian. Club: Cosmopolitan. Author books including: Europe and the United States, 1950; Foreign Policy Without Fear, 1953; The Nature of the Non-Western World, 2d edit., 1966; New

Patterns of Democracy in India, rev. edit., 1969; Builders of Emerging Nations, 1961; West and Non- West: New Perspectives, 1963; The United States and the New Nations, 1964; The UN Today, 1965. Contbr. jours. Home: 70 E 96th St New York City NY 10028

DEAN, WALTER CLARK, retired mfg. exec.; b. Albion, Mich., Oct. ., 1898; s. George E. and Belle A. (Clark) D.; B.A., Albion Coll., 1921, D. Bus. Adminstrn. (hon.), 1960; B.S., U. Mich., 1922; m. Mate W. Wonsey, June 14, 1923; children—Ethel, Dagmar, Joanna, Jon. With Westinghouse Electric & Mfg. Co., East Pittsburgh, Pa., 1922-24; with Union Steel Products Co., Albion, 1924-68, v.p., gen. mgr., 1930, pres., gen. mgr., 1932-63, chmn. bd., 1962-68. Mayor, Albion, 1945-46. Hon. trustees Albion Coll. Mem. Sigma Chi. Methodist. Mason. Home: Haven Lane Albion MI 49224

DEAN, WILLIAM TUCKER, legal educator; b. Chgo., Aug. 31, 1915; s. William Tucker and Martha (Boldt) D.; A.B., Harvard, 1937, M.B.A., 1947; J.D., U. Chgo., 1940; m. Ann Coulson, May 15, 1943; children—Jonathan, Robert Coulson, Tobias, Sheila. Admitted to D.C. bar, 1940, N.Y. bar, 1949, also U.S. Supreme Ct.; atty. bituminous coal div. Dept. Interior, 1940-41; legal adviser fuel sect. OPA, 1941-42; atty. anti-trust div. Dept. Justice, 1943; asst. prof. law U. Kan. Law Sch., 1946-47; asst., then asso. prof. law Instr., Washington and Lee U., 1913-14; admitted to Md. bar, 1915, practiced in Frederick, 1915-38; prof. law, 1958—; gen. counsel, dir. Geotechnics and Resources, Inc., 1959-63; asso. dir. research N.Y. State Law Revision Commn., 1963-66; justice Village of Cayuga Heights, N.Y., 1962—. Co-chmn. N.Y. State Citizens Com. for Liquor Law Revision, 1964. Democratic candidate for county judge Tompkins County, 1963, 67. Served to capt. AUS, 1942-46. Decorated Army Commendation ribbon. Mem. Tompkins County Magistrates' Assn. (pres. 1969), Assn. Bar City N.Y., Am., N.Y. State bar assns., Order of Coif, Phi Beta Kappa, Phi Kappa Phi. Mem. United Ch. Christ. Author: (with C.O. Gregory and others) Illinois Annotations to Restatement of Torts, 1942; also numerous articles. Editor: Annual Survey American Law, 1950-53; Survey of New York Law, 1950-53; mem. adv. bd. Am. Jour. Legal History, 1957—. Home: 206 Overlook Rd Ithaca NY 14850

DEAN, WINTON BASIL, author; b. Birkenhead, Eng., Mar. 18, 1916; s. Basil Herbert and Esther (Van Gruisen) D.; B.A., King's Coll., Cambridge (Eng.) U., 1938, M.A., 1941; m. Thalia Mary Shaw, Sept. 4, 1939; children—Brigid (dec.), Stephen, Diana (dec.), Diana (adopted). Ernest Bloch prof. music U. Cal. at Berkeley, 1965-66. Mem. music panel Arts Council, London, 1957-60. Mem. Handel Opera Soc., Royal Mus. Assn. (council 1965—, v.p. 1970—). Author: The Frogs of Aristophanes (translation of choruses to music of Walter Leigh), 1937; Bizet, 1948; Carmen, 1949; Introduction to the Music of Bizet, 1950; Franck, 1950; Puccini (The Heritage of Music), 1951; Handel's Dramatic Oratorios and Masques, 1959; Shakespeare and Opera, 1964; Georges Bizet, His Life and Work, 1965; Handel and the Opera Seria, 1969; Beethoven and Opera (The Beethoven Companion), 1971. Home: Hambledon Hurst Gadalming Surrey England

DEANE, FREDERICK, Jr., banker; b. Boston, Aug. 5, 1926; s. Frederick and Julia (Coolidge) D.; B.A., Harvard, 1948, M.B.A., 1951; m. Dorothy Legge, Dec. 21, 1948; children—Dorothy Porcher, Eleanor Dodds, Frederick III. Asst. to pres. Bank of Va., 1953-56, v.p., 1956-59, sr. v.p., 1959-64, exec. v.p., 1964-67, pres., 1967-69, vice chmn., 1969—; exec. v.p. Va. Commonwealth Bankshares, Inc., 1963-65, pres., 1965—; dir. Mut. Insurers, Inc., Wards Co., Inc. Pres. Richmond Area Assn. Retarded Children, 1958-62; active United Givers Fund; v.p., mem. finance com. Richmond Symphony, 1958-65. Trustee Mus. Fine Arts; bd. dirs., mem. exec. com., past pres. Blue Cross Va. Served to 1st lt. AUS, 1944-47, 1st lt., 1951-53. Mem. Young Presidents Orgn., Assn. Res. City Bankers, Richmond Soc. Financial Analysts Fedn. Episcopalian. Clubs: Harvard of Va. (past v.p., pres. bus. sch. sect.); Hasty Pudding Inst. 1770, Delphic (Harvard); Commonwealth, Country of Virginia (Richmond); Harvard, Brook (N.Y.C.). Home: 110 W Hillcrest Av Richmond VA 23226 Office: 800 E Main St Richmond VA 23214

DEANE, HERBERT ANDREW, educator; b. Bklyn., May 26, 1921; s. Andrew and Annette (Franzen) D.; A.B., Columbia, 1942, Ph.D., 1953; postgrad. Harvard, 1946-47. Mem. faculty Columbia, 1948—, prof. govt., 1961—, vice provost acad. planning, 1968, Lieber prof. polit. philosophy, 1969—. Cons. legal and polit. philosophy Rockefeller Found., 1952-53. Served with USNR, 1942-46. Rockefeller fellow, 1958-59; Guggenheim fellow, 1960-61. Mem. Am. Polit. Sci. Assn., Am. Soc. Polit. and Legal Philosophy, Inst. Internat. de Philosophie Politique, Acad. Polit. Sci., Phi Beta Kappa. Democrat. Club: Century Assn. (N.Y.C.). Author: The Political Ideas of Harold J. Laski, 1955; The Political and Social Ideas of St. Augustine, 1963. Editor Polit. Sci. Quar., 1963—, Jour. History Ideas, 1961—. Home: 423 W 120th St New York City NY 10027

DEANE, JOHN RUSSELL, Jr., army officer; b. San Francisco, June 8, 1919; s. John Russell and Margaret (Wood) D.; B.S., U.S. Mil. Acad., 1942; M.B.A., George Washington U., 1964; grad. Command and Gen. Staff Coll., 1953, Armed Forces Staff Coll., 1955, Nat. War Coll., 1959; m. Elizabeth Fitzgerald Heard, June 4, 1942; children—John Russell III, Nancy H. (Mrs. Carl J. Kreitler, Jr.), Margaret A., C. Richard, Elizabeth H. Commd. 2d lt. U.S. Army, 1942, advanced through grades to maj. gen., 1967; asst. div. comdr. operations Hdqrs. 82d Airborne Div., Ft. Bragg, N.C., 1965-66; chief of staff Hdqrs. Field Force I, U.S. Army, Vietnam, 1966; asst. div. comdr. 1st Inf. Div., 1966; comdg. gen. 173d Airborne Brigade, Vietnam, 1966-67; dir. doctrine and systems Office Asst. Chief of Staff for Force Devel., Washington, 1967-68; comdg. gen. 82d Airborne Div., Ft. Bragg, 1968-70; dir. Def. Spl. Projects Group, Washington, 1970—. Decorated D.S.C. with oak leaf cluster, D.S.M. with oak leaf cluster, Silver Star with 2 oak leaf clusters, Legion of Merit with 2 oak leaf clusters, D.F.C., Bronze Star with oak leaf cluster, Joint Service Commendation medal, Army Commendation medal, Purple Heart, Air medal with 24 oak leaf clusters (U.S.), Vietnam Service Medal, Rep. of Vietnam Campaign Medal with device, Nat. Legion of Honor 5th Class, Gallantry Cross with palm and gold star, Medal of Honor (Vietnam). Mem. Assn. U.S. Army. Clubs: Foxfire Golf and Country (Pinehurst, N.C.); Army and Navy (Washington). Home: 4924 Ft Sumner Dr Washington DC 20016 Office: Defense Spl Projects Group Washington DC 20305

DEANE, MARTHA, see Taylor, Marian Young.

DEANE, MICHAEL BENJAMIN, pub. relations and mgmt. cons.; b. Aug. 4, 1918; s. Benjamin and Homer and Alice Bertha (Zak) D.; A.B., Bates Coll., 1936; LL.B., Georgetown U., 1941; m. Beatrice Sterman, Nov. 15, 1940; childrenNancy Joanne, Jeffrey Michael. With Dept. Commerce, 1936-37; economist U.S. Tariff Commn., 1937-41, adv. com. to Council Nat. Def., 1940; bus. economist OPA, 1942-43; dir. allocations div., France, distrbn. div., Rome, Italy, UNRRA, 1945-47; pres. Mercury Trade and Devel. Corp., N.Y.C., also Deane Internat., Washington, 1947-49; coordinator export requirements Office Internat. Trade, Dept. Commerce, 1949; spl. asst. ECA mission to Greece, Athens, 1949-50, spl. adviser small bus. to U.S. spl. rep., Paris, 1950-53; asst. to pres. Coca Cola Export Corp., 1953- 55; exec. v.p. Am. Watch Assn., Inc., 1955-58; pres. Michael B. Deane Assos., Washington, 1958-; past pres. Malaysian Trading & Devel. Co., Ltd., Korean Trade and Devel Co., Ltd., Rec. Arts Internat., Inc. Mem. Railroad Emergency Bd., 1964-. Alternate del. Democratic Nat. Conv., 1960. Served to 2d lt. USAAF, 1943-45. Mem. Washington Trade Assn. Execs. Clubs: National Press, National Capital Democratic, Circus Saints and Sinners, Georgetown University, Aero, Bates College, Propeller (Washington); Sugar (N.Y.C.). Home: 3315 Fessenden St NW Washington DC 20008. Office: Nat Press Bldg NW Washington DC 20004

DEANE, STEPHEN RUSSELL, psychologist; b. Leeds, Me., Nov. 17, 1911; s. Stephen Homer and Alice May (Gould) D.; A.B., Bowdoin Coll., 1934; A.M. Harvard, 1941; Ph.D., U. Md., 1949; m. M. Ruth Weller, Aug. 1, 1936; childrenDeborah, Ruth Deane, Nancy Alice. Instr. psychology Westbrook Jr. Coll., 1938-43; asst. dir. vets. testing clinic U. Md., 1947-49; asso. prof. psychology Simmons Coll., Boston, 1949-51, prof., 1951—, chmn. div. philosophy, psychology and edn., 1953—. Lectr. indsl. psychology Northeastern U.; lectr. psychology Boston chpt. Am. Inst. Banking; staff asso. Div. Instl. Programs NSF, 1965-66. Chmn., Inter-group Relations Council Greater Boston, Fair Housing Practices Com., Wellesley, Mass. Mem. Democratic Town Com. Wellesley. Served as lt. (j.g.) USNR, 1944-46. Mem. Am., Eastern, Mass. psychol. assns., Mass. Adult Edn. Assn. (pres.), Am. Assn. U. Profs., Adult Edn. Soc. U.S. Home: 37 Kirkland Circle Wellesley Hills MA 02181 Office: Simmons College Boston MA 02115

DEANGELI, MARGUERITE, writer; b. Lapeer, Mich., Mar. 14, 1889; d. Shadrach G. and Ruby A. (Tuttle) Lofft; student pub. schs.; m. John de Angeli, Apr. 2, 1910; children—John, Arthur, Ted, Maurice, Nina (Mrs. Alfred Kuhn). Author, illus. children's books: The Door in the Wall, 1949; Just Like David; Marguerite de Angeli's Book of Nursery and Mother Goose Rhymes; Black Fox of Lorne, 1956; The Old Testament Selected and Illustrated, 1960; Marguerite de Angeli's Favorite Hymns, 1963; The Goose Girl, 1964; Turkey for Christmas, 1965; (autobiography) Butter at the Old Price, 1971. Home: 2601 Parkway Philadelphia PA 19130

DEANS, HARRY ALEXANDER, educator; b. Dallas, June 17, 1932; s. Herbert Ambrose and Marie (Cooke) D.; B.A., Rice Inst., 1953, B.S., 1954, M.S., 1956; Ph.D., Princeton, 1960; student Tech. Hochschule, Hanover, Germany, 1956; m. Karolyn Ann Kaspar, Sept. 20, 1956; children—Lauren, Daniel Michael, Melissa. Mem. faculty Rice U., Houston, Tex., 1959—, prof. chem. engring., 1968—. Cons. to industry; Fulbright lectr., Israel, 1964. Recipient Brown Teaching award Rice U., 1970. Mem. Am. Inst. Chem. Engrs. Author, patentee in field. Home: 1724 Milford St Houston TX 77006

DEARBORN, HENRY, former fgn. Service officer; b. Lawrence, Mass., Jan. 30, 1913; s. Dr. Henry Follansby and Grace Elizabeth (Valpey) D.; grad. Phillips Acad., Andover, Mass., 1932; A.B., Dartmouth, 1936; M.A., Yale, 1938; grad. Nat. War Coll., 1959; m. Maria Rosa Pareja, Nov. 16, 1946; children—Pamela M., Henry M. Vice consul Am. consulate, Barranquilla, Colombia, 1941-42, Manta, Ecuador, 1942-44; country desk officer for Ecuador, Dept. State, 1944-47, for Argentina, 1947-52, officer charge River Plate affairs, 1952-54, dep. dir. Office S.A. affairs, 1955; 1st sec., consul Am. embassy, Lima, Peru, 1956-58; detailed to Nat. War Coll., 1958-59; counselor of embassy, Ciudad Trujillo, Dominican Republic, 1959-60, consul gen., Ciudad Trujillo, 1960- 61; counselor of embassy, Bogota, Colombia, 1961-67; minster-counselor embassy, Mexico, 1967-69; ret. Mem. Kappa Sigma Address: 7005 Beechwood Dr Chevy Chase MD 20015

DEARDEN, BASIL, film producer, dir.; b. Westcliff-on-Sea, Essex, Eng. Engaged in prodn., direction, writing motion pictures, now with Ealing Studios; dir. films including: Train of Events, The Blue Lamp, Pool of London, I Believe in You, The Gentle Gunman, The Square Ring, The Rainbow Jacket, The Ship That Died of Shame, Smallest Show on Earth, Violent Playground, Sapphire, League of Gentlemen, Man in the Moon, Victim, Life for Ruth, The Mind Benders, Woman of Straw, Masquerade, Khartoum, Walk in the Shadow, The Assassination Bureau, The Man Who Haunted Himself. Address: care United Artists Corp 729 7th Av New York City NY 10019*

DEARDEN, DOUGLAS MOREY, educator; b. Echo, Utah, Aug. 25, 1923; s. Morey Thomas and Melba Viola (Richins) D.; student Kansas City (Mo.) Jr. Coll., 1940-41, U. Colo., 1942-43; B.A., U. Utah, 1947, M.A., 1949; postgrad. U. Cal. at Berkeley, 1949-50; Ph.D., U. Minn., 1959; m. Fay Rose Steuer, Oct. 9, 1948; children—Holly Kay, Mark Douglas, Laurie Ann. Grad. teaching asst. U. Utah, 1947-49; instr. U. Minn., 1950-51, prof., 1952—. Served with USNR, 1943-46, 51-52. Recipient Tozer Found. grant field studies biology, 1958. Mem. A.A.A.S., Nat. Assn. Reesearch Sci. Teaching, Phi Sigma, Phi Delta Kappa, Sigma Xi. Contbr. articles profl. jours. Home: 2912 Orchard Av North Minneapolis MN 55422

DEARDEN, JOHN, educator; b. Lancashire, Eng., Nov. 19, 1919; s. Ernest and Florence (Curwen) D.; came to U.S., 1924, naturalized, 1933; B.A., Am. Internat. Coll., Springfield, Mass., 1945; M.B.A., U. Pa., 1946, C.P.A., 1948; M.A., Harvard, 1964; m. Helen-Marie Borden, June 25, 1945; childrenJohn Curwen, Robert George, Thomas Allen, Rachel Guerin, Ruth Anne. Instr. accounting U. Pa., 1947-49; mem. central finance staff Ford Motor Co., 1949-59; mem. faculty Harvard, 1959—, Herman C. Krannert prof. bus. adminstrn., 1969—. Served with USNR, 1943- 46. Mem. Am. Inst. C.P.A.'s, Am. Accounting Assn., Financial Execs. Inst., Beta Gamma Sigma, Beta Alpha Psi. Autbor: (with R. N. Anthony) Accounting Problems and Cases, 1961; Cost and Budget Analysis, 1962; (with R.N. Anthony & R.V. Vaneil) Management Control Systems, 1965; (with F.W. McFarlan) Management Information Systems, 1966; Computers in Business Management, 1966; Essentials of Cost Accounting, 1969; (with McFarland and Zani) Computer Based Information Systems, 1970. Home: 33 Summit Rd Lexington, MA 02173. Office: Morgan Hall Soldiers Field Boston, MA 02163

DEARDEN, JOHN FRANCIS, cardinal; b. Valley Falls, R.I., Oct. 15, 1907; s. John S. and Agnes (Gregory) D.; grad. St. Mary's Sem., Cleve., 1929, N.Am. Coll., Rome, Italy, 1934; S.T.D., Gregorian Univ., Rome, 1934. Ordained priest Roman Catholic Ch., 1932; rector St. Mary's Sem. Cleve., 1944-48; apptd. papal chamberlain with title very rev. monsignor, 1945; consecrated coadjutor bishop Pitts., titular bishop Sarepta, 1948; bishop Pitts., 1950-58; archbishop Archdiocese Detroit, 1959—; named to Coll. Cardinals, 1969. Mem. Nat. Conf. Cath. Bishops (pres. 1966-71). Address: 1234 Washington Blvd Detroit MI 48226

DEARDEN, WILLIAM EDGAR CHAMBERS, chocolate co. exec.; b. Phila., Sept. 14, 1922; s. William Edgar Chambers and Nellie (Maloney) D.; B.S. in Econs., Albright Coll., 1944; postgrad. Harvard Bus. Sch., 1944-45, Temple U., 1953-54; m. Mary Kline, July 10, 1944; children—Bonnie Lynne (Mrs. Peter Larson), Pamala Kay. Sales rep. Dun & Bradstreet, Inc., Reading, Pa., 1946-50, mgr., Trenton, N.J., 1950-51; asst. bus. mgr. Milton Hershey Sch., Hershey, Pa., 1953-57, bd. mgrs., 1964-; with Hershey Foods Corp., 1957-, dir. sales and marketing, 1965- 67, v.p. sales and marketing, 1967—, also dir.; v.p., dir. Hershey Chocolate Can. Ltd., 1967-; dir. Hershey Trust Co., San Giorgio Macaroni, Inc., Delmonico Foods, Inc., H.B. Reese Candy Co., Inc., David & Frere Ltd. Bd. mgrs. M.S. Hershey Found., 1964—; trustee Albright Coll. Served to lt. USNR, 1943-46, 51-53. Named Alumnus of Year, Milton Hershey Sch., 1964. Mason (Shriner), Rotarian (past pres. Hershey). Home: 405 Homestead Rd Hershey PA 17033 Office: Hershey Foods Corp Hershey, PA 17033.

DEARING, GEORGE BRUCE, univ. vice chancellor; b. Erie County, Pa., Jan. 11, 1918; s. James Roscoe and Clara (Patterson) D.; A.B., Allegheny Coll., 1939, LL.D. (hon.), 1965; M.A. in English, State U. Ia., 1940, Ph.D., 1942; M.A. in Psychology, Swarthmore Coll., 1954; student Inst. Coll. and U. Adminstrs., Harvard Bus. Sch., 1958; m. Betty Boltz, June 29, 1940; children—Mary Susan, James Bruce. Instr. English, U. Minn., 1942-43, Cornell U., 1946-47; asst. prof. English, Swarthmore Coll., 1947-50, from asst. to asso. prof., 1952-57, dir. Bell Program in Liberal Arts for Execs., 1956-57; vis. prof. English, U. Mass., summer 1956; prof. English, dean Sch. Arts and Sci., U. Del., 1957-65; pres. State U. N.Y. at Binghamton, 1965-71; vice chancellor acad. programs State U. N.Y., Albany, 1971—. Active Boy Scouts Am. Bd. dirs. Am. Humanities Center 1958—. Served with USNR, 1943-46, 50-52; capt. Res. Am. Council Learned Soc. faculty study fellow, 1952-53. Mem. Coll. English Assn. (dir. 1951-52, 60-63, pres. 1953), Assn. Land Grant Colls. and State Univs. (chmn. div. arts and scis. 1963), Modern Lang. Assn., Nat. Council Tchrs. English, Am. Assn. U. Profs., Eastern Assn. Coll. Deans, Am. Conf. Acad. Deans, Soc. Advancement Edn. (trustee 1966), Phi Beta Kappa, Psi Chi. Episcopalian. Contbr. articles profl. jours. Home: Heritage Village Albany NY 12186

DEARING, VINTON ADAMS, educator; b. San Francisco, July 30, 1920; s. Henry H. and Estelle (Sosso) D.; A.B., Harvard, 1940, M.A., 1942, Ph.D., 1949; m. Marion Elizabeth Miser, Dec. 3, 1946; childrenHenry, Mary. Mem. faculty U. Cal. at Los Angeles, 1949-, prof. English, 1963-68, prof. English and computer applications in lit., 1969-. Served AUS, 1942-46. Guggenheim fellow, 1959-60; IBM Corp. research grantee, 1967. Mem. Bibliog. Soc., Modern Lang. Assn., Soc. Bib. Lit., A.A.A.S., Assn. Machine Translation. Author: A Manual of Textual Analysis, 1959. Textual editor: The Works of John Dryden, 1956-. Home: 10542 Garwood Pl Los Angeles CA 90024

DEARING, WARREN PALMER, govt. official; b. Palo, Ia., Aug. 17, 1905; s. John Anthony and Laura (Williams) D.; A.B., State Coll. of Wash., 1927; M.D. cum laude, Harvard, 1931; m. Gladys Snowman Proctor, Sept. 5, 1931; childrenEleanor Jean (Mrs. James W. McKinster), John Proctor, James Palmer, Albert Seward. Engaged as poliomyelitis and Tb field investigator with U.S.P.H.S., 1934-41; detailed to O.C.D. as asst. chief med. officer and later chief med. officer, 1941-44; personnel officer health div., U.N.R.R.A., Washington, D.C., North Africa, Europe, 1944-45; dep. chief div. of pub. health methods, 1945- 46, chief div.. commd. officers, 1946-48, dep. surgeon gen., 1948-57; asst. dir.-health ODM, 1957-58; dir. health services OCDM, 1958-61; exec. dir. Group Health Assn. Am., Inc., 1961-71. Mem. Pres.'s Consumer Adv. Council 1965-66. Diplomate Am. Bd. Preventive Medicine (founders group). Fellow Am. Pub. Health Assn. (med. care sec.), A.M.A. (ho. of dels. 1948-56); mem. Assn. Mil. Surgeons U.S., Am. Soc. Pub. Adminstrn., Group Health Assn. Am., A.A.A.S., Consumer Fedn. Am. (v.p. 1969—, bd. dirs. 1970—), Med. Soc. D.C. Club: Army-Navy (Washington). Home: 6900 Millwood Rd Bethesda MD 20034. Office: 1321 14th St NW Washington DC 20005.

DEARING, WILLIAM HILL, educator, physician; b. Memphis, Dec. 3, 1908; s. William Hill and Theresa Irene (Trenham) D.; A.B., U. Pa., 1930, M.A., 1934, M.D., 1934; Ph.D., U. Minn., 1941; m. Edith Wintersteen, Aug. 29, 1936; children—Jane C., John C. (dec.), Carl B. Intern medicine Geisinger Meml. Hosp., Danville, Pa., 1934-35, asso. medicine, 1935-36; fellow medicine Mayo Found., U. Minn., 1936-39, mem. faculty, 1942—, prof. medicine, 1962—; 1st asst. medicine Mayo Clinic, 1939-41, cons. medicine, 1941—, head sect., 1956—, mem. bd. govs., 1955-60. Diplomate Am. Bd. Internal Medicine (subspeciality gastroenterology). Fellow A.C.P.; mem. A.M.A., Central Soc. Clin. Research, Central Clin. Research Club, Am. Fedn. Clin. Research, Am. Gastroenterology Soc., Minn. Soc. Internal Medicine, A.A.A.S. Presbyn. Contbr. articles profl. jours. Home: Rochester Towers Sunny Slopes Rochester MN 55901 Office: Mayo Clinic Rochester MN 55901

DEARSTYNE, HOWARD BEST, educator; b. Albany, N.Y., Aug. 2, 1903; s. Charles and Lottie (Best) D.; A.B., Columbia, 1925, postgrad., 1925-28; diploma, Bauhaus, Dessau, Germany, 1932; postgrad. Bauhaus, Berlin, 1932-33; m. Barbara Louise Timmons, Oct. 5, 1946. Archtl. designer Wallace K. Harrison and J.A. Fouilhoux, N.Y.C., 1935-39, Raymond Loewy and Antonin Raymond, 1940-41; exhibited photography one man shows Va. Mus. Fine Arts, 1951, Art Inst. Chgo., 1962, U. Mich. Art Mus., 1962, Bloomfield (Mich.) Art Assn., 1963, U. Mich. Extension Service and Grad. Study Center, Dearborn, 1963, Andrew Dickson White Mus. Art, Cornell U., 1963, Grand Rapids Art Galley, 1963, Twentiety Century Gallery, Williamsburg, 1963, Randolph Macon Woman's Coll., Lynchburg, 1963, Hollins Coll., 1963, Peninsula Arts Assn., Newport News, 1964, Richmond Profl. Inst., 1964, Longwood Coll., 1964, Howard U., 1964, Krannert Art Mus. U. Ill., Urbana, 1964, U. Tex., Autin, 1964, Tex. A. and M. U., 1964, Ariz. State U., 1965, U. Utah, 1965, U. Ore., 1965, Ft. Worth Art Center, 1965, M. H. DeYound Meml. Mus., San Francisco, 1966, U. Okla., 1966, Mills Coll., 1966, Ill. Inst. Tech., 1967, Tex. Technol. Coll., 1967, Wheaton Coll., Norton, Mass., 1967, Fisk U., 1968, Grand Valley State Coll., Allendale, Mich., 1968, Spelman Coll., Atlanta, 1968; exhibited group shows 2d Armory Exhbn., N.Y.C., 1945, Mus. Modern Art Shows, 1946, 50, 51, 57, 58,-59, 60, 62, Los Angeles County Mus., 1950, George Eastman House, 1959, 63- 64; faculty Black Mountain Coll., N.C., 1941-42; resident architect, tchr. arch. Lawrence Coll., Appleton, Wis., 1943-44; head dept. design Cranbrook Acad. Art, Mich., 1944-46; faculty Coll. William and Mary, 1946-57; asso. prof. dept. arch. Ill. Inst. Tech., 1957-; asst. archtl. records editor Colonial Williamsburg, 1946- 56; Fellow Graham Found. Advanced Studies Fine Arts, 1969—. Mem. A.I.A., Coll. Art Assn. Am., Soc. Archtl. Historians (past dir.), Assn. Collegiate Schs. Arch. (past Com. chmn.). Author: (with A. Lawrence Kocher) Colonial Williamsburg/ Its Buildings and Gardens, 1949, Shadows in Silver-A Record of Virginia, 1850-1900, 1954. Asso. editor Inland Architect, 1967-68. Translator: (with Hilla Rebay) Point and Line to Plane, 1947, The Non-Objective World, 1959. Contbr. articles to mags. Home: 60 E 32d St Chicago IL 60616.

DEARTH, ROBERT ALFRED, advt. exec.; b. Cleve., Feb. 4, 1920; s. Thomas Gregg and Ethel May (Henry) D.; A.B. in Fgn. Service, George Washington U., 1941; grad. study Coll. Coll., 1941, Western Res. U., 1946; m. Regina E. Miller, Jan. 9, 1943; childrenRobert Alfred, Gregg M., Jeffrey L. Copywriter, McCann-Erickson, 1945-55; v.p. Ross Boy, Inc., Detroit, 1955-61; pres. Morse Internat., N.Y.C., 1961; sr. v.p. Kenyon & Eckhardt, Detroit, 1961-63, then exec. v.p.; sr. v.p. D.P. Bro. co., 1967-. Pres. Conn. Universalist Conv., 1961. Mem. Mich. Consumers Council, 1970—; pres. Camp Oakland Youth Programs, Inc., Oxford, Mich. Adviser Republican Nat. Campaign Com., 1952; state chmn. U.S. senator Robert Griffin campaign, 1966.

Served to lt. comdr. USNR, World War II. Mem. Alpha Delta Sigma, Acacia. Unitarian. Clubs: Players (N.Y.C. and Detroit); Darien (Conn.) Country; Orchard Lake Country (Mich.). Editor: Land of the Free (Freedoem Found. award), 1947. Composer: Caught in a Whirling Wind, 1945. Home: 310 Martell Dr Bloomfield Hills MI 48013 Office: Gen Motors Bldg Detroit MI 48202.

DEASON, WILLARD, govt. ofcl.; b. Stockdale, Tex., Jan. 3, 1905; s. Horace M. and Nettie (Key) D.; B.S., S.W. Tex. State Coll., 1930; LL.B., San Antonio Law Sch., 1934; m. Jeanne FitzPatrick, Apr. 8, 1945; childrenDiann, Patrick Lyndon. Tchr. social sci. Alamo Heights Jr. High Sch., San Antonio, 1930- 34; admitted to Tex. bar, 1934; practice in Houston, 1934-35; jr. atty. Fed. Land Bank, Houston, 1934-35; adminstrv. asst. to state dir. Tex. Nat. Youth Adminstrn., 1935-37, dep. state adminstr., 1937-42; sales mgr. radio sta. KTBC, Austin, Tex., 1946-48; mgr., owner radio sta. KVET, Austin, 1949-65; commr. ICC, Washington, 1965—. Mem. adv. com. M Mut. Network Affiliates, 1952-59. Mem. adv. com. Austin Bd. Edn., 1950-58; mem. U.S. Nat. Commn. Pan Am. Ry. Congress Assn.; mem. Council Adminstrv. Conf. U.S. presdl. elector for Tex., 1960. Bd. dirs. Austin Better Bus. Bur. Served to comdr. USNR, 1942-46. Mem. Tex. Assn. Broadcasters (past pres., dir.), Austin C. of C. (bd. dirs.). Episcopalian. Kiwanian. Home: 6101 Kennedy Dr Chevy Chase, MD 20015. Office: ICC 12th and Constitution Av Washington DC 20423

DEASY, CORNELIUS MICHAEL, architect; b. Mineral Wells, Tex., July 19, 1918; s. Cornelius and Monetta (Palmo) D.; B. Arch., U. So. Cal., 1941; m. Lucille Laney, Sept. 14, 1941; children—Diana, Carol, Ann. Practice architecture, Los Angeles, 1946—; partner Robert D. Bolling, 1960—; prin. works include prin. offices First Western Bank & Trust Co., Lincoln Savs. & Loan Assn., Booth Meml. Hosp., Meml. Auditorium, Mulholland Jr. High Sch. Vice pres. Los Angeles Beautiful; dir. Regional Plan Assn. Fellow A.I.A. (past pres., dir. So. Cal. chpt., chmn. com. research). Home: 11100 Valley Spring Lane North Hollywood CA 91602 Office: 3121 Temple St Los Angeles CA 90026

DEASY, MARY MARGARET, author; b. Cin., May 20, 1914; d. William P. and Clara L. (Woelfel) Deasy; Mus. B., Coll. Conservatory Music, U. Cin., 1935. Mem. Authors Guild. Author: The Hour of Spring, 1948; Cannon Hill, 1949; Ella Gunning, 1950; Devil's Bridge, 1952; The Corioli Affair, 1954; The Boy Who Made Good, 1955; O'Shaughnessy's Day, 1957; The Celebration, 1963; also numerous short stories. Address: 3218 Griest Av Cincinnati OH 45208

DEATHERAGE, FRED E. educator; b. Waverly, Ill., Dec. 30, 1913; s. Fred E. and Marian Eve (Sevier) D.; A.B., ILL. Coll.; 1935, D. So., 1960; A.M., U. Ill., 1936; Ph. D., U. Ia., 1938; fellow Ohio State U., 1940-42; m. Nellie Lou Carothers, Jan. 3, 1942; children—Fred Sevier, Catherine Margaret, Marilyn Nan. Instr. biochemistry U. Ia., 1938-40; chemist Kroger Food Found Cin., 1942-46; asst. prof. Ohio State U., 1946-48, asso. prof., 1949-51, prof., chmn. dept. agrl. biochemistry, 1951-64, prof., 1964—; asst. dept. animal sci. Ohio Agrl. Expt. Sta., 1949-51, asso. 1951-53, prof., 1953- -; food scientist, technologist AID. Brazil, 1964-68. Mem. Am. Chem. Soc., Am. Inst. Nutrition, Inst. Food Technologists, A.A.A.S., Am. Oil Chemists Soc., Am. Soc. Biol. Chemists, Am. Soc. Animal Sci., Phi Beta Kappa, Sigma Xi, Sigma Pi, Phi Lambda Upsilon. Home: 4310 Colerain Av Columbus OH 43214

DEATLEY, LINDLEY SHAFER, chem. co. exec.; b. Kansas City, Mo., Aug. 2, 1912; s. Edward E. and Ella (Shafer) DeA.; B.S. in Chem. Engring., U. Kan., 1933; m. Julia Ellen Wilson, Nov. 20, 1937; children—Linda Ellen (Mrs. Robert D. Miller), William B. Chemist, Thompson-Hayward Chem. Co., Kansas City, Kan., 1934-36, chief chemist, 1938-42, lab. dir., 1942-51, dir. research and chem. engring., 1951-53, v.p. research devel. and prodn., 1953-65, v.p. research and devel., 1965-69, sr. v.p., dir. research and devel., 1969—; chem. engr. Puritan Compressed Gas Corp., 1936-38. Registered profl. engr., Mo., Kan. Recipient Alpha Chi Sigma award U. Kan., 1933. Fellow A.A.A.S.; mem. Am. Inst. Chem. Engrs. (chmn. Kansas City sect. 1958), Am. Chem. Soc. (chmn. 1949), Sci. Research Soc. Am. (br. pres. 1954), Tech. Socs. Council Kansas City Area (chmn. 1948), Nat., Mo. socs. profl. engrs., Entomology Soc. Am., Weed Soc. Club: Indian Hills Country (Prairie Village, Kan.). Home: 6601 Woodson Dr Shawnee Mission KS 66202 Office: 5200 Speaker Rd Kansas City KS 66206

DEATLY, WILLIAM HENRY, ins. and trust.; b. N.Y.C., Oct. 30, 1903; s. William Henry and Kathryn Agnes (Ackerson) D.; student Pace Inst., 1923-26; m. Bernice Louise Henry, June 17, 1927 (dec. Apr. 1940); 1 son, Richard Henry; m. 2d, Helen Louise Swope, Oct. 4, 1947. Accountant, Ernst & Ernst, N.Y.C., 1926-33; comptroller Title Guarantee Co., N.Y.C., 1933-37; v.p. 1937-50, trustee, 1941—, v.p., gen. mgr. 1943-50, pres., 1950-64, exec. v.p. adminstrn. and finance Title Ins. & Trust Co., Los Angeles. C.P.A., N.Y. Cal. Episcopalian. Clubs: California (Los Angeles); Union League (N.Y.C.). Home: 560 Orange Grove Circle Pasadena CA 91105 Office: 433 S Spring St Los Angeles CA 90013

DEATON, CHARLES, architect, indsl. designer; b. Clayton, N.M., Jan. 1, 1921; s. Charles Elmer and Nina Maude (Utter) D.; ed. pub. schs.; m. Zada Sue Davis, May 9, 1942 (div. May 1947); 1 son, Robert Earle; m. 2d, Ida Richardson, May 22, 1948 (div.); children—Claudia, Charles, Snow; m. 3d, Jacklyn Kay Spinney, Aug. 1, 1970. Aircraft illustrator, engr. Lockheed Aircraft Corp., also Curtis-Wright Corp., 1941-43; pvt. practice architecture and indsl. design, Chgo. and N.Y.C., 1943-49, St. Louis, 1951-55, Denver, 1955—; prin. archtl. works include Central Bank & Trust Co., Denver, 1957, Wyo. Nat. Bank, Casper, 1962, Sculptured House, 1966, Sports-Complex, Kansas City, 1967; design includes bank vault equipment, office furniture, comml. lighting equipment; chief designer Bank Bldg. Corp., St. Louis, 1949-52; tchr. design Franklin Sch. Profl. Arts. N.Y.C., 1946-49. Recipient Horatio Alger award, 1969. Patentee in field. Address: Genesee Mountain Golden CO 80401

DEATS, PAUL KINDRED, Jr., educator, clergyman; b. Graham, Tex., Oct. 1, 1918; s. Paul Kindred and Agnes (Craig) D.; A.A., Tarleton (Tex.) State Coll., 1937; B.A., So. Meth. U., 1939; B.D., Union Theol. Sem., N.Y.C., 1943; Ph.D. (Gen. Edn. Bd. fellow, Rockefeller fellow, Kent fellow), Boston U., 1954; m. Ruth Miller Zumbrunnen, Sept. 10, 1941; children—Patricia Zee (Mrs. Alain Jehlen), Carolyn Kay, Frances Ann (Mrs. Donald Poe, Jr.), Randall Kin. Ordained to ministry Methodist Ch., 1944; asso. minister Highland Park Meth. Ch., Dallas and Met. Duane Meth. Ch., N.Y.C., 1939-41, 41-42; dir. Wesley Found., U. Tex., 1942-51; dir. United Ministry, Boston U., 1953-55, asst. prof. religion in higher edn., 1954-58, asso. prof. religion in higher edn. and social ethics, 1958-63, prof. social ethics, 1963—, chmn. div. theol. and religious studies Grad. Sch., 1969—. Chmn. dept. social relations Mass. Council Chs., 1964-68; mem. Gen. Commn. on Ch.-Govt. Relations, 1965-68. Trustee Grumman Found. Am. Assn. Theol. Schs. fellow, 1961-62. Mem. Am. Soc. Christian Ethics, Soc. for Sci. Study Religion, Am. Anthrop. Assn., Am. Sociol. Soc. Democrat. Author: (with others) The Responsible Student, 1957; (with H.E. Stotts) Methodism and Society: Guidelines for Strategy, 1962. Home: 106 Berkeley St West Newton MA 02165 Office: 745 Commonwealth Av Boston MA 02215

DEAVER, DARWIN HOLLOWAY, utility exec.; b. Topeka, Oct. 6, 1914; s. Glenn Harry and Mabel (Holloway) D.; Ph.B., Washburn Coll., 1935; M.B.A., Harvard, 1937; m. Jane Harriet Miller, Apr. 26, 1941; children—James Miller, Robert Holloway Henry Crandon. Investment analyst Delafield & Delafield, N.Y.C., 1937-39, Continental Casualty Co., Chgo., 1939-41, Harris Hall & Co., Chgo., 1946-49; asst. to pres. Automatic Electric Sales Corp., Chgo., 1949-50, supply sales mgr., 1953-55, pres., 1955-62; exec. v.p., dir. Automatic Electric Co., 1962-64, pres., dir., 1964-67; exec. v.p. mfg. United Utilities, Inc., Kansas City, Mo., 1967- -, also dir.; dir. North Electric Co., United Computing Systems, Inc., Rixon Electronics Inc., United Bus. Communications, Inc. Bd. dirs. Rehab. Inst. Served to lt. USNR, 1941-45, as lt. comdr., 1950-52. Republican. Episcopalian. Clubs: Kansas City; Chicago (Chgo.); Glen View (Golf, Ill.); Mission Hills Country. Home: 1902 W 69th Terrace Shawnee Mission KS 66208 Office: PO Box 11315 Plaza Station Kansas City MO 64112

DE BAKEY, MICHAEL ELLIS, surgeon; b. Lake Charles, La., Sept. 7, 1908; s. Shaker Morris and Rehelga (Zerba) De B.; B.S., Tulane U., 1930, M.D., 1932, M.S., 1935; LL. D., 1965; Docteur Honoris Causa, U. of Lyon, France, 1961, U. of Brussels (Belgium), 1962, U. of Ghent, 1964, U. Athens, 1964; D.H.C., U. of Turin (Italy), 1965; LL.D., Lafayette Coll., 1965; m. Diana Cooper, Oct. 15, 1936; children—Michael Maurice, Ernest Ochsner, Barry Edward, Denis Alton. Intern Charity Hosp., New Orleans, 1932-33, asst. surgery, 1933-35; asst. surgery U. Strasbourg, 1935-36; instr. surgery Tulane U., 1937-40, asst. prof., 1940-46, asso. prof., 1946-48; prof. surgery, chmn. dept. Baylor U., 1948—, v.p. med. affairs, 1968—, chief exec. officer Coll. Medicine, 1968-69, pres. Coll. of Medicine, 1969—; surgeon-in-chief Ben Taub Gen. Hosp., 1963—; sr. attending surgeon Meth. Hosp.; cons. surgery VA, St. Elizabeth's, M.D. Anderson, St. Luke's, Tex. Children's hosps.; clin. prof. surgery U. Tex. Dental Br., Houston; cons. Tex. Inst. Rehab. and Research, Brooke Gen. Hosp., Brooke Army Med. Center, Ft. Sam Houston, Tex.; cons. surgery Walter Reed Army Hosp., Washington. Mem. of med. adv. com. Sec. Def., 1948-50; chmn. com. surgery NRC, 1953, mem. exec. com., 1953; mem. com. med. services, Hoover Commn. Chmn. bd. regents Nat. Library Medicine, 1959. Past mem. nat. adv. heart council NIH; mem. Nat. Adv. Health Council, 1961-65, Nat. Adv. Council Regional Med. Programs, 1965—, Nat. Adv. Gen. Med. Scis. Council 1965; mem. Program Planning Com., Com. Tng., Nat. Heart Inst., 1961—; mem. civilian health and med. adv. council Office Asst. Sec. Def.; chmn. Pres.' Commn. Heart Disease, Cancer and Stroke, 1964. Served as col. Office Surgeon General, AUS, 1942-46, now colonel in the Reserve; cons. to the surgeon gen., 1946—. Awarded Legion of Merit, 1946; Rudolph Matas award, 1954; Hektoengold medal. A.M.A.; Internat. Soc. Surgery Distinguished Service award, 1957; recipient of the Modern Medicine award, 1957, Roswell Park medal, 1959; A.M.A. Distinguished Service award, 1959; Leriche award, Internat. Soc. Surgery, 1959; Great Medallion, U. Ghent, Belgium, 1961; Grand Cross of Order Leopold, Belgium, 1962; Albert Lasker award for clin. research, 1963; Order Merit, Chile, 1964; St. Vincent prize med. scis. U. Turin, 1965; Orden del Libertador Gen. San Martin, Argentina, 1965; Centennial medal Albert Einstein Med. Center, 1966; Gold Scalpel award Internat. Cardiology Found., 1966; Distinguished Service prof. Baylor U., 1968; numerous others. Diplomate Nat. Bd. Med. Examiners, Am. Bd. Surgery, Am. Bd. Thoracic Surgery. Fellow A.C.S., Inst. of Medicine Chgo. (hon.); mem. Am. Coll. Cardiology (hon. fellow), Royal Soc. Medicine, Halsted Soc., Am. Heart Assn., So. Soc. Clin. Research, A.A.A.S., Southwestern Surg. Congress (pres. 1952), Soc. Vascular Surg. (pres. 1953), A.M.A., Am. So., Western Surg. assns., Am. Assn. Thoracic Surgery (pres. 1959), Internat. Cardiovascular Soc.(pres. 1958, North Am. chpt. 1964), Mexican Acad. Surgery (hon.), Soc. Clin. Surg., Soc. U. Surgs., Internat. Soc. Surgery, Soc. Exptl. Biology and Medicine, Bio-med. Engring. Soc. (bd. dirs. 1968), Houston Heart Assn. (mem. adv. council 1968-69), Sociedad Nacional de Cirugia (Cuba), C. of C., Sigma Xi, Alpha Omega Alpha. Democrat. Episcopalian. Club: University (Washington). Author: (with Robert A. Kilduffe) Blood Transfusion, 1942; (with Gilbert W. Beebe) Battle Casualties, 1952; (with Alton Ochsner) Textbook of Minor Surgery, 1955; (with T. Whayne) Cold Injury, Ground Type, 1958. Editor: Yearbook of Surgery, 1958—. Chmn. adv. editorial bd. Medical History of World War II. Home: 5323 Cherokee St Houston TX 77005

DEBARDELEBEN, ARTHUR, lawyer; b. Great Falls, Mont., July 12, 1918; s. John Arthur and Antoinette (Merselis) DeB.; Ph.B., U. Wis., 1940, LL.B., 1947; m. Edith June Gunther, Feb. 25, 1956. Admitted to Wis. bar, 1947, since practiced in Park Falls. Bd. regents U. Wis., 1959-68, pres. bd. regents, 1964-67; mem. Wis. Coordinating Com. Higher Edn., 1959-67. Presdl. elector, 1964. Served with AUS, 1941- 45. Mem. Am. Arbitration Assn. (nat. panel), Am., 15th Jud. Circuit (pres. 1959-60) bar assns., State Bar Wis., Am. Acad. Polit. and Social Sci., Am. Civil Liberties Union, Am. Judicature Soc. Author: (with Walter P. Metzger, Sanford H. Kadish, Edward J. Bloustein) Dimensions of Academic Freedom, 1969. Mem. bd. Wis. Law Rev., 1940-41. Address: Park Falls WI 54552

DE BARDELEBEN, BAILEY THOMAS, transp. exec.; b. Anniston, Ala., Apr. 8, 1908; s. Henry T. and Lulie (Thomas) De B.; student Ala. Poly. Inst., 1927-30; m. Mildred Edmonson, Oct. 23, 1935; children-Jill, Lane Thomas. Purser, S.S. H.F. De Bardeleben, 1930-32, 3d mate, purser, 1932; asst. to traffic mgr. De Bardeleben Coal Corp., Birmingham, Ala., 1932-36, mgr. bunker div., Mobile, 1936-39, v.p., dir., 1948-58; pres., dir. De Bardeleben Marine Corp., 1959-66; mgr. Tex. div. Coyle Lines, 1939-43, gen. mgr. operations, New Orleans, 1943-49, dir., 1946-66, pres., 1949-66; pres. Bolivar Terminal Co., Houston, 1944-66; Alacoal Barge Corp., Birmingham, 1957-66, W.G. Coyle & Co., Inc., New Orleans, 1954-66, Tampa Terminals, Inc., 1964-66; pres., dir. Bailey Barge Line, Inc., Metairie, La., 1966- -, Star Towing Co., Inc., 1966-69 Bailey Coke Transport, Inc., 1968—, Mem. Am. Waterways Operators (chmn., past regional v.p.), Intracoastal Canal Assn. La. and Tex. (v.p. 1955), C. of C. (chmn. waterways devel. com. 1953). Episcopalian (vestryman, treas., trustee ch. sch.). Clubs: Boston, Pickwick (New Orleans); Metairie (La.) Country. Home: 104 Magnolia Dr Metairie LA 70005 Office: PO Box 9386 Metairie LA 70005

DEBARDELEBEN, NEWTON HANSON, banker; b. Birmingham, Ala., Jan. 19, 1915; s. Henry T. and Donie (Drane) DeB.; A.B., U. N.C., 1936; LL.B., Yale, 1939; m. Virginia Swann, Apr. 10, 1940; children—Newton Hanson, Cathrine Swann. Admitted to Ala. bar, 1939; asso. Cabaniss & Johnston, Birmingham, 1939-42; asst. to exec. v.p. DeBardeleben Coal Corp., Birmingham, 1945-48, exec. v.p., 1948, pres., 1949-62; v.p. 1st Nat. Bank of Birmingham, 1962-67, exec. v.p., 1967-68, pres., dir., 1968-69, vice chmn., 1969—; mem. exec. com. Crawford Johnson Co.; dir. First Nat. Bank Birmingham, Mead Corp., Anderson Electric Corp., Ala. Great So. R.R., Russell Mills, Inc. Bd. dirs. Children's Hosp., Baptist Hosps. Found. Birmingham. Mem. Birmingham Area C. of C. (dir.), Order of Coif, Phi Delta Phi, Sigma Alpha Epsilon. Episcopalian. Rotarian. Clubs: Redstone; Mountain Brook; Birmingham Country. Home: 2824 Cherokee Rd Birmingham AL 35223 Office: First Nat Bank Bldg Birmingham AL 35202

DE BARY, WILLIAM THEODORE, educator; b. Bronx, N.Y., Aug. 9, 1919; s. William Emil and Mildred (Marquette) de B.; B.A., Columbia, 1941, M.A. (fellow Am. Council Learned Socs. 1947-48), 1948, William Bayard Cutting traveling fellow, also Fulbright scholar in China, 1948-49, Ph.D., 1953; Henry Evans traveling fellow, Harvard, 1941-42; m. Fanny Brett, June 16, 1942; children—Mary Brett, Paul Ambrose, Catherine Anne, Mary Beatrice. Mem. faculty Columbia, 1949—, prof. Chinese and Japanese, 1959-66, chmn. dept., 1960-66, chmn. univ. com. Oriental studies, 1950—, Oriental records editor Records of Civilization, 1952—, Horace Carpentier prof. Oriental studies, 1967—. Chmn. exec. com. univ. senate, 1968-70, provost, v.p. acad. affairs, 1971—. Dir. Cath. Commn. Intellectual and Cultural Affairs, 1960—. Served to lt. comdr. USNR, 1943-45; PTO. Mem. Assn. Asian Studies (dir. 1961-64, pres. 1969-70), China Soc., Japan Soc. N.Y. (dir. 1964-66), Am. Council Learned Socs. (chmn. subcom. Chinese thought). Co-author: Sources of Japanese Tradition, 1958; Sources of Indian Traditions, 1958; Sources of Chinese Tradition, 1960. Translator: Five Women Who Loved Love (Ihara Saikaku), 1956. Editor: Approaches to the Oriental Classics: Asian Literature and Thought in General Education, 1959; A Guide to Oriental Classics, 1964; Approaches to Asian Civilizations, 1964; The Buddhist Tradition, 1969; Self and Society in Ming Thought, 1969. Home: 98 Hickory Hill Rd Tappan NY 10983 Office: Columbia U New York City NY 10027

DEBBINS, WILLIAM, educator; b. Flint, Mich., Mar. 28, 1927; s. Joseph Michael and Nell (Hyde) D.; A.B., Central Mich. U., 1952; M.A., Syracuse U., 1953, Ph.D., 1959; m. Solvita Kalnins, May 30, 1953; children—Paul Alexander, Katherine Kaija. Instr., Syracuse U., 1956-59, vis. prof., 1965; asst. prof. Elmira Coll., 1959-62; asso. prof. Cornell Coll., Mt. Vernon, Ia., 1962-65, Erastus Burroughs Soper prof. philosophy, 1965—. Vis. prof. Northwestern U., 1966. Councilman, Mt. Vernon, 1967-; alternate del. Republican Nat. Conv., 1968. Served with USAAF, 1945-47. mem. Am. Assn. U. Profs., Am. Philos. Assn., Mind Assn., Philosophy Sci. Assn. Author: (with T.V. Smith) Constructive Ethics, 1961. Editor, contbr. Essays in Philosophy of History, 1966; Aphorisms, 1967. Home: 824 Summit Av Mount Vernon IA 52314

DE BEER, GAVIN RYLANDS, biologist, author; b. London, Eng., Nov. 1, 1899; s. Herbert Chaplin and Mabel (Rylands) de B.; M.A., U. Oxford (Eng.), 1924, D.Sc., 1932; Sc.D. (hon.), U. Cambridge (Eng.), 1958; D. és Lettres (hon.), U. Lausanne (Switzerland), 1950; D. de L;Univ. (hon.), U. Bordeaux (France), 1961; m. Cicely Glyn Medlycott, Mar. 20, 1925. Fellow Merton Coll., U. Oxford, 1923-38, sr. lectr. zoology, 1926-38; prof. embryology Univ. Coll., U. London, 1945-50; dir. Brit. Museum (Natural History), 1950-60, Thomas Nelson & Sons, pubs., 1960-67. Pres. XV Internat. Congress Zoology, 1958. Served to lt., Grenadler Guards, Brit. Army, 1918-19; BEF in France and Germany; served to lt. col. Grenadier Guards, 1939-45; ETO. Medallist, Royal Soc., 1958, Soc. de'Acclimatation, Paris, France, 1954; created knight, 1954; recipient Kalinga prize UNESCO, 1968. Fellow Royal Soc., Soc. Antiquaries, Linnean Soc. (pres. 1946-49, medallist 1958); hon. mem. zool. socs. France, Belgium, India; corr. mem. Acad. des Scis., Paris, Soc. d'Histoire de Geneva, Soc. Vaudoise d'Histoire Soc. Neuchateloise d'Histoire. Author numerous works on zoology, embryology, palaeontology, genetics, evolution, history of sci., lit. history, biography, mil. history, alpine history. Address: La Colline 1880 BEX Switzerland

DEBELAK, WILLIAM F., food co. exec.; b. Chgo., Jan. 21, 1914; s. Frank and Mary D.; B.S., U. Ill., 1936; J.D., Chgo. Kent Coll. Law; m. Beatrice McLaughlin, Mar. 16, 1943; 1 dau., Kim M. Sec. Quaker Oats Co., Chgo., 1950-59, sec., 1959-. Bd. dirs. Med. Center YMCA, Chgo. Served to lt. col. AUS, 1941-46. Mem. Am., Chgo. bar assns., Am. Soc. Corporate Secs. Home: 3217 Hartzell St Evanston, IL 60201. Office: Merchandise Mart Plaza Chicago IL 60654

DE BENEDETTI, SERGIO, physicist; b. Florence, Italy, Aug. 17, 1912; s. Guido and Amelia (Passigli) DeB.; Ph.D., U. Florence, Italy, 1933; m. Emma Falco, Apr. 10, 1944; children—Lydia, Vera, Gilbert. Came to U.S., 1940, naturalized, 1946. Asst. prof. U. Padua, Italy, 1933-38; research fellow Curie Lab., Paris, 1938-40; asst. Bartol Found., Swarthmore, Pa., 1940- 42; asso. prof. Kenyon Coll., Gambier, O., 1943-44; sr. physicist Monsanto Chem. Co., Dayton, O., 1944-45; prin. physicist Oak Ridge Nat. Lab., 1946-48; asso. prof. Washington U., St. Louis, 1948- 49; prof. physics Carnegie-Mellon U., Pitts., 1949—; staff Manhattan Project, 1941-45. Cons. AEC. Fulbright fellow U. Turin (Italy), 1956-57. Fellow Am. Phys. Soc.; mem. Fedn. Am. Scientists (nat. council 1961). Author: Nuclear Interactions, 1964. Bd. editors Nuclear Instruments and Methods, 1960-63; Review Modern Physics and Nuclear Instruments and Methods, 1962-64. Contbr. articles to profl. Jours., U.S., France, Italy. Home: 122 Hastings St Pittsburgh PA 15206

DE BESCHE, HUBERT WATHIER AUGUST, Swedish diplomat; b. Frösö, Jämtlands län, Sweden, July 7, 1911; s. Hubert W. and Ebba A. (Fröberg) de B.; degree in law, U. Stockholm, 1935; student U. Grenoble (France), U. Heidelberg (Germany); m. Eva Rhedin, Mar. 21, 1946; childrenCaroline, Gunilla. Joined Swedish Fgn. Ministry, 1936; assigned London, Eng., 1937-40; assigned Fgn. Ministry, 1940-49, charge Commn. Trade and Commerce, 1947-49; econ. counselor embassy, Washington, 1949-53; head trade dept. Fgn. Ministry, 1953-56; dep. sec. gen. Fgn. Ministry, 1956-64; Swedish ambassador to U.S., 1964- . Mem. steering bd. for trade OEEC, 1956-60; vice chmn. trade com. OECD, 1960-63; chmn. prep. com. European Free Trade Assn., Stockholm, 1959; chmn. Swedish trade delegations to Finland, Spain, U.K., 1954-55, to Gen. Agreement Tariffs and Trade, 1955-60; vice chmn. negotiations Free Trade Area, Paris, France, 1956-58; vice chmn. Swedish delegation European Free Trade Assn., 1960-63. Decorated knight comdr. Order North Star (Sweden); knight grand cross Iranian Order Homayoun; Portuguese Order Christ; Order Merit (Chile), numerous other decorations. Home: 3900 Nebraska Ave NW Washington DC 20016 Office: 2249 R St NW Washington DC 20008

DEBEVOISE, ELI WHITNEY, lawyer; b. N.Y.C., Dec. 14, 1899; s. Thomas M. and Anne (Whitney) D.; A.B., Yale, 1921; LL.B., Harvard, 1925; m. Barbara Clay, June 23, 1923 (div); children—Elizabeth Anne (Mrs. Harold H. Healy, Jr.), Thomas M. II; m. 2d, Agnes Holder, Feb. 2, 1966. Master, Hotchkiss Sch., Lakeville, Conn., 1921-22; admitted to N.Y. bar, 1926; asso. Davis, Polk, Wardwell, Gardiner & Reed, 1926-31; partner Debevoise, Plimpton, Lyons & Gates, and predecessors, N.Y.C., 1931—. Dir. Bank of N.Y., Bank of N.Y. Co., Inc., St. Joseph Lead Co., Westvaco Corp. Embree lectr. Yale, 1953; lectr. on German postwar devel. 1953—. Chmn. Alien Enemy Hearing Bd., N.Y.C., 1942-45; mem. Nat. Appeal Bd., 1943-45; gen. counsel Office U.S. High Commr. Germany, 1951-53, acting dep. high commr., 1952- 53; mem. N.Y. Spl. Legislative Com. on Integrity and Ethical Standards in Govt., 1954; chmn. N.Y. State Task Force on Youth and Juvenile Delinquency, 1959-60; chmn. Gov. Con. to Rev. N.Y. Laws and Procedures in Human Rights Area, 1967-68; del. Conf. on Germany and Western Europe, Bruges, 1955,

Internat. Commn. Jurists, Athens, 1955, Lagos, 1961. Rio de Janeiro, 1962, Bangkok, 1965, Geneva, 1966, Dakar, 1967, Stockholm, 1967, Strasburg, 1968. Trustee Rockefeller U., Russell Sage Found. (hon.); bd. dirs. Free Europe, Inc., N. Jersey Conservation Found., N.Y. Assn. Blind (pres. 1946-51). Served as 2d lt. F.A., U.S. Army, 1918; mem. Squadron A, N.Y. Militia, 1927-29. Mem. Assn. Bar City of N.Y., Am., N.Y. State, N.Y. County, Internat. bar assns., Am. Bar Found., Am. Law Inst., Internat. Commn. Jurists (bd. dirs., pres. Am. Assn.), Internat. Law Assn. Clubs: University (pres.), Century, Downtown Assn., Union, Yale (N.Y.C.); Metropolitan (Washington). Home: 870 United Nations Plaza New York City NY 10017 Office: 320 Park Av New York City NY 10022

DEBEVOISE, KENDALL BUSH, lawyer; b. Bklyn., Dec. 13, 1913; s. Charles L. and Marguerite R. (Bush) DeB.; B.A., Amherst Coll., 1935; LL.B., Yale, 1938; m. Elizabeth Watson, May 18, 1940; childrenKendall W., Susan W., Malcolm B. Admitted to N.Y. bar, 1938, since practiced in N.Y.C.; partner firm Breed, Abbott & Morgan, 1947—; lectr. antitrust law N.Y. Practising Law Inst. Dir. Union Camp Corp., Montclair Savs. Bank. Mem. Montclair (N.J.) Bd. Edn., 1954-57, pres., 1956- 59. Alumni trustee Amherst Coll., 1951-57, life trustee, 1959—. Mem. Am., N.Y. State (chmn. antitrust sect. 1963) bar assns., Bar Assn. City N.Y., Phi Beta Kappa. Delta Kappa Epsilon. Clubs: Wall Street, University (N.Y.C.) ; Montclair Golf. Contbr. articles to profl. jours.) Home: 58 Edgemont Rd Montclair NJ 07042 Office: 1 Chase Manhattan Plaza New York City NY 10005

DEBEVOISE, THOMAS MCELRATH, lawyer; b. N.Y.C., Aug. 10, 1929; s. Eli Whitney and Barbara (Clay) D.; B.A., Yale, 1950; LL.B., Columbia, 1954; m. Ann Taylor, Nov. 1951; childrenEli Whitney II, Albert Clay, Thomas McElrath III, Ann Elizabeth. Admitted to N.Y. bar, 1954, Vt. bar, 1957; admitted to D.C. bar, 1963; asst. U.S. Atty. So. Dist. N.Y., 1954-56; pvt. practice law, Woodstock, Vt., 1957-59; dep. atty. gen. Vt., 1959-60, atty. gen., 1960- 62; asst. gen. counsel Fed. Power Commn., 1962-64; pvt. practice law, D.C., 1964; partner Debevoise, & Liberman, Washington, 1965—. Mem. Fed. Power, Fed., Am., Vt., D.C. bar assns., Assn. Bar City N.Y., Phi Delta Phi. Republican. Episcopalian Mason. Clubs: Lakota, National Lawyers Century, City Tavern. Home: 3411 Volta Pl NW Washington DC 20007 Office: Shoreham Bldg Washington DC 20005.

DE BILLY, GILLES, lawyer; b. Levis, Que., Can., Apr. 4, 1920; B.A., Laval U., 1939, LL.L., 1942. Admitted to Que. bar, 1942; partner firm Gagnon, de Billy, Cantin & Dionne. Mem. Canadian, Que. bar assns. Office: 100 d'Youville Quebec 4 Quebec Canada*

DE BILLY, JACQUES, lawyer; b. Levis, Que., Can., June 25, 1916; LL.L., Laval U., 1938. Admitted to Que. bar, 1938; partner firm Gagnon, de Billy, Cantin & Dionne, Que. Mem. Que., Canadian bar assns., Fedn. Ins. Counsel. Office: 100 d'Youville Quebec 4 Quebec Canada*

DE BLIJ, HARM JAN, educator; b. Schiedam, Netherlands, Oct. 9, 1935; s. Hendrik and Nelly (Erwich) de B.; B.Sc., U. Witwatersrand (Johannesburg, S.Africa), 1955; M.A., Northwestern U., 1957, Ph.D., 1959; m. Katherine Ruth Powers, Dec. 27, 1964; children—Tanya Powers, Hugh James. Lectr., U. Natal Pietermaritzburg, S.Africa, 1959-60; asst. prof. Northwestern U., Evanston, Ill., 1960-61; from asst. prof. to prof. and asso. dir. African Studies Center, Mich. State U., East Lansing, 1961-68; prof., chmn. dept. geography U. Miami, Coral Gables, Fla., 1968—; author TV series on Africa, 1962-67. Cons. publishers, govt. agys. Fellow, Northwestern U. African studies program, 1958-59. Fellow African Studies Assn., Am. Geog. Soc.; mem. Orgn. for Tropical Studies (bd. dirs. 1971—), Assn. Am. Geographers (councillor 1970—, steeing com. Southeastern div. 1971—), Nat. Council for Geographic Edn. (officer 1970—), Miami Geog. Soc. (exec. bd. 1970—), Sigma Xi. Author: Africa South, 1962; Dar es Salaam: a Study in Urban Geography, 1963; A Geography of Subsaharan Africa, 1964; Systematic Political Geography, 1967; Mombasa: an African City, 1968; Geography: Regions and Concepts, 1971. Editor: The Jour. of Geography, 1970—. Home: 4850 Biltmore Dr Coral Gables FL 33146

DE BLOOM, CARL GEORGE, Jr., newspaper editor; b. Columbus, O., Jan. 25, 1918; s. Carl George and Elizabeth (Jones) DeB.; ed. pub. schs.; m. Betty Jane Ayres, Jan. 25, 1940; 1 son, Gary G. Mem. Staff Columbus Dispatch, 1936—, chief Washington bur., 1960-66, mng. editor, 1966-68, exec. mng. editor, 1968-69, exec. editor, 1969—; dir. Dispatch Printing Co.; pres. of Dispatch Features, Inc. Trustee, v.p. Dispatch Charities. Served to 2d lt., inf. Aus, 1943-45. Mem. Sigma Delta Chi. Methodist. Home: 7836 Riverside Dr Dublin OH 43017 Office: 34 S 3d St Columbus OH 43215.

DEBOCK, FLORENT ALPHONSE, home bldg. co. exec.; b. LaLouviere, Belgium, Feb. 3, 1924; s. Benoit and Elvire (Verbeke) DeB.; Tchr. diploma, Inst. Ste. Marie, Arlon, Belgium, 1944; Accountant diploma, Inst. Prefessionel Superieur de Belgigue, 1953; postgrad. La Salle Extension U., Chgo., 1956; m. Mary C. Murray, July 2, 1960; 1 son, Mark Steven. Came to U.S., 1954, naturalized, 1959. Govt. auditor U.S. Army Audit Agy., Engr. Procurement Center, Europe, 1946-54; auditor Touche, Ross, Bailey & Smart, N.Y.C., 1954-61; controller Armor Elevator Co. and affiliates, Queens, N.Y., 1962-64; controller subsidiary of Eaton, Yale & Towne, Dusseldorf, Germany, 1964-67; group controller bus. furnishings group Litton Industries, N.Y.C., 1967-68; controller Levitt & Sons, homebuilding div. Internat. Tel. & Tel. Co., Lake Success, N.Y., 1969—. Served with inf., Belgian Army, 1945-46. Decorated War of 1940-45 Commemorative medal, 1940-45 Vol. medal. C.P.A., D.C. Mem. Am. Inst. C.P.A.'s, N.Y. State Soc. C.P.A.'s, Nat. Assn. Accountants, ITT Exec. Assn. Democrat. Roman Catholic. Home: 9102 Colonial Rd Brooklyn NY 11209 Office: Lakeville Rd Lake Success NY 11403

DE BOER, SACO RIENK, city planner, landscape architect; b. The Netherlands, Sept. 7, 1883; s. Rienk Kornelis and Asselina (Rinsma) De B.; student Engring. Inst., The Netherlands, 1900-03; spl. studies in Germany, 1903-05, and in Eng., 1922; m. Anna Sophie Elizabeth Koster, Feb. 24, 1910; children—Elizabeth Thelma, Richard James. Came to U.S., 1908, naturalized, 1914. Engaged in engring., Colo., 1909-10; landscape architect for numerous instns., pvt. estates, subdivs. and schs. landscape architect and city planning cons., Denver, 1910—; city planning cons., Boulder, Colo., 1928—; city planning for Greeley, Colo., Johnstown, Colo., Grand Junction, Colo., Albuquerque, Cheyenne, Wyo., 1927-34, Englewood, Colo., Sidney, Neb., Las Cruces, N.M.; studies for Douglas and Arapahoe counties, Colo.; regional plan, Grand Junction, 1928, Denver, 1930; cons., planner State of Wyo., 1927-34; Boulder City nr. Hoover Dam, U.S. Bur. Reclamation, 1930-31; cons. planner for Dept. Agr., 1928-32; Nat. Park Service, 1933; cons. Casper (Wyo.) Mountain Park System; state planner Nat. Resources Bd., N.M., Wyo. and Utah, 1934—; studies for Ogden, Utah, Provo, Utah, Salt Lake City, 1942-43; city plans for Aurora, Golden, Boulder, Greenwood Village, Cherry Hills Village (Colo.), Moscow, Ida.; park system, Colorado Springs, Colo.; city plans Brainerd, Minn., Scottsbluff, Neb., Idaho Falls, Ida., Grand Island, Neb., Trinidad, Colo., Glenwood Springs, Colo., Glendive, Mont., Bozeman, Mont.; mil. posts at Fort Bliss, Tex., White Sands Proving Grounds and Holliman Air Base, New Mexico Park and Recreation Plan for Ft. Collins, Colo.; Central Bus. Dist. Plan Ft. Collins; city plans Carriczo, N.M., Arvada, Colo., Kimball, Neb.; landscape plan Interstate Highway Number 70 (Colo.). Fellow Am. Soc. Landscape Architects; mem. Colo. State Planning Bd., Colo. Soc. Engrs. (life), Am. Inst. Planners (pres. Colo.), A.I.A. (hon.), Am. Soc. Planning Ofcls. (hon.), Am. Inst. City Planning, Netherlands Inst. for City Planning and housing. Clubs: Rotary (Denver); Netherlands-America Found. (N.Y.); 100,000 Miles by Air Club. Author: Studies in City Planning-Shopping Districts; Around the Seasons. Contbr. to jours. Home: 501 E Iliff Av Denver CO 80210 Office: 515 E Iliff Av Denver CO 80210

DEBOLT, ORVILLE LAWRENCE, former found. exec.; b. Barry County, Mich., Apr. 9, 1908; s. Wesley C. and Edith (Warren) DeB.; m. Maxine A. McNames, Sept. 14, 1932; children—Barbara A. (Mrs. William Herberg), Robert. With W.K. Kellogg Found., Battle Creek, Mich., 1939-70, asst. sec., 1955-70, treas., 1954- 70. Conglist. (v.p. bd., chmn. finance com. 1962—). Mason (32), Rotarian. Home: 39 Lakeside Dr Battle Creek MI 49015 Office:

DE BONVOISIN, BARON PIERRE, banker; b. Verviers, Belgium, Nov. 23, 1903; s. Paul and Cecile (Modera) B.; Docteur En Droit, 1926; C.R.B. fellow, Princeton and Harvard, 1927- 29; m. Elisabeth Galopin, July 26, 1933; children—Marie-Cecile (Countess Herve d'Ursel), Pierre-Alexandre, Benoit, Marie-Francoise. With Nat. City Bank of N.Y., Brussels, Belgium, 1929-34; head legal dept. Bangue Belge pour l'Etranger, Brussels, 1934-35; charge de mission Nat. Bank of Belgium, 1935-38; joint mgr. Inst. de Reescompte et de Garantie, 1935-38; mem. mng. com. Banque de la Societe Ger Banque de la Societe Generale de Belgique, Brussels, 1938-44, mng. dir., 1944-46, vice chmn. bd., 1946- 51, chmn. 1951-63, hon. chmn., 1963-; hon. chmn. Belgian-Am. Banking Corp., Belgian Am. Bank and Trust Co., Banque Belge, Ltd., London, Banque Belge (Far East), Banque du Congo; chmn. Banque Italo-Belge, Cie Immobiliere de Belgique, Credit Foncier de Belgique, Credit Foncier International; prof. money and banking U. Louvain (Belgium). Decorated comdr. Ordre Equestre de. St. Gregoire le Grand, officer Order of Leopold, Order Royal du Lion, chevalier Order de la Couronne Order Au merite de la Republique Italienne, Order du Cedre de Liban; grand officer Ordre Equestre du Saint Sejulere de Jerusalem; recipient Medaille Commemorative de la Guerre, 1940-45. Home: 30 Blvd St Michel Brussels Belgium Office: 3 Montagne du Paro Brussels Belgium

DE BORCHGRAVE, ARNAUD, editor lectr.; b. Brussels, Belgium, Oct. 26, 1926; s. Count Baudouin and Audrey (Townshend) de B.; student Maredsous, Belgium, 1936-39, King's Sch., Canterbury, Eng., 1940-42; m. Dorothy Solon, Apr. 1950; 1 son, Arnaud; m. 2d, Eileen Ritschel, Mar. 31, 1959; 1 dau., Trisha; m. 3d, Alexandra D. Villard, May 10, 1969. Free- lance writer Eastern Europe, 1946-47; staff United Press, Western Europe, 1947-51, mgr. Benelux Countries, 1949-51; European Corr. Newsweek, Paris, North Africa, Middle East, Indo-China War, 1951-54, asso. editor fgn. reports, N.Y.C., 1954-55, gen. editor, fgn. editor, 1955, sr. editor, 1955-59, chief fgn. corr., 1959-62, mng. editor internat. edits., 1962-63, chief Newsweek Corr., 1964-. Served with Brit. Royal Navy, 1942-46. Decorated Medaille Maritime Belge. Clubs: Racquet and Tennis; Overseas Press; Traveller's (London, Eng.); Federal City (Washington). Home: 270 Park Av New York City NY 10022 Office: 444 Madison Av New York NY 10022

DEBRAH, EBENEZER MOSES, diplomat; b. Koforidua, Ghana, July 9, 1928; s. Moses Kwasi and Mary (Osei) D.; B.A., U. Ghana, 1954; LL.D., Wilberforce U., 1969, Cedar Crest Coll., 1970, Benedict Coll., 1971; m. Teresa Baffoe, Aug. 7, 1956; children—Kofi, Stella, Yaw, Kwasl. Tutor, Abuakwa State Coll., Kibi, Ghana, 1951; asst. publs. officer Dept. Information Services, 1954- 55; asst. sec. Dept. Def. and External Affairs, 1955-57; 1st sec. embassy Ghana, Liberia, 1957-59, Cairo, Egypt, 1959-60; counsellor embassy Ghana, Washington, 1960-62; dir. Asia and Middle East affairs Ministry Fgn. Affairs, Accra, 1962-63; A.E. and P. of Ghana to Ethiopia, 1963-67, to U.S., 1967—. Mem. Ghana delegation African Summit Meeting, Orgn. African Unity, 1963; leader Ghana delegation First Meeting Transp. and Communications Commn., 1964; Ghana chief del. Commn. of Refugees, 1964; leader Ghana delegation 2d Meeting Def. Commn., 1965; mem. Ghana delegation 2d Summit Meeting, Accra, 1965; chmn. com. legal experts to draw up draft conv. relating to status refugees in Africa, 1966; mem. 3d Summit Meeting, Addis Ababa, 1966; leader 8th Session UN Econ. Commn. for Africa, Lagos, 1967; leader 8th session Council Ministers, 1967; mem. Inaugural Meeting Econ. Community W. Africa, Interim Council Ministers, 1967. Home: 2929 Benton Pl NW Washington DC 20008 Office: 2460 16th St NW Washington DC 20009

DEBRAY, REGIS, author Border; Young Man in the Know; Essays on Latin America; Revolution in the Revolution: Armed and Political Struggle in Latin America. Address: care Grove Press 80 University Pl New York City NY 10003*

DEBRE, MICHEL JEAN PIERRE, French govt. ofcl.; b. Paris, Jan. 15, 1912; s. Robert Debre and Mlle. Debat-Ponsan; student Lycee, Paris; grad. Cavalry Sch., Saumur; LL.D., diploma Ecole Libre des Sciences Politiques; m. Anne-Marie Lemaresquier, 1936; children—Vincent, Francois, Jean-Louis, Bernard. Apptd. magistrate Council of State, 1934; sec.-gen. Commn. for Customs, 1937; mem. staff minister finances, 1938; spl. commr. Republic for Angers region, 1944-45; charge reform pub. functions cabinet pres. Provisional Govt. (de Gaulle), 1945-46; sec.-gen. German and Austrian affairs Fgn. Ministry, 1947; mem. Senate for Indre-et-Loire, 1948, 55; minister of justice De Gaulle Cabinet, 1958; premier of France, 1959-62; elected deputy La Reunion, 1963-66, 67-68; minister of economy and finance, 1966; minister fgn. affairs, 1968-69; minister nat. def., 1969—. Served from lt. to maj., cav., French Army, 1939-44; mem. Franch Resistance, 1940. Decorated Legion of Honor, Croix de Guerre, Rosette of Resistance, Medal of Escaped Prisoners. Roman Catholic. Author books on govt. Address: Palais-Bourbon Paris France

DE BREMAECKER, JEAN-CLAUDE, educator; b. Antwerp, Belgium, Sept. 2, 1923; s. Paul J.C. and Berthe (Bouché) De B.; came to U.S., 1948, naturalized, 1963; M.S. in Mining Engring., U. Louvain (Belgium), 1948; M.S. in Geology, La. State U., 1950; Ph.D. in Geophysics, U. Cal. at Berkeley, 1952; m. Arlene Ann Parker, Nov. 29, 1952; childrenChristine, Suzanne. Research scientist, sr. research scientist Inst. pour la Recherche Sci. in Afrique Centrale, Bukavu, Congo, 1952-58; Boese postdoctoral fellow Columbia, 1955-56; postdoctoral fellow Harvard, 1958-59; faculty Rice U., Houston, 1959—, prof. geophysics, 1965-; parttime with br. astrogeology U.S. Geol. Survey, Flagstaff, Ariz., 1964—. Research asso. U. Cal. at Berkeley, 1966, Chmn., Citizens for McCarthy, Houston, 1968; mem. Houston com. to End the War in Vietnam; Ams. for Democratic Action. Served with Belgian Army, 1944-45. Mem. Am. Geophys. Union. Seismol. Soc. Am., Soc. Exploration Geophysicists, Internat. Assn. Seismology and Physics of Earth's Interior (asso. sec. gen. 1963—), UN Assn, Houston (dir.); Houston Council Human Relations, Am. Civil Liberties Union. Unitarian. Home: 2506 Addison St Houston TX 77025

DE BRETTEVILLE, CHARLES, banker; b. San Francisco, Mar. 11, 1913; s. A. and Clarisse (Lyons) de B.; A.B., Stanford, 1934; postgrad. Harvard Sch. Bus. Adminstrn., 1936; m. Frances Mein, June 28, 1938; children—Leslie (Mrs. Hall), Peter, Frances (Mrs. Edward McC. Blair), Charles. Pres., dir. Spreckels Sugar Co., San Francisco, 1951-62; Spreckels Cos., 1949-62; pres., dir. Bank of Cal., San Francisco, 1962-67, pres., chief exec. officer, 1963-70; chmn., chief exec. officer, 1970—; dir. Shell Oil Co., Western Union Telegram Co., Safeway Stores, Inc., Pacific Gas & Electric Co., Amfac, Ridder Publs. Served from lt. to lt. comdr., USNR, 1942-46. Clubs: Cypress Point; Pacific Union; San Francisco Golf; Burlingame Country; California (Los Angeles); Brook, Links (N.Y.C.). Home: Canada Rd Woodside Redwood City CA 94062 Office: 400 California St San Francisco CA 94104

DEBREU, GERARD, educator, economist; b. Calais, France, July 4, 1921; s. Camille and Fernande (Decharne) D.; student Ecole Normale Supérieure, Paris, France, 1941-44, Agrége de L'Universite, 1946; D. Sc., U. Paris, 1956; m. Francoise Bled, June 14, 1945; children—Chantal, Florence. Came to U.S., 1950. Research asso. Centre Nat. De La Recherche Sci., Paris, 1946-48; Rockefeller fellow, U.S., Sweden and Norway, 1948-50; research asso. Cowles Commn., U. Chgo., 1950-55; asso. prof. econs. Cowles Found., Yale, 1955-60; fellow Center Advanced Study Behavioral Scis., 1960-61; vis. prof. econs. Yale, fall 1961; prof. econs. U. Cal. at Berkeley, 1962—; Guggenheim fellow, vis. prof. Center Operations Research and Econometrics, U. Louvain 1968-69; Erskine fellow U. Canterbury, summer 1969. Served with French Army, 1944-45. Fellow Am. Acad. Arts and Scis., Econometric Soc. (v.p. 1969-70); mem. Am. Econ. Assn. Author: Theory of Value, 1959. Asso. editor Internat. Econ. Rev., 1959- 69. Home: 267 Gravatt Dr Berkeley CA 94705

DE BROCA, PHILIPPE CLAUDE ALEX, film producer; b. Paris, Mar. 15, 1933; s. Yvor and Suzanne (Barrault) de B.; ed. Ecole nationale de photographie et de cinèmatographie; m. Michèle Heurtaux, Dec. 21, 1961. Formerly asst. to film execs. including Henri Decoin, Georges Lacombe, Claude Chabrol, Francois Truffaut; film producer, 1959-; motion pictures include Cartouche, The Man from Rio, The Five Day Lover, The Love Game, Male Companion. Home: 29 rue Victor-Hugo Carréres-sur-Seine, France. Office: Sociêt Andrè Bernheim 55 avenue George-V Paris 8e, France.*

DE BROGLIE, LOUISE VICTOR PIERRE RAYMOND, French physicist; b. Dieppe, France, Aug. 15, 1892; s. Victor and Pauline (d'Armaille) de B.; Baccalaureat, Sorbonne U., Paris, 1909; license in sci., U. Paris, 1913, Docteur es Sciences, 1924. Lectr. faculty scis. U. Paris 1926-28, prof. theoretical physics Henri Poincare Inst., 1928-, founder center of studies in applied mathematics, 1943; established concept of connection between particles and waves known as de Broglie wave length, 1923, established theory of photon, 1943. Counselor French High Commn. Atomic Energy, 1945. Served with radio- telegraph br., French Engring. Corps, 1913-19. Decorated Albert I Grand Prize of Monaco, 1932, also Order Leopold of Belgium; recipient Nobel prize in physics, 1929, Henri Poincare medal Academie des Sciences, 1929, Kalinga prize, 1952, grand prize Soc. Engrs. of France, 1953. Mem. Academie des Sciences (sec. 1942-), Academic Francaise, Institut France, Royal Soc. (London). Author: Matter and Light, 1946; The Revolution in Physics, A Non-Mathematicla Survey of Quanta, 1953. Home: 94 rue Perronet 11 rue Peirre Curie Paris Ve, France*

DE BRUYN, PETER PAUL HENRY, anatomist, educator; b. Amsterdam, Holland, July 28, 1910; s. Henry and Marianne (van den Nieuwenhuysen) DeB.; M.D., U. Amsterdam, 1938, Stokvis fellow, 1938; m. Jeannette Meershock, Sept. 6, 1931; children—Anneke, Yolande. Came to U.S., 1941, naturalized, 1947. Asst. in histology Histological Lab., U. of Amsterdam, 1936-39; instr. anatomy U. Chgo., 1941, successively asst. and asso. prof., prof., 1952—, chmn. dept., 1946-61. Served as med. officer, Dutch Army, 1939-40. Fellow A.A.A.S.; mem. Am. Assn. Anatomists, Am. Soc. Naturalists, Inst. Med., Am. Soc. Zoologists, Internat. Soc. Cell Biology. Club: Quadrangle. Author articles in profl. jours. Home: 5201 S Cornell Av Chicago IL 60615

DEBRUYN, PHILIP LOUIS, educator; b. George, Republic S. Africa, May 7, 1921; B.S., U. Stellenbosch, 1940, M.S., 1944; Sc.D., Mass. Inst. Tech., 1952; m. Johanna W. Kamerling, Dec. 7, 1953; childrenLillian A., Karen L., Lucia J., Eric C. H. Came to U.S., 1945, naturalized, 1954. Asst. prof. mineral engring. Mass. Inst. Tech., Cambridge, 1949-56, asso. prof., 1956-62, prof. metallurgy, 1962-. Mem. Am. Inst. Mining and Metall. Engrs., Am. Chem. Soc., Sigma Xi. Home: 71 Moore Rd Wayland MA 01778 Office: 77 Massachusetts Av Cambridge MA 02139

DE BRUYN KOPS, JULIAN, lawyer; b. Savannah, Ga., Nov. 9, 1908; s. Julian and May (Woodberry) de B.K.; A.B., Harvard, 1929, LL.B., 1932; m. Mary Virginia Thompson, July 1, 1939; children—Julianna, Virginia, Julian III. Admitted to Md. bar. 1932, Ohio bar, 1946; practice of law, Balt., 1932-41, also service with U.S. Govt., 1934-35; counsel Dayton Power & Light Company, Dayton, Ohio, 1946-69, now general counsel, since 1969—. Served with AUS, 1941-36. Mem. Am., Ohio, Dayton bar assns. Clubs: Lawyers, Engineers (Dayton). Home: 3 Forrer Blvd Dayton 19 OH Office: 25 N Main St Dayton 1 OH

DEBUS, ALLEN GEORGE, educator; b. Chgo., Aug. 16, 1926; s. George Walter William and Edna Pauline (Schwenneke) D.; B.S., Northwestern U., 1947; A.M., Ind. U., 1949; Ph.D., Harvard, 1961; postgrad. U. Coll. London (Eng.), 1959- 60; m. Brunilda Lopez-Rodriguez, Aug. 25, 1951; children—Allen Anthony George, Richard William, Karl Edward. Research chemist Abbott Labs., North Chicago, Ill., 1951-56; asst. prof. U. Chgo., 1961-65, asso. prof. history, 1965-68, prof., 1968-. Social Sci. Research Council fellow, 1959-60; Fulbright fellow, 1959-60; Fels Found. fellow, 1960-61; Guggenheim fellow, 1966-67; overseas fellow Churchill Coll., Cambridge (Eng.) U., 1966-67, 69; research grantee Am. Philos. Soc., 1961-62, NIH, 1962-70, NSF, 1961-63, 71—, Am. Council Learned Socs., 1966, 70, 71. Mem. History Sci. Soc. (mem. council 1962-65), Soc. Study Alchemy and Early Chemistry (mem. council 1967—), Am. Assn. for History Medicine, Brit. Soc. for History Sci., Internationale Paracelsus Gesellschaft, Am. Chem. Soc. (asso. mem. history of chemistry div., exec. com. 1969—), A.A.A.S., Renaissance Soc., Am. Soc. Med. History of Chgo. (mem. council), Am. Hist. Assn.; corr. mem. Académie Internat. d'Histore de la Médicine. Author: The English Paracelsians, 1965, 66; (with Robert P. Multhauf) Alchemy and Chemistry in the 17th Century, 1966; The Chemical Dream of the Renaissance, 1968; Science and Education in the 17th Century, 1970. Editor: World Who's Who in Science from Antiquity to the Present, 1968; editor reprint: Theatrum Chemicum Britannicum Britannicum (1962), 1967. Contbr. articles profl. jours. Patentee in field. Home: 85 Bent Creek Ridge Deerfield IL 60015 Office: Dept of History U Chgo Chicago IL 60637

DEBUS, KURT HEINRICH, govt. ofcl.; b. Frankfort Main, Germay, Nov. 29, 1908; s. Heinrich P.J. and Melly (Graulich) D.; M.S. in Elec. Engring., Darmstadt (Germany) Tech. U., 1936, Ph.D. in Elec. Engring., 1939; LL.D., Rollins Coll., 1967; m. Irmgard Helene

Brueckmann, June 30, 1937; childrenUte, Sigrid (Mrs. William R. Northcutt). Came to U.S., 1945, naturalized, 1959. Assistant professor elec. engineering Darmstadt Tech. U., 1939-42; test engr., later flight test dir. Peenemuende Rocket Center, 1942-45; dep. dir. guidance and control div., later staff asst. to Wernher von Braun rocket research and devel. div., U.S. Army Ordnance, 1945-52; dir. missile firing lab. Army Ballistic Missile Agy., 1952-60; dir. Launch Operations Center, NASA, 1960-63, John F. Kennedy Space Center, NASA, 1963—, member of management council Office Manned Space Flight, 1962—, mem. sr. council Office Space Sci., 1962; Recip. Exceptional Civilian Service award, 1959; Frank A. Scott Gold Medal award, Am. Ordnance Assn., 1964; NASA Outstanding Leadership award, 1964; Pioneer Windrose award, Order Diamond, 1965; AAS Space Flight award, 1968; Career Service award Nat. Civil Service League, 1969; Distinguished Service Medal NASA, 1969, Apollo Achievement award, 1969; Americanism medal D.A.R., 1969; Nat. Space Hall of Fame, 1969; Achievement award Interagy. Data Exchange Program, 1969. Fellow Am. Inst. Aeros. and Astronautics; mem. Am. Ordnance Assn. (life), Nat. Geog. Soc., Brit. Interplanetary Soc. (adv. bd. 1968), German Soc. Rocket Tech. and Space Flight (hon.), Hermann Oberth Gesellschaft (hon.), Deutsche Gesellschaft fur Raketentechnikünd Raumfahrt (hon.), Instrument Soc. Am. (hon.), M.B.L.S. (adv.). Home: 100 North Riverside Dr Patrick AFB, FL Office: Kennedy Space Center, FL

DEBUSK, MANUEL CONRAD, lawyer, coll. trustee; b. Grosvenor, Tex., June 13, 1914; s. Elias C. and Ollie (Lewis) DeB.; B.A., Tex., Technol. Coll., 1933; LL.B., So. Meth. U., 1941; m. Edith Mann, June 13, 1941. Admitted to Tex. bar, 1942, adminstrv. asst. FHA, Washington, Dallas, 1934-41; spl. agt. FBI, 1941-46; prtner DeBusk & DeBusk, Dallas, 1946—. Chmn. bd. Debusk Corp.; pres. Fairfield Housing Corp., Lincoln Housing Corp., Tex. Mortgage Liquidation Corp.; v.p. Teeling Mortgage Co., Inc., Trinity Mortgage Co. of Dallas, Killeen Savs. & Loan Assn., Waco Savs. & Loan Assn. Mem., chmn. coordinating bd. Tex. Colls. and Univs., 1969—. Exec. sec. Dallas County Democratic Party, 1955-63. Bd. dirs., chmn. bd. trustees Tex. Technol. Coll., 1959-65. Mem. Am., Tex. bar assns., Tex., Nat. mortgage bankers assns., Nat. Lefthanded Golf Assn. (past pres.), Cosmopolitan Internat. (past internat. pres.). Home: 7365 Elmridge Dr Dallas TX 75240 Office: 1st Nat Bank Bldg Dallas TX 75202

DEBUSK, ROGER WOODSON, hosp. adminstr.; b. Winfield, Kan., Jan. 28, 1908; s. Burchard W. and Sarah M. (Druley) DeB.; B.A., U. Ore., 1929, M.D., 1933; m. Mary L. Stauffer, Apr. 5, 1952; chilren by previous marriage—Susan (Mrs. Larry Johnson), Paul W., Sarah (Mrs. Wayne Hill). Intern U. Wis. Gen. Hosp., 1933-34, chief resident, 1934-39; asst. dir. St. Luke's Hosp., N.Y.C., 1939-41; dir. Evanston (Ill.) Hosp., 1941-49, Samuel Merritt Hosp., Oakland, Cal., 1952-54, Grace Hosp., Detroit, 1954-. Chmn. adv. bd. Mich. Bd. Nursing, 1965-66; trustee Mich. Med. Service, 1959-65. Mem. Soc. Med. Adminstrs., Sigma Nu, Nu Sigma Nu. Home: 123 Cloverly Rd Grosse Pointe Farms MI 48236 Office: Grace Hosp 4160 John R St Detroit MI 48201

DEBUTTS, HARRY ASHBY, retired business exec.; b. Delaplane, Va., Oct. 13, 1895; s. Dulany F. and Emma Virginia (Ashby) de Butts; B.S., Virginia Military Institute, Lexington, 1916; m. Margaret Ross Blair, June 7, 1922 (dec.); 1 dau., Frances Van Meter (Mrs. George M. Page); m. 2d Mary Moore Glascock, Mar. 7, 1956. With Southern Railway System since July 6, 1916, beginning as student apprentice, became track supervisor, Strasburg, Va., 1919, trainmaster, Sheffield, Ala., 1921, div. supt., Selma, Ala., 1924, same, Macon, Ga., Alexandria, Va., Greensboro, N.C., 1924-29; gen. supt., Danville, Va., 1930, gen. mgr., Charlotte, N.C., 1934, v.p. in charge operation, Washington, 1937, pres., dir. 1952-62, chairman of bd., 1962-63; director of the Southern Railway, also Woodward & Lothrop, Inc., Washington, Riggs Nat. Bank, Washington. Mem. exec. com. Virginia Historical Society; member exec. com. Geo. C. Marshall Research Found. Served as 1st lt. USMC, World War. Mem. Va. Hist. Soc. (exec. com.), Kappa, Alpha, Episcopalian. Mason. Clubs: Chevy Chase, Metropolitan (Washington); Commonwealth (Richmond, Va.). Home: Upperville VA

DEBUTTS, JOHN DULANY, telephone co. exec.; b. Greensboro, N.C., Apr. 10, 1915; s. Sydnor and Mary Ellen (Cutchin) deB.; B.S. in Elec. Engring., Va. Mil. Inst., 1936; LL.D., Knox Coll., 1966, Northwestern U., 1966; LL.D., Loyola U., Chgo., 1967; m. Gertrude Willoughby Walke, Nov. 4, 1939; children—Gertrude (Mrs. Tyler Cain), Mary (Mrs. R. Collins Couch). With Chesapeake & Potomac Telephone Co., 1936-49, 51-55, 59-62, v.p. operating and engring., dir., 1959-62; with Am. Tel.&Tel. Co., N.Y.C., 1949-51, 55-57, asst. v.p. govt. relations, Washington, 1957-58; gen. mgr. N.Y. Telephone Co., 1958-59; pres., dir. Ill. Bell Telephone Co., 1962-66; exec. v.p. Am. Tel.&Tel. Co., N.Y.C., 1966-67, vice chmn. bd. dirs., 1967--; dir. Southwestern Bell Telephone Co., N.Y. Telephone Co., Sears Roebuck & Co., 1st Nat. City Bank N.Y., Kraftco Corp. Chmn. bd. Nat. Jr. Achievement, 1967—. Hon. trustee Chicago Mus. Sci. and Industry; mem. bd. visitors Va. Mil. Inst.; hon. life mem. bd. lay trustees Loyola U., Chgo.; trustee Joint Council on Econ. Edn. Mem. O.R.C., 1936-39, U.S. N.G., 1939-40. Recipient Silver Beaver award Boy Scouts Am., 1965; silver plaque Nat. Conf. Christians and Jews, 1966. Mem. Western Soc. Engrs., Armed Forces Communications and Electronics Assn., Navy League U.S., Kappa Alpha, Beta Gamma Sigma (hon.). Republican. Episcopalian. Clubs: Chicago, Commercial (Chgo.); Old Elm (Ft. Sheridan, Ill.); Princess Anne Country (Virginia Beach, Va.); Metropolitan (Washington); Economic, University (N.Y.C.); Commonwealth (Richmond, Va.); Links. Home: 200 E 66th St New York City NY 10021 Office: 195 Broadway New York City NY 10007

DE CAPRILES, MIGUEL lawyer; b. Mexico City, Mexico, Nov. 30, 1906; s. Abraham M. and Cristina Treserra de C.; came to U.S., 1920, naturalized, 1932; B.S. cum laude, New York U., 1927, A.M., 1931, J.D., 1935; also post-grad. work law; m. Dorothy Hafner, Sept. 22, 1938; children—Thomas, Cristina (Mrs. James P. Carney). Adminstrv. officer, N.Y.U., 27-42, mem. faculty econs. dept., 1928-42, on leave of absence, 1942-45, mem. law faculty 1945—, dir. Inter-Am. Law Inst., 1947-57, asso. dean Law Sch., 1948-63, vice dean, 1963-64, dean, 1964-67, v.p., sec., gen. counsel univ., 1967—, dir. office instnl. research and ednl. planning, 1953-56; vis. prof. U. Cla., 1949, Stanford, 1950. Admitted to N.Y. bar, 1936, U.S. Supreme Ct. bar, 1964; counsel to bd. trustees, Hofstra Coll., 1936-38; spl. asst. to atty. gen., war div., U.S. Dept. Justice, 1942-45. Cons. N.Y. Joint Legislative Com. Study Revision Corp. Laws, 1959—; treas. Inst. Jud. Adminstrn. 1952—. Active in amateur fencing, U.S. Olympic Coms. mem. U.S. Olympic and Internat. Teams, 1932-51; winner of several nat. championships, 1931-47; pres. Amateur Fencers League of Am., 1949-53; asso. counselor Fedn. Internationale d'Escrime, 1961-64; mem. exec. com. Pan Am. Sports Orgn., 1967—. Decorated comdr. Ordre du Mérite Sportif (France); recipient Alumni Meritorious Service award N.Y.U., 1938. Fellow Consular Law Soc.; mem. Assn. Bar City N.Y., Am., Inter-Am. N.Y. State bar Assns., Internat. Law Assn., Am. Soc. Internat. Law, Am. Econ. Assn., Am. Acad. Polit. and Social Sci., N.Y. County Lawyers Assn., Am. Fgn. Law Assn., Am. Assn. Comparative Study of Law (pres. 1960-65), Phi Beta Kappa Assos. Clubs: Century, New York University, Fencers. Co-author: New York University Self Study, 1956; author Modern Financial Accounting, 1962. Contbr. econ. and legal publs. Home: 37 Washington Sq W New York City NY 10011 (summer) Wayne ME Office: 40 Washington Sq New York City NY 10012

DE CARLO, CHARLES, steel co. exec.; b. N.Y.C., Sept. 2, 1919 s. John and Bertha (Cervenka) de C.; evening student N.Y. U. Grad. Sch. Bus. Adminstrn.; m. Esther M. Nicholson, June 3, 1944; children—Deborah, (Mrs. Danel R. Thompson), Barbara, Charles, Valerie. With Reynold & Co., N.Y.C., 1936-50, security analyst, 1941-50; with Jones & Laughlin Steel Corp., 1950—, treas., 1967—. Served with AUS, 1942-45. Mem. N.Y. Soc. Security Anlysts. Republican. Episcopalian. Clubs: Duquesne, Wildwood Golf. Home: 1060 Covington Pl Allison Park PA 15101 Office: 3 Gateway Center Pittsburgh PA 15230

DE CARVALHO, ELEAZER SEGUNDO ALFONSO, orch. condr.; b. Iguatu, Ceará, Brazil, June 28, 1915; s. Manuel Alfonso and Daila (Mandonca) de C.; student City Sch. for Apprentice Seamen, Fortaleza, 1926-27, Sch for Ordinary Seamen, Angra do Reis, 1927-28; grad. Instituto Rio Branco, 1934; grad. Nat. Sch. Music, U. Brazil, 1934, diploma as condr. and composer, 1940. Tuba player, orch. of Teatro Municipal, Rio de Janeiro, condr. opera, 1942-44; mem. Brazilian Symphony Orch., permanent asst. condr., 1941—; condr. Beethoven program, sponsorship Municipal Dept. Culture, Sao Paulo, Brazil, 1945; asst. tgn. class in conducting Berkshire Music Center, 1946—; mus. dir. condr. St. Louis Symphony Orch., 1963; guest condr. Boston Symphony Orch., N.Y. Philharmonic Symphony, Cleve. Orch., Colorado Springs Symphony. Mem. Nat. Acad. Art in Brazil (permanent chair). Compositions: (opera) The Discovery of Brazil, 1939, Tiradentes, 1940; The White Symphony (premiered 1944), other chamber works. Home: Rua Alvaro Alvim 24 Rio de Janeiro Brazil Office: St Louis Symphony 812 Olive St St Louis MO*

DE CAULP, WILLIAM EDGAR, corp. lawyer; b. N. Little Rock, Ark., May 18, 1920; s. Arthur Gray and Ruth (Paine) DeC.; student Little Rock Jr. Coll., 1937-39; B.A. cum laude, U. Ark., 1948, LL.B. cum laude, 1950; m. F. Irene Kountoupis, June 29, 1946; 1 dau., Bobara Elizabeth. Admitted to Ark. bar, 1950, S.C. bar, 1951, N.Y. bar, 1956; staff atty. Dyke Assos., Inc., Little Rock, 1950; asso. atty. Talley & Owen Little Rock, 1950; asst. to gen. counsel W.Va. Pulp & Paper Co., Charleston, S.C. and N.Y.C., 1951-57; asst. counsel The Stanley Works, New Britain, Conn., 1957-60, asst. sec., 1960, asst. gen. counsel, 1960-62; counsel, asst. sec. Union Camp Corp., 1962-65; secretary, general counsel Fafnir Bearing Co., 1965—. Past chmn. Berlin (Conn.) Republican Town Com. Corporator New Britain Gen. Hosp. Served with USNR, 1942-47. Mem. Am. Bar. Assn., Phi Alpha Theta past chpt. pres.), Phi Alpha Delta, Omicron Delta Kappa (past pres. Ark.). Conglist. Home: Oxyoke Dr Kensington CT Office: 37 Booth St New Britain CT

DE CHANT, JOHN ALOYSIUS, govt. ofcl., author; b. Milw., June 21, 1917; s. John Henry and Frances Irene (McGee) De C.; Ph.B. in Journalism, Marquette U., 1939; m. Mary Elizabeth Knoernschild, May 30, 1944; children—John David, Robert Thomas, Michael Patrick, Richard Dennis, James Francis. Publicity dir. Milw. Council of Catholic Charities, 1939-40; news editor, columnist, editorial writer The New World, 1940-41; asst. dir. pub. relations Nat. Cath. Community Service, Washington, 1941-42; chief field information War Assets Adminstrn., 1946; dir. community relations Aircraft Industries Assn., Washington, 1946-47, Hill & Knowlton, Inc., N.Y.C., 1947-49; field counseling officer office small bus., ECA, Washington 1949; sr. pub. relations cons. Office Civil Def., NSRB, 1950- 51; dir. pub. affairs FCDA and adminstr. Nat. Civil Def. Pub. Edn. Program, Washington, 1951-54; exec. dir. Am. Heritage Found., N.Y.C., 1954-55; v.p. Crusade for Freedom, 1956; established pub. relations counseling firm under own name; head John A. De Chant & Assos., 1957-64; dir. information Bur. Employment Security, Dept. Labor, 1965-68; spl. asst., manpower information dir., 1969—. Mem. Nat. Def. Exec. Res., Office Emergency Planning, 1962-. Vice pres. Marine Corps War Meml. Found.; chmn. Fed. Service Overseas Fund Campaign and Washington dir. Crusade for Freedom. Served as capt. USMCR, 1942-46; PTO. Decorated Navy Ribbon with 4 battle stars; recipient Nat. Air Council fellowship, 1947; Distinguished Service award, FCDA; gold medal, Swedish Civil Def. League. Mem. Pub. Relations Soc. Am., Marine Corps Res. Officers Assn. (exec. council 1950-54), Am. Legion, Sigma Delta Chi. Club: Nat. Press (Washington). Author: (with Richard Hubler) Flying Leathernecks, 1944; Devilbirds-Marine Aviation in World War II, 1947; Modern U.S. Marine Corps, 1966. Home: 9213 Farnsworth Dr Potomac MD 20854 Office: US Dept Labor Washington DC 20525

DECHANT, TONY T., farm orgn. official; b. Munjor, Kan., June 13, 1915; s. Joseph C. and Rosa (Leiker) D.; student St. Joseph's Coll., Hays, Kan., 1930-35; m. Agnes Bailey, June 20, 1939; children—Maurice Lyle, Karen. Farming, trucking, transfer work, 1932-36; accountant auto sales co., 1936; county supr., state property officer, state payroll officer, regional property officer Nat. Youth Adminstrn., Topeka, Denver, 1937-42; accountant. Nat. Farmers Union, 1942—, pres., 1966—; chmn. bd. Nat. Farmers Union Property & Casualty Co., Nat. Farmers Union Life Ins. Co., Nat. Farmers Union Service Corp., Nat. Farmers Union Standard Ins. Co. Mem. Nat. Export Expansion Council; bd. dirs. interagy. com. on food and agr. orgn. FAO; mem. Pres.'s Com. on Employment Handicapped; trustee Am. Freedom from Hunger Found., Joint Council on Econ. Edn., v.p. CARE; mem. pub. adv. com. on U.S. Trade Policy; mem. Commn. on Agrl. Credit; mem. Adv. Com. on Overseas Coop. Devel.; chmn. Farmers Ednl. Found.; mem. Com. for Nat. Health Ins. Mem. Internat. Fedn. Agrl. Producers (exec. com.), Nat. Assembly for Social Policy and Devel. (corporate mem.). Roman Catholic. Democrat. K.C. Home: 3330 E Tennessee Av Denver CO 80209 Office: PO Box 2251 Denver CO 80201

DE CHASCA, EDMUND, educator; b. Coban, Guatamala, June 17, 1903; s. Adolf von Trzaska, and Maria (Villela) C.; came to U.S., 1919, naturalized, 1941; B.A., Wooster Coll., 1928; M.A., U. So. Cal., 1929; Ph.D., U. Chgo., 1941; m. Edith Sexton, Aug. 27, 1933; children—Daniel, Edmund. Head, modern langs. Blackburn Coll., 1930-42, Romance langs. Wittenberg, Coll., 1942-43; asst. prof. Romance Oberlin Coll., 1943-44; asso. prof. Spanish U. So. Cal., 1944-47, U. Toronto, 1947-50, U. Chicago, 1950-53; professor of Spanish literature University of Iowa, 1953—, chairman department Romance langs., 1953-67; vis. prof. U. Chgo., summers 1947-48. Guggenheim fellow, 1971. Mem. Modern Lang. Assn. Am., Am. Assn. Tchrs. Spanish, Asociacion Internacional de Hispanistas; corr. mem. Hispanic Soc. Am. Clubs: University Athletic. Author: Lope de Rueda's Comedia de los engaados, 1941; Estructura y forma en el Poema de Mio Cid; El arts Juglaresco UN el Cantar de Mio Cid; Registro de fórmulas verbales en el Cantar de Mio Cid; and numerous articles on hispanic subjects. Editor: Alarcón's Sombrero de tres picos, 1952. Office: Schaeffer Hall U of Ia Iowa City IA

DECHAZEAU, MELVIN GARDNER, educator; b. Olympia, Wash., Mar. 20, 1900; s. Melvin and Estella (Lucas) deC.; A.B., U. Wash., 1924, M.A., 1925; M.A., Harvard, 1927, Ph.D., 1930; m. Eunice Storey, June 1, 1929; 1 dau., Marian (Mrs. David R. Holmes). Prof. econs. U. Va., 1930-46; prof. marketing U. Chgo., 1946- 48; prof. Sch. Bus. and Pub. Adminstrn., Cornell U., Ithaca, N.Y., 1948- -, acting dean, 1952-53, prof. emeritus, 1970—, coordinator Exec. Devel. Program, 1955-69. Econ. adviser, dir. non-mil. div. OPM, OPACS, WPB, 1940-44; cons. ECA, 1948-49; mem. sr. staff Council Econ. Advisers, 1953-54; cons. Dept. Justice, 1965—; dir. Nat. Bur. Econ. Research, Inc., 1955-65; mem. research staff Com. Econ. Devel., 1945-48; cons. U.S. C. of C., 1960-61; Fulbright lectr., Copenhagen, 1954-55. Author: (with Daugherty and Stratton) Economics of the Iron and Steel Industry, 1937; (with A.E. Kahn) Integration and Competion in the Petroleum Industry, 1959. Editor, contbr. Regulation of Business Investment, 1954. Home: 119 The Knoll Ithaca NY 14850

DECHERD, H. BEN, newspaper exec.; b. Dallas, Mar. 14, 1915; s. Henry Benjamin and Fannie (Dealey) D.; B.A. in Govt., U. Tex., Austin, 1936; m. Isabelle Thomason, Dec. 17, 1938; children—Dealey (Mrs. H. David Herndon), Robert W. With A.H. Belo Corp., pub. Dallas Morning News, Tex. Suburban Dailies and Tex. Almanac; owner radio-TV stas. WFAA, TV sta. KFDM, Beaumont, Tex., 1936, 38—, v.p., sec., 1960-64, chmn. exec. com., 1964-68, chmn. bd., 1968—; with Balt. Sunpapers, 1937. Past pres. Family Guidance Center, Incarnation Bay Sch., S.W. Sch. Printing, St. Marks Sch. Tex.; bd. dirs. Central Bus. Dist. Assn., Dallas Zool. Soc., Dallas Symphony Orch., Southwestern Legal Found., St. Marks Sch. Tex.; trustee Dallas Hist. Soc., Tex. Research Found. Served to lt. col., inf., AUS, 1942-46. Decorated Bronze Star. Mem. Tex. Daily Newspaper Assn. (past pres.), Phi Beta Kappa, Phi Delta Theta. Episcopalian. Clubs: City, Dallas Country, Northwood, Petroleum, Idlewild (Dallas). Home: 4305 Belclaire Av Dallas TX 75205 Office: Dallas Morning News Dallas TX 75222

DECHERT, ROBERT lawyer, govt. ofcl.; b. Phila., Nov. 29, 1895; s. Henry Taylor and Virginia Louise (Howard) D.; grad. Lawrenceville (N.J.) Sch., 1912; A.B., U. Pa., 1916, LL.B., 1921, LL.D. (hon.), 1958; U.S. Army student, St. John's Coll., Oxford (Eng.) U., 1919; m. Helen Hope Wilson, May 24, 1922 (dec. Oct. 1950); children—Peter, Hope (Mrs. Michael C. Mitchell), Marion Godey (Mrs. Donald F. Dixon); m. 2d, Helen Branson, Dec. 1, 1951. Admitted to Pa. Pennsylvania bar, 1921, and began practice at Phila.; asso. Hepburn, Dechert & Norris, 1921-27; mem. faculty U. of Pa. Law Sch., 1923-42; v.p., counsel Penn Mut. Life Ins. Co., 1927-30, counsel, 1930-48, gen. counsel, 1949-56, 59-65, trustee, 1959-69; mem. Dechert, Price & Rhoads 1930—; dir. Fidelity Bank, Phila., 1932-37, 59—; gen. counsel Dept. of Def. Washington, 1957-59. Cons. Office Gen. Counsel, ECA, 1949-50; mem. Pa. Bd. Law Examiners, 1933-39, 70—. Trustee U. Pa., 1928—; mem. Bd. of Law, 1928—, chmn., 1952-56; of Libraries, 1956-65, mem. Bd. of Social Work 1945—, chmn., 1945-52, chmn. Ednl. Policy Com. 1959-67; mem. Bd. Wistar Inst. of Anatomy and Biology, 1967--; trustee Lawrenceville (N.J.) Sch., 1929--; bd. dirs. YMCA Phila., 1936—, pres. 1947-50; bd. dirs. United Fund Phila. 1930—, gen. campaign chmn. 1942; chmn. Asso. Services for Armed Forces, Inc., 1950-51; mem. bd. govs., mem. corp. U.S.O., 1951-70, chmn. exec. com., 1951-55; bd. dirs., mem. exec. com. United Def. Fund, 1951-55; chmn. J. C. Brown Library Assos., Providence, 1962-65; pres. World Affairs Council Phila. 1963-65. Served from 2d lt. inf. to capt., U.S. Army World War I. Decorated D.S.C. Mem. Am. (ho. of dels. 1948-49, 51-55), Pa. (ho. of dels. 1966-69), Phila. bar assns., Ins. Fedn. Pa. (dir., pres. 1947-49), Assn. Life Ins. Counsel (pres. 1946-47), S.R., Order of Coif, Phi Beta Kappa, Delta Psi. Coif. Republican. Episcopalian. Clubs: Philadelphia, Grolier. Contbr. articles, publs. in field of law, ins. and rare Am. books. Home: 663 Dodd's Lane Gladwyne PA 19035 Office: Three Penn Center Philadelphia PA 19102

DECHERT, W. CORNELL, corp. exec.; b. Harrisonburg, Va., Feb. 4, 1907; s. Daniel Orville and Edith Hastings (Cornell) D.; A.B., Cornell U., 1928; M.A. N.Y.U., 1935; m. Mary Jane Davis, Mar. 29, 1937; childrenMary (Mrs. Frank Goldring) (dec.), William Davis. Asst. sec., asst. treas. Tex. Gulf Producing Co., N.Y.C., 1933-37; economist Fed. Res. Bank, San Francisco, 1938-40, Dept. Commerce, 1941-42, WPR, 1942-43, Lend-Lease Adminstrn., 1943-45; central field commnr. for Africa and Middle East, Office Fgn. Liquidation, Cairo, Egypt, 1946- 47; economist Am. Mission for Ald to Greece, Athens, 1948, ECA office Spl. Rep., Paris, France, 1948-52, ECA mission to London, Eng., 1953; with Knoll Internat., Inc., N.Y.C., 1953—, pres. 1960, also dir.; pres. Art Metal Inc., Jamestown, N.Y., 1962-68, also dir.; trustee UN We Believe, Studio 95, Mem. Cornell U. Council, Cornell Club N.Y., Phi Beta Kappa, Delta Upsilon. Episcopalian. Home: Quaker Bridge Rd Croton-on-Hudson NY 10520 Office: Knoll Internat 320 Park Av New York NY 10022

DE CHIRICO, GEORGIE, artist; b. Volos, Thessaly, Greece, July 10, 1888; s. Evaristo and Gemma de Chirico; studied with pvt. art tchrs.; grad. Polytechnic Inst., Athens, 1906; student Acad. Fine Arts, Munich; m. Isabella Far. Painter townscapes, Italy and Paris; exhibited Salon des Independants, 1913; founded metaphysical school with Carlo Carra, Italy, 1917; designed sceneery and costumes, ballet and operatic prodns.; other work includes lithographs, murals, book illus., fabric designs; paintings include Melancholy, 1912, Delights of the Poet, 1913, Lassitude of the Infinite, 1913, Joye and Enigmas of a Strange Hour, 1913, Anxious Journey, 1913, The Square, 1913 (still life) Turin, Spring, 1914, Portrait of Guillaume Apollinaire, 1914, Inconsistencies of the Thinker, 1915, Hector and Andromache, 1916, Evangelical Still Life, 1917, Metsphysical Interior with Waterfall, 1918, Roman Villa and Knights, 1922, Autoritratto, 1924. Author: Gustave Courbet, 1925; Piccolo Trattatodi Technica Pittorica, 1928; (novel) Hebdomeros, 1929; (autobiography) Memorie della mia Vita, 1945; Commedia dell'arte moderna, 1945. Home: 31 Piazza di Spagna Rome, Italy

DECICCO, JOHN, educator, mathematician; b. Bklyn., Apr. 5, 1911; s. Joseph and Catherine (Riccio) DeC.; B.S., Bklyn. Coll., Coll. City N.Y., 1933; Ph.D., Columbia, 1938; m. Laura Mary Welsh, Oct. 10 1941. Tutor, instr. Bklyn. Coll., 1933-40; instr. Ill. Inst. Tech., 1940-45, asst. and asso. prof., 1945-49; vis. asso. prof. Columbia, 1946-47; prof. math., chmn. dept. DePaul U., Chgo., 1949-62; prof. math. Ill. Inst. Tech., Chgo., 1962—; reviewer Der Zentralblatt Fur Mathematik; Math. Reviews, Providence; book reviewer Math. Jour. Recipient award of honor for research Coll. City of N.Y., 1944; named to Wisdom Hall Fame, 1970. Mem. Am. Math Soc., Math. Assn. Am. (vis. lectr. 1963- 68), Tensor Soc. Japan, Sigma Xi. Author: Geometry and Dynamics, 1947; also articles. Home: 7363 S Coles Av Chicago IL 60649

DECIO, ARTHUR JULIUS, mfg. co. exec.; b. Elkhart, Ind., Oct. 19 1930; s. Julius A. and Lens (Alesia) D.; student DePaul U., 1949-50; m. Patricia George, Jan. 6, 1951; children—Terrnce, Jamie, Linda, Jay, Leigh Allison. Pres. Skyline Corp., Elkhart, 1956-59, pres., chmn. bd., 1959—; dir. St. Joseph Valley Bank, Elkhart Hotel Corp. Chmn., Elkhart County United Fund, 1966; mem. adv. council Coll. Bus. U. Notre Dame. Bd dir., past pres. Jr. Achievement Elkhart County; bd. dirs. United Community Services Elkhart County, Elkhart Urban League; trustee LaLumiere Sch., La Porte, Inc.; mem. pres.'s council Marmion Mil. Acad., Aurora. Ill. dir. Elkhart Gen. Hosp., Inc. Recipient Alumni Achievement award Marmio Mil. Acad., 1964; golden Plate award Acad. Achievement, Dallas, 1967. Mem. Young

Pres. orgn., Mobile Home Mfrs. Assn. (dir., chmn. Washington com., pres.). Roman Catholic. Elk. Home: 3215 Greenleaf Blvd Elkhart IN 46514 Office: 2520 ByPass Rd Elkhart IN 46514

DECK, ARTHUR CLARENCE, editor; b. Salt Lake City, Feb. 20, 1908; s. Jacob Conrad and Dorothea (Hegemeier) D.; student U. Utah, 1924-28; m. Winnifred Willey, Dec. 28, 1936; children—Stephanie Ann, Churchill John Willey. Exec. editor Salt Lake Tribune, Salt Lake City, 1950—; bd. dirs. Newspaper Agy. Corp. Mem. C. of C. (dir. treas.), Am. Soc. Newspaper Editors, Beta Theta Pi, Theta Tau, Sigma Delta Chi. Club: Alta (Salt Lake City). Home: 767 10th Av Salt Lake City UT 84103 Office: 143 S Main St Salt Lake City UT 84110

DECK, JOSEPH FRANCIS, educator, chemist; b. St. Louis, Mar. 19, 1907; s. Michael and Anna (Westerheide) D.; A.B., St. Louis U., 1928, M.S., 1930; Ph.D., U. Kan., 1932; m. Lillian M. Schwalbe, June 30, 1937; childrenJerry Bothe, Mary Victory, Peter Mitchel. With Stewart Inso Board Co., S. St. Joseph, Mo., 1932-36; quality supr. U.S. Gypsum co., 1936; Faculty U. Santa Clara (Cal.), 1936-, prof. chemistry, 1945-, chmn. dept., 1936-; Lectr., U. San Francisco, summers 1948, 49; research chemist Richmond Chase Co., 1940-49, Moyer Chem. Co., 1957-59, Food Machinery Corp., 1959-61. Named Chemist of Year, St. Louis U. Chemists Club, 1965. Mem. Am. Assn for Advancement Scis., Am. Chem. Soc., Inst. Good Tech. Albertus Magnus Guild, Cal. Assn. Chemistry Tchrs., Sigma Xi. Rotarian (past pres. Santa Clara). Research on organic syntheses involving heterocyclic compound, free radicals. Home: 937 Morse St San Jose, CA 95126. Office: Dept Chemistry U Santa Clara CA 95053

DECK, RAYMOND HENRY, ins. co. exec.; b. St. Louis, June 26, 1922; s. Clement H. and Emma (Grimm) D.; B.S. in Commerce magna cum laude, St. Louis U., 1948; m. Veronica Abbick, Feb. 7, 1946; children—Barbara A., Raymond Henry, Michael C., Mark J., Kevin F., Mary V. Gen. mgr. Hardware Muts., Sentry Ins. Co., Stevens Point, Wis., 1941-60, v.p. data processing, 1960-62; sr. v.p. control Am. Mut. Ins. Group, Wakefield, Mass., 1962-65; sr. v.p., comptroller Hartford Ins. Group (Conn.), 1965—; dir. Hartford Fire Ins. Co. and subsidiaries. Trustee St. Joseph Coll., W. Hartford. Served to lt. (j.g.) USNR, 1943-46. Home: 47 W Hill Dr West Hartford CT 06119 Office: Hartford Plaza Hartford CT 06115

DECKER, ALONZO GALLOWAY, Jr., mfg. co. exec.; b. Baltimore County, Md., Jan. 18, 1908; s. Alonzo Galloway and Fanny F. (Fox) D.; student Balt. Poly. Inst., 1922-26; E.E., Cornell U., 1929; m. Virginia Gent. Cons. engr., export sales dept. Black & Decker Mfg. Co., 1930, various positions mfg. divs. including engring. and research, v.p. charge mfg. and dir., 1940-54, v.p., dir., 1954-56, exec. v.p., dir. 1956-60, pres., dir. 1960-68, chief exec. officer, 1964-68, chmn. bd., pres., chief exec. officer, 1968—, also dir. subsidiary cos.; dir. AMF Inc., Monumental Life Ins. Co., Monumental Corp., First Nat. Bank Md., Western Md. Ry. Co., Balt. Gas & Electric Co., Balt. br. Fed. Res. Bank Richmond, 1952-53; dir. Fed. Res. Bank Richmond, 1954, dep. chmn., 1955-58, chmn., 1959-62. Pres. Indsl. Corp. Balt, 1956-59, dir., 1959—; chmn. Baltimore County Plan Bd., 1955-59; mem. Greater Balt. Com. chmn. Balt. County March Dimes, 1950, A.R.C., 1953; Md. Vol. State chmn. Savs. Bonds program, 1966-70. Trustee Md. Acad. Scis., Union Meml. Hosp., Johns Hopkins U.; dir. Balt. chpt. A.R.C., 1954-59. Mem. Cornell Soc. Engrs., Sigma Alpha Epsilon. Democrat. Episcopalian. Clubs: Greenspring Valley Hunt; Baltimore Country; Maryland; Union League. Home: Broadway Rd Lutherville MD 21093 Office: Towson MD 21204

DECKER, BERNARD MARTIN, U.S. dist. judge; b. Highland Park, Ill., Apr. 2, 1904; s. Martin C. and Florence (Bryant) D.; student Northwestern U., 1922-23; A.B., U. Ill., 1926; LL.B., Harvard, 1929; m. Louise Armstrong, Aug. 15, 1928; children—Janine L. (Mrs. Jack G. Collins), Martin C. II. Admitted to Ill. bar, 1929; law clk. Ralph J. Dady, 3d and 4th dists. Appellate Ct. Ill., 1938-43; gen. practice law firm Decker & Decker, Waukegan, Ill., 1929-51; judge Circuit Ct., 17th Circuit Ill., 1951-57; presiding judge, 19th Circuit, 1957-62; U.S. judge No. Dist. Ill., Chgo., 1962—. Chmn. organizing com. Ill. Jud. Conf., 1957, mem. exec. com., 1958-62, chmn. conf., 1959; exec. com. Nat. Conf. State Trial Judges, 1961-63, del., 1961, 62; mem. com. ct. administrn. U.S. Cts., 1968. Pres. bd. edn. Waukegan Twp. High Sch., 1946-49; mem. citizens com. U. Ill., 1960—. Mem. Am. Judicature Soc., Harvard Law Soc. Chgo. (pres. 1964- 65), Am., Ill., Lake County (pres. 1955) bar assns., Phi Beta Kappa, Delta Tau Delta. Home: 1500 N Sheridan Rd Waukegan IL 60085 Office: US Ct House 219 S Dearborn St Chicago IL 60604

DECKER, CHARLES LOWMAN, ret. army officer; b. Oskaloosa, Kan., Oct. 18, 1906; s. Charles Edward and Monica (Lowman) D.; student U. Kan., 1923-25; B.S., U.S. Mil. Acad., 1931; J.D., Georgetown U. 1942; LL.D., St. Edwards U. 1943, John Marshall Law Sch. 1964; m. Suzanne Marie Louise Mineraut, June 14, 1941. With Panama Canal Dept., 1934-36; instr. English and law U.S. Mil. Acad., 1936-39; commd. 2d lt. U.S. Army, 1931, advanced through grades to maj. gen., 1961; founder, 1st comdt. judge Adv. Gen.'s Sch., 1951-55; judge adv. gen. for internat. affairs, mil. affairs, mil. justice, appellate div. and legal assistance, U.S. Army, Washington, 1957-61; judge adv. gen. U.S. Army, 1961-63, ret.; dir. Nat. Defender Project, 1964-70. cons. Adminstrn. Criminal Justice, 1970—. Admitted to Kan. bar, 1942. Adviser pres.'s Commn. Law Enforcement and Adminstrn. Justice, 1966-67; adv. council Nat. Commn. Reform Fed. Criminal Law, 1967—. Mem. council progress U. Kan. Decorated D.S.M., Bronze Star, Legion of Merit. Named Outstanding Alumnus of Year Georgetown Law Center, 1961; recipient citation for distinguished service U. Kan., 1963; award for pub. service Nat. Bar Assn., 1967. Mem. Am. Bar Assn. ho. of dels., (past chmn. criminal law and legal edn.). Nat. Lawyers Club, Judge Advs. Assn. (dir.), Pi Sigma Mu, Delta Theta Phi. Presbyn. Club: Army-Navy. Co-author: Serviceman and the Law. Home: 4200 Cathedral Av NW Washington DC 20016 Office: Georgetown Law Center 506 E St NW Washington DC 20001

DECKER, DONALD GILMORE, univ. adminstr.; b. Elizabeth, Colo., Jan. 7, 1914; s. Sidney and Nellie (Gilmore) D.; B.S. Eastern Mich. U., Ypsilanti, 1935; M.A., Colo. State Coll., 1937; Ph.D., Columbia, 1943; Sc.D. (hon.), Mich. State Normal U., 1951; m. Doris Ritter, Dec. 23, 1937 (dec. 1953); 1 dau., Judith C. (Mrs. John Gilbert); m. 2d, Doris Stricklan, Mar. 14, 1955. Faculty U. No. Colo., 1937—, prof. sci. edn., 1948—, chmn. div. sci., 1948-54, dean of coll., 1955-70, provost 1970—, dean Sch. Ednl. Charge and Devel., 1971—; research asso. bur. ednl. research and sci. teaching Columbia Tchrs. Coll. 1940-43; research asso. Manhattan project, Oak Ridge, 1943-45. Mem. council instrn. Colo. Dept. Edn., 1958- -; adv. com. Colo. Com. Study Edn. Beyond High Sch.; adv. bd. Colo. Senate Com. on Edn., 1959—; mem. Sci. Materials Center, 1959—, Ednl. Policies Commn., 1960—; adv. bd. Products Design Co., 1959—. Mem. Nat., Colo. (pres. sci. sect. 1944) edn. assns., Nat. Sci. Tchrs. Assn. (pres. 1959-60), Nat. Assn. Research Sci. Teaching, Internat. Council Elementary Sci., Colo. Schoolmasters Club, Lambda Sigma Tau, Sigma Phi Epsilon. Rotarian. Mem. Bd. Editors L.W. Singer Science Series, Grades 1-9, 1957-59. Ednl. collaborator Coronet Films, 1958—. Contbr. articles to ednl. jours. Home: 1427 Glenmere Rd Greeley CO 80631

DECKER, FRANZ PAUL, symphony condr.; b. Cologne, Germany, June 22, 1923; s. Caspar and Elisabeth (Scholz) D.; grad. high sch.; student State Inst. for Mus. Edn., Cologne; M.Conducting, U. Cologne; m. Christa Terka, May 26, 1969; 1 dau., Arabella. Choir dir., asst. condr. Municipal Theater, Giessen, 1944; condr. opera, Cologne, 1945; municipal dir. music, Krefeld, from 1946; prin condr. State Opera house, Wiesbaden, 1950-53; permanent dir. Municipal Symphony Orch., Wiesbaden, 1953-56; generalmusikdirektor, Bochum, 1956-62; chief condr., artistical dir. Rotterdam Philharmonic Orch., 1962-67; permanent condr., mus. dir. Montreal (Can.) Symphony Orch., 1967—. Recipient Edgar Roquette Pinto medal (Brazil), 1963, Herscheppend Schep Ik medal (Netherlands), 1968. Rotarian. Club: Chaine des Rotisseurs. Composer symphonies, opera, oratories, chamber music. Home: 3590 Ridgewood Montreal Quebec Canada

DECKER, FREDERIC CHARLES, magazine pub.; b. S. Bend, Ind., June 3, 1916; s. Charles Abram and Edith Gertrude (Heffer) D.; m. Lorayne Lutsch, Feb. 15, 1941; children-William F., Craig D., Keith P., Michael J. Pub. Printers Ink mag., N.Y.C., Consumer Advt., Bus. Advt. mags., 1960-; v.p. Physicians Information Exchange, Inc.; pub. Marketing Communications Magazine, N.Y.C., New Products Report, coll. texts, bus. books; v.p. vision, Inc., 1963-65; pres. Decker Communications, Inc., 1965—. Trustee Inst. Advanced Marketing Studies, also trustee of American Health Foundation. Mem. Am. Advt. Federation, Am. Bus. Press, Direct Mail Advt. Assn., Mag. Pubs. Assn. Writer Weekly column. Home: High Ridge Rd Brookfield Center, CT 06805. Office: 501 Madison Av New York City, NY 10022.

DECKER, FREEMAN BERNARD, educator; b. Arlington, Neb., Feb. 26, 1908; s. Bernard and Keoka (Hagenbuck) D.; A.B., Wayne State Tchrs. Coll., 1930; M.A., U. Neb., 1945, Ed.D., 1956; m. Constance Herndon, July 14, 1931; children—Karen, Judith. Prin., Carroll (Neb.) High Sch., then photographer, Wayne, Neb., 1935-38; county supt. schs., Wayne, 1938-43; dep. Neb. Dept. Pub. Instrn., 1943-51, state supt. schs., 1951-55, commr. edn., 1955-62; co-ordinator state colls., 1962; now dir. publs. Wayne (Neb.) State Coll. Home: 200 Blaine St Wayne NB 68787

DECKER, GEORGE HENRY, assn. exec.; b. Catskill, N.Y., Feb. 16, 1902; s. Gordon H. and Mary (Napier) D.; B.S., Lafayette Coll., Easton, Pa., 1924; grad. Inf. Sch., Ft. Benning, Ga., 1932, Command and Gen. Staff Sch., Ft. Leavenworth, Kan., 1937; D. Sc., Lafayette Coll., 1953; LL.D., St. Peters Coll., 1959; Litt. D., Pa. Mil. Coll., 1961; m. Helen E. Inman, June 2, 1926; childrenJane E., James I. Commd. 2d lt., inf., U.S. Army, 1924, advancing through the grades to general, 1956; served with 26th Inf., Plattsburgh, N.Y., 1924-28; 35th Inf., Schofield Barracks, Hawaii, 1928- 31; 29th Inf., Ft. Benning, Ga., 1932-35; 7th Inf., Vancouver Barracks, Wash., 1935-36; 10th Inf., Ft. Thomas, Ky., 1937-40; 39th Inf., Ft. Bragg, N.C., 1940; hdqrs. 9th Div., Ft. Bragg, 1940-41; hdqrs. I Corps, Columbia, S.C., 1941; War Dept. Gen. Staff, 1941-42; dep. chief of staff, Third Army San Antonio, Tex., 1942-43; dep. chief of staff, Sixth Army, 1943-44, chief of staff Sixth Army, May 1944-Jan. 1946; dep. comdr. and chief of staff U.S. Army Pacific, 1946-48; comdg. gen., 5th Inf. Div., July 1948-Mar. 1950, budget officer Dept. of Army, 1950-52, comptroller, 1952-55; comdg. gen. VII Corps, 1955-56; dep. comdr. in chief European Command, 1956-57; comdr. in chief UN Command, comdr. U.S. Forces, Korea, comdg. gen. 8th U.S. Army, 1957-59; vice chief staff U.S. Army, 1959-60, chief staff, 1960-62, retired, 1962; pres. Mfg. Chemists Assn., 1963-69. Decorated Distinguished Service Medal with oak leaf cluster, Silver Star, Legion of Merit, Bronze Star (U.S.); also decorations from govts. of Argentina, Colombia, France, Germany, Greece, Italy, Korea, Peru, Philippines, Thailand, Venezuela. Mem. Phi Gamma Delta. Episcopalian. Mason. Home: 2101 Connecticut Av Washington DC 20015

DECKER, GEORGE NIXON, mfg. co. exec.; b. Springfield, Mass., Sept. 27, 1914; s. George Henry and Mary (Nixon) D.; student Rochester (N.Y.) Sch. Commerce, 1932-33, Ohio U., 1934-35, Niagara U., 1935-37; m. Rosemary Agnes Charlotte Morgan, Apr. 8, 1939; children—Sharon Lee, Robert Charles. Accountant, Van Vechten Milling Co., Rochester, N.Y., 1937-38; self employed grain broker Decker Grain Co., Rochester, 1938-40; supr. gen accounting IBM Corp., Rochester, 1940-43; successively asst. comptroller, comptroller, v.p., first v.p. Kellogg div. Am. Brake Shoe Co., Rochester, 1943-59, pres. Kellogg div., Oxnard, Cal., 1959-62, pres. Abex Corp. Group Aerospace Cos., Oxnard, 1962-70; pres., chief exec. officer GMW Internat., Inc., Camarillo, Cal., 1971—, also dir.; dir. Flying Flags Recreation Co., Buellton, Cal. Active in County Republcan Club. Mem. Oxnard C. of C., Financial Execs. Inst. Club: Las Posas Country. Home: 123 Vientos Rd Camarillo CA 93010 Office: PO Box 1015 Camarillo CA 93010

DECKER, HAROLD, business exec.; b. Chgo., Dec. 16, 1903; s. Victor Hugo and Mary Isabelle (Mullins) D.; student Kenyon Coll., 1921-22, U. Okla., 1922-25; grad. Advanced Mgmt. Program, Harvard, 1949; m. Martha Jessica McGinnis, July 3, 1927; 1 dau., Sandra Ann (Mrs. Michael F. Frost). Petroleum engr. Skelly Oil Co., Okla., 1930-33, prodn. supt., Tex., 1933-37; div. prodn. supt. Gulf Coast, southwestern Tex. area Seaboard Oil Co., 1937-45; asst. mgr. Pan Am. Prodn. Co., Houston, 1945-47, v.p., gen. mgr., dir., 1947-49; pres., dir. Houston Oil Co. of Tex., 1950-56; pres. East Tex. Pulp & Paper Co., 1953-54, v.p., 1954-56, cons., dir., 1957—, chmn. exec. com., 1964—; pvt. oil operator, cons., Houston, 1964—; dir. chmn. bd. Empire state Oil Co., 1969-71; past pres. Highland Oil Co., Frio Pipe Line Co., past gen. mgr. oil div. Herman Brown & George R. Brown (partnership); dir. Haliburton Oil Well Cementing Co., Duncan, Okla., Tex. Gulf Sulphur Co. Mem. Am. Petroleum Inst. (dir.) Am. Inst. Mining and Metall. Engrs., Ind. Petroleum Assn. Am. (pres. 1962-63, dir.), Tex. Mid-Continent Oil and Gas Assn. (dir.), Sigma Alpha Epsilon. Clubs: Burning Tree (Washington); Houston, Ramada, Houston Country (Houston). Home: 7 Pine Hill Lane Houston TX 77019 Office: Bank Southwest Bldg Houston TX 77002

DECKER, JAMES H., dir. univ. athletics; b. Elmira, N.Y., Aug. 27, 1911; s. Charles Harvey and Marion (Gordon) D.; B.S., Syracuse U., 1932; m. Eleanor Brant, June 26, 1937; childrenNancy Lee (Mrs. Robert Moore), James H. With Elmira Star-Gazette, 1932-35; with Syracuse U., 1935-, now dir. athletics. Active Syracuse Regatta Assn. Served with USNR, 1942-46. Mem. Psi Upsilon. Home: 115 Nottingham Rd Syracuse, NY 13210.

DECKER, JOHN LAWS, physician; b. Bklyn., June 27, 1921; s. John William and Margaret (Laws) D.; B.A., U. Richmond, 1942; M.D., Columbia, 1951; m. Lucille Macbeth, Nov. 13, 1954; children—Virginia Elliott,David Laws, Margaret Cauthorn Susan Curtis. Intern asst. resident, chief resident medicine Presbyn. Hosp., N.Y.C., 1951-55; research fellow medicine Mass. Gen. Hosp., 1955-58; instr. medicine Columbia Coll. Physicians and Surgeons, 1954- 55; tutor med. scis. Harvard Med. Sch., 1957-58; from instr. to asso. prof. medicine U. Wash. Med. Sch., 1958-65; chief arthritis and rheumatism br., Nat. Inst. Arthritis and Metabolic Disease, NIH, Bethesda, Md., 1965—. Cons. U.S. Army, 1962—. Served to lt. USNR, 1942-46. Docorated Purple Heart. Fellow A.C.P.; mem. A.M.A., Am. Rheumatism Assn. (chmn. editorial com. Primer on Rheumatic Diseases 1963-64), Am. Fedn. Clin. Research, Phi Beta Kappa, Alpha Omega Alpha, Omicron Delta Kappa, Phi Gamma Delta, Nu Sigma Nu. Contbr. articles to profl. jours. Mem. editorial bd. Arthritis and Rheumatism, 1961-. Home: 4703 Broad Brook Dr Bethesda, MD 20014. Office: Nat Institutes Health Bethesda, MD 20014.

DECKER, JOSEPH JACOB, plumbing and heating co. exec.; b. Bklyn., Apr. 13, 1915; s. Joseph and Eva (Jancsics) D.; student pub. schs.; m. Margaret Elizabeth Struthers, June 28, 1945; children—Susan M., Gary J. Trainee, Am. Radiator & Standard San. Corp. (co. name changed to Am. Standard, Inc. 1957), N.Y.C., 1934-38, with sales dept., 1938-54, mgr. comml. devel., 1954-56, asst. to pres., 1956-57, pres. air conditioning div., 1957-58, pres. plumbing and heating div., 1959-67, mgr. product coordination, 1967-69, dir. operations plumbing and heating bus., 1969-71, dir. Far Eastern plumbing and heating, 1971—. Served to capt. USAAF, 1942-45. Mem. Gas Appliance Mfrs. Assn. (past pres.), Am. Arbitration Assn. Clubs: Engineers', Union League (N.Y.C.); Country of Darien (Conn.). Home: 12 Scout Trail Darien CT 06820 Office: 40 W 40th St New York City NY 10018

DECKER, R. G., savs. and loan assn. exec. Exec. v.p. Pomona First Fed. Savs. and Loan Assn. Office: 399 N Arey Av Pomona CA 91766*

DECKER, RALPH WINFIELD, educator; b. Dunmore, Pa., July 3, 1908; s. David John and Maud M. (Jackson) D.; diploma Wyo. Sem., 1928; A.B., Wesleyan U., Middletown, Conn., 1932, postgrad., 1932-33; M.A., Boston U., 1936, S.T.B.Cum laude, 1937, Ph.D., 1941; Beebe fellow U. Berlin, 1938-39; D.D., Cornell Coll., 1961; L.H.D., Pfeiffer Coll., 1965; m. Elvira Doris Krotzer, Oct. 12, 1932; 1 son Ralph Winfield. Ordained to ministry United Meth. Ch., 1935, deacon, 1936, elder, 1937; pastor South Meth. Ch., Middletown, 1929-34, asst. minister Ch. of Covenant, Boston, 1935-37; pastor North Meth. Ch., Fall River, Mass., 1937-38, Meth. Ch., Bourne, Mass., 1938; prof. Bible, philosophy Union Coll., Barbourville, Ky., 1939-40; pastor Parkman St. Meth. Ch., Dorchester, Mass., 1941-44; instr. N.T., religious edn. Boston U., 1941- 44, asst. prof., 1944-45, dir. religious edn., 1944-45, prof. N.T. lit., 1945-50, registrar, 1942-50; pastor Meth. Ch., Edgartown, Mass., 1946; pres. Wyo. Sem., 1950-59, dir. ednl. instns. Meth. Ch., 1959-68; dean, prof. N.T., Scarritt Coll., Nashville, 1969—. Mem. Order DeMolay, Sigma Nu. Home: 4322 Signal Hill Dr Nashville TN 37205

DECKER, ROBERT B., trust co. exec. Sr. v.p., comptroller Marine Midland Grace Trust Co., N.Y.C. Office: 140 Broadway New York City NY 10015*

DECKER, ROBERT DAVID, coll. pres.; b. Hays County, Tex., Nov. 10, 1922; s. C.M. and Grace E. (Springall) D.; B.S., Tex. A. and M. U., 1948, M.Ed., 1954, Ph.D., 1958; m. Jacqueline Ractor, Dec. 21, 1947; children—David, Lynn, Jack. Tchr. vets. agrl. course Hays County, 1948-49, San Marcos (Tex.) High Sch., 1949-55; research asst. Tex. A. and M. U., 1955-57; asst. prof. agrl. econs. and econs. Sul Ross State Coll., Alpine, Tex., 1957-59, asso. prof., registrar, 1959-61; dean admissions, registrar Odessa (Tex.) Coll., 1961-66; asst. to chancellor Minn. State Coll. System, 1966-67, acting chancellor, 1967-68, asst. chancellor, 1968; pres. Bemidji (Minn.) State Coll., 1968—. Served to 1st lt. AUS, 1942-46; lt. col. Res. Mem. Nat., Minn. edn. assns., Phi Delta Kappa. Methodist. Rotarian, Mason. Contbr. articles profl. jours. Home: Rural Route 6 Bunchberry Lane Bemidji MN 56601

DECKER, ROBERT WAYNE, educator, geophysicist; b. Williamsport, Pa., Mar. 11, 1927; s. P. Harold and Catherine T. (Sullivan) D.; B.S., Mass. Inst. Tech., 1949, M.S., 1951; D.Sc. (Sinclair fellow), Colo. Sch. Mines, 1953. Asst. geologist Bethlehem Steel Co., Venezuela, 1949; geophysicist New World Exploration Co., Reno, 1952-54; asst. prof. Dartmouth, 1954-61, asso. prof., 1961-67, chmn. dept. geology, 1963-65, prof., 1967—; geophysicist U.S. Geol. Survey, 1957—; asso. prof. Inst. Tech. Bandung, Indonesia, 1959-60. Participant Internat. Symposium on Volcanology in New Zealand, 1965; chmn. geophysics group Surtsey Research Conf., Reykjavik, Iceland, 1967. Am. Philos. Soc. and NSF grantee 1966-68; NSF grantee for seismic studies on Mt. Rainier Volcano, 1968—. Fellow Geol. So. Am., Am. Geophys. Union (sect. v.p.); mem. Seismol. Soc. Am., A.A.A.S., Sigma Xi. Editor: Catalog of Active Volcanoes of the World, 1968; Am. adv. editor Bull. Volcanologique, 1967. Contbr. articles prof. jours. Home: 2 Kingsford Rd Hanover NH 03755

DECKER, WALTER O., packing co. exec.; b. Piqua, O., 1899. Pres., dir. Val Decker Packing Co., Piqua; pres. Arrow Products Inc.; dir. Miami Citizens Nat. Bank and Trust Co. Home: 1208 Broadway Piqua OH 45356 Office: 727 E Ash St Piqua OH 45356*

DECKER, WAYNE LEROY, meteorologist, educator; b. Patterson, Ia., Jan. 24, 1922; s. Albert Henry and Effie (Holmes) D.; B.S., Central Coll., Pella, Ia., 1943; postgrad. U. Cal., Los Angeles, 1943-44; M.S., Ia. State U., 1947, Ph.D., 1955; m. Martha Jane Livingston, Dec. 29, 1943; 1 dau., Susan Jane. Meteorologist, U.S. Weather Bur., Washington, Des Moines, 1947-49; mem. faculty U. Mo. at Columbia, 1948—, prof. meteorology, 1958-67, prof., chmn. dept. atmospheric sci., 1967—, chmn. grad. program in atmospheric sci., 1960-67. Mem. Am. Meteorol. Soc. (vis. scientist 1959- -), Am. Geophys. Union, Am. Agronomy Soc., A.A.A.S., Sigma Xi, Gamma Sigma Delta. Home: 1007 Hulen Dr Columbia MO 65201

DECKER, WILLIAM C., business exec.; b. York, Pa., Dec. 26, 1900; s. Jacob E. and Laura (Flinchbaugh) D.; B.S., Pa. State Coll., 1922; postgrad. Columbia, 1924- 25; M.B.A., Harvard, 1927; LL.D., Alfred U., 1950; D. Eng. (hon.), Clarkson Coll. Tech., 1956; children—Thomas, Karen. Chem. engr. Western Elec. Co., 1922-25; sales engr. Brown Co., 1927- 30, sales mgr., 1930, treas., 1936, v.p. 1941; pres., dir. Corning Glass Works, 1946-61, chief exec. officer, 1957-60, chmn. bd., chief exec. officer, 1961-64, chmn. exec. com., 1964-65, hon. vice chmn. bd., 1966-71, hon. chmn. bd., 1971—, also dir.; dir. Pitts. Corning Corp. Mem. U.S. Commn. on Coinage. Trustee Corning Glass Works Found. Recipient Distinguished Alumnus award Pa. State U., 1955. Clubs: Cotton Bay (Bahamas); Fifth Avenue, Link, University (N.Y.C.): Corning Country; Elmira (N.Y.) Country; Augusta Nat. Golf; Lyford Cay (Nassau, Bahamas). Home: 5 E 5th St Corning NY 14830 Office: Corning Glass Works Corning NY 14830

DECLARIS, NICHOLAS, educator, elec. engr.; b. Greece, Jan. 1, 1931; s. Elias and Helen (Georgiu) DeC.; B.S., Tex. A. and M. Coll., 1952; M.S., Mass. Inst. Tech., 1954, Sc.D., 1959; m. Joan Giuffre, July 25, 1956; 1 son, John William. Research engr. Cal. Research Corp., 1952; research asst., fellow Mass. Inst. Tech., 1952-56; asst. prof. to asso. prof. elec. engring. Cornell U., 1956-64, prof. Elec. Engring. and applied mathematics, 1964-67; prof., head dept. elec. engring., research prof. Inst. for Fluid Dynamics and Applied Mathematics of

U. Md., 1967—. Cons. Gen. Elec. Co., IBM Corp., Westinghouse Corp., AVCO; reviewer Mathematics Reviews, 1962-65. Fellow I.E.E.E. (asso. editor Circuit Theory Trans. 1958-66); mem. Am. Math. Soc., Soc. Indsl. and Applied Mathematics, Am. Soc. Engring. Edn. Author: (with R.E. Kalman) Aspects of Network and System Theory, 1971. Editor: Electrical Science Series, 1966—. Contbr. articles profl. jours. Home: Beaufort Dr Fulton MD 20759 Office: Elec Engring Dept Univ Maryland College Park MD 20742

DE CONDE, ALEXANDER, educator, historian; b. Utica, N.Y., Nov. 13, 1920; s. James A. and Mary (Tofani) De C.; A.B., San Francisco State Coll., 1943; M.A., Stanford, 1947, Ph.D. in History, 1949; m. Jeanne Doris Seeger, Sept. 1945 (div.); children—Alexander Christopher, Keith Thomas, Kenneth Paul, Stephen Frederick. Instr. Stanford, 1947-48; from asst. prof. to asso. prof. Whittier Coll., 1948-52; asst. prof. Duke, 1952-57; asso. prof. U. Mich., 1957-61; prof. history U. Cal. at Santa Barbara, 1961—, chmn. dept., 1964-67; Fulbright lectr. Center Am. Studies, Rome, Italy, 1965; lectr. sr. seminar U.S. Fgn. Service Inst., summer 1963; reader Am. history Ednl. Testing Service, Princeton, N.J., 1960-62. Bd. dirs. Internat. Social Sci. Inst., Santa Barbara, 1963-68. Served to lt. USNR, 1943-46; PTO. Guggenheim fellow, 1960, 67-68; grantee Am. Philos. Soc., 1963, Social Sci. Research Council, 1951, 56; named faculty research lectr. U. Cal. at Santa Barbara, 1967. Mem. Orgn. Am. Historians, Am. Hist. Assn. (co-recipient annual award Pacific Coast br. 1949; chmn. Beveridge prize com. 1965-68), UN Assn. (1st v.p. Santa Barbara 1963), Am. Assn. U. Profs., Soc. Historians Am. Fgn. Relations (pres. 1968-69), Phi Alpha Delta, Delta Sigma Phi. Democrat. Club: Montecito (Cal.) Country. Author: The Quasi-War: The Politics and the Undeclared War with France, 1797- 1801, 1966; Herbert Hoover's Latin American Policy, 1951; New Interpretations in American Foreign Policy, rev. edit., 1961; Entangling Alliance, Politics and Diplomacy under George Washington, 1958; The American Secretary of State: An Interpretation, 1962; A History of American Foreign Policy, 2d edit., 1971; (With R. N. Current) United States History, 1967; Decisions for Peace: The Federalist Era. Editor, contbr.: Isolation and Security, Ideas and Interests in Twentieth Century American Foreign Policy, 1957; editor: (with A. Rappaport and W. R. Steckel) Patterns in American History, 2 vols., 1965, rev., 1 vol. edit., 1969; co-editor: Essays Diplomatic and Undiplomatic of Thomas A. Bailey), 1969. Mem. adv. bd. America; History and Life: A Guide to Periodical Literature, 1963-68; cons. editor Wadsworth Pub. Co.; contbr. Ency. Britannica, Am. Ency., Colliers Ency., profl. jours.; editorial bd. The Historian. Home: 1367 Plaza de Sonadores Santa Barbara CA 93103

DE CONINGH, EDWARD HURLBUT, mfg. co. exec.; b. Chgo., July 2, 1902; s. Frederic Benjamin Edward and Lucy (Peck) de C.; A.B., Princeton, 1922; student U. Grenoble (France), 1922; B.S., Mass. Inst. Tech., 1925; m. Virginia Scott Mueller, Nov. 7, 1927 (dec. 1964); childrenMary (Mrs. Oliver F. Emerson), Edward Hurlbut, Virginia Frank; m. 2d. Martha Hooker Washburn, 1965. Began his career as an apprentice, American Steel Foundries, 1925; sec. Laudryette Mfg. Co., Cleve, 1926-27; tech. editor Dust Recovering and Conveying Co., Cleve., 1928-33; partner, chief engr. Mueller Electric Co. (now Mueller Electric Co., Inc.), 1933-66, chmn. bd., 1966-; dir. Emerson Press, Inc., Midwest Screw Products, Inc. Pres. Cleve. Welfare Fedn., 1956-59; campaign chmn. Cleve. United Appeal, 1961, 62; pres. Cleve. Community Chest, 1964-65, Vice Chmn. trustees Smith Coll.; trustee Greater Cleve. Asso. Found., Cleveland Inst. Music, Case Western Res. Univ., Laurel Sch. Recipient Outstanding Service award Cleve. Welfare Fedn., 1959, Distinguished Service award Cleve. United Appeal, 1963; 1967 Cleve. medal for pub. service. Mem. Phi Beta Kappa, Tau Beta Pi, Chi Phi. Clubs: Cleveland Skating, Kirtland Country, Union, University (Cleve.). Home: 23799 Stanford Rd Shaker Heights, OH 44122. Office: 1583 31st St Cleveland OH 44114.

DECOSSE, ALME, bishop; b. Somerset, Man., Can., June 21, 1903; s. Anthyme and Amelia (Allaire) D.; B.A., St. Boniface Coll., Man., 1922; license in philosophy Maj. Sem., Laval U., 1923; D.Th., 1926. Ordained priest Roman Cath. Ch., 1926; sec. Chancery Archdiocese of St. Bonaface, 1926-44, also chaplain Old Folk's Home, 1926-42; founder, pastor Treherne (Man.) Parish, 1944-46; pastor Ste. Elisabeth Parish, 1946-48; rector Maj. Sem., 1948-53; apptd. Bishop of Gravelbourg, Sask., Can., 1953, consecrated, 1954; made Domestic Prelate by Rome, 1952. Home: Bishop's Residence Gravelbourg Sasketchwan Canada

DECOSTA, EDWIN J., physician, surgeon; b. Chgo., 25, 1906; s. Lewis M. and Grace (Myers) DeC.; B.S., U. Chgo., 1926; M.D., Rush Med. Coll., 1929; m. Mari H. Bachrach, Jan. 5, 1935 (dec. 1970); children—Mari Jane (Mrs. David M. Terman Catherine (Mrs. Stuart Burstein), Louise (Mrs. Burton W. Wides), John Lewis; m. 2d, Alyce H. Heller, Feb. 1, 1971. Intern Cook County Hosp., Chgo., 1929-30, resident obstetrics and pathology, 1930-32; resident gynecology Michael Reese Hosp., Chgo., 1932-33; attending Passavant Meml. Hosp., Cook County Hosp.; prof. obstetrics and gynecology Northwestern U. Med. Sch., 1946—. Served as officer USNR, 1940-46. Diplomate Am. Bd. Obstetricians and Gynecologists (examiner 1955—). Mem. Am., Chgo. gynecol. socs., Am., Central assns. obstetricians and gynecologists, Am. Coll. Obstetricians and Gynecologists, A.C.S., A.M.A., Ill., Chgo. med. socs., Central Travel Club, Chgo. Inst. Medicine, Pan-Pacific Surg. Assn., Pan-Am. Med. Assn., Phi Beta Kappa, Sigma Xi, Alpha Omega Alpha; hon. mem. Ark., Neb. obstet. and gynecol. socs., Am.-Brit. Cowdray Med. Soc., Tex. Assn. Obstretricians and Gynecologist. Author: (with J.I. Brewer) Gynecology, 4th edit., 1967. Home: 799 Highland Pl Highland Park IL 60035 Office: 707 N Fairbanks Ct Chicago IL 60611

DECOSTA, FRANK AUGUSTUS, coll. dean; b. Charleston, S.C., Apr. 12, 1910; s. Benjamin Rhodes and Anna (Harrenburg) DeC.; A.B., Lincoln U., 1931; A.M., Columbia, 1938; Ph.D., U. Pa., 1954; m. Mabel Beautine Hubert, Jan. 10, 1934; children—Miriam D. (Mrs. Russell B. Sugarman), Frank Augustus. Prin. Avery Inst., Charleston, S.C., 1936-41; dean Grad. Sch., S.C. State Coll., Orangeburg, 1945-55, Morgan State Coll., Balt., 1964—; with statis. office Ministry Edn., Kaduna, Nigeria, 1962-64; cons. S.C., Ala., Md., N.J. depts. edn., 1945—, Middle States Assn. Colls. and Secondary Schs., 1966—, U.S. Office Edn., 1965—, Phelps-Stokes Fund. Recipient Distinguished Service award State Dept., 1964. Mem. Alpha Phi Alpha, Sigma Pi Phi. Democrat. Methodist. Mason. Home: 2711 Elsinore Av Baltimore MD 21216

DECOSTA, LALER COOK, coll. dean; b. Charleston, S.C., Sept. 25, 1917; s. Benjamin Robert and Gertrude (Cook) DeC.; B.S., in Agr., S.C. State Coll., 1941, M.S., 1951; Ph.D., Cornell U., 1956; m. Geraldine Stevenson, May 4, 1940; children—Laler Cook II, Gerald Stevenson. Tchr. vocational agr., 1941- 42; mem. faculty S.C. State Coll., Orangeburg, 1946-50, 56-, dean agr. and home econs., 1959-. Served to capt. AUS, 1942-46, 50-53. Decorated Bronze Star with oak leaf cluster, Combat Inf. badge with 2 stars. Fellow Gen. Ed. Bd., 1953. Mem. Soc. Animal Prodn., Soc. Dairy Sci., Am. Grassland Council, Alpha Phi Alpha. Methodist. Mason. Author: Utilization of Antibiotics and Fat by Growing and Fattening Swine, 1953. Home: Belleville Rd Orangeburg, SC 29115.

DECOSTER, CYRUS COLE, educator; b. Leesburg, Va., Sept. 21, 1914; s. Cyrus C. and Jeane Brulay) Dec.; A.B., Harvard, 1937; M.A., U. Chgo., 1940, Ph.D., 1951; m. Barbara Krause, Dec. 28, 1948; childrenJanine B., David C., Kenneth B., James K. Instr. romance llangs. Carlston Coll., 1946-48, asst. prof., 1948-56, asso. prof., 1956-57; prof. romance langs. U. Kan., Lawrence, 1957-69, chmn. dept., 1962-65, prof. Spanish, Northwestern U., Evanston, Ill. 1969—. Served to lt. USNR, 1941-46. Author: Correspondencia Inedita de Don Juan Valera, 1956; Obras Desconocidas de Juan Valera, 1965. Editor: Juan Valera, Articulos De "El Contemporáneo," 1966. Home: 6 Martha Lane Evanston IL 60201

DECOURSEY, ELBERT, pathologist; b. Ludlow, Ky., Apr. 12, 1902; s. William and Mary (Carter) DeC.; A.B., U. Ky., 1924, Sc.D. (hon.), 1955; M.D., Johns Hopkins, 1928; LL.D. (hon.), Baylor U., 1959; m. Esther Fertig, June 16, 1928. Intern Brooke Army Hosp., Ft. Sam Houston, Tex., 1929; commd. 1st lt., M.C., U.S. Army, 1929, advanced through grades to maj. gen., 1954; asst. curator Army Med. Mus., 1935-39; dir. 9th Army Area Lab., Ft. Lewis, Wash., 1941-43, 18th Med. Gen. Lab., Oahu, Hawaii, 1943-46; lab. cons. PTO, 1944-46; dir. Army group Joint Commn. for Investigation Effects of Atomic Bomb, Nagasaki, Japan, 1945-46; various med.-mil. positions, 1946—, including Operation Crossroads, Bikini, 1946; ret., 1959; dir., exec. com. Usaa Life Ins. Co.; dir. sci. research Trinity U. San Antonio, 1959-68, prof. biology, 1961-68; cons. eye pathology Robert Green Meml., Hosp., San Antonio; clin prof. ophthalmology U. Tex. Med. Sch., San Antonio; clin. prof. pathology Baylor U. Coll. Medicine; civilian cons. USAF Lackland Hosp., 1961—; staff physician San Antonio State Hosp., 1969—. First vice chmn. bd. mem. exec. com. United Services Automobile Assn., 1963-67. Bd. dirs. Nat. Bd. Med Examiners, 1948-55; dir., mem. exec. com. Tex. div. Am. Cancer Soc.; pres. Bexar Cancer Soc.; dir. Tex. Heart Assn.; pres. San Antonio Heart Assn. Chmn. San Antonio Com. 100. Dir., trustee Morningside Manor, 1967—; adv. bd. S.W. Tex. Meth. Hosp., San Antonio Med. Found.; pres., chmn. bd. Jackson-Todd Meml. Cancer Found. Decorated Legion of Merit, 1945; recipient Caldwell award, 1963. Diplomate Am. Bd. Pathology. Fellow Coll. Am. Pathologists, A.C.P.; mem. Am. Assn. Pathology and Bacteriology (treas. 1953-61), A.A.A.S. Am. Hosp. Assn. (chmn. com. edn., council research and edn. 1959-61), Sigma Xi. Clubs: St. Anthony, Rotary (dir.); Cosmos (Washington); San Antonio Country. Author: Atlas of Ophthalmic Pathology (with J. E. Ash), rev. edit. 1942; also book chpts. Bd. editors Am. Jour. Clin. Pathology, 1950-55; mil. medicine. cons. Tex. Jour. Medicine. Contbr. profl. publs. Home and Office: 114 Brandon Dr W San Antonio TX 78209 ☆

DECOURSEY, JAMES H., Jr., lt. gov. Kan.; b. Kansas City, Kan., July 7, 1932; s. James H. and Jenny (Mathews) DeC.; B.S. in Finance, U, Notre Dame, 1954; J.D., U. Kan., 1960; m. Joyce Ann Brewer, Aug. 16, 1958; childrenJames H. III, Tim, Mary, Ted. Admitted to Kan. bar, 1960; pvt. practice, Kansas City, 1960- 67; alternate rep. for gov. Kan. to Ozark Regional Commn., 1967-68; spl. asst. to gov. Kan. on urban and community affairs, 1967-68; lt. gov. Kan., 1968-. Partner Apex Investment Co.; sec., dir. S & S Grain, Inc.; dir. Security Nat. Bank, Kansas City, Kan., Centennial State Bank, Mission, Kan., DeCoursey-Breidenthal Investment Co. Mem. pub. affairs com. Partner of Alliance Program; past chmn. Govtl. Affairs Com., Kansas City, Kan.; chmn. Kan. Vehicle Reciprocity Commn., Kan. Legislative Coicil, Kan. Interstate Coop. Commn.; v.p. Pub. Affairs Com., Kansas City, Kan. Bd. dirs. St. Margaret's Hosp. Sch. Nursing; hon. dir. Rockhurst Coll.; mem. pres. council St. Mary Coll., Leavenworth, Kan. Mem. Am., Wyandotte County, Kan. Bar Assns., Kansas. City C. of C. (past bd. dirs.). Democrat. Elk. Home: 6914 W 52d Pl Mission, KS Office: Statehouse Topeka, KS 66612.

DECOURSEY, RUSSELL MYLES, former educator, zoologist, b. Indpls., Jan. 17, 1900; s. Arthur I. and Sarah E. (Sims) DeC.; A.B. (Edward Rector scholar), DePauw U., 1923; M.A., U. Ill., 1925, Ph.D., 1927; children—Lowell A., Marilyn J. (Mrs. Donald B. Richardson). Asst. prof. entomology La. State U., 1927-29; mem. faculty U. Conn., Storrs; 1929-70, prof. zoology and entomology, 1932-70, head dept., 1932-64 prof. emeritus, 1970—. Fellow A.A.A.S.; mem. Entomol. Soc. Am., Soc. Systematic Zoology, Am. Inst. Biol. Scis., Conn. Entomol. Soc. (past pres.), Am. Soc. Zoologists, Am. Assn. U. Profs., Conn. Pub. Health Assn., Sigma Xi. Author: El Humano Organismo, 1966; The Human Organism, 3d edit., 1968; (with F. Dolyak) Laboratory Manual of Human Anatomy and Physiology, 2d edit., 1964; also articles. Home: Storrs Heights Rd Storrs CT 06268

DE CREEFT, JOSE, sculptor; b. Guadalajara, Spain, Nov. 27, 1884; s. Mariano and Rosa (Champane) de C.; student sculpture Augustina Querol Studio, Madrid, 1903-04, Academie Julien, Paris, 1906-07, Maisons Greber, Paris, 1910- 14; m. Alice Carr, May 15, 1928; children—William, Nina; m. 2d, Lorraine Helen Goulet, Nov. 12, 1941; 1 dau. Dona Maria. Came to U.S. 1929, naturalized, 1940. Exhibited in Seattle, 1929, Kennedy Galleries, N.Y.C. 1969, annually at Georgetta Passedolt Gallery, N.Y.C., 1936-49, also Fine Arts Pavilion N.Y. World's Fair, 1964, White House Festival of Arts, Washington, 1965; tchr. sculpture Art Students League; tchr. New Sch. Social Research, N.Y.C., 1934-62, Norton Sch. of Art, W. Palm Beach, Fla., winter 1948-49, 1950-51, Skowhegan (Me.) Sch. Painting and Sculpture, summer 1948-49. Commd. Alice in Wonderland 16 foot Bronze group, N.Y., 1960, ceramic mural Bronx Municipal Hosp. Center, 1961, mosaic Bronx Municipal New Nurses Residence and Sch., 1963, bronze relief Pub. Health Lab., Bellevue Hosp., N.Y.C., 1967; rep. permenent collections Met. Art. Mus., Whitney Mus. Am. Art, Mus. Modern Art, Phila. Mus. Art, Bklyn. Mus., Pa Acad., Seattle Art Mus., San Francisco Mus. of Art. Recipient 1st prize for sculpture (Torso) Acad. Julien, 1906, Met. Mus. Art (Maternity, granite), 1942, Pa. Acad. (head of Rachmaninoff, beaten lead), 1945; anonymous prize (figure, Maturity), Audubon Artists, 1956, gold medal, first prize, 1957; award Nat. Sculpture Soc., 1969; commd. Poet by Fairmont Park Art Assn., 1950; Ford Found. award, retrospective exhibit, 1961. N.A. Fellow Nat. Sculpture Soc., Sculptor's Guild, Fedn. Modern Painters and Sculptors; mem. Acad. Arts and Letters, Artists' Equity (dir.), Audubon Artists (dir.), Am. Assn. U. Profs., Internat. Assn. Plastic Arts. Biography: Jose de Creeft, by Jules Campos; book: Jose Creeft, 1949, Home and studio: 241 W 20th St New York City NY 10011 ☆

DECTER, MIDGE, editor, writer; b. St. Paul, July 25, 1927; d. Harry and Rose (Calmenson) Rosenthal; student U. Minn., 1945-46, Jewish Theol. Sem. Am., 1946-48; m. Norman Podhoretz, Oct. 21, 1956; children—Rachel, Naomi, Ruth, John. Asst. editor Midstream mag., 1956-58; mng. editor Commentary, 1961-62; editor Hudson Inst., 1965-66, CBS Legacy Books, 1966- 68; exec. editor Harper's mag., 1969—. Author: The Liberated Woman and Other Americans, 1971. Contbr. articles to popular publs. Home: 924 West End Av New York City NY 10025 Office: 2 Park Av New York City NY 10016

DEDEO, JOSEPH ERMENEGILDO, advt. exec.; b. Newark, Sept. 18, 1937; s. Joseph S. and Clara (Veneziano) DeD.; grad. The Delbarton Sch., 1955; B.A. in Psychology, Princeton, 1959; m. Esther Ellen Dadigam, July 19, 1969. With Young & Rubicam Inc., N.Y.C., 1961—, account supr., 1968-69, v.p., mgr. Far East and Pacific area, Sydney, Australia, 1969—. Clubs: Princeton (N.Y.C.); American (Sydney). Home: 23 Alton St Wollahra Sydney Australia Office: 47 Macquarie St Sydney 2000 Australia

DEDEZADE, M. HALID, banker. Vice chmn. Turkish Bank of Nicosia (Cyprus) Ltd. Office: PO Box 1742 Nicosia Cyprus*

DEDMON, EMMETT, author, editor; b. Auburn, Neb., Apr. 16, 1918; s. Roy Emmett and Cora Christine (Frank) Deadman; A.B., U. Chgo., 1939; m. Claire Catherine Lyons, June 19, 1945; 1 son, Jonathan, Asst. fgn. editor Chgo. Times; 1940; columnist, critic Book Week, lit. supplement Chgo. Sun, 1946-47; lit. editor Chgo. Sun-Times, 1947, drama critic, 1950, asst. Sunday editor, 1953, asst. mng. editor, 1955-58, mng. editor, 1958-62, exec. editor, 1962-65, editor, 1965-68, v.p., editorial dir. Chgo. Sun-Times and Chgo. Daily News, 1968—, Mem. newspaper mgmt. bd. Field Enterprises, Inc. Served with USAAF, 1940-45; P.O.W., 1943-45. Decorated Air medal Mem. nat. acad. council Valparaiso U.; pres. YMCA Met. Chgo., 1965-68. trustee U. Chgo., Chgo. Hist. Soc. Mem. Am. Socc. Newspaper Editors, Soc. Am. Historians, Air Force Assn., Sigma Delta Chi, Phi Kappa Psi. Lutheran. Clubs: Chicago Press, Arts, Tavern, Chicago, Economic. Author: Duty to Live, 1946; Fabulous Chicago, 1953; Great Enterprises, 1957; A History of The Chicago Club, 1960. Home: 1420 Lake Shore Dr Chicago IL 60610 Office: 401 N Wabash Chicago IL 60611

DEDUVE, CHRISTIAN RENE, educator, scientist; b. Thames-Ditton, Eng., Oct. 2, 1917; s. Alphonse and Madeleine (Pungs) de D.; M.D., U. Louvain (Belgium), 1941, M.Sc., 1946; Dr. honoris causa, univs. Turin, Leiden and Sherbrooke; m. Janine Herman, Sept. 30, 1943; children—Thierry, Anne, Francoise, Alain. Prof. physiol. chemistry U. Louvain Med. Sch., 1947; prof. biochemistry Rockefeller U., N.Y.C., 1962—. Recipient Prix des Alumni, 1949, Prix Pfizer, 1957, Prix Francqui, 1960, Prix Quinquennal Belge des Sciences Médicales, 1967 (Belgium); Gairdner Found. Internat. award merit (Can.), 1967. Mem. Royal Acad. Medicine, Royal Acad. Belgium, Am. Chem. Soc., Biochem. Soc., Am. Soc. Biol. Chemistry, Pontf Acad. Sci. Am. Soc. Cell Biology, Soc. Chem. Biol., Soc. Beige Biochem., Sigma Xi; fgn. mem. Am. Acad. Arts and Scis. Address: 80 Central Park W New York City NY 10023

DEE, RUBY, actress; b. Oct. 27, Cleve.; d. Marshall Edward and Emma (Benson) Wallace; B.A., Hunter Coll., 1945; apprentice Am. Negro Theatre, 1941-44; m. Ossie Davis, Dec. 9, 1948; children—Nora, La Verne, Guy. Stage appearances include Jeb, 1946, Raisin in the Sun, 1959, Purile Victorious, 1961, others; appeared on Off-Broadway as Lena in Boesman and Lena, 1970, others; motion pictures include The Jackie Robinson Story, Take a Giant Step, St. Louis Blues, Raisin in the Sun, Purile Victorious; numerous TV appearances. Recipient (with husband) Frederick Douglass award N.Y. Urban League for bringing a sense fervor and pride to countless millions, 1970. Mem. N.A.A.C.P., CORE, Student Non-Violent Coordinating Com., S.C.L.C. Address: Cooly Pl Mount Vernon NY 10550*

DEEDY, JOHN GERARD, Jr., editor; b. Worcester, Mass., Aug. 17, 1923; s. John G. and Grace R. (McDonough) D.; A.B., Holy Cross Coll., 1948; certificate, Institut du Pantheon, Paris, 1949; A.B., Trinity Coll., Dublin, 1949, M.A., 1957; m. Mary M. Noonan, Apr. 22, 1949; children—Mary Joan, John J., Justine A., Paul V. Reporter, corr. Boston Post, Boston Globe, Worcester Telegram, 1940-51; founding editor Cath. Free Press, Worcester, 1951-59; editor Pitts. Cath., 1959-67; mng. editor Commonweal, N.Y.C., 1967—. Served with USAAF, World War II. Recipient Pro Ecclesia et Pontifice Pope Pius XII, 1954. Author: (with Jack Frost) The Church in Worcester New England, 1957; (with Martin Marty, David Silverman) The Religious Press in America, 1963; Eye on the Modern World, 1965; The Vatican, 1970. Home: 4 Bayard St Larchmont NY 10538 Office: 232 Madison Av New York City NY 10016

DEEGAN, JAMES WAYNE, indsl. engr., educator; b. Peterson, Ia., Aug. 3, 1912; s. James Bonson and Eva May (Underwood) D.; B.S., U. Ia., 1934, M.S., 1935; m. Margaret Albright, Oct. 3, 1936; children—James Lewis, Robert Wayne. Jr. design engr. John Deere Harvester Co., 1935-36; indsl. engr. Owens-Ill. Glass Co., 1936-40; sr. indsl. engr. Nat. Supply Co., 1940-43; staff engr. Armstrong Cork Co., Lancaster, Pa., 1943-49; prof. indsl. engring., chmn. dept. mech. engring. U Ia., 1949-62; coordinator placement Coll. Engring. U. Ia., Iowa City, 1953-68, chmn. indsl. and mgmt. engring. dept., 1962-71, prof. indsl. and mgmt. engring., 1971—. Sec., Nat. Council Indsl. Engring. Acad. Dept. Heads, 1967, vice chmn., 1968, chmn., 1969. Registered profl. engr., Pa. Mem. Am. Soc. M.E., Nat. Soc. Profl. Engrs., Ia. Engring. Soc., Iowa City Engrs. Club, Am. Soc. for Engring. Edn., Am. Inst. Indsl. Engrs. (nat. dir. sr-student chpt. relations, 1965-67), Sigma Xi, Tau Beta Pi, Pi Tau Sigma. Presbyn. (elder). Rotarian. Author (with J.K. Louden) Wage Incentives. Contbr. articles to profl. publs. Home: 250 North St Iowa City IA 52240

DEEGAN, THOMAS JOSEPH, Jr., mgmt. adviser; b. Bklyn., July 11, 1910; s. Thomas Joseph and Bertha (Berckmeier) D.; A.B., Fordham, 1934, L.H.D., 1964; LL.D., U. Tampa, 1963, L.I.U., 1964; m. Alice Russell, Dec. 30, 1939; children— Mavourneen Maura, Thomas Joseph 3d, Deirdre Gael (dec.), Christopher, Timothy John, Michael Nicholas, Mary Angela, and Cecily Ann. Engaged as reporter for N.Y. Times, 1932-38; pub. relations bus., 1938-42; pub. relations officer to Gen. R.W. Johnson, 1942-43; dir. pub. relations Am. Airlines, 1944-45; with C. & O. Railway, 1946-54, v.p., 1949-54, also dir. mem. exec. com.; v.p., dir. mem. exec. com. Alleghany Corp., 1954-59; v.p. staff NY Central Railroad, 1954-57; chmn. Thomas J. Deegan Co., Inc., mgmt. counsel to corps., N.Y.C., 1957—; vice chmn., dir., mem. exec. com. Interpublic, Inc., 1966-68, v.p. dir. Fifth Av. Assn.; dir. Gen. Battery Corp., Av. of the Ams. Assn., Am. Information Services Inc., Gt. Western Ranches, Tower Capital Fund dir., mem. exec. com. Bank of Commerce. Founder, chmn. exec. com. N.Y. World's Fair 1964-65 corp.; v.p. Nat. Museum of Racing, Inc. Mem. Adv. bd. N. Am. sect. Vatican Radio. Bd. dirs. Saratoga Center for performing Arts, Inst. for Ecumenical Research, Regional Plan Assn. Boy's Club Am., Boy Scouts Am.; visitors U.S. Naval Acad., 1962-65; mem. nat. bd. Am. Cancer Soc. trustee John Fitzgerald Kennedy Library, Internat. Coll. Beirut, Alfred E. Smith Found. Finch Coll. Decorated Knight Grand Cross Holy Sepulchre, Knight Malta. Mem. Marketing Execs. Soc. (past pres.), Friendly Sons Saint Patrick (steward), Pub. Relations Soc. Am., Pub. Relations Soc. N.Y., Internat. Pub. Relations Assn., Soc. Silurians, Sigma Delta Chi. Clubs: Nat. Press (Washington): Overseas Press, Racquet and Tennis, Sky, Hemisphere (N.Y.C.); Stanwich (Greenwich, Conn.). Home: 577 Round Hill Rd Greenwich CT 06830 Office: Time and Life Bldg Rockefeller Center New York City NY 10020

DEELEY, WILLIAM RADCLIFFE, retail food distbn. co. exec.; b. Mt. Vernon. O., Sept. 27, 1922; s. Benjamin Charles and Frances (Radcliffe) D.; B.S., La. State U., 1948; m. Shirley Jane Edwards, June 22, 1956; 1 son, William Radcliffe II. Enlisted U.S. Army, 1942, discharged, 1945; commd. 2d lt. 1949, advanced through grades to capt., 1954; resigned 1957; pres., chief exec. officer, Alpha Beta Acme

Markets, Inc., La Habra, Cal., 1957—. Bd. dirs. La Habra Boys Club, North Orange council Boy Scouts Am. Mem. La Habra C. of C. (bd. dirs.). Episcopalian. Office: 777 S Harbor Blvd La Habra CA 90631

DEEMS, MERVIN MONROE, educator, clergyman; b. Balt., Feb. 22, 1899; s. (James) Harry and Mary (Adams) D.; A.B., Johns Hopkins, 1921; Th.M., So. Bapt. Theol. Sem., 1924; Ph.D., U. Chgo., 1928; m. Cleta Merie Naylor, Apr. 30, 1924; children—Margaret Cox, Mary Howland. Asst. prof. history William Jewell Coll., Liberty, Mo., 1924-26; asst. prof. history and religion Carleton Coll., Northfield, Minn., 1928-31; Albert Kahn fellow, 1931-32; pastor, Norway, Me., 1932-36; Waldo prof. ecclesiastical history and missions Bangor (Me.) Theol. Sem., 1936-43, dean, prof. Christian history, Fogg prof. sacred rhetoric, 1954-68, dean, prof. emeritus, 1968—; Protestant minister, Castine, Me., 1968—; prof. history early Christianity and missions Chgo. Theol. Sem., Federated Theol. Faculty, U. Chgo., 1943-54; lectr. ch. history Union Theol. Sem., N.Y.C., summer, 1948; Samuel Harris lectr. Bangor Theol. Sem., 1952; vis. prof. religion Pomona Coll., Claremont, Cal., 1953, Pacific Sch. Religion, Berkeley, Cal., summer 1960. Pres. Me. Council Chs., 1960-64; mem. exec. com., bd. dirs. Me. conf. United Chs. Christ, 1965-71, mem. hist. commn., 1965—, chmn., 1969-71. Pres. bd. trustees Me. Christian Assn. U. Me., 1958-60. Mem. Am. Ch. History Soc., Congl. Ch. Hist. Soc. (pres. 1965-69), Boston Seaman's Friend Soc. (bd. govs. 1970—), Phi Beta Kappa, Delta Upsilon. Rotarian. Conglist. Clubs: Apollos (Chgo.); Castine Mens. Author chpts. books, also reports. Editor: Chgo. Theol. Sem. Register, 1947-54; Bangor Sem. Alumni Bull., 1954-68. Contbr. religious periodicals. Home: Box 61 Castine ME 04421

DEEMS, RICHARD EMMET, mag. pub. exec.; b. N.Y.C., Jan. 19, 1913; s. Walter A. and Marie (Neufeld) D.; m. Jean S.; one dau., Cynthia. Propr. Interstate News Service, 1930-32; with the circulation dept. New Yorker mag., 1932-33; circulation mgr. Esquire mag., 1933-39; with Harper's Bazaar, 1939-52, advt. mgr., 1947-52; v.p. charge advt. Hearst mags., 1952-55, exec. v.p., 1955-60, pres., 1960—; dir. Hearst Corp., Nat. Mag. Co., London. Trustee William Randolph Hearst Found., The Hearst Found. Inc., Advt. Ednl. Found., People-to-People, Rochester Inst. Tech. Mem. Advt. Fedn. Am., Advt. Council (dir.), Mag. Pubs. Assn. (dir.), Confrerie des Chevaliers du Tastevin. Clubs: Detroit Athletic; Bohemian (San Francisco); Madison Square Garden (N.Y.C.); Waccabuc (N.Y.) Country; Everglades (Palm Beach, Fla.). Home: East Ridge Rd Waccabuc NY 10597 Office: 959 8th Av New York City NY 10019

DEENER, DAVID RUSSELL, coll. adminstr.; b. Weverton, Md., Jan. 8, 1920; s. Russell Marcellus and Josephine (Main) D.; B.A., U. Pitts., 1941, M.A., 1948; Ph.D., Duke, 1951; m. Helen Ruth Buchner, Jan. 30, 1943; children—Karen Lee (Mrs. David Depp), Helen Jane (Mrs. Charles Johnson). Adminstrv. asst. War Dept., 1941-42; instr. U. Pitts., 1946-48; part-time instr. Duke, 1948-50, research asso., 1951-52, exec. sec. Commonwealth Studies Center, also vis. asso. prof., 1957-58; mem. faculty Tulane U., 1952—, prof. polit. sci., 1957—, chmn. dept., 1964- 66, dean Grad. Sch., 1966—, also provost, 1967—; head dept. polit. sci. Newcomb Coll., 1960-64, acting dean, 1965- 66. Cons. Brookings Instn., 1951, Inst. Pub. Adminstrn., 1960-61, Nat. Inst. Mental Health project, 1960-67; editorial adviser Hauser Press, 1958—. Mem. New Orleans Met. Area Com., 1966—; adv. com. fgn. relations U.S. State Dept., 1969—; chmn. elect Council Grad. Schs. in U.S.; mem. com. visitors Vanderbilt U. Grad. Sch. Bd. visitors U.S. Army Transp. Sch., Ft. Eustis, Va. Served to lt. USNR, 1942-45. Mem. Am. Soc. Internat. Law (v.p. 1964-65); Am. polit. Sci. Assn., Phi Beta Kappa. Democrat. Mem. Ch. of Brethren. Club: Cosmos (Washington). Author: The United States Attorneys General and International Law, 1957; also articles. Editor, contbr.; Canada-United States Treaty Relations, 1963, de Lege Pactorum, 1970. Home: 7733 St Charles Av New Orleans LA 70118

DEER, JAMES WILLIS, lawyer; b. Reading, Pa., Mar. 14, 1917; s. Irvin E. and Rosemary (French) D.; A.B; Oberlin Coll; 1938; J. D., U. Mich., 1941; m. Marion M. Hawkinson, July 31, 1943; 1 dau., Ann Marie. Admitted to Ohio bar, 1941, N.Y. State bar, 1948; legal staff SEC, 1942-45; practice in N.Y.C., 1948-; mem. firm Holtzmann, Wise & Shepard, 1954—; chmn. bd. Western Auto Supply Corp., 1960; sec., dir. Am. Diversified Enterprises, Inc., 1951—; sec. Tele-register Corp., 1953-69, DuBois Chems., Inc. 1960-62, Ogden Corp. dir. A D Industries, Inc., Arts Way Mfg. Co., Inc. Mem. Am., N.Y. State bar Assns., Phi Beta Kappa, Phi Alpha Delta. Home: 611 Shore Acres Dr Mamaroneck NY 10543 also: 221 NW 17th St Delray Beach FL 33444 Office: 30 Broad St New York City NY 10004

DEERE, DON UEL, engring. educator; b. Corning, Ia., Mar. 17, 1922; s. Oral Uel and Wilma (Hanna) D.; student N.W. Mo. State Coll., 1939-41; B.S., Ia. State Coll., 1943; M.S., Colo. U., 1948-49; Ph.D., U. Ill., 1955; m. Carmen Pilar Garcia, Aug. 15, 1944; children—Diana, Don William Jr. Mining engr. Phelps Dodge Corp., 1943-44; exploration engr. Potash Co. Am., 1941-46; asst. prof., then asso. prof. civil engring. U. P.R., 1946-51, head dept., 1949-51; mem. faculty U. Ill. at Urbana, 1955—, now prof. civil engring. and geology; cons. to industry, govt.; spl. research rock constrn. Mem. Nat. Acad. Sci., Am. Soc. C.E., Geol. Soc. Am., Am. Geophys. Union, Am. Inst. Profl. Geologists, Assn. Engring. Geologists, Am. Inst. Mining Engrs., Am. Soc. Testing Materials, Nat. Acad. Engring., Sigma Xi, Phi Kappa Phi, Tau Beta Pi. Home: 2210 Fletcher St Urbana IL 61801

DEERING, FERDIE JACKSON, editor; b. Denison, Tex., Oct. 24, 1910; s. Norman Henry and Hattie (Brand) D.; student East Central State Coll., 1928-31; m. Flora Mildred Jennings, May 3, 1935; children—Cheryl Beth (Mrs. Richard Ralph Wilson), Robert E. Reporter Ada (Okla.) Evening News, 1931-32; advtg. salesman Denison (Tex.) Herald, 1932-33; night editor Ada News, 1934-37; asso. editor The Farmer-Stockman, Oklahoma City, 1937-42; editor, 1943-67, editor, mgr., Oklahoma City, Okla., 1967—; editor, mgr. RX Golf and Travel mag., 1967-68; editor Oklahoma's Orbit mag., 1961-69; mem. mgmt. com. Okla. Pub. Co., 1948—, dir., asst. sec., 1958—. Vice chmn. gov. bd. Baptist Meml. Hosp., Oklahoma City; bd. dirs. U. Okla. Research Inst. Mem. State Farm Mag. Bur. (dir. 1967—), Agrl. Pub. Assn. (dir. 1967—), Okla. City C. of C. (v.p. 1962-63), Am. Agrl. Editors Assn. (pres. 1951). Republican. Baptist. Clubs: Sirloin Okla. (pres. 1957-58); Quail Creek Golf and Country (Oklahoma City). Home: 3232 Whippoorwill Rd Oklahoma City OK 73120 Office: 500 N Broadway Oklahoma City OK 73125

DEERING, FRED, oil co. exec.; b. McAlester, Okla., Jan. 10, 1925; s. Freddie Lee and Lillie Mae (Phillips) D.; childrenJohn, Elizabeth Ann, Susan Lynn, Robert Lantz, Michael Lee. With Warren Petroleum Corp., 1950-60 comptroller, 1958-60; with Gulf Oil Corp., 1960—, comptroller, 1968-. Served with USAAF, 1943-45. Mem. Am., Pa. insts. C.P.A.'s Am. Petroleum Inst., Am. Mgmt. Assn. Home: 1465 Mohican Dr Pittsburgh PA 15228 Office: P O Box 1166 Pittsburgh, PA 15230.

DEERINGER, JACK MORGAN, univ. dean; b. Lockport, N.Y., Jan. 16, 1915; s. Henry William and Agnes Ethel (Morgan) D.; A.B., Hobart Coll., 1936; M.Ed., U. Buffalo, 1948, Ed.D., 1953. Tchr. high sch. English, also dept. chmn. pub. schs., N.Y. State, 1936-43; curriculum coordinator Lockport pub. schs., 1946-51; admissions counselor U. Buffalo, 1951-52, dean students, 1952-58; dean coll. Corning (N.Y.) Community Coll., 1958-61; asso. dean acad. affairs State U. N.Y. at Albany, 1961-62, acad. dean. 1962-. Pres., bd. dirs. Albany Sch. Practical Nursing. Served with AUS, 1943-46. Mem. N.Y. State Assn. Deans and Guidance Personnel, N.Y. State Tchrs. Assn., N.E.A., Assn. Higher Edn., Phi Delta Kappa, Theta Delta Chi. Home: 8 Bain Dr Delmar, NY also; 39 Waterman St Lockport NY 14094 Office: 223 Western Av Albany NY 12203

DEES, BOWEN CAUSEY, inst. pres. b. Batesville, Miss., July 20, 1917; s. John Simeon and Ida Lea (Causey) D.; A.B., Miss. Coll., 1937, D.Sc., 1963; Ph.D., N.Y.U., 1942; m. Sarah Edna Sanders, Aug. 25, 1937; 1 dau., Sarah Edna. Grad. asst. physics N.Y.U., 1937-43; prof. physics Miss. Coll., 1943-44; instr. elec. communications Radar Sch., Mass. Inst. Tech., 1944-45; asst. prof. physics Rensselaer Poly. Inst., 1945-47; physicist, then div. chief sci. and tech. div., gen. hdqrs. SCAP, Tokyo, Japan, 1947-51; program dir. fellowships NSF, 1951-56, dep. asst. dir. sci. personnel and edn., 1956-59, asst. dir. 1959-63, asso. dir. for edn., 1963-64, asso. dir. planning, 1963-66; v.p. U. Ariz., 1966-68, provost acad. affairs, 1968-70; pres. Franklin Inst., Phila., 1970—. Mem. adv. com. U.S. Army Command and Gen. Staff Coll., 1967- 69; mem. sci. information council NSF, 1970—. Trustee Sci. Service. Fellow A.A.A.S.; mem. Am. Phys. Soc., Am. Assn. Physics Tchrs., Am. Soc. Engring. Edn., Sigma Xi. Democrat. Clubs: Poor Richard, Midday (Phila); Cosmos (Washington). Author: Fundamentals of Physics, 1945. Contbr. articles tech., ednl. jours. Address: Franklin Inst Philadelphia PA 19103

DEES, JAMES WILTON, ret. chem. co. exec.: b. Hazlehurst, Miss., Dec. 19, 1910; s. Frank and Georgia (Bass) D.; B.S., Millsaps Coll., 1935; m. Effie Ragsdale, Aug. 7, 1935; 1 son, Wilton Frank. With E.I. duPont de Nemours & Co., 1935- 42, mgr. Old Hickory chem. plant, 1942-45; with Stauffer Chem. Co., 1945- 69, dir. employee relations, 1954-64, v.p., 1964-69. Mgmt. rep. chem. sec. ILO, 1962. Active local Community Fund. Mem. Mfg. Chemists Assn., N.A.M., Am. Mgmt. Assn., Personnel Mgmt. Assn., Kappa Sigma. Clubs: N.Y. Athletic; Shenorock Shore (Rye, N.Y.). Home: Sneads Island Rd Rt 2 Box 397 Palmette FL 33561 Office: 299 Park Av New York City NY 10017

DEESE, JAMES EARLE, educator; b. Salt Lake City, Dec. 14, 1921; s. Thomas D. and Serena Jane (Johnson) D.; A.B., Chapman Coll., 1944; A.M., Ind. U., 1946, Ph.D., 1948; m. Ellin Ruth Krauss, Dec. 24, 1948; childrenElizabeth Ellin, James Lawrence. From asst. prof. to prof. psychology Johns Hopkins Balt., 1948- -. Vis. prof. U. Cal. at Berkeley, 1958-59; cons. editor Jour. Exptl. Psychology, Psychol. Rev. Fellow Soc. Exptl. Psychologist, Am. Psychol. Assn. (dir.); mem. Eastern Psychol. Assn. (pres. 1966-67), Linguistic Soc. Am. Democrat. Unitarian. Club: 14 West Hamilton Street. Author: How to study, 1957; Psychology of Learning, 3d edit. (with S.H. Hulse), 1967; Principles of Psychology, 1964; The Structure of Associations in Language and Thought, 1965; General Psychology, 1967; Psycholinguistics, 1969; contbg. author Introduction to Psychology (C.T. Morgan), 1955. Asso. editor Jour. Exptl. Psychology, 1963-68; editor: Psychol. Bull.; 1968—. Home: 216 Longwood Rd Baltimore MD 21210

DEEVEY, EDWARD SMITH, Jr., biologist; b. Albany, N.Y., Dec. 3, 1914; s. Edward Smith and Villa (Augur) D.; B.A., Yale, 1934, Ph.D., 1938; m. Georgiana Baxter, Dec. 24, 1938; childrenRuth Newcomb, Edward Brian, David Kevin. Instr. biology Rice Inst., Houston, 1939-43; research asso. biology Woods Hole Oceanographic Instn., 1943-46; asst. prof. biology Yale, 1946-51, asso. prof., 1951-57, prof., 1957-68; dir. Geochronometric Lab., 1951-62; Killam research prof. biology Dalhousie U., Halifax, N.S., Can., 1968-. Sect. head environmental and systematic biology Nat. Sci. Found., 1967- 68; member Fisheries Research Board Canada, 1969-; NSF sr. postdoctoral fellow, Fulbright travel grantee U. Canterbury, Christ church, New Zealand, 1964-65. Recip. Fulbright research award Denmark, 1953-54; Guggenheim fellow, Denmark, 1953-54. Fellow Am. Assn. Advancement of Sci. Geological Society Am.; member Am. Soc. Limnology and Oceanography, Ecol. Soc. Am. (pres. 1969-70), Anthrop. Assn., Soc. Am. Archeologists, Soc. Am. Naturalists. Club: Cosmos (Washington). Home: Shad Bay Halifax Co NC also: Sheldon Pl Pine Orchard, Branford, CT 06405 Office: Dept of Biology Dalhousie U Halifax, Nova Scotia Canada.

DEFALCO, LAWRENCE MICHAEL, bishop; b. McKeesport, Pa., Aug. 25, 1915; s. Rosario and Margret (Desmone) DeF.; student St. Vincent's Coll., Latrobe, Pa., 1933-35, St. John's Mission Sem., Little Rock, 1935-42; J.C.L., Gregorian U., Rome, Italy, 1955. Ordained priest Roman Catholic Ch., 1942; asst. pastor St. Patrick's Fort Worth, 1942-52, pastor, 1962; asst. pastor Sacred Heart Cathedral, Dallas, 1952; vice chancellor Dallas-Fort Worth Diocese, 1952-55, sec. Marriage Tribunal, 1955-62; pastor Our Lady Perpetual Help Ch., Dallas, 1956-62; bishop of Amarillo, Tex., 1963-. Home: 1800 N Lake St Amarillo, TX 79107 Office: 1800 N Spring St Amarillo, TX 79107.

DEFELITTA, FRANK PAUL, producer, writer, dir.; b. N.Y.C., Aug. 3, 1921; s. Pat and Genevieve (Sibillo) D.; student N.C. U., 1939, New Sch. Social Research, 1948; m. Dorothy Gilbert, Aug. 4, 1945; children—Eileen, Raymond. Dir.-writer CBS, 1950-57; dir. programming Nat. Telefilms Assos., 1959-61; producer, writer, dir. NBC, from 1962; now producer, dir., writer Universal Studios; film documentaries include Music of the South, 1955, (sci. series) Conquest, 1957, (natural sci. series) Adventure, 1953-55, (hist. series) Odyssey, 1958, The Chosen Child (Writers Guild award), 1962, Emergency Ward (Emmy award), 1962, Experiment in Excellence (Sch. Bell award), 1963, Battle of the Bulge, 1964, The Stately Ghosts of England, 1944, The World of the Teenager (Robert J. Flaherty award), 1966. Served to capt. USAAF, 1941-45; ETO Decorated D.F.C., Air medal (5), Presdl. citation; recipient Peabody award, 1954, 63, Ohio State U. award, 1957, Thomas Alva Edison award, 1958; CINE gold medal (2); Brotherhood award of Nat. Conf. Christians and Jews for film Mississippi- A Self Portrait; George Washington Honor medal of Freedoms Found. for film The American Image. Mem. Writers Guild Am., Dirs. Guild Am. Author (films) The First of January, 1970; The Savage Is Loose, 1971. Home: 3008 Paulcrest Dr Los Angeles CA 90046

DEFEO, SULLIVAN S., banker; b. Paterson, N.J., 1907. Sr. v.p., comptroller First Nat. Bank Passaic County, N.J.; dir. First Savs. & Loan Fairlawn. Home: 393 Cedar Hill Av Wyckoff NJ 07481 Office: 515 Union Blvd Borough Totowa NJ 07512*

DEFEO, VINCENT JOSEPH, educator, biologist; b. N.Y.C., Oct. 1, 1925; s. Salvadore Francis and Teresa (Catalano) DeF.; B.S., Juniata Coll., 1949; M.S., Rutgers U., 1951; Ph.D., Ohio State U., 1954; postdoctoral Johns Hopkins, 1955; m. Elizabeth Ann Walling, Sept. 20, 1952; children—Steven V., Ronald M. Asst. prof. physiology Ohio State U., 1954-55; USPHS fellow Carnegie Inst. of Washington at Balt., 1955-57; asst. prof. anatomy U. Ill., 1957-63; vis. prof. anatomy U. Tenn. Med. Unit, 1961; USPHS postdoctoral tng. neuroendocrinology U. Cal. at Los Angeles, 1959, electon microscopy Washington U., 1963; asst. prof. to asso. prof. anatomy and obstetrics/gynecology Vanderbilt U. Sch. Medicine, 1963-66; asso. prof., asso. chmn. anatomy U. Hawaii, 1966-68, prof., 1968—, chmn. dept., 1969—. Mem. Soc. Study Reprodn., Soc. Study Fertility, Endocrine Soc., Am. Assn. Anatomists, Assn. Anatomy Chairmen, Am. Physiol. Soc., Am. Soc. Cell Biology, A.A.A.S., Pan Am. Assn. Anatomy, Sex Information and Edn. Council U.S., Soc. Developmental Biology, Assn. Am. Med. Colls. Research and publs. on nervous and hormonal control reprodn., biology of implantation and embryo spacing, uterine decidualization, biol. clocks in reproductive phenomena. Home: 1941 Ualakaa St Honolulu HI 96822

DEFERRARI, ROY JOSEPH coll. prof.; b. Stoneham, Mass., June 1, 1890; s. Augustino and Mary (Crovo) D.; A.B., Dartmouth, 1912; M.A. and Ph.D., Princeton; m. Evelyn Mary Biggi, Dec. 30, 1920; childrenAustin John, Mary Evelyn. Instr. in Latin and Greek, Princeton, 1915-18; instr. in same, Catholic U., Washington, D.C., 1918-20, asso. dean of Grad. Sch., 1930-38, sec. gen., 1938-67. Instr. in military studies, Princeton U. Ground School, World War. Fellow Medieval Acad. America. Mem. mng. com. American Sch. Classical studies, Athens, Rome; dir. affiliation The Cath. University of Am. Mem. Am. Philol. Assn., Linguistic Soc. America, Classical Assn.. Middle Atlantic States. Catholic. Author several books latest of which are: College Organization and Administration, 1947; Marian Latin Serfes (4 vols.), 1950-53; Lexicon, Latin- English of St. Thomas Aquinas, 1953; Early Christian Biography, 1952; Minor Works of St. Augustine, 1953; Memoirs of the Catholic U. of Am. 1918-1960, 1961; Theological Treatises of St. Ambrose, 1961. Editor: Catholic U. Patristic Studies (100 vols.), 1922-45; Catholic U. Studies in Mediaeval and Renaissance Latin (30 vols.); Catholic Univ. Classical studies vols.); Complete Index of Summa Theologica of St. Thomas, 1956; Sources of Catholic Dogma, 1957; Latin-English Dictionary of St. Thomas, 1960. Editorial director The Fathers of the Church (50 volumes). Contbr. to Commonwealth, Cath. Ednl. Rev., Classical Weekly. Home: 1303 Quincy St NE Washington DC 20017*

DEFFERRE, GASTON, mayor of Marseilles, France; b. 1910; ed. Coll. de Nimes, Aix-en- Provence U. Practiced law, Marseilles before World War II; active in Brutus resistance orgn., 1940-44; dir. Le Provencal, 1944; mayor Marseilles, 1945, 53—. Dep. from Bouches du Rhne to Constituent Assemblies, 1945-46, Nat. Assembly, 1946-58; sec. of state Presidence du Conseil, 1946; under-sec. of state Overseas France, 1945-46; minister Mcht. Marine, 1950-51; minister Overseas France, 1956-57; senator, 1959- 62; dep. Nat. Assembly, 1962—. Socialist candidate for pres. Republic, 1964. Decorated officer Legion d'Honneur, Croix de Guerre, Rosette de la Resistance, King's medal for Courage in Cause of Freedom. Address: 52 Traverse Nicholas Marseilles France

DEFLEUR, MELVIN LAWRENCE, educator, sociologist; b. Portland, Ore., Apr. 27, 1923; s. Robert H. and Dorothy (Foster) DeF.; B.S. cum laude, St. Louis U., 1949; M.S., U. Wash., 1952, Ph.D., 1954; m. Lois Begitske, Dec. 5, 1961. Faculty, Ind. U., 1954-63; prof. U. Ky., 1963-67; prof. Wash. State U., Pullman, 1967—, chmn. dept. sociology, 1968—. Fellow Am. Sociol. Assn.; mem. Pacific Sociol. Assn., So., Argentine sociol. socs., Internat. Institut de Sociologie. Author: (with Otto N. Larsen) The Flow of Information, 1958; Techicas y Metodos de Investigacion Social, 1965; Theories of Mass Communication, 2d edit., 1970; (with others) Sociology: Man in Society, 1971. Home: 107 Viento Dr Pullman WA 99163

DEFLIESE, PHILIP LEROY, accountant; b. Queens County, N.Y., Feb. 11, 1915; s. Philip and Frances (Ankenbrand) D.; B.B.A., Coll. City N.Y., 1938, M.S., 1940; C.P.A., 1947; m. Pauline Harnisch, Apr. 28, 1946; children—Philip Leroy, Robert Wayne, Jeanne Marie. Tchr. accounting Grover Cleveland High Sch., N.Y.C., 1938-42; asst. prof. Adelphi U., 1947-48; adj. prof. Pace U., 1950-56; with Lybrand, Ross Bros. & Montgomery, C.P.A.'s, 1942—, partner, 1956—, now mng. partner, chmn. exec. com., nat. dir. accounting, auditing and SEC Services, 1962-68. Mem. N.Y. State Bd. C.P.A. Examiners, 1964-69. Active local Boy Scouts Am., 1927-54, recipient Silver Beaver award, 1947. Served to lt. USNR, 1942-46. Mem. Am. Inst. C.P.A.'s (chmn. accounting principles bd. 1971—, past chmn. auditing procedure com.) N.Y. State Soc. C.P.A.'s (past chmn. com. accounting procedure), Am. Accounting Assn., Nat. Assn. Accountants. Clubs: Lawyers, Harbor View, Union League, Hemisphere, Board Room (N.Y.C.); Garden City Country; Lake George. Author: (with N.J. Lenhart) Montgomery's Auditing, 8th edit., 1957. Contbr. articles prof. jours. Home: 63 Princeton St Garden City NY 11530 also: Boston Landing NY 12814 Office: 1251 Av Americas New York City NY 10019

DEFOE, WILLIAM MARTIN, shipbldg. co. exec.; b. Bay City, Mich., July 11, 1920; s. Harry Joseph and Maude (Currey) D.; student Bay City Jr. Coll., 1937-39, U. Mich., 1939; m. Mildred Louise Mann, Aug. 8, 1970; 1 dau., Barbara Jo (Mrs. Robert C. Bishop). With Defoe Shipbldg. Co., Bay City, 1939—, chmn. bd., 1962—; dir. Aerospace Am., Inc., Fed. Res. Bank Detroit. Chmn., dir. Defoe Found.; trustee Greater Mich. Found.; bd. dirs. Citizens Research Council Mich. Served to lt. (j.g.) USNR, 1944-46. Mem. N.A.M. (past bd. dirs.), Mich. Mfrs. Assn. (sr. v.p.), Bay Area C. of C. (past pres.), Newcomen Soc., Soc. Naval Architects and Marine Engrs., Naval Engrs. Soc. Republican. Episcopalian. Elk. Clubs: Bay City Country; Saginaw (Mich.), Saginaw Bay Yacht. Home: 2323 Nurmi Dr Bay City MI 48706 Office: Defoe Shipbldg Co Foot of Adams St Bay City MI 48706

DE FORCE CLYDE, corp. exec.; b. Santa Monica, Cal., Oct. 21 1907; s. Albert Clyde and Lena (Kruger) de F.; m. Ercel Grant-Cooper, Oct. 16, 1936. With Wilcox Drake & Co., Los Angeles, mem. N.Y. Stock Exchange, 1929-31; with Standard Oil Co. of Cal., 1931-32; with A.O. Slaughter, Anderson & Fox, mem. N.Y. Stock Exchange, 1933-36; with Wm. Wrigley Jr. Co., Chgo., 1936- , v.p., 1958-; dir. Wrigley Co., Ltd., London, Eng., Deutsche Wrigley G.M.B.H., Dusseldorf, Germany and Wrigley Co. A/B, Wrigley S/A, France, Wrigley Espana. Served with 512th F.A., 3d Army, AUS, World War II. Home: 67 Cadogan Gardens London S W 3, England Office: Wrigley Co Ltd London, England.

DEFORD, DONALD DALE, univ. adminstr.; b. Alton, Kan., Dec. 28, 1918; s. Harvey Dale and Helena (Hadley) DeF.; A.B., U. Kan., 1940, M.A., 1947, Ph.D., 1948; m. Leora Miriam Adams, June 21, 1942; children—Ruth Irene, David Lynn. Mem. faculty Northwestern U., 1948—, prof. chemistry, 1960—, chmn. dept., 1962-69, asst. to provost, 1969-70, asso. dean faculties, 1970-71, asst. v.p. research, 1971—. Served to maj. AUS, 1941-46. Mem. Am. Chem. Soc., Instrument Soc. Am., Phi Beta Kappa, Sigma Xi, Alpha Chi Sigma, Phi Lambda Upsilon. Home: 619 Juniper Rd Glenview IL 60025 Office: Rebecca Crown Center Northwestern U Evanston IL 60201

DEFORD, MIRIAM ALLEN, (Mrs. Maynard Shipley), writer; b. Phila., Aug. 21, 1888; d. Moise and Frances (Allen) deFord; student Wellesley Coll., 1907-08; A.B., Temple U., 1911; grad. study, U. Pa., 1911-12; m. W. Armistead Collier, Feb. 14, 1915 (div.); m. 2d, Maynard Shipley, Apr. 16, 1921 (dec. 1934). Staff writer Phila. N. Am., 1906-07, 08-11, Asso. Advt., Boston, Mass., 1912-13; reporter Ford Hall Open Forum, Boston, 1912-15; pub. stenographer and writer for house organs, San Diego and Los Angeles, 1915-17; editor house organ, Balt., 1917; ins. claim adjuster, Balt., Chgo., San Francisco, 1918-23; staff corr. Federated Press, 1921-56, Labor's

Daily, 1956-58, San Jose Reporter, 1959; contbr. biog. dictionaries British Authors of 19th Century, American Authors, 1600- 20th Century Authors; British Authors to 1800, European Authors, 1000-1900. Recipient Essay award Com. Econ. Devel., 1958. Fellow Am. Humanist Assn.; mem. Mystery Writers Am. (bd. mem.), Sci. Fiction Writers Am., Rationalist Press Assn. (London, Eng.), Authors Guild, Poetry Soc. Am. Secularist. Author: Love Children (biog.), 1931; Children of Sun (poems), 1939; Who Was When? A Dictionary of Contemporaries, rev. edit., 1949; They Were San Franciscans (biography), rev. edit., 1947; Shaker with the Wind (novel), 1942; Psychologist Unretired; Lillien J. Martin (biography), 1948; Up-Hill All the Way; Maynard Shipley (biography), 1956; The Overbury Affair (Edgar award Mystery Writers of Am.), 1960; Penultimates, (poetry) 1962; Stone Walls; Prisons from Fetters to Furloughs 1964; Murderers Sane and Mad (award Mystery Writers Am.), 1965; The Theme is Murder (stories), 1967; Thomas Moore, 1967; The Real Bonnie and Clyde, 1968; Xenogenesis (sci. fiction), 1969; On Being Concerned (biography), 1969; The Real Ma Barker, 1970; Elsewhere, Elsewhen, Elsehow (sci. fiction), 1971. Contbr. stories, articles, verse to mags.; rep. by stories in O. Henry Meml. Prize Vol., "The Silver Knight," 1930; "Pride," 1934; verse in over 50 anthologies; also numerous short stories in anthologies. Publ. asso.; The Humanist. Editor: Anthology, Space, Time and Crime, 1964. Address: Ambassador Hotel 55 Mason St San Francisco CA 94102

DEFORD, SARA WHITCRAFT, educator; b. Youngstown, O., Nov. 9, 1916; d. Union Corwin and Grace (Whitcraft) de Ford; A.B., Mt. Holyoke Coll., 1936, M.A., 1938; Ph.D., Yale, 1942. Instr. English, Barnard Coll., 1942-46; asst. prof., Goucher Coll., Towson, Md., 1946-50, asso. prof., 1950-57, prof. English, 1957- -; vis. prof. Tsuda College, Tokyo, 1969-70. Nurse's aide A.R.C., 1950—. Recipient Eugene F. Saxton Meml. fellowship, 1948; Fulbright lectr., Japan, 1954, 61-62. Mem. Nat. Council Tchrs. English, Medieval Acad. Am., Coll. English Assn., Am. Assn. U. Profs., Am. Assn. U. Women. Mem. Soc. of Friends. Home: 921 Dulaney Vally Ct Towson MD 21204

DEFORE, DON J., actor; b. Cedar Rapids, Ia., Aug. 25, 1917; s. Joseph E. and Albia (Nezerka) DeF.; student U. Iowa, Pasadena Community Sch. Theater 1934-37; m. Marion Holmes, February 14, 1952; children—Penny Lu, David, Dawn, Ronnie, Amy N. Began in stock, touring cos.; appeared on Broadway in Where Do We Go From Here, Steel, Male Animal; motion picture debut We Go Fast, 1941, others include Male Animal, City Without Men, Human Comedy, Thirty Seconds Over Tokyo, Affairs of Susan, You Came Along, Ramrod, Romance on the High Seas, One Sunday Afternoon, My Friend Irma, Dark City, Time To Love, Battle Hymn, Southside 1-1000. Without Reservations, It Happened on Fifth Avenue, A Guy Named Joe, Facts of Life, She's Working Her Way through College, Too Late for Tears, A Girl in Every Port, numerous others; TV show Ozzie and Harriet; co-star TV series Hazel; owner Silver Banjo Restaurant, Disneyland; pres. D4 Prodns., Inc., producing motion pictures, 0V. Trustee, Nat. TV Acad. Mem. Acad. TV Arts and Scis. (pres. 1954-56). Mason (32, Shriner). Author: With All My Love, Penny, 1965. Office: care Academy Television Arts and Sciences 7188 Sunset Blvd Hollywood CA 90046 also: Silver Banjo Disneyland Anaheim CA 92802

DE FOREST, GIDEON KNAPP, physician; b. N.Y.C., May 12, 1906; s. Edward Layton and Margie Duryea (Bliven) de F.; student Hotchkiss Sch., 1921-25; B.S., Yale, 1929, M.D., 1932; m. Isabel Shaw, children—Mott Layton, Margie Duryea, Caroline, Isabel; m, 2d, Anna Orr, 1947; 1 son, Douglas Orr; m. 3d, C. Ellen Keith Riese, 1959; 1 dau., Ellen L.; 1 step-dau., Alida Elizabeth. Intern internal medicine New Haven Hosp., 1932-34; Milbank Fund fellow. 1934, 1942-43; pvt. practice, Concord, Mass., 1934-42, New Haven, since 1942; fellow Saybrook Coll., Yale, 1944, clin. instr. preventive medicine sch. medicine, 1944-47, asst. clin. prof. medicine 1947-53, asso. clin. prof. medicine, 1953—; medical director Arthritis and Rheumatism Found., 1950-54, member bd. of govs. 1961—; director of the arthritis clinic Grace-New Haven Hosp., 1951—; cons. VA Hosp., W. Haven, Conn., State Conn. Office Tb Control. Hosp. Care and Rehabilitation; member out-patient staff Mass. Gen. Hosp., Boston, 1934-42. Mem. b. trustees Concord Acad., 1941-42; dir. United Fund, New Haven. Mem. St. Anthony, Torch Honor Soc., Nu Sigma Nu. Episcopalian. Club: Yale (N.Y.C.). Author articles med. jours. Home: Dromara Rd Guilford CT 06437 Office: 309 Edwards St New Haven CT 06511

DE FOREST, ROY D., artist; b. N. Pltte, Neb., Feb. 11, 1930; s. Roy Henry and Oma (Woods) De F.; A.A.A., Yakima Jr. Coll., 1950; student Cal. Sch. Fine Arts, 1950- 52; A.B., San Francisco Art Inst., 1953, M.A., 1958. One man exhbns. include East & West Gallery, San Francisco, 1958, 55, Dilexi Gallery, San Francisco, 1960, 61, 63, 66, Stonecourt Gallery, Yakima, 1960, Allan Frumpkin Gallery, N.Y.C., 1968, San Francisco Art Inst., 1969, Hansen Fuller Gallery, San Francisco, 1971, Cal. Palace Legion Honor, San Francisco, 1971; asst. prof. art U. Cal. at Davis, 1965—. Mem. artists council San Francisco Art Assn. Bd. dirs. Web Found., 1966—. Served with AUS, 1953-55. Recipient Neallie Sullivan award San Francisco Art Inst. Home: Box 47 Port Costa CA 94569 Office: Univ of Cal Davis CA

DE FOSCHI, FELIX F., banker. Vice pres., comptroller Conn. Savs. Bank of New Haven. Office: 47 Church St Box 208 New Haven CT 06501*

DEFRANCIS, JOHN, educator; b. Bridgeport, Conn., Aug. 31, 1911; s. Frank and Rose (Mastroni) DeF.; B.A., Yale, 1933; M.A., Columbia, 1941, Ph.D., 1948; m. Katharine Gerry Wilson, Aug. 20, 1938; 1 son, Charles Alexander. Instr., Yale, 1943-45; asst. prof. Johns Hopkins, 1947-54; asso. prof. Quinnipiac Coll., 1956-61; research prof. Seton Hall U., 1962-66; prof. U. Hawaii, Honolulu, 1966—. Mem. Assn. for Asian Studies, Am. Oriental Soc., Linquistic Soc. Am., Chinese Lang. Tchrs. Assn. Author: Nationalism and Language Reform in China, 1950; (with E-tu Zen Sun) Chinese Social History, 1956; Beginning, Intermediate and Advanced Chinese, Character Texts, and Readers, 12 vols., 1963-68. Editor: Jour. of Chinese Lang. Tchrs. Assn., 1968—. Asso. editor: Jour. of Am. Oriental Soc., 1950-55. Home: 1923 Uluwehi Pl Honolulu HI 96822

DE FRANCO, BONIFACE FERDINAND LEONARDO BUDDY, clarinet player; b. Camden, N.J., Feb. 17, 1933. Winner Tommy Dorsey amateur contest; performed with Billy Krechner, Phila., Scat Davis, 1939, Gene Krupa, 1941-42, Ted Fio Rito, 1942, Charlie Barnet, 1943-44, Tommy Dorsey, 1944-46, 47-48, Boyd Raeburn, Cal., 1946-47; with various small groups, N.Y.C., Chgo.; with Count Basie, 1950; formed own band, 1951, quartet, 1952, toured Europe with Jazz Club USA, 1954; appeared motion picture film, Wild Party, 1956; recorded Cross Country Suite, also performed with Nelson Riddle at Hollywood Bowl; recital tour Tri- State Musical Festival, Enid, Okla., also Rose Festival, Portland, Ore.; recordings with Art Tatum, Oscar Peterson. Recipient Down Beat Poll award, 1945-54, Down Beat Critics award, 1953, 54, Metronome Poll award, 1950-55, Musicians Poll award Ency. Jazz, 1956. Address: 3921 Hillcrest Dr Los Angeles CA 90008*

DEFRANK, VINCENT, condr.; b. L.I. City, N.Y., June 18, 1915; s. Nicholas and Della (Proudford) DeF.; student Juilliard Sch. Music, 1934-46, Ind. U., 1950-52; m. Jean Marie Martin, Aug. 26, 1960; children—Vincent Nicholas, Philip Martin. Cellist Detroit Symphony Orch., 1939-40, St. Louis Symphony, 1947-50; condr. Memphis Symphony Orch., 1952—; music supr. Memphis-Hebrew Acad., 1969—; mem. adv. panel Tenn. Arts Commn., 1970—; condr. Memphis Civic Ballet, Memphis Opera Theatre, Tenn. All-State Orch., Sewanee Summer Music Center, Jackson Symphony, Nashville Little Symphony. Served with AUS, 1940-45. Mem. Memphis Music Inc., Am. Symphony Orch. League, Nat. Rifleman Assn. Club: Petroleum (Memphis). Office: Crosstown Sta Box 4682 Memphis TN 38104

DE FUNIAK, WILLIAM QUINBY, legal author, former educator, b. Birmingham, Ala., Nov. 16, 1901; s. Ernest and Florence (Quinby) de F.; J.D., U. Va., 1924; LL.M., U. San Francisco, 1947; m. Eleanor Slater, Oct. 30, 1932; children—Olivia, William Slater, Frederick. Admitted to Ky. bar, 1923, Cal. bar, 1933; practice of law, 1924-36; asst. editor in chief Callaghan & Co., Chgo., 1937-41; prof. law U. San Francisco, 1941-66; prof. law U. Pacific, Sacramento, 1968-71; vis. prof. law U. London, Edinburgh, 1963, U. Ariz., 1966-67. Served with War Relocation Authority, 1942; USCGR, 1943-45. Named Ky. col. Mem. Cal., Ky. bar assns. Democrat. Episcopalian. Clubs: Scribes, Commonwealth. Author: Am. Notaries Manual, 1942; Principles of Community Property, 3d edit., 1971; Cases and Materials on Community Property, 2d edit., 1969; Handbook of Modern Equity, 2d edit., 1956; American- British Dictionary, 1963-67; Cases on Equitable Relief, 1964-65; co- author; Cyclopedia of Federal Procedure, 1943-44, 51-52; Municipal Corporations, 1949; Wisconsin Pleading and Practice; Illinois Pleading and Practice; Michigan Pleading and Practice. Editor annual supplement Cyclopedia of Federal Prodecure, 1945-48; Callaghan's Michigan Digest, 1941-42; Callaghan's Iowa Digest, 1941. Contbr. to legal encys., legal periodicals. Address: 223 Trevethan Av Santa Cruz CA 95060

DE FURIA, GUY G., lawyer; b. Phila., Nov. 13, 1904; A.B., U. Pa., 1925, LL.B., 1928. Admitted to Pa. bar, 1928, U.S. Supreme Ct. bar, 1937; from asst. dist. atty. to 1st asst. dist. atty., Delaware County, Pa., 1932-44; asst. counsel U.S. Senate Select Com. on Censure, 1954; now partner firm Fronefield, de Furia & Petrikin, Media. Fellow Am. Coll. Trial Lawyers; mem. Am., Pa., Delaware County bar assns., Phi Beta Kappa, Order of Coif. Office: 107 W 3d St Media PA 19063*

DE GAETANO, ARMAND LEONARD, educator; b. Corigliano, Italy, Jan. 4, 1913; s. Francesco and Antonietta (Toto) De G.; came to U.S., 1925, naturalized, 1937; B.S.S., Coll. City N.Y., 1939; M.A., Columbia, 1948, Ph.D., 1954; m. Carolyn Alice Hall, Aug. 26, 1947; children—Mark, Douglas. Instr. biology, Italian and Spanish, N.Y.C. schs., 1939-42, 45-48; mem. faculty Wayne State U., Detroit, 1948—, chmn. Italian area, 1965—, prof. Italian and Spanish, 1968—, mem. grad. studies com., 1956—, mem. lang. and lit. com. Italian area studies dept. sociology, 1957—, chmn. Italian sect. Lang. Lab., 1948—, acting chmn. dept. Spanish and Italian, 1961. Bd. dirs. P.T.A. Mason Sch., Grosse Pointe, Mich., 1959-61. Served to 1st lt., inf. AUS, 1942-46. Decorated knight Order Merit Italian Republic; named hon. citizen Carunchio, Italy, 1944. Am. Philos. Soc. grantee, 1963-64. 65, 70, Fulbright fellow, 1964; fellow, grantee Wayne State U., 1963, 68. Mem. Am. Assn. Tchrs. Italian (pres. 1966-68, dir. Italian flood relief fund 1966-68), Renaissance Soc. Am., Modern Lang. Assn., Dante Soc., Am. Assn. U. Profs., Am. Italian Hist. Assn., Mich. Fgn. Lang. Assn. (exec. council 1968—). Contbr. articles profl. jours. Home: 2119 Beaufait Dr Grosse Pointe MI 48236 Office: Romance-Germanic Dept Wayne State U Detroit MI 48202

DEGARA, PAUL FREDERICK, physician, educator; b. Meran, Austria, Nov. 11, 1902; s. Geza and Rosemary (Polla) deG.; M.D., U. Heidelberg (Germany), 1926, J. Padua (Italy), 1927; m. Ruth Horstmann, Mar. 9, 1929; children—Beatrice (Mrs. Seymour R. Glanz), Renata (Mrs. Albert F. Cafiero). Came to U.S., 1939, naturalized, 1944. Asst. prof. U. Greifswald (Germany), 1929-32, U. Milan (Italy). 1935-38; instr. N.Y.U. Sch. Medicine, 1939-40; from instr. to clin. prof. emeritus Cornell U. Med. Coll., 1940—. Chmn. bd. Allergy Found. Am., 1969—. Fellow A.M.A., Am. Acad. Allergy, Am. Coll. Allergists (pres. 1969-70); mem. N.Y. State, Westchester, West Coast allergy socs., Vienna Med. Soc. Author numerous articles in field. Home: 876 James St Pelham Manor NY 10803 Office: 133 E 58th St New York City NY 10022

DEGARMO, E. PAUL, educator; b. Lucerne, Mo., Jan. 29, 1907; s. Arthur and Editha (Snider) DeG.; B.S., U. Wash., 1930; M.S., Cal. Inst. Tech., 1937; m. Mary Elizabeth Turner, Dec. 26, 1934; childrenRichard William, David Arthur. Indsl. engr. Converse Co., Inc., Seattle, 1930-31, Firestone Tire & Rubber Co., Los Angeles, 1934-37; faculty U. Cal. at Berkeley, 1937—. instr. to asso. prof., 1937-50, prof. indsl. and mech. engring., 1950—, chmn, dept., 1957-60. Dir. welding research contracts OSRD, 1943-47, cons. engr. Mem. Nat. Soc. Profl. Engrs., Am. Soc. M.E., Am. Welding Soc. (Lincoln medal 1948), Am. Inst. Indsl. Engrs., Am. Soc. Metals, Phi Beta Kappa, Sigma Xi,Sigma Alpha Epsilon. Author: (with B.M. Woods) Introduction to Engineering Economy, 1942; (with F. Jonassen) Technical Lettering, 1941, 43; Materials and Processes in Manufacturing, 1957, 62, 69; Engineering Economy, 1960, 68. Contbr. articles to profl. jours. Home: 299 Grizzly Peak Blvd Berkeley CA 94708

DE GAUTIER, FELISA, city ofcl., mem. Democratic Nat. Com.; b. Ceiba, P.R., Jan. 9, 1897; d. Enrique Rincon Plumey and Rita Marrero Rivera; LL.D., Marymount Coll., Milw., 1958; L.H.D. Temple U., 1960; m. Jenaro Gautier, Mar. 23, 1940. City mgr., San Juan P.R., 1946-61, 69—, mayor, 1961-69. Founder pres. San Juan Xmas Festival Fund. Mem. directive Popular Dem. Party P.R., pres. municipal com., 1948-69; mem. Dem. Nat. Com. for P.R. Bd. dirs. Med. Center San Juan Recipient Woman of Am. award Union Am. Women, 1954; Golden Medal Honor, Don Quixote medal, Daus. Charity medal (Spain); Jean of Arc medal (France); Holden Medal of Honor (Ecuador); Bolivar medal (Venezuela); Fed. Women's Club Am. medal, Jane Adams medal (San Juan); Nat. Order Honor and Merit Haiti; Order Merit (Israel); Sacred Sepulchre medal (Vatican). Mem. City Mgrs. Assn., Mayor Assn., Fedn. Women's Club (Coadjutant founder P.R. chpt.), Mayor's Assn. P.R., (past pres.), Union Mujeres Americanas (coadjutant founder), Alianza Interamericana (coadjutant founder). Address: Caleta de San Juan 51 San Juan PR 00909

DEGENSTEIN, LESTER ERNEST, stock broker; b. Phila., Apr. 1, 1903; s. David and Bertie (Beckman) D.; student U. Pa., 1923; m. Lila Rosin, Apr. 4, 1953; 1 son, Lee. Partner, Newburger-Loeb & Co., Phila., N.Y.C., 1936-39; sr. partner Content Hano & Co., 1939-41, Newburger Hano & Co., 1941-47, Zuckerman Smith & Co., N.Y.C., 1948—; dir. Rosenau Bros. Asst. treas. Lexington Sch. for Deaf, N.Y.C., 1960—; chmn. finance com. Maternity Center Assn., 1955—. Served to maj. USAAF, World War II. Home: 33 E 70 St New York City NY 10021 Office: 30 Broad St New York City NY 10004

DE GEORGE, RICHARD THOMAS; educator; b. N.Y.C., Jan. 29, 1933; s. Nicholas and Carmelina (D'Ippollto) De G.; B.A., Fordham U., 1954; Ph.B., U. Louvain (Belgium), 1955; M.A., Yale, 1958, Ph.D., 1959; m. Fernande I. Melanson, June 15, 1957; children—Rebecca, Anne Marie, Catherine. Faculty, U. Kan., 1959—, prof. philosophy, 1964—, chmn. dept., 1966—; lectr., sr. research fellow Columbia, 1965-66; asso. Inst. E. European Studies, Fribourg, Switzerland, 1962-63; Research fellow Yale, 1969-70. Served to 1st lt. AUS, 1955-57. Fulbright fellow, 1954-55; Ford fellow, 1962-63; recipient Hope Teaching award U. Kan., 1965; Nat. Endowment for Humanities fellow, 1969- 70. Mem. Am. Philos. Assn., Metaphys. Soc. Am., Am. Assn. for Advancement Slavic Studies. Author: Patterns of Soviet Thought, 1966; The New Marxism, 1968; Soviet Ethics and Morality, 1969; A Guide to Philosophical Bibliography and Research, 1971; also articles. Editor: Ethics and Society, 1966; Classical and Contemporary Metaphysics, 1962; editor, contbr.: Reflections on Man, 1966. Home: 945 Highland Dr Lawrence KS 66044

DE GERENDAY, LACI ANTHONY, sculptor; b. Budapest, Hungary, Aug. 17, 1911; s. Ladislaus and Helen (Jiraszek) deG.; came to U.S., 1912, derivative citizenship; student S.D. Sch. Mines, 1929-30, Ursinus Coll., 1930-31, N.A.D., 1932-34, Beaux-Arts Inst., 1934-35; m. Mary Ellen Lord, Dec. 19, 1939; 1 dau., Lynn. Exhibited group shows N.A.D., Pa. Acad. Design, Phila. Mus., Cin. Art Mus., Mus. Ariz., San Francisco Art Mus., Modern Art Mus., Grand Central Gallery, Feragil Gallery, Art Assn. Newport (R.I.), Nat. Sculpture Soc. bas-relief show, French Art Gallery, Archtl. League Gold Medal Exhbn., Acad. Arts and Letters, Nat. Arts Club, Corning Glass Mus., Boston Mus., N.Y. Coliseum, Rockefeller Center, Allied Artists, Smithsonian Inst., Sculpture Center, N.Y.C.; executed Farragut medal N.Y. U. Hall Fame; bas-reliefs Chgo. Hotel; equestrian portrait Mus. of Africa, Algiers; large reliefs Post Office Tell City, Ind., Ct. House Aberdeen, S.D.; medal for Am. Inst. E.E.; portraits and creative sculpture pieces in pvt. collections; bronze relief Killearn Gardens, Tallahassee; design for Corning Glass; large relief in bronze St. Francis of Assisi Sch., Torrington, Conn.; silver coin Nat. Commemorative Soc., Mermaid Fountain, N.Y.C. Garden, Bronze relief Bklyn. Community Coll., others. Served with combat engrs. AUS, ETO, MTO 1943-46. Recipient citation City N.Y.; Ellen Speyer award N.A.D., 1947, 62; Lindsey Morris Meml. award Allied Artists, 1969; prize Nat. Sculpture Soc., Bennett award, 1963; 1st sculpture prize N.J. Art Assn. Fellow Nat. Sculpture Soc. (council). Address: 22-27 76th St Jackson Heights NY 11370

DE GIVENCHY, HUBERT, fashion designer; b. Beauvais, France, Feb. 21, 1927; s. Lucien and Béatrice (Badin) Taffin de G.; ed. Ecole nationale supérieure des beauxarts; Faculty of Law, U. Paris. Apprenticeship fashion houses of Piquet, Lelong, Fath and Schiaparelli; opened his own fashion house, Paris, 1952. Address: 3 Av George-V Paris, France.*

DEGLER, CARL NEUMANN, educator, author: b. Orange, N.J., Feb 6, 1921; s. Casper and Jewell (Neumann) D.; A.B., Upsala Coll., N.J., 1942, L.H.D., 1969; M.A., Columbia, 1947, Ph.D., 1952; m. Catherine Grady, Nov. 19, 1948; children—Paul Grady, Suzanne Catherine. Instr., Hunter Coll., 1947-48, N.Y.U., 1947- 49, Adelphi Coll., 1950-51, Coll. City N.Y., 1952; mem. faculty Vassar Coll., 1952-68, prof. history, 1962-68, chmn. dept., 1966-68; prof. Am. history Stanford, 1968—; vis. prof. Columbia Grad. Sch. 1963-64, Stanford, summer 1964. Mem. com. examiners in history Grad. Record Exam., 1970—, Served with AUS, 1942-45; CBI. Am. Council Learned Socs. fellow; 1964- 65. Mem. Am., So. hist. assns., Econ. History Assn., Am. Studies Assn., Orgn. Am. Historians (exec. bd. 1970—), Am. Assn. U. Profs. Author: Out of our Past, 1959; rev. edit., 1970; Neither Black Nor White, 1971; Age of Economic Revolution, 1967; Affluence and Anxiety, 1968. Editor: Pivotal Interpretations of American History, 1966; Women and Economics (C.P. Gilman), 2d edit., 1970; The New Deal, 1970. Bd. editors Am. Quar., 1967-70, Jour So. History, 1967—. Home: 907 Mears Ct Stanford CA 94305

DEGLIHAN, ANTHONY HENRY, chemist, educator; b. Chicago, 1928; B.S. in Physics, Yale, 1950; Ph.D. in Chemistry, Harvard, 1956; m. Sally Ann Jones, July 5, 1957; children--Kenneth J., Nancy A. Chemist, Acme Chem. Co., Blue Island, Ill., 1950-51; director of Reseach Lab., Indsl. Chemicals Corp., Cambridge, Mass., 1956-60; project coordinator environmental sect. Steinmetz Assos., Chgo., 1960-61; v.p. for reseach Bauer Bros. Chem. Co., Inc., Memphis, 1961-64; asst. prof. chemistry Washington U., St. Louis, 1964-66, asso. prof., 1966-70, prof., 1970--, head of chemistry dept., 1970-71. Vis. prof. So. Ill. U., summer 1967, U. of Ore., 1969. Scoutmaster, Boy Scouts America, University City, Mo., 1968-70. Bd. dirs. Rest Haven Home for Elderly, 1960-61; trustee of the Lutheran Hosp., 1965-71. Served from lt. to capt., AUS, 1951-53. Mem. Am. Chem. Soc., Sci. Research Soc. Am. (chpt. treas. 1967), Sigma Xi. Author: (with others) Basic Inorganic Chemistry, 1971. Contbr. articles to profl. jours., encys., also chpts. to books. Home: Fairfax Apts 7291 Windermere Dr University City MO 63105 Office: Dept Chemistry Washington University St Louis MO 63130

DEGNAN, HERBERT RAYMOND, leasing co. exec.; b. N.Y.C., Mar. 16, 1921; s. John T. and Florence R. (Schoonmaker) D.; student Columbia, 1938-40, postgrad., 1946-48; B.S., St. John's Coll., 1943; LL.B., Fordham U., 1955; m. Gertrude J. Fretterd, Oct. 3, 1943; children—Donald J., Regina (Mrs. Timothy Greiner), Raymond H., Robert W. Accountant Scovell Wellington Co., N.Y.C., 1946-55; admitted to N.Y. bar, 1955; atty. Seghers & Reinhart, N.Y.C., 1955-57; sr. v.p., dir. Empire State Bldg. Corp., N.Y.C., 1957-62; v.p., dir. Nat. Car Rental System, N.Y.C., 1962-65; chief exec. officer, dir. 1st Fed. Savs. & Loan Assn., Tampa, Fla., 1965-67; pres., dir. Bermec Corp., N.Y.C., 1967—. Served to lt. comdr. USNR, 1943-45. Decorated Bronze Star. Mem. Am., N.Y. State bar assns., N.Y. State Soc. C.P.A.'s, Am. Inst. C.P.A.'s, Skull and Circle, Delta Phi. Home: 97 Salem Rd Westwood NJ 07675 Office: 40 Bennett Rd Englewood NJ 07631

DEGNAN, THOMAS LEONARD, lawyer; b. Waseca, Minn., Jan. 18, 1909; s. John James and Martha (Kurkowski) D.; student St. Mary's Coll., Winona, Minn., 1925-27; J.D., Georgetown U., 1930; m. Nan Glennon, Sept. 24, 1938; children—Nancy (Sister Nancy), Martha, Denise. Admitted to Minn. bar, 1930, N.D. bar, 1933; with firm Sexton, Mordaunt, Kennedy & Carrol, St. Paul, 1930-38; founder, 1938, since sr. partner firm Degnan, McElroy, Lamb & Camrud, Grand Forks, N.D. Mem. N.D. Jud. Council, 1961-63; mem. N.D. Med. Center Advisory Bd., 1963-67, N.D. Judicial Survey Commission, 1965-67. Director No. Supply Co., Grand Forks Indsl. Found., Dakota Reddy-Mix Co., Davis Jewelry Co. Pres. Young Dems., N.D., 1940-44, nat. committeeman, 1944-48. Bd. dirs. St. James High Sch., 1954-56; past pres., dir. Grand Forks Community Chest. Mem. Am., N.D. (pres. 1960-61), First Dist. (pres. 1957-59), Grand Forks County (pres. 1952-53) bar assns., Edward Douglas White Law Club, Pierce Butler Law Club, Grand Forks C. of C. (past pres., dir.), Sigma Nu Phi. Elk (past exalted ruler). Home: 210 27th Av S Grand Forks ND 58201 Office: 1st Nat Bank Bldg Grand Forks ND 58201

DEGOTTEX, JEAN, artist; b. Sathonay, 1918. First pictures Show Fauve influence; 1st non- figurative paintings shown Galerie Denise Rene, 1949 participant Salon de Mai; one-man exhbns. Galerie Kleber, Galerie L'Etoile Scallee, Galerie Rive Driote, Galerie Fournier (all Paris). Address: care Galerie Denise Ree 123 Rue La Boetie Paris 8e France*

DEGRAAF, DONALD EARL, educator; b. Grand Rapids, Mich., June 17, 1926; s. Benjamin and Mary (Stonehouse) DeG.; A.B., Calvin Coll., 1948; B.S. in Elec. Engring., U. Mich., 1947, M.S., 1950, Ph.D. in Physics, 1957; m. Malois Wieland, Aug. 20, 1948; children—Daniel M., Gwen L., David P. With dept. physics U. Mich., Flint, 1957—, asso. prof., 1961-67, prof., 1967—, chmn. dept., 1965-70, 71—; vis. prof. edn. research center Mass. Inst. Tech., Cambridge, 1970-71. Cons. on coll. physics curriculum devel. Corp. mem. Inter-Varsity Christian Fellowship, 1968—, chmn. faculty com., 1970—. Served to lt., USNR, 1944-46, 53-55. Fellow Am. Sci. Affiliation; mem. Am. Phys. Soc., Am. Assn. Physics Tchrs., A.A.A.S. Mem. Christian Reformed Ch. Home: 1909 Proctor St Flint MI 48504

DEGRAAFF, FRANCES, educator; b. Leiden, Holland, Oct. 11, 1904; d. Willem Hendrik and Franziska (Levy) DeGraaff; Ph.D., U. Leiden, 1933. Came to U.S., 1939, naturalized, 1944. Tchr., Reed Coll., Portland, Ore., 1940-41, Black Mountain (N.C.) Coll., 1941-44, Wells Coll., Aurora, N.Y., 1945-47; faculty Bryn Mawr (Pa.) Coll. and Haverford Coll., 1947—, prof. Russian, chmn. dept., 1964-. Mem. Modern Lang. Assn., Am. Assn. Tchrs. Slavic ane East Eu opean Langs. Author: Sergej Etsenin, A Biographical Sketch, 1966. Home: 10 Railroad Av Haverford, PA 19041 Office: Bryn Mawr Coll Bryn Mawr, PA 19010.

DE GRAFF, ARTHUR CHRISTIAN, med. educator; b. Paterson, N.J., Dec. 3, 1899; s. Christian and Trina (Cooper) D.; B.S., N.Y.U., 1920, M.D., 1921; m. Dorothy Dodd, June 30, 1926; children—Arthur Christian, Elliott Dodd, Eric William. Intern, resident physician Bellevue Hosp., N.Y.C., 1921-24; instr. medicine Univ. and Bellevue Med. Coll., 1923-24; Crile research fellow physiology Western Res. U., 1924-25; instr. physiology N.Y.U. Med. Coll., 1925-27, Samuel A. Brown prof. therapeutics, 1932—; specialist heart disease; vis. physician Bellevue Hosp., 1936—; cons. div. internal medicine Meadowbrook Hosp., Hempstead, L.I.; cons. medicine Nassau Hosp., St. Agnes Hosp., White Plains, N.Y.; cons. cardiologist Hackensack (N.J.) Hosp., Mount Vernon (N.Y.) Hosp., Manhattan VA Hosp., United Hosp., Port Chester, N.Y., Yonkers (N.Y.) Gen. Hosp., Rockaway Beach (N.Y.) Hosp., Lawrence Hosp., Bronxville, N.Y.; mem. cons. staff N.Y. Infirmary, Phelps Meml. Hosp., Ossining, N.Y.; chmn. med. bd. Irvington House; attending physician med. service Univ. Hosp., N.Y.U. Med. Center. Past pres. U.S. Pharmacopoeia. Fellow A.C.P., Am. Coll. Cardiology; mem. Am. Soc. Exptl. Therapeutics, A.M.A., Soc. Exptl. Biology and Medicine, Am. Fedn. Clin. Research, Am. Physiol. Soc., Am. Soc. Clin. Investigation, New York Acad. Med., N.Y. Heart Assn. Am. Therapeutic Soc. (past pres.), New York County, Westchester County med. socs., Am. Heart Assn. (council basic scis.), Biometric Soc., Arthritis and Rheumatism Found., Harvey Soc., Soc. Alumni Bellevue Hosp., Sigma Xi, Alpha Omega Alpha, Editor: Annual Review of Medicine; editorial bd. Am. Heart Jour., Clin. Pharmacology and Therapeutics. Home: 55 Crestwood Av Tuckahoe NY 10707 Office: 850 Park Av New York City NY 10021

DEGRAFF, HERRELL, food economist, executive; b. Murray, N.Y., Aug. 12, 1908; s. Franklin Hamilton and Martha Louise (Furguson) DeG.; B.S., Cornell, 1937, Ph.D., 1941; post doctoral study U. Chicago, 1941-42; m. Gladys M. Poole, July 10, 1930; children—Peter Herrell, Sara Kathryn. With elec. appliance co., Rochester, N.Y., 1927-30, sales officer mgr. Batavia br., 1929-30; with G. E. Barrett & Co., Elmira (N.Y.) ty., 1930-31; investment salesman Varn Claus, 1931-33; mem. faculty Cornell, 1940-62, prof. agrl. econs. until 1951, H. E. Babcock prof. food econs., sch. nutrition, 1951-62; exec. v.p. Am. Meat Inst., 1962-63, pres., 1963—. Mem. bd. trustees Mutual of New York, 1969—. Student rural econ. conditions in Mexico (spl. fellowship, Rochefeller Found.), 1949; dir. econ. studies Am. Nat. Cattlemen's Assn., 1957-61; econ. cons. Nat. Assn. Food Chains, 1959-62; econ. cons. to sec. U.S. Dept. Agr., 1955- 60; cons. Rockefeller Found. Agrl. Program in Mexico, 1952, Columbia, 1953; mem. consumer issues com. U.S. C. of C., 1967—; mem. agrl. bd. Nat. Acad. of Sci.-NRC, 1968—. Faculty rep. bd. trustees Cornell, 1949-54. Mem. Am. Enterprise Assn. (adv. bd. 1953-62, chmn. 1958-62), Phi Kappa Phi, Alpha Gamma Rho, Alpha Zeta. Clubs: University (Chgo.); Cornell (N.Y.); Capitol Hill (Washington). Home: R R 1 Valparaiso IN 46383 Office: 59 E Van Buren St Chicago IL 60605

DEGRAFF, JOHN TELLER, lawyer; b. Amsterdam, N.Y., May 25, 1902; s. Edward T. and Anna V. (Taylor) DeG.; B.S. magna cum laude, St. Lawrence U., 1922; LL.B., Albany Law Sch., 1925; m. Audrey B. Brown, Aug. 18, 1923; children—John T., Richard, David A.; m. 2d, Pauline R. Gibson, Apr. 15, 1970. Admitted to N.Y. State bar, 1925; mem. firm DeGraff, Foy, Conway and Holt-Harris, Albany; counsel N.Y. State Legislative Commn. Extension Civil Service, 1939-41. Mem. N.Y. State Bd. Law Examiners, 1940-49, pres., 1949-69; chmn. Nat. Conf. Bar Examiners, 1951-52, N.Y. State Tenure Commn., 1944-61. Trustee St. Lawrence U., 1959—. Mem. Am. (ho. dels.), N.Y. State (v.p. 1955-61) bar assns., Am. Law Inst., Phi Beta Kappa. Tau Kappa Alpha, Alpha Tau Omega. Justinian. Clubs: Albany Country; Ft. Orange; Mill Reef. Home: 136 State St Albany NY 12207 Office: 90 State St Albany NY 12207

DEGRAND, R.L., savs. and loan assn. exec. Exec. v.p. Piasa First Fed. Savs. and Loan Assn., Alton, Ill. Office: State and Wall Sts Alton IL 62002*

DEGRANDI, JOSEPH A., lawyer; b. Hartford, Conn., 1927; B.S., Trinity Coll., Hartford, 1949; M.S., George Washington U., 1950, LL.B., 1952. Admitted to D.C. bar, 1952, U.S. Supreme Ct. bar, 1956; now mem. firm Browne, Beveridge & DeGrandi, Washington. Mem. Am., Inter-Am., Fed., bar assns., Bar Assn. D.C. (dir. 1968-69, chmn. patent, trademark and copyright law sect. 1967-68), Am. Patent Law Assn., Patent Lawyers Club Washington (pres. 1959), Am. Judicature Soc., Thomas More Soc. Am., Nu Beta Epsilon. Office: Browne Beveridge & DeGrandi Fed Bar Bldg W 1819 H St NW Washington DC 20006*

DEGRAVELLES, CHARLES, Republican committeeman. Chmn. Republican State Central Com., La. Address: 409 Azalea St Lafayette LA 70501

DE GRAVELLES, WILLIAM DECATUR, Jr., physician; b. Jennings, La., Feb. 20, 1928; s. William Decatur and Ara May (Zenor) deG.; B.S., S.W. La. Inst., 1949; M.D., Tulane U., 1952. Intern Charity Hosp. La., New Orleans, 1952-53; splty. tng. in phys. medicine, rehab. N.Y.U., Bellevue Med. Center, N.Y.C., 1953-56; practice medicine, specializing in phys. medicine and rehab.; dir. rehab. service Duke Med. Center, Durham, N.C., 1956-58; chief phys. medicine and rehab. Ia. Meth. Hosp., Des Moines, 1958—; chief phys. medicine and rehab. Younker Meml. Rehab. Center, Des Moines, 1958—, med. dir., 1958—. Med. cons. Easter Seal's Camp Sunnyside, Des Moines; chmn. med. adv. com. Polk County (Ia.) Nat. Found., 1958-65; mem. Gov's Com. on Employment Handicapped; bd. dir. Ia. Easter Seal Soc.; mem. Ia. regional adv. group Regional Med. Program Heart Disease, Cancer and Stroke. Bd. dirs. Goodwill Industries, Inc., Des Moines. Named Ia. Physician of Year, Gov.'s Com. on Employment Handicapped, 1969; recipient citation for meritorious service Pres.'s Com. on Employment of the Handicapped. Diplomate Am. Bd. Phys. Medicine and Rehab. Mem. A.M.A., Ia., Polk County med. socs., Muscular Dystrophy Assn. Am. (med. adviser Polk County chpt.), Nat. Multiple Sclerosis Soc. (chmn. med. adv. com. central Ia. chpt. 1958- 66), Ia. Rehab. Assn. (past dir., past pres.). Home: 6024 Ronwood Dr Des Moines IA 50312 Office: Ia Meth Hosp 1200 Pleasant St Des Moines IA 50308

DEGRAY, EDWARD JOHN, broadcasting exec.; b. Bronx, N.Y., June 11, 1916; s. Michael and Lillian (Cassano) D.; A.B., U. N.C., 1937; children—Richard E., Doris A. Robert J., Barbara S., Janet M. Accountant CBS, N.Y.C., 1937-40; office mgr., auditor, mgr. personnel sta. WBT, Charlotte, N.C., 1940-45; bus. mgr., asst. sec.-treas. Jefferson Standard Life Ins. Co., Charlotte, 1945-46, nat. sales mgr., dir., asst. gen. mgr., sec.-treas., 1946-48; exec. asst. to v.p. CBS, Inc., N.Y.C., 1948-51, sta. relations rep., coop. sales mgr., 1951-53, dir. sta. relations, supr. charge coop. sales, 1953- 55; rep. Vitapix-Guild Films, N.Y.C., 1955; nat. dir. radio sta. relations ABC, N.Y.C., 1955-56, v.p. charge radio sta. relations, 1956- 57, v.p. charge stations, 1957-58, pres. ABC radio network, 1957-60; pres. DeGray & Assos., 1960—; chmn. exec. com., dir. Broadcast Editorial Reports, Inc.; gen. mgr. KHOW, Denver, pres., treas. Trans- Tel Corp., WXTV Channel 41, 1969—; dir. Lin Broadcasting Co. Mem. nat. adv. council Nat. Pollution Found. Mem. Internat. Radio and TV Soc. Clubs: Variety Internat. (Charlotte); Heights Casino Tennis (Bklyn.); Seventh Regiment Tennis (N.Y.C.). Home: 220 Hartsdale Av White Plains NY 10606 Office: 4 W 58th St New York City NY 10019

DE GRAZIA, ALFRED, educator, behavioral scientist; b. Chgo., Dec. 29, 1919; s. Alfred J. and Katherine (Lupo) de G.; A.B., U. Chgo., 1939, Ph.D., 1948; student Columbia Law Sch., 1940-41; m. Jill B.L. Oppenheim, May 11, 1942; childrenCatherine (Mrs. Dante Matelli), Victoria F., Jessica M., Paul R., John S., Carl M., Christopher. Mem. faculty Northwestern U., 1948, U. Minn., 1948-50, Brown U., 1950-52, Stanford, 1952-57; prof. social theory in govt. N.Y. U., 1959-, dir. research program rep. govt., 1966- ; vis. lectr. U. Istanbul (Turkey), U. Rome (Italy), U. Gothenburg (Sweden), U. Bombay (India); cons. in field, 1948-. Chmn. bd. Princeton Information Tech., Inc., 1967-; adv. bd. Simulmatics Corp., 1967. Mem. U.S. delegation to UNESCO, 1960. First pres. Found. Vol. Welfare, 1957- 59. Chmn. research com. N.Y.C. Republican Party, 1961; cons. Rep. Nat. Com., 1964. Served to capt. AUS, 1942-46; ETO. Decorated Bronze Star. Mem. Am. Polit. Sci. Assn. (exec. council 1962-64), Mediterranean Social Sci. Research Council, Internat. Polit. Sci. Assn., Am. Fedn. Scientists, Am. Assn. Pub. Opinion Research. Author: Public and Republic, 1949; Elements of Political Sci., 1952, World Politics, 1949; The Western Public, 1954; The American Way of Government, 1957; Grass Roots Private Welfare, 1958; American Welfare, 1960; Science and Values in Administration, 1961; Political Behavior and Organization, 2 vols., 1962; Apportionment and Representative Government, 1963; Republic in Crisis; Congress Against the Executive Force, 1965; The Velikovsky Affair, 1966; Congress and the Presidency; The Role in Modern Times, 1965; (poetry) Passage of the Year, 1967. Editor; Congress; First Branch of Government, 1966. Founder, editor jour. Am. Behavioral Scientist, 1957-66. Designer computerized reference retrieval system in social scis., Universal Reference System, 1962-67. Home: 16 Linden Lane Princeton NJ 08540 Office: 2 Washington Sq Village New York City NY 10012

DEGRAZIA, ETTORE TED, artist; b. Morenci, Ariz., June 14, 1909; s. Domenico and Lucia (Gagliardi) DeG.; B.A., U. Ariz., 1944, B.S., M.A., 1945; m. Marion Sheret, June 14, 1946. Exhibited in numerous one man shows, 1932—; works have appeared in Ariz. Hwys. and other mags.; important collections include Kino Collection, scenes from life of Jesuit priest Father Eusebio Kino, Way of the Cross; paintings depicting 15 Stas. of the Cross presented to Newman Catholic Student Center, U. Ariz., 1964; painting Los Ninos reproduced as UNICEF greeting card, 1960. Recipient Achievement award U. Ariz., 1968. Mem. Sinfonia. Author: Ah- Ha-Toro, 1967; Yaqui Easter, 1968; The Rose and the Robe, 1968. Built Gallery in the Sun, 1965. Address: 6300 N Swan Tucson AZ 85718

DE GRAZIA, SEBASTIAN, educator, author; b. Chgo., Aug. 11, 1917; s. Alfred Joseph and Catherine Cardinale (Lupo) de G.; A.B., Ph.D., U. Chgo; m. Miriam Lund Carlson; children—Alfred Joseph III, Margherita, Sebastian; m. 2d, Anna Maria d'Annunzio di Montenevoso (div. 1967); children—Marco, Tancredi. With FCC 1941-43, OSS, 1943-45; mem. faculty U. Chgo., 1945-50; cons. bus. firms, state and U.S. Govt., 1947—; mem. faculty Princeton, 1957; dir. research study time, work and leisure Twentieth Century Fund, 1957-61; prof. politics Rutgers U., 1962—; vis. prof. U. Florence (Italy), 1950-52, U. Madrid (Spain), 1963, John Jay Coll. Criminal Justice, City U. N.Y., 1967—. Grantee Am. Philos. Soc., Social Sci. Research Council, Am. Council Learned Socs.; Fulbright prof. Mem. Am. Polit. Sci. Assn., Am. Soc. Polit. and Legal Philosophy, Assn. Internationale de Sci. Politique. Clubs: Quadrangle (Chgo.); Nassau (Princeton). Author: The Political Community, 1948; Errors of Psychotherapy, 1953; Of Time, Work and Leisure, 1962. Home: 12 Chestnut St Princeton NJ 08540 Office: Eagleton Inst Rutgers U New Brunswick NJ 08903

DEGROFF, HAROLD MILLER, educator, aero. engr.; b. Toledo, May 10, 1920; s. Harold M. and Marjorie (Lantz) DeG.; B.S. in Aero. Engring., Rensselaer Poly. Inst., 1946; Ph.D., Cal. Inst. Tech. 1950; m. Sarah E. Meek, Aug. 24, 1947; children—Thomas Dudley, Katherine Harriet, Joseph Edward, Mary, Judith. Design engr. NEPA div. Fairchild Airplane Co., 1949-51; prof. Purdue U., 1951-54, head Sch. Aero. and Engring. Scis., 1954-66, exec. asst. to dean engring., 1966-67; pres., dir. Midwest Applied Sci. Corp.; pres. dir. Araneida, Inc. Served to ensign USNR, 1942-46. Mem. Am. Soc. Engring. Edn., Am. Inst. Aeros. and Astronautics, Sigma Xi, Tau Beta Pi, Delta Chi. Rotarian. Home: R R 10 Lafayette IN 47906 Office: 1205 Kent Av West Lafayette IN 47906 0478600 PO Box 761 Estes Park CO 8051

DEGROOT, ALFRED THOMAS, educator; b. Hunters Mills, Va., Oct. 30, 1903; s. Harry Thomas and Margaret Sarah (Dunlap) DeG.; student Lynchburg (Va.) Coll., 1922-25; A.B., Butler U., 1926, A.M., 1927, B.D., 1929; certificate U. Grenoble (France), 1928; Ph.D., U. Chgo., 1939; m. Beulah Mary Richey, June 19, 1928; 1 dau., Patricia Rose. Asst., then asso. prof. O.T. langs. and lit., Butler U., 1929-33; ordained to ministry Christian Ch., 1926, and served as minister, Spencer, Ind., 1933- 36, Kalamazoo, (Park St. Ch. of Christ), 1936-41; prof. of history of religions, Drake U., 1941-45; dean Chapman Coll., Los Angeles, 1945- 49; staff lectr. Overdale Coll. Birmingham, Eng., 1948; dean, Grad. Sch., Tex. Christian U., 1949-56, distinguished prof. ch. history, 1956-69; dean of ship World Campus Afloat, fall 1967-68. Hon. archivist Faith and Order Commn. World Council of Chs. 1953—. Mem. Am. Soc. Ch. History, Soc. Am. Historians, Phi Kappa Phi, Tau Kappa Alpha. Author several books including; The Literature of the Churches of Christ in Great Britain and Ireland, 1950; (with W.E. Garrison), The Disciples of Christ. A History. (Christian Bd. publ.), 1948; You Can Live Forever, 1953; The Restoration Principle, 1960; Disciple Throught: A History, 1965; Extra Ecclesiam Nulla Salus, 1968; Church Unity; An Annotated Outline of the Growth of the Ecumenical Movement, 1969. Editor microfilms of internat. ch. history records. Home: PO Box 761 Estes Park CO 80517 ☆

DEGROOT, DON FERDINAND, TV exec.; b. Holland, Mich., Aug. 17, 1911; s. Ferdinand H. and Wilhelmina (Knopf) DeG.; A.A., Flint (Mich.) Jr. Coll., 1930; m. Iola Shirley, Oct. 20, 1934; children—Ted E., Douglas A., John D. With WFDF, Flint, Mich., 1930-41; radio dir. Holden-Graham-Clark Advt. Agy., 1941; with WWF AM-FM-TV (formerly WWJ-The Detroit News at W45D), 1941-46, 49—, asst. gen. mgr., Detroit, 1952-69, v.p., 1971—, gen. mgr., 1969—; progrm mgr. WBAL, Balt., 1946-47; sta. mgr. WTAC, Flint, 1948-49. Bd. dirs. Broadcast Music. Chmn. Mich. industry adv. com. CONELRAD, 1960-61; v.p. Mich. Radio and TV Brotherhood Week, 1961; pres. Farmington Area Community Fund, 1954-56; TV chmn. Detroit United Found. Torch Dr., 1954. Mem. Mich. Assn. Broadcasters (pres. 1961), Broadcast Pioneers (chmn. Mich. chpt. 1958-59), Mich. Asso. Press Broadcasters (pres. 1957-58), Mich. Assn. Broadcasters (v.p. 1952), Detroit C. of C., Adcraft Club Detroit. Clubs: Detroit Athletic, Economic, Press, Orchard Lake Country (Detroit). Home: 30225 Ardmore St Farmington MI 48024 Office: 622 Lafayette Blvd Detroit MI 48231

DEGROOT, MORRIS HERMAN, educator, statistician; b. Scranton, Pa., June, 8, 1931; s. Archibald L. and Florence (Dinner) DeG.; B.S., Roosevelt U., 1952; M.S., U. Chgo., 1954, Ph.D., 1958; m. Dolores Pine, Sept. 7, 1952; children—Jenny, Jeremy. Mem. faculty Carnegie-Mellon U., and predecessor, 1957—, prof. math. statistics, head dept. statistics, 1966—. Fellow Am. Statis. Assn. (asso. editor jour. 1970—, book rev. editor 1971—), Inst. Math. Statistics; mem. Am. Math. Soc., A.A.A.S., Am. Assn. U. Profs. Author: Optimal Statistical Decisions, 1969; also articles, Home: 1236 Murdoch Rd Pittsburgh PA 15217

DEGROOT, WILLARD GERALD, investment banker; b. Holland, Mich., Aug. 19, 1917; s. John and Anna (Nyboer) DeG.; A.B., Hope Coll., Holland, 1939; M.B.A., Northwestern U., 1940; m. Barbara Riley, children—John Sheldon, Wendy (Mrs. William W. Drewry III). With Bateman Eichler, Hill Richards, Inc. (formerly Bateman, Eichler & Bingham, Inc.) Los Angeles, 1946—, exec. v. pres., 1957-60, pres., 1960-66, chmn. bd., chief exec. officer, 1966—; dir. Applied Magnetics Corp., also of Volk-McLain Communities, Inc. Bd. fellow Claremont Univ. Coll.; bd. dirs. Los Angeles Orthopaedic Hosp., So. Cal. Bldg. Funds. Served to lt. comdr. USNR, World War II. Mem. Investment Bankers Assn. Am. (chmn. Cal. group, mem. nat. bd. govs.), Bond Club Los Angeles, Nat. Assn. Securities Dealers. Clubs: Stock Exchange, California (Los Angeles); Annandale Golf (Pasadena, Cal.). Home: 3 Oak Knoll Terrace Pasadena CA 91106 also: 2020 S Pacific Av Oceanside CA 92054 Office: 453 S Spring St Los Angeles CA 90013

DEGUEFE, TAFFARA, banker; b. Ankober, Ethiopia, June 15, 1926; s. Deguefe and Erguetc. Gabre (Mariam) Belaineh; B.Com., U. B.C., 1951; diploma law, U. Coll. of Addis Ababa, 1955; m. Laurie A. Paterson, Mar. 17, 1958; children—Belaineh, Taitu. Atty. State Bank of Ethiopia, 1952-55; dir. gen. Civil Aviation of Ethiopia, 1955-57; mgr. State Bank Br., Khartoum, Sudan, 1958-60; gen. mgr. State Bank of Ethiopia, 1961-63; gen. mgr., dir. Comml. Bank of Ethiopia, Addis Ababa, 1964—; chmn. Savs. and Mortgage Co. Hon. treas. Ethiopian Red Cross Soc. Decorated Officer Star of Ethiopia, Officer and Comdr. Order of Menelik II (Ethiopia). Mem. Am. Judicature Soc., Inst. Bankers of London, Am. Acad. Polit. Sci., Ethiopian Chamber of Commerce, Industry and Agr. (pres.), Ethopian Bankers Assn. (pres.). Club: Rotary (Addis Ababa). Author: Capital Formation in Ethiopia, 1958. Contbr. articles profl. mags. Home: Lideta Woreda Airport Zone Box 1374 Addis Ababa Ethiopia Office: Haile Selassie I Square Addis Ababa Ethiopia

DE GUIGNE, CHRISTIAN, III, chem. corp. exec.; b. San Mateo, Cal., Aug. 26, 1912; s. Christian and Marie Louis (Elkins) de G.; student Gunnery Sch., Washington, Conn., Hun Sch., Princeton, N.J., 1930-32, Harvard, 1932-33; m. Eleanor Christenson, July 27, 1935; children—Christian IV, Charles. With Stauffer Chem. Co. and subsidiaries, San Francisco, 1934—, v.p., dir., pres., chmn., 1953—; dir. Bank Cal., The Pacific Tel. & Tel. Co. Dir. Stanford Research Inst.; chairman bd. of govs. Internat. Sci. Found. Clubs: Pacific Union, Bohemian (San Francisco); Burlingame (Cal.) Country; Capitol Hill (Washington); Racquet and Tennis, The Brook (N.Y.) Home: 891 Crystall Springs Rd San Mateo CA 94402 Office: 636 California St San Francisco CA 94119

DEGUISTI, DOMINIC LAWRENCE, educator; b. Treviso, Italy, Mar. 30, 1911; s. Angelo L. and Angela (DeNegri) DeG.; came to U.S., 1916, naturalized, 1925; B.S., Coll. of St. Thomas, St. Paul, 1936; M.S., U. Mich., 1938; Ph.D. (DuPont fellow), U. Wis., 1943; m. Dorothy Zelinski, Sept. 18, 1938; children—Lenore (Mrs. Antoine Noujaim), Angelo, Peter. Instr., Coll. of St. Thomas, 1936-38, asst. prof., 1942-43, 46-47; asst. in helminthology U. Mich. Biol. Sta., 1939-41, 46-51; instr., asst. prof. N.Y.U. Coll. Medicine, N.Y.C., 1943-46; research asso. U. Minn. Coll. Medicine, 1946-47; asst. prof. Catholic U. Am., Washington, 1947-49; asso. prof. dept. biology Wayne State U., Detroit, 1949-57, prof. dept. biology and Sch. Medicine dept. microbiology, 1957—, chmn. dept. biology, 1967—. Markle Found. fellow to Central Am., 1945, Fulbright Research fellow to Naples, Italy Zool. Sta., 1952, La. State U. fellow to Caribbean, 1957. Fellow N.Y. Acad. Scis., A.A.A.S.; mem. Am. Soc. Parasitologist (mem. council 1964-67), Am. Soc. Tropical Medicine and Hygiene, Internat. Coll. Tropical Medicine, Am. Soc. Zoology, Am. Soc. Protozoology, Am. Micros. Soc. (mem. council 1963-69, v.p., 1965, pres. 1966), Helminthology Soc. Washington, Mich. Acad. Sci., Arts and Letters, Mich. Entomol. Soc. (pres. 1954), Sigma Xi. Home: 18233 Pennington St Detroit MI 48221

DEHAAN, NORMAN RICHARD, architect; b. Chgo., July 8, 1927; s. Peter Arend and Clara Anna (Nordstrom) DeH.; student Ill. Inst. Tech., 1944-45; m. Christopher Welles, Dec. 1957 (div. Jan. 1963). Art dir. Country Life Ins. Co., Chgo., 1947-48; archtl. and interior designer Sidney Morris & Assos., Chgo., 1948-53; designer, architect UN Korean Reconstrn. Agy., 1953-54; archtl. adviser Office of Pres. Korea, 1953-55; asst. dir. design Container Corp. of Am., Chgo., 1955-57; project dir. AID, Korea, 1958-61; est. Norman DeHaan Asso., Chgo., 1964—; pres. Norman DeHaan Asso., Inc., 1967—; design adviser Korean Tourist Service, Ltd., 1964—, Korea Trade Promotion Corp., 1967—. Regional rep. Nat. Accessions Com., Dept. of State's Art in Embassies Program. Dir. Lake Michigan Regional Planning Council. Bd. dirs. Mod-Am. Ballet; trustee Chgo. Sch. Architecture Found. Served with USNR, 1945-46; with C.E., U.S. Army, 1950-52. Mem. A.I.A., Am. Inst. Interior Designers (chmn. bd.). Clubs: Cliff Dwellers, Arts (Chgo.). Home: 237 Menomonee St Chicago IL 60614 Office: 8 E Hubbard St Chicago IL 60611

DEHART, THOMAS ALAN, fgn. service officer; b. Upland, Cal., July 21, 1926; s. Harry O. and Nora M. (Moreland) DeH.; B.A., Whittier Coll., 1951; m. Elaine Mary McGoran, Feb. 15, 1963; children—Thomas Alan, Lynn Rene, Mary Catherine, James Patrick. Vice-consul, Munich, Germany, 1952-55; vice-consul, Hong Kong, 1955-57; Chinese lang. student, 1957-59; consul Am. embassy, Taipei, Taiwan, Formosa, 1959-63; dep. dir. visa office, Dept. State, 1963-66; prin. officer, Adelaide, Australia, 1967-68; chief consular sect. Am. consulate gen., Hong Kong, 1968—. Served with USMC, 1942-45. Mem. Asm. Fgn. Service Assn. Home: care Dept State Foreign Service Washington DC 20521 Office: American Consulate General Hong Kong British Crown Colony

DE HARTOG, JAN, writer; b. Haarlem, Holland, Apr. 22, 1914; s. Arnold Hendrik and Lucretia (Meyjes) de H.; student Amsterdam Naval Coll., 1930; m. Marjorie E. Mein, Sept. 1961; children—Sylvia, Arnold, Nicholas, Catherine, Eva, Julia. Author: (plays) Skipper Next to God, 1946; This Time Tomorrow, 1947; The Fourposter, 1951; William and Mary, 1964; (novels) The Lost Sea, 1951; The Distant Shore, 1952; The Little Ark, 1954; A Sailor's Life, 1956; The Spiral Road, 1957; The Inspector, 1960; Waters of the New World, 1961; The Artist, 1963; The Hospital, 1964; The Call of the Sea, 1966; The Captain, 1966; The Children, 1968; The Peaceable Kingdom, 1971; (musical) I Do Do, 1966. Mem. Soc. of Friends. Office: Atheneum Publs New York City NY 10001

DE HAVEN, GLORIA, actress, singer; b. Los Angeles, July 23, 1925; d. Carter and Flora (Parker) De Haven; grad. Mar-Ken Profl. Sch., Hollywood, Cal., 1943; m. John Payne (marriage dissolved); 2 sons, 2 daus.; m. 2d, Martin Kimmel (marriage dissolved); m. 3d, Richard Fincher (marriage dissolved). Theatrical appearances include Seventh Heaven, 1955; (stock) The Unsinkable Molly Brown, 1963; films include Susan and God, 1940; Best Foot Forward, 1943; Two Girls and a Sailor, 1944; Step Lively, 1944; Broadway Rhythm, 1944; The Thin Man Goes Home. 1944; Summer Holiday, 1948; Summer Stock, 1950; Three Little Words, 1950; I'll Get By, 1950; Two Tickets to Broadway, 1951; So This is Paris, 1954; The Girl Rush, 1955; numerous TV appearances in U.S. and Eng., also nightclub appearances. Home: 50 Sedgwick Av Darien CT Office: care Martin Bregman 630 3d Av New York City NY 10017*

DEHAVEN, WILLIAM LOY, speciality meat co. exec.; b. Ft. Wayne, Ind., Mar. 24, 1936; s. John R. and Juanita (Loy) DeH.; student Ind. U., 1956-58; B.S., U. Evansville, 1960; m. Julie Ann Sobosan, Apr. 27, 1957; children—Matthew, Jennifer, Melissa, Cynthia. Accounting mgr. Magnavox Co., Ft. Wayne, Greeneville, Tenn., 1960-68; corporate controller Peter Eckrich & Sons, Ft. Wayne, 1969—. Mem edn. com. Taxpayers Research Assn., 1969—. Served with U.S. Army, 1954-56. C.P.A., Ind. Mem. Nat. Assn. Accountants (v.p., dir.), Ind. Assn. C.P.A.'s, Adminstrv. Mgmt. Soc., Ft. Wayne C. of C. Home: 4118 Roxton Lane Fort Wayne IN 46805 Office: 3515 Hobson Rd Fort Wayne IN 46805

DE HAVILLAND, OLIVIA MARY, actress; b. Tokyo, Japan, July 1, 1916; d. Walter Augustus and Lilian Augusta (Ruse) de H. (parents British subjects); ed. in schools and convent in Calif.; awarded scholarship Mills College, m. Marcus Goodrich, Aug. 26, 1946 (div.); 1 son. Benjamin Briggs Goodrich; m. 2d, Pierre Galante, Apr. 2, 1955; 1 dau., Gisele. Naturalized Am. Citizen, 1941. Pres. Jury Cannes Film Festival, 1966. Made stage debut as Hermia in Midsummer Night's Dream (Max Reinhardt prodn.), Hollywood Bowl, 1934; 1st motion picture in same role, 1935; starred in pictures, including: Captain Blood, Anthony Adverse, Robin Hood, Gone With the Wind (her performance nominated for Acad. award), Strawberry Blonde, Hold Back the Dawn (her performance nominated for Acad. award), Princess O'Rourke, To Each His Own (received Acad. award for best actress performance, 1946), Dark Mirror, Snake Pit (performance nominated for Acad. award; also received N.Y. Critics award), The Heiress (received 2n Acad. award for best actress performance, 1949. New York Critics award), The Snake Pit (Laurel award, best performance 1948-53), My Cousin Rachel, 1952, Not As A Stranger, 1954. Ambassador's Daughter, 1955 (Belgian Critics Prix Femina), Proud Rebel, 1957, Light in the Piazza, 1961, Lady in a Cage, 1963, (films and filming award), Hush, Hush Sweet Charlotte, 1964, The Adventurers, 1969; Pope Joan, 1971; summer stock; What Every Woman Knows (Westport, Conn., Easthampton, L.I.), 1946; Candida, 1951; 245 performances Transcontinental Tour, 1951-52; 100 performances Juliet, 1951, Toured Army and Navy hosps, in U.S., Alaska, Aleutians, South Pacific, 1943-44. Recipient Women's Nat. Press Club award, presented by Pres. Truman, 1950; for best female performance); play A Gift of Time, Screen Actors Guild, Acad. of Motion Picture Arts and Scis. Democrat. Episcopalian. Author: Every Frenchman Has One, 1962. Address: BP 156-16 Paris France

DEHAY, JOHN CARLISLE, Jr., lawyer; b. Jones Prairie, Tex., Mar. 30, 1922; s. John Carlisle and Valda (Drury) DeH.; B.B.A., So. Meth. U., 1949, LL.B., 1949; m. Barbara Jean Smith, Nov. 30, 1956; 1 dau., Leslie. Admitted to Tex. bar, 1948; mem. legal dept. Employers Casualty Co., Dallas, 1949-51; pvt. practice law Gardere, Porter & DeHay, Dallas, 1951—. Dir. Tex. Assn. Def. Counsel, 1968. Served with AUS, 1942-45. Decorated B.S.M. Mem. Am. Coll. Trial Lawyers, Am., Dallas bar assns. Baptist. Clubs: Woodvale Fishing (Mineola, Tex.), Dallas Idlewild (Dallas). Home: 3201 Villanova St Dallas TX 75225 Office: Republic Bank Bldg Dallas TX 75201

DEHENNIN, HERMAN, diplomat of Belgium; b. Lier, Belgium, July 20, 1929; s. Alexander and Florence (Brehmen) D.; D. in Law, U. Leuven (Belgium), 1951; m. Margaret Donvil, Nov. 17, 1954; children—Philip, Steven. Lawyer, Leuven, 1953-54; attache, Belgian Ministry Fgn. Affairs, Brussels, 1954-56; 3d sec., Belgian embassy, The Hague, 1957-59; 2d then 1st sec. Belgian embassy, New Delhi, India, 1960- 63; 1st sec. Belgian embassy, Madrid, Spain, 1963-65; charge d'affairs of Belgium, Brazzaville, 1965-66; Belgian ambassador, Rwanda, 1966-70; econ. minister Belgian embassy, Washington, 1970—. Served as lt. Belgian Army, 1951-53. Decorated officer Order Leopold of Belgium. Home: 4949 Quebec St NW Washington DC 20016 Office: 3330 Garfield St NW Washington DC 20008

DEHLENDORF, ROBERT OLIVER, II, communications services exec.; b. St. Louis, May 13, 1931; s. Robert Oliver and Louise (Bertram) D.; B.A., Amherst Coll., 1953; M.B.A. with high distinction, Harvard, 1955; m. Patricia Ann Landis, June 20, 1953 (dec. June 1971); children—Deborah L., Scott R. Controller, treas. Kimball Mfg. Co., San Rafael, Cal., 1958-59; v.p., treas. Microwaves Electronic Corp., Palo Alto, Cal., 1959-64; pres., chief exec. officer Arcata Nat. Corp., Menlo Park, Cal., 1964—; dir. Opportunity Funding Corp., Washington, 1970—. Mem. Stanford-Mid Peninsula Urban Coalition, 1969—, exec. com. Pres.'s Adv. Council Minority Bus. Enterprise, 1969—; mem. adv. bd. Stanford Grad. Sch. Bus., exec. council Harvard Bus. Sch. Assn. Served with AUS, 1955-58. Office: 2750 Sand Hill Rd Menlo Park CA 94025

DEHNER, DOROTHY, painter, sculptor; b. Cleve.; d. Edward P. and Louise (Uphof) Dehner; student U. Cal. at Los Angeles, then Art Student's League, 1927-31; study and research abroad; B.S. in Art, Skidmore Coll., 1955; m. David Smith; m. 2d, Ferdinand Mann, Sept. 9, 1955; stepchildren—Irwin Mann, Abigail Mann Thernstrom. Lectr. Skidmore Coll., 1947, 54; worked Atelier 17, 1952-55; tchr. Indian Hill Music Workshop, Stockbridge, Mass., 1953-54, Barnard Sch. for Girls, N.Y.C., 1954-56; exhibited with David Smith, Albany inst., 1947, 1953; one-man shows Albany Inst. 1953, Rose Fried Gallery, N.Y.C., 1952, U. Va. Mus. Fine Art, 1954, Chgo. Art Inst., 1955, Willard Gallery, N.Y.C., 1955, 57, 60, 63, 66, 70. Wittenborn's Gallery, 1956, Gres Gallery, Washington, 1959, (retrospective) Jewish Mus., N.Y. 1965; one-man traveling show to 20 colls. and museums, 1953-54, 63-64; exhibited in group shows Whitney Mus. Am. Art (watercolors) 1951, 52, 53, (sculpture), 1960, 63, Bklyn. Mus. Internat. Watercolor show, 1953, 55, 59, Mus. Modern Art, 1952, 54, 59-71, Met. Mus., N.Y.C., 1953, also important museums U.S.A., France; show Am. Sculptors Gallery Bernard, Paris, Italy, Holland, Germany, Eng., London, New Sculpture group Stable Gallery, N.Y.C.; works in permanent collection Met. Mus., N.Y.C., State Dept., Columbia, Jewett Art Center, Wellesley Coll., Munson Williams Proctor Inst., Utica, N.Y., Mus. Modern Art, Columbus Gallery Fine Art, Hyde Collection, Glens Falls, N.Y., 1st Nat. Bank, Chgo., Biria Acad. Art, Calcutta, India, Seattle Art Mus., Minn. Mus. Art, various colls., others. Appeared on radio NBC Art Forum WOR interview, 1949-50. Fellow Tamarind Workshop, 1965. Recipient 1st prize for drawing Audubon Ann., 1947; Art U.S.A., 1959; 1st prize for sculpture Kane Meml. Exhbn., Yaddo Found. Mem. Sculptors Guild, New Sculpture group Fedn. Am. Painters and Sculptors. Author art criticism Archtl. Forum, 1947. Home: 33 Fifth Av New York City NY 10003 Studio: 41 Union Sq New York City NY 10003

DE HOFFMANN, FREDERIC, nuclear physicist; b. Vienna, Austria, July 8 1924; s. Otto and Marianne (Halphen) de H.; B.S., Harvard, 1945, M.A., 1947, Ph.D. (fellow NRC, 1946-48), 1948; m. Patricia Lynn Stewart, June 10, 1953. Came to U.S., 1941, naturalized, 1946. Staff mem. Los Alamos Sci. Lab., 1944-46, 48-55, alternate asst. dir., 1950-51; cons. AEC, 1947-48, com. sr. responsible reviewers, 1947-51, cons. Joint Congl. Com. Atomic Energy, 1954; asst. v.p. nuclear planning Convair, San Diego, Cal. (div. Gen. Dynamics Corp), 1955, v.p. Gen. Dynamics Corp., 1955-67, also gen. mgr. Gen. Atomic div., 1955-59, pres., 1959-67; pres. Gen. Atomic Europe, Zurich, Switzerland, 1960-67; v.p. Gulf Oil Corp., also pres. Gulf Gen. Atomic and Gulf Gen. Atomic Europe, 1967-69; chancellor Salk Inst. Biol. Studies, 1970—; dir. Gulf Mineral Resources, So. Cal. Nat. Bank, So. Cal. 1st Nat. Corp. Hon. prof. theoretical physics U. Vienna, 1968. Sci. sec. UN Internat. Conf. Peaceful Uses Atomic Energy, 1955. Governing bd. Courant Inst. Math., N.Y.U., 1968—; dir. Atomic Indsl. Forum, 1962-70. Trustee Salk Inst., Scripps Clinic and Research Found., 1956-66. Decorated gt. comdr. Cross Medal, Cross Sci. and Arts (Republic Austria). Fellow Am. Phys. Soc., Am. Nuclear Soc. (bd. dirs. 1964-67); mem. Harvard Alumni Assn. (dir. 1961-64), Sigma Xi. Rotarian. Author: Introduction to the Theory of Neutron Diffusion (with K. M. Case and G. Placzek), Vol. 1, 1954; Mesons and Fields (with H. A. Bethe and S. S. Schweber) Vols. 1 and 2, 1955. Home: 9736 LaJolla Farms Rd La Jolla CA 92037 Office: PO Box 1809 San Diego CA 92112

DEHONEY, WILLIAM WAYNE, clergyman; b. New Raymer, Colo., Aug. 22, 1918; s. William Warren and Ruby (Northup) D.; student Baylor U., 1938-39; A.B., Vanderbilt U., 1941; B.D., So. Bapt. Theol. Sem., 1946; D.D. (hon.) Union U., 1964; LL.D., Atlanta Law Sch., 1965; m. Lealice Bishop, Aug. 24, 1944; childrenRebecca Ann, Katherine Elaine, William Wayne. Ordained to ministry Bapt. Ch., 1940; rural pastor in Tenn., 1940-43; pastor 1st Bapt. Ch., Rogersville, Tenn., 1945-48, Immanuel Bapt. Ch., Paducah, Ky., 1948-50, Central Park Bapt. Ch., Birmingham, Ala., 1950-57, 1st Bapt. Ch., Jackson, Tenn., 1957-67, Walnut St. Bapt. Ch., Louisville, 1967—. Pres. So. Bapt. Conv., 1964-66; mem. exec. com- Bapt. World Alliance. Mem. Tenn. Govs. Commn. Human Relations; exec. com. Nat. Citizens' Com. Community Relations; North Am. Coordinator for Crusade of the Americas. Trustee Union U.; chmn. bd. trustees Clear Creek Bapt. Sch. Pineville. Mem. Sigma Nu. Rotarian. Author: Challenges to the Cross, 1962; Homemade Happiness, 1963; African Diary, 1966; Disciples in Uniform, 1967; Baptists See Black, 1969; Set the Church Afire, 1970. Home: 2103 High Ridge Rd Louisville KY 40207 Office: 3d and St Catherine Louisville, KY 40202.

DEHORITY, EDWARD HAVENS, govt. ofcl.; b. Elwood, Ind., Aug. 6, 1899; s. Edward C. and Myrtle (Powell) DeH.; B.S., Ind. U., 1921; M.B.A., Harvard, 1923; m. Gladys M. Vermillion, Feb. 11, 1926; 1 son, Edward Havens II. Asst. cashier First Nat. Bank, Elwood, 1924-33; bank supr., also sec. for Commn. Financial Instns. Ind., 1933-40; with FDIC, 1940—, chief examiner, 1964—, spl. asst. to bd. dirs. 1969—, ret., 1971; co- organizer Inter Agy. Sch. for bank examiners, 1952. Served with U.S. Army, 1918. Mem. Beta Theta Pl. Author papers in field. Home: 3810 52d St N W Spring Valley, Washington, DC 20016 Office: 550 17th St N W Washington, DC 20429.

DEIBLE, CLARENCE RICHARD, glass co. exec.; b. Warren County, Pa.; ed. Carnegie Inst. Tech. Vice pres. Glass Containers Corp., Knox, Pa. Mason (Shriner), Elk. Address: care Glass Containers Inc Knox, PA 16232.

DEIGERT, ROBERT CAMPBELL, architect; b. St. Louis, June 15, 1908; s. Edward Frederick and Agnes (Kludt) D.; student U. Mich., 1928-29; B.F.A., Yale, 1933; m. Joan Lozier Thomas, Dec. 19, 1943; childrenRobert Campbell, Alison Lozier, Joan Braddock. Chief architect Yale Expdn. to Doura Europos, Mesopotamia, 1931-32; indsl. design asso. Harold Van Doren Assos., 1934- 37; individual practice architecture, Detroit, Toledo, 1937-42, Washington, 1945-46; sr. partner Deigert & Assos., architects and engrs., Washington, Asheville, N.C., 1946-. Chmn. bd. dirs. Primary Day Sch., Washington. Served to lt. col. USAAF, 1942-45. Decorated Legion of Merit. Mem. A.I.A., Acoustical Soc. Am. Clubs: Biltmore Forest Country; Mountain City (Ashville); Kenwood Country (Washington). Important works include Royal Netherlands Chancery, Washington, Water Pollution Lab. Center U.S. Dept. Health, Edn. and Welfare, Narragansett, R.I., Fed. Narcotics Labs., Lexington, Ky., Hdqrs., Studios, Program Recording and Distbn. Center, Voice of Am., Washington, Audio Visual Communication Center Ohio State U., Electronics Lab., Cheltenham, Md. army, navy bldgs., U.S. Embassy, Mogadiscio, Somalia, hdqrs. Nat. Arboretum, Washington. Home: 18 Forest Rd Asheville NC 28803 Office: 16 All Souls Crescent Biltmore NC 28803

DEIGHTON, LEE CECIL, former publisher; b. Seattle, Oct. 7, 1906; s. Cecil Harrison and Eva (Willcuts) D.; B.S., U. Minn., 1926; m. Bethana Bucklin, Sept. 2, 1933; children—Eve, Mark, Jane. Dir. Harcourt, Brace & Co., 1943-53; v.p. Sci. Research Assos., 1954-56; dir. Macmillan Co., also v.p. charge ednl. dept., 1957-61, exec. v.p., 1961-62, pres., 1962-65, chmn. bd., 1965-71; sr. v.p. Crowell, Collier & MacMillan, Inc., 1966-71. Pres. Am. Ednl. Publishers Inst., 1967-68. Mem. Phi Delta Kappa, Phi Kappa Psi. Editor-in-chief Ency. Edn. 1967-71. Home: Round Hill Dr Briarcliff Manor NY 10510

DEIHL, R.H., savs. and loan assn. exec. Pres., mgr. Home Savs. and Loan Assn., Los Angeles. Office: 761 S Broadway Los Angeles CA 90014*

DEILY, CURTIS R., banker. Cashier, Nat. Savs. & Trust Co., Washington. Office: New York Av at 15th St NW Washington DC 20005*

DEIN, RAYMOND CHARLES, educator; b. Powell, Neb., June 26, 1905; s. Charles Jacob and Anna Barbara (Grim) D.; B.Sc. in Bus. Adminstrn., U. Neb., 1930, M.A., 1935; Ph.D., U. Minn., 1944; m. Jane Howard, Sept. 3, 1942; 1 dau., Ellen. Asst. instr., then instr. accounting U. Neb., 1930-38; instr. accounting U. Minn., 1939-42; price analyst OPA, 1942-44; asst., then asso. prof. accounting U. Ark., 1945-46; asst. prof. accounting U. Wis., 1946-48; asso. prof. accounting U. Neb., 1948-51, prof., 1951-. Mem. Am. Accounting Assn. (dir. research 1960, pres. 1962), Am., Midwest econ. assns., Phi Beta Kappa, Beta Gamma Sigma, Sigma Alpha Epsilon. Author articles in field. Home: 1916 Dakota St Lincoln, NB 68502.

DEINERT, HERBERT, educator; b. Wiedenbrück, Germany, Dec. 13, 1930; came to U.S., 1954, naturalized, 1959; Ph.D., Yale, 1960; m. Waltraut von der Emde, 1957; children—Erika, Mark. Mem. faculty U. Ga., Athens, 1959-61, Duke, 1961-65; mem. faculty Cornell U., Ithaca, N.Y., 1965—, asso. prof. 1965—, chmn. dept. German lit., 1968—. Mem. Modern Lang. Assn., Am. Assn. Tchrs. German. Home: 130 Honness Lane Ithaca NY 14850

DEINES, HARRY J., advt. exec.; b. Loveland, Colo., Nov. 5, 1909; s. John Henry and Mary (Maseka) D.; B.S. in Mech. Engring., U. Colo.; advanced mgmt. Harvard; m. Eleanor Vrooman, Sept. 17, 1932; children—Gretchen Susan (Mrs. Charles Langston), Mark Edward, Katrina (Mrs. Kurt Dahl), Stephen John. Advt. mgr. Gen. Electric Co., 1930-45; v.p. Fuller & Smith Ross, 1945- 49; gen. advt. mgr. Westinghouse Electric Corp., 1949-53; v.p. J. Walter Thompson, N.Y.C., 1953-56, Fuller & Smith & Ross, N.Y.C., 1956- 59; exec. v.p., dir. Campbell, Mithun, Inc., Mpls., 1959—. Clubs: Canadian (N.Y.C.); Minneapolis; Denver Athletic; Farmington, (Charlottesville, Va.). Home: 29 Crestmoor Dr Denver CO Office: 200 Fillmore St Denver CO 80206

DEINES, JOHN MICHAEL, dentist; b. Lincoln, Neb., Apr. 19, 1916; s. John George and Anna (Bauer) D.; D.D.S., U. Neb., 1939; m. Lucille Margaret McDonnell, Feb. 3, 1940; children—Anna Margaret (Mrs. Frank Yon), John McDonnell. Intern, USPHS, Galveston, Tex., Seattle, 1939-41; gen. practice dentistry, Seattle, 1945—. Served with AUS, 1941-45. Fellow Am. Coll. Dentists, Internat. Coll. Dentists; mem. Am. Dental Assn. (pres. 1970-71), Washington Dental Assn. (pres. 1958-59), Delta Sigma Delta. Republican. Roman Catholic. Lion (pres. 1962). Clubs: Assembly (pres. 1962-63), Washington Athletic (Seattle). Home: 2437 Interlaken Blvd E Seattle WA 98102 Office: 227 Broadway E Seattle WA 98102

DEINHARDT, FRIEDRICH WILHELM, microbiologist, educator; b. Gueterslob, Germany, May 26, 1926; s. Walter Ernst and Luise (Fischer) D.; student U. Gottingen, 1946-48, U. Zurich, 1948; M.D., U. Hamburg, 1951; m. Jean Bannister Brown, July 2, 1959; children—Tobias Friedrich, Nicholas George. Came to U.S., 1954, naturalized, 1961. Intern, resident internat. medicine, pathology U. Hosp., Hamburg, 1951-54; research fellow, asst. prof. Childrens Hosp., U. Pa., Phila., 1954-61; asso. prof., chmn. dept. microbiology Presbyn. St. Lukes Hosp., U. Ill., 1961-66, prof. microbiology, 1966—; cons. NIH, Surg. Gen. U.S. Army, Bd. Health Chgo. Served with German Army, 1943-45. Fellow Am. Acad. Microbiology; mem. Am. Assn. Immunology; mem. Am. Soc. Clin. Investigation. Home: 1431 Judson Av Evanston IL 60201 Office: Presbyn St Luke's Hosp 1753 W Congress Pkwy Chicago IL 60612

DEINLEIN, VICTOR E., diversified industry exec.; b. Chgo., 1910; grad. Northwestern U., 1932. With Yawman & Erbe Mfg. Co., until 1941; with Acme Visible Records Inc., Crozet, Va., 1945—, v.p. sales, 1961-64, pres., chief exec. officer, 1964-70, chmn. bd., chief exec. officer, 1970—, also dir.; dir. Citizens Bank of Charlottesville (Va.); pres., dir. Acme-Seeley Bus. Systems Ltd., Acme Datagraphic Bus. Systems, Dataflow Autographic, Jackson Metal Industries, Ltd. Home: 2 Lake Rd Farmington Charlottesville VA 22901 Office: Acme Visible Records Inc Crozet VA 22932*

DEISCHER, CLAUDE KNAUSS, educator, chemist; b. Emmaus, Pa., Oct. 14, 1903; s. Jonathan R. and Blanche H. (Knauss) D.; tchr. certificate Kutztown State Coll.; B.S., Muhlenberg Coll., 1925, Lehigh U., 1927; M.S., U. Pa., 1928, Ph.D., 1933; m. Dorcas S.E. Heil, Sept. 14, 1929; 1 son, Harry. Tchr. in Emmaus (Pa.) schs., 1921-27; mem. faculty U. Pa., 1928—, asso. prof. chemistry, 1953-71, prof. emeritus, 1971—, asst. chmn. dept., 1952-65, acting chmn., fall 1962, acting curator Edgar F. Smith collection history chemistry, 1955—; lectr. in field, 1928—. Mem. Moravian Ch., 1928—. Mem., sec. provincial elders conf. No. Province, 1956-70. Trustee Moravian Coll., 1956-70, Linden Hall Sch. Girls, 1956—. Recipient award excellence undergrad. teaching U. Pa., 1959. Fellow Soc. Am. Studies; mem. Am. Chem. Soc. (treas. Phila. 1953-55; bd. dirs. 1953—, chmn. 1958; Service award Phila. 1959), Am. Inst. Chemists (chmn. Phila. 1961-62; Service award Phila. 1963, Honor Scroll award Phila. 1964), History Sci. Soc., Moravian Hist. Soc., Pa. German Hist. Soc., Moravian Music Found., A.A.A.S., Sigma Xi, Alpha Chi Sigma, Phi Lambda Upsilon. Club: Faculty Senate University of Pa. (sec. 1962-63). Author articles in fields. Home: 158 Idris Rd Merion Station PA 19066 Office: Chem Dept Univ Pennsylvania Philadelphia PA 19104; also: 69 W Church St Bethlehem PA 18018

DEISS, JOSEPH JAY, author, former business exec.; b. Twin Falls, Ida., Jan. 25, 1915; s. Joseph John and Charlotte (Neilson) D.; B.A., U. Tex., 1934, M.A., 1935; m. Catherene Dohoney, Aug. 3, 1937; children—John Casey (dec.), Susanna (Mrs. Eric Chivian). Co-editor Report of Pres.'s Commn. on Farm Tenancy, 1937; editor Handbook on Edn. and War, 1942, Execs. War Digest, 1944-45; bus. cons., N.Y.C., 194647; partner Med. and Pharm. Information Bur., N.Y.C., 1950-54; pub. relations cons. Charles Pfizer, Inc., N.Y.C., 1950-54; author, 1954—. Vice dir. Am. Acad. Rome (Italy), 1965-69. Recipient Distinguished Alumnus award U. Tex., 1970 ; decorated Cavaliere Ordine della Stella della Solidarita Italiana, 1971. Mem. Author's Guild, Phi Gamma Delta. Author: A Washington Story (novel), 1950; The Blue Chips (novel), 1957; The Great Infidel Frederick II of Hohenstaufen (hist. novel), 1963: Captains of Fortune—Profiles of Six Italian Condottieri, English edit., 1965, Am. edit., 1967; Herculaneum-Italy's Buried Treasure (archaeology) (0ne of 12 outstanding books of year BBC list; Hist. Book Club Gt. Britain 1968), 1966; The Roman Years of Margaret Fuller (biography) (one of 100 outstanding books Book World), 1969. contbr. pamphlets U.S. govt., articles nat. mags. Home: Thoreau House Wellfleet MA 02667 Office: care Thomas Y Crowell Co Inc 201 Park Av S New York City NY 10003

DEISS, WILLIAM PAUL, Jr., physician, educator; b. Shelbyville, Ky., Feb. 1, 1923; s. William Paul and Florence (Schilling) D.; B.S., U. Notre Dame, 1942; M.D., U. Ill., 1945; m. Bettye Jane Baker, May 5, 1948; children-Diana Elizabeth, William David, Paula Jane. Intern, U. Wis., 1945-46, resident, fellow in medicine, 1948-54; asst. prof., asso. prof. medicine Duke, 1954-58, asst. prof. biochemistry, 1954-58; asso. prof., prof. medicine and biochemistry Ind. U., 1958-68; prof., chmn. dept. medicine U. Tex., Galveston, 1968—; mem. adv. com. NIH. Served from 1st lt. to capt., M.C., U.S. Army, 1946-48. Fellow A.C.P.; mem. Am. Fedn. Clin. Research (past sec.-treas.), Am. Soc. Clin. Investigation, Assn. Am. Physicians, Endocrine Soc., Am. Clin. Climatol. Soc., Central Soc. Clin. Research. Contbr. articles profl. jours. Home: 7618 Beluche St Galveston TX 77550

DEITRICK, JOHN ENGLISH, physician; b. Watsontown, Pa., Apr. 13, 1905; s. Edgar Dentler and Capitola H. (Heine) D.; B.S., Princeton, 1929; M.D., Johns Hopkins, 1933; m. Dorothy Geib, May 9, 1936; children—Sarah, John, William. Intern Johns Hopkins Hosp., 1933-34; resident medicine N.Y. Hosp., 1934-36; asst. Cornell Med. Coll., 1934-36, instr., 1936-42, asst. prof. clin. medicine, 1942- 44, asso., 1944-52; dir. 2d Cornell Med. Div., Bellevue Hosp., N.Y.C., 1946-49; dir. survey med. edn. A.M.A. and Assn. Am. Med. Colls., 1949- 52; Magee prof. medicine Jefferson Med. Coll., Phila., 1952-57; dean prof. medicine Cornell U. Med. Coll., 1957-69; exec. dir. Assn. Med. Schs. Greater N.Y., 1969—; pres. N.Y. Acad. Medicine, 1970; attending physician N.Y. Hosp., N.Y.C. Dir. Prudential Ins. Co., Prudential Life Ins. Co., Newark. Bd. Dirs. Phila. div. Am. Cancer Soc. Diplomate Nat. Bd. Med. Examiners. Fellow A.C.P.; mem. A.M.A., Harvey Soc., Pa., Phila. County med. socs., N.Y. Acad. Medicine, Coll. Physicians Phila., Assn. Am. Physicians, Assn. Am. Med. Colls. (pres. 1963-64), Phi Beta Kappa, Sigma Xi. Clubs: Century Assn. University (N.Y.C.). Author: Medical Schools in the United States at the Mid-Century (with Robert C. Berson, M.D.), 1953. Home: 69 Rocklege Bd Bronxville NY Office: New York Acad Medicine New York City NY 10029

DEITRICK, JOHN ROBERT, pub. relation exec.; b. Coudersport, Pa., May 20, 1919; s. Gordon V. and Elizabeth (Jenkins) D.; B.A. in Journalism, Pa. State U., 1941; m. Jane Roeting, Jan. 8, 1949; children—Lynn, Barbara, Dana. Reporter, Waynesboro (Pa.) Record-Herald, 1941-42, A.P., 1946-52; with Allied Pub. Relations, Inc., N.Y.C., 1952—, exec. v.p., 1957, pres., 1957—. Mem. Automobile Mfrs. Assn., Pub. Relations Soc. Am., Nat. Def. Transp. Assn. Clubs: Overseas Press (N.Y.C.); Nat. Press (Washington). Home: 33 Rangs Dr Merrick NY 15566 Office: 250 Park Av New York City NY

DEITRICH, JONATHON ALLEN, educator, biologist; b. Ames, Ia.; B.A., Ia. State U., 1936, M.A., 1937, Ph.D. with honors, 1940; m. Ann Ross, Mar. 23, 1946; children--Edward, Thomas A., Mark. Instr., Ia. State U., 1946-47; asst. prof. biology Johns Hopkins, 1947-50, asso. prof., 1950-62, prof., 1962--, chmn. dept., 1963-69; vis. lectr. Stanford, 1970-71. Active Boy Scouts Am., 4-H Club. Served with AUS, 1940-46. Mem. Am. Soc. Biologists, Md. Soc. Cell Biologists, Am. Soc. Exptl. Biology, Internat. Union Biologists, A.A.A.S., Am. Acad. Arts and Scis., Phi Beta Kappa. Home: 48936 W Hancock Blvd Baltimore MD 20206

DEITRICK, WILLIAM HENLEY, architect; b. Danville, Va., Mar. 5, 1895; s. William H. and Lito (Townes) D.; A.B., Wake Forest Coll., 1916; student Columbia, 1922- 24; m. Elizabeth Hunter, Nov. 27, 1920. Prin. Newnan (Ga.) High Sch., 1916-17; bldg. contractor, 1919-22; architect, N.C., 1927-59; projects Western N. C. San., N.C. State Fair Arena, N.C. State Coll. Student Union Bldg., elementary and high schs.; architect Wake Forest Coll., 1931-50; asso. with John A. Park, Jr. & Co., 1967-. Pres. N. C. Design Found., N.C. State Coll., 1959-62; chmn. Raleigh Hist. Sites Com., 1965-68; pres. Raleigh Hist. Sites Found., 1965-68, chmn. 1967; Gov.'s Com. Beautification, treas., 1967, 68, 69—. Served as 2d lt. F.A., AUS, 1917-19. Co-winner gold medal in engrng. from N.Y. Archtl. League, 1953, first honor award in merit, 1955, 2 awards of merit, 1957. Fellow A.I.A. (chmn. South Atlantic regional conf. 1956), N.C. State Art Soc. (chmn. bd. 1949). Home: 1900 McDonald Lane Raleigh NC 27608 Office: 115 W Morgan St Raleigh NC 27601

DEITZ, AARON, physician; b. Washington, June 29, 1906; s. Max and Rosalie (Feldman) D.; A.B., U. Pa., 1928; M.D., Jefferson Med. Coll., 1932; m. Margaret S. Oxenburg, July 2, 1933; children—Robert David, Beverly (Mrs. Jerome Stanbury). Intern Gallinger Municipal Hosp., Washington; practice in Hyattsville, Md., 1933—; health officer, Hyattsville, 1942-43; organizer, dir. Casualty Sta. for Def. Hyattsville, 1942-43; med. examiner Draft Bd. I, 1942-43; obtained original grant for Prince Georges Hosp., Cheverly, Md., 1944, chief staff, 1946-48, 52, chief gen. medicine, 1952-70. Chmn. bd. Md. Bd. Health and Mental Hygiene, 1959-66. Dir. Citizens Bank Md., Riverdale, Md., Md. Bldg. & Loan Assn. Pres. Social Service League Prince George County, 1952-55. Mem. alumni adv. council bd. trustees Jefferson Med. Coll., 1966-67. Served with M.C., USNR, 1942. Mem. Jefferson Med. Coll. Alumni Assn. (founder, 1st pres. D.C., Va. and Md. chpt. 1962), Md. Med. and Surg. Faculty, D.C. Med. Soc. (asso.), Royal Soc. Health (London, Eng.), So. Med. Soc. Democrat. Jewish religion. Home: 7011 Forest Hill Dr Hyattsville MD 20782 Office: 3700 East-West Hwy Hyattsville MD 20782

DEITZ, PURD EUGENE, retired ch. ofcl.; b. York, Pa., Oct. 22, 1897; s. Harry William and Ada Gertrude (Gilbert) D.; A.B., Ursinus Coll., 1918, D.D., 1937, postgrad. Edinburgh U., 1931-32; m. Thisbe Elizabeth Shultz, Dec. 1, 1923; children—Barbara Jane (Mrs. Paul Frederick Mehl), James Gilbert. Ordained to ministry Evang. and Reformed Ch., 1921; pastor Fourth Reformed Ch., Dayton, O., 1921-25, Trinity Reformed Ch., Phila., 1925-38; prof. practical theology Eden Theol. Sem., Webster Groves, Mo., 1938-50; gen. sec. Bd. Nat. Missions, Evang. and Reformed Ch., 1950-62, gen. sec. div. of Church Extension United Ch. Bd. Homeland Ministries, 1962-69. Mem. Nat. Council Chs. Christ U.S. (chmn. div. home missions, v.p. 1954-57). Author: (hymn) We Would Be Building, 1935; (textbook) Christ's Life and Ours, For Every Time of Need. Home: 203 Sylvan Rd Bloomfield NJ 07003

DEJAGER, HAROLD GLEN, packing co. exec.; b. Orange City, Ia., Nov. 12, 1941; s. Pierce and Edna (Schreur) DeJ.; A.A., Northwestern Coll., 1961; B.S., U. S.D., 1963; m. Beverly Kay Eckhoff, May 27, 1966; children—Daniel L., Debra L. Summer accounting trainee No. Natural Gas Co., Omaha, 1962; accountant Peat, Marwick, Mitchell & Co., Omaha, 1963-66; office mgr. Needham Packing Co., Inc., Sioux City, Ia., 1966-68, corporate accountant, 1968, controller, 1968—. C.P.A. Mem. Beta Gamma Sigma. Home: 2635 S Lyon St Sioux City IA 51106 Office: Badgerow Bldg Sioux City IA 51101

DEJARDIN, DONALD ARTHUR, athletic mgr.; b. N.Y.C., Jan. 29, 1936; s. Alphonse Anthony and Grace Cecilia (McGirr) D.; B.S., U.S. Military Acad., 1958; M.B.A., Duquesne U., 1964; m. Sondra Lee Kamerer, June 14, 1958; children—Laura Lynn, Katherine Bryn, Julia Ann, Bradford John. Purchasing mgr. Westinghouse Electric, Pitts., 1961-65; mgmt. cons. Boeing Co., Cocoa Beach, Fla., 1965-66; purchasing exec. Westinghouse Electric, Phila., 1966-68; gen. mgr. Carolina Cougers, Greensboro, N.C., 1968-70, Phila. 76ers, 1970—. Initiated regional concept in profl. basketball. Home: 302 Oak Lane Newtown Square PA 19073 Office: The Spectrum Philadelphia PA 19148

DEJARMON, LEMARQUIS, coll. dean; b. Popular Bluff, Mo., Oct. 20, 1916; s. Burrell Franklin and Tessie (Britt) DeJ.; A.B., Howard U., 1946; J.D., Western Res. U., 1948; LL.M., N.Y.U., 1962; m. Elva Lianne Pegues, June 10, 1942; 1 dau., Michelle Renee. Asst. finance officer Nat. Youth Adminstrn., Youngstown, O., 1940-41; admitted to Ohio bar, 1949, S.C. bar, 1955, N.C. bar, 1962, U.S. Supreme Ct. bar, 1960; prof. law S.C. State Coll., Orangeburg, 1948-55; dean, prof. N.C. Central U., Durham, 1955—; partner firm Pearson, Malone, Johnson & DeJarmon, Durham, 1968—. Mem. adv. com. U.S. Senate Labor Com., 1959-60; mem. N.C. Criminal Code Commn., 1971—, N.C. Gen. Statute Commn., 1971—; cons. student rights and responsibilities to various colls., univs.; mem. N.C. adv. com. U.S. Commn. on Civil Rights, 1967—, Durham Com. Negro Affairs, 1958—, Human Relations Council, Durham, 1966—, N.A.A.C.P., 1940—. Bd. dirs. Found. Community Devel., Durham, Orange-Chatham Legal Aid Clinic. Served with AUS, 1942-46; ETO. Recipient Plaque of Dedication, N.C. Central U. Law Jour., 1969. Mem. Southeastern Lawyers Assn. (past pres.), Am. Bar Assn., Nat. Bar Assn. (exec. com.), Am. Judicature Soc., Phi Beta Sigma. Contbr. Ency. Internationale,— Grolier, 1968, Legal Aspects of Civil Rights Movement, 1965, All Deliberate Speed, 1969, also to several law revs., publs. Home: 125 Masondale Av Durham NC 27707

DE JONG, GARRIT, Jr., educator; b. Amsterdam, Holland, Mar. 20 1892; s. Gerrit and Lijda Marianna (Kuiper) de J.; came to U.S., 1906, naturalized, 1913; A.B., U. Utah, 1920, A.M., 1925; post grad. Nat. U. of Mexico, summer 1921, U. Munich (Germany), 1926-27; Ph.D., Stanford, 1933; m. Rosabelle Winegar, Sept. 14, 1911; children—William Gerrit (dec.), Belle Felice (Mrs. Dean E. Van Wagenen), Nola Eloise (Mrs. Clyde E. Sullivan), Carma (Mrs. Richard L. Anderson); m. 2d, Thelma Bonham, Sept. 28, 1951. Pvt tchr., music (piano and organ), 1910; instr. music and langs. Murdock Acad., Beaver, Utah, 1916-18; instr. modern langs. Latter-day Saints U., Salt Lake City, 1919-25; asso. prof. modern langs. Brigham Young U., Provo, Utah, 1925-27, prof., 1927—, dean Coll. Fine Arts, 1925-59. Dir. Centro Cultural Brasil-Estados Unidos, Santos, Brazil, 1947-48. Mem. gen. ch. music com. Ch. of Jesus Christ of Latter-day Saints; gen. bd. Deseret Sunday Sch. Union, 1933-68. Univ. fellow, Stanford, 1931-32; recipient Karl G. Maeser Teaching award Brigham Young U., 1960, Distinguished Service award, 1967. Fellow Utah Acad. Scis., Arts and Letters; (past pres.; award distinguished services 1953), mem. Modern Lang. Assn. Am., Am. Assn. Tchrs. Spanish and Portuguese, Am. Musicol. Soc., Internat. Soc. Musicologists. Republican. Author: The Elements of Musicality in the Literary and Critical Works of Otto Ludwig, Greater Dividends from Religion, 1950; Living the Gospel, 1957; The Testimony of President H. J. Grant, 1965; The Gospel Today, 1966; Four Hundred Years of Brazilian Literature, 1969. Composer choral orchestral and chamber music. Home: 640 N University Av Provo UT 84601

DE JONG, MEINDERT, author; b. Wierum, The Netherlands, 1910; A.B., Calvin Coll.; m. Hattie Overeinder. Recipient Nat. Book Award for children's lit., 1968. Author: Dirk's Dog Bello; The Cat That Walked a Week; Smoke Above the Lane; Good Luck Duck; The Tower by the Sea; Shadrach; Hurry Home, Candy; The Wheel on the School, The Little Cow and the Turtle; The House of Sixty Fathers: Along Came a Dog; The Mighty Ones; The Last Little Cat; Nobody Plays with a Cabbage; The Singing Hill; Journey From Peppermint Street; Far Out the Long Canal; Puppy Summer. Address: 1150 Griswold St SE Grand Rapids MI*

DEJONG, RUSSELL MELSON, physician, educator; b. Orange City, Ia., Mar. 12, 1907; s. Dr. Conrad and Cynthia J. (Bursma) DeJ.; A.B., U. Mich., 1929, M.D., 1932, M.S., 1936; m. Madge Anna Brook, Apr. 23, 1938; childrenMary Cynthia, Constance Jacqueline, Russell Nelson. Intern Univ. Hosp., Ann Arbor, 1932-33, asst. resident neurology, 1933-34; instr. med. sch. U. Mich., 1934-37, asst. prof., 1937-41, asso. prof., 1941-50, prof., chmn. dept. neurology, 1950—; mem. adv. bd. SSS 1940-45; cons. neurology VA Hosp., Ft. Custer, Mich. 1946—; neurology, psychiatry Surgeon Gen., U.S. Army, Far East Command, 1949; cons. USPHS, Nat. Inst. Neurol. Disease and Blindness; mem. Med. adv. bd. Nat. Multiple Sclerosis Soc.; Am. del. World Fedn. Neurology and Internat. Neurol. Congress, 1961-65. Bd. dirs. Nat. Muscular Dystrophy Research Found., Inc. Diplomate Am. Bd. Psychiatry and Neurology (dir., pres. 1957-58). Mem. A.M.A., Am. Neurol. Assn. (pres. 1964-65), Pan-Am. Congress Neurology (v.p. 1963-67), Am. Psychiat. Assn., Research Nervous and Mental Disease, Am. Assn. History Medicine, Am. Acad. of Neurology (1st v.p. 1961-63), Am. League against Epilepsy (pres. 1954-55), Central Neuropsychiat. Assn. Mich. Soc. of Neurology and Psychiatry, Sigma Xi, Phi Kappa Phi, Alpha Omega Alpha, Phi Chi. Republican. Presbyn. Author: Neurologic Examination. Editor of U. Hosp. Bull., 1937- 51; editor-in-chief Neurology, 1951—. Home: 1526 Harding Rd Ann Arbor MI 48104

DE JONGH, THEUNIS WILLEM, banker; b. Gouda, Rep. S. Africa, Dec. 15, 1913; s. Petrus Johannes and Rachel (Wium) De J.; B.Sc., U. Stellenbosch, 1934, M.Sc., 1936; M.A., Columbia, 1940; D.C.S., U. Pretoria, 1941; m. Anna Francina Visser, Nov. 8, 1941; children—Laetitia, Petrus, Elizabeth, Andries, Theunis. Chief statistician Indsl. Devel. Corp. S. Africa, Johannesburg, 1942-45; head dept. research S. African Res. Bank, Pretoria, 1946-62, exec. asst., 1962-67, gov., 1967—; chmn. Nat. Finance Corp. S.Africa, 1967—. Home: 134 Eastwood St Pretoria South Africa Office: Church Sq Pretoria South Africa

DEJOSE, JOHN S., lawyer, banker; b. N.Y.C., Nov. 28, 1919; s. Thomas Dominic and Rose (Muscorella) DeJ.; B.A. magna cum laude, Hofstra U., 1941; LL.B., Cornell U., 1943; m. Grace Carolyn Cancellieri, Nov. 26, 1944; children—Carol Ann, John Philip, Valerie Jean. Admitted to N.Y. bar, 1943; asso. firm White & Case, N.Y.C., 1943-64, Sprague, Dwyer, Aspland & Tobin, Mineola, N.Y., 1964-68; v.p., gen. counsel Bankers Trust Co., N.Y.C., 1968—. Activities fund raising local Boy Scouts Am., 1960-64; mem. Syosset (N.Y.) Citizens Planning Commn., 1968; bd. dirs., mem. finance com. Speedwell Services Children, N.Y.C., 1968-69. Trustee Hofstra U. Recipient George M. Estabrook Distinguished Service award Hofstra U., 1969. Mem. Am. (com. on banking 1969), N.Y. State bar assns., Assn. of Bar City, N.Y., Cornell Law Assn., Hofstra Alumni Assn. (v.p., exec. com. 1958-59). Republican. K.C. Clubs: Hofstra Univ., Hofstra Century. Home: 567 Split Rock Rd Syosset NY 11791 Office: 280 Park Av New York City NY 10017

DE KIEWIET, CORNELIS WILLEM U. pres., historian; b. Rotterdam, Holland, May 21, 1902; A.B., U. Witwatersrand (Johannesburg, South Africa), 1923, A.M., 1924; Ph.D., U. London, 1927; student U. Paris, 1927-28, U. Berlin, 1928-29; LL.D., Syracuse U., 1951, N.Y.U., 1951, Hull U., Eng., McGill U., Northwestern U., 1958; L.H.D., Hobart and William Smith Colls., 1952, Colgate U., 1959; Litt.D., Rennes U., France, 1958; Natal U., Durban, S.A., 1960; m. Lucas Marian Hejinian, Aug. 22, 1930; children—Marie, Christina (dec.), John. Naturalized U.S. citizen, 1939. Teacher Afrikaans and history Southern Rodesia, 1923-25; asst. prof. history, State U. Ia., 1929- 35; asst. prof. history, State U. Ia., 1929-35, asso. prof., 1935-37, prof., 1937-41; prof. modern European history, Cornell U. since 1941, dean coll. arts and scis., 1945-48, provost, 1948-49, acting pres., Cornell U., 1949-51, pres. U. Rochester, Rochester, N.Y., 1951- 61, pres. emeritus, 1961—. Mem. bd. dirs. George Eastman House, Lincoln-Rochester Trust Co. Board trustees Corning Mus. Glass, Chmn. com. on edn. in tropical Africa NRC, 1960—, mem. council on higher edn. N.Y. University Commn. on Human Resources and Advanced Tng., 1951-54; adv. com. under developed areas Mut. Security Agy., 1950-52; mem. Ford Found. African screening com.; Can.-U.S. com. Am. Council Edn. Decorated Officer Legion of Honor. Mem. Am. Hist. Assn., Am. Council Learned Socs. (chmn. bd. dirs. 1952-54), Assn. Am. Universities (pres. 1956-58), Assn. Colleges and State New York (sec.- treas. 1953). Council Fgn. Relations, Inc., Phi Beta Kappa. Clubs: Century, University, Country, Genesee Valley. Author: British Colonial Policy and the South African Republics (London), 1929; The Imperial Factor in South Africa (Cambridge), 1937; A Hist. of So. Africa (Oxford), 1941; The Anatomy of South African Misery, 1956; also articles on profl. subjects. Co-editor Dufferin- Carnarvon correspondence. Home: 22 Berkeley St Rochester NY 14607

DEKKER, MARCEL, pub. co. exec.; b. Amsterdam, Holland, Feb. 12, 1931; s. Maurits and Rozetta S. (Roos) D.; came to U.S., 1939, naturalized, 1945; B.S., N.Y. U., 1957; m. Harriett Gromb, July 21, 1967; children—Russell Maurits, David Robert, Jacqueline. Advt. and import mgr. Intersci. Pub. Co., N.Y.C., 1958-62; pres., chief exec. officer Marcel Dekker, Inc., N.Y.C., 1963—; mng. dir. Marcel Dekker, Ltd., Maidenhead, Berks, Eng., 1968—. Served with USAF, 1951- 55. Clubs: West Park Tennis (N.Y.C.); New Rochelle (N.Y.) Tennis. Home: 146 Cat Rock Rd Cos Cob CT 06807 Office: 95 Madison Av New York City NY 10016

DEKKER, MAURITS, co. exec.; b. Amsterdam, Holland, Mar. 18, 1899; s. Marcus and Elisabeth (Pekel) D.; Ph.D., U. Amster, 1923; m. Rozetta Sophia Roos, July 2, 1925; children—Elisabeth Emma, Andrew, Marcel. Came to U.S., 1939, naturalized, 1945. Founder, pres. Dekker & Nordemann, Amsterdam, 1928—, Elsevier Pub., N.Y.C., 1940—, Intersci. Pubs., Inc., N.Y.C., 1940—; v.p. John Wiley & Sons, 1961-64; chmn. Marcel Dekker, Inc., N.Y.C., 1965—, Maurits Dekker Assos., 1965—. Chmn. bd. dirs. Dekker Fund., 1961—. Fellow A.A.A.S., N.Y. Acad. Scis., Am. Inst. Chemists; mem. Am. Chem. Soc., Internat. Sci. Publs. Assn., Am. Arbitration Assn. (arbitrator). Club: Netherland of New York. Maj. internat. sci. editor, 1939—. Home: 60 Heights Rd Plandome NY 11030 Office: 95 Madison Av New York City NY 10016

DEKNATEL, FREDERICK BROCKWAY, art historian; b. Chgo., Mar. 9, 1905; s. Frederick H. and Wilfreda (Brockway) D.; A.B., Princeton, 1928; Ph.D., Harvard U., 1935; L.H.D., Alfred U., 1966; m. Virginia Herrick, June 22, 1931; childrenJohn H., William B., Charles Y. Instr., tutor Harvard, 1932-40, asso. prof. fine arts, 1940-46, prof., 1946-, William Dorr Boardman prof., 1955-, chmn. dept., 1944-49. Pres. Coll. Art Assn., 1947-48. Decorated knight 1st class Order St. Olaf (Norway). Author: Edvard Munch, 1950. Home: 146 Brattle St Cambridge MA 02138

DEKNATEL WILLIAM FERGUSON architect; b. Chgo., May 29, 1907; s. Frederick H. and Wilfreda (Brockway) D.; A.B., Princeton, 1929; Taliesin fellow, Ecole des Beaux Arts, Paris, France, 1932, Diplomé parle Gouvernement, 1936; m. Geraldine Eager, Apr. 17, 1930; children—Diane (Mrs. Emery Pierson), Frederick Henry II. Architect, 1936—; dir. Mackie-Lovejoy Co., Chgo., 1932-60, pres., 1949-60; dir. Setwell Co., Chgo., 1932—, chmn., treas., 1949- -, pres., 1967—; chmn., treas. Elting, Deknatel & Assos., Inc., 1960-62; co-principal Urban Renewal Planning Assos., 1961-67; v.p. The Clearing, 1951-56, dir., 1951-58. Chmn. planning for services com. Welfare Council Met. Chgo., 1956-59; dir. Nat. Fedn. Settlements and Neighborhood Centers, 1959-67, v.p., 1964-67, chmn. civil rights com., 1964-67; chmn. Near West Side Planning Bd., 1949-50, vice chmn., 1950-56, exec. com., 1956-62; vice chmn. West Central Planning Assn., 1954-64. Trustee Hull House Assn., 1939—, pres., 1953-56, 61-62, hon. pres., 1964. Registered architect, Ill., Wis., Mich. Mem. A.I.A., Soc. Contemporary Am. Art (pres. 1951-53), Lambda Alpha. Clubs: University (Chgo.); Anglers (N.Y.); Arts. Home: 1310 N Ritchie Ct Chicago IL 60610 Office: 79 W Monroe St Chicago IL 60603

DE KONING, PAUL, mfg. exec.; b. Quincy, Ill., Oct. 2, 1901; s. Gysbert and Lena J. (Meves) D.; B.A., Ore. U., 1924; m. Emma Jean Sies, Sept. 8, 1926; children—Robert Paul, John Meves. Adjustment mgr. Jantzen Inc. (formerly Jantzen Knitting Mills), 1924-26, collection mgr., 1926-28, export sales mgr., 1928-30, asst. prodn. mgr., 1935-39, prodn. mgr., 1939-45, v.p., gen. mgr., 1945-56, pres., 1956-67, chmn. bd., 1966-68, now ret.; sales mgr., dir. Jantzen (Australia), Ltd., 1930-35; dir. Portland br. First Nat. Bank of Ore., Rotarian. Club: Waverly Country. Home: 6817 S E Pine Ct Portland OR 97215 Office: Jantzen Inc Jantzen Center Portland OR 97208

DE KOONING, ELAINE, artist; b. N.Y.C., Mar. 12, 1920; d. Charles Frank and Mary Ellen (O'Brien) Fried; hon. degree Western Coll. Women, Oxford, O., 1964; m. William de Kooning, Dec. 9, 1943. One-woman shows include Stabe Gallery, N.Y.C., 1954, 56, Tibor de Nagy Gallery, N.Y.C. 1957, Graham Gallery, N.Y.C. 1960, 61, 63, 65. U. N.M., 1957, Mus. N.M., Santa Fe, 1959, Gump's, San Francisco, 1959, Washington Gallery Modern Art (presdl. portraits), 1964, Lyman Allen Mus., New London, Conn. (retrospective), 1959; rep. permanent collections Mus. Modern Art. Loeb Center, N.Y.C., also pvt. collections; tchr. U. N.M., 1959, Pa. State U., 1960, Contemporary Art Assn., Houston, 1952, U. Cal. at Davis, 1963-64, Yale, 1967, Carnegie-Mellon U., 1969-70, U. Pa., 1970—, Wagner Coll., 1970—. Home: 51 Raynor St Freeport NY 11520 Office: care Graham Gallery 1014 Madison Av New York City NY 10021

DE KOONING, WILLEM, artist; b. Rotterdam, Holland, Apr. 24, 1904; s. Leendert and Cornelia (Nobel) de K.; student Acad. Fine Arts, Rotterdam, 1916-24; m. Elaine Marie Fried, Dec. 7, 1943. Painter mural Hall of Pharm., N.Y. World's Fair, 1939; faculty Black Mountain Coll., N.C., 1948, Yale, 1950-51; one- man show Egan Gallery, 1948, 51, Sidney Janis Gallery, 1953, 56, 59, 62, Paul Kantor Gallery, 1961, M. Knoedler & Co. Inc., 1967, 69, others; paintings included collections Mus. Modern Art, St. Louis Mus., Chgo. Art Inst., pvt. collections Nelson Rockefeller, Mrs. John D. Rockefeller, III. Recipient Logan purchase prize Chgo. Art Inst., 1951. Author articles popular, profl. publs. Office: M Knoedler Co 21 E 70th St New York City NY 10021 •

DE KOSTER, LESTER RONALD, librarian, educator; b. Zeeland, Mich., Apr. 21, 1915; s. Cornelius C. and Sarah (Cass) De K.; A.B., Calvin Coll., Grand Rapids, Mich., 1937; M.A. in Philosophy, U. Mich., 1942, M.A. in L.S., 1955; Ph.D. in L.S., 1964; student U. Chgo., 1952; m. Ruth Jane DeVries, June 6, 1941; children—Leslie Ann, Paul, Mark, Stephen. Tchr., English and speech South High Sch., Grand Rapids, 1937-47; asst. prof. speech Calvin Coll., 1947-69, dir. library coll. and sem., 1951-69; adj. prof. librarianship Western Mich. U., 1969—; tchr.. evening schs., 1955—. Precinct del. Kent County, also Mich. Democratic convs., 1954—; exec. com. Kent County Dem. Com., 1958—. Served to lt. (j.g.) USNR, 1943-45. mem. Evangelical Press Assn., Religious Press Assn., Am. Soc. Reformation Research. Mem. Christian Reformed Ch. Author: All Ye That Labor, 1956; Communism and Christian Faith, 1962; Vocabulary of

Communism, 1964; The Christian and the John Birch Society, 1966; The Citizen and the John Birch Society, 1968. Editor; (Phelps) Speaking in Public, 1958. The Banner, 1969—. Asso. editor Reformed jour., 1957-69. Home: 2800 Thornapple River Dr S E Grand Rapids MI 49506

DEKOVIC, GENE, communications cons.; b. Chgo., June 9, 1922; s. Charles W. and Lillian (Hill) D.; student Northwestern U., 1940-42, Inst. Design, 1946-48, U. Chgo., 1955-59; m. Margery Jean Walker, July 14, 1945; 1 son, Barry Walker. Photographer, R. R. Donnelley & Sons, Chgo., 1945-46; prodn. mgr. Schnell Mills, Inc., advt., Chgo., 1946-48; asst. advt. mgr. Gaylord Prodns., Chgo., 1948-49; salesman Warren, Wetherell & Assos., Chgo., 1949-51; partner, bus. mgr. Dekovic-Smith Design Orgn., Chgo., 1951-57; owner Gene Dekovic, communication research-planning, Chgo., 1957-; tchr. bus. communication Western Electric Grad. Tng. Center, 1958, U. Chgo., 1958-59; tchr. mass communication media Columbia Coll., Chgo., 1963-, trustee, 1965-; cons. pubs. elementary and high sch. textbooks, 1957-; spl. research ednl. efficiency textbooks. Served to 1st lt., navigator, USAAF, 1942-46; German prisoner of war. Mem. Soc. Typographic Arts (pres. 1964-65), Soc. Gen. Systems Research, Internat. Soc. Gen. Semantics. Home: 1817 Tanglewood Dr Glenview, IL 60025 Office: 540 N Lake Shore Dr Chicago, IL 60611.

DEKSNYS, ANTHONY LOUIS, bishop; b. Buteniskis, Lithuania, May 9, 1906; s. Stasys and Venceslava (Kiliute) D.; Ph.D., U. Fribourg, Switzerland, 1940; S.T.L., Sem. and Theol. U., Kaunas, Lithuania, 1931. Came to U.S., 1941, naturalized, 1946. Ordained priest Roman Cath. Ch., 1931; asst. pastor Panevezys and Birzai, Lithuania, 1931-36; asst. pastor, Chgo., 1941, Mt. Carmel, Pa., 1942; pastor Immaculate Conception Parish, East St. Louis, Ill., 1943-69; bishop for Lithuanians in West Europe, Rome, Italy, 1969—. Dir. Resettlement, Belleville Diocese, 1967- 69. Mem. Am. Lithuanian Cath. Priest League (v.p. 1941-69). K.C. Address: Piazza Asti 25 00182 Rome Italy

DE LA BURDE, ROGER ZYGMUNT, UN ofcl.; b. Katowice, Poland, Sept. 22, 1931; s. Rudolph Z. and Helena (Swiatek) de la B.; M.S., Ph.D., Krakow (Poland) U.; M. Engring. in Indsll. Mgmt., Krakow Poly. Inst., 1956; Ph.D. in Engring., Tech. Hochschule Aachen (Germany), 1961; m. Brigitte E. Stoltenberg, June 7, 1958; children—Clette-Alison, Corinna-Margot. Mgr. internat. div. Krakow Mfg. Co., 1952-56; scientist Roswell Park Meml. Inst., Buffalo, 1956-59; project leader Armour & Co., Chgo., 1959-61 sr. scientist Philip Morris Corp., 1961-68; dir. Fed. Inst. Indsl. Research, Lagos Nigeria, 1968- 69. Dir. Consol. Industrials, Inc., Richmond, Va., Parachemicals Ltd., Ikeja, Nigeria, Recipient Polish Nat. Tech. award, 1952, U.S. Hide Assn. award, 1961, Philip Morris Patent award, 1967, citation Fgn. Trade Bd., 1955. Fellow A.A.A.S., Am. Inst. Chemists, Inst. Director (London); mem. Am. Chem. Soc., Research Soc. Am. (hon.). Author 1 book, also brochures and articles. Home: 1617 Pope Av Richmond VA Office: Fed Inst Indsl Research Oshodi Nigeria

DELACATO, CARL HENRY, educator; b. Pottstown, Pa., Sept. 10, 1923; s. Ercole S. and Julia (de Bartolomeo) D.; B.S. in Edn., W. Chester State Coll., 1945; M.S. in Edn., U. Pa., 1948, Ed.D., 1952; m. Janice E. Fernstrom, June 20, 1951; children—Elizabeth F., Carl Henry, David F. Asst. headmaster Chestnut Hill Acad., Phila., 1945-64; founder, dir. Chestnut Hill Reading Clinic, 1948; prof. Avery Postgrad. Inst., Phila., 1963—; prof., chmn. dept. developmental edn. U. Plano, 1965—; asso. dir. Inst. Para Le Orgn. Neurologica, Buenos Aires, 1967—; asso. dir. Insts. Achievement Human Potential, Phila., 1953—. Vice pres. U.S. World Orgn. Human Potential. 1968—; mem. Pa. Commn. Human Potential; mem. Gov. Sergipe (Brazil) Commn. Human Potential. Dir. Insts. Achievement Human Potential, Dallas Acad., Insts. Achievement Human Potential, San Antonio, Centro de Reabilitacao N.S. de Gloria, Sao Paulo, Brazil, Internat. Rehab. Forum. Recipient Diploma de Honra Ho Merito, Piracicba, Brazil, 1965, Diploma de Reconheciemen, to Sao Paulo, 1965, Diploma Socio-Benmento, Porto Allegra, Brazil, 1965, Diploma e Medalha Comemorativa de APAE, Rio de Janeiro, 1965, gold medal honor (Brazil), 1960, statuette with pedestal Internat. Rehab. Forum, 1966, 1st Trailblazer award U. Plano, 1966. Club: Phila. Cricket. Author: The Treatment and Prevention of Reading Problems, 1959; Diagnosis and Treatment of Speech and Reading Problems, 1963; Elementary School of the Future, 1964; A New Start For the Child With Reading Problems, 1970; also numerous articles. Address: Thomas Rd Philadelphia PA 19118

DE LA CHAPELLE, CLARENCE EWALD, physician, educator; b. N.Y.C., Dec. 6, 1897; s. Maximilien G. Hugo and Mathilde (Koenig) de la C.; student St. Johns Coll., Fordham U., 1916-18; B.S., N.Y. U., 1921, M.D., 1922; m. Lillian L. Buckmann, Jan. 29, 1925; children—Donald Clarence, Norman Frederic. Instr. in pathology N.Y.U. Coll. of Medicine, 1924-26, instr. in medicine, 1926-32, asst. prof., 1932-38, acting chmn. dept. medicine, 1937-38, prof. clinical medicine, 1938-48, asst. dean, 1942-45, asso. dean, 1945-48, dir. postgrad. div., 1945-48, prof. medicine N.Y.U. Post Grad. Med. Sch., asso. dean, 1948-63, cons. postgrad. med. edn., 1963—; dir. Div. Affiliated and Regional Hosps., N.Y. U. Med. Center, 1950-63; asso. vis. physician Lenox Hill Hosp., 1933-45, chief cardiac clinic, 1933-45, attending cardiologist, 1945-48, dir. medicine, 1948-60, cons. physician, 1960—; physician Bellevue Sch. Nursing, 1925-45; cons. physician St. Lukes Hosp., Newburgh, N.Y., 1933-52, Fitkin Meml. Hosp., Neptune, N.J., 1945-51; cons. physician in internal medicine Vassar Bros. Hosp., Poughkeepsie, N.Y., 1948-63; cons. med. end. Surgeon Gen. USAF, 1958-64; cons. cardiologist Community Hosp., Glen Cove, 1945-52, 58—, New Rochelle (N.Y.) Hosp., 1950—. Nassau Hosp, Mineola, 1950-52, North Shore Hosp., Manhasset, 1955—. Mem. administrs. med. adv. panel FAA, 1965-68. Commd. lt. comdr. USNR, 1933-37; cons. in cardiology SSS, cons. and adviser to war dept. in profl. edn., 1942-44. Diplomate Am. Bd. of Internal Medicine. Fellow A.M.A., A.C.P., Acad. of Medicine (v.p. 1964-66); mem. Am. Heart Assn. (dir. 1937-48, 55-57), Interam. Soc. Cardiology (dir. 1960-68), Am. Assn. Pathologists and Bacteriologists, N.Y. Heart Assn. (council 1928-45, bd. of dirs., 1945—, v.p. 1947-49), Internat. Acad. Pathology, Harvey Soc., N.Y. Pathol. Soc., Sigma Xi, Alpha Omega Alpha. Club: University. Contbr. Profl. publs. Mem. editorial bd. Am. Heart Jour., 1946-50, Circulation, 1950-61. Home: 300 E 33d St New York City NY 10016 Office: 140 E 54th St New York City NY 10022

DE LA CHAPELLE, RICHARD, investment banker; b. Ottawa, Ill., Jan. 21, 1900; s. Jean and Berthe (Salembier) de La C.; ed. pub. schs.; m. Frances Barr Malone, Feb. 12, 1931 (dec. 1965); childrenAnne, Richard, Peter, Frances, Jeanne, Helene; m. 2d, Gertrude E. Nolan, 1967. Pres. and dir. Lee Higginson Corp., N.Y.C., 1948-64; partner, mem. exec. com. Dean Witter & Co., 1964- 68; sr. v.p. Dean Witter & Co., Inc., 1968—; dir. Household Finance Corp., Chgo. Served to 2d lt. A.C., U.S. Army, World War I. Clubs: Links, Down Town Assn., N.Y. Stock Exchange Lunch (N.Y.C.); Englewood (N.J.). Home: 200 E 66th St New York City NY 10021 also Halsey Lane Remsenburg NY 11960 Office: 14 Wall St New York City, NY 10005.

DE LA COLINA, RAFAEL, Mexican ambassador; b. Tulancingo, Hidalgo, Mexico, Sept. 20, 1898; s. Manuel and Maria (Riquelme) C.; B.S., Nat. U. Of Mexico, 1915, Fng. Service Officer, 1918; m. Ruth Rosecrans, Dec. 24, 1920 (dec.); childrenRuth (Mrs. Francis W. Silk), Rafael; m. 2d, Amanda Steinmeyer, July 22, 1944. Chancellor, Mexican consulate, Phila., 1918; vice-consul, St Louis, 1922; chief adminstrv. sect., Consular Dept., Fgn. Office, Mexico City, 1923; consul of Mexico, Boston, 1924-25, New Orleans, 1926-27, Laredo, Tex., 1928-29, Los Angeles, 1930-31; chief of consular dept., Fgn. Office, Mexico City, 1932; chief Bur. of Licenses, Govt. of the City of Mexico, 1933; consul-gen., San Antonio, Tex., 1934-35, N.Y.C., 1936-42; minister-counselor, Mexican embassy, Washington, 1943-44, E.E. and M.P., 1944-48, charge d'Affaires and interim, Aug.-Dec. 1948, A.E. and P., 1949-53; permanent rep. of Mexico to UN, 1953-59; Mexican ambassador to Canada, 1959-62; Mexican ambassador to Japan, Tokyo, 1962-64, to OAS, 1965—. Mem Mexican delegation as del., UNRRA, Atlantic City, 1943 (elected v.p. 1st session), Montreal, Can., 1944, Interim Commn., (Food and Agr. Orgn.), Washington, 1944-45, Interam. Econ. and Financial Tech. Com., Washington, 1943-45; as alternate del., Security Council U.N., N.Y. C., 1946, P.I.C.A.O. (Caribbean regional meeting), Washington, 1946; adviser, U.N.C.I.O., San Francisco, 1945; dep. sec. gen. Interam. Conf. on Problems of War and Peace, Mexico City, 1945; Mex. rep. Com. of Experts (U.N. Security Council), 1946; Mex. alternate del. U.N. Security Council, 1946; Mex. del. Provisional Internat. Civil Aviation Orgn., 1946, U.N. Gen. Assembly, N.Y.C., 1946, (alternate) Gen. Assembly, 2d Session, Lake Success, N.Y., 1947, 2d Extraordinary Session, Lake Success, Apr.-May 1948; Mex. rep. (alternate) Council of Orgn. of Am. States (Consejo de la Organización de los Estados Americanos), Washinton, May-July 1948; Mexican del. of Japanese Peace Conf., San Francisco, 1951, 2d spl. Inter Am. Conf., Rio de Janeiro, 1965; acting chief of the Mexican delegation, VII to XIII. Gen. Assembly of UN; chief Mexican delegation spl. commn. amendments to Charter OAS, Panama City, 1966; chief Mexican del. Intelsat Conf., Washington, 1969-70. Decorated Order of the Merit (Chile); Order Honneur et Merite (Haiti); Order of the Merit Juan Pablo Duarte (Dominican Republic); Order of Vasco Nuez de Balboa (Panama); Imperial Order Rising Sun (Japan). Mem. Acad. of History (Mexico). Amer. Soc. Internat. Law, Mexican Acad. Internat. Law. Clubs: International (Washington). Address: 2440 Massachusetts Av NW Washington DC 20008

DELACORTE, GEORGE THOMAS, Jr., publisher; b. N.Y.C., June 20, 1894; s. George T. anc Cecelia (Koeing) D.; student Harvard, 1910-11; A.B., Columbia, 1913; m. Margarita von Doenhoff, Aug. 30, 1912 (dec.); childrenAlbert, Margarita, Malcolm, Consuelo, Marianne, Victoria; m. 2d, Valerie Hoecker, May 15, 1959. Chmn. bd. Dell Pub. Co., Inc., N.Y.C., Dell Books, Laurel Books, Delacorte Press books and 25 mags. Republican. Clubs: University, Harvard (N.Y.C.). Home: 998 Fifth Av New York City NY 10012 Office: 750 3d Av New York City NY 10012

DELACOUR, JEAN THEODORE, naturalist; b. Paris, France, Sept. 26, 1890; s. Theodore and Marguerite (Rousseau) D.; ed. Jesuit Sch., Rue de Madrid, Paris; Lic.S., U. of Lille, 1914; unmarried. Naturalized citizen of U.S., 1946-. Engaged in work as naturalist since 1908; maintained home, Chateau de Clères, Normandy, as site of gardens and buildings for living collections of rare animals and birds obtained on own expeditions and by special collectors throughout world, 1919-39; the collections were practically destroyed with records and library during World War II, now restored; ex- dir. dept. history, sci., arts Los Angeles County. Research asso. Am. Mus. Natural History, N.Y.C., 1942-60; collaborator Fish and Wildlife Service, Dept., Interior pres. Ligue Francaise pour la Protection des Oisenux; v.p. Société Nationale d'Acclimatation de France, Avicultural Soc. London; pres. Avicultural Soc. Am.; mem. com. Am. Com. for Internat. Wild Life Protection; council Zool. Soc. London (hon.), Société Ornithologique et Mammalogique de France (editor 1920-40), Société Zoologique de France; v.p. Council Internat. de la Chasse (v.p.), Académie des Sciences, Arts et Belles-Lettres de Rouen, N.Y. and Phila. zool. socs., Brit. Ornithologists Union, Ornithol. Soc. Japan. Roman Catholic. Clubs: Knickerbocker, Century Assn., Explorers, Coffee House (N.Y.C.); Cal. (Los Angeles). Editor: L'Oiseau et la Revue Française d'Ornithologie (mag.), 1920-40. Author: numerous scientific books and articles relating to ornithology and mammalogy published in learned journals of France, Eng., U.S. and Germany. Home: 538 S Flower St Los Angeles CA 90017 Retired.

DELACY, PHILLIP HOWARD, educator; b. Seattle, May 4, 1913; s. John Byron and Abbie (Green) DeL.; A.B., U. Wash., 1932, A.M., 1933; Ph.D., Princeton, 1936; m. Estelle Allen, Dec. 19, 1936. Instr. classics Princeton, 1936-38; asst. prof. classics Stanford, 1938-40; instr. Latin, U. Chgo., 1940-43, asst. prof., 1943-49, prof. classics, chmn. dept. Washington U., 1949-61, acting dean Coll. Liberal Arts, 1958, asso. dean, 1959-60; prof. classics Northwestern U., 1961- 65; vis. prof. classics Cornell U., Ithaca, N.Y., 1958-59, prof. 1965-67; prof. classical studies, chmn. dept. U. Pa., 1967—. Guggenheim fellow, 1960-61. Mem. Am. Philol. Assn. (pres. 1966-67), Am. Assn. U. Profs., Archaeol, Inst. Am., Classical Assn. Middle West and South (pres. 1963-64), Soc. for Ancient Greek Philosophy (pres. 1962-64), Phi Beta Kappa. Author: Philodemus: On Methods of Inference (with Estelle DeLacy), 1941; (with B. Einarson) Plutarch Moralia, Vol. 7, 1959, Vol. 14, 1967; also articles in prof. jours. Editor: Transactions and Proceedings of the American Philological Assn., vols. 80-83, 1949-52; Philological Monograph XV. Acting editor Classical Jour., vol. 51, 1955-56. Home: 4062 Irving St Philadelphia PA 19104

DELAFIELD, CHARLES BARBER, elec. exec.; b. Riverdale-on-Hudson, N.Y., June 28, 1905; s. Frederick Prime and Elsie (Barber) D.; student Harvard, 1927; m. Helen Thorndike, Nov. 8, 1927; children—Eleanor, Harriet. Salesman Coffin & Burr, Inc., investment bankers, N.Y.C., 1927-33; mgr. pub. utility dept. Kidder, Peabody & Co., Investment bankers and brokers, N.Y.C., 1935-42; financial cons. Ill. Power Co., Decatur, Ill., 1942-43, asst. to pres., 1943-45, v.p., asst. to pres., 1945-46; asst. to pres. Consol. Edison Co., N.Y., N.Y.C., 1946-48, asst. v.p., 1948-50, v.p., 1950- 69, treas., 1968-69; chmn., dir. Peerage Properties, Inc., partner Carfield Assos.; dir. Nashua Corp., First Investors Life Ins. Co., Fifth Av. Assn., de Vegh Mutual Fund, Simplex Wire & Cable Co. Dir., vice chmn. Asso. Hosp. Service of N.Y., Trustee New Eng. Fund, 1961- 66, Muttontown Village, L.I., 1955-61, 69—, Eastwood Sch., Oyster Bay, L.I., 1952-55; pres. bd. govs. Hundred Year Assn. of N.Y., 1951-56; pres. dir. Community Hosp. at Glen Cove, 1960-68; dir. Edison Electric Inst., 1949-58, 61-69; adv. com., dir. Delafield Family Assn. Dir. Nat. Assn. Electric Cos., 1952- 68. Mem. Am. Gas Assn., N.Y. Soc. Security Analysts, Inc., West Side Assn. Commerce (v.p., dir. 1953-69). Clubs: Harvard, Piping Rock, Union, Recess (N.Y.C.); Edgartown Yacht (Mass.); Leash; Mill Reef (Antiga). Home: RFD 1 Syosset NY 11791

DELAFIELD, EDWARD COLEMAN, broker; b. Westhampton Beach, L.I., N.Y., July 10, 1877; s. Maturin Livingston and Mary Coleman (Livingston) D.; A.B., Princeton, 1899; m. Margaretta Stockton Beasley, Apr. 30, 1900; children—Maturin Livingston, II, Margaretta Stockton, Edward C., Mary; m. 2d, Clelia C. Benjamin, Feb. 4, 1928; children—Clelia, Walter Benjamin, Cynthia. V.p. and pres. Franklin Trust Co. from 1914, merged with The Bank of America, May 1, 1920, of which was pres.; dir. and mem. exec. com. City Bank Farmers Trust Co.; resigned as v.p. City Bank Farmers Trust Co., 1937; became sr. partner stock exchange firm Delafield & Delafield; trustees Greenwich Savs. Bank; dir. Cerveceria Corona, Inc., and Cerveceria Nacional Dominicana, Inc. Mem. bd. Meml. Center Cancer and Allied Diseases; mem. exec. com. and trustee Sloan-Kettering Inst. for Cancer Research. Served as major, later lt. col. 9th C.A.C., N.Y.G.; reserve list Oct. 8, 1919, Col. Finance Dept. U.S. Army, ret. Mem. N.Y. State Mil. Rifle Teams, Nat. matches, 1918-19. Decorated Knight Comdr. Order Crown of Italy. Pres. and dir. Delafield Family Assn. Fellow Corp. N.Y. Bot. Gardens, Am. Mus. Nat. History; mem. A.A.A.S., N.Y. Hist. Soc. (patron), Pilgrims Soc., Soc. of Colonial Wars, Soc. of the Cincinnati, Soc. War of 1812, St. Nicholas Society, S.R., N.Y. Soc. of Mil. and Naval Officers World War I, N.Y. Geneal. and Biol. Soc. (life), N.Y. Zool. Soc. (life), Soc. Descendants Signers of Declaration of Independence, Descendants of Colonial Lords of Manors in America, Brooklyn Institute of Arts and Science (life). Republican. Episcopalian. Clubs: Union, Down Town, Contemporary, Onteora (dir.). Home: 834 Fifth Av New York City NY 10021 Office: 140 Broadway New York City NY 10005

DELAFIELD, JAMES POTT, mgmt. cons.; b. Bedford, Mass., Jan. 8, 1911; s. Tallmadge P. and Eleanor (Pott) D.; B.A., U. Va., 1932; m. Marina Batty, June 24, 1939; children—George Mason, Ann (Mrs. Boyle). Asso. Grand Union Food Chain, 1932-41; advt. exec. Benton & Bowles, 1945-46; with Gen. Foods Corp., White Plains, N.Y., 1946-66, marketing mgr. Maxwell House div., 1947-52, marketing mgr. Birds Eye div., 1952-55, v.p. sales and customer services, 1955-59, v.p. corp. gen. mgr. and pres. internat. div., 1960- 66, dir. internatl. devel., 1965-66; gen. partner Knight & Gladieux, mgmt. cons., 1967-69; pres., dir. Francois L. Schwartz, Inc., N.Y.C., 1969—; pres., dir. Wilson Anchor Sleeve, Inc., Darien, Conn.; pres. D & H Corp., Darien, Hayfield Enterprises, Inc., Darien, Wilcott, Internat., Inc., Darien, 1968—. Mem. Delafield Family Assn. (v.p., dir.), Clubs: Union League (N.Y.C.); Wee Burn (Darien, Conn.); Coral Beach Tennis (Bermuda); Sunapee Country (N.H.). Home: 15 Midbrook Lane Darien CT 06820 also King Ridge Rd New London NH Office: 500 Fifth Av New York City NY 10036 also 576 Post Rd Darien CT 06820

DE LA GARZA, ELIGIO, congressman; b. Mercedes, Tex., Sept. 22, 1927; s. Dario and Elisa (Villarreal) de la G.; student Pan Am. Coll., Edinburg, Tex., 1947-48; LL.B., St. Mary's U., San Antonio, 1951; m. Lucille Alamia, May 29, 1953; children—Jorge Luis, Michael Alberto, Angela Dolores. Admitted to Tex. bar, 1951; mem. Tex. Ho. of Reps. from Hidalgo County, 1953-64; mem. 89th-92d Congresses 15th Dist. Tex. Served with USNR, World War II, with AUS, Korea. Democrat. Home: 1812 Cummings St Mission TX 78572 Office: House Office Bldg Washington DC 20515

DELAGI, EDWARD FRANCIS, physician; b. N.Y.C., Nov. 4, 1911; s. Michael Nicholas and Angela (Ciani) D.; B.S., Fordham U., 1934; M.D., Hahnemann Med. Coll., 1938; m. Westa Vespa, Feb. 16, 1941; children—West Ann (Mrs. Richard Hanafin), Edwina (Mrs. Donald Askew). Intern Fordham Hosp., Bronx, N.Y., 1938-40; resident Bronx VA Hosp., 1951-54; chief phys. medicine and rehab. Bronx VA Hosp., 1946-56; dir. phys. medicine and rehabilitation Misericordia Hosp., Bronx, 1958-65; attending physician Bronx Municipal Hosp. Center, 1956—; cons. phys. med. and rehabilitation No. Westchester Hosp., Misericordia Hosp., Bronx, St. Joseph's Hosp., Yonkers, N.Y.; asst. prof. dept. rehabilitation medicine Albert Einstein Coll. Med., Bronx, 1950-55, asso. prof., 1959, 64, prof., 1964—. Served with AUS, 1941-45. Decorated Bronze Star. Fellow A.C.P., Am. Acad. Phys. Medicine and Rehab., N.Y. Acad. Medicine; mem. A.A.A.S., Am. Congress Phys. Medicine, N.Y. Acad. Sci. Home: 73 Heatherdell Rd Ardsley NY 10052 Office: Dept Rehabilitation Medicine Albert Einstein College of Medicine 1300 Morris Park Av Bronx NY 10461

DE LAGUNA, FREDERICA ANNIS, anthropologist; b. Ann Arbor, Mich., Oct. 3, 1906; d. Theodore and Grace (Andrus) de Laguna; A.B., Bryn Mawr Coll., 1927; Ph.D. in Anthropology, Columbia, 1933. Asst., Am. sect. U. Pa. Mus., 1930-35; asso. soil conservationist U.S. Dept. Agr., 1935-36; mem. faculty Bryn Mawr Coll., 1938-, successively lectr., asst. prof., asso. prof., 1938-55, prof. anthropology, 1955-, chmn. dept. sociology and anthropology, 1952-66, chmn. dept. anthropology, 1966—; leader archaeol. and ethnol. expdns. to Alaska, 1930, 31, 32, 35, 49, 50, 52, 54, 58, 60, 68, Ariz., 1941; co-leader Danish Nat. Mus. Alaska expdn., 1933. Served from lt. (j.g.) to lt. comdr., USNR, 1942-45. NRC fellow, 1936; Rockefeller postwar fellow, 1945; Wenner-Gren fellow, 1949; Social Sci. Research Council faculty fellow, 1962-63. Fellow Am. Anthrop. Assn. (exec. bd. 1956-59; pres.-elect 1965-66; pres. 1966-67), Soc. Am. Archaeology, Arctic Inst. N. Am., A.A.A.S.; mem. Soc. Pa. Archaeology, Phila. Anthrop. Soc., Am. Ethnol. Soc., Sigma Xi. Home: 221 Roberts Rd Bryn Mawr PA 19010

DELAHANTY, DONALD D., educator, veterinarian. Prof. vet. surgery, dir. large animal hosp. Cornell U., Ithaca, N.Y. Office: Vet Coll Cornell U Ithaca NY 14850*

DELAHAY, PAUL, educator; b. Sas Van Gent, Netherlands, Apr. 6, 1921; s. Jules and Helene (Flahou) D.; B.S. in Gen. Engring., U. Brussels, 1941, M.S. in Chemistry, 1945; M.S. in Elec. Engring., U. Liege, 1944; Ph.D. in Chemistry, U. Ore., 1948; m. Yvonne Courroye, 1962. Came to the U. S., 1946, naturalized, 1955. Instr. chemistry U. Brussels, 1945- 46; research asso. U. Ore., 1948-49; faculty La. State U., 1949-65, prof. chemistry, 1955-56, Boyd prof. chemistry, 1956-65; prof. of chemistry N.Y.U., N.Y.C., 1965—. Guggenheim fellow Cambridge (Eng.) U. 1955-56, N.Y. U., 1971-72; Fulbright prof. Sorbonne, Paris, France, 1962-63. Recipient medal U. Brussels, 1963, Heyrovsky medal Czechoslovak Acad. Sci., 1965. Mem. Am. Chem. Soc. (award pure chem. 1955; Southwest award 1959), Electrochem. Soc. (Turner prize 1951; Palladium award 1967; chmn. theoretical div. 1957-59), A.A.A.S., Am. Phys. Soc., Internat. Union Pure and Applied Chemistry (chmn. commn. electrochem. data 1959-63; titular mem. analytical sect. 1961-65), Sigma Xi. Author: New Instrumental Methods in Electrochemistry, 1954; Instrumental Analysis, 1957; Double Layer and Electrode Kinetics, 1965. Editor: Advances in Electrochemistry, 1961—. Home: 1 Washington Square Village New York City NY 10012

DE LAITTRE, JOHN, cons.; b. Mpls., Sept. 7, 1907; s. Karl and Rosamond (Little) De L.; B.A., Harvard, 1929, LL.B., 1933; m. Carolyn Erminger, Apr. 30, 1934; childrenCorinne, Carolyn, Lila. Admitted to Minn. bar, 1933; asso. Kingman, Cross, Morley, Cant & Taylor, Mpls., 1933-40; with Farmers and Mechanics Savs. Bank of Mpls., 1940-62, pres., 1957-62; mem. Fed. Home Loan Bank Bd., 1962-66; exec. v.p. Mortgage Bankers Assn. Am., 1966-68. Asst. to dir. fgn. operations A.R.C., 1943. Mem. Nat. Assn. Mut. Savs. Banks (pres. 1959). Clubs: Chicago; Minneapolis; Metropolitan, Capitol Hill (Washington); Kitchi Gammi (Duluth, Minn.); Harvard (N.Y.C.). Home: 2800 R St NW Washington, DC 20007.

DELAKAS, DANIEL LIUDVIKO, educator; b. Springfield, Mass., Aug. 25, 1921; s. Alexander and Eva (Poska) D.; student Smith Coll., summers 1936-40, U. Rochester, 1940-42; A.B., Bklyn. Coll., 1946; postgrad. Columbia, 1946; doctorate U. Paris (France), 1948; diploma U. Firenze (Italy), 1957; fellow Harvard from Northwestern U., 1954; m. Mimi Cordich, July 22, 1945; 1 son, David Mark. From lectr. to asst. prof. Northwestern U., 1948-56; prof. Romance langs. Ripon (Wis.) Coll., 1956—, chmn. dept., 1956-69; vis. summer prof. U. Wash., 1960, U. Me., 1961, U. Besançon (France), 1962, 63, Stillman Coll., Tuscaloosa, Ala., 1964, Tufts U., 1965, U. Toulouse (France), 1966, 68, U. Alaska, 1967. Reader French advanced placement Ednl. Testing Service, 1958-63; cons., fgn. lang. editor Sci. Research Assos., 1963-65; academic dir. Academic Year Abroad, Inc., Paris, 1969-70; cons., conf. participant UNESCO, Paris, 1970. Mem. charter com., constn. writer, regional pres. N.E. Wis. Fgn. Lang. Orgn. (New-Flo), 1968-69; exec. com. Insts. Coll. Teaching as a Career, Marquette U.-U. Wis. at Madison, 1960- 63. Served with USAAF, 1942-43. Decorated Presdl. citation, Bronze Star; named chevalier Palmes Académiques, 1967. Mem. Am. Assn. U. Profs., Modern Lang. Assn. (co-editor annual French 17th Century Studies 1952- -), Wis. Assn. Presidents and Deans, Am. Assn. Tchrs. French, Am. Assn. Tchrs. Italian, Internat. Comparative Lit. Assn., Assn. Internat. des etudes françaises, Assn. Internat. des Docteurs de l'Univ. de Paris (nat. exec. sec.), Phi Sigma Iota. Contbr. to yearbooks, encys. Home: 416 Woodside Av Ripon WI 54971

DELALIO, LOUIS DANTE, electronics co. exec.; b. Farmingdale, N.Y., Sept. 1, 1926; s. Leon and Emma (Ampolini) D.; B.Elec. Engring., Rensselaer Poly. Inst., 1950; grad. student Bklyn. Poly. Inst., C. W. Post Coll.; m. Marilyn Margaret Heggie, Sept. 25, 1955; childrenDenise Deborah, Louis, John. Project engr., then group leader Sperry Gyroscope Co., 1950-53, head dept. gyro mechanisms, 1953-54; br. head Norden KeTay Co., 1954-57; chief engr., v.p. Filtors, Inc., div. Deutsch Co., 1957-65, pres., 1965-. Mem. sci. council Rensselaer Poly. Inst., 1962-. Served with USNR, 1944-47. Mem. Nat. Assn. Relay Mfrs. (pres. 1965-66, bd. dirs. 1966-67), I.E.E.E., Am. Mgmt. Assn., Huntington (N.Y.) C. of C., Rensselaer Assos. (bd. govs. 1965-66), Rensselaer Alumni Assn, L.I. (pres. 1962-63), Sigma Xi, Tau Beta Pi. Patentee magnetic amplifier and saturable reactor. Office: 65 Daly Rd East Northport NY 11731

DELAMATER, EDWARD DOANE, microbiologist, educator; b. Plainfield, N.J., Jan. 24, 1912; s. Van Ness and Jacqueline (Newton) DeL.; student Oberlin Coll., 1930-32; student Johns Hopkins, 1932-37, M.A., 1937; Ph.D., Columbia, 1941, M.D., 1942; m. Jean Edgar, Jan. 31, 1943; children—Gretchen, Peter, David; m. Margaret Henderson Turner, Feb. 25, 1961; children—Margaret, Anna. Intern New York Hosp., N.Y. City, N.Y., 1941, Steptoe Valley Hosp., Ely, Nev., 1942; asst. in botany Johns Hopkins, 1933-36; asst. dermatology Columbia, 1936-42; mycologist Vanderbilt Clinic Med. Center, 1936-42; fellow dermatology Mayo Clinic, 1946-47; asst. prof. bacteriology and mycology Mayo Found., U. Minn., 1947-48, mycologist, 1946-48; asso. research prof. dermatology U. Pa., 1948-51, research prof., 1951-63, asso. research prof. microbiology, 1950-51, research prof., 1951-63, dir. sect. cytology and genetics dept. physiology, 1953-63; prof., chmn. dept. microbiology N.Y. Med. Coll., 1963-66; dean Coll. Sci., Fla. Atlantic U., 1966-68, Dist. U. prof. of sci. 1968—; cons. Pepper Lab., Univ. Hosp., 1958-63, to lab. Smith, Kline & French Labs., Phila., 1948-51; cons. Office Surgeon Gen., 1948- 63; Children's Hosp., Phila., 1949—, VA, 1954-63; cons. in microbiology and mycology at Skin and Cancer Hospital of Phila., 1958-63. Mem. med. adv. bd. East Pa. chapter Nat. Multiple Sclerosis Soc., 1955-63. Served as capt. M.C., USAAF, 1942-46. John Simon Guggenheim Meml. Found. fellow, 1953. Fellow A.C.P., N.Y. Acad. Scis., N.Y. Acad. Medicine, Royal Soc. Health; mem. Am. Acad. Microbiology, Am. Assn. Cancer Research, Am. Genetic Assn., Biol. Stain Commn., Bot. Soc. Am., Genetics Soc. Can., Phila. Dermatol. Soc., Soc. Am. Bacteriologists, others. Mycol. Soc. Am., Genetics Soc. Am., A.A.A.S., A.M.A., Torrey Bot. Club, Am. Soc. Human Genetics, Sigma Xi; affiliate Royal Soc. of Medicine. Asso. editor Mycopathologia et Mycologia Applicata. Sic. advisor Mikroskopie, 1954-63. Home: 888 Oleander Av Boca Raton FL 33432

DELAMATER, JAMES NEWTON, educator, physician; b. North Plainfield, N.J., Jan. 24, 1912; s. Van Ness and Jacqueline M. (Newton) DeL.; student Va. U., 1930-31; A.B., Stanford, 1934, M.D., 1938; m. Harriet French, Sept. 1, 1934; childrenSteven French, Anne Terry, Sarah Van Ness. Intern Los Angeles County Gen. Hosp., 1937-39, resident in medicine, 1939-41; pvt. practice medicine, Los Angeles, since 1946; asst. prof. bacteriology U. So. Cal. Sch. Medicine, 1945, asso. prof., 1946, asso. prof. medicine, asso. dean, 1949-52, clin. prof. medicine, 1952—; affiliated Huntington Meml., Los Angeles County Gen. hosps.; epidemiologist Los Angeles County Med. Research Found., 1947—; med. cons. M.C., U.S. Army. Served from lt. (j.g.) to comdr. M.C., 1941-45. Fellow A.C.P., Los Angeles Acad. Medicine; mem. A.M.A., A.A.A.S., Am. Geriatrics Soc., Am. Soc. Tropical Medicine and Hygiene, Holland Soc. N.Y., Alpha Omega Alpha, Sigma Xi. Republican. Presbyn. Clubs: University, Athletic (Pasadena); Hewlett; Toastmasters. Contbr. articles med. jours. Home: 1064 Sierra Madre Blvd San Marino CA 91108 Office: 48 N El Molino Av Pasadena CA 91101

DE LANCEY, WILLIAM JOHN, lawyer, steel corp. exec., b. Chgo., June 2, 1916; s. John Richmond and Louise Ella (Hart) De L.; B.A., U. Mich., 1938, J.D., 1940; m. Sally Ann Roe, July 10, 1940; childrenAnn Louise, Mark Roe. Admitted to N.Y. bar, 1941, Ohio bar, 1953; with Cravath, de Gersdorff, Swaine & Wood, now Cravath, Swaine & Moore, N.Y.C., 1940-52; with Republic Steel Corp., Cleve., 1952-, gen. counsel, 1959—, v.p., 1961—, also dir., v.p. Beatrice Pocahontas Co.; dir. Reserve Mining Co., Liberia Mining Co., Ltd., Republic Supply Co. Dir., also mem. exec. com. Goodwill Industries, Cleve., bd. dirs. Marymount Hosp., Cleve.; trustee Cleve. Inst. Music. Served as lt. (j.g.) USNR, 1943-45. Mem. Am. Bar Assn. (adv. com. for corporate debt financing project; mem. council, sect. corp., banking and bus. law, Am. Social Health Assn. (bd. dirs.), Order of Coif, Phi Beta Kappa, Phi Kappa Phi, Phi Eta Sigma. Episcopalian (sr. warden). Editor Mich. Law Review, 1939-40. Home: 2952 Kingsley Rd Shaker Heights OH 44120 Office: Republic Bldg Cleveland OH 44115

DELANCIE, RICHARD, profl. services co. exec.; b. Berkeley, Cal., May 9, 1915; s. Harry S. and Anna (Zaro) DeL.; A.B., U. Cal., Berkeley, 1940; postgrad., 1948-51; m. Marlene Falkenheim, June 28, 1950; children—Nicolas, Steven, Philip. Asst. mgr., econ. planning dept. Pacific-Alaska div. Pan Am. World Airways, San Francisco, 1946-48; operations analyst Western Air Def. Force, 1952-54; operations analyst URS Systems Corp. (formerly United Research Services, then URS Corp.), San Mateo, Cal., 1954-58, pres., 1958-71, chmn. bd., chief exec. officer, 1971, chmn. exec. com., vice chmn. bd., 1971—. Exec. com. Stanford Mid-Peninsula Urban Coalition. Served from ensign to lt. comdr., USNR, 1942-46, lt. comdr., 1951-52. Mem. Operations Research Soc., Inst. Mgmt. Scis., Econometric Soc., Inst. Math. Statistics, San Mateo Area Bus. Leadership Council, Intergroup Relations Assn. No. Cal. (pres.), Am. Civil Liberties Union (bd. dirs. No. Cal.), Phi Mu Epsilon. Home: 521 Dorchester Rd San Mateo CA 94402 Office: 155 Bovet Rd San Mateo CA 94402

DELANEY, GEORGE A., engr.; b. Centerview, Mo., Feb. 11, 1895; s. John and Jessie (Hering) D.; B.S., U. Mo., 1917; m. Barbara A. Stoye, June 30, 1945. Draftsman Savage Arms Corp., Sharon, Pa., 1919-20; product engr. Paige-Detroit Motor Car Co., 1920-23, exptl. engr., 1923-25, asst. chief engr., 1925- 27; exptl. engr. Graham Motors Corp., Detroit, 1927-34; elec. engr. Pontiac Motor div. Gen. Motors Corp., Pontiac, Mich., 1934-39, asst. chief engr., 1939-42, 45-47, chief engr., 1947-56; cons. Automobile Mfrs. Assn., Inc., 1959-65, Pioneer Engring. and Mfg. Co., 1965- ; supervising engr. aircraft Fisher Body div. Gen. Motors Corp., Detroit, 1942-45. Served as 1st lt. F.A., U.S. Army, 1917-19. Recipient honor award for distinguished service in engring. U. Mo., 1956. Mem. Am. Standards Assn. (dir. 1953-56), Soc. Automotive Engrs. (pres. 1956), Am. Ordnance Assn., Engring. Soc. Detroit. Home: 37 Cambridge Pleasant Ridge MI 48069

DELANEY, GEORGE PHILIP, govt. ofcl.; b. Washington, Feb. 20, 1909; s. George Patrick and Agnes E. (Connery) D.; student Emerson Prep. Sch., Washington, Mt. St. Mary's Coll., Emmitsburg, Md., Harvard, 1945-46; m. Margaret D. Mulholland, July 1947; childrenTimothy, Hannah Kevin, Mary Margaret. Engaged as apprentice molder, U.S. Navy Yard, Washington, 1928-38; internat. rep., Molders Internat., Cin., 1938-42, 47-48; labor specialist, Civilian Prodn. Adminstrn., Washington, 1946-47; with Lustron Corp., Columbus, O., Mar.-July 1948; chief of mission, liaison sect., E.C.A., July-Oct. 1948; internat. rep. AFL-CIO, Washington, October 1948; now spl. asst. to sec., coordinator internat. labor affairs Dept. Labor. Workers delegate from U.S. to Internat. Labor Orgn. Served as molder, U.S. Navy, 1942-45. Mem. Internat. Molders and Foundry Workers Union. Democrat. Roman Catholic. K.C., Elk. Home: 2946 McKinley St NW Washington, DC 20015.

DELANEY, HAROLD, coll. dean; b. Phila., Aug. 24, 1919; B.S., Howard U., 1941, M.S., 1943, Ph.D. in Organic Chemistry, 1958; married; 2 children. Asst. prof. chemistry Agr. and Tech. Coll. N.C., 1945-48; mem. faculty Morgan State Coll., Balt., 1948—, now dean, prof. chemistry. Mem. Am. Chem. Soc. Office: Morgan State Coll Baltimore MD 21212*

DELANEY, JAMES J., congressman; b. N.Y.C., Mar. 19, 1901; married; 1 son, Patrick. Asst. dist. atty. Dist. atty's. Office, Queen's County, N.Y., 9 years; mem. 79th, 81st-87th Congresses, 7th Dist. N.Y.; mem. 88th to 92d Congresses, 9th N.Y. Dist. Democrat. Home: Long Island City NY 11101 Office: House Office Bldg Washington DC 20515

DELANEY, JOHN, educator; b. Geneseo, N.Y., Oct. 2, 1910; s. William J. and Mary (Kiel) D.; student State Normal Sch., Geneseo, 1930-33; B.S., N.Y. State Coll. for Tchrs., Albany, 1934; Ph.D., Cornell U., 1948; m. Ellen Prescott, Aug. 20, 1937; children—Mary Ellen, Thomas John. Instr. Cornell U., 1935-36, 41-42; mem. gen. edn. bd. Rockefeller Found., 1936-37; instr. edn. State Normal Sch., Cortland, N.Y., 1937; supr. Ithaca (N.Y.) Pub. Schs., 1937-41; successively instr., supr. student teaching, dir. placement, chmn. dept. edn. State U. Coll., Oneonta, N.Y., 1942—; cons. N.Y. State Edn. Dept., 1936-41. Mem. Mus. Natural History, Nat. Audubon Soc., Am. Assn. Sch. Adminstrs., N.E.A. Democrat. Roman Catholic. Author: Elementary School Inventory, 1940; The Theory and Practice of Elementary Education in New York State, 1941. Home: 6 N Belmont Circle Oneonta NY 13820

DELANEY, ROBERT MICHAEL, educator, physicist; b. Wood River, Ill., Nov. 13, 1931; s. James Martin and Florence (Paul) D.; B.S., St. Louis U., 1953, Ph.D., 1958. Instr. physics St. Louis U., 1957-60, asst. prof., 1960-65, asso. prof., 1965-68, prof., 1968—, mem. univ. council, 1969—, mem. exec. com. univ. council, 1969-71, mem. com. on rank and tenure, 1970—. Mem. Am. Phys. Soc., Am. Assn. Physics Tchrs., Sigma Xi, Pi Mu Epsilon. Roman Catholic. Home: 3423B Grand Forest Dr St Louis MO 63103

DELANEY, SHELAGH, writer; b. North of Eng., Nov. 25, 1939; d. Joseph Paul and Elsie (Twemlow) Delaney; ed. high sch.; 1 dau., Charlotte Jo. Author play, A Taste of Honey, performed Theatre Workshop, London, 1958; author play The Lion in Love, performed Royal Court Theatre, London, 1960 (Ency. Britannica award for best play 1960-62). Author: Sweetly Sings the Donkey, 1963. Office: care of Hope Leresche and Steele 11 Jubilee Pl London SW3 England also care of CMA 555 Madison Av New York City NY 10022

DELANEY, WILLIAM FRANCIS, Jr., ins. exec.; b. Newark, Sept. 8, 1917; s. William F. and Viola (Kelly) D.; student Ecole Albert de Mun Nogent sur Marne, France, Douai Sch., Eng.; Sch. certificate Oxford and Cambridge; A.B., Princeton U., LL.B., Harvard, student N.Y. U., Practicing Law Inst., Ins. Soc. of N.Y.; m. Virginia Beers; childrenMarcia, Gayle. Studied law, Paris, France; admitted to N.Y. bar, also U.S. Supreme Ct.; atty.-at-law Irving Trust Co., N.Y.C., 1936- 43; gen. counsel Am. Internat. Underwriters Corp. Group, 1943-46; N.Y. reinsurance mgr. Fairfield & Ellis, 1946-54; pres. Delaney Offices, Inc., N.Y., 1954-; reins. intermediary and cons. for U.S. and world wide; reins. lectr. Ins. Soc. N. Y. Mem. Am. Fgn. Law Assn., Internat. Assn. Ins. Counsel, Ins. Soc. of N.Y. Roman Catholic. Clubs: Princeton Alumni, Drug and Chemical, Reinsurance, Deal Golf. Author: Reinsurance Laws of South America and Mexico. Contbr. ins. publs. Home: 215 Elberon Av Allenhurst NJ 07711 Office: 99 John St New York City NY 10038

DELANO, FRANK ELMER, advt. exec.; b. East Orange, N.J., May 23, 1911; s. Frank Elmer and Lyda May (Cahill) D.; B.S., Lehigh U., 1933; student Duke U., 1932, N.Y. Law Sch., 1933-34; m. Rosalie Jean Leistikow, Aug. 31, 1939; 1 son, Frederick Cahill. Radio mgr., exec. Young & Rubicam, advt., 1933-40, 1941-42, 1945-47; account exec. Warwick & Legler, advt., 1940-41; now vice chmn. bd., dir. Foote, Cone, Belding, advt., N.Y. City. Served as lt. aviation, U.S. Navy, 1942-45; lt. U.S.N.R. Member S.A.R., E. Africa Profl. Hunters Assn., Conseil Internat. de la Chasse, Assn. des Chasseurs et Pecheurs Gabonais. Republican. Clubs: Camp Fire of Am., American Yacht (Rye, N.Y.). Home: Manursing Island Rye NY 10580 Office: 200 Park Av New York City NY 10017

DELANO, LESTER ALMY, Jr., advt. exec.; b. New Bedford, Mass., Nov. 28, 1928; s. Lester A. and Beatrice (Thomas) D.; student Amherst Coll., Brown U.; M.A., U. Chgo.; m. Margaret Dent (div.); 1 dau., Leslie. Marketing cons., Chgo., 1950 54; v.p. North Advt., Inc., Chgo., 1955-60; pres. Dodge & Delano, Inc., N.Y.C., 1961—. Served with USNR, 1945-48. Author: Creative Advertising Planning. Home: 530 Park Av New York City NY 10021 Office: 130 E 59th St New York City NY 10022

DELANO, VICTOR, pub. co. exec.; b. Washington, Dec. 20, 1919; s. Harvey and Marcia (Murdock) D.; B.S. in Elec. Engring., U.S. Naval Acad., 1941; M.S., Mass. Inst. Tech., 1949; student Indsl. Coll. Armed Forces, 1961-62; m. Jacqueline Stinson, June 23, 1951; children—Katherine Stinson, Harvey II. Commd. ensign U.S. Navy, 1941, advanced through grades to capt., 1959; asst. to dir. Navy Long Range Objectives Group. 1959-61; comdr. Amphibious Squadron 8, 1965-66, chief of staff amphibious force Atlantic Fleet, 1966-67, head Congl. and Policy Coordination br., Washington, 1967-69; dir. Wichita Eagle & Beacon Pub. Co., Inc. (Kan.), 1957—, treas., 1963—, pres., 1970—. Decorated Bronze Star medal, Legion of Merit (2). Mem. Naval Inst., Naval Hist. Found., Sigma Xi. Clubs: Chevy Chase (Md.); Army and Navy (Washington); University (San Francisco); Princess Anne Country, Wichita. Home: 711 Pyle Rd Bethesda MD 20034

DELANY, FRANK JOSEPH, lawyer; b. Chgo., Apr. 18, 1910; s. Frank and Estil M. (Wood) D.; grad. Loyola Acad., Chgo., 1927; A.B., Georgetown U., 1927-31; LL.B. cum laude, Harvard , 1934; m. Anne E. Clark, Jan. 29 1944; childrenFrank Joseph, Richard, Gael, Julianne. Admitted to Ill. bar, 1934; practiced with Hopkins, Starr & Godman, later Dickinson, Sprowl, Norville & James, Chgo., until 1939; atty. U.S. Dept. Labor, Chgo., 1939-43; faculty Loyola U. Sch. of Law, 1935-39; became faculty mem. and mem. adv. bd. Inst. Pub. Adminstrn., Loyola U., 1939; solicitor Post Office Dept., 1946-51, pvt. practice law, Washington, 1951—; now mem. firm Delany, Robertson & Anderson; also cons. on def. matters Gen. Services Adminstrn. Bd. dirs. Friends of Law Library Congress. Served from pvt. to 2d lt. USMCR 1943-46. Fellow Internat. Acad. Trial Lawyers; mem. Am., Fed. (nat. pres. 1951-52, dir.), Chgo. bar assns., Bar Assn. D.C., Fed. Bar Found. (dir.), Am. Cath. Sociol. Soc., Cath. Council on Working Life. Democrat. Roman Catholic. Clubs: University (Washington); Congressional Country; Chicago Athletic Assn. Home: 3821 Jenifer St NW Washington DC Office: 815 15th St NW Washington, DC 20005.☆27

DELANY, KEVIN F.X., journalist-writer; b. Bklyn., Aug. 26, 1927; s. John J. and Anna C. (Gallagher) D.; A.B., Williams Coll., 1950; M.S. in Journalism, Columbia, 1952, M.A. in Polit. Sci., 1962. Reporter, columnist N.Y. World Telegram & Sun, 1955-57; reporter, assignment editor CBS News, 1957-63, Hong Kong corr., 1958-59; with Peace Corps, 1963-70, dir., Thailand, 1968-70; writer, cons. fgn. affairs, 1971—. Served with USNR, 1945-46, 52-55. CBS News fellow, 1960-61. Address: 3025 Orchard Lane NW Washington DC 20007

DE LA OSSA, ERNEST GEORGE, food and drug co. exec.; b. Colon, Panama, Oct. 31, 1915; s. Ernesto and Estella Irene (Kerns) de la O.; B.A., Columbia, 1937; m. Bonnie Eleanor Slattery, July 15, 1950; children—Donna Andrea (Mrs. Walter B. Hultin), Richard William, William Haynie, Robin Lynn Estella. With R.H. Macy & Co., 1937-42; with NBC, 1942-55, gen. mgr. radio and TV sta., 1953-55; chmn. Latin Am. planning and policy com. W. R. Grace & Co., also v.p., dir. P.R., Mexican, Cuban, Colombian affiliates and v.p. Grace paper div., 1955-61; v.p. overseas operations Internat. Paper Co., 1961-62; v.p. mgmt. planning Federated Dept. Stores, Inc., 1962-64; pres. internat. operations Foremost Foods Co., 1964-70; pres. Foremost Internat., San Francisco, 1970—; dir. Foremost McKesson, Inc. Mem. salary stablzn. bd. U.S. Dept. Labor. Bd. dirs. Latin Am. Inst.; mem. Am.-Korean Found. Inc., Agribusiness Council Inc.; adv. council Japan U.S. Econ. Relations. Mem. N.Y. Personnel Mgmt. Assn. (past pres.), Am. Mgmt. Assn., Sales Execs. Club N.Y., Commerce and Industry Assn. N.Y. (chmn. personnel relations com.), Pan Am. Soc., Columbia Alumni Assn. (permanent pres. class 1937), Am. Arbitration Assn., U.S. C. of C. (chmn. budget com.), Midwest Coll. Placement Assn. Clubs: Hyde Park Golf and Country (Cin.); Westchester Country (Rye, N.Y.); Larchmont (N.Y.) Yacht; Pelham (N.Y.) Country; Rotary (N.Y.C.). Home: 1435 Southdown Rd Hillsborough CA 94010 Office: Crocker Plaza 1 Post St San Francisco CA 94104

DELAP, TONY, artist; b. Oakland, Cal., Nov. 4, 1927; s. Truman Henry and Catherine (Yontz) D.; A.A., Menlo Jr. Coll., 1947; student Claremont Grad. Sch., 1947-49; m. Kathleen Rose Campbell, Dec. 27, 1964; children—Kelly Rose, Jack Henry. Exhbtd. group shows San Francisco Museum, Oakland Museum, Whitney Museum, U. Ill., Museum Modern Art N.Y., Los Angeles County Museum, Pasadena Museum; exhbtd. one-man shows Dilexi Gallery, San Francisco, Robert Elkon Gallery, N.Y.C., Felix Landau Gallery, Los Angeles, U. Cal. at Irvine; rep. permanent collections Whitney Museum, Museum Modern Art N.Y.C., Walker Art Inst., Tate Gallery, London; asso. prof. U. Cal. at Irvine, 1965—. Home: 225 Jasmine St Corona del Mar CA 92625 Studio: 959 W 17th St Costa Mesa CA 92627

DELAPENA, HARVEY V., Jr., banker. Vice pres. Bank N.Y. Office: 48 Wall St New York City NY 10015*

DELAPLAINE, EDWARD SCHLEY, author, jurist; b. Frederick, Md., Oct. 6, 1893; s. William T. and Fannie (Birely) D.; B.A., Washington and Lee U., 1913; student Washington and Lee U. Law Sch., 1913-14, U. Md. Law Sch., 1914-15. Admitted to Md. bar, 1915, and practiced law in Frederick, 1915-38; mem. Md. Ho. of Dels., 1916-18, chmn. com. on amendments to state constn., 1918; mem. state councils sect. Council of Nat. Def., Washington, 1918; city atty. Frederick, 1919-22; codified Frederick City Code, 1920; admitted to practice before Supreme Ct. U.S., 1932; U.S. concillation commr., 1934-38; county atty. Frederick County, 1935-38; counsel to Bd. County Commrs., Frederick County, 1935-38; apptd. chief judge 6th Jud. Circuit and asso. judge Ct. Appeals of Md., 1938, to serve until election, 1942, elected for term, 1942-57, apptd. asso. Judge Ct. of Appeals Md. from 3d Appellate Jud. Circuit, 1945-56; v.p. Gt. So. Printing & Mfg. Co. (pub. Frederick News and Frederick Post), 1955—. Mem. First Conf. of Chief Justices, St. Louis, 1949. Sec. Frederick County Chpt. A.R.C., 1921-38; treas. Frederick chpt. Wakefield Nat. Meml. Found., 1926-27; mem. Md. Tercentenary Commn., 1927-34; pres. Roger Brooke Taney Home, Inc. 1929-46; treas. Roger Brooke Taney Nat. Meml. Found. 1933-46; mem. Bicentennial Com. Frederick, 1944- 45; mem. United Citizens League, Balt. (war service council 1944- 45; hon. pres. 1946-53); trustee C. Burr Artz Library of Frederick, 1935-49. Mem. Md. and Va. Potomac River Commn., 1958; hon. mem. Lincoln Sesquicentennial Commn. 1959, vice chmn. Md. Civil War Centennial Commn., 1959-65; v.p. Francis Scott Key Meml. Found., Inc.; mem. Gov.'s Star-Spangled Banner Sesquicentennial Commn., 1963-64, Frederick City and County Human Relations Council, 1965. Recipient Distinguished Service award U. Md., 1963, Mem. S.A.R. (pres. Sgt. Lawrence Everhart chpt. 1926-28), Am., Md., Frederick County bar assns., Am. Judicature Soc., Nat., Md., Columbia, Frederick County, Montgomery County hist. socs., Mil. Order Loyal Legion U.S., Lincoln Group of D.C., Star-Spangled Banner Flag House Assn. Baltimore (life mem. 1929), Lafayette Meml. Assn. (pres.), John Hanson Soc. Md. (hon.), Phi Beta Kappa, Delta Sigma Rho, Omicron Delta Kappa (hon. 1939). Republican. Episcopalian. Kiwanian (hon.). Author: Roger B. Taney: His Career as a Lawyer, 1918; Thomas Johnson, Maryland and the Constitution, 1925; The Life of Thomas Johnson, 1927; The Dred Scott Case, 1934; Francis Scott Key, Life and Times, 1937; Religious Liberty and the Courts, 1944; Francis Scott Key and the National Anthem, 1947; The Origin of Frederick County, Maryland, 1949; Lincoln's Companions on the Trip to Antietam, 1954; Maryland in Law and History, 1964; John Frederick Amelung, Maryland Glassmaker, 1971. Contbr. to Dictionary of Am. Biography, Dictionary of Am. History. Home: 308 Upper College Terrace Frederick MD 21701 Office: Pythian Castle Bldg Frederick MD 21701

DELAPLANE, STANTON HILL, newspaper columnist; b. Chgo., Oct. 12, 1907; s. Frank Hugh and Marion (Hill) D.; student Hyde Park (Chgo.), Santa Barbara (Cal.), Monterey high schs., 1922-26; m. Miriam Moore, Dec. 6, 1940 (div. 1958); children—Kristin Moore, Thomas; m. 2d, Susan Aven, Feb. 2, 1961; children—Andrea Aven, John Berry Hill. Editor Aperitif Mag. (pub. by Baroness Emily Von Romberg), 1933-36; reporter San Francisco Chronicle since 1936, editor women's dept., 1937, now columnist; also columnist Chronicle

Features, San Francisco, Organizer Cal. Young Democrats and editor The Young Democrat, 1933-34. Served to lt. comdr. USMC, Maritime Commn., Washington, D.C., 1942-44. U.S. war corr., San Francisco Chronicle, 1944-45; accredited corr. U.N. Conf., 1945. Recipient Pulitzer prize for regional reporting of movement of Cal.-Ore. border countries to secede and form the 49th state, 1941, Nat. Headlines journalism award for feature series titles, Ding Dong Daddy of the D Car Line, 1946; Nat. Headlines award 1959; 1st Ann. Writers award for best N. Am. article on sea travel Transpacific Passenger Conf. Club: San Francisco Press (pres. 1970-71, dir.). Author: Pacific Pathways. Contbr. to Reader's Digest, North American Newspaper Alliance, etc. Home: Tiburon CA 94920 Office: San Francisco Chronicle San Francisco CA 94103

DELAPLANE, WALTER HAROLD, coll. ofcl.; b. Toledo, Feb. 2, 1907; s. Ralph Nichols and Zoe (Emerson) D.; A.B., Oberlin Coll., 1929, A.M., 1931; Ph.D., Duke U., 1934; m. Florence Elizabeth Hine, Sept. 8, 1934; children—Charles Thorne, Walter Harold. Instr. econs. Duke U., 1934-40, asst. prof., 1940-43, asst. to dean of Grad. Sch., 1937-43; fgn. econ. adminstr., economist and chief, Iberian Sect., Blockade Div., 1943-45; vis. prof. econs. Nat. U. of Paraguay, 1945-46; lectr. Colegio Libre, Buenos Aires, 1946; prof. econs. and head dept. St. Lawrence U., 1946-48; prof. econs. and head dept. Tex. A. and M. Coll., 1948-53, dean sch. arts and scis., 1953-58; dean coll. arts and scis., So. Meth. U., 1958-62; v.p. acad. affairs U. Ariz., 1962—. Mem. Am. Econ. Assn., Econ. History Assn., Am. Assn. U. Profs., So. Acad. Deans Conf. (chmn.) 1961, Am. Acad. Polit. and Social Sci., Latin American Studies Assn., Phi Beta Kappa, Phi Kappa Phi. Conglist. Kiwanian. Contbr. Six Faces of Mexico, 1966. Contbr. articles profl. jours. Home: 5820 Mina Vista Tucson AZ 85718

DELAPP, GEORGE LESLIE, bishop; b. East Delavan, Wis., Nov. 4, 1895; s. Lawson LeGrand and Carrie Elizabeth (West) DeL; ed. high sch., Mpls., extension courses U. of Minn., YMCA Am. Inst. Bankers, Graceland Coll.; m. Ardyce Lucille Case, July 25, 1926; children—Cloely Anne, Patricia Lucile, George Leslie. Clk. First Nat. Bank, Mpls., 1913-17; connected with F.A. Bean Properties, Inc. (farming operations), 1918-28; bishop Minn. dist. Reorganized Ch. of Jesus Christ of Latter Day Saints, 1926-28, bishop of Lamoni (Ia.) Stake, 1928- 31, counselor to presiding bishop, hdqrs. Independence, Mo., 1931-40, presiding bishop and trustee in trust, 1940-66; now bishop. Commr. Jackson County Sports Complex Authority (Mo.). Former trustee Kansas City Gen. Hosp. and Med. Center. Served with AUS, 1917-18. Author: Quarterly materials (Herald Pub. House), 1941-42. Home: 6200 E 23d St Independence MO 64055 Office: The Auditorium Independence MO 64051

DELAPPE, IRVING PIERCE, govt. ofcl., scientist; b. Boston, Oct. 28, 1915; s. Stephen Pierce and Sedley (Kirkpatrick) D.; S.B., Harvard, 1942, A.M., 1946, Ph.D., 1953; m. Virginia R. Hebert, Sept. 19, 1942; children—Diane (Mrs. Manfred Eickholz), Virginia, Stephen. Teaching fellow biology Harvard, 1947-48, teaching asst. tropical medicine Med. Sch., 1947-48, asst. epidemiology exotic diseases Sch. Pub. Health, 1948; asst. prof. bacteriology and pub. health Mich. State U., 1948-54; dir. tech. information Am. Cyanamid Co., N.Y.C., 1954-60; chief biochemistry and physiology, extramural programs Nat. Inst. Allergy and Infectious Diseases, NIH, 1960—. Mem. Sigma Xi. Clubs: Harvard Varsity, Harvard (Boston and Washington); Sierra (regional chmn. 1961-66); Potomac Appalachian Trail (Washington). Author: (with Hawkins and Lindquist), Introduction to Parasitology 1953; also articles. Home: 8907 Ridge Pl Bethesda MD 20034 Office: Nat Inst Allergy and Infectious Disease Nat Insts Health Bethesda MD 20014

DE LARENTA, OSCAR, fashion designer; b. Santo Domingo, Dominican Republic, July 22, 1932; s. Oscar and Maria Antonia (deFiallo) de LaR.; student Santo Domingo U., also Academia de San Fernando, Madrid, Spain; m. Francoise deLanglade, Oct. 31, 1967. Asst. to Castillo at Lanvin, Paris; designer Elizabeth Arden, N.Y.C.; now designer Oscar de La Renta, Inc., N.Y.C.; owner specialty store in Santo Domingo. Active Rehab. Center for Mentally Retarded Children, Santo Domingo. Recipient Coty awards, 1967, 68, Golden Tiberius award, 1968. Home: 138 1/2 E 80th St New York City NY 10021 Office: 550 7th Av New York City NY 10009

DE LARROCHA, ALICIA DE LA CALLE, pianist; b. Barcelona, Spain, May 23, 1923; d. Eduardo and Ma Teresa (de la Calle) de Larrocha; ed. pvt. schs.; m. Juan Torra, June 21, 1950; children—Juan Francisco, Alicia. Concert appearances in Europe, South and Central Am., South Africa, Middle East, U.S., Japan; dir. Academia Marshall, Barcelona, 1959—, mem. teaching staff internat. course Spanish music, 1959—, mem. bd. dirs., 1968—. Recipient Grand Prix du Disque, Paris, France, 1960; Gold medal Academia Marshall, 1943; Harriet Cohen Internat. Music award, 1956; Paderewski Meml. medal, London, Eng., 1961; Internat. Edison award, Amsterdam, Holland, 1968; decorated Order Civil Merit (Spain), 1962. Home: 117 Infanta Carlota Barcelona Spain

DE LA TORRE, REY, classic guitarist. Address: care Ermine Kahn Artist Mgmt 111 W 57th St New York City, NY 10019.*

DELATOUR, HUNTER L., lawyer; b. Bklyn, Jan. 16, 1887; s. George L. and Rebecca S. (Holcomb) D.; LL.B., N.Y. Law Sch., 1906, LL.D., 1964; m. Margery Dohrman, June 1, 1915; children—Hunter L., Robert J. Admitted to N.Y. bar, 1909; practice law, Bklyn., now mem. firm Delatour & Miller; chmn. adv. com. Title Guarantee & Trust Co., 1950-; trustee King's County Trust Co., 1955-67; pres. N.Y. Law School, 1962-66. Trustee Village Thomaston, Great Neck, N.Y., 1934-; mem. town bd. No. Hempstead, N.Y. 1934-38; mem. Ethics Com. County Nassau, 1964-. Dir. Legal Aid Soc. of Nassau County, 1952—. Fellow Am. Bar Assn., mem. N.Y. State (pres. 1954), Nassau (pres. 1943), Bklyn. (pres. 1943-46) bar assns., Assn. Bar City N.Y., Great Neck Library Assn. (pres. 1947-51), New Eng. Soc. of Bklyn. (pres. 1935-37). Episcopalian (chancellor of diocese 1953- —, mem. standing com. of diocese, & trustee of estate). Club: Brooklyn. Home: 5 Buckingham Pl Great Neck NY 11021 Office: 185 Montague St Brooklyn NY 11201

DELAUER, RICHARD D., aerospace co. exec.; b. Oakland, Cal., Sept. 23, 1918; s. Michael and Matilda (Giambruno) DeL.; A.B., Stanford, 1940; B.S., U.S. Naval Postgrad. Sch., 1949; Aero. Engr., Cal. Inst. Tech., 1950, Ph.D., 1953; m. Ann Carmichael, Dec. 6, 1940; 1 son, Richard Daniel. Structrual designer Glenn L. Martin Co., Balt., 1940-42; design engr. Northrop Co., Hawthorne, Cal., 1942; commd. ensign USN, 1942, advanced through grades to comdr., 1958; assignments in U.S., 1943-58; ret., 1966; lab. dir. Space Tech. Labs., El Segundo, Cal., 1958-60, Titan Program dir., 1960- 62, v.p., dir. ballistic missile program mgmt., 1962-66; v.p., gen. mgr. systems engrng. and integration div. TRW Systems Group, Redondo Beach, Cal., 1966-68, v.p., gen. mgr., TRW Systems Group, 1968-70; exec. v.p. TRW, Inc., Redondo Beach, 1970—; vis. lectr. U. Cal., Los Angeles. Chmn., Long Beach Met. Area, Nat. Alliance Businessman, 1968-69, chmn. Region IX, 1970. Vice chmn. bd. overseers Johnston Coll., U. of Redlands; mem. adv. council Stanford U. Sch. Engrng. Fellow Am. Inst. Aeros. and Astronautics, Am. Astron. Soc.; mem. Nat. Acad. Engrng., A.A.A.S., Aerospace Tech. Council, Aerospace Industries Assn., Sigma Xi. Author: (with R.W. Bussard) Nuclear Rocket Propulsion, 1958, Fundamentals of Nuclear Flight, 1965. Home: 2222 Av of the Stars Los Angeles CA 90067 Office: One Space Park Redondo Beach CA 90278

DELAUNAY, SONIA TERK, artist; b. Ukrainem Russia, 1885; m. Robert Delaunay, 1910 (dec.) Greatly influencd by Cubism; paintings include Prismes Electriques; also works in bookbinding, collages, fabric design and illus. poem Transsiberien; a founder First Salon des Realites Nouvelles; reprospective exhbns. in museums of Grenoble, Bielefeld, Turin, Lyon and Paris. Address: 18 Rue Quartre Vents Paris 5e, France.*

DELAUP, PAUL SIDNEY, educator, physicist; b. New Orleans, Sept. 1, 1902; s. Sidney Philip and Gabrielle (Roux) D.; E.E., Tulane U., 1923, M.S., 1925; Ph.D., U. Chgo., 1930; m. Marie Louise Dessommes, Aug. 16, 1934. Instr. physics and astronomy U. Chgo., 1931-32; instr. physics Tulane U., New Orleans, 1929-30; former head of dept., prof. of physics U. of Southwestern La., ret. 1971. Recipient Palmes Academiques (France). Mem. La. Acad. Scis. (past pres.), Am. Phys. Soc., Am. Assn. Physics Tchrs., Sigma Xi, Sigma Pi Sigma. Roman Catholic. Home: 132 Gen Gardner St Lafayette LA 70501

DE LAURENTIIS, DINO, motion picture producer, distbr.; b. Torre Annunziata, Italy, Aug. 8, 1919; s. Rosario Aurelio and Giuseppina (Salvatore) DeL.; ed. high sch. and comml. sch., Naples, also Centro Sperimentale di Cinematografia Rome; m. Silvana Magnano, July 17, 1949; childrenVeronica, Rafaella, Federico, Francesca. Mem. actor's sch., Expt. Film Center, Rome, 1937- 39; organized first film prodn. co., 1941; now owner Dino De LaurentiisCinematografica S.p.A.; productions include Bitter Rice, 1952. Ulysses, 1955, War and Peace, 1956, La Strada (Acad. award), 1956, Nights of Cabiria (Acad. award), 1957, This Angry Age, 1958; The Tempest, 1959, Under Ten Flags, 1960, The Best of Enemies, 1962, Barabbas, 1962; Three Faces of a Woman (Soraya), 1964, The Bible, 1966, Barbarella, 1967; Anzio, 1967; Waterloo, 1970. Office: Via Pontima km 23 270 Rome, Italy

DE LAVALLADE, CARMEN, dancer; b. Los Angeles, Mar. 6, 1931; d. Leo Paul and Grace (Grenot) de Lavallade; student Los Angeles City Coll., 1950-51; m. Geoffrey Holder, June 26, 1955; 1 son Leo. Trained with Lester Horton Dance Theatre, 1948- 54, with Carmelita Maracci, 1951-54; Broadway appearance in House of Flowers, 1955; with Met. Opera, 1956, 58, N.Y. City Center Opera, 1962- 65; appeared Spoleto Festival of Two Worlds, 1958-59, 65, Kennedy Meml. Concert, Dallas, 1964; numerous concert and TV appearances, 1955-; toured S.E. Asia with de Lavallade-Ailey Am. Dance Company for State Dept., 1963; formed Am. Dance Quartet. Bd. dirs. Am. Guild Musical Artists. Recipient Dance Mag. award for 1966, 1967. Address: 164 W 88th St New York City, NY 10024.

DE LA VERGNE, JULES KRISTIAN, architect; b. New Orleans, Aug. 17, 1911; s. Hugues Jules and Marie Louise (Schmidt) de la V.; B.Arch., Notre Dame U., 1933; postgrad. Harvard, 1933-34; m. Betty Parham Felder, Oct. 27, 1936; children—Paulette (Mrs. Frank B. Stewart, Jr.), Jules Christian. Partner, Wogan, Bernard & de la Vergne, 1946-48; owner Jules K. de la Vergne & Assos., New Orleans, 1948—. Mem. Pub. Affairs Research Council La., 1962—; mem. Com. for Better La., 1964—; mem. Isaac Delgado Mus. Art Assn., 1957—; bd. dirs. Spring Fiesta, 1963-65; mem. Met. Crime Commn., 1968, Vice Pres., dir. Alumni Bd. U. Notre Dame. Served to lt. USNR, World War II. Mem. A.I.A., La. Architects Assn., La. Landmarks, Soc. Archtl. Historians New Orleans C. of C., Internat. House, S.A.R., Soc. War 1812, Navy League U.S., Soc. of the Founders of New Orleans, France-Amerique de la Louisiane, Inc. (past pres.). Clubs: Plimsoll, Serra (past pres.), Notre Dame (past pres.), Pickwick, Stratford, Pendennis, Round Table (New Orleans); Lake Shore (Slidell). Home: 5811 Hurst St New Orleans LA 70115 Office: Pere Marquette Bldg New Orleans LA 70112

DELAY, ROBERT FRANCIS, advt. exec.; b. Beresford, S.D., Jan. 4, 1919; s. John A. and Rosalie M. (Burns) DeL.; student S.D. State Coll., 1941; m. Bonnie C. Nelson, Jan. 24, 1942; 1 son, Stephen. Advt. mgr. Victor Animatograph Corp., Davenport, Ia., 1946-49; advt. mgr., pub. relations dir. Am. Air Filter Co., Inc., Louisville, 1949-55; v.p. Burnett & Logan, Inc., Chgo., 1955- 57; account exec. Waldie & Briggs, Chgo., 1957-59; pres. Direct Mail Advt. Assn., Inc., N.Y.C., 1959—. Served from 2d lt. to lt. col., Aus, 1941-46. Decorated Bronze Star. Mem. Assn. Indsl. Advertisers (dir.), Am. Advt. Fedn. (dir.), Sigma Delta Chi. Home: 31 Stony Brook Rd Westport CT 06880 Office: 230 Park Av New York City NY 10017

DELAYO, LEONARD JOSEPH, ednl. adminstr.; b. N.Y.C., Feb. 14, 1921; s. Anthony and Mary (Antonucci) DeL.; B.S., U. N.M., 1949; M.A., Tchrs. Coll., Columbia, 1949; m. Helen Griffith, Apr. 25, 1946; children—Leonard Joseph, Donna Marie, Dianne. Tchr. pub. schs., Albuquerque, 1949-50; prin. Sandia Base Schs., Albuquerque, 1950-1958; exec. sec. Tchrs. Assn. Baltimore County, Md., 1959-63; supt. of pub. instrn. State of N.M., Santa Fe, 1963—. Chmn. Govs. Com. to Investigate State Hosp. for Mental Defectives, 1956; Govs. Commn. Mental Health, 1964; bd. mgrs. N.M. Congress Parents and Tchrs., 1952-58; mem. of Gov.'s coms. TV, 1963—, State Commn. Children and Youth, 1967—, Vocational Rehab., 1964—; mem. Nat. Adv. Com. on Guidance and Counseling. Served with USMCR, 1943-46. Mem. Council Chief State Sch. Officers (dir. 1971—), N.M., nat., U.N.M. edn. assns., Albuquerque Pub. Schs. Edn. Assn. (past pres.), Phi Delta Kappa (past pres. U.N.M.), Kappa Delta Pi. Clubs: Rotary, Optomist (past v.p.) (Albuquerque). Home: 114 La Paloma Santa Fe NM 87501 Office: State Dept Edn Sante Fe NM 87501

DELBRUCK, MAX, scientist; b. Berlin, Germany, Sept. 4, 1906; s. Hans and Lina (Thiersch) D.; Ph.D., U. Göttingen 1930; m. Mary Bruce, August 2, 1941; children—Jonathan, Nicola, Tobias and Ludina. Came to the United States, 1937, naturalized, 1945. Prof. biology Calif. Inst. Tech. since 1947. Recipient Nobel prize in physiology and medicine, 1969. Mem. Nat. Acad. Sci. Home: 1510 Oakdale St Pasadena CA 91106

DEL CANTO SCHRAMM, JORGE, economist; b. Santiago, Chile, May 28, 1916; s. Gabriel Hermogenes Del Canto Aguirre and Clara Schramm Goessling; student Sch. Econs., U. Chile, 1935-38; grad. student U. Cal. at Berkeley, 1939-42, also other U.S. univs. in summers; m. Blanca DePallens Paulsen, Sept. 16, 1944; children—M. Elena, M. Isabel, M. Christina. Officer, Chilean Fgn. Office, 1937-38; prof. Sch. Econs., U. Chile, 1942—; adviser Central Bank of Chile, 1942-46; officer Internat. Monetary Fund, 1946—, dir. Western hemisphere dept., 1957—; lectr. fgn. univs. Recipient award as best grad. student Sch. Econs., U. Chile, 1938, named hon. acad. mem. faculty econs., 1958. Author several papers. Home: 5412 Christy Dr Springfield Washington, DC 20016. Office: 19th and H Sts Washington DC 20431

DELCHAMPS, ALFRED FREDERICK, food chain store exec.; b. Mobile, Jan. 25, 1895; s. Alfred W. and Annie Marie (Theuer) D.; ed. Mobile pub. schs.; LL.D. (hon.), Huntingdon Coll., Montgomery, Ala., 1955; m. Lucile Crowell, June 19, 1930; children—Alfred Frederick, Margaret (Mrs. Edward W. Young), Lucile (Mrs. Richard T. Nelson). Partner Delchamps Grocery Co., Mobile, 1921-46; pres. Delchamps, Inc., Mobile, 1946-65, chmn. bd., 1965—; dir. First Nat. Bank Mobile. Mem. bd. edn. Mobile County Schs., 1946-58, pres., 1950-52, 56-58; pres. Indsl. Devel. Bd. Mobile, 1970—; 1st v.p. Mobile County Found. Pub. Higher Education, 1962—. Trustee Bellingrath-Morse Found., Mobile, 1951—; life mem. bd. Huntingdon Coll., 1948—; bd. dirs. United Funds and Council Am., 1958-64, sec. bd., 1963-64. Served with U.S. Army, 1917-19. Named Mobilian of Year, 1950. Mem. Nat. Assn. Food Chains, Super Market Inst., Mobile Area C. of C. (pres. 1960-62, bd. dirs. 1959—) Religious-Heritage of Am. (dir.). Methodist (chmn. trustees). Clubs: Lions, Mobile Country, Athelstan (Mobile); International Trade; Bienville. Home: 2559 S Delwood Dr Mobile AL 36606 Office: 305-307 N Water St Mobile AL 36601

DELCHAMPS, O.H., Jr., business exec.; b. Mobile, Ala., 1938. Pres., Delchamps, Inc., Mobile; dir. Mchts. Nat. Bank Mobile. Home: 116 W Pinebrook Dr Mobile AL 36608 Office: 305 N Water St Mobile AL 36601*

DELCHAMPS, O.H., Sr., business exec.; b. Mobile, Ala., 1900. Vice chmn. bd. Delchamps, Inc., Mobile. Home: 2557 S Delwood St Mobile AL 36606 Office: 305 N Water St Mobile AL 36601*

DELCHER, EDWIN G., mfg. co. exec.; b. Balt.; grad. bus. adminstrn. Loyola Coll., Balt. Controller, Martin-Marietta Corp., 1961-66; financial v.p., treas. Black & Decker Mfg. 1966—. Mem. Financial Execs. Inst., Md. Assn. C.P.A.'s. Address: Black & Decker Mfg Co E Pennsylvania Av Towson MD 21204

DEL CHIARO, MARIO A., educator; A.B., U. Cal. at Berkeley, 1950, M.A., 1951, Ph.D., 1956. Prof. art, chmn. dept. art U. Cal. at Santa Barbara. Office: Dept Art U Cal Santa Barbara CA 93106*

DE LEEUW, HENDRIK, journalist, author; b. Amsterdam, Netherlands, July 18, 1891; s. Gerrit and Estelle (van Gelder) de L.; attended Amsterdam S. and H.; m. Bess Bogel, Oct. 11, 1931. Came to U.S., 1912, naturalized, 1923. Began career as world traveler, 1912; sent by Firestone Tire & Rubber Co. to Far East as spl. rep., 1920-28; chmn. Queen Wilhelmina Fund for Bklyn., Queens, L.I., 1940; joined OWI as head Netherlands sect., 1942, since with another br. U.S. Govt. Made expdns. to Dutch Borneo, Surinam, Netherlands Guiana, with film records of travels, used for lectr. purposes; gave series TV lectures on WNBT; radio commentator NBC, WOR, WMCA, WEVD, WNYC, 1930—. Mem. Am. Acad. Polit. Sci., A.R.C. (life), L.I., N.Y. hist. socs., Brooklyn Heights Assn., Soc. Am. Travel Writers. Author: Crossroads of the Java Sea, 1931; Crossroads of the Caribbean Sea, 1935; Crossroads of the Zuider Zee, 1938; Crossroads of the Buccaneers, 1937; Java Jungle Tales, 1934 (juvenile); Cities of Sin, 1933; Sinful Cities of the Western World, 1934; Flower of Joy, 1939; Peewee the Mousedeer, 1943 (juvenile); History of Colonies; American Morals, A Survey and a Report, 1949; Fallen Angels, 1953; Crossroads of the Mediterranean, 1954; The Underworld Story, 1955; Conquest of the Air, 1959; Fallen Angels, 1960; From Flying Horse to Man in the Moon, 1963. Contbr. mags., sci. and travel publs., newspapers and syndicates. Address: 15 Oliver St Brooklyn NY 11209

DELEEUW, KAREL, educator; b. Chgo., Feb. 20, 1930; B.S., U. Chgo., 1950, M.S., 1951; Ph.D. in Math., Princeton, 1954; married; 3 children. Instr. in math. Dartmouth, 1953-55; research instr. U. Wis., Madison, 1955-57; from asst. prof. to prof. Stanford, 1957—. Mem. Inst. for Advanced Study, 1960-61. Mem. Am. Math. Soc. Office: Dept Math Stanford U Stanford CA 94305*

DELEHANTY, EDWARD JOHN, investment co. exec.; b. Wallingford, Conn., Oct. 14, 1929; s. Robert Thomas and Bertha (Slanec) D.; A.B., Clark U., Worcester, Mass., 1951; m. Margaret Marshall, July 18, 1969; children—Marke Cheryl, Dana Keith, Jeffrey Dean, Robin Lee. Agt., agy. supr., regional tng. supr., gen. agt. Paul Revere Life Ins. Co., Worcester, 1951-64; v.p., dir. agys. Boston Mut. Life Ins. Co., 1964-65; v.p., dir. Mut. Fund Assoc., Inc., San Francisco, 1965-68, exec. v.p., 1968-70; v.p., dir. Putnam Mgmt. Co., Boston, 1970—. Mem. alumni com. Clark U., 1962-65. Mem. Newcomen Soc., Sales and Marketing Execs. Internat. Mason. Club: Commonwealth (San Francisco). Home: 5 Countryside Rd Littleton MA 01460 Office: 265 Franklin St Boston MA 02110

DE LEMOS, GASTON PEREIRA, psychiatrist; b. Lisbon, Portugal, Oct. 22, 1923; s. Eurico de Cruz Pereira and Ernestina de Lemos Pereira; student U. Lisbon, 1941-42; M.D., U. Coimbra, 1948; student Lisbon Inst. Tropical Medicine, 1948-49, Washington Sch. Psychiatry, 1958-62; m. Hilda Fisher; 3 children. Came to U.S., 1949, naturalized 1959. Intern St. Luke's Hosp., New Bedford, Mass., 1949-50; psychiat. resident Taunton (Mass.) State Hosp., 1953-55, Bowman Gray Sch. Medicine, 1955-56, Spring Grove State Hosp., Balt., 1956-57; dir. adult sect. Fairfax (Va.) County Mental Health Center, 1957-60; dir. Montgomery County (Md.) Dept. Mental Health, 1958-62; chief psychiat. cons. Christ Child Center Emotionally Disturbed Children, Rockville, Md., 1958-62; clin. dir., supt. Huntington (W.Va.) State Hosp., 1963-69; dir. Day Care Service, S. Fla. State Hosp., Hollywood, 1969-71; dir. drug abuse dept. Meml. Hosp., Hollywood, 1971—; guest cons. Peace Corps, Nigeria, 1962. U.S. rep. Fronte Unida Angolana, Pro-Angolan Independence Party, 1962-63, League Angolan Citizens, 1962-63. Mem. Am. Psychiat. Assn., N.Y. Acad. Sci., A.M.A., Fla., Broward County psychiat. socs., World Fedn. Mental Health, Order Portuguese Physicians. Roman Catholic. Club: Emerald Hills Country. Contbr. profl. jours. Home: 3341 N 41st Ct Hollywood FL 33021 Office: 3601 Johnson St Hollywood FL 33021

DELFORGE, RALPH HENRY, elec. equipment co. exec.; b. Green Bay, Wis., June 2, 1920; s. Edward J. and Ottilia (Wirth) D.; B.S. cum laude, Marquette U., 1949, J.D., 1950; m. Barbara K. Gannon, June 8, 1950; children—Kathleen M., Michele M., Dean P., Drew J. Sec., asst. treas. Milw. Braves, Inc., 1961-65; treas. Car Lease Co., Milw., 1965-67; asst. sec. Globe-Union, Inc., Milw., 1967; controller internat. div. Cutler-Hammer, Inc., Milw., 1967-70, treas., 1970—; dir. Cutler-Hammer Internat. Finance, Inc., Cutler-Hammer Can., Ltd., Cutler-Hammer Mexicana, S.A., Cutler-Hammer Centro-americana, S.A. Mem. Holy Family Parish Edn. Bd., 1969-70. Served to 1st lt. USAAF, 1941-46. Mem. Wis. Bar Assn., Wis. Mfrs. Assn., Financial Execs. Inst., Delta Theta Phi, Beta Gamma Sigma. Club: Milwaukee Athletic. Staff mem. Marquette Law Rev., 1949-50. Home: 5134 N Ardmore Av Milwaukee WI 53217 Office: 4201 N 27th St Milwaukee WI 53216

DELGADO, JOSE MANUEL RODRIQUEZ, educator, neurophysiologist; b. Ronda, Spain, Aug. 8, 1915; s. Rafael R. Amerigo and Amada Delgado; M.D., Madrid (Spain) U., 1940, D.Sc., 1942; m. Caroline Stoddard, May 26, 1956; children—Jose Carlos, Linda Amada. Came to U.S., 1950. Asso. prof. Madrid U. Sch. Medicine, 1942-46; vis. fellow Yale Med. Sch., 1936-38, mem. faculty, 1950—, prof. physiology, 1965—. Author: Physical Control of the Mind: Toward a Psychocivilized Society. Devel. electrodes for permanent implantation in brain; devel. methods radio stimulation brain; also study social behavior in colonies of monkeys and chimpanzees. Office: 333 Cedar St New Haven CT 06510

DEL GIUDICE, AMORE, hosp. supt.; b. Waterbury, Vt., Oct. 31, 1913; s. Alfonso and Sebastiana (Imbruglia) Del G.; B.S., U. Vt., 1936, M.D., 1939; m. Helen E. Chubb, Oct. 1940; children—Richard, Joan; m. 2d, Marie Maschino Berning, Dec. 5, 1953. Intern Vassar Bros. Hosp., Poughkeepsie, N.Y., 1939-40; resident psychiatrist Binghamton (N.Y.) State Hosp., 1946-51; asst. dir. St. Lawrence State Hosp., Ogdensburg, N.Y., 1961-66; dir. Middletown (N.Y.) State Hosp., 1966—. Served with M.C., AUS, 1940-46. Diplomate Am. Bd. Psychiatry and Neurology. Mem. A.M.A., Am. Psychiat. Assn., N.Y. State, Orange County med. socs., Med. Supts. Mental Hosps. Assns. Home: Middletown State Hosp Middletown, NY 10940.

DEL GRECO, FRANCESCO, physician; b. Lanciano, Italy, Aug. 23, 1923; s. Gaetano and Gilda (Borga) del G.; M.D., U. Rome, 1946; postgrad. Northwestern U., 1959-61; m. Gerrie Flynn, June 23, 1956; 1 son, Paul. Came to U.S., 1951, naturalized, 1959. Intern Univ. Hosp., Rome, 1946-50, resident, 1950-51; practice medicine, Cleve., 1951-57, Chgo., 1957—; research fellow Cleve. Clinc, 1951-54, asst. staff, 1955-57; vol. asst., research fellow Postgrad. Med. Sch. U. London, St. Thomas Hosp., 1954-55; intern Passavant Meml. Hosp., Chgo., 1957-58, resident, 1958-60, adj. staff, 1960-64, attending staff, 1964—, head artificial kidney unit, 1958—, dir. Clin. Research Center, 1961—; attending staff VA Research Hosp., Chgo., 1960—, asso., 1960-61; asst. prof. medicine Med. Sch. Northwestern U., Chgo., 1961-64, asso. prof., 1964-67, prof., medicine, 1967—. Med. adv. bd. Ill. Kidney Found. Danish Govt. scholar, 1951; Nat. Heart Inst. NIH fellow, 1952-53. Mem. Am. Physiol. Soc., Soc. Exptl. Biology and Medicine, Central Soc. Clin. Research, Am. Soc. Artificial Internal Organs, Council on Circulation, Council on Arteriosclerosis, Am. Heart Assn., Am. Fedn. Clin. Research, A.A.A.S., A.M.A., Central Research Club., Am., Internat. socs. nephrology, Am. Soc. Clin. Pharmacology and Therapeutics, N.Y. Acad. Scis. Office: Passavant Meml Hosp Chicago IL 60611

DE LIAGRE, ALFRED GUSTAV ETIENNE, Jr., theatrical producer, dir.; b. Passaic, N.J., Oct. 6, 1904; s. Alfred and Frida (Unger) de L.; A.B., Yale University, 1926; m. Mary M. Howard; children—Nicolas, Christina. In various businesses, including banking real estate, publishing aviation, free-lance writing, 1926-31; began career in theatre as asst. stage mgr. with Jane Cowl in Twelfth Night, 1930. Co-producer and dir. (with Richard Aldrich) Three Cornered Moon, 1933, numerous others; producer and dir. (lates); Yes, My Darling Daughter, 1937; Voice of the Turtle (Critics Prize play), 1943; The Druid Circle, 1947; The Madwoman of Chaillot, 1948; Second Threshold, 1950; Cupid and Psyche (in London), 1951; The Deep Blue Sea, 1952; Escapade, 1953; The Golden Apple 1954; producer Janus, 1955; Nature's Way, 1957; Girls in 509, 1958; J.B., 1959; Kwamina, 1961; also of Photo Finish, 1963; (play) The Irregular Verb to Love, 1963. Chmn. Sch. of the Drama, Yale U. council; chmn. theatre div. Salvation Army; trustee Guild Hall of East Hampton; v.p. Actors Fund Am.; dir. Nat. Repertory Theatre, Am. Shakespeare Festival Theatre and Acad., Council Living Theatre; v.p. Am. Theatre Wing. Decorated Chevalier French Legion of Honor. Recip. Pulitzer prize for play, 1959. Mem. Am. Theatre Soc. (mem. bd. trustees), Nat. Book Committee, France-American Society, League New York Theatres (gov.), Com. Theatrical Producers (dir.), Renaissance Found., A.N.T.A., Nat. Cultural Center, Beta Theta Pi. Clubs: Maidstone, Pundits, Century Assn., River. Editor: Sportman Pilot, 1929. Home: 322 E 57th St New York City NY 10022 Office: 55 W 42d St New York City NY 10036

DE LIMA, OSCAR ABENUN, bus. exec.; b. N.Y.C., Apr. 16, 1898; B.S., Mass. Inst. Tech., 1919; S.B., Harvard, 1919; m. Suzanne Hume, Nov. 30, 1937; children—Suzanne Abenun, Elizabeth Abenun, Virginia Abenun. Mining engr., explorer, 1919- 25; bldg. constrn., 1924-28; hotel corp. exec., hotel industry cons., 1928—; pres., dir. Roger Smith Hotels Corp. and affiliated corps., 1931- 62, chmn. bd. dirs., 1962—; pres., dir. Hadley Falls Hotel Co., Hexanite Corp., Minex Corp.; exec. v.p., dir. Nat. Hotel of Cuba Corp., 1939-43; pres. Balneario Sol, Arena y Mar, S.A., 1940-43; dir., mem. exec. com. Nat. Bank of Westchester, Peoples Nat. Corp.; dir. Park Crescent Hotel, Inc. Mem. com. initiative and liaison Forum Internat. pour la Paix, 1951-54; vice chmn. UN Guide Service, 1952-53, chmn., 1954-55; dir., mem. exec. com. Am. Assn. UN, 1946- 64, exec. v.p., 1951-57, acting pres., 1957-58, chmn. bd. govs., 1952-54, chmn. bd. dirs., 1954-58, chmn. exec. com., 1960-64; chmn. exec. com. UN Assn. USA, 1964-69, vice chmn., 1969—; mem. exec. com. of Speaker Services for the UN, 1958-68; mem. UN Com. City N.Y.; mem. drafting com. and mem. exec. com. Commn. to Study Orgn. Peace; mem. presidium Zagreb, Yugoslavia Conf. Peace and Internat. Cooperation, 1951; del. Nat. Conf., U.S. Nat. Commn. for UNESCO, 1951; chmn. Conf. U.S. Responsibility for World Leadership, 1952; mem. U.S. delegation to W.I. Conf., 1946, 48; mem. Nat. Citizens' Commn. on Internat. Cooperation, 1964-65, Nat. Com. on Urban Devel., 1965. A founder Highlands Mus. and Biol. Sta., 1927; treas., dir. Geneva (Switzerland) Sch. Internat. Studies, 1926-30; bd. mgrs. Sevilla Home for Children, 1938-42; adv. council Caribbean Interim Tourist Com., 1948-52, Caribbean Tourist Assn., 1952-60. Dir. Stamford Mus. and Nature Center 1958—; dir. Stamford Forum for World Affairs, 1962—; exec. com. Citizens Action Council Improvement Stamford, 1966-70; bd. overseers U. Conn.'s Bartlett Arboretum 1967—. With tech. sect. Office of the U. S. Naval Attache, attached to Brit. Admiralty, London, 1942-43; tech. sect., readiness div. Comdr. Naval Forces in Europe, 1943; mine warfare sect. Office Chief Naval Operations, 1943-44; war plans officer Comdr. Minecraft, U.S. Pacific Fleet, 1944-45, rep. this command on staff Comdr.-in-Chief, 1945; cons. Dept. of State, 1946-47, U.S., U.K., French and Netherlands sects. Caribbean Commn. 1946-60; comdr. USNR, ret. Registered profl. engr., Conn. Mem. Soc. Am. Mil. Engrs., Soc. Harvard Engrs., Scientists, Am. Inst. Mining and Metall. Engrs. (asso.), Am. Math. Soc., Operations Research Soc. Am., Council Fgn. Relations. Home: 2901 High Ridge Rd Stamford, CT 06903. Office: 106 7th Av New York City NY 10011

DELISIO, STEPHEN SCOTT, lawyer; b. San Diego, Dec. 30, 1937; s. Anthony J. and Emma (Cheney) DeL.; student Am. U., 1958-59; B.A., Emory U., 1959; LL.B., Albany Law Sch., 1962; LL.M., Georgetown U., 1963; m. Margaret I. Winter, June 26, 1964; children—Anthony W., Stephen Scott, Heather E. Admitted to Alaska bar, 1964; practice in Fairbanks, 1963—; asst. dist. atty., Fairbanks, 1963-65; asso. McNealy & Merdes, 1965-66; lectr. U. Alaska, 1965-67; partner Merdes, Schaible, Staley & DeLisio, 1966—; city atty., Fairbanks, 1967-70, Barrow, 1969—, Ft. Yukon and North Pole, 1970—. Sec. U. Alaska Heating Corp., Inc.; sec.-treas. Trans-Alaska Electronics, Inc., Baker Aviation, Inc. Precinct committeemann Republican Party, 1970- -. Pres. Tanana Valley State Fair Assn.; v.p. Fairbanks Mental Health Assn., Fairbanks United Good Neighbors Fund; bd. dirs. Fairbanks Montessori Assn., Greater Fairbanks Community Hosp. Found. Recipient Jaycee Distinguished Service award, 1968. Mem. Am., Alaska, Tanana Valley bar assns., Am. Trial Lawyers Assn., Am. Judicature Soc., U.S. (past dir.), Alaska (past pres.), Fairbanks (past pres.) Jaycees, Chi Phi, Pi Sigma Phi. Author: (with others) Law and Tactics in Federal Criminal Cases, 1964. Home: 5102 Shorecrest Dr Anchorage AK 99502 Office: 700 H St Anchorage AK 99501

DELISLE, JACQUES, lawyer; b. Montreal, Que., Can., May 4, 1935; s. Roch and Cecile (Miller) D.; B.A., Quebec Jesuits Coll., 1954; LL.L., Laval U., 1958; postgrad. Paris U., 1958-59, U. Toronto, 1959-60; m. Nicole Rainville, Sept. 17, 1960; children-Elene, Jean. Called to bar, Que., 1958; practice in Quebec, 1960—; partner Letourneau, Stein, Marsheille, Delisle & Larue, 1960— tchr. Law Faculty, Laval U. Mem. Canadian, Quebec, Quebec Jr. (past pres.) bar assns. Home: 1240 DeSamos St Sillery Que Canada Office: 65 Ste Anne St Quebec 4 Que Canada

DELL, GABRIEL, actor; Broadway appearance in The Sign in Sidney Brustein's Window, 1964.*

DELL, ROBERT MERRITT, educator; b. N.Y.C., Oct. 5, 1920; s. Frederick C.J. and Grace (Merritt) D.; A.B., Franklin and Marshall Coll., 1942; M.A., Columbia Tchrs. Coll., 1947, diploma in teaching, 1949; Ph.D., N.Y. U., 1960; m. Mary Frances Grunitz, June 8, 1946; children—Blair Kenneth, Douglas Frederic. Instr., Manhattan Coll., 1946-49; mem. faculty Pace Coll., N.Y.C., 1948-67, prof., English, 1960- 67, chmn. dept., 1963-67; div. head arts and scis. Pace Coll. Westchester, Pleasantville, N.Y., 1967-68, chmn. depts. English, Speech, Drama, also Fgn. Langs., 1968—; vis. prof. Poole, Eng., 1961-62; adj. prof. English, Columbia Coll. Pharm. Scis., 1964-71. Mem. Nat. Bd. Rev. Motion Pictures. Served to lt. USNR, 1942-46. Mem. Am. Assn. U. Profs., Coll. English Assn., Nat. Council Tchrs. English, Conf. English Edn., Bronte Soc., Lambda Chi Alpha, Phi Delta Kappa. Contbr. profl. jours. Home: 121 Croton Av Mount Kisco NY 10549 also Delwood Corinth VT 05039 Office: Pace Coll Westchester Bedford Rd Pleasantville NY 10570

DELLA CASA, LISA, opera singer; b. Burgdorf, Switzerland, Feb. 2, 1921; d. Francesco Robert and Margarete (Mueller) Della Casa; ed. pub. schs., Switzerland, conservatorium at Bern; m. Dragan Debelevic, Dec. 5, 1949; 1 dau., Wesna. Mem. Vienna State Opera, 1947—, Metropolitan Opera, N.Y.C., 1953- -; has appeared at Festival of Salzburg, Bayreuth, Covent Garden, London, La Scala, Milan, Paris, Hamburg, München, Zurich, Geneva, Monte Carlo, Edinburgh. Home: Schloss Gottlieben Thurgau Switzerland also Krapfenwaldgasse 51 Vienna 191 Austria

DELLA-CIOPPA, GUY, radio exec.; b. Phila., Aug. 17, 1914; s. Thomas Edmund and Nellie Harper (Gill) Della-C.; B.S., U. Pa., 1937; m. Flora Darrah Cooper, Aug. 24, 1940; 1 dau., Margaret Neila Darrah. Actor, radio writer, 1937; producer C.B.S., 1938-40, Henry Souvaine, Inc., N.Y. City, 1940; producer C.B.S., N.Y. City, 1941-42, asst. to chmn. bd., 1947-48, asso. dir. programs, Hollywood, Cal., 1948-50, dir. network radio and TV programs, 1951, v.p. radio div. 1952-58, vice pres. program dir. Hollywood TV City, 1958-67; vice pres., mem. bd. dirs. CBS, 1967—. Served as chief tactical radio operations Psychol. Warfare Div., SHAEF, O.W.I.-OSS, 1943-46. Awarded Bronze Star. Mem. Beta Gamma Sigma, Theta Xi. Club: Mask and Wig (Phila.). Home: 3274 Oakdell Rd North Hollywood CA 91604 Office: 7800 Beverly Blvd Los Angeles CA 90036

DELLENBACK, JOHN RICHARD, congressman; b. Chgo., Nov. 6, 1918; s. William H. and Margaret (Albright) D.; B.S. in Applied Econ. Sci., Yale, 1940; J.D., U. Mich., 1949; m. Mary Jane Benedict, Sept. 10, 1948; children—Richard Ludlow, David Albright, Barbara Clare. Bus. tng. student Gen. Electric Co., 1940-42; instr. bus. law Ore. State U., 1949-50, asst. prof., 1950-51; admitted to Ore. bar; partner in law with Frank J. Van Dyke, Medford, Ore., 1952-66; mem. Ore. Ho. Reps., 1960-66; mem. 90th-92d Congresses, 4th Dist. Ore. Dir. Radio Medford, Inc. Mem. Ore. Bd. Bar Examiners. Pres. United Medford Crusade, Jackson County Cancer Soc.; moderator Ore. Synod United Presbyn. Ch.; mem. permanent jud. commn. Gen. Assembly United Presbyn. Ch., mem. commn. ecumenical mission and relations. Bd. dirs. Medford YMCA, Kiwanis Found. Del. Republican Nat. Conv., 1964, 68. Served to lt. comdr. USNR, 1942-46. Named Jr. First Citizen, Medford Jr. C. of C., 1953. Mem. Am., Ore., Jackson County bar assns., Medford C. of C. (bd. dirs.), Phi Gamma Delta, Phi Alpha Delta. Kiwanian (pres. Medford), Mason, Elk. Clubs: Rogue Valley Univ.; Rogue Valley Country. Home: 6903 Crail Dr Bethesda, MD 20034; also 300 Windsor Av Medford OR 97501 Office: House Office Bldg Washington DC 20515

DELLER, ALFRED, singer; b. Margate, Kent, Eng., May 31, 1912; s. Thomas William and Mary (Cave) D.; ed. secondary schs., Eng.; m. Kathleen Margaret Lowe, June 5, 1937; children—Mark, Simon, Jane. Lay-clk. Canterbury Cathedral, 1940- 47; vicarchoral St. Paul's Cathedral, 1947-61; soloist inaugural concert BBC program, Third, 1946; formed vocal ensemble Deller Consort, 1950; title role Oberon premier performance Britten's opera A Midsummer Night's Dream, 1961; solo concert tours U.S., 1955, 57, 59, 62, Deller Consort tours U.S., 1964, 66, 69; European festival performances include Edinburgh, York, Aldeburgh, London, Vienna, Holland, Royal Danish, Strasbourg. Hon. music adviser U. Kent. Mem. Inc. Soc. Musicians, Assn. English Singers and Speakers. Club: Catch of Am. (pres.). Address: Barton Cottage The Street Kennington Ashford Kent England

DELLEUR, JACQUES WILLIAM, educator; b. Paris, France, Dec. 30, 1924; s. Georges Leon and Simone (Rossum) D.; came to U.S., 1952, naturalized, 1957; Civil and Mining Engr., Nat. U. Columbia, 1949; M.S. in Civil Engring., Rensselaer Polytech. Inst., 1950; Dr. Engring. Sci., Columbia, 1955; m. DeLores Ann Horne, June 18, 1957; children—James Robert, Anne Marie. Civil engr. R.J. Tipton and Assos., 1950-52; from research asst. to instr. civil engring. and engring. mechanics Columbia, 1952-55; mem. faculty Purdue U., 1955—, prof. hydraulic engring. and hydrology, 1963—, head hydromechanics and water resources area, 1965—, asso. dir. Water Resources Research Center, 1971—; Grenoble (France), 1961-62; research hydrology French Nat. Hydraulics Lab., Chatou, 1968-69. Mem. Am. Soc. C.E. (chmn. fluid dynamics com. 1964-66, task com. mechanics of turbulence, 1964-69, task com. hydraulics of bridges 1963- 68), Am. Soc. M.E., Am. Geophys. Union, Am. Soc. Engring. Edn., Internat. Assn. Hydraulic Research, Internat. Assn. Sci. Hydrology. Author articles, reports in field. Home: 124 Mohican Pl West Lafayette IN 47906 Office: Sch Civil Engring Purdue Univ Lafayette IN 47907

DELLINGER, BROWER, mining engr.; b. Westfield, N.J., Mar. 19, 1913; s. Lester Earl and Alice (Brower) D.; grad. Stanford, 1936; postgrad. U. Hawaii, 1943; m. Jane L. Parsons, June 29, 1940; 1 son, Brower II. Underground shift boss Empire Mines, Grass Valley, Cal., 1937, mining engr., 1938-42, supt. North Star Mine, 1947-48, asst. gen. mgr., 1949-52; supt. operations Newmont Mining Corp., Goldfield, Nev., 1945-47; mgr. Spokane Idaho Mines, Kellogg, Ida., 1952-54; supt. exploration NL Industries (formerly Nat. Lead Co. Salt Lake City, 1954-56; mgr. Monticello uranium plant, 1956-58, asst. plant mgr. MacIntyre Devel., Titanium div. NL Industries, Tahawus, N.Y., 1958-65, plant mgr., 1965-67; mgr. mining and exploration dept. NL Industries, N.Y.C., 1968—; dir. Albany Trust Co. Cal. dir. for Bells of Freedom, 1952. Served to lt. USNR, 1942-45; PTO. Mem. Soc. Mining Engrs. of Am. Inst. Mining, Metall. and Petroleum Engrs. (past pres.), Mining and Metall. Soc. Am. Lion. Clubs: Mining, Bankers Am. (N.Y.C.); University (Salt Lake City). Contbr. articles profl. jours. Home: 23 Concord Lane Convent NJ 07961 Office: NL Industries 111 Broadway New York City NY 10006

DELLINGER, DAVID, editor, printer; b. Wakefield, Mass., Aug. 22, 1915; s. Raymond Pennington and Marie E. (Fiske) D.; B.A., Yale, 1936, student Yale Div. Sch., 1937-38; Henry fellow New Coll., Oxford (Eng.) U., 193637; student Union Theol. Sem., N.Y.C., 193940; m. Elizabeth Peterson, Feb. 4, 1942; children—Patchen, Ray, Natasha (Mrs. Val Burd), Daniel, Michele. Asso. minister Jube Meml. Ch., Newark, 1939-40; partner Libertarian Press, workers coop., Glen Gardner, N.J., 194667; editor and pub. Liberation, 1956—. Chmn. Nat. Mblzn. Commn. End War in Vietnam, 1967—; coordinator Fifth Av. Vietnam Peace Parade Com. 1965—; mem. Bertrand Russell War Crimes Tribunal, 196667. Poynter fellow journalism Yale, 1969. Mem. Internat. Assn. Sociology Coop. (bd. dirs.), Berzelius and The Colony Found. (Yale), Phi Beta Kappa. Author: Cuba: America's Lost Plantations, 1961. Contbr. Seeds of Liberation, 1964; Nonviolence in America, 1966; Telling It Like it Was-The Chicago Riots, 1969; Against The Crime of Silence, 1969; Collected Essays—Revolutionary nonviolence, 1970; The People vs. the United States of America, 1971. Office: 339 Lafayette St New York City NY 10012

DELLIQUADRI, PARDO FREDERICK, univ. dean; b. Pueblo, Colo., Jan. 20, 1915; s. Colombo Frederick and Rose Marie (Russo) D.; B.A. cum laude, U. Colo., 1938; M.S. in Social Work, U. Neb., 1941; m. Velma Lee Ingram, Sept. 9, 1939; children—Toni Cheryl, Lyn Christine, Geri Martha. WPA investigator in Wyo., 1938-39; research Brookings Instn., 1940; pub. welfare childrens worker, Yakima, Wash., 1941; state statistician Wyo. Pub. Welfare Dept., 1942, dir. childrens div., 1946-48; supt. child welfare Ill. Dept. Pub. Welfare, 1948-50; dir. div. children and youth Wis. Dept. Pub. Welfare, 1950-60; dean N.Y. Sch. Social Work, Columbia, 1960-67; dean Sch. Social Work, U. Hawaii, 1967-68; chief U.S. Children's Bur., Washington, 1968-69; dean Sch. Social Welfare, U. Wis., Milw., 1969—. Exec. sec. Ill. Com. Children and Youth, 1948, Wis. Com. Children and Youth, 1950-60; tech. adv. com. White House Conf. Children and Youth, 1950; adv. council child welfare U.S. Congress, 1958-59; UN social welfare adviser to El Salvador, 1959; U.S. rep. Inter-Am. Children's Inst., Montevideo, Uruguay, 1958-61, v.p., 1959-61; vice chmn. U.S. delegation Pan Am. Child Congress, Bogata, 1959; U.S. exec. bd. UNICEF, 1961-69; mem. of Mayor N.Y.C. Com. Pub. Welfare, 1961-67; mem. bd., exec. com. N.Y. Citizens Com. Children, 1961-67; ad hoc com. Dept. Health, Edn. and Welfare, 1961; panel tng. grants Pres.'s Commn. Juvenile Delinquency, 1962-66, chmn., 1963-66; chmn. adv. group N.Y. State Legislative Com. on Child Care, 1965-67; chmn. N.Y. Adv. Welfare Study Com., 1965-66; del. White House Conf. on Children, 1970-71; program chmn. Nat. Conf. Social Welfare, 1970-71; exec. bd. Wis. Welfare Council, 1969; cons. Community Research Assos., N.Y.C., 1970—. Mem. task force on leisure Nat. Council Chs. U.S.A., 1965-67; U.S. del. UN Conf. for Internat. Ministers Social Welfare, 1968. Served to lt. USNR, 1942-46. Recipient FONEME Internat. award on youth, Milan, Italy, 1968; Norlin medal, 1969. Mem. Am. Pub. Welfare Assn. (chmn. membership com. 1950-52, dir. 1952, 54, 57, chmn. self-study com. 1965), Child Welfare League Am., Am. Assn. Social Workers (chmn. nominating com. 1954-55), Council Social Work Edn. (chmn. career com. 1961-67, chmn. com. on adminstrn. 1968-69, chmn. dean's steering com. 1971, Nat. Assn. Social Workers (chmn. Wis. 1957-59), Am. Council Nationality Services, Nat. Conf. Social Work (v.p. 1960-61, chmn. program com.), confs. social welfare Wyo., Ill., Wis., N.Y., Wis. P.T.A. (life), Alumni Assn. U. Colo. (pres. Northeastern chpt.), Phi Beta Kappa. Office: Sch Social Work U Wis Milwaukee WI 53201

DELLMUTH, CARL K., banker; b. Camden, N.J., Nov. 10, 1908; s. Enos Bowen and Florence Davis (Kugler) D.; A.B., Swarthmore Coll., 1931; m. Margaret Ball, Apr. 2, 1934; children—Carl Sturges, Nancy Gail. Dir., athletics and phys. edn., 1941-49; exec. sec. Pa. Bankers Assn., 1949-53; sr. v.p. Fidelity Bank, 1953-64, exec. v.p., 1964-66, pres. 1966—, chmn. bd., 1971—, also dir.; vice chmn., dir. Fidelity Internat. Corp., Phila., Fidelity Bldg. Corp., Phila., Globe Ticket Co., Phila., Fidelity Internat. Bank, N.Y. Bd. mgrs. Franklin Inst.; bd. dirs. Southeastern Pa. Econ. Devel. Corp., Walter E. Hering Found., Barnwell Found.; bd. mgrs. Swarthmore Coll., Franklin Inst. Mem. Res. City Bankers Assn., World Affairs Council, A.I.M., Kappa Sigma. Republican. Methodist. Home: 323 Swarthmore Av Swarthmore PA 19081 Office: Fidelity Bank Broad and Walnut Sts Philadelphia PA 19109

DELLO JOIO, NORMAN, composer; b. N.Y.C., Jan. 24, 1913; s. Casimir and Antoinette (Garramone) Dello Joio; student All Hallows Inst., 1926-30, Coll. City N.Y., 1932-34, Inst. Mus. Art, 1936, Juilliard Grad. Sch., 1939-41, Yale Sch. Music, 1941; Mus. D. (hon.), Colby Coll., Lawrence Coll.; Mus. D. (hon.), U. Cin., 1967, St. Mary's Coll., 1969; m. Grayce Baumgold, June 5, 1943; children—Victoria, Justin, Norman Adrian. Tchr. composition, Mannes Coll. Music; 1945—; commentator Met. Opera broadcasts. Chmn. planning com. Ford Found. Composer: Ballet On Stage!, 1944; Ricercari (for piano and orch.), 1946; Variations- Chaccone-Finale, 1947; Diversion of Angeles (dance), 1948; Concerto for Clarinet and Orch., 1949; New York Profiles (for orch.), 1949; The Triumph of St. Joan, (opera), 1950; Psalm of David (chorus and orch.), 1950; Song of Affirmation (soprano, chorus, narrator, orchestra), 1950; The Tall Kentuckian (score for musical play), 1952; Song of the Open Road (chorus), 1952; The Ruby (opera), 1953; The Lamentation of Saul, 1954; The Trial at Rouen (opera), 1955; Mediations on Ecclesiates, 1956; Air Power, symphonic suite, 1956; Ballad of the 7 Lively Arts, 1957; To St. Cecilia, 1958; Blood Moon (opera); also Variations and Fantasy for Piano and Orchestra, 1961; score Anthony and Cleopatra; Variants on Mediaeval Tune for Symphonic Band; Songs of Adieu, score The Louvre, NBC TV, 1965 (Emmy award), Beyond Every Horizon (for Symphonic band), Antiphonal Fantasy (organ, brass, strings), 1965, Songs of Walt Whitman for Orch. and Chorus, 1966; Capriccio (for piano) 1968; Fantasies on Theme of Haydn, 1968; Time of Snow (ballet) 1968; Proud Music of the Storm (chorus, brass, organ) 1967; Days of the Modern (chorus, brass, percussion), 1968; Evocations (chorus, orch.), 1970; Psalm of Peace (chorus, organ, french horn, trumpet), 1971; Mass (chorus, organ, brass). Mem. research adv. council U.S. Office Edn.; adv. council State U. N.Y., Potsdam; chmn. policy com. contemporary music Ford Found. Bd. dirs. Am. Music Center. Recipient Elizabeth Sprague Coolidge award, 1937; Town Hall Composition award, 1941; 2 Guggenheim fellowships, 1943, 1944, grant Am. Acad. Arts and Letters, 1945; N.Y. Music Critics Circle award, 1949, 58, Pulitzer prize for music, 1957. Mem. League Composers (dirs.), Broadcast Music, Inc., Nat. Inst. Arts and Letters (mem. council). Club: Century. Home: 1115 Fifth Av New York City NY 10029 also East Hampton Long Island NY 11937

DELLOW, REGINALD LEONARD, advt. exec.; b. Detroit, Sept. 13, 1924; s. Reginald C. and Ethel (White) D.; student Wayne State U., 1941-43; B.S., Detroit Inst. Tech., 1946; m. Betsy Ann Paton, Feb. 26, 1949; children—John Paton, Elizabeth Diana, Tracy Susannah. Research dir., asst. to media dir. D. P. Brother & Co., Detroit, 1948-53; dir. media and research Allman Co., Detroit, 1953-56; exec. v.p. Grant Advt., Inc., Chgo., 1956—. Pres. Chgo. agy. Media Group,

1960. Named Media Man of Month, Apr. 1960; recipient Advt. award Am. Legion, 1958. Mem. Am. Marketing Assn. (pres. Mich. chpt. 1955, mem. nat. conv. com. 1963, 66, treas. Chi chpt. 1969-70), Alpha Gamma Upsilon (pres. 1946), Omega Alpha Pi (pres. 1945). Republican. Mem. Christian Scientist Ch. Club: Union League (Chgo.). Home: 900 Green Bay Rd Winnetka IL 60093 Office: 10 S Riverside Plaza Chicago IL 60606

DELMAR, BRUCE EUGENE, aero. engr.; b. Pasadena, Cal., July 19, 1913; s. Algernon and Belle (Rogers) DelM.; student U. Cal. at Los Angeles, 1931-33; B.S., U. Cal., 1937; m. Mary Van Ness, Apr. 1, 1939; children—Patricia Jean, Marna Belle. Aircraft tooling engr. Douglas Aircraft Co., Santa Monica, Cal., 1933-37, aircraft stress analyst, 1937-38, research engr., 1938-40, cabin supercharging engr., 1940-43, asst. mech. design engr., 1943-44, mech. test engr., 1944-46, preliminary design engr., 1946-48; spl. projects engr., 1948-51; grad. sch. lectr. Guggenheim Aero. Lab., Cal. Inst. Tech., 1943-48; founder, pres., treas. DelMar Engring. Labs., Inc., Los Angeles and Santa Monica, Cal., 1952—; founder, pres. Aeroplastics Corp., Venice California, 1956—, Avionics Research Products Corp., El Segundo, Cal., 1958—, Del Mar Sci. Found (ednl.), Los Angeles, specialist in high altitude and high speed target aircraft design; pres. Electromation Co., Los Angeles. Mem. Los Angeles regional export expansion council U.S. Dept. Commerce, 1966—. Founder, life asso. Los Angeles Music Center; founder, life mem. U. Cal. at Los Angeles Meml. Activities Center; counsellor Jr. Achievement. Licensed pvt. airplane and helicopter pilot, profl. engr., Cal. Asso. fellow Inst. Aero. Scis.; mem. Am. Soc. M.E. (recipient nat. jr. award 1945), Am. Helicopter Soc., Strategic Industries Assn. (dir. 1962—), Am. Ordnance Assn., Cal. Riviera Home Owners Assn. (dir. 1963—), U. Cal. Alumni Assn., Bruin Bench. Presbyn. (elder). Clubs: Riviera Country, Pacific Palisades; El Dorado Country (Palm Desert, Cal.). Contbr. engring. jours. Patentee. Home: 1175 Corsica Dr Pacific Palisades CA 90272 Office: 6901 Imperial Hwy Los Angeles Internat Airport Los Angeles CA 90009

DEL MAR, ROLAND HADDAWAY, army officer; b. Attica, Ind., Feb. 11, 1908; s. Carlos Florio and Mabelle Antoinette (Leonard) del M.; student Coll. of Wooster, 1930; grad. Cav. Sch., 1942, Command and Gen. Staff Coll., 1945. Armed Forces Staff Coll., 1950, Army War Coll., 1954, Command Mgmt. Sch., 1956; m. Elizabeth Kathryn Adams, Oct. 11, 1930; 1 dau., Mareen Duvall (Mrs. John L. Braddock). With Internat. Harvester Co., 1928-41; commd. capt. U.S. Army, 1941, advanced through grades to maj. gen., 1962; asst. div. comdr. 4th Armored Div., 1956; readiness officer AFSE (NATO), Naples, 1958-59, operations officer, 1959-60; comdg. gen. Combat Command A, 1st Armored Div., 1960-61, Antilles Command, P.R., 1961-63; dir. Inter. Am. Def. Coll., 1963-66, Latin Am. Cons. Chmn. Md. Comm. Latin Am. Affairs. Trustee Charles Delmar Found., Coll. of Wooster, Americas Found., Internat. Inst. Americas. Decorated Legion of Merit, Bronze Star medal, DSM, Army Commendation, UN medal. Mem. Am. Legion, Md., Frederick County hist. socs., S.A.R., Chevalier du Tastevin, Soc. Internat. Devel., Inter. Am. Acad., Latin Am. Studies Assn., Inter-Am. Council, Southeastern Conf. on Latin-America Studies. Mem. Mil. Order World Wars. Mem. P.E. Ch. Mason (Shriner), Rotarian, Nat. Sojourneur. Clubs: Explorers (Washington); Casanova (Va.) Hunt. Home: Route 1 Oakland Knoxville MD 21758 Office: 520 N St NW Washington DC 20024

DEL MONACO, MARIO, opera singer; b. Florence, Italy, July 27, 1915; student Conservatory of Pesaro, also student art, Pesaro; scholarship Conservatorio Rossini, Pesaro; m. Rina Fedora; children—Giancairo, Glaudio. Profl. debut, Milan, 1941; dramatic tenor; appeared La Scala, Milan, also opera houses in Rome, Naples, Barcelona, Lisbon, Stockholm, Covent Garden in London, Buenos Aires, Rio de Janeiro, Mexico City; Am. debut as Radames in Aida, San Francisco Opera Co., 1950; debut Met. Opera, 1950, mem. company, 1951—; recorded operatic roles, including Calaf in Turandot, Otello, Duke in Rigoletto, Canio in Pagliacci, others; also appeared in motion pictures, TV. Address: care Metropolitan Opera Assn 147 W 39th St New York City NY 10018

DELMORE, JOHN ROBERT, govt. ofcl.; b. Mpls., Nov. 20, 1915; s. John James and Anna Lillian (Griffin) D.; B.S. cum laude, Marquette U., 1945; m. Marian Louise Julien, June 17, 1939; children—Joan (Mrs. Michael J. Myles), John Thomas, Michael, Lynne Ann. With Pabst Brewing Co., 1938-41; chief accountant Grede Foundries, 1941-45; accountant Arthur Andersen & Co., C.P.A.'s, 1945-53; controller Henry Disston & Sons, Inc., 1953-54; with Gen. Acctg. Office, 1954-59, asst. dir. civil accounting and auditing div., 1955-59; asst. commnr. Pub. Housing Adminstrn., 1959-61; dir. Office Audits, Office Sec. Dept. Commerce, 1961-70, spl. asst. to the asst. controller for auditing, 1971—. Recipient Outstanding Service award Gen. Accounting Office, 1957, 58, Commerce Dept., 1964, 65. C.P.A., Wis. Mem. Am. Accounting Assn., Am. Inst. C.P.A.'s, Wis. Soc. C.P.A.'s, Alpha Kappa Psi, Alpha Sigma Nu, Beta Gamma Sigma, Beta Alpha Psi. Roman Catholic. Club: Lakewood Country. Home: 4503 Edgefield Rd Kensington MD 20795 Office: USAEC Germantown MD

DELO, DAVID MARION, coll. pres.; b. Mt. Morris, Ill., Dec. 20, 1905; s. Frank Sherman and Ina Salome (Colburn) D.; A.B., Miami U., Oxford, O., 1926, LL.D. (hon.), 1956; M.A., U. Kan., 1928; Ph.D., Harvard, 1935; postgrad. Northwestern U., 1930-31; Sc.D. (hon.), Hartwick Coll., 1954; L.H.D., Rollins Coll., Winter Park, Fla., 1968; LL.D., U.S. Fla., 1969; m. Elsie Muriel Crooker, June 17, 1933; children—Diana, David Michael, Virginia Ann. Geologist, So. Crude Oil Purchasing Co., 1928-29; instr., Washington U., St. Louis, 1929-30, Northwestern U., 1930-32; chmn. dept. geology, Lawrence Coll., Appleton, Wis., 1934-37; chmn. dept. geology and geography, Knox Coll. 1937-46, certified instr. civilian pilot tng. program, 1939-43; tech. aide, Office Sci. Research and Devel., 1944-46; chief, sci. manpower br., Research and Devel. Div., Gen. Staff, Dept. of the Army, 1946-49; exec. dir. Am. Geol. Inst., exec. sec. div. geol. and geog. NRC, 1949-52; cons. on sci. manpower Research and Devel. Command, USAF, 1951; pres. Wagner Luth. Coll., 1952-58; pres. U. Tampa (Fla.), 1958-71, chancellor, 1971—. Holder of grand-in-aid, NRC, 1936 (com. tng. in geology, 1946; com. on geologic personnel 1948). Recipient George Washington medal Freedoms Found., 1966. Pres. Fla. Assn. Colls. and Univs., 1964-65; chmn. Ind. Colls. and Univs. of Fla., 1966-68. Fellow Geol. Soc. Am.; mem. Assn. Geol. Tchrs. (pres. 1952), Phi Beta Kappa, Sigma Xi, Beta Theta Pi. Kiwanian. Club: Cosmos (Washington). Author of books, including Phacopid Trilobites of North America, 1940; Scientists in Uniform, 1948; also articles. Co-author: Years of This Land, 1943. Home: 52 W Davis Blvd Tampa FL 33606

DELOACH, CARTHA DEKLE, corp. ofcl.; b. Claxton, Ga., July 20, 1920; s. Cartha Calhoun and Eula Mary (Dekle) DeL.; B.A., Stetson U., 1942, student Law Sch., 1941-42, J.D. (hon.), 1966; U.D. (hon.), Lincoln Coll., 1968; m. Barbara Owens, Apr. 22, 1945; children—Barbara Elaine, Cartha Dekle, Thomas O., Theresa M., Gregory D., Sharon Marie, Mark Christopher. With FBI, 1942- -, asst. dir., 1959-65, asst. to dir., 1965-70; v.p. corporate affairs Pepsico, Inc., Purchase, N.Y., 1970—. Bd. dirs. J. Edgar Hoover Found., 1964—; bd. of dirs. Banking Instns., Damon Runyon Cancer Meml. Fund. Served with USNR, 1944-46. Recipient Dist. Alumni award Stetson U., 1958; Pres.' Medal, St. John's Coll., 1967; George Washington Honor medal, Freedoms Found., 1967, 68, 69; Man of Year, Nat. Assn. State Dirs. Vets. named Man of Year, Nat. Assn. State Dirs. Vets. Affairs, 1964. Mem. Am. Legion (dept. comdr. 1958, nat. vice comdr. 1959, chmn. nat. pub. relations commn. 1959—; Man of year award 1963), Stetson U. Alumni Assn. (dist. Alumnus award 1966), Pi Kappa Phi, Phi Alpha Delta. Home: 96 Perkins Rd Greenwich CT 06830

DELON, ALAIN, actor; b. Sceaux, France, Nov. 8, 1935; s. Fabien and Edith (Arnold) D.; ed. Catholic Boarding Sch., Bagneux, France; m. Francine-Nathalie Canovas, Aug. 13, 1964 (div.); 1 son, Anthony. Motion picture appearances include Quand la Femme S'en Mele, 1957, Sois Belle et Tais- Toi, 1957, Faibles Femmes, 1958, Le Chemin des Ecoliers, 1959, Plein Soleil, 1959, Rocco et Ses Freres, 1960, Quelle Joie de Vivre, 1961, Les Amours Célèbres, 1961, L'Eclipse, 1961, Le Diable et Les Dix Commandements, 1962, Le Guépard, 1962, Mélodie en Sous Sol., 1962, La Tulipe Noire, 1963, Les Félins, 1963, L'Insoumis, 1964, La Rolls Royce Jaune, 1964, Once A Thief, 1964, Les Centurions, 1965, Paris Brule-t- Il?, 1965; Texas Across the River, 1966; Les Aventuriers, 1966; stage appearance in Dommage Qu'Elle Soit Une P........, 1961; Histoires extraordinaires, Le Samourai, Diaboliquement votre, La Motocyclette, 1967; Adieu l'Ami, les Yeux crevés, La Piscine, 1968; Jeff, 1969. Served with French Marine Corps, 1953-55; Indo- China. Club: Monte Carlo Yachting. Home: 3 rue Francois ler Paris 8 France Office: care Georges Beaume 58 rue Pierre-Charron Paris 8 France

DE LONG, CHARLES EDWARD, lawyer; b. Annville, Pa., Sept. 6, 1918; s. William Francis and Florence (Wagenhurst) DeL.; A.B., U. Pa., 1938; postgrad. Yale, 1938-39; LL.B., Harvard, 1946; m. Helen Lillian Fraser, Dec. 6, 1958; 1 son, Robert Fraser. Admitted to Pa. bar, 1947; atty. SEC, Washington, 1947-48; practiced in Phila., 1948-64; partner Pepper, Hamilton & Scheetz, 1960- 64; asst. sec. Certain-teed Products Corp., Valley Forge, Pa., 1964-65, sec., res. counsel, 1965—; Sec. Modular Scis., Inc., Valley Forge, Pa., 1970—; dir. Sun Pipe Line Co., 1960-64. Bd. dirs. Greater Phila. Council Chs. Served with AUS, 1941-45; PTO. Mem. Am., Pa., Phila. bar assns., Phi Beta Kappa. Republican. Presbyn. Club: Harvard (Phila.). Home: 370 Belrose Lane Radnof PA 19087 Office: care of Certain-Teed Products Corp Valley Forge PA 19481

DE LONG, EARL HOWARD, univ. dean; b. Kirkland, Ill., Mar. 9, 1909; s. John E. and Jennie (Whipple) De L.; B.A., Northwestern U., 1929, M.A., 1930, Ph.D., 1933; m. 2d, Gladys Pember Berenguer, Feb. 15, 1946; children—William B., James V., John P.; 1 stepdau., Linda P. Berenguer. From instr. to asso. prof. polit. sci. Northwestern U., 1933-41; staff analyst and exec. U.S. Civil Service Commn., 1941-43, VA, 1945-48, Office Sec. Def., 1948- 50, CIA, 1950-59; tech. dir. Spl. Operations Research Office, Am. U., 1959-63, dean Sch. Govt. and Pub. Adminstrn., 1963—. Served with USMCR, 1943-45. Mem. Am. Polit. Sci. Assn., Am. Soc. Pub. Adminstrn., Phi Beta Kappa, Delta Sigma Rho, Phi Gamma Delta. Republican. Methodist. Home: 1602 N Greenbrier St Arlington VA 22205 Office: Am U Washington DC 20016

DELONG, VAUGHN RUSSELL, govt. ofcl.; b. Corning, O., Jan. 24, 1903; s. George W. and Addie Mary (Moore) DeL.; A.B., Ohio Wesleyan U., 1923; A.M., Ohio State U., 1929; student U. Pitts., N.Y. U.; children by former marriage—Merrill B., Jan; m. 2d, Ilse Margarete Schulte; children—Peter W., Gwynne Elizabeth. Tchr., Ashland, Ky., 1923-26, prin., 1927-29; prin., Ellwood City, Pa., 1929-32, supt. schs., 1932-38; supt. schs., Oil City, Pa., 1938-43; edn., cultural relations officer mil. govt., Hesse, Germany, 1945-48, chief, 1948-49; officer charge German cultural and social relations Dept. State, 1949-52, chief program devel. Internat. Ednl. Exchange Service, 1952-56, dir. cultural planning and coordination, 1956-58; consul gen., Edinburgh, Scotland, 1958-63; program officer Bur. of Internat. Edn., Dept. Health, Edn. and Welfare, 1963-65, dir. overseas assistance and tng. br., div. fgn. studies U.S. Office Edn., 1965-66, chief of overseas assistance and tng., 1966-67, sr. staff asst. Office Internat. Affairs, 1967-69, dep. dir., 1971—, dir. internat. orgns. and communications staff, 1969-70, acting spl. asst. to Sec. Internat. affairs, 1970-71. Mem. U.S. delegation Conf. Cultural Relations and Internat. Coop., UNESCO, 1955; adviser U.S. delegation cultural experts conf. NATO, 1956; alternate U.S. delegation Edinburgh (Scotland) Film Festival, 1963, chmn., 1964, 66; adviser U.S. delegation 44th session ECOSOC, 1968. Served from capt. to maj., AUS, 1943-46; Mil. Govt. for Germany. Decorated Croix de Guerre (Belgium); commendable service award Dept. State. Home: 6771 Brigadoon Dr Bethesda MD 20034 Office: Internat Affairs Dept Health Edn and Welfare Washington DC 20201

DELOREAN, JOHN ZACHARY, automobile co. exec.; b. Detroit, Jan. 6, 1925; s. Zachary R. and Katherine (Pribak) DeL.; B.S. in Mech. Engring., Lawrence Inst. Tech., 1948; M.A. in Indsl. Engring., Chrysler Inst., 1952; M.B.A., U. Mich., 1957; m. Kelly Harmon. Engr., Chrysler Corp., 1948-52, Packard Motor Co., 1952-56; dir. advanced engring. Pontiac Motor div. Gen. Motors Corp., 1956-59, asst. chief engr., 1959-61, chief engr., 1961-65, gen. mgr., 1965-69, v.p. corp., 1965—, gen. mgr. Chevrolet div., 1969—. Mem. bd. dirs. Mich. United Fund, Oakland U. Mem. Soc. Automotive Engrs., Am. Soc. Body Engrs., Engring. Soc. Detroit, Indsl. Math. Soc., Mich. Profl. Engrs., Detroit Inst. Arts. Clubs: Bloomfield Hills Country; Detroit Athletic (gov.); Augusta Nat. Golf. Home: Box 427 Bloomfield Hills MI 48013 Office: Chevrolet Div Gen Motors Corp Gen Motors Bldg Detroit MI 48202

DE LORENZO, ANTHONY GEORGE, pub. relations exec.; b. Edgerton, Wis., Aug. 26, 1914; s. Joseph and Anna (Pipitoni) DeL.; B.A., U. Wis., 1936; D.Sc. in Bus. Adminstrn., Cleary Coll., 1958; m. Josephine Paratore, Sept. 28, 1940; children—Annette M., Anthony J., Josephine M., Peter M. Editorial staff Racine Jour.-Times, 1933-35; staff United Press Assn., Madison, Wis., also Milw., Chgo., 1935-41, automotive editor, Mich. mgr., Detroit, 1941- 44; pub. relations staff various accounts Kudner Agy., Inc., advt., 1944- 49; staff dept. pub. relations Gen. Motors Corp., Detroit, 1949-56, v.p. charge pub. relations staff, 1957—. Mem. board U. Wisconsin Found., 1962. Recipient U. of Wis. Dist. Achievement in Journalism citation, 1958. Member of U. Wis. Alumni Assn. (nat. president 1965-66), Public Relations Soc. Am., Sigma Delta Chi. Roman Catholic. Clubs: National Press, 1925 F Street (Washington); Detroit, Detroit Athletic, Recess (Detroit); Flint City, Flint Golf; University (N.Y.C.). Home: Birmingham MI 48012 Office: 3044 W Grand Blvd Detroit MI 48202

DELORIA, VINE, Jr., author Custer Died for Your Sins; We Talk You Listen, 1970. Address: care Macmillan Co 866 3d Av New York City NY 10022*

DE LOS ANGELES, VICTORIA, concert and opera singer; b. Barcelona, Spain, Nov. 1, 1924; d. Bernardo and Victoria (Garcia) Lopez; student Conservatorio de Liceo, Barcelona; m. Enrique Magrina Mir, Nov. 20, 1948; two children—John Enrique, and Alejandro. Concert debut as soprano, 1944; Carnegie Hall debut, 1950; Met. Opera debut in Faust, 1951; has also sung opera in La Scala, Covent Garden Theatre, Staatsoper (Vienna), Grand Opera (Paris), Colon (Buenos Aires), Royal Opera (Stockholm) Brussells, (Copenhagen), Liceo (Barcelona), others; concerts in U.S., Can., Australia, S. and C.A., S. Africa, festivals in Europe. Recipient Conservatorio Liceo gold medal, Barcelona, 1943, 1st prize Internat. Contest, Geneva, Switzerland, 1947, Ofelia Nieto, Spain, 1946, 1st Critics prize, Buenos Aires, 1951, 53; decorated cross Lazo de Dama de la Orden de Isabel la Católica (Spain), 1957; Decoration with the Gold medal of Barcelona, 1958, Silver medal, 1959; cravate du commandeur Education Civique (France); Banda de la Orden Civil de Alfonso X; medal Premio Roma, 1969. Home: 57 Avenida de la Victoria Barcelona Spain Office: care Hurok Attractions 711 Fifth Av New York City NY 10022

DE LOS REYES, JOSEPH MANUEL, surgeon, assn. ofcl.; b. Cuba, Oct. 12, 1903; s. Joseph Manuel De Los Reyes and Ernestina De Leon De Los Reyes; B.S., Casado Acad. (Havana, Cuba), 1919, Lafayette Coll., Pa., 1924; M.D., Jefferson Med. Coll., 1928, Havana U., 1929; m. Pearl Westbrook, June 21, 1926; children—Peria Mercedes (Mrs. Gordon Stice), Kathleen (Mrs. George Smith), Mary Jo (Mrs. Frederick Weller). Came to U.S., 1922, naturalized, 1939. Surgeon, United Fruit Co., Cuba, Guatemala and Honduras, 1930-33; cons. surgeon Hollywood Presbyn., French, St. Francis, Sunset West, Glendale Meml., Norwalk State, Behrens Meml., Camarillo State hosps., City of Los Angeles Fire and Police depts.; sr. surgeon California Luth., Queen of Angeles, Santa Monica, Culver City hosps.; surgeon All Nations Clinic. Adv. bd. dirs. Imperial Bank Cal., Los Angeles. Pres. Cal. Bd. Med. Exam., 1958; med. adv. com. Los Angeles County; nat. coordinator Assn. Operating Room Nurses; mem. Gov.'s Com. Physically Handicapped; gen. lectr. Inst. World Affairs, Internat. Relations, U. So. Cal. Mem. speaker's bur., v.p. County Assembly, pres. 20th Congl. Dist. Republican Party. Bd. govs. Zool. Soc. Los Angeles; adv. council bd. trustees Jefferson Med. Coll. Recipient Americanism award, 1963. Fellow A.C.S., Internat. Coll. Surgeons (gen. chmn. 1958-62, regent; pres.-elect 1966; N. and Central Am. and Caribbean Fedn. sec.); mem. A.M.A. (chmn. sci. program 1952), Cal., Los Angeles (past v.p., past sr. councilor) med. assns., Assn. Mil. Surgeons, Cuban Med. Assn., Cuban Surg. Soc., Medical- Dental Vets. Los Angeles (v.p.), Am. Med. Authors Soc., Alumni Assn. Jefferson Med. Coll. (v.p.), Pan Am. Friendship Club, Kappa Delta Rho, Phi Rho Sigma, Theta Nu Epsilon. Mason. Clubs: Jesters, Los Angeles Trojan. Surg. editor Western Ann. Medicine and Surgery; guest editor Am. Legion News. Home: 401 Meadow Grove Circle Pasadena CA 91103 Office: 2010 Wilshire Blvd Los Angeles CA 90057

DELOUGAZ, PINHAS PIERRE, educator, archaeologist; b. Russia, July 16, 1901; s. Simon and Zipporah (Silverman) D.; student U. Paris (France) 1922-26, U. Chgo., 1939-42; m. Nathalie Poliakoff, 1943 (div. 1969). Came to U.S., 1938, naturalized, 1944. Archtl. asst. Harvard-Baghdad Sch. Expdn., Nuzi, Iraq, 1928-29; field asst. Oriental Inst. Iraq Expdn., 1929-31, dir. excavations at Khafaje, Iraq, 1931-37, field dir. Iraq Expdns., 1948-61, dir. Israel Expdn., 1952—, dir. Iraq Expdn., 1961—, curator inst. museum, 1944—, dir. archaeol. reconaissance expdn., 1961-62; field dir. Univ. Mus. of U. Pa.-Am. Sch. Oriental Research joint expdn., Khafaje, 1937-38; mem. faculty U. Chgo., 1949-67, prof. archaeology, 1960-67, chmn. com. archaeol. studies, 1950-67; prof. Near Eastern archaeology U. Cal. at Los Angeles, 1967—, dir. Mus. Cultural History, 1970—. dir. joint Iranian expdn., 1968—, U. Cal. at Los Angeles, 1967. Mem. Am. Oriental Soc. (past mem. exec. com.), Archaeol. Inst. Am., Am. Assn. Museums, Internat. Inst. Conservation, Am. Assn. U. Profs. Author: The Temple Oval at Khafajah, 1940; Pottery from the Diyala Region, 1952; Piano-Convex Bricks and the Methods of Their Employment and The Treatment of Clay Tablets in the Field, 1933; (with S. Lloyd) Pre-Sargonid Temples in the Diyala Region, 1942; (with R. C. Haines) A Byzantine Church at Khirbat al-Karak, 1960; (with Hill and Lloyd) Private Houses and Graves in the Diyala Region, 1967; also articles. Home: 10990 Massachusetts Av Los Angeles CA 90024

DELP, GEORGE C., mfg. exec.; b. Lancaster, Pa., Aug. 27, 1908; s. John S. and Martha (Zimmerman) D.; student Lancaster Bus. Coll., 1924-27; m. Grace M. Butz, Apr. 12, 1928; children—Gervasse, Georgia, Germaine, Gemma, Glenna, Greta. Asst. to gen. mgr., Mountville (Pa.) Mfg. Co., 1928-33; asst. to mgr. farm machinery div. Dellinger Mfg. Co., Lancaster, 1933-40; gen. mgr., sec. and treas., New Holland (Pa.), 1940-47, pres. of New Holland, 1940-47, pres. of New Holland div. Sperry Rand Corp., 1947-68, pres. of corp., 1968—; pres. Stated Equipment Co., Inc., Lancaster, Pa., 1944—; pres. Lancaster-Lincoln-Mercury Co., 1962—, Equipment Finance, Inc., Lancaster, 1962—. Bd. dirs. of St. Joseph's Hosp., Lancaster; chmn. Lancaster Airport Authority. Clubs: Canadian (N.Y. C.); Hamilton, Lancaster (Pa.) Country; Skytop (Pa.); Pine Valley Golf (N.J.); Chicago; Saucon Valley (Pa.); Indian Creek (Fla.). Home: 1905 Millersville Pike Lancaster PA 17303 Office: New Holland Div Sperry Rand Corp New Holland PA 17557

DELP, MAHLON HENRY, physician; b. Lenora, Kan., Nov. 26, 1903; s. Henry Alexander and Alice Belle (Breeden) D.; B.S., M.D., U. Kan., 1934; m. Florence Elizabeth Aldrich, Nov. 15, 1924; 1 dau., Virginia Elizabeth. Intern U. Kan. Med. Center, 1934-35, resident internal medicine, 1935-38, asso., 1938-42, asst. prof., 1942-48, asso. prof., 1948-51, prof., 1951-60, chmn. dept. postgrad. med. edn., asst. dean, 1952-60, Bohan prof. medicine, 1960—, chmn. dept. internal medicine, 1960-69; pvt. practice internal medicine, Kansas City, Kan., 1938—. Served from maj. to col. M.C., U. S. Army, 1942- 46. Diplomate Am. Bd. Internal Medicine. Fellow A.C.P.; mem. A.M.A., Kansas City Acad. Medicine, Am. Clin. Climatol. Soc., Delta Upsilon, Phi Chi, Alpha Omega Alpha. Republican. Episcopalian. Club: Milburn Country. Co-author: Physical Diagnosis (textbook). Contbr. med. jours. Home: 6131 Terrydale Rd Merriam KS 66203 Office: University of Kansas Medical Center Kansas City KS 63103

DEL REGATO, JUAN ANGEL, physician, radio-therapeutist and oncologist; b. Camaguey, Cuba, Mar. 1, 1909; s. Juan and Damiana (Manzano) del Rl; student U. Havana, 1930; M.D. U. Paris (France), 1937, Laureat, 1937; Dr.S., Colo. Coll., 1969; m. Inez Johnson, May 1, 1939; children—Ann Cynthia (Jaeger), Juanita Inez (Peters), John Carl. Came to U.S., 1937, naturalized, 1941. Asst., Radium Inst., U. Paris, 1934-37, Chgo. Tumor Inst., 1938; radiotherapeutist Warwick Cancer Clinic, Washington, 1939- 40; research Nat. Cancer Inst., Balt., 1941-43; chief dept. radiotherapy Ellis Fischel State Cancer Hosp., Columbia, Mo., 1943-48; dir. Penrose Cancer Hosp., Colorado Springs, Colo., 1949—; prof. clin. radiology U. Colo. Med. Sch., 1950—. Mem. Nat. Adv. Cancer Council, Bethesda, Md., 1967—; cons. Fitzsimmons Army Hosp., Denver, VA Hosp. Denver; mem. med. adv. com. Milheim Found., Denver. Mem. adv. com. atomic energy U. P.R. Decorated Order of Carlos Finlay of Cuba; recipient Gold medal Radiol. Soc. North Am., 1967, Gold medal Inter-Am. Coll. Radiology, 1967, Gold medal Am. Coll. Radiology, 1968. Fellow A.M.A., Am. Coll. Radiology (bd. chancellors); mem. Nat. Acad. Medicine of France (Laureat 1948), Radiol. Soc. North Am. (v.p. 1959-60), Am. Roentgen Ray Soc., Am. Radium Soc. (v.p. 1963-64, treas. 1966-68, pres. 1968-69, chmn. exec. com. 1971—), Assn. Am. Med. Colls., Internat. Club Radiotherapists (pres. 1962-65), Inter-Am. Coll. Radiology (pres. 1967- 71), Am. Soc. Therapeutic Radiologists (sec. 1958-68, historian 1968—); hon. mem. Rocky

Mountain, Pacific N.W., Tex., Ore., Minn. radiol. socs., radiol. socs. Cuba, Mexico, Panama, Ecuador, Peru, Paraguay, Can., Argentina, Buenos Aires (Argentina). Club: Cheyenne Mountain Country (Colorado Springs). Author: (with L.V. Ackerman, M.D.) Cancer; Diagnostic Treatment and Prognosis, 1947, 54, 62, 70. Editor: Cancer Seminar, 1960—. Contbr. articles profl. jours. Home: 2 E Columbia St Colorado Springs CO 80907 Office: Penrose Cancer Hosp 2215 N Cascade Av Colorado Springs CO 80907

DELSOL, ROBERT CHARLES, corp. exec.; b. Montreuil-s/Bois, France, Apr. 14, 1908; s. Raoul and Jeanne (Daniel) R.; student Universite de Paris, 1926-28; M.S., Conservatoire Nat. des Arts et Metiers, 1931; m. Denise Massard, Feb. 6, 1935; children—Bernard, Edmee. Engr., Usines a Gaz de Gennevilliers until 1946; chief engr. Gaz de France, 1946-55, dir. research, new techniques, 1955-64, insp. gen., 1964—; hon. pres. Groupe Europeen des Recherches Gazières; adminstr. Methane Transport, Gas Marine, Chaleur et Industrie, Société Francaise et de Realisations d'Equipments Gaziers; membre comité directeur Assn. pour le Dévelopement de l'Enseignement et des Recherches for Faculté des Scis. Paris, Assn. Francaise des Techniciens du Petrole, Revue Générale de Thermique. Pres. Assn. Technique de l'Industrie du Gaz en France, 1961-62; v.p. Union Internationale de l'Industries du Gaz, 1963-67; v.p. Assn. Nationale de la Recherche Technique, 1960-63; mem. sci. Action Com. for Nat. Defense, 1962—; pres. Centre de Perfectionnement tecqnique, 1964—; pres. sect. energie solaire de la Sté Fse. des Thermiciens, 1966—, Assn. Francaise pour l'Etude et le Developpement de l'Energie Solaire, 1966—. Decorated chevalier Legion of Honor, officer Academic Palms, officer Research and Investigation, officer Comml. and Indsl. Merit, chevalier Maritime Merit. Clubs: Rotary (past pres. Nord de Paris); Circle Interallie; Golf du Coudray. Home: 5 rue Philibert Delorme Paris 17 France Office: 23 rue Philibert Delorme Paris France

DELSON, ELIZABETH, artist; b. N.Y.C., Aug. 15, 1932; d. Julius and Emmy (Haas) Pfannmuller; B.A., Smith Coll., 1954; m. Sidney L. Delson, Sept. 10, 1955; children—Karen Lee, Sara Jeanne, Matthew Robert. Shows include: USIA Travelling Exhibit, 1962-64, Bklyn. Museum Nat. Print Exhbn., 1966, L.I.U., 1969, others; instr. graphic. arts Pratt Inst. 1962-66; one man exhbn. Hicks St. Gallery, 1964, L.I.U., 1969, Paerdegat Library, 1971, others; represented in collections N.Y. Pub. Library, L.I.U., U. So. Ill., Boston Pub. Library, Bklyn. Mus. Recipient medal of honor for graphics Audubon Artists, 1961. Mem. Soc. Am. Graphic Artists, League Present Day Artists, Audubon Artists, Artists Equity Assn. Address: 625 3d St Brooklyn NY 11215

DELSON, GEORGE VICTOR, investment banker; b. N.Y.C., May 18, 1922; s. Israel S. and Celia (Weinstein) D.; B.B.A., Coll. City N.Y., 1947; m. Gertrude Schwartz, Apr. 19, 1947; children-Janis, Lawrence. Partner, Jerome G. Futerman & Co., C.P.A.'s, N.Y.C., 1948-55; pvt. practice tax s N.Y.C., 1958—; exec. v.p., tax counsel, dir. Cantor, Fitzgerald & Co., 1955-56; partner Hanigsberg, Delson, & Broser, C.P.A.'s, N.Y.C., 1958—; exec. v.p., tax counsel, dir. Cant Inc., Investment bankers, N.Y.C. and Beverly Hills, Cal., 1970—; faculty Tax Workshop Sch., N.Y.C., 1955-58; admittefi1952; dir. Seaboard Life Ins. Co. Am., 1960-65, Rapid-Am. Corp., 1963—. Seminar leader N.Y. State Soc. C.P.A.'s Tax Seminars; panelist Hofstra U. Conf. on Acquisitions and Mergers. Served with arty., AUS, 1943-46. C.P.A., N.Y., Cal. Mem. Am. Inst. C.P.A.'s, N.Y. State, Cal. socs. C. P.A.'s, Fed. Tax Forum (dir.), Am. Retail Fedn. Contbr. articles profl. jours. Home: 135 E 83d St New York NY 10028 Office: 1345 Av of Americas New York NY 10019 also 711 Fifth Av New York NY 10022

DELSON, MAX, lawyer; b. N.Y.C., May 26, 1903; s. Louis and Ethel (Naumoff) D.; A.B., Columbia, 1924, LL.B., 1926; LL.D. (hon.), Chungang U., Seoul, Korea; m. Dorothy Haupt, Dec. 23, 1932; children—Arthur K., Mary Ellen, Amy Louise. Admitted to N.Y. bar, 1926, Fed. bar, 1931; sr. partner firm Delson & Gordon, N.Y.C., 1927; counsel in U.S. for several fgn. govts. Pres., Great Eastern Small bus. Investment Corp.; chmn. bd. Leisure & Learning, Inc. Bd. dirs. N.A.A.C.P.; hon. trustee Chungang U.; coop. edn. adv. com. Manhattan Community Coll. Mem. Am., N.Y. bar assns., Bar Assn. City N.Y., Internat. Law Assn., Am. Acad. Polit. and Social Sci., Delta Sigma Rho. Home: 77 Park Av New York City NY 10016 Office: 230 Park Av New York City NY 10017

DELSON, ROBERT, lawyer; b. N.Y.C., July 18, 1905; s. Louis and Ethel (Naumoff) D.; A.B., Cornell, 1926; LL.B., Columbia, 1928; m. Marjorie Feldman, Dec. 25, 1941; children—Eric Robert, James Lewis. Admitted to N.Y. State bar, 1929, since practiced in N.Y.C.; asso. with Wise & Seligsberg, attys., 1929-31; asso. gen. counsel, Consol. Film Industries, Inc. and Republic Pictures Corp., 1931-37; asso. firm Delson & Gordon, 1937-45, mem. firm 1945—; specialist in internat. pub. and pvt. law and internat. econ. devel. 1939—. Counsel in U.S. several fgn. govts.; gen. counsel Internat. League Rights of Man, Am. Com. on Africa. Bd. dirs. Am. Friends Wilton Park. Mem. Internat. Law Assn., Am. Soc. Internat. Law, Am. Civil Liberties Union, Am., Internat. bar assns., Am. Arbitration Assn., Fgn. Policy Assn., N.Y. State Bar Assn., Columbia, Cornell alumni assns., N.Y. County Lawyers Assn., Consular Law Soc., Am. Law Inst., U.S. Com. Inter-Am. Assn. Democracy and Freedom, Am. Fgn. Law Assn., Phi Beta Kappa, Phi Beta Kappa Assos. Author articles profl. jours. Home: 11 E 86th St New York City NY 10028 Office: 230 Park Av New York City NY 10017 also: 1900 L St NW Washington DC 20036

DE LUCA, JOHN ROBERT, corp. exec.; b. N.Y.C., Jan. 18, 1922; s. Louis Otto and Rose (Galdi) DeL.; B.B.A., Manhattan Coll., 1948; M.S., Columbia, 1949; m. Rosemarie Anne LaSala, May 1, 1954; children—Elaine, Nora-Jean, Mark, Brian, John Francis. Div. budget mgr. RCA, Harrison, N.J., 1949-54; mgr. budgets Standard Brands, Inc., N.Y.C., 1954-58; div. controller Sperry Rand Corp., N.Y.C., 1958-61; controller Interchem. Corp., N.Y.C., 1961-67; v.p. finance Shulton, Inc., 1967—. Vice pres. Mayfair Knollwood Civic Assn., 1954-55; mem. Budget Com. Town Greenberg, N.Y., 1954-55. Served to 2d lt. USAAF, 1942-45. Recipient Spl. Service award Am. Mgmt. Assn., 1965. Mem. Financial Execs. Inst., Nat. Assn. Accountants, Am. Mgmt. Assn. (chmn. finance seminars). Home: 680 Cheyenne Dr Franklin Lakes NJ 07417 Office: Shulton Inc Clifton NJ 07015

DELUCA, JOSEPH RUDOLPH, air force officer; b. Greenville, Pa., Sept. 3, 1918; s. Pasquale and Concetta (Catullo) DeL.; grad. Profl. Sch. Accounting, Cleve., 1938, Air War Coll., 1957; B.A., U. Md., 1961; M.A., George Washington U., 1963; m. Doris Colleen Hays, Jan. 22, 1944; children—Pat Bryan, Joel Ronald, Kathy Doreen, Barbara Colleen, Teresa Marie, Michael Joseph, Tina Diane, Marisa Joan. Commd. 2d lt. USAAF, 1942, advanced through grades to maj. gen. USAF, 1967; served in Europe, Pacific and Conus; dir. budget Headquarters U.S. Air Force, Pentagon, Washington, 1971—. Decorated D.S.M., Legion of Merit, Joint Staff Commendation medal; recipient Eugene M. Zukert Mgmt. award sec. air force, 1968. Mem. Air Force Assn. Home: 25 Westover Av Bolling AFB Washington DC 20335 Office: Hdqrs USAF Pentagon Washington DC

DELUCA, PETER J., lawyer; b. N.Y.C., Oct. 15, 1927; s. Thomas A. and Madeline (Insard) DeL.; LL.B. cum laude, N.Y. Law Sch., 1953; m. Marie Joan Macchia, Sept. 18, 1954; 1 son, David Laurence. Admitted to N.Y. bar; practice in N.Y.C.; mem. firm Cravath, Swaine & Moore, 1953-59; with Pepsi Co., Inc., N.Y.C., 1959—, v.p., 1963-65, v.p., gen. counsel, sec., 1965—; dir. Wilson Sporting Goods Co., Pepsi-Cola, Ltd. of Bermuda, Pepsi- Cola Italia, Wilson Sporting Goods Co. Served with U.S. Mcht. Marine, 1945-47. Mem. N.Y. State Lawyers Assn., N.Y. State, Westchester County bar assns., Delta Theta Phi, Sigma Pi Phi. Democrat. Clubs: Internat., N.Y. Athletic. Home: 360 E 72d St New York City NY 10027 Office: 500 Park Av New York City NY 10022

DELUCCIA, EMIL ROBERT, engr.; b. Brighton, Mass., Sept. 20, 1904; s. Emil James and Edna Laura (Hewes) de L.; B.S. in Civil Engring., Mass. Inst. Tech., 1927; m. Margaret McCutcheon, Jan. 16, 1932; children—Margaret Crichton, Jane Hewes. Surveyman and transitman Met. Water Supply Commn., Enfield, Mass., 1927-29; engr. designer Stone and Webster Engring. Corp., 1929- 31; engr. inspector and designer U.S. Engr. Office, Charleston, W. Va., 1931-33; asso. engr. and chief of design sect., U.S. Engr. Office, Huntington, W.Va., 1933-38; Fed. Power Commn., 1938-51; v.p., chief engr. Pacific Power & Light Co., 1952-66, senior vice president, 1966-69; pres. Ore. Grad. Center and Cons. Engr., 1969—; sr. engineer cons. on dams and Hydroelectric projects, 1938-40, chief, power supply branch, Nat. Defense Power staff, 1940-41; asst. dir. Nat. Defense Power staff and asst. chief Bur. of Elec. Engring. (also consultant on power to O.P.M. and W.P.B.), chief Bur. of Power since 1944. Joined Pacific Power & Light Co. as gen. engring. cons. and mgr. Yale hydroelectric project and others, 1951. U.S. del. Internat. Conf. on High Dams, Stockholm, 1948, Internat. Conf. on High Tension Elec. Systems, Paris, 1948; chief U.S. delegation Internat. Conf. High Tension Lines, Paris, 1950; U.S. del. World Power Conf., London, Eng., 1950; U.S. ofcl. Negotiation Treaty with Canada for division of water at Niagara Falls; cons. to UN, Japan, 1961, AEC, Nat. Security Resources Bd.; chmn. Internat. Passamaquoddy Bd. Engrs.; chairman of U.S. Com. on Large Dams. Served with R.O.T.C., Mass. Inst. Tech., 2d lt., O.R.C., 1927; commd. capt. and advanced through grades to lt. col., AUS 1942-45; with SHEAF, European Theater, Jan.-Nov. 1944; ret. as lt. col., O.R.C., 1956. Mem. Tech. Indsl. Disarmament Com. for German and Japan Elec. Power Industry. Decorated Europe-Africa-Middle East ribbon with one star, Legion of Merit, Am. Campaign Ribbon, Victory Medal, World War II; named Oregon Engineer of Year, 1962. Registered profl. engr., D.C., Ore.; Fellow I.E.E.E., Am. Soc. C.E.; mem. Soc. of Am. Mil. Engineers (dir.; recipient of the Goethals Medal award 1963), A.I.M., Vets. of Fgn. Wars, Am. Geophys. Union, Am. Legion, Internat. Assn. High Tension Lines, International Assn. Hydraulic Research, Internat. Assn. Large Dams Mason (Shriner). Clubs: Army-Navy Country (Arlington, Va.); Cosmos (Washington); Arlington, University, Waverly Country (Portland). Home: 1225 S Skyland Dr Lake Oswego OR 97034 Office: Ore Grad Center Beaverton OR

DELUCE, DANIEL, fgn. corr.; b. Yuma, Ariz., June 8, 1911; s. Robert and Myrtle (Hickey) De L.; B.A., U. Cal. at Los Angeles, 1934; m. Alma Chalupnik, Oct. 21, 1936. With A.P. since 1929, with exception of one year as reporter Los Angeles Examiner (1934-35), assigned to Balkan bur., May 1939, covered war in Poland, Albanian front during Axis-Greek war, Anglo-Soviet occupation Iran, Anglo-Chinese defeat in Burma, 1942, Allied victory campaign in Tunisia, entered Italy with British Eighth Army, D-Day, 1943, obtained first interviews with Tito's partisan forces on Yugoslav soil during that month, entered Rome with U.S. Fifth Army, June 4, 1944, entered Warsaw after its liberation with first press party from Moscow; covered Palestine war, 1948; bur. chief in Germany, 1950-56, gen. exec., 1956-65, asst. gen. mgr., 1965—. Mason. Awarded Pulitzer prize, 1944, for distinguished telegraphic reporting of internat. affairs; Nat. Headliners' award for fgn. reporting, 1948. Contbr. Free Men are Fighting (O. S. Gramling, 1942). Address: care Associated Press 50 Rockefeller Plaza New York City NY 10020

DE LUE, DONALD HARCOURT, sculptor; b. Boston, Oct. 5, 1897; m. Martha Naomi Cross, Oct. 5, 1933. Prin. works: four large granite panels representing Law and Justice and 2 large marble panels of Am. Eagle for Fed. Ct. House, Phila.; large marble fountain, male figure of Triton for gardens of Fed. Res. Bank, Phila.; figure of Alchemist for U. of Pa. Chemistry Bldg.; completed six large granite panels for Harvey S. Firestone Meml., Akron, O.; two panels, Josiah Willard Gibbs and Benjamin Franklin, New Sci. Engring. Bldg., Carnegie Inst. of Tech.; figure in bronze Spirit of Am. Youth, 2 allegorical figures U.S. and France in limestone, 2 bronze meml. urns. U.S. Mil. Cemetery Meml. at Omaha Beach, St. Laurent, Normandy, France; Edward Hull Crump Meml., portrait statue bronze; granite seat with meml. figures Inspiration and Achievement, Memphis; Am. Eagle in marble for Fed. Res. Bank, Boston; Figure of Creation, nickel bronze relief for Jr. High Sch., N.Y.C.; Stas. of the Cross (14), marble for Loyola Sem., Shrub Oak, N.Y.; granite panel Athletic for Phys. Culture Bldg., U.S. Naval Acad.; symbolic figure Life and Healing, marble panel for Abraham Jacobi Hosp., N.Y.; 2 figures in granite U.S. and France for St. Laurent, Normandy, France, U.S. Mil. Cemetery; sculptor Boy Scout Meml., Washington; theme figure The Rocket Thrower, 45 ft. high, N.Y. World's Fair, 1964; 2 Angels- bronze, 12 ft. bronze door Woodmont Shrine; George Washington at Prayer statue at Valley Forge; Green Beret bronze 12 ft. high at Fort Bragg, N.C., George Washington portrait statue; 14 stations of the cross for Sisters of St. Joseph, Toronto, Can., Confederate Soldier, Gettysburg, Pa.; 2 figure group bronze, Miss. State Meml. at Gettysburg, Pa., numerous others; also several urns, portrait statues, medals, panels, murals, etc. Chmn. Com. on art Hall of Fame for Great Ams. N.Y.U. Recipient Avery Prize, Archtl. League, 1942, Gold medal, 1951; Lindley Morris prize, Nat. Sculpture Soc., 1942, N. A., 1943 Guggenheim fellow, 1943-44; Henry Hering Meml. Gold medal, twice 1960; gold medal Nat. Sculpture Soc.; Herbert Adams gold medal Nat. Sculpture Soc.; Samuel B. Morse gold medal N.A.D. Fellow Am. Numismatic Soc. (J. Sanford Saltus medal), Nat. Sculpture Soc. (pres. 1945-46-47); mem. Inst. Arts and Letters, Am. Artists Profl. League (bd.), Allied Artists Am., N.A.D., Royal Soc. of Arts, Am. Inst. Commemorative Art (hon.). Adv. editor Am. Artist Mag. Address: 82 Highland Av Leonardo NJ 07737

DELUGACH, ALBERT LAWRENCE, newspaper reporter; b. Memphis, Oct. 27, 1925; s. Gilbert and Edna (Short) D; B. Journalism. U. Mo., 1951; m. Bernice Goldsein, June 11, 1950; children—Joy, David, Daniel Sharon. Reporter, Kansas City (Mo.) Star, 1951-60. St. Louis Globe Democrat, 1960-69, St. Louis Post Dispatch, 1969-70; investigative reporter Los Angeles Times, 1970—. Served with USNR, 1943-46. Recipient Pulitzer prize for spl. local reporting, 1969. Mem. Sigma Delta Chi. Home: 17144 Nanette Granada Hills CA 91344 Office: Los Angeles Times Los Angeles Times Square Los Angeles CA

DELUIGI, JANICE WEIL LEFTON, painter, sculptor; b. Indpls., Nov. 27, 1915; d. Nathan Charles and Rosalind (Whitman) Weil; student Art Inst. Chgo., 1952, 62-64, U. Chgo., 1959; certificate Accademia di Brera, Milan, Italy, 1965; also pvt. studies in Japan, Italy, Austria; diploma Instituto Nazionale Per L'Istruzione E L'Addestramento Nel Settore Artigiano, Venice, Italy, 1970; m. Ludovico DeLuigi, June 24, 1965; children (by previous marriage)—Larry, Margo. One man shows Ruth Dickens Gallery, Chgo., 1951, Sherman Hotel, Chgo., 1953, Wurlitzer Bldg., Chgo., 1955, Riccardo's Gallery, Chgo., 1959, Mdse. Mart, Chgo., 1960, Morrison Hotel, Chgo., 1961, Monroe Gallery, Chgo., 1961, Lake Meadows Gallery, Chgo., 1961-62, McCormack Pl. Gallery, Chgo., 1962, Chgo. Pub. Library, 1962, Juster Gallery, N.Y.C., 1961, Galerie Ror Volmar, Paris, France, 1964, Galleria d'Arte Il Camino, Rome, Italy, 1964, Galleria Santa Croce, Florence, Italy, 1964, Fondazione Cini, Venice, Italy, 1964, USIS, Milan, 1964; exhbt. group shows including Art Inst. Chgo., Ill. State Fair, U. Ill., U. Chgo., Northwestern U., Roosevelt U., Evanston (Ill.) Art Center, Artists League Midwest; exhibited sculpture work murano glass Biennale Venice, Italy International Art EXhibition; rep. numerous pvt. collections, U.S. and Italy; tchr. painting, sculpture, history art George Williams Coll., Chgo., 1962, Contemporary Art Workshop, Chgo., 1962-64; tchr. painting, sculpture history art Fondazione Cini, Venice, 1964-66, prof. art, 1966—. Commn. from Italian Government for the John F. Kennedy Meml. Monument in Italy, Milan, 1967. Recipient 1st prize Internat. Painting and Sculpture, Fruili-Venezia Giulia, 1971; others. Mem. Arts Club Chgo., Renaissance Soc. of U. Chgo., Artists Equity Assn., Alumni Assn. Sch. Art Inst. Chgo. Address: Piscina San Moise 2053 San Marco 30124 Venice Italy

DE LUIGI, VICO, artist; b. Venice, Italy; s. Mario De Luigi; ed. Accademia Belle Arti 981; extensive studies art movements and techniques, U.S. and Europe; m. Janice Lefton. Painter, U.S., Europe; dir. Am. Sch. Venice, Cini Found., 1966—; exhibited Drake Hotel Art Gallery, Chgo., 1967; represented in permanent collections Galleria d'Arte il Traghetto, Venice, Galleria d'Arte il Canale, Accademia-Galleria il Cavallino, San Marco, Italy, Galleria S. Croce, Florence, Italy, Galleria il Cannocchiale, Galleria Naviglio, Milan, Italy, Galleria Venezia Ravagnan, Piazza San Marco, Venice; one man shows Sci. Fiction Internat. Festival, Trieste, 1969, Milano-Sagittarius Art Gallery, 1970, Casa Italiana, Columbia U., 1971; represented in numerous pvt. collections U.S., Italy. Important works include: (with Marlo De Luigi) Leonardo Da Vinci's Panels of main entertaining room; (with Janice Lefton) Kennedy Monument, Kennedy Farm Found., Milan. Address: Piscina San Moise 2053 S Marco Venice 30124 Italy

DELUISE, DOM, actor; b. Bklyn., Aug. 1, 1933; s. John and Virgette (DeStefano) De L.; student Tufts Coll.; m. Carol Arata, Nov. 23, 1965; children—Peter John, Michael Robert. Actor off-Broadway plays All in Love, Another Evening with Harry Stoones, Mad Wednesday; actor Broadway plays Here's Love, Gypsy, The Last of the Red Hot Lovers; regular TV series The Entertainers, The Dom De Luise Show, appeared TV shows The Dean Martin Show, Carol Burnett Show, Glen Campbell Show, Merv Griffin Show, Tonight Show, Dick Cavett Show, Mike Douglas Show; actor movies including Fail Safe, The Glass-Bottom Boat, Norwood, Who is Harry Kellerman?, The Twelve Chairs, Ever Little Crook and Nanny. Home: 1186 Corsica Dr Pacific Palisades CA 90272 Office: care William Morris Agy Inc 151 El Camino Beverly Hills CA 90212

DEL VALLE, JUAN, paper co. exec.; b. Colon, Panama, Mar. 4, 1933; s. William Andrew and Vina (Saunders) del V.; B.S., Yale, 1953; M.B.A., Harvard, 1958; m. Wendy Hobart, Sept. 4, 1954; children—Cristina Cross, Tracy Saunders. With Weyerhaeuser Co., 1958-62; with Boise Cascade Corp., 1962—, v.p., 1967- 71, sr. v.p., 1971—; v.p., dir. Miramachi Timber Recources Ltd., Newcastle, N.B.; pres. Ont.-Minn. Pulp and Paper Co. Ltd. Trustee Pacific U., Forest Grove, Ore. Served with USNR, 1953-56. Home: 4317 SW Bernard Dr Portland OR 97201 Office: 1600 SW 4th St Portland OR 97201

DELVAUX, PAUL, artist; b. Antheit, Belgium, Sept. 23, 1897; s. Jean and Laure (Jamotte) D.; ed. Anthenaeum of St. Gilles, Brussels; m. Anne-Marie De Martelaere, Oct. 25, 1952. Prof. Painting Ecole Nat. Superieure d'Architecture et Arts Decorarifs a La Cambre, Brussels, 1950-62; prin. exhbns. include Belgium, London, Holland, Mexico, N.Y.C., Buenos-Aires, Venice, Helsinki, Congo, Sao Paulo, Saarbrucken, Basel, S. Africa, Germany, Paris, Can., U.S.; personal summation of works: to create for another human being an emotion through the art of painting. Recipient prize Acad. Picard, Belgium, 1938, Reggi prize, Emilia, Italy, 1955, Fait medal Brussels World's Fair, 1958, Painters prize Province Liege, 1960, Career Dedication prize, 1965; decorated knight Order Leopold; officer Order de la Couronne, 1962, grand officer, 1962. Mem. Royal Acad. Fine Arts Belgium. Address: 34A Av des Companules 1170 Brussels Belgium also Noordduinen St Idesbald Belgium

DELZA, ELIZABETH MUNSON, dancer, choreographer, educator; b. Russia; d. Solomon and Eva (Katcher) Hurwitz; dance tng. Neighborhood Playhouse, N.Y.C., 1917-24, Dalcroze Sch., Paris and N.Y.C., 1922-23; Gurdjieff Inst., Fontainbleau, France, 1925-48; pupil of Jessmin Howarth, Margot Duncan, Anna Duncan, Mary Porter Beegle, Alma Frank, Azuma; music pupil of Sandra Levitski, Carol Robinson, Gertrude Wollner, Yella Pessl, Ralph Lawton, Thomas de Hartmann; auditor Wanda Landowska seminar, 1944; scholarship Seymour Sch. Mus. Re-edn., N.Y.C., 1924; m. Gorham B. Munson, Apr. 2, 1921. Festival dancer Neighborhood Playhouse, 1922-28, 34; debut as soloist own concert group Guild Theatre, N.Y.C., 1933; dir. dance Walden Sch., N.Y.C., 1925-35, Elizabeth Delza Sch. Dance, 1936—; dir., dancer Assn. Music and Art, Cape Cod, Mass., 1940; choreographer, tchr. movement drama dept. U. Cal. at Davis, 1967; concerts various cities and colls., 1933—; concerts include modern dance forms, ancient sacred dances, dances with modern poetry, dances with contrapuntal music, dance dramas. Recipient citation drama dept. U. Cal. at Davis, 1967. Mem. Am. Dance Guild, Poetry Soc. Am. Contbr. magazines. Home: Hotel Wellington 7th Av at 55th St New York City NY 10019 Office: care Carnegie Hall New York City NY 10019

DELZELL, CHARLES FLOYD, educator; b. Klamath Falls, Ore., Mar. 6, 1920; s. William Abner and Edith May (White) D.; B.S., U. Ore., 1941; M.A., Stanford, 1943, Ph.D., 1951; postgrad., Instituto Italiano per gli Studi Storici, Naples, Italy, 1948-49; m. Eugenia May Robertson, Mar. 21, 1948; children—William Robertson, Charles Neal, Pauline Ethel. Curator, Mediterranean Area collections Hoover Instn., Stanford, 1946-49; asst. prof. history U. Hawaii, 1949-50; instr. history U. Ore., 1950-51; asst. prof. history Vanderbilt U., 1952-55, asso. prof., 1955-61, prof., 1961—, chmn. dept., 1970—, Harvie Branscomb distinguished prof. history, 1970-71. Mem. Pres. Hoover's Spl. Food Mission to Europe, 1946; vis. prof. history U. Ore., summer 1963, Stanford, summer 1966. Served with AUS, 1943-45. Fulbright research scholar, Italy, 1964-65. Mem. Am. (George Louis Beer prize), So. (exec. council 1969-71, chmn. European history sect. 1963-64) hist. assns., Am. Assn. U. Profs., Soc. for Italian Hist. Studies (pres. 1968-69), Phi Beta Kappa, Phi Alpha Theta, Sigma Nu. Methodist. Mason. Club: University (Nashville). Author: Mussolini's Enemies: The Italian Anti-Fascist Resistance, (Borden award Hoover Instn. and Library, Stanford), 1961; Mediterranean Fascism, 1919-1945, 1970; Italy in Modern Times, 1963, The Unification of Italy, 1859-1861, 1965; (with John L. Snell) The Meaning of Yalta, 1956; (with Hans A. Schmitt) Historians of Modern Europe, 1971; also articles. Home: 2303 Bernard Av Nashville TN 37212

DELZELL, MARK WILSON, educator; b. Lincoln, Neb., Oot. 21, 1904; s. William Newton and Dora (Wilson) D.; A.B., Peru (Neb.) State Tchrs. Coll., 1925; A.M., Columbia Tchrs. Coll., 1928; Ph.D., Neb. U., 1946; m. Nettie Mae Dennis, June 13, 1930; children—Dora Lee, Donald Dennis, Allen Wilson. Prin., sci. tchr. Clay Center (Neb.) High Sch., 1925-27, supt. pub. schs., 1928-36; instr. U. Neb., 1936-42; prof. edn. U. S.D., 1946-51, dean Sch. of Edn., dir. summer session, 1951-69, prof. edn., since 1969—. Served as capt. USAAF, 1942-46. Mem. N.E.A., S.D. Edn. Assn. (pres. 1967), Phi Delta Kappa. Rotarian. Home: 526 N Dakota St Vermillion SD 57069

DE MACAYA, MARGARITA ORTIZ, diplomat; b. San Jose, Costa Rica, Jan. 16, 1916; d. Ernesto Ortiz Emilia (Alvarado) de Macaya; grad. Colegiodu Buestra Senora de Sion; married; children—Ernesto, Carlos. Del. of Costa Rica to Inter-Am. Commn. Women, 1950-; del. and/or head numerous internat. confs. Pres. Garden Club Costa Rica, 1946-58; mem. adminstrv. bd. dirs. Nat. Museum, 1950-58; mem. com. cultural assistance Ministry Pub. Edn. Costa Rica, 1951-58; pres. Nat. Assn. Sch. Trustees, 1952-58; founder-mem., mem. exec. bd. Girls Lyceum, Anastasio Alfara, 1952-58; mem. Bd. Protection Aboriginal Race, 1952-58; founder, pres. Nat. Bd. Social Welfare, 1954-58; mem. Sociol. and Archeol. Study Mission to Central Am., 1956; mem. Boston League Voters, 1960-63; mem. Latin Am. Assn., Harvard, 1960-63; counsel gen. Costa Rica, Boston, 1962-67. Trustee Middle Am. Sports Found., 1968—. Address: 950 25th St New York City NY 10001

DEMAILLY, CHARLES FORBES, corp. exec.; b. Boston, Nov. 7, 1918; s. Charles G. and Elizabeth Claire (Forbes) DeM.; B.S., Mass. Inst. Tech., 1940; m. E. Eleanore Clark, Sept. 28, 1940; children—Claire (Mrs. Edward K. Prohl), Marianne (Mrs. Kevin G. Barbera), Charles Forbes; m. 2d, Beatrice Kinnear, 1967. Supt., then asst. mgr. J.C. Rhodes & Co., New Bedford Mass., 1946-56; with Plymouth Cordage Industries, Inc., Boston, 1956—, exec. v.p., gen. mgr., 1958-61, pres., 1961-, also dir.; v.p. Plymouth Cordage Co., Boston and Plymouth, Mass., 1961-64, pres., 1964—, also dir.; exec. v.p. Emhart Corp., Bloomfield, Conn., 1966-67; pres. Plymouth div. Emhart Corp., 1967—; dir. Plymouth Cordage Co. Can., Ltd., PCI de Mexico SA de CV., Mchts. Nat. Bank of New Bedford. Served to maj., ordnance dept., AUS, 1941-45. Mem. Alpha Tau Omega. Republican. Unitarian. Clubs: Algonquin (Boston); New Bedford Yacht; Wamsutta. Home: 20 Pleasant St South Dartmouth MA 02714 Office: Indsl Park New Bedford MA 02745

DE MAIO, D. ANTHONY, banker. Sr. v.p. Green Point Savs. Bank, Bklyn. Office: 807 Manhattan Av Brooklyn NY 11222*

DEMAMBRO, GENE, machinery mfr.; b. Boston, Sept. 19, 1907; s. Anthony and Elizabeth (Bastianelle) DeM.; LL.B., Detroit Coll. Law, 1932; m. Ruth Jessica Williams, Dec. 9, 1948; children—Gene Brian, David William. Toolmaker apprentice, foreman prodn. engring. Ford Motor Co., 1924-32; admitted to Mich. bar, 1932; sr. partner DeMambro & Chapman, Detroit, 1933-43; pres. Curtis Machine Corp., Jamestown, N.Y., 1946-56; pres., dir. Standard Portable Products Co., 1947—, Lincoln Park Industries, Detroit, 1948- 54; v.p. Carborundum Co., Niagara Falls, N.Y., 1955-59; pres. Classic Enterprises, Inc., 1959—; pres., dir. Mayville Plastics, Inc., (N.Y.), 1963—, Campbell-Rice Inc., 1968—, Gene D. Realty, Inc., Mayville (N.Y.) Wire Forms Co., Inc., 1970—; pres. Bowling Assos., Inc.; partner law firm DeMambro, Ford & Lundine, Mayville; pres., dir. Linkay Assos. Inc., 1970—; dir. Dowcraft Inc., Ellison Bronze Co., Jamestown. Mem. Indsl. Devel. Commn. Jamestown, 1955-59. Field adviser Small Bus. Adminstrn., 1955-59. Served as comdr. USNR, 1943-46. Recipient citation Navy Dept. Mem. C. of C. (v.p., dir. 1956). Republican. Mason (32, Shriner). Club: Exchange (pres. 1939) (Lincoln Park, Mich.); Moon Brook Country (Jamestown, N.Y.). Home: Wooglin Beach Mayville NY 14757 (winter) Lakeview Apts Sweetwater Dr Boca Raton FL 33432 Office: Standard Portable Products Co Mayville NY 14757

DEMARAY, CALVIN DORR, clergyman, coll. pres.; b. Nashville, Mich., Oct. 21, 1901; s. Charles H. and Harriet (Bassett) D.; student Greenville Coll., Ill., 1919-22; A.B., U. Mich., 1924, A.M., 1927; student U. So.Cal., 1936-39; Litt.D., Seattle Pacific Coll., 1946; m. L. Grace Vore, Aug. 26, 1925; children—Dr. Donald E., Wendell A., Margaret Brown. Prof. speech Adrian Coll., Mich., 1924-27, Sterling Coll., Kan., 1927-30; prof. speech and English, Los Angeles Pacific Coll., 1930-41, dean of students, 1936-41, pres., 1941-48; pastor Seattle Pacific Coll. Ch., 1948-59, pres. Seattle Pacific Coll., 1959-68, pres. emeritus of coll., 1968—. Ordained to ministry Free Meth. Ch., 1941. Trustee, Pacific Sci. Found., King's Garden, Inc. Mem. Am. Assn. Sch. Adminstrs., Pi Kappa Delta. Rotarian. Home: 1705 NW 193d St Seattle, WA 98177.

DE MARCO, JEAN ANTOINE, sculptor; b. Paris, France, May 2, 1898; s. Antoine and Maria Angela (Bordone) de M.; student Ecole Nationale des Arts Decoratifs, Paris; m. Clara Fasano, 1936. Came to U.S., 1928, naturalized, 1944. Formerly instr. sch. fine arts of Boston Mus.; instr. sculpture Bennett Jr. Coll. Milbrook N.Y., Columbia U., now at N.A.D., N.Y.; exhbns. Am., France; sculptor Chimes Tower, Whitemarsh Park Meml., Prospectville, Pa., Court of Nations, N.Y. World's Fair, also post offices, Weldon, N.C., Danville, Pa.; sculpture, relief portraits in Chamber of Congress, Washington; sculpture in Cathedral Assumption of Blessed Virgin Mary, Balt.; War Meml. of West Coast at Presidio, San Francisco; Francis Schiervier Hosp., Bronx; War Meml. at Howard Hall Notre Dame U.; 2 chapels at Nat. Shrine Immaculate Conception; others; represented in permanent collections Met. Mus., N.Y.C., Bklyn. Mus. Arts, Norfolk (Va.) Mus. Art and Sci. Served as cpl. Italian Army, World War I. Decorated Croix de Guerre. Won nat. competition for relief to decorate facade, New War Dept. Bldg., Washington; silver medal Art Assn., New Rochelle, N.Y.; Saltus gold medal for artistic merit, Cannon prize, N.A.D.; Lindsey Morris Meml., Louis Bennett prizes, Nat. Sculpture Soc.; grant and citation Nat. Inst. Arts and Letters, N.Y.; Joseph Mayer prize Audubon Artists Soc.; Herbert Adams Meml. medal, Henry Herring citation Nat. Sculpture Soc.; Medal of Merit, Am. Acad. Arts and Letters; Gold medal Archtl. League of N.Y.; Daniel Chester French award Allied Artists Am., Elizabeth Watrous gold medal N.A.D., 1966. N.A. Mem. emeritus Nat. Sculpture Soc. (Henry Herring medal); mem. Nat. Inst. Arts and Letters. Roman Catholic. Home: Cervaro Prov-Frosinone, Italy. Office: Nat Acad Design 1083 Fifth Av New York City NY 10028

DE MARCO, ROLAND R., ret. coll. pres.; b. Mt. Morris, N.Y., July 21, 1910; s. Marion and Mary (Scalzette) De M.; diploma Geneseo State Tchrs. Coll., 1930; B.S., N.Y. State Coll. for Tchrs., 1934; A.M., Columbia, 1937, Ph.D. (Kappa Delta Pi scholar 1939-40), 1942; student U. Munich, 1937, Shrivenham Am. U., Eng., 1945, Officers Candidate Sch., San Antonio, 1944, Air Intelligence Sch., Orlando, Fla., 1944; LL.D., Chungang U., Seoul, Korea, 1959; D.Litt., Sung Kyun Kwan U., Seoul, 1969; m. Lydia Hees, June 23, 1934; children—Richard, Ronald, Lynn. Instr., Gowanda Pub. Schs., 1930-34; dir. social studies East Islip (N.Y.) High Sch., 1934-38; instr. social sci. Coll. of Charleston, summer 1939, Columbia, 1939-40, vis. prof. history summers 1946, 1947; prof. history, head dept. social sci. Ala. State Tchrs. Coll., 1940-46; curriculum cons. Jackson County (Ala.) Schs., 1942-43; head hist. dept. Finch Jr. Coll., N.Y.C., 1946-49, pres. dep., dean, 1949, adminstrv. head, 1949-50, pres., 1950-52, pres. Finch Coll., 1952-69, pres. emeritus, cons., 1969—. Pres. All-Am. Open Karate Championship, 1965—; pres. Karate Championship N. AM., 1967—. Exec. vice chmn. and chmn. ednl. adv. com. Am.-Korea Found., 1953- 64, pres., 1964-68, hon. chmn., 1968—; trustee Allen-Stevenson Sch. for Boys, pres. bd., 1956-58; dir., treas. Council Higher Ednl. Instns., N.Y.C.; bd. dirs. Am. Behavioral Scis., 1967—. Served to 1st lt. USAAF, 1943-46; asst. prisoner of war officer, 1st air div., 8th Air Force, 1945; adminstrv. and counter intelligence officer, European Air Transport Service, Wiesbaden, Germany, 1945-46. Decorated Order Cultural Merit Nat. Medal (Korea); named hon. citizen of Seoul, Korea, 1964, knight officer Order of Merit (Republic Italy). Mem. Am. Hist. Assn., Am. Acad. Polit. and Social Sci., N.E.A., Nat. Council Social Studies, N.Y. Assn. Deans and Guidance, Soc. Advancement Edn., Acad. Polit. Sci., Academia Tiberina, Phi Delta Kappa, Kappa Delta Pi. Clubs: Carom, Incorporated, University (N.Y.C.). Author: The Italianization of African Natives, 1943; also pamphlet. Contbr. to School and Society, Ednl. Register, Am. Rev. Address: 35 E 85th St New York City NY 10028

DEMAREE, KENNETH BROWDER, book pub.; b. Matsuyama, Japan, Jan. 16, 1904; s. Thomas Walter Bascomb and Gania (Holland) D. (parents Am. citizens); student Ky. Wesleyan Coll., 1920-23; B.A., U. So. Cal., 1924; M.A., U. Mich., 1928; student U. N.C., 1932-33; m. Mildred Cameron, Aug. 19, 1935; 1 son, Allan Thomas. Tchr., Cynthiana (Ky.) High Sch., 1924-26, U. Miss., 1926-28, Wentworth Mil. Acad., Lexington, Mo., 1928-29, Mont. State Coll., 1929- 34; field rep. to editor McGraw-Hill Book Co., 1934-43; editor Harper & Bros., N.Y.C., 1946-58, mgr. coll. dept., 1959-62, dir., 1960-62; v.p. W.W. Norton & Co., 1962—, dir., 1964—; dir. Nat. Book Co. Served to maj. AUS, 1943-46. Mem. Am. Math. Assn., Am. Inst. Biol. Scis. Republican. Episcopalian. Clubs: Ponte Vedra (Fla.); Silver Spring (Ridgefield, Conn.). Home: 791 N Wilton Rd New Canaan CT 06840 Office: 55 Fifth Av New York City NY 10002

DEMAREST, GEORGE STUART, educator; b. Roselle Park, N.J., Aug. 9, 1906; s. George L. and Ethel L. (Johnson) D.; Litt. B., Rutgers U., 1928, M.A., 1938; m. Grace Banker, June 18, 1931; children—Muriel Ann, Donald B. (dec.). Editor, Rahway (N.J.) Record, 1928-30; editor publs. Rutgers U., 1930, mem. faculty, 1935—, chmn. dept. English, 1945-58, prof. English, 1951—, dean Univ. Coll., 1965-69. Mem. Am. Assn. U. Profs., Modern Lang. Assn., Theta Chi. Republican. Presbyn. Author articles. Home: 323 Tuttle Pky Westfield, NJ 07090.

DEMAREST, MICHAEL HENRY SAMUEL, magazine editor; b. W. Hempstead, L.I., N.Y., July 31, 1924; s. Donald DeGray and Ruth (Wood) D.; student Magdalen Coll., Oxford (Eng.) U., 1941-42; m. Madeleine Mayer Fite, Jan. 17, 1947; children—Michele, Hugh, David, Timothy. Asso. editor N.Y. Acad. Scis., 1946, San Francisco Argonant, 1947-49; reporter, columnist Santa Rosa (Cal.) Press Democrat, 1950-54; writer Time mag., 1954-58, fgn. corr., London, Eng., 1958-61, asso. editor, 1961-63, sr. editor, 1964-70; exec. editor Playboy Mag., 1970—. Served with U.S. Merchant Marine, 1942-45. Club: Jack's (London). Home: 1240 N Sheridan Lake Forest IL 60045 Office: 919 N Michigan Av Chicago IL 60611

DE MARINIS, FRANK, geneticist, educator; b. Bari, Italy, Dec. 14, 1912; s. Paul and Rosina (LaGioia) De M.; came to U.S., 1921, naturalized, 1955; A.B., Western Res. U., 1936, M.A., 1937, Ph.D., 1940; m. Mary Roberta Zullo, June 19, 1937; children—Roselynn (Mrs. Kenneth Deyo). June M. (Mrs. H. Wagner), Norma J. (Mrs. J. McCann), Paul M. Asst. biology Western Res. University, 1937-40; research chemist Petri Wine Lab. 1940-41, S.K. Wellman Co., 1941-45, Aluminum Co. Am., 1945-46; asst. prof. biology Fenn Coll., Cleve., 1946-50, prof., chmn. dept., 1950-65; prof. Cleve. State U., 1965—, chmn. biology dept., 1965-7o. Guest researcher in genetics Konan U., Japan, 1970, U. Barcelona, Spain, 1971; vis. prof. U. Rome, Italy, 1971. Cons. OSRD, 1944; participant radioactive fallout study for AEC, Nev. Test Site, 1957; sr. scientist USPHS Res., 1957—; dep. sci. attache Am. embassy, Rome, Italy, 1960-62; mem. adv. bd. Air Pollution Control Cleve., 1960; mem. heredity clinic Cleve. Met. Hosp., 1957-58; vis. scientist Ohio Acad. Sci.-NSF, 1963; off-site surveillance USPHS-AEC, Las Vegas, 1963, Dribble project USPHS-AEC, Hattiesburg, Miss., 1964. Mem. work group fed. and state policies, plans, and procedures Great Lakes Basin Commn. Fellow A.A.A.S., Ohio Acad. Sci.; mem. Am. Chem. Soc., Soc. Devel. and Growth, Genetics Soc. of Am., Soc. of Human Genetics, N.Y. Acad. Scis., Commd. Officer Assn. USPHS, Nat. Assn Standard Med. Dictionary, Sigma Xi. Club: American (Rome). Contbr. articles sci. jours., coll. manuals. Home: 2611 Exeter Rd Cleveland OH 44118

DEMARIS, OVID, (Ovide E. Desmarais), author; b. Biddeford, Me., Sept. 6, 1919; s. Ernest J. and Aurore (Casavant) D.; A.B., Coll. Ida., 1948; student Syracuse U. Law Sch., 1948- 49; M.S., Boston U., 1950; m. Inez E. Frakes, May 15, 1942; children—Linda Lee (Mrs. John Teixeira), Peggy Ann (Mrs. Benjamin Cabral). Reporter, Quincy (Mass.) Patriot-Ledger, 1949-50, Boston Daily Record, 1950, Boston bur. U.P., 1950-52; advt. copy chief Los Angeles Times, 1953-59; free-lance writer, 1959—. Served with USAAF, 1940-45. Author: Ride the Gold Mare, 1957; The Hoods Take Over, 1957; The Lusting Drive, 1958; The Slasher, 1959; The Long Night, 1959; The Extortioners, 1960; The Enforcer, 1960; The Gold-Plated Sewer, 1960; Lucky Luciano, 1960; The Dillinger Story, 1961; The Lindbergh Kidnaping Case. 1961; Candyleg, 1961; Chip's Girl, 1961; The Parasites, 1962; (with Ed Reid) The Green Felt Jungle, 1963; The Organization, 1964 (reissued as Fatal Mistake 1966); (with Garry Wills) Jack Ruby, 1968; Captive City, 1969; America the Violent, 1970; Poso del Mundo, 1970; Inside Howard Hughes, 1971. Address: care Scott Meredith Lit Agency 580 Fifth Av New York City NY 10036 also PO Box 6071 Santa Barbara CA 93111

DEMARS, RICHARD BRUCE, constrn. co. exec.; b. Indpls., Sept. 6, 1918; s. Arch E. and Lillian B. (Dearmyer) DeM.; B.S., Purdue U., 1940; m. Joy Geupel, Nov. 30, 1940; children—Dan Richard, Elizabeth Ann (Mrs. Gilbert P. Hammond, Jr.). Gen. foreman maintenance Delco-Remy div. Gen. Motors Corp., 1940-44; bldg. supt. L.S. Ayres & Co., 1946-51; exec. Carl M. Geupel Constrn. Co., Inc., 1951-65; pres. Geupel DeMars, Inc., Indpls., 1965—; pres. bd. dirs. Citizens Gas & Coke Utility; dir. Hoosier Motor Club. Mem. Met. Devel. Commn. Indpls., 1968—; dir. United Fund Greater Indpls., 1967—; pres., dir. Central Ind. council Boy Scouts Am., 1965-66. Vice chmn. bd. dirs. Community Hosp. Indpls., 1968—; trustee Arthur Jordan Found., 1965—; chmn. bd. trustees Hanover Coll., 1971. Served with Corps of Engrs., AUS, 1944-46. Mem. Indpls. C. of C. (pres. 1971), Phi Kappa Psi. Republican. Presbyn. (elder). Home: 1011 W 52d St Indianapolis IN 46208 Office: 1919 N Meridian St Indianapolis IN 46202

DEMARS, VERNON ARMAND, architect, educator; b. San Francisco, Feb. 26, 1908; s. Louis Avila and Bessie (Willis) DeM.; A.B., U. Cal., 1931; m. Elizabeth Ann Bates, Apr. 20, 1939. Regional architect FSA, San Francisco, 1937-42; chief housing standard sect. Nat. Housing Agy., Washington, 1942-43 vis. prof. Mass. Inst. Tech., 1946-49; prof. architecture U. Cal. at Berkeley, 1952—, chmn. dept., 1959-61; architect assn. for 100 Memorial Dr. Apts., Cambridge, Mass., Easter Hill Village, Richmond, Cal., Student Center, Auditorium-Theatre, Wurster Hall, U. Cal. at Berkeley, Golden Gateway Center, San Francisco, Miliani Newtown, Oahu, Hawaii, Old Sacramento Historic Area, Library at Coll. Arts and Crafts, Oakland, Cal., Library, Mt. Angel Abbey, Ore.; cons. Dept. State, Marshall Plan housing for miners in Ruhr, 1952; U.S. del. Italian-American Planning Seminar, Italy, 1955. Trustee of San Francisco Museum of Art. Served to lt. (s.g.) USNR, 1943-45. Fellow A.I.A. Home: 240 The Uplands Berkeley CA 94705

DE MARTINI, JOSEPH, artist; b. Mobile, Ala., July 20, 1896, Painter, exhibiting, 1941—; resident artist U. Georgia, 1953-54; in exhbns. of Mus. Modern Art, Carnegie Inst., Whitney Mus. Am. Art, Corcoran Art Gallery Art, Pa. Acad. Fine Arts, Art Inst. Chgo., Worcester (Mass.) Mus. Art, Va. Mus. Fine Arts; represented in collections of Mus. Modern Art, Met. Mus. Art, Boston Mus. Fine Arts, Brooks Meml. Mus. (Memphis), Farnsworth Mus., Rockland, Me., U.S. Dept. State., IBM, Ency. Brit., Michener Coll. U. Tex., Phillips Meml. Coll., Washington. Recipient Palmer Award, 1950, Jennie Sesnan Gold Medal, Pa. Acad. Fine Arts, 1952; Guggenheim Fellowship, 1951. Mem. Audubon Assn. N.A. Home: 2 Hamilton Av Weehawken NJ 07087 Studio: 103 W 27th St New York City NY 10001

DEMARTINO, FRANCESCO, educator; b. Naples, Italy, May 31, 1907; s. Armando and Elisa (Angrisani) DeM.; Laureate in Jurisprudence; m. Teresa Angrisani, Nov. 25, 1936 children—Armando, Guido, Antonino, Elisa, Laura. Staff prof. history Roman law U. Naples. Del. Parlement, 1948—; ex sec. Italian Socialist Party; v.p. cabinet, 1969—. Home: 258 Aniello Falcone Naples, Italy. Office: 476 Via de Corso Rome Italy

DEMAY, KENNETH DISOSWAY, architect; b. N.Y.C., May 6, 1932; s. Harry Disosway and Estella (de Paz y Mino) DeM.; student USCG Acad., 1950-52; B.Arch. with honors, Pratt Inst., 1956; M.Arch., Harvard, 1953; m. Katherine Hollier Mosedale, Dec. 15, 1956; children—Dwight Hamilton, Mason Kenneth, Thayer Copley. Prin., Sasaki, Dawson, DeMay Assos., Inc., Watertown, Mass., 1963—; asst. dean Pratt Inst. Sch. Architecture, Bklyn., 1956-59; chief critic in architecture Pratt Inst. Evening Sch., 1958-59; vis. design critic Harvard Grad. Sch. Design, 1961-65; vis. lectr., critic New Eng. Bd. Higher Edn., U. Va., Boston Archtl. Center, La. State U. Served as 2d lt., C.E., U.S. Army, 1956. Recipient Pratt Inst.- A.I.A. medal, 1956, citation Progressive Architecture, Engring. Scis. Center, U. Colo., 1963, Design award for housing complex U. R.I., 1965, award of merit HFA, 1964, 1st honor award U.S. Bur. Higher Edn., 1966, 1st prize Copley Sq. Competition, Boston, 1965, Design in Steel citation Am. Iron and Steel Inst., 1971. Registered profl. architect, Mass., R.I., N.Y., Conn., Del., Va., Ky., Ia., Ind., Colo. Mem. A.I.A., Boston Soc. Architects, Nat. Trust Historic Preservation, Soc. Archtl. Historians, Ky. Hist. Soc., Nat. Audubon Soc. Club: Windsor. Important works include Engring. Scis. Center, U. Colo., Marine Family Housing, housing complex U. R.I., MacMaster U. Men's Residence, Providence Coll. Library, Brandeis U. dormitories, U. Rochester Sci. Complex, U. Va. Fine Arts Center, Wightman Tennis Center, Weston, Mass. (award excellence Am. Inst. Steel Constrn. 1970), Tobin Sch., Cambridge, Mass., Loomis Sch. Library and dormitories, St. Mark's Sch. Library, Portsmouth Abbey adminstrn. bldg., Barrington Coll. phys. edn. bldg., Ramapo Coll. of N.J., Regis Coll. sci. bldg. Home: 201 Kent Rd Waban MA 02168 Office: 23 Main St Watertown MA 02172

DE MAYNADIER, ALAIN, banker; b. Paris, France, July 12, 1929; s. George du Rieu and Jacqueline (Douard de Fleurance) deM.; B.A., Coll. Wooster, 1961; M.A., Cornell U., 1964; divorced; children-Patrick, Philip. Came to U.S., 1957, naturalized, 1961. With Morgan Guarantee Trust, N.Y.C., 1963-66; territorial asst. Central Nat. Bank, Cleve., 1966-67; with Provident Nat. Bank, Phila., 1967—, sr. v.p., 1969—; pres., dir. Provident Internat. Corp.; dir. Arrendadora de Mexico, S.A., Mexico City. Mem. Am. Econ. Assn., Am. Finance Assn. Clubs: Racquet, Art Alliance (both Phila.). Home: 341 S 25th St Philadelphia PA 19103 Office: Provident Nat Bank Brad and Chestnut Sts Philadelphia PA 19101

DEMBER, WILLIAM NORTON, educator, psychologist; b. Waterbury, Conn., Aug. 8, 1928; s. David and Henrietta (Siegel) D.; A.B., Yale, 1950; M.A., U. Mich., 1951, Ph.D., 1955; m. Cynthia Fox, Dec. 21, 1958; children—Joanna, Laura, Gregory. Instr. dept. psychology U. Mich., 1954-56; asst. prof. Yale, 1956-59; mem. faculty U. Cin., 1959—, prof. psychology, asst. dean, grad. sch., 1965-67, prof., head dept. psychology, 1968—. Mem. Am. Psychol. Assn., A.A.A.S. Author: Psychology of Perception, 1960; Visual Perception, 1964; General Psychology, 1970; also articles. Developed and tested theory motivation applying to behavior human beings and animals. Home: 920 Oregon Trail Cincinnati OH 45215

DEMBERGH, ROBERT CHARLES, banker; b. Phila., June 19, 1921; s. Charles N. and Margaret (Jonson) D.; B.S., Lehigh U., 1947; postgrad. U. Pa., 1949-50, Temple U., 1950- 51; m. Katherine Ann McCoy, Oct. 10, 1942; children—Peter J., Christian T. With Land Title Bank & Trust Co., 1947-52; asst. cashier First Nat. Bank Phila., 1953-55; v.p. First Pa. Banking & Trust Co., 1955-56; pres. Bank of Pa., Reading, 1966—; dir. Union Fidelity Corp. Phila. Chmn. promotion and tng. United Community Services Berks County, 1968. Bd. dirs. Reading Hosp., Muhlenburg Assos. Served with USNR, 1942-45. Clubs: Camden (Me.) Yacht; Merion Cricket (Haverford, Pa.); Meridian (Phila.); Berkshire Country, Wyomissing (Reading). Home: N Tulpehocken Rd Greenfields Reading, PA 19601. Office: 50 N 5th St Reading PA 19603

DEMBLING, PAUL GERALD, lawyer, govt. ofcl.; b. Rahway, N.J., Jan. 11, 1920; s. Simon and Fannie (Ellenbogen) D.; B.A., Rutgers U., 1940, M.A., 1942; J.D., George Washington U., 1951; m. Florence Brotman, Nov. 22, 1947; children—Ross Wayne, Douglas Evan, Donna Stacy. Grad. asst., teaching fellow Rutgers U., 1940-42; economist, salary and wage analyst Office Chief Transp. Dept. Army, 1942-45; admitted to D.C. bar, 1952, since practiced in Washington; indsl. relations NACA, 1945-51, spl. counsel, legal adviser, gen. counsel, 1951-58; asst. gen. counsel, dir. legislative affairs NASA, 1958-63, dep. gen. counsel, 1963-67, gen. counsel, 1967-69, chmn. bd. contract appeals, 1958-61, vice chmn. inventions and contbns. bd., 1959-67; mem. and alternate rep. U.S. Delegation to UN Legal Subcommittee Com. on Outer Space, 1964-69; gen counsel U.S. Gen. Accounting Office, 1969—; professorial lectr. George Washington U. Law Sch., 1965—. Vice pres. Merrimack Civic Assn., 1956-57; bd. dirs. Merrimack Park Recreation Assn., 1956-59, 61- 64. Recipient Meritorious Civilian Service award War Dept., 1945; Distinguished Service award NASA, 1968. Asso. fellow Am. Inst. Aeros, and Astronautics (chmn. com. law and sociology 1969—); mem. Am., Fed. (nat. council 1963—) bar assn., Internat. Inst. Space Law (pres. Am. assn. 1970), Nat. Lawyers Club, Nat. Contract Mgmt. Assn., Phi Delta Phi. Editor-in-chief, Fed. Bar Jour., 1962-69, Contbr. articles profl. jours. Home: 6303 Tone Dr Bethesda, MD 20034 Office: 441 G St NW Washington DC 20548

DEMBNER, S. ARTHUR, mag. pub.; b. N.Y.C., Oct. 7, 1920; s. Jack Dembner; A.B. (evenings), New Sch. Social Research, 1950; m. Dec. 5, 1948; 3 children. Account exec. Modern Mdse. Bur., 1945-47; circulation exec. Time, Inc., 1947-52; with Newsweek mag., 1952—, circulation dir., 1961—, v.p., 1962—, mem. exec. com., 1969—, dir., 1969—, also pub. book div.; sr. v.p. Newsweek, Inc., 1971—; mng. dir. Art New mag. Chmn. bd. govs. Direct Mail Advt. Assn., 1959-60; chmn. com. advisers on direct mail Dept. Agr., 1956-58; adv. com. sales and subscriptions Com. Econ. Devel., 1960. Chmn. Vols. in Politics, N.Y.C., 1953. Bd. dirs. Encampment for Citizenship. Served to capt. USAAF, World War II. Mem. Advt. Fedn. Am., Hundred Million Club (past pres.), Sales Promotion Execs. Assn., Mag. Pubs. Assn. (chmn. circulation com.). Club: Players. Editor: Modern Circulation Methods. Home: 140 Cabrini Blvd New York City NY 10033 Office: Newsweek Inc 444 Madison Av New York City NY 10022

DEMBO, LAWRENCE SANFORD, educator; b. Troy, N.Y., Dec. 3, 1929; s. Irving and Mildred (Spiwak) D.; B.A., Syracuse U., 1951; M.A., Columbia, 1952; Ph.D., Cornell U., 1955; m. Royce Benderson, Mar. 15, 1953. Instr. English, Cornell U., 1959-60; asst. prof. U. Cal. at Los Angeles, 1960-65; Fulbright lectr., Montpellier, France, 1963; prof. English, U. Wis., 1965—. Served to lt. (j.g.) USNR, 1956-59. Guggenheim fellow, 1968-69. Author: Hart Crane's Sanskrit Charge, a Study of the Bridge, 1960; The Confucian Odes of Ezra Pound, a Critical Appraisal, 1963; Conceptions of Reality in Modern American Poetry, 1966, Nabokov, The Man and His Work, 1967; Criticism, Speculative and Analytical Essays, 1968. Editor Contemporary Literature, 1966—. Home: 5 Beach St Madison WI 53705

DEMBOWSKI, PETER FLORIAN, educator; b. Warsaw, Poland, Dec. 23, 1925; s. Wlodzimierz and Henryka (Sokolowski) D.; B.A. with honors, U. B.C., 1952; Doctorat d'Universite, U. Paris (France), 1954; Ph.D., U. Cal. at Berkeley, 1960; m. Yolande Jessop, June 29, 1954; children—Anne, Eve, Paul. Instr. French, U. B.C., 1954-56; asst. prof. French, U. Toronto, 1960-63, asso. prof., 1963-66; mem. faculty U. Chgo., 1966—; prof. French, 1970—, dean students, div. humanities, 1968-70. Served with Polish Army, 1944-46. Decorated Cross of Valor, Cross of Service with swords (Poland); Guggenheim fellow, 1970-71. Mem. Modern Lang. Assn., La Societe de Lingsuistique Romane. Author: La Chronique de Robert de Clari, 1963; Jourdain de Blaye, 1969; Ami et Amile, 1969. Home: 5447 S Kenwood Av Chicago IL 60615

DEMCOE, JOHN WILLIAM, railroad ofcl.; b. Kenora, Ont., Can., Apr. 18, 1912; s. William and Annie (Mylebroder) D.; B.S. in Civil Engring. (Gold medallist 1939, Isbestor scholar 1937-38), U. Man., 1939; m. Lydia Janet Robertson, Apr. 28, 1939; children—John Robertson, William James. With Canadian Nat. Rys., 1939-67, gen. mgr., Monoton, 1961-62, v.p. transp. and maintenance, 1962-67, v.p., 1969—, also v.p. subsidiaries and affiliates; v.p., gen. mgr. Grand Trunk Western R.R., 1967-69. Registered profl. engr., Ont. Mem. Toronto Ry. Club (past dir.), Canadian Ry. Club, Profl. Engrs. Soc. Ont., Engring. Inst. Can., Am. Ry. Engring. Assn., Am. Assn. R.R. Supts., Canadian C. of C. Clubs: Boulevard (Toronto); Mount Royal Curling, Summerlea Golf and Country (Montreal). Home: 75 Glengarry Av Mount Royal Montreal Quebec Canada Office: CN Hdqrs 935 Lagauchetiere W Montreal Quebec Canada

DE MENIL, DOMINIQUE, educator; b. Paris, France, Mar. 23, 1908; d. Conrad and Louise (Delpech) Schlumberger; B.A., U. Paris, 1927; postgrad. math. and physics; m. John de Menil, May 9, 1931; children—Christophe (Mrs. Christophe de Menil Thurman), Adelaide, George, Francois, Philippa. Came to U.S., 1941, naturalized, 1962. Art collector, 1945—; acting chmn. art history dept. U. St. Thomas, Houston, 1964, chmn. dept., 1965-69, dir. Inst. for Arts, 1968—; organizer exhbns., 1964—. Trustee Mus. Fine Arts, Houston. Home: 3363 San Felipe Rd Houston, TX 77029.

DE MENIL, JOHN, corp. exec.; b. Paris, France, Jan. 4, 1904; s. Georges Menu and Madeleine (Rougier) de M.; B.A., U. Paris, 1922, grad. Sch. Polit. Sci., 1925, B.Law, 1935; m. Dominique Schlumberger, May 9, 1931; children—Christophe (Mrs. Christophe Thurman), Adelaide, Georges, Francois, Philippa (Mrs. Francesco Pellizzi). Came to U.S., 1941, naturalized, 1962. Vice pres. Banque Nat. pour le Commerce et l'Industrie, Paris, 1932-38; pres. Schlumberger Overseas and Schlumberger Surenco, Houston, 1941-57; chmn. exec. com., dir. Schlumberger Ltd., Houston, 1958-68, chmn. bd., 1968-70; dir. Bank of S.W., Istel Fund, Inc. Trustee Mus. Primitive Art, N.Y.C., Mus. Modern Art, Inst. Internat. Edn., Inst. Religion, Houston, R.I. Sch. Design, Providence; v.p. Internat. Council Museum of Modern Art. Clubs: Ramada, River Oaks Country, Petroleum (Houston). Home: 3363 San Felipe Rd Houston TX 77019 also 111 E 73d St New York City NY 10021

DE MENT, JACK ANDREW, research chemist, author tech. books; b. Portland, Ore., Feb. 6, 1920; s. Andrew Thomas and Bernadine (Michaels) De M.; student Reed Coll., 1938-41; D.Sc. (hon.), Western States Coll., 1955. Chemist and metallurgist, Mont. Assay Office, 1941, asst. spectroscopist, Charlton Labs., Portland, 1941- 42; research chemist, asso. editor, Mineralogist Mag., Portland, 1940- 51; research chemist and head, De Ment Labs., Portland, 1941—; research asst. U. Ore. Sch. Dentistry, 1948-50, research cons. biophysics and pharmacology, 1961-66; co-investigator USPHS, 1953-58; pres. of Polyphoton Corp., 1963—; sci. ed. Prevue Mag., 1958-65; research cons. Ultra-Violet Products, Inc., Los Angeles, 1942-50. Cons. Sec. of War, Project Crossroads (spent 2 mos. at Bikini atomic bomb tests), 1946; mem. Pres.' Conf. Tech. Distbn. Research, 1957; del. 1st Nat. Laser Safety Seminar, Orlando, Fla., 1966. Research: named and established fluorochemistry, 1942; formally enunciated First Law of Fluorescence (De Ment's Absorption Law), new tests for uranium and ores; invented new weapons, radiological, new methods for radioactive decontamination; several hundred discoveries and inventions described in over 300 papers in sci. jours.; U.S. and fgn. patents granted on new laser systems; holds or has filed 100 patents, assigned two dozen to AEC. Student of human strength, 1936-41. Recipient Wisdom Award of Honor, 1970. Diplomate Nuclear Physics, Am. Bd. Bio-Analysts. Fellow Am. Coll. Med. Technologists; mem. Profl. Execs. Hall of Fame, Sigma Xi. Author: (with H.C. Dake) Fluorescent Light and Its Applications, 1941; (with H. C. Dake) Uranium and Atomic Power, 1941 (rev. edn., 1945); Fluorescent Chemicals and Their Applications, 1942; (with H. C. Dake) Ultraviolet Light and Its Applications, 1942; Fluorochemistry, 1945; Rarer Metals, 1946 (English edition 1949); (with H. C. Dake) Handbook of Uranium Minerals, 1947, rev. edit., 1949; Handbook of Fluorescent Minerals, 1947; New Horizons in Cancer Control, 1954; Ultraviolet Light in Crime Detection, 1957. Author of prize essay Gravity Research Found., 1951. Contbr. other books and encys. Laser research, color radiography. Inventor fluidic optics; optoexplosive systems (explotron) separating blast-free light from explosions. Home: 4847 SE Division Portland OR 97206

DEMENT, WILLIAM CHARLES, educator, psychiatrist; b. Wenatchee, Wash., July 29, 1928; s. Charles Frederick and Kathryn (Severyns) D.; B.S. cum laude, U. Wash., 1951; M.D. with honors in Physiology, U. Chgo., 1955, Ph.D. (USPHS postdoctoral research fellow), 1957; m. Eleanor Weber, Mar. 23, 1956; children—Cathy, Elizabeth, Nicky. Rotating intern Mt. Sinai Hosp., N.Y.C., 1957-58, research fellow, 1958-63; mem. faculty Stanford Med. Sch., 1963—, prof. psychiatry, 1967—, dir. Sleep Lab., 1963—, dir. Sleep Disorder Clinic, 1970—; chief editor, founder Sleep Revs. Project of Brain Information Services, 1969—; Thomas W. Salmon lectr. N.Y. Acad. Medicine, 1969. Recipient Harry Ginsburg Meml. prize U. Chgo., 1955. Mem. Am. Psychiat. Assn. (Hofheimer prize 1964), Am. Psychol. Assn. (co-recipient 2d prize annual research award div. psycholopharmacology 1970), Assn. Psychophysiol. Study Sleep (co-founder), Western EEG Assn., Psychiat. Research Soc., N.Y. Acad. Sci., Am. Psychosomatic Soc., Am. Psychopathol. Assn., Soc. Psychophysiol. Research, Soc. Neurosci., Sigma Xi (nat. lectr. 1970). Editorial bd. Jour. Nervous and Mental Disease, Science. Home: 440 Gernona Rd Stanford CA 94305

DEMERATH, NICHOLAS JAY, sociologist, planning cons.; b. Kewanee, Ill., Nov. 15, 1913; s. Nicholas Jay and Gertrude Wells (Doyle) D.; A.B., DePauw U., 1934; M.A., Harvard, 1938, Ph.D., 1942; m. Helen Louise Titus, May 10, 1935; children—Nicholas Jay III, Julia Wells, Jeffrey Titus. Asst. prof. Tulane U., 1940-42; social sci. analyst U.S. Dept. Agr., Nat. Housing Agy., 1942-44; prof. sociology U. N.C., 1946-56; vis. prof. U. Birmingham (Eng.), 1948, Harvard, summer 1952; dir. Social Sci. Inst., Washington U., St. Louis, 1956-62, chmn. dept. sociology and anthropology, 1956-59, prof. sociology, 1956—; cons. Ford Found. (India), 1965-66; dir. St. Louis Human Devel. Corp., Mark Twain State Bank, St. Louis; cons. Am. Council on Edn., U.S. Dept. State, World Health Orgn., NIH, USAF, N.C. Planning Bd., Oak Ridge Nat. Lab. Adviser to pres. P.I., 1945-46; mem. delegation Philippine Republic to UNRRA Gen. Assembly, 1946; adviser to dir. gen. Pan Am. Sanitary Bur., 1958-59; Ford Found. vis. prof. Ind. U., 1961. Bd. dirs. St. Louis Group Health Assn. Mem. Soc. Applied Anthropology (pres. 1958), Am. Sociol. Assn. Clubs: Harvard (N.Y.C.); Cosmos (Washington). Author, editor: The Urban South; Human Relations and Organizational Performance; Human Adaptation to Disasters; Power, Presidents, and Professors: Studies of University Adminstration; Institution Building in Higher Education. Home: River Downs Farm Golden Eagle IL 62036 Office: Washington U St Louis MO 63130

DEMERE, MCCARTHY, plastic surgeon; b. Memphis, Jan. 20, 1918; s. Clifton and Leona (McCarthy) DeM.; B.S. with honors in biology. Southwestern Coll., 1939; M.D., U. Tenn., 1942; LL.B., U. Memphis, 1960; m. Ruth Mary Pidgeon, May 23, 1953; children—McCarthy, Michael, Patrick, Marie. Intern, resident surgery Barnes Hosp., St. Louis, 1942-44; surgical resident St. Luke's Hospital, N.Y.C., 1946-47; fellow plastic surgery Washington U., St. Louis, 1947-50; pvt. practice plastic surgery, Memphis, 1950—; mem. staff St. Joseph, Meth., LeBonheur hosps.; asso. staff Bapt. Hosp.; instr. surgery and plastic surgery U. Tennessee Medical School, 1950-62, asst. prof. surgery, 1962—; instr. law Memphis State U. Law School. Consultant USPHS Hosp., 1950- 59, 60—, U.S. Naval Hosp., 1950-59; guest lectr. plastic surgery Paris, Barcelona and Geneva, 1955; panelist Law Sch. Week, Houston, 1960. Chairman of adv. council Memphis Juvenil Ct. Campaign mgr. for Chancellor Hoffmann, Memphis, 1958; del. Democratic Nat. Conv., 1960. Bd. dirs. Memphis Boys Town, 1956—, Memphis Symphony Soc., 1958-59; founding mem., bd. dirs. Little City of Mid-South for Retarded Children, 1959; pres. Sertoma Projects, Inc., sponsoring Boys Town and Girls Club, 1958; sponsor grad. class U. Tenn. Med. Sch., 1952, 54, 55; chmn. bd. dirs. U. Interfaith Assn. Served to capt., M.C., AUS, 1944-46. Decorated Croix de Guerre (Luxembourg). Diplomate Am. Bd. Plastic Surgery, Am. Bd. Surgery. Fellow Am., Internat. colls. surgeons, Legal Sci. Inst. (founding mem.), Am. Acad. Ophthalmology and Otolaryngology, Southeastern Surg. Soc. (sr.); mem. Am., Southeastern (founding mem., bd. dirs., pres. 1964-65) socs. plastic and reconstructive surgery, A.M.A., Am. Soc. Head and Neck Surgeons, Am., Tenn. bar assns., Am. Legion, Nat. Honor Soc. (charter), Chi Beta Phi, Kappa Alpha (pres. 1957- 59), Delta Theta Phi (pres. 1958-59), Phi Chi. Clubs: University; Tenn. Sertoma (pres. Memphis 1960-61, internat. award for outstanding service 1958). Author sci. papers in field. Developed original methods total ear and eyelid reconstrn., research carcinogenesis implated polymer plastics. Home: 826 Reddoch Memphis TN 38117 Office: 1460 Madison Memphis TN 38104

DEMETRIOS, BISHOP (born Demetrios Makris) titular bishop of Olympus; b. Glossa, Island of Skopelos, 1910; s. Thomas and Helen (Lolios) Makris; grad. theol. sch. Nat. U. Athens, 1932. Ordained deacon, 1931; ordained priest Greek Orthodox Ch., 1936, served at Halkis, Island of Euboia, 1936-38; assigned Greek Orthodox Community, Pensacola, Fla., 1938-40, Worcester, Mass., 1940-44; also tchr. theology and other subjects Greek Orthodox Theol. Sem., instr., 1944-50, asst. dean. 1946-50; chancellor Arch-diocese, 1950; consecrated Titular Bishop of Olympus, 1951; former bishop Western States Diocese. Contbr. religious publs. Address: 180 Pond St Jamaica Plain MA 02130

DEMETRIOU, ANGELO JOHN, food service exec.; b. Chgo., Jan. 11, 1937; s. John Louis and Angeline (Katsulos) D.; B.S.C., DePaul U., 1958; postgrad. Northwestern U., 1965, Loyola U., Chgo., 1966; m. Judith A. Schroeder, Oct. 14, 1961; children—Kristine, Nicole. Social worker, Cook County, Ill., 1961-62; mgmt. trainee Amsted Industries, Chgo., 1963-64, cost accountant, 1964-66, asst. plant controller, 1966-68; controller Szabo Food Service, Lyons, Ill., 1968—. Mem. Am. Hellenic Edn. and Philanthropic Assn., Chgo., 1965—. Served with AUS, 1958-60. Mem. Planning Execs. Inst., Data processing Mfrs. Assn., Am. Inst. Corp. Controllers, Nat. Assn. Accountants. Office: 4242 S 1st Av Lyons IL 60534

DEMETZ, PETER, educator; b. Prague, Czechoslovakia, Oct. 21, 1922; s. Hans and Anna (Brod) D.; Dr.phil., Charles U., Prague, 1948; M.A., Columbia, 1954; Ph.D., Yale, 1956; m. Hana Mueller, Apr. 21, 1950; children—Anne-Marie Bettina. Came to U.S., 1952, naturalized, 1958. Editor, Radio Free Europe, 1950-52; instr. German, Yale, New Haven, 1956-58, asst. prof., 1958-60, asso. prof., 1960-62, prof. German and comparative lit., 1962- -, chmn. dept. German, 1963-69. Yale Morse fellow, 1959-60, Guggenheim fellow, 1965-66. Recipient Golden Goethe medal (Germany). Mem. Modern Lang. Assn., Am. Assn. Tchrs. German, P.E.N., Berliner Akademie der Künste. Author: René Rilkes Prager Jahre, 1953; Marx, Engels und die Dichter, 1959. Am. edit., 1967, Spanish edit., 1968; Theodor Fontane, 1964. Editor: Twentieth Century Views: Brecht, 1961; (with W.T.H. Jackson) An Anthology of German Literature, 1967; Post-War German Literature, 1970, German edit., 1970. Contbr. articles profl. jours. Home: 126 Ridgewood Av North Haven CT

DEMICHEAL, DONALD ANTHONY, mag. editor; b. Louisville, May 12, 1928; s. Joseph and Ernestine Elizabeth (Lefler) DeM.; student Ind. U., 1957-59, U. Louisville, 1960; m. Anna Elizabeth Murphy, June 5, 1948; children—David Sidney, Deborah Ann. Profl. musician on drums and vibraharp, 1944—; leader band, 1951- 60; author jazz criticism, 1959—; mem. staff Down Beat mag., 1960-67, editor-in-chief, 1961-67; editor Actual Specifying Engr. mag., 1967—, editor, asso. pub., 1971—; music editor Scholastic Roto, 1968-69; music columnist Youth Enterprises Syndicate, 1969—. Author: (with Alan Dawson) A Manual for the Modern Drummer, 1962. Editor, compiler: Jazz Record Review, Vols. 5-8, 1961-64. Home: 1935 W 101st Pl Chicago IL 60643 Office: 1801 Prairie Av Chicago IL 60616

DEMICK, ALVIN, publisher; b. N.Y.C., Jan. 24, 1926; s. Solomon and Martha (Schneider) D.; B.A., Fordham U., 1949; m. Theresa Ugo, Apr. 29, 1967. Promotions dir. Anti- Defamation League, N.Y.C., 1956-65; pub. Arts mag., N.Y.C., 1965—. Served with USNR, 1943-45. Address: 229 E 25th St New York City NY 10010

DEMIKHOV, VLADIMIR PETROVICH, surgeon; b. Moscow, 1916; ed. First Medical Inst.; m.; 2 children. Exptl. work Vishnevsky Surg. Inst., USSR Acad. Med. Scis., after World War II; developed technique for replacement hearts and lungs of dogs with hearts and lungs of other dogs, replacement heart of a dog with mechanical instrument; established lab. First Med. Inst., Moscow; successfully grafted head of one dog to neck of another, 1954; demonstrated transplantation of dog's heart Leipzig U., 1958; demonstrated head grafting of dogs, resulting in two-headed dogs. Inst. Reconstructive Plastic Surgery, N.Y.U.-Bellevue Med. Center, 1959. Recipient Academician Burdenko prize for giving dogs a second or auxiliary heart, 1951. Address: Organ Transplantation Laboratory First Medical Inst Moscow, USSR.*

DE MILHAU, JOHN WADDINGTON, banker; b. N.Y.C., Oct. 23, 1910; s. Louis J. deG. and Renee Noel (Gourd) de M.; grad. Middlesex Sch., Concord, Mass., 1928; student Harvard, 1932; m. Dorothea M. Harrison, Sept. 9, 1939; 1 son, David Livesey. With Harris Forbes & Co., N.Y.C., 1930-31, Chase Harris Forbes Corp., 1931-33, Chase Nat. Bank, 1933-55; with Chase Manhattan Bank, 1955-68, sr. v.p., 1962-68; now exec. v.p., dir. Altgelt & Co., Inc. Mem. Investment Bankers Assn. Am. (bd. govs. 1963-66). Clubs: Bond, Municipal Bond (past pres.), Municipal Forum, Harvard, N.Y. Yacht, Wall Street (N.Y.C.); Riverside Yacht; Innis Arden Golf (Old Greenwich, Conn.). Home: Grosset Rd Riverside, CT 06878. Office: 45 Wall St New York City NY 10005

DE MILLE, AGNES, choreographer; d. William Churchill and Anna (George) de Mille; A.B. cum laude, U. Cal.; Litt.D. (hon.), Mills Coll., 1952, Russell Sage Coll., 1953, Smith Coll., 1954, Western Coll., 1955, Hood Coll., 1957, Northwestern U., 1960, Goucher Coll., 1961, Clark U., 1962, U. Cal. at Los Angeles, 1964, Franklin and Marshall, 1965, Western Mich. U., 1967, Nosson Coll., 1971; m. Walter F. Prude, June 14, 1943; 1 son, Jonathan. Dance recitalist, U.S., Eng., France, Denmark, 1928-42; choreographer and dancer The Black Crook, 1929; choreographer; (film) Romeo and Juliet, 1936, (musicals) Nymph Errant, 1933, Hooray for What, 1937, Oklahoma, 1943, One Touch of Venus, 1943, Bloomer Girl, 1944, Carousel, 1945, Brigadoon, 1947, Gentlemen Prefer Blondes, 1949, Paint Your Wagon, 1951, The Girl in Pink Tights, 1954, Goldilocks, 1958, Juno, 1959, Kwamina, 1961; (ballets) OBeah Black Ritual, 1940, Three Virgins and a Devil, 1942, Drums Sound in Hackensack, 1941, Rodeo, 1942, Tally-Ho, 1944, Fall River Legend, 1948, The Harvesting According, 1952; Oklahoma (film), 1955; The Bitter Wierd, 1962; The Wind in the Mountains, 1965; The Four Mary's, 1965; The Golden Age, 1967; A Rose for Miss Emily, 1970; choreographer, dir. Allegro, 1947; dir. Rape of Lucrecia, 1949, Out of this World, 1950, Come Summer, 1969; choreographer, (musical) 110 In the Shade, 1963. Head dance and theatre co. Agnes de Mille Dance Theatre, presented by S. Hurok, 6 mos. tour, 126 cities, 1953-54; Omnibus lectrs. and ballets, 1956-57. Recipient N.Y. Critics prize, 1942-46, Donaldson award, 1943-47, Madamoiselle merit award, 1944, Antoinette Perry award, 1947, 62, Lord and Taylor award, 1947, Dancing Masters award of merit, 1950; Dance Mag. award, 1957; Capezio award, 1966; named Woman of Year by Am. Newspaper Womans Guild, 1946. Mem. Soc. Stage Dirs. and Choreographers (pres. 1965-66). Author: Dance to the Piper, 1952; And Promenade Home, 1958; To A Young Dancer, 1962; The Book of the Dance, 1963; Lizzie Borden Dance of Death, 1968; Dance In America, 1970; Russian Journals, 1970. Contbr. Good Housekeeping, Esquire, Horizen, Vogue, Atlantic Monthly, McCalls mags.

DEMING, FLOYD ALLYN, r.r. ofcl.; b. St. Paul, Aug. 15, 1921; s. Floyd Asa and Hazel (Jefferson) D.; grad. high sch.; m. Phyllis Ann Sweeney, May 13, 1944 (dec. May 1970); children—Candace (Mrs. Scott D. Miller), Scott Phillip, Paige Ann (Mrs. T.R. Finlay), Kevin Patrick, Amy Jo. Stenographer, Ajax Transfer Co., South St. Paul, Minn., 1938-40; premium clk. Minn. Mut. Life Ins. Co., St. Paul, 1940-42; asst. to offce mgr. Ralph Equipment Co., St. Paul, 1945-47; sec. to claim agt. N.P. Ry., St. Paul, 1947-50, chief clk. claim dept., 1950-62, personal sec. to v.p., 1962-66, personal sec. to pres., 1966-67, corporate sec., 1967-70; asst. sec., dir. shareholder relations Burlington No. Inc., St. Paul, 1970—; sec. No. Airmotive, Inc., Duluth Union Depot & Transfer Co., Lemhi Telephone Co., Plum Creek Lumber Co.; asst. sec. BN Transport Inc., Walla Walla Valley Ry. Co., Spokane, Portland & Seattle Ry. Co.; Glacier Park Co. Served with USCGR, 1942-45. K.C. Home: 1362 W Eldridge Av St Paul MN 55113 Office: 176 E 5th St St Paul MN 55101

DEMING, OLCOTT HAWTHORNE, diplomat; b. Westchester, N.Y., Feb. 28, 1909; s. William Champion and Imogen (Hawthorne) D.; A.B., Rollins Coll., 1935; postgrad. U. Tenn., 1935-37; m. Louise Bennett Macpherson, June 2, 1937; children—Rust Macpherson, John Hawthorne, Rosamond Bennett. Research asst. TVA, Knoxville, 1935-37; instr. Spanish, English, Fairfield Country Day Sch., also Edgewood Sch., Greenwich, Conn., 1937-41; del. New Edn. Fellowship Conf., Ann Arbor, 1940; edn. program officer Co-ordinator Inter-Am. Affairs, Washington, 1941-43; with Dept. State, 1943- 48, exec. sec. interdepartmental com. sci. and cultural cooperation, 1947-48; mem. internat. secretariat UN organizing conf., San Francisco, 1945; apptd. fgn. service officer, 1948; 1st sec., consul, Bangkok, Siam, 1948-51, Tokyo, Japan, 1951-53; assigned Bur. UN Affairs, Dept. of State, 1953-57, spl. asst., 1956-57; counsellor Am. embassy, Tokyo, consul gen., Okinawa, 1957-59; dir. Office Eastern and So. African Affairs, Dept. of State, 1959-62; Am. Ambassador to Uganda, 1963-66; assigned to Dept. of State, Washington, 1966-69, coordinator nat. interdepartmental seminar, 1966-69; Diplomat in residence U. N.C., Chapel Hill, 1966-67; dir. Fgn. Student Service Council, 1969—. Leader student groups to Europe, Expt. in Internat. Living, Putney, Vt., 1938-40. Trustee Rollins Coll., Winter Park, Fla. Mem. Am. Soc. Internat. Law, Am. Fgn. Service Assn., Asiatic Soc. Tokyo. Clubs: Metropolitan (Washington); Chevy Chase (Md.); City Tavern (Georgetown). Editor Jour. of Siam Soc., 1948-50. Home: 1510 Dumbarton Rock Ct Washington DC 20007 Office: Fgn Student Service Council Washington DC 20009

DEMING, QUENTIN BURRITT, medical educator; b. N.Y.C., July 24, 1919; s. Harold Simpson and Katherine (Burritt) D.; A.B., Dartmouth Coll., 1941; M.D., Columbia, 1943; m. Vida Ginsberg, July 5, 1949; children—Lilith, Maeve. Intern Presbyn. Hosp., N.Y.C., 1944, resident, 1946-47; John and Mary Markle scholar med. sci. Stanford and Columbia, 1950-55; mem. Columbia research service Goldwater Meml. Hosp., 1953-58; mem. faculty Albert Einstein Coll. Medicine, Bronx, N.Y., 1958—, now prof. medicine, dir. program research aging; mem. staff Bronx Municipal Hosp. Center. Served with M.C., USNR, 1944-46. Mem. Assn. Am. Physicians, Am.,

Western Socs. clin. investigation, Harvey Soc. Home: 150 E 89th St New York City NY 10028 Office: Albert Einstein Coll Medicine Bronx NY 10461

DEMING, WILLIAM EDWARDS, math. statistician; b. Sioux City, Ia., Oct. 14, 1900; s. William Albert and Pluma Irene (Edwards) D.; B.S., U. Wyo., 1921, LL.D., (hon.), 1958; M.S., U. Colo., 1924; Ph.D., Yale, 1928; student U. London, 1936; m. Agnes Bell, June 14, 1922; m. 2d, Lola E. Shupe, Apr. 2, 1932; children—Dorothy, Diana, Linda. Instr. elec. engring., U. of Wyo., 1921-22; instr. physics, Colo. Sch. of Mines, 1922- 23, asst. prof., 1923-24; asst. prof., U. of Colo., 1924-25; instr. Yale, 1925-27; physicist U.S. Dept. of Agr., 1927-39; math. adviser Bur. of Census 1939—; adviser in sampling Bur. of Budget, 1942-53; spl. lectr. maths. Nat. Bur. Standards, 1930-40; head dept. maths. and statistics Grad. School, U.S. Dept. of Agr., 1933-53; cons. to sec. of war, 1940—; cons. in statis. techniques Govt. of India, 1947, 1950, 1951-71; cons. to Supreme Command, Tokyo, 1947, 50; cons. also lectr. Union of Japanese Scientists and Engrs., 1950-52, 55-56, 60—; cons. Central Statis. Office, 1960—, Govt. Turkey, 1960-69. Mem. UN subcommn. on statis. sampling, 1947-52; prof. statistics grad. sch. bus. adminstrn. N.Y.U., 1948—. Recipient Shewhart medal, Am. Soc. Quality Control, 1955; 2d Medal Sacred Treasure, Emperor of Japan, 1960; Merit medal Am. Soc. Testing and Materials, 1969. Fellow Inst. Math. Statistics (pres. 1945), Royal Statis. Soc. London (hon.), Am. Statis. Assn., Am. Soc. for Quality Control; hon. life mem. Japan Statis. Assn., Union of Japanese Scientists and Engrs., German Statis. Soc.; mem. Philos. Soc. Wash. (treas. and corr. sec. 1940-43), Biometric Soc., Internat. Statis. Inst., Market Research Council, World Assn. for Pub. Opinion Research, Phi Beta Kappa, Sigma Xi, Phi Kappa Phi, Kappa Sigma. Episcopalian. Club: Cosmos. Author: Theory of Sampling, 1950, others; also papers on statistics and sampling. Editor: Papers by Bayes, 1940, others. Composer of several masses and canticles. Home: 4924 Butterworth Pl Washington DC 20016 Office: 100 Trinity Pl New York City NY 10006

DEMING, WILLIS RILEY, business executive; b. Ada, O., Nov. 28, 1914; s. Cliffe and Okla (Riley) D.; B.A., Ohio State U., 1935, J.D., 1938; m. Dorothy Arline Hill, Aug. 19, 1950 (div. Aug. 1971); children—Susan Elizabeth, Deborah Anne, David Riley; m. 2d, Constance S. Mori, Nov. 6, 1971; Admitted to Ohio bar, 1938, Cal. bar, 1947, D.C. bar, 1957; pvt. practice, Columbus, O., 1938-39; casualty claim examiner Am. Surety Co., N.Y.C., 1939-41; chief bds. and claims rev. br. San Francisco Port Embarkation, 1946-47; mem. firm Treadwell and Laughlin, San Francisco, 1947-54, Brobeck, Phleger & Harrison, San Francisco, 1954-56, Washington, 1956-60; pvt. practice, Washington, 1961-62; v.p., sec. Matson Navigation Co., San Francisco, 1962-71, gen. counsel, 1967-71, now sec. v.p., sec., gen. counsel Alexander Baldwin, Inc., Honolulu, 1968—. Served to lt. col. AUS, 1941-46. Mem. Am., Fed., Hawaii bar assns., State Bar Cal. Republican. Methodist. Clubs: Stock Exchange (San Francisco); Oahu Country (Honolulu); Metropolitan, Army and Navy (Washington). Home: 1526 Lau Kahi St Honolulu HI 96814 Office: 822 Bishop St Honolulu HI 96813

DEMIREL, SULEIMAN, Turkish govt. ofcl.; b. 1924; ed. Istanbul Tech. U. (Turkey). Engr. in U.S., 1949-51, 54-55; with dir.-gen. of elec. studies, Ankara, Turkey, 1950-52; in charge of bldg. various hydro-electric schemes, 1952-54; head Dept. of Dams; dir. gen. water control, 1954-55; Eisenhower fellow for study in U.S., 1955; dir. State Hydraulics Adminstrn., Turkey, 1955-60; tchr. engring. Middle East Tech. U., 1960-64; engring. cons., 1961-65; pres. Justice Party of Turkey, 1964—; dep. prime minister of Turkey, 1965, prime minister, 1965-71. Address: care Justice Party Ankara Turkey*

DEMLER, MARVIN CHRISTIAN, air force officer; b. North Tonawanda, N.Y., Oct. 23, 1909; s. Ernest Frederick and Bertha (Krull) D.; B.S. in Mech. Engring., N.Y.U., 1931, Aero. E., 1934, D.Sc., 1967; grad. Air Corps Flying Tng. Center, 1931-32; M.S., U. Mich., 1941; student Harvard Sch. Bus. Adminstrn., 1951; m. Willena Mayverette Brown, July 15, 1933; children—James Carl, Roger Lee. Commd. 2d lt., Air Corps, U.S. Army, 1931, advanced through grades to maj. gen. USAF, 1958; aero. engr., pilot, 1932—; chief staff 316th Bomb Wing, Okinawa, 1945-46; chief Power Plant Lab., chief aero. div., chief staff and vice comdr. Wright Air Devel. Center, 1949-54; asst., dep. comdr. Air Research and Devel. Command, 1954-58; dir. research and devel. Hdqrs. USAF, 1958-60, dir. systems devel., 1960-61, dir. of advanced tech., 1960-61; comdr. research and tech. div., AFSC, 1962-67; sr. mem. UN Command Component, Mil. Armistice Commn., Korea, 1967; comdr. Chanute (Ill.) Tech. Tng. Center, 1967-69; asst. for arms control Joint Chiefs of Staff, 1969—. Decorated Legion of Merit with 2 clusters, D.S.M., Bronze Star medal Joint Commendation medal. Fellow Am. Inst. Aeros. and Astronautics; mem. Zeta Psi. Lutheran. Home: 30 Westover Av Bolling Air Force Base Washington DC 20332

DEMMLER, RALPH HENRY, lawyer; b. Pitts., Aug. 22, 1904; s. Otto and Maud (Theobald) D.; A.B., Allegheny Coll., Meadville, Pa., 1925, LL.D., 1965; LL.B., U. Pitts., 1928; m. Catherine Hollinger, Oct. 5, 1929; 1 son, John Henry. Admitted to Pa. bar, 1928, Pa. and U.S. cts.; faculty fellow Law Sch., U Pitts., 1928-30; practiced law in Pitts., 1928-53; partner firm Reed, Smith, Shaw & McClay, 1948-53, 55—; chairman U.S. SEC, 1953-55; dir. Mesta Machine Co., Duquesne Light Co., Hammermill Paper Co. Mem. Sch. Bd. of Ross Twp., 1933-45, Allegheny County, Pa., 1938-45. Trustee Allegheny College, 1957—, chmn. bd., 1968—. Fellow Am. Bar Found.; mem. Am., Pa., Allegheny County bar assns., Am. Law Inst., Order of Coif, Phi Beta Kappa, Delta Theta Phi, Delta Sigma Rho, Phi Gamma Delta. Presbyn. Mason. Clubs: Duquesne (dir.), Rolling Rock, University (Pitts.); Metropolitan (Washington). Home: Washington Plaza 1420 Centre Av Pittsburgh PA 15219 Office: Union Trust Bldg Pittsburgh PA 15219

DE MONTEBELLO, GUY-PHILIPPE LANNES, museum dir.; b. Paris, France, May 16, 1936; s. Roger L. and Germaine (de Croisset) de M.; came to U.S., 1951, naturalized, 1955; B.A. magna cum laude, Harvard, 1961; postgrad., N.Y.U. Inst. Fine Arts, 1961-63; m. Edith Bradford Myles, June 24, 1961; children—Marc, Laure, Charles. Asso. curator European paintings Met. Mus. Art, N.Y.C., 1963-69; dir. Mus. Fine Arts, Houston, 1969—. Mem. adv. bd. trustees Alley Theater, Houston. Served to 2d lt. AUS, 1956-58. Woodrow Wilson fellow, 1961-62. Mem. Coll. Art Assn., Am. Assn. Mus., Am. Assn. Mus. Dirs., Houston C. of C. (cultural affairs com.). Author: Peter Paul Rubens, 1969; contbr. to mus. bulls., various exhbn. catalogs. Home: 3440 Wickersham Houston TX 77027 Office: PO Box 6826 Houston TX 77005

DEMOREST, JEAN-JACQUES, educator; b. Lille, France, Oct. 31, 1920; s. Don Louis and Louise (Dury) D.; B.A., Ohio State U., 1940. M.A., 1940; Licence es lettres, Sorbonne, 1946; Ph.D., Princeton, 1949; m. Karin E. Rosenthal, June 6, 1964. Instr. Duke U., 1948, asst. prof., 1950-53, assoc. prof., 1953-56; asso. prof. Cornell, 1956, prof., chmn. dept. romance lit., 1957-68; vis. prof. Harvard, 1967-68, prof. Romance langs., 1968—. Mem. cabinet French minister of nat. edn., 1964. Served as officer Free French Forces, 1941-47. Decorated Officer Legion of Honor, Médaille de la Résistance, Croix de Guerre (France), Fulbright research scholar, Paris, 1951-52; Guggenheim fellow, 1960; Am. Council Learned Socs. fellow, Paris, 1963-64. Mem. Association des Francais Libres, Modern Lang. Assn. Am., Am. Assn. Tchrs. French. Author: Dans Pascal, 1953; Les Passionnés ont vécu, 1956; Pascal Ecrivain, 1957. Translator: The French and The Republic (by Charles Moraze), 1958. Editor: Studies in XVIIth Century French Literature. Address: Harvard U Dept Romance Langs Cambridge MA 02138

DEMOREST, WILLIAM JENNINGS, real estate exec.; b. N.Y.C., Apr. 18, 1890; s. Henry C. and Annie (Lawrie) D.; student Trinity Sch.; M.E., Columbia, 1913; Dr. Humanities, Piedmont Coll., 1961; m. Wealthy Albro Lewis, June 29, 1918; children—Dilys (Mrs. Samuel F. Peirce), William Jennings, Annie Lawrie (Mrs. Spencer M. Hurtt), Carolyn A. (Mrs. T.H. Tenney, Jr.). With Whitney Co., 1914; sec., v.p. Cushman & Wakefield, Inc., 1919-30; v.p. Wm. A. White & Sons, N.Y.C., 1939-43, pres., 1943-63, vice chmn., chmn. exec. com., 1964—; v.p., dir. Coliseum Exhbn. Corp., 1955—; dir., mem. finance com. Home Life Ins. Co.; trustee, mem. mortgage com. Greenwich Savs. Bank of N.Y. Past gov., sec., v.p. Real Estate Bd. of N.Y., pres., 1935-36; dir. Citizens Housing and Planning Council. Realty Adv. Bd. on Labor Relations, 1934-37, Citizens Budget Com., 1935; vice chmn. adv. com. World's Fair, 1939; gen. chmn. Met. Fair Rent Com., 1945-48; chmn. bldg. com. Interch. Center, 1955-59; mem. finance com. Com. Econ. Devel., 1962. Chmn. Community Chest drive, Rye, N.Y., 1937. Mem. zoning bd. appeals, Rye, 1944-56; past mem. Mayor's Com. for Removal Elevated Structures, N.Y.C.; mem. finance com. Bd. Nat. Missions, United Presbyn. Ch. U.S., 1933-55; past gov. 42d Street Property Owners Assn. Bd. mgrs. Jerry McAuley Cremorne Mission; trustee Columbia U. Club Found.; Univ. Devel. Com., Columbia. Served to capt. U.S. Army, World War I. Mem. Inst. Real Estate Appraisers, Soc. Older Grads. Columbia U. (pres.), Laymen's Movement for a Christian World (dir.), C. of C. State N.Y., Huguenot Soc., Pilgrims U.S., St. Andrews Soc., Psi Upsilon. Presbyn. (elder; pres. bd. trustees). Clubs: University, Columbia University (governor) (N.Y.C.); Apawamis; Misquamicut (Watch Hill, R.I.). Home: Upper Dogwood Lane Rye, NY 10580. Office: 51 E 42d St New York City NY 10017

DEMOS, PETER THEODORE, prof. physics, dir. Lab. Nuclear Sci., Mass. Inst. Tech. Address: Cambridge, MA 02139.*

DEMOSS, RALPH DEAN, microbiologist, educator; b. Danville, Ill., Dec. 29, 1922; s. Guy and Ruby (Walker) DeM.; A.B., Ind. U., 1948, Ph.D., 1951; student Clemson Coll., 1943, St. Louis U., 1943-44; m. Patricia H. Day, June 2, 1946; children—Susan L., G. Newton, Guy R., Kurt S. AEC postdoctoral fellow Brookhaven Nat. Lab., 1951-52; asst. prof. McCollum-Pratt Inst., Johns Hopkins, 1952-56; asso. prof. microbiology U. Ill., Urbana, 1956-59, prof. microbiology, 1959—, head dept. microbiology, 1971—; mem. microbiology tng. com. NIH, 1967-69, chmn., 1969-71. Served with AUS, 1942-46; ETO. Mem. Am. Soc. Microbiology, Am. Acad. Microbiology, Am. Soc. Biol. Chemists, A.A.A.S., Soc. Gen. Microbiology, Sigma Xi. Research and publs. in field of microbial biochemistry and physiology. Editor: Jour. of Bacteriology, 1965-70. Home: 45 Golf Dr Mahomet IL 61853 Office: Dept of Microbiology U Ill Urbana IL 61801

DE MOTT, BENJAMIN HAILE, educator, author; b. Rockville Centre, N.Y., June 2, 1924; s. D. Gerard and Janet (Sanders) DeM.; B.A., George Washington U., 1949; Ph.D., Harvard, 1953; M.A., Amherst Coll., 1960; D.Litt., Franklin and Marshall Coll., 1970; m. Margaret Jane Craig, June 22, 1946; children—Joel, Thomas, Benjamin, Megan. Teaching fellow Harvard, 1950; instr., prof. English Amherst (Mass.) Coll., 1951—; columnist Harper's, Am. Scholar, 1962-64; vis. prof. Mass. Inst. Tech., 1962; Fulbright prof. Birmingham (Eng.) U., 1965; vis. prof. Utah U., 1966, Yale University, 1968-70; writer Nat. Ednl. TV, 1964, also cons.; mem. Columbia Seminar Am. Civilization; cons. Office Edn., Carnegie Commn. Ednl. TV; Soc. Mag. Writers, Inst. for Services to Edn., Newton, Mass., N.Y. State Arts Council, Nat. Endowment for Arts, Am. Council Learned Socs., Danforth, Rockefeller founds.; exec. com. Tchrs. and Writers Collaborative, N.Y.C. Bd. acad. advisers Marlboro Coll.; ednl. adv. com. Guggenheim Found. Recipient Harbison award for distinguished teaching Danforth Found., 1969; Guggenheim fellow, 1964, 69. Mem. PEN, Modern Lang. Assn., Phi Beta Kappa. Club: Century. Author: (novels) The Body's Cage, 1959; A Married Man, 1968; (essays) Hells & Benefits, 1962. You Don't Say, 1966; Supergrow, 1969; Surviving the Seventies, 1971. Mem. bd. editors: College English, 1964-70. Contbr. articles profl. jours. Home: 22 Hitchcock Rd Amherst MA 01002

DEMOYER, ROBERT, engring. educator; b. Tamagua, Pa., Jan. 30, 1907; s. John William and Flora Estelle (Baker) DeM.; C.E., Lehigh U., 1929; M.S. in Civil Engring., Swarthmore Coll., 1938; m. Ruth Mildred Ellicott, Dec. 20, 1935; 1 son, Robert. Constrn. insp. Reading R.R. Co., 1929-33; draftsman Pa. Dept. Hwys., 1933-34; from asst. prof. to prof. civil engring. Pa. Mil. Coll., 1935-42; mem., faculty Lafayette Coll., 1942—, prof. civil engring., 1953—, head dept., 1953—, Simon Cameron Long prof., 1953—. Registered profl. engr., Pa. Fellow Am. Soc. C.E.; mem. Am. Soc. Engring. Edn., Am. Concrete Inst., Am. Soc. Photogrammetry, Am. Rd. Builders Assn., Tau Beta Pi. Republican. Presbyn. Clubs: Lafayette Faculty; Country of Northampton County (Pa.). Home: 2419 Woodridge Terrace Easton PA 18042

DEMPESY, COLBY WILSON, educator; b. Chgo., Mar. 12, 1931; B.A., Oberlin Coll., 1952; M.A., Rice Inst., 1955, Ph.D. in Physics (Shell Oil Co. fellow), 1957; married; 4 children. Instr. physics Amherst Coll., 1957-58, asst. prof., 1958-63, asso. prof., 1963-69, prof., 1969—. Mem. Am. Phys. Soc., Am. Assn. Physics Tchrs. Office: Physics Dept Amherst Coll Amherst MA 01002*

DEMPEWOLFF, RICHARD FREDERIC, editor, author; b. N.Y.C., Oct. 30, 1914; s. Augustus Frederick and Katherine (Rübsamen) D.; B.S., Middlebury Coll., 1936; m. Rita Mary Fitzpatrick, Oct. 16, 1939; 1 dau., Judith Ann. Researcher, writer Lit. Digest, 1936-38; mng. editor True, 1938-40; press and edn. editor Newsweek, 1940-42; article editor Pic, 1946-48; Eastern editor Popular Mechanics, 1949-62, exec. editor, 1962-67; editor Sci. Digest, 1967—; fgn. corr., Venezuela, 1950, Japan, 1951; mem. Deepfreeze I, Byrd Expdn. to Antarctica, 1955-56, Deepfreeze VI Expdn. to Antarctica, 1960-61. Served to lt. (j.g.) USNR, 1942-46. Mem. Nat. Assn. Sci. Writers, Am. Soc. Mag. Editors, Sigma Delta Chi, Kappa Delta Rho. Clubs: Overseas Press (N.Y.C.); National Press (Washington). Author: Famous Old New England Murders, 1942; Animal Reveille, 1943; Precut House, 1955; Adventure with Nature Craft, 1959. Home: 7 Bedford Rd S Chappaqua NY 10514 Office: 224 W 57th St New York City NY 10019

DEMPSEY, EDWARD WHEELER, anatomist; b. Buxton, Ia., May 15, 1911; s. Aid Sell and Julia (Wheeler) D.; A.B., Marietta Coll., 1932, D.Sc., 1954; Sc.M., Brown U., 1934, Ph.D., 1937; A.M., Harvard, 1946; m. Betsey Mills Beach, June 13, 1936; children—Charles Gates, Julia Wheeler, Richard Clinton. Fellow NRC, NRC, Harvard Med. Sch., 1937-38, instr. physiology, 1938-41, asso. in anatomy, 1941-42, asst. prof., 1942-46, asso. prof., 1946-50; prof. anatomy and head dept. Washington U., St. Louis, 1950- 66, dean sch. medicine, 1958-64; prof. anatomy, chmn. dept. Coll. Phys. and Surg., Columbia, 1966—; spl. asst. sec. Dept. Health, Edn., Welfare, 1964-65; mem. Pres.' Commn. Heart Disease, Cancer, Stroke, 1964; mem. Nat. Adv. Health Council, 1961-64, Nat. Adv. Council Gen. Med. Scis., 1966-70. Mem. Am. Assn. Anatomists, Am. Physiol. Soc., Assn. for Study of Internal Secretions, Soc. Exptl. Biology and Medicine, Am. Acad. of Arts and Scis., Biol. Stain Commn., Histochem. Soc. Contbr. articles med. and biol. jours. Asso. editor Endocrinology Mag., 1943-44, mng. editor, 1945-52. Home: 75 East End Av New York City, NY 10028. Office: 630 W 168th St New York City NY 10032

DEMPSEY, ERNEST COOK, lawyer; b. Cleve., 1890; A.B., Kenyon Coll., 1911, LL.D., 1945; B.A., Yale, 1912; LL.B., Harvard, 1916. Admitted to Ohio bar, 1917; mem. firm Squire, Sanders and Dempsey, Cleve. Office: 1800 Union Commerce Bldg Cleveland OH 44115*

DEMPSEY, FRANK JOSEPH, librarian; b. San Francisco, Nov. 8, 1925; s. Frank Joseph and Ruth M. (McPhedran) D.; B.A., U. Cal. at Berkeley, 1950, B.L.S., 1953. Reference librarian Newark Pub. Library, 1953-54; tng. officer, head librarian Oakland (Cal.) Naval Supply Center, 1954-58; asst. city librarian Berkeley (Cal.) Pub. Library, 1958-62, city librarian, 1962—; instr. reading improvement Oakland City Coll., 1957-58, U. Cal. at Berkeley Extension, 1966-67. Mem. Berkeley Workreation Council. Bd. dirs. Friends of Cal. Libraries, Concert Theater, Inc., 1964-65, v.p. Berkeley chpt. A.R.C., 1971-72. Served with USNR, 1950-52. Recipient Superior Accomplishment award U.S. Naval Supply Center, 1956. Mem. A.L.A. (chmn. friends of libraries com.), Cal. Library Assn. (chmn. pub. relations com.), Pub. Library Execs. Central Cal. (pres. 1964-65), East Bay Library Council (chmn. 1965-66), Urban League. Democrat. Author: (with Craig McMicken) A Review of Library Administration, 1961. Contbr. numerous articles and book revs. profl. jours., Ency. Americana. Home: 3456 16th St San Francisco CA 94114 Office: 2090 Kittredge St Berkeley CA 94701

DEMPSEY, JACK, owner Jack Dempsey Restaurant, N.Y.C.; former world's heavyweight boxing champion; mem. staff Ill. Comml. Men's Assn., Chgo., 1972—. Address: 1619 Broadway New York City NY 10019* also c/o Ill Comml Men's Assn 180 N Michigan Av Chicago IL 60601

DEMPSEY, JAMES HOWARD, Jr., lawyer; b. Cleve., Oct. 18, 1916; s. James Howard and Ada (Hunt) D.; B.A., Yale, 1938, LL.B., 1941; m. Julia C. Bolton, Aug. 2, 1942; children—Julia B. (Mrs. Howard E. Cox, Jr.), Melissa Hunt. Admitted to Ohio bar, 1941; practiced in Cleve. 1945—; gen. partner Squire, Sanders & Dempsey, Cleve., 1958—; dir. Maynard H. Murch Co., Cleve., 1963—. Mayor, Hunting Valley Village, 1952-58. Trustee Cleve. Mus. Art, U. Hosps., Home for Aged Women, Lake View Cemetery Assn., Episcopal Diocese Ohio. Served to lt. comdr., USNR, 1941-45. Mem. Am., Ohio, Cleve. bar assns. Clubs: Yale (N.Y.C.); Union, Tavern, Kirtland, Chagrin Valley Hunt. (Cleve.). Home: River Rd Chagrin Falls OH 44022 Office: Union Commerce Bldg Cleveland OH 44115

DEMPSEY, JAMES RAYMON, aero. engr.; b. Red Bay, Ala., Oct. 4, 1921; s. Newman W. and Maude (Berry) D.; student U. Ala., 1937-39; B.S., U.S. Mil. Acad., 1943; M.S., U. Mich., 1947, D.Engring. (hon.), 1964; m. Dolores Barnes, Jan. 19, 1934; children—Susan, David Barnes, Anne. Commd. 2d lt. U.S. Army, 1943, advanced through grades to lt. col. USAF, 1951; with photo reconnaissance squadron, Eng., France, World War II, squadron comdr., 1945; guided missiles project officer, then chief guided missile projects Research and Devel. Directorate, Air Force Hdqrs., 1948- 49; exec. officer to Dep. Chief Staff for Devel., 1950-51; chief project sect. Air Force Missile Test Center, Patrick AFB, Fla., then operations officer missile test range, 1951-53, resigned 1953; asst. to v.p. planning Convair div. Gen. Dynamics Corp., 1953-54, dir. Atlas program, 1954-57, mgr. Convair-Astronautics div., 1957-58, v.p. Convair div., 1958-61, sr. v.p. Gen. Dynamics Corp., pres. Gen. Dynamics Astronautics, 1961-65, pres., Gen. Dynamics Convair, 1965-66; v.p. missiles, space and electronics group Avco Corp., 1966-68, v.p., group exec. govt. products group, 1968—. Decorated Air Medal with clusters, D.F.C. (U.S.); Croix de Guerre (France). Fellow Am. Inst. Aeros. and Astronautics, Am. Astronaut. Soc.; mem. Air Force Assn. (dir. 1958-59), NASA (spl. com. on space tech.), Soc. Advancement Mgmt. Clubs: Essex County; Burning Tree. Rotarian. Home: Hickory Hill Road Manchester MA 01944 Office: 201 Lowell St Wilmington MA 01887

DEMPSEY, JOHN, cons., former gov. Conn.; b. Cahir, Ireland, Jan. 3, 1915; s. Edward P. and Ellen (Luby) D.; came to U.S., 1925, naturalized, 1931; student Providence Coll., 1934-36; LL.D., St. Anselm's Coll., Manchester, N.H., 1962, Providence Coll., 1963, U. Hartford, 1963, Fairfield U., 1966, U. Bridgeport, Trinity Coll., 1967; L.H.D., Am. Internat. Coll., 1966, St. Joseph Coll., 1970; m. Mary M. Frey, Nov. 11, 1918; children—Edward, Margaret (Mrs. Donald Seligman), John, Kevin. Mem. Putnam (Conn.) City Council, 1936-42, alderman-at-large, 1946-48; mgr. Putnam Water Dept., 1940-46; field rep. Congresswoman Mrs. Chase G. Woodhouse, 1945-50; mayor of Putnam 1948-61; mem. Conn. Gen. Assembly, 1949-55, asst. minority leader Ho. of Reps., 1951, minority leader, 1953; exec. aide to Gov. Ribicoff, 1955-58; lt. gov. Conn., 1958-61; gov. of Conn., 1961-71; cons. in environmental programs So. New Eng. Telephone Co., 1971—. Chmn., New England Governors' Conf., 1963-65. Past mem. of Conn. Devel. Commn. Past Democratic town chmn., Putnam. Active fund raising Jimmy Fund Hosp., A.R.C., Little League Baseball. Decorated comdr. Order Merit (Rep. of Korea); comdr. Order of Merit (Government of Italy); recipient Golden Eagle award Fraternal Order Eagles, 1959; Americanism award Am. Legion, 1956; Veritas award for dist. pub. service Providence Coll. Alumni Assn., 1959; Dist. Service award as mayor of Putnam, Vets. Fgn. Wars, 1953, Meritorious award as mayor of Putnam, 1954-59, Dist. Service award, 1949, 59; Hwy. Safety award All State Ins. Co., 1958; honored for outstanding leadership to people and community during floods, 1955; named No. 1 Legislator, Conn. Ho. of Reps., 1953; Americanism award Conn. Valley council B'nai B'rith, 1964; Adult Americanism award D.A.R., 1964; named National St. Jude Man of the Year, 1966; John F. Kennedy Meml. award, 1970; others. Mem. Putnam C. of C. (past dir.), Foresters of Am. Catholic. K.C. (4), Elk, Rotarian (hon.). Club: Putnam Irish-American. Home: 53 Neptune Dr Mumford Cove Groton CT 06340 Office: So New Eng Telephone Co New London CT

DEMPSEY, JOHN CORNELIUS, mfg. co. exec.; b. Cleve., July 14, 1914; s. John Henry and Anna Gertrude (Donavon) D.; student John Carroll U., 1932-35; children—Virginia Agnes (Mrs. William J. McNamara), Patricia Marie, Mary Therese, Maureen Anne, Judith Marie, Michael Henry. With U.S. Steel Corp., Cleve., 1932-40; auditor Ernst & Ernst, Cleve., 1940-45; asst. comptroller Werner G. Smith, Cleve., 1945; sec. Greif Bros. Corp., Delaware, O., 1946—, chmn. bd., chief exec. officer, 1947—. Trustee Central Ohio council Boy Scouts Am.; trustee St. Ann Maternity Hosp., Cleve. City Hosp., chmn. bd. trustees, 1949. Home: East Olentangy River Rd Route 4 Delaware OH 43015 Office: 621 Pennsylvania Av Delaware OH 43015

DEMPSEY, JOSEPH E., investment exec.; b. Hudson Heights, N.J., Apr. 27, 1902; s. Joseph A. and Cora (Schoonmaker) D.; B.S., Northwestern U.; m. Ethel Armstrong, June 23, 1927; children—Joseph, Carol, Robert. With Harris Trust & Savs. Bank. Chicago, 1924-29, Foreman State Corp., 1929-32; chmn. Dempsey & Co.; dir. Ohio Gas Co., Admiral Corp. Clubs: Union League, Attic, Skokie Country, Bond (Chgo.). Home: 756 Valley Rd Glencoe IL 60022 Office: 135 S LaSalle St Chicago IL 60603

DEMPSEY, MICHAEL RYAN, aux. bishop; b. Chgo., Sept. 10, 1918; s. Edward A. and Mary C. (Ryan) D.; M.A., St. Mary Lake Sem., Mundelein, Ill., 1942, S.T.L., 1943. Ordained priest Roman Catholic Ch., 1943; asso. pastor St. Mary Lake Ch., Chgo., 1944-62; tchr. theology Mundelein Coll., Chgo., 1946-58; asso. pastor St. Francis de Paula Ch., Chgo., 1962-64; pastor Our Lady of Lourdes Ch., Chgo., 1965—; vicar del. Archdiocese Chgo., 1966—, aux. bushop, 1968—, coordinator inner city apostolate, 1967—. Nat. dir. Campaign for Human Devel., 1970—. Home: 1444 S Keeler Av Chicago, IL 60623. Office: 4 N Cicero Av Chicago IL 60644

DEMPSEY, THOMAS L., business exec.; b. Cleve., 1926; B.S. in Commerce, Cleve. State U., B. Elec. Engring., 1950; married. Various positions in solar engring. and welding fields, 1950-57; v.p. Indsl. Pub. Co., Cleve., 1957-64; v.p. indsl. pub. Pittway Corp., Northbrook, Ill., 1964-68, exec. v.p. Indsl. div., 1968-69, pres. Indsl. Pub. div., 1969-70, corporate v.p., 1970—. Office: Pittway Corp 601 Skokie Blvd Northbrook IL 60062*

DEMPSEY, WILLIAM JAMES, lawyer; b. Brooklyn, N.Y., February 22, 1906; s. John Joseph and Kathryn Theresa (McCarthy) D.; B.S., Coll. of Arts and Scis. Georgetown U., 1927, M.A., Graduate Sch., same, 1929, LL.B., Law Sch., same, 1931; m. Mildred Christine Garrett, Jan. 17, 1931; children—William James, Jr. (dec.), John Joseph, II, Mary Catherine, Joanne (now Mrs. William J. Walsh). Teacher mathematics and physics, Georgetown Coll., 1927-29, asst. prof. math., 1929-31; admitted to bar, D.C., 1930, N.Y. State, 1932, Supreme Ct. U.S., 1935; practiced law, New York, 1931-32; atty., P.W.A., 1933-34, counsel, 1934-37; asst. gen. counsel, Fed. Power Commn., 1937; spl. counsel, Fed. Communications Commn., 1937-38, gen. counsel, 1938-May 1940; pvt. practice law, Washington, D.C., since May 1940; mem. Dempsey & Koplovitz prof. fed. communications law. grad. sch. law dept. Georgetown U., 1954-56. Mem. Am., D.C., Fed. Communications, Fed. bar assns. Clubs: University, Columbia Country (Washington), Burning Tree Golf. Roman Catholic. Democrat. Home: 4935 Linnean Av NW Washington DC 20008 (summer) Santa Fe NM 87501 Office: 821 Fifteenth St NW Washington DC 20005

DEMPSTER, EVERETT ROSS, educator, research geneticist; b. San Francisco, Mar. 17, 1903; s. Milen Ross and Amy (Cotrel) D.; B.S., U. Cal. at Berkeley, 1927, Ph.D., 1941; m. Lauramay Tinsley, Oct. 8, 1927; children—Iris Alberta (Mrs. John K. Green), Philip Tinsley. Engr., Magnavox Co., Oakland, Cal., Chgo., Ft. Wayne, Ind., 1927-31; with Grigsby Grunow Co., Chgo., 1931; chief engr. Magnavox (Great Britain), Ltd., London, 1932-33; teaching asst., instr., asst. prof., asso. prof., prof. genetics dept. U. Cal. at Berkeley, 1935- -, chmn. dept., 1963-70, now prof. emeritus; research engr. NACA, 1942-45; asso. statistician NDRC, 1945; cons. dept. exptl. statistics N.C. State Coll., 1954; cons. AEC, 1967. Mem. A.A.A.S., Genetics Soc. Am., Am. Soc. Human Genetics, Am. Soc. Naturalists. Home: 15 El Toyonal St Orinda CA 94563 Office: Genetics Dept U Cal Berkeley CA 94720

DEMPSTER, RICHARD VREELAND, power tool co. exec.; b. E. Rutherford, N.J., May 28, 1928; s. Frank Vreeland and Hazel (Miller) D.; B.B.A. Pace Coll., 1951; A.M.P. Harvard Bus. Sch., 1969; m. Jean Van Osten, Apr. 28, 1951; children-Denise, Diana, Donna. With The Black & Decker Mfg. Co., Towson, Md., 1964—, v.p. indsl. and constrn. divs. 1964-68, v.p. marketing, 1968-70, v.p. operations 1970—. Served with AUS, 1945-47. Mem. Power Tool Inst., (pres. 1969—), Am. Supply and Machinery Mfr.'s Assn. (bd. dirs. 1966- -). Clubs: N.Y. Athletic; Baltimore Country; Eagles Nest Country (Phoenix, Md.); Hunt Valley Country (Cockeysville, Md.). Home: 6902 Charles Ridge Rd Ruxton MD 21204 Office: Black & Decker Mfg Co Towson MD 21204

DEMSKE, JAMES MICHAEL, coll. pres.; b. Buffalo, Apr. 10, 1922; s. Albert J. and Augusta (Nagel) D.; A.B., Canisius Coll., Buffalo, 1947; Ph.L., Woodstock (Md.) Coll., 1951; S.T.L., U. Innsbruck (Austria), 1958; Ph.D., U. Freiburg (West Germany), 1962. Fingerprint technician FBI, 1942-43; joined Soc. of Jesus, 1947, ordained priest Roman Cath. Ch., 1957; instr. philosophy St. Peter's Coll., Jersey City, 1951-54; prof. theology, dir. students Bellarmine Coll., Plattsburgh, N.Y., 1963-66; pres. Canisius Coll., 1966- -. Bd. dirs. Greater Buffalo Devel. Found.; trustee Buffalo United Fund, Buffalo Studio Arena Theatre, Buffalo Philharmonic. Served to capt. AUS, 1943-46. Mem. Buffalo Area C. of C. (dir.), Buffalo and Erie County Hist. Soc., Buffalo Fine Arts Acad., Buffalo Soc. Natural Scis. Author: Introductory Metaphysics, 1955; Encounters with Silence, 1960; Sein, Mensch Und Tod, 1963; Being, Man and Death, 1970. Home: 2001 Main St Buffalo, NY 14208.

DEMUS, JOERG, pianist; b. St. Poelten, Austria, Dec. 2, 1928; s. Dr. Otto and Erika (Budik) D.; ed. high sch. and coll., Vienna; student Vienna State Acad. for Piano, also with Edwin Fischer, Walter Gieseking. Piano debut, Vienna Musikverein, 1943; recital tours, Italy, 1948, 49, South Am., 1951, 54; 1st Am. debut, 1955, annual tours; recordings Westminster, Decca Records, Deutsche Grammophon. Recipient Busoni award, Bolzano, 1956; Harriet Cohen Bach medal, London, 1958. Home: Doeblinger Hauptstrasse 77a Vienna 19 Austria Office: care Joerg Demus Doeblinger Hauptstrasse 77A A 1190 Vienna Austria

DEMUTH, LAURENCE WHEELER, Jr., lawyer, utilities exec.; b. Boulder, Colo., Nov. 22, 1928; s. Laurence Wheeler and Eugenia (Roach) DeM.; A.B., U. Colo., 1951, LL.B., 1953; m. Margaret Evelyn Glasebrook, Jan. 17, 1956; children—Debra Lynn, Laurence Wheeler III, Brant Hill. Admitted to Colo. bar, 1953, since practiced in Denver; asso. firm Akolt, Shepherd & Dick, 1953-60, partner, 1961-67; v.p., gen. counsel Mountain States Tel. & Tel. Co., Denver, 1968—. Precinct committeeman Jefferson County (Colo.) Republican Party, 1956-67, dist. capt., 1966-70. Trustee Temple Hoyne Buell Found., Arthur Cerasa Found. Served with USAF, 1954-56. Mem. Am., Colo., Denver bar assns., Order of Coif, Phi Beta Kappa, Phi Delta Phi, Sigma Alpha Epsilon, Kappa Kappa Psi, Pi Gamma Mu. Presbyn. Home: 970 Front Range Rd Littleton CO 80120 Office: Mountain States Tel & Tel Co 931 14th St Denver CO 80202

DEMUTH, RICHARD HOLZMAN, internat. ofcl.; b. N.Y.C., Sept. 11, 1910; s. Leopold and Dora (Holzman) D.; A.B., Princeton, 1931; LL.B., Harvard, 1934; m. Eunice Burdick, June 14, 1947; 1 dau., Nancy Chase. Admitted to N.Y. bar, 1934; law clk. to Circuit Judge Julian W. Mack, 1934-35; asso. Simpson Thacher & Bartlett, 1935-39; spl. asst. to U.S. atty. gen. Office Solicitor Gen., 1939-42; sr. officer Internat. Bank Reconstrn. and Devel., 1946—, now dir. devel. services dept., mem. pres.'s council. Mem. adv. com. Woodrow Wilson Sch. Pub. and Internat. Affairs, Princeton, 1957-66; governing bd. Internat. Inst. Ednl. Planning. Mem. budget com. Health and Welfare Council, Nat. Capital Area, 1960-64. Served from 2d lt. to lt. col., AUS, 1942-46. Decorated Legion of Merit; recipient Fay diploma Harvard Law Sch. Mem. Assn. Bar City N.Y., Soc. Internat. Devel. Clubs: Metropolitan (Washington); Princeton (N.Y.C.). Home: 5404 Bradley Blvd Bethesda, MD 20014. Office: 1818 H St NW Washington DC 20433

DENAVASQUES, EMILIO, Spanish diplomat; b. Madrid, Spain, Mar. 23, 1904; s. Emilio and Angela (Ruiz de Velasco) deN.; student Instituto Catolico de Artes e Industrias, 1912-19, U. Madrid, 1919-23; LL.D., Ecole Libre des Scis. Politiques, Paris, 1923; m. Maria Elisa Bertran, Aug. 1, 1935; childrenPilar (Mrs. Juan Antonio Ansaldo y Bernaldo de Quiros), Maria Elisa (Mrs. Javier Aguirre), Mercedes (Mrs. Rafael Aguire), Joaquin, Teresa, Maria Pia. Sec. consulates, Marseilles and Tangier, legation, Paraguay, embassy, Paris, 1929-33; sec. Spanish Commn. Soc. Nations, 1933-34; dir. gen. Commercio y Politica Arancelaria, 1938; first sec. Spanish embassy, Lisbon, 1940-42; Jefe del Servicio de Tratados de Comercio Ministry Fgn. Affairs, 1943, dir. gen. Politica Economica, 1944- 47; subsecretario de Economia Exterior y Comercio, 1947; minister, The Hague, 1948-50; ambassador, Buenos Aires, 1950; under-secretary fgn. affairs de Asuntos Exteriores, 1951-55; inspector gen. de Servicios Ministry Fgn. Affairs, 1956—; ambassador, Rome, 1956-; dir. Diplomatic Sch., 1959—. Pres. Iberia Airlines Spain, also Calatrava; dir. Ensidesa, Cros. Decorated Cruz de Guerra, Red Crosses Mil. Merit, Gran Cruz de Isabel la Catolica, Cristo de Portugal, Merito de la Republica Argentina, del Merito del Peru, Gran Cruz del Nilo de Egipto, del Cedro del Libano, Comendador de Numero de Carlos III. Mem. Royal Acad. Jurisprudence. Home: 31 Avenida de Miraflores Madrid-20, Spain.

DENBEAUX, FRED, educator, writer; b. St. Louis, May 8, 1914; s. Ralph and Margaret (Langanke) D.; B.A., Elmhurst (Ill.) Coll., 1936; B.D., Union Theol. Sem., N.Y.C., 1939, St.M., 1940; m. Jane van Voorst, June 9, 1937; children—Mark, Andrea. Social worker Bklyn. Children's Aid Soc., 1937-39; ordained to ministry United Presbyn. Ch. USA., 1940; pastor in Rebersburg, Pa., 1940-42; tchr. theology Dana Hall Schs., Wellesley, Mass., 1946-50; faculty Wellesley Coll., 1946-, prof. religion, 1958—, chmn. dept., 1955—, chmn. bd. preachers, 1964—; vis. prof. Brown U., 1960-61; vis. lectr. Trinity Coll., 1962-63. Served as chaplain AUS, 1942-46. Author: Understanding the Bible, 1958; The Art of Christian Doubt, 1960; Guide to the Old Testament, 1964; Introduction to New Testament, 1965; Guide to the New Testament, 1965; The Premature Death of Protestantism, 1967; also articles. Home: 9 Lovewell Rd Wellesley MA 02181

DENBY, CHARLES, lawyer; b. Tientsin, China, Jan. 21, 1901 (parents Am. citizens); s. Charles and Martha (Orr) D.; A.B., Princeton, 1922; LL.B., Harvard, 1925; m. Rosamond Reed, Feb. 26, 1927; children—Peter, Reed. Admitted to Pa. bar, 1927; practice in Phila., 1927-36, Pitts., 1936—; partner firm Reed, Smith, Shaw & McClay, 1936—. Dir. Old Republic Ins. Co. Asst. adminstr. Lend-Lease Adminstrn., World War II. Chmn. Pitts. Symphony Soc., 1967—. Clubs: Duquesne (Pitts.); Allegheny Country (Sewickley); Century Assn. (N.Y.C.); Metropolitan (Washington). Home: 632 Pine Rd Sewickley, PA 15143. Office: Union Trust Bldg Pittsburgh PA 15219

DENBY, EDWIN ORR, writer; b. Tientsin, China, Feb. 4, 1903 (parents U.S. citizens); s. Charles and Martha (Orr) D.; grad. Hotchkiss Sch., 1918; student Harvard, 1919-22, Schule Hellerau-Laxenburg (Austria), 1925-27. Dancer, State Theatre, Darmstadt, Germany, 1928-29, with Claire Eckstein, Berlin and Munich, Germany, 1930-33, with Marietta von Meyenburg, Switzerland, 1935; dancer, collaborator text N.Y. musical Horse Eats Hat, 1936; choreographer Negro ballet Knickerbocker Holiday, 1938; dance critic Modern Music, 1936-42, N.Y. Herald Tribune, 1942-45; contbr. magazines in field, 1946—. Guggenheim fellow, 1948; recipent award Poets' Found., 1965, Dance mag., 1966. Mem. P.E.N. Author: (dance criticism) Looking at the Dance, 1949; (poems) In Public, In Private, 1948, Mediterranean Cities, 1956; (dance and art) Dancers, Buildings and People in the Streets, 1965; (librettos) Die Neue Galathee, 1928; The Second Hurricane, 1937. Address: 145 W 21st St New York City, NY 10011.

DENBY, JAMES ORR, museum dir.; b. Am. Legation, Peking, China, Aug. 30, 1896; s. Charles and Martha (Orr) D.; A.B., Princeton, 1919; A.M., George Washington U., 1921; m. Phyllis Douglas Cochran, Feb. 19, 1927; children—George Cochran, Douglas. Third sec. Embassy, Tokyo, Japan, 1921-23; 3d sec. Legation, Athens, Greece, 1923-27; 2d sec. Legation, Peiping, China, 1927-30; 1st sec. Legation, Dublin, Irish Free State, 1930-36; consul, Capetown, South Africa, 1936-43; assigned to State Dept., Washington, 1943, 1949-56; counselor Legation, Vienna, Austria, 1946; dir. Mus. of Soc. of Cincinnati, 1954-66. Served in Intelligence Corps, U.S. Army, 1914-18. Decorated Chevalier of the French Legion of Honor. Clubs: Metropolitan (Washington); Quadrangle (Princeton); City (Capetown); Meath Hunt (Dublin). Home: Upperville VA 22176 Office: 2118 Massachusetts Av Washington DC 20008 (winter) 24 Wentworth St Charleston SC 29401

DENDY, MARSHALL COLEMAN, ch. ofcl.; b. Lavonia, Ga., June 4, 1902; s. Samuel Knox and Josey (Wilkes) D.; A.B., Presbyn. College of S.C., 1923; B.D., Columbia Sem., Decatur, Ga., 1926; M.A., U. Tenn., 1944; D.D., King Coll., Bristol, Tenn., 1942; m. Nan McElroy Copeland, June 30, 1926; children—Nancy (Mrs. Dallas M. Ryle, Jr.), Marshall Coleman. Ordained to ministry Presbyn. Ch., 1926; supt. home missions Augusta (Ga.) Presbytery, 1926-28; pastor, Crawfordville, Ga., 1926-28, Newberry, S.C., 1928-31, Gainesville, Ga., 1931-38, Knoxville, Tenn., 1938-42, Orlando, Fla., 1942-52; exec. sec. Bd. Christian Edn., Presbyn. Ch. U.S., 1953-68. Trustee Agnes Scott Coll.; bd. dirs. Presbyn. Center, Atlanta. Moderator Presbyn. Synod of Fla., 1948, Gen. Assembly of Presbyn. Ch. U.S., 1967. Pres. Community Chest, Orlando, 1949. Mem. Fellowship of St. James, Pi Kappa Phi, Phi Kappa Phi. Mason (K.T.), Kiwanian (pres. Gainesville 1937, Orlando 1950). Author: Changing Patterns in Christian Education, 1964; A Study of the Catechism for Families, 1966; also articles, editorials. Address: 1717 Gay Dr Orlando FL 32803

DENECKE, ARNO HARRY, state justice; b. Rock Island, Ill., May 7, 1916; s. Harry and Gertrude (Etzel) D.; A.B., U. Ill., 1937, LL.B., 1939; m. Selma Rockey, Oct. 20, 1945; children—Virginia, David, William, John, Anne. Admitted to Ill. bar, 1939, Ore. bar, 1946; mem. law dept. Montgomery Ward Co., Chgo. and Oakland, Cal., 1939-41; mem. firm Mautz, Souther, Spaulding, Denecke & Kinsey, Portland, Ore., 1947-58; circuit judge State Ore., Portland, 1959-62; asso. justice Supreme Ct. Ore., 1963—. Mem. sch. bd., Portland, 1957- 58. Trustee Reed Coll., Portland, 1958—. Served from pvt. to maj., AUS, 1941-45. Mem. Am. Bar Assn. Episcopalian. Home: 2830 Bolton Terrace S Salem OR 97302 Office: Supreme Court of Oregon Salem OR 97310

DENEEN, JAMES ROBERT, educator; b. Mpls., Mar. 28, 1928; s. James A. and Margaret (Simpson) D.; B.A., St. Meinrad Coll.; M.A., Cath. U. Am.; Ph.D., Ind. U. Ordained priest Roman Cath. Ch.; supt. Cath. schs., Evansville, Ind., 1957-67; chmn. supt. div. Nat. Cath. Ednl. Assn., 1967-69; sr. program dir. Ednl. Testing Service, Princeton, N.J., 1969—; mem. faculty Ind. U., 1966-67, Fordham U., 1968—. Asso. dir. Com. on Edn., 1968-; cons. Ford Found., 1969. Bd. dirs. Community Action Program, Human Relations Commn., Clergy Dialogue, Rehab. Center. Author: New Patterns for Catholic Education, 1968. Contbr. profl. jours. Address: Educational Testing Service Princeton, NJ 08540.

DENEGRE, GEORGE, lawyer; b. New Orleans, Oct. 10, 1923; s. Thomas Bayne and Alma (Baldwin) D.; B.A., Yale, 1943; LL.B., Tulane U., 1948; m. Gayle Stocker, Oct. 4, 1950; children—Stanhope Bayne-Jones, Gayle Stocker, George, John Gayle. Admitted to La. bar, 1948; with firm Chaffe, McCall, Toler & Philips, 1948-49; asso. firm Jones, Walker, Weachter, Poitevent, Carrère & Denègre, New Orleans, 1949-52, partner, 1952—; chmn. exec. com., dir. La. & So. Life Ins. Co.; sec., dir. Canal Barge Co., Inc., Central Gulf S.S. Corp.; dir. Dr. G. H. Tichenor Antiseptic Co., Bank New Orleans & Trust Co.; chmn. bd., dir. Geocom., Inc. Bd. dirs., pres. La. Assn. Mental Health, 1960-61; bd. dirs., sec. Greater New Orleans, Inc.; bd. dirs. Internat. House, 1964, Met. Crime Commn., 1965, Eugenie and Joseph Jones Family Found. Served to lt. USNR, 1943-46. Mem. Am., La., New Orleans, Maritime bar assns. Clubs: Metropolitan (Washington); Racquet and Tennis (N.Y.C.); Boston, Pickwick, Louisiana, Stratford (New Orleans). Home: 1525 Webster St New Orleans, LA 70118. Office: La and So Life Bldg New Orleans LA 70112

DENEUVE, CATHERINE, (de Dorleac, Catherine), actress; b. Paris, Oct. 22, 1943; d. Maurice Dorleac and Renee Deneuve; ed. Lycee La Fontaine, Paris; 1 son, Christian Vadim. Motion picture appearances include les Petitis Chats, 1956; les Collegiennes, 1956; Les portes claquent, 1960; les Parisiennes, 1961; Et Satan conduit le bal, 1962 Vacances portugaises, 1963; le Vice et la Vertu, 1963; les Parplunies de Cherbourg, 1964; la Chasse al'homme, 1964; les Plus belles escrogueries de monde, 1964; un Monsieur de compagnie, 1964; Repulsion, 1965; Coeur a la gorge, 1965. Home: 77 Saint-Fargeau Paris France Office: care of William Morris Orgn 83 rue du Faubourg-Saint-Honore Paris 8 France*

DENFELD, LOUIS EMIL, retired naval officer; b. Westboro, Mass., Apr. 13, 1891; s. Louis E. and Etta May (Kelley) D.; A.M., Naval Acad., 1912; m. Rachel Metcalf, June 5, 1915. Commd. ensign, June 1912 and advanced through grades to admiral; served in Virginia, Ark., Paducah, and N.J., 1912-17; on Destroyers Ammen and Lamberton on escort duty during World War I; comd. Destroyers Wadsworth and Brooks and Submarine S-24, 1919-29; aide to Chief of Bur. of Navigation, 1929-31; staff of Comdr. Battle Force and Comdr. in Chief, U.S. Fleet, 1931-33; Bur. of Navigation, 1933-35; comd. Destroyer Div. 11, Battle Force, 1935-37; adminstrative aide to Chief of Naval Operations, 1937-39; comd. Destroyer Div. 18 and Destroyer Squadron 1, 1939-41; special naval observer in London, Chief of Staff for Comdr. Support Force, Atlantic Fleet, 1941; asst. chief naval personnel, Bur. of Naval Personnel, Navy Dept., 1942-44; comdr. battleships, Div. 9, Pacific, 1945; chief of Naval Personnel, 1945-47; comdr.-in-chief Pacific and U.S. Pacific, 1947; chief of naval operations, and mem. Joint Chiefs of Staff, 1947-49; ret. as adm., 1950; cons. Sun Oil Co., 1950-71. Decorated D.S.M., Legion of Merit with Gold-Star. Episcopalian. Clubs: Chevy Chase (Md.); Army-Navy, Metropolitan, Carlton, 1925 F Street. Home: 9 Charles St Westboro MA 01581

DENHAM, HARRY CLAYTON, physician, surgeon; b. Vanceburg, Ky., June 17, 1918; s. Henry Harvey and Elizabeth (Bertram) D.; B.S., U. Ky., 1941; M.D., U. Louisville, 1944; m. Minkie Clarke, Sept. 15, 1944; childrenJohn Reis, Cynthia Clarke. Surg. resident Louisville Gen. Hosp., 1944-46, 48-49; pvt. practice surgery, Maysville, Ky., 1949-; surgeon Denham Med. Clinic. Dir. State Nat. Bank, Maysville. Mem. Council Higher Edn. Ky., Maysville Sch. Bd. Trustee U. Ky. Del. Democratic Nat. Conv., 1960. Served to capt., M.C., AUS, 1947-48. Mem. Am., Ky. med assns. Address: Maysville, KY 41056

DEN HARTOG, JACOB PIETER, engr.; b. Java, East Indies, July 23, 1901; s. Marten and Elisabeth (Schol) Den H.; E.E., U. Delft, Holland, 1924, Dr. Tech. Sci. (hon.), 1967; Ph.D., U. Pitts., 1929; A.M. (hon.), Harvard, 1942; D.Engring. (hon.), Carnegie Inst. Tech., 1962; D.Sc., University Ghent (Belgium), 1966, Salford U., 1970; m. Elisabeth Stolker, July 29, 1926; children—Martin Dirk, Stephen Ludwig. Came to U.S., 1924, naturalized, 1930. Engr. Westinghouse Research Labs., Pitts., 1924-32; asst. prof. mech. engring. Harvard, 1932-36, asso. prof., 1936-41; became prof. Mass. Inst. Tech., 1945, head dept. mech. engring., 1954-58. Served with USN, 1941-45; now capt., USNR, ret. Fellow Am. Inst. Aeros. and Astronautics, Brit. Inst. M.E.; mem. Am. Soc. M.E. (hon.), Japan Soc. M.E. (hon.), Am. Soc. Naval Engrs., Royal Inst. Engrs. (Dutch), Nat. Acad. of Sci., Am. Inst. Cons. Engrs. Author: Mechanical Vibrations, 1934, 41, 46, 54; Mechanics, 1948; Strength of Materials, 1949; Advanced Strength of Materials, 1952. Home: Barnes Hill Rd Concord MA 01742 Office: Mass Inst Tech Cambridge MA 02139

DENHOF, MIKI, graphic designer; b. Triste, Italy, Jan. 1, 1912; d. Bernard and Olga (Krieger) Bardach; ed. Vienna, Austria, also Reiman Sch. Art, Berlin, Germany; m. Hans Denhof, Aug. 27, 1933 (div.). Came to U.S., 1938, naturalized, 1944. Asst. to art dir. Esquire mag., 1940-44; art dir. J. Walter Thompson, advt., 1944-45; promotion art dir. Conde Nast Publs., 1945-55; art editor Glamour mag., 1955-60, art dir., 1960-70; asso. editor House and Garden mag., 1970—; work rep. Art Dirs. shows, also permanent graphic arts file Mus. Modern Art. Recipient awards Am. Graphic Arts Soc. Mem. Met. Mus. Art, Mus. Modern Art, Met. Opera Guild. Home: 227 Central Park W New York City NY 10024 also 17 Barns Lane Easthampton Long Island NY 11937 Office: Conde Nast Publs Inc 420 Lexington Av New York City NY 10017

DENHOLM, CHARLES JOSEPH, army officer; b. Pitts., Sept. 20, 1914; s. Charles Jefferson and Mary Johnna (Lutz) D.; B.S., U.S. Mil. Acad., 1938; postgrad. Armed Forces Staff Coll., 1951, Army War Coll., 1955; m. Elizabeth Humphreyson, Feb. 9, 1941; childrenElizabeth (Mrs. Thomas Mazza), Charles J., Eleanor. Commd. 2d lt. U.S. Army, 1938, advanced through grades to maj. gen., 1961; adviser Mil. Assistance Adv. Group, Iran, 1960-61; Nat. Security Agy., Ft. Meade, 1961-62; chief staff 2d Army, 1962; assigned Office Asst. Chief Staff Intelligence, Dept. Army, 1962-65; comdg. gen. U.S. Army Security Agy., Arlington, Va., 1965—. Decorated D.S.C., D.S.M., Silver Star medal with cluster, Legion of Merit with cluster, Bronze Star medal with cluster, Purple Heart with cluster, Croix de Guerre, Combat Inf. Badge. Home: Quarters 1 Arlington VA 22212 Office: Hdqrs US Army Security Agy Arlington Hall Sta Arlington VA 22212

DENHOLM, FRANK EDWARD, congressman; b. Brookings, S.D., Nov. 29, 1923; s. John James and Laura Anne (Mathias) D.; B.S., S.D. State U., 1956; J.D., U. S.D., 1962; postgrad. pub. adminstrn., U. Minn., 1956-57; m. Mildred Therese Niehaus, June 12, 1950.

Engaged as farmer, 1945-56, in interstate truck transp. bus., 1946-53, auctioneer, 1948-56; sheriff Day County, S.D., 1950-53; agt. FBI, 1956-61; admitted to S.D. bar, 1962; mem. firm Denholm & Glover, Brookings, 1962—; lectr. S.D. State U., 1962-66; corp. counsel cities Brookings, Volga and White, 1962-71; mem. 92d Congress 1st Dist. S.D. Mem. Am., S.D. bar assns., Am. Judicature Assn., Am. Trial Lawyers Assn., U.S., Brookings chambers commerce, S.D. Sheriffs and Police Officers Assn., Nat. Sheriffs Assn., Phi Delta Phi. Democrat. Elk, Kiwanian. Home: 2127 Elmwood Dr Brookings SD 57006 Office: House Office Bldg Washington DC 20205

DENIKER, PIERRE GEORGES, psychiatrist; b. Paris, France, Feb. 16, 1917; s. Georges and Marguerite (Delgobe) D.; M.D., Faculties Sciences and Medicine, Paris, 1945; m. Nadine Vincent, Dec. 6, 1941. Extern Paris hosps., 1938; intern Seine Psychiat. Hosps., 1946; chief clinic Faculty Medicine of Paris, 1949-52, asst. Psychiat. Clinic, 1952—, med. surp. Psychiatric Hospitals, 1950- -; prof. psychiatry U. of Paris, 1961; researcher psychopharmacology. Reporter for the French Psychiat. Congress, 1953, Brazilian Psychiat. Congress, 1956, 2d Internat. Congress Psychiatry, 1957, World Congress Psychiatry, 1961, 66, 71; mem. council Order of Physicians; mem. Nat. Com. Neurophysiology and Psychopharmacology, 1961. Served as capt. French Combat Forces, 1939-45. Decorated Croix de Guerre, Public Health Cross, Chevalier de la Legion d'Honneur; also recipient Albert Lasker prize, 1957. Corr. Fellow Am. Psychiat. Assn.; mem. Medio-Psychol. Soc., Med. Legal Soc., Internat. Soc. Criminology, Internat. Coll. Neuro-Psycho-Pharmacology (sec.). Author: (with Prof. Delay): On Psychiatric Chemotherapies, 1961. Home: 17 rue de la Ville-l'Evque Paris 8 France Office: 1 rue Cabanis Paris 14e France

DENIS, LAURENT G., educator; b. Montreal, Can., Feb. 21, 1932; s. Lucien and Germaine (Langlois) D.; B.A., Loyola Coll., Montreal, 1954; B.L.S., McGill U., 1955, M.L.S., 1965. Cataloguer, Nat. Library Can., 1955-56; asst. chief librarian Coll. Militaire Royal de St.-Jean, 1956-61; dir. Ecole de Bibliothéconomie, U. Montreal, 1961-70; prof. Sch. Library Sci. U. Toronto, 1970—. Mem. Canadian, Am., Que. library assns., Assn. Canadienne des Bibliothecaires de Langue Francaise, Inst. Profl. Librarian Ont. Author reports, editor profl. proc. Home: 8 Kingsgrove Blvd Toronto 590 Ontario Canada Office: 140 St George St Toronto 181 Ontario Canada

DENISCO, STANLEY GABRIEL, advt. exec.; b. N.Y.C., Sept. 24, 1918; s. Fred and Mamie (Brancato) DeN.; B.A., Fordham U., 1940; M.A., N.Y. U., 1948, Ph.D., 1962; m. Marie LaRegina, Sept. 14, 1941; children—Ann Marie (Mrs. Basil Labbate), Richard Kim, Christopher. Chemist, Sheffield Farms, 1940-42, Best Foods, 1942-44; asso. research dir. Standard Brands, 1944-51; v.p., mgr. sci. dept. Ted Bates & Co., Inc., 1951—. Mem. A.A.A.S., Am. Chem. Soc., Am. Oil Chemists Assn., Inst. Food Technologists. Home: 24 Monroe St Pelham Manor NY 10803 Office: 666 Fifth Av New York City NY 10019

DENISE, MALCOLM LAWRENCE, lawyer; b. Decatur, Mich., Oct. 29, 1913; s. Malcolm F. and Margaret E. (Lawrence) D.; A.B., U. Mich., 1935, J.D., 1937; m. Shirley T. Verner, May 21, 1938; children—Richard Malcolm, Douglas Theodore, Jerome Robert, David James, Sharon Lee. Admitted to Mich. bar, 1937; asso. Lucking, Van Auken & Sprague, 1937-41, I. A. Capizzi, 1941-46; dir. indsl. relations legal dept. Ford Motor Co., Dearborn, Mich., 1946-48, asso. counsel indsl. relations, 1948-55, gen. indsl. relations mgr. labor relations, 1955-59, v.p., 1959—. Apptd. industry mem. nat. WSB, 1951, chmn. industry mems. 1952; mem. employer delegation Internat. Labor Conf., 1962, 63; mem. nat. adv. health council USPHS, 1965-67. Mem. Am., Mich. (chmn. labor law sect. 1956-57), Detroit bar assns., Indsl. Relations Research Assn., Am. Mgmt. Assn. (v.p. personnel div. 1970—), Alpha Kappa Lambda. Clubs: Detroit Boat-Detroit Athletic, Detroit Press. Home: 1 Stratford Pl Grosse Pointe MI 48230 Office: The American Rd Dearborn MI 48121

DENISE, THEODORE CULLOM, educator; b. Whitewater, Wis., Mar. 9, 1919; s. Malcolm F. and Margaret E. (Lawrence) D.; B.A., U. Mich., 1942, M.A., 1947, Ph.D., 1955; m. Kathleen W. Cowles, Oct. 4, 1942; children—Patricia B., (Mrs. Nicholas White), Theodore Cullom. Teaching fellow U. Mich., 1946-48; mem. faculty Syracuse U., 1948—, asso. prof. philosophy, 1959-64, prof. philosophy, 1964—, chmn. dept., 1959—, dir. liberal studies Inst. Univ. Adminstrs., 1961-63, dir. of semester in Italy, 1967-68. Served with AUS, 1942-46. Member of Assn. Symbolic Logic, Am. Philos. Assn., Am. Assn. U. Profs., Alpha Kappa Lambda. Author: (with others) Great Traditions in Ethics, 1953; (with S. P. Peterfreund) Contemporary Philosophy and Its Origins, 1967. Editor: (with M. H. Williams) Retrospect and Prospect, 1956. Contbr. philos. jours. Home: 301 Haddonfield Dr DeWitt NY 13214 Office: Dept Philosophy Syracuse U Syracuse NY 13210

DENISEN, ERVIN LOREN, educator; b. Austin, Minn., Nov. 10, 1919; s. Alfred J. and Emma (Hansen) D.; B.S., U. Minn., 1941; M.S., Ia. State U., 1947, Ph.D., 1949; m. Virginia Peyton, May 8, 1943; children—Kathryn Ann, Peggy Jane, Mary Clare. County 4-H Agt. Douglas County, Alexandria, Minn., 1939; voc. agrl., sci. tchr. Watertown, Minn., 1941-42; with Ia. State U., 1946—, instr., 1946-49, asst. prof., 1949-59, asso. prof., 1959-65, prof. hort. dept., 1965—, chmn. dept. hort., 1967—; hort. cons. U.S. AID to Uruguay, 1963; cons. hort. articles World Book Encyclopedia. Bd. dirs. Iowa Arboretum Inc. Served to capt. USAAF, 1942-46. Mem. Am. Soc. Hort. Sci. (chmn. edn. sect. 1970), Am. Soc. Plant Physiologists, Am. Inst. Biol. Sci., A.A.A.S., Ia. Acad. Sci., Weed Sci. Soc. Am., Am. Hort. Soc., Sigma Xi, Phi Kappa Phi, Gamma Sigma Delta. Developed Cyclone (1959) and Stoplight (1971) strawberry varieties; developed Amethyst raspberry, 1968; patentee strawberry harvesters. Author: Principles of Horticulture, 1958; author (with H. E. Nichols); Laboratory Manual in Horticulture, 1962. Home: 2137 Friley Rd Ames IA 50010

DENISON, EDWARD FULTON, economist; b. Omaha, Neb., Dec. 18, 1915; s. Edward Fulton and Edith Barbara (Brown) D.; student Central YMCA Coll., Chicago, 1932-34, Loyola U., Chicago, 1935; A.B., Oberlin Coll., 1936; A.M., Brown U., 1938; Ph.D., 1941; fellow in econs. Brookings Instn., 1939-40; grad. Nat. War Coll., 1951; m. Elsie Lightbown, June 14, 1941; children—Janet (Mrs. Howell), Edward. Instr., Brown U., 1940-41; economist., nat. income div., Office of Bus. Econ., U.S. Dept. Commerce, 1941-47, acting chief, nat. income div., 1948, asst. dir. Office of Bus. Econs., 1949-56; economist Com. Econ. Devel., 1956-62; member of the senior staff of Brookings Institution, 1962—; vis. research prof. U. Cal. at Berkeley, 1966-67; chief aggregates unit, U.S. Strategic Bombing Survey, Germany, 1945; lectr. Am. U., Washington, 1946. Chmn. exec. com. Conf. Research Income and Wealth, 1957-59. Mem. Internat. Assn. for Research in Income and Wealth, Conf. Research Income and Wealth, 1957-59. Recipient Woytinsky award, 1967. Fellow Am. Statis. Assn.; mem. Internat. Assn. for Research in Income and Wealth, Conf. on Research in Income and Wealth, Am. Econ. Assn. Club: Sherwood Forest (Md.). Author: The Sources of Economic Growth in the United States and the Alternatives Before Us, 1962; Why Growth Rates Differ, 1967. Home: 560 N St SW Washington, DC 20024. (summer) Sherwood Forest Annapolis MD 21405

DENISON, JAMES HENRY, univ. ofcl.; b. Mt. Sterling, O., Jan. 8, 1907; s. George and Margaret Olive (Warren) D.; A.B., Defiance Coll., 1928; m. Mary Kendrew, Apr. 3, 1937; 1 dau., Jane Kendrew. Mem. editorial staff Toledo Times, 1928-31, Detroit Free Press, 1931-40; dir. information Mich. War Council, 1940- 43; adminstrv. asst. to gov. Mich., 1945-47; asst. pres., dir. univ. relations Mich. State U., 1947-69, cons. to pres., 1969—, asso. prof., 1947-49, prof., 1949—. Mem. Joint Council Ednl. TV, 1950-59, vice chmn., 1952-59; mem. information com. Joint Office Instl. Research, 1958-64, chmn., 1960-64; cons. Dept. Def., 1953-54. Mem. nat. budget com. Community Chests and Councils Am., 1953-57; mem. East Lansing Planning Commn., 1958-69, chmn., 1962-68. Bd. dirs. Mich. United Fund, 1953-68. Served to capt. AUS, 1943-45. Decorated Bronze Star medal. Mem. Assn. State Univs. and Land-Grant Colls. (chmn. information com. 1957-61), Am. Coll. Pub. Relations Assn. (trustee-at-large 1962-64, exec. com. 1962-66, pres. 1964-65), Pub. Relations Assn. Mich., Newbury (Eng.) Operatic Soc. (v.p. 1966—), Fusalier, Mil. Order Fgn. Wars, Sigma Delta Chi. Author: (with A. L. Hunter) Administration and Financing of Educational Education, 1958. Club: University (East Lansing, Mich.). Home: 819 Southlawn East Lansing MI 48823

DENISON, RICHARD DAVID, food co. exec.; b. Detroit, Oct. 19, 1929; s. Donald Goodrich and Adeline (Smith) D.; B.A., Amherst Coll., 1951; M.B.A., U. Chgo., 1956; m. Katherine C. Redmon, Nov. 29, 1952; children—Thomas, Charles, Mary, Stephen. With Harris Trust and Savs. Bank, Chgo. 1953-57; with Glore Forgan Wm. R. Staats, Inc., Chgo., 1957-65, partner, 1963-65; with Quaker Oats Co., Chgo., 1965—, treas., 1966—. Served as lt. (j.g.) USCGR, 1951-53. Mem. Investment Analysts Soc. Chgo. Home: 525 Ash St Winnetka, IL 60093. Office: Merchandise Mart Chicago IL 60654

DENISON, ROBERT HOWLAND, paleontologist; b. Somerville, Mass., Nov. 9, 1911; s. William Kendall and Florence Letchworth (Howland) D.; A.B., Harvard, 1933; M.A., Columbia, 1934; Ph.D., 1938; m. Marion Swift, June 29, 1940 (div. 1948); children—John Howland, David Oldmixen; m. 2d Mary S. Maynard, Aug. 3, 1965. Asst. curator in mus. Dartmouth, 1937-47, instr. zoology, 1938-42, asst. prof., 1943-47; paleontologist African expdn. U. Cal., 1947-48; curator fossil fishes Field Mus. Nat. History, Chgo., 1948-70, research asso., 1971—; lectr. evolutionary biology U. Chgo., 1965—; field trips in U.S., Can., Europe, Africa, 1931—. Guggenheim fellow, 1953-54. Fellow Geol. Soc. Am.; mem. Soc. Vertebrate Paleontology (pres. 1962-63), Am. Soc. Zoologists. Contbr. profl. jours. Home: 717 Park Av Winnetka, IL 60093. Office: Field Mus Natural History Chicago IL 60605

DENIUS, FRANKLIN WOFFORD, lawyer; b. Athens, Tex., Jan. 4, 1925; s. S. F. and Frances (Cain) D.; B.B.A., LL.B., U. Tex.; m. Charmaine Hooper, Nov. 19, 1949; children—Frank Wofford, Charmaine. Admitted to Tex. bar, 1949, since practiced in Austin; partner Clark, Thomas, Harris, Denius & Winters, 1949—. Sec.-treas., dir. Telcom Corp.; dir. So. Union Gas Co., Aztec Oil & Gas Co., Delhi-Australian Petroleum Ltd., Capital Nat. Bank Austin. Chmn. United Fund Spl. Schs. div., 1960, Pacesetters div., 1961, Schs. div., 1964; 1st v.p. United Fund; chmn. steering com. Sch. Bond Campaign, trustee Austin Ind. Sch. Dist., 1964. Pres. Young Men's Bus. League Austin; pres., exec. council Austin Ex-Students Assn. U. Tex. Served with AUS, 1943-45. Decorated Silver Star medal with two oak leaf clusters, Purple Heart; recipient Outstanding Young Man of Austin award Jr. C. of C., 1959. Mem. Am., Tex., Travis County bar assns. Presbyn. (deacon; elder). Mason. Clubs: Longhorn (past pres.), West Austin Optimists (past dir.), Headliners (v.p.; sec. bd. trustees; mem. exec. com.). Home: 3703 Meadowbank Dr Austin, TX 78703. Office: PO Box 1148 Austin TX 78767

DENIUS, HOMER RAINEY, electronics co. exec.; b. Appomattox, Va., Jan. 31, 1914; s. Frank E. and Margaret (Watters) D.; student U. Cin.; D.Sc., Fla. Inst. Tech., 1964; m. Grace Evelyn Pence, June 26, 1936; children—Chris F., Sandra Jeanne (Mrs. Robert Keeley), Homer R. Vice pres., dir. engring., dir., Melpar, Inc., then exec. electronic engr. Am. Type Founders Corp.; dir. quality control Magnavox Corp.; comml. engr. Ken-Rad Tube Co.; with Crosley Corp.; co-founder Radiation Inc., 1950, pres., 1950-62, chmn., 1961-69; chmn. Electro-Sci. Mgmt. Corp., 1968—. Trustee Fla. Inst. Tech.; established Denius Found., 1961. Sr. mem. I.E.E.E.; mem. Instrument Soc. Am. Mason (32). Methodist. Clubs: Yacht (N.Y.C.); Yacht (St. Petersburg, Fla.); Coral Reef Yacht: Eau Gallie Yacht (commodore 1966); Yacht (Biscayne Bay). Home: 2105 SE 18th St Fort Lauderdale FL 33316 Office: 2170 SE 17th St Fort Lauderdale FL 33316

DENK, HORST GEORGE, food co. exec.; b. Wiesbaden, Germany, Oct. 29, 1929; s. Kurt A. and Anne Marie (Badde) D.; student U. Mainz, 1949-50, Marquette U., 1951-53, U. Detroit, 1962-63; m. Ruth Erna Schreyer, Sept. 12, 1953; 1 dau., Susanne Romy Thelen. Came to U.S., 1954, naturalized, 1959. Foreman, asst. gen. prodn. mgr. Am. Bakeries Co., Chgo., 1954-63; bread prodn. mgr., v.p. bakery prodn. Ward Foods, Inc., N.Y.C., 1963-67; v.p. mfg. Sunshine Biscuits, Inc., N.Y.C., 1967, v.p. operations, 1968, exec. v.p., 1968-69, pres., chief exec. officer, 1969-71, also dir.; chmn. bd. Humpty Dumpty Foods, 1969-70; pres. chief exec. officer Denk Baking Corp., 1971—; pres. H.R.S. Enterprises, Inc., DBC Enterprises, Inc.; dir. 563 Park Corp. Mem. Young Pres. Orgn., Am. Soc. Bakery Engrs., Met. Bakery Prodn. Club (past pres.), Newcomen Soc. Rotarian. Club: N.Y. Athletic. Home: 563 Park Av New York City NY Office: 3240 Bronx Blvd Bronx NY 10467 also Windswept Meadows Farm Callicoon Center NY 12724

DENKER, DAVID DANIEL, coll. pres.; b. Denver, Colo., Apr. 23, 1915; B.A., Yale, 1948. Ph.D., 1951; m. Jane Sibley Gurley, Mar. 10, 1943; children—Joel Sibley, Michael Porter, Dana Whitford, Cornelia Canwell. Mem. staff N.Y. Times. 1933-45; tchr., dir. Yale Am. Studies Fgn. Scholars, 1948-55; instr. history Yale, also Rockefeller fellow, 1951-52; mem. faculty Rutgers U., 1952-67, asst. to pres., prof. history, 1958-67; pres. N.Y. Med. Coll., 1967-69; v.p. Pratt Inst., 1970—. Trustee Rutgers Prep. Sch., 1966. Served with AUS, 1942-45. Ford Found. study and lecture grantee, 1962, 65, 66, N.Y. Med. Coll. study and lecture grantee, 1969-70; Fulbright scholar, dir. 2d annual seminar Am. studies, Manila, Philippines, 1965. Mem. Phi Beta Kappa. Clubs: Elizabethan (bd. govs. 1948) (New Haven); Yale (N.Y.C.). Editor: Seven Summers: A History of American Studies for Foreign Scholars at Yale, 1955; Higher Education in the United States, 1960. Home: 675 Easton Av Somerset NJ 08873 Office: Washington Av and Willoughby Av Brooklyn NY 11205

DENKEWALTER, ROBERT GEORGE, pharm. co. research chemist; b. Chgo., Mar. 3, 1918; s. Walter E. and Katherine (Kelly) D.; B.S., Loyola U., Chgo., 1939, D.Sc. (hon.), 1969; Ph.D., U. Chgo., 1943; m. Rosemary Conley, June 19, 1943; children—Kathleen (Mrs. Michael D. Rayburn, Jr.), Eric Charles, Elizabeth (Mrs. W. Gregoire Ryberg, Jr.), Paul E., Mary G. With Merck & Co., Inc., 1943—, v.p. devel. research, 1969—. Asst. dist. chmn. Boy Scouts Am., 1964-66. Mem. Am. Chem. Soc., Am. Inst. Chemists, N.J., N.Y. acads. scis., Soc. Chem. Industry, Assn. Research Dirs. (pres. 1966), A.A.A.S. Research synthesis enzyme ribonuclease. Home: 620 Standish Av Westfield, NJ 07090. Office: Merck Sharp & Dohme Research Labs Rahway NJ 07065

DENMAN, BEN PITTMAN, ins. co. exec.; b. Brownwood, Tex., Apr. 23, 1916; s. Walter Gilbert and Marcia Kathryn (Pittman) D.; B.B.A., U. Tex., 1942; m. Elizabeth Nell Dyess, Feb. 17, 1943; children—William Edwin, Marajen. Sec.-treas. J. R. Beadel and Co., wholesale grocers, Brownwood, Tex., 1945-51; with Southwestern Life Ins. Co., Dallas, 1951—, agy. v.p., 1962-68, exec. v.p., 1969—. Served to lt. comdr. USNR, 1942-45. C.L.U. Mem. Phi Eta Sigma, Beta Gamma Sigma, Lambda Chi Alpha. Clubs: Friars, Rotary, Texas Cowboys (Dallas); University Texas (Austin). Home: 7173 Kendallwood Dr Dallas TX 75240 Office: Southwestern Life Insurance Co 1807 Ress Av Dallas TX 75221

DENMAN, JOE C., Jr., forest industry exec.; b. Lufkin, Tex., Sept. 30, 1923; B.S. in Architecture, Tex. A. and M. U., m. Virginia Cox, Jan. 10, 1948; children—Joe C. III, Elizabeth Anne, Ginia Geanette. With Temple Industries, Inc., Diboll, Tex., 1950—, prodn. mgr., 1955-60, v.p., 1961-64, corporate v.p., 1964-66, exec. v.p., 1967—; dir. Diboll State Bank, Tex. Gypsum Co., Woodward, Inc., Topaz Oil Co., Chattanooga Container Co., Tex. Southeastern R.R. Mem. adv. bd. dirs. Salvation Army. Served with A.C., USNR, 1943-46. Mem. Lufrin C. of C. (dir. 1966-68), So. Forest Product Assn. (pres. 1969-70), Tau Beta Pi. Home: 702 Nelson Dr Diboll TX 75941 Office: Temple Industries Inc Diboll TX 75941

DENMAN, LEROY GILBERT, Jr., lawyer; b. San Antonio, Feb. 18, 1918; s. Leroy Gilbert and Mary Louise (Carter) D.; B.A., U. Tex., 1936, LL.B., 1939; m. Fannie Lee Harvin, June 7, 1939; children—Margaret Emily, Deirdre. Admitted to Tex. bar, 1939; mem. firm Denman, Franklin, Denman, San Antonio, 1939-41, 46—; spl. asst. U.S. Ambassador, Guatemala, C.A., 1941-45, Buenos Aires, Argentina, 1945-46. Chmn. San Antonio Loan & Trust Co.; dir. First Nat. Bank of San Antonio, Kleberg First Nat. Bank, Deltec Internat. Ltd. Trustee Southwest Found. Research and Edn. Served with AUS, 1945. Home: 109 W French Pl San Antonio TX 78212 Office: 711 Navarro St San Antonio TX 78205

DENMARK, BERNHARDT, corp. exec.; b. Bklyn., June 6, 1917; s. William M. and Kate (Lazarus) D.; A.B., N.Y.U., 1941; postgrad. Am. U., 1941-42, Nat. Inst. Pub. Affairs, 1941-42; m. Muriel Schechter, Sept. 22, 1943; children—Richard J., Karen. Vice pres. sales Telecoin Corp., N.Y.C., 1946-49; v.p. sales Internat. Latex Corp., N.Y.C., 1949-55; marketing mgr. Playtex Co., N.Y.C., 1955-59, v.p., gen. mgr. family products div., 1959-63, v.p. marketing, 1963-65, pres. Playtex div., 1965-67; pres. Internat. Playtex Corp., N.Y.C., 1968-69, chmn. bd., 1969; exec. v.p. Glen Alden Corp., N.Y.C., 1969—, also dir.; mem. exec. com.; dir. Stanley Warner Corp., Schenley Industries, BVD Corp. Served to capt. AUS, 1942-46. Clubs: Fairview Country (Greenwich, Conn.); City Athletic (N.Y.C.). Home: 24 Dorchester Dr Port Chester NY 10573 Office: 350 Fifth Av New York City NY 10001

DENNEN, IRWIN HAROLD, mfg. co. exec.; b. Oak Park, Ill., Dec. 24, 1925; s. Louis and Fannie (Freedman) D.; B.S. in Engring., U. Mich., 1947, M.S., 1948; J.D., DePaul U., 1952; m. Beverly Anne Aune, May 19, 1962; children—David Lewis, Michael John, Anne Katherine, Martha Lee. With Pettibone Mulliken Corp., Chgo., 1948-59, Tee Pak Inc., Chgo., 1959-60, Beardsley & Piper, Chgo., 1960-64; v.p., gen. mgr. Clyde Iron Works, Inc., Duluth, Minn., 1965-67; pres. Di Arco div. Houdaille Industries, Lake City, Mich., 1968-70, Pratt & Whitney div. Colt Industries, Hartford, Conn., 1970—. Served to lt. (j.g.) USNR, 1942-46. Mem. Am. Foundrymens Soc. (pres. Chgo. chpt. 1962, nat. bd. dirs. 1963), Am. Mgmt. Assn., Nat. Machine Tool Builders, Machinery and Allied Products Inst. Home: 7 Saddleridge St West Simsbury CT 06092 Office: Pratt & Whitney Charter Oak Blvd West Hartford CT 06092

DENNES, WILLIAM RAY, educator; b. Healdsburg, Sonoma County, Cal., Apr. 10, 1898; s. Edward Frederick and Harriet (Ray) D.; A.B., U. Cal. at Berkeley, 1919, M.A., 1920, LL.D., 1966; D.Phil., Oxford U., Eng., 1923; LL.D., N.Y. U., 1951; m. Margaret Munroe Stevenson, June 22, 1923; children—Richard, Margaret (Mrs. Edwin Honig). Mills fellow in philosophy, U. Cal., 1920, instr. philosophy, 1923-24, asst. prof., 1924- 27, asso. prof., 1927-32, 33-36, prof., 1936—, chmn. dept., 1941-43, 44-48, Mills prof. intellectual and moral philosophy, civil polity U. Cal. at Berkeley, 1958-65, emeritus, 1965—, dean grad. div., 1948-55; asso. prof. philosophy Yale, 1932-33; vis. prof. philosophy, Harvard, 1935, Stanford, 1941, 43; Woodbridge Meml. lectr. in philosophy Columbia, 1958; vis. prof. philosophy So. Ill. Univ., 1966; vis. prof. philosophy U. Va., 1967, U. Cal., Santa Cruz, 1970-71. Served with USN, 1918-19; asst. dir. Manhattan Dist. Los Alamos Project, 1943. Awarded Univ. medal, U. of Cal., 1919; Rhodes Scholarship, Corpus Christi Coll., Oxford, 1920-23; Guggenheim fellowship in Germany and Eng., 1929-30. Pres. assn. grad. schs. Assn. Am. Univs., 1952; chmn. grad. council Assn. Land-Grant Colls. and Univs., 1952; mem. Conf. on Sci., Philosophy and Religion, 1952. Fellow Royal Soc. Arts, A.A.A.S.; mem. Am. Philos. Assn. (pres. Pacific div. 1945), Mind Soc. Gt. Britain, Phi Beta Kappa (pres. Alpha chpt. Calif., 1941-42), Alpha Kappa Lambda. Democrat. Club: Faculty (Berkeley). Author books in field; (latest) Naturalism and the Human Spirit (with John Dewey and others), 1944; Civilization and Values, 1945; East-West Philosophy (with others), 1951; Symbols and Values (with others), 1954; Some Dilemmas of Naturalism, 1960; C.I. Lewis on the Morally Imperative, 1969; co-author 18 vols. in philosophy, U. Cal. Publs., co-editor, 1941-60. Home: 15 Eucalyptus Rd Berkeley CA 94705 ☆

DENNEY, CORWIN D., corp. exec.; b. 1921; B.S. in Aero. Engring., U. Mich., 1943; widower; children—Caroly, Mary, Anne, Des Cyane. Chief helicopter engr., power plant and project engr. Marquardt Corp., Van Nuys, Cal., 1946-48; pres. Am. Helicopter Co., Manhattan Beach, Cal., 194854; pres. MidContinental Mfg. Co., 195459; with Automation Industries Inc., 1959—, now chmn. bd., pres., chief exec. officer, dir.; pres. G & H Tech. Inc., Automation Forster Inc.; chmn. bd. Vitro Corp. Am. Address: 1901 Building Century City Los Angeles, CA 90067.*

DENNEY, DONALD BEREND, educator; b. Seattle, Apr. 3, 1927; s. John Edwin and Catherine Boswell (Macgowan) D.; B.Sc., U. Wash., 1949; Ph.D., U. Cal., Berkeley, 1952; m. Dorothy Ziebell, Aug. 24, 1956. Research chemist E.I. duPont, 1952-53; with Hickrill Chem. Found., Katonah, N.Y., 1953-54; mem. faculty Rutgers U., 1955—, prof. chemistry, 1962—; cons. various chem. cos. Mem. NIH Medicinal Panel B, 1965-69. Served with USCGR, 1944-45. A.P. Sloan fellow, 1955-59. Mem. Am. Chem. Soc., Phi Beta Kappa. Editor: Techniques and Methods in Organic and Organometallic Chemistry, 1970; editorial bd. Phosphorus, 1971—. Home: 1884 Mountain Top Rd Somerville NJ 08876

DENNEY, GEORGE COVERT, Jr., govt. ofcl.; b. Pitts., July 18, 1921; s. George Covert and Ruth (Crowthers) D.; B.S., Waynesburg Coll., 1942; LL.B., Harvard, 1948; M.A., Columbia, 1950; m. Alice McCauley, Apr. 13, 1946; children—Christopher Stock, Jill McCauley. Admitted to Mass. bar, 1948, D.C. bar, 1961; fgn. affairs

officer State Dept., 1950-52; asst. gen. counsel Office Dir. Mut. Security, Exec. Office Pres., 1953-54; dep. asst. gen. counsel internat. matters Office Sec. Dept. Def., 1954-56; cons. com. fgn. relations U.S. Senate, 1956-62; dep. dir., bur. intelligence and research State Dept., 1963—. Fellow Inst. Current World Affairs, N.Y.C., 1962-63. Served to lt. USNR, 1942-46. Mem. Am. Bar Assn., Am. Soc. Internat. Law. Home: 2604 36th St NW Washington, DC 20007. Office: Bur Intelligence and Research Dept of State Washington DC 20505

DENNEY, KENNETH DUANE, mfg. and service co. exec.; b. Plattsburg, O., May 27, 1923; s. Clark E. and Edith (Yeoman) D.; student Office Tng. Sch., Columbus, O., 1942-43, Franklin U., Columbus, 1946-49; m. Patricia A. Nisley, Aug. 30, 1946; children—Susan A., Diane L. Vice pres. finance, dir., mem. exec. com. Automation Industries, Inc., Los Angeles, 1949—. Served with USNR, 1943- 46. Decorated Bronze Star medal with 4 oak leaf clusters. Mem. Financial Execs. Inst. (Los Angeles chpt.), Am. Mgmt. Assn., Nat. Office Mgmt. Assn. Mason (Shriner), Lion, Elk. Home: 146 Via Monte D'Oro Redondo Beach CA 90277 Office: 1901 Bldg Century City Los Angeles CA 90067

DENNEY, LAWRENCE VINCENT, ex-govt. ofcl.; b. Washington, Apr. 5, 1910; s. Harry and Mar E. (O'Connell) D.; LL.B., Columbus U., 1934, B.C.S., 1938; m. Suemary Hite, Oct. 17, 1939; children—Lawrence, Thomas, James, Edward, Susan. Adm. to D.C. bar; practice, Washington, 1934-35; with audit and claims div. Gen. Accounting Office, 1935-42, atty. Office Gen. Counsel, 1942-51, asst. gen. counsel, 1951-57, dir. claims div., 1957-68. Mem. Fed. Bar Assn. Home: 4535 48th St NW Washington DC 20016 Retired Oct. 1, 1968.

DENNEY, REUEL NICHOLAS, educator, author; b. N.Y.C., Apr. 13, 1913; A.B., Dartmouth, 1932; m. Ruth Lois Norton, July 1, 1938; 1 son, Randall. Asso. editor Fortune mag., 1945-47; asst. prof. social scis. U. Chgo., 1947, advanced to prof.; now prof. Am. studies U. Hawaii. Guggenheim fellow, 1941. Mem. bd. Hawaii Found. on Culture and Arts, 1966. Fellow Nat. Inst. Arts and Letters; mem. PEN Internat. (pres. Hawaii, 1970—). Club: Waikiki Yacht. Author: The Connecticut River, 1939; (with David Riesman, Nathan Glazer) The Lonely Crowd, 1950; Astonished Muse, 1957; In Praise of Adam, 1961; Conrad Aiken, 1964. Adv. bd. Jour. Social History, 1968—. Home: 2957 Kalakaua Av Honolulu HI 96815

DENNEY, ROBERT VERNON, judge; b. Council Bluffs, Ia., Apr. 11, 1916; s. Arthur J. and Helen (Weaver) D.; student Peru State Tchrs. Coll., 1933-34, U. Neb., 1934-36; LL.B. cum laude, Creighton U., 1939; m. Ruth Conklin, Dec. 21, 1940; children—Vernon, David, Michael, Deborah Admitted to Neb. bar, 1939; practice in 45—; Neb., 1939-40, 45—; spl. agt. FBI, 1940-41; atty. Jefferson County, Neb., 1947, Fairbury, 1951; mem. 90th-91st Congresses 1st Dist. Neb.; U.S. dist. judge, Neb., 1971—. Pres. Fairbury Indsl. Devel. Corp., 1960; mem. Fairbury Sch. Bd., 1956. Chmn. Jefferson County Republican Com., 1960, Neb. Rep. Party, 1960-64. Served to lt. col. USMCR, 1942-45; PTO. Decorated Bronze Star. Mem. Fairbury C. of C. (past pres.), Am. Legion (past post comdr.), V.F.W. Mason (K.T., Shriner), Lion. Clubs: Fairbury Executives (pres.), Fairbury Country (pres.). Presbyn. (elder). Home: 3020 Paddock Rd Apt 018D Omaha NB 68124 Office: PO Box 1297 Downtown Sta Omaha NB 68101

DENNEY, WALTER RAYMOND, lawyer; b. Smith County, Tenn., Apr. 10, 1900; s. Walter R. and Nancy (Alexander) D.; LL.B., Vanderbilt U., 1925; m. Katherine White, Feb. 26, 1925; children—Dan White, Nancy Alexander. Admitted to Tenn. bar, 1924; practicing lawyer, Nashville, 1925-; mem. Denney, Leftwich, Lackey & Chernau; lectr. law Vanderbilt U. Law School. Dir. Fidelity Fed. Savs. & Loan Assn., Attys. Title Co. Del. Nat. Democratic Conv., Chgo., 1944. Chmn. Tenn. Commn. for Ltd. Constl. Conv. Bd. dirs. Tenn. Children's Home Soc. Fellow Internat. Acad. Trial Lawyers, Am. Coll. of Trial Lawyers; mem. Tenn. (pres. 1949-50), Nashville Am. bar assns., Sigma Alpha Epsilon. Clubs: Bell Meade Golf and Country; Cumberland. Lion. Home: Ellendale Dr Nashville TN 37205 Office: 218 3d Av N Nashville TN 37203

DENNIG, LOUIS SCHAEFER, Jr., banker; b. St. Louis, Feb. 7, 1926; s. Louis Schaefer and Marie (Disbrow) D.; A.B., Princeton, 1948; m. Geraldine Martha Froemke, June 27, 1952; children—Louis III, Elizabeth, Gerald, Corinne, Marie, August. With Merc. Trust Co., St. Louis, 1948—, asst. v.p., 1958-59, v.p., 1959-69, sr. v.p., chief lending officer, 1970—; dir. Valley Dolomite Corp., Greer Spring Co., Smith & Davis Mfg. Co., (all St. Louis). Bd. dirs., exec. com. Blue Cross; bd. dirs. Mary Inst., St. Louis. Served to lt. (j.g.) USNR, 1944-46. Home: 26 The Orchards St Louis MO 63132 Office: 721 Locust St St Louis MO 63101

DENNING, JAMES EDWIN, film, TV exec.; b. N.Y.C., Nov. 25, 1912; s. John Joseph and Estelle (McCoy) D.; A.B., Columbia, 1935, LL.B., 1938; m. Catherine E. Manton, Jan. 20, 1940; children—Peter, Anne, Jeffrey, Gale, Sara. Admitted to N.Y. bar, 1938, Cal. bar, 1966; atty. U.S. Dept. Justice, 1938-39; with firm Townley, Updike & Carter, N.Y.C., 1939-44; sec., gen. counsel Press Wireless, Inc., 1944-47; dir. indsl. relations RCA Communications, Inc., 1947-51; sr. atty. NBC, Inc., N.Y.C., 1951-54, mgr., then dir. talent and program contract operations, 1955-57, v.p. talent and program adminstrn., 1957-59; v.p. MCA-TV, Ltd., 1959-65, Universal City Studios (Cal.), 1963-65, MCA Entertainment, Inc., 1965—, Cinematique, Ltd., 1965—, Universal TV, 1966—; v.p., sec., then pres. MCA Tech., Inc., 1967—; lectr. law of corps., agy. and partnerships N.Y.U., 1946-48. Mem. exec. bd. Alfred W. Dater council Boy Scouts Am., 1952-63, bd. dirs. Darien chpt. A.R.C., 1961-62, Darien Fund, 1954-63. Mem. Republican Town Meeting, Darien, 1951-63, moderator, 1955- 58; chmn. Darien Town Govt. Study Commn., 1961-63. Mem. Darien Rep. Town Com., 1960-62. Mem. Nat. Acad. TV Arts and Scis., Assn. Motion Picture and TV Producers, Am. Arbitration Assn. (nat. panel arbitrators), Am., Beverly Hills, Los Angeles County bar assns., Los Angeles Copyright Soc., Town Hall. Club: Cave Des Roys. Home: 13167 Boca de Canon Los Angeles CA 90049 Office: 100 Universal City Plaza Universal City CA 91608

DENNING, JOSEPH P., bishop; b. Flushing, N.Y., Jan. 4, 1907; s. Philip and Bridget (Cunningham) D.; Cathedral Coll., Bklyn., 1926; M.A., St. Mary's Sem., Balt., 1932; D.D. (hon.), St. John's U., LL.D. (hon.), Litt.D. (hon.), St. Francis Coll. Ordained priest Roman Cath. Ch.; tchr. Cathedral Coll., 1933-53; pastor Queen of Angeles Ch., Long Island City, 1953-60, Queen of Martyrs Ch.; 1960—; aux. bishop Bklyn., 1959—. Mem. all sessions Vatican II. Address: 110-06 Queens Blvd Forest Hills NY 11375

DENNING, RICHARD, (Louis Albert Denninger), actor; b. Poughkeepsie, N.Y., Mar. 27, 1914; s. Louis Andrew and Anna Marie (Bohrmann) Denninger; M.A. in Bus. Adminstrn. magna cum laude, Woodbury Coll., 1934; m. Evelyn F. Ankers, Sept. 6, 1942; 1 dau., Diana Dee. Actor Paramount Pictures, Hollywood, Cal., 1936-45; free-lance actor stage, screen, radio and TV, 1945—; motion pictures include Adam Had Four Sons, Beyond the Blue Horizon, An Affair to Remember, Day The World Ended, Black Scorpion, Gun That Won the West, Seven Were Saved, Crooked Web, Lady Takes a Flyer, Desert Hell, Emergency Squad, Golden Gloves, Black Beauty; star TV series Mr. and Mrs. North, The Flying Doctor, Michael Shayne, Karen; featured actor as the governor in Hawaii Five-O, 1968—. Mem. exec. bd. Maui council Boy Scouts Am., 1970—. Adv. bd. Woodbury Coll. Served with USNR, 1942-45. Mem. Gamma Sigma Pi, Phi Gamma Kappa. Mem. Christian Ch. (deacon). Clubs: Maui Country; Newport Sailing; Kamadle Skin Divers. Office: Armstrong-Deuser Agy 449 S Beverly Dr Beverly Hills CA 90212

DENNIS, CARTER WILLIAM, meat packing co. exec.; b. Red Oak, Ia., Jan. 30, 1907; s. Lloyd J. and Irene (Carter) D.; student S.D. State Coll., 1926-29; m. Ebba Evers, June 13, 1931; children—Diane Kay, Carter Ray. With Ia. Pub. Service Co., 1929-33; organized, 1933, since pres. Dennis Refrig. Supply Co., Sioux City, Ia., 1933; an organizer S.C. Dressed Beef Co., Sioux City, 1954, pres., 1954-60; organizer S.C. Dressed Pork, Inc., Sioux City, 1957, MID Packing Co., Luverne, Minn., 1962, since pres., dir.; dir. Northwestern Bell Telephone Co., Home Fed. Savs. & Loan Assn., Sioux City, First Nat. Bank, Sioux City. Gov. Ia. rep. to Mo. River's State Conn., 1958; bd. dirs. Ia. Devel. Commn., 1958. Bd. dirs. United Community Fund, Sioux City. Mem. U.S., Sioux City (past pres.) chambers commerce, Nat. Assn. Refrig. Wholesalers (past v.p.). Mason (Shriner). Home: 5200 Country Club Blvd Sioux City, IA 51104. Office: 1200 Bluff Rd Sioux City IA 51107

DENNIS, CLARENCE, surgeon; b. St. Paul, June 16, 1909; s. Warren Arthur and Clara May (Van Orman) D.; B.S., Harvard, 1931; M.D., Johns Hopkins, 1935; M.S., U. of Minn., 1938, Ph.D., 1940; m. Eleanor Mary Smith, June 17, 1939; children—Jane E. (Mrs. James J. Smith), Richard, James, David. Trained in surgery under Dr. O. H. Wangensteen, U. of Minn., 1935-40, in physiology with Dr. M. B. Visscher, 1938-39, instr. in physiology, 1938-39, in surgery, 1940-41, asst. prof., 1941-44, asso. prof., 1944-47, prof. surgery, 1947-51; prof. surgery, chmn. dept. State U. N.Y. Downstate Med. Center; surgeon-in-chief Kings County Hosp.; State U. Hosp. Diplomate Am. Bd. Surg., Fellow A.C.S. (past gov.); mem. Am. Heart Assn., Am. Soc. for Artificial Internal Organs (past pres.), Internat., N.Y. (past pres.) surg. socs., Soc. Vascular Surgery (past pres.) N.Y. (past pres.), Bklyn. (past pres.) surg. socs., Am. Assn. Surgery Trauma, Am. Assn. Thoracic Surgery, Soc. U. Surgeons, Am. Sug. Assn. (v.p.), Soc. Clin. Surgery, Soc. Exptl.. Biology and Medicine, N.Y. Cancer Soc. (past pres.), Internat. Cardiovascular Soc., Soc. Surgery Alimentary Tract, N.Y. Soc. Thoracic Surgery, Soc. U. Surg. Chmn. (past pres.). Contbr. articles to profl. publs. and textbooks. Home: 989 Edgewood Av Pelham Manor NY 10803 Office: State U NY Downstate Med Center 450 Clarkson Av Brooklyn NY 11203

DENNIS, CLYDE AVERY, educator; b. Bloomdale, O., Feb. 23, 1900; s. Charles Ellsworth and Etta Mae (Frederick) D.; B.S., Coll. of Wooster, 1923; M.S., Ohio State U., 1928, Ph.D., 1937; m. Helen Good, Aug. 26, 1924; 1 dau., Patricia Ann (Mrs. Harry Cole). Instr., Bloomdale High Sch., 1923-24; from instr. to prof. biology Tusculum Coll., Greenville, Tenn., 1924-44, chmn. dept., 1937-44, v.p., 1944-45; field rep. Curtis Pub. Co., 1945-48; chmn. dept. biology, prof. Millikin U., 1948-61, dean Coll. Arts and Sci., 1961-66, former prof. biology. Mem. Sigma Xi, Phi Kappa Phi. Republican. Presbyn. Rotarian. Author: sci. papers. Home: 1850 Spittler Dr Decatur IL 62521

DENNIS, DAVID WORTH, congressman; b. Washington, June 7, 1912; s. William Cullen and Agenes (Barker) D.; grad. Sidwells Friends Sch., Washington, 1929; A.B., Earlham Coll., 1933; LL.B., Harvard, 1936; m. Tresa Marie Justice, Dec. 3, 1938; children—William Cullen II, Martha Ellen. Admitted to Ind. bar, 1936; asso. firm Rupe, Brown & Reller, Richmond, Ind., 1936-39; pros. atty. 17th Jud. Circuit, Wayne County, Ind., 1939-43; asso. firm Ross, McCord, Ice & Miller, Indpls., 1943-44; partner firms Dennis & Dennis, Richmond, Ind., 1947-62, Dennis, Dennis & Puckett, Richmond, 1962-67, Dennis, Dennis & Reinke, 1967-69, Dennis, Dennis, Reinke & Vertesch, Richmond, 1969-71; mem. Ind. Ho. of Reps. from Wayne County, 1947- 49; joint rep. Wayne and Union counties, 1953-59; mem. 91st-92d Congresses 10th Dist. Ind. Served to 1st lt. J.A.G.D., AUS, 1944-46; PTO, 1945-46. Mem. Am., Ind., Indpls., Wayne County bar assns., Ind., Am. trial lawyers assns., Nat. Assn. Def. Lawyers Criminal Cases, Am. Soc. Internat. Law, Wilderness Soc. Republican. Clubs: Capitol Hill (Washington); Tourist, Rotary (Richmond); Columbia (Indpls.). Home: 610 W Main St Richmond IN 47374 Office: Longworth Ho Office Bldg Washington DC 20515

DENNIS, EARL AUBREY, former fgn. service res. officer; b. Bloomdale, O., June 9, 1902; s. Charles E. and Etta Mae (Frederick) D.; A.B., Coll. of Wooster, 1925; Ph.D., U. Chgo., 1934; m. Dorothy Mae Donley, July 26, 1928; 1 dau., Anne Elaine. Sci. tchr. Lodi (Ohio) High Sch., 1926-27; instr. biology Tusculum Coll., Greeneville, Tenn., 1927-28, Allegheny Coll., Meadville, Pa., 1928-31; grad. asst. zoology, U. Chgo., 1931-34; asst. prof., biology, Am. U., Washington, 1935-40, asso. prof., 1941-42, prof., 1942-46, chmn. dept., 1935-46, dean coll. arts and scis., 1944-45; on leave to serve as civilian instr. biology, Biarritz Am. Univ., France, 1945-46; adviser, sci. and tech. sect., Office Internat. Information and Cultural Affairs, U.S. Dept. of State, 1946; acting asst. chief div. Internat. Exchange of Persons, office of Ednl. Exchange, Dept. of State, 1947-48; pub. affairs officer, and attache of Embassy, Wellington, New Zealand, 1949-51; chief Brit. Commonwealth and No. European br. Internat. Information Adminstrn., Dept. of State, 1951-53; pub. affairs officer Am. embassy, Copenhagen, Denmark, 1953-56; chief, study programs div., Internat. Ednl. Exchange Service, Dept. State, 1956- 59; pub. affairs officer Am. Embassy, Stockholm, Sweden, 1959-64; coordinator binat. programs Bur. Ednl. and Cultural Affairs, Dept. State, 1965-67; chief overseas assistance and tng. br., div. fgn. studies Dept. Health, Edn. and Welfare, 1967-69, now ret. Fulbright Found., Wellington 1949-51, Copenhagen, 1953-56; mem. Fulbright Commn., Sweden, 1959-65. Home: 4838 Butterworth Pl Washington DC 20016

DENNIS, EDWARD WIMBERLY, physician; b. Macon, Ga., July 31, 1923; s. John Cobb and Helen (Wimberly) D.; B.S. in Medicine, Emory U., 1947, M.D., 1949; m. Beatrice L. Forrest, May 28, 1948; children—Sara Margaret, Edward Forrest, Kathleen Laurie, Kenrick Johnson. Life Ins. Med. Research Fund student fellow, 1946-48; intern, then resident medicine U. Mich. Hosp., 1949-53; mem. faculty Baylor U. Coll. Medicine, Houston, 1954—, prof. medicine, 1967—; chief med. cardiology service Meth. Hosp., Houston. Mem. planning com., conf. program dirs. Nat. Heart Inst., 1956-59. Bd. dirs. Houston Heart Assn. Diplomate Am. Bd. Internal Medicine. Fellow A.C.P., Am. Coll. Cardiology, Am. Heart Assn. (council clin. cardiology), Am. Coll. Angiology; mem. Am. Fedn. Clin. Research (councillor 1956-59, vice chmn. 1959-60, chmn. So. sect. 1960-61), Tex. Club Internists, Nat. Acad. Medicine Brazil (hon.). Author articles, chpts. in books. Home: 12214 Boheme St Houston TX 77024 Office: 6516 Bertner St Houston TX 77025

DENNIS, G. W., pres., publisher Halifax (N.S.) Chronicle-Herald. Address: care Chronicle-Herald Argyle St Halifax Nova Scotia Canada*

DENNIS, GEORGE WILLIAM, banker; b. Bklyn., Oct. 23, 1923; s. George William and Edith L. (Brown) D.; B.B.A., St. Johns U., 1949; postgrad. Rutgers U., 1965; m. Catherine L. Mullen, May 30, 1949; childrenGeorge William III, Raymond P., Karen, Victoria, Donovan P. Sr. accountant Haskins & Sells, C.P.A.'s, N.Y.C., 1947-59; auditor Hanover Bank, N.Y.C., 1959-61; gen. auditor Mfrs. Hanover Trust, N.Y.C., 1961—. Pres., treas. Willistons Baseball League, Inc.; trustee Nassau County Police Boys Club. Served with USAAF, 1942- 45. Decorated Air medal with two oak leaf clusters; recipient Carolina Conf. Found. award, 1962. Mem. Am. Inst. C.P.A.'s, N.Y. State Soc. C.P.A.'s, Am. Inst. Banking, Bank Adminstrn. Inst. (chmn. audit commn., dir.), Am. Legion. Home: 528 Marcellus Rd Williston Park, NY 11596. Office: 4 New York Plaza New York City NY 10004

DENNIS, GLENN STANLEY, corp. exec.; b. Atlantic City, Jan. 6, 1928; s. Henry U. and Lois (Hamerle) D.; B.A., Syracuse U., 1951; J.D., U. Mich., 1956; m. Miriam Hopkins, Aug. 23, 1952; children—Stephen Hopkins, Julie Elizabeth. Admitted to N.Y. bar, 1956; asso. atty. firm Wiser, Shaw, Freeman, Van Graafeiband, Harter & Rochester, 1956-59; corp. counsel Sealtest Foods div. Nat. Dairy Products Corp., 1960-66; gen. counsel, sec. Alco Product, Inc., 1966-69; formerly sr. atty. Caterpillar Tractor Co. Vice pres. Ramsey (N.J.) Republican Club, 1967-68; mem. town council, Ramsey, 1968-69. Served with USNR, 1945-46, USAF, 1951-53. Mem. Assn. Bar City N.Y., N.Y. State, Ill., Peoria bar assns., Alpha Sigma Phi, Phi Alpha Delta. Republican. Presbyn. Rotarian. Home: 906 W Kensington Dr Peoria IL 61614

DENNIS, JAMES LOUDON, med. educator; b. Oklahoma City, Aug. 8, 1913; s. William Bates and Artie (Abernathy) D.; B.S., U. Okla., 1936, M.D., 1940; m. Virginia Roueche, June 15, 1940; children—William H., James R., Constant Marie. Intern Highland-Alameda County Hosp., Oakland, Cal., 1941-42; resident medicine Merced County (Cal.) Hosp., 1941-43; resident pediatrics U. Tex. Med. Br., Galveston, 1950-52; asst. prof. pediatrics U. Tex. Med. Sch., 1952-54; dir. edn. Children's Hosp., Med. Center No. Cal., Oakland, 1955-62; prof. pediatrics U. Ark. Med. Sch., 1962-64; dean, dir. U. Okla. Med. Center, 1964-70, v.p. Med. Center affairs, 1967-70; v.p. for health scis. U. Ark., Little Rock, 1970—. Mem. Nat. Adv. Commn. Health Facilities, 1968-69; cons. Cal. Dept. Pub. Health, 1959-62, Am. Legion Child Welfare Com., 1962-69; mem. nat. com. Pediatric Research Edn. and Practice, 1961—; chmn. Okla. Commn. Med. Research, 1964-70, Okla. Commn. Handicapped, 1965-70; cons. Nat. Found., Com. Hosp. Care Children. Bd. dirs. Okla. Med. Research Found., 1964-70, Okla. Health Sci. Fedn., 1965-70. Served with M.C., USNR, 1943-46. Decorated Bronze Star. Diplomate Am. Bd. Pediatrics. Fellow Am. Acad. Pediatrics; mem. A.M.A. (council sci. assembly 1965— chmn. sect. pediatrics 1966), So. Soc. Pediatric Research, A.A.A.S., Am. Pub. Health Assn., Oklahoma City C. of C. (dir. 1969-70), Cal. Acad. Medicine, Sigma Xi, Alpha Omega Alpha, Alpha Kappa Kappa. Democrat. Methodist. Rotarian. Club: Commonwealth (San Francisco). Contbr. numerous articles in field. Home: 2617 Shenandoah Valley Dr Little Rock AR 72207 Office: 4301 W Markham Little Rock AR 72201

DENNIS, JOE, educator; b. Sherman, Tex., Dec. 5, 1911; s. Elbert Leander and Maude Clay (Bernard) D.; B.A., Austin Coll., 1933, D.Sc. (hon.), 1965; M.A., U. Tex., Med. Sch., 1937, Ph.D., U. Tex., 1942; m. Jeanette Wallis, Aug. 25, 1935; children—Nancy Clay, Linda Joan, Susan Moon. Tutor biol. chemistry U. Tex. Med. Sch., 1934- 36, instr., 1936-38; instr. chemistry Tex. Tech. U., 1938-41, asst. prof. chemistry, 1941-45, asso. prof., 1945-47, prof. chemistry, 1947-50, 69—, prof., head dept. chemistry and chem. engring., 1950-60, head dept. chemistry, 1960-69. Fellow A.A.A.S. (S.W. div. pres. 1955); mem. Am. Chem. Soc., Am. Inst. Chemistry, Sigma Xi, Phi Kappa Phi. Presbyn. Home: 2718 29th St Lubbock TX 79410

DENNIS, JOHN MURRAY, educator, physician; b. Willards, Md., Jan. 31, 1923; s. John Murray and Betty (Hearne) D.; B.S., U. Md., 1943, M.D., 1945; m. Mary Helen France, Oct. 8, 1947; children—Lori Ann, John Murray, Patrick France, Terry Elizabeth. Intern U. Md. Hosp., 1945- 46, resident radiology, 1948-50; fellow radiology U. Pa., 1950-51; mem. faculty U. Md. Sch. Medicine and Hosp., 1951—, prof., head dept. radiology, 1953—; cons. Mt. Wilson State Hosp., Balt. City Hosps., Fort George G. Meade Hosp. Pres. Md. div. Am. Cancer Soc., 1962-65, bd. dirs. Md. div., 1955—, nat. bd. dirs., 1965-69. Served with AUS, 1946-48. Recipient Div. award outstanding service Am. Cancer Soc., 1966. Fellow Am. Coll. Radiology (vice chmn. council 1966-68, chmn. 1968-70, exec. com. bd. chancellors 1970—); mem. Med. and Chirurgical Faculty Md. (council 1968—, vice chmn. council 1970-71), Am. Roentgen-Ray Soc., Radiol. Soc. N.Am.; hon. mem. Rocky Mountain Radiol. Soc., Ind. Roentgen Soc. Home: 803 Huntsman Rd Towson MD 21204 Office: 22 S Green St Baltimore MD 21201

DENNIS, KENNETH RALPH, constrn., land devel. co. exec.; b. Martins Ferry, O., Oct. 17, 1925; s. Ralph L. and Helen M. (McKim) D.; B.S. in Math., Miami U., Oxford, O., 1946; postgrad. Ohio State U., 1948-50; m. Judi Kay Espe, Apr. 30, 1955. Comml. audit mgr. Arthur Andersen & Co., Cin., 1950-65; controller Del E. Webb Corp., Phoenix, 1966—. Served with USNR, 1944-47. Mem. Am. Inst. C.P.A.'s, Ohio Soc. C.P.A.'s Nat. Assn. Accountants, Beta Alpha Psi, Beta Gamma Sigma. Optimist. Home: 3512 E Pasadena Av Phoenix AZ 85018 Office: 3800 N Central Av Phoenix AZ 85012

DENNIS, LAWRENCE, writer; b. Atlanta, Ga., Dec. 25, 1893; s. George and Mary (Smith) D.; student Phillips Exeter Acad., 1913-15; A.B., Harvard, 1920; m. Eleanor Simson, 1933 (div.); children—Emily (Mrs. Dermot Harvey), Laura (Mrs. Mark Dollard); m. 2d, Mrs. Dora Shuser Burton. In U.S. diplomatic service 1920-27, serving in Port au Prince (Haiti), Bucharest (Rumania), Managua (Nicaragua), Tegucigalpa (Honduras); was charge d'affaires for periods in Rumania, Honduras, Nicaragua; condr. peace conf. and first phase Am. Intervention in Nicaragua, 1926, during revolution; assigned to Am. embassy, Paris, June 1927, when resigned to enter banking; with J. & W. Seligman & Co., bankers, N.Y.C., 1927-30; brokerage business E. A. Pierce & Co., N.Y.C., 1936- 39; writer since 1930; propr., editor and pub. The Weekly Foreign Letter, N.Y.C., 1939-43, Appeal to Reason (weekly news analysis), since April 1946. Served at Plattsburg, 1915-17; commd. 2d lt. U.S. Army, Aug, 1917; served in A.E.F., 1918-19; hon. disch. as 1st lt., Aug. 1919. Club: Harvard (N.Y.C.). Author: Is Capitalism Doomed? 1932; The Coming American Fascism, 1936; The Dynamics of War and Revolution, 1940; A Trial on Trial (with Maximillian J. St. George), 1946; Operational Thinking for Survival, 1968. Home: 300 Riverside Dr New York City NY 10025

DENNIS, PATRICK, see Tanner, Edward Everett 3d.

DENNIS, RICHMOND BRAMWELL, corp. exec.; b. Mobile, Dec. 14, 1920; s. James Albert and Belva (Morris) D.; student Spring Hill Coll., Mobile, Loyola U., New Orleans; B.B.A., Tulane U., 1949; m. Barbara Anne Deasy, July 26, 1958. With Weis Fricker Mahogany Co., Pensacola, Fla., 1949-50, Otis J. Chamberlain, C.P.A., New Orleans, 1950-51; successively audit, budget mgr., accounting mgr., regional controller, financial analysis mgr. Montgomery Ward & Co., Chgo., 1951-66; controller Laclede Steel Co., St. Louis, 1966, treas., 1966, v.p., 1967-70; v.p. finance and adminstrn. Automobile Club So.

Cal., Los Angeles, 1970—. Served with USNR, 1941-46; PTO. Mem. Financial Execs. Inst. Home: 985-B S Orange Grove Blvd Pasadena CA 91105 Office: 2601 S Figueroa St Los Angeles CA 90007

DENNIS, ROBERT MILLARD, lawyer; b. Cin., Nov. 15, 1917; s. Fred and Jessie (Jones) D.; student Xavier U., 1938-39, U. Cin., 1938-45, U. Ala., 1943; J.D., Chase Coll., 1942; m. Shirlee Hayes, July 9, 1949; children-Sally Ann, David Brian. Admitted to Ohio bar, 1942; practice in Cin., 1946—; asso. Rendigs & Fry, 1946-53; partner Rendigs, Fry, Kiely & Dennis, 1953—; lectr. Chase Coll. Sch. Law. Founder, pres., chmn. bd. United Cerebral Palsy of Cin. and Ohio, Childrens Dental Care Found.; pres. Ednl. Devel. Found.; pres., chmn. bd. Cin. Citizens Police Assn. Served to capt. USAAF, 1942-45. Decorated D.F.C., Air Medal with eight oak leaf clusters. Mem. Am., Ohio, Cin. bar assns., Soc. Hosp. Attys., Def. Research Inst., Fedn. Ins. Counsel, Greater Cin. C. of C., Cin. Hist. Soc., Newcomen Soc. N. Am., Phi Alpha Delta. Clubs: Cincinnati Country, University, Cincinnati Athletic, Hundred (sec.) (Cin.). Home: 2265 Grandin Rd Cincinnati OH 45208 Office: Central Trust Tower Cincinnati OH 45202

DENNIS, ROGER PETER, educator; b. Suring, Wis., Oct. 4, 1915; s. Thomas Joseph and Gertrude Minerva (Wilbur) D.; A.B., St. Norbert Coll., W. De Pere, Wis., 1939; M.A., U. Wis., 1950; Ph.D., Mich. State U., 1960; m. Myra Elizabeth Zimplemann, May 24, 1911; 1 dau., Michele Marie (Mrs. Gary C. Fawcett). Supr. music Vilas County, Eagle River, Wis., 1939-43; dir. music Eagle River High Sch., 1945-47, Shawano (Wis.) High Sch., 1950-52; chmn. dept. music Wis. State U., Oshkosh, 1952—, prof. music, 1962—. Justice of peace, Vilas County, 1945-50. Nat. patron Delta Omicron; bd. dirs. Oshkosh Civic Symphony. Mem. Wis. Arts Council, Civic Music Assn. (bd. dirs.), Nat. Assn., Schs. Music, Music Educators Nat. Conf., Nat. Assn. Humanities Edn., Wis. Music Educators Conf., Wis. Sch. Music Assn., Assn. Wis. State Univs. Faculties, Assn. Wis. Coll. and U. Music Adminstrs., Lincoln Fellowship Wis. Republican. Lutheran. Composer commd. Concerto for Puppets and Orchestra, 1961. Home: 1503 Lake Breeze Rd Oshkosh WI 54901

DENNIS, SANDY, actress; b. Hastings, Neb., Apr. 27, 1937; d. Jack Dennis; student Neb. Wesleyan U., U. Neb.; studied acting Herber Berghof Studio, N.Y.C.; m. Gerry Mulligan, June 1965. Stage debut in Bus Stop, Palm Beach, Fla.; appeared on Broadway in Burning Bright, 1960, Face of a Hero, 1960, The Complaisant Lover, 1961, A Thousand Clowns, 1962, Any Wednesday, 1964; film debut in Splendor in the Grass, 1961, later appeared in Who's Afraid of Virginia Woolf?, 1965, Up the Down Staircase, 1967, The Fox, 1967; Sweet November, Daphne in Cottage D, The Millstone, also appeared in A Hatful of Rain, Thank You All Very Much, That Cold Day in the Park, The Out-of-Towners. Recipient Tony awards for A Thousand Clowns, 1963, Any Wednesday, 1964, Oscar award as best supporting actress for Who's Afraid of Virginia Woolf?; Moscow Film Festival best-actress award for Up the Down Staircase, 1967. Address: care Creative Management Associates Ltd 555 Madison Av New York City NY 10022*

DENNIS, WALTER EUGENE, broker; b. Bklyn. Nov. 24, 1905; s. Charles E. and Edith (Jenkinson) D.; student pub. schs.; m. Eleanor Pierce Very, May 17, 1928; 1 dau., Patricia D. Whittenberger. With Chase-Manhattan Bank, N.Y.C., 1926-68, successively credit man, asst. mgr. credit dept., asst. cashier, asst. v.p., v.p., 1926-54, exec. v.p., 1956-66, dir., 1966-67; v.p. Paine, Webber, Jackson & Curtis, Inc., N.Y.C., 1968—; dir. Bucyrus- Erie Co., Milw., SuCrest Corp., N.Y.C., Allied Stores, N.Y.C., Essex Internat., Inc., Ft. Wayne, Ind. Pres. Beekman Downtown Hosp., N.Y.C. Clubs: River, Recess (N.Y.C.); Arcola Country (Paramus, N.J.). Home: 4 Dogwood Lane Tenafly NJ 07670 Office: 140 Broadway New York City NY 10005

DENNIS, WARD BRAINERD, aerospace co. exec.; b. Detroit Lakes , Minn., Aug. 28, 1922; s. Fred and Laura (Bergseng) D.; B. Aero. Scis., U. Minn., 1943; M.S., U. Mich., 1947; postgrad. Johns Hopkins, 1948-50; m. Bette Mae Evans, Mar. 16, 1948; childrenKaren Christine, Patrick Ward. With Bell Aircraft Co., 1944-45, Cornell Aero. Lab., 1945-46; asst. prof. U.S. Naval Postgrad. Sch., 1947-50; with Rand Corp., 1950-53; with Northrop Corp., 1953-, v.p. corp. devel. planning, 1963-. Home: 16632 Adlon Rd Encino CA 91316 Office: 1800 Century Park E Century City Los Angeles CA 90067

DENNIS, WAYNE, former psychologist, educator; b. Washington County, O., Sept. 1, 1905; s. Samuel R. and Mary V. (Fox) D.; A.B., Marietta Coll., 1926; A.M., Clark U., 1928, Ph.D., 1930; Social Sci. Research Council fellow, Yale, 1936-37; m. Marsena Anne Galbreath, Mar. 19, 1928 (dec. July 1965); children—Mary, Anne, James Gill; m. 2d, Margaret Wallihan Hudson, Mar. 18, 1970. Asst. prof., U. Va., 1929-42; vis. prof. Clark U., 1937-38; prof., head dept. psychology La. State U., 1942-46, U. Pitts., 1946-51; prof. psychology Bklyn. Coll., 1951-70, chmn., 1951-62; exec. officer doctoral program gen. psychology U. City N.Y., 1962-64, vis. prof. Am. U. of Beirut, 1955-56, 58-59. Served as lt. USNRF, 1943-46; head, Human Engring. sect., Spl. Devices Div., Office of Naval Research. Fellow Am. Psychol. Assn., Interam. Soc. Psychology, Gerontol Soc., Soc. for Research in Child Devel.; mem. Eastern Psychol. Assn., Phi Beta Kappa, Sigma Xi. Author: The Hopi Child, 1940; Group Values Through Children's Drawing, 1966. Co-author: Current Trends in Psychology, 1947. Current Trends in Social Psychology, 1948; Current Trends in Industrial Psychology, 1949; Current Trends in the Relation of Psychology to Medicine, 1950; Current Trends in Psychological Theory, 1951. Editor: Readings in Child Psychology, 1951, rev., 1963; Readings in the History of Psychology, 1948, Readings in General Psychology, 1949, (with Ihsan Al-Issa) Cross Cultural Studies of Behavior, 1970; Historical Readings in Child Psychology, 1971. Editor Psychol. Bull., 1953-58. Home: Sam Hill Doswell VA 23047

DENNIS, WILLARD KELSO, librarian; b. Odebolt, Ia., Apr. 21, 1916; s. Homer E. and Madge (Kelso) D.; A.B., S.W. Mo. State Coll., 1937; B.L.S., U. Ill., 1939; m. Lorene Brown, Dec. 26, 1938. Tchr. social studies, Stockton, Mo., 1937-38; asst. adult edn. Ill. State Library, Springfield, 1939-40; librarian Parks Air Coll., East St. Louis, Ill., 1940-45, Beech Aircraft Corp., Wichita, Kan., 1945-47, S.W. Regional Library, Bolivar, Mo., 1947-63, Kansas City (Kan.) Pub. Library, 1963—. Mem. Mo. Libraries Plan Commn., 1953-54, Mo. Library Devel. Commn., 1955- 63, Kan. Library Systems Adv. Council, 1966—; sec.-treas. Mo. Libraries Film Coop., 1953-63; pres. S.W. Mo. Library Service, Inc., 1957-63; mem. grant area 2 com. Kan. State Library. Mem. A.L.A. (regional processing com. RTSD 1960-68), Mo. Library Assn. (pres. 1954, co chmn. legislative com. 1957; gov.'s com. libraries in Kan. 1963—). Methodist. Contbr. articles to aviation and library publs. Home: 985 Hillcrest Dr Kansas City KS 66102 Office: 625 Minnesota Av Kansas City KS 66101

DENNISON, BYRON LEE, educator, elec. engr.; b. Clarksburg, W. Va., Dec. 8, 1930; s. Raymond Lewis and Edna (Sturm) D.; B.S. in Elec. Engring., W. Va. U., 1953; M.S. in Elec. Engring., Va. Poly. Inst., 1962; Ph.D. in Elec. Engring., Worcester Poly. Inst., 1967; m. Betty Jean Davis, July 4, 1954; children—Diane Lee, Shirley Joanne. Sr. engr. govt. and indsl. div. Philco. Corp., Phila., 1953-58; asst. asso. prof. Va. Poly. Inst., Blacksburg, 1958-66; prof. Lowell (Mass.) Tech. Inst., 1966—, head dept. elec. engring., 1967—; cons. Polysci. Corp., Blacksburg, 1961-63, Worcester Found. Exptl. Biology, Shrewsbury, Mass., 1966-68. Registered profl. engr., Mass., Va., W. Va. Mem. I.E.E.E., Am. Soc. Engring. Edn., Simulation Councils, Sigma Xi, Eta Kappa Nu, Phi Kappa Phi. Research devel. math. model for motor activity of cat iris. Home: 70 Patten Rd Forge Village MA 01828 Office: Lowell Tech Inst 1 Textile Av Lowell MA 01854

DENNISON, CHARLES STUART, chem. co. exec.; b. N.Y.C., Mar. 21, 1918; s. Charles Stuart and Charlotte (Irwin) D.; student Columbia, N.Y.U.; m. Carol Frances Krueger, June 6, 1951; children—Laura Hardie, Deborah Irwin. Exec. trainee Gen. Motors Corp., 1935-39; asst. mgr. advt. and sales promotion U.S. Steel Export Co., 1939-42; export sales mgr., acting gen. sales mgr. Willys Overland Motors, Inc., 1946-51; mng. dir. Olin Mathieson Ltd., also E. R. Squibb Ltd., London, Eng., 1951-57; v.p. Chrysler Export Corp., 1957-58; v.p. overseas Internat. Minerals & Chem. Corp., Skokie, Ill., 1958-70; dir. Internat. Minerals & Chems., Ltd., London, Eng., (ANZ) Pty. Ltd., Australia, (Bahamas) Ltd.,(Can.) Ltd., (Panama), Corommandel Fertilisers, Ltd., Secunderabad, India, Compagnie Senegalaise des Phosphates de Taiba, Dakar, Azufrera Intercontinental S.A. de C.V., Mexico, until 1970. Mem. Pres.'s Sci. Adv. Com. Panel on World Food Supply; mem. exec. com. FAO Industry Coop. Program, Rome, until 1970; mem. industry adv. com. FAO, Rome; mem. steering com. Pacific Basin Econ. Coop. Council; mem. council Soc. for Internat. Devel.; mem. com. on Internat. Devel. Inst., Nat. Acad. Scis.; mem. Council Fgn. Relations; mem. fgn. relations task force White House Conf. on Youth; chmn. com. on tech. Council of Americas; bd. advisers Assn. Internat. des Etudiants en Scis. Economiques et Commerciales; adv. com. on application sci. and tech. to devel. Latin Am., Orgn. Am. States. Trustee Agrl. Devel. Council; bd. dirs. Overseas Devel. Council, Agribus. Council. Served to capt., parachute inf., AUS, World War II. Decorated Bronze Star, Combat Inf. badge; comdr. Order Merit (Senegal), N.A.M.. (mem. pres.'s adv. group for internat. affairs) Internat. C. of C. (vice chmn. devel. com. U.S. council), English Speaking Union, Asia Soc. (chmn. India council). Clubs: Metropolitan (N.Y.C.); Racquet (Chgo.); Internat. (Washington); American (London). Home: 45 E 89th St New York City NY 10028 Office: 485 Lexington Av New York City NY 10017

DENNISON, DAVID MATHIAS, theoretical physicist; b. Oberlin, O., Apr. 26, 1900; s. Walter and Anna (Green) D.; A.B., Swarthmore Coll., 1921, D.Sc. (hon.), 1950; Ph.D., U. Mich., 1924; m. Helen Lenette Johnson, Aug. 28, 1924; children—Edwin Walter, David Severin. Gen. Edn. Bd. fellow, Inst. for Theoretical Physics, Copenhagen, Denmark, 1924-26; Guggenheim fellow, 1940; prof. physics U. Mich., 1935-66, Harrison M. Randall prof. physics, 1966-70, emeritus, 1970—, chmn. dept., 1955-65, Henry Russell lectr., 1952; cons. OSRD, 1942- 45. Recipient Distinguished Faculty Achievement award, 1963. Fellow Am. Phys. Soc., Am. Optical Soc.; mem. Nat. Acad. Scis., Phi Beta Kappa, Sigma Xi, Phi Kappa Phi. Research in theory of infra red spectra, molecular structure, specific heat of hydrogen. Home: 2511 Hawthorn Rd Ann Arbor MI 48104

DENNISON, DAVID SHORT, Jr., govt. ofcl.; b. Poland, Ohio, July 29, 1918; s. David Short and Cordelia (Whitman) D.; student Western Reserve Acad., 1936; A.B., Williams Coll., 1940; LL.B., Western Reserve U. Sch. Law, 1945; m. Margaret Gillmer Kroehle, Sept. 7, 1946; children—Jennie, David Whitman. Admitted to Ohio bar, 1946, D.C. bar, 1959; pvt. practice, Waren, O., 1946-70; mem. Ohio 85th Congress, 1957-58; cons. U.S. Civil Rights Commn., 1959; mem. FTC, 1970—. Chmn. Trumbull County (O.) Republican Central and Exec. Coms., 1964-66, mem. Ohio Republican Central Com., 1966-70; mem. Trumbull County Bd. Elections, 1964-68. Trustee Western Reserve Acad. Served with Am. Field Service, World War II. Home: Columbia Plaza 500 23d St NW Washington DC 20037 Office: Fed Trade Commn Washington DC 20580

DENNISON, RAYMOND ALEXANDER, educator; b. Sedalia, A.B., Miami U., Oxford, O., 1936; M.S., State U. Ia., 1940, Ph.D., 1942; m. Mary L. Grumbein, Dec. 26, 1942; childrenDaniel, John, Carolyn. Research asst. U. Ia., 1938-42; asso. prof. U. Fla., 1946- 53, prof., 1953-, head dept. food technology and nutrition, 1956-66, chmn. food sci. dept., 1966-. Served with USNR, 1942-46. Fellow A.A.A.S.; mem. Inst. Food Technologists, Am. Soc. Plant Physiologists, Am. Soc. Hort. Sci., Am. Chem. Soc., Sigma Xi. Presbyn. Home: 4961 NW 8th Av Gainesville FL 32601

DENNISON, ROBERT LEE, pub. co. exec.; b. Warren, Pa., Apr. 13, 1901; s. Ludovici Waters and Laura Florence (Lee) D.; B.S., U.S. Naval Acad., 1923; M.S., Pa. State Coll., 1930; D. Eng., Johns Hopkins, 1935; m. Mildred Fenton Mooney Neely, May 10, 1937; children—Lee, Robert Lee. Commd. ensign USN, 1923, advanced through grades to adm., 1959, served with Atlantic, Pacific and Asiatic fleets, commd. U.S.S. Ortolan, 1935-37, U.S.S. Cuttlefish, 1937- 38, U.S.S. John D. Ford, 1940-41, U. S.S. Missouri, 1947-48; mem. joint war plans com. of Joint Chiefs of Staff, 1944-45; asst. chief of Naval Operations (polit.-mil. affairs), 1945-47; naval aide to Pres. of U.S., 1948-53; comdr. Cruiser Div. 4, U.S. Atlantic Fleet, 1953-54; dir. Strategic Plans Div., asst. chief naval operations (plans and policy), Office Naval Operations, 1954-56; mem. joint strategic plans com. of Joint Chiefs of Staff; comdr. First Fleet, U.S. Pacific Fleet, 1956-58; DCNO (Plans and Policy), Navy Dept., 1958-58; comdr.-in-chief US Naval Forces, Eastern Atlantic and Mediterranean, 1959-60, Atlantic and U.S. Atlantic Fleet. Supreme Allied Comdr. Atlantic, 1960- 63; chief of staff of comdr. submarines, East Australia and Comdrs. Allied Naval Forces, East Australia, 1942; chief of staff Amphibious Forces U.S. Pacific Fleet, 1942-43; chief staff to comdr. 9th Amphibious Forces, 1943; v.p. dir. The Copeley Press, Inc., 1964—. Decorated D. S.M., Legion Merit; Gold Star in lieu of 2d Legion of Merit; Am. Def.; Asiatic-Pacific Area, 2 Stars, Philippine Def. with Star; Navy Unit Commendation (U.S.S. Pennsylvania); Navy Occupation Service medal (European Clasp), Nat. Def. Service medal; Army Distinguished Unit Citation (Philippines) Am. Area; World War II Victory (U.S.); Order of British Empire; Grand officer of the Order of Naval Merit (Brazil); Comdr. of the Order of the Crown (Belgium); Comdr. Legion of Honor (France); Grand Cross Order of Orange-Nassau (The Netherlands), Grand Cross Mil. Order of Aviz (Portugal). Mem. Sigma Xi. Clubs: New York Yacht; Metropolitan, Chevy Chase, Army Navy (Washington). Home: 5040 Westpath Terrace Washington, DC 20016 Office: 1629 K St NW Washington DC 20006

DENNISTON, ALFRED BENJAMIN, state ofcl.; b. Mt. Pleasant, Pa., Sept. 27, 1904; s. Samuel Lowry and Elouise (Reppert) D.; B.S., U.S. Mil. Acad., 1928; M.S., U. Mich., 1934; m. Frances Reeder Wilson, Aug. 25, 1928; children—Carol D. (Mrs. George W. Campbell), Kendall D. (Mrs. Charles K. Newman). Commd. 2d lt. U.S. Army, 1928, advanced through grades to maj. gen., 1956; mem. faculty Army War Coll., 1950-53, dep. q.m. gen., 1953-58, comdg. gen. q.m. tng. command, 1958-62; ret. 1962; asst. dir. indsl. devel. Office Gov. Va., Richmond, 1962-65, coordinator civil def., dir. emergency planning 1965—. Decorated Legion of Merit with 2 oak leaf clusters (U.S.), Order of Orange (Nassau, Holland). Home: Tattoo Hill Route 2 Chesterfield VA 23832 Office: Midlothian Pike Richmond VA 23225

DENNISTON, JOSEPH CHARLES, physician; b. Rochester, N.Y., Nov. 1, 1914; s. Frank J. and Anna (Rigney) D.; A.B., Holy Cross Coll., 1936; M.D., Tufts U., 1940; m. Dorothy Quinn, June 23, 1938; children—Dorothy, Anne, Madelyn, Joseph, Mary, Intern Nassau Hosp., Mineola, N.Y., 1941-42; resident pediatrics St. Josephs Hosp., Louisville, 1952-54; gen. practice medicine, Russellville, Ky., 1946-52; practice pediatrics, Lewisburg, Ky., 1954-59; practice medicine, specializing in mental retardation, 1959-63, Butlerville, Ind., 1967-70; supt. Hissom Meml. Center, 1963-64, Hosp. for Mentally Retarded, Georgetown, Del., 1964-65; dir. Bur. Services for Mentally Retarded State Pa., Harrisburg, 1965-67; supt. Caro (Mich.) State Home and Tng. Sch., 1970—. Asso. clin. prof. pediatrics U. Okla. Med. Sch. Mem. adv. bd. Childrens Bur. Dept. Health, Edn. and Welfare, Washington. Served to capt. USAAF, 1942-46; PTO. Recipient Community Service awards Lewisburg, 1957. Mem. A.M.A., Am. Acad. Pediatrics. Lion. Home: RR 1 North Vernon IN 47265 Office: Caro State Home and Training School Caro MI 48723

DENNLER, CARL, Jr., educator; b. Washington, Mo., Oct. 15, 1923; s. Carl L. and Lona (Rogers) D.; B.S. in Bus. Adminstrn., U. Mo., 1948, M.A. in Econs., 1950; Ph.D. in Accounting, U. Wis., 1962; m. Mary Jeanne McDonald, June 3, 1951; children—McDonald K., Christine D. Instr., then asst. prof. U. Me., 1952-57; asso. prof. W.Va. U., 1957-63; mem. faculty U. Mass., 1963—, chmn. accounting dept. Sch. Bus. Adminstrn., 1966—, prof. accounting, 1968—. Served with USAAF, 1943-46. Mem. Am. Accounting Assn., Am. Econ. Assn., Beta Gamma Sigma, Beta Alpha Psi, Tau Kappa Epsilon. Kiwanian. Home: 25 Bellview Circle Amherst MA 01002

DENNLER, WILLIAM H., exec. v.p. Gen. Electric Co. Address: 570 Lexington Av New York City NY 10022*

DENNSTEDT, FREDERICK DEVERE, oil co. exec.; b. Harmony, Minn., Sept. 23, 1918; s. Frederick William and Ida Henrietta (Bruflodt) D.; B. Chem. Engring., U. Minn., 1948; grad. Advanced Mgmt. Program, Harvard, 1958; m. Marjorie Ernst, July 7, 1948; children—Frederick Ernst, Sara Elizabeth. With Esso Standard Oil Co., 1948-61, asst. gen. mgr. Baton Rouge refinery, 1959-61; with Humble Oil & Refining Co., 1961-64, v.p. mfg. dept., 1962-63, v.p. supply and transp. dept., 1963-64, v.p. refining, Houston, 1969—; refining coordinator Standard Oil Co. (N.J.), 1964-68; logistice operations mgr., 1968-69. Mem. Am. Petroleum Inst. Home: 623 Saddlewood St Houston TX 77024 Office: 800 Bell St Houston TX 77002

DENNY, CHARLES RUTHVEN, radio exec.; b. Balt., Apr. 11, 1912; s. Charles Ruthren and Beulah (Byrd) D.; A.B., Amherst Coll., 1933, hon. LL.D., 1948; LL.B., Harvard, 1936; m. Elizabeth Marie Woolsey, Dec. 31, 1937; children—Alison Byrd, Christine, Charles (dec.). Admitted to D.C. bar, 1936, and practiced with firm of Covington, Burling, Rublee, Acheson and Shorb, Washington, 1936-38; atty., U.S. Dept. of Justice, 1938-41; spl. asst. to Atty. Gen., 1941-42; asst. gen. counsel Fed. Communications Commn., 1942, gen. counsel, 1942-45, commr., 1945- 46, acting chmn., 1946, chmn., 1946-47; v.p. NBC, 1947- 56, exec. v.p. operations, 1956-58; v.p. RCA, 1958—; chmn. bd. RCA Internat. Ltd. (Bermuda), RCA Internat. Ltd. (U.K.), RCA Ltd. (Can.), RCA Ltd. (U.K.), RCA S.A. de C.V. (Mexico); pres. RCA Internat. Devel. Corp.; dir. RCA Global Communications, Inc., Hertz Internat., Ltd., RCA Taiwan Ltd. Chmn. Internat. Telecommunications Confs., 1947. Democrat. Home: Pine Island Rye NY 10580 Office: RCA 30 Rockefeller Plaza New York City NY 10020

DENNY, ROBERT STANLEY, church exec.; b. Somerset, Ky., July 23, 1914; s. A.S. and Ada Thurston D.; B.S. in Bus., U. Ky., 1937, J.D., 1939; L.H.D., Georgetown (Ky.) Coll., 1961; m. Mary Gunn Webb, Aug. 1939 (dec. Jan. 1959); children—Robert Stanley, Julia Webb, Allie Gunn; m. 2d, Jane Ray Bean, Dec. 19, 1959. Ordained minister Bapt. Ch., 1939; Bapt. student dir. La. State U., 1939-41; dir. religious activities Baylor U., Houston, 1941- 45; asso. dept. student work Bapt. Sunday Sch. Bd., Nashville, 1945-56; asso. sec. Bapt. World Alliance, 1956-69, gen. sec., 1969—. Home: 3501 N Vermont St Arlington VA 22207 Office: 1628 16th St N W Washington DC 20009

DENNY, WAYNE BELDING, educator; b. Oberlin, O., Feb. 4, 1914; s. Walter Bell and Mabel (Stevens) D.; B.A., Oberlin Coll., 1935; postgrad. N.Y. State Coll. Tech., Albany, summers 1934-35, Columbia, summers 1936-39; Ph.D., Yale, 1941; postgrad. Case Inst. Tech., 1947-48; m. Clara Guerry, June 17, 1939; children—Walter Bell, John Guerry. Instr. math. Bethlehem Central High Sch., Delmar, N.Y., 1935-38; instr. physics Emory U., 1941-43; asst. prof. physics Oberlin Coll., 1943-48; asso. prof. physics Grinnell (Ia.) Coll., 1948-50, prof., 1950—; research asso. Argonne Nat. Lab., summers 1955-56; vis. lectr. physics Neb. Wesleyan U., summer 1961; Fulbright vis. prof. physics Robert Coll., Istanbul, Turkey, 1958-59; vis. prof. physics U. N.D., summers 1963-64; Fulbright vis. prof. physics Ahmednagar Coll., India, 1965-66; U.S. AID cons. in physics, India, summers 1965-68; vis. prof. physics Silliman U., Dumaquete City, Philippines, 1971-72. Mem. Ia. Acad. Sci., I.E.E.E., Am. Assn. Physics Tchrs., Audio Engring. Soc., Am. Assn. U. Profs. Conglist. Contbr. articles profl. jours. Home: 1409 Park St Grinnell IA 50112

DENNY, WILLIAM DOUGLAS, educator; b. Seattle, July 2, 1910; s. Frank William and Ruby (Van Ornum) D.; A.B., U. Cal. at Berkeley, 1931, M.A., 1933; fellow Am. Acad. Rome, 1939-41; m. Jeanne Gilbert Moyle, July 20, 1940; childrenGail, Leila. Instr., Harvard, 1941-42; instr. Vassar, 1942-45; prof. music U. Cal. at Berkeley, 1945—. Home: 2910 Garber St Berkeley CA 94705

DENNY-BROWN, DEREK ERNEST, physician; b. Christchurch, New Zealand, June 1, 1901; s. Charles and Marian F. (Denny) Denny-B.; M.B., U. New Zealand, 1924, M.D., 1946; Ph.D., Oxford U. (Beit Research fellow), 1928; A.M. (hon.), Harvard, 1943; LL.D. (honorary), Wayne State University, 1959; D.Sci., Otago U., N.Z., 1969; m. Sylvia Summerhayes, Mar. 17, 1937; children—Bruce Charles, Martin John, Myles Robert, John Summerhayes. Came to U.S., 1941, naturalized, 1952. House officer, registrar, later vis. physician Nat. Hosp. Nervous Diseases, London, Eng., 1928-41; neurologist St. Bartholomews Hosp. and Coll., London, 1935-41; prof. neurology Harvard, 1941-46, James Jackson Putnam prof. neurology since 1946; dir. neurological unit, neurologist-in-chief. Boston City Hosp., 1941-67, pres. med. staff, 1966; chief sect. neurophysiology N.E. Primaic Research Center, 1967—. Chmn. bd. cons. Nat. Inst. Neurol. Disease and Blindness, 1965-66. Served with Royal Army M.C., 1939-41, IndiaBurma, 1945-46, advancing from maj. to brig. gen. Decorated Officer Order Brit. Empire; Order Unanue (Peru). Recipient Sherrington medal Royal Soc. Medicine (London), 1962; Jacoby award, American Neurol. Assn., 1968; Modern Medicine award for distinguished achievement, 1965. Fellow Royal Coll. Physicians; hon. mem. Can., German, Mexican, Peruvian neurol. socs.; mem. Physiol. Soc., Am. Neurol. Assn. (past president), Royal Society Medicine of London (hon. fellow), Assn. Am. Physicians, Assn. Brit. Neurologists, Mass. Med. Soc., Boston Soc. Psychiatry and Neurology (past pres.), Am. Assn. Neuropathologist (past pres.), Phila. Neurological Soc. (hon.), Neurological Soc. Paris (hon.), Swiss

Neurological Soc. (corres. mem.). Author articles and books. Home: 3 Mercer Circle Cambridge MA 02138 Office: New Eng Primate Research Center Southborough MA 01772

DENOUE, JEHAN, internat. diplomatic agt.; b. Etretat Seine Inf. France, June 17, 1907; s. Vicomte Achille and Vicomtess Beatrice Ellen (Reid) de N.; student Ecole des Roches, France, 1919-24, Ecole des Sciences Politiques, Paris, 1926-29, Faculte de la Sorbonne, 1926-29; m. Isabelle Decazes de Glucksbierg. June 1948 (dec. Nov. 1968). Ofcl. lectr. in U.S. and Can., as v.p. of the Sauvegarde de l art Francais and rep. the Demeure Historque of France, 1937, 38, 39; ofcl. lectr. Fedn. of Alliance Francaise in U.S. and Can., 1940-41; head of French lang. dept., Rollins Coll., Fla., 1941-42: vis. lectr. and prof., Middlebury Coll., summer 1941-42; mem. U.N. Preparatory Commn., London, 1946, 1st session of gen. assembly, London, Jan. 1946; chief of protocol UN, N.Y.C., 1946-62, chief of protocol European office, Geneva, 1962-67. E.E. and M.P. Order Malta to Switzerland, 1967-71, to Ethiopia, 1971—. Served as French liaison officer with 1st Coldstream Guards in France, Flanders and Dunkirk, 1940, and with 1st British Inf. Div. in Tunisia, Ital (Anzio), 1943-44; French Allied Mil. Govt. officer in U.S. 5th Army in Italy (French corps), 1944; chief staff officer of gen. comdg. French sect. Allied Central Commn. in Italy, 1944-45 and of gen. comdg. Air Div. Allied Control Commn., Berlin, Germany, 1945. Awarded French Croix de Guerre, Am. Bronze Star. Roman Catholic. Club: Jockey (Paris). Home: 8 rue Robert de Traz Geneva Switzerland

DENOVO, JOHN AUGUST, educator; b. Galva, Ill., Nov. 5, 1916; s. August and Paula (LaMantia) DeN.; B.A., Knox Coll., Galesburg, Ill., 1938; M.A., U. Minn., 1940; Ph.D., Yale, 1948; postdoctoral student Harvard, 1956-57, Johns Hopkins, 1957; m. E. Jeanne Humphreys, Dec. 22, 1948; children—Anne, Jay. Teaching asst. U. Minn., 1939-41; asst. in instrn. Yale, 1947; from instr. to prof. Am. history Pa. State U., 1948-64; prof. Am. history, U. Wis., 1964—; vis. lectr. George Washington U., summer 1949; vis. asso. prof. U. Wis., summer 1961; vis. prof. Cornell U., 1963-64. Served to lt. USNR, 1941-45. Grantee Social Sci. Research Council, summer 1956, 59; Ford Found. fellow, 1956-57; Faculty fellow Assn. Middle Eastern Studies, summer 1963; Rockefeller fellow, 1966-67. Mem. Soc. Historians Am. Fgn. Relations, Am. Hist. Assn., Orgn. Am. Historians, Am. Assn. U. Profs., Middle East Studies Assn., Phi Alpha Theta (Book prize 1964). Author: American Interests and Policies in the Middle East, 1900-1939, 1963; also articles, chpts. in books. Home: 216 Walnut St Madison WI 53705

DENOYER, JOHN MILFORD, geologist; b. Kalaw, Burma, May 19, 1926 (parents Am. citizens); s. Andrew J. and Mary (Gibbs) DeN.; A.B., Chico State Coll., 1953; M.A., U. Cal. at Berkeley, 1955, Ph.D., 1958; m. Doris H. Hoffman, Nov. 3, 1951; children—Barbara J., Linda A., Perry H., Emily J. From instr. to asso. prof. U. Mich., Ann Arbor, 1957-65, acting head acoustics and seismics lab., 1963-65; staff mem. Inst. for Def. Analyses, Washington, 1962-63; dep. dir. Nuclear Test Detection, Advanced Research Projects Agy., Washington, 1965-67; asst. dir. research U.S. Geol. Survey, Washington, 1967-69; dir. Earth Observations Programs Hdqrs. NASA, Washington, 1969—. Served with AUS, 1944-46, 50-51. Recipient Henry Russel award U. Mich., 1964. Fellow A.A.A.S. (mem. council 1968); mem. Am. Geophys. Union (mem. council 1968-70), Seismol. Soc. Am., Geol. Soc. Am., Acoustical Soc. Am., Sigma Xi. Home: 4835 Drummond Av Chevy Chase MD 20015 Office: Earth Observations Programs Hdqrs NASA Washington DC 20546

DENSEN, PAUL MAXIMILLIAN, health adminstr.; b. N.Y.C., Aug. 1, 1913; s. Charles Edwin and Carrie (Weinberg) D.; A.B., Bklyn.Coll., 1934; D.Sc., Johns Hopkins, 1939; M.A. (hon.), Harvard, 1968; m. Elizabeth A. Reed, Dec. 19, 1939; childrenRebecca E. (Mrs. John Rothfuss), Peter. From instr. to asso. prof. preventive medicine Vanderbilt U. Med. Sch., 1939-46; chief div. med. research statistics VA, Washington, 1946-49; asso. prof., then prof. biometry Grad. Sch. Pub. Health, U. Pitts., 1949-54; dir. div. research and statistics Health Ins. Plan Greater N.Y., 1954-59; dept. commnr. N.Y.C. Dept. Health, 1959-66; dept. adminstr. N.Y.C. Health Services Adminstrn., 1966-68; dir. Harvard Center Community Health and Med. Care, 1968-; prof. community health Harvard Sch. Pub. Health, 1968—. Fellow Am. Statis. Assn., Am. Pub. Health Assn., A.A.A.S.; mem. Am. Epidemiological Soc., Biometric Soc., Internat. Epidemiological Soc., DElta Omega. Home: 46 Gardner Rd Brookline MA 02146 Office: 643 Huntington Av Boston MA 02115

DENSLOW, JOHN STEDMAN, osteopath; b. Hartford, Conn., Dec. 19, 1906; s. George H. and Maud (Stedman) D.; D.O., Kirksville (Mo.) Coll., 1929; m. Mary Jane Laughlin, Aug. 22, 1934; children—Martha, George, Peter. Asst. dir. clinic, Chgo. Coll. Osteopathy, 1933- 38; pvt. practice, Kirksville, since 1938; prof. osteopathic teohnic, Kirksville Coll. Osteopathy and Surgery since 1940, chmn. dept. osteopathic technic, dir. research affairs, 1938-65, v.p. coll., 1965—; dir. of Still Meml. Research Trust. Mem. USPHS Rev. Com. Basic and Spl. Project Grants for M.D. and D.O. Schs. Mem., chmn. Mo. Bd. Health; mem. Mo.. Gov.'s Adv. Council for Comprehensive Health Planning, cons. USPHS Nat. Center for Health Statistics. Mem. Am. Physiol. Soc., Am. Assn. Osteopathic Colls. (V.P.), Am. Osteopathic Assn., Mo. Assn. Osteopathic Physicians and Surgeons. Episcopalian. Rotarian Home: Thousand Hills Farm Kirksville MO 63501

DENSMORE, MORRIS AUBREY, banker; b. East Noel, N.S., Can., June 3, 1923; s. Alfred and Nellie (Harvey) D.; naturalized U.S. citizen, 1944; A.B., Bowdoin Coll., 1947; postgrad. Boston U., 1947-48; M.B.A., Harvard, 1950; m. Arline Helen Thurlow, July 27, 1946; children—Gregory Bruce, Jeffrey Brown, Martha Dole, Comml. rep. New Eng. Tel. & Tel. Co., Boston, 1947-48; with trust dept. First Nat. Bank Portland (Me.), 1950-64; v.p., sr. trust officer Old Kent Bank & Trust Co., Grand Rapids, Mich., 1964-70, sr. v.p., 1969-70; sr. v.p. Union Bank Los Angeles, 1970-71, exec. v.p., 1971—; former dir. Fed. Loan & Bldg. Assn., Portland. Pres. Me. Estate Planning Council, 1963; chmn. Bowdoin Coll. Alumni Fund, 1965-66. Treas., bd. dirs. Grand Rapids Symphony Soc., 1967-70, Mary Free Bed Hosp. and Rehab. Complex, 1966-70; bd. dirs. jr. Achievement Grand Rapids, 1967-68, Grand Valley council Boy Scouts Am., 1968-70; corporator Me. Med. Center, 1962—. Served to lt. comdr. USNR, 1943-46. Mem. Am. Inst. Banking, Zeta Psi. Conglist. Home: 605 Chiswick Rd Palos Verdes Estates CA 90274 Office: 445 Figueroa St Los Angeles CA 90017

DENSMORE, PARK, steel co. exec.; b. Monrovia, Cal., Aug. 27, 1927; s. Ralph A. and Margaret (Kennedy) D.; B.A. in Bus., U. Mont., 1953; m. Grace M. Barrett, Aug. 30, 1952; childrenPeggy, Joy B., Park S. Cost accountant Northrop Aircraft Co., 1953-55; with Earle H. Jorgensen Co., Los Angeles, 1955—, controller, 1965—. Served with USNR, 1946-48. Mem. Financial Execs. Inst. Club: Cabrillo Beach Yacht (commodore 1968). Home: 3645 Via Palomino Palos Verdes Estates CA 90247 Office: 10650 S Alameda St Los Angeles CA 90044

DENSTEDT, ORVILLE FREDERICK, educator, biochemist; b. Blyth, Ont., Can., Mar. 2, 1899; B. Sc., U. Man., 1929; Ph.D. in Biochemistry, McGill U., 1937; married in 1938; two children. Asst., Pacific Fisheries Expt. Sta., 1929-32; mem. faculty McGill U., 1937-68, Gilman Cheney prof. biochemistry, 1965-68, emeritus prof. biochemistry, 1968—. Fellow N.Y. Acad. Sci.; mem. Am. Soc. Biol. Chemists, Chem. Inst. Can.; emeritus mem. Canadian Physiol. Soc. (past pres.), Canadian Fedn. Biol. Socs., Canadian Biochem. Soc. (past pres.), Canadian Nutrition Soc., Internat. Soc. Hematology, Am. Soc. Hematology, Canadian Inst. Food Tech. (past pres.), Corp. Profl. Chemists Province of Que. Address: 4167 Grand Blvd Montreal Quebec Canada

DENT, ALBERT WALTER, univ. pres.; b. Atlanta, Sept. 25, 1904; s. Albert and Daisey (Thomas) D.; A.B., Morehouse Coll., 1926, LL.D., 1947; LL.D., Bishop Coll., 1969, Tulane U., 1969; m. Ernestine J. Covington, June 23, 1931; childrenThomas Covington, Benjamin Albert, Walter Jesse. Auditor, Atlanta Life Ins. Co., 1926; v.p., Safety Constrn. Co., Houston, 1927-28; alumni sec., Morehouse Coll., 1928-31; supt., Flint-Goodridge Hosp. of Dillard U., 1932-41; bus. mgr. Dillard U., 1935-41, pres., 1941-69. cons. Health Edn. Authority of La., 1969—. U.S. del. World Health Assembly, 1948, 55, 58; cons. health adv. com. fgn. Operations Adminstrn., 1954. Dir. So. Regional Council, 1944-, v.p., 1952-65; dir. Nat. Orgn. Pub. Health Nursing, 1944-50, Com. for Nation's Health 1946-52, Nat. Health Council, 1949- (pres. 1953-55), United Negro Coll. Fund; Mem. Commn. on Health Careers, 1958—; La. adr. com. Civil Rights Commn. 1959—; bd. dirs. Nat. Med. Fellowship, Inc., 1959- ; bd. assos. Chgo. Theol. Sem.,1962-; mem. Nat. Commn. Community Health Services, 1962—, Fed. Hosp. Council 1946-50, 61—. Bd. trustees Meharry Med. Coll., 1951-54; mem. com. on fellowships Ford Found., 1951-54. Fellow Am. Coll. Hosp. Adminstr.; mem. Assn. Colls. and Secondary Schs. for Negroes (pres. 1948-49). Am. Hosp. Assn. (commn. hosp. care), U.S. Children's Bur. (commn. on Children and Youth), Nat. Planning Assn. (com. on South, exec. com. 1952-), Nat. Tb Assn. (pres. 1965-66), Nat. Student Health Assn. (pres. 1942-48), Nat. Conf. Hosp. Adminstrs. (chmn. 1936-42), Morehouse Coll. Alumni Assn. (pres. 1936- 39), Omega Psi Phi (past grand basileus). Home: 2401 Gentilly Blvd New Orleans LA 70122

DENT, ELLSWORTH CHARLES, ednl. film cons.; b. Dunlap, Kan., Dec. 9, 1899; s. William Ellsworth and Emma Rosetta (Rake) D.; B.S., Kan. State Tchrs. Coll., 1923; postgrad. U. Kan., 1926-31; m. Dorothy Mabel Adam, July 25, 1931. Dir. bur. visual instrn. U. Kan., Lawrence, 1923-33; visual instrn. cons. Brigham Young U., 1933-34; dir. div. motion pictures Dept. Interior, Washington, 1934-36; ednl. dir. RCA, Camden, N.J., 1936-43; gen. mgr. Soc. Visual Edn., Inc., Chgo., 1943-46; dir. distbn. Coronet Films, Chgo., 1946-57, v.p. Esquire, Inc., 1957-69, exec. v.p. Esquire Education Group, 1969-70; v.p. Coronet Films, 1957-64, senior vice president, 1964-69. Recipient Distinguished Alumnus of Year award Kan. State Tchrs. Coll., 1961, Man of Year award Ill. Audio-Visual Assn., 1961. Mem. Nat. Edn. Assn. (dir. exhibitors assn. 1957-61, pres. 1959- 60), Nat. Audio-Visual Assn. (chmn. edn. com. 1953-69), Am. Assn. Sch. Adminstrs., Soc. Motion Picture and Television Engrs., Sigma Tau Gamma (pres. 1925-35; Distinguished Achievement award 1971), Phi Delta Kappa, Kappa Delta Pi, Acacia. Clubs: Executives (Chgo.); Army and Navy Country (Washington). Author: The Audio Visual Handbook, 6th edit., 1949. Home: 9414 Drake Av Evanston IL 60203 Office: 65 E South Water St Chicago IL 60601

DENT, FREDERICK BAILY, textile co. exec.; b. Cape May, N.J., Aug. 17, 1922; s. Magruder and Edith (Baily) D.; grad. St. Paul's Sch., 1940; B.A., Yale, 1943; m. Mildred C. Harrison, Mar. 11, 1944; children—Frederick Baily, Mildred Hutcheson, Pauline Harrison, Diana Gwynn, Magruder Harrison. Dirs., Joshua L. Baily & Co., Inc., N.Y.C., 1946-47; pres. Mayfair Mills, Arcadia, S.C., 1947—, also dir.; dir. Gen. Electric Co., S.C. Nat. Bank. Chmn. Spartanburg County Planning and Devel. Commn., 1960—. Trustee, treas. Inst. Textile Tech.; trustee Spartanburg Day Sch. Served with USNR, 1943-46. Mem. S.C. Textile Mfrs. Assn. (dir.), Am. Textile Mfrs. Inst. (dir.), Bus. Council. Episcopalian. Home: 19 Montgomery Dr Spartanburg SC 29302 Office: Mayfair Mills Arcadia SC 29320

DENT, HARRY SHULER, govt. ofcl.; b. St. Matthews, D., Feb. 21, 1930; s. Hampton N. and Sallie (Prickett) D.; B.A., Presbyn@J Hampton N. and Sallie (Prickett) D.; B.A., Presbyn. Coll., Clinton, S.C., 1951; LL.B., George Washington U., 1957, LL.M., 1959; m. Betty Francis, Aug. 16, 1951; children—Harry Shuler, Dolly, Virginia, John. Washington corr. several S.C. newspaper and radio stas., 1954; adminstv. asst. to U.S. Senator Strom Thurmond, 1955-65; admitted to S.C. bar, 1957; practice in Columbia and St. Matthews, 1965-68; chmn. S.C. Republican Party, 1965-68; dept. counsel to President Nixon, 1968—. Pres. S.C. State Soc., Washington, 1960; founder, chmn. Senate Staff Prayer Breakfast Group, 1962. Active S.C. Rep. campaigns, 1964-68. Baptist (deacon, trustee). Served with AUS, 1951-53; Korea, maj. Res. Home: 4617 Perry Ct Columbia SC 29206 Office: The White House Washington DC 20500

DENT, JOHN H., comgressman; b. Johnetta, Pa., Mar. 10, 1908; s. Samuel and Genevieve Dent; student pub. schs., Pa.; m. Margaret R. Dent, Apr. 4, 1924; childrenPatricia (Mrs. Donald Sarp), John Frederick. Mem. local council United Rubber Workers, 1923-27, then pres. of local, mem. exec. council, also mem. internat. council; mem. Pa. Ho. of Reps., 1934-36, mem. Senate, 1936-58, floor leader; mem. 85-91st congresses, 21st Dist. Pa. Served with Air Corps, USMC, 1924-28. Democrat. Office: House Office Bldg Washington DC 20525

DENT, JOHN WILLIAM, marble co. exec.. b. Cartersville, Ga., Nov. 11, 1905; s. Frederick William and Pearl (Dodd) D.; student N. Ga. Coll.; m Charlotte Flemister, June 1930; 1 dau., Sue brook (Mrs. Elliott Phillips). With Ga. Marble Co., Atlanta, 1947—, pres., 1955-67, now chmn. bd., 1967—, also dir., mem. exec. com., dir., mem. exec. com. Atlantic Steel Co., Fulton Fed. Savs. & Loan Assn.; dir. Atlanta & West Point R.R. Co., Jim Walter Corp., Ga. Internat. Corp., Abby Internat. Corp. Mem. Ga. C. of C. (past pres.), Marble Inst. Am. (past pres.), Nat. Assn. Marble Producers (pres.). Presbyn. (elder). Clubs: Capital City, Commerce, Peachtree Golf (Atlanta); Cartersville (Ga.) Country. Home: 557 W Main St Cartersville GA 30120 Office: 11 Pryor St Atlanta GA 30303

DENT, THOMAS ASHLEY III, diversified mfg. cos.; s. Ashley, Jr. and Louise McAllister (Young) D.; grad. Hotchkiss Sch., 1940; B. Mech. Engring., Cornell U., 1944; m. Geraldine K. Tyner, June 26, 1948; children—Daubray, Thomas H., Alexandra. With U.S. Gypsum Co., 1946-56, asst. mgr. engring., Chgo., 1954-56; with Ruberoid Co. (became div. of General Aniline & Film Corp. 1967), 1957- 67, asst. v.p. operations, 1961-64, v.p., 1964-67; v.p. GAF Corp., 1967-68, v.p. tech. services, 1969—. Committeeman Hopewell Twp. (N.J.), 1966-70, mayor of Hopewell Township, 1969; chmn. Hopewell Twp. Municipal Utilities Authority, 1965-70. Served to lt. (j.g.) USNR, 1943-46. Mem. Kappa Alpha. Home: Amwell Rd Hopewell NJ 08525 Office: GAF Corp 140 W 51st St New York City NY 10039

DENT, V. EDWARD, advt. and communications co. exec.; b. Green Bay, Wis., Oct. 17, 1918; s. Florian E. and Loretta M. (Castona) D.; B.S., U. Wis., 1940. Mng. editor pharmacy publs. McGraw-Hill Co., N.Y.C., 1946-49; exec. v.p. L.W. Frohlich and Co. Intercon Inter Inc., N.Y.C., 1949-; exec. dir. Nat. Sci. Network, N.Y.C., 1964-. Served to 1st lt. AUS, 1941-46; PTO. Mem. Mus. Modern Art, Clarion Concerts, Mus. Primitive Art. Mem. Nat. Assn. FM Broadcasters, Pharm. Advt. Club N.Y.C. Club: University (N.Y.C.). Home: 159 E 63d St New York City NY 10022 Office: 34 E 51st St New York City NY 10022

DENTAN, ROBERT CLAUDE, clergyman, educator; b. Rossville, Ind., Nov. 27, 1907; s. Claude Gavin and Maud (Parry) D.; A.B., Colo. Coll., 1928; B.D., Berkeley Divinity Sch. (fellow), 1932, S.T.D., 1954; student of American Sch. of Oriental Research, Jerusalem, 1932-33; Ph.D., Yale, 1946; m. Dealome Knox, July 21, 1934 (dec. Sept. 1970); 1 son, Robert Knox. Ordained deacon, P.E. Ch., 1932, priest, 1934; priest in charge, St. John's Ch., Donora, Pa., 1934-36; rector, St. John's Ch., New Haven, 1936-43; prof., lit. and interpretation of the O.T., Berkeley Div. Sch., 1943-54; asst. Christ Church, New Haven, 1943-54; prof. O.T. lit and interpretation, Gen. Theol. Sem., N.Y.C., 1954—. Trustee Berkeley Div. Sch., 1954-58, Am. Schs. of Oriental Research, 1954-56; dir. Am. Sch. Oriental Research, Jerusalem, 1956-57, mem. Jerusalem Sch. com., 1957—. Mem. Am. Bible Soc. (board mgrs. and translations com. 1959—), Nat. Council Chs. (Standard Bible Com. 1961—), Conn. Acad. Arts and Scis., Nat. Assn. Profs. Hebrew, Soc. Bibl. Lit. and Exegesis. Am. Oriental Soc., Am. Acad. of Religion, Phi Beta Kappa. Author: Preface to Old Testament Theology, 1950; The Holy Scriptures: a Survey, 1950; Commentary on Zechariah 9-14 and Malachi, in The Interpreter's Bible.; Redemption and Revelation, 1951; The Apocrypha, Bridge of the Testaments, 1954; The Design of the Scriptures, 1961; 1-2 Kings, 1-2 Chronicles (Layman's Bible Commentary); The King and His Cross, 1965; The Knowledge of God in Ancient Israel, 1968. Editor: The Idea of History in the Ancient Near East, 1955; Journal of Biblical Literature, 1950-54, editorial bd., 1966-70. Contbr. Ency. Brit., Ency. Americana, Interpreters' Dictionary of the Bible, Oxford Annotated Bible, N.Y. Times Book Review, others. Address: 175 9th Av New York City NY 10011

DENTON, CHARLES MANDAVILLE, salt co. exec.; b. Glendale, Cal., June 22, 1924; s. Horace Bruce and Marguerite (Mandaville) D.; student U. Cal., 1942, Okla. A. and M. Coll., 1943; B.A. in Journalism, U. So. Cal., 1949; m. Jean Margaret Brady, Dec. 10, 1955; children—Charles Mandaville II, Margot Elizabeth. Reporter, San Fernando Valley Times, N. Hollywood, Cal., 1949-50, U.P., Los Angeles, 1950-52; reporter, sportswriter, columnist I.N.S., Los Angeles, 1952-59; reporter, feature writer, TV editor-columnist Los Angeles Examiner, 1959-62; free-lance TV and mag. writer 1962-63; reporter Los Angeles Times, 1963; columnist San Francisco Examiner, from 1963; now communications dir. Leslie Salt Co., San Francisco. Pres. Greater Los Angeles Press Club Welfare Found., 1961. Served with USNR, 1943-46. Mem. Phi Beta Kappa, Phi Kappa Phi, Sigma Delta Chi, Blue Key. Clubs: Greater Los Angeles Press (pres. 1955-57), Tiburon Peninsula, Bohemian. Author: (with Dr. W. Coda Martin) A Matter of Life, 1964. Home: 40 Seafirth Rd Tiburon CA 94965 Office: Leslie Salt Co 505 Beach St San Francisco CA 94133

DENTON, FRANK RICHARD, former business exec.; b. Arkansas City, Kan., July 16, 1899; s. Albert Hamilton and Alice Emily (Young) D.; student Culver Mil. Acad., 1914-18, Cum Laude, 1948; student University of Kansas, 1920-22; LL.D., Washington and Jefferson College, 1948, Allegheny College, 1958; D.Sc., University of Pittsburgh, 1958; m. Elizabeth Moorhead Bovard, April 28, 1932 (dec. Apr. 1964); children—Frank Richard, James; m. 2d, Constance Connelly Casey, Apr. 19, 1965; stepchildren—Joan Casey Leisure, Samuel B. Casey, Rosemary Casey Carter. Dir., former chief exec. Mellon Nat. Bank & Trust Co., Pitts.; dir. emeritus Pitts. Baseball Club, Gulf Oil Corporation, Pitts.; dir. Trailmobile Finance Company, Pullman, Inc. Mem. Business Council. Trustee Kan. Endowment Assn.; trustee emeritus U. Pitts.; dir. Culver Edn. Found.; board member nat. council Nat. Planning Bd. Dir. Regional Indsl. Devel. Southwestern Pa. Served as 2d lt. F.A., U.S. Army, 1918. col. to brig. gen. Gen. Staff Corps, 1942-45. Decorated D.S.M.; recipient citation for distinguished service U. Kan., 1954. Mem. Sigma Chi. Republican. Presbyn. Clubs: Duquesne, Pittsburgh Golf (Pitts.); Rolling Rock, Laurel Valley Golf (Ligonier); Paradise Valley Country (Phoenix); Bear River (Brigham City, Utah). Home: Ligonier PA 15658 Office: Mellon Nat Bank & Trust Co Pittsburgh PA 15230

DENTON, IRA CLAUDE, banker; b. Belen, Miss., Apr. 1, 1906; s. Ira Claude and Birdie (Partee) D.; B.A. and B.S.C., U. Miss., 1928; LL.B., U. Memphis, 1932; m. Margaret Mason, Apr. 24, 1934; children—Ira Claude, Margaret Mason (Mrs. Robert Khayat). Bookkeeper trust dept. First Nat. Bank, Memphis, 1929- 32, former sr. v.p., sr. trust officer, exec. head, now ret.; pres. Commercial Title Guaranty Co., Memphis; dir. Nat. Toddle House Corp., Dobbs Houses, Inc., Wm. A. Webster Co. Pres., Memphis Travelers Aid; v.p., bd. dirs. H.W. Durham Home for Aged; trustee C.M. Gooch Found. Mem. Am., Tenn. (sect. pres.) bankers assns., Am., Tenn., Shelby County bar assns., Delta Theta Phi. Evangelical (deacon). Home: 176 E Chickasaw Pkwy Memphis TN 38111 Office: 12 S Main St Memphis TN 38101

DENTON, THOMAS RALSTON, corp. exec.; b. Amherst, N.S., Can., July 24, 1934; s. Harvey LeRoy and Evelyn (Powell) D.; B.A., Acadia U., 1955; LL.B., Dalhousie U., 1958; m. June Lillian Smith, Sept. 3, 1957; children—Peter, Janet, Sarah, Paul, Thomas. Called to Alta. bar, 1959; practice law Macleod, Dixon, Calgary, 1958-60; asst. sec., asso. counsel Home Oil Co., Ltd., Calgary, 1960-67; sec. BACM Industries, Ltd., Winnipeg, Can., 1967—, v.p., 1970—; dir. Con-Force Ltd., Consol. Concrete Ltd., BACM Ltd., Standard Gen. Constrn. Ltd., Engring. Bldgs. Ltd., B-A Constrn. Ltd. Served with Royal Canadian Naval Res., 1953-66. Decorated Canadian Forces Decoration. Mem. Canadian Bar Assn. Presbyn. Home: Twin Oaks River Rd RM of St Andrews Manitoba Canada Office: 1500 Plessis Rd Winnipeg 25 Manitoba Canada

DENTON, WILLARD KIRKPATRICK, banker; b. N.Y. City, Mar. 9, 1899; s. Charles Allen and Mabel (Kirkpatrick) D.; grad. Washington Irving High Sch., Tarrytown, N.Y., 1917; student various courses in banking and economics, Columbia U. and Am. Savings and Loan Inst.; m. Faith de Baubigny, Feb. 15, 1947; 1 son, Willard K. Clerk, R.R. Co-op. Bldg. and Loan Assn., N.Y. City, 1921-23, asst. treas., 1923, treas. and dir. 1924, vice pres.-treas. and dir., 1924-30; spl. deputy supt. of banks for State of N.Y., 1930-38; exec. v.p. and trustee Metropolitan Savings Bank, N.Y. City, 1938-42, became pres. and trustee Mar. 1942; became pres. and trustee Manhattan Savings Instn., May 1942; pres. and trustee Manhattan Savs. Bank July 1942—, chmn. of the bd. trustees, March 1967—. (this bank formed by successive combination of Metropolitan Savings Bank, Manhattan Savings Instn. and Citizens Savings Bank); mem. advisory bd. Chemical Bank & Trust Co.; mem. bd. dirs. Savings Bank Trust Co.; chmn. Fed. Deposit Ins. Corp. Com. of Assn. of Mutual Savings Bank; mem. Fed. Deposit Ins. Corps Savings Banks Council; mem. council of adminstrn. N.Y. Savings Assn. Trustee Nat. Fund Med. Edn.; mem. bd. dirs. YMCA; mem. N.Y. Cancer Com., N.Y. Bus. Development Corp. Served as seaman 2d class, U.S. Navy, 1918-19; lt. (j.g.). U.S. Coast Guard, 1941-42. Chmn. exec. com. Group IV, Savings Banks Assn., State of N.Y. Mem. N.Y. War Finance Com. (mem. exec. com.; exec mgr.; chmn. N.Y. Co.), 1944-45. Mem. East Side C. of C. (dir.),

Fifth Avenue Assn. (dir. 1958), Am. Legion. Mason. Clubs: Union League (N.Y.C.); Economic of N.Y. (treas.). Home: Succabone Rd Mt Kisco NY 10549 Office: 385 Madison Av New York City NY 10017

DENTON, WINFIELD K., lawyer; born Evansville, Ind., Oct. 28, 1896; s. George K. and Sara Linda (Chick) D.; A.B., DePauw U.; J.D., Harvard; m. Grace Abernethy, Dec. 27, 1927; childrenBeth (Mrs. Jim Bamberger), Mary, Sara (Mrs. L. Fried). Admitted to Ind. bar, practiced in Evansville; prosecutor Vanderburgh County, Ind.; mem. Ind. State Legislature, caucus chmn., 1939, minority leader, 1941; mem. 81st, 82d, 84th-89th U.S. Congresses, from eighth congressional district Indiana; attorney at law Denton, Gerling, Grove & Moore. served as 2d lieutenant, Aviation Corp., U.S. Army, World War I; from maj. to lt. col., USAAF, World War II; judge adv. gen. dept. Mem. Am. Legion, Vets. Fgn. Wars, Phi Kappa Psi. Democrat. Mason (32, K.T., Shriner). Elk. Home: 937 Powell Av Evansville IN 47713 Office: Old Nat Bank Bldg Evansville IN 47708

DENUNZIO, RALPH DWIGHT, investment banker; b. White Plains, N.Y., Nov. 17, 1931; s. Frank and M. Winifred (Sandbach) DeN.; A.B., Princeton, 1953; m. Jean A. Ames, Sept. 25, 1954; children—David Ames, Peter Dwight, Thomas Richard. With KP, Inc., and predecessor, 1953—, exec. v.p., 1968—, chmn. exec. com., 1970—, also dir.; pres., dir. Ralwin Realty Corp.; dir. Dreyfus Offshore Trust N.V. Bd. govs. N.Y. Stock Exchange, 1968—, vice chmn. bd., 1969-71, chmn. bd., 1971—. Past trustee Vis. Nurse Service N.Y. Gov. Investment Bankers Assn. Republican. Catholic. Clubs: Bond (past officer, gov.), Wall Street, Lunch (N.Y.C.); Princeton (N.J.) Quadrangle (trustee); Stanwich (Greenwich, Conn.); Riverside Yacht. Home: Bridle Path Lane Riverside CT 06878 Office: 20 Exchange Pl New York City NY 10005

DENURE, CHARLES LAVERN, coll. dean; b. nr. S. Wayne, Wis., Dec. 21, 1922; s. Charles Franklin and Hilma (Hanson) D.; B.S., Wis. State Tchrs. Coll., 1948; M.S., U. Wis., 1954, Ph.D., 1961; m. Mary I. Kindschi, July 7, 1948; children—Charles George, Robert James, John Michael. Tchr. secondary schs., Flushing, Mich., 1948-49, Oconto, Wis., 1949-52; tchr. Wis. State U., Platteville, 1952-64, dean, 1964—. Served with USNR, 1942-46. Mason. Home: 190 Preston Dr Platteville WI 53818

DENYAR, EDGAR JAMES, railroad ofcl.; b. Montreal, Que., Can., July 31, 1910; s. Harry Peerless and Mary (Widowson) D.; grad. O'Sullivan Bus. Coll., Montreal, 1928; extension student Sir George Williams U., Montreal, 1930; m. Judith Harquil, Mar. 29, 1969; children—Brian Edgar, Roy Alan. With Montreal & So. Counties Ry., St. Lambert, Que., 1926, Canadian Govt. Merchant Marine and Canadian Nat. (West Indies) Steamships Ltd., 1926- 29; with Canadian Nat. Ry. Co., 1929—, sr. asst. treas., 1952-58, treas., 1958—, also treas. subsidiaries in Can. and asst. treas. U.S. subsidiaries; treas. Toronto Terminals Ry. Co., No. Alta. Rys. Co., Shawinigan Falls Terminal Ry. Co. Active local welfare and charity campaigns. Mem. Assn. Am. Railroads, Canadian Ry. Club. Mem. United Ch. Can. Clubs: Mount Stephen (Montreal); Country of Montreal (St. Lambert Que.). Home: 3555 Coote des Neiges Rd Apt 705 Montreal Quebec Canada Office: PO Box 8100 Montreal Quebec Canada

DENZ, DONALD F., business exec.; B.B.A., St. Bonaventure U., 1953. Accountant, Pontiac Auto Transport, 1955-58; supr. indsl. accounting Twin Industries, 1958-63; supr. corporate accounting S.M. Flickinger Co. Inc., Buffalo, 1963-68, asst. controller, 1968-69, controller, 1969—. Served to 1st lt. AUS, 1953-55. Office: 45 Azalea Dr Buffalo NY 14240*

DEOME, KENNETH BENTON, cancer researcher; b. Kalkaska, Mich., 1906; A.B., Albion Coll., 1928; M.S., Mich. State Coll., 1934; Ph.D., U. Cal. at Berkeley, 1938. Instr., then asst. pof., asso. prof. comparative pathology, div. vet. sci. U. Cal. at Berkeley, 1938-50, dir. Cancer Research Genetics Lab., prof. zoology, 1950—, exec. sec. cancer research coordinating com.; research anatomist Sch. Vet. Medicine, U. Cal., Davis. Home: 671 Florence Av Oakland CA 94618 Office: Cancer Research Genetics Lab Univ Cal Berkeley CA 94720

DEONIS, JUAN, newspaperman; b. N.Y.C., Oct. 22, 1927; s. Federico and Harriet (Wishneff) D.; B.A., Williams Coll., 1948; M.S., Columbia, 1951; m. Marcia McCarthy, June 19, 1952; children—Juan Francisco, Francesca, Teresa, Harriet Ann, Alexandra. With U.P.I. in Boston, N.Y.C., Rio de Janeiro and Buenos Aires, 1951-57; mem. staff N.Y. Times, 1957—, corr.. Buenos Aires, 1958-61, Rio de Janeiro, 1961-67, UN, 1967-69, Mexico, 1969—. Served with USNR, 1945-46. Recipient Ed Stout Meml. award Overseas Press Club, 1963; Maria Moors Cabor award Columbia, 1963. Home: 118 Old Stage Rd Centerville MA 02632 Office: New York Times 229 W 43d St New York City NY 10036

DE PALMA, ANTHONY FREDERICK, orthopedist; b. Phila., Oct. 12, 1904; s. Pascal and Lucia (Finoia) De P.; student U. Md.; M.D., Jefferson Med. Coll., Phila., 1929; m. Vivienne Muti, Jan 3, 1934; children—Bruce, Barton, Brian. Intern Phila. General Hosp., 1929-31, chief orthopedic surgeon 1951—; orthopedic tng. N.J. Orthopedic Hosp., Orange, 1932-37, attending orthopedic surgeon, 1936-45; attending orthopedic surgeon, 1936-45; attending orthopedic surgeon. cons. Newark Meml. Hosp., 1938-45, Columbus Hosp., Newark, 1938-45, Newton (N.J.) Meml. Hosp., 1938-45; cons., orthopedic surgeon Crippled Children's Country Home, Westfield, N.J., 1938-45; chief orthopedic surgeon U.S. Naval Hosp., Phila., 1945-46, M.E. Hosp., Phila. 1946—; cons. orthopedic surgeon Valley Forge Gen. Hosp., Phoenixville, Pa., 1947-48; chief orthopedic surgeon St. Agnes Hosp., Phila., 1948-51; James Edwards prof. orthopedic surgery, head dept. Jefferson Med. College and Hosp., Phila., 1950—. Diplomate Am. Bd. Orthopedic Surgeons. Fellow Am. Acad. Orthopedic Surgery, A.C.S.; mem. A.M.A., Pa., Phila. Co. med. socs., Am. Assn. Phys. Anthropologists, Coll. Physicians Phila., N.Y. Acad Scis., Am. Orthopaedic Assn., Assn. Bone and Joint Surgeons, Alpha Omega Alpha. Club: Orthopedic (Phila.). Author: Surgery of the Shoulder, 1950; Diseases of the Knee, 1954; Management of Fractures and Dislocations, 1959. Contbr. articles profl. publs. Address: 248 S 21st St Philadelphia PA 19103

DEPALMA, JOHN T., banker; b. N.Y.C., 1911; grad. Rutgers Grad. Sch. Banking, 1954. Pres., treas. Kings Lafayette Bank, Bklyn.; chmn. Kings Lafayette Corp. Home: 31 Churchill Rd Cresskill NJ 07626 Office: 342 Fulton St Brooklyn NY 11201*

DEPALMA, JOSEPH ANTHONY, bishop; b. Walton, N.Y., Sept. 4, 1913; s. Vincenzo and Concetta (Dursi) DeP.; student Rome (N.Y.) Free Acad., 1927-31, Divine Heart Coll., Donaldson, Ind., 1937-38, Sacred Heart Theoligate, Hales Corner, Wis., 1939-45. Ordained priest Roman Cath. Ch., 1944; bishop, 1967; superior Sacred Heart Novitiate, Ste. Marie, Ill., 1945-52, Sacred Heart Theoligate, 1952-55; provincial superior N. Am. province Priests of Sacred Heart, 1955-59, superior gen., 1959-67; bishop of deAar, C.P., S. Africa, 1967—. Address: 1 Van Riebeeck St DeAar CP South Africa

DEPALMA, SAMUEL, fgn. service officer; b. Rochester, N.Y., June 22, 1918; s. Nicholas and Rose (Freda) DeP.; A.B., U. Rochester, 1940; postgrad. Am. U., 1940-41; m. Grace E. Kilbourne, July 5, 1941; children—Cynthia M., Winifred R. Econ. analyst, later air intelligence specialist, USAAF, 1941-45; expert internat. orgn. affairs Dept. of State, 1945-54; officer charge UN Gen. Assembly affairs, 1955-56, dep. dir. Office UN Polit. and Security Affairs, 1956-58; polit. officer U.S. delegation, Paris, 1958-61; counselor polit. affairs The Hague, Holland, 1961-63; chief office Polit. Affairs U.S. Arms Control and Disarmament Agy., 1963-66, asst. dir. U.S. Arms Control and Disarmament Agy., 1966-69; asst. sec. U.S. Dept. of State, 1969—. Adviser U.S. delegations numerous internat. confs. Mem. Am. Fgn. Service Assn., Council on fgn. Relations, Phi Beta Kappa. Home: 6707 Rannoch Rd Bethesda MD 20014 Office: care US Dept State Mailroom Washington DC 20525

DE PARIS, WILBUR, orch. leader, trombonist; b. Crawfordsville, Ind., Sept. 20, 1900; s. Sidney Gibney and Frances (Hyatt) de P.; grad. Crawfordsville High Sch., 1919; m. Barbara Nickerson, Oct. 30, 1958 (div. 1968); children—Steven, Melanie, Todd, Karen. Played with father's band, 1907-17, Original Blue Rythm Band, 1931, Benny Carter, 1930, Noble Sissle, 1931-32, Teddy Hill, 1938, Louis Armstrong, 1938-39; Ella Fitzgerald, 1940-41, Duke Ellington, 1945-46; band with brother Sidney de Paris, 1944; played for Guy Lombardo, Jones Beach, N.Y., summer 1965; various shows Midwest and Toronto, Can., 1966; toured Europe, 1961; in Africa for State Dept., 1957; own band at Cannes Festival, 1960. recording artist for Atlantic Records. Mem. Sons of Indiana. Jazz composer. Address: 55 W 19th St New York City NY 10011

DEPASQUALE, JOSEPH, musician; b. Phila., Oct. 14, 1919; s. Horace and Rosa (Lanza) dep.; grad. Curtis Inst. Music, 1942; m. Maria M. von Leuchtenberg de Beauharnais, Aug. 7, 1949; children—Maria Alexandra, Elizabeth Ann, Joseph Serge, Charles Nicholas. Mem. All-Am. Youth Orch., 1941, ABC Symphony Orch., 1945-47; 1st violist Boston Symphony Orch., 1947-64; prin. violist Phila. Orch., 1964—; mem. various chamber music groups, Boston, 1948-60; formed (with brothers) dePasquale String Quartet, 1963, concertized in North and South Am.; solo performances with orchs. in U.S. and Can., recitals in U.S. and Bermuda; tchr. Hart Sch. Music Hartford, Conn., 1947-50, Boston Conservatory. 1947-48, New Eng. Conservatory, 1948-64, Tanglewood Summer Music Sch., 1947-64, Curtis Inst. Music, 1964—; recording artist for RCA, Columbia, Boston records. Served with USMCR, 1942-45. Decorated Star Italian Solidarity, Pres. Italian Republic, 1969. Mem. N.Y., Phila. musicians unions, Italian Am. Soc. Phila. Republican. Roman Cath. Home: 532 General Lafayette Rd Merion PA 19066 Office: Acad of Music Locust and Broad Sts Philadelphia PA 19102

DEPATIE, DAVID HUDSON, motion picture co. exec.; b. Los Angeles, Dec. 24, 1930; s. Edmond LaVoie and Dorothy (Hudson) DeP.; student U. of South, 1947-48; A.B., U. Cal. at Berkeley 1951; m. Beverly Dee McKay, Nov. 26, 1965; children—David Hudson, Steven Linn, Michael Linn. With Warner Bros. Pictures, Inc., 1951-63, v.p., gen. mgr. comml. and cartoon films div., 1963; pres. DePatie-Freleng Enterprises, Inc., Van Nuys, Cal., 1963—; producer Pink Panther and Inspector theatrical cartoon series, TV series The Super 6, Super President, The Road Runner, Here Comes the Grump, and the Pink Panther Show; The Ant and the Aardvark, The Tijuana Toads, also Merry Melodies and Looney Tunes cartoon series; TV live- action and animation sp. Goldilocks; Dr. Dolittle TV series; Dr. Seuss Cat in the Hat TV spl. Mem. Acad. Motion Picture Arts and Scis. (Oscar award for Pink Panther 1964), Soc. Motion Picture Editors, Phi Gamma Delta. Republican. Episcopalian. Home: 15980 Valley Wood Rd Sherman Oaks CA 91403 Office: 6859 Hayvenhurst Av Van Nuys CA 91406

DE PAUR, LEONARD, condr.; mus. dir. De Paur Inf. Chorus; condr. Orch. New World, Cin. Symphony, Lena Concerts, N.Y.C., Hancock Summer Festival, Me., Philharmonic Hall, N.Y.C.; arranger, condr. Green Pastures; arranged music for Pension Fund Concerts. Address: 746 St Nicholas Av New York City NY *

DEPAUW, GOMMAR ALBERT, educator; b. Stekene, Belgium, Oct. 11, 1918; s. Desire and Anna (Van Overloop) De P.; Diplomate Classical Humanities, Coll. St. Nicholas, Belgium, 1936; J.C.B., U. Louvain, 1943, J.C.L., 1945; Juris Canonici Dr., Cath. U. Am., 1953, Came to U.S., 1949, naturalized, 1955. Ordained priest Roman Cath. Ch., 1942; parish priest, chaplain Cath. Social Action, Chent, Belgium, 1945-49, N.Y.C., 1949-52; with Mount St. Mary's, Emmitsburg, Md., 1952, successively prof. moral and fundamental dogmatic theology and canon law, sem. div., asso. prof. philosophy coll. div., 1952—, dean studies, maj. sem. div., 1954-64, mem. council adminstrn., 1957—. Theol. adviser II Vatican Ecumenical Council, 1962-65; founder- pres. Cath. Traditionalist Movement, Inc., 1965—. Served with Inf. M.C., Belgian Army, 1939-45. Decorated Honor cross Free Polish Forces. Mem. Cath. Theol. Soc. Am., Canon Law Soc. Am., Am. Cath. Philos. Assn., Nat. Cath. Ednl. Assn., Am. Assn. U. Pros. Author: The Educational Rights of the Church, 1953; Chronica Ephemerides Theologicae Lovanienses; Homiletic and Pastorial Review. Co-author: Encyclopedic Dictionary of the Bible, New Catholic Ency. Address: Pan Am Bldg 200 Park Av New York City NY 10017*

DEPEW, JOSEPH WILLIAM, lawyer; b. Slater, Mo., Sept. 17, 1889; s. James Pendelton and Emma (Hesser) DeP.; LL.B., Ill. Wesleyan U., 1914; m. Finney Rozetta McKim; 1 dau., Johanna Audre (Mrs. Barry W. McLeane). Admitted to Ill. bar, 1914; practice in Bloomington, 1920—; mem. firm DePew, Grimes & DePew, 1966—; asst. states atty. McLean County, 1920-24, states atty., 1928-32; arbitration Indsl. Commn. Ill., 1946-49; mem., atty. War Price and Radion Bd., McLean County, World War II; atty. Twp. of City of Bloomington, 1937-59. Trustee, legal counsel Baby Fold, Normal, Ill., 1946—; life mem. adv. bd. Salvation Army. Recipient Distinguished Service award City Bloomington, 1969. Served to 2d lt., inf., U.S. Army, 1917-19. Mem. McLean County Bar Assn., Am. Legion, Tau Kappa Epsilon. Republican. Mason. Home: 1710 N 5th St Springfield IL 62702 Office: 317 N Main St Bloomington IL 61701

DEPEYSTER, FREDERIC AUGUSTUS, surgeon; b. Chgo., Nov. 8, 1914; s. Frederic A. and Florence (Bryant) deP.; B.A., Williams Coll., 1936; postgrad. med. sch. Harvard, 1938; M.D., U. Chgo., 1940; m. Marjorie Shay, June 18, 1948; children—Frances Lee, Deborah. Intern Presbyn. Hosp., Chgo., 1940-41; surg. officer Peter Bent Brigham Hosp. & Children's Hosp., both Boston, 1941-43; resident surgeon Presbyn. Hosp., Chgo., 1946-48, Nicholas Senn fellow, 1948; Am. Cancer fellow U. Ill., 1949; practice medicine, specializing in surgery, Chgo., 1945—; sr. attending surgeon Presbyn.-St. Luke's Hosp., Chgo., 1948-62, chmn. gen. surgery sect., 1970—; mem. staff Cook County Hosp., Ravenswood Hosp. (both Chgo.); mem. faculty surgery dept. U. Ill. Med. Sch., Chgo., 1946-71, prof., 1969-71; prof. surgery Rush Med. Coll., Chgo., 1971—. Mem. Winnetka Community House Council, 1950-51; pres. 13th Gen. Hosp. Assn., 1949-50; sec. treas. Presbyn. Hosp. Staff, 1957-59; v.p. Presbyn.-St. Luke's Hosp. Staff, 1968-70, pres., 1970-72; chmn. bd. dirs. Med. and Nursing Services of Mid-America, A.R.C., 1964-66. Bd. dirs. Bishop Anderson Found., Chgo., 1950-69; trustee Rush Med. Coll., 1957-70. Served to maj., M.C., AUS, 1943-46. Decorated Bronze Star, Sec. of War Commendation. Diplomate Am. Bd. Gen. Surgery. Mem. A.M.A., A.C.S., Ill., Chgo. surg. socs., Internat. Soc. Surgery, Soc. Surgery Alimentary Tract (founder mem.), Central Surg. Soc., Western Surg. Assn., Nat. Soc. Med. Research, Rush Med. Coll. Alumni Assn. (pres. 1961-66), Am. Soc. Cancer Research, Sigma Xi, Alpha Omega Alpha. Clubs: University, Williams (Chgo.). Contbr. profl. jours. Home: 696 Prospect Av Winnetka IL 60093 Office: 1725 W Harrison St Chicago IL 60612

DEPHILLIPS, FRANK ANTHONY, educator; b. N.Y.C., Sept. 20, 1908; s. Antonio and Caroline (Salerno) DeP.; B.S.S., Coll. City N.Y., 1932; M.A., N.Y. U., 1943; Ph.D., Fordham U., 1953; m. Elena Proto, Aug. 20, 1932; 1 dau., Elaine (Mrs. Marc Patterson, Jr.). Tchr. Pub. Sch. 19, N.Y.C., 1935-36, Newtown High Sch., 1936-38; instr. Coll. City N.Y., 1936-39; prof. mgmt. and indsl. relations N.Y. U., 1937-61, vice chmn. dept., 1957-59; asst. to dean Coll. Bus. Adminstrn., St. John's U., Jamaica, N.Y., 1961-63, prof. mgmt., 1961—, chmn. dept. mgmt. grad. and undergrad., 1966-69; with human relations tng. CBS, 1959-60; tng. cons. to Columbia Records, 1964-; cons. human relations and supervisory tng. Pa. RR., N.Y. Trust Co., Esso of N.J., USAAF; cons. Lorenz-Schneider Corp., Yorkshire Food Sales Corp., Bowery Savs. Bank, N.Y.C. Certified psychologist, N.Y. State. Mem. Am., N.Y. State psychol. assns., Am. Assn. U. Profs., Acad. Mgmt., Alpha Kappa Psi, Phi Kappa Delta. Co-author: Fundamentals of Management Training. 1960; also articles. Home: 208-08 42d Av Bayside NY 11361 Office: St John's U Jamaica NY 11432

DEPIERO, NICHOLAS G., physician; b. New Castle, Pa., Nov. 29, 1915; s. Sebastiano and Theresa (Ferraro) DeP.; B.S., Geneva Coll., Beaver Falls, Pa., 1933-37; M.D., Hahnemann Med. Coll., 1942; postgrad. student, Temple U., U. Pa., N.Y.U.; m. Marion V. Marcyan, Feb. 14, 1953; children—Nicholas A., Roberta Ann, Christopher Michael. Intern, then resident anesthesiology Huron Rd. Hosp., Cleve., 1942-44; mem. staff Marymount Hosp., Cleve., 1950—, dir. anesthesiology, 1950—, dir. med. edn., 1961—. Trustee Anesthesia Found. Served to capt. AUS, 1944-46; ETO. Decorated Bronze Star; cavalier Grand Cross Republic of Italy. Diplomate Am. Board Anesthesiology. Fellow Am. Coll. Anesthesiologists; mem. Am. (asst. treas. 1960-61, treas. 1961-65, pres. 1966-67), Ohio (pres. 1964-65, sec.-treas. 1957-64, 1968—), Internat. socs. anesthesiologists, World, Pan Am. med. assns., N.Y. Acad. Sci., Assn. Hosp. Dirs. Med. Edn., World Fedn. Socs. Anesthesiologists, A.M.A., Cleve. Acad. Medicine, Cleve. Med. Library Assn. Home: 10710 Cardinal Lane Brecksville OH 44141 Office: 9710 Garfield Blvd Garfield Heights OH 44125

DE PINIES, JAIME, Spanish diplomat; b. Madrid Spain, Nov. 18, 1917; s. Vicente and Mercedes (Rubio) De P.; high sch. degree, licenciate in law, Faculty of Law, U. Madrid, 1941; m. Luz Bianchi, Dec. 30, 1954: children—Jaime, Pablo. With law div. Bank of Spain, 1941-45; joined Spanish fgn. service, 1944; sec. embassy in Cuba, 1945-47, Great Britain, 1947-48, Washington, 1948-52, Panama 1953, Costa Rica, 1953, Manila, 1956; mem. Spanish delegations to XI, XII, XIII, XIV, XV gen. assemblies UN, also ECOSOC, OACI, others; dir. N.A. div. Ministry Fgn. Affairs, Madrid, 1957- 60; dep. permanent rep. Spain to UN, 1960—. Fought in Spanish Civil War, 1936-39. Decorated Order Isabella the Catholic, award Civil Merit (Spain); Red Cross (Cuba). Home: 817 Fifth Av New York City NY Office: Mission of Spain to UN United Nations 820 Second Av New York City NY 10017

DEPODWIN, HORACE J., univ. dean; b. Bklyn., Oct. 28, 1922; s. Thaddeus and Lena (Kornat) DeP; A.B., Middlebury (Vt.) Coll.; A.M., Ph.D., Columbia; m. Carolyn Prudence Ohlander, June 19, 1948; childrenAndrew, Elizabeth Margaret, David. Prof. econs., dean Grad. Sch. Bus., Rutgers State U.; mgr. econ. research Gen. Electric Co.; pres. Horace J. DePodwin Assos., Inc.; dir. Nortek Corp., Mutual Benefit Fund, vice chmn., dir Rutgers Minority Investment Co., adviser Commonwealth P.R.; cons. on GATT negotiations for U.S. Govt. Trustee Sales Execs. Found.; bd. dirs. Interracial Council on Bus. Opportunity; chmn. N.J. Task Force on Vocational Tng. In Corrections Instns. Served with inf. AUS, World War II. Decorated Bronze Star, Combat Inf. badge. Mem. Am. Econ. Assn., Am. Statis. Assn., Am. Assn. U. Profs. Author; Discharging Business Tax Liabilities, 1954; also articles. Home: 145 Wyoming Av Maplewood NJ 07040 Office: 18 Washington Pl Newark NJ 07102 also 350 Fifth Av New York City NY 10001

DE POIX, VINCENT PAUL, naval officer; b. Los Angeles, Aug. 13, 1916; s. Elzear Paul and Grace (Howard) deP.; B.S. in Elec. Engring., U.S. Naval Acad., 1939; student U.S. Naval Postgrad. Sch., 1944-46; M.S. in Aero. Engring., Mass. Inst. Tech., 1946; m. Betty Ann Rose, Feb. 25, 1942; children—Suzanne, Carole (Mrs. McGarvey), Christopher, Peter. Commd. ensign U.S. Navy, 1939, advanced through grades to vice adm., 1969; served in U.S.S. Mpls. and U.S.S. Sicard, 1939-41; flight tng., 1941-42; fighter pilot Fighting Squadron Six on U.S.S. Enterprise, PTO, 1942-43; comdg. officer Fighting Squadron 172, 1948-50; first comdg. officer U.S.S. Enterprise, 1st nuclear aircraft carrier, 1960-63; comdr. Carrier Div. 7, 1966-67; asst. dep. chief naval operations (Devel.), 1967-69, dep. dir. (administrn., evaluation and mgmt.) Office Dir. Def. Research and Engring., OSD, 1969-71; comdr. 2d fleet, Norfold, Va., 1971—. Decorated D.S.M., Legion of Merit, Air medal, Purple Heart. Home: Georgia House US Naval Base Norfolk VA Office: Comdr Second Fleet FPO New York City NY

DEPOL, JOHN, artist; b. N.Y.C., Sept. 16, 1913; s. Joseph Zangrando and Theresa (Mariani) DeP.; student Art Students League N.Y., Sch. Tech., Belfast, No. Ireland; m. Thelma June Roth, May 31, 1946; 1 dau., Patricia Gail. Free lance wood engraver, printmaker, illustrator; prints represented permanent collections Cin. Mus., Library of Congress, N.Y. Pub. Library, Met. Mus. of Art, Syracuse U. Library, and others. Served with USAAF, 1943-45. Recipient Richard Comyn Eames Mus. purchase prize, 1952, Kate W. Arms Meml. prize, 1955, 56, Albany Print Club Purchase prize, 1968, John Taylor Arms Meml. prize NAD, 1968, others; creator of Woodcut Soc. presentation print, 1952. Miniature Print Soc. presentation print, 1953, Albany Print Club presentation print, 1958-59. A.N.A. Mem. Art Students League (life), Soc. Am. Graphic Artists, Albany Print Club. Address: 280 Spring Valley Rd Park Ridge NJ 07656

DE POOL, MANUEL E., banker. Asst. gen. mgr. Banco de Reservas de la Republica Dominicana, Santo Domingo. Office: Isabel La Catolica No 71 Santo Domingo Dominican Republic*

DEPPEN, MARGARET MARY, univ. dean; b. Ft. Wayne, Ind., Mar. 17, 1910; d. John H. and Mary (Funck) Deppen; B.A., St. Mary-of-the-Woods Coll., 1933; M.S., Ind. U., 1948. Sec. Lincoln Nt. Life Ins. Co., Ft. Wayne, 1933-37, U.S. R.R. Retirement Bd. Washington, also San Francisco, Chgo., 1937-42, Armour Research Found., Ill. Inst. Tech., Chgo., 1946-47; club worker U.S.O., Mass., Brazil, S.A., 1942-45, A.R.C., Korea, 1951-55; head residence Stephens Coll., 1948-51; dean of women Ohio U., 1952—, also asso. dean students, dir. student activities. Mem. Nat., Ohio assns. deans and counselors of women, League Women Voters, St. Mary-of-the-Woods Alumnae Assn. Home: 2 Evans St Athens OH 45701

DEPPERMANN, WILLIAM HERMAN, pub. relations exec.; b. Indpls., May 15, 1903; s. Otto Frederick and Anna (Klotz) D.; student Ind. U.; m. Margaret Little, Sept. 17, 1937; children—Stephen Rolfe, Daniel Robert. Reporter Indpls. Star, 1921-24; advt. mgt., publicity agt. various motion picture theaters, 1925-32; in sales promotion Western Union Telegraph Co., 1932-39; in charge of newsstand promotion Reader's Digest, 1939-42; account exec. Steve Hannagan Pub. Relations; dir. pub. relations Olin Industries, 1951-55; dir. pub. relations Link-Belt Co., 1955-61; account exec. Hill & Knowlton, Inc., 1961—, v.p. subsidiary H & K Marketing Services Inc. Mem. pub. relations conf. Nat. Safety Council. Author: Shooter's Choice, 1952. Founder, editor, pub. Practical Pub. Relations. Home: 24 Old Mill Rd Chappaqua NY 10514

DE PRE, JACQUELINE, violoncellist; b. 1945; ed. London Cello Sch.; pupil of William Pleeth at Guildhall Sch. Music: pupil of Paul Tortelier, Paris, France, also Rostropovich, Moscow, USSR. Debut, Wigmore Hall, London, 1961; now soloist with prin. English orchs. and conductors at Royal Festival Hall, Royal Albert Hall, also Bath and Edinburgh festivals; concerts in Berlin, Paris, Rotterdam, Stravanger, U.S. and USSR, recording artist for Angel Records. Recipient Suggia Internat. Cello award, 1956. Address: care Ibbs and Tillett Ltd 124 Wigmore St London W1 England*

DE PREE, WILLARD AMES, fgn. service officer; b. Zeeland, Mich., Nov. 1, 1928; s. Adrian and Edith (Kroeze) De P.; B.A. with honors, Harvard, 1950; Rotary Found. fellow, U. Coll. Wales, 1950-51; M.A., U. Mich., 1952; postgrad. Northwestern U., 1960-61; m. Elisabeth Pierrou, Aug. 18,1956; children—Carin, Thomas, Peter, Birgitta, Susan. With U.S. Fgn. Service, 1956-70, vice consul, Cairo, 1957-58; 2d sec., Cyprus, 1958-60; assigned State Dept., 1961-64; 1st sec., Accra, 1964-68; counselor of embassy, Freetown, Sierra Leone, 1968-70; sr. seminar in fgn. policy State Dept., 1970-71; teaching fellow polit. sci. U. Mich., 1952-53. Served with AUS, 1954-56. Recipient Meritorious Honor award State Dept., 1966. Home: 143 Centennial St Zeeland MI 49464 Office: Fgn Service Inst Dept of State Washington DC 20521

DEPREIST, JAMES ANDERSON, conductor; b. Phila., Nov. 21, 1936: s. James Henry and Thel (Anderson) DeP.; B.S., U. Pa., 1958, M.A., 1961; student Phila. Conservatory Music, 1959-61; m. Betty Louise Childress, Aug. 10, 1963. Music dir. Comtemporary Music Guild, Phila., 1959-62; v.p. charge music Allen's Lane Art Center, Phila., Am. specialist music for State Dept., 1962-63; conductor-in-residence, Bangkok, Thailand, 1963-64; asst. conductor to Leonard Bernstein and N.Y. Philharmonic Orch., 1965-66; music dir., conductor sta. WCAU-TV, Phila., Music-Specials series, 1965, 66; music dir., summer music program Westchester County, N.Y., 1965, 66. Recipient 1st prize gold medal Dimitri Metropoulos Internat. Music Competition for Conductors, 1964. Mem. Sigma Pi Phi. Composer; (ballet scores) vision of America, 1960, Tendrils, 1961, A Sprig of Lilac, 1964; (theme music) Eye on N.Y., series WCBS-TV, 1965; (concert) Requim, 1965.‡

DEPROSPO, NICHOLAS DOMINICK, educator, biologist; b. Bronx, N.Y., July 16, 1923; s. Domenick and Lucy (Riccio) DeP.; B.A., N.Y. U., 1946, M.A., 1947, Ph.D., 1957; m. Margaret Joyce Bing, Dec. 31, 1960; 1 son, Douglas Francis. Instr., L.I. U., summer 1947; mem. faculty Seton Hall U., 1947—, acting dean Coll. Arts and Scis., 1958—, prof., 1959—. Served with AUS, 1943-46. Recipient Founders Day award N.Y. U., 1958. Mem. A.A.A.S., Am. Soc. Zoologists, Am. Inst. Biol. Scis., N.J. Acad. Sci., Am. Assn. U. Profs., Assn. Advisers Health Professions (sec.), Sigma Xi, Alpha Epsilon Delta (Hon.). Republican. Roman Catholic. K.C. Author: Guide to Chordate Anatomy, 1962. Home: 917 Sheridan St Union NJ 07083 Office: Seton Hall U South Orange NJ 07079

DEPUY, CHARLES HERBERT, educator, chemist; b. Detroit, Sept. 10, 1927; s. Carroll E. and Helen (Plehn) DeP.; B.S., U. Cal., Berkeley, 1948; A.M., Columbia, 1952; Ph.D., Yale, 1953; m. Eleanor Burch, Dec. 21, 1949; children—David Gareth, Nancy Ellen, Stephen Bailey, Katherine Louise. Asst. prof. chemistry Ia. State U., 1953-59, asso. prof., 1959-62, prof., 1962-63; prof. chemistry U. Colo., Boulder, 1963—, chmn. chemistry dept., 1966-68; vis. prof. U. Ill., summer 1954; vis. prof. U. Cal., Berkeley, summer 1960; NIH sr. postdoctoral fellow U. Basel, Switzerland, 1969-70. Cons. A.E. Staley Co., 1956—, Marathon Oil Co., 1964—; Served wih AUS, 1946-47. Fellow A.A.A.S., Chem. Soc. London; mem. Am. Chem. Soc. (mem. exec. com. organic div., chmn. Colo. sect.), Sigma Xi. Author: with Kenneth L. Rinehart) Introduction to Organic Chemistry, 1967; (with Orville L. Chapman) Molecular Reactions and Photochemistry, 1970. Mem. adv. bd. Jour. of Organic Chemistry, 1969—. Contbr. articles profl. jours. Home: 1509 Cascade Av Boulder CO 80302

DEPUY, WILLIAM EUGENE, army officer; b. Jamestown, N.D., Oct. 1, 1919; s. Richard Merrill and Ruth (Tweed) DeP.; B.A., S.D. State U., 1941; postgrad. Command and Gen. Staff Coll., 1945-46, Armed Forces Staff Coll., 1953, Brit. Imperial Def. Coll., 1960; m. Marjory Walker, June 8, 1951; children—William Eugene, Joslin, Daphne. Commd. 2d lt. U.S. Army, 1941, advanced through grades to lt. gen., 1969; mil. attaché, Budapest, Hungary, 1949-50; with Office Chief Staff, Washington, 1956-59; comdg. officer 1st Battle Group, 30th Inf., 3d Inf. Div., 1961-62; Dir. Spl. Warfare Office Dept. Chief Staff for Mil. Operations, Washington, 1962-63; Dir. Plans and Programs Office Asst. Chief Staff for Force Devel., Washington 1963-64; Asst. Chief Staff Operations J3, U.S. Mil. Assistance Command, Vietnam, 1964-66; Comdg. Gen. 1st Inf. Div., Vietnam, 1966-67; spl. asst. counterinsurgency and spl. activities Office Joint Chiefs Staff, Washington, 1967-69; with Office Chief Staff Army, Washington, 1969—. Decorated D.S.C. with oak leaf cluster, D.S.M. with 2 oak leaf clusters, Silver Star with 2 oak leaf clusters, Legion of Merit, D.F.C., Bronze Star, Air medal with 20 oak leaf clusters, Purple Heart with oak leaf cluster, Combat inf. badge; Legion of Honor, Croix de Guerre (France); Gallantry Cross with palm, Nat. Order 5th class (Republic of Vietnam). Episcopalian. Home: Quarters 10 Fort McNair Washington DC 20024 Office: Asst Vice Chief Staff Army Pentagon Washington DC 20310

DERAMUS, WILLIAM NEAL, III, railroader; b. Pittsburg, Kan., Dec. 10, 1915; s. William Neal and Lucile Ione (Nicholas) D.; A.B., U. of Mich., 1936; LL.B., Harvard, 1939; m. Patricia Howell Watson, Jan. 22, 1943; children—William Neal IV, Patricia Nicholas, Jean Watson, Jill Watson. Transp. apprentice Wabash R.R. Co., St. Louis, 1939-41, asst. trainmaster, 1941-43; asst. to gen. mgr. K.C.S. Ry. Co., Kansas City, Mo., 1946-48, asst. to pres. C.G.W. Ry. Co., Chgo., 1948, pres., dir., 1949-57, chmn. exec. com., 1954-57; pres., dir. M.-K.-T. R.R., 1957-61; chmn. bd. MAPCO, Inc., Tulsa, 1960—; pres. Kansas City So. Lines (Mo.), 1961-68, chmn. bd., 1966—; pres. Kansas City So. Industries, Inc. (Mo.), 1962-66, chmn. bd., 1966—; dir. City Nat. Bank & Trust Co., Employers Reins, Corp., BMA Corp. (all Kansas City, Mo.). Trustee Wayland Acad., Beaver Dam, Wis. Served from capt. to maj., Transp. Corps, Mil. Ry. Service AUS, 1943-46; overseas, India, 1943-45. Mem. Beta Theta Pi. Clubs; Chicago (Ill.); Kansas City, River, Mission Hills Country, Mercury, Saddle and Sirloin, Rotary (Kansas City). Home: 1030 W 55th St Kansas City MO 64113 Office: 114 W 11th St Kansas City MO 64105

DERBER, MILTON, educator; b. Providence, June 19, 1915; s. Harry and Sophie (Kalman) D.; student Springfield (Mass.) Jr. Coll., 1932-33; A.B., Clark U., 1936; A.M., U. Wis., 1937, Ph.D., 1940; m. Zelda Trenner, June 14, 1940; children—Clara Gail, Charles. Social Sci. Research Council fellow, 1936- 39; research asso. 20th Century Fund, 1939-40; economist U.S. Bur. Labor Statistics, 1940-41, 46-47; field examiner NLRB, 1941-42; economist OPA, 1942-43; economist and research dir. Nat. War Labor Bd., 1943-45; coordinator of research Inst. Labor and Indsl. Relations, U. Illinois, 1947-58, asso. prof. labor and indsl. relations, 1947-49, prof. 1949—, acting dir., 1951-52. Chief economist Pres.'s Fact- Finding Bds., Gen. Motors and Pacific Coast Longshore Labor Disputes, 1945-46; vice chmn., project dir. Ill. Gov.'s Adv. Commn. on Labor-Mgmt. Policy for Pub. Employees, 1966. Mem. Indsl. Relations Research Assn. (editor 1948-50, mem. exec. bd. 1959-61), Am. Assn. U. Profs. (pres. U. Ill. chpt. 1959-60), Am. Civil Liberties Union. B'nai B'rith. Contbg. author: How Collective Bargaining Works, 1942. Author: Labor-Management Relations under Industry-Wide Bargaining, 1955; co- author The Local Union-Management Relationship, 1960; Plant Union- Management Relations, 1965, Research in Labor Problems in the United States, 1967; The American Idea of Industrial Democracy, 1865-1965, 1970. Editor: Termination Report of Nat. War Labor Board, 1948. Co-editor: Problems and Policies of Dispute Settlement and Wage Stabilization during World War II, 1950; Labor and the New Deal, 1957. Project coordinator; Labor-Management Relations in Illini City, 1953. Home: 607 W Hessel Blvd Champaign IL 61820

DERBY, DONALD, univ. dean; b. N.Y.C., May 14, 1908; s. Chester Cawthorne and Amy (Holiday) D.; A.B., Bowdoin Coll., 1931; A.M., Harvard, 1934, Ph.D. in History, 1940; m. Cordelia Evelyn Pass, Apr. 13, 1946; children—Cordelia Evelyn, Amy Priscilla. Research, writing Nat. Archives, Washington, 1946-47; dean adminstrn., prof. history Am. U., 1947-, v.p., dean faculties, 1960-68. Secretary of the U., 1968—. Served with Signal Corps, M.T., AUS, 1942-46. Mem. Phi Beta Kappa. Contbr. articles profl. jours. Home: 4700 Reservior Rd Washington DC 20007

DERBY, STANLEY KINGDON, educator, physicist; b. Bangor, Mich., Sept. 12, 1920; s. Glenwood Robert and Hazel (Sheffield) D.; B.S., U. Chgo., 1944; M.S., U. Mich., 1948, Ph.D., 1957; m. Jean Graham, Dec. 9, 1943; children—Linda Jean (Mrs. Michael B. Monroe), Robert Graham, Kenneth David. Mem. faculty Western Mich. U., 1955—, asst. prof. physics, 1955-60, asso. prof., 1960-64, prof., 1964—. Examiner undergrad. record exam. natural scis. area Ednl. Testing Service (Princeton, N.J.). Active Boy Scouts Am. Served to 1st lt., USAAF, 1943-46. Mem. Am. Assn. Physics Tchrs. Research on emission spectroscopy. Home: 1308 Bretton Dr Kalamazoo MI 49007

DERBYSHIRE, HARRY S., business exec.; B.S., Drexel Inst. Tech., 1948. Mem. staff Lybrand, Ross Bros. & Montgomery, C.P.A.'s, 1948-52; asst. chief accountant Kaiser Metal Products Co., 1952-55; chief dep. controller City of Phila., 1955-58; div. controller Raytheon Co., 1958-65; corporate controller Hoffman Electric Co., 1965-67; controller Whittaker Corp., Los Angeles, 1967—, v.p., 1970—. C.P.A., Pa. Office: 9229 Sunset Blvd Los Angeles CA 90069

DE REGNIERS, BEATRICE SCHENK, author, editor; b. LaFayette, Ind., Aug. 16, 1914; d. Harry and Sophia (Feinstein) Freedman; student U. Ill., 1931-33; Ph.B., U. Chgo., 1935, student Grad. Sch., 1936-37; postgrad. U. Toulouse (France), summer 1935, The Sorbonne, Paris, France, 1935-36; M. Ed., Winnetka (Ill.) Grad. Tchrs. Coll., 1941; m. Francis de Regniers, May 3, 1946. Mem. Eloise Moore Dance Group, Chgo., 1942-43; copywriter Scott Foresman & Co., Chgo., 1943-44; welfare officer UNRRA, Egypt, 1944-46; copywriter Am. Book Co., N.Y.C., 1948-49; dir. ednl. materials Am. Heart Assn., N.Y.C., 1949-61; editor Lucky Book Club of Scholastic Book Services, N.Y.C., 1961—. Recipient Jr. Book award Boys Club Am., 1960, Most Distinguished Work of Fiction for Younger Children Award Ind. U. Writers Conf., 1964. Mem. Authors Guild Am., Loose-enders. Author: The Giant Story, 1953; What Can You Do With a Shoe?, 1955; A Little House of Your Own, 1955; Was It a Good Trade?, 1956; A Child's Book of Dreams, 1957; Something Special, 1958; Cats Cats Cats Cats Cats, 1958; What Happens Next?, 1959; The Snow Party, 1959; The Shadow Book (also co-designer), 1960; Who Likes the Sun?, 1961; The Little Book (also illustrator), 1961; The Little Girl and Her Mother, 1963; May I Bring a Friend? (Caldecott award), 1964; The Abraham Lincoln Joke Book, 1965; David and Goliath, 1965; How Joe the Bear and Sam the Mouse Got Together, 1965; Penny, 1966; Circus, 1966; The Giant Book, 1966; The Day Everybody Cried, 1967; Willy O'Dwyer Jumped in the Fire 1968. Catch a Little Fox, 1969; Poems Children Will Sit Still For, 1969; The Boy, the Rat, and the Butterfly, 1971; Little Red Riding Hood Retold in Verse for Boys and Girls to Read Themselves, 1972. Home: 180 W 58th St New York City NY 10019 Office: 50 W 44th St New York City NY 10036

DERESIEWICZ, HERBERT, educator; b. Brno, Czechoslovakia, Nov. 5, 1925; s. William and Lotte (Rappaport) D.; B.M.E., Coll. City N.Y., 1946; M.S., Columbia, 1948, Ph.D. (Univ. fellow 1949-50), 1952; m. Evelyn Aetman, Mar. 12, 1955; children—Ellen, Robert, William. Sr. staff engr. Applied Physics Lab., Johns Hopkins, 1950-51; mem. faculty Columbia, 1951—, prof. mech. engring., 1962—; cons. stress analysis, vibrations, elastic contact, wave propagation, mechanics granular and porous media. Served with AUS, 1946-47. Fulbright sr. research scholar, Italy, 1960-61; Fulbright lectr., Israel, 1966-67. Mem. A.A.A.S., Am. Soc. M.E., Seismol. Soc. Am., N.Y. Acad. Scis., Sigma Xi. Contbr. profl. jours. Home: 336 Broad Av Englewood NJ 07631 Office: SW Mudd Bldg Columbia Univ New York City NY 10027

DERGE, DAVID RICHARD, univ. ofcl.; b. Kansas City, Mo., Oct. 10, 1928; s. David Richard and Blanche (Butterfield) D.; A.B., U. Mo., 1940; A.M., Northwestern U., 1951, Ph.D., 1955; m. Elizabeth Anne Greene, Sept. 4, 1951; children—David Richard III, Dorothy Anne. Instr. U. Mo., 1954-56, Northwestern U., summer 1955; mem. faculty Ind. U., 1956—, prof. polit. sci., 1965—, dean adminstrn., exec. v.p., 1968—. Pres. Behavioral Research Assos., 1968—. Mem. U.S. Adv. Commn. Internat. Ednl. and Cultural Affairs, 1969; White House cons. Exec. Office of President, 1970; cons. higher and internat. edn. Dept. Health, Edn. and Welfare, 1971; sec., dir. Midwest Univs. Consortium for Internat. Activities, 1967—. Mem. City Council, Bloomington, Ind., 1964-67. Served with USNR, 1946-48. Grantee Social Sci. Research Council, 1957, Eagleton Inst. Practical Politics, 1959, Citizenship Clearing House, 1961; recipient Sigma Delta Chi Teaching award, 1963; Weatherly Distinguished Teaching award Ind. U., 1964; named Outstanding Young Man Ind., Ind. Jr. C. of C., 1963. Mem. Am. Polit. Sci. Assn., U.S. Naval Inst., Phi Beta Kappa, Pi Sigma Alpha, Alpha Pi Zeta, Kappa Sigma. Presbyn. Clubs: Columbia (Indpls.); Bloomington Squash Racquets. Author: Public Leadership in Indiana, 1969; Institution Building and Rural Development, 1968; The World of American Politics, 1968; also articles. Home: Woodruff Lane Bittner Woods Bloomington IN 47401

DERGE, GERHARD JULIUS, metallurgist; b. Lincoln. Neb., Feb. 11, 1909; s. Matt L. and Wilma (Gesell) D.; A.B., Amherst Coll., 1930; Ph.D., Princeton, 1934; m. Katharine McKechnie, Oct. 27, 1937; childrenPortia, Jeffrey. Staff metals research lab. Carnegie-Mellon U, 1934—, asst. prof. metall. engring., 1939-45, asso. prof. 1945-49, prof., 1949—. Fellow Am. Inst. Mining, Metall. and Petroleum Engrs. (chmn. Iron and steel div. Metall. Soc. 1961, Hunt award 1950), Am. Soc. Metals; mem. Am. Chem. Soc., Am. Ceramic Soc., Am. Soc. for Testing and Materials, Iron and Steel Inst., London. Editor: Transactions of Metallurgical Society, 1958-69; Metallurgical Transactions, 1970—. Contbr. tech. publs. Patentee in field. Home: 8 Longfellow Rd Pittsburgh PA 15215

DER HAROOTIAN, KOREN, sculptor; b. Ashodvan, Armenia, Apr. 2, 1909; s. Haroutun and Nevart (Mouradian) Der Haroutunian; student pub. Schs., Worcester Art Mus. Sch.; m. Hermine Ohanesyan, May 13, 1939. Came to U.S., 1921, naturalized, 1954. Sculptor, painter; works exhibited one man show Caz- Delbos Galleries, N.Y.C., 1929, Jamaica (B.W.I.) Museum, 1931, 34, 38, 43, Worcester (Mass.) Art Museum, 1932, Kraushaar Galleries, N.Y.C., 1945, outdoor exhbn., N.Y.C., 1948, Art Alliance, Phila., 1950. Zwemmer Gallery, London, 1964, Armenian Gen. Benevolent Union Gallery, N.Y.C., 1965, Rockland Community College, Suffern, N.Y., 1967. Contemporaries Gallery, N.Y.C., 1967; two man show Gallery Ten, Inc., Mt. Vernon, N.Y., 1958; works exhibited annual and group shows Whitney Mus. Am. Art, Pa. Acad. Fine Arts, Chgo. Art Inst., Neb. U., Worcester, Cranbrook, Springfield, Toledo, Cin. museums, Des Moines Art Center, Ohio U., Phila. Mus. Art, Audubon Artsist exhbns., Sculptors Guild exhbns., John Herron Art Inst., Indpls., various London (Eng.) galleries, Royal Acad., London, 1964, 65, Royal Glasgow (Scotland) Inst., 1964; works owned by and permanently exhibited Met. Mus. Art, N.Y.C., Worcester Art Mus., Jamaica (B.W.I.) Mus., Pa. Acad. Fine Arts, Whitney Mus. Am. Art, N.Y.; perm. colls. Ariz. State Coll., Newark Art Mus., Bezelel Nat. Mus., Israel, Jerusalem Museum Art, Israel, Our Lady, Queen Angels Seminary, Albany, N.Y.; private collections U.S., England, W. Indies; exhibited work in marble United States Pavilion, Brussels World's Fair, 1958, USIS, Florence, Italy, 1963: commissioned to carve figure Christ and 4 martyrs for Diocese building Armenian Ch. and Cultural Center, N.Y.C., 1959, Beaver for Bernard Baruch City Coll., 1962, 1st prize Springfield Art Assn., 1944; Gold medal Audubon Artists 7th Ann. Exhbn., 1949; 1st prize sculpture, 8th Ann. Exhbn., 1950; commn. Phila. Internat. Sculpture Exhbn., 1949; Fairmount Park Art Assn., 1950; George D. Widener Meml. Gold Medal, Pa. Acad. Fine Arts, 1954, monetary award, Nat. Inst. Arts and Letters, 1954, Medal of Honor, Gruppo Donatello, Florence, 1962. Mem. Fedn. Modern Painters and Sculptors, Internat. Platform Assn. Address: RFD 9 W Castle Rd Orangeburg NY 10962

DE RIVAS, CARMELA FODERARO, psychiatrist; b. Cortale, Italy, Nov. 25, 1920; d. Salvatore and Mary (Vaiti) Foderaro; came to U.S., 1935, naturalized, 1942; student U. Pa., 1940-42; M.D., Women's Med. Coll. Pa., 1946; m. Aureliano Rivas, Oct. 30, 1948; children—Carmen, Norma, Sandra, David. Intern women's Med. Coll. Pa. Hosp., 1946; gen. practice Phila. and Tex., 1947-49; mem. staff Norristown (Pa.) State Hosp., 1949—, supt., 1963-70; asso. psychiatry U. Pa., 1963—; psychiatrist Penn Found. for Mental Health, Sellersville, Pa., 1970—; Mem Conjoint Mental Health Bd., 1961—; mem. adv. bd. Montgomery County Mental Health Clinics, 1968—. Named to Hall of Fame, S. Phila. High Sch., 1968; recipient citation Women's Med. Coll.Pa., 1968. Diplomate Am. Bd. Psychiatry and Neurology. Fellow Am. Psychiat. Assn., Pa. Psychiat. Soc. (councillor 1967—); mem. Phila. Psychiat. Soc., Assn. Med. Supts. Mental Hosps., A.M.A., Montgomery (bd. dirs., past pres.), Pa. med. socs. Home: 700 Joseph Dr Wayne PA 19087 Office: Penn Found for Mental Health Sellersville PA 18960

DERMAN, CYRUS, math. statistician; b. Phila., July 16, 1925; s. Samuel and Bessie (Segal) D.; A.B., U. Pa., 1948, A.M., 1949; Ph.D., Columbia, 1954; m. Martha Winn, Feb. 24, 1961; childrenAdam Jason Winn, Hester Beth Rebecca. Instr. Syracuse U., 1954-55; faculty Columbia, 1955-, prof. operations research, 1965—; vis. prof. Israel Inst. Tech., Halfa, 1961-62, Stanford, 1965-66. Fellow Inst. Math. Statistics, Am. Statis. Assn.; mem. Internat. Assn. Statistics in Phys. Scis. Author: (with Morton Klein) Probability and Statistical Inference for Engineers, 1959, Finite State Markovian Decision Processes, 1970. Research and publs. on theory of Markov chains, Brownian motion, statis. inference, mgmt. sci. and operations research. Home: 15 Pond Hill Rd Chappaqua NY 10514 Office: Mudd Bldg Columbia New York City NY 10027

DERMER, OTIS CLIFFORD, chemist, educator; b. Hoytville, O., Nov. 11, 1909; s. George Abraham and Iva (Darrow) D.; B.S., Bowling Green State U., 1930, D.Sc. 1960; Ph.D., Ohio State U., 1934; m. Verne Hughes, May 22, 1935; children—Carmen (Mrs. Richard A. Lehnert), Richard, Verne Allen (Mrs. N. Ospovat). Mem. faculty Okla. State U., 1934—, prof. chemistry, 1946—, chmn. dept., 1949—. Cons. Cities Service Research and Devel. Co., 1944-54, Dow Chem. Co., 1955-69. Mem. Am. Chem. Soc. (chmn div. chem. edn. 1949), Okla. Acad. Sci. (pres. 1946), Am. Assn. U. Profs., A.A.A.S., Chem. Soc. (London), Sigma Xi, Phi Lambda Upsilon, Phi Kappa Phi. Contbr. articles profl. jours. Home: 623 Harned Dr Stillwater OK

DERMODY, THOMAS HENRY, mfg. co. exec.; b. East Orange, M.J., Nov. 21, 1909; s. Thomas H. and Margaret C. (Connell) D.; grad. St. Benedict's Prep. Sch., Newark, 1927; B.C.S., N.Y. U., 1932; m. Helen R. Ryan, June 22, 1931; children—Mary L. (Mrs. Robert J. Teuscher), Thomas H., Helen E. With Ruberoid Co., S. Bound Brook, N.J., 1941—, mgr. central accounting office, 1941-43, comptroller, 1943—, v.p., 1957-63, v.p. finance, 1963-66, sr. v.p., 1966-67, also dir., mem. exec. com.; v.p. finance GAF Corp., N.Y.C. C.P.A.. N.Y. Mem. Nat. Assn. Accountants. Home: 1145 Hillside Av Plainfield NJ 07060 Office: 140 W 51st St New York City NY 10020

DERMOTA, ANTON, tenor; b. Kropa, Jugoslavia, 1912; m. Hilda Dermota. Tenor, Vienna State Opera; concert, recital, oratorio, opera singer in Europe, Australia, America; recording artist. Address: Hagenberggasse 36 Vienna 13 Austria*

DER NERSESSIAN, SIRARPLE educator; b. Constantinople, Turkey, Sept. 5, 1896; d. Mihran and Akabie (Ormanian) Der Nersessian; Licence és Lettres, Sorbonne, 1920, Diplme d'Etudes Supérieures, 1921, Docteur és lettres, 1936; Dipme de l'Ecole des Hautes Etudes, Paris, 1926; Litt. D., Wilson Coll., 1948; L.H.D., Smith Coll., 1957. Came to U.S., 1930. Chargée de Conférence Temporaire, Ecole des Hautes, Etudes, Paris, 1926-29; vis. lectr. dept. of art Wellesley Coll., 1930-34, asso. prof., 1934-37, Clara Bertram Kimball prof. art, chmn. dept., and dir. Farnsworth Museum, 1937-46; prof. Byzantine art and archeology, Dumbarton Oaks, Washington, also mem. faculty arts and scis. Harvard, 1946-67, prof. emeritus, 1967—. vis. lect. N.Y. Univ., 1931 and 1936, Ecole Libre des Hautes Etudes, N.Y.C., 1942. Recipient Prix Fould, Institut de France, Académie des Inscriptions et Belles Lettres and Prix de l'Association des Etudes Grecques. Fellow Medieval Acad.; mem. Archeol. Inst. Am., Coll. Art Assn., Société National des Antiquaries de France, Soc. of Byzantine Studies (Athens), Am. Assn. Women. Author: Manuscrits arméniens illustrés des XII, XIII, XIV siécles de la Bibliothéque des Pères Mekhitharistes de Venise, 1936-37; L'illustration de Roman de Barlaam et Joasaph, 1937; Armenia and the Byzantine Empire, 1945. Contbr. profl. jours. Home: 3245 S St NW Washington DC 20007 Office: 1703 32d St NW Washington DC 20007

DE ROCHEMONT, LOUIS, motion picture producer; b. Chelsea, Mass., Jan. 13, 1899; s. Louis L. G. and Sarah Wilson (Miller) de R.; ed. pub. schs., Winchester, Mass., Naval Aviation School, Mass. Inst. Tech., and Naval Cadet Sch., Harvard 1917-18; L.H.D., U. N.H., 1944, Bates College: m. Virginia Shaler, Sept. 12, 1929; children—Louis, Virginia. Served as line officer, U.S. Navy until resignation, 1923; on staff Internat. Newsreel, 1923-27; asst. editor Pathé News, 1927-29; dir. and producer Twentieth Century-Fox; joined TIME Inc., 1934: co-founder, 1st producer The March of Time, 1934-43; directed and produced, The Ramparts We Watch, 1940; now executive producer of RD-DR Corp. producer: The Fighting Lady, 1944 (special award from N.Y. film critics); The House on 92d Street, 1945: 13 Rue Madeline, 1946; Boomerang, 1946; Lost boundaries (received eleven major awards), 1949; The Whistle at Eaton Falls. 1951; Walk East on Beacon, 1952, 1952; Cinemiracle Windjammer; Manona String; The Roman Spring of Mrs. Stone; Parlons Francis; pres. of Louis de Rochemont Asso., Inc., film pup.; The Earth and its People (integrated series ednl. film.) 1948; Martin Luther, 1953; Animal Farm, 1954; Cinerama Holiday, 1955. Decorated Order of St. Olav. 1959. Recipient of the Academy Award for best documentary, 1944; received Order of Liberation from King Haakon of Norway, 1948. Home: Blueberry Bank Newington NH 03871 Office: 22 W 46th St New York City NY 10017

DE ROCHEMONT, RICHARD GUERTIS, motion picture, TV producer; b. Chelsea, Mass., Dec. 13, 1903; s. Louis L.G., and Sarah Wilson (Miller) de R.; ed. pub. schs., Cambridge Latin Sch.; A.B., Harvard, 1928; m. Helen Bentley Bogart, Apr. 11, 1924. Reporter, N.Y. American, 1928, N.Y. Sun, 1929; fgn. editor Movletone Newsreel, 1930-31; dir. for France, Fox Movietone, 1931-34; gen. fgn. mgr., The March of Time, 1934-40, mng. editor, The March of Time (div. of Time, Inc.), 1940-43, producer March of Time, 1943-52; ind. producer for Dept. of State, Ford Found., N.B.C., etc., 1952-53; v.p. J. Walter Thompson Co., N.Y.C., 1953-55; pres. Vavin, Inc., 1955—; war corr. Life, accredited to Fr. Army 1939-40; war corr. March of Time, accredited U.S. Forces, 1944-45. Won Motion Picture Acad. award for prodn. of A Chance to Live, 1949. Awarded Chevalier du Merite Agricole, 1938, promoted to officier, 1959; decorated Officier de la Legion d'Honneur, 1945 (France), Officier Ordre du Merite Touristique, 1959 (France). Mem. France Forever (nat. pres. 1943-46.). Episcopalian. Clubs: Paris-American (pres. 1962-64), Harvard, Williams, Sky, Coffee House, Explorers (N.Y.C.); Societe des Amis des Bouviers de Flandres, Cercle Interallié (Paris); Overseas Press of America (gov. 1940-43, 48, 57-63; trustee corrs. fund 1945—). Home: Box 101 RR 5 Flemington NJ 08822 Moulin de Coutant Pont-Levoy (Loir-et-Cher) France Office: 236 E 46th St New York City NY 10017

DE ROO, REMI JOSEPH, bishop; b. Swan Lake, Man., Can., Feb. 24, 1924; s. Raymond and Josephine (de Pape) DeR.: student St. Boniface (Man.) Coll.; S.T.D., Angelicum U., Rome, Italy. Ordained priest Roman Cath. Ch., 1950; curate Holy Cross Parish, St. Boniface, 1952-53; sec. to archbishop of St. Boniface, 1954-56; diocesan dir. Cath. action Archdiocese St. Boniface, 1953-54; exec. sec. Man. Cath. Con., 1958; pastor Holy Cross Parish, 1960-62; bishop of Victoria, B.C., Can., 1962—. Canadian episcopal rep. Internat. Secretariat Apostleship See, 1964—; pres. episcopal office Mass Media Communications. Address: 740 View St Victoria British Columbia Canada

DEROSIER, ARTHUR HENRY, Jr., univ. dean; b. Norwich, Conn., Feb. 18, 1931; s. Arthur Henry and Rose (Raymond) DeR.; B.S., U. So. Miss., 1953; M.A., U. S.C., 1955, Ph.D., 1959; m. Dora Delores Jordan, Feb. 23, 1952; children—Deborah Ann, Marsha Carol, Charles Arthur, Melissa Estelle. Asst. prof. history The Citadel, 1956-57, Converse Coll., Spartanburg, S.C., 1957-59; asst. prof. U. So. Miss., 1959-60, asso. prof., 1960-64, prof., 1964-65; asso. prof. history U. Okla., 1965-67, asst. dean Grad. Coll., 1966-67; dean Grad. Sch., prof. history E. Tenn. State U., Johnson City, 1967—. Vis. prof. history U. Mass., summer 1964; prof. history, ednl. TV series on Am. history, 1966-71. Active numerous Indian philanthropies. Served with USAF, 1948-52. Southern fellow, 1958; Am. Philos. Soc. grantee, 1964. Mem. Am. Hist. Assn., Orgn. Am. Historians, So., Western hist. assns., Council Grad. Schs. U.S. Democrat. Rotarian. Author: Through the South with a Union Soldier, 1969; The Removal of the Choctaw Indians, 1970. Contbr. articles to hist. jours. Home: 1304 Buffalo St Johnson City TN 37601

DE ROUGEMONT, DENIS, author; b. Neuchatel, Switzerland, Sept. 8, 1906; s. Georges and Alice (Bovet) de R.; lit. and philos. studies Neuchatel, Vienna and Geneva, 1929; m. Anahite Repond, Feb. 2, 1952; children—Nicholas, Martine. Pub. Paris, 1931—; active in creation personalist, 1932—; lectr. French lit. U. Frankfurt (Germany), 1935-36; lectr. l'Ecole libre des Hautes-Etudes, N.Y.C., 1942; script writer Voice Am., 1942-43; active in creation European federalists movement, 1946-50; founder, 1950, since dir. Centre Européan de la Culture, Geneva, Switzerland; pres. exec. com. Congres pour la Liberté de la Culture, 1951-66; pres. Association Européenne des Festivals de Musique, 1951—, Tables Rondes du Conseil de l'Europe, 1953, 55; prof. Inst. universitaire d'Etudes Europeénnes, Geneva, 1963—. Recipient prix Schiller, 1960, prix E. Delacroix, 1957, prix de Monaco, 1963; Grand prix Littéraire de Genève, 1967; Paul Tillich award, 1969; Prix Robert Schuman, 1970. Author: le Payasan du Danube, 1932; Politique de la Personne, 1934; Penser avec les mains, 1936; Journal d'un intellectuel en chmage, 1937; Journal d'Allemagne, 1938; L'Amour et l' Occident, 1939 (pub. in English as Love in the Western World, 1940, Passion and Society, 1940); Nicolas de Flue, 1939; Mission Démission de la Suisse; The Heart of Europe, 1941; La part de Diable, 1944 (pub. English as The Devil's Share, 1945, Talk of the Devil, 1946); Les Personnes du Drame, 1946 (pub. English as Dramatic Personages 1964); Lettres sur la Bombe Atomique, 1946 (pub. English as The Last Trump 1946); Vivre en Amerique, 1947; Doctrine Fabuleuse, 1947; Suite Neuchateloise, 1948; L'Europe en Jeu, 1948; Journal des Deux Mondes, 1948; La Confédération Suisse, 1953; L'Aventure Occidentale de l' Homme, 1957 (pub. in English as Man's Western Quest, 1957); Comme toi-meme, 1961 (pub. English as Love Declared 1963, The Myths of Love 1964), Vingt- Huit Siécles d'Europe, 1961 (pub. English as The Idea of Europe 1966); Les Chances de l'Europe, 1962 (pub. English as The Meaning of Europe 1965); The Christian Opportunity, 1963; La Suisse on l'histoire d'un peuple heureux, 1965; Journal d'un Epoque, 1968; Lettre Ouverte aux Européens, 1970; Le Cheminement des esprits, 1970. Address: Ferney-Voltaire (Ain) France

DEROUNIAN, STEVEN BOGHOS, judge; b. Sofia, Bulgaria, Apr. 6, 1918; s. Boghos and Eliza (Aprahamian) D.; brought to U.S., 1921, derivative citizen; A.B., N.Y. U., 1938; LL.B., Fordham U., 1942; m. Emily Ann Kannard, Aug. 20, 1947; children—Ann Ashby, Steven Blake, Eleanor Kannard. Admitted N.Y. bar, 1942; practiced in Mineola, N.Y., Garden City, N.Y.; former mem. law firm Derounian, Candee, Guardino Murphy; mem. 83d-87th U.S. Congresses, 2d Dist. N.Y., mem. 88th Congress 3d Dist. N.Y.; mem. Com. on ways and means; Justice Supreme Ct. State of N.Y., Councilman, mem. bd. Town of North Hempstead, N.Y., 1948-52; chmn. Cancer Crusade, North Hempstead, 1952. Served to capt. inf., 103rd Div., AUS, 1942-46; maj. Res. Decorated Purple Heart, Bronze Star with cluster, Combat Infantryman's badge. Mem. Am., N.Y. State, Nassau County bar assns., V.F.W., Am. Legion, Res. Officers Assn., Delta Theta Pi. Republican. Mason, Elk Club: Garden City Golf. Home: 15 Carteret Pl Garden City NY 11530 Office: Supreme Ct Mineola NY 11501

DERR, ROBERT JAMES, ins. co. exec.; b. Sterling, Neb., Oct. 21, 1919; s. Herbert S. and Emma (Mahler) D.; student U. Neb., 1938-41, also Los Angeles City Coll., U. So. Cal., U. Cal. at Los Angeles and Berkeley.; m. A. Jean Lavender, Jan. 10, 1942; children—Virginia Hall, Barbara, Thomas. Mfg. engr. Lockheed Aircraft Co., 1941-47; with Indsl. Indemnity Co., San Francisco, 1947—, exec. v.p., 1968-69, pres., 1970—, also dir., mem. exec. com. Guest lectr. Am. Mgmt. Assn., Stanford Grad. Sch. Bus., 1957-58. Bd. assos. Golden State Coll.; dir., past pres. Western Ins. Information Service; trustee Ins. Edn. Assn. Republican. Methodist. Clubs: Jonathan, California (Los Angeles); Sierra, Commonwealth, Stock Exchange, World Trade (San Francisco); Round Hill Country (Alamo, Cal.). Home: 2525 Round Hill Dr Alamo CA 94507 Office: 255 California St San Francisco CA 94111

DERRICK, CHARLES LUTHER, utilities exec.;b. Washington, July 27, 1902; s. Luther Lee and Mary (Colison) D.; E.E., Lehigh U., 1923; m. Malvina S. De Hart, Oct. 29, 1926; children—Marilyn E. (Mrs. Edwin F. Aune), Kenneth C. Engr., Pub. Service Electic & Gas Co., N.J., 1923-42; supt. engring. Hartford Electric Light Co. (Conn.), 1942-52, v.p., 1952-64, pres., 1964-68, now chmn., chief exec. officer also bd. dirs. Past dir. Mitchell House of Hartford. Fellow I.E.E.E.; mem. Edison Elctric Inst. (past chmn. equipment com.). Greater Hartford C. of C. (dir.). Clubs: Lions (past pres.), City (past pres.), Hartford Engineers (Hartford); Golf of Avon (past pres.), Hartford. Home: 81 Waterside Lane West Hartford CT 06007 Office: 176 Cumberland Av Wethersfield CT 06109

DERRICK, CLARENCE, educator; b. New Britain, Conn., Apr. 8, 1912; s. Clarence and Eva (Reid) D.; A.B., Trinity Coll., Hartford, Conn., 1935; M.A., Western Res. U., 1945; Ph.D., U. Chgo., 1953; m. Mary Elizabeth Tyler, July 4, 1945; children—Mary T., Thomas J. Tchr. Avon (Conn.) Old Farms Sch., 1935-41, Univ. Sch., Shaker Heights, O., 1941-47; asst. dir., dept. exams. Chgo. Bd. Edn., 1948-49; supr. humanities sect. Ednl. Testing Service, Princeton, N.J., 1949-53; prof. humanities, chmn. dept. U. Fla., 1953-. Home: 1818 NW 21st Terrace Gainesville FL 32601

DERRICK, HUGH REID, Bus. exec.; b. Trenton, N.J., Sept. 16, 1910; s. Clarence and Eva (Reid) D.; B.S., Va. Poly. Inst., 1931; m. Mary Rau, June 23, 1934 (dec. July 19, 1957); 1 dau., Alice Dearing (Mrs. James D. Reynolds); m. 2d, Margaret S. Towles, Sept. 6, 1958. Distbn. supt., mgr. Ala. Gas Corp., Tuscaloosa, 1931-38, mgr., Gadsden, Montgomergy plants, 1938-43, v.p., dir. corp., 1948-53, pres., 1953-56, now dir.; dir. Laclede Gas Co., 1956—, chief exec. officer, chmn. bd., 1968- ; v.p., gen. mgr. Chattanooga Gas Co., 1946-48; chmn bd. St. Charles Gas Corp.; dir. Am. Investment Co., Boatmen's Nat. Bank of St. Louis. Bd. of dirs. City Art Mus.; mem. Civic Progress, Inc., St. Louis. Served with USNR, World War II. Mem. Am., So. gas assns., Ind. Natural Gas Assn. Am. (dir.). Clubs: Bogey, Racquet, Noonday, University (St. Louis). Home: 4 N Kingshighway St Louis MO 63108 Office: 720 Olive St St Louis MO 63101

DERRICK, JOHN RAFTER, med. educator; b. Clayton, Ga., Jan. 17, 1922; B.S., Clemson Coll., 1943; M.D., Tulane U., 1946; married; 6 children. Instr. chest and cardiovascular surgery Sch. Medicine, Emory U., 1956-57; asso. prof. thoracic surgery, acting chief div. thoracic and cardiovascular surgery U. Tex. Med. Br., 1957-69, prof., chief div., 1969—. Served with USAF, 1947-49. Mem. Assn. Thoracic Surgery, Am. Coll. Angiology, Am. Coll. Cardiology, A.C.S., Am. Fedn. Clin. Research, Am. Heard Assn., A.M.A., Soc. Univ. Surgeons, Soc. Vascular Surgery, Internat. Cardiovascular Soc. Office: Div Thoracic and Cardiovascular Surgery U Tex Galveston TX 77550*

DERRICK, LELAND EUGENE, coll. dean; b. Hollis, Okla., Apr. 14, 1901; s. Joseph Edward and Ada (Magee) D.; B.A., U. Tex.,1926, M.A., 1930, Ph.D., 1940; m. Delia May Thomas, Apr. 14, 1923; children—Leland Eugene, Gus Wilburn. Prin Sherwood (Tex.) Pub. Sch., 1922-24, supt., 1924-25; with S.W. Tex. State Coll. (new S.W. Tex. State U.), 1926—, instr., asst. prof., asso. prof., 1926-40, prof. English, 1940—, dir. dept., 1954-58, now v.p. and dean Grad. Sch., also acting pres. of coll., 1968-69. Served to maj. USAAF, 1942-45; lt. col., 1951-52. Mem. Coll. English Assn. (pres. Tex. div. 1958-59), Coll. Tchrs. English (dir. Tex. Conf. 1956-59), Assn. Tex. Grad. Schs. (pres. 1961-62), Am. Legion. Methodist. Mason, Rotarian. Home: Box 440 San Marcos TX 78666

DERRICK, ROYDEN GLADE, steel co. exec.; b. Salt Lake City, Sept. 7, 1915; s. Hyrum H. and Margaret (Glade) D.; H.H.D., U. Utah, 1965; m. Allie Olson, May 27, 1938; childrenLinda (Mrs. Roger Wood), James Royden, David Glade, Bruce Glade. Pres., gen. mgr. Western Steel Co. and subsidiary Steel Erection & Rigging Co.; pres. Bonneville Life Ins. Co. 1958-65; chmn. bd. Bonnsville-Sylvan Life Ins. Co., 1965—, Salt Lake City br. Fed. Res. Bank of San Francisco. dir. Salt Lake City Depot & R.R. Co. mem. trade mission to So. India. Dept. Commerce, 1959; mem. Study Team to Bolivia Dept. State, 1964. Mem. Salt Lake City Met. Water Bd., 1957-58; dir. Utah Citizens Rate Assn., 1959-; mem. Central Utah Water Conservancy Dist. Bd., 1964—. Bd. regents U. Utah, 1957-65, chmn. bd., 1959-65. Mem. Nat. (regional v.p. 1964-66), Utah (dir., past pres.) Mfrs. assns., Salt Lake City C. of C. (bd. govs. 1960- 63), Nat. Assn. Partners of the Americas (chmn. bd.). Mem. Ch. of Jesus Christ of Latter-Day Saints (mem. gen. superintendency Deseret Sunday Sch. Union). Club: Fort Douglas. Home: 2051 Princeton Salt Lake City UT 84108 Office: Crandall Bldg Salt Lake City UT 84101

DERRY, JOHN ALVIN, engring. adminstr.; b. Uhrichsville, O., May 9, 1907; s. John Frank and Minnie Dorothy (Fox) D.; B.S., Rose-Hulman Inst., Terre Haute, Ind., 1929; m. Kathryn Elisabeth Stroup, July 5, 1930 (dec. Apr. 6, 1952); children—Josephine Amanda, Stephen Michael, Brian John; m. 2d. M. Virginia Krieg-Jackson, Apr. 3, 1954. Student eng. Ohio Bell Telephone Co., 1929; chief substation supr., electrification constrn., Pa. R.R. Co., 1930-36, regional constrn. engr. Rural Electrification Adminstrn., 1936-42. Active duty as 1st lt., O.R.C., U.S. Army, 1942-46; advanced through grades to lt. col. C.E.; office chief engrs., Manhattan Engring., Dist. (atomic bomb project) nuclear reactor pilot plant and electromagnetic separations plant, Oak Ridge, Los Alamos weapons lab., Comdr. Gen. L. R. Groves staff, Washington and Bikini; asst. to gen. mgr. A.E.C., Feb. 1947, coordinator Spl. Assignments, div. of prodn., 1949-50, exec. officer div. of biology and medicine, 1950, chief project A and mgr. San Francisco office, divs. research and prodn., 1950-52, asst. dir. prodn., 1953; dir. div. of constrn. and supply, 1954-61, dir. div. of constrn., 1961—. Decorated Legion of Merit, Army Commendation ribbon with oak leaf cluster, Am. Theatre and World War II medals; recipient merit citation, Nat. Civil Service League, 1956, citation for exceptional achievement AEC, 1958, Honor Alumnus award Rose Poly. Inst., 1968. Registered prof. engr., D.C. Mem. I.E.E.E., Sigma Nu. Lutheran. Club: Kenwood Golf and Country (Washington). Home: 5723 Ogden Washington DC 20016

DERRYBERRY, EVERETT, univ. pres.; b. Columbia, Tenn., Oct. 11, 1906; s. Felix Oscar and Bonnie Everett (McDonald) D.; B.A., U. of Tenn., 1928; B.A., U. of Oxford, Eng. (Rhodes sohoiar), 1932, M.A., 1939; D. Litt., U. Chattanooga, 1965; LL.D., Pepperdine Coll., 1967; m. Joan Pitt- Rew, Aug. 5, 1933; children—Walter Everett, June Elizabeth. Prof. of English, Burritt Coll., Spencer, Tenn., 1932-33; head dept. of English, U. Tenn. Jr. Coll., 1933-38; head dept. langs. and lit. Murray (Ky.) State Coll., 1938-40; pres. Tenn. Technol. U., Cookeville, since Dec. 1940. Regional dir., U.S.O. and Nat. War Fund, 1943-46. Chmn. Tenn. Edn. Legislative Com., 1943, 44, 45; adv. bd. Tenn. Congress P.T.A.; sec. Conf. on Pub. Instns. in So. States, 1949; mem. Tenn. Jud. Council; pres. Tenn. Water Safety Congress, 1951; chmn. council univ. pres.'s Tenn. Bd. Edn. Recipient Outstanding Civilian Service medal U.S. Dept. Army, 1968. Mem. Am. Assn. U. Profs., Nat. Council English Tchrs., U. of Tenn. Alumni Assn. (pres. 1946) Tenn. Coll. Assn. (pres. 1945), So. Assn. Colls. (commn. on higher edn.), Phi Delta Kappa, Sigma Chi, Phi Kappa Phi, Pi Kappa Delta, Omicron Delta Kappa, Kappa Delta Pi. Rotarian, Lion. Address: Tenn Technol U Cookeville TN 38501

DERRYBERRY, JAMES WARD, corp. exec.; b. Denver, July 10, 1927; s. Charles Wayne and Wilda Gertrude (Wallace) D.; B.A. in Econs., Psychology and Sociology, Yale, 1951; m. Nancy Lynn Hill, Jan. 26, 1957; children—Ann Page, Cathrine Wallace, Amy Jane. Vice-pres., dir. Pacific Coast Holdings, Inc., Pacific Coast Holdings Ins. Co., Pacific Coast Holdings Mgmt. Corp., Pacific Coast Holdings Morgage Co., (all San Francisco), 1968—, Pacific Coast Holdings Advisers, Inc., Pacific Coast Holdings Capital Co., San Francisco, 1971—; pres., dir. Bell Savs. and Loan Assn., San Mateo, San Rafael and Burlingame, Cal., 1968—. Fund chmn., dir. A.R.C.; active Cancer Fund, United Crusade, Yale Alumni Schs. Com. Councilman, vice-mayor Chico City; county chmn., nat. committeeman Young Republicans Cal.; mem. County Republican Central Com. Trustee St. Stephen's Parish Day Sch., Belvedere, Cal.; dir. Marin City Boys Club. Served with AUS, 1945-47. Mem. Soc. Indsl. Realtors. Clubs: Commonwealth, The Family, Bankers. Home: 1470 Vistazo West Tiburon CA 94920 Office: Bank of Am Center San Francisco CA 94104

DERRYBERRY, MAYHEW, pub. health educator; b. Columbia, Tenn., Dec. 25, 1902; s. James Marshall and Mary Katherine (Hardison) D.; A.B., U. Tenn., 1925; M.A., Columbia Tchrs. Coll., 1927; Ph.D., N.Y. U., 1933; m. Helen W. Fosdick, July 5, 1930. Asso. dir. research Am. Child Health Assn., N.Y.C., 1925- 35; sec. to san. supt. N.Y.C. Health Dept., 1935-36; sr. pub. health statistician USPHS, 1936-42, chief health edn. service, 1942-63; health edn. adviser to India, AID, 1963-66; prof. in residence Sch. Pub. Health, U. Cal. at Berkeley, 1966-71, ret., 1971; research asst. N.Y. U., 1932-36. Recipient Elizabeth Prentiss award health edn. Cleve. Health Mus. 1950; Meritorious Service award USPHS, 1968. Fellow Am. Pub. Health Assn. (gov. council, chmn. health edn. sect.); hon. fellow Soc. Pub. Health Educators (pres. 1950). Author: (with P. Van Ingen and G. T. Palmer) Health Protection of Preschool Child, 1931. Home: 1401 Walnut St Berkeley CA 94709

DERSHOWITZ, ALAN MORTON, educator, lawyer; b. Bklyn., Sept. 1, 1938; s. Harry and Claire (Ringel) D.; B.A. magna cum laude, Bklyn. Coll., 1959; LL.B. magna cum laude, Yale, 1962; M.A. (hon.), Harvard, 1967; m. Sue Barlach, June 21, 1959; children—Elon Marc, Jamin Seth. Admitted to D.C. bar 1963, Mass. bar, 1968, also U.S. Supreme Ct.; law clk. to chief judge David L. Bazelon, U.S. Ct. Appeals, 1962-63, to justice Arthur J. Goldberg, U.S. Supreme Ct., 1963-64; mem. faculty Harvard, 1964—, prof. law, 1967—. Cons. to dir. Nat. Inst. Mental Health, 1967-69, Pres.'s Commn. Civil Disorders, 1968, Pres.'s Com. Causes Violence, 1968, N.A.A.C.P. Legal Def. Fund, 1967-68. Bd. dirs. Am. Civil Liberties Union, 1968-71. Mem. Order of Coif, Phi Beta Kappa. Jewish religion. Author: (with others) Psychoanalysis, Psychiatry and the Law, 1967; also articles. Editor-in-chief Yale Law Jours., 1961-62. Home: 21 Robinson St Cambridge MA 02138

DERTHICK, LAWRENCE GRIDLEY, Sr., ednl. exec.; b. Hazel Green, Ky., Dec. 23, 1906; s. Henry J. and Pearl S. (Derthick) D.; A.B., Milligan Coll., 1927, LL.D., 1953; A.M., U. Tenn., 1930; student Columbia, 1939; LL.D., U. Chattanooga, 1954, Franklin Coll., 1957. Kent State U., 1958, Boston U., 1959, Fairleigh Dickinson U., 1960; Sc.D. Edn., U. Me., 1958; Ed.D., R.I. Coll. Edn., 1958; L.H.D., Yeshiva U., 1959; Dr. Pub. Service (hon.), Ohio Wesleyan U., 1959; Ed.D., Bryant Coll., 1960; m. Helda Lee Hannah, Sept. 16, 1927; children—Lawrence Gridley, Alan Wendell, Louann. Tchr. and prin. consol. schs., Greene County, Tenn., 1927-29; prin. Joint City-County High Sch., Clarksville, Tenn., 1930-35; state high sch. visitor East Tenn., prof. edn. East Tenn. State Coll., Johnson City, 1935-39; asst. supt. charge instrn. Nashville pub. schs., 1939-42; supt. city schs., Chattanooga, 1942-56; U.S. commr. edn. Dept. Health Edn. and Welfare, Washington, 1956-60; asst. exec. sec. for profl. devel. and instructional services N.E.A., 1961—; chief ednl. br. Office Mil. Govt. for Bavaria, 1948-49. Dir. Internat. Textbook Co. Chmn. of Interdeptl. Com. on Edn. Activities in Internat. Orgns.; chmn. U.S. Office Edn. team to study schs. of Soviet Union, 1958. Mem. U.S. nat. commn. for UNESCO, 1957-60; U.S. del. 1st Regional Edn. Seminar, sponsored by South Pacific Commn., Brisbane, Australia, 1959; mem. Pres's Com. on Employment Physically Handicapped; mem. com. on sch. service Boy Scouts Am.; adv. com. on sch. relations Girl Scouts U.S.A.; life mem. Nat. Congress Parents and Tchrs.; bd. dirs. Fgn. Study League; mem. Fulbright Bd. Fgn. Scholarships, 1957-60; Tenn. del. White House Conf. on Edn., 1955. Recipient medal Honor for Distinguished Service, U.S. Dept. Health, Edn. and Welfare, 1960; medal for Distinguished Service, Tchrs. Coll., Columbia U., 1967. Mem. N.E.A. (life mem.; adviser ednl. policies commn.), Tenn. Edn. Assn., Am. Assn. Sch. Administrs. (mem. yearbook commn. 1948, chmn. 1953; pres. 1953-54; chmn. com. for advancement sch. adminstrn. 1955-57), Newcomen Soc., Phi Kappa Phi, Kappa Delta Pi, Phi Delta Kappa. Co-author: Be Safe and Live; contbr. numerous edn. and other publs. Office: 1201 16th St NW Washington DC 20036

DERUJINSKY, GLEB W., sculptor; b. Smolensk, Russia, Aug. 13, 1888; s. Wladimir F. and Sophia A. (Artzimovitch) D.; ed. Imperial Acad. of Art, Petrograd, Russia; grad. in law U. Petrograd, 1912; m. Alexandra N. Michailoff, May 7, 1924 (dec. Aug. 1956); children—Gleb, Natalie; m. 2d, Natalie Tarby, Nov. 21, 1956. Came to U.S., 1919, naturalized citizen, 1933. Began as sculptor in Petrograd, 1915; exhibited in Russia, London, Brussels, Paris, and under auspices of Nat. Acad. Design (N.Y.C.), and Art Inst. Chgo. Works in perm. colls. of Met. Mus. Art, San Diego Mus., Toledo. Represented by fountain (Europa), N.Y. World Fair. 1939. 14 Stas. of the cross. at Cardinal Hayes Memorial Chapel, 1942; 8 medallions carved in wood, Postmaster General's office. Washington; 3 reliefs, Chemical Engring. Bldg., Cornell U.; 4 wood statues, Ch. of Assumption, Westport, Conn.; memorial bust Franklin D. Roosevelt for Hyde Park Library Court; Crucifixion (in wood), Kent Sch., Conn.; Madonna and Child in mahogony for Jesuit Ch., India; bronze bust of

Dr. Charles May at N.Y. Med. Acad.; teak wood carving meml., Harvard Club, N.Y.; bronze group (Ecstasy) Brookgreen Gardens, South Carolina, also stone carving Samson and the Lion, Diona hunting with dog in bronze; 14 stations of the Cross for private chapel for Cardinal Spellman, N.Y.C.; bronze bust Theodore Roosevelt, Panama Law Adminstrn. Bldg.; Stas. of Cross, House of Theology, Cin.; 4 statues for Ch. of St. Vincent Ferrer, N.Y.C. St. Joseph for St. Mary's Ch., Flushing, N.Y.; statues in marble Cathedral of Immaculate Conception. Washington; Franz Liszt statue Haifa (Israel) Music Museum. Recipient awards, most recent; Sculpture prize Am. Artists Profl. League, Allied Artists; Henry Hering medal, 1960, 61. Daniel Chester French Prize, 1962, Bronze Medal of Honor. Nat. Arts Club, 1961, 64, Gold medal Allied Artists Am., 1966. Pauline Law prize, 1968. N.A. Mem. Nat. Acad. Fine Arts, Nat. Sculpture Soc. (spl. citation. emeritus mem.), N.A.D., Allied Artists (emeritus) Am. Artists Profl. League (medal for sculpture). Mem. Greek Orthodox Ch. N.A. Address: 29 W 65th St New York City NY 10023 ☆

DERVAUX, PIERRE JEAN EMILE, opera condr.; b. Juvisey-sur-Orge, Jan. 3, 1917; m. Arlette Madres, Apr. 27, 1953; children—Jean Pierre, Marie Christine (by prev. marriage), Thiery. Profl. musician, 1931-44; pianist, orch. leader Opera Comique, 1945-53; v.p. Concerts Pasdeloup, 1948-52; toured Am., South Africa, Centra Am., Scandinavia, Hungary, Israel, Spain, S.Am., Gt. Britain, USSR; now condr. Lyric Opera, Chgo. Mem. bd. Conservatoire National of Music. Decorated Legion of Honor. Clubs: Tennis, Artists. Home: 81 Avenue Victor Hugo Paris 16e France Office: care Luric Opera of Chicago 10 N Michigan Av Chicago IL*

DERWINSKI, EDWARD JOSEPH, congressman; b. Chgo., Sept. 15, 1926: s. Casimir Ignatius and Sophia (Zmijewski) D.; B.Sc. in History, Loyola U., 1951; m. Patricia Vander Giessen; children—Maureen Sue, Michael Stephen. Pres. W. Pullman Savs. & Loan Assn., 1946—, dir. 1949—; rep. 24th Dist., Ill. Gen Assembly, 1957-58; mem. 85th-92d Congresses, 4th Dist. Ill. Served with inf., Aus. 1945-46; now maj. in Res. Named one of ten Outstanding Young Men of Chgo., 1959, 61. Mem. V.F.W., Polish Highlanders (nat. dir.), Cath. War Vets., Polish Alma Mater, Am. Legion, Polish Legion Am. Vets (past state vice comdr.), Amvets, Polish Roman Cath. Union, Polish Nat. Alliance. Republican. Roman Catholic. Moose, K.C., Kiwanian. Home: 515 E 160th Pl South Holland IL 60473 Office: 2441 Vermont St Blue Island IL 60406

DERY, TIBOR, author; b. Budapest, Hungary, Oct. 18, 1894; s. Karoly and Ernestine (Rosenberg) D.; m. Elisabeth Hulman, Nov. 11, 1955. Recipient Kossuth prize, 1948. Mem. acads. Berlin, Mainz and Hamburg. Author: The Unfinished Sentence; Answer; The Excommunicator; Mr. G.A. in X; The Giant; The Portuguese Princess; The Old Woman and the Horse; Theokritos in New-Pest; The Double Shout; The Giant Baby; No Verdict; Niki; (poetry) The Animals of the Clouds. Address: II Lotz Károly 20 Budapest Hungary

DERZON, GORDON M., physician. Asst. commr. Kings County Hosp. Center, Bklyn. Office: 451 Clarkson Av Brooklyn NY 11203*

DESAI, KANTILAL THAKORDAS, legal cons.; b. Surat, India, May 23, 1903; s. Thakordas Jekisondas and Chanda (Vakilna) D.; student Elphinstone Coll., 1920-22; B.S., Wilson Coll., 1924; LL.B., Govt. Law Coll. India, 1926; m. Vina Markandrao Mehta, Mar. 1, 1933; children—Sujata (Mrs. Manohar), Sadhana, Dipika (Mrs. Shah). Named solicitor, 1928, advocate, 1930; practice before Bombay (India) High Ct., 1930-57, judge, 1957-60; chief justice Gujarat (India) High Ct., 1961-63; legal cons., 1963—; vice chmn. State Bank India, Bombay, 1966-70; chmn. marine services enquiry coms. Govt. India, 1968-69; chmn. Bennett Coleman & Co. Ltd., Bombay; dir. Press Trust India Ltd., Garware Nylons Ltd. Chmn. bd. visitors St. George's Hosp., Bombay. Home: 265 12th Rd Khar Bombay 52 India Office: 19 Nanabhai Lane Fort Bombay India

DESALVO, ALFRED, finance co. exec.; b. N.Y.C., Dec. 26, 1919; s. Anthony and Alvina (Gatalano) DeS.; B.B.A., Coll. City N.Y., 1941; grad. Advanced Mgmt. Program, Harvard, 1965; m. Thelma Lambert, Dec. 7, 1945; children—Keith Alan, David Anthony. With C.I.T. Financial Corp., 1957—, treas., 1964- -, v.p., 1965—; dir. Service Fire Ins. Co., Service Casualty Ins. Co. Bd. dirs. Eastern Property Owners Assn., Garden City, 1966—. Served to col. USAAF and USAF, 1941-46, 51-53. Mason. Home: 97 Transverse Rd Garden City NY 11530 Office: 650 Madison Av New York City NY 10022

DESAN, WILFRID, educator; License en Philosophie, Lille (France) U.; Ph.D., Harvard. Taught at Kenyon Coll., Harvard U.; now prof. philosophy Georgetown U. Author: The Tragic Finale; The Planetary Man (A Noetic Prelude to a United World); The Marxism of Jean-Paul Sarte. Office: Dept Philosophy Georgetown Univ Washington DC 20007

DE SANCTIS, EDWARD L., bank exec. Auditor, security officer Oneida Nat. Bank & Trust Co. Central N.Y. Office: 268 Genessee St Utica NY 13503*

DE SANTILLANA, GLORGIO DIAZ, historian of science; b. Rome, Italy, May 30, 1902; s.David and Emilia (Maggiorani) de S.; grad. Rome U., 1925; m. Dorothy Hancock Tilton, Sept. 1, 1948. Came to U.S., 1936, naturalized, 1945. Instr. Rome U., 1929-32; lectr. New Sch. for Social Research, 1936-37; vis. lectr. Harvard, 1937-39; mem. faculty Mass. Inst. Tech., 1941—, prof. history and philosophy of sci., 1954—, now emeritus; Fulbright fellow in Italy, 1954- 55. Mem. Am. Acad. of Arts and Sciences, History of Sci. Soc. Club: Somerset (Boston). Author: Aspects of XIX Century Rationalism, 1941; Galileo's Dialogue of the Great World Systems, 1953; The Crime of Galileo, 1955; The Age of Adventure, 1956; The Origins of Scientific Thought, 1961; Reflections and Ideas, 1968; Hamlet Mill, 1969. Home: Curtis Point Prince St Beverly MA 01915

DE SANTIS, VINCENT PAUL, educator, historian; b. Birdsboro, Pa., Dec. 25, 1916; s. Antonio and Martha Mae (Templin) DeS.; B.S., W. Chester (Pa.) State Coll., 1941; Ph.D., Johns Hopkins, 1952; m. Helene O'Brien, June 24, 1946; childrenVincent, Edmund, Philip, John. Mem. faculty U. Notre Dame, 1949-, prof. history, 1962-, Chmn. dept., 1963—; summer vis. prof. Johns Hopkins, 1954, Bklyn. Coll., 1961, Georgetown U., 1962; vis. prof. U. Genoa, 1967-68. Mem. Cath. Commn. on Intellectual & Cultural Affairs. Served to capt. AUS, 1941-45. Recipient R.D.W. Connor award N.C. Lit. and Hist. Assn., 1959; award Am. Philos. Soc., 1955, 62, 63, Distinguished Alumni award W. Chester State Coll., 1970. Guggenheim fellow, 1960-61; Fulbright lectr., 1967-68, Mem. Orgn. Am. Historians, Nat. Geog. Soc., Soc. Am. Historians, Am. Cath. (pres. 1963-64), So. hist. assns., Am. Studies Assn., Am. Assn. U. Profs. Author: Republicans Face the Southern Question, 1959. Co-author: Our Country, 1960; America's Ten Greatest Presidents, 1961; The Democratic Experience, 1963; The Gilded Age, 1963; America Past and Present, 1968. Compiler: The Gilded Age, 1971. Home: 1236 E Madison St South Bend IN 46617

DESAUTEL S, CLAUDE JOHN, pub. relations exec.; b. Montreal, Que., Can., June 8, 1921 (parents U.S. citizens); s. Victor Joseph andCedia (Brault) D.; B.S. in Fgn. Service Georgetown U., 1949; m. Yvette Poirer, Sept. 5, 1949; childrenMark G., Suzanne M., John C., Claire E. Exec. asst. to Congressman Wayne Aspinall, 1949-61; spl. asst. at White House, 1961-66; exec. asst. to postmaster gen., 1966-68; spl. asst. to chmn. Democratic Nat. Com., 1968-69; pres. Desautels Assos., pub. relations, 1969—. Vice pres. Silver Spring (Md.) Jr. C. of C., 1954-58. Vice chmn. Montgomery County (Md.) Com. Kennedy for President, 1960; Kennedy coordinator Democratic Nat. Conv., 1960; advance coordinator Kennedy-Johnson campaign, 1960. Served with AUS, 1942-46; PTO. Mem. Delta Sigma Pi (pres. Washington Alumni club 1951-54). Roman Catholic, Clubs: Federal City, Nat. Communications. Home: 3910 Woodlawn Rd Chevy Chase MD 20015

DESCH, CARL WILLIAM, banker; b. N.Y.C., Oct. 3, 1915; s. William and Marie (Mayerhofer) D.; A.B., Columbia, 1937, M.A., 1939; m. Katherine Woerner, Aug. 31, 1940; children—Carol J. (Mrs. Russell R. Desoe) Carl William, Barbara K. With First Nat. City Bank, N.Y.C., 1939—, v.p., 1955-58, cashier, 1958-65, sr. v.p., cashier, 1965- -; sec., treas., First Nat. City Corp.; dir. Advance Mortgage Corp. Mem. Commnrs. adv. council charities registration N.Y. State Dept. Social Welfare, 1966—; chmn. major gifts div. Greater N.Y. chpt. A.R.C., 1967, mem. bd. dirs. and exec. com.; pres. Alumni Fedn. Columbia U.; Vice pres. Assn. of Alumni Columbia Coll.; pres. Nat. City Ednl. and Charitable Found. pres. First Nat. City bank Found. Served with USAAF and AUS, 1943-46. Mem. Am. Soc. Corp. Secs., N.Y. C. of C. Clubs: University (N.Y.C); Garden City Country. Home: 121 Wilson St Garden City NY 11530 Office: 399 Park Av New York City NY 10022

DESCH, THEODORE EDWARD, railroad ofcl., lawyer; b. Chgo., Oct. 1, 1931; s. Louis G. and Dorothy (Prieb) D.; A.B., U. Ill., 1952, LL.B., 1954; m. Donna K. Thorsell, Feb. 3, 1951; children—Theodore M. (Dec. 1968), Steven R., Katherine S., Gregory S. Admitted to Ill. bar, 1954; asst. gen. atty. C., R.I.&P. Ry., 1956-59, gen. atty., 1959-65, gen. counsel, 1965-68, v.p. and gen. counsel, 1968-70, vice chmn. bd., chief exec. officer, dir., 1970—. Dir. Heritage Bank of Addison, Ill. Served to 1st lt., inf., U.S. Army, 1954-56. Mem. Am., Ill., Chgo. bar assns., Delta Sigma Phi, Phi Alpha Delta. Lutheran. Mason. Clubs: Union League (Chgo.); Capitol Hill (Washington). Home: 129 Springwood Dr Naperville IL 60540 Office: 139 W Van Buren St Chicago IL 60605

DESCHATELETS, JEAN PAUL, senator; b. Montreal, Que., Oct. 9, 1912; s. Sigefroy and Fabiola (Dequoy) D.; ed. St. Mary's Coll., Montreal, Valleyfield Sem., U. Montreal; m. Fernande Dufresne, Nov. 11, 1939; children—Helen, Bernard, Andree. Called to bar Que., 1937; enforcement counsel for Que. W.P.T.B., 1942-51; permanent sec. Que. Assn. Architects, 1952-53; later liaison officer with R.C.M.P. for black market investigations for Montreal and Western Que.; mem. Ho. of Commons for Maisonneuve Rosemont, 1953-65; minister pub. works, 1963-65; mem. Senate of Can., 1966—, dep. govt. leader, 1966, speaker, 1968—; mem. Canadian Parliament Delegation to Commonwealth Parliament Conf. to New Delhi, Pakistan and Ceylon, 1957. Liberal. Roman Catholic. K.C. Club: Reform. Address: The Senate Ottawa Ontario Canada*

DE SCHAUENSEE, MAX, music critic; b. Rome, Italy, Dec. 5, 1899; s. Frederic and Matilda Dale (Toland) de S.; student Curtis Inst. Music, 1925-27. Came to U.S., 1913, naturalized, 1923. Appeared in Am. premieres of Kovenchina (Moussorgsky), 1928, Demon (Rubenstein), Phila., 1929, as Radames in Aida, Atlantic City, 1934; asst. music critic Phila. Pub. Ledger, 1940- 42; music critic Evening Bull., Phila., 1942-. Appearances on Met. Opera Quiz, 1950-. Served with USCGR, World War II. Author: (poems) Viareggio and Other Poems, 1926; The Collector's Verdi and Puccini, 1962. Contbr. to Musical Am., Opera News, High Fidelity. Home: 135 S 18th St Philadelphia PA 19103 Office: Phila Bulletin 30th and Market Sts Philadelphia PA 19101

DESCHLER, LEWIS, parliamentarian; b. Chillicothe, O., Mar. 3, 1905; s. Joseph Anthony and Lillian Louise (Lewis) D.; student Miami U., Oxford O., 1922-25, LL.D., 1963; student George Washington U., 1925; M.P.L., J.D., Nat. U., 1932, LL.D., 1947; m. Virginia A. Cole, Jan. 18, 1931; children—Lewis II, Joan Mari (Mrs. William B. Eddy). Admitted to D.C. bar in 1934, U.S. Supreme Ct. bar, 1937; apptd. messenger at speakers table, U.S. Ho. of Reps., Dec. 1925; apptd. asst. parliamentarian U.S. Ho. of Reps., Jan. 1927, parliamentarian, 1928—. Served as asst. sec. Am. Group of Interparliamentary Union Con., London, July 1930. Recipient Gov.'s award, Ohio, 1970, 1st Annual John W. McCormack award, 1970. Mem. Nat. Portrait Gallery, Delta Tau Delta. Editor: House Rules and Manual, 1929-71. Home: Bethesda MD 20014 Address: Speakers Rooms Ho of Reps Washington DC 20515

DESCHRYVER, HUBERT, Belgium diplomat; b. Ghent, Belgium, June 15, 1929; s. August Edmond and Maria (Scheerders) DeS.; Dr. of Law, U. Ghent, 1953; m. Simonetta Jung, Oct. 1, 1962. Atty., 1953; joined Belgian Fgn. Service, 1954; attache Belgian embassy, Rio de Janeiro, 1957-59; vice consul, Milano, 1960-63; consul Naples, 1963-64; counselor of Belgian embassy to Holy See, 1964-68; consul gen. of Belgium in San Francisco, 1968—. Decorated cavaleiro do Cruzeiro do Sul Brazil; officer Crown (Belgium); comdr. Gregorius Magnus (Vatican). Clubs: World Trade, Commonwealth, Press (San Francisco). Home: 52 Kwaadham Ghent Belgium Office: 100 Bush St San Francisco CA 94104

DESCHWEINITZ, KARL, Jr., eductor; b. Phila., Mar. 16, 1920; s. Karl and Jessie (Dickson) deS.; B.A., Dartmouth Coll., 1941; Ph.D., Yale U., 1949; m. Margery Anne Skinner, Aug. 8, 1945; children—Ellen, Deborah, Anne. Prof. econ. Northwestern U., 1949-67; prof. econ. and law, 1967—. Served with AUS, 1943-45. Mem. Am. Polit. Sci. Assn., Am. Economic Assn., Am. Assn. U. Profs., Am. Civil Liberties Union. Author: Industrialization and Democracy, 1964; Man and Modern Society, 1953. Home: 2676 Orrington Av Evanston IL 60201

DESCIPIO, FRANK, physician. Asst. commr. Goldwater Meml. Hosp., N.Y.C. Office: Welfare Island New York City NY 10017*

DESCLEE DE MAREDSOUS, CHARLES, elec. utility exec.; b. Brussels, Belgium, Oct. 9, 1916; s. Benoit and Anne-Marie (Capelle) D. de M.; Lic. in Econs., U. Louvain, 1941, LL.D., 1938; m. Bernadette Chaudoir, Dec. 4, 1945; children—Isabelle, Pascale, Philippe, Sybille, Bruno. Econ. adviser Ministry Econ. Affairs, Brussels, 1945-46; econ. attaché Belgian embassy, London, 1946-47; chargé de mission Ministry of Colonies, Kinshasa, 1948-49; mgr. H. Desclee & Co. S.A., Bruges, 1949-56; dir., mem. exec. com. Electrobel, 1956—; mng. dir. Desclee Frères & Co., Brussels, 1958—; dir. G.B. Enterprises, E.B.E.S., Intercom, dir. Nederlandse Credit Bank, Amsterdam; mem. supervisory bd. Bank Lambert, 1965—. Decorated officer Leopold Order, officer Couronne Order. Mem Belgian Soc. Security Analysts (chmn.). Club: Guides Officer's (Brussels). Home: 16 Avenue de Tervueren 1040 Brussels Belgium Office: 32-36 Avenue de Tervueren 1040 Brussels Belgium

DE SEGONZAC, ADALBERT RENE DE BARDON, journalist; b. Paris, France, July 25, 1912; s. Jean Ludovic and Daisy Mathilde (d'Erlanger) de S.; m. Marie-Madeleine duCailar, Jan. 29, 1943; children—Lionel, Catherine, Laurence-Diane, Jean-Renaud. Reporter. L'Intransigeant, 1932-33, Le Jour, Paris, 1934-35; asst. bur. chief London, Eng. for Paris-Soir, 1936-39, chief corr., London, 1945-56, chief corr. North Am., Washington, 1956—. Served with French Army, 1939- 40; mem. Free French Air Force, 1941-44; prisoner of war in Germany. Decorated officer Legion of Honor, Croix de Guerre with 5 clusters (France); D.F.C. (Eng.). Clubs: Federal City, Overseas Writers, National Press (Washington). Author: Visa for Peking, 1956. Home: 5100 Loughboro Road NW Washington DC 20016 Office: Nat Press Bldg Washington DC 20004

DE SELDING, EDWARD BERTRAND, investment banker; b. Summit, N.J., June 15, 1926; s. Edward Fitzgerald and Alene (Rockwell) deS.; B.A., Yale U., 1950; m. Joan Bulkley, Oct. 21, 1950; children—Peter, Ann, Edward Bertrand, Jr. with Spencer Brask & Co., Inc., N.Y.C., 1950—, partner, 1962-68, v.p., dir., 1968-71, sr. v.p., dir., 1969—. Served with USAAF, 1944-46. Mem. Nat. Assn. Securities Dealers Inc. (chmn. dist. 12 com. 1971), Bond Club N.Y. (sec. 1967-68). Republican. Episcopalian (vestryman 1961-63, 67-69). Clubs: Yale, Lunch (N.Y.C.); Tokeneke (gov. 1970—). Home: 18 Fox Hill Lane Darien CT 06820 Office: 60 Broad St New York City NY 10004

DESER, STANLEY, educator, physics; b. Rovno, Poland, Mar. 19, 1931; s. Norman and Miriam (Melamed) D.; came to U.S., 1941, naturalized, 1946; B.S. summa cum laude, Bklyn, Coll., 1949; M.A., Harvard, 1950, Ph.D., 1953. Mem. Inst. for Advanced Study, Princeton 1953-55, Parker fellow, 1953-54, Jewett fellow, 1954-55, NSF postdoctoral fellow, mem. Inst. Theoretical Physics, Copenhagen, Denmark, 1955-57; lectr. Harvard, 1957- 58; mem. faculty Brandeis U., 1958—, prof. physics, 1965—, chmn. dept., 1969-71; vis. scientist European Center Nuclear Research, Geneva, Switzerland, 1962- 63; Fulbright and Guggenheim fellow, vis. prof. Sorbonne, Paris, France, 1966-67. Mem. Am. Phys. Soc. Spl. research theoretical physics, field theory, relativity. Mem. editorial bd. Jour. Math. Physics, 1961-64. Home: 45 Whitney Rd Newtonville MA 02160 Office: Physics Dept Brandeis Univ Waltham MA 02154

DE SEVERSKY, ALEXANDER P., see Seversky, Alexander P., de.

DESFOR, MAX, news photographer; b. Bronx, N.Y., Nov. 8, 1913; s. Benjamin and Anna (Bick) D.; student Brooklyn Coll. of City Coll. of N.Y.; m. Clara Mehl, July 29, 1934; 1 son, Barry David. Joined Asso. Press. N.Y.C., 1933, trans. to Baltimore bur. as staff photographer, 1938, Washington, 1939, photo editor, Washington, 1942-44; war corr. (photographer), attached to Navy (Adm. Nimitz command, Pacific); made landing with Marines, Yokosuka, Japan, Aug. 1945; covered Japan surrender, War Crimes Trials in Manila, disturbances in India, 1946; transferred to Rome, 1949; covered Korean War, 1950-51. Awarded Pulitzer prize for photography, 1951; Graflex Diamond award, 1951; 1st prize and hon. mention in Editor and Publisher contest; prize awards in White House News Photographers Assn. contest and Nat. Press Photographers Assn. contest. Mem. Nat. Photographers Assn., White House News Photographers Assn. Club: Overseas Press; Tokyo Correspondents. Home: 139-26 Coolidge Av Jamaica NY 11435 Office: 50 Rockefeller Plaza New York City NY 10020

DESHAZO, THOMAS GORDON, govt. ofcl.; b. nr. Fredericksburg, Va., Sept. 29, 1922; s. Roberson and Carrie (Jones) DeS.; B.S. in Commerce, U. Va., 1949; m. Dorothy Bridgman Hawkins, May 31, 1952. Asst. nat. bank examiner, 1949-55, nat. bank examiner, 1955-62; chief nat. bank examiner of U.S., 1962-63; dep. comptroller of currency U.S. Treasury Dept., Washington, 1963—. Served with USAAF, 1941-45. Recipient Meritorious Service award U.S. Treasury Dept., 1968. Mem. U. Va. Alumni Assn. (life). Home: 4217 University Dr Fairfax VA 22030 Office: U S Treasury Dept Washington DC 20220

DESHLER, JAMES II, corp. ofc.; b. New Brunswick, N.J., Apr. 20, 1909; s. George R. and Mabel (Dixon) D.; A.B., Williams Coll., 1931; LL.B., N.J. Law Sch., 1934; m. Caryle L. Quackenboss, June 15, 1934; 1 dau., Elaine. Admitted to N.J. bar, 1934, master-in-chancery N.J., 1938; asso. Hicks, Kuhlthau & Thompson, 1934-38, partner Hicks, Kuhlthau, Thompson & Deshler, 1938- 41; asst. sec., asst. to gen. counsel Johnson & Johnson, New Brunswick, N.J., 1941-45; asst. sec. Indsl. Tape Corp., Ethicon Suture Corp., Atlantic Diesel Corp., 1941-45; asst. sec. Ortho Pharm. Corp., 1941-45; sec., dir., 1945-47; pres., dir. Edgar Bros. Co., 1947-54; chmn. Minerals & Chem. Philipp Corp., Menlo Park, N.J., 1954-63, pres., dir., chmn. exec. com., 1963-64, vice chmn., 1964-67; chmn. Chemstone Corp., Menlo Park, N.J., The Cuyahoga Lime Co., (Cleve.), Porocel Corp. (Little Rock), Eastern Magnesia Talc Co., Johnson, Vt., 1967-70; chmn. minerals and chems. div. Engelhard Minerals & Chems. Corp., 1967-69, dir., mem. exec. com., 1967-71; dir. Engelhard Industries, Inc., Newark, Vamistor Corp., Cedar Knolls, N. J., 1965—. Dir. Nat. Conf. Christians and Jews, 1962—; dir., v.p. Community Chest, 1940-41; v.p., dir. New Brunswick chpt. A.R.C., 1940- 41. Trustee Rutgers Prep. Sch., New Brunswick, N.J., 1959—. Mem. Upper Raritan Watershed Assn. N.J., N.J., Middlesex County bar assns., Newcomen Soc., Gargoyle Soc., Zeta Psi. Episcopalian. Clubs: Union League, Delray Beach Yacht, Colonia Country, Somerset Hills Country, Country of Florida, Ekwanok Country, Essex Hunt, Williams; Little (Golf Stream, Fla.); Ocean (Fla.). Home: Oldwick NJ 08858 also Village of Golf FL 32955 Office: Engelhard Minerals & Chems Corp Menlo Park Edison NJ 08817

DESHONG, ANDREW WALTER, business exec.; b. New Boston, Tex., Sept. 26, 1908; s. Andrew Wesley and Lottie (West) DeS.; student Paris Jr. Coll., 1925-26; B.S. in Journalism, So. Meth. U., 1929; m. Dorothy Rose, Apr. 20, 1935; children—Dorothy Margaret (Mrs. Charles T. McGregor III), Andrew Walter III. Reporter, bus. editor, asst. city editor Dallas Times Herald, 1929-36; pub. relations mgr. Dallas C. of C., 1936-41, indsl. devel. mgr., 1945-47, asst. gen. mgr., 1953-61, v.p., gen. mgr., 1961-71; exec. Eare Hays Enterprises, Inc.; asst. to div. mgr. Tex. div. N.Am. Aviation, Inc., 1941-45; indsl. devel. mgr. Republic Nat. Bank, 1947-48; asst. to div. mgr. Chance Vought Aircraft div. United Aircraft Corp., Dallas, 1948-53. Bd. dirs. State Fair of Tex. Mem. Am. (v.p. 1968-69), So. (pres. 1966-67) assns. C. of C. execs. Episcopalian. Home: 5510 Nakoma St Dallas TX 75209 Office: 1507 Pacific St Dallas TX 75201

DE SICA, VITTORIO, actor, director; b. Sora, Caserta, Italy, July 7, 1902; m. Giuditta Rissone, 1937; 1 child. Appeared first in revues; in films, 1917—, plays 1923—; own film company 1933—; dir. film Red Roses, 1939, others The Children are Watching Us, 1942, Shoe Shine, 1946, The Bicycle Thief, Miracle in Milan, Umberto D, Indiscretion of an American Wife, The Roof, Neapolitan Gold, The Bigamist, Bocaccio 70, 1962; Anatomy of Love; Bay of Naples; Two Women; Yesterday, Today and Tomorrow (Acad. award as best fgn. lang. film 1965), A Young World, 1966, After the Fox, 1966; appeared in The Amorous Adventures of Moll Flanders, 1965; comedy actor Bread, Love and Dreams, 1954. Address: care Jos Burstyn Inc 113 W 42d St New York City NY 10018*

DE SILVA, CARL H., educator. Prof., chmn. dept. mech. engring. Wayne State U. Office: 5980 Cass Av Detroit MI 48202*

DE SIMONE, DANIEL V., govt. ofcl.; b. Chgo., May 4, 1932; s. James L. and Helen Catherine (Lattanzio) DeS.; B.S. in Elec. Engring. with highest honors, U. Ill., 1956; LL.B., N.Y. U., 1960, J.D., 1967; m. Virginia Carey, Aug. 13, 1955; children—Jane Ellen, James Michael, Daniel Carey. Teaching asst. U. Ill., 1954-56; engr. and atty. Bell Telephone Labs., 1956-62; admitted to N.Y. bar, 1960; U.S. Supreme Ct., 1964; cons. internat. and legislative matters to commnr. patents, Washington, 1962-63; cons. to Asst. Sec. Commerce for sci. and tech., also to Office Tech. Services, Washington, 1963-64; dir. Office Invention and Innovation, Nat. Bur. Standards, 1964—, dir. Study of Nat. Conversion to Metric System for U.S. Congress, 1969—; advises dept. sci. affairs OAS, 1968—. Exec. dir. Nat. Inventors Council, 1963—; mem., reporter Interagy. Com. on Intellectual Property in East-West Trade, 1963; mem. Sec. Commerce's panel on venture capital, 1968-70; exec. sec. panel invention and innovation Dept. Commerce, 1965-66; mem. U.S. delegation East-West Patent Conf., Geneva, Switzerland, 1964. Recipient Outstanding Achievement award I.E.E.E., 1956, Ford Found. fellowship grant, 1963, Gold Medal award for distinguished achievement in fed. service, 1969. Served with USAF, 1948-52. Mem. I.E.E.E. (chmn. U. Ill. br., 1955-56), Am., Inter-Am. bar assns., N.Y. U. Law Rev. Assn., Tau Beta Pi, Eta Kappa Nu. Contbr. N.Y. Times and other publs. Editor, author: Improving the National Climate for Invention and Innovation, 1964; Technological Innovation; Its Environment and Management, 1967; Education for Innovation, 1968. Home: 2433 N Quantico St Arlington VA 22207 Office: Nat Bur Standards Washington DC 20234

DESIMONE, HERBERT FLORIE, govt. ofcl.; b. Providence, Sept. 5, 1929; s. Florie and Lena (Capuano) DeS.; A.B., Brown U., 1951; LL.B., Columbia, 1954; m. Sally A. Reynolds, Nov. 12, 1955; children—Herbert Florie, Douglas Roy, Deborah Maria. Admitted to R.I. bar, 1954; partner firm DeSimone & DeSimone, Providence, 1954-66; gen. counsel R.I. Dept. Bus. Regulation, 1959-60; atty. gen. R.I., 1967-70; asst. sec. of transp., sec. for environment and urban systems, 1971—. Chmn. New Eng. Assn. Attys. Gen., 1967—; exec. com. Nat. Assn. Attys. Gen., 1968-70, chmn. Gov. R.I. Com. Crime, Delinquency and Criminal Administrn. 1968-70, Gov. R.I. Task Force Reviso Criminal Laws R.I., 1968-70. Mem. N. Providence Republican Town Com., 1952-68; mem. R.I. Rep. Central Com., 1956—, mem. exec. com., 1960—. Mem. Am., R.I. bar assns., Brown U. Alumni Assn., Columbia U. Alumni Assn., Aurora Civic Assn. K.C. Club: Brown of R.I. Home: 557 Fruit Hill Av North Providence RI 02911 Office: 400 7th St SW Washington DC 20590

DESJARDINS, PAUL J.R., educator; b. Rochester, N.Y., Mar. 5, 1921; s. Charles B.R. and Edna (Jacques) D.; A.B., Yale, 1942, M.A., 1951, Ph.D., 1958; postgrad. Louvain U., Belgium, 1951; m. Rosemary M. Desjardins, June 16, 1955; children—Margaret H.R., Alexander C.R. Instr. philosophy Yale, 1953-55; mem. faculty Wheaton Coll., Norton, Mass., 1955-57; asst. prof. Haverford (Pa.) Coll., 1958-64. asso. prof., 1964-68, prof., 1968—; mem. nat. selection com. grad. fellowship Danforth Found., 1962-66; cons. Japan Soc., 1965-66. Served with USNR, 1942-46, Kent fellow; Am. Council Learned Socs. fellow Mem. Am. Philos. Assn., Metaphys. Soc. Am., Grange, Phi Beta Kappa. Republican. Roman Catholic. Clubs: Fullerton, Oriental (Phila.); Elizabethan. Address: Haverford Coll Haverford PA 12941

DESKINS, WILBUR EUGENE, educator, mathematician; b. Morgantown, W.Va., Feb. 20, 1927; s. Wilbur Lawrence and Avis (Creasy) D.; B.S., U. Ky., 1949; M.S., U. Wis., 1950, Ph.D., 1953; m. Barbara Brown, Apr. 18, 1953; children—Lucinda Eugenie, Samantha Eugenie. Teaching asst., U. Wis., 1949-51, fellow, 1951-52, teaching asst., 1952-53, instr., 1953; instr. Ohio State U., 1953-55, asst. prof., 1955-56; asst. prof. Mich. State U., East Lansing, 1956-59, asso. prof., 1959-63, prof. math., 1963-71; prof. math., chmn. dept. U. Pitts., 1971—. Mem. Am., London math. socs., Math. Assn. Am., A.A.A.S. Author: Abstract Algebra, 1964. Research and articles on algebra and group theory. Office: Univ Pittsburgh Pittsburgh PA 15213

DESLOGE, BERNARD FARRAR, engr.; b. St. Louis, Mar. 12, 1927; s. Joseph and Anne Kennett (Farrar) D.; Yale, 1949; m. Miriam Thomas, Oct. 19, 1952; childrenJulie, Gaines, Lucy. Pres. Minerva Oil Co., St. Louis; trustee St. Joseph Lead Co. Home: 7345 Westmoreland St Louis MO 63130 Office: 314 N Broadway St Louis MO 63102

DESLOGE, JOSEPH, engr.; b. St. Louis, Jan. 26, 1889; s. Firmin and Lydia (Davis) D.; A.M., St. Louis U., 1909; B.S., Mass. Inst. Tech., 1912; m. Anne Farrar, Oct. 10, 1922 (dec.); children—Joseph, Anne (Mrs. Louis Werner, II), Bernard, Zoe (Mrs. Samuel Fordyce); m. 2d, Marie Saalfrank, Oct. 26, 1953. Pres. Killark Electric Mfg. Co., 1913—; Minerva Oil Co., 1940—; dir. St. Joseph Lead Co. Pres. United Charities, 1942-43. Served as lt. French Army, World War I. Decorated Croix de Guerre, Legion of Honor (France); named Papal Chamberlain. Mem. Mo. Hist. Soc. (past pres.), St. Louis Acad. Sci. (past pres.), A.A.A.S., Am. Inst. Mining and Metall. Engrs., Am. Geog. Soc. Home: Florissant MO 63031 Office: 3940 Easton Av St Louis MO 63113

DESLOGE, TAYLOR STITH, steel co. exec.; b. St. Louis, June 16, 1921; s. George T. and Madeleine (Stith) D.; A.B., St. Louis U., 1942; LL.B., Washington U., 1948; m. Marian Falk, July 7, 1950; childrenM. Lindsay, Madeleine G., Stephen F., G. Taylor, M. Allan, Phillip G., Judeth C. With Gen. Steel Industries, Inc., Granite City, Ill., 1955- asst. treas., 1955-61, sec., treas., 1961-66, v.p., treas., 1966-. Vice pres. St. Louis Heart Assn., 1962-63, dir., 1960-63; mem. adv. bd. St. John's Hosp., St. Louis, 1959—. Served to capt. AUS, 1942-46. Mem. Financial Execs. Inst. Home: 18 Kingsbury Pl St Louis MO 63112 Office: 1 Memorial Dr St Louis MO 63102

DESMARAIS, OVIDE E., author; b. Biddeford, Me., Sept. 6, 1919; s. Ernest J. and Aurore (Casavant) D.; A.B., Coll. Ida., 1948; student law, Syracuse U.; M.S., Boston U., 1950; m. Inez E. Frakes, May 15, 1942; children—Linda Lee (Mrs. John Teixcira), Peggy Ann (Mrs. Benjamin Cabral). Reporter, Quincy (Mass.) Patriot Ledger, 1949-50, U.P., Boston, 1950-51; advt. copy chief Los Angeles Times, 1953-59; self- employed writer, 1959—. Served with USAAF, World War II. Mem. Authors Guild. Author: Ride The Gold Mare, 1957; The Hoods Take Over, 1957; The Lusting Drive, 1958; The Slasher, 1959; The Long Night, 1959; The Extortioners, 1960; The Enforcer, 1960; Lucky Luciano, 1960; The Gold-Plated Sewer, 1960; Candyleg, 1961; The Lindberg Kidnapping Case, 1961; Dillinger Story, 1961; The Parasites, 1962; Capo Mafioso; (with Ed Reid) The Green-Felt Jungle, 1963; The Organization (reissued as Fatal Mistake 1966, The Contract 1970), 1964; (with Garry Wills) Jack Ruby, 1968; Captive City, 1969; America the Violent 1970; Poso del Mundo, 1970. Address: PO Box 6071 Santa Barbara CA 93105

DE SMEDT, ADOLPHE THEODORE, shipping line exec.; b. Bronx, N.Y., Apr. 29, 1917; s. Albert and Mary (de Ruyffelaere) De S.; ed. pub. schs.; m. Elenor Schneier, Nov. 15, 1940; childrenWilliam Harold, Robert Theodore. With U.S. Lines, 1937- 42, 45-48; with Isbrandtson Co., Inc., 1948-60, v.p., 1954-60; v.p. Am. Export Lines, Inc., 1961-64; exec. v.p. Am. Export Isbrandtsen Lines, Inc., 1964-67, pres., 1967, now chmn. exec. com., mem. bd. dirs.; pres. Isthmian Lines, Inc., 1968—. Active local Boy Scouts Am. Served with USAAF, 1942-45. Mem. Nat. Def. Transp. Assn. (pres. N.Y. chpt. 1962-63), Am. Arab Assn. (bd. dirs.), Am. Israeli Assn. (bd. dirs.). Mem. Reformed Ch. Clubs: Foreign Commerce, Rudder, Propeller (N.Y.C.). Home: 4 Sleepy Hollow Rd Upper Saddle River NJ 07458 Office: 26 Broadway New York City NY 10004

DESMET, RICHARD M., savs. and loan holding co. exec.; b. Detroit, June 13, 1915; s. Richard and Emma (Loosevelt) DeS.; B.A., U. So. Cal., 1940; m. Minabel Layton, May 4, 1942; childrenFrederic, Sylvia, Stephen. Mgr. audit div. John I. Bolen Assos., 1948-57; treas. Am. Savs. & Loan Assn., 1957-59; exec. v.p. Financial Fedn., Inc., Los Angeles, 1959—, also dir.; pres. Financial Facts, Inc., Los Angeles, Affiliated Properties, Inc., Financial Appraisals, Inc., Affiliated Escrow, Inc.; dir. Sequoia Savs. & Loan Assn., Fresno; instr. Pasadena City Coll. C.P.A., Cal. Mem. Am. Inst. C.P.A.'s, Cal. Soc. C.P.A.'s, Am. Accounting Assn., Nat. Assn. Accountants, Financial Execs. Inst. Rotarian. Home: 930 N Chester Av Pasadena CA 91104 Office: 615 S Flower St Los Angeles CA 90017

DESMOND, ALICE CURTIS (Mrs. Thomas C. Desmond), writer; b. Southport, Conn., Sept. 19, 1897; d. Lewis Beers and Alice (Beardsley) Curtis; grad. Miss Porter's Sch., Farmington, Conn., 1916; student Parson's Art School, N.Y.C., 1920; Litt.D., Russell Sage College, 1946; m. Thomas C. Desmond, Aug. 16, 1923. Vice-pres., and dir. T.C. Desmond & Co., Inc., Colonial Terraces Corp. Has made three world tours. Recipient of Juvenile award of Nat. League of Am. Pen Women, 1949. Hon. fellow Rochester Mus. Arts and Sciences, 1946. Fellow Soc. of Am. Historians; mem. Nat. League of Pen Women, Am. Anthrop. Assn., Am. Folk Lore Soc., Nat. Assn. U. Women, Soc. Mayflower Descendants, Colonial Dames Am., D.A.R., Daus., Founders and Patriots America, N.Y. State Hist. Assn., Soc. Woman Geographers, Federated Garden Clubs of N.Y. State (hon.), Internat. Mark Twain Soc. (hon.), N.A.D., Am. Water Color Soc., N.Y. Soc. Artists, Photog. Soc. Am., Royal Photog. Soc. Gt. Britain, Am. Numismatic Assn., Am. Philatelic Soc. Nat. Assn. Women Artists, Print Club of Albany, Authors League of Am., Pen and Brush, Nat. Grange. Episcopalian. Clubs: Women's National Republican, Colony, Junior League, Collectors (N.Y.C.); also Ossoli (Newburgh, N.Y.). Author: Far Horizons, 1931; South American Adventures, 1934 (both books endorsed by Carnegie Endownment for Internat. Peace as promoting internat. good will and several hundred copies placed by Carnegie Endowment in "Internat. Alcoves" of pub. and other libraries); The Lucky Llama, 1939; Soldier of the Sun, 1939; Feathers, 1940; For Cross and King, 1941, Jorge's Journey, 1942 (translated into Portuguese and Swedish, also German; German edit. 1959); Martha Washington, 1942; The Sea Cats, 1944; Glamorous Dolly Madison, 1946; The Talking Tree, 1949 (translated into Swedish, 1956); Alexander Hamilton's Wife, 1952; Barnum Presents; General Tom Thumb, 1954 (translated into French and Dutch languages, 1956); Bewitching Betsy Bonaparte, pub, 1958; George Washington's Mother, 1961; Teddy Koala; Mascot of the Marines, 1962; in Anthologies; Roads to Travel, 1936; Boys of the Andes, 1941; Wonder and Laughter, 1947; Adventures in Reading Exploration, 1947; People and Progress, 1947; Told Under Spacious Skies, 1952; A Book of Gladness, 1953; Your Flag and Mine, 1960; American Backgrounds, 1959; Sword and Pen for George Washington, 1964; This is Our Land, 1965; Cavalcades, 1965; Marie Antoinette's Daughter, 1967, Cleopatra's Children, 1971. Contbr. articles, fiction, verse, to newspapers and mags. Home: PO Box 670 Newburgh NY 12550

DESMOND, ALTON HAROLD, educator; b. Springfield, Vt., Aug. 3, 1922; s. Harold Michael and Louisa (Hilliard) D.; B.S., Hartwick Coll., 1949; Sc.M., Brown U., 1951, Ph.D., 1954; m. Dorothy Ann Garfield, Apr. 23, 1945; 1 dau., Jane Carol. Asst. prof. zoology George Washington U., 1953-59, asso. prof., 1959-63, prof., 1963—, chmn. dept. biol. scis., 1969—. Cons. to McGraw Hill Pub. Co., Indian Govt. Civil Service Commn., Bur. Higher Edn. Div. Grad. Programs of Dept. H.E.W.; mem. biology sect. Nat. Sci. Found. Panel for Evaluating Nat. Sci. Found. Fellows, 1962. Dir. Arlington (Va.) Ballet Workshop, 1960-69. Served with USCG, 1942-46. Recipient F.W. Miller award Hartwick Coll., 1949; Eli Lilly fellow, 1952-53. Fellow Am. Acad. Forensic Sci.; mem. A.A.A.S., Am. Soc. Zoologists, Am Micros. Soc., Am. Assn. Univ. Profs., Am. Soc. Cell Biologists, Am. Inst. Biol. Scis., Sigma Xi. Research on effect of azo dyes and their components on liver of rat. Home: 4907 Erie St Annandale VA 22003 Office: 2029 G St NW Washington DC 20006

DESMOND, CHARLES S., lawyer; b. Buffalo, N.Y., Dec. 2, 1896; s. Patrick and Katherine (Jordan) D.; A.B., Canisius Coll., Buffalo, 1917, A.M., 1918; LL.B., U. Buffalo, 1920; hon. degrees sev. colls. and univs.; m. Helen Marie Ryan, June 28, 1928 (dec. 1958); children—Ryan, Sheila, Kathleen, Patricia. Admitted to N.Y. bar, 1920; asso., later partner Thomas C. Burke, Buffalo, 1920-40; apptd. to N.Y. State Supreme Court, Jan. 1940; elected asso. judge Ct. Appeals, State N.Y., 1941-54, 1955-60, chief judge, 1961-66; mem. law faculty Cornell U., State U. N.Y., has lectured various law schools. Chmn. N.Y. Jud. Conf., 1960-66, Pres. Legal Aid Soc., Buffalo. Chmn. adv. bd. Sisters Hosp. of Buffalo. Served in USMC, 1918. Mem. N.Y. State Bd. of Social Welfare, 1936-40; Chmn. bd. Canisius Coll.; mem. adv. council U. Notre Dame Law Sch. Mem. Am., N.Y. State and Erie Co. bar assns., Am. Law Inst., Order of the Coif, Phi Delta Phi. K.C. Clubs: Fort Orange (Albany); Buffalo, Buffalo Athletic (Buffalo); Wanakah Country. Author two books on law, also articles and revs. Home: Eden NY 14057 Office: Western Bldg Buffalo NY 14202

DESMOND, JOHN JACOB, architect; b. Denver, Apr. 5, 1922; s. Timothy and Rose (Devorak) D.; B.Arch., Tulane U., 1943; M.Arch., Mass. Inst. Tech., 1948; m. Blanche Russell, Sept. 29, 1951; children—John Michael, Russell, Margaret. Archtl. draftsman Skidmore, Owings & Merrill, N.Y.C., 1947; archtl. designer, draftsman A. Hays Town, 1949-50; architect Desmond & Davis, 1954-58, Desmond-Miremont-Burks, Baton Rouge, Hammond, La., 1959—. Bd. dirs. La. Council Music and Performing Arts, 1968. Served to lt., USNR, 1943-46. Recipient archtl. awards profl. orgns. Fellow A.I.A.; mem. La. Architects Assn., La. Landmarks Assn., Soc. Archtl. Historians, Nat. Trust Historic Preservation. Author: Louisiana's Antebellum Architecture, 1970. Principal works include Southeastern La. Coll. Cafeteria, Hammond (1st honor award Gulf States region, Nat. Merit award A.I.A.), 1956; St. Thomas More Ch. and Sch., Baton Rouge (honor award Gulf States region A.I.A.), 1960; Cath. Student Center, Southeastern La. Coll. (honor award Gulf States region A.I.A.), 1960; La. State Library, Baton Rouge (nat. A.I.A.-A.L.A. award, honor award Gulf States region A.I.A.), 1954; Union Bldg., La. State U., Baton Rouge (1st honor award Gulf States region A.I.A.), 1963; Cath. Life Center, Baton Rouge (honor award Gulf States region A.I.A.), 1964; additions to Grace Meml. Episcopal Ch., Hammond (honor award Gulf States region A.I.A.), 1967; D.C. Reeves Elementary Sch., Ponchatoula, La. (honor award Gulf States regional Nat. Honor award A.I.A.), 1968; Tangopahoa Parish Courthouse, Amite, La. (honor award A.I.A. and Office Civil Def.), 1969. Home: 905 Greenlawn St Hammond LA 70401 Office: 703 Laurel St Baton Rouge LA 70802

DESMOND, PAUL BREITENFELD, saxophonist; b. San Francisco, Nov. 25, 1924; studied clarinet San Francisco Polytechnic High, also San Francisco State U. Joined Jack Finci, 1950, Alvino Rey, 1951, Dave Brubeck, 1951; recorded albums with Brubeck and with own groups; toured Eng. with Brubeck, also Europe, Middle East, 1958; toured Eng. with Nat Jazz Festival show, 1959. Recipient Down Beat Critics award, 1953, Readers' Poll award, 1955-59, 62-65, Metronome Poll award, 1955-56, Playboy Poll award, 1957-60. Address: 27 Deming St San Francisco CA 94114*

DESMOND, ROBERT WILLIAM, educator, newspaperman; b. Milw., July 31, 1900; s. William John and Lillian Amy (Wilce) D.; A.B., U. of Wis., 1922; certificate Sch. of Internat. Studies, Geneva, Switzerland, 1929; M.A., U. Minn., 1930; Ph.D., U. London, Sch. of Econ. and Polit. Sci., 1936; m. Dorothy Christian, 1927 (div.); 1 son, Richard; m. 2d Emily V. Wall, 1949; children—Christopher, Carolyn. With Milw. Jour., 1922-25, Miami (Fla.) Herald, 1925-26, N.Y. Herald (Paris ed.) 1926-27, Christian Sci. Monitor, 1933-38 (London bur., 1936); taught journalism U. Mich. 1927- 28, U. Mjnn. 1928-32, Medill Sch. of Journalism, Northwestern U., 1938- 39; prof. journalism, U. Cal. at Berkeley, 1939-68, prof. emeritus, 1968—, chmn. dept., 1939-54, 1962-63, also 1967, acad. dir. Fgn. Assignment tour, Europe, 1952; Louisville Courier- Jour., summer, 1955; Fulbright lectr. U. Amsterdam, 1955-56, U. Baghdad, Iraq, 1965-66, U. Teheran (Iran), 1968- 69; spl. rep. and lectr. Internat. Center for Advanced Instruction in Journalism, U. Strasbourg, France, 1956, 58, 60; on fgn. news desk, N.Y. Times, summer 1941; news commentator,radio station KSFO, San Francisco, Cal., 1941-42; on staff San Francisco Chronicle, 1968, San Diego Union, 1969—; columnist Copley News Service, 1971—. Served AUS, NATO USA, ETO, 1943-44; attached to O.W.I. and UN Information Office, 1944-45; mem. UNESCO commn. on tech. needs of mass media, 1947. Cons. Ency. Americana, 1959-60, Internat. Press. Inst., Zurich, 1960-62, Hartford (Conn.) Times, summer 1964. Recipient citations U. Cal., Cal. Senate, 1968. Mem. Am. Assn. Schs. and Depts. Journalism (pres. 1947), Assn. Edn. Journalism, Sigma Delta Chi. Author: Press and World Affairs 1937; and others, (UNESCO brochure) Professional Training of Journalists, 1949. Contbr. to mags. Home: 314 Ricardo Pl LaJolla CA 92037 ☆

DESMOND, THOMAS CHARLES, retired engr.; b. Middletown, N.Y., Sept. 15, 1887; s. Thomas Henry and Katherine (Safried) D.; A.B. magna cum laude, Harvard, 1908; S.B. in C.E., Mass. Inst. Tech., 1909; L.H.D., Union Coll. 1939; m. Alice B. Curtis, Aug. 16, 1923. Engaged in Constrn. work in various parts of U.S., 1909-14; pres. T. C. Desmond & Co., engrs. and contractors, N.Y. since 1914, pres. Colonial Terraces Corp. Mem. N.Y. State Senate, 1930-58. Nat. treas. Roosevelt Non-Partisan League, 1916; pres. N.Y. Young Republican Club, 1926-29; del. Rep. Nat. Conv., Ka Kansas City, Mo., 1928, Phila., 1940; mem. N.Y. Rep. Co. Com., 1915-30. Trustee or officer several profl., sci or ednl. instns. Mem. bd. mgrs. N.Y. Bot. Garden, N.Y.C. Trustee Theodore Roosevelt Assn.; mem. nat. adv. com. White House Conf. Aging, 1959. Mem. vis. com. bd. overseers dept. of astronomy Harvard; mem. at large nat. council Boy Scouts Am.; mem. adv. bd. Inst. Nutrition Scis., Columbia, 1959-; life mem. governing bd. Mass. Inst. Tech. Recipient Silver Antelope award Boy Scouts Am., 1947; Brotherhood Award, 1956, Distinguished Service award N.Y. chpt. N.Y. Soc. Profl. Engrs., 1958; 1957 annual award Gerontological Research Found.; N.Y. State YMCA youth and govt. award, 1958; 1959 Ann. War Meml. award N.Y. Young Rep. Clubs, Eloise Payne Luauer medal, Garden Club Am., 1961. Mem. Nat. Geriatrics Soc. (hon.), Am. Astron. Soc., Astron. Soc. of the Pacific, Nat. Municipal League, State Soc. Profl. Engineers, C. of C. State New York, Acad. Scis., Am. Acad. Polit. and Social Sci., Royal Astron. Soc. of Can., Harvard Engring. Soc., Am. Soc. C.E. (life), Nat. Inst. Social Scis., A.A.A.S., Phi Beta Kappa, Phi Beta Kappa Assos., Sigma Alpha Epsilon. Mason (K.T.), Elk. Clubs: Newburgh City, Powelton; University, Union League, Union, Engineers, Harvard, Technology, Tuxedo, City, Century, Explorers (N.Y.C.); Harvard (Boston). Fort Orange (Albany); Adirondack; Lake Placid. Contbr. articles to mags. Owner and developer pvt. arboretum containing nearly 800 species trees and shrubs. Recipient medal award Fed. Garden Clubs of N.Y. State, 1950; large gold medal award Mass. Hort. Soc., 1950; Mass. Inst. Tech. Silver Stein Award, 1952; N.Y. Hort. Soc. Amateur award, 1971. Address: 94 Broadway Newburgh NY 12553 ☆

DESOBRY, WILLIAM ROBERTSON, army officer; b. Manila, P.I., Sept. 11, 1918; s. Elmer C. and Emily (Dorsey) D.; B.S., Georgetown U., 1941; grad. Command and Gen. Staff Coll., 1952, Army War Coll., 1965, Nat. War Coll., 1959; m. Jacqueline Keyes, Aug. 22, 1942; children—Mrs. William Chescavage, Virginia R., Nancy K., Geoffrey K., Leslie M., William R. Commd. 2d lt. U.S. Army, 1941, advanced through grades to maj. gen., 1969; comdg. officer 20th Armored Inf. Bn., 1944-45; dir. personnel U.S. Forces Austria, 1948; comdg. officer combat 2d Armored Div., Germany, 1955-56; chief of staff 2d Armored Div., 1956-57; sr. advisor ARVN IV Corps, South Vietnam, 1965-68; comdg. gen. 1st Armored Div., 1969-70; comdg. gen. Armor Center, comdr. Armor Sch., Ft. Knox, Ky., 1971—. Decorated D.S.M., Silver Star, Legion of Merit with oak leaf cluster, Bronze Star, Air medal with 10 oak leaf clusters, Purple Heart. Office: Office Commanding General Armor Center Fort Knox KY 40121

DESPRES, EMILE, economist; b. Chgo., Sept. 21, 1909; s. Emile and Irma Helen (Rosenthal) D.; student Riverdale (N.Y.) Country Sch., 1922-25; S.B., Harvard, 1930, resident cons. Grad. Sch. Pub. Adminstrn., 1937-38; L.H.D., Williams Coll., 1970; m. Joanna Hitt Eakin, Dec. 22, 1939; children—Lani (Mrs. David A. Burack), John, Charles. Spl. fgn. exchange analyst Fed. Res. Bank, N.Y.C., 1930-37, Held fgn. research div., 1938-39; econ. adviser to chmn. bd. govs. Fed. Res. System, Washington, 1939-41; mem. bd. analysts, dir. econ. divs., alternate mem. joint intelligence staff U.S. Joint Chiefs Staff, O.S.S., 1941-44; adviser on German econ. affairs Dept. State, 1944-45; mem. faculty Williams Coll., 1946-61, prof. econs., chmn. dept. 1950-61; prof. econs., Stanford, 1961—; vis. research prof. Brookings Instn., 1967-68. Mem. financial adv. mission Chinese Nat. Govt., 1941; mem. Am. del. to Potsdam Conf., 1945, office program rev. E.C.A., Paris, summer 1948; attached to Am. Embassy, Belgrade, for econ. aid program to Yugoslavia, summer 1951; fiscal and monetary advisor Pakistan Planning Bd., 1955-56, dir. Inst. Devel. Econs., Karachi, Pakistan, 1959-64. Mem. Council Fgn. Relations, Am. Econ. Assn. Club: Century Assn. Home: Grove Ct Portola Valley CA 94025

DESPRES, LEO ARTHUR, educator; b. Lebanon, N.H., Mar. 29, 1932; s. Leo Arthur and Madeline (Bedford) D.; B.A., U. Notre Dame, 1954, M.A., 1956; Ph.D., Ohio State U., 1960; m. Loretta A. LaBarre, Aug. 22, 1953; children—Christine, Michelle, Denise, Mary Louise, Renee. Research asso. Columbia Psychiat. Inst. and Hosp., 1957-60; postdoctoral fellow Social Sci. Research Council, Guyana, 1960-61; asst. prof. Ohio Wesleyan U., 1961-63; mem. faculty Case Western Res. U., Cleve., 1963—, prof. anthropology, 1967—, chmn. dept., 1968—. Cons. in field. Fulbright scholar U. Guyana, 1970-71. Mem. Am. Anthrop. Assn., Am. Ethnol. Soc., African Studies Assn., Central States Anthrop. Soc. (exec. com.), Am. Assn. U. Profs. (pres. elect univ. chpt.). Author: Cultural Pluralism and Nationalist Politics in British Guyana, 1968. Home: 2832 Berkshire Rd Cleveland Heights OH 44118 Office: Dept Anthropology Case Western Res U Cleveland OH 44106

DESPRES, LEON MATHIS, lawyer, city ofcl.; b. Chgo., Feb. 2, 1908; s. Samuel and Henrietta (Rubovits) D.; Ph.B., U. Chgo., 1927, J.D., 1929; m. Marian Alschuler, Sept. 10, 1931; children—Linda Baskin, Robert Leon. Admitted to Ill. bar, 1929; pvt. practice law, Chgo., 1929-; trial examiner NLRB, Chgo., 1935-37; instr. U. Chgo., 1936, U. Wis., summers 1946-49; alderman 5th Ward City Chgo., 1955-. Mem. Am., Ill., Chgo. bar assns., Order Coif, Phi Beta Kappa. Home: 1220 E 56th St Chicago IL 60637 Office: 77 W Washington St Chicago IL 60602

DESROSIER, NORMAN WILFRED, food co. exec.; b. Athol, Mass., Dec. 6, 1921; s. Wilfred H. and Leona (Hachey) D.; B.S., U. Mass., 1947, M.S., 1948, Ph.D., 1949; m. Ann Colwell O'Brien, June 22, 1946; children—Nancy John, James, Brian. Prof. food sci. and tech. Purdue U., 1949-63; dep. sci. dir. Q. M. Food and Container Inst. Armed Forces, 1957-59; dir. research Beech-Nut Life Savers, Inc., 1963, v.p., 1963-65; dir. research Nabisco, N.Y., 1965—. Sci. cons. European productivity agy. O.E.E.C., 1958—; mem. U.S. atoms for peace program European Nuclear Energy Agy., 1960—. Bd. dirs. 2d v.p. Q. M. Corps Research and Devel. Assos.; vice chmn. food industry com. Nutrition Found.; bd. dirs. Nabisco-Astra Devel. Corp. Served with inf. AUS, World War II; ETO. Decorated Purple Heart, Bronze Star medal, Combat Inf. badge; Croix de Guerre (France). Mem. Assn. Research Dirs., Inst. Food Technologists, Am. Inst. Biol. Scis., Am. Chem. Soc. Author: Technology of Food Preservation, 3d edit., 1970; Attack on Starvation, 1962. Co-author: Radiation Technology in Food, Agriculture and Biology, 1961; Economics of New Food Product Development, 1971. Home: 509 Fowler Av Pelham Manor NY 10803 Office: Nabisco Research Center Fair Lawn NJ 07410

DESRUISSEAUX, PAUL, lawyer, bus. exec., Canadian legislator; b. Sherbrooke, Que., Can., May 1, 1905; s. Geoffroy Francois and Sarah (Gauthier) D.; grad. St. Charles Coll., 1928; Montreal Coll., 1931; grad. law U. Montreal, 1931-34; postgrad. Babson Inst., 1935, Harvard, 1935-36; LL.D., U. Sherbrooke, 1964; m. Celine Duchesne, June 16, 1945; children—Louis (dec.), Francois, Helene, Pierre. Admitted to Que. bar, 1934, practiced in Sherbrooke; sr. mem. Desruisseaux, Fortin, Rouillard until 1960; created King's counsel, 1948, Queen's counsel, 1953; senator div. Wellington, 1966—; past chmn. La Tribune, Inc., CHLT, CHLT-FM and CHLT-TV, 1955-66, Melchers Distilleries Ltd.; past pres. Que. Telemedia, Inc., Telegram Printing & Pub. Co., Ltd., Delta Services, Inc., Radio and TV Sherbrooke, Inc.; pres. Desmont Research and Devel. Inc., Cablevision, Desruisseaux Corp.; v.p. Cinema Premier, Inc., 1953, Societe Tele-Cinema, Inc., 1954; pres. Cinema Plaza, Inc.; dir. Laurentien Gas Co. Ltd., Walter M. Lowney Co., Ltd., Westmount Life Assurance Co., Ltd., Canadian Gen. Electric Co., Ltd., Royal Bank of Can., Que. Asst. commr. Catholic Scouts of Sherbrooke, 1937-39. Mem. Canadian World Federalist Parliamentary Assn.; mem. Canadian br. Commonwealth Parliamentary Assn.; mem. Canadian group Inter- parliamentary Union; mem. NATO Parliamentary Assn. Bd. govs. Sherbrooke Hosp.; pres. Sherbrooke Red Cross Soc., 1954-57; bd. govs., trustee U. Sherbrooke, 1957-59, v.p. bd. trustees, 1957—; bd. regents U. Ottawa, 1960; chmn. hon. bd. govs. Que. Assn. Retarded Children, 1961—. Served with Royal Canadian Army, 1942-45, asst. judge adv., 1943-45. Recipient medals Latin union, l'Alliance Francaise; Bene Merenti medal; decorated comdr. Royal Order St. Gregoire Great; Knight Magistral Order Malta. Mem. Sherbrooke C. of C. (past dir.), Sherbrooke Fusiliers (hon. mem. Officers Club), A.I.M. (mem. pres.' council), P.Q. C. of C. (gov.), Canadian Research Assn., Canadian Assn. Advancement Sci., Canadian, St. Francis (past counsellor, past treas.) bars, Canadian Daily Newspaper Pubs. Assn. (dir.), Canadian Press (dir.). Roman Catholic. Clubs: Hillcrest Ski (co- founder; life mem.) (North Hatley); Sherbrooke Social, Sherbrooke Country; Garrison (Quebec); Canadian (N.Y.C.); St. James's, St. Denis, Montreal (Montreal). Home: 405 Victoria St Sherbrooke Quebec Canada also 3 Westmount Sq Westmount Montreal Quebec Canada also Chateau Laurier Ottawa Ontario Canada

DESSART, DONALD JOSEPH, educator; b. Green Bay, Wis., Apr. 2, 1928; s. Eli Joseph and Mary Octavia (Warrichaiet) D.; B.S., U. Wis., 1950, M.S., 1955; Ph.D., U. Md., 1961; m. Gloria Jean Clemons, June 17, 1950; children—Mary, Thomas, Jean, Brian, Ruth Anne. Tchr. math. Escanaba, Mich., 1953-54, Madison, Wis., 1954-56; prof. State U. N.Y. at Oneonta, 1956-62; prof. math., math. edn. U. Tenn., Knoxville, 1962—. Served with USNR, 1950-53; Korea. Decorated 6 Battle Stars; named Danforth Tchr., 1959-60. Mem. Am. Ednl. Research Assn., A.A.A.S., Math. Assn. Am., Nat. Council Tchrs. Math., Tenn. Math. Tchrs. Assn. (pres. 1967-69), Phi Beta Kappa, Sigma Xi, Phi Delta Kappa, Phi Eta Sigma, Phi Kappa Phi, Pi Mu Epsilon. Episcopalian. Contbr. articles profl. math., ednl. jours. Home: 8012 Bennington Dr Knoxville TN 37919

DESSAUER, JOHN HANS, chemist; b. Aschaffenburg, Germany, May 13, 1905; s. Dr. Hans and Bertha (Thywissen) D.; B.S., Inst. Tech., Munich, Germany, 1924-26; M.S., D.Eng., Inst. Tech., Aachen, Germany, 1929; L.H.D. (hon.), Le Moyne Coll., 1963; m. Margaret B. Lee, June 29, 1935; children—John Philip, Margot, Thomas David. Came to U.S., 1929, naturalized, 1936. Chemist, Ansco, Binghamton, N.Y., 1929-35; chemist Haloid Co., Rochester, N.Y., 1935-38, research dir., 1938-46, v.p. charge research and product devel., dir., 1946-59 (name changed to Haloid Xerox, Inc., 1958), exec. v.p. research and advanced engineering div. Xerox Corp., 1959-68, vice chmn. bd., until 1970, dir. Mem. N.Y. State Adv. Council for Advancement Indsl. Research and Devel.; mem. adv. council N.Y. State Tech. Services Program; bd. overseers chemistry vis. com. Harvard Coll.; mem. engring, adv. com. mech. and aerospace scis. dept. U. Rochester; Bd. dirs. Rochester Regional Research Council, St. Mary's Hosp., Rochester; trustee Rochester Mus. and Sci. Center. Fellow Photog. Soc. Am., N.Y. Acad. Scis., Am. Inst. Chemists; mem. Am. Chem. Soc., Nat. Acad. Engring. (mem., councilor exec. com.). Roman Catholic. Co-author: Xerography and Related Processes. Home: Twin Oaks Pittsford NY 14534 also Hillsboro Beach FL Office: 57 Monroe Av Pittsford NY 14534

DESSEL, NORMAN FRANK, educator; b. Ida Grove, Ia., July 9, 1932; s. Joseph A. and Lela (Bright) D.; B.A., U. Ia., 1955, M.A., 1957, Ph.D., 1961; m. Marydale Merrill, Sept. 3, 1955; children—Diana Elizabeth, Dirk Norman, Jennifer Leigh. Prof. physics San Diego State Coll., 1961-68, prof., head phys. sci., 1968—; cons. phys. optics USN Electronics Lab., San Diego, 1961-69; Columbia U./U.S. AID prof. physics Patna U., India, 1965. Bd. dirs. San Diego County council Boy Scouts Am. Served with USAF, 1953-55. Mem. N.Y. Acad. Sci., Am. Optical Soc., Delta Tau Delta, Sigma Pi Sigma, Phi Mu Alpha, Phi Delta Kappa. Republican. Methodist (trustee). Author: (with Nehrich and Voran) Lasers, 1968. Contbr. articles profl. jours. Home: 6443 Lance Ct San Diego CA 92120

DESSLER, ALEXANDER JACK, educator; b. San Francisco, Oct. 21, 1928; s. David Alexander and Julia (Shapiro) D.; B.S., Cal. Inst. Tech., 1952; Ph.D., Duke, 1956; m. Lorraine Hudek, Apr. 18, 1952; children—Pauline Karen, David Alexander, Valerie Jan, Andrew Emory. Sect. head Lockheed Missiles and Space Co., 1956-62; prof. Grad. Research Center, Dallas, 1962-63; prof., chmn. space sci. dept. Rice U., 1963-69, prof. space sci, 1970—; sci. adviser Nat Aeros. and Space Council, 1969-70. Served with USNR, 1946-48. Recipient Outstanding Young Scientist award Tex. wing Air Force Assn., 1963. Fellow Am. Geophys. Union (Macelwane award 1963); mem. Am. Astron. Soc., Internat. Sci. Radio Union, Internat. Assn. Geomagnetism and Aeronomy (chmn. Commn. VIII Upper Atmospheres). Editor Jour. Geophys. Research, 1965-69; Revs. of Geophysics and Space Physics, 1969- -; The John Wiley Space Science Text Series; adv. bd. Planetary and Space Sci. Home: 5126 Loch Lomand Dr Houston, TX 77035.

DESSUREAULT, JEAN MARIE, senator, lumber dealer; b. Ste. Genevieve de Batiscan, Que., Dec. 30, 1888; s. Aime and Marie-Anne (Rousseau) D.; ed. Sacred Heart Coll., St. Anne de la Perade and Victoriaville, Que.; m. Aurore Vallee, June 30, 1913 (dec. 1954); children—Louise (Mrs. Will C. Kelliher), Marthe (Mrs. Kenneth F. Brown), Suzanne (Mrs. Robert M. Ross), Claire (Mrs. Martin Garneau); m. 2d, Elise Dion, Sept. 21, 1957. Pres., J.M. Dessureault, Inc.; propr. J.M. Dessureault Lumber Co.; v.p. La Banque Canadienne Nationale, 1944-64, Quebec Land & Realty Co., La Compagnie de Courtage Immobilier de Quebec Ltee; dir. Trust Gen. du Can., Hotel Windsor, Montreal; mem. Senate of Can., 1945—. Alderman, Quebec City, 1922-26. Bd. govs. Sch. Commerce, Laval U. Decorated chevalier l'Ordre Equestre du St. Sepulcre de Jerusalem. Apptd. hon. lt. col. Que. Regt., 1937. Liberal. Roman Catholic. Clubs: Quebec Garrison; Reform; University. Home: 1270 Holland Av Sillery Quebec Canada Office: 2601 Tadoussac St Quebec Quebec Canada*

DESTINE, JEAN-LEON, choreographer, dancer, tchr.; b. St. Marc, Haiti, Mar. 26, 1928; s. Leon and Lucienne (Joseph) D.; student Lycee Petion, Port-au-Prince, Haiti, 1940-43, Ethnol. Inst., Haiti, 1941-42. Came to U.S., 1944, permanent resident, 1947. Choreographer, dancer; founder, dir. Troupe Nationale Folklorique, Haiti's Internat. Expn., 1950; choreographer, dancer Troubled Island (N.Y.C. Opera), 1949-50, Witch Doctor (motion pictures), 1950-51, Cantiones Unidas, 1957; artistic dir., choreographer, lead dancer Jean-Leon Destine Afro-Haitian Dance Co. appearing U.S., Canada, Europe, Asia, Latin-Am.; pres., dir. Destine Dance Co., Ltd. Hon. cultural attache in U.S. for Rep. of Haiti. Decorated chevalier Order Honneur et Merite, Haitian Govt., 1951, officer, 1958; Rockefeller Found. scholar, 1944-46. Address: 676 Riverside Dr New York City NY 10031

DESTLER, CHESTER MCARTHUR, educator; b. Wyncote, Pa., July 27, 1904; s. Lewis Wesley and M. Louise (Griesemer) D.; A.B., cum laude, Coll. of Wooster, 1925; A.M., U. Chgo., 1928, Ph.D. (Henry Milton Wolf fellow Am. history), 1932; m. Katharine Hardesty, Sept. 9, 1936; children—Paul Lewis, Irving McArthur, Anne Louise, William Wallace. Instr. history Coll. of the Ozarks, 1925-28; research asst. U. Chgo., 1930-31; asst. prof. history Albion Coll., 1931- 34; prof. history Ga. Tchrs. Coll., 1934-41, dir. jr. div., 1935-41; prof. U. System of Ga., 1937-41, Tulane U., summer 1940, U. N.C., summer 1941, Elmira Coll., 1941-42, Cornell, summer 1942, 52; prof., chmn. dept. history Conn. Coll., 1942-54, Charles J. MacCurdy prof. Am. history, 1949-54; vis. prof. Yale, 1945, 50-51, Cornell U., 1953. Mem. ednl. bd. Miss. Valley Hist. Review, 1946-49, Soc. Edn., 1946-51; mem. ednl. adv. bd. Am. Heritage, 1946-49. Fellow Berkeley Coll., Yale, 1945-46, 66-70, asso. fellow, 1946-66, 71—; Library of Congress fellow in Am. civilization, 1945-46; recipient Everett Edwards award in agrl. history for 1957. Pres. Ga. Council Social Studies, 1939-41. Mem. Assn. for Study Conn. History (pres. 1970-71), Agrl. Hist. Soc., Conn. Hist. Soc., Orgn. Am. Historians, Am., New Eng. Hist. Assn., N.E. Assn. Social Sci. Tchrs. (pres., 1950-51) Phi Beta Kappa. Democrat. Conglist. Author: American Radicalism, 1865-1901; Essays and Documents, 1946; Joshua Coit, American Federalist, 1962; Henry Demarest Lloyd and the Empire of Reform, 1963; Roger Sherman and Independent Oil Men, 1967. Sr. editor Studies in Social Progress, 1938. Editor: The Democratic Process, 1948; Liberalism As A Force in History, 1953. Contbr. hist. and econ. jours. Home: 97 Meadowbrook Rd West Hartford CT 06107

DESTON, RAYMOND, life ins. exec.; b. Fall River, Mass., Aug. 16, 1906; s. Sidney and Elizabeth (Turner) D.; A.B., Bowdoin Coll., 1930; m. Dorrance Harwood Chase, Mar. 21, 1937; children—Nancy (Mrs. Charles L. Sullivan III), Diana (Mrs. C. J. Andrade), Pamela (Mrs. Richard C. Conard), Elizabeth. With John Hancock Mut. Life Ins. Co., 1933-56, successively agt., Boston, supr., agy. asst., supr. field tng., gen. agt., San Francisco, 1933-56, Western v.p., 1956-59; v.p., dir. agys. West Coast Life Ins. Co., 1959-61; resident v.p. Continental Assurance Co., 1961-71, ret.; cons., 1971—. Served to lt. USNR, 1943-46; chief central information div., research and analysis br. OSS, Washington. C.L.U. Mem. Los Angeles Life Underwriters Assn., Am. Soc. Chartered Life Underwriters, Phi Beta Kappa, Zeta Psi. Home: 710 S St Andrews Pl Los Angeles CA 90005 Office: 600 S Commonwealth Av Los Angeles CA 90005

DE STWOLINSKI, GAIL ROUNCE BOYD, educator; b. Sidney, Mont., Nov. 8, 1921; d. Harold Lowell and Alice (Hardenburgh) R.; Mus.B., U. Mont., 1943; M.Music Theory, Eastman Sch. Music U. Rochester, 1946, Ph.D. in Music Theory, 1966; m. David Robinson Boyd, Sept. 4, 1943 (dec. 1944); 1 son, David Robinson; m. 2d, Louis Charl de Stwolinski, June 15, 1951. Instr., U. Okla., 1946, asst. prof. music theory, 1949-55, asso. prof., 1955-66, prof., 1966—, chmn. dept. music theory and composition, 1953-60. Adviser, cons. in field. Recipient Regents award superior teaching, 1966; named David Ross Boyd prof., 1970. Mem. Okla. Music Tchrs. Assn., Okla. Theory Roundtable, Music Tchrs. Nat. Assn. Music Educators Nat. Conf., Am. Assn. U. Profs., Mortar Bd., Pi Kappa Lambda, Mu Phi Epsilon, Kappa Kappa Gamma. Democrat. Contbr. articles to mus. jours. Home: 1037 Cruce St Norman OK 73069

DESWARTE, WILLEM PIETER ALBERIC, airlines exec.; b. Brussels, Belgium, Sept. 6, 1906; s. Alberic and Lea (Bonneels) D.; Docteur en droit, Brussels U., Lic.Sci.Politiques, Lic. sc. Financieres; diploma Bur. Internat. Studies, Geneva; Dr. Hon. Causa, Acad. Internat. Law, Mexico; m. Irene Tesch, 1940. Asso. Batonniere Order Belgian Advicates, 1929-33; sec. gen. to adminstr., dir. l'Innovation, 1933-45; pres. Belgian Maritime Tribunal, London, 1945-46; counsellor Ministry of Finance, 1946-47; chief of Cabinet of Prime Minister, 1947, Cabinet of Minister of Interior, 1947-49; dir.-gen., pres. Sabena Airlines, Brussels, 1949—. Vice chmn. Belgian Assn. Civil Rights Movement; pres. Belgian sect. World Assn. World Federalists. Served with Belgian Army; capt. Res. Decorated comdr. Order Orange-Nassau, officer Order of Crown, chevalier Legion of Honour, comdr. Order of Leopold, Cross of Voluntary Escapers in War, France-Germany Star, Brit. Def. of Britain Medal. Mem. Inst. Air Transport (v.p.). Mem. Belgian Socialist Party. Author: La limitation des dividendes, 1942; L'impot sur le capital applique aux societes par actions, 1946. Home: 33 rue Cardinal Mercier 1000-Brussels Belgium Office: 35 rue Cardinal Mercier 1000-Brussels Belgium

DE TARNOWSKY, PIERRE A., pharm. co. exec. Formerly sr. v.p. Warner-Lambert Pharm. Co.; pres., chief exec. officer Armour Pharm. Co., also v.p. Armour & Co., 1963—; group v.p., dir. Armour-Dial, Inc. Address: 1500 N Lake Shore Dr Chicago IL 60610

DETERLING, RALPH ALDEN, Jr., surgeon, educator; b. Williamsport, Pa., Apr. 29, 1917; s. Ralph Alden and Edith Pauline (Ritter) D.; A.B., Stanford, 1938, M.D., 1942; M.S. in Surgery, U. Minn., 1946, Ph.D., 1947; m. Mary Ann Gilson, June 21, 1947; children—Ralph III, William R., John S., Paul A. Intern, Hosp. U. Pa., 1941-42, resident, 1942-43; fellow surgery Mayo Found., 1943-47; staff physician Nopeming Sanatorium, 1947; asst. attending surgeon Presbyn. Hosp., N.Y.C., 1948-50, asso. attending surgeon, 1950-59; surg. cons. U.S. Naval Hosp., St. Albans, Manhattan VA Hosp., N.Y.C., Paterson (N.J.) Gen. Hosp.; asso. surgeon attending Francis Delafield Hosp., N.Y.C.; asst. prof. surgery Columbia Coll. Phys. and Surg., 1948- 50, asso. prof., 1950-54, asso. clin. prof. surgery, 1954-59, dir. surg. research labs.; prof., chmn. dept. surgery Tufts U. Sch. Medicine, Boston, 1959—; surgeon-in-chief New Eng. Med. Center Hosps., 1959—; dir. first surg. service Boston City Hosp., 1959-70, dir., 1970—; cons. Newton- Wellesley, Boston VA, Mt. Auburn, St. Elizabeth's, Lemuel Shattuck hosps. Diplomate Nat. Bd. Med. Examiners, Am. Bd. Surgery, Am. Bd. Thoracic Surgery. Fellow A.C.S., Am. Coll. Chest Physicians; mem. Am., N.Y. thoracic socs., Harvey Soc., Whipple Soc., Colombian (hon.), Brazilian (hon.) colls. surgeons N.Y. Soc. Cardiovascular Surgery (sec.-treas. 1957, v.p.), Med. Strollers (pres. 1957), Soc. Vascular Surgery, Internat. (treas.-gen. 1953, 57, sec.-gen. 1961, 63, 65, v.p. 1969, pres. 1969-71, New Eng. cardiovascular socs., N.Am. chpt. pres. 1965), A.A.A.S., Am. Soc. Artificial Internal Organs, angiology socs. Argentina (hon.), Uruguay (hon.), Brazil (corr.), N.Y. acads. medicine, Soc. U. Surgeons, N.Y. Acad. Scis., Internat. Soc. Surgery, Am. Assn. Thoracic Surgery, Am., Mass. heart assns., Am. Philatelic Soc., Stanford, Mayo Found. alumni assns., Assn. Surgeons Gt. Britain and Ireland (corr.), Am. Acad. Arts and Scis., Am. Surg. Assn., Mass. Med. Soc., New Eng., Boston (pres. 1970), St. Paul (hon.), N. Pacific (hon.), N.Y. surg. socs., Nat. Surg. Soc. Cuba (hon.), Phi Beta Kappa, Sigma Xi (chpt. sec.), Alpha Omega Alpha, Alpha Kappa Kappa. Contbr. articles to med., sci. jours. Home: 43 Scotch Pine Rd Weston MA 02193 Office: 171 Harrison Av Boston MA 02111

DETERT, GUNTHER RICHARD, lawyer; b. Jersey City, Nov. 11, 1912; s. Richard and Hedwig (Lohmann) D.; A.B., Stanford, 1933; LL.B., U. Cal., 1936; postgrad. U. Munich (Germany), 1937; m. Marie-Louise Whittell, Feb. 20, 1941; children—Marie- Louise K. (Mrs. Thomas H. Garrett), Sandra L. (Mrs. Thomas M. Cover). Partner firm Sedgwick, Detert, Moran & Arnold, and predecessors, San Francisco, 1948—. Mem. Am., San Francisco (dir. 1941-42, 45-46, 67-68) bar assns., Def. Counsel Assn., Am. Bd. of Trial Attys., Internat. Assn. Ins. Counsel, State Bar Cal., Cal. Vintage Wine Soc. (pres.), Napa Valley Wine Library Assn. (pres.), San Francisco Wine & Food Soc., Alpha Kappa Lambda, Phi Alpha Delta. Club: San Francisco Barristers (pres. 1941). Home: 2533 Filbert St San Francisco CA 94123 Office: 111 Pine St San Francisco CA 94104

DETGEN, EDWARD JOSEPH corp. ofcl.; b. N.Y.C., Nov. 17, 1911; s. Richard Joseph and Mary Josephine (Bannon) D.; B.S., Georgetown U., 1934; m. Benedicta Gannon, Sept. 10, 1938; children—John Peter, Mildred Mary, Edward Joseph, Virginia Lambert. Chief spltys. div. U.S. Dept. Commerce, 1939-42; dir. containers div. WPB, 1943-45; sales mgr. Owens-Corning Fiberglas Corp., 1945-54, v.p., gen. sales mgr., 1954-58; v.p., gen. mgr. home bldg. products div., 1958-66, v.p. nat. affairs, 1966—. Trustee Nat. Housing Center; bd. dirs. Urban Inst. Mem. Producers Council, Nat. Sales Execs., Home Improvement Council (dir.). Clubs: Chevy Chase, International (Washington); Prince George Yacht. Home: 7400 Helmsdale Bethesda MD 20034 Office: 900 17th St NW Washington DC 20006

DETHIER, VINCENT GASTON, educator; b. Boston, Feb. 20, 1915; s. Jean Vincent and Marguerite Frances (Lally) D.; A.B., Harvard, 1936, A.M., 1937, Ph.D., 1939; Sc.D. (hon.), Providence Coll., 1964; Ohio State U., 1970; m. Lois E. Check; children—Jehan Vincent, Paul. Harvard fellow Atkins Inst. of Arnold Arboretum, Soledad, Cuba, 1939-40; instr. biology John Carroll U., Cleve., 1939-41, asst. prof., 1941-42; prof. zoology Ohio State U., 1946- 47; asso. prof. biology Johns Hopkins, 1947-51, prof., 1952-58; prof. zoology U. Pa., 1959-67, prof. psychology, 1959-67, asso. Neurol. Inst., 1959-67; prof. biology Princeton, 1967—. Hixon lectr. Cal. Inst. Tech., 1949; speaker Internat. Congress Entomology, Amsterdam, 1951; Belgian-Am. Ednl. Found. fellow Belgian Congo, 1952; sr. Fulbright research scholar London Sch. Hygiene and Tropical Medicine, 1954; Guggenheim fellow, Netherlands, 1964-65; cons. Ednl. Testing Service, Princeton, N.J., Canadian Def. Bd., Office Surgeon Gen., U.S.; dir. research Internat. Centre Insect Physiology and Ecology, Nairobi, Kenya. Served as maj. AUS, World War II. Fellow Entomol. Soc. Am., Nat. Acad. Sci., Am. Acad. Arts and Scis., Royal Entomol. Soc. London (hon.); mem. A.A.A.S., Am. Soc. Zoologists, Soc. Gen. Physiologists, Am. Physiol. Soc., Am. Soc. Naturalists. Author: Chemical Insect Attractants and Repellents, 1951; (with Stellar) Animal Behavior; Physiology of Insect Senses; To Know a Fly; Fairweather Duck; (with Villee) Biological Principles and Processes. Editorial bd. Jour. Comparative Physiol. Psychology. Contbr. Insect Physiology (editor K.D. Roeder), 1953; also various periodicals. Home: Stony Ford Pretty Brook Rd Princeton NJ 08540

DETHMERS, JOHN R., lawyer; b. Plessis, Ia., Oct. 15, 1903; s. Roy P. and Agnes (DeRoos) D.; student Hope Coll., 1921-24, LL.D., 1954; LL.B., U. Mich., 1927, LL.D., 1959; J.D., Detroit Coll. Law, 1947, LL.D., 1967; m. Aleen DeJong, April 4, 1931; children—John Robert, David Conrad, Marjorie Aleen. Admitted to Mich. bar, 1927; practice law, Holland, Mich., 1927-45; pros. atty. Ottawa County, Mich., 1931-38; chief asst. atty. gen. Mich., 1943-44; atty. gen. Mich., 1945-46; apptd. Supreme Ct. Mich., 1946, 1st permanent chief justice, 1956-62, chief justice, 1967-69, mem. Supreme Ct. Mich., until 1971; partner firm Parmenter, Forsythe, Rude & Dethmers, Muskegon, Mich., 1971—. Chmn., Republican State Central Com., 1942-45. Mem. bd. Mus. Youth Internat., Salme, Mich.; chmn. finance bd. Blue Lakes (Mich.) Art and Music Camp. Mem. Am. Bar Assn. (vice chmn. sect. jud. adminstrn. 1959-63), Am. Judicature Soc. (chmn. bd. 1961-63), Nat. Conf. Chief Justices (chmn. 1957-58), Scribes, Delta Theta Phi. Presbyn. K.P. Mason, Rotarian. Contbr. articles to profl. jours. Home: 3920 Highgate Rd Muskegon MI 48441 Office: Nat Lumberman's Bank Bldg Muskegon MI 49440

DETHY, RAY CHARLES, univ. dean; b. Louisville, Nov. 3, 1929; s. Raymond A. and Ellen (Beach) D.; B.Sc., Ohio State U., 1951, M.A., 1959, Ph.D., 1963; m. Gloria A. Hegenberger, June 6, 1953 (div.); children—David Lee, Stephen Ray, Christine Elise. Elementary tchr., Whitehall, O., 1954, football and track coach, tchr. Latin, 1955-56, supt. schs. Knox County, O., 1956-57; asst. supt. schs., Newark, O., 1957-60; asst. to dean Ohio State U., 1960-63; asso. prof., chmn. depts. instrn. and adminstrn. Northeastern U., 1963-65, prof. edn., dir.

grad. sch. edn., dir. Urban Edn. Center, 1965-69; dean Sch. of Edn., St. John's U., 1969—; incorporating mem. Edn. Devel. Center, Boston; partner GDH Assos., Boston. Vice pres. Plymouth County Hosp. Served with AUS, 1951-53. Mem. Phi Delta Kappa. Lion. Author: (with R. Ostrander) A Values Approach to Educational Adminstration, 1969. Home: 33-24 Parsons Blvd Flushing NY 11354 Office: St John's Univ Jamaica NY 11432

DETJEN, GUSTAV, Jr., bus. exec.; b. Germany, 1905; s. Gustav and Martha (Lueders) D.; ed. Pace Coll.; m. Marion L. Kirby, Sept. 16, 1944; children—Christine Marion (Mrs. William H. Westendorf), Theodore Gustav, James Thomas, Louise Harriet. Came to U.S., 1926, naturalized, 1932. Pres., dir. Detjen Corp., 1938—. Mem. Entomol. Soc. Am., A.A.A.S., N.Y. Acad. Sci., Franklin D. Roosevelt Philatelic Soc. (pres.), Ferrary Soc. (pres.), Mennonite. Stamp editor various newspapers. Editor: Fireside Chats. Home: RD 1 Pleasant Valley NY 12659 Office: Pleasant Valley NY 12659

DETJENS, JOHNS, III, apparel co. exec.; b. N.Y.C., Feb. 24, 1935; s. John and Estelle (Skinner) D.; B.A., Princeton, 1956; LL.B., Yale, 1961; m. Stephanie Williams, June 10, 1960; children—Karen Elise, Courteneay Elizabeth. Asso. firm Simpson, Thacher & Bartlett, N.Y.C., 1961-64; staff asst. to pres. Warnaco Inc., Bridgeport, 1964-67, sec., gen. counsel, 1967-70, sr. v.p. group operations, 1970—. Served with AUS , 1956-58. Home: 72 Marsh Rd Easton CT 06425 Office: 350 Lafayette St Bridgeport CT 06604

DETLEFSEN, GUY-ROBERT, mgmt. exec.; b. Chgo., May 3, 1919; s. Gustav C. and Elsa L. (Larrieu) D.; B.A. cum laude, Harvard, 1941; m. Merry Campbell, May 30, 1941; children—Guy-Robert, Keith Campbell, Joan Andre. With shipbldg. div. Bethlehem Steel Co., Quincy, Mass., San Francisco, 1941-44; research tech. Pillsbury Co., 1945-52, dir. comml. research and devel., 1952-58, v.p. growth and tech., 1959-66, v.p. comml. devel. div., 1966-69; exec. v.p., gen. mgr., dir. Maple Island, Inc. , Mpls., 1970—; dir. Webster Lumber Co., St. Paul. Dir. research adv. council Nat. Indsl. Conf. Bd. Mem. Am. Marketing Assn. (award for product testing 1949, past v.p. marketing mgmt. div.), Am. Econ. Assn. Home: 4290 Cottonwood Lane Village of Deephaven Excelsior MN 55331 Office: 2815 Blaisdell Av S Minneapolis MN 55408

DE TOLEDANO, RALPH, see Toledano, Ralph de.

DE TOLNAY, CHARLES ERICH, art historian; b. Budapest, Hungary, May 27, 1899; s. Arnold and Anna (Pilk) deT.; student U. Vienna, 1918-19, 23-25, U. Berlin, 1920-21, U. Frankfurt am Main, 1922; Ph.D., U. Vienna, 1925; D.Litt., Rome U., 1964; Budapest U., 1970; m. Rina Ada Clara Bartolucci, 1930. Came to U.S., 1939, naturalized, 1945. Research, Rome and Florence, Italy, 1925- 28; lectr. history of art U. Hamburg, 1929-33, Sorbonne, Paris, France, 1934-39; vis. lectr. fine arts U. London, 1935, U. Gand, 1936, U. Utrecht, 1937, Collège de France, 1948, Sorbonne, 1950, U. Basle 1951; vis. prof. Columbia, 1954-64; dir. Casa Buonarroti, Florence, 1965—. Prof., Hamburg U., 1957; vis. lectr. Princeton, 1958; mem. Inst. Advanced Study, Princeton, N.J. 1939-48; travel and study, Europe. Recipient Lauréat de l'Académie des Inscriptions et Belles-Lettres, Inst. France, Paris, 1937. Guggenheim fellow, 1948-49, 53-54. Mem. Coll. Art Assn., Accademia di S. Luca, Accademia N. dei Lincei, Accademia dell'Arte del Disegno (hon.). Author: The Youth of Michael Angelo, 1943; The Sistine Ceiling, 1945; The Medici Chapel, 1948; History and Technique of Old Master Drawings, 1943; The Drawings of Pieter Bruegel the Elder, 1952; The Tomb of Julius II, 1954; Michelangelo, The Final Period, 1960; also other books. Contbr. articles to U.S., European jours. Home: Casa Buonarroti Via Ghibellina 70 Florence Italy

DE TONNANCOUR, PAUL ROGER GODEFROY, library adminstr.; b. Fall River, Mass., May 22, 1926; s. R. Godefroy and Emilie (St. Germain) de T.; A.B. cum laude, Providence Coll., 1952; M.S., Simmons Coll., 1953; postgrad. Western Res. U., U. So. Cal.; m. Mary E. Fenno, Apr. 9, 1955; children—Paul Godefroy, Camille Marie. Asst. librarian Enoch Pratt Library, Balt., 1953-54; chief librarian, tech. analyst Armco Steel Corp., Balt., 1954-56; dir. research library Gen. Dynamics, Ft. Worth div., 1956—, dir. tech. information programs, 1964—; cons. Modern Lang Assn. Am., U.S. Office Edn. on sci. information personnel. John Cotton Dana lectr., 1966. Singer, Ft. Worth Opera Assn. Chorus. Active United Fund and Community Council; mem. exec. com. Big Bros. Tarrant County. Trustee Cosmopolitan Internat., 1961-63. Served with USNR, 1943-46. Named Boss of Year, Am. Bus. Women's Assn., 1965. Mem. A.L.A., A.A.A.S., Am., Nat. mgmt. assns., Ft. Worth Art Assn., Spl. Libraries Assn., Am. Soc. Information Sci., Delta Epsilon Sigma. Episcopalian. Mason. Club: Fort Worth Boat. Author: The Exploitation of Technical Information, 1966; co-author: Science Information Personnel, 1963. Contbr. articles profl. jours. Home: 6332 Genoa Rd Ft Worth TX 76116 Office: PO Box 748 Ft Worth TX 76101

DETREVILLE, ROBERT TREAT PAINE, physician, found. exec.; b. Beaufort, S.C., Feb. 19, 1925; s. Benjamin Ellis and Ruth Claghorn (Saffold) DeT.; B.S., The Citadel, 1948; M.D., Med. Coll. S.C., 1948; Sc.D. in Indsl. Medicine, U. Cin., 1956; grad. Sch. Aviation Medicine; m. Janice Suzanne Mundy, Nov. 26, 1953; children—Suzanne, Anne Hamilton, Janice Mundy, Nancy Beaumont, George Mundy. Rotating intern St. Francis X. Infirmary, Charleston, S.C., 1947-48, Roper Hosp., Charleston, 1948-49; practice gen. medicine, Charleston County, 1949-51; commd. 1st lt. USAF, 1951, advanced through grades to maj. M.C., 1957; chief phys. standards Surgeon Gen.'s Office, hdqrs. Air Material Command, Wright-Patterson AFB, O., 1952-53, dep. chief profl. services div., 1956-59; chief Aerospace Med. Br., Norton AFB, Cal., 1959-60; chief health and safety, ballistic systems div. Air Force Systems Command, Inglewood, Cal., 1960-61; asst. clin. prof. indsl. health U. Cin., 1958-59, asst. prof. indsl. health, dept. preventive medicine and indsl. health Coll. Medicine, 1961-63; vis. lectr. occupational medicine U. Cal. Med. Center, Los Angeles, 1960-61; co. physician Ethyl Corp., 1961-62, asst. med. dir., 1962-63; mng. dir. Indsl. Hygiene Found. Am., Mellon Inst., Pitts., 1963-68; pres. Indsl. Health Found. Am., Inc., 1968—; adj. prof. occupational medicine U. Pitts. Grad. Sch. Pub. Health, 1963- -; cons. staff div. medicine dept. occupational health West Pa. Hosp., 1963—. USAF liaison mem. NRC Com. on Toxicology, 1956- 60. Diplomate occupational medicine Am. Bd. Preventive Medicine. Fellow Am. Acad. Occupational Medicine (chmn. publs. com. 1962-65), Indsl. Medicine Assn. (chmn. com. indsl. hygiene and clin. toxicology 1960-62), A.C.P., Am. Coll. Preventive Medicine; mem. Aerospace Med. Assn., Air Force Assn., A.A.A.S., Am. Indsl. Hygiene Assn., A.M.A., Assn. Mil. Surgeons, Pa. Med. Assn., Allegheny County Med. Soc. Episcopalian. Editorial bd. Jour. Occupational Medicine, 1961- 67. Home: 730 13th St Oakmont PA 15139 Office: 5231 Centre Av Pittsburgh PA 15232

DETTMER, ROGER CHRISTIAN, newspaper columnist; b. Cin., Aug. 2, 1927; s. Christian Herman and Cornelia (Van Schouwen) D.; student U. Cin., 1945-47, Columbia, 1947; B.A., U. Mich., 1950. Asst. mgr. Cin. Symphony Orch., 1950-51; music writer N.Y. Herald-Tribune, 1951-53; music and theatre critic Chgo. Today (formerly Chicago's American), 1953—; adviser, instr. Rockefeller Found. project tng. music critics U. So. Cal., 1965-68; writer Opera mag., London, Eng., 1960—, Recordo Geijitsu, Tokyo, Japan, 1968—; free-lance mag. writer, 1950—. Mem. theater adv. panel Ill. Arts Council. Co-recipient Feature Div. award A.P., 1965. Mem. Music Critics Assn. (v.p. 1956), Phi Beta Kappa; hon. mem. Phi Kappa Phi, Theta Alpha Phi. Presbyn. Office: 445 N Michigan Av Chicago IL 60611

DETWEILER, JOSEPH HALL, mfg. exec.; b. Aurora, Ill., Aug. 12, 1920; s. Harry Rutt and Verne (Hall) D.; B.S., Princeton, 1941; I.A., Harvard, 1943, M.B.A., 1946; m. Catherine Ann Lawrence, Apr. 19, 1945; children—Peter Hall, Steven Lawrence, Nancy Ross, Carol Norton. Engr., Lockeed Aircraft, 1941-42; accountant Arthur Andersen & Co., 1946-48; cons. Sanderson & Porter, 1948-49; treas. Argus Cameras, Inc., Ann Arbor, Mich., 1949-55, v.p., 1955-57, v.p. Argus Cameras div. Sylvania Electric Products, Inc., 1957- 59; dir. corporate planning Louis Allis Co., Milw., 1959-61; financial v.p. Hamilton Mfg. Co., Two Rivers, Wis., 1961-63, exec. v.p., 1963-65; treas., dir., v.p. finance Kroehler Mfg. Co., Naperville, Ill., 1965—. Past chmn. Ann Arbor Republican Com. Served as lt. USNR, 1943-46. C.P.A., Mich. Mem. Financial Execs. Inst. Club: Ruth Lake Country. Home: 57th St nr County Line Rd Hinsdale IL 60521 Office: Kroehler Mfg Co Naperville IL 60540

DETZER, KARL WILLIAM, writer; b. Fort Wayne, Ind., Sept. 4, 1891; s. August J. and Laura (Goshorn) D.; m. Clarice Nissley, Nov. 26, 1921; children—Karl (dec.), Mary-Jane (Mrs. J.C. Moench). Reporter, photographer Ft. Wayne newspapers, 1909-16, advt. writer, Chgo., 1920-23; screen play writer and tech. dir., Hollywood, 1934-36; roving editor Reader's Digest, 1939-42, 46—; pub. Enterprise-Tribune, Leland, Mich., 1947-51. Pres., Leland Harbor Corp., 1963—. Mem. Mich. State Corrections Council, 1948-49; chmn. Mich. Citizens Com. on Reorgn. State Govt., 1950-51; spl. adviser to Mil. Govt., Berlin, Germany, 1948. Served from pvt. to capt., inf. U.S. Army, 1916-1919; from maj. to col. Gen. Staff Corps., AUS, 1942-46. Decorated D.S.M. Mem. Authors League Am., Internat. Assn. City Mgrs., Mich. State Police (hon.), V.F.W. (hon. life Floyd Gibbons Post, N.Y.C.). Democrat. Unitarian. Clubs: Deadline (N.Y.C.); National Press, Overseas Press. Author: books and screen plays; latest book Myself When Young, 1968. Contbr. articles to leading mags. Home: Leland MI 49654 Office: The Reader's Digest Pleasantville NY 10570

DEUPREE, CHARLES LAMAR, assn. exec.; b. New Orleans, Feb. 2, 1917; s. Elijah Julius and Della (Morgan) DeuP.; B.B.A., U. Tex., 1940; m. Grace Fisher, Mar. 26, 1946; children—Della Grace (Mrs. Lawrence M. Ryan), Anne Colista (Mrs. John A. Richardson), Cecilia Valerie, Elisabeth Frances. Independent oil operator and owner; exec. v.p. Assn. Oilwell Servicing Contractors, Dallas, 1961—. Mem. exec. com. petroleum sect. Nat. Safety Council, 1966- -. Bd. dirs. Tex. Safety Council. Served from pvt. to capt., AUS, 1942- 46; ETO. Decorated Purple Heart, Bronze Star medal. Mem. Am. Soc. Assn. Execs., Tex. Soc. Assn. Execs. (v.p. 1966, pres. 1967—, dir. 1964—), U.S. C. of C., Patriotic Soc. Colonial Wars (founder Tex. gentleman council 1966, registrar 1968, treas. 1969), La. Petroleum Council (safety adv. com. 1966—), Am. Petroleum Inst., Assn. Petroleum Writers, Ind. Petroleum Assn. Am. (cost study com.), Sigma Nu; hon. mem. Internat. Petroleum Expn. and Congress. Episcopalian. Mason (32, Shriner), Rotarian. Home: 4414 Alta Vista Lane Dallas TX 75229

DEUPREE, MARVIN MATTOX, accountant; b. Woodbine, Ia., Oct. 8, 1917; s. Archie Orin and Pearl (Mattox) D.; B.A. with high distinction, State U. Ia., 1941; M.B.A. with distinction, Wharton Sch. of U. Pa., 1948; m. Katherine Anita Beard, Aug. 18, 1951; children—Marvin Mattox, Meredith Ann. With Arthur Andersen & Co., C.P.A.'s, 1948—, partner, 1960—, mem. policy com. on accounting and auditing, 1962—. Instr. accounting U. Pa., 1947-48. Served as officer USNR, 1943-46. C.P.A., N.Y., Ill., Mich., La., Ia., Va., N.C. Mem. Am. Inst. C.P.A.'s, N.Y. State, Ill. socs. C.P.A.'s, Nat. Assn. Accountants, Am. Accounting Assn. Episcopalian. Clubs: Wall Street (N.Y.C.), Executives, University (Chgo.). Contbr. articles to profl. jours. Home: 999 Castlegate Ct Lake Forest IL 60045 Office: 69 W Washington St Chicago IL 60602

DEUPREE, RICHARD REDWOOD, corp. official; b. Norwood, Va., May 7, 1885; s. Richard Overton and Susan Elizabeth (Redwood) D.; ed. pub. schs., Covington, Ky.; m. Martha Rule, Oct. 18, 1913 (died Aug. 1943); children—Richard Redwood, John Rule, James Young, Elizabeth (Mrs. Richard E. Goldsmith); m. 2d, Emily Powell Allen, Dec. 26, 1944; stepchildren—Mrs. Polk Laffoon III, Mrs. Jason Ellis. Clerk S. Cincinnati & Covington St. Ry. Co., 1901-05; with The Procter & Gamble Co., 1905—, becoming pres., 1930, now hon. chmn. bd.; dir. Cin. Bell Inc.; mem. dirs. advisory council Morgan Guaranty Trust Co.; trustee Equitable Life Ins. Co. Ia. Hon. trustee Children's Hospital; co-chmn. War Chest, 1942, gen. chmn., 1945. Civilian chmn. Army-Navy Munitions Bd., 1946-47; apptd. mem. President's Com. on Fgn. Aid, 1948; chmn. United Community Campaigns of Am., 1959; mem. Citizens Adv. to Pres. on Mut. Security Program; hon. mem. Bus. Council. Former mem. vis. com. Harvard Bus. Sch.; mem. Cin. Music Hall Assn. Mem. Christian Ch. Clubs: Queen City, Commercial, Commonwealth, Camargo, Cincinnati Country (Cin.). Home: 6305 Park Rd Indian Hill Cincinnati OH 45243 Office: 301 E 6th St Cincinnati OH 45202

DEUPREE, RICHARD REDWOOD, Jr., lawyer; b. Cin., Oct. 3, 1914; s. Richard Redwood and Martha (Rule) D.; A.B., Princeton, 1936; LL.B., Harvard, 1939; m. Ann Taylor, Nov. 5, 1937; children—Thomas R., Susan (Mrs. John M. Jones), Richard Redwood III, Caleb T. Admitted to Ohio bar, 1939; since practiced in Cin.; partner firm of Dinsmore, Shohl, Coates & Deupree, and predecessors, 1946—. Dir. Johnson Paper Co. Chmn. finance com. Episcopal Diocese So. Ohio, 1957-61. Mem. Indian Hill Village Council, 1961-65, vice mayor, 1963-65. Vice pres., trustee Children's Hosp., Cin.; trustee Pub. Library Cin. and Hamilton County. Served with USNR, 1943-45; PTO. Mem. Am., Ohio, Cin. bar assns. Clubs: Queen City, Cin. Country. Home: 963 Hill St Cincinnati OH 45202 Office: Fifth Third Center Cincinnati OH 45202

DE URZAIZ, LUIS, educator, tech. inst. exec.; b. Vigo, Spain, Sept. 1, 1896; s. Gen. Luis and Filomena (Duran) de U.; diploma in bus. econs., U. Neuchatel, 1916; guest, polit. sci., philosophic and pure sci., Columbia, 1925-26; m. Elizabeth Norcott, Sept. 12, 1929; 1 son, Louis C. Came to U.S., 1925, naturalized, 1939. Prof. econs. and bus. Central Coll. of High Econ. Studies, Madrid, Spain, 1919; charge stock exchange dept., banking, Credit Lyonnais, Madrid, 1918-23; asst. to Brocker Sangrador, Stock Exchange of Madrid, 1923-25; commr. of Spanish govt. in U.S.A., 1925-26; engr. Ford Motor Co., Detroit and Barcelona, 1927-29; pres. Nat. Tech. Inst., N.Y.C., 1929—; dir. Luis de Urzaiz Assos.; pres. Midwestern Technical Inst., Chgo., Natec Publications, Inc., 1961—; v. p. Spanish Inst., N.Y.C. Licensed aviation pilot. Mem. Am. Soc. Engring. Edn. Club: The Wings (N.Y.C.). edited, Archtl. Drafting. Collector of Old Master and Modern paintings. Home: Meads Mountain Rd Woodstock NY 12498

DEUSCHLE, KURT WALTER, physician, educator; b. Kongen, Germany, Mar. 14, 1923; s. John and Marie (Schaefer) D.; came to U.S., 1924, naturalized, 1949; B.S. cum laude, Kent State U., 1944; M.D., U. Mich., 1948; m. Lois E. Bittinger, Aug. 16, 1946; children—Kurt J., Sally, James. Intern Colo. Gen. Hosp., Denver, 1948-49; resident medicine, fellow oncology Upstate Med. Center of State U. N.Y. at Syracuse, 1950-52, instr. medicine, 1954-55; asst. prof. pub. health and preventive medicine Cornell Med. Coll., 1955-60; prof., chmn. dept. community medicine U. Ky., 1960-69; Lavanburg prof., chmn. and dir. dept. community medicine Mt. Sinai Sch. of Medicine of City U. N.Y., 1968—. Mem. tech. bd. Milbank Meml. Fund; mem. tuberculosis control adv. com. Center Disease Control Dept. HEW; cons. manpower intelligence Nat. Insts. Health; mem. Inst. of Medicine of Nat. Acad. Scis. (Washington). Served with AUS, 1943-46. Commonwealth Fund sr. health fellow, 1966-67. Fellow Am. Coll. Preventive Medicine; mem. A.M.A., Am. Pub. Health Assn., Am. Thoracic Soc., Assn. Tchrs. Preventive Medicine, Internat. Epidemiol. Assn., N.Y. County, N.Y. State med. socs., Alpha Omega Alpha. Author: (with J. Adair) The People's Health: Anthropology and Medicine in a Navajo Community, 1970. Contbr. to Medicine in the Ghetto (ed. John Norman), 1969, Community Medicine: Teaching, Research and Health Care (ed. Lathem and Newberry), 1970. Home: 251 Ancon Av Pelham NY 10803 Office: 19 E 98th St New York City NY 10029

DEUSING, MURL, producer; b. Milw., Sept. 5, 1908; s. Henry and Olga (Henning) D.; B.E., U. Wis., 1933; m. Mildred Nickels, May 25, 1928. Asst. curator edn. Milw. Pub. Mus., 1932-45, curator edn., 1945-59; during this period adminstr. audiovisual library serving Milw. schs., also pioneered mus. TV Programs; photographer wild life Walt Disney's True Life Adventures, Zoo Parade, Warner Bros., also lectr. wild life and travel, 1939—; owner Murl Deusing Film Prodns., classroom teaching films, 1946- -; dir. Mus. Sci. and Natural History, St. Louis, 1959-61; producer tv programs Nat. Ednl. TV and Radio Center, N.Y.C., 1961—; producer Murl Dausing Safari TV series, 1964—. Recipient Distinguished Alumnus award U. Wis.-Milw. Alumni Assn., 1971. Mem. A.A.A.S., Wis. Soc. Ornithology (past pres.), Am. Assn. Museums (counselor 1959), Izaak Walton League (past nat. dir., past sec. Wis.), Midwest Mus. Conf. (past pres.), Acad. Sci. St. Louis, Wis Acad. Sci., Nat. Conservancy, Wilderness Soc., Nat. Parks Assn. Author: Soil, Water and Man, 1936. Address: 5325 W Van Beck Av Milwaukee WI 53220

DEUTCH, MURRAY, music publishing co. exec.; b. Bronx, N.Y., Mar. 23, 1920; s. Hyman and Yetta Deutch; ed. pub. schs.; m. Pamela Walker, Nov. 8, 1947; children—Howard Roy, Lisa Faith. Formerly gen. profl. mgr. So. Music Co., then v.p. Jubilee Records; now exec. v.p. United Artists Music Companies, N.Y.C. Served with AUS, World War II. Home: 15 Steven Dr Hewlett NY 11557 Office: 729 7th Av New York City NY 10019

DEUTSCH, ADOLPH, banker; b. Budapest, Hungary, Oct. 25, 1881; s. Bernard and Mary (Adelberg) D.; A.B., U. Budapest, 1900; m. Erzsi Sugar; children—Robert S., Alfred L., Charles L. Pres. Am. Savs. & Loan Assn., Detroit, 1947- 62, former chmn. bd., dir.; pres., dir. Moore, Deutsch & Co., Detroit, 1931—; v.p., dir. Citizens Mortgage Corp., Detroit. Mason (Shriner). Club: Knollwood Country. Home: 19211 Prairie St Detroit MI 48221

DEUTSCH, ALFRED LEONARD, savs. and loan assn. exec.; b. N.Y.C., Apr. 13, 1914; s. Adolph and Nina (Warady) D.; B.A., U. Mich., 1934; LL.B., Detroit Coll. Law, 1937; m. Bernice Roseberg, Sept. 17, 1946; children—Robert J., Dennis B., Morris H. Formerly with Am. Savs. & Loan Assn., Detroit, exec. v.p., 1955- 62, pres., dir.; chmn. bd. Citizens Mortgage Corp., Detroit, 1965—; vice chmn. bd. FHLB Indpls., 1964—; admitted to Mich. bar, 1937. Chmn. finance com., dir. Mich. Council Econ. Edn., 1963—. Bd. dirs. Children's Orthogenic Sch., Detroit, 1957—, pres., 1960—; bd. dirs. Tb and Health Soc. Detroit, 1963—, Boys Com. Detroit, 1962—; chmn. Detroit Allied Jewish Campaign, 1967; pres. Deutsch Family Found., 1965—. Served to 1st lt. AUS, 1942-46. Mem. Mich. Bar Assn., Mortgage Bankers Am., Econ. Club Detroit, Greater Detroit Bd. Commerce, Phi Epsilon Pi. Clubs: Franklin Hills Country (Franklin, Mich.); Savoyard, Standard-City (Detroit). Home: 1200 Ardmoor Dr Birmingham MI 48010

DEUTSCH, BABETTE, (Mrs. Avrahm Yarmolinsky), writer; b. N.Y.C., 1895; A.B., Barnard Coll. (Columbia), 1917, Litt. D., 1946. Lectr. English, Columbia, 1944-68, sr. lectr., 1969—. Hon. cons. Library of Congress, 1961-66. Mem. Nat. Inst. Arts and Letters, P.E.N. Author: Banners (verse), 1919; Honey Out of the Rock (verse), 1925; A Brittle Heaven (novel), 1926; In Such a Night (novel), 1927; Potable Gold (criticism), 1929; Fire For the Night (verse), 1930; Epistle to Prometheus (verse), 1931; Mask of Silenus (novel), 1933; This Modern Poetry (criticism), 1935; One Part Love (verse), 1939; Heroes of the Kalevala (juvenile), 1940; It's a Secret! (juvenile), 1941; Walt Whitman, Builder for America (juvenile), 1941; The Welcome (juvenile), 1942; Rogue's Legacy (novel), 1942; Take Them, Stranger (verse), 1944; The Reader's Shakespeare (criticism), 1946; Poetry in Our Time (criticism), 1952, 56, 63; Animal, Vegetable, Mineral (verse), 1954; Poetry Handbook, 1957, 62, 69; Coming of Age: New and Selected Poems, 1959, 64; Collected Poems, 1919-1962, 63; I Often Wish (juvenile), 1966; The Collected Poems of Babette Deutsch, 1969. Co-author: The Steel Flea (juvenile), 1943; Tales of Faraway Folk (juvenile), 1952; More Tales of Faraway Folk (juvenile), 1963. Editor: The Poems of Samuel Taylor Coleridge (criticism), 1967. Translator several vols. verse including The Twelve by Alexander Blok, Eugene Onegin by Pushkin, Poems from The Book of Hours by Rilke, 1941; Two Centuries of Russian Verse, 1966; There Comes a Time (juvenile), 1969. Home: 300 W 108th St New York City NY 10025

DEUTSCH, EBERHARD PAUL, lawyer; b. Cin., Oct. 31, 1897; s. Gotthard and Hermine (Bacher) D.; student Tulane U., 1924-25; J.D. (hon.), U. Messina (Sicily), 1943; m. Rhea Loeb, Aug. 1, 1929 (dec. Mar. 1961); 1 son, Brunswick G. Admitted to La. bar, 1925, since practiced in New Orleans; spl. asst. to atty. gen. U.S. on Texas City Disaster litigation, 1950-53; prin. legal adviser to Gen. Mark W. Clark in Mil. Adminstrn. of Austria, 1945-46, also chmn. Allied Legal Directorate; dir. The Vernon Bank; chmn. Dixie Ship Repair Co. Bd. dirs. Isaac Delgado Mus. ,New Orleans. Lt. F.A., U.S. Army, 1917-19, col., Gen. Staff Corps, 1942-46. Decorated Silver Star, Bronze Star, Legion of Merit, Purple Heart; Gold Cross of Merit (Austria); Croix de Guerre with palm and fourragere. Mem. Internat., Fed., Am. (chmn. admiralty and maritime law com. 1961-62, chmn. com. peace and law through UN 1962-63, 65-68, chmn. com. law treaties 1967; mem. com. abuse of process, com. marine resources, council sect. internat. and comparative law), La. (chmn. com. law reform), New Orleans bar assns., Assn. Bar City N.Y., Am. Judicature Soc. (dir. 1935- 56), Maritime Law Assn., Am. Soc. Internat. Law, Met. Crime Commn., Miss. Valley Assn., New Orleans Philharmonic Symphony Soc., Notaries Assn. New Orleans, Tulane Alumni Fund, Indian Soc. Internat. Law, Am. Arbitration Assn., Am. Civil Liberties Union, Am. Soc. Legal History, Assn. Average Adjusters, Assn. Am. Indian Affairs, Assn. U.S. Army, Bur. Govt. Research, Consular Corps New Orleans (hon consul gen. Republic Austria), Escoffiers, Fgn. Relations Assn. (dir.), France Amerique de la Louisiane. Grand Consistory La.,

Information Council of Ams., Internat. Legal Aid Assn., La. Free Enterprise Assn., La. Assn. Def. Counsel, La. Civil Service League, La. Hist. Soc., La. U. Found., Research Fellows Southwestern Legal Found., Assn. ICC Practitioners, Bd. Trade, C. of C., Alumni Assn. Tulane U., Scribes, Athence Louisianais, Audubon Soc., Confrerie des Chevaliers du Tastevin, English Speaking Union, Fellowship U.S.-Brit. Comrades, Heroes of '76, Hon., Order of Blue Goose Internat., Order of Lafayette Inter-Am. Bar Assn., Le Petit Theatre du Vieux Carre, Met. New Orleans Safety Council, Mil. Govt. Assn., Mil. Order World Wars, Nat. Aero. Assn., Nat. Geog. Soc., Opera House Assn., Zool. Soc., Res. Officers Assn., Selden Soc., Council for a Better La., Internat. Soc. Mil. Law, Shakespeare Soc. New Orleans, Internat. Law Assn., Nat. Trust Historic Preservation (mem. nat. devel. com.), Nat. Waterways Conf., V.F.W., Vets. World War I U.S., U.S. Internat. Sailing Assn., Blue Key, 33d Div. War Vets. Assn., Phi Delta Phi. Mason (Shriner, Sojourner), Elk; mem. B'nai B'rith. Clubs: Army and Navy, Insurance, International House, (dir. and mem. of exec. com.), Press, University. Athletic, Knife and Fork, Petroleum, Round Table, Southern Yacht, Mariners, Opera (New Orleans); Downtown Athletic (N.Y.C.); Petroleum (Houston); Propeller U.S.; Skyriders; City (Baton Rouge); National Lawyers (Washington); Tulane Side Lines; Lamplighter; Plimsoll. Editor: The Internat. Lawyer. Home: Pontchartrain Hotel New Orleans LA 70140 Office: Hibernia Bank Bldg New Orleans LA 70112

DEUTSCH, ELIOT, educator, editor; b. Gary, Ind., Jan. 8, 1931; s. Adolph and Pearl (Sandler) D.; B.S., U. Wis., 1952; postgrad. Harvard, 1952-53; Ph.D., Columbia, 1960; m. Sanna Saks, July 15, 1957; 1 son, Adley. Prof. philosophy, chmn. dept. Rensselaer Poly. Inst., 1960-67; prof. philosophy U. Hawaii, 1967—; editor Philosophy East and West; dir. 6th East-West Philosophers' Conf. Served with AUS, 1953-55. Faculty fellow Am. Inst. Indian Studies, 1963-64. Mem. Soc. Asian and Comparative Philosophy (sec.), Inst. Religion and Social Change (dir.), Am. Philos. Assn., Assn. Asian Studies, Metaphys. Soc. Am., Aesthetics Soc. Author: Bhagavad Gītā, 1968; Advaita Vedanta, 1969; Humanity and Divinity, 1970; (with I.A.E. Van Buitenen) A Source Book of Advaita Vedānta, 1971. Home: 4837 Kolohala St Honolulu HI 96816

DEUTSCH, GEORGE S., diversified industry exec.; b. 1924; B.Sc., U. Manchester (Eng.), 1944; married. Research asst. Dunlop Rubber Co. Ltd., Eng., 1944-46; sales dir. Crowther Ltd., Leicester, Eng., 1946-55; v.p. S.Am. div. W.R. Grace & Co., 1955-61; mng. dir. Lessona Ltd., Eng., 1966, v.p. marketing, 1966-67; v.p. Amerace Corp., N.Y.C., 1966-68; v.p. Amerace Esna Corp., N.Y.C., 1968-69; sr. v.p., 1969—; pres. A & A Sales Co. Home: 249 E 48th St New York City NY 10017 Office: 245 Park Av New York City NY 10017*

DEUTSCH, JAN GINTER, educator; b. Katowice, Poland, May 25, 1935; s. Fred J. and Stella (Storch) D.; came to U.S., 1939, naturalized, 1953; B.A., Yale, 1955, LL.B., 1962, Ph.D., 1962; B.A., Clare Coll., Cambridge, Eng., 1957, M.A., 1963; m. Barbara V. Weiss, May 26, 1961. Admitted to D.C. bar, 1963, Ohio bar, 1965; practiced in Cleve., 1964-66; law clk. Justice Potter Stewart, U.S. Supreme Ct., 1962-64; asso. Jones, Day, Cockley & Reavis, 1964-66; asst. prof. Yale Law Sch., New Haven, 1966-67, asso. prof., 1967-68, prof., 1968—; exec. v.p. Devel. Techs., Inc., Washington, 1969-70; cons. President's Commn. on Law Enforcement Adminstrn. of Justice, summer 1966, President's Task Force on Communications Policy, summer 1968. Justice of Peace, Woodbridge, Conn., 1969-71. Mem. Democratic Party Com., Woodbridge, 1968-69. Bd. dirs. Council on Econ. Priorities, 1969-70. Served with AUS, 1957-58. Mem. Am. Bar Assn., Phi Beta Kappa. Home: 18 Pleasant Hill Rd Woodbridge CT 06525 Office: Yale Law Sch New Haven CT 06520

DEUTSCH, JOHN JAMES, economist, univ. ofcl.; b. Quinton, Sask., Can., Feb. 26, 1911; s. Carl and Elizabeth (Frehs) D.; B.Com. in Commerce and Econs., Queen's U., 1935; LL.D., St. Mary's U., Halifax, N.S., Can., 1956, McGill U., U. Winsdor (Ont.), 1964, Sir George Williams U., York U., U. Calgary, McMaster U., U. Man., U. Toronto; m. Stephanie Heagerty, June 1, 1940; 1 dau., Mary. Research asst. dept. econ. research Bank of Can., Ottawa, Ont., 1936-42; asst. dir. research Rowell-Sirois Commn. on Dominion-Provincial Relations, 1937-40 (on loan); lectr. econs. Queen's U., Kingston, Ont., 1940, prof. econs., 1959-63, vice prin. adminstrn., 1959-62, vice prin., 1962-63, prin.-elect, prof. econs., 1967, prin., vice chancellor, 1968—; spl. asst. to undersec. state for external affairs Govt. of Can., Ottawa, 1942-44; mem. editorial staff, econ. adviser Winnipeg (Man.) Free Press, 1945-46; dir. internat. econ. relations div. Ottawa Dept. Finance, 1946-53, asst. dept. minister finance, 1953-56, sec. treas. bd., 1954-56; prof., head dept. econs. and polit. sci. U. B.C., Vancouver, 1956-59; chmn. Econ. Council of Can., Ottawa, 1963-68. Dir. Internat. Nickel Co. Can. Ltd., Canadian Imperial Bank of Commerce. Mem. Royal Commn. on Nfld. Finances, 1957; chmn. Natural Gas Distbn. Enquiry Commn. of Greater Winnipeg, 1958; econ. adviser Spl. Senate Com. on Manpower and Employment, 1960-61; chmn. Royal Commn. on Higher Edn. in N.B., 1961-62; mem. Spl. Com. on Inquiry into Unemployment Ins. Act, 1961-62; spl. adviser to a study on Maritime Union, 1968-70; mem. Ont. Govt. Commn. to Plan Post-Secondary Edn. for Next 20 Years, 1969—; chmn. com. to advise Ont. Govt. on province's future energy needs, 1971—. Bd. govs. U. Ottawa, 1965—. Recipient Vanier medal, 1968; named companion Order of Can. Fellow Royal Soc. Can.; mem. Canadian Polit. Sci. Assn., Canadian Inst. Pub. Adminstrn. Roman Catholic. Clubs: Rideau (Ottawa); Cataraqui Golf and Country (Kingston), Author: (with others) The Canadian Economy; Selected Readings, The American Economic Impact on Canada. Home: Summerhill Queens U Kingston Ontario Canada

DEUTSCH, KARL WOLFGANG, polit. scientist; b. Prague, Czechoslovakia, July 21, 1912; s. Martin M. and Maria (Scharf) Deutsch; J.U.C., German U. Prague, 1934; Dr. Law and Polit. Sci., Charles U., Prague, 1938; Ph.D., Harvard, 1951; M.A. (hon.), Yale, 1958; m. Ruth Slonitz, Apr. 2, 1936; children—Mary Elizabeth, Margaret, Beatrice Hope. Came to U.S., 1938, naturalized, 1948. Instr. to prof. Mass. Inst. Tech., 1942- 52, prof. history and polit. sci., 1952-58; prof. polit. sci. Yale, 1958-67; now asso. fellow Silliman Coll.; prof. of govt. Harvard, 1967—, faculty asso. Harvard Center Internat. Affairs, 1969—; vis. prof. Princeton, 1953- 54, U. Chgo., 1954, Yale, 1957-58, Heidelberg U., 1960, Mass. Inst. Tech., 1960-61, Harvard, 1961, Frankfurt U., 1968, Geneva U., 1970, 71, U. Mannheim, 1971; Stanfield prof. internat. peace Harvard, 1971; specialist U.S. Dept. State, India, 1963, Germany, Czechoslovakia, Poland, 1967. Fellow Center for Advanced Study in the Behavioral Scis., Stanford, Cal., 1956-57. Awarded Sumner prize polit. sci., Harvard, 1951; Guggenheim fellow, 1954, 71. Fellow Am. Acad. Arts and Sci., Conf. on Sci., Philosophy and Religion; mem. Am. Political Science Assn. (pres. 1969-70), Internat. Polit. Sci. Assn. (v.p. 1970-71), New Eng. Polit. Sci. Assn. (pres. 1964-65), Am. Unitarian Assn., Am. Acad. Arts and Scis. Author: Nationalism and Social Communication, 1953, rev. 1966; (with others) Political Community and the Northern Atlantic Area, 1957, The Nerves of Government, 1963, rev. edit. 1966; (with others) Modern Political Systems; Europe, 1968; (with others) World Handbook of Political and Social Indicators, 1964; Arms Control and the Atlantic Alliance, 1967; (with others) France, Germany and the Western Alliance, 1967; The Analysis of International Relations, 1968; Nationalism and its Alternatives, 1969; Politics and Government: How People Decide Their Fate, 1970; (with R.L. Merritt) Nationalism and National Development: An Interdisciplinary Bibliography, 1970. Mem. edit. bd. Behavioral Sci. Home: 25 Lakeview Av Cambridge MA 02138

DEUTSCH, MARTIN, physicist; b. Vienna, Austria, Jan. 29, 1917; s. Felix and Helena (Rosebach) D.; S.B., Mass. Inst. Tech., 1937, Ph.D., 1941; Docteur honoris causa, U. Algiers, 1959; m. Suzanne Zeitlin, June 6, 1939; children—L. Peter, Nicholas A. Came to U.S., 1935, naturalized, 1941. Instr., Mass. Inst. Tech., 1941-44, asst. prof., 1945-49, asso. prof., 1949-53, prof., 1953—; mem. Los Alamos Sci. Lab., 1944-46; Guggenheim fellow, 1953-54,60-61; cons. Mem. Am. Phys. Soc., A.A.A.S., Am. Acad. Arts and Scis., Soc. Francaise de Physique, Fedn. Am. Scientists (v.p. 1956), Nat. Acad. Sci. Home: 43 Reservoir St Cambridge MA 02138

DEUTSCH, MORTON, psychologist, educator; b. N.Y.C., Feb. 4, 1920; s. Charles and Ida (Prager) D.; B.S., Coll. City N.Y., 1939; M.A., U. Pa., 1940; Ph.D., Mass. Inst. Tech., 1948; m. Lydia S. Shapiro, June 1, 1947; children—Anthony Charles, Nicholas Andrew. Asst. to asso. prof. psychology N.Y. U., 1948-56; dir. research interpersonnel processes Bell Telephone Labs., Murray Hill, N.J., 1956-63; prof. psychology, edn. Tchrs. Coll. Columbia, N.Y.C., 1963—; cons. Nat. Inst. Mental Health, VA. Trustee Marshall Fund; bd. sponsors Nat. Com. Sane Nuclear Policy. Served to 1st lt. USAAF, 1942-45. Decorated D.F.C. with cluster, Air medal with three clusters; recipient A.A.A.S. Socio-Psychology prize, 1961, Samuel Flowerman Meml. award, 1963, Hovland Meml. award, 1967, Kurt Lewin Meml. award, 1968. Mem. Soc. Psychol. Study Social Issues (past pres.), Am., N.Y. State (past pres.), Eastern (pres. 1968-69), psychol. assns., Am. Sociol. Assn., A.A.A.S. Author: Inter-racial Housing, 1951; Research Methods in Social Relations, 1951; Preventing World War III; Some Proposals, 1962; Theories in Social Psychology, 1965. Home: 161 W 86th St New York City, NY 10024.

DEUTSCH, ROBERT WILLIAM, physicist; b. Far Rockaway, N.Y., Mar. 21, 1924; s. Nathan and Lena (Berger) D.; B.S., Mass. Inst. Tech., 1948; Ph.D., U. Cal., 1953; m. Florence Kadish, Sept. 11, 1949; children—Jane Lisa, David Jeffrey. Physics cons. Martin-Marietta Corp., Balt., 1962-64; pres. Gen. Physics Corp., Columbia, Md., 1966—, also prof., chmn. dept. nuclear sci. and engring. Cath. U. Am., 1964—. Served with AUS, 1943-46. Mem. Am. Nuclear Soc. (chmn. Washington sect.), Am. Phys. Soc., Am. Assn. Univ. Profs., A.A.A.S. Contbr. articles profl. jours. Research on tng. of nuclear power plant personnel. Home: 8502 Arbor Wood Rd Baltimore MD 21208 Office: Gen Physics Corp Banneker Bldg Columbia MD 21043

DEUTSCH, SID, educator, bioengr.; b. N.Y.C., Sept. 19, 1918; s. Elias and Gussie (Hazen) D.; B.E.E., Cooper Union, 1941; M.E.E., Bklyn. Poly. Inst., 1947, D.E.E., 1955; m. Ruth Appleman, Nov. 15, 1941 (div. June 1969); children—Alice, Phyllis, Naomi. Designer, Fairchild Camera & Instrument Co., N.Y.C., 1943-44; instr. Madison Inst., Newark, 1946-50; engr. Poly. Research & Devel. Co., Bklyn., 1950-54; mem. faculty Bklyn. Poly. Inst., 1954—, prof. elec. engring., 1962—; cons. Lewyt Mfg. Corp., 1958-60; affiliate Rockefeller Inst., 1961-64. Mem. adult edn. com. Roslyn (N.Y.) pub. schs., 1955-58. Served with USNR, 1944-46. Fellow Soc. Information Display; mem. I.E.E.E., Sigma Xi, Tau Beta Pi, Eta Kappa Nu. Author: Theory and Design of TV Receivers, 1951; Models of the Nervous System, 1967. Patentee pseudorandom dot scan for TV. Home: 205 W 89th St New York City NY 10024 Office: 333 Jay St Brooklyn NY 11201

DE VALERA, EAMON, pres. of Ireland; b. New York City, Oct. 14, 1882; s. Vivion and Catherine (Coll) De V.; ed. National Sch., Bruree, Christian Brothers' School, Charleville, Blackrock Coll. and National U. of Ireland; degrees conferred; B.A., B.Sc., H.Dip. in Edn., LL.D., Ph.D., Sc.D. H.C.; m. S. Ni Flhannagāin, Jan. 8, 1910; children—Vivion, Máirin Eamonn, Brian (dec.), Ruaidhri, Emer (wife of Brianō Cuiv), Toirleach. Joined Irish Vols. at Found., 1913, served as pres., 1917-21; adj. Dublin Brigade, 1915-16, and comdt. in Irish Nat. Insur., 1916; sentenced to death, sentence commuted to penal servtude for life, released in Gen. Amnesty, June 1917, again imprisoned, May 1918; escaped from Lincoln Gaol, Feb. 1919; vis. U.S. and raised loan of six million dollars for Irish Republican Govt., 1919-20; pres. of the Irish Republic, 1919-22; pres. Sinn Féin, 1917-26 (when Fianna Fáil was founded); pres. Fiana Fáil, 1926-59, leader opposition Irish Free State Parliament, 1927-32; Parliamentary representative for Clare, 1917-59, also for East Mayo, 1918-21, M.P. for Down (Northern Ireland), 1921-29, South Down (Northern Ireland), 1933-37; president Exec. council, Irish Free State, and minister for external affairs, Mar. 1932- Dec. 1937; Taoiseach (thē0shēk)0(Head of govt.), 1937-48, 1951-54, 57- 59; pres. of Ireland, 1959—; minister for external affairs, Govt. of Ireland, 1937-48; minister for edn., 1939-40; leader of opposition in Dāil Eireann, 1948-51, 54-57. Pres. of council League Nations sessions, Sept. and Oct. 1932; pres. Assemby of League of Nations, 1938. Chancellor of Nat. U. of Ireland, 1921—. Recipient Grand Cross of the Order of Pius IX, 1933, also Grand Cross of the Order of Charles, 1961; also Supreme Order of Christ, 1962. Rejected Anglo-Irish Treaty in Dail Eireann, Dec. 1921-Jan. 1922. Address: Aras an Uachtarain Dublin Ireland.

DE VALOIS, NINETTE, choreographer; b. Baltyboys, Ireland, June 6, 1898; d. Thomas Robert Alexander and Elizabeth Graydon (Smith) Stannus; studied dancing with Enrico Cecchetti; Mus.D. (hon.), U. London, 1947; D. Litt. (hon.), Reading U., 1951, Oxford U. 1955; Mus. D., Sheffield U., 1955, Trinity Coll., Dublin, 1957; A.F.D., Smith College, 1957; LL.D., Aberdeen, 1958; m. Arthur Blackall Connell, 1935. Appeared as dancer London theatres, 1914-20; toured Europe with Diaghilev Russian Ballet, also appeared Covent Garden, 1923-25; partner Anton Dolin, 1926- 28; dir. ballet Abbey Theatre, Dublin, 1928-31; dir. Vic-Wells Ballet, 1931; dir. Sadler's Wells Ballet (now The Royal Ballet), 1931; founder, 1931, since dir. Sadler's Wells Ballet School (now The Royal Ballet School); organized Nat. School Ballet, Turkey, 1947. Decorated Comdr. Order Brit. Empire, 1947, Dame Comdr. Order Brit. Empire, 1951; Legion of Honor (France), 1950. Mem. Royal Acad. Dancing (v.p.). Author: Invitation to the Ballet, 1937; Come Dance With Me, 1957. Office: care of Royal Ballet Sch 153 Talgarth Rd London W14 England

DEVAN, CHRISTOPHER BARTRAM, librarian; b. Plainfield, N.J., Nov. 15, 1926; s. Samuel Arthur and Winifrede (Richards) D.; B.A., George Washington U., 1950; M.S. in L.S., U. Ill., 1954; m. Margaret Brice Brown, Feb. 23, 1963; children—Cathryn Allison, Elizabeth Anne, Caroline Gatewood, William Arthur, Margaret Richards. Asst. field dir. A.R.C., 1952-53; br. librarian Milw. Pub. Library, 1954-57; county librarian Greene County Library, Springfield, Mo., 1957-60; county and extension librarian pub. libraries, Springfield and Greene County, 1960-61; coordinator pub. library service Chester County Library, West Chester, Pa., 1961-63; asst. dir. Wilmington (Del.) Inst. Free Library, 1963-64; dir. libraries Wilmington Inst. Free Library and New Castle County Free Library, 1964-70; dir. Cuyahoga County Pub. Library, Cleve., 1970—. Served with AUS, 1945-46, 50-51. Mem. Am. (council 1966-70), Del. (pres. 1968-69), Ohio library assns., Middle Atlantic Regional Library Fedn. Episcopalian. Kiwanian. Home: 17855 Lake Rd Lakewood OH 44107 Office: 4510 Memphis Av Cleveland OH 44144

DEVAN, EUGENE MCCAIN, Jr., apparel mfg. co. exec.; b. Mobile, Ala., Nov. 24, 1928; s. Eugene McCain and Gladys Marie (Biggio) DeV.; B.S., U. Ala., 1961; m. Eloise McCullough, Sept. 24, 1947; children—Marcia Susan, Marilyn (Mrs. Stephen Joseph Uurtamo). Treas., Devan-Horner, Inc., supermarkets, Mobile, 1947-58; sr. auditor Arthur Andersen & Co., Atlanta, 1961-63; controller Phila. Carpet Co., 1963-64; sr. v.p. Jackson-Atlantic, Inc., Atlanta, 1964-68; treas., controller Oxford Industries, Inc., Atlanta, 1968—. C.P.A., Ga. Recipient certificate for highest cumulative average Beta Alpha Psi, 1961, scholarship key Delta Sigma Pi, 1961. Mem. Financial Execs. Inst., Am. Inst. C.P.A.'s, Ga. Soc. C.P.A.'s, Beta Alpha Psi. Clubs: Civitan, Athletic (Atlanta). Home: 1490 Montevallo Circle Decatur GA 30033 Office: 222 Piedmont Av Atlanta GA 30312

DEVANEY, MARK JOSEPH, former corp. exec.; b. Cin., Aug. 19, 1906; s. John and Ellen (Nolan) D.; B.B.A., U. Cin., 1931; m. Dorothea M. Caemmerer, Nov. 26, 1936; 1 son, Mark Joseph. Auditor, Am. Airlines, Inc., Chgo., 1932-34, chief accountant Nat. Distillers Products Corp., N.Y.C., 1934-51, asst. comptroller, 1951-53, comptroller, 1953-63; v.p., controller Nat. Distillers & Chem. Corp., 1963-70, also mem. mgmt. com. Mem. arbitration panel N.Y. Stock Exchange. Mem. East Coast adv. com. U. Cin. Trustee Bd. Edn., Merrick, L.I., 1944-52, pres., 1945-46, 48-52. Mem. Quarter Century Wireless Assn. (dir., treas.), Financial Execs. Inst. Clubs: Larchmont (N.Y.) Shore (dir.). Home: 8 Wagon Wheel Rd Mamaroneck NY 10543

DEVANS, FRANK E., lawyer; b. East Bethany, N.Y., Aug. 3, 1893; s. Edward J. and Rose (Ashley) D.; LL.B., Albany Law Sch., 1917; m. Ruby H. Knox, Mar. 24, 1956. Admitted to N.Y. bar, 1919 and since practiced in Rochester; mem. Nixon, Hargrave, Devans & Doyle and predecessor firms, 1927—; dirs., adv. bd., Lincoln Rochester Trust Co.; hon. dir. Sybron Corp. Mem. Am., N.Y. State, Rochester bar assns., Am. Legion. Club: Rochester Country. Home: 51 Pelham Rd Rochester NY 14610 Office: 1 Exchange St Rochester NY 14614

DE VARON, JOSE KURT PAWOLLECK, indsl. exec.; b. Madrid, Spain, Aug. 4, 1914; s. Jose Varon Y Caballero and Elsa Pawolleck; came to U.S., 1924, naturalized, 1931; A.B., magna cum laude, Harvard, 1938, LL.B., 1941;m. Lorna Cooke, May 14, 1944; children—David, Joanna, Christina, Alexander Mark. Admitted to Mass. bar, 1942; with Eastern Gas and Fuel Assos., Boston, 1941-70, v.p., gen. counsel, 1963-65, sr. v.p. law, stockholder relations and public relations, 1965-70; pres. Rocky Mountain Energy Co., 1970—; sec. gen. counsel, dir. Atlantic Bulk Trading Corp., Castner, Curran & Bullitt, Inc.; gen. counsel, sec., clk. Boston Gas Co.; sec., clk., asst. treas., dir. Boston Tow Boat Co.; sec., dir. Conn. Coke Co., Eastern Ocean Transp. Corp., Mystic Steamship Corp.; v.p., sec., dir. Eastern Marine Leasing Corp.; dir. Midland Enterprises. Bd. dirs. Cambridge Soc. Early Music, Internat. Inst. Girls in Spain; trustee Longy Sch. Music; v.p., dir. World Affairs Council. Served with inf. AUS, 1942-45, Decorated Bronze Star with oak leaf cluster. Mem. Am., Boston bar assns., Am. Soc. Internat. Law, Boston Com. Fgn. Relations, Phi Beta Kappa. Clubs: Engineers; Union, St. Botolph (Boston). Home: 94 Lakeview Av Cambridge MA 02138 Office: 621 17th St Denver CO 80202 also 345 Park Av New York City NY 10022 and Prudential Tower Boston MA 02199

DEVAULT, VIRGIL THOMAS, physician; b. White County, Ind., July 16, 1901; s. Thomas and Bertha (Summers) D.; B.S., Ind. U., 1927, M.D., 1929; M.D., San Marcos U., Lima, Peru, 1934; postgrad. in surgery, London, Heidelberg, Munich, Edinburgh, Vienna, 1935; m. Arilla Spence, June 23, 1930. Intern, Gorgas Hosp., Panama C.Z., 1929-30; chief med. officer Anglo-Ecuadorian Oil Field, ltd., Salinas, Ecuador, 1930; asst. resident surgeon St. Agnes Hosp., Balt., 1930-31; chief surgeon Williston (N.D.) Clinic, 1931-32; chief surgeon, med. officer Compania Petrolera Lobitos, Ltd., Peru, 1932- 34, 36-37; chief surgeon, dir. Anglo-Am. Hosp. and Clinc, Lima, 1937- 50; mem. dir. Fgn. Service and Dept. State, Washington, 1950-63, med. dir. all personnel State Dept. and agys., 1952-63; capt. USPHS Res., 1950-59; internat. rep. A.M.A., Chgo., 1965-67, dir. dept. internat. health, 1967-70; internat. exec. sec. Internat. Coll. Surgeons, Washington, 1971—. Mem. adv. bd. CARE-Medico, 1961—. Bd. dirs. Music Research Found., Inc., Internat. Mus. of Surg. Sci. and Hall of Fame, Chgo.; trustee German Med. Soc. Chgo. Ednl. Found. Recipient diploma of honor Municipality San Isidro, Peru, 1946; decorated knight comdr. Orden del Sol, Orden Daniel Carrion (both Peru). Fellow A.C.S. (mem. internat. relations com. 1964—), Internat. Coll. Surgeons (dir. Gen. North Am. Fedn. 1961-64, asso. internat. sec. gen. 1964-65, mem. qualifications council 1965—, v.p. U.S. sect. 1969—), Sociedad de Cirugia de Madrid (hon.); mem. Pan Am. Med. Soc. (v.p. 1958, trustee 1959-64, pres. 1963-64), Am. Hosp. Assn., A.M.A., Washington Med. Soc., Am. Med. Soc. Vienna (life, chmn. surg. group Vienna 1935), Accion Medico del Peru, Assn. Mil Surgeons, Internat. Med. Assn., Am. Soc. Peru (gov. 1938, pres. 1940), Pan Am. Assn., Inc. (trustee 1952—), Indiana Soc., Theta Kappa Psi. Baptist. Mason (33). Clubs: Lima Country, Lima Golf (Peru); Cosmos (Washington); Explorers (N.Y.); Lake Shore (Chgo.); Pan Am. Clipper. Contbr. med articles to profl. pubs. Home and office: Westchester Apts 3900 Cathedral Av NW Washington DC 20016

DEVCICH, MICHAEL MILES, textiles co. exec.; b. Hoboken, N.J., Nov. 8, 1911; s. Christopher and Mary (Devcich) D.; grad. high sch.; m. Mary Kalugera, Nov. 9, 1941; children—Richard M., Carol M. With Pacific Mills, N.Y.C., 1929—, v.p. charge merchandising, 1956-59, exec. v.p. merchandising, 1959-66, pres., 1966-68; exec. v.p. Burlington Worsted div. Burlington Industries, 1968- -. Clubs: Ridgewood (N.J.) Country, Englewood Yacht. Home: 15 N Saddle Brook Dr Ho-Ho-Kus, NJ 07423. Office: 1290 Av of Americas New York City NY 10019

DEVEAU, THOMAS C., hotel exec.; b. Schenectady, June 19, 1906; s. Thomas R. and Anne (Hughes) D.; A.B., Cornell U., 1927; m. Elizabeth Reardon, July 27, 1929; children—Thomas C., John R. Gen. mgr. Sheraton-Biltmore Hotel, Providence, 1948-52; gen mgr. Sheraton-Mt. Royal Hotel, Montreal, Can., 1952-56; v.p., gen. mgr. Park Sherton Hotel, N.Y.C., 1956-62; Midwest div. mgr., v.p. Sheraton Corp. Am., 1962—. Mem. Canadian (past v.p.) R.I. (past pres.), Montreal (past pres.), Am., Greater St. Louis hotel assns., Sigma Nu. Address: Sheraton-Jefferson Hotel St Louis MO 63101

DE VEER, WILLIAM KIPP, banker; b. Hoboken, N.J., Nov. 18, 1914; s. William H. and Henrietta (Kipp) de V.; A.B., N.Y.U., 1936, LL.B., 1940, J.D., 1968; m. Frances Hutchison, June 9, 1945; children—William H., Nancy K. Admitted to N.Y. bar, 1941; with Bank of Manhattan Co., 1935-37, Empire Trust Co., 1938-42, Chase Nat. Bank, 1946; pres., dir. Financial Consultants, Inc., Miami, Fla., 1946-65; v.p. First Nat. Bank, Palm Beach, Fla., 1955-57, pres., dir., 1965—; pres., dir. Arthur V. Davis Co., 1959-65; dir. Am.-Bankers Life Assurance Co., Oceanography Devel. Corp. Mem. Palm Beach Civic Assn., 1955—. Trustee Bassett Found., Janet R. and Wiley R. Reynolds Jr. Found. Served to lt. comdr. USNR, 1942-46. Mem. Phi

Delta Phi. Episcopalian. Clubs: Miami, (Miami); Everglades, Beach Breakers Golf, Palm Beach Sailfish, Ocean Old Guard Society Palm Beach Golfers (Palm Beach, Fla.). Home: 220 Orange Grove Rd Palm Beach FL 33480 Office: 255 S County Rd Palm Beach FL 33480

DE VELDER, MARION, clergyman; b. Boyden, Ia., Jan. 28, 1912; s. Franklin Dirk and Aartje (Ver Hoef) de V.; A.B., Central Coll., Ia., 1934, D.D., 1950; B.D., New Brunswick Theol. Sem., N.J., 1937; postgrad. U. Chgo. Div. Sch., summers 1944, 45, Preaching Workshop, 1956; m. Mable Edith Wandscheer, Aug. 15, 1935; children—Mark Elton, Mary Ellen, Anne Christine. Ordained to ministry Reformed Ch., 1937; sutdent pastor, Griggstown, N.J., 1935-37; minister North and Southampton Ref. Ch., Churchville, Pa., 1937-39, Hope Ref. Ch., Holland, Mich., 1939-51, 52-59, Central Reformed Ch., Grand Rapids, 1959-61; stated clk. Reformed Ch. Am., 1961-68, gen sec., 1968—; tchr. Western Theol. Sem., Holland, Mich., 1944, 45, 54, 55, 57; speaker Ch. of Air, CBS, 1946-59. Dir. United Advance Fund, Ref. Ch. Am., 1946-49; chmn. commn. United Approach, 1949-52; pres. Gen. Synod, Ref. Ch. Am., 1958-59 mem. labor mediation panels, Mich., 1942, 46. Mem. gen. bd. Nat. Council Chs., 1961—, rec. sec., 1966-69, chmn. gen. adminstrn. and finance com., 1969—; exec. com. World Alliance Ref. Chs., 1961—; bd. dirs. Religion in Am. Life, 1961; exec. com., vice chmn. U.S. Conf., World Council Chs. Rotarian (pres.) Holland 1955-56. Contbr. articles mags., sermons religious publs. Home: 506 Heights Rd Ridgewood NJ 07450 Office: 475 Riverside Dr New York City NY 10027

DEVENING, ROBERT RANDOLPH, food co. exec.; b. San Francisco, Mar. 8, 1942; s. John I. and Jean (Devening) Bolen; grad. Phillips Andover Acad., 1959; A.B. in Internat. Relations, Stanford, 1963; M.B.A., Harvard, 1966; m. Susan Church Willis, Feb. 8, 1964; children—Jennifer McQueen, Brian Willis, Jason Bolen. With Price Waterhouse & Co., C.P.A.'s, 1963-64, Applied Power Industries, Inc., Milw., 1966-67; with Jos. Schlitz Brewing Co., 1967- 70, dir. distbn. planning and research, 1969-70; controller Fairmont Foods Co., Omaha, 1970—. Pres. Stanford Alumni Club Wis., 1968; sec.- treas. Harvard Bus. Sch. Club Milw., 1968-69. Mem. Delta Tau Delta. Home: 8414 Hickory St Omaha NB 68124 Office: 3201 Farnam St Omaha NB 68101

DEVENOW, CHESTER, mfg. co. exec.; b. Detroit, Mar. 3, 1919; s. Samuel E. and Bessie (Aronow) D.; B.A., N.Y. U., 1941; postgrad. Harvard Law Sch., 1941-42; m. Marilyn S. Fruchtman, Apr. 20, 1947; children—Mark Stephen, Jeffrey, Sara, Susan. Pres., dir. Globe-Wernicke Industries, Inc., 1954-67; pres., chief exec. officer, dir. Sheller-Globe Corp.; chmn. bd. Superior Coach Corp.; pres. Community Improvement Corp. Toledo; dir. Merg. Nat. Bank, Miami, GAC Corp. Trustee Blue Cross Northwest Ohio, Riverside Hosp. Served to 1st lt. AUS, 1942-45. Decorated Bronze Star. Clubs: Glengarry Country (Holland, O.); Town (Toledo); Belmont Country; Brynwyck Golf. Home: 3000 Valleyview Dr Toledo OH 43615 Office: 1505 Jefferson Av Toledo OH 43624

DEVEREAUX, HELENA TRAFFORD, (Mrs. James Fentress), found. and ednl. cons.; b. Phila., Feb. 2, 1885; d. Arthur Trafford and Betsy (Blyton) Devereux; ed. Phila. Normal Sch., Temple U., U. Pa.; m. James Fentress (dec.). Founder dir. Devereux Schs., in Devon, Berwyn, Paoli, Malvern, Glenmore (all Pa.), Santa Barbara, Cal., Tex., Mass., Conn., and Arizona; adminstrv. cons. to Devereux Found., which operates Devereux Schools for Dynamic Edn., also the Dr. G. Henry Katz Research Dept. and Dr. Clinton P. McCord Tng. Center. Hon. fellow Am. Physchiatric Assn. (life mem.), Phila. Assn. Psychoanalysis (affiliate), Psychoanalytic Soc. Phila. (affiliate), Am. Assn. Mental Deficiency (life), P.E.O., Delta Kappa Gamma (hon.). Address: 556 S Waterloo Rd Devon PA 19333

DEVEREUX, EDWARD CLIFTON, Jr., educator, sociologist; b. Great Neck, N.Y., Sept. 14, 1912; s. Edward Clifton and Annabel (Rickert) D.; grad. Phillips Exeter Acad., 1930; A.B., Harvard, 1934, M.A., 1938, Ph.D., 1950; m. Edwina Embree, May 16, 1942; children—Catherine Day, John Rickert. Instr. sociology U. Toronto, 1940- 42; asst. prof. sociology Princeton, 1945-50 research asso. Columbia, 1949-50, asso. prof., 1950-55; prof. child devel. and family relations Cornell U., 1955—, chmn. dept., 1966—; Fulbright research scholar U. Frankfurt (Germany), 1956-57. Pres., bd. dirs. Tompkins County Mental Health Assn., 196163. Served to lt. USNR, 1942-45. Recipient Burgess award Nat. Council Family Relations, 1960. Mem. Am. Sociol. Assn., Nat. Council Family Relations. Unitarian (trustee 1966-69). Asso. editor Jour. Marriage and The Family, 1965-69, Child Devel., 1969—. Home: 416 Cayuga Heights Rd Ithaca NY 14850

DEVEREUX, LAWRENCE HACKETT, indsl. exec.; b. N.Y.C., Aug. 14, 1929; s. Philip L. and Agnes (Hackett) D.; A.B., Holy Cross Coll., 1951; M.B.A., N.Y.U. Grad. Sch. Bus., 1958; m. Alice Fraser, Nov. 17, 1956; children-Lawrence, Elizabeth, Alison. Asst. treas., asst. controller, Hewitt Robins, 1956-65; asst. comptroller, Ingersoll Rand Corp., 1965-68; v.p., controller Amerace Esna Corp., N.Y.C., 1968—. Served to 1st lt. USMC, 1951-53. Mem. Financial Execs. Inst. Club: Union League (N.Y.C.). Home: 6 Birchwood Lane Westport CT 06880 Office: 245 Park Av New York NY 10017

DEVETZI, VASSO, pianist; b. Salonika, Greece, Sept. 9, 1929; s. Constantin and Marie (Koulis) D.; laureate Govt. Conservatory Greece, 1942; grad. U. Salonika, 1945; student Acad. Margerite Long-Jacques Thibaud, Paris, 1951. Concert pianist, 1955—; soloist Gt. Symphonic Concerts, Paris, 1951—; numerous recitals throughout Europe, U.S., S. Am.; rec. artist His Master's Voice, Philips. Recipient gold cross Efpiia (Greece), 1965; medal art and lit. Paris, 1960; Internat. Grad Prix of Record, Paris, 1963, 70. Address: 14 rue du Dobropol Paris 17e France

DE VILLAFRANCA, GEORGE WARREN, educator; b. Meriden, Conn., Nov. 21, 1923; s. Jose Francisco and Ruth (Pease) de V.; B.S., Yale U., 1948, Ph.D., 1953; m. Suzanne E. Crane, July 26, 1947 (dec. Nov. 1960); children—Suzanne C., Ruth P., George W.; m. 2d, Erica Satzinger, July 13, 1965. Instr. R.I. State Coll., 1948; instr. zoology Smith Coll., 1951-54, asst. prof., 1954-59, asso. prof., 1959-63, prof., 1963—, asst. to pres., 1961-66, chmn. dept. biol. sci., 1968—; cons. NSF, 1968. Served with USAAF, 1943-46. Lalor Found. fellow, 1953, 56; Am. Cancer Soc. fellow, 1954-55. Mem. Am. Soc. Zoologists, Biophys. Soc., Soc. Gen. Physiologists, A.A.A.S., Sigma Xi. Home: 88 N Elm St Northampton MA 01060

DEVIN, WILLIAM AUGUSTUS, Jr., lawyer; b. Oxford, N.C., May 21, 1904; s. William Augustus and Virginia Hunter (Bernard) D.; A.B., U. N.C., 1926, postgrad. law sch., 1926-28; m. Margaret Peyton Jarboe, Apr. 30, 1935; children—Virginia Peyton, William Augustus III, Robert Spotswood, Margaret Lewis. Admitted to N.C. bar, 1928; practiced in Durham, 1928-30, Hickory, 1930-40; N.C. gen. counsel Home Mortgage Co., N.C. Mortgage Corp., Mortgage Service Corp., 1930-40; head atty. HOLC, Washington, 1940-42; counsel R.F.C., Washington, 1942- 51, asst. gen. counsel, 1951-57; asst. gen. counsel Fed. Facilities Corp., Washington, 1954-57; asst. chief counsel, office def. lending Dept. Treasury, 1954-57, chief counsel, 1957-64, spl. asst. to gen. counsel, 1964—; gen. counsel War Damage Corp. 1957-60. Mem. N.C. Bar Assn., N.C. State Bar, Kappa Sigma, Phi Delta Phi. Episcopalian. Clubs: Monogram (U. N.C.); Manor Country (Norbeck, Md.). Home: 1519 Red Oak Dr Silver Spring MD 20910 Office: Main Treasury Bldg Washington DC 20224

DEVINATZ, ALLEN, educator, mathematician; b. Chgo., July 22, 1922; s. Victor and Kate (Bass) D.; B.S., Ill. Inst. Tech., 1944; A.M., Harvard, 1947, Ph.D., 1950; m. Pearl Moskowitz, Sep. 16, 1956; children—Victor Gary, Ethan Sander. Instr., Ill. Inst. Tech., 1950-52; NSF Postdoctoral fellow, 1952-53; fellow Inst. for Advanced Study, 1953-54; asst. prof. U. Conn., 1954-55; faculty Washington U., St. Louis, 1955-67, prof., 1961-67; prof. math. Northwestern U., Evanston, Ill., 1967—. Sr. NSF Postdoctoral fellow, 1960-61. Mem. Am. Math. Soc., Sigma Xi, Tau Beta Pi. Contbr. articles profl. jours. Home: 626 La Vergne Av Wilmette IL 60091 Office: Dept Math Northwestern U Lunt Bldg Evanston IL 60201

DEVINE, C. ROBERT, pub. co. exec.; b. Clarksburg, W.Va., June 13, 1917; s. James J. and Frances M. (Ryan) D.; grad. Princeton, 1938; m. Louise C. Williams, Mar. 27, 1943; children—Mallory C., Rodney W., Ian C. Promotion, research dir. U.S. News Pub. Co., 1946-48, asst. advt. dir., 1948-55; exec. bus. dept. Reader's Digest, N.Y.C., 1955-58, advt. dir. Internat. Editions, 1958-60, asst. gen. mgr., 1960-66, dep. gen. mgr. Internat. editions, 1966, now v.p., dir. pub. relations Reader's Digest Assn., Inc. Dir., mem. finance com. Met. Opera Assn. Trustee Vail-Deane Sch. Served from pvt. to maj., AUS, World War II. Decorated Bronze Star medal. Mem. Sales Exec. Club, Internat. Advt. Assn. (pres.), 1962-64, (dir. at large), Internat. C. of C., Mag. Pubs. Assn. (chmn. internat. com. 1964- -), Mil. Order Fgn. Wars, N.A.M. (mem. pres.'s adv. group for internat. affairs), Pub. Relations Soc. Am., N.Y. Grand Jury Assn. Republican. Episcopalian. Rotarian. Clubs: Squadron A, Dutch Treat; Union, River (N.Y.C.). Home: 105 E 67th St New York City NY 10021 Office: 200 Park Av New York City NY 10017

DEVINE, DAVID FRANCIS, ins. co. exec.; b. Boston, Feb. 26, 1929; s. John Morrison and Marguerite (Curley) D.; A.B., Harvard, 1952; m. Marie Carol Young, Nov. 8, 1952; children—Carol Frances, Deborah Marie, Marcia Calder, Amy Elizabeth. Group rep. John Hancock Mut. Life Ins. Co., 1954-56; with Boston Mut. Life Ins. Co., 1956—, v.p., corp. sec., 1967—; sec., treas., dir. Boston Mut. Equity Growth Fund, Inc.; dir. Boston Mut. Sales Corp. Asst. dist. commr. Town of Needham, Boston council Boy Scouts Am., 1961-68; mem. finance com. Town of Needham. Served with USMCR, 1952-54; lt. col. Res. Mem. Life Office Mgmt. Assn., Am. Mgmt. Assn., Marine Corps Res. Officers Assn. (past pres. Tripoli chpt.). Clubs: Harvard (Boston); Needham Pool and Racquet. Home: 141 Dawson Dr Needham MA 02192 Office: 156 Stuart St Boston MA 02116

DEVINE, FRANK JAMES, fgn. service officer; b. Albany, N.Y., June 30, 1922; s. Frank James and Margaret (Groat) D.; B.B.A., Rensselaer Poly. Inst., 1943; postgrad. U. Wis. 1953-54, Nat. War Coll., 1961-62; m. Barbara Eleanor Ryan, Aug. 26, 1953; children—Margaret Rose, Frank James III, Penelope Anne. Certifying officer Panama Air Depot, Curundu, C.Z., 1946-47; joined U.S. fgn. service, 1948; assigned Barranquilla, Columbia, 1948-50, Montevideo, Uruguay, 1951-53, Santiago, Chile, 1955- 56; spl. asst. Bur. Inter-Am. Affairs, State Dept., 1957-61; 1st sec. Am. embassy, Lisbon, Portugal, 1962-65; counselor embassy, Santo Domingo, 1966-70, minister-counselor embassy, Caracas, Venezuela, 1970—. Served with AUS, 1943-46. Mem. Am. Fgn. Service Assn., Sigma Xi (asso.). Address: Am embassy Caracas Venezuela Office: Dept of State Washington DC 20525

DEVINE, GREGORY S., ry. exec.; b. Rahway, N.J., Mar. 20, 1906; s. Gregory and Mary (Barry) D.; student St. Viator's Coll., Northwestern U. Medill Sch. Journalism; m. Ursula Baumann, Dec. 27, 1933; children—Barry, Jon, Suzi; v.p. coal traffic and devel. Chesapeake & Ohio Ry. Co., 1957-60, sr. v.p., 1960- 63, exec. v.p., 1963-64, pres., 1964-71, dir., mem. exec. com., 1964—, chief exec. officer, 1966-71, chmn. exec. com., 1971—; pres., dir., chief exec. officer Balt. & Ohio R.R. Co. until 1971, chmn. bd., 1971—; bd. dirs. Western Maryland Ry. Co., Western Pocahontas Corp., Washington & Old Dominion R.R., Nicholas, Fayette & Greenbrier Rd., Lake Erie Coal Co., Kanawha-Ohio Corp., Ft. St. Union Depot Co. Dir. Nat. Coal Policy Conf. Mem. Assn. of Am. RRs. Clubs: Chicago Athletic; Sky. Pinnacle (N.Y.C.); Union, Pepper Pike, Westwood Country, Clifton (Cleve.). Home: 11610 Harborview Dr Cleveland OH 44102 Office: Chesapeake & Ohio Ry Co Terminal Tower Cleveland OH 44101

DEVINE, JOHN FRANCIS, advt. exec.; b. N.Y.C., Oct. 18, 1916; s. Patrick F. and Anne (Quinn) D.; Ph.B., Holy Cross Coll., 1937; LL.B., Columbia, 1940; m. Rita Kathryn Keating, Feb. 2, 1952; children—Patrick Francis II, Mary Ann. Admitted to N.Y. bar, 1940; atty. J. Walter Thompson Co., N.Y.C., 1946- 53, exec. rev. bd., 1953-55, v.p., 1954—, adminstr. radio and TV, 1955- 60, gen. counsel, 1960-65, adminstrv. v.p., 1964—, sec., 1964-65, dir., 1965—, mem. exec. com., 1966—, exec. v. p. corporate adminstrn., 1969—. Served from ensign to lt. USNR, 1942-45. Decorated knight Equestrian Order of Holy Sepulchre of Jerusalem. Mem. Bar Assn. City N.Y., Soc. Friendly Sons of St. Patrick. Democrat. Roman Catholic. Clubs: Westchester Country, Apawamis (Rye, N.Y.); Holy Cross College (N.Y.C.). Home: Hunter Lane Rye NY 10580 Office: 420 Lexington Av New York City NY 10017

DEVINE, JOSEPH LAWRENCE, drama critic; b. N.Y.C., Sept. 21, 1935; s. John Justin and Hazel (Tippit) DeV.; student Georgetown U., 1953-54, U. Mich., 1954; B.S. in Journalism, Northwestern U., 1957; m. Genevieve Christian, Apr. 29, 1959 (div. 1968); children—John Justin II, Ellen Morse; m. 2d, Lucy Memory Williamson, July 26, 1968. Drama critic Miami (Fla.) Herald, 1962-67; entertainment editor, drama and film critic Los Angeles Herald- Examiner, 1967-68; entertainment editor, drama critic Detroit Free Press, 1968—. Served with AUS, 1958-62. Mem. Beta Theta Pi, Sigma Delta Chi. Home: 1050 Van Dyke Detroit MI 48214 Office: 321 W Lafayette Blvd Detroit MI 48231

DEVINE, MATTHEW LANZA, corp. exec.; b. Salt Lake City, Dec. 17, 1905; s. James and Annie B. (Lanza) D.; B.S., Northwestern U., 1928; LL.B., Georgetown U., 1937; m. Mary Ann Brailsford, Sept. 5, 1928; children—Michael Brailsford, Beatrice Ann (Mrs. David Dellett). Admitted to D.C. bar, 1937, Ill. bar, 1938; engr. Am. System of Reinforcing & Graver Tank & Mfg. Co., Chgo., 1929-33; adminstr. engring. PWA, Washington, 1933-40; mem. mgmt. research group, exec. dept. Gen. Electric Co., Princeton, N.J., 1946-47; sr. asso. Cresap, McCormick & Paget, N.Y.C., Chgo., 1948-49, partner, 1950-60; pres., chief exec. officer, dir. Amphenol Corp. (merged with Bunker-Ramo Corp. 1968) 1960-67, chmn. bd., chief exec. officer, 1967-68, dir., 1968—; dir., Arvin Industries, Inc., Bresnehan Computer Leasing Corp., Sargent-Welch Sci. Co., ILG Industries Inc. Pres. U. Chgo. Cancer Research Found., now vice chmn.; trustee Better Govt. Assn. Served as col. control div. A.S.F., AUS, 1941-45. Decorated Legion of Merit. Mem. Theta Tau, Phi Delta Theta. Clubs: Economic, Sunset Ridge Country, Chicago (Chgo.). Home: 848 Ash St Winnetka IL 60093

DEVINE, RICHARD JOSEPH, univ. dean; b. N.Y.C., Apr. 10, 1929; s. Joseph Leo and Mary (Ballard) D.; B.A. in Philosophy, Mary Immaculate Coll., Northampton, Pa., 1951; M.A. in English, Niagara U., 1957; S.T.D., U. Fribourg (Switzerland), 1963. Joined Congregation of Mission, 1950, ordained priest Roman Cath. Ch., 1955; instr. English, Niagara U., 1959-60, asst. to pres. for devel., 1957-59, dir. student activities, 1959-60; prof. theology Mary Immaculate Sem. and Coll., 1963-66, dir. students, 1963-66; dean Grad. Sch. Arts and Scis., St. John's U., Jamaica, N.Y., 1966-68, dean St. John's Coll., 1968—. Mem. Cath. Theol. Soc. Am. Home: St John's Univ Jamaica NY 11432

DEVINE, SAMUEL LEEPER, congressman; b. South Bend, Ind., Dec. 21, 1915; s. John Francis and Kittie Marie (Leeper) D.; student Colgate U., 1933-34, Ohio State U., 1934-37; LL.B. cum laude, U. Notre Dame, 1940; m. Betty Galloway, Aug. 24, 1940; children—Lois Collins, Joyce Morrell, Carol. Admitted to Ohio bar, 1940; spl. agt. FBI, Dept. Justice, 1940-45; with Hamilton & Kramer, Columbus, 1948-55; pros. atty. Franklin County, O., 1955-58; mem. Ohio Legislature, 1951-55; mem. 86th-92d Congresses 12th Dist. Ohio. Past chmn. Ohio Un-Am. Activities Commn. Mem. Charity Newsies, Soc. Former FBI Agts., Ohio Assn. Football Ofcls., Varsity O Assn. Republican. Methodist. Mason (Shriner). Club: Columbus Country. Home: 195 N Roosevelt Av Columbus OH 43209 Office: Rayburn House Office Bldg Washington DC 20515

DEVINE, THOMAS JOHN, textile industry exec.; b. N.Y.C., Nov. 14, 1927; s. Thomas and Mary Ellen (O'Rourke) D.; B.A. in Bus. Edn., Hunter Coll., N.Y.C., 1950; m. Jean M. Commorato, Feb. 14, 1953; children—Susan, Diane, Thomas John, Laura, Terence. With Arthur Andersen & Co. C.P.A.'s, N.Y.C., 1951-58; asst. comptroller Metro-Goldwyn-Mayer Inc., 1958-64, comptroller, asst. treas., 1964-69; v.p. Finance, dir. Monroe Group, Inc., N.Y.C., 1969—. Served with USNR, 1945-46, 50-52. C.P.A. N.Y., N.J. Mem. Am. Inst. C.P.A.'s N.Y. State, N.J. socs. C.P.A.'s, Am. Accounting Assn. Contbr. articles to profl. jours. Office: 124 W 36th St New York City NY 10018

DEVINE, WALTER JOSEPH, Jr., odd-lot dealer; b. Phila., Oct. 21, 1908; s. Walter Joseph and Ruby S. (Rudrauff) D.; student Peirce Sch. Bus. Adminstrn., Phila., 1927-28, Wharton Sch. U. Pa., eves. 1928-31; m. Doris M. Coady, May 25, 1934; children—Karen E. (Mrs. Walter C. Janney III), Doris R. (Mrs. John C. Elwell). With H.T. Greenwood & Co., Phila., 1936-59, resident partner, 1951-59; self-employed, Phila., 1959—; mem. Phila., Balt., Washington Stock Exchange, 1938—, mem. com. admissions, 1965—, vice chmn. com., 1968, mem. com. floor procedure, 1965-70, chmn. com., 1968, bd. govs., 1965—. Clubs: Union League (Phila.). Aronimink Golf. Home: 428 Louella Av Wayne PA 19087 Office: 17th St and Stock Exchange Pl Philadelphia PA 19103

DEVINO, WILLIAM STANLEY, educator, economist; b. Burlington, Vt., Nov. 17, 1926; s. William Arthur and Elaine Anna (Blaise) D.; B.A., U. Vt., 1951; M.A., U. Conn., 1953; Ph.D., Mich. State U., 1959; m. Raphaella Frances Gillespie, Aug. 27, 1948; children—Bonnie Ann, Denise Marie. Instr. econs. Mich. State U., 1955-57, Ford Found. dissertation fellow econs., 1957-58, research asso. Sch. Labor and Indsl. Relations, 1958-59, lectr. econs., 1959-60; faculty U. Me., Orono, 1960—, prof. bus. and econs., 1963—, dir. Sch. Bus. Adminstrn., 1963-65, dean Coll. Bus. Adminstrn., 1965—. Cons. Mich. Senate Labor Com., 1955; mem. Gov. Mich. Task Force on Labor, 1959; participant Ford Found. Workshop Unemployment Problems and Policy, Goucher Coll., summer 1962; mem. arbitration roster Fed. Mediation and Concilation Service. Served with AUS, World War II. Mem. Am. Arbitration Assn. (nat. labor panel), Am. Econ. Assn., Indsl. Relations Research Assn. Author: Exhaustion of Unemployment Benefits During a Recession, 1960; co-author: A Study of Textile Mill Closings in Selected New England Communities, 1966. Contbr. articles to profl. jours. Home: 358 Howard St Bangor ME 04401

DEVITT, EDWARD JAMES, dist. judge; b. St. Paul, May 5, 1911; s. Thomas Phillip and Catherine Ethel (McGuire) D.; LL.B., U. N.D., 1935, B.S., 1936, also LL.D.; m. Marcelle M. LaRose, Apr. 22, 1939; children—Marcelle Terese, Timothy Patrick. Admitted to D.C., Minn., Ill. and N.D. bars; practiced in East Grand Forks, Minn., 1935-39, St. Paul, 1946—; municipal judge, 1935-39; asst. atty. gen., Minn., 1939-42; instr. law U. N.D., 1935-39, St. Paul Coll. Law, 1945—; mem. 80th Congress, 4th Minn. Dist.; probate judge Ramsey County, St. Paul, 1950-54; U.S. dist. judge, 1954—. Bd. dirs. Fed. Judicial Center. Served as intelligence officer USNR, 1942-46. Decorated Purple Heart. Fellow Am. Bar Found.; mem. Am., Minn., Ramsey County bar assns., Am. Judicature Soc., Am. Legion, V.F.W., D.A.V., Order of Coif, Blue Key, Phi Delta Phi, Beta Gamma Sigma, Delta Sigma Rho. Republican. Roman Catholic. K.C. Club: Athletic (St. Paul). Author: (with Blackmar) Federal Jury Practice and Instructions. Home: 1676 S Mississippi River Blvd St. Paul, MN 55116. Office: Federal Courts Bldg St Paul MN 55101

DEVITT, JAMES E., ins. co. exec.; b. St. Paul, July 23, 1920; s. Louis J. and Gertrude (Cavanaugh) D.; B.B.A., U. Minn., 1942; LL.B., Harvard, 1949. Admitted to Minn. bar; practice in St. Paul, 1949-51; with Northwestern Nat. Life Ins. Co., Mpls., 1951-56, group sec., 1952-56; with Mut. of N.Y., N.Y.C., 1956—, v.p. health ins., 1965-67, v.p. underwriting, 1967-69, sr. v.p., 1969—. Served to capt., inf., AUS, World War II. Mem. Beta Gamma Sigma. Clubs: Harvard (N.Y.C.); Gardiner's Bay Country (Shelter Island, N.Y.). Home: 215 E 79th St New York City NY 10021 also Dinah Rock Rd Shelter Island Heights NY 11965 Office: 1740 Broadway New York City NY 10019

DEVITT, JOHN HARDEN, paper mfg. co. exec.; b. Conneaut, O., June 8, 1903; s. Duff and Henrietta (Harden) D.; student pub. schs.; m. Edith Rust, 1921; 1 son, Robert Duff. With Hammermill Paper Co., Erie, Pa., 1922—, pres., 1963—, chief exec. officer, 1965—, chmn. bd., chmn. exec. com., 1969—, also dir.; dir. Am. Sterilizer Co., Grays Harbor Paper Co., Gen. Pub. Utility, N.Y., 1st Nat. Bank, Erie. Bd. dirs. Am. Paper Inst., N.Y.C.; bd. incorporators Hamot, St. Vincent's hosps., Erie; mem. lay adv. bd. Gannon Coll., Erie. Mem. Nat. Assn. Accountants (past nat. pres.). Republican. Episcopalian. Clubs: Erie, Kahkwa (Erie). Home: 5275 Wolf Rd Erie PA 16505 Office: East Lake Rd Erie PA 16507

DEVLIN, BERNADETTE JOSEPHINE, mem. Brit. parliament; b. Cookstown, No. Ireland, Apr. 23, 1947; d. John James and Elizabeth Bernadette Devlin; ed. Queens U., Belfast; 1 daughter. Participated in No. Ireland's first massive civil rights demonstration, 1968; co-organizer People's Democracy at Queens U., 1968, Young Socialists Alliance march from Belfast to Londonderry, 1969; M.P. from No. Ireland, 1969—; tried and sentenced to prison, 1970; served 4 months in Armagh Prison, 1970. Roman Catholic. Author: The Price of My Soul, 1969. Address: House of Commons London S W 1 England*

DEVLIN, COLUMBIA JOHN, clergyman; b. Phila., Oct. 24, 1922; s. Hugh Edward and Mary Elizabeth (McCusker) D.; student St. Francis Coll., Loretto, Pa., 1941-44; B.A., Cath. U. Am., 1945, S.T.L., 1950, M.A., 1951. Ordained priest Roman Cath. Ch., 1949; instr.

history St. Francis Prep. Sch., Spring Cove, Pa., 1951-53, St. Thomas More High Sch., Phila., 1953-56; acad. dean St. Francis Coll., 1956-59; pres., 1959-62; pres . Coll. of Steubenville (O.), 1962-69; minister provincial Sacred Heart Province 3d Order Regular St. Francis, Pitts. Bd. govs. Pa. Com. Edn., 1961. Mem. Citizens Adv. Planning Com. Steubenville. Mem. Nat. Cath. Edn. Assn., Am. Council Edn., N.E.A., Francescan Ednl. Conf., Steubenville C. of C. Lion. Address: 601 Pitcairn Pl Pittsburgh PA 15232

DEVLIN, EDWARD JAMES, indsl. financial exec.; b. Evanston, Ill., Dec. 27, 1925; s. Edward J. and Lucille (Emory) D.; B.S., Northwestern U., 1950, grad. student, 1951; m. Anita Landucci, Feb. 4, 1959; children—Lisa Maria, Michael Scott. Domestic and internat. operations Ford Motor Co., 1952-66; corporate controller Polaroid Corp., 1966-68; v.p. finance and adminstrn. Consol. Cigar Corp.-Gulf & Western Corp., N.Y.C., 1969—; Served to 2d lt. F.A. Parachute Inf., AUS, 1944-48. Mem. Financial Execs. Inst., Sigma Chi. Home: 10 Deerwood Rd Westport CT 06880 Office: 1 Gulf and Western Plaza New York City NY 10023

DEVLIN, JOHN H., steel co. exec.; b. 1921; B.B.A., U. Ill., 1943; married. With Libby, McNeill & Libby, 1946-47, Laramore & Douglas, 1947-51; with Fansteel Inc., North Chicago, Ill., 1951—, v.p. adminstrn. and finance, 1963—. Served with AUS, 1943-46. C.P.A., Ill. Office: 1 Tantalum Pl North Chicago IL 60604*

DEVLIN, JOHN HERBERT, brewing co. exec.; b. Toronto, Can., Mar. 23, 1920; s. Charles D. and Florence Devlin; ed. Upper Can. Coll., Toronto; m. Margaret Lorraine Hopkins, Mar. 8, 1947; children—Julie, Jane, Lesley. Advt. mgr. Duplate Can. Ltd. and Asso. Companies, Toronto, 1946-53; gen. sales mgr. Smith & Stone Ltd., Toronto, 1953-59; exec. v.p. then pres. Rock City Sakes Ltd., 1959; pres. Rothmans of Pall Mall Can., Ltd., 1959; chmn. bd., chief exec. officer Canadian Breweries Ltd.; chmn. Carling Brewing Co.; dir. Rothmans Group Services, S.A., Luxembourg, Rock City Tobacco Co. (1960) Ltd., Crown Life Ins. Co.; mem. Toronto adv. bd. Royal Trust Co. Bd. dirs. Art Gallery Ontario, Ontario, Rothmans Art Gallery, Stratford; bd. govs. Dominion Drama Festival. Served to flight lt. Royal Canadian Air Force. Mem. Anglican Ch. Clubs: Badminton and Racquet, Royal Canadian Yacht (Toronto). Home: 240 Dunvegan Rd Toronto 7 Ontario Canada Office: 75 Dufflaw Rd Toronto 19 Ontario Canada*

DEVLIN, PAUL, investment banker; b. Chgo., Jan. 5, 1903; s. John L. and Carmen (Blesch) D.; student U. Ill., 1926; m. Mary L. Brinkmann, July 5, 1924; children—Mary Lou (Mrs. Edward J. O'Rourke), Joann (Mrs. C. Henry Roath). With Blyth & Co., Inc., N.Y.C., 1924—, now chmn. bd., mem. exec. com.; dir. Banque Blyth & Cie, Paris. Clubs: N.Y. Stock Exchange Lunch, Bond, 29 (N.Y.C.); Apawamis (Rye, N.Y.); Ocean, Delray Yacht, Country of Fla. (Delray Beach, Fla.); Old Baldy (Saratoga, Wyo.); Blind Brook (Portchester, N.Y.). Home: 4 Plymouth Rd Rye NY 10580 Office: 14 Wall St New York City NY 10005

DEVLIN, WALTER J., distilling co. exec.; b. High Bridge, N.J., Oct. 23, 1915; s. John and Anna (Sheehan) D.; grad. Lawrenceville Sch., 1933; A.B., Princeton, 1937; LL.B., Harvard, 1940; m. Genevieve Dickson, Dec. 29, 1945; children—John, Patricia, Peter, Mary Sean. With Lindabury-DePue-Faulks, Newark, 1940-42, RFC, N.Y.C., 1942-43; with Fleischmann Distilling Corp., N.Y.C., 1943—, asst. to pres., 1946-53, v.p., 1953-65, exec. v.p., 1965—. Mem. Distilled Spirits Inst. (chmn. bd.), Distillers Feed Research Council (dir.), Ky. Distillers Assn. (dir.). Home: 125 Crescent Lane East Hills Roslyn NY 11576 Office: 625 Madison Av New York City NY 10022

DEVOE, ARTHUR GERARD, physician; b. Seattle, Mar. 24, 1909; s. Ralph Godwin and Frances Reba (Gerard) D.; A.B., Yale, 1931; M.D., Cornell, 1935; D.Med. Sci., Columbia, 1940; m. Margaret Stobie, Jan. 21, 1939; children—Gerard Ely, David Ramsay, Ralph Godwin. Intern Bellevue Hosp., N.Y.C., 1935-37; resident ophthalmologist Presbyn. Hosp., 1937-40, dir. Inst. Ophthalmology, 1959—; dir. eye service Bellevue and Univ. Hosps., 1950; asso. in ophthalmology Coll. Phys. and Surg., Columbia, 1942-50; prof. ophthalmology and chmn. dept. N.Y. U. Post Grad. Med. Sch. 1950-59, Columbia, 1959—; sr. cons. U.S. Vets. Hosp., Manhattan, 1955; research com. Nat. Council to Combat Blindness. Served with M.C., AUS, 1942-46. Diplomate Am. Bd. Ophthalmology (mem. bd.). Fellow A.C.S., N.Y. Acad. Medicine; mem. A.M.A., N.Y. Acad. Scis., Societe Francais d'Ophthalmologie, Am. Ophthal. Soc., Am. Acad. Ophthalmology and Otolaryngology, Assn. for Research in Ophthalmology, Pan Am. Ophthal. Soc., Beta Theta Pi. Club: Century Assn. (N.Y.C.). Contbr. articles to sci. jours. Home: 35 Woodmill Rd Chappaqua, NY 10514. Office: 635 W 165th St New York City NY 10032

DE VOGELAERE, RENE J., educator. Prof. math. U. Cal. at Berkeley. Office: 301 Campbell Hall U Cal Berkeley CA 94720*

DEVOL, KENNETH STOWE, educator; b. Los Angeles, Apr. 3, 1929; s. Howard Putnam and Gladys (Harris) D.; A.B., U. So. Cal., 1951, M.S., 1954, Ph.D., 1965; m. Shirley May Dixon, Dec. 30, 1951; children—Sharon Marie, Randall Putnam. Instr. jour. Van Nuys (Cal.) High Sch., 1953-55; chmn. journalism Los Angeles Valley Coll., 1955-61; asst. prof. San Fernando Valley State Coll., 1961-65, asso. prof., 1965-69, prof., chmn. jour., 1969—; judge news awards Radio-TV News Assn. So. Cal., 1969; judge Nat. Acad. TV Arts and Scis., 1971. Mem. Assn. for Edn. in Journalism (mem. exec. com. 1970-71), Am. Soc. Schs. and Depts. of Jour., Am. Assn. U. Profs., Am. Civil Liberties Union, Sigma Delta Chi, Kappa Tau Alpha. Author: (with Esther Davis) Writing Style For Journalists, 1962; Mass Media and the Supreme Court: The Legacy of the Warren Years, 1971. Home: 16953 Superior St Sepulveda CA 91343 Office: 18111 Nordhoff St Northridge CA 91324

DEVOLLD, WALTER LEONARD, educator; b. Zanesville, O., Nov. 20, 1911; s. Leonard and Louise (Haarer) DeV.; B.A., Ohio State U., 1935, M.A., 1937, B.Ed., 1940; Ph.D., Western Res. U., 1958; m. Mary Edith Wall, Sept. 6, 1942. Instr. German, St. John's Mil. Acad., Delafield, Wis., 1940-46; asst. prof. Tex. A. and M. U., 1946-47; mem. faculty Kent State U., 1947—, chmn. dept. Germanic and Slavic langs., 1965—, prof. German, 1968—. Mem. Am. Assn. Tchrs. German, Am. Assn. U. Profs., Ohio Modern Lang. Tchrs. Assn. (pres. 1969-70). Home: 3573 Summit Rd Ravenna OH 44266 Office: Kent State Univ Kent OH 44242

DEVONS, SAMUEL, educator, physicist; b. Bangor, N.Wales, U.K., Sept. 30, 1914; s. David Isaac and Edith (Edlestein) D.; B.A., Trinity Coll., Cambridge (Eng.) U., 1935, M.A., Ph.D. (Exhbn. 1851 scholar), 1939; M.Sc., Manchester (Eng.) U., 1959; m. Celia Ruth Toubkin, Sept. 7, 1938; children—Susan Danielle, Judith Rosalind, Amanda Jane, Cathryn Ann Julie. Came to U.S., 1959. Sr. sci. officer Air Ministry, Ministry Supply, U.K., 1939-45; fellow, dir. studies, lectr. physics Trinity Coll., 1946-49; prof. physics Imperial Coll., London, Eng., 1950-55; Langworthy prof. physics, dir. phys. labs. U. Manchester, 1955-60; prof. physics Columbia, 1960—, chmn. dept., 1963-67. Royal Soc.-Leverhulme vis. prof., Andhra, India, 1967-68. Mem. Tech. Assistance-UNESCO Team of UN to S. Am., 1957. Served with RAF, 1944-45. Recipient Rutherford medal and prize Inst. Physics, U.K., 1970. Fellow Phys. Soc. London (past v.p.), Royal Soc. London, Am. Phys. Soc. Author: Excited States of Nuclei, 1949. Editor: Biology and the Physical Sciences, 1969; High Energy Physics and Nuclear Structure, 1970. Home: Lewis Rd Irvington-on-Hudson NY 10533 Office: Dept Physics Columbia U New York City NY 10027

DEVOR, JOHN WESLEY, educator; b. Custer County, Neb., July 19, 1901; s. John William and Rhoda Ann (Gilmore) D.; student Central Coll., McPherson, Kan., 1920-22; A.B., U. Kan., 1924, M.A., 1929; Ph.D., U. Chgo., 1952; m. Lois Blanche Batchelder, Dec. 25, 1924. Tchr. pub. schs., Rankin, Okla., Covert, Kan., Belle Plaine, Kan., Wichita, Kan., 1919-48; asso. prof. Asbury Coll., 1948-52, prof. edn., 1952-53, chmn. div. edn. and psychology, 1954-56; prof. edn. Am. U., 1956-59, chmn. dept. edn., 1959-60, chmn. div. edn., 1960-67, prof. edn., 1967-71, also dir. secondary edn., 1967-70, prof. emeritus edn., 1971—. Mem. Nat. Commn. Tchr. Edn. and Profl. Standards. Mem. Am. Assn. U. Profs., Assn. Higher Edn., Am. Assn. Sch. Adminstrs., N.E.A., Assn. Supervision and Curriculum Devel., Nat. Sci. Tchrs. Assn. (regional dir. 1949-52), Assn. Tchr. Educators (pres. Ky. 1954-55, chmn. com. on arrangements nat. workshop 1955), Nat. Soc. Study Edn., D.C. Edn. Assn., Fed. Schoolmen's Club. Methodist (vice chmn. ofcl. bd.). Author: Learning Experiences for Student Teachers, rev. edit., 1958; Guide for Supervising Teachers, 1957; The Experience of Student Teaching, 1964. Contbr. articles ednl. jours. Home: 6560 Montezuma Rd San Diego CA 92115

DEVORE, BOYD IRVEN, educator; b. Joy, Tex., Oct. 7, 1934; s. Boyd Irven and Clara (Hurt) DeV.; B.A., U. Tex., 1956; M.A., U. Chgo., 1959, Ph.D., 1962; M.A. (hon.), Harvard, 1966; m. Nancy Marie Skiles, Apr. 20, 1956; children—Gregory Irven, Marie Claire. Baboon research, Kenya, 1959; asst. prof. anthropology U. Cal., Berkeley, 1960-61; fellow Miller Inst. Basic Research, 1961-62; fellow Center for Advanced Study in Behavioral Scis., Palo Alto, Cal., 1962-63; Bushman research, Botswana, 1963-64, 67-68; lectr. anthroplogy Harvard, 1963-66, asso. prof., 1966-69, prof., 1969—; cons. NIH, Edn. Devel. Center, Cambridge, Mass., Danforth Found., St. Louis, Nat. Humanities Faculty, Concord, Mass. Recipient Walker prize for meritorious sci. investigation and discovery Museum of Sci., Boston, 1970. Fellow A.A.S., Am. Acad. Arts and Scis., Am. Anthrop. Assn. (mem. exec. bd.). Author: (with S. Eimerl) The Primates, 1965. Editor: Primate Behavior, 1965; (with R.B. Lee) Man the Hunter, 1968. Home: 33 Hurlbut St Cambridge MA 02138

DEVORE, GEORGE WARREN, educator, geologist; b. Laramie, Wyo., Apr. 29, 1924; s. George W. and Isabella (Norene) DeV.; B.S., U. Wyo., 1948, M.A., U. Chgo., 1950, Ph.D., 1952; m. jean Marie Bowen, Sept. 12, 1952; children—Jeffrey Steven, Carol Kimberly. Geologist, U.S. Geol. Survey, 1946-64; instr., then asst. prof. geology U. Chgo., 1950-60; mem. faculty Fla. State U., 1960—, prof. geology, chmn. dept., 1963-. Served with USAAF, 1943-46. Fellow Mineral Soc. Am.; mem. Clay Mineral Soc., A.A.A.S., Norsk Geologische Forening, Sigma Xi. Home: 2350 Armistead St Tallahassee, FL 32302.

DE VORE, THOMAS FRANKLIN, ins. co. exec.; b. Huron, S.D., June 28, 1929; s. Hubert Marlo and Lora (Coursey) De V.; grad. high sch.; m. Margaret Antonia Sahene, Nov. 15, 1952; children—Christopher Franklin, Leslie Frances, Stephanie Lynn, Jeffrey Michael. Employment mgr. O'Keefe & Merritt Co., Los Angeles, 1953-54; dir. personnel Price-Pfister Brass Mfg. Co., Los Angeles, 1954-55; adminstrv. v.p. Occidental Life Ins. Co. Cal., Los Angeles, 1955-71, v.p., mng. dir. for Japan, 1971—; Transam. Ins. Corp. Cal., Los Angeles, 1970-71. Cons. Jr. Achievement, 1966—, Los Angeles County Heart Assn., 1970-71; active United Crusade, 1968—. Served with USAF, 1949-52. Home: 631 E Athens St Altadena CA 91001 Office: 1150 S Olive St Los Angeles CA 90015

DEVOS, RICHARD MARVIN, chem. co. exec.; b. Grand Rapids, Mich., Mar. 4, 1926; s. Simon C. and Ethel R. (Dekker) DeV.; student Calvin Coll., 1946; m. Helen J. Van Wesep, Feb. 7, 1953; children—Richard Marvin, Daniel George, Suzanne Cheryl, Douglas Lee. Partner, Wolverine Air Service, 1946-49; pres. Ja-Ri Corp., 1949—, Amway Corp., 1959—, Amway of Can. Ltd., 1964—, Amway Pty. Ltd., Australia, 1970—; dir. Cascade/Data Computer Systems, Inc. Bd. dirs., past pres. Kent County Tb and Emphysema Soc.; pres., bd. dirs. Grand Rapids Jr. Achievement, 1966-67; bd. dirs., mem. exec. com. Nat. Jr. Achievement; trustee Am. Econ. Found.; bd. advisers St. Mary's Hosp.; bd. dirs. Wedgewood Acres. Served with USAAF, 1944-46. Recipient Alexander Hamilton award Econ. Edn. from Freedoms Found.; Distinguished Salesman of Year award Grand Rapids Sales and Marketing Execs. Mem. Grand Rapids C. of C. (bd. dirs.), Sales and Marketing Execs. (bd. dirs.). Mem. Reformed Ch. (elder, chmn. finannce com.) Home: 7154 Windy Hill Rd Grand Rapids MI 49506 Office: 7575 E Fulton Rd Ada MI 49301

DEVOSS, JAMES THOMAS, assn. exec.; b. Ocheyedan, Ia., Mar. 22, 1916; s. Jesse Franklin and Ada Calista (Johnson) DeV.; student U. Ia., 1933-37; B.S., U. Md., 1958; m. Dorothy Alberta Durr, Oct. 10, 1938; children—Richard Allan, Robert Neal, Rosalie Jean. Circulation supr. Des Moines Register and Tribune, 1938-40; commd. 2d lt., inf. ORC, 1937; called to active duty, 1941, advanced through grades to col., 1961; grad. Command and Gen. Staff Coll., 1953; mem. mil. staff Big Three Conf., Bermuda, 1953; spl. security officer U.S. Army, Pacific, 1949-52, U.S. Forces, Austria, 1954- 55, SHAPE, 1955-58, Joint Chief Staff and sec. def., 1958-61; ret., 1961; asst. exec. sec. Am. Philatelic Soc., 1961-63, exec. sec., 1963—. Decorated Legion of Merit; recipient McCoy award Am. Philatelic Congress, 1953, 59, John N. Luff award Am. Philatelic Soc., 1955, 58, Tilleard medal Royal Philatelic Soc., 1957; Jere Hess Barr award Am. Philatelic Congress, 1959; Hanford cup Garfield-Perry Stamp Club, Cleve., 1964; Outstanding Achievement in Philately award, 1967. Fellow Royal Philatelic Soc.; mem. Am. Philatelic Soc., Am. Philatelic Congress, Collectors Club N.Y. Presbyn. Rotarian. Contbr. profl. handbooks. Editor Am. Philatelic Congress Book, 1953. Home: 9 Nittany View Circle State College PA 16801 Office: PO Box 800 State College PA 16801

DE VOURSNEY, ANDREW MERLE, air lines exec.; b. Butte, Mont., May 28, 1913; s. Andrew M. and Anna Louise (Wrightson) De V.; A.B., U. Wis., 1935; postgrad. Harvard, 1947; m. Pauline I. Knoernschild, July 29, 1937; children—Robert M., John A., Suzanne M., Andrea J. Investment analyst, Milw., 1935-40; route devel. mgr. United Air Lines, 1944-48, asst. to v.p. in charge finance and property, 1948-50, treas., 1950—, v.p. treas., 1958-61, sr. v.p. econ. planning, 1962—; dir. Scott, Foresman & Co. Clubs: Inverness (Ill.) Golf; International (Washington). Home: 1727 W Banbury Rd Inverness IL 60067

DEVOY, FRANCIS STANLEY, banker; b. Bklyn., Dec. 14, 1908; s. George M. and Edna (Smith) DeV.; grad. Rutgers U. Grad. Sch. Banking, 1941; prestandard and standard certificate, Am. Inst. Banking, 1932; m. H. Shirley Keeler, July 14, 1934; children—Susan (Mrs. Raymond K. Helling), Carolyn (Mrs. Thomas L. Holmes). With Rochester Savs. Bank (N.Y.), 1928—, asst. treas., 1941-49, treas., 1949-51, v.p., 1951-57, v.p., treas., 1957- 67, exec. v.p., 1967-70, pres., trustee, chief exec. officer, 1970-71, vice chmn. bd., trustee, chief exec. officer, 1971—. Bd. mgmt. Rochester YMCA, 1967—; co-chmn. North of Main Devel. Corp., 1970—; treas. Endowment Fund, chmn. devel. com. Fairport Bapt. Home, 1970—; mem. finance com. Monroe County Bapt. Assn. Mem. Nat. Assn. Mut. Savings Banks (mem. com. mortgage investments), Savs. Banks Assn. N.Y. mem. mortgage and real estate com.), Rochester C. of C. Republican. Baptist. Mason. Clubs: Rochester, Monroe Golf (Rochester). Home: 201 Nob Hill Rochester NY 14617 Office: 40 Franklin St Rochester NY 14604

DEVRIES, BERNARD JERIN, architect; b. Chgo., June 21, 1909; s. Christian W.B. and Johana (Zicterman) DeV.; student Mich. State U., 1929-30; B.S. in Architecture, U. Mich., 1934; m. Jean Ann Frissel, June 27, 1936; 1 dau., Jo-Ann C. Asst. engr. City of Ann Arbor (Mich.), 1934-37; designer Lewis J. Sarvis, architect, Battle Creek, Mich., 1937-38; pvt. practice architecture Bernard J. DeVries (now DeVries Assos., Inc.), architects and planners, Muskegon, Mich., 1938—; profl. community planner; architect Gen. Telephone Co. Mich., Master City Plan Muskegon, CBD Redevel. Plan Muskegon, Muskegon Marquette Urban Renewal Project. Mem. Mich. State Bd. Registration for Architects. Commr. Muskegon City Planning Commn., 1944—, chmn., 1947—; commr. Muskegon Bd. Appeals, 1954—; charter mem. Muskegon Community Services Planning Council, 1963—, dir., 1963; founder, charter mem. Lake Michigan Region Planning Council, Inc., 1960—, vice chmn., 1964—, chmn. Mich. delegation, 1961—. Recipient Distinguished Service award Jr. C. of C., 1943, hon. mention Am. Gas Assn. Residence Competition, 1939, Mich. Sch. Bds. Sch. Design Competition, 1963; named Muskegon's Mr. Planner, Muskegon Chronicle, 1963. Registered architect, Mich. Fellow A.I.A. (sec., dir. Western Mich. chpt. 1945-47, v.p. Grand Valley chpt. 1963, pres. 1964); mem. Mich. Soc. Architects (bd. mem. 1967—, gold medal 1966), Am., Mich. (founder, charter dir. 1956, bd. mem. 1967—, pres.) socs. planning ofcls., Mich. Assn. of Professions (charter), Muskegon C. of C. (Builders award 1956). Kiwanian. Clubs: Muskegon Century, Muskegon Yacht. Co-author: Dunes Area Regional Planning, 1962; Regional Highways and Population Growth Report, 1963. Home: 1907 Hoyt St Muskegon MI 49442 Office: Hackley Union Nat Bank Muskegon MI 49440

DEVRIES, HENRY P., lawyer; b. Willemstad Curacao, N.W.I., Dec. 21, 1911; s. Hendrik Pieter and Emma (Riedel) deV.; brought to U.S., 1917, naturalized, 1935; A.B., Columbia, 1934, LL.B., 1937; m. Irene Hamar, May 26, 1943; 1 dau., Diane Elvira. Admitted to N.Y. bar, 1937; asso. Sullivan & Cromwell, N.Y.C., 1937-48; spl. asst. atty. gen., State N.Y., 1947; faculty mem., sch. law Columbia 1948—, prof. law, 1952—, dir. InterAm. Law Center, 1965—; vis. prof., univs. Sao Paulo and Brazil, 1954; Inter-Am. Acad. Internat. Juridical Sci., 1966; counsel to Baker, McKenzie & Hightower, N.Y.C., 1960—. Asso. dir. Parker Sch. Foreign and Coop. Law, 1954—. Mem. Faculty of Comparative Law, Strasbourg, France, since 1960. Served as lt. col. AUS, 1942-46. Decorated Officer, Order of Leopold, Belgium; Commander, Order of Oranje-Nassau, the Netherlands. Member Association Bar City of New York, American Bar Association, American Foreign Law Association (dir.), Council on Fgn. Relations, Am. Soc. Internat. Law, Phi Beta Kappa. Author: Counseling in International Transactions, 1948; Recent Developments in Private International Law in the U.S., 1949; Nationalization; The French Experience, 1950; European Legal Systems, 1951; The French Legal System (with Rene David), 1958, rev. edit., 1966; Inter-American Legal Studies, 1959, 2 vols. 1961, 1 vol., 1964; The Law of the Americas, 1965; Foreign Law and American Lawyer, 2 vols., 1969. Address: 350 Park Av New York City NY 10022

DE VRIES, PETER, writer, editor; b. Chgo., Feb. 27, 1910; s. Joost and Henrietta (Eldersveld) deV.; A.B., Calvin Coll., 1931; student Northwestern U., summer 1931; m. Katinka Loeser, Oct. 16, 1943; children—Jan, Peter Jon, Emily, Derek. Editor community newspaper, Chgo., 1931; free lance writer since 1931; asso. editor Poetry Mag., 1938, co- editor, 1942; mem. editorial staff New Yorker Mag., 1944—. Mem. Nat. Inst. of Arts and Letters. Author: No But I Saw The Movie, 1952; The Tunnel of Love, 1954; Comfort Me with Apples, 1956; The Mackerel Plaza, 1958; The Tents of Wickedness, 1959; Through the Fields of Clover, 1961; The Blood of the Lamb, 1962; Reuben, Reuben, 1964; Let Me Count the Ways, 1965; The Vale of Laughter, 1967; The Cat's Pajamas and Witch's Milk, 1968; Mrs. Wallop, 1970; Into Your Tent I'll Creep, 1971. Home: 170 Cross Highway Westport CT 06880 Address: care New Yorker Mag 25 W 43d St New York City NY 10036

DE VYVER, FRANK TRAVER, univ. prof.; b. Mt. Vernon, N.Y., May 14, 1904; s. Frank Oscar and Lillian Adith (Buchanan) deV.; A.B., Oberlin Coll., 1926, M.A., 1927; M.A., Princeton, 1930, Ph.D., 1935; m. Marion Anna Roth, June 28, 1928; 1 dau., Virginia Harriet. Research asst. in labor problems, Inst. Research in Social Scis., U. Va., 1928-30; instr. econ. Princeton, 1930-35; instr. Duke U., 1935, asst. prof., 1937, asso. prof., 1939, prof. econs., 1942—. chmn. dept. econs. and bus. adminstrn., 1957-64, vice provost, 1960-69; Fulbright lectr. U. Sidney Law Sch., 1956-57, U. Western Australia, 1964; vis. prof. U. Natal, summers 1964, 67; vis. lectr. Monash U., Australia, 1969, 72; trustee Joint Council Econ. Edn., 1962-70; part-time supr. merit examinations, State of N.C. 1938-56. Indsl. relations and personnel dir. Erwin Mills, Inc., Durham, N.C., 1942-55; v.p., 1945-55. Mem. bd. trustees Watts Hosp., Durham, N.C.; mem. Durham County Hosp. Commn. Mem. Econ. History Assn., Am., So. (pres. 1960-61) econ. assns., Indsl. Relations Research Assn., Phi Beta Kappa. Democrat. Presbyn. Home: 8 Sylvan Road Durham NC 27701

DEW, CHARLES BURGESS, historian, educator; b. St. Petersburg, Fla., Jan. 5, 1937; s. Jack Carlos and Amy (Meek) D.; A.B., Williams Coll., 1958; Ph.D., Johns Hopkins, 1964; m. Robb Reavill Forman, Jan. 26, 1968. Instr. Wayne State U., 1963-64, asst. prof., 1964-65; asst. prof. La. State U., 1965- 68; asso. prof. U. Mo., Columbia, 1968—; vis. asso. prof. U. Va., 1970-71. Recipient Fletcher Pratt award N.Y. Civil War Round Table, 1966, award of merit Am. Assn. for State and Local History, 1967. Mem. Am. Hist. Assn., Orgn. Am. Historians, Phi Beta Kappa, Delta Psi. Author: Ironmaker to the Confederacy: Joseph R. Anderson and the Tredegar Iron Works, 1966. Home: 512 Maplewood Dr Columbia MO 65201

DE WAART, EDO, orch. condr.; b. Amsterdam, Netherlands, June 1, 1941; s. Marinus and Jacoba (Rose) de W.; soloist degree oboe Montessori Mulo, Amsterdam Music lyceum, 1962; studied orchtl. conduction J. Spaanderman, Amsterdam, also with Franco Ferrara; m. Rick Nicolet, May 27, 1970; children by previous marriage—Marjolein, Boris. Substitute 1st oboe Concergebonn Orch.; asst. condr. N.Y. Philharmonic Orch., 1965-66, Concertgeb. Orch., Amsterdam; prin. condr. Rotterdam Philharmonic Orch.; artistic dir. Netherlands Wind Ensemble; guest condr. Dutch, Brit. orchs., also Chgo. Symphony, Los Angeles Philharmonic Orch., Santa Fe Opera. Recordings with Philips Records. Recipient 1st prize D. Mitropeulos competition for condrs., 1964. Address: 93 Weerdestein Amsterdam Holland

DE WAHL, DAVID ALLEN, lawyer, mfg. co. exec.; b. Mpls., June 3, 1924; s. Arvid Rutherford and Gertrude Sophia DeW.; B.A., U. Minn., 1946; LL.B., Harvard, 1949; m. Lois Martha Dann, July 24, 1953; children—David Allen, Elizabeth Ann, Duncan Comrie. Admitted to N.Y. bar, 1949; asso. firm Sullivan & Cromwell, N.Y.C., 1949-52; atty. Am. Standard, Inc. (formerly Am. Radiator & Standard San. Corp.), N.Y.C., 1952- 55, asst. sec., 1955-60, sec., 1960-66, v.p., gen. counsel, sec., 1966- -. Mem. Am. Bar Assn., Assn. Bar City N.Y., Phi Beta Kappa. Club: Harvard (N.Y.C.); Sleepy Hollow Country. Home: 652 Long Hill Rd Briarcliff Manor NY 10510 Office: 40 W 40th St New York City NY 10018

DEWALD, FRANKLIN KENNETH, govt. ofcl.; b. Ft. Wayne, Ind., Jan. 20, 1910; s. Frank and Madeline (Petgen) DeW.; LL.B., Ind. Law Sch., 1935, J.D., 1937; m. Elizabeth Nunnally, Dec. 29, 1936; children—Nancy (Mrs. Cyrus Stewart), Marybeth (Mrs. Gerald Piatt), Franklin Kenneth. Admitted to Ind. bar, 1935, U.S. Supreme Ct. bar, 1960; practiced in Indpls., 1935-42; state supr. accounting, state property accountant, state personnel dir., state dir. tng. and re-employment WPA, Ind., 1935-42, nat. dir. tng., Washington, 1942-43, personnel dir., 1943; asst. personnel dir. OPA, 1943-44; personnel dir., bur. ordnance Navy Dept., 1946-51, asst. dir. adminstrv. div., 1951-55; dir. dept. civilian personnel div. Exec. Office of Sec., Navy Dept., 1955-60; dir. Civil Service Commn. Mich., 1960-70; personnel adminstr. U.S. Dept. Labor, Washington, 1970—. Pres. dist. chpt. Civil Service Assembly, Md., Va., D.C., 1951-52. Served as lt. USNR, 1944-46. Mem. Soc. Advancement Mgmt., Soc. Personnel Adminstrn., Pub. Personnel Assn. (mem. exec. council 1965-67, pres. elect 1968, pres. 1969), Sigma Delta Kappa. Rotarian. Home: 3001 Veazey Terrace NW Washington DC 20008 Office: US Dept Labor 1726 M St NW Washington DC

DEWALL, RICHARD ALLISON, surgeon; b. Appleton, Minn., Dec. 16, 1926; s. Herman H. and Grace G. (Gardner) DeW.; B.A., U. Minn., 1949, B.S., 1950, B.M., 1952, M.D., 1953, M.S. in Surgery, 1960; m. Diane B. Prettyman, Oct. 24, 1952; children—Beth B., Amy, Melissa. Research asst. dept. surgery U. Minn., 1954-56, instr. surgery, 1960, asst. prof., 1962; research fellow Am. Heart Assn., 1956-58; advanced research fellow, 1958-60, established investigator, 1960-62; prof. surgery, chmn. dept. Chgo. Med. Sch., 1962-66; chief surgery Cox Heart Inst., Kettering, O., 1966—; staff Kettering Hosp.; coordinator surgery residency tng. program Kettering Meml. Hosp., 1968—. Recipient award U.S. Jr. C. of C., 1957. Diplomate Am. Bd. Surgery, Am. Bd. Thoracic Surgery. Fellow A.C.S., Am. College Cardiology; mem. Soc. for Thoracic Surgery, A.M.A., Am. Coll. of Chest Physicians, A.A.A.S. (co-recipient Ida B. Gould Meml. award 1956), Soc. Univ. Surgeons, Am. Assn. Thoracic Surgery, Dayton Surg. Soc., Nu Sigma Nu, Sigma Chi. Research on perfusion techniques as an aid to open cardiac surgery. Home: 247 Northview Rd Dayton OH 45419 Office: Fidelity Med Bldg Dayton OH 45402

DEWAR, HENRY HAMILTON HAL, investment banker; b. Chgo., Mar. 26, 1902; s. Hamilton and Mary (Kinney) D.; A.B., U. Tex., 1923; m. Hallie Ball, Oct. 14, 1927; children—Robert Ball, Hallie Ball (Mrs. Keene Ferguson), Marion Cooke (Mrs. Michael Bell). Engaged as employee of Guaranty Co. of New York, 1923-24, J.E. Jarratt Co., San Antonio, 1924-29; mgr. bond dept., Alamo Nat. Co., 1929-31; partner, Dewar, Robertson and Pancoast, San Antonio, 1932-67, Hornblower & Weeks-Hemphill, Noyes, 1967—. Chmn. Tex. Dist. Investment Bankers Conf., 1938-39; mem. Nat. Com. of Securities Industry for War Financing, 1942; mem. financial adv. com. Com. for Econ. Devel., 1945. Mem. N.Y. Stock Exchange, gov., 1958-61; mem. Am. Stock Exchange, 1949-67; mem. Assn. Stock Exchange Firms (bd. govs. 1950- 52); mem. finance dept. com. U.S. C. of C.; mem. investment banking div. Voluntary Credit Restraint Com. Trustee, mem. bd. govs. S.W. Research Inst., 1954—, vice chmn., 1962-66. Pres. United Fund of San Antonio, 1957; mem. Tex. Commn. on Higher Edn. (vice chmn. 1956-60); mem. Tex. Bd. of Edn. Investment Adv. Com., 1960; mem. Commn. on Goals for South Higher Edn., 1961; mem. So. Regional Edn. Bd., 1966—. Mem. Investment Bankers Assn. of Am. (v.p. 1944-48; pres. 1948-49; gov. 1943-50), Tex. Investment Bankers Assn. (pres. 1931-32), Nat. Assn. Securities Dealers (mem. bd. govs. and exec. com. 1940-42; chmn. 1942), Delta Tau Delta, Beta Gamma Sigma. Clubs: San Antonio Country, Order of Alamo, Argyle (San Antonio), Racquet and Tennis (N.Y.C.); Bohemian (San Francisco). Home: 10 Ironwood Rd San Antonio TX 78212 Office: Milam Bldg San Antonio TX 78205

DEWAR, MICHAEL JAMES STEUART, educator; b. Ahmennagar, India, Sept. 24, 1918; s. Francis and Nan (Keith) D.; B.A., Oxford (Eng.) U., 1940, D.Phil., 1942, M.A., 1943; m. Mary Williamson, June 3, 1944; children—Robert Berridale Keith, Charles Edward Steuart. Came to U.S., 1959. Imperial Chem. Industries fellow Oxford U., 1945; phys. chemist Courtaulds Ltd., 1945-51; prof. chemistry, head dept. Queen Mary Coll., U. London (Eng.), 1941-59; prof. chemistry U. Chgo., 1959-63; Robert A. Welch prof. chemistry U. Tex., 1963—; Reilly lectr. U. Notre Dame, 1951; Tilden lectr. Chem. Soc. London, 1954; vis. prof. Yale, 1957; Falk-Plaut lectr. Columbia, 1963; William Pyle Phillips visitor Haverford Coll., 1964, 70; Arthur D. Little vis. prof. Mass. Inst. Tech., 1966; Marchon vis. lectr. U. Newcastle (Eng.), 1966; Glidden Co. lectr. Kent State U., 1967; Grehm lectr. Eldg. Technische Hochschule, Zurich, Switzerland, 1968; Barton lectr. U. Okla., 1969; Distinguished vis. lectr. Yeshiva U., 1970; Kahlbaum lectr. U. Basel (Switzerland, 1970; cons. to industry. Recipient Harrison Howe award Am. Chem. Soc., 1961. Fellow Royal Soc., Am. Acad. Arts and Scis., Chem. Soc. London; mem. Am. Chem. Soc., Sigma Xi. Author: Electronic Theory of Organic Chemistry, 1949; Hyperconjugation, 1962; Introduction to Modern Organic Chemistry, 1965; Computer Compilation of Molecular Weights and Percentage Compositions of Organic Compounds, 1969; The Molecular Orbital Theory of Organic Chemistry, 1969; also articles. Home: 6808 Mesa Dr Austin TX 78731.

DEWAR, ROBERT EARL, chain store exec.; b. Traverse City, Mich., Nov. 20, 1922; s. Floyd C. and Irlene (Nash) D.; student Alma Coll., 1940-42; LL.B., Wayne State U., 1948; postgrad. U. Mich. Grad. Sch. Bus. Adminstrn., 1963; m. Nancy Jane Miller, Sept. 26, 1944; children—Robert Earl, Jane Elizabeth, John. Admitted to Mich. bar, 1948; gen. practice law, Detroit, 1948-49; with S. S. Kresge Co., 1949—, asst. v.p. finance, 1963-65, v.p. finance, 1965-66, adminstrv. v.p., 1966—, exec. v.p. adminstrn. and finance, 1968-70, pres., 1970—, also dir. Trustee Detroit Inst. Cancer Research. Served as pilot USNR, 1942-45. Decorated Air medal (2). Mem. Financial Execs. Inst., Delta Theta Phi, Omicron Delta Kappa. Presbyn. Home: 22236 Nottingham Dr Birmingham MI 48016 Office: 2727 2d Av Detroit MI 48232

DEWART, LESLIE SUTHERLAND, educator, philosopher; b. Madrid, Spain, Dec. 12, 1922; s. Gerardo and Adamina (Duarte) Gonzalez; B.A., U. Toronto, 1951, M.A., 1952, Ph.D., 1954; m. Joanne McWilliam, Aug. 19, 1954; children—Leslie, Elizabeth, Sean, Colin. Teaching fellow dept. philosophy St. Michaels Coll., U. Toronto, 1952-54, asst. prof., 1956-61, asso. prof., 1961-68, prof. faculty Theology, 1968-69, prof. dept. religious studies, 1968—, prof. Inst. Christian Thought, 1969—, chmn. combined depts. religious studies, 1970-71; instr. dept. philosophy U. Detroit, 1954-56; prof. Toronto Grad. Sch. Theol. Studies (now Toronto Sch. Theology), 1968—. Served to flying officer RCAF, 1942-47. Recipient Can. Council Research grant, 1970. Mem. Societe Europeenne de Culture, Canadian Soc. for Study Religion. Author: Christianity and Revolution, 1963; The Future of Belief, 1966; The Foundations of Belief, 1969; Religion, Language and Truth, 1970. Asso. editor: Continuum, 1964-71; Internationale Dialog Zeitschrift, 1967—; Concurrence, 1968-70. Contbg. editor: The Ecumenist, 1968—. Editorial bd. Studies in Religion-Sciences Religeuses, 1970—. Contbr. articles profl. jours. Home: 313 Oriole Pkwy Toronto 7 Ontario Canada

DEWASNE, JEAN, artist; b. Lille, France, 1921; student Ecole Nat. des Beaux Arts, Paris. First abstract paintings, 1943; a founder Realities Nouvellos; 1st one- man show Galerie Denise Rene, Paris, 1949; founder Atelier d'Art Abstrait, 1950; organizer Lectures on Abstract Art; inventor Anti-Sculptures; exhbns. throughout Europe, N. and S. Am. Address: care Realites Nouvelles Sta 18 Rue Quatre Vents Paris 5e France*

DEWBERRY, LAWRENCE GLENN, Jr., steel co. exec.; b. Atlanta, Sept. 7, 1919; s. Lawrence Glenn and Florence (Bowen) D.; student Atlanta div. U. Ga., 1939-40; Asso. Sci. in Indsl. Tech., So. Tech. Inst., 1949; m. Sylvia Snow, Aug. 14, 1942; children—Lawrence Glenn III, Lewis S. With Atlantic Steel Co., Atlanta, 1949—, v.p. operations, 1961-63, exec. v.p., 1963-65, pres., 1965—, also dir.; chmn. exec. com., dir. Atlantic Bldgs. Systems, Inc., Dir. Atlanta Freight Bur., Better Bus. Bur. Met. Atlanta, Jr. Achievement. Served to capt., F.A., AUS, 1941-46. Mem. N.A. M., Am. Iron and Steel Engrs. (dir.), Am. Iron and Steel Inst., Ga. Bus. Industries Assn. (past pres., dir.). Methodist (chmn. bd. trustees). Rotarian. Home: 2470 Tanglewood Rd Decatur GA 30033 Office: 1300 Mecaslin St N W Atlanta GA 30318

DEWEERD, HAROLD, banker; b. Holland, Mich., Jan. 21, 1907; s. Henry J. and Martha (Tietsema) D.; student Parsons Bus. Sch., 1924-25; m. Doris Faye Crouse, Dec. 3, 1938; children—William, James. With KVP Sutherland Paper Co., Kalamazoo, 1925-67, sec., asst. to pres., 1925-51, sec. co., 1951- 67; sec. Am. Nat. Bank, Kalamazoo, 1967—. Home: 339 Oak Grove Av Parchment MI 49004 Office: American National Bank Kalamazoo MI 49003

DEWEESE, DAVID DOWNS, physician and surgeon; b. Columbus, O., Mar. 16, 1913; s. Bernard D. and Vilette Downs (Gilfillan) DeW.; A.B., U. Mich., 1934, M.D., 1938; m. Mary Dorothy Jones, June 24, 1938; children—Diane Downs, Dana Evelyn (both adopted). Intern U. Hosp., Ann Arbor, Mich., 1938-39, resident otolaryngology, 1939-40; instr. otolaryngology U. Mich. Med. Sch., 1941- 44; instr. otolaryngology U. Ore. Med. Sch., 1944-45, clin. prof., 1951- 61, chmn. dept. otolaryngology, 1958—, prof., 1961—; otolaryngologist Portland (Ore.) Clin., 1944-61. Bd. dirs. Portland Center for Hearing and Speech, 1947—, pres., 1949-59, med. dir., 1958—; chmn. communicative disorders research tng. com. NIH, 1965- 66, mem. adv. council Nat. Inst. Neurol. Diseases and Stroke, 1968-70. Trustee, Marylhurst Coll., 1965—. Jr. fellow A.C.S.; mem. A.M.A., Ore., Multnomah County med. socs., Ore. Acad. Ophthalmology and Otolaryngology (pres. 1958), Pacific Coast Oto- Ophthal. Soc. (pres. 1964), Am. Laryngol., Rhinol., Otol. Soc., Am. Acad. Ophthalmology and Otolaryngology (2d v.p. 1957-58), Portland Acad. Medicine, Am. Otol. Soc., Am. Broncho-Esophageal Assn., Am. Laryngol. Assn., Soc. Univ. Otolaryngologists (pres. 1968), Sigma Chi, Nu Sigma Nu (nat. pres. 1959- 60), Alpha Omega Alpha. Clubs: Waverly Country, Golf, Multnomah Athletic, Rotary, Arlington. Sr. author: Textbook of Otolaryngology, 1960. Editorial bd. A.M.A. Archives of Otolaryngology, 1961-64. Home: 1200 S W 61st Dr Portland OR 97221

DEWEESE, MARION SPENCER, educator, surgeon; b. Corydon, Ind., Aug. 17, 1915; s. Arville Otis and Vergie (Jenkins) DeW.; B.A., Kent State U., 1935; M.D., U. Mich., 1939, M.S. in Surgery, 1948; m. Helen Sosnoski, June 25, 1941; children—Diane Hope, Dawn Cheryl, Pamela Lea. Intern, then resident gen. surgery U. Mich. Hosp., 1939-41, 45-48; instr., then asst. prof. surgery U. Mich. Med. Sch., 1948-51; pvt. practice gen. surgery, San Diego, 1951-53; asso. prof., then prof. surgery U. Mich. Med. Sch., 1953-64; prof. surgery, chmn. dept. U. Mo. Med. Sch., 1964—, also W. Alton Jones dist. prof.; chief surgery Ann Arbor VA Hosp., 1953-56. Served to lt. col., M.C., AUS, 1941-45. Mem. A.C.S., Am., Central, Western, So. surg. assns., Soc. Vascular Surgery, A.M.A. Contbr. profl. jours. Home: 807 Stewart Rd Columbia MO 65201

DE WELDON, FELIX WEIHS, sculptor; b. Vienna, Austria, Apr. 12, 1907; s. Ignaz Weihs and Fredericka (Wenger) de W.; came to U.S., 1937, naturalized, 1945; A.B., Marchetti Coll., Vienna, Austria, 1922-25; M.A., M.S., U. of Vienna (Acad. of Creative Arts, Sch. of Architecture), 1927, Ph.D., 1929; postgrad. study in art and architecture, Paris, Rome, Florence, Oxford; m. Margot Kraemer, June 19, 1944. Public monument sculptor, portrait painter; exhibited Vienna, 1925-28, Paris Salon, 1929-30, Cairo, 1932- 33, Royal Acad. (London), 1934-37, Montreal, 1938, Architectural League (New York), 1939, Art Assn. (Newport, R.I.), 1948; executed World War I Monument, Belleau Wood, France; King George VI (coronation bust), 1937; Prime Minister Mackenzie King, Can., 1938; USMC War Memorial (Iwo Jima Flag Raising), Washington, 1954; Nat. Monument for Malayasia, Kuala Lumpur, Malaya; Truman Monument, Athens, Greece; bronze statue of Speaker Rayburn, Bonham, Tex., 1959; equestrian statue Simon Bolivar, 1958; Red Cross Monument, 1959 (both Washington); bronze Pres. Kennedy, 1966, gold medal Pres. Johnson, 1966 (both White House, Washington D.C.); equestrian statue of Gen. Garcia, Havana, Cuba, 1958; bronze monument to Adm. Richard E. Byrd for Washington, 1961; bronze of Sgt. Alvin York, Nashville, Tenn.; bronze of Pres. Andrew Jackson, Columbia, S.C. Mem. Commn. of Fine Arts of U.S., 1950-63. Served USN World War II. Mem. Am. Fedn. of Arts, Metropolitan Mus. of Art, English Speaking Union. Home: 2132 Bancroft Pl NW Washington DC 20008 also: Beacon Rock Harrison Av Newport RI 02840 Office: 219 Randolph Place NE Washington DC 20002

DEWELL, WILBUR, cosmetic co. exec.; b. Cushing, Ia., Dec. 1, 1890; s. George Allen and Agnes Woodside (Moore) D.; student Morningside Coll., Sioux City, Ia.; m. Minna Ehlers, Nov. 24, 1909; 1 son, Lloyd (dec.). Sales mgr. Churchill Drug Co., Burlington, Ia., 1922-27; with McKesson & Robbins, Inc., 1927-56, v.p., 1934-56, dir., 1943-56; gen. mgr. McKesson Labs., Bridgeport, Conn., 1929-56; with Lanolin Plus, Inc., Newark (merged to form Bishop Industries, Inc., 1962), 1958—, chairman of the board, now dir.; director Frough Constrn. Co., N.Y.C. and Bridgeport, Savoy Industries, Inc., L. I. City, N.Y. Named Ky. col., 1941. Mason (Shriner), Rotarian. Home: 494 Hill Farm Rd Fairfield CT 06430 Office: 2345 Vauxhall Rd Union NJ 07083

DEWEY, BRADLEY, Jr., chem. exec.; b. Pitts., Apr. 10, 1916; s. Bradley and Marguerite (Mellon) D.; B.S., Harvard, 1937; Sc.D., Mass. Inst. Tech., 1940; m. Jane Holcombe, Aug. 10, 1940; children—Margot, Bradley III, John Holcombe, Carolyn, Joan. With Dewey & Almy Chem. Co., Cambridge, Mass., 1940-56, v.p., 1951-56, dir., 1952-56; pres. Cryovac div. W. R. Grace & Co., Duncan, S.C., 1956-64; Sr. v.p. chem. group. W.R. Grace & Co., 1964-67; pres. Thermal Dynamics Corp., West Lebanon, N.H., 1968—. Served as capt. C.W.S., AUS, 1943-45. Mem. Am. Chem. Soc., Am. Inst. Chemists, Am. Inst. Chem. Engrs., Soc. Chem. Industry, Sigma Xi, Alpha Chi Sigma. Home: 43 Occom Ridge Hanover NH 03755 Office: Thermal Dynamics Corp West Lebanon NH 03784

DEWEY, CHARLES SCHUVELDT, ret. banker; b. Cadiz, O., Nov. 10, 1880; s. Albert B. and Louise (Schuveldt) D.; student St. Paul's Sch., Concord, N.H., 1896-1900; Ph.B., Yale, 1904; m. Suzette deM. Hall, Dec. 20, 1905 (dec. Dec. 1956); children—Suzette D. (Mrs. Frederick Alger), Charles S., Louise (Mrs. Edward B. Smith), A. Peter; m. 2d, Elizabeth Zolnay Smith, June 3, 1959. Vice pres. No. Trust Co., Chgo., 1920-24; asst. sec. treasury charge fiscal affairs, 1924-27; financial adviser Republic Poland, 1927- 31; dir. Bank of Poland, 1927-31, hon. life dir.; v.p. Chase Nat. Bank, 1945-50; agt. gen. Joint Congl. Com. Fgn. Econ. Cooperation, 1946-50; mem. Washington Nat. Monument Soc., 1960—. Nat. treas. A.R.C., 1927, chmn. D.C. chpt., 1957-61, now mem. exec. com.; pres. Washington Hosp. Center, 1951-57; mem. adv. com. Export-Import Bank of Washington, 1947. Mem. U.S. Ho. of Reps. from 9th Ill. Dist., 1941-45. Served with USNRF, 1917-19. Decorated grand officer Legion of Honor (France); grand comdr. Polonia Restituta (Poland); grand comdr. Crown of Rumania; grand comdr. Order St. Sava (Yugoslavia). Mem. S.A.R., Delta Psi. Republican. Episcopalian. Clubs: Chicago, Society of Cincinnati, Metropolitan (Washington). Home: 3539 Williamsburg Lane N W Washington DC 20008 Office: Washington Nat Monument Soc Interior Bldg Washington DC 20240

DEWEY, CHESTER ROBERT, banker; b. Mazon, Ill., Aug. 21, 1888; s. Robert Hall and Ida Josephine (Burleigh) D.; A.B., U. of Ill., 1908, LL.B., 1909; m. Helen L. Capron, Feb. 1, 1913; children—Chester Robert (dec.), Frederick Capron (dec.), Helen Elizabeth (Mrs. Harlan P. Wallingford), Priscilla Anne (Mrs. Eugene S. Dewey). Admitted N.Y. bar, 1910, and began practice with Wilmer, Canfield & Stone, later Satterlee, Canfield & Stone, N.Y.C.; moved to Utica, N.Y., 1913; mem. Dunmore & Ferris, 1916, Dunmore, Ferris & Dewey, 1917-32; pres. Citizens Trust Co., Utica, 1928-31; vice chmn. First Citizens Bank & Trust Co., Utica, 1931-33; pres. Grace Nat. Bank of New York, 1933-54; partner Ferris, Hughes, Dorrance & Groben, 1954—; pres. Homestead Aid Assn., Utica, 1929-33; pres. Trust Co.'s Assn. N.Y., 1930-33; pres., chmn., dir. Utica Fire Ins. Co.; mem. bd. dirs. Ogden Grain Co. Trustee Hamilton Coll. Mem. Venezuelan C. of C. (past pres.), Am. Arbitration Assn., S.A.R., Am., N.Y. State bar assns., N.Y. State Bankers Assn. (past pres.). Republican. Presbyn. Mason (32, Shriner). Clubs: Illini, India House (N.Y.C.); Fort Schuyler (Utica); Scarsdale Golf; Yahnundasis Golf. Home: 1609 Sherman Dr Utica NY 13501 Office: First Nat Bank Bldg Utica NY 13501

DEWEY, EDWARD RUSSELL, found. exec.; b. Elmira, N.Y., May 2, 1895; s. Edward Wilkins and Harriet (Russell) D.; S.B. cum laude, Harvard, 1920; m. Elenore Stratton, Sept. 22, 1922; children—Barbara, Edward; m. 2d, Catherine Doak, Feb. 13, 1935. Dir. Found. for Study of Cycles, 1940-67, exec. v.p., 1963-67, vice chmn., 1967-69, pres., 1969—; adj. research prof. acad. disciplines U. Pitts., 1965—; adminstr. Comité international de Recherche et d'tude de Facteurs d l'Ambiance, association internationale á but scientifique, Brussels, 1968—. Fellow World Acad. Art and Sci.; mem. Am. Statis. Assn., Soc. Biol. Rhythm, A.A.A.S., N.Y. Acad. Scis., Internat. Soc. Biometeorology, Soc. Mayflower Descs. Republican. Conglist. Clubs: Faculty (Pitts); Cosmos (Washington); Harvard (Pitts., N.Y.C.). Author: (with E. F. Dakin) Cycles: The Science of Prediction; (with Og Mandino) Cycles: Mysterious Forces That Trigger Events, Cycles: Selective Writings. Editorial bd. Jour. Interdisciplinary Cycle Research, 1970—. Contbr. articles to profl. jours. Home: RD 1 East Brady PA 16028 Office: 124 S Highland Av Pittsburgh PA 15206

DEWEY, ERNEST WAYNE, educator; b. Hutchinson, Kan., May 20, 1925; s. Ernest A. and Violet (Hampton) D.; B.A., U. Kan., 1949, M.A., 1950; Ph.D., U. Tex., 1954; m. Helen Josephine Scamell, Apr. 11, 1949; children—Ernest Ralph, William Frederick, James Franklin. Vis. instr. U. Kan., 1953-54; asst. prof. Okla. State U., 1954-58, asso. prof., 1958-60; prof., chmn. philosophy U. S.D., 1960-66; prof., chmn. philosophy U. Toledo, 1966—; symposia-review editor Philosophy Forum, 1970—. Served with AUS, 1943-46. Mem. Am. Assn. U. Profs., Am., Ohio Philosoph. Socs., Southwestern Philosoph. Soc. (sec. treas. 1957-58, editor Newsletter 1957-59), Am. Soc. for 18th Century Studies, Phi Alpha Theta, Pi Gamma Mu. Democrat. Home: 2227 Drummond Rd Toledo OH 43606

DEWEY, HORACE WILLIAM, educator; b. Mpls., May 20, 1920; s. Horace Elliot and Carol (McCurdy) D.; LL.B., U. Mich., 1950, Ph.D., 1955; m. Margaret Ann Avery, Feb. 1, 1942; children—James William, Margaret Carol (Mrs. James D. Huber), John Elliott, Russell Avery. Mem. faculty U. Mich., 1948—, prof. Slavic langs. and Russian history, 1961—; cons. in field, 1960—; active summer exchange programs, 1966—. Served with AUS, 1943-46. Mem. Am. Assn. Advancement Slavic Studies, Medieval Soc. Am., Am. Assn. Tchrs. Slavic and E. European Langs. Author: (with John Mersereau, Jr.) Reading and Translating Contemporary Russian, 1963; Muscovite Judicial Texts, 1488-1556, 1966. Home: 2301 Woodside St Ann Arbor MI 48104.

DEWEY, HOWARD EUGENE, ins. co. exec.; b. Fredonia, N.Y., July 15, 1915; s. Russell A. and Dora (Pickett) D.; grad. high sch.; m. Winifred E. Cole, Oct. 15, 1938; children—Juanita Lesh, Paul H., Shelia E. Griffen. With Mut. of Omaha, 1938—, v.p. sales, 1955-64, sr. v.p. sales and agy. mgmt., 1964-69, sr. regional v.p., Ariz., Scottsdale, 1969—. Home: 12821 N 67th St Scottsdale AZ 85254 Office: 77 3d Av W Scottsdale AZ 85251

DEWEY, LAWRENCE R., cons.; b. Des Moines, May 19, 1901; s. Clyde Russell and Lola Mae (Williams) D.; B.S., U.S. Mil. Acad., 1924; grad. Cav. Sch., 1930, Signal Sch., 1931, Nat. War Coll., 1947; m. Florence Powers, Dec. 22, 1931; children—Lawrence R., Florence Powers, Donald H., Elizabeth H. Commd. 2d lt. Cav., U.S. Army, 1924, advanced through grades to maj. gen., 1954; assigned 26th Cav., Ft. Stotsenburg, P.I., 1933-35; a.d.c., 1935-39; 3d Cav., Ft. Myer, Va., 1939-40; operations officer and exec. officer 82d Reconnaissance Bn., 2d Armored Div., Ft. Benning, Ga., 1940-41, operations officer 2d Armored Div., Ft. Benning, 1942, chief staff 2d Armored Div., Morocco, 1942; operations officer 1st Armored Div., Tunisia, 1943; chief staff 1st Armored Div., Morocco, 1943-44; combat command comdr. 1st Armored Div., 1944-45; operations officer U.S. Constabulary ETO, 1946; student, instr. Nat. War Coll., 1946-50; staff officer Standing Group, NATO, 1950; asst. div. comdr. 1st Armored Div., Ft. Hood, Tex., 1951; chief staff 9th Corps, 8th Army, Korea, 1951-53; chief mgmt. div. Office Army Comptroller, 1953-55; became asst. comptroller of army, 1955; chief Joint Am. Mil. Mission for Aid to Turkey, 1955-57; dir. Mil. Assistance Div., Hdqrs. U.S. European Command, 1957-59; chief U.S. Army Audit Agy., Washington, 1959-61; with CIA, Washington, 1961-63; cons. Research Analysis Corp., McLean, Va.; now cons. in pvt. practice. Decorated D.S.M.

with cluster, Silver Star with cluster, Legion Merit with two clusters, Bronze Star medal, Purple Heart. Address: 3201 Juniper Lane Falls Church VA 22044

DEWEY PHELPS publisher; b. Mpls., Mar. 23, 1928; s. Maurice Adams and Alice (Wheelwright) D.; student Dartmouth, 1947-48; m. Jennifer Owings, June 25, 1966; children by previous marriage—Richard, Susan, Kimberley, Peter. Promotion dir. San Francisco Chronicle, 1953-60; press relations mgr. Los Alamos Sci. Lab., 1960-62; promotion mgr. Chgo. Daily News/ Chgo. Sun Times, 1962-63; promotion dir. San Francisco Chronicle, also gen. mgr. Chronicle Features Syndicate, 1963-65; promotion dir. San Francisco Newspaper Printing Co., 1965-70; gen. mgr. Chronicle Books div. Chronicle Pub. Co., 1965—. Mem. Western Book Pubs. Assn. (dir. 1970—). Home: 4625 Paradise Dr Tiburon CA 94920 Office: 54 Mint St San Francisco CA 94103

DEWEY ROBERT EUGENE educator, philosopher; b. Vermillion, S.D., Aug. 11, 1923; s. Ziba Norman and Mary (Eskelson) D.; A.B., U. Neb., 1943; M.A., Harvard, 1947, Ph.D., 1949; m. Mary Ellen Sim, Dec. 24, 1943; children—Barbara Lynn, Christopher Sim. Asst. prof. U. Md., 1949-52; vis. lectr. Goucher Coll., 1952; research fellow Inst. Philos. Research, San Francisco, 1952-55; lectr. Mills Coll., 1955; asst. prof. Dartmouth, 1955-58; asso. prof. U. Neb., 1958-62, prof. philosophy, chmn. dept., 1962—. Served to 1st lt., F.A., AUS, 1943-46; ETO. Mem. Am. Philos. Assn., Mountain Plains Philos. Conf., Am. Assn. U. Profs., Phi Beta Kappa, Phi Sigma Tau. Unitarian. Contbr. articles profl. publs. Editor: Problems of Ethics, 1961. Home: 441 Steinway Rd Lincoln NB 68505.

DEWEY ROBERT F., banker; b. Woodstock, Ill., May 13, 1909; s. Harry A. and Beatrice (Dietz) D.; A.B., U. N.C., 1930; J.D., U. Chgo., 1934; m. Edythe Boyce, Oct. 17, 1936. Admitted to Ill. bar, also Ariz. bar; practice in Chgo., 1934-48; v.p., trust officer First Nat. Bank Ariz., Phoenix, 1950-61; sr. v.p., sr. trust officer Bank of Cal., N.A., San Francisco, 1961-67, exec. v.p., chief adminstrv. officer, 1967—. Pres. Ariz. Corp. Fiduciary Assn., 1959. Served to maj. USAAF, 1942-45. Mem. Am., Ill., San Francisco, Ariz. bar assns., Cal. Bankers Assn. (chmn. trust div. 1965-66), No. Cal. Trust Companies Assn. (pres. 1964-65), Phi Beta Kappa, Phi Gamma Delta. Clubs: University, California Golf, The Family (San Francisco). Home: 882 Green St San Francisco CA 94111. Office: 400 California St San Francisco CA 94120

DEWEY, THOMAS EDMUND, lawyer; b. Owosso, Mich., Mar. 24, 1902; s. George Martin and Annie (Thomas) D.; A.B., U. Mich., 1923, LL.M., 1937; LL.B., Columbia, 1925; LL.D., Tufts Coll., 1937, Brown U., 1938, Dartmouth, 1939, St. Lawrence U., 1941, N.Y.U., 1942, Union Coll., 1943, Alfred U., 1945, Fordham, 1946, Colgate, 1947, Hamilton Coll., 1947, Columbia, 1947, Williams Coll., 1949, St. Bonaventure, 1950, Yeshiva U., 1951, U. Rochester, 1957; m. Frances E. Hutt, June 16, 1928; childrenThomas E., John Martin. Admitted to N.Y. bar, 1926; asso. Larkin, Rathbone & Perry, 1925-27; with McNamara & Seymour, 1927-31; chief asst. U.S. atty., So. Dist. of N.Y., 1931-33, U.S. atty., 1933; pvt. practice, 1934- 35; counsel to Assn. of Bar in N.Y. in removal of Municipal Justice Harold L. Kunstler, 1934; spl. prosecutor Investigation of organized Crime, N.Y., 1935-37; elected dist. atty. N.Y. County, 1937; Republican candidate for gov. State of N.Y., 1938, elected gov., 1942, reelected, 1946, 50; Rep. nominee for pres. U.S., 1944, 48; mem. law firm Dewey, Ballantine, Bushby, Palmer & Wood, N.Y.C., 1955—. Awarded Medal for Excellence, Columbia U., in recognition pub. service, 1936; Cardinal Newman Distinguished Service award U. Ill., 1939, various other awards. Trustee N.Y. Heart Assn., N.Y. YMCA, Roosevelt Hosp., N.Y.C. Fellow Am. Coll. Trial Lawyers; mem. Am., N.Y. State bar assns., Assn. Bar City N.Y., N.Y. County Lawyers Assn., Council Fgn. Relations, Pilgrims, Phi Mu Alpha, Phi Delta Phi. Episcopalian. Mason (33). Clubs: Links, Blindbrook, Recess, Downtown Assn., City Midday, Hill; Augusta Nat., Indian Creek. Author: The Case Against the New Deal, 1940; Journey to the Far Pacific, 1952; Thomas E. Dewey on the Two Party System, 1966. Contbr. to mags. Home: 141 E 72d St New York City NY 10021 Office: 140 Broadway New York City NY 10005 Died Mar 16 1971

DEWHURST, COLLEEN, actress; b. Montreal, Can.; student Downer Coll., Milw., then at Am. Acad. Dramatic Art; pupil of Harold Clurman and Joseph Anthony; m. James Vickery, 1947 (marriage dissolved); m. 2d, George C. Scott; 2 sons. First profl. appearance in The Royal Family, 1946; Broadway appearances include Desire Under the Elms, 1952, Tamberlain the Great, 1956, Camille, 1956, The Eagle Has Two Heads, 1957, The Country Wife, 1957, All the Way Home, 1960, Great Day in the Morning, 1962, Ballad of the Sad Cafe, 1963, also off Broadway roles and appearances with N.Y. Shakespeare Festival; motion picture appearance in The Nun's Story, 1959; numerous TV appearances, 1957—. Recipient Obie award, 1957, 63; Lola D'Annunzion award, also Tony award, 1961; Sylvania award, 1960. Address: Riverdale NY 10471*

DEWHURST, JOHN DAVIS, govt. ofcl.; b. Metheum, Mass., Feb. 21, 1921; s. Thomas and Isabella (McPhee) D.; student Hillyer Coll., 1940-41; m. Shirley J. Studley, Feb. 21, 1942; children—John, Terry Paul. Tool and die apprentice Underwood Corp., 1939-41; toolmaker United Aircraft Corp., 1941; president of Arrow Tool Co., Inc., Wethersfield, Conn., 1942-69; v.p., treas., dir. Mechtron Instrument Corp., Wethersfield, 1956-69; plant mgr. Norden Instrument Corp., White Plaines, N.Y., 1950- 51; dep. dir. adminstrn. Selective Service System, Washington, 1970—. Mem. Fed. Com. Apprenticeship, 1960-70; mem. U.S. Trade Mission to Yugoslavia, 1958; bus. and def. services industry adv. com. Dept. Commerce, 1955-70; Fed. Govt. Com. Adminstrn. Tng. Programs, 1967-68; pres. Wethersfield Indsl. Park, 1965-70; chmn. Conn. exec. reserve association Department Commerce. Trustee Central Conn. Tool and Die Industries Group Ins. Trust, 1952-69. Bd. founders U. Hartford. Served with USNR, 1943-45. Recipient numerous award for activities in apprenticeship and training fields. Mem. Am. Soc. Tool and Mfg. Engrs., Nat. Tool, Die and Precision Machining Assn. (pres. 1961-62, trustee 1952-69), Central Conn., Western Mass. tool and die mfrs. assns., Am. Standard, Assn. (dir. 1961-63). Wethersfield Businessmens and Civic Assn., Wethersfield C. of C. (pres. 1965-67). Author articles, handbooks. Office: 1724 F St NW Washington DC

DEWHURST, MARGARET GRANT, (Mrs. J. Fredario Dewhurst), assn. exec.; b. Foxburg, Pa., d. Thomas Byron and Mary Elizabeth (Thomas) Grant; A.B., Sweet Briar Coll., 1915; A. M., Columbia, 1917, Ph.D., 1938; m. Albert Marsh, 1917; 1 dau., Leslie Grant (Mrs. Leslie C. Bigelow); m. 2d, Harold O. Schneider, 1927 (dec.); children—Margaret (Mrs. L. M. Voight, Junior), and Harold; m. 3d, J. Frederic Dewhurst, April 16th, 1966. Member of the research staff inquiry committee assembling data for Paris Peace Conf. under Col. E. M. House, 1917-18; statis. research Fed. Res. Bank, N.Y.C., 1919; editorial work on diary and documents of Paris Peace Conf. by David Hunter Miller, legal adviser Am. Commn. to Negotiate Peace, 1920-24; course in corp. finance and banking, mem. investment adv. and sales dept. Guaranty Co. of N.Y., 1924-27; research staff Rockefeller Liquor Control Study Com. (study legislation U.S. and Europe on control of mfr. and sale alcohol), 1932; asso. dir. econ. research 20th Century Fund, N.Y.C., 1933-35; research, European survey com. on social security, Social Sci. Research Council, 1935-38; asso. dir. Nat. Orchestral Survey sponsored by Carnegie Corp., 1938-39; exec. sec. Berkshire Music Center, Tanglewood, Mass., 1939-43; sec. Koussevitzky Music Found., Inc., 1942-; dir. research and statis. services USO, 1943- 45; dean, asst. to dir. Eastman Sch. Music, U. Rochester, 1945-46; econ. affairs officer, also chief studies unit of econ. and social council of UN, 1946-55; gen. sec. World Brotherhood, 1955-; exec. dir. Council on World Tensions, Inc., since 1960. Organizer of several conferences on world tensions. Executive sec. Am. Internat. Music Fund, Inc. Mem. Am. Statis, Assn., Am. Academy Polit. and Social Science, Phi Beta Kappa. Episcopalian. Club: Cosmopolitan (N.Y.C.). Author: More Security for Old Age, 1937; Old Age Security; Social and Financial Trends, 1939; (with H. S. Hettinger) America's Symphony Orchestras and How They are Supported, 1940. Editor: South Asia Pacific Crisis; 1964. Co-editor: Stock Market Control Security Markets. Home: 23 Braeburn Dr Princeton NJ 08540.

DEWILDE, BRANDON, actor; b. N.Y.C., Apr. 9, 1942; s. Frederic and Eugenia (Wilson) deW.; grad. high sch. Broadway appearances include Member of the Wedding, 1950, Mrs. McThing, 1952, The Emperor's Clothes, 1953, Comes a Day, 1958; motion pictures include Shane, 1951, Member of the Wedding, 1952, Night Passage, 1956, Goodbye, My Lady, 1955, The Missouri Traveler, 1957, Blue Denim, 1959; Hud, 1963; In Harms Way, 1965; Race of Hairy Men, 1965, frequent TV appearances, including starring role in Jamie, 1953. Youngest recipient Donaldson award, 1950. Address: New York City NY 10001

DE WIND, ADRIAN WILLIAM ANDREWS, lawyer; b. Chgo., Dec. 1, 1913; s. Norman and Ethel (Andrews) De W.; student Lakefield (Ont.) Prep. Sch., 1925-29; A.B., Grinnell Coll., Ia., 1934; student, U. Paris, Sorbonne, 1932-33; LL.B., Harvard, 1937; m. Joan Elizabeth Mosenthal, June 21, 1941; childrenBarbara (Mrs. Edward Fiske Mooney), Adrian William Andrews, Susan (Mrs. Robert R. Kesner), John. With Sage, Gray, Todd & Sims, N.Y.C., 1937-43; with U.S. Treasury Dept., 1943-48, asst. tax legislative counsel 1945-47, tax legislative counsel, 1947-48; mem. firm Paul, Weiss, Goldberg, Rifkind, Wharton & Garrison 1948—; dirs. Randolph Computer Corp. Lectr. taxation, N.Y.U. Sch. Law, 1948-54; chief counsel, subcom. on adminstrn. of internal revenue laws, com. on ways and means, Ho. of Reps., Washington 1951-52; chmn. adv. group on city taxation to N.Y.C. Council Pres., 1966; mem. adv. group to Commr. Internal Revenue, 1966-67; mem. Mayor's Task Force on N.Y. Constnl. Conv., 1967; del. Democratic Nat. Conv., 1968. Bd. dirs. Revlon Foundation, Inc., N.A.A.C.P. Legal Def. and Ednl. Fund, Inc. (mem. exec. com.), Met. Applied Research Center, Inc., Nat. Com. Against Discrimination in Housing. Mem. President's Task Force on Tax Policy, 1961. Trustee Harvard Law School Assn. of N.Y. C., Inc. Mem. Am. Law Inst., Am. Bar Assn. (sect. on taxation), Am. bar Found., N.Y. County Lawyers Assn., Assn. Bar City N.Y., N.Y. State Bar Assn. (exec. com. tax sect.; mem. spl. com. on exempt orgns.), Fed. Bar Council. Club: Metropolitan. Contbr. articles in legal periodicals. Home: 37 W 12th St New York City NY 10011 also Sherman Ct 06784 Office: 345 Park Av New York City NY 10022

DE WINDT, EDWARD MANDELL, mfg. co. exec.; b. Great Barrington, Mass., Mar. 31, 1921; s. Delano and Ruth (Church) deW.; student Williams Coll., 1939-41; m. Betsy Bope, June 21, 1941; children—Pamela, Delano II, Dana, Elizabeth, Edward Mandell. With Eaton Corp., Cleve., 1941—, gen. mgr. stamping div., 1954-59, v.p. sales, 1959-61, group v.p. internat., 1961-66, pres., 1967-69, chmn. bd., 1969—, also dir.; mem. exec. com. Mogul Corp.; mem. exec. com., dir. Ohio Bell Telephone Co.; dir. Am. Can Co., Cleve. Trust Co., Diamond Shamrock Co. Trustee Cleve. Ednl. Television Assn., Cleve. State U., Hawken Sch., Cleve., Berkshire Sch. (Mass.), Cleve. Clinic; bd. dirs. Soc. Christians and Jews; bd. dirs., mem. exec. com. Greater Cleve. Growth Assn. Mem. Soc. Automotive Engrs., N.A.M. (dir.), Soc. Cin., Am. Soc. Corporate Execs., Am. Ordnance Assn., Bus. Council. Clubs: Union, Tavern, Pepper Pike Country, Kirtland (Cleve.); Detroit Athletic; Bloomfield Hills (Mich.) Country; Laurel Valley, (Ligonier, Pa.); Links (N.Y.C.). Home: 25299 Cedar Rd Lyndhurst OH 44124 Office: 100 Erieview Plaza Cleveland OH 44114

DEWINDT, HAROLD CLIFFORD, clergyman; b. Grand Rapids, Mich., Jan. 23, 1911; s. Justus Christopher and Amy (Tuinman) DeW.; A.B., Hope Coll., 1933; Th.B., Princeton, 1936; A.M., Columbia, 1941; D.D. (hon.), Trinity U., 1946; LL.D., Parsons Coll. 1958; m. Esther A. Maurits, June 13, 1936; 1 son, David Maurits. Ordained to ministry of Presbyn. Ch., 1936; served as minister First Ch., Morrisville, Pa., 1935- 37, Webb Horton Meml. Ch., Middletown, N.Y., 1937-42, West-Park Ch. N.Y. C., 1943-53, Kirk in the Hills, Bloomfield Hills, Mich, 1953—. Vice-moderator of N.Y. Presbytery, 1953-54; trustee ch. erection fund, Gen. Assembly of Presbyn. Ch. U.S.A., 1951-55; mem. bd. mgrs., joint dept. evangelism, Nat. Council of Chs.; mem. gen. council Synod of Mich., also Presbytery of Detroit. Clubs: Bloomfield Hills Country, Forest Lake Country, Home: West Long Lake Rd Bloomfield Hills MI 48013

DEWING, ARTHUR STONE utilities exec.; b. Boston, Apr. 16, 1880; s. Charles Hamlet and Eliza Williams Stone (Paine) D.; A.B., Harvard, 1902, A.M., 1903, Ph.D., 1905; postgrad. U. Munich, Germany; m. Frances Hall Rousmaniere, June 3, 1910; children—Mary Stone (Mrs. Lloyd L. Morain), Abigail Starr (Mrs. Stuart B. Avery, Jr.), Ruth Rousmaniere (Mrs. James D. Ewing). Asst. in philosophy, Harvard, 1902-11, instr. in econ., 1911-12, 1919-20, asst. prof. econs., 1920-22, asso. prof. finance, 1922-27, prof., 1927-33; pres. Portland, Chatham, Hazardville and Jewett City Water cos., Ill. Gas Co., Eastern Ill. Gas & Securities Co., Pinetum, Inc. (N.H.), Wetmore Gas Producing Co.; pres. Granite State Gas & Elec. Co., Edward Durant Investment Co.; bd. dirs. Fall River Gas Co., Keene N.H. Sentinel Pub. Co., others; chmn. Old Colony R.R. Bondholders Protective Committee. Mem. of bd. of visitors classical art Boston Museum of Fine Arts. Fellow Am. Acad. Arts, Scis., Am. Numismatic Soc. (Greek numismatics (past pres.), Royal Numismatic Soc.; mem. The Am. Friends of Greece, Mass. Hist. Soc., N.E. Hist. Geneal. Soc., Mass. Soc. Mayflower Descs., Soc. for Preservation of N.E. Antiquities (past pres.), Archeol. Inst. Am. (past pres. Boston soc.). Republican. Author books including: Life as Reality, 1910; Corporate Promotions and Reorganization, 1914, Reprinted in American Life and Culture, 1969; Financial Policy of Corporations, 1920, 5th rev. edit. 1953; The Corporation—A Study of Its Financial Structure, 1934. Address: 8 Willard St Cambridge MA 02138 Died Jan. 20, 1971

DEWIRE, JOHN WILLIAM, educator, physicist; b. Milton, Pa., June 12, 1916; s. John W. and Ella Mae (Aunkst) DeW.; B.S., Ursinus Coll., 1938; Ph.D., Ohio State U., 1942; m. Ruth Hale, Mar. 20, 1943; children—Susan (Mrs. James Hosek), William H. Asso. scientist OSRD, Princeton, 1942-43, Los Alamos Sci. Lab., 1943-46; mem. faculty Cornell U., 1946—, prof. physics, 1957—. NSF sr. postdoctoral fellow, 1960-61; Fulbright scholar, 1967-68. Home: 148 Pine Tree Rd Ithaca NY 14850.

DEWITT, BRYCE SELIGMAN, educator, physicist; b. Dinuba, Cal., Jan. 8, 1923; s. Lewis Lipman and Honor (Pettit) Seligman; S.B., Harvard, 1943, Ph.D., 1950; m. Cécile Andrée Paule Morette, May 2, 1951; children—Nicolette, Jan, Christiane, Abigail. Sr. research physicist U. Cal. Radiation Lab., Berkeley and Livermore, 1952-55; mem. faculty U. N.C., 1956-, Agnew Hunter Bahnson, Jr. prof. physics, 1964-; mem. Inst. Advanced Study, Princeton, 1949-50,54,64,66; Fulbright lectr., Bombay, India, 1952, Osaka, Japan, 1964; dir. research Inst. Field Physics, U.N.C., 1956-. Served as aviator USNR, World War II. Fellow Am. Phys. Soc.; mem. Internat. Com. Relativity and Gravitation, Phi Beta Kappa, Sigma Xi. Author: Dynamical Theory of Groups and Fields, 1964. Home: Route 5 Chapel Hill NC 27514

DEWITT, HARRY KEATOR, hospital supply co. exec.; b. Schenectady, Feb. 22, 1907; s. Norman and Susan (Keator) DeW.; B.A., Union Coll., Schenectady, 1929; m. Harriet B. Rogers, Aug. 5, 1933; 1 dau., Nancy (Mrs. Paul Minus). With N.Y. Telephone Co., 1928-41; with Am. Hospital Supply Corp., 1941—, pres. hospital supply div., corporate v.p., 1959-61, group v.p., 1961-63, exec. v.p. corp., 1963-64, pres., 1964—, chief exec. officer, 1965—, also dir. Trustee, bd. sec. Nat. Coll. Edn. Mem. Hosp. Industries Assn. (past pres.). Presbyn. Clubs: Chicago, Economic, Glenview. Home: 140 Appletree Rd Winnetka IL 60093 Office: 1740 Ridge Av Evanston IL 60204

DEWITT, JOHN DOYLE, ins. exec.; b. Sully, Ia., June 25, 1902; s. Henry and Lola Belle (Forsyth) DeW.; student Drake U., 1921-24; LL.D., 1955; LL.D. (hon.), Trinity Coll., 1962; L.H.D. (hon.), U. Hartford, 1964; m. Marjorie Aileen Everett, Oct. 3, 1927; children—John Doyle, Patricia Ann (Mrs. Brig Barnum Elliott). Claim adjuster, Travelers Ins. Cos., Hartford, Des Moines office, 1925, transferred to home office, 1927, claim examiner, 1929, asst. mgr. life, accident, and group claim dept., 1933, supervising adjuster in charge met. N.Y., 1937, asst. mgr. home office, 1939, sec. in charge all claim depts. 1943, asst. to pres. 1945, v.p., asst. to pres. Travelers Ins. Co., Travelers Indemnity Co., Travelers Fire Ins. Co., Charter Oak Fire Ins. Co., 1950- 52, pres., dir., 1952-64, chmn. bd., chief exec. officer, 1964-68, chairman of the board of directors, 1964-70; pres. Eastern Life Claim Conf., 1939-40; chmn. exec. com. of International Claim Assn. 1942-43, pres., 1943-44; dir. Chase Manhattan Bank, N.A., Hartford Nat. Bank & Trust Company, Veeder Industries, Inc., also So. N.E. Telephone Co., United Aircraft Corp., Trustee Nat. Safety Council, Herbert Hoover Birthplace Found., YMCA Greater Hartford; a founder, regent U. Hartford; corporator Mt. Sinai Hosp.; corporator Saint Francis Hospital; trustee Rensselaer Poly. Inst. Conn., Inc., Hartford Grad. Center; dir. Hartford Hosp. Served in USN, World War I. Recipient of the Freedoms Found. Honor Medal award, 1950; spl. award Conn. League Hist. Socs., 1961; Drake U.'s Alumni Distinguished Service award, 1968. Fellow Am. Numis. Soc.; mem. Hartford C. of C. (Certificate of Merit award), Hartford Numis Soc. Republican. Methodist. Clubs: Hartford, Ekwanok Country, Links, Golf (Hartford); Economic, Twentieth Century, Accident and Health (N.Y.C.); Nat. Golf (Augusta, Ga.). Home: 111 Stoner Dr West Hartford CT 06007

DEWITT, PAUL BURTON, lawyer; b. Sheldon, Ia., Apr. 15, 1910; s. Jesse Arthur and Pearl (Monk) DeW.; A.B., A.M., U. Ia., 1931; A.M., Harvard, 1934; LL.B., U. Mich., 1937; m. Else Hvistendahl, May 31, 1943; 1 son, Jon Lance. Admitted to Ia. bar, 1937, N.Y. bar, 1969; practiced with Shull and Marshall, Sioux City, 1937-38; chief legislative drafting bur. and state law librarian, State of Ia., 1939-40; asst. sec. Am. Judicature Soc., Ann Arbor, Mich., 1941; reporter, rules com., Supreme Ct. Ia., Des Moines, 1941-42; exec. sec. Assn. of Bar City of N. Y. 1945—; sec. Nat. Conf. of Judicial Councils since 1941. Served as lt. USNR, 1942-46, now lt. comdr. Recipient medal Assn. of the Bar City of New York, 1970. Mem. Am. (alternate del. to U.N., 1946, sec. spl. com. on improving judicial adminstrn., chmn. sect. of bar activities, 1947-49; dir. state coms., sect., jud. adminstrn., 1948-51; mem. Ho. of Dels.), Ia. (sec. 1941-42) bar assns., Phi Beta Kappa, Phi Delta Theta. Episcopalian. Clubs: Century Coffee House (N.Y.). Editor Annual Handbook Nat. Conf. of Jud. Councils. Home: 1601 E 20th St New York City NY 10010 Office: 42 W 44th St New York City NY 10036

DEWITT, ROBERT LIONNE, Jr., bishop; b. Jamaica Plain, Mass., Mar. 12, 1916; s. William Judson and Ethel (Furness) DeW.; B.A., Amherst Coll., 1937; B.D., Episcopal Theol. Sch., Cambridge, Mass. 1940; D.D., Va. Theol. Sem., 1961, Amherst Coll., 1962, Phila. Div. Sch., 1965; L.H.D., Temple U., 1965; m. Barbara Anne De Yoe, June 15, 1939; children—Rebecca (Mrs. Thomas Kershner), Laurence B., Kathrina, John, Robert Lionne. Ordained to ministry Episcopal Ch., 1940; curate Christ Ch., Oranbrook, Mich., 1940-44, rector, 1948-60; rector St. Luke's Ch., Ypsilanti, Mich., 1944-48; suffragan bishop Mich., 1960-64; bishop coadjutor of Pa., 1964; bishop of Pa., 1964—. Chmn. home dept., exec. council P.E. Ch., 1964—; chmn. citizens adv. com. integration Bd. Edn. Phila., 1965—. Recipient Fellowship award Fellowship Commn., 1966. Mem. Newcomen Soc., English Speaking Union. Home: Mather Rd East of Morris Rd Ambler PA 19002. Office: 202 W Rittenhouse Sq Philadelphia PA 19103

DEWITT, ROSCOE PLIMPTON, architect; b. Dallas, Feb 18, 1894; s. Edgar A. and Imogene (Walker) DeW.; A.B., Dartmouth, 1914; Harvard U., 1917; M.A. in architecture; hon. M.A., Dartmouth Coll., 1937; m. Elizabeth Boyd Newcomb, 1943; children by previous marriage—Sylvia Louise (Mrs. Tom Ferguson), Elizabeth Frances (Mrs. Julian Acker). Engaged in practice architecture, Dallas, 1919—; architect Parkland, Meml. Hosp., Neiman Marcus Preston Center, Neiman Marcus Dallas, Wynnewood Housing Project, Wynnewood and Varsity Village Shopping Centers, Woodrow Wilson, Sunset high schs., So. Meth. U. adminstrn. bldg., stadium and library, Highland Park Meth. Ch. and High Sch., Tex. & Pacific R.R. Hosp., Marshall, Texas, also schs. at Athens, Cameron, Galveston, Harlingen, Kaufman, Temple, Denison, Mexia and other cities in Texas, Pampa (Tex.) Post Office, Sam Rayburn Library, Bonham, Tex., Carswell AFB Hosp., Sheppard AFB Hosp., Mil. Housing Project, Laughlin AFB, St. Vincent's Hosp., Jacksonville, Fla., remodeling the Cannon House Office bldg., D.C.; asso. architect extension of East front of Capitol and James Madison Meml. Bldg. of Library of Congress, Washington Mus. of Fine Arts, Dallas, Fed. Housing Group, Dallas; Tex. Bldg. at Tex. Centennial expn. (1936); Music Bldg., Tex. Woman's Coll., Avion Village housing project, Grand Prairie, Tex., Mercy, Psychiat., Mound Park hosps., St. Petersburg, Fla.; office bldgs. Nat. Cash Register Co., Dallas, Republic Ins. Co., Los Angeles, Dallas, N.Y.C., St. Paul Hosp. Chapel, Convent and Clinic, Dallas, Presbyn. Hosp., Dallas; cons. architect Hotel Dieu Hosp., New Orleans. Bd. dirs. Dallas Civic Opera. Served as 2d lt., capt. C.A.C., U.S. Army, World War I; capt. to lt. col. C.A.C., World War II. Fellow A.I.A. (past pres. Dallas chpt.); asso. personal mem. Am. Hosp. Assn.; mem. Am. Fedn. Arts, Tex. Soc. Architects, Soc. Am. Mil. Engrs., Royal Soc. Arts, Am. Assn. Hosp. Planning, Phi Delta Theta. Clubs: Dallas Athletic, Dallas Country, Brookhollow Golf, City (Dallas); Harvard (N.Y.C.); Cosmos (Washington). Home: 4657 Mockingbird Lane Dallas TX 75209 Office: 2025 Cedar Springs Rd Dallas TX 75201 also 425 13th St NW Washington DC 20004

DEWITT, WILLIAM ORVILLE, baseball club exec.; b. St. Louis, Missouri, August 3, 1902; s. William Joseph and Lulu May (Sowash) D.; student St. Louis University, 1925-27, Law School, 1928-31, Washington U., 1927-28; m. Margaret Holekamp, Mar. 21, 1936; children—Joan, Donna Dorothy, William O. Office boy for St. Louis Browns, 1916; stenographer St. Louis Cardinals, 1917-25, treas., 1926-35, v.p., 1936; v.p., gen. mgr. St. Louis Browns, 1936-48, pres., 1949- 51, v.p., 1952-53; asst. gen. mgr. N.Y. Yankees, 1954-56; baseball coordinator, 1957-59; pres. Detroit Baseball Co., 1959-60; v.p., gen. mgr. Cin. Baseball Club Co., 1960-61; pres., gen. mgr. Cincinnati Reds, 1961-66; baseball cons. 1967—. Admitted to Mo. bar, 1931, Fed. bar, 1958. Named Maj. League Exec. Yr., 1944. Mem. Mo. Bar Assn., Bar Assn. St. Louis, Delta Theta Phi, Alpha Sigma Nu. Mason (Shriner). Presbyn. Clubs: University (St. Louis); Queen City, Cincinnati Country (Cin.); Bankers, Commonwealth. Home: 2841 Ambleside Pl Cincinnati OH 45208 Office: Central Trust Tower Cincinnati OH 45202

DEWOLF, L. HAROLD, clergyman, educator; b. Columbus, Neb., Jan. 31, 1905; s. Lotan R. and Elsie (Cook) DeW.; student York Coll., 1920-22; A.B., Neb. Wesley U., 1924, S.T.D., 1948; S.T.B., Boston U., 1926, Ph.D., 1935; postgrad. U. Neb., 1929-30; m. Martha P. Monkman, Aug. 5, 1925 (dec. Feb. 1939); children—Donald J., Elaine L. (Mrs. Francis V. Lombardi); m. 2d, Madeleine E. Marsh, June 15, 1940; children—Daniel L., Edward M. Ordained to ministry Meth. Ch., 1926; pastor Neb. Conf., 1926-31, Dracut, Mass., 1931-36; from lectr. to prof. philosophy Boston U., 1934-44, prof. systematic theology Sch. Theology, 1944-65, univ. lectr., 1960-61; dean, prof. systematic theology Wesley Theol. Sem., 1965—; vis. prof. U. So. Cal., summer 1950; spl. cons. theol. edn. Central and East Africa for Meth. Ch. and Internat. Missionary Council, 1955-56, for World Council of Chs., 1962-63, East and Southeast Asia for Found. for Theol. Edn. in Southeast Asia, 1967; vis. lectr. Wellesley Coll., 1957-58; faculty Meth. Theol. Inst., Lincoln Coll., Oxford. Eng., 1958; Cole lectr. Vanderbilt U., 1960; Colliver lectr. on Christian Edn., Coll. of the Pacific, 1960; Mendenhall lectr. DePauw U., 1962; spl. lectr. Facultad Evangelica de Teologia, Buenos Aires, 1963. Mem. nat. bd. SANE, 1961—. Mem. Am. Theol. Soc. (pres. 1961-62), Am. Soc. Christian Ethics Am. Acad. of Religion, Am. Assn. U. Profs., Phi Kappa Phi, Pi Kappa Delta. Author: Issues Concerning Immortality in Thirty Ingersoll lectures, 1896-35, 1935; The Religious Revolt Against Reason, 1949; A Theology of the Living Church, 1953, rev. edits., 1967, 69; Trends and Frontiers of Religious Thought, 1955; The Case for Theology in Liberal Perspective, 1959; Present Trends in Christian Thought, 1960; The Enduring Message of the Bible, 1960; Teaching Our Faith in God, 1963; A Hard Rain and A Cross, 1966; Responsible Freedom Guidelines to Christian Action, 1971; chpts. in books, articles. Home: 4435 Albermarle St N W Washington DC 20016

DEWS, PETER BOOTH, med. researcher, educator; b. Eng., Sept. 11, 1922; s. George Ashley and Ella (Booth) D.; came to U.S., 1948, naturalized, 1957; M.B., Ch.B., U. Leeds (Eng.), 1944; Ph.D., U. Minn., 1952; M.A. (hon.), Harvard, 1959; m. Grace Miller, Dec. 6, 1949; childrenPamela, Kenneth, Alan, Michael. House physician Grimsby (Eng.) Dist. Hosp., 1944-45; lectr. pharmacology U. Leeds, 1945-47; Wellcome research fellow, Tuckahoe, N.Y., 1948-49; fellow, then research asso. physiology and biometrics Mayo Clinic, Rochester, Minn., 1950-52; instr. to asso. prof. pharmacology Harvard Med. Sch., Boston, 1953-62, Stanley Cobb prof. psychiatry and psychobiology, 1962-. Mem. adv. coms. NIH, USPHS. Fellow of Am. Adad. of Arts and Scis., mem. Physiol. Soc., Am. Soc. Pharmacology and Exptl. Therapeutics. Editorial bd. jours. in field. Contbr. articles profl. jours. Home: 181 Upland Rd Newtonville MA 02160 Office: 25 Shattuck St Boston MA 02115

DEWSBURY, EDWIN L., banker. Sr. v.p. Dime Savs. Bank Bklyn. Office: 9 De Kalb Av Brooklyn NY 11201*

DEXTER, BYRON, editor; b. Newark, Dec. 9, 1900; s. James Leonard and Mary Gordon (Bourne) D.; A.B., Princeton, 1923; m. Jeannette Thurber Pruyn, 1927 (div.); children—Joan Gordon (Mrs. D. Blackmer), Dierdre Pruyn (Mrs. S. Maiarkey); m. 2d, Jane Wilson, 1940 (div.); m. 3d, Lorraine Le Huray Commons, 1944. Reporter, Atlanta Jour., 1923; staff mem. Charles Scribner's Sons, 1924-27; circulation mgr., asst. editor, New Republic, 1928-31, 34-42; asst. editor Fgn. Affairs, 1943, mng. editor, 1949-55; editor Let's Talk About, monthly discussions of fgn. affairs, 1952-55; editor Vermonter mag., 1966. Mem. Council Fgn. Relations. Clubs: Century, Woodstock Country, Princeton of N.Y. Editor: The Arabs: (with Philip K. Hitti) A Short History, 1943. Author: The Years of Opportunity: The League of Nations 1920-26, 1967. Contbr. to Clausewitz and Soviet Strategy in the Soviet Union 1922-62 (editor Philip E. Mosely), 1962. Contbr. to periodicals. Home: Wicklow Farm South Woodstock VT 05071

DEXTER, HOWARD WAYNE, meat packing co. exec.; b. Vinton, Ia., Mar. 30, 1909; s. John Albert and Minnie (Standard) D.; student Gates Coll., 1928; m. Gail Smith, Nov. 15, 1931; children—Gerry, Mary (Mrs. Richard Dean Rice), Margaret (Mrs. Randy Bray). With Rath Packing Co., Houston, 1928-30, Dallas, 1930-33, Waterloo, Ia., 1933—, asst. to controller, 1943-47, asst. controller, 1947-54, controller, 1954—, treas., 1967—. Mem. finance com. Girl Scouts U.S.A., Waterloo. Mem. Financial Execs. Inst., Am. Meat Inst. (chmn. com. on standard costs), Nat. Assn. Accountants (past pres. Waterloo chpt., nat. dir.), Waterloo C. of C. (tax study com.). Republican. Methodist. Club: Knife and Fork (dir. Waterloo). Home: 3233 Terrace Dr Cedar Falls IA 50613. Office: Rath Packing Co Elm and Sycamore Sts Waterloo IA 50704

DEXTER, JOHN, theatrical dir.; b. Derby, Eng., Aug. 2, 1925; s. Harry James and Rose Dexter. Asso. dir. English Stage Co., 1957-63, Nat. Theatre, 1963-67, 71—; prodn. include St. Joan, 1963, Hobson's Choice, 1964, Othello, 1964, Royal Hunt of the Sun, 1964, Armstrong's Last Goodnight, 1965, Black Comedy, 1965, A Bond Honoured, 1966, The Storm, 1966, Yes and After, 1957, Purgatory, 1967, Each His Own Wilderness, 1958, Chicken Soup with Barley, 1958, Roots, 1959, I am Talking About Jerusalem, 1960, The Kitchen, 1961, Jackie the Jumper, 1963, The Keep, 1961, Squat Betty and The Sponge Room, 1962, Toys in the Attic, 1960, South, 1961, My Place, 1961, England Our England, 1962, Half A Sixpence, 1963, Wise Child, 1967, Do I Hear a Waltz?, 1965, Chips with Everything, 1962, White Lies and Black Comedy, 1967, The Unknown Soldier and his Wife, 1967; (opera) Benvenuto Cellini, 1966; (films) Virgin Soldiers, 1968, Sidelong Glances of a Pigeon Kicker, 1970, I Want What I Want, 1970; (plays) A Woman Killed With Kindness, 1971, Tyger, 1971. Address: care London Internat Famous 11-12 Hanover Sq London W 1 England

DEXTER, JOHN BONDY, fgn. service officer; b. Great Falls, Mont., June 17, 1923; s. John and Ruth (Bondy) D.; B.A., Harvard, 1947; Postgrad. Cornell U., 1952-53, Yale, 1953-54; m. Elizabeth Koupal, Feb. 14, 1952; childrenSusan, Martha, Emily, Catherine, John Robin. Joined U.S. Fgn. Service, 1947; vice consul, Canton, China, 1947-49, Instanbul, Turkey, 1949-50, Hong Kong, 1950-52; 2d sec. embassy, Rangoon, Burma, 1954-56; consul, attache U.S. Resident Delegation and Consulate Gen., Geneva, Switzerland, 1958-59; internat. economist Office Chinese Affairs, State Dept., 1960-61, officer-in-charge Burmese affairs, 1961-64, Republic of China affairs, 1964, dep. dir. Office of S.E. Asian Affairs, 1964-65; assigned to Nat. War Coll., 1965-66; dep. chief of mission Am. embassy, Singapore, 1966-68; dep. regional dir. internat. security affairs Office of Def. Sec., 1968-69; country dir. for Thailand and Burma, State Dept., 1969—. Served with AUS, 1943-45. Mem. Am. Fgn. Service Assn. Home: 6310 E Halbert Rd Bethesda MD 20014 Office: Dept State Washington DC 20520

DEXTER, LEWIS, physician; b. Concord, Mass., Mar. 1, 1910; s. Smith Owen and Helen (Denison) D.; B.A., Harvard, 1932, M.D., 1936; m. E. Cassandra Kinsman, Dec. 12, 1941; childrenLewis, Smith Owen, Cassandra Kinsman. Intern Presbyn. Hosp., N.Y.C. 1936-38; staff mem. Peter Bent Brigham Hosp. 1941—, physician 1952—; faculty mem. Med. Sch., Harvard, 1941- -; tutor medicine 1948—; prof. medicine Peter Bent Brigham Hosp., 1969—; pvt. practice Boston. Fellow A.C.P. under Doctor Bernardo A. Houssay, Inst. Physiology, Buenos Aires, Argentina, 1940-41. Diplomate Am. Bd. Internal Medicine. Fellow A.C.P., Am. Coll. of Cardiology; mem. Am. Soc. Clin. Investigation, Assn. Am. Physicians, Am. Heart Assn., Am. Physiol. Soc., Am. Acad. Arts and Scis. Club: Interurban Clin. Mem. editorial bd. Circulation, Am. Heart Jour. Home: 108 Upland Rd Brookline MA 02146 Office: 721 Huntington Av Boston MA 02115

DEXTER, RICHARD NORMAN, educator, physicist; b. Ashland, Wis., Nov. 22, 1927; s. Stephen Torrey and Mildred (Carlstrom) D.; B.S., Mich. State U., 1949; M.S., U. Wis., 1951, Ph.D., 1955; m. Gladys Ruth Eastman, Dec. 20, 1958; children—Carol, Beth, Andrea, Matthew. Staff mem. Lincoln Lab., Mass. Inst. Tech., 1952-55; mem. faculty U. Wis., 1955—, prof. physics, 1961- -; staff mem. Lincoln Lab., summer 1958, 61, IBM Research Lab., summer 1964. Served with USNR, 1945-46. Sloan fellow, 1955-58. Fellow Am. Phys. Soc.; mem. Sigma Xi. Mem. editorial bd. Revs. of Sci. Instruments, 1958-61. Research exptl. solid state physics. Home: 4034 Mandan Circle Madison WI 53711.

DEXTER, ROBERT REGINALD, aero. exec.; b. Jersey City, Sept. 1, 1908; s. Reginald James and Agnes (Paul) D.; B.S., N.Y. U., 1930, A.E., 1932; m. Isabella McConnell, June 15, 1935; children—Barbara Ann, Robert R., Reginald Thomas. Mem. sales dept. Sun Oil Co., N.Y.C., 1932-34; sales engr. Fred Buse, Inc., N.Y., 1934-36; research worker Staff Inst. Aero. Scis., N.Y.C., 1936-39; dir. Paul Kollsman Library, dir. tech. information service, 1939-43, now sec., asst. dir. U.S. panel mem. to NATO adv. group aero. research and devel., 1957-69, sec. and adminstr. tech. information programs, 1967—; exec. sec. Internat. Council Aero. Scis., 1964—, editor ICAS Procs. Paris, 1964, London, 1966. Fellow Am. Inst. Aeros. and Astronautics, A.A.A.S., Royal Aero. Soc. (London), Canadian Aeros. and Space Inst. (hon.); mem. Soc. Automotive Engrs., Aviation-Space Writers Assn., Engrs.' Council Profl. Devel. (asst. sec.), Internat. Council Aero. Scis. (exec. sec.). Methodist. Asso. editor Jour. Aero Space Scis., 1943-62; tech. editor Aero Space Engring., 1942-46, tech. adviser, 1946-62. Home: 64 Underhill Rd Ossining NY 10562 Office: 1290 Av Americas New York City NY 10019

DEY, CHARLES FREDERICK, coll. dean; b. Newark, Dec. 15, 1930; s. Elbert William and Eleanor Rose (Faatz) D.; B.A., Dartmouth, 1952; M.A., Harvard, 1957; m. Phoebe Ann Evans, Dec. 22, 1956; children—Penelope, Robin Evans, Andrew MacDougald, Thomas Ridgeway. Tchr. history Phillips Acad., Andover, Mass., 1956-60; asst. dean Dartmouth, 1960-62, asso. dean, 1962-66, dean Tucker Found., 1967—. Asso. rep. Peace Corps, Philippine Islands, 1962-63; dir. project A Better Chance, also trustee. Trustee Kimball Union Acad. Served to lt. USNR, 1953-56. Danforth Found. Underwood fellow, 1971-72. Mem. Casque and Gauntlet, Beta Theta Pi. Episcopalian (vestryman). Author: ABC Report, 1964. Home: 36 N Main St Hanover NH Office: College Hall Hanover NH 03755

DEY, JOSEPH CHARLES, Jr., sports exec.; b. Norfolk, Va., Nov. 17, 1907; s. Joseph Charles and Martha Lillian (Holt) D.; student U. Pa., 1925-27; m. Rosalie Moran Knapp, Jan. 29, 1937; 1 son, Edward Knapp. Newspaper Sports writer, 1923- 34; exec. dir. U.S. Golf Assn., 1934-69; commr. tournament players div. Profl. Golfers Assn. Am. 1969—. Sec. World Amateur Golf Council 1958-69. Served as lt. USNR, World War II. Mem. Sigma Alpha Epsilon. Republican. Episcopalian. Clubs: Creek (Locust Valley); Union League (N.Y.C.); Royal and Ancient Golf (St. Andrews, Scotland). Home: Factory Pond Rd Locust Valley NY 11560. Office: 60 E 42d St New York City NY 10017 also Profl Golfers Assn Am Box 12458 Palm Beach Gardens FL 33403

DE YOUNG, HERBERT CORNELL, lawyer; b. Harvey, Ill., Feb. 16, 1904; s. Frederic Robert and Miriam (Cornell) De Y.; A.B., U. Chgo., 1925, J.D., 1928; m. Virginia Winston, Dec. 28, 1940; children—James Winston, Laura Cornell. Admitted to Ill. bar, 1928; asso. firm Miller, Gorham, Wescott & Adams, and predecessors, Chgo., 1928-34, partner, 1934—. Mem. Ill. Com. on Adoption Laws, 1957- 59, Ill. Commn. Higher Edn., 1959—, Mayor Chgo Adv. Com. Tb. Bd. dirs. Tb. Inst. of Chgo. and Cook County, 1936—, exec. com., 1937—, pres., 1946-56; bd. dirs. Welfare Council Met. Chgo., 1954—, exec. com., 1956, 59-61, treas. 1959-61. Elected citizen fellow Inst. Medicine, Chgo., 1950. Mem. Nat. Tb Assn. (bd. dirs. 1947—, exec. com. 1956—, pres. 1960-61), Chgo. Law Inst. (bd. mgrs. 1940-47, sec. 1941-46, pres. 1947). Home: 336 Raleigh Rd Kenilworth IL 60043 Office: 1 N LaSalle St Chicago IL 60602

DEYOUNG, RUSSELL, rubber co. exec.; b. Rutherford, N.J., Apr. 3, 1909; s. Abram and May (Thompson) DeY.; B.S., Akron U., 1932, D.Sc., 1960; M.S., Mass. Inst. Tech., 1940; m. Lois E. Biship, May 1, 1937; children—Bruce Russell, Ralph Earl, Janet Lois (Mrs. James Mungo). With Goodyear Tire & Rubber Co., Akron, O., 1928—, v.p. 1956-58, pres., 1958-64, chmn. bd., chief exec. officer, 1964—; dir. Lykes-Youngstown Corp., Kennecott Copper Corp., Aluminum Co. Am., Rubber Mfrs. Assn. Mem. nat. adv. council Jr. Achievement, 4-H Found. Mem. corp. Mass. Inst. Tech.; mem. Bus. Council. Trustee Conf. Bd. Mem. N.A.M. (dir.), Soc. Automotive Engrs. Clubs: Laurel Valley (Latrobe, Pa.); Union (Cleve.), University (N.Y.C.); Portage Country (Akron); Congress Lake (Hartville, O.). Home: 910 Eaton Av Akron OH 44303 Office: 1144 E Market St Akron OH 44316

DE ZENDEGUI, GUILLERMO, editor; b. La Habana, Cuba, Feb. 28, 1912; s. Rafael and Maria del Loreto (Carbonell) de Z.; B.A., Belen High Sch., 1920; Dr. Social and Polit. Scis., U. Havana, 1937, J.D., 1939, Journalism Degree, 1940; m. Beatriz Lugris, Dec. 28, 1944; 1 son, Guillermo. Journalist, writer, 1937—; pres. Cultural Com. Municipal Govt., Havana, 1950-52; gen. dir. Nat. Inst. Culture, Cuba, 1954-58; dep. dir. dept. cultural affairs OAS, 1964—; editor-in-chief Americas, Washington, 1963—. Decorated Order of C.M. de Cespedes (Cuba); Orden Petión at Bolivar (Haiti); Order of Cristóbal Colón (Dominican Republic); Orden of Isabel La Católica (Spain). Author: Panorama de Sociología Cubana, 1948; Ambito de Martí, 1953; also essays. Home: 5205 Massachusetts Av Washington DC 20036 Office: 1725 I St NW Washington DC 20006

DEZENDORF, JAMES CORKISH, lawyer; b. Portland, Ore., June 7, 1910; s. James N. and Hattie (Corkish) D.; LL.B., U. Ore., 1932; m. Nancy Bennett Richards, Apr. 10, 1940; children—Elizabeth Ann, James Nelson, Lee Richards. Admitted to Ore. bar, 1932, since practiced Portland; partner McColloch, Dezendorf, Spears & Lubersky and predecessor firms, Portland. Sec., dir. Nicholas Ungar, Inc., Beebe Co., Inc., Country Gas, Inc., Domestic Gas Co., Domestic Indsl. Gas. Co.; dir. MacDonald Andrews Co., Inc., Portland; v.p., dir. Chicona Farms, Inc., Gile Investment Co. Mem. Nat. Conf. Commrs. Uniform State Laws, 1941—, pres., 1957-59; mem. U.S. delegation The Hague Conf. on Pvt. Internat. Law, 1960, 64, 68; mem. Am. delegation to 2d Diplomatic Conf. on Internat. Sale of Goods, The Hague, 1964; Am. rep. Internat. Inst. for Unification of Pvt. Law, Rome, 1959, 63, 68; mem. adv. com. U.S. Sec. State on Pvt. Internat. Law, 1959—; mem. permanent editorial bd. on Uniform Comml. Code, 1959—. Mem. Internat., Am., Multnomah bar assns., Ore. State Bar, Am. Law Inst. (exec. com., dir., treas.), Am. Judicature Soc. Clubs: Arlington, Astoria Golf and Country, International, Multhomah Athletic, Racquet, University, Waverley Country. Home: 1929 S W Carter Lane Portland OR 97201 also Green Pastures PO Box 77 Gearhart OR 97138 Office: Pacific Bldg Portland OR 97204

DEZUTTER, HENRY WAYNE, educator; b. Chgo., July 23, 1941; s. Henry M. and Evelyn (Dammer) DeZ.; student Williams Coll., 1959-61; B.A., U. Mich., 1963; M.S. in Journalism, Northwestern U., 1965; m. Janet Ann Hertler, Feb. 16, 1963; children—Christopher Blake, Maxwell Tobin. Edn. writer Chgo. Daily News, 1966-70; tchr. Malcolm X Coll., Chgo., 1970—, also coordinator communications Media Inst., 1970—. Cofounder, editor Chgo. Journalism Rev., 1968. Office: Malcolm X Coll 1900 W Van Buren Chicago IL 60612

DHARMAPUTRA, GARNAWAN, Indonesian diplomat; b. Bandung, Indonesia, Jan. 12, 1926; s. R. Suhardjawikarta and Dewi (Kurniasih) D.; Dr., Gadjah Mada U., Indonesia, 1955; postgrad., U. Cal. at Berkeley, 1956-57; grad. 1st Asian Fgn. Service Course, Manila, 1967, sr. diplomatic course, Djakarta, 1968; m. Semiarti Pjunaedi, Dec. 15, 1955 (div. 1967); children—Geofano, Budiati. 2d, then 1st sec. Indonesian embassy, Belgrade, Yugoslavia, 1960-64; counselor Indonesian embassy, Kuala Lumpur, Malaysia, 1968-70, Washington, 1970—; lectr., Djaja Baja U., 1967-68. Leader Indonesian govt. team to gen. elections in Sarawak, Malaysia, 1970. Mem. exec. bd. Indonesian Students Youth Assn., 1952-55, World U. Service, Indonesian com., 1953-55; Cal.-Indonesia Inst., Indonesia, 1954-57. Served with Students Corps, War of Independence, 1946-49. Trans. into Indonesian: The Proper Study of Mankind (Stuart Chase), 1964. Home: 4981 Battery Lane Bethesda MD 20014 Office: 2020 Massachusetts Av Washington DC 20036

DIACONESCU, GHEORGHE, ambassador of Romania to UN; b. Mar. 12, 1915; ed. Sch. Law Iasi U. In Supreme Ct. and Gen. State Pros. Magistracy until 1954; minister justice, 1951-61; ambassador to Poland, 1961-66; ambassador Romania to UN, 1966—. Prof. law Bucharest U. Address: 60 E 93d St New York City NY 10028*

DIAKITE, YORO, Mali army officer and govt. ofcl. Formerly dir. Mil. Sch. at Kali; 1st v.p. mil. com. Nat Liberation, 1968—; prime minister provisional govt. Mali, 1968-69; prime minister, minister of transport, telecommunications and tourism, 1969-70; minister of interior, security and def., 1970-71; premier minister of def., 1971—. Address: Bamoko Republic of Mali*

DIAL, WILLIAM HENRY, banker; b. Lake City, Fla., Dec. 12, 1907; s. John Clarke and Katie Belle (Woltz) D.; LL.B., U. Fla., 1932; m. Grace Franklin, Feb. 9, 1935; children—Joan (Mrs. E. Daniel Ruffier), Patricia (Mrs. Peter Vig). Admitted to Fla. bar, 1932; practiced in Orlando, 1932-58; mem. firm Akerman, Dial & Akerman; atty. Fla. Bankers Assn., 1946-58; exec. v.p. First Nat. Bank, Orlando, 1958-61, pres., 1961-68, chmn. bd., 1968—, also dir.; chmn. bd. First at Orlando Corp.; dir. Seaboard Coast Line Industries, Seaboard Coast Line R.R., So. Bell Tel. & Tel., Fla. Gas Co., Fla. Gas Utilities Co., Fla. Gas Transmission Co., Winter Park, 1st Nat. Bank of Leesburg, Citizens Bank of Gainsville, Fla. Chmn. bd. United Appeal, Orange County, 1961; mem. Fla. Council 100, 1962—; mem. Fla. Road Bd., 1955-58, Fla. Bd. Control, 1953-54; former mem. regional adv. com. 6th Nat. Bank Region, Comptroller of Currency, treas. Central Fla. Devel. Com., 1963; mem. adv. bd. Fla. Inst. Tech., 1967—. Served to lt. col. AUS, World War II. Mem. Orange County Bar Assn. (past pres.), Orlando Area C. of C. (past pres.), Am., Fla. (pres. 1966-67) bankers assns. Presbyn. (deacon). Rotarian. Clubs: Orlando Country, Bay Hill, Executives, University, Citrus. Author: Florida Banking Code, 1953; History of the Banking Laws of Florida, 1953. Home: 1132 Country Club Dr Orlando FL 32804 Office: PO Box 3833 Orlando FL 32802

DIAMANDIS, PETER GEORGE, publisher; b. Newark, Nov. 26, 1931; s. Peter G. and Agnes (Yeamans) D.; B.S., Bucknell U., 1953; postgrad. Coll. City N.Y., 1957; m. Joan Lafferandre, Apr. 2, 1955; children—Peter, Christian, Cameron, Hollis, T.G., Jason. Account exec. Grey Advt., N.Y.C., 1957-59; sr. v.p. The Lampert Agy., Inc., N.Y.C., 1962-70; pub. Mademoiselle mag., N.Y.C., 1970-71; dir. Worldwide Indorsements, Inc. Dir. Consumers Ecol. Council. Dir. Coty Awards Found. Served with USNR, Korea. Mem. Advt. Club N.Y., Sales Execs. Club. Independent. Mem. United Ch. of Rowayton. Home: 50 Rowayton Av Rowayton CT 06853 Office: 420 Lexington Av New York City NY 10017

DIAMANDOPOULOS, PETER, educator; b. Irakleion, Crete, Greece, Sept. 1, 1928; s. Theodore George and Rita (Mouzenides) D.; came to U.S., 1948, naturalized, 1964; diploma with honors, Athens Coll.,' 1947; B.A. cum laude, Harvard, 1951, M.A., 1956, Ph.D., 1957; m. Jamie Gay Hitchcock, Aug. 9, 1963; children-Theodore, Cybele, Ariadne. Instr. philosophy Bates Coll., 1958; instr., then asst. prof. philosophy U. Md., 1958-62; mem. faculty Brandeis U., 1962—, prof. philosophy, 1965—, dean faculty, 1965—; dir. studies Adlai Stevenson Inst., Chgo., 1968—. cons. history of sci. Smithsonian Instn., 1959-61. Mem. Am. Philol. Assn., Am. Philos. Assn., Mind Assn., Aristotelian Soc. Home: Prudential Center Apts Boston MA 02199 Office: Brandeis Univ Waltham MA 02154

DIAMANT, ALFRED, educator; b. Vienna, Austria, Sept. 25, 1917; s. Ignatz and Julia (Herzog) D.; came to U.S., 1940, naturalized, 1942; student Textilschule Vienna, 1935-36; A.B. with highest honors, Ind. U., 1947; M.A., Yale, 1948, Ph.D., 1957; m. Mary Ann Redmon, Mar. 18, 1943; children—Steven R., Alice L. Textile engr., Austria, Yugoslavia, U.S., 1935-38, 40- 42; from instr. to asso. prof. polit. sci. U. Fla., 1950-60; prof. polit. sci. Haverford Coll., 1960-67, chmn. dept., 1963-67; prof. polit. sci. Ind. U. Bloomington, 1967—, dir. grad. studies, 1969-71, sr. research asso. European adminstrn. research project, 1966-70, dir. West European studies program, 1971—. Vis. asso. prof. polit. sci. Yale, 1958-59, Columbia, summer 1961; vis. prof. Ruhr U. Bochum, 1966-67. Mem. program com. Comparative Adminstrn. Group, 1963-70; cons. U.S. Office Edn., 1965-66. Served to 1st lt. AUS, 1942-45. Tchr. study grantee Danforth Found., 1955; Fulbright travel grantee, 1966. Mem. Am. Polit. Sci. Assn., Am. Soc. Pub. Adminstrn., Am. Assn. U. Profs. (chmn. Haverford Coll. chpt. 1962-64), Phi Beta Kappa. Democrat. Episcopalian. Author: Austrian Catholics and the First Republic: Democracy, Capitalism and the

Social Order, 1918-34, 1960 (trans. into German, Italian 1964); Modellbetrachtung der Entwicklungsverwaltung, 1967; co-author: Temporal Dimensions of Development Administration,, 1970; Frontiers of Developmental Administration, 1971. Asso. mng. editor Jour. Politics, 1950-55; editorial bd. Jour. Politics, 1968—, Jour. Comparative Adminstrn., 1968—. Contbr. chpts. to 5 books, articles to profl. jours. Home: 2033 Montclair Av Bloomington IN 47401

DIAMOND, BERNARD LEE, educator, psychiatrist; b. San Francisco, Dec. 8, 1912; s. Leon Isaac and Rose (Cohen) D.; A.B., U. Cal. at Berkeley, 1935; M.D., U. Cal. at Berkeley and San Francisco, 1939; m. Ann Landy, Feb. 10, 1946; children—Joan (Mrs. Menachem Katz), Lynn (Mrs. Alan Feiger), Larry, Lisa, Judy, Jan. Intern, resident psychiatry U. Mich. Neuropsychiat. Inst., 1938- 40, 41-42; grad. San Francisco Psychoanalytic Inst., 1952; pvt. practice psychiatry and psychoanalysis, San Francisco, 1945-64; faculty U. Cal. at Berkeley, 1963—, prof. criminology and law, 1964—, clin. prof. psychiatry, 1968—, acting dean Sch. Criminology, 1969-70. Mem. Cal. Commn. Insanity and Criminal Offenders, 1960-63. Bd. dirs. Wright Inst., Berkeley. Served to lt. col. M.C., AUS, 1940-41, 42-45. Recipient J. Elliot Royer award U. Cal., 1964. Fellow A.A.A.S., Am. Psychiat. Assn. (Isaac Ray award 1968), Am. Orthopsychiat. Assn. (chmn. com. social issues 1967-68, bd. dirs.), Am. Sociol. Assn., Am. Coll. Psychiatrists; mem. Am., Internat. psychoanalytic assns., Group for Advancement Psychiatry, Am. Acad. Forensic Scis., Med. Correctional Assn., A.M.A., No. Cal. Psychiat. Soc. (past pres.), San Francisco Psychoanalytic Inst. and Soc. (past pres.) Contbr. articles to profl. jours. Home: P O Box 518 Ross CA 94957 Office: Sch Criminology U Cal Berkeley CA 94720

DIAMOND, DAVID LEO, composer; b. Rochester, N.Y., July 9, 1915; s. Osias and Anna (Schildhaus) D.; student Cleve. Inst. of Music, 1927-29, Eastman Sch. of Music (U. of Rochester), 1930-34, Am. Conservatory, Fountainebleau, France, Summers, 1937 and 1938, New Music and Dalcroze Inst., N.Y. C., 1934-36. Tchr. of composition Met. Music Sch., N.Y.C., 1950; lectr. on Am. music Seminar in Am. Studies, Schloss Leopoldskron, Salzburg, Austria, 1949; Slee prof. music U. Buffalo, 1961, 63; prof. composition Manhattan Sch. Music, N.Y.C., 1965-67, also chmn. of dept. of composition; Fulbright prof. U. Rome; Compositions include 8 symphonies, concertos, 11 string quartets, chamber music, preludes and fugues, sonatas, choral music and songs, scores for motion pictures, and other forms of instrumental music. Composer music for Columbia recording albums, Romeo and Juliet, The Tempest Overture, Fourth Symphony, Fourth String Quartet; composer and condr. original score for Margaret Webster prodn. of The Tempest, 1944-45; also incidental music for Tennessee Williams prodn., The Rose Tattoo; Setting of Licoln's Gettysburg Address "This Sacred Ground," 1962. Works performed by major orchs. and other well known music orgns., throughout U.S. and abroad. Recipient of numerous awards and prizes, 1935—; Prix de Rome; Paderewski award; Guggenheim fellow, 1938, 42,58; Juilliard Pub. award; Stravinsky award A.S.C.A.P. Mem. Nat. Inst. of Arts and Letters. Contbr. to Modern Music, Decision, N.Y. Herald Tribune, Musical Quarterly, Music Jour. Home: 249 Edgerton St Rochester NY 14607.

DIAMOND, FREDA, designer, home furnishings cons., lectr.; b. N.Y.C.; d. Jack and Ida (Levine) Diamond; grad. Woman's Art Sch., Cooper Union; study archtl. , decorative design in France, Eng., Italy, Belgium, Sweden, Denmark; m. Alfred Baruch. Designer, home furnishings cons., stylist, coordinator dept. stores and mfrs. in U.S., Mexico, Europe; designs displayed Mus. Modern Art, N.Y.C., Toledo Mus., Akron (O.) Art Inst., Avery Mus., Hartford, Conn., also Paris Expn. Sent to Italy as tech. adviser rehab. of Italian craftsmen after World War II; went to Japan as adviser to Japanese Govt. on handcraft and small industries for Am. market, 1957,68; adviser for Am. trade and indsl. devel. with Israel, 1969. Mem. Am. Inst. Decorators, Am. Soc. Indsl. Designers, Nat. Home Fashions League, Fashion Group. Author: The Story of Glass, 1953. Contbg. author: Your Future in the Fashion World. Address: 140 E 37th St New York City NY 10016

DIAMOND, LOUIS KLEIN, educator, physician; b. N.Y.C., May 11, 1902; s. Lazer and Lena (Klein) D.; A.B., Harvard, 1923, M.D., 1927; m. Flora Kaplan, July 2, 1929; childrenJared Mason, Susan Judith. Successively intern, asst. resident, chief resident pediatrics Children's Hosp., Boston, 1927-31, asso. med. chief, 1955-68, chief hematology div., 1951-68; fellow in hematology, 1927-28, 31-33; dir. Blood Grouping Lab., Boston, 1947—; prof. pediatrics Harvard Med. Sch., 1963-68, emeritus prof., 1968-; prof. U. Cal. Med. Sch., San Francisco Med. Center, 1968—. Med. dir. blood program A.R.C., 1948-51, bd. dirs. Met. Boston chpt., 1964-. Recipient Karl Landsteiner award Am. Assn. Blood Banks, 1963, Distinguished Pub. Service in Sci. medal Theodore Roosevelt, 1965, 4 awards sci. research Joseph P. Kennedy, Jr. Meml. Found., 1966; Carlos J. Finlay gold medal Cuban Govt., 1951; award of merit Netherland Red Cross, 1959; George R. Minot lectr. A.M.A., 1965; Rachford Meml. lectr. Children's Hosp., Cin., 1966. Mem. Am. Pediatrics Soc. (pres. 1968-69), Am. Acad. of Pediatrics (Mead Johnson award 1946). Soc. Clin. Investigation, Internat., Am. hematology socs., Soc. Pediatric Research, Mass. Med. Soc., Am. Acad. Arts and Scis., Internat. Transfusion Soc. Author: Erythroblastosis Fetalis, 1958; Atlas of Blood in Children, 1944; also numerous articles. Home: 1333 Jones St San Francisco CA 94109.

DIAMOND, MARTIN, educator; b. N.Y.C., Dec. 19, 1919; s. George and Rose (Desowitz) D.; A.M., U. Chgo., 1952, Ph.D., 1956; L.H.D., Hartford U., 1968; m. Bess Sohn, Aug. 7, 1940 (div. 1969); children—Katherine, Thomas; m. 2d, Ann Stuart Sheldon, Mar. 7, 1970. Instr., asst. prof. Ill. Inst. Tech., 1952-55; from lectr. to asst. prof. U. Chgo., 1952-58; faculty Claremont Men's Coll. and Claremont Grad. Sch., 1958-71, Wohlford prof. Am. polit. instns., 1963-71; prof. polit. sci. No. Ill. U., Dekalb, 1971—. Served with U.S. Mcht. Marine, 1943- 45. Center Advanced Study Behavioral Scis. fellow, 1960-61; Rockefeller fellow, 1963-64; Relm Found. fellow, 1966-67. Mem. Am., Western, So. Cal. polit. scis. assns., Pi Alpha Sigma. Author: (with W.M. Fisk, H. Garfinkel) The Democratic Republic, 1966, 2d edit., 1970; (with others) Essays in Federalism, 1961. Editor: (with M. Frisch) The Thirties: A Reconsideration, 1968. Address: No Ill U DeKalb IL 60115

DIAMOND, MURRAY ALLEN, hosp. exec.; b. Phila., Mar. 2, 1910; s. Edward L. and Rose (Roth) D.; B.S., Tulane U., 1933, M.D., 1936; M.P.H., Johns Hopkins, 1947; m. Irene Roth, June 14, 1936; children—Stephen P., Richard D. Intern, Trinity Hosp., Bklyn., 1936-37; sr. intern USPHS Hosp., Lexington, Ky., 1937-39, staff physician internal medicine, 1938-39; psychiat. fellow U. Colo., 1939-40; psychiat. resident USPHS Hosp., Ft. Worth, 1940-42, clin. dir., 1942-44; practice medicine specializing in psychiatry, New Orleans, 1947-49, N.Y.C., 1949-53, Lexington, 1953-57, Washington, 1962- -; exec. officer, chief psychiat. service USPHS Hosp., New Orleans, 1944- 46; regional mental health cons. Dept. Health. Edn. and Welfare, Region I and II, N.Y.C., 1946-47; dir. edn. USPHS Hosp., Lexington 1949-51, clin. dir., 1951-54, med. officer-in-charge, 1958-62; asst. chief div. hosps. USPHS, Washington, 1954-55, spl. asst. to surgeon gen. for health preparedness, 1955, dep. chief div. personnel Office Surgeon Gen., 1955- 58, asst. surgeon gen. for personnel, 1962-66; exec. dir. Touro Infirmary 1966—; instr. psychiatry Tulane U. Sch. Medicine, 1944-46, clin. prof. psychiatry, 1967—, adj. prof. Sch. Pub. Health and Tropical Medicine, 1967—; asso. prof. psychiatry U. Ky. Sch. Medicine, 1960-62. Recipient USPHS Commendation medal, 1962, USPHS Meritorious medal, 1966. Diplomate Am. Bd. Psychiatry and Neurology. Fellow Am. Psychiat. Assn., Am. Pub. Health assns., A.C.P., A.A.A.S.; mem. A.M.A., Am. Hosp. Assn., Am. Soc. Pub. Adminstrn., Soc. for Personnel Adminstrn., Nat. Health Council (dir.), Armed Forces Relief and Benefit Assn. (v.p.), Alpha Omega Alpha. Mason (32, Shriner), Lion. Home: 2423 Oriole St New Orleans LA 70122 Office: 1401 Foucher St New Orleans LA 70115

DIAMOND, SIGMUND, educator, editor; b. Balt., June 14, 1920; s. Isidor and Yetta (Mirtenbaum) D.; A.B., Johns Hopkins, 1940; Ph.D. in History, Harvard, 1953; m. Shirley Welson, Jan. 4, 1945; children—Stephen Mark, Betty. With U.S. Govt., 1942-43; internat. rep. UAW-CIO, 1943-47; lectr. Am. history Sarah Lawrence Coll., 1955-56; mem. faculty Columbia, 1955-, prof. hist. sociology, 1964-; editor Polit. Sci. Quar., 1963-. Fellow Center Advanced Study Behavioral Scis., 1959-60; sr. research fellow Newberry Library, 1967. Mem. Am. Hist. Assn., Am. Sociol. Assn., Econ. History Assn. Author: The Reputation of the American Businessman, 1955. Editor: The Nation Transformed, 1963. Home: 15 Claremont Av New York City NY 10027.

DIAMOND, WILLIAM, banker; b. Balt., Dec. 20, 1917; s. Isidor and Yetta (Mirtenbaum) D.; A.B., Johns Hopkins, 1937, Ph.D., 1942; m. Lois Marie Wilhelm, Oct. 28, 1946. With Bd. Econ. Warfare, also FEA, 1942-46, UNRRA, 1946-47; with World Bank, 1947-62; dir. devel. finance companies dept. Internat. Finance Corp., 1962-68; dir. devel. finance cos. dept. World Bank, 1968- ; dep. dir. Fgn. Trade Adminstrn. Greece, 1947-48; mem. staff Econ. Devel. Inst., World Bank, 1956-58. Mem. Phi Beta Kappa. Clubs: Cosmos, Internat. (Washington). Author: Economic Thought of Woodrow Wilson, 1943; Czechoslovakia Between East and West, 1947; Development Banks, 1957; also articles. Editor: Development Finance Companies; Aspects of Policy and Operation, 1968. Home: 3315 Garfield St NW Washington DC 20008 Office: 1818 H St NW Washington DC 20433

DIAMOND, WILLIAM DOSSETT, physician; b. Beulah, Miss., Jan. 29, 1920; s. Wright Wiley and Laura (Walley) D.; B.A., U. Ala., 1941; M.D., U. Tenn., 1944; m. Ethel Boyce Warr, June 15, 1943; childrenElizabeth, Jean, Frederick. Intern Meth. Hosp., Memphis, 1944-45; resident pediatrics John Gaston Hosp., Memphis, 1947-49; pvt. practice pediatrics, Tex., 1950-60; pediatrician United Mine-Workers Am., Ala., 1960-62, Firestone plantations Co., West Africa, 1963-65; with Mich. Dept. Mental Health, 1965-, med. supt. Mt. Pleasant State Home and Tng. Sch., 1966-. Served with M.C., USNR, 1945-46, 50-51. Diplomate Am. Bd. Pediatrics. Mem. Sigma Chi. Address: Mount Pleasant State Home and Tng Sch Mount Pleasant MI 48858.

DIANA, LEWIS, educator; A.B., Harvard; M.A., Ph.D., U. Pitts. Prof. sociology and anthropology, chmn. dept. sociology and anthroplogy Va. Commonwealth U., Richmond. Office: Va Commonwealth U Richmond VA 23220*

DIAZ, AGUSTIN, hosp. adminstr. Exec. dir. Hosp. Dr. Alejandro Ruiz Soler, Bayamon, P.R. Office: Rd 2 KM 8HM2 Bayamon PR 00619*

DIAZ, ALIRIO, composer; b. Carora, Venezuela, 1923; student guitar, composition, history and aesthetics of music, Caracas Conservatory; scholarship, Madrid Conservatory (first and extraordinary prizes); student Andres Segovia's advanced courses classical guitar, Acad. Musicale Chigianam Siena. Debut, Caracas, 1950; asst. prof. to Segovia, 1955—; recital and concert tours France, Germany, Israel, Spain, Italy, Belgium, N. and S.Am., Eng., Australia. Recipient order Del Maestro Libertador Andres Bello (Venezuela). Address: (a) 30 Via Nobili Rome, Italy*

DIAZ, JOAQUIN BASILIO, educator; b. Arecibo, P.R., Apr. 15, 1920; s. Joaquin Diaz de Haro and Juanita (Reina) D.; student Washington and Jefferson Coll., 1936-38; A.B., U. Tex., 1940; Ph.D., Brown U., 1945; m. Eleanore Ursillo, Sept. 30, 1944; children—Joan Marguerite, Ronald P. Asst. prof. math. Carnegie Inst. Tech., 1946-47, Brown U., 1947-50; research asso. Inst. Fluid Dynamics and Applied Math. of U. Md., 1950-51, asso. research prof., 1951-56, research prof., 1956-66; vis. prof. math. Mass. Inst. Tech., 1956-57; prof. math., chmn. dept. U. Cal. at Riverside, 1966-67; Albert Einstein prof. sci. and math. Rensselaer Poly. Inst., 1967—. Cons. A.E.C., 1951-56, Naval Ordnance Lab., 1955-68; mem. com. basic research, advisory to U.S. Army Research Office, Nat. Acad. Sci.-Nat. Research Council, 1964-70; mem. com. math., adv. to Office Naval Research, Nat. Research Council, 1968-71. Mem. Am. Math. Soc. (council (1966-68), Am. Assn. U. Profs., Phi Beta Kappa, Sigma Xi. Asst. editor of proc. Am. Math. Soc., 1949-52, proc. Conf. Differential Equations, U. Md., 1955; mng. editor proc. contbns. to Partial Differential Equations, 1962-66; editor proc. Symposium on Fluid Dynamics and Applied Math., 1961; editorial bd. Jour. Math. and Mechanics, Ind. U., 1966-68, Applicable Analysis: an Internat. Jour., 1970—. Home: 17 Chestnut Hill S Loudonville NY 12211 Office: Rensselaer Polytechnic Institute Troy NY 12181

DIAZ, JUSTINO, bass; b. San Juan, P.R., Jan 29, 1940; s. Justino Diaz-Morales and Gladys Villarini; student U. P.R., 1958-59, New Eng. Conservatory Music, 1959-62; m. Anna Aragno, Oct. 3, 1967, 1 dau., Natascia. Appearances with New Eng. Opera Theatre, 1961, Opera Co. Boston, 1966, Am. Opera Soc., 1963-64, 69, Dallas Civic Opera, New Orleans Opera Co., Balt. Opera Co., N.Y.C., Cleve., Boston and, (Eng.), Phila., Chgo. symphony orchs., N.Y., Los Angeles Philharmonic orchs., also Spoleto, Casals and Salzburg festivals and La Scala, Milan, Italy, Gran Teatro del Liceo, Barcelona, Spain, Teatro Colon, Buenos Aires, Argentina; leading bass Met. Opera Co., 1963—; rec. artist for Columbia, London, Vanguard, ABC records. Recipient Handel medalion, N.Y.C., 1966; recipient Family of Man citation Soc. Family of Man, 1966. Mem. Alpha Beta Chi. Club: Dutch Treat (N.Y.C.). Home: 165 West End Av New York City NY 10023 Office: Metropolitan Opera Co Lincoln Center New York City NY 10023

DIAZ, MANUEL, steamship co. exec.; b. 1921; B.A., Dartmouth, 1942; married. Mgr. steamship cargo services to Spain. Mediterranean and Cuba, Garcia & Diaz, 1946-58; v.p. traffic U.S. Atlantic ports to W. Coast S. Am. and Caribbean, 1952-63; w.p. T.J. Stevenson & Co., 1963-65; pres., dir. W. Coast Lines, Inc., 1965-67; exec. v.p. Am. Export Industries Lines Inc., 1967, pres., chief exec. officer, now chmn. exec. com.; pres. Am. Export Freight Inc. Address: 26 Broadway New York City NY 10004*

DIAZ-COLLER, CARLOS, physician; b. Villahermosa, Tabsco, Mexico, Sept. 2, 1916; s. Jose Diaz- Coller and Maria Gonzalez; M.D., Army Med. Sch., Mexico, 1945; M.P.H., Harvard, 1948; m. Anna Maria de la Garza, Dec. 17, 1945; childrenCarlos, Jose Alberto, Mario, Juan Antonio and Anna Maria Elisa (twins). Del. from Mexico, WHO, 1956, 57, 58; exec. bd. alternate WHO, 1956-57, v.p. exec. bd., 1958-59; del. from Mexico to directing council Pan-Am. San. Orgn., 1956, 57, exec. com. 1957-58, pres. exec. com., 1958- 59; del. from Mexico, XV Pan Am. San. Conf., 1958; dir. div. exptl. studies in pub. health Ministry Pub. Health and Welfare, Mexico, 1957, 58; now chief dept. of profl. edn. and editorial and reference services Pan Am. Health Orgn. of WHO. Pub. health supr. Mexican Army, 1948-56; dir. Sch. Pub. Health, Mexico, 1953. Mem. Mexican Pub. Health Soc. (pres. 1957-58), Am. Pub. Health Assn., Nat. Geog. Soc. Editor Jour. of Mexican Pub. Health Soc., 1955-58. Home: 3505 Dundee Driveway Chevy Chase MD 20015. Office: 525 23d St N W Washington DC 20037.

DIAZ ORDAZ, GUSTAVO, pres. of Mexico; b. 1911; ed. Instituto de Ciencas y Artes Oaxaca, Colegio del Estado de Puebla. Legal, Judicial posts, Puebla, Tlatlangui and Tehuacan, 1937; dep. to Fed. Legislative Assembly, senator, 1946-52; former prof. adminstrn. and labor law Puebla U.; chief officer Secretariat of Govt., 1952-58, sec. Govt., 1958, later minister of interior; candidate Partido Revolucionario Institucional for Presidency of the Republic, 1963; elected pres., July 5, 1964. Address: Office of the president State Capital Mexico City Mexico*

DIBBLE, CHARLES ELLIOTT, anthropologist, educator; b. Layton, Utah, Aug. 18, 1909; s. George Elliott and Ella Annice (Tolman) D.; B.A., U. Utah, 1936; M.A., Nat. U. Mexico, 1938, Ph.D., 1942; m. Audrey Nelson, Dec. 16, 1936; children—Nelson, Ella, Charlene, Carlos. Faculty U. Utah, Salt Lake City, 1939—, prof. anthropology, 1952—, head dept., 1960-64; vis. prof. U. Minn., 1957, 59; spl. research Nahautl lang. Recipient Distinguished Research Prof. award U. Utah, 1970. Fellow Hist. Soc. N.M.; mem. Am. Anthrop. Assn., Sociedad Mexicana de Antropologia, Inst. Andean Research, Asociacion Internacional de Nahuatlatos, Phi Beta Kappa, Sigma Xi, Phi Kappa Phi. Author: El Codice en Cruz, 1942; El Codice Xolotl, 1951; Codice de 1576, 1963. Co-translator; Florentine Codex Volumes, 1950-69. Home: P O Box 216 North Salt Lake UT 84054 Office: U Utah Salt Lake City UT 84112

DIBBLE, LEWIS ACKER, Jr., metal fabricating co. exec.; b. Waterbury, Conn., July 20, 1921; s. Lewis Acker and Lillie (Kneringer) D.; grad. Kent (Conn.) Sch., 1939; B.S., Yale, 1942; m. Loraine H. Cadwell, Dec. 26, 1942; children—Lewis Acker III, Ellen H., Peter C., Elizabeth P., Laura M., Edward K. Benjamin C. With Risdon Mfg. Co., Naugatuck, Conn., 1946—, pres., 1961- 70, chmn. bd., 1971—; trustee Naugatuck Savs. Bank; dir. C. Cowles & Co., New Haven; mem. adv. bd. Colonial Bank and Trust Co., Naugatuck. Chmn. Bd. Edn., Naugatuck; past v.p., dir. Naugatuck YMCA; past chmn. Naugatuck chpt. A.R.C.; former vice chmn. Conn. Pub. Expenditure Council; trustee Waterbury Hosp.; past v.p. McTernon Sch., Waterbury. Mem. Mfrs. Assn. Conn. (past dir.), Naugatuck (dir.), Conn. (past dir.) chambers commerce. Elk (dir.). Clubs: Highfield (Middlebury, Conn.); Waterbury. Home: 510 Church St Naugatuck CT 06770 Office: Risdon Mfg Co Risdon St Naugatuck CT 06770

DIBNER, BERN, elec. engr.; b. Lisianka, Ukraine, Aug. 18, 1897; s. David and Hannah (Goodman) D.; came to U.S., 1904, naturalized, 1913; E.E., Poly. Inst. Bklyn., 1921, D.Eng., 1959; student U. Zurich, Switzerland, 1936-37, Columbia, 1940-41; m. Barbara Druss, Apr. 15, 1923; 1 son, David. Engr., Adirondack Power & Light Corp., Schenectady, 1921-23, Electric Bond & Share Co., N.Y.C., 1923-24; founder, chmn. bd. Burndy Corp., Norwalk, Conn., 1924—. Cons. elec. equipment commn. Smithsonian Instn.; founder Burndy Library, 1936. Fellow Brandeis U., Pierpont Morgan Library. Trustee U. Bridgeport, Yale Med. Library. Served with S.A.T.C., World War I, from capt. to lt. col., USAAF, 1942-45. Decorated Bronze Star medal. Registered profl. engr., N.Y., Conn. Fellow I.E.E.E., Acad. Arts and Scis.; mem. History Sci. Soc. (council), Soc. History Tech. (pres.), Elec. Hist. Found. (chmn.), Am. Technion Soc., Tau Beta Pi, Eta Kappa Nu. Author: Leonardo da Vinci, Military Engineer, 1946; Moving the Obelisks, 1950; Heralds of Science, 1955; Agricola on Metals, 1958; The Atlantic Cable, 1959; Darwin of the Beagle, 1960; Oersted and the Discovery of Electromagnetism, 1961; The Victoria and the Triton, 1962; The New Rays of Prof. Roentgen, 1963; Alessandro Volta and The Electric Battery, 1965; A Letter from Galilee, 1967. Home: 23 E Meadow Rd Wilton CT 06897 Office: Burndy Corp Norwalk CT 06850

DICARLO, LOUIS MICHAEL, educator; b. N.Y.C., Jan., 17, 1903; s. Amedeo and Theresa (Glacomo) DiC.; B.A., Union Coll., 1932; certificate of proficiency Clarke Sch. for Deaf, 1936; M.S., Mass. State U., 1937; Ed.D., Columbia, 1948; m. Marian E. Warcup, Sept. 17, 1947. With N.Y. State Police, 1923-26; social worker, 1932-35; tchr. pub. schs., New Rochelle, N.Y., 1938-47; faculty Ind. U. 1942; faculty dept. audiology and speech pathology Syracuse U., 1947—, prof., 1952—, chmn. dept., 1952-62, asso. clin. prof. rehabilitation medicine Upstate Med. Sch., Syracuse, 1959—; vis. prof. audio and speech pathology U. Hawaii, 1964-65; vis. prof. Ithaca Coll., 1968-69; chief audiology and speech pathology VA Hosp. Syracuse, N.Y. State Crippled Children's Assn., Sunnyview Orthopaedic and Rehabilitation Hosp., Schenectady; with Gordon D. Hoople Hearing and Speech Center; dir. speech pathology Syracuse Rehab. Center; cons. Pineland Hosp. and Tng. Center, Pownal, Me. Bd. dirs. United Cerebral Palsy Assn. of Syracuse; auxiliary bd. Graham Alexander Assn. Served with U.S. Army, 1919-23; with AUS, 1942-45. Recipient Archibold high scholarship prize, Warner prize. Fellow Am. Speech and Hearing Assn.; mem. Am., N.Y. State, Syracuse psychol. assns., Alexander Graham Bell Assn. for Deaf, Speech Assn. Eastern States, Acoustical Soc. Am., Nat. Council Psychol. Aspects of Disability, Am. Assn. Mental Deficiency, Council Exceptional Children (Hammond prof. 1960), N.Y. State Speech and Hearing Assn. (pres.). Author: Speech after Laryngectomy, 1958; Our Educational Dilemma; The Deaf, 1964. Contbr. articles profl. jours., fiction to mags. Home: 1030 E Genesee St Syracuse NY 13210

DICHTER, ERNEST, cons. psychologist; b. Vienna, Aug. 14, 1907; s. William and Mathilde (Schneider) D.; Ph.D., U. of Vienna, licenciés es lettres, Sorbonne; m. Hedy Langfelder, 1935; children—Thomas William, Susan Jane. Research psychologist, J. Stirling Getchell, Inc., advt. agy. N.Y.; now pres. Inst. for Motivational Research, Inc.; cons. psychologist on programs, CBS; ind. cons. psychologist; pub. Findings. Introduced "dept- interviewing" into marketing research, adapted numerous clin. techniques to gen. consumer testing. Mem. Am. Psychol. Assn. Author: The Psychology of Radio Commercials, chapter in Radio Research, 1943-44; Television Research, series of 9 articles in Tide mag., 1945; The Psychology of Everyday Living, 1946; Motivational and Market Behavior, chpt. on testing techniques, 1958; The Strategy of Desire, 1960; Handbook of Consumer Motivations, 1964; Motivating Human Behavior, 1971. Frequent speaker acad., bus. and advt. groups; contbr. articles on market research. Home: Croton-on-Hudson NY 10520

DICK, ALBERT BLAKE, II, mfr.; b. Chgo., Mar. 10, 1918; s. Albert Blake and Helen (Aldrich) D.; student Yale, 1938-39; m. Elisabeth York, Sept. 14, 1940; children—Albert Blake IV, John Howard, Frederick Aldrich; m. 2d, Susan Drake Bent, Aug. 20, 1960. With A. B. Dick Co., 1939-, holding various positions in purchasing, mfg., sales, and controllers divs., dir., 1946- -, treas., 1947-60, pres.,

1947-61, chmn., 1961—; dir. No. Trust Co., Commonwealth Edison Co., First Nat. Bank of Lake Forest (Ill.), First Nat. Bank of Lake Bluff (Ill.). Trustee Ill. Inst. Tech.; chmn. bd. trustees, chmn. exec. bd. Rush-Presbyn.-St. Luke's Med. Center; v.p., dir. Lake Forest Hosp. Served in USN, 1942-45. Mem. Hosp. Planning Council (v.p., dir.). Clubs: Economic, Executives, Chicago, Attic, Commercial, Racquet (Chgo.); Onwentsia (Lake Forest); Metropolitan (Washington); Fifth Avenue (N.Y.C.); Shoreacres (Lake Bluff); Cotton Bay (Eleuthera, Bahamas); Old Elm (Ft. Sheridan, Ill.). Home: 1550 N Green Bay Rd Lake Forest IL 60045. Office: 5700 W Touhy Av Chicago IL 60648

DICK, BERTRAM GALE, Jr., educator; b. Portland, Ore., June 12, 1926; s. Bertram Gale and Helen (Meengs) D.; B.A., Reed Coll., 1950; B.A. (Rhodes scholar) Wadham Coll., Oxford (Eng.) U., 1953, M.A., 1958; Ph.D., Cornell U., 1958; m. Ann Bradford Volkmann, June 23, 1956; children—Timothy Howe, Robin Louise, Stephen Gale. Research asso. U. Ill., 1957-59; mem. faculty U. Utah, 1959—, prof.physics, 1965—, chmn. dept., 1964-67; cons. Minn. Mining and Mfg. Co., 1960-67; vis. prof. Technische Hochschule, Munich, 1967-68. Served with USNR, 1944-46. Mem. A.A.A.S., Am. Phys. Soc., Sierra Club, Phi Beta Kappa, Sigma Xi. Research in theory solid state. Home: 1377 Butler Av Salt Lake City UT 84102.

DICK, EDISON bus. exec.; b. Lake Forest, Ill., June 29, 1900; s. Albert Blake and Mary Henrietta (Mathews) D.; A.B., Yale, 1922; postgrad. Magdalen Coll., 1923; m. Jane Warner, Sept. 23, 1930; children—Marion (Mrs. James T. Last), Letitia (Mrs. William C. Ellis), Edison Warner. With A.B. Dick Co., Chgo., 1923—, v.p., 1934-47, chmn. exec. com., 1954—, also dir.; dir. Upper Av. Nat. Bank. Vice pres., bd. dirs. Woman's Hosp. and Maternity Center, 1968—; bd. dirs. Passavant Hosp., 1930—, pres., 1947-62, chmn. bd. 1962—; bd. dirs. Allendale Assn.; trustee Ravinia Festival. Served as comdr. USNR, 1942-45. Mem. Orchestral Assn. Republican. Presbyn. (elder). Clubs: Yale, Chicago Commercial, Commonwealth (Chgo.); Onwentsia; Old Elm. Home: 612 Woodland Rd Lake Forest IL 60045 Office: 5700 W Touhy Av Chicago IL 60648

DICK, GEORGE WILLIAM, ins. co. exec.; b. Ravenna, O., Mar. 29, 1916; s. Floyd W. and Myrtle J. (Engle) D.; B.A. in Bus. Adminstrn., Antioch Coll., 1939; postgrad. Oberlin Coll., Boston U.; m. Helen Hettler, July 19, 1946; children—Deborah Anne, Jeffrey William, Michael Thomas. Various field sales and mgmt. positions, IBM, to 1956, dir. marketing VISIrecord, Inc., N.Y.C., 1957; v.p. marketing Am. Mut. Liability Ins. Co., Wakefield, Mass., 1957-60; v.p. electronic data processing div. RCA, 1960-62; exec. v.p., dir., mem. exec. com. CEIR, Inc., Washington, 1962-64; chmn., pres., dir. Am. Research Bur., Inc., 1964-66; v.p. Sterling Inst., Washington, 1966-68; v.p. field manpower devel. Met. Life Ins. Co.; N.Y.C., 1968-70, v.p. marketing systems, 1970—; dir. Colormedia Communication Corp. Active various charities. Bd. dirs. UN Tourism Council. Served as aviator USNR, 1942-45. Mem. Def. Orientation Conf. Assn., Am. Mgmt. Assn., Soc. Controlled Property Casualty Underwriters. Clubs: Ponte Vedra, Georgetown. Contbr. articles to profl. publs. Home: 40 Fairfield Dr Short Hills NJ 07078 Office: 1 Madison Av New York City NY 10010

DICK, JANE WARNER, (Mrs. Edison Dick), civic worker; b. Lake Forest, Ill., June 6, 1906; d. Ezra Joseph and Marion (Hall) Warner; A.B., U. Chgo., 1958; L.H.D. (hon.) Lake Forest Coll. 1964; m. Edison Dick, Sept. 23, 1930; children—Marnie (Mrs. James Theodor Last), Letitia (Mrs. William Corson Ellis), Edison Warner. U.S. rep. Social Commn. UN Econ. and Social Council, 1961-65; spl. adviser U.S. delegation 16th. 17th, 19th gen. assemblies U.N., alternate rep. 18th gen. assembly. Chmn. women's division Stevenson for Gov. Com., 1948; vice chmn. Nat. Vols. for Stevenson, 1952; nat. co-chmn. Stevenson for Pres. Com., 1955-56, Vols. for Stevenson-Kefauver. 1956; chmn. adv. bd. Ill., Kennedy for President, 1960. Dir. Ill. Children's Home and Aid Soc., Immigrants Service League, Mental Health Soc. Greater Chgo., Chgo. Council Fgn. Relations; mem. regional adv. bd. Inst. Internat. Edn.; gov. Menninger Found.; mem. nat. bd. Am. Assn. for UN; mem. Ill. Bd. Pub. Welfare Commrs., 1949-53; dir. Ill. Welfare Found., 1951-58; mem. women's bd. U. Chgo., Field Mus. Natural History; nat. bd. Nat. Council Women U.S., U.S. Com for Refugees, Nat. Social Welfare Assembly. Mem. League Women Voters. Home: 612 Woodland Rd Lake Forest IL 60045

DICK, JOHN KENNETH, corp. exec.; b. London, Eng., Apr. 5, 1913; s. John and Beatrice May (Chitty) D.; grad. high sch.; chartered accountant, 1936; m. Pamela Madge Salmon, June 6, 1942; children—Anthony James (dec.), Peter Stuart, Christopher John. Partner Messrs. Mann Judd & Co., London, 1947-57; mng. dir. Mitchell Cotts Group, Ltd., London, 1957—, dep. chmn., 1964-66, chmn., 1966—; mem. Commonwealth Devel. Corp., 1967—. Mem. Brit. Nat. Export Council, 1968-71; chmn. Com. for Middle East Trade, 1968-71. Fellow Inst. Chartered Accountants, Royal Soc. Arts; mem. City London Soc. (gov. 1961—). Clubs: City, Caledonian (London); Rand (Johannesburg). Home: Langleys Queens Dr Oxshott Surrey England Office: Mitchell Cotts Group Ltd Cotts House Camomile St London EC3 England

DICK, ROBERT FRANK, mgmt. cons.; b. St. Louis, Sept. 21, 1913; s. William Jarvis and Rosabel (Schleicher) D.; student Westminister Coll., 1931-33, B.S. in Commerce, Northwestern U., 1935; M.B.A. with distinction, Harvard, 1937; m. Katherine Morton, Jan. 5, 1939 (div. Jan. 1969); children—Ann, Stratford, Elizabeth; m. 2d, Charlotte Patterson Henry, July 1969. Instr. advt. and marketing Northwestern U., 1937-39; mgmt. cons. Booz, Allen & Hamilton, 1939-42, Fry, Lawson & Co., 1942-46; v.p., partner George Fry & Assos., Chgo., 1946-51, exec. v.p., 1958-59, pres., 1959-68, also dir.; vice chairman of bd. Fry Consultants, 1969—; v.p. Ill. Tool Works, 1951-58; dir. Pyle-Nat. Co., 1958-70, Curtiss Candy Co., 1957-60; adv. bd. Atwood Vacuum Machine Co., 1959, Corry-Jamestown Corp., 1962—, Riverside Paper Co., 1969—, Hurst Perf. Inc. Div. Sunbeam Corp., 1970—. Mem. Am. Mgmt. Assn. (planning council 1956-59; award for contbn. mgmt. practices 1960), Profl. Pres. Assn., Phi Delta Theta. Episcopalian. Clubs: University, Attic (Chgo.); Harvard (N.Y.C.). Author articles in field. Home: 223 E Delaware Pl Chicago IL 60611 Office: 10 S Riverside Plaza Chicago IL 60603

DICK, ROSS MELVIN, newspaperman; b. Moline, Ill., Oct. 4, 1912; s. Ross C. and Frances A. (Peterson) D.; B.A., Beloit Coll., 1937; m. Shirley W. Kretschmer, June 21, 1940; children—Susan W., Mar. B., Ross E. Reporter Beloit (Wis.) bur. Rockford Newspapers, Inc., 1937, Rockford (Ill.) Morning Star, 1938; joined state news desk Milw. Jour., 1941, became state editor, 1945, bus.-financial editor, 1946—. Mem. Soc. Am. Bus. Writers (pres. 1968), Sigma Delta Chi. Conglist. Club: Milwaukee Press (pres. 1949-50). Home: 5662 N Consaul Pl Milwaukee WI 53217. Office: 333 W State St Milwaukee WI 53203

DICK, WILLIAM WHITE, Jr., army officer; b. Montgomery, Ala., Feb. 8, 1910; s. William W. and Marguerite (Buist) D.; B.S., U.S. Mil. Acad., 1931; grad. F.A. Sch., 1935; m. Frances Halliday Lawson, June 9, 1933. Commd. 2d lt. U.S. Army, 1931, advanced through grades to lt. gen., 1962; battery officer, Ft. Hoyle, Md., 1931-34, Hawaii, 1935-37; instr. U.S. Mil. Acad., 1937-41; bn. comdr., chief of staff 25th Inf. Div., PTO, 1941-45, arty. exec. officer, arty. comdr. 25th Inf. Div., Korea, 1950-51; personnel staff officer Hdqrs. Dept. Army, 1951-52; comdg. gen. 31st Inf. Div. Arty., 1952-54; arty. comdr. chief of staff, 7th Army, Germany, 1954-56; army dep. Hdqrs. Joint Task Force 7, Washington, 1956-58; dir. spl. weapons Office Chief of Research and Devel., Hdqrs. Dept. of Army, 1958-60, dep. chief Research and Devel., 1960-61; comdg. gen. 3d Inf. Div., 1961-62, U.S. Army Air Def. Command, 1962-63; chief of research and devel. Dept. Army, 1963-66; comdr. Allied Land Forces (NATO), S.E. Europe. Home: 879 Mithat Pasha Ismir Turkey

DICKASON, DON LINTON, lawyer; b. Okemah, Okla., Dec. 10, 1906; s. Simon Milton and Linnie (Kellerman) D.; LL.B., U. Okla., 1929; m. Mabel Townsend, Dec. 24, 1943. Admitted to Okla. bar, 1929, N.M. bar, 1932; practice in Okmulgee, Okla., 1929-31, Albuquerque, 1932-; partner firm Rodey, Dickason, Sloan, Akin & Robb, and predecessors, 1957—. Dir. First Nat. Bank, Albuquerque. Chmn. Albuquerque Personnel Bd., 1947-57; mem. Albuquerque Civic Auditorium Bd., 1950-51; pres. Albuquerque Game Protective Assn., 1940-41; chmn. com. to select site for Bernalillo County (N.M.) Juvenile Detention Home, 1939; chmn. Albuquerque Charter Revision Com., 1965. Mem. N.M. Senate, 1937-48, majority floor leader, 1942-48; mem. exec. com. Dem. County Central Com., 1952-62. Adv. bd. Albuquerque Salvation Army; dir. Bernalillo County Tb Assn., pres., 1960-62; bd. dirs. Albuquerque Wild Life and Conservation Assn. Mem. Am., N.M. bar assns., Am. Judicature Soc., Fedn. of Ins. Counsel, C. of C., Taxpayers Assn. N.M., U. Okla. Alumni Assn., Lawyers Club (past pres.), U. Okla. Law Sch. Assn. Mem. Christian Ch. Mason, Elk (past state pres., past dist. dep., past exalted rule), Rotarian. Club: Petroleum (Albuquerque). Home: 1800 Mesa Vista Rd NE Albuquerque NM 87103 Office: First Nat Bank Bldg PO Box 1888 Albuquerque NM 87103

DICKE, ROBERT HENRY, educator, physicist; b. St. Louis, May 6, 1916; s. Oscar H. and Flora (Peterson) D.; A.B., Princeton, 1939; Ph.D., U. Rochester, 1941; m. Annie Currie, June 6, 1942; children—Nancy Jean (Mrs. John Rapoport), John Robert, James Howard. Microwave radar devel. Radiation Lab., Mass. Inst. Tech., 1941-46; physics faculty Princeton, 1946—, Cyrus Fogg Brackett prof. physics, 1957- -, chmn. physics dept., 1967-70. Mem. adv. panel for physics NSF, 1959- 61; chmn. adv. com. atomic physics Nat. Bur. Standards, 1961-63; mem. com. on physics NASA, 1963-70, chmn., 1963-66; chmn. physics adv. panel Com. on Internat. Exchange of Persons (Fulbright- Hays Act), 1964-66; chmn. adv. com. on radio astronomy telescopes NSF, 1967, 69. Recipient Nat. medal Sci., 1970. Mem. Nat. Acad. Scis., Am. Geophys. Union, Am. Phys. Soc., Am. Astron. Soc., Am. Acad. Arts and Scis. (Rumford medal 1967). Author: (with Montgomery, Purcell) Principles of Micro-wave Circuits, 1948; (with J.P. Wittke) An Introduction to Quantum Mechanics, 1960; The Theoretical Significance of Experimental Relativity, 1964; Gravitation and the Universe, 1970. Home: 321 Prospect Av Princeton NJ 08540

DICKE, ROBERT JEROME, educator; b. Sheboygan Falls, Wis., June 16, 1912; s. William Charles and Anna Louise (Kerskamp) D.; B.S., U. Wis., 1940, Ph.D. in Entomology, 1943; m. Hermine Marie Prisland, Aug. 24, 1940; children—Robert Ted, William John, Mary Hermine, Katherine Anna. Mem. Faculty U. Wis., 1946—, prof. entomology, 1952—, chmn. dept., 1959-68; spl. research med. entomology, insect morphology. Served to lt. (s.g.) USNR, 1943-46. Fellow A.A.A.S.; mem. Entomol. Soc. Am., Wis. Acad. Scis., Arts and Letters (sec.-treas. 1952-56, pres. 1959). Home: 3717 Council Crest Madison, WI 53711.

DICKELMAN, HOWARD C., food chain exec.; b. Exeland Wis., Sept. 27, 1918; s. Lawrence Henry and Elsia (Skode) D.; student Marguette U., 1937-38; m. Dorothy Finkler, Dec. 16, 1939; children—Judith (Mrs. William Strenger), James, Vicki (Mrs. James Price). Sales rep. Chgo. div. Gen Foods Corp., 1939-46; with Schultz Sav-O Stores, Inc., Sheboygan, Wis., 1946—, pres., gen. mgr., 1967—; dir., v.p., mem. exec. com., chmn. budget and finance com. Topco Assos., Inc. Adv. bd to sec. agr. Wis.; dir. econ. stblzn; Sheboygan. Trustee Topco Trust. Served with USNR, 1944-46. Mem. Sheboygan C. of C. (dir.). Roman Catholic (counselor). Elk, Rotarian. Clubs: Pine Hills Country (Sheboygan); Sheboygan Economics (pres., bd. dirs. 1968- 69). Home: 629 Green Pl Kohler WI 53044 Office: 2215 Union Av Sheboygan WI 53081

DICKEN, SAMUEL NEWTON, educator, geographer; b. nr. Colfax, Ky., Jan. 26, 1901; s. William F. and Sarah W. (Harry) D.; A.B., Marietta Coll., 1924, D.Sc. (hon.), 1964; Ph.D., U. Cal., 1930; m. Emily F. Puehler, Jan. 23, 1929; 1 son, Charles Francis. Geographer, Ky. Geol. Survey, Frankfort, 1927, 28; instr., U. Minn., 1929-34, asst. prof. geography, 1934-39, asso. prof., 1939-46, prof., 1946-47; prof. geography U. Ore., Eugene, 1947—, head. dept., 1947-63. Geomorphologist, Soil Conservation Service, Washington, 1937-38; cons. Army Air Forces, 1942, 43; O.S.S., 1944; head. geog. and geol. br. Biarritz Am. U., 1945, 46. Fellow Am. Geog. Soc.; mem. Assn. Am. Geographers (editorial bd. Ann. 1952, 53), Assn. Pacific Coast Geographers (pres. 1951-52), Phi Beta Kappa, Sigma Xi. Author: Regional Economic Geography; Oregon Geography; Human Geography, Cultural Geography; Pioneer Trails of the Oregon Coast; also monographs, bulls. Contbr. articles to profl. jours. Home: 2385 Madrona Dr Eugene OR 97403

DICKENS, ANTHONY S., physician. Dir., Jersey City Med. Center. Office: 50 Baldwin Av Jersey City NJ 07304*

DICKENS, CLAUDE, Jr., utility exec.; b. Springfield, Mo., Nov. 10, 1925; s. Claude Stephen and Dora Edith (Carden) D.; B.S. in Edn., S.W. Mo. State Coll., 1949; M.Ed., U. Mo., 1955; m. Norma Pauline Dalton, Dec. 23, 1947; children—David Andrew, Ann Elizabeth, Steven Lawrence. Personnel dir. City Utilities, Springfield, 1951-55, comptroller, 1956-59, asst. gen. mgr., 1960-63; controller, sec.-treas. City Pub. Service Bd., San Antonio, 1963—. Served with USMC, 1944-46. Rotarian, Optimist. Home: 112 Atwater Dr San Antonio TX 78213 Office: 145 Navarro St San Antonio TX 78206

DICKENS, MILTON, educator; b. St. Louis, July 25, 1908; s. Andrew and Della (Williams) D.; student Ill. Wesleyan U., 1925-27; A.B., U. So. Cal., 1930; A.M., Syracuse U., 1932, Ph.D., 1939; m. Jennette Holmes, Sept. 15, 1928; children—Justin Kirk, Eve Shelley. Instr. speech Syracuse U., 1930-38, asst. prof., 1939-43; statis. analyst Douglas Aircraft Co., 1943-45; asst. prof. speech U. So. Cal., 1946-47, asso. prof., 1947-50, prof., 1950—, head dept., 1950-61, chmn. div. communication, 1954—; vis. prof., acting cir. Center for Communication Research, U. Tex. 1967-68. Mem. Speech Assn. Am. (mem. Legislative assembly 1963-65, mem. exec. council), Western Speech Assn. (pres. 1956), Am. Assn. U. Profs., Phi Beta Kappa, Sigma Xi, Phi Kappa Phi, Delta Sigma Rho, Pi Kappa Delta, Theta Chi. Author: Speech: Dynamic Communication, 1954, rev., 1963; Guidebook for Speech Practice, 1961. Contbr. articles profl. jours. Home: 5255 Veronica St Los Angeles, CA 90008.

DICKENSON, ALBERT VICTOR, musician; b. Xeniz, O., Aug. 6, 1906; s. Robert Clarke and Lou (Alexander) D.; m. Rachel Otealia Foye, June 18, 1932. Played trombone with Claude Honkins, 1930, Benny Carter, 1930, Sidney Bechet, 1940. Count Basie, 1940, also various small bands; European tours. 1950, 60, Australia and Japan, 1960; now mem. Bobby Hackett Quintet; recording artist for numerous companies. Recipient Esquire Silver award, 1946, 47. Address: 774 E 225th St New York City NY 10466

DICKENSON, FREDERICK ROSS, found. exec.; b. Hamilton, Ont., Can., Mar. 24, 1904; s. Frederick Henry and Emily (Brierly) D.; B.Sc., U. Toronto, 1924; m. Olive Sinclair, Nov. 5, 1927; childrenJoyce Sinclair, Jane Sinclair, Frederick Ross. Came to U.S., 1924, naturalized, 1938. Sales staff Am. Blower Corp., Detroit, 1924-32, dist. mgr., Cleve., 1932-36, asst. sales mgr., 1936-39, dir. indsl. relations, 1939-44, works mgr., 1944-46; exec. v.p. Townsend Co., New Brighton, Pa., 1946-48, pres., dir., 1948-68, ret., 1968; mgmt. cons., 1968. Pres. dir. New Life Found., Inc., St. Petersburg, Fla., 1971—. Club: Duquesne (Pitts.). Home: 220 Pine Rd Belleaire Clearwater FL 33516

DICKERMAN, MARION, educator; b. Westfield, N.Y., Apr. 11, 1890; d. Edwin Hull and Emily (Willey) Dickerman; student Wellesley Coll., 1907-09; A.B., Syracuse U., 1911, Pd.B., 1912, A.M., 1912. Instr., Canisteo (N.Y.) High Sch., 1912-13, Fulton HIgh Sch., 1913-18; dean N.J. State Normal Sch., Trenton, 1920-21; instr. Bryn Mawr (Pa.) Coll. Summer Sch., 1922, 23; instr. Todhunter Sch., N.Y.C., 1922-27, prin., 1927-39; asso. princ. Dalton Schs., 1939-42; dir. pub. edn. Am. Arbitration Assn., 1942-44; instr. Hunter Coll., 1944-45. Panel mem. region 2 Nat. Labor Bd.; ednl. dir. Marine Hist. Assn., Mystic, Conn., 1945-62, now cons. edn. dept.; mem. State Mus. Com.; v.p. Nat. Sci. for Youth Found., New Canaan Nature Center. Alternate, Democratic Nat. Convs., 1928, 32, 36, 40, mem. Com. on Resolutions, 1940. Mem. Pres.'s Commn. to Study Indsl. Relations in Gt. Britain and Sweden, summer 1938, Conf. on Children in a Democracy, Apparel Industry Com., Bd. Edn. Served in record dept. Endell St. Mil. Hosp., London, Eng., 1918-19. Mem. Am. Assn. U. Women (pres. N.Y. br. 1938-39), New Canaan Hist. Soc. (v.p.). Democrat. Episcopalian. Club: Cosmopolitan. Co-author: Who's Who in Labor. Lectr., writer on current ednl., polit. topics. Home: Sunset Hill Rd New Canaan CT 06840 Office: Marine Mus Mystic CT 06355

DICKERSON, CLAUDE WYATT, Jr., corp. exec.; b. Roanoke, Va., Aug. 25, 1924; s. Claude Wyatt and B. M. (Kirkwood) D.; student Duke, 1942-43; Tulane U., 1943-44; m. Nancy Hanschman, Feb. 24, 1962; children—Elizabeth, Ann, Jane, Michael and John. Pres. bd. dirs. Consol. Finance Co., 1953-57; chmn. bd. Conn. Telephone & Electric Co., 1956-57; pres., chmn. Cherry Smash Corp., 1957-63; pres., chmn. First Capital Corp., 1963-70, Liberty Equities Corp., 1966—; chmn. bd. Pioneer Products, Inc., 1967-70, Salem Pipe Co., 1967-70, Ferro Pipe Co., 1967-70, Internat. Seafood U.S. Aluminum Co., 1968-70, Smithfield Packing Co., Inc., 1969; mem. exec. com., dir. Allied Capital Corp., 1967-69; pres. Dickerson & Co. Inc., 1970—. Cons. to various corps., 1957—. Chmn., Lincoln Centennial, 1961, Civil War Centennial Com., 1961-62. Served with USNR, 1942-45. Clubs: Federal City (founder, v.p., gov.), 1925 F Street (Washinton). Home: Merrywood McLean VA 22101 Office: 1140 Connecticut Av Washington DC 20036

DICKERSON, EARL BURRUS, lawyer; b. Canton, Miss., June 22, 1891; s. Edward and Emma (Garrett) D.; A.B., U. Ill., 1914; J.D., U. Chgo. 1920; H.H.D., Wilberforce U., 1961; m. Kathryn Kennedy, June 15, 1930; 1 dau., Diane. Admitted to Ill. bar, 1920; exec. v.p. Supreme Life Ins. Co. of Am., 1954-55, gen. counsel, 1921-55, gen. mgr., 1955-62, pres., also chief exec. officer, 1955-71, chmn. bd., 1971—; asst. corp. counsel City of Chgo., 1923-27; asst. atty. gen., Ill., 1933-39; mem. city Council City Chgo., 1939-43. Dir. Hyde Park Fed. Savs. & Loan Assn., South Side Bank and Trust Co. Dir. S.E. Chgo., Commn., 1953—; mem. Pres.'s Com. Fair Employment Practice, 1941-43. Trustee La Rabida Jackson Park Sanitarium. Served as lt. inf., AEF, World War I. Recipient citation for pub. service Alumni Assn. U. Chgo., 1961. Mem. Chgo. Urban League (past pres.), N.A.A.C.P. (dir.), Am., Nat., Ill. State, Cook County, Chgo. bar assns., U. Ill. Alumni Assn., Northwestern U. Alumni Assn., U. Chgo. Law Sch. Assn., Am. Legion (founder), Kappa Alpha Psi (past grand polemarch). Episcopalian. Club: City. Home: 4800 Chicago Beach Dr Chicago IL 60615 Office: 3501 Martin Luther King Jr Dr Chicago IL 60653

DICKERSON, ELBERT LEE, coll. adminstr.; b. Okolona, Ark., Jan. 17, 1918; s. Thomas G. and Maude (Van Meter) D.; B.A., Henderson State Coll., 1939; M.Ed., U. Ark., 1955, Ed.D., 1958; m. Edna Mae Walker, Dec. 22, 1946; children—Richard L., Kathy Lynn. Tchr. pub. schs. Ark., 1939-41; accountant firm W.W. Findley Co., Little Rock, 1945-47; prin. Chidester, Ark. high sch., 1947-51, supt. schs., 1952-56; research asst. U. Ark., 1956-58; dean Sch. Edn., Midwestern U., Wichita Falls, Tex., 1958-69, dean Grad. Sch., 1969—. Served with AUS, 1941-45, 51-52, 61-62; ETO. Mem. Phi Delta Kappa (pres. U. Ark. chpt. 1957-58, pres. Texhoma Field chpt. 1971-72), Kappa Delta Pi. Home: 4502 Dunbarton St Wichita Falls TX 76302

DICKERSON, FREDERICK REED, lawyer, educator; b. Chgo., Nov. 11, 1909; s. Fred George and Rena (Reed) D.; grad. Lake Forest Acad., 1927; A.B., Williams Coll., 1931; LL.B., Harvard, 1934; LL.M. (Univ. fellow 1938-39), Columbia U., 1939, J.S.D., 1950; m. Jane Morrison, June 14, 1939; children—Elizabeth Ann (Mrs. David D. Brown), John Scott, Martha Reed. Admitted to Mass. bar, 1934, Ill. bar, 1936, U.S. Supreme Ct. bar, 1943; asso. firm Goodwin, Procter & Hoar, Boston, 1934-35, McNab, Holmes & Long, Chgo., 1936-38; asst. prof. law Washington U., St. Louis, 1939- 40, U. Pitts., 1940-42; atty. OPA, 1942-47; asst. legislative counsel U.S. Ho. of Reps., 1947-49; chmn. com. on codification Joint Army-Air Force Statutory Revision Group, dep. asst. gen. counsel U.S. Dept. Def., 1949-58; prof. law Ind. U., 1958—, asso. dean, 1971—. Pres., F. G. Dickerson Co., Chgo., 1948—; chmn. commn. on uniform laws State of Ind., 1969—; cons. Dept. Def., 1958-59, 66, FAA, 1960-65, Dept. Transp., 1967- 69, Commn. on Govt. Procurement, 1971—; lectr. Northwestern U., 1938, Am. U., 1956, 58, Practising Law Inst., 1961. Cons. Pres.'s Com. on Consumer Interests, 1967-68. Recipient Distinguished Civilian Service award Dept. Def., 1957; Ford Found. law faculty fellow Harvard, 1961-62. Mem. Am. Law Inst., Nat. Legislative Conf., Am. (chmn. standing com. law and tech. 1968- 69, chmn. standing com. legislative drafting 1969—), Ind. bar assns., Order Coif, Phi Alpha Delta, Phi Gamma Delta. Presbyn. (elder). Author: Products Liability and the Food Consumer, 1951; Legislative Drafting, 1954; Fundamentals of Legal Drafting, 1965. Editor: Legal Problems Affecting Private Swimming Pools, 1961; Product Safety in Household Goods, 1968; Cases and Materials on Legislation, 1968; mem. editorial bd. Jurimetrics Jour., 1962—. Home: 870 Woodscrest Dr Bloomington IN 47401

DICKERSON, GEORGE WILLIAM, army officer; b. Warrenton, Va., Aug. 29, 1918; s. Broadus Charles and Ada Monte (Davis) D.; B.S., Va. Poly. Inst., 1941; M.S., Ohio U., 1956; M.B.A., George Washington U., 1963; m. Lois Ann Wood, Apr. 22, 1946. Commd. 2d lt. U.S. Army, 1941, advanced through grades to brig. gen., 1967; served with 24th Div., PTO, 1942-45; in ofr. Army Sch. System, 1946-50; condr. Inf. Bn., Austria, 1950-53; mil. prof. Ohio U., 1953-56; regtl. comdr., Korea, 1957-59; mem. staff Dept. Army and Joint Chiefs Staff, 1959-63, NATO, 1963-66; prof. Army War Coll., 1967; comptroller Continental Army Command, 1967-68; comdg.

gen. 3d Brigade, 82d Airborne Div., Vietnam, 1967-69; comptroller U.S. Army, Europe, 1970—; instr. U. Md. Overseas Div., 1957-59. Active Girl Scouts, Boy Scouts Am. Decorated D.S.M., Silver Star, D.F.C., Soldier's Medal, Bronze Star with 2 oak leaf clusters, Air medal with 18 oak leaf clusters, Joint Service Commendaion medal, Army Commendation medal with 2 oak leaf clusters. Mem. Assn. U.S. Army, Phi Kappa Phi, Alpha Kappa Psi, Omicron Delta Kappa. Baptist. Rotarian. Contbr. articles service jours. Home: 86 Culpeper St Warrenton VA 22186 Office: Hdqrs US Army Europe Comptroller APO New York City NY 09403

DICKERSON, HARVEY, lawyer; b. Ely, Nev., June 3, 1905; s. Denver S. and Una (Reilly) D.; student U. Nev., 1930-31; LL.B., Southeastern U. 1941; m. Virginia Shephard, Oct. 27, 1938; children—Carol, Denver Shepard, Valerie, Donald Charles. Admitted to Nev. bar, 1941, practiced in Las Vegas, 1942—; chief dep. U.S. marshal, Nev., 1933-34; floor sec. Sen. McCarran, 1935- 38; jr. tax expert CAA, 1939; adminstrv. asst. WPA, 1940; atty. gen. Nev., 1955-58, 63-70; city atty. North Las Vegas, Nev., 1961—. Past dist. gov. Boy Scouts Am.; mem. Gov.'s Crime Commn., 1969—; chmn. Pvt. Investigator Licensing Bd., 1969—. Mem. Clark County Democratic Central Com.; candidate lt. gov. Nev., 1949, U.S. senator 1956, gov., 1958; mem. exec. com. Dem. party, 1960-61. Mem. Am. (hon. dels. 1955-56), Nev. (dist. gov. 1944-49, pres. 1953) bar assns., Am. Judicature Soc. Kiwanian (pres. 1948). Club: Boulder-Vegas Shrine (past pres.). Home: 2030 Ives Av Reno NV 89503 Office: 105 N Sierra St Reno NV 89501

DICKERSON, NANCY HANSCHMAN, news corr.; b. Milw.; d. Frederick R. and Florence (Conners) Hanschman; student Clarke Coll., Dubuque, Ia.; grad. U. Wis., 1948; postgrad. Harvard; H.H.D., Am. Internat. Coll., Springfield, Mass.; m. Claude Wyatt Dickerson, Feb. 24, 1962; children—Elizabeth, Ann Jane, Michael, John. Sch. tchr., Milw.; staff asst. Senate Fgn. Relations Com., Washington; prod. CBS News, 1956-60, corr., 1960-63; news corr. NBC, 1963-70; reporter Pres. Kennedy's funeral, Republican and Democratic convs., Civil Rights March on Washington, Kennedy, Johnson and Nixon inaugurations; represented Pub. Broadcasting Corp. on all-network Conversation with Pres. Nixion, 1970. Recipient Collegian award LaSalle Coll., Phila.; Spirit of Achievement award Albert Einstein Coll., Yeshiva U.; Sigma Delta Chi award Boston U.; Pioneer award New Eng. Women's Press Assn. Mem. Radio-Television News Analysts. Club: National Press (past v.p.). Home: Merrywood Chain Bridge Rd McLean VA 22101 Office: 1750 Pennsylvania Av NW Washington DC 20006

DICKERSON, NORVIN KENNEDY, contractor; b. Louisville, Mar. 3, 1917; s. Norvin Kennedy and Clara (Mertinkate) D.; ed. pub. schs., Louisville; m. Sara McCarten Craig, June 7, 1939; children—Norvin Kennedy, Ann Gillam. From gen. supt. to Southeastern mgr. R. B. Tyler Co., Louisville, 1935-45; founder, Dickerson Inc., Monroe, N.C., 1945, pres., 1945-58, chmn. bd., 1958—; dir. Am. Bank & Trust Co. Monroe, Am. Comml. Agy., Charlotte, N.C., Comml. Products Inc., Monroe, Contractors & Materials Inc., Columbia, S.C., Indsl. Ventures, Inc., Monroe; owner Sally Mae Farms, Sally Mae Greenhouses; co-owner Ridgewood Devel. Co., Monroe, Monroe Motels. N.C. Banking Commn. Mem. regional bd. dirs. Boy Scouts Am., past pres. Central N.C. council; found. mem. Wingate Coll.; mem. N.C. State Engring. Found.; mem. found. U. N.C. at Charlotte; trustee U. N.C. Mem. Asso. Gen. Contractors Am. (hon. life dir.; dir past chmn. hwy. div.; past pres. Carolinas br. Clubs: Charlotte City; City, Sphinx (Raleigh); Country N.C. (Pinehurst); Rolling Hills Country (Monroe, N.C.). Home: 2001 Griffith Rd Monroe, NC 28110. Office: Box 400 Monroe NC 28110

DICKERSON, RICHARD EARL, educator, chemist; b. Casey, Ill., Oct. 8, 1931; s. Earl Samuel and Zelda Lorraine (Claypool) D.; B.S. in Chemistry, Carnegie Inst. Tech., 1953; Ph.D. in Phys. Chemistry, U. Minn., 1957; m. Lola Mae Hulderson, June 9, 1956; children—Ian Michael, Daniel Scott, Lise Ann, Sara Jean, Joyce Leah. NSF postdoctoral fellow Leeds (Eng.) U., 1957; NSF/NIH postdoctoral fellow Cambridge (Eng.) U., 1958-59; asst. prof. chemistry U. Ill., 1959-63; mem. faculty Cal. Inst. Tech., 1963—, prof. chemistry, 1968—. Mem. Am. Soc. Biol. Chemists, Am. Crystallographic Assn., Am. Inst. Physics, A.A.A.S., Sigma Xi, Alpha Tau Omega. Democrat. Unitarian. Author: (with I. Geis) The Structure and Action of Proteins, 1969; Molecular Thermodynamics, 1969; (with others) Chemical Principles, 1970. Home: 620 S Sierra Bonita Pasadena CA 91106

DICKERT, HERMAN ALONZO, former educator, textile engr.; b. Newberry, S.C., Jan. 16, 1903; s Alonzo Haskum and Mattie D. (Lominack) D.; A.B., Newberry Coll., 1923, D.Sc. (hon.), 1955; A.M., U.N.C., 1925; m. Mabel Elizabeth Couch, Sept. 28, 1927; children—Sally Lou (Mrs. Ariel V. Colin), Martha Couch (Mrs. Robert B. Nelson). With chemistry food nutrition lab. N.C. State Dept. Agr., 1924-25; with E.I. du Pont de Nemours & Co., 1925-31, 1934- 45, tech. service rep., 1945; established textile lab. Burlington Mills, 1931-33; prof. textile engring. Ga. Inst. Tech., 1958-70, dir. A. French Textile Sch., 1945-58; textile cons.; spl. lectr. Technion-Israel Inst. Tech., Haifa, 1964. Mem. adv. subcom. on fibers, fabrics, com. q.m. problems, Nat. Research Council, 1948-51; mem. tech. subcom. Dept. of Agr. cotton and cotton-seed research and marketing adv. com., 1958-60. Licensed profl. textile engr., Ga. Fulbright lectr. U. Barcelona, Tarassa, Spain, 1963-64. Mem. Am. Assn. U. Profs., Am. Assn. Textile Chemists and Colorists (sec. Southeastern sect. 1951), Nat. Council Textile Edn. (v.p. 1951-52, pres. 1952- 53), Textile Operating Execs. Ga. (sec., treas. 1951-59), Phi Psi. Lutheran. Mason. Club: Ga. Tech. Faculty. Home: 1059 Citadel Dr NE Atlanta GA 30324

DICKEY, CHARLES DENSTON, Jr., paper co. exec.; b. N.Y.C., Jan. 15, 1918; s. Charles Denston and Catherine Dunscomb (Colt) D.; grad. St. Paul's Sch., 1936; B.A., Yale, 1940; m. Helen Barrett Lynch, Nov. 29, 1947; children—Charles Denston III, Helen B., Sylvia L., Catherine S., Robert M. Spl. agt. FBI, 1941-43; with Scott Paper Co., 1946—, asst. v.p., 1956-57, v. p., 1957-67, exec. v.p., 1967-68, pres., 1969—, now chief exec. officer, also dir.; dir. B.C. Forest Products Ltd., Vancouver, INA Corp., Phila., J.P. Morgan & Co., Inc., Morgan Guaranty Trust Co. of N.Y. Trustee U. Pa., Phila., St. Timothy's Sch., Stevenson, Md. Home: 649 Dorset Rd Devon PA 19333 Office: Scott Paper Co Philadelphia PA 19113

DICKEY, ERVIN JOHN, Jr., ins. co. exec.; b. Atlanta, 1919; ed. U. Va., 1942; m. Dorothy Ann Davis, 1943; 1 son, Trent Stevenson. Pres., dir. Agrl. Ins. Co., Am. Empire Ins. Co. Sioux Falls; dir. adjustment bur. Channing Financial Corp.; dir. Marine Midland No. N.Y., Hungerford & Holbrook Co. Trustee House of Good Samaritan Hosp., Clarkson Coll., Potsdam, N.Y. Mem. Mem. Am. Ins. Assn. (exec. com.). Clubs: Metropolitan (N.Y.C.); Capital City (Atlanta); Black River Valley (Watertown, N.Y.). Home: 221 Clinton St Watertown NY 13601 Office: 215 Washington St Watertown NY 13601

DICKEY, FRANCIS GEORGE, hosp. supt.; b. Balt., Nov. 12, 1909; s. Philip Sadtler and Anna (Bode) D.; B.A., Johns Hopkins, 1932; M.D., U. Md., 1935; m. Martha A. Dillhofer, Sept. 7, 1940; children—Martha Anne (Mrs. Bruce A. Pottle), Susan Jane (Mrs. Thomas W. Smith), David Sadtler, Mary Frances. Intern, then resident internal medicine Univ. Hosp., Balt., 1935-39; fellow gastroenterology Univ. Hosp., Phila., 1939-40; pvt. practice, Balt., 1940-42, 46-52; with VA, 1952—, supt. St. Louis VA Hosp., 1964-70; supt. VA Center, Martinsburg, W.Va., 1970—; attending physician Ft. Howard VA Hosp., Balt., 1947-52; asst. prof. medicine U. Md. Med. Sch., 1954-57, Marquette U. Med. Sch., 1960-62. Mem. Fed. Exec. Bd., St. Louis, 1964—, mem. policy com., chmn. equal opportunity com., 1966-67. Served to lt. col., M.C., AUS, 1942-45; PTO, CBI. Mem. A.M.A., Med. and Chirurgical Faculty Md. Address: VA Center Martinsburg WV 25401

DICKEY, FRANK, mfg. exec.; b. Harvey, Ia., Oct. 2, 1907; s. William Raymond and Clara Myrtle (Woodyard) D.; student pub. schs.; m. Lela Knight, Sept. 3, 1928 (dec. March 4, 1965); children—Margaret Jane (now Mrs. Martin Johnson), Jere F.; m. 2d, Doris Penn, Feb. 5, 1966. Employed with Deere & Co., Moline, Ill., 1928—, successively foundry pieceworker, foreman, head time study dept., supt., factory mgr., 1928-56, v.p. in charge indsl. relations and personnel, 1956-59, v.p. in charge govt. and minority relations, 1969—, also dir. Home: 1800 7th St East Moline IL 61265 Office: John Deere Rd Moline IL 61265

DICKEY, FRANK GRAVES, ednl. ofcl.; b. Wagoner, Okla., Dec. 1, 1917; s. Joseph Stone, Jr., and Katherine (Bridges) D.; A.B., Transylvania Coll., 1939; M.A., U. Ky., 1942, Ed.D., 1947; LL.D., Berea College, Jacksonville University, Loyola Univ., New Orleans, Louisiana; D.Litt., Transylvania College; D. Humane Letters, Findlay Coll.; m. Elizabeth Joan Drymon, Oct. 18, 1940; children—Frank Graves, Jooeph Terry, Ann Elizabeth. Tchr. pub. schs., Lexington and Fayette Co., Ky., 1939-43; successively instr., asst. prof., asso. prof. edn. U. Ky., 1947-49, prof. edn., dean coll. edn., 1949-56; pres., 1956-63; exec. dir. So. Assn. Colleges and Schools, 1963- 65; exec. dir. Nat. Commn. Accrediting, 1965—. Mem. exec. com. So. Regional Edn. Bd., 1962-63; Army Adv. Panel on R.O.T.C. Affairs, 1961- 63; bd. curators Transylvania Coll., 1959-63; bd. dirs. Ky. Heart Assn., 1959-63, Ky. Soc. Crippled Children, 1959-63; v.p. Internat. Conv. Disciples of Christ, 1964-66. Member board of visitors Air University. Served as master sgt. with U.S. Army, 1943-46. Fellow edn. Harvard, 1952- 53. Recipient Alma Magna Mater award U. Ky., 1962, Distinguished Alumnus award, 1965. Mem. Am. Council Edn. (dir., exec. com., chmn. commn. accreditation service experiences), N.E.A., Ky. Edn. Assn., S.A.R., S.R., Order Ky. Cols., Newcomen Soc., Delta Pi Epsilon, Phi Delta Kappa, Kappa Delta Pi, Omicron Delta Kappa, Kappa Alpha, Alpha Zeta, Alpha Phi Omega. Mem. Disciples of Christ. Clubs: Kenwood Country, Spindletop. Author: (with others) Principles of Supervision; Principles of Student Teaching. Office: 1785 Massachusetts Av NW Washington DC 20036

DICKEY, IMOGENE BENTLEY, educator; b. Nashville, Sept. 30, 1908; d. Thomas Clay and Emogene (Rountree) Bentley; B.A., E. Tex. State U., 1930; M.A., George Peabody Coll. Tchrs., 1932, Ph.D., 1941; m. Charles Lively Dickey, June 28, 1960. Tchr. pub. elementary schs., Paris, Tex., 1927-30, pub. high sch., 1930-34; tchr. English and Spanish, Paris Jr. Coll., 1934-42, dean of coll., 1942-44; prof. English N. Tex. State U., 1944—, dean of women, 1944-68; lectr. in field. Mem. Am. Assn. U. Women, Tex. Tchrs. Assn., Nat., Tex. assns. women deans and counselors, Denton C. of C., N.E.A., S. Central Modern Lang. Assn., Tex. Assn. Coll. Tchrs., Tex. Conf. Coll. Tchrs. English, Delta Kappa Gamma, Pi Gamma Mu, Kappa Delta Pi. Author: Early Literary Magazines of Texas, 1970. Home: 1803 Greenwood St Denton TX 76201

DICKEY, JAMES, poet, critic; b. Atlanta, Feb. 2, 1923; s. Eugene and Maibelle (Swift) D.; student Clemson Coll., 1942; B.A., Vanderbilt U., 1949, M.A., 1950; m. Maxine Syerson, Nov. 4, 1948; children—Christopher Swift, Kevin Webster. Poet in residence Reed Coll., Portland, Ore., 1963-64, San Fernando (Cal.) Valley State Coll., 1964-65, U. Wis., 1966; cons. in poetry Library of Congress, 1966-68; now writer in residence and Prof. of English at U. of S. C. Served with USAAF and USAF, World War II. Korea. Decorated Air medal. Recipient Union League prize, 1958, Vachel Lindsay award, 1959, Longview award, 1959; Melville Cane award, 1965-66. Sewanee Rev. fellow, 1954-55; Guggenheim fellow, 1962-63; Nat. Inst. grant of $2500, 1966. Author: (poems) Into The Stone, 1960, Drowning with Others, 1962, Helmets, 1964, Two Poems of the Air, 1964, Buckdancer's Choice, 1965 (Nat. Book Award of poetry 1966); (criticism) The Suspect in Poetry, 1964; (criticism) The Suspect in Poetry, 1964; Poems, 1957-67; Babel to Byzantium, 1968; (novel) Deliverance, 1970. Address: 4620 Lelias Ct Lake Katherine Columbia SC 20540 Office: Library of Congress Washington DC 20540

DICKEY, JAY W., lawyer; b. Ft. Worth, Sept. 14, 1906; s. Thomas Marvin and Gertrude (Harris) D.; LL.B., U. Ark., 1934; m. Margaret Lillian Rowell, June 17, 1933; children—Barbara (Mrs. Edwin Adams McCain), Jay W. Admitted to Ark. bar, 1934, since practiced in Pine Bluff; partner Rowell, Rowell & Dickey, 1934-64; sr. mem. firm Dickey, Dickey & Drake, 1964—; city atty., Pine Bluff, 1936-48. Vice pres., dir. Guaranty Fed. Savs. & Loan Assn.; dir. Jefferson Abstract Co., Holsum Baking Co. Mem. Ark. Legislative Council, 1947-49; mem. Ark. Stadium Commn., 1957-67. Bd. dirs. Ark. Sports Hall of Fame, Cotton Bowl Athletic Assn.; trustee U. Ark. Recipient SSS medal, 1946. Mem. Am., Ark., Jefferson County bar assns., Pine Bluff C. of C., Blue Key. Methodist. Mason, Kiwanian. Author: Dickey's Digest of the Ordinances of the City of Pine Bluff, 1947. Home: 47 So Pines Dr Pine Bluff AR 71601 Office: 216 E 5th Av Pine Bluff AR 71601

DICKEY, JOHN HORACE, lawyer; b. Edmonton, Alta., Can., Sept. 4, 1914; s. Horace Arthur and Catherine (Macdonald) D.; B.A., St. Mary's U., 1936; LL.B., Dalhousie U., 1940; m. Eleanor Joyce Carney, Apr. 18, 1959; children-Thomas, Michael, John Robert, Stephen, Gregory. Called to bar, N.S., 1940, since practiced in Halifax; partner McInnes, Cooper & Robertson, 1947—. Pres. N.S. Pulp, Ltd.; dir. Fraser-Brace Maritimes, Ltd., Dover Mills, Ltd., Atlantic Trust Co. Canadian rep. Econ. and Social Council of UN, 1950; mem. Canadian Delegation to UN, 1950. Mem. Canadian Ho. of Commons rep. Constituency Halifax, 1947-57; parliamentary asst. to minister Def. Prodn. and minister Trade and Commerce, 1952-57. Chmn. bd. Mt. St. Vincent U. Served to maj. Canadian Army, 1942-47. Apptd. Queen's Counsel, 1957. Mem. Canadian Bar Assn. (past v.p.), N.S. Barristers Soc. (past pres.), Liberal Fedn. Can. (v.p.). Home: 1532 Larch St Halifax N S Canda Office: PO Box 730 1673 Bedford Row Halifax N S Canada

DICKEY, JOHN SLOAN, educator; b. Lock Haven, Pa., Nov. 4, 1907; s. John W. and Gretchen (Sloan) D.; A.B., Dartmouth Coll., 1929; J.D., Harvard, 1932; m. Christina M. Gillespie, Nov. 26, 1932; children—Sylvia Alexander, Christina Louise (Mrs. Stewart P. Stearns, Jr.), John Sloan, Jr. Admitted to Mass. bar, 1932, practiced Boston, 1932; asst. to commr., Mass. Dept. of Correction, 1933; asst. to asst. sec. of state and asst. to legal adviser, U.S. Dept. State, 1934-36; law practice with Gaston, Snow, Hunt, Rice & Boyd, Boston, 1936-40; special asst. to sec. of state, 1940; spl. asst. to Coordinator of Inter-Am. Affairs, 1940-44, and detailed to U.S. Dept. State as chief World Trade Intelligence div. Dir. Office Pub. Affairs, Dept. State, 1944-45, and served as public liaison officer, U.S. delegation, U.N. Conf. on Internat. Orgn., San Francisco, 1945; lectr. in Am. fgn. policies, Sch. Advanced Internat. Studies, Washington, 1944-45; pres. Dartmouth Coll., 1945-70, pres. emeritus, Bicentennial prof. pub. affairs, 1970—. Trustee Rockefeller Found., Charles F. Kettering Found. Sr. vis. fellow Council on Fgn. Relations, 1971-72. Mem. Phi Beta Kappa. Contbg. author: The Secretary of State. Editor: The United States and Canada. Contbr. law and fgn. affairs jours. Address: Dartmouth Coll Hanover NH 03755

DICKEY, LLOYD BLACKWELL, educator, physician; b. Racine, Wis., Apr. 7, 1894; s. George Harry and Agnes Margaret (Thomson) D.; A.B., Fargo Coll., 1915; M.A., U. Ill., 1917; B.S., U. Minn., 1921, B.M., 1922, M.D. cum laude, 1923; m. Marion Marie Treadwell, Mar. 16, 1935; children—Barbara Dickey Douglass, Thomas Lloyd, Patricia Marion (Mrs. William Hubenette). Instr. anatomy U. Minn., 1919-21; asst. in morphology Marine Biol. Sta., U. Wash., summer 1921; chief Children's Clinic, Stanford U. Med., 1928- 49; vis. pediatrician in Tb, San Francisco Hosp., 1928-59; vis. physician Arequipa Sanatorium, 1934-57; intern Stanford U. Hosp., 1923 24, asst. resident pediatrics, 1924-25, resident pediatrics, instr., 1925-26, asst. prof. pediatrics, 1926-28, asso. prof., 1928-52, prof., 1952-59, prof. emeritus, 1959—, acting exec. head dept. pediatrics, 1955. Cons. pediatrics Presbyn. Med. Center and Children's Hosp., San Francisco, Kaiser Hosp., San Rafael, Cal., also Permanente Medical Group, 1959-71, Marin County Health Dept., 1971—. Served as pvt. with U.S. Army, 1918. Fellow emeritus Am. Thoracic Soc., Am. Acad. Pediatrics, Am. Coll. Chest Physicians, A.M.A.; mem. Gamma Alpha, Sigma Xi, Alpha Omega Alpha, Pi Gamma Mu, Sigma Chi, Nu Sigma Nu. Author numerous papers in field. Home: 113 Garden Av San Rafael CA 94903 Office: 99 Montecillo Rd San Rafael CA 94903

DICKEY, PARKE ATHERTON, educator, geologist; b. Chgo., Mar. 3, 1909; s. Samuel and Louise Parke (Atherton) D.; student Lincoln U. (Pa.), 1924-26; Ph.D. in Geology, Johns Hopkins, 1932; m. Janet McCleery Woods, Dec. 28, 1935; children—Margaret (Mrs. Theodore E. Wilde), Louise (Mrs. David J. Pinkow), Andrew W., Thomas M. Geologist, Lago Petroleum Co., Maracaibo, Venezuela, 1930-31, Tropical Oil Co., Colombia, 1932-38, Pa. Geol. Survey, Pleasantville, 1938-42, Forest Oil Co., Bradford, Pa., 1942-44, Quaker State Oil Refining Co., Bradford, 1942-46; head, geol. research Carter Oil Co., Tulsa, 1946-58; supr. exploration Creole Petroleum, Maracaibo, 1958-60; mgr. geol. div. Jersey Prodn. Research Co., Tulsa, 1960-61; prof. geology, head, dept. earth scis. U. Tulsa, 1961—; tchr. Oil and Gas Cons. Internat., Tulsa, 1969—; petroleum cons. various cos. Dir. First Bank Owasso (Okla.), Petroleum Resources, Inc., Wichita, Kan. Trustee Collinsville (Okla.) Meml. Hosp. NSF grantee, 1968-70, Fed. Water Quality Adminstrn. grantee, 1970-71. Mem. Soc. Petroleum Engrs. (dir. Midcontinent sect.), Colombian Geol. Soc. (corr.), Tulsa Geol. Soc. (pres. 1958), Am. Assn. Petroleum Geologists (research com. 1958, distinguished lectr. 1946), Am. Inst. Mining and Metall. Engrs., Geol. Soc. Am., Am. Geophys. Union. Author: Geology of Titusville, 1941; Geology of Oil City, 1942; also articles. Home: Route 1 Box 1193 Owasso OK 74055

DICKEY, PAUL SMITH, former meter co. exec.; b. Monticello, Ind., Sept. 21, 1903; s. Frank T. and Eva (Smith) D.; B.S. in Mech. Engring., Purdue U., 1925, D. Engring., 1953; m. Annabelle Phillips, Oct. 21, 1937; children—John P., Nancy J., Mary Ann, William P. With Bailey Meter Co., Cleve., 1925—, v.p., 1947- 55, pres., chmn., 1955-70, also dir.; dir. Bailey Meter Co. Ltd., Montreal, Montreal, Can Can. Trustee Fenn Edn. Found.; past chmn. Euclid Gen. Hosp. Assn.; nat. counselor Purdue Research Found. Mem. Sci. Apparatus Makers Assn. (pres.), Cleve. Engring. Soc., Am. Soc. M.E., Soc. Naval Architects and Marine Engrs., Instrument Soc. Am., Sigma Xi. Patentee instruments, automatic control systems. Home: 16224 Brewster Rd Cleveland OH 44112

DICKEY, RAYMOND ROOSEVELT, lawyer; b. Washington, June 10, 1917; s. Raymond B. and Rose (Maxwell) D.; student George Washington U., 1934-36; LL.B., Southeastern U., 1940; m. Hilda Finch; children—Susan Jean (Mrs. Leslie Bonde), Diane, David Raymond, Douglas Finch, Christopher Bruce. Admitted to D.C. bar, 1940, also U.S. Supreme Ct.; expert antitrust div. Dept. Justice, 1938-40; trade regulations, then Washington editor Research Inst. Am., 1940-42; editor in chief Modern Plastics mag., 1942-43; mgr. plastics div. Monroe Auto Equipment Co. (Mich.). 1943-44; partner firm Buckley & Danzansky, Washington, 1945-47; chief counsel U.S. Senate Small Bus. Com., 1947-49; spl. adviser to U.S. Ambassador Harriman under Marshall Plan, Paris, 1949- 50; partner firm Danzansky & Dickey, Washington, 1950-53, 54-69; gen. counsel USIA, 1953-54; sr. partner firm Danzansky, Dickey, Tydings, Quint & Gordon, 1969—; mem. Atty. Gen.'s Com. to Study Anti-trust Laws, 1953-55. Treas., dir., counsel San Juan (P.R.) Racing Assn., 1954—. Pub. mem. fgn. service selection panel USIA, 1954. Served with AUS, 1943. Mem. Delta Tau Delta. Republican. Episcopalian. Clubs: Nat. Lawyers, Capitol Hill, Nat. Press, Capital Yacht, International (Washington); Dorado Beach Golf and Tennis (P.R.). Home: 6912 Armat Dr Bethesda MD 20034 Office: 1120 Connecticut Av NW Washington DC 20036

DICKEY, ROBERT, III, mfg. co. exec.; b. Pitts., Jan. 28, 1918; s. Robert and Mary Appleby (Hugus) D.; B.S. in Mech. Engring., Princeton, 1939; m. Elizabeth Priscilla Beckwith, May 11, 1942; children—Diana Beckwith, Susan Scott, Robert IV. Jr. engr. United Engring. & Foundry Co., Pitts., 1939-42; engr. H.H. Robertson Co., Ambridge, Pa., 1946-48; with Dravo Corp., Pitts., 1948-51, 52-56, 62—, exec. v. p., 1962-64, pres., 1964—. also chief exec. officer, dir., chmn. exec. com.; with Union Barge Line Corp., Pitts., 1956—, pres., 1961-62, chmn., 1964—, also dir.; pres. So. Transfer Co., Pitts., 1961-62, chmn., 1964—, also dir.; exec. v.p. Dravo Can. Ltd., 1963-64, pres., 1964—, also dir.; exec. v.p. Dravo Constrn. Ltd., 1963-64, pres., 1964—, also dir.; pres., dir. Potomac Sand & Gravel Co., 1963—; chmn. Dravo Pty., Ltd.; dir. Zeni-McKinney-Williams, Pitts. Nat. Bank, Joy Mfg. Co. Exec. com. Allegheny Conf. on Community Devel. Bd. dirs. Pitts. United Fund; trustee E. Liberty Presbyn. Ch., Shadyside Hosp., Pitts. Served to lt. comdr. USNR, 1942-46, 51-52. Decorated Legion of Merit. Clubs: Pittsburgh Golf, Fox Chapel Golf, Duquesne (Pitts.); Laurel Valley Golf (Ligonier, Pa.); Rolling Rock. Home: 705 Devonshire St Pittsburgh PA 15213 Office: 1 Oliver Plaza Pittsburgh PA 15222

DICKIE, GEORGE THOMAS, educator, philosopher; b. Palmetto, Fla., Aug. 12, 1926; s. George Harrison and Emily (Brown) D.; A.B., Fla. State U., 1949; Ph.D., U. Cal. at Los Angeles, 1959; m. Ruth Joyce Petty, Aug. 5, 1950; children—Garrick George, Blake Allen. From instr. to asso. prof. Wash. State U., 1956-64; asso. prof. U. Houston, 1964-65; mem. faculty U. Ill. at Chgo. Circle, 1965—, prof. philosophy, 1967—. Served with USMC, 1944-46. Mem. Am. Philos. Assn., Am. Soc. Aesthetics (trustee 1966- 1966- 69). Democrat. Contbr. profl. jours. Home: 1506 Wesley St Evanston, IL 60201. Office: Dept Philosophy U Ill Chgo Circle Chicago IL 60680

DICKIE, HELEN AIRD, med. educator; b. N. Freedom, Wis., Feb. 19, 1913; s. Robert Bruce and Anna (Adams) Dickie; B.A., U. Wis., 1935; M.D., 1937. Intern, chest resident Los Angeles County Hosp., 1937-40; resident medicine U. Wis. Med. Sch., 1940-42, staff instr.

medicine, 1942-43, asst. prof., 1943-45, asso. prof., 1945-55, prof. medicine, 1955—; cons. VA Hosp. Fellow A.C.P.; mem. Central Soc. Clin. Research, Am. Thoracic Soc., Am. Fedn. Clin. Research, Wis. Tb and Respiratory Diseases Assn. (pres. 1968, dir.), Alpha Omega Alpha. Research on farmer's lung, tuberculosis, acute histoplasmosis, spontaneous mediastinal emphysema. Home: 501 Clifden Dr Madison WI 53711

DICKINSON, ALFRED JAMES, realtor; b. Eufaula, Ala., Dec. 19, 1916; s. Alfred J. and Bertha (Trotter) D.; B.A., U. Richmond (Va.), 1937; M.B.A., Harvard, 1939; m. Elsie Vick Mattingly, Mar. 21, 1942; children—Alfred James IV, Paul Mattingly, Elsie Stringfellow, Mary Bridgers. Asst. to comptroller Virginia-Carolina Chem. Corp., Richmond, Va., 1939-41, v.p., 1952-56, v.p., asst. to pres., 1956-57; v.p. Freeport Sulphur Co., 1957-60; exec. v.p. W. M. Brown & Son, Inc., Richmond, 1960-63; pres. Alfred J. Dickinson, Inc., Richmond, 1963—. Spl. agt. FBI, 1941-44. Served as capt. USMCR, 1944-46. Mem. Harvard Bus. Sch. Alumni Assn., Phi Beta Kappa, Omicron Delta Kappa, Phi Gamma Delta. Baptist. Clubs: Country of Virginia, Commonwealth. Home: 6101 Three Chopt Rd Richmond VA 23226 Office: 4900 Augusta Av Richmond VA 23230

DICKINSON, ALICE BRAUNLICH, educator; b. N.Y.C., Apr. 11, 1921; d. Hans and Dorothy (Harding) B.; B.A., U. Mich., 1941, Ph.D., 1952; M.A., Columbia, 1947; m. David J. Dickinson, Dec. 10, 1944; children—Sara, Dan. Asst. project engr. Sperry Gyroscope Co., Garden City, N.Y., 1942-44;; mem. staff Mass. Inst. Tech. Radiation Lab., Cambridge, Mass., 1944-45; lectr. Pa. State U., 1950-56; vis. prof. U. Baroda, India, 1962, 68, U. Aligarn, India, 1961-62; mem. faculty Smith Coll., 1959—, prof., chmn. math. dept., 1970—; cons. Hampshire Coll., 1965-68. Recipient Hampshire Coll. Founders award, 1970. Mem. Ely Ringing Guild, Am. Assn. U. Women. Author: Differential Equations: Time and Motion, 1971. Home: Graves Rd Ashfield MA 01330 Office: Tyler Annex Smith Coll Northampton MA 01060

DICKINSON, CALVIN L., chem. co. exec.; b. Wilmington, N.C., Aug. 2, 1914; s. John B. and Sallie (Duncan) D.; B.A., Wake Forest Coll., 1936; M. Chem. Engring., N.C. State Coll., 1942; m. Dorothy Dockery, Sept. 9, 1940; children—Calvin L., James D. Mgr. Houston plant organic chem. div. Diamond Alkali Co., 1951-53; with Am. Potash & Chem. Corp., 1953-70, v.p. mfg., 1963-70; v.p. mfg., engring., purchasing and distbn. Velsicol Chem. Corp., Chgo., 1970—. Home: 505 N Lake Shore Dr Chicago IL 60611 Office: 341 E Ohio St Chicago IL 60611

DICKINSON, DAVID FRANKLIN, educator, chem. engr.; b. Coffeyville, Kan., Jan. 28, 1914; s. Frank Harland and Jennie (Morgan) D.; A.B., Kan. State Tchrs. Coll., 1934, M.S., 1936; Ph.D. in Chem. Engring., Ia. State U., 1941; m. Mildred Ione Jeffers, Dec. 27, 1950; 1 dau., Sharon Lee. Research chemist Maytag Co., Newton, Ia., 1941-43; jr. engr. Mathieson Alkali Works, Niagara Falls, N.Y., 1943-46; project leader Armour Research Found., Chgo., 1946-47; asst. prof. chem. engring. Mich. State U., 1947-51; asst. prof., head dept. chemistry and chem. engring. Ind. Tech. Coll., Ft. Wayne, 1951-54; asso. prof. chem. engring. U. Tulsa, 1954-56; prof. chem. engring. U. N.M., 1956-58; resident research asso. chem. engring. and reactor engring. Argonne Nat. Lab. (Ill.), 1957-58; prof., chemn. dept. nuclear engring. U. Nev., Reno, 1958—, supr. reactor facility. Mem. Am. Chem. Soc., Am. Soc. Metals, Am. Inst. Chem. Engrs., Am. Soc. Engring. Edn., Nat. Soc. Profl. Engrs., Am. Nuclear Soc., Navy League, Sigma Xi, Kappa Mu Epsilon, Phi Kappa Phi, Phi Sigma Pi, Phi Lambda Upsilon, Sigma Pi Sigma, Sigma Tau. Clubs: Lions, President's (Reno). Home: 785 W 12th St Reno NV 89503

DICKINSON, DWIGHT, fgn. service officer; b. Annapolis, Md., Dec. 13, 1916; s. Spencer Edward and Laetitia (Thompson) D.; grad. Lawrenceville Sch., 1936; B.A., Harvard, 1940; m. Eleanor Anderson Hoge, May 23, 1942; children—Spencer Edward, Philip Lloyd. Third sec., second sec. Am. embassy, Mexico City, Mexico, 1946-49; vice consul Am. consulate gen.., Curacao, N.W.I., 1949- 51; assigned State Dept., Washington, 1951, 54, 5658, Nat. War Coll., 1958-59, second sec., 1st sec. Am. embassy, Beirut, Lebanon, 1954-56, counselor of embassy, for polit. affairs, Rabat, Morocco, 1959-62; polit. adviser U.S. Mission to UN, 1962-66; political adviser, with personal rank of minister U.S. Mission to North Atlantic Treaty Orgn., 1966-67; dep. chief mission Am. embassy, Rabat, 1967-70; ambassador to Togo, 1970—; mem. U.S. del. 15th-20th gen. assemblies. 1960-65, alt. U.S. rep. trusteeship council, 1964-65, mem. vis. mission Naura and New Guinea, 1965. Lt. comdr. USNR, 1941-46. Mem. Fgn. Service Assn. Office: care Dept of State Washington DC 20525

DICKINSON, EDWIN WALTER, artist, painter; b. Seneca Falls, N.Y., Oct. 11, 1891; s. Edwin Henry and Emma Sofia (Carter) D.; professional art student Pratt Inst., Art Students League of N.Y., Nat. Acad. of Design, 1910-13; pupil of William M. Chase and Charles W. Hawthorne, 1912-14; studied in Paris, 1919-20; m. Frances Foley, Oct. 31, 1928; children—Helen F., Edwin C. Instr. painting and drawing Buffalo Fine Arts Acad., 1915; instr. Art Student League of N.Y., 1922-23 and since 1945; instr. Stuart School, Boston, 1940-41; instr. Assn. for music and art on Cape Cod, 1942; instr. Art Inst. of Buffalo, 1939; instr. Cooper Union, 1945-49, Art Sch. Bklyn. Museum 1949—. Columbia, 1957. Exhibited The Carnegie Internationals, Mus. of Modern Art, Luxembourg Mus., Paris, 1920. Had one-man exhbns. Albright Art Gallery, Buffalo, 1926; Wood Meml. Gallery, Rochester, 1940; Farnsworth Mus., Wellesley Coll., 1941; Passedoit Gallery, N.Y.C., 1936-43; Mus. Modern Art. Represented in permanent collections Mus. Modern Art, Bowdoin Coll., Albright Art Gallery, Mus. of Fine Arts (Springfield, Mass.). Met. Mus. of Art, N.A.D., others. Served as radio operator U.S. Navy, 1917-19. Awarded 2d Altman prize by Nat. Acad. Design. 1929, 1st prize portrait, 1949, grant for art, Nat. Inst. of Arts & Letters, 1954, Medal for Art, The Century Assn., 1956; Benjamin Altman prize for landscape, 1958; Medalist Brandeis U., 1959, Artists Fellowship, 1962; Ford Found. grant for art, 1959; Brevoort-Eickenmeyer prize Columbia Univ., 1965. Mem. Nat. Institute Arts and Letters (v.p.), Fed. Modern Painters and Sculptors, Artists Equity Assn., N.A.D., Am. Acad. Arts and Letters. Clubs: The Beachcombers (Provincetown, Mass.); The Patteran (Buffalo). Home: 420 W 119th St New York City NY 10027 also Wellfleet MA 02667

DICKINSON, ERNEST MILTON, educator; b. Boston, O., May 12, 1905; s. Ernest Samuel and Mary Lily (English) D.; D.V.M., Ohio State U., 1927; M.S., Ore. State U., 1935; m. Celeste Snyder, Sept. 30, 1927; children—Milton Zan, Bess Celeste. Asst. prof. Ore. State U., Corvallis, 1927-36; asso. prof., 1938-41, prof., 1941—, head dept. vet. medicine, 1955-70; veterinarian U. Cal. at Berkeley, 1936-38. Cons. U.S. Dept. Agr., Agrl. Research Service, Dept. Interior, Wildlife Service, Dept. Health, Edn. and Welfare, NIH, USPHS. Recipient Meritorius Service award Ore. Turkey Industry, 1947; Dedicated Service award Ore. Poultry and Hatchery Assn., 1970. Fellow A.A.A.S.; mem. Am. (chmn. poultry disease sect. 1942-45), Ore. vet. med. assns., Am. Assn. Avian Pathologists, Poultry Sci. Assn., U.S. Animal Health Assn., Wildlife Disease Assn., Sigma Xi, Gamma Sigma Delta. Mason. Research avian diseases, coccidiosis, pullorum diseases, salmonellosis, erysipelas, ornithosis, fowl pox. Contbr. articles to sci. jours. Home: 231 NW 30th St Corvallis OR 97330

DICKINSON, FAIRLEIGH STANTON, Jr., mfg. co. exec., state senator; b. Rutherford, N.J., Dec. 9, 1919; s. Fairleigh Stanton and Grace Bancroft (Smith) D.; B.A. cum laude, Williams Coll., 1941; m. Mary Elizabeth Harrington, June 25, 1946; children—Ann Bancroft, Tracy Harrington. With the firm of Becton, Dickinson & Co., Rutherford, 1941—, pres., 1948—, also chmn. bd., chief exec. officer. dir.; chmn. bd., dir. Nat. Community Bank, Rutherford. Chmn. Bergen chpt. Nat. Conf. Christians and Jews, 1962—. Mem. N.J. Senate, 1967—. Trustee Bennington Coll.; trustee Kent Sch., Fairleigh Dickinson U. Served to lt. comdr. USCGR, 1941-46. Decorated Order Vasco Nunez de Balboa (Panama). Mem. Phi Beta Kappa, Delta Upsilon. Clubs: University, N.Y. Yacht, Williams (N.Y.C.); Edgartown (Mass.) Yacht; St. Croix (Virgin Islands) Yacht. Home: 160 Fairmount Rd Ridgewood NJ 07450 Office: Becton Dickinson and Co Rutherford NJ 07070

DICKINSON, FRANCIS HERMAN, paper and pulp co. exec.; b. Cabano, Que., Can., Jan. 19, 1914; s. Frank Elwood and Bertha Blanch (Mitchell) D.; ed. LaSalle Extension U., N.Y.U. night courses; m. Irene Delphia Carter, July 28, 1944; children—Diane Susan, Deborah Irene. Cost accountant Fraser Cos. Ltd., Edmundston, N.B., Can., 1933-41; cost accountant, cost and statistics mgr. Westvaco Corp., N.Y.C., 1946-56, comptroller, 1970—; comptroller-mgr. finance, sec.-treas. Hide & Dauch Paper Co. Can. Ltd., Toronto, Ont., 1956-62; controller, treas. Demtar Constrn. Materials Ltd., Montreal, 1962-70; dir. Corrugated Paper Box Ltd., H & D Boxes Ltd., 1960-62, Mathieu Lumber Co. Ltd., 1968-70. Served to capt. Canadian Army, 1942-46. Mem. Financial Execs. Inst. (dir. 1960-62, 69-70), N.A.M., Tax Found., Am. Paper Inst. Club: Sleepy Hollow Country (Scarborough, N.Y.). Home: 2 Manor Close North Tarrytown NY 10591 Office: Westvaco Corp 299 Park Av New York City NY 10017

DICKINSON, FRANKLYN, former electric utility exec.; b. St Paul, July 3, 1902; s. Frederick and Marie (Tenner) D.; student U. Minn., 1922-23; grad. exec. program bus. adminstrn., Columbia, 1952; m. Leone Rohloff, Nov. 27, 1929. With No. States Power Co., 1923-28, Ala. Power Co., 1928-37; with Ohio Edison Co., 1937-70, gen. mgr. charge sales, 1954-61, v.p. charge sales, 1962-70; 1962-70 cons. Def. Electric Power Adminstrn., 1951-52. Mem. Sales Execs. Conf., Ohio, Akron chambers commerce. Theta Chi. Presbyn. Mason (Shriner). Clubs: Portage Country; Akron City. Home: 98 Greencrest Terrace Akron OH 44313

DICKINSON, FRED EUGENE, educator; b. Buena Vista, Minn., Dec. 29, 1912; s. Ralph Herman and and Eddie Elizabeth (Speelman) D.; student Bemidji (Minn.) State Coll., 1930- 32; B.S. in Forestry, U. Minn., 1938; M.S. in Forest Products, Mich. State U., 1941; postgrad. U. Cal. at Los Angeles, 1942; Ph.D. in Forest Products Econs., Yale, 1951; m. Doris Elida Vance, Dec. 31, 1938; children—Robert Vance, Thomas Edward, Roger Eugene. Forestry foreman Civilian Conservation Corps, 1938-39; teaching asst. Mich. State U., 1939-41; dir. div. forestry and lumbering Lassen Jr. Coll., Susanville, Cal., 1941-42; technologist U.S. Forest Products Lab., Madison, Wis., 1942-45; civilian packaging specialist War Dept., ETO, 1945; asst. prof. lumbering, then asso. prof. Yale, 1945-52, also part-time research technologist Office Naval Research at univ., 1946-51; asso. prof. wood utilization, chmn. dept. wood tech. U. Mich., 1952-55; prof. forestry, dir. forest products lab., U. Cal. at Berkeley, 1955—. Mem. com. on forestry research agrl. bd. NRC-Nat. Acad. Scis., 1964-66; mem. ofcl. U.S. delegation Fifth FAO Conf. Wood Tech., 1963. Recipient Heinrich Christian Burckhardt medal Faculty of Forestry, U. Güttingen, 1970. Fellow Internat. Acad. Wood Sci. (pres. bd. adv. 1969—), Soc. Am. Foresters (asso. editor Journal of Forestry 1960-66); mem. Forest Products Research Research Soc. (pres. 1963-64), Internat. Union Forest Research Orgns. (chmn. working group on terminology, sect. 41, 1966—), Soc. Wood Sci. and Tech. (dir. visting scientist program 1960-62), Sigma Xi. Republican. Lutheran. Editorial bd. Wood and Sci. Tech. Quar. Home: 1265 Contra Costa Dr El Cerrito CA 94530 Office: 1301 S 46th St Richmond CA 94804

DICKINSON, JOHN BREWER, Jr., former accountant; b. Morehead City, N.C., Sept. 7, 1917; s. John Brewer and Sallie (Duncan) D.; student Wake Forest Coll., 1936-40; m. Helen Carol Swart, July 26, 1941; children—John Brewer III, Duncan B. Staff accountant A. M. Pullen & Co., C.P.A.'s, Greensboro, N.C., 1945-50, asst. mgr., Winston-Salem, N.C., 1951-52, partner-in-charge Charlotte N.C., 1952-69, mem. exec. com., 1958-68, chmn. mgmt. service com., 1960- 64. Sec., v.p. N.C. Bd. C.P.A. Examiners, 1958-60, pres. 1960-61. Mem. budget com. Charlotte United Appeal, 1954-55, Charlotte Solicitation Rev. Bd., 1956-58. C.P.A., Va., N.C. Mem. Am. Inst. C.P.A.'s (past chmn. N.C. membership com., mem. mgmt. services com.), N.C. Assn. C.P.A.'s (past mem. fed. taxation com.), Nat. Assn. Accountants, Sigma Phi Epsilon. Democrat. Methodist (steward). Clubs: Star Hill, Morehead Country, Dune's. Home: Surf Song Cottage Route 1 Morehead City NC 28557

DICKINSON, JOSHUA CLIFTON, Jr., museum dir., educator; b. Tampa, Fla., Apr. 28, 1916; s. Joshua Clifton and Mary (Martin) D.; student U. Va., 1936-39, Cornell U., summer 1939; B.S., U. Fla., 1940, M.S., 1946, Ph.D., 1950; m. Lucy Freeman Jackson, Apr. 13, 1936; children—Joshua Clifton III, Martin Freeman, Susan Ellissa. Faculty, U. Fla., 1946—, asso. prof. zoology, 1954—; curator Fla. State Mus., 1952—, chmn. natural scis., 1952-60, dir., 1960—. Research fellow Harvard, 1951-52; vis. investigator Woods Hole Oceanographic Inst., 1952; expdns. to Honduras, 1947, Bahamas, 1960-67, Jamaica, 1962, Baffin Is., 1955, Sombrero Is., 1963, Navassa Is., 1965. Chmn., Fla. commn. Archives and History, 1964—; mem. mus. adv. panel Nat. Endowment for Arts, 1970—. Served to comdr. USCGR, 1942-45. Grantee Nat. Park Service, 1952-54, NSF, 1955-57. Mem. Am. Ornithologists Union, Am. Soc. Naturalists, Am. Assn. Museums (council 1963—, sec. 1970—), A.A.A.S., Am. Soc. Zoologists, Wilson Soc., Dirs. Systematic Collections, Am. Assn. Sci. Mus. Dirs. (v.p. 1967-69), Sigma Xi, Phi Sigma, Alpha Tau Omega. Democrat. Rotarian (pres. Gainesville 1967-68). Contbr. monographs, sci. papers to profl. lit. Home: 1804 S W 35th Pl Gainesville FL 32601 Office: Fla State Mus U Fla Museum Rd Gainesville FL 32601

DICKINSON, LEVI CALL, lawyer; b. Algona, Ia., June 7, 1905; s. Lester Jesse and Myrtle (Call) D.; LL.B., George Washington U., 1930; m. Marion Carmichael, June 8, 1929; children—Levi Call, Roderick C., Nancy Jane. Admitted to Ia. bar, 1930, since practiced in Des Moines; sr. partner Dickinson, Throckmorton, Parker, Mannheimer & Raife; instr. taxation Drake U., 1941- 42. Mem. Am., Ia., Polk County bar assns., Sigma Chi. Conglist. Club: Des Moines. Home: 405 37th St Des Moines IA 50312 Office: Fleming Bldg Des Moines IA 50309

DICKINSON, PERRY GEORGE, lawyer; b. Cuyahoga Falls, O., May 16, 1926; s. Robert E. and Isa M. (Starkey) D.; B.S., Kent State U., 1955; J.D., Akron U., 1960; m. Clementine Bosko, June 29, 1949; children—Kurt, Caroline. Admitted to Ohio bar, 1960; spl. agt. FBI, 1960-62; practice in Ravenna, 1962—; acting judge Municipal Ct., 1970—. Police prosecutor, 1965-69; asst. county prosecutor, 1969-70; prof. law Kent State U., 1962-64; mem. Ohio Criminal Justice Com., 1964—; spl. counsel Ohio atty. gen. Kent State U., 1970—. Chmn. Cancer Drive, 1963; sec. bd. Boys Club; bd. dirs. Cancer Soc. Served with USMCR, 1944-46. Decorated Purple Heart. Mem. Am., Ohio, Portage County bar assns. Democrat. Roman Catholic. Kiwanian. Home: 3917 New Milford Rd Rootstown OH 44272 Office: 250 S Chestnut St Ravenna OH 44266

DICKINSON, PETER MALCOLM DE BRISSAC, author; b. Zambia, Dec. 16, 1927; s. Richard Sebastian Willoughby and Nancy (Lovemore) D.; student Eton, 1941-46, King's Coll., Cambridge, 1948-52; m. Mary Rose Barnard, Apr. 26, 1953; children—Philippa, Polly, John, James. Asst. editor Punch mag., London, Eng., 1952-69. Author crime novels and children's books, including The Old English Peep-show, 1969; Sleep and His Brother, 1970; Emma Tupper's Diary, 1971. Named Brit. Crime Novelist of Year, Crime Writers Assn. 1969, 70. Address: 33 Queensdale Rd London W 11 England

DICKINSON, PORTER, newspaper publisher; b. Glasgow, Ky., Mar. 10, 1906; s. Michael Hall and Emma Raus (Smith) D.; student U. Wash., 1925-26; m. Eleanor Roberts, July 26, 1930; 1 son, Robert Brewster. Pub. emeritus Honolulu Star-Bull., 1927—; pres. Hawaii Newspaper Agy., 1962—; v.p., dir. Guam Publs., Inc., 1970—, Mariana Publs., Inc., 1970—, Huntington Pub. Co. (W.Va.); dir. C. Brewer & Co., Ltd., First Hawaiian Bank; hon. consul of Finland for Hawaii, 1961—. Chmn. adv. bd. Hawaii Salvation Army, 1949-51, 67. Bd. dirs. Better Bus. Bur. Decorated Order Finnish Lion. Mem. Honolulu C. of C. (pres. 1952-53), Am. Newspaper Pub. Assn., Hawaii Newspaper Publishers Assn., Cal. Newspaper Pubs. Assn. Republican. Rotarian (pres. Honolulu 1947- 48, dist. gov. 1951-52), Mason (Jester). Home: 2003 Kalia Rd Honolulu HI 96815 Office: PO Box 3080 Honolulu HI 96802

DICKINSON, RAYMOND L., former philanthropic cons.; b. Shellsburg, Ia., Feb. 2, 1890; s. Herbert and Nellie Isabel (Sherman) D.; student Tilford Collegiate Acad., Ia. State Tchrs. Coll.; B.S. in Civil Engring., Ia. State Coll., 1915; L.H.D., Muskingum Coll., 1953; m. Kathleen Miller, Oct. 6, 1917; children—Richard L., Mary Louise (Mrs. Richard S. Bentley), Robert M. Prin. schs., Brandon, Ia., 1908-11; community sec. Cedar Falls, Ia., 1915-16; instr. math. Ia. State Tchrs. Coll., Cedar Falls, 1916-17; indsl. sec., exec. sec. South Side br., exec. sec. Central br., asso. gen. exec. YMCA, Columbus, O., 1917-32; exec. sec. Community Fund, Columbus, 1932-33; exec. Ohio area nat. Council YMCA's, 1934-42, exec. v.p., N.Y.C., 1942-56, nat. treas., 1956-66; philanthropic cons. Hanover Bank, N.Y.C., 1956-59. Hon. mem. Springfield Coll. Corp. Mem. Protestant Council; mem. world's com. YMCA, 1947-57, hon. life mem. nat. bd. Trustee Springfield Coll. Mem. Assn. Secs. YMCA, Tau Beta Pi. Phi Kappa Phi, Sigma Delta Chi. Republican. Rotarian. Club: Quill (N.Y.C.). Home: 160 Cabrini Blvd New York City NY 10033

DICKINSON, ROBERT SMITH, flour milling co. exec.; b. Columbus, Neb., Jan. 22, 1889; s. Richard Storrs and Mary Leona (Holden) D.; B.A., Doane Coll., Crete, Neb., 1910; m. Carrie Hazel Clark, Dec. 20, 1913; children—Jean, Robert Hugh, Ann Marie, Sheila, Rae Leona. With Ravenna Mills (Neb.), 1910-20; with Con-Agra, Inc. (formerly Neb. Consol. Mills Co.), Omaha, 1920-71, chmn. bd., hon. chmn. until 1971. Home: 417 Happy Hollow Blvd Omaha NB 68106 Died July 12, 1971.

DICKINSON, SIDNEY EDWARD, painter; b. Wallingford, Conn., Nov. 28, 1890; s. Charles Henry and Mary Lord (Thorn) D.; studied under George Bridgman and William M. Chase, Art Student's League, New York, and under Douglas Volk, National Academy of Design; m. Mary Watson, August 1, 1928; children—Thorn Watson, Nathaniel Rogers. Instructor Art Students' League, 1919-20 and since 1943; instr. New School of Design, 1924-26, National Academy Design, 1928-30, 1939- 42. Represented in permanent collection, Corcoran Gallery, Washington, D.C., by "Portrait of the Artist"; Art Institute Chicago, " Unrest "; City Art Museum, St. Louis, "The Young Painter"; Houston Art Mus., "Portrait of the Artist"; Davenport Municipal Gallery, "Mary"; The Allentown (Pa.) Museum, "Mary and The Studio "; portrait of Mrs. High, High Mus. Art, Atlanta; portrait Samuel H. Kress, Nat. Gallery, Washington; also represented permanent collection Dallas Mus. Awarded 3d Hallgarten prize, Nat. Acad. Design, 1917; Philadelphia prize, Pa. Acad. Fine Arts, 1923; Popular prize, Corcoran Gallery, 1924; 1st Hallgarten prize, Nat. Acad. Design, 1924; Beck gold medal, Pa. Acad. Fine Arts, 1924; Bronze Medal, Allied Artists of America, 1929; Walter Lippincott prize, Pa. Acad., 1931; 1st prize, Nat. Arts Club, 1932; Maynard portrait prize, Nat. Acad. Design, 1933; 1st Altman prize, Nat. Acad. Design 1936; medal of honor Allied Artists of America, 1937; Maynard portrait prize, Nat. Acad. Design, 1938; Carnegie prize Nat. Acad. Design, 1942. A.N.A., 1921, N.A., 1927; hon. mention Carnegie Inst., 1948; Century Assn. medal, 1959. Mem. Allied Artists America, Nat. Inst. Arts and Letters, Century Assn., Lotos Club. Address: 155 Washington Av Pleasantville NY 10570

DICKINSON, WILLIAM BOYD, newspaper editor; b. Kansas City, Mo., May 18, 1908; s. William Boyd and Alice G. (Hillman) D.; A.A., Kansas City Jr. Coll., 1927; A.B., U. Kan., 1929; Nieman fellow Harvard, 1939-40; m. Aileen Robinson (dec.); m. 2d, Joan S. Younger; children—William Boyd III, Beverly (Mrs. Robert J. Albertson), Theresa Joan, Rosalind Alice, Diana Mary. Reporter Kansas City Star, 1929-30; with U.P.I., 1930-49, successively mgr. burs., Denver, Mpls., N.Y.C., bus. rep., Chgo., news editor, London, S.W. Pacific mgr. and war corr., 1930-47, fgn. news editor, N.Y.C., 1947-49; Phila. Evening and Sunday Bull., 1949—, news editor, Washington bur. chief, asso. city editor, 1949-56, asst. mng. editor, 1956-59, mng. editor, 1959-69, exec. editor, 1969—. Mem. Asso. Press Mng. Editors Assn. (past pres.). Am. Soc. Newspaper Editors (dir.), Phila. Press Assn., Sigma Delta Chi, Delta Tau Delta. Clubs: National Press (Washington); Franklin Inn, Midday (Phila.). Home: 2219 Spruce St Philadelphia PA 19103 Office: 30th and Market Sts Philadelphia PA 19101

DICKINSON, WILLIAM BOYD, Jr., editor; b. Kansas City, Mo., Feb. 21, 1931; s. William Boyd and Aileen (Robinson) D.; A.B., U. Kan., 1953; student George Washington U. Law Sch., 1957-58; m. Betty Ann Landree, Feb. 1, 1953; children—William Boyd IV, David Alan. With U.P.I., 1955-59, mem. staff overnight desk, Washington, 1957-59; staff writer Editorial Research Reports, Washington, 1959-66, editor, 1966—; v.p. Congl. Quar., Inc., 1972—; acted as discussion leader Am. Press Inst., 1966—. Winston Churchill Traveling fellow, summer 1968. Served with AUS, 1953-55. Mem. Internat. Press Inst., English-Speaking Union (dir. Washington chpt.), Alpha Tau Omega, Omicron Delta Kappa. (Washington). Supervisory editor Congl. Quarterly's Congress and the Nation, Vol. II, Congl. Quar.'s Complete Guide to Congress. Home: 5430 N 22d Rd Arlington VA 22205 Office: 1735 K St NW Washington DC 20006

DICKINSON, WILLIAM HALE, Jr., clergyman; b. Paris, Tex., July 20, 1913; s. William Hale and Lucy (Davidge) D.; B.A., So. Methodist U., 1935; B.D., Perkins Sch. Theology, 1946; D.D. (hon.), Tex. Wesleyan Coll., 1959; m. Nina Rebecca Sadler, June 22, 1937; children—James Walter, Lucy Ann. Ordained to ministry Meth. Ch., 1936; pastor in Tex., 1936-43; asso. charge pastoral ministry Highland Park Meth. Ch., Dallas, 1946-58, pastor in charge, 1958—. Mem. bd. publns. Meth. Ch. Mem. planning com. Goals for Dallas; participant Am. Assembly, 1966, Pub. Affairs Inst., 1967. Bd. dirs. Timberlawn

Found., Meth. Hosp., Dallas; bd. govs. So. Meth. U.; bd. trustees, exec. com. Southwestern U. Served as chaplain AUS, 1943-46. Decorated Legion of Merit, Bronze Star; Croix de Valor (Italy); named Distinguished Alumnus So. Meth. U. Mem. Blue Key. Home: 3932 Purdue St Dallas TX 75225 Office: 3300 Mockingbird Lane Dallas TX 75205.

DICKINSON, WILLIAM HAROLD, mfg. co. exec.; b. Ft. Worth, Nov. 16, 1910; s. John William and Harriet (Dickey) D.; B.S. in Elec. Engring., Tex. A. and M. U., 1930; m. Mary Kathryn Border, Aug. 19, 1953; children—Elaine (Mrs. Thomas Anthony Phillips), Thomas William, Robert William. With Westinghouse Electric Corp., 1930-56, supr. naval ordnance, Detroit, 1943-45, supt. fgn. mfg., Pitts., 1945-50, dir. mfg. engring., 1950-56; with A.O. Smith Corp., Tipp City, O., 1956-60, 69—, works mgr. Electric Motor div., gen. mgr., 1957-60; v.p., gen. mgr. Power Controls div. Midland-Ross Corp., Owosso, Mich., 1960-68; v.p., dir. Midland-Ross of Can. Ltd., 1965-60; dir. Dolly Toy Co., Tipp City, O., 1957—; dir. Tipp City Shopping Center, 1960—, v.p., 1969—. Adviser on electric mfg. industry to Govt. of India, 1949, Mem. adv. bd. Owosso Coll., 1965-69; YWCA 1968-69; chmn. Owosso drive United Fund, 1968-69, v.p., dir. Shiawassee County, (Mich.) United Fund, 1968-69; trustee Owosso Meml. Hosp., 1961-70, pres., 1964-67. Mem. Soc. Automotive Engrs. Methodist (ofcl. bd., trustee, pres. bd. trustees 1965-67). Clubs: Troy Country; Detroit Athletic. Address: 1031 Cloverdale Dr Troy OH 45373

DICKINSON, WILLIAM LOUIS, congressman; b. Opelika, Ala., June 5, 1925; s. Henry K. and Bernice (Lowe) D.; LL.B., U. Ala., 1950; m. Mary Patterson Stanfield, 1948; children—Chris, Mike, Tara, William Louis. Admitted to Ala. bar, 1950; practiced in Opelika, 1950-63; judge Opelika City Ct., 1951-53; judge Ct. Common Pleas, 1953-59; judge Juvenile Ct. Lee County, 1953-59; judge Fifth Judicial Ct. Ala., 1959-63; asst. v.p. So. Ry. System, Montgomery, 1963-64; mem. 89th-92d Congresses, 2d Dist. Ala. Chmn. Ala. Rep. Congl. Delegation. Chmn. Opelika Bd. Edn., 1960-61; mem. Gov's..Indsl. Com. of 100, 1963-64; dir. Lee Country Civil Defense, 1961-62. Pres. bd. dirs. Ala. Mental Health Assn., Lee County Mental Health Clinic; bd. dirs. Lee County Rehab. Center. Served with USNR, World War II. Named Man of Year Opelika Jr. C. of C., 1960, One of Four Outstanding Young Men in Ala., 1960. Mem. Ala. Bar Assn., Ala. Alumni Assn., Sigma Alpha Epsilon. Mason, Kiwanian, Elk. Home: 6301 Beachway Dr Falls Church VA 22041 Office: House Office Bldg Washington DC 20515

DICKINSON, WILLIAM REYNOLDS, lawyer; b. Chgo., May 8, 1913; s. William Reynolds and Anna (Wilson) D.; A.B., magna cum laude, Yale, 1934, LL.B., 1937; m. Anne L. Knowles, July 22, 1945; children—Amy T., Anna W. (Mrs. Richard B. Platt), William Reynolds. Admitted to Ill. bar, 1938; with Wilson & McIlvaine, Chgo., 1937—, partner, 1952—. Pres., dir. Chicago Summer Resort Co.; pres., dir. State Safety Co.; director KEY Television, Inc., Pres., trustee Chgo. Zool. Soc.; sec., bd. dirs. Schweppe Found., Chgo.; bd. dirs. Field Mus.. National History, Children's Meml. Hosp. Served to lt. USCGR, 1942-46. Mem. Am., Ill., Chgo. bar assns., Am. Judicature Soc., Phi Beta Kappa, Zeta Psi. Clubs: Legal, Law, Attic, Casino, Commercial (Chgo.); Old Elm (Ft. Sheridan, Ill.); Onwentsia (Lake Forest, Ill.); Shoreacres (Lake Bluff, Ill.); Valley of Montecito (Santa Barbara, Cal.). Home: 770 W Westleigh Rd Lake Forest IL 60045 Office: 135 S LaSalle St Chicago IL 60603

DICKISON, WALTER LEE, coll. dean; b. Montrose, Mo., Oct. 19, 1913; s. C. Bernice and Zetta (Harvey) D.; B.S. in Edn., Central Mo. State Coll., 1941; B.S. in Pharmacy, U. Colo., 1949, M.S., 1956, Ph.D., 1957; m. Virginia Black, June 25, 1939; children—James Edwin, Jane Elizabeth. Instr. pharmacy U. Colo., 1949-51, 55-57; pharmacist Stanton Drug Co., 1951-55; faculty Southwestern State Coll., Weatherford, Okla., 1957—, prof. pharmacy, 1959-65, dean Sch. Pharmacy, 1965—. Served to lt. USCGR, 1942-46. Mem. Am. Pharm. Assn., Am. Assn. Colls. Pharmacy. Baptist. Rotarian (pres. 1964-65). Home: 711 E Arlington St Weatherford OK 73069

DICKLER, GERALD, lawyer; b. N.Y.C., Aug. 20, 1912; s. Michael and Lillian (Fishoff) D.; A.B., Columbia, 1931, LL.B., 1933; m. Ruth A. Crohn, June 1, 1933; children—Abby Catherine (Mrs. Lawrence S. Pratt), Jane Frances (Mrs. Richard N. Lebow), Susan. Admitted to N.Y. bar, 1934, since practiced in N.Y.C.; asso. Weil, Gotshal & Manges, 1933-36; pvt. practice, 1936-58; partner Hall, Dickler & Howley and predecessor firm, 1959—. Sec., dir., mem. exec. com. Capital Cities Broadcasting Corp. Trustee Walden Sch., N.Y.C., 1938-42. Served with USNR, 1944-46. Mem. Bar Assn. City N.Y., Acad. TV Arts and Scis. Author: Man on Trial, 1962. Home: 120 E 81st New York City NY 10028 Office: 460 Park Av New York City NY 10022

DICKMAN, FRANCOIS MOUSSIEGT, fgn. service officer; b. Iowa City, Ia., Dec. 23, 1924; s. Adolphe Jacques and Henriette Louise (Moussiegt) D.; B.A., U. Wyo., 1947; M.A., Fletcher Sch. Law and Diplomacy, Medford, Mass., 1948; m. Margaret Hoy, June 3, 1947; children—Christine, Paul. Research asst. Brookings Instn., Washington, 1950; with U.S. Fgn. Service, 1951—; consular/comml. officer, Barranquilla, Colombia, 1952-54; Arabic lang. trainee, 1955-57; econ./comml./consular officer, Khartoum, Sudan, 1957-60; UAR-Syrian affairs desk officer Dept. State, 1961-65; econ. officer, Tunis, Tunisia, 1965-68; student U.S. Army War Coll., Carlisle, Pa., 1968-69; econ. counselor, Jidda, Saudi Arabia, 1969—. Served with AUS, 1943-46, 50-51. Recipient Dept. State Meritorious Honor award, 1965. Mem. Am. Fgn. Service Assn., U. Wyo. Alumni Assn., Phi Beta Kappa, Phi Kappa Phi. Home: 1407 Sheridan Av Laramie WY 82070 Office: Am Embassy Jidda Saudi Arabia APO New York City NY 09697

DICKMAN, JOSEPH LAWRENCE, air force officer; b. Tampa, Fla., Mar. 23, 1917; s. Frederick Thibaut and Hayes (Lawrence) D.; B.S., U.S. Mil. Acad., 1939; grad. Air Command and Staff Sch., 1948, Air War Coll., 1951, Nat. War Coll., 1956; m. Helen Elizabeth Taylor, Apr. 13, 1940; children—Joseph Taylor, John Frederick. Commd. 2d lt. U.S. Army 1939, advanced through grades to maj. gen. USAF, 1965: assigned 8th Air Force, also 15th Air Force, ETO, 1942- 45, hdgrs. USAF, 1951-56, 60-61, U.S. Air Forces, Europe, 1956-60; exec. asst. to sec. air force, 1961-63; comdr. Duluth Air Def. Sector. 1963- 64, Hdgrs. N.Am. Air Def. Command, 1964-67; comdr. Eastern NORAD Region and 1st Air Force, 1967-70; with Hdqrs. Aerospace Def. Command, Ent AFB, Colo., 1970-71; Hdqrs. Def. Nuclear Agy., Washington, 1971—. Decorated Legion of Merit with oak leaf cluster, D.F.C. with oak leaf cluster, Air medal with 4 oak leaf clusters, Purple Heart, Air Force Commendation medal. Mem. Air Force Assn. Home: 26 Westover Av Bolling AFB Washington DC 20332 Office: Hdqrs Def Nuclear Agy Washington DC 20305

DICKMANN, DALE SIDNEY, mfg. co. exec.; b. St. Louis, Dec. 31, 1931; s. Walter F. and Wilma (Bergman) D.; B.S., B.A., U. Mo., 1953; m. Gloria Ann McCrome, Sept. 24, 1955; children—Mark Allen, Barbara Ann, Beth Ann. Mem. factory controller's staff Sears, Roebuck & Co., Chgo., 1955-65; controller Kellwood Co., St. Louis, 1966—. Served with USAF, 1953-55. Home: 1616 Bennett St Warson Woods MO 63122 Office: 9909 Clayton Rd St Louis MO 63124

DICKS, JOHN BARBER, educator; physicist; b. Natchez, Miss., Mar. 10, 1926; s. John Barber and Pauline (Merrill) D.; B.S., U. of South, Sewanee, Tenn., 1948; Ph.D., Vanderbilt U., 1955; m. Joan Balfour Payne, Aug. 26, 1952; children—Ian, Ayers Merrill, Agnes, Josephine. Asso. prof. Tenn. Technol. U., Cookeville, 1953-54; asst. prof., asso. prof. U. of South, 1954-64; prof. physics U. Tenn. Space Inst., Tullahoma, 1964—. Pres. J.B. Dicks & Assos., 1967—. Chmn. steering com. Symposium on Engring. Aspects of Magnetohydrodynamics, 1971. Asso. fellow Am. Inst. Aeros. and Astronautics; mem. Am. Phys. Soc., Am. Assn. U. Profs. (Tenn. state chmn. 1962-64), Am. Soc. Mech. Engrs. (sec. energetics div. 1971), Sigma Xi, Sigma Pi Sigma. Contbr. articles profl. jours. Home: 3 Oklahoma Av Sewanee TN 37375

DICKSON, ALAN T., textile mfr.; b. Charlotte, N.C., 1931. grad. N.C. State Coll., 1953; student Harvard Grad. Sch. Bus. Adminstrn., 1955. Chmn., dir. Am. & Efird Mills, Inc., Mt. Holly, N.C.; dir. Wilson Sales Co.; dir. Charlotte bd. N.C. Nat. Bank. Home: 512 Museum Dr Charlotte NC 28207 Office: American & Efird Mills Inc P O Box 507 Mount Holly NC 28120*

DICKSON, CARROLL J., lawyer; b. Mpls., Aug. 6, 1905; LL.B., U. Minn., 1927; LL.M., Columbia, 1930. Admitted to Minn. bar, 1927, N.Y. bar, 1933; now mem. firm Havens Wandless, Stitt & Tighe, N.Y.C. Mem. Am. Bar Assn., Assn. Bar City N.Y., Phi Delta Phi. Office: 99 Park Av New York City NY 10016*

DICKSON, CARTER, see Carr, John Dickson.

DICKSON, ELEANOR COWPER, petroleum co. exec.; b. Jersey City, May 13, 1916; d. George W. and Eleanor Sophia (Morris) Dickson; student Barnard Coll., 1932-34, N.Y.U., 1948. Stenographer, sec. to asst. gen. counsel, sec. to gen. counsel, sec. to chmn. bd., asst. sec. Standard-Vacuum Oil Co., 1935-55, sec., 1957; now sec. Mobil Petroleum Co., Irvington, N.Y. Mem. Budd Lake Civic Assn. Republican. Presbyn. Home: 7 Lakeview Av Budd Lake NJ 07828 Office: 150 E 42d St New York City NY 10017

DICKSON, EVELYN WIGHT (Mrs. Carroll Dickson), civic worker; b. Bklyn., Dec. 16, 1899; d. J. Sherman and Ida (Robins) Wight; student Bryn Mawr Coll., 1916-18; m. Carroll J. Dickson, Sept. 27, 1932; 1 dau., Patricia D. Edgar. Chmn. A.R.C. Nurses Aides, Bklyn. chpt., 1942-45; dir. visiting Nurses Assn. Bklyn., 1946-70; dir. Bklyn. Inst. Arts and Scis., 1948—; governing com. Bklyn. Children's Mus., 1948—, chmn. com., 1960-68; sec., finance chmn. Nursing Service Com. for Civil Def., Greater City N.Y., 1952-55; chmn., mem. bd. regents Sch. Nursing Com., L.I. Coll. Hosp., Bklyn., 1952-54; governing mem. Bklyn. Acad. Music, 1955-67; women's com. chmn. Boston Symphony Orch. Concerts in Bklyn., 1955-58; dir. State League Nursing, 1956-58. Mem. Nat. Council Women U.S. Club: Civitas of Bklyn. (pres. 1953-55). Address: 160 Henry St Brooklyn NY 11201

DICKSON, GEORGE EDMOND, coll. dean; b. Seattle, Jan. 6, 1918; s. Charles Edmond and Blanche Erwin (Crane) D.; B.A., Central Wash. Coll. Edn., 1940; M.A., Stanford, 1948, Ed.D., 1949; m. Dorothy O'Nita Brown, Aug. 27, 1940; children—Charles Brown, Dean Edmond. Tchr. pub. schs., Pasco, Wash., 1940- 41, Toppenish, 1941-42, Wapato, 1945-47; dir. student teaching, asso. prof. elementary edn. Central Wash. Coll. Edn., 1949-53; asst. prof. elementary edn. Ohio State U., 1953-56, asso. prof. elementary and higher edn., 1956-57; prof. edn., dean Coll. Edn., U. Toledo, 1957—. Dir. Internat. Research Project on Characteristics Tchr. Education Students in British Isles and U.S.; dir. Research Projects of Devel. Ednl. Specifications for a Model Tchr. Edn. Program; mem. Ednl. Study Team to Israel. Served with USAAF, 1942-46; ground sch. instr. Primary Flight Sch., 1942-44; information and edn. specialist Scott Field, Ill., 1945-46. Mem. Ohio, N.W. Ohio edn. assns., Assn. Supervision and Curriculum Devel., Assn. Higher Edn., Am. Ednl. Research Assn. Am. Assn. U. Profs., Am. Assn. Sch. Adminstrs., Asso. Orgns. for Tchr. Edn. (past chmn. nat. council), Nat. Council for Accreditation of Teacher Edn., Phi Kappa Phi, Phi Delta Kappa, Kappa Delta Pi. Author: (with I. Miller, L. Tomlinson) Guidebook for Elementary Student Teachers, 1958; (with others) The Characteristics of Teacher Education Standards in the British Isles and U.S., 1965; Educational Specifications for a Comprehensive Elementary Teacher Education Program, Vols. 1 and 2, 1968; (with others) The Feasibility of Education Specifications for a Comprehensive Elementary Teacher Education Program, 1969; also articles ednl. publs. Home: 2733 Middlesex Dr Toledo, OH 43606.

DICKSON, GEORGE HENRY, packing co. exec.; b. Westburn, Man., Can., July 4, 1915; s. George A. and Lillian E. (McLachlan) D.; B.Sc. in Agr., Ont. Agrl. Coll., 1938; m. Margaret Eleanor Leggatt, May 18, 1938; children—Beverly Anne (Mrs. Ian G. Monteith), George Kent. With Can. Packers Ltd., Toronto, 1938—, gen. mgr., 1960-62, exec. v.p., 1962—, also dir.; chmn. bd. Beardmore Leather Co., Collis Leather Co., Anglo Canadian Leather Company; vice pres. Calgary Packers; dir. of Can. Packers (U.K.) Ltd., Can. Packers N.Y. and Los Angeles, John Loudon & Co., Wilsil Ltd., Parent Goyer & Cie, York Farms, York Trust & Savs. Corp. Mem. Agrl. Inst. Can., Am. Mgmt. Assn., Toronto Bd. Trade, Profl. Agrologists Can., Am. Meat Inst. Club: St. George's Golf and Country. Home: 5 Edenbridge Dr Islington Ontario Canada Office: Canada Packers Ltd 2200 St Clair Av W Toronto 9 Ontario Canada

DICKSON, JOHN, chem. engring and constrn. co. exec.; b. Whitinsville, Mass., Feb. 1, 1929; s. John and Clara (Mellor) D.; B.S., U. R.I., 1951; m. Doris Lyon, Aug. 27, 1949; children—Alan W., Scott C. Accountant, York Corp (Pa.), 1951-53; Ford Motor Co., Chester, Pa., 1953-55; controller IRC Inc., Phila., 1955-64; controller Badger Co., Cambridge, Mass., 1964—; owner Lost River Valley Campground, North Woodstock, N.H., 1970—. Served with AUS, 1946-47. Mem. Nat. Assn. Nat. Accountants, Financial Execs. Inst. Home: 51 Forest Av Cohasset MA 02025 Office: 1 Broadway Cambridge MA 02142

DICKSON, PAUL, educator; b. Lakeland, Fla., Sept. 9, 1905; s. David B. and Coral (Patrick) D.; student Stetson U., 1922-26; Ph.D. cum laude, Ludwigs- Maxmillians U., Munich, Germany, 1951; M.A., Columbia, 1954, Ed.D., 1960; m. Anna Elizabeth Clarke, May 24, 1930; children—Elizabeth Anne (Mrs. Tabor Tucker), David Franklin. Clk., Lincoln Hotel, Indpls., 1927- 28; chief clk. Statler Hotel, St. Louis, 1928-33; Commd. 1st lt. U.S. Army, 1934-38; exec. asst. mgr. Southwest Hotels Co., Memphis and Kansas City, Mo., 1938-39; gen. mgr. Commonwealth Hotel, Kansas City, Mo., 1939-40; returned to active duty as capt. U.S. Army, 1940, advanced through grades to col., 1953; various assignments U.S. mil. schs. and inf. divs., 1940-45; prof. mil. sci. and tactics Denver pub. schs., 1945- 47; assigned U.S. Army Europe, 1947-49; mem. faculty U.S. Mil. Acad., 1949-55; ret., 1956; dean Munich Campus U. Md., 1957-61; asso. prof. fgn. lang. edn. Fla. State U., 1961-63, prof., 1963-69, dir. staff devel. Pinellas County schs., Fla, 1969—. lang. cons. south Fla. Edn. Center, 1962-64; adv. council N.E. Conf. lang. cons. S. Fla. Edn. Center, 1962-64; adv. council N.E. Conf. Teaching Fgn. Langs, 1963-67. Decorated Bronze Star; Medaille de Reconnaissance (France); named officer d'Academie Francaise. Mem. Modern Lang. Assn. Am. (regional fgn. lang. cons. 1963—), Am. assn. tchrs. French, German, Spanish and Portuguese, Nat., Fla. (pres. modern lang. sect. 1965-68) edn. assns., Assn. Higher Edn., South Atlantic Modern Lang. Assn., Assn., Supervision and Curriculum Devel., So. Humanities Conf., Pi Kappa Phi. Episcopalian (lay reader, vestryman, clk. deacon). Author: Das Amerikabild in der deutschen Emigrantenliteratur seit, 1933, 1951; Visible Vocabulary to Accompany German Military Readings, 1954; Foreign Language Instruction, 1960; Ins Deutsche Hinein!, 1963; Articulated Language Learning, 1964; Foreign Language Education, 1966. Editor: Deutsche Sprachlehre, 1954; German Military Readings, 1954. Home: 216 Harrison Av Belleair Beach FL 33523

DICKSON, WILLIAM MACLEAN, educator; b. Lordsburg, N.M., Dec. 15, 1925; s. Robert Henry and Christina Ellen (Maclean) D.; B.A., U. Minn., 1949; M.S., Utah State U., 1953, Ph.D., Stanford, 1962; m. Carolyn M. Brainard, Sept. 6, 1947 (dec.); children—James Maclean, Elizabeth Helen, Andrea Ellen; m. 2d, Janet L. Scott, Dec. 21, 1968. Analyst, Lockheed Missiles and Space Co., 1960-62; asso. prof. polit. scis. Utah State U., 1962-63; dean Coll. Bus., Econs. and Govt., also dir. Inst. Bus., Econs. and Govt. Research, U. Alaska, 1963-65; commr. econ. devel. State of Alaska, 1965-66; prof. polit. sci. Western Washington University, Bellingham, 1967-68; vis. prof. dept. econs. and commerce Simon Fraser U., Burnaby, B.C., Can., 1968—, chairman of the M.B.A. program, 1969—. Cons. Oceanic Found., Honolulu, Alaskan Fedn. Natives. Chairman Gov. Alaska Advisory Commission Employment; chmn. prodn. task force group Emergency Resources Planning Com. Alaska. Served to capt., inf., U.S. Army, World War II, Korea. Decorated D.F.C. with 2 oak leaf clusters, Air Medal with 9 oak leaf clusters, Combat Inf. badge. Mem. Am. Polit. Sci. Assn., A.A.A.S., Am. Assn. U. Profs. Contbr. profl. jours. Home: 1202 Bartlett Coquitlaw British Columbia Canada Office: Dept Econs and Commerce Simon Fraser U Barnaby 2 British Columbia Canada

DICKSON, WILLIAM P., Jr., lawyer; b. Norfolk, Va., Dec. 11, 1915; s. William Petty and Nellie Tate (Talbot) D.; LL.B., U. Va., 1938; m. Caroline E. Sand, May 3, 1945; children—Caroline Tate (Mrs. Curtis B. Snyder), Mary Petty. Admitted to Va. bar, 1938; practice in Norfolk; mem. Wilcox, Savage, Lawrence, Dickson & Spindle. Chmn. Conf. Va. Bar Presidents, 1956-59; spl. regional com. World Peace through Law; adv. com. to spl. Com. on Atomic Attack, 1960-61. Trustee Norfolk Gen. Hosp., pres. elect, 1970-72; bd. dirs., vice chmn. Blue Cross Va.; bd. dirs. Blue Shield Va. trustee, sec.-treas. Mary F. Ballantine Home for Aged; trustee, sec. Jackson Field Home for Girls; pres. Norfolk Servicemens Club; pres., co-founder Downtown Norfolk Assn.; mem. nat. com. Community Chests and Councils Am., 1957-58. Served to lt. USNR, 1941-46; PTO. Decorated Bronze Star, Purple Heart. Mem. Am. (ho. of dels. 1960—, chmn. spl. com. on retirement-benefits, bd. govs. 1969—), Va. (pres. 1959-60), Norfolk-Ports-mouth (pres. 1955-56), bar assns., Va. State Bar (chmn. sect. on estates and property), Am. Legion, U. Va. Alumni Assn. (pres. 1970-71), Delta Phi, Phi Delta Phi. Episcopalian. Clubs: Norfolk Sports, Princess Ann Country, Norfolk German Press of Virginia, Farmington Country, Commonwealth. Home: Linkhorn Shores Virginia Beach VA 23451 Office: Va Nat Bank Bldg Norfolk VA 23510

DICUS, CLARENCE HOWARD, Jr., lawyer; b. Poplar Bluff, Mo., Apr. 26, 1921; s. Clarence H. and Lena (Hardey) D.; A.B., U. Mo., 1941; J.D., Harvard, 1947; m. Edith Helen George, June 20, 1942; children—Linda Ornes, Laurie, Stephen, Paul, Todd, Kent, Brian. Admitted to Mo. bar, 1947, since practiced in Kansas City; partner firm Dietrich, Davis, Burrell, Dicus & Rowlands, 1957—. Pres. Naturalization Council of Kansas City, 1951, Unity Soc. Practical Christianity, 1957. Bd. dirs. Citizens Assn. Kansas City, 1964—. Served to comdr. USNR, 1942-45. Fellow Am. Coll. Probate Counsel; mem. Am., Kansas City bar assns., Lawyers Assn. Kansas City (v.p. 1963), Estate Planning Council Kansas City (pres. 1963), Pi Kappa Alpha. Clubs: University (Kansas City); Ward Parkway Country. Home: 8816 Iroquois Trail Kansas City MO 64114 Office: Dwight Bldg Kansas City MO 64105

DICUS, JOHN CARMACK, savs. and loan assn. exec.; b. Hutchinson, Kan., May 16, 1933; s. George Byron and Desda (Carmack) D.; B.S., U. Kan., 1955; m. Barbara Elizabeth Bubb, Feb. 4, 1956; children—Debra Elizabeth, John Bubb. With Capitol Fed. Savs. & Loan Assn., Topeka, 1959—, exec. v.p., 1963- 69, pres., 1969—. Chmn. Shawnee Country chpt. A.R.C., 1965; treas. Jayhawk area council Boy Scouts Am., 1967-68. Served to lt. (j.g.) USNR, 1956-59. Mem. U.S. Savs. and Loan League (past dir.), Topeka C. of C. (dir. 1962, v.p. 1965-66, 71), U. Kan. Alumni Assn. (pres. Shawnee County chpt. 1966), Kansas C. of C. (dir.), Phi Delta Theta. Episcopalian (vestry). Mason (32, Shriner, Jester), Rotarian (past dir.). Clubs: Topeka Country (bd. dirs., pres. 1968). Home: 1524 Lakeside Dr Topeka KS 66604 Office: 700 Kansas Av Topeka KS 66603

DICUS, R. EARL, bishop Episcopal Ch. Address: PO Box 6885 San Antonio TX 78209*

DIDDLE, ALBERT WASHINGTON, educator, physician; b. Hamilton, Mo., July 1, 1909; s. Jesse Albert and Laura (Edwards) D.; A.B., U. Mo., 1930, M.A., 1933; M.D., Yale, 1936; m. R. J. King, Jan. 10, 1942; children—Jane Ellen, John Allen. Research asst. anatomy U. Mo., 1931-33, Yale, 1933-36; resident obstetrics and gynecology U. Ia. Hosps., 1937-40, asso., 1940-42; clin. instr. postgrad. obstetrics Ia. Health Dept., 1940-42; asso. prof. Southwestern Med. Coll., 1945-48; prof., chmn. dept. obstetrics and gynecology Meml. Research Center, U. Tenn., 1956—; cons. gynecology br. 10, VA, 1946-48, Area V, 1948-58. Grand program sec. 3d Am. Congress Obstetrics and Gynecology, 1947. Served to lt. comdr., M.C., USNR, 1942-46. Rollins scholar U. Mo., 1931. Diplomate Am. Bd. Obstetrics and Gynecology (asso. examiner), Nat. Bd. Med. Examiners. Mem. Am. Coll. Obstetricians and Gynecologists, Am., Central (exec. council 1954-57, 59, -61) assns. obstetricians and gynecologists, Continental, Kansas City (hon.) gynecol. socs., E. Tenn. (pres. 1960) obstet. and gynecol. socs., Knoxville Surg. Soc. (pres. 1955-56), James Fitzgerald Obstetric and Gynecologic Travel Club, Sigma Xi, Phi Beta Pi. Author numerous articles in field. Home: 7209 Sheffield St Knoxville TN 37919

DIDIO, LIBERATO JOHN ALPHONSE, educator, anatomist; b. Sao Paulo, Brazil, May 7, 1920; s. Pascoal and Lydia (Cacace) DiD.; B.S., U. Sao Paulo, 1939, M.D. summa cum laude, 1945, M.S. summa cum laude, 1949, Ph.D. summa cum laude, 1951; postgrad. Nat. Coll. War, Rio de Janeiro, 1957; m. Lydia S. Silva, Mar. 12, 1960; children—Vera, Rubens, Lydia N.S., Arthur S. Instr. physiology Faculty Medicine U. Sao Paulo, Brazil, 1942-43, instr. anatomy, 1943-45, asst. prof. anatomy, 1945-51, asso. prof., 1952-53, intern dept. tropical medicine U. Hosp. Faculty Medicine, 1944-45, tchr. chemistry Roosevelt State Coll., Sao Paulo, 1943-44; prof., chmn. dept. topog. anatomy Faculty Ciencias Medicas, Cath. U. Minas Gerais, 1954-55, chmn. dept. anatomy med. sch. Belo Horizonte, U. Minas Gerais, 1954-63; dir. Inst. Morphology, 1962-63; prof. anatomy Med. Sch., Dental Sch., Grad. Sch. Northwestern U., Chgo., 1963-67; prof. anatomy, chmn. dept. Med. Coll. Ohio, Toledo, 1967—. Vis. prof. U. Messina, Italy, 1955, U. Brazil, 1957, U. Parma,

Italy, 1958; vis. prof. anatomy, Rockefeller Found. fellow Sch. Medicine U. Wash., 1960-61; guest investigator Rockefeller Inst. Med. Research, N.Y.C., 1961, Med. Sch. Harvard, 1961. Co-chmn. 41st Session 7th Internat. Congress Anatomy, N.Y.C., 1960, chmn. session on heart and arteries, Leningrad, 1970; del. Internat. Congress for Electron Microscopy, Phila., 1962, 8th Internat. Congress Anatomy, Wiesbaden, Germany, 1965; del., co-chmn. Session on Embryology I Panam. Congress Anatomy, Mexico City, 1966; chmn. sect. meeting Chgo. Heart Assn. U. Chgo., 1967; adj. prof. biology U. Toledo, Bowling Green U., 1967. Seminars at numerous univs. U.S., South Am.; cons. Escola Medica do Rio de Janeiro, Ency. Brit., Inst. Med. Research Toledo Hosp., Pan Am. Health Orgn. Recipient William H. Rorer award Am. Coll. Gastroenterology, 1970; named Outstanding Educator of Am., 1971. Fellow A.A.A.S., mem. Am. Assn. Cell Biology, Am. Assn. Anatomists, Am. Assn. U. Profs., Anat. Soc. Gt. Britain and Ireland, Assn. Am. Med. Colls., Electron Microscopy Soc. Am., Internat. Assn. Dental Research, Internat. Coll. Surgeons, N.Y. Acad. Scis., Pan Am. Assn. Anatomy (pres.) Midwest Soc. Anatomists, numerous others, Sigma Xi. Contbr. articles to profl. jours. Home: 4375 Sheraton Rd Toledo OH 43615

DIEBENKORN, RICHARD CLIFFORD, Jr., painter; b. Portland, Ore., Apr. 22, 1922; s. Richard Clifford and Dorothy (Stephens) D.; B.A., Stanford, 1949; student U. Cal. at Berkeley, 1943, Cal. Sch. Fine Arts, 1946; M.A., U. N.M., 1952; m. Phyllis Gilman, June 16, 1943; children—Gretchen Gilman, Christopher James. Tchr., San Francisco Art Inst., 1959-67; prof. art U. Cal. at Los Angeles, 1967—; artist-in-residence Stanford, 1963-64; one man shows Cal. Palace of Legion of Honor, San Francisco, 1948-60, San Francisco Mus. Art, 1954, Oakland Mus., 1956, Pasadena Mus. Art, 1959, Phillips Meml. Gallery, Washington, 1961, Nat. Acad. Arts and Letters, N.Y.C., 1962, Carnegie Inst., Pitts., 1962, Washington Gallery Modern Art, 1964, Jewish Mus., N.Y.C., 1965, Tate Gallery, London, Eng., 1964, De Young Mus., San Francisco, 1963, others; group show at Venice Biennale, 1968; works represented in permanent collections Toronto Mus., Nelson Gallery, Kansas City, Phoenix Mus., Albright Gallery, Buffalo, Oberlin Coll. Gallery, San Francisco Mus. Art, Pasadena Art Mus., Phillips Meml. Gallery, Carnegie Inst. Mem. Nat. Found. on Arts and the Humanities, Nat. Inst. Arts and Letters. Author: Drawing, 1965. Home: 334 Amalfi Dr Santa Monica, CA 90403. Office: Dept Art U Cal Los Angeles CA

DIEBOLD, ALBERT RICHARD, pharm. co. exec.; b. Cleve., Jan. 13, 1906; s. Albert Henry and Treva (Couch) D.; grad. Hotchkiss Sch., Lakeville, Conn., 1924; student Princeton, 1929; m. Dorothy Roosen, June 5, 1930; children—Albert Richard, Diane Treva (Mrs. Frank Gavel), Dudley George. Mem. N.Y. Stock Exchange, also firm Bell & Beckwith, Toledo, 1929-38; engaged in drug and cosmetic bus., 1939-42, 45-61; pres. Diebold Products, Inc., N.Y.C., 1941—, Double-D Ranch, Inc., Loxahatchee, Fla., 1958—; chmn. bd. Rad, Inc., N.Y.C., 1950—; owner Toplands Farm, Holstein cattle, Roxbury, Conn., 1945—; dir. Am. Home Products Corp. Bd. dirs. Christian Herald Assn. Served to maj. AUS, 1942-45. Clubs: N.Y. Yacht, Racquet and Tennis (N.Y.C.); Bath and Tennis, Everglades (Palm Beach, Fla.). Home: 35 Sutton Pl New York City NY 10022 also Toplands Farm Roxbury CT 06783 and 400 S Ocean Blvd Palm Beach FL 33480 Office: 375 Park Av New York City NY 10022

DIEBOLD, CHARLES ROBERT, lawyer, banker; b. Buffalo, Feb. 14, 1912; s. Charles and Lillian (Tinnerman) D.; LL.B., U. Buffalo, 1935; m. Mary J. Kittinger, June 9, 1934; children-Charles III, Peter D., David K., Mary D. Admitted to N.Y. bar, 1935, since practiced in Buffalo; partner Diebold & Millonzi, 1936- -; pres., chmn. bd. Western N.Y. Savs. Bank of Buffalo, 1948-70; now trustee; pres., chief exec. officer First Empire State Corp., 1970—; v.p., dir. Dickenson Mines, Ltd., Can.; dir. Mfrs. & Traders Trust Co., Buffalo Ins. Co. Vice chmn. State U. Constrn. Fund, 1967—; mem. Niagara Frontier Transp. Authority, 1967—; chmn. Buffalo Municipal Housing Authority, 1960-62. Pres. Deaconess Hosp., Erie County Soc. for Prevention Cruelty to Animals; treas., bd. dirs. N.Y. State Thruway Authority, 1961-64; bd. dirs. Research Found. State U. N.Y., Health Research; trustee State U. N.Y., Randolph Childrens Home. Mem. Am., N.Y. State, Erie County bar assns., Buffalo Area C. of C. (past pres.), Nat. Assn. Mut. Savs. Banks (past pres.), Savs. Banks Assn. N.Y. State (past pres.). Episcopalian. Mason (33) Clubs: Buffalo Country, Midday, Saturn (Buffalo); Canadian (N.Y.C.), Cherry Hill of Canada (Ridgeway, Ont., Can.); Ontario, Granite Seigniory, Jockey (dir.) (Toronto, Can.); Augusta (Ga.) National Golf; Fort Orange (Albany); Fort Erie (Ont.) Jockey (bd. dirs.). Home: 75 Nottingham Terrace Buffalo NY 14216 Office: One M & T Plaza Buffalo NY 14240

DIEBOLD, JOHN, bus. exec.; b. Weehawken, N.J., June 8, 1926; s. William and Rose (Theurer) D.; B.S. (Regtl. Acad. award), U.S. Mcht. Marine Acad., 1946; B.A. in Econs. with high honors, Swarthmore Coll., 1949; M.B.A. with distinction, Harvard, 1951; LL.D., Rollins Coll., 1965; Sc.D., Clarkson Coll., 1965; D. Engring., Newark Coll. Engring., 1970; m. Doris Hackett, Nov. 22, 1951; 1 dau., Joan. With Griffenhagen & Assos., mgmt. cons., N.Y.C., also Chgo., 1951-57, owner, 1957—, merged with Louis J. Kroegar & Assos. to become Griffenhagen-Kroeger, Inc., 1960; founded Diebold Group, Inc., mgmt. cons., N.Y.C., 1954, pres., chmn. bd., 1954—; founded Diebold Europe S.A., also Mgmt. Sci. Tng. Inst., 1958; founded John Diebold Inc., mgmt. and investment, 1967, chmn., 1967—; chmn. Diebold Venture Capital Corp., 1968—, Diebold Computer Leasing, Inc., 1967—, Gemini Computer Systems, Inc., 1968—, Intermodal Transp. Systems, Inc., 1969—; dir. Genesco. Mem. Sec. Labor Adv. Com. Manpower and Automation, 1962, Pres. Kennedy's Com., Dept. Labor's 50th Anniversary, 1963; mem. U.S. delegation UN Sci. Conf., Geneva, Switzerland, 1963 ; mem nat. adv. council Peace Corps, 1965—; mem. com. on human values Nat Council Chs., 1965—; mem. Com. on 2d Regional plan for N.Y.C., 1966—; vice chmn. Nat. Com. on U.S.- China Relations, 1969—; sec. Bus. Council for Internat. Understanding, 1970—. Chmn. vis. com. Sch. Bus. Administrn., Clarkson Coll., 1961-66; vice chmn. vis. com. econs. Harvard, 1963-69,70—; adv. council inst. for Crippled and Disabled N.Y.C., 1957—; mem. U.S. adv. com. European Inst. Bus. Adminstrn., 1965—; bus. adv. com. Grad. Sch. Indsl. Adminstrn., Carnegie-Mellon U., 1969—; trustee Freedom House, 1969—, Com. for Econ Devel., 1970—; bd. dirs. Am. Council on Germany, 1970—; pub. mem. Hudson Inst. Served with USNR, World War II. Decorated grand officer Order of Istiqlal (Jordan); grand cross Eloy Alfaro Found. (Panama); cross Order St. Martin (Vienna). Named one of ten outstanding young men U.S. Jr. C. of C., 1962. Mem. Internat. Cybernetics Assn. (dir. 1965—), Soc. History Tech. (exec. council), Council Fgn. Relations, Young Pres.'s Orgn., U.S.C. of C. (council on trends and perspectives 1969—), Inst. Dirs. (London). Clubs: Harvard Business School (dir.), Economic, Union League. Harvard (N.Y.C.); Metropolitan (Washington). Chicago. Author: AutomationThe Advent of the Automatic Factory, 1952; Beyond Automation, 1964; Man and the Computer—Technology as an Agent of Social Change, 1969; Business Decisions and Technological Change, 1970; also articles. Home: 1 East End Av New York City, NY 10021. Office: 430 Park Ave New York City NY 10022

DIECKMAN, PAUL WILLIAM, clergyman, educator; b. East Mauch Chunk, Pa., June 1, 1907; s. John William and Anna Catherine (Goodhardt) D.; A.B., Muhlenberg Coll., 1929, LL.D., 1957; grad. Phila. Luth. Theol. Sem., 1932, B.D., 1933, S.T.M., 1935; D.D., Wagner Coll., 1951; m. Ruth La Belle Rickert, Sept. 2, 1931. Ordained to ministry Luth. Ch., 1932; pastor St. Peter's Ch., Easton, Pa., 1932-35, Redemption Ch., Phila., 1935-41, Holy Communion Ch., Detroit, 1941-45; univ. pastor Luth. students, Greater Chgo., 1945-47; asst. to pres. Wagner Coll., S.I., N.Y., 1947-48, adminstrv. asst., 1948-50, v.p., 1950-51, 67—; pastor Grace Luth. Ch., Lakeland, Fla., 1951-52; pres. Midland Coll., Fremont, Neb., 1952- 67. Mem. adv.bd First Nat. City Bank, 1968—. Pres., Neb. Assn. Ch. Colls., 1953-55, Neb. Ind. Coll. Found. 1954-58, Neb. Assn. Colls. and Univs., 1962-63; mem. Commn. on Pub. Information, 1959-61, Commn. on Christian Higher Edn., 1959-62, Nat. Luth. Council, 1965-66, Nat. Luth. Campus Ministry, 1966—. Mem. United Luth. Ch. Am. (pres. Mich. synod 1944-45), Nat. Luth. Ednl. Assn. (pres. 1965-66), Kappa Phi Kappa. Rotarian. Club: Neb. Schoolmasters. Author: Preparation for What?, 1949. Home: 1100 Clove Rd Staten Island NY 10304

DIECKMANN, HERBERT, educator; b. Duisburg, Germany, May 22, 1906; s. Gottfried and Amanda (Wehrhahn-MacDonald) D.; Ph.D., U. Bonn, 1930; student U. Heidelberg, 1925-26. 1927-28 U. Paris. 1926-27, U. Minich, 1928-29; M.A., Harvard, 1950; Doctor Letters (hon.), U. Exeter (Eng.), 1965; m. Liselotte Neisser, May 1930 (div. 1955); children—Beate, Martin; m. 2d, Jane Kennan Marsh, June, 1959; children—Margaret K., Judith R. Came to United States, 1938, naturalized, 1945. Fellowship Notgemeinschaft Deutscher Wissenshaft. 1930-33; Subvention Dutch Emergency Council for Refugees, 1933-34. Guggenheim fellow, 1948, 1949, 1951; lectr. Turkish State U., Istanbul, 1934-37; asst. Prof. Washington U., St. Louis. 1938-46, asso. prof., 1946-48, prof., chmn. dept. Romance Langs., 1948-49; asso. prof. of French, Harvard, 1950-52, became prof. and chmn. of dept. of Romance Languages, 1952, Smith Professor of French and Spanish langs., 1957-65; prof. French and comparative lit. Cornell U. Ithaca, N. Y. 1966—, Avalon Foundation prof., 1967—, Society for Humanities senior fellow, 1969-70. Fulbright lectr., 1956-57. Decorated Legion of Honor (France). Mem. Am. Acad. Arts and Scis., Modern Lang. Assn. Am., Phi Beta Kappa (hon.). Home: 115 Oak Hill Rd Ithaca NY 14850

DIECKMANN, LISELOTTE, educator; b. Frankfurt, Germany, Oct. 31, 1902; d. Max and Emma (Hallgarten) Neisser, Ph.D., U. Heidelberg (Germany), 1927; m. Herbert Dieckmann, May 28, 1930 (div.); children—Beate (Mrs. Max Goree), Martin. Came to U.S., 1938, naturalized, 1944; lectr. German and Greek, U. Istanbul (Turkey), 1934-37; mem. faculty Washington U., St. Louis, 1943- -, prof. German, 1957—, chmn. dept., 1963-67. Guggenheim fellow, 1955- 56; Carnegie intern Yale, 1956-57. Hon. mem. Phi Beta Kappa; mem. Modern Lang. Assn. Author articles problems symbolism. Home: 6906 Columbia Pl St Louis, MO 63130.

DIEDERICH, JOHN THOMAS, lawyer; b. Newport, Kentucky, Mar. 10, 1888; s. Frederick and Minnie (Diederich) D.; LL.B., Centre Coll., 1910; m. Ada Murphy, July 18, 1917. Admitted to Ky. bar, 1910, Supreme Ct., 1928; practice of law, Ashland, Ky., 1910—; city atty., 1912-18, city solicitor, 1922-34. Pres. Ashland Indsl. Corp.; chmn. Third Nat. Bank, Ashland. Delegate Republican National Convention, 1932, 52, Rep. State Chmn., 1955-56; mem. Rep. Nat. Com. for Ky., 1956-65. Chairman of the advisory board of Our Lady of Bellefonte Hosp. Served from pvt. to lt., U.S. Army, 1918- 19. Mem. Ky. Oil and Gas Assn. (pres. 1949-50), Am., Ky., Boyd County bar assn. Presbyn. Mason (Shriner). Home: 2100 Lexington Av 41101 Office: P O Box 1689 Ashland KY 41101

DIEDERICHS, JOHN KUENSTING, appliance co. exec.; b. Chgo., July 16, 1921; s. John Peter and Clara H. (Kuensting) D.; A.B., U. Chgo., 1943; m. Janet Barbara Wood, Sept. 26, 1953. Sales adminstr. Pan Am. World Airways, Chgo., 1946-49, Pan Am. Grace Airways, 1949-52; mem. cons. staff Booz, Allen & Hamilton, mgmt. cons., Chgo., 1952-55; dir. techno-econ. research, mgmt. research Ill. Inst. Tech. Research Inst., 1956-62; v.p. Edwin C. Johnson & Assos., mgmt. cons., 1962-63; v.p. research, corp. devel. Chgo. Mill & Lumber Co., 1962-65; dir. corporate planning Sunbeam Corp., Chgo., 1965—; Served to lt. USNR, 1943-56. Clubs: Chicago; Economic; Internat.; Omega. Home: 229 E Lake Shore Dr Chicago, IL 60611. Office: 5400 W Roosevelt Rd Chicago IL 60650

DIEFENBACH, ALLAN BERLEMAN, lawyer; b. Bluffton, Ind., May 18, 1909; s. Howard Berleman and Josephine C. (Zartman) D.; A.B. cum laude, Heidelberg Coll., 1931; J.D., U. Mich., 1934; postgrad. U. Akron. Admitted to Ohio bar, 1934, since practiced in Akron; partner firm Alpeter, Diefenbach & Davies, 1935—. Dir. Fair Finance Co. Exec. com. Gov. Ohio Traffic Safety Conf., 1959-61; organizing pres. Greater Akron Council Chs., 1947- 50; mem. com. Akron Pub. Sinking Fund, 1937-44; chief tng. officer Summit County Civil Def., 1943-45. Trustee Ohio Presbyn. Homes, Heidelberg Coll.; bd. visitors law sch. U. Mich., 1963-66. Fellow Am. Bar Found.; mem. Am., Ohio (pres. 1959-60), Akron (Charles Travers Grant Meml. prize 1942, 56, pres 1952-53) bar assn., Am. Judicature Soc., Nat. Huguenot Soc. (past counselor gen.), Pi Kappa Delta, Tau Kappa Alpha. Republican. Presbyn. Kiwanian. Clubs: Franklin, City (Akron). Home: 356 S Rose Blvd Akron OH 44313 Office: Second Nat Bldg Akron OH 44308

DIEFENBACH, ROBERT L., sec.-treas. Hotel and Restaurant Employees and Bartenders Internat. Union. Home: 810 Old Orchard Cincinnati OH 45230 Office: Transit Bldg 6 E 4th St Cincinnati OH 45202*

DIEFENBACH, VIRON LEROY, assn. exec.; b. Balt., Feb. 9, 1922; s. William Lewis and Ardie Gertrude (Von Wachter) D.; student Western Md. Coll., 1940-42, Pratt Inst. Engring., 1943, Harvard, 1944; D.D.S., U. Md., 1949; M.P.H., U. Pitts., 1954; m. Adele Larson, Apr. 18, 1956; children—Kathryn Louise, Arthur Karl. Dental intern USPHS Hosp., Norfolk, Va., 1949-50, various clin. assignments, 1950-52, dental pub. health field tng., 1952-53, asst. regional dental cons. USPHS, Chgo., Office Personnel, Office Surgeon Gen., USPHS, Washington, 1955-56, information dir. div. Dental Pub. Health, 1957-59, regional dental cons. USPHS, Denver, 1959-61, dep. chief div. Dental Health, Bethesda, Md., 1962-65, acting chief and dir., 1966, asst. surgeon gen. USPHS, 1966-70; asst. exec. dir. Am. Dental Assn., 1970—. Served with AUS, 1942-44; with USPHS, 1949-70. Recipient Scholarship Gold medal U. Md., 1949, Meritorious Service medal USPHS, 1966. Diplomate Am. Bd. Dental Pub. Health. Fellow Am. Pub. Health Assn. (past sect. chmn., sec.), A.A.A.S., Am. Coll. Dentists; mem. Commd. Officers Assn. USPHS (mem. exec. bd., past chmn. bd.), Am. Dental Assn., Am. Assn. Pub. Health Dentists, Fedn. Dentaire Internationale. Democrat. Home: 1405 N Sandburg Terrace Chicago IL IL 60610 Office: 211 E Chicago Av Chicago IL 60611

DIEFENBAKER, JOHN GEORGE, ex-prime minister Can.; b. Grey County, Ont., Can., Sept. 18, 1895; s. William Thomas and Mary Florence (Bannerman) D.; B.A., U. Sask. 1915, M.A., 1916, LL.B., 1919; LL.D., McMaster U., Dartmouth, McGill U., U. B.C., U. N.B., St. Mary's U., Wesleyan U., Laval U., U. Punjab, U. Delhi, U. Toronto, Royal Mil. Coll., Ont., U. Montreal, Mich. State U., Princeton, Assumption U., Wayne State U. Meml. U., St. Johns, Nfld., Dr. Sacred Letters, Victoria Coll, Toronto; D.C.L., U. Western Ontario, Mount Allison U., Depauw U., Acadia U., U. Sask. Bishiop's U., Litt.D., Dropsie Coll., H.H.D., Okla. U., m. Edna May Brower, June 29, 1929 (dec. 1951); m. 2d, Olive Evangeline Freeman Palmer, 1953. Called to Sask. bar, 1919, B.C., 1951, Alta., 1954; created King's Counsel, 1929; practiced in Prince Albert. Sask., 1922-57; mem. Diefenbaker, Cuelenaere & Hall, 1948-57. Active polit. field, 1925—; elected mem. Ho. of Commons, 1940, 45, 49, 53, 57, 58, 62, 63; prime minister Can., 1957-63; leader of Opposition, Govt. Can., 1963-67. Adviser Canadian Conservative Party of UN orgn., San Francisco, 1945; Canadian Parliament del. chmn. Parliamentary Assn. Conf. Ottawa, 1943, del., Bermuda, 1946, New Zealand, Australia, 1949; mem. NATO Parliamentary Conf., Paris, 1955. Hon. freeman City of London; hon. fellow Bar Ilan U., Israel. Chancellor U. Sask. Served as lt. C.E.F., 1916-17. Fellow Royal Soc. Arts, Royal Soc. Can., Royal Archtl. Inst. Can.; mem. Canadian Bar Assn. (v.p. 1934-42), Law Soc. Upper Can. (hon. bencher), Illustre Nacional Colegio de Abogados (hon.), Gray's Inn (hon. bencher). Baptist. Mem. Progressive Conservative Party. Mason (33, Shriner). Kiwanian. Club Albany (Toronto). Address: 115 Lansdowne Rd Ottawa Ontario Canada

DIEFENDERFER, WILLIAM EDGAR, aircraft corp. exec.; b. Tamaqua, Pa., Aug. 12, 1916; s. William Henry and Esther (Miller) D.; B.S. in Mech. Engring., Pa. State U., 1938; m. Eva Pearl Dericott, Sept. 11, 1940 (dec.); children—Barbara, William Robert; m. 2d, Francesca Balliano, Dec. 27, 1968. Mem. faculty Pa. State Univ., 1938-41; with Hamilton Standard, div. United Aircraft Corp., 1941—, pres., 1961, v.p. corp., 1965-67, group v. p., since 1967- -; advisory board Hartford Nat. Bank & Trust Co.; dir. So. New Eng. Telephone Co., CG Fund, Inc. Mem. Hartford area adv. bd., indsl.-profl. advisory council Pa. State U.; corporator Health Care Facilities Council Greater Hartford, St. Francis Hosp. Registered prof. engr., Conn. Mem. Pi Kappa Phi. Phi Eta Sigma, Pi Mu Epsilon, Pi Tau Sigma, Tau Beta Pi. Home: 671 Ridge Rd Wethersfield CT 06109 Office: United Aircraft Corp East Hartford CT 06108

DIEFFENDERFER, JOHN C., Jr., bus. exec.; b. Easton, Pa., May 8, 1924; s. John Calvin and Helen Adelaide (Aiken) D.; B.A., summa cum laude, Amherst Coll., 1948; postrad. Brasenose Coll., Oxford U. (Eng.), 1948-49; LL.B., Yale, 1952; m. Joyce Mary VanDyk (Div. 1965); children—Anne Leslie, Susan Carol, John Calvin III; m. 2d, Denise Goés Penna, Dec. 29, 1965. Admitted to Ohio bar, 1953, Ill. bar, 1955; atty., law firm, 1952-54; account exec., then agy. mgr. ins. co., 1954- 57; cons., then asso., mgmt. cons., 1957-61; asst. dir. for planning evaluation, then asso. mission dir. AID, Rio de Janeiro and dir. N.E. Brazil program AID, Recife, Brazil, 1962-64; exec. dir., adv. com. on pvt. enterprise in fgn. aid AID, Washington, 1964-65; successively dir. vols., v.p. personnel, v.p. overseas operations, sr. v.p. operations Internat. Exec. Service Corps, Inc., 1965-68; sr. asso. Mgmt. Cons., 1968- 69, v.p., resident mgr. N.Y., 1969-70, chmn., 1970—. Served to capt. AUS, 1943-46. Decorated Air medal with oak leaf cluster. Mem. Phi Beta Kappa, Phi Delta Phi, Psi Upsilon. Home: 65 Heritage Hill Rd New Canaan CT 06840

DIEHL, HAROLD SHEELY, physician, pub. health adminstr.; b. Nittamy, Pa., Auq. 4, 1891; s. William Kleinfelter and Annie Belle (Sheely) D.; B.A., Gettysburg (Pa.) Coll., 1912, Sc.D., 1935; postgrad. Syracuse U., summer 1914; M.D., U. Minn., 1918, M.A., 1921; m. Julia Louise Mills, Sept. 7, 1921; children—Annabelle Louise, Antoni Mills. Asst. prin., tchr. math. high sch., Fulton, N.Y., 1912-14; asst. prof. preventive medicine, pub. health U. Minn., 1921-24, asso. prof., 1924-29, prof., 1929-58, dean med. scis., 1935-58; sr. v.p. for reasearch and med. affairs, dep. exec. v.p. Am. Cancer Soc., 1958-68, now spl. cons. med. and sci. affairs. Dir. no. div. A.R.C. Commn. to Poland, 1919-20; mem. sub-com. on med. edn. Nat. Def. Council, 1939-40; mem. directing bd. Procurement and Assignment Services for Physicians, Dentists and Veterinarians, War Manpower Commn., 1941-46; mem. med. adv. com. United Mine Workers Welfare Fund, 1947-57; mem. adv. com. on health resources Office Def. Moblzn. 1950-57, vice chmn., 1953-57; mem. nat. adv. com. Selective Service on Physicians, Dentists, and Allied Specialists, 1950- 57; mem. med. adv. com. U.S. Office Vocational Rehab. 1954-58; hon. cons. Surgeon-Gen. Navy, 1955-58; mem. U.S.A. com. Internat. Union Against Cancer, 1958-64; mem. adv. com., cancer control USPHS, 1958-64; mem. pres.'s com. on Heart Disease and Cancer, 1961; vice chmn. Nat. Interagy. Council on Smoking and Health, 1964-68; mem. Nat. Adv. Food and Drug Council, 1964- 67. Mem. U.S. delegation to World Health Assembly, 1954, 55, 58. Bd. dirs. Planned Parenthood, N.Y.C. Served with M.C., U.S. Army, 1918-19. Decorated Medal of Polonia Restituta, 1921. Recipient Ed Hitchcock award Am. Coll. Health Assn., 1961. Fellow Am. Pub. Health Assn. (gov. council 1946-50), A.M.A. (chmn. sec. preventive, indsl. medicine and pub. health 1939-40); mem. Assn. Am. Med. Colls. (exec. council 1938-40, 1956-47, v.p. 1955-56), Minn. Med. Assn. (chmn. com. on med. edn. and hosps. 1940-58), Minn. Pub. Health Conf. (hon. life), Central Soc. Clin. Research, A.A.A.S., Minn. Acad. Sci., Minn. Acad. Medicine, Am. Student Health Assn. (pres. 1927-29; sec.-treas. 1934-35), Phi Beta Kappa, Sigma Xi, Phi Delta Theta, Nu Sigma Nu, Alpha Omega Alpha. Republican. Conglist. Clubs: University (N.Y.C.); Campus (U. Minn., pres. 1934-35). Author: (with R.E. Boynton) Healthful Living for Nurses, 1944, Personal Health and Community Hygiene, 1951; (with Anita Laton, Franklin Vaughn) Health and Safety for You, 1954, 3d edit., 1969; Healthful Living, 8th edit., 1968; Tobacco and Your Health—The Smoking Controversy, 1969. Editorial bd. Jour. Lancet, 1930—; adv. editorial bd. Med. World News, 1962-71. Contbr. articles to profl. jours. Home: 11 Riverside Dr New York City NY 10023 Office: 219 E 42d St New York City NY 10017 ☆

DIEHL, HARVEY CLARENCE, Jr., educator; b. Detroit, Nov. 2, 1910; s. Harvey Clarence and Ella F. (Straass) D.; B.S., U. Mich., 1932, Ph.D., 1936; m. Helen Louise Clark, June 21, 1936; children—Margaret Sue, Byron Clark, Rosemary, Barbara Lyon, Harvey R., Elizabeth Ann. Instr., Cornell U., 1936-37, Purdue U., 1937-39; asst. prof. Ia. State Coll., 1939-42, asso. prof., 1942- 47, prof., 1947-65, Distinguished prof., 1965—. Recipient Fisher award in analytical chemistry Am. Chem. Soc., 1956, Ia. medal from Ia. section, 1961; ann. award Assn. Analytical Chemists, 1966. Mem. Am. Chem. Soc., Am. Assn. U. Profs., A.A.A.S., Ia. Acad. Sci, Sigma Xi, Phi Lambda Upsilon, Alpha Chi Sigma. Author: Applications of the Dioximes to Analytical Chemistry, 1940; (with H. H. Willard) Advanced Quantitative Analysis, 1942, Electrodeposition, 1947; (with Smith) Quantitative Analysis, 1952; Quantitative Analysis, Elementary Principles and Practice, 1970. Home: 3310 Oakland St Ames IA 50012

DIEHL, VAL BURL, biscuit co. exec.; b. Mitchell, S.D., Sept. 4, 1916; s. Maurice Blake and Alene (Wallace) D.; B.S., Dakota Wesleyan U., 1938; student Navy Supply Corps Sch., 1943, advanced mgmt. program Harvard, 1962; m. Mary Ellen Condon, Sept. 7, 1940; children—Barbara Mae (Mrs. W. Wilson), James Maurice, Julie Ann. Distbr., Royal Typewriter Co., Mankato, Minn., 1940-42; with Nat. Biscuit Co., 1942-43, 46—, asst. dir. internat. operations, 1954-56, chmn. Nabisco Foods Eng., 1956-61, asst. to pres. Nat. Biscuit Co., N.Y.C., 1961-62, v.p. internat. div., 1963, now exec. v.p., also dir.

subsidiary cos., Eng., France, Italy, Can., Nicaragua, Panama. Served to lt. USNR, 1943-45. Republican. Roman Catholic Clubs: Fifth Avenue (N.Y.C.), Maplewood (N.J.) Country. Home: 315 Wychwood Rd Westfield NJ 07090 Office: 425 Park Av New York City NY 10017

DIEHL, WALTER JOSEPH, banker; b. Nashville, Apr. 6, 1897; s. Adam and Mollie (Back) D.; student pub. schs., Nashville; m. Hazelle Slayden, Mar. 3, 1924; children—Ann (Mrs. Miles Marvin McInnis, Jr.), Walter Joseph, Slayden. Clk., Cumberland Valley Nat. Bank (merger Am. Nat. Bank 1922), Nashville, 1915-22, mgr. Cumberland Valley Office, 1922-27; asst. cashier 3d Nat. Bank, Nashville, 1927-28, cashier, 1929-46, sr. v.p., 1947-49, chmn. bd., 1950-64, sr. chmn. bd., 1964-70, hon. chmn. bd., 1970—, also dir., mem. exec. com., mem. trust bd. Chmn. bd. commrs. Nashville Housing Authority, 1946-61; treas. Tenn. Tb. Assn., 1935-59. Bd. dirs. Bill Wilkerson Hearing and Speech Center, 1953; bd. dirs. Middle Tenn. Heart Assn. Served with USNRF, 1918-19. Mem. Am. (past exec. council), Tenn. (past pres., exec. council, Fifty Year Club) bankers assns., Tenn. Taxpayers Assn. (exec. council), Nashville Clearing House Assn. (past pres.), Nashville C. of C. (past treas.), Tenn. Bus. Men's Assn. (past dir.), Tenn. Hist. Soc., Soc. Amateur Chefs. Methodist. Mason (32). Clubs: Cumberland, Belle Meade Country, Cedar Creek. Home: 4215 Harding Rd Nashville TN 37205 Office: 201 4th Av N Nashville TN 37219

DIEHM, VICTOR CHRISTIAN, broadcasting co. exec.; b. Sparrows Point, Md., Nov. 7, 1902; s. Christian O'Brien and Mary (Hackman) D.; student U. Md., 1925, Peabody Conservatory Music, 1925; Dr. Art of Oratory, Staley Coll., 1954; m. Hazel Virginia Loose, Dec. 19, 1936; children—Elizabeth Anne (Mrs. Richard I. Bernstein), Victor Christian. Entered radio broadcasting in Balt., 1926; with Steinman Group, Lancaster, Pa., 1931-46; owner WAZL and WAZL-FM, Hazleton, Pa., 1946—; formed Vic Diehm Radio Group, 1948, operated radio stas. in Biddeford, Me., Boston, Allentown, Pa., Meadville, Pa., Tallahassee, Fla., 1948-60; pres., chief exec. officer MBS, N.Y.C., 1969—; dir. Nat. Diversified Industries, Inc., Juniper Road Reality, Inc., Pocono Downs Raceways, Inc. Mem. Pa. Indsl. Devel. Authority, 1955—; Pa. lay del. Nat. Am. Cancer Soc. Bd., 1971-73. Candidate Pa. Senate, 1966. Past trustee Bloomsburg (Pa.) State Coll. Recipient Coronet Mag. award for outstanding pub. service, 1950, V.F.W. Nat. award for distinguished local service, 1962; named Pa. Broadcasters ambassador of good will; Vic Diehm Day in Pa. proclaimed by gov., Nov. 6, 1969. Mem. Nat. (dir.), Pa. (past pres.) assns. broadcasters, Radio Advt. Bur. (past chmn.), Pa. C. of C. (v.p.). Methodist. Mason (Shriner, Jester), Elk, Kiwanian. Home: Frederick Dr Conyngham PA 18219 Office: 135 W 50th St New York City NY 10020

DIEKHOFF, JOHN SIEMON, educator; b. Ann Arbor, Mich., Oct. 23, 1905; s. Tobias Johann Casjen and Julia Catherine (Schacht) D.; A.B., U. Mich., 1926, M.A., 1927; postgrad. Oxford U., 1927-28; Ph.D., Western Res. U., 1937; L.H.D., Rutgers U., 1959; m. Vera Ethel Johnston, Dec. 20, 1929. Instr. rhetoric U. Mich., 1928-29; instr. English, Oberlin Oberlin Coll., 1929-40; asst. asso. prof. English, Queens Coll., 1940-51; dir. Center for Study Liberal Edn., Chgo., 1951-53; prof. edn., dir. instnl. research Hunter Coll., 1953-56; dean Cleve. Coll., Western Res. U., 1956-63; prof. higher edn. U. Mich., Ann Arbor, 1963- 65; prof. English, asso. dean faculty Western Res. U. Cleve., 1965-67, acting dean Grad. Sch., 1967; vice provost Case Western Res. U., 1967-70, prof. emeritus, 1970—; vis. lectr., prof., univs. Louisville, Mich., Chgo. Research cons. bd. higher edn., N.Y.C., 1947, 50; mem. commn. trends in edn. Modern Language Assn., 1954-57, mem., chmn., 1965-70; cons., staff assn. N.Y. state com. White House Conf. Edn., 1956; mem. governing bd. Center Study Liberal Edn. for Adults, 1956-59; mem. commn. colls. and univs. North Central Assn., 1958-65. Served from pvt. to capt. AUS, 1943-46. Rockefeller Found. fellow humanities, 1948-49. Mem. Modern Lang. Assn., Milton Soc. Am. (pres. 1957-58), Coll. English Assn., Nat. Council Tchrs. English, Theta Chi, Phi Delta Kappa, Phi Kappa Phi. Author: Milton on Himself, 1939; Milton's Paradise Lost, A Commentary, 1946; Democracy's College, 1950; The Domain of the Faculty, 1956; (with Marjorie B. Smiley) Prologue to Teaching, 1959; A Maske At Ludlow, 1968; (with Ida Long Rogers) Roger Private Higher Education in Tennessee, 1970. Editorial Bd. Prose Works of John Milton, 1948-62, 65—. Office: Case Western Res U Cleveland OH 44106

DIEM, BUI, diplomat of Vietnam; b. Phu-Ly, N. Vietnam, Oct. 1, 1923; s. Bui Ky and Le Thi (Sau) D.; grad. Math., U. Hanoi; m. Vu Thi Kim Ngoc; children—Bui Ngoc Luu, Bui Ngoc Giao, Bui Han. Participated in fight against Communism, 1945; stayed inside Communist zone N. Vietnam until 1949; escaped and joined Nationalist Zone, 1949; student in France, Switzerland and Eng., 1951-53; asst. minister def., 1953; head Vietnamese del. mil. and def. problems during negotiations with French Govt., 1953; mem. Vietnamese delegation to Geneva Conf., 1953; engaged in pvt. bus., also prof. math., 1955-63; dep. sec. gen. Council of Notables of Vietnam, 1963-64; fact finding tour around world, 1964; sec. of state at the prime minister's office, 1965; spl. asst. to prime minister, 1965-66; sec. state fgn. affairs, 1966-67; mem. Vietnamese del. Manila Conf., 1966; ambassador of Vietnam to U.S., 1967—. Home: 4535 32d St NW Washington DC 20008 Office: 2251 R St NW Washington DC 20008

DIEM, WILLIAM, journalist. Editorial writer Cleve. Plain Dealer. Office: 1801 Superior Av Cleveland OH 44114*

DIEMAND, JOHN ANTHONY, insurance; b. Phila., Pa., Jan. 19, 1886; s. Francis and Margaret (Elchele) D.; student Girard Coll., Phila., 1894-1908; LL.D., Jefferson Med. Coll. and Med. Center, 1951, Bucknell U., 1955, St. Joseph's Coll., 1956, U. Pa., 1957; D.Sc. in Commerce, Drexel Inst. Tech., 1951; Doctor of Science, Habnemann Medical College, 1960; m. Mabel Cameron, June 30, 1909; children—Christine Cameron (Mrs. H. W. Kuehn), John Anthony. Stenographer Phila. Casualty Co., 1904-10; Fidelity & Deposit Co., 1910- 13; Surich Gen. Accident & Liability Ins. Corp., 1913-28; Home Indemnity Co., 1928-33; exec. v.p. Indemnity Ins. Co. of North America, 1933-41; v.p. Ins. Co. of North America, 1938-41, pres., 1941-61, chmn. bd., chief exec. officer, 1961-64, former chmn. exec. com., dir.; chmn. bd., chmn. exec. com., chief exec. officer Life Ins. Co. N. Am., 1961—; pres., dir. Old Phila. Redevel. Corp., dir. Phila. Electric Co., Central Penn. Nat. Bank, Phila. Saving Fund Soc. Trustee Abington Meml. Hosp.; trustee Temple U., Girard Coll., Williamson Free Sch. of Mech. Trades. Recipient George Henry Ryne award Fedn. Ins. Counsel, 1936; Isaiah Van Sant Williamson award, 1957; Powell award, 1959; Nat. award Nat. Conf. Christians and Jews, 1955; Gold Medal award Pennsylvania Society, 1959. Republican. Mem. Ref. Ch. Clubs: Union League, Racquet (Phila.); Drug and Chem., India House (N.Y.); Rittenhouse. Home: Boxley Farm Buckingham PA 18912 Office: 1600 Arch St Philadelphia PA 19103

DIENER, BERT, food broker, artist; b. N.Y.C., Mar. 21, 1915; s. Frederick and Lena (Rublin) D.; B.S., U. Va., 1937; m. Hermine Van Baarn, Nov. 14, 1940; children—Francine Carol, Fredric Jay. Partner, Gold-Rose Diener, N.Y.C., 1939-45, Rich-Diener, N.Y.C., 1945-63; pres. Pratico-Diener Corp., Fort Lee, N.J., 1963-68, exec. v.p. Pratico, Diener & Stein, Inc., 1968-69; exec. v.p. Diener & Stein, Inc., 1969—. Exhibited in one man shows Southhold Gallery, L.I., 1967, Frankel Gallery, Roslyn, N.Y., 1968, Center Art Gallery, N.Y.C.; three man show Sears-Vincent Price Gallery, Chgo., 1969; exhibited in group show Grand Prix International D'Art Contemparin De la Principaute de Monaco, 1970; pres. Telestar Products Corp., Grovery Industry Services, Inc.; mem. marketing adv. com. U.S. Banknote Corp. Mem. Grocery Mfrs. Reps. N.Y.C. (past pres.), Nat. Food Brokers Assn. (past dir.), Assn. Food Distbrs. (past chmn. brokers div.), Composers, Authors, Artists of Am., Sales Execs. Club N.Y. Republican. Club: New York Athletic. Pub., editor: Grocery Industry Directory Met. N.Y., 1961-65. Home: 177 E 75th St New York City NY 10021 Office: 140 Sylvan Av Englewood Cliffs NJ

DIENER, DAVID EPHRAIM, advt. exec.; b. N.Y.C., Mar. 9, 1919; s. Isaac and Lina (Schwartzfeld) Schwartzfeld) D.; student George Washington U., 1940; B.S., City Coll. N.Y., 1941; m. Esther Moskowitz, Oct. 15, 1950; children—Jonathan, Bart, Michael. Copywriter, Columbia Pictures Corp., with Republic Pictures Corp., 1946- 47, United Artists Corp., 1947; with Monroe Greenthal Co., Inc., N.Y.C., 1947-66, v.p., 1956-64, pres., 1964-66; pres. Diener-Houser-Greenthal Co., Inc., N.Y.C., 1966—. Served to capt. AUS, 1941-46; ETO. Author: (play) Even to the Knife, 1942; (with Leon Roth) (musical) Hizzoner the Mayor, 1948. Office: 25 W 43d St New York City NY 10036

DIENER, JOAN, (Mrs. Albert Marre), actress, singer; b. Cleve., Feb. 24, 1936; student Sarah Lawrence Coll.; m. Albert Marre; 1 son, 1 dau. N.Y.C. acting debut Season in the Sun, N.Y.C., 1950; appeared in Kismet, N.Y.C., 1954, London, 1955, Man of La Mancha, N.Y.C., 1966, 67, London, 68, Paris, 69, appeared on TV, London, Eng., 1959; operatic roles Germany, Italy, 1959-60; TV appearances include: 54 Street Revue, 1951-52; Androcles and the Lion, Omnibus, 1956, Cry for All, N.Y.C., 1970. Recipient Theatre World award for performance Kismet, 1954, Donaldson award Season in the Sun. Mem. Am. Fedn. TV and Radio Artists, Am. Guild Variety Artists, Screen Actors Guild, Actors' Equity Assn.

DIENNER, JOHN ASTOR, patent lawyer; b. Elkhart, Ind., Sept. 22, 1886; s. Christian King and Susan (Christophel) D.; ed. pub. schs., Elkhart; B.S. in Elec. Engring., Purdue U., 1910, E.E., 1913, hon. Dr. Engring, 1939; LL.B., George Washington U., 1913; studied patent law Georgetown U., M.L.D., 1913; LL.D., John Marshall Law Sch. Chgo., 1960; m. Pearl J. Calhoun, July 27, 1915; children—John Astor, Ann Calhoun. Began in employ of Home Telephone Co., 1904; with signal dept., N.Y. Central R.R., 1903-06; Union Switch & Signal Co., 1908-09; with Gen. Elec. Co., 1910; asst. examiner U.S. Patent Office, 1910-14; practiced law with Brown, Hanson & Boetteher, 1914-19; mem. Brown, Boettcher & Dienner, 1919-27; mem. firm Brown, Jackson, Boettcher & Dienner, 1927-69, Johnson, Dienner, Emrich, Verbeck & Wagner, 1969—. Dir. Purdue Research Found. (Lafayette, Ind.), Clark Equip. Co. Mem. Patent Adv. Panel, AEC, 1960. Mem. Patent Office Adv. Com., 1960; del. of U.S. to Conf. for Revision of Internat. conv. for Protection of Indsl. Porperty by negotiation of a new treaty, London, 1934; accredited rep. of U.S. to German Govt. for Berlin Congress of AIPPI, 1936. Apptd. by Sec. Hopkins, spl. counsel for Dept. of Commerce to present evidence on the U.S. Patent System before the Temp. Nat. Econ. Com., 1939; cons. Dept. of Commerce, 1942- 43; mem. penicillin adv. com. for OSRD, 1944; spl. lectr. John Marshall Law Sch., 1941-67, trustee, 1960-68. Fellow Royal Soc. London; mem. Newcomen Soc. London, Am. Inst. of Chemists, Am. Inst. E.E., Chgo. Patent Law Assn. (pres. 1936), Am. Patent Law Assn. (pres. 1945), Am. Bar Assn. (chmn. patent sect., 1942- 43), Internat. Assn. for Protection of Indsl. Property (mem. bd. dirs. 1934-35, pres. 1935-43), Am. Judicature Soc., Acad. of Polit. Sci. (life), Franklin Inst., Art Inst. Chgo., Western Soc. Engrs., Nat. Rifle Assn. (life), Delta Tau Delta (life mem., pres., Chgo. Alumni chpt. 1938), Phi Delta Phi, Tau Beta Pi, Eta Kappa Nu (hon.). Republican. Episcopalian. Clubs: Union League Chgo.; University (Evanston); Westmoreland Country. Home: 1034 Sheridan Rd Evanston IL 60202 Office: 53 W Jackson Blvd Chicago IL 60604

DIENSTFREY, HARRIS DAVID, editor; b. N.Y.C., May 14, 1934; s. Joseph Leon and Elizabeth (Hertz) D.; B.A., U. Chgo., 1954, M.A., 1956; m. Jane Winborne Olds, May 29, 1970; stepchildren—Elizabeth Tobier, Natalie Tobier, Lincoln Tobier. Asst. editor Commentary mag., 1959-61; editor Center for Urban Edn., 1965-68; co-founder, editor-in-chief Outerbridge & Dienstfrey, N.Y.C., 1969—. Served with AUS, 1956-58. Home: 75 Prospect Park W Brooklyn NY 11215 Office: 200 W 72d St New York City NY 10023

DIEPENBROCK, ALOYSIUS I., lawyer; b. San Jose, Cal., Feb. 8, 1893; s. M. H. and Clara L. (Coolet) D.; A.B., U. Cal. at Berkeley, 1915, J.D., 1917; m. Lydia F. Krause, Aug. 22, 1921; children—Louise Guard, John V., R. James, Virginia Wood. Admitted to Cal. bar, 1917, since practiced in Sacramento; member firm Diepenbrock, Wulff, Plant & Hannegan and predecessor firms, 1919—; director Lucky Stores, Inc. Mem. State Bar Cal., Sacramento County Bar Assn., Phi Delta Phi, Kappa Alpha. Clubs: Sutter (Sacramento); Del Paso Country. Home: 1400 N St Sacramento CA 95814 Office: 455 Capitol Mall Sacramento CA 95814

DIEPENBROCK, VICTOR LEO, lawyer; b. San Francisco, Dec. 8, 1905; s. Melchoir H. and Louise (Coolot) D.; A.B. cum laude, U. Santa Clara, 1928; J.D., U. Cal. at Berkeley, 1931; m. Betty D. Buckley, June 2, 1934; children-Anthony C., Katherine D. Stillman, Elizabeth V., John E., Robert P. Admitted to Cal. bar, 1931, since practiced in Sacramento; asso. Devlin, Devlin & Diepenbrock, 1931-37; partner Diepenbrock, Wulff, Plant & Hannengan and predecessor firms, 1937—; prof. law McGeorge Coll. Law, 1933-41. Pres. Stanford Lathrop Meml. Home; bd. dirs. Archbishop Hanna Center for Boys. Mem. Am., Sacramento County bar assns., State Bar Cal., Nat. Assn. Trial Counsel, Phi Delta Phi. Republican. Roman Catholic. Clubs: Serra (past pres.), Sutter (Sacramento). Home: 1881 8th Av Sacramento CA 95818 Office: 455 Capitol Mall Sacramento CA 95814

DIERCKS, FREDERICK OTTO, govt. ofcl.; b. Rainy River, Ont., Can., Sept. 8, 1912 (parents Am. citizens); s. Otto Herman and Lucy (Plumkett) D.; B.S., U.S. Mil. Acad., 1937; M.S. in Civil Engring., Mass. Inst. Tech., 1939; M.S. in Photogrammetry, Syracuse U., 1950; m. Kathryn Frances Transue, Sept. 1, 1937; children—Frederick William, Lucy Helena. Commd. 2d lt. U.S. Army, 1937, advanced through grades to col., 1952; comdg. officer U.S. Army Map Service, Washington, 1957-61; dir. U.S. Army Coastal Engring. Research Center, Washington, 1964-67; ret., 1967; asso. dir. U.S. Coast and Geodetic Survey (now Nat. Ocean Survey), Rockville, Md., 1967—. U.S. mem. commn. cartography Pan Am. Inst. Geography and History, OAS, 1961-67, alternate U.S. mem. directing council, 1970—. Decorated Legion of Merit (U.S.); grand cross Order of King George II (Greece); most Exalted Order of White Elephant (Thailand). Registered profl. engr., D.C. Fellow Am. Soc. C.E.; mem. Am. Soc. Photogrammetry (pres. 1970-71, dir.), Sigma Xi. Republican. Presbyn. Mason. Home: 9313 Christopher St Fairfax VA 22030 Office: 6001 Executive Blvd Rockville MD 20852

DIERCKS, H. ROBERT, corp. exec.; b. Mpls., 1913; ed. U. Minn., 1937. Exec. v.p., dir. Cargill, Inc.; pres., dir. Cargill Cal., Inc.; v.p., dir. Kerr Gofford & Co.; dir. Rogers Terminal & Shipping Corp., Greenwich Marine, Inc., Soo Line R.R. Co. Bd. dirs. Chgo. Bd. Trade. Home: 4505 Browndale Av Minneapolis MN 55424 Office: Cargill Bldg Minneapolis MN 55402*

DIES, DOUGLAS HILTON, assn. exec.; b. St. Paul. Sept. 9, 1913; s. Edward Jerome and Mareeta (Cole) D.; A.B., Harvard, 1934; postgrad. Oxford U., 1934-35; m. Mary Frances Doreen Harding, Nov. 25, 1939; children—Harding Mogridge, Andrea Frances. Editorial staff Grand Forks (N.D.) Herald, summer 1933, Mpls. Star, summer 1934, London Sunday Chronicle, summer 1935; staff London bur. U.P., 1935-38, Knoxville (Tenn.) Jour., 1938-40; pub. relations dept. Westinghouse Electric Co., 1940-41; staff A.P., Cleve., 1941-42; pub. relations staff U.S. Bd. Econ. Warfare, Washington, 1942-43; pub. relationist, Washington, 1946—; asso. world trading corps. 1947—; asst. to pres. Nat. Inst. Oilseed Products, 1947—; Washington rep. Pillsbury Co., 1956-64, East Asiatic Co., 1956—, Woodward & Dickerson, Inc., 1958; asst. sec., bur. raw materials Am. Vegetable Oils and Fats Industries, 1961-62, sec., 1962—; exec. sec. Am. Council Ind. Labs., 1963—. Guest lectr. George Washington u. Sch. Fgn. Trade. Mem. Adv. com. State Tech. Services Act D.C. Mem. Republican City Com., Alexandria, 1958-61. Served from ensign to lt. comdr., USNR, 1943-46. Mem. S.R. (gov. D.C., 1956-65), Mil. Order World Wars, Sigma Alpha Epsilon. Episcopalian (vestryman). Clubs: Harvard (N.Y.C., Washington); University, Oxford-Cambridge (Washington). Editor: Chemurgie Digest, 1940-58. Home: 505 Robinson Ct Alexandria VA 22302 Office: 1026 17th St N W Washington DC 20036

DIES, EDWARD JEROME, author, publicist; b. nr. Springfield, Ore., May 23, 1891; s. Allen and Martha (Hilton) D.; ed. pub. schs. and under pvt. tutor; studied finance and economics two years; m. Mareeta Cole, May 29, 1912; 1 son, Douglas. Corr. United Press Assn., 1910-11; staff corr. A.P., 1911-19; reported anti- govt. activities, World War; spl. writer Canadian govt., Canadian rys. and Hudson's Bay Co., 1920-21; publicity advt. counsel Chgo. Bd. of Trade, 1922-35; owner and editor Nat. Syndicate Service, officer and pub. relations adviser to various corps. and assn., 1922—; econ. cons. to industries. Dir. Fedn. of Am. Bus., 1931- 33; mem. bd. govs. Nat. Farm Chemurgic Council, 1941-55; mem. Cereal Industries Com. of Fed. Food Adv. Bd., 1942-43; mem. nat. panel of arbitrators, Am. Arbitration Assn., N.Y., 1948—. Fellow Royal Econ. Soc., London, Internat. Inst. of Arts and Letters; mem. Huguenot Soc., Am. Acad. Polit., Soc. Sci., Am. Econ. Assn., Am. Soc. Internat. Law, Authors League Am., Soc. Midland Authors, S.R., Hereditary Order Descs. of Colonial Govs., Pi Gamma Mu. Episcopalian (vestryman). Clubs: Union League (mem. bd. of dirs. 1938-41) (Chgo.); National Press, Capitol Hill (Washington); City Tavern (Georgetown); Author: The Wheat Pit, 1925; Solving the Form Riddle, 1926; The Plunger, 1929; Skylines (short history arch.), 1930; Where Trade Tides Converge (Brochure), 1930; Der Speculant (hist. novel pub. in Germany), 1931; Street of Adventure, 1935; Soybeans: Gold From The Soil, 1942; Titans of The Soil, 1949 (pub. in various Oriental langs. through Dept. State); Behind the Wall Street Curtain, 1952. Contbr. to gen., financial and bus. mags. Home: 2111 Jefferson Davis Hwy Arlington VA 22202 Office: TWA Bldg Washington DC 20036

DIETEL, WILLIAM MOORE, educator; b. Islip, N.Y., Aug. 14, 1927; s. Frederick W. and Zillah (Vannuccini) D.; A.B., Princeton, 1950; M.A., Yale, 1952, Ph.D., 1959; m. Linda Remington, June 16, 1951; children—Elizabeth Lynn, Cynthia Lynn, Lisa Remington, John Frederick and Victoria Moore. Began as instructor history extension sch. U. Conn., 1952-53; instr. history U. Mass., 1954-59, asst. prof., 1959; asst. dean coll., asst. prof. humanities Amherst Coll., 1959-61; former principal Emma Willard Sch., Troy, New York. Member of the advisory council dept. religion Princeton. Served with USNR, 1945-46. Mem., Nat. Assn. Prins. Schs. for Girls, Headmistresses Assn. of the East. Clubs: Quadrangle (Princeton); University (N.Y.C.).

DIETER, GEORGE E. Jr., univ. dean; b. Phila., Dec. 5, 1928; s. G. Ellwood and Emily (Muench) D.; B.S. in Metall. Engring., Drexel Inst. Tech., 1950; Sc.D., Carnegie Inst. Tech., 1953; m. Nancy Joan Russell, June 21, 1952; children—Carol Joan, Barbara June. Research engr. E.I. duPont Engring Research Lab., Wilmington, Del., 1955-59, research supr., 1959-62; prof., head dept. metall. engring. Drexel Inst. Tech., 1962-69; dean Coll. Engring. Drexel U., 1969—; cons. in field. Mem. AUS, 1953-55. Mem. Am. Inst. M.E., Am. Soc. for Metals, Am. Soc. Engring. Edn., A.A.A.S., Franklin Inst., Sigma Xi, Tau Beta Pi. Author: Mechanical Metallurgy, 1961. Home: 621 Braeburn Lane Narberth PA 19072 Office: Drexel U 32 and Chestnut Sts Philadelphia PA 19104

DIETERLE, DONALD LYLE, educator, accountant; b. Sterling Ill., Nov. 27, 1908; s. John George and Edith Marie (Carolus) D.; B.S., U. Ill., 1930, M.S., 1931, grad. study, 1931-32; m. Mary Elizabeth Paul, Dec. 20, 1935; 1 son, Donald Paul. Instr. accounting U. Ill., 1930-32; auditor RFC, 1932-35; prof. accounting Southeastern U., Washington, 1932-35; asst. financial examiner SEC, 1935; partner Dieterle & Cinkoske, C.P.A.'s, Bloomington, Ind., 1935—; prof. accounting Ind. U., 1935—, asso. dir. engring., sci. sci. mgmt. war tng. program, 1941-45, dir. small bus. programs, 1945—, chmn. dept. accounting, 1955-67. Sec.-treas. Bus. & Real Estate Trends, Inc., Bloomington, 1949—; sec.-treas., dir. Universal Life & Accident Ins. Co., Bloomington, 1955—; treas. Univ. Underwriting Co., Inc.; partner Cardinal Oil Co.; dir., mem. exec. and finance coms. Gt. No. Life Ins. Co., Indpls.; v.p., treas., dir. Mohawk Oil Co., Inc. Mem. bd. certified accountants, Ind., 1948—. Served as lt. (j.g.), Supply Corps, USN, 1935-41. C.P.A., Ill., Ind. Mem. Am. Inst. Accountants (bd. examiners 1954-55), Ind. Soc. of Chgo., Am. Accounting Assn., Nat. Accounting Assn., C.P.A. Examiners, Financial Execs. Inst., C. of C., Beta Alpha Psi, Acacia, Beta Gamma Sigma, Alpha Kappa Psi. Presbyn. Mason (Shriner), Rotarian. Club: Columbia (Indpls.). Author: (with J.K. Lasser, others) Tax Accounting Methods, 1952; C.P.A. Coaching Problems, revised edit., 1954; (with Seawell) CPA Problems, 1959. Home: 520 S High St Bloomington IN 47401

DIETHELM, GEORGE EDWARD, lawyer, refining co. exec.; b. Toledo, June 23, 1908; s. Gotthard and Mary (Nolan) D.; A.B., St. John's Coll., 1929; LL.B., U. Mich., 1932; m. Margaret C. Whitney, Apr. 11, 1942; 1 dau., Margaret M. Admitted to Ohio bar, 1932, N.Y. bar, 1934; asso. Milbank, Tweed, Hope & Webb, N.Y.C., 1932-35; mem. law dept. Am. Sugar Refining Co. (now Amstar Corp.), N.Y.C., 1935-42, 45-53, gen. counsel, 1953—, v.p., 1957—. Served from 1st lt. to lt. col. USAAF, 1942-45. Mem. Pilgrims of U.S. Roman Catholic. Clubs: Union (N.Y.C.); Creek, Piping Rock (Locust Valley, N.Y.); Metropolitan (Washington). Home: Locust Valley NY 11560 Office: 1251 Av of Americas New York City NY 10020

DIETRICH, HENRY BUCKLEY, steel construction exec.; b. Balt., Oct. 27, 1903; s. Andrew and Susanna (Wilcox) D.; student Army and Navy Prep. Sch., Balt., Lehigh U.; m. Elizabeth Tubman, Oct. 27, 1928; 1 dau., Mary Elizabeth (Mrs. C. Herbert Wineholt, Jr.); m. 2d, Mary Perry, Apr. 6, 1956. With Dietrich Brothers, Inc., Balt., 1926—, successively salesman, purchasing agent, 1929-44, pres., treas.,

1944—; dir. Arlington Fed. Savs. & Loan Assn., Md. Nat. Bank (Balt.); mem. Md. adv. bd. Liberty Mut. Ins. Co. Coordinating Council fund-raising campaigns YMCA, Balt., mem. constrn. and civic dept. com. nat. chamber, Washington; bd. dirs. Balt. Safety Council, Franklin Sq. Hosp., Balt. Mem. Am. Inst. Steel Constrn. (pres.). Episcopalian. Clubs: Baltimore Country; Princess Anne Country (Virginia Beach, Va.); Seaview Country (Absecon, N.J.). Home: St Thomas Lane Owings Mill MD 21117 Office: 2700 Loch Haven Rd Baltimore MD 21218

DIETRICH, JOHN ERB, educator; b. Spokane, Nov. 13, 1913; s. John Hassler and Louise Ernestine (Erb) D.; B.A., U. Wis., 1937, M.A., 1941, Ph.D., 1945; m. Lois Gernhardt, Apr. 13, 1949; children—Lisa, John. Instr., asso. dir. univ. theatre Purdue U., 1937-41, also dir. Lafayette (Ind.) Little Theatre Assn.; asst. prof., asso. dir. theatre U. Wis., 1945-47, asso. prof., asso. dir. theatre, 1947-52, prof., asso. dir. theatre, also prodn. dir. WHA-TV, 1952-55; prof., dir. theatre Ohio State U., 1955-59; prof. speech, head dept. Mich. State U., 1959-64, asst. provost, dir. ednl. devel., 1964—. Trustee Milton (Wis.) Coll. Mem. Speech Assn. Am. (pres. 1959), Am. Ednl. Theatre Assn. (bd. research 1954-57, exec. com. 1955-58), Am. Nat. Theatre and Acad. (dir. 1960), Central State Speech Assn. (pres. 1953), Speech Assn. Eastern States, Phi Eta Sigma, Pi Epsilon Delta., Delta Sigma Rho. Author: Play Direction, 1953; Practical Speaking for the Technical Man, 1958. Home: 6150 Brich Row Dr East Lansing MI 48823

DIETRICH, MARLENE, actress; b. Berlin, Germany; d. Edward and Josephine (Felsing) von Losch; ed. Augusta Victoria Sch., Berlin; m. Rudolf Sieber, May 13, 1924; 1 dau., Maria. Began as violinist; debut as actress in "Broadway," Berlin; 4 years with Max Reinhardt; later in "The Blue Angel" (motion picture); came to U.S., 1930, and since starred in motion pictures, including: Golden Earrings, Martin Boumagnac (French). Foreign Affair, Stage Fright, No Highway in the Sky, Rancho Notorious; also appears in night clubs and theatres. Recipient Spl. Tony award, 1967-68. Author: Marlene Dietrich's ABC, 1962. Toured Army Service Camps, Europe, 1945.

DIETRICH, ROBERT LEE, mfg. co. exec.; b. Wheeling, W.Va., May 28, 1921; s. Donald C. and Elsie (McKelvey) D.; B.S., Carnegie Mellon U., 1943; m. Carolyn L. Gibb, Feb. 19, 1944; children—Kimberly Ann (Mrs. W.T. Martin), Donald Gibb, John Scott. With Dow Chem. Co., Midland, Mich. and Madison, Ill., 1943-55; with Olin Mathieson Chem. Co., East Alton, Ill. and N.Y.C., 1955-62; with Celanese Corp., 1962-67, v.p. mfg. and tech., 1967—. Bd. dirs. Found of U. N.C. Home: 45 E 89th New York City NY 10028 Office: Celanese Corp 522 Fifth Av New York City NY 10036

DIETRICH, WILLIAM GALE, lawyer, shopping center exec.; b. Kansas City, Mo., Mar. 6, 1925; s. Roy Kaiser and Gale (Gossett) D.; A.B., Yale, 1948, LL.B., 1951; m. Marjorie Nell Reich, July 14, 1945; children—Meredith Gale, Ann Elizabeth, Walter Reich. Admitted to Mo. bar, 1951, since practiced in Kansas City; partner firm Dietrich, Davis, Burrell, Dicus & Rowlands and predecessor firms, 1953—; project dir., gen. counsel Blue Ridge Shopping Center, Inc., Kansas City, Mo., 1955—, pres., gen. mgr., 1964—; pres. gen. mgr. Blue Ridge Tower, Inc., Kansas City, 1967—. Served to 1st lt. AUS, 1943-46; PTO. Mem. Am., Kansas City bar assns., Mo. Bar, Blue Ridge Mall Merchants Assn. (bd. dirs. 1958—), Internat. Council Shopping Centers (past dir. for Mo., Kan., Ia.), Lawyers Assn. Kansas City, Phi Beta Kappa, Phi Delta Phi. Episcopalian (vestry). Rotarian. Clubs: University, Mission Hills Country, County, Yale (Kansas City, Mo.). Home: 1000 Huntington Rd Kansas City, MO 64113. Office: 55 Blue Ridge Mall Kansas City MO 64133 also Dwight Bldg Kansas City MO 64105

DIETSCH, ROBERT WILLIAM, journalist; b. Cleve., Oct. 23, 1919; s. William and Emma (Schurig) D.; B.A. magna cum laude, Western Res. U., 1941; m. Paulene F. Gatz, Dec. 24, 1942; children—John, Deborah, Douglas, Craig. Asst. city editor, then asst. bus. editor Buffalo Evening News, 1948-51; World news editor, then bus. editor Cleve. Press, 1951-61; bus. editor Scripps-Howard Newspapers, Washington, 1961—. Mem. South Euclid-Lyndhurst (O.) Sch. Bd., 1958-61. Bd. dirs. Cleve. World Affairs Council, 1955-59, Cleve. chpt. Am. Civil Liberties Union, 1959-61. Served with USAAF, 1942-45. Fellow Internat. Press Inst., 1959; recipient award Cleve. Newspaper Guild, 1955, 57, 59. Mem. Nat. Soc. Bus. Editors, Phi Beta Kappa, Sigma Delta Chi. Clubs: National Press (Washington). Home: 5303 Elliott Rd Washington, DC 20016. Office: 1013 13th St N W Washington DC 20005

DIETTRICH, SIGISMOND DE RUEDESHEIM, geographer; b. Budapest, Hungary, Feb. 7, 1906; s. Anthony Maxmillian and Julia (Papp) D.; A.B., U. Budapest, 1927, A.M., 1928; Ph.D., Clark U. (univ. fellow), 1931; summer student U. Chgo., 1929; D.Sc., Royal Hungarian Palatine-Joseph U., Budapest, 1936; m. Iren Dokupil, July 27, 1932; 1 dau., Rosemary. Came to U.S., 1928, naturalized, 1938. Mem. faculty U. Fla., 1931-59, head geography sect., div. geography and geology, 1942-44, acting chmn., 1944-45, chmn., 1945- 48, head prof. dept. geography, 1948-59, chmn. war training courses in geography, 1943-44; spl. cons. O.S.S., Aug.-Sept. 1943; regional geographer U.S. bd. on geog. names Dept. Interior, 1944; geographer, asst. to chief div. geography and cartography Dept. State, 1944-1945; educationist Dept. State, 1945-50; cons. Nat. Lexicographic Bd., Ltd., N.Y., 1952—; chmn. social scis. Inter-Am. U. P.R., San Juan Campus, 1962-66, chmn. dept. geography, 1966-68, asso. dean faculty, 1968-70, coordinator univ. spl. programs, 1970 —, asst. to sr. v.p. for acad. affairs, 1971—, chmn. com. on acad. affairs Met. br., 1962-66, mem. acad. council and univ. council 1963-66, acad. senate, 1966—; Fulbright vis. prof. U. Dacca, Pakistan, 1959-61, U. Edinburgh, Scotland, U. Bonn, West Germany, 1961. Del. to Pax Romana Congresses, Bologna, Italy, 1923, Warsaw, Poland, 1927; rep. U.F. 4th Pan-Am. consultation on geography, Pan-Am. Inst. Geography and History, Mexico City, 1955; travel fellow attending 9th Gen. Assembly, 18th Internat. Geog. Congress, Rio De Janeiro, 1956; rep. Inter. Am. U. at 20th Internat. Geog. Congress, London, 1964; mem. symposium on colonization and settlement Internat. Geog. Congress, Dublin, 1964. Mem. So. Work Conf. Com. on Resources Use Edn., 1947-49; mem. Govs. Com. on Resources Use Edn., 1948-59; mem. Assn. Am. Geographers (chmn. S.E. sect. 1948-49), Nat. Council Geography Tchrs. (chmn. com. on conservation, resource use edn. 1954-60), Am. Geog. Soc. of N.Y., Am. Acad. Polit. and Social Scis., Fla. Acad. Scis. (v.p. 1953, pres. 1954), Soil and Crop Sci. Soc. Fla., Delta Tau Kappa (chancellor for P.R. and Caribbean). Dir. St. Patricks Choir, Gainesville, Fla., 1931-53, 1956-59. Author several books, several leaflets and articles. Address: P O Box 1293 Hato Rey PR 00919 ☆

DIETZ, ALBERT GEORGE HENRY, educator; b. Lorain, Ohio, Mar. 7, 1908; s. Peter and Adele (Grevsmuhl) D.; A.B., Miami U., 1930; Sc.D., Mass. Inst. Tech., 1941; m. Ruth Avery, Sept. 9, 1936; children—Margaret, Henry Avery. With dept. bldg. engring. and constrn., Mass. Inst. Tech., Cambridge, 1934-62, asst., instr., 1936-41, asst. prof., 1941-46, asso. prof., 1946-50, prof., 1950- 62, prof. bldg. engring. depts. civil engring. and architecture, 1962—, dir. plastic research lab., 1946-62. on leave of absence to Forest Products Labs. as sr. cons. engr., 1942; field service cons. office Field Service OSRD, 1944-45; cons. constrn. and materials, 1940—. Mem. Engring. Edn. Mission to Japan; 1952. Chmn. bldg. research adv. bd. Nat. Acad. Sci.-NRC. Recipient John Derham Internat. award Plastics Inst. Australia, 1962; New England award Engring. Socs. New Eng., 1968. Fellow A.A.A.S., Am. Acad. Arts and Scis.; mem. Am. Soc. Testing Materials, hon., Richard L. Templin award 1948, award merit 1957, Soc. Plastics Industry, Am. Soc. C.E., Am. Soc. M.E., Soc. Engring. Edn., Forest Products Research Soc., Soc. Plastics Engrs. (past nat. dir.), Boston Soc. Civil Engrs., Desmond Fitzgerald award 1945, 56, Bldg. Research Inst. (past dir.), Phi Beta Kappa Assos., Phi Beta Kappa, Sigma Xi, Tau Beta Pi. Author: Dwelling House Construction, 1946: Materials of Construction: Wood, Plastics, Fabrics, 1949 (with Marcia Koth, Julio Silva) Housing in Latin America, 1965; Plastics for Architects and Builders, 197O. Editor: Engineering Laminates, 1949; composite, engineering Laminates, 1970. Contbr. articles to profl. jours. Home: 19 Cambridge St Winchester MA 01890 Office: Mass Inst Tech Cambridge IL 61238

DIETZ, ARTHUR TOWNSEND, educator; b. Mt. Vernon, N.Y., Oct. 30, 1923; s. William Arthur and Adele (Dods) D.; B.A., Wesleyan U., 1946; M.A., Princeton, 1948, Ph.D., 1953; m. Mary Edmunds Archer, June 29, 1946; children—Adele Archer (Mrs. Robert Steele Watson), Laura Townsend, Amelia Edmunds. Instr. Princeton, 1948-49; instr. Wesleyan U., 1949-53; asst. prof. econs., 1953-54; asst. prof. Emory U., 1954-56, asso. prof., 1956-59, prof., 1959—, dir. M.B.A. program, 1959—, Mills Bee Lane lectr. finance and banking, 1970—; cons. in field. Trustee Cousins Mortgage and Equity Investments. Served with AUS, 1944-45. Woodrow Wilson fellow, 1946-47. Mem. Am., So. econ. assns., Am., So. finance assns., Phi Beta Kappa, Beta Gamma Sigma. Author: An Introduction to the Antitrust Laws, 1951; Education for Business Beyond High School, 1957; Capital Budgeting, 1968. Contbr. articles profl. jours. Home: 3300 Wood Valley Rd NW Atlanta GA 30327

DIETZ, CECIL EUGENE, journalist; b. Cookeville, Tenn., Apr. 7, 1925; s. Harry Denney and Emma Jane (Bilbrey) D.; B.S., Tenn. Tech. Inst., 1950; m. Imogene Rockwell, June 29, 1946; children—Charles Harold, Cecil Burton, Brenda Carol, Wallace Wordsworth, Franz Gerald. With Nashville Tennessean, 1950-70, edn. editor, 1962-70; publns. dir., journalist-in-residence Peabody Coll. Tchrs., 1970—, exec. producer, writer films, 1970—; regional editor Nat. Ednl. TV, 1965-68. Served with USNR, 1943-46. Recipient Tenn. Sch. Bell award, 1962. Democrat. Methodist (adminstrv. bd. 1968-72). Home: 3614 Woodmont Blvd Nashville TN 37215

DIETZ, CHARLES C., gas co. exec.; b. 1921; B.B.A., Pace Coll., 1943; married. With Bklyn. Union Gas Co., 1940—, chief accountant, 1956-62, asst. comptroller, 1962-69, comptroller, 1969—. Served with AUS, 1942-45. Office: 195 Montague St Brooklyn NY 11201

DIETZ, DAVID HENRY, editor, author; b. Cleve., Oct. 6, 1897; s. Henry William and Hannah (Levy) D.; A.B., Western Res. U., 1919, Litt.D., 1948; LL.D., Bowling Green State U., 1954; m. Dorothy B. Cohen, Sept. 26, 1918; children—Doris Jean, Patricia Ann, David Henry. Editorial staff Cleve. Press, 1915—; sci. editor Scripps-Howard Newspapers, 1921—. Lectr. gen. sci. Western Res. U., 1927-50. Pres., Shaker Heights Library Rd.; mem. subcom. on publicity, div. med. sci. NRC, 1940-46; cons. Surg. Gen. U.S. Army, 1944-47; at Bikini with Army-Navy Task Force One for atomic bomb test, as news corr., radio commentator, summer 1946. Trustee Mt. Sinai Hosp., Cleve. Recipient numerous awards including Pulitzer prize for journalism, 1937, Albert Lasker Med. Journalism award, 1954, Ohioana Career medal, 1958, James T. Grady award, 1961. Fellow Am. Geog. Soc., Royal Astron. Soc., A.A.A.S., Ohio Acad. Sci., Sigma Delta Chi; mem. Nat. Assn. Sci. Writers (charter, 1st pres.), Am. Astron. Soc., Astron. Soc. Pacific, Sociét é Astronomique de France, Sigma Xi, Zeta Beta Tau (v.p.), Omicron Delta Kappa (hon.). Clubs: Rowfant Oakwood, Mid-Day, City, (Cleve.); National Press (Washington). Author: The Story of Science, 1931; Medical Magic, 1937: Atomic Energy in the Coming Era, 1945 (transl. into 13 langs.); Atomic Science, Bombs and Power, 1954; All About Satellites and Space Ships, 1958; All About Great Medical Discoveries, 1960; All About the Universe, 1965; Stars and the Universe, 1968. Contbr. atomic bomb article Ency. Brit., 1946 edit., also Brit. Book of Year, 1946. Home: 2891 Winthrop Rd Shaker Heights OH 44120 Office: Cleve Press Bldg Cleveland OH 44114

DIETZ, FRANK TOBIAS, educator; b. Bridgeport, Conn., Aug. 13, 1920; s. Frank Charles and Otillia (Wasserman) D.; B.S., Bates Coll., 1942; M.A., Wesleyan U., Middletown, Conn., 1946; Ph.D., Pa. State U., 1951; m. Thera Louise Bushnell, Feb. 24, 1945; children—Martha (Mrs. Peter Bradley), Thomas Frank. Instr. physics Pa. State U., 1947-49, research asst., 1949-51; asso. underwater acoustics Woods Hole (Mass.) Oceanographic Inst., 1951-54; asst. prof. physics, research asso. phys. oceanographer U. R.I., 1954-56, asst. prof. physics, 1956-58, asso. prof., 1958-64, prof., 1964-68, prof. physics and oceanography, 1968—; vis. asso. prof. marine sci. U. Miami, 1963-64. Served with USNR, 1944. Mem. Am. Assn. Physics Tchrs., Acoust. Soc. Am., Am. Geophys. Union, Delta Phi Alpha, Sigma Xi, Pi Mu Epsilon, Phi Kappa Phi. Home: 28 Spring Hill Rd Kingston RI 02881

DIETZ, HOWARD, librettist; b. N.Y.C., Sept. 8, 1896; student Towsend Harris Hall, Hall, 1911-13, Columbia, 1913-17; m. Tanis Montagu, 1937; 1 dau., Liza (Mrs. Christopher Shaw); m. 2d, Lucinda Goldsborough Ballard, July 31, 1951; stepchildren—Robert F.R. Ballard, Jenifer Ballard (Mrs. Walter Romberg). Began as newspaper reporter; dir. publicity and advertising Goldwyn Pictures Corp., N.Y.C., 1918-24, continuing since merger into Metro-Goldwyn-Mayer, 1924, apptd. v.p., 1940. Screen and radio chmn. U.S. Treasury, 1941-58. Served with U.S.N., 1917-19. Author: June Goes Downtown, 1923; Dear Sir (with Jerome Kern), 1924; Merry-Go-Round (with Morris Byskind), 1927; The Little Show, 1929; Second Little Show, 1930; Three's a Crowd, 1930; Bandwagon (with George S. Kaufman), 1932; Flying Colors, 1932; Revenge With Music, 1934; At Home Abroad, 1935; Follow the Sun (prod. in Eng.), 1936; Between Between the Devil, 1937; Dancing in the Streets, 1943; Jackpot, 1944; Sadie Thompson (with Reuben Mamoulian), 1944; Inside U.S.A., 1948; Fledermaus (for Met. Opera Co.), 1950; The Bandwagon (motion picture), 1953; The Gay Life, 1961; Jennie (play), 1963; also English adaption of Puccini's La Boheme Songs (with Arthur Schwartz) Bell for Adano. Contbr. to periodicals. Mem. A.S.C.A.P. Clubs: Regency, Sands Point Golf. Address: 47 Cow Neck Rd Sands Point NY 11050

DIETZ, JAMES STRATTON, ret. naval officer; b. Washington, Mar. 25, 1911; s. George Tucker and Irene Mae (Stratton) D.; B.S., U.S. Naval Acad., 1933; grad. Indsl. Coll. Armed Forces, 1949-50, Advanced Mgmt. Program, Harvard, 1955; m. Rosalie Jensine Godhart, July 18, 1936; children—Rosalie Johanna, James Stratton, Margaret Grace. Commd. ensign U.S. Navy, 1933, advanced through grades to rear adm.; cashier Bank of Am. Samoa, 1938; supply officer U.S.S. Alaska, 1944; fighting afloat, Iwo Jima and Okinawa, 1945; dir. Navy Subsistence, 1945-49; comdg. officer Naval Supply Depot, Yokosuka, Japan, 1952-54; dir. Naval Pay, 1955; planner, later exec. officer Naval Supply Center, Norfolk, Va., 1950-59; comdg. officer Navy Finance Center, Cleve., 1959-62; comdr. Def. Indsl. Supply Center, Phila., 1962-64; comdr. Def. Gen. Supply Center, Richmond, Va., 1964-65; comdg. officer U.S. Naval Supply Center, Norfolk, Va., 1965-68, retired, 1968. Navy rep. to Japan-Wide Commodore Perry Centennial Celebration, 1954. Chmn. Loudon County chap. A.R.C., 1969—; pres. Loudoun County chpt. Va. Museum, 1969—. Decorated Bronze Star, Legion of Merit with star; Joint Service Commendation medal. Mem. U.S. Naval Inst., Nat. Def. Transp. Assn. Clubs: Army and Navy (Washington); Army-Navy Country (Arlington, Va.); Loudoun Hunt (Leesburg, Va.). Address: Fancy Free Route 2 Lovettsville, VA 22080.

DIETZ, PAUL, mfg. exec.; b. Blumenau, Brazil, June 14, 1903; s. Peter and Adele (Grevesmuehl) D.; A.B., Miami U., Oxford, O., 1925; postgrad. Friederich-Wilhelm U., Breslau, Germany, fellow Inst. Internat. Edn., Carnegie Found., 1926; m. Hannalene Margaret Gray, June 8, 1940; children—Patricia Karen, Paul Michael, Jonathan Lee, Hannalene Margaret. Came to U.S., 1905, naturalized, 1908. Factory rep. B.F. Goodrich Co., internat. div., Mexico, 1930-32, China mgr. internat. div., 1932-42; export mgr. Industries Group Allis-Chalmers Mfg. Co., 1943-57; asso. dir. sales Allis Chalmers Internat., 1957-62, dir. sales engring. products, 1962-64; v.p. Allis-Chalmers Mfg. Co., Milw., 1964—; past v.p., dir. Allis Chalmers de Mexico, S.A.; past dir. Allis Chalmers Gt. Brit., Ltd. Dir. Nat. Fgn. Trade Council. Mem. Am. Troop, Shanghai Vols., 1933-42. Mem. N.A.M. (internat. relations com.), U.S. C. of C., Milw. Fgn. Policy Assn. (dir. 1956-60), Milw. World Trade Club (pres. 1956), Phi Beta Kappa, Tau Kappa Alpha, Sigma Delta Chi. Rotarian (pres. West Allis, Wis. 1953-54). Home: Murray Hill Blvd Murray Hill NJ 07974 Office: 100 Church St New York City NY 10007

DIETZ, ROBERT HENRY, architect, educator; b. Crofton, Neb., Jan. 26, 1912; s. Jacob and Frances (Huennekens) D.; B.Arch., U. Wash., 1941; m. Arch., M. I. T., 1944; D.Sc., Univ. of Neb. 1967; m. Sara J. Perkins; children—Alan, Carl, Earl. Supr., estimator various bldg. contractors, Seattle, 1937-39; draftsman Paul Hayden Kirk, architect, Seattle, 1940; with radiation lab. Mass. Inst. Tech., 1942-43, OSRD, Princeton, 1943-45; designer, draftsman, supr. Anderson & Beckwick, Cambridge, Mass., 1945-47; pvt. practice architecture, Seattle, 1947-52; partner Waldron & Dietz, Architects, Seattle, 1952-68; instr. architecture U. Wash., 1947-48, asst. prof., 1948-53, asso. prof., 1953-58, prof., 1958-62, dean Coll. Architecture and Urban Planning, 1962—. Sec. Nat. Archtl. Accrediting Bd., 1963-64, pres., 1964—; mem. design standards adv. bd. Seattle Civic Center and World Fair, 1957; mem. Gov. Wash. Planning Adv. Council, 1964; mem. Nat. Commn. on Archtl. Barriers, 1966; mem. com. on urban technology Nat. Research Council, 1967. Recipient numerous A.I.A. honor awards. Fellow A.I.A. (chmn. research com., past v.p. Wash.); mem. Assn. Collegiate Schs. Architecture (exec. com.). Contbr. articles to ednl., archtl. mags. Home: 11828 84th St N E Kirkland, WA 98033. Office: Coll Architecture and Urban Planning U Wash Seattle WA 98105

DIETZ, WILLIAM STEPHENS, mgmt. cons.; b. Cin., July 27, 1915; s. William C. F. and Bertha (Stephens) D.; A.B., Dartmouth Coll., 1936; m. Elizabeth Brandt, May 7, 1941 (div. 1969); children—Stephens Marsh, Kristin Ellen. With advt. dept. Proctor & Gamble Co., 1938-46; asst. advt. mgr. Albers div. Carnation Co., 1946- 48; account exec. Ted Bates Advt. Agy., 1948-53; v.p. charge account mgmt. Ogilvy, Benson & Mather, 1953-55; with Kenyon & Eckhardt, Inc., 1955-69, exec. v.p., 1963-67, chmn. bd., 1967-69, also dir., mem. exec. com.; mgmt. cons. Arthur D. Little, N.Y.C., 1969- -. Chmn. bd. dirs. Am. Youth Hotels, Inc. Served to lt. USNR, 1943-45. Mem. Phi Beta Kappa. Unitarian (trustee). Club: University (N.Y.). Home: 305 E 86th St New York City NY 10028 Office: 630 Fifth Av New York City NY 10020

DIETZE, GOTTFRIED, educator; b. Kemberg, Germany, Nov. 11, 1922; s. Paul and Susanne (Pechstein) D.; came to U.S., 1949; Dr.Jur., U. Heidelberg (Germany), 1949; Ph.D., Princeton, 1952; S.J.D., U. Va., 1961. Instr. polit. sci. Dickinson Coll., 1952-54; mem. faculty Johns Hopkins, 1954—, prof. polit. sci., 1962—; vis. prof. U. Heidelberg, 1956, 58-60, Brookings Instn., 1960-61, 67. Mem. Am. Polit. Sci. Assn., Am. Soc. Polit. and Legal Philosophy, Deutsche Gesellschaft für Amerikastudien, Acad. Human Rights, Mont Pelerin Society. Lutheran. Author: Ueber Formulierung der Menschenrechte, 1956; The Federalist, 1960; In Defense of Property, 1963 (Monks award); Magna Carta and Property, 1965; America's Political Dilemma, 1968; Youth, University and Democracy, 1970; Ueber Bedeutungswandel der Menschenrechte, 1971. Editor: Essays on the American Constitution, 1964. Office: Johns Hopkins Univ Baltimore MD 21218

DIETZEL, PAUL FRANKLIN, football coach; b. Fremont, O., Sept. 5, 1924; s. Clarence Harlan and Catherine (Bihmer) D.; student Duke, 1942-43; B.S. in Edn., Miami U., Oxford, O., 1948; m. Anne Wilson, Sept. 25, 1944; children—Stephen Paul, Katherine Anne. Asst. Football coach U.S. Mil. Acad., West Point, N.Y., 1948, 53-54, named head football coach, 1962; asst. football coach U. Cin., 1949-50, U. Ky., Lexington, 1951-52; head football coach La. State U., Baton Rouge, 1955-61; now athletic dir., head football coach U. S.C., Columbia. Served with USAAF, 1943-46. Decorated Air medal with ofk leaf cluster; named Coach of Year, 1958. Mem. Am. Football Coaches Assn. (trustee, sec. bd trustees; nat. pres. 1969), Fellowship Christian Athletes (nat. pres. 1963-65), Omicron Delta Kappa, Kappa Delta Pi. Author: Wing T and the Chinese Bandits, 1959. Contbr. articles to profl. publs. Home: 327 Harrow Dr Whitehall Columbia SC 29210

DIETZGEN, JOSEPH EUGENE, business exec.; b. Lugano, Switzerland, Nov. 20, 1917; s. Eugene and Magdalena (Janssen) D.; B.S., Mass. Inst. Tech., 1941; m. Caroline Paterson, Feb. 7, 1942; m. 2d, Marion Boyd Donaldson, Nov. 25, 1967. Came to U.S., 1938. With Eugene Dietzgen Co., Chgo., 1941—, pres., dir., 1943—. Mem. Am. Soc. M.E., Am. Congress Surveying and Mapping. Clubs: Arts of Chicago, Exmoor Country. Home: 1010 Mt. Pleasant Rd Winnetka, IL 60093. Office: 2421 Sheffield Av Chicago IL 60614

DIEZ DE MEDINA, RAUL, diplomat of Bolivia; b. La Paz, Bolivia, Aug. 16, 1914; s. Eduardo and Etelvina (Guachalla) Diez deM.; B.A. Colegio Nacional Ayacucho, La Paz, 1927; M.S., Georgetown U., 1932; m. Mariya Leudinskas, Feb. 12, 1950; children—Richard, Marlyn, Christina, Michael Anthony, Diana. Attache, Bolivian legation, Washington, 1929; sec. Bolivian delegation Pan-Am. Arbitration and Conciliation Conf., 1929; sec. spl. mission to Cuba, 1929; 2d sec. legation, Washington, 1930; Latin Am. editor Washington Sunday Star, 1930-37; 1st sec. embassy, Washington, 1937; charge d'affaires of Bolivia in U.S., 1938; del. VIII Pan Am. Sci. Conf., 1940; counselor delegation II Cont. Fgn. Minister Am. Republics, 194O; de, Inter-Am. Econ. and Financial Com., 1940; counselor spl. mission to Mexico, 1940; counselor embassy, Washington, 1941, minister counselor, 1946; del. Internat. Labor Conf., 1946, council UNRRA, 1946; ambassador to UN Palestine Commn., also vice chmn. comm., 1948; dir. dept. pub. information Pan Am. Union, 1948; ambassador V Gen. Assembly UN, 1950; alternate exec. dir. Internat. Bank Reconstrn. and Devel., 1951; pres. Copesa, La Paz, 1955; dir. Pan Am. Union Office in Bolivia, 1958—; ambassador, rep. Bolivia council OAS, 1964—, vice chmn. council,

1966; ambassador, del. X-XII meeting consultation fgn. ministers, OAS rep, Argentina, 1969. Author: Autopsy of the Monroe Doctrine, 1934; The United States Versus Eruope in Latin America, 1937; also articles under pen name Gaston Nerval. Home: 9210 Cedar Way Bethesda MD 20014 Office: 760 Av de Mayo Buenos Aires Argentina

DIEZ SALAZAR, JORGE, formerly consul gen. of Peru in San Francisco. Address: 785 Market St San Francisco CA 94103*

DIFFENDERFER, HAROLD BOSSLER, savs. and loan assn. exec.; b. Middletown, Pa., Feb. 7, 1904; s. William H. and Annie Fletcher (Bossler) D.; B.S. in Econs., Wharton Sch. of U. Pa., 1925; m. Ethel Kendig, Apr. 2, 1927; 1 dau., Diana (Mrs. William Kelly). With Conway Corp., 1927-30; spl. dep. Pa. Banking Dept., 1931- 35; dist. examiner FHLB of N.Y., 1936-40; v.p., treas., 1941-53; pres., dir. County Fed. Savs. and Loan Assn., Rockville Centre, N.Y., 1954—. Mem. adv. council L.I. Better Bus. Bur., 1962—. Mem. Insured Savs. and Loan Assns. Nassau and Suffolk Counties (pres. 1959—), U.S., N.Y. State (past bd. dirs.). savs. and loan leagues. Club: Rockville Links. Home: 125 Lincoln Av Mineola NY 11501 Office: 53 N Park Av Rockville Centre NY 11571

DIFFORD, WINTHROP CECIL, univ. dean; b. East Liverpool, O., Nov. 12, 1921; s. Lionel Cecil and Pamela (Grice) D.; B.S., Mt. Union Coll., 1942; postgrad. Ohio State U., 1942-43; M.S., W.Va. U., 1947; Ph.D., Syracuse U., 1954; m. Nedra Arline Erisman, Nov. 28, 1944; children—Pamela Arline (Mrs. Clyde Hinkle), Phyllis Ann, Kenneth Edel. Asst. area engrng. geologist Neb., area engrng. geologist Colo., U.S. Bur. Reclamation, 1948-51; asst. state geologist, Harrisburg, Pa., 1955-56; prof., chmn. dept. geology Dickinson Coll., 1954-65; E.L. Phillips Found. intern acad. adminstrn. U. R.I., 1965-66; asst. dean grad. studies U. Bridgeport, Conn., 1966- 68; dean Grad. Coll., dir. summer session Wis. State U., Stevens Point, Wis., 1968—; vis. scientist Am. Geol. Inst.; cons. in S.Vietnam under U.S. AID Higher Edn. contract; cons. U.S. Naval Oceanographic Office; v.p. Inst. Oceanographic Communication. Vice pres. Stevens Point Anti- Tb. Assn.; bd. dirs. Portage County Humane Soc., Riverwoods Assn. Served with USNR, World War II, Korean Conflict. Fellow Geol. Soc. Am.; mem. Marine Tech. Soc. (past vice chmn. edn. com.), Sigma Xi, Sigma Gamma Epsilon, Phi Delta Kappa. Mason, Rotarian. Author: (with R. Jankowski) Introduction to Oceanography-Science of the Seventies, 1967. Editor: Proceedings of Nat. Conf. in the Concept of a Sea-Grant College, 1965. Home: 3131 Dan's Dr Stevens Point WI 54481

DIFRANCO, LORETTA, lyric coloratura; b. Bklyn., Oct. 28, 1942; d. Philip Carl and Lavinia (Russo) DiFranco; student Hunter Coll., Julliard Sch. of Music. Formerly mem. chorus Met. Opera Assn., N.Y.C., now performing soloist; performances in Paris, France, also summer concerts, Lewisohn Stadium, 1966; mem. various choruses, festivals and concert series, including Empire State Music Festival, Mozard Opera Festival, Chautauqua, N.Y., 1964; also performed on radio and TV. Recipient 1st prize Met. Opera Nat. Auditions, 1965; Kathryn Turney Long scholar, 1965-66; recipient Stuart and Irene Chambers award, 1965; Martha Baird-Rockefeller Fund for Music, 1964. Mem. Am. Guild Mus. Artists. Home: Brooklyn NY

DI FURIA, GIULIO, hosp. supt., psychiatrist; b. Ariano, Irpino, Italy, Oct. 24, 1925; s. Oto Maria and Vincenza (Scauzillo) di F.; M.D., Bologna (Italy) U., 1951; m. Marion Ann Rampuli, Mar. 27, 1955; children—Renzo, Diane, Robert, Richard, Julieann, Paul. Came to U.S., 1953, naturalized, 1959. Chief hosp. services Medfield State Hosp., Harding, Mass., 1957-58; mem. staff Western State Hosp., Fort Stellacoom, Wash., 1958—, supt., 1963—; asst. clin. prof. psychiatry and pharmacology U. Wash. Sch. Medicine, 1965—. Recipient citation for outstanding service to Wash. in mental health, 1964. Fellow Am. Psychiat. Assn., Am. Geriatric Soc., N. Pacific Soc. Neurology and Psychiatry; mem. Am. Assn. Med. Supts. Mental Hosps. (mem. council 1971—). Contbr. profl. jours. Address: 34 Country Club Dr SW Tacoma WA 98498

DIGGES, SAM COOK, broadcasting exec.; b. Columbia, Mo., Jan. 8, 1916; s. Charles William and Frances (Cook) D.; B.A. in Journalism, U. Mo., 1937; m. Carol Jean Ellis, Dec. 16, 1961; 1 son by previous marriage, Sam Cook. Advt. salesman, columnist Washington Daily News, 1937-42; time salesman sta. WMAL/WMAL- TV, Washington, 1942-49; with CBS, Inc., 1949—, gen. mgr. sta. WCBS-TV, N.Y.C., 1954-58, adminstrv. v.p. CBS Films Inc., N.Y.C., 1958-67, exec. v.p. CBS-owned AM stas. CBS Radio div., 1967-70, pres. CBS Radio div., 1970—; dir. Stephens & Towndrow Co. Ltd., Can., 1967—. Bd. curators Stephens Coll., 1970—; bd. advisers Bedside Network, Vets. Hosp. Radio and TV Guild, 1970—; bd. dirs. N.Y.C. Jr. Achievement, 1967—, Radio Advt. Bur., 1969—. bd. dirs. N.Y.C. chpt. Assn. Help Retarded Children, 1962-66. Served with U.S. Merchant Marine, 1944-45. Recipient plaque Assn. Help Retarded Children, 1957, Letchworth Village chpt. N.Y. State Assn. Retarded Children, 1962; Humanitarian award Sisterhood for Retarded Children, 1963. Mem. Internat. Radio and TV Soc. (pres. 1963-65, bd. govs. 1959-71), Nat. Acad. TV Arts and Scis. (bd. trustees 1966-67, bd. govs. N.Y.C. chpt. 1965-67), Broadcast Pioneers, TV Pioneers, Phi Delta Theta, Alpha Delta Sigma. Republican. Lutheran. Clubs: Woodway Country (Darien, Conn.); Variety (N.Y.C.). Home: 134 Foxwood Rd Stamford CT 06903 Office: 51 W 52d St New York City NY 10019

DIGGS, BERNARD JAMES, educator, philosopher; b. Norfolk, Va., July 11, 1916; s. Bernice James and Annie (Petree) D.; B.S., U. Va., 1937, M.A., 1939; postgrad. U. Toronto, 1939-40; Ph.D., Columbia, 1946; m. Fanny Robinson Hoxton, Dec. 26, 1942; children—Llewellyn Hoxton, Anne Marie. Mem. faculty U. Ill., 1946—, prof. philosophy, 1963—, chmn. dept., 1963-69. Served with USMCR, 1942-46. Grantee Ford Found., 1953-54. Mem. Am. Philos. Assn., Assn. Symbolic Logic, Am. Soc. Polit. and Legal Philosophy, Am. Assn. U. Profs. Author: Love and Being: An Investigation into the Metaphysics of St. Thomas Aquinas, 1947. Home: 2206 S Lynn St Urbana, IL 61801.

DIGGS, CHARLES C., Jr., congressman; b. Detroit, Dec, 2, 1922; s. Charles C. and Mayme E. (Jones) D.; student U. Mich., 1940-42, Fisk U., 1942-43, Wayne U. Sch. Mortuary Sci., 1945-46, Detroit Coll. Law, 1951-52; m. Anna Johnson; children by previous marriage—Charles III, Denise, Alexis. Former pres. House of Diggs. Inc., funeral Home; pres., treas. Detroit Met. Mutual Assurance Co.; v.p. Diggs Enterprises. Mem. Mich. State Senate, 1951-54; mem. 84th-92d Congresses, 13th Mich. Dist. Served as 2d lt. USAAF, 1943-45. Mem. Am. Legion. Democrat. Baptist. Mason, Elk. Office: 2464 Rayburn House Bldg Washington DC 20515

DIGGS, LEMUEL WHITLEY, physician, educator; b. Hampton, Va., Jan. 9, 1900; s. Chaplin Spencer and Ruby (Hudgins) D.; A.B., Randolph Macon Coll., Ashland, Va., 1921, A.M., 1922; M.D., Johns Hopkins, 1926; m. Beatrice Moshier, Apr. 10; children—Walter, Alice, John, Margaret. Intern and Asst. resident in medicine, U. Rochester, Strong Meml. Hosp., 1926-28; instr. of medicine in charge course in clin. pathology, U. Rochester, 1928- 29; asst. prof. pathology, U. Tenn., Memphis, 1929-36, asst. prof. medicine, 1936-38, asso. prof. medicine, 1938-44, prof. medicine, 1947-63, Goodman prof. medicine, 1963—; Instr. in English, Randolph Macon Coll., 1921-22; instr. chemistry, Mt. Vernon Coll., 1923; with Internat. Health Bur. malaria survey, 1924; physician, du Pont de Nemours Powder Plant, Millington, Tenn., 1941; pvt. med. practice, Whitehaven, Tenn., 1942-45; instr. courses in hematology to med. officers, World War II; cons. in clin. pathology, T.V.A., 1936- 45; fellow in trop. medicine, Guatemala, 1943; vis. prof. medicine, U. of Rochester, summer 1944; clin. pathologist Cleve. Clinic Found., 1945-47; cons. to staff Armed Forces Inst. of Pathology, 1951; cons. in hematology VA, 196d—. Mem. bd. govs. St. Jude Hosp. Diplomate in clin. pathology. Mem. Memphis, Shelby County med. socs., A.M.A., Am. Soc. Clin. Pathologists (council hematology; recipient Ward Burdick award 1964), So. Med. Assn., Coll. Am. Pathologists,' internat. Soc. Hematology, Memphis Acad. of Medicine (pres. 1962), Phi Beta Kappa, Sigma X; Alpha Omega Alpha, Sigma Upsilon, Tau Kappa Alpha. Author: papers on Sickle Cell Anemia, blood banking and blood preservation; Morphology of Human Blood Cells: Laboratory Procedures in City of Memphis Hospitals; Basic Medical Laboratory Procedures. Co- author: Textbook of Clinical Pathology (with Miller). Asst. in revision of Gould's Medical Dictionary. Editor: Manual of Approved Laboratory Procedures, T.V.A., 1943. Mem. bd. editors Am. Jour. Clin. Pathology, 1958. Contbr. Medical Physics. Home: 7340 LaGrange Rd Cordova TN 38018 Office: 800 Madison Memphis TN 38103 ☆

DIGGS, WALTER WHITLEY, health adminstr.; b. Memphis, June 8, 1932; s. L. W. and Beatrice (Moshier) D.; B.S., Washington and Lee U., 1954; M.H.A., U. Minn., 1956; m. Ann Carol Thobae, Nov. 19, 1958; children—Jennifer, Thomas, Andrew. Adminstrv. resident Stormont-Vail Hosp., Topeka, 1955-56; asst. chief personnel records div., also adminstrv. officer dependents unit U.S. Naval Hosp., Chelsea, Mass., 1957-59, adminstrv. asst. outpatient service Johns Hopkins Hosp., Balt., 1959-61, asst. adminstr. Wilmer Ophthalmological Inst., 1962-66; adminstr. hosps. and clinics Med. Coll. Ga., Eugene Talmadge Meml. Hosp., Augusta, 1966- 70; asst. dir. health care programs Med. Coll. Ga., 1970—, also asst. prof.; asst. prof. Ga. State U. Program Hosp. Adminstrn.; adj. faculty Ga. Tech. Program Hosp. and Med. Systems, 1967-70. Pres. August Civic Ballet, Inc., 1969—, Augusta Speech and Hearing Center, 1970—. Sec. bd. trustees St. Joseph's Hosp., Augusta; bd. dirs. Augusta Red Cross Served to lt. (j.g.), Med. Service Corps, USNR, 1956-59. Mem. Ga. League Nursing, Am., Ga. hosp. assns., Am. Coll. Hosp. Adminstrs., Am. Pub. Health Assn. Home: 2708 Bellevue St Augusta GA 30904 Office: 1459 Gwinnett St Augusta GA 30902

DIGIA, ROBERT M., mfg. co. exec.; b. N.Y.C., Aug. 24, 1924; S. Mauro and Margaret (Giglio) DiG.; B.S., N.Y. U., 1950; m. Rita B. Welsh, Nov. 16, 1958; children—Robert M., Kenneth W. Prin., Haskins & Sells, C.P.A.'s, N.Y.C., 1955-65; controller Ogden Corp., 1965—. C.P.A., N.Y. Mem. Am. Inst. C.P.A.'s, N.Y. State Soc. C.P.A.'s, Financial Execs. Inst. Home: 28-27 208th St Bayside, NY 11360. Office: 161 E 42d St New York City NY 10017

DI GIORGIO, J.S., bus. exec.; b. Washington, 1901; m.; 2 children. Chmn. exec. com., dir. Di Giorgio Corp.; dir. N.Y. Fruit Auction Corp., N.Y.C. Club: Commercial (San Francisco). Office: 1 Maritime Plaza San Francisco CA 94111

DIGIORGIO, ROBERT, food co. exec.; b. N.Y.C., Dec. 2, 1911; s. Salvatore and Marie (Meyer) Di G.; A.B., Yale, 1933; B.L., Fordham U., 1936; m. Eleanor Vollmann, Jan. 20, 1940 (div); children—Ann, Barbara, Christine, Dorothy; m. 2d, Patricia Kuhrts Sharman, Aug. 7, 1964. Admitted to N.Y. bar, 1937; with Di Giorgio Corp., San Francisco, 1937—, pres., 1962-71, chmn. bd., chief exec. officer, 1971—; dir., mem. exec. com. Bank of Am.; dir. Broadway-Hale Stores, Inc., Pacific Telephone & Telegraph Company (all San Francisco), Union Oil Co., Cal., Newhall Land & Farming Co. Clubs: Yale (N.Y.C.); California (Los Angeles); Pacific-Union, Commercial (dir., past pres.), Commonwealth, Bohemian, Golf (San Francisco). Office: One Maritime Plaza San Francisco CA 94111

DIKE, PHIL, artist, educator; b. Redlands, Cal., Apr. 6, 1906; s. Andrew Noble and Jennie E. (Twigg) D.; student Chouinard Art Inst., 1924-28, Art Students League, 1928, Am. Acad., Fontainbleau, France, 1930; m. Betty Love Woodward, June 17, 1933; 1 son, Philip Woodward. Color cons. Walt Disney, 1935-45; instr. figure painting Chouinard Art Inst., 1945- 50; instr. painting Scripps Coll., 1950, now prof. emeritus art Scripps Coll. and Claremont Grad. Sch. Exhbns. Carnegie, 1936, 37, 50, Chgo. Art Inst., Pa. Acad. Fine Arts, Salon, Paris, France, Met. Mus. Art, 1951, Nat. Acad. Works in permanent collection Met. Mus. Art, Wood Mus., Santa Barbara Mus. Awarded 1st prize oil painting, Golden Gate Expn., 1940; Medal Achievement, Pepsi Cola, 1946; Hatfield prize, 1946; Dana Mention, Pa. Acad. Fine Arts, 1947; Nat. Acad. Water Color prize, 1950, 58; 1st prize, Cal. Water Color Soc., 1931, Cole prize, 1952, Pottinger award, 1953, Brugger award, 1957, 66; 1st prize Watercolor Butler Inst. Am. Art, 1959; Albert Dorne purchase prize Am. Water Color Soc., 1960; Grumbacher prize Cal. Water Color Soc., 1960; Paul B. Remmy Meml. award, Am. Water Color Exhbn., 1962, John L. Ernst award, 1965; purchase prize Springfield Nat. Watercolor Exhbn., 1967, Cal. Nat. Watercolor Exhbn., 1969. Nat. Academician; mem. Am. (hon. v.p. 1954), Cal., West Coast (v.p. 1964-65) water color socs. Club: Watercolor (Phila.). Home: 3110 Forbes Av Claremont CA 91711

DIKER, CHARLES MICHAEL, toy hobby and craft co. exec.; b. Bklyn., Dec. 5, 1934; s. Daniel and Helen (Hoffner) D.; B.A., Harvard, 1956, M.B.A., 1958; m. Valerie Tishman, June 25, 1959; children—Bruce Daniel, Patricia Helen, Mark Norman. Asst. to pres. Revlon Inc., 1958-63, marketing mgr. fragrance div., 1963-65, dir. marketing fragrance div., 1965-68, v.p. marketing, 1968-69; pres. Aurora Products Corp., West Hempstead, N.Y., 1969—. Mem. Hobby Industry Assn. (dir.), Toy Mfg. Assn. (dir.). Clubs: Harmonie, Harvard (N.Y.C.); Century Country (Westchester). Home: 1095 Park Av New York City NY 10028 Office: 44 Cherry Valley Rd West Hempstead NY 11552

DILATUSH, LUTHER COX, credit co. exec.; b. Mercerville, N.J., July 30, 1910; s. Forman W. and Emma (Anderson) D.; B.S. in Commerce, Rider Coll., 1930; postgrad. Grad. Sch. Banking, Rutgers U., 1954; m. Louise A. Kapp, Oct. 29, 1937; 1 dau., Gayle (Mrs. McDonnell). Vice pres. Am. Nat. Bank & Trust Co., Chgo., 1949-58; v.p., sr. trust officer Mchts. Nat. Bank, Indpls., 1958-62; sr. v.p. Md. Nat. Bank, Balt., 1962-69; v.p. Comml. Credit Co., Balt., 1970—. Trustee Harriet Lane Home of Johns Hopkins Hosp.; bd. dirs. Balt. Symphony Orch. Assn.; pres., bd. dirs. Assn. Ind. Colls.; trustee, treas. Md. Inst. Coll. Art. Mem. Inst. Chartered Financial Analysts, Am. Mgmt. Assn., Nat. Indsl. Conf. Bd., Balt. Soc. Financial Analysts, Balt. Wine and Food Soc. (dir.). Clubs: Merchants, Hunt Valley Golf, Center (Balt.). Home: 12 Nantucket Garth Phoenix City MD 21131 Office: 300 St Paul Pl Baltimore MD 21202

DILL, LEONARD CARTER, Jr., ednl. adminstr.; b. Phila., Aug. 3, 1906; s. Leonard Carter and Amanda (Vansant) D.; A.B., U. Pa., 1928; m. Helen L. Richardson, Sept. 24, 1929; children—Leonard Carter III, Julie D. with E.W. Clark & Co., Phil., 1929-33, L.C. Dill Jr. & Co., investments, 1933-40; pres., also dir. Beaver Constrn. Co., 1935-45, exec. sec. Gen. Alumni Soc., U. Pa., 1940-65, dir. alumni relations, 1960-65, asst. to pres. com. relations; pub., bus. mgr. The Pennsylvania Gazette, Phila., 1945-65, The General Magazine and Historical Chronicle, 1940-58; chmn. bd. Bailey, Banks & Biddle Co., Phila.; dir. Cons. Mut. Project dir. Peace Corps, India. Pres. Organized Classes, U. Pa., 1938; chmn. Lower Merion Twp. (Pa.) Republican Com., 1960-64; pres. Am. Alumni Council, 1952-53; exec. bd. CARE, Phila; bd. West br. YMCA. Trustee Phila. Community Coll., Brandywine Battle Field Park Comm. Mem. Hist. Soc. Pa., Zool. Soc. Phila., Pa. Acad. Fine Arts, Phila. Museum of Art, Franklin Inst., Beta Theta Pi, Alpha Beta Chi. Presbyn. Clubs: Midday (pres.) (Phila.); Merion Cricket (Haverford, Pa.); University (N.Y.C.). Home: Maybrook Cottage Penn Rd Wynnewood PA 19096 Office: U Pa Philadelphia PA 19104

DILL, WILLIAM RANKIN, univ. dean; b. Sewickley, Pa., Aug. 18, 1930; s. Frederick Hayes and Caroline (Rankin) D.; A.B., Bates Coll., 1951; M.S., Carnegie Inst. Tech., 1953, Ph.D., 1956; postgrad. U. Oslo, 1953-54; m. Jean McLeod, June 13, 1953; children-Jens McLeod, Holly Ruth, Harrison Rankin, Cynthia Wightman. Sr. research fellow Grad. Sch. Indsl. Adminstrn., Carnegie Inst. Tech., Pitts., 1955-56, asst. prof., 1956-60, asso. prof., 1960-65, asst. dean, 1959-62, asso. dean, 1962-65; program dir. edn. research and devel. IBM Corp., White Plains, N.Y., 1965-70; dean Grad. Sch. Bus. Adminstrn., N.Y.U., N.Y.C., 1970—. Trustee Bates Coll.; bd. advisers Ecology Forum, Grad. Sch. Bus., Atlanta U. Fulbright scholar, 1953-54; Ford Found. Faculty Research fellow, 1964-65. Mem. Am. Psychol. Assn., Inst. Mgmt. Scis., Assn. Computing Machinery, A.A.A.S., Phi Beta Kappa, Sigma Xi, Delta Sigma Rho. Unitarian. Author: The New Managers, 1962; The Carnegie Tech. Management Game, 1964. Home: 101 Greenridge Av White Plains NY 10605 Office: 100 Trinity Pl New York NY 10006

DILLARD, ALLYN, lawyer, bus. exec.; b. Norfolk, Va., Feb. 2, 1905; s. George Mason and Elizabeth (Allyn) D.; LL.B., U. Va., 1927; m. Frances E. Pratt, Apr. 30, 1938; 1 dau., Frances Allyn. Admitted to Va. bar, 1927, N.Y. bar, 1929; asso. Mitchell, Capron, Marsh, Angulo & Cooney, and predecessors, N.Y. City, 1929-45; sec. Reynolds Metals Co., and affiliates, 1945-71; dir. Reynolds Metal Co., 1959—. Pres. Richmond Area Community Council, 1957- 59. Mem. Am. Soc. of Corporate Secs., Inc., Va. State Bar Assn., Newcomen Soc. N.Am., Kappa Alpha, Phi Delta Phi. Club: Country of Virginia. Democrat. Episcopalian. Home: 9 Oak Lane Richmond VA 23226

DILLARD, DUDLEY, economist, educator; b. Ontario, Ore., Oct. 18, 1913; s. John James and Frances (Cunning) D.; B.S., U. Cal., 1935, Ph.D., 1940; vis. scholar Harvard, 1939, Columbia, 1940; m. Louisa Gardner, August 22, 1939; children—Lorraine Gardner, Amber Frances. Teaching asst. U. Cal., 1935- 36, Flood fellow in econs., 1936-37, research asst., 1937-38, teaching asst., 1938-39; Newton Booth Travelling fellow, 1939-40; instr. econs. U. Colo., 1940-41, U. Del., 1941-42; asst. prof. U. Md., 1942-45, asso. prof. 1945-47, prof. since 1947, head dept. econs. since 1951; vis. asso. prof. econs. Columbia, 1948-50, vis. prof., summer, 1955, 1958. Cons. U.S. Army, 1945-46. Chmn. Gov.'s Com. on Employment in Maryland; mem. Gov.'s Adv. Com. on Manpower Devel. and Training, 1962—. Mem. U.S. exec. bd. Am. College in Paris, 1966. Mem. Am. Econ. Assn., Econ. History Soc., Am. Assn. U. Profs., Phi Beta Kappa, Pi Gamma Mu, Beta Gamma Sigma, Beta Alpha Psi. Club: Cosmos (Washington, District of Columbia). Author: The Economics of John Maynard Keynes, 1948; (with others) Post-Keynesian Economics, 1954; Economic Development of North Atlantic Community, 1967. Editorial bd. Jour. Econ. History, 1948-54. Contbr. profl. jours. Home: 7007 Forest Hill Dr College Heights Estates Hyattsville MD 20781 Office: Dept Econs U Md College Park MD 20742

DILLARD, HARDY CROSS, judge; b. New Orleans, Oct. 23, 1902; s. James Hardy and Avarene Lippincott (Budd) D.; grad. Va. Episcopal Sch., 1919; B.S., U.S. Mil. Acad., 1924; student U. Va., 1919-20, 1924-27, LL.B., 1927; student U. Paris, 1930-31; LL.D. (hon.), Tulane U., 1971; m. Janet Gray Schauffler, Nov. 16, 1934 (dec. July 1970); children—Joan Jarvis, Hardy Schauffler. Admitted to Va. bar, 1927; practiced in N.Y., 1929-30; Carnegie endowment fellow in Internat. law, U. Paris, 1930-31; acting asst. prof. law, U. Va., 1927-29, acting asso. prof. law, 1931-33, asso. prof., 1933-38, prof., 1938-58, James Monroe prof., 1958-70, asst. dean, 1937-40, dean of Law Sch., 1963-67; judge Internat. Ct. Justice, The Hague, 1970—; mem. arbitral tribunal Beagle Channel Case between Chile and Argentina, 1971; dir. Inst. Pub. Affairs, 1938-42; vis. prof. law Columbia, 1962-63; maj. 1942, lt. col., 1942, col., 1943, U.S. Army, comd. and staff assignments, European and Far Eastern Theatres, 1943-45; cons. Brookings Instn., 1947-50; dir. studies Nat. War Coll., 1946, mem. bd. cons., 1951-54, cons., 1956- -; cons., lectr., Western Germany, 1950; Fulbright lectr. Oxford, summer 1953; Carnegie lectr. Hague Acad. Internat. Law, 1957; mem. com. to study non-tech. instrn. in armed forces Sec. of Def., 1961-62; Tucker lectr. Washington and Lee U.; Sibley lectr. U. Ga.; Bailey lectr. La. State U., others. Trustee Va. Episcopal Sch., 1952-61; mem. adv. council U.S. Air Force Acad. Mem. Commn. Constl. Revision for Va., 1968. Decorated Legion of Merit with Oak Leaf Cluster, Bronze Star medal; recipient Raven award, 1957, Thomas Jefferson award, 1967; Distinguished Civilian award U.S. Air Force, 1970. Fellow Am. Bar Found.; mem. Am., Va., W.Va. bar assns., Am. Soc. Internat. Law (pres. 1962-63), Am. Law Inst. (mem. council), Am. Soc. Polit. and Legal Philosophy, Order of Coif, Phi Beta Kappa, Beta Theta Pi, Phi Delta Phi, Omicron Delta Kappa. Democrat. Episcopalian. Clubs: Colonnade, Farmington. Contbr. articles and reviews to numerous profl. jours. Adv. editor Va. Quarterly Rev., 1937-70. Editorial bd. Am. Jour. Internat. Law. Editor: Va. Bar News, 1956-62; Proceedings of Inst. of Pub. Affairs, 8 vols. Home: 1221 Rugby Rd Charlottesville VA 22903 Office: The Peace Palace The Hague Netherlands

DILLARD, KATHERINE SHANNON RAWLINGS, (Mrs. Tom Clinton Dillard), editor; b. Sulphur, Okla., Oct. 13; d. Frank Hill and Floy (Dickinsheets) Rawlings; student Tex. Christian U., 1938-39; m. Tom Clinton Dillard, Sept. 5, 1942; 1 dau., Shannon Howard (Mrs. Shyam H. Gurbaxani). Feature editor, soc. and amusements editor Ft. Worth Star-Telegram, 1937-42; feature writer, asst. to city editor San Antonio Light, 1942-45; feature writer Dallas Morning News, 1945-47, women's editor, 1947—. Mem. women's bd. Dallas Civic Opera. Recipient Matrix award Theta Sigma Phi, 1969. Mem. Nat. Soc. Interior Designers, Nat. Home Fashions League, Fashion Group Inc., Delta Kappa Gamma, Theta Sigma Phi. Methodist. Clubs: Dallas Athletic, Lakewood Country. Home: 7022 Merrilee Lane Dallas TX 75214 Office: Communications Center Dallas TX 75214

DILLARD, ROBERT CARL, supermarket chain exec.; b. Prattville, Ala., Apr. 9, 1931; s. Joseph Samuel and Marie (Meek) D.; student Auburn U., 1948-49, Huntington Coll., 1951-52; A.A., Marshall U., 1955; student U. Pitts., 1958-59; m. Wanda Charlene Cahpman, Aug. 5, 1951; children—William Douglas, Robin Renee. Supr. accounting The Kroger Co., Charleston, W.Va., 1955-58, Pitts., 1958-59, Detroit, 1959-60, dir. accountant, 1960-61; with Hudson-Thompson & Co., Montgomery, Ala.,1961-64, controller, 1961-64; treas., controller M. Loeb Co., Chgo., 1964-66; controller, treas. New England Grocer Supply Co., Worcester, Mass., 1966-68; dir. finance and adminstrn.

A.J. Bayless Markets Inc., Phoenix, Ariz., 1968—, v.p., 1970—, sec., treas., 1968—. Co-chmn. Concerned Bus. Com. 1970. Bd. dirs. Ariz. Easter Seal Soc. Served with USMCR, 1949-51. Lion. Home: 2423 E Lincoln Circle Phoenix AZ 85016 Office: 111 E Buckeye Rd Phoenix AZ 85004

DILLARD, ROBERT LIONEL, Jr., lawyer, life ins. co. exec.; b. Corsicana, Tex., Sept. 30, 1913; s. Robert Lionel and Mattie Sam (Jack) D.; B.S. in Commerce, So. Meth. U., 1934, J.D., 1935; LL.M., Harvard, 1936; m. Dundee Sheeks, Jan 3O, 1937; children—Robert Lionel III, Diane (Mrs. Richard Day), Deborah (Mrs. John B. Cullen III). Admitted to practice before the Tex. bar, 1935; with firm Saner, Saner & Jack, Dallas 1936-41; asst. city atty., Dallas, 1941-45; with Southland Life Ins. Co., Dallas, 1945—, v.p., gen. counsel, sr. v.p., gen. counsel, 1968-70, exec. v.p., gen. counsel, 1970—, also dir., city atty., Carrollton, Tex., 1947—. Mem. bd. edn. Dallas Ind. Sch. Dist., 1953-62, pres., 1961-62; trustee pub. television, Dallas, 1960- -; pres. Dallas Council Social Agys., 1963-65; pres. Dallas Council Camp Fire Girls, 1960-61, chmn. nat. bd., 1965—. Sec., mem. exec. com. Dallas Symphony Orch. Recipient Distinguished Law Alumnus award So. Meth. U., 1958, Distinguished Alumnus award, 1963. Fellow Am. Bar Found.; mem. Am. (ho. of dels. 1956-58), Inter-Am., Tex., Dallas bar aasns., Am. Judicature Soc., Nat. Legal Aid Soc., Assn. Life Ins. Counsel, Life Insurers Conf., Tex. LIfe Conv. (chmn. legislative com), Alpha Tau Omega, Delta Theta Phi (past dist. chancellor), Order Woolsack. Methodist (chmn. ofcl. bd., tchr. adult Sunday sch.). Mason (33; grand master Tex., 1961-62). Author articles in field. Home: 6624 Lakewood Blvd Dallas TX 75214 Office: 1105 Southland Center Dallas TX 75201

DILLARD, WILLIAM ELBERT, ret. railroad exec.; b. Buena Vista, Ga., Feb. 13, 1898; s. Joseph Demps and Ella Jane (Mathis) D.; student pub. schs., Ellaville, Ga.; m. Elizabeth Pace, Jan. 1, 1919; children—Jane (Mrs. B. Ellis deTreville), Sara (Mrs. T. F. Morrison, Jr.), William Elbert, James C. With C. of Ga. Ry., 1915-68, successively ticket clk., agt.-operator, chief clk., freight agt., trainmaster, div. supt., gen. supt., gen. mgr., v.p., 1915-54, pres., dir., mem. exec. com. Savannah, Ga., 1954-68, dir., 1968—; past pres., dir., mem. exec. com. Ocean S.S. Co. of Savannah, Southwestern R.R.; past pres., dir. Albany Passenger Terminal Co., C. of Ga. Motor Transport Co., Chatham Terminal Co., Empire Land Co., Macon Terminal Co.; past v.p., dir. Atlanta Terminal Co.; dir. Wrightsville & Tennille R.R., Savannah & Atlanta Ry., Savannah Bank & Trust Co. Mem. exec. adv. com. Historic Savannah. Bd. dirs. YMCA Savannah, Goodwill Industries of Central Coastal Empire; trustee, mem. exec. com., vice chmn. bd. St. Joseph's Hosp; trustee Shorter Coll., Rome, Ga. Mem. Newcomen Soc. North Am., English Speaking Union. Baptist. Clubs: Commerce (Atlanta); Oglethorpe, Rotary, Savannah Golf; Forest City Gun. Home: 5721 Sweetbriar Circle Savannah GA 31406 Office: 227 W Broad St Savannah GA 31406

DILLAVOU, GEORGE JACKSON, univ. dean; b. Billings, Mont., May 18, 1922; s. R. Clarke and Louise (Bradford) D.; A.B., U. Ill., 1946; M.A., Columbia U., 1951; Ph.D., U. Chgo., 1970. Instr. Tex. A. & M. Coll., 1946-50; tchr. Jefferson High Sch., Port Arthur, Tex., 1951; instr. speech and English, U. Md., 1953-55, dir. N. Atlantic div., 1956-60; dir. field services U. Chgo., 1960-62; coordinator field services U. Ariz., 1962-64; dir. Continuing Edn. dir. Roosevelt U., 1966-70; dean Coll. Continuing Edn., 1970-71; dean Univ. Extension, U. R.I., Providence, 1971—; cons. spl. degree programs for adults. Mem. nat. adv. council Coll.-Level Examination Program, Coll. Entrance Examination Bd. Bd. dirs. Adult Edn. Council Greater Chgo. Served with AUS, 1942-45. Carnegie U. Adminstrn. fellow, 1964. Mem. Adult Edn. Assn., Assn. Univ. Eve. Coll., Nat. Univ. Extension Assn., Speech Communication Assn., Phi Sigma Kappa. Mason (Shriner). Author: The Swarthmore Chautauqua: An Adult Education Enterprise, 1970. Home: 4030 N Clarendon Av Chicago IL 60613 Office: Univ Rhode Island Providence RI 02908

DILLE, EARL KAYE, elec. utility exec.; b. Chillicothe, Mo., Apr. 25, 1927; s. George Earl and Josephine Christina (Kaye) D.; B.S., U.S. Naval Acad., 1950; M.S., St. Louis U., 1961; m. Martha Virginia Merrill, Sept. 8, 1951; children—Thomas Merrill, James Warren. With Union Elec. Co., St. Louis, 1957—, exec. v.p., 1970—; dir. Elec. Energy, Inc., Mo. Power & Light Co., Mo. Edison Co. Dir. Civic Employment Corp., 1970-71. Served with USN, 1950-57; comdr. Res. Mem. Engrs. Club St. Louis, I.E.E.E., Sigma Xi. Episcopalian. Mason. Clubs: Bellerive Country, Noonday, St. Louis (St. Louis). Home: 310 Woodside Dr Kirkwood MO 63122 Office: 1 Memorial Dr St Louis MO 63166

DILLE, GUY, wholesale trade co. exec.; b. Rochester, Pa., July 25, 1929; s. Guy Burdette and Sadie (Gorby) D.; B.B.A., Geneva Coll., 1955; m. Dorothy Reed, Apr. 4, 1959; children—Gail Lynn, Guy Burdette, Gregg, Gwen, Gary. Staff accountant Arthur Young & Co., Pitts., 1955-58; with Williams & Co., Inc., Pitts., 1958—, asst. treas., 1962-68, treas., 1968—. Served with USAF, 1948-52. Mem. Am., Pa. insts. C.P.A.'s, Nat. Assn. Accountants. Home: 641 Ryland Park Pittsburgh PA 15237 Office: 901 Pennsylvania Av Pittsburgh PA 15233

DILLE, JAMES MADISON, educator; b. Omaha, Neb., June 9, 1907; s. James Madison and Luella (Butterfield) D.; student Creighton U., 1926-27; B.A., U. Neb., 1930, M.S., 1933; Ph.D., Georgetown U., 1935; M.D., U. Ill., 1945; m. Mary Elizabeth Pugh, June 9, 1935; children—Russell Meredith, Janet Leona, Jean Louella. Faculty dept. pharmacology, Univ. of Washington, 1935—, prof. and chairman dept. pharmacology, sch. medicine, 1945—. Mem. Am. Soc. Pharmacology and Exptl. Therapeutics, Soc. Exptl. Biology and Medicine, Western Pharmacology Soc., Sigma Xi, Alpha Omega Alpha, Phi Sigma. Home: 3045 NE 185th St Seattle WA 98155

DILLE, JOHN FLINT, Jr., editor, publisher, broadcasting exec.; b. Chgo., Nov. 14, 1913; s. John Flint and Phoebe Minerva (Crabtree) D.; A.B., U. Chgo., 1935, A.M. 1956; Litt.D., Tri-State Coll., Ind., 1965; m. Jayne Paulman, Apr. 9, 1938; children—John Flint III, Joanne Paulman. Producer newspaper features Nat. Newspaper Syndicate, Chgo., 1935-52; pres. Communicans Group, pubs. daily Elkhart (Ind.) Truth, operates WSJV-TV, South Bend- Elkhart, WTRC-AM- FM, Elkhart, 1953—; pres. WKJG, Inc. (TV-AM), Ft. Wayne, Ind., 1957—; dir. First Nat. Bank Elkhart, Hotel Elkhart Corp. Chmn. bd. govs. ABC-TV Affiliates Assn. Mem. univ. cabinet, citizens bd., vis. com. on U. Chgo.; vice chmn. Ind. Toll Rd. Commn., 1961-66. Bd. dirs. United Health Found. Served to lt. comdr. USNR, World War II. Mem. Am. Soc. Newspaper Editors, U. Chgo. Alumni Assn. (pres.), Nat. Assn. Broadcasters (chmn. joint bd. dirs. 1965-67), Broadcast Pioneers (v.p.), Chief Execs. Forum (V.p.), Elkhart C. of C. (past pres., dir.), Alpha Delta Phi, Sigma Delta Chi. Episcopalian (past vestry). Clubs: Congressional Country, National Press, International (Washington); Elcona Country (dir. Elkhart incorporator); University (Chgo.); Lost Tree (North Palm Beach, Fla.). Home: 1 Holly Lane Elkhart IN 46514 Office: Communicana Bldg Elkhart IN 46514

DILLE, ROBERT CRABTREE, newspaper syndicate exec.; b. Chgo.; s. John Flint and Phoebe (Crabtree) D.; A.B., U. Chgo., 1944, postgrad., 1944; grad student Northwestern U., 1949; m. Virginia L. Nichols, July 26, 1945; children—Lorraine Virginia, Robert Nichols Flint. Copywriter, Homer J. Buckley & Assos., 1944; membership dir. Nat. Safety Council, 1945-46; dir. sales markets, methods Ency. Britannica, 1946-48; pres. Robert C. Dille & Assos., 1948- 52; promotion mgr. Nat. Newspaper Syndicate, Chgo., 1952, mgr., 1953, sec., treas., 1953—, gen. mgr., 1956-57, pres., 1957—, also editor; dir. John F. Dille Co., Buck Rogers Co., Truth Pub. Co., Elkhart, Ind., WSJV-TV, South Bend. Vice chmn. U. Chgo. Alumni Fund; exec. com. Alumni Found. U. Chgo. Mem. Nat. Newspaper Promotion Assn., U. Chgo. Alumni Senate (life), A.I.M., Aircraft Owners and Pilots Assn., Alpha Delta Phi, Order Owl and Serpent. Rep. Clubs: Tower, Antique Automobile, Economic (Chgo.). Home: 1631 E Ridgewood Lane Glen Oaks Acres Glenview IL 60025 Office: 20 N Wacker Dr Chicago IL 60606

DILLE, ROLAND PAUL, coll. pres.; b. Dassel, Minn., Sept. 16, 1924; s. Oliver Valentine and Eleanor (Johnson) D.; B.A. summa cum laude, U. Minn., 1949, Ph.D., 1962; m. Beth Hopeman, Sept. 4, 1948; children—Deborah, Martha, Sarah, Benjamin. Instr. English, U. Minn., 1953-56; asst. prof. St. Olaf Coll., Northfield, Minn., 1956-61; asst. prof. English, Cal. Lutheran Coll., Thousand Oaks, Cal., 1961-63; mem. faculty Moorhead (Minn.) State Coll., 1963—, pres., 1968—. Bd. dirs. KFME-TV, Fargo, N.D. Served with inf. AUS, 1944- 46. Mem. Assn. Minn. Colls. (pres. 1969-70), Nat. Council Tchrs. English, Phi Beta Kappa. Author: Four Romantic Poets, 1969. Home: 516 9th St S Moorhead MN 56560

DILLENBACK, LEMUEL CROSS, educator; b. Cobleskill, N.Y., Apr. 7, 1890; s. Jonas and Helen (Spraker) D.; A.B., Carnegie Inst. Tech., 1913, A.M., 1914; m. Hazel McIntosh Soper, Nov. 29, 1919; children—Mary Louise (Mrs. James Pierce Butler Jr.), Lemuel Cross. Instr. architecture U. Ill., 1915-17, asst. prof., 1920-23, asso. prof., 1923-25, prof., 1925-30; prof. architecture Columbia, 1930-34; prof. architecture Syracuse U., 1934-58, acting dir. dept., 1936, dir., 1937-45, dean Coll. Fine Arts and dir. Sch. Architecture, 1945-58. Served to lt. comdg. officer USAAF, World War I. Recipient Merit award Carnegie Alumni Fedn., 1955. Registered Architect, N.Y. Fellow A.I.A. (pres. Central N.Y. chpt. 1946-47), Syracuse Soc. Architects (v.p. 1937-38, pres. 1942-43), Sigma Nu, Phi Kappa Phi, Sigma Upsilon Alpha, Alpha Chi Tau, Tau Sigma Delta. Republican. Lutheran. Rotarian. Home: 570 Cumberland Av Syracuse NY 13210

DILLENBERGER, JOHN, educator, clergyman; b. St. Louis, July 11, 1918; s. Charles and Bertha (Hoffmann) D.; B.A., Elmhurst Coll., 1940, D.D., 1959; B.D., Union Theol. Sem., 1943; Ph.D., Columbia, 1948; D.D., U. Vt., 1957; S.T.D., Ch. Divinity Sch. Pacific, 1965, Ripon Coll., 1966; L.H.D., U. San Francisco, 1966; m. 2d, Jane Daggett Karlin, July 19, 1962; children (by previous marriage)—Eric John, Paul Gregor. Ordained to ministry, United Ch. of Christ, 1943; tutor asst. theology Union Theol. Sem., N.Y.C., 1947-48; instr. religion Princeton, 1948-49; asst. prof. religion Columbia, 1949-52, asso. prof., 1952-54; asso. prof. theology Harvard Div. Sch., 1954-57, Parkman prof. theology, 1957-58; Ellen S. James prof. systematic and hist. theology, grad. sch. and seminary Drew U., Madison, N.J., 1958-62; prof. hist. theology, dean grad. studies San Francisco Theol. Sem., San Anselmo, Cal., 1962-64; dean, pres., prof. hist. theology Grad. Theol. Union, Berkeley, Cal., 1962—. Served as lt. Chaplain's Corps, USNR, 1943-46. Fellow Soc. for Religion in Higher Edn. Author: God Hidden and Revealed, 1953; (with Claude Welch) Protestant Christianity: Interpreted Through Its Development, 1954; Protestant Thought and Natural Science, 1960; Contours of Faith, 1969. Editor: Martin Luther: Selections from his Writings, 1961; John Calvin: Selections from His Writings, 1971. Chmn. editorial bd. Library of Protestant Thought, 1958—. Home: 1536 LeRoy Berkeley CA 94708

DILLER, PHYLLIS, actress, authoress; b. Lima, O., July 17, 1917; d. Perry Marcus and Frances Ada (Romshe) Driver; student Sherwood Music Conservatory, Chgo. 1935-37, Bluffton (O.) Coll., 1938-39; m. Sherwood Anderson Diller, Nov. 4, 1939 (div. Sept. 1965); children—Peter III, Sallee, Suzanne, Stephanie, Perry; m. Warde Donovan, Oct. 7, 1965. Theatrical prodns. include Dark at the Top of the Stairs, 1961, Wonderful Town, 1962, Happy Birthday, 1963; numerous appearances TV and radio, concerts, supper clubs and hotels, 1955—; producer, author Phyllis Diller Shows, 1963, 64; recording artist for Verve Records; pres. Eldorado Enterprises, Inc., 1964—, BAM Prodns., Ltd., 1965, PhilDil Prodns., Ltd., 1966; head Phyllis Diller King Exotic Plants. Motion pictures include Boy Did I Get a Wrong Number!, 1966, Eight on the Lam, 1967; star The Pruitts of Southampton, TV series, 1966-67. Recipient Recipient Star of Yr. award Nat. Assn. Theatre Owners. Hon. life mem. San Francisco Press and Union League Club. Author: Phyllis Diller Tells All About Fang, 1963; Phyllis Diller's Housekeeping Hints, 1966; Phyllis Diller's Marriage Manual; The Complete Mother. Accompanied Bob Hope entertainment group to South Vietnam, Christmas, 1966. Office: care Frank Liberman & Assos 9255 Sunset Blvd Los Angeles CA 90069

DILLER, THEODORE CRAIG, lawyer; b. Pitts., Aug. 3, 1904; s. Theodore and Rebecca (Craig) D.; Ph.B., Kenyon Coll., 1925; LL.B., Harvard, 1928; m. Barbara Cox, May 16, 1936; children—Anne Cox (Mrs. Keir B. Sterling), Rebecca Crossette (Mrs. James Robert Howe), Deborah Howard. Admitted to Pa. bar, 1928, Ill. bar, 1929; practice in Chgo., 1929—; partner firm Lord, Bissell & Brook, 1946—. Sec. Magnaflux Corp., 1940-59. Mem. Am., Ill., Chgo. bar assns., Law Club Chgo., Legal Club Chgo. Republican. Episcopalian. Clubs: University. Mid-Am. (Chgo.) Home: 416 Cumnor Rd Kenilworth IL 60043 Office: 135 S LaSalle St Chicago IL 60603

DILLER, WILLIAM F., educator, zoologist; b. Lancaster, Pa., July 26, 1902; s. William F. and Lida (Schofield) D.; A.B., Franklin and Marshall Coll., 1923; Ph.D., U. Pa., 1928; m. Irene Corey, June 18, 1938. Instr. zoology U. Pa., 1923- 25, Franklin and Marshall Coll., 1925-27, U. Pa., 1927-30; asst. prof. zoology Dartmouth, 1931-39; faculty zoology U. Pa., Phila., 1939-42, 46—, prof., 1958—. Vis. scientist Johns Hopkins Zool. Lab., 1939. Sterling Research fellow Yale, 1930-31; fellow by courtesy Laboratoire Arago, Sorbonne, Banyuls, 1939; USPHS fellow Central Coll., Bangalore, India, 1955. Mem. Am. Soc. Zoologist, Am. Soc. Protozoologists, A.A.A.S., Am. Soc. Naturalists, Am. Micros. Soc., Phi Beta Kappa, Sigma Xi. Research, numerous publs. on nuclear behavior and genetics one-celled animals, including finding that these organisms may develop either bisexually or by self-fertilization. Home: 2417 Fairhill Av Glenside PA 19038 Office: Leidy Lab U Pa 38th and Woodland Av Philadelphia PA 19104

DILLEY, ROY THOMAS, ret. banker; b. Loogootee, Ind., Feb. 23, 1906; s. William H. and Maud C. (Cropp) D.; grad. Am. Inst. Banking, 1944, Am. Bankers Assn. Grad. Sch. Banking, Rutgers U., 1946; m. Viola L. McDaniel, Oct. 6, 1928; children—Richard H., Elizabeth A., John W. With Fletcher Trust Co., 1923- 55, auditor, 1943-50, controller, 1950-55; comptroller, v.p. Am. Fletcher Nat. Bank & Trust Co. (merger Am. Nat. Bank & Fletcher Trust Co.), 1955- 67, v.p. finance, 1967-71; ret., 1971; former lectr. Ind. U. Extension, Central States Sch. Banking, U. Wis. Bd. govs., finance com. bd. dirs. Community Hosp. of Indpls.; mem. finance and budget com. Am. Cancer Soc. Mem. Financial Execs. Inst. Am. (pres. Indpls. chpt. 1959-60), Am. Inst. Banking (pres. Indpls. chpt. 1942-43), Nat. Assn. Bank Auditors and Comptrollers (state v.p. 1946-48), Indpls. Conf. Bank Auditors and Comptrollers, Indpls. C. of C. Club: Hillcrest Country. Home: 5320 E 10th St Indianapolis IN 46219

DILLIARD, IRVING, journalist, educator; b. Collinsville, Ill., Nov. 27, 1904; s. James Irving and Mary Beedle (Look) D.; A.B., U. Ill., 1927; grad. student Harvard 1928-29, Nieman fellow, 1939; Litt.D., MacMurray Coll., 1951; LL.D., Colby Coll., 1953; L.H.D. New Sch. for Social Research, 1954; D.C.L., Brandeis U., 1956; L.H.D., So. Ill. U., 1958; LL.D., Washington U., St. Louis, 1961; m. Dorothy Alice Dorris, June 20, 1931; children—Doris Lee (Mrs. James V. Sprong), Mary Sue (Mrs. Ernest L. Schusky). Corr. St. Louis Post-Dispatch, 1923, reporter, 1927-30, editorial writer, 1930-49, 57-60, editor, editorial page 1949-57; corr. The Christian Science Monitor, 1928-38. Commd. capt., AUS, July 12, 1943; Sch. Mil. Govt. Charlottesville, Va.; assigned to Surpeme Hdqrs., AEF, 1944; major, 1945; lt. col., Nov. 1945; 6870 DISCC, 3rd U.S. Army; Info. Control Div., Mil. Govt., Bavaria, 1945-46; adv. editor The Stars and Stripes, Germany, 1946. James lectr. U. Ill., 1949; Lovejoy lectr. Colby Coll., 1953; Brandeis lectr. Brandeis U., 1953; Kappa Tau Alpha lectr. U. N.M., 1954; Allen lectr. U. Ore., 1955; Hogate lectr. DePauw U., 1956; White lectr. U. Kan., 1957; Mellett lectr. U. Nev., 1958; lectr. Salzburg seminar in Am. Studies, Austria, 1960, 66; regents lectr. U. Cal., 1963; Ferris prof. Princeton, 1963—; Edward L. Bernays lectr. Boston U., 1971. Trustee U. Ill., 1961-67. Decorated Bronze Star; Mil. Div. Order British Empire; Medaille de la Reconnaissance Francaise; chevalier Legion of Honor; Florina Lasker award, 1958; Am. Bar Assn. Silver Gavel award, 1959. Trustee Ill. Hist. Library, 1938-45; trustee Collinsville (Ill.) Meml. Pub. Library, 1936—, pres. 1957—. Mem. Sigma Delta Chi (nat. pres. 1940- 41, F., 1951), Alpha Kappa Lambda (nat. pres. 1936-38), Phi Beta Kappa (senator 1958-70, nat. historian 1970—), Am. Newspaper Guild (hon. withdrawal), Ill. Library Assn. (pres. trustees 1940-41), Ill. State Hist. Soc. (pres. 1947-48). Clubs: Town and Gown (St. Louis); Press, Army and Navy (Washington). Author: The Development of a Free Press in Germany: An Aspect of American Military Government, 1949; I'm from Missouri, 1951. Editor: Mr. Justice Brandeis, Great American, 1941; The Spirit of Liberty: Papers and Addresses of Learned Hand, 1952; One Man's Stand for Freedom: Mr. Justice Black and Bill of Rights, 1963. Contbr. articles to Dictionary of American History; Ency. of the Social Sciences; Missouri-A Guide to the Show Me State; Ency. Britannica, Dictionary of Polit. Sci., also to mags. Home: 407 Crestwood Dr Collinsville IL 62234

DILLIN, SAMUEL HUGH, U.S. judge; b. Petersburg, Ind., June 9, 1914; s. Samuel E. and Maude (Harrell) D.; A.B. in Govt., Ind. U., 1936, LL.B., 1938; m. Mary Eloise Humphreys, Nov. 24, 1949; 1 dau., Patricia Jane. Admitted to Ind. bar, 1938; partner firm Dillin & Dillin, Petersburg, 1938-61; U.S. dist. judge So. Dist. Ind., 1961—. Sec. Pub. Service Commn. Ind., 1942; mem. Interstate Oil Compact Commn., 1949-52, 61. Mem. Ind. Ho. of Reps. from Pike and Knox County, 1937, 39, 41, 51, floor leader, 1951; mem. Ind. Senate from Pike and Gibson County, 1959, 61, floor leader, pres. pro tem, 1961; candidate for gov. Ind., 1956. Served to capt. AUS, 1943-46. Mem. Am. Bar Assn., Am. Judicature Soc., Delta Tau Delta, Phi Delta Phi. Democrat. Presbyn. Club: Indianapolis Athletic. Home: 4710 Laurel Circle North Dr Indianapolis In 46226 Office: Federal Bldg Indianapolis IN 46204

DILLING, MILDRED, harpist; b. Marion, Ind.; d. Frank M. and Rachel (Freel) Dilling; student harp, N.Y.C., with Henriette Renie, Paris; m. Clinton W. Parker, Oct. 9, 1943 (dec. 1948). European debut, Salle Erard, Paris; Am. debut, Aeolian Hall, N.Y.C.; concerts in Europe, N. and S. Am., Can., Middle and Far East and Near East; numerous recitals, symphony, radio and TV appearances; starred in film Adventures in Music, 1940; organized 1st harp sextet to play Radio City Music Hall; 1st harpist to play on radio in Ireland; 7 engagements at White House; teacher of the harp, Indiana University School of Music, 1948. Hon. mem. Sigma Alpha Iota. Editor, collector: Old Tunes for New Harpists, 2d edit., 1956; 30 Little Classics, 2d 3dit., 1954. Owner largest pvt. collection harps ever assembled. Home: 400 E 52 St New York City NY 10022 also (summer) Ohayo Mountain Woodstock NY 12498 Office: 400 E 52d St New York City NY 10022

DILLINGER, JOSEPH ROLLEN, educator, physicist; b. Carbondale, Ill., May 20, 1916; s. Isaac Roland and Minnie (Etherton) D.; B.Ed., So. Ill. U., 1938; Ph.D. in Physics, U. Wis., 1947; m. Martha J. Freeman, June 6, 1942; children—James R., Ellen M., Thomas E. Mem. staff radiation lab. Mass. Inst. Tech., 1941-46; mem. faculty U. Wis., 1947—, prof. physics, 1960—. Mem. Am. Phys. Soc., Am. Assn. Physics Tchrs. (treas. 1962-66). Research on photoelectric and thermionic emission; devel. power pulse generators and gas discharge tubes; low temperature physics. Home: 2001 Van Hise Av Madison WI 53705

DILLINGHAM, HOWARD IRVING, former coll. pres.; b. Elba, N.Y., Oct. 11, 1904; s. James Irving and Sara Rossin (Keates) D.; B.S., Wharton Sch., U. Pa., 1927; M.S., Ph.D., Syracuse U., 1938; L.H.D., Alfred U., 1967; LL.D., Pratt Inst., 1967; m. Josephine Hammond, 1929 (dec.); children—Elizabeth D. Kress, Carol Ann D. Rivet; m. 2d, Dorothy King Hoyt, 1962. Mdse. mgr. Gorham Co., Providence, 1927-32; dir. Auburn (N.Y.) Collegiate Center, 1933-37; dean Rider Coll., Trenton, N.J., 1938-44; headmaster Manlius Sch., 1944-50, Riverside Mil. Acad. 1950-51; asst. to pres. Ithaca Coll., 1951-53, v.p., 1953-57, pres., 1957-70, pres. emeritus, 1970—. Dir. Tompkins County Trust Co., Ithaca Savs. & Loan Assn. Mem. Sigma Phi Epsilon, Phi Delta Kappa. Rotarian. Address: 1 Ladoga Landing Rd Myers NY 14866

DILLINGHAM, LOWELL SMITH, corp. exec.; b. Honolulu, June 17, 1911; s. Walter Francis and Louise (Gaylord) D.; grad. Middlesex Sch., Concord, Mass., 1930; student Harvard, 1934; m. Harriet Barbour, June 12, 1936; children—Gail Louise (Mrs. William C. Bartholomay), Heather Barbour. With the firm of Dillingham Corp. and subsidiaries, Honolulu, 1934—, pres., 1955-71, chmn., chief exec. officer, 1971—, also dir.; dir. Bank of Hawaii, B.F. Dillingham Co., Ltd., Hawaiian Western Steel, Ltd., Oahu Sugar Co., Ltd., Pioneer Mill Co., Hawaiian Cement Corp., Bank of Am. NT & SA, Bankam. Corp., Western Air Lines, Inc., Times Mirror Inc.; pres., dir. Hawaiian Land Co., Ltd. Pres. emeritus, dir. Maunalani Hosp.; trustee Punahou Sch., Com. for Econ. Devel., Pacific Tropical Garden. Mem. Honolulu C. of C., Hawaiian Sugar Planters Assn. Clubs: Oahu Country, Pacific, Outrigger Canoe (Honolulu); Pacific Union (San Francisco); A.D. (Harvard). Home: 3330 Tantalus Dr Honolulu HI 96822 Office: Ala Moana Bldg PO Box 3468 Honolulu HI 96801

DILLMAN, BERYL REESE, educator; b. Central, Ind., Oct. 1, 1918; s. Clifford Kingsley and Bertha (Eickelberger) D.; A.B. in Chemistry, Olivet Nazarene Coll., 1949; M.Ed., U. Ill., 1952, Ed.D., 1959; m. Hazel Blanton, June 18, 1944; children—Carolyn (Mrs. Jann Pence), Ruth Ann. Tchr. Manteno, Ill., high sch., 1949-52, prin., 1952-57; asso. in ednl. research U. Ill., Urbana, 1957-59; asst. prof. edn. U. Cal. at Santa Barbara, 1959-64; asso. prof. No. Ill. U., Dekalb, 1964-66; prof., chmn. div. edn., psychology Olivet Nazarene Coll., Kankakee, Ill., 1966-68; prof., dir. tchr. edn. Pasadena (Cal.) Coll.,

1968—; Mem. Ill. Dept. Edn. evaluation teams, 1966-68, Nat. Council for Accreditation evaluation teams, 1967—; cons. to pub. schs. Treas. Manteno council Boy Scouts Am., 1954-57; pres. El Encanto Heights Home Owners Assn., Goleta, Cal., 1963-64. Named Outstanding Alumnus Year, Olivet Nazarene Coll., 1968. Mem. N.E.A., Cal. Tchrs. Assn., Phi Delta Kappa, Phi Delta Lambda, Kappa Delta Pi. Mem. Ch. Nazarene. Contbr. profl. jours. Home: 1700 E Mendocino St Altadena CA 91001 Office: 1539 E Howard St Pasadena CA 91104

DILLMAN, H. GRANT, journalist; b. Columbus, O., May 4, 1918; s. Herschel G. and Daisy (Fothergill) D.; student Franklin U., 1939-40; m. Jeanne L. Ford, 1940; 1 dau., Mrs. Daniel F. Kunkle; m. 2d, Audrey Maslow, June 30, 1945; children— Darryl, Craig. With Columbus (O.) Dispatch, 1938-42; with pub. relations dept. Curtiss-Wright Corp., 1942; with UPI, 1942—, Ohio legislative corr., 1942-43, mgr. Columbus bur., 1944, with Washington staff, 1945—,editor night news, 1950-63, Washington news editor, 1963—. Club: Gridiron. Home: 5161 N 38th St Arlington VA 22207 Office: Nat Press Bldg Washington DC 20004

DILLMAN, L. THOMAS, physicist; b. Huntington, Ind., Au. 26, 1931; s. Lloyd Everett and Nancy (Walther) D.; B.A., Manchester Coll., 1953; M.S., U. Ill., 1955, Ph.D., 1958; m. Mary Alice Bagwell, Apr. 18, 1954; children—John Mark, Anne Elizabeth, Mary Susan, Bradford Louis. Research asst. Los Alamos (N.M.) Sci. Lab, summer, 1958; prof. physics Ohio Wesleyan U., 1958—; lectr. physics U. Ill., summers 1960-61; health physics research Oak Ridge Nat. Lab., summers 1967—, cons. Health Physics div. Oak Ridge (Tenn.) Nat. Lab., 1967—. Mem. Am. Phys. Soc., Am. Assn. Physics Tchrs., Health Physics Soc., Soc. Nuclear Medicine (Mem. med. internal radiation dose com. 1968—), Nat. Council on Radiation Protection (mem. com. 33, 1969—), Sigma Xi. Contbr. articles health physics, nuclear medicine, nuclear gamma-ray spectroscopy. Home: 184 W Lincoln Av Delaware OH 43015

DILLON, MRS. C. DOUGLAS, museum trustee; b. South Bend, Ind., Aug. 3, 1910; d. John Chess and Alice (Chalifoux) Ellsworth; grad. Miss Porter's Sch., Farmington, Conn., 1926; m. C. Douglas Dillon, Mar. 10, 1931; children—Phyllis Ellsworth (Mrs. Mark Collins), Joan Douglas (Princess Joan de Luxembourg). Trustee Museum of Modern Art, N.Y.C., 1959—. Past mem. Fine Arts Com. for State Dept.; mem. vis. com. Western European Arts, Met. Mus., N.Y.C. Home: Far Hills NJ 07931

DILLON, CLARENCE DOUGLAS, ex-govt. ofcl.; b. Geneva, Switzerland, Aug. 21, 1909; s. Clarence and Anne McE. (Douglass) D.; grad., Groton Sch., 1927; A.B., Harvard, 1931; LL.D., N.Y. U., 1956, Lafayette Coll., 1957, U. Hartford, 1958, Columbia U., 1959, Harvard, 1959, Williams Coll., 1960, Rutgers U., 1961, Princeton, 1961, U. Pa., 1962; m. Phyllis C. Ellsworth, Mar. 10, 1931; children—Phyllis Ellsworth (Mrs. Mark Collins), Joan Douglas (Princess Joan de Luxembourg). Mem. New York Stock Exchange, 1931-36; dir. U.S. & Foreign Securities Corp. and U.S. & Internat. Securities Corp., 1937-53, pres., 1937-53, pres., dir., 1967-71, chmn. bd., 1971—; v.p., dir. Dillon, Read & Co., Inc., 1938-53, chmn. bd. 1946-53; A.E. & P. to France, 1953-57; under sec. of state for econ. affairs, 1958-59, under sec. of state, 1959-60; sec. of treasury, 1960-65; dir. Chase Manhattan Bank, Am. Tel. and Tel. Co. Pres. Met. Mus. Art, N.Y.C., 1970—; bd. govs. N.Y. Hosp. Met. Mus. (on leave). pres. bd. overseers Howard Coll. Served from ensign to lt. comdr., U.S. N.R., 1941-45. Awarded Air Medal, Legion of Merit. Mem. Soc. Colonial Wars N.Y. Clubs: Racquet and Tennis, Knickerbocker, Links, River, Recess, Century, Pilgrims (N.Y.C.); Metropolitan (Washington). Office: 757 Fifth Av New York City NY 10022

DILLON, CONLEY HALL, educator; b. Lawrence County, O., Oct. 19, 1906; s. Elmer Wesley and Ottie Olive (Hall) D.; A.B., Marshall Coll., 1928; A.M., Duke, 1933, Ph.D., 1936; m. Virginia Bull, Dec. 29, 1934; children—Carol, Conley. Prin., Lorado (W.Va.) Grade Sch., 1928-29; asst. prin., athletic coach, tchr. social sci. Chapmanville (W.Va.) High Sch., 1929-32; teaching fellow polit. sci. Duke, 1934; instr. polit. sci. Marshall Coll., Huntington, W.Va., 1934-45, asst. prof., 1935-36, asso. prof., head dept., 1937-41, prof., 1941; prof. govt., politics U. Md., College Park. Cons., Gov. W.Va., 1961-68, Huntington Prodn. Pool, 1955-57, Appalachian Regional Commn., 1968—; state, fed. assignments OPA, 1942- 46, OPS 1951-53; mem. forum faculty U.S. Office Edn., 1936-37; mem. Am. Com. in Geneva, 1937; mem. Prince Georges County Study Commn., 1966- 68. Bd. dirs. Marshall Foundation. Mem. Am. So. polit. sci. assns., Am. Soc. for Pub. Adminstrn., Am. Soc. Internat. Law, Am. Assn. U. Profs., Alpha Sigma Phi, Pi Sigma Alpha, Phi Kappa Phi. Democrat. Conglist. Author: International Labor Conventions: Their Interpretations and Revision, 1942; Government and Labor in Action, 1951; The Area Redevelopment Administration: New Patterns in Developmental Administration, 1964; co- author Introduction to Political Science, 1958. Editor: Official Papers and Messages of J. Millard Towers, 2 vols., 1967. Home: 1754 Overlook Dr Silver Spring MD 20903 Office: U Md College Park MD 20740

DILLON, DONALD, editor; b. Washington, Sept. 24, 1914; s. Morris Nixon and Bertha Florence (Porter) D.; student La. State U., 1933-34, U. N.M., 1934-35, U. Philippines, 1935; m. Marie Faulhaber, Sept. 12, 1942; children—Richard, Kathleen. With U.P.I. (formerly United Press Assns.), Manila, P.I., 1935, corr. Far Eastern countries, 1935-40, N.Y.C., 1941-50, editor for Europe, Asia, Africa and Australia, 1951—. Presbyn. Home: 541 Monroe Ct River Edge NJ 07661 Office: UPI 220 E 42d St New York City NY 10017

DILLON, GEORGE CHAFFEE, mfg. co. exec.; b. Kansas City, Mo., Oct. 29, 1922; s. Edward J. and Mary (Coon) D.; B.S., Harvard, 1944, M.B.A., 1948; m. Joan Alamo Kent, Sept. 11, 1948; children—Kenty, Courtney, Emily. Adminstrv. asst. J. A. Bruening Co., Kansas City, Mo., 1948-53; with Butler Mfg. Co., Kansas City, Mo., 1951—, treas., 1960—, v. p., 1961-63, exec. v. p., 1963-67, pres., 1967—. Formerly treas. bd. trustees, then chmn. Midwest Research Inst., Kansas City, Mo.; chmn. bd. dirs. Kansas City area council Boy Scouts Am., 1958—. Served to lt. (s.g.) USNR, 1943-46. Mem. Mo. C. of C. (bd. dirs. 1959—). Home: 600 Westover Rd Kansas City MO 64113 Office: BMA Tower-Penn Valley Park Kansas City MO 64141

DILLON, GEORGE SANFORD, mfg. co. exec.; b. Bklyn., Sept. 12, 1917; s. Harry J. and Anna (Sanford) D.; B.S., Syracuse U., 1939; LL.B., Cornell U., 1946; m. Jane Gardner, Oct. 24, 1942; children—Judith Ann, Peter G., George Sanford, Nancy Louise. Admitted to N.Y bar, 1946; with firm Shearman & Sterling, N.Y.C., 1946-62; with Air Reduction Co., Inc., 1962—, exec. v.p., 1963- 64, pres., 1964—, chief operating officer, 1964-68, chief exec. officer, 1968—, dir., 1963—; trustee Dry Dock Savs. Bank. Trustee Syracuse U. Served to lt. (s.g.) USNR, 1942-45. Mem. Assn. Bar City N.Y., Mfg. Chemists Assn., Am. Iron & Steel Inst. Clubs: Links (N.Y.C.); Sleepy Hollow Country (Scarborough-on-Hudson, N.Y.); Pacific-Union (San Francisco). Home: Todd Lane Briarcliff Manor NY 10510 Office: 150 E 42d St New York City NY 10017

DILLON, GERALD F., clergyman; b. Providence, R.I., Jan. 22, 1905; s. James Francis and Katherine Mary (O'Rourke) D.; student Providence (R.I.) Coll., 1922-24, LL.D., 1940; postgrad. Am. Coll., U. Louvain (Belgium), 1924-30; M.A., Catholic U. Am., Washington, D.C., 1931. Ordained priest of Roman Catholic Ch., 1930; asst. pastor St. Johns Ch., Providence, 1931-39; prof. Cath. Teachers Coll., Providence, summer sessions 1931—; dean of men Cath. U. Am., 1939-46, on leave of absence for naval service, 1942-45; vice rector Our Lady of Providence Sem., Warwick Neck, R.I., 1946; prof. chaplain Salve Regina Coll., Newport, R. I.; pastor St. Joseph's Ch., Newport. Served with U.S.N.R., 1942-45. Decorated Victory and Am. Theatre medals, Asiatic-Pacific Theater ribbon with seven stars, Philippine Liberation ribbon with two stars, Navy Unit Commendation and Commendation with two combat devices. Address: St Joseph's Ch Newport RI 02840

DILLON, JESSE WILLIAM, govt. ofcl.; b. Dillonsmill, Va., July 15, 1904; s. Dr. Charles Lewis and Janie Elizabeth (Goggin) D.; student Fork Union Mil. Acad.; LL.B., U. Richmond, 1931; m. Margaret Knight, May 30, 1931; children—Peter L. P., Margaret Burroughs (Mrs. Eugene G. Bowles, Jr.), Julie Maupin (Mrs. Antony M. DeVilbiss). Admitted to Va. bar; staff Dept. Taxation, Richmond, 1928-33; dist. counsel HOLC, 1933-34; supr. div. inheritance and gift taxes Commonwealth of Va., 1934-45, sec. to gov., 1945-47, sec. Commonwealth, 1945-47, state treas., 1947-57, chmn. compensation bd., 1955-57; mem. Va. Corp. Commn., 1957—, chmn., 1971—. Sec., Democratic Central Com. Va. Trustee U. Richmond, also vice rector; trustee Fork Union (Va.) Mil. Acad. Mem. Delta Theta Phi, Kappa Alpa, Omicron Delta Kappa. Methodist (steward). Club: Country of Virginia. Home: 5 Highland Rd Richmond VA 23229 Office: Blanton Bldg Richmond VA 23219

DILLON, JOHN ANDREW, Jr., univ. dean; b. Pawtucket, R.I., Sept. 24, 1923; s. John Andrew and Helen (Tiernan) D.; Sc.B. in Physics, Fordham U., 1947; Sc.M., Brown U., 1949, Ph.D., 1954; m. Mary Leona Naughton, Sept. 12, 1953; children—John Andrew III, Mary Elizabeth. Instr., Fairfield (Conn.) U., 1949-51, Providence Coll., 1951-52; research physicist Air Force, Cambridge (Mass.) Research Center, 1953-54; asst. prof. physics, asst. to dean coll., asso. prof. physics, prof., exec. officer dept. Brown U., 1954-66; vis. prof. R.I. Coll., 1960-61; resident fellow Pembroke Coll., 1960-66; prof. physics, dean Grad. Sch., U. Louisville, 1966—. Vis. prof. Cavendish Lab., Cambridge (Eng.) U., 1963. Counselor, Oak Ridge Asso. Univs., 1966—. Served with USAAF, 1943-46. Fellow Am. Phys. Soc., Am. Assn. Physics Tchrs.; mem. Am. Vacuum Soc. (sr., chmn. thin film div. 1966-67, chmn. edn. com. 1967—70), R.I. Acad. Scis. (v.p. 1966, exec. council 1963-66), Am. Inst. Physics (regional counselor 1963-66), Louisville C. of C., English Speaking Union, Monumental Brass Soc. (Eng.), Sigma Xi, Kappa Delta Pi. Editor: Jour. Thin Solid Films, 1966—. Contbr. articles to profl. jours. Home: 2540 Dundee Rd Louisville KY 40205

DILLON, JOHN FORREST, IV, lawyer; b. Alexander City, Ala., Nov. 15, 1930; s. John Forrest III and Virginia (Henderson) D.; B.S. in Law, U. Ala., 1953, J.D., 1954; m. Elizabeth Carrington Millar, Dec. 30, 1953; 1 dau., Elizabeth Breckinridge. Admitted to Ala. bar, 1954; asso. firm LeeMaistre, Clement & Gewin, Tuscaloosa, 1954; partner firm Dillon, Kelley & Barnes, and predecessor firm, Alexander City, 1958—, sr. partner, 1969—; trial counsel Central of Ga. Ry. Co. Past mem. exec. com. Ala. Jr. Bar Assn. Mem. Alexander City Lay Citizens Edn. Study Com.; adv. com. Russel Hosp., Alexander City. Served to 1st lt. AUS, 1954-57. Mem. Am., Ala., Tallapoosa bar assns., Am. Arbitration Assn., Ala. Trial Lawyers Assn., Ala. Def. Lawyers Assn., Alexander City C. of C. (past bd. dirs.), Phi Delta Phi, Phi Delta Theta. Democrat. Episcopalian (past sr. warden). Club: Willow Point Golf and Country (past pres., chmn. bd.) (Alexander City). Home: 903 Woodland Rd Alexander City AL 35010 Office: Wilbanks Bldg Alexander City AL 35010

DILLON, JOHN HENRY, cons. physicist; b. Ripon, Wis., July 10, 1905; s. Frank George and Hattie (Barnes) D.; A.B., Ripon Coll., 1927, Sc.D. (hon.), 1950; Ph.D., U. Wis., 1931; M.S. (hon.), Lowell Technol. Inst., 1951; D.Sc. (hon.), Southeastern Mass. U., 1971; m. Bernice Olmsted, June 18, 1935 (dec. Aug. 1960); m. 2d, Rena Quinn Perkson, Apr. 4, 1963; stepchildren—Howard N. Perkson, Pamela Perkson Brown. Physics research group Firestone Tire & Rubber Co., 1931-37, head physics div., 1937-45, asst. dir. research, 1945-46; dir. research Textile Found. and Textile Research Inst., 1946-51; dir. Textile Research Inst., Princeton, N.J., 1951-59, pres., 1959-70, hon. fellow, 1971; vis. lectr. Princeton, 1947-71, prof. dept. chem., 1952-71; cons. physicist, 1971—; lectr. Clemson U., 1971—. Chmn. Gordon Research Conf. Textiles, 1949; chmn. physicists group Nat. Acad. Sci.- NRC adv. panels to Nat. Bur. Standards, 1961-63. Trustee Phila. Coll. Textiles and Sci.; trustee Ripon Coll. Recipient Harold DeWitt Smith Meml. medal, 1955. Fellow Am. Phys. Soc. (chmn. div. high polymer physics 1944), The Textile Inst. (Eng.); mem. Am. Inst. Physics (gov. bd. 1957-59), Am. Assn. Textile Chemists and Colorists, Am. Assn. Textile Technologists, Am. Chem. Soc., Am. Soc. Testing Materials, Fiber Soc. (hon. mem.; pres. 1961-62), Soc. Rheology (pres. 1957- 59), Nat. Council Textile Edn. (pres. 1958-59), Soc. Chem. Industry Gt. Britain, Phi Beta Kappa, Sigma Xi. Club: Nassau. Author numerous articles in sci. and trade jours. Mem. editorial bd. Jour. Applied Polymer Sci., 1960-71. Holder U.S. and fgn. patents. Address: Bayshore Estates Bayview CT Route 2 Seneca SC 29678

DILLON, JOHN JOSEPH, lawyer; b. Indpls., Aug. 1, 1926; s. John J. and Margaret (Sweeney) D.; student Xavier U., 1949; LL.B., Ind. U., 1952; m. Anna C. Dean, Jan. 19, 1957; children—Ann Margaret, John Joseph, Denise Marie. Admitted to Ind. bar, 1952; formerly mem. firm Dulberger, Dillon, Bulen & Heeter, Indpls.; counsel Indpls. Legal Aid Soc., 1953-56; city atty. Indpls., 1956-64; atty. gen. Ind., 1965-69; mem. firm Dillon, Kelley, McCarty, Haramon & Cohen, Indpls. Pres. Marian Coll. Assos., Indpls., 1963. Bd. dirs. Indpls. Legal Aid Soc., 1963—, also pres. Vice chmn. bd. trustees Marian Coll. Served with USAAF, World War II. Mem. Am., Ind. bar assns., Lawyers Assn. Indpls., 500 Festival Assns., Ind. U. Law Sch., Indpls. Alumni Assn. (pres.), Aircraft Owners and Pilots Assn., Sigma Delta Kappa. Democrat. Home: 320 E Kessler Blvd Indianapolis IN 46220 Office: 120 E Market St Indianapolis IN

DILLON, NEAL, lawyer; b. Maxville, O., Jan. 5, 1925; s. Samuel H. and Annabelle (Wolfe) D.; student Ind. Tech. Coll., 1942-43; A.B., Ohio U., Athens, 1949; J.D. cum laude, Ohio State U., 1952; m. Fern Elizabeth Devol, June 30, 1944; children—Lisa Diane, Steven Matthew, Craig Knowlton. High sch. tchr., Murray City, O., 1944-45; admitted to Ohio bar, 1952; practiced in Cleve., 1952-53, Logan, 1953—; dir. Logan Broadcasting Co., Wanco Investments, Inc., Well Investments, Inc., Hayden Dillon, Inc. City solicitor, Logan, 1958-61. Chmn. bd. Hocking County chpt. A.R.C., 1957. Served with AUS, World War II. Mem. Am., Ohio, Hocking County bar assns., Am. Judicature Soc., Am. Trial Lawyers Assn., Hocking County Farm Bur., Order of Coif, Delta Theta Phi, Alpha Gamma Upsilon. Republican. Methodist (trustee). Kiwanian. Club: Logan Trade. Home: Route 2 Logan OH 43138 Office: 82 1/2 E Main St Logan OH 43138

DILLON, PAUL WASHINGTON, mfg. exec.; b. Sterling, Ill., June 3, 1883; s. Washington Moorehead and Sarah Jane (Martin) D.; student Shattuck Mil. Acad., Faribault, Minn., 1901-03; m. Crete Blackman, Nov. 16, 1904 (dec.); children—Crete Blackman (Mrs. John W. Bowman) (dec.), Margaret (Mrs. Goddard), Washington Martin. With Northwestern Steel & Wire Co. (formerly Northwestern Barb Wire Co.), dir., 1908—, pres., 1920-38, 40-51, treas. 1921-48, chmn. bd., 1938- -; dir. Parrish-Alford Fence & Machine Co., Northwestern Products Corp., Sterling, Illinois. Served as capt., U.S. Army, World War I. Presbyn. Clubs: Rock River Country (Sterling); Union League (Chgo.). Home: 1005 E 3d St Sterling IL 61081 Office: Northwestern Steel & Wire Co Sterling IL 61081

DILLON, RAY EARNEST, merchandising exec.; b. Sterling, Kan., July 30, 1897; s. John S. and Daisy (Hogsett) D.; student pub. schs.; m. Stella A. Schmitt, June 24, 1923; children—Ray Ernest, Richard W. With J.S. Dillion & Sons Stores Co., Inc. (co. name changed to Dillon Cos., Inc.), Hutchinson, Kan., 1921—, now chmn. bd.; dir. Hutchinson Nat. Bank & Trust Co. Pres. Super Market Inst., 1953-54; also dir. Served with 35th Div., U.S. Army in France, World War I. Mem. Nat. Assn. Food Chains (dir.). Home: 301 W 20th St Hutchinson KS Office: 2700 E 4th St Hutchinson KS 67501

DILLON, RAY EARNEST, Jr., supermarket exec.; b. Hutchinson, Kan., May 7, 1924; s. Ray Earnest and Stella A. (Schmitt) D.; student Kan. U.; m. Betty L. Lay, June 22, 1946; children—Diane, Ray Earnest III, Janet Lou. With J.S. Dillon & Sons Stores Co. (now Dillon Cos., Inc.), Hutchinson, 1946—, pres., 1962—. Mem. Kan. C. of C. (bd. dirs.). Home: 201 Kisiwa Hutchinson KS 67501 Office: 2700 E 4th St Hutchinson KS 67501

DILLON, RICHARD HUGH, author, librarian; b. Sausalito, Cal., Jan. 16, 1924; s. William T. and Alice M. (Burke) D.; A.A. with hon. mention, U. Cal. at Berkeley, 1943, A.B. with honors in History, 1948, M.A., 1949, B.S. in L.S., 1950; m. Barbara A. Sutherland, June 9, 1950; children—Brian, David, Ross. Head, Sutro Library, San Francisco, 1953—; tchr. summer sessions U. Cal. at Los Angeles, 1964, U. San Francisco, 1959—, U. Hawaii, 1962. Served with inf. AUS, World War II; ETO. Decorated Purple Heart; recipient awards of merit Cal. Hist. Soc., also Am. Assn. State and Local History for all-around research and publishing; Laura Bride Powers award for distinguished service to city of San Francisco, 1970. Mem. Western History Assn., Cal. Hist. Soc., Phi Beta Kappa. Author: Embarcadero (2d place nonfiction Phelan awards 1959), 1959; The Gila Trail, 1960; Shanghaiing Days, 1961; California Trail Herd, 1961; The Hatchet Men, 1962; Meriwether Lewis (Gold medal Commonwealth Club Cal. 1966), 1965; J. Ross Browne, 1965; The Legend of Grizzly Adams, 1966; Fool's Gold (silver medal Commonwealth Club Cal. 1967), 1967; Humbugs and Heroes, 1970. Home: 98 Alta Vista Av Mill Valley, CA 94941. Office: 2130 Fulton St San Francisco CA 94117

DILLON, RICHARD THOMAS, legal educator; b. Tampa, Fla., Jan. 7, 1927; s. Charles Ira and Mary Ellen (Moody) D.; B.S. cum laude, U. Tampa, 1953, L.H.D., 1969; J.D., Stetson U., 1957; LL.M., N.Y.U., 1961; m. Betty Vallejo, June 18, 1948; 1 dau., Brenda Jan. Admitted to Fla. bar, 1957; mem. faculty Stenotype Inst. Tampa, 1951-54, Fla. Central Coll., Tampa, 1954-57, U. Tampa, 1955-57; prof. law Stetson U., St. Petersburg, Fla., 1957—, dean, 1968—; lectr. in field. Mem. Com. 100, St. Petersburg. Bd. dirs. Nat. Police Resources Devel. Corp., Law Center Found, St. Petersburg; v.p. Walola Chapel and Retreat, Winter Haven, Fla. Served with USNR, 1944-46. Ford Found. fellow, 1961-63; recipient Distinguished Alumni award Stetson U., 1971. Mem. Am. Bar Assn., Fla. Bar, Am. Judicature Soc., Am. Assn. U. Profs., Am. Trial Lawyers Assn., Am. Acad. Polit. and Social Sci., Tau Kappa Epsilon, Phi Alpha Delta. Democrat. Baptist. Home: 620 63d St South St Petersburg FL 33707

DILLON, ROBERT E., corp. exec.; b. Titusville, Pa., Oct. 31, 1904; s. John T. and Catherine F. (Hanley) D.; student Amherst Coll.; m. Marion A. McNulty, June 29, 1926; children—Robert E., James M. Vice pres. Struthers Wells Corp., Warren, Pa.; pres., chmn. bd. Lake Erie Engring. Corp., Buffalo; chmn. United Steel of Am., Inc., N.Y.C., Mapes & Sprowl Steel Co., Union, N.J., Am. Steel & Aluminum Corp., Cambridge, Mass., also Hartford, Conn.; chmn. dirs. trust investment com., dir., mem. exec. com. Marine Midland Trust Co., Dunlop Tire & Rubber Corp. Mem. Temp. Emergency Relief Adminstrn. N.Y. State, 1930-33; chmn. Erie County Emergency Relief Bd., 1931-35; cons. Def. Plant Corp., Washington, 1942-43; mem. NLRB, 1942-45; adv. bd. Rochester Ordnance Dist. Mem. Buffalo council N.Y. State Commn. Human Rights; pres. Children's Aid Soc., Soc. Prevention Cruelty to Children Erie County, 1958-68; chmn. Buffalo finance com. Amherst Coll.; chmn. pub. relations Child Welfare League Am., Inc., N.Y.; trustee Millard Filmore Hosp., D'Youville Coll., Erie Community Coll., St. Bonaventure U.; finance bd. Children's Hosp., Buffalo. Pres. The Robert E. Dillon Found. Mem. Am. Ordnance Assn. (dir.), Archaeol. Inst. Am. (pres. Western N.Y.), Psi Upsilon. Clubs: Buffalo; Saturn, Metropolitan (N.Y.C.); Cumberland (Portland, Me.). Home: 82 Meadow Rd Buffalo NY 14216 Office: Marine Trust Bldg Buffalo NY 14203

DILLON, THOMAS CHURCH, advt. exec.; b. Seattle, Mar. 27, 1915; s. Thomas J. and Clarissa (Church) D.; student Harvard, 1933-36; m. Georgiana Adams, Nov. 8, 1939 (dec. May 1964); children—Thomas Adams, Victoria Caroline, George Anthony; m. 2d, Patricia Doran, 1965. With Batten, Barton, Durstine & Osborn, Inc., 1938—, successively copy writer, Mpls., creative head, San Francisco, Los Angeles, 1938- 48, v.p., 1948-59, mgr. Los Angeles office, 1957-58, treas., dir., 1958- -, exec. v.p., 1959-64, gen. mgr., 1962—, pres., 1964—, chief exec. officer, 1967—; v.p. treas. BBDO Internat., Inc., 1960-67, vice chmn., 1967-71, pres., chief exec. officer, 1971—. Bd. dirs. Advt. Research Found. Clubs: Advertising of N.Y., Economic, Harvard (N.Y.C.). Home: Sleepy Hollow Rd New Canaan CT 06840 Office: 383 Madison Av New York City NY 10017

DILLON, W. MARTIN, steel and wire mfg. exec.; b. Sterling, Ill., Mar. 19, 1910; s. Paul Washington and Crete (Blackman) D.; grad. Culver Mil. Acad., 1929; student Babson Inst., 1929-30; m. Helene Reynolds, June 20, 1931; children—Peter W., Margo (Mrs. James Lexvold), Gale (Mrs. Philip Inglee). Sec. Parrish Alford Fence & Machine Co., Rock Falls, Ill., 1930, pres., 1936—; asst. to pres. Northwestern Steel & Wire Co., 1939-48, 1948—, pres., 1951—; pres. Northwestern Products Co., 1950—. Mem. C. of C., Am. Iron and Steel Inst., Nat. Assn. Mfrs. Clubs: Union League (Chgo.); Rock River Country (Rock Falls, Ill.). Home: P O Box 537 Sterling IL 61081 Office: Northwestern Steel & Wire Co Sterling IL 61081

DILLON, WALTER STANLEY, newspaper editor; b. Reading, Pa., Feb. 23, 1893; s. William Henry and Margaret Amanda (McKinney) D.; grad. high sch.; m. Irene Catharine Leas, Jan. 28, 1929. Reporter, Reading Times, Reading Telegram, Reading Eagle, 1912-26; asst. city editor Reading Eagle, 1926-33, city editor, 1933-34, mng. editor, 1934-67, editor, 1967—. Home: 216 Amherst Av Lincoln Park PA 15207 Office: 30 N 4th St Reading PA 19601

DILLWAY, ROBERT B., government ofcl.; b. Washington, Nov. 10, 1924; s. Robert Gardiner and Ida Louise (Clark) D.; B.S. in Mech. Engring., B.S. in Math., U. Mich., 1945; M.S. in Physics, U. Ill., 1951,

Ph.D., 1953; m. Delva Dorothea Powell, Nov. 1, 1947 (dec. Mar. 1971); children—Ronald Clark, Blair Brewster, Robert Keith; m. 2d, Beverly A. Mercer, Aug. 14, 1971; stepchildren—Theodore A., Lauren D., Brian P. Engr., Carrier Corp., 1945-46; tchr. math U. Syracuse, 1945-46; engr. Research Assos., Inc., Washington, 1946-48; with Rocketdyne div. N. Am. Aviation, Inc., 1953-64, mgr. nuclear and elec. propulsion, 1957- 64; indsl. cons., nuclear propulsion project Los Alamos Sci. Lab., 1954- 55; corp. dir. research and tech., market planning N. Am. Aviation Inc., 1964-68; dep. dir. Office of Program Appraisal, also asst. to Sec. of Navy, U.S. Navy Dept., Washington, 1968-69; dep. comdr. for labs., Army Material Command, Washington, 1969; bd. dirs. H. A. Hill, Inc., 1965- -; extension prof., engring. dept. U. Cal. at Los Angeles, 1953-66. Mem. Nat. Aero. Assn. (mem. Timers chpt. bd. 1961-66, astronautics dir. 1961- 66, sr. v.p. 1966), Am. Soc. M.E. (chmn. aviation and space div. 1964, chmn. adv. com. 1966, pres. industry dept. 1970—), Am. Inst. Aeros. and Astronautics, Am. Arbitration Assn. Author: Introduction to Fluid Mechanics, 1965. Home: 3425 Barger Dr Falls Church VA 22044 also 20557 Wells Dr Woodland Hills CA 91364 Office: Army Material Command Washington DC 20315

DILS, ROBERT EARL, coll. dean; b. Miamisburg, O., July 6, 1919; s. Elmer Earl and Irene (Warner) D.; student Wittenberg Coll. (O.), 1937-42; B.S., Colo. A. and M. Coll., 1946, M.F., 1947; Ph.D., Mich. State U., 1952; m. Nedra Eve Daley, Dec. 24, 1942; children—Lynn Marie (Mrs. James N. Buchanan), Janet Carol, Kristin Jean. From instr. to asso. prof. Mich. State U., 1947-55; asso. prof. Sch. Natural Resources, U. Mich., 1955-58; prof. Colo. State U., Ft. Collins, 1958-69, asso. dean Coll. Forestry and Natural Resources, 1966-69, dean, 1969—; cons. FAO, El Salvador and Argentina, U. of Andes, Venezuela, U.S. AID, Taiwan; participant UN-USSR Seminar, Moscow; Antarctic visitor NSF. Del., Internat. Union Forest Research Orgns., Vienna, 1961; vis. scientist, lectr. Soc. Am. Foresters- NSF, 1960-61. Chmn. steering com. Future Ft. Collins, 1970—. Trustee Colo. State U. Research Found. Served with Weather Services, AUS, 1942- 46. Fulbright research scholar New Zealand, 1964-65. Fellow Soc. Am. Foresters, Soil Conservation Soc. Am.; mem. Am. Geophys. Union, Antarctica Soc., A.A.A.S., Sigma Xi. Contbr. articles profl. jours. Home: 705 Cherokee Dr Fort Collins CO 80521

DILTS, C. GORDON, lawyer; b. Winnipeg, Man., Can., Apr. 19, 1921; B.A., U. Man., 1942, LL.B., 1948; partner firm Thompson, Dewar, Sweatman, Winnipeg, Man. Lectr. Man. Law Sch., 1953—. Mem. Man. Law Soc., Man., Canadian bar assns. Office: 500 Montreal Trust Bldg Winnipeg 2 Manitoba Canada*

DI LUZIO, FRANK C., business exec. Vice pres. E.G. & G. Inc. Office: Crosby Dr Bedford MA 01730*

DILUZIO, NICHOLAS ROBERT, educator, physiologist; b. Hazleton, Pa., May 4, 1926; s. Nicholas and Carmela (Searfella) D.; B.S., U. Scranton, 1950; Ph.D. (USPHS fellow), U. Tenn., 1954; m. Gertrude Alma Dezangattis, June 10, 1948; children—Nicholas Mark, Tamara Ann, Daniel Val. Investigator, Dorn Lab. for Med. Research, Bradford, Pa., 1954, Oak Ridge Nat. Lab., 1956, U.S. Naval Radiol. Def. Lab., 1958; mem. faculty U. Tenn. Med. Units, Memphis, 1955-68, prof., 1962-64, chmn. physiology and biophysics dept., 1965-68; prof., chmn. dept. physiology Tulane U. Med. Sch., 1968—. Mem. Tenn. Adv. Com. on Atomic Energy, 1958-68; mem. sci. adv. bd. Nat. Council on Alcoholism, 1963-68. Recipient Lederle Med. Faculty award, 1958-61. Mem. A.A.A.S., Am. Physiol. Soc., Am. Heart Assn., Radiation Research, Transplantation Soc., Soc. for Exptl. Biology and Medicine, Reticuloendotheliel Soc. (pres. 1966-68). Editor: Advances in Experimental Medicine and Biology. Contbr. articles profl. jours. Patentee in field. Home: 732 Fairfield Av Gretna LA 70053 Office: Tulane U Sch Medicine New Orleans LA 70112

DILWORTH, JOSEPH RICHARDSON, investment banker; b. Hewlett, N.Y., June 9, 1916; s. Dewees Wood and Edith (Logan) D.; A.B., Yale, 1938, LL.B., 1942; m. Elizabeth Cushing, June 15, 1940; children—Joseph Richardson, Melissa McKay (Mrs. Herbert Gold), Alexandra Cushing, Charles Dewees. Admitted to Conn. bar, 1942; buying dept. Kuhn, Loeb & Co., 1946-51, partner, 1951- 58; with Rockefeller Family & Assos., 1958—; chmn. bd. Rockefeller Center, Inc.; dir. R.H. Macy & Co., Inc., Internat. Basic Economy Corp., Chase Manhattan Bank, Diamond Shamrock Corp., Chrysler Corp., Selected Risk Investments, Omega Fund Inc. Mem. Council Fgn. Relations. Successor trustee Yale Corp.; trustee Colonial Williamsburg Found.; pres., trustee Inst. for Advanced Study; trustee, v.p. Met. Mus. Art; trustee Rockefeller U., Carnegie Found. for Advancement Teaching. Served as lt. comdr. USNR, 1942-45. Mem. Am. Legion, Pilgrims of U.S., Phi Beta Kappa. Republican. Clubs: Links, Brook, Century Assn. (N.Y.C.); Beden Brook (Princeton). Home: 141 Hodge Rd Princeton NJ 08540 Office: 30 Rockefeller Plaza New York City NY 10020

DILWORTH, RICHARD HANSON, banker; b. Harrisonburg, Va., Oct. 24, 1927; s. Thomas Burt and Helen (Lewis) D.; B.A., U. Va., 1949; postgrad. Stonier Grad. Sch. Banking, Rutgers U., 1956-58; m. Joan Faith Parker, Sept. 26, 1953; children—Faith Parker, Jennifer Lewis, Richard Hanson. With United Va. Bank, Richmond, 1951—, exec. v.p. in charge comml. banking group, 1971—. Lectr. banking Am. Inst. Banking, Nat. Comml. Lending Sch., Va.-Md. Sch. Bank Mgmt., S.C. and W.Va. Banking Schs. Pres., United Givers Fund Richmond, 1970, Big Bros. Richmond, 1965; chmn. loan com. Va. Indsl. Devel. Corp., 1962-63. Bd. dirs. United Givers Fund Richmond, Richmond Area Community Council, United Community Funds and Councils Va. Served with USN, 1945-47. Recipient Meritorious Ser. award Richmond C. of C., 1960. Mem. Robert Morris Assos. (pres. Carolina-Virginias chpt. 1970-71), Navy League U.S., English Speaking Union. Republican. Episcopalian. Contbr. articles on credit adminstrn., statement analysis, loan procedure profl. jours., chpts. to textbooks. Home: 65 Old Mill Rd Richmond VA 23226 Office: 900 E Main St Richmond VA 23219

DILWORTH, RICHARDSON, lawyer; b. Pitts., Aug. 29, 1898; s. Joseph R. and Annie H. (Wood) D.; student St. Marks Sch., Southboro, Mass., 1911-17; A.B., Yale, 1921, LL.B. cum laude, 1926; m. Elizabeth Brockie, May 20, 1922; children—Patricia Anne, Brockie, Warden; m. 2d, Ann K. Hill, Aug. 6, 1935; children—Deborah, Richardson. Admitted to Pa. bar, 1927, since practiced in Phila.; partner Dilworth, Paxson, Kalish, Kohn & Dilks, 1938-55; specialist trial law; dist. atty. Phila., 1952-55. Dir. Lincoln Nat. Bank, Phila. Democratic candidate for gov. Pa., 1950, 62; mayor Phila., 1955-62 Pres., Phila. Bd Edn., pres. U.S. Conf. Mayors, 1960. Trustee Pa. State U.; bd. dirs. phila. Contributionship. Served with USMC, A.E.F., 1918, to maj. USMCR, World War II. Decorated Purple Heart, Silver Star. Recipient Phila. award, 1968. Member Phila. Bar Assn. (past gov., past chmn. disciplinary com.), Scroll and Key Soc., Order Coif, Delta Kappa Epsilon. Clubs: Philadelphia, Racquet (Phila.); Racquet and Tennis (N.Y.C.). Home: 225 E Washington Sq Philadelphia PA 19106

DIMAGGIO, FRANK LOUIS, educator; b. N.Y.C., Sept. 2, 1929; s. Serafino and Maria (Barbuto) DiM.; B.S., Columbia, 1950, M.S., 1951, Ph.D., 1954; m. Irene C. Koehn, Dec. 15, 1963; children—Samuel, Peter. Prof. civil engring. Columbia, 1956—; cons. in field, 1958—. Served with AUS, 1954-56. Mem. Am. Soc. Civil Engrs., Sigma Xi. Home: 138 Van Orden Av Leonia NJ 07605 Office: Dept Civil Engring and Engring Mechanics Columbia Univ New York City NY 10027

DIMAN, WILLIAM ALEXANDER, life ins. co. exec.; b. Greenwood, Miss., Mar. 31, 1917; s. Harry and Wheat (Burkhalter) D.; diploma Bentley Sch. Accounting, 1936-38; student Life Office Mgmt. Inst., 1948-53, Mass. Inst. Tech., 1958, Aspen Inst., 1968; m. Lisbeth H. Schafer, Sept. 2, 1939; children—Charles N., Alice B. (Mrs. Alexander H. Pratt, Jr.), Margaret C. (Mrs. John R. Sattelmair). Auditor, Charles F. Rittenhouse & Co., C.P.A.'s, Boston, 1938-42; with John Hancock Mut. Life Ins. Co., 1942—, controller, 1964—; dir. John Hancock Advisers, Inc., John Hancock Distbrs., Inc., John Hancock Realty Devel. Corp.; trustee Newton Savs. Bank. Alderman, City of Newton, Mass., 1952-55, 62-63. Treas., Rebecca Pomeroy Found.; trustee Newton Cemetery Corp. Served to lt. USNR, 1944-46. C.P.A., Mass. Fellow Life Office Mgmt. Assn.; mem. Am. Inst. C.P.A.'s, Financial Execs. Inst. (pres. Boston chpt.). Home: 645 Centre St Newton MA 02158 Office: 200 Berkeley St Boston MA 02117

DI MARCA-RELLI, CORRADO, see Marca-Relli, Corrado di.

DIMARCO, F.A., banker. Vice pres., cashier First Nat. Bank of Tampa (Fla.). Office: 414-16 Franklin St Tampa FL 33601*

DI MATTEO, DOMINICK, Jr., food. co. exec. Sr. v.p. Fisher Foods, Inc. Office: 5300 Richmond Rd Bedford Heights OH 44105*

DIMICHAEL, SALVATORE GEORGE, assn. exec., psychologist; b. N.Y.C., Apr. 21, 1914; s. George and Carmela (Pellettiere) DiM.; B.S. cum laude, Fordham Coll., 1935; M.A., Fordham U., 1939, Ph.D., 1943; m. Eleanor Marie Gasparovich, June 1, 1946; children—Nicholas James, Carmelita, Stephen M. Asst. dir., supr. teaching methods AAF Instrs. Sch., St. Louis, 1942-43; asst. prof., dir. tchr. tng. St. Louis U., 1943-44; cons., psychol. services Vocational Rehab. Adminstrn., U.S. Dept. Health, Edn. and Welfare, Washington, 1944-53, regional rep., 1957-66, regional asst. commr., 1966- 67; exec. dir. Inst. Crippled and Disabled, 1968—; lectr. psychology, supr. counsel-trainees Cath. U. Am., 1946-53; exec. dir. Nat. Assn. for Retarded Children, N.Y.C., 1954-57. Exec. sec. Nat. Psychol. Research Council for the Blind, 1949-53. Exec. com. Pres.' Com. Employment Handicapped. Recipient Family Action award Nat. Catholic Welfare Conf., 1955; Merit award Phi Mu Sigma, 1956; Encaenia award Fordham Coll., 1960. Diplomate Am. Bd. Examiners in Profl. Psychology. Fellow Am. Psychol. Assn. (pres. div. psychologists in rehab. 1961-62), Am. Assn. on Mental Deficiency; mem. Am. (pres. div. rehabilitation counseling 1957-58), D.C. (pres.) personnel and guidance assns., Am. Cath. Psychol. Assn. (pres. 1958-59), Nat. Vocational Guidance Assn. Author: Vocational Rehabilitation: AMajor Social Force, 1964. Mem. editorial adv. bd. Personnel and Guidance Jour., 1959-62, Jour. of Rehab., 1963-69. Home: 13-38 Parsons Blvd Whitestone, NY 11357. Office: 324 E 24th St New York City NY 10010

DIMKE, GERTRUDE, recording sec. Gen. Orgn. Christian Chs. Internat. Address: 221 Ohmer Av PO Box 19136 Indianapolis IN 46319*

DIMLER, ROBERT JULIUS, chem. researcher; b. Pekin, Ill., Sept. 28, 1914; s. Paul John and Amelia (Dietrich) D.; B.S., Bradley U., 1936; M.S., U. Wis., 1938, Ph.D., 1940; m. Elizabeth Ruth Dregne, June 23, 1941; children—Bruce G., Paul T., Steven R. Alumnae Research Found. fellow and scholar U. Wis., 1936-38, research asst. biochemistry, 1938-40, postdoctoral research asst., 1940-41; with Dept. Agr., 1941—. chief cereal properties lab. No. Marketing and Nutrition Research Div., 1960-64, dir. div., 1964—; parttime instr. carbohydrate chemistry Bradley U., 1947-63. Active local YMCA, Boy Scouts Am. Recipient Superior Service award Dept. Agr., 1962; Distinguished Alumnus award Bradley U., 1966. Mem. Am. Chem. Soc. (chmn. Peoria 1959), Am. Assn. Cereal Chemists, Sigma Xi, Phi Kappa Phi. Mem. United Ch. Christ. Rotarian. Contbr. articles in field. Home: 2532 N Rockwood Dr Peoria, IL 61604. Office; 1815 N University St Peoria IL 61604

DIMMOCK, DAVID LACKLAND, advt. exec.; b. N.Y.C., Apr. 3, 1930; s. Marion Stuart and Marian (Winstead) D.; grad. Phillips Exeter Acad., 1948; B.A. in Econs., Princeton, 1952; m. Martha V.A. Powell, May 10, 1958; children—David Lackland, Andrew Stuart, Kate Van Antwerp. With Compton Advt. Inc., N.Y.C., 1955—, sr. v.p., 1968—. Mgr., New Canaan (Conn.) Boys' Baseball Team; mem. exec. com. Princeton Class of 1952. Served with USNR, 1952-54. Mem. Phi Beta Kappa. Clubs: Princeton (N.Y.C.); Field (New Canaan). Home: 156 Parish Rd New Canaan CT 06840 Office: 625 Madison Av New York City NY 10022

DIMOCK, EDWARD JORDAN, judge; b. Elizabeth, N.J., Jan. 4, 1890; s. George Edward and Elizabeth (Jordan) D.; student Pingry Sch., Elizabeth, N.J., 1901-06; A.B., Yale, 1911; hon. mem. Princeton, 1910; LL.B., Harvard, 1914; m. Constance Bullard, June 20, 1912; children—Constance D. (Mrs. Frank H. Ellis), Mary D. (Mrs. Mary D. Robbins), Elizabeth D. (Mrs. William B. Ryan), Lucy D. (Mrs. Lieberfeld), Emily D. (Mrs. Ignatius G. Mattingly). Admitted to N.Y. bar 1914; mem. law firm Hawkins, Delafield & Longfellow, N.Y.C., 1918-41; state reporter editing ofcl. law reports State N.Y., Albany, 1942-45; chmn. appeal bd. Office Contract Settlement, Washington, 1945-48, mem. appeal bd., 1948-51; U.S. dist. judge So. N.Y., 1951-61, sr. dist. judge, 1961-70. Lectr. law municipal corps. Yale Law Sch., 1941-46. Asso. fellow Berkeley Coll., Yale. Chmn. joint com. N.Y.C. Bar Assns., 1937-39, Yale Alumni U. Fund, 1938-40; rep. U.S. Dist. Cts. 2d Circuit on Jud. Conf., 1957-59. Pres. emeritus Miss Hall's Sch., Pittsfield, Mass. Mem. Assn. Bar City N.Y. (exec. com. 1938-42), N.Y. State, Fed., Sullivan County, Am. Ho. of Dels. 1943, bd. editors Jour. 1944-68, bd. govs. 1948-51) bar assns., Am. Law Inst. (mem. council), N.Y. County Lawyers Assn., Psi Upsilon. Democrat. Episcopalian. Clubs: Century, Yale Round Table (N.Y.C.), Elihu, Elizabethan (Yale). Home: Hartwood R 1 Monticello NY 12701

DIMOCK, GEORGE EDWARD, Jr., educator, Classicist; b. New Haven, Dec. 19, 1917; s. George Edward and Imogen (Kinsey) D.; grad. Andover Acad., 1935; A.B., Yale, 1939, M.A., 1940, Ph.D., 1949; m. Mary Teleki Mesier, July 2, 1946; children—George Edward, Peter Henry, Bridget. With Hartwood Syndicate (N.Y.), 1946-48; instr., then asst. prof. Yale, 1948-55; mem. faculty Smith Coll., 1955—, prof. Classics, 1961—. Am. Council Learned Socs. fellow, 1960; Guggenheim fellow, 1964. Mem. Am. Philol. Assn., Classical Assn. New Eng. Author articles. Home: 62 Revell Av Northampton, MA 01060.

DIMOCK, MARSHALL EDWARD, educator; b. San Bernadino, Cal., Oct. 24, 1903; s. Milton Edward and Anne (Behrens) D.; B.A., Pomona Coll., Claremont, Cal., 1925; Ph.D., Johns Hopkins, 1928; m. Lucy Butler Stotesbury, Sept. 14, 1926 (dec.); children—Milton Marshall, Mark, Marianne; m. 2d, Gladys Gouverneur Ogden, June 29, 1940; 1 son, Davis Ludlow. Instr. polit. sci., U. Cal. at Los Angeles, 1928-30, asst. prof. 1930-32; asso. prof. pub. adminstrn., U. of Chgo., 1932-41; lectr. Sch. of Pub. Law and Administrn., N.Y. U., 1941-44, prof., head of govt. dept., 1955-62; 2d asst. sec. of labor, 1938-40; asso. commr., Immigration and Naturalization Service, Dept. of Justice, 1940-42; dir. Recruitment and Manning Orgn. and asst. dept. war shipping adminstr., 1942-44; prof. polit. sci., Northwestern U., 1944-1948; rep. tech. assistance bd., UN (Turkey), 1953-54; co.-dir. Pub. Adminstrn. Inst. for Turkey and Middle East, 1953-54; cons. Adminstrv. Staff Coll., Eng., 1954; Ford vis. prof. pub. adminstrn. Internat. Christian U., Tokyo, 1966-67; vis. prof. U. Va., Mich., P.R., Carleton Coll., U. Ankara, Fla. State U., Adminstrv. Staff Coll. (Eng.), U. Colo., Indian Inst. Pub. Adminstrn. Fellow Social Sci. Research Council, 1932-33. Made studies for Sec. of War on Panama Canal enterprises and inland waterway transp., 1933-35; cons. Nat. Resources Com., 1935-39; chmn. Sec. of Labor's Commn. on Immigration Adminstrn., 1938-39; cons. War Department, 1944, Gen. Accounting Office, 1946-48; office of Sec. of Def., 1948- 49. Mem. Vt. State Legislature, 1949-50. Fellow (council mem. 1955- 59) A.A.A.S.; mem. Internat. Inst. Adminstrv. Scis., Royal Inst. Pub. Adminstrn. (London), Internat., Am. polit. sci. assns., Unitarian Universalist Assn. (moderator 1961-64), Am. Soc. Pub. Adminstrn., Soc. for Advancement of Mgmt. (pres. Washington Chapt., 1941-42; nat. dir. 1942-43; nat. v.p. 1945-46), Am. Econ. Assn., Pi Sigma Alpha (nat. pres. 1962-64). Dir., mem. exec. com. United Seamen's Service (chmn. 1946-56). Pres. Shinner Found., 1947-50. Unitarian. Rotarian. Author: several books; later ones: (with Gladys Ogden Dimock) American Government in Action, 1951; Business and Government, 1957; Free Enterprise and the Administrative State, 1951; (with Gladys Dimock) Pub. Administration, 4th edit., 1969. A Philosophy of Administration, 1958; Administrative Vitality, 1959; The New American Political Economy, 1962; Creative Religion, 1963; The Japanese Technocracy, 1968. Editor Goals for Political Science, 1951. Home: Scrivelsby Bethel VT 05032

DIMOCK, ROSS ALBERT, govt. ofcl.; b. Stanley, Wis., July 11, 1917; s. Albert and Maude (Covert) D.; student U. Ida., 1935; m. Ellen Marie Scott, Sept. 30, 1938; children—Roy Scott, Mary Ellen (Mrs. Lawrence Schaad), Nancy Ann, Richard Ross. With Dept. Agr., 1937—, asst. dir. sales Fed. Crops Ins. Corp., 1956-61, dir. sales mgmt., 1961—. Active local Boy Scouts Am., YMCA. Served with USNR, 1946-47. Recipient Outstanding Performance award Dept. Agr., 1955, 56. Presbyn. (past trustee). Home: 13104 Jingle Lane Silver Spring, MD 20906. Office: South Agr Bldg Washington DC 20250

DIMOND, JOHN HENRY, state justice; b. Valdez, Alaska, Dec. 28, 1918; s. Anthony Joseph and Dorothea Frances (Miller) D.; B.Applied Chemistry, Cath. U. Am., 1941, LL.B., 1948; m. Roberta Gene Dooley, Jan. 11, 1946; children—Anthony Joseph, Patricia Helen, Timothy Robert. Admitted to Alaska bar, 1948; asst. atty. gen. Territory Alaska, 1949-52; gen. practice, Juneau, 1953- 59; justice Supreme Ct. Alaska, 1959—. Served with AUS, 1942-46; PTO. Decorated Silver Star, Purple Heart, Bronze Star. Mem. Am. Judicature Soc. Democrat. Catholic. Elk. Home: 506 5th St Douglas AK 99824 Office: Pouch U State Capitol Juneau AK 99801

DIMPFL, RICHARD ALBERT, airline exec.; b. Rochester, N.Y., July 3, 1917; s. Albert and Irene (Virkus) D.; B.A., Swarthmore Coll., 1939; M.B.A., U. Chgo., 1949; postgrad. Loyola U., Chgo., 1949-51; J.D., U. Md., 1953; m. Lorraine Marie Smith, Feb. 13, 1943. Admitted to Colo. bar, 1958; U.S. Dist. Ct. Colo., Supreme Ct. U.S.; with United Air Lines, Chgo., 1947—, asst. to exec. v.p., 1966-68, asst. sec. corp., 1968-69, sec. corp., 1970—; lectr. William Rainey Harper Coll., Palatine, Ill. Served to col. USAAF, 1942-47, USAF, 1951-53. Decorated Commendation medal. Mem. Am. Bar Assn., Am. Soc. Corporate Secs., Phi Delta Theta. Home: 4 Barrow-on-Duxbury Rolling Meadows IL 60008 Office: PO Box 66100 Chicago IL 60666

DINBERGS, ANATOL, Latvian fgn. service officer; b. Riga, Latvia, Mar. 3, 1911; s. Alfred and Marie (Iocz) D.; LL.M., U. Latvia, 1936; Ph.D., Georgetown U., 1953; m. Ruth Bauer, June 10, 1949; children—Anatol Alfred, Andrew M. Joined Latvian fgn. service, 1932; sec. legal dept. Ministry Fgn. Affairs, 1934- 37; Latvian vice consul, N.Y.C., 1937-41; attache Latvian embassy, Washington, 1941-48, 1st sec., 1954, counselor, 1955-70, charge d'affaires, 1970—. Home: Office: Latvian Legation Washington DC 20011

DINCE, ROBERT REUBEN, educator; b. N.Y.C., Dec. 27, 1924; s. Robert R. and Irene (Hess) D.; B.S., Rutgers U., 1945; M.A., U. Cal. at Los Angeles, 1950; Ph.D., Cornell U., 1960; m. Miriam Konvitz, May 23, 1947; 1 dau., Anna Katherine. Jr. exec. textile industry, 1946-50; instr. Cornell U., 1950-53; asst. prof. U. Ga., Athens, 1953-60, asso. prof., 1960-63, prof., head dept. banking and finance, 1963—. Regional econ. adviser, 6th nat. bank region, comptroller of currency Treasury Dept.; econ. cons. Nat. Broiler Marketing Assn. Served with AUS, 1943. Ford Found. grantee, 1960, 61, 63, 66. Mem. Am., So. (pres. 1970) Finance Assns., Am., So. econ. assns. Club: Classic City Tennis (Athens). Asso. editor So. Jour. of Bus. Contbr. articles to profl., sci. jours. Home: 323 Riverview Rd Athens GA 30601

DINE, JIM, painter; b. Cin., June 16, 1935; ed. U. Cin., Boston Museum Sch.; B.F.A., Ohio U. Tchr. Yale, 1965; prod. Happenings, including Car Crash, 1960; exhibited in one-man shows since 1959, including N.Y.C., Milan, Brussels, Paris; exhibited in groups shows Venice, London, Dallas, Buenos Aires, Phila., Pasadena, The Hague, Tokyo, Buffalo, Stockholm, Chgo., London, N.Y.C.; represented in permanent collections Brandeis U., Mus. Modern Art, Guggenheim Mus., Albright Mus., N.Y.U., others. Artist in residence Oberlin Coll., 1965, Cornell U., 1966-67; instr. Royal Coll. Art, London, 1967-68. Address: care Sidney Janis Gallery 15 E 57th St New York City NY 10022

DINEEN, ROBERT EMMET, lawyer; b. Syracuse, N.Y., Aug. 12, 1903; s. Laurence and Mary (Donaber) D.; certificate in law, Syracuse U., 1924; LL.D., Syracuse U., 1966; m. Carolyn Bareham, Apr. 27, 1937; children—Carolyn, Kathryn, Robert E. II. Claim and legal dept. Aetna Life Ins. Co., Aetna Casualty & Surety Co., Syracuse, N.Y., 1924-25, Lumber Mut. Casualty Co., Saranac Lake, N.Y., 1925-26; admitted to N.Y. bar, 1926, Wis. bar, 1951; asso. Bond, Schoeneck & King, Syracuse, 1926- 43, mem. firm, 1934-43; supt. ins. N.Y. State, 1943-50; former pres., chmn. and chief exec. officer Northwestern Mut. Life Ins. Co., Milw., 1950-68. Mem. Nat. Assn. Ins. Commrs. (pres. 1946-47, cons. 1968—), 1968— Am., Wis. bar assns., Phi Delta Phi. Home: 3909 N Murray Milwaukee WI 53211 Office: 633 W Wisconsin Av Milwaukee WI 53203

DINERMAN, HELEN SCHNEIDER, sociologist; b. N.Y.C., Dec. 25, 1920; d. Maurice and Lillian (Blau) Schneider; A.B., Hunter Coll., 1940; M.A., Columbia, 1948; m. James Dinerman, May 20, 1945; children—Robert, Alice. Analyst for the OWI, 1942-44; with Bur. Applied Social Research, Columbia, 1944-47; sci. dept. Am. Jewish Com., 1947-48; chmn. Internat. Research Assos., Inc.; dir. Internat. Research Assos. Compania Anonima (Venezuela), 1957. Mem. World (past officer), Am. (past officer) assns. pub. opinion research, Soc. Psychol. Study Social Issues, Am. Sociol. Soc., Phi Beta Kappa.

Author: The New Men of Power (with Mills and Schneider), 1949; also articles Public Opinion Quarterly, chpt. Research for Action, chpt. The Corporation and Its Publics. Home: 179 E 70th St New York City NY 10021 Office: 1270 Av of the Americas New York City NY 10020

DINGELL, JOHN DAVID, Jr., congressman; b. Colorado Springs, Colo., July 8, 1926; s. John D. and Grace (Bigler) D.; B.S. in Chemistry, Georgetown U., 1949, LL.B., 1952; m. Helen Patricia Henebry, June 25, 1952; children—John David III, Christopher, Jeanne Patricia, Jennifer Eilen. Park ranger U.S. Dept. Interior, 1948-52; admitted to D.C. bar, 1952, admitted Mich. bar, 1953; research asst. U.S. Dist. Judge Levin, 1952-53; asst. pros. atty., Wayne County (Mich.), 1953-55; mem. 84th to 88th Congresses, 15th Dist. Mich., mem. 89th to 92d Congresses, 16th Dist. Mich., mem. migratory bird conservation commn. Served as 2d lt. inf., AUS, 1945-46. Mem. Nat. Rifle Assn. (dir.), Delta Theta Phi. Home: Dearborn MI 48121 Office: Ho of Reps Washington DC 20515

DINGEMAN, JAMES HERBERT, indsl. exec.; b. Detroit, July 31, 1917; s. Harry J. and Bessie (Schafer) D.; LL.B., U. Detroit, 1939; m. Ann R. McGillivray, Apr. 26, 1941; children—Patricia D. (Mrs. Thomas J. Moran), James Herbert, Peter J., Mary Ann. Admitted to Mich. bar, 1939; practice in Detroit, 1939-43; mem. firm Dingeman & DeGalan, 1939-43; legal adviser Fed.-Mogul Corp., Detroit, 1943-46, asst. dir. indsl. relations, 1946-60, dir. orgn. planning exec. devel., 1960-68, sec. 1965-68; v.p. legal and corp. planning affairs, sec. Parke, Davis & Co., 1968-70, group v.p. legal and corp. planning affairs, sec., 1970—, dir. 1970—; v.p. Warner-Lambert Co., 1970—. Instr. Detroit Coll. Law, 1940, Walsh Inst. Accountancy, 1945. Founder Little League Baseball, Grosse Pointe Farms, 1952, pres., 1954- 55; area chmn. United Fund, 1965. Mem. Republican Finance Com., 1950-63; councilman, Grosse Pointe Farms, 1966—, mayor pro-tem, 1969. Mem. Am., Mich., Detroit bar assns., N.A.M., Assn. Gen Counsel, Am. Soc. Corporate Secs., Am. Mgmt. Assn., Greater Detroit C. of C., Lambda Sigma (past nat. pres.), Delta Theta Phi. Clubs: Detroit, Detroit Country, Cardinal (Detroit); Otsego Ski (Gaylord, Mich.); Detroit Athletic. Home: 4 Radnor Circle Grosse Pointe Farms MI 48236 Office: PO Box 118 GPO Detroit MI 48232

DINGLE, JOHN FREDERICK, mfg. co. exec.; b. Irvington, N.J., Apr. 2, 1923; s. Charles W. and Dorothy L. (White) D.; B.Sc., Rutgers U., 1943; M.B.A. with distinction, Harvard, 1947; m. Barbara Ann Russell, Apr. 10, 1960; children—Laurie Jane, Robert John, Peter Charles, Sarah Ann, Russell Earl, Jonathan. With Norton Co., Worcester, Mass., 1947—, asst. controller, 1954-63, controller, 1964-71, v.p., controller, 1971—. Served to lt. USNR, 1943-46. Mem. Nat. Assn. Accountants, Financial Execs. Inst., Phi Beta Kappa, Alpha Sigma Phi. Home: 7 Wyndhurst Dr Holden MA 01520 Office: 1 New Bond St Worcester MA 01606

DINGLE, JOHN HOLMES, physician, educator; b. Cooperstown, N.D., Nov. 24, 1908; s. John Geech and Harriet (Holmes) D.; Ph.C., B.S., U. Wash., 1930, M.S., 1931; Sc.D., Johns Hopkins, 1933; M.D., Harvard (James Jackson Cabot fellow 1936-39, Francis Weld Peabody fellow in medicine 1940-42), 1939; m. Doris V. Brown, Jan. 18, 1946; children—Eva M., David R. Asst., McDermott Found., U. Washington, 1929-31; asst. bacteriologist State Dept. Health, Md., 1933; bacteriologist Upjohn Co., Kalamazoo, 1933-35; house officer in medicine Infants and Children's Hosp., Boston, 1939-40; asst. depts. of medicine, bacteriology and immunology Harvard, 1940-41, instr. bacteriology and immunology, 1940-42, instr. dept. medicine, 1941-42, asso. medicine, 1942-46; asst. physician Boston City Hosp., 1941-46; prof. preventive medicine Sch. Medicine, Western Res. U., 1946—, asso. prof. medicine, 1946-65, prof. medicine, 1965—, asso. physician Univ. Hosps., Cleve., 1946-68, physician, 1968—. Cons. to Sec. of War on epidemeic diseases, 1941-44; mem. Commn. on Acute Respiratory Diseases, Armed Forces Epidemiol. Bd., 1942-55, dir., 1942-55, asso. mem., 1955—; mem. Armed Forces Epidemiol. Bd., 1951-67, pres., 1955-57; mem. bd. cons. med. and pub. health Rockefeller Found., 1952-55; mem. Cleve. Health Council, 1946-68. Served from maj. to lt. col. M.C., AUS, 1944-46. Decorated Legion of Merit; recipient Albert Lasker award, 1959; James D. Bruce Meml. award; Outstanding Civilian Service award Dept. Army, 1967. Mem. A.A.A.S., Am. Assn. Immunologists (v.p. 1956, pres. 1957), Am. Soc. Microbiology, Assn. Tchrs. Preventive Medicine, Am. Fedn. Clin. Research, Am. Soc. Clin. Investigation, Soc. Exptl. Biology and Medicine, Assn. Am. Physicians, Central Soc. for Clin. Research (v.p. 1958, pres. 1959), Am. Epidemiol. Soc. (pres. 1958), Am. Clin. and Climatol. Assn., Harvey Soc., Nat. Acad. Scis., Phi Beta Kappa, Sigma Xi, Alpha Omega Alpha. Home: 2344 Roxboro Rd Cleveland Heights, OH 44106. Office: 2064 Abington Rd Cleveland OH 44106

DINGLEDY, PAUL GEORGE, pub. relations exec.; b. Youngstown, O., Oct. 25, 1903; s. George L. and Antonia (Boehme) D.; B.S., U. Ill., 1925, M.S., 1929; m. Martha Beadel, Sept. 14, 1935 (dec. 1966); children—Frances (Mrs. Robert R. Barker), Edward B., Louise O. (Mrs. David R. Rose), Maryann (Mrs. Geoffrey K. Barnes); m. 2d, La Verne Haddad, Nov. 26, 1969. Test, Pa.-Ohio Power & Light Co., 1925-26; sales engr. Pa. Power Co., 1926-28, asst. to v.p., gen. mgr., 1931-50, asst. to pres., 1950-53, dir., 1950-62, v.p., 1953-62; sales engr. Ohio Edison Co., 1929-41, v.p. 1962-70, ret., 1970; pub. relations counselor, 1970—. Pres. Community Chest New Castle, Pa., 1947-51, Greater New Castle Assn., 1953-54. Mem. Alpha Delta Phi, Tau Beta Pi. Republican. Presbyn. Club: City (Akron). Home: 2344 Banbury Rd Akron OH 44313

DINGMAN, MAURICE J., Cath. bishop Diocese Des Moines. Address: PO Box 1816 180 37th St Des Moines IA 50312*

DINGMAN, MICHAEL DAVID, holding co. exec.; b. New Haven, Sept. 29, 1931; s. James Everett and Amelia (Williamson) D.; student U. Md.; m. Jean Hazlewood, May 16, 1953; children—Michael David, Linda Channing, James Clifford. Gen. partner Burnham & Co., investment bankers, N.Y.C., 1964-71; pres., dir., chief exec. officer Equity Corp., N.Y.C., 1970—; chief exec. officer, dir. Bell Intercontinental Corp., N.Y.C., 1970, pres., 1970-71, chmn. bd., 1971—; pres. Frye Industries, Inc., 1970-71, dir., 1970—, chmn. bd., 1971—; dir. United Bd. & Carton Corp., Wheelabrator Corp., Allied Equities Corp., Chappaqua Oil Corp., Temple Industries, Inc., Neonex Internat., Ltd. (Can.), Wheelabrator-Allevard (France). Mem. I.E.E.E. Clubs: Recess, Board Room (N.Y.C.); Basin Harbor (Vt.); Mt. Kisco (N.Y.) Country. Home: 55 Cowdin Circle E Chappaqua NY 10514 Office: 299 Park Av New York City NY 10017

DINGMAN, REED OTHELBERT, surgeon, educator; b. Rockwood, Mich., Nov. 4, 1906; s. Wilbert Alva and Gertrude (Scherer) D.; A.B., U. Mich., 1928, D.D.S., 1931, M.S., 1932, M.D., 1936. m. Thelma Agnes Muir, Nov. 24, 1932; children—David Lyons, Sue Muir, Sally Fae. Oral and plastic surgeon Gelsinger Meml. Hosp., Danville, Pa., 1937-39; pvt. practice oral and plastic surgery, Washington, 1939-40; asst. prof. oral surgery U. Mich., 1940-45, asso. prof., 1945-65, prof. surgery, head sect. plastic surgery Med. Sch., 1965—; head sect. plastic surgery VA Hosp., Ann Arbor, Mich.; chief dept. plastic surgery St. Joseph Mercy Hosp., Ann Arbor. Diplomate Am. Bd. Oral Surgery, Am. Bd. Plastic Surgery (chmn. 1964-65). Fellow A.C.S., Am. Coll. Dentists; mem. Am. Dental Assn., A.M.A., Am. Soc. Oral Surgeons, Am. Soc. Plastic and Reconstructive Surgery (pres., dir. found., pres. 1963-64), Am., Western surg. socs., Am. Assn. Plastic Surgery, Am. Cleft Palate Soc., Am. Soc. Maxillo-facial Surgeons, Am. Soc. Trauma. Club: Barton Hills Country. Author: (with Paul Natvig) Surgery of Facial Fractures; co-author: Plastic Surgery. Editor: Jour. Oral Surgery 1948-52; asso. editor Jour. Plastic and Reconstructive Surgery. Contbr. articles to med., dental publs. Home: 1029 Chestnut Rd Ann Arbor MI 48104 Office: 221 N Ingalls St Ann Arbor MI 48104

DINGMAN, ROY ALBERT, former mfg. exec.; b. Plymouth, Wis., Nov. 13, 1904; s. Buel H. and Carolyn (Suhrke) D.; B.A., U. Wis., 1928; m. Garnett Enarson, Aug. 22, 1929 (dec. June 1969); 1 son, Douglas A.; m. 2d, Clara Pollock, May 16, 1970. Vice pres. indsl. relations Commonwealth Edison Co., Chgo., 1928-48; dir. indsl. relations Weyerhaeuser Co., 1948-56; v.p. indsl. relations A.O. Smith Corp., Milw., 1956-66, v.p. corporate relations, 1966-70. Vice pres., dir. Wis. Bd. Vocational, Tech. and Adult Edn., 1968-70; treas., dir. Wis. Higher Ednl. Aids Bd., 1968-70; dir. Wis. Coordinating Council for Higher Edn., 1968-70; bd. dirs. United Community Fund, Milw., 1966-70. Bd. dirs., pres. Milw. Urban League, 1960-66; v.p. bd. dirs. Wis. Council of Safety, 1968-70. Clubs: Milw. Country, University (Milw.); Union League (Chgo.). Home: 2806 W Magee Rd Tucson AZ 85704

DINGMAN, WILLIAM ELLSWORTH, banker; b. Grand Rapids, Mich., Jan. 4, 1898; s. William Ellsworth and Anna (Bradley) D.; student Ferris Inst., Big Rapids, Mich., 1915-16, 18- 19; m. Jean Johnson, Aug. 5, 1922 (dec. Mar. 1968); m. 2d, Elizabeth McKnight, Apr. 19, 1969. Cashier, Bank of Commerce, Hamtramck, Mich., 1924-30, dir., 1926—, v.p., cashier, 1930-43, exec. v.p., 1943-54, pres., 1954-67, chmn. bd., cons., 1967—. Vice pres., treas., bd. dirs. Hamtramck Bd. Commerce; treas., bd. dirs. United Community Services. Mem. Am. (past com. chmn.), Mich. (past com. chmn.) bankers assns., Newcomen Soc. Kiwanian. Clubs: Red Run Golf (Royal Oak, Mich.); Economic, Recess (Detroit). Home: 641 Dewey St Birmingham MI 48009 Office: 11300 Jos Campau St Hamtramck MI 48212

DINIELLI, NICHOLAS ANTHONY, canteen co. exec.; b. Jersey City, Apr. 4, 1930; s. Felix and Josephine (Rella) D.; B.B.A., Pace Coll., 1952; M.B.A., Rutgers U., 1962; m. Jeanne Frances Elphinstone, Oct. 14, 1951; children—Jacqueline, Constance, Philip. With budget and financial analysis dept. Getty Oil Co., N.Y.C., 1952-61; mgr. accounting, taxes, consolidations, ins. Fed. Electric Corp., Paramus, N.J., 1962-67; mgr. financial controls ITT World Hdqrs., N.Y.C., 1967-70; controller Canteen Corp., subsidiary ITT, Chgo., 1970—; lectr. corporate accounting Upsala Coll., East Orange, N.J., 1965-67. Served with USNR, 1947-53. Mem. Financial Execs. Inst. Home: 1315 N Chestnut Av Arlington Heights IL 60004 Office: Canteen Corp Merchandise Mart Chicago IL 60654

DININ, BENJAMIN GEORGE, physician, hosp. adminstr.; b. N.Y.C., Dec. 29, 1909; s. Louis and Rebecca (Edison) D.; A.B., U. Ala., 1930; M.D., Duke, 1933; m. Isabelle Louise Long, Dec. 19, 1941; children—James D., John R. Intern in internal medicine Duke Hosp., Durham, N.C., 1933-34, in obstetrics and gynecology N.Y. Hosp., N.Y.C., 1934-35, in pediatrics Jewish Hosp., Bklyn., 1935-36; sr. resident communicable diseases Kingston Av. Hosp., Bklyn., 1936-40, acting dep. med. supt. 1936-40, dep. med. supt., 1947-49; exec. physician Triboro Hosp., Jamaica, N.Y., 1940-41; dep. med. supt. City Hosp., Welfare Island, N.Y.C., 1941-47; med. supt. Cumberland Hosp., Bklyn., 1949-54, Met. Hosp., N.Y.C., 1954-57; gen. med. supt. N.Y.C. Dept. Hosps., 1957-59; med. dir. Grasslands Hosp., Valhalla, N.Y., 1959—; commr. Dept. Hosps., Westchester County, 1966—; lectr. Sch. Pub. Health and Adminstrv. Medicine, Columbia, 1959—. Mem. Westchester County Com. on Alcoholism, Westchester County Com. on Narcotics; hosp. rep. Westchester Council Social Agys. Bd. dirs. Westchester Heart Assn., Tb and Respiratory Disease Assn. Lower Hudson Valley; bd. mgrs. Westchester County Dept. Labs., 1959—, Bellevue Hosp. Schs. Nursing, 1957-59. Served to maj., M.C., AUS, 1942-46. Diplomate Nat. Bd. Med. Examiners. Fellow Am. Pub. Health Assn.; mem. A.M.A., N.Y. State (Mem. council com. on hosp. and profl. relations), Westchester County (hosp. com.) med. socs. Am. Coll. Hosp. Adminstrs., Am., N.Y. State, Westchester County (past pres.) hosp. assns., Duke Med. Alumni Assn. Mason. Home: Hammond House Rd Valhalla, NY 10595. Office: Grasslands Hospital Valhalla NY 10595

DINITZ, SIMON, educator; b. N.Y.C., Oct. 29, 1926; s. Morris and Dinah (Schulman) D.; student City Coll., N.Y., 1943-44; B.A., Vanderbilt U., 1947; M.A., U. Wis., 1949, Ph.D., 1951; m. Mildred H. Stern, Aug. 20, 1949; children—Jeffrey, Thea, Risa. Successively scholar, teaching asst., research asst., fellow U. Wis., 1947-50; mem. faculty Ohio State U., 1951—, prof. sociology, 1958—, research asso. psychiatry, 1956—; vis. lectr. U. Wis., summers 1951, 52; vis. prof. U. So. Cal., summer 1968, U. Wis., summer 1969, Tel Aviv U., Tel Aviv, Israel, 1970; cons. UN Social Def. Research Inst., Rome, Italy, 1970. Mem. Mayor Columbus Faculty Com. Urban Disorders, 1967-68, Ohio Tech. Adv. Com. Aging, 1967—, Ohio Task Force Community Mental Health, 1965- 66; faculty Hillel Found., Ohio State U., 1967—. Trustee Alvis House, Buckeye Boys Ranch, Columbus Community Mental Health Center. Served with USNR, 1945-46. Recipient Hofheimer prize Am. Psychiat. Assn., 1968, Outstanding Teaching award Ohio State U., 1968. Fellow Am. Sociol. Assn., Am. Psychopathol. Assn.; mem. Ohio Valley Sociol. Soc. (v.p. 1968), Am. Soc. Criminology (pres. 1970-71), Soc. Study Social Problems, Phi Beta Kappa (hon.). Co-author: Social Problems, 1964; Schizophrenics in the Community, 1967; Women After Treatment, 1968; Critical Issues in the Study of Crime, 1968; Deviance, 1969; also articles. Home: 298 N Cassady St Columbus OH 43209

DINKEL, THOMAS ARTHUR, banker; b. Denver, June 20, 1928; s. Thomas A. and Edith (Thompson) D.; B.A., U. Colo., 1952; grad. Am. Inst. Banking, 1963; m. Rosemarie Kreig, May 4, 1956; children—Susan (Mrs. Walter Snyder), Michael Alan. With Central Bank & Trust Co., Denver, 1952—, mortgage loan officer, 1960-69, asst. v.p. mortgage loan div., 1969—. Served to sgt. AUS, 1946-48: Japan. Mem. Am. Inst. Banking (pres. 1970-71), Denver Home Builders Assn., Mortgage Bankers Assn., Alpha Kappa Psi, Pi Kappa Alpha. Mason, Elk. Home: 8651 Circle Dr Westminster CO 80030 Office: Central Bank & Trust Co 15th and Arapahoe Sts Denver CO 80020

DINKELOO, JOHN GERARD, architect; b. Holland, Mich., Feb. 28, 1918; s. William and Bessie (Brouwer) D.; student Hope Coll., 1936-39; B.Arch. in Archtl. Engring., U. Mich., 1942; m. Thelma Ann Van Dyke, Jan. 30, 1943; children—Carter John, Janje, Dirk Van Dyke, Tessa, Christian Van Dyke, Hanni, Kaaren. Designer, Skidmore, Owings & Merrill, Chgo., 1942-43, chief prodn., 1946-50; partner Eero Saarinen & Assos., Birmingham, Mich. and Hamden, Conn., 1959-66, Kevin Roche-John Dinkeloo and Assos., Hamden, 1966—; prin. works include TWA Terminal at Kennedy Airport, 1961, Dulles Airport, 1962, CBS Hdqrs. Bldg., N.Y.C., 1965, Oakland (Cal.) Mus., 1967, Ford Found. Adminstrn. Bldg., N.Y.C., 1967, Gateway Arch, Jefferson Nat. Expansion Meml., St. Louis, 1965, Morse and Stiles colls., Yale, 1963. Trustee Hope Coll. Served as officer USNR, 1943-46. Recipient Bard award for Ford Found. Bldg., 1968. Mem. A.I.A. Devel. structural neoprene plazing gaskets, laminated metalized heat reflecting glass, exposed structural bldg. components of corrosion resistant steel. Home: 145 Blue Trail Hamden, CT 06518. Office: 20 Davis St Hamden CT 06517

DINKELSPIEL, MARTIN JERROLD, lawyer; b. San Francisco, Nov. 30, 1898; s. Henry George Washington and Estelle (Jacobs) D.; student U. Cal., 1916-19; LL.B., Harvard, 1922; m. Frances Delmore Lederman, June 20, 1929; children—Peter, Marcia. Admitted to Cal. bar, 1921; partner Dinkelspiel & Dinkelspiel, San Francisco, 1924—; vice consul, Thailand, 1922-32, consul, 1932-41, consul gen., 1947-67. Mem. Cal. Commn. Uniform State Laws, 1944-59, chmn., 1940-59 mem. Cal. Commn. Interstate Cooperation, 1949-59; bd. mgrs. Council State Govts. Laws, 1951-53, life mem., 1961—; mem. Gov.'s Adv. Com. on Children and Youth; bd. dirs. Cal. Assn. Mental Health. Chmn. Native Sons and Daus. Homeless Children Com., 1931-46; mem. Cal. Citizens Com. Adoptions. Decorated Order of Crown of Thailand. Fellow Am. Bar Assn.; mem. Cal., San Francisco bar assns., Nat. Legal Aid Soc., Am. Law Inst., Am. Judicature Soc. (dir. 1957-61), Am. Arbitration Assn. (dir. 1956-), Harvard Law Sch. Assn. (council 1955- 58), Am. Counsel Assn. (pres. 1946-48). Mason. Home: 110 Palo Alto Av San Francisco CA 94114 Office: 111 Pine St San Francisco CA 94111

DINKELSPIEL, RICHARD COLEMAN, lawyer; b. Oakland, Cal., Feb. 13, 1913; s. Edward and Ellen (Gaines) D.; A.B., U. Cal., 1934, J.D., 1937; m. Miriam Cutter, Dec. 9, 1939; children—Susan (Mrs. Fritz Stern), Robin (Mrs. Anthony Miller), Joan, Anne, Richard Coleman. Admitted to Cal. bar, 1937; city judge Suisun, Cal., 1937-42; practice law, Suisun, 1937-42, San Francisco, 1946—; partner Dinkelspiel, Steefel, Levitt, Weiss & Donovan; justice of peace, Suisun Twp., 1939-42; gen. counsel Cal. State Sheriffs Assn., 1953—, chmn. citizens adv. com. to review lien laws Cal. Legislature, 1963-64. Chmn. Adv. Com. to State Senate on Lien Law Revision, 1965-69; mem. Gov.'s Adv. Com. Children and Youth, 1967—; co-chmn. Gov.'s Commn. on Family, 1966; co-chmn. San Francisco Lawyers Com. for Urban Affairs, 1968-70. Served from lt. to lt. col., AUS, 1942-46. Recipient award of pub. recognition St. Thomas More Soc., 1970. Mem. Bar Assn. San Francisco (pres. 1968, dir.), State Bar of Cal., Am. Bar Assn., Nat. Conf. Bar Presidents, St. Thomas More Soc. San Francisco (pres. 1960), Sigma Alpha Epsilon, Phi Delta Phi. Clubs: Commonwealth (Quar. chmn. 1969), Commercial, Meadow, The Family. Home: Box 511 Kentfield CA 94904 Office: 235 Montgomery St San Francisco CA 94104

DINKINES, FLORA, educator; b. McLoud, Okla., Apr. 6, 1910; d. John W. and Sophia (Washecheck) D.; B.S. in Math., Fla. State Coll. for Women, 1929; M.S. in Math., U. Mich., 1940; Ph.D., U. Chgo., 1951; postgrad. U. Tex. at Austin, 1937-38. Tchr. pub. schs., Jupiter, Pensacola, Hollywood, Fla., 1929-42; instr. U. S.C., 1942-43, adj. prof., 1943-45; student asst. U. Chgo., 1946-47; instr. U. Ill. at Chgo., 1951-52, asst. prof., 1952-59, asso. prof. math., 1960-64, prof., 1964—; instr. math. Fla. State Coll. for Women, summer 1930, U. Tex. at Austin, summer 1938; asst. prof. NSF Inst., Washburn U., summer 1959, asso. prof., summer 1963. Mem. Am. Math. Soc. Author: Elementary Concepts of Modern Mathematics, 1964. Contbr. articles profl. jours. Home: 1528 E 86th Pl Chicago IL 60619

DINKLER, CARLING, Jr., hotel co. exec.; b. Atlanta, Aug. 10, 1919; s. Carling and Alice (Huthnance) D.; student U. Ga., 1937, Loyola U., New Orleans, 1938; m. Cornelia Vandagaer, June 26, 1939; children—Gayonne (Mrs. Harold Pate), Carling III, Derek and Kendel. With the Dinkler Hotels Corp., Atlanta; chmn. bd. Dinkler Plaza Hotel, Atlanta; now vice consul of Monaco, Miami, Fla. Clubs: Atlanta Country, Peachtree Golf (Atlanta); Indian Creek Country, Surf, La Gorce Country (Miami, Fla). Home: 720 NE 69th St Miami FL 33138

DINNICK, JOHN SAVERY, investment banker; b. Toronto, Ont., Can., Oct. 29, 1911; s. Wilfrid and Alice Louise (Conlin) D.; student St. Andrew's Coll., 1924-26, Upper Can. Coll., 192630, Trinity Coll., U. Toronto, 193133; m. Marion Jean Tope, Oct. 10, 1936; children—Martha, Sarah, Victoria. With McLeod, Young, Weir & Co. Ltd., Toronto, 1933—, pres., 1960—, chmn. bd., 1970—, also dir.; dir. Great Lakes Power Corp., Canron Ltd., Holland Life Ins., Photo Engravers & Electrotypers Ltd. Bd. dirs. Donwood Found. Served with RCAF, 1940-45. Mem. Investment Dealers Assn. Can. (pres. 1969-70). Club: Canadian (past pres.) (Toronto). Home: 5 Wychwood Park Toronto 176 Ontario Canada Office: 50 King St W Toronto 110 Ontario Canada

DINSMORE, JOSEPH CAMPBELL, lawyer; b. Cin., Mar. 29, 1899; s. Frank Forbus and Mary Evelyn (Campbell) D.; A.B., Harvard, 1921, LL.B., 1924. Admitted to Ohio bar, 1925; asso. Dinsmore, Shohl & Sawyer, Cin., 1925-33; partner Dinsmore, Shohl, Barrett, Coates & Deupree and predecessors, Cin., 1934-64, Dinsmore & Dinsmore, 1964-66. Hamilton County rep. Ohio State Gen. Assembly, 1927-28, 29-30; mem. Hamilton County (O.) Republican Club. Trustee Cin. Law Library Assn., 1939—, pres., 1965-57. Mem. Am., Ohio, Cin. (pres. 1958- 59) bar assns., Cincinnatus Assn. (pres. 1932-33). Presbyn. (trustee 1942-51, pres. bd. 1943-51). Clubs: Lawyers, Country, Queen City, Racquet, Commonwealth (Cin.). Home: 331 E 4th St Cincinnati OH 45202 Office: 2608 Carew Tower Cincinnati OH 45202

DINSMORE, RAY PUTNAM, engring. mgmt. cons.; b. Tewksbury, Mass., Apr. 24, 1893; s. Hiram Putnam and Susan (Toye) D.; B.S. in Chem. Engring., Mass. Inst. Tech., 1914; D. Eng. (hon.), Case Sch. of Applied Sci., Cleve., 1940; m. Violet Cowie, Sept. 24, 1919; children—Ruth H. (Ayers), Ray Putnam. Tech. staff, Goodyear Tire & Rubber Co., Ohio, 1914-16, asst. chemist, Can., 1916-19, chief chemist, Cal., 1919-21, chief chemist, research dir., Ohio, 1921-32, asst. factory mgr., 1932-39, mgr. devel. dept., 1940-43, v.p., 1943-61, dir., 1960-64, cons., 1961-67. Asst. dep. rubber dir., 1942-43, organized synthetic rubber research and devel. program for govt. and co. Pres. Nat. Adv. Council for Gifted, 1961-63. Term mem. Mass. Inst. Tech. Corp., 1954-59; trustee Kent State U., 1959-66. Recipient Colwyn Medal awarded by Inst. Rubber Industries, 1947; Charles Goodyear medal, Am. Chem. Soc., 1955. Pres. Am. sect. Sociéte de Chimie Industrielle, 1958, chmn. bd. dirs., 1959. Fellow Am. Inst. Chemists, Inst. of Rubber Industries (Brit.), Royal Soc. of Arts (Brit.), A.A.A.S., mem. Am. Chem. Soc. (councilor 1922-25, chmn. Akron section, vice chmn. rubber div., 1925-26, chmn. rubber div., 1926-27), Am. Inst. Chemist, 1953, (pres. 1955, 56; chmn. bd., 1956-57), N.Y. Acad. Scis., Am. Inst. Chem. Engrs. (chmn. profl. devel. com.; recipient Founder's Award 1964), Agr. Research Inst. (bd. govs. 1954-59), Ohio Acad. Scis., Soc. Automotive Engrs., Alpha Chi Sigma. Clubs: Chemists, Akron University (hon. mem.), Portage Country (hon. mem.). Contributed numerous articles on rubber to sci. mags.; lectr. rubber industry, 7th Found. lectr. Econ. and Phys. Aspects of GR-S Modifications, 1952. Home: 795 Merriman Rd Akron OH 44303 Office: 9 Overwood Rd Akron OH 44313

DINTZIS, HOWARD MARVIN, scientist; b. Chgo., May 28, 1927; s. Harry and Bertha (Horwitz) D.; B.S., U. Cal. at Los Angeles, 1948; Ph.D., Harvard, 1953; D.Sc. (hon.), Lawrence U., 1964; m. Renee

Zlochover, June 16, 1951; children—William Stephen, Joanne Beth, Suzanne Martha. Research fellow chemistry Yale, 1953-54; NRC and Rockefeller Research fellow physics U. Cambridge (Eng.) 1954-56; asst. prof. chemistry Cal. Inst. Tech., 1956-58; sr. research asso. biology Mass. Inst. Tech., 1958-61; prof. biophysics, dir. dept. Johns Hopkins Sch. Medicine, 1961—; spl. research structure and synthesis proteins and nucleic acids. Mem. Phi Beta Kappa, Sigma Xi. Home: 4413 Norwood Rd Baltimore MD 21218

DINWIDDIE, DONAL, editorial exec.; b. Cin., Feb. 17, 1919; s. Courtenay and Susan (Ellis) D.; student U. Va., 1936-40; m. Nancy Lewis, June 24, 1942; children—John Cary, Anne Courtenay. Editor, Altavista (Va.) Jour. newspaper, 1940-41; mng. editor Sci. & Mechanics Pub. Co., Chgo., 1946-58, editor, v.p., 1958-60; mng. editor Popular Mechanics mag., Chgo., 1960-62, editor Chgo., N.Y.C., 1962-65; editorial dir. Consumers Union of U.S., pubs. Consumer Reports, Mt. Vernon, N.Y., 1965—. Pres. Ravinia Civic Assn., Highland Park, Ill., 1959-66; v.p. Highland Park Safety Council, 1960-62. Served to capt. AUS, 1941-46. Mem. Headline Club Chgo., Chgo. Press Club, Sigma Delta Chi. Contbr. articles profl. jours. Office: 256 Washington St Mount Vernon NY 10550

DINWOODEY, DEAN, former editor, pub.; b. Idaho Falls, Ida., Nov. 2, 1899; s. Charles Eugene and Lucy (Dean) D.; A.B., U. Utah, 1922; LL.B., George Washington U., 1929; LL.D., Brigham Young U., 1959; m. Edith Austin, Dec. 23, 1925; children—Margaret Jean, Judith Austin, David Taylor. Sec. Swiss-German Mission, Church of Latter Day Saints, 1924-25; mem. editorial staff U.S. Daily, 1926-33; editor United States Law Week, 1933-64, Labor Relations Reporter, 1937-64. Pres., editor-in-chief, Bur. Nat. Affairs, Inc., 1933-64, chmn. bd., 1960-69; dir. Tax. Mgmt., Inc., Fisher-Stevens, Inc., Auerbach Corp. Mem. Bar D.C., Bar Supreme Ct. of U.S., Am. Bar Assn., Nat. Lawyers Club, Pi Kappa Alpha, Pi Delta Epsilon. Clubs: Nat. Press, Cosmos, Columbia Country (Washington). Home: 9600 Hillridge Dr Kensington MD 20795

DIONISIJE, (see Milivojevich, Dionisije), Bishop of Serbian Ch. in U.S. and Can.

DIONNE, RENE W., lawyer; b. Que., Can., July 21, 1933; B.A., Garnier Coll., 1952; LL.L., Laval U., 1956; postgrad. Acad. Internat. Law, Holland. Admitted to Que. bar, 1957; partner firm Gagnon, de Billy, Cantin & Dionne. Mem. Canadian, Que. bar assns. Office: 100 d'Youville Quebec 4 Quebec Canada *

DIORI, HAMANI, pres. Niger; b. June 16, 1916; ed. Victor Ballot Sch., Dahomey, Ecole William Ponty, Senegal. Dep. Niger Ty., French Nat. Assembly, 1946-51, 56-58, v.p., 1957; prime minister Republic of Niger, 1958-60, pres., 1960—, also pres. Council of Ministers, minister fgn. affairs. Address: Office of the President Niamey Niger*

DIPPOLD EDWIN WALTER, assn. exec.; b. N.Y.C., Mar. 20, 1930; s. Herman George and Margaret (Bagnall) D.; student Pace Coll., 1952; m. Alice M. Jasper, May 4, 1952; children—Edwin Walter, William Louis, Dale Ellen, Nancy Ann. Accountant, Pogson, Peloubet & Co., C.P.A.'s, N.Y.C., 1955-63; v.p., sec. Am. Arbitration Assn., 1963—. Served to lt. USNR, 1952-55. C.P.A., N.Y. Mem. Am. Inst. C.P.A.'s, N.Y. State Soc. C.P.A.'s. Home: 19 Cedar Dr Massapequa NY 11759 Office: 140 W 51st St New York City NY 10020

DIPRIMA, RICHARD CLYDE, educator, mathematician; b. Terre Haute, Ind., Aug. 9, 1927; s. Clyde and Ethel (Phillips) DiP.; B.S., Carnegie Inst. Tech., 1950, M.S., 1951, Ph.D., 1953; m. Maureen P. Clune, Nov. 27, 1954; children—Shivaun, Richard Clyde. Research asso. Mass. Inst. Tech., 1953-54; research fellow Harvard, 1954-56; research physicist Hughes Aircraft Co., 1956- 57; mem. faculty Rensselaer Poly. Inst., 1957—, prof. math., 1962—, asso. dean Grad. Sch., 1968—, chmn. Faculty Council, 1969-70; cons. to industry, 1961—; Fulbright lectr. Wiezmann Inst. Sci., Rehovoth, Israel, 1964-65. Mem. budget com. Troy United Fund, 1960-64; mem. adv. bd. Albany Diocesan Office Health and Social Services, 1966-70, v.p., 1969-70. Served with AUS, 1946-48. Mem. Am. Math. Soc., Am. Math. Assn., Soc. Indsl. and Applied Math. (mem. council 1970—), Am. Assn. U. Profs., Am. Acad. Mechanics, Soc. for Natural Philosophy, Am. Soc. M.E., Sigma Xi. Author: Elementary Differential Equations and Boundary Value Problems, 1965, 2d edit., 1969; Elementary Differential Equations, 1965, 2d edit. 1969; Introduction to Differential Equations, 1970. Home: 3 Meadowbrook Lane Troy NY 12180

DIRAC, PAUL ADRIEN MAURICE, prof. mathematics; b. Bristol, Eng., Aug. 8, 1902; s. Charles Adrien Ladislas and Florence Hannah (Holten) D.; B.Sc., Bristol Univ., 1921; Ph.D., Cambridge Univ., 1926; m. Margit Wigner, 1937. Fellow St. John's Coll., Cambridge, 1927—, Succession prof. of mathematics, Cambridge U., Eng., 1932-69; prof. physics Fla. State U., 1971—; vis. lectr. U. Wis., Apr.-June, 1929, U. Mich., summer 1929, Princeton U., Oct.-Dec., 1931; mem. Inst. for Advanced Studies, 1947-48, 58-59. Awarded Nobel Prize for Physics (with E. Schrodinger), 1933. Fellow Royal Soc. of London (Eng.). Author: Principles of Quantum Mechanics, 1930. Home: 7 Cavendish Av Cambridge England Office: Fla State U Tallahassee FL

DIRANI, AFIFA MAHMOUD, Lebanese diplomat; b. Kasrnaba, Lebanon, May 25, 1940; d. Mahmoud H. and Rasmieh (Rasmieh) Dirani; B.A., Beirut Coll. for Women, 1962; M.A., Am. U. Beirut, 1964, postgrad., 1964-66; Arabic asst. for research and editing German Inst. for Oriental Studies, Beirut, part time, 1963-66; tchr. Arabic lit. sr. high sch., Lebanon, 1963; tchr. Arabic, Fgn. Service Inst., Beirut, 1964-66; cultural counselor Lebanese embassy, Washington, 1966—. Author, editor: Diwan Ibn Az-Zaqqaq al-Balanci 1964. Home: 2401 Calvert St NW Washington DC 20008 Office: 28th St NW Washington DC 20008

DIRKS, HOWARD MEISER, corp. ofcl.; b. New Albany, Ind., Feb. 2, 1908; s. Louis Herman and Blanche (Meiser) D.; A.B. cum laude, Ind. U., 1929; m. Miriam Brown, July 18, 1931; children—Richard Alan, Robert Brown. Personnel dept. Marmon Motor Car Co., Indpls., 1929-31; mem. Emergency Work Com., Inc. (affiliate C. of C.), also work dir. Fed. Emergency Relief Adminstrn., Indpls., 1931-34; personnel mgr. Arvin Industries, Inc., Franklin, Ind., 1934-36, plant supt., 1937-38; dir. indsl. relations Perfect Circle Corp., Hagerstown, Ind., 1938-47; v.p. personnel Carrier Corp., Syracuse, N.Y., 1947-60; v.p. personnel Harris Intertype Corp., Cleve., 1960—. Mem. Machinery and Allied Products Inst. (indsl. relations council), Am. Mgmt. Assn. (council), Phi Beta Kappa, Delta Chi, Beta Gamma Sigma. Presbyn. Mason. Club: Country (Cleve.). Author articles on personnel relations. Home: 28600 Bolingbrook Rd Pepper Pike Village Cleveland OH 44124 Office: 55 Public Sq Cleveland OH 44113

DIRKS, JOHN EDWARD, found. exec.; b. Ia., July 18, 1919; s. John and Henrietta (Smit) D.; B.A., U. Dubuque, 1940; student McCormick Theol. Sem., Chgo., 1940-42; B.A., Yale, 1943; Ph.D., Columbia, 1947; m. Annabelle B. Voigt, June 14, 1943; children—Christopher, Timothy, Nicholas, Rebecca. Ordained to ministry United Presbyn. Ch., 1947; mem. religious teaching staff Columbia, 1944-49; prof. philosophy Lake Forest (Ill.) Coll., 1949-55; asso. dir., commn. on higher edn. Nat. Council Chs., 1953-54; Stephen Merrill Clement prof. christian methods, Yale Div. Sch., 1955-67, staff spl. research project Edward W. Hazen Found., 1955-60; vice pres. Danforth Found., St. Louis, 1967—; founder, editor Christian Scholar, until 1967, sec. univ. tchrs. com. World Student Christian Fedn., Geneva, Switzerland, 1953-60. Trustee Am. U., Cairo, Egypt. Mem. Am. Philos. Soc., Nat. Assn. Bibl. Instrs., Nat. Assn. Coll. and U. Chaplains. Author: The Critical Theology of Theodore Parker, 1947. Home: 7419 Cromwell Dr Clayton MO 63105 Office: 222 S Central Av St Louis MO 63105

DIRKSEN, CHARLES JOSEPH, coll. dean; b. Springfield, Ill., Aug. 27, 1912; s. Frank Theodore and Mary (Cloney) D.; B.S.C., St. Louis U., 1935, M.S.C., 1938; grad. student University of Illinois, 1936; LL.D., University of Santa Clara, 1965; m. Rita Seneker, Aug. 16, 1941; children—Charles, Frank, Victor, Mary Lula (dec.), Mary Rita (dec.), John. Instr. econs. St. Louis U., 1937-38; research and cons., St. Louis, 1934-37; charge nat. advt. San Jose Evening News, 1940-42; dean Coll. Bus. Adminstrn., U. of Santa Clara since 1942, dean Grad. Sch. Bus., professor marketing; asst. director war training program; dir. Newcomb Hotel Interests. Dir. Santa Clara Co. Pub. Opinion Panel; mem. editorial bd. and book review editor Jour. of Marketing since 1945. Commr. Cal. State Scholarship and Loan Commission, chairman, 1969—. Member board of trustees Serra Medical Hospital, 1967—. Member Am. Marketing Assn., Am. Statis. Assn., A.A.A.S., Nat. Sales Exec. Assn., Cath. Econ. Assn., Newcomen Soc., Am. Econ. Assn., American Association College Schs. Business (president 1965-66, chairman of past presidents' council 1966—), Beta Gamma Sigma (national dir. since 1963). Clubs: Rotary, Commonwealth. Author: (with others) Cases in Marketing, 3d edit., 1964, 4th edit., 1971; Principles of Sales Mgmt.; Advertising Principles and Problems, 1959, rev. 1964; Readings in Marketing, 1963, rev. 1968; History of AACSB, 1966; Readings in Marketing II, 1968; Advertising Principles III, 1968. Contributor articles profl. publs. Home: 1465 Calaveras Av San Jose CA 95126 Office: Grad Sch Bus U Santa Clara Santa Clara CA 93153

DIRLAM, ARLAND AUGUSTUS, architect; b. Somerville, Mass., Oct. 17, 1905; s. Frederick William and Lena Scafe (Charlton) D.; B.S., Tufts, 1926, L.H.D., 1953, M.Arch., Harvard, 1929, traveling fellow, 1929-30; spl. courses Ecole des Beaux Arts, Am. Acad. Rome; Doctor Fine Arts (hon.), Simpson Coll., 1968; m. Catherine V. Price, Dec. 16, 1933 (dec. July 1966); m. 2d, Grace Raymond Baker, Oct. 27, 1967. Architect, Mass., 1931—, specializing church and coll. architecture; pres. Arland A. Dirlam, Inc., Boston, 1956—; projects include Gordon Coll. and Divinity Sch., Wenham (Mass.) Library, also buildings for Tufts U., U. N.H., Colby Jr. Coll., Lawrence Acad., Green Mountain Jr. Coll.; designed War Meml. Tower at Cathedral Pines; lectr. architecture Boston U., Inst. Social and Religious Studies N.Y.; tech. adviser bur. ch. bldg. Nat. Council Chs. Christ Am.; dir. Wesleyan Assn.; corporate mem. Morgan Meml. Dir. Marblehead Trust Co. Dir. Marblehead Scholarship Found.; trustee, incorporator New Eng. Deaconess Hosp.; incorporator New Eng. Bapt. Hosp. Registered architect, Mass., R.I., Conn., Me., Vt., N.H., N.Y., Va. Served as lt. comdr. USNR, World War II; mem. Fgn. Liquidations Commn., 1945. Recipient distinguished service key Tufts Coll., J. Harleston Parker gold medal Boston Soc. Architects, 1952, 1st prize Religious Arts Guild Am. Unitarian Assn., hon. mention award Ch. Archtl. Guild Am., 1954. Corp. mem. Open Ch. Found. Fellow Internat. Inst. Arts and Letters; mem. Am. Soc. Ch. Arch. (dir.), A.I.A., Ch. Archtl. Guild Am. (dir., past pres.), Boston Soc. Architects, Mass. Assn. Architects, Beaux Arts Inst. Design, Marblehead Hist. Soc. (dir.), Newcomen Soc., Am. Arbitration Assn., Alpha Tau Omega. Republican. Methodist. Mason (33 degree). Clubs: Harvard, Boston Tufts (past pres.) Boston Yacht (Boston). Contbr. relgious mags. Home: 18 Park Lane Marblehead MA 01945 Office: 739 Boylston St Boston MA 02116

D'ISA, FRANK ANGELO, engring. educator; b. Youngstown, O., Mar 30, 1921; s. Gustave and Rose (Tanzola) D'I.; B.S., Youngstown U., 1943; M.S. in Mech. Engring., Carnegie Inst. Tech., 1947; Ph.D., U. Pitts., 1960; m. Mary Kathryn Buckley, Dec. 30, 1950; children—Nancy Judith, Jane. Faculty William Rayen Sch. Engring., Youngstown U., 1947-, chmn. dept. mech. engring., 1956—, prof., 1960—. Served with AUS, 1943-46. Registered profl. engr., Ohio. Mem. Am. Soc. M.E. (certificate high regard Youngstown chpt. 1961), Nat., Ohio, Mahoning Valley socs. profl. engrs., Am. Soc. Engring. Edn., Sci. Research Soc. Am., Pi Tau Sigma, Sigma Tau, Roman Catholic. Author: Mechanics of Metals, 1968. Home: 4120 Lockwood Blvd Youngstown OH 44511

DISALLE, MICHAEL VINCENT, lawyer, former gov. Ohio; b. N.Y.C., Jan. 6, 1908; s. Anthony and Assunta (D'Arcangelo) DiS.; student Central Cath. High Sch., Toledo; J.D., Georgetown U., 1931; LL.D., Notre Dame U., 1949, Miami U., 1959, Bowling Green State U., U. Toledo, Kent State U., U. Akron, 1960; D.H.L., Ohio U., 1963; M.S. (hon.), U. Bridgeport, 1951; m. Myrtle Eugene England, Dec. 19, 1929; children—Antoinette, Barbara, Constance, Diana, Michael E. Admitted to Ohio bar, 1932, and began practice in Toledo; sr. mem. DiSalle, Green & Haddad; asst. dist. counsel Home Owners Loan Corp., 1933-35; mem. Ohio Ho. of Reps., 1937; asst. city law dir. City of Toledo, 1939- 41, mem. city council, 1942-47, vice mayor, 1944-48, mayor (city mgr.), 1948-50; dir. price stblzn., Washington, 1950-52; apptd. dir. econ. stblzn., 1952; gov. Ohio, 1958-63; practice law, Columbus, O., 1963- 66, Washington, 1966—; Counsel Chapman, Duff & Lenzini, Washington, 1966—. Distinguished prof. U. Mass. Originator, first chmn. Toledo Labor-Mgmt. Citizens Com. (Toledo Plan), 1945 (plan has been adopted by other cities for mediation labor disputes); an organizer and 1st pres. Ohio Assn. Municipalities, 1949; chmn. adv. bd. U.S. Conf. Mayors, 1949; del. Internat. Union Cities, Geneva, 1949. Mem. Pres.'s Adv. Com. on Intergovtl. Affairs, 1961-63. Served in Ohio N.G., World War II. Named outstanding man of year Jr. C. of C., 1944, outstanding alumnus Georgetown Student Bar Assn., 1962; recipient award Interfaith Movement, 1962. Mem. Am., Fed., Ohio, Columbus, Toledo bar assns., Bar Assn. D.C., Delta Theta Phi. Democrat. Roman Catholic. Home: 2510 Virginia Av NW Washington DC 20006 Office: Pennsylvania Bldg Washington DC 20004

DI SANT'ANGELO, GIORGIO, designer; b. Florence, Italy, May 5, 1939; s. Domingo Imperatrice and Leila (Ratti) de S.; B.A., Coll. Nat. Domingo Faustina Sarmiento, Argentina, 1956; student architecture and indsl. design, U. Arch. Buenos Aires, 1956-60. Indsl. design studio, Argentina, 1960-61; free-lance architect and indsl. designer, Rome; tchr. indsl. design (furniture, ceramics) Rodari (Argentina) Sch. Design, 1959; textile designed Gloria Buse Studio, N.Y.C., 1962; textile designer, stylist Ameritex, N.Y.C., 1962, Marcus Bros., N.Y.C., 1963; indsl. designer and decoration Carribean Hotel, Nassau; free-lance accessories designer, 1966; propr. Sant' Angelo Ready to Wear, 1966-67, Di Sant'Angelo, Incorporated, 1968—. Served as lt. Argentine Army. Recipient 1st prize ceramics, Argentina, 1959, 1st prize sculpture, Argentina, 1968. 1st prize animation, 1961; Spl. Coty award, 1968; 1970. Coty award womens fashion ``Winnie''. Mem. Fashion Designers Am. (council 1969). Address: 24 E 38th St New York City NY 10016

DISCHER, SISTER MARTHA, hosp. adminstr.; b. Louisville, Ky., Apr. 17, 1928; d. Louis J. and Evelyn (King) Discher; B.S., Spalding Coll., 1949; M.S., St. Louis University, 1964. Tchr. in secondary schools, Memphis, Tenn., Bellaire, Ohio, 1958-62; adminstrv. resident Mt. Carmel Hosp., Columbus, O., 1963-64, St. Mary's Hosp., Evansville, Ind., 1963-64; asst. adminstr. St. Joseph Infirmary, Louisville, 1964, adminstr., 1965-69; faculty mem. hosp. adminstrn. program Xavier U., Cin., 1970; sr. hosp. adminstr. Ky. Dept. Health Med. Care Div., Frankfort, 1971—. Mem. Am. Coll. Hosp. Adminstrs. Mem. Sisters of Charity of Nazareth. Home: 311 E Main St Frankfort KY 40601 Office: Ky Dept Health Med Care Div 275 E Main St Frankfort KY 40601

DI SCIPIO, ALFRED, entertainment co. exec.; b. Chelsea, Mass., Feb. 23, 1927; s. Attilio and Adeline (Pote) di S.; B.S. in Elec. Engring., Northeastern U., 1950; M.B.A., N.Y. U., 1955; student Ohio State U.; m. Corinne J. Capone, Sept. 3, 1949; children—Lawrence, Christine, Diane, Robert. Product dir. Chicopee Mills, Inc. div. Johnson & Johnson, N.Y.C., 1950-56; mgmt. cons. McKinsey & Co., Inc., N.Y.C., 1956-59; v.p. marketing and comml. devel. Internat. Tel. & Tel. Corp., N.Y.C., 1959-61; pres. ITT Information Systems div., 1961-62; group v.p. consumer products div. Singer Co., N.Y.C., 1963-67, group v.p. N. Atlantic consumer products group, 1967-70; exec. v.p., dir. Filmways, Inc., N.Y.C., 1970—; dir. Singer Co., Singer Sewing Machine Co. Mem. Northeastern U. Corp. Served with USNR, 1945-46. Recipient Alumni award Northeastern U., 1950. Mem. Am. Mgmt. Assn., Sales Execs. Club of N.Y., Friars Nat. Assn., also fraternities Phi Kappa Phi, Tau Beta Pi, Eta Kappa Nu, Knight of Holy Sepulchre. Clubs: Westchester Country; New York University, N.Y. Athletic (N.Y.C.). Home: Upland Dr Greenwich CT 06830 Office: 540 Madison Av New York City NY 10022

DISERNIA, PATRICIA SUE RHINEHEARDT, publisher; b. Richmond, Va., Oct. 20, 1927; d. John Pascal and Margaret (Ballard) Rhineheardt; student U. N.C., 1941-43; B.A., U. Md., 1945; m. Eugene Anthony diSernia, Apr. 2, 1949; 1 son, David Rudolph. With George Jensen, Inc., N.Y.C., 1945-46, M.C. Flynn, Inc., N.Y.C., 1946-49; asst. fashion editor Girl Scouts U.S.A., 1950-52, fashion and merchandising editor, 1952-57, fashion and merchandising dir., 1957-67, editor in chief Am. Girl and Leader mags., 1967—. Cons. in product devel.; nat. polit. speech writer. Mem. Fashion Group, Advt. Women N.Y., League Women Voters (v.p. local chpt.). Home: 656 Westbury Av Westbury NY 11590 Office: 830 3d Av New York City NY 10118

DISMUKES, WILLIAM PAUL, educator; b. Nashville, Tenn., June 30, 1903; s. William Marcus and Florence (Roberts) D.; A.B., Vanderbilt U., 1926, A.M., 1927; Ph.D., U. Ill., 1936; summer study Sorbonne, 1925, 55, U. Chgo., 1928, U. Heidelberg, 1931, Alliance Francaise, 1933, Middlebury, 1941, Nat. U. Mexico, 1944, U. San Carlos, Guatemala, 1959, Linguistic Inst. U. Tex., 1960, Linguistic Inst. U. Ind., 1964; m. Ruth Hood, June 23, 1931; 1 son, William Paul. Instr. French, Vanderbilt U., 1927-30; asst. in French and Italian, U. Ill., 1930-36, instr. 1936-37; asst. prof. French, U. Miami, 1937-39, asso. prof., 1939-40, prof. Romance langs., 1940-69, prof. Romance langs. emeritus, 1969—, dean div. adult edn., 1947-50, chmn. dept. modern langs., 1951-61. Sec. Jr. Mus. Miami, 1953-55. DDecorated Croix de Chevalier dans L'Ordre des Palmes Académiques. Chmn. Coral Gables UN Assn. Mem. Am. Assn. Tchrs. French (past pres., sec., treas. Fla. chpt.; nat. trustee 1969—), Am. Assn. Tchrs. Italian, Am. Assn. Tchrs. Spanish and Portuguese, Modern Lang. Assn., South Atlantic Modern Lang. Assn. (pres., 1958), Am. Assn. U. Profs. (chpt. pres. 1960), Am. Assn. UN (former v.p. Fla. chpt.), Assn. U. Evening Colls., Dante Soc. Greater Miami (past pres.), Phi Beta Kappa (past pres. Phi Beta Kappa Assn. of Greater Miami), Beta Theta Pi, Phi Kappa Phi, Sigma Delta Pi, Pi Delta Phi (past nat. v.p.), Sigma Upsilon. Democrat. Episcopalian (exec. bd. Diocese S. Fla. 1948-51, sr. warden 1960). Club: Century (Coral Gables). Home: 3633 Harlano St Coral Gables FL 33134

DISNEY, DORIS MILES, (Mrs. George J. Disney), writer; b. Glastonbury, Conn., Dec. 22, 1907; d. Edward Lucas Hart and Elizabeth Anne (Malone) Miles; ed. pub. schs., Conn.; m. George J. Disney, June 19, 1936 (dec.); 1 dau. Elizabeth Miles. Democrat. Roman Catholic. Club: Woman's. Author: books among which: Family Skeleton, 1949 (Crime Club publs.) Fire at Will, 1949; Look Back on Murder, 1950; Straw Man, 1951; Heavy Heavy Hangs, 1952; Do Unto Others, 1953; Prescription: Murder, 1953; The Last Straw, 1954; Room for Murder, 1955; Driven to Kill; Unappointed Rounds, Method in Madness, My Neighbor's Wife, Black Mail; Dark Lady, 1960; Mrs. Meeker's Money, 1961; No Next of Kin; Shadow of A Man; At Some Forgotten Door; The Magic Grandfather. Home: 373 Main St Farmington CT 06032☆

DISNEY, ROY O., motion picture exec.; b. Chgo., 1893; s. Elias and Flora (Call) D.; m. Edna Francis, Apr. 11, 1925; 1 son, Roy Edward. Chmn. bd., dir. Walt Disney Prodns., Burbank, Cal. Trustee Cal. Inst. Arts. Office: 500 S Buena Vista St Burbank CA 91505

DISNEY, VIRGIL HAWTHORN, engineer; b. Moberly, Mo., Nov. 28, 1913; s. Harve Adam and Dollie (Hawthorn) D.; A.A., Moberly Jr. Coll., 1933; B.S., U. Mo., 1936; grad. study Ill. Inst. Tech.; m. Esther A. Ruediger, July 18, 1942; children—Diane Clare, Virginia Ann, Dorothy Jo. Test engr. Gen. Electric Co., 1936-37; elec. engr. Am. Can. Co., 1937-41; instr. Ill. Inst. Tech., 1941-42, mgr. elec. engring. Armour Research Found., 1949-59, dir. Elec. Engring. div., 1959-62; v.p. Ill. Inst. Tech. Research Inst., 1962-70; project engineer C. G. Conn, Elkhart, Ind., 1942-46; section head Curtiss Wright, Columbus, O., 1946-47; project engr. Sperry Gyro Co., Great Neck, L.I., 1947-49; dir. research Bank Adminstrn. Inst., 1970—. Mem. I.E.E.E. Eta Kappa Nu, Tau Beta Pi, Rho Epsilon. Home: 40 S Stough St Hinsdale IL 60521 Office: 10 W 35th St Chicago IL 60610

DISOSWAY, GABRIEL POLLION air force officer; b. Pomona, Cal., June 11, 1910; s. Wilbur Frotheringham and Elizabeth (Forrest) D.; student U. Okla., 1927-28; grad. U.S. Mil. Acad., 1933; m. Dorothy Ford, May 1, 1937; children—Judith (Mrs. William R. Hanna), John Ford. Commd. 2d lt. F.A., U.S. Army, 1933, advanced through grades to gen. USAF, 1963; student flying schools, Randolph and Kelly fields, San Antonio, 1935; primary flying instr., Randolph AFB, 1938-42, also flight comdr., stage comdr.; comdr. fighter group, dep. comdr. 26th Fighter Command, Panama, 1943-44, trainer First Brazilian Fighter Group; comdr. Ephrata (Wash.) Army Air Base, 1944; operations officer 312th Fighter Wing, Far East, later comdg. officer, 1945; comdr. 311th Fighter Group, 1945; liaison officer Third Amphibious Marine Corps, Tientsin, China, 1945; asst. comdr. Barksdale AFB, La., 1946; student Air War Coll., Ala., 1947-48; head tng. div. Directorate Tng. and Requirements Office, Washington, 1948-50; dir. tng. office dep. chief staff for personnel Hdqrs. USAF; comdr. Flying Tng. Air Force, Air Tng. Command, Waco, Tex., 1952-57; USAF in Europe, 1957-60; sr. Air Force mem. Weapons System Evaluation Group, office Sec. Def., 1960-61; vice comdr. Tactical Air Command, 1961-62; dep. chief staff Operations Hdqrs. USAF, Washington, 1962-63, dep. chief staff programs and requirements, 1963; comdr. in chief U.S. Air Forces in Europe, 1963-65; comdr. USAF Tactical Air Command, Langley AFB, Va.,

1965-68; sr. v.p. LTV Aerospace Corp., Dallas, 1968—. Decorated Legion of Merit, Bronze Star medal, Air Medal, D.S.M. (U.S.); Cloud and Banner, Glorious Tripod (China); Mil. Medal, Order So. Cross (Brazil); Republic of Vietnam Air Force Distinguished Service Order; D.S.M. (upon retirement); D.F.C. Address: 13710 Spruce Wood Dallas TX 75240

DISSMEYER, EDWARD FREDERICK, former utility co. exec.; b. Firth, Neb., Oct. 18, 1901; s. George and Augusta (Petz) D.; B.S. in Elec. Engring., U. Neb., 1925; m. Ethyl E. Copley, Aug. 4, 1928; children—Joan L. (Mrs. Ronald N. Bartell), George E. With Westinghouse Electric and Mfg. Co., Pitts., 1925-26, Commonwealth Power Corp., Jackson, Mich., 1926-28, Stevenson & Wood, Jackson, 1929, Allied Engrs., Inc., Jackson, 1930-31, Comsumers Power Co., Grand Rapids, Mich., 1931-35, Commonwealth & So. Corp., Jackson, 1935-49; treas., dir. Commonwealth Assos. Inc., Jackson, 1949-52; with Ohio Edison Co., Akron, 1952-69, v.p., 1960-69; dir. Commonwealth Services Inc., N.Y.C., 1951-52. Adv. com. Coll. Engring., U. Akron. Registered profl. engr., Mich., Ohio, Ill. Fellow I.E.E.E.; mem. Nat., Ohio socs. profl. engrs. Clubs: City, Fairlawn Country (Akron); Bras Coupe Fishing and Hunting (Que., Can.). Home: 1854 Brookfield Dr Akron OH 44313

DISSMEYER, VIRGIL M., banker. Sr. v.p., cashier Northwestern Nat. Bank Mpls. Office: 7th and Marquette Sts Minneapolis MN 55440*

DI STEFANO, GIUSEPPE, tenor; b. 1921. Debut in Manon, 1946, since has appeared with opera cos. throughout world, including Chgo. Lyric Opera, Met. Opera, N.Y.C., La Scala, Milan; Berlin debut, 1966; tour of U.S. and Can. with Viennese Opera Co., 1967; rec. artist on Columbia, H.M.V., Decca, Deutsche Grammophon, Ricordi. Address: Via Palatino 10, Milan, Italy.

DISTLER, THEODORE AUGUST, ednl. cons.; b. Bklyn., Nov. 22, 1898; s. Ernst Frederick and Marie (Kossman) D.; student Stevens Sch., N.J., 1914-18, Brown U., Providence, R.I., 1918-19; B.S., N.Y.U., 1922, M.A., 1932; hon. degrees 36 colls. and univs.; m. Alice Boxold, June 30, 1923; children—Theodore Alden, Paul Antonie, George Ernest. Mem. faculty N.Y.U., 1922-25, sec. com. on admissions, 1925-26, 28-29, asst. dir. student welfare, 1926-28, dir. student welfare, 1928-29, dir. student personnel, 1929-34, instr. personnel adminstrn., summer, 1932; dean Lafayette Coll., Easton, Pa., 1934-41; pres. Franklin and Marshall Coll., 1941-54, pres. emeritus, 1965—; pres. Assn. Am. Colls., 1954-65; pres. Commn. of Ind. Colls. and Univs., 1966-67; adminstrv. cons. Service Assn. Am. Colls., 1968-70. Gen. chmn. Easton Community Chest, 1941; pres. Lancaster Community Chest, 1949; vice chmn. Lancaster Redevel. Authority, 1967. Bd. dirs. Temple U., 1945-54; bd. regents Mercersburg Acad.; bd. visitors Davidson Coll.; mem. corp. Lancaster Theol. Sem.; mem. adv. council Nat. Merit Scholarship Sem. Corporator Presbyn. Ministers Fund (bd. dirs. 1945—), Pa. Assn. Colls. and Univs. (pres. 1946). Mem. Eastern Assn. Coll. Deans and Advisers of Men (pres. 1933-34, mem. exec. com. 1929-36), Soc. for Promotion Engring. Edn., Am. Acad. Polit. and Social Sci., Acad. Polit. Sci., Assn. Sch. and Coll. Placement (v.p. 1941), Scabbard and Blade, Phi Beta Kappa, Zeta Psi, Phi Delta Kappa, Tau Kappa Alpha. Clubs: Hamilton (Lancaster, Pa.); Century (N.Y.C.). Address: 548 N Duke St Lancaster PA 17602

DITTES, JAMES EDWARD, educator; b. Cleve., Dec. 26, 1926; s. Mercein Edward and Mary (Freeman) D.; A.B., Oberlin Coll., 1949; B.D., Yale, 1954, M.S., 1955; Ph.D., 1958; m. Frances Martha Skinner, Mar. 20, 1948; children—Lawrence William (dec.), Nancy Eleanor, Carolyn Ann, Joanne Frances. Instr., Am. Sch., Talas Turkey, 1950-52; ordained to ministry United Ch. Christ, 1954; mem. faculty Yale, 1955—, prof. psychology of religion, 1967—, dir. grad. studies, 1968—. Chmn. Council on Grad. Studies in Religion in U.S. and Can., 1970—. Served with USNR, 1945-46. Guggenheim fellow, 1965-66; Fulbright Research fellow, Rome, Italy, 1965-66. Fellow Am. Psychol. Assn.; mem. Soc. Sci. Study Religion (exec. sec. 1959-63; editor jour. 1966- 71; pres. 1971-73). Author: The Church in the Way, 1967; Minister on the Spot, 1970; (with Robert Menges) Psychological Studies of Clergyman, 1965. Home; 107 Westminster St Hamden CT 06518 Office: 409 Prospect St New Haven CT 06510

DITTMAN, DUANE ARTHUR, univ. adminstr.; b. Yonkers, N.Y., Nov. 19, 1924; s. Willis Arthur and Marion (Wilson) D.; B.A., Colgate U., 1950; m. Virginia Scott, May 31, 1952; children—D. Scott, Sharon J., Douglas A., Donna L. Coll. rep. Am. Book Co., N.Y.C., 1950-52; asst. sales mgr. Krementz & Co., Newark, 1952-55; asst. dir. devel. Colgate U., Hamilton, N.Y., 1955-58; dir. devel. St. Lawrence U., Canton, N.Y., 1958-63, v.p., 1963—. Dir. First Nat. Bank of Canton. Served with USNR, 1943-47. Recipient Maroon citation Colgate U., 1970. Mem. Am. Coll. Pub. Relations Assn. (trustee 1966-68, sec. 1969, pres. 1970-71), Beta Theta Pi. Presbyn. (elder). Rotarian. Home: 38 Judson St Canton NY 13617 Office: St Lawrence U Canton NY 13617

DITTMAN, MARION MARTHA, editor; b. Chgo., Feb. 24, 1909; d. Ernest C. and Lydia (Karau) Dittman; B.A., M.A., Northwestern U. Formerly editor North Shore News; editorial room staff U. Chgo. Press; editor trade books Rand McNally & Co.; sr. editor Childcraft, Field Enterprises Ednl. Corp., Chgo.; editor publs. A.L.A., Chgo., now mng. editor pub. dept. Mem. Chgo. Children's Reading Round Table, Women's Nat. Book Assn., Classical Club of Chgo., Midland Authors, Chgo. Council on Foreign Relations, Alumna Am. Sch. Classical Studies (Athens, Greece), Phi Beta Kappa, Delta Zeta. Home: 5831 N Kostner Av Chicago IL 60646 Office: Am Library Assn 50 E Huron St Chicago IL 60611

DITTMER, ALMA AUGUST, educator; b. Salt Lake City, May 27, 1908; s. August A. and Sophie (Bull) D.; A.B., U. Utah, 1936; M.A., Columbia, 1938; Ph.D., U. Rochester, 1949; m. Veda Faye Kartchner, May 31, 1938; children—A. Lowell, Ruth Ellen (Mrs. Wm. Richard Wood), N. Kent, Phil H., Veda Kaye, Valorie Debra. Tchr., dir. music dept. E. Carolina Tchrs. Coll., Greenville, N.C., 1938-43; asst. prof. music Kent (O.) State U., 1946-48; tchr., dir. music dept. Ricks Coll., Rexburg, Ida., 1948-56; asso. prof., prof. music Utah State U., Logan, 1956—. Mem. Nat. Assn. Tchrs. Singing, Am. Choral Dirs. Assn., Music Educators Nat. Conf. Mem. Ch. of Jesus Christ of Latter-day Saints. Composer 3 string quartets, 1 clarinet quartet, 1 brass sextet, choral works and arrangements. Home: 1828 N 12th E Logan UT 84321

DITTMER, CLARENCE CHRISTIAN, bus. exec.; b. Bklyn., Jan. 2, 1895; s. Joseph and Catherine Dorothy (Bauer) D.; B.C.S., N.Y. U., 1921; m. Marie Edith Hachtmann, June 15, 1921; children—Clarence Paul, Luther Albert. Asst. Sec. Advt. Men's League of N.Y.C., 1914-15; purchasing and sales agt. Student Vol. Movement for Fgn. Missions and Fgn. Missions Conf. of N.A., 1915-27; sales mgr. religious book dept. Doubleday Doran Co., 1927-31, Long and Smith, 1931-33; sales rep., Round Table Press, 1934-42, Augsburg Pub. House, 1934-44; pres., treas. Carroll Good, Inc., 1936—. Army field clerk, adj. gen. dept. U.S. Army, World War I. Former treas. Luther League of N.Y. State; former pres. Luther League Am.; former mem. bd. dirs. United Lutheran Pub. House; bd. dirs. Paradise Falls Luth. Assn.; treas., mgr. Paradise Falls Resort, 1949- 51; treas. Missionary Edn. Movement for U.S. and Can., 1946-48. Mem. Luth. Soc. N.Y., Beta Gamma Sigma. Home: 1751 W 9th St Brooklyn NY 11223 also Paradise Falls Resort Cresco PA 18326 Office: 17 Park Pl New York City NY 10007

DITZEN, LOWELL RUSSELL, clergyman, ch. ofcl.; b. Kansas City, Kan., Feb. 16, 1913; s. Paul Henry and Emma (Brenner) D.; student Park Coll., Parkville, Mo., 1929-31, D.D., 1943; B.A., William Jewell Coll., 1933, Litt.D., 1961; B.D., McCormick Theol. Sem., 1942; L.H.D., Hope Coll., 1961; LL.D., Central Coll., 1957; m. Virginia Stuart, Aug. 19, 1933 (div. 1964); children—Lowell Stuart, Deborah; m. 2d, Eleanor Davis Tydings, Dec. 15, 1966. Ordained to ministry Presbyn. Ch., 1936; minister Pullman Presbyn. Ch. Chgo., 1934-38, South Shore Presbyn. Ch., Chgo., 1938-42; asst. minister Brick Presbyn. Ch., N.Y.C. 1942-43; minister 1st Presbyn. Ch., Utica, N.Y., 1943-50, Ref. Ch., Bronxville, N.Y., 1950-62; dir. Nat. Presbyn. Center, Washington, 1963—; preacher, minister in charge Village Chapel, Pinehurst, N.C., 1965-66. Coll. preacher Cornell U., Hamilton Coll., Union Theol. Sem., others; lectr. univs. and colls., India, 1957, Am. U., Wesley Sem., Washington, 1964; exchange preacher, Europe, Far and Near East; moderator Utica Presbytery, 1950; commr. to Presbyn.-Ref. World Alliance, 1948, 54, 61, 62; del. World Council Chs., 1948; v.p. Am. Com. on Interchange of Preachers, 1958-66. Mem. N.Y. Council Mental Hygiene, 1951-56; program com. YMCA, N.Y.C., 1959-63. Recipient Freedoms Found. awards, 1951-71; citation for outstanding service to Am., D.A.R., 1957. Mem. Newcomen Soc. Eng. Clubs: Kenwood Country; Cosmos. Author: Personal Security Through Faith, 1954; You Are Never Alone, 1956; Secrets of Self- Mastery, 1958; The Storm and the Rainbow, 1959; Handbook of Church Administration, 1962; Jesus and Our Human Needs, 1963; Handbook for the Chuch Secretary, 1963; Benjamin Goodall Symon, Jr. (a biography), 1964; The Minister's Desk Book, 1968. Asst. editor Toward a More Efficient Church, 1940. Contbr. articles, sermons to profl. publs. Radio, tv broadcasting including The Art of Living, NBC, 1963-64; host NBC Issues, 1969—. Home: 2474 Tracy Pl NW Washington DC 20008 Office: 4125 Nebraska Av NW Washington DC 20016

DIVALL, ROBERT KEITH, hosp. supply co. exec.; b. Oak Park, Ill., Sept. 29, 1923; s. Robert George and Elizabeth (O'Keefe) DIV.; B.S. cum laude, U. Ill., 1945; m. Ann Sterchy, Oct. 27, 1951; childrenLinda Ann, Jeanne Renee, Diane Carol. Pub. accountant Arthur Andersen & Co., Chgo., 1945-51; comptroller, asst. treas. Central Sci. Co., Chgo., 1951-56; treas., controller Benjamin Electric Co., Chgo., 1956-59; controller Lytle Corp., Chgo., 1959; controller Am. Hosp. Supply Corp., Evanston, Ill., 1959-66, v.p., treas., 1966-. Served with USAAF, 1943. Mem. Financial Execs. Inst., Am. Inst. C.P.A.'s, Alpha Kappa Psi, Beta Gamma Sigma. Home: 708 WaPella Av Mount Prospect, IL 60056. Office: 1740 Ridge Av Evanston IL 60201

DIVELY, GEORGE SAMUEL, mfg. co. exec.; b. Claysburg, Pa., Dec. 17, 1902; s. Michael A. and Martha A. (Dodson) D.; B.S. in E.E., U. Pitts., 1925, D.Sc. in Engring. (hon.), 1962; M.B.A., Harvard, 1929; D. Eng. (hon.), Case Inst. Tech., 1961; m. Harriett G. Seeds, June 30, 1933 (dec. Aug. 1968); 1 son, Michael A.; m. 2d, Juliette Gaudin, Feb., 1969. With Harris-Intertype Corp., 1937—, successively asst. to sec.-treas., asst. treas., sec.-treas., dir., v.p. and gen. mgr. 1937- 47, pres., 1947-54, chief exec. officer, 1952-68, chmn. bd., 1954—; dir. Warner & Swasey Co., Central Nat. Bank, Cleve., White Motor Corp. Trustee, vice chmn. Case Western Res. U.; co-founder, chmn. Corporate One Per Cent Program for Higher Edn.; vis. com. Harvard Grad. Sch. Bus. Adminstrn. Fellow Am. Mgmt. Assn. (dir.); mem. Nat. Printing Equipment Assn. (dir.), Greater Cleve. Growth Assn. (dir.). Mason. Clubs: Pepper Pike Country, The Country, Shaker Heights Country, Union, Harvard (Cleve.); Harvard (N.Y.C); Royal Palm Yacht and Country (Fla.). Author: The Power of Professional Management. Home: 20776 Brantley Rd Shaker Heights OH 44122 Office: 55 Public Sq Cleveland OH 44113

DIVER, WILLIAM, educator; b. Chgo., July 20, 1921; B.A., Lawrence Coll., 1942; M.A., Harvard, 1947; Ph.D., Columbia, 1953. Instr. English, Ripon (Wis.) Coll., 1947- 49; tchr. Latin, Blake Sch., Minn., 1954-55; from asst. prof. to prof. linguistics Columbia, 1955—. Served from ensign to lt. (j.g.), USNR, 1942-45. Decorated Legion of Merit. Mem. Societe de Linguistique de Paris. Office: Philosophy Hall Columbia Univ New York City NY 10027

DIVERS, WILLIAM KEEVENY, bus. exec.; b. Cin., Apr. 12, 1905; s. William Reilly and Grace (Keeveny) D.; LL.B., U. Cin., 1928, LL.M., 1930; m. Minna Rosenbaum, Aug. 27, 1935; children—Lois (Mrs. Harry R. Alward), Diane (Mrs. Hugh R. Kincaid). Admitted to Ohio bar, 1928; mem. Divers & Warm, Cin., 1928-33; asst. pros. atty., 1931-32; mem. legal staff Fed. Emergency Pub. Works Adminstrn., Washington, D.C., 1933-34, 37, Columbus, 1935-36; mem. legal staff U.S. Housing Authority, 1938, regional dir. 15 mid-west states, 1939-40, asst. gen. counsel, spl. asst. to ir. dir. fed. housing div. Fed. Works Agy., 1941; regional rep. Nat. Housing Agy., 1942-43; spl. asst. to Nat. Housing Expediter, 1946; asst. adminstr. Nat. Housing Agy., 1947; former chmn. Fed. Home Loan Bank Bd.; chmn. exec. com. Savs. & Loan Found., Inc. Democrat. Roman Catholic. Club: Cosmos. Home: 10654 Montrose Av Bethesda MD 20014 Office: 1111 E St Washington DC 20004

DIVINE, ROBERT ALEXANDER, educator; b. Bklyn., May 10, 1929; s. Walter E. and Emily (Mable) D.; B.A., Yale, 1951, M.A., 1952, Ph.D., 1954; m. Barbara C. Renick, Aug. 6, 1955; children—J. Douglas, Elisabeth T., Richard L., Kirk M. Instr., U. Tex., Austin, 1954-47, asst. prof., 1957-61, asso. prof., 1961-63, prof. history, 1963—, chmn. dept. history, 1963-68; fellow Center for Advanced Study in Behavioral Scis., Stanford, Cal., 1962-63; Albert Shaw lectr. in diplomatic history Johns Hopkins, 1968. Mem. Orgn. Am. Historians, Am. Hist. Assn. Democrat. Methodist. Author: American Immigration Policy, 1924-52, 1957; The Illusion of Neutrality, 1962; The Reluctant Belligerent, 1965; Second Chance, 1967; Roosevelt and World War II, 1969. Home: 2402 Rockingham Circle Austin TX 78704

DIVINE, THOMAS FRANCIS, educator; b. Kansas City, Mo., Aug. 23, 1900; s. James Francis and Agnes (Herson) D.; A.B., St. Louis U., 1923, A.M., 1924; Ph.D., U. London, Sch. Econ. (Eng.), 1938; Geneva Inst. Internat. Relations, summers 1935- 37. Entered Soc. of Jesus, 1917; ordained priest, 1930; instr., Loyola U. (Chgo.), 1924-26, Creighton U. (Omaha), 1926-27; asst. prof. soc. scis. and asst. dean, Rockhurst Coll. (Kansas City), 1931-32; instr., Marquette U. (Milw.), 1933-34, asst. prof. econ., 1938-42, dean Coll. Bus. Adminstrn., prof. econs., 1942-59; prof. econs. St. Louis U., 1960-63; prof. econs. Marquette U., 1963—, editor Marquette Bus. Rev., 1963—. Dir. Marquette Labor Coll., 1941-49, Marquette Inst. Indsl. Relations, 1941-49. head econs. dept., 1942-48; vice pres. Council for a Lasting Peace, 1943, pres. 1945; part-time pub. mem. Nat. War Labor Bd., Region 6, 1943-44; pub. panel mem. 1944-45; mem. Nat. Panel Arbitrators (Am. Arbitration Assn.); dir. Citizens Conf. on Internat. Econ. Union, 1947- 52. Mem. Cath. Econ. Assn. (pres. 1943; exec. council 1944-46), Am. Econ. Assn., Econometric Soc., Am. Inst. Mgmt. (asso.), Am. Assn. Collegiate Schs. Bus. (exec. com. 1953-56), Royal Econ. Soc. (England), Mid-West Econ. Assn., Beta Gamma Sigma (nat. exec. com. 1955-63). Author tariff pamphlet and mag. articles; also (book) Interest: An Historical and Analytical Study in Economics and Modern Ethics, 1959. Editor-in-chief Rev. Soc. Economy, 1947-59. Contbr. to book, encys. Home: 1131 W Wisconsin Av Milwaukee WI 53233

DIVINE, WILLIAM ROBINSON, railroad ofcl.; b. Los Angeles, Sept. 13, 1915; s. Thomas J. and Lucy A. (Robinson) D.; B.A., Pomona Coll., 1937; M.A., U. Cin., 1939; J.D., George Washington U., 1947; m. Leir O. Clifford, Feb. 23, 1941; children—William Robinson, Suzanne (dec.), Phillippe Alvin. Admitted to D.C. bar, 1947; with Bur. Budget, 1941-51, chief mgmt. improvement staff, 1948-51; dir. budget and mgmt. U.S. Regional Office, Paris, France, 1951- 54; v.p. Lester B. Knight and Assos., cons. engrs., Chgo., 1954-56; asst. comptroller So. Ry. System, 1956-61, comptroller, 1961-70, v.p., 1967-70; v.p. finance Penn Central Transp. Co., 1971—. Adj. prof. bus. finance and data processing Am. U. Sch. Bus. Adminstrn., 1951-65; mem. orgn. planning council Nat. Indsl. Conf. Bd., 1963—. Mem. Financial Execs. Inst. (pres. Washington chpt. 1965-66), Soc. Advancement Mgmt. (pres. Washington chpt. 1961-62, internat. pres. 1964-65, chmn. bd. 1965-66), Am. Mgmt. Assn., U.S. C. of C., Phi Beta Kappa, Order of Coif. Clubs: University, Internat. (Washington); Commerce (Atlanta, Ga.); Congressional Country (Bethesda, Md.). Editor George Washington U. Law Rev., 1946-47. Home: The Barclay Rittenhouse Sq E Philadelphia PA 19103 Office: 6 Penn Center Plaza Philadelphia PA 19104

DIWOKY, ROY JOHN, petroleum exec.; b. Council Bluffs, Ia., Dec. 4, 1910; s. Adolph and Ann (Koncal) D.; B.S., State U. Ia., 1933, M.S., 1934; student Harvard Bus. Sch., 1948; m. Doris M. Hendricks, Apr. 17, 1933; childrenRoy James, Linda. With Standard Oil Co. (Ind.), Whiting (Ind.) Refinery, 1935-49, asst. gen. supt., 1948-49; exec. asst. to pres., dir., v.p. Pan-Am. So. Corp., New Orleans, 1949, exec. v.p. and dir., 1950-56; gen. mgr. mfg. Am. Oil Co., 1956-57; pres., dir. Commonwealth Oil Refining Co., Inc. 1957-61; pres., chief exec. officer Crown Central Petroleum Corp., 1961-67, now cons. and dir.; treas., sec., dir. Liquilux Gas Service, Inc., also Bottle Service, Inc., 1968—. Mem. Am. Petroleum Inst. (mem. gen. refining com.), Am. Chem. Soc., Am. Inst. Chem. Engrs., New Orleans C. of C., Nat. Petroleum Refiners Assn. (dir.), 25 Yr. Club Petroleum Industry, Phi Gamma Delta. Clubs: International House, Petroleum (New Orleans); The Chicago (Ill.); Dorado Beach (San Juan, P.R.); Deportivo, Yacht (Ponce, P.R.); Maryland, Baltimore Country; Ridglea Country (Ft. Worth). Home: 919 Old Lake Houston, TX 77027. Office: 8904 Lawndale Houston TX 75211

DIX, CHARLES HEWITT, educator; b. Los Angeles, Mar. 27, 1905; s. Charles Arthur and Florella (Hewitt) D.; B.S., Cal. Inst. Tech., 1927; M.A., Rice Inst., 1928, Ph.D., 1931; m. Josephine Bayley Weber, Nov. 5, 1970. Instr. math. Rice Inst., 1929-34; research geophysicist Humble Oil Co., 1934-37; geophysicist Socony-Vacuum Oil Co., 1939-41; chief geophysicist United Geophys. Co., 1941-48, v.p., 1942-48; mem. faculty Cal. Inst. Tech., 1948—, prof., geophysics, 1953—; cons. in field. Fulbright fellow, 1963-64. Mem. Am. Phys. Soc., Am. Geophys. Union, Seismol. Soc. Am., Soc. Exploration Geophysicists (hon.), A.A.A.S., Phi Beta Kappa, Sigma Xi. Author: Seismic Exploration for Oil, 1952. Home: 82 S Santa Anita Av South Pasadena CA 91107 Office: 1201 E California St Pasadena CA 91109

DIX, GEORGE EVERTSON, art dealer; b. Evanston, Ill., Apr. 6, 1912; s. George Evertson and Janet (Dortch) D.; A.B., Yale, 1934, M.A., 1942; student U. Berlin, 1934- 35. Tchr. German, Middlesex Sch., 1936-38; asst. dir. Am. British Art Center, N.Y.C., 1946-47; operator George Dix Gallery, 1947-48; co-dir. Durlacher Bros., 1948-67; now engaged as private art dealer, 1967-. Served to lt. USNR, 1942-46. Episcopalian. Clubs: Knickerbocker, Century Assn. (N.Y.C.); Metropolitan (Washington). Home: 19 E 55th St New York City, NY 10022.

DIX, ROBERT CLINTON, publisher; b. Wooster, O., Aug. 5, 1908; s. Emmett C. and Edna (Voorhees) D.; student Ohio Wesleyan U., 1926-28; B.A., U. Wis., 1931; LL.D., Kent State U., 1961; m. Helen Westcott, June 15, 1938; children—Robert Clinton, David, Timothy, Darcy, Kristina. Co-publisher Record-Courier, Kent-Ravenna, O., 1933-40; pub. Record-Courier, daily newspaper, Kent-Ravenna, O., 1940—; dir. First Nat. Bank & Trust Co., Ravenna, O., First Fed. Bank, Kent, O., Wooster (O.) Record, Defiance (O.) Crescent News, Martins Ferry and Bellaire (O.) Time-Leader, radio sta. WWST, Wooster radio sta. WRAD, Radford, Va., Alliance (O.) Rev., Ashland (O.) Times-Gazette, Frankfort (Ky.) State Journal, WKNT-AM and FM, Kent, O. Bd. trustees Kent State U. Mem. Aviation Writers, Am. Newspaper Pubs. Assn., Am. Soc. Newspaper Editors, Inter-Am. Press, Inland Press, Omicron Delta Kappa, Signa Delta Chi, Phi Gamma Delta. Methodist. Rotarian (past pres. Kent). Home: 517 Edgewood Dr Kent OH 44240 Office: N Chestnut St Ravenna OH 44266

DIX, WILLIAM SHEPHERD, librarian; b. Winchester, Va., Nov. 19, 1910; s. William Shepherd and Loula (Henson) D.; B.A., U. Va., 1931, M.A., 1932; Ph.D., U. Chgo., 1946; LL.D., U. Fla., 1967; Litt.D., Washington Coll., 1971; m. Jane Griffin, June 6, 1935; children—William S., Griffin, Martha. Master Darlington Sch. Boys, 1932-39; instr. English, dir. com. on private research Western Res. U., 1940-42; instr. English, Williams Coll., 1942-44; research asso. Radio Research Lab., OSRD, Harvard, 1944-46, instr. English, 1946-47; asst. prof. English, Rice Inst., 1947-48, asso. prof. and librarian, 1948-53; librarian Princeton, 1953-56, librarian and lectr. in English, 1956—. Chmn. U.S. Nat. Commn. UNESCO, 1959-61; mem. U.S. delegation Gen. Conf. UNESCO, Paris, 1958, vice chmn. delegation, 1960; mem. Govt. Adv. Com. Internat. Book and Library Programs; adv. council on grad. edn. U.S. Office Edn. Bd. dirs. Council on Library Resources, Inc.; vice chmn. bd. dirs. Franklin Book Programs, Inc. Recipient Melville Dewey award, 1969; Lippincott award, 1971. Mem. Am. (pres. 1969-70), N.J. (recipient Distinguished Service award 1969) library assns., Assn. Coll. and Reference Libraries, Assn. Research Libraries (chmn. 1962), Am. Assn. U. Profs., Phi Beta Kappa. Presbyn. Clubs: Grolier, Century (N.Y.C.). Contbr. articles profl. jours. Home: 94 McCosh Circle Princeton NJ 08540 Office: Princeton U Library Princeton NJ 08540

DIXON, ANDREW DERART, medical educator; b. Balfast, No. Ireland, Oct. 27, 1925; s. Andrew and Martha (Stewart) D.; Licentiate in Dental Surgery, Queens U., Belfast, 1948, B.Dental Surgery, 1949, M.Dental Surgery, 1953, B.S. (Nuffield Found. dental fellow), 1954, D.Sc., 1965; Ph.D., U. Manchester, 1958; m. Mary Elizabeth Henderson, Oct. 14, 1948; children—Penelope Jane, Melinda Sara, Alison Mary. Asst. lectr. anatomy U. Manchester, 1954-56, lectr., 1956-62, sr. lectr., 1962-63; vis. asso. prof. anatomy U. Ia., 1959-61; prof. dental sci. U. N.C., Chapel Hill, 1963-65, prof. dental sci., prof. anatomy, 1965-69, prof. oral biology, prof. anatomy, 1969—, asst. dean, coordinator research Sch. Dentistry, 1966-69, dir. Dental Research Center, 1967—, asso. dean research, 1969—. Fulbright Sr. Travel award, 1959-61, Commonwealth Fund Travel fellow, 1961. Mem. Anat. Soc. Gt. Britain and Ireland, Am. Assn. Anatomists, Brit. Dental Assn., Internat. Assn. Dental Research, Electron Microscopy Soc. Am., A.A.A.S., Am. Soc. Cell Biology, N.Y. Acad. Sci., Interat. Soc. Craniofacial Biology, Sigma Xi, Omicron Kappa Upsilon, Psi

Omega. Author: (with J. H. Scott) Anatomy for Students of Dentistry, 3d edit., 1971. Contbr. numerous articles to profl. jours. Studies on early devel. and growth of the jaws, sex chromatin in oral smears as a diagnostic tool, nerve supply to oral mucous membrane, facial tissues and temporomandibular joint, facial skeltal growth, trigeminal pathway, including trigeminal ganglion, using histological, histochem. and electron microscopy methods. Home: 1514 Cumberland Rd Chapel Hill NC 27514

DIXON, ARTHUR GEORGE JOHN, engring. exec.; b. E. St. Louis, Ill., June 13, 1897; s. Robert John and Wilhelmina (Schlosser) D.; B.S. in Engring., U. Ill., 1924; m. Dorothy Jane McConnell, June 16, 1928; children—David Arthur, Diana Jane. With Modine Mfg. Co., Racine, Wis., 1926—, successively engr., sales mgr., sec. corp., 1926-54; v.p. engring. and research, 1954-57, exec. v.p., 1957-60, pres., 1960-63, vice chmn. bd. 1963—, also dir. Mem. fed. industry adv. coms. Pres., Village of North Bay, Wis. Served with USMC, World War I. Mem. Am. Legion. Mason, Rotarian. Club: Racine Country. Home: 401 Cross Creek Rd Racine WI 53402 Office: 1500 DeKoven Av Racine WI 53403

DIXON, DANIEL BRADY, lawyer; b. Pitts., Nov. 11, 1912; s. Daniel J. and Julia (Brady) D.; B.S. in Bus. Adminstrn., U. Pitts., 1935, LL.B., 1938; m. Mary Elizabeth Mattas, June 29, 1940; children—Daniel M., Noel L., Julie A. Admitted to Pa. bar, 1938, since practiced in Pitts.; sr. partner firm Rose, Schmidt & Dixon, 1965—. Served with AUS, 1943-46. Mem. Pa. Bar Assn. (chmn. mineral law sect. 1961-65, mem. council real property, probate and trust sect. 1966—, ho. dels. 1966—), Teutonia Maenner Chor. Elk. Club: Pitts. Press. Home: 617 McCully St Pittsburgh PA 15243 Office: Oliver Bldg Pittsburgh PA 15222

DIXON, DEAN, conductor; b. N.Y.C.; grad. Juilliard Sch. Music, Columbia U., also student with Albert Stoessel; m. Baroness Mary Mandelen. Juilliard Fellowship in conducting, 1936-39; Rosenwald Fellowship, 1945-47. Has appeared as conductor of many leading orchestras in U.S. and Europe, including N.Y. Philharmonic Symphony, N.B.C. Symphony, Boston Symphony, Goteborg Symphony in Sweden (of which he has been resident condr.), Rundfunk Symphony Orch., Hessian Radio Orch. Recorded in works by Schubert, Tchaikovsky.

DIXON, FRANK JAMES, educator; b. St. Paul, Mar. 9, 1920; s. Frank James and Rose Augusta (Kuhfeld) D.; B.S., U. Minn., 1941, M.B., 1943, M.D., 1944; m. Marion Edwards, Mar. 14, 1946; children—Janet Wynne, Frank, Michael. Intern U.S. Naval Hosp., Great Lakes, Ill., 1943-44; research asst. dept. pathology Harvard, 1946-48; instr. dept. pathology Washington U., 1948- 50, asst. prof., 1950-51; prof., chmn. dept. pathology U. Pitts. Med. Sch., 1951-60; chmn. dept. exptl. Pathology Scripps Clinic and Research Found., La Jolla, Cal., 1961—; chmn. biomed. research depts., 1970—; research asso. dept. biology U. Cal. at San Diego, 1961-64, prof. in residence in dept. biology, 1965-68, adj. prof. dept. pathology, 1968—; sci. adviser NIH, Nat. Found., Helen Hay Whitney Found., Allergy Found. Am., Baylor U. Sch. Medicine, Sloan Kettering Inst. Mem. expert adv. panel on immunology WHO. Served with MC, USNR. Recipient Theobald Smith award, 1952; Parke-Davis award exptl. pathology, 1957; Distinguished Achievement award Modern Medicine, 1961; Martin E. Rehfuss award in internal medicine, 1966; Von Pirquet medal Ann. Forum on Allergy, 1967; Bunim medal Am. Rheumatism Assn., 1968; Gairdner Found. Internat. award, 1969; Mayo Soley award Western Soc. Clin. Research, 1969. Mem. N.Y., Acad. Scis. Western Assn. Physicians, Western Soc. Clin. Research, Soc. Exptl. Biology and Medicine, Internat. Acad. Pathology, A.A.A.S., Am. Soc. Clin. Investigation, Am. Acad. Allergists, Interurban Path. Soc., Am. Assn. Pathology and Bacteriology, Am. Soc. Exptl. Pathology (pres. 1966), Am. Assn. Immunologists, Am. Assn. for Cancer Research, Sigma Xi, Nu Sigma Nu, Alpha Omega Alpha. Contbr. articles profl. jours. Editor: Advances in Immunology. Editorial bd. Jour. Exptl. Medicine, Jour. Immunology, Am. Jour. Pathology, Cellular Immunology, Perspectives in Biology and Medicine, Hosp. Practice. Home: 2355 Avenida de La Playa LaJolla CA 92037 Office: 476 Prospect St LaJolla CA 92037

DIXON, GEORGE FRANCIS, Jr., mfg. exec.; b. Jersey City, Feb. 24, 1918; s. George F. and Frances (Martin) D.; B.S., U.S. Mil. Acad., 1940; M.S., Cornell U., 1947; D.Eng., Grenoble U., France, 1949; m. Lottie Ivy Carter, Dec. 1, 1950; children—George Francis III, Richard Elliott, Marshall Lawrence, Charlotte Ivy. Dist. engr. Vicksburg Dist. Corps Engrs., 1949-53; pres. Dart Truck Co., Kansas City, Mo., 1955-57, also dir.; with Carlisle Corp. (Pa.), 1954—, pres., 1957-70, chmn., 1970—, also dir.; dir. Dauphin Deposit Trust Co., Harrisburg, Pa. Trustee Dickinson Sch. Law. Served at lt. col. AUS, World War II; div. engr., comdg. officer 65th Engrs., 25th Inf. Div. Mem. Am. Soc. C.E., Assn. Grads. U.S. Mil. Acad. (trustee), Soc. Automotive Engrs., Soc. Am. Mil. Engrs. Home: R D I Boiling Springs PA 17007 Office: Carlisle Corp Carlisle PA 17013

DIXON, GEORGE HALL, banker; b. Rochester, N.Y., Oct. 7, 1920; s. George H. and Frances (Wheeler) D.; B.S., Wharton Sch., U. Pa., 1942; M.B.A., Harvard, 1947; m. Marjorie Freeman, Apr. 3, 1948; children—George E., Andrew T., Candis H. With Brown Bros. Harriman & Co., N.Y.C., 1947-50; gen. partner Davis & Davis, Providence, 1950-56; v.p. finance, treas. Sperry & Hutchinson Co., N.Y.C., 1956-68; pres., dir. First Nat. Bank Mpls., 1968—; dir. Otter Trail Power Co., Fergus Falls, Minn., Soo Line R.R., Mpls., Donaldson Co., Mpls., Internat. Multifoods, Mpls., Honeywell Co., Mpls. First Computer Corp., First Bank System, Inc., Mpls. Trustee Carleton Coll. Served to capt. AUS, 1943-46. Mem. Assn. Res. City Bankers. Presbyn. Clubs: University, (N.Y.C.); Minneapolis, Minikahda, Harvard Business Sch. Alumni (Mpls.). Home: 1510 Mt Curve Av Minneapolis MN 55403 Office: 120 S 6th St Minneapolis MN 55402

DIXON, GEORGE S., lawyer; b. Detroit, Mar. 4, 1906; A.B., U. Mich., 1929, LL.B., 1930. Admitted to Mich. bar, 1930; mem. firm Matheson, Dixon & Bieneman, Detroit. Mem. Am., Detroit bar assns., State Bar Mich., Motor Carrier Lawyers Assn. Office: One Woodward Av Detroit MI 48226*

DIXON HAROLD CHRISTOPHER, advt. exec.; b. N.Y.C., Aug. 28, 1923; s. George T. and Catharine (Meyer) D.; student High Point (N.C.) Coll., 1940-41, U. N.C., 1941-42; m. Mary Alice Casey, Dec. 13, 1944; children—Donna (Mrs. Charles Restivo), Mary Anne, Christine, Susan. Copywriter, Eves & Price, San Diego, 1948-50; free-lance writer, also with Am. Plywood Assn., Tacoma, 1950-52; copy chief, partner Condon Co., Tacoma, 1952-62; exec. v.p., creative dir. Cole & Weber, Seattle, 1962—, also mem. exec. com.; advt.-marketing lectr. Bd. dirs. Tacoma Art Mus. Served with USNR, 1942-48. Decorated D.F.C., Air medal. Mem. U.S. Plol Assn., Sigma Sigma. Club: Woodbrook Hunt (Tacoma). Home: 14302 Spanaway Loop Tacoma WA 98444 Office: 3100 S 176th St Seattle WA 98188.

DIXON, HARRY STERLING, cons. engr.; b. Woodland, Cal., Nov. 30, 1910; s. Thomas H. and Persis Harris (Kimball) D.; A.B., Stanford, 1931, Engr., 1936; Ph.D., Purdue U., 1952; m. Helen C. Knox, June 23, 1937; children—Caroline P. (Mrs. David A. Zlotnick), Diane K. (Mrs. Hugh G. Orr), Harry Sterling, Charles L. Transitman, insp. U.S. Bur. Pub. Roads, 1931; asst. engr. Reclamation Dist. 108, Cal., 1934-37; instr. elec. engring. Purdue U., 1937-42; vis. research engr. Gen. Electric Co., Nela Park, 1941; elec. test engr. Douglas Aircraft Co., 1942-44; elec. design engr. North Am. Aviation, Inc., 1944-45; prof., chmn. dept. elec. engring. N.D. Agr. Coll., 1945-51; lectr. U. Cal., 1951-52, 56-57; prof., chmn. dept. elec. engring. Newark Coll. Engring., 1952-56; cons. engr., 1957—; UNESCO internat. expert U. Lagos, Nigeria, 1964-65. Registered engr., Cal., N.D. Fellow A.A.A.S.; mem. I.E.E.E. (sr.), Illuminating Engring. Soc., Am. Soc. Engring. Edn., Am. Arbitration Assn. (nat. panel arbitrators), Nat. Soc. Profl. Engrs. (pres. N.D. soc. 1949), Aircraft Owners and Pilots Assn., Sigma Xi, Tau Beta Pi, Eta Kappa Nu, Sigma Pi Sigma. Presbyn. (elder). Mason (Shriner). Clubs: Commonwealth (San Francisco); Ikoyi (Lagos, Nigeria); Afro-Latin Flying (Oakland, Cal.). Contbr. tech. hand books and periodicals. Home: 950 Creston Rd Berkeley CA 94708 Office: 995 Market St San Francisco CA 94103

DIXON, IVAN N., III actor; b. N.Y.C., Apr. 6, 1931; s. Ivan N. Dixon; B.A. in Polit. Sci., N.C. Coll. Negroes; postgrad. student theatre, Western Res. U.; m. Berlie Ray, June 1, 1954; children—Ivan N., Gail C., A. Kimara. Broadway appearances include The Cave Dwellers, A Raisin in the Sun; films include Something of Value, 1956, Raisin in the Sun, 1959, Nothing But A Man, 1963, A Patch of Blue, 1965; TV appearances include Studio I, DuPont Show of the Month, Twilight Zone, Laramie, Have Gun, Will Travel, The Defenders, The New Breed, Cain's Hundred, Perry Mason, The Fugitive, The Eleventh Hour, Dr. Kildare, Alcoa Presents, Outer Limits. Address: 2345 Hanning Av Altadena, CA 91002.

DIXON, JAMES ALEXANDER, lawyer; b. Burkesville, Ky., July 4, 1900; s. James Abijah and Ella Nora (Walker) D.; A.B., U. Ky., 1920; student Harvard Law Sch., 1922-24; m. Ruth B. Richards, Sept. 10, 1926; 1 son, James Addison. Admitted to Ky. bar, 1924, Fla. bar, 1925; mem. firm Dixon, Bradford, Williams, Mckay & Kimbrell, Miami, Fla. Mem. Internat. Assn. Ins. Counsel, (v.p. 1957-58), Fed. Communications Bar Assn. Am., Fla., Dade County (dir.) bar assns., Fla. Bar, Harvard Law Sch. Assn. (council), Harvard Law Sch. Assn. Fla. (pres. 1956-58). Club: Indian Creek Country, Surf (Miami Beach). Contbr. tech. articles legal publs. Home: 10585 N E 6th Av Miami FL 33138 Office: Dade Fed Office Bldg Miami FL 33132

DIXON, JAMES PAYSON, Jr., coll. pres.; b. Portsmouth, N.H., Mar. 15, 1917; s. James Payson and Mary (Russell) D.; B.S., Antioch Coll., 1939; M.D., Harvard, 1943; M.S., Columbia, 1947; m. Edla Denton Mills, Aug. 31, 1941; children—Linn, Russell M., Pamela, Deborah, Donna, Peter C. Intern, Boston City Hosp., 1944; fellow W.K. Kellogg Found., 1945-46, Rockefeller Found., 1946-47; med. dir. Denver Gen. Hosp., 1947-48; asso. prof. preventive medicine and pub. health U. Colo.; mgr. health and hosps., Denver, 1948-52; prof. pub. health and preventive medicine U. Pa., 1952-59; commr. health, Phila., 1952-59; pres. Antioch Coll., 1959—, also trustee. Overseer, Coll. of V.I.; trustee Goddard Coll. Served from surgeon to med. dir. USPHS, 1952-54, asst. dir. clin. center NIH. Diplomate Am. Bd. Preventive Medicine and Pub. Health. Author pub. health, social welfare and ednl. articles. Home: Glen Helen House Antioch Coll Yellow Springs OH 45387

DIXON, JAMES WILLIAM, Jr., educator; b. Wingate, Tex., July 12, 1913; s. James William and Mary (Longley) D.; A.B., Baylor U., 1934, M.A., 1935; Ph.D., U. Wis., 1955; m. Lenora Cornwell, June 2, 1938. Tchr. pub. schs., Tex., 1935-42; mem. faculty Baylor U., 1942—, prof. geology, 1942—, chmn. dept., 1942—; cons. in field, 1948—; engaged in farming, 1963—. Fellow Tex. Acad. Scis.; mem. Nat. Assn. Geology Tchrs. Baptist. Contbr. profl. jours. Home: Route 2 Box 665 Waco TX 76710

DIXON, JEANE L., author, lectr., real estate broker, columnist; m. James L. Dixon. Pres., founder Children to Children Inc.; author articles, books; exponent of extrasensory perception (subject of book A Gift of Prophecy). Chmn. Christmas Seal campaign, Washington, 1968. Recipient Loreto Internat. award Loreto Shrine in Italy; Internat. L'Enfant award Holy Family Adoption League; named Woman of Year, Internat. Orphans. First Anglo hon. Navajo princess. Mem. Nat. League Am. Pen. Women, A.S.C.A.P., Internat. Platform Assn. Club: Internat. (Washington). Author: My Life and Prophecies; Reincarnation and Prayers to Live By. Address: 1144 18th St N W Washington DC 20036

DIXON, JOHN ALDOUS, surgeon, ednl. adminstr.; b. Provo, Utah, July 16, 1923; s. Henry Aldous and Lucille (Knowlden) D.; student Weber Coll., Ogden, Utah, 1940-42, Ida. State U., 1942; B.S., U. Wash., 1943; M.D., U. Utah, 1947; m. Karma Jeppsen, Sept. 28, 1944; children—Stephen, Kay, Lisa. Surg. resident U. Rochester Med. Center, 1947-50; pvt. practice surgery, Odgen, Utah, 1953- 68; part-time tchr. U. Utah Med. Sch., 1953-68, asso. clinical prof. surgery, 1965-68, asso. prof. surgery, 1968-70, prof. surgery, 1970—, exec. v.p. of univ., 1970—, head surg. gastroenterology, div. gastroenterology, dept. internal medicine; spl. cons. medical affairs U. Utah, 1965-67; chief of surgery Dee Hosp., 1965-67. Chmn. Utah Bd. Health, 1960-63. Bd. regents U. Utah, 1963-66; bd. dirs. Utah chpt. Am. Cancer Soc., 1956-67. Mem. Ogden City Council, 1956. Served with USNR, 1943-46; served to capt. USAAF, 1951-53. Diplomate Am. Bd. Surgeons. Fellow A.C.S.; mem. Am. Gastroenterological Assn., Soc. for Surgery of Alimentary Tract, Western Surg. Assn., Utah Soc. Bio-med. Researcgh, Alpha Omega Alpha, Phi Kappa Phi. Contbr. Am. Med. Jour. Home: 2989 Sherwood Dr Salt Lake City UT Office: 210 Park Bldg Salt Lake City UT 84112

DIXON, JOHN JAMES, radio broadcasting exec.; b. Elkhorn, Wis., Dec. 30, 1910; s. John and Elizabeth (Edwards) D.; B.A., U. Wis., 1930, M.A., 1931; m. Louise Frances Farnsworth, July 11, 1936; children—Sara (Mrs. Donald T. Woodford), John F., Richard E. Announcer, program dir. radio sta. WCLO, Janesville, Wis., 1934-39; program dir. radio sta. WROK, Rockford, Ill., 1939-43, comml. mgr., 1943-54, gen. mgr., 1954-60; owner, pres., gen. mgr. WAPL. Appleton, Wis., 1960—; co-owner, sec.-treas., dir. WLBK, DeKalb, Ill., 1959-65; owner, pres. WAPL-FM, Appleton, Wis., 1965—. Mem. nat resolutions com. A.R.C., 1949, 53, vice chmn. Outagamie County chpt., chmn., 1964-65; bd. dirs. Appleton YMCA, United Community Services Appleton, Appleton Taxpayer's Assn., Valley Dist. council Boy Scouts Am. Mem. bd. regents Wis. State Univs. Recipient Freedoms Found. award for radio series What Price Am., 1952. Mem. Appleton C. of C., Sigma Phi, Phi Delta Kappa. Conglist. Rotarian. Author: (with John Dixon) How to Speak, 1951. Home: 1815 Reid Dr Appleton WI 54910 Office: 103 W College Av Appleton WI 54910

DIXON, JOHN M., business exec.; married. With H.K. Porter Co., Inc., Pitts., 1962—, controller, 1964—. Office: H K Porter Co Porter Bldg Pittsburgh PA 15219*

DIXON, JOHN MORRIS, magazine editor; b. Long Branch, N.J., June 22, 1933; s. Abram C. and Emily (Minton) D.; B.Arch., Mass. Inst. Tech., 1955; m. Carol Ruth Nipomnich, Dec. 27, 1959; children—Peter, Susannah. From asst. editor to sr. editor Progressive Architecture, 1960-65; sr. editor Archtl. Forum, 1965—. Served to 1st lt. AUS, 1955-57. Mem. A.I.A. (chmn. exhibits com. N.Y. chpt. 1964-65, co-chmn. visitors com. N.Y. chpt. 1965-66, chmn. pub. relations com. N.Y. chpt. 1970-71). Author: Architectural Design Preview, U.S.A., 1962; (with N. White and E. Willensky) A.I.A. Guide to New York City, 1967. Home: 75 Prospect Park W Brooklyn NY 11215 Office: 130 E 59th St New York City NY 10022

DIXON, JOHN ROBERT, educator; b. Akron, O., Oct. 19, 1930; s. Otis D. and Sara (Griffith) D.; B.S., Mass. Inst. Tech., 1952, M.S., 1953; Ph.D., Carnegie Inst. Tech., 1961; m. Shirley Troescher, Mar. 25, 1951; children—Randal John, Linda Jo, Michael Andrew. Engr., Jarl Extrusions, Inc., Rochester, N.Y., 1955-57; project engr. Jos. Kaye Co., Cambridge Mass., 1957-58; asst. prof. Carnegie Inst. Tech., Pitts., 1960-61; asso. prof. Purdue U., 1961- 64; asso. prof. Swarthmore (Pa.) Coll., 1964-66; prof., head mech. engring. dept. U. Mass., Amherst, 1966—. Served with AUS, 1953-55. Mem. Am. Soc. Mech. Engrs., Am. Soc. Engring. Edn., Sigma Xi, Tau Beta Pi. Author: Programmed Introduction to Probability, 1964; Deisgn Engineering, 1967. Home: 20 Grantwood Dr Amherst MA 01002

DIXON, JOHN WAINWRIGHT, corp. exec.; b. Lexington, Ky., Mar. 12, 1920; s. Thomas H. and Mary (Edmonds) D.; student George Washington U., 1948-49; A.B., U. Houston, 1948; M.A., U. Miami (Fla.), 1951; m. Doris I. Sowell, May 13, 1961; children—Jacqueline P., Frederick D.R., Clinton M. Asst. to v.p. planning Convair Gen. Dynamics, San Diego, 1956-61; asst. comptroller, dir. systems planning Office Asst. Sec. Def., Washington, 1961-62; dir. planning Ling Temco Vought, Inc., Dallas, 1962-67, v.p. planning, 1967-69; chmn., pres. LTV Electrosystems, Inc. (subsidiary Ling-Tempco-Vought, Inc.), 1969—. Mem. Dallas Council World Affairs. Served with AUS, 1941-46. Mem. Air Force Assn., Aerospace Industries Assn., Am. Ordnance Assn., U.S. Army Assn., Phi Beta Kappa. Club: Dallas Economists (pres. 1968). Home: 5106 Kelsey Rd Dallas TX 75214 Office: PO Box 6030 Dallas TX 75222

DIXON, JOSEPH ARDIFF, educator; b. Phila., Nov. 4, 1919; s. Joseph Francis and Mabel Alberta (Miltenberger) D.; B.S., Pa. State U., 1942, M.S., 1945, Ph.D., 1947; m. Marjorie Jane Watts, Apr. 17, 1942; children—Kathleen (Mrs. Walter Swift). Brian Gilbert. With U.S. Dept. Agr., 1942-44; mem. faculty Pa. State U., 1947-51, 55—, prof. chemistry, 1962—, head dept., 1971—; with Cal. Research Corp., Richmond, 1951-52; mem. faculty Lafayette Coll., 1952-55. Mem. Am. Chem. Soc., A.A.A.S, Sigma Xi. Contbr. articles sci. jours. Home: 1000 Plaza Dr State College PA 16801

DIXON, LLOYD A., Jr., mfg. exec.; b. Oshkosh, Wis., Aug. 16, 1920; s. Lloyd A. and Ruth (Shobert) D; B.S. in Indsl. Engring., Pa. State U., 1942; m. Charlotte Lowe, Aug. 22, 1942; children—Lloyd A. III, Peter L. Chief engr. Pitts. DuBois Co., DuBois, Pa., 1940-44, exec. v.p., 1944-47, gen. mgr. Pitts. DuBois div. Rockwell Mfg. Co., Pitts., 1947-50; asst. v.p. Rockwell Mfg. Co., 1950-52, v.p., 1952-64; v.p. W.E. Bowler Co., 1954-64, Valve Products, Inc., 1955-64; pres., dir. Automatic Voting Machine Co. (now AVM Corp.), 1964—, Jamestown, N.Y., Jamestown Metal Products Co., 1964-69, Am. Locker Co., Jamestown, 1964—, Canadian Locker Co., Toronto, Ont., Can.; pres. Knowles Fisher Co., Signore Inc., dir. Penn Lincoln Hotel. Mem. school bd., DuBois, 1948-50; planning commr. Churchill Borough, Pa., 1954-57. Bd. dirs. Columbia Hosp., Jamestown United Fund. Mem. Am. Water Works Assn., Am. Petroleum Inst., Am. Gas Assn., A.I.M., Am. Soc. M.E., Nomads, Am. Inst. Indsl. Engrs. (dir.). Episcopalian (mem. vestry). Home: 65 Terrace Av Lakewood NY 14750 Office: AVM Corp Box 1000 Jamestown NY 14701

DIXON, PAUL RAND, govt. ofcl.; b. Nashville, Sept. 29, 1913; s. James David and Sarah (Munn) D.; A.B., Vanderbilt U., 1936, LL.B., U. Fla., 1938; m. Doris Busby, Oct. 11, 1939; children—David Leslie, Paul Randall. Asst. football coach U. Fla., 1936-38; admitted to Tenn. bar, Fla. bar; trial atty. FTC, 1938-57, chmn., 1961-70, commr., 1970—; chief counsel, staff dir. subcom. antitrust and monopoly U.S. Senate, 1957-61. Area rep. Glen Mar Park Council, Bethesda, Md., 1955-56. Mem. alumni bd. dirs. Vanderbilt U. Served with USNR, 1942-45. Mem. Fed., Am. bar assns., Tenn. Soc. (pres. Washington 1958-59, exec. bd. 1960-61), Vanderbilt U. Alumni Assn. (pres. Washington 1954-55), Nat. Lawyers Club, Phi Delta Phi, Alpha Tau Omega. Democrat. Methodist. Mason. Clubs: Naval Officers, Kenwood Golf and Country (Bethesda); Nashville Quarterback. Home: 5911 Carlton Lane Glen Mar Park Washington DC 20016 Office: Fed Trade Commn Washington DC 20580

DIXON, ROBERT JAMES, air force officer; b. N.Y.C., Apr. 9, 1920; s. William H. and Mary A. (Smith) D.; grad. Collegiate Sch. for Boys, N.Y.C., 1937; A.B., Dartmouth, 1941; grad. Air War Coll., 1959; m. Lamana M. Kelly, July 19, 1958; children—Kelly Lee, Thomas Fries, Roland Cahill, Mary Lucinda. Enlisted RCAF, 1941, commd. pilot officer, 1942, trans. USAAF, 1943, advanced through grades to lt. gen. USAF, 1970; served as pilot ETO, World War II, 4th Fighter Wing, Korea, vice comdr. 7th Air Force, Vietnam, 1969-70; comdr. 45th Air Div., Loring AFB, Me., 1965-67; dep. chief staff personnel Hdqrs. USAF, Washington, 1970—. Mem. U.S. Olympic Com., 1967-69. Bd. dirs. Army/Air Force Exchange Service, 1967-69. Decorated D.S.C., D.S.M., Legion of Merit, D.F.C., Bronze Star; recipient Zuckert Mgmt. award USAF, 1969. Mem. Phi Gamma Delta. Club: Dartmouth (Washington). Home: 67 Westover Av Bolling AFB Washington DC 20332 Office: The Pentagon USAF-AF/DP Washington DC 20330

DIXON, ROBERT LIVINGSTON, educator; b. Ann Arbor, Mich., Aug. 3, 1909; s. Robert Livingston and Mabel Gladys (Wyckoff) D.; A.B., U. Mich., 1930; M.B.A., 1931; Ph.D., Yale, 1941; m. Marie Elizabeth Clark, Jan. 22, 1932; 1 dau., Anne Marie. Instr. accounting Yale, 1932-37; asst. prof. U. Chgo., 1938-41; asso. prof. U. Mich., 1942-47, prof. accounting, 1948—; Australian Soc. Accountants-Commonwealth Bank guest lectr. in Australia, 1957, Am. Inst. C.P.A.'s distinguished vis. prof., 1969-70. C.P.A., Ill. Hon. fellow Australian Soc. Accountants; mem. Am. Accounting Assn. (dir. research 1944-46, pres. 1949), Am. Inst. C.P.A.'s, Mich. Assn. C.P.A.'s, Financial Exec. Inst., Delta Sigma Pi, Tau Kappa Epsilon, Beta Gamma Sigma, Beta Alpha Psi. Rotarian. Author: Make or Buy Decisions in Tooling for Mass Production, 1961; (with W.A. Paton) Essentials of Accounting, 1966; Executive's Accounting Primer, 1971. Editor: Introductory Accounting. Editor of The Accounting Rev., 1947-48. Contbr. to Accountants' Handbook. Home: 1365 Chalmers Dr Ann Arbor MI 48104

DIXON, ROGER COIT, fgn. service officer; b. Hanover, N.H., July 13, 1914; s. Frank Haigh and Alice Lester (Tucker) D.; grad. Phillips Exeter Acad., 1932; A.B., Princeton, 1936, Ph.D., 1942; m. Ruth Priest, Dec. 27, 1960; children—Michael A. Strong, Ann S. Dixon, Peter T. Strong. With anti-trust div. Dept. Justice, 1940-42, USAAF intelligence, 1942-45, Dept. State, 1946-63; counselor embassy for econ. affairs of Am. embassy, Copenhagen, 1963-67; counselor security trade control U.S. Mission to O.E.C.D., Paris, France, 1967—. Grad. fellow Brookings Instn., 1940-41. Mem. Am. Econ. Assn. Home: 107 Av Henri Martin Paris 16e France Office: American Embassy Paris France

DIXON, STEWART STRAWN, lawyer; b. Evanston, Ill., Nov. 5, 1930; s. Wesley M. and Katherine (Strawn) D.; B.A., Yale, 1952; LL.B., U. Mich., 1955; m. Romayne Wilson, June 24, 1961; children—Stewart Strawn, John Wilson, Romayne Warren. Admitted to Ill. bar, 1957; mem. firm Kirkland, Ellis, Hodson, Chaffetz & Masters, Chgo., 1957-67; partner Wildman, Harrold, Allen & Dixon, Chgo., 1967—. Del. Republican Ill. State Nominating Conv., 1964; treas. 43d Ward Regular Rep. Orgn. of Chgo., 1964—. Pres. bd. dirs. Infant Welfare Soc. Chgo., 1969—; bd. dirs. Chgo. Fed. Soc., Chgo. Latin Sch. Served with AUS, 1955-57. Mem. Am., Ill., Chgo. bar assns., Am. Judicature Soc., Am. Acad. Matrimonial Lawyers, Northwestern U. Assn. Clubs: Onwentsia (Lake Forest, Ill.); Racquet, Casino, Saddle and Cycle, University (Chgo.). Home: 6 E Scott St Chicago IL 60610 Office: 6 N Michigan Av Chicago IL 60602

DIXON, THOMAS FRANCIS, aviation co. exec.; b. Nashville, Mar. 15, 1916; s. Sam Jones and Mary (Francis) D. B.S. in Engring., Vanderbilt U., 1938; B.S. in Chem. Engring., M.S., U. Mich., 1940; M.S. in Aero. Engring., Cal. Inst. Tech., 1945; m. Margaret Ann Donovan, July 6, 1943; children—Thomas A., Neil E., Nancy A., Jane E. Vice pres. research & engring. Rocketdyne div. N.Am. Aviation Co., 1946-60; dep. asso. adminstr. NASA, 1961-63; vice pres. N.Am. Aviation, Inc., 1963-67; chmn. bd. Airtronics, Inc., 1967-69, pres., 1969—. Served to lt. comdr. USNR, World War II. Recipient Robert M. Goddard Meml. award Am. Rocket Soc., 1957; Louis W. Hill Space Transp. award Inst. Aero. Scis., 1961. Fellow Am. Inst. Aeros. and Astronautics; mem. Soc. Automotive Engrs. Home: Route 1 Box 58 Broad Run VA 22041

DIXON, VERNON, film set decorator; b. Pietermaritzburg, S. Africa, Feb. 11, 1915; s. Frederick and Francis (Crouch) D.; ed. in S. Africa; later student Poly. Art and Display Schs., London. Set decorator motion pictures, 1945—, latest being The Private Life of Sherlock Holmes, 1969, The Adventurers, 1968, The Battle of Britain, 1967, Oliver 1967, You Only Live Twice, 1966; Nicholas and Alexandra, 1970; Lamb, 1971. Recipient Acad. Motion Picture Arts and Scis. award for best set decoration for Oliver, 1969. Asso. Guild Film Art Dirs. (Brit.). Address: 10 Courtlands Castlebar Hill London W5 England

DIXON, WILFRID JOSEPH, educator; b. Portland, Ore., B.A., Ore State Coll., 1938; M.A., U. Wis., 1939; Ph.D., Princeton, 1944; m. Eva Milne, Sept. 3, 1938; children—Janet (Mrs. Robert M. Elashoff), Kathleen (Mrs. Costas Hercules). Asst. prof. mathematics U. Oklahoma, 1942-44, 45-46; member joint Army-Navy Target Group, Washington and Guam, 1944- 45; asso. prof., then prof. math. U. Ore., 1946-55; prof. preventive medicine U. Cal. at Los Angeles, 1955-67, prof., chmn. dept. biomath., 1967—; cons. NIH, 1960—, NRC, 1948—, NSF, 1968—, Cal. Dept. Mental Hygiene and Pub. Health, 1963—, VA, 1967—. Fellow A.A.A.S.; mem. Inst. Math. Statistics, Am. Statis. Assn. (v.p. 1969-70). Author: (with F.J. Massey) Introduction to Statistical Analysis, 3d edit., 1969; also articles. Asso. editor Biometrics, 1955-65, Annals of Math. Statistics, 1955-58. Home: 433 25th St Santa Monica, CA 90402 Office: Univ Cal Los Angeles CA 90024

DIXON, WILLIAM CORNELIUS, lawyer; b. Dexter, N.Y., July 1, 1904; s. Frank and Celia (Potter) D.; A.B., U. Mich., 1926, LL.B., 1928; m. Arvilla Pratt, Nov. 20, 1934; children—Anne Arvilla, Nancy Cornelia. Admitted to Ohio bar, 1928, Cal. bar, 1948, bar Supreme Ct. U.S.; asso. with firm Holliday-Grossman-McAfee, Cleve., 1928-32; asst. dir. law, Cleve., 1932-33; practiced law, Cleve., 1933-38, judge Supreme Ct. Ohio, 1938; spl. asst. to atty. gen. U.S. in anti-trust div., 1944-54; with anti-trust div. Dept. Justice, 1945; chief asst. trial sect. anti-trust div., 1945. Legal adviser and mem. Joint War and State Depts. Zaibatsu Mission to Japan, 1946; apptd. chief West Coast offices Anti-trust Div., 1946, chief trial counsel for Govt. U.S. versus Standard Oil Co. Cal. et al, 1948, chief Los Angeles Office, 1948-54; pvt. law practice, Los Angeles, 1954-59, 63—; spl. asst. atty. gen. Cal., 1959, in charge state anti-trust enforcement, 1959-63. Dir. relief for Ohio under Emergency Relief Act, 1938-39. Moderator Los Angeles Assn. Congl. Churches, 1957; moderator Congl. Conf. So. Cal. and S.W., 1960; mem. constn. commn. United Ch. of Christ; mem. United Ch. Bd. for Homeland Ministries, 1962-65. Mem. Cal., Los Angeles bar assns., Delta Sigma Rho, Pi Kappa Alpha. Democrat. Home: 1188 Romney Dr Pasadena CA 91105 Office: Subway Terminal Bldg 417 S Hill St Los Angeles CA 90013

DIXON, WILLIAM JAMES, railroad exec.; b. Pitts., Dec. 6, 1918; s. William Robinson and Blanche (Juhling) D.; B.S. in Civil Engring., Carnegie Inst. Tech., 1940; certificate transp., Yale, 1941; m. Helen Marshall Starkey, Sept. 30, 1950; 1 dau., Angie Louise. Asst. transp. insp. New Haven R.R., 1946-47; spl. engr. B. & O. R.R., 1948-55, dep. supr. methods research engr., Balt., 1955-57, research engr., 1957-61, indsl. engr., 1961, dir. indsl. engring., 1962-64; gen. mgr. indsl. engring. B. & O. R.R. -C. & O. Ry., Balt., 1964-65, asst. to pres. C.R.I. & P.R.R., Chgo., 1965-67, v.p. exec. dept., 1967-69, sr. v.p., 1969-70, pres., 1970—. Served to capt. AUS, 1941-46, 51-52. Registered profl. engr., Pa. Mem. Am. Soc. C.E., Am. Ry. Engring. Assn., Operations Research Soc. Am., Inst. Mgmt. Scis., Ry. Systems and Mgmt. Assn., Sigma Xi, Tau Beta Pi, Phi Kappa Phi, Pi Delta Epsilon. Home: 610 Sunrise Av Lake Bluff IL 60044 Office: 139 W Van Buren St Chicago IL 60605

DIXON, WILLIAM ROBERT, composer, trumpeter; b. Nantucket, Mass., Oct. 5, 1925; student Boston U., also Hartnett Sch. Music. Formerly free-lance arranger and trumpeter, N.Y.C.; leader own group, 1950—; work with Cecil Taylor, 1959—; player own works, 1962—; an organizer October Revolution Concert, 1964; parttime tchr. trumpet, composition and painting; one- man shows, N.Y.C.; recording artist for Savoy Records. Served with AUS. Address: 5404 W Touhy Av Chicago IL 60648*

DIXSON, ROBERT JOHN, corp. exec., lawyer; b. Bklyn., July 3, 1907; s. John J. and Catherine (Woelfel) D.; LL.B., St. John's U., 1929, LL.D., 1969; m. Margaret Ott, June 4, 1932; 1 son, Robert John. Admitted to N.Y. bar, 1930; law faculty St. John's U., 1930-42; law firm Vollmer, Wildermuth & Dixson, 1930-42; dir. indsl. relations Chicopee Mfg. Corp., 1944-49; asst. gen. counsel Johnson & Johnson, New Brunswick, N.J., 1942-45, exec. asst. dir. overseas operations, 1949-54, dir. overseas operations, 1954-57, dir., 1952—, mem. exec. com., 1961—; pres. Johnson & Johnson Internat., 1957- 61, vice chmn., 1961—; dir. First Bank & Trust, Boynton Beach, Fla. Former mem. Export-Import U.S.; dir. Far East-Am. Council Commerce and Industry. Mem. council St. Johns U., Bklyn.; v.p. bd. govs. Muhlenberg Hosp., Plainfield, N.J.; conferee USAF War Coll., 1961. Trustee Francis E. Parker Meml. Home, Robert Wood Johnson Found.; Johnson Found.; Am. Inst. Free Labor Devel. Recipient Pietas medal St. Johns U., 1965. Mem. Am., N.Y., Nassau County bar assns., Am. Judicature Soc., Nat. Fgn. Trade Council (chmn.), Internat. Mgmt. Assn., Internat. C. of C. (U.S. Council), Nat. Council Cath. Men, Phi Delta Phi. Clubs: Union League (N.Y.C.); Bay Head (N.J) Yacht; Plainfield (N.J) Country; Garden City (N.Y.) Golf; Capitol Hill (Washington); Ekwanok Country (Manchester, Vt.); Gulf Stream (Fla.) Bath and Tennis, Little (Gulf Stream); Baltusrol Golf (Springfield, N.J.). Contbr. articles to profl. jours. Home: 1779 Sleepy Hollow Lane Plainfield NJ 07060 Office: 501 George St New Brunswick NJ 08902 also 2665 N Ocean Blvd Gulf Stream FL 33480

DIZ, ADOLFO CESAR, economist, educator; b. Buenos Aires, Argentina, May 12, 1931; s. Agustin and Elisa (Aristizabal) D.; C.P.A., U. Buenos Aires, 1951, Licenciate Econs., 1952; M.A. in Econs., U. Chgo., 1957, Ph.D., 1966; m. Martha E. Solari, July 18, 1959; children—Agustin, Joaquin I., Diego A., Rodrigo A. Came to U.S., 1966. Inst. statistics U. Buenos Aires, 1951-59; prof. statistics and econometrics U. Tucuman (Argentina), 1959- 63, prof. monetary theory, 1964-66, dir. Inst. Econ. Research, 1959-66; exec. dir. Internat. Monetary Fund, 1966-. Mem. Am. Econ. Assn., Econometric Serv., Associacón Argentina de Economnia Politica, Inst. de Sci. Econommique Apliques. Roman Cath. Author articles in field. Home: 8506 W Howell Rd Bethesda MD 20034 Office: Internat Monetary Fund 19 and H St Washington DC 20431

DIZARD, WILSON PAUL, Jr., fgn. service officer; b. N.Y.C., Mar. 6, 1922; s. Wilson Paul and Helen Marie (Oliver) D.; B.S., Fordham Coll., 1947; posgrad. Columbia, 1947-49; m. Lynn Margaret Wood, Mar. 11, 1944; children—John William, Stephen Wood, Wilson Paul III, Mark Christopher. Writer, editor Time Inc., N.Y.C., 1947-51; with Dept. State, 1951—; vice consul, Istanbul, Turkey, 1951-53; with USIA, 1953—; chief Greece-Turkey-Iran br., 1953-55; information officer Am. Embassy, Athens, Greece, 1955-60; pub. affairs officer Consulate-Gen., Dacca, 1960-62; spl. asst. dep. dir., 1964-65; asst. dep. dir., 1966-67; 1st sec. Embassy, Warsaw, Poland, 1968-70; asst. dir. Pub. Affairs Office, Saigon, Vietnam, 1970—; mem. U.S. delegation and exec. asst. to conf. dir. Internat. Telecommunications Satellite Conf., Washington, 1968-69. Bd. advisers Internat. U. Communications, Washington; cons. Carnegie Found. Commn. on Ednl. TV. Served with AUS, 1943-46. Research asso. Center Internat. Studies Mass. Inst. Tech., 1962-63; recipient distinguished alumni award Fordham Coll., 1962. Club: International (Washington). Author: The Strategy of Truth, 1961; Television—A World View, 1966. Contbr. articles profl. jours. Home: 2811 28th St NW Washington DC 20008 Office: JUSPAO Am Embassy Saigon Dept State Washington DC 20520

DJAPARIDZE, DAVID, philologist, educator; b. Koutais, Georgia, Russia, Apr. 23, 1921; s. Alexander and Olga (Iosseliani) D.; diploma de l'Ecole des Langues Orientales Vivantes, 1948; Licence ès lettres, 1948; m. Justina Besharov, July 24, 1954; 1 son, Ludwig. Came to the U.S., 1958. Began as librarian charge Slavic and E. European collections Ecole Nationale des Langues Orientales Vivantes, Paris, France, 1948-58; vis. lectr. U. Oxford (Eng.), 1951, 52, 53; mem. learned council Inst. Study USSR, Munich, Germany, 1955-56; charge de cours Ecole des Hautes Etudes, Sorbonne, Paris, 1956, 57, dir. d'etudes, 1957—; vis. lectr. Ecole Militaire, 1956; vis. prof., curator Slavic collection Ind. U., 1959-60; vis. prof. sr. fellow Council Humanities, Princeton, 1960-61, prof. Slavic langs. and lits., 1961—, chmn. program, 1961-63; vis. prof. Columbia U., N.Y.C., 1967, summer 68, State U. of N.Y., Albany, 1969-70. Rockefeller fellow, 1953-54. Mem. Mediaeval Acad. Am., Am. Assn. Advancement Slavic Studies, Linguistic Soc. Am. Author: Medieval Slavic Manuscripts, 1957. Contbr. specialized jours. Home: 340 Riverside Dr New York City, NY 10025; (summer) Trabo Milton-on-Hudson NY 12547 Office: East Pyne Bldg Princeton U Princeton NJ 08540

DJERASSI, CARL, educator, chemist; b. Vienna, Austria, Oct. 29, 1923; s. Samuel and Alice (Friedmann) D.; naturalized U.S. citizen, 1945; A.B. summa cum laude, Kenyon Coll., 1942, D.Sc. (hon.), 1958; Ph.D., U. Wis., 1945; D.Sc. (hon.), Nat. U. Mexico, 1953; m. Norma Lundholm; children— Pamela, Dale. Research chemist Ciba Pharm. Products, Inc., Summit, N.J., 1942- 43, 45-49; asso. dir. research Syntex, Mexico City, 1949-52, research v.p., 1957-60; v.p. Syntex Labs., Palo Alto, Cal., 1960-62; v.p. Syntex Research, 1962-68, pres., 1968—; chmn. bd. dirs. Zoecon Corp., Syva Co.; dir. Syntex Corp.; prof. chemistry Wayne State U., 1952-59, Stanford, 1959—; Andrews lectr. U. New South Wales, Australia; Debye lectr. Cornell U.; Reynaud lectr. Mich. State U.; Venable lectr. U.N.C.; Edgar Fahs Smith Meml. lectr. U. Pa.; O.H. Smith lectr. Okla. State U.; Stieglitz lectr. U. Chgo.; Bachman lectr. U. Mich., Mack lectr. Ohio State U.; ann. chemistry lectr. Royal Swedish Acad. Engring. Recipient Intrasci. Research Found. award, 1969; Freedman Patent award Am. Inst. Chemists, 1971. Mem. Nat. Acad. Scis., Am. (award pure chemistry 1958, Baekeland medal 1959, Fritzsche award 1968), British (Centenary lectr. 1964; hon. fellow), Swiss, German chem. socs., Am. Acad. Arts and Scis., German Acad. Natural Scientists, Am. Acad. Pharm. Scis., Brazilian Academy Scis., Mexican Acad. Sci. Investigation, Am. Soc. Biol. Chemists, Am. Pugwash Com., Phi Beta Kappa, Sigma Xi, Phi Lambda Upsilon (hon.). Author 6 books. Editorial bd. Jour. Organic Chemistry, 1955-59, Tetrahedron, 1958—, Steroids, 1963—, Proceedings of Nat. Acad. Scis., 1964-70, Jour. Am. Chem. Soc., 1966—, Organic Mass Spectrometry, 1968—. Contbr. numerous articles profl. jours. Office: Dept Chemistry Stanford U Stanford CA 94305

DJILAS, MILOVAN, author, politician; b. 1911; ed. Belgrad (Yugoslavia) U. Mem. Communist Party, 1932; imprisoned, 1932-35; mem. Central Com. Communist Party, 1938, mem. Politburo, 1940; minister, head Parliament, v.p. Yugoslavia until 1954; expelled from party, 1954; imprisoned, 1956- 61, 62-66. Author: Essays, 1941-46, 1947; Struggle of the Communist Party of Yugoslavia, 1948; On National History as an Educational Subject, 1949; Lenin and the Realations Between Socialist States, 1950; On New Roads to Socialism, 1956; Reflections on Various Questions, 1951; On the Aggressive Pressure of the Soviet Bloc against Yugoslavia, 1951; The Legend of Njegos, 1952; The New Class, 1957; (in English) Land Without Justice, 1958, Montenegro, 1964; Conversations with Stalin, 1962; The Leper and Other Stories, 1964; Njegos, 1966; The Unperfect Society, 1969; Izqubljeni Raj, 1970; Under the Colors, 1971; The Stone and the Violets, 1972. Address: care Harcourt Brace Jovanovich Inc 757 3d Av New York City NY 10017

DLAMINI, MBONI NAPH, Swaziland diplomat; b. Nkhungwini, Swaziland, Nov. 20, 1928; s. Majozi and Lontombi (Simelane) D.; diploma in internat. relations, econs. and internat. relations, econs. and internat. law, U. Oxford (Eng.), 1968; m. Joyce Simangele, Jan. 16, 1964; children—Ketsiwe, Muzi, Gaciniwe. High sch. tchr., Swaziland, 1958-62; headmaster Jurniz Secondary Sch., Ntshanini, Swaziland, 1963-66; counsellor Swaziland Mission to UN, 1968-69; ambassador, permanent rep. to UN, N.Y.C., 1970—. Office: 866 UN Plaza New York City NY 10017

DOAN, CHARLES AUSTIN, med. research; b. Nelsonville, O., June 5, 1896; s. Robert Austin and Lelia Minturn (Welch) D.; B.S., Hiram (O.) Coll., 1915-18; postgrad. U. Cin., 1919; M.D., Johns Hopkins, 1923; Harvard Med. Sch., summer, 1920; Peter Bent Brigham Hosp., Boston, summer, 1922; Sc.D. (hon.), Ohio State U., 1964; m. Margaret Dixon Riggs, May 28, 1926; children—Elizabeth, Ellen Virginia. Resident house officer, Johns Hopkins Hosp., 1923; research asst., asst. prof. Thorndike Meml. Labs. Harvard Med. Sch., 1924-25; asso. Rockefeller Inst. Med. Research, 1925-30; prof. of med. and dir. dept. med. and surg. research, Ohio State U., 1930-36, chmn. Dept. of Medicine and dir. of med. research, 1936-44, dean Coll. of Medicine, prof. medicine, dir. Health Center, dir. med. research, 1944-61, dean and prof. of med. emeritus, 1961—, dir. div. hematology, 1961-66; tech. dir. A.R.C. Blood Donor Center, 1942-45, med. dir., 1947- 57; chmn. Region No. 8 (Ohio and Pa.) Grad. War Med. Meeting Commn.; chmn. Commn. on Sci. Work, O.S.M.A., 1942-45; expert cons. Surgeon Gen., Dept. of Army. Served with M.C., U.S. Army, advancing to sgt. in charge Bacteriol. Lab., 1917-June 1919; lt. col. Med. Corps Res., A.U.S., 1940-42. Mem. sub-com. on blood and blood derivitives A.R.C.; chmn. hematology study sect. Nat. Insts. Health, USPHS, mem. com. on blood and blood forming orgns of panel on clin. physiology NRC, also com. on growth; mem. panel on blood and blood forming orgns Med. Adv. Bd. Master A.C.P. (gov. for Ohio ,1948; chmn. bd. govs., 1st v.p.); mem. Am. Assn. Anatomists, Harvey Soc., Soc. Exptl. Biol. and Medicine, Central Soc. Clin. Research (pres. 1939-40), Am. Soc. Clin. Investigation, Am. Soc. Exptl. Pathology, Am. Soc. Clin. Pathology, Ohio Acad. Scis. (v.p. 1936, pres. 1937), Assn. Am. Physicians, Ohio Pub. Health Assn. (past pres.), Internat. R-E Society (past pres.), Am. Soc. Hematology (pres. 1963-64), Phi Beta Kappa, Phi Chi, Pi Kappa Delta, Sigma Xi, Alpha Omega Alpha. Mem. Disciples of Christ Ch. Mason (33, K.T.). Contbr. on scientific research in hematology and tuberculosis. Home: 4935 Olentangy Blvd Columbus OH 43214 Office: 3600 Olentangy River Rd Columbus OH 43214☆

DOAN, HERBERT DOW, chem. engr.; b. Midland, Mich., Sept. 5, 1922; s. Leland Ira and Ruth (Dow) D.; student Cranbrook Prep. Sch., 1937-41; B.Sc. in Chem. Engring., Cornell U., 1949; m. Donalda Mary Lockwood, July 27, 1946; children—Jeffrey William, Christine Mary, Michael Alden, Ruth Alden. Tech. service and devel. Dow Chem. Co., Midland, Mich., 1950, purchase analyst, 1951-52, exec. research, 1953-56, mgr. chems. dept., 1956-61, exec. v.p., 1961-62, pres., 1962-70, now only dir.; dir. Dow Badische Co., Dow Corning Corp., Am. Research & Devel., Chemical State Savs. Bank. Mem. chem. subcom. Nat. Indsl. Pollution Control Council, Dept. Commerce. Exec. com. Mich. United Fund. Mem. bd. fellows Saginaw Valley Coll.; mem. pres.'s council Cal. Inst. Tech.; adv. council Grad. Sch. Bus. Adminstrn., Mich. State U.; mem. Cornell U. Engring. Council; trustee Citizens Research Council Mich., Dow Found. Mem. Am. Inst. Chem. Engrs., Am. Chem. Soc., Mfg. Chemists Assn., Mich. C. of C. (mem. bd.). Rotarian. Home: 3801 Valley Dr Midland MI 48640 Office: Dow Chemical Co Midland MI 48640

DOAN, HOWARD WILLIAM, ret. army officer; b. La Salle, Ill., Mar. 18, 1907; s. Howard Frank and Gertrude (Hoeshelt) D.; B.S., Drake U., 1928; M.D., U. Ia., 1932; M.P.H., U. Cal. at Berkeley, 1949; m. Dorothy J. Havens, Mar. 10, 1943; children—Jacqueline Jean, Robert Havens, Julie Dianne. Commd. 1st M.C., U.S. Army, 1933, advanced through grades to maj. gen., 1962; dep. surgeon gen. U.S. Army, 1961-63; exec. dir. Armed Forces Dependent Med. Care Program, 1963-64, ret., 1964; dir. dept. hosps. and med. facilities A.M.A., Chgo., 1964-68; dir. Colo.-Wyo. Regional Med. Program, 1968—. Chmn. Def. Med. Material Bd., 1961-63. Decorated Legion of Merit, Bronze Star, Army Commendation medal, D.S.M. Fellow Am. Pub. Health Assn.; mem. A.M.A. (sec. council on med. service), Am. Hosp. Assn., Am. Coll. Hosp. Adminstrs. Home: 1501 S Kenton Aurora CO 80010 Office: 2045 Franklin St Denver CO 80220

DOAN, LELAND IRA, chem. co. dir.; b. North Bend, Neb., Nov. 9, 1894; s. Ira and Hester (Spencer) D.; student U. Mich., 1913-16; D.E. (hon.), Case Inst. Tech., 1952; LL.D. (hon.), Kalamazoo Coll., 1955, Central Mich. Coll., 1956, Earlham Coll., 1957, Alma Coll., 1963; D.Sc. in Bus. Adminstrn., Cleary Coll., 1957; D.H.L., Findlay Coll., 1962; LL.D. (hon.), Northwood Inst., 1967; m. Ruth Alden Dow, Apr. 7, 1917 (dec.); children—Leland Alden, Dorothy (Doan) Arbury, Herbert Dow; m. 2d, Mildred Mellus, 1950. With Dow Chem. Co., 1917, beginning in sales dept., successively asst. sales mgr. and gen. sales mgr., v.p. and sec., 1938-49, pres., 1949-62, chmn. exec. com., 1962-70, dir., 1935—; dir. Nat. Bank Detroit. Mem. Nat. Indsl. Conf. Bd. Recipient Chem. Industry medal Am. sect. Soc. Chem. Industry, 1964. Mem. Mfg. Chemists Assn., Sigma Chi. Presbyn. Mason (33). Clubs: Detroit Athletic; Chemists (N.Y.C.); Bohemian (San Francisco); Surf (Miami, Fla.); Midland. Home: 3701 Valley Dr Midland MI 48640 Office: Dow Chem Co Midland MI 48640

DOAN, MILES J., utility exec.; b. Bay City, Mich., June 22, 1917; s. Howard and Ida (Schuman) D.; A.A., Bay City Jr. Coll., 1937; B.A., M.B.A., U. Mich., 1941; m. Lynne Phelps, Dec. 15, 1945; 1 dau., Lynnette. Accountant, Arthur Andersen & Co., Chgo., 1941-42, 46-49; with Cin. Gas and Electric Co., 1949—, financial v.p., sec., 1963-65, financial v.p., 1965-70, sr. v.p., 1970—, also dir. Bd. trustees Salmon P. Chase Coll. Sch. Law, Cin., 1962—; bd. dirs. The Children's Protective Service, 1967—; mem. finance com. Cin. Community Chest and Council, 1964—. Served to lt. USNR, 1942-46, C.P.A., Ill. Mem. Am. Inst. C.P.A.'s, Ohio Soc. C.P.A.'s, Am. Gas Assn., Edison Electric Inst. Mason. Home: 5741 Pinehill Lane Cincinnati OH 45238 Office: 139 E 4th St Cincinnati OH 45202

DOBBIE, GEORGE HERBERT, textile mfg. co. exec.; b. Galt, Ont., Can., Nov. 15, 1918; s. George Alexander and Edith (Scott) D.; student Bishop Ridley Coll., 1934-35, McGill U., 1936-39; m. Marie L. Reiser, Mar. 15, 1941; children—George C., Murray S., Brian II, Alexander M. With Newlands & Co., Galt, 1939—, sales mgr. hand knit div., 1947-51, pres., 1951—; pres., chmn. Dobbie Industries, Ltd., Dobble Glemoit, Lit.; dir. Dominion Life Assurance Co., Waterloo, Ont., Can., Can. Trust Co., London, Ont., Domtar, Ltd., Montreal, Que., Can. Gov., Waterloo U. Served from pvt. to capt. Royal Canadian Army, 1941-45. Mem. Canadian Woolen and Knit Goods Mfrs. Assn. (pres. 1956-58), Primary Textiles Inst. Can. (chmn.). Home: 45 Blair Rd Galt Ontario Canada Office: Water St Galt Ontario Canada

DOBBIN, GEORGE F., constrn. co. exec. Pres., Aberthat Constrn. Co., Boston. Office: 60 State St Boston MA 02109*

DOBBIN, TILTON HEMSLEY, banker; b. Lawyers Hill, Md., Apr. 9, 1917; s. Robert A. and Maria Kerr (Hemsley) D.; grad. Boys' Latin Sch., Balt., 1936; m. Julia Morris Bruce, Feb. 14, 1942; children—Mary Greeley, Robert, Douglas Seddon, Elizabeth Hemsley, Frances Key. With Balt. Nat. Bank, 1936-40, 45-49; asst. cashier Mellon Nat. Bank, Pitts., 1949-53; asst. treas. Olin Mathieson Chem. Corp., Balt., 1953-57; v.p. Balt. Nat. Bank, 1957-60; pres. Md. Nat. Bank, 1960—, also chmn. exec. com., dir.; dir. Md. Shipbldg. & Drydock Co., Md. Casualty Co., Fidelity & Deposit Co. Md., Title Guarante Co. Md., Balt., Am. Gen. Ins. Co., Houston, So. Md. Agrl. Assn., Bowle, Balt. br. Fed. Res. Bank Richmond. Trustee Greater Balt. Med. Center, Washington Coll., Chestertown, Md., Westminster Sch., Simsburg, Conn., Goucher Coll. Served with USNR, 1940-45. Episcopalian. Clubs: Merchants, Maryland (Balt.); Green Spring Valley Hunt (Garrison, Md.). Home: Golf Course Rd Owings Mills MD 21117 Office: Md Nat Bank Baltimore MD 21203

DOBBINS, CHARLES GORDON, educator, editor; b. Greensboro, Ala., Aug. 15, 1908; s. John Gordon and Mantie Edgar (Wolf) D.; A.B., Howard Coll., 1929; M.A., Columbia, 1931; postgrad. U. Wis., 1931-33; L.H.D., Judson Coll., 1967; Litt.D., Jamestown Coll., 1971; m., 1935; 1 son, Peter Young; m. 2d, Sylvie Buffet, Dec. 21, 1963. Reporter Birmingham Age-Herald, 1929; instr. English, U. Wis.,

1931-34; dir. Fed. Emergency Relief Adminstrn. Transient Camp, Ft. McClellan, Ala., 1935; dist. dir. Nat. Youth Adminstrn., Gadsden, Ala., 1936; asst. to pres. Ala. Coll., 1936-39; editor, pub. Anniston (Ala.) Times, 1939-42; editor Montgomery (Ala.) Advertiser, 1946-47; editor, pub. Montgomery Examiner, 1947-55; staff asso. Am. Council on Edn., 1956-62, dir. commn. on fed. relations, 1962-63, exec. sec., 1963—, dir. acad. adminstrn. internship program, 1967—. Pres. Ala. Press Assn., 1942. Bd. dirs. Nat. Home Library Found. Dir. OPS, Ala., 1951-53; mem. Nat. Planning Assn. (Com. of South), 1946-55, Ala. Bd. Edn., 1951-59; bd. visitors Fla. Presbyn. Coll., 1968—. Served with USNR, 1942-46. Mem. Omicron Delta Kappa, Sigma Delta Chi, Sigma Nu. Democrat. Baptist. Club: Army-Navy (Washington). Author: American Council on Education: Leadership and Chronology, 1918-1968, 1968. Editor: Educational Record, 1968—; The Strength to Meet our National Need, 1956; Expanding Resources for College Teaching, 1956; Higher Education and the Federal Government; Programs and Problems, 1963; The University, The City, and Urban Renewal, 1964. Co-editor; Whose Goals for American Higher Education?, 1968. Contbr. articles to Colliers, London Economist, Ency. Americana, others. Home: 1545 18th St N W Washington DC 20036 Office: 1 Dupont Circle Washington DC 20036

DOBBINS, CRIS, business exec.; b. Denver, Colo., Jan. 8, 1904; s. George S. and Julia Josephine (Spillane) D.; B.B.A., U. Denver, 1927, LL.D., 1967; m. Elvira Mae Bjork, Oct. 19, 1930; children—Christopher, Michael A., Felicity Anne. Asst. sales mgr. Colo., Portland Cement co., Denver, 1930-41, sales mgr., 1941-43; asst. to pres. Ideal Cement Co., Denver, 1943-44, v.p., gen. mgr., 1944-48, exec. v.p., gen. mgr., 1948-52, pres., 1952-67; chmn., pres. Ideal Basic Industries, Inc., 1968-70, chmn., chief exec. officer, 1970-71, dir., chmn., 1971—; chmn., dir. Am. Crystal Sugar Co., Brown Palace Hotel Co., Denver br. Fed. Res. Bank, Kansas City; dir. Am. Smelting & Refining Co., Colo. & So. Ry. Co., Burlington No., Inc., Ideal Corp. Chmn., trustee Boettcher Found.; trustee Tax Found., Denver Mus. Natural History; bd. dirs. Air Force Acad., Central City Opera House Assn.; Am. Mining Congress (pres. 1968-71), Conf. Bd.; pres., treas., bd. dirs. Dobbins Found. Mem. adv. bd. Denver Area council Boy Scouts Am.; mem. Nat. Indsl. Pollution Control Council, chmn. bldg. materials subcouncil, 1970. Mem. Most Venerable Order Hosp. St. John of Jerusalem, Alpha Kappa Psi, Beta Gamma Sigma (hon.). Republican. Episcopalian. Clubs: Denver Athletic, Denver, Denver Country; Pacific-Union (San Francisco; Burlingame Country (Cal.); Garden of the Gods (Colorado Springs, Colo.); Chicago; Buck's (London); Eisenhower Golf (life, Air Force Acad.); Wigwam; Mile High; Tower; Balboa (Mazatlan, Mexico). Home: 770 High St Denver CO 80218 Office: 821 17th St Denver CO 80202

DOBBINS, EMERY EARL, advt. co. exec.; b. Bedford, Ind., Aug. 8, 1914; s. Emery Earl and Hazel (Johnson) D.; B.S., Northwestern U., 1937; m. Marilynn J. Piper, Dec. 16, 1945. With advt. dept. Butler Bros. Chgo., 1937-38; asst. advt. mgr. Barrett div. Allied Chem. & Dye Co., 1938-40; advt. mgr. Adams Mfg. Co., 1940-48; founder Dobbins, Woodward & Co., S. Orange., N.J., 1948, pres., 1948-60; pres. Buchen Advt., Inc., N.Y.C., 1960-68, chmn. bd., 1968—, also dir.; dir. Swan Mfg. Corp., Hagen Comm. Corp. Trustee Garden State Ballet Found. Served with USAAF, 1942-45. Mem. N.Y. Advt. Club, Sigma Alpha Epsilon, Sigma Delta Chi. Clubs: Union League (N.Y.C.); Chicago Athletic Assn. Home: 90A Heritage Village Southbury CT 06488 Office: 280 Park Av New York City NY 10017

DOBBINS, GAINES STANLEY, clergyman, educator; b. Langsdale, Miss., July 29, 1886; s. Charles Wesley and Letitia (Gaines) D.; B.A., Miss. Coll., Clinton, 1908; Th.D., So. Bapt. Theol. Sem., Louisville, Ky., 1914; M.A., Columbia, 1925; D.D., Miss. Coll., 1915, LL.D., 1947; m. May Virginia Riley, Dec. 1910; children—Gaines Stanley, Riley Franklin, Charles Austin. Ordained Baptist ministry, 1914; pastor Gloster, Miss., 1914, New Albany, Miss., 1915; mem. editorial staff So. Bapt. Sunday Sch. Bd., 1915-20; prof. religious edn. and ch. adminstrn., So. Bapt. Theol. Sem., 1920-56, treas., 1933-42; acting pres., 1950- 52, dean Sch. Religious Edn.; distinguished prof. ch. adminstrn. Golden Gate Bapt. Theol. Sem., Mill Valley, Cal., 1956-66; lectr. Samford U., Birmingham, Ala., 1967—; guest lectr. prof. Ruschlikon Bapt. Sem., Zurich, Switzerland, Instituto Filadelfia, Rivili-Turin, Italy, Nigerian Bapt. Theol. Sem., Ogbomosho. Chmn. commn. Bible study and membership tng. Bapt. World Alliance. Recipient Mullins award for Distinguished Denominational Service, So. Bapt. Theol. Sem., 1966. Mem. Am. Acad. Polit. and Social Sci. Author several books, later ones are: Building Better Churches, 1947; Evangelism According to Christ, 1949; The Churchbook, 1951; Winning the Children, 1953; Building A Better Sunday School; The Years Ahead; A Ministering Church, 1960; Guiding Adults in Bible Study; The Church at Worship, 1962; Great Teachers Make a Difference, 1965; Learning to Lead, 1968; also brochures on religious topics. Contbr. Bapt. Sunday Sch. Bd., Nashville. Home: 2121 Ridgeview Dr Birmingham AL 35216 ☆

DOBBINS, INNES WILSON, Jr., banker; b. Fulton, Ky., Feb. 16, 1908; s. Innes Wilson and Mignonne (Murphey) D.; A.B., U. Louisville, 1930; m. Anne Cooper Parker, Oct. 26, 1935; children—Anne Cooper, Innes Wilson III, Stephen A. With mortgage loan and trust dept. Ky. Trust Co., Louisville, 1931-33; with Liberty Nat. Bank and Trust Co., Louisville, 1933—, exec. v.p., 1965-68, pres., 1968—; dir. Liberty Nat. Bank & Trust Co., Bus. Devel. Corp. (all Louisville). Cons. Louisville Urban Renewal Com., 1963—; mem. Mayor Louisville Com. Urban Renewal, 1954—, Louisville Health and Welfare Council, 1964—, Louisville Govt. Venter Study Com., 1965—; chmn. civic center com. Louisville Central Area, 1966—; mem. consumer relations com. Ky. Emergency Resource Planning Com., 1964; mem. athletic com. U. Louisville, 1965. Pres. Louisville Family and Children's Agy., 1952—, bd. dirs., 1956—; chmn. bd. dirs. U. Louisville Assos., 1966—; bd. dirs. Louisville Central Area, 1966—; mem. president's civic council Bellarime coll., 1964—. Mem. Louisville C. of C. (bd. dirs.), Delta Upsilon. Presbyn. Mason (32). Clubs: Louisville Country, Pendennis, Wynn- Stay (Louisville). Home: 347 Mockingbird Valley Rd Louisville KY 40207 Office: 416 W Jefferson St Louisville KY 40202

DOBBINS, JAMES JOSEPH, artist; b. Woburn, Mass., Aug. 12, 1924; s. William John and Delia (Feeney) D.; student Cornell Coll., Mt. Vernon, Ia., 1945; B.S., Mass. Coll. Art, 1951; student Boston U. Grad. Sch. Edn., 1951-52; m. Dorothy Esther Fitzpatrick, Jan. 20, 1951; chiidren-Patricia, William, Mary, James Joseph, Rita, Mark, Dorothy, Christopher, John, Maura. Tchr., Boston pub. schs., 1952; editorial cartoonist Lowell (Mass.) Sun, 1952- 53, N.Y. Daily News, 1953, Boston Post, 1953-556, Boston Herald Traveler, 1956-70. Original drawings donated to Syracuse U. Library. Served with USNR, 1943-45. Decorated D.F.C., Air medal; recipient two Freedoms Found. 1st prizes, 14 honors medals; Christopher Lit. awarrd, 1958; grand prize Internat. Competition, Wayne State U., 1960; certificate of merit Syracuse U., 1969; named Outstanding Young Man, Boston Jaycees, 1957. Mem. Nat. Cartoonist Soc., Assn. Am. Editorial Cartoonists. Democrat. Catholic. Club: Boston Press (pres. 1967-68). Author: Dobbins Diary of the New Frontier, 1964. Home: 94 Church St Winchester MA 01890 Offiice: 300 Harrison St Boston MA 02106

DOBBS, HUBERT LEE, hosp. adminstr.; b. Cameron, Tex., Feb. 3, 1908; s. S.H. and Velma (Fuller) D.; grad. Bus. Coll., 1928; LL.D. (hon.), Georgetown (Ky.) Coll., 1960; m. Eugenia Cook, Dec. 22, 1934; children—Velma Gene (Mrs. James Wright), Hubert Lee. Adminstr., Ky. Baptist Hosp., Louisville, 1935—; exec. dir. Hosp. Commn. Ky., 1951—, Hosp. Commn. of Ky. Baptist Hosps., 1965—; pres., Ky. Bapt. Hosps., Inc., 1969—. A founder Blue Cross-Blue Shield programs, 1935, bd. dirs., 1935—. Fellow Am. Coll. Hosp. Adminstrs.; mem. Ky. Hosp. Assn. (past pres.), Am. Hosp. Assn., Am. Protestant Hosp. Assn. (pres. 1962—). Baptist. Mason, Rotarian. Club: Big Spring Golf (Louisville). Home: 2539 Seneca Dr Louisville KY 40205 Office: 810 Barret Av Louisville KY 40204

DOBBS, MATTIWILDA, opera and concert singer, coloratura soprano; b. Atlanta, Georgia; d. John Wesley and Irene Ophelia (Thompson) Dobbs; B.A. with honors, Spellman Coll., Atlanta, 1946; M.A., Tchrs. Coll. Columbia, 1948; studied voice with Mme. Lotte Leonard, N.Y.C., 1946-50; student Mannes Music Coll., 1948-49, Berkshire Music Festival, 1949; studied French music with Pierre Bernac, Paris, 1950-52; m. Luis Rodriguez Garcia, Apr. 4, 1953 (dec. June 26, 1954); m. 2d, Bengt Janzon, Dec. 23, 1957. Appeared Dutch Opera, Holland Festival, 1952, also recitals, Holland, Paris, Stockholm; appeared LaScala Opera, Milan, Italy, 1953, also concerts Eng., France, Italy, Scandinavia, Austria, Belgium; command performance Covent Garden, London, 1954; concert tours, U.S., 1954—, Australia, 1955, 59, Israel, 1957, 59, USSR, opera and concerts, 1959, Hamburg State Opera, 1961-62; United States opera debut, San Francisco Opera, 1955; debut Met. Opera, N.Y.C., 1956. Recipient 2d prize Marian Anderson awards, 1947; John Hay Whitney fellow, Paris, 1950; 1st prize Internat. Competition Mus. Performers, Geneva Conservatory Music, 1951. Conglist. Home: Vastmannagatan 50 Stockholm Sweden Office: care Michael O'Daniel Am Program Bur 59 Temple Pl Boston MA 02111

DOBBS, RUFUS HOWARD, Jr., life ins. exec.; b. Atlanta, May 16, 1906; s. Rufus Howard and Viola (Coffey) D.; student Ga. Mil. Acad., 3919-23, Emory U., 1923-25; m. Helen Woodward, June 4, 1926. Joined Life Ins. Co. of Ga., 1925, asst. treas., 1928-30, treas., 1930-52, 1st v.p., 1947, now chmn. bd., dir.; dir. Atlanta Gas Light Co., Rich's Dept. Store, Trust Co. Ga., So. Bell Telephone & Telegraph Co. Treas. Atlanta Florence Crittenden Home, 1952; mem. Fulton County (Atlanta) Bd. Health, 1951-61, chmn. 1956-61; v.p. Atlanta Community Services, Inc., 1959; vice chmn. Atlanta chpt. A.R.C. Trustee Emory U., Agnes Scott Coll. Served as capt. A.A.F., 1942-45; with Air Tech. Services Command, 1944. Mem. Am. Life Conv. (pres. 1964- 65), Life Insurers Conf., Atlanta C. of C. (pres., 1952), Alpha Tau Omega. Methodist. Mason (Shriner). Clubs: Rotary (pres. 1956), Athletic, Capital City, Piedmont Driving, Commerce, Atlanta Athletic (Atlanta). Home: 3905 Tuxedo Rd NW Atlanta GA 30305 Office: 600 West Peachtree St NE Atlanta GA 30308

DOBELL, BYRON MAXWELL, editor; b. Bronx, N.Y., May 30, 1927; s. Jacob and Marie (Schaeffer) D.; A.B., Columbia, 1947; m. Edith Spielberg, 1952 (div. 1957); m. 2d, Ande Rubin, 1958 (dec. 1967); 1 dau., Elizabeth; m. 3d, Elizabeth Rodgers Dempster, 1969. Picture editor U.S. Camera, 1952-55; asso. editor Popular Photography, 1956-57; feature editor Pageant, 1957-58, This Week, 1958-60; sr. editor Time-Life Books, 1960-62, asso. dir. editorial planning, 1971—; mng. editor Esquire mag., 1962-67; editor-in-chief Book World, weekly lit. supplement Chgo. Tribune and Washington Post, 1967-69; editor-in-chief book div. McCall Pub. Co., 1969-71. Bd. dirs. Am. Inst. Graphic Arts, 1971—. Served with AUS, 1946-47. Clubs: P.E.N., Coffee House (N.Y.C.). Editor: Life Pictorial Atlas of the World; Life Guide to Paris. Home: 150 E 69th St New York City NY 10021 Office: Time-Life Bldg Rockefeller Center New York City NY 10020

DOBEY, JAMES KENNETH, banker; b. Vallejo, Cal., June 20, 1919; s. Austin E. and Margaret (Hansen) D.; A.B., U. Cal. at Berkeley, 1940; postgrad. Rutgers U., 1956; m. Jean Smith, Apr. 18, 1942; children—James A., Peter M. With Shell Oil Co., Comml. Credit Corp., 1940-42; with Wells Fargo Bank, San Francisco, 1946—, exec. v.p., 1965—; dir. Wells Fargo & Co. Asso., Golden Gate Coll. Bd. govs. Bay Area Council; bd. dirs. Golden Gate chpt. A.R.C. Served to capt. airborne inf., AUS, 1942-46. Mem. Assn. Res. City Bankers, Delta Chi. Clubs: Family; Peninsula Golf and Country (San Mateo). Home: 3033 Atwater Dr Burlingame CA 94010 Office: 464 California St San Francisco CA 94104

DOBIE, ERNEST WILLIAM, Jr., former naval officer, instrument corp. exec.; b. Oakland, Cal., July 31, 1916; s. Ernest William and Harriet (Colbath) D.; student U. Cal. at Berkeley, 1935-36; B.S. in Elec. Engring., U.S. Naval Acad., 1940; M.S. in Chem. Engring., Cornell U., 1946; grad. Naval War Coll., 1960; m. Geraldine Frances Bonnnington, May 3, 1943; children—Robert A., Sharon A., Christine M., Donna C. Commd. ensign USN, 1940, advanced through grades to rear adm., 1965; assigned gunnery dept. U.S.S. Minneapolis, 1940-44; gunnery officer U.S.S. New Jersey, 1946-47; tech. supr. Navy Spl. Weapons Unit 471, Albuquerque, 1948-50; liaison officer with comdr.-in-chief, Pacific for atomic bomb tests, Eniwetok, 1950-51; comdg. officer U.S.S. Lofberg, 1952-53; ordnance officer on staff comdr. Cruiser-Destroyer Force, Pacific, 1954-56; exec. officer Navy Spl. Project (Polaris) field office with Lockheed Missile and Space Div., 1957-59; comdr. Destroyer Div. 112, 1960-61; comdg. officer U.S.S. Mount Baker, 1961-62; head surface ship anti-submarine warfare devel. br. Office Dep. Chief Naval Operations (devel.), 1962-63; comdr. Destroyer Squadron 2, 1963-64; dir. tech. appraisals and requirements Office Div. Anti-Submarine Warfare Programs, 1964-65; dir. undersea and strategic warfare devel. Office Dept. Chief Naval Operations (devel.), 1965-67, dep. dir. anti-submarine warfare programs, 1967-68; comdr. Cruiser-Destroyer Flotilla 2, 1968-70; insp. gen. U.S. Pacific Fleet, 1970-71; ret., 1971; mgr. advanced systems planning Chesapeake Instrument Corp., 1971—. Decorated Legion of Merit, Bronze Star (2) with combat V. Home: 1720 Long Green Dr Annapolis MD

DOBLER, DONALD WILLIAM, coll. dean; b. Rocky Ford, Colo., Apr. 18, 1927; s. William L. and Anna (Nelson) D.; B.S. in Engring., Colo State U., 1946-50; M.B.A., Stanford, 1958, Ph.D., 1960; m. Elaine Carlson, Dec. 27, 1951; Children-Kathleen, David Daniel. Application and sales engr. Westinghouse Elec. Corp., Phila., 1950-53; mgr. purchasing and materials FMC Corp., Green River, Wyo., 1953-57; guest lectr. Stanford Sch. Bus., 1960; asst. prof. mgmt. State U. Utah, Logan, 1960-63, assoc. prof., 1964-66, head dept. bus. adminstrn., 1964-66; vis. prof. mgmt. Dartmouth 1963-64; dean Coll. Bus., Colo. State U., Ft. Collins, 1966—, Dir. U. Nat. Bank, 1967—; pres. Parklane Arms, Inc., 1967—; part-time mgmt. cons., 1960—. Mem. Colo. Gov.'s Adv. Com., 1968—, Ft. Collins Mayor's Budget Com., 1968—. Mem. Acad. Mgmt., Nat. Assn. Purchasing Mgmt. (nat. com. profl. end. 1967—), Am. Prodn. and Inventory Control Soc., Green River C. of C. (pres. 1955), Am. Assn. Collegiate Schs. Bus., Sigma Tau, Phi Kappa Phi. Rotarian. Author: Purchasing and Materials Management: Text and Cases, 1965. Contbg. author to mgmt. books. Contbr. to profl. jours. Home: 1505 Lakeside Dr Ft Collins CO 80521

DOBLER, WILLIAM O., newspaper editor; b. St. Joseph, Mo., Mar. 18, 1926; s. William O. and Rose (Beardsley) D.; B.A., U. Neb., 1950; m. Mary Nancy McMullen, Aug. 21, 1948; children-James, Lisa, Gregory, Christine. Reporter, Lincoln (Neb.) Star, 1950-57, editorial page editor, 1957-59, editor, 1959—. Pres. Lincoln Park and Recreation bd., 1970; pres. Lincoln Hosp. and Health Council, 1970; pres. Lincoln Children's Zoo Assn., 1970; vice chmn. Pius X Found., 1970. Served with USNR, 1944-46. Mem. Am. Soc. Newspaper Editors, Sigma Delta Chi (pres. Neb. 1958). Roman Catholic (mem. Neb. Cath. Conf., v.p. parish council 1970). Elk. Club: Lincoln Serra (pres. 1967-68). Home: 3411 Stockwell St Lincoln NB 68506 Office: The Lincoln Star 926 P St Lincoln NB 68501

DOBLES SANCHEZ, LIC LUIS, diplomat of Costa Rica; b. Milw., June 2, 1925; s. Luis Dobles and Trina Sanchez; student U. Cal. at Berkeley, 1946; m. Elza Villela, May 29, 1948; children—Maria Christina, Pedro, Luis, Elza, Maria Gabriela. Chief of protocol, 1950-53; ambassador to Brazil, 1935-55, to Peru, 1960-62; dep. minister fgn. affairs, 1966-68; ambassador to UN, 1968-71. Mgr. Metaltica (iron works). Mem. Coffe Bd. Costa Rica; mem. Chamber of Agr. Recipient decorations from Brazil, Peru, Ecuador, China, King of Italy. Mem. C. of C., (bd. dirs.), Chamber Sugar Producers. Mem. Unificacion Nacional Party Costa Rica. Home: PO Box 1518 San Jose Costa Rica

DOBLIN, JAY, designer, educator; b. N.Y.C, Dec. 10, 1920; s. Frank C. and Evelyn (McElroy) D.; grad. Pratt Inst., 1942; m. Annette Woodward, Mar. 27, 1949. Indsl. designer, devel. work govt. projects, camouflage Raymond Loewy Assos., N.Y.C., 1942-49, exec. designer, 1952-55; indsl. designer Singer, Frigidaire, Schick, Coca Cola, Shell Oil Co., Nat Biscuit Co., 1945-49, Carl Otto, 1949-52; dir. Inst. Design, Ill. Inst. Tech., 1955-69, prof., 1955-69; sr. v.p., dir. Unimark Internat. Chgo. Chmn. indsl. design dept. night sch. Pratt Inst.; lectr. Recipient honor student award Pratt Inst., 1942, Kaufmann Internat. Design award Internat. Inst. Edn. Fellow Indsl. Design Socs. of Am. (pres. 1956, dir.), Internat. Council Socs. Indsl. Design (v.p.), Internat. Design Conf. (dir.); mem. Indsl. Design Educators Assn. (past pres.). Author: Perspective—A New System for Designers, 1955; 1OO Great Product Designs, 1970. Home: 2235 N Cleveland Av Chicago IL 60614

DOBRIANSKY, LEV EUGENE, educator, economist; b. N.Y.C., Nov. 9, 1918; s. John Eugenia (Greshchuk) D.; B.S., N.Y.U. (Charles Hayden Meml. scholar 1937-41), 1941, M.A., 1943, Hirshland polit. sci. fellow, 1943-44, Ph.D., 1951; LL.D., Free Ukrainian U. at U. Munich (Germany), 1952; m. Julia Kusy, June 20, 1946; children—Larisa Eugenia, Paula Jon. Mem. faculty N.Y.U., 1942-48; asst. prof. econs. Georgetown U., 1948-52, asso. prof., 1952-60, prof., 1960-, acting chmn. dept., 1953-54, exec. mem. Inst. Ethnic Studies, 1957—, dir. Inst. on Comparative Econ. and Polit. Systems, 1970—; faculty Nat. War Coll., 1957-58; lectr. on Soviet Union, Communism, U.S. fgn. policy. Chmn. Nat. Captive Nations Com., Inc.; mem. Economists Nat. Com. on Monetary Policy; strategy staff mem. Am. Security Council, 1962—, econs. editor Washington Report; cons. Corpus Instrumentorum, Kreber Found.; mem. Am. Com. to Aid Katanga Freedom Fighters, Emergency Com. Chinese Refugees; planning mem. Freedom Studies Center., Boston. Asst. sec. Republican Nat. Conv., 1952, adviser Rep. Nat. Com., 1956, mem. Com. on Program and Progress of Rep. Party, 1959; asst. to chmn. Rep. Nat. Conv., 1964; vice chmn. nationalities div. Rep. Nat. Com., 1964. Chmn., Ukrainian Catholic Studies Found., 1970—. Lt. col. (res.) 352d Mil. Govt. Civil Affairs, 1958; col. U.S. Army Reserves, 1966. Recipient Freedoms Found. award, 1961; Shevchenko Freedom award Shevchenko Meml. Com., 1964; Shevchenko Sci. Soc. medal, 1965; Hungarian Freedom Fighters' Freedom award, 1965; Latvian Pro Merito medal, 1968; Freedom Acad. award, Korea, 1969; Wisdom award of honor Cal., 1970. Mem. Free World Forum (exec. com.), Acad. Polit. Sci., Nat. Acad. Econs. and Polit. Sci., Am. Assn. U. Profs., Am. Acad. Polit. and Social Sci., Am., Cath. econ. assns., Am. Finance Assn., Nat. Soc. Study Edn., Shevchenko Sci. Soc., Ukrainian Congress Com. Am. (chmn.), N.Y.U. U. Alumni Assn., Gold Key Soc., Beta Gamma Sigma, Delta Sigma Pi. Clubs: Capitol Hill, International, University (Washington). Author: A Philosophico-Economic Critique of Thorstein Veblen, 1943; The Social Philosophical System of Thorstein Veblen, 1950; Free Trade Ideal, 1954; Communist Takeover on Non-Russian Nations in USSR, 1954; (co-author) The Great Pretense, 1956; Veblenism: A New Critique, 1957; Captive Nations Week Resolution, 1959; The Crimes of Khrushchev, 1959; (co-author) Decisions for a Better America, 1960; Vulnerabilities of USSR, 1963; Nations, Peoples, and Countries in the USSR, 1964; The Vulnerable Russians, 1967; U.S.A. and the Soviet Myth, 1971. Editor: Europe's Freedom Fighter; Taras Shevchenko, 1960; asso. editor Ukrainian Quar., 1946-62, chmn. editorial bd., 1962—. Contbr. to Peace and Freedom Through Cold War Victory, 1964. Author articles in field. Home: 4520 Kling Dr Alexandria VA 22312 Office: Georgetown U Washington DC 20007

DOBRINER, WILLIAM M., educator, sociologist; b. Springfield, Mass., Oct. 28, 1922; s. J.E. and Marion (Mann) D.; A.B., Hofstra Coll., 1948; M.A., Columbia, 1950, Ph.D., 1956; m. Eileen P. Phypers, Sept. 2, 1950; children—Gail Evans, Jill Hampton, Scott Blackwell. Lectr. sociology Hofstra Coll., 1948—, mem. faculty, 1950-71, prof. sociology, chmn. dept., 1965-69; Charles A. Dana prof. sociology Lafayette Coll., Easton, Pa., 1971—; vis. prof., grad studies div. Coll. Arts and Scis., City U., 1959-67; vis. prof. U. Vt., 1969-70. Served with USAAF, 1942-45. Mem. Am., Eastern sociol. assns., Alpha Kappa Delta (N.E. regional rep. 1970—). Author: The Suburban Community, 1958; Class in Suburbia, 1963; Social Structures and Systems, 1969. Home: 152 Pennsylvania Av Easton PA 18042

DOBROVOLNY, JERRY STANLEY, engring. educator; b. Chgo., Nov. 2, 1922; s. Stanley and Marie Barone D.; B.S. in Mech. Engring., U. Ill., 1943, M.S., 1947; m. Joan Gretchen Baker, June 14, 1947; children—James Lawrence, Janet Lee. Faculty U. Ill. at Urbana, 1945—, asso. prof. Coll. Engring., 1957—, prof., head dept. gen. engring., 1959—; geophys. research engr. Ill. Geol. Survey, summers 1949-52; design and traffic survey engr. Ill. Div. Hwys., summers 1948, 53, 54; cons. soil mechanics, 1955—. Mem. Ill. Adv. Council on Vocational Edn., 1969-72, Nat. Adv. Council on Vocational Edn., 1970-72. Past pres. Champaign County Young Rep. Club; mem. Champaign County Rep. Central Com. Served to sgt., C.E., AUS, 1942-44. Recipient Arthur L. Williston award Am. Soc. Engring. Edn., 1970. Registered profl. engr. Fellow A.A.A.S.: mem. Am. Legion, 40 and 8, History of Sci. Soc., Ill. Acad. Sci., Am. Soc. Engring. Edn. (Arthur Williston award 1971), Am. Assn. Petroleum Geologists, Soc. Am. Mil. Engrs., Am. Soc. C.E., Am. Tech. Edn. Assn. (trustee 1965-68, 69—, pres. 1967-68), Nat., Ill. (v.p.), Champaign County socs. profl. engrs., Newcomen Soc. N.Am., Signa Xi, Scabbard and Blade, Sigma Iota Epsilon, Tau Nu Tau. Author: (with others) Basic Drawing for Engineering Technology; (with R.P. Hoelscher and C.H. Springer) Graphics for Engineers, 1968. Home: 1104 S Prospect Av Champaign IL 61820 Office: Coll Engring U Ill Urbana IL 61801

DOBROVOLSKY, SERGEI PAVLOVICH, educator; b. Vladivostok, Russia, Oct. 8, 1908; s. Paul and Claudia (Politova) D.; came to U.S., 1941, naturalized, 1946; diploma Faculty of Law,

Harbin, Manchuria, 1931; M.A., Columbia, 1942, Ph.D., 1949. Accountant, sales rep. bus. firms in China, 1931-41; research Nat. Bur. Econ. Research, 1942-45, OSS, 1945-46; instr. Columbia, 1946-47; lectr. Swarthmore Coll., 1947-48; asst., then asso. prof. Wayne U., 1948- 57; prof. econs. Rensselaer Polytech, Inst., 1957—, head dept., 1957-67; vis. prof. econ. Rice U., Houston, 1963-64. Fellow Social Sci. Research Council, 1947. Mem. Am. Econ. Assn., Am. Finance Assn., Econometric Soc. Author: Corporate Income Retention, 1951; (with others) Trends in Capital Formation and Financing in Manufacturing and Mining, 1960; The Economics of Corporation Finance, 1971; also articles profl. jours. Home: 111 Sandra Dr Troy NY 12180

DOBRYNIN, ANATOLY FEDOROVICH, Soviet diplomat; b. 1919; grad. tech. coll.; M.S. in History; m. Irina Nikolaevna; 1 dau., Yelena. Mem. Soviet Diplomatic Service, 1944—; asst. to dep. minister fgn. affairs,1949-52, counselor Ministry Fgn. Affairs, 1955, 60-61, head Am. dept., 1960-62; counselor Soviet embassy, Washington, 1952-54, minister-counselor, 1954-55; adviser Soviet delegation 11th session UN Gen. Assembly, 1956; mem. Soviet delegation London Conf. on Suez Canal, 1956; mem. secretariat UN, 1957, undersec. without portfolio, 1957; undersec. charge dept. polit. and security council affairs secretariat UN, 1957-60; ambassador to U.S., 1962—. Lecture course on Soviet-Am. relations State Inst. Internat. Relations, Moscow. Address: 1125 16th St NW Washington DC 20036

DOBSON, ELEANOR ROBINETTE see Kewer, Eleanor Dobson.

DOBSON, GWEN ARMSTRONG, journalist; b. Fairfax County, Va., May 17, 1930; d. J. Sherman and Helen V. (Dove) Armstrong; grad. high sch.; m. Robert V. Dobson, Feb. 26, 1949; children—Micahel C., Robyn Leslie, John Lindsey. Gen. reporter Alexandria (Va.) Gazette, 1947-50, women's editor, 1956-61; Sunday women's editor The Washington Star, 1961-64, women's editor, 1964—. Mem. Women's Nat. Press Club, Am. Newspaper Women's Club (pres.). Home: The Meadows Delaplane VA 22025 Office: 2d and Virginia Av SE Washington DC 20003

DOBSON, HERBERT GORDON, mgmt. cons.; b. Can., Dec. 19, 1900; s. Joseph Brent and Minnie (Steeves) D.; student pub. schs. of N.B.; m. Frances Garland Roberts, June 21, 1930; children—Ann Garland, Jane Frances. Came to U.S., 1918, naturalized, 1938. Auditor Can. Nat. Rys., 1918-20; insp. Bank Am. Nat. Trust Savs. Assn., Los Angeles, 1920-43; v.p., controller Occidental Life Ins. Co., Los Angeles, 1943-62, sr. v.p., 1962-65; pres. Angeles/Cardillo Travel Agy., 1965-67; mgmt. cons., 1969—. Pres. Episcopal Ch. Home for Children, 1965-69, 70—; coordinator Episcopal Ch. Cathedral Project, 1970—. Home: 2690 E California St San Marino CA 91108

DOBSON, PAUL ARTHUR, walnut grower; b. Ulysses, Neb., Apr. 1, 1897; s. Park George and Carey Maude (Palmer) D.; A.B., U. Neb., 1920; m. Elizabeth Brown, Sept. 24, 1921; children—Edward Brown, Jerome John, Cynthia J. (Mrs. Glenn Hamilton). Pres. Emporer Grape Growers Assn., 1943-45; dir. Sequoia Walnut Growers Assn., 1945—; pres. Diamond Walnut Growers, Inc., 1955-65, mem. bd. dirs., 1946—; mem. nat. research and marketing adv. com. U.S. Dept. Agr., 1958-64; mem. Fed. Farm Credit Bd., 1967—; mem. exec. bd. Nat. Council of Farmer Coops., 1960-67, 1st v.p., 1961-62; exec. com. Agrl. Council of Cal., 1959-65, v.p., 1959-60. Office: 1050 S Diamond St Stockton CA 95201

DOBSON, PHILIP E., clergyman, ednl. adminstr.; b. N.Y.C., Sept. 13, 1909; s. James and Margaret (Smith) D.; student Seton Hall Coll., 1928-29; A.B., Woodstock (Md.) Coll., 1935, M.A., 1936; LL.D., St. Peters Coll., 1953. Mem. Soc. of Jesus (Jesuits) 1929—; dir. Xavier Inst. Indsl. Relations, N.Y.C., 1938-39; ordained priest Roman Cath. Ch., 1942; asso. dir. Crown Heights Labor Sch., Bklyn., 1944-46; arbitrator, meditator indsl. relations, N.Y.C. area; condr. pub. forums labor-mgmt. problems; founder, dir. inst. indsl. relations St. Peter's Coll., 1946-52; pres. Canisius Coll., 1952- 59; dean sch. bus. Fordham U., 1959-63, asst. to pres. for constrn. Lincoln Sq., Fordham, 1963-66, dir. Intown div., 1964-66; dean Coll. Bus. Adminstrn., Cath. U. P.R., Ponce, 1966-70; v.p. devel. and pub. relations Bayamón Central U., Bayamón, P.R., 1970—. Exec. com. bd. trustees Community Chest; chmn. pub. service div. 1958 United Community Chest-Red Cross Appeal; bd. dirs. Childrens Aid Soc. Received Catholic Action award K.C., Robert V. Kinkead award for fight against communism in labor movement. Mem. Buffalo Soc. Nat. Scis. (bd. mgrs.); hon. mem. Alpha Kappa Psi, Beta Alpha Sigma, Beta Gamma Sigma. Address: Bayamón Central U Bayamón PR 00919

DOBSON, RICHARD PORTWAY, tobacco co. exec.; b. Bristol, Eng., Feb. 11, 1914; s. John Frederic and Dina (Portway) D.; B.A. with Honors, King's Coll., Cambridge (Eng.) U., 1935; m. Emily Margaret Carver, May 3, 1946. With Brit.-Am. Tobacco Co., Ltd., London, 1935—, dir., 1955—, dep. chmn., 1962-68, vice chmn., 1968-70, chmn., 1970—. Served to flight lt. RAF, 1941-45. Club: United University (London). Author: China Cycle (Macmillan Centenary award 1946), 1946. Home: 16 Marchmont Rd Richmond upon Thames Surrey England Office: 7 Millbank London SW1 England

DOBSON, WILLIAM DAVIS, dairy products exec.; b. Hartford City, Ind., Apr. 2, 1906; s. Walter Norton and Adeline Catherine (Hunt) D.; student Washington U., 1929; M.B.A. with high distinction, Harvard, 1936; m. Ann Dawson, July 10, 1956. Various positions Sandusky Cooperage & Lumber Co., St. Louis, 1929-34; successively trainee, asst. gen. sales mgr., asst. to gen. mgr., mgr. San Jose sales dist. and mfg. operations Golden State Co., Ltd., San Francisco, 1936-39; gen. sales mgr. No. Cal. fresh milk and ice cream div. Carnation Co., Oakland, 1939-41, gen. sales mgr. So. Cal., 1941-42, gen. sales mgr. U.S. Fresh Milk and Ice Cream div., 1942-51, asst. v.p., 1951—, also chmn. jr. bd. dirs.; exec. v.p. Gen. Milk Co. (internat. div. Carnation Co.), 1951-65, pres., 1965—; dir. Gen. Milk Co., Carnation Co. Mem. Harvard Bus. Sch. Assn., Internat., Am. mgmt. assns., Phi Lambda Epsilon, Kappa Alpha. Clubs: Los Angeles Country; Harvard of Southern Cal., Harvard Business School of Southern Cal. Home: 16115 Anoka Dr Pacific Palisades CA 90272 Office: 5045 Wilshire Blvd Los Angeles CA 90036

DOBY, JOHN THOMAS, educator, social psychologist; b. Gray, Ky., May 29, 1920; s. Daniel W. and Minnie (Farris) D.; A.B., Union Coll., Barbourville, Ky., 1946; M.S., U. Wis., 1950, Ph.D., 1956; m. Rose C. Hopper, Dec. 21, 1942; children—Mary Catherine, Nancy Hopper. Partner Hopper-Graybeal Co., Cobin, Ky., 1948; teaching asst. U. Wis., 1949-50; asso. prof. sociology Wofford Coll., 1950-56, prof., 1956-58; asso. prof. sociology and anthropology Emory U., 1958-63, prof., 1963—, chmn. dept., 1961-69; cons. Engring. Expt. Sta., Ga. Inst. Tech., 1960-62, Ednl. Testing Service, Princeton, N.J., 1969—; vis. prof. U. Ga., summer 1960. Dir. Gt. So. Devel. Co. Mem. adv. bd. mental health div. Ga. Dept. Health, 1966—; chmn. community mental health programs, profl. adv. bd. Ga. Mental Health Assn., 1960-62. Chmn. trustees Spartanburg Mental Health Clinic, 1956-58, chmn. sci. and tech. adv. com. on mental retardation Ga. State Dept. Health, 1964-65. Served to maj. USAAF, 1941-46; PTO. Fellow Am. Social. Assn.; mem. So. Sociol. Soc. (exec. com. 1961-63, pres. 1969-70), So. Soc. Philosophy and Psychology, A.A.A.S., Alpha Kappa Delta, Pi Gamma Mu. Methodist (gen. supt. 1960-61). Author: Introduction to Social Psychology, 1966. Editor, co-author: Introduction to Social Research, 1954, 2d edit., 1967; also articles. Home: 1897 Breckenridge Dr Atlanta GA 30345 Office: Emory U Atlanta GA 30322

DOBYNS, BROWN MCILVAINE, educator, surgeon; b. Jacksonville, Ill. May 14, 1913; s. Henry D. and Leah (McIlvaine) D.; B.A., Ill. Coll., 1935; M.D., Johns Hopkins, 1939; M.S., U. Minn., 1944, Ph.D., 1946; m. Mary Meredith Davis, Sept. 21, 1940; children—Mary Meredith, Courtney S., Brown McIlvaine. Intern surgery Johns Hopkins Hosp., 1939-40; fellow surgery Mayo Found., 1940-43; resident surgery Kahler Hosp., Mayo Clinic, 1943-45, 1st asst. surgery, 1945-46, asst. surg. staff, 1946; research fellow surgery, med. sch. Harvard, 1946-48, asst. prof. surgery, 1948-51; grad. asst. surgery Mass. Gen. Hosp., 1946-48, asst. surgery, 1946-51; asso. prof. surgery Western Res. U. Med. Sch., 1951-58, prof. surgery, 1958—; asst. chief surg. service Cleve. Met. Gen. Hosp., 1951-66, asso. chief surgical service, 1967—; asst. surgeon Univ. Hosp., Cleve., 1951—; Fulbright lectr., Australia, 1966. Mem. fellowship subcom. Com. on Growth, NRC, 1950-54; mem. fellowship com. Nat. Sci. Found., 1954-61, chmn., 1955-61; adv. screening com. med. scis. (Fulbright), 1955-58; adv. com. research on etiology cancer Am. Cancer Soc., 1956-59, chmn. adv. com. on instnl. grants, 1963-65; mem. Dernham Scholarship Com. for Cal., 1964—. Recipient Van Meter Prize Am. Goiter Assn., 1946, award of merit Am. Thyroid Assn., 1954. Diplomate Am. Bd. Surgery. Fellow A.C.S.; mem. Soc. Univ. Surgeons, Am. Soc. Clin. Investigation, Am., Central surgical assns., Am. Thyroid Assn. (pres. 1956-57), Internat. Soc. Surgeons, Cleve. Surg. Soc. (pres. 1966-67), Halstead Soc., Société Internationale de Chirurgie, A.A.A.S., Endocrine Soc., Sigma Xi. Home: 2904 Huntington Rd Shaker Heights OH 44120 Office: 3395 Scranton Rd Cleveland OH 44109

DOBYNS, EDWARD PERRIN, fgn. service officer; b. Mexico, Mo., June 19, 1916; s. Carl Francis and Josephine Mary (Verhoff) D.; B.S., Georgetown U., 1943; m. Rosemary Theresa Nechkash, June 3, 1941; children—Mary Josephine (Mrs. Roston Miller), Edward Perrin, Donna Elizabeth (Mrs. John A. Gulley, Jr.). With Dept. State, 1939—; adminstrv. officer, analyst fgn. service planning, 1939-49; adminstrv. officer Am. embassy, Ireland and Denmark, 1949-54; chief diplomatic and consular br., chief div. program rev., spl. internat. activities rev. Office of Budget, 1954-58; fgn. service officer, 1955—; mem. 12th Fgn. Service Selection Bd., 1958; fgn. service insp. Fgn. Service Inspection Corps, 1958-61, guest lectr. Fgn. Service Inst.; counselor embassy for adminstrn. Am. embassy, Madrid, 1961-64; exec. dir. Bur. African Affairs, Dept. State, 1964-69; exec. dir. Am. Fgn. Service Assn., 1969; chief career mgmt. and assignment div. Office of Personnel, 1970-71; consul gen., Monterrey, Mexico, 1971—. Mem. 20th Fgn. Service Selections Bd., 1966; mem. bd. examiners for Fgn. Service, 967. Bd. dirs., pres. State Dept. Credit Union. Served to lt. (j.g.), USNR, World War II. Mem. Am. Fgn. Service Assn., Internat. Good Neighbor Council. Clubs: Club de Campo, Am. Men's (Madrid, Spain); Rotary (Dublin, Ireland, Copenhagen, Denmark, Monterrey, Mexico). Home: Rio Volga 117 Colonia Del Valle Monterrey Mexico Office: Am Consulate Gen Apartado Postal 152 Monterrey Mexico

DOBYNS, HENRY FARMER, educator, anthropologist; b. Tucson, July 3, 1925; s. Henry Farmer and Susie Kell (Comstock) D.; B.A., U. Ariz., 1949, M.A., 1956; Ph.D., Cornell U., Ithaca, N.Y., 1960; m. Mary Faith Patterson, Aug. 9, 1968; children—Henry F., William C., Martha S., Mark McC., York H. Research asso. Ariz. State Mus., 1950-51, 58-59; research anthropologist Hualapai Tribe of Ariz., 1952-57; successively research asso., sr. research asso., lectr. sociology and anthropology Cornell U., 1959-66; prof. anthropology, chmn. dept. U. Ky., 1966-70; prof. anthropology Prescott (Ariz.) Coll., 1970—; cons. in field. Democratic precinct chmn. Fayette County (Ky.), 1968-70. Served with AUS, 1943-44. Co-recipient Anisfield-Wolf award Sat. Rev., 1968. Fellow A.A.A.S., Am. Anthrop. Assn.; mem. Soc. Applied Anthropology (Malinowski award 1951). Author: The Social Matrix of Peruvian Indigenous Communities, 1964; (with R.C. Euler) The Ghost Dance of 1889 Among the Pai Indians of Northwestern Arizona, 1967. Editor: (with M.C. Vazquez) Migracióne e Integración en el Perú, 1963. Address: Center for Man and Environment Prescott Coll Prescott AZ 86301

DOBZHANSKY, THEODOSIUS, educator; b. Nemirov, Russia, Jan. 25, 1900; s. Gregory and Sophie (Voinarsky) D.; grad. U. Kiev, 1921; D.Sc. (hon.), U. São Paulo, Brazil, 1943, Coll. Wooster (O.), 1945, U. Munster (Germany), U. Montreal (Can.), 1958, U. Chgo., 1959, U. Sidney, Australia, 1960, Oxford (Eng.) U., 1964, Louvain U., 1965, Columbia, 1964, Kalamazoo Coll., 1965, Clarkson Coll. Tech., 1965, U. Mich., 1966, U. Syracuse, 1967, U. Cal. at Berkeley, 1968, U. Padua (Italy), 1968, Northwestern U., 1968; D.H.L. (hon.), U. Cal., 1968, Wittenberg U., 1970, St. Mary's Coll., 1971; m. Natalie Sivertzev, Aug. 8, 1924; 1 dau., Sophie. Came to U.S., 1927, naturalized, 1937. Asst. prof. zoology Polytechnique Inst., Kiev, 1921-24; lectr. genetics U. Leningrad, 1924-27; fellow int. edn. bd., 1928-29; asst. prof. genetics Cal. Inst. Tech., 1930-36; prof., 1936-40; prof. zoology Columbia, 1940, later DaCosta prof. zoology; prof. Rockefeller Inst., N.Y.C., 1962-71; adj. prof. U. Cal. at Davis, 1971—; exchange prof. U. Sao Paulo, Brazil, 1943, 48-49. Recipient G. Elliott prize and medal Nat. Acad. Sci., Kimber prize, 1958; Guggneheim fellow, 1959; recipient Nat. Medal of Science, 1964; Addison Emery Verrill medal, 1966; Distinguished Achievement in Sci. award Am. Mus. Natural History, 1969. Mem. Nat., Royal Danish, Royal Swedish, Brazilian acads. scis., Academia dei Lincei, Italy, Royal Soc., London, Eng., Am. Philos. Soc. Am. Soc. Zoologists, Am. Soc. Genetics, Am. Soc. Naturalists, Am. Soc. for Study Evolution. Author: Genetics and Origin of Species, 1937, 3d edit., 1951; Evolution, Genetics and Man, 1955; Mankind Evolving, 1962; Biology of Ultimate Concern, 1967; Genetics of the Evolutionary Process, 1970. Address: 2122 Espana Ct Davis CA 95616

DOCKERAY, JAMES CARLTON, educator, economist; b. Grand Rapids, Mich., Aug. 16, 1907; s. Floyd Carlton and Katherine Caroline (Eddy) D.; B.A., Ohio Wesleyan U., 1929; M.A., Ohio State U., 1931, Ph.D., 1936; m. Isabel Ruth McRoberts, Sept. 2, 1935; children—George Carlton, William Floyd, Susan Ruth. Student accountant Chesapeake & Potomac Telephone Co., 1929-30; asst. econs. Ohio State U., 1931-35; instr. Ia. State Tchrs. Coll., 1935-36; asso. prof. econs. and bus. adminstrn. James Millikin U., 1936-42; prof. finance U. Md., 1942-46; fiscal and financial economist Dept. Commerce, 1946-61; professorial lectr. George Washington U., 1946-55, prof. finance, 1955—, chmn. dept. govt. and bus., 1955—, asst. dean Sch. Govt. Bus. and Internat. Affairs, 1964-66, dean Sch. Govt. and Bus. Adminstrn., 1966—; lectr. Grad. Sch. Banking, Rutgers U., 1952-55; dep. mem. FHLB, 1938; cons. statis. control div. USAAF, 1943-45. Mem. Am. Econ. Assn., Am. Finance Assn., Washington Soc. Investment Analysts. Author: Public Utility Taxation in Ohio, 1938; (with W.W. Husband) Modern Corporation Finance, 6th edit., 1966. Home: 4010 Van Buren St University Park Hyattsville MD 20782 Office: George Washington U Washington DC 20006

DOCKERTY, MALCOLM BIRT, physician; b. Cardigan, Prince Edward Island, Can., Sept. 19, 1909; s. Robert Alexander and Addie May (Birt) D.; student Prince of Wales Coll., Charlottetown, Prince Edward Island, 1925-28, hon. diploma; M.D. C.M., Dalhousie U., Halifax, N.S., 1934; M.S. (fellow pathology), U. Minn., 1937; LL.D., Prince of Wales U., 1967; m. Marjorie Stoddart, Dec. 29, 1937; 1 adopted son, John Malcolm. Came to U.S., 1934, naturalized, 1939. Intern Victoria Gen. Hosp., Halifax, Can., 1933-34; faculty grad. sch. U. Minn., 1938—, successively instr., asst. prof., asso. prof., prof. Mayo Found., 1953—; head surg. pathology sect. Mayo Clinic, 1956—, head dept. surgical pathology, 1958—. Civilian cons. Armed Forces Inst. Pathology. Mem. Central Assn. Obstetricians and Gynecologists, Am., Minn. socs. clin. pathologists, Am. Assn. Pathologists and Bacteriologists, N.S. Med. Soc., St. Paul Surg Soc., Izaak Walton League Am., Sigma Xi. Home: 1344 2d St NW Rochester MN 55901 Office: Mayo Clinic Rochester MN 55901

DOCKING, ROBERT BLACKWELL, gov. of Kan.; b. Kansas City, Mo., Oct. 9, 1925; s. George and Mary Virginia (Blackwell) D.; B.S. with honors, U. Kan., 1948; grad. Grad. Sch. Banking, U. Wis.; m. Meredith Martha Gear, 1950; children— William Russell, Thomas Robert. With Union State Bank, Arkansas City, Kan., 1956- 59, pres., 1959—; mayor Arkansas City, 1963-66; gov. Kan., 1967—. Former chmn. Interstate Oil Compact Commn.; chmn. Midwest Gov.'s Conf., 1971. Mem. Kan. Bank Mgt. Commn. Mem. City Comn. Arknasas City, Winfield, 1963-66. Past pres. Community Chest, pres. United Fund; chpt. chmn. A.R.C., 1961. Chmn. Douglas County Dem. Party, 1954-56; v.p. Kan. Democratic Vets., 1957. Served from pvt. to 1st lt., USAAF, 1943-46. Named Young Man of Year, Kan. Jr. C. of C., 1959. Mem. Arkansas City C. of C. (pres.), Am. Legion (comdr. Arkansas City, Kan.), Cowley County Bankers Assn., Am. Bankers Assn., Ind. Oil and Gas Assn., Kan. Livestock Assn., Internat. Platform Assn., Am. G.I. Forum, Am. Assn. for UN, U. Kan. Alumni Assn., Am. Assn. Criminology, Beta Theta Pi, Beta Gamma Sigma, Delta Sigma Pi. Mason (32, Shriner), Elk, Eagle, Rotarian. Home: 925 N 2d St Arkansas City KS 67005 also Cedar Crest Executive Mansion Topeka KS 66603 Office: State Capitol Bldg Topeka KS 66612

DOCKSON, ROBERT RAY, savs. and loan exec.; b. Quincy, Ill., Oct. 6, 1917; s. Marshall Rayand Letah (Edmondson) D.; A.B., Springfield Jr. Coll., 1937; B.S., U. Ill., 1939; M.S. in Fgn. Service, U. So. Cal., 1940, Ph.D., 1946; m. Katheryn Virginia Allison, Mar. 4, 1944; 1 dau., Kathy Kimberlee. Lectr., U. So. Cal., 1940-41, 45-46, prof., head dept. marketing, 1953-59, dean Sch. Bus. Adminstrn. and prof. bus. econs., 1959-69, dir. Inst. Bus. Econs.; pres. Cal. Fed. Savs. & Loan Assn., Los Angeles, 1970—, vice chmn. bd., 1969-70, also dir.; instr. at Rutgers U., 1946-47, asst. prof., 1947-48, dir. Bur. Bus. and Econ. Research, 1947-48; economist Western home office Prudential Ins. Co., 1948-52, Bank of Am., San Francisco, 1952-53; econ. cons., 1953-57; dir. Hoffman Electronics, Foremost-McKesson, Inc., Bekins Co., Pacific Lighting Corp., Blue Chip Stamps, Olga Co.; adv. bd. Investment Co. Am. Am. specialist for U.S. Dept. State; mem. Town Hall, 1954—, bd. govs., 1963-65, hon. bd. govs., 1965—, pres., 1961-62. Mem. Greater Los Angeles chpt. Nat. Safety Council. Mem. bd. Journey for Perspective Found. bd. dirs. So. Conf. Christians and Jews; mem. Regional Export Expansion Council of So. Cal., Los Angeles, 1962—, chmn. 1962-65; bd. trustees John Randolph Haynes and Dora Haynes Found., Orthopaedic Hosp., Rose Hills Meml. Park Assn., Cal. Council for Econ. Edn.; bd. govs. Goodwill Industries of So. Cal.; v.p., mem. exec. com., bd. govs. So. Cal. chpt. Arthritis Found.; bd. councilors Grad. Sch. Bus. Adminstrn., U. So. Cal. Served from ensign to lt., USNR, 1942-44. Recipient Asa V. Call Achievement award; decorated Star of Solidarity by the Govt. of Italy. Mem.. Cal. (dir.), Los Angeles (dir.) chambers commerce, Am. Econ. Assn., Am. Finance Assn., Am. Mgmt. Assn., Am. Marketing Assn., Am. Arbitration Assn., Newcomen Soc. North Am., Phi Kappa Phi, Beta Gamma Sigma. Rotarian. Clubs: Bohemian, Los Angeles, Los Angeles Country, One Hundred, Lincoln, Jonathan, Silver Dollar. Home: 1642 Camino Lindo South Pasadena CA 91030 Office: 5670 Wilshire Blvd Los Angeles CA 90036

DOCKSTADER, FREDERICK J., museum dir.; b. Los Angeles, Feb. 3, 1919; s. Fred and Dorothy D.; A.B., A.M., Ariz. State Coll.; Ph.D., Western Res. U., 1951; m. Alice Elizabeth Warren, Dec. 25, 1951. Tchr., Flagstaff (Ariz.) city schs., 1936-41, Cranbrook (Mich.) schs., 1942-50; staff ethnologist Cranbrook Inst. Sci., 1950-52; faculty, also curator anthropology Dartmouth, 1952-55; asst. dir. Mus. Am. Indian, Heye Found., N.Y.C., 1955-60, dir., 1960—; adv. editor Ency. Americana, 1957—; commr. U.S. Indian Arts and Crafts Bd., 1955-67; vis. prof. art and archeology Columbia, 1961-64. Mem. N.Y. State Mus. Adv. Council, 1960-65. Fellow Rochester Mus. Arts and Scis. Recipient 1st prize silversmithing Cleve. Mus. Art, 1950. Fellow A.A.A.S., Cranbrook Inst. Sci., Am. Anthrop. Assn.; mem. Soc. Am. Archeology. Club: Cosmos. Author: The Kachina and the White Man, 1954; Indian Art in America, 1960; Indian Art in Middle America, 1964; Kunst in Amerika: I, 1965; Indian Art in South America, 1967; Kunst in Amerika: II, 1968; Kunst in Amerika: III, 1969; (with Ferdinand Anton) Pre-Columbian Art, 1968. Compiler: The American Indian in Graduate Studies, 1957. Home: 165 W 66th St New York City NY 10023 Office: Museum Am Indian Heye Foundation Broadway at 155th St New York City NY 10032

DOCZI, GEORGE FREDERIC, architect; b. Budapest, Hungary, May 5, 1909; s. Dr. Imre and Jolan (Kohn) D.; M.A. in architecture, Royal Poly. U., Budapest, 1933; advanced design studies Royal Acad., Stockholm, 1944; postgrad. Royal Poly. U., Stockholm, 1948; m. Aina Matilda Belfrage, June 15, 1946; 1 dau., Ann Christine. Came to U.S., 1946, naturalized, 1961. Archtl. designer, Hungary, 1933-37, Sweden, 1937-46, Iran, 1952-56; asso. Litchfield-Whiting-Panero & Severud, N.Y.C., 1953-57, Harmon, Pray & Detrich, Seattle, 1966—; instr. architecture Los Angeles City Coll., 1961; lectr. Royal Acads. Art, Stockholm and Copenhagen, 1959; paintings, drawings and illustrations exhibited Sweden, Hungary, U.S. Recipient 2d prize Budapest Dept. Pub. Works for resort hotel Isle of St. Margit, Budapest, 1932, 1st prize for resort hotel Hagyvillam, Visegrad, Hungary, 1933, hon. mention for Royal Acad. Arts, Stockholm, 1944. Mem. A.I.A., Common Cause. Illustrator, author children's book: Csoppseg, 1940. Paintings and drawings in permanent exhbn. Pacific Sci. Center, Seattle. Home: 6837 47th St NE Seattle WA 98115 Office: 2230 8th Av Seattle WA 98121

DODD, CHARLES GARDNER, phys. chemist; b. St. Louis, Jan. 26, 1915; s. Harry Gardner and Ruth Esther (Hauskins) D.; B.S. with distinction, Rice U., 1940; M.S., U. Mich., 1945, Ph.D., 1948; m. Edel Marie Bovbjerg, June 10, 1943; children—Sally Little, Karen Elise, Mary Bartlett, Frederick Porter. Chem. engr. Freeport Sulphur Co., New Orleans, 1940-42; instr. chemistry, research investigator war research project U. Mich., 1942-47; asst. prof. dept. ceramics Pa. State Coll. Sch. Mineral Industries, 1947- 48; sr. phys. chemist Fed. Bur. Mines, Bartlesville, Okla., 1948-52; research asso. Continental Oil Co., Ponca City, Okla., 1952-55; asso. prof. dept. chemistry Lehigh U.,1955-56; Erle P. Halliburton prof. petroleum engring. U. Okla. 1956-62; chief advanced materials research sect. Owens-Ill. Tech. Center, Toledo, 1962-68; asso. prin. scientist Philip Morris Research Center, 1968—. Chmn. 8th Nat. Clay Conf., U. Okla., 1959. Fellow A.A.A.S., Am. Inst. Chemists; mem. Mineral. Soc. Am., N.Y. Acad. Scis., Clay Minerals Soc., Am. Ceramic Soc., Am. Vacuum Soc., Am.

Chem. Soc. (past mem. exec. com. div. colloid chemistry), Am. Crystallographic Assn., Mineral. Soc., Phi Beta Kappa, Sigma Xi, Phi Lambda Upsilon, Tau Beta Pi, Phi Kappa Phi. Unitarian. Author sci., tech. articles. Home: 509 West Drive Circle Richmond VA 23229 Office: 210 E Main St Richmond VA 23219

DODD, DAVID LEFEVRE, educator; b. Berkeley County, W.Va., Aug. 23, 1895; s. David Henry and Mary Virginia (Shaffer) D.; B.S., U. Pa., 1920; M.S. Columbia, 1921, Ph.D., 1930; m. Elise Marguerite Firor, Aug. 9, 1924; 1 dau., Barbara Anderson. Research asst. to economist Nat. Bank of Commerce, N.Y.C., 1921-22; instr. econs. Columbia, 1922-25, instr. finance, 1925-30, asst. prof. finance, 1930-38, asso. prof., 1938-47, prof., 1947- 61, prof. finance emeritus, 1961—, charge courses bus. and econs., 1926-45, asso. dean Grad. Sch. Bus., 1948-52; cons. expert on valuation of securities, pvt. clients, 1928—. Ltd. partner Newman & Graham 1950- 58, gen. partner Graham-Newman & Co., 1958-59; dir. Criterion Ins. Co., Govt. Employees Ins. Co., Govt. Employees Life Ins. Co., Govt. Employees Corp. (vice chmn. profit-sharing plan of all cos. listed 1960- 63). Mem. investment com. Social Sci. Research Council, 1959-56. Served from boatswain to lt. (j.g.) USN, 1917-19. Mem. Am-Finance Assn. (v.p. 1946-47), N.Y. Soc. Security Analysts, Beta Gamma Sigma, Phi Gamma Delta, Alpha Kappa Psi, Phi Chi Theta. Author: Stock Wattering, 1930; (with Benjamin Graham, Sidney Cottie, Charles Tatham) Security Analysis, 4th rev. edit., 1962. Home: 39 Claremont Av New York City NY 10027

DODD, EDWARD BENTON, cartoonist; b. La Fayette, Ga., Nov. 7, 1902; s. Jesse Mercer and Effie (Cooke) D.; student Ga. Inst. Tech., 1921-22, N.Y. Art Students League, 1923-24, under Daniel Beard; m. Miriam Croft, Feb. 26, 1938 (dec. 1943); m. 2d, Elsa Norris, July 25, 1958 (div. 1968). Instr., dir. Dan Beard Camp for Boys, 1920-38; instr. outdoor activities N.Y. Mil. Acad., Cornwall, N.Y., 1926-27; comml. artist, N.Y.C., 1929-30; drew humor panel Back Home Again, United Feature Syndicate, 1930-45; cartoonist Mark Trail, Pubs.-Hall Syndicate, 1946—. Recipient award for service to conservation Nat. Forestry Assn.; outstanding cartoon strip Sigma Delta Chi, 1948; for conservation wildlife, Wis. Humane Soc.; for conservation edn. Detroit Sportsman's Congress; hon. chmn. Nat. Wildlife Week, 1952-53; Conservation award, Nat. Wildlife Fedn., 1967. Mem. Outdoor Writers Am., Delta Tau Delta. Presbyn. Clubs: National Press (N.Y.C.); Homosassa, Piedmont Driving (Atlanta). Author: Mark Trail's Book of North American Mammals; Mark Trail Outdoor Tips; Flapfoot; Chipper; Today's World of Conservation; Mark Trail's Fishing Tips; Mark Trail's Hunting Tips; Mark Trail's Camping Tips. Contbr. articles to popular publs. Address: Lost Forest Sandy Springs GA 30328 Office: 30 E 42d St New York City NY 10017

DODD, EDWARD HOWARD, Jr., pub., author; b. N.Y.C., June 25, 1905; s. Edward Howard and Mary Elizabeth (Leggett) D.; grad. Hotchkiss Sch., Lakeville, Conn., 1924; A.B., Yale, 1928; m. Roxana Foote Scoville, Aug. 6, 1932 (div. May 1950); children—Louise Armstrong, Roxana Foote, Edward H. III; m. 2d Camille O. Gilpatric, Oct. 1952. Cruised through South Seas on small schooner, 1928-29; with Dodd, Mead & Co., pubs., 1929—, head editorial dept., 1937—, dir., 1938—, v.p., 1941, pres., 1953-57, chmn., 1966—, chmn. editorial bd., 1957-66; with Office Strategic Services, Washington, 1942-45. Trustee Marlboro Sch. Music. Served with Squadron A, 101st Cav., N.Y. N.G. 3 yrs. Mem. Elihu Soc., Alpha Delta Phi. Clubs: Century, Yale (New York). Author: Great Dipper to Southern Cross: The Cruise of the Schooner "Chance" through the South Seas, 1930; The First Hundred Years: A History of Dodd, Mead & Co., 1939; Of Nature, Time and Teale, 1960; Tales of Maui, 1964; Polynesian Art, 1967. Address: 79 Madison Av New York City NY 10016

DODD, EDWIN DILLON, container mfr.; b. Point Pleasant, W.Va., Jan. 26, 1919; s. David Rollin and Mary Grace (Dillon) D.; B.S., B.A., Ohio State U., 1941; Indsl. Adminstr., Harvard, 1943; LL.D., U. Toledo, 1970; m. Marie Marshall, Apr. 18, 1942; 1 dau., Marjorie Lee (Mrs. Jay Wannamaker). Engr. airplane div. Curtiss-Wright Corp., 1941-42; pub. relations rep. Owens-Ill. Glass Co., 1946-49, pub. relations dir., 1949- 54, prodn. mgr. Libbey Glass div., 1954-56, factories mgr., 1956-58, v.p., asst. gen. mgr. Owens-Ill. Paper Products div. (formerly Nat. Container Corp.), 1958, gen. mgr. paper products dir., 1959-61, forest products div., 1961-64; exec. v.p. Owens-Ill., Inc., Toledo, 1964- 68, pres., 1968—, dir., 1966—, gen. mgr. forest products div., 1961- 68; chmn. bd. Bahamas Agrl. Industries Ltd., 1966-68, pres., 1962-66, dir., 1962—; pres. Forest Products Corp., 1959-68, also dir.; pres. Sabine River & No. R.R., 1966-68, dir. 1966—; pres. Valdosta So. R.R. Co., 1961-68, dir., 1966; pres. Marinette, Tomahawk & Western R.R. Co., 1961-68, dir., 1966-; pres., chmn. bd. Owens-Ill. Timber Corp., 1962-68, dir., 1962—; dir. O.I. Overseas Capital Corp., Ohio Bell Telephone Co., Toledo Trust Co., Goodyear Tire & Rubber Co., Nat. Petro Chems. Corp. Chmn. Fourdinier Kraft Bd. Inst., Inc. Past pres. Toledo Bd. Edn.; mem. Toledo-Lucas County Port Authority; mem. Pres.'s Indsl. Pollution Control Council, 1970—. Bd. dirs. Florence Crittenton Home; trustee Inst. Paper Chemistry, Nat. Center for Solid Waste Disposal, Toledo Hosp.; asso. trustee Toledo Boys' Club; mem. devel. fund Ohio State U.; bd. visitors Berry Coll. Served as maj. AUS, 1943-46. Decorated Legion of Merit; Mil. Merit Medal (P.I.). Recipient Distinguished Citizen award Toledo Jr. C. of C., 1955, Ohio Jr. C. of C., 1955. Mem. Toledo C. of C., Fibre Box Assn. (dir. 1960-68; pres. 1965), Internat. Corrugated Case Assn. (pres. 1967, dir. 1967—), Nat. Paper Board Assn. (dir. 1964-68), Am. Paper Inst. (dir. 1966-68), Newcomen Soc. N.Am., Nat. Municipal League (regional v.p. 1967, council), Nat. Indsl. Conf. Bd., Harvard Bus. Sch. Assn. (exec. council 1968—), Phi Gamma Delta. Presbyn. Clubs: Harvard Business School, Toledo, Toledo Country; Mid-America (Chgo.); Cloud (N.Y.C.); Inverness; Lyford Cay (Bahamas). Home: 5029 Corey Rd Toledo, OH 43623. Office: Owens-Ill Inc Madison Av Toledo OH 43601

DODD, LAMAR, artist and art educator; b. Fairburn, Ga., Sept. 22, 1909; s. Francis Jefferson and Etta Irene (Cleveland) D.; student Ga. Sch. of Tech., 1926- 27, Art Students League of N.Y., 1929-33; L.H.D., LaGrange Coll., 1949; A.F.D., U. Chattanooga, 1959. M. Mary Lehmann, Sept. 25, 1930; 1 dau., Mary Irene. Art teacher Five Points Alabama, 1927-28; asst. mgr. Spivy-Johnson Co., Birmingham, Ala., 1933-37; asso. prof. art U. Ga., 1937-40, prof. art, 1940—, head dept. fine arts, 1960—. Chmn. Georgia Art Commn. Mem. Com. on arts U.S. Dept. State. Numerous awards and prizes 1936-57; 2d award, Painting of The Year, Pepsi-Cola Art Exhibition, 1947; Virginia Biennial Purchase Award, 1948; 1st purchase prize Southeastern Art Exhibition, 1949; Grant, Nat. Inst. of Arts and Letters, 1950; Grumbacher Oil Award, Fla. Internat. Exhibit, 1952; Edwin Palmer Memorial Prize, N.A.D., 1953; 1st transparent watercolor prize, Southeastern Art Assn. Exhbn. 1953. Exhbn. Am. Art (N.Y. World's Fair), 1940. Exhibited throughout U.S. 1930-57; Whitney Mus. Ann. Exhbn. (1937- 57), Neb. Ann. Exhbn. (1940), Carnegie Internat. (Pittsburgh, 1936), N.Y. World's Fair (1939, 1940), San Francisco Fair (1939); work represented in Met. Museum, N.Y.C., by "Stand, Sea and Sky," also in collections of Telfair Acad., Savannah, High Mus., Atlanta, Pa. Acad. Fine Arts, Whitney Mus. Am. Art, many pvt. collections, One man shows: various mus. and galleries, such as Corcoran Museum, Washington, D.C., 1942; Grand Central Art Gallery, N.Y., Rochester Meml. Art Gallery, 1949; Witte Meml. Mus., San Antonio, 1951; and many others. Nat. Academician. Mem. Phi Kappa Phi, Sphinx. Author articles on art subjects. Home: 590 Springdale Athens GA Address: U Ga Athens GA 30601☆

DODD, ROBERT BRUCE, physician, educator; b. Fairbury, Neb., Apr. 12, 1921; s. Cyrus Milo and Blanche (Kohl) D.; student U. Chgo., 1939-41; M.D., U. Neb., 1945; m. Mary Elinor Karll, Dec. 30, 1949; children—Hollyce Ann (Mrs. Thomas Gregory Rose), Robert Bruce, David Karll. Intern, Research and Edn. Hosps. U. Ill., 1945-46; dir. anesthesia Columbia Hosp., Milw., 1948-49; trainee in anesthesia Mass. Gen. Hosp., 1950-51, asst. anesthetist, 1951; practice medicine specializing in anesthesiology, Milw., 1948-49, Dallas, 1951-53, Balt., 1953-56, St. Louis 1956-69, Springfield, Ill., 1969—; instr., asso. prof. anesthesiology Southwestern Med. Sch. U. Tex., Dallas, 1951-53; prof., head dept. anesthesia Sch. Medicine U. Md., 1953-56; Henry E. Mallinckrodt prof. anesthesiology, head div. anesthesiology Sch. Medicine, Washington U., 1956-69, anesthesiologist-in-chief Barnes Hosp., 1956-68; cons. VA Hosps., Dallas, McKinney, Tex., 1951-53, USPHS Hosp., Balt., 1955-56, VA Hosp., St. Louis City Hosps., 1956-69; clin. prof. anesthesiology So. Ill. U. Sch. Medicine, Carbondale, 1969—; anesthesiologist Meml. Hosp., Springfield, 1969—. Served with M.C., AUS, 1946-48. Mem. A.M.A., Am. (2d v.p., 1967-68), St. Louis (past pres.) socs. anesthesiologists, Internat. Anesthesia Research Soc., Assn. U. Anesthetists (past treas.), Sangomon County Med. Soc., So. Med. Assn. (past sect. chmn.), Alpha Omega Alpha, Author: Diethyl Ether, 1962. Contbr. articles to profl. jours. Home: 2178 Huntleigh Rd Springfield IL 62704 Office: Meml Hosp Springfield IL 62702

DODD, WILLIAM JOSEPH, lawyer; b. Liberty, Tex., Nov. 25, 1909; s. Daniel David and Virginia 1 (Sapp) LL.B., La. State U., 1947, grad. student speech, 1937, LL.D., 1968; LL.D. (hon.), N.W. State Coll., 1968; m. Verone Ford, Aug. 27, 1939; children—William Ford, Leonard Bruce. Admitted to La. bar, 1947, since practiced in Baton Rouge; partner firm Dodd, Hirsch, Barker, Avant & Wall, 1952—; partner Overton & Dodd, farm operations, 1948—. Mem. La. House of Reps. from Allen Parish, 1940-48; lt. gov. La., 1948-52, auditor La., 1956-60; pres. La. Bd. of Education; supt. of public education, State Louisiana, 1964—. Mem. La. Democratic Central Com., 1952-56, 60—. Dir. Civil Def. La., 1950; rep. Gov. La. on La. Tidelands Claim, Washington, 1948-50. Mem. Am., La. bar assns., Am. Judicature Soc., La. Tchrs. Assn. (pres., council), La. P.T.A. (legislative chmn.), Northwestern State Coll. Alumni Assn. (v.p.). Served with AUS, 1942-45. Elk. Mason (Shriner). Baptist. Home: 429 Government St Baton Rouge LA 70802

DODDS, HAROLD WILLIS, former univ. pres.; b. Utica, Pa., June 28, 1889; s. Samuel and Alice (Dunn) D.; A.B., Grove City (Pa.) Coll., 1909; LL.D., 1931; A.M., Princeton, 1914, LL.D., 1957; Ph.D., U. Pa., 1917; LL.D., Yale, 1933, Dickinson U., Am. U. Rutgers U., N.Y. U., Harvard, Williams Coll., 1934, U. Cin., 1935, U. Pa., 1936, Dartmouth, 1937, Purdue U., 1938, Tulane U., 1941, Tusculum, 1945, U. N.C., 1946, Oberlin Coll., 1947, Toronto U., 1947, Washington and Lee U., 1949, U. Glasgow, 1951, Brown U., 1954, U. Cal., U. Mich., McGill U., 1955, Dropsie Coll., Colgate U., 1957, U. B.C., 1958, U. Manchester, 1959, U. N.B., Centre Coll., 1963; D.C.L., U. Pitts., 1957; D.Social Sci., Laval U., 1952; Litt.D., Columbia, 1934, Hahnemann Med. Coll., 1937, U. Hawaii, 1949; L.H.D., Hobart Coll., 1936, Bucknell U., 1958; H.H.D., Coll. Wooster, 1938; m. Margaret Murray, Dec. 25, 1917. Instr. econs., Purdue U., 1914-16; exec. sec. U.S. Food Adminstrn., Pa., 1917-19; asst. prof. polit. sci. Western Res. U., 1919-20; sec. Nat. Municipal League, 1920- 28, editor Nat. Municipal Rev., 1920-33; prof. politics Princeton, 1927-34, pres. univ., 1933-57. Electoral adviser Govt. Nicaragua, 1922-24; tech. adviser pres. Tacna-Arica Plebiscitary Commn., 1925-26; chief adviser pres. Nat. Bd. Elections Nicaragua, 1928; cons. Cuban Govt. in election law and procedure, 1935. Chmn., Pres.'s Com. on Integration Med. Services of Govt., 1946; mem. Pres.'s Adv. Commn. on Universal Tng., 1947; chmn. task force on personnel, 2d Hoover Commn., 1954-55; chmn. Am. delegation Anglo.-Am. Conf. on Refugee Problem, Bermuda 1943. Named comdr. Order of King Leopold, 1937. Mem. Am. Acad. Arts and Scis., Am. Philos. Soc., Phi Beta Kappa. Presbyn. Clubs: Athaeneum (London, Eng.); Century, Princeton (N.Y.C.); Nassau (Princeton). Author: Out of This Nettle...Danger, 1943; The Academic President—Educator or Caretaker?, 1962; also numerous articles, surveys and reports in polit. sci. Home: 87 College Rd W Princeton NJ 08540

DODDS, JOHN WENDELL, educator; b. Grove City, Pa., July 20, 1902; s. Samuel and Alice (Dunn) D.; B.A., Coll. of Wooster, 1924, Litt.D., 1945; M.A., Yale, 1927, Ph.D., 1932; L.H.D., Ohio Wesleyan U., 1964; m. Marjorie Jane Krantz, June 18, 1928; children—John Arthur, Christopher Deis. Faculty dept. English, U. Pitts, 1927-37; asso. prof. English, Stanford U., 1937-39, prof., 1939-67, dir. of spl. programs in humanities, dean Sch. of Humanities, 1942-48, Jackson Eli Reynolds prof. humanities, 1962-67, now emeritus; vis. lectr., cons. humanities Emory U., 1952; vis. prof. U. Hawaii, summer 1953, sr. cons. humanities Ednl. Radio and TV Center, Ann Arbor, 1955-58; bd. dirs. Wenner-Gren Found., 1954—, pres., 1965—; editorial adv. bd. World Book Ency., 1963-68. Trustee Coll. of Wooster (Ohio), 1966—, also Mills Coll., Oakland, Cal., 1943-53, Pomona Coll., Claremont Coll., 1955-68. Chmn. editorial bd. Pacific Spectator 1946-56. Fellow Guggenheim Found., 1947-48, Viking Fund, 1948. Mem. Modern Lang. Assn., Am. Assn. U. Profs., Am. Council Learned Socs. (chmn. Pacific Coast com. for humanities 1943-58), Phi Beta Kappa (Senator United chpts. 1952-70), Delta Sigma Rho. Presbyn. Club: Authors' (London). Author: Thomas Southerne, Dramatist, 1933; Thackeray: A Critical Portrait, 1941; The Age of Paradox: a Biography of England, 1841-1851, 1952; American Memoir, 1961; Everyday Life in Twentieth Century America, pub. 1965. Editor: An Oxford Anthology of English Prose (with Arnold Whitridge), 1935; Types of English Fiction (with Hardin Craig), 1940; Modern Brit. and Am. Plays (with W.H. Durham), 1947. Home: 729 Frenchman's Rd Stanford University CA 94305

DODDS, ROBERT JAMES, Jr., lawyer; b. Pitts., Mar. 5, 1916; s. Robert James and Agnes Julia (Raw) D.; grad. Shady Side Acad., Pitts., 1933; A.B., Yale, 1937; LL.B., U. Pa., 1940; m. Kathryn Moore Bechman, June 6, 1942 (dec. Sept. 1943); 1 son, Robert James III; m. 2d, Virginia T. Enright, Feb. 13, 1961; children—Dana, Anthony. Admitted Pa. bar, 1940, since practiced Pitts.; mem. firm Reed, Smith, Shaw & McClay; gen. counsel U.S. Dept. Commerce, 1959-61; dir. Herbick & Held Printing Co., Spang & Co., Buyers Purchasing Digest Co., Fisher Sci. Co., Haugh & Keenan Transfer & Storage Co., Power Control Corp., Internat. Staple & Machine Co. Trustee Shady Side Acad., Children's Hosp. of Pitts., U. Health Center Pitts.; bd. dirs., Blue Cross Western Pa., Health Center Hosp. Service Corp., Pitts. YMCA. Served from pvt. to maj., inf. AUS, 1941-45; ETO. Decorated Bronze Star medal. Mem. Am., Pa., Allegheny County bar assns., Am. Judicature Soc. Presbyn. (trustee) Clubs: Duquesne (Pitts.), Pitts. Athletic Assn.; Longue Vue Country, Rolling Rock, Yale (N.Y.C.); Metropolitan (Washington). Home: 1740 Beechwood Blvd Pittsburgh PA 15217 Office: Union Trust Bldg Pittsburgh PA 15219

DODGE, CHARLES GRANVILLE, ret. army officer, assn. exec.; b. Maplewood, N.J., Mar. 12, 1907; s. Eben Grant and Sue Tyler (Hyde) D.; B.S., U.S. Mil. Acad., 1930; grad. advance equitation course, Cav. Sch., 1936, Command and Gen. Staff Coll., 1941, Nat. War Coll., 1951; m. Elizabeth Febiger Marrack, Aug. 16, 1935; childrenSue Hyde, Charles Tyler. Commd. 2d lt., cav., U.S. Army, 1930, advanced through grades to lt. gen., 1963; troop officer, then instr. maths. and horsemanship U.S. Mil. Acad., instr. motors and weapons Cav. Sch., dir. dept. weapons Tank Destroyer Sch., chief staff Tank Destroyer Center, 1930-44; chief staff 8th and 2d armored divs., 1944-46; dep. G-1 Third U.S. Army, 1946-47; dir. U.S. element Allied Commn., also asst. dep. U.S. Commr. Austria, 1947-49; assigned Gen. Staff, Dept. Army, chief Mediterranean and Middle East br. operations div., 1949; exec. sec. weapons systems evaluation group, Office Sec. Def., 1951-53, comdg. officer Combat Command C. 2d Armored Div., 1953-55; dep. chief staff for operations Hdqrs. 7th U.S. Army, 1955-56; chief U.S. Army Adv. Group, Air U., 1956-58; dep. chief legislative liaison Office Sec. Army, 1958-59; asst. div. comdr. 1st Cav. Div., 1960, comdg. gen. of div., 1960; asst. chief of staff for res. components Dept. of Army, Washington, 1961, chief of information, 1961-63; comdg. gen, 5th U.S. Army, Chgo., 1963-66, ret.; exec. v.p. Assn. U.S. Army, Washington, 1966-. Decorated The Distinguished Service medal, The Legion of Merit, Bronze Star medal (U.S.); War Cross (Czechoslovakia); Order Orange Nassau, Knight Comdr. with swords (Netherlands); Croix de Guerre with palm (France); Order of Leopold with palm, Croix de Guerre with palm, (Belgium). Home: 8125 Dunsinane Ct McLean, VA 22101. Office: 1529 18th St NW Washington DC 20036

DODGE, CHARLES MALCOLM, educator, composer; b. Ames, Ia., June 5, 1942; s. Albert Francis and Constance (Ruth) D.; B.A. with honors and high distinction in music, U. Ia., 1964; M.A., Columbia, 1966, D.M.A., 1970; m. Mary Van Beuren King, Aug. 5, 1966 (div. 1971); children— Rachael Constance, Baird Willard. Compositions have been performed by Univ. Symphony Orch., Iowa City, 1963, Nat. Gallery Art, 1964, Group Contemporary Music, Columbia, 1964, Tanglewood, Lenox, Mass., 1960, Composer's Forum, N.Y.C., 1965, Columbia Group, 1965, Tanglewood Festival Am. Music, 1965, Library of Congress, Coolidge Festival, 1970. Instr. music Columbia, 1967, asst. prof., 1970—; instr. Princeton, 1969. Woodrow Wilson fellow, 1964-65; Lydia C. Roberts fellow, 1965-66. Recipient Broadcast Music awards, 1963, 64, 66, 67; 1st pl. Joseph H. Bearnes prize, 1964, 67, Raphael Sagalyn award, 1964; commd. Fromm Music Found., 1965, Contemporary Music Soc., Koussevitzky Found., 1969. Mem. Am. Soc. U. Composers, Am. Composers Alliance (pres. 1971-73), Phi Beta Kappa, Pi Kappa Lambda, Phi Eta Sigma. Composer: Textures for Orchestra, 1962; Duo for Flute and Piano, 1963; Composition in Five Parts of Cello and Piano, 1964; Composition for Oboe, Violin, Contrabass, Horn and Piano, 1964; Folia and Rota for Orch., 1966; Changes, 1970. Home: 502 W 113th St New York City NY 10025 Office: Columbia U Music Dept New York City NY 10027

DODGE, CLEVELAND E., financier; b. N.Y.C., Feb. 5, 1888; s. Cleveland H. and Grace (Parish) D.; A.B., Princeton, 1909, Ph.D., 1959; LL.D. Presbyn. Coll., 1941, N.Y. U., 1952, Columbia, 1954; L.H.D., Springfield Coll., 1951; Litt.D., U. Ariz., 1958; m. Pauline Morgan, 1919; children—Elizabeth (Mrs. Bolling W. Haxall), Cleveland E., Joan (Mrs. Frederic Rueckert, Jr.). With Phelps Dodge Corp.; N.Y.C., 1910-67, v.p., 1924-61, now hon. dir.; trustee Atlantic Mut. Ins. Co. Trustee Tchrs. Coll. Columbia, Grant Found.; hon. trustee Am. Mus. Natural History; nat. bd. dirs., mem. exec. com. internat. com. YMCA; bd. dirs. YMCA Greater N.Y., pres. 1925-35; bd. dirs. Near East Found., pres. 1930- 53); bd. dirs. Council Chs. City N.Y.; emeritus dir. Internat. House. Chmn., Bronx Adv. Planning Bd., 1938-44; mem. U.S.O., N.Y. Com. Served with 304th F.A., U.S. Army, 1917-19. Decorated Cross of Grand Comdr., Royal Order George I, 1953 (Greece); Order of Homayoun, 1955 (Iran). Recipient Russell Colgate citation as layman of year, 1954. Mem. Am. Inst. Mining, Metall. and Petroleum Engrs., Mining and Metall. Soc. Am. (pres. 1937). Presbyn. Clubs: University, Princeton, Pinnacle (N.Y.C.). Home: Dodgewood Rd Riverdale New York City, NY 10471. Office: 641 Lexington Av New York City NY 10022

DODGE, CLEVELAND EARL, Jr., mfg. co. exec.; b. N.Y.C., Mar. 7, 1922; s. Cleveland Earl and Pauline (Morgan) D.; grad. Hotchkiss Sch., 1939; B.S. in Mech. Engring., Princeton, 1943; m. Phyllis Boushall, Dec. 19, 1942; children—Alice, Sally Mole, Cleveland III. With DeLaval Steam Turbine Co., 1942, Gen. Electric Co., 1946-51; v.p., dir. Warren Wire Co., Pownal, Vt., 1951-55; pres., dir. Dodge Industries, Inc., Hoosick Falls, N.Y., 1955-67; v.p., dir. Engineered Yarns, Inc., 1962-68; pres. Internat. Dodge, Inc., 1968—, also treas., dir.; pres. Dodge Machine Co., 1968—, also dir.; chmn. bd. Dant Ltd., Uxbridge, U.K., 1969-71; dir. Phelps Dodge Corp.; dir. Nat. Comml. Bank & Trust Co., Albany, N.Y., also mem. regional bd., Hoosick Falls br. Trustee Bennington Mus., Cleveland H. Dodge Found. Served to lt. USNR, World War II. Mem. Soc. Plastics Industry, Princeton Engring. Assn., Princeton Rowing Assn. Episcopalian. Kiwanian. Clubs: Laurentian Lodge (Shawbridge, Que., Can.); Princeton (N.Y.C.). Home: Quarry Hill Farm Pownal VT 05261 Office: Internat Dodge Inc Hoosick Falls NY 12090

DODGE, ERNEST STANLEY, museum dir., writer; b. Trenton, Me., Mar. 18, 1913; s. George Flint and Beatrice Marion (Dolliver) D.; spl. student anthropology Harvard, 1937-38; M.A. (hon.), Marlboro Coll.; D.Litt., Boston U.; m. Irene Doucette, Dec. 23, 1938; children—Rebecca Ann, Ernest Stanley; m. 2d, Elisabeth Shrigley Wheeler, Nov. 24, 1965. Mus. asst. Peabody Mus. of Salem, Mass., 1931-37, asst. curator, 1937-43, curator, 1943-46, asst. dir., 1946-50, dir., 1950—; Lowell lectr., 1962; sr. specialist East-West Center, 1968. Guggenheim fellow, 1960-61. Trustee, pres. Ropes Mem.; trustee Penobscot Marine Mus., Fruitlands Mus., Merrimack Textile Mus.; councillor Essex Inst.; adviser Robert Bennet Forbes House, Woodbridge House, Salem Home for Aged Women, Oxford Coll. Barges Preservation Trust. Fellow Am. Anthrop. Assn.; Am. Acad. Arts and Sci., Royal Anthrop. Inst., Royal Geog. Soc.; mem. Mass. Hist. Soc., Colonial Soc. Mass., Am. Folklore Soc., Am. Antiquarian Soc., Am. Ethnological Soc., C. of C. (dir. 1953-55, 66-68), Soc. History Discoveries (pres. 1965-67), Am. Soc. Ethno History (pres. 1966-67). Unitarian. Clubs: Grolier (N.Y.); Odd Volumes (Boston). Author: Gourd Growers of the South Seas, 1943; Northwest By Sea, 1961; New England and the South Sea, 1965; Beyond the Capes, 1971; also sci., hist. and popular articles. Editor: The American Neptune. Home: 161 Essex St Salem MA 01970 Office: Peabody Museum Salem MA 01970

DODGE, GUY HOWARD, educator; b. Jefferson, O., Oct. 4, 1910; s. Guy B. and Jennie S. (Bragg) D.; A.B., Western Res. U., 1933; A.M., Harvard, 1937, Ph.D., 1942; A.M., Brown U., 1951; m. Dorothea K. Zantiny, Aug. 15, 1942; one dau., Dorothea Lynn. Instr. tutor Harvard, 1939-40; instr. Brown U., Providence, 1941—, asst. prof., 1944-48, asso. prof., 1948-51, prof., 1951—, chmn. dept. polit. sci., 1950-62. Sheldon traveling fellow in France, Harvard, 1938-39, Fulbright fellow, France, 1949-50, 63-64. Mem. Am., New England (exec. council 1950-51, v.p., 1956-57, pres. 1957- 58) polit. sci. assns., Am. Soc. Polit. and Legal Philosophy, Institut Internat. de Philosophie Politique, Soc. French Hist. Studies, Am. Assn. U. Profs., Am. Hist. Assn., Lambda Chi Alpha, Phi Beta Kappa. Club: Faculty.

Author: Political Theory of the Huguenots of the Dispersion, 1947; Jean-Jacques Rousseau: Authoritarion Libertairan?, 1971; also articles and revs. in polit. sci. mags. Home: 94 Miller Av Rumford RI 02916

DODGE, JAMES AUGUSTUS, Jr., investment banker; b. Chester, Pa., Jan. 29, 1916; s. James Augustus and Ethyl (McQuire) D.; B.S. in Commerce, Northwestern U., 1938; postgrad. advanced mgmt. program Harvard, 1960; m. Ruth E. Dunham, June 14, 1941; children—Susan D., Deborah D., Meredith D. With Pet Milk Co., St. Louis, 1938-70, past pres. milk Products, Inc., P.R.; account exec. Stifel, Nicolaus & Co., investment bankers, St. Louis, 1970—. Mem. Grocery Mfrs. Assn., Evaporated Milk Assn. (v.p. dir.). Home: 2 Bennington Lane Landue MO 63124 Office: 1 N Brentwood St Louis MO 63105

DODGE, JOHN VILAS, editor; b. Chgo., Sept. 25, 1909; s. George Dannel and Mary Helen (Porter) D.; B.S., Northwestern U., 1930; postgrad. U. Bordeaux, France, 1930-31; m. Jean Elizabeth Plate, Aug. 17, 1935; children—Ann, John M., Gerald C., Kathleen. Free-lance writer, 1931-32; editor Northwestern U. Alumni News and ofcl. publs. of Northwestern, 1932-37; exec. sec. Northwestern U. Alumni Assn., 1937-38; asst. editor Ency. Brit., asso. editor Brit. Book of Year, 1938-43; asso. editor Ten Eventful Years (4 vol. history 1937-46), 1947; asst. editor Ency. Brit., 1946-50, mng. editor, 1950-60, exec. editor, 1960-64, sr. v.p.-editorial, 1964-65, sr. editorial cons., 1965-70, v.p. internat. editorial, 1970—, editor Brit. World Lang. Dictionary, 1954. Editorial counselor Ency. Universalis, Paris. Served from pvt. to 1st lt. A.A.A., M.I., AUS, 1944-46. Recipient staff citation War Dept. Mem. Sigma Delta Chi. Home: Shurmer Rd Northbrook IL 60062 Office: 425 N Michigan Av Chicago IL 60611

DODGE, L.L., mfg. co. exec.; b. Wis., May 25, 1905; s. Allen and Abigail Dodge; m. Edna B. Dodge, Sept. 8, 1928; 1 son, John A. With Gen. Motors Corp., 1926-48; with Dana Corp., Toledo, 1948-71, v.p., finance sec., until 1971; dir. Chelsea Prod., Inc., Gen. Drop Forge Corp. Mem. Soc. Automotive Engrs., Am. Mgmt. Assn. Home: 5411 Olde Post Rd Toledo OH 43606 Office: 4100 Bennett Rd Toledo OH 43612

DODGE, PHILIP ROGERS, physician; b. Beverly, Mass., Mar. 16, 1923; s. Israel R. and Anna (McCarthy) D.; student U. N.H., 1941-43, Yale, 1943-44; M.D., U. Rochester, 1948; m. Martha Hoyt, Aug. 25, 1947; children—Susan, William, Judith. Intern, Strong Meml. Hosp., 1948-49; asst. resident neurology Boston City Hosp., 1949-50, resident, 1950, sr. resident, 1951-52; practice medicine, specializing in neurology, Boston, 1956-67, St. Louis, 1967—; teaching fellow neurology Harvard Med. Sch., 1950, 51-53, instr. neurology, 1955-58, asso. in neurology, 1958-61, asst. prof., 1962-67; asst. neurologist Mass. Gen. Hosp., 1956-59, dir. pediatric neurology program, 1958-67, asso. neurologist, 1959-63, asso. pediatrician, 1961- 62, pediatrician, 1962-67, investigator Joseph P. Kennedy, Jr. Meml. Labs. for Study Mental Retardation, 1962-67, neurologist, 1963-67; pediatric neurologist Boston Lying-In Hosp., 1961-67; cons. in neurology Walter E. Fernald State Sch. for Retarded Children, 1963-67; med. dir. St. Louis Childrens Hosp., 1967—; asso. neurologist Barnes Hosp., 1967- -; prof., head Mallinckrodt Dept. Pediatrics, Washington U. Sch. Medicine, 1967—, prof. neurology, 1967—. Vis. scientist Clin. Research Center, U. P.R., 1965-66, hon. vis. prof. physiology, 1967; cons. collaborative project on cerebral palsy Nat. Inst. Neurol. Diseases and Blindness, 1958—; bd. dirs., chmn. research adv. com. Mass. Soc. for Prevention Cruelty to Children, 1961-67; mem. sci. research adv. bd. Nat. Assn. for Retarded Children, 1963-67. Dir. Central Midwestern Regional Lab., Inc., 1967-70. Served from 1st lt. to maj., M.C., U.S. Army, 1950- 56. Diplomate Am. Bd. Psychiatry and Neurology. Mem. St. Louis Med. Soc., Am. Pediatric Soc., Am. Acad. Neurology (past com. chmn.), Am. Neurol. Assn., Assn. for Research in Nervous and Mental Disease, Soc. Pediatric Research, Soc. Biol. Psychiatry, St. Louis Soc. Neurol. Scis., Alpha Omega Alpha. Editorial bd. Jour. Developmental Medicine and Child Neurology, 1965—, Jour. Pediatrics, 1970—, Pediatric Research, 1970—; Current Problems in Pediatrics, 1969—. Contbr. articles profl. jours. Home: 909 Lay Rd St Louis MO 63124 Office: 500 S Kingshighway St Louis MO 63110

DODGE, WASHINGTON, investment advisor; b. San Francisco, Sept. 23, 1907; A.B., Yale, 1929; m. Helen K. Hubbard, 1932; m. 2d, Helen M. Brown, 1941. Financial editor Time mag. and editorial assignments for Archtl. Forum and Fortune mags., N.Y.C., 1929-33; pub. relations Barrett Co., 1933-37; author bus. commentary, "Washington Dodge's Letter," 1937-57; investment adv. 1937—; partner Arthur Wiesenberger & Co., mem. N.Y. Stock Exchange, 1941-44, Roberts, Rutter & Co., 1944-69, Clark Dodge & Co., 1969—; dir. 417 Park Av. Corp. Mem. Native Sons Golden West, Skull and Bones, Alpha Delta Phi. Clubs: Grolier, Racquet and Tennis (N.Y.C.); Maidstone (East Hampton); Seven Lakes (Palm Springs). Home: 417 Park Av New York City NY 10022

DODGE, WENDELL PHILLIPS, editor, explorer, ethnologist; b. Manchester, New Hampshire, Aug. 12, 1883; son of Arthur Pillsbury and Elizabeth Ann (Day) D.; student Art Inst., Chgo. Musical Coll. (Chgo.); Chase Sch., Nat. Acad. Design, Art Students League (N.Y.); civil engring., N.Y.U., 1903-06; m. Clothilde Beatrice Masson, June 23, 1908; children—Wendell Phillips (dec. May 25, 1947), Richard William. Numerous indsl., comml., reportorial assignments, 1905-13; founder, propr., The World Wide News Service, 1913, gen. mgr. mng. editor; contbr. mags., U.S. and fgn.; founder-dir. Am. Theater in Paris, 1929; produced several plays, 1919-32; directed Mlle. Lucienne Boyer, Escudero, Nikita Balieff, 1934; London Intimate Opera Co., N.Y.C. and Canada, 1937-38; produced Explorers T.V. Program, WNBT, N.Y.C. 1949. Explored Dead Sea, and site Gomorrah in Jordan Valley; Syrian and Red Deserts; excavated mounds of Balawat, east of Monsulate site of Ninevah, also vicinity of Baghdad; excavations at tomb of Cyrus on Plain of Pasargadae, 1900-01; organized and directed P'an Ku Exploration and Exhbn. Co., Far East and Near East expdns., 1939. Mem. Am. adv. bd., Yenching U., Peiping, China. Fellow Royal Geographical Society (London); Egyptian Geographical Soc. (Cairo); mem. several profl. assns. Clubs: Lambs, Explorers (past dir.), Arm0 and Navy, Circumnavigators; The Silurians. Completed History of Bahai Revelation and Ency. of Religion begun by father. Author several books and plays, latest: Sweeney Todd, 1959; Short History of the Arctic, published 1963; series on exploration; also articles; contbr. articles on shipbuilding and shipping, New Internat. Year Book, 1946, 1951—; The Book of Knowledge (articles on explorations of the year, 1951—); editor Marine News, 1943-50; editor Explorers Jour., 1945-54; Circumnavigators Log., 1953, 62-63. Address: Army and Navy Club of NY 4 W 43d St New York City NY 10036

DODGEN, HAROLD WARREN, educator; b. Blue Eye, Mo., Aug. 31, 1921; s. James Monroe and Lora (Myers) D.; student Long Beach Jr. Coll., 1939-41; B.S., U. Cal. at Berkeley, 1943, Ph.D., 1946; m. Harriet Keddie Ralston, Jan. 20, 1945; children—Cynthia Jeanne, Gilbert Keddie, Stephen LaRele. Research asst. Manhattan Dist. Project, U. Cal. at Berkeley, 1943-46; post-doctorate fellow Inst. Nuclear Studies, U. Chgo., 1946-48; asst. prof. chemistry State Coll. Wash., 1948-52, asso. prof., 1952-59, prof. chemistry, 1959-63, prof. chemistry and physics, 1963—, dir. Nuclear Reactor Project, 1954-68, chmn. chem. physics program, 1968—. Fellow Am. Inst. Chemists; mem. Am. Chem. Soc., Am. Phys. Soc., Am. Nuclear Soc., Am. Assn. U. Profs., A.A.A.S., Phi Beta Kappa, Sigma Xi, Alpha Chi Sigma. Home: 1607 Fisk St Pullman WA 99163

DODRILL, FOREST DEWEY, surgeon; b. Webster Springs, W.Va., Jan. 26, 1902; s. John Leonard and Rebecca (Hamrick) D.; A.B., W.Va. U., 1925; M.D., Harvard, 1930; M.S., U. Mich., 1944; m. Adris Twork, 1938; children—Judith Ann, Christine Rebecca, Mary Sue. Surgeon, pioneer in development heart-lung machine for open cardiac surgery. Diplomate Am. Bd. Surgeons, Am. Bd. Thoracic Surgeons. Fellow A.C.S.; mem. Mich. Heart Assn. (pres. 1958), A.M.A., Am. Assn. Thoracic Surgery. Methodist. Home: 225 Woodberry Dr Bloomfield Hills MI 48013 Office: 306 David Whitney Bldg Detroit MI 48226

DODSON, A.A., business exec. Controller, Emporium Capwell Co., San Francisco. Office: 835 Market St San Francisco CA 94103*

DODSON, CHARLES RUSSELL, petroleum co. exec.; b. Washington, Sept. 1, 1907; s. Gilbert R. and Martha G. (Shackelford) D.; B.S., U. Md., 1930; M.S., Mass. Inst. Tech., 1932; postgrad. U. Cal., Berkeley, 1932-34, Dartmouth, 1955-57; m. Mary- Bell Reynolds, Aug.22, 1942; children-Anne (Mrs. Edward Gould), Gilbert E., Norman R. With Gen. Electric Co., Lynn, Mass., 1930-32; instr. U. Cal., Berkeley, 1932-35; with York Ice Machinery Co. (Pa.), 1935-36; dir. prodn. tech. lab. Standard Oil Co. of Cal., 1936-42, staff petroleum engr., 1942-45, div. petroleum engr., 1945-47; prof., head dept. petroleum engring. U. So. Cal., 1947-52; partner Stanley, Stolz & Dodson, cons. petroleum engrs., Los Angeles, 1951-53; v.p. petroleum dept. First Nat. City Bank, N.Y.C., 1954-59; mgr. petroleum dept., sr. v.p. natural resources United Cal. Bank, Los Angeles, 1959-70; v.p. Investors Diversified Services, Inc., Mpls., 1970—; pres. IDS Oil Programs, Inc., Los Angeles, 1970—; dir. Ladd Petroleum Corp., Western Crude Oil, Inc., Denver, Mut. Exploration Funds, Inc.; cons. petroleum engr., 1947-54. Chmn. Eagle Scout Recognition Dinner, 1968. Mem. adv. bd. S.W. Legal Found. Distinguished lectr. Am. Inst. Mining, Metall. and Petroleum Engrs., 1966. Registered profl. engr., Cal. Mem. Am. Inst. Mining, Metall. and Petroleum Engrs. (treas., dir.), Petroleum Prodn. Pioneers (v.p., dir.), Am. Mining Congress, Am. Petroleum Inst., Soc. Petroleum Engrs., Town Hall, Los Angeles C. of C., Sigma Xi, Tau Beta Pi (trustee exec. council), Phi Kappa Phi, Phi Epsilon Tau, Omicron Delta Alpha. Republican. Clubs: Annandale Country (Pasadena, Cal.); California, Los Angeles Country, Petroleum (Los Angeles); Pauma (Cal.) Valley Country. Contbr. articles profl. jours. Home: 521 Montana Av Santa Monica CA 90403 Office: 6151 W Century Blvd Los Angeles CA 90045

DODSON, DAN WILLIAM, educator; b. nr. Mt. Vernon, Tex., June 4, 1907; s. George Franklin and Beulah (Crump) D.; A.B., McMurry Coll., 1931, LL.D., 1957; M.A., So. Meth. U., 1936; Ph.D., N.Y.U., 1941; m. Evelyn Foreman, June 7, 1937; children—Beverly Ann, Dan William Jr. Instr. McMurry Coll., 1931-35; faculty N.Y.U., 1936-, successively teaching fellow, instr., asst. prof., asso. prof. sociology, 1936-50, prof., 1950-, dir. Center for Human Relations and Community Studies, 1956—; participant numerous neighborhood area and sch. surveys. Mem. Mayor's Com. on Unity (dir. 1944-48), 1944-53; mem. exec. bd. Save the Children Fedn.; dir. Citizens for All-Day Neighborhood Sch.; adv. bd. Child Guidance League; adv. com. AFL-CIO Community Service Activities, 1956-; adv. com. human relations Boys Clubs Am.; mem. nat. council, nat. com. on voluntary training Greater N.Y. council Boy Scouts Am.; mem. com. relations com. Girl Scouts Am. Mem. research com. Youth Bd., N.Y.C., Bd. govs. Ethical Culture Schs.; mng. trustee E. George Payne Ednl. Sociology Found. trustee Methodist Theological Seminary of Ohio. Recipient Florina Lasker award Great N.Y. Urban League, 1954; 1st Good Neighbor award N.Y.C. Mission Soc.; Ernest O. Melby award in human relations N.Y.U. Alumni Assn. Fellow Am. Sociology Soc.; mem. N.E.A. Assn. Supervision and Curriculum Devel. (chmn. human relations com.), Am. for Democratic Action, Soc. Study Edn., Soc. Study Social Problems, Soc. Psychol. Study Social Issues, Nat. Assn. Intergroup Relations Ofcls., Nat. Conf. Christians and Jews (exec. bd. Manhattan-Westchester area), Council on Am. Unity (chmn. bd.), Brotherhood-In-Action (bd.), Nat. Council Chs. of Christ Am. (com. on gen. program, field and planning; com. on racial and cultural relations), Nat. Social Welfare Assembly, Pub. Edn. Assn., Urban League Greater N.Y. (exec. bd.), Alpha Kappa Delta, Phi Delta Kappa. Methodist. Author chpts. in books Editor Jour. Ednl. Sociology, 1943—. Home: 17 Odell Av Yonkers NY 10701 Office: New York U Washington Sq New York City NY 10003

DODSON, EDWARD GRIFFITH, Jr., lawyer; b. Norfolk, Va., Feb. 11, 1914; s. Edward Griffith and Harriotte Jones (Winchester) D.; B.A., U. Va., 1937, LL.B., 1937; m. Mary Archer Talcott, Oct. 26, 1940; children—Elizabeth Archer, Harriotte Winchester (Mrs. E.R. McDannald), Edward Griffith III. Admitted to Va. bar, 1937, since practiced in Roanoke; asso. Cocke, Hazlegrove & Shackelford, 1937-42, 46-47; sr. partner Dodson, Pence, Coulter, Viar & Young and predecessor firm, Roanoke, Va., 1948—; substitute justice Juvenile and Domestic Relations Ct., 1947-48,. Dir., past chmn. Roanoke bd. Bank Va.; dir. Richardson- Wayland Elec. Corp., Bank of Va. of Southwest, Bank of Va. Roanoke Valley. Mem. Roanoke Youth Commn., 1946-49, Charter Study Commn., 1961; pres. Roanoke City-County Pub. Forum, 1948-49; pres. Roanoke Guidance Center, 1963-64; mem. Roanoke Charter Commn., 1965. Mem. Va. Ho. of Dels., 1948-54. Past bd. dirs. A.R.C.; bd. dirs., past v.p. Family Service Assn.; past bd. dirs. Children's Home Soc., Travelers Aid Soc.; mem. social planning council Roanoke Community Fund; past vice chmn. adv. com. Sch. Social Work, Va. Commonwealth U. trustee Episcopal High Sch., 1965-71; pres. bd. trustees Diocese S.W. Va.; vice chmn. Roanoke Valley Mental Health-Mental Retardation Services Bd. Served to lt. USNR, 1942-46. Mem. Am., Va. (past v.p.), Roanoke (past pres.) bar assns., Va. State Bar (pres. 1961-62), Roanoke Jr. C. of C. (past pres.), Va. Inland Sailing Assn., Newcomen Soc., Delta Kappa Epsilon, Phi Delta Phi. Democrat. Episcopalian. (past vestryman, sr. warden). Clubs: Roanoke German, Shennandoah. Home: PO Box 1045 Roanoke VA 24005 Office: Southwest Virginia Bldg Roanoke VA 24005

DODSON, JACK, actor; b. Pitts., May 16, 1931; s. John M. and Margaret (Smeaton) D.; B.F.A. in Drama, Carnegie Inst. Tech., 1953; m. Mary I. Weaver, Aug. 28, 1959; children—Cristina, Amy Elizabeth. Appeared U.S. premieres of Chemin de Fer, 1969, The Quare Fellow, 1958, A Penny for a Song, 1962, The Balcony, 1960, Infancy, 1962, revivals of Under Milkwood, 1961, Our Town, 1959, Pullman Car Hiawatha, 1962, Six Characters in Search of an Author, 1963-64, Hughie, 1964-65; appearances nationwide TV programs, 1959—; co-star The Andy Griffith Show, CBS-TV, 1966-68; co-star of Mayberry R.F.D., CBS-TV, 1968-71. Recipient Gold medal award Freedoms Found., 1949. Founding mem. Assn. Producing Artists. Home: Van Nuys CA 91408 Office: 1880 Century Park E Los Angeles CA 90067

DODSON, MARWIN REYNOLDS, ins. exec.; b. Norwood, O., Nov. 25, 1909; s. Edwin L. and Margrette C. (Cosby) D.; B.S., U. Mich., 1932; m. Virginia Eckert, June 23, 1933; 1 son, Reynolds Edwin. Asst. actuary Ohio Nat. Life Ins. Co., Cin., 1934-43, actuary, 1944-46, v.p., actuary, 1946-47, exec. v.p., 1947-56, pres., 1956-70, chmn., chief exec. officer, 1971—; dir. First Nat. Bank Cin. Dir. U. Cin. Fellow Soc. Actuaries; mem. Phi Beta Kappa, Alpha Kappa Psi, Phi Kappa Phi, Triangle. Episcopalian. Mason (32, Shriner). Clubs: Cincinnati Country, Queen City, Commercial (Cin.) Home: 2444 Madison Rd Cincinnati OH 45208 Office: Box 237 Cincinnati OH 45201

DODSON, OSCAR HENRY, numismatist, mus. dir.; b. Houston, Jan. 3, 1905; s. Dennis S. and Margaret (Sisk) D.; B.S., U.S. Naval Acad., 1927; grad. U.S. Naval Postgrad. Sch., 1936; M.A. in History, U. Ill., 1953; m. Pauline Wellbrock, Dec. 17, 1932; 1 son, John Dennis. Commnd. ensign USN, 1927, advanced through grades to rear adm., 1957; mblzn. planning officer Bur. Naval Personnel, 1945-48; comdg. officer U.S.S. Thomas Jefferson, 1949-50; prof. naval sci. U. Ill., 1950-53; comdr. Landing Ship Flotilla, Atlantic Fleet, 1954-55; chief staff U.S. Naval mission to Greece, 1955-56; chief staff 1st Naval Dist., Boston, 1956-57; ret., 1957; asst. prof. history U. Ill., 1957-59; dir. Money Mus., Nat. Bank Detroit, 1959-65; dir. Classical and European Culture Mus., U. Ill. Urbana, 1966—. Mem. numis. adv. com. Smithsonian Instn., 1946; mem. Ann. Assay Commn., 1948; mem. U. Ill. Found.; visited numis. socs. under auspices State Dept., U.S.S.R., Finland, Poland, Austria, Denmark, 1959. Decorated Silver Star. Fellow Am., Royal (London) numis. socs.; mem. Am. Numis. Assn. (life, Farran Zerbe award 1968, bd. govs. 1950-55, pres. 1957-61), Am. Mil. Inst., Am. Hist. Assn., Archeaol. Inst. Am., Am. Assn. Museums, Internat. Council Museums, U. Ill. (life, Loyalty award 1966), U.S. Naval Acad. alumni assns. Rotarian. Clubs: Yacht (N.Y.C.); Army-Navy Country (Washington); Circumnavigators, Torch. Author: Money Tells the Story, 1962. Contbr. articles to profl., numis. jours. Office: Lincoln Hall U Ill Urbana IL 61801

DODSON, RAYMOND M., educator, chemist; b. W. Hazleton, Pa., July 8, 1920; s. Curvin E. and Lena (Correll) D.; B.S. summa cum laude, Franklin and Marshall Coll., 1942; postgrad. U. Wis., 1944; Ph.D., Northwestern U., 1947; m. Margaret Ann Ward, Feb. 6, 1943; children—Karen L. (Mrs. Terry Bloom), Steven R., Debra L., Rebecca D. Asst. prof. U. Minn., 1947-51; chemist G.D. Searle and Co., Chgo., 1951-55, asst. dir. chem. research, 1956-60; prof. chemistry U. Minn., 1960—. Mem. endocrinology study sect. NIH, 1962-66. NRC fellow, 1946-47. Mem. Am. Chem. Soc., A.A.A.S., N.Y. Acad. Sci., Chem. Soc. (London, Eng.), Phi Beta Kappa, Sigma Xi. Co-inventor syncromate, cronolone, 1959; dir. research aldactone (spironolactone), 1956-59, microbiol. aromatization steroids, 1960, reactions sulfur monoxide, 1967, reactions of disulfur monoxide, 1970. Home: 189 Logan Pky Minneapolis MN 55432

DODSON, RICHARD WOLFORD, educator chemist; b. Kirksville, Mo., Jan. 15, 1915; s. Roy B. and June Florence (Jones) D.; student N.E. Mo. State Tchrs. Coll., 1932-34; B.S., Cal. Inst. Tech., 1936; Ph.D. (Am. Can Co. fellow), Johns Hopkins, 1939; m. Mary Ellen Stout, Aug. 25, 1937; children—Robert Kemble, Don Charles. Staff mem. NDRC projects Cal. Inst. Tech. and Northwestern, 1940-43; group leader, asst. div. leader Los Alamos Lab., 1943-45; asst. prof. chemistry Cal. Inst. Tech., 1946-47; asso. prof. chemistry Columbia, 1947-53, prof. 1953—; acting chmn., later chmn. chemistry dept. Brookhaven Nat. Lab., 1947- 68, sr. chemist, 1948—. Sec. gen. adv. com. AEC, 1951-56. NRC fellow Cal. Inst. Tech., 1940. Mem. Am. Phys. Soc., Am. Chem. Soc., A.A.A.S. Contbr. articles to profl. jours. Home: 407 Middle Rd Bayport NY 11705 Office: Brookhaven Nat Lab Upton NY 11973

DOE, RICHARD PHILIP, educator, physician; b. Mpls., July 21, 1926; s. Richard Harding and Ruth Elizabeth (Schoen) D.; B.S., U. Minn., 1949, M.B., 1951, M.D., 1952, Ph.D., 1966; m. Shirley Joan Cedarleaf, Sept. 15, 1950; children—Nancy Jean, Charles Jeffrey, Robert Bruce. Intern, Oakland (Cal.) Hosp., 1951-52; resident internal medicine Mpls. VA Hosp., 1952-55, chief chemistry sect., 1956-60, chief metabolic endocrine sect., 1960-69; head metabolic endocrine sect. U. Minn. Hosp., 1969—; faculty U. Minn. Med. Sch., Mpls., 1955—, prof. medicine, 1969—. Served with USNR, 1944-46. USPHS grantee, 1958—. Mem. Am. Soc. Clin. Investigation, Central Soc. Clin. Research, Endocrine Soc., Internat. Soc. Study Biol. Rythms. Home: 5613 Hawkes Dr Edina MN 55436 Office: Box 57 Univ Minn Hosps Minneapolis MN 55455

DOELZ, PAUL RUDOLPH, investment exec.; b. Mpls., Sept. 19, 1899; s. Otto R. and Johanna (Gerbig) D.; B.S., U. Minn., 1921; m. Grace Tangen, 1923; 1 dau., Nancy Grace. Br. mgr. Mpls. office Blair & Co., N.Y.C., 1922-31; pres., dir. Kalman & Co., Mpls.-St. Paul, 1948-67; chmn. bd. Dain, Kalman & Quail Co., Mpls., 1967-70, also dir.; past chmn. Ind. Gen. Corp., Valparaiso, Ind.; chmn. bd. Mpls. Gas Co., Domain Industries; past dir. Bliss & Laughlin (Oak Brook, Ill.). Asso. Mem. N.Y. Stock Exchange. Mem. Upper Research and Devel. Council. Clubs: Minneapolis, Minikahda. Home: 2540 Cedar Shore Dr Minneapolis MN 55416 Office: 110 S 6th St Minneapolis MN 55402

DOENGES, BYRON FREDERICK, univ. dea; b. Ft. Wayne, Ind., June 18, 1922; s. Arthur Phillip and Elise (Mesing) D.; diploma Internat. Bus. Coll., 1941; A.B., Franklin (Ind.) Coll., 1946; M.B.A., Ind. U., 1948, Ph.D., 1962; m. Elaine Aiken, June 15, 1947. Instr., headmaster boarding dept. Punahou Sr. Acad., Honolulu, 1948-50; dir. scholarships and loans Ind. U. at Bloomington, 1951-56, asst. dean Coll. Arts and Scis., 1955-65; prof. econs., dean Coll. Liberal Arts, Willamette U., 1965—. Program devel. head Title II Nat. Def. Edn. Act, U.S. Office Edn., Washington, 1958-59; asso. dir. Salzburg (Austria) Seminar Am. Studies, 1962-64; mem. Higher Commn. N.W. Assn. Secondary and Higher Schs., 1968—; mem. exec. bd. N.W. Assn. Pvt. Colls. and Univs., 1967—. Bd. dirs. Salem Art Assn. Served with USNR, 1943-46. Mem. Am. Econ. Assn., Assn. Liberal Edn. (Great Britain), Soc. Internat. Develop., Western Econ. Assn., Lambda Chi Alpha (mem. nat. fellowship bd. 1965—), Pi Gamma Mu, Omicron Delta Kappa. Rotarian. Contributor profl. journals. Spl. research internat. capital movements, econs. higher edn. Home: 735 Tillman Av SE Salem OR 97302

DOENGES, NORMAN ARTHUR, educator; b. Ft. Wayne, Ind., Aug. 23, 1926; s. Arthur Philip and Elsie (Mesing) D.; B.A., Yale, 1947, Balliol Coll., Oxford (Eng.) U., 1949; M.A., Princeton, 1951, Ph.D., 1954; Fulbright scholar Am. Sch. Classical Studies, Athens, Greece, 1951-52; m. Pamela Lee Wiegand, Aug. 23, 1952; children—Cynthia Lee, Stephanie Lynn, Jonathan Philip. Instr., Princeton, 1949-50, 52-53; mem. faculty Dartmouth, 1955—, prof. classics, 1965—, chmn. dept., 1959-63, 67—, chmn. humanities div., 1963-67, asso. dean faculty, 1964-66. Served with AUS, 1953-55. Mem. Am. Philol. Assn., Soc. Promotion Hellenic Studies, Classical Assn. Can., Classical Assn. New Eng. (sec.- treas. 1963-68). Home: 34 Rip Road Hanover NH 03755

DOENGES, WILLIAM CONRAD, mem. Dem. Nat. Com.; b. Maple Park, Ill., May 24, 1907; s. Rudolph Conrad and Lulu (Soland) D.; A.B., Oklahoma City U., 1929; m. Elizabeth Shannon, Oct. 23, 1929; children—William Soland, Robert Shannon, James, Rebecca. Pres. Doenges Inc., Tulsa, 1946-; v.p. Heildis, Inc., Tulsa 1948—; ind. oil and gas producer, Okla., Kan. and Tex., Den-Tex Oil Co., Dallas;

partner Shibley Oil Co., Bristow, Okla., Langford Oil Co., Dewey, Okla.; dir. Home Savs. & Loan Assn., Bartlesville, Okla., Century Geophys. Co., Inc., Tulsa, Bartlesville Ford Inc., Coffeyville Motor Co., Tonkawa Motor Co. Mem. Democratic Nat. Com. for Okla., 1951—. Trustee Oklahoma City U. Mem. Nat. (dir.), Okla. (pres.) amateur athetic unions, Olympic Com., Sigma Alpha Epsilon. Home: Box Z Bartlesville OK 74003 also 5th and Detroit Tulsa OK 74120

DOERFLER, LEO G., educator; b. N.Y.C., June 25, 1919; s. Gustav S. and Anna (Steiner) D.; A.B., N.Y.U., 1939; M.S., Washington U., St. Louis, 1941; Ph.D., Northwestern U., 1948; m. Alice Laura Turecheck, Dec. 19, 1943; children—Dennis Lee, Donald Lee, David Lee, Ann Laura. Tchr.- psychologist Ia. Sch. Deaf, Council Bluffs, Ia., 1941-43; instr. audiology Northwestern U., 1946-48; prof. audiology Sch. Medicine, dir. doctoral program bioacoustics U. Pitts., 1948—; dir. dept. audiology Eye and Ear Hosp., Pitts., 1948—; cons. in field, 1946—. Bd. dirs. Cerebral Palsy Assn. Pitts., 1958—. Served with AUS, World War II. C.C. Bunch fellow Northwestern U., 1946-47. Fellow A.A.A.S., Am. Speech and Hearing Assn. (pres. 1967); mem. Am. Bd. Examiners in Speech Pathology and Audiology (pres. 1960), Sigma Xi. Contbr. profl. jours. Inventor D-S test for psychogenic deafness. Home: 4533 Barlind Dr Pittsburgh, PA 15227. Office: Eye and Ear Hosp Pittsburgh PA 15213

DOERFLINGER, WILLIAM MAIN, editor; b. Bklyn., July 30, 1910; s. William Frederic and Lilian Rose (Main) D.; B.A. with highest honors, Princeton, 1931, M.A., 1932; M.A., Harvard, 1939; m. Joy Homer, June 28, 1940 (dec. 1946); 1 dau., Katharine Homer; m. 2d, Anne Homer Warner, Oct. 21, 1950; 1 son, Thomas Main. Asst. editor Macmillan Co., 1935-38; relief work in China, 1939; mng. editor Am. Mercury, 1940-41; asso. editor E.P. Dutton & Co., Inc., 1942, 45-50, sr. editor, 1953—; news editor, war corr. overseas br. OWI, 1942-45; information officer Am. embassy, Rome, Italy, 1950-53. Mem. Phi Beta Kappa. Club: Overseas Press of Am. Author: The Middle Passage (Roland Barker), 1939; Shantymen and Shantyboys: Songs of the Sailor and Lumberman, 1951. Home: Canfield Rd Convent, NJ 07961. Office: 201 Park Av S New York City NY 10003

DOERGE, JOHN OTTO, investmen banker; b. Cleve., Nov. 26, 1922; s. Otto J. and Freda (Genzell) D.; student Kenyon Coll., 1941-44, Wharton Sch. Finance, U. Pa., 1953; children—Diane, Douglas, David, Dan, John. With Saunders, Stiver & Co., Cleve., 1946—, v.p., 1951-57, pres., 1957—, also dir.; dir. Bally Mfg. Corp., Bonne Bell, Inc., Boston Capital Corp., ComCorp., Inc., Diamond Truing Systems, Inc., Formigli Corp., Hickok Mfg. Co., Inc., Mobil Townes Corp., P.J. Parker, Inc., Progressive Plastics Co. Trustee Kenyon Coll. Served with USNR, 1944-46. Mem. Investment Bankers Assn. Am. (past gov. No. Ohio group), Young Pres.'s Orgn., C. of C. Clubs: Bond, Westwood Country, Union (Cleve.); Indian Creek Country, Jockey (dir.) (Miami, Fla.); Ocean Reef (dir.) (Key Largo, Fla.); Wall Street (N.Y.C.). Home: 21831 Avalon Dr Rocky River OH 44116 Office: One Terminal Tower Cleveland OH 44113

DOERING, GRACE BERNARDINA (Mrs. John W. McCord), lawyer; b. Cleve., June 16, 1890; d. Anton and Frances J. (Langer) Doering; A.B., Case Western Res. U., 1911; J.D., magna cum laude, Baldwin Wallace Coll., 1925; LL.M., Cleve.-Marshall Law Sch., 1927; m. John W. McCord, July 25, 1957. Instr. pub. high schs., Ohio, 1911-19; staff Albuquerque Morning Jour., 1920; admitted to N.M., bar, 1925, Ohio bar, 1931, U.S. Supreme Ct. bar, 1960; with John F. Simms, N.M., 1925-26; law asst. Ct. Appeals, 8th Dist. Ohio, 1926-33; asso. Doering, Doering & Doering, 1933—. Prof. appellate practice and procedure Grad. Sch., Cleve.-Marshall Law Sch., 1933-38; asst. dir. law City of Cleve., 1935-42; regional atty. OPA, 1942. Pub. mem. 5th regional tripartite panel Nat. Labor Bd., 1943-45; v.p. Nat. Assn. Women Lawyers Found., 1956-57. Trustee Legal Aid Soc. Recipient recognition awards for civic and profl. activities, including citation bd. govs. Case Western Res. U., 1963. Fellow Ohio State Bar Found.; mem. Nat. Assn. Women Lawyers (pres. 1957-58, del. ho. of dels. to Am. Bar Assn. 1958-59) Am. (1st woman assembly del. to ho. dels. 1957), Fed., Ohio, Cleve., Cuyahoga (trustee 1938-49, life) bar assns., Internat. Assn. Women Lawyers, Am. Judicature Soc., Cleve. Law Library, Citizens League, League Women Voters, Bus. and Profl. Women (hon.), Am. Assn. U. Women, Alumnae Assn. Flora Stone Mather Coll. Case Western Res. U., Nat. Women's Party, Czechoslovak Soc. Am. (hon.), Nat. Conf. Bar, Cleve. Women Lawyers Assn. (pres. 1954-56), Phi Beta Kappa, Phi Delta Delta. Clubs: Women's City, College (hon.) (Cleve.). Contbr. articles to profl. pubs. Home: 14269 Cedar Rd Cleveland OH 44121 also Del Sur Grande Big Sur CA 93920 also McCord AK Office: 5484 Broadway Cleveland OH 44127

DOERING, JOHN ADAM, hosp. adminstr.; b. Bryn Athyn, Pa., June 15, 1905; s. Charles E. and Lucy Lyons (Cooper) D.; M.D., Hahnemann Med. Coll., 1931; m. Katherine Macbeth Boggess, Mar. 24, 1934; children—Barbara (Mrs. L.W. Riley), Katherine D. (Mrs. Charles Lehman), John C., James A. Intern Shadyside Hosp., Pitts., 1931-32, resident, 1932-36; pvt. practice psychiatry, Pitts., 1936-42; dir. Del. State Mental Hygiene Clinics, 1946-48; with VA hosps., 1949—, dir. VA Hosp., Coatesville, Pa., 1960-66, VA Hosp., Roseburg, Ore., 1966—. Asso. psychiatry U. Pa., 1960-66. Mem. Portland Fed. Council; chmn. Central Douglas Combined Fed. Campaign. Served to maj., M.C., AUS, 1942-45; ETO. Diplomate Am. Bd. Psychiatry and Neurology. Mem. A.M.A., Am. Psychiat. Assn., Am. Coll. Hosp. Adminstrs., Assn. Med. Supts. Mental Hosps., Ore. Assn. Hosps., So. Ore. Hosp. Council, Fed. Hosp. Inst. Alumni Assn. Address: VA Hosp Roseburg OR 97470

DOERING, OTTO CHARLES, Jr., lawyer; b. Wilmette, Ill., Oct. 29, 1904; s. Otto Charles and Mabelle Ione (Montgomery) D.; LL.B., Cornell U., 1927; m. Lucy S. Thomas, June 9, 1927; children—Rogers Montgomery, Paul Edward, Otto Charles III. Admitted to N.Y. bar, 1927, since practiced in N.Y.C.; mem. firm Donovan, Leisure, Newton & Irvine, 1935—. Dir. Diamond Distbrs., Inc. Pres., Field Photo Meml. Home, Reseda, Cal. Bd. dirs. Internat. Rescue Com., Am. Friends of Captive Nations. Served to lt. col. AUS, 1942-45. Decorated Legion of Merit (U.S.); Order Brit. Empire; Order White Elephant (Thailand). Mem. Am. Bar Assn., Assn. Bar City N.Y., N.Y. County Lawyers Assn. Clubs: Downtown Athetic (N.Y.C.); St. Andrew's Golf (Hastings-on- Hudson, N.Y.); Lake Placid (N.Y.). Home: 137 Fort Hill Rd Scarsdale NY 10583 Office: 2 Wall St New York City NY 10005

DOERING, WILLIAM VON EGGERS, educator, organic chemist; b. Ft. Worth, June 22, 1917; s. Carl Rupp and Antionette (von Eggers) D.; B.S., Harvard, 1938; Ph.D., 1943; m. Ruth Haines, 1947 (div.1954); children—Christian, Peter, Margaretta; m. 2d, Sarah Cowles Bullitt, Nov. 30, 1969. Faculty, Columbia, 1943-52; prof. Yale, 1952-67, dir. div. sci., 1962-65; prof. Harvard, 1967—, Mallinkrodt prof., 1968—. Research chemist Nat. Def. Research Council, Harvard, 1941-42, Polaroid Corp., 1943, Office Prodn. Research and Devel., 1944-45; dir. Hickrill Chem. Research Found., Katonah, N.Y., 1947-59; cons. Upjohn Co., 1956—, Procter & Gamble Co., 1958—. Chmn., Council for Livable World, Washington, 1962—. Recipient John Scott award City of Phila., 1945; Pure Chemistry award Am. Chem. Soc., 1953; Synthetic Organic chem. mfrs. Assn. medal for creative work in synthetic organic chemistry, 1966; Hofmann medal German Chem. Soc., 1962; William C. DeVane medal Yale Phi Beta Kappa, 1967; Theodore William Richards medal, 1970. Mem. Nat. Acad. Sci., Am. Acad. Arts and Scis. Contbr. articles to profl. jours. Hon. regional editor Tetrahedron, 1958-60. Office: Harvard U 12 Oxford St Cambridge MA 02138

DOERMER, RICHARD T., banker; b. Ft. Wayne, Ind., Dec. 12, 1922; s. John S. and Kathryn (Morris) D.; B.S., U. Notre Dame, 1943; LL.B., Cornell U., 1949; m. Mary Louise McNabb, June 18, 1949; children-Richard D., Kathryn A. Admitted to Ind.bar, 1949, practiced in Ft. Wayne until 1956; pres., dir. Ind. Bank & Trust Co., Ft. Wayne, 1957—; dir. Kendallville Bank & Trust Co., Decatur Bank & Trust Co., Frances Slocum Bank, Wabash, Ind., Avis Indsl. Corp., Detroit, Pierce Gov. Co., Upland, Ind.; chmn. bd. First Equity Security Life Ins. Co., Anderson, Ind., Marion Malleable Iron Works, Inc. (Ind.) Pres., bd. dirs. Ft. Wayne Cath. Social Services; treas. Allen County United Fund. Trustee St. Francis Coll., Ft. Wayne. Served to lt. (j.g.), USNR, 1943-46. Named Ft. Wayne area Outstanding Young Man of Year, 1956; Man of Year Met. Notre Dame Club Ft. Wayne, 1960. Mem. Ft. Wayne Press Club (bd. dirs.), Ind. Bankers Assn. (chmn. small bus. com.), Ind., Am. bar assns. Roman Catholic. K.C. (4!). Home: 5310 Centruy Ct Fort Wayne IN 46807 Office: 915 S Clinton St Fort Wayne IN 46802

DOERNER, ERWIN J., lawyer; b. St. Louis, Aug. 23, 1897; LL.B., Washington U. Admitted to Okla. bar, 1921; mem. firm Doerner, Rinehart & Stuart, Tulsa, now Doerner, Stuart, Saunders, Daniel & Langenkamp. Mem. Am., Okla., Tulsa County bar assns., Am. Coll. Trial Lawyers. Office: 1200 Atlas Life Bldg Tulsa OK 74103

DOERR, ROBERT EDWARD, dental educator; b. Traverse City, Mich., Aug. 9, 1921; s. Harry B. and Neva Elizabeth (Sessions) D.; B.S., Western Mich. U., 1943; D.D.S., U. Mich., 1950, M.S., 1953; m. Mary Jane Blanchard, Sept. 22, 1945; children—M. Kathleen, Thomas R., Diana B. Asst. prof. dentistry U. Mich., 1953-57, asso. prof., 1957-61, prof., sec. dental faculty, 1961- -, asso. dean, 1962—. Cons. dental edn. Pan Am. Health Orgn., 1963, 64; mem. rev. panel for constrn. schs. dentistry Bur. State Services, Dept. Health Edn. and Welfare, 1964-67, mem. dental edn. rev. com. Bur. Health Professions Edn. and Manpower Training, 1968—; adv. com. dental div. Mich. Dept. Health, 1964-68; cons. Council on Dental Edn. Am. Dental Assn., 1968—. Trustee bd. edn., Ann Arbor, 1965-68. Served with AUS, 1943-46. Fellow Am. Coll. Dentists; mem. Am., Mich. dental assns., Am. Acad. Dental Practice Adminstrn., Am. Assn. U. Profs., Am. Assn. Dental Schs., Internat. Assn. Dental Research, Omicron Kappa Upsilon, Delta Sigma Delta, Phi Kappa Phi. Presbyn. Rotarian. Co- author: Operative Dentistry, 1966. Contbr. papers to profl. publs. Home: 2108 Shadford Rd Ann Arbor MI 48104

DOERSCHUK, ERNEST EDWIN, Jr., librarian; b. Sugar Creek, O., Dec. 14, 1914; s. Ernest Edwin and Minnie (Strome) D.; B.A., Oberlin Coll., 1937; B.S., Western Res. U., 1938; m. Helen Elizabeth Monks, Sept. 3, 1938; children—Ernest Edwin III, Peter M. Library asst. N.Y. Pub. Library, 1938-46; tech. librarian VA, N.Y.C., 1946-48; librarian Lancaster (Pa.) Free Pub. Library, 1948-57; dir. extension div. State Library Pa., Harrisburg, 1957-63, library devel. dir., 1963-64, state librarian, 1964—. Mem. Lancaster County Community Council, 1952-57. Served to 1st lt. AUS, 1942-46. Mem. Am., Pa. (past pres.) library assns., Pa. Assn. for Adult Edn. (past pres.), Am. Legion, Phi Beta Kappa. Mem. United Ch. of Christ (sec.). Home: 145 Kready Av Millersville PA 17551 Office: State Library Harrisburg PA

DOFT, FLOYD SHELTON, biochemist; b. Griswold, Ia., May 19, 1900; s. Edgar William and Sarah Elizabeth (Shelton) D.; A.B., Simpson Coll., 1921, Sc.D., 1952; Ph.D., Yale, 1926; m. Frances Pauline Fisk, Nov. 26, 1935; one stepson, Leon W. Research asst. Yale, 1923-24, Cheney fellow, 1924- 26, traveling fellow guest at Carlsberg Lab., Copenhagen, Denmark, 1926-27; asst. in physiology, Harvard, 1927-29; Eli Lilly fellow Yale, 1929-31; instr. in biochemistry and exptl. pathology U. Rochester, 1931-37; mem. staff NIH, 1937-62, chief biochemistry and nutrition lab., asst. dir. Exptl. Biology and Medicine Inst., 1947-50; acting dir., 1950-51; asso. dir. in charge research, Nat. Inst. Arthritis and Metabolic Diseases, 1951-53, dir., 1953-62, cons., 1962—; vis. prof. Einstein Coll. Medicine, 1962-66. Sci. adv. com. Vitamin Found., 1954-57, Nutrition Found., 1956-63, Nat. Better Bus. Bur., 1958—; mem. Nat. adv. council Monell Chem. Senses Center, U. Pa., 1968-; chmn., devel. council Simpson Coll., 1961-66; v.p. bd. trustees Biol. Abstracts, 1963-65; mem. food and nutrition bd. NRC, 1962-66; chmn. adv. com. on research Bur. Comml. Fisheries, 1963-66. Organizer, mem. U.S. Sci. Mission to USSR, 1960. Served with U.S. Army, 1918. Recipient D.S.M., USPHS, 1962. Diplomate Am. Bd. Nutrition. Fellow Am. Inst. Chemists, A.A.A.S., Washington Acad. Scis.; mem. Nat. Assn. Standard Med. Vocabulary (cons. 1962—), Internat. Union Nutrition (U.S. nat. com. 1961-65, vice chmn. 1961-63), Am. Chem. Soc., Am., Internat. socs. hematology, Soc. Am. Inst. Nutrition (pres. 1960-61), Exptl. Biology and Medicine, Am. Soc. Biol. Chemists, Wash. Acad. Medicine, Am. Rheumatism Assn., Pan Am. Med. Assn. (N.Am. v.p. nutrition), Internat. Platform Assn., Nat. Trust Hist. Preservation, Sigma Xi, Delta Upsilon, Epsilon Sigma, Gamma Alpha, Alpha Chi Sigma. Clubs: Cosmos, Farmington Country (Charlottesville). Asst. editor: Nutrition Reviews, 1944-47; asso. editor Jour. Nutrition, 1951-55. Contbr. numerous articles to various sci. jours. Home: 6416 Garnett Dr Chevy Chase MD 20015 Office: Nat Insts Health Bethesda MD 20014

DOGGETT, AUBREY CLAYTON, Jr., mortgage banker; b. Greensboro, N.C., Nov. 8, 1928; s. Aubrey Clayton and Ann (Blevins) D.; B.S., U. N.C., 1950; m. Judy Perier, July 26, 1952; children—Aubrey Clayton III, Kathryn Ann, Russell, Robert, Karen Michelle. Salesman, Richardson Realty, Inc., Greensboro, 1950, 52-53; reviewing appraiser Prudential Ins. Co. Am., Greensboro, 1953-58; exec. v.p., dir., mem. exec. com. Key Co., Greensboro, 1958-63; v.p. mortgage loan dept. Wachovia Bank & Trust Co., Winston-Salem, N.C., 1963-66, sr. v.p., 1969—; pres. Wachovia Mortgage Co.; pres., trustee Wachovia Realty Investments; dir. N.C. Title Co. Mem. Winston-Salem Real Estate Bd. Mem. Gov. N.C. Com. Low Income Housing, 1969; chmn. ad hoc com. Winston-Salem Model Cities Commn.; mem., past chmn. N.C. Housing Adv. Council; mem. Winston-Salem Housing Found. Exec. Bd.; chmn. Greater Greensboro Open Golf Tournament, 1960. Served to 1st lt. USMCR, 1950-52. Mem. mortgage bankers assns. Carolinas (pres., dir. 1970), Am. (Washington com., mortgage market com.), Winston-Salem C. of C., S.A.R., Sigma Chi. Episcopalian. Clubs: Greensboro Country; Old Town. Home: 2813 Galsworthy Dr Winston-Salem NC 27106 Office: PO Box 3174 Winston-Salem NC 27102

DOGGETT, JOSEPH MCSWAIN, educator; b. Piedmont, S.C., June 21, 1908; s. Alexander McBee and Betty Mae (Corbin) D.; A.B., Wofford Coll., 1930; M.A., Peabody Coll., 1937, Ph.D., 1950; postgrad. Harvard, Vanderbilt U., U. London (Eng.), Oxford (Eng.) U., also British Mus., Bibliothique Nat., Paris, France; m. Katherine Brewer, Apr. 6, 1942; 1 son, Joseph Brewer. Prin. Pelzer (S.C.) Pub. Schs., 1930-37; staff English dept. Erskine Coll., 1937-39, Peabody Coll., 1939-41, 46; asst. prof. English, Fla. State U., 1946-56; vis. prof. U. Houston, 1954-56, prof. English, 1958—, chmn. dept., 1959-69; vis. prof. U. Hawaii, 1957-58; spl. research lit. periodicals, Queen Anne period. Lectr., adminstrv. aide Civil Service Adminstrn., Atlanta and 5th Dist., 1942; field dir., field supr. A.R.C. Field Service, London, S. Eng. and Wales, 1942-45, chmn. Leon (Fla.) County chpt., 1951-53, exec. bd. Harris County (Tex.) chpt., 1956—. Named as Distinguished Son of South Carolina, 1966. Mem. Modern Lang. Assn., Nat. Council Tchrs. English, S. Central Coll. English Assn. (regional pres. 1960-61), Conf. Coll. Tchrs. English (pres. 1961-62), Modern Humanities Research Assn., Alpha Phi Omega, Kappa Phi Kappa, Pi Gamma Mu, Phi Kappa Phi (chpt. pres. 1964-65), Phi Eta Sigma (hon. mem.), Sigma Tau Delta, Phi Kappa Tau. Methodist (ofcl. bd.). Clubs: Churchill, Embassy (London); Torch (pres. chpt. 1971-72) (Houston). Author: A College Forum, 1962; also articles. Home: Oaklane Manor 2414 Rosamond St Houston TX 77006

DOHENY, DAVID ARMOUR, lawyer; b. Cobourg, Ont., Can., July 2, 1931; s. Clarence William and Kate (Armour) D.; brought to U.S., 1931, naturalized, 1955; A.B. cum laude, Williams Coll., 1953; LL.B., Harvard, 1958; m. Olga Kean, June 13, 1959 (div.); children—John Douglas Armour, Jennifer. Admitted to Ill. bar, 1959, Fla. bar, 1966; asso. Taylor, Miller, Busch & Magner, Chgo., 1958-63; asst. gen. counsel Am. Photocopy Equipment Co., Evanston, Ill., 1963-65; sec., gen. counsel legal dept. Gen. Devel. Corp., Miami, Fla., 1966-68, v.p., sec., gen. counsel, 1968—. Republican precinct capt., Chgo., 1962-65. Vice pres., bd. dirs. Greater Miami Philharmonic Soc. Served with C.E., U.S. Army, 1953-55. Mem. Am., Fla., Chgo., Dade County bar assns., Lincolns Inn Soc., N.Y. Geneal. and Biog. Soc., Am. Soc. Corporate Secs. (v.p. Southeastern regional group), Zeta Psi. Episcopalian. Club: University (Miami). Home: 3471 Main Hwy Miami FL 33133 Office: 1111 S Bayshore Dr Miami FL 33131

DOHENY, WILLIAM JOSEPH, jurist, educator, author; b. Merrill, Wis., May 30, 1898; s. William R. and Bridget (O'Connor) D.; J.U.D. (Dr. Roman and Canon Law), Cath. U. Am., 1927. Entered Congregatio a Sancta Cruce, 1919; ordained priest Roman Cath. Ch., 1924; title of monsignor conferred, 1948; asst. superior Fgn. Mission Sem., Washington, 1925-28, acting superior 1928-29; superior Holy Cross Internat. Coll., Rome, Italy, 1929-34, Sem. of Our Lady of Holy Cross, North Dartmouth, Mass., 1934-35, Sem. of Our Lady of Holy Cross, North Easton, Mass., 1935- 37, Holy Cross Coll., Cath. U. Am., 1937-41; asst. superior gen. Congregation of Holy Cross, Washington and N.Y.C., 1941-45, gen. supr. studies, 1945—; prof., legal ethics U. Notre Dame, 1945-48. Admitted as adv. and atty., Sacred Roman Rota and Apostolic Signatura, 1932; asso. justice Tribunal of Sacred Roman Rota, Vatican City, 1948—, presiding judge Vatican City, 1960—; legal expert 2d Vatican Council, 1952—; judge Appellate Court of Vatican City. Consultor Sacred Congregation of the Sacraments, 1950—, Sacred Congregation of the Rites, 1950—. Charter mem. Riccobono Seminar of Roman Law, Washington. Hon. life mem. Canon Law Soc. of Am. (1st pres., 1938). K.C. Author: Church Property: Modes of Acquisition, 1927; Canonical Procedure in Matrimonial Cases, 1937, Canonical Procedure in Matrimonial Cases, Vol. II, 1946; Practical Manual for Marriage Cases, 1938; Practical Problems in Church Finance, 1941; The Pater Noster of St. Teresa, 1942; Give Us This Day Our Daily Bread, 1944; Our Life in Christ, 1945; Papal Documents on Mary, 1954. Home: Palazzo delle Congregazioni Piazza San Callisto 16 Rome Italy Office: Tribunal of the Sacred Roman Rota Palazzo della Cancelleria Vatican City Vatican State

DOHERTY, EDMOND JOHN, librarian; b. N.Y.C., Dec. 9, 1933; s. George Doherty and Marie Eloise (Ducote) D.; B.A., St. Martin's Coll., Olympia, Wash., 1955; M.L.S., Rutgers U., 1960; m. Frances Jeffreys, Aug. 1, 1959; children—Edmond John, Elizabeth, Margaret, Katharine. Librarian intern East Orange (N.J.) Pub. Library, 1958-61; br. librarian Free Library, Phila., 1961- 66; dir. Reading (Pa.) Pub. Library, 1966—. Pres. Community Welfare Assn. Berks County, 1966-69; chmn. summer opportunities program Econ. Opportunity Council Berks County, 1968-69, chmn. planning com., 1969; vice chmn. planning div. United Way of Berks County, 1970—. Served with AUS, 1955-57. Mem. Am. (chmn. legislative com., adult services 1968-69), Pa. (com. chmn.) library assns., Fgn. Affairs Council Reading and Bucks County (mem. bd. 1969—). Home: 733 N 4th St Reading PA 19601 Office: Reading Pub Library 5th and Franklin Sts Reading PA 19602

DOHERTY, EDWARD J., clergyman, editor, author; b. Chgo., Oct. 30, 1890; s. James E. and Ellen (Rogers) D.; ed. pub. and parochial schs., Chgo., St. Phillip's Acad., Granville, Wis.; m. Marie Ryan, Dec. 15, 1914 (dec. Oct. 1918); 1 son, Edward J.; m. 2d, Mildred Frisby, July 16, 1919 (dec. Mar. 1939); 1 son, Jack Jim; m. 3d, Baroness Catherine de Hueck, June 25, 1943. Asso. with Chicago newspapers, 1906-24 (with interludes in Tampico, Mex., and Hollywood, Cal.); mem. staff N.Y. Daily News, formerly city editor N.Y. Am.; staff writer Liberty Mag.; war corr.; editorial writer Chgo. Sun, 1941-46; ordained priest Byzantine Rite Catholic Ch., 1969; editor Restoration, publ. of Madonna House, Combermere, Ont., Can. Author: Broadway Murders; Gall and Honey (autobiography), 1941; Splendor of Sorrow, 1946; Tumbleweed, 1947; Martin, 1948; Captain Marooner (with Louis B. Davidson), 1952; True Devotion to Mary, a Nun with A Gun, 1959; I Cover God, 1962; King of Sinners, 1963; others. Home: Madonna House Combermere Ontario Canada also Madonna House Winslow AZ 86047

DOHERTY, EDWARD WOODS, fgn. service officer; b. St. Louis, Apr. 18, 1914; s. George Paul and Irene Elizabeth (Woods) D.; B.S., St. Louis U., 1935; M.B.A., Harvard, 1937; student New Sch. Social Research, 1938-39; m. Georgie Virginia Hazard, July 2, 1947; children—Christopher Hazard, Moira Elizabeth. Research economist Scudder, Stevens & Clark, 1937-39; instr. econs., sociology Manhattanville Coll. Sacred Heart, 1939-40; economist Dept. Commerce, O.P.A., 1941-42; economist Office Financial and Develop. Policy, Dept. State, 1946-49, asst. chief Financial Affairs div., 1947- 49, officer in charge econ. affairs Office N.E. Asian Affairs, 1949-51, chief Functional Intelligence div., 1951-56; fgn. service officer, 1956—, assigned Nat. War Coll., 1957-58; chief econ. affairs sect. U.S. Mission Berlin, 1958-60; counselor embassy for economic affairs Am. embassy, Tokyo, Japan, 1960-63; minister-counselor and dep. chief mission Am. embassy, Seoul, Korea, 1963-66; mem. policy planning council Dept. State, Washington, 1966-69; Am. consul gen., Munich, Germany, 1969—; exec. sec. for joint Phillippine-Am. Finance Commn. Manila, 1947. Served with USN, 1942-46. comdg. officer LSM 98, 1944-45. Roman Catholic. Club: Harvard (N.Y.C.). Author: (with others) Principles of Political Geography, 1957. Home: 8 Munich 81 Opitzstrasse 8 Munich Germany Office: 8 Munich 22 Koeniginstrasse 5 Munich Germany

DOHERTY, HERBERT JOSEPH, Jr., educator, historian; b. Jacksonville, Fla., Feb. 4, 1926; s. Herbert Joseph and Marie (Bishop) D.; B.A., U. Fla., 1948, M.A., 1949; Ph.D., U.N.C., 1953. Mem. faculty U. Fla., 1949-50, 53—, chmn. social scis., 1963—, prof. history and social sci., 1964—; lectr. Far East div. U. Md., 1959-60, European div., 1960-61. Mem. adv. commn. Fla. Bd. Archives and History, 1968-70; adv. bd. Fed. Records Center, Atlanta, 1967-71, adv. council Fed. Regional Archives, 1971—. Served with USAAF, 1944-46. Mem. Am. Assn. U. Profs., Orgn. Am. Historians, Am., So., Fla. (bd. dirs. 1962-68, 70-72, pres. 1968-70, editor quar. 1962-64) hist. assns.,

Phi Beta Kappa, Phi Kappa Phi, Phi Alpha Theta, Delta Tau Delta, Fla. Blue Key. Democrat. Author: Richard Keith Call: Southern Unionist, 1961; The Whigs of Florida, 1845-1854, 1959; also articles. Home: 415 NE 5th Av Gainesville FL 32601

DOHERTY, JAMES EDWARD III, educator, physician; b. Newport, Ark., Nov. 22, 1923; s. James Edward and Ida Josephine (Parish) D.; B.S. Medicine, U. Ark., 1944, M.D., 1946; m. Margaret Walton Croskeys, June 5, 1948; children—Richard Edward, Margaret Elise. Intern, Columbus (Ga.) City Hosp., 1946-47; resident internal medicine U. Ark. Sch. Medicine, 1949-52, instr. medicine, 1952-53, asst. prof., 1953-61, asso. prof., 1962-68, prof., 1968—, dir. cardiology div., 1969—; chief cardiology sect. VA Hosp., Little Rock, 1956-58. Del., U.S. Pharmacopeial Conv., 1970; mem. so. regional research and adv. com. Am. Heart Assn., 1969-70. Bd. dirs. Ark. Heart Assn., 1960—, sec., 1955-56, pres., 1959-60. Served with AUS, 1943-46, USAF, 1947-49. Diplomate Am. Bd. Internal Medicine (cardiovascular disease). Mem. A.C.P., Am. Coll. Cardiology (gov. Ark. 1962-65, 68-71), Soc. Nuclear Medicine, N.Y. Acad. Scis., A.M.A., So. Soc. Clin. Investigation, Sigma Xi, Alpha Omega Alpha, Alpha Epsilon Delta, Sigma Chi. Mason. Clubs: Medical Center Camera, Raquet. Pioneer research tritium labelled digoxin. Contbr. articles to profl. publs. Home: 48 Wingate Dr Little Rock AR 72205

DOHERTY, JAMES JOHN, Jr., elec. mfg. co. exec.; b. Brockton, Mass., June 11, 1911; s. James John and Agnes C. (Shaughnessy) D.; A.B., Dartmouth, 1933; M.B.A., N.Y.U., 1950; m. Ethelmae Brady, Oct. 10, 1936; 1 dau., Deborah K. With Western Electric Co., 1946—, works mgr., Oklahoma City, 1960-63, v.p. mfg., 1963—; dir. Nassau Smelting & Refining Co. Mem. bd. visitors Emory U.; mem. adv. council Bus. Information Center at Ga. State U. Served to lt. col. AUS, 1941-46. Mem. Phi Beta Kappa. Rotarian. Clubs: Commerce, Stadium, Capital City, Dunwoody Country (Atlanta). Home: 5587 Trowbridge Dr NE Atlanta GA 30338 Office: 600 W Peachtree St NW Atlanta GA 30308

DOHERTY, JOSEPH E., engring. systems co. exec.; b. 1929; B.B.A., St. Johns U., 1951; married. Auditor, Combustion Engring. Co., 1953-60; accountant Vitro Corp. Am., N.Y.C., 1960-66, asst. controller, 1966-67, controller, 1967-69, treas., controller, 1969—. Served with AUS, 1951-53. Office: 90 Park Av New York City NY 10016*

DOHERTY, LOUIS W., lawyer; b. Springfield, Mass., June 30, 1898; s. James L. and Harriet I. (Madigan) D.; A.B., Bowdoin Coll., 1919; LL.B., Harvard, 1922; m. Mary C. Spence, Feb. 15, 1931; children—James L., Paul S. Admitted to Mass. bar, 1922; mem. McCarthy & Doherty, 1922-42, Gordon, Doherty, Bulkley & Godfrey, 1943-54, Doherty and Murphey, 1955-67, Doherty, Wallace, Pillsbury and Murphy, 1967—; was U.S. commr., 1928-44; dir. Springfield Safe Deposit and Trust Co., Moore Drop Forging Co.; trustee Springfield Instn. Savs. Mem. Springfield (Mass.) Fire Commn., 1925-35, chmn., 1931-35. Chmn. bd. Bay Path Jr. Coll., 1949-70. Served as 2d lt., inf., U.S. Army, 1918. Mem. Am., Mass. bar assns., Delta Kappa Epsilon. Clubs: Colony (Springfield); Longmeadow (Mass.) Country. Home: 118 Farmington Av Longmeadow MA 01106 Office: 1387 Main St Springfield MA 01103

DOHERTY, PAUL E., lawyer; b. Bklyn., 1910; B.S., Wesleyan U., 1930; LL.B., St. Lawrence U., 1933, J.S.D., 1935. Admitted to N.Y. bar, 1934, N.J. bar, 1943; mem. firm Whitman & Ransom, N.Y.C.; judge N.J. State Div. Tax Appeals, 1958—. Commr. Hudson County, (N.J.) Bd. Taxation, 1942-52, pres., 1954-58. Mem. Assn. Bar. City N.Y., Hudson County, N.J. State, Am. bar assns., Phi Delta Phi. Office: 522 Fifth Av New York City NY 10036*

DOHERTY, RICHARD P., economist, indsl. relations and tv exec.; b. Wilton, N.H., May 5, 1905; s. Edward and Myra J. (Duval) D.; A.B. magna cum laude, Clark U., 1925; A.M., Brown U., 1926, grad. fellow, 1927-28; m. Dorothea M. Sullivan, May 30, 1933; 1 dau., Judith Dale. Prof. econs. Boston U., 1928-46, head dept., 1940-45; v.p., dir. labor relations Nat. Assn. Radio and TV Broadcasters, 1946-54; pres. TV-Radio Mgmt. Corp., 1954—, TV-Radio Properties Corp., 1964—. U.S. mgmt. del. ILO, Geneva, Switzerland, 1949-67; mgmt. mem. Internat. Social Security Experts Com., 1962-70; industry mem. WSB, 1951-52; founder, exec. dir. Indsl. Relations Council Met. Boston, 1940-46; industry adviser Pres. Truman's Labor Mgmt. Conf., 1945. Dir. Mass State Civil Def., 1941-45; chmn. East Coast Civil Def. Council, 1942-45. Awarded Pres. Certificate of Merit for civil def., 1945. Mem. Am. Econs. Assn., Am. Assn. Bus. Economists, Broadcast Pioneers, Broadcasters club Assn., Phi Beta Kappa. Clubs: Circumnavigators, Broadcasters (Washington). Author: Interpretation Business and Financial Conditions, 1934; Structure American Business, 1937; Economic Organization of Society, 1939; Essentials of Collective Bargaining, 1946; Broadcasting and Business Cycles, 1950; Taft Hartley Act and Broadcasting Industry, 1948; Wage Policy and Administration, 1954; Pitfalls in Collective Bargaining, 1955; TV: America's Growth Industry, 1964; Appraisal of the International Labor Organization, 1965. Contbr. articles to profl. jours. Home: Bleak House Downs Dennis MA 02638 Office: 1735 DeSales St NW Washington DC 20036

DOHERTY, WILLIAM THOMAS, Jr., educator; b. Cape Girardeau, Mo., Mar. 30, 1923; s. William Thomas and Kittie (Baird) D.; A.B., B.S., S.E. Mo. State Coll., 1943; M.A., Am. U., 1950; Ph.D., U. Mo., 1951; m. Dorothy Ashley Huff, Aug. 13, 1947; children—Victor Sargent, Dorothy Ashley, Catherine Baird, Julia Holbrook, William Thomas III. Instr. history Westminster Coll., Fulton, Mo., 1947-48, Christian Coll., 1949-50, U. Mo., 1948-49, 50-51; asst. prof. history U. Miss., 1951-53; asst. prof., then asso. prof. history U. Ark., 1953-56; asso. prof. history U. Miss., 1956-58, prof., chmn. dept. history, 1958-61; prof. history, dir. Ford Found. 3 yr. Master's program Kan. State U., Manhattan, 1961-63; prof. history, chmn. dept. W.Va. U., Morgantown, 1963-. Mem. Miss. Hist. Commn., 1958-61. Mem. Am., So., Miss. Valley hist. assns., Am. Assn. U. Profs. Author: Louis Houck: Missouri Historian and Entrepreneur, 1960. Editor: Minerals, Vol. IV in Conservation History of the United States, 1971; Berkeley, U.S.A.: A Bicentennial History of a Virginia and West Virginia County 1772-1972, 1972. Home: 140 Waitman St Morgantown WV 26505

DOHL, PAUL RAYMOND, food and beverage co. exec.; b. Syracuse, N.Y., Mar. 9, 1927; s. John Paul and Alberta (Swortwood) D.; student State Tchrs. Coll., Fredonia, N.Y., 1943-45, St. Bonaventure U., 1948-49; LL.B. cum laude, Albany Law Sch., 1952; LL.M., N.Y. U., 1958; m. Carol C. Christine, Mar. 31, 1962; children—Michael, Nancy, Stephen, Karen Ann. Admitted to N.Y. State bar, 1952; atty. Norwich Pharmacal Co. (N.Y.), 1952-54, asst. sec., 1954-58, sec., gen. counsel, 1958-62; v.p., gen. counsel Heublein, Inc., Hartford, Conn., 1962-71, group v.p., also pres. Heublein Internat., Ltd., 1971—; dir. Hamm Brewing Co., United Vintners, Inc. Mem. Am. (trade regulation and product liability coms.), N.Y. State bar assns., Greater Hartford C. of C., Conn. Opera Guild, Wadsworth Atheneum. Clubs: City (Hartford); Golf (Avon, Conn.). Home: Talcott Notch Rd Farmington CT 06032 Office: 330 New Park Av Hartford CT 06101

DOHLMAN, CLAES HENRIK, physician; b. Uppsala, Sweden, Sept. 11, 1922; s. Gosta Fritz and Ebba Gustava (Ribbing) D.; M.D., U. Lund, 1950, Ph.D., 1957; m. Carin Björklund, Apr. 24, 1948; children—Lena, Jan, Ebba, Henrik, Piter, Erik. Came to U.S., 1958, naturalized, 1965. Resident in ophthalmology U. Lund, 1950-52; asst. surgeon Univ. Eye Clinic, Lund, Sweden, 1954-58; research asso. Retina Found., Boston, 1958-62; fellow in ophthalmology Mass. Eye & Ear Infirmary, Boston, 1958-63, asst. in ophthalmology, 1963-66, dir. cornea service, 1964—, asst. surgeon, 1966—. Dir. dept. cornea research Retina Found., 1962—; asso. prof. ophthalmology Harvard Med. Sch., 1969—. Served as lt. comdr. Swedish Navy, 1948. Decorated Order of Vasa; recipient New Eng. Ophthal. Soc. award, 1966. Friedenwald award for research in ophthalmology, 1971; USPHS, John A. Hartford Found., Mass. Lions Eye Research Fund, Inc. grantees. Fellow Am. Acad. Ophthalmology and Otolarngology; mem. Assn. Research in Ophthalmology, New Eng. Ophthal. Soc., Deutsche Ophthalmologische Gesellschaft. Contbr. articles to profl. jours. Home: 206 Pleasant St Arlington MA 02174 Office: 20 Staniford St Boston MA 02114

DOHRENWEND, CLAYTON OLIVER, engr., coll. ofcl.; b. New Britain, Conn., May 20, 1909; s. Frank Henry and Lena (Splettstoeszer) D.; C.E., Rensselaer Poly. Inst., 1931, M.C.E., 1935, M.S., 1937; Ph.D., U. Mich., 1940; m. Ruth Evans, Mar. 19, 1932; children—Robert Evans, John Clayton. Instr. civil engring. Rensselaer Poly. Inst., Troy, N.Y. 1931-37, prof. head dept. mechanics, 1950 -52. dir. grad. div., 1952-57, chmn. sci. faculty, 1955-58, dean Grad. Sch., 1952- 59, dean Sch. Sci., 1958-59, provost of sch., 1959—, v.p., 1960- ; asst. prof. U. Conn., 1939-41; instr. civil engring., Armour Coll. Engring., also staff mem. Armour Research Found., Chgo. 1937-39, chmn. engring. mechanics research sects., Armour Research Found., Ill. Inst. Tech., 1941-45, cons. in mechanics, 1945-46, also dir. mechanics, Ill. Inst. Tech., 1945-46; research cons. and asst. dir. research Midwest Research Inst., Kansas City, 1946-49. Registered profl. engr., Mo., Conn. Fellow Am. Soc. M.E.; mem. Am. Soc. C.E., Soc. Exptl. Stress Analysis, Am. Soc. Engring. Edn., Sigma Xi, Tau Beta Pi. Home: 5 Carla Lane Troy NY 12180

DOHRS, FRED E., educator, geographer; b. Chgo., Nov. 21, 1917; s. Fred L. and Zora (Stevens) D.; student Mich. State U., 1936-38; B.S., Northwestern U., 1942, M.A., 1948, Ph.D., 1950; m. Mary Ellen Green, Apr. 7, 1955; children—Anne, Larry. Terrain analyst Corps Engrs., Germany, 1946-47; mem. faculty Wayne State U., 1950—, prof. geography, 1960—, chmn. dept., 1956—; vis. prof. polit. geography U.S. Naval War Coll., 1958- 59; cons. environments Gen. Motors Co. Tech. Center, 1961-63; dir. policy and research in communist areas Radio Free Europe, 1963-64. Served to maj. USAAF, World War II; ETO; colonel USAF Reserve, Carnegie fellow, 1948. Fellow Royal Geog. Soc., Nat. Council Geog. Edn.; mem. Assn. Am. Geographers, Sigma Xi. Author: Outside Readings in Geography, 1955; Northern Ireland, 1967; Introduction to Geography, 1967; Physical Geography, 1967; Cultural Geography, 1967; Economic Geography, 1968. Home: 1919 Cedar Hill Dr Royal Oak MI 48067 Office: Dept Geography Wayne State Univ Detroit MI 48202

DOI, JAMES ISAO, educator; b. Stockton, Cal., Feb. 28, 1923; s. Giochi and Asako (Asahi) Doi; student Muskingum Coll., 1943-44; M.A., U. Chgo., 1950, Ph.D., 1952; m. Mary Yamashita, July 11, 1945; 1 dau., Mary Margaret. Asst. to textbooks and curriculum officer CID-GHQ-SCAP, Occupation of Japan, 1946- 48; research asst. dept. edn. U. Chgo., 1951; budget analyst, asst. to chancellor N.M. Bd. Ednl. Finance, Santa Fe, 1952-56, asst. chancellor, 1956-57; dir. instl. research, asso. prof. edn. U. Colo., 1957- 60, asso. provost, 1960-63, prof. edn. and sociology, 1962-63; dir. instnl. research, prof. edn. N. Y. U., 1963-64; prof. higher edn. U. Mich., Ann Arbor, 1964-71, dir. Center for Study Higher Edn., 1970-71; dean Coll. Edn., U. Rochester (N.Y.), 1971—. Dir. studies Colo. Assn. State-Supported Instns. Higher Edn., 1957-60; cons. U.S. Office Edn., 1965-67. Served with AUS, 1945- 46. Mem. Am. Ednl. Research Assn., Assn. Higher Edn., Assn. Instnl. Research (exec. com. 1965-67), Am. Soc. Pub. Adminstrn., Am. Assn. U. Profs., Soc. Coll. and U. Planners, Phi Beta Kappa. Contbr. articles to profl. jours. Address: College of Education Univ of Rochester Rochester NY 14627

DOIG, ANDREW T., trust co. exec. Sr. v.p. County Trust Co., White Plains, N.Y. Office: 235 Main St White Plains NY 10602*

DOIG, JAMESON WALLACE, educator; b. Oakland, Cal., June 12, 1933; s. James Rufus and Mary (Jameson) D.; A.B., Dartmouth, 1954; M.P.A., Princeton, 1958, M.A., 1959, Ph.D., 1961; m. Joan Nishimoto, Oct. 8, 1955; children—Rachel, Stephen, Sarah. Research asst. N.J. Republican Com., 1957; staff mem. Brookings Instn., 1959-61; asst. prof. to prof. politics Princeton, 1961—; cons. Fels Fund, 1966-68, Guggenheim Found., 1970-71; vis. prof. John Jay Coll. Criminal Justice, 1967-68, 70-71. Mem. adv. com. Gov. N.J., 1966-69. Served to lt. (j.g.) USN, 1954-56. Mem. Am. Polit. Sci. Assn., Am. Soc. Pub. Adminstrn. Author: Metropolitan Transportation Politics and the New York Region, 1966; (with D.E. Mann) The Assistant Secretaries, 1965; (with D.T. Stanley and D.E. Mann) Men Who Govern, 1967. Home: 12 College Rd Princeton NJ 08540 Office: Woodrow Wilson School Princeton NJ 08540

DOISY, EDWARD ADELBERT, educator; b. Hume, Ill., Nov. 13, 1893; s. Edward Perez and Ada (Alley) D.; A.B., U. Ill., 1914, M.S., 1916, Ph.D., Harvard, 1920; D.Sc., Washington U., 1940, Yale, 1940, U. Chgo., 1941. Central Coll. 1942, U. Ill., 1960, Gustavus Adolphus Coll., 1963; LL.D., St. Louis U., 1955; Docteur Honoris Causa, U. Paris, 1945; m. Alice Ackert, July 20, 1918 (dec. 1964); children—Edward Adelbert, Robert Ackert, Philip Perez, Richard Joseph; m. 2d, Margaret McCormick, Apr. 19, 1965. Asst. in biochemistry, Harvard Med. Sch., 1915-17; instr., asso. and asso. prof. biochemistry, Washington U. Sch. of Medicine, 1919-23; prof. biochemistry, dir. dept. St. Louis U. Sch. Medicine, 1923-65, Distinguished Service prof. biochemistry, emeritus, also dir. emeritus Edward A. Doisy dept. biochemistry, 1965—, adminsrv. bd.; dir. dept. biochemistry, biochemist St. Mary's Hosp., St. Louis, 1924—. Served to 2d lt. U.S. Army, 1917-19. Several named lectures at various univs. and soc. meetings. Recipient Gold medal St. Louis Med. Soc., 1935; Philip A. Conné medal Chemists Club N.Y., 1935; St. Louis award, 1939; Willard Gibbs medal, 1941; Am. Pharm. Mfg. Assn. award, 1942; Squibb award, 1944; shared Nobel Prize in Physiology and Medicine with Dr. Henrik Dam, 1943. Mem. League of Nations com. for standardization sex hormones, London, 1932, 35. Mem. Am. Soc. Biol. Chemists (council 1926-27, 34-37, 40-45, pres. 1943-45), Am. Chem. Soc., Nat. Acad. Scis., Am. Philos. Soc., Pontifical Acad. Scis., Am. Acad. Arts and Scis., Phi Beta Kappa, Sigma Xi, Phi Kappa Phi, Alpha Omega Alpha. Author: Sex and Internal Secretions (with Edgar Allen and Charles H. Danforth), 1939. Contbr. articles on blood buffers, sex hormones, vitamin K, and antibiotic compounds to profl. jours. Home: 4B Colonial Village Ct Webster Groves MO 63119 Office: 1402 S Grand Blvd St Louis MO 63104 ☆

DOKU, HRISTO CHRIS, dental educator; b. Istanbul, Turkey, Apr. 17, 1928; s. Anastas C. and Despina M. (Zumbuli) D.; certificate of physics, chemistry, biology U. Istanbul, 1947, D.D.S., 1951; D.M.D., Tufts U., 1958, M.S.D., 1960; 1 dau., Deadra. Instr. oral surgery Sch. Dental Medicine, Tufts U., Boston, 1957-59, asst. prof., 1959-63, asso. prof., 1963-67, prof., 1967—, chmn. dept. oral surgery, 1965, asst. dean for hosp. and clin. affairs, 1966—; vis. surgeon Boston City Hosp.; chief dental service New Eng. Med. Center Hosps.; cons. VA Hosp., Boston. USPHS Tchr. trainee, 1958-60. Served with Turkish Air Force. Recipient Hatton award Internat. Assn. Dental Research, 1960. Mem. Omega Kappa Upsilon. Contbr. articles to profl. jours. Home: 37 Maugus Hill Rd Wellesley Hills MA 02181

DOLAN, HARRY EDWARD, Jr., author, playwright; b. Pitts., Nov. 5, 1927; s. Harry Edward and Walse (Jones) D.; certificate in writing Harvard Extension, 1959; m. Claire Louise Pyburn, Feb. 4, 1954; children—Rodger, Kevin, Mark, Stacey, Linda. Editor, Boston Sun, 1960—; editor mag. Los Angeles Next Week, 1964—. Dir. Douglass House Found., Los Angeles, 1967—. Pres. Frederick Douglass Writers' Workshop, 1966—. Bd. dirs. Frederick Douglass House. Served with USCGR, 1947-51. Mem. Writers Guild Am., West, Inc. Author: (TV, Losers Weepers, 1967; Julia; Love American Style; (documentary) Hold Tight My Hand, 1966; Tell It Like It Is; The Negro in the Navy; (play) Nat. Turner. Contbr. stories to popular mags.; anthologies. Home: 11119 S Van Ness Av Inglewood CA 90303 Office: 1690 E 103d St Los Angeles CA 90002

DOLAN, JOHN WILLIAM, Jr., naval officer; b. Jeffersonville, Ind., July 29, 1915; s. John William and Mary (Doyle) D.; B.S., U.S. Naval Acad., 1939; M.S., Mass. Inst. Tech., 1944; grad. Advanced Mgmt. Program, Harvard, 1962; m. Dorothy Louise Haas, June 5, 1941; children—Susan M., Mrs. Robert Lewis Millham. Commd. ensign U.S. Navy, 1939, advanced through grades to rear adm., 1967; repair and constrn. ships, 1944-63; comdr. San Francisco Naval Shipyard, 1963-65, Long Beach (Cal.) Naval Shipyard, 1965-67; fleet maintenance officer U.S. Atlantic Fleet, 1967-70; dep. comdr. Naval Ships System Command, Washington, 1970—. Decorated Legion of Merit. Mem. Am. Soc. Naval Engrs., Soc. Naval Architects and Marine Engrs. Home: 2111 Jefferson Davis Hwy Arlington VA 22202 Office: Dep Comdr Naval Ships System Command Washington DC

DOLAN, JOSEPH FRANCIS, corp. exec.; b. Woodhaven, N.Y., Nov. 21, 1921; s. Joseph and Helen (Carlin) D.; A.B., LL.B., St. John's U., 1947; m. Martha McMillen, July 3, 1959; children—Thomas, Peter. Admitted to Colo. bar, 1949; atty. U.S. Dept. Justice, Washington, 1947-51; practice of law, Denver, 1953-60, mem. firm Collins, Henry & Dolan, 1955-60; asst. dep. atty. gen. U.S., 1961-65; adminstrv. asst. to U.S. Senator Robert Kennedy, 1965-68; pres. Shakey's Inc., Englewood, Colo., 1969—; dir. Gt. Western United Corp., Denver. Mem. Colo Legislature, 1959-61; asst. counsel spl. U.S. Senate Com. Investigating Lobbying and Campaign Finance, also asst. to Sen. John F. Kennedy, 1956-57; chief counsel House Select Com. on Lobbying Activities, 1950; mem. Colo. Commn. for Promotion Uniform State Laws, 1955-65. Served with AUS, World War II. Author legal articles. Home: 4101 S Colorado Blvd Englewood CO 80110 Office: 333 W Hampden Englewood CO 80110

DOLAN, LOUIS E., corp. exec.; b. Youngstown, O., 1920; LL.B., Western Res. U., 1947. Exec. v.p., sec., gen. counsel, dir. Gamble-Skogmo, Inc., now vice chmn.; chmn. John Alden Life Ins. Co.; dir. Kissell Co. Home: Route 3 Box 775 Excelsior MN 55331 Office: 15 N 8th St Minneapolis MN 55403*

DOLAN, MARGARET BAGGETT, (Mrs. Charles E. Dolan), nursing educator; b. Lillington, N.C., Mar. 17, 1914; d. John Robert and Allene (Keeter) Baggett; A.A., Anderson Coll., 1932; diploma in nursing Georgetown U., 1935; B.S., U. N.C., 1944; M.A., Columbia, 1953; LL.D., Duke, 1970; m. Charles E. Dolan, June 3, 1941. Staff nurse Instructive Vis. Nurse Soc., Washington, 1935-36; epidemiol. nurse Tb studies USPHS, 1936-41; staff nurse supr. City Health Dept., Greensboro, N.C., 1941-43; Tb nursing cons. USPHS, 1945-46; supr., spl. cons. Balt. County Health Dept., Towson, Md., 1947-50; asso. prof. U. N.C. Sch. Pub. Health, 1950-59, prof., head dept. health nursing, 1959—. Mem. N.C. Med. Care Commn.; bd. dirs. Nat., N.C. Tb assns.; mem. Pres.'s Adv. Com. Health Resources, 1962-68; com. social ins. and taxes Pres.'s Commn. Status Women, 1962-64; mem. Nat. Adv. Council for Nurse Tng., 1964-68; mem. Nat. Commn. to Study Nursing Edn.; pres. Nat. Health Council, 1969-70; mem. health ins. benefits adv. council Social Security Adminstrn., 1968—. Bd. dirs. Nat. Assembly Soc. Policy and Devel. Past pres. Am. Jour. Nursing Co. Fellow Am. Pub. Health Assn. (mem. governing council; mem. exec. bd. 1968—); mem. Am. (pres. 1962-64, dir. 1964-68), N.C. (bd. dirs.) nurses assns., Nat. League Nursing, Am. Assn. U. Profs., Am. Nat. Council Health Edn. of Pub. (dir.), League Women Voters, Phi Theta Kappa, Kappa Delta Pi, Delta Omega, Sigma Theta Tau (nat. treas. 1968—). Democrat. Episcopalian. Home: 34 Mt Bolus Rd Chapel Hill NC 27514

DOLAN, PATRICK, co. director; b. Eng., Aug. 14, 1911; s. Joseph Thomas and Mary Josephine (Hayes) D.; student St. Joseph's Coll., Upholland, Lancashire, Eng., 1924-29; m. Britta Salen, Mar. 5, 1949; children—Patrick Sean, Christina Lisa. Came to U.S., 1929, naturalized. naturalized. With Chgo. Times, 1936-38, CBS, 1938-41; European v.p. Foote, Cone & Belding Inc., 1946-48; chmn. Patrick Dolan & Assos., pub. relations, N.Y.C., London, also chmn. Dolan, Davies, Whitcombe & Stewart, advt., London, 1949-60; pres. Batten, Barton, Durstine & Osborn Internat. Inc., N.Y.C., 1960-67, Malta Free Port, 1968—; chmn. Moray Firth Maltings Ltd., Inverness, Scotland, 1968—; dir. Combustion Combustion Power, Inc., Palto Alto, Cal. Cons. Brit. Fishing Industry, 1955-58, Western Region Govt. Nigeria, 1958-63, Dutch Bulb Industry, 1948-60, U.K. Horserace Betty Levy Bd., 1963-67, State Dept., 1965-69, Hambro Bank, London, 1967—. 1967—. Served with OSS, AUS, 1941-46; ETO. Decorated Legion of Merit; comdr. Order White Lion (Czechoslovakia). Democrat. Roman Catholic. Clubs: President's (Washington); Boodle's, Royal Thames Yacht, Pilgrims, Special Forces Ends of Special Forces Ends of Earth, American (London); Sky (N.Y.). Home: 165 E 66th St New York City NY 10021 also 34 South St London WI England Carldane Ct Much Hadham Much Hadham Herts England

DOLAN, PHILIP HILARY, librarian; b. Cambridge, Mass., July 5, 1914; s. Jeremiah M. and Catherine Gleason (Riley) D.; A.B. cum laude, Harvard, 1935, Ed.M., 1937; S.B., Columbia, 1942. Asst. librarian Newton (Mass.) Free Library, 1937-41; chief circulation Harvard Coll. Library, 1946-49; dir. Cambridge Pub. Library, 1949-70, dir. emeritus, 1970—; cons. in field, 1958—. Pres. Nalod Assos., 1968—. Active local Mental Health Assn., Council Youth and Leisure Time. Served with AUS and USAAF, 1942-46. Mem. Am., New Eng., Mass. library assns., N.E.A., Adult Edn. Assn., Phi Delta Kappa. Contbr. periodical lit. Editor, compiler municipal reports. Home: 381 173d Av North Redington Beach FL 33708

DOLAN, ROBERT EMMETT, composer, conductor; b. Hartford, Conn., Aug. 3, 1908; s. Lawrence and Marion (Lynch) D.; student Loyola Coll., Montreal, Can.; m. Vilma Ebsen, June 24, 1933 (div. Jan. 1948); 1 son, Robert Emmett; m. 2d, Nan Martin, Mar. 17, 1948;

1 son, Casey Martin. Musical dir. radio programs, 1934—; member faculty music Columbia U., 1964—; composer, condr. Broadway prodns., 1935—, latest being Juno, 1958-59, Foxy, 1963-64; composer, condr. Paramount Studios, Hollywood, Cal., 1941-51, prod., 1951-56; prodns. include White Christmas, 1954, Anything Goes, 1955; TV prodns. include Acad. Awards shows, 1956, 58, Aladdin, 1957, numerous specials. Recipient Exhibitor Laurel, So. Cal. Motion Picture Council, 1954, Box Office award, 1954. Mem. A.S.C.A.P., Acad. Motion Picture Arts and Scis. (past chmn. music br., bd. govs.), Screen Composers Assos. (past v.p.), Dramatists Guild, Composers and Lyticists Guild Am. Composer: (songs) Little by Little, 1929, Big Movie Show in the Sky, 1949, Talk to Me Baby, 1964; (Broadway musical comedies) Texas, Li'l Darlin', 1949, Foxy, 1964; (motion picture scores) Going My Way, Bells of St. Mary's, Three Faces of Eve, Mr. Peabody and the Mermaid, The Great Gatsby, numerous others; (TV film scores) The World of Jacqueline Kennedy, The World of Sophia Loren, The World of Jimmy Doolittle, The World of Billy Graham, The World of Maurice Chevalier, The World of Darryl Zanuck. Author: Music in Moder Media, 1967.‡

DOLAN, ROBERT FRANCIS, mfg. co. exec.; b. Wayland, Mass., Dec. 29, 1904; s. John Edward and Mary A. (Golding) D. student U. N.H. With Fokker Aircraft Corp., 1928- 34, Douglas Aircraft Corp., 1934-46; with Joslyn Mfg. & Supply Co., Chgo., 1946—, formerly pres., chmn. bd., now dir. Home: 260 E Chestnut St Chicago IL 60611 Office: 155 N Wacker Dr Chicago IL 60606

DOLAN, THOMAS JAMES, educator, cons. engr.; b. Chgo., Dec. 29, 1906; s. Thomas Charles and Elizabeth Bertha (Ringler) D.; B.S. in Civil Engring. U. Ill., 1929, M.S., 1932; m. Virginia Bess Fisher, Nov. 27, 1929; children—Cynthia Bess (Mrs. R.J. Gabrielli), Thomas James. Faculty U. Ill., 1929—, successively instr., asst. prof. dep. theoretical and applied mechanics, asso. prof., 1929-49, research prof., 1949-52, prof., head dept., 1952- 70. Dir. Packer Engring. Assos.; cons. numerous large corps. Project dir. coop. research programs, pressure vessel research com. Office Naval Research; mem com. NRC; mem. U.S. Nat. Commn. for Theoretical and Applied Mechanics, 1963—, Research Devel. Bd.; cons. mathematics, phys. sci. and engring. div. NSF; mem. U.S. Army Materials and Mechanics Research Council; mem. com. on materials evaluation techniques NRC. Served as capt. Ordnance Dept., AUS, 1942-45, charge gun tube mfg. and subcontracting Watertown Arsenal. Recipient R.L. Templin award, 1952, C.B. Dudley medal Am. Soc. Testing Materials, 1954. Fellow Am. Soc. Testing Materials (dir. 1962-65), Am. Soc. M.E. (chmn. Central Ill. sect. 1949, nat. v.p., 1958-60); mem. soc. Exptl. Stress Analysis (pres. 1952), Am. Soc. Engring. Edn., Sigma Xi, Theta Tau, Phi Eta Sigma, Chi Epsilon, Tau Beta Pi. Club: Urbana Golf and Country. Contbr. numerous tech. papers on materials, stress, failure analysis. Am. editor Applied Materials Research (internat. jour.). Home: 510 S Highland Av Champaign IL 61820 Office: 212 Talbot Lab Urbana IL 61801

DOLAN, THOMAS PAUL, publisher; b. Norwood, N.Y., May 12, 1919; s. John J. and Catherine (McCormick) D.; B.A., Rider Coll., 1941; student Harvard Bus. Sch., 1943, U. Notre Dame Law Sch., 1946; m. Margaret M. Brunet, Oct. 12, 1946; children—Ann, Cathy, Betsy. With Gannett Co., Inc., 1947- -, now dir.; v.p., pub. Courier-News Co., Plainfield, N.J., 1965-70; pres. Westchester Rockland Newspapers, White Plains, N.Y., 1970—; dir. Nat. Bank Westchester. Bd. dirs. N.Y. Med. Coll. Served to capt. USAAF, 1941-45. Mem. N.Y. State Pubs. Assn. (dir.), Sigma Delta Phi, Delta Sigma Pi. Clubs: Sleepy Hollow Country, Whippoorwill Country, Metropolitan. Home: 3 Suzanne Lane Pleasantville NY 10570 Office: 8 Church St White Plains NY 10602

DOLAN, WINTHROP WIGGIN, educator; b. Agawam, Mass., Mar. 13, 1909; s. Edwin Bailey and Marion (Wiggin) D.; B.A., Denison U., 1930; A.M. in Math., Harvard, 1937; Ph.D., U. Okla., 1947; m. Thelma Miller, Nov. 21, 1933; children—Kathleen (Mrs. J.C. Huneke), Edwin, John. Dean, Bacone (Okla.) Jr. Coll., 1931-42; asst. prof. math. Denison U., 1943-45, U. Okla., 1947-48; prof. math. Linfield Coll., McMinnville, Ore., 1948-, dean faculty, 1949-54, 59-65, 68-69, acting pres., 1968, vice pres., 1968—; asst. dir. Linfield Research Inst., 1956-59, trustee, 1963—. Mem. Math. Assn. Am., Ore. Acad. Sci. (pres. 1963-64), Phi Beta Kappa, Sigma Xi, Am. Commons Club, Pi Mu Epsilon, Sigma Pi Sigma. Baptist. Author articles. Address: Linfield Coll McMinnville OR 97128

DOLAND, DILMAN JOHN, educator; b. Onslow, Ia., Dec. 31, 1920; s. Forrest W. and Elizabeth (Corbitt) D.; B.A., Grinnell Coll., 1948; Ph.D., Syracuse U., 1953; m. Kathleen Teresa Dolan, Mar. 17, 1950. Psychol. cons. to mgmt. Rohrer, Hibler & Replogle, Cleve., 1952-53; instr. psychology Smith Coll., 1953-55, asst. prof. 1955-60, asso. prof., 1960-70, prof., 1970—, chmn. dept., 1962-68, 1971—; psychol. cons. Crow Tribe of Indians, 1968-69. Mem. Health Com. Assn. on Am. Indian Affairs, 1970—. Served with USNR, 1942-45. Mem. Eastern, Am. psychol. assns., Phi Beta Kappa, Sigma Xi. Home: 25 Tyler Ct Northampton MA 01060

DOLAR, RAYMOND EDWARD, communications co. exec.; b. Chgo., Sept. 14, 1910; s. Edward and Antoinette (Holpuch) D.; student Northwestern U., N.Y.U.; m. Arona Stefanik, Jan. 1, 1936. With Gen. Telephone & Electronics Corp., 1931- 66, controller, 1939-66; v.p., controller Gen. Telephone Co. Fla., Tampa, 1966—. Chmn. Roslyn (N.Y.) Water Dist., 1951-66; pres. Nassau County Village Ofcls. Assn., 1965-66; ethics com. Town N. Hempstead, N.Y. 1963-66. Mayor, Village E. Hills, N.Y. 1953-66. Mem. U.S. Ind. Telephone Assn., Financial Execs. Inst., N.Y. Soc. C.P.A.'s, Fla. Telephone Assn. (dir. 1967-69). Clubs: Palma Ceia (Tampa, Fla.); Nassau (N.Y.) Country. Home: 4501 Watrous Av Tampa FL 33609 Office: 610 Morgan St Tampa FL 33601

DOLBIER, MAURICE, (Wyman), journalist, author; b. Skowhegan, Me., May 5, 1912; s. Elmer and Melissa (Jones) D.; student pub. schs., Skowhegan, Whitehouse Acad. Dramatic Arts, Boston; m. Mary Helen Brown; children—Cordelia, Stephanie, Mary Melissa. Formerly dir. Sta. WABI, Bangor, Me.; lit. editor Providence Jour., 1967—; mem. book rev. staff N.Y. Herald Tribune, N.Y.C., 1956- 66, daily book critic N.Y. World Jour. Tribune, 1966- 67. Author: (juveniles) Jenny, The Bus That Nobody Loved, 1944; The Magic Shop, 1946; The Half-Pint Jinni, and Other Stories, 1948; Torten's Christmas Secret, 1951; A Lion in the Woods, 1955; (humor) Nowhere Near Everest, 1955; All Wrong on the Night, 1966; (novels) Benjy Boone, 1967, The Mortal Gods, 1971; also plays. Club: Players. Office: Providence Jour Co 75 Fountain St Providence RI 02902

DOLCH, WILLIAM LEE, educator; b. Kansas City, Mo., July 11, 1925; s. Bruce Eugene and Mary (Mullinnix) D.; B.Ch.E., Purdue U., 1947, M.S., 1949, Ph.D., 1956; m. Elaine Thome Byers, June 27, 1948; children—Kathryn Marie, Eric Alan. Research asst. Civil Engring. Sch. and Joint Hwy. Research Project, Purdue U., 1959-56, asst. prof., 1956-60, asso. prof., 1960-64, prof. engring. materials, 1964—; cons. problems of cement and concrete. Served with USN, 1944-46. Recipient Dudley medal Am. Soc. for Testing and Materials, 1966; Wason medal, Am. Concrete Inst., 1968. Mem. Am. Soc. for Testing and Materials, Hwy. Research Bd., Am. Concrete Inst., Sigma Xi. Research engring. materials, especially portland cement, concrete, aggregates. Home: 1407 N Grant St West Lafayette IN 47906 Office: Civil Engring Sch Purdue U Lafayette IN 47907

DOLCI, DANILO, writer; b. Sesana, Trieste, June 28, 1924; s. Enrico and Mely (Kontely) D.; ed. Dept. Architecture, U. Rome (Italy), Milan (Italy) Poly.; m. Vincenzina Mangano, 1954; 5 children, 5 stepchildren. Sec. Nomadelphia (Christina communal village near Modena, Italy), from 1950; workman- resident villages Trappeto, then Partinico (both Sicily), from 1952, now head Centro Studie Iniziatve Partinico. Recipient Premio della Bonta, Milan, 1954; Lenin Peace prize, 1957; Sonning prize, 1971. Lecture tour U.S., 1967, 70, 71. Author: The Outlaws of Partinico, 1955; Report from Parlermo, 1956; Waste, 1960; A New World in the Making, 1964; Inventare il futuro, 1968; The Man Who Plays Alone, 1970; Il limone lunare, 1970; Non sentite l'odore del fumo? (Can't You Smell the Smoke?), 1971. Office: Largo Scalia 5 Partinico Palermo Italy

DOLCIANI, MARY PATRICIA, educator; b. N.Y.C., Mar. 3, 1923; B.A., Hunter Coll., 1944; M.A. (Erastus Brooks fellow), Cornell U., 1945, Ph.D. (Olmstead fellow), 1947. Instr. math. Hunter Coll., N.Y.C., 1945, from asst. prof. to prof. math., 1955—, also chmn. dept. math.; instr. Vassar Coll., 1948-50, asst. prof., 1950-55. Mem. Am. Math. Soc., Math. Assn., Canadian Math. Congress, London Math. Soc. Office: 695 Park Av New York City NY 10021*

DOLE, HOLLIS MATHEWS, govt. ofcl., geologist; b. Paonia, Colo., Sept. 4, 1914; s. Edwin Engart and Mary Velma (Mathews) D.; B.S., Ore. State Coll., 1940, M.S., 1942; student U. Cal., 1941, U. Utah, 1951-52; m. Ruth Josephine Mitchell, Sept. 29, 1942; children—Michael Hollis, Stephen Eric. With U.S. Bur. Mines, 1942, U.S. Geol. Survey, 1946; staff Ore. Dept. Geology and Mining Industry, 1946-69, successively field geologist, geologist, asst. dir., 1946-55, acting dir., 1955-56, state geologist, 1956-69, 1956—; asst. sec. mineral resources Dept. Interior Washington, 1969—; instr. geology Vanport Coll., Ore. Extension, 1949-52; adj. prof. Portland State U., 1969—. Mem. Ore. and Cal. Revested Lands Adv. Bd. Served from ensign to lt. USNR, 1942-46. Mem. Soc. Mining Engrs. of Am. Inst. Mining, Metall. and Petroleum Engrs., Am. Assn. Petroleum Geologists, Geol. Soc. Am., Soc. Econ. Geologists, Assn. Am. State Geologists, Ore. Acad. Sci., Sigma Xi, Sigma Gamma Epsilon, Kappa Kappa Psi, Delta Sigma Phi. Republican. Presbyn. Home: 4201 Massachusetts Av NW Washington DC 20016 Office: Dept Interior 18th and C Sts Washington DC 20240

DOLE, MALCOLM, physical chemist; b. Melrose, Mass., Mar. 4, 1903; s. William Andrews and Grace Weld (Soper) D.; A.B., A.M., Harvard, Ph.D., 1928; m. Frances Hibbard Page, Oct. 27, 1928; children—Priscilla Page, Malcolm. Research phys. chemist, Rockefeller Inst. for Med. Research, 1928-30; instr. Northwestern U., 1930-35, asst. prof., 1935-38, asso. prof. 1938-43, on leave of absence 1943-45, prof., 1945-69, prof. emeritus, 1969—, chmn. Materials Research Center, 1964-68; Robert A. Welch prof. chemistry Baylor U., Waco, Tex., 1969—; dir. Nat. Def. Research Com. Lab., Dugway Proving Ground, 1943-44; research physicist radiation lab. U. Cal. and Oak Ridge, 1944-45; cons. Oak Ridge Nat. Lab., 1953-63, NSF, 1962-65; hon. mem. faculty U. San Marcos (Lima, Peru), U. Chile. Mem. phys.-chemistry adv. panel Office Naval Research, 1948-50. Trustee Gordon Research Conf., 1958-61. Awarded Army-Navy certificate of appreciation, 1948. Mem. Electrochem. Soc. (v.p. 1940), Assn. Harvard Chemists (pres. 1942-43). Episcopalian. Clubs: Ridgewood Country; Sheridan Shore Yacht. Author: Experimental and Theoretical Electrochemistry, 1935; The Glass Electrode, 1941; Introduction to Statistical Thermodynamics, 1954. Contbr. sci. articles to profl. jours. Asso. ditor Chem. Revs., 1956-59. Home: 5813 Mt Terminal Dr Waco TX 76710

DOLE, ROBERT J., U.S. senator; b. Russell, Kan., July 22, 1923; s. Doran R. and Bina Dole; student U. Kan., U. Ariz.; A.B., Washburn Municipal U., Topeka, 1952, LL.B., 1952; m. Phyllis E. Holden; 1 dau., Robin. Admitted to Kan. bar; mem. Kan. Ho. of Reps., 1951; pvt. practice law, Russell, Kan., 1953-61; Russell County atty., 1953-61; mem. 87th Congress 6th Dist. of Kan., mem. 88th-90th congresses, 1st Dist. Kan.; now mem. U.S. Senate from Kan. Chmn., Republican Nat. Com., 1970—. Served with AUS, World War II. Decorated Bronze Star with cluster. Mem. Am. Legion, Vets. Fgn. Wars, 4-H Fair Assn., Kappa Sigma. Methodist. Mason (Shriner), Elk, Kiwanian. Home: Russell KS 67665 Office: New Senate Office Bldg Washington DC 20510

DOLE, VINCENT PAUL, educator, med. research exec.; b. Chgo., May 8, 1913; s. Vincent Paul and Anne (Dowling) D.; A.B., Stanford, 1934; M.D., Harvard, 1939; m. Elizabeth Ann Strange, May 23, 1942 (div. 1965); children—Vincent Paul, Susan, Bruce; m. 2d, Marie Nyswander, 1965. Intern, Mass. Gen. Hosp., Boston, 1940-41; staff Rockefeller U., 1941—, mem., prof., 1951—. Developer methadone maintenance treatment program for heroin addiction. Office: Rockefeller U 66th and York Av New York City NY 10021

DOLEMAN, EDGAR COLLINS, army officer; b. Washington, Sept. 8, 1909; s. Edgar Bradley and Rosalie (Rollins) D.; B.S., U. S. Mil. Acad., 1933; m. Dorothy Elizabeth Devery, June 22, 1935; children—Robert Dunk, Edgar Collins, William Henry. Commd. 2d lt. U.S. Army, 1933, advanced through grades to lt. gen., 1963; chief mil. mission to Bolivia, 1945-48; dep. for research and evaluation Command and Gen. Staff Coll., 1952; dep. comdt. Army War Coll., 1956-59; asst. chief staff intelligence U.S. Army, Pacific, 1959-60; comdg. gen. 8th Inf. Div., 1961; asst. chief staff operations U.S. Army Europe, 1961- 63; asst. chief staff intelligence U.S. Army, 1964-65; comdg. gen. I U.S. Corps, 1965; dep. comdr. in chief U.S. Army, Pacific, 1965—. Dist. chmn. N. Atlantic council Boy Scouts Am., 1960-61, v.p., 1962-63, mem. Aloha council, 1965-68. Decorated D.S.C., D.S.M., Legion of Merit, Silver Star, Bronze Star, Purple Heart with cluster; Condor Andes (Bolivia); Legion of Honor (France). Home: 9 Palm Circle Dr Ft Shafter HI 96823 Office: Hdqrs USARPAC APO San Francisco CA 96558

DOLIN, ALBERT HARRY, dept. store exec., lawyer; b. Chgo., Nov. 28, 1913; s. Harry and Esther (Kiltsky) D.; B.S., Northwestern U., 1936; LL.B., Loyola U., Chgo., 1943; m. Rivy Hoffing, June 14, 1936; 1 son, Barry M. Admitted to Ill. bar, 1943; gen. counsel Goldblatt Bros., Inc., Chgo., 1951-63, financial v.p., sec., 1963-68, exec. v. p., 1968—; dir. Prospect Plaza State Bank, Mt. Prospect, Ill., 1961-63. Chmn. taxation com. State St. Council, Chgo., 1960-; gen. counsel Chgo. Heart Research Found., 1962—; chmn. appeal bd. SSS, No. Jud. Dist. Number 4. Trustee Goldblatt Bros. Found., 1968—, Spertus Coll. Judaica, Cancer Research Found., U. Chgo., 1963—; bd. dirs. Jewish Vocational Service, 1968-69, Highland Park (Ill.) Hosp., 1956-61, Civic Fedn. Chgo., 1956—, Jewish Home for Aged, Chgo., 1961-67; bd. govs. State of Israel Bonds, 1961-67. Mem. Am., Ill., Chgo. bar assns., Am. Technion Soc. (bd. dirs.). Jewish religion (chmn. trustees synagogue 1960-63, pres. temple 1957-60). Clubs: Covenant (Chgo.); Green Acres Country (Northbrook, Ill.). Home: 68 Lakeview Terrace Highland Park IL 60035 Office: 333 S State St Chicago IL 60604

DOLIN, ANTON, dancer, choreographer; b. Sussex, Eng., July 27, 1904; s. George H. and Helen Maude (Healey) Kay; ed. pvt. tutors; dramatic tng. with Italia Conti; ballet tng. with Grace Cone, Princess Seraphine Astafleve and Bronislava Nyinskao; unmarried. Began as actor, 1915; danced, acted leading role in Ballerina, London, 1933, and in Precipice, London, 1934; founder, dir., prin. dancer Markova-Dolin Ballet, 1935-38; toured with Original Ballet Russe, Australia, 1939; premier danseur or guest artist Ballet Theatre, until 1946; dancer, choreographer ballet in revue Seven Lively Arts, N.Y.C., 1944-45; organizer, dancer new Markova-Dolin group, touring U.S., C.Am., Mexico, 1945-48; guest artist Original Ballet Russe, 1946-47; founded (with Markova) group that became London's Festival Ballet, 1949, artistic dir., prin. dancer, 1949-61; formed and toured with Stars of Ballet, 1961; dir., choreographer Rome Opera Ballet, 1962. Creator of Diaghileff ballets; Train Bleu, Le Bal, Zepher and Flore, Le Facheaux, Fils Prodigue, Les Biches. Own choreographys: David, Job (creation) Nightingale and the Rose, Rhapsody in Blue, Quintet, N.Y.C., 1940; Capriocioso and Pas de Quatre, Chgo., 1940. Has danced and acted in many motion pictures. Lectured at Oxford and Cambridge univs. and on radio in England, Australia and U.S. Author: Divertissement, 1930; Ballet Go Round, 1938; Pas de Deux: the Art of Partnering, 1949; Alicia Markova, 1953; Autobiography, 1960. Home: 99 Madison St New Bedford MA 02740 Office: 300 E 57th St New York City NY 10022

DOLKART, JOEL, lawyer, corp. exec.; b. N.Y.C., 1916; grad. Coll. City N.Y., 1937; J.D., N.Y.U., 1940; m. Ruth Marcus, 1941; children—Martha Ellen Bernstein, Andrew Lance. Partner firm Strasser, Spiegelberg, Fried & Frank, N.Y.C., partner Simpson, Thatcher & Bartlett, N.Y.C., 1967—; gen. counsel, mem. exec. com., dir. Gulf & Western Industries, Inc.; gen. counsel, dir. Ward Foods, Inc., H.C. Bohack Corp.; dir. Honolulu Iron Works Co., Honolulu and Philippines, Madison Sq. Garden Corp. Served to capt. USAAF, 1941-45. Home: 2 E 88th St New York City NY 10028 Office: 1 Battery Park Plaza New York City NY 10004

DOLL, A. ROBERT, lawyer; b. Tampa, Fla., Apr. 21, 1927; B.A., Coll. William and Mary, 1949, B.C.L., 1951. Admitted to Va. bar, 1951, Ky. bar, 1954, D.C. bar, 1962; mem. firm Greenebaum, Grissom, Doll, Matthews & Boone, Louisville; atty. Office of Chief Counsel Bur. Internat. Revenue, Washington and Louisville, 1951-54. Mem. Am., Ky., Louisville bar assns. Office: 614 Kentucky Home Life Bldg Louisville KY 40202*

DOLL, HARRY LEE, bishop; b. Martinsburg, W. Va., July 31, 1903; s. Harry Lee and Milicent Scott (Jones) D.; student U. W.Va., 1921-22, William and Mary Coll., 1928-30; B.D., Va. Theol. Sem., 1933, D.D., 1945; m. Delia Francis Gould. Oct. 11, 1935; children—Millicent Scott, Mary Chotard, Rebecca Tidball. Ordained to ministry P.E. Ch., 1932; asst. rector Ch. of Epiphany, Washington, 1933-35; rector Christ Ch., Alexandria, Va., 1935-39, Trinity Ch., Houston, 1939-42, St. Paul's Ch., Balt., 1942-55; suffragan bishop Diocese Md., 1955-58, bishop coadjutor, 1958-63, bishop, 1963—. Chmn. dept. Christian edn. Diocese Tex., 1939-42, chmn. dept. mission, mem. exec. bd., 1940-42; mem. exec. council Diocese Md., 1945-55, chmn. bd. Christian edn., 1949-55. Dir. YMCA, 1955-61; v.p. bd. trustees Ch. Home and Hosp., 1953-63; pres. bd. trustees, chaplain St. Paul's Sch. for Boys, 1942-55; pres. bd. trustees Benevolent Soc. City and County of Balt., 1942-55; trustee Gen. Theol. Sem., 1965-68, Phila. Divinity Sch. Mem. Council Chs. and Christian Edn. Md. and Del. (pres. 1954, 57). Rotarian. Home: 3601 N Charles St Baltimore MD 21218 Office: 105 W Monument St Baltimore MD 21201

DOLLAHON, JAMES CLIFFORD, coll. dean; b. Roswell, N.M., Sept. 27, 1930; s. Robert Wentworth and Annie (Calloway) D.; B.S., N.M. State U., 1952; M.S., U. Fla., 1956, Ph.D., 1958; m. Mary Kathryn Floyd, July 17, 1954; children—Grace Ann, James Floyd. Research asst. U. Fla., 1954-58; asst. prof. animal sci. Miss. State U., 1958-60; asst. prof. genetics Wis. State U., 1960-62, chmn. dept. animal sci., 1962-64, dean Coll. Agr., 1944—; pres. Reata Assos. Asst. dir. Agriservices Found., 1970—. Bd. dirs. Wis. R.E.C. Youth Found., v.p., 1971—. Served with USAF, 1952-54. Mem. Am. Soc. Animal Sci., Am. Genetics Assn., Sigma Xi, Phi Delta Kappa, Alpha Zeta, Phi Sigma, Gamma Sigma Delta, Sigma Alpha Epsilon. Methodist. Home: PO Box 4 River Falls WI 54022

DOLLAND, JOSEPH FRANK, mfg. co. exec.; b. Mystic, Ia., June 25, 1922; s. Joseph F. and Mary (Grenko) D.; B.A., State Coll. Ia., 1943; postgrad. Harvard Grad. Sch. Bus. Adminstrn., 1943-44; Indsl. Engr., Chgo. Indsl. Engring. Coll., 1947; m. Edna E. McLain, Sept. 11, 1948; children—Deanna, David, Debra, Dorothy, Denise. Gen. mgr. Magnavox Co., Greenville, Tenn., 1952- 53; v.p. mfg. O.A. Sutton Corp., Wichita, Kan., 1955-58; with North Electric Co., Galion, O., 1958-68, exec. v.p., 1965-68; exec. v.p. Consol. Aluminum Co., Jackson, Tenn., 1968-69, pres., 1969-70; v.p. mfg. and engring. Barnes Mfg. Co., Mansfield, O., 1971—. Served to lt. USNR, World War II. Mem. Indsl. Council, V.F.W. Roman Catholic. Club: Country. Home: RFD 1 Box 561 Galion OH 44833 Office: 651 N Main St Mansfield OH 44902

DOLLAR, HERBERT STANLEY, Jr., shipping and lumber exec.; b. Oakland, Cal., May 18, 1915; s. R. Stanley and Esther (Johnson) D.; student Hill Sch., Pottstown, Pa., Stanford U.; m. Nancy Ferguson, Aug. 1, 1942; children—Deborah, Robert Stanley III, Daphne. Pres., dir. The Robert Dollar Co., Dollar Assos., Inc.; chmn. San Francisco and Oakland Helicopter Airlines, Inc.; owner West of Eng. S.S.; dir. Security Pacific Nat. Bank, States Steamship Co., Protection & Indemnity Assn. Ltd., Rayonier, Inc. Trustee San Francisco Maritime Mus.; dir. Nat. Fgn. Trade Council, Inc. Served from pvt. to maj., F.A., AUS, World War II. Clubs: Pacific-Union, Bohemian, St. Francis Yacht (San Francisco); Claremont Country (Oakland, Cal.); India House (N.Y.C.). Home: Box 757 Walnut Creek CA 94597 Office: 311 California St San Francisco CA 94104

DOLLARD, STEWART EDWARD, coll. ofcl.; b. Chgo., Sept. 14, 1905; s. Joseph A. and Josephine (Kelley) D.; student St. Mary of the Lake Sem., Mundelein, Ill., 1924-25; A.B., St. Louis U. 1928, A.M., 1930, Ph.D., 1934; S.T.L., St. Mary's Coll., St. Marys, Kan., 1937. Entered Soc. of Jesus, 1925. Instr. in philosophy, West Baden Coll., West Baden Springs, Ind., 1937-42, asso. prof., 1942-46, asso. dean, 1941-46; dean Grad. Sch., Loyola U., Chgo., 1946-65, dir. grad. students, 1965—. Mem. Jesuit Ednl. Assn., Nat. Cath. Ednl. Assn., Assn. Am. Colls., Am. Cath. Philos. Assn. Home: Loyola U 6525 N Sheridan Rd Chicago IL 60626 Office: 820 N Michigan Av Chicago IL 60611

DOLLE, JAMES ARTHUR, architect; b. Erie, Pa., Apr. 2, 1931; s. Bernard Charles and Gladys (Novotny) D.; B. Archtl. Engring., Wash. State U., 1954; m. Malander Dolle, June 12, 1954; 1 dau., Catherine Anne. Draftsman, John W. Maloney, Arch., Seattle, 1954, Edwin C. French, Arch., Roswell, N.M., 1955; project mgr. Day W. Hilborn, Arch., Vancouver, Wash., 1956-62; partner firm Nelson, Walla & Dolle, Architects and Planners, AIA, Vancouver, 1962—; also sec. treas., N.W.D., Inc., Vancouver, 1967—. Bd. dirs. Children's Home Soc. Washington, Catholic Children's Services Clark County. Served to 1st lt. USAF, 1954-56. Mem. A.I.A., Vancouver C. of C. (bd. dirs.).

Roman Catholic. Kiwanian, Elk. Club: Royal Oaks (Vancouver). Home: 3407 I St Vancouver WA 98663 Office: 202 W 8th St Vancouver WA 98660

DOLLE, WILLIAM L., mfr. machine tools; b. Cin., Dec. 4, 1901; s. Louis J. and Augusta (Lodge) D.; student Georgetown U., 1919-22; Ph.B., Xavier U., Cin., 1925; m. Mildred Roberts, Oct. 14, 1926; 1 son, 3 daughters. With Lodge and Shipley Co., Cin., 1923-71, beginning as apprentice, successively asst. supt., sec., v.p., 1923-41, pres., 1941-66, chmn. bd., 1966-71. Home: 8420 Annwood Rd Largo FL 33540

DOLLEY, JAMES CLAY, economist, educator; b. Lebanon, Ill., Sept. 29, 1900; s. James Clay and Mary (Turnley) D.; A.B., McKendree Coll., 1919; A.M., U. Ill., 1923; Ph.D., U. Cal., 1928; m. Lois Dee, July 5, 1922; 1 dau., Norma Lee. High sch. instr. and athletic coach, Sparta, Ill., 1919-20, Granite City, Ill., 1920-22, Harrisburg, Ill., 1923-26; teaching fellow econ. U. Cal., 1926-28; asst. prof. bus. adminstrn. U. Tex., 1928-29, asso. prof. banking and investments, 1929-35, prof., 1935—, v.p., prof. banking, 1945-52, acting pres., 1952-53, v.p. for fiscal affairs, 1955-60, vice chancellor fiscal affairs, 1960-66; econ. adviser Fed. Res. Bank, Dallas, Tex., 1943-44, dir. research, 1944-45; dir. Austin Nat. Bank, pres., 1953-54. Pres. United Fund of Austin, 1954-55. Chmn. Franklin Lindsay Student Aid Fund, 1961—. Mem. Am. Econ. Assn., Royal Econ. Soc. (Eng.), Southwestern Social and Polit. Sci. Assn., Am. Finance Assn. (v.p. 1940-41), Economists Nat. Com. Monetary Policy, Newcomen Soc., Nat. Coll. Athletic Assn. (v.p. 1937-41), Southwestern Athletic Conf. (pres. 1943-44), Austin (Tex.) C. of C., Financial Analysts Fedn. (v. p. 1966-67), Beta Gamma Sigma, Delta Sigma Pi. Clubs: Artus, Town and Gown, 40 Acres. Author: Principles of Investment, 1940. Contbr. articles to nat. econ. publs. Home: 2106 Elton Lane Austin TX 78703

DOLLEY, ROBERT DAVID, internat. affairs cons.; b. Lebanon, Ill. May 11, 1903; s. James Clay and Mary Miller (Turnley) D.; B.S., Bradley U., 1927; postgrad. Harvard, 1927; student U. Tenn., 1932; M.S., Colo. State U., 1934; m. Martha Denbeaux, Sept. 12, 1925; children—Robert David, William Clay. Adminstr. pub. schs., Jacksonville, Fla., 1925-37, Fla. Dept. Edn., 1937-46; dir. summer sch., U. Fla., Daytona Beach, 1938- 45; Fla. dir. War Manpower Tng., 1940-46; spl. rep. I.I.A.A. to Republic of Panama, 1946-47; asst. to pres. U. Miami, 1948-49; asst. supt. schs., Miami, Fla., 1950-52; chief edn. field party, U.S. Office Edn., Saudi Arabia, 1952-54; spl. adviser edn. ICA, Indonesia, 1954-55; chief edn. adviser U.S. Operations Mission to Paraguay, S.A., 1953-57; chief Far East-So. Asia br., edn. div. ICA, Washington, 1957-58; chief edn. adviser U.S. Operations Mission, Republic of Colombia, S.A., 1958-64; became mgr. instrnl. contracts A.I.D. projects in sci. edn. for colls. and univs. in Ind., 1964; field service coordination in India, 1964. Decorated by Minister Edn. and Culture for service to Republic of Paraguay. Mem. Nat. Assn. State Suprs. Ind. Edn. (past pres.), Am. (chmn. div. internat. edn.), Fla. (past pres.) vocational assns., Am. Fgn. Service Assn., Diplomatic and Consular Officers Ret., Iota Lambda Sigma, Eta Ma Pi, Phi Kappa Psi. Home: 695 Timuquana Dr Merritt Island FL 32952

DOLLMEYER, WALKER GEORGE, former mfg. operations cons.; b. Freeport, Ill., Sept. 14, 1902; s. George Joseph and Nellie (Walker) D.; B.S. in Metallurgy, U. Wis., 1924; m. Martha Bergland, Jan. 1, 1927 (dec. Mar. 1966); m. 2d, Grace Charles Wallace, Sept. 16, 1967. Prodn. mgr. Interstate Drop Forge Co., Milw., 1924-29; supt. forge div. Davenport Locomotive Corp., (Ia.), 1929-31; asst. works mgr. J.G. Brill Co. (ACF-Brill), Phila., 1931-41; works mgr. Lockheed Aircraft Corp., Burbank, Cal., 1941-47; v.p. mfg., dir. Toledo Scale Co., dir. Toledo Scale Co. Can., Ltd., Windsor, Ont., Can., 1947-56; v.p. operations, dir. Solar Aircraft Co., San Diego, 1956-60; dir. Electronics Systems Devel. Corp., Ventura, Cal., 1958-60; v.p. operations Lycoming div. Avco Corp., Stratford, Conn., 1960-66; mfg. operations cons. 1966-70. Mem. Phi Sigma Kappa. Episcopalian. Rotarian, Mason (32). Clubs: Asheville (N.C.) City, Country of Asheville; Biltmore Forest Country. Address: 61 Hilltop Rd Biltmore Forest Asheville NC 28803

DOLMATCH, THEODORE BIELEY, publisher; b. N.Y.C., Apr. 22, 1924; s. Aaron and Diana (Bieley) D.; B.A., N.Y.U., 1947, M.A., 1948; student Columbia, 1948-50; m. Blanche Ormont, Dec. 28, 1948; children—Karen Ann, Stephen Joseph. Tchr. Queens Coll., 1948-50; asst. supr. Sch. Gen. Studies, Bklyn. Coll., 1950-55; publs. bus. mgr. Am. Mgmt. Assn., 1955-62; pres. Pitman Pub. Corp., N.Y.C., 1962-71; pres. Intext Publishers Group, N.Y.C., also Intext Ednl. Devel. Group, N.Y.C., 1971—; dir. Steck-Vaughn Publishing, Austin, Tex. Pres. Abbott House (children's home). Author (sometimes under pseudonym Stephen Josephs) articles. Editor: Revolution in Training, 1962. Home: 112 Holly Pl Briarcliff Manor NY 10510 Office: 257 Park Av S New York City NY 10010

DOLMETSCH, CARL RICHARD, Jr., educator; b. Kingston, Pa., July 5, 1924; s. Carl Richard and Margaret (Hollister) D.; B.A., Drake U., 1948, M.A., 1949; Ph.D., U. Chgo., 1957; m. Joan Downing Feb. 7, 1948; children—Carl Richard III, Christoph. Instr., Drury Coll., 1949-51; high sch. tchr., Oak Park, Ill., 1951-56; asst. prof. Drake U., 1956-59; asst. prof. Coll. William and Mary, Williamsburg, Va., 1959-63, asso. prof., 1963-67, prof., 1967—, chmn. dept. English, 1970—; John Hay fellow Columbia, 1954-55; Fulbright-Hays lectr. Free U. Berlin, Germany, 1964-66; lectr. Falkenstein Seminar in Am. Studies, W. Germany, 1966, 69, 71. Served with USAAF, 1943-45. Mem. Modern Lang. Assn., Am. Assn. U. Profs., Deutsch Gesellschaft für Amerikastudien, Tau Kappa Epsilon. Democrat. Author: The Smart Set: A History and Anthology, 1966. Co-editor: The Poems of Charles Hansford, 1961. Contbr. to Literatur und Sprache der Vereinigten Staaten, 1969. Contbr. articles profl. jours. Home: 108 Hermitage Rd Williamsburg VA 23185

DOLNICK, BERNARD, educator, county ofcl.; b. Chgo., Aug. 18, 1915; s. Ben and Bertha (Balter) D.; B.A., U. Chgo., 1939, M.B.A., 1949; m. Florence Mary Kagan, Oct. 17, 1942; 1 dau., Bonnie Sue; m. 3d, Karel Ann Brown, Oct. 8, 1969; children—Karla M., Bena Tonya. Adminstr. asst. to dep. dir. Ill. Dept. Pub. Welfare, Chgo., 1950-52; bus. mgr. Ill. Neuropsychiat. Inst., 1952-53, spl. dep. dir., 1953; asst. commr. Ind. Div. Mental Health, Indpls., 1953-56; supt. Ft. Wayne State Hosp. and Tng. Center, 1956-65; acting dir. Ind. Div. Mental Retardation, 1961-62; instr. Purdue U., 1958-60, adj. prof., 1962—; commr. Ind. Dept. Correction, 1965- 67; asso. prof. dept. police adminstrn. Ind. U., 1967-71; dir. Youth Services Dept., Cook County Sheriff Dept., vis. asso. prof. U. Ill. Circle Chgo., 1971—. Past mem. adv. com. on youth to assist Allen Circuit and Juvenile Cts.; mem. Nat. Com. Mental Retardation Council of State Govts.; mem. Ft. Wayne Community Services Study, 1959-60; mem. Ind. Gov.'s Subcom. on Phys. and Mental Health of Aged and Aging, 1953-65; mem. adv. com. mentally retarded, div. spl. edn. Ind. Dept. Pub. Instrn., 1959-65; past mem. Ft. Wayne Mayor's Youth Commn.; past mem. exec. com. Allen County Econ. Opportunity Council; past mem. exec. com. Allen County chpt. March Dimes. Served with USAAF, World War II. Recipient Dept. Pub. Welfare spl. citation for services at Ill. Neuropsychiat. Inst., 1952; citation for meritorious service to People of State of Ind., 1956; citation Parents and Friends Ft. Wayne State Schs., 1958; Alumnus award-citation for pub. service U. Chgo., 1959; Distinguished Service award Frontiers Club Ft. Wayne, 1961; named Sagamore of Wabash, 1963. Fellow Am. Assn. Mental Deficiency; mem. Am. Soc. Pub. Adminstrn., Internat. Assn. Police Profs., Am. Assn. U. Profs. Contbr. articles to profl. jours. Home: 1700 E 56th St Chicago IL 60637 Office: Cook County Sheriff Dept Civic Center Chicago IL 60602

DOLPH, JOHN MATHER, Jr., assn. exec.; b. Phila., Apr. 3, 1928; s. John Mather and Margaret (Ormsby) D.; B.A., Wesleyan U., 1951; m. Mary Jean Harold, June 20, 1953; children—John Mather III, Andrew Harold. Free-lance writer, N.Y.C., 1951-52; successively producer-dir., program dir. WCAU-TV, Phila., 1952-60; dir. network sports CBS-TV, N.Y.C., 1960-69; commr. Am. Basketball Assn., N.Y.C., 1969—. Radio and television cons.; lectr. Active Boy Scouts Am. Active in presdl. campaigns for John F. and Robert F. Kennedy. Served with AUS, 1946-48. Mem. Nat. Acad. TV Arts and Scis. (bd. govs. N.Y. chpt.), Nat. Sportscasters and Sportswriters Assn., Phi Nu Theta. Democrat. Clubs: New York Athletic (N.Y.C.); Greenwich (Conn.) Country; (Palm Bay Miami, Fla.). Home: 84 Meadow Rd Riverside CT 06878 Office: 1700 Broadway New York City NY 10019

DOLPH, WILBERT EMERY, lawyer; b. Palatka, Fla., Dec. 29, 1923; s. Wilbert Emery and Ophelia (Reynolds) D.; student U. Ariz., 1941-42, LL.B., 1949; m. Roberta Hundley; children—Wilbert Emery III, Kenneth Alan, Scott Marshall, Cheryl. Admitted to Ariz. bar, 1949; asst. city atty., Tucson, 1949-50; asst. atty. Ariz., 1950-51; practice in Tucson, 1951—; partner firm Bilby, Thompson, Shoemhair & Warnock, 1953—; counsel jud. com. Ariz. Senate, 1952. Pres. Pima County Young Democrats, 1952-53; v.p. Ariz. Young Democrats, 1952-53. Trustee Ariz. Sonora Desert Mus.; bd. dirs. Ariz. Heart Assn., Tucson Festival Soc., Ariz. Children's Home Assn., Tucson YMCA. Served with USNR, 1942-43, to capt. USMCR, 1943-46. Decorated Air medal. Mem. Am., Ariz., Pima County (exec. com.) bar assns., Ariz. Cattle Growers Assn., R.R. Trial Lawyers Assn., Am. Bd. Trail Advocates, Navy League, Phi Delta Phi, Sigma Chi. Episcopalian (vestry). Clubs: Old Pueblo, Mountain Oyster, Graduate, Skyline Country (Tucson). Home: 6145 Mina Vista St Tucson AZ 85718 Office: Valley Nat Bldg Tucson AR 85701

DOLSON, CHARLES HERBERT, air line exec.; b. St. Louis, May 13, 1906; s. Frank Edward and Hattie Mae (Harbison) D.; B.S. in C.E., Washington U., 1928; m. Bonnie Gooch, May 27, 1935 (dec.); m. 2d, Clara Allison, Aug. 30, 1962. Test pilot Curtiss Wright Airplane Co., St. Louis, 1930-31; pilot Am. Airlines, Inc., 1931-34, Delta Air Lines, Inc., Atlanta, 1934-40, chief pilot, 1940-42, 1945-47, operations mgr., 1947-48, v.p. operations, 1948-59, exec. v.p., 1959-65, pres., 1965-70, chief exec. officer, 1966—, also chmn. bd., 1970—, dir., 1955—; dir. Trust Co. of Ga., Fla. Nat. Banks of Fla., Inc. Served as lt. comdr. USNRF, 1928-30, 42-45. Mem. Nat. Aviation Club, Soc. Automotive Engrs., Alpha Tau Omega. Elk. Home: 660 W Conway Dr NW Atlanta GA 30327 Office: Delta Air Lines Inc Atlanta Airport Atlanta GA 30320

DOLSON, HULL PLATT, investment mgmt. co. exec.; b. Oakland, Cal., Oct. 31, 1914; s. Frederick C. and Theckla L. (Johnson) D.; A.B. in Econs., Stanford, 1936; m. Frances Marie Gignoux, May 7, 1944; 1 son, Hull Eric. Security analyst Wells Fargo Bank, San Francisco, 1937-49; with First Nat. Bank Ore., Portland, 1949-69, v.p., mgr. investment dept., 1950-64, sr. v.p. bond and investment depts., 1964-69; v.p. Transam. Investment Counselors, Inc., 1969-70, exec. v.p., pres., 1970; chmn., chief investment officer, dir. Transam. Investment Mgmt. Co., 1971—; dir. Bumble Bee Seafoods, Transam. Investment Research Co., Transam. Capital Fund, Transam. Investors Fund. Mem. Lake Oswego (Ore.) City Council, 1954-55, mem. Lake Oswego Sch. Bd., 1959-63, chmn., 1963. Served to lt. USNR, 1943-45; PTO. Chartered financial analyst, 1963. Mem. Fedn. Financial Analysts, Security Analysts San Francisco. Clubs: Stock Exchange, California (Los Angeles); Arlington (Portland, Ore.). Address: Occidental Center 1150 S Olive St Los Angeles CA 90015

DOMAN, GLENN JOSEPH, child devel. worker, author; b. Bucks County, Pa., Aug. 26, 1919; s. Joseph Jay and Helen (Gould) D.; ed. Drexel Inst., 1938; P.R.I., U. Pa., 1940; Sc.D. (hon.) U. Plano (Tex.), 1965; Diploma de Honra Jo Meyto, Piracasa, Brazil, 1965; Deploma de Reconhecimento, Sao Paulo, Brazil 1965; Diploma Socio-Benmento, Porto Alegre, Brazil, 1965; Diploma de Medaina Comemorativa De APAE, Rio de Janeiro, Brazil, 1965; m. Hazel Katie Massingham, Sept. 16, 1944; children—Bruce K., Janet J., Douglas Mac. Mem. staff Temple U. Hosp., 1941, Pa. Hosp., 1945; dir. Norwood Rehab. Center, 1948-55; founder dir. Insts. Achievement Human Potential, 1955—; asso. dir. Centro de Reabilitacao N.S. da Gloria, Rio de Janeiro, 1959—; prof. Avery Postgrad. Inst., Phila., 1963—; prof. human potentil U. Plano, 1965—; asso. dir. Inst. Para La Orgn. Neurologica, Buenos Aires, 1967—; pres. World Orgn. Human Potential 1968—. Trustee U. Plano; dir. Insts. Achievement Human Potential, U.S. Army and Navy Legion of Valor, Maimon Found., Buenos Aires, Noss Senhora de Gloria, Rio de Janeiro, Internat. Rehab. Forum. Mem. Gov. Pa. Commn. Human Potential; mem. Gov. Serpige (Brazil) Commn. Human Potential. Served with AUS, World Was II. Decorated D.S.C., Silver Star, Bronze Star; Mil. Cross (Eng.); Croix de Guerre (Luxembourg)); recipient Outstanding Phys. Therapist award Alumni Assn. U. Pa. Sch. Phys. Therapy, 1951; Roberto Simonsen medal social service to Brazil, 1959; gold medal honor (Brazil), 1960; Trailblazer award U. Plano, 1965; statuette with pedestal Internat. Acad. Neurol. Orgn., 1965; knight Order So. Cross (Brazil), 1966. Mem. Phila. Athenaeum, Army and Navy Legion Valor (past nat. comdr.). Clubs: British Officers (Phila.); Metropolitan (N.Y.C.). Author: Nose is Not Toes, 1964; How to Teach Your Baby to Read, 1964; also numerous articles. Address: 8801 Stenton Av Philadelphia PA 19118

DOMANDI, MARIO, educator; b. N.Y.C., Feb. 5, 1929; s. Santo and Filomena (Ciancimino) D.; B.A., St. John's U., 1950; postgrad. U. Rome, 1950-51; M.A., Columbia, 1952, Ph.D., 1960; m. Agnes Koerner, June 22, 1952; 1 dau., Mary Charlotte. Prof. Italian, Vassar Coll., Poughkeepsie, N.Y., 1956—, dean of freshman, 1961-64, Dante Antolini prof. Italian studies, 1969—. Vis. prof. modern langs. State U. N.Y. Coll. at Purchase, 1970—. Served with AUS, 1952-54. Mem. Renaissance Soc. Am., Am. Hist. Assn., Modern Lang. Assn. Editor: (Guicciardini) History of Florence, 1970. Translator: Ernst Cassirer's The Individual and the Cosmos in Renaissance Philosophy, 1964. Address: Vassar Coll Poughkeepsie NY 12601

DOMANSKA, JANINA, book illustrator; b. Warsaw, Poland; d. Wladystaw and Jadwiga (Muszynska- Videra) Domanska; ed. Acad. Fine Arts, Warsaw; m. Jerzy Lakowski, Dec. 23, 1954. Came to U.S., 1952, naturalized, 1964. Tchr. art in Italy, 1949-51; group exhbns. include Roman Found. Fine Arts, 1951, internat. Exposition Biennale, Genoa, Italy, 1951; one man exhbns. include Galleria San Bernardo, Rome, Italy, 1948, Studio 3, Kew Gardens, N.Y., 1959; three one man exhbns. Lynn Kottler Galleries, N.Y.C.; rep. permanent collections Mus. Modern Art, Warsaw, pvt. galleries, Rome; illustrator for book pubs., mags., 1959—. Recipient 1st prize All Poland Exhibit, 1946. Illustrator: (juveniles) Mischievous Meg (award 8th Ann. Book Jacket Competition), 1963, I Like Weather (a notable book of year Chgo. Tribune), 1963, The Golden Seed (1st class certificate Printing Industries Met. N.Y.), 1963, The Coconut Thieves (Herald Tribune Children's Spring Book Festival award), 1964; The Trumpeter of Krakow, 1966. Author, illustrator: Why so Much Noise?, 1965; Palmiero and the Ogre (honor book Book Week 1967 Spring Children's Book Festival), 1967. Address: 3 Sweetcake Mountain Rd New Fairfield CT 06810

DOMAR, EVSEY DAVID, educator, economist; b. Lodz, Poland, Apr. 16, 1914; s. David O. and Sarah (Slonimsky) Domashevitsky; student State Faculty of Law, Harbin, Manchuria, 1930-31; B.A., U. Cal. at Los Angeles, 1939; M.A., U. Mich., 1941; postgrad. U. Chgo.; M.A., Harvard, 1943, Ph.D., 1947; m. Carola Rosenthal, Apr. 16, 1946; children—Erica, Alice. Came to U.S., 1936, naturalized, 1942. Teaching fellow U. Mich., 1940-41, lectr., summer 1946, teaching fellow Harvard, 1941-43; economist Bd. Govs. Fed. Res. System, 1943-46; lectr. George Washington U., summer 1944; asst. prof. econs. Carnegie Inst. Tech., 1946-47; asst. prof. econs., research asso. Cowles Commn., U. Chgo., 1947-48; asso. prof. polit. economy Johns Hopkins, 1948-55, prof., 1955-58, dir. Russian studies Operations Research Office, 1949-51; vis. prof. Mass. Inst. Tech., 1957, prof. econs., 1958—; vis. lectr. U. Buffalo, 1949; vis. asso. prof. Russian Inst., Columbia, 1951-55; vis. Fulbright prof. Oxford U., 1952- 53; vis. prof. Stanford, summer 1957, Harvard, summer 1958, 62, Universidad de Los Andes, Bogota, Colombia, summer 1965, U. Cal. at Los Angeles, summer 1968; research asso. Harvard Russian Research Center, 1958—; exec. com. Conf. Research in Income and Wealth, 1966-68; cons. Rand Corp., 1951—; lectr. Centro de Estudios Monetarios Latino- americanos, Mexico City, 1954; cons. fgn. study, research fellowship program Ford Found., 1954-58; chmn. com Slavic grants Am. Council Learned Socs., 1960-62; fellow Center for Advanced Study in Behavioral Scis., Stanford U., 1962-63; John R. Common award Omicron Delta Epsilon, 1965. Trustee Omicron Delta Epsilon. Fellow Am. Acad. Arts and Scis., Econometric Soc.; mem. Am. Econ. Assn. (exec. com. 1963- 65, v.p.1970), Royal Econ. Soc., Assn. for Comparative Econs. (pres. 1970), Am. Assn. U. Profs., Phi Beta Kappa, Pi Gamma Mu. Author: Essays in the Theory of Economic Growth, 1957; also articles profl. jours. Mem. bd. editors Am. Econ. Review, 1957-59, The American Economist, 1963—. Home: 264 Heath's Bridge Rd Concord MA 01742 Office: Dept Econs E52-371 Mass Inst Tech Cambridge MA 02139

DOMAREKI, JOSEPH THEODORE, artist; b. Newark, May 17, 1914; s. Michael and Anna (Siarkewicz) D.; B.A., Newark State Coll., 1937; M.A., U. Ia., 1947; m. Helen Louise Sauer, June 25, 1937; children—Beverly Ann, Gregory Joseph, George Wayne, Wesley Mark. One-man exhbns.; Contemporary Arts, Inc., N.Y.C., 1949-53, La. State Mus., Shreveport, 1954, Castellane Gallery, N.Y.C., 1961, Swain's Gallery, 1955, Artist Gallery, 1959, Seton Hall U., South Orange, New Jersey, 1965; paintings exhibited; traveling exhbn. Mus. Modern Art, Sao Paulo, Brazil, Honolulu Acad. Arts, Chgo. Art Inst., Butler Art Inst., Youngstown, O., Nat. Acad., Nat. Arts Club Delgado Mus., New Orleans, State Mus., Trenton, N.J., N.J. State Mus., Montclair (N.J.) Mus., U. Wis., Newark Mus., Albright Assn., Am. Petroleum Inst. Club: Yale. Mus., Buffalo, Art USA at Madison Sq. Garden, 1960, U. Ia. annual, 1959, Gallery 64, also Am. Art Today, N.J. Pavilion, Pavilion of Fine Arts, all N.Y. Worlds Fair 1964-65; rep. permanent collections. Navy Dept. in Pentagon Bldg., Columbia (S.C.) Mus. Fine Arts. art dept. of U. Ia., St. Casimir Parish Hall, Newark, Newark State Coll., Sinclair Research Center, Tulsa, Seton Hall U., South Orange, N.J., Niagara (N.Y.) U., Broad Nat. Bank, Newark, St. Lukes Episcopal Ch., Haworth, N.J., Davy Jones, N.Y., Union County Ct. House, Elizabeth N.J., Monmouth Coll., West Long Branch, N.J., Walton Labs., Irvington, Newark Brush Co., Kenneworth, also pvt. collections. Head art dept. Sch. Dist. South Orange and Maplewood, N.J.; vis. artist Chataugua (N.Y.) Arts Festival. Served to lt. (s.g.), combat artist, USNR, World War II; lt. comdr. Res.; ret. Decorated Air medal (Navy); recipient medal of honor Knickerbocker Artists Ann. Nat. Exhbn., N.Y.C., 1955, 63, Nat. Cath. Arts Soc., 1957, Audubon Artists Annual, 1961; John J. Newman Meml. medal, Nat. Soc. Painters Casein, 1962; Agnes B. Noyes award, 1965; Best prof. comparative religion Dropsie Coll., Phila., 1944-59; prof. in Show, Westfield Art Assn. N.J. Exhbn., 1969. Mem. Audubon Artists (pres. 1963-painting Kusciusko Found., N.Y.C., 1949, Samuel Shore Purchase award, 1963; Nat. Arts Club award, 1965. Mem. Audubon Artists (pres. 1963-67), Nat. Art Edn. Assn., N.J. Vocational and Arts Assn. (past pres.), Nat. Soc. Painters in Casein (pres. elect, dir.) Asso. Artists N.J. (dir., v.p. elect), Knickerbocker Artists, N.J. Water Color Soc., Nat. Soc. Arts and Letters (hon.), Am. Legion. Club: Salmagundi. Home: 1482 Fox Trail Mountainside NJ also 11 Sunset Lane Monmouth Beach NJ 07750 Office: Bd Edn South Orange Maplewood NJ 07040

D'OMBRAIN, GEORGE LEE, univ. dean; b. Walton, Eng., July 7, 1911; s. Cyril Wilberforce and Marjorie Lee (Anderson) d'O.; B.Sc., Imperial Coll. Sci., U. London, 1931, diploma, 1932, Ph.D., 1935; asso. City and Guilds Inst., 1931; m. Cathleen Gertrude Cullen, July 1, 1935; children—Katharine M. (Mrs. Katharine M. Grant), Antony J., Nicholas J. Chmn. elec. engring. Alexandria (Egypt) U., 1948-49; chmn. elec. engring. Battersea Coll., U. London, 1949-58; chmn. elec. engring. McGill U., 1958-68, dean Faculty Engring., 1968—, Macdonald prof., 1959—, also mem. bd. govs.; cons. to pvt. cos. in automatic control, 1968—. Bd. dirs. Newman Assn. Research fellow Harvard, 1967-68. Fellow English Inst. Elec. Engrs.; mem. I.E.E.E. (sr.), Engring. Inst. Can., Corp. Engrs. Que. Author: Plant and Process Dynamic Characteristics, 1957. Patents and publs. in automatic process control. Home: 1550 McGregor Av Montreal 109 Quebec Canada

DOMEIER, J.L., savs. and loan assn. exec. Pres., Oak Park Fed. Savs. and Loan Assn. Office: 1001 Lake St Oak Park IL 60301*

DOMENICALI, CHARLES ANGELO, educator, physicist; b. Albuquerque, Dec. 27, 1917; s. Pietro Luca and Angelina (Selva) D.; B.S., U. N.M., 1939; Ph.D., Mass. Inst. Tech., 1949; m. Maxine Elinor Lind, Mar. 11, 1944; children—Dena Ann, Peter Lind, Donna Lynne. Physicist, U. N.M., 1942; research asso. magnetism Mass. Inst. Tech., 1947-49; asso. prof., chmn. physics dept. Alfred (N.Y.) U., 1949-52; research physicist, sect. head Franklin Inst. Labs., Phila., 1952-55, cons., 1965; research physicist, head solid state physics sect. Honeywell Research Center, Hopkins, Minn., 1955-57, sr. research physicist, 1957-61; vis. lectr. elec. engring. U. Minn., 1959; prof. physics Ariz. State U., Tempe, 1961-63; research physicist Union Carbide Research Inst., Tarrytown, N.Y., 1963-64; prof. physics Temple U., Phila., 1965—, chmn. physics dept., 1965-68. Mem. Am. Phys. Soc., Am. Assn. Physics Tchrs. Contbr. articles profl. jours. Home: 919 Coates Rd Meadowbrook PA 19046 Office: Physics Dept Temple U Philadelphia PA 19122

DOMIAN, OTTO EMIL, educator; b. Lester Prairie, Minn., Feb. 16, 1901; s. Louis E. and Emilia (Meyer) D.; B.A., Hamline U., 1921; M.A., U. Minn., 1928, Ph.D., 1951; m. Edna F. Bezanson, June 20, 1923; children—Louis A., Norma E. (Mrs. John J. Magnuson). Tchr., prin., supt. Minn. schs., 1921-44; supt. schs., St. Louis, Park, Minn., 1944-48; faculty U. Minn., 1948—, prof. edn., 1954- -, dir. Bur. Field Studies and Surveys, 1951-68, asso. dean Coll. Edn., 1968—. Chief UNESCO Ednl. Mission to Brazil, 1963. Mem. Nat., Minn. edn. assns., Am., Minn. assns. sch. adminstrs., Nat., Minn. socs. study edn., Nat. Council Schoolhouse Constrn., Nat., Minn. assns. sch. bus. ofcls.,

Phi Delta Kappa. Author: (with Roscoe V. Cramer) Administration and Supervision in the Elementary School, 1960; (with Robert J. Keller) Comprehensive Educational Survey of Kansas, 5 vols., 1960; School District Organization for Missouri, 1968; Education: South Dakota; A Statewide Study of the Public Schools, 1969; An Assessment of Elementary and Secondary School Services and Needs by Minnesota Planning Regions, 1970; also sch. surveys. Home: 6801 Olympia St Golden Valley MN 55427 Office: Univ Minnesota Minneapolis MN 55455

DOMINCOVICH, RUTH, educator; b. Phila., Mar. 25, 1915; d. Harry Anthony and Margaretta (Lickfield) Domincovich; A.B., Radcliffe Coll., 1937; A.M., U. Pa., 1938, Ph.D., 1947; student summer lang. schs., Middlebury Coll., 1940-46. Tchr. French, Latin and English, Friends' Select Sch., Phila., 1939-43; instr. Spanish, Agnes Scott Coll., 1943-45; asst. instr. Spanish, U. Pa., 1945-46; from instr. to asst. prof. fgn. langs. Temple U., 1947-55; mem. faculty Drew U., 1955—, prof. Spanish, 1966—; instr. French, acting dean women Juniata Coll., Huntingdon, Pa., summer 1950. Mem. Sigma Delta Pi. Mem. Soc. of Friends (clk. Summit monthly meeting 1968—). Home: 381 Woodland Rd Madison NJ 07940

DOMINGO, PLACIDO, tenor; b. Madrid, Spain; s. Placido and Pepita (Embil) D.; student Conservatory in Mexico City; m. Marta Domingo; children—Jose, Placido, Alvaro Maurizio. Operatic debut, 1961; star tenor with opera cos. including Met. Opera (debut 1968), La Scala, Covent Garden, Hamburg State Opera, Vienna State Opera, N.Y.C. Opera, San Francisco Opera, Nat. Hebrew Opera in Tel-Aviv; leading roles 50 operas including Ernani, Andrea Chenier, Pagliacci, Tosca, Roberto Devereux, Don Carlo, La Traviata, Manon Lescaut, Il Trovatore, Carmen, La Boheme, Aida, Lucia di Lammermoor and Don Rodrigo. Recordings for RCA. Address: care Met Opera Co Lincoln Center New York City NY 10023

DOMINGUEZ, ADOLFO G., consul gen. of Mexico in San Francisco. Address: 870 Market St San Francisco CA.*

DOMINICK, BAYARD, II, investment banker; b. Stamford, Conn., Feb. 14, 1914; s. Gayer Gardner and Eleanor (Hoyt) D.; grad. St. Mark's Sch., Southborough, Mass., 1933; B.A., Yale, 1937; m. Elizabeth Yallalee, June 29, 1937; children—Joan, Gayer Gardner, II, Margrett Pryce, Edward Hoyt, Wilder Bellany. With Dominick & Dominick, 1937—, partner, 1938—; chmn. Dominick & Dominick, Inc. Pres. The Dominick Fund, Inc.; past gov. N.Y. Stock Exchange. Trustee Roosevelt Hosp., Union Theol. Sem. Mem. Pilgrims of U.S. Clubs: Union, Links. Home: Huckleberry Hill Rd New Canaan CT 06840 Office: 14 Wall St New York City NY 10005

DOMINICK, DAVID DEWITT, govt. ofcl.; b. Phila., Jan. 24, 1937; s. DeWitt and Elizabeth (Pullman) D.; grad. Pomfret Sch., 1955; B.A., Yale, 1960; J.D., U. Colo., 1966; m. Mary Helen Stein, Sept. 8, 1966; children-Christopher, Andrew (stepchildren), DeWitt. Admitted to Colo. bar, 1966, Wyo. bar, 1966; legislative asst. U.S. Senator Clifford P. Hansen, Wyo., 1966-69; commr. Fed. Water Quality Adminstrn., Dept. Interior, 1969—. Served to capt. USMCR, 1960-63. Mem. Am. Bar Assn., Wyo. Wildlife Fedn., Wyo. Hist. Soc. Sierra Club. Contbr. articles profl. jours. Home: 6806 Wemberly Way McLean VA 22101 Office: Fed Water Quality Adminstrn Dept Interior Washington DC 20242

DOMINICK, PETER HOYT, U.S. senator; b. Stamford, Conn., July 7, 1915; s. Gayer G. and Eleanor (Hoyt) D.; A.B., Yale, 1937; LL.B., 1940; m. Nancy Parks, July 12, 1940; children—Peter Hoyt, Michael P., Lynne B., Alexander S. Admitted to N.Y. bar, 1940, Colo. bar, 1946; asso. Carter, Ledyard & Milburn, N.Y.C., 1940-42, White & Holland, Denver, 1946-47; partner Holland & Hart, 1947-61; atty., Cherry Hills, Colo., 1947-56; mem. Ho. Reps., Colo. Gen. Assembly, 1955-58, 58-61; mem. 87th Congress 2d Dist. Colo.; U.S. senator from Colo., 1961--. Officer, trustee Denver Art Mus.; trustee Arapahoe County Mental Health Center. Served from aviation cadet to capt., USAAF, 1942-46. Decorated Air medal with cluster, D.F.C. Mem. Am., Colo., Denver bar assns., Vets. Fgn. Wars, Res. Officers Assn. Episcopalian. Home: 5050 E Quincy St Englewood CO 80110 Office: Senate Office Bldg Washington DC 20510

DOMINIS, JOHN, photographer; b. Los Angeles, June 27, 1921; s. Paul and Mamie (Ostoja) D.; student U. So. Cal., 1943; m. Frances Clausen, Nov. 10, 1949; children—Paul, Dori, Greg. Freelance photographer, Japan, 1947-48; staff photographer Life mag., 1949—, assigned Hong Kong, 1956-62, Korean War, 1950, Vietnam, 1961; contbr. numerous Life books. Served with USAAF, 1943-46. Named Photographer of Year, U. Mo. Sch. Journalism, 1966. Author: (photobook) The Forbidden Forest, 1948. Home: Contentment Island Darien CT 06820 Office: Time-Life Bldg Rockefeller Center New York City NY 10020

DOMINO, ANTOINE, (Fats), pianist, singer, songwriter; b. New Orleans, Feb. 26, 1928. Pianist since youth; tours with group in clubs, for dances, in theaters; composer blues; appeared in film The Girl Can't Help It; recording artist.*

DOMINO, EDWARD FELIX, educator, pharmacologist; b. Chgo., Nov. 20, 1924; s. James I. and Mary (Dolerzek) D.; B.S., U. Ill. at Urbana, 1948, B.S., at Chgo., 1949, M.S. in Pharmacology, M.D., 1951; m. Antoinette Kaczorowski, Nov. 20, 1948; children—Karen Barbara, Laurence Edward, Debra Ann, Kenneth Edward, Stephen Edward. Rotating intern Presbyn. Hosp., Chgo., 1951-52; mem. faculty U. Ill., 1951-53; mem. faculty U. Mich. Med. Sch., 1953—, prof. pharmacology, 1962—; dir. neuropsychopharmacology div. Lafayette Clinic, Detroit, 1967—; vis. prof. in neuropsychopharmacology Wayne State U., 1959—; study sect. pharmacology and chemistry Nat. Inst. Mental Health, 1965-69; vis. pharmacologist U.S.-USSR Cultural Exchange Program, 1971. Served with USNR, 1944-46. Recipient Sigma Xi prize medicine, 1951; Research award Mich. Soc. Neurology and Psychiatry, 1955; Sci. Exhibit 1st prize Am. Soc. Anesthesiologists, 1963; Sci. Exhibit certificate merit A.M.A., 1964; Kravkov Meml. medal, acad. bd. Inst. Pharmacology and Chemotherapy of Acad. Med. Scis. USSR, 1968. Fellow A.A.A.S.; mem. Am., Central encephalographic socs., Am. Soc. Pharmacology and Exptl. Therapeutics, N.Y. Acad. Scis., Washtenew County Med. Soc., Soc. Exptl. Biology and Medicine, Internat. Brain Research Orgn., Soc. Psychophysiol. Research, Am. Coll. Neuropsychopharmacology (councilor 1969-71), Soc. Biol. Psychiatry, Am. Coll. Clin. Pharmacology and Chemotherapy, Nat. Assn. Standard Med. Vocabulary, Sigma Xi (councilor 1961-63), Alpha Omega Alpha. Author articles in field. Editorial bd. Jour. Pharmacology and Exptl. Therapeutics, 1958-65, Jour. Neuropharmacology, 1962—; cons. editor Psychophysiology, 1968—. Home: 3071 Exmoor St Ann Arbor MI 48104

DOMINY, FLOYD E., former govt. ofcl., rancher, cons.; b. Hastings, Neb., Dec. 24, 1909; s. Charles M. and Emma (Shay) D.; student Hastings Coll.; B.A., U. Wyo., 1932, postgrad., 1932- 33, LL.D., 1966; postgrad. Columbia, 1944; m. Alice M. Criswell, Dec. 23, 1929; children—Janice Elaine DeBolt, Charles Elgin, Ruth Ellen Swart. Vocational agr. tchr. Hillsdale High Sch., 1933-34; county agrl. agt. Campbell County, Gillette, Wyo., 1934-38; field rep. western div. A.A.A., Washington, 1938-42; asst. dir. food supply div. Office Coordinator Inter-Am. Affairs, Washington, 1942-44; chief allocation and repayment br., asst. dir. div. irrigation Bur. Reclamation, Dept. Interior, 1946-53, chief div. irrigation, 1953-57, asso. commr., 1957-59, commr., 1959-69; cons. land and water resources; owner, operator Angus cattle farm, Shenandoah Valley, Va. Served as lt. USNR, 1944-46. Decorated knight comdr. Order Isabel the Catholic (Spain), Star Order Thailand; recipient Distinguished Service award Dept. Interior, 1966; named Pub. Works Man of Year, Am. Pub. Works Assn., 1966. Mem. Sigma Xi, Phi Kappa Phi, Alpha Zeta. Mason, Lion (past pres. Gillette). Home: Bellevue Farm White Post VA 22663

DOMKE, CLIFFORD HOWARD, lawyer; b. Chgo., Oct. 20, 1910; s. Paul O. and Margaretha O. (Geise) D.; A.B., U. Mich., 1932, J.D., 1935; m. Elizabeth Jane Whiting, Aug. 30, 1934; children—Carol D. (Mrs. Thomas R. James), Nell D. (Mrs. James P. Revel). Admitted to N.Y. bar, 1938; mem. firm Robert H. Montgomery, N.Y.C., 1936-41; partner Dunnington, Bartholow & Miller, N.Y.C., 1941-47, Bisbee, McKone, Badgley & McInally (name changed to Domke, Marcoux, Allen & Beaman), Jackson, Mich., 1948—. Dir. Aeroquip Corp., Jackson, 1966—, Libbey-Owens-Ford Co., Toledo, 1969—, Nat. Bank Jackson, 1963—. Trustee Ella Sharp Mus. Assn., Jackson Found. Served to lt. comdr. USNR, 1944-46. Mem. Am., Jackson County (pres. 1964), Mich. (chmn. taxation sect. 1970-71), Fed., Internat. bar assns., Assn. Bar City N.Y., Internat. Fiscal Assn., Am. Coll. Probate Counsel. Home: 5700 Browns Lake Rd Jackson MI 49201 Office: Domke Marcoux Allen & Beaman City Bank Bldg Jackson MI 49201

DOMKE, HERBERT REUBEN, state ofcl.; b. Hillsboro, Kan., Apr. 6, 1919; s. Henry and Lydia (Steltzer) D.; student Wright Jr. Coll., Chgo., 1935-37; S.B., U. Chgo., 1939, M.D., 1942; M.P.H., Harvard, 1949, Dr.P.H., 1959; m. Joan Marie Sullivan, June 14, 1946; children—Catherine (Mrs. James Teague), Jane Alice, Elizabeth Marie, Henry Francis. Intern Billings Meml. Hosp., Chgo., 1942-43, Chgo. Meml. Hosp., 1943-44; chief med. officer Chgo. Health Dept., 1944-47; health commr. St. Louis County Health Dept., 1949-58; dir. Pitts.-Allegheny County (Pa.) Health Dept., 1959-66; dir. Health and Hosps., St. Louis, 1966-70; dir. Mo. Div. Health, Jefferson City, 1971—; instr. U. Chgo., 1944-46; asst. prof. Washington U., St. Louis, 1949-58, prof. pub. health, prof. medicine, 1966; adj. asso. prof. U. Pitts., 1959-66; clin. prof. preventive medicine St. Louis U., 1966. Mem. Pa. Gov.'s Commn. Health Services for Appalachia, Mo. Gov.'s Council Comprehensive Health Planning, Mo. Air Conservation Commn., med. adv. com. Mo. Div. Welfare, Bi-State (Mo.-Ill.) Regional Med. Program; mem. commn. to USSR urban health planning, 1966; co-founder Conf. Urban Health Providers; pres. U.S. Conf. City Health Officers, 1968-70; ex officio chmn. Mo. Nursing Home Adv. Council. Bd. dirs. Blue Cross Western Pa., St. Louis Tb Health Soc., Pitts. Tb League, Pitts. United Mental Health Services, St. Louis Hosp. Planning Commn.; trustee Cancer Research Center, Columbia, Mo. Med. dir. USPHS, 1966—. Recipient Mayor's Civic award City of St. Louis, 1970; Milton research fellow Harvard Sch. Pub. Health, 1948-49. Mem. A.M.A., Am. (com. evaluation and standards), Mo. pub. health assns., A.A.A.S. (mem. commn. air conservation), Nat. Med. Assn. (recipient presdl. award 1967), Mo. Pan Med. Assn. Club: University (St. Louis). Contbr. articles to pub. health jours. Editorial bd. Pub. Health Reports, 1960-68. Home: Route 2 New Bloomfield MO 65063 Office: Missouri Div Health 221 W High St Jefferson City MO 65101

DOMMEN, ARTHUR JOHN, newspaper corr.; b. Mexico City, Mexico, June 24, 1934; s. John Henry and Sarah (Hall) D.; came to U.S., 1941, naturalized, 1958; B.Sc., Cornell U., 1955. Mem. staff U.P.I., 1957- 63, bur. chief, Hong Kong, 1961-63; mem. staff Los Angeles Times, 1965- -, bur. chief, New Delhi, India, 1966-68, Saigon, Vietnam, 1968—. Served with AUS, 1955-57. Press fellow N.Y. Council Fgn. Relations, 1963-64. Author: Conflict in Laos, The Politics of Neutralization, 1964. Home: 8 Av de Jurigoz 1006 Laussane Switzerland Office: Caravelle Hotel Saigon Vietnam

DOMMEYER, FREDERICK CHARLES, educator; b. Warrington, Fla., Jan. 12, 1909; s. Frederick Charles and Christine Barbara (Levy) D.; A.B., Union Coll., Schenectady, 1932; M.A., Brown U., 1935, Ph.D., 1937; fellow R.I. English Speaking Union, Oxford (Eng.) U., 1933-34; m. Mariam Pankov, July 1, 1937; children—Barbara Pauline, Carl Dennis, Curt John. Instr. philosophy Brown U., 1937-38, Syracuse U., 1938-44; asst. prof., then asso. prof. philosophy St. Lawrence U., 1944-58, head dept., 1944-58; prof. philosophy, San Jose (Cal.) State Coll., 1958—, head dept., 1958-65. Licensed minister Universalist Ch., 1959. Mem. Am. Philos. Assn., Internat. Phenomenological Soc., Parapsychology Assn. Author and editor several books in philosophy and parapsychology. Contbr. articles profl. jours. Home: 1352 Happy Valley Av San Jose CA 95129

DOMONKOS, ANTHONY NICHOLAS, physician, educator; b. South Bend, Ind., May 29, 1912; s. Anton and Justina (Godollei) M.; student Northwestern U., 1930-32; M.D., Kiralyi Magyar Pazmany Peter Tudomanyegyetem, Budapest, Hungary, 1939; m. Dorothy E. Parrish, June 7, 1940; 1 dau., Dita (Mrs. Eugene Altman). Intern Univ. Hosp., Budapest, 1937-39, Conemaugh Valley Meml. Hosp., 1940-41; grad. student dermatology Columbia Coll. Phys. and Surg., 1946- 49; asst. dermatologist Vanderbilt Clinic, 1946-49; attending dermatologist Presbyn. Hosp., N.Y.C., 1969—; clin. prof. dermatology Columbia Coll. Phys. and Surg., 1969—; mem. staff Doctors Hosp., N.Y.C., 1966—. Mem. subcom. drug efficiency study NRC-Nat. Acad. Sci., 1966-68. Served to maj., M.C., USAAF, 1942-46. Decorated Bronze Star; medal Order Cristobal Columbo (Dominican Republic), 1967. Fellow A.C.P.; mem. N.Y. County, N.Y. State med. socs., A.M.A., Am. Acad. Dermatology and Syphilology, Am. Acad. Dermatology (v.p. 1966, bd. dirs. 1965-68, chmn. spl. course dermatologic X-ray physics and treatment 1966-70), Met., N.Y. State dermatol. socs., Am.-Hungarian Med. Assn. (chmn. sci. program 1965, v.p. 1967), N.Y. Acad. Medicine (chmn., sec.-treas. sect. dermatology 1967-68), World Med. Assn., Soc. Investigative Dermatology, Am. Dermatol. Assn. (treas. 1967—), Internat. Soc. Tropical Dermatology; hon. mem. Iranian Soc. Dermatology and Venereology; corr. mem. Soc. Venezolana de Dermatologia, Australasian Coll. Dermatologists, Verereologia y Leprologia. Author, co-author 3 textbooks on dermatology, also sci. articles. Home: 1075 Park Av New York City NY 10028 Office: 115 E 61st St New York City NY 10021

DOMS, KEITH, librarian; b. Endeavor, Wis., Apr. 24, 1920; s. Reinhard Edward and Lillian (Gohlke) D.; B.A., U. Wis., 1942, B.L.S., 1947; m. Margaret Ann Taylor, Apr. 1, 1944; children—Peter Edward, David Laurance. City librarian Concord (N.H.) Pub. Library, 1947-51; dir. Grace A. Dow Meml. Library, Midland, Mich., 1951-56; asso. dir. Carnegie Library of Pitts., 1956-64, dir., 1964-69; dir. Free Library of Phila., 1969—; cons. pub. library devel. programs and pub. library bldgs.; specialist, dir. library seminar for state dept., Pakistan, 1964; pres. Pitts. Regional Library Center, 1967-69. Pres. United Mental Health Services of Allegheny County, 1963- 65, Pa. Home Teaching Soc., 1969—; mem. Gov.'s Council on Library Devel., 1968—. Bd. visitors Grad. Sch. Library and Information Scis., U. Pitts.; mem. Museum Council; bd. dirs. Reading is Fundamental Found., Freedom to Read Found. Served with AUS, 1942- 46. Mem. A.L.A. (mem. council 1960-63, exec. bd., 1963-67, v.p. 1970-71, pres. 1971-72; chmn. com. on Freedom access to libraries 1966-68, coordinating com. on library services to disadvantaged 1968-70, pres. library adminstrn. div. 1963- 64), Pa. Library Assn. (pres. 1961), World Affairs Council Phila. (bd.), Internat. Fedn. Library Assns. (bldgs. com.), Spl. Library Assn., Beta Phi Mu (pres. 1962-64). Clubs: Pittsburgh Bibliophiles, Philobiblon, Franklin Inn, Art Alliance, Sunday Breakfast; Science and Arts (Germantown). Contbr. articles tech. lit. Home: 3101 W Coulter St Philadelphia PA 19129 Office: 3 Logan Sq Philadelphia PA 19103

DON, MEYER, business exec. Pres., Edward Don and Co., Chgo. Office: 2201 S LaSalle St Chicago IL 60616*

DONACHIE, ROBERT JAMES, mgmt. cons.; b. Kingston, Pa., Apr. 7, 1928; s. Bernard A. and Ruth M. (Kelly) D.; B.S. cum laude, U. Scranton, 1952; m. Ann B. Flood, June 7, 1952; children—Robert, Judith, Mark. Auditor, plant accountant, adminstrv. asst. to dir. ceramic research Corning Glass Works, 1952-58; asst. controller, treas., treas.-controller, v.p. Clark Bros. Co. div. Dresser Industries, Olean, N.Y., 1958-64; v.p., controller Dresser Industries, Inc., 1964-66; mgmt. cons., Dallas, 1966—; exec. v.p., dir. Earth Resources Co. (Nev.); v.p., sec., treas., dir. Graystone Drilling Co.; sec., dir. Delta Refining Co., Vitro Minerals Corp.; tchr. mgmt. information systems St. Bonaventure U., 1960. Bd. dirs. YMCA. Served with USNR, 1946-48. Recipient Lybrand Silver medals Nat. Assn. Accountants, 1959, 64. Mem. Nat. Assn. Accountants (v.p.), Am. Mgmt. Assn., Financial Execs. Inst. Contbr. articles profl. publs. Home: 4243 Bobbitt Dr Dallas TX 75229 Office: 6116 Central Expressway N Dallas TX 75206

DONADIO, JAMES V., lawyer; b. Branford, Conn., Dec. 3, 1905; LL.B., U. Ind., 1928. Admitted to Ind. bar, 1927; mem. firm Ice, Miller, Donadio & Ryan, Indpls. Fellow Am. Coll. Trial Lawyers; mem. Am., Ind., Indpls. bar assns. Office: Fidelity Bldg 111 Monument Circle Indianapolis IN 46204*

DONAGAN, ALAN, educator, philosopher; b. Melbourne Australia, Feb. 10, 1925; s. Harry Cyril and Ruby Evaline (Evans) D.; B.A., Queen's Coll., U. Melbourne, 1946, M.A., 1951; B.Phil., Oxford (Eng.) U., 1953; m. Barbara Lynn Galley, Aug. 18. 1951. Came to U.S., 1956. Lectr. philosophy U. Western Australia, 1946-48, Univ. Coll., Canberra, Australia, 1949-51, sr. lectr., 1955; vis. asst. prof. U. Minn., 1953-54, asst. prof., 1956-57, asso. prof., chmn. dept. philosophy, 1957-61; prof. philosophy, chmn. dept. Ind. U., 1961-65; prof. philosophy U. Ill., 1965-70; prof. philosophy U. Chgo., 1970—. Mem. Am. Philos. Assn. (mem. nat. lectureships com.), Mind. Assn., Aristotelian Soc. Author: The Later Philosophy of R.G. Collingwood, 1962; (with Barbara L. Donagan) Philosophy of History, 1965; also articles in profl. jours. Home: 453 E Park Pl Chicago IL 60637

DONAGHY, WILLIAM ANDREW, clergyman; b. New Bedford, Mass., Nov. 13, 1909; s. James J. and Rose (King) D.; student Holy Cross Coll., 1927-29, St. Stanislaus Novitiate, Lenox, Mass., St. Louis U., 1935-36; M.A., Weston (Mass.) coll., 1935; L.H.D., Georgetown U., 1956. Entered Soc. of Jesus, 1929, ordained priest Roman Cath. Ch., 1941; instr. poetry Holy Cross Coll., 1937-38; asso. editor America, 1942; ascetical studies Our Lady of Martys Tertianship, Auriesville, N.Y., 1943; retreat master Campion Hall, North Andover, Mass., 1944-46; spiritual dir. theologians Weston Coll., 1946-48; superior Campion Hall, 1948-54; pres. Holy Cross Coll., 1954-60; later engaged in spiritual retreat work; became prof. theology Boston Coll., Chestnut Hill, Mass., 1961. Mem. Cath. Poetry Soc. Am. (v.p. 1956). Author: Hear Ye Him, 1948; That We May Have Hope, 1954. Contbr. America, Thought, Rev. for Religious.

DONAHO, GLYNN ROBERT, ret. naval officer; b. George, Tex., Mar. 25, 1905; s. George Robert and Ennis Cornelius (McGill) D.; B.S., U.S. Naval Acad., 1927; postgrad. applied communications, 1935-36; grad. Nat. War Coll., 1951; m. Louise S. Stebbings, Nov. 26, 1932. Commd. ensign U.S. Navy, 1927, advanced through grades to vice adm., 1964; comdr. Mil. Sea Transp. Service, 1964-67; ret., 1967; pres. Oetiker, Inc., Livingston, N.J., 1868. Decorated Navy Cross (4), Silver Star medal (2), D.S.M. Mem. Navy League, Sons Republic Tex. Baptist. Mason (Shriner). Clubs: N.Y. Yacht; Army-Navy Country (life) (Arlington, Va.); Army and Navy (Washington). Home: 6251 Old Dominion Dr Vinson Hall McLean VA 22101

DONAHOE, FRANCIS MARION, savs. and loan exec.; b. Salem, Ore., June 16, 1907; s. Thomas Malcolm and Florence (Coffman) D.; A.B., U. Wash., Seattle, 1930; m. Nan Saunders, Oct. 17, 1931; children—Nancy (Mrs. John J. Wall), Thomas S., Francis C., Kathleen. Asst. mgr. Olympia (Wash.) Fed. Savs. and Loan, 1935-44; exec. sec. Capitol Savs. & Loan Assn., Olympia, 1944-51; sr. v.p. Fed. Home Loan Bank of San Francisco, 1951-53, pres., 1953—, also chmn. bd., Vice pres. Cal. Tax Payers Assn., 1970—, also mem. bd. dirs. Bd. dirs. Downtown Assn. San Francisco. Mem. San Francisco C. of C. (v.p. 1964-67), Cal. (pres. 1962), U.S. (legislative com.) savs. and loan leagues, Savs. and Loan Found. (trustee), Stock Exchange Club San Francisco (bd. dirs.). Kiwanian. Home: 431 Hillcrest Rd San Mateo CA 94402 Office: 700 Market St San Francisco CA 94102

DONAHUE, CHARLES, lawyer; b. Portland, Me., Aug. 14, 1912; s. Charles Louis and Helen Katherine (Cunningham) D.; grad. Canterbury Sch., New Milford, Conn., 1930; A.B., Princeton, 1934; LL.B., Harvard, 1937; m. Bertha Halsted Terry, Nov. 14, 1942 (div.); children—William Halsted, Christopher Cunningham, Charles, Helen Cunningham, Peter Waldron; m. 2d, Jeanne Coleman Small, June 6, 1968. Admitted to Me. bar, 1937, D.C. bar, 1938; atty. Nat. Cath. Welfare Conf., 1938-39, Dept. Labor, 1939-43, 46-49; labor counsel U.S. Senate Majority Policy Com., 1949; asst. solicitor of labor for employment security, 1949-51, asst. solicitor of labor for legislation, 1951-52; research dir. United Assn. Plumbers and Pipefitters, 1953-61; became solicitor of labor Dept. Labor, 1961; now in pvt. practice law. Served to capt. AUS, 1943-46. Mem. Am., Fed. bar assns., U.S. Judge Advocates Assn., Indsl. Relations Research Assn., Internat. Soc. Labor Law and Social Legislation (exec. com.), Princeton Alumni Assn., Harvard Law Sch. Alumni Assn., Nat. Lawyers Club. Club: Nat. Press. Author labor law rev. articles. Home: 3034 Dent Pl N W Washington DC 20007

DONAHUE, DONALD JORDAN, metal co. exec.; b. Bklyn., July 5, 1924; s. John F. and Florence (Jordan) D.; B.A., Georgetown U., 1947; M.B.A., N.Y. U., 1951; m. Mary Meyer, Jan. 20, 1951; children—Mary G., Judith A., Donald Jordan, Thomas, Nicholas P. With Chem. Corn Exchange Bank, N.Y.C. 1947-49; with Am. Metal Climax Inc., N.Y.C., 1949—, treas., 1957—, v.p., 1963-65, exec. v.p., 1965-69, pres., 1969—, also dir., mem. finance and exec. com.; dir. Tsumeb Corp. Ltd., Copper Co. Ltd., DCL Inc. Bd. dirs. Pine St. Fund, Sogen Fund. Served with AUS, 1943-46. Clubs: Manhasset Bay (N.Y.) Yacht; University. Home: 86 Barkers Point Rd Port Washington NY 11050 Office: 1270 Av of Americas New York City NY 10020

DONAHUE, HAYDEN HACKNEY, psychiatrist; b. El Reno, Okla., Dec. 4, 1912; s. Henry Hilton and Mamie (Hackney) D.; student U. S.D., 1930-31; student U. Kan., 1932-34, B.S., 1939, M.D., 1941; m.

Helen Patricia Toothaker, Feb. 22, 1947; children—Erin Kathleen, Kerry Shannon, Patricia Marie. Intern, U. Ga. Medicine Hosp., 1941-42, USAAF Sch. Aviation Medicine, 1943; chief hosp. operations VA, Washington, 1946; asst. mgr., acting mgr. VA Hosp., North Little Rock Ark., 1946-49; dir. edn. and research Ark. State Hosp., 1949-51; asst. med. dir. Tex. Bd. Hosps. and Spl. Schs., 1951-53; dir. mental health Okla., 1953-59; asst. supt., dir. projects Ark. State Hosp., 1959-61; supt. Central State Griffin Meml. Hosp., Norman, Okla., 1961—. Chief cons. psychiatry Okla. State Penitentiary, 1964—; cons. psychiatry USAF Hosp., Tinker Field, 1964—, Okla. Crime Bur., 1964—; asst. dir. Okla. Dept. Mental Health, 1967-70, dir., 1970—; asso. prof. psychiatry Ark. Sch. Med., 1949-51, 60-61; lectr. legal medicine U. Tex. Sch. Law, 1952-53; cons. asst. prof. neurology and psychiatry U. Okla. Sch. Medicine, 1954- 58, asso. prof. psychiatry, 1958-67, clin. prof. psychiatry behavioral scis., 1967—; instr. psychology Okla. State U., 1958-59; mem. faculty Southwestern Homicide Inst., U. Okla.-U. Tex., 1953—. Mem. Okla. Med. Research Commn., 1963—, Gov. Okla. Adv. Mental Health Planning Com., 1963-68, Gov. Okla. Com. Alcoholism, 1962-70, Okla. Mental Health Planning Com., 1963-68, Adv. Com. to Mental Health Authority, 1963—, Okla. and Ark. Govs. Commn. White House Conf. Aging, 1959-61, 69; nat. adv. council White House Conf. on Aging, 1959-61, chmn. sect. mental health and aging, 1960-61, vice chmn. Okla. com. White House Conf. Children and Youth, 1959, 69—; adviser to Okla. com. Pres.'s Com. on Employment Handicapped, 1957-59, 61—; rep. 2d Latin Am. Seminar Mental Health, WHO, Buenos Aires, 1963; council mental health tng. and research So. Regional Edn. Bd., 1954-59; co-chmn. sect. pvt. and pub. mental hosps. 2d Nat. Conf. Mental Illness and Health, Chgo., 1964; sec. sect. psychopharmacology U.S.-Mexican Psychiat. Conf., 1963; mem. exec. com. Okla. Crime Commn., 1969—; chmn. Crime Commn. Com. on Juvenile Delinquency, Okla. Council on Juvenile Delinquency Planning, 1969—; mem. Mental Health Authority, Okla. Alcohol Authority 1970—, Okla. Drug Treatment and Rehab. Authority, Com. Reorgn. Exec. Govt. Okla., 1971—, Health Planning Council, 1965-69, med. adv. bd. United Cerebral Palsy Assn. Okla., 1969—. Bd. dirs., v.p. Okla. Alcoholism Council; bd. dirs. Sr. Citizens Okla.; bd. dirs., treas. Pan Am. Tng. Exchange in Psychiatry, 1961-65; bd. dirs. Wesley Found., U. Okla., 1962—, chmn., 1963-68; bd. dirs. Assn. Med. Supts. Mental Hosps. Served with M.C., USAAF, 1942-46. Recipient Outstanding Service awards Okla. Mental Health Assn., 1962, Okla. Psychol. Assn., 1962; Leadership and Teaching award Psychiat. Tech. Assn., Ark.; Donahue Appreciation Day proclaimed in Okla., 1959. Fellow Am. Psychiat. Assn. (pres. Okla. dist. br. 1963, del. Okla. 1969—, chmn. budget com., treas. 1968—), Am. Assn. Mental Deficiency, Am. Geriatrics Soc., A.A.A.S., Coll. Am. Psychiatrists (a founder, regent 1965—); mem. Mid-Continent, Okla. (pres. 1962-66) psychiat. assns., Am. Med. Correctional Assn., Nat. Acad. Religion and Mental Health, Nat., Okla. (pres. 1969) rehab. assns., Am., Okla. (chmn. council pub. health 1962-, ho. of dels. 1964-67) med. assns., Nat. Assn. Mental Health (nat. profl. adv. council 1959-68), Nat. Assn. Mental Hosp. Program Dirs. (organizing com. 1958-59), Brookings Inst. Mental Health and Govt., Norman C. of C. (dir.). Methodist (steward). Rotarian. Contbr. articles to med. and profl. jours. Home: 107 State Dr Norman OK 73069 Office: Box 151 Norman OK 73069

DONAHUE, JACK CLIFFORD, author; b. Waco, Tex., Dec. 6, 1917; s. Jackson Washington and Bertie Beatrice (Knight) D.; student Baylor U., 1935-36; m. Novelia Ellen Sellingsloh, Feb. 16, 1940; children—Michael David, Terence Holman, Brian Robin. Exec. city editor Houston Press, 1953-56; mng. editor Houston Post, 1958-60, Los Angeles Mirror, 1960-62. Author: Someone to Hate; The Confessor, 1963; Erase My Name, 1964; DivorceAmerican Style, 1967; also numerous essays, short stories, TV plays. Home: 1260 Laurel Av Los Angeles CA 90046

DONAHUE, JAMES KENNETH, educator; b. New Haven, Conn., Dec. 16, 1904; s. James S. and Mitilda (Lutz) D.; B.A., U. Ia., 1930; M.A., Princeton, 1932, Ph.D., 1933; LL.D., Hamilton Coll., 1968; m. Esther Mary Lawshe, June 13, 1936; children—Susan Spencer, Jeffrey Hayes. Research asso. biology Princeton, 1933-35; prof. biology Coll. Charleston (S.C.), 1935-49; prof. biology, chmn. dept. Utica Coll., Syracuse U., 1950-62, dean coll., 1963, pres., 1964-70, pres. emeritus, 1970—; vis. prof. biology Hamilton Coll., 1970-71. Trustee Utica Pub. Library, 1963—, St. Luke's Hosp., Utica, 1962—; bd. dirs. Utica Coll. Found., 1963—. Served to lt. USCGR, 1940-42. Mem. A.A.A.S. Clubs: Fort Schuyler (Utica); Princeton (N.Y.C.). Author articles marine endocrinology. Home: 30 Marvin St Clinton NY 13323

DONAHUE, JOHN FRANCIS, investment co. exec.; b. Pitts., July 28, 1924; s. John H. and Margaretta (Bailey) D.; B.S., U.S. Mil. Acad., 1946; m. Rhodora Jacob, Dec. 26, 1946; children—Kathy, Christopher, Maribeth, Rhodora, Patricia, William, Theresa, Thomas, Susan, Carol, Maureen, Rebecca, Gregory. Commd. 2d lt. USAF, 1946, advanced through the grades to 1st lt., 1948, ret., 1950; v.p. King Merritt & Co., 1950-55; pres., dir. Boston Fund. Fund, Inc., Pitts., 1955—, Federated Plans, Inc., 1958-67, Federated Investors, Inc., Pitts., 1958—, Federated Research Corp., 1958-65, Federated Growth Fund, 1960-69, Empire Fund, Inc., 1961—, Second Empire Fund, Inc., 1964—, Presdl. Exchange Fund, Inc., 1965—, Pacific Standard Fund, Inc., 1965—, Third Empire Fund, Inc., 1965—, Fourth Empire Fund, Inc., 1965—, Fifth Empire Fund, Inc., 1966—, Sixth Empire Fund, Inc., 1966—, Second Presdl. Exchange Fund, Inc., 1965—, Fifth Presdl. Fund, Inc., 1966—, Federated Dual-Exchange Fund, 1966—, Am. Leaders Fund, Inc., 1968—, Lutheran Brotherhood Securities Corp., 1969—, Federated Securities Corp., 1969—; chmn. bd., dir. Mut. Fund for Investing in U.S. Govt. Securities, Inc., 1969—, Federated Research Corp., 1965—, Luth. Brotherhood Fund, Inc., 1966—; dir. Century Savs. & Loan Assn. Mem. United Smoke council Allegheny Conf. on Community Devel. Mem. West Point Soc. of Western Pa. Clubs: Pittsburgh Field, Duquesne (Pitts.). Home: 1054 Beechwood Blvd Pittsburgh PA 15206 Office: 421 7th Av Pittsburgh PA 15219

DONAHUE, JOHN LEO, Jr., lawyer; b. Phila., July 10, 1920; s. John Leo and Florence (O'Neill) D.; A.B., U. Ariz., 1942, LL.B., 1949; postgrad. Harvard Grad. Sch. Bus. Adminstrn., 1943, U. Santa Clara Law Sch. 1946-47; m. Charlotte Ann Taylor, Oct. 30, 1950; children-Maureen, John Christopher, Hugh O'Neill, Mary Jayne. Admitted to Ariz. bar, 1949, also U.S. Supreme Ct.; dep. county atty., Pima County, 1949-50; practiced in Tucson, 1950-70; sr. partner firm Robertson & Fickett, Pima County, Ariz., 1967—; lectr. various estate planning councils, Ariz. State Tax Inst., Ariz. Law Inst. (dir. 1963—); pres. So. Ariz. Estate Planning Council, 1962-63. Bd. dirs., vice chmn. bd. St. Mary's Hosp., 1964-70. Served to lt., Supply Corps, USNR, 1942-46; PTO. Mem. Tucson Symphony Assn. (bd. dirs. 1962- 70), Ariz. (founding chmn. liason com. with Internal Revenue Service), Pima County bar assns. Home: 5441 E Burns St Tucson AZ 85711 Office: P O Box 2268 Tucson AZ 85702

DONAHUE, KENNETH, museum dir.; b. Louisville, Jan. 31, 1915; s. Samuel J. and Ida (Walton) D.; A.B., U. Louisville, 1936; A.M., N.Y.U., 1942, grad. student, 1946- 47; m. Daisy Cain, Aug. 13, 1940; children—L. Nicaea, Craig R. Lectr. Mus. Modern Art, 1938-43; research fellow Am. Council Learned Societies, Italy, 1947-49; lectr., curatorial asst. Frick Collection, 1949-53; curator John & Mable Ringling Mus. Art, Sarasota, Fla., 1953-57, dir. mus., 1957-64; dep. dir. Los Angeles County Mus. Art, 1964-66, dir., 1966—. Mem. art adv. panel to commr. internal revenue, 1970—. Served with AUS, 1943-45. Mem. Assn. Am. Museums (dir.), Coll. Art Assn. (v.p. 1969—, dir.), Assn. Art Mus. Dirs. Author articles profl. jours. Home: 245 S Westgate Los Angeles CA 90049 Office: 5905 Wilshire Blvd Los Angeles CA 90036

DONAHUE, ROBERT FRANCIS, mfg. co. exec.; b. Evanston, Ill., June 26, 1926; s. Orville J. and Winifred (Gorman) D.; B.S.C., De Paul U., 1950; C.P.A., U. Ill., 1956; M.B.A., U. Chgo., 1966; m. Suzanne Walsh, Nov. 22, 1951; children—Robert Francis, Nancy Sue. Auditor, Peat, Marwick, Mitchell & Co., Chgo., 1950- 57; asst. treas. Calumet & Hecla, Inc., Evanston, 1957-65, controller, 1965-69; asst. controller Universal Oil Products Co., 1969—. Served with USNR, 1944-46. Mem. Financial Execs. Inst., Am. Inst. C.P.A.'s, Ill. Soc. C.P.A.'s. Home: 1224 Western Av Northbrook IL 60062 Office: 30 Algonquin Rd Des Plaines IL 60016

DONAHUE, ROBERT WILLIAM, petroleum co. exec.; b. Chgo., Apr. 25, 1916; s. Frank H. and Hattie (Rogers) D.; B.S., Purdue U., 1941; m. Carolyn Maloy, Nov. 7, 1942; children—Ann (Mrs. Leonard Giunta), Mary (Mrs. Stephen O'Neill), Katherine, Patricia, Margaret, Richard. With Sun Oil Co., 1941—, dir. comml. devel., 1964-67, dir. purchasing, 1967-70, exec. v.p. products group, dir., 1970—. Mem. Am. Chem. Soc., Am. Petroleum Inst., Soc. Automotive Engrs. Republican. Roman Catholic. Home: 1777 Hamilton Dr Valley Forge PA 19481 Office: 1608 Walnut St Philadelphia PA 19103

DONAHUE, STEPHEN J., ret. bishop; ordained priest Roman Cath. Church, May 25, 1918; apptd. aux. bishop of N.Y., 1934, now ret. Home: 207 W 96th St New York City NY 10025

DONAHUE, THOMAS MICHAEL, educator; b. Healdton, Okla., May 23, 1921; s. Robert Emmett and Mary (Lyndon) D.; A.B., Rockhurst Coll., 1942; Ph.D., Johns Hopkins, 1947; m. Esther Marie McPherson, Jan. 1, 1950; children-Brian M., Kevin E., Neil M. Research asso., asst. prof. Johns Hopkins, 1947-51; asst. prof. U. Pitts., 1951-53, asso. prof., 1953-57, prof., 1957—, dir. Lab. Atmospheric and Space Sci., 1966—, dir. Space Research Coordination Center, 1970—; mem. plantetary atmosphere subcom. NASA Office Space Scis. and Applications steering com.; mem. atmospheric scis. adv. panel NSF; mem. rocket research com. and contamination com. Nat. Acad. Scis. Served with AUS, 1944-46. Guggenheim fellow U. Paris, 1960. Fellow Am. Phys. Soc.; mem. Am. Geophys. Union. Editor: Space Research X, 1969. Home: 110 Hodil Terrace Pittsburgh PA 15238

DONAHUE, THOMAS REILLY, trade union ofcl.; b. N.Y.C., Sept. 4, 1928; s. Thomas Reilly and Mary E. (Purcell) D.; B.A., Manhattan Coll., 1949; J.D., Fordham U., 1956; m. Natalie A. Kiernan, Nov. 11, 1950; children—Nancy Angela, Thomas Reilly III. Dir. edn. local 32B, Bldg. Service Employees Internat. Union, AFL-CIO, 1949-52; dir. contract dept., 1952-57; European labor program coordinator Free Europe Com., Inc., Paris, France, 1957-60; asst. to pres. Bldg. Service Employees' Internat. Union, 1960-67; asst. sect. for labor-mgmt. relations Dept. Labor, 1967- 69; exec. sec. Service Employees Internat. Union, 1969-71, 1st v.p., 1971—. Bd. dirs. Muscular Dystrophy Assns. Am. Served with USNR, 1945-46. Democrat. Home: 7210 Extair Rd Bethesda MD 20014 Office: 900 17th St N W Washington DC 20006

DONAHUE, WILMA THOMPSON, gerontologist; b. Mitchellville, Ia., Dec. 4, 1900; d. William James and Lynn (Roller) Thompson; A.B., U. Mich., 1926. M.A., 1927, Ph.D., 1937; D.Sc. (hon.), Institutum Divi Thomae, 1967; m. Lester J. Donahue, Nov. 3, 1922. Mental hygienist Student Health Service, U. Mich., 1935-45, chief psychologist Psychol. Clinic, 1938-45, dir. bur. psychol. service Inst. Human Adjustment, 1945-48, dir. electronic reader research project, 1948-51, chmn. and research psychologist div. gerontology Inst. Human Adjustment, 1948—; co-dir. Inst. Gerontology, U. Michigan-Wayne State U., 1966—; mem. of adv. com. 2d Internat. Gerontological Congress, 1951; editorial bd. Geriatrics and Gerontol. Soc. Newsletter. Chmn. Governor's Interdepartmental Com. on Aging, 1953-54; dir. Multi-U. Sponsored Program in Social Gerontology; mem. U. Mich. Ann. Conf. on Aging; mem. Legislative Adv. Council on Problems of Aging, 1956-60; chmn. Mich. Commn. Aging, 1961—; Nat. Adv. Com. Aging, Dept. Health, Edn., Welfare, 1965; nat. adv. com. on housing for the elderly Housing and Home Finance Agency, 1956-60, U.S. Dept. of Housing and Urban Development, 1967—. Mem. research com. Gerontol. Research Found.; mem. bd. Kirkpatrick Meml. Recipient ann. award for distinguished work gerontology Gerontol. Research Found., 1957; Harry J. Kelley award Mich. Soc. Gerontology, 1966. Diplomate Clinical Psychology. Member A.A.A.S., Am., Mich. psychol. assns., Midwestern Assn. Coll. Psychiatrists and Clin. Psychologist (past pres.), Gerontol. Soc. (v.p. 1960-61), Adult Edn. Assn. U.S.A. (chmn. com. on aging), Nat. Psychol. Research Council for Blind (past chmn.), Mich. Soc. Gerontology (pres. 1957), Phi Kappa Phi, Phi Beta Kappa, Sigma Xi. Author: (with C. Tibbitts) Aging in Todays Society, pub. 1960. Editor: Measurement of Student Adjustment and Achievement (with Clyde H. Coombs, Robert M. W. Travers), 1949; Psychological Diagnosis and Counseling of the Adult Blind (with Donald Dabelstein.) 1950; Rehabilitation of the Older Worker (with J. Rae Jr., Coll. Served as comdr. USNR, 1942-45; overseas. Mem. Acad. Polit. R. Berry), 1953; Education for Later Maturity, 1954; Housing the Aging, 1954; (with C. Tibbitts) New Frontiers of Aging, 1957, Aging in The Modern World, 1957; (with W. Hunter, D. Coons, H. Maurice) Free Time; Challenge to Later Maturity, 1958; (with C. Tibbitts) Aging Around the World-Social and Psychological Research, 1961; (with R. H. Williams and C. Tibbitts) Psychological and Social Processes of Aging, 1961. Co- editor: Politics, 1962. Home: Box 147 Ann Arbor MI 48107

DONALD, DAVID HERBERT, author, educator; b. Goodman, Miss., Oct. 1, 1920; s. Ira Unger and Sue Ella (Belford) D.; student Holmes Jr. Coll., 1937-39; A.B., Millsaps Coll., 1941; A.M., U. Ill., 1942, Ph. D., 1946; teaching fellow U. N.C., 1942; M.A. (hon.), U. Oxford, 1959; m. Aida DiPace, 1955; 1 son, Bruce Randall. Research asst. history U. Ill., 1943-45, research asso., 1946-47; fellow Social Sci. Research Council, 1945-46; instr. history Columbia, 1947-49; asso. prof. history Smith Coll., 1949-51, asst. prof. history Columbia Grad. Faculty, 1951-52, asso. prof., 1952-57, prof. history 1957-59; prof. history Princeton, 1959-62; prof. Am. history Johns Hopkins, Balt., 1962—, Harry C. Black prof., 1963—, dir. Inst. So. History, 1966—. Vis. asso. prof. Amherst Coll., 1950; Fulbright lectr. Am. history U. Coll. North Wales, 1953-54; mem. Inst. Advanced Study, 1957-58; Harmsworth prof. Am. history Oxford U., 1959-60; John P. Young lectr. Memphis State U., 1963; Walter Lynwood Fleming lectr. La. State U., 1965. Guggenheim fellow, 1964-65; fellow Am. Council Learned Socs., 1969- 70, Center for Advanced Study Behavioral Scis., 1969-70, George A. and Eliza G. Howard fellow, 1957-58; Nat. Endowment for Humanities sr. fellow, 1971-72. Fellow Am. Acad. Arts and Scis.; mem. Orgn. Am. Historians, Am., So. (v.p. 1968, pres. 1969) hist. assns., Soc. Am. Historians, Mass. Hist. Soc., Am. Antiquarian Soc., Phi Beta Kappa, Phi Kappa Phi, Pi Kappa Delta, Pi Kappa Alpha, Omicron Delta Kappa. Episcopalian. Clubs: Cosmos, Johns Hopkins. Author: Lincoln's Herndon, 1948; Divided We Fought, A Pictorial History of the War, 1861-1865, 1952; Inside Lincoln's Cabinet: The Civil War Diaries of Salmon P. Chase, 1954; Lincoln Reconsidered: Essays on the Civil War Era, 1956, rev. 1961; A Rebel's Recollections (G.C. Eggleston 1959); Charles Sumner and the Coming of the Civil War, 1960 (Pulitzer prize in biography 1961); (with J.G. Randall) Why the North Won the Civil War, 1960; The Civil War and Reconstruction, 2d edit. 1961, rev., enlarged edit., 1969; The Divided Union, 1961; The Politics of Reconstruction, 1863-67, 1965; The Nation in Crisis, 1861-1877, 1969; Charles Sumner and the Rights of Man, 1970; The South Since the War (Sidney Andrews), 1970. Gen. editor: The Making of America Series; Documentary History of American Life; co-editor (with wife) The Diary of Charles Francis Adams, 2 vols., 1964. Contbr. articles to periodicals. Home: 6 St Martin's Rd Baltimore MD 21218

DONALD, RICHARD HEMPSTEAD, govt. ofcl.; b. Johannesburg, S.Africa, Nov. 3, 1922 (parents Am. citizens); s. George Kenneth and Cherry (Hempstead) D.; grad. Kent Sch., 1940; B.A., Yale, 1944; student State Dept. Chinese Lang. and Area Studies Sch., 1956-58; m. Jean Randolph Plass, Aug. 25, 1944; children—Christopher H., Susan L., Ann Randolph, Nancy Hempstead. With U.S. Fgn. Service, 1946—; served in El Salvador, Germany, Japan, Colombia, Taiwan, Hong Kong, Singapore; dep. dir. Asian Communist Affairs, 1966-68, dir. E.Asian Regional Affairs, 1968-69, counselor Am. embassy, Djakarta, Indonesia, 1970—. Mem. State Dept. Sr. Seminar in Fgn. Policy, 1969-70. Served to 1st lt. AUS, 1943-46. Recipient Superior Honor award State Dept., 1966. Address: care State Dept Washington DC 20520

DONALDSON, COLEMAN DUPONT, cons. engr.; b. Phila., Sept. 22, 1922; s. John W. and Renee (duPont) D.; B.S. in Aero. Engring., Rennselaer Poly. Inst., 1943; M.A., Princeton, 1954, Ph.D., 1957; m. Barbara Goldsmith, Jan. 17, 1945; children—B. Beirne, Coleman duPont, Evan F., Alexander M., William F. Staff NACA, Langley Field, Va., 1943-44, head aerophysics sect., 1946- 52; gen. aerodynamics USAC, Wright Field, O., 1945-46; aerodynamic evaluation Bell Aircraft, Niagara Falls, N.Y., 1946; sr. cons., pres. Aero Research Assos. of Princeton (N.J.), 1955—; cons. missile guidance and control, Gen. Precision Equipment Corp., 1957-68; cons. magnetohydro- dynamics Thompson Ramo Wooldridge, Inc., 1958-61; cons. aerodynamic heating, gen. aerodynamics Martin Marietta Corp., 1955—; gen. editor Princeton series on high speed aerodynamics and jet propulsion, 1955-64; cons. boundary layer stability, aerodynamic heating, missile and ordnance systems dept., Gen. Electric Co., 1956—; cons. Grumman Aerospace Corp.; Robert H. Goddard vis. lectr. with rank of prof. Princeton U.; dir. Princeton Bank & Trust Co. Mem. research and adv. subcom. on fluid mechanics NASA. Mem. adv. council dept. aerospace and mech. scis., Princeton. Asso. fellow Am. Inst. Aeros. and Astronautics; Am. Phys. Soc., Inst. Navigation, Acad. Applied Sci., N.Y. Acad. Scis., Sigma Xi, Delta Phi. Author articles on aerodynamics. Home: 162 Library Pl Princeton NJ 08540 Office: 50 Washington Rd Princeton NJ 08540

DONALDSON, EDWARD ENSLOW, educator; b. Wenatchee, Wash., Mar. 7, 1923; s. George Howard and Milbra (Enslow) D.; B.S., Wash. State U., 1948, Ph.D. in Physics, 1953; m. Helen Virginia Voss, Apr. 28, 1946; 1 dau., Dinah Lee. Physicist, Gen. Electric Corp. Hanford Labs., Richland, Wash., 1953-57; asst. prof. physics Wash. State U., Pullman, 1957-64, asso. prof., 1964- 67, prof., chmn. dept., 1967—. Vis. prof. U. Liverpool (Eng.), 1968, program chmn. surface physics symposium Wash. State U., 1963-70. Served with AUS, 1943-45; ETO. Sr. mem. Am. Vacuum Soc. (dir. 1966-68, sr.); mem. Am. Phys. Soc., Am. Inst. Physics, Am. Assn. Physics Tchrs., A.A.A.S., Sigma Xi. Contbr. articles in field to profl. jours. Home: 500 Water St Pullman WA 99163

DONALDSON, ETHELBERT TALBOT, educator; b. Bethlehem, Pa., Mar. 18, 1910; s. Francis and Anne H. (Talbot) D.; B.A., Harvard, 1932; Ph.D., Yale, 1943; m. Christine H. Hunter, June 24, 1941 (div. 1967); 1 dau., Deirdre H.; m. 2d, Jacqueline Sissa Filson, Mar. 23, 1967 (div. 1969). Tchr. French, English, Latin and Greek, Kent Sch., Conn., 1932-38, 1939-40; faculty Yale, 1946-67, 70—, research instr. to asso. prof., 1946-56, prof., 1956-66, Bodman prof. English, 1966-67, 70—, acting master of Saybrook Coll., Yale, 1963; prof. English, Columbia, 1967-70; visiting prof. Guggenheim fellow U. Coll., London, 1951-52; Am. Council Learned Soc. fellow 1961-62. Served from pvt. to capt., USAAF, 1943-46. Mem. Modern Lang. Assn. Am., Conn. Acad. Arts and Scis. (pres. 1966-67), Phi Beta Kappa. Clubs: Savage, Athenaeum (London). Author: Piers Plowman: The C-Text and Its Poet, 1949. Author articles in field. Editor: Chaucer's Poetry, 1958. Home: 123 York St New Haven CT 06511

DONALDSON, FRANK ARTHUR, Jr., mfg. co. exec.; b. Mpls., Aug. 19, 1919; s. Frank Arthur and Ruth (Chase) D.; A.B., Harvard, 1942; m. Irene Elizabeth Sweeney, Mar. 1, 1954; children— Frank Arthur III, John Andrew. With Donaldson Co., Inc., Mpls., 1942—, v.p., 1947-51, pres., 1951—, gen. mgr. 1951—; dir. Graco, Inc., North Central Co., St. Paul, First Nat. Bank of Mpls., Marquette Corp., Minn. Natural Gas Co., Mpls. Trustee Jr. Achievement Greater Mpls., Blake Sch., Hopkins, Minn.; dir. Abbott-Northwestern Hosp., Mpls., N. Star Research and Devel. Inst., Mpls. Served with USNR, 1944-45. Mem. St. Paul, Greater Mpls. (bd. dirs.) chambers commerce, Soc. Automotive Engrs. Clubs: Minneapolis, Minikahda (Mpls.); Desert Forest (Carefree, Ariz.). Home: 2764 W Lake of Isles Blvd Minneapolis MN 55416 Office: 1400 W 94th St Minneapolis MN 55431

DONALDSON, GORDON, educator; b. Winnipeg, Man., Can., July 1, 1922; s. Joseph Hamilton and Catherine (McIntosh) D.; B.Commerce, U. Man., 1942; M.A., U. Toronto, 1944; M.B.A., U. Chgo., 1948; D.C.S., Harvard, 1956; m. Eileen Johanna Steel, May 28, 1948; children—Patricia Catherine, Robert Gordon, Mary Louise, Richard Eric. Asso. prof. finance U. Man. Sch. Commerce, 1944-55; faculty Harvard Grad. Sch. Bus. Adminstrn., 1955—, prof. bus. adminstrn., 1963-68, Willard Prescott Smith prof. corporate finance, 1969—. Mgmt. cons., 1950—; dir. XTRA, Inc., Boston. Served with RCAF, 1943-44. Asso. fellow Dudley House, Harvard. Mem. Am. Finance Assn. Author: (with Hunt, Williams) Basic Business Finance, 1958; Corporate Debt Capacity, 1961; Strategy for Financial Mobility, 1969. Contbr. articles to profl. jours. Mem. editorial bd. Harvard Bus. Rev., 1961—. Home: 95 Upland Rd Concord MA 01742 Office: Harvard Bus Sch Boston MA 02163

DONALDSON, JAMES BOWIE, univ. dean, physician; b. Clydebank, Scotland, Apr. 11, 1916; s. David and Mary (Bowie) D.; came to U.S., 1923, naturalized, 1930; M.D., Temple U., 1944; m. Catharine Prestwood, June 16, 1945; children—Barbara Anne (Mrs. Joseph P. Conlon, Jr.), James Bowie, Catharine Lynn, Carol Ann, Patricia Lynn, Peter Marshall. Intern Presbyn. Hosp., Phila., 1944-45, resident, 1945-46, 48-49; practice internal medicine, Phila., 1949—; mem. staff Phila. Gen., Temple U. and Presbyn. hosps.; cons. VA Hosp., Phila., 1953-59; acting chmn. dept. medicine Hahnemann Med. Coll., 1958- 59; mem. faculty Temple U. Med. Sch., 1952—, prof. medicine, 1966—, asso. dean, 1967—; chief staff Temple U. Hosp., 1967—; 1st guest med. speaker Alaska, 1959. Served with

M.C., USNR, 1946-47. Recipient Legion of Honor, Chaplain of Four Chaplains, 1968. Diplomate Pan Am. Med. Assn. Mem. A.M.A., Internat. Soc. Internal Medicine, Pa. Thoracic Soc., A.C.P., Phila. Coll. Physicians, Am. Coll. Cardiology, A.A.A.S., Pa. (del. 1963, 66, 67, 68, 69, 70), Phila. County (bd. dirs. 1962—, chmn. pub. relations com. 1962-68, dir.-at- large 1969—) med. socs., W. Phila. Med. Assn. (past. pres.), St. Andrew's Soc. Mason (32). Clubs: Union League, Bachelors Barge (Phila.). Contbr. profl. jours. Home: 714 Woodcrest Rd Radnor PA 19087 Office: 3401 N Broad St Philadelphia PA 19140

DONALDSON, JOHN WILLSON, army officer; b. Ft. Oglethorpe, Ga., Feb. 7, 1924; s. Thomas Quinton and Elizabeth (Rumbough) D.; B.S., U.S. Mil. Acad., 1944; diploma in French civilization Sorbonne U., Paris, 1946-47; M.A. in Fgn. Affairs, George Washington U., 1963; m. Margarethe Rose Zauner, May 24, 1948; children—John Willson, Steven Rumbough. Commd. 2d lt. U.S. Army, 1944, advanced through grades to brig. gen., 1969; dep. comdr. 32d Inf., also G-3 7th Inf. div., Korea, 1961-62; mem. Joint Staff, Washington, 1963-66; chief of staff 7th Inf. Div., Korea, 1961-62; mem. staff group of chmn. Joint Chiefs Staff, Washington, 1967-68; comdr. 11th Light Inf. Brigade, Vietnam, 1968-69; chief of staff, asst. div. comdr. Am. Div., Vietnam, 1969-70; mem. Joint Staff, Washington, 1971—; asst. prof. French and German langs. U. Md., 1961-62, 65; asso. prof. French, George Washington U., 1966. Active Waynewood Citizens Assn. Decorated Silver Star with oak leaf cluster, D.F.C. with oak leaf cluster, Bronze Star with 2 oak leaf clusters, Legion of Merit with 3 oak leaf clusters, Air medal with 28 oak leaf clusters, Joint Services Commendation medal, Army Commendation medal, Purple Heart, Combat Inf. badge with oak leaf cluster. Mem. Assn. U.S. Army, Assn. Grads., U.S. Mil. Acad., Rainbow Div. Vets Assn., U.S. Modern Pentathlon and Biathlon Assn., 1st Inf. Div. Soc. Home: 818 Elaine Ct Alexandria VA 22308 Office: Hdqrs 1st US Army Ft George G Meade MD 20755

DONALDSON, LAUREN R., educator; b. Tracy, Minn., May 13, 1903; s. Russell C. and Jessie M. (Moses) D.; A.B., Intermountain Union Coll., 1926; M.S., U. Wash., 1931, Ph.D., 1939; D.Sc. (hon.), Rocky Mountain Coll., 1958, Hamline U., 1965; m. Lenora E. Carney, June 25, 1927; children—John Russell, Joann Lauren. Prin. and tchr. sci. and athletics Shelby (Mont.) High Sch., 1926-30; summer mem. staff Mont. Dept. of Fish and Game, 1926-31; asst. to asso. prof. fisheries U. Wash., Seattle, 1932- 48, prof. 1948—, dir. Applied Fisheries Lab., 1943-57, Lab. Radiation Biology, 1958-66. Asst. prof. U. Ore., summer 1941; biologist Wash. Dept. Fish, summers 1942-43; chief div. radiobiology Operation Crossroads, 1946, Bikini Sci. Resurvey, 1948; radiobiol. observer Operation Sandstone (Eniwetok), 1948, biologist Operation Ivy, 1952; dir. U. Wash. radiobiol. studies Pacific weapons testing program, 1954-64; rep. AEC, Japan, 1954; lectr. U. Oslo (Norway), 1952, U. Helsinki (Finland), 1959; cons. fisheries U.S. Fish and Wildlife Service, 1935-40, Internat. Pacific Salmon Fisheries Commn., 1941- 43; cons. biol. effects radiation Gen. Electric Co., Richland, Wash., 1947-56, mineral metabolism Gen. Mills, Inc., 1963—, planning Nat. Fisheries Center aand Aquarium, U.S. Fish and Wildlife Service, 1965-66. Mem. Seattle Civil Def. Bd., 1946-50; chmn. Wash. Gov.'s Adv. Com. on Fisheries, 1957-64; chmn. Aquarium com. Oceanographic Commn. Wash., 1967—; mem. Bonneville regional adv. council U.S. Dept. Interior, 1968—; sci. adv. group Internat. Atlantic Salmon Found., 1970—. Mem. Am. Fisheries Soc., Wildlife Soc., A.A.A.S., Phi Sigma, Sigma Xi. Contbr. numerous articles to profl. jours. and reports on fisheries mgmt. and radiobiology. Home: 6201 51st NE Seattle WA 98105 Office: Fisheries Center U Wash Seattle WA 98105

DONALDSON, MARJORIE CATHERINE, librarian; b. Milw., June 15, 1911; d. Robert Sample and Lenore (Okey) Donaldson; B.A., Rutgers U., 1933. State traveling library, Des Moines, 1933-38; state dir. Ia. WPA Library Project, 1938-39; asst. librarian Ames (Ia.) Pub. Library, 1939-44; with Pasadena (Cal.) Pub. Library, 1944—, city librarian, 1956—. Recipient Woman of Year award Women's Civic League, Pasadena, 1957, sec., 1958—. Mem. Cal. Library Assn. (pres. pub. libraries sect. 1960), Pub. Library Execs. of So. Cal. (pres. 1957), Pasadena Municipal Employees Assn. (dir. 1952-53), Bus. and Profl. Women's Club (local pres. 1949-50), C. of C., P.E.O. (chpt. pres. 1947). Republican. Presbyn. Clubs: Zonta (pres. 1964-65), Women's City (dir. 1950-56, pres. 1955-56) (Pasadena). Home: 1183 Romney Dr Pasadena CA 91105 Office: 285 E Walnut St Pasadena CA 91101

DONALDSON, RICHARD MIESSE, oil co. exec., lawyer; b. Columbus, O., Apr. 8, 1929; s. Maynard McClure and Mary Ann (Miesse) D.; B.S., Northwestern U., 1950; J.D., U. Mich., 1953; LL.M., Harvard, 1957; m. Carolyn Jean Cray, Aug. 30, 1952; children—Nancy Ann, Susan Beth, Richard Cray. Admitted to Ohio bar, 1953; spl. partner McAfee, Hanning, Newcomer, Hazlett & Wheeler, Cleve., 1957-67; gen. partner Squire, Sanders & Dempsey, Cleve., 1967-70; v.p., gen. counsel Standard Oil Co. (Ohio), Cleve., 1970—. Trustee Children's Aid Soc. of Cleve., 1965—, pres., 1967-69; trustee Planned Parenthood of Cleve., 1966—, Cleve. Council World Affairs, 1970—; com. mem. Young Life in Cleve., 1970—, chmn., 1971-72. Mem. Rocky River (O.) Bd. Edn., 1962-69, pres. bd., 1965-68. Served to capt. J.A.G.D., USAF, 1953-56. Mem. Am., Ohio, Cleve. bar assns. Republican. Mem. United Ch. of Christ (mem. session). Clubs: Cleve. Yachting, Midday (Cleve.). Home: 21418 Kenwood Av Rocky River OH 44116 Office: Midland Bldg Cleveland OH 44115

DONALDSON, ROBERT CHARLES, educator; b. San Francisco, Jan. 28, 1924; s. Donald and Cora Priscilla (Donaldson) Wood; student U. Ariz., 1942; B.A., U. So. Cal., 1950, M.A., 1951; Ph.D., U. Mich., 1954; Fulbright scholar U. Brussels, 1953-54; m. Margery Johnson, Apr. 6, 1950; children—Diane Margery, Robert Charles. Asst. prof. Eastern Ky. State Coll., 1954-57; asst. prof. history Sacramento State Coll., 1957-62, asso. prof., 1962-67, prof., 1967—, chmn. dept., 1969—, chmn. acad. senate, 1968-69, coll. ombudsman, 1969-70. Senator, Acad. Senate of Cal. State Colls., 1969—. Served with AUS, 1943-46. Mem. Am. Hist. Assn., Am. Civil Liberties Union, Phi Kappa Phi, Phi Alpha Theta, Blue Key. Democrat. Home: 3852 El Ricon Way Sacramento CA 95825

DONALDSON, RODGERS, aircraft corp. exec.; b. Pitts., Sept. 6, 1908; s. John Speer and Isla Flora (Rodgers) D.; grad. Phillips Exeter Acad., 1926; B.S., Harvard, 1930; LL.B. cum laude, Boston U., 1933; m. Leslie Robinson Fisher, Oct. 26, 1940; 1 son, Rodgers. Admitted to Mass. bar, 1933, Cal. bar, 1956; asso. Choate, Hall & Stewart, Esquires, Boston, 1933-39; partner, Cunningham & Donaldson, Pittsfield, Mass., 1939-42; counsel Lockheed Aircraft Corp., Dayton, O., 1942; asst. mgr. Eastern dist., Dayton and Washington, 1942-45, mgr., N.Y.C., then asst. chief counsel, chief counsel, 1954-65, v.p., chief counsel, 1965-68, v.p., gen. counsel, 1968-71, sr. counselor, 1971—; gen. counsel, sec. Am. Optical Co., Southbridge, Mass., 1949-54. Bd. dirs. Los Angeles Met. YMCA, Hollywood Presbyn. Hosp.; trustee All Nations Found. Mem. Los Angeles Com. on Fgn. Relations. Republican. Methodist. Rotarian. Clubs: Wings, Harvard (N.Y.C.); Los Angeles Country. Home: 651 S Beverly Glen Blvd Los Angeles CA 90024 Office: Lockheed Aircraft Corp Burbank CA 91503

DONATH, FRED ARTHUR, geologist; b. St. Cloud, Minn., July 11, 1931; s. Arnold C. and Elizabeth (Crary) D.; B.A., U. Minn., 1954; M.S., Stanford, 1956, Ph.D., 1958; m. Mavis Eleanor Hagen, July 19, 1952; children—Robert William, Deborah Ann. Faculty, San Jose (Cal.) State Coll., 1957-58; faculty Columbia, N.Y.C., 1958-67, prof. geology, 1966-67; prof., head dept. U. Ill., Urbana, 1967—. Vis. lectr. Am. Geol. Inst., 1966—, Am. Geophys. Union, 1967—. Recipient Semicentennial medallion Rice U., 1962. Fellow geol. socs. Am., London, A.A.A.S.; mem. Am. Geophys. Union (sec. tectonophysics sect. 1964-68), Am. Assn. Petroleum Geologists (lectr. continuing edn. program 1965—, Phi Beta Kappa, Sigma Xi. Asso. editor Geol. Soc. Am., 1963—, Tectonophysics, 1963—. Contbr. articles to profl. lit. Fundamental research in exptl. high pressure geophysics; mechanics deformation of earth's crust; design of high pressure equipment. Home: 2021 Cureton Dr Urbana IL 61801

DONATI, ENRICO, painter, corp. exec.; b. Milan, Italy, Feb. 19, 1909; s. Federico and Marianna (Vita) D.; D.Econs. and Social Scis., U. Pavia (Italy), 1929; m. Claire Javal, 1934; children—Marina (Mrs. Serge Lier), Sylviane (Mrs. Philippe Mathieu); m. 2d, Adele Schmidt, 1965; 1 d., Alyssa Donati. Came to the U.S., 1934, naturalized, 1945. Mem. Surrealist group until 1950; one-man shows include New Sch. Social Research, 1942, Passedoit Gallery, N.Y.C., 1942, 44, G Pl. Gallery, Washington, 1944, Chgo. Arts Club, 1944, 59, Durand Ruel, N.Y.C., 1945- 47, 49, Syracuse U., 1947, Galerie Drouant, Paris, France, 1947, Paul Rosenberg Gallery, N.Y.C., 1950, Galleria del Milione, Milan, 1950, Obelisco, Rome, Italy, 1950, Iolas Gallery, N.Y.C., 1952, Cavalino, Venice, Italy, 1952, 53, Naviglio, Lilan, 1953, Betty Parsons Gallery, N.Y.C., 1954, 55, 57, 59, 60, Palais des Beaux-Arts, Brussels, Belgium, 1961, Neue Galerie, Munich, Germany, 1962, Staempfli Gallery, N.Y.C., 1962, 63, 66, J. L. Hudson Gallery, Detroit, 1964, 66, Mass. Inst. Tech., 1964, Obelisk Gallery, Washington, 1965; rep. permanent collections Am. Republic Ins. Co., Des Moines, Mus. Modern Art, Whitney Mus., Washington U., St. Louis, Mus. Fine Arts, Houston, Muses Royaux des Beaux-Arts de Belgique, Brussels, Mus. Internat. Center Aesthetic Research, Turin, Italy, Albright-Knox Art Gallery, Detroit Inst., Arts, U. Mich. Art Gallery, Balt. Mus. Art, Newark Mus., Galleria Nazionale d'Arte Moderna, Rome and Milan, Mitchener Found., Allentown, Pa., Olsen Found., Guliford, Conn., IBM Corp., Mass. Inst. Tech., Chase Manhattan Bank, Rockefeller Inst., C. Friedrich von Stemens Stiftung. Munich, Indian Head Mills collection, N.Y.C., Mich. Consol. Gas Co., Detroit, J. L. Hudson Co., Palm Beach Co., Johns Hopkins Hosp., Yale Art Gallery, Anderson Clayton Co., Houston, Washington Gallery Modern Art, Tougaloo (Miss.) Coll., also numerous pvt. collections; vis. lectr. Yale, 1960- 62. Mem. jury Fulbright Scholarship Program, 1954-56, 63-64; mem. Yale Council Arts and Architecture, 1962-69. Adv. bd. regents Brandeis U., 1956—. Chmn. bd., chief exec. officer Houbigant, Inc., perfumes and cosmetics, 1965—; pres. Donrico, Inc., designing and printing, 1940-. Chmn. nat. com. Univ. Art Mus., U. Cal. Berkeley. Served as lt. Italian Mountain Troops. Decorated cavaliers Della Corona D'Italia. Club: Stamford (Conn.) Yacht. Home: 953 Fifth Ave New York City NY 10021 also 428 N Wilton Rd New Canaan CT 06840 Office: 539 W 45th St New York City NY 10036

DONATI, PINE, musician; b. Verona, Italy, May 9, 1907; s. Felice and Dorina (Maceri) D.; student Liberal Arts Sch., Verona, Italy, Verdi Conservatory of Milan; protege Riccardo Zandonai; m. Maria Canigila, Sept. 3, 1939; 1 son, Paolo. Gen. mgr. Teatro Arena, Verona, Italy; gen. mgr. Teatro Communale, Bologna; artistic dir. Teatro San Carlos, Lisbon, Portugal; musical asst. to gen. mgr. Lyric Opera, Chgo. 1958; conducted operas, Italy, France, Spain, Portugal, S.A., Egypt; composer symphonic music, chamber music; composer opera in two acts Corradino lo Svevo, 1932, three acts Lancilotto del Lago, 1939. Served with Italian Army, 1927. Recipient Commendatore dell'Italia, King Umberto of Italy, 1937; Cavaliere della Cultura, Lisbon, 1946. Contbr. articles Italian newspapers. Address: Via Lisbona 11 Rome Italy

DONATO, ANTHONY, educator, composer, condr., violinist; b. Prague, Neb., Mar. 8, 1909; s. Anthony and Milada (Maresh) D.; student U. Neb., 1926-27; Mus.B., Eastman Sch. Mus., 1931, Mus.M., 1937, Ph.D., 1947; m. Carolyn C. Scott, Dec. 30, 1931. Head violin dept., Drake U., 1930-37, Ia. State Tchrs. Coll., 1937-39, U. Tex., 1939-47; prof. theory and composition, Northwestern U., 1947—, conductor Univ. Chamber Orch., 1947-58. Fulbright grantee to lecture on contemporary Am. music in Eng., 1951-52. Mem. Music Tchrs. Nat. Assn. Am. Composers and Condrs., Am. Assn. U. Profs., A.S.C.A.P., Internat. Soc. for Contemporary Music, Phi Mu Alpha, Pi Kappa Lambda, Sigma Phi Epsilon. Mason. Recipient numerous awards and commissions. Compositions include works for orchestra, band, chorus, opera, various chamber combinations, piano, organ, solo voice and various instruments with piano. Author: Preparing Music Manuscript, 1962. Contbr. profl. jours. Home: 9317 Kedvale Av Skokie IL 60076 Office: Northwestern U Evanston IL 60201

DONATONI, FRANCE, composer, educator; b. Verona, Italy, June 9, 1927; s. de Silvio and Dolores (Stefanucci) D.; ed. in music composition; m. Susan Park, Sept. 20, 1958; children—Roberto, Renato. Composer, prof. harmony, counterpoint and composition G. Verdi Conservatory, Milan, Italy. Address: via Capri 20 20131 Milan Italy

DONAVAN, GEORGE E., banker. Sr. v.p. First Nat. Bank Jackson, Miss. Office: 248 E Capitol St Jackson MS 39205*

DONCEEL, JOSEPH FLORENT, educator; b. Antwerp, Belgium, Sept. 16, 1906; s. Armand and Marie (Vernimmen) D.; Docteur en Philosophicum, Louvain, Belgium, 1934-55; asst. prof. philosophy Loyola Coll., Balt., 1940-44; from asst. prof. to prof. philosophy Fordham U., N.Y.C., 1944—. Author: Philosophical Psychology, 1955; Philosophical Anthropology, 1965; A Marechal Reader, 1970 Home: Fordham U Bronx N Y 10458

DONEGAN, CHARLES EDWARD, legal educator; b. Chgo., Apr. 10, 1933; s. Arthur C. and Odessa (Arnold) D.; B.S.C., Roosevelt U., 1954; M.S., Loyola U., 1959; J.D., Howard U., 1967; LL.M., Columbia, 1970; m. Patty Lou Harris, June 15, 1963. Pub. sch. tchr., Chgo., 1956-59; with Office Internal Revenue, Chgo., 1959-62; labor economist U.S. Dept. Labor, Washington, 1962-65; legal intern U.S. Commn. Civil Rights, Washington, summer 1966; admitted to N.Y. and D.C. bars, 1968; asst. consul N.A.A.C.P. Legal Def. Fund, N.Y.C., 1967-69; lectr. law Baruch Coll., N.Y.C., 1969-70; asst. prof. law State U. N.Y. at Buffalo, 1970—. Active Americans for Democratic Action. Ford Found. scholar, 1965-67. Mem. Am., Nat. bar assns., Bar Assn. City N.Y., Bronx and Harlem Lawyers, Nat. Conf. Black Lawyers (bd. organizers), Roosevelt, Loyola, Howard and Columbia alumni assns., Alpha Phi Alpha. Home: 309 North St Buffalo NY 14201

DONEGAN, DOROTHY, pianist; b. Chgo., Apr. 6, 1926; d. Ella Day Donazell; scholarship, Chgo. Mus. Coll., 1942-44; student U. So. Cal., 1953-54; m. John T. McClain, Dec. 7, 1948; 1 dau., Jan. Gave half classical-half jazz concert at Orchestra Hall, Chgo., 1942; appeared at Chgo. Stadium, 1943, Embers Club, N.Y.C., 1954—; appeared in motion picture Sensations of 1945; now appearing as jazz artist, San Juan, P.R. Mem. musical com. City of Hope; artist patron Boy Scouts Am. Episcopalian. Author: Dorothy Donegan's Musical Compositions, 1942-54; Piano Boogie, 1939; Kilroy Was Here, 1947; DDT Blues, 1953. Home: 500 E 33d St Chicago IL 60615 Office: 745 Fifth Av New York City NY 10022

DONEGAN, E. CARY, Jr., advt. exec.; b. Bridgeport, Conn., Oct. 15, 1921; s. Earl C. and Marian (Meath) D.; Ph.B. in Commerce, U. Notre Dame, 1943; m. Nancy Caroline White, Nov. 28, 1964. Sales exec. Am. Newspaper Advt. Network, N.Y.C., 1946-48, Cowles Pub. Co., N.Y.C., 1949-51, Hearst Mags., N.Y.C., 1951-52; v.p. Motion Pictures for Television, Inc., N.Y.C., 1952-54; v.p. sales C & C Television, Inc., N.Y.C., 1954-56; pres. Universal Graphics Corp., N.Y.C., 1964—, Cydon Enterprises, Inc., N.Y.C., 1961—, Woods, Donegan and Co., Inc., N.Y.C., 1956—; dir. Heartland Properties, Inc., Campus Lodge, Inc. Served with USNR, World War II; ETO, PTO. Decorated King Peter Freedom medal, Count de Savoya decoration. Club: Meadow (Southampton, N.Y.). Home: Ochre Lane Southampton NY 11968 also 12 Beekman Pl New York City NY 10022 Office: 400 Madison Av New York City NY 10017

DONEGAN, HORACE WILLIAM BADEN, clergyman; b. Eng., May 17, 1900; s. Horace George and Pembroke (Hand); came to U.S., 1910, naturalized, 1919, student St. Stephen's College; Oxford U.; B.D., Episcopal Theol. Sem. Cambridge, Mass., 1927; student Harvard Divinity Sch.; D.D., N.Y.U., 1940. Trinity Coll., U. of South; S.T.D., U. Kings Coll., Halifax, 1960, Hobart Coll., Gen. Theol. Sem., Columbia U., 1960; D.C.L., Nashotah, 1956; D.D., Bard Coll., 1957; Ordained to ministry P.E. Ch. as deacon 1927, priest 1928; asst. All Saints Ch. Worcester, Mass., 1927-29; rector Christ Ch., Balt., 1929-33, St. James Ch., N.Y.C., 1933-47; consecrated suffragan bishop Diocese of N.Y., 1947, bishop coadjutor, 1949, diocesan, 1950. Pres., Episcopal Mission Soc., House of Redeemer N.Y., Bd. Deaconesses N.Y., Widows and Orphans Fund, St. Hilda's and St. Hugh's Sch.; hon. pres. Seamen's Ch. Inst. Trustee Bard Coll., Seminario del Caribe; chmn. Gen. Theol. Sem. Decorated Legion of Honor, France. Recipient Grand Cross St. Joanikije, 1956; Sublime Prelate, Order St. John of Jerusalem, 1956; comdr. Order Brit. Empire, 1957; Silver medal of Red Cross of Japan, 1959; Grand Knight Order St. Dennis; Holy Panagia of Armenian Ch. Churchill fellow Westminster Coll. Club: Pilgrims (v.p.), Union League, Century Assn. (N.Y.C.); R.A.C., London Union. Home: The Bishop's House Cathedral Heights New York City NY 10025 Office: Synod House Cathedral Heights New York City NY 10025

DONEGAN, THOMAS JAMES, lawyer; b. Bklyn., Feb. 27, 1907; s. Thomas James and Mary F. (Carey) D.; A.B., Columbia, 1929; LL.B., Fordham U., 1931; m. Dorothy N. Reynolds, May 2, 1936; 1 son, Thomas James. Admitted to N.Y. bar, 1932, also U.S. Supreme Ct., Fed. Bar So. and Eastern Dist. N.Y.; practice in N.Y.C., 1932-33, 46-57; with Fed. Bur. Investigation, 1933-46; spl. asst. to atty. gen. U.S., 1947-57; chmn. interdeptl. com. internal security Nat. Security Council, 1953-54; chmn. personnel security adv. com. Exec. Office of Pres., 1957-67; became dir. investigation div. Indian Claims Commn., Washington, 1967. Lt. USNR, 1937-40. Mem. Am. Bar Assn. Address: 3743 McKinley N W Washington DC 20506

DONELAN, JOSEPH FRANCIS, Jr., fgn. service officer; b. N.Y.C., Feb. 16, 1918; s. Joseph Francis and Mary Rose (Sheeran) D.; student Coll. City N.Y., 1935-42; B.S., Georgetown U., 1947; M.A., George Washington U., 1967; m. Lucille Ann Florey, June 13, 1942; children—Jo Ann, Sharon Mary, Barbara Lee, Kathleen. With Auchincloss, Parker & Redpath, securities, N.Y.C., 1936-41; mgmt. analyst USAF, 1946-49; mgmt. analyst Dept. State, 1949-52, mgmt. officer, adminstrv. officer Am. embassy, Paris, 1952-56, dir. finance Dept. State, 1956-57, dep. budget and finance officer, 1957-58; prin. officer, Am. consul Am. Consulate, Nagoya, Japan, 1958-61; consul gen. Am. embassy, Tokyo, 1961; counselor embassy Am. embassy, New Delhi, 1961-63; assigned to Nat. War Coll., Washington, 1963-64; exec. dir. Arms Control and Disarmament Agy., 1964-67; fgn. service insp., 1967-68; controller for intrastructure NATO, 1968-69; dep. asst. sec. state for budget and finance, 1969-71, asst. sec. state for adminstrn., 1971—. Served to capt. AUS, 1941-46. Mem. Am.-Japan Soc. (v.p. Nagoya, Japan). Rotarian. Address: 9220 E Parkhill Dr Bethesda MD 20014

DONELSON, LEWIS R., III, lawyer; b. Memphis, Oct. 9, 1917; s. Lewis R., Jr. and Katharine (Campbell) D.; grad. cum laude, Choate Sch., 1934; B.A. with distinction, Southwestern at Memphis, 1938; LL.B., Georgetown U., 1941; m. Janice Ost, Feb. 3, 1945; children—Janice, Lewis R. IV, Loring. Accountant, FHA, 1938-41; admitted to Tenn. bar, 1940, D.C., bar, 1941; atty. CAB 1941-42; law clk. to circuit ct. judge, Cin., 1943-44; pvt. practice, Memphis, 1944—; partner firm Heiskell, Donelson, Adams, Williams & Wall, and predecessors, 1954—. Mem. Tenn. Civil Rights Commn., 1961-62; dir. Program of Progress, Memphis, 1965-66. Bd. dirs. Republican Assn. Shelby County, 1960—, pres., 1962, 63, 65; Tenn. chmn. Citizens for Eisenhower, 1956; del. Rep. Nat. Conv., 1964; campaign mgr. Rep. candidate for U.S. Senate, 1964; mem. Tenn. Rep. Exec. Com., chmn. call and rules com.; mem. Memphis City Council, 1967—. Bd. dirs., treas. Southwestern at Memphis, 1961—; bd. dirs. Shelby United Neighbors, 1958—, pres., 1962. Named to Southwestern at Memphis Hall Fame, 1963. Mem. Am., Tenn., Shelby County bar assns., Omicron Delta Kappa, Sigma Alpha Epsilon. Presbyn. (elder). Rotarian. Contbr. articles on tax to profl. jours. Home: 134 E Cherry Dr Memphis TN 38117 Office: First Nat Bank Bldg Memphis TN 38103

DONEN, STANLEY, film producer, dir.; b. Columbia, S.C., Apr. 13; s. Mortie and Helen Donen; ed. U. S.C. Dir. films including: Fearless Fagan, Give the Girl a Break, Royal Wedding, Love Is Better Than Ever, Deep in My Heart, Seven Brides for Seven Brothers, Funny Face, Kiss Them for Me; co-dir. Singin' in the Rain, It's Always Fair Weather, On the Town; producer-dir. Pajama Game, Indiscreet, Damn Yankee, Once More with Feeling, Surprise Package, The Grass is Greener, Charade, Arabesque, Two for the Road, Bedazzled, Staircase. Office: care Universal Pictures 445 Park Av New York City NY 10022*

DONENFELD, IRWIN, pub. and distbg. co. exec.; b. N.Y.C., Mar. 1, 1926; s. Harry and Gussie (Weinstein) D.; B.A., Bates Coll., 1946; m. Alice Ray Greenhaum, Apr. 7, 1963; children—Rita Lynn, Amy Ruth, Ben Allen, Harry Lawrence. With Nat. Periodical Publs., Inc., 1948—, exec. v.p., 1964—; v.p., sec., dir. Independent News Co. Chmn. 3d Century Fund, Columbia Grammar Sch., N.Y.C., 1966—, trustee, 1966—; N.Y. chmn. Am. Med. Center, Denver, 1964, trustee, 1966—, v.p., 1967—. Served with USAAF, 1942-43. Home: 215 E 61st New York City NY 10021 Office: 575 Lexington Av New York City NY 10022

DONER, DEAN BENTON, educator; b. Brookings, S.D., May 1, 1923; s. David Benton and Edna (Beals) D.; B.S., S.D. State U., 1947; M.F.A., U. Ia., 1948, Ph.D., 1953; m. Lois Jacobsen, Dec. 23, 1944; children—Kalia Louise, Margaret, Lauren Elizabeth. Instr. English, U. Ida., 1950-53; instr., prof. English, asso. dean Sch. Humanities, Purdue U., 1953-67; dean Coll. Liberal Arts and Scis., prof. English, U. Ill., Chgo. Circle, 1967—; vis. prof. U. Hamburg, 1967; faculty

Salzburg Seminar in Am. Studies, 1967. Served with USAAF, 1943-46. Democrat. Unitarian. Contbr. short stories, poems, article to mags. Home: 2513 Park Pl Evanston IL 60201 Office: Box 4348 Chicago IL 60680

DONER, MARY FRANCES, author; b. Port Huron, Mich.; d. James and Mary Jane (O'Rourke) Doner; ed. Immaculate Heart Convent and Western High Sch., Detroit, St. Clair (Mich.) High Sch., Columbia, Began writing for pulps after leaving coll.; staff writer Dell Pub. Co., N.Y.C., 8 yrs.; music reporter, Boston Traveler, 2 yrs.; contract writer for several pulps in N.Y.C., for Alfred H. King, Penn Pub. Co.; contract writer Doubleday & Co., 1940—, for novels of Great Lakes country; speaker Living Literature, Boston U., 1939, Boston Book Fair, 1938, Meet the Author series, Boston Pub. Library, 1946; tchr. creative writing, Boston Center for Adult Edn., 1943-45, Ludington (Mich.) High Sch., Jr. High and Pub. Library, 1964—. Hon. mem. Internat. Mark Twain Soc., Ladies Library Assn., Port Huron, Mich.; mem. Internat. Inst. of Arts and Letters, Author's League, Pen and Brush Club (N.Y.C.). Author: several novels, later ones; Ravenswood, 1948; Cloud of Arrows, 1950; The Host Rock, 1952; The Salvager, 1958; The Shores of Home, 1961; While the River Flows, 1962; The Wind and the Fog, 1963; Cleavenger Va. Castle, 1968; Pere Marquette-Soldier of the Cross, 1969; Return A Stranger, 1970. Contbr. over 250 short stories and serials to mags. some transcribed into Braille. Home: 210 N Lewis St Ludington MI 49431 ☆

DONER, WILFRED B., advt. exec.; b. Detroit, Nov. 5, 1914; s. Nathan and Regina (Sobel) Silberstein; A.B., U. Wis., 1936; m. Rolla Jacob Friedman, Mar. 19, 1964; children (by previous marriage)—Judith Anne (Mrs. Edward Berne), Frederick Nathan, Mary Alice. Partner Fink & Doner, 1937-43; pres. W. B. Doner & Co., advt. agy., 1943-68, chmn. bd., 1968—; v.p., dir. Mich. Chandelier Co. Bd. dirs. Project Hope; nat. dir., dir. Mich. chpt. Nat. Multiple Sclerosis Soc. Clubs: Franklin Hills Country, Great Lakes, Standard. Home: 27530 Fairway Hills Dr Franklin MI 48025 Office: First Nat Bank Bldg Detroit MI 48226

DONEY, WILLIS FREDERICK, Jr., educator; b. Pitts., Aug. 19, 1925; s. Willis Frederick and Ora (Powell) D.; B.A., Princeton, 1946, M.A., Ph.D., 1949; M.A., Dartmouth, 1966. Instr. Cornell U., 1949-52; vis. lectr. U. Mich., 1952; asst. prof. Ohio State U., 1953-56, 57-58; George Santayana fellow, 1956-57; mem. faculty Dartmouth, 1958—, prof. philosophy, 1966—; vis. lectr. Harvard, 1963. Author articles on 17th Century philosophy. Editor: Descartes: A Collection of Critical Studies, 1967. Home: N Main St Norwich VT 05055 Office: Philosophy Dept Dartmouth Coll Hanover NH 03755

DONG, PHAM VAN, prime minister Democratic Republic North Viet Nam. Address: Hanoi Democratic Republic of North Viet Nam*

DONGUS, GUSTAV HERMAN, lawyer; b. Indpls., Aug. 20, 1909; s. Gustav A. and Caroline (Riker) D.; A.B., Butler U., 1932; LL.B., Harvard, 1935; m. Margaret K. Lewis, Dec. 26, 1936; children—Jane Rainier, Steven (dec.). Admitted to Ind. bar, 1935, U.S. Supreme Ct. bar, 1946; practice in Indpls. 1935—; now partner firm Dongus, Ging, Stein, Cregor & Messick. Bd. mgrs. Childrens Bur. Indpls. Orphan Asylum, 1950-59. Govt. appeal agt. Selective Service Bd. Served to lt. comdr. USNR, World War II. Mem. Am., Ind., Indpls. (pres. 1960) bar assns., Harvard Law Sch. Assn. Ind. (pres. 1951-52), Lawyers Assn. Indpls. (pres. 1947), Newcomen Soc. N.Am., Sigma Nu, Phi Kappa Phi. Clubs: Indianapolis Athletic; Lawyers (pres. 1958). Home: 7414 N Meridian St Indianapolis IN 46260 Office: One Indiana Sq Indianapolis IN 46204

DONIACH, SEBASTIAN, educator. Prof. applied physics Stanford. Office: Dept Physics Stanford U Stanford CA 94305*

DONLAN, CHARLES JOSEPH, aero. engr.; b. Lawrence, Mass., July 15, 1916; s. Thomas Francis and Mary Anne (Tierney) D.; B.S. in Aero. Engring., Mass. Inst. Tech., 1938; extension grad. student, U. Va.; m. Marguerite Anne Phelan, Feb. 7, 1942; children—Charles Joseph, Richard Michael (dec.). With NASA, and predecessor, 1938—, tech. asst. to asso. dir. Langley Research Center, 1955-58, asst. mgr. space task group, 1958, asso. dir. research and devel. Project Mercury, 1959-61, asso. dir. Langley Research Center, 1961-67, dep. dir., 1967-68; asso. adminstr. manned space flight (tech.) NASA Hdqrs., Washington, 1968—, acting dir. Space Shuttle program, 1970—. Mem. Peninsula Airport Commn. for City Hampton, Va., 1961-68. Mem. subcom. stability and control NACA, 1955-58, mem. research airplane panel, 1952-58; spl. duty Mut. Weapons Def. Program. Recipient Outstanding Leadership medal NASA, 1963. Fellow Am. Astronautical Soc.; asso. fellow Am. Inst. Aero. and Astronautics, Tau Beta Pi. Contbr. articles in field. Home: 1113 Colingwood Rd Alexandria VA 22308 Office: NASA 400 Independence Washington DC 20003

DONLEAVY, JAMES PATRICK, writer; b. Bklyn., Apr. 23, 1926; student Trinity Coll., Dublin, Ireland; m. Mary Wilson Price; children—Philip, Karen. Served with USNR, World War II. Author: The Ginger Man (novel, later adapted as play), 1955; Fairy Tales of New York (drama), 1960; A Singular Man (novel, later adapted as play), 1963; Meet My Maker the Mad Molecule (short stories, sketches), 1964; The Saddest Summer of Samuel S. (novella, later adapted as play), 1966; The Beastly Beatitudes of Balthazar B. (novel), 1968, The Onion Eaters (novel), 1971; The Plays of J.P. Donleavy, 1972. Home: Balsoon House Bective County Meath Ireland

DONLEVY, THEODORE WILLIAM lawyer, corp. exec.; b. Kent, O., 1922. Home: 23 Beacon St Boston MA 02107

DONLEY, EDWIN I., army officer; b. Buchanan, Mich., May 9, 1918; s. Rolla Edward and Bernice (Bird) D.; B.S., U.S. Naval Acad., 1940; M.B.A., U. Mich., 1949; grad. Indsl. Coll. Armed Forces, 1961; m. Marion Miller, Aug. 2, 1940; children—Steven E., Kevin M., Douglas. Commd. 2d lt. U.S. Army, 1941, advanced through grades to maj. gen., 1970; supply and maintenance adviser Rep. of Korea Army Mil. Adv. Group, 1961-63; student officer U.S. Army Logistics Mgmt. Center, Ft. Lee, Va., 1963; Pershing Project mgr. U.S. Army Missle Command, Redstone Arsenal, Ala., 1963-66, dep. comdr. land combat systems, 1966-67; comdg. gen. U.S. Army Mobility Equipment Command, St. Louis, 1967-68; dep. comdg. gen. supply and maintenance U.S. Army Communication Zone, Europe, 1968-69; comdg. gen. U.S. Army Materiel Command, Europe, 1969, U.S. Army Missile Command, Redstone Arsenal, 1969—. Pres. Tenn. Valley council Boy Scouts Am.; spl. mem. bd. dirs. Huntsville (Ala.) Community Council. Decorated Legion of Merit with 2 oak leaf clusters, Bronze Star. Mem. Assn. U.S. Army, U.S. Naval Acad. Alumni Assn. Rotarian. Clubs: Willowbrook Country (Huntsville); Army-Navy Country (Arlington, Va.). Home: 1 Wadsworth Dr Redstone Arsenal AL 35808 Office: Hdqrs US Army Missile Command Redstone Arsenal AL 35809

DONLON, MARY H., judge; b. Utica, N.Y.; d. Joseph M. and Mary (Coughlin) Donlon; LL.B., Cornell U., 1921; LL.D., Skidmore Coll., 1947; Litt. D., Nazareth Coll., 1951, Marquette U., 1961; m. Martin J. Alger. Admitted to N.Y. State bar 1921, since practiced in N.Y.; mem. firm Burke and Burke, N.Y.C., 1928-44. Apptd. chmn. State Indsl. Bd., N.Y., 1944, chmn. State Workmen's Compensation Bd., 1945-55; apptd. by Pres. Eisenhower judge U.S. Customs Ct., 1955. Guest West Germany govt. for tour Germany, 1952. Trustee Cornell U., 1937—; mem. adv. council on social security 80th Congress. Mem. Am., N.Y.C. bar assns., N.Y. County Lawyer's Assn., Internat. Assn. Indsl. Accidents Bds. and Commns. (pres. 1948), Am. Assn. U. Women, Fedn. Bus. and Profl. Women (rep. Rep. Nat. Conv., 1952). Republican (co-mgr. Dewey-for-Gov. campaign, 1942; nat. adv. com. Citizens for Eisenhower, 1952; N.Y. State del.-at-large, Rep. Nat. convs., 1944, 48). Club: Cosmopolitan. Mary Donlon Workmen's Compensation Fund, lectures, N.Y. State Sch. Indsl. and Labor Relations, Cornell U., 1945. Dormitory at Cornell U. named in her honor Home: 3024 E 6th St Tucson AZ 85716 Office: US Customs Ct 1 Federal Plaza New York City NY 10007

DONLON, SEAN, Irish diplomat; b. Ireland, 1940; student St. Finian's Coll., Mullingar, 1953-58, Maynooth Coll., 1958-60; B.A., U. Coll., Dublin, 1960; m. Paula Doyle, 1964; children—Monica, Brendan. Adminstrv. officer Irish Dept. Finance, Dublin, 1961-63; 3d sec. Irish Dept. Fgn. Affairs, 1963-64; 1st sec. embassy of Ireland, Bonn, 1964-69; consul gen. of Ireland, Boston, 1969—. Decorated Verdienstkreuz Erste Klasse (Germany). Office: 437 Boylston St Boston MA 02116

DONNAHOE, ALAN STANLEY, newspaper exec.; b. Asheville, N.C., Aug. 27, 1916; s. Paul Albert and Kate (Stanley) D.; student pub. schs.; m. Elsie Pitts, 1938; children—Kate Stanley (Mrs. C. Porter Vaughan III), Maureen. Dir. research Richmond (Va.) C. of C., 1936-46, asst. exec. mgr., 1946-50; exec. sec. Richmond Inter-Club Council, 1938-41, Va. Soc. Pub. Accountants, Richmond, 1946-50; dir. research Richmond Newspapers, Inc., 1950-55, v.p., 1956-59, exec. v.p., asst. pub., 1959-66, pres., 1966—, also dir.; pres., chief exec. officer Media Gen., Inc., 1969—; pres., dir. Southeast Media, Inc., Media Gen. Financial Daily, Metro Guide, Inc., WRNL, Inc., Westover Pub. Co., Capitol Ins. Co., Yellow Tavern Corp. (all Richmond, Va.), Cablevision of Fredericksburg, Inc. (Va.), Tribune Co., Tampa, Fla.; dir. Security Fed. Savs. & Loan Co., UVB/State Planters, Beacon Press, (all Richmond, Va.), Evening News Pub. Co., Fidelity Engravers (both Newark, N.J.), Piedmont Pub. Co., Winston-Salem, N.C., Garden State Paper Co., Garfield, N.J., Morgan Mills, Lititz, Pa., WFLA, Inc., Tampa, Fla., Instant Type, Inc., Greensboro, N.C., Newspaper Preprint Corp., N.Y.C. Mem. bus. adv. com. U.S. Bur. Labor Statistics, 1948-49, U.S. Bur. Census, 1948-49; mem. Tax Study Commn., 1963-64, Va. Met. Area Commn., 1966-67, fiscal study com. Va. Adv. Legislative Com., 1959—. Bd. dirs., past pres. Richmond Eye Hosp.; pres. RPI Found., Richmond; bd. dirs. Richmond Meml. Hosp., Better Richmond, Inc., United Givers Fund, Richmond; pres. Collegiate Schs., 1967-68, now dir.; past pres. River Rd. Civic Assn. Served from pvt. to 1st lt., C.E., AUS, 1943-46; ETO; as 1st lt., Gen. Staff, U.S. Army, 1950-52. Mem. U.S., Richmond (pres. 1968) chambers of commerce, Va. State Bar. Contbr. articles to profl. jours. Home: 8912 Alendale Rd Richmond VA 23229 Office: 333 E Grace St Richmond VA 23219

DONNAHOO, ROBERT W., govt. ofcl.; b. Spartansburg, S.C., Oct. 8, 1911; s. Charles and Agatha (Pope) D.; m. Dorothy V. Watson, July 4, 1934 (dec.); m. 2d, Hallie Jean Cochran, July 2, 1938; 1 son, Robert. Indsl. textile engr. Inman Mills, 1930-36; rep. C.I.O., 1936-38, AFL, 1938-42; tech. commr. U.S. Conciliation Service, 1942-47; commr. Fed. Mediation and Conciliation Service, 1947-54, dir. Region II, 1954—. Home: 212 Thomas Av Riverton NJ 08077 Office: Mall Bldg 4th and Chestnut St Philadelphia PA 19106

DONNALLY, BAILEY LEWIS, physicist, educator; b. Deatsville, Ala., June 22, 1930; s. Bailey Lewis and Alice (Bell) D.; B.S., Auburn U., 1951, M.S., 1952; Ph.D., U. Minn., 1961; m. Patricia Joan Biesecker, Sept. 3, 1955; children—Bailey Lewis, Brian Earl, Diane Mae. Instr., asst. prof. physics Coll. St. Thomas, 1955-61, chmn. dept., 1959-61; asst. prof. physics Lake Forest (Ill.) Coll., 1961-63, asso. prof., 1963-66, prof., chmn. physics dept., 1966—. Vis. prof. Auburn U., summer 1961; vis. fellow Yale, 1966-67. Recipient Distinguished Service citation Am. Assn. Physics Tchrs., 1969. Fellow Am. Phys. Soc., A.A.A.S.; mem. Am. Assn. Physics Tchrs. (pres. 1970), Am. Assn. U. Profs., Am. Inst. Physics (bd. govs.), So. Assn. Sic. and Industry (hon.), Photog. Soc. Am., Commn. on Coll. Physics, Sigma Xi, Sigma Pi Sigma, Pi Mu Epsilon, Tau Beta Pi, Phi Kappa Phi. Contbr. articles profl. jours. Patentee in field. Home: 383 E Illinois Rd Lake Forest IL 60045

DONNAY, JOSEPH DESIRE HUBERT, crystallographer, ret. educator; b. Grandville, Belgium, June 6, 1902; s. Désiré Mathieu Joseph and Marie Madeleine (Doyen) D.; Candidat Ingénieur, U. Liége, 1922, Ingénieur civil des Mines, 1925; Ph.D., Stanford, 1929; m. Marie Madeleine Hennin, Dec. 23, 1931; children—Robert, Nicole; m. 2d, Gabrielle Eva Hamburger, July 25, 1949; children—Albert H., Victor J. Came to U.S., 1925; naturalized, 1939. Belgian-Am. Ednl. Found. fellow, Stanford, 1925-26, 1927-29; engr. Financo, Rabat, French Morocco, 1929-30; research asso., Stanford, 1930- 31, Harvard, summer 1937; asso. Johns Hopkins, 1931-39; prof. agrégé, U. Laval, Que., 1939-40, professeur titulaire, 1940-42 (on leave of absence, 1942-45); research chemist Expt. Sta., Hercules Powder Co., 1942-45; vis. prof. Johns Hopkins, 1945, prof. crystallography and mineralogy, 1946-71, emeritus, 1971—; professeur ordinaire U. Liége, 1946-47, prof. honoraire, 1948—; Fulbright lectr. Sorbonne, 1958-59. U.S.A. voting delegate to 1st Internat. Congress on Crystallography, 1948, substitute del. to 2d Internat. Congress, Stockholm, 1951; del. Nat. Acad. Sci.-NRC to Gen. Assembly Internat. Union Crystallography, Paris, 1954, Montreal, 1957, Moscow, 1966; U.S.A. Nat. Com. on Crystallography, 1948- 53, 56-61, 64-67. Fellow Geol. Soc. Am. (v.p. 1953), Mineral Soc. Am. (pres. 1953, Roebling medal 1971); corr. mem. Soc. Royale des Scis. de Liége, Geol. Soc. Belgium (v.p., 1946-47); mem. Assn. fr. de Crist. (v.p. 1959-60), French Mineral. Soc. (v.p. 1949), Am. Soc. for X-ray and Electron Diffraction (sec. 1944-46), Crystallographic Soc. Am. (v.p. 1946- 48, pres. 1949), Am. Crystallographic Assn. (council 1950, pres. 1956), Phi Beta Kappa, Sigma Xi. Author: Spherical Trigonometry after the Cesaro Method, 1945; Crystal Data, 1954, 63. Inventor diamond switch hwy. intersection system, 1968. Contbr. articles to sci. jours. Philologist. Home: 320 Cote St-Antoine Rd Montreal 217 Quebec Canada

DONNELL, EDWARD S., retail chain store co. exec.; b. Cleve., Sept. 16, 1919; s. Luke and Maybell Donnell; ed. Duke, 1941; m. Rose Kueffner, Oct. 25, 1941; children—William, Ann, Sally, Mark. With B.F. Goodrich Co., 1941-46; with Sears, Roebuck & Co., 1946-62, group mgr., Los Angeles, 1961-62; v.p., Eastern regional mgr. Montgomery Ward & Co., Balt., 1962-64, exec. v.p., 1964-66, pres., Chgo., 1966—; dir. Pennwalt Corp. Mem. Pi Kappa Alpha. Clubs: Chicago, Indian Hill, Economic, Commercial. Home: 1207 Whitebridge Hill Winnetka IL 60093 Office: 918 Chicago Av Chicago IL 60611

DONNELL, FORREST C., lawyer, ex-gov.; b. Quitman, Mo., Aug. 20, 1884; s. John Cary and Barbara Lee (Waggoner) D.; A.B., U. Mo., 1904, LL.B., 1907, LL.D., 1960; LL.D., Westminster Coll., Mo., 1941; m. Hilda Hays, Jan. 29, 1913; children—Ruth, John Lanier. Admitted to Mo. bar, 1907, practiced in office of Selden P. Spencer, St. Louis, 1907-11; mem. Spencer & Donnell, 1911-25, Spencer, Donnell & McDonald, 1925-28, Holland, Lashly & Donnell, 1928-33, Donnell & McDonald, 1933-41; in pvt. practice law, St. Louis, 1951-56; mem. firm Donnell, Schoenbeck & Donnell, St. Louis, 1956-67, Donnell, Schoenbeck & La Tourette, 1967; individual practice law, 1967—. Pres. Assn. Young Republicans Mo., 1916; chmn. bd. mgrs. Mo. Sch. for Blind, 1931-34; former trustee State Hist. Soc. Mo.; chmn. bd. Downtown Y.M.C.A., 1932-35; mem., former chmn. St. Louis adv. bd. Salvation Army; pres. Mo. Sunday Sch. Council Religious Edn., 1929-31; pres. St. Louis City Evangelization Union of M.E. Ch., 1930-34; former chmn. St. Louis World Court Com.; del. from Mo. to Gen. Conf. Methodist Ch., Atlantic City, N.J., 1932. Elected gov. of Mo., 1941-45; elected U.S. senator from Mo., 1945-51. Bd. trustees Jefferson Nat. Expansion Meml. Assn. Mem. Am. Bar Assn. (mem. first Ho. of Dels.; chmn. sect. com. on coordination of state and local bar assns., 1936-37; mem. com. Am. Citizenship 1934-35; mem. com. legal aid, 1920-28, etc.), Mo. Bar, Am. Law Inst., Assn. Bar City N.Y., Bar Assn. St. Louis, Mo. Acad. Squires, Order of Coif, Phi Beta Kappa, Kappa Sigma, Phi Delta Phi. Republican. Methodist. Mason (33); Past Grand Master of Grand Lodge of Masons of Mo.; Dep. for Mo. of Scottish Rite, 1937-39. Clubs: Noonday, Scottish Rite (St. Louis). Home: 245 Union Blvd St. Louis, MO 63108. Office: 611 Olive St St Louis MO 63101

DONNELL, FRANKLIN HUNKINS, corp. exec.; b. Los Angeles, Sept. 6, 1904; s. John Tilden and Stella (Hunkins) D.; student Harvard (mil.) Sch. of Los Angeles; m. Emily White, June 25, 1926; 1 son, Franklin H. Sales rep. Frick, Martin & Co., investments, Los Angeles, 1922-25; stock dept. mgr. Stevens, Page & Sterling, investments, Los Angeles, 1926; v.p. Jones, Hubbard & Donnell, mem. Los Angeles Stock Exchange, 1927-31; rep. Dean Witter-Wm. Cavalier & Co., Los Angeles, 1932-41; with Metal Products Engring., Inc., Los Angeles, 1942—, v.p., 1942-43, pres., 1943-54, chmn., 1954—; v.p., dir., chmn. finance com. Consolidated Electrodynamics Corp., Pasadena, Cal., 1946-60; pres., dir. Con-Vac Realty, Rochester, N.Y., 1953-56; v.p., dir. Electro Data Corp., Pasadena, 1954-56, Consolidated Systems Corp., Monrovia, Cal., 1959-61; chmn. investment com. Bell & Howell Retirement Trust, 1961-69, Lear Siegler Profit Sharing Trust, 1965- -; dir. of Anadex Corp., Los Angeles. Dir. Bel Air Assos. (pres. 1963-65); trustee Descanso Gardens; bd. dirs. Historic Los Angeles Assn. Mem. Asso. Cal. Inst. Tech. (v.p., dir.), Friends Harvey Mudd Coll. (founding mem.), Cal. Mfrs. Assn., C. of C., S.A.R. Republican (finance com. So. Cal. 1934-60). Episcopalian (vestryman). Clubs: Bel Air Country, California, Lincoln, Men's Garden (Los Angeles). Home: 635 Carcassonne Rd Bel Air Los Angeles CA 90024 Office: 360 N Sierra Madre Villa Pasadena CA 91109

DONNELL, JAMES C., II, bus. exec.; b. Findlay, O., June 30, 1910; s. Otto Dewey and Glenn (McClelland) D.; A.B., Princeton, 1932; m. Dolly Louise DeVine, July 2, 1932; 1 dau., Susan (Mrs. Harry W. Konkel). Mgr. crude oil sales Marathon Oil Co., Findlay, 1932-36, dir., 1936—, v.p., 1937-48, pres., 1948—; dir. Mountain Fuel Supply Co., 1st Nat. Bank, Findlay, O., Nat. City Bank Cleve., Armco Steel Corp., Libbey-Owens-Ford Co., Phelps Dodge Corp., N.Y. Life Ins. Co. Mem. world council, nat. council YMCA. Mem. Am. Petroleum Inst., Am. Assn. Petroleum Geologists, Nat. Petroleum Council, The Conf. Bd., Sigma Xi, Phi Beta Kappa. Republican. Presbyn. Elk. Clubs: Country (Findlay, O.); Princeton, Links, University (N.Y.C.); Duquesne (Pitts.); Union (Cleve.); Inverness (Toledo); Detroit; Bohemian (San Francisco). Home: 839 S Main St Findlay OH 45840 Office: 539 S Main St Findlay OH 45840

DONNELL, JOHN RANDOLPH, petroleum exec.; b. Findlay, O., June 22, 1912; s. Otto Dewey and Glenn (McClelland) D.; B.S., Case Inst. Tech., 1934; m. Margaret Louise Watt, Feb. 1, 1939; children—John Randolph, Ann (Mrs. R. Kennedy Davis), William Watt, Thomas Blakeman, Richard Holmes. Spl. rep. Marathon Oil Co., Findlay, 1938, asst. to mgr. prodn., 1944-50, treas., 1950-54, v.p., dir., 1954—, v.p. charge internat. activities, 1961-65, sr. v.p. internat., 1965-67, sr. v.p. corporate planning, 1967-69, sr. v.p. finance and planning, 1969—; pres. Marathon Internat. Oil Co., 1961-67; dir. First Nat. Bank Findlay, 1939—, chmn. bd., 1947—; dir. Toledo Trust Co. Pres., Bd. Edn. Findlay, 1944-54. Trustee Case Western Res. U., Cleve. Regional chmn. Boy Scouts Am., 1953- 56, now mem. nat. exec. bd. Mem. Sigma Xi, Tau Beta Pi. Presbyn. Home: 2200 S Main St Findlay OH 45840 Office: 539 S Main St Findlay OH 45840

DONNELLAN, KEITH SEDGWICK, educator, philosopher; b. Washington, June 25, 1931; s. John S. and Louise (Nuckolls) D.; B.A., U. Md., 1953; M.A., Cornell U., 1954, Ph.D., 1961; m. Susan Patton, Sept. 6, 1952; children—Kevin Keith, Scott Sedgwick. From instr. to prof. philosophy Cornell U., Ithaca, N.Y., 1958-70; prof. philosophy U. Cal. at Los Angeles, 1970—. Vis. prof. Harvard, 1961-62, 68, summer 1969, Mass. Inst. Tech., 1968, U. Cal. at Los Angeles, 1966 U. Mich., summer 1966, Stanford, summer 1968. Served to 1st lt. USAF, 1956-58. Mem. Phi Beta Kappa, Phi Kappa Phi. Co-editor Philos. Rev., 1962-63, 65, 67, 68-69. Contbr. articles to profl. jours. Office: Dept Philosophy Univ Cal Los Angeles CA 90024

DONNELLAN, THOMAS A., bishop; b. N.Y.C., Jan. 24, 1914; s. Andrew and Margaret (Egan) b.; A.B., St. Joseph's Sem., 1939; J.C.D., Cath. U. Am., 1942. Ordained priest Roman Catholic Ch., 1939; vice chancellor Archdiocese N.Y., 1947-50; synodal judge Marriage Tribunal, 1950-58; chancellor Archdiocese N.Y., 1958-62; rector St. Joseph's Sem., 1962-64; bishop of Ogdensburg, N.Y., 1964-68; archbishop of Atlanta, 1968—. Decorated knight comdr. Knights Holy Sepulchre. Address: 136 W Wesley Rd NW Atlanta GA 30305

DONNELLEY, DIXON, govt. ofcl.; b. Forest Hills, N.Y., July 29, 1915; s. Patrick John and Katherine Marie (Dixon) D.; student Columbia, 1934-37; m. Lucia Tarquinio de Sousa, Mar. 27, 1943; 1 dau., Leigh Patricia. Jr. reporter N.Y. Daily News, 1936-37; city editor Havana (Cuba) Post, 1937-40; asst. city editor Washington Daily News, 1941-42; news editor Office Coordinator Inter-Am. Affairs 1942; press attache Am. embassy, Mexico City, 1946-47; asst. pub. affairs officer Am. embassy, Santiago, Chile, 1947-48; press attache Am. embassy, Buenos Aires, Argentina, 1948-50; information officer Am. republics area State Dept., 1950; editor, pub. Vision News mag., Rio de Janeiro, Brazil, 1950-52; mem. pub. relations staff Creole Petroleum Corp., 1954-55; editorial dir. com. juvenile delinquency U.S. Senate, 1955; pub. relations dir. Kefauver Presdl. Campaign, 1955-56; cons. information Pres. Com. Scientists and Engrs., 1956-58; spl. asst. to under sec. state, 1958-61; spl. asst. to sec. treasury, Treasury Dept., 1961-66; asst. sec. of state for pub. affairs, Dept. State, 1966-69; spl. asst. to sec. treasury, Treasury Dept., 1969-70. Del. numerous nat. and internat. confs. Served with USAAF, 1942-46. Mem. Fgn. Service Assn. Clubs: Nat. Press, Federal City (Washington); Overseas Press (N.Y.C.). Author: Establishing and Operating a Small Newspaper, 1946; also mag. articles. Home: 4100 Cathedral Av Washington DC 20016

DONNELLEY, GAYLORD, printing exec.; b. Chgo., May 19, 1910; s. Thomas E. and Laura L. (Gaylord) D.; A.B., Yale, 1931; LL.D., Wabash Coll., 1965; m. Dorothy W. Ranney, May 4, 1935; children—Elliott R., Strachan, Laura Gaylord, Naomi Williams. With

R.R. Donnelley & Sons Co., Chgo., 1932—, v.p. 1947-52, pres., 1952-64, chmn. bd., 1964—; dir. Reuben H. Donnelley Corp., Dun & Bradstreet, Inc., Borg-Warner Corp., First Nat. Bank Chgo., First Chgo. Corp. Mem. Ill. Nature Preserves Commn., Gov.'s Adv. Council State of Ill.; mem. exec. com. Chgo. Community Trust. Chmn. bd. trustees U. Chgo.; trustee Sarah Lawrence Coll., Newberry Library, United Presbyn. Found., Ducks Unlimited, Inc., Nat. Recreation and Park Assn.; bd. dirs. Community Fund Chgo., Research Found. Served as lt. comdr. USNR, 1942-45. Decorated Purple Heart. Mem. Nat. Alliance Businessmen (mem. bd. Chgo. met. area), N.A.M. (dir.), C. of C. U.S. (policy com.). Republican. Presbyn. Home: Almond Rd Libertyville IL 60048 Office: 2223 King Dr Chicago IL 60616

DONNELLY, CHARLES EDWARD, lawyer; b. Oswego, N.Y., Aug. 1, 1890; s. Charles Edward and Elizabeth (Henrick) D.; LL.B., U. So. Cal., 1912; m. Dorcas Metcalf, Apr. 21, 1920; children—George Swanwick, Margaret E. (Mrs. Ellsworth H. Kendig), Charles Edward. Admitted to Cal. bar, 1912, since practiced Los Angeles; with Donnelly, Clark, Chase & Haakh and predecessor firms, 1914—; dir., sec. Union Security Co., Los Angeles; dir., counsel Fitger Cal. Co.; v.p., counsel, dir. Kelco Co.; sec., dir. Asso. Investment Corp.; dir. Scotia Marine Products Ltd., Sixth and Spring Corp., Metalite Co.; mem. panel arbitrators N.Y. Stock Exchange. Trustee Pomona Coll. Mem. Delta Theta Phi, Mason (32). Clubs: California, Athletic, Stock Exchange (Los Angeles); Pacific Coast (Long Beach, Cal.); Irvine Coast Country. Newport Harbor Yacht (Newport Beach, Cal.). Home: 139 S Irving Blvd Los Angeles CA 90004 Office: 600 S Spring St Los Angeles CA 90014

DONNELLY, EDWARD JOHN, cons. engr.; b. Balt., June 12, 1915; s. John Joseph and Agnes (Tarr) D.; B.Engring., Johns Hopkins, 1937; D.Sc. (hon.), Loyola Coll., Balt., 1967; m. Anne B. Lawrence, July 6, 1940; children—Anne Lawrence (Mrs. Stephen D. Langhoff), Kathleen Patricia (Mrs. William J. Solomon), Sharon Elizabeth, Deborah Anne. With J.E. Greiner Co., Inc., Balt., 1937—, chmn. bd., 1970—; chmn. exec. com., dir. Easco Corp., Balt., 1969—, vice chmn., 1970—; chmn., dir. Greiner AG, Zug, Switzerland; chmn. bd. Greiner Environmental Systems, Inc., Diversified Services Corp., Balt., Diversified Services Ins. Agy., Inc., Balt.; pres. Sea, Inc., Balt.; dir. Whiteford, Falk & Mask, Inc., Balt. Mem. president's bd. Loyola Coll., 1956—, chmn., 1965—, trustee, 1967—; bd. dirs. King St. Ferdinand III Coll. Scholarship Fund, Harrisburg, Pa., 1962—, Golfers Charitable Assn., 1967—; trustee Bon Secours Hosp., 1963—; bd. mgrs. Md. Gen. Hosp., 1963—; exec. com. Catholic Youth Orgn. Retreat House, Sparks, Md. Served to lt. USNR, 1943-45. Decorated knight Equestrian Order Holy Sepulchre Jerusalem. Mem. Balt. Symphony Orch., Balt. Mus. Art, Am. Arbitration Assn., Am. Inst. Cons. Engrs., Am. Soc. C.E., Nat., Md. socs. profl. engrs., Soc. Am. Mil. Engrs., Cons. Engring. Council Md., Md. Assn. Engrs., Engring. Soc. Balt., Internat. Bridge Tunnel and Turnpike Assn., Prestressed Concrete Inst., Hwy. Research Bd. (div. pres. 1964, bd. dirs. 1968—), Am. Road Builders Assn. Clubs: Maryland, Baltimore Country, Center, Johns Hopkins, Advertising (Balt.); Annapolis (Md.) Yacht; Seaview Country (Absecon, N.J.). Home: 117 St Albans Way Baltimore MD 21212 Office: 201 N Charles St Baltimore MD 21201

DONNELLY, FREDERICK STOCKHAM, Jr., bldg. materials co. exec.; b. Balt., Dec. 23, 1919; s. Frederick Stockham and Catherine (Wright) D.; B.A., Swarthmore Coll., 1941; m. Margaret Frances Dougherty, Jan. 3, 1942; children—Kate Purnell (Mrs. Robert Hickey), Margaret Wolfe (Mrs. Peter P. Brubaker), Susan Wright. With Armstrong Cork Co., 1941—, gen. sales mgr., 1964-65, treas., 1966- 67, v.p., gen. mgr. internat. operations, 1968—. Bd. dirs. Lancaster County chapter Am. Red Cross. First v.p. Lancaster County Council Alcoholism, 1966—. Served to lt. USNR, 1942-45. Mem. Kappa Sigma. Club: Lancaster Country. Home: Carriage House 202 N President Av Lancaster PA 17603 Office: Armstrong Cork Co Liberty and Charlotte Sts Lancaster PA 17604

DONNELLY, GEORGE EDWARD, newspaper exec.; b. Wellesley, Mass., Feb. 22, 1913; s. John Joseph and Mary Ellen (Doocey) D.; S.B., Mass. Inst. Tech., 1936; grad. Air Force Mgmt. Course, Harvard, 1942; m. Thelma Louise Carson, Mar. 5, 1946; children—Mary Kathleen, Patricia Ann, Nancy Louise. Cadet engr. Babcock Wilcox Co., 1936-38; adminstrv. asst. N.Y. Daily News, 1938-42, asst. bus. mgr., 1946-55, bus. mgr., asst. treas., 1955-62, gen. mgr., sec., dir., 1962—; treas. Chicago-Tribune-N.Y. News Syndicate; treas., dir. WPIX, TV, Inc.; v.p., dir. News Bldg. Corp.; v.p. News Syndicate Co., Inc.; pres., dir. Daniels & Kennedy, Inc.; asst. treas., dir. Ill. Atlantic Corp.; dir. Newsynd Radio Relay, Inc. V.p., dir. Joseph M. Patterson Charitable Found.; mem. exec. com. MIT Alumni Center N.Y. Served from pvt. to maj., USAAF, 1942-46. Registered profl. engr., Ohio. Mem. Pubs. Assn. N.Y.C. (chmn. 1961-63), News Welfare Assn. (dir.), Am. Soc. M.E., Am. Soc. Safety Engrs. Clubs: Engineers, Advertising, MIT (N.Y.C.); Overseas Press, Union League, Canadian. Home: 84 Oriole Way Westbury NY 11590 Office: 220 E 42d St New York City NY 10017

DONNELLY, HAROLD COOPER, govt. ofcl.; b. Lynn, Mass., Feb. 1, 1910; s. Thomas L. and Nellie (Cooper) D.; B.S., U.S. Mil. Acad., 1933; m. Dorothy E. Bishop, Feb. 16, 1934; children—Margaret (Mrs. Peter J. Hino), Judith (Mrs. Warren A. Samouce). Commd. 2d lt. U.S. Army, 1933, advanced through grades to lt. gen. USAF, 1964; dep. chief of staff, chief staff CBI, 1945-46; mil. exec. to undersec. office Sec. Air Force, 1950-51; chief plans br. SHAPE, 1954- 57; asst. dept. chief staff for plans and programs Hdqrs. USAF, 1957-60; comdr. field command Def. Atomic Support Agy., 1960-63, dir. agy., 1964-68; asst. dep. chief staff research and devel. Hdqrs. USAF, 1963-64; ret., 1968; mgr. Albuquerque operations office U.S. AEC, 1968- -. Dir. Albuquerque Nat. Bank. Mem. regional com. on sci. adminstrn. U. N.M.; mem. Nat. Council on Crime and Delinquency, Gov.'s Com. Tech. Excellence in N.M.; v.p. Kit Carson council Boy Scouts Am.; chmn. fed. exec. bd. Albuquerque-Santa Fe Fed. Assn.; mem. Armed Forces Adv. Com., Albuquerque. Chmn., Presbyn. Hosp. Center Found.; bd. dirs. United Community Fund. Mem. Council on Fgn. Relations. Club: Albuquerque Country. Home: 204 16th St SW Albuquerque NM 87104 Office: U S AEC P O Box 5400 Kirtland AFB-East Albuquerque NM 87115

DONNELLY, HAROLD GEORGE, educator; b. Detroit, Apr. 21, 1912; s. John and Sarah Elizabeth (Roth) D.; B.S., Wayne State U., 1936; M.S., U. Mich., 1938, Ph.D., 1951; m. Dorothy Ruth Flemming, Apr. 13, 1938; children—Richard George, Edwin Harold. Instr. chem. engring. Wayne State U., Detroit, 1936-37, asst. prof., asso. prof., prof. chem. engring., 1938-53, prof., head dept. chem. engring., metall. engr., 1953-69, sr. prof. chem. engring., 1969—, U. rep. AEC Nuclear Sci., Engring. Fellowship Program; asst. dir. research Compressed Indsl. Gases, Inc., Detroit, 1937-38; cons. various indsl. firms; v.p., dir. Apex Chem. Mfg. Co., Detroit, Spectrum Assos., Inc., Fraser, Mich.; dir. Cheradco, Inc. Chmn. Architects, Profl. Engrs. and Land Surveyors Council on Registration State Mich., 1961-62. Registered profl. engr., Mich. Fellow Am. Inst. Chemists; mem. Am. Inst. Chem.E. (past com. chmn., sec.), Am. Soc. Engring. Edn. (com. chmn.), Am. Chem. Soc., A.A.A.S., Engring. Soc. Detroit (past com. chmn.), Sigma Xi, Theta Tau (past nat. grand vice regent), TAu Beta Pi, Phi Lambda Upsilon, Alpha Sigma Mu. Presbyn. (ruling elder). Patentee in field. Home: 1241 Falcon Av Dearborn MI 48128 Office: 664 Putnam Av Detroit MI 48202

DONNELLY, JOSEPH FRANCIS, clergyman; b. Norwich, Conn., May 1, 1909; s. John E. and Bridget M. (Shea) D.; B.A., St. Mary U., Balt., 1930, M.A., 1931; LL.D., Fairfield (Conn.) U., 1952. Ordained priest Roman Catholic Ch., 1934; asst. pastor, Waterbury, Conn., 1934-44; chaplain Highland Heights Ch., New Haven, 1944-58, St. John the Baptist Ch., New Haven, 1958; aux. bishop Archdiocese Hartford, Conn., 1964—, vicar gen., 1965—, dir. Diocesan Labor Inst., 1942-64. Hearing officer region I, NWLB, 1943-45; vice chmn. Conn. Bd. Mediation and Arbitration, 1943, chmn., 1949-65; arbitrator Am. Arbitration Assn., 1953—, Nat. Acad. Arbitrators, 1957- -; chmn. bd. ethics New Haven, 1960—; mem. New Haven Redevel. Agy., 1962—; commr. New Haven Housing Authority, 1963—. Chmn. exec. com. bd. trustees St. Raphael Hosp., New Haven, 1960—. Recipient Peter McGuire Meml. award Conn. Fedn. Labor, 1954, Distinguished Service award Conn. Fedn. Tchrs., 1956, Conn. Outstanding Citizen award Grand Lodge Sons of Italy, 1957, Veritas award Providence Coll. Alumni Assn., 1964, McAuliffe medal award Diocesan Labor Inst., 1965. Home: 55 Mumford Rd New Haven CT 06515 Office: 700 Middletown Av North Haven CT 06473

DONNELLY, JOSEPH PETER, historian, educator; b. O'Connor, Neb., Sept. 20, 1905; s. Peter Thomas and Bridget Ann (Mawe) D.; A.B., St. Louis U., 1928, M.A., 1929, Ph.D., 1940; S.T.L., St. Mary's Coll., 1937. Joined S.J., 1923; asst. prof. history Regis Coll., 1940-43; asso. prof. history St. Louis U., 1943-55, dir. libraries, 1946-55; asso. prof. Marquette U., 1955-56, prof. history, 1956—, chmn. dept. history, 1960—. Mem. Am., Mo. hist. assns., A.L.A., Orgn. Am. Historians, Spl. Libraries Assn. Home: 201 Dempster Evanston IL 60201

DONNELLY, KENNETH GERALD, educator; b. Bklyn., Jan. 17, 1937; s. William Joseph and Anne Frances (McLaughlin) D.; student Mother of Savior Sem., 1957-58; B.A., Cath. U., 1960, M.A. (univ. fellow), 1961; Ph.D. (univ. fellow), U. Pitts., 1964; m. Carole Anne Dieter, Jan. 20, 1962; children—Carole, Andrew, Patrick, Edwin. Instr. Gallaudet Coll., Washington, 1961-62, asst. prof., 1964, asso. prof., 1965; dir. speech and hearing services Cath. Charities, Rockville Centre, N.Y., 1966-67; asso. prof. speech and theater arts U. Cin., 1967-69, prof., 1969—, head dept., 1969—. Fellow Am. Speech and Hearing Assn.; mem. Ohio Speech and Hearing Assn., Societe Internationale d'Audiologie, Acad. Rehabilitative Audiology, Nat. Rehab. Assn. Author: Hearing Therapy for Young Deaf Adults, 1964; Hearing and Speech: A Manual for Orientation, 1964. Home: 1069 Meadowind Circle Cincinnati OH 45231

DONNELLY, MARJORIE MORRISON, (Mrs. James Ford Donnelly, Jr.), state govt. ofcl.; b. Hawthorne, Fla., Aug. 30, 1919; d. Columbus Franklin and Blanche (Sparkman) Morrison; B.S. in Home Econ., Fla. State Coll. Women, 1940; M.S. in Nutrition, U. Tenn., 1945; m. James Ford Donnelly, Jr., Jan. 14, 1961 (dec. June 1966). Dir. nutrition services Fla. Bd. Health, Jacksonville, 1948-58; regional nutrition cons. children's bur. Dept. Health, Edn. and Welfare, Denver, 1958-61; specialist charge foods and nutrition N.C. Agrl. Extension Service, Raleigh, 1966—; TV lectr., 1965—. Mem. Raleigh Woman's Club, 1962—. Served with USPHS, 1945-47. Named N.C. Dietitian of Year, N.C. Deitetic Assn., 1969. Fellow Am. Pub. Health Assn.; mem. Am. Dietetic Assn. (pres.), Am. Home Econ. Assn. Democrat. Methodist. Home: 2325 Champion Ct Raleigh NC 27606 Office: 213 Ricks Hall NC State U Raleigh NC 27607

DONNELLY, ROBERT CLINTON, banker; b. Toledo, Apr. 9. 1926; s. Orra C. and Enid (George) D.; student U. Toledo, 1947-50; grad. Bank Adminstrn. Inst., U. Wis., 1967; m. Lois Jean Grappy, Oct. 2, 1959. Process engr. A.O. Smith Corp., Toledo, 1950-55; asst. auditor Toledo Trust Co., 1956-68; auditor Union Commerce Bank, Cleve., 1968—. Served with inf., AUS, 1944-46; PTO. Mem. Bank Adminstrn. Inst., Am. Inst. Banking, Fraternal Order of Police Assn. Mason (Shriner). Home: 4920 Devon Dr North Olmsted OH 44070 Office: 917 Euclid Av Cleveland OH 44101

DONNELLY, ROBERT LEO, rubber co. exec.; b. Springfield, Mass., May 9, 1925; s. Leo Joseph and Ruth Gertrude (Meramble) D.; B.A. with honors, U. Conn., 1951, LL.B., 1955; m. Elizabeth Anne Lyons, Nov. 29, 1947; 1 son, Robert Leo. With Ernst & Ernst, Hartford, Conn., 1951-59; with Armstrong Rubber Co., West Haven, Conn., 1959—, sec., corp. atty., 1966—; admitted to Conn. bar, 1955. Served with AUS, 1943-46. C.P.A., Conn. Mem. Am. Bar Assn., Am. Inst. C.P.A.'s. Home: 680 S Greenbrier Dr Orange CT 06477 Office: 500 Sargent Dr New Haven CT 06507

DONNELLY, RUSSELL JAMES, educator, physicist; b. Hamilton, Ont., Can., Apr. 16, 1930; s. Clifford Ernest and Bessie (Harrison) D.; B.Sc., McMaster U., 1951, M.Sc., 1952; M.S., Yale, 1953, Ph.D., 1956; m. Marian Card, Jan. 21, 1956; 1 son, James. Faculty, U. Chgo., 1956-66, prof. physics, 1965-66; prof. physics, chmn. dept. U. Ore., Eugene, 1966—; co-founder Pine Mountain Obs., 1967—. Cons. Gen. Motors Co. Research Labs., 1958-68, NSF, 1968—; spl. research physics fluids, especially hydrodynamic stability and superfluidity. Bd. dirs. U. Ore. Devel. Fund. Alfred P. Sloan fellow, 1959-63. Fellow Am. Phys. Soc. (exec. com. div. fluid dynamics 1966—, sec-treas. 1967-70, vice-chmn. 1970-71); mem. Am. Assn. U. Profs., A.A.A.S., Am. Assn. Physics Tchrs., Am. Astron. Soc. Episcopalian. Clubs: Cosmos (Washington); Town (Eugene). Contbr. papers to profl. lit. Editor: (with Herman, Prigogine) Non-Equilibrium Thermodynamics Variational Techniques and Stability, 1966; (with Parks, Glaberson) Experimental Superfluidity, 1967. Asso. editor Physics of Fluids, 1966-68. Home: 2175 Olive St Eugene, OR 97405.

DONNELLY, THOMAS CLAUDE, former univ. pres.; b. Rockcastle, W.Va., Apr. 1, 1905; s. Hugh Parker and Rose Etta (Parsons) D.; A.B. magna cum laude, Marshall Coll., 1926, Litt.D., 1953; A.M., N.Y. U., 1928, Ph.D., 1930; m. Mabel Stanley, Dec. 21, 1928 (dec. June 1936); 1 son, Thomas Alan; m. 2d, Dorothea Berry, Dec. 17, 1938. Coll. instr., N.Y. U., 1930; prof. polit. sci., N.M. State Tchrs. Coll., 1931-33, Marshall Coll., 1933-35; prof. govt., head dept., U. N.M., 1935-42, 1945-47, dean Coll. Arts and Scis., 1947-52, dir. div. govt. research, 1945-47, dir. summer session; pres. N.M. Highlands U., 1952-70. Dist. information exec. Office of Price Adminstrn., 1942, regional information exec., 1943, dir. field operations, 1944; dep. administr. O.P.A. for information, 1944; asst. adminstr. O.P.A., 1945; mem. N.M. Merit System Commn., 1939; mem. N.M. Bd. Suprs., Courtesy and Information div., 1940; mem. N.M. Little Hoover Commn., 1951-52; cons. Princeton Surveys, 1950. Mem. Am. Polit. Sci. Assn., Western Polit. Sci. Assn. (pres. 1948-49), Am. Soc. Pub. Adminstrn., Phi Kappa Phi, Kappa Delta Pi, Pi Gamma Mu, Pi Sigma Alpha. Editor: Rocky Mountain Politics, 1940. Author: The Government of New Mexico, 1945. Co-author: The 1928 Campaign, 1931; New Mexico History and Civics, 1933; The 1932 Campaign, 1935; The Story of New Mexico, 1936. Home: 3117 San Joaquin SE Albuquerque NM 87106

DONNELLY, THOMAS JOSEPH, lawyer; b. Pitts., Mar. 4, 1925; s. Thomas E. and Ruth L. (Beitzer) D.; student Mass. Inst. Tech., 1943-44; B.S. in Engring., U. Mich., 1946, J.D., 1950; m. Marilyn A. Pfohl, Apr. 16, 1955; children—Thomas C., Elizabeth A., Daria, Heather, Michael, Marilyn, Peter. Student engr. Westinghouse Electric Corp., 1946-47; admitted to Pa. bar, 1951, since practiced in Pitts.; dir. Presdl. Exchange Fund, Inc., Pabst Brewing Co., Empire Fund, Inc., Pension Leaders Fund, Inc., Federated Research Corp., Federated Investors, Inc., Boston Fund. Fund, Inc., Second Presdl. Exchange Fund, Inc., Third Empire Fund, Inc., Fourth Empire Fund, Inc., Fifth Empire Fund, Inc., Sixth Empire Fund, Inc., Fifth Presdl. Exchange Fund, Inc., Federated Dual- Exchange Fund, Inc., Am. Leaders Fund, Inc., Fund for U.S. Govt. Securities, Inc. Trustee Carlow Coll., Pitts. Dir. Young Republicans Allegheny County, 1954-55. Served as apprentice seaman USNR, 1943-46. Mem. Barristers Soc., Am., Pa., Allegheny County bar assns., Tau Beta Pi. Roman Catholic. Clubs: Toastmasters, University of Mich. Lawyers (Ann Arbor, Mich.); University, Duquesne. Home: 1085 Shady Av Pittsburgh PA 15232 Office: Union Trust Bldg Pittsburgh PA 15219

DONNELLY, THOMAS RENN, Jr., service orgn. exec.; b. Steubenville, O., May 23, 1939; s. Thomas Renn and Flora (Conti) D.; B.S. in Chem. Engring., Princeton, 1961; m. Marie Christine McCafferty, Feb. 23, 1963; children—Thomas Renn III, Derek Sevier, Terence Reese. Sales rep. Johns Manville Sales Corp., 1960-63; sales engr. Air Products & Chems., Inc., 1963-65; supr. Air Products & Chems., Inc., Allentown, Pa., 1965-67; dir. adminstrn. U.S. Jaycees, 1967-68, exec. v.p., 1969-70; bd. dirs. Nat. Center for Voluntary Action, 1970, exec. v.p., 1970—; pres. T.R. Donnelly & Asso., Inc., 1970—. Sec.-treas. War Meml. Found. Mem. Nat. council Boy Scouts Am., 1969—. Bd. dirs. Tulsa Council Chs., 1968-70, Citizens for Justice with Order, 1969—, Tulsa A.R.C., 1969—, Nat. Conf. Christians and Jews, 1969—; pres. trustees On the Bricks, halfway house for ex-convicts, 1968-71; bd. advisers Boys Clubs Am., 1968-70. Named one of outstanding young men in Am., 1966. Mem. Am. Soc. Assn. Execs., Tulsa C. of C. Presbyn. (deacon 1968-70). Mailing address: Office: 1735 Eye St NW Washington DC 20006

DONNELLY, TOM, journalist; book editor Washington News. Office: 1013 13th St Washington DC 20005 *

DONNEM, ROLAND WILLIAM, business exec.; b. Seattle, Nov. 8, 1929; s. William Rolland and Mary Louise (Hughes) D.; B.A., Yale, 1952; J.D. magna cum laude, Harvard, 1957; m. Sarah Brandon Lund, Feb. 18, 1961; children—Elizabeth Prince, Sarah Madison. Admitted to N.Y. bar, 1958, Supreme Ct. bar, 1963, D.C. bar, 1969; with Davis, Olk & Wardwell, N.Y.C., 1957-63, 64-69; law sec. appellate div. N.Y. Supreme Ct., N.Y.C., 1963-64; dir. policy planning antitrust div. Justice Dept., Washington, 1969-71; v.p., sec., gen. counsel Standard Brands, Inc., N.Y.C., 1971—. Chmn. pub. utilities com. Spring Valley-Wesley Heights Citizens Assn., Washington, 1970. Served from ensign to lt. (j.g.) USNR, 1952-54. Mem. Fed., Am., N.Y. State bar assns., Fed. Bar Council, Bar Assn. D.C., Am. Law Inst., Am. Judicature Soc., Nat. Panel Arbitrators, Am. Arbitration Assn. Republican. Presbyn. Clubs: Yale, Lunch (N.Y.C.); University (Washington). Contbr. articles to profl. jours. Office: 625 Madison Av New York City NY

DONNER, ARVIN NEHEMIAH, educator; b. Dayton, Wis., Mar. 25, 1898; s. Henry Albert and Carrie Belle (Burnham) D.; student Lawrence Coll., 1915-17, U. Minn., 1920-22, Columbia, 1930; B.S., State U. Ia., 1927, M.A., 1928, Ph.D., 1937; m. Florence Myrtle Graham, June 4, 1922; 1 son, Arvin Nehemiah. High sch. tchr., Mason City, Ia., 1920; elementary sch. prin., Ft. Madison, Ia., 1920-23, jr. high sch. prin., 1923-27; platoon sch. prin., Port Arthur, Tex., 1928-32, jr. high sch. prin., 1932-36, sr. high sch. prin., 1937-39; asso. prof. edn. U. Houston, 1939-42; asst. supt. schs., Houston, 1942-45; dir. Sch. Edn., Grad. Sch., U. Houston, 1945-50, dean Coll. Edn., 1950-66, prof. adminstrn. and supervision, 1966-68, dean, prof. emeritus, 1968—. Vis. summer prof. U. Ia., 1937-38, U. Ark., 1929; Ind. State Tchrs. Coll., 1948, U. Tex., 1949. Mem. Am. Assn. Sch. Adminstrs. Phi Delta Kappa, Kappa Delta Phi, Phi Kappa Phi. Contbr. to ednl. yearbooks, jours. Home: 3706 Murworth St Houston TX 77025

DONNER, FREDERIC G., found. exec.; A.B., U. Mich., 1923. With Gen. Motors Corp., 1926-27, asst. treas. 1934-37, gen. asst. treas. 1937-41, v.p. 1941-56, exec. v.p., chmn. financial policy com., 1956-58, chmn., bd., chief exec. officer, 1958-67, dir., 1942—, mem. finance com., 1958—; chmn. bd. Alfred P. Sloan Found., 1968—; dir. Communications Satellite Corp. Home: Port Washington NY 11050 Office: 630 Fifth Av New York City NY 10020

DONNER, HENRY FREDERICK, univ. prof.; b. Wilson, N.Y., Sept. 1, 1902; s. Henry and Louise (Mary) (Schultz) D.; B.S., U. Mich., 1925, M.S., 1927, Sc.D., 1936; m. Florence L(itchard) Mudge, July 30, 1927. Testman, Gen. Electric Co., Schenectady, N.Y., 1925-26; research astronomer, Lamont-Hussey Obs., U. Mich., Bloemfontein, S. Africa, 1927-33; field asst. U.S. Geol. Survey, Colo., summer 1936; instr. geology Western Res. U., 1936-38, asst. prof. geology, 1938-43, asso. prof. geology, acting head dept., 1943-45, asso. prof. geology and astronomy; acting head dept. geology, geography and dept. astronomy, 1945-46, prof. geology and astronomy, head dept. geology, geography and head dept. astronomy, until 1961, prof. geology, until 1968, prof. emeritus geology, 1968—. Discovered 1057 new double stars, Lamont-Hussey Obs., 1927-33. Fellow Ohio Acad. Sci., Geol. Soc. Am.; mem. Am. Geophys. Union (life), Am. Assn. Petroleum Geologists, Sigma Xi. Republican. Methodist. On sabbatical leave Feb.-Oct. 1948, travel and study in Africa; drove car from Algiers south through Africa to Cape Town; made 200 double star measures at Lamont-Hussey Obs. Author: Geology of the McCoy Area, Eagle and Routt Counties, Colo., 1949. Home: 3094 E Overlook Rd Cleveland Heights OH 44118

DONNER, MARTIN WALTER, physician; b. Leipzig, Germany, Sept. 5, 1920; s. Walter T. and Else (Ruehl) D.; M.D., U. Leipzig Med. Sch., 1945; m. Adelheid I. Wimmer, Apr. 28, 1951; children—Cornelia, Stephanie, Thomas. Resident in internal medicine U. Hosp., Leipzig, 1945-50; resident fellow Radiology Center, Cologne, 1950-54; resident Mound Park Hosp., St. Petersburg, Fla., 1954-57; radiologist Johns Hopkins Hosp., Balt., 1957—, asso. prof. radiol. scis., 1964-68, prof. radiology, 1966—, dir. div. diagnostic radiology, 1967—, prof. radiol. sci., 1968—; vis. investigator Carnegie Inst. Washington; vis. prof. Free U. of Berlin, State U., Ohio U., Heidelberg. Fellow Am. Coll. Radiology; mem. A.M.A., Radiol. Soc. N.Am., Md. Radiol. Soc., Md. Med. and Chirurgical Faculty, Johns Hopkins Med. Soc., Assn. U. Radiologists, German Soc. Internal Medicine, German Soc. Radiology. Editorial staff Am. Jour. Med. Sci., 1961-68. Home: 317 Southwind Rd Baltimore MD 21204 Office: Johns Hopkins Hosp 606 N Broadway Baltimore MD 21205

DONOGHUE, DENIS, prof. modern English and Am. lit. Univ. Coll., Dublin, Ireland. Author: The Third Voice; Connoisseurs of Chaos; The Ordinary Universe, 1968. Address: Univ Coll Dublin, Ireland.

DONOHEW, JACK NORMAN, air force officer; b. Slater, Mo., Oct. 15, 1911; s. Edward Grant and Myrtle Belle (Agee) D.; B.S. in Chem. Engring., U. Mo., 1933; B.S., U.S. Mil. Acad., 1937; M.A. in Internat. Affairs, George Washington U., 1963; grad. numerous service schs. including Nat. War Coll.; m. Dorothy Ella Harman, July 2, 1938; children—Jack Norman, Kenyon Edward. Commd. 2d lt. U.S. Army, 1937, advanced through grades to maj. gen. USAF, 1962; various assignments, U.S. and Alaska, 1937-44; assigned Hdqrs. USAAF, 1944-45, Joint Chiefs Staff, 1945; mem. staff and faculty Air Command and Staff Sch., 1946-49; dir. air targets, dep. for intelligence Hdqrs. FEAF, Tokyo, Japan, 1950; comptroller Hdqrs. 13th Air Force, Clark AFB, Philippines, 1950-52; comdr. Clark AFB, 1952-53; chief programming div., asst. for programming, dep. chief staff operations Hdqrs. USAF, 1954- 56, dep. asst. programming, 1956-57, dep. dir. programs, dep. chief staff plans and programs, 1957-59; dir. Joint Programs Office, Joint Staff, Joint Chiefs Staff, 1959-61; comdr. Air Command and Staff Coll., 1961-63; chief staff U.S. So. Command, Quarry Heights, C.Z., 1963-66; dir. Inter-Am. Def. Coll., Ft. McNair, Washington, 1966-67; comdt. Air War Coll., Maxwell AFB, Ala., 1967—. Decorated Legion of Merit with 4 oak leaf clusters, D.F.C., Air medal. Mem. Am. Ordnance Assn., Assn. Grads. U.S. Mil. Acad., Tau Beta Pi. Home: Quarters 336 Maxwell AFB AL 36113 Office: Office Commandant Air War Coll Maxwell AFB AL 36112

DONOHO, CLIVE WELLINGTON, Jr., educator; b. Nashville, Tenn., Jan. 16, 1930; s. Clive Wellington and Daisy (Hill) D.; B.S., U. Ky., 1952; M.S., N.C. State U., 1958; Ph.D., Mich. State U., 1960; m. Cynthia Debish, May 21, 1955; children—Gary Hill, Anne Nell, Theresa Carroll, Glen Thomas. Asst. prof. Ohio State U., 1960-64, asso. prof., 1964-66, prof., 1966-67; prof., head dept. N.C. State U., 1967—. Served with USAF, 1952-56. Mem. Am. Inst. Biol. Scis., Am., Internat. socs. hort. sci., Sigma Xi, Alpha Zeta. Research, publs. horticultural research. Home: 3328 Thomas Rd Raleigh NC 27607

DONOHO, PAUL LEIGHTON, educator, physicist; b. Ft. Worth, Sept. 7, 1931; s. David H.L. and Martelle (Hicks) D.; B.A., Rice U., 1952; Ph.D., Cal. Inst. Tech., 1958; m. Julia A. Haas, Aug. 14, 1954; children—David, Andrew, Julia. Mem. tech. staff Bell Telephone Labs., Inc., Murray Hill, N.J., 1957-59; prof. physics Rice U., Houston, 1959—; maitre de Conferences Associe, U. Grenoble, France, 1967-68; cons. Alpine Geophys. Assos., Inc., 1961-67, U.S. Army Missile Command, 1965—, U. Tex. Med. Br., 1966—; vis. scientist in physics Am. Inst. Physics, 1966—. Mem. Am. Phys. Soc., A.A.A.S., Am. Assn. Physics Tchrs., Colloque Ampere, Phi Beta Kappa, Sigma Xi. Republican. Methodist. Home: 5183 Huckleberry St Houston TX 77027

DONOHOE, HUGH ALOYSIUS, bishop; b. San Francisco, June 28, 1905; s. Patrick and Frances Catherine (Brogan) D.; M.A., Catholic U., Washington, 1933, Ph.D., 1936. Consecrated bishop of San Francisco, auxiliary bishop, 1947, bishop of Stockton Cal., 1962-69; bishop of Fresno, 1969—. Democrat. Home: 1113 W Celeste St Fresno CA 93705

DONOHOE, LAWRENCE E., Jr., lawyer; b. Winnfield, La., June 15, 1927; J.D., La. State U., 1951. Admitted to La. bar, 1951; partner firm Davidson, Meaux, Onebane & Donohoe, Lafayette. Mem. Lafayette, La. State (mem. jr. bar com. on pub. relations 1955, com. on selection of judges 1955), Am. bar assns., Order of Coif, Gamma Eta Gamma. Office: 201 W Main St Lafayette LA 70501*

DONOHUE, ALBERT F., investment banker; b. Scott, N.Y.,Sept. 1, 1909; s. Jeremiah G. and Mary J. (Sweeney) D.; A.B., U. Mich., 1932, LL.B., 1936; m. Barbara A. Braun, Oct. 17, 1935; children—James, Thomas, Mary, John. Admitted to N.Y. bar; investment banker since 1936; asso. Kidder, Peabody & Co., N.Y.C. 1944- -, partner, 1950—, v.p., dir., 1957—; dir. Giant Food Properties, Inc., Washington, also Handy Andy, Inc., San Antonio, Tex., Alterman Foods, Inc., Atlanta, others. Mem. Am., N.Y. bar assns., Bar Assn. City N.Y. Roman Catholic. Clubs: St. Andrews Golf (Hastings, N.Y.); Bronxville (N.Y.) Field; Shenorock Shore (Rye, N.Y.); Bond, Recess (N.Y.C.). Home: 9 Essex Pl Bronxville NY 10708 Office: 20 Exchange Pl New York City NY 10005

DONOHUE, CARROLL JOHN, lawyer; b. St. Louis, June 24, 1917; s. Thomas M. and Florence (Klefisch) D.; A.B., Washington U., 1939, LL.B. magna cum laude, 1939; m. Juanita Maire, Jan. 4, 1943; children—Patricia Carol (now Mrs. Stevens), Christine Ann (Mrs. Smith), Deborah Lee. Admitted to Mo. bar, 1939; asso. law firm Hay & Flanagan, St. Louis, 1939-42, law firm Salkey & Jones, 1946-49; partner Husch, Eppenberg, Donohue, Elson & Jones, 1949-63; sr. partner Husch, Eppenberger, Donohue, Elson & Cornfeld, St. Louis, 1963—. Campaign chmn. A.R.C., St. Louis County, 1950; mem. adv. com. Child Welfare, St. Louis, 1952-55, exec. com. Slum Clearance, 1949, bond issue com., 1955, St. Louis County Bond Issue screening and supervisory coms., 1955-61, county citizen's com. for better law enforcement, 1953-56; chmn. com. on immigration policy, 1954- 56. Mayor, Olivette, Mo., 1953-56; chmn. County Bd. Election Commrs., St. Louis County, 1960-65; chmn. speakers com. Non-Partisan Ct. Plan. Served to lt. USNR, 1942-45. Decorated Bronze Star medal, Navy and M.C. medal. Mem. Mo. (past mem. bd. govs., chmn. annual meeting, editor jour. 1940-41), Am., St. Louis (past pres., v.p., treas.) bar assns., Order of Coif, Omicron Delta Kappa, Sigma Phi Epsilon, Delta Theta Phi. Clubs: Missouri Athletic, Creve Coeur Racquet (St. Louis). Author articles in fleid. Home: 23 Heather Hill Lane Olivette, MO 63132. Office: Buder Bldg 7 N 7th St St Louis MO 63101

DONOHUE, EUGENE JAMES, corp. exec.; b. Bklyn., Nov. 22, 1923; s. Francis L. and Genevieve (Fitzgerald) D.; B.B.A., Manhattan Coll., 1947; m. Patricia Gentle, May 16, 1945. Staff accountant Haskins & Sells, C.P.A.'s, 1947-57, prin., 1947-61; treas., v.p. Ogden Corp., N.Y.C., 1962-68, sr. v.p., 1968—; chmn., pres. Ogden Mgmt. Corp.; dir. Avondale Shipyards, Inc., Shaker Savs. Assn., ABC Consol. Corp., Better Built Machinery Corp., Ogden Foods Corp., Ogden Devel. Corp., Internat. Products Corp., Internat. Terminal Operating Co., Jarcho Bros., Inc., Luria Bros. Co., Inc., Lipsett, Inc., Odgen Am. Corp., Odgen Tech Labs, Inc., Ogden Recreation, Inc., Tillie Lewis Foods, Inc. Served with USAAF, 1943-46. C.P.A., N.Y., Mich. Mem. Am. Inst. (dir., v.p. N.Y. chpt.). Office: 161 E 42d St New York City NY 10017

DONOHUE, F. JOSEPH, lawyer; b. Lynn, Mass., Jan 15, 1900; s. James J. and Gertrude Elizabeth (Powers) D.; A.B., Catholic U., 1922, LL.B., 1925; m. Martha Vey Apperson, Aug. 23, 1948. Instr. econs. and banking Catholic U., 1922-30, Am. Inst. Banking, 1922-30; admitted to D.C. bar, 1925, since practiced in Washington; partner firm Donohue, Kaufmann, Shaw & Kligman; prof. law Columbus U., Washington, 1936-40. Dir. First Nat. Bank Washington, Miami Nat. Bank (Fla.). Mem. D.C. Bd. Commrs., 1951- 53, pres. bd., 1952-53. Chmn. D.C. delegation to Democratic Nat. Conv., 1952; vice chmn. Stevenson-Kefauver Campaign Com., 1956; chmn. Inaugural Parade, 1961; mem. D.C. Dem. Central Com. Served with USAAF, World War II. Decorated Bronze Star. Fellow Am. Coll. Trial Lawyers; mem. Am. (chmn. spl. com. retirement benefits, standing com. fed. legislation), D.C. bar assns., Am. Thrift Assembly (chmn.). Club: Nat. Lawyers (treas.) (Washington). Home: 3141 O St N W Washington DC 20007 Office: 503 D St N W Washington DC 20001

DONOHUE, FRANCIS MICHAEL, Jr., stock broker; b. N.Y.C., Aug. 9, 1931; s. Frank Michael and Mary (Marvel) D.; A.B., Princeton, 1953; m. Audrey McMillan Furber, Sept. 22, 1956; children—Cornelia Furber, Susan Buttler, Francis Michael IV. With Laird, Bissell & Meeds, Inc., Wilmington, Del., 1955—, exec. v.p., 1968—, also dir.; dir. Corp. Ser. Co., Wilmington. Served with USMCR, 1953-55. Republican. Episcopalian. Clubs: Wilmington (bd. govs.), Wilmington Country (bd. dirs.); Pine Valley (N.J.) Golf, Delaware Turf (Stanton, Del.). Home: Marshall Bridge Rd Kennett Square PA 19348 Office: 300 Delaware Av Wilmington DE 19801

DONOHUE, HAROLD DANIEL, congressman; b. Worcester, Mass., June 18, 1901; s. Cornelius and Margaret (Lyons) D.; grad. Northeastern U., 1925. Admitted to Mass. Bar, 1926; practiced in Worcester; mem. 80th- 92d Congresses, 4th Dist. Mass. Alderman, pres. bd., acting mayor, Worcester. Served to lt. comdr. USNR, 1942-45. Trustee Worcester City Hosp., Belmont Hosp. Mem. Mass., Worcester County bar assns., Am. Legion, World War II Vets. Assn. (Worcester). Democrat. Roman Catholic. Elk, K.C. Home: 82 Forest St Worcester MA 01609 Office: 390 Main St Worcester MA 01608

DONOHUE, JAMES CHANDLER, educator, clergyman; b. Norwich, Conn., Feb. 8, 1925; s. James J. and Sarah (Bowman) D.; A.B., St. Bernard's Sem., Rochester, N.Y., 1946; S.T.B., St. Mary's Sem., Balt., 1950; Ph.D., Cath. U. Am., 1957. Ordained priest Roman Catholic Ch., 1950; asst. pastor, Balt., 1950- 57; asst. supt. schs. Archdiocese of Balt., 1957-60, supt., 1960-65; co-dir. dept. edn. Nat. Cath. Welfare Conf. (now U.S. Cath. Conf.), 1965-66, dir. div. elementary and secondary edn., 1966—. Cons., U.S. Office Edn.; mem. Bishop's Commn. on Ecumenism and Cath. Edn.; mem. Pres.'s Com. for Employment Handicapped; mem. Working Group representing Bishop's Com. for Ecumenical and Interreligious Affairs and Nat. Council Chs.; mem. adv. council Fgn. Study League, Salt Lake City; mem. nat. adv. bd. Reading is Fundamental Com.; corp. mem. Nat. Assembly for Social Policy and Devel., Inc. Bd. dirs. Mt. St. Agnes Coll., Balt.; trustee Religious Educators Found., Washington, Joint Council Econ. Edn., N.Y.C. Elevated to rank of papal chamberlain, 1963. Mem. Nat. Cath. Edn. Assn. (sec. supts. dept. 1963-65), N.E.A., Religious Edn. Assn. (dir.), Am. Assn. Sch. Adminstrs. Editorial adv. bd. Cath. Sch. Jour. Home: 4001 14th St N E Washington, DC 20017. Office: 1312 Massachusetts Av N W Washington DC 20005

DONOHUE, JERRY, educator; b. Sheboygan, Wis., June 12, 1920; s. Jerry and Leila Marian (Bishop) D.; A.B., Dartmouth, 1941, M.A., 1943; Ph.D., Cal. Inst. Tech., 1947; m. Patricia Ann Schreier, Feb. 10, 1945; children—Terence, Nora. Instr. chemistry Dartmouth, 1941-43; sr. research fellow Cal. Inst. Tech., 1947-52; prof. chemistry U. So. Cal., 1953-66, U. Pa., 1966—. Mem. Am. Crystallographic Assn., Phi Beta Kappa, Sigma Xi. Office: Dept Chemistry Univ Pa Philadelphia PA 19104

DONOHUE, MARK, paper co. exec.; b. Quebec, Que., Can., Sept. 8, 1909; s. Joseph Timothy and Emilie (Normandin) D.; B.A., Laval U., 1931, L.L.L., 1934; postgrad. Harvard, 1934-35; m. Lucile Tessier, Sept. 30, 1939; children—Thomas, Charles, Louise, Patricia. Called to Que. bar, 1934; pres. Donohue Bros., Ltd., Clermont, Charlevoix, 1959-67, now chmn. exec. com. Trustee Laval U. Mem. Canadian Bar Assn. Home: 150 Laurier Av Quebec 4 Quebec Canada Office: 500 est Grand Allée Quebec 4 Quebec Canada

DONOUGH, ROBERT JOHN, banker; b. Lebanon, Pa., July 20, 1924; s. Leroy B. and Kathryn (Karch) D.; B.S., Lebanon Valley Coll., 1945; M.B.A., Harvard, 1947; m. Margaret Joyce Foote, Jan. 24, 1945; children—Robert John, Michael Leroy, James Philip, Kathleen Mary. With State Bank Albany (N.Y.), 1947- -, cashier, 1964—, also v.p. Active Albany Community Chest. Served with USNR, 1942-45, 51-53. Mem. Financial Execs. Inst. (sec.-treas. 1967). Club: Fort Orange (Albany). Home: 4 Red Oaks Dr Latham, NY 12110. Office: 69 State St Albany NY 12201

DONOVAN, ALLEN FRANCIS, aero. engr.; b. Onondaga, N.Y., Apr. 22, 1914; s. Paul Andrew and May (Hudson) D.; B.S., U. Mich., 1936, M.S., 1936, D. Engring. (hon.), 1964; m. Beverly Fay, Aug. 14, 1940 (div. Dec. 5, 1949); 1 son, Allen Michael; m. 2d, Doris Mildred Efram, Apr. 17, 1953; children—Kathryn Ellen, Marshall Stephen. With Curtiss-Wright Corp., Glenn L. Martin, Stinson Aircraft, Vultee Aircraft, 1936-46; head aero. mechanics dept. Cornell U. Aero. Lab., 1946-55; dir. aero. research and devel. staff Space Tech. Labs., Inc., 1955-58, v.p., 1958-60; sr. v.p. tech., Aerospace Corp., 1960—. Cons. Pres.'s Sci. Adv. Com.; mem. Air Force Sci. Adv. Bd., 1948-57, 59-68. U.S. del. Geneva Conf., 1959. Recipient U.S. medal for exceptional civilian services, 1968; recipient Sci. award Air Force Assn. Fellow Am. Inst. Aeros. and Astronautics; mem. Nat. Acad. Engrs. Editor vols. on high speed aerodynamics, jet propulsion. Author tech. papers on space vehicles, aeronautics. Home: 4033 via Marina Marina del Rey CA 90291 Office: 2350 E El Segundo Blvd El Segundo CA 90245

DONOVAN, BARBARA MAUD, (Mrs. Cornelius Peter Donovan), editor; b. Summit, N.J., Aug. 19, 1934; d. Rodney Fielding and Maud (Grebbin) Starkey; student Traphagen Sch. Fashion, 1954-56, Fashion Inst. Tech., 1956-58; N.Y. Sch. Interior Design, 1964; m. Cornelius Peter Donovan, Mar. 23, 1968. Copy editor Vogue Pattern Book, 1958-60; beauty editor Vogue mag., 1961; dir. womens services Bartell Media Corp., 1961-66; editor-in-chief Bride's mag., N.Y.C., 1966—. Adv. bd. Lab. Inst. of Mdsg. Mem. Nat. Council of Women, 1967—, Nat. Council on Family Relations, 1966—. Bd. dirs. Pan Pacific and S.E. Asia Womens Assn. Recipient Alma award, 1968. Mem. Fashion Group, Cosmetic Career Women, Nat. Home Fashions League, Am. Soc. Mag. Editors, Nat. Soc. Interior Designers (press mem.), Am. Inst. Interior Designers, Am. Women in Radio and TV, Intercorporate Group, Viviane Woodward Council Fine Arts, Met. Mus. Art, Mus. Modern Art. Beauty cons., author: The ABC's of Beauty, 1963; also various sales booklets, advt. campaigns. Home: 220 E 60th St New York City NY 10021 Office: 420 Lexington Av New York City NY 10017

DONOVAN, CHARLES ANDREW, information tech. co. exec.; b. Boston, Sept. 17, 1921; s. Joseph Daniel and Katherine Josephine (Flaherty) D.; A.B magna cum laude, Boston Coll., 1942; m. Barbara Anne Brawley, June 17, 1948; children—Katherine J., Joseph D., Regina L., Charles B. Accountant, New Eng. Electric Co., 1942-44; auditor Arthur Young & Co., Boston, 1944-52; account mgr. Electronics Corp. of Am., Cambridge, Mass., 1952-56; asst. treas., asst. sec. Tracerlab/Keleket Co., Waltham, Mass., 1956-57; account/C.P.A. prin., 1957-58; controller, dir. adminstrn., asst. treas., treas. Itek Corp., Lexington, Mass., 1958—; v.p., treas. Itek Leasing Co.; treas. Univis, Inc., Univis Optical Co., White Haines Corp., Itek Bus. Products, Ltd., Itek Internat. Corp. Mem. Financial Execs. Inst., Am. Inst. C.P.A.'s, Boston Coll. Alumni Assn. (sec., dir. 1969-70), St. Vincent de Paul Soc., Holy Name Soc. Clubs: Treasurer's, Skating (Boston). Home: 3 Glenburnie Rd Roslindale MA 02131 Office: 10 Maguire Rd Lexington MA 02173

DONOVAN, CHARLES FRANCIS, ednl. adminstr.; b. Boston, Mar. 28, 1912; s. John J. and Mary E. (Doyle) Donovan; A.B., Boston Coll., 1933; A.M., Fordham U., 1938; S.T.L., Weston (Mass.) Coll., 1944; Ph.D., Yale, 1948. Joined Soc. of Jesus, 1933; ordained priest Roman Catholic Ch., 1943; faculty Boston Coll., 1938-39, 48—, prof. edn., 1948—, chmn. dept., 1948-63, dean Sch. Edn., 1952-66, acad. v.p. univ., 1961-68, sr. vice pres., dean faculties, 1968—. Adviser Jesuit higher edn. in New Eng. Mem. New Eng. Assn. Coll. Tchrs. Edn. (past pres.), Mass. Council Tchr. Edn. (past pres.), New Eng. Tchr. Preparation Assn. (past pres.), Assn. Higher Edn. (planning com. 1957, exec. com. 1963-67), Am. Assn. Colls. Tchr. Edn. (exec. com. 1963-67), Jesuit Edn. Assn. Contbr. articles profl. jours. Address: Boston Coll Chestnut Hill MA 02167

DONOVAN, CLEMENT HAROLD, educator; b. Canton, N.Y., Oct. 21, 1911; s. Daniel and Nora (MacSweeney) D.; B.S., St. Lawrence U., 1931; Ph.D., U. N.C., 1940; m. Elizabeth Whitbeck, Nov. 30, 1935; 1 son, Michael. Mem. faculty U. Fla., 1940—, prof. econs., 1948—, chmn. dept., 1952-70; vis. prof. U. Khartoum (Sudan), 1964-65; Fulbright vis. lectr., India, 1958-59; dir. Fla. Inst. Pub. Affairs, 1967—. Served with USNR, 1942-46. Mem. Am. Econ. Assn., Nat. Tax Assn., Phi Beta Kappa, Beta Gamma Sigma. Home: 1110 NW 36th Rd Gainsville FL 32601

DONOVAN, DENNIS FRANCIS, judge; b. Champion, Mich., Apr. 9, 1889; s. Michael and Mary (Harrington) D.; LL.B., U. Mich., 1913; m. Alice Gertrude Flaherty, Dec. 2, 1916; children—Mary Gertrude (Mrs. A.C. Kelly), Dennis Francis. Admitted to Mich. bar, 1913, Minn. bar, 1914, since practiced in Minn.; U.S. dist. judge, District of Minn., 1945—, now U.S. dist. sr. judge Minn. Mem. Minn. State Eleventh Judicial Dist., Am. bar assns. Democrat. Roman Catholic. Rotarian (past pres.) Clubs: Kitchi Gammi, Athletic, Minnesota (St. Paul); Minneapolis. Home: Madonna Towers Rochester MN 55901 Office: Federal Bldg Duluth MN 55802

DONOVAN, EDWARD, sports exec. Gen. mgr. N.Y. Knickerbockers Profl. Basketball Team. Address: 307 W 49th St New York City, NY 10019.*

DONOVAN, EGBERT HERBERT, clergyman; b. Buffalo, Jan. 15, 1913; s. James D. and Laura-Mary (Thompson) D.; A.B., St. Vincent Coll., Latrobe, Pa., 1936; M.A., 1940; M.Ed., Cath. U. Am., 1945; Ed.D. (hon.), St. Francis Coll., 1968; LL.D. (hon.), Seton Hill Coll., 1969. Headmaster St. Vincent Prep. Sch., Latrobe, Pa., 1945-54; dean of men St. Vincent Coll., 1957-62; chaplain Pa. State U., 1962-67; archabbot, chancellor St. Vincent Archabbey and Coll., Latrobe, 1967—. Bd. dirs. St. Vincent Coll., 1947-62, 67—. Mem. Nat. Newman Chaplains Assn., Am. Benedictine Acad., Conf. Major Superiora of Men. K.C. Address: St Vincent Archabbey Latrobe PA 15650

DONOVAN, EILEEN ROBERTA, ambassador; b. Boston, Apr. 13, 1915; d. William Francis and Mary (Barry) Donovan; grad. Girls Latin Sch., Boston, 1932; B.S. in Edn., Boston Tchrs. Coll., 1936, Ed. M., 1937; postgrad. Sch. Mil. Govt., U. Va., also Civil Affairs Tng. Sch., U. Mich., 1944-45; M. Pub. Adminstrn. (Fgn. Service Inst. fellow 1956), Harvard, 1957. Tchr. history pub. schs., Boston, 1938-43; fgn. service officer Dept. State, 1948—; 2d sec., vice consul Office U.S. Polit. Adviser, Tokyo, Japan, 1948-49; staff Bur. Far Eastern Affairs, Japan-Korea Pub. Affairs, 1949-52; State Dept. mem. Ednl. Exchange Survey Mission to Japan, summer 1949; 2d sec., consul Am. Embassy, Manila, P.I., 1952-54; consul U.S. consulate gen., Milan, Italy, 1954-56; chief So. Europe br. Bur. Intelligence and Research, Washington, 1957-59; detailed Sr. Seminar in Fgn. Policy, State Dept., 1959; prin. officer, Am. consul, Barbados, W.I., 1960-62, U.S. consul gen. Barbados and The Windward and Leeward Islands, W.I., 1962-65; asst. dir. Office Caribbean Affairs, Dept. State, 1965-69; U.S. ambassador to Barbados, also U.S. spl. rep. to Antigua, Dominica, Grenada, St. Kitts-Nevis-Anguilla, St. Lucia, St. Vincent, 1969—. Served from pvt. to capt. WAC, 1943-46; civilian adviser Japanese women's and secondary edn. to Supreme Comdr. Allied Powers, Tokyo, 1946-48. Recipient Fed. Women's award, 1969. Address: American Embassy care US Naval Facility FPO New York City NY 09553

DONOVAN, GEORGE, constrn. co. exec. Chmn., Donovan Constrn. Co., St. Paul. Office: 1080 Montreal Av St Paul MN 55102*

DONOVAN, GEORGE FRANCIS, educator; b. Rockland, Mass., Dec. 1, 1901; s. John Joseph and Catherine (Smith) D.; A.B., Boston Coll., 1925, A.M., 1927; A.M., Harvard, 1929; Ph.D., St. Louis U., 1931; m. Margaret Mary Ryan, Sept. 7, 1931. Instr. Rockhust Coll., 1927-29; teaching fellow St. Louis U., 1929-31; pres. Webster Coll., 1931-48; br. chief ednl. and cultural relations U.S. Mil. Govt., Germany, 1948-49; adviser pub. affairs Dept. State, Wiesbaden, Germany, 1949-51; sr. adviser U.S. High Command, Germany, 1951-52; cultural affairs attache Am. embassy, India, 1952-53; dir. higher edn. program Cath. U. Am. Grad. Sch. Arts and Scis., Washington, 1954-66; chmn. dept. edn. Marquette U., Milw., 1966—, also dir. tchr. edn. 1966—. Cons. study coll. bds. trustees N. Y. State Bd. Regents, 1964-65; pres. Cath. Conf. Indsl. Problems; coordinator U.S. Peace Corps tng. program for coll. and univ. tchrs. overseas Georgetown U., summer 1964. Mem. Am., Cath. hist. assns., Am. Acad. Polit. and Social Sci., Am. Polit. Sci. Assn., Am. Assn. U. Profs., Cath. Assn. Internat. Peace, Nat. Fedn. Cath. Alumni (pres. St. Louis 1939-40, regional dir. 1940- 41), Nat. Cath. Ednl. Assn. (chmn. coll. and univ. dept. Eastern regional unit, mem. exec. com. coll. and univ. dept. 1961—), N.E.A. (mem. com. on fraudulent schs. Assn. for Higher Edn. 1955-57), Alpha Sigma Nu. Democrat. Roman Catholic. Lion. Clubs: Harvard (Milw.), Serra (v.p. 1946). Author: The Pre-Revolutionary Irish in Massachusetts, 1620-1775; Developments in the Accreditation of Teacher Education in the United States, 1957; Selected Readings for the College and University Officer of Administration, 1961; The Faculty Manual in American Colleges and Universities, 1966, rev. 3d edit., 1969; Selected Annotated Readings on Accreditation in Higher Education, 1966; Vatican Council II; Challenge to Education, 1967. Co-author: The Road Ahead; Quality of College Teaching and Staff, 1961; Church-Related Boards Responsible for Higher Education, 1964. Editor: Higher Education Book Review, 1960; College and University Student Personnel Services, 1962; Selected Problems in the Administration of American Higher Education, 1964; College and University Inter-institutional Cooperation, 1965; Vatican II Council-Its Challenge to Education, 1967; (with W. Hugh Stickler) Representative Questions Asked in Comprehensive Doctoral Examinations in the Area of Higher Education, 1967. Home: 7851 N Links Circle Fox Point, WI 53217. Office: Marquette U Milwaukee WI 53233

DONOVAN, GERALD, lawyer; b. Providence, Aug. 3, 1891; s. Joseph and Margaret Barrett (Fitzgerald) D.; A.B., Brown U., 1912; J.D., N.Y. U., 1916; m. Louise Priddie, Oct. 27, 1920; children—Richard, Geraldine (Mrs. Robert Lenehan), William, Daniel Gerald. Admitted to N.Y. bar, 1916, R.I. bar, 1917; asso. Nicoll, Anable, Fuller & Sullivan, N.Y. C., 1919-24, and successor firms, now Sullivan, Donovan, Hanrahan, McGovern & Lane; atty. for N.Y. Soc. Prevention of Cruelty to Children, 1932—. Dir., past pres. Home for Aged of New Rochelle, N.Y. Served as maj. F.A., U.S.

Army Res., World War I. Mem. Assn. Bar City N.Y., N.Y.U. Law Alumni Assn. (dir., past pres.), Phi Beta Kappa. Roman Catholic. Clubs: Brown University (dir.), Down Town Assn., Links, Wykagyl Country, Garden City Golf (N.Y.C.); The Dundas, Pt. Judith Country (Narragansett, R.I.). Home: 40 Brewster Terrace New Rochelle NY 10804 Office: 70 Pine St New York City NY 10005

DONOVAN, HEDLEY WILLIAMS, journalist; b. Brainerd, Minn., May 24, 1914; s. Percy Williams and Alice (Dougan) D.; A.B. magna cum laude, U. Minn., 1934; B.A., Oxford U. (Rhodes scholar), 1936; Litt.D., Pomona Coll., Boston U., Mt. Holyoke Coll.; L.H.D., Southwestern at Memphis, Rochester U.; LL.D., Carnegie-Mellon U.; m. Dorothy Hannon, Oct. 18, 1941; children—Peter Williams, Helen Welles, Mark Vicars. Reporter, Washington Post, 1937-42; writer, editor Fortune mag., N.Y. C., 1945-51; asso. mng. editor, 1951-53, mng. editor, 1953-59; editorial dir. Time, Inc., 1959-64, editor-in-chief, 1964—, dir., 1962—. Trustee N.Y.U., U. Minn. Found., Carnegie Endowment for Internat. Peace; bd. visitors Air Force Systems Command. Served to lt. comdr. USNR, 1942-45. Recipient Outstanding Achievement award U. Minn. Alumni, 1956. Mem. Council Fgn. Relations (dir.), Phi Beta Kappa, Delta Upsilon. Clubs: University, Manhasset Bay Yacht, Century, Sands Point Golf. Home: Harbor Rd Sands Point NY 11050 Office: Time and Life Bldg Rockefeller Center New York City NY 10020

DONOVAN, JAMES ALPORT, Jr., govt. ofcl.; b. Buffalo, May 25, 1916; s. James Alport and Laura S. (Hickok) D.; B.A., Yale, 1937, postgrad. Grad. Sch., 1937-40, Linguistic Inst., U. Mich., summer 1938; m. Abbie Daggett Morse, July 18, 1939; children—Peter Morse, Patrick James. Translator, spl. agt. FBI, 1941-46; with State Dept., 1946—, staff dir. U.S. Adv. Commn. Internat. Ednl. and Cultural Affairs, 1960—; instr. German, George Washington U., 1947-49. Mem. Alexandria (Va.) Sch. Bd., 1961-67; chmn. Alexandria Adv. Com. Adult Edn., 1964-67. Trustee Greater Washington Ednl. TV Assn., 1964-67. Recipient Meritorious Service award State Dept., 1959. Mem. Soc. Former Spl. Agts. FBI, Assn. Higher Edn., Thoreau Soc. Author articles. Home: 25 W Glebe Rd Alexandria VA 22305 Office: Dept of State Washington DC 20520

DONOVAN, JAMES NORTON, financial exec.; b. Toronto, Ont., Can., Aug. 28, 1921 (parents U.S. citizens); s. James Michael and Cornelia (Smith) D.; B.S., U. Cal. at Berkeley, 1947; M.B.A., 1949; m. Mary Elizabeth Carter, Dec. 6, 1944; 1 dau., Elizabeth Lathrop. Accountant, Houston, Cossar & Bartlett, Toronto, 1940-42; pub. accountant McLaren, Goode, West & Co., San Francisco, 1947-52; chief accountant, asst. controller Varian Assos., Palo Alto, Cal., 1952-57, treas., 1957—. Served with USNR, 1942-44; USMCR, 1944-46. C.P.A., Cal. Mem. Am. Inst. C.P.A.'s. Home: 1035 Trinity Dr Menlo Park CA 94025 Office: 611 Hansen Way Palo Alto CA 94303

DONOVAN, JOHN ANTHONY, bishop; b. Chatham, Ont., Can., Aug. 5, 1911; s. John J. and Mary C. (O'Rourke) D.; B.A., Sacred Heart Sem., 1932; postgrad. N.A. Coll., Rome (Italy), 1936; J.C.L., Pontifical Athenaeum of Lateran, Rome, 1947; LL.D., U. Detroit, 1952. Ordained priest Roman Cath. Ch., 1935, domestic prelate, 1949; pastor St. Aloysius' Ch., Detroit, also chancellor Archdiocese of Detroit, 1951-58, St. Veronica's Ch., East Detroit, 1958- 67; Titular Bishop of Rhasus and Auxiliary Bishop of Detroit, 1954-67; Vicar General, Archdiocese of Detroit, 1959-67; bishop of Toledo, 1967- - Address: 2116 Parkwood Toledo OH 43620

DONOVAN, JOHN CHAUNCEY, educator; b. N.Y.C., Feb. 9, 1920; s. Michael James and Myrtie (Tucker) D.; A.B., Bates Coll., 1942; M.A., Harvard, 1948, Ph.D., 1949; m. Beatrice Florence Witter, Sept. 9, 1947; children—Caarey, Christine Martha, John. Teaching fellow Harvard, 1946-49; mem. faculty Bates Coll., 1949-59, prof. govt., chmn. social sci. div., 1957-59; administrv., asst. to U.S. Senator Muskie, 1959-62; exec. asst. to sec. labor Wirtz, 1962-65; DeAlva Stanwood Alexander prof. govt. Bowdoin Coll., 1965—, chmn. dept. govt. and legal studies, 1967-69. Chmn. New Eng. Regional Manpower Adv. Com., Me. Bd. Arbitration and Conciliation, 1955-56; chmn. Me. Adv. Council on Vocational Edn. Chmn. Me. Democratic Com., 1957- 58; candidate for U.S. Congress, 2d dist. Me., 1960. Overseer Bates Coll. Served with USNR, World War II; PTO. Mem. Am. Polit. Sci. Assn., Phi Beta Kappa. Author: The Politics of Poverty, 1967; The Policy Makers, 1970. Contbr. articles profl. jours. Home: 56 Federal St Brunswick ME 04011

DONOVAN, JOHN DENNIS, educator, sociologist; b. Peabody, Mass., Feb. 15, 1918; s. John A. and Ellen T. (Broderick) D.; A.B., Boston Coll., 1939, M.A. (O'Malley fellow 1939-41), 1941; Ph.D. (Univ. fellow 1941-42, Robert Treat Paine fellow 1942-43), Harvard, 1951; m. Mary F. Phipps, Jan. 21, 1950; children—Christine E., John Dennis. From instr. to asst. prof. Fordham U., 1946-52; asso. prof., then prof. Boston Coll., 1952—, chmn. dept. sociology, 1958-65; vis. research prof. U. Louvain (Belgium). Mem. U.S. Bishops Com. on Liturgical Adaptation, 1967-69. Dir. Greater Boston Urban League, 1958-60; dir. family life bur. Nat. Cath. Welfare Conf., 1960- 62. Served to capt. AUS, 1943-46. Mem. Am. Sociol. Assn., Am. Cath. Sociol. Soc. (pres. 1958). Author: The Academic Man in the Catholic College, 1964. Asso. editor: Sociology of Edn., Sociol. Analysts; editor Contemporary Problems in Sociology: A Seminar Series. Author numerous articles on sociology of religion. Home: 12 Coulton Park Needham MA 02192 Office: Boston Coll Chestnut Hill MA 02167

DONOVAN, JOHN F., constrn. co. exec. Pres., Donovan Constrn. Co., St. Paul. Office: 1080 Montreal Av St Paul MN 55102*

DONOVAN, JOSEPH JEREMIAH, clergyman, educator; b. San Francisco, Feb. 25, 1897; s. Jeremiah and Brigid (Kelly) D.; A.B., Gonzaga U., 1918, A.M., 1919; postgrad. in theology and canon law, U. Innsbruck, Austria, 1922-26; Ph.D., Gregorian U., Rome, 1938. Entered Soc. of Jesus, 1912, ordained priest, 1925; dean studies, regent Sch. Law, Loyola U. of Los Angeles, 1927-31, regent Sch. Law, 1931—. Mem. Am. Judicature Soc., Am. Irish Hist. Soc. (v.p. Cal. 1926-30), Assn. Law Librarians, Legal Aid Found. Los Angeles (dir.). Democrat. Home: 1901 Venice Blvd Los Angeles CA 90006 Office: 1440 W 9th St Los Angeles CA 90015

DONOVAN, LEITCH, singer, composer. Recording artist for Warner Bros. Records. Compositions include: Sunshine Superman; There is a Mountain; Mellow Yellow (Jay award 1967), Catch the Wind. Address: care Sid Maurer Maurer Productions 850 7th Av New York City NY 10019

DONOVAN, RICHARD FRANK, composer, condr., music educator; b. New Haven, Conn., Nov. 29, 1891; Mus.B. Sch. Music Yale, 1922; student Inst. Mus. Art, N.Y. C., 1914-18; M.A. (hon.), Yale, 1947; m. Grace Revere, 1919; children—Richard, David. Tchr. music, Taft Sch., 1920-23, Smith Coll., 1923-28; also instr. Inst. Mus. Art, 1925-28; asst. prof. theory of music, Yale Sch. of Music, 1928-40, asso. prof., 1940-47, prof., 1947-54, Battell prof. theory music, 1954-60, Battell prof. emeritus theory music, 1960—; lectr. theory music Finch Jr. Coll., N.Y.C., 1926-40; condr. Bach Cantata Club New Haven, 1933-44; condr. New Haven Symphony Orch. 1936-51; mem. staff Middlebury Coll. Composers Conf., summers 1946, 47; organist, choirmaster Christ Ch., New Haven, 1928-66; vis. faculty, U. So. Cal., summer, 1948, 64. Dir., Yaddo Corp., mem. music com. of Yaddo Music Festivals. Composer: Works for orchestra, chamber music, choral, organ, piano music and songs, several recordings. Recipient Naumburg Recording award, 1962, Waite award Am. Acad. Arts and Letters, 1963. Mem. Am. Composers Alliance (pres. 1961-64). Home: Hamden CT 06514

DONOVAN, ROBERT JOHN, journalist; b. Buffalo, Aug. 21, 1912; s. Michael J. and Katherine (Sullivan) D.; Litt.D. (hon.), Am. Internat. Coll., 1962; m. Martha Fisher, May 9, 1941; children—Patricia, Peter, Amy. Mem. staff Buffalo (N.Y.) Courier-Express, 1933-37; with N.Y. Herald Tribune, 1937- 63, on European edit., 1945, mem. Washington Bur., 1947-63, chief, 1957- 63; chief Los Angeles Times, Washington bur., 1963-70, asso. editor newspaper, Los Angeles, 1970—. Served AUS, WW II; staff Stars and Stripes in Paris. Mem. White House Corrs. Assn. (pres. 1954). Clubs: Federal City (Washington); Gridiron, National Press. Author: The Assassins, 1955; Eisenhower: The Inside Story, 1956; My First Fifty Years in Politics (with Joseph W. Martin, Jr.), 1960; PT 109: John F. Kennedy in World War II, 1961; The Future of the Republican Party, 1964; also mag. articles. Home: 5100 Brookeway Dr Washington DC 20016 Office: Los Angeles Times Washington Bureau 1700 Pennsylvania Av NW Washington DC 20006

DONOVAN, STANLEY JOSEPH, former air force officer; b. Portland, Me., Oct. 5, 1910; s. James and Blanche (O'Neill) D.; B.S., U.S. Mil. Acad., 1934; student AC Advanced Flying Sch., 1936; m. Margaret Roblee, June 28, 1943; children—Diana G., Sheila M., Frederic S. Commd. 2d lt. U.S. Army, 1934, advanced through grades to lt. gen. USAF, 1953; staff Office Chief of AC, Washington, 1941-42, 12th Bomber Command, 1942; comdr. 97th Bomb Group, 1943; mem. War Dept. Gen. Staff, 1944-45; air attache Am. embassy, Argentina, 1945-48; assigned War Plans Hdqrs., USAF, Washington, 1948-52; comdr. 40th Bomb Wing, SAC, 1953, comdr. 14th Air. Div., 1953-55; dep. chief Joint U.S. Mil. Group, Spain, 1955-58; chief, 1958-60; dep. for operations Hdqrs. TAC, 1960-63; chief Joint U.S. Mil. Group and Mil. Assistance Adv. Group, Spain, 1963-66; comdr. 16th Air Force, 1966-67; became U.S. rep. to permanent mil. deps. group Central Treaty Orgn., Ankara, Turkey, 1 1967. Decorated Silver Star, Legion of Merit, D.F.C., Air Medal, D.S.M. Clubs: Army-Navy (Washington); American (Madrid, Spain) (dir. 1957—).

DONOVAN, WILLIAM ALLAN, lawyer; b. N.Y.C., Apr. 24, 1926; s. Gerald and Louise (Priddle) D.; student Stevens Inst. Tech., 1943-44; B.S. in Elec. Engring., Northwestern U., 1946, J.D., 1950; A.B., Brown U., 1947; m. Barbara Laier, May 13, 1950; children-Eve, Louise, Homer Carey. Admitted to N.Y. bar, 1951, since practiced in White Plains; mem. firm McCarthy, Fingar, Gaynor & Donovan and predecessor firms, 1951—. Sec. dir. Am. Precision Industries, Inc. Mem. Am. Bar Assn., S.A.R., Sons Confederate Vets. Home: 27 New York Av White Plains NY 10606 Office: 175 Main St White Plains NY 10601

DONWORTH, CHARLES TENNEY, judge; b. Seattle, Feb. 15, 1892; s. George and Emma Laura (Tenney) D.; grad. Phillips Andover Acad., 1910; A.B., Yale, 1914; LL.B., U. Wash., 1916; m. Evelyn Carey, Feb. 5, 1918 (dec. 1934); children—Charles Carey, Mary Evelyn (Mrs. Lincoln Wayland Craighead); m. 2d, Dorothy Lee Griffin, Dec. 28, 1945. Admitted to Wash. State bar, 1916, practiced in Seattle, 1916-49, mem. firm Donworth, Donworth & Smith, 1942-49; asst. corp. counsel Seattle, 1920-23, judge Supreme Ct. of Wash., 1949-67, pro tem judge, intermittently, 1968—, chief justice, 1956-57. Served as 1st lt. inf. U.S. Army, 1917-19. Recipient Carkeek prize U. Wash. Law Sch., 1916. Mem. Am. Wash., Seattle (pres. 1934) bar assns., Am. Judicature Soc., Phi Delta Phi, Order of Coif. Club: Rainier (Seattle). Home: 2227 S Water St Olympia WA 98501

DOOB, JOSEPH LEE, mathematician, educator; b. Cin., Feb. 27, 1910; s. Leo and Mollie (Doerfler) D.; A.B., Harvard, 1930, M.A., 1931, Ph.D., 1932; m. Elsie Haviland Field, June 26, 1931; children—Stephen, Peter, Deborah. Faculty U. Ill., 1935—, successively asso., asst. prof., asso. prof., 1935-45, prof. math., 1945—. Mem. Nat. Acad. Scis., Am. Acad. Arts and Scis. Home: 208 W High St Urbana IL 61801

DOOB, LEONARD WILLIAM, psychologist; b. N.Y.C., Mar. 3, 1909; s. William and Florence (Lewis) D.; A.B., Dartmouth, 1929; A.M., Duke, 1930; postgrad. U. Frankfurt, Germany, 1930-32; Ph.D., Harvard, 1934; m. Eveline Bates, Mar. 21, 1936; children—Christopher Bates, Anthony Newcomb, Nicholas Ellsworth. Asst. instr. psychology Duke, 1929-30; instr. sociology Dartmouth, 1932-33; mem. faculty Yale 1934—, prof. psychology, 1950- -, also div. social scis., chmn. African studies. Investigator Senate Munitions Com., 1934; chief analysis sect. Coordinator Inter-Am. Affairs, 1940-42; chief cons. psychologist M.I., G-2, War Dept., 1942- 43; chief bur. overseas intelligence O.W.I., 1943-44, policy coordinator overseas br., 1944-45; mem. adv. bd. Inst. for Propaganda Analysis, 1938- 40; sr. staff mem. com. on human environments in Africa, Nat. Acad. Scis., 1958-60; vis. research prof. Univ. Coll., Dar es Salaam, Tanzania, 1967-68. Fellow Guggenheim Meml. Foundation, 1960-61. Certified psychologist, Conn. Mem. Am. Acad. Arts and Scis., African Studies Assn., Phi Beta Kappa, Sigma Xi. Author: Propaganda: Its Psychology and Technique, 1935; Competition and Cooperation (with M.A. May), 1937; Frustration and Aggression (with J. Dollard and others), 1939; The Plans of Men, 1940; Public Opinion and Propaganda, 1948; Social Psychology, 1952; Becoming More Civilized, 1960; Communication in Africa, 1961; Patriotism and Nationalism, 1964; Ants Will Not Eat Your Fingers, 1966; A Crocodile Has Me By the Leg, 1967; Patterning of Time, 1971. Editor: Reducing Conflict in Africa, 1970. Editor Jour. Social Psychology, 1965—. Contbr. tech., psychol. jours. Home: Clark Rd Woodbridge CT 06525 Office: 333 Cedar St New Haven CT 06510

DOOCY, FRED J., bank ofcl.; b. Hartford, Conn., May 5, 1913; student Am. Inst. Banking, Rutgers U. Grad. Sch. Banking; m. Mary O'Keefe, June 1944; children—Virginia, Eileen, Fred, Catherine, Paul. Head bookkeeper, teller Hartford Nat. Bank, 1931-42, asst. treas., 1945-50; sec. Hartford Nat. Bank & Trust Co., 1950-59, v.p., 1959—; asst. to pres. Hartford Nat. Corp., 1970—. Mem. Conn. Senate, 1958-67, past pres. pro-tem; lt. gov. Conn., 1967-68. Mem. South Windsor Bd. Edn., also town treas. Served with USAAF, 1942-45. Recipient Citizen of Year award South Windsor Lions Club, 1963. Mem. Am. Legion, East Hartford C. of C. (past pres.). Rotarian. Address: 2093 Ellington Rd South Windsor CT 06074

DOODY, JOHN RAYMOND, electronic co. exec.; b. Chgo., Nov. 26, 1918; s. James E. and Catherine (Neville) D.; C.P.A., U. Ill., 1948; m. Frances Rieder, June 23, 1945; children—Robert, Nancy, Suzanne, John F., David. With Warwick Mfg. Co., 1953-63, Maloney Products, Inc., 1963-66; treas. Chamberlain Mfg. Corp., Elmhurst, Ill., 1966-69, v.p., gen. mgr. Perma Power div., Chgo., 1969—. Area chmn. Experiment in Internat. Living, 1968-70. Treas., Park Forest, Ill. 1952-54. Home: 1029 N Knight St Park Ridge IL 60068 Office: 5740 N Tripp St Chicago IL 60646

DOODY, JOHN ROBERT, shoe co. exec.; b. Joplin, Mo., Nov. 21, 1930; s. Patrick John and Anna (Gibbs) D.; B.S., U. Mo., 1957; m. Mary Ann Goold, Nov. 24, 1962; children—John Robert, Gregory Lawrence, Elizabeth Ann. Profl. accountant Ernst & Ernst, St. Louis, 1957-65, mgr. nat. tng. program, Cleve., 1965; sec., controller Brown Shoe Co., Inc., St. Louis, 1966-70, v.p. finance, sec., 1970—. Bd. dirs. Greater St. Louis council Girl Scouts Am., 1967. Served with USAF, 1951-55. Mem. Financial Execs. Inst., Am. Inst. C.P.A.'s, Tax Execs. Inst., Am. Soc. Corp. Execs. Home: 405 Spring Valley Ct St Louis MO 63017 Office: 8350 Maryland Av St Louis MO 63105

DOODY, THOMAS CLARE, educator, chem. engr.; b. San Rafael, Cal., Oct. 13, 1901; s. Michael C. and Caroline E. (Blaney) D.; B.S., U. Cal. at Berkeley, 1924, M.S., 1925, Ph.D., 1938; m. Catherine C. Clarke, Aug. 27, 1939. Chemist, Barium Products, Inc., Modesto, Cal., 1926-29; chem. engr., termite investigations com. U. Cal. at Berkeley, 1930-34; prof. Poly. Coll. Engring., Oakland, Cal., 1938-39; from asst. prof. to prof. N.C. State Coll., 1939-47; asso. prof. chem. engring., Purdue U., 1947-53, prof., 1964-70, prof. emeritus, 1970—; adviser Taiwan Provincial Coll. Engring., Formosa, 1953-56; asso. prof. Colo. Sch. Mines, 1956-57; cons. Ind. Bd. Profl. Engrs. Registered profl. engr., Ind. Mem. A.A.A.S., Am. Soc. Engring. Edn., Am. Chem. Soc., Am. Inst. Chem. Engrs., Sigma Xi. Author: (with Merle Randall) Service of Paints on Wood Treated with Termite Repellents, 1938; Octahedral Arsenious Oxide, 1939; Liquid Mercury and Dilute Solutions of Sodium in Mercury Forced Convection, 1953. Contbr. Termites and Termite Control, 1934. Home: 2105 Indian Trail Dr West Layfayette IN 47906 Office: Sch Chem Engring Purdue Univ Lafayette IN 47907

DOOHER, MUREDACH JOSEPH, editor; b. Ireland, Oct. 22, 1913; s. James Francis and Mary Elizabeth (Nixon) D.; came to U.S., 1923, naturalized, 1938; grad. St. Benedict's Coll. Prep. Sch. Newark, 1931. Editor, Am. Mgmt. Assn., N.Y.C., 1937-56; exec. editor Dun's Rev., N.Y.C., 1956-61; editor indsl. and bus. books McGraw-Hill Book Co., Inc., 1961—. Mem. Indsl. Relations Research Assn. Republican. Roman Cath. Editor: Rating Employee and Supervisory Performance, 1950; The A.M.A. Handbook of Wage and Salary Administration, 1950; The Supervisor's Management Guide, 1949; The Management Leader's Manual, 1947; The Development of Executive Talent, 1952; Effective Communication on the Job, 1956; Selection of Management Personnel, 1957. Author essays and verse in British and Am. periodicals. Home: 242 Carmita Av Rutherford NJ 07070 Office: McGraw Hill Book Co 330 W 42d St New York City NY 10036

DOOLE, GEORGE ARNTZEN, Jr., aviation co. exec.; b. Quincy, Ill., Aug. 12, 1909; s. George Andrew and Naomi (Arntzen) D.; B.S., U. Ill., 1931; M.B.A., Harvard, 1939; with Pan Am. World Airways, N.Y.C., 1934-53, regional dir. Middle East and Asia, 1946-53; pres., dir. The Pacific Corp., Washington, 1953—; mng. dir., chief exec. officer, dir. Air Am., Inc., Air Asia Co., Ltd., Washington, 1953—; pres., dir. DHM Co., Quincy, Ill., 1949—; dir. Civil Air Transport Co. Ltd., Taiwan, 1955—, Air Am., Ltd., Hong Kong, Thai-Pacific Services Co. Ltd., Bangkok. Mem. U.S. presdl. team during negotiation 1st Air Transport Services agreement between U.S. and India, 1946. Gov. adm. Bristol Hosp., Istanbul, Turkey, 1946-51. Served from cadet to col. USAF, World War II, Korea. Decorated Order of Cedars (Lebanon). Mem. Am. Inst. Aero. and Astronautics, Nat. Aero. Assn. Clubs: Wings, Harvard (N.Y.C.); Army and Navy, Aero. (Washington); Chevy Chase (Chevy Chase, Md.); St. George's (Beirut, Lebanon). Home: 4000 Cathedral Av NW Washington DC 20016 Office: 1725 K St NW Washington DC 20006

DOOLEN, PAUL DWIGHT, ins. co. exec.; b. Vernon, Ill., Feb. 24, 1905; s. Isham Willis and Rose (Arnold) D.; B.S., U. Ill., 1927; LL.B., Harvard, 1931; m. Martha Estine Lewis, Oct. 20, 1934; children—Mark Lorimer, Deborah (Mrs. Robert Ittel). Admitted to Ill. bar, 1932, Fed. bar, 1935, U.S. Supreme Ct. bar, 1944; mem. firm Seago & Doolen, Chgo., 1931-36, Decker & Doolen, Waukegan, Ill., 1936-43; counsel A.E. Staley Co., Decatur, Ill., 1944-48, sales mgr., 1948-52; pres. Constn. Life Ins. Co., Chgo., 1953-62, now vice chmn., dir.; vice chmn. bd. Bankers Life & Casualty Co., Chgo., 1952-65, chmn. exec. com., 1965—, also vice chmn. bd., dir.; dir. Bankers Multiple Life Ins. Co., Dubuque, Ia., Protection Mut. Life Ins. Co., Phila., Gotham Life Ins. Co., Hempstead, N.Y., Union Bankers Life Ins. Co., Dallas, Western Am. Life Ins. Co., Dallas, Citizens Bank & Trust Co., Park Ridge, Ill. Mem. Delta Tau Delta. Clubs: Harvard, Sky Line, Chicago Curling (Chgo.). Home: 51 E Hwy 22 Barrington IL 60010 Office: 4444 W Lawrence Av Chicago IL 60630

DOOLEY, ARCH RICHARD, educator; b. Oklahoma City, Feb. 1, 1925; s. Archibald E. and Grace (Moore) D.; A.B., Yale, 1944; M.B.A., Harvard, 1950, D.C.S., 1960; m. Patricia Folts, Sept. 5, 1953; children—Arch Richard, Christopher Folts. Asst. prof. Oklahoma City U., 1946-47; asst. prof., asst. dean bus. U. N.C., 1950-54; mem. faculty Harvard Grad. Sch. Bus. Adminstrn., 1954—, prof., 1965—, Jesse Philips prof. mfg., 1969—; mem. vis. faculty Keio (Japan) U., U. Western Ont., Inst. Panamericano de Alta Direccion des Empresa (Mexico), Exec. Tng. Inst. Philippines, Singapore Mgmt. Inst., U. de Carabobo (Venezuela); cons. to govt. and industry, 1962—. Served as officer USNR, World War II. Mem. Acad. Mgmt., Beta Theta Pi. Author: Business Management Credit Bureaus, 1953; (with others) Casebooks in Production Management-Basic Problems, Concepts and Techniques, rev. edit., 1968; Production Operating Decisions in the Total Business Strategy, 1964; Operations Planning and Control, 1964; Wage Administration and Worker Productivity, 1964. Home: 21 Summit Rd Lexington MA 02173 Office: Harvard Business Sch Soldiers Field Boston MA 02163

DOOLEY, DELMER JOHN, found. exec.; b. Ramona, S.D., Mar. 15, 1920; s. Frank M. and Theresa (DeRungs) D.; B.S., S.D. State U., 1948; M.S., Colo. State U., 1952; Ed.D., U. Mo., 1964; m. Thalia Elma Doty, June 12, 1952; children—Douglas John, Alan Patrick. Vocational agr. instr., Platte, S.D., 1949-53, Lakeview, Ore., 1953-55; with Near East Found., 1955—, exec. dir., 1964—. Mem. exec. com. Am. Council Vol. Agys., 1965—, treas, 1970—. Exec. bd. Morris-Sussex council Boy Scouts Am., 1968—, dist. vice chmn. 1967-69, dist. chmn., 1969-71. Bd. dirs. Overseas Laymen. Served with USAAF, 1942-45. Decorated Independence medal King Hussein of Jordan. Mem. Middle East Inst., Soc. Internat. Devel., People-to-People, Am. Legion, Alpha Tau Alpha, Phi Delta Kappa. Roman Catholic. Rotarian. Home: 116 DeForest Av Hanover NJ 07936 Office: 54 E 64th St New York City NY 10021

DOOLEY, EDMUND JAMES, newspaper editor; b. Albany, Ore., July 23, 1914; s. John F. and Julia A. (Dorgan) D.; B.A., Ore. State U., 1938; m. Marjorie Cranna, Oct. 22, 1943; children—Nancy A., James B., Michael C. Successively sports reporter, news reporter, desk editor Portland Oregonian, 1938-42; news editor, then mng. editor Denver Post, 1946-56; editor weekly Pacific Bus., San Francisco, 1956-57; mem. staff San Francisco Examiner, 1957—, editor, 1962—. Bd. dirs. San Francisco Boys Club. Served with USAAF, 1942-46. Mem. A.P. Mng. Editors Assn., Am. Soc. Newspaper Editors, Sigma Delta Chi (past pres. No. Cal. chpt.), Beta Theta Pi. Roman Catholic. Home: 25 Turnsworth Av Redwood City CA 94062 Office: San Francisco Examiner 110 Fifth St San Francisco CA 94103

DOOLEY, EDWARD W., advt. agy. exec. Sr. v.p. J. Walter Thompson Co., N.Y.C. Office: 420 Lexington Av New York City NY 10017*

DOOLEY, EDWIN BENEDICT, former congressman; b. Bklyn., Apr. 13, 1905; s. Joseph Augustus and Isabelle (Delaney) D.; A.B., Dartmouth, 1927; LL.B., Fordham U., 1930; m. Harriette M. Feeley, Oct. 7, 1926 (dec. Jan. 1952); 1 son, Edwin Benedict; m. 2d, Anita M. Gillies, 1955 (dec. 1962); m. 3d, Margaret Sheefel Bailhe, Jan. 9, 1964. Feature writer N.Y. Sun, 1927-38; v.p. Don Spencer Co., advt. agy., 1938-42; dir. pub. relations Gen. Foods Corp., 1942-46; asso. Inst. Pub. Relations, 1946-48; exec. dir. N.Y. State div. Am. Cancer Soc., 1948-50; dir. pub. relations and advt. Health Ins. Plan Greater N.Y., 1950-55; mem. 85th to 87th Congresses, 26th Dist. N.Y. State; v.p. Jones, Brakeley & Rockwell. Chmn., N.Y. State Athletic Commn., 1966—; mem. N.Y. State com. Nat. Capitol Sesquicentennial Commemoration, 1951; pub. relations com. Boy Scouts Am., 1948-50. Mayor, Mamaroneck, N.Y., 1950-56. Bd. dirs. Community Chest. Republican. Clubs: Dartmouth (pres. Westchester 1953-54); Touchdown (chmn. 1945-46), Orienta Beach, University (Mamaroneck); N.Y. Athletic. Home: 810 Oakwood Rd Mamaroneck NY 10543

DOOLEY, GEORGE ELIJAH, med. adminstr.; b. Hopland, Cal., Dec. 25, 1918; s. Franklin Wayne and Mary Catherine Dorathea (Hageman) D.; B.S., St. Mary's Coll., Cal., 1939; M.S., George Washington U., 1966; postgrad., Nat. War Coll., 1960-61; m. Helen Ursula Fitch, July 28, 1945; children—Jeffrey Earle, Jill (Mrs. Michael Crane). Joined USMC, 1939, commd. 2d lt., 1940, designated Naval aviator, 1941, advanced through grades to brig. gen., 1966; served to PTO, World War II; staff officer Hdqrs. Marine Corps, Washington, 1957-60; comdg. officer Marine Aircraft Group 13, Hawaii, 1961-63; staff officer Fleet, Marine Force, Atlantic, 1963-65; chief of staff Fleet Marine Force, Atlantic, Norfolk, Va., 1965-66; asst. dep. chief of staff Hdqrs., Washington, 1966-68; chief of staff 3d Marine Amphibious Force, Danang, Vietnam, 1968-70; comdg. gen. Landing Force Tng. Command, Pacific, 1970; ret., 1970; adminstr. Kensington Med. Group, San Diego, 1971—. Sec.-treas. Kensington Investment Corp., San Deigo. Decorated D.S.M., Silver Star, Legion of Merit, D.F.C., Air medal (U.S.); Nat. Order 5th class, Gallantry cross with palm (Vietnam); Korean Chung Moo. Mem. Del Mar C. of C., Del Mar Civic Assn., Med. Group Mgmt. Assn., Navy League, Med. Adminstrs. Cal., Del Mar Thoroughbred Club. Roman Catholic. Rotarian. Club: Cuyamaca (San Diego). Home: 2055 Seaview Del Mar CA 92014 Office: 4193 Adams Av San Diego CA 92116

DOOLEY, JIM, football coach; b. Stoutsville, Mo., Feb. 8, 1930; grad. U. Miami (Fla.), 1952; m. Elaine Elliott; children—Jim, Pat, Tim, Bill, Lisa Ann. Player, def. halfback Chgo. Bears, Nat. Football League, 1952-53, offensive end, 1953-62, asst. coach, 1963-68, head coach, 1968—. Served with USAF, 1955-56. Home: Arlington Heights IL 60004 Office: Chgo Bears Football Club Inc 173 W Madison St Chicago IL 60602

DOOLEY, THOMAS PRICE, educator, b. Elberton, Ga., Oct. 12, 1904; s. William and Lois (Hardy) D.; B.A., Morehouse Coll., Atlanta, 1927; M.S., State U. Ia., 1931, Ph.D., 1939; summer student U. Detroit, 1928, Columbia, 1942; m. Eula Mae Muckleroy, May 30, 1941; children—Lois Marie, Thomas Price. Prof. biology Ark. State Coll., Pine Bluff, 1929-32; mem. faculty Prairie View (Tex.) A. and M. Coll., 1934—, prof. biology, 1942—, spl. research genetics, cytology, antibiotics. Chmn. region 6 on Study Undergrad. Biol. Edn. Tex. Colls., 1966-69. Mem. A.A.A.S., Am. Genetics Assn., Am. Microscopic Soc., Nat. Inst. Sci., Nat. Assn. Research Sci. Teaching, Tex. Acad. Sci. (v.p. biol. sect. 1967-68), Sigma Xi, Beta Kappa Chi, Beta Beta Beta. Home: Box 2726 Prairie View TX 77445

DOOLEY, WILLIAM EDWARD, baritone; b. Modesto, Cal., Sept. 9, 1932; s. Andrew Taylor and Irma (Cornwell) D.; B.A., Eastman Sch. Music, 1954; postgrad. Acad. Music, Munich, Germany, 1956-57; m. Chardelle Hayward, July 14, 1957. Mem. Heidelberg (Germany) Opera, 1957-59, Bielefeld (Germany) Opera, 1959-62, Deutsche Opera Berlin (Germany), 1962—, Met. Opera, N.Y.C., 1963—, Salzburg (Austria) Festival, 1964—; recording artist for RCA Victor. Served with AUS, 1954-56. Fulbright scholar, 1956; recipient Best Singer award Theatre des Nations, Paris, France, 1961, Berlin Culture award, 1964. Home: Glockenturmstrasse 28 Berlin 19 West Germany Office: care Metropolitan Opera Company New York City NY 10023

DOOLEY, WILLIAM GROVER, banker; b. Chgo., Dec. 4, 1893; s. Thomas J. and Ellen (O'Connor) D.; A.B., Loyola U., Chgo., 1914, LL.B., 1917; m. Marie O'Connell, Nov. 10, 1917 (dec. Nov. 1918); 1 dau., Marie (Mrs. Richard Ballschmider); m. 2d, Mary J. Hopkinson, Nov. 16, 1924; children—William J., Barbara, Josephine (Mrs. Leo Blaber), Richard. Vice pres., dir. Liberty Nat. Bank, Chgo., 1919-34; v.p., dir. Sears Bank & Trust Co., Chgo., 1934-52, pres., dir., 1953-59, vice chmn., dir., 1959—; dir. Wis. Tool & Die Corp. Founder, 1st pres. Greater Lawndale Conservation Commn., 1954; active Cath. Charities Chgo. Trustee Midwest Chgo. Boys Club. Mem. Chgo. (past dir.), West Side (past pres.) bankers assns. Clubs: Executives, Bankers (Chgo.). Home: 617 Ashland Av River Forest IL 60305 Office: 3401 Arthington St Chicago IL 60624

DOOLING, JOHN FRANCIS, Jr., U.S. judge; b. Bklyn., June 13, 1908; s. John Francis and Anna Clothilde (Conlan) D.; A.B. cum laude, St. Francis Coll., Bklyn., 1929; LL.B. magna cum laude, St. Johns U., 1932, Harvard, 1934; m. Marie Dorothea Elizabeth Bernard, Apr. 24, 1937; children—Julienne (Mrs. Eugene B. Nann), Deborah (Mrs. Paul P. Fitzgerald), Peter, Ann, Marie. Admitted to N.Y. bar, 1934; with firm Sullivan & Cromwell, N.Y.C., 1934-61; U.S. judge Eastern Dist. N.Y., 1961—. Trustee Vassar Coll., 1965-69. Mem. Am. Law Inst., Assn. Bar City N.Y. (chmn. com. state legislation 1951-53, com. cts. superior jurisdiction 1957- 60). Home: 621 2d St Brooklyn NY 11215 Office: US Court House 225 Cadman Plaza E Brooklyn NY 11201

DOOLITTLE, ARTHUR KING, chem. engr.; b. Oberlin, O., Nov. 15, 1896; s. Frederick Giraud and Maud (Tucker) D.; A.B., Columbia, 1919, B.S., 1920, Chem. E., 1923; m. Dortha Bailey, Aug. 8, 1923; children—Robert Frederick II, Elizabeth May (Mrs. Donald Charles Peckham). Research engr. Dorr Co., Westport, Conn., 1923-25; plant engr. Sherwin-Williams Co., Chgo., 1925-29, chief lacquer div., Newark, 1929-31; devel. engr. spray drying Bowen Research Corp., N.Y.C., 1931; dir. lacquer research Bradley Vrooman Co., Chgo., 1931-32; tech. head coatings research Carbide & Carbon Chems. Co., South Charleston, W.Va., 1932-44, asst. dir. research, 1944-55, sr. scientist, 1955-61; pres. Arcadia Inst. for Sci. Research, Inc., Charleston, W.Va., 1959—; cons., 1959—; partner Dorr Consultants, N.Y.C., 1959-61; prof. chemistry Drexel Inst. Tech., Phila., 1961-64. Mem. adv. bd. chem. engring. dept. Princeton, 1955-58. Served to 2d lt. A.S., AUS, 1917-19. Decorated Croce di Cavaliere al Merito Della Republica Italiana (Italy), 1967. Registered profl. engr., W.Va., N.Y., N.J., Del. Mem. Am. Inst. Chem. Engrs. (dir. 1951-54, v.p., 1955, chmn. Charleston sect. 1943-44), A.A.A.S. (chmn. mgmt. com. Gordon Confs., 1955-56, adv. bd. 1950-58), Am. Chem. Soc. (chmn. paint plastics and printing ink div. 1952-53, div. councilor 1952-56, council com. on Nat. meetings and div. activities 1952-56, adv. bd. indsl. and engring. chemistry 1954-56), Order of Daedalians, Sigma Xi, Phi Beta Kappa, Tau Beta Pi, Phi Lambda Upsilon, Chi Beta Phi, Alpha Chi Rho. Clubs: Columbia University (N.Y.C.); Quiet Birdmen, Cosmos (Washington). Author: The Technology of Solvents and Plasticizers, 1954; also articles in sci. jours. Contbr. to Ency. of Chem. Tech., 1954. Patentee in field. Home: 406 Osborne Lane Wallingford PA 19086

DOOLITTLE, GEORGE LEO, former lumber mcht.; b. Colfax, Ia., July 30, 1899; s. James M. and Ruth Locke (Kapple) D.; student N.M. Mil. Inst., 1916-17; B.S., U.S. Mil. Acad., 1920; m. Rosalie Furry, Sept. 2, 1925; children—Jeannette L. (Mrs. Donald C. Ingram), James M. II, George Leo. Commd. 2d lt. C.A., U.S. Army, 1920, ret. as 1st lt., 1923; served from 1st lt. to maj. C.E., U.S. Army, 1942-46; asst. dist. engr., Albuquerque, 1942- 43; supply div. Office Chief Engrs. Washington, 1943-46; instr. N.M. Mil. Inst., 1923-24; with Albuquerque Lumber Co., 1924-68, pres., 1942-64, chmn. bd., 1964-68; pres. Fir- Pine Lumber Co., Albuquerque, 1948-68, Constrn. Supply Co., Farmington, N.M. 1952-68; sec. Alco Devel. Co., 1960-68; dir., mem. adv. bd. Mountain States Tel.&Tel. Co. Chmn., Armed Forces Adv. Com., 1964. Chmn., Community Chest. Mem. N.A.M. (dir.), Newcomen Soc., Mountain States Lumber Dealers Assn. (dir.), Southwest Wholesale Distbrs. Assn. (dir.), Albuquerque C. of C. (dir.). Episcopalian (vestry). Mason. Club: Albuquerque Country (pres.). Home: 1617 San Cristobal Rd S W Albuquerque NM 87104 Office: Sunshine Bldg Albuquerque NM 87101

DOOLITTLE, GILLUM HOTCHKISS, lawyer; b. Burton, O., Aug. 14, 1883; s. James Clement and Philena (Townsley) D.; A.B., Western Res. U., 1906, LL.B., 1908; m. Marta E. Habicht, June 8, 1912; children—Marloe J. (Mrs. James Jamieson), Philene (Mrs. Carl Engel), Bruce F. Admitted to Ohio bar, 1908, since practiced in Akron; dir. law City Akron, 1932-33; partner firm Buckingham, Doolittle & Burroughs, 1934—. Summit County (Ohio) Republican Exec. Com., 1925-35, Ohio Rep. Finance Com., 1934. Fellow Ohio Bar Assn. Found.; mem. Am., Ohio (past mem. exec. com.), Akron (past pres.) bar assns., Am. Judicature Soc., Akron C. of C. (mem. bd.). Home: 3466 W Bath Rd Akron OH 44313 Office: 1 Cascade Plaza Akron OH 44308

DOOLITTLE, J. WILLIAM asst. sec. manpower and reserve affairs Dept. of Air Force. Address: 4238 50th St Washington DC 20016.*

DOOLITTLE, JAMES, educator; b. Morristown, N.J., Oct. 8, 1917; s. James and Mabel Vescelius (Jenkins) D.; grad. Phillips Exeter Acad., 1935; A.B., Princeton, 1939, M.A., 1942, Ph.D., 1948; m. Pauline G. Snow, Dec. 11, 1944; children—Janet V., Ellen R., Patricia S., Sarah A., John P., Peter M. Tchr., Thacher Sch., Ojai, Cal., 1939-40; instr. modern langs. Princeton, 1946-49; asst. prof., prof. Romance langs. Ohio State U., 1949-61; prof., head dept. Romance langs. and lits. U. Cin., 1961-65; prof. dept. fgn. and comparative lit. U. Rochester, 1965—. Travel grantee Am. Philos. Soc., 1955; postdoctoral fellow Ohio State U., 1959-60; Guggenheim fellow, 1965-66; Am. Council Learned Socs. fellowship grantee, 1968. Mem. Modern Lang. Assn. Am. Author: Rameau's Nephew: A Study of Diderot's Second Satire, 1960; Afred de Vigny, 1967. Home: 338 Hollywood Av Rochester NY 14618

DOOLITTLE, JAMES HAROLD, aviator, ins. co. exec.; b. Alemeda, Cal. Dec. 14, 1896; s. Frank H. and Rosa C. (Shepherd) D.; A.D., U. Cal., 1918 (1922); fellow aero. engring. Mass. Inst. Tech., 1924, M.S., 1925, Sc.D., 1926; m. Josephine E. Daniels, Dec. 24, 1917; children—James H., John P. Aviator, U.S. Army, 1917-30; resigned 1930; maj. Res. Corps; mgr. aviation dept. Shell Petroleum Corp., 1930-40, apptd. mem. Army AC Investigating Com. (Baker Bd.), 1934; apptd. maj. USAAF, 1940, lt. col. to maj. gen., 1942, lt. gen., 1944; comdr. 12th Air Force in North Africa, Strategic Air Force, 15th and 8th Air Forces, comdr. 8th Air Force, Okinawa, 1945; inactive duty, 1946-58, ret., 1959; v.p., dir. Shell Oil Co., 1946-58, dir., 1946-67; chmn. bd., dir. Space Tech. Labs., 1959-63; cons. TRW Systems, 1962-66; dir. Tele-Trip Co., Inc., Companion Life, Mut. of Omaha, United Benefit Life Ins. Co., Mut. Omaha Growth and Income Funds; trustee Aerospace Corp., 1963-69, chmn. bd. trustees, chmn. exec. com., 1965-69. Pres., Air Force Assn., 1946- 47, chmn., 1948-49; apptd. chmn. Sec. War's Bd. on Enlisted Men- Officer Relationships; mem. NACA, 1948-56, chmn. 1956-58; adviser to Com. on Nat. Security Orgn. and Joint Congl. Aviation Policy Bd.; mem. adv. bd. Nat. Air Mus., Smithsonian Inst., 1956-65; chmn. Pres.'s Airport Commn., 1952, Pres.'s Task Group on Air Inspection, Stassen Disarmament Com., 1955, Pres.'s Bd. on Fgn. Intelligence, 1955-65, Air Force Sci. Adv. Bd. 1955-58; mem. Def. Sci. Bd., 1957-58, Pres.'s Sci. Adv. Com., 1957-58, Nat. Aeros. and Space Council, 1958. Decorated Congl. Medal of Honor, D.S.M. with oak leaf cluster, Silver Star, D.F.C. with two oak leaf clusters, Bronze Star, Air medal with three oak leaf clusters; Bolivian Order of Condor medal, Yon-Hwei Class III; grande officier French Legion d'Honneur, Croix de Guerre with palm; knight comdr. Order of the Bath; grande officer Order of Crown with Palm and Croix de Guerre with palm (both Belgium), 1948. Recipient Harmon Internat. Aviation award; winner Schneider Trophy Race, 1925; awarded Mackay trophy, 1926; Harmon trophy, 1930; winner Bendix Trophy Race, Burbank, Cal. to Cleve., 1931; winner Thompson Trophy Race, 258.68 miles per hr., 1932; also set world's high speed record for landplanes, 1932. Fellow Inst. Aero Scis. (pres. 1940, hon.), Royal Aero. Soc.; mem. Nat. Aero. Assn. Clubs: Explorers, Boone and Crockett, Bohemian, Army and Navy, Wings, Lotos. Contbr. sci., aero. articles to profl. jours. Home: 233 Marguerita Av Santa Monica CA 90402 Office: 5225 Wilshire Blvd Los Angeles CA 90036

DOOLITTLE, JONATHAN EDISON, former telephone co. exec.; b. Wallingford, Conn., Oct. 19, 1905; s. Dexter O. and Amelia P. (Pinard) D.; A.B., Yale, 1926; m. Catherine Lochhead, July 21, 1928; children—Jonathan Edison, Robert L. Joined So. New Eng. Telephone Co., 1926, successively statistician, gen. personnel supr., gen. accounting supr., 1926-47, comptroller, 1947-64, v.p., 1955-64, became adminstrv. v.p., 1965; dir. Tradesmen Nat. Bank, Internat. Silver Co., So. New Eng. Telephone Co. Dir. Conn. Med. Service.

DOOLITTLE, ROBERT FREDERICK, lawyer; b. Oberlin, O., June 14, 1902; s. Frederick Giraud and Maude (Tucker) D.; grad. Ethical Culture Sch., N.Y.C., 1919; A.B. magna cum laude, Harvard, 1923. LL.B., 1930; LL.D., Youngstown State U., 1968; m. Gretchen Reller, Oct. 11, 1958. Admitted to the N. Y. State bar, 1932, Ohio bar, 1953; asso. with Taylor, Blanc, Capron & Marsh, N.Y.C., 1930-32; with firm Cotton, Franklin, Wright & Gordon (name now Cahill, Gordon, Sonnett, Reindel & Ohl), 1932- 42; counsel for Baldwin Locomotive Works (name changed to Baldwin-Lima-Hamilton Corp., Dec. 1950), Phila., 1946-48, v.p., counsel, 1948-52; v.p. Baldwin Locomotive Sales Corp., Baldwin Locomotive Works of Can., Baldwin Locomotive Internat., Inc., 1948-52; asst. gen. counsel, asst. sec. Youngstown Sheet and Tube Co. (O.), 1952-59, gen. counsel, corp. sec., 1959-67, v.p., 1964-67, dir., 1967-69; counsel to law firm, Baker, Hostetler & Patterson, Cleve., 1967—. Bd. dirs. World Affairs Council Phila., 1951-52; mem. Gov.'s Com. on Water Resources, Ohio, 1954-58; mem. adv. council Ohio Water Commn., 1966-67; chmn. adv. council task force on financing State Water Mgmt. Plan, 1966-67; mem. Gov.'s Com. Emergency Resource Planning, Ohio, 1966-67. Mem. Ohio Bd. Regents for Higher Edn., 1963—, vice chmn., 1966—; trustee, v.p. Arcadia Inst. Sci. Research; trustee, mem. exec. com. Cleve. Council on World Affairs. Maj., U.S. Army, July 1942, to lt. col., June 1944; assigned by War Dept. to Office Contract Settlement, Exec. Office Pres., Washington, 1944; disch., 1945; asst. gen. counsel, later gen. counsel, Office Contract Settlement, 1945-46. Mem. Am. Judicature Soc., Am., N.Y. State, Ohio, Cleve. bar. assns., Ohio Mfrs. Assn. (trustee 1955-67, pres. 1965-67, exec. com. 1957—), Youngstown Symphony Soc. (dir. 1953-67), N.A.M. (edn. policy com.), Am. Iron and Steel Inst., Phi Beta Kappa, Phi Delta Phi. Conglist. Clubs: Youngstown Country; Merion Cricket (Haverford, Pa.); Merion Golf (Ardmore, Pa.); Rittenhouse (Phila.); Harvard (N.Y.C.); Chagrin Valley Hunt; Kirtland Country, Union (Cleve.). Home: Berkshire Rd Gates Mills OH 44040 Office: Union Commerce Bldg Cleveland OH 44115

DOOLY, OSCAR EARLE, investment broker; b. Talbotton, Ga., June 5, 1900; s. Oscar Earle and Ada Belle (Lummus) D.; student Riverside Mil. Acad., Gainesville, Ga., 1917-18; m. Constance Davenport, May 16, 1923; 1 dau., Caren (Mrs. Richard L. Tatum). Pres., Oscar E. Dooly Assos., Inc., real estate, Miami, Fla., 1930—; chmn. bd. Dooly, Gerrish & Co., investments. Chmn. finance com., past pres. Orange Bowl Com. Chmn. U. Miami. Recipient Gold Medal award of merit U. Miami. Mem. Miami, Miami Beach bds. realtors, Fla. (dir.), Miami, Miami Beach chambers commerce, Fla. Assn. Realtors, Nat. Assn. Real Estate Bds., Fla. Security Dealers Assn., Nat. Assn. Securities Dealers, Soc. Colonial Wars, S.A.R. Mason. Clubs: LaGorce Country Club (past pres.), Bath, Indian Creek Country (Miami Beach); Miami (past pres.); Bankers of Am. (N.Y.C.); Capital City (Atlanta); River (Jacksonville). Home: 1291 N E 96th St Miami, FL 33138. Office: 25 S E 2d Av Miami FL 33131

DOORLEY, JOSEPH ALOYSIUS, Jr., mayor of Providence; b. Providence, Sept. 12, 1930; s. Joseph Aloysius and Nora (Cannon) D.; A.B., U. Notre Dame, 1953; LL.B., Boston Coll., 1958; m. Claire Walsh, June 13, 1953; children—Joseph Aloysius III, Michael, Brian, Dennis, Carleen, Patricia Mary. Research technician for R.I. Devel. Council, 1955; adminstrv. asst. to gov. R.I., 1956-58; admitted to R.I. bar, 1958; practice in Providence, 1959-64; adminstrv. asst. for legislative affairs to gov. R.I., 1961-62; councilman, Providence, 1963-64; mayor of Providence, 1965—. Chmn. ex officio Bd. Hosp. Commrs. Providence, Charles H. Smith Estate, Providence Sinking Fund Commn.; mem. Providence City Plan Commn.; chmn. Dexter Donation Trust; mem. human resources devel. com. U.S. Conf. Mayors; mem. pub. ofcls. adv. council Office Econ. Opportunity. Chmn. registration drive R.I. Kennedy for Pres., 1960; mem. Democratic Nat. Com. for R.I. Mem. Am., R.I. bar assns., Notre Dame Alumni Assn., St. Pius Holy Name Soc. K.C. Home: 97 Hilltop Av Providence RI 02908 Office: City Hall Providence RI 02903

DORAIN, PAUL BRENDEL, educator, chemist; b. New Haven, Aug. 30, 1926; s. Hugh Alfred and Marion (Burritt) D.; B.S., Yale, 1950; Ph.D., Ind. U., 1954; m. Elsie Vega Ahlberg, Aug. 19, 1950; children—Melanie, Douglas. Postdoctoral fellow U. Chgo., 1954-56; solid state physicist Aero. Research Lab. USAF, Dayton, O., 1956-58; mem. faculty Brandeis U., 1958—, prof. chemistry, 1967—, co-chmn. chemistry dept., 1970—. Vice pres. Norfolk Fellowship Found., 1968—; founding mem. Laymen's Legislative League, 1967. Served with USNR, 1944- 46. Mem. Am. Phys. Soc., Sigma Xi. Author: Symmetry in Inorganic Chemistry, 1964. Research optical and magnetic properties of solids. Home: 31 Locust Av Lexington MA 02173 Office: Dept Chemistry Brandeis U Waltham MA 02154

DORAN, ADRON, univ. pres.; b. Graves County, Ky., Sept. 1, 1909; s. Edward C. and Elizabeth (Clemons) D.; B.S., Murray State Coll., 1932, M.A., 1948, LL.D., 1970; Ed.D., U.Ky., 1950; LL.D., Ashland Coll., 1967, Eastern Ky. U., 1970; m. Mignon McClain, Aug. 23, 1931. Tchr., basketball coach, prin. Boaz (Ky.) High Sch., 1932-35, Sylvan Shade (Ky.) High Sch., 1935-38; prin. Wingo (Ky.) High Sch., 1938-48; editor Fulton (Ky.) Daily Leader, 1946-48; vis. prof. U. Ga. Coll. Edn., 1951; dir. div. tchr. edn. and certification Ky. Dept. Edn., 1952-54; pres. Morehead (Ky.) State U., 1954—. Mem. White House Conf. on Edn., 1954, So. Regional Conf. on Edn. Beyond High Sch., 1958, dir. first 3 legislative work confs., 1952- 54; assisted formation Western Interstate Commn. Higher Edn., 1950-52; mem. Eastern Ky. Regional Planning Commn., 1957—; adv. com. Council State Govts., 1948; mem. Pres.'s Council on Higher Edn., Nat. Adv. Council on Edn. Professions Devel., 1967, Edn. Commn. of States, 1968; exec. com. So. Regional Edn. Bd.; mem. adv. com. on edn. to Appalachian Commn.; chmn. N.E. Gateway (Ky.) Tourist Com. Mem. Ky. Ho. of Reps. from Graves County, 1944-51, chmn. edn. com., 1944-50, speaker of house, 1950-51, mem. legislative research commn., 1950-51. Bd. govs. Stennett Settlement Sch., Leslie County, Ky., 1948-50; exec. com. Blue Grass council Boy Scouts Am., 1954—. Bd. dirs. Ohio Valley Coll., Parkersburg, W. Va.; trustee Ohio Valley Coll. Recipient award of merit Ky. Assn. Colls., Secondary and Elementary Schs., 1946; Outstanding Service to Soil Conservation Dists. award. Soil Conservation Dists. Ky., 1958; named Kentuckian of Year, Ky. Press Assn., 1959; Ky. col., Ark. traveller, La. col., Neb. adm., Okla. commodore; named Boss of Year, Morehead Jr. C. of C., 1967; recipient Distinguished Kentuckian award, 1966, Horatio Alger award, 1971, Distinguished Service award for achievements field edn., 1969, Distinguished Civilian award 1st Army, 1971. Mem. Nat. (chmn. legislative commn. 1965—), Ky. (dir., past pres., Lincoln key award 1959), First Dist. (past pres.), Eastern Ky. (past pres.) edn. assns., Morehead C. of C. (dir., Man of Year award 1959), Ky. Assn. Future Homemakers Am. (hon.), Phi Delta Kappa, Kappa Delta Pi. Mem. Ch. of Christ. Kiwanian. Home: 328 University Blvd Morehead KY 40351

DORAN, AMBROSE BENEDICT, mfg. co. exec.; b. N.Y.C., July 10, 1915; s. William T. and Johanna Ethel (Finotti) D.; A.B., Dartmouth, 1937; M.B.A., Harvard, 1939; m. Marjorie Westgate, Aug. 28, 1937; children—Marianne (Mrs. Robert Steinhacker), Linda (Mrs. William T. MacCary) (dec.), Patricia (Mrs. Fred Schaum), Kathleen. Employed with the Chatham Process Corp., 1939-40; asst. to v.p. Gen. Foods Corp., 1940-45; v.p. Thorsen Products Corp., 1945-55; co. acquired by Union Camp Corp., 1956, gen. mgr. chem. div., 1958—, v.p. corp., 1964—, also dir. Home: 248 S Mountain Av Montclair NJ 07042 Office: 1600 Valley Rd Wayne NJ 07470

DORAN, CHARLES EDWARD, textile mill products exec.; b. Hartford, Conn., Mar. 31, 1928; s. Charles Edward and Josephine Catherine (Masher) D.; B.A., Hamilton Coll., 1951; M.A., Yale, 1952; m. Anne Marie McGovern, May 18, 1957; children—Charles Francis, John Francis, Pamela Anne. Trainee Gen. Elec. Co., 1953-56, financial mgmt. positions, 1956-65; asst. treas. Collins & Aikman Corp., N.Y.C., 1965-71, treas., 1971—. Served with USNR, 1946-48. Mem. Phi Beta Kappa. Club: Yale (N.Y.C.). Home: 10 Hardscrabble Circle Armonk NY 10504 Office: 210 Madison Av New York City NY 10016

DORAN, JAMES R., newspaper man. Editor Harrisburg Patriot News. Address: 859 Country Club Rd Capitol Hill Harrisburg PA 17110*

DORAN, MADELEINE, educator; b. Salt Lake City, Aug. 12, 1905; d. Frank and Nellie May (Kunkel) Doran; student San Diego State Coll., 1923-25; B.A., Stanford, 1927, Ph.D. (univ. fellow, 1928-30), 1930; M.A., U. Ia., 1928; postgrad. U. Coll. U. London, 1933; D.Litt., Wheaton (Mass.) Coll., 1963. Instr. English, Wellesley Coll., 1930-33, Mary Whiton Calkins vis. prof., 1957; instr. English, U. Wis., Madison, 1935-39, asst. prof., 1939-47, asso. prof., 1947-51, prof., 1951—, Ruth C. Wallerstein prof. English lit., 1967—, prof. Inst. for Research in Humanities, 1970—; vis. prof. Stanford, spring 1960; grantee Huntington Library, winters 1960, 64; fellow Folger Shakespeare Library, spring 1964. Fellow Am. Council Learned Socs., 1933-34, Am. Assn. U. Women, 1946-47; Guggenheim fellow, 1967-68. Mem. Modern Lang. Assn. Am. (exec. council 1964-67), Am. Assn. U. Women, Shakespeare Assn. Am., Renaissance Soc. Am. (mem. council 1963-64, 67-68, 69-70), Am. Assn. U. Profs., Malone Soc., Madison Lit. Club, Nature Conservancy, Nat. Parks Assn., Audubon Soc., Am. Museum Natural History, Save-the-Redwoods League, Phi Beta Kappa. Author: Books 2, 3, Henry VI: Their Relation to the Contention and the True Tragedy, 1928; The Text of King Lear, 1931; Endeavors of Art: A Study of Form in Elizabethan Drama, 1954. Editor: If You Know Not Me (by Thomas Heywood), 1934; A Midsummer Night's Dream (Shakespeare), 1959. Contbr. articles, revs. on Shakespeare, Elizabethan drama, Renaissance in profl. jours. Home: 4238 Wanda Pl Madison WI 53711

DORAN, PAUL RICHARD, educator; b. Wilkinsburg, Pa., Jan. 10, 1920; s. Paul Richard and Dora Margaret (Heffernan) D.; B.A., Cath. U., 1940; M.A., U. Pa., 1945, Ph.D., 1971. Mem. Bros. Christian Schs., 1935-71; tchr. LaSalle High Sch., Phila., 1940-43, chmn. English dept., 1945-49; tchr. West Phila. Cath. High Sch., 1944-45; asst. prof. LaSalle Coll., 1949, chmn. English dept., 1950-56, dean Sch. Arts and Scis., 1956-69, asso. prof., 1958—. Mem. Modern Lang. Assn., Nat. Council Tchrs. English, Coll. English Assn., Eastern Assn. Deans and Advisers Students, Assn. Higher Edn., Pa. Deans Liberal Arts Colls. Address: LaSalle Coll Philadelphia PA 19141

DORAN, ROBERT C., advt. agy. exec.; b. Boone, Ia., 1928; grad. Ia. State U., 1949. Exec. v.p., mgr. Griswold-Eshleman Co., Chgo. Mason. Home: 1098 Forest Hill Rd Lake Forest IL 60045 Office: 1 E Wacker Dr Chicago IL 60601*

DORATI, ANTAL, composer, condr.; b. Budapest, Hungary, Apr. 9, 1906: s. Alexander and Margit (Kunwald) D.; student of composition and piano, Acad. of Music, Budapest, diploma, 1924; student U. Vienna, 1923-25; D. Music Macalester Coll. 1957; Klara Korody, July 14, 1929; 1 dau., Antonia Klara. Came to U.S., 1934, naturalized, 1947. Condr., Budapest Royal Opera House, 1924-28, Dresden State Opera, 1928-29, Munster State Opera, 1929-32, Ballet Russe de Monte Carlo, 1933-37; mus. dir. original Ballet Russe, 1938-40, Ballet Theatre, 1940-44; mus. dir. Dallas Symphony Orch., 1945-49; mus. dir. Mpls. Symphony Orch., 1949-60; chief condr. BBC Symphony Orch., London, 1962-66; chief condr. Stockholm Philharmonic, 1966--; music dir. Washington Nat. Symphony, 1969—; guest condr. all maj. orchestras, U.S., Europe, Latin Am., Australia. Compositions include string quartet, quintet for oboe and strings, divertimento for small orchestra, three An. serenades for string orchestra, cello concerto; 2 Hungarian Peasant Tunes for violin and piano, 1945; arranger La Vie Parisienne by Offenbach, for New Opera Co., 1941; The Way of the Cross (Cantata); The Two Enchantments of Li Tai Pe, (lyric scene for baritone and small orchestra); Symphony (for large orch.); Missa brevis (for mixed choir and percussion instruments); Magdalena (ballet); 7 Pieces for Orchestra; Octet for Strings; Madrigal Suite (chorus and orch.), Largo Concertato for String Orchestra, Chamber Music for Soprano and String Orchestra; ballet arrangements include: Graduation Ball, Bluebeard, Helen of Troy, Pavillon, Fair at Sorochinsk, Harvest Time. Records for Mercury Recording Co. EMI, Philips, RCA- Victor, Decca. Home: Via del Foraggi 74 Rome Italy Office: care Hurok Attractions 730 Fifth Av New York City NY 10019

DORBURN, FREDERICK JOHN diversified mfg. co. exec.; b. Cin., May 21, 1910; grad. Phillips Acad., Andover, Mass., 1927; B.S., Princeton, 1931; postgrad. Mass. Inst. Tech., 1931-33; m. Jean R. Holland, June 16, 1935; children--Lois A., Andrew M., James. Salesman, Brown Mfg. Co., Boston, 1932-33; jr. engr. Ball Metals Co., Carson City, Nev., 1933-36, engr., 1936-37, sr. engr., 1937-40; project engr. Kingston Engring. Co., Los Angeles, 1940-43; with dept. engring. City of Denver, 1946-50, dep. head, 1950-52; 2d v.p. Johnson Mfg. Co., Kansas City, Kansas, 1952-54, v.p. for engring., 1954-57; v.p. research Consol. Industries, Inc., South Bend, Ind., 1957-60, exec. v.p., 1960-65, pres., 1965-70, chmn. bd., chief exec. officer, 1970--, also dir.; dir. ABC Chem. Co., 2d Nat. Bank, Country Food Storage Co., Providence Indsl. Corp. (Ind.), Wilson Investment Co., Inc., Hammond Life Ins. Co., Inc. (Ind.), Prudential Ins. Co., Haverford Mfg. Co., Leader Pub. Co. Pres., Dewey High Sch., Kansas City, Mo., 1953-54; fund chmn. local div. Salvation Army, 1959-60. Mem. South Bend Republican Com., 1964-68. Bd. dirs. Ind. council Boy Scouts Am., 1969-71; trustee Lovell Found. Served to lt., Corps Engrs., AUS, 1943-45. Decorated Bronze Star medal. Member N.A.M., South Bend C. of C. (v.p. 1963-65, dir. 1965-70), Am. Mgmt. Assn., Ind. Engrs. America. Trustee Coshocton Animal Welfare League, Curry Home for the Aged. Named Man of Year, Coshocton Junior Chamber of Commerce, 1968. Mem. Coshocton C. of C. (vice president 1967-68, pres. 1969-70), English Speaking Union, Coshocton Sertoma Club, Nat. Assn. Mfrs., Sales Executives Institute, Phi Beta Kappa, Sigma Chi, Phi Mu. Democrat. Mem. Christian Ch. (lay leader). Mason (32, Shriner). Clubs: Coshocton Country, Coshocton City, Running Deer Country. Home: 2d Av Coshocton OH Office: 3d Av Coshocton OH

DORCUS, ROY MELVIN, univ. dean; b. Frederick, Md., Feb. 9, 1901; s. Charles W. and Emma (Feiser) D.; A.B., Johns Hopkins, 1922, A.M., 1924, Ph.D., 1925; m. Mildred Day, Sept. 8, 1925. Instr. psychology Johns Hopkins, 1925-28, asso. prof., 1928-37; asso. prof. psychology U. Cal. at Los Angeles, 1937- 45, prof. 1949—, also prof. psychology of medicine, dean life sci. div., 1950—. Mem. Am. Psychopathol. Assn., Am., Western, So. Cal., Cal. State psychol. assns., Brit. Soc. Med. Hypnosis, Soc. Exptl. and Med. Hypnosis, Am. Eugenics Soc., Geriatrics Assn., Cal. Soc. Mental Hygiene, Sigma Xi, Pi Gamma Mu, Sigma Phi Epsilon. Democrat. Lutheran. Author: Abnormal Psychology, 1950; Handbook on Employee Selection, 1950; Hypnosis and Its Therapeutic Applications, 1955. Editor Jour. Psychology, Jour. Exptl. Hypnosis. Contbr. articles on psychology to profl. jours. Home: 1242 A B Berkely St Santa Monica CA 90404

DORE, VINCENT CYRIL, clergyman, coll. chancellor; b. New Haven, Jan. 31, 1900; s. John Joseph and Catherine Theresa (McMahon) D.; A.B., Providence Coll., 1925, LL.D., 1945; A.M., Cath. U. Am., 1927; S.T.L., Dominican Inst. Theology, Washington, 1929; LL.D., Bryant Coll., 1958, Brown U., Salve Regina Coll. 1964, Stonehill Coll., 1965; S.T.M., Rome, 1965; Ed.D., Suffolk U., 1952; Ph.D., R.I. Coll. 1962. Joined Dominican Order, 1921; ordained priest Roman Catholic Ch., 1928; tchr. Aquinas High Sch., Columbus, O., asst., acting chaplain Ohio State Penitentiary, 1929-31; prof. sociology Providence Coll., 1931-41, treas., 1941-45, dean of studies, 1945-57, v.p. charge acad. affairs, 1950-61, religious superior Dominican community, 1956-61, dean faculty, 1957-61, pres., 1961-65, chancellor, 1965—. Cons. indsl. and labor relations; mem. Dominican ednl. ann. conf. com., 1945—; del. Coll. Entrance Exam. Bd., 1945-57. Mem. Minimum Wage Bd. for R.I. Retail Stores, 1940-41; chmn. Minimum Wage Bd. for R.I. Restaurants and Hotel Restaurants, 1941-50; arbiter R.I. Dept. Labor, 1938—; mem. R.I. Com. on Practical Nursing; mem. exec. bd. R.I. World Affairs Council, Urban League R.I., United Fund R.I., Progress for Providence, R.I. Council Community Services; mem. Com. of 100, R.I. White House Conf. Steering Com., industry council com. Am. Cath. Sociol. Soc., 1945—; mem. adv. com. on edn. handicapped children and youth U.S. Office Edn., 1964—; v.p. United Fund Southeastern New Eng., 1969—. Bd. dirs. Hosp. Service Corp. R.I., R.I. Health Facilities Planning Council, Research and Design Center; bd. dirs., incorporator R.I. Group Health Assn., 1968—; trustee New Eng. Colls. Fund. Recipient certificate Am. Arbitration Assn., 1944, White House Conf., 1950; certificate distinction Dept. War, A.S.T.P., World War II; U.S. Army Outstanding Civilian Service award, 1962; Georgetown U. 175th Anniversary medal honor, 1963; Pontifical Benemerenti medal, 1958; Roger Williams award for distinguished service Greater Providence C. of C., 1968; citation of honor Urban League R.I., 1971; mem. R.I. Heritage Hall Fame, 1971. Mem. Am. Assn. Deans, Nat. Cath. Edn. Assn. (exec. bd.), New Eng. Assn. Colls. and Secondary Schs. (com. on instns. of higher learning, 1947-51) Internat. Assn. U. Presidents, Eastern Assn. Deans, Newcomen Soc. N.Am., Delta Epsilon Sigma (nat. exec. com.), Alpha Epsilon Delta. Address: Providence Coll Providence RI 02908

DOREMUS, ROBERT BARNARD, univ. dean; b. Newton, Mass., May 19, 1915; s. Robert Proudfit and Eleanor (Barnard) D.; A.B., Harvard, 1935, A.M., 1936, Ph.D., 1940; m. Betty Bartlett Holt, Apr. 26, 1941 (dec. May 1970); children—John Barnard, Andrew Bartlett. Faculty U. Wis., 1940-42, 46—, prof. English, 1953—, asst. dir. freshman English, 1946-47, asst. dean Coll. Letters and Sci., 1947- 50, asso. dean, 1950—. Served to capt. USAAF, 1942-46. Mem. Modern Lang. Assn. Author: Writing College Themes, 1960. Editor: (with Lacy and Rodman) Patterns in Writing, rev. edit., 1963. Home: 18 Appomattox Ct Madison WI 53705

DORF, ERLING, geologist; b. Nysted, Neb., July 19, 1905; s. Alfred T. and Thyra Axelsen (Dreier) D.; B.S., U. Chgo., 1925, Ph.D., 1930; m. Ruth Kemmerer, Apr. 3, 1934; children—Thomas (dec.), Norman Kemmerer, Robert Erling, Martha Dreier. Asst. instr. U. Chgo., 1926-27, fellow geology, 1928- 30; instr. Princeton, 1926-3O, asst. prof., 1930-40, asso. prof., 1936-45, prof. geology, 1946—, curator paleobotany, 1930—. Research asst. Carnegie Inst. of Washington, 1926-45; lectr. U. Pa., 1936-42, Princeton Adult Sch., 1964—; research curator Phila. Acad. Sci., 1936-46; prof. geology Wagner Free Inst. Sci., 1948—; vis. lectr., Villanova U., 1961-67; vis. prof. Rutgers U., 1967-70; dir. NSF summer geol. conf., Mont., 1964—; paleobot. cons., U.S. Nat. Mus.; chmn. com. on paleobotany NRC, 1941-46; bd. dirs. Princeton chpt. A.R.C., 1942-53, 60-66, vice chmn. 1964; mem. Princeton Twp. Bd. Health, 1960—; trustee Princeton Community Players, 1950-53, 56-58, Princeton Country Day Sch., 1946-56; cons. Ednl. Testing Service, 1969—; U.S. del. Indian Sci. Congress, 1953; sci. collaborator Nat. Park Service, 1954-58. Fellow A.A.A.S. (council 1947-57), Geol. Soc. Am., Paleontol. Soc. Am. (v.p. 1943), Bot. Soc. Am.; mem. Nat. Assn. Geology Tchrs. (v.p. east sect. 1956-57, pres. 1957- 58; Neil Miner award, 1963, Ralph Digman award 1967), Am. Assn. U. Profs., N.J. Geol. Soc., N.J. Acad. Sci., Internat., Am. assns. plant taxonomists, Yellowstone-Bighorn Research Assn. (council 1961- -, pres. 1964), Am. Inst. Biol. Scis., Am. Geol. Inst., Atlantic Coastal Plain Assn., Paleobot. Soc. India (hon.), Royal Danish Acad. Arts and Scis. (fgn.), Sigma Xi, Kappa Epsilon Pi, Alpha Tau Omega. Club: Nassau (pres. 1961). Author: Pliocene Floras of Cal., 1933; Upper Cretaceous Floras of Rocky Mountain Region, 1942. Contbr. articles to geol. and bot. jours. Home: 283 Mercer Rd Princeton NJ 08540

DORFMAN, ALBERT, physician; b. Chgo., July 6, 1916; s. Aron and Anna (Schwartzman) D.; S.B., U. Chgo., 1936, Ph.D., 1939, M.D., 1944; m. Ethel Steinman, Sept. 1, 1940; children—Abby, Julie. Instr. biochemistry U. Chgo., 1939-42, asst. prof. pediatrics, 1948-53, asso. prof., 1953-57, prof., 1957—, also chmn. pediatrics dept.; dir. LaRabida-U. Chgo. Inst., 1957—, Richard T. Crane prof. pediatrics, 1965—. Chief biochemistry Army Med. Sch., Washington, 1946-48; dir. Joseph P. Kennedy, Jr., Mental Retardation Research Center, 1965—; dir. La Rabida-U. Chicago Inst. Recipient E. Mead Johnson award for research in pediatrics, 1957. Mem. Am. Chem. Soc., Am. Soc. Biol. Chemists, Soc. Exptl. Biology and Medicine, Am. Acad. Arts and Scis., Am. Heart Assn., Am. Rheumatism Soc., Soc. Pediatric Research, Am. Pediatric Soc., Am. Council Rheumatic Fever. Contbr. articles to sci. jours. Home: 2231 E 67th St Chicago IL 60649

DORFMAN, JOSEPH, univ. prof.; b. Ramanovska, Russia, Mar. 27, 1904; s. Mendel and Etta D.; A.B., Reed Coll., 1924; A.M., Columbia 1925, Ph.D., 1935; m. Sarah Sorrin, June 11, 1932; children—Susan Lois, Mark Harris. Economist, Nat. Indsl. Conf. Bd., 1927-29; asso. Economist Columbia, 1931-36; lectr., 1936-40; asst. prof. 1940-46, asso. prof. 1946-48, prof. 1948—. Received 1st award of Seligman prize, Columbia, for A Doctoral Dissertation of Distinguished Scholarship, 1937; awarded 2 yr. grant Rockefeller Found. for study Development Am. Economic Thought, 1945; Guggenheim fellow, 1953-54; Ford Faculty Research fellow, 1959-60, Mem. Evolutionary Econs. Assn. (exec. bd. 1965-66, pres. 1969), Am. Econs. Assn. (supervising com. history assn.). Wrote intro. 1937 edit. Thorstein Veblen's Imperial Germany and Industrial Revolution. Author: Thorstein Veblen and His America, 1934; Economic Mind in American Civilization (5 vols.), 1946-59; (with R. G. Tugwell) Early American Policy, 1960; (with others) Institutional Economics, 1963. Editor: Relation of the State to Industrial Action and Economics and Jurisprudence (H.C. Adams), 1955; Types of Economic Theory: From Mercantilism to Institutionalism (W.C. Mitchell), Vol. 1, 1967, Vol. 2, 1969. Contbr.: Chief Justice Marshall: A Reappraisal, 1956; articles to Am. Econ. Rev., Econ. Jour., Jour. Polit. Economy, Am. Hist. Rev., other tech. jours. Mem. editorial bd. Papers of Alexander Hamilton. Mem. adv. bd. Jour. History Polit. Economy, Jour. Econ. Issues, Polit. Sci. Quar. Home: 39 Claremont New York City NY 10027

DORFMAN, LEON MONTE, educator; b. Winnipeg, Man., Can., June 9, 1922; s. Gabriel and Dora (Gorin) D.; B.S., U. Man., 1944; M.A., U. Toronto (Ont., Can.), 1945, Ph.D., 1947; m. Lorraine Rose, Aug. 1, 1948; children—Gail Anne, Amy Rachel, David Alan. Came to U.S., 1947, naturalized, 1949. Postdoctoral fellow U. Rochester, 1947-49; research asso. Gen. Electric Co., Schenectady, 1950- 57; sr. chemist, group leader Argonne (Ill.) Nat. Lab., 1957-64, now cons.; prof. chemistry Ohio State U., Columbus, 1964—, chmn. chemistry dept., 1968—; prof. chemistry U. Toronto, 1967. Vis. research prof. Hebrew U. of Jerusalem, 1969. Chmn. Gordon Conf. on Radiation Chemistry, 1966. Guggenheim fellow, 1971—. Mem. Am. Chem. Soc., Am. Phys. Soc., Radiation Research Soc. Author: (with M.S. Matheson) Pulse Radiolysis, 1969. Home: 1514 A Lafayette Dr Columbus OH 43220 Office: 140 W 18th Av Columbus OH 43210

DORFMAN, RALPH ISADORE, biochemist; b. Chgo., June 30, 1911; s. Aron and Anna (Schwartzman) D.; B.S. in Chemistry, U. Ill., 1932; Ph.D. in Physiol. Chemistry and Pharmacology, U. Chgo., 1934; m. Adeline Smith, Sept. 5, 1933 (dec. 1964); children—Gerald Allen, Ronald Arthur; m. 2d, Margaret Cameron, Feb. 11, 1965. Research fellow physiol. chemistry U. Chgo., 1932-33, research asst., 1933-35; instr. pharmacology La. State U., 1935-36; instr. physiol. chemistry Yale, 1936- 39, asst. prof., 1939-41; asst. prof. biochemistry Western Res. U., 1941- 50, asso. prof., 1950-51; asso. dir. labs. Worcester Found. Exptl. Biology, Shrewsbury, Mass., 1951-56, dir. lab., 1956-64; prof. (affiliate) chemistry Clark U., 1955-64; research prof. biochemistry Boston U., 1951-67; dir. Inst. Hormone Biology, 1964-69, sr. v.p. Syntex Research Center, Palo Alto, Cal., 1964—; vis. prof. pharmacology Stanford U. Sch. Medicine, 1967—. Recipient Distinguished Service award Medical Alumni U. Chgo., 1967. Fellow N.Y. Acad. Sci., A.A.A.S., Am. Acad. Arts and Scis., Chilean Med. Assn. (hon.); mem. Am. Chem. Soc., Soc. Exptl. Biology and Medicine, Am. Assn. Cancer Research, Am. Soc. Biol. Chemists, Endocrine Soc. (council), Pan Am. Med. Assn., Danish Soc. Endocrinology, Mexican Endocrine Soc., Argentinian Soc. Endocrinology and Nutrition (hon.), Statistical Soc., Sigma Xi, Phi Lambda Epsilon. Home: 10465 Berkshire Dr Los Altos Hills CA 94022 Office: Syntex Research Center Stanford Indsl Park Palo Alto CA 94022

DORFMAN, ROBERT, economist, educator; b. N.Y.C., Oct. 27, 1916; s. Samuel M. and Mina (Gordon) D.; B.A., Columbia 1936, M.A., 1937; Ph.D., U. Cal., 1950; m. Nancy Schelling, Nov. 6, 1949; children—Peter J., Ann Elizabeth. With Bur. Labor Statistics, 1939-41, OPA, 1941-43; faculty U. Cal., 1950-55; faculty Harvard Cambridge, Mass., 1955—, prof. econs., 1957—. Mem Pres.'s Com. To Appraise Employment and Unemployment Statistics, 1962. Served as operations analyst USAAF, World War II. Ford Found. faculty research fellow. Fellow A.A.A.S., Econ. Soc.; mem. Am. Econ. Assn., Operations Research Soc. Am. (council 1959-62), Econometric Soc. (council 1961—), NRC, Am. Statis. Assn., Inst. Mgmt. Scis. (pres. 1965). Author: Application of the Linear Programming to the Theory of the Firm, 1951; (with P. O. Steiner) Economic Status of the Aged, 1956; (with P. A. Samuelson, R. Solow) Linear Programming and Economic Analysis, 1958; (with others) Design of Water Resource Systems, 1962; The Price System, 1964. Editor: Measuring Benefits of Goverment Investments, 1965. Home: 81 Kilburn Rd Belmont MA 02178

DORFMAN, SAUL, educator, musician; b. Chgo., May 18, 1912; s. Louis and Hilda (Goldenberg) D.; student U. Chgo., 1940-42; student Leipzig (Germany) State Conservatory of Music, 1930-32, State Coll. Music (Berlin, Germany), 1932-33; m. Helen Gordon, July 17, 1941; 1 son, Marc. Piano soloist Chgo. Symphony Orchestra, 1926, 1934; concerts, Germany, 1930-33; appeared concerts also soloist various symphony orchestras U.S.; numerous appearances pianist, lectr. TV also radio; prof., chmn. piano dept. Chgo. Musical Coll., Roosevelt U., 1945—; music dir. Beth Emet Synagogue, Evanston, Ill., 1951—. Recipient Gold medal, Am. Conservatory of Music, 1925; Chicagoland Piano Playing Tournament Grand prize, 1927. Mem. Am. Assn. U. Profs., Music Tchrs. Nat. Assn., Soc. Am. Musicians, Nat. Guild Piano Tchrs. Jewish religion. Contbg. editor Piano Quar. Home: 3132 W Birchwood Av Chicago IL 60645

DORFMEYER, ROBERT EDWARD, mfg. co. exec.; b. Woodville Twp., O., Dec. 27, 1916; s. John and Caroline (Stausmire) D.; B.S. in Bus., Bowling Green State U., 1940; J.D., Cleve.-Marshall Law Sch., 1944; m. Ruth Pearl Spackman, Aug. 25, 1945; children—Nancy, Martha, Robert Edward. Admitted to Ohio bar, 1944; with Glidden Co., 1940—, v.p. corp. devel., 1962—, dir., 1965—. Trustee Bowling Green State U. Recipient Meml. award Chem. Marketing Research Assn., 1970. Mem. Cleve. Bar Assn., Am. Mgmt. Assn., Bldg. Research Inst., Phi Alpha Chi, Sigma Alpha Epsilon, Delta Theta Phi. Home: 3595 Eldorado Dr Rocky River OH 44116 Office: Glidden Co Commerce Bldg Cleveland OH 44115

DORGAN, JOHN JOSEPH, Jr., oil co. exec.; b. Providence, Sept. 1, 1923; s. John Joseph and Isabelle Regina (Carroll) D.; A.B., Harvard, 1944, M.B.A., 1948; m. Cynthia Codrington, June 8, 1946; children—Carroll S., Elizabeth B., Peter M., John C. Economist, Continental Oil Co., 1948-51, asst. to pres., 1952-54, landman, 1954-56, dir. credit and ins., 1956-57, asst. treas., 1957-58, treas., 1958-64, coordinator plant food projects and activities, 1964- 65, v.p., 1965-69, dir. supply and transp., 1970—; petroleum economist Petroleum Adminstrn. for Def., Washington, 1951-52. Mem. Am. Petroleum Inst., Ind. Petroleum Assn. Am., Nat. Assn. Creditmen. Home: 42 Avenue Rd London England Office: Conoco Europe Berkeley Square House London England

DORIAN, FREDERICK, educator, musicologist; b. Vienna, Austria, July 1, 1902; s. Alois and Therese Neumann (Deutsch) D.; Ph.D., U. Vienna, 1925; m. Sadie Pearlman, Aug. 8, 1940. Came to U.S., 1936, naturalized, 1940. Music critic Berlin Morgenpost, 1930-34, Frankfurter Zeitung, Paris, 1934-35, Neues Wiener Journal, Vienna, 1935-36; prof. music Carnegie-Mellon U., 1936-71, prof. emeritus, 1971—, Andrew Mellon lectr. in music, 1971-72; music editor Pitts. Symphony Program Mag., 1952—. Recipient research award A. W. Mellon, 1958-61; Research award Pitts. Foundation, 1966-67. Mem. Internat. Soc. Contemporary Music, Am. Musicol. Soc., Internat. Soc. Musicology. Author: The Fugue in the Works of Beethoven, 1927; History of Music in Performance, 1942; Musical Workshop, 1947; Commitment to Culture, 1964. Home: 4921 Forbes Av Pittsburgh PA 15213

DORION, NOEL, lawyer; b. Charlesbourg, Que., Can., July 24, 1904; s. Charles F. X. and Rose de Lima (Racine) D.; B.es A., Petit Seminiare de Quebec, 1923; LL.M., Laval U., 1927, J.D., 1954; m. Olga Malherbe, June 7, 1932; children—Louis, Henri. Sr. crown pros., 1936-39, 49-58; tchr. criminal law Laval U., 1948-50; batonnier Dist. Que., batonnier gen., Province Que., 1954-55; mem. Ho. of Commons for Bellechase, 1958-62; also sec. state for Can., chmn. Privy Council for Can.; now mem. law firm Dorion, Dorion & Bernier. Del. Que. bar to Stage Conf., Paris, 1953, 54; mem. bar discipline bd. for Que., 1956--. Alderman Ste. Foy City, 1943-50. Mem. Young Bar Assn. Que. (pres. 1933-34). Conservative. Roman Catholic. Clubs: Quebec Garrison; Cercle Universitaire. Home: 2590 Chemin St Louis Rd Ste Foy Quebec Canada Office: 80 St Pierre St Quebec Canada

DORIOT, GEORGES F., educator, corp exec.; b. Paris, France, Sept. 24, 1899; s. Auguste Frederic and Berthe Camille F (Baelher) D.; student Lynton Coll., Kent, Eng.; B.S., U. Paris, 1915; student Harvard, 1921, M.A., 1942; L.H.D., Union Coll., 1938; LL.D., Emerson Coll., 1955, Ohio U., 1962; M.S., Lowell Inst. Tech., 1952; m. Edna Allen, Dec. 20, 1930. Came to U.S., 1921. Asst. dean Harvard Bus. Sch., 1926-31, asso. prof., 1926-29, prof. indsl. mgmt., 1929-66, prof. emeritus, 1966—; pres., dir. Am. Research & Devel. Corp.; adv. dir. Nat. Shawmut Bank, Boston; chmn., dir. European Enterprises Devel. Co.; dir., mem. exec. com. Ionics Inc., dir., mem. exec. com. Canadian Enterprise Devel. Corp., Kendall Co., Textron Inc.; dir. Textron Atlantic Inc., Sun Life Assurance Co. Can. (U.S.), Tech. Studies, Inc. Adviser dir. Institut European d'Administration des Affaires-INSEAD. Trustee, v.p. Franklin Found.; trustee Geo-Transport Found. New Eng., Inst. for Future. Served to brig. gen. U.S. Army, 1941-47. Decorated D.S.M.; comdr. Legion Honor (France), comdr. B.E., G.O. du Merite Recherche et Invention

(France); Outstanding Civilian Service medal (U.S. Army). Clubs: Harvard, Brook (N.Y.C.); Somerset (Boston). Home: 12 Lime St Boston MA 02108 Office: 200 Berkeley St Boston MA 02116

DORKIN, FREDERIC EUGENE, mfg.; b. Bridgeport, Conn., Feb. 1, 1932; s. William and Selma (Kraus) D.; A.B., Dartmouth, 1953; LL.B., Duke, 1956; LL.M., George Washington U., 1968; m. Harriette A. Garfinkel, June 14, 1959; children— Rosalyn Gail, David Ira, Deborah Ruth. Admitted to Conn. bar, 1956; atty. SEC, Washington, 1956-57; pvt. practice law, Bridgeport, Conn., 1960-61; asst. sec. CT Corp. System, N.Y.C., Washington, 1961-68; asso. counsel, asst. sec. Susquehanna Corp., Alexandria, Va., 1968-69; sec., counsel Microdot Inc., Greenwich, Conn., 1969—; dir. Clyde Iron Works, Inc., Wiley Mfg. Co. Served with Judge Adv. Gen. Corps, AUS, 1957-60. Mem. Am. Soc. Corporate Secs., Phi Delta Phi, Tau Epsilon Phi. Home: 30 Druid Hill Dr Parsippany NJ 07054 Office: 475 Steamboat Rd Greenwich CT 06830

DORLAND, GILBERT MEDING, steel co. exec.; b. N.Y.C., Nov. 26, 1912; s. Gilbert Grant and Louise (Eckhardt) D.; student Rensselaer Poly. Inst., 1931-32; B.S., U.S. Mil. Acad., 1936; M.S. in Civil Engring., U. Cal. at Berkeley, 194O; m. Lillian Okkerse, Mar. 21, 1937; children—Gilbert N., John H., Peter G., Richard L., Diane L. Commd. 2d lt. U.S. Army, 1936, advanced through grades to col., 1944; with Manhattan Dist., C.E., Armed Forces Spl. Weapons Project, Oak Ridge and Albuquerque, 1946-50; asst. dist. engr. Alaska Dist., C.E., 1950-52, dist. engr. Nashville Dist., 1952-56; ret., 1956; exec. v.p. Nashville Bridge Co., 1956-61, pres., 1962-69; pres. Bessemer Galvanizing Works (Ala.), 1962-68; v.p. Torres Mexicannas, S.A., 1962-68; exec. v.p. Carolina Steel Corp., Greensboro, 1969- 7O, pres., 1971—; dir. First Am. Nat. Bank, Nashville, 1961-69; Greensboro dir. Wachovia Bank & Trust Co., 1971—. Pres. Middle Tenn. council Boy Scouts Am., 1954-56, now mem. Nat. council; past chmn. Tenn.-Tombigbee Waterway Devel. Authority; pres. Cumberland Valley Assn., 1968-69; chmn. nat. com. Nat. Rivers and Harbors Congress, 1967-69. Mem. engring. mgmt. adv. council Vanderbilt U., 1967-69. Bd. dirs. Mississippi Valley Assn., 1957-69, Greater Greensboro Housing Found., Inc. Decorated Legion of Merit, Bronze Star medal, Order Brit. Empire; recipient Outstanding Civilian Service award Dept. Army, 1968. Registered profl. engr., Tenn. Fellow Am. Soc. C.E.; mem. Nat. Soc. Profl. Engrs., Soc. Am. Mil. Engrs., Am. Ordnance Assn., Am. Mgmt. Assn., Am. Inst. Steel Constrn. (dir. 1959—, 1st v.p. 1969—), Nat. Waterways Conf. (pres. 1963-65 dir.). Episcopalian. Kiwanian (past pres. Nashville). Club: Greensboro Country. Home: 1916 Granville Rd Greensboro NC 27408 Office: P O Box 20888 Greensboro NC 27420

DORMAN, BERNHARDT LOUIS, mech. engr.; b. Chgo., July 30, 1907; s. Alexander and Bessie (Weissman) D.; student Butler U., 1923; B.S. in Mech. Engring., Purdue U., 1928, D.Engring. (hon.), 1960; m. Stella Berkowitz, Apr. 7, 1935; children—Burton Paul, Myron David, Robert Alan. Chief engr. Paragon Vaporizer Corp., Chgo., 1931-33; devel. engr. Internat. Harvester Co., 1934-43; v.p. test engring. Aerojet-Gen. Corp., Azusa, Cal., 1943- 64, v.p. future operations, 1964-67, v.p. procurement and materiel, 1968—; asst. adminstr. for industry affairs NASA, 1967-68; pres. Aerojet Investments, Ltd., 1969—. Recipient fellowship award Am. Rocket Soc., 1955. Mem. Am. Inst. Aeros. and Astronautics, Instrument Soc. Am., Tau Beta Pi. Office: 9100 E Flair Dr El Monte CA 91731

DORMAN, DAN EDWARD, banker; b. Topeka, Kan., Jan. 6, 1911; s. Roy N. and Elizabeth (Downey) D.; student pub. schs., also spl. banking courses; m. Mary R. Chadwick, May 22, 1948; 1 son, Dan Edward (dec.). Clerk First Nat. Bank & Trust Co., Tulsa, 1928-36; salesman Frick Reid Supply Corp., Okla., also Tex., 1938; asst. bank examiner 12th Fed. Res. Dist., San Francisco, 1941-48; asst. v.p. First Nat. Bank of Hawaii (now First Hawaiian Bank), Honolulu, 1948-51, v.p., 1952-57, exec. v.p., 1958-62, pres., 1962-68, chmn. bd., 1969-71, also dir.; dir. Honolulu Painting Co., Ltd., Honsador, Lumber Dry Kilns, Ltd., Universal Motor Co., Ltd., Hawaii Islanders, Inc. Bd. regents Chaminade Coll., trustee Friends Library of Hawaii, Hawaii Vets. Meml. Fund. Served with AUS, 1943-46. Mem. Honolulu C. of C. (bd. dirs.), Navy League. Methodist. Clubs: Oahu Country, Outrigger Canoe (Honolulu). Home: 2003 Kalia Rd Honolulu HI 96815

DORMAN, GERALD DALE, physician; b. Beirut, Lebanon, Nov. 12, 1903 (parents Am. citizens); s. Harry Gaylord and Mary Bliss (Dale) D.; grad. Phillips Acad., Andover, Mass., 1921; B.A., Harvard, 1925; M.D., Columbia, 1929; m. Georgia Foster White, June 29, 1929 (dec. Oct. 1960); children—Gerald Huntington, Dale Foster (Mrs. Samuel E. Shaw II); m. 2d, Lois R. Ackerman, Mar. 24, 1962. Intern St. Luke's Hosp., N.Y.C., 1930-31, mem. fracture and surg. clinic, 1931-42; mem. surg. staff St. Mary's Hosp. Children, N.Y.C., 1932-38, Seaside Hosp., New Dorp, S.I., 1934-41; asst. med. dir. N.Y. Life Ins. Co., 1945-47, med. dir. charge employees welfare, 1947-60, 2d v.p., med. cons., 1961-68. Cons. R.R. Retirement Bd.; bd. dirs. N.Y.C. Cancer Com.; chmn. N.Y.C. Cancer Research and Grants Com.; cons. nat. planning com. health and med. care for White House Conf. Aging, 1961; pres. N.Y.C. div. Am. Cancer Soc., 1970—; planning com., forum mem. White House Conf. on Children, 1970. Bd. dirs. Am. Middle East Relief; trustee Damascus Coll. Served to lt. col., M.C., AUS, 1942-45. Diplomate Am. Bd. Preventive Medicine in occupational medicine. Fellow N.Y. Acad. Medicine, Indsl. Med. Assn.; mem. A.M.A. (trustee 1960-68, sec. treas. 1966-67; pres. 1969-70), N.Y. State (pres. 1st dist. br. 1960-61; councillor; chmn. workmens compensation and commn. med. service 1954-61; trustee 1963-68), N.Y. County (pres. 1955-56, trustee 1955-60; chmn. bd. 1960-61) med. socs., World Med. Assn. (chmn. council 1964-65, 66-68; exec. dir. finance 1968—, acting sec. gen. 1969—, sec.-treas. U.S. Com. Inc. 1962-65), Nat Health Council (dir. 1962-68), N.Y.C. Bd. Trade, U.S. C. of C. Conglist. Home: 500 E 77th St New York City NY 10021 Office: 10 Columbus Circle New York City NY 10019

DORMAN, GLADYS M., lawyer; b. Bklyn., July 18, 1911; d. Benjamin N. and Blanche (Rosenthal) Dorman; B.A., Cornell U., 1931; M.A., Columbia, 1933; LL.B., Bklyn. Law Sch., 1936; m. Benjamin R. Raphael, Feb. 12, 1939; children—Stephen M., Alan H. Admitted to N.Y. bar, 1936; practice of law, 1936—; partner Raphael & Dorman, Bklyn., 1950—. Chmn. Jewish Day for Blind, 1955; Mem. Bd. Higher Edn. City N.Y. 1949-68. Mem. exec. bd. Dem. Women's Workshop. Recipient medal of Honor, Brooklyn Coll., 1964, Kingsboro Coll., 1968. Mem. Bklyn. Bar Assn. (trustee 1966—), Bklyn. Women's Bar Assn. (pres. 1944-46), Fedn. Jewish Philanthropy, Philonomic Council. Club: Brooklyn Lawyers (v.p. 1945-46; dir. 1946-70). Contbr. articles legal pubs. Home: 8801 Shore Rd Brooklyn iY 11209 Office: 26 Court St Brooklyn NY 11201

DORMAN, MAURICE HENRY, gov. gen. Malta; b. Stafford, Eng., Aug. 7, 1912; s. John Ehrenfried and Madeleine Louise (Bostock) D.; M.A., Magdalene Coll., Cambridge (Eng.) U., 1935; LL.D. (hon.), Royal U. Malta, 1964; D.C.L. (hon.), U. Durham (Eng.), 1961; m. Florence Monica Churchward Smith, Dec. 4, 1937; children—John, Joanna, Elisabeth (Mrs. George Latham), Sibella. Adminstrv. officer Tanganyika Terr., 1935-40, clk. council, 1940-45; asst. to lt. gov. Malta, 1945-47; prin. asst. sec. Palestine, 1947-48; asst. sec. social services dept. Colonial Office, London, 1948-50; dir. social welfare Gold Coast, Accra, 1950-52; colonial sec. Trinidad and Tobago, 1952-55, also acting gov. Trinidad; gov., comdr. in chief, vice adm., Sierra Leone, 1956-61, gov. gen., 1961-62; gov. Malta, 1962-64, gov. gen., 1964—. Named knight grand cross Most Distinguished Order St. Michael and St. George, 1956; knight grand cross Royal Victorian Order, 1961; knight Most Venerable Order St. John, 1957; companion Most Distinguished Order St. Michael and St. George, 1955; recipient gran croce Al Merito Melitenese, Sovereign and Mil. Order Malta, 1966. Clubs: Athenaeum, East India, Sports (London): Casino Maltese (Valletta). Home: The Old Manor Overton Marlborough Wiltshire England Office: The Palace Malta

DORMAN, ROLAND F., ins. co. exec.; b. Rocky Mount, N.C., 1924. Vice pres., actuary Aetna Ins. Co., Hartford, Conn. Home: 18 Drumlin Rd West Simsbury CT 06092 Office: 55 Elm St Hartford CT 06115*

DORN, CHARLES MEEKER, educator; b. Mpls., Jan. 17, 1927; s. Melville Wilkinson and Margaret (Meeker) D.; B.A., M.A., George Peabody Coll. Tchrs., 1950; Ed.D., U. Tex., 1959; m. Virginia Josephine Coble, July 11, 1947; children—Mary Jan, Charles Meeker. Asst. prof. art Union U., Jackson, Tenn., 1950-54; instr. art and edn. Memphis State U., 1954-57, lectr. edn. U. Tex., 1957- 59; head art dept. Nat. Coll. Edn., Evanston, Ill., 1959-61; asso. prof. art No. Ill. State U., 1961-62; exec. sec. Nat. Art Edn. Assn., Washington, 1962-70; prof., chmn. dept. art San Fernando Valley State Coll., Northridge, Cal., 1970—. Served with AUS, 1945-46. Recipient 25th Anniversary award for distinguished service Nat. Gallery Art, 1966. Mem. Nat. Com. Art Edn., Nat. Art Edn. Assn., N.E.A., Phi Delta Kappa, Kappa Phi Kappa. Home: 3530 Cody Rd Sherman Oaks CA 91403 Office: 18111 Nordhoff Northridge CA 91324

DORN, JOHN EMIL, educator; b. Chgo., Apr. 10, 1909; s. John and Agusta Alice (Reindl) D.; B.S., Northwestern U., 1931, M.S., 1932; D.Sc. (hon.), 1971; Ph.D., U. Minn., 1936; m. Virginia Alice Henneman, Feb. 22, 1937; children—John Robert, Michael Raymond. Research asst. chemistry Northwestern U., 1931-32; teaching asst. U. Minn., 1932-36; postdoctoral research fellow Battelle Meml. Inst., 1936-38; asst. prof. mech. engring. U. Cal., 1938-41; 42-45, asso. prof. phys. metallurgy, 1945-48, prof. materials sci., 1949—; research metallurgist Dow Chem. Co., 1941-42; speaker sci. confs. Recipient Charles B. Dudley medal Am. Soc. Testing Materials, 1958, Henry Marion Howe medal Am. Soc. Metals, 1959, Albert Easton White distinguished tchrs. award Am. Soc. Metals, 1964, medal Societe Francaise de Metallurgie, 1968; Miller research prof., 1962-63. Fellow Am. Inst. Mining and Metall. Engrs., Am. Soc. Metals (chmn. Golden Gate chpt. 1946, nat. trustee 1947-49); mem. Sigma Xi. Editor: The Mechanical Behavior of Metals of Elevated Temperatures, 1961. Contbr. articles profl. jours. Home: 95 Evergreen Dr Orinda CA 94563 Office: Univ California Berkeley CA 94720

DORN, LOWELL MINNIS, ret. life ins. co. exec.; b. Des Moines, Ia., Dec. 2, 1906; s. Clinton R. and Elizabeth (Minnis) D.; B.A., Drake U., 1928; M.A., U. Toronto, 1930; m. Ariel Corry, June 16, 1931; children—Robert L., Sharon L. (Mrs. John E. Alspach), Kirk L. With N.Y. Life Ins. Co., 1930-71, asso. actuary, 1945- 47, actuary, 1947-71, 2d vice pres., 1953-59, v.p., 1959-61, v.p., chief actuary, 1961-64, sr. v.p., chief actuary, 1964-71. Former exec. v.p. Assos. U. Toronto. Fellow Soc. Actuaries; mem. Am. Acad. Actuaries, Canadian Inst. Actuaries, Phi Beta Kappa. Presbyn. (elder). Home: 1952 Sharon St Boca Raton FL 33432

DORN, OTTO AUGUST, publisher; b. Ft. Wayne, Ind., Aug. 17, 1900; s. Louis and Marie (Roeder) D.; student Concordia Coll., 1914-18, Northwestern U., 1926-27, U. Chgo., 1928-29; LL.D., Valparaiso U., 1955; m. Mildred Hasenbank, Dec. 25, 1931; children—Robert, Richard. With S.F. Bowser Co., Ft. Wayne, 1918-20, Gen. Electric Co., 1920-22, News Sentinel, 1922-23, Suedhoff Ross Advt. Co., 1923-25, Walther League, Chgo., 1925-41; asst. gen. mgr. Concordia Pub. House, St. Louis, 1941-45, gen. mgr., 1945—; mem. bd., v.p. Concordia Hist. Inst. Mem. Protestant Ch. Owned Pubs. Assn. (dir.). Home: 9006 Whitehaven Dr St Louis MO 63123 Office: 3558 S Jefferson St Louis MO 63118

DORN, WILLIAM JENNINGS BRYAN, U.S. congressman; b. Greenwood, S.C., Apr. 14, 1916; s. Thomas Elbert and Pearl (Griffith) D.; ed. pub. schs. Greenwood, S.C.; LL.B. (hon.), Lander Coll., Greenwood, S.C., 1965; LL.B. (hon.), Clemson U., 1970; m. Millie Johnson; children—Briana Pearl (Mrs. Wade Batson), Oliva Byrd, Debbie Gail, William Jennings Bryan, II, Johnson Griffith. Mem. Ho. of Reps. of S.C., 1939-40; mem. S.C. State Senate, 1940-42; mem. 80th, 82d to 92d U.S. Congresses, 3d S.C. dist., 1946—. Served as cpl. in USAAC, 1942-45; ETO. Mem. Am. Legion, Vets. Fgn. Wars, Air Force Assn., Farm Bur., Woodman of World, Grange. Democrat. Baptist. Mason. Home: RFD 1 Greenwood SC 29646 Office: House of Representatives Washington DC 20515

DORNBERGER, WALTER ROBERT, rocket develop. engr.; b. Giessen, Hesse, Germany, Sept. 6, 1895; s. Hermann and Hedwig (Roltsch) D.; A.B., Tech. U., Berlin-Charlottenburg, 1927, A.M., 1930; Eng.D. (hon.) Tech. U., Berlin, 1935; m. Alice Raeder, Sept. 3, 1932 (dec. 1961). Br. chief German Bd. Ordnance (started devel. solid rockets 1930), 1930-32, group chief (started devel. liquid fuel rockets 1932), 1932-37, div. chief, 1937-43; established Army Guided Missile Exptl. Sta., Peenemuende, Germany, 1936, and served as mil. and tech. chief, 1936-44; commr. German Armed Forces for entire guided missile program, Berlin, 1944; prisoner of war in Eng., 1945-47; guided missile cons. as German specialist USAF, Hdqrs., A.M.C., Wright Patterson AFB, Dayton, 1947-50; guided missile cons. Bell Aircraft Corp., Buffalo; retired as v.p., chief scientist Bell Aerosystems Co. div. Bell Aerospace Corp., 1965. Entered German Army, 1914, commd., 1915, and advanced through grades to lt. gen., 1945, ret. 1947. Decorated Knight Cross of the War Merit Cross, Iron Cross (1st and 2d class), eleven other war and merit awards; Grand award German Bd. Ordnance for outstanding work in weapon devel., 1943. Came to U.S., 1947. Fellow Am. Astronautical Soc., asso, fellow Inst. Aerospace Scis.; mem. Am. Rocket Soc. Home: Back Creek Rd Boston MA 02191

DORNBUSCH, SANFORD MAURICE, educator; b. N.Y.C., June 5, 1926; s. Meyer and Gertrude (Weisel) D.; A.B., Syracuse U., 1948; M.A., U. Chgo., 1950, Ph.D., 1952; m. Barbara Anne Farnham, Feb. 28, 1950; children—Jeffrey Neil, Steven Samuel. Instr. sociology Syracuse U., 1948-49, U. Ill., 1950-51. Ind. U., 1950- 52; research asso. U. Chgo., 1951-52; asst. prof. U. Wash., 1952-54, asso. prof., 1958-59; asst. prof. Harvard, 1955-58; head dept. sociology Stanford, 1959-64, prof., 1959—, asso. dean Sch. Humanities and Scis., 1961-62, chmn. senate acad. council, 1970-71, research asso. Center for Research and Devel. in Teaching; vis. prof. sociology U. Ibadan (Nigeria), 1966-67. Cons. Social Sci. Research Council; mem. behavioral scis. fellowship panel NIH, 1961-67; editorial cons. sociometry, 1957-60. Chmn. regional selection com. Woodrow Wilson Nat. Fellowship Found. 1963-66. Served as pvt. AUS, 1943-44; served with USNR, 1945-46. Grantee NSF, NIH; fellow, Center Advanced Study Behavioral Scis., 1954-55; faculty research fellow Social Sci. Research Council, 1958-59; hon. univ. fellow U. Chgo., 1949-50. Fellow Am. Sociol. Assn. (chmn. methodology sect.), African Studies Assn.; mem. Am. Assn. U. Profs. (chpt. pres. 1968-69), Pacific Sociol. Assn. (pres. 1963-64), Am. Statistical Assn., Soc. Study Social Problems. Author: A Primer of Social Statistics, 1955; Popular Religion, 1958. Cons. editor sociology McGraw-Hill Book Co., 1958-62. Home: 841 Pine Hill Rd Stanford CA 94305

DORNFELD, ERNST JOHN, zoologist; b. Milw., Apr. 6, 1911; s. Ernst Philip and Gertrude (Krubsack) D.; B.S., Marquette U., 1933; M.A., U. Wis., 1935, Ph.D., 1937; m. Lorena Sue Ferguson, Aug. 18, 1945; children—Ernst Guy, Susan, Ruth, Margaret, Carl. Instr. histology and embryology U. Okla. Med. Sch., 1937-38; instr. zoology Ore. State U., 1938-42, asst. prof., 1942- 45, asso. prof., 1945-50, prof., 1950—, chmn. dept., 1952—. Adv. com. Am. Cancer Soc., 1958-61. Recipient Carter award, 1947. Mem. Am. Soc. Zoologists, Western Soc. Naturalists, A.A.A.S., Ore. Acad. Sci., Am. Assn. U. Profs., Am. Soc. Cell Biology, Soc. Gen. Physiologists, Sigma Xi, Phi Kappa Phi. Researcher cellular biology. Home: 3415 Crest Dr Corvallis OR 97330

DORNIN, MARSHALL EDGAR, naval officer; b. Berkeley, Cal., Jan. 25, 1908; s. Nelson Edgar and Susan (Edson) D.; B.S., U.S. Naval Acad., 1930; grad. U.S. Naval Postgrad. Sch., 1939, Naval War Coll., 1951; m. Nova Lane, Dec. l4, 1935; children—Marcia and Margot (twins). Commd. ensign U.S. Navy, 1930, advanced through grades to rear adm., 1957; served in battleships and destroyers, 1930-41; staff comdr. service force U.S. Atlantic Fleet, 1941-43; comdr. U.S.S. Abbot, 1943-44; assigned Bur. of Ordnance, Navy Dept., 1945-47; staff comdr. in chief U.S. Atlantic Fleet, 1947-49; comdr. Destroyer Div. 162, 1950-51; assigned Naval Gun Factory, Washington, 1951-53; comdr. naval transport, 1953-54; naval liaison officer to Congress, 1955-56; comdr. U.S.S. Des Moines, 1956-57; asst. chief for plans Bur. Naval Personnel, Navy Dept., 1957-59; comdr. Destroyer Flotilla 3, 1959-61; supt. U.S. Naval Postgrad. Sch., 1961-63; Comdr. Cruiser-Destroyer Force, U.S. Pacific Fleet, 1963-65; comdr. Operational Test and Evaluation Force, 1965-67; comdt. 11th Naval Dist., San Diego, 1967—. Decorated Legion of Merit with oak leaf cluster, Bronze Star with oak leaf cluster. Home: 867 Harbor View Pl San Diego CA 92106 Office: Commandant Eleventh Naval District San Diego CA 92130

DOROUGH, CHARLES DWIGHT, educator; b. Gober, Tex., Apr. 14, 1912; s. Charles Deets and Maude (Scott) D.; B.A., U. Tex., 1936, M.A., 1936, Ph.D., 1946; m. Ivy Anderson, Dec. 28, 1937; children—Catherine Elaine, Charlotte Diane. Prin., Harrison Sch., Fannin County, 1934; investigator for atty. gen. Tex., 1935-37; instr. English, N.W. Mo. State Tchrs. Coll., 1937-38, U. Ark., 1938-41; tutor English, U. Tex., 1941-42, grad. fellow, 1942-43, instr. communications naval personnel, 1943-44; asst. prof. English, Memphis State Coll., 1944-46; asso. prof. English, Birmingham-So. Coll., 1946-48; asso. prof. English, U. Houston, 1948-51, prof., 1951—, chmn. dept., 1954-58, asst. dean, 1951-56, asso. dean arts and scis., 1956- 58, asso. dean grad. div., 1958-59. Mem. Modern Lang. Assn., Am. Assn. U. Profs., So. Central Modern Lang. Assn., Coll. Conf. Tchrs. of English, Nat., Houston councils tchrs. English, Am. Studies Assn., Coll. English Assn., Phi Delta Kappa, Phi Kappa Phi, Phi Eta Sigma. Club: Torch (Houston). Author: Mr. Sam, 1962; Automated Instruction of Remedial English, 1963. Editor: An Invitation to Philosophy (Winifred E. Garrison), 1970. Home: 5330 Jackwood Houston TX 77035

DORR, GOLDTHWAITE HIGGINSON, lawyer; b. Newark, Oct. 21, 1876; s. John Van Nostrand and Nancy (Higginson) D.; A.B., Harvard, 1897; LL.B., Columbia, 1904; m. Virginia Elbert, Sept. 18, 1905 (dec. Jan. 1963); children—Russell Higginson, John Van Nostrand II, Katharine Goldthwaite. Admitted to bar N.Y., 1904; lectr. Harvard, 1899, Columbia U. Law Sch., 1906-14; engaged in practice law, N.Y., 1904—; asst. U.S. atty., N.Y., and spl. asst. to U.S. atty.- gen. Dept. of Justice at various times from 1906-21; acted as expert for President Hoover's Commn. on Law Observance in U.S., 1930-31; counsel cotton textile industry in NRA code formulation and adminstrn.; engaged in gen. econ. survey of Turkey for Turkish govt., 1934; adviser Nfld. govt. as to econ. survey of Nfld., 1940; v.p., dir., gen. counsel Dorr Co., Inc., chmn. bd. Cotton Textile Inst., 1935; withdrew from practice to act as spl. asst. to sec. of war, 1942; returned to practice in N.Y.C., 1945; now mem. firm Mudge, Rose, Guthrie & Alexander. Alternate to Sec. War, Cabinet Com. on Palestine, 1946; cons. to sec. of state, 1947; Am. del. to Internat. Refugee Council, 1948; cons. War Dept. on Germany, 1948-49, Japan, 1950; mem. med. services com. Hoover Commn. on Orgn. of Exec. Br. of Govt.; rep. Dept. Def. Council of Fgn. Ministers, Paris, 1949; Am. rep. Tripartite Conf. Migration Problems, Paris, 1950. Bd. dirs. Near East Found.; chmn. bd. Robert Coll., 1952-55; past chmn. Am. Sch. Prehistoric Research; fellow Am. Bar Found.; vis. com. dept. anthropology, also Peabody Mus., Harvard. Served as seaman, U.S. Navy, Spanish- Am. War; asst. dir. munitions, War Dept., World War I. Awarded D.S.M., Medal of Merit. Mem. Am. Acad. Polit. Sci., Am. Bar Assn., Assn. Bar City of N.Y., Am. Ordnance Assn., Bus. Hist. Soc., Municipal Art Soc., Soc. Bus. Adv. Professions. Clubs: Harvard, Century Assn., Downtown Assn. (N.Y.C.); Cosmos, Metropolitan (Washington). Home: 1192 Park Av New York City NY 10028 Office: 10 Broad St New York City NY 10005

DORR, HAROLD EDWARD, oil co. exec.; b. N.Y.C., Apr. 30, 1910; s. Edward Charles and Lillian (Keyser) D.; student Columbia, Pace Inst.; grad. Advanced Mgmt. Program, Harvard, Columbia; m. Marjorie Marie Sievers, Nov. 24, 1934; children—George Harold, Robert Harold, William Harold. Formerly with Sinclair Oil Co., and affiliates and subsidiaries, asst. comptroller parent co., 1957-62, comptroller; v.p. Sinclair Colombian Oil Co., Inc., Sinclair Kuwait Trading Co., Inc.; dir. Sinclair Belgium, S.A., Sinclair Colombian Oil Co., Inc., Sinclair Caribbean Oil Co., Sinclair Cuba Oil Co., S.A., Sinclair Kuwait Trading Co., Inc., Sinclair Libyan Oil Co., Sinclair Petroleum Co., Inc., Sinclair Venezuelan Oil Co. Mem. Am. Petroleum Inst., Tax. Execs. Inst., Nat. Tax Assn., Fed. Tax Forum, Comptrollers Inst. Home: 62-43 Alderton St Forest Hills NY 11375 Office: 600 Fifth Av New York City NY 10020

DORR, HAROLD M., univ. dean; b. Chadwick, Mich., Jan. 16, 1897; s. Foster P. and Berlie (McVicar) D.; A.B., U. Mich., 1923, A.M., 1929, Ph.D., 1933; m. H. Barbara Johnston, Apr. 29, 1932; 1 stepdau., Janette J. Prin., Lake City (Mich.) High Sch., 1923-27; supt. schs., Lake City, 1927-28; asst. in polit. sci. U. Mich., 1928-29, instr. 1929-35, asst. prof., 1935-39, asso. prof., 1939-44, prof., 1944- 68, prof. emeritus, 1968—, acting chmn., 1948, dir. summer session, 1950-67, dean of statewide edn., 1956-67. Served with O.T.C., Camp Hancock, Ga., 1918. Mem. City Charter Study Commn., Wartime Housing Commn., Selective Service Local Bd. 85, Washtenaw County; chmn. Social-Civic Com., Mich. Council on Adult Edn.; cons. and spl. adv. to numerous civic orgns. and govtl. agys.; chmn. Ann Arbor Twp. Planning Commn. Vis. expert (C.A.D.), Mil. Govt. for Germany, 1949; govtl. specialist Dept. of State (HICOG), assigned to Germany, summer 1950. Mem. Conf. Mid-West Polit. Scientists (pres. 1949-50), Am. Assn. U. Profs. (council 1951-54), Am. Polit. Sci. Assn. (com. advancement teaching), Am. Soc. Pub. Administrs., Am. Acad. Polit. and Social Sci. (spl. editor Annals, vol. 249), Mich. Acad., Schoolmasters Club, Sigma Delta Kappa, Phi Kappa Phi, Pi

Sigma Alpha. Republican. Clubs: Research, Quadrangle, University, Rotary (dist. gov. 1934-55). Author books. Editor: Michigan Constitutional Convention of 1835-36; Debates and Proceedings; Governing Postwar Germany. Contbr. articles and papers to profl. jours. Home: 493 Orchard Hills Dr Ann Arbor MI 48104

DORR, JOHN A., Jr., geologist, educator; b. Grosse Pointe Park, Mich., Oct. 25, 1922; s. John A. and Velma (Read) D.; B.S., U. Mich., 1947, M.S., 1949, Ph.D., 1951; m. Ruth Muriel Pritchett, Nov. 4, 1943; children—John A. III, James, Robin. Curator vertebrate paleontology Carnegie Mus., Pitts., 1951-52; prof. U. Mich., Ann Arbor, 1952—, chmn. geology dept., 1966—, research asso. Mus. Paleontology, 1952—, dir. Geol. Expdns., 1965—. Fellow Geol. Soc. Am.; mem. Soc. Vertebrate Paleontology (past pres.), Soc. for Study Evolution, Mich. Acad. Sci., Sigma Xi. Contbr. articles profl. jours. Home: 291 Gralake St Ann Arbor MI 48103

DORRA, HENRI, art historian; b. Alexandria, Egypt, 1924; s. Clement and Aimee (Castro) D.; B.Sc., U. London (Eng.), 1944; S.M., A.M., Harvard, 1950, Ph.D., 1953; m. Mary Lawrence Tonetti, 1965. Came to the U.S., 1947, naturalized, 1953. Asst. dir. Corcoran Gallery Art, 1954-61, Phila. Mus. Art, 1961-62; exec. v.p. Art Assn. Indpls., 1962-63; faculty U. Cal. at Los Angeles, 1963-65; prof. U. Cal., Santa Barbara, 1965—. Trustee Santa Barbara Mus. Art. Recipient Bowdoin prize Harvard, 1948; student fellow Met. Mus. Art, 1951-52. Mem. Am. Assn. Museums, Coll. Art Assn., Club: Harvard (N.Y.C.). Author: (with John Rewald) Georges Seurat, 1959; The American Muse, 1961, also articles. Address: U Cal Santa Barbara CA 93106

DORRANCE, GEORGE MORRIS, Jr., banker; b. Phila., Dec. 28, 1922; s. George Morris and Emily (Fox) D.; grad. Westminster Sch., 1942; A.B., U. Pa., 1949, M.B.A., 1951; m. Carter Rogers, June 20, 1947; children—Mary Irwin, George Morris III. With Fed. Res. Bank, Phila., 1949-51; with Phila. Nat. Bank, 1951—, pres., 1964—, also dir.; dir. Kewanee Oil Co., Arbuthnot Latham & Co., Ltd., Penn Va. Corp., R. R. Donnelly & Sons Co., Provident Mut. Life Ins. Co., Phila., Rohm and Haas Corp., Asso. Hosp. Service of Phila. Banque Worms & Cie, Paris, Joh. Berenberg, Gossler & Co., Hamburg, Germany. Sec.-treas. Southeastern Pa. Devel. Fund. Trustee Inst. for Cancer Research; trustee Am. Oncologic Hosp. Served with USAAF, 1943-46. Mem. Res. City Bankers Assn. (dir.). Republican. Episcopalian. Office: Phila Nat Bank Broad and Chestnut Sts Philadelphia PA 19101

DORRANCE, JOHN THOMPSON, Jr., food processing exec.; b. Cinnaminson, N.J., Feb. 7, 1919; s. John Thompson and Ethel (Mallinckrodt) D.; grad. St. George's School, Newport, R.I., 1937; A.B., Princeton, 1941; children—John Thompson, III, Bennett, Mary Alice and Keith Bassett, Langdon Mannion. with Campbell Soup Co., 1946—, asst. treas., 1950, asst. to the pres., 1955, chmn. bd., 1962—, also dir.; v.p. dir. Joseph Campbell Co., 1953-61 dir. John Wanamaker, Phila., Morgan Guaranty Trust Co. of N.Y., J.P. Morgan & Co., Inc.; trustee Penn Mut. Life Ins. Co., estate John T. Dorrance. Trustee Family Counseling Service Ch. Farm Sch., Paoli, Pa.; v.p. Inst. Medical Research. Served as capt. AUS, World War II. Mem. Soc. Cin. Republican. Clubs: Union (N.Y.C.); Philadelphia, Rittenhouse, Corinthian Yacht, Racquet (Phila.); Gulph Mills (Pa.) Golf; Pine Valley (N.J.). Golf. Nat. Golf Links of Am. (Scuthampton, N.Y.). Home: Monk Rd Gladwyne PA 19035 Office: Campbell Pl Camden NJ 08101

D'ORSA, CHARLES SALVATORE, ret. army officer; b. Mezzoiuso, Sicily, Italy, Jan. 16, 1911; s. Nicola and Caterina (Schiro) D'O.; came to U.S., 1911, naturalized, 1922; B.S., U.S. Mil. Acad., 1932; student Inf. Sch., Ft. Benning, Ga., 1936-38, Command and Gen. Staff Coll., 1942, Army War Coll., 1950-51; m. Rose Marie Onorato, Apr. 21, 1935 (dec. Oct. 1969); 1 dau., Catherine Diane (Mrs. William M. Shields). Commd. 2d lt. inf., U.S. Army, 1932, advanced through grades to maj. gen., 1962; assigned 26th Inf., 1932-36, 66th Inf., 1938-40; mem. faculty Inf. Sch., 1940-42; assigned 5th Army, N. Africa and Italy, World War II; with U.S. Occupation Forces, Vienna, Austria, 1945-47, Hdqrs. 6th Army, 1947-49, Army Field Forces, Ft. Monroe, Va., 1949-50, Joint Chiefs Staff, Washington, 1951-52; comdr. 180th Inf. Regt., 45th Div., Korea, 1952-53; sr. adviser Korean Tng. Center, 1953; pres. Inf. Bd., Ft. Benning, 1953-56; assigned Hdqrs. NATO, Naples, Italy, 1936-58; comdg. gen. U.S. Forces, Berlin, Germany, 1958-60; comdr. Combat Devel. and Exptl. Center, Ft. Ord, Cal., 1960-62; comdg. gen. Inf. Tng. Center, Ft. Jackson, S.C., 1962-64; dep. comdg. gen. U.S. Army Ryukyu Islands/IX Corps, Okinawa, 1964-66; comdg. gen. VI U.S. Army Corps, Battle Creek, Mich., 1966-68; dep. comdg. gen. 1st U.S. Army, Ft. Meade, Md., 1968-70, ret., 1970. Decorated Legion of Merit with 4 oak leaf clusters, Bronze Star, Combat Inf. badge, UN medal (U.S.); Croix de Guerre with gold star (France); Order Brit. Empire; grand officer Italian Crown; Polish Gold Cross Merit with crossed swords; Ulchi Mil. Distinguished Service medal with silver star (Korea); Philippine Legion Honor; Papal Knight St. Gregory. Address: 1600 S Eads St Arlington VA 22202

DORSCHEL, QUERIN PETER, lawyer; b. Green Bay, Wis., Feb. 8, 1898; s. Peter Frank and Pauline (Schumacher) D.; B.S., Marquette U., 1920; LL.B., U. Chgo., 1934; m. Philemene Connell, 1927; m. 2d, Gertrude Reiss Corbett, Feb. 21, 1939. Pvt. practice pub. accounting, auto financing, Milw., Chgo., 1920-32; admitted to Ill. bar, 1934; counsel, sec. Ill. Power & Light Corp. and subsidiaries, 1934-39; partner Pam, Hurd & Reichmann, now Schiff, Hardin, Waite, Dorschel & Britton, Chgo., 1939—; dir. Ill. Power Co., C. Reiss Coal Co. Bd. dirs. Cath. Charities Archdiocess Chgo.; lay trustee Loyola U. Mem. Am., Ill., Chgo. bar assns. Clubs: Chicago, University, Glen View Country. Home: 1242 Lake Shore Dr Chicago IL 60610 Office: 231 S LaSalle St Chicago IL 60604

DORSETT, JAMES K., Jr., lawyer; b. Spencer, N.C., Nov. 15, 1916; B.A., Davidson Coll., 1938; J.D., U. N.C., 1941; m. Anna Lee Smith, 1950; children—James K. III, Anna Lee, Rush Terrell, Stuart Battle. Admitted to N.C. bar, 1941; practice in Raleigh; mem. firm Smith, Anderson, Dorsett, Blount & Ragsdale. Exec. v.p., gen. counsel Wachovia Corp., 1970—; dir. Occidental Life Ins. Co. N.C.; mem. Raleigh bd. Wachovia Bank & Trust Co. Mem. bd. visitors Davidson Coll., St. Andrews Presbyn. Coll. Mem. Am. (state chmn. Jr. Bar Conf. 1948-49), N.C. (pres. 1950-60), Wake County (exec. com. 1947-48) bar assns., Am. Counsel Assn., Internat. Assn. Ins. Counsel, Phi Beta Kappa, Order Coif, Omicron Delta Kappa, Phi Delta Phi. Clubs: Sphinx, Carolina Country. Editor-in-chief N.C. Law Rev., 1940-41. Office: Wachovia Bank Bldg Raleigh NC 27601

DORSEY, ARNOLD GEORGE, (Englebert Humperdinck), singer; b. Eng. 1937. Numerous night club appearances; records include Release Me; There Goes My Everything; The Last Waltz; Am I That Easy to Forget; Engelbert Humperdinck; Sweetheart; We Made It Happen. Address: Dorsey Brothers Music Co 63a Frith St London W1 England*

DORSEY, BOB RAWLS, oil co. exec.; b. Rockland, Tex., Aug. 27, 1912; s. Elias Leon and Lillie (Rawls) D.; B.S. in Chem. Engring., U. Tex., 1940; D. Sc., U. Tampa (Fla.); m. Angelina Johnapelus, May 11, 1941; children—Michael Rawls, James Thomas, Ellen. Engr., Gulf Oil Corp., Port Arthur, Tex., 1940-48, coordinator mfg. dept., Pitts., 1955- 58, adminstrv. v.p., 1958-60, sr. v.p., 1961, exec. v.p., 1962-65, pres., 1965—, also dir.; mgr. Gulf Refining Co., Puerto La Cruz, Venezuela, 1948-55; dir. Gen. Foods Corp., Gulf Oil Co., Allegheny Ludlum Industries, Inc., Corpus Christi Bank & Trust. Mem. pres.'s council Cal. Inst. Tech.; mem. Allegheny Conf. Community Devel. Trustee Southwest Research Inst., U. Pitts., Mercy Hosp. Recipient Distinguished Engring. Grad award U. Tex., 1965. Mem. Am. Petroleum Inst. (bd.), Pitts C. of C. Clubs: Duquesne, Pittsburgh Athletic Assn. (Pitts.); Rolling Rock. Home: 102 Pheasant Dr Pittsburgh PA 15238 Office: Gulf Bldg 7th Av Pittsburgh PA 15230

DORSEY, CHARLES HOWARD, Jr., former newspaper editor; b. Balt., May 2, 1904; s. Charles Howard and Leila Risteau (Walter) D.; grad. Balt. City Coll., 1923; A.B., Johns Hopkins, 1927; m. Emma Beck Deputy, Nov. 21, 1933; 1 son, John Russell. Instr. philosophy Johns Hopkins Coll. for Tchrs., 1930-31; reporter Balt. Evening Sun, 1931-32, 33-42, acting asst. city editor, 1942; asst. mng. editor Balt. Sun (morning), 1942-47, mng. editor, 1947-66, asso. editor, 1966-69; v.p. A.S. Abell Co., pub. Balt. Sun papers, 1956-69. Mem. Kappa Alpha. Democrat. P.E. ch. Clubs: Maryland, Tudor and Stuart (Balt.); National Press (Washington). Home: 14 Bouton Green Village of Cross Keys Baltimore MD 21210

DORSEY, EARL A., distillery co. exec.; b. Louisville, 1915. Sr. v.p., dir. Brown-Forman Distillers Corp.; v.p., dir. Jack Daniel Distillery, Ashbourne Realty & Land Redevel. Corp.; treas. Canadian Mist Distillers, Ltd. Office: 1908 Howard St Louisville KY 40210

DORSEY, EUGENE CARROLL, Newspaper publisher; b. Springfield, Ill., Feb. 27, 1927; s. Prentiss Eugene and Reta Mae (Bennett) D.; B.S. in Journalism, U. Ill., 1949; m. Rita LaVerne Sutzer, June 18, 1949; children-David Eugene, Philip Alan. Writer radio sta. WDZ, Decatur, Ill., 1949-51; program dir. radio sta. WSOY, Decatur, 1951-57; gen. mgr. radio sta. WVLN, Olney, Ill., 1957-59; gen. mgr. Eve. and Sunday Jour., E. St. Louis, Ill., 1959-63; with Ida. Statesman, Boise, 1963—, pub., 1966—. Dir. Federated Publns., 1967—, v.p., 1969—. Served with USNR, 1945-46. Named Outstanding Young Man of Olney, 1958, Outstanding Young Man of E. St. Louis, 1961, Outstanding Young Man of Ill., 1961. Pres. E. St. Louis C. of C., 1961-62, Boise United Fund, 1968-69, Boise YMCA, 1966-67. Vice chmn. trustees Coll. of Ida.; bd. dirs. Boise A.R.C., Boise United Fund, Boise Jr. Achievement. Mem. Am. Soc. Newspaper Editors, Ida. (bd. dirs.), Boise chambers commerce, Sigma Delta Chi. Presbyn. (elder). Rotarian (v.p. Boise) Home: 4018 Edgemont Boise ID 83704 Office: 300 N 6th St Boise ID 83701

DORSEY, GRAY LANKFORD, educator; b. Hamilton, Mo., Feb. 16, 1918; s. Claude Purdue and Mary Alice (Lankford) D.; student Baker U., 1936-38; A.B. in Journalism, U. Kan., 1941; LL.B., Yale, 1948, J.S.D., 1950; m. Jeanne DeVall, Jan. 1, 1942; 1 dau., Deborah DeVall. Editor, pub. Cameron (Mo.) Sun, 1940-42; mem. faculty Washington U., St. Louis, 1951—, Nagel prof. jurisprudence and internat. law, 1962—; vis. prof. Nat. Taiwan U., also Soochow U., Taipei, Taiwan, China, 1952-53; lectr. philosophy U. Hawaii, summer 1959; fellow Center Advanced Study Behavioral Scis., Stanford, 1960-61; admitted to Mo. bar, 1956; cons. field of antitrust law. Served to lt. (s.g.) USCGR, 1942-46, to maj. U.S. Army Res., 1956-62. Fellow Am. Council Learned Socs., 1948-50. Mem. Am., St. Louis bar assns., Mo. Bar, Am. Soc. Internat. Law, Internat. Assn. Legal Philosophy and Social Philosophy (pres.). Contbr. publs. in field. Editor: Constitutional Freedom and the Law, 1965; Validation of New Forms of Social Organization, 1968. Home: 8 Conway Springs Dr Chesterfield MO 63017 Office: Law Sch Washington U St Louis MO 63130

DORSEY, GREGORY FREDERICKchemist, educator; b. Chicago, 1928; B.S. in Physics, Yale, 1950; Ph.D. in Chemistry, Harvard, 1956; m. Sally Ann Jones, July 5, 1957; children--Kenneth J., Nancy A. Chemist, Acme Chem. Co., Blue Island, Ill., 1950-51; director of Reseach Lab., Indsl. Chemicals Corp., Cambridge, Mass., 1956-60; project coordinator environmental sect. Steinmetz Assos., Chgo., 1960-61; v.p. for reseach Bauer Bros. Chem. Co., Inc., Memphis, 1961-64; asst. prof. chemistry Washington U., St. Louis, 1964-66, asso. prof., 1966-70, prof., 1970--, head of chemistry dept., 1970-71. Vis. prof. So. Ill. U., summer 1967, U. of Ore., 1969. Scoutmaster, Boy Scouts America, University City, Mo., 1968-70. Bd. dirs. Rest Haven Home for Elderly, 1960-61; trustee of the Lutheran Hosp., 1965-71. Served from lt. to capt., AUS, 1951-53. Mem. Am. Chem. Soc., Sci. Research Soc. Am. (chpt. treas. 1967), Sigma Xi. Author: (with others) Basic Inorganic Chemistry, 1971. Contbr. articles to profl. jours., encys., also chpts. to books. Home: Fairfax Apts 7291 Windermere Dr University City MO 63105 Office: Dept Chemistry Washington University St Louis MO 63130

DORSEY, HUGH MANSON, Jr., lawyer; b. Atlanta, Mar. 29, 1912; s. Hugh Manson and Adair (Wilkinson) D.; grad. Woodberry Forest Prep. Sch., 1929; A.B., Emory U., 1933, LL.B., 1935; m. Laura L. Whitner, Dec. 21, 1935; children—Mary Adair (Mrs. James T. Sisk, Jr.), Laura W. (Mrs. Thomas N. Rains), Hugh Manson III, Rufus Thomas IV. Admitted to Ga. bar, 1935; practice in Atlanta, 1936—; partner firm Hansell, Post, Brandon & Dorsey, and predecessors, 1959—. Past pres. Atlanta Legal Aid Soc. Fellow Am. Coll. Trial Lawyers, Inst. Jud. Adminstrn.; mem. Am., Ga. (pres. 1963-64), Atlanta (exec. com. 1942-52) bar assns., State Bar Ga. (pres. 1963-64), Lawyers Club Atlanta, Am. Judicature Soc., Phi Beta Kappa, Chi Phi, (nat. pres. 1943-47), Omicron Delta Kappa. Presbyn. (elder). Clubs: Atlanta Athletic (past pres.), Piedmont Driving (Atlanta). Home: 51 28th St N W Atlanta GA 30309 Office: First Nat Bank Bldg Atlanta GA 30303

DORSEY, JOHN MORRIS, educator, author; b. Clinton, Ia., Nov. 19, 1900; s. Edward William and Anna Elizabeth (Looney) D.; A.B., U. Ia., 1925, M.D., 1925, M.S., 1927; m. Mary Louise Carson, Oct. 26, 1926; children—John Morris, Edward Carson. Intern, U. Ia. Hosps., 1925-26; resident psychiatrist U. Ia., State Psychopathic Hosp., instr. psychiatry, 1926-28; asst. dir. Mich. State Psychopathic Hosp., 1928-35; asso. prof. U. Mich. Med. Sch., 1933-38, lectr. postgrad. medicine, 1938-48; cons. psychiatrist Wayne County Juvenile Ct., Detroit, 1929-35, 37-50; tng. psychiatrist Children's Center, Detroit, 1938-48; psychiatrist, head Wayne State U. Mental Hygiene Service, 1938-40, chmn. dept. psychiatry, 1946-61, also professorial lectr.; psychiatrist Purdue U. Sch. Survey Com.; dir. Child Guidance Div., Children's Fund of Mich., 1945-54, Univ. prof. Wayne State U., 1961—. Ednl. dir. Children's Center, 1944-50; med. dir. McGregor Center, hosp. for rehab. and health edn.; chief cons. neurology and psychiatry, Dearborn VA Hosp.; staff physician Harper Hosp.; psychiatrist Children's Hosp.; chmn. dept. psychiatry Detroit Receiving Hosp. Rockefeller Found. grantee, 1935- 37. Mem. Highland Park Bd. Edn. (pres. 1944, 50, 54); mem. City-County Mental Health Bd. Trustee Luella Hannan Meml. Home, John Scudder Found. for Old People. Commd. 1st lt. Med. Res. Corps. Diplomate Am. Bd. Psychiatry and Neurology. Mem. A.M.A., Am. Psychiat. Assn., Am. Psychol. Assn., Am. Psychopathol. Assn., Am. Assn. Mil. Surgeons, A.A.A.S., Am. Psychoanalytic Assn., Mich. Soc. Neurology and Psychiatry (pres.), Am. Med. Writers Assn., Am. Coll. Psychoanalysis, U. Mich. Research Club, Sigma Xi, Alpha Kappa Delta, Nu Sigma Nu, Sigma Chi, Alpha Omega Alpha. Republican. Clubs: Torch, Detroit Boat, Prismatic (Detroit); Ann Arbor Golf and Outing. Author: The Foundations of Human Nature, 1935; The Use of the Psycho-Analytic Principle in Child Guidance Work, 1949; (with Walter H. Seegers) Living Consciously: The Science of Self; Illness of Allness, 1965; American Government, 1969; Psychology of Emotion, 1971; Psychology of Language, 1971. Editor: The Letters of Thomas Jefferson and his Personal Physician Robley Dunglison; The Growth of Self-Insight (Franklin Lecture Series). Contbr. to Modern Marriage, 1950; also to jours. Home: 65 Moss Av Highland Park MI 48030 Office: David Mackenzie Hall Wayne State U Detroit MI 48202

DORSEY, JOHN RUSSELL, journalist; b. Balt., Dec. 17, 1938; s. Charles Howard and Emma (Deputy) D.; A.B., Harvard, 1961. Mem. staff Balt. Sun, 1962—, Sunday Sun book rev. editor, 1967-69. Democrat. Episcopalian. Clubs: Maryland, Harvard (Balt.). Home: 1619 Park Av Baltimore MD 21217 Office: Baltimore Sun Calvert and Centre Sts Baltimore MD 21203

DORSEY, LEO PATRICK, lawyer; b. Towanda, Pa., s. Patrick D. and Margaret M. (Moore) D.; A.B., U. Pa., 1920; LL.B., Harvard, 1923; m. Ruth E. Knickerbocker, Oct. 25, 1923; children—L. L. Dean, John D., Robert K. Admitted to N.Y. bar, 1925, since practiced in N.Y.C.; mem. firm Dorsey, Burke & Griffin, and predecessors; now counsel Boal, Doti, Fitzpatrick & Hart, N.Y.C.; N.Y. State counsel HOLC, 1933-37; mortgage commr. N.Y. State, 1937-39. Bd. dirs. Queens council Boy Scouts Am. Mem. Am., Internat., N.Y. State bar assns., Bar Assn. City N.Y. Home: 1102 Shore Rd Douglaston NY Office: 116 John St New York City NY 10038

DORSEY, MONTGOMERY, lawyer; b. Denver, Sept. 11, 1900; s. Clayton Chauncey and Marguerite (Montgomery) D.; student Hotchkiss Sch., Lakeville, Conn., 1915-18; A.B., Yale, 1922; LL.B., Denver U., 1925; m. Margaret Owen, Nov. 25, 1935. Admitted to Colo. bar, 1925; practice of law with Hughes & Dorsey, Denver, 1925—; chmn. bd., chmn. exec. com. First Nat. Bank of Denver, First Nat. Bancorp., Inc.; dir., mem. exec. com. Denver Tramway Corp., Rio Grande Industries, Inc.; dir. Denver & Rio Grande Western R.R. Co. Bd. dirs., v.p., A.V. Hunter Trust; chmn., trustee Laurence Phipps Found. Mem. Am., Colo., Denver bar assns. Clubs: Denver, Country, Athletic, 26 (Denver); Mile High; Garden of Gods (Colorado Springs). Home: 177 Race St Denver CO 80206 Office: 635 17th St Denver CO 80202

DORSEY, PETER, lawyer; b. Mpls., Aug. 22, 1922; s. James Emmett and Mary (Toomey) D.; A.B., Harvard, 1947, LL.B., 1949; children—Sheila, Cynthia, Justin, Sage. Admitted to Minn. bar, 1949; with firm Dorsey, Marquart, Windhorst, West & Halladay, and predecessors, Mpls., 1949—, jr. partner, 1956-59, gen. partner, 1959—; gen. counsel Minn. Twins Baseball Club, 1962—, Super Valu Stores, Inc., Hopkins, Minn., 1965—. Chmn. Legal task force Urban Coalition Mpls., 1969-70. Bd. dirs. Minn. Theatre Co. Found., Guthrie Theatre, 1963-69, mem. exec. com., 1964-68, exec. v.p., 1966-68. Served to 1st lt., airborne inf., AUS, 1942-46. Mem. Am. Bar Assn., Am. Civil Liberties Union (pres. Minn. br. 1963-65, dir.), Minn., Hennepin County bar assns., Mpls. C. of C. (Distinguished Service award 1966), Am. Trial Lawyers Assn. (Merit award 1966). Clubs: Harvard of Minn. (pres. 1965-66), Minneapolis. Home: 1916 Irving Av S Minneapolis MN 55403 Office: First Nat Bank Bldg Minneapolis MN 55402

DORSEY, RAY, newspaperman; b. Phila., July 29, 1913; s. Rudolph Raymond and Marjorie (Conner) D.; B.A., Dartmouth, 1936; M.S. in Journalism, Columbia, 1937; m. Bettie Arnette Brunn, Oct. 27, 1940; 1 son, Noel Michael. Gen. assignment and beat reporter Cleve. Plain Dealer, 1937-46, city hall reporter, 1946-56, polit. editor, 1956-63, asso. editor, editorial writer, 1964, chief editorial writer, editor editorial page, 1964—. Mem. 1967 Pulitzer Prize Journalism Jury. Trustee Cuyahoga unit Am. Cancer Soc. Mem. Nat. Conf. Editorial Writers, Am. Soc. Newspaper Editors, Alpha Sigma Phi. Home: 30200 Ednil Dr Bay Village OH 44140 Office: 1801 Superior Av NE Cleveland OH 44114

DORSEY, RHODA MARY, coll. adminstr.; b. Boston, Sept. 9, 1927; d. Thomas Francis and Hedwig (Hoge) Dorsey; B.A. magna cum laude, Smith Coll., 1949; B.A., Cambridge (Eng.) U., 1951, M.A., 1954; Ph.D., U. Minn., 1956; LL.D., Nazareth Coll. Rochester. Mem. faculty Goucher Coll., Towson, Md., 1954—, prof. history, 1965-68, dean, v.p., 1968—; lectr. history Loyola Coll., Balt., 1958-62, Johns Hopkins, 1960-61. Mem. Gov. Md. Adv. Com. for Register Hist. Sites in Md. Trustee Park Sch. Mem. Am., (com. on films), So. hist. assns., Orgn. Am. Historians (commn. on status women in profession), A.A.A.S. (com. on minorities in sci.), Md. Hist. Soc. (publs. com.). Club: Smith (Balt.). Chmn. bd. editors Md. Hist. Mag. Home: 502 Goucher Blvd Towson MD 21204

DORSEY, THOMAS ANDREW, clergyman, composer; b. Villa Rica, Ga., July 1, 1899; s. Thomas Madison and Etta (Plant) D.; student Chgo. Music Coll.; M.A., Baptist Tng. Sch., 1941; D. Gospel Music Creation (hon.), Simmons Art and Music Inst., Charleston, S.C., 1944; m. Kathryn Mosely, Feb. 17, 1941; children—Thomas Madison, Doris Mary. Ordained to ministry Bapt. Ch., 1964; mus. dir., asst. minister Pilgrim Bapt. Ch., Chgo., 1932—; pres. Nat. Conf. Gospel Choirs, 1932—; speaker Evangelistic campaigns throughout U.S., 1933—; music dir. Congressman William L. Dawson's meeting hdqrs., Chgo., 1963—. Recipient awards Lyon & Healy Music Co., N.A.A.C.P., Urban League, Nat. Assn. Musicians. Author: (non-fiction) My Ups and Downs, 1943. Composer music for TV serial, Ordeal by Five, 1959, also over 400 gospel songs, including Peace in the Valley, 1937, Precious Lord Take My Hand, 1932. Home: Chicago IL Office: 4154 S Ellis Av Chicago IL 60653

DORSEY, THOMAS BROOKSHLER, newspaper exec.; b. Keokuk, Ia., Apr. 30, 1928; s. Frank Blinn and Johanna (Brookshier) D.; student DePauw U., 1946-47, State U. Ia., 1947- 50; m. Helen Danner, June 30, 1951; children—Diana, Frank Blinn. Corr., Des Moines Register, 1949-51; chief European corr. Times Pub. Co., 1954-56; nat. affairs editor Am. Weekend, Washington, 1956-57; editor, gen. mgr. N.Y. Herald Tribune News Service, 1957-59; v.p. Barnet & Reef Assos., Inc., N.Y.C., 1959-63; v.p., dir. internat. div. John Moynaham & Co., N.Y.C., 1963; dir., editor Newsday Spls. (syndicate) Newsday Inc., 1964-69; editor Chgo. Tribune-N.Y. News Syndicate, Inc., N.Y.C., 1969—. Served with USAF, 1951- 54. Mem. Aviation/Space Writers Assn., Internat. Radio and TV Soc., Sigma Delta Chi. Clubs: Nat. Press (Washington); Deadline (exec. bd. dir.). Home: 301 E 64th St New York City NY 10021 Office: 220 E 42d St New York City NY 10017

DORSKIND, BENJAMIN, advt. exec.; b. Warsaw, Poland, Aug. 15, 1897; s. Solomon and Eva (Danziger) D.; came to U.S., 1901, naturalized, 1914; ed. pub. schs., N.Y.C.; m. Rose Friedman, June 1, 1920; children—Albert, Robert; m. 2d, Anne M. Meyer, Feb. 25, 1950. With Brown Advt. Agy., 1919-21; organizer Diener and Dorskind, 1921, chmn. bd., 1956—. Mem. Bklyn. Draft Bd., 1941-46. Home: 123 W 57th St New York City NY 10019 Office: 1501 Broadway New York City NY 10036

DORSKIND, ROBERT, advt. exec.; b. N.Y.C., May 25, 1925; s. Benjamin and Rose (Friedman) D.; student Clemson U., 1945, N.Y.U., 1947; m. Doris Weiss, Apr. 7, 1945; children—Bruce, Glenn. With Diener & Dorskind, N.Y.C., 1946—, exec. v.p., 1952-56, pres., 1956—; publisher Met. Golfers Annual, 1963- -; sec.-treas. Eldor Pub. Co., 1964—; sec. Programs Internat., 1964—; treas. Classified Mgmt., 1968—; pub. relations dir. Met. Profl. Golfers Assn.; pub. Met. Rev. of 1970. Served with AUS and USAAF, 1943-45. Recipient plaque Met. Profl. Golfers Assn., 1965, 66. Club: Pine Hollow Country (bd. govs. 1969—, chmn. admissions, 1970). Home: 205 Birch Dr Roslyn NY 11576 Office: 1501 Broadway New York City NY 10036

DORST, JOHN PHILLIPS, educator, physician; b. Cin., July 8, 1926; s. Stanley Elwood and Mary (Conway) D.; student Princeton, 1944, 47-48, U. Cin., 1946, Pomona Coll., 1948-49; M.D., Cornell U., 1953; m. Marcia Louise Kinney, June 17, 1950; children—Stanley Kinney, Nancy, John Radcliffe, Margaret. Rotating intern U. Ia. Hosps., 1953-54; resident radiology VA Hosp., Mpls., 1955, State U. Ia. Hosps., 1955-58; fellow pediatric radiology U. Cinn. Coll. Medicine, 1958-59, from asst. prof. to asso. prof. radiology, also from instr. to asst. prof. pediatrics, 1959-66; mem. faculty Johns Hopkins Med. Sch., 1966—, prof. radiology, 1970—, asso. prof. pediatrics, 1967—; radiologist Johns Hopkins Hosp., 1966—. Mem. com. child abuse Md. Dept. Social Services. Served with AUS, 1944-46. Fellow Am. Coll. Radiology; mem. Radiol. Soc. N.Am., Am. Roentgen Ray Soc., Soc. Pediatric Radiology, Sigma Xi. Home: 304 Northway Baltimore MD 21218

DORST, STANLEY ELWOOD, physician; b. Cin. July 20, 1897; s. John Louis and Florence May (Elwood) D.; A.B., Wittenberg Coll., 1919, Sc.D., 1948; M.D., U. Cin., 1923, L.H.D., 1962; LL.D., Xavier U., 1963; m. Mary Conway, Oct. 1926; 1 son, John Phillips; m. 2d, Emma H. Prince, Apr. 11, 1935. Intern Lakeside Hosp., Cleve., 1923-24; resident physician Cleve. Clinic Hosp., 1924-26; asst. prof. medicine U. Cin., 1926-30, asso. prof., 1930-53, prof., 1953—, dean Coll. Medicine, 1940-63 dean emeritus, 1963—; asst. attending physician, Cin. Gen. Hosp., 1926-30, attending physician 1930—, chief physician to out-patient dispensary, 1930-41; dir. Louis Kuhn Meml. Lab., 1926-37; cons. internist Children's Hosp., 1935-61; chmn. directing med. staff Cin. Gen. Hosp. and Christian R. Holmes Hosp. 1940-63; cons. med. edn., 5th Service Command, 1942-46. Pres., mem. exec. council Assn. Am. Med. Colls.; mem. adv. council Am. Specialty Bds. Medicine, 1949-60. Served as 2d lt., Inf., U.S. Army, 1918-19. Recipient Abraham Flexner award Assn. Am. Med. Colls., 1967. Diplomate Am. Bd. Internal Medicine. Mem. Am. Soc. for Clin. Investigation, Central Soc. Clin. Research, A.A.A.S., A.M.A., (commn. for study of British medicine, 1949-50), Alpha Omega Alpha, Sigma Xi, Pi Kappa Epsilon, Alpha Kappa Kappa, Beta Theta Pi. Clubs: University, Literary (Cin.). Author section on diseases of hypersensitivity in Reimann's System of Treatment; section on body weight in Ency. Medicine. Contbr. numerous articles to sci. jours. Home: 2401 Ingleside Av Cincinnati OH 45206

DORTCH, CARL RAYMOND, assn. exec.; b. nr. Madisonville, Ky., Sept. 14, 1914; s. Walter B. and Delia (Baldwin) D.; A.B., DePauw U., 1936; M.A. in Pub. Adminstrn., U. Cin., 1938; m. Anna Gale Greenland, Nov. 17, 1950; children—Walter A., David J. With Indpls. C. of C., 1936—, asst. gen. mgr., 1950-62, gen. mgr., 1962-64, exec. v.p., 1964—. Bd. dirs. Indpls. chpt. A.R.C., Bd. Fundamental Edn., Central Ind. council Boy Scouts Am., Flanner House, Urban League Indpls., Starlight Musicals, United Fund Greater Indpls., Indpls. Sci. and Engring. Found.; bd. advisers Jr. Achievement, 1963—, Christian Theol. Sem. Served as 1st lt. USAAF, 1943-45. Recipient John N. VanDerVries award U.S. C. of C., 1947, Distinguished Service award U.S. Jr. C. of C., 1949; named Man of Year, Indpls. Times, 1956. Mem. Am. C. of C. Execs. (bd. dirs.), Ind. Commerce Execs. Assn. (past pres.), DePauw Alumni Assn., Edward Rector Alumni Assn. (past pres.). Presbyn. Mason, Kiwanian. Clubs: Southern, Indianapolis Press, Indianapolis Athletic (bd. dirs.), Columbia, Meridian Hills Country (Indpls.). Home: 7031 Washington Blvd Indianapolis IN 46220 Office: 320 N Meridian St Indianapolis IN 46204

DORTICOS, TORRADO OSVALDO, pres. Cuba; b. 1919; student Havana U. Admitted to bar and practiced law; leader Castro revolutionary movement in Cienfuegos, 1957- 58, imprisoned, Dec. 1958; escaped and fled to Mexico, returned upon success of revolution; minister revolutionary laws, 1959; pres. Cuba, 1959—. Mem. Cuban Nat. Bar Assn. (v.p.). Address: Palacio Presidencial Havana Cuba *

DORVILLIER, WILLIAM JOSEPH, editor, pub.; b. North Adams, Mass., Apr. 24, 1908; s. Joseph and Aurise (Champagne) D.; student N.Y.U.; m. Mary Elizabeth Johnson, Oct. 1, 1938; 1 son, William Clay. With North Adams Transcript; editor S. Am. desk A.P., N.Y.C., then corr. A.P. and U.P.I., Caribbean area; accredited war corr., World War II; editor Puerto Rico World Jour., 1940-43, 44-45, 56-57, Washington corr., 1945-53; founder Dorvillier News Letter, weekly bus. and econ. publ., 1953; founder San Juan Star, 1959, editor, pub., 1959—; pres., dir. Star Pub., editor, pub., 1959-67; past pres., dir. Star Pub. Corp.; now chmn. bd. Dorvillier News Agy., Inc.; news dir. WAPA-TV, 1969—. Chmn. information and edn. com. United Fund P.R.; chmn. adv. com. Civil Air Patrol. Recipient Pulitzer prize for distinguished editorial writing, 1961. Mem. Sigma Delta Chi. Club: Nat. Press (Washington). Author: Workshop U.S.A., The Challenge of Puerto Rico, 1962. Office: Dorvillier News Agy Inc P O Box 9174 Santurce PR 00908

DORWART, HAROLD LAIRD, former educator; b. Greenville, Pa., Aug. 27, 1902; s. George Wilson and Clara (Laird) D.; A.B., Washington and Jefferson Coll., 1924, D.Sc., 1968; Ph.D. in Math., Yale, 1931; m. Carolyn Frances Yeisley, Jan. 2, 1933; 1 son, Roger Wilson. Asst. to instr. math. Yale, 1924-28; instr. Williams Coll., 1928-30, 31-35; from asst. prof. to prof. math. Washington and Jefferson Coll., 1935-49; Seabury prof. math., chmn. dept. Trinity Coll., Hartford, Conn., 1949-67, dean of the coll., 1967-68. Mem. Am. Math. Soc., Math. Assn. Am. (bd. govs. 1948-51), Phi Beta Kappa, Sigma Xi. Author: The Geometry of Incidence, 1966; Configurations, 1968. Contbr. numerous articles profl. jours. Home: 54 Willieb St Glastonbury CT 06033

DOSE, WILLIAM N., food co. exec.; b. Chgo., 1907; B.S., Northwestern U., 1929. Accountant, Duhne, Bauer & Co., 1929-30, Consol. Electric & Gas Co., 1930-33; auditor Frazer & Torket, C.P.A.'s, 1933-42; with Carnation Co., 1942—, asst. controller, 1947-54, gen. controller, 1954-67, v.p., controller, 1967—. Home: 1541 Greenbriar Rd Glendale CA 91207 Office: 5045 Wilshire Blvd Los Angeles CA 90036*

DOSKOCIL, KARL VACLAV, psychiatrist; b. Prague, Czechoslovakia, Jan. 6, 1921; s. Jan and Albina (Feiglova) D.; B.S. Real Gymnasium (Czechoslovakia), 1941; M.D., Johan Wolfgang Goethe U. (Germany), 1950; m. Mary Tola, June 20, 1954; children—Karl Andrew, Patricia Gail, Frank Alan, John Melvin. Intern St. Vincent's Hosp., Hanau M., Germany, 1950-51; intern St. Joseph's Infirmary, Louisville, 1951-52; resident in psychiatry University Hosp., Louisville, 1952-53, Dorothea Dix Hosp., Raleigh, N.C., 1953-54, Eastern State Hosp., Williamsburg, Va., 1954-55, chief male service, 1955-57; chief med. staff Ky. State Hosp., Danville, 1957-59, clin. dir., 1959-61; chief psychiatrist S.C. State Hosp., Columbia, S.C., 1961-65, dir. profl. services, 1965-69, supt., 1969—; teaching cons. William S. Hall Psychiatric Inst., Columbia; cons. Mid-Carolina Council on Alcoholism, Columbia. Mem. Assn. Med. Supts., Am. Psychiatric Assn., Am., S.C. med. assns., Columbia Med. Soc., S.C. Mental Health Assn., Mid-Carolina Council Alcoholism. Roman Catholic. Home: 1426 Summerville Av Columbia SC 29201 Office: PO Box 119 Columbia SC 29202

DOSS, BOWMAN, former ins. exec.; b. Waiteville, W.Va., Feb. 29, 1908; s. Charles Hubert and Martha Jane (Jarvis) D.; student Alderson-Broaddus Coll., Philippi, W.Va., 1927-29; m. Hallie Dransfield, June 16, 1934; children—Charles, Jerry. Tchr. schs., 1928-33; with Nationwide Mut. Ins. Cos. (formerly Farm Bur. Ins. Cos.), 1932—, beginning as solicitor for agt., successively agt., dist. sales mgr., spl. agt., state agt., asst. supt. agts., asst. sec., agy. v.p., 1934-55, 1st v.p. Nationwide Mut. Ins. Co., Nationwide Mut. Fire Ins. Co., Nationwide Gen. Ins. Co., Nationwide Life Ins. Co., Columbus, O., 1956-64, pres., gen. mgr., dir., 1964-70; pres. Nationwide Ins. Cos., 1964-70, Nationwide Devel. Co., Heritage Securities, Inc.; pres., dir. Nationwide Consumer Services, Inc.; pres., chmn. Allnations, Inc.; pres., dir. Nationwide Communications, Inc.; dir. Comml. Standards Ins. Co., Ft. Worth, Norlie, Inc., Seattle, No. Life Ins. Co., Seattle, Mich. Life Ins. Co., Royal Oak, Mich.; dir. W. Coast Life Ins. Co., San Francisco. Chmn. exec. com. ins. sect. Internat. Coop. Alliance; dir., chmn. Coop. League U.S.A. Mem. exec. bd. Devel. Com. Greater Columbus. Trustee Children's Hosp., Columbus, Alderson-Broaddus Coll., Philippi, W.Va. Mem. Columbus Area C. of C. (exec. bd.). Methodist (ofcl. bd.). Home: 1438 Sherbrooke Pl Columbus OH 43209

DOTEN, ROGER DOLPH, lawyer; b. Albion, Neb., Dec. 24, 1903; s. Frank Andrew and Mary Barker (Dolph) D.; A.B., U. Mich., 1925, LL.B., 1927; m. Mollie O. Burton, Nov. 27, 1932; 1 son, David Roger. Admitted to Ill. bar, 1927; partner Dent, Dobyns & Freeman, 1927-31, Dent, Weichelt & Hampton, 1931-50, Dent, Hampton & Doten, Chgo., 1950—. Mem. Am., Chgo. bar assns., Internat. Ins. Counsel, Pi Kappa Alpha, Gamma Eta Gamma. Episcopalian. Mason. Home: 840 Romona Rd Wilmette IL 60091 Office: 209 S LaSalle St Chicago IL 60604

DOTI, JOSEPH E., lawyer; b. N.Y.C., May 23, 1915; LL.B., Fordham U., 1936. Admitted to N.Y. bar, 1937; now partner firm Boal, Doti, Fitzpatrick & Hart, N.Y.C. Office: 44 Wall St New York City NY 10005*

DOTSON, GEORGE EDGAR, educator; b. Milton, Ore., Sept. 15, 1904; s. Eli E. and Dora E. (Edgar) C.; A.B., San Diego State Coll., 1926; A.M., Stanford, 1927, Ed.D., 1939; m. Gladys Aileen Fisher, Aug. 15, 1931; 1 son, Robert E. Instr. phys. edn. La Jolla Jr.-Sr. High Sch., San Diego, 1927-30; dir. activities Oceanside-Carlsbad Union High Sch., 1930-35; registrar, dir. student personnel San Diego State Coll., 1936-42; pres. Long Beach City Coll., 1942-64, asst. supt., 1951-61; dir. ednl. services, prof. edn. Cal. State Coll. at Long Beach, 1964-67, prof. edn., 1964-71; dep. supt. Long Beach Unified Sch. Dist., 1962- 64; on leave to Stanford, 1935-36. Rotarian. Home: 1230 Los Altos Av Long Beach CA 90815

DOTT, ROBERT HENRY, Jr., educator; b. Tulsa, June 2, 1929; s. Robert Henry and Esther Edgerton (Reed) D.; student U. Okla., 1946-48; B.S., U. Mich., 1950, M.S., 1951; Ph.D. (AEC fellow), Columbia, 1955; m. Nancy Maud Robertson, Feb. 1, 1951; children—James, Karen, Eric, Cynthia, Brian. Exploration geologist Humble Oil & Refining Co., Ariz., Ore., Wash., 1954-56, So. Cal., 1958; mem. faculty U. Wis.-Madison, 1958—, prof. geology, 1966—; vis. prof. U. Cal. at Berkeley, 1969; lectr. Tulsa U., 1969. Cons. Roan Selection Trust, Ltd., Zambia, 1967. Served to 1st lt. USAF, 1956-57. Recipient Outstanding Tchr. award Wis. Student Assn., 1969. Fellow Geol. Soc. Am.; mem. Am. Assn. Petroleum Geologists (President's award 1956), Soc. Econ. Paleontologists and Mineralogists (sec.-treas. 1968-70), A.A.A.S., Internat. Assn. Sedimentologists, Sigma Xi. Unitarian. Author: (with R.L. Batten) Evolution of the Earth, 1971. Contbr. articles profl. jours. Office: Univ Wisconsin Madison WI 53706

DOTTER, CHARLES THEODORE, radiologist, educator; b. Boston, June 14, 1920; s. John Maury and Rosalind (Allin) D.; A.B., Duke, 1941; M.D., Cornell U., 1944; m. Doris Pamela Beattie, Sept. 30, 1944; children—Barbara Allin, Jeffrey Churchill, Jane Huntington. Intern U.S. Naval Hosp., St. Albans, N.Y., 1944-45, intern medicine N.Y. Hosp., 1946-47, resident radiology, 1947- 50, asst. attending radiologist, 1950-52; instr. medicine Cornell U. Med. Coll., 1948-52, instr. radiology, 1948-51, asst. prof. radiology, 1951-52; prof. radiology Med. Sch., U. Ore., head dept. radiology U. Ore. Med. Sch. Hosps. and Clinics, 1952—. Served as lt. (j.g.) USNR, 1944- 46; bn. surgeon 1st Div. USMC, China, 1945-46. Diplomate Am. Bd. Radiology. Fellow Am. Coll. Radiology; mem. Am. Roentgen Ray Soc., A.M.A., Am. Heart Assn., I.E.E.E., Radiol. Soc. N.Am., Pacific N.W. Radiol. Soc., Ore. Radiol. Soc., Assn. U. Radiologists, Ore., Multnomah County med. socs., Am. Fedn. Clin. Research, Western, N.W. Socs. clin. research, Portland Acad. Medicine, Ore. Thoracic Soc., Am., Ore. State heart assns., Internat. Cardiovascular Soc., Portland Heart Club, Soc. Chmn. Acad. Radiology Depts., Am. Coll. Chest Physicians, Czechoslovak Med. Soc. J.E. Purkyne. Clubs: Explorers of Mexico; Mazamas; Portland City; Am. Alpine. Author: (with Israel Steinberg) Anglocardiography (Vol. XX, Annals Roentgenology), 1951. Editorial bd. Circulation. publ. Am. Heart Assn., 1954-58. Contbr. sci. articles profl. jours. Research into cardiac disease and physiology by radiological means. Home: 4004 S W Greenleaf Dr Portland OR 97221

DOTTERWEICH, FRANK HENRY, educator, engr.; b. Balt., Dec. 11, 1906; s. Frank Edward and Dolly Wilson (White) D.; B.E., Johns Hopkins, 1928, Ph.D., 1937; m. June Ramsay Smith, May 16, 1946. Cadet engr. Consol. Elec. Light and Power Co., Balt., 1928-29, gen. foreman, 1929-30, asst. to gen. supt. gas operations, 1930-32; profl. athlete and chem. instr. Balt. Poly. Evening High Sch., 1932-34; instr. and coach in phys. edn., grad. student, Johns Hopkins, 1934-37; asso. prof. Tex. A. and I. U., 1937-40, prof., 1940—, dir. div. engring., 1944-67, dean Sch. Engring., 1967-71, prof., 1971—; cons. petroleum, natural gas and chem. engr., 1940—. Tech. cons. natural gas and natural gasoline Petroleum Adminstrn. for War, Washington, 1942-45. Profl. engr., Tex. Mem. So. Gas Assn. (hon. life), Am. Inst. Mining, Metall. and Petroleum Engrs., Am. Inst. Chem. Engrs., Am. Petroleum Inst., Am. Chem. Soc., Nat. Assn. Corrosion Engrs., Am. Gas Assn., Kappa Sigma, Sigma Tau. Lutheran. Mason. Contbr. petroleum and natural gas engring. publs. Mem. Am. Olympic Lacrosse team, 1928. Address: care Tex A & I U Kingsville TX 78363

DOTTS, HAROLD WILLIAM, pub. relations exec.; b. Corydon, Ia., May 7, 1904; s. William E. and Pauline (Goodell) D.; A.B., Simpson Coll., 1926; postgrad. Harvard Bus. Sch., 1936; m. Evelyn Dosey, Oct. 10, 1931; children—Harold W., Robert D., Dorothy Catherine; m. 2d, Glady Carlisle, Dec. 26, 1965. With Jewel Tea Co., Barrington, Ill., 1926-53, successively salesman, asst. mgr., br. and dist. mgr., asst. gen. sales mgr., gen. sales mgr. and v.p., 1942-53; pres. Stonegate China Co., 1953-62; exec. dir. Nat. Home Service Assn., 1962-68; with Knox Assos., Oak Brook, Ill., 1968-70; pub. relations dir. Northwest Trust & Savs. Bank, Arlington Heights, 1970—. Trustee Simpson Coll., Northwest Community Hosp. Mem. Am. Soc. Assn. Execs., Nat. Premium Sales Execs. Epsilon Sigma. Republican. Clubs: Chicago Sales Executives (pres. 1948-49), Nat. Sales Executive (dir. 1950-54), Economic, Home: 1015 S Highland Arlington Heights IL 60005 Office: 311 S Arlington Heights Rd Arlington Heights IL

DOTTS, RICHARD DORIAN, ins. co. exec.; b. Omaha, Feb. 13, 1919; s. William G. and Edith L. (Usher) D.; student Tex. A. and M. U., 1942, U. So. Cal., 1947-48; m. Westa E. Mauger, July 12, 1941; children—Richard Edmund, Westa Suzanne (Mrs. Maurice John Jorden, Jr.). With Pacific Mut. Life Ins. Co., Los Angeles, 1939—, treas., 1957-62, v.p., treas., 1962-65, v.p. adminstrn., 1965-66, financial v.p., 1966-67, exec. v.p., 1967—. Finance chmn., bd. dirs. YMCA; chmn. exec. com. Cal. Heart Assn. Served with USNR, 1942-45. Recipient Distinguished Service award Am. Heart Assn., 1965. Mem Assn. Cal. Life Ins. Cos. (treas.). Methodist. Lion. Club: Jonathan. Home: 3620 Amesbury Rd Los Angeles CA 90027 Office: 523 W 6th St Los Angeles CA 90054

DOTY, DAVID SINGLETON, lawyer; b. Anoka, Minn., June 30, 1929; s. Walter H. and Miriam (Singleton) D.; B.A., U. Minn., 1961, LL.B., 1961; m. Mary Wagner, Dec. 23, 1952; children—Laura Mary, John Wagner, Robert Singleton. Admitted to Minn. bar, 1961; practiced in St. Paul, 1961, Mpls., 1962—; mem. firm Felhaben, Larson & Fenlon, 1961; mem. firm Erickson, Popham, Haik & Schnobrich, 1962-65, jr. partner, 1965-67, sr. partner, 1967-68, prin., 1968—; instr. labor law William Mitchell Coll. Law, 1965-66; gen. counsel Twin Cities Area Met. Transit Commn. Dir. Popham, Haik, Schnobrich, Kaufman & Doty, Ltd. Republican ward chmn., 1970. Trustee Mpls. Library Bd., 1971—. Served from 2d lt. to capt. USMC, 1952-58. Mem. Am., Minn. (com. chmn.), Hennepin County (com. chmn.) bar assns. Club: Minneapolis Athletic, 6 O'Cclock (Mpls.). Home: 146 W Rustic Lodge Av Minneapolis MN 55409 Office: F and M Bank Bldg Minneapolis MN 55402

DOTY, FRANKLIN AHASUERUS, coll. dean; b. Omaha, Apr. 11, 1912; s. Frank and Lulu May (Quistgard) D.; A.B., U. Omaha, 1934; M.A., U. Ia., 1937, Ph.D., 1946. High sch. tchr., Webster City, Ia., 1937-40; asst. prof. to prof. social sci. and history U. Fla., Gainesville, 1946-58, chmn. dept. social sci., 1961-64, asst. dean acad. affairs, 1964-66, dean Univ. Coll., 1966-71. Served with AUS, 1942-45. Mem. Am. Hist. Assn., Am. Guild Organists (past chpt. dean). Author: (with W.G. Carleton) Social Science Syllabi, 1955. Contbr. articles profl. jours. Home: 3300 S W 4th Ct Gainesville FL 32601

DOTY, JAMES EDWARD, coll. pres.; b. Lakewood, O., May 8, 1922; s. Ordello Luce and Margaret (McCurdy) D.; A.B., Mt. Union Coll., Alliance, O., 1944, D.D., 1965; S.T.B. cum laude, Boston U., 1947, Ph.D., 1959; D.D., DePauw U., 1966; m. Mary Merciel Smith, Sept. 8, 1943; children—Mark Allen, David Wesley, Martha Suzanne. Ordained to ministry Methodist Ch., 1945; pastor in Salem, Mass., 1947-51, Lynn, Mass., 1951-57; founder, dir. Greater Lynn Pastoral Care and Counselling Center, 1954-57; dir. pastoral care and counselling Ind. Area Meth. Ch., 1957-66; pres. Baker U., 1966—; mem. staff Boston Center Adult Edn., 1949-53; spl. lectr. Union Theol. Sem., Buenos Aires, Argentina, 1962, Meth. Theol. Sem., Sao Paulo, Brazil, 1962, Epworth Theol. Sem., Salisbury, Rhodesia, 1963, Meth. Theol. Sem., Mulungwishi, Congo, 1964, Trinity Theol. Coll., Singapore, 1967. Mem. first Student Christian Movement Conf. in postwar Germany, Heidelberg U., summer 1947; del. World Family Life Consultation, Birmingham, Eng., 1966; mem. World Meth. Council, London, Eng., 1966; v.p. Sch. Bd. Pike Twp., Marion County, Ind., 1960-66. Recipient Alumni award of year Mt. Union Coll., 1963; Alumni award of merit Boston U., 1969. Mem. Clin. Pastoral Edn. Inst., Am. Assn. Pastoral Counselors (bd. dirs.), Acad. Religion and Mental Health, Am. Psychol. Assn., Sigma Alpha Epsilon, Zeta Chi. Club: University (Kansas City, Mo.). Author: The Pastor as Agape Counselor, 1964; Postmark Lambarene: A Visit with Albert Schweitzer, 1965. Editor: Authentic Man Encounters God's World, 1967; Students Search For Meaning, 1971. Home: 505 8th St Baldwin City KS 66006

DOTY, PAUL MEAD, Jr., chemist, educator; b. Charleston, W. Va., June 1, 1920; s. Paul Mead and Maud Katherine (Stewart) D.; B.S., Pa State Coll., 1941; M.A., Columbia, 1943, Ph.D., 1944; m. Margaretta Elenor Grevatt, Oct. 31, 1941; 1 son, Gordon Sutherland; m. 2d. Helga Boedtker, Feb. 27, 1954; children—Marcia, Rebecca, Katherine. Instr., research asso. Poly. Inst., Bklyn., 1943-45, asst. prof. chemistry, 1945-46; asst. prof. chemistry U. Notre Dame, 1946-48; asst. prof. Harvard, 1948-50. asso. prof. chemistry, 1950-56, prof. biochemistry, 1956—, chmn. dept. biochemistry and molecular biology; Harvey lectr., 1959-60. Rockefeller fellow Cambridge U., Eng., 1946- 47; Guggenheim fellow, 1958: recipient Pure Chemistry award Am. Chem. Soc., 1956. Fellow (sr.) Soc. of Fellows, Harvard, Nat. Acad. Scis; mem. Fedn. Am. Scientists, Am. Acad. Arts and Sci., Am. Chem. Soc., Biophys. Soc. Am. Soc. Biol. Chemists. Author research papers. Editor Jour. Polymer Sci., 1945-61; editorial bd. Jour. Molecular Biology. Home: 4 Kirkland Pl Cambridge MA 02138

DOTY, RICHARD MARTIN, wine co. exec.; b. Hastings, Neb., Oct. 20, 1918; s. Ralph H. and Elsie (Martin) D.; B.S., U. Neb., 1939, LL.B., 1942; m. Julia Cook, Jan. 21, 1950. Admitted to Cal. bar, 1948; with firm Pilsbury, Madison & Sutro, San Francisco, 1948-58; v.p., sec., gen. counsel, dir. United Vintners, Inc., San Francisco, 1958—. Served to 1st lt. AUS, 1942-46, 50-52. Mem. Beta Theta Pi, Phi Delta Phi. Clubs: St. Francis Yacht, Olympic, Villa Taverna (San Francisco). Home: 1000 Vallejo St San Francisco CA 94105 Office: 601 4th St San Francisco CA 94107

DOTY, ROBERT CLARK, fgn. corr.; b. Evanston, Ill., Apr. 7, 1915; s. Samuel Stranahaan and Helen Douglas (Clark) D.; student Northwestern U., 1933-34; m. Mary Woodward Warner, July 16, 1935; children—Elizabeth (Mrs. E. R. Speare), Mark Woodward. With City News Bur., Chgo., Ill. 1937-39; staff Courier Jour., Louisville, 1939-42, Ky. state capital bur., 1946, Washington bur., 1947; dir. pub. relations Internat. Refugee Orgn., Geneva, Switzerland, 1947-50; with N.Y. Times, 1950—, staff, N.Y.C., 1950-51, Paris bur., 1951-53, chief corr. Middle East, 1953-55, chief corr., Paris, 1958-63, chief corr., Rome, 1964—. Served as capt. AUS, 1942-45. Mem. Sigma Chi. Home: Via Gregoriana 25 Rome Italy Office: Via di Propoganada Fide 27 Rome Italy

DOUBET, EARL WESLEY, machinery co. exec.; b. Peoria, Ill., Aug. 13, 1926; s. Earl Wesley and Julia (Petzing) D.; diploma in Civil Engring., Ore. State Coll., 1944; B.S.C., Bradley U., 1948; postgrad. Mass. Inst. Tech., 1966; m. Norma Mae Hill, Jan. 28, 1951; children—Earl Wesley III, Steven H. Sales mgr. Caterpillar Tractor Co., Ltd., Glasgow, Scotland, 1959-61; European sales mgr. Caterpillar Overseas SA, Geneva, Switzerland, 1961-63, sales mgr., 1963-65; pres. Caterpillar Americas Co., Peoria, 1965-66; v.p. Towmotor Corp., Cleve., 1966-68, exec. v.p., 1968-70; mgr. new products Caterpillar Tractor Co., Peoria, 1970—. Served with AUS,

194-46. Mem. Nat. Alumni Assn. Bradley U. (dir.). Presbyn. Mason (Shriner). Home: 906 W Kensington Dr Peoria IL 61614 Office: 100 NE Adams St Peoria IL 61602

DOUBLEDAY, NELSON, publisher; grad. Princeton, 1954. With Doubleday & Co., Inc., 1954-56, 59—, now v.p., sec., dir. trade publ. div. Served with USAF, 1956-59.*

DOUCE, WILLIAM CLARK, petroleum co. exec.; b. Kingman, Kan., Dec. 9, 1919; s. William Thew and Grace (Griswold) D.; B.S., U. Kan., 1942; m. Willene Brady Magruder, June 14, 1943; children—Terri (Mrs. David Rolf Balstad), William Clark. With Phillips Petroleum Co., various locations, 1942—, mgr. chem. dept., 1966-69, sr. v.p., 1969—, also dir., mem. exec. com.; dir. various subsidiary cos. City commr. City Bartlesville, Okla., 1951-56; pres. Okla. Safety Council, 1969; mem. Okla. Crime Commn., 1968-71; chmn. Bartlesville Community Relations Commn., 1971; chmn. adv. bd. Greater Univ. Fund, U. Kan., 1970—; mem. Pres.'s adv. Council Bartlesville Wesleyan Coll., 1970—. Bd. dirs. Nat. Safety Council; trustee Jane Phillips Meml. Hosp. Center, Bartlesville. Mem. chambers commerce Bartlesville (pres. 1967-68), Okla. (v.p.), Am. Petroleum Inst., Soc. Chem. Industry, Mfg. Chemists' Assn., Nat. Assn. Mfrs., Theta Tau, Phi Gamma Delta, Tau Beta Pi, Sigma Tau. Presbyn. Mason (Shriner, Jester); mem. Order De Molay. Club: Hillcrest Country (Bartlesville). Home: 3425 Hawthorne Ct Bartlesville OK 74003 Office: Phillips Bldg Bartlesville OK 74004

DOUD, ROBERT SKINNER, banker; b. N.Y.C., Mar. 22, 1931; s. Walter E. and Mary A. (McInerney) B.; B.S., Fordham U., 1955; m. Sheila C. McHugh, June 15, 1957; children-Robert H., Paul, Shieila. Sr. accountant Price Waterhouse & Co., N.Y.C., 1955-62; v.p. Franklin Nat. Bank, Westbury, N.Y., 1962-69; v.p., controller Security Nat. Bank, Melville, N.Y., 1969—; lectr. Nassau chpt. Am. Inst. Banking. Vice pres. St. Joseph's Sch. Bd., 1968- 70. Served with U.S. Army, 1950-52. C.P.A.., N.Y. Mem. Am. Inst. C.P.A.'s, N.Y. State Soc. C.P.A.'s, Bank Adminstrn. Inst. K.C. Home: 1383 Noel Av Hewlett NY 11557 Office: Route 110 and Pinelawn Rd Melville NY 11746

DOUDNA, QUINCY VON OGDEN, univ. pres.; b. Poynette, Wis., Jan. 16, 1907; s. Frank I. and Lenore (Emery) D.; B.A., Carroll Coll., 1927, LL.D. (hon.), 1960; M.A., U. Wis., 1930, Ph.D., 1948; m. Winifred Zimmerman, Mar. 22, 1930; children—Lonnie Bruce, Gary Kent. Sci. tchr. Antigo (Wis.) High Sch., 1927-34; supervising prin. Lone Rock (Wis.) High Sch., 1934- 37; prin. Richland County (Wis.) Normal Sch., 1937-40, Door Kewanee Rural Normal Sch., Algoma, Wis., 1940-45; dir. rural edn. Wis. State Coll., Stevens Point, 1945-47, dean adminstrn., 1947-56; specialist tchr. edn., Lima, Peru, 1950-51; cons. tchr. edn., Alexandria and Cairo, Egypt, 1953, Rubio, Venezuela, 1954, U.S. Office Edn., 1954; pres. Eastern Ill. U., Charleston, 1956-71; cons. edn., W.I., 1960-62. Dir. Charleston Nat. Bank. Mem. Phi Delta Kappa, Kappa Delta Phi, Alpha Phi Omega, Phi Theta Pi. Methodist. Rotarian. Contbr. articles profl. jours. Home: 933 11th St Charleston IL 61920

DOUDOROFF, MICHAEL, educator; b. Petrograd, USSR, 67 Nov. 14, 1911; s. Boris and Natalie (Shulgin) D.; came to U.S., 1923, naturalized, 1928; A.B., Stanford, 1933, M.A., 1934, Ph.D., 1939; m. Mary Gottlund, July 15, 1934 (div. 1944); 1 son, Michael John; m. 2d, Rita Whelton, Oct. 10, 1944 (dec. 1951); m. 3d, Olga Lott, Aug. 15, 1952. Mem. faculty U. Cal. at Berkeley, 1940—, prof. bacteriology, 1952—, research prof. Miller Inst., 1960-62, prof. molecular biology, 1964—; spl. research microbiol. physiology and metabolism, enzymology. Recipient Sugar Found. award, 1947; Guggenheim fellow, 1949-50; spl. fellow NIH, 1963. Mem. Nat. Acad. Scis., Am. Soc. Biol. Chemists, Soc. Am. Microbiologists, Soc. Gen. Physiologists.

DOUDS, CHARLES TUCKER, former govt. ofcl.; b. Plumville, Pa., Apr. 11, 1898; s. James Bothel and Margaret Jane (Morrow) D.; B.S., Pa. State U., 1922; M.A., Columbia, 1929; m. Ella Anna Fowler, June 11, 1926; 1 son, Charles Fowler. Sec., U. Rochester YMCA, 1922-28; staff, student div. Nat. Council YMCA, 1929-32; sec. Pa. Com. for Old Age Security, 1933-34, Agrl. Adjustment Adminstrn., 1935-36; regional dir. Nat. Labor Relations Bd., 1937-42, asst. dir. field div., 1942, regional dir. N.Y., 1942-57, regional dir. Newark, N.J., 1957-58; chief labor manpower div. Fgn. Econ. Adminstrn., Washington, 1946-47; dir. bur. mediation State of Pa., 1958-69. Labor arbitrator, cons. Better Govt. Assos., Harrisburg; chief of staff Gov.'s Commn. to Revise Pub. Employe Law, 1968. Served with U.S. Army, 1918. Alumni rep. on bd. trustees Pa. State Univ. Mem. Am. Soc. Pub. Adminstrn., Assn. Labor Meditation Agys. (pres. 1965- 66), Nat. Acad. Arbitrators, Am. Arbitration Assn. Presbyn. Club: Penn State (pres. Harrisburg area 1967-68). Home: 2912 Russell Rd Camp Hill PA 17011

DOUGAL, IRWIN ADELBERT, educator, elec. engr.; b. Dunlap, Ia., Nov. 22, 1926; s. Adelbert Isaac and Goldya (White) D.; B.S., Ia. State U., 1952; M.S., U. Ill., 1955, Ph.D., 1957; m. Margaret Jane McLennan, Sept. 3, 1951; children—Catherine Ann, Roger Adelbert, Leonard Harley, Laura Beth. Radio engr. Collins Radio Co., Cedar Rapids, Ia., 1952; research asst., research asso., asst. prof., asso. prof. U. Ill., Urbana, 1952-61; prof., mem. grad. faculty, dir. labs. for electronics and related sci. research U. Tex., Austin, 1961-67, prof., dir.-designate Electronics Research Center, 1969—; asst. dir. def. research and engring. for research Office Sec. Def., Washington, 1967-69; cons. Tex. Instruments, Inc., Dallas, Gen. Dynamics Corp., Ft. Worth, U. Cal. Los Alamos Sci. Lab. Faculty sponsor U. Tex. Conservative Democrats Club, 1966-67. Served with USAF, 1946-49. Recipient Teaching Excellence awards U. Tex. Students Assn., 1962, 63, Spl. award for outstanding service as program chmn. S.W. I.E.E.E. Conf. and Exhbn., 1967. Registered profl. engr., Tex. Fellow Am. Phys. Soc.; mem. I.E.E.E. (sr.), Am. Soc. Engring. Edn., Soc. Engring. Sci., Nat. Soc. Profl. Engrs., Sigma Xi, Phi Kappa Phi, Tau Beta Pi, Eta Kappa Nu, Pi Mu Epsilon, Phi Eta Sigma. Presbyn. (elder). Contbr. articles profl. jours. Home: 6115 Rickey Dr Austin TX 78731

DOUGALL, HERBERT EDWARD, educator; b. Merritton, Ont., Can., Oct. 20, 1902; s. Hugh Shaw and Eleanor (Taylor) D.; student Collegiate Inst. London, Ont., 1916-18; Collegiate Inst., Hamilton, 1918-20; B.A., U. Toronto, 1925; M.B.A., 1926; Ph.D., Northwestern U., 1930; Social Sci. fellow, France and England, 1931-32; m. Louise Alice Perkins, Aug. 21, 1929; children—Eleanor Louise, Jean Anne. Came to U.S., 1925, naturalized, 1936. Successively instr. in econ. and finance, asst. prof., asso. prof. Northwestern U., 1927-42, prof. finance 1942-46; dir. undergrad. div. Sch. Commerce, 1939-44, dir. summer session, 1944- 46; prof. finance, grad. sch. bus., Stanford U, 1946-53, C.O.G. Miller prof. finance, 1953-68, prof. finance emeritus, 1968—; cons. finance. Dir. Am. Express Funds, San Francisco. Tech. advisor to Pres. Emergency R.R. Bd., 1937. Trustee Coll. Retirement Equities Fund, 1955-59. Mem. nat. adv. com. Loeb awards in financial journalism, 1958—. Ford Found. faculty fellow in bus., 1959-60. Mem. Am. Economic Assn., Am. Finance Assn. (v.p. 1949), Western Econ. Assn., Western Finance Assn., Delta Sigma Pi, Beta Gamma Sigma. Presbyn. Rotarian. Clubs: University (Palo Alto, Cal.); Faculty (Stanford). Author: Corporate Financial Policy (with H. G. Guthmann), 1940-62; Problems in Corporation Finance (with H. W. Torgerson), 1941-51; Investments, 1952-68; Capital Markets and Institutions, 1965-70. Contbr. Ency. Brit., articles to econ. and financial publs. Home: 15 Holden Ct Portola Valley CA 94025

DOUGAN, ROBERT ORMES, librarian; b. Ilford, Essex, Eng., Aug. 21, 1904; s. Hugh and Rebecca (Ormes) D.; diploma librarianship, Univ. Coll., London, 1929; M.A., Trinity Coll., U. Dublin (Ireland), 1954; m. Olive Constant McMicken, Oct. 3, 1929 (dec. Jan. 1963); m. 2d, Margaret Truax Hunter, Jan. 21, 1964. Came to U.S., 1958, naturalized, 1964. Partime librarian Royal Hist. Soc., London, 1925-35; bibliog. research worker, cataloguer E.P. Goldschmidt and Co., Ltd., London, 1926-40; librarian Sandeman Pub. Library, Perth, Scotland, 1945-52; dep. librarian Trinity Coll., 1952-58; librarian Henry E. Huntington Library and Art Gallery, San Marino, Cal., 1958—; lectr. for Foras Eireann, Dublin, 1955-58; organizer 2 Scottish book exhbns. Festival of Britain, 1950-51. Mem. Cal. Adv. Council Edn. Librarianship, 1962-65. Served to flight lt. RAF, 1941-45. Fellow Library Assn. U.K.; mem. Bibliog. Soc. U.K., A.L.A. (chmn. rare books sect. 1964-65), Internat. Bibliophile Assn. Presbyn. (elder). Club: Grolier. Home: 855 S Orange Grove Blvd Pasadena CA 91105 Office: 1151 Oxford Rd San Marino CA 91108

DOUGHERTY, CHARLES GIBBS, ins. co. exec., lawyer; b. Norfolk, Va. Nov. 21, 1907; s. William Brewer and Elizabeth Selden (Gibbs) D.; B.S., U. Va., 1929, LL.B., 1931; m. Mary Holland, Nov. 11, 1947; children—Mary Elizabeth, Charles William. Admitted to Va. bar, 1930, N.Y. bar, 1933; asso. law firm Gibboney, Johnston, and Flynn, N.Y.C., 1931-32; asso. Met. Life Ins. Co., N.Y.C., 1932—, asst. gen. counsel, 1946-47, asso. gen. counsel, 1948-50, 2d v.p., 1950-55, v.p., 1956-63, sr. v.p., 1963-65, exec. v.p., 1965—. Served with USNR, 1942-46. Mem. Assn. Life Ins. Counsel (past pres.), Am., N.Y. bar assns., Better Bus. Bur. Met. N.Y. (dir.), N.Y. C. of C. (v.p.), Ins. Soc. N.Y., Pilgrims of U.S., Phi Beta Kappa, Phi Delta Phi, Order of Coif, Raven Hon. Soc., Kappa Sigma. Episcopalian (vestryman). Clubs: University, Church (N.Y.C.); Scarsdale Golf; Priness Anne Country (Virginia Beach, Va.). Home: 200 E 66th St New York City NY 10021 Office: One Madison Av New York City NY 10010

DOUGHERTY, CHARLES JOSEPH, utility exec.; b. Clayton, Mo., Apr. 29, 1919; s. Harry J. and Loretto (Grace) D.; B.S.C., St. Louis U., 1941, LL.B., 195O; m. Suzanne L. Hamilton, May 1, 1943; children—Charles H., Mary Suzanne, Amy Louise. Admitted to Mo. bar, 1950; with Union Electric Co., St. Louis, 1941—, gen. counsel, 1964, exec. v.p., 1964-66, pres., dir., 1966—, chief exec. officer, 1968—; dir. Electric Energy, Inc., Boatmen's Nat. Bank St. Louis. Vice pres. Civic Progress, Inc., 1969—. Trustee Mo. Pub. Expenditure Survey, 1966—, Govtl. Research Inst., 1967—; bd. dirs. Jr. Achievement Mississippi Valley, Inc. 1968—; mem. exec. bd. St. Louis Area council Boy Scouts Am., 1966—. Served with USMCR, 1942-46. Recipient St. Louis U. Alumni Merit award, 1966. Mem. Am. Bar Assn., Mo. Bar, Bar Assn. St. Louis, C. of C. Met. St. Louis (dir. 1962—, pres. 1970), Nat. Assn. Electric Cos. (dir. 1968—), Edison Electric Inst. (dir. 1968—), Alpha Sigma Nu. Clubs: St. Louis (dir. 1968—), Old Warson Country (St. Louis); Stadium; Bogey; Noonday; Links (N.Y.C.). Home: 18 Huntleigh Woods St Louis MO 63131 Office: PO Box 87 1 Memorial Dr St Louis MO 63166

DOUGHERTY, DAVID MITCHELL, educator; b. Wilmington, Del., Aug. 6, 1903; s. George Myers and Jennie (Mitchell) D.; A.B., U. Del., 1925; A.M., Harvard, 1927, Ph.D., 1932; student U. Paris, 1923-24, 29; m. Edna M. Rettew, June 22, 1927 (dec. 1963); children—David M. Jr., Philip R.; m. 2d, Jean Bruere Jones, May 15, 1964. Tchr., Manlius (N.Y.) Sch., 1926-28; instr. French, Mass. Inst. Tech., 1929-30; instr. and tutor romance langs., Harvard, 1929-31; asst. prof., asso. prof., prof. romance langs. Clark U., 1931-46, chmn. dept., 1942-46, dir. A.S.T.P. Unit, 1943-44, chmn. Acad. Council, 1943-45; dir. U. Del. Jr. Year Plan, Paris, 1939, Geneva, 1946-47; prof. romance langs. U. Ore., 1947—, head dept. fgn. langs., 1947-64, dir. Nat. Def. Edn. Act. summer inst., Tours, France, 1961-68, officer modern and classical langs. div., 1964- 67, head dept. romance langs., 1967-69. Decorated Chevalier Legion of Honor, Medal of the City of Tours (France). Mem. Modern Lang. Assn. Am., Medieval Acad. Am., Am. Assn. Tchrs. French (pres. 1966-70), Am. Assn. Tchrs. Spanish, Philol. Assn. Pacific Coast (pres. 1961-62), Société Roncesvals, Theta Chi. Episcopalian. Author: Political Literature in France under Charles V. and Charles VI; Year Abroad (with R. Picard and L. Wawrzyniak), 1953; (with D. Hernried) Perspectives de la littérature française 1961. Editor: (with E. B. Barnes) La Geste de Monglane, 1966; book revs. Contbr. articles to ednl. jours. Home: 2829 Central Blvd Eugene OR 97403

DOUGHERTY, JAMES HENRY, educator; b. Fayettee, Mo., Jan. 5, 1901; s. James Lee and Minnie (White) D.; B.S., Northeast Mo. State Coll., 1925; Ph.D., U. Mo., 1933; m. Elizabeth Estelle Hurtt, Aug. 10, 1927; children—James Henry, Charles Raymond. Tchr., prin. Mo. elem. schs., 1918-22; prin. New Franklin (Mo.) pub. schs., 1923-25, supt., 1925-27; supt. Ashland (Mo.) pub. schs., 1927-30; asso. supt. Columbia (Mo.) pub. schs. 1932-37; prof. edn. Christian Coll., Stephens Coll., 1932-37; prof. edn. U. Mo., summers 1931-40; asso. prof. Tex. Christian U., 1937-40, prof., 1940-41; prof. chmn. dept. elementary edn. N. Tex. State U., 1941—; cons. Mo. Dept. Curriculum Study, 1936-37, Johnson, Anderson and Wilbarger counties (Tex.), 1946-53, Sherman, Denison and Plano (Tex.) pub. schs., 1952-66. Mem. Tex., Nat. elem. sch. prins., Assn. Suprs. and Curriculum Devel., N.E. Mo. State Tchrs. Assn. (v.p.), Denton C. of C., Kappa Delta Pi, Phi Delta Kappa. Mem. Christian Ch. Kiwanian (dir. 1957-59, 1969—). Author: Elementary School Organization and Managment, 1936. rev. edit., 1950; Some Facts Concerning Teaching of Arithmetic, 1933; Guide to Healthful Living in Elementary Schools, 1946; Natural Phenomena as Explained by Children, 1966. Home: 401 Normal Av Denton TX 76201

DOUGHERTY, JOHN JOSEPH, clergyman; b. Jersey City, Sept. 16, 1907; s. John J. and Christina (Farrell) D.; A.B., Seton Hall U., 1930; student U. Propaganda, Rome, Italy, 1930-32; S.T.L., Gregorian U., Rome, 1934; student Pontifical Bibl. Inst., Rome, 1934-37, D.S.S., 1948; L.H.D. (hon.), U. Detroit, 1960; LL.D., Rutgers U., 1962, St. Peter's Coll., 1964, St. Ambrose Coll., 1964. Ordained priest Roman Cath. Ch., 1933, papal chamberlain, 1954, domestic prelate, 1958, titular bishop of Cotenna and auxiliary to archbishop of Newark, 1963—; pastor St. Rose of Lima Ch., Short Hills, N.J., 1969—; prof. of sacred scriptures Immaculate Conception Sem., Darlington, N.J., 1937-59; radio broadcasting CBS, NBC, ABC, 1946—, TV broadcasting CBS, NBC, 1951—; regent Inst. Judaeo-Xtian Studies, Seton Hall U., 1954-59, pres. univ., 1959-69. Mem. Vatican Commn. on Radio and TV, 1956-60. Bd. dirs. Cath. Bibl. Assn., 1957—, UNDA (Internat. Assn. Cath. Radio and TV), 1956—, UNA-USA; mem. Nat. Citizens Commn. Internat. Coop., 1965; mem. Adv. Com. Edn. of the Deaf, 1966; vice chmn. com. of dept. internat. affairs U.S.C.C., 1969; trustee Council Religion and Internat. Affairs, 1971—. Decorated Star of Solidarity (Republic Italy), recipient Freedoms Found. medal, 1953; award Cath. TV Arts 1959; Ann. Americanism award B'nai B'rith, 1965; citation Nat. Conf. Christian and Jew 1965. Author: Searching the Scriptures, 1959. Address: 50 Short Hills Av Short Hills NJ 07078

DOUGHERTY, JOHN L., newspaper editor; b. Bradford, Pa., May 24, 1918; s. John L. and Edith (Larson) D.; B.A., Alfred U., 1939; postgrad. (Nieman fellow), Harvard, 1956; m. Mary Loise Hoag, June 19, 1944; children—Brian M., Ann E., Martha L. Reporter, Salamanca (N.Y.) Republican Press, 1935-39; with Rochester (N.Y.) Times-Union, 1939—, telegraph editor, 1952-56, city editor, 1956-62, asst. mng. editor, 1962-66, mng. editor, 1966—; discussion leader Am. Press Inst., Columbia, 1961—. Vice pres. Friends Rochester Pub. Library, 1966-69. Mem. bd. Safety Fund Met. Rochester. Served to 1st lt. AUS, 1942-47. Decorated Bronze Star. Mem. Soc. Nieman Fellows, N.Y. State A.P. Assn. (pres. 1970—), A.P. Mng. Editors Assn., Sigma Delta Chi. Home: 265 Idlewood Rd Rochester NY 14618 Office: 55 Exchange St Rochester NY 14614

DOUGHERTY, JOSEPH CHARLES, Jr., educator; b. Phila., July 14, 1920; s. Joseph Charles and Mary (McGonigal) D.; B.A., St. Charles Coll., Overbrook, Pa., 1944; M.A., Georgetown U., 1948, Ph.D. (fellow 1949-50), 1955; m. Cecilia M. Fleming, June 19, 1965; children—Moya, Joseph III, Gerard. Instr., Villanova U., 1950-51; intelligence analyst Dept. Def., 1955-62; lectr. U. Md., 1962- 65; prof. St. Leo (Fla.) Coll., 1965-67; prof. history and polit. sci., chmn. dept. U. Scranton, 1967-70; cons. faculty mem. U.S. Army Command and Gen. Staff Coll., 1968—; adj. faculty mem. U.S. Army Civil Affairs Sch., 1967—. Moderator, Young Republicans, U. Scranton. Served with AUS, 1944-46, 51-53. Mem. Am. Polit. Sci. Assn., Am. Hist. Soc., Dag Hammarskjold Soc., Phi Alpha Theta, Pi Gamma Mu. K.C. (4). Author: Political Thought of George Bernard Smith as Expressed in His Drama, 1948; Genesis of Social Security Act of 1935, 1955; The Angry Sixties, 1970. Home: 119 Spring St Clarks Green PA 18411 Office: Univ Scranton Scranton PA 18510

DOUGHERTY, RICHARD, journalist, author; b. Bolivar, N.Y., Aug. 7, 1921; s. John Peter and Elizabeth (Crelly) D.; A.B., Columbia, 1948; m. Cynthia Abbott, Apr. 23, 1966; 1 dau, by previous marriage, Lisa. Reporter, N.Y. Herald Tribune, 1948-51; press officer N.Y.C. Govt., 1951-56; corp. pub. relations counsel, 1956-60; nat. polit. writer Washington Bur., N.Y. Herald Tribune, 1964-66; N.Y. bur. chief Los Angeles Times, 1966—. Served with USAAF, 1942-45. Democrat. Club: Century Assn. (N.Y.C.). Author: (novels) A Summer World, 1960, Duggan, 1962, The Commissioner, 1962, We Dance and Sing. 1971; (play) Fair Game for Lovers, 1964. Home: 164 E 72d St New York City NY 10021 Office: United Nations Plaza New York City NY 10017

DOUGHERTY, RUSSELL ELLIOTT, air force officer; b. Glasgow, Ky., Nov. 15, 1920; s. Ewell Walter and Bess (House) D.; A.B., Western Ky. U., 1941; J.D., U. Louisville, 1948; m Geralee Shaaber, Apr. 26, 1943; children—Diane Ellen (Mrs. James R. Streicker), Mark Elliott, William Bryant. Admitted to Ky. bar, 1948, also U.S. Supreme Ct.; commd. 2d. lt. USAAF, 1943, advanced through grades to lt. gen., USAF, 1970; various staff and command assignments in Far East Air Forces, SAC, U.S. European Command, World War II; dir. European region Office of Sec. of Def., 1965-67; dep. chief of staff for plans and operations Hdqrs. USAF, 1967—. Planned Operation Powerflight Mission, 1957; U.S. planner Stanleyville (Republic Congo) Rescue Operation, 1964. Decorated D.S.M., 2 Legion of Merit (3), Bronze Star. Mem. Ky. Bar Assn., Omicron Delta Kappa, Phi Alpha Delta, Lambda Chi Alpha. Home: 201 1st St W Barksdale AFB LA 71110 Office: Comdr 2d Air Force Barksdale AFB LA 71110

DOUGHERTY, THOMAS FRANCIS, histologist; b. Forman, N.D., Mar. 27, 1915; s. Thomas Francis and Mary (Brandenburg) D.; B.S., U. Minn., 1936, A.M., 1937, Ph.D., 1942; fellow Donner Found., 1942-43; m. Jean Ann Hay, Apr. 5, 1941; children—Michael Bruce, Ann Marie. Instr. in anatomy Yale Sch. of Medicine, 1943-47; prof. anatomy (histology) U. Utah, 1947, now chmn. dept. anatomy, dir. radiobiology lab., 1954—; cons. Surgeon Gen. of U.S. Army. Mem. Reticulendothelial Soc. (pres. 1957), Am. Assn. Cancer Research, Am. Assn. Study Internal Secretions, Am. Assn. Anatomists, Internat. Soc. Hematology, Soc. Exptl. Biology and Medicine, Phi Sigma Kappa. Democrat. Home: 1097 Bonneville Dr Salt Lake City UT 84108

DOUGHERTY, WILLIAM H., banker; b. Liberty Borough, Pa., 1930; grad. U. Pitts., 1952. Exec. v.p. N.C. Nat. Bank, Charlotte, NCNB Corp.; pres., dir. NCNB Properties Inc.; dir. NCNB Mortgage Corp., Stephenson Finance Co., Am. Comml. Agy. Inc., Factors, Inc., Cato Stores, Inc. Home: 3801 River Ridge Rd Charlotte NC 28211 Office: 200 S Tryon St Charlotte NC 28201*

DOUGLAS, BRUCE LEE, oral surgeon; b. N.Y.C., July 14, 1925; s. William and Carrie (Basescu) D.; A.B., Princeton, 1947; D.D.S., N.Y. U., 1948; certificate in Oral Surgery, Columbia, 1951, M.A., 1955, diploma in Higher Edn., 1957; M.P.H., U. Cal. at Berkeley, 1962; m. Frederica Ann Schneider, May 27, 1954; children—Clifford, Steven, Jennifer. Dental intern Queens Gen. Hosp., Jamaica, N.Y., 1948-49; oral surgery resident Queens Hosp. Center, Jamaica, 1953-54; practice oral surgery, Rego Park, N.Y., 1954- 59, Chgo., 1962—; Fulbright prof. Japan, 1959-61; prof. U. Ill. Colls. Dentistry and Medicine, 1962—, Rush Med. Coll., 1970—; chmn. dept. dentistry Presbyn.-St. Luke's Hosp., Chgo., 1968—; WHO cons. to Colombia and Venezuela, 1964-69. Bd. dirs. Com. on Ill. Govt., Ind. Democratic Coalition, Ind. Precinct Orgn., Ind. Voters Ill.; mem. Ill. Ho. of Reps. 11th Dist., 1971—. Bd. dirs. Chgo. Easter Seal Soc. Served with USNR, 1943- 45, to lt., Dental Corps, 1951-53. Diplomate Am. Bd. Oral Surgery. Fellow Am. Pub. Health Assn., Internat. Coll. Dentists, Chgo. Inst. Medicine (bd. govs.), Am. Dental Soc. Anesthesiology (past pres.); mem. Am. Dental Assn., Am. Pub. Health Assn., Am. Assn. Hosp. Dentists (pres. elect), Sigma Xi, Phi Delta Kappa, Omicron Kappa Upsilon. Author: Guide to Hospital Dental Procedure, 1964; Dental Care for Special Patient, 1966; Introduction to Hospital Dentistry, 1970. Contbr. articles profl. jours. Home: 841 Castlewood Terrace Chicago IL 60640 Office: 4753 N Broadway Chicago IL 60640

DOUGLAS, CATHLEEN CURRAN HEFFERNAN, (Mrs. William O. Douglas), wife of Supreme Ct. Justice, conservationist; b. Apr. 30, 1943; d. Curtis V. and Mary (Curran) Heffernan; ed. Maryhurst Coll., Am. U.; m. William O. Douglas. Active in work with emotionally disturbed girls, urban problems, preservation of natural scenic resources. Address: Washington DC 20013*

DOUGLAS, CLAUDE ELMER, truck co. exec.; b. Northampton, Mass., Dec. 16, 1922; s. Claude Elmer and Dorothy (Hillenbrand) D.; B.A., Colgate U., 1945; M.A., U. Mass., 1951; m. Ann Elizabeth Robinson, Oct. 7, 1961; children—Claudia Anne, John Robinson. Economist, U.S. Govt., 1951-52; divisional controller White Motor Corp., Cleve., 1953-61, treas., 1961-69, pres., now v.p., treas. Served to lt. (jg.) USNR, 1943-45. Home: 2581 Stratford Rd Cleveland Heights OH 44118 Office: 100 Erieview Plaza Cleveland OH 44114

DOUGLAS, DONALD WILLS, ret. aircraft mfr.; b. Bklyn., Apr. 6, 1892; s. William Edward and Dorothy (Locker) D.; prep. edn., Trinity Chapel Sch., N.Y.C.; student U.S. Naval Acad., 1909-12; B.S., Mass. Inst. Tech., 1914; m. 2d, Marguerite Tucker, Mar. 6, 1954; children (by previous marriage—Donald Wills II, William Edward, Barbara

Jean, James Sholto, Malcolm Angus. Chief engr. Glenn L. Martin Co., aircraft mfrs., Los Angeles, 1915-16; chief civilian aero. engr. U.S. Signal Corps, 1916-17; chief engr. Glenn L. Martin Co., Cleve., 1917-20; pres. Douglas Co., Santa Monica, Cal., 1920-28; pres. Douglas Aircraft Co., 1928-57, chmn. bd., chief exec. officer, 1957-67; hon. chmn. bd. McDonnell Douglas Corp., 1967—. Recipient USAF Exceptional Service award French Legion of Honor, Comdr. Order House of Orange and Nassau (Netherlands). Mem. Delta Psi. Republican. Episcopalian. Club: Los Angeles Yacht. Home: 4 Crest Rd E Rolling Hills CA 90274

DOUGLAS, DONALD WILLS, Jr., aerospace corp. exec.; b. Washington, July 3, 1917; s. Donald Wills and Charlotte Marguerita (Ogg) D.; student Stanford, 1934-38; m. Molly McIntosh, May 1, 1939; children—Victoria, Holly; m. 2d Jean Ashton, Aug. 17, 1950. Engr., Douglas Aircraft Co., Inc., Santa Monica, Cal., 1939-43, chief flight test group 1943-51, dir. contract adminstrn., 1948, in charge research labs. Santa Monica div., 1949, v.p. mil. sales, 1951-57, pres., 1957-67; pres. Douglas Aircraft Co. div. McDonnell Douglas Corp. (merger Douglas Aircraft Co., Inc. and McDonnell Co.), 1967-68, v.p. adminstrn. parent co., also mem. exec. com., dir., 1968—; chmn. pres. Douglas Aircraft Co., Can., Ltd., 1968—; dir. Hilton Hotels Corp. Mem. exec. com. Nat. Export Expansion Council; dir. Danish-Am. Trade Council, 1966—; mem. St. Louis Area council Boy Scouts Am. Mem. Pres.'s council St. Louis U.; trustee Air Force Museum Found. Decorated chevalier Legion of Honor (France); officiale Order Merit (Republic of Itlay). Asso. fellow Am. Inst. Aeros. and Astronautics; mem. Nat. Indsl. Conf. Bd., Aerospace Industries Assn. (bd. chmn. 1964), Nat. Def. Transp. Assn. (nat. v.p. 1958-63), Air Force Assn., Am. Ordnance Assn. (St. Louis v.p. 1969—), Assn. U.S. Army, Nat. Security Indsl. Assn. (trustee). Newcomen Soc. N.Am., Navy League U.S. (life), St. Louis Com. Fgn. Relations, Los Angeles World Affairs Council (dir. 1966-69), Phi Gamma Delta. Clubs: St. Louis, Bellerive Country (St. Louis); Los Angeles Country, California, Los Angeles Yacht, Los Angeles, Transpacific Yacht (Los Angeles); Burning Tree, Nat. Aviation, Federal City (Washington); St. Francis Yacht (San Francisco). Home: 2122 S Mason Rd St Louis MO 63131 Office: McDonnell Douglas Corp Box 516 St Louis MO 63166

DOUGLAS, FRED ROBERT, petroleum co. exec.; b. Newark, Apr. 25, 1924; s. Nathan and Sara (Schneider) D.; B.S. in Chem. Engring., Newark Coll. Engring., 1945; M.S. in Chem. Engring., Poly. Inst. Bklyn., 1949; m. Lenore Berger, Mar. 20, 1954; children—Neil Richard, David Nathaniel. Asst. to prodn. mgr. Bristol-Myers Corp., N.Y.C., 1948-52; chem. engr. Jefferson Chem. Co. Inc., N.Y.C., 1952-53; sr. research chem. engr. Texaco Inc., Beacon, N.Y., 1953—. Pres. Hudson Valley Community Concerts Assn., 1968-69. Served with AUS, 1945-47. Named Engr. of Distinction, Engrs. Joint Council, 1970. Mem. Am. Assn. Cost Engrs. (nat. sec. 1968-69), Research Soc. Am. (treas. br. 1958-59). Contbr. articles profl. jours. Home: Watch Hill Dr Fishkill NY 12524 Office: Texaco Inc PO Box 509 Beacon NY 12508

DOUGLAS, GEORGE F., business exec.; b. Fayetteville, Ark., Feb. 3, 1915; B.S., U. Ark., 1940; 4 children. With Consol. Aircraft Co., 1940-42, Interstate Engring. Corp., 1942-46, N.Am. Aviation Co., 1946-53; with Northrop Corp., Los Angeles, 1953—, v.p. engring. Norair div., 1957-62, gen. mgr., corporate v.p. Ventura div., 1962-67, pres. Northrop Carolina, 1967-69, sr. v.p. adminstrn., Los Angeles, 1969—. Names to U. Ark. Engring. Hall of Fame, 1969. Asso. fellow Am. Inst. Aero. and Astronautics; mem. Am. Ordnance Assn., Armed Forces Mgmt. Assn., Nat. Security Assn. Office: 1800 Century Park East Los Angeles CA 90067

DOUGLAS, GILBERT FRANKLIN, obstetrician and gynecologist; b. Pushmatah, Ala., Jan. 13, 1888; s. George Washington and Sarah Belinda (Grace) D.; grad. Meridian Coll.; M.D., U. Ala., 1910; m. Mary Rachael Griffin, June 26, 1912; children—Mary Elizabeth, Gilbert Franklin, Sarah Frances, George Capers, Lillian Miriam (Mrs. J.W. Berg, Jr.), William Wesley. Asst. physician East Miss. Insane Hosp., Meridian, 1911-16; postgrad. tng. N.Y. Polyclin. Med. Sch. and Hosp., 1914, 17, Harvard Grad. Sch. Medicine, 1916, N.Y. Lying-In Hosp., 1917, U. Paris (France), 1919; staff South Highlands Infirmary, Birmingham Bapt. Hosps., U. Hosp., Carraway Methodist Hosp., East End Meml. Hosp. (all Birmingham); asso. prof. clin. gynecology Med. Coll. Ala.; mem. editorial council, head sect. gynecol. surgery Am. Jour. Proctology. Served from 1st lt. to capt., M.C., U.S. Army, 1917-19; maj. Res. Recipient citation and bronze plaque Internat. Exec. Council, U.S. sect. Internat. Coll. Surgeons, 1956. Diplomate Am. Bd. Obstetrics and Gynecology. Fellow Internat. Coll. Surgeons (chmn. bd. regents U.S. sect., v.p., trustee), A.C.S., Southeastern Surg. Congress (pres. 1948-49, past chmn. state exec. com.), Am. Soc. Study Sterility, Internat. Fertility Assn., Am. Coll. Obstetrics and Gynecology; mem. A.M.A., So. Med. Assn., Med. Assn. Ala., Jefferson County Med. Soc. (pres. 1949), Temple Academia (Bologna, Italy), Central, Ala. (pres. 1946) assns. obstetricians and gynecologists, Birmingham Obstet. and Gynecol. Soc., Birmingham Acad. Surgeons, So. Soc. Cancer Cytology, Am. Cancer Soc. (chmn. Jefferson County adv. com.), Soc. Obstetricians and Gynecologists Dominican Republic. Methodist (steward). Contbr. numerous med. articles to profl. publs. Home: 212 Mecca Av Birmingham AL 35209 Office: 1923 14th Av S Birmingham AL 35205

DOUGLAS, GORDON, film dir.; b. N.Y.C. Formerly actor in Hal Roach stock co.; writer, collaborator Topper series, Housekeeper's Daughter; dir. 30 shorts in Our Gang series; recent films include: I Was a Communist for the FBI, Come Fill the Cup, Mara Maru, Iron Mistress, She's Back on Broadway, So This Is Love, The Charge at Feather River, Them, Young at Heart, McConnell Story, Sincerely Yours, Santiago, The Big Land, Bombers B-52, Ford Dobbs, Yellowstone Kelly, Rachel Cade, Gold of 7 Saints, Follow That Dream, Call Me Bwana, Rio Conchos, Robin and the Seven Hoods, Sylvia, Harlow, Stagecoach, Way Way Out, In Like Flint, Chuka, Tony Rome, The Detective, Lady in Cement, Barquero, They Call Me Mr. Tibbs. Address: care 20th Century Fox 444 W 56th St New York City NY 10019*

DOUGLAS, GORDON WATKINS, obstetrician, gynecologist, educator; b. Midlothian, Va., June 2, 1921; s. Vivian T. and Virginia (Watkins) D.; A.B., Princeton, 1942; M.D., Johns Hopkins, 1945; m. Elizabeth Burnside, Mar. 28, 1945; children—Gordon Watkins, Laurel, Virginia, Andrew. Intern, Johns Hopkins Hosp., 1945- 46; resident obstetrics and gynecology Bellevue Hosp., N.Y.C., 1948-52, vis. obstetrician and gynecologist, service dir., 1956—; asst. to asst. prof. N.Y. U. Coll. Medicine, 1949-56, prof., chmn. dept. obstetrics and gynecology, 1956—, Markle Scholar med. sci., 1952-57; attending staff, dir. gynecology service Univ. Hosp., N.Y.C., 1956—; cons. obstetrics and gynecology Knickerbocker Hosp., N.Y.C., United Hosp., Port Chester, N.Y. Diplomate Am. Bd. Obstetrics and Gynecology (pres. 1970—). Fellow Am. Coll. Obstetricians and Gynecologists, A.C.S., N.Y. Acad. Medicine, Am. Gynecol. Soc., Am. Assn. Obstetricians and Gynecologists, N.Y. Acad. Scis.; mem. N.Y. Obstet. Soc., Soc. Alumni Bellevue Hosp., A.M.A., N.Y. State, County med. socs. Clubs: Princeton, Century (N.Y.C.). Contbr. articles to med. jours. Home: 940 Highland Av Pelham NY 10803 Office: 550 First Av New York City NY 10016

DOUGLAS, HELEN GAHAGAN, (Mrs. Melvyn Douglas), author, lectr.; b. Boonton, N.J., Nov. 25, 1900; d. Walter and Lillian Rose (Mussen) Gahagan; student Barnard Coll., 1920- 22; m. Melvyn Douglas, Apr. 5, 1931; children—Peter Gahagan, Mary Helen. Actress N.Y.C., starred in plays including Young Woodley, 1925, Enchanted April, 1925, Trelawney of the Wells, 1926, Tonight or Never, 1930, Mary Queen of Scotland, 1934, First Lady, 1952; opera singer European tour, 1928-30, 37; star motion picture She, 1935; mem. 79th to 81st congresses from 14th dist. Cal., mem. fgn. affairs com., co-author McMahon-Douglas Bill; U.S. del. UN Gen. Assembly, 1946. Mem. nat. adv. com. WPA, 1939; del. of Jane Addams Peace Assn. to Soviet-Am. Women's Conf., Moscow, USSR, hon. co-chmn. Women's Internat. League for Peace and Freedom, 1964. Del. Dem. Nat. Conv., Dem. Nat. Committeewoman from Cal., 1940; vice chmn. Dem. state central com., chmn. women's div., 1941-44. Named Woman of Year, N.Y. Hadassah, 1945, 1 of 12 Outstanding Women of Year, Nat. Council Negro Women, 1945. Mem. Nat. Women's Trade Union League Am. Author: The Eleanor Roosevelt We Remember, 1963. Address: 50 Riverside Dr New York City NY 10024

DOUGLAS, JAMES HENDERSON, Jr., lawyer; b. Cedar Rapids, Ia., Mar. 11, 1899; s. James Henderson and Inez (Boynton) D.; A.B., Princeton, 1920; studied Corpus Christi Coll. (Cambridge U.), 1 year; LL.B., Harvard, 1924; LL.D., Princeton, 1960, Grinnell Coll., Lake Forest (Ill.) Coll.; m. Grace Farwell McGann, Nov. 26, 1927 (dec. Feb. 1949); children—James Henderson III, Robert Stuart, John Bruce, David Ogden; m. 2d, Elinor Thompson Donaldson, Sept. 2, 1950. Admitted to Ill. bar, 1925, D.C. bar, 1945, practiced in Chgo.; asso. Winston, Strawn & Shaw until 1929; with Field, Glore & Co., investment bankers, 1929-32; fiscal asst. sec. of treasury, 1932-33; under-sec. Dept. Air Force, 1953- 57, sec. of air force, 1957-59; dep. sec. of def., 1959-61, mem. firm Gardner, Carton, Douglas, Chilgren & Waud, 1934—; dir. Met. Life Ins. Co., Am. Airlines. Trustee U. Chgo., 1933—; mem. Grad. Council of Princeton, 1933-45; vice chmn. Ill. Pub. Aid Commn., 1941-43; pres. Chgo. council Boy Scouts Am., 1941, also mem. nat. exec. bd.; pres. Community Fund Chgo., 1949-52. Treas. Republican Program Com., 1939. Commd. 2d lt. inf., U.S. Army, 1918; served at Camp Hancock, Ga.; col. chief of staff, Air Transport Command, 1942-45. Decorated D.S.M.; recipient Medal of Freedom, 1960. Hon. fellow Corpus Christi Coll.; mem. Am., Ill., Chgo. bar assns. Republican. Presbyn. Clubs: Commercial, University, Chicago (Chgo.); Onwentsia (Lake Forest); Royal and Ancient Golf Club of St. Andrews (Scotland); Metropolitan (Washington). Home: 1 Stonegate Road Lake Forest IL 60045 Office: 1 First National Plaza Chicago IL 60670

DOUGLAS, JAMES MARSH, lawyer; b. St. Louis, Jan. 6, 1896; s. Walter Bond and Francesca (Kimball) Douglas; LL.B., Washington U., St. Louis, 1921, LL.D., 1968; LL.D., Westminster Coll., 1958; m. Mary Lumaghi, Aug. 5, 1939; 1 son, James Kimball. Admitted to Mo. bar, 1917, U.S. Supreme Ct. bar, 1932; began practice in St. Louis, 1921; asso. with law firm Nagel & Kirby; city councilor, Florissant, Mo., 1933-35; judge Circuit Ct., St. Louis, 1935-37; apptd. judge Supreme Ct. of Missouri, 1937, to fill unexpired term, elected, 1938, for term expiring 1944, reelected under Non-Partisan Ct. Plan known as Mo. Plan of Jud. Tenure for a term expiring 1954, chief justice, 1943- 45, resigned, 1949; re-entered law practice as partner Thompson, Mitchell, Douglas, Neill & Guerri, St. Louis; chmn. Jud. Conf. of Mo., 1943-45; chmn. Appellate Jud. Commn. of Mo., 1943-45; lectr. med. jurisprudence Washington U. Med. Sch., 1929-37; spl. counsel to atty. gen. Mo. on edn. beyond high sch., 1962-64. Orgn. dir. St. Louis Ednl. TV Commn. KETC, 1955-57; Mo. chmn. Nat. Library Week. Pvt. Battery A, Mo. Natl. Guard, 1913-17; Mexican border service, 1916; entered 1st O.T.C., Ft. Riley, Kan., 1917; 1st lt. 342d F.A., 89th Div. AEF (St. Mihiel sector, Army of Occupation). Mem. Mo. Def. Council, 1941- 45; bd. dirs. St. Louis Crime Commn.; chmn. task force on legal services and procedure 2d Hoover Commn., 1954-55; sponsor mem. Civic Progress, Inc. of St. Louis; mem. orgn. com., bd. mem. United Fund of St. Louis, 1955; bd. dirs. St. Louis SymPhony Soc.; trustee Washington U., 1950-66, chmn. bd., 1954-61, 1st vice chmn., 1961-66, trustee emeritus, 1967—; trustee St. Louis Children's Hosp., 1951-55; mem. U.S. Territorial Expansion Commn., 1950—, chmn. exec. com.; trustee Jefferson Nat. Expansion Meml. Assn. Recipient citation merit U. Mo. Alumni Assn., 1966; hon. col. on staff gov. Mo., 1953-57, 61-65. Fellow Am. Bar Found.; mem. Am. (chmn. sect. jud. adminstrn. 1950-51; ho. of dels. 1952-54; chmn. jud. selection 1950-59; adv. bd. Am. Bar Jour.), Mo. (dir. dept. of judiciary, 1956-57), St. Louis bar assns., Lawyers Assn. St. Louis (award of honor 1951), Am. Judicature Soc. (dir. 1955-57), Am. Law Inst., Mo. Hist. Soc. (pres. 1940-44; trustee, 1950-59; life mem.). Inst. Jud. Adminstrn., Assn. Bar City N.Y. (asso.), Omicron Delta Kappa (hon.), Order of Coif, S.R., Alpha Tau Omega, Phi Delta Phi (nat. pres. 1931-33). Democrat. Episcopalian. Clubs: Round Table, University, Noonday. Author articles legal mags. Home: 6336 Wydown Blvd St Louis MO 63105 Office: 705 Olive St St Louis MO 63101

DOUGLAS, JAMES STUART, banker, rancher; b. N.Y.C., June 20, 1922; s. Lewis Williams and Peggy (Zinsser) D.; grad. Groton (Mass.) Sch., 1940; student Amherst Coll., 1941; m. Mary Peace Hazard, Mar. 9, 1946; children—James Stuart V, Peter Hazard, Bronwyn MacGregor, Morgan Peace. With So. Ariz. Bank & Trust Co., Tucson, 1946—, exec. v.p., 1963-68, pres., 1968—, also dir. Pres. Devel. Authority for Tucson's Economy, 1970-71, adv. council, 1971-72; Metro chmn. Nat. Alliance of Businessmen; gen. chmn. fund drive United Community Campaign, 1970-71, pres., 1971-72. Served to 1st lt. USAAF, World War II. Decorated Air medal with 3 oak leaf clusters. Mem. U.S. Equestrian Team Assn., Ariz. Bankers Assn. (pres. 1965-66, mem. exec. council), So. Ariz. Cutting Horse Assn. (pres.), Tucson C. of C. (pres. 1971-72). Home: 4761 E Fort Lowell Rd Tucson AZ 85712 Office: 150 N Stone Av Tucson AZ 85702

DOUGLAS, JESSE, mathematician, educator; b. N.Y.C., July 3, 1897; s. Louis Douglas and Sarah (Kommel) D. B.S., Coll. City N.Y., 1916; Ph.D., Columbia, 1920; m. Jessie Nayer, June 30, 1940 (dec. 1955); 1 son, Lewis Philip. Instr. math. Columbia, 1920-25, lectr., 1951- 55; NRC fellow Princeton, 1926-27, Harvard, 1927, Chgo., 1928, Paris, 1928-30; asst. prof. math. Mass. Inst. Tech., 1930-34, asso. prof., 1934- 37; researcher Inst. Advanced Study, Princeton, 1934-35, 38-39; Guggenheim fellow 1940-42, asst. prof. math. Bklyn. Coll., 1942-46; prof. Coll. City N.Y., 1955—, City U. N.Y., 1963—. Recipient Fields medal Internat. Congress Mathematicians, Oslo, Norway, 1936; Townsend Harris medal Assn. Alumni Coll. City N.Y., 1939. Fellow Am. Acad. Arts and Scis.; mem. Am. Math. Soc. (council mem. 1935-38, Bocher prize 1943), Math. Assn. Am., Nat. Acad. Scis., Sigma Xi, Phi Beta Kappa. Asso. editor Transactions Am. Math. Soc., 1930-32, 36-40. Contbr. articles to various Am., European math. jours. Home: Butler Hall 88 Morningside Dr New York City NY 10027

DOUGLAS, JOHN, consultant, educator; b. E. Orange, N.J., July 15, 1929; s. Matthew and Sarah (Smith) D.; student Rutgers U., eves., 1947-48; A.B., Heidelberg (O.) Coll., 1952; M.B.A., Ohio State U., 1955; Ph.D., Cornell U., 1960; m. Marilyn Jean Thomas, Dec. 31, 1952; children—Sara Lee, John Thomas. Instr., Coll. Commerce, W.Va. U., 1955-57; lectr. Elmira (N.Y.) Coll., 1957-60; asst. prof. Sch. Bus. Adminstrn., Wayne State U., 1960-62; prof. bus. adminstrn., chmn. dept. Coll. Bus. and Econs., U. Ky., 1964- 68; cons. to industry, 1960—. Bd. dirs. Ch. Community Service, Inc., 1966-68. Served with AUS, 1952-54. Mem. Acad. Mgmt. (pres. Midwest div. 1969), Indsl. Relations Research Assn., Soc. Applied Anthropology. Presbyn. (elder). Co-author: Marketing Management: A Behavioral Systems Approach, 1966; Human Behavior in Marketing, 1967. Home: 341 Glendover Rd Lexington KY 40503

DOUGLAS, JOHN GRAY, geologist, educator; b. Balt., Aug. 1, 1900; s. Eugene and Ethel (Gray) D.; A.B. in Biology, Johns Hopkins, 1921, Ph.D. in Geology and Paleontology, 1928; m. Violet Anath Marshall, May 28, 1936. Geologist, Venezuela Gulf Oil Co., 1924-25, 26-27; paleontologist Lago Petroleum Corp., Venezuela, 1928-31; asso. prof. geology U. N.C. 1931-34; geologist Mene Grande Oil Co., Venezuela, 1934-55; asso. prof. geology U. Miss., 1955-56, prof., 1956-70, prof. emeritus, 1970—, chmn. dept. geology, 1956-65. Fellow Geol. Soc. Am.; mem. Am. Assn. Petroleum Geologists, A.A.A.S., Am. Assn. U. Profs., Miss. Geol. Society, Sigma Xi, Gamma Alpha, Sigma Gamma Epsilon. Episcopalian. Contributor articles to profl. jours. Home: Leighton Rd Oxford MS 38655 Office: U Miss University, MS 38677.

DOUGLAS, JOHN JAY, communications co. exec.; b. Chgo., Oct. 4, 1916; s. Charles G. and Martha (Brown) D.; Ph.B., U. Wis., 1939; m. Jeanne M. McGauran, June 3, 1944; children—Charles Gardner, John Jay, Steven Anthony, Thomas Slade, Mary Jeanne, Ann Elizabeth, Patricia Mary. With Gen. Telephone System cos., 1940—; pres. Lenkurt Electric Co., San Carlos, Cal., 1959-63, exec. v.p. finance Gen. Telephone & Electronics Corp., N.Y.C., 1963—, also dir.; pres. Anglo-Canadian Telephone, also dir. several subsidiary and affiliated cos.; dir. MFB Mut. Ins. Co.; mem. Grand Central adv. bd. Chem. Bank N.Y. Trust Co., N.Y.C. Named Industry Man of Year, San Francisco Peninsula Mfrs. Assn., 1963. Mem. Am. Inst. C.P.A.'s, Delta Upsilon. Republican. Roman Catholic. Clubs: Scarsdale Golf (Hartsdale, N.Y.); Economic (N.Y.). Home: 15 Taunton Rd Scarsdale NY 10583 Office: 730 3d Av New York City NY 10017

DOUGLAS, JOHN WALDO, aluminum foil mfg. exec.; b. N.Y.C. Feb. 25, 1907; s. Archibald and Edith (Douglas) D.; Ph.B., Yale, 1929; m. Priscilla Alden Lieb, June 22, 1939; children—John W., Stuart, Alexander. With Marc Eidlitz & Son, gen. contractor, N.Y.C., 1930-33, Beryllium Corp., N.Y.C., 1933-34, Phelps Dodge Copper Products Co., N.Y.C., 1934-37 Revere Copper & Brass, Inc., N.Y.C., 1937-41; with OPM, Washington, 1941, chief brass mill br., asst. dir. copper div. WPB, 1942-44; founder Republic Foil, Inc. (co. merged with Nat. Steel Corp., Pitts. 1968), Danbury, Conn., 1945, pres., dir., 1945-69; ltd. partner Dryden & Co., N.Y.C.; dir., mem. exec. com. Barden Corp.; dir. Danbury Indsl. Corp., Savs. Bank of Danbury; mem. adv. com. Danbury office City Trust Co. Mem. prime aluminum products industry adv. com. Dept. Commerce: mem. Am. Marketing Team to Italy, sponsored FOA, 1954. Trustee Danbury Hosp. Mem. Mfrs. Assn. Conn. (past pres., dir.), Danbury C. of C., Aluminum Assn. (hon., past pres., chmn. bd.). Author: Government Administration to Cooper Industry World War II, 1950. Home: Long Meadowhill Rd Brookfield Center CT 06805 Office: 8 West St Danbury CT 06810

DOUGLAS, JOHN WOOLMAN, lawyer; b. Phila., Aug. 15, 1921; s. Paul Howard and Dorothy Sybil (Wolff) D., grad. Deerfield (Mass.) Acad., 1939; B.A., Princeton, 1943; LL.B., Yale, 1948; D. Phil. (Rhodes scholar), Oxford (Eng.) U., 1950; m. Mary Evans St. John, July 14, 1945; children—Katherine St. John, Peter Roderick. Admitted to bar, 1948; law clk. to U.S. Supreme Ct. Justice Burton, 1951-52; with firm Covington & Burling, Washington, D.C., 1950- 51, 52-63, 66—; asst. atty. gen. civil div. Dept. Justice, 1963-66. Served with USNR, 0D 1943-46. Mem. Am. Bar Assn. Democrat. Presbyn. Home: 5700 Kirkside Dr Chevy Chase MD 20015 Office: 888 16th St N W Washington DC 20006

DOUGLAS, KENNETH JAY, food co. exec.; b.Harbor Beach, Mich., Sept. 4, 1922; s. Harry Douglas and Xenia (Williamson) D.; student U. Ill., 1940-41, 46-47; LL.B., Chgo. Kent Coll. Law, 1950; grad. Advanced Mgmt. Program, Harvard, 1962; m. Ann Elizabeth Schweizer, Aug. 17, 1946; children-Connie Ann, Andrew Jay. Admitted to Ill. bar, 1950, Ind. bar, 1952; spl. agt. FBI, 1950-54; dir. indsl. relations Dean Foods Co., 1954-64, v.p. finance and adminstrn., 1964-70, chmn. bd. dirs., 1970—. Served with USRN, 1944-46. Mem. Phi Eta Sigma, Phi Delta Phi. Republican. Clubs: Chicago, Economic, Executives (bd. dirs.) (Chgo.); Oak Park (Ill.) Country; River Forest Tennis. Home: 711 Keystone Av River Forest IL 60305 Office: 3600 N River Rd Franklin Park IL 60131

DOUGLAS, KIRK, actor, motion picture producer; b. Amsterdam, N.Y., Dec. 9, 1918; s. Harry and Bryna (Sanglel) Danielovitch; A.B., St. Lawrence U., 1938, D. Fine Arts (hon.), 1958; student Am. Acad. Dramatic Arts, 1939-41; m. Diana Dill (div. Feb. 1950); children—Michael, Joel; m. 2d, Anne Buydens, May 29, 1954; children—Peter, Eric Anthony. Appeared on Broadway in Spring Again, Three Sisters, Kiss and Tell, Wind is Ninety, Alice in Arms, Man Bites Dog; motion pictures include Strange Love of Martha Ivers, Letters to Three Wives, Ace in the Hole, Bad and the Beautiful, 20,000 Leagues Under the Sea, Ulysses, Lust for Life, Gunfight at the O.K. Coral, The Vikings, The Devil's Disciple, Town Without Pity, Lonely are the Brave, One Flew Over the Cuckoo's Nest (stage play based on Ken Kesey's novel), Seven Days in May, In Harms Way, Heroes of Telemark, Cast a Giant Shadow, The War Wagon, The Brotherhood, numerous others; pres. Bryna Co. Mem. heart com. Motion Picture Industry. Nominated for Acad. Award; 1949, 52, 56; recipient N.Y. Film Critics award, also Hollywood, Fgn. Press award, 1956, Heart and Torch award Am. Heart Assn., 1956; spl. award of merit George Washington Carver Meml. Found., 1957; Cecil B. DeMille award for contbns. in entertainment field, 1967. Mem. UN Assn., (dir. Los Angeles chpt.). State Dept.-USIA tours of S.Am., Far East, Europe. Office: Bryna Co 141 El Camino Beverly Hills CA 90212

DOUGLAS, LEWIS WILLIAMS, former ambassador; b. Bisbee, Ariz., July 2, 1894; s. James Stuart and Josephine Leah (Williams) D.; B.A., Amherst Coll., 1916; postgrad. Mass. Inst. Tech., 1916-17; LL.D., Amherst Coll., Harvard, 1933, Queens Coll., Princeton, Brown, N.Y. and Wesleyan univs., 1938, U. Ariz., 1940, Leeds (Eng.), 1948, U. Bristol, St. Andrews, London, 1949, Edinburgh, Birmingham, Glasgow, 1950, U. Cal., McGill U., Columbia, Dalhousie, 1951; D.C.L., Oxford (Eng.), 1948; m. Peggy Zinsser, June 19, 1921; children—James Stuart, Lewis W., Sharman. Instr., Amherst Coll., 1920; mem. Ariz. Ho. of Reps., 1923-25; mem. 70th to 73d Congresses (1927-33), at large, Ariz.; resigned to become dir. budget, 1933-34; v.p., dir. Am. Cyanamid Co., 1934- 38; prin., vice chancellor McGill U., Montreal, Que., Can., 1938-39; pres. Mut. Life Ins. Co. of N.Y., 1940-47, chmn. bd., 1947-59, chmn. exec. com. bd. dirs., dir., 1959—; hon. chmn. So. Ariz. Bank & Trust Co.; dir. Western Bancorp., Newmont Mining Corp., Union Corp., Ltd. Dep. war shipping adminstr., 1942-44; spl. adviser to Gen. Clay, German Control Council, 1945; ambassador to Gt. Britain, 1947-50; chmn. Nat. Policy Bd. Pres., chmn. Am. Assembly, Alfred P. Sloan Found. Bd. dirs. Am. Mus. Nat. Hist.; trustee emeritus Amherst Coll.; pres., trustee Acad. Polit. Sci., U.S. Churchill Found. Nat. chmn. Am. Shakespeare Festival Theatre and Acad.; hon. pres. Nat. Soc. for Prevention Blindness; mem. adv. bd. Meml. Hosp. Served to 1st lt. F.A., U.S. Army, World War I; AEF in France. Decorated citation from Gen. Pershing; Croix de Guerre, Grand Croix de l'Order de la Couronne (Belgium); Grand Croix de la Legion d'Honneur (France); hon. knight grand cross Order Brit. Empire. Mem. English-Speaking Union (hon. chmn.), Nat. Inst. Social Scis. (v.p.), Am. Philos. Soc. (trustee). Democrat. Episcopalian. Home: Sonita AZ 85637 Office: care So Ariz Bank & Trust Co Tucson AZ 85702 also 1740 Broadway New York City NY 10019

DOUGLAS, LLOYD VIRGIL, bus. educator; b. Brandon, Ia., Aug. 4, 1902; s. Delbert G. and Dora E. (Lizer) D.; B.S., State U. Ia., 1923, A.M., 1928, Ph.D., 1936; postgrad. Ia. State Coll., summer 1925; m. Grace A. Waddell, Aug. 26, 1925. High sch. bus. tchr., Jefferson, Ia., 1923-25; head dept. bus. edn. U. No. Ia., 1937-70, prof. emeritus, 1970—; summer grad. lectr. Okla. A. and M. Coll., 1941, State U. Ia., 1946, State U. Colo., 1949, U. Wis., 1950, Northwestern U., 1951; recruiting specialist 8th U.S. Civil Service Dist., St. Paul, 1942; supr. U.S. Naval Tng. Sch., Ind. U., 1942-44; distinguished prof. Mich. State U., summer 1958; vis. prof. No. Ill. U., 1970-71. Chmn. practical arts com. Ia. Secondary Sch. Coop. Curriculum program, 1946-48; chmn. Ia. research com. United Bus. Edn. Assn. Bus. edn. curriculum cons. Ia. secondary schs.; mem. Nat. Policies Commn. Bus. and Econ. Edn. Recipient John Robert Gregg award, 1960; Representative Citizen award Cedar Falls C. of C., 1966. Mem. N.E.A. (bd. 1950-53), United Bus. Edn. Assn. (pres. 1953-54), North Central Bus. Edn. Assn. (pres. 1967), Nat. Bus. Tchrs. Assn. (bd. 1942-48, v.p. 1949), Internat. Soc. for Bus. Edn. (council, 1948-49), Nat. Assn. Bus. Tchr. Tng. Instns. (dir. 1941-43), Central Comml. Tchrs. Assn. (pres. 1940), Future Bus. Leaders Am. (trustee 1957-67), Am. Vocational Assn. (research com.); Ia. Edn. Assn., Ia. Bus. Edn. Assn. (pres. 1947-48), Cedar Falls C. of C. (pres., 1945-47), Pi Omega Pi (nat. pres. 1941-44, nat. organizer, 1944-46), Delta Pi Epsilon (nat. research awards com., 1945-48), Kappa Delta Pi. Lion (pres. 1949-50). Author: (with others) Modern Business, 1948; Business Education, 1963; other textbooks. Contbr. profl. mags. and yearbooks. Home: 114 W 19th St Cedar Falls IA 52405

DOUGLAS, MELVYN, actor; b. Macon, Ga., Apr. 5, 1901; s. Edouard G. and Lena (Shackelford) Hesselberg; m. Helen Gahagan, Apr. 5, 1931; children—Gregory, Peter Gahagan, Mary Helen. Began as actor, 1919; appeared in stock with Jessie Bonstelle; played in "Free Soul", "Jealousy", "Tonight or Never", N.Y.C.; played in motion pictures As You Desire Me, She Married Her Boss, etc.; Time Out for Ginger, Broadway, cross country tour and Australia, 1953-55. Co-producer ex-G.I. hit mus. rev., "Call Me Mister"; actor, producer, dir. (motion pictures) Blandings Builds His Dream House, 1947, The Great Sinner, 1948, Carriage Entrance, 1949, On the Loose, 1951, Billy Budd, 1962, Hud, 1963 (recipient Acad. award for best supporting actor 1963); The Americanization of Emily, 1964; appeared in Rapture, 1965, Hotel, 1967; I Never Sang For My Father (nominated for Acad. award); also (stage shows) Two Blind Mice, 1949, Bird Cage, 1950, Let Me Hear the Melody, 1951; Little Blue Light, 1951; Glad Tidings, 1951-52; Time Out for Ginger, 1953-55; Inherit the Wind, 1955- 56; Waltz of the Toreadors, N.Y.C. and on tour; The Gang's All Here, 1959-60; The Best Man, 1960-61; appeared in Do Not Go Gentle Into the Night, CBS-TV, 1967, Spofford, on Broadway, 1967-68. Mem. follow-up program White House Conf. on Children in a Democracy, mem. State Relief Commn., State Dept. Soc. Welfare. Del. Nat. Conv., 1940; mem. nat. com. La Guardia-Norris Independent Voters Com.; state chmn. (Cal.). Apptd. head Arts div. Office Civilian Def. Served from pvt. to maj. AUS, 1942-46; CBI. Recipient Tony award for best actor on Broadway, 1960. Mem. Players, Screen Actors Guild (dir.), Res. Officers Assn. Address: William Morris Agy 1740 Broadway New York City NY 10019

DOUGLAS, MIKE, TV personality; b. Chgo. Aug. 11, 1925; s. Michael Delaney and Gertrude (Smith) Dowd; grad. high sch.; m. Genevieve Purnell, 1943; children—Michele and Christine (twins), Kelly Anne. Appeared on The Irish Hour, Chgo.; appeared supper clubs and radio programs also on TV show Kay Kysers Kollege of Musical Knowledge, Hollywood, Cal.; host Hi Ladies, also appeared on TV variety show NBC's Club 60, Chgo.; master of ceremonies afternoon TV show, Cleve., now on network TV as The Mike Douglas Show. Recipient Emmy award, 1967. Served with USNR, World War II. Address: care Westinghouse Broadcasting Co 1619 Walnut St Philadelphia PA 19103*

DOUGLAS, MURRAY ALANSON, educator; b. Syracuse, N.Y., May 7, 1915; s. William Lewis and Lily Belle (Devereaux) D.; B.S., Wayne State U., 1936; M.A., Ohio State U., 1940; Ph.D., 1956; m. May Martha Richardson, Aug. 30, 1940; 1 dau., Sara May Douglas (Mrs. Paul Garbarini). Art tchr. Brookside Sch. Cranbrook, Bloomfield Hills, Mich., 1936-50; prof. art edn. Wayne State U., Detroit, 1950—, chmn. dept., 1962—; exhibited in internat. and local exhibits; ceramics represented to permanent collections Detroit Inst. Arts, Syracuse Mus., others. Served with AUS, 1944-46. Recipient award Mich. Craftsmen, 1955, Nat. Ceramics Show, 1947. Mem. Nat., Mich. art edn. assns., Mich. Potters Assn., Am. Assn. U. Profs. Home: 4717 Olivia Av Royal Oak MI 48073 Office: Arts Bldg Wayne State U Detroit MI 48202

DOUGLAS, PAUL HOWARD, educator, former U.S. senator; b. Salem, Mass., Mar. 26, 1892; s. James Howard and Annie (Smith) D.; A.B., Bowdoin Coll., 1913; A.M., Columbia, 1915, Ph.D., 1921; postgrad. Harvard, 1915-16; LL.D., MacMurray Coll., Bates Coll., DePaul, St. Ambrose, Lake Forest Coll., William and Mary U., Oberlin Coll., New Sch. for Social Research, Bowdoin Coll., U. Rochester, Knox Coll., Bryant Coll., Bucknell U., Amherst; Litt.D., Rollins Coll.; L.H.D., Lincoln Coll., U. So. Ill., U. Ill., m. Dorothy S. Wolff, 1915; children—Helen (Mrs. Paul Klein), John, Dorothea (Mrs. Robert John), Paul; m. Emily Taft, 1931; 1 dau., Jean (Mrs. Edward Bandler). Instr. econs. U. Ill., 1916-17; instr., asst. prof. econs. Reed Coll., Portland, Ore., 1917-18; asso. prof. econs. U. Wash., 1919-20; asst. prof. indsl. relations U. Chgo., 1920-23, asso. prof. 1923-25, prof. 1925-48; U.S. senator, 1948-66; faculty New Sch. Social Research, N.Y.C., 1966-69. Vis. prof. Amherst Coll., 1924-27. Indsl. relations work with Emergency Fleet Corp., 1918-19; acting dir. Swarthmore Unemployment Study, 1930; sec. Pa. Commn. on Unemployment, 193O; econ. adviser N.Y. Commn. on Unemployment 1930; Guggenheim fellow, 1931; mem. Ill. Housing Commn., 1931-33; mem. Consumers' Adv. Bd., NRA, 1933-35, Adv. Com. to U.S. Senate and Social Security Bd. on Fed. Social Security System, 1937; chmn. Pres.'s Commn. on Urban Problems, 1967-68. Del.-at-large Democratic Nat. Convs., 1948, 52, 56, 64, 68; alderman 5th ward Chgo. City Council, 1939-42. Chmn. bd. trustees Freedom House, 1967—. Served from pvt. to lt. col. USMCR, 1942-46. Decorated Bronze Star. Recipient Sidney Hillman award, 1957; John F. Kennedy award Cath. Interracial Council, 1970. Fellow Econometric Soc., Am. Acad. Arts and Scis.; mem. Am. (pres. 1947), Royal econ. assns., Am. Statis. Assn., Am. Philos. Soc., Phi Beta Kappa, Delta Upsilon. Unitarian. Clubs: Federal City (Washington); Chicago Literary. Author: American Apprenticeship and Industrial Education, 1921; (with others) Worker in Modern Economic Society, 1923; Wages and the Family, 1925; (with others) Adam Smith (1776-1926), 1928; Real Wages in the United States (1890-1926), 1930; Economy in the National Government, 1932; America in the Market Place, 1966; Standards of Unemployment Insurance, 1933; The Theory of Wages, 1934; Controlling Depressions, 1935; Social Security in the United States, 1936; Ethics in Government, 1952; In Our Time, 1968. Co-Author: Movement of Real Wages (1926-28), 1930; The Problem of Unemployment, 1931. Contbr. to Am. Econ. Rev., Jour. Polit. Economy. Polit. Sci. Quar., others. Home: 2909 Davenport St N W Washington DC 20008

DOUGLAS, PAUL WOLFF, mining co. exec.; b. Springfield, Mass., Sept. 12, 1926; s. Paul Howard and Dorothy (Wolff) D.; A.B., Princeton, 1948; student Leeds (Eng.) U., 1948; m. Colette Smith, Nov. 19, 1926; children—Philip Lee Breton, Carolyn Jory, Christine Sanders, Paul Harding. Dir. internal finance sect. ECA Mission to France, 1948-52; with Freeport Minerals Co., 1952—, exec., v.p., dir., 1970—; chmn., joint mng. dir. Sulphur Export Corp., 1963—. Chmn. Community Planning Bd. N.Y.C., 1967-68. Served with USNR, 1944-46. Home: 25 Charlton St New York City NY 10014 Office: 161 E 42d St New York City NY 10017

DOUGLAS, RICHARD HERBERT, educator; b. Edmonton, Alta., Can., Sept. 20, 1919; s. Ancus W. and B. Elizabeth (Cope) D.; B.Sc. (hons. physics), U. Alta., 1941; M.Sc., U. Toronto, 1947; Ph.D., McGill U., 1957; m. Alison Boyd McBride, May 24, 1944; children—Alison Elizabeth, Kenneth Boyd. With Meteorol. Service Can., 1941-60, also research asso. McGill U., 1954-60; asso. prof. meteorology McGill U., 1960-65; prof., chmn. dept. agrl. physics Macdonald Coll. of McGill U., 1965—. Canadian, Royal meteorol. socs., Sigma Xi. Home: 6890 Monkland Av Montreal 262 Quebec Canada

DOUGLAS, RICHARD MATEER, educator; b. Cleve., May 27, 1922; s. Richard Steele and Mary (Mateer) D.; A.B., Princeton, 1943; Ph.D., Harvard, 1956; m. Elizabeth Lida Woodward, Sept. 12, 1947; children—David, Andrew, Samuel. Instr., Coll. of Wooster, 1947-49; instr. Brown U., 1953-55; asso. prof. Amherst Coll., 1955-62; prof. history, chmn. dept. humanities Mass. Inst. Tech., Cambridge, 1962—; cons. Edn. Devel. Center, Cambridge; curriculum devel. Newton (Mass.) Pub. Schs. Mem. Newton Sch. Com., 1968—. Served to capt. USMCR, 1943-46. Mem. Am. Acad. Arts and Scis., Am. Renaissance Soc., Am. Hist. Assn., Phi Beta Kappa. Author: Jacopo Sadeleto: Humanist and Reformer, 1959. Home: 97 Hillside Av West Newton MA 02165 Office: Mass Inst Tech Cambridge MA 02139

DOUGLAS, ROBERT ALDEN, educator; b. High Point, N.C., Dec. 4, 1925; s. Elwood Leigh and Ethel May (Kelley) D.; B.S. in Engring. Mechanics, Purdue U., 1951, M.S., 1952, Ph.D., 1956; m. Irmgard Signus, May 1, 1948; children—Sylvia, Vivian, Robert. Supr. devel. group Danly Machine Specialties, Inc., Chgo., 1956-58; mem. faculty N.C. State U., 1958—, asso. prof., 1958-63, prof., 1963—, asso. head dept. engring. mechanics, 1966—; dep. chief party U.S. Engring. Team, Kabul, Afhanistan, 1964-66; cons. Packer Assos., Chgo., 1958—. Served to 1st lt. AUS, 1944-45. Mem. N.Y. Acad. Scis., A.A.A.S., Am. Soc. Metals, Am. Soc. M.E., Soc. Exptl. Stress Analysis. Author: Introduction to Solid Mechanics, 1963; patentee apparatus for manufacture diffraction gratings. Home: 3712 Horton St Raleigh NC 27607

DOUGLAS, SAMUEL HORACE, educator; b. Ardmore, Okla., May 10, 1928; s. Harrison and Corine (Gunn) D.; B.S., Bishop Coll., 1950; M.S., Okla. State U., 1959, Ph.D. (NSF fellow), 1967; divorced; children—Carmen, Samuel, Emanuel. Asst. prof. math. Prairie View (Tex.) A. and M. U., 1959-63, chmn. dept., 1962-63; prof. math. Grambling (La.) Coll., 1967—, chmn. dept., 1967—. Cons. Com. Undergrad. Program Math.; mem. Panel Spl. Problems Minority Groups; dir. summer and Inservice Insts. Math., 1968, 69, 70, 71. Recipient Disntinguished Service award Pi Mu Epsilon, 1970. Mem. Math. Assn. Am. (vis. lectr., vice chmn. La.-Miss. sect.), Am. Math. Soc., Pi Mu Epsilon, Alpha Phi Alpha. Home: Box 564 Grambling LA 71245

DOUGLAS, SCOTT, dancer; b. El Paso, Tex., June 16, 1927; s. William Oren and Alberta (Celum) Hicks; grad. high sch., El Paso; studied dance with Karma Deane, Lester Horton, Ruth St. Denis, Willam Christenson. Mem. San Francisco Ballet, 1947-50, Ballet Theater, 1950-58, prin. dancer, 1955-58, premier danseur Met. Opera, N.Y.C., 1958—; Jerome Robbin's Ballets: U.S.A., 1961; mem. Glen Tetley Dance Co.; ret. 1969; ballet master Netherlands Dans Theatre, HET Nat. Ballet Amsterdam, Den Norske Opera, Oslo. Served with USNR, World War II. Home: 15 W 9th St New York City NY 10011

DOUGLAS, SHELDON J., supermarket exec.; b. Portland, Ore., Dec. 14, 1920; s. Lysle V. and Celonise (De Grandpre) D.; B.A. in Econs., Reed Coll., 1943; m. Manesa O. Winters, Aug. 26, 1946; children—Shellie A., Steven J., Ronald P., Robert P., Sheree M. Accountant, Safeway Stores, Portland, 1943-46, office mgr., 1947-54, staff asst. to v.p., controller, Oakland, Cal., 1954-59, controller N.Y. div. Jersey City, 1959-61, asst. corporate controller. Oakland, 1961-65; v.p., controller, treas. Allied Supermarkets, Inc., Detroit, 1965-66, sr. v.p., 1966—. Roman Catholic. Home: 22641 N Nottingham Dr Birmingham MI 48010 Office: 8711 Meadowdale Detroit MI 48228

DOUGLAS, THOMAS CLEMENT, Canadian govt. ofcl.; b. Falkirk, Scotland, Oct. 20, 1904; s. Thomas and Annie (Clement) D.; B.A.; Brandon Coll., Manitoba, Can., 1930; M.A., McMaster U., Hamilton, Ont., 1933; postgrad. U. Chgo., 1931; m. Irma M. Dempsey, Sept. 3, 1930; children—Shirley Jean (Mrs. Donald Sutherland), Joan Diane (Mrs. T.H. Tulchinsky). Ordained to ministry Baptist Ch., 1930; served in Weyburn, Sask., 1930-35; rep. Constituency of Weyburn to Parliament, 1935-44; mem. Legislative Assembly for Weyburn to 1961; premier of Sask., 1944-61, minister pub. health for Sask., 1944-49, minister coops., 1949-60; elected federal leader New Democratic Party, founding conv., Ottawa, 1961, served until 1971. Home: 404 Laurier Av E Ottawa Ontario Canada

DOUGLAS, THORNTON STONE mfg. exec.; b. Lima, O., Apr. 1, 1932; B.S., U. San Francisco, 1954; M.S., Stanford University, 1956; m. Rosemarie Lois Brown, May 15, 1955; 1 son, Anthony Robinson. Sales rep. Ames-Brockton Fabricated Products, Akron, O., 1956-58, sales mgr. Coshocton, Ohio, 1959-61, gen. manager plant, 1961-68, v.p. sales, 1968--. Instr. bus. Coshocton Jr. College, 1968-69. Mem. Coshocton C. of C. (vice president 1967-68, pres. 1969-70), English Speaking Union, Coshocton Sertoma Club, Nat. Assn. Mfrs., Sales Executives Institute, Phi Beta Kappa, Sigma Chi, Phi Mu. Democrat. Mem. Christian Ch. (lay reader). Mason (32, Shriner). Clubs: Coshocton Country, Coshocton City, Running Deer Country. Home: 2d Av Coshocton OH Office: 3d Av Coshocton OH

DOUGLAS, WALTER SPALDING, civil engr.; b. Cranford, N.J., Jan. 22, 1912; s. Walter Jules and Elizabeth Appleton (Spalding) D.; grad. Phillips Exeter Acad., 1929; B.A., Dartmouth, 1933; M.S. in Civil Engring., Harvard, 1935; m. Jean Gairdner Moment, May 6, 1938; children—David, Joanne, Nancy. Structural steel detailer Nashville Bridge Co., 1935-37; asst. to chief engr. N.Y. World's Fair, Inc., 1937-39; asso. engr. Parsons, Brinckerhoff, Hall & Macdonald, N.Y., 1939-42, 46-52, partner Parsons, Brinckerhoff, Quade & Douglas, 1952—, sr. partner, chmn. bd., 1966—. Trustee Hillside Cemetery, Plainfield, N.J.; bd. govs. Muhlenberg Hosp., Plainfield, 1950—, pres., 1958-59. Served to lt. comdr. USNR, 1942-45. Recipient citation Engring. News-Record, 1966, Moles Assn. award for Outstanding Achievement in Constrn., 1970. Fellow Am. Soc. C.E. (James Laurie prize 1969); mem. Am. Inst. Cons. Engrs. (pres v.p.), Soc. Am. Mil. Engrs., Nat. Acad. Engring. Clubs: Down Town Association (N.Y.C.); Plainfield Country; Conanicut Yacht (Jamestown, R.I.); Olympic (San Francisco). Prin. works include responsibility for design, constrn. mgmt. San Francisco Bay Area Rapid Transit System, design Combat Operations Center, N.Am. Air Def., Colo. Home: 1796 Fernwood Lane Plainfield NJ 07060 Office: 111 John St New York City NY 10038

DOUGLAS, LORD WILLIAM SHOLTO, (Douglas of Kirtleside), Marshalof the Royal Air Force; b. Oxford, Eng., Dec. 23, 1893; s. Robert Langton and Margaret (Cannon) D.; student Tonbridge Sch., 1908- 13, Lincoln Coll., Oxford (hon. fellow), 1913-14; m. Hazel Walker. 1955; 1 dau., Katharine Ann. Joined Royal Arty., trans. to R.A.F., 1914; comd. fighter squadrons, France, 1917-18; comdg. officer R.A.F., Sudan, 1929- 32; instr. Imperial Defence Coll., 1932-36; dir. staff duties, Air Ministry, 1936-37, asst., chief, Air Staff, 1937-40, deputy chief, 1940, air officer comdr-in-chief Fighter Command, 1940-42, Middle East Command, 1942-44, Coastal, 1944-45; air comdr.-in-chief, British Air Force of Occupation, Germany, 1945-46; comndr.-in-chief mil. gov. British zone in Germany, 1946-47; dir. British Overseas Air Corps, 1948-49; chmn. British European Airways, 1949-64, Horizon Asso. Travel, Ltd., 1964—. Decorated Knight Grand Cross, Order of the Bath, Mil. Cross, D.F.C., Legion of Merit (chief comdr.), Naval D.S.M.; created a peer, 1948. Mem. Internat. Transp. Assn. (pres. 1956-57). Author: Years of Combat, 1963; Years of Command, 1966. Home: Shepherds Holt Denham Buckinghamshire England

DOUGLAS, WILLIAM C., bus. exec. Past hon. chmn. Punta Alegre Sugar Corp., N.Y.C.; now hon. chmn., dir. Bangor Punta Corp.; dir. Baragua Sugar Estates. Address: care of Bangor Punta 1 Greenwich Plaza Greenwich CT 06830

DOUGLAS, WILLIAM KENNEDY, physician; b. Estancia, N.M., Sept. 5, 1922; s. Leo Arthur and Maude Wise (Kennedy) D.; student U. N.M., 1939-41; B.S., Tex. Western Coll., 1946; M.D., U. Tex. 1948; M.P.H., Johns Hopkins, 1954; m. Marguerite Wade McIlroy, Aug. 17, 1946; 1 son, Wade. Wade, Intern Wayne Gen. County Hosp. and Infirmary, Eloise, Mich., 1948-49; commd. 1st lt., M.C., USAF, 1949, advanced through grades to colonel, 1964, rated chief flight surgeon, 1965; assigned San Antonio, 1949-50, Nfld., 1950- 53, Balt., 1953-54, Langley AFB, Va., 1954-55, Andrews AFB, Md., 1955- 57, Hdqrs. USAF, 1957-59; flight surgeon astronauts Project Mercury NASA. 1959-62; asst. dept. for bioastronautics Hdqrs. Air Force Missile Test Center, 1962-65; dep. for bioastronautics Hdqrs Eastern Test Range, 1965-66; asst. dep. chief staff bioastronautics and medicine Hdqrs. Air Force Systems Command, Andrews AFB, Washington, 1966-68; Command, Andrews AFB, Washington, 1966-68; chief central aeromed. services USAF, Europe, 1968—. Decorated Legion of Merit. Diplomate aviation medicine Am. Bd. Preventive Medicine. Fellow A.C.P., Aerospace Med. Assn; mem. Am. Inst. Aeronautics and Astronautics, Assn. Mil. Surgeons, A.M.A., Internat. Acad. Astronautics, Sigma Chi. Home: 216 N St Vrain El Paso TX 79901 Office: USAF Hospital Box 700 APO New York City NY 09220

DOUGLAS, WILLIAM ORVILLE, asso. justice U.S. Supreme Ct.; b. Maine, Minn., Oct. 16, 1898; s. William and Julia Bickford (Fiske) D.; B.A., Whiteman Coll., 1920, LL.D., 1938; LL.B., Columbia, 1925; M.A. (hon.), Yale, 1932; LL.D., Wesleyan U., 1940, Washington and Jefferson Coll., 1942, William and Mary Coll., 1943, Rollins Coll., 1947, Nat. U., 1949, New Sch. for Social Research, 1952, U. Toledo, 1956, Bucknell U., 1958, Dalhousie U., 1958, Colby Coll., 1961; m. Mildred Riddle, Aug. 16, 1923; children—Mildred Riddle (Mrs. Norman T. Read), William Orville; m. 2d, Mercedes Hester, Dec. 14, 1954 (div. 1963); m. 3d, Joan Martin, Aug., 1963 (div.); m. 4th, Cathleen Heffernan, July, 1966. Instr. high sch. Yakima, Wash., 1920-22; admitted to N.Y. bar, 1926; practiced N.Y.C., 1925-27; mem. law faculty, Columbia, 1925-28, Yale, 1928-34; bankruptcy studies, Yale Inst. Human Relations and US Dept. Commerce, 1929-32; sec. Com. on Bus. of Fed. Cts., Nat. Commn. on Law Observance and Enforcement, 1930-32; dir. protective com. study, Securities and Exchange Commn., Washington, 1934-36, commr. and chmn., 1936-39; asso. justice U.S. Supreme Ct., 1939—. Served as pvt. U.S. Army, 1918. Mem. Royal Geog. Soc. (London), Beta Theta Pi, Phi Alpha Delta, Delta Sigma Rho, Phi Beta Kappa. Democrat. Presbyn. Mason. Clubs: Yale; Himalayan (Delhi, India); University (Washington); Overseas Press. Author: Various law case books; also Of Men and Mountains, 1950; Strange Lands and Friendly People, 1951; Beyond the High Himalayas, 1952; North from Malaya, 1953; An Almanac of Liberty, 1954; We The Judges, 1955; Russian Journey, 1956; The Right of the People, 1958; Exploring the Himalaya, 1958; West of the Indus, 1958; My Wilderness: East to Katahdin, 1960; My Wilderness: The Pacific West, 1961; A Living Bill of Rights, 1961; Democracy's Manifesto, 1962: The Anatomy of Liberty, 1963; Mr. Lincoln and the Negroes, 1963; Freedom of the Mind, 1963; A Wilderness Bill of Rights, 1965; The Bible and the Schools, 1966; Farewell to Texas, 1967; Towards a Global Federalism, 1968. Contbr. law jours. Home: Goose Prairie Washington DC 20013 Office: US Supreme Ct Washington DC 20543

DOUGLAS, WILLIAM WILTON, educator; b. Glasgow, Scotland, Aug. 15, 1922; M.B., Ch.B., Glasgow U., 1946, M.D., 1949; married; 2 children. Lectr. physiology Aberdeen U. (Scotland), 1947-48; staff mem. med. research council, physiol. and pharmacological div. Nat. Inst. Med. Research, Eng., 1950-56; vis. asso. in pharmacology, Coll. Physicians and Surgeons, Columbia, 1952-53; asso. prof. Albert Einstein Coll. Medicine, N.Y.C., 1956-58, prof., 1958-69; prof. pharmacology Yale, 1969—. Served as maj. Royal Army, 1948-50. Mem. Am. Physiol. Soc., Am. Soc. Pharmacology, Canadian, Brit. pharmacological socs. Office: Dept Pharmacology Yale New Haven CT 06520*

DOUGLASS, ALFRED EUGENE, mfg. exec.; b. Allentown, Pa., Jan. 16, 1888; s. William Merton and Helen Louise (Billings) D.; student Mercersburg (Pa.) Acad., 1906; m. Jean Melicent Ellis, Dec. 7, 1907 (dec.); child:en—Alfred Eugene, Donald Stoughton, Elizabeth Laurene (Mrs. Max Hess). Supr. Allentown Portland Cement Co., 1912-18, pres., dir., 1939-51, chmn., 1951-57, chmn. exec. com., 1957-61; mgr. crushing dept. Fuller-Lehigh Co., Fullerton, Pa., 1918-25; v.p., gen. mgr. Fuller Co., machinery mfrs., Catasaugua, 1926-29, pres., 1929-39, dir., chmn. exec. com., 1939- 54, pres., 1954-57, chmn. bd., 1957—; dir. emeriti First Nat. Bank Allentown. Mem. C. of C., Am. Soc. Mech. Engrs. Republican. Episcopalian. Elk. Clubs: Livingston, Lehigh Country (Allentown); Catasauqua, Lehigh Valley Engineers. Home: 2302 Hamilton St Allentown PA 18104

DOUGLASS, EARL LEROY, clergyman; b. McKeesport, Pa., Aug. 22, 1888; s. Elisha Peairs and Elvira (Weddle) D.; grad. Mercersburg Acad., 1909; A.B., Princeton, 1913; grad. Union Theol. Sem., 1916, postgrad., 1923-25; D.D., Tusculum Coll., 1931, Wooster Coll., 1936; Litt.D., Catawba Coll., Salisbury, N.C., 1941; m. Lois Haler, Sept. 4, 1913; children—Elisha P., Dorothy (Allen). Ordained to ministry, Presbyn. Ch., 1917; pastor First Ch., Tonawanda, N.Y., 1917-23, Poughkeepsie, N.Y., 1925-31, Summit Ch., Germantown, Phila., 1931-45. Trustee Mercersburg Acad., 49 years; chmn. Gen. Assembly's Com. on Tercentenary of Westminster Assembly, 1942-43; chmn. Gen. Assembly's Com. to revise the Intermediate Catechism, 1944-47. Recipient George Washington Honor medal Freedoms Found. of Valley Forge. Mason. Clubs: Authors' League (N.Y.C.); Union League (Phila.); Princeton (N.Y.C., Phila.); Nassau, S.R. (Princeton). Author: Prohibition and Common Sense, 1931; The Faith We Live By, 1937; The Douglass Sunday School Lessons (34 edits. of ann. commentary on Internat. Sunday Sch. Lessons); The Douglass Devotional, 1964. Syndicates two religious features in 104 newspapers. Contbr. revs. and articles to religious mags. Home: 41 Armour Rd Princeton NJ 08540

DOUGLASS, HILTON LEE, lawyer, bus. exec.; b. Van Buren, Ark. Jan. 12, 1905; s. George Lee and Pearl (McEachin) D.; LL.B., U. Kan., 1926; m. Marian Cooke, Dec. 5, 1928; children—Diane Lee (Mrs. John Arthur Philbin), George Lee. Admitted to Okla. bar, 1925; asst. county atty., Pushmataha County, Antler, 1926-28; pvt. practice, Hugo, 1928-30, Oklahoma City, 1930—; mem. firm Cantrell, Douglass, Thompson & Wilson, attys., v.p. Lyon Devel. Co., 1946—; pres. Marian Land Co., Comml. Bldg. Co., Park View Homes, Inc. Mem. Oklahoma City Park Bd. Served as lt. comdr., Amphibious Forces, 1943-46. Recipient Philippines Liberation Medal for assault landing on Luzon; Asiatic-Pacific medal for landing on Iwo Jima. Mem. Am., Okla., Oklahoma County bar assns., Delta Upsilon, Phi Alpha Delta, Sachem. Episcopalian (chancellor). Kiwanian. (pres. Oklahoma City 1965). Clubs: Oklahoma City Golf and Country, Beacon, Men's Dinner. Home: 6815 N Country Club Dr Oklahoma City OK 73116 Office: First Nat Bldg Oklahoma City OK 73102

DOUGLASS, INMAN HARRY, educator; b. Kaufman, Tex.; s. Harry and Zula (Norwood) D.; student So. Meth. U.; m. Dixie Taylor, Apr. 14, 1929; 1 dau., Katherine (Mrs. Robert Burks). Pub. accountant, tax accountant U.S. Govt., 1933-42; Christian Sci. practitioner, 1942—; rep. Christian Sci. Ch. in Washington, 1955-59, nat. bd. dirs., 1961-70; tchr., Dallas, 1970—. Office: Davis Bldg Dallas TX 75202

DOUGLASS, JOSEPH HENRY, govt. ofcl.; b. Washington, June 26, 1917; s. Haley George and Evelyn (Dulaney) D.; A.B., Fisk U., 1937, M.A., 1941; Ph.D., Harvard U., 1946; m. Katherine Washington, Nov. 19, 1938; children—Betty, Jo Ann. Dean Fayetteville State Coll., 1947-54; Fulbright lectr. Cairo Sch. Social Work, Cairo, Egypt, 1952-53; spl. rep. of sec., asst. to asst. sec. Program Analysis Office, Dept. Health, Edn. and Welfare, Washington, 1954-61; program, policy coordinator chief interagy. br. Nat. Inst. Mental Health, Bethesda, Md., 1961-68; exec. dir., policy adviser White House Conf. on Children and Youth, 1968-70; exec. dir. President's Com. Mental Retardation, 1971—. Sr. cons. Acad. for Ednl. Devel., N.Y.C. Bd. dirs. Human Resources Found. N.Y.; profl. bd. Acad. Religion and Mental Health N.Y.; bd. dirs. Am. Soc. Health Assn. N.Y. Trustee African Art Museum, Washington, Nat. Conf. Christians and Jews. Fellow Am. Sociol. Soc., Royal Geog. Soc.; mem. Royal Acad. Promotion Health (London, Eng.). Author: Racism in America, 1965. Home: 3314 16th St NE Washington DC 20018 Office: 7th and D Sts SW Washington DC 20201

DOUGLASS, KINGMAN, Jr., investment banker; b. Chgo., Sept. 29, 1923; s. Kingman and Helen Field (James) D.; grad. St. Mark's Sch., 1942; A.B., Yale, 1948; m. Marlan Phelps, Jan. 1, 1949; children—Louise James, Kingman Scott, Timothy Phelps, Robert Dun, Kathryn Cowles. Office mgr. Dun & Bradstreet Inc., 1948-57; loan officer Harris Trust & Savs. Bank, 1957-61; v.p., dir. A. G. Becker & Co., Inc., Chgo., 1961-65; sr. v.p., dir. Glore Forgan, William R. Staats, Inc., 1965-66, exec. v.p. head midwestern div., 1966- 71, also mem. exec. com.; resident partner Kuhn, Loeb & Co., 1971—; dir. U.S. Reduction Co., East Chicago, Ind., Admiral Corp., Chgo., also VSI Corp., Pasadena, Cal. Trustee Chgo. Sunday Evening Club, Presbyn.-St. Luke's Hosp.; trustee, chmn. finance. comm. Ill. Children's Home and Aid Soc. Presbyn. (elder). Clubs: Chicago, Attic (Chgo.); Onwentsia (Lake Forest); Old Elm. Home: 20 E Laurel Av Lake Forest IL 60045 Office: 135 S LaSalle St Chicago IL 60603

DOUGLASS, LATHROP, architect; b. Kansas City, Mo., Sept. 5, 1907; s. Willard R. and Floyd (Smith) D.; A.B., Yale, 1929, B.F.A. with honors, 1932; student Fontainebleau (France), 1931; m. Dorothy Duncan Howe, Sept. 10, 1937; children—Rebecca Lanier, LathroP Howe. Site planner, designer, 1934-39; housing control architect N.Y. State Housing Bd., 1940-41; asst. chief engr. charge design Army Middle East Repair Bases, 1942-43; practicing architect, 1945—; pres. Lathrop Douglas S.A.R.L., Paris, planning consultants; cons. Eastern ShopPing Centers, Esso Italiano (Rome, Italy) Internat. Petroleum, AEC, 1951-52, others; works include Cross County Center, N.Y., Prince Georges Plaza, Washington, regional shopping centers and dept. stores U.S., P.R., Europe, Creole Bldg. and Luz Electrica Bldg., Caracus, Venezuela, Esso Bldgs., Paris, Bogota, Colombia, Antwerp, Belgium, Tysons Corner Center, Washington, Plaza Las Americas, San Juan, P.R., Parly 2, La Belle Epine, Paris; new town centers, Creteil, Pontoise; urban redevel., New Haven, Chapel Square, New Haven, Main Pl., Buffalo, Greenwich (Conn.) Sta. Plaza. Lectr., Internat. Council Shopping Centers. Mem. Internat. bd. Temple Understanding, Dir. N.Y. Bd. Trade; mem. pub. adv. panel Fed. Bldgs. Program, 1966-68. Recipient 1st Medal award Festival Internat. d'Architecture, Paris, 1956. Fellow Internat. Inst. Arts and Letters. A.I.A. (dir. N.Y. chpt. 1958-62, treas. 1966-67, v.p. 1967- 68, pres. 1968-69); mem. Nat. Inst. Archtl. Edn. (treas. 1961-63 trustee), N.Y. State Assn. Architects. Am. Soc. C.E., St. Nicholas Soc., Sigma Xi (asso.). Clubs: University, Yale (N.Y.C.); Bellehaven (Greenwich). Author mag. articles; illustrator geology textbooks. Home: 501 Lake Ave Greenwich CT 06830 Office: 521 Fifth Av New York City NY 10017 also 33 rue Galilee Paris XVI France

DOUGLASS, PAUL F., lawyer, former univ. pres.; b. Corinth, N.Y., Nov. 7, 1904; s. Rev. George C. and Mabel (Parker) D.; A.B., Wesleyan U., 1926, LL.D., 1946; A.M., U. Cin., 1929, Ph.D. (Taft fellow), 1931; student U. Chgo., 1928, U. Berlin, 1931-33. Reporter Cin. Post, 1926-27, ednl. editor, 1927-28; corr. Chgo. bur. Christian Sci. Monitor, 1928-30; dir. study of cts. of ltd. jurisdiction and Cin. Municipal Ct. for Inst. of Law, Johns Hopkins U., in Hamilton County, O., 1930-31; ordained to ministry M.E. Ch., 1933; pastor Meth. Ch., Poultney, Vt., 1933-41; pres. Am. U., Washington, 1941-52; prof. polit. sci. Rollins Coll., also dir. Center for Practical Politics (Falk Found.), 1956-71; dir. Mgmt. Corp. of Americas. Adviser to pres. of Republic of Korea and counsel to ministry of fgn. affairs, 1952-55; chmn. nat. adv. com. on recruitment, tng. and placement recreation personnel Nat. Recreation Assn., 1952-58; v.p., chmn. finance com. Am. Recreation Found., 1960-65; mem. Pa. Gov.'s Recreation Council, 1956-58; chmn. Settlement Ho. Study Com., United Community Services, Wash., 1951-53; chmn. Christian Friends of Korea; trustee Nat. Recreation and Park Assn., 1965—; chmn. task force on leisure Nat. Council of Chs., 1965-67; mem. arbitration panel Fed. Mediation and Conciliation Service. Awarded the Haakon VII Cross (Norway), 1948; Order of Ascending Star with Rosette (China), 1948; Order of Taiguk (Korea), 1950. Admitted Vt., D.C. bars. Mem. Vt. Ho. Reps., 1937-39, 39-41, Vt. Senate, 1941-43. Mem. numerous profl. assns. and orgns., past officer several. Clubs: University, National Press, Cosmos, Metropolitan (Washington). Author several books, later ones including Six Upon the World, 1954; The Group Workshop Way, 1956; Communication through Reports, 1957; Teaching for Self Education at a Life Goal, 1960; How to be an Active Citizen, 1960; The ABC of Industrial Parks, 1960; Inside Isthmus America, 1971. Editor several books, latest, Recreation in Age of Automation, 1957. Contbr. to Ency. Americana. Home: Grand View Farm Granville NY Office: West Pawlet VT 05775

DOUGLASS, RAYMOND DONALD, prof. math.: b. Gorham, Me., Dec. 29, 1894; s. Edward K. and Josephine (Chick) D.; A.B., U. of Maine, 1915, A.M., 1916. Sc.D., 1943; Ph.D., Mass. Inst. Tech., 1931; m. Ollave Norton, Feb. 2, 1918; children—Charlotte (Mrs. Wilbard Mott), Eleanor, Marjorie (Mrs. Charles Humphreys). Prin. high sch., Mass., 1916-17; sub-master, high sch., N.H., 1917-18; successively instr., asst. prof., asso. prof., prof. math. Mass. Inst. Tech., 1919—. Mem. bd. examiners Math. Coll. Examination Bd. Cons. Chem. Warfare Service, Nat. Defense Research Com. Bd. dirs. Boston Center for Adult Edn., Adult Edn. Council of Greater Boston. Served with U.S. Navy, 1918-19; cons. Chem. Warfare Service since 1930, state coordinator (Mass.) 1941-43, war man-power bd. (Mass.) 1941-46; war tng. programs, 1941-45; cons. camouflage sect., N.D.R.C., 1943-45. Recipient citation Army Signal Corps, commendation N.D.R.C., The Charles Francis Park Gold medal. Mem. Am. Math Assn., Am. Math. Soc., Am. Soc. Engrng. Edn., Mass. Coaches Assn., Mass. Track and Field Ofcls. Assn., Phi Beta Kappa, Sigma Xi, Delta Tau Delta. Republican. Mem. Methodist Ch. Mason (grand comdr. Grand Commandry of K.T. 1962). Clubs: Bellingham Navy; Gridiron (Greater Boston); Five-O (Cambridge, Mass.); Lexington Minute Men. Author: Calculus and its Applications, 1947; Elements of Nomography, 1947; Graphical Mathematics sect. of Engineers Handbook, 1950; Analytic Geometry, 1950; Encyclopedia of Science and Technology (nomography). Home: 18 Oak Av Belmont MA 02178 Office: Massachusetts Institute of Technology Cambridge MA 02139

DOUGLASS, ROBERT RAYMOND, univ. prof.; b. Florence, Ala., Oct. 30, 1901; s. William Shelbourne and Mary Cornelia (Clark) D.; A.B., U. Ala., 1921; B.L.S., Peabody Coll., 1935; A.M., Colo. State Coll., 1939; Ph.D., U. Chicago, 1957. Prin., Grenola (Kan.) High Sch., 1921-22; tchr. Latin, Atlanta pub. schs., 1922-25; teacher-librarian in high sch., Weslaco, Tex., 1926-28; sch. librarian, Mercedes, Tex., 1928-34; asst. librarian N. M. Mil. Inst., Roswell, 1935-39; instr. in library service North Tex. State Coll., Denton, 1939-41; asst. prof. Peabody Library Sch., 1941-44; asso. prof. and acting dir. George Peabody Coll., 1945-47; prof. library sci. U. Tex., 1948-70, dir. library sch., 1948-68. Chmn. Tex. Council Library Edn., 1948-51. Mem. A.L.A. (exec. bd. library edn. div. 1954-57, 61-63, pres. 1961-62), Assn. Coll. and Reference Libraries, Southwestern, Tex. (exec. bd. 1955-56, 62-64, pres. 1962-63) library assns., Spl. Libraries Assn., Council on Library Edn. (chmn. 1950-51), Assn. Am. Library Sch. (exec. bd. 1947-49), Am. Assn. U. Profs., Phi Kappa Sigma. Democrat. Home: 1707 Westover Rd Austin TX 78703

DOUMA, JOHN HENRY, oil co. exec.; b. Oilfields, Cal., July 20, 1914; s. Hendrick J. And Geertje (Kok) D.; B.S. in Petroleum Engrig., U. Cal. at Berkeley, 1938; m. Eloise Moore, Aug. 20, 1939; children—Sharon Wilma, Robert Warren. With Barnsdall Oil Co., (merged with Sunray Oil Corp., 1950); 1938-50, supt. mid-continent div., 1948-50; with Sunray Oil Corp., 1950-55, (merged with Mid-Continent Petroleum Corp. to become Sunray Mid-Continent Oil Co., 1955, name changed to Sunray DX Oil Co., 1962), mgr. engrng., 1954-55; v.p., mgr. Western div., Denver, 1960-63, v.p. prodn. dept., 1963-66, sr. v.p. extractive, 1966-68, co. merged with Sun Oil Co., 1968, dir., sr. v.p. extractive DX div. Sun Oil Co., 1968-70, dir., v.p. prodn., 1970—. Mem. Internat. Oil and Gas Ednl. Center of Southwest Legal Inst. Bd. dirs. Internat. Petroleum Expn. Mem. Independent Petroleum Assn. Am. (bd. dirs.), Western Oil and Gas Assn. (bd. dirs.), Am. Petroleum Inst., Soc. Petroleum Engrs. of Am., Inst. Mining, Metall. and Petroleum Engrs., Rocky Mountain Oil and Gas Assn. (bd. dirs.) Mid-Continent Oil and Gas Assn. Clubs: Dallas Petroleum, Brook Hollow Golf. Home: 7210 Stonetrail Dallas TX 75230

DOUTT, JOHN THOMPSON, educator; b. Rochester, Pa., Jan. 10, 1918; s. Frank W. and Ella (Thompson) D.; A.B., Muskingum Coll., 1939; M.B.A., Harvard, 1941; Ph.D., U. Pitts., 1957; m. Mary Malinda Hogsett, Jan. 29, 1944; children—Mary Malinda (Mrs. David A. Tillyer), John Thompson, Christine Louise. Shop supt. Babcock & Wilcox Tube Co., Beaver Falls, Pa., 1941-46; asst. prof. Geneva Coll., 1946-50; asst. prof. U. Rochester, 1950-53; asst. prof. U. Pitts., 1953-57; asso. prof. U. Colo., 1957-61; prof., chmn. prodn. dept. Kent (O.) State U., 1961-66, prof., chmn. mgmt. dept., 1966—, chmn. community relations com., 1966—. Mem. Acad. of Mgmt., Am. Assn. U. Profs. (pres. Kent State U. chpt. 1970), Beta Gamma Sigma. Author: (with John R. Kline) Small Business in The Rocky Mountain West, 1962. Contbr. articles profl. jours. Home: 455 Harvey St Kent OH 44240

DOUTT, RICHARD LEROY, educator, entomologist; b. La Verne, Cal., Dec. 6, 1916; s. Mace and Adele (Bussey) D.; B.S., U. Cal. at Berkeley. 1939, M.S., 1940, Ph.D., 1946; LL.B., San Francisco Law Sch., 1959, J.D., 1968; m. Lucinda Margaret Killian, Mar. 21, 1942; children—Richard Jonathan, Jeffrey Thomas. Admitted to Cal. bar, 1960. Faculty, U. Cal. at Berkeley, 1946—, prof. entomology, 1960—, chmn. div. biol. control, 1964-69, acting dean Coll. Agrl. Scis., 1969-70; mem. firm Foley, Saler & Doutt, Albany, Cal., 1960-67. Served to lt. comdr. USNR, 1941-45. Fellow Cal. Acad. Scis.; mem. A.A.A.S., Entomol. Soc. Am., Ecol. Soc. Am., Cal. Bar Assn., Sigma Xi. Democrat. Contbr. articles to profl. jours. Home: 41 Millside Lane Mill Valley CA 94941 Office: 1050 San Pablo Av Albany CA 94706

DOVAT, ERNEST CHARLES, banker; b. Knoxville, Tenn., Sept. 20, 1905; s. Adrian Paul and Alice (Durham) D.: student spl. bus. courses, Am. Inst. Banking. Auditor, controller, asst. v.p. East Tenn. Nat. Bank, Knoxville, 1924-33; cashier Park Nat. Bant, Knoxville, 1933-64, v.p., sr. v.p., 1949-64, chmn. bd., chief exec. officer, 1964—, also dir.; dir. Appalachian Nat. Life Ins. Co. Mem. adv. bd. Carson Newman Coll., 1964—. Trustee, chmn. bd. Ft. Sanders Presbyn. Hosp., Knoxville, 1956-63. Served as capt. AUS, 1942-44. Club: City, Home: Route 12 Knoxville TN 37918 Office: Park National Bank Knoxville TN 37901

DOVENMUEHLE, GEORGE HENRY, mortgage banker; b. Chgo., Jan. 29, 1895; s. Henry C. and Louise K. (Hoffman) D.; A.B., Yale, 1916; m. Mary E. Dyer, June 8, 1922; children—George Henry, Elizabeth D. Asst. mgr. H.F.C. Dovenmuehle & Son, wholesale shoes, Chgo. 1916-24; chmn. Dovenmuehle, Inc., since 1924. Trustee Cancer Found., U. Chgo.; bd. dirs. Metropolitan Housing Council. Served as capt. 344th Inf., U.S. Army, 1917-19. Mem. Mortgage Bankers Assn. Am. (past bd. dirs.), Chgo. Assn. Commerce and Industry (bd. dirs.), Chgo. Real Estate Bd. (v.p. 1935), Chgo. Mortgage Bankers Assn. (past pres.), Alpha Delta Phi. Republican. Conglist. Clubs: Chicago Athletic Assn., Indian Hill; Commercial. Home: 92 Indian Hill Rd Winnetka IL 60093 Office: 135 S La Salle St Chicago IL 60603

DOVER, EUGENIA RUBLE, librarian; b. Lott, Tex., Aug. 13, 1900; d. Robert and Mary (McCreary) Ruble; student Baylor U., 1916-19, Cadek Conservatory Music, Chattanooga, 1926-29; charter certification med. librarianship, Med. Library Assn., 1954; m. John Earl Dover, Oct. 7, 1919; 1 son, John Earl. Library asst. St. Louis Pub. Library, 1941-44; asst. librarian Temple U., Schs. Dentistry and Pharmacy, 1945-5O; asst. librarian N.Y. Med. Coll.-Flower and Fifth Av. Hosps., 1950-53, librarian, 1953—. Mem. Med. Library Assn. Home: 616 E Lincoln Av Mt Vernon NY 10552 Office: NY Med Coll Flower and Fifth Av Hosps New York City NY 10029

DOVER, JAMES BURRELL, ins. co. exec.; b. Dawson, Ala., June 2, 1927; s. Doyle and Essie (Rucks) D.; B.S., U. Ala., 1957; m. Margaret Moody, Aug. 7, 1954; children—Suzanne, James Donaldson. Chief examiner Ala. Ins. Dept., 1957-61; with Am. Amicable Life Ins. Co., Waco, Tex., 1961—, asst. sec., 1965-69, sec., 1969—; sec., dir. U.S. Life Ins. Co., Waco, 1968—, Alico Mgmt. Co., Waco, 1968—. Served with USNR, 1950-52; Korea. Home: 640 Cardinal St Waco TX 76710 Office: 425 Austin St Waco TX 76703

DOW, ALDEN BALL, architect; b. Midland, Mich., Apr. 10, 1904; s. Herbert Henry and Grace A. (Ball) D.; student U. Mich., 1923-26, D.Arch. (hon.), 1960; B.Arch., Columbia, 1931; A.F.D. (hon.), Hillsdale Coll., 1960, Albion Coll., 1964, Mich. State U., 1966; m. Vada Bennett, Sept. 16, 1931; children—Michael Lloyd, Mary Lloyd, Barbara Alden. Architect, pres. Alden B. Dow Assos., Inc., Midland, 1933—. Mem. Mich. Cultural Commn., 1961-63, Mich. Council for Arts, 1963-65, mem. environmental arts com., 1967. Pres., Herbert H. and Grace A. Dow Found. Diplome de Grand Prix for residential architecture in U.S., Paris Internat. Expn., 1937. Registered architect, Ariz., Ohio, Mich., N.Y., N.C., Tex., Fla. Fellow A.I.A. (pres. Saginaw Valley chpt. 1948-49); mem. Nat. Council Archtl. Registration, Am., Mich. (past pres., dir.) socs. architects, Mich. Engrng. Soc., Guild for Religious Architecture, Archtl. League N.Y., Theta Delta Chi, Alpha Rho Chi. Clubs: Country (Midland, Mich.); Saginaw (Mich.); Saginaw Bay Yacht (Bay City, Mich.). Author: Reflections, 1970. Home: 315 Post St Midland MI 48640

DOW, CHARLES WILLIAM, finance exec.; b. Marion, Ia., May 10, 1906; s. Lewis C. and Alice (Lillie) D.; B.S., Ia. State U., 1929. With Equitable Life Assurance Soc., N.Y.C., 1935-56, pres., 1956; with C.I.T. Financial Corp., 1957-71, formerly chmn. finance com. Bd. dirs. Huntington Hosp.; chmn. bd. govs. Human Resources Center. Home: Blueberry Hill Northport NY 11768

DOW, DAVID, educator; b. Ann Arbor, Mich., Aug. 24, 1912; s. Earl Wilbur and Sybil Mathilda (Pettee) D.; A.B., U. Mich., 1933, J.D., 1936; m. Sarah Pierce, Aug. 16, 1939 (dec. 1948); children—Philip Summer, Alice Pettee; m. 2d, Bneta Peterson, July 1, 1950; 1 dau., Jean. Admitted to N.Y. bar, 1938, practiced in N.Y.C., 1938-43; asst. to dir. Los Alamos Labs., 1944-45; asso. prof. law U. Neb., 1946-47, prof. law, 1947- -, acting dean Law Sch., 1954-55, former dean. Recipient Distinguished Teaching award U. Neb., 1957. Mem. Am., Neb. bar assns., Phi Beta Kappa, Phi Kappa Sigma. Home: 2710 Sewell St Lincoln NB 68502

DOW, DONOVAN WILLIAM, educator, biologist; b. Ames, Ia. Instr., Ia. State U., 1946-47; asst. prof. biology Johns Hopkins, 1947-50, asso. prof., 1950-62, prof., 1962--, chmn. dept., 1963-69; vis. lectr. Stanford, 1970-71. Active Boy Scouts Am., 4-H Club. Served with AUS, 1940-46. Mem. Am. Soc. Biologists, Md. Biologists, A.A.A.S., Am. Acad. Arts and Scis., Phi Beta Kappa.

DOW, EDWARD FRENCH, educator; b. Falmouth, Me., Apr. 19, 1901; s. William Edward and Mabel (French) D.; B.S., Bowdoin Coll., 1925; A.M., Harvard, 1926, Ph.D., 1932; m. Amy Burnell, June 30, 1930; children—Ruth, Mary, Jean, David, Instr. polit. sci. Case-Western U., 1926-27, Dartmouth, 1927-28; asso. prof. govt. U. Me., Orono, 1929-38, prof. govt., 1938- 66, prof. polit. sci., 1966-69, head dept. history, govt., 1932-66, originator, dir. pub. mgmt. program, 1945-66, vis. prof. polit. sci., 1971-72; prof. bus. adminstrn. Husson Coll., Bangor, Me., 1969-71; dir. New Eng. Mgrs. Inst., 1946-66. Trial justice, Penobscot County, 1942-54; chmn. Me. Personnel Bd., 1941-46; chmn. Employees Retirement System Me., 1942- 46. Mem. Internat. City Mgrs. Assn. (hon.), Am. Polit. Sci. Assn., Phi Kappa Phi. Author monographs including: County Government in Maine, 1952. Contbr. articles to various publs. Home: 30 N Main St Orono ME 04473

DOW, FREDERICK WARREN, educator; b. Boston, Aug. 2, 1917; s. Frederick Vincent and Marcia (McMahon) D.; B.S. in Chemistry, Boston Coll., 1940; M.S. in Physical Chemistry, U. Mass., 1942; A.M. in Ednl. Psychology, Yale, 1950, Ph.D. in U. Adminstrn., 1955; m. Patricia Rathbone, Sept. 2, 1944; children—Meryl (Mrs. Richard Wayne Brand), Frederick Warren, Bradford Rathbone, Martha Treleven. Various mgmt. positions Dow Chemical Co., 1950-67, mng. dir., France, 1963-66, gen. mgr. Latin Am., Pacific, Office of Asso. Cos., Midland, Mich., 1966-67; Hayes Healy prof. marketing Grad. Sch. Bus., U. Notre Dame, 1967—; sr. partner Dow Kennedy and Asso., mgmt. cons., Notre Dame. Served to maj. AUS, 1942-46. Decorated Air medal, Bronze Star. Mem. Am. Chemical Soc., Sigma Xi, Phi Kappa Phi. Clubs: Union League (N.Y.C.); Travelers (Paris). Home: 1804 E Jefferson South Bend IN 46617 Office: College Business Administration Univ Notre Dame Notre Dame IN 46556

DOW, HAROLD EUGENE, former ins. exec.; b. New Haven, Sept. 1, 1912; s. Milton W. and Madeline M. (Young) D; B.S. summa cum laude, Harvard, 1933, M.A., 1935; M.A., U. Vt., 1934; m. Phyllis I. Bickford, Sept. 17, 1938; children—Ronald R., Carolyn L., Barbara B., Marilyn G. With Prudential Ins. Co. Am., 1935-70, asst. actuary, 1947-49, asso. actuary, 1949-50, 2d v.p., 1590-57, v.p. charge Northeastern home office, Boston, 1957-62, sr. v.p. planning and devel. dept., Newark, 1962-66, sr. v.p. ins. services, 1966-70. Mem. Harding Twp. Zoning Bd. Fellow Soc. Actuaries; mem. Phi Beta Kappa. Presbyn. (pres. bd. trustees). Clubs: Canoe Brook Country; Harvard of N.J.

DOW, HERBERT HENRY, corp. ofcl.; b. Midland, Mich., Aug. 6, 1927; s. Willard Henry and Martha (Pratt) D.; grad. Hotchkiss Sch.; B.S., Mass. Inst. Tech., 1952; m. Barbara Clarke, Sept. 16, 1951; children—Dana, Willard Henry II, Pamela. With Dow Chem. Co., Midland, Mich., 1952—, dir., 1953—, sec., 1968—, also sec. exec. com., mem. finance com.; dir. First Nat. Bank & Trust Co. Midland. Home: 2301 W Sugnet Rd Midland MI 48640 Office: Dow Chemical Co Midland MI 48640

DOW, JAMES WILSON, physician, educator; b. Worcester, Mass., Sept. 8, 1917; s. Edwin Arthur and Lily (Caton) D.; B.S., Harvard, 1941; M.D., Tufts U., 1944; m. Helen Louise Pollard, Mar. 10, 1945; children-Duncan, Kate; m. 2d, Beverly Anne Brooks, May 26, 1967;

1 son, James Bichanan. Intern R.I. Hosp., Providence, 1944-45; resident Lahey Clinic, Boston, 1945-46, House Good Samaritan, Brookline, Mass., 1946-47, Peter Bent Brigham Hosp., Boston, 1947-49; practice medicine specializing in cardiology and biomed. engring., Boston, 1948-58, Phila., 1958-62. Chgo., 1966—; instr. medicine, dir. Circulation Lab., Children's Med. Center, Boston, 1949- 51; asst. prof. medicine Tufts Med. Sch., also dir. Circulation Lab., Boston Cityy Hosp., 1953-58; adj. prof. med. sci., dir. biomed. engring. tng. program Drexel Inst. Tech., 1960-62; head biophys. scis. sect. tng. br. Nat. Inst. Gen. Med. Scis., NIH, 1962-66; prof. medicine U. Ill. Med. Center, 1966-70; prof. bioengring., head bioengring. program, prof. biomed. engring., prof. medicine U. Ill. at Chgo. Circle Coll. Engring., 1966—; chmn. biomed. engring. Rush Presbyn. St. Luke's Med. Center, Chgo., 1970—. Home: 495 Sheridan Rd Evanston IL 60202 Office: 1752 W Congress Pky Chicago IL 60612

DOW, JOHN GOODCHILD, congressman; b. N.Y.C., May 6, 1905; s. Joy Wheeler and Elizabeth (Goodchild) D.; A.B., Harvard, 1927; M.A., Columbia, 1937; m. Harriet Dow, Oct. 18, 1930; children—Thomas, Diantha (Mrs. Walter B. Schull), Sophia. Engaged as systems analyst for industry, 1930-64; asst. mgr. systems and procedures ACF Industries, Inc., 1961-64; mem. 89th, 90th and 92d Congresses, 27th Congl. Dist. N.Y.; staff aide to various congressmen, 1969-70. Chmn. zoning Bd. Appeals, Grand View, N.Y., 1963-64. Chmn. Rockland County Mental Health Fund drive, 1958; dep. dir. civil def., Grand View, 1951-64. Dem. candidate for N.Y. State Senate, 1954, N.Y. State Assembly, 1956, supr. Orangetown, N.Y., 1963; chmn. Orangetown Dem. Com., 1957-62; del. Dem. Nat. Conv., 1968. Episcopalian. Home: MD 16 Grand Av Newburgh NY 12550 Office: House Office Bldg Washington DC 20515

DOW, JOHN RENEAU, bakery exec.; b. Oak Bluffs, Mass., May 3, 1898; s. Ernest Wentworth and Carrie Ann (Reneau) D.; A.B., William Jewell Coll., 1922; m. Marjorie Reed, June 1, 1923. Comml. air pilot, 1920-21; mgr. Grennan Bakers, Inc., St. Louis, 1925-26; gen. supt. prodn. Schulze Baking Co., Kansas City, Mo., 1927-35; gen. mgr. sales, prodn. Inter-state Bakeries Corp., 1935-39, v.p., 1940-47, dir., 1943—, exec. v.p., 1940-57, pres., 1957-64, vice chmn., chief exec., 1964, chmn. bd., chief exec., 1956- -, chmn. exec. com., 1967—; chmn. bd., dir. Interstate Brands Corp., 1970—; dir. Starlight Theater Assn. (Kansas City), Commerce Trust Co. (Kansas City). Vice pres., mem. exec. com. Am. Royal. Served as 2d lt. AUS, U.S. Army, 1918-19. Dir. Midwest Research Inst., Kansas City; trustee U. Mo. at Kansas City. Mem. N.A.M., Am. Bakers Assn. (bd. dirs., chmn. bd. govs., exec. com.), Am. Inst. Baking (Chgo. bd. dirs., exec. com.), Kansas City Crime Commn. (bd. dirs.), Phi Gamma Delta. Conglist. Clubs: Saddle and Sirloin (bd. dirs.), Kansas City (v.p.), U. (Kansas City, Mo.); Rancheros Visitadores (Santa Barbara, Cal.); Kansas City 711, River; Mission Hills Country. Home: 6401 Sagamore Rd Mission Hills Shawnee Mission, KS 66208. Office: 12 E Armour Kansas City MO 64111

DOW, LOUIS ARNOLD, educator; b. Shelbyville, Ind., Apr. 25, 1927; s. James Amie and Emma (Alfrey) D.; B.S., Ind. U., 1949, M.B.A., 1951, Ph.D., 1954; children by previous marriage—Christopher Louis, Scott Stuart, Shannon Michal; m. 2d, Mary Carolyn Green, June 1, 1967; 1 son, Louis Ramsey. Teaching fellow marketing and econs. Ind. U., 1951-53; asst. prof. econs. U. Ark., 1953-55; asst. prof. econs. U. Okla., 1955-61; asso. prof. econs. N.C. State U., Raleigh, 1961-66; prof. econs. Ga. State Coll., 1966-67; prof. econs. U. Houston, 1967-70, chmn. dept. econs., 1968-70; vis. prof. econs. U. Ala., Birmingham, 1970-71, prof. econs., 1971—; lectr. Middle-Mgmt. Program, USAF, Tinker AFB, 1960; prin. investigator for area devel. study in Western N.C. for Dept. Commerce, 1962-64; NSF vis. scientist Ark. State U., 1970. Served with USNR, 1945. Mem. Am., So. econ. assns., Southwestern Social Sci. Assn., Beta Gamma Sigma, Omicron Delta Epsilon, Lambda Chi Alpha. Democrat. Unitarian-Universalist. Author: Business Fluctuations in a Dynamic Economy, 1968. Contbr. articles profl. jours. Home: 3045 Sterling Rd Birmingham AL 35213

DOW, ROBERT NESBITT, Jr., pub. relations cons.; b. Jacksonville, Fla., Oct. 10, 1917; s. Robert Nesbitt and Louise (Haile) D.; student pub. schs.; m. Martha Ayres Sayer, Jan. 15, 1942; children—Cameron Sayer, Robin Haile, Lauren Ainsley. With Jacksonville Jour., 1935-59, mng. editor, 1950-59, editor-in-chief, 1959; dir. pub. relations Hubbard, Duckett Mason & Dow, Inc., 1959—. Col. Fla. N.G., 1946—. Served as maj. USAAF, 1942-45. Decorated D.F.C. with oak leaf cluster, Air medal. Recipient Distinguished Service award U.S. Jr. C. of C. Presbyn. Club: University. Home: 2750 San Fernando Rd Jacksonville FL 32217 Office: 1420 Flagler Av Jacksonville FL 32202

DOW, STERLING, historian; b. Portland, Me., Nov. 19, 1903; s. Sterling Tucker and Alice (Verrill) D.; A.B., Harvard, 1925; Fiske Scholar, Trinity Coll., Cambridge, Eng., 1925-26; A.M., Harvard, 1928, Ph.D., 1936; student Am. Sch. Classical Studies, Athens, Greece, 1931-36 (Guggenheim fellow, 1934- 35, excavated at Corinth, 1934); LL.D., U. Cal. at Berkeley; Litt.D., St. Francis Coll.; L.H.D., Boston Coll.; m. Elizabeth Sanderson Flagg, 1931; children—Elizabeth, Sterling III. Instr., tutor Harvard, 1936-41, asso. prof., 1941-46, prof. history and Greek, 1946-49, John E. Hudson prof. archaeology, 1949- 70, prof. emeritus, 1970—; vis. prof. Greek civilization and history Boston Coll., 1970—; Sather prof. U. Cal. at Berkeley, 1964; Ann. prof. Am. Sch. Classical Studies, Athens, 1966-67. Served OSS, Washington and Cairo, 1942-44; war archivist, Harvard, 1944-45. A founder Tchrs. of Classics in New Eng., pres. 1947-60, Am. Research Center in Egypt, trustee, 1950-53. 55-59; trustee Byzantine Inst., Radcliffe Coll., 1953-59, El Centro Arqueologico Hispano-Americano; adv. bd. Guggenheim Found., 1955-67. Recipient Guggenheim fellowship, 1959, 66-67. Mem. Archaeol. Inst. Am. (pres. 1946-48, hon. pres. 1949—), Am. Philol. Assn., Classical Assn. New Eng. (pres. 1955-56), Am. Classical League, Soc. for Promotion Hellenic Studies (hon. life London, Eng.), Soc. Promotion Roman Studies (hon. Am. sec.), Cambridge (William and Frances White Emerson scholar), Mass. hist. socs., Council Basic Edn., Deutsches Archaeologisches Inst. (hon.), Phi Beta Kappa (hon.) Club: Tavern (Boston) Author: various monographs and articles in archaeol., hist. and philol. jours. in U.S. and abroad. Home: 159 Brattle St Cambridge MA Office: Widener Library 690 Cambridge MA 02138

DOW, WILBUR EGERTON, Jr., lawyer; b. Bklyn., Aug. 5, 1906; s. Wilbur Egerton and Minnie Chloe (Oltman) D.; student U. Wash., 1925-28, U. So. Calif., 1931-32; LL.B., N.Y. U., 1934; m. Ruth Elizabeth Paul, Sept. 2, 1931; children—William Paul, Lynn Elizabeth, Ruth Lee. Admitted to N.Y. bar, 1936; specializing in admiralty, N.Y.C., 1936—. Mcht. marine license unlimited master; N.Y. harbor, Hudson River pilot; officer, dir. s.s. cos.; leader Dow Expdn. to Magnetic North Pole, 1954. Pres. bd. trustees Sailors Snug Harbor. Mem. Soc. Naval Architects and Marine Engrs., Maritime Law Assn., Assn. Bar City of N.Y., Am. Bar Assn., Marine Soc. City N.Y. (pres.), Delta Tau Delta. Clubs: Down Town Assn. (N.Y.C.). Home: 38 Sherwood Rd Short Hills NJ 07078 also Pine Point Lake George NY 12845 Office: 80 Broad St New York City NY 10004

DOW, WILLIAM GOULD, elec. engr., educator; b. Faribault, Minn., Sept. 30, 1895; s. James Jabez and Myra Amelia (Brown) D.; B.S., U. Minn., 1916, E.E., 1917; M.S.E., U. Mich., 1929; m. Edna Lois Sontag. Oct. 24, 1924 (dec. Feb. 1963); children—Daniel Gould, David Sontag; m. 2d, Katherine Bird Keene, Apr. 2, 1968. Diversified engring. and bus. experience, 1917-26; faculty, dept. elec. engring. U. Mich., Ann Arbor, 1926-65, prof. elec. engring., 1945-65, chmn. dept. elec. engring., 1958-64, prof. emeritus, 1966—, sr. research geophysicist Space Physics Research Lab., 1966-71; electronics cons. Nat. Bur. Standards, 1945-55; research staff, Radio Research Lab., Harvard, 1943-45, assignment U.K., winter 1944-45; sci. adv. com. Harry Diamond Labs., 1953-64. Mem. vacuum tube devel. com. NDRC, World War II; European vacuum tube research survey, 1953; mem. rocket and satellite research panel, 1946-60, U.S. tech. panel on rocketry, IGY, 1956-59. Served as lt. C.E., U.S. Army, World War I. Recipient medal, award in elec. engring. edn. I.E.E.E., 1963. Fellow I.E.E.E. (bd. editors 1941-54); mem. Am. Phys. Soc., Am. Inst. Aerons. and Astronautics, Am. Soc. Engring. Edn., Am. Welding Soc., Nat. Electronics Conf. (dir. 1949-52, chmn. bd., 1951) , A.A.A.S., Engring. Soc. Detroit, Sigma Xi, Tau Beta Pi, Eta Kappa Nu. Mason. Club: Cosmos (Washington). Author: Fundamentals of Engineering Electronics, 1937, rev. 1952; Very High Frequency Techniques (co-author), 2 vols., 1947. Contbr. tech. articles in field. Home: 915 Heatherway Ann Arbor MI 48104

DOWD, DAVID JOSEPH, banker; b. Long Island City, N.Y., June 6, 1924; s. David Joseph and Elsie (Schaeffler) B.; B.S. in Bus. Adminstrn., N.Y. U., 1949; m. Carol Velonis, Sept. 25, 1959; children-Laury, David, Patrick, Carol. Asst. v.p. Irving Trust Co., N.Y.C., 1952-64; v.p. Franklin Nat. Bank, N.Y.C., 1964-66; sr. v.p. Security Nat. Bank, Huntington, N.Y., 1967—; Pres., Suffolk County council Boy Scouts Am., 1969-70. Served with USMCR, 1942- 45, 51-52. Mem. L.I. Bankers Assn. (dir. 1969—), Empire State C. of C. (dir. 1969—). Home: Springwood Path Laurel Hollow NY 11791 Office: 345 Main St Huntington NY 11701

DOWD, FRED A., banker; b. Owen County, Ky., 1906. Chmn. bd., dir. First Nat. Bank of Cin.; dir. Midland Guardian Co., Cin. Gas. & Electric Co., Vulcan Corp., CNO and Tex Pacific R.R., William Powell Co. Clubs: Cin. Country, Queen City, Bankers. Home: The Edgecliff 2200 Victory Pkwy Cincinnati, OH 45206. Office: 4th and Walnut Sts Cincinnati OH 45201

DOWD, JAMES EDWARD, stock exchange exec.; b. Cambridge, Mass., May 18, 1922; s. Batholomew J. and Sarah E. (Connolly) D.; A.B., Boston Coll., 1944, LL.B., 1949; postgrad. Georgetown Sch. Fgn. Service, 1944; m. Marguerite A. O'Donoghue, May 5, 1951; children—Jane E., James Edward, Ann E. Admitted to Mass. bar, 1949; practiced in Boston, 1949-50; asso. Langan, Lawless & Dempsey, 1949- 50; trial atty. SEC, Boston, 1951-55, chief enforcement atty., 1957-65, regional adminstr., 1966-69; pres. Boston Stock Exchange, 1969—, chmn. bd. Boston Stock Exchange Clearing Corp.; br. operating mgr. Westinghouse Electric Corp., N.Y.C., 1955-57. Pres., dir. Charitable Irish Soc.; 1969. Served to 1st lt. AUS, 1943-46. Mem. Am., Fed. bar assns. Home: 50 Princeton Rd Arlington MA 02174 Office: 53 State St Boston MA 02109

DOWD, JOHN COOKE, advt. exec.; b. Lowell, Mass., Mar. 23, 1901; s. Michael Joseph and Della Agatha (Cooke) D.; grad. Harvard, 1920; m. Marguerite McCann, Dec. 15, 1930; children—John Cooke, Carol, Roger, Michael, Paul. Newspaper work Boston Herald Traveler, Manchester (N.H.) Union-Leader, Worcester (Mass.) Post, Washington Post, Lawrence (Mass.) Sun-Telegram, 1920-26; pres. Dowd & Ostreicher, Inc., advt. agy., Boston. 1926-39: pres. Dowd Advt., Boston, 1939—; dir. Charlestown Savs. Bank (Mass.). Trustee Boston Municipal Research Bur., Simmons Coll.; bd. dirs. St. Elizabeth's Hosp., Boston; pres. bd. trustees Cushing Hall, Inc., Boston. Served with USMCR, 1918. Mem. Beacon Soc. Boston. Clubs: Harvard, N.Y. Athletic, Canadian (N.Y.C.); Weston (Mass.) Golf; Algonquin, Harvard (Boston). Home: 192 Meadowbrook Rd Weston MA 02193 Office: 4780 Prudential Tower Boston MA 02199

DOWD, JOSEPH F., trust co. exec. Auditor, L.I. Trust Co., Garden City, N.Y. Office: 1401 Franklin Av Garden City NY 11530*

DOWD, LAURENCE PHILLIPS, educator; b. Ft. Monroe, Va., Oct. 21, 1914; s. William Stuart and Julia (Phillips) D.; B.A., U. Wash., 1938; M.A., U. Hawaii, 1949; Ph.D., U. Mich., 1954; m. Juliet Irene Rudolph, Sept. 7, 1938; children—William L. (dec. 1965), Richard S., Judith I. (Mrs. Stewart Rush). With Lewers & Cooke, Ltd., Honolulu, 1939-40; instr. to asso. prof. U. Wash., 1940-41, 46, 50-55; lectr., dir. Mich. Bus. Execs. Research Conf. of U. Mich., 1957-60; prof. world bus., also dir. Center for World Bus. of San Francisco State Coll., 1960-71, prof. world bus., 1970—; vis. prof. U. Ore., 1969-70. Cons. Far East Trade Promotion, Port of Seattle, 1955-57; trustee Wash. State Internat. Trade Fair, 1950-55; cons. trans-Pacific trade research project Bur. Bus. Research of U. Hawaii, 1962-64. Served from 2d lt. to maj., AUS, 1941-45. Mem. Am. Econ. Assn., Am. Marketing Assn., Assn. Edn. Internat. Bus., Phi Beta Kappa, Beta Gamma Sigma, Phi Kappa Phi. Author: The European Economic Community: Implications for Michigan Business, 1961; Principles of World Business, 1965. Editorial review bd. of Jour. Marketing, 1958—. Home: 3047 Hillside Dr Burlingame CA 94010 Office: San Francisco State Coll San Francisco CA 94132

DOWD, PATRICK JOSEPH, mfg. co. exec.; b. St. Louis, Aug. 22, 1912; s. John William and Lillie (Kanzow) D.; student Washington U., St. Louis; C.P.A., Ark., 1942; grad. Advanced Mgmt. Program, Harvard, 1953; m. Mary Coleman, June 17, 1939; children—Patrick Coleman, Anne Claire. With Monsanto Co., St. Louis, 1941—, treas., 1958—, v.p., 1964—, sec. finance com., 1963-67; pres., dir. Monsanto Internat. Finance Co., 1965—; dir. St. Louis Fed. Savs. & Loan Assn., Mfrs. Bank & Trust Co., St. Louis. Chef chems. br. OPA, 1952. Commr. St. Louis Planned Indsl. Expansion Authority, 1967-69. Bd. dirs. St. Louis Heart Assn.; trustee John and Olga Queeny Ednl. Found. Mem. Am. Inst. C.P.A.'s, Mo. Soc. C.P.A.'s, Financial Execs. Inst., Newcomen Soc. N. Am. Clubs: Mo. Athletic, St. Louis (charter) , Washington U., Harvard Business School (St. Louis) . Home: 246 Woodbourne Dr St Louis MO 63105 Office: 800 N Lindbergh Blvd St Louis MO 63166

DOWD, PAUL L., dept. store exec.; b. Charlestown, Mass., May 5, 1909; s. Joseph and Theresa (Dineen) D.; A.B., Harvard, 1930; m. Mary E. Maguire; children—Paul L., Mary Anne (Mrs. John Deyst), Joseph J., John F., Thomas B., Dennis M., Nora E., Patricia. With R.H. White Co., Boston, 1930-46, div. mdse. mgr., 1943-44; with Filene's, Boston, 1946-56, gen. mgr. Worcester (Mass.) store, 1948-55, mem. mgmt. bd., 1952-56, div. mdse. mgr., Boston, 1955-56; v.p. charge merchandising and publicity Lansburgh's, also gen. mdse. mgr. Lansburgh's, Washington and Langley Park, Md., 1956-59; v.p., gen. mdse. mgr. Loveman, Joseph & Loeb, Birmingham, Bessemer and Montgomery, Ala., 1959-61, pres., 1961-64; v.p. City Stores Co., 1962; pres., mng. dir. Gertz Dept. Stores in L.I., div. Allied Stores CorP., 1964—; v.p. Allied Stores Corp.; tchr. in field. Participant numerous civic activities, Worcester, Birmingham and Jamaica, N.Y. Mem. mcht. adv. council N.Y.U. Sch. Retailing. Served to lt. USNR, 1944-46. Recipient Retail Citizenship award Reader's Digest. 1961, Monte Meacham award of Children's Theatre Conf., Am. Ednl. Theatre Assn., 1962. Club: N.Y. Athletic. Author articles, chpts. in field. Home: 215 Manhasset Woods Rd Manhasset NY 11030 Office: Gertz Dept Store 162-10 Jamaica Av Jamaica NY 11432

DOWD, THOMAS NATHAN, lawyer; b. Sioux City, Ia., Mar. 29, 1917; s. Daniel Thornton and Eva (Willett) D.; A.B., George Washington U., 1939, J. D. with distinction, 1942; m. Mary Catherine Majure, July 18, 1940; children—Margaret Majure (Mrs. Thomas Randall Isgrig), Catherine Eva. Admitted to D.C. bar, 1942, Md. bar, 1958, also U.S. Supreme Ct.; with FBI, 1939-4O; practice in Washington, 1942—; partner firm Pierson, Ball & Dowd, and predecessor, 1945—; general counsel, dir. Potomac Nat. Bank. Served to maj. USMCR, 1942-46. Mem. Am., D.C., FCC bar assns., Phi Beta Kappa, Order of Coif, Phi Eta Sigma, Phi Delta Delta, Pi Kappa Alpha. Clubs: Metropolitan, Congressional Country (Washington); Potomac Hunt, Potomac Polo (owner) (Md.). Operator horse and Angus cattle farm, 1958—. Home: Belvedere Farm Route 3 Gaithersburg MD 20760 Office: Ring Bldg 1200 18th St NW Washington DC 20036

DOWDALL, RICHARD JAMES, lawyer; b. Los Gatos, Cal., July 9, 1925; s. James Reginald and Grace (Pitts) D.; student U. Utah, 1945-46, Ariz. U., Tempe, 1946-47; LL.B., U. Ariz., 1954; m. N. Beryl Tolliver, Aug. 5, 1946; children-Reginald James, Jacquelyn Ann, Douglas Allen, Cynthia Lea. Admitted to Ariz. bar, 1954, since practiced in Tucson; mem. firm Dowdall, Harris, Hull & Terry and predecessor firms, 1954—. Pres., trustee Sch. Bd., 1963—; pres. Ariz. Sch. Bd. Assn., 1970—. Mem. Am., Ariz., Pima County bar assns., Am. Judicature Soc. Home: 1321 Via Caballo Tucson AZ 85704 Office: 250 N Church St Tucson AZ 85701

DOWDEN, RAYMOND BAXTER, educator; b. Coal Valley, Pa., Dec. 25, 1905; s. Samuel Louis and Catherine (Baxter) D. B.A., Carnegie Inst. Tech., 1930; fellow Tiffany Found., Oyster Bay, N.Y., 1931-32; m. Anne Ophelia Todd, Apr. 1, 1934. Tchr., Cherry Lawn Sch., Darien, Conn., 1934-35. Carnegie Inst. Tech., 1930-33; designer Westinghouse Electric Co., 1930; part-time designer Petgen Stained Glass Co., Pitts., 1928-30; part-time tchr. Manchester Ednl. Center, Pitts., 1930-33; tchr., pub. relations dir., 1928; trustee Starr Commonwealth for Boys, Albion, Mich., 1945-55; prof. art Cooper Union Sch. Art and Architecture, N.Y.C., 1936-70, head dept., 1945-67, prof. emeritus, 1970—; dir. Yale-Norfolk (Conn.) Art Sch., 1952-59; free-lance advt., design, illustration, 1936—; works exhibited Soc. Ind. Artists, N.Y.C., G.R.D. Gallery, N.Y.C., Whitney Mus. Biennial, Internat. Water Color shows, Chgo., Elliott Gallery, Pitts., Carnegie Inst., Gulf Gallery, Pitts.; designer Murals for Westinghouse at Chgo. Worlds Fair, 1933, Murals for West Side Center, N.Y.C., stained glass windows St. Mary's Ch., Homestead, Pa. Trustee Mus. Illustration Art. Mem. Am. Inst. Graphic Arts, Tau Sigma Delta. Club: Art Directors (ex-officio mem. scholarship com.) (N.Y.C.). Home: 205 W 15th St New York City NY 10011

DOWDEY, CLIFFORD SHIRLEY, Jr., author; b. Richmond, Va., Jan. 23, 1904; s. Clifford Shirley and Bessie (Bowis) D.: grad. John Marshall High Sch., Richmond, Va., 1921; student Columbia, 1923-25; Litt.D., Ripon Coll.; m. Frances Wilson. July 13, 1944; children—Frances, Sarah. Reporter, book reviewer Richmond News Leader, 1925-26; editorial staff Munseys and Argosy (mags.), book reviewer for N.Y. Sun, 1926-28, editor pulp mags. Dell Pub. Co., 1928- 29, 1933-35; free lance writer, 1929-33, 1935—; lect. in creative writing U. Richmond; has lived in Va., Fla., Conn., Ariz., Tex., Calif., N.C. and N.Y.C., doing research and writing. Guggenheim fellow., 1938. Mem. Soc. Am. Historians. Episcopalian. Author books including: Bugles Blow No More (novel), 1937; (history) Experiment in Rebellion, 1946; Weep for My Brother (novel), 1950; (novel) Jasmine Street 1952; The Proud Retreat, 1953; (history) The Land They Fought For; The Story of the South as the Confederacy, 1832-1865, 1955; The Great Plantation, 1957; History: Death of a Nation, 1958; Lee's Last Campaign (history), 1960; The Wartime Papers of R.E. Lee (editor, writer), 1961; The Seven Days (history), 1964; Lee (1 vol. biography), 1965; The Virginia Dynasties (history), 1969; The Golden Age (history), 1970. Saturday Rev., McCall's, Ladies Home Jour., Holiday, American Heritage, Atlantic MMonthly. Author originals to motion pictures. Home: 2504 Kensington Av Richmond VA 23220

DOWDLE, JOHN WESLEY, Jr., corp. exec.; b. Rome, Ga., Mar. 8, 1926; s. John Wesley and Lucille (Field) D.; B.S., U.S. Mcht. Marine Acad., 1946; LL.B., U. S.C., 1952; LL.M., Georgetown U., 1955, S.J.D., 1958; m. Virginia Louise Sandy, Nov. 23, 1950; children—John Wesley III, Jason Earl, Merriman Lee. Admitted to S.C. bar, 1951, N.C. bar, 1961; atty. Chief Counsel's Office, Internal Revenue Service, Washington, 1955-60; tax atty. R.J. Reynolds Tobacco Co., Winston-Salem, N.C., 1960-62, tax mgr., 1962-70, asst. sec., 1963-70, asst. treas., 1968-70; treas. R.J. Reynolds Industries, Inc., Winston-Salem, 1970—; dir. 1st Union Nat. Bank, Winston-Salem. Mem. N.C. Tax Study Commn., 1963-65. Served to lt. USNR, 1952-54. Mem. Tax Execs. Inst. (v.p. 1967-68). Republican. Episcopalian. Rotarian. Home: 2836 Fairmont Rd Winston-Salem NC 27106 Office: RJ Reynolds Industries 4th and Main Winston-Salem NC 27102

DOWDY, ANDREW HUNTER, physician; b. Longwood, Mo., Nov. 24, 1904; s. Nathaniel M. and Emmaa (Patterson) D.; A.B., Central Coll., 1929; M.D., Washington U., 1931; D.Sc., Central Coll., 1957; m. Helen M. Brandes, August 28, 1930; children—Andrew Hunter, Robert Alan. Intern internal medicine Henry Ford Hosp., Detroit, 1931-34, intern radiology 1934-36, resident radiology, 1936-37; instr., later prof., chmn. dept. radiology, chief radiologist sch. medicine and dentistry U. Rochester, 1937-48, dir. AEC project, 1946-48; dir. Manhattan project, 1943-46; chmn. dept. radiology sch. medicine, U. Cal. at Los Angeles, 1948-66, prof., 1948—, chief radiation biology div. AEC 1948-55, cons., 1955-62. Mem. panel appraisers Handbook Biol. Data, 1950; mem. radiol. safety adv. com. Calif. State Disaster Council, 1950-56, chmn. subcom. radiation exposure; mem. civil def. Cal. State Evaluation Bd. 1951-55. Recipient Certificate of Appreciation for work on gas gangrene U.S. Army-Navy, 1948. Diplomate Am. Bd. of Radiology (certificate of appreciation, 1963). Pan-Am. Med. Assn. Fellow A.A.A.S., Am. Coll. Radiology (gold medal, 1970); mem. Am. Thermographic Soc. (charter), nat., state, local gen. and spl. med. assns. Author many publs. in field cancer theraphy and research, radiology and radiation biology. Home: 1984 Stradella Rd Los Angeles CA 90024

DOWDY, GEORGE THEODORE, educator, economist; b. nr. Eastover, S.C., Mar. 11, 1913; s. William W., Sr., and Alice L. (Shiner) D.; B.S., S.C. State A. and M. Coll., 1937; M.S., Ohio State U., 1947, Ph.D., 1952; m. Ruth B. Ball, Apr. 29, 1939; children—Ann Brenda (Mrs. James A. Brown), George T. With S.C. State Extension Service, 1937-43; county extension agt. Tuskegee Inst., 1947—; cons. O.E.O., 1966, various corps.; dir. Tuskegee Fed. Savs. & Loan Assn. Served with U.S. Army, 1944-46. Mem. Am., So. agrl. econs. assns., Internat. Agr. Assn., Am., So. econ. assns., Assn. Social Sci. Tchrs. (dir., past pres.), Ala. Assn. Coll. Tchrs. and Adminstrs. (pres. 1958-60). Mason

(Shriner, 32). Author: Dictionary of Agricultural Economics and Related Terms, 1966. Contbr. articles profl. jours. Home: 309 Bibb St Tuskegee Institute AL 36088

DOWDY, GEORGE WINSTON, merchant; b. Youngsville, N.C., Mar. 10, 1904; s. Norman Austin and Cora Agnes (Wicker) D.; student pub. schs.; m. Ruth Virginia Crowell, Sept. 29, 1929; children—George Winston, Ruth Crowell. Salesman, then dept. mgr., asst. in buying Belk-Leggett Co., Durham, N.C., 1919-25, asst. mgr., Danville, Va., 1925-27; mgr., treas. Belk's Dept. Store, Concord, N.C., 1927-33; gen. mgr. Belk Bros. Co., Charlotte, N.C., 1933- 68, exec. v.p., 1953-68, chmn. bd. 1968—, also dir.; chmn. bd. Belk Stores Services, Inc., 1969—; past pres: Inter-City Advt. Co., Charlotte; dir. Belk Stores Reciprocal Ins., First Union Nat. Bank N.C., Belk-Doughton Co. (Elkin, N.C.), Belk-Hudson Co. (Orangeburg, S.C.); exec. com. The Belk Stores. Hon. mem. N.C. Gov. Council Occupational Health; mem. U.S. Trade Commn. to Italy, 1956; former vice commr. Housing Authority, Charlotte. Hon. mem. bd. dirs. Mecklenburg County exec. council Boy Scouts Am. Commr. com. Queen's Coll., trustee, past chmn. bldg. com. Decorated French Order Merite Commercial, 1957; named North Carolinian of Year, Alpha Kappa Psi, 1954, Retailer of Year N.C. Mchts. Assn., 1957; recipient Algernon Sidney Sullivan award Queen's Coll., 1954; Silver Beaver award Boy Scouts Am. Mem. Charlotte C. of C. (past pres., dir., exec. com.), Nat. Retail Mchts. (pres. 1958, dir. N.C. 1963—; gold medal 1964), N.C. (past pres.), Charlotte (past pres.) mchts. assns., United Arts Council, Alpha Kappa Psi. Methodist. Mason (Shriner). Clubs: Charlotte Country, Charlotte City, Good Fellows (dir.). Quail Hollow (Charlotte). Home: 1871 Cassamia Pl Charlotte NC 28211 Office: 115-127 E Trade St Charlotte NC 28201

DOWDY, JOHN, congressman; b. Waco, Tex., Feb. 11, 1912; s. Carroll Vernard and Lula Mae (Jamison) D.; student East Tex. Bapt. Coll., 1929-31; m. Mary Ellen Fite, Sept. 14, 1932 (dec. Dec. 6, 1943); children—Carol Sue (Mrs. Forrest Earl Roberts, Jr.), John; m. 2d, Johnnie D. Riley, Aug. 20, 1946. Admitted to Tex. bar, 1940; practiced law, Athens, 1940-52; dist. atty. 3d jud. dist. of Tex., 1944-52. Mem. 82d (elected spl. election 1952) also 83d to 92d Congresses, 2d Dist. Tex. Democrat. Methodist. Odd Fellow. Kiwanian. Home: Athens TX 75751 Office: House Office Bldg Washington DC 20525

DOWDY, JOHN WESLEY, clergyman, educator; b. Albertville, Ala., Jan. 7, 1912; s. Sherman and Beulah Bee (Strange) D.; A.B., Okla. Baptist U., 1934, D.D., 1960; Th.B., So. Bapt. Theol. Sem., Louisville, 1939, Th.M., 1940; Th.D., Central Baptist Theol. Sem., Kansas City, 1945; M.R.E., 1948; m. Floy Weaver Thurston, Apr. 2, 1930; children—John Wesley, David, Floyd William, Paul Philip. Ordained elder, ministry of Baptist Church, 1933, served pastorates in Shawnee, Okla., 1933-34, Haskell, Okla., 1934-36, English, Ky., 1936-39, Wheatley, Ky., 1939-4O; asst. exec. sec. Ky. Baptist Gen. Assn., Louisville, 1940-43; asst. gen. supt. Mo. Baptist Gen. Assn., Kansas City, 1943-45; prof. systematic theology Central Baptist Theol. Sem., 1945-48; pres. S.W. Baptist Coll., Bolivar, Mo., 1948-61; pastor 1st Bapt. Ch., Guthrie, Okla., 1961—. Moderator Central Bapt. Assn.; bd. dirs. Bapt. Gen. Conv. of Okla. Mem. Logan County Hosp., Assn.; chmn lay adv. bd. Alverno Heights Hosp.; chmn. Guthrie Human Relations Com. Bd. dirs. United Community Chest Fund; trustee Okla. Bapt. U. Decorated Order of Red Cross of Constantine. Democrat. Mason (33, Shriner) ; mem. Order of Eastern Star, DeMolay Legion Honor (hon. life) , Rotarian. Home 410 E Mansur St Guthrie OK 73044 Office: First Bapt Ch Guthrie OK 73044

DOWDY, LEWIS CARNEGIE, coll. pres.: b. Eastover, S.C., Sept. 1, 1917; s. William Wallace and Alice (Shivar) D.; A.B., Allen U., 1939, Litt.D., 1962; M.A., Ind. State Coll., 1949; Ed.D., Ind. U., 1965; m. Elizabeth Smith, June 26, 1943; children—Lewis Carnegie Lemuel, Elizabeth. Sch. prin., Eastover, Aiken. S.C., 1939-51; faculty A. and T. Coll., Greensboro, N.C., 1951—, dean instr., 1960-64, pres., 1964—. Pres. Greensboro Human Relations Coll.; active United Fund Greensboro, Greensboro Community Council. Mem. N.C.Coll. and Univs. Assn., Nat. Assn. State Univs. and Land-Grant Colls. (exec. com., chmn. council of presidents) , N.E.A., N.C. Tchrs. Assn., Assn. Social Sci. Tchrs., Nat. Soc. Study Edn., Greensboro C. of C., Kappa Delta Pi, Sigma Rho Sigma, Alpha Kappa Mu. Democrat. Baptist. Rotarian. Club: Greensboro Men's. Author articles. Home: 900 Bluford St Greensboro NC 27411

DOWE, THOMAS WHITFIELD, coll. dean; b. Eagle Pass, Tex., Jan. 26, 1919; s. James Watson and Bertie E. (Brown) D.; B.S., Tex. A. and M. U., 1942; M.S., Kan. State U., 1947, Ph.D., 1954; m. Elizabeth Ann Faubion, May 29, 1943; children—Kelly Ann, Thomas Whitfield, Leslie Elizabeth. Asst. prof. S.D. State U., 1947; asso. prof. U. Neb., 1948-51, prof., 1954-58; dir. Agr. Expt. Sta. U. Vt., Burlington, 1958-65, dean Coll. Agr. and Home Econs., dir. Agr. Expt. Sta., 1965—, also prof. animal and dairy sci. Corporator, Burlington Savs. Bank. Served to capt. AUS, 1942- 46: ETO. Decorated Bronze Star medal. Mem. Am. Soc. Animal Sci., Sigma Xi, Gamma Sigma Delta. Home: 55 Crescent Rd Burlington VT 05401

DOWELL, DAWSON ARNOLD, educator, physician; b. Hamlin, Kan., Feb. 14, 1906; s. George W. and Emily (Arnold) D.; student Washburn Coll., 1923-26; B.S., Creighton U., 1929, M.D., 1931; m. Anna Clara Shaeffer, Oct. 6, 1934; children—Mary Susan, George William, Kathleen Helen, John Arnold, Margaret Ann, Patricia Elizabeth, Teresa Jane. Intern Creighton Meml. St. Joseph's Hosp., Omaha, 1931-32; resident radiology Creighton U. Allied Hosps., 1932-36; practice radiology, Omaha, 1937-42; mem. faculty Creighton U. Sch. Medicine, 1948—, prof. radiology, chmn. dept., 1963—; dir. dept. radiology Creighton Meml. St. Joseph's Hosp., 1963—; cons. VA; mem. staff Douglas County, Bergen hosps. Served with M.C., AUS, 1942-46; MTO. Fellow Am. Coll. Radiology; mem. A.M.A., Am. Roentgen Ray Soc., Am. Radium Soc., Radiol. Soc. N.Am., Am. Assn. U. Profs., Am. Assn. Study Neoplastic Diseases, V.F.W., Phi Rho Sigma, Alpha Omega Alpha, Alpha Sigma Nu. Democrat. Home: 426 N 38th St Omaha NB 68131

DOWELL, DUDLEY, former ins. exec.; b. Little Rock, Ark., Aug. 24, 1903; s. Martin L. and Sallie E. (Pearson) D.; grad. Little Rock High Sch.; LL.D., U. Ark., 1948; m. Elizabeth Smith, Aug. 27, 1926; children—Dudley, Dana. Clk. N.Y. Life Ins. Co., Little Rock, 1921-25, cashier, Jackson, Miss., 1925-27, asst. mgr., Little Rock, 1927-29. mgr., Butte, Mont., 1929-36, mgr., Seattle, 1936-39, supr. Allegheny dept., Pitts., 1939-41, insp. of agys., 1941, supt. agys., home office, 1941, asst. v.p., 1942, v.p. 1943-45, v.p. in charge agys., N.Y.C., 1945-54, exec. v.p., 1954-62, pres., 1962-69, dir., 1958—, chmn. exec. com., 1959-69; mem. adv. bd. dirs. Worthen Bank & Trust Co., Little Rock. Mem. bd. Ark. Council on Econ. Edn.; mem. devel. council U. Ark.; trustee Ark. Arts Center. Pres. Little Rock Underwriters Assn., 1928, Butte Life Underwriters Assn., 1936, Seattle Mgrs. and Gen. Agts. Assn., 1937, Life. Ins. Agy., Mgmt. Assn., 1948. Episcopalian. Clubs: Church, University (N.Y.C.); Eden Isle Country (Heber Springs, Ark.,) Country, Capitol (Little Rock, Ark.). Home: Route 2 Box 338C Eden Isle Heber Springs AR 72543 Office: Worthen Bank Bldg Little Rock AR 72201

DOWELL, JOHN CARSON, tire co. exec.; b. Vandalia, Mo., Nov. 13, 1909; s. George F. and Effie (Creach) D.; B.A., Mo. Valley Coll., 1933; student Northwestern U., 1935; m. Mary Lou Harkness, Feb. 5, 1948; children—Kay Lynn (Mrs. Robert Kopsack), Carlene, John C. Asst. to treas., instr. acctg. Mo. Valley Coll., 1933-35; with Goodyear Tire & Rubber Co., Akron, Ohio, 1935-54, store supr., 1952-54; with The Kelly-Springfield Tire Co., Cumberland, Md., 1954—, asst. sales mgr., 1954-58, asst. to pres., 1959-61, v.p. custom brand sales, 1961-63, exec. v.p., 1963-69, pres., 1970—; dir. Liberty Trust Co. of Md., Queen City Brewing Co., Chesapeake and Potomac Tel. Co. of Md. Chmn. jud. selection commn. 4th Jud. Circuit Md., 1971; pres. Allegany County Econ. Devel. Co., 1967-68; pres. County United Fund, 1966. Mem. adv. bd. Sacred Heart Hosp.; trustee Md. State Colls. Mem. Sigma Nu. Democrat. Presbyn. Mason (Shriner). Club: Center. Home: 4 Forest Dr Cumberland MD 21502 Office: PO Box 300 Cumberland MD 21502

DOWEY, EDWARD ATKINSON, Jr., educator; b. Phila., Feb. 21, 1918; s. Edward Atkinson and Margaret (Turner) D.; B.A., Lafayette Coll., 1940, then D.D.; B.D., Princeton Theol. Sem., 1943; M.A., Columbia, 1947; Th.D., U. Zurich, 1949; D.D., Lewis and Clark Coll.; m. Lois Montgomery, Jan. 22, 1954; children—Edward Montgomery, Elizabeth Margaret. Ordained to ministry United Presbyn. Ch.; instr. Lafayette Coll., 1949-51; asst. prof. Columbia, 1951-53; asso. prof. McCormick Theol. Sem., 1953-56; prof. history Christian doctrine Princeton Theol. Sem., 1956—; vis. lectr. Princeton, Drew Theol. Sem., Bryn Mawr Coll., San Francisco Theol. Sem. Trustee Lafayette Coll.; bd. dirs. Presbyn. Life, Westminster Found. at Princeton U. Served to lt. USNR, 1943-46. Guggenheim fellow, Zurich, 1961-62. Mem. Am. Soc. Ch. History, Presbyn. Hist. Soc., Zwingliverein (Zurich) , Phi Beta Kappa. Democrat. Author: The Knowledge of God in Calvin's Theology, 1952; Commentary on the Confession of 1967, 1968. Contbr. articles profl. jours. Home: 52 Mercer St Princeton NJ 08540

DOWGRAY, JOHN GRAY LAIRD, Jr., educator, univ. ofcl.; b. Kansas City, Mo., Jan. 10, 1922; s. John Gray Laird and Mabel (Holmes) D.; student Rockhurst Coll., 1939-41; A.B. with distinction in History, U. Kansas City, 1947; M.S., U. Wis., 1947, Ph.D. in History, 1956; m. Joanne Carol Dooley, Jan. 17, 1971; children by previous marriage—John Gray Laird III, Laurie Louise. Instr. history U. Mo. at Kansas City, 1952-56, asst. prof., 1956-59, asso. prof., 1959-63, prof., 1963-69, coordinator grad. studies, 1961-64, dean grad. studies, 1964-65, dean faculties, 1965-69; v.p. acad. affairs U. Tulsa, 1969—. Mem. Orgn. Am. Historians, Am. Studies Assn. Home: 6234 S 72d E Av Tulsa OK 74145

DOWLER, FRANCIS WALTON, lawyer; b. London, Ont., Can. June 19, 1917; s. Robert Henry and Margaret Katherine (Peart) D.; B.A. with honours in Bus., U. Western Ont., 1941; LL.B., Osgoode Hall Law Sch., 1944; m. Dorothy Louise Davis, July 7, 1951; children—Sandra Margaret Louise, Sheila Bernice, Daphne Louise. Read law with Fraser, Beatty, Tucker, McIntosh & Stewart, 1941- 44; called to bar Ont., 1944, named Queen's counsel, 1959; practice in London, 1947—; partner Ivey & Dowler, 1951—. Mem. Delta Upsilon. Mem. United Ch. of Can. Clubs: London, London Hunt and Country. Home: 968 Wellington St London 11 Ontario Canada

DOWLER, LLOYD, coll. dean; b. Chugwater, Wyo., Nov. 1, 1911; s. Hamilton R. and Gertrude (Leggitt) D.; B.S., U. Wyo., 1935, M.S., 1941; m. Goldie Blanche Smith, Mar. 3, 1935; 1 dau., Mary Dolores. Tchr. vocational agr. Wyo., 1935-43; state supr. agrl. edn., Carson City, Nev., 1946-48; intermediate vocational instr. Fresno State Coll., 1948-51, dean agr., 1951-60, now head dept. agr., dean Farm Sch., dean Sch. Agr. Mem. Cal. State Bd. Agr., 1964-67. Served with USNR, 1943-46. Mem. Farm Bur., Am. Assn. U. Profs., Cal. Soc. Ednl. Adminstrs., Cal. State Employees Assn., Assn. Cal. State Coll. Instrs., Cal. Agrl. Tchrs. Assn. Mason (Shriner). Home: 887 Swift Fresno CA 93704

DOWLIN, CHARLES EDWIN, state librarian; b. Laird, Colo., June 3, 1933; s. Ross Everett and Fern May (Peterson) D.; B.S., U. Colo., 1955, M. Personnel Services, 1956; M.A., U. Denver, 1963; m. Clara May Nichol, Sept. 5, 1960; children—Patrick Edwin, Kerry Anne. Successively inventory control clk., prodn. control clk., statistician Sundstrand Aviation, Denver, 1959-62; library trainee VA Hosp., Denver, 1962-63; city librarian Provo City Corp., Utah, 1963-67; head, catalog center, State Library Ohio, 1967-68, head, library devel., 1968-70; state librarian N.M. State Library, Santa Fe, 1970—. Served with AUS, 1956-59. Mem. A.L.A., N.M. Library Assn., Delta Sigma Pi. Rotarian. Contbr. articles to profl. jours. Home: 2104 Calle Tecolote Santa Fe NM 87501 Office: PO Box 1629 Santa Fe NM 87501

DOWLING, ALLEN VINCENT, financial editor; b. Madison, Neb., Feb. 4, 1913; s. William L. and Willa C. (Allen) D.; student Neb. State U., 1932, U. Md., 1933-35; m. Gretchen L. Hastings, June 8, 1940; children—Patrick Allen, Mary M., Martha A. Newspaper editor and reporter, Washington, Chgo., Detroit, N.Y.C., Omaha, 1935-46; pub. relations in motion pictures and utilities, 1946-49; mgr. agencies Ohio Nat. Life Ins. Co., 1949-53; v.p., dir. mem. exec. com. Franklin Life Ins. Co., Springfield, Ill., 1954-58; pres. North Am. Accident Ins. Co., Chgo., 1958-60, North Am. Co. for L., H. & A. Ins., 1960, Chgo. Nat. Life Ins. Co., Mgmt. Assos. North Am.; chmn. North Am. Mgmt. Corp., City Investment Assos.; pres. Chgo. Mgmt. Corp., 1962- 67; financial editor Los Angeles Herald-Examiner, Hearst Corp., 1967—. First appointee, dir. gen. services State of Ill. Past dir. Neb. Resources Found. Clubs: Bob O' Link Golf, Pine Tree Golf. Home: 156 S Swall Dr Beverly Hills CA 90211 Office: 1111 S Broadway Los Angeles CA 90015

DOWLING, DAN, cartoonist; b. O'Neil, Neb., Nov. 16, 1906; s. Harry Purcell and Claudia (Blair) D.; student U. Cal. at Berkeley, 1924-28; m. Harriet Kelly, Jan. 6, 1943; children—Daniel Blair, Karen Blair. Newspaper reporter, Chgo., 1931-33; artist N.Y. Asso. Press, 1933-36; cartoonist Omaha World-Herald, 1937-48; contbr. N.Y. Herald Tribune, 1946-48, staff and syndicated cartoonist, 1949-67; now editorial cartoonist Kansas City Star. Served as capt. inf., AUS, 1942-46. Recipient Christopher medal, 1956; Freedom Found. award, 1956; award Sigma Delta Chi, 1961. Mem. Assn. Am. Editorial Cartoonists (pres. 1956-58), Beta Theta Pi. Clubs: Omaha Country, (Omaha); Ardsley Country (Irvington, N.Y.). Home: 6401 Ensley Lane Shawnee Mission KS 66208 Office: Kansas City Star Kansas City MO 66101

DOWLING, EDDIE, actor, producer, dir.; b. Woonsocket, R.I., Dec. 9, 1894; s. Charles and Bridget Goucher; ed. pub. schs.; D.H.L., Mt. Mary Coll., Cath. U., Washington; m. Ray Dooley; children—John G., Mary Maxine. Sang with St. Paul's Cathedral Choir on world tour; first stage appearance New England Stock Co.; appeared in #24She Took a Change,#25 "Velvet Lady," "Ziegfeld Follies" (1918, 19, 20); "The Girl in the Spotlight," "Blaze of Glory," "Love's Old Sweet Song," "Purple Dust," "Our Town"; produced and played in "Thumbs Up," "Here Come the Clowns," "The Time of Your Life,"; produced "His Double Life," "Big Hearted Herbert," "Richard II," "Shadow and Substance," "Madame Capet," "The White Steed." Wrote and played in "Girl Behind the Gun#25, #24Rainbow Man#25; wrote and produced #24Sidewalks of New York#25 wrote, produced and played in #24Sally, Irene and Mary #25 and #24Honeymoon Lane#25; producer, dir. The Righteous are Bold, 1956; star and dir. Mr. Dooley, 1957; prod. plays by new authors for various univs. and colls.; pres. Eddie Dowling Prodns., Eddie Dowling, Inc. Recipient Drama Critics' award for #24Shadow and Substance,#25 1938, #24The White Steed," 1939; both Pulitzer prize and Drama Critics' award for "The Time of Your Life," 1940; Critic's Circle Award for "The Glass Menagerie," 1943; directed "The Iceman Cometh." Organizer, 1st pres., U.S. Camp Shows, Inc. Discovered Kate Smith, Maurice Evans, Paul Vincent Carroll. Also produced, wrote and directed Chrysler-Ziegfeld Radio Follies. Chmn. State and Screen Div. of Nat. Dem. Party, 1932, 36, 40. Roman Catholic Clubs: Lambs, Dutch Treat; Savage (London); Chinese (Hong Kong). Seven new plays to be produced for a new circuit, Coll. Theatre in Fla. and Ga., 1961. Home: 1 Washington Square Village New York City NY 10012 Office: 130 W 56th St New York City NY 10019

DOWLING, HARRISON KENNETH diversified mfg. co. exec.; b. Cin., May 21, 1910; grad. Phillips Acad., Andover, Mass., 1927; B.S., Princeton, 1931; postgrad. Mass. Inst. Tech., 1931-33; m. Jean R. Holland, June 16, 1935; children--Lois A., Andrew M., James. Salesman, Brown Mfg. Co., Boston, 1932-33; jr. engr. Ball Metals Co., Carson City, Nev., 1933-36, engr., 1936-37, sr. engr., 1937-40; project engr. Kingston Engring. Co., Los Angeles, 1940-43; with dept. engring. City of Denver, 1946-50, dep. head, 1950-52; 2d v.p. Johnson Mfg. Co., Kansas City, Kansas, 1952-54, v.p. for engring., 1954-57; v.p. research Consol. Industries, Inc., South Bend, Ind., 1957-60, exec. v.p., 1960-65, pres. 1965-70, chmn. bd., chief exec. officer, 1970--, also dir.; dir. ABC Chem. Co., 2d Nat. Bank, Country Food Storage Co., Providence Indsl. Corp. (Ind.), Wilson Investment Co., Inc., Hammond Life Ins. Co., Inc. Pres., Dewey High Sch., Kansas City, Mo., 1953-54; fund chmn. local div. Salvation Army, 1959-60. Mem. South Bend Republican Com., 1964-68. Bd. dirs. Ind. council Boy Scouts Am., 1969-71; trustee Lovell Found. Served to lt., Corps Engrs., AUS, 1943-45. Decorated Bronze Star medal. Member N.A.M., South Bend C. of C. (v.p. 1963-65, dir. 1965-70), Am. Mgmt. Assn., Ind. Engrs. Soc. (program com. 1961-62), Princeton Alumni Assn. Episcopalian. Rotarian, Optimist. Clubs: South Bend Golf; 1947-50, asso. prof., 1950-62, prof., 1962--, chmn. dept., 1963-69; vis. lectr. Stanford, 1970-71. Active Boy Scouts Am., 4-H Club. Served with AUS, 1940-46. Mem. Am. Soc. Biologists, Md. Biologists, A.A.A.S., Am. Acad. Arts and Scis., Phi Beta Kappa. Home: 48936 W Hancock Blvd Baltimore MD 20206

DOWLING, JAMES WILSON, shoe co. exec., lawyer; b. Ozark, Ala., July 24, 1912; s. James Roscoe and Frances (Wilson) D.; B.S. in Commerce, N.Y. U., 1948, J.D., 1950; m. Velma Vavra, Jan. 8, 1947. Group chief, intelligence div. Treasury Dept., N.Y.C., 1946-51; admitted to N.Y. bar, 1951; chief investigator subcom. adminstrn. Internal Revenue Law, U.S. Ho. of Reps. Ways and Means Com., 1951-52; practiced in N.Y.C., and Binghamton, N.Y., 1952-60; asst. sec., counsel Endicott Johnson Corp., 1961-66, sec., chief counsel, 1967—. Mem. Broome County Charter Commn., 1962-63; town atty., Vestal, N.Y., 1963-64. Served to 1st lt. AUS, 1943-46; CBI. Mem. N.Y. State, Broome County bar assns., Broome County C. of C. Home: 113 Eldredge Dr Vestal NY 13850 Office: 1100 E Main St Endicott NY 13760

DOWLING, JOHN CLARKSON, educator; b. Strawn, Tex., Nov. 14, 1920; s. Albert Clarkson and Georgia Anna (Turrill) D.; B.A., U. Colo., 1941; M.A., U. Wis., 1943, Ph.D., 1950; m. Constance Guinevere Ford, Dec. 26, 1949; 1 son. Robert Clarkson. Instr. Spanish and Portuguese, U. Wis. at Madison, 1951-53; prof. Spanish, head dept. fgn. langs. Tex. Tech. Coll. at Lubbock, 1953-63; prof., chmn. dept. Spanish and Portuguese, Ind. U., Bloomington, 1963—; vis. prof. Romance langs. U. Tex., fall 1957. Served to lt. (s.g.) USNR, 1942-46. Albert P. Markham traveling fellow, 1950-51; Guggenheim fellow, 1959-60. Mem. Modern Lang. Assn. Am., Am. Assn. Tchrs. Spanish and Portuguese, Tex. Fgn. Lang. Assn. (pres. 1954-55), Hispanic Soc. of Am. (corr. mem.). Author books, articles. Spl. research Spanish golden age, 18th Century in lit., Spanish theatre. Home: 105 Hampton Ct Bloomington IN 47401

DOWLING, JOHN E., business exec.; b. East Orange, N.J., 1931; grad. Gannon Coll., 1954. Vice pres., corporate controller Zurn Industries, Inc., Erie, Pa. Mem. Nat. Assn. Accountants, Am. Inst. C.P.A.'s. Home: 4415 Briggs Av Erie PA 16504 Office: 5601 New Perry Hwy Erie PA 16509*

DOWLING, P. BRUCE, conservationist, assn. exec.; b. Sept. 20, 1926; s. Paul Phillips and Jean (Crowe) D.; B.S. in Edn., Pa. State U., 1951, M.S. in Zoology, 1952; m. Elinor L. Ralston, May 31, 1949; children—Dawn Karen, Laurie Lane. High sch. tchr., 1950; instr. Pa. State U., 1951-52; biologist Mo. Conservation Commn., Mt. Vernon and St. Charles, 1953-58; Midwest field dir. Nature Conservancy, 1957-59, asst. dir. for natural areas, 1959-64; v.p. Natural Area Council, Inc., N.Y.C., 1964—; v.p., exec. dir. America the Beautiful Fund, Washington, 1965—. Spl. instr. Washington U., 1957-58, Mich. State U., 1962; cons. Ford Found., World Wildlife Fund, also to state and fed. natural area systems, colls. and univs. Served with AUS, 1944-46; PTO. Loeb fellow Harvard, 1971-72. Fellow A.A.A.S. (sec. council study commn. natural areas as research facilities); mem. Ecol. Soc. Am., Wildlife Soc., Am. Ornithologists Union, Am. Inst. Biol. Scis., Am. Soc. Mammalogists. Contbr. articles to sci. jours. Home: 3505 Cameron Mills Rd Alexandria VA 22305 Office: Shoreham Bldg Washington DC 20005

DOWLING, ROBERT WHITTLE, real estate exec.; b. N.Y.C., Sept. 9, 1895; s. Robert Emmet and Minetta (Link) D.; ed. Cutler Sch., N.Y.C., D.F.A., Adelphi Coll., 1961, Fairleigh Dickinson U., 1963; L.H.D., Dowling Coll., 1969; LL.D., Ithaca Coll., 1970; m. Ethel Robertson, June 1920 (div. 1931); m. 2d, Alcie Bevier Hall, Jan. 5, 1934 (div. 1968); 1 dau., Ruth Alice; m. 3d, Audrey A. Reber, Feb. 9, 1968. Engaged in real estate and bldg. bus., N.Y.C., 1918—; with firms including U.S. Realty & Improvement Co., N.Y. Dock Co., Starrett Bros. & Eken, Inc., 1943; pres., dir. City Investing Co., 1943-60, chmn., 1966-70, chmn. exec. com., 1970—; chmn. Pierre Hotel, 1967— housing and planning cons. real estate projects, Parkchester (mem. bd. design), Stuyvesant Town, Clinton Hill, Peter Cooper Village, Fordham Hill; dir. Gen. Devel. Corp., United Artists Corp., Knickerbocker Investing Co., French & Co., Hotel Waldorf-Astoria Corp., Chemway Corp., N.Y. Airways, Ednl. Broadcasting Corp., 1st Nat. City Bank Trust Bd., Xicom Inc., Home Ins. Co., R.H. Macy & Co., Inc., Hilton Hotels Internat., trustee Emigrant Savs. Bank; owners rep., Pitts., Gateway Center; cons. Canadian Pacific Ry., Penn Central Company. Hon. chmn. N.Y. Bd. of Trade. Chmn., dir. Citizens Budget Commn.; mem. N.Y.C. Off-Track Betting Corp., N.Y. State Commn. on Powers Local Govt.; vice chmn. D.C. Auditorium Commn.; hon. trustee Nat. Urban League; mem. Am. Com. To Preserve Abu-Simbel; co- chmn., dir. Nat. Conf. Christians and Jews; nat. chmn. fund raising campaign Urban League, 1948; chmn. Borough of Manhattan Planning Bd. Dir. UN Assn. U.S.; member Mayor's Com. Off Street Parking. Trustee St. Johns Guild. Dir. Regional Plan Assn., Commerce abd Industry Assn., Am. Arbitration Assn., Boy Scouts Am. Mem. nat. shrines adv. bd.

Dept. Interior; chmn. adv. com. arts John F. Kennedy Center for Performing Arts, 1959-67, trustee, 1968—; chmn., trustee Dowling Coll. (formerly Adelphi-Suffolk, endowed by, named for him), 1968—. Inst. on Man and Sci., 1968—; hon. chmn. ANTA. Bd. overseers Harvard Coll.; chmn. bd. design Penn Central Park, Pitts.; co-chmn. trustee Inst. Internat. Edn.; chmn. exec. com. chmn., founder Fed. Hall, N.Y.C.; preserved and established Ft. Clinton, N.Y.C.; trustee Carnegie Hall Corp., Carnegie Hall Soc. Balloon tng. corps Columbia U. unit, U.S. Army, World War I, on spl. assignment by naval cons. bd., USN; served as first frogman of U.S. Navy. Decorated Cross of Chevalier of Legion of Honor; Order of Merit, Republic of Germany; Brazilian Order of So. Cross; recipient Medal of City of N.Y.; medal for invention of all-glass doors by Glass Inst.; spl. award Nat. Conf. Christians and Jews; Antoinette Perry award; Lambs club award for achievements in theatre; certificate of merit C. of C. U.S. Mem. Nat. Inst. Social Sci. (v.p.). Democrat. Clubs: N.Y. Athletic, Knickerbocker, Racquet and Tennis, Tuxedo. Am. Nat. long distance swimming champion, 1916. Home: Pierre Hotel 2 E 61st St New York City NY 10021 Office: 767 Fifth Av New York City NY 10022

DOWLING, WALTER, former U.S. ambassador; b. Atkinson, Ga., Aug. 4, 1905; s. Walter and Alice (Benton) D.; A.B., Mercer U., 1925; LL.D., Seoul Nat. U., 1959, Mercer U., 1961, U. Md., 1962; m. Alice Jernigan, Dec. 17, 1930; children—Patricia Dowling (Mrs. Philip Winterer), Michael. Bank clk., 1925-29; sec., 1929-31; fgn. service officer, 1931—, student Fgn. Service Sch., 1931-32, vice consul Oslo, 1932-36, Lisbon, 1936-38, 3d sec., Rome, 1938-41, 2d sec., 1941, 2d. sec. and vice consul, Rio de Janeiro, 1941-44, fgn. service officer Office U.S.Rep., Adv. Council for Italy, 1944, 2d sec. and consul, Rome, 1945, asst. chief, div. So. European Affairs, Dept. State, 1945-47, assoc. chief, 1947-49, acting chief, 1949, counselor of legation, Vienna, 1949, U.S. dep. high commr. for Austria, 1950, rank of minister, 1952, dep. high commr. for Germany, 1953, minister Am. embassy, Bonn, 1955-56, ambassador to Korea, 1956-59, asst. sec. state for European affairs, 1959, U.S. ambassador to West Germany, 1959-63, now dir. gen. Atlantic Inst., Paris. Chmn. internat. council Mus. Modern Art, N.Y.C. Bd. dirs. Nat. Carl Schurz Assn., Phila. Recipient Grand Cross of Merit, Fed. Republic Germany, Gold Badge Order of Merit (Republic of Austria). Mem. Atlantic Council U.S. (gov.), Council Fgn. Relations, Pi Kappa Alpha. Clubs: Metropolitan (Washington); The Brook; Oglethorpe (Savannah, Ga.). Address: 244 Oglethorpe Av E Savannah GA 31401

DOWNE, EDWARD R., Jr., communications and pub. conglomerate exec.; grad. U. Mo. Sch. of Journalism, 1952. Editorial, promotion positions True and Argosy mags.; organized mail order firm, 1957; acquired various mags., including Family Weekly, Ladies Home Jour., others; now chmn. bd., pres. Downe Communications, Inc.; chmn. bd. Bartell Media Corp. Address: 641 Lexington Av New York City NY 10022

DOWNER, J. R., union ofcl.; Sec., Internat. Assn. Bridge, Structural and Ornamental Iron Workers AFL-CIO. Office: 3615 Oliver St St Louis MO 63108*

DOWNER, JOSEPH PLATT, oil co. exec.; b. Coblenz, Germany, July 11, 1922 (parents U.S. citizens); s. John Walter and Gladys (Trevor) D.; B.S. cum laude, Harvard, 1943, M.B.A., 1948; m. Jannett Lord Tucker, Dec. 30, 1949; children—Jannett Trevor, William Tucker, John Ashton. Asst. to v.p. for coordination and planning Continental Oil Co., 1948-52; mgr. oil dept. Wertheim & Co., Dallas and N.Y.C., 1952-59; with Sinclair Oil Corp., 1959-69, exec. v.p., 1968-69, chmn. finance com., 1966-69, also dir.; exec. v.p. internat. div., dir. Atlantic Richfield Co., 1969—. Treas., Village of Oyster Bay Cove, N.Y., 1965-69. Trustee East Woods Sch., Oyster Bay Cove, Trinity Sch., N.Y.C., Trinity Pawling Sch., Pawling, N.Y. Served to capt. AUS, 1943-46. Mem. Am. Petroleum Inst. Republican. Episcopalian (vestryman, treas.). Clubs: Economic, Harvard (N.Y.C.); Army Navy (Washington); A.D. (Cambridge, Mass.); Cold Spring Harbor (N.Y.) Beach. Home: Cove Edge Rd Oyster Bay Cove RFD Syosset NY 11791 Office: 277 Park Av New York City NY 10017

DOWNER, MARION, author. Recipient 1964 Children's Spring Book Festival award for Shadow of a Bull. Author: Story of Design, 1963; Roofs Over America, 1967; Long Ago in Florence; The Story of Della Robbia, 1968. Address: care Lothrop Lee & Shepard 381 Park Av S New York City NY 10016*

DOWNER, SAMUEL FORSYTHE, bus. exec.; b. Monongahela, Pa., Aug. 12, 1918; s. Eliphalet Kern and Elizabeth (Forsythe) D.; B.S.C. cum laude, Ohio U., 1940; postgrad. Harvard Grad. Sch. Bus. Adminstrn., 1945, grad. Advanced Mgmt. Program, 1964; m. Jessie Cooper, Aug. 24, 1940; children—Benita E. (Mrs. John B. Rountree III), Philip Stuart. Office, credit mgr. Jessop Steel Co., Washington, Pa., 1942-44, asst. to pres., 1946-47, asst. gen. sales mgr., 1947-48; resident rep. Burroughs Corp., Colorado Springs, Colo., 1948-56; chmn. Puffer Merc. Co., Colorado Springs, 1951-53; asst. v.p. Exchange Nat. Bank, 1956-57, v.p. 1957-60; sec. Continental Can Co., 1960-64; v.p. finance LTV Aerospace Corp., Dallas, 1965—, also treas., dir.; v.p., sec.-treas., dir.,mem. exec. com. Kentron Hawaii, Ltd.; dir. Service Tech. Corp., Park Towers, Inc. Fund chmn., chpt. chmn. exec. com. Pike's Peak chpt. A.R.C., 1948-60, Midwest adv. council, 1950-54, nat. bd. govs., 1954-60; chmn. bd. trustees Colorado Springs Child Guidance Clinic, 1953; vis. com. Coll. Bus. Adminstrn., Ohio U., 1963-66. Served with USNR, World War II; PTO. Recipient Exceptional Service award USAF. Mem. Def. Orientation Conf. Assn. (dir.), Am. Pub. Health Assn. (nat. adv. com. on finance), Assn. U.S. Army (adv. bd. dirs., v.p.), Colo. Soc. C.P.A.'s (recognition), Omicron Delta Kappa. Clubs: Lancers, Nanhook Yacht. Home: Park Towers 3310 Fairmont St Dallas TX 75201 Office: LTV Tower P O Box 5003 Dallas TX 75222

DOWNES, DAVID ANTHONY, coll. dean; b. Victor, Colo., Aug. 17, 1927; s. David Michael and Julia (Zitnik) D.; B.A. cum laude in English, Philosophy and Lit., Regis Coll., Denver, 1949; M.A. in English Lang. and Lit., Marquette U., 1950; Ph.D. in Victorian Lit., U. Wash., 1956; m. Audrey Romaine Ernst, Sept. 7, 1949; children—Mary Kathryn, Jane Frances, Daniel Ross, Michelle Marie. Instr. Gonzaga U., 1950-53; asst. prof.,then asso. prof. Seattle U., 1953-64, prof. English, chmn. dept., 1964-68; dean Sch. Humanities and Fine Arts, prof. English, Chico (Cal.) State Coll., 1968—; vis. lectr. TV sta. KCTS, Seattle, 1957-63; dir. Nat. Def. Edn. Act Summer English Inst., Seattle U., 1965. Recipient 5 research and pub. grants. Mem. Modern Lang. Assn., Nat. Council Tchrs. English, Am. Conf. Acad. Deans. Author: Gerard Manley Hopkins, A Study of His Ignation Spirit, 1960; Victorian Portraits: Hopkins and Pater, 1965; The Temper of Victorian Belief: Studies in the Religious Novels of Pater, Kingsley and Newman, 1971.

DOWNES, EDMUND WILLIAM, newspaper exec.; b. Hartford, Conn., Oct. 23, 1920; s. William H. and Katherine L. (Delaney) D.; B.S., Hillyer Coll., Hartford, Conn., 1956; m. Mary Alice Moore, June 5, 1947; children—Donald W., Maryanne M., Elizabeth J. With Hartford Courant Co., 1952—, pres., 1968—, also dir.; dir. Conn. Bank and Trust Co., Hartford, Greater Hartford Corp. Mem. Glastonbury (Conn.) Redevel. Agy. Bd. dirs. Jr. Achievement Hartford; trustee Central Conn. Communities, Civic and Charitable Corp., Hartford Courant Found., Eastern States Exposition; bd. corporators Hartford Hosp., Mt. Sinai Hosp. Served with USAAF, 1942-46. Mem. Conn. Daily Newspaper Assn. (exec. bd.). Home: 39 High Rdge South Glastonbury CT 06073 Office: 285 Broad St Hartford CT 06101

DOWNES, EDWARD OLIN DAVENPORT, music historian, critic, radio broadcaster; b. Boston, Aug. 12, 1911; s. Edwin Olin and Marian Amanda (Davenport) D.; student Columbia, 1929-30, Manhattan Sch. Music, 1930-32, U. Paris (France), 1932-33, U. Munich (Germany), 1932, 34-36, 38-39; Ph.D., Harvard, 1958; m. Mildred Fowler Gignoux, Oct. 23, 1943 (div. Aug. 1954). Asst. music critic N.Y. Post, 1936-38; music critic Boston Evening Transcript, 1939-41; commentator, asst. program mgr. radio sta. W67Ny. N.Y.C., 1941-42; intelligence analyst and editor OSS, Dept. State, also War Dept., 1943-46; program annotator, lectr. music Boston Mus. Fine Arts, 1946-50; lectr. music Wellesley Coll., 1948-49; prof. music history U. Minn., 1950-55, and Ph.D. Grad. Center Queens Coll. of City U. N.Y., 1966—; asst. music critic N.Y. Times, 1955-58; quizmaster Met. Opera broadcasts, 1958—; program annotator N.Y. Philharmonic- Symphony Soc., 1960—; intermission host N.Y. Philharmonic Symphony broadcasts, 1964-66, First Hearing Broadcast series Sta. WQXR, N.Y.C., 1968—. lectr. music series Met. Mus. Art, 1960-66; faculty Master Classes Bayreuth (West Germany) Festival, 1959-65. Served with AUS, 1942-45. Mem. Am. (council 1958-60, 69-71), Internat. musicol. socs., Gesellschaft fuer Musikforschung, Soc. Theatre Research (Eng.), Am. Soc. Theatre Research, Am. Council Learned Socs., Coll. Music Soc., Am. Music Library Assn., Società Italiana di musicologica, Socété Belge de Musicologie, Internat. Fedn. for Theatre Research, Assn. for Recorded Sound. Author: Adventures in Symphonic Music, 1943. Translator Verdi: The Man in His Letters, 1942. Editor: (with H.C. Robbins Landon) Temistocle (opera by Christian Bach), 1965. Address: care Souvaine Assos 135 Central Park W New York City NY 10023

DOWNEY, FRANK PATRICK, machine mfg. exec.; b. St. Joseph, Mo., Feb. 10, 1909; s. Frank P. and Susan (Fahey) D.; m. Noel Calhoun, Apr. 18, 1967; 1 son, Thomas P. Vice Pres. Am. Machine and Foundry Co., 1944-62, exec. v. p., 1962-63, vice chmn., 1963-65; dir.; pres., dir. AMF Pinspotters, Inc.; v.p., dir. Nat. Bowling and Billiard Corp., Tempered Maple Corp.; dir. AMF Pinspotters (Can.), Ltd., Voit Rubber Co., Ben Hogan Co. Clubs: Meadowbrook; Nassau Country (Glen Cove, N.Y.); Pinnacle (N.Y.C.). Home: Wolver Hollow Rd Upper Brookville NY 11771 Office: 261 Madison Av New York City NY 10016

DOWNEY, FREDERICK A., corp. exec.; b. 1928; ed. Pace Inst. m. With Warnaco Inc., 1951—, treas., 1963-69, sr. v.p., 1969—. Address: 350 Lafayette St Bridgeport CT 06604

DOWNEY, FRED MCEWEN, chain drug co. exec.; b. Pleasantville, Tenn., Feb. 12, 1906; s. William Lee and Minnie (Little) D.; grad. Max Morris Coll. Pharmacy, Macon, Ga., 1926; m. Lorraine Church Beasley, June 11, 1932; 1 son, Fred McEwen. Mgr., Coble's Drug Store, Centerville, Tenn., 1926-29; with Peoples Drug Stores Inc., Washington, 1929—, v.p., 1956-66, exec. v.p., 1966-70, vice chmn. bd., 1970-71, ret., 1971. Dir. Washington Restaurant Assn., 1951-66, treas., 1959; mem. Washington Bd. Trade. Bd. dirs. York County (Pa.) Community Chest, 1946- 51, pres., 1949-51; bd. dirs. York and Adams Counties council Boy Scouts Am., 1946-51; adv. com. food service tech. program No. Va. Tech. Coll. Mem. D.C. Pharm. Assn., Friendly Sons St. Partick, Newcomen Soc. N. Am. Mason, Rotarian. Clubs: Kenwood Golf and Country (Bethesda, Md.); University (Washington). Home: 5200 Brittany Dr S St Petersburg FL 33715

DOWNEY, GLANVILLE, educator; b. Balt., June 14, 1908; s. Emory Kelly and Katherine Joyce (Glanville) D.; A.B., Princeton, 1931, Ph.D., 1934; m. Sarah Sawyer Atherton, Aug. 9, 1942; children—Katherine Glanville, Sarah Sawyer (Mrs. Darold E. Maxwell). Mem. archaeol. expdn. to Antioch, Syria, 1932; asst. Gennadius Library, Am. Sch. Classical Studies, Athens, 1934-35, mem. exec. com., 1957-61, mem. mng. com., 1956—; mem. Inst. Advanced Study, Princeton, 1935-40; librarian Sch. Fine Arts, Yale, 1940- 42; fellow Dumbarton Oaks Research Library and Collection of Harvard, Washington, 1945-46, asst. prof. Byzantine literature, 1946-51, asso. prof. 1951-60, prof. 1960-64; bd. scholars Dumbarton Oaks, 1953-65; Guggenheim fellow, mem. Inst. for Advanced Study, Princeton, 1956-57; Bedell lectr. Kenyon Coll. 1956; vis. lectr. Princeton U., 1957-58; guest prof. Princeton Theol. Sem., 1957-59; prof. Grad. Sch. Theology, U. of South, 1960-61, 64; asso. sect. history and lit. Royal Belgian Acad., 1965—; mem. editorial bd. of Greek and Byzantine Studies, 1958—, of Neo-Hellenika, 1968—; acting librarian Dumbarton Oaks, 1961-64; prof. history and classical studies Ind. U., Bloomington, 1964—. Served with Signal Corps, AUS, 1942-45. Mem. Am. Philol. Assn., Archaeol. Inst. Am. (exec. com. 1961), Mediaeval Acad. Am. (council 1961-64), German Archaeol. Inst. (corr.), Am. Hist. Assn., Am. Numismatic Soc., U.S. Nat. Com. for Byzantine Studies, Center for Neo-Hellenic Studies (asso.), Classical Assn. (Gt. Britain), Soc. for Promotion Roman Studies (London), Phi Beta Kappa. Episcopalian. Author: A Study of the Comites Orientis and the Consulares Syriae, 1939; Greek and Latin Inscriptions in Antioch-on-the- Orontes, II- III, 1938, 41; Constantinople in the Age of Justinian, 1960; Belisarius, Young General of Byzantium, 1960; A History of Antioch in Syria from Seleucus to the Arab Conquest, 1961; Antioch in the Age of Theodosius the Great, 1962; Aristotle, Dean of Early Science, 1962; Ancient Antioch, 1963 (Arabic translation 1969); Gaza in the Early Sixty Century, 1963; Stories from Herodotus, 1965; The Late Roman Empire, 1969. Editor, translator Procopius Buildings (with Dewing), 1940; Chronicle of John Malalas, Books VIII-XVIII (with Spinka), 1940; editor-in- chief Am. Jour. Archaeology, 1949-52, adv. editor 1953—; asso. editor Archaeology, 1948-52, editor, translator Mesarites, Description of the Church of the Apostles, 1957; co-editor: Themistii Orationes Qui supersunt, 2 vols., 1965-70. Contbr. articles to profl. jours., ency. Home: 2621 Fairoaks Lane Bloomington IN

DOWNEY, JOHN ALEXANDER, physician; b. Regina, Sask., Can., Sept. 16, 1930; s. John Stuart and Victoria (McKenzie) D.; B.Sc. in Medicine, U. Man., 1953, M.D., 1954; D.Phil., U. Oxford (Eng.), 1962; m. Elsie Winnifred Waterman, July 16, 1952; children—Richard Stuart, Susan Elizabeth, Robert John, Jennifer Alison. Came to U.S., 1954. Intern Vancouver Gen. Hosp., 1953-54; resident physician Columbia Presbyn. Med. Center, N.Y.C., 1954-56, 57- 59; resident physician (jr. and sr.) Peter Bent Brigham Hosp., Boston, 1956-57, 59-60; research fellow Christ Ch., Oxford U., 1960-62; mem. faculty Columbia Coll. Physicians and Surgeons, 1962—, prof. rehab. medicine, 1967—; dir. rehab. medicine Blythdale Children's Hosp., Valhalla, N.Y.; vis. scientist dept. human physiology and pharmacology U. Adelaide (S. Australia). Presbyn. (ruling elder). Home: 51 Willow Rd Closter NJ 07624 Office: 180 Fort St Washington Av New York City NY 10032

DOWNEY, JOHN CHARLES, educator, zoologist; b. Eureka, Utah, Apr. 12, 1926; s. John Charles and Cleone (Owens) D.; B.S., U. Utah, 1949, M.S., 1950; Ph.D., U. Cal. at Davis, 1957; m. Norine Margaret Simpson, June 25, 1949; children—John Charles III, Michael, Mary Ann, Dennis James, Patrick Joseph. Faculty, U. Utah, 1947-52, instr. biology, 1951-52; faculty U. Cal. at Davis, 1952-56; asst. prof. zoology So. Ill. U., Carbondale, 1956-61, asso. prof., 1961-66, prof., 1966-68; prof., head dept. biology U. No. Ia., Cedar Falls, 1968—. Recipient research grants Am. Philos. Soc., 1959, NSF, 1959-61, 62, 64-66, 66-68. Mem. Soc. Study Evolution, Lepidopterists Found., Pacific Coast Entomologists Soc., Lepidopterists Soc. (sec. 1964-71), Soc. Systematic Zoologists (charter mem.), Entomologists Soc. Am., So. Cal., Ill., Ia. acads. scis., Sigma Xi, Phi Sigma, Phi Kappa Phi. Publs. on variation and evolution using insects, especially butterflies as the tool organism; studies of population dynamics showing how host-plants, parasites and symbiotic associations can influence evolution; studies on mimicry; sound prodn. in immature stages of butterflies. Home: 333 Martin Rd Waterloo IA 50701 Office: U No Ia Dept Biology Cedar Falls IA 60613

DOWNEY, JOHN FRANCIS, lawyer; b. Sacramento, Dec. 31, 1914; s. Stephen W. and Persis (McIntire) D.; B.A., Stanford, 1936; LL.B., U. So. Cal., 1938; m. Betty Werner, Oct. 16, 1943; children-Barbara, Michael, Cynthia, David, Kathryn, Eve, Stephen, John, Richard, Thomas, Dennis. Admitted to Cal. bar, 1938; practiced in Visalia, 1938-39; fed. conciliation commr., Tulare County, Cal., 1939-40; partner Downey, Brand, Seymour & Rohwer, Sacramento, 1946—; tchr. McGeorge Coll. Law, 1946-47. Vice-chmn. Capitol Bldg., Planning Commn., State Cal., 1960-67. Mem. adv. bd. Sacramento State Coll., 1956—, now chmn.; mem. Human Relations Com. Sacramento County, 1963-68. Bd. dirs. Sacramento State Coll. Found.; vice chmn. chancellor's adv. council Cal. State Colls. Served to maj., C.E., AUS, 1940-45. Decorated Bronze Star medal with oak leaf cluster, Purple Heart, Fellow Am. Coll. Trial Lawyers, Am. Bar Found.; mem. Sacramento County Bar Assn. (pres. 1959), Sacramento Legal Aid Soc. (pres. 1956). Rotarian (pres. Sacramento 1958). Club: Sacramento Univ. (pres. 1953). Home: 3850 W Land Park Dr Sacramento CA 95822 Office: Crocker-Citizens Bank Bldg 1007 7th Av Sacramento CA 95814

DOWNEY, JOSEPH FRANCIS, priest, educator, editor; b. Lima, O., Oct. 16, 1916; s. Thomas and Anna Elizabeth (Ley) D.; Litt.B., Xavier U., Cin., 1939; M.A., Loyola U., Chgo., 1946, M.Ed., 1951; S.T.L., W. Baden (Ind.) Coll., 194Q. Joined Soc. of Jesus, 1935, ordained priest Roman Cath. Ch., 1948; tchr. English and Latin, St. Xavier High Sch., Cin., 1942-45; lectr. theology Loyola U., Chgo., 1950-51; asst. dean Coll. Arts and Scis., U. Detroit, 1951-53; registrar, instr. edn. and ch. history St. Mary of the Lake Sem., Mundelein, Ill., 1953-58; dean Coll. Arts and Scis., John Carroll U., Cleve., 1958-62, trustee univ., 1958-62; asst. provincial Detroit province Soc. of Jesus, 1962-69, vice-provincial Detroit province, 1965, 66; mng. editor America newsweekly, N.Y., 1969—. Participant Pugwash Conf., 1958, 3d Nat. Inst. for Deans, 1961; mem. Ohio Council Advanced Placement, 1959-62; mem. liberal arts com. Cleve. Council Higher Edn., 1960-62. Editor: Prose and Poetry for Enjoyment, rev. edit., 1953. Address: 106 W 56th St New York City NY 10019

DOWNEY, MORTON, company exec., b. Wallingford, Conn., Nov. 14, 1901; s. James Andrew and Elizabeth (Cox) D.; m. Ann Van Gerbig, Feb. 5, 1970. Cons., Coca-Cola Co. Decorated Grand Cross of Merit of Soverign Order of Malta. Roman Catholic. Clubs: Madison Square Garden, River (N.Y.C.); Everglades (Palm Beach). Address: care Arthur Stryker 125 E 50th St New York City NY 10022

DOWNEY, STEPHEN WHEELER, army officer; b. Sacramento, June 1, 1916; s. Stephen Wheeler and Edith (Jennings) D.; student N.M. Mil. Inst., 1931-36; B.A., Stanford, 1939; m. Dorothy May Wilder, Sept. 6, 1947; 1 dau., Dianne. Commd. 2d. lt. Cav. Res., 1937, U.S. Army, 1939, advanced through grades to maj. gen., 1967; served in SHAPE Hdqrs., 1958-61, 62-64; comdr. 4th Armored Div., 1968-70; faculty Army War Coll., 1955-58; chief of staff Central Army Group NATO, 1970—. Decorated D.S.M., Silver Star medal, Legion of Merit with three oak leaf clusters, Bronze Star, Army Commendation medal, Purple Heart. Mem. Phi Gamma Delta. Home: 1300 41st St Sacramento CA 95819 Office: Hdqrs Central Army Group NATO APO New York City NY 09099

DOWNEY, WILLIAM F., lawyer; b. Wallingford, Conn., Sept. 28, 1932; s. John E. and Mary (O'Connell) D.; B.A., Yale, 1954; M.B.A., Harvard, 1956; LL.B., N.Y.U., 1964; m. Eugenia Olekshy, May 20, 1966. With First Nat. City Bank, N.Y.C. and Singapore, 1958-59, Morgan Guaranty Trust Co., N.Y.C., 1959- 64; admitted to N.Y. bar, 1964, since practiced in N.Y.C.; mem. firm Lovejoy, Wasson, Lundgren & Ashton 1964—. Dir. Inflight Motion Pictures, Inc., Armour and Co., 1969-70; sec., dir. Uncle John's Restaurants, Inc., 1967-68, Gen. Host Corp., 1968—. Served with AUS, 1956-57. Home: 333 E 55th St New York City NY 10022 Office: 250 Park Av New York City NY 10017

DOWNING, EDWARD D., wire co. exec.; B.S., City Coll. N.Y., 1934; LL.B., N.Y. U., 1943; m. Mary M. Downing; children—Peter E., Alison M. (Mrs. Jeffrey W. Kolb). Admitted to N.Y. bar, Ind. bar, practice in N.Y.C., 1946-53; counsel Servo Corp. Am., 1953-55; asst. sec. Miles Labs., Inc., 1955-65; sec., gen. counsel Essex Internat., 1965- 67, v.p.-legal, sec., 1968—. Bd. dirs. Ft. Wayne Fine Arts Found., Ft. Wayne Art Inst. Served with USNR, 1943-46. Clubs: Summit, Ft. Wayne Country. Home: 4001 N Washington Rd Fort Wayne IN 46804 Office: 1601 Wall St Fort Wayne IN 46804

DOWNING, GLENN, oil co. exec. Vice pres., treas. Douglas Oil Co. Cal. Office: 530 W 6th St Los Angeles CA 90014*

DOWNING, HAROLD SEARS, advt. exec.; b. Pitts., Feb. 4, 1893; s. A. U. and Stella (Sears) D.; A.B., U. Pitts., 1915; m. Linda Johnston, Oct. 1, 1917; children—Betty Jane (Mrs. J.R. Overend), Harold Sears, Mary Louise (Mrs. M.L. Warner), Robert Stanley, William Johnston. With Walker & Downing, advt. agy., Pitts., 1916—; owner Walker and Downing Indsl. div., 1938—; pres., treas. Downing Indsl. Ad., Inc., 1956-67, chmn., treas., 1967—. Mem. Phi Gamma Delta. Republican. Presbyn. Clubs: Duquesne, University; Pittsburgh Athletic Assn. Home: 825 Morewood Av Pittsburgh PA 15213 Office: Oliver Bldg Pittsburgh PA 15222

DOWNING, JAMES BARTHOLOMEW, investment co. exec.; b. Yonkers, N.Y., July 7, 1901; s. P.J. and Ellen (O'Sullivan) D.; student N.Y.U. Sch. Commerce, 1920-23; m. Ann H. Saunders, Nov. 26, 1932 (dec. Dec. 1966); 1 dau., Genevieve Lee. Auditor Lehman Bros., N.Y.C., 1923-29; with Lehman Corp., N.Y.C., 1929—, treas., 1946-68, sec., 1957-58, v.p., 1958—; v.p., dir. Gas Properties, Inc., Club: Montclair (N.J.) Country. Home: 935 Park Av New York City, NY 10028. Office: 1 S William St New York City NY 10004

DOWNING, MARJORIE, educator; b. N.Y.C., Mar. 16, 1917; d. Charles Aloysius and Margaret (Ohland) Coogan; B.A., Coll. Mt. St. Vincent, 1938; M.A., Catholic U. Am., 1939; Ph.D., Yale, 1942; m. Francis Downing, Sept. 8, 1952; children—Francis, Nicholas. Instr. Barnard Coll., 1942-47; asst. prof., asso. prof. Bklyn. Coll., 1947-61; dean Sarah Lawrence Coll., 1961-65; dean faculty Scripps Coll., Claremont (Cal.) Colls., 1965-71, prof. English, 1971—. Mem. Com. Profl. Women for Los Angeles Philharmonic. Mem. Mod. Lang.

Assn., Western Assn. Schs. and Colls. (dir. Western region), Comparative Edn. Soc. Home: 1055 Dartmouth Av Claremont CA 91711

DOWNING, PAUL H., cons. on horse-drawn transp.; b. N.Y.C., Feb. 10, 1898; s. George Henry and Magdalena (von Ronnberg) D.; student Sedgewick Inst., Gt. Barrington, Mass., 1914-15; m. Clarisse Spencer DeBost, May 14, 1921; children—Clarissa (Mrs. Bidwell Moore), William DeBost, Paul Mayhew. Various positions Columbia Fire Extinguisher Co., 1919-28; mgr. S.I. officer N.Y. Title & Mortgage Co., 1928-33; real estate dept. Central Savs. Bank, N.Y.C., 1933-42; dir. St. George, Staten Island Bldg., Loan; carriage cons. Colonial Williamsburg, Mt. Vernon Ladies Assn.; mus. curator Smithsonian Instn., Nat. Park Service; cons. on horse-drawn transp; Bd. dirs. (hon.) Breakers Stable, Newport, R.I. Served with Nat. Guard on Mexican Border 1916-17; from 2d lt. to capt., cav., U.S. Army, World War I; maj. to lt. col., A.C., AUS, 1942-45. Granted Freedom of Worshipful Co. Coach Makers and Coach-Harness Makers, London, Eng., 1965. Mem. Staten Island N.Y. (asso. life), Buffalo hist. socs. (v.p., dir., chmn. carriage com.), Richmondtown Restoration (trustee, bd. dirs.), Carriage Assn. Am. (v.p.), Grand Jurors Assn. Episcopalian. Mason. Clubs: Staten Island Tennis and Cricket; Richmond County Country; Bay Head (N.J.) Yacht; Richmond County Yacht (commodore); Mohawk (Schenectady); Genessee Valley, Rochester Country (Rochester, N.Y.). Editor: The Carriage Jour. Home: 157 N Saint Austins Pl Staten Island, NY 10310.

DOWNING, REGINALD HORTON, educator; b. New Germany, N.S., Can., Nov. 19, 1908; s. William Peers and Laura (Chesley) D.; B.A., Acadia U., 1930; M.S., W.Va. U., 1932, Ph.D. in Math., 1934; m. Helen Dolores Chesner, July 19, 1949; 1 dau., Joan Laureva. Came to U.S., 1930, naturalized, 1942. Instr. math., research asso. Bur. for Govt. Research, W.Va. U., 1934-38; instr. math. Purdue U., Lafayette, Ind., 1938-42; dynamics engr. Kaiser Fleetwings, Inc., Bristol, Pa., 1942-47; asso. prof. Air Force Inst. Tech., Wright- Patterson AFB, O., 1947-49, head dept. faculty, 1949-51, dean Resident Coll., 1951-58, dean faculty, 1958-61, dean Sch. Engring., 1961-69, dir. for acad. affairs, 1969—. Bd. dirs. Honor Seminars of Met. Dayton; adv. bd. Arctic Environmental Engring. Lab., U. Alaska. Fellow A.A.A.S.; mem. Math. Assn. Am., Am. Math. Soc., Am. Inst. Aeros. and Astronautics, Am. Soc. for Engring. Edn., Assn. for Higher Edn., Am. Assn. U. Profs., Tau Beta Pi. Home: 432 Avon Way Kettering OH 45429 Office: Air Force Institute of Technology Wright-Patterson AFB OH 45433

DOWNING, ROBERT WOODLING, r.r. ofcl.; b. Sewickley, Pa., Sept. 18, 1913; s. James A. and Hattie (Wragg) D.; B.S. in Civil Engring., Yale, 1935; m. Mary A. Matthews, Aug. 7, 1937; children—Nancy J., Robert M., Susan E. Asst. on engr. corps, asst. supr. track Pa. R.R., 1935-38; rodman C., M., St.P. & P. R.R., 1938; asst. to supt., dist. roadmaster, trainmaster, div. supt., asst. to pres. Great Northern Ry., 1938-58, v.p., 1958-67, exec. vice pres., 1967-70; exec. v.p. Burlington No., Inc., St. Paul, 1970-71, pres., 1971—; chmn. C. & S. Ry. Co., 1971—, Ft. Worth & Denver Ry., 1971—. Served to lt. comdr. USNR, 1941-45. Home: 2028 Upper St Dennis Rd St Paul MN 55116 Office: 176 E 5th St St Paul MN 55101

DOWNING, THOMAS NELMS, congressman; b. Newport News, Va., Feb. 1, 1919; s. Samuel and Lucille (Nelms) D.; B.S., Va. Mil. Inst., 1940; LL.B., U. Va., 1947; m. Virginia Dickerson Martin, Feb. 17, 1947; children—Susan Nelms, Samuel Dickerson Martin. Admitted to Va. bar, 1947; substitute judge Municipal Ct., City of Warwick (now Newport News), 1953-58; mem. 86th to 92d Congresses, 1st Dist. Va., mem. mcht. marine and fisheries com. sci. and astronautics com., chmn. subcom. NASA legislative oversight. Bd. visitors Mcht. Marine Acad., Kings Point, N.Y. Served to maj. Cav., 3d Army, AUS, World War II. Decorated Silver Star, five campaign battle stars. Mem. Am. Legion, Am., Va. State, Hampton, Newport News-Warwick (past pres.) bar assns., Red Men's Assn., Young Dems. Va., Am. Legion, V.F.W. Democrat. Episcopalian (trustee). Elk, Jr. O.U.A.M. Clubs: Propeller, Lions (Newport News). Home: 27 Indigo Dam Rd Newport News VA 23606 Office: House Office Bldg Washington DC 20515

DOWNS, DAVID LEE, mfg. co. exec.; b. Phila., Nov. 23, 1929; s. Malcolm C. and Kathryn (Bensinger) D.; A.B., Princeton, 1951; m. Mary-Theresa Whipple, July 6, 1957; children—David Lee, John L., Elizabeth C. With Mfrs. Hanover Trust Co., N.Y.C., 1955-69, v.p. comml. lending, 1967-69; exec. v.p. corporate finance Topper Corp., Elizabeth, N.J., 1969—, also dir. Served to lt. (s.g.) USNR, 1951-54. Republican. Clubs: Gipsy Trail (Carmel, N.Y.); Pelham Country (Pelham Manor); Princeton (N.Y.C.); Cloister Inn (Princeton, N.J.). Home: 14 Witherbee Av Pelham Manor NY 10803 Office: 107 Trumbull St Elizabeth NJ 07206

DOWNS, HUGH MALCOLM, radio and TV broadcaster; b. Akron, O., Feb. 14, 1921; s. Milton Howard and Edith (Hick) D.; student Bluffton (O.) Coll., 1938-39, Wayne State U., 1940-41, Columbia, 1955-56; m. Ruth Shaheen, Feb. 20, 1944; children—Hugh Raymond, Deirdre Lynn. Staff announcer radio sta. WLOK, Lima O., 1939, program dir., 1939-40; staff announcer radio sta. WWJ, Detroit, 1940-42, NBC, Chgo., 1943-54; free-lance radio and TV broadcaster, 1954—; programs include Home Show, 1954-57, Sid Caesar's Hour, 1956-57, Concentration, 1958-68, Jack Paar show Tonight, 1957-62; host Today Show, 1962—; spl. cons. UN on refugee problems Middle East, 1961—. Chmn. bd. Raylin Prodns., Inc., 1960—. Recipient Fame award as best announcer of year, 1959-64. Address: NBC 30 Rockefeller Plaza New York City, NY 10020.

DOWNS, JAMES CHESTERFIELD, Jr., property mgmt.; b. Des Moines, Oct. 18, 1905; s. James Chesterfield and Frieda (Braun) D.; student U. Ill., 1923-25; D.C.S., U. Fla., 1952; m. Florence Finn, June 20, 1929; children—James Anthony, Carolyn, Suzanna. Asso. Edward C. Waller, Chgo., 1926-28; mgr. property mgmt. Baird & Warner, 1929-31; with Foreman Nat. Bank, 1931; pres. Real Estate Research Corp., 1931-56, chmn. bd. dirs.,1956- -; mgr. br. office Draper & Kramer, 1931-33; v.p. Dayton Keith & Co., Chgo., 1933-38; spl. lectr. univs. Fla., Leland Stanford, Notre Dame; dir. Chgo. Title & Trust Co., Goldblatt Bros. Dept. Stores, Chgo., J.M. Foster, Inc. Housing and redevel. coordinator City of Chgo., 1954-57; chmn. lay bd. consultors Mercy Hosp. Bd. dirs. Ednl. Facilities Lab., Inc.; mem. bd. Chgo. City Coll.; trustee U. Chgo., 1957—. Certified property mgr. Mem. Chgo. Assn. Commerce and Industry (dir.), Inst. Real Estate Mgmt. (pres. 1938-39), Theta Chi. Democrat. Roman Catholic. Clubs: Commerical (pres. 1960), Mid-America, Economic (pres. 1959), Chicago (Chgo.). Author: Principles of Real Estate Management, 1950. Home: 1000 Lake Shore Dr Chicago IL 60611 also Chesterbrook Elburn IL 60119 Office: 72 Adams St Chicago IL 60603

DOWNS, JOHN A., constrn. co. exec.; b. Watervliet, N.Y., Aug. 11, 1915; B.S. in Civil Engring., U. N.H., 1937; M.S., Mass. Inst. Tech., 1938; m. Ruth E. Crosby, Dec. 20, 1941; children—Michael, James, Sally, Robert, Nancy. With Great Lakes Dredge & Deck Co., Downers Grove, Ill., 1960—, pres., 1966—, also dir. Served to maj., C.E., AUS, 1941-45. Home: 4827 Saratoga Av Downers Grove IL 60515 Office: 228 N LaSalle St Chicago IL 60616

DOWNS, KENNETH THORNTON, corp. exec.; b. Downs, Ill., June 26, 1909; s. Carey Alfred and Alma Mae (Washburn) D.; student U. Mont., 1926-28; grad. Command and Gen. Staff Sch., Ft. Leavenworth, 1943; m. Harriette Clarke, Apr. 20, 1934 (div. 1946); children—Michael Kenneth Lionel, Julie Alma (Mrs. Charles Garcia); m. 2d, Marie Therese Suzanne Laudet, Jan. 20, 1948; children—Terry William David, Lawrence Alfred. Journalist, 1928-41, chief Paris bur. Internat. News Service, 1936-40; staff U.S. Mil. Govt. and Fgn. Service, 1948-50; pub. affairs officer, Berlin, Germany, 1948-51; exec. Time, Inc., 1951-58; asst. dir. OCDM, 1958-61; v.p. internat. div. Selvage & Lee, Inc., 1961-64; pres. Downs & Roosevelt, Inc., pub. relations counsel, 1964—. Served from capt. to lt. col., AUS, 1942-46. Decorated Silver Star; Croix de Guerre with palm and gold star (France); recipient George Holmes Meml. award for reporting, 1939; award for fgn. corr. Sigma Delta Chi, 1940; Atlantic City Headliners award for war corr., 1941. Mem. Kappa Sigma, Sigma Delta Chi. Clubs: Chevy Chase (Md.); Army and Navy, Nat. Press (Washington); Union; Overseas Press (N.Y.C.). Home: 2837 49th St N W Washington DC 20007 Office: Time and Life Bldg New York City NY 10020

DOWNS, LENTHIEL HOWELL, educator; b. Goshen, N.Y., May 26, 1915; s. Leon Hamilton and Mabel Augusta (Howell) D.; B.A., Tusculum Coll., 1936; M.A., U. Ia., 1937, Ph.D., 1940; grad. student, Sorbonne, Paris, France, 1950-51; m. Marguerite Tomasini, June 10, 1952 (div. 1958); children—Richard Laurence, Christopher Marc. Prof. English, Presbyn. Coll., 1940-42; asst. prof. English, U. Tulsa, 1946-47; mem. faculty Denison U., 1947—, prof. English, 1956—, chmn. dept., 1963-65. Mem. Modern Lang. Assn., Coll. English Assn. Author: (with Edward A. Wright) A Primer for Playgoers, 2d edit., 1969. Home: Box 423 Granville, OH 43023.

DOWNS, ROBERT BINGHAM, librarian; b. Lenoir, N.C., May 25, 1903; s. John McLeod and Clara Catherine (Hartley) D.; A.B., U.N.C., 1926, LL.D., 1949; B.S., Columbia, 1927, M.S., 1929; Litt.D., Colby Coll., 1944; D.L.S., U. Toledo, 1953: L.H.D., Ohio State U., 1963, So. Ill. U., 1970; m. Elizabeth Crooks, Aug. 17, 1929; children—Clara (Mrs. Wm. J. Keller), Mary Roberta (Mrs. Terence A. Andre). Asst., U.N.C. Library, 1922-26, N.Y. Pub. Library, 1927-29; librarian Colby Coll., Waterville, Me., 1929-31; asst. librarian U.N.C., 1931-32, librarian and asso. prof. library sci., 1932-34, librarian, prof., 1934-38; dir. libraries N.Y. U., 1938-43; dir. Library and Library Sch., prof. library sci. U. Ill., Urbana, 1943-58, dean library adminstrn., 1958- 71, asso. Columbia Sch. Library Service, 1942-43; cons. Kabul U., Afghanistan, 1963. Chmn. A.L.A. Bd. on Resources Am. Libraries, 1939-42, 1945-50; pres. Assn. Coll. and Reference Libraries, 1940-41; spl. cons. civil information and edn. sect. SCAP, Japan, 1948, 1950; vis. chief Union Catalog Div., cons. in bibliography Library of Congress, 1949; adviser Nat. Library and Nat. U. Mexico, 1952; library adviser to Turkish Govt., 1955,68,71. Recipient Clarence Day award, 1963, Joseph W. Lippincott award, 1964. Mem. Am. (1st v.p. 1951-52, pres. 1952-53), Ill. (pres. 1955-56), Southeastern library assns., Am. Assn. U. Profs., Bibliog. Soc. Am., Soc. Midland Authors, Phi Beta Kappa, Beta Phi Mu, Phi Kappa Phi. Democrat. Clubs: Rotary, Dial, Caxton, University (Urbana). Author: The Story of Books, 1935; Resources of Southern Libraries, 1938; Resources of New York City Libraries, 1942; Am. Library Resources, 1951-62; Books that Changed the World, 1956; Molders of the Modern Mind, 1961; Famous Books, Ancient and Medieval, 1964; (with others) Family Saga, 1958; Resources of North Carolina Libraries, 1965; How To Do Library Research, 1966; Resources of Missouri Libraries, 1966; Resources of Canadian Academic and Research Libraries, 1967; Books That Changed America, 1970. Editor: Library Specialization, 1941; Union Catalogs in the United States, 1942; Status of American College and University Librarians, 1958; The First Freedom, 1960; The Bear Went Over the Mountain, 1964; (with Frances B. Jenkins) Bibliography, Current State and Future Trends, 1967; Famous American Books, 1971. Contbr. articles to library jours. Home: 708 W Pennsylvania Av Urbana IL 61801

DOWNS, THOMAS JOSEPH, lawyer; b. Terre Haute, Ind., Mar. 7, 1904; s. James Edward and Mary Gertrude (Cannon) D.; student Ind. State U., 1922-23; J.D., Georgetown U., 1928; m. Frances M. Mayrose, June 2, 1931; children—Sara Ann (Mrs. Eugene P. O'Brien), Ellen (Mrs. Daniel de la Torre). Admitted to Ill., D.C. bars; partner Downs & Scheib, 1942-50, Downs, Johnson & Zahler, Chgo. and Washington, 1950-53, Thomas J. Downs, Chgo. and Washington, 1953-70, Downs & Pierce, 1970—. Pub. adminstr. Cook County, 1957-62; mem., v.p. Med. Center Commn., 1953—. Asst. atty. gen. Ill., 1968—. Delegate Republican Nat. Conv., 1940, 48, 56, 60, 68; Rep. nominee 2d Ill. Dist. U.S. Congress 1942, 44. Recipient 175th Anniversary medal of Honor, Georgetown U. Sch. Law, 1964, Mem. Am., Ill., Chgo. bar assns., Bar Assn. 7th Fed. Circuit, Am. Judicature Soc., Delta Chi. Clubs: Union League, South Shore Country, Executives, Press (Chgo.). Home: 300 N State St Chicago IL 60610 Office: 135 S LaSalle St Chicago IL 60603 also 1830 Jefferson Pl Washington DC 20036

DOWNS, WILBUR GEORGE, educator, physician; b. Perth Amboy, N.J., Aug. 7, 1913; s. James Cloyd and Mabel Lulu (Lehman) D.; A.B., Cornell U., 1935, M.D., 1938; M.P.H., Johns Hopkins, 1941; M.A. (hon.), Yale, 1964; m. Helen Martley Geer, Sept. 20, 1940; children—Helen (Mrs. Christian J. Haller III), Anne (Mrs. James A. Carroll), William M., Isabel. Mem. staff Rockefeller Found., 1941-61, asso. dir., 1961-71, dir. virus program, div. biomed. scis., 1961-71; prof. epidemiology Yale Med. Sch., 1964-71. Mem. standing adv. com. Med. Research Brit. Caribbean, 1956—; expert panel arthropod-borne viruses WHO, 1956—; commn. for malaria Armed Forces Epidemiological Bd., 1965—. Bd. dirs. Hartley House, N.Y.C. Served with AUS, 1942-46. Diplomate Am. Bd. Preventive Medicine. Mem. Am., Royal socs. tropical medicine and hygiene, Am. Pub. Health Assn. Home: 10 Halstead Lane Branford CT 06405 Office: Yale Arbovirus Research Unit 60 College St New Haven CT 06510

DOWNS, WILLIAM RANDALL, Jr., news corr.; b. Kansas City, Kan., Aug. 17, 1914; s. William R. and Katherine Lee (Tyson) D.; A.B., U. Kan., 1937; m. Rosalind Gerson, Dec. 18, 1946; children—William R., Karen Louise, Adam Michael. Began career as fgn. corr. United Press, London, 1939-42; with CBS, 1942-62, in Moscow, 1943, war corr. Europe and Far East, 1944- 46, Bikini Atomic Test, 1946, Berlin, 1948-50, Korean War, 1950, Washington, 1950-53, Rome, 1953-56, diplomatic corr., 1956-62; free- lance writer, 1962-63; corr. ABC News, 1964—. Recipient Headliners award, 1945; Overseas Press Club award for best fgn. radio reporting, 1949. Mem. Overseas Writers. Clubs: Nat. Press, Overseas Press. Contbr. to various publs., including Newsweek, This Week mag. Home: 5535 Warwick Pl Chevy Chase MD 20015 Office: ABC News 1124 Connecticut Av Washington DC 20015

DOWNSBROUGH, GEORGE ATHA, electronic co. exec.; b. Firthcliffe, N.Y., Feb. 14, 1910; s. Ernest and Ethel (Atha) D.; B.S., Rutgers U., 1931, M.S., 1933, Ph.D., 1936; m. Margaret E. McDougall, July 24th, 1948; children—George A., Bruce Owen. Sr. physicist Johns Manville Co., Manville, N.J., 1936-40; physicist Bur. Ordnance, Navy Dept., Washington, also Norfold, Va., 1940-42; v.p., gen. mgr. Boonton Radio Corp. (N.J.), 1942-44, pres., gen. mgr., 1944-50, pres., dir., treas., 1950-56, pres., dir., 1956-63; asst. to pres. Am. Radiator & Standard San. Corp., N.Y.C., 1963-65; v.p. tech. products div. Singer Co., N.Y.C., 1965-68, v.p. and chief tech. officer, 1968-70; pres. HRB Singer, State College, Pa., 1970—. Trustee Riverside Hosp., Boonton. Mem. I.R.E., Am. Phys. Soc., A.A.A.S., Sci. Apparatus Makers Assn. Home: 495 Pepperidge Tree Terrace Smoke Rise Butler NJ 07405 Office: HRB Singer State College PA 16801

DOWS, DAVID ALAN, educator; b. San Francisco, July 25, 1928; s. Samuel Randall and Rita M. (Bowers) D.; B.S., U. Cal. at Berkeley, 1952, Ph.D., 1954; m. Wena Hunt Waldner, July 29, 1950; children—Janet Louise, Carol Marie, Joyce Ellen. Instr. chemistry Cornell U., 1954-56; instr. U. So. Cal., Los Angeles, 1956-57, asst. prof., 1957-59, asso. prof., 1959-63, prof. chemistry, 1963—, chmn. dept., 1966—; NATO prof. 1970; cons. Los Alamos Nat. Lab. NSF fellow, 1962-63. Fellow Chem. Soc. London; mem. Am. Chem. Soc., Am. Phys. Soc., Phi Beta Kappa. Contbr. articles profl. jours. Office: U So Cal Chemistry University Park Los Angeles CA 90007

DOWSON, GRAHAM RANDALL, diversified co. exec.; b. Westcliff, Eng., Jan. 13, 1923; s. Cyril James and Dorothy (Foster) D.; ed. U. Pensacola; m. Fay Valerie Weston, Aug. 28, 1954; children—Deborah Randall, Sally Randall. With U.S. Steel Corp., Columbia Steel Co.; broadcaster Midsouth Broadcasting System, 1949-52; dir. A.C. Nielson Co., Chgo., 1952-58; with The Rank Orgn., 1958—, now dep. chief exec., also dir. subsidiary cos. Served as pilot RAF, 1940- 46. Mem. Royal Aero Club. Clubs: Carlton (London, Eng.); Royal London Yatch; Royal Air Force Yacht; Royal Cork Yacht. Home: 20 Raynham St Norfolk Crescent London England Office: 38 South St London W1 England

DOXIADIS, CONSTANTINOS APOSTOLOS, architect-planner; b. Stenimachos, May 14, 1913; s. Apostolos and Evanthia (Mezeviri) D.; grad. architect-engr., Tech. U. Athens, 1935; Dr. Ing. Mit Auszeichnung, Berlin-Charlottenburg (Germany) U., 1936; LL.D., Swarthmore Coll., 1962, Mills Coll., 1964, U. Mich., 1967, Tulane U., 1968, Kalamazoo Coll., 1968; D.Sc., Detroit Inst. Tech., 1966, U. Pitts., 1967; D.F.A., U.R.I., 1966; D.H., Wayne State U., 1964; L.H.D., No. Mich. U., 1965, Case Western Res. U., 1969; m. Emma Scheepers, Apr. 30, 1940; children—Evanthia, Calliope, Eufrosyne, Apostolos. Chief town planning officer Greater Athens Area, 1937-38; head dept. regional and town planning Greek Ministry Pub. Works, 1939-45; lectr., acting prof. town planning Tech. U., Athens, 1939-43; prof. ekistics Grad. Sch. Ekistics, Athens Tech. Inst., also chmn. bd., 1958—; minister, permanent sec. Greek Housing Reconstrn., 1945-48; minister-coordinator Greek Recovery Program, 1948-51; pres. Doxiadis Assos., cons. devel. and ekistics, Athens, 1951—; vis. lectr. U. Chgo., Yale, Harvard, Princeton, Swarthmore Coll., Mass. Inst. Tech., Ga. Inst. Tech., Dublin, Mich., N.Y., Oxford, Trinity colls. Participant numerous internat. dels., also cons. Decorated Greek Mil. Cross, 1941; officer Order Brit. Empire, 1945; mem. Order Cedar (Lebanon), 1958; Royal Order of Phoenix (Greece), 1960; Yugoslav Flag Order with Golden Wreath, 1966; recipient Sir Patrick Abercrombie prize Internat. Union Architects, 1963; Cali de Oro award Soc. Mexican Architects, 1963; award of excellence Indsl. Designers Soc. Am., 1965; Aspen award humanistic studies Colo., 1966. Mem. Soc. Internat. Devel., Am. Mgmt. Assn., Am. Soc. Testing and Materials, Internat. Fedn. Housing and Planning, Am. Inst. Planners, Am. Soc. Planning Ofcls., Greek Tech. Chamber, Inter-Am. Planning Soc.; hon. corr. fellow Royal Incorp. Architects of Scotland; hon. corr. mem. Town Planning Inst. Gt. Britain Author: Raumordnung im Griechischen Stadtebau, 1937; A Simple Story (in Greek), 1945; Ekistic Analysis (in Greek), 1946; Destruction of Towns and Villages in Greece, 1946; A Plan for the Survival of the Greek People (with others), 1947; March of the People (in Greek), 1949; Our Capital and its Future (in Greek), 1960; Architecture in Transition (in English), 1963; Urban Renewal and the Future of the American City (in English), 1966; Between Dystopia and Utopia (in English), 1966; Ekistics, an Introduction to the Science of Human Settlements (in English), 1968; reports problems of devel. and ekistics in 36 countries. Home: 2 Strat Syndesmou Athens 136 Greece Office: 24 Strat Syndesmou Athens 136 Greece

DOYLE, ARTHUR JOSEPH, steel co. exec.; b. Cleve., Aug. 28, 1908; s. Arthur Leo and Kathryn (Sullivan) D.; ed. privately; m. Helen L. Holloway, June 26, 1937; children—Charles J., Mary Lorine (Mrs. Gerald L. Sauter, Ann (Mrs. J. Orin Anderson). With Youngstown Steel Door Co., Cleve., 1937—, v.p., 1958-66, pres., 1966—; v.p. subsidiary Camel Sales Co., Cleve., 1951-65, pres., 1965-66; pres. subsidiary Camel Co. Ltd., Cleve., 1962—. Mem. Cleve. Advt. Club. Clubs: Chicago Athletic Assn.; Youngstown (O.); Union, Clevelander, Cleveland Athletic (Cleve.); Mt. Stephen (Montreal, Que., Can.). Home: 762 Kenwood Dr Gates Mills, OH 44040. Office: 590 The Arcade Cleveland OH 44114

DOYLE, BERTRAM WILBUR, ret. bishop; b. Lownesboro, Ala., July 3, 1897; s. Henry Sebastian and Anna Magnolia (Walker) D.; A.B., Ohio Wesleyan U., 1921; A.M., U. Chgo., 1924, Ph.D., 1934; D.D., Lane Coll., 1934; Doctor of Laws (hon.), Miles Coll., 1958; D.D., Ohio Wesleyan U., 1962; m. Pansy Ray Stewart, August 12, 1918; children—Vera Corinne, Annie Glenn, Grace Margaret, Pansy Henrietta, Bertram Wilbur. Tchr. Samuel Houston Coll., 1921-22, Claflin Coll., 1922-24, Clark Coll., 1924-25; dean Paine Coll., 1925-27; tchr. Fisk U., 1927-37, personnel dean, 1928-30; ordained to ministry Christian M.E. Ch., 1925; pastor Orangeburg, Allendale, S.C., Nashville, Goodlettsville, Tenn.; faculty summer schs. Atlanta U., 1939, Hampton Inst., 1940-41; dean Louisville Municipal Coll., 1942-50; sec. edn. Christian M.E. Ch., 1937-50; elected bishop 7th dist., 1950, 6th dist., 1954, 8th dist., 1958, 2nd dist., 1966; mem. exec. com. World Meth. Council, 1951-71; sr. bishop Christian M.E. Church, 1962-70; chmn. Christian M.E. delegation to World Meth. Conf., Oslo, 1961, London, 1966. Chmn. bd. trustees Tex. Coll., 1958-66. Mem. Nat. Council Christian Chs. (gen. bd. 1950—; mem. constituting conv. 1950; v.p. at large 1966-69), Nat. Assn. Deans and Registrars (pres. 1948), Nat. Protestant Council Higher Edn. (sec. exec. com. 1948-50), New Deal Progressive League, Phi Beta Kappa, Kappa Alpha Psi, Sigma Pi Phi. Author: Etiquette of Race Relations in the South, 1937. Editor: A Study of Negro Business and Employment in Louisville, 1944. Contbr. articles to mags. Home: 1982 Madison Lane Gary IN 46407

DOYLE, DANIEL MORAN, banker; b. Chgo., Apr. 28, 1929; s. Lawrence Joseph and Mary Margaret (Moran) D.; A.B. with honors, U. Ill., 1956; grad. Stonier Grad. Sch. of Banking of Rutgers U., 1963; m. Martha Clare Rogers, Sept. 5, 1959; children—M. Clare, Ann Rogers. Asst. cashier Fed. Res. Bank of Chgo., 1961-64, asst. v.p., 1964-68, v.p., 1968-69, sr. v.p. Detroit br., 1969—. Trustee Mich. Hosp. Service, 1971—. Served with inf. AUS, 1951-53. Decorated Bronze Star, Purple Heart. Mem. Econ. Club Detroit (asst. treas.), Phi Beta Kappa, Phi Alpha Theta. Office: 160 W Fort St Detroit MI 48231

DOYLE, DONALD EARL, banker; b. N.Y.C., Apr. 24, 1930; s. Earl S. and Sadie (Harrigan) D. B.C.S. cum laude, Benjamin Franklin U., 1952; M.C.S., 1953; grad. Bank Adminstrn. Inst., U. Wis., 1960; m. Barbara A. Rollins, Oct. 13, 1956; children—Diane Marie, Steven Brian, Deborah Ann. With Lincoln Nat. Bank, Washington, 1948-58, auditor, 1954-58; bank consol. with Riggs Nat. Bank, 1958, auditor, 1967-70, v.p., gen. auditor, 1970—. Mem. Am. Inst. Banking (pres. Washington 1960-61, mem. faculty Washington 1962—). Office: Riggs Nat Bank 9th and F Sts NW Washington DC 20004 Mailing Address:

DOYLE, EDWARD ALLEN, clergyman, dean.; b. Columbia, S.C., July 14, 1914; s. Alexander Calhoun and Lillian Catherine (Allen) D.; A.B., Georgetown U., 1935; student Spring Hill Coll., 1938-40; S.T.L., St. Mary's Coll., 1947; Ph.D., Cath. U. Am., 1952. Ordained priest Roman Cath. Ch., 1946; tchr. St. Charles Coll., Grand Coteau, La., 1939-40; dir. dramatics Jesuit High Sch., New Orleans, 1940-43; dean faculties, sch. arts and scis. Loyola U., New Orleans, 1952-65, bd. dirs., 1952-66, acad. v.p., 1965-66; dir. studies New Orleans Province Jesuit Ednl. Assn., Ponchatoula, La., 1966-67, prin. Jesuit High Sch., New Orleans, 1967-68, pres.- prin., 1968-71, pres., 1971—. Mem. La. com., commn. on secondary schs. So. Assn. Colls. and Schs.; mem. secondary sch. commn. Jesuit Ednl. Assn., 1969—; mem. Archdiocesan Adv. Council, New Orleans, 1969—. Bd. trustees Spring Hill Coll., Mobile, Ala.; bd. dirs. Citizens for Advancement of Pub. Edn., 1965-66; rep. Nat. Cath. Edn. Assn., 4th Nat. Conf. Citizenship, 1950; chmn. Conf. Acad. Deans So. States, 1959. Pres. New Orleans Children's Bur., 1956-57. Served as lt. O.R.C., U.S. Army. Mem. Jesuit Ednl. and Lit. Soc. (dir. higher edn. New Orleans province 1959-61), Assn. Collegiate Deans, Assn. Deans Jesuit Colls., Assn. Higher Edn. N.E.A., Soc. Advancement Edn., Nat. Soc. Study Edn., Blue Key, Alpha Sigma Nu, Kappa Delta Pi, Delta Epsilon Sigma. Author: The Status and Functions of the Departmental Chairman of Colleges of Liberal Arts, 1952; chpt. in Functions of The Dean of Studies in Higher Education, 1957. Address: Jesuit High School PO Box 19145 New Orleans LA 70179

DOYLE, EDWARD JOSEPH, retired marine corps officer; b. Wharton, N.J., May 6, 1918; s. Joseph Augustus and Edna Josie (Hanschka) D.; B.A., Dartmouth Coll., 1940; M.A., George Washington U., 1963; m. Jane Louise Singleton, Aug. 16, 1941; children—Bonnie Lynn (Mrs. Peter Charles O'Reilly), Edward Joseph. Joined USMC, 1941, commd. 2d lt., 1941, advanced through grades to brig. gen., 1967; naval flight tng., 1943; dir. Mid East, Africa, South Asia div. Joint Staff, Washington, 1969-70; retired, 1971. Decorated Legion of Merit (3), Bronze Star, D.F.C. (3), Air medal (5). Roman Catholic. Club: Army/Navy Country (Washington). Address: Audubon Lane Port Royal Plantation Hilton Head SC 29928

DOYLE, FRANK C., lighting co. exec.; b. Highland, Wis., 1909; married. With A.O. Smith Corp., Milw., until 1945; with Thomas Industries, Inc., Louisville, 1945—, now sec., treas. Home: 4039 St Ives Ct Louisville KY 40207 Office: 207 E Broadway Louisville KY 40202*

DOYLE, HAROLD C., lawyer; b. Yankton, S.D., Nov. 25, 1926; s. Harold A. and May (Carlon) D.; student Creighton U., 1947; LL.B., S.D. U., 1950; m. Norma Ann German, May 23, 1953; children—Elizabeth May, Patrick Harold, Nora Ann, Mary Ellen. Admitted to S.D. state bar; gen. practice of law in Yankton, 1950-61; states atty. Yankton County, 1957-61; U.S. atty. Dist. S.D., 1961-69; partner firm May Boe & Johnson, Sioux Falls, 1969—. County chmn. Democratic Party, Yankton, 1955-60. Served with USNR, 1944-46. Mem. Yankton Jr. C. of C. (pres. 1954), Delta Tau Delta, Phi Delta Phi. Elk, K.C. Home: 2107 S Phillips Av Sioux Falls SD 57105 Office: 412 W 9th St Sioux Falls SD 57104

DOYLE, JAMES ALEXANDER, lawyer; b. Thedford, Neb., Jan. 19, 1904; s. John and Hattie (Beckhoff) D.; Ph.B., Creighton U., 1924; LL.B., U. of Neb., 1933; LL.M., Harvard, 1942; m. Amelia Brosius, June 9, 1927; children—James Alan, Katherine Ann. Supt. Thomas County High Sch., Thedford, Neb., 1927-30; admitted to Neb. bar; law clerk to U.S. Circuit Judge, Omaha, 1933-35; prof. law U. Neb., 1936-43; asst. reviser Neb. Statute Commn., Lincoln, 1941-43; regional atty. U.S. Dept. of Agr., Lincoln, Neb., 1943-44, Chgo., 1944-45; asso. solicitor, Washington, 1945-48, spl. cons. to solicitor on litigation, 1948; dean Creighton U. Sch. of Law, Omaha, Neb., 1948-70, dean emeritus, 1970—; also arbitrator in labor disputes. Fellow Harvard Law Sch., 1937-38. Pres. Legal Aid Soc. Omaha, Inc. Mem. Am. Law Inst., Am., Neb. bar assns., Order of Coif, Phi Delta Phi, Alpha Sigma Nu. Roman Catholic. Rotarian. Contbr. articles to Neb. Law Rev. Home: 9468 Dewey Av Omaha NB 68114

DOYLE, JAMES ALOYSIUS, assn. exec.; b. Pitts., Mar. 20, 1921; s. James A. and Anna Sophia (Holthaus) D.; B.A., Queens Coll., N.Y.C., 1943; m. Ethel Miriam Clancey, Oct. 3, 1943; children—John Kevin, Elizabeth Marie, Brian James, Peter, Thomas. Editor, promotion mgr., circulation dir. Howes Pub. Co., Inc., N.Y.C., 1946-58; publicity chmn. Am. Assn. Textile Chemists and Colorists, 1955-58; exec. sec. Cath. Press Assn. U.S., Inc., 1958—. Served as sgt., AUS, 1944-46, 1st lt., 1951-52. Mem. Alumni Assn. Queens Coll. (1st pres. 1946-47, dir. 1947-50). Club: Overseas Press (N.Y.C.). Home: 25 Gregory Av Merrick NY 11566 Office: 432 Park Av S New York City NY 10016

DOYLE, JAMES EDWARD, U.S. judge; b. Oshkosh, Wis., July 6, 1915; s. James Edward and Agnes (McCarthy) C.; A.B., U. Wis., 1937; LL.B., Columbia, 1940; m. Ruth Bachhuber, Aug. 10, 1940; children—Mary Eileen (Mrs. James Pickman), James Edward, Catherine Margaret, Anne Malloy. Admitted to Wis. bar, 1940, also U.S. Supreme Ct.; atty. criminal div. Dept. Justice, 1940-41; law clk. to asso. justice James F. Byrnes, U.S. Supreme Ct., 1941-42; cons. Office War Moblzn. and Reconversion, 1945; asst. to counselor State Dept., 1945-46; asst. U.S. atty., Madison, Wis., 1946-48; partner firm LaFollette, Sinykin & Doyle, Madison, 1948-65; U.S. judge Western Dist. Wis., 1965—; lectr. U. Wis. Law Sch., 1951-53, 58. Nat. co-chmn. Americans for Democratic Action, 1953-55. Chmn. Wis. Democratic Party, 1951-53; exec. dir. Nat. Stevenson for Pres. Com., 1960. Served to lt. USNR, 1942-45. Mem. Am. Law Inst., Dane County Bar Assn. (pres. 1962-63). Bd. editors Columbia Law Rev., 1938-40. Home: 1114 Mohican Pass Madison WI 53711 Office: US District Ct Madison WI 53701

DOYLE, JAMES EDWIN, (Ned), advt. exec.; b. N.Y.C., Oct. 23, 1902; s. William Joseph and Josephine (Huttenbrauch) D.; student Hamilton Coll., 1920-22; LL.B., Fordham U., 1931; m. Helen Aisley; 1 son, Anthony Edwin; m. 2d, Marion E. Lance, May 26, 1945 (div. Jan. 1966); children—Michael Varian, Ellin Downey; m. 3d, Margaret Rivelli, Aug. 14, 1967. Advt. mgr. Look mag., 1937-42; account exec., vp. Grey Advt. Agy., 1945-49; exec. v.p. Doyle, Dane, Bernach, advt. agy., N.Y.C., from 1949, formerly chmn. exec. com., now bd. dirs.; owner Floridians basketball team. Mem. bus. adv. com. on mgmt. improvement State of N.Y. Trustee Hamilton Coll. Served as capt. USMC, 1942-45. Mem. Nat. Football League Alumni Assn. (hon.), Alpha Phi, Chi Psi. Club: Farmington Country (Charlottesville, Va.). Home: 242 E 19th St New York City NY 10003 also Fire Island Biscayne FL 33149 Office: 20 W 43d St New York City NY 10036 also 1674 Meridian Miami Beach FL 33139

DOYLE, JAMES N., corp. exec.; b. Lachine, Can., 1916; ed. McGill U., 1937. Vice pres., gen. counsel, sec., dir. Steinberg's Ltd.; sec. dir., Steinberg's Shopping Centres Ltd.; sec., gen. counsel, dir. Ivanhoe Corp.; sec. Steinberg Properties Ltd.; sec., dir. Steinberg Realty Ltd.; dir. Cartier Sugar Ltd., Phenix Mills Ltd. Chmn., Retail Council Can. Home: 100 Sunnyside Av Westmount 6 Quebec Canada Office: 110 Cremazie Blvd W Montreal 5 Quebec Canada

DOYLE, JOHN VINCENT, bus. exec.; b. Oak Park, Ill., Oct. 31, 1922; s. J. Frederick and Elizabeth (Meyers) D.; student Northwestern U., 1941-42, Internat. Corr. Schs., 1942-44, Columbia 1945-46, N.Y. U., 1947-48; m. Frances G. Jiranek, Feb. 10, 1945; children—Kathleen Frances, Virginia Marie, Frederick Charles. Promotion copywriter Chgo. Tribune-N.Y. News Syndicate, N.Y.C., 1946-47; copywriter O.S. Tyson, Inc., N.Y.C., 1947- 48, Batten, Barton, Durstine & Osborn, N.Y.C., 1948-51; sr. v.p., dir. account mgmt. Campbell-Ewald Co., Detroit, 1951-68; dir. marketing Florists Transworld Delivery Assn., Detroit, 1968—. Bd. dirs. United Community Services, Detroit, 1963—. Trustee Cranbrook Inst. Sci., Bloomfield Hills, Mich., 1964—. Served with USCGR, 1942-45. Mem. Mich State C. of C. (past dir.). Clubs: Recess, Adcraft (Detroit). Home: 578 Woodway Ct Bloomfield Hills MI 48013 Office: 900 W Lafayette Detroit MI 48226

DOYLE, JOSEPH, educator; b. Jersey City, Dec. 13, 1915; s. Joseph A. and Mary A. (Kelsey) D.; grad. Newark Acad., 1933; A.B., Princeton, 1937; A.M., Columbia, 1941, Ph.D., 1952; m. Alice Valentine Pulsifer, May 23, 1942; children—Valentine, Allen Pulsifer. Instr. French, Peekskill Mil. Acad., 1938-39; asst. English, Columbia, 1941-43, instr., 1947-48; asst. prof. English, Washington and Jefferson Coll., 1948-50; dean prof. lit. Washington Coll., Chestertown, Md., 1953-58; acad. dean Am. Internat. Coll., Springfield, Mass., 1958-60; prof. English, U. Hartford, 1960—, dean Sch. Arts and Scis., 1960-66. Served to lt. (s.g.), USNR, 1943-46. Mem. Eastern Assn. Deans (exec. com. 1956-58, v.p. 1958-59, pres. 1959-62), Am. Assn. U. Profs., Modern Lang. Assn., Coll. English Assn., Nat. Council Tchrs. English, Assn. Higher Edn. Unitarian. Contbr. articles, poems to profl. jours. Home: 80 Kane St West Hartford CT 06119 Office: 200 Bloomfield Av West Hartford CT 06107

DOYLE, JUSTIN J., lawyer; b. Rochester, N.Y., Dec. 29, 1904; s. Joseph P. and Catherine (McCarthy) D.; student Dartmouth, 1923-24; A.B., U. Rochester, 1927; LL.B., Harvard, 1930; m. Jane M. Kreag, June 11, 1943; children—Carol E., Justin P. Admitted to N.Y. State bar, 1930; practiced in Rochester, 1930—; sr. mem.firm Nixon, Hargrave, Devans & Doyle, 1946—. Dir. Rochester Telephone Corp., Bausch & Lomb, Inc. Served with USAAF, World War II. Mem. Am., N.Y. State, Rochester (past v.p.) bar assns., N.Y. State Automobile Assn. (past v.p., dir.), Phi Beta Kappa, Alpha Delta Phi. Home: 327 Allen's Creek Rd Rochester, NY 14618. Office: 1 Exchange St Rochester NY 14614

DOYLE, LEE THOMAS, army officer; b. Lakewood, O., Apr. 14, 1926; s. Leo P. and Mae (Scanlon) D.; B.S., U.S. Mil. Acad., 1948; M.A. in English, U. Pa. 1961; M.S., in internat. Affairs, George Washington U., 1968; m. Johnsie Loftin, Oct. 3, 1953; children—Thomas, Adrian, Timothy, Aimee. Commd. 2d lt. U.S. Army, 1948, advanced through grades to col., 1969; asst. 3d Armored Div., 1956-57; from instr. to asso. prof. English, U.S. Mil. Acad., 1961- 64; plans officer 8th U.S. Army, 1964-65; then asst. exec. officer procurement, edn., research and tng. div. Office Asst. Sec. Manpower and Res. Affairs, Washington; chief Procurement edn., research and tng. div. Office Asst. Sec. Manpower and Res. Affairs, 1969—. Home: 7804 Kincardine Ct Alexandria, VA 22310. Office: The Pentagon Washington DC 20301

DOYLE, MARION WADE, (Mrs. Henry Grattan Doyle), civic worker; b. Cambridge, Mass., Oct. 30, 1894; d. John F. and Joanna T. (Phelan) Sharkey; grad. Cambridge Latin Sch., 1911; A.B. cum laude in Romance Langs., Radcliffe Coll., 1914; L.H.D., Am. U., 1955; m. Henry Grattan Doyle, Sept. 15, 1917 (dec. 1964); children—Henry Grattan, Marion (Mrs. Charles Campbell, Jr.), Robert Carr. Mem. D.C. Bd. Edn., 1929-49, pres., 1935-49; regional dir. Nat. League Women Voters, 1929-31, nat. exec. v.p., 1931-33; exec. dir. Washington Self-Help Exchange, 1939-45, now pres.; chief employe relations personnel div., Dept. Treasury, 1945- 47; mem. 4th Regional Loyalty Bd., Civil Service Commn., 1948-52; mem. Nat. Loyalty Rev. Bd., 1952-53; asst. to dir., also rep. for orgns., White House Conf. on Edn., 1954-55, U.S. Office of Edn., 1955-57, chmn. D.C. com. 1960 White House Conf. on Children and Youth; chmn. nat. capital area Ten Yr. Program for Radcliffe Coll.; chmn. adv. com. D.C. Juvenile Ct., 1951-53, 57-59; chmn. D.C. Commr's. Youth Council, 1953-56, hon. chmn., 1959—; v.p., later pres. D.C. Commrs.' War Hospitality Com., 1946-47, chmn. successor orgn. D.C. Armed Services Hospitality Com., 1950-54, also pres. Recreation Services (its operating agy.) until 1954, when retired from office, remaining as mem. com.; treas. Chevy Chase Civilian Def. Com.; past sec. Chevy Chase Women's Club; served as pres. Chevy Chase Community Council; active in community orgns., including Vis. Nurse Assn.; bd. dirs. Catholic Charities, Archdiocese Wash., 1962—. Recipient various awards and honors, including certificate of merit D.C. Commrs., 1954, citation as distinguished alumna Radcliffe Coll., 1954, John Benjamin Nichols award D.C. Med. Soc., 1955; achievement award Corrections div. United Community Services D.C., 1956; Nat. Brotherhood award Nat. Conf. Christians and Jews, 1959; Catholic Youth Orgn. award, 1960. Mem. D.C. League Women Voters (past pres.), Radcliffe Coll. Alumnae Assn. (bd. mgmt. 1964-67), Columbian Women of George Washington U. (past pres.), Kappa Delta Pi, Delta Kappa Gamma. Club: Twentieth Century (hon.). Contbr. articles to ednl. jours. Home: 5500 33d St Washington DC 20015

DOYLE, MORRIS MCKNIGHT, lawyer; b. Bishop, Cal., Jan. 4, 1909; s. Guy P. and Helen (McKnight) D.; A.B., Stanford, 1929; LL.B., Harvard U., 1932; L.H.D., Nat. Coll. Edn., 1965; m. Juliet H. Clapp, Sept. 15, 1934; children—Barbara (Mrs. George Roupe), Thomas M. Admitted to Cal. bar, 1932; asso. firm McCutchen, Olney, Mannon & Greene, San Francisco, 1932-42; Partner McCutchen, Thomas, Matthew, Griffiths & Greene, San Francisco, 1942-58, McCutchen, Doyle, Brown & Enersen, 1958—. Trustee Stanford (pres. bd. trustees 1962-65), James Irvine Found., Alta Bates Community Hosp.; dir. Stanford Research Inst. Council Financial Aid Edn. Fellow Am. Bar Found., Am. Coll. Trial Lawyers; mem. Am., Cal., San Francisco bar assns., Bar Assn. City N.Y., Am. Law Inst., Am. Judicature Soc. Clubs: Pacific Union, Bohemian, Commonwealth (San Francisco). Home: 36 El Camino Real Berkeley, CA 94705. Office: 601 California St San Francisco CA 94108

DOYLE, MORTIMER BERNARD, forest products industry exec., engrng. co. exec, assn. exec.; b. N.Y.C., Oct. 15, 1916; s. James Joseph and Theresa (Hanrahan) D.; student bus. mgmt. and law LaSalle Extension U., 1947-50; m. Joyce Solomon, Dec. 5, 1942; children—Stephen Paul, Kenneth Anthony. Advt. rep. Gerlach Barklow Co., Joliet, Ill., 1945-46; asst. sales mgr. O'Sullivan Rubber Corp., Winchester, Va., 1946-47; dir. devel N.A.M., 1947-57; exec. v.p. Nat. Forest Products Assn., Washington, 1957-68; pres., chmn. bd. Timber Engrng. Co. Washington, 1957-68; exec. v.p. S.W. Forest Industries, Inc., Phoenix, 1968—. Chmn. lumber survey com. U.S. Dept. Commerce, 1957-65. Served with USMCR, 1936-45; col. Res., 1946-70. Decorated Purple Heart; recipient Distinguished Service award Middle Atlantic Lumbermen's Assn., 1960, Leadership plaque Life Mag., 1960; Mem. U.S. C. of C. (past chmn. assn. com., Distinguished Service award 1962), Am. Soc. Assn. Execs.(pres., dir., exec. com., Key Man award 1964), Washington Trade Assn. Execs., Forest Industries Council (council, past chmn. exec. com.), Washington Bd. Trade, Civil War Round Table. Nat. Assn. Execs. Club. Clubs: International, Capitol Hill, Columbia Country (Washington); Paradise Valley Country (Scottsdale, Ariz.); Phoenix Executives; Congressional Country (Potomac, Md.). Home: 7526 N Eucalyptus Dr Scottsdale AZ 85253 Office: 3443 N Central Av Phoenix AZ 85012

DOYLE, ROBERT EDWARD, educator; b. Valley Stream, N.Y., Dec. 25, 1929; s. John Joseph and Madeliene (Kappe) D.; B.S., Iona Coll., 1951; M.S., N.Y.U., 1956, Ph.D., 1963. Tchr. math. West Hempstead (N.Y.) High Sch., 1955-57; asst. prof. Iona Coll., 1957-63; asst. prof. St. John's U., 1963-64, asso. prof., 1964-67, prof. counselor edn., chmn. dept. counselor edn., 1967—; cons. N.Y.C. Bd. Edn. Served with AUS, 1952-55. Mem. Nat. Cath. Guidance Conf. (pres. 1968-70), N.Y. State Assn. Counselor Educators and Suprs. (pres. 1969-70), Am. Psychol. Assn., Am., N.Y. State personnel and guidance assns., Nat. Vocational Guidance Assn., Am. Sch. Counselors Assn. Author: Career Patterns of Alumni of a Men's Liberal Arts Coll., 1963. Office: St John's U Jamaica NY 11432

DOYLE, ROBERT WALTER, clergyman; b. Torrington, Conn., July 30, 1908; s. Moses W. and Mary J. (McElhone) D.; student Spring Hill Coll., Mobile, Ala., 1927-28. St. Thomas Sem., Hartford, Conn., 1928-29, St. Mary's Sem., Balt., 1929-35. Ordained priest Roman Cath. Ch., 1935, papal chamberlain, 1954, domestic prelate, 1957; asst. pastor St. Peter's Ch., also prin. St. Peter's Sch., Hartford, 1935-46; asst. supt. schs. Archdiocese of Hartford, 1946- 51, supt. schs., 1951-61; pastor St. Augustine's Ch., Hartford, 1961-68. Sacred Heart Ch., Wethersfield, 1968—. Archdiocesan consultor, 1963—. Home: 56 Hartford Av Wethersfield, CT 06109.

DOYLE, ROGER HART, lawyer; b. New Orleans, July 6, 1919; s. John Warren and Stella (Vaughn) D.; J.D., Tulane U., 1947; m. Mary Eleanor Boylan, Apr. 10, 1944; children-Mary Katharine (Mrs. Edward Alden McLellan, Jr.), Pamela. Admitted to La. bar, 1947, since practiced in New Orleans; partner firm Doyle, Smith, Doyle & Watters, 1947—. Served to capt. USAF, 1941-45. Decorated D.F.C., Air medal with seven oak leaf clusters. Mem. Am., La., New Orleans bar assns., Order of Coif. Democrat. Episcopalian. Clubs: Lawn, Tennis, Plimsol, Crillo, Petroleum, Recess (New Orleans). Mem. student bd. editors Tulane Law Rev., 1946-47. Home: 1629 4th St New Orleans LA 70130 Office: 225 Baronne St New Orleans LA 70112

DOYLE, THOMAS RALPH, food retailing co. exec.; b. Waterville, N.Y., July 21, 1914; s. Thomas A. and Elizabeth (Carney) D.; student merchandising, accounting, Columbia, N.Y.U.; m. Lois H. Benton, Oct. 16, 1937; children—Eleanor (Mrs. James W. Dye), Diane (Mrs. Richard Rolfe), Nancy E. With Grand Union Co., 1934—, sr. v.p. supermarket operations, 1968- -. Home: 11 Shaw Rd Woodcliff Lake, NJ 07680. Office: 100 Broadway East Paterson NJ 07407

DOYLE, WILFRED EMMETT, bishop; b. Calgary, Alta., Can., Feb. 18, 1913; s. John Joseph and Mary (O'Neill) D.; B.A., U. Alta, 1935; D.C.L., U. Ottawa, Ont., Can., 1949. Ordained priest Roman Cath. Ch., 1938; chancellor Archdiocese Edmonton, Alta., Can., 1949-58; bishop Nelson, B.C., Can., 1958—. Chmn. bd. govs. Notre Dame U. Nelson. Address: 813 Ward St Nelson British Columbia Canada

DOYLE, WILLIAM ALEXIUS, Jr., newspaperman; b. Jersey City, Oct. 5, 1924; s. William A. and Mary Ellen (Murtha) D.; B.S., Fairleigh Dickinson Coll., 1950; m. Dolores Rita Mahoney, Sept. 29, 1951; children—William Alexius III, Kevin G., Robert P., Elizabeth M. Reporter, Jersey Observer, Hoboken, N.J., 1948-51; financial writer N.Y. World-Telegram, 1951-57, investment columnist, 1957-66; bus. editor N.Y. News, N.Y.C., 1966—; syndicated columnist United Features Syndicate, N.Y.C., 1958—. Mem. Soc. Am. Bus. Writers (pres.), N.Y. Financial Writers Assn., Boat Loaders of Am., Hatch 1. Office: 800 Investors Bldg Minneapolis MN 55402

DOYLE, WILLIAM EDWARD, U.S. circuit judge; b. Denver, Feb. 5, 1911; s. William R. and Sarah (Harrington) D.; A.B., U. Colo., 1940; J.D., George Washington U., 1937; m. Helen Sherfey, Mar. 4, 1939; children—Michael J., Susan Kathleen. Admitted to Colo. bar, 1938; dep. dist. atty., Denver, 1938-41; Pvt. practice, Denver,1941-43, 46-58; dist. ct. judge, Denver, 1948-49; chief dep. dist. atty., Denver, 1948-52; justice Supreme Ct. Colo., 1959-61; U.S. dist. judge, Colo., 1961-71; U.S. circuit judge, Denver, 1971—; part-time tchr. law Westminister Coll. Law, 1946- 56, U. Denver Coll. Law, 1956—; vis. lectr. U. Colo., 1953. Served with AUS, 1943-45; ETO. Mem. Am., Colo., Denver (trustee) bar assns., Colo. Mental Health Assn., U.S. Jud. Conf. (chmn. magistrates com.), Order Coif, Pi Sigma Alpha, Phi Alpha Delta. Democrat. Roman Catholic. Contbr. articles legal jours. Home: 3555 Belcaro Dr Denver CO 80209 Office: US Courthouse Denver CO 80202

DOYLE, WILLIAM LEWIS, biologist; b. Bklyn., May 19, 1910; s. William John and Elizabeth (Lewis) D.; student Dickinson Coll., 1927-29; M.A., Johns Hopkins, 1932, Ph.D. (Bruce fellow), 1934; Gen. Edn. Bd. fellow, Cambridge U., 1935-36; m. Margot E. Metcalfe, Aug. 7, 1937; 1 dau., Katharine. Asst. prof. biology Bryn Mawr Coll., 1937-42; civilian with OSRD, 1942-45; dir. toxicity lab. U. Chgo., 1945-46, asso. prof. anatomy, 1945-50, prof. anatomy, 1950—, asso. dean div. biol. sci., 1958-61, coordinator med. scis., 1969-71. Dir. Mt. Desert Island Biol. Lab., 1964-67, pres., 1970—; sci. attaché Am. Embassy, Stockholm, 1951-52. Mem. Electron Microscope Soc. Am., Am. Assn. Anatomists, Am. Physiol. Soc., Am. Soc. Zoologists, Histochem. Soc. (pres. 1961-62), Soc. Study Devel. and Growth, Phi Beta Kappa, Sigma Xi. Editorial bd. Physiol. Zoology, 1955—. Home: 5545 Dorchester Av Chicago IL 60637

DOYLE, WILLIAM THOMAS, educator, physicist; b. New Britain, Conn., Dec. 5, 1925; s. Thomas William and Kathleen (McConn) D.; Sc.B. in Physics, Brown U., 1951; M.A., Yale, 1952, Ph.D., 1955; m. Barbara May Grant, June 16, 1951; children—Peter, Jeffrey. Mem. faculty Dartmouth, 1955—, prof. physics, 1964—, chmn. dept., 1967—. Served with USNR, 1943-46. NSF predoctoral fellow, 1953-54, 54-55, postdoctoral fellow, 1958-59. Mem. Am. Phys. Soc., A.A.A.S., Sigma Xi. Home: 6 Tyler Rd Hanover, NH 03755.

DOYLE, WILLIAM THOMAS, newspaperman; b. Oakland, Cal., May 22, 1925; s. Albert Norman and Catherine (Stein) D.; B.Journalism, U. Nev., 1950; m. Claire Louise Wogan, Sept. 1, 1946; children—Patrick, Lawrence, Brian, Carrie. Reporter, Richmond (Cal.) Independent, 1950-53; reporter Oakland (Cal.) Tribune, 1953-62, asst. state editor, 1962-64, telegraph editor, 1964- 67, financial editor, 1967—. Pres. Richmond Jr. C. of C., 1957-58; bd. dirs. Cath. Social Service Contra Costa County (Cal.), 1959-62; mem. Richmond Schs. Citizens Adv. Com., 1969. Served with USAAF, 1943-45. Recipient award for best financial sect. daily newspaper Cal., Cal. Newspaper Pubs. Assn., 1968, 70; Hughes fellow Rutgers U., 1969. Mem. Marine Exchange San Francisco Bay Area, Sigma Delta

Chi. Club: Contra Costa (Cal.) Press (Best News Story award 1945, pres. 1965). Home: 2728 Del Monte Av El Cerrito CA 94530 Office: 401 13th St Oakland CA 94604

DOYLE, WILSON KEYSER, evangelist; b. Balt., Jan. 3, 1903; s. W. Harvey and Edith (Griffith) D.; A.B., U. N.C., 1924; Ph.D., Johns Hopkins, 1936. Instr. polit. sci. U. Ala., 1936-43; research asso. U. Va., 1945-47; head dept. pub. adminstrn., Fla. State U., 1947-49, dean sch. pub. adminstrn., 1949-59; mem., founder Gospel Witness Assn. Tech. con. to Commn. To Study Hospitalization of Indigents in Va., 1945; mem. Com. Va. Adv. Legislative Council, 1945; tech. cons. to joint house and senate tax survey com. State of Fla., 1949, League of Va. Counties, 1945-47, Fla. Legislative Com. on Govtl. Reorgn., 1949, Fla. Adv. Council County Officers and Employees, 1951, gov. of Fla., 1949-51; chmn. steering com. of Joint Legislative Com. on Fees, Compensation, and Duties of County Officers, 1952-53; ednl. adviser Fla. Girls State, Boys State, 1950-59; cons. to Fla. Council Higher Edn., 1954-56. Gov.'s Com. on Fiscal Affairs, 1955; cons. mem. industry adv. com. Fla. Devel. Commn., 1955-59. Mem. Phi Beta Kappa. Author: Independent Commissions in the Federal Government, 1939; co-author: The Government and Administration of Florida, 1954. Editorial bd. Jour. Politics, 1954-56. Address: Greenwood VA 22943

DOZER, DONALD MARQUAND, educator; b. Zanesville, O., June 7, 1905; s. Perley Walter and Minnie Bell (Marquand) D.; A.B., Coll. Wooster, 1927; A.M., Harvard, 1930, Ph.D., 1936; (postgrad. Ohio State U., summers 1927, 28; m. Alice Louise Scott, Aug. 2, 1941; children—Charles, Jane, Hilary. Tchr. history and debating Wooster (O.). High Sch., 1927-29; asst. history U., 1934-45; jr. archivist Nat. Archives, Washington, 1936-37; dept., Harvard U. and Radcliffe Coll., 1930-34; instr. history Boston U., 1934-35; jr. archivist, Nat. Archives, Washington, 1936-37; instr. history U. Md., 1937-42; research analyst Coordinator of Information. OSS, 1941-43; liaison officer Office Lend-Lease Adminstrn., 1943-44; fgn. trade analyst. FEA, 1944; research analyst and asst. chief div. Am. Republics Analysis and Liaison, Dept. State, 1944-47, acting chief, div. research for Am. Republics, Office Intelligence Research, 1947-49, coordinator spl. intelligence project involving Latin Am. area for Joint Chiefs of Staff in Office of Intelligence Research, 1949-51, asst. to chief Div. Hist. Policy Research, Hist. Div., Office of Pub. Affairs under Asst. Sec. Pub. Affairs, 1951-56; State Dept. rep. spl. conf., Panama, C.Z., 1948; asst. tech. sec. U.S. delegation 9th Internat. Conf. Am. States, Bogota, Colombia, 1948. Lectr. Strategic Intelligence Sch., Nat. Mil. Establishment, Washington, 1949-51; lectr. Latin Am. Area study program Dept. Internat. Relations and Orgn. and Dept. History, Am. U., Washington, 1949-59; cons. on Latin Am., Brookings Instn., 1950-51; lectr. dept. history Coll. Spl. and Continuation Studies, U. Md., and Montgomery Jr. Coll., Takoma Park, 1956-59; asso. prof. history U. Cal., Santa Barbara, 1959-64, prof., 1964—. Cons. Center for Strategic Studies, Georgetown U., 1964, 66-67. Past mem. alumni bd. Coll. Wooster. Relm Found, fellow, 1963, 66; Fullbright lectr. to Argentina, 1971. Mem. Conf. on Latin Am. Studies, Am. Hist. Assn., Pacific Coast Council on Latin Am. Studies (governing bd. 1964-67, chmn. 1969-70), Am. Revolution Bicentennial Commn. of Cal. (vice chmn.), Geog. Soc. Lima (corr.), Phi Beta Kappa, Omicron Delta Kappa (hon.), Delta Sigma Rho. Christian Scientist. Author: Are We Good Neighbors?, 1959, 61; Latin America; An Interpretive History, 1962; (with others) Trouble Abroad, 1965; The Monroe Doctrine: Its Modern Significance, 1965; (with others) Latin America: Politics, Economics and Hemisphere Security, 1965: Editor: The Conferences at Cairo and Tehran, 1961; also numerous articles Am. fgn. policy, Latin- Am. Relations and hist. subjects in jours. and revs. Home: 421 Miramonte Dr Santa Barbara CA 93105

DOZIER, CRAIG LANIER, educator; b. Spartanburg, S.C., June 14, 1920; s. Edwin Jordan and Lucy (Ladshaw) D.; B.A., U. Wis., 1947; M.A., U. Md., 1951; Ph.D., Johns Hopkins, 1954; m. Virginia Alice Neely, June 11, 1956; children—John Craig, David Ladshaw. Asst. prof. U. S.C., 1954-56, Rollins Coll., 1957-59; asso. prof. La. Poly. Inst., 1959-60; asso. prof. geography U. N.C. at Greensboro, 1960-69, prof., 1969—. Served with USAAF, 1942-45; ETO. Mem. Assn. Am. Geographers, Wilderness Soc., Latin Am. Studies Assn., Conf. Latin Am. Geographers, Southeastern Conf. Latin Am. Studies, Kappa Sigma, Gamma Theta Epsilon. Democrat. Episcopalian. Author: Indigenous Tropical Agriculture in Central America, 1958; Land Development and Colonization in Latin America: Case Studies of Peru, Bolivia and Mexico, 1969. Home: 1614 N College Park Dr Greensboro NC 27403

DOZIER, WILLIAM, TV exec.; b. Omaha, Feb. 13, 1908; s. Robert C. and Emma (McElroy) D.; A.B., Creighton U., 1929; m. Katherine Foley, Sept. 14, 1929; 1 son, Robert J.; m. 2d, Joan Fontaine, May 2, 1946; 1 dau., Deborah Leslie (div. 1950); m. 3d, Ann Rutherford, 1953. Rep. writers artists agy., 1935; head story and writing dept. Paramount Studios, Hollywood, Cal., 1941-44; prodn. exec. RKO-Radio Pictures, Universal-Internat. Pictures, producer Columbia Pictures, 1944-51; program exec. CBS, N.Y.C., 1951-54, exec. dir. story dept., exec. producer, 1958, v.p. charge programs Hollywood, CBS-TV, 1958-60; v.p. charge prodn. Screen Gems, 1960-64; pres. Greenway Prodns., 1964—. Home: 826 Greenway Dr Beverly Hills CA 90210 Office: MGM Studios Culver City CA 90230

DOZORETZ, LOUIS, mental hosp. dir.; b. Bucharest, Rumania, Mar. 17, 1922; s. Morris and Sonya (Fishman) D.; came to U.S., 1922, naturalized, 1928; student Coll. City N.Y., 1938-40; B.A., N.Y.U., 1943; M.D., Middlesex U., Waltham, Mass., 1947; m. Bernice Fleischman, Jan. 6, 1940; children—Shari Lynne, Mark Jeremy, David Michael. Rotating fellow, intern Gouverneur Hosp., N.Y.C., 1947-48; resident psychiatrist Buffalo State Hosp., 1948-51; sr. psychiatrist, 1951-53, supervising psychiatrist, 1953-58; supervising psychiatrist Central Islip (N.Y.) State Hosp., 1958-61, clin. asst. dir., 1961-63, asso. dir., 1963-65; dir. Binghamton (N.Y.) State Hosp., 1965—; asst. psychiatry U. Buffalo Sch. Medicine, 1956-59. Asso. examiner com. certification mental hosp. adminstrs. Am. Psychiat. Assn., 1966—; chmn. area regional com. Mental Health and Retardation, 1968. Served with AUS, 1945-46. Certified mental hosp. adminstr. Mem. World Med. Assn., Assn. Med. Supts. Mental Hosp. (treas. N.Y. State chpt. 1967-70), A.M.A., N.Y. State Med. Soc., Am. Psychiat. Assn., World Med. Assn., Broome County Med. Soc., Am. Geriatrics Soc., Med. Correctional Assn., A.A.A.S., N.Y. Acad. Sci., Am. Assn. Advancement Psycotherapy, Am. Group Psychotherapy Assn., Am. Profl. Practice Assn., World Fedn. Mental Health. Rotarian. Office: Binghamton State Hosp Binghamton NY 13901

DRABKIN, DAVID LION, biochemist; b. Mohilev, Russia, May 3, 1899; (parents Am. citizens); s. Harry and Rose (Drabkin) D.; A.B., Coll. City N.Y., 1919; M.D., Cornell U., 1924; Nat. Research Council fellow Yale, 1924-26; Guggenheim fellow Johns Hopkins, 1940-41; m. Stella M. Friedman, May 1, 1926. Faculty, U. Pa., 1926—, successively instr. biochemistry sch. medicine, asst. prof., asso. prof., 1926-46, prof., chmn. dept. biochemistry Grad. Sch. Medicine, 1946-68, prof. emeritus biochemistry, Sch. Dental Med., 1968- -; cons. Army Postgrad. Sch. Med. Army Med. Center, Washington, VA Hosp., Coatesville, Pa.; mem. panel for establishment nat. hemoglobin standard Nat. Research Council. Recipient Townsend Harris medal for notable achievement City Coll. N.Y., 1969. Mem. Soc. Am. Biol. Chemists (historian), Am. Inst. Nutrition, Soc. Exptl. Biology and Medicine, Phi Beta Kappa. Sigma Xi. Author: Thudichum-Chemist of the Brain, 1958. Home: 2404 Pine St Philadelphia PA 19103

DRACHKOVITCH, MILORAD M., educator, author; b. Belgrade, Yugoslavia, Nov. 8, 1921; s. Milorad and Jovanka (Milanovitch) D.; A.B. in Polit. Sci., U. Geneva (Switzerland), 1949, Ph.D., 1953; m. Jelena Dzigurski, Aug. 5, 1956; children—Radoye, Alexandra. Came to U.S., 1958, naturalized, 1965. Dir. studies Coll. Europe, Bruges, Belgium, 1957-58; vis. asst. prof. polit. sci. U. Cal. at Berkeley, 1959-60; fellow Russian Research Center, Harvard, 1960-61; sr. fellow Hoover Instn. War, Revolution and Peace, also lectr. polit. sci. Stanford, 1961—. Mem. Am. Polit. Sci. Assn., Am. Assn. Advancement Slavic Studies. Author: Les socialismes francais et allemand et le problème de la querre, 1870-1914, 1953; De Karl Marx á Léon Blum, 1954; United States Aid to Yugoslavia and Poland, 1963: Editor: (with B. Lazitch) Comintern: Historical Highlights, 1966; Marxism in the Modern World, 1966; Marxist Ideology in the Contemporary World, 1966; Revolutionary Internationals, 1864-1943, 1966; Yearbook of International Communist Affairs, 1966; Fifty Years of Communism in Russia, 1968. Home: 923 Casanueva Pl Stanford, CA 94305.

DRACHLER, NORMAN, sch. supt.; b. Poland, May 20, 1912; (Am. citizen); B.A., Wayne State U., 1936, M.A., 1939; Ph.D., U. Mich., 1951; m. 1937; 3 children. Tchr. Detroit Pub. Schs., 1936-46, asst. prin. elementary sch., 1946-53, prin., 1953-57; resident dir. edn. Citizens Study Edn. Needs, 1957-59; exec. adminstrv. asst. Detroit Pub. Schs., 1959-61, asst. supt., 1961-66, acting supt., 1966-67, supt., 1967—; cons. U.S. Office Edn., 1967—. Recipient Human Relations award U. Detroit, 1967; Human Right award Commn. Community Relations, 1967; Distinguished Alumnus award Wayne State U., 1969. Mem. Am. Assn. Sch. Adminstrs., Assn. Supervision and Curriculum Devel. (chmn. com. ethnic bias 1969—), Nat. Assn. Temple Edn. (pres. 1957-59), Phi Kappa Phi. Office: 5057 Woodward Detroit MI 48202*

DRACKETT, ROGER, mfg. exec.; b. Cin., Feb. 20, 1910; s. Harry Rogers and Stella (Moorman) D.; B.S., Ohio State U., 1932; M.B.A., Harvard, 1934; m. Jeanne Herbstriet, Nov. 2, 1935; children—Cecile Stewart (Mrs. Michael A. Schacht), Sallie Bolton (Mrs. Alexander T. Van Rensselaer), Harry Rogers III. Various positions Drackett Co., Cin., 1934-48, pres., dir. 1948-69, chmn., 1969—; sr. v.p. Bristol-Myers Co., 1967—; dir. Bristol-Myers Co., N.Y.C., Cin. Gas & Electric Co., Fifth Third Bank, Taft Broadcasting Co. (all Cin.). Trustee Children's Hosp., Cin. Clubs: Bankers, Queen City, Camargo (Cin.). Home: 9200 Old Indian Hill Rd Cincinnati OH 45243 Office: 5020 Spring Grove Av Cincinnati OH 45232

DRAGNICH, ALEX N., educator; b. Republic, Wash., Feb. 22, 1912; s. Nick D. and Stella (Knezevich) D.; student Linfield Coll., McMinnville, Ore., 1933-35; B.A., U. Wash., 1938; M.A., U. Cal. at Berkeley, 1939, Ph.D., 1945; m. Adele Louise Jonas, Mar. 25, 1937; children—Alix Sandra, Paul Nicholas, George Stephen. Propaganda and orgns. analyst Dept. Justice, 1942-44; research analyst OSS, 1942-45; asst. prof. polit. sci. Case-Western U., 1945-47; cultural attache, pub. affairs officer Am. embassy, Belgrade, Yugoslavia, 1947-50; mem. faculty Vanderbilt U., 1950—, prof. polit. sci., 1952—, chmn. dept., 1965-69; Chester W. Nimitz prof. U.S. Naval War Coll., 1959-60; summer tchr. univs. Mont., Alta. Mem. Nashville Community Relations Conf., Nashville Council Fgn. Relations. Ford Faculty fellow, 1955-56; Social Sci. Council fellow, 1952-53. Mem. Am., So. polit. sci. assns., Am. Assn. U. Profs., Phi Beta Kappa. Democrat. Author: Tito's Promised Land, 1954; Major European Governments, rev. edit., 1970. Co-editor, co-author: Government and Politics, rev. edit., 1971. Contbr. profl. jours. Home: 2001 21st Av S Nashville TN 37212

DRAGO, RUSSELL STEPHEN, chemist, educator; b. Turners Falls, Mass., Nov. 5, 1928; s. Stephen R. and Lillian (Pucci) D.; B.S., U. Mass., 1950; Ph.D., Ohio State U., 1954; m. Ruth Ann Burrill, Dec. 30, 1950; children—Patricia, Stephen, Paul, Robert. Mem. faculty U. Ill. at Urbana, 1955—, prof. chemistry, 1965—; cons. Am. Cyanamid, 1957—. Mem. Am. Chem. Soc. (award research inorganic chemistry 1969), Chem. Soc. (London). Author: (with T.L. Brown) Experiments in General Chemistry, 3d edit., 1970; Physical Methods in Inorganic Chemistry, 1965; Prerequisites for College Chemistry, 1966; (with N.A. Matwiy off) Acids and Bases, 1958.) Contbr. articles profl. jours. Home: 3308 Lakeshore Dr Champaign IL 61820 Office: Noyes Lab U Ill Urbana IL 61820

DRAGSTEDT, LESTER REYNOLD, educator; b. Anaconda, Mont., Oct. 2, 1893; s. John A. and Caroline (Selene) D.; B.S., U. Chgo., 1915, M.S., 1916, Ph.D., 1920; M.D., Rush Med. Coll., 1921; Doctor honoris causa, U. Guadalajara, 1953, U. Lyon (France), 1950; D.Sc., U. Fla., 1969; m. Gladys Shoesmith, 1922; children—Charlotte Gladys (Mrs. Thomas E. Jeffrey), Carol Maxine (Mrs. Robert N. Stauffer), Lester R. II, John. Instr. pharmacology State U. Ia., 1916-17, asst. prof. physiology, 1917-19; asst. prof. physiology U. Chgo., 1919-23; prof. physiology and pharmacology Northwestern U. Med. Sch., 1923-25; asso. prof. surgery U. Chgo., 1925-30, then Thomas D. Jones Distinguished Service prof., past chmn. dept., now prof. emeritus; research prof. surgery U. Fla., 1960, prof. physiology, 1968—; hon. prof. surgery U. Guadalajara, 1953; attending surgeon Billings Hosp., 1927-60; surgeon res. USPHS; pres. Chgo. Surg. Soc., 1944-45. Served to lt., M.C., U.S. Army, 1918-19. Decorated Royal Order of North Star (Sweden); recipient Distinguished Service award, gold medal A.M.A., 1963; Julius Friedenwald medal Am. Gastroenterol. Assn., 1964; gold medal Malmo Surg. Found., Sweden, 1st Distinguished award Alumni Assn. Rush Med. Coll., others. Fellow Royal Coll. Physicians and Surgeons of Can. (hon.), Internat. Coll. Surgeons (hon.), Royal Coll. Surgeons Eng. (hon.), Internat. Surg. Soc. (hon.); mem. Nat. Acad. Scis., A.C.S., Am. Gastroenterol. Assn., A.M.A. (gold medal, 1950; chmn. sect. on physiology and pathology 1960-61), A.C.P., Internat. Surg. Soc., Am. Physiol. Soc., Soc. for Exptl. Biology and Medicine, Nat. Soc. for Med. Research (pres.), Inst. Medicine Chgo., Am. Surg. Assn. (1st Distinguished Service award and gold medal 1970), Soc. for Clin. Surgery, Nat. Acad. Medicine Mexico, Gastroent. Assn. Mexico, Phi Beta Kappa, Sigma Xi, Phi Chi, Alpha Omega Alpha. Club: Quadrangle. Contbr. articles to sci. jours. Developed and introduced operations of vagotomy; discovered a hormone, lipocaic, also cause of duodenal and gastric ulcers. Home: 2224 N W 11th Av Gainesville FL 32601

DRAHMANN, JOHN B., educator; B.S., St. John's U., Minn., 1943; Ph.D., St. Louis U., 1952. Prof. physics, dir. div. maths. and phys. scis., also chmn. dept. physics U. Santa Clara, dean Coll. Scis., 1968—. Address: Univ Santa Clara Santa Clara, CA 95053

DRAINE, DONALD PATRICK, educator; b. Chgo., Apr. 9, 1928; s. Harry John and Anne (Ambuehl) D.; A.B., U. Notre Dame, 1950, M.A., 1957; grad. student Harvard, 1955; Ph.D., U. Mich., 1969. Instr. philosophy U. Notre Dame, 1954-57; instr. philosophy, counselor St. Edward's U., Austin, Tex., 1957-60; dean students, asst. prof. philosophy U. Portland, 1960-62, dean Grad. Sch., 1966-67, also dir. instl. research, research adminstrn., dir. sr. coll. program Regional Edn. Lab. for the Carolinas and Virginia, 1967-69; grad. fellow Center Higher Edn., U. Mich., 1962-64; dir. acad. planning Minn. Higher Edn. Coordinating Commn., 1970—. Exec. sec. com. sem. programs Holy Cross Fathers, 1965-66. Recipient Dockweiler medal U. Notre Dame, 1950; named Hon. Texan, 1962, Carnegie fellow U. Mich., 1962-64. Mem. Assn. Inst. Research, Am. Acad. Polit. and Social Scis., Am. Assn. Higher Edn., Nat. Cath. Edn. Assn., Phi Kappa Phi. Author articles. Address: Capital Square 550 Cedar St Paul MN 55101

DRAINVILLE, ROBERT, business exec.; b. Woonsocket, R.I., Mar. 11, 1918; B.S. in Accounting, Hill Coll., 1940; m. Adrienne C. Bonneau, Apr. 18, 1942; children—Jocelyn (Mrs. Peter Himes), Richard. With Bachmann Uxbridge Worsted Co., Uxbridge, Mass., 1956-61; asst. treas. Whitin Machine Works, Whitinsville, Mass., 1961-66; controller White Consolidated Industries, Inc., Cleve., 1966-71, v.p., controller, 1971—. Mem. finance com. town Uxbridge, 1946-50. Club: Avon (O.) Oaks Country. Home: 7858 Normandie Blvd Cleveland OH 44130 Office: 11770 Berea Rd Cleveland OH 44111

DRAKE, ALFRED CAPURRO, actor, singer; b. N.Y.C., Oct. 7, 1914; s. John Mario and Elena (Maggiolo) Capurro; A.B., Bklyn. Coll., 1935; m. Harvey Brown, Mar. 10, 1944; children—Candace, Samantha. Staring roles include Kiss Me Kate, 1948, Right You Are, 1951, The Gambler, 1952, Kismet, 1954, Kean, 1961 (all Broadway); played Hajj in Kismet, London, Eng., 1955-56; English Version of Rugantino, 1964. Recipient Variety Critics Award for Curley in Oklahoma, 1944, Donaldson Award for Petrucchio in Kiss Me Kate, 1948, Perry, Variety Critics, and Donaldson awards for Hajj in Kismet, 1953. Address: care Elias A Jacobs 595 Madison Av New York City NY 10022

DRAKE, CHARLES LUM, educator; b. Ridgewood, N.J., July 13, 1924; s. Ervin Thayer and Elizabeth (Lum) D.; B.S. in Engring., Princeton, 1948; Ph.D., Columbia, 1958; m. Martha Ann Churchill, June 24, 1950; children—Mary Aiken, Caroline Elizabeth, Sarah Ruth, Susannah Churchill. Research asso. Lamont Geol. Obs., Columbia, 1948-56, sr. scientist, 1956-58, became mem. faculty univ., 1958, prof. geology, chmn. dept., 1967, acting asst. dir. Lamont Geol. Obs., 1963-65; now with dept. geology Dartmouth Coll., Hanover, N.H. Mem. coms. Nat. Acad. Sci.; cons. NSF, 1964-68. Trustee, Village S. Nyack, N.Y., 1963-65, 66-69, dep. mayor, 1968-69. Served with AUS, 1943-46. NSF postdoctoral fellow, 1965-66. Mem. Am. Geophys. Union, A.A.A.S., Am. Assn. Petroleum Geologists, Geol. Soc. Am., Seismol. Soc. Am., Royal Astron. Soc., Soc. Exploration Geophysicists, Marine Tech. Soc., Sigma Xi. Home: RFD 1 East Thetford VT 05043

DRAKE, CHARLES WARREN, aircraft mfg. exec.; b. Troy, O., Dec. 6, 1909; s. Charles M. and Anna (Scott) D.; grad. high sch.; m. Beverly Buerlot, Apr. 11, 1953; children—Linda Bay, William Warren, Peter Frank, Scott Christopher. Clk., Hobart Bros. Co., Troy, O., 1927-28; mfg. dept., prodn. mgr. Waco Aircraft Co., 1928-34; prodn. mgr., factory mgr. Beech Aircraft Corp., Wichita, Kan., 1935-39; with McDonnell Aircraft Corp. (co. name changed to McDonnell Douglas Corp.). St. Louis, 1940—, successively factory mgr., dir. mfg. adminstrv. v.p., 1940-49, mfg. v.p., 1949-63, v.p. operations, 1963-69, v.p. mfg. and quality assurance, 1969—, mem. exec. com., 1952-61. Alderman, City of Huntleigh. Mem. Am. Ordnance Assn. (regional v.p. 1963-64), St. Louis, St. Louis County chambers commerce. Presbyn. Mason. Clubs: St. Louis, Old Warson Country (St. Louis). Home: 2832 S Lindbergh St Louis, MO 63131. Office: PO Box 516 St Louis MO 63166

DRAKE, CLIFFORD BARNES, marine corps officer; b. N.Y.C., Nov. 7, 1918; s. Leon Andrew and Nellie Maude (Barnes) D.; B.A. in Physics, U. Cal. at Los Angeles, 1940; M.A., Stanford, 1951; student U.K. Joint Services Staff Coll., 1957, Nat. War Coll., 1963; m. Margery Forbes Jones, Feb. 9, 1943; children—Christopher Barnes, Caroline Forbes. Commd. 2d lt. USMC, 1940, advanced through grades to maj. gen., 1967; service U.S.S. California, Pearl Harbor, 1941; bn. comdr. 4th Marine Div., 1943- 45, 2d Marine div., 1951-53; adminstrv. aide to Vice Chief Naval Operations, 1948-50; personnel dept. Hdqrs., USMC, 1953-56; rep. Brit. Joint Amphibious Warfare Command, 1956-59; asst. manpower coordinator Hdqrs. USMC, 1959-61; regtl. comdr. 3d Marine Div., 1961-62; dir. Command and Staff Coll., 1964-66; dir. USMCR, 1966-68; dep. comdr. XXIV Corps, Vietnam, 1968-69; asst. chief staff operations and tng. Hdqrs. USMC, 1969—. Decorated Navy D.S.M., Legion of Merit, Bronze Star, campaign and fgn. decorations. Mem. Marine Corps Assn., Pearl Harbors Survivors Assn., Sigma Nu. Home: 208 S St Asaph St Alexandria VA 22314 Office: Hdqrs Marine Corps Washington DC 20380

DRAKE, DIXIE, assn. exec.; b. Iron City, Ga., Jan. 22, 1909; d. Henry T. and Mary F. (Barber) Drake; A.A., Andrew Coll., Cuthbert, Ga., 1928; B.C.S., Ga. Evening Coll., Atlanta, 1947; M.A., Emory U., 1952. Asso. with John T. Goree, atty.-at-law, Donalsonville, Ga., 1928-32; admitted to Ga. bar, 1930; ct. reporter Pataula Jud. Circuit, Ga., 1932; chief clk. Office Atty. Gen. Ga., 1933-38; with firm Powell, Goldstein, Frazer & Murphy, Atlanta, 1939-49; exec. dir. League of Women Voters of Ga., 1949-52; orgn. sec., program-orgn. sec., asst. exec. sec. League Women Voters of U.S., Washington, 1952-58, exec. sec., 1958-66, exec. dir., 1966-70, spl. asst. to pres. and bd., 1970—. Trustee Phi Chi Theta Found., 1966-67. Mem. Pi Sigma Alpha, Phi Chi Theta (dist. dir. 1963-64; pres. Washington alumnae chpt. 1963-64), Delta Sigma Gamma. Home: 2501 Q St NW Washington DC 20007 Office: 1730 M St NW Washington DC 20036

DRAKE, DOROTHY MARGARET, librarian; b. Canton, Ill.; d. Carl and Amanda (Erickson) Drake; A.B., Knox Coll., 1925; M.A., Claremont Coll., 1947; grad. work U. Chgo., U. So. Cal., U. Cal. at Los Angeles, Librarian Venice High Sch., Los Angeles, 1927-30, 31-35, George Washington High Sch., Los Angeles, 1934- 38; acting librarian Knox Coll., 1930-31; librarian Scripps Coll., 1938- 70, head librarian, emeritus, 1970—; lectr. San Jose State Coll., 1939; organized deptl. library at UN, 1949. Mem. Nat. Com. on Non-Western Materials. Mem. adv. council Univ. So. Cal. Library Sch., 1961-64. Mem. Mayor's exec. com. Sister-City Program, 1961—; mem. Bd. Town Affiliation, Chmn. of Civic Symphony Assn., Claremont, Cal., 1947; mem. bd. Pacific Coast Browning Found., 1956—. Recipient alumni achievement award Knox Coll., 1950. Mem. A.L.A. (council, div. exec. bd. 1961-64), Cal. Library Assn. (pres. coll. univ. and research librarians, 1952; chmn. publs. committee 1959-62; program coordinator ann. conf. 1961), Los Angeles City Schs. Library Assn. (pres. 1928-30), Am. Assn. U. Profs., Am. Assn. UN (dir. Pomona Valley chpt. 1958-61), Pasadena (pres. 1945), San Antonio (pres. 1947, 58-59) library clus, Mortar Bd., Am. Assn. UN (exec. bd. Pomona Valley 1958-61), Phi Beta Kappa, Delta Sigma Rho, Pi Beta Phi. Methodist (ofcl. bd.; trustee). Contbr. articles to profl. periodicals. Home: 1030 N College Av Claremont CA 91711 Office: Scripps Coll Library Claremont CA 91711

DRAKE, DOROTHY MAY, retired librarian; b. Hailey, Ida., May 22, 1910; d. William Todd and May (Ringgold) Drake; B.A., U. Cal., 1932, certificate librarianship, 1933. With Sacramento City Library, 1933-43, 44-48; city librarian, Sacramento, 1958-66, city-county librarian, 1966-71. Mem. Historic Landmarks Commn., 1955-60. Bd. dirs. Vol. Bur., 1968, Travelers Aid Soc. Sacramento, 1960-62, Regional Arts Council, 1968. Mem. adv. council edn. for librarianship U. Cal., 1968-71. Mem. Am., Cal. (2d v.p. 1958, council 1970-71) library assns., Women's Overseas Service League, League Women Voters, Am. Assn. U. Women. Club: Zonta Internat. Home: 2516 52d St Sacramento CA 95817

DRAKE, SIR ERIC, oil co. exec.; b. Rochester, Eng., Nov. 29, 1910; s. Arthur William Courtney and Ethel (Davidson) D.; M.A., Pembroke Coll., Cambridge (Eng.) U., 1935; m. Rosemary Moore, Aug. 15, 1935; children—Anna Pauline Rosalind (Mrs. Robert Freer), Felicity Katharine (Mrs. Peter Low); m. 2d, Margaret Elizabeth Wilson, Sept. 14, 1950; children—John Arthur Courtney, William Eric. Mng. dir. Brit. Petroleum Co. Ltd., 1958—, dep. chmn., 1962-69, chmn., 1969—. Mem. council Chamber Shipping U.K., 1958—, v.p., 1963, pres., 1964; gen. com. Lloyd's Register Shipping, 1960—; Com. on Invisible Exports, 1969—. Ct. Hon. petroleum adviser to Brit. Army, 1971—. Gov. London Sch. Econs. and Polit. Sci., 1963—. Decorated comdr. Brit. Empire, 1952; comdr. Ordre de la Couronne, Belgium, 1969; Knight Grand Cross Order Merit, Italy, 1970. Fellow Inst. Chartered Accountants. Home: The Old Rectory Cheriton nr Alresford Hampshire England Office: Britannic House Moor Lane London E C 2 England

DRAKE, ERVIN MAURICE, composer; b. N.Y.C., Apr. 3, 1919; s. Max and Pearl (Cohen) Druckman; B.S., Coll. City N.Y., 1940; m. Ada Sax, May 28, 1947; children—Linda Shifra, Besty Jennifer. Composer: I Believe, 1953, Tico Tico, 1943, One God, 1954, Al Di La, 1962, Come to the Mardi Gras, 1947, Perdido, 1942, A Room Without Windows, 1964, It Was A Very Good Year (Grammy award), 1965, Father of Girls, 1968; composer-lyrist The Bachelor TV Musical Comedy, 1956; writer, asso. producer Yves Montand on Broadway, 1962; librettist, lyricist, composer Her First Roman, 1968; author, composer, producer numerous TV programs including ABC-TV Series' It Was A Very Good Year, 1971. Recipient Sylvania award as composer-lyrist The Bachelor, 1956; Emmy nomination writer-asso. producer Yves Montand on Broadway, 1962; recipient Christopher award, 1953; nomination Nat. Acad. Recording Arts and Sci. as composer-lyrist What Makes Sammy Run for best score from Broadway musical, 1964. Mem. A.S.C.A.P. (exec. v.p.), Am. Guild Authors and Composers, Writers Guild Am., Authors League, Dramatists Guild, Am. Arbitration Assn. Clubs: Lake Success Golf, Spalding Hole-In-One. Office: 34 W 53d St New York City NY 10019

DRAKE, EVERETT COLEMAN, merchandising exec.; b. Huntsville, Ala. Mar. 4, 1918; s. Robert Coleman and Annie M. (Blount) D.; student pub. schs.; m. Helen Elizabeth Braly, Apr. 15, 1937; children—Everett C., James David, Donna Elizabeth. With M. Lowenstein & Sons, Inc., N.Y.C., 1946-64, comptroller, 1957-59, pres., dir., 1959-64; pres. Blue Ridge Mfrs., Inc., 1964—, Imperial Shirt Co., 1964—, Bates Fabrics, 1968—; pres., dir. Imperial Reading Corp.; exec. v.p., chief exec. officer Bates Mfg. Co., Inc., 1968—. Mason (Shriner). Clubs: Union League (N.Y.C.), Garden City Golf. Home: 1519 Hawkins Av Baldwin NY 11510 Office: 1290 Av of the Americas New York City NY 10019

DRAKE, FRANCIS EDWARD, Jr., utility co. exec.; b. Lynn, Mass., Sept. 11, 1915; s. Francis Edward and Grace (Johnson) D.; B.S. in Elec. Engring., Columbia, 1937; m. Dorothy M. Edwards, Sept. 2, 1938; children—Francis Edward III, Gurden Edwards. With Rochester Gas & Electric Corp. (N.Y.), 1937—, exec. v.p., 1965-67, pres., chief exec. officer, 1967-68, chmn. bd., chief exec. officer, 1968—; pres., dir. Canadea Power Corp.; dir. McCurdy & Co., Lincoln-Rochester Trust Co. Dir. Bur. Municipal Research. Trustee Rochester Inst. Tech. Registered profl. engr., N.Y., Pa. Mem. Am. Inst. E.E., Nat. Soc. Profl. Engrs., Rochester C. of C. (trustee). Home: 90 Knollwood Dr Rochester, NY 14618. Office: 89 East Av Rochester NY 14604

DRAKE, FRANK DONALD, astronomer; b. Chgo., May 28, 1930; s. Richard Carvel and Winifred Pearl (Thompson) D.; B. Engring. Physics, Cornell U., 1952; M.A., Harvard, 1956, Ph.D., 1958; m. Elizabeth Buckner Bell, Mar. 7, 1953; children—Stephen David, Richard Procter, Paul Robert. Mem. Harvard Radio Astronomy Project, 1955-58; dir. Astron. Research Group, Ewen-Knight Corp., 1958; asst., asso. scientist Nat. Radio Astronomy Obs., 1958-63, head telescope operations div. and sci. services div., radio studies Venus and Jupiter; chief lunar and planetary scis. sect. Jet Propulsion Lab., 1963-64; asso. prof. astronomy Cornell U., Ithaca, N.Y. 1964-66, prof., 1966—, chmn. dept., 1968-71, asso. dir. Center for Radiophysics and Space Research, 1965—, dir. Arecibo Inospheric Obs., 1966-68, dir. Nat. Astronomy and Ionosphere Center, 1971—; mem. sci. adv. bd. Ryan Aero. Co., 1964-68; mem. NRC, 1969-71; adviser govt. coms. on space research and astronomy. Mem. Am. Astron. Soc., I.E.E.E., Internat. Astron. Union, Internat. Sci. Radio Union, Sigma Xi, Tau Beta Pi. Author: Intelligent Life in Space, 1962. Home: 121 Pine Tree Rd Ithaca NY 14850

DRAKE, GEORGE ALBERT, coll. dean, historian; b. Springfield, Mo., Feb. 25, 1934; s. George Bryant and Alberta (Stimpson) D.; A.B., Grinnell (Ia.) Coll., 1956; Fulbright scholar, U. Paris, 1956-57; A.B. (Rhodes scholar), Oxford U., 1959, M.A., 1963; B.D., U. Chgo., 1962, M.A., 1963, Ph.D. (Rockefeller fellow), 1965. Instr. history Grinnell Coll., 1960-61; asst. prof., asso. prof. history Colo. Coll., Colorado Springs, 1964—, acting dean of Coll., 1967-68, dean, 1969—. Trustee Grinnell Coll. Mem. Am. Hist. Assn., Am. Ch. History Soc., Am. Conf. Acad. Deans. Home: 1820 N Prospect St Colorado Springs CO 80907

DRAKE, GEORGE FRANCIS, educator. Prof. romance langs. Washington and Lee U., Lexington, Va. Office: Dept Romance Langs Washington and Lee U Lexington VA 24450*

DRAKE, HARRINGTON, publishing co. exec.; b. Kansas City, Mo., Sept. 2, 1919; s. Embree and Orpha (Anderson) D.; B.A., Colgate U., 1941; m. Shirley Grant, Feb. 18, 1942; children—Ted G., Jeffrey, Anderson. With Reuben H. Donnelley Corp., N.Y.C., 1947—; pres., chief exec. officer, 1968—; dir. Reuben H. Donnelley Corp., Dun & Bradstreet, Inc. Served to lt. col. USAAF. World War II. Decorated Air medal with cluster. Home: Harbor Point Riverside CT 06878 Office: 825 3d Av New York City NY 10022

DRAKE, JERRY EDWARD, consultant; b. Edna, Tex., Sept. 22, 1907; s. Robert Alonzo and Clara (Bronaugh) D.; B.A., So. Methodist U., 1929; B.B.A., 1946; M.B.A., N. Tex. State U., 1949; Ph.D., U. Tex., 1956; m. Jean Gray, Apr. 20, 1940; children— Jean Elizabeth (Mrs. John M. Watson), Mary Dianne, Alice Lynn, Jerry Edward. Salesman advt. Dallas Dispatch, 1929, Dallas Times Herald, 1930-31; grad. mgr. publs. So. Meth. U. Student's Pub. Co., 1931-46; indsl. cons. Drake Research and Cons. Service, Dallas, 1956—; instr. marketing So. Meth. U., Dallas, 1946-50, asst. prof., acting chmn. marketing, 1950-56, asso. prof., chmn. marketing, 1956-58, prof., chmn. marketing, 1958-70; marketing research cons., 1956—. Research grantee Dallas County Home Builders, 1955-56. Mem. Am. Marketing Assn., Nat. Marketing Theory Seminar, Advt. Fedn. Am., Dallas Advt. League, Dallas Sales and Marketing Execs. Club, Alpha Kappa Psi, Alpha Delta Sigma (nat. v.p. 1957-61). Methodist. Mason (Shriner). Author: (with Frank Millar) Marketing Research, 1969. Home: 3409 Wentwood Dr Dallas TX 75225

DRAKE, JOHN GIBBS ST. CLAIR, educator, anthropologist; b. Suffolk, Va., Jan. 2, 1911; s. John Gibbs St. Clair and Bessie Lee (Bowles) D.; B.S., Hampton Inst., 1931; postgrad U. Chgo., 1937-40, 46-47, Ph.D. in Anthropology, 1954; m. Elizabeth Dewey Johns, June 17, 1942; children—Sandra, Carl J. Instr. sociology and anthropology Dilliard U., 1935-37, 41-42; Julius Rosenwald fellow U. Chgo., 1937-38, 47-48; asso. dir. Ill. Commn. Condition Urban Colored Pop., 1940-41; statis. medd. div. U.S. Maritime Service, N.Y.C., 1943-45; asst. prof. sociology and anthropology Roosevelt U., Chgo., 1946-48, asso. prof., 1948-54, prof. sociology, 1954-69; now prof. anthropology and sociology Stanford, dir. undergrad. program African and Afro-Am. studies; Rosenwald fellow for study of race relations in Great Britain, 1947-49; vis. lectr. social anthropology Boston U., 1953; research asso. Twentieth Century Fund's Survey of Tropical Africa, 1953-54; vis. prof. social scis. U. Liberia, Rep. of Liberia, W. Africa, 1954, studied impact of press, film and radio on W. Africa, under grant from Ford Found., 1954-55; cons. Ford Found. African fellowship tng. program, 1955-57; prof., chmn. dept. sociology U. of Ghana, 1958-61; vis. prof. of sociology Stanford U., 1963, 65; Peace Corps tng. staff for Ghana, 1961, 62, 64, for Sierra Leone, 1966; vis. prof. Columbia U., 1967, U. Ghansa, 1965. Ofcl. U.S. representative 1st World Festival of Negro Arts, Dakar, Senegal, 1966, Social Science Research Council fellow, 1965. Fellow Am. Anthrop. Assn., African Studies Assn. U.S.A.; mem. Internat. Soc. for Study Race Relations, Am. Soc. African Culture, Phi Beta Sigma. Author: (with Horace R. Cayton) Black Metropolis, 1943 (selected for 1946 honor roll Schomburg coll. N.Y.C. Pub. Library, as race relations book of the year; also Anisfeld Wolf award as one of two books contbg. most to race relations for year 1945), rev. and repub. as Harper Torchbook, 1962; (with Peter Omari) Social Work in West Africa, 1963; Race Relations in a Time of Rapid Social Change, 1966; also articles profl. publs. Office: Stanford U 245 Leland Av Palo Alto CA 94305

DRAKE, JOHN WALTER, educator; b. Detroit, Feb. 10, 1932; s. John Alfred and Eleanor Bryan (Smith) D.; B.S. magna cum laude, Yale, 1954; Ph.D., Cal. Inst. Tech., 1958; m. Pamela Elizabeth Grunau, Dec. 3, 1960; children—Juliet Anne, Jonathan Andrew, Nicholas. Research asso., instr. microbiology U. Ill., Urbana, 1958-59, asst. prof., 1959-64, asso. prof., 1964-69, prof., 1969—, chmn. genetics program, 1969—. Fulbright fellow Weizmann Inst., Israel, 1957-58; Guggenheim fellow Lab. Molecular Biology, Cambridge, Eng., 1964-65; USPHS Spl. fellow U. Edinburgh (Scotland), 1971-72. Mem. Genetics Soc. Am., Am. Soc. Microbiology, Environmental Mutagen Soc. (councillor), A.A.A.S. Author: Molecular Mechanisms of Mutation, 1970. Research and publs. in embryology, virology, genetics. Office: Dept Microbiology U Ill Urbana IL 61801

DRAKE, ORMOND JOHN, coll. adminstr.; b. Blissfield, Mich., Apr. 15, 1906; s. Herbert Ralston and Alice M. (Mickle) D.; A.B., U. Mich., 1929, A.M., 1930; Litt.D., 1964; m. Frances Mack Summers, Sept. 3, 1932 (div.); 1 dau., Diana Mack; m. 2d, Leila Ettinger, Nov. 7, 1947 (div.); m. 3d, Georgette Newman, Aug. 7, 1968. Instr. in speech Mich. State Coll., 1930-36, N.Y. U., 1936-37; advanced instr. English, Princeton, 1937-38; asst. prof. speech N.Y. U., 1937, chmn. dept. speech and dramatics, 1937-40, asso. prof. speech and dir. admission, Coll. of Arts and Sci. and Coll. of Engring., 1940-45, asst. dean Coll. of Arts and Sci., 1945-54, asst. sec. univ., 1954-56, asso. dean Sch. of Continuing Edn., also prof. speech (on leave), 1954—, and dir. pub. occasions. Dir. Town Hall, 1956-71. Moderator, radio program Archives, WNBC, 1956, TV programs, univ. sta., WATV, 1954-56, Am. in the Making, WCBS, 1955, The Way to Go, WCBS, 1956—, Our Nation's Roots, WCBS, 1957; also appears on other TV programs. Cons. bus. speaking Hayden Stone, Hornblower & Weeks. Member bd. Performing Arts Repertory Theatre Found.; mem. bd. overseers Dropsia College. Mem. Nat. Assn. Tchrs. Speech, Phi Beta Kappa, Delta Sigma Rho, Tau Kappa Alpha, Pi Kappa Delta, Phi Mu Delta. Republican. Presbyn. Clubs: N.Y. U. Faculty (pres. 1945-46); Roundout Valley; Lotos. Co-author; Handbook in Objective Speaking, 1947. Home: Canal St Fort Plain NY 13339 Office: 123 W 43d St New York City NY 10036

DRAKE, PAUL WOODHULL, architect; b. Morristown, N.J., July 31, 1897; B.Arch., Cornell U., 1921. With Ludlow & Peabody, 1922-24, Voorhees, Gmelin & Walker, 1924-25, McKim, Mead & White, 1925-26; now mem. firm Drake, Convery & Cueman and predecessor firms, architects; principal architectural works include Masonic Temple, Morristown, 1930, Welfare Home, Morris County, 1953, Presbyn. Ch., (with Charles A. Scheuringer), 1954, First Nat. Iron Bank, Morristown, also Sperry & Hutchinson Co., office and warehouse, Natick, Mass., 1959, Short Hills County Day Sch., N.J., 1961; asst. prof. Drew U., 1942-43; lectr. high schs., service clubs. Pres. Nat. Council Archtl. Registration Boards, 1963; mem. N.J. Bd. Architects, 1953-60; mem. zoning bd., Madison, N.J., 1950-53. Recipient Award of Merit, N.J., Soc. Architects, 1950, First Nat. Bank of Highland Park, 1951, Kirch Furniture Store, 1953. Fellow A.I.A. (v.p. N.J. 1939-41, pres. 1941-43). Address: 7 Shadylawn Dr Madison NJ 07940*

DRAKE, RALEIGH MOSELEY, psychologist; b. Odell, Neb., Jan. 17, 1902; s. Fred Ellis and Mae Nellie (Moseley) D.; B.B.A., Boston U., 1926, A.M., 1930; Ph.D., U. London, 1931; studied violoncello with Hane Hess, Chgo., and Alwin Schroeder, Boston; m. Irene Greenleaf, June 6, 1925 (dec. Apr. 1964); children—Dorothy Emma (Mrs. Donald Hubbard), Raleigh Moseley, Irene Mae (Mrs. C.L. Callaway); m. 2d, Elma Brenner German, Aug. 20, 1966. Asst. in psychology Boston U., 1927; asso. prof. psychology Wesleyan Coll., Macon, Ga., 1931-41; prof. psychology and head dept. of psychology and philosophy Mary Washington Coll., U. Va., 1941-47; prof. psychology Kent State U. 1947—, head dept., 1947-61; instr. U. Ga., summers 1939, 40. Mem. ednl. psychology com. Ga. Project Progressive Edn. Assn., Mem. Am. Psychol. Assn. Mem. United Ch. of Christ. Kiwanian. Author books including outlines and workbooks of social, child, adolescent, abnormal, ednl. and applied psychology; Drake Musical Aptitude Tests, 1954. Asso. editor Jour. of Musicology; editor and pub. Student-Tchr. Aide in Psychology, 1935—. Contbr. chpts. in various publs. including: Ency. of Psychology, 1948. Home: 2864 Lakeland Pkwy Cuyahoga Falls OH 44224

DRAKE, RICHARD BRYANT, educator; b. Ames, Ia., Aug. 5, 1925; s. G. Bryant and Alberta (Stimson) D.; A.B., Doane Coll., 1948; M.A., U. Chgo., 1950; Ph.D., Emory U., 1957; m. Julia Leland Angevine, Sept. 5, 1945; children—Elisabeth, John Bryant, Margaret Ellen. Prof. history Piedmont Coll., Demorest, Ga., 1950-53; instr. history Agnes Scott Coll., Decatur, Ga., 1955-56; instr. history and polit. sci. Berea (Ky.) Coll., 1956-57, asst. prof., 1957-61, asso. prof., 1961-67, prof. 1967—, dept. chmn., 1958—. Served with USNR, 1943-48. Mem. Am., So. hist. assns., Am. Studies Assn. (past div. pres.), Am. Assn. U. Profs., Assn. Am. Historians. Democrat. Conglist. Author: Outline History of Appalachian America, 1960; An Appalachian Reader, 1970. Contbr. articles profl. jours. Home: 110 Van Winkle Grove Berea KY 40403

DRAKE, RICHARD MATTHEWS, educator; b. Albia, Ia., May 25, 1906; s. Frank E. and Nellie (Mason) D.; student Ft. Dodge (Ia.) Jr. Coll., 1924-25; B.S. in Math., Physics, Edn., U. Minn., 1928, M.A., Ph.D. in Math. Ednl. Psychology, Enl. Adminstrn., 1938; m. Lillian M. Berg, June 26, 1929; children—Richard Matthews, Katharine. Instr. math. Antigo (Wis.) pub. schs., 1928-32; instr. edn., also chmn. math. dept. Lab. Sch., U. Minn., 1932-39; asst. prof. edn. U. Buffalo, 1939-42, asso. prof., 1942-44, co- ordinator inst. ASTRP, 1944-45, prof. edn., 1944-45, asst. dean Coll. Arts and Scis., also dir. tutorial instrn., 1948-54, acting dean students, 1949-50, dir. self appraisal Coll. Arts and Scis., 1952-54, dir. Office Instl. Research, also prof. higher edn., 1954-55; vis. prof. edn. U. Minn., summer 1946-47; v.p., prof. higher edn. U. Kansas City, 1955-56, acting chancellor, 1956-57, chancellor, 1957-61; provost Fairleigh Dickinson U., 1962-71; cons. Ford Found. Fund for Advancement of Edn., 1961-62. Dir. Truman Library, 1958-61. Mem. Phi Delta Kappa, Sigma Nu. Author: (with Harl R. Douglass and V. R. Walker) Survey Test in Plane Geometry, 1939; (with T. H. Fenske and A.W. Edson) Arithmetic in Agriculture, revised edit., 1931; Self Appraisal of the College of Arts and Sciences, 1934; also numerous articles. Contbr. Ency. Ednl. Research, 1950. Home: 1286 River Rd Teaneck NJ 07666 Office: Fairleigh Dickinson U Teaneck NJ 07073

DRAKE, ROBERT MORTIMER, Jr., engring. exec.; b. Eagle Cliff, Ga., Dec. 13, 1920; s. Robert Mortimer and Elizabeth Margaret (Foushee) D.; B.S. in Mech. Engring., U. Ky., 1942; M.S. in Mech. Engring., U. Cal. at Berkeley, 1946, Ph.D., 1950; m. Jane Mardelle Smith, Aug. 19, 1944; children—Dianne Elizabeth, Kevin Robert. Asso. prof. mech. engring. U. Cal. at Berkeley, 1947-55; engine design cons. aircraft gas turbine div. Gen. Electric Co., 1954-56; prof. mech. engring. Princeton, 1956-63, chmn. dept., 1957-63; vis. prof. U. Ky., Lexington, 1964-65, prof. mech. engring, 1965—, chmn. dept. mech. engring., 1966-67, dean Coll. of Engring., 1966-71, dir. office of research and engring. services 1966-71; v.p. research and devel. Combustion Engring. Inc., 1971—. Cons. Air Preheater Corp., NSF; dir. Intertech Corporation (N.J.). Mem. Ky. State Bd. Registration Profl. mem. Ky. Commn. on Coal Research, 1970—, Ky. Commn. on Sci. and Tech., 1970—. Served to capt. USAAF, 1942-47. Registered profl. engr., Cal., Ky. Asso. fellow Am. Inst. Aeros. and Astronautics; mem. Am. Soc. M.E., Am. Soc. Engring. Edn., Nat., Ky. socs. profl. engrs., Sigma Xi, Tau Beta Pi, Pi Tau Sigma, Omicron Delta Kappa. Club: Lexington (Ky.) Country. Author: (with E.R.G. Eckert) Introduction to Transfer of Heat and Mass, 1950, Heat and Mass Transfer, 1959; Analysis of Heat and Mass Transfer, 1970; also numerous articles. Cons. editor: McGraw Hill Book Co., 1958-66. Editorial adv. bd. Internat. Jour. Heat and Mass Transfer, 1960-70. Home: 30 Mallard Dr Farmington CT 06032

DRAKE, WILLIAM EARLE, educator; b. Asheville, N.C., Sept. 25, 1903; s. John Robert and Irene Temperance (Ingle) D.; A.B., U. N.C., 1924, A.M., 1928, Ph.D., 1930; m. Zelma Mae Paxton, Aug. 20, 1926; children—William Earle, Dennis Clemens, Caroline Imogene. Prin., Murphey Sch., Orange County, N.C., 1924-26; supt. Columbia (N.C.) schs., 1926-28; teaching fellow U. N.C., 1928-30; asst. prof. Pa. State Coll., 1930-39; asso. prof. U. of Mo., 1939-44, prof. edn., head dept. of history and philosophy of edn., 1944-57; prof. history and philosophy of edn. U. Tex., Austin, 1957—, chmn. dept., 1959-70; vis. lectr., summers U. N.C., 1936, U. Ill. 1953, U. Tex., 1955. Mich. State U., 1966. Auburn U., 1968. Pres., bd. dirs. Columbia Coop. Market, 1943-50; nat. sec.-treas. Philosophy of Edn. Soc., 1950-60; pres. Pa. Fedn. of Tchrs., 1936-39; pub. panel mem. Nat. War Labor Bd., Region IX, 1944- 45; arbitrator indsl. disputes Am. Bd. Arbitration. Prof. Shrivenham Am. U., England, U.S. Army, E.T.O., 1945-44. Recipient Alphonso Smith research prize, social scis. U.N.C., 1930. Fellow A.A.A.S., Nat. Philosophy of Edn. Soc. (pres. S.W. 1961-62), Internat. Inst. Arts and Letters; mem. John Dewey Soc., Soc. for Advancement Edn., Am. Assn. U. Profs., Am. Civil Liberties Union, Nat. Soc. Coll. Tchrs. of Edn. (exec. com. 1957-60). Tex. Tchrs. Assn., Phi Delta Kappa, Alpha Pi Zeta, Alpha Phi Omega. Mason, Kiwanian. Author: The American School in Transition, 1955; Higher Education in North Carolina Before 1860, 1964; Intellectual Foundations of Modern Education, 1967. Co-author: Sociological Foundations of Education, 1942; Significant Aspects of American Life and Postwar Education, 1944; Teaching World Affairs in American Schools, 1956; American Education, Volume I, 1958; Automation and Society, 1959; The Challenge of Science Education, 1959; The Heritage of American Education, 1961; Teaching in America, 1962. Editor: Sources for Intellectual Foundations of Modern Education, 1967; also numerous mag. articles Mem. editorial bd. Ednl. Theory. Home: 5806 Trailridge Circle Austin TX 78731

DRAKE, WILLIAM FRANK, Jr., lawyer; b. St. Louis, Mar. 29, 1932; s. William Frank and Beatrice (Olmmstead) D.; B.A., Principia Coll., 1954; LL.B., Yale, 1957; m. Mary Baldwin Clarke, June 14, 1955; children-Stephen C., Peter O., Thomas W. Admitted to Pa. bar, 1958; practice in Phila., 1958-68, Valley Forge, 1968—; mem. firm Montgomery, McCracken, Walker & Rhoads, 1958-68; v.p., gen. counsel Alco Standard Corp., 1968—. Served with U.S. Army, 1957-58. Mem. Am., Pa., Phila. bar assns. Christian Scientist. Clubs: Union League (Phila.); Merion Cricket (Haverford, Pa.). Home: Ithan PA 19085 Office: Alco Standard Corp Valley Forge PA 19481

DRAKE, WILLIAM PLUMMER, chem. mfg. exec.; b. Bath, Me., Jan. 18, 1913; s. Frederick E. and Henrietta Barker (Plummer) D.; grad. Deerfield Acad., Mass., 1932, Bowdoin Coll., 1936; m. Margaret Maynadier Hardcastle, June 19, 1937; children—James B., Margaret (Mrs. S. Hoyt Peckham), Anne (Mrs. Gerard W. Dowd), Sally, William Plummer. With Pennwalt Corp. (formerly Pennsalt Chems. Corp.), 1934—, successively student trainee, salesman, sales mgr. chem. specialities dept., asst. v.p., v.p. sales, v.p. and gen. mgr. indsl. chems. div., exec. v.p., dir., pres., 1955-69, chmn., chief exec. officer, 1969—; dir. Bath Industries, Inc., INA Corp., Marcor, Inc., First Pennsylvania Banking & Trust Co., First Pa. Corp., Berwind Corp., Fabricke Van Chemische Prodn. Vondelingenplaat (Holland). Dir. rubber, chems. and drug. div. OPS, 1952. Dir. Old Phila. Devel. Corp., Urban Coalition Phila. Trustee Bowdoin Coll., Baldwin Sch., Bryn Mawr, Pa., Deerfield Acad. Mem. Am. Ordnance Assn. (dir. Phila. 1955), Mfg. Chemists Assn. (dir.), Phila. C. of C. (dir.), Psi Upsilon. Episcopalian. Clubs: Union League, Urban, Bowdoin (Phila.); Sailing of the Chesapeake; Corinthian Yacht (Phila.). Home: Berwyn PA 19312 Office: Pennwalt Bldg Philadelphia PA 19102

DRAKE, WILLIAM WHITING, Jr., aerospace co. exec.; b. N.Y.C., Sept. 7, 1922; s. William Drake and Heather (Goodwin) D.; B.S., Principia Coll., Elash, Ill., 1944; student Harvard, 1946-47, Brown U., 1947-48; m. Ruth Arlene Carey, Jan. 14, 1946; children—David Chisholm, Jonathan Carey, Pamela Jane. Mem. staff Mass. Inst. Tech., 1948-49, Los Alamos Sci. Lab., 1949-52; asst. to v.p. Europe Raytheon Co., Lexington, Mass., 1952-60; v.p. adminstrn., treas. Aerospace Corp., El Segundo, Cal., 1960—. Vice chmn. S.W. Los Angeles area United Way, 1968; chmn. S.W. Los Angeles area United Crusade, 1966; dist. chmn. Boy Scouts Am., 1966- 68, also rep.,

1967—. Served with USNR, 1943-45. Mem. I.E.E.E., Am. Phys. Soc. Home: 400 Bay View Dr Manhattan Beach CA 90266 Office: 2350 E El Segundo Blvd El Segundo CA 90045

DRAKEFORD, JOHN WILLIAM, educator, psychologist; b. Sydney, Australia, Sept. 26, 1914; s. Walter and Elsie (Curtis) D.; B.A., U. Sydney, 1949; Dip. Edn., Sydney Tchrs. Coll., 1950; B.D., New South Wales Bapt. Sem.; M.A., Tex. Christian U., 1958, Th.M., 1960; D.Religious Edn., Southwestern Sem., 1956, Ed.D., 1967; m. Robina Bailie, Dec. 13, 1941; children—Warwick, Brenton. Came to U.S., 1934, naturalized, 1964. Ordained to ministry Baptist Ch., 1941; pastor in Australia, 1937-42, Haberfield, New South Wales, 1949-54; prof. psychology Southwestern Sem., 1954—. Served with Australian Army, 1943-45. Author: Counseling for Church Leaders, 1961; Red Blueprint for the World, 1962; Psychology in Search of a Soul, 1964; The Home: Laboratory of Life, 1965; The Great Sex Swindle, 1967; Integrity Therapy, 1967; The Awesome Power of the Listening Ear, 1967; Farewell to the Lonely Crowd, 1969; This Insanity Called Love, 1969; Games Husbands and Wives Play, 1970—; co-author: An Introduction of Pastoral Counseling, 1959; Religion and Medicine, 1967; Forbidden Love, 1971. Home: 3228 Spanish Oak Dr Fort Worth TX 76109

DRALLE, LEWIS ARNOLD, historian, educator; b. Ottawa, Ill., Apr. 23, 1908; s. Henry Thomas and Ida (Suehr) D.; A.B., U. Chgo., 1939; M.A., U. Cal., Los Angeles, 1948, Ph.D., 1952; m. Mildred Adams Pascoe, Oct. 21, 1955. Lectr. history U. Cal., Los Angeles, 1950-52, vis. asso. prof., summer 1960, vis. prof., 1962; asst. prof., prof. State Coll. Ark., 1955-63; vis. asso. prof. history U. Tex., summer 1958; prof. history Wichita (Kan.) State U., 1963—, chmn. history dept., 1965—; mem. editorial com. Univ. Press Kan. Served with AUS, 1941-45. Fellow, Folger Shakespeare Library, Washington, summer 1967. Mem. Conf. Brit. Studies (rec. sec.), Am. Com. Irish Studies, Am. Assn. U. Profs. Editor: (with John Carswell) The Political Journal of George Bubb Dodington, 1965. Home: 2200 N Fountain Wichita KS 67208

DRAPANAS, THEODORE, educator, physician; b. Buffalo, Feb. 20, 1930; s. Thomas and Anasthasia (Tsiros) D.; M.D., U. Buffalo, 1952; m. Arlene Ann Thrun, June 25, 1954; children—Carol Ann, Mark Thomas, Wendy. Intern, resident surgery E.J. Meyer Meml. Hosp., Buffalo, 1952-58; asst. prof. surgery State U. N.Y., Buffalo, 1959-64; prof. surgery U. Pitts. Sch. Medicine, 1964-68; Henderson prof., chmn. dept. surgery Tulane U. Sch. Medicine, 1968—; practice medicine, specializing in surgery, New Orleans, 1968—; surgeon-in-chief Tulane div. Charity Hosp. of La. Mem. bd. examiners Am. Bd. Surgery; mem. com. on trauma Nat. Acad. Scis.-NRC, 1969—; mem. surgery study sect. NIH, 1969—; mem. adv. com. on trauma Surgeon Gen.'s Office, Dept. Army, 1970—; mem. surgery adv. com. FDA, 1971—. Served with M.C., U.S. Army, Res. Recipient Gold Key award as outstanding man of year Buffalo Jr. C. of C., 1961. Mem. A.C.S., Am., Central, So. surg. assns., Soc. U. Surgeons (sec.), Soc. Clin. Surgery, Soc. Vascular Surgery, Am. Assn. Thoracic Surgery, Am. Assn. Surgery of Trauma, A.A.A.S., Internat. Soc. Surgery, James IV Assn. Surgeons, Assn. Am. Med. Colls. (rep.), Phi Beta Kappa. Editor: Surgery, 1971—. Contbr. articles profl. jours. Home: 2929 Prytania St New Orleans LA 70115 Office: 1430 Tulane Av New Orleans LA 70112

DRAPEAU, JEAN, mayor of Montreal; b. Montreal, Que., Can., Feb. 18, 1916; s. J. N. and Berthe (Martineau) D.; Arts degree, U. Montreal, 1938, student Faculty Law, 1938-41; hon. degrees U. Moncton, 1956, U. Montreal, 1964, McGill U., 1965, Sir George Williams U., Laval U., 1967; m. Marie-Claire Boucher, July 27, 1945; 3 sons. Admitted to Montreal bar, 1943, began practice specializing in comml. and corp. law; became mayor Montreal for 1st time, 1954, re-elected, 1960, 62, 66, 70. Founder Montreal Civic Party, 1960; sr. Canadian rep. Internat. Bur. Exhbns., 1967. Apptd. Queen's counsel, 1961. Created companion Order Can., 1967; recipient Indsl. Devel. award Trade and Industry Dept. 10 Canadian Provinces, 1965; Gold medal Royal Archtl. Inst. Can., 1967. Hon. mem. Am. Bar Assn., numerous other nat. and internat. orgns. Home: 5700 des Plaines Av Montreal Quebec Canada Office: City Hall Montreal Quebec Canada

DRAPER, BRICE MARCHBANKS, ret. ins. co. exec.; b. Memphis, Jan. 19, 1908; s. Brice M. and Mary (Raines) D.; student Southwestern Coll., Memphis, 1926-27, Northwestern U., 1928- 29; m. Anne Elizabeth Gilliland, Aug. 17, 1929; children—Brice Marchbanks, Martha Louise. With Hartford Fire Ins. Co., 1927-69, exec. v.p., 1964-69. Home: 310 Cedar Key Circle Atlantis FL 33460

DRAPER, CHARLES STARK, cons. aero. engr.; b. Windsor, Mo., Oct. 2, 1901; s. Charles Arthur and Martha Washington (Stark) D.; student U. Mo., 1917-19; A.B., Stanford U., 1922, B.S. in Elec. Chem. Engring., Mass. Inst. Tech., 1926, M.S. in Aero. Engring., 1928, Sc.D. (physics), 1938; hon. degree Eidgenossische Technische Hochschule, Zurich, Switzerland, 1967; m. Ivy Willard, Sept. 7, 1938; children—James, Martha, Michael, John Clayton. Operated lab. to develop infra-red signaling devices for U.S. Navy, 1927; research asst. in aero. engring., Mass. Inst. Tech., 1929-30, research asso., 1930-35, asst. prof., 1935-38, asso. prof., 1938- 39, prof., 1939—, head aeros. and astronautics dept., until 1966, now prof. emeritus, dir. Charles Stark Draper Lab. (formerly Instrumentation Lab.), pres. lab., 1970—; Wilbur Wright Meml. lectr. Royal Aero. Soc., May 1955, Wright Brothers lectr., 1966. Mem. Sci. Adv. Bd.; cons. U.S. Navy, also U.S. Air Force, and comml. orgns. in field of aeros. and control. Commnd. 2d lt., U.S. Army Air Corps. Tng. Center, Brooks Field, Tex., 1926, Training Middletown Air Depot, 1931-32, 1935, Wright Field, Ohio, 1936, 1st lt. A.C. Reserve, 1926-42. Awarded Exceptional Civilian Service award Dept. of Air Force, 1951. Navy Distinguished Pub. Service award, 1956; Airpower award of Mass. Wing, Air Force Assn.; Thurlow award, Inst. Navigation; Airpower trophy Air Force Assn.; Godfrey L. Cabot award Aero club New England, 1959; Potts medal, 1960; Navy Distinguished Pub. Service award Dept. Navy, 1961; Golden Plate award Acad. Achievement, 1961; Mo. Honor award U. Mo., 1962; Nat. Soc. Profl. Engrs. award, 1962; Louis W. Hill Space Transp. award, 1962; Comdrs. award Ballistic System div. USAF, 1964; Montgomery award Nat. Soc. Aerospace Profls. and Aerospace Mus., 1963; Nat. Sci. medal Presdl. award, 1965, Vincent Bendix award, 1966, Guggenheim medal, 1967; Distinguished Pub. Service medal NASA, 1968; J. B. Laskowitz Gold medal N.Y. Acad. Scis., 1968; Exceptional Civilian Service award USAF, 1968, 69; Sylvanus Albert Reed Award, Inst. Aero Scis., Medal for Merit, Naval Ordnance Devel. award for devel. of major improvements in antiaircraft fire control equipment, N.E. Award for 1947 given by Engring. Socs. of N.E.; NASA Pub. Service award, 1969, Apollo Achievement award, 1969; Elmer A. Sperry award, 1970; Founders medal Nat. Acad. Engring., 1970; Thomas D. White Nat. Def. award USAF Acad., 1970; Lovelace award Am. Astron. Soc., 1971. Fellow N.Y. Acad. Scis., Am. Phys. Soc., Am. Acad. Arts and Sci., Am. Soc. M.E., (Holley medal, 1957), I.E.E.E., Am. Inst. Aeros. and Astronautics, A.A.A.S., Am. Astron. Soc., Nat. Acad. Engring.; hon. fellow Canadian Astronautical Soc., Inst. Aero. Scis., Brit. Instn. Mech. Engrs., Brit. Interplanetary Soc., Royal Aero. Soc.; mem. German Soc. Guidance and Nav. (hon.), Brit. Inst. Nav. (hon.), Am. Soc. Engring. Edn., Internat. Acad. Astronautics (pres.), Soc. Automotive Engrs., Nat. Inventors Council (chmn.), Nat. Acad. Scis. Am. Ordnance Assn. (Blandy medal, 1958), Am. Inst. of Cons. Engrs., Sigma Xi. Contbr. articles in field of aero. instruments in tech. jours. Home: 62 Bellevue St Newton MA 02158 Office: Mass Inst Tech Instrumentation Lab 68 Albany St Cambridge MA 02139

DRAPER, EARLE SUMNER, planning, housing cons.; b. Falmouth, Mass., Oct. 19, 1893; s. Frederic Ward and Bertha (Sumner) D.; grad. high sch., Milford, Mass., 1911; B.S., Mass. State Coll., Amherst, Mass., 1915; Dr. Landscape Architecture (hon.). U. of Mass., 1950; studied and traveled in Europe, 1922; m. Norma Farwell, May 26, 1917; children—Frederic Farwell, Earle Summer, Norman Claflin (killed in action 1944), Charles Alfred. Norma (dec. 1934); m. 2d, Elizabeth Jordan. Landscape architect, Cambridge, Mass., 1915; settled at Charlotte, N.C., 1917; pioneer in landscape architecture in southern states. Prin. works include: T.V.A. projects; estates and towns throughout the South. Vis. prof. Lowthorpe Sch. of Landscape Architecture, 1931-32, Harvard U. Sch. of Landscape Architecture, 1932. Dir. land planning and housing T.V.A., 1933-37, dir. dept. of regional planning studies, TVA, 1937-40; asst. adminstr. Fed. Housing Adminstrn, 1940-41, dep. commr., 1942-45; in own office, housing and planning cons., since 1945. Cons. Nat. Resources Com. and the Md. State Planning Bd. on Balt.-Washington- Annapolis Area Report, 1936-37, Ga., Ala. State Planning Bds., 1937; acting regional counselor, Southeast, Nat. Resources Planning Bd., 1937-40; lectr. in field. Fellow Am. Soc. of Landscape Architects (former v.p., dir.); mem. Am. Inst. of Planners (pres. 1940-42), Am. Soc. of Plan Ofcls. (past bd. dirs.). Phi Kappa Phi, Alpha Sigma Phi. Mason. Clubs: Cosmos, Congressional Country (Washington). Contbr. to publs. Home: 936 E Causeway Blvd Vero Beach FL 32960 ☆

DRAPER, FREDA, opera and concert singer; b. Kansas City, Mo.; d. Frederick and Leila (Burleigh) Faulkner; student Chgo. Mus. Coll.; studied voice Edna Forsythe, Kansas City, Mo.; operatic work Dino Bigalli, Chgo.; scholarship pupil Mary Garden; m. Vernon Gerhardt, 1947. Tour soloist Ballet Russe de Monte Carlo, Chgo. Opera Co., 1937-42; sang world premier Bride of Bagdad, winner Am. Opera Soc.'s 1st award, 1940; vocal faculty Northwestern U., 1941- 44; with Chgo. Opera Co., 1937-42; appeared as soloist with leading symphony orchs. U.S., guest nat. radio programs; made seven months tour P.I. as soloist before armed forces, 1945; appeared in concert and opera on 3 continents, 1952-55; coached oratorio with Chas. Baker, N.Y.C.; light opera appearances St. Louis Municipal Opera, Hollywood Prodns., Inc. Recipient Presdl. citation, Medal of Freedom, 1947; Hon. Dau. Mark Twain award for contbr. to Am. music. Hon. mem. Women's C. of C. Kansas City, Sigma Alpha Iota; internat. hon. mem. Beta Sigma Phi. Home: 33052 Big Sur St Dana Point CA 92629

DRAPER, FREDERICK GAYLORD, former govt. ofcl.; b. Rochester, N.Y., Dec. 25, 1909; s. Herbert Stone and Gertrude (Beebe) D.; B.S., Sheffield Sci. Sch., Yale, 1931; m. Blanche Caroline Miller, Feb. 5, 1944; 1 son, Gaylord DeWitt. With Congoleum- Nairn Inc., 1931-42, Office Mil. Govt. Germany, Berlin, 1946-49, Office U.S. High Commr. Germany, 1949-50, chief reparations and restitution bd., property div. ECA/MSA mission to Turkey, 1950-52, chief tech. assistance div. Office Indsl. Resources MSA/FOA/ICA, Washington, 1953- 61; with Office Tech. Coop. and Research, AID, 1961-67, dep. dir. indsl. devel., 1961-68. Adviser U.S. delegations numerous UN Internat., indsl. devel. meetings, Sec. North Arlington Parish Council, 1969-71. Served to maj. AUS, 1942-46. Mem. Soc. Internat. Devel. Lutheran (councilman 1963-66). Clubs: Yale (Washington); Goose Creek Country (Leesburg, Va.). Home: 1546 Northgate Sq Reston VA 22070

DRAPER, GEORGE WILLIAM, govt. ofcl.; b. Easton, Pa., Aug. 10, 1920; s. George William and Grace (Collins) D.; LL.B., Howard U., 1947; LL.M., N.Y.U., 1948; m. Be sie Carrolle Thornton, Sept. 6, 1940; children—George William Thornton Collin, Wesley Robert. Admitted to Mo. bar, 1950, also U.S. Supreme Ct.; asst. prof. law Lincoln U. Law Sch., St. Louis, 1948-50; mem. firm Witherspoon, Lewis & Draper, St. Louis, 1950-52; asst. circuit atty. Office Circuit atty., St. Louis, 1952-55; mem. Draper & Martin, St. Louis, 1955-57; chief trial asst. circuit atty. Office Circuit Atty., St. Louis, 1957-60; asst. atty. gen. chief criminal appeals div., Mo., 1960-64; dir. legal services St. Louis Human Devel. Corp., also instr. Washington U. Law Sch., 1964-65; former chief counsel Office Met. Devel., Dept. Housing and Urban Devel.; now dep. exec. dir. Equal Employment Opportunity Commn. Pres. Tamarack Triangle Civic Assn., Silver Spring, Md., 1966—. Mem. Mo., St. Louis bar assns., Lawyers Assn. Mo., N.A.A.C.P. (life), Sigma Delta Tau, Alpha Phi Alpha. Democrat. Episcopalian. Home: 13312 Bea Kay Dr Silver Spring MD 20904 Office: 1800 G St N W Washington DC 20006

DRAPER, MAURICE LEE, church ofcl.; b. Arma, Kan., Aug. 25, 1918; s. Earl Theodore and Olive Irene (Pruden) D.; A.A., San Bernardino Valley Coll., 1935-37, Denver U., 1939, U. Ala., 1945, Kansas City U., 1950; B.A., William Jewell Coll., 1957; M.A., U. Kan., 1964; m. Olive Ruth Willis, Apr. 28, 1940; children—David Lee, Edward Alan, Janette Louise. Domestic field missionary Reorganized Ch. of Jesus Christ, Latter Day Saints, 1937-47, mem. council Twelve Apostles, 1947-58, pres. Australasian Mission, 1952-56, mem. 1st presidency, 1958-. Past pres. Community Music Assn., Independence. Trustee Mo. Heart Assn., School of Restoration, Independence, also Independence Sanitarium and Hosp. Author: Why I Belong, 1958; Marriage in the Restoration, 1968; The Gifts and Fruit of the Spirit, 1969. Co-editor The Saints Herald, also The Restoration Witness. Contbr. articles to religious publs. Home: 2815 Maybrook Av Independence MO 64057 Office: The Auditorium Independence MO 64051

DRAPER, NORMAN RICHARD, educator, statistician; b. England, Mar. 20, 1931; s. Norris and Helen (Draper); came to U.S., 1955; B.A., Cambridge (Eng.) U., 1954, M.A., 1958; Ph.D., U. N.C., 1958. Tech. officer, statistician plastics div. Imperial Chem. Industries, 1958-60; mem. Math. Research Center, U. Wis., 1960-61, mem. faculty, 1961—, prof. statistics, 1966—; vis. prof. Imperial Coll., London, fall 1967, 68. Fellow Royal Statis. Soc., Am. Statis. Assn.; mem. Inst. Math. Statistics, Biometric Soc., Am. Soc. Quality Control (sr. mem.; lectr. 1963—). Author: (with H. Smith) Applied Regression Analysis, 1966; (with G.E.P. Box) Evolutionary Operation, 1969; (with W. E. Lawrence) Probability: An Introductory Course, 1970. Address: 1210 W Dayton St Madison WI 53706

DRAPER, ROBERT FARGO, mfg. co. exec.; b. Deerfield, Wis., Dec. 3, 1913; s. M.H. and Helen (Fargo) D.; student U. Wis., 1934; m. Louise Heins, Sept. 13, 1927; children-Linda (Mrs. Charles T. Sprague), Elizabeth (Mrs. T.C. Martin), Robert Fargo II. Br. mgr. Sherwin Williams Co., LaCrosse, Wis., 1939-41; buyer Montgomery Ward & Co., Chgo., 1947-50; exec. engr., sales mgr. Regal Ware, Inc., Chgo., 1951-54; v.p., marketing dir. Nat. Presto Industries, Inc., Eau Claire, Wis., 1955-61; pres. Schick, Inc., N.Y.C., 1961-63, John Oster Mfg. Co., 1964-67, Sunbeam Appliance Co., 1967-69; exec. v.p., dir. Sunbeam Corp., 1969—. Bd. dirs. U. Wis. Found., Wis. Alumni Research Fund. Mem. Jr. C. of C. (bd. dirs.), Milw. Met. C. of C. (bd. dirs.), U. Wis. Alumni Assn. (pres.), Nat. Housewares Mfrs. Assn. (pres.). Home: 549 E 7th St Hinsdale IL 60521 Office: 5400 W Roosevelt Rd Chicago IL 60650

DRAPER, THEODORE, author; b. Bklyn., Sept. 11, 1912; s. Samuel and Annie D.; B.S.S., Bklyn. Coll.; 1 son, Roger. Writer; research fellow Hoover Instn. on War, Revolution and Peace Stanford (Cal.) U., 1963—; mem. Inst. for Advanced Study, Princeton, 1968—. Author: The Six Weeks' War, 1944; The Roots of American Communism, 1957; American Communism and Soviet Russia, 1960; Castro's Revolution: Myths and Realities, 1962; Castroism, Theory and Practice, 1965; Abuse of Power, 1967; Israel and World Politics, 1968; The Dominican Revolt, 1968; The Rediscovery of Black Nationalism, 1970. Contbr. to magazines Encounter, Commentary, Polit. Sci. Quar., Dissent, others. Address: Institute for Advanced Study Princeton NJ 08540

DRAPER, VERDEN ROLLAND, accountant; b. St. Louis, Feb. 23, 1916; s. Neal McLain and Florence (Meyers) D.; B.S., Washington U., St. Louis, 1938; m. Eileen Ogden, Aug. 18, 1940; children—Mallen, Eileen Ann, Cynthia, Patti, Verden. With Price Waterhouse & Co., C.P.A.'s, St. Louis, 1938-51, Tulsa, 1951-55, Pitts., 1955-60, Buffalo, 1960—; mem. of faculty Washington U., St. Louis U., U. Tulsa. Pres. Better Bus. Bur. Western N.Y. Served with USNR, World War II. Mem. Am. Inst. C.P.A.'s Mo., Okla., Pa., N.Y. State socs. C.P.A.'s, Am. Accounting Assn., Beta Gamma Sigma, Omicron Delta Kappa, Delta Sigma Pi (Alumnae award, 1938), Alpha Kappa Psi (hon.), Theta Xi. Presbyn. Clubs: Buffalo Country (past treas., gov.), Buffalo; Niagara. Author: (with Robert H. Irving) Accounting Practices in the Petroleum Industry, 1958. Contbr. articles profl. publs. Home: 129 Greenaway Rd Eggertsville NY 14226 Office: Marine Trust Bldg Buffalo NY 14203

DRAPER, WILLIAM FRANKLIN, artist, portrait painter; b. Hopedale, Mass., Dec. 24, 1912; s. Clare Hill and Matilda Grace (Engman) D.; student Pomfret (Conn.) Sch., 1927- 31, Harvard, 1931-33, Nat. Acad. Design, 1933-34, Grande Chaumiere, Paris, 1935, Art Student's League, N.Y.C., 1937; m. Barbara Cagiati, Oct. 7, 1944; children—William Franklin, Francesca Cagiati, Margaret Joy. Instr. Art Students League N. Y., 1965—. Exhibited Nat. Gallery, Washington, Met. and Nat. Acad. Design, Chgo. Art Inst., Inst. Modern Art, Mus. Fine Arts, Boston, Nat. Gallery, London; works include 3 murals Bencroft Hall, U.S. Naval Acad., portraits Pres. John F. Kennedy, Mohammed Rega Pahlevi, Shah of Iran, Sen. Leverett Saltonstall, Roy Larsen, Gov. Endicott Peabody of Mass., Richard Rodgers, Terrence Cardinal Cooke, Pres. Nathan Pusey of Harvard, Pres. Sarah Gibson Blanding of Vassar Coll., Gen. Bedell Smith, Dr. Charles Mayo, Bishop Angus Dun, Sec. of State Dulles, Sec. of Treas. Dillon, John D. Rockefeller III, Ambassador Joseph Kennedy, others; represented Chrysler perm. coll.; one man shows N.Y.C., Boston, St. Louis. Served as lt. comdr., ofcl. combat artist, U.S.N.R., 1942-46. Awarded Bronze Star. Clubs: Harvard, Century Assn. Home: 160 E 83d St New York City NY 10028 Studio: 535 Park Av New York City NY 10021

DRAPER, WILLIAM HENRY, Jr., investment banker, corp. exec.; b. N.Y. City, Aug. 10, 1894; s. William Henry and Mary Emma (Carey) D.; A.B., N.Y.U., 1916, M.A., 1917, LL.D. (hon.), 1949, U. Louisville, 1948, Duke, 1950; m. Katharine Louise Baum, September 7 1918 (dec.); children—Dorothy H. (Mrs. Phillips Hawkins), Katharine L. (Mrs. George Haimbaugh), William Henry III; m. 2nd Eunice Barzynski, March 12, 1949. National City Bank, N.Y.C., 1919-21; asst. treas. Bankers Trust Co., 1923-27; joined Dillon, Read & Co., investment bankers, N.Y.C., 1927, v.p. 1937-53; trustee L.I. R.R., 1950, chmn. L.I. Transit Authority, 1951; exec. officer, chmn. bd. Mexican Light & Power Co., 1954-59; partner firm Draper, Gaither & Anderson, 1959-67. Chmn. bd. Combustion Engring., Inc., 1960-64; dir. Ins. Securities Trust Fund, US Leasing Corp., Cosmodyne Corp. Mem. Pres.'s Adv. Com. Selective Service, Washington, 1940; mem. Joint Army and Navy Com. Welfare and Recreation, 1941. Hon. chmn. Population Crisis Com.; spl. cons. Internat. planned parenthood Fedn.; U.S. rep. UN Population Commn., 1969—. Mil. govt. adv. Sec. State, Moscow Conf. Fgn. Ministers, 1947; under sec. army, 1947-49; U.S. spl. rep. Europe, rank Ambassador, Jan. 1952-June 1953. Trustee The Kosciuszko Found. Served as maj. Infantry, U.S. Army, World War I; chief staff, 77th div. O.R.C., 1936-40; active duty inf. Gen. Staff, U.S. Army, Washington, 1940-41; comd. 136th Inf. Regt., 33d Inf. Div., 1942-44. P.T.O., 1943-44; in charge contract termination War Dept., 1944; chief econ. div. Control Council for Germany, 1945-46; econ. adv. to comdr. in chief EUCOM, 1947; now maj. gen. U.S.A.R. Decorated Legion of Merit, 1943 (Navy), 1945; Selective Service medal, 1946; D.S.M. (U.S.), 1948; Order of Orange Nassau (Netherlands), 1949; Medal for Freedom, (U.S.), 1953; Great Cross Order of Merit (Italy), 1954. Mem. Council Fgn. Relations, Acad. Polit. Science, Am. Legion (co. comdr. 1932-34), Planned Parenthood Fedn. (vice chmn.), Soc. Am. Magicians. Psi Upsilon Republican. Presbyn. Clubs: Bond, Recess, Downtown Athletic, Brook (N.Y.C.); Army and Navy, Metropolitan (Washington). Home: 2202 Foxboro Pl NW Washington DC 20007 Office: 1835 K St N W Washington DC 20006

DRATZ, HENRY MARTIN, physician; b. Rockeville Center, N.Y., Mar. 2, 1920; s. B. Martin and Katherine (Mess) D.; M.D., Duke, 1944; m. Dorothy Deaton, Dec. 27, 1942. Intern, resident neurosurgery Duke Hosp., 1944-50; physician VA, 1953—, regional med. dir. region 5, Washington, 1969—. Served to capt. M.C., AUS, 1951-52. Home: 1700 S Joyce St Arlington VA 22202 Office: VA Central Office Washington DC 20420

DRAUS, FRANK JOHN, educator; b. Dupont, Pa., Oct. 30, 1929; s. John and Helen (Gola) D.; B.S., Alliance (Pa.) Coll., 1951; M.S., Duquesne U., 1953, Ph.D., 1957; m. Patricia Kagrise, Oct. 20, 1956; children—Julia, John, Peter, Elizabeth. Mem. faculty U. Pitts. Sch. Dental Medicine, 1956—, prof. biochemistry, 1965—, head dept., 1966—. Cons. to industry; temporary adviser WHO, 1969. Adv. mem. bd. trustees Alliance Coll., 1963—. Recipient Distinguished Alumni award Alliance Coll., 1963. Fellow Am. Inst. Chemists; mem. Am. Chem. Soc., Internat. Assn. Dental Research, N.Y. Acad. Scis., A.A.A.S., Am. Dental Assn. (asso.), Alliance Coll. Alumni Assn. (pres. 1961-65, bd. dirs. 1965-70), Sigma Xi, Omicron Kappa Upsilon. Author articles in field. Home: 1024 Dale Dr Pittsburgh PA 15220

DRAWDY, SHERMAN, banker; b. Groveland, Fla., Oct. 6, 1903; s. Andrew Jackson and Ellen (Raulerson) D.; student pub. schs.; m. Fairy Hester, 1923; children—Ullainee (Mrs. George A. Sancken, Jr.), Charlotte (Mrs. J. Tobin Barrett, Jr.). Clk., cashier Bank of Groveland, 1921-26; bank examiner State of Fla., 1926-33; examiner FDIC, 1933-34; examiner Fed. Res. Bank of Atlanta, 1934-36; v.p., cashier Ga. R.R. Bank & Trust Co., 1936-47, pres., dir. 1947-69, chmn., chief exec. officer, 1960—; chmn., chief exec. ofcr. Ga. R.R. and Banking Co., First R.R. and Banking Co. of Ga.; chmn. bd., chief exec. officer, dir. First Ga. Devel. Corp., Augusta; chmn. Peoples Am. Bank of Atlanta, Southeastern Newspapers, Inc., Castleberry Food Co., Cato Stores, Inc., Charlotte, N.C., Piedmont Ins. Co., Atlanta, Cullum's, Inc., Augusta, Ga., Ga.-Carolina Brick & Tile Co., N. Augusta Banking Co., Pilgrim Health & Life Ins. Co. Augusta. Trustee Ga. Found. Ind. Colls., Shorter Coll., Rome, Ga., St. Joseph's Hosp., Augusta. Mem. Am. (past treas.), Ga. (past pres.) bankers assns., Ga. State C. of C. (dir.). Clubs: Pinnacle (Augusta, Ga.); Ponte Vedra

(Fla.); Augusta (Ga.) Country; Capitol City (Atlanta); Kiwanis. Home: 3008 Park Av Augusta GA 30904 Office: 699 Broad St Augusta GA 30903

DRAY, SHELDON, educator, physician; b. Chgo., Nov. 20, 1920; s. Harry and Sarah (Zaas) D.; B.S. in Chemistry, U. Chgo., 1941; M.D., U. Ill., 1946, M.S., 1947; Ph.D. in Biol. Chemistry, U. Minn., 1954; m. Margaret Berman, Mar. 7, 1953 (div.); children—Tevian Gordon, Nancy Laraine; m. 2d, Marjory J. Nadherny, Nov. 19, 1968. Intern U. Ill. Research and Ednl. Hosps.,1946- 47; med. officer USPHS, 1947-65; prof. microbiology, chmn. dept. U. Ill. Coll. Medicine, 1965—; cons. immunology sect. WHO, 1964—, Nat. Bd. Med. Examiners. Served with AUS, 1943-46. Mem. Am. Assn. Immunologists (sec.-treas. 1964-70), Am. Soc. Human Genetics, Am. Chem. Soc., A.A.A.S., Internat. Union Immunological Socs. (mem. council 1969—), Soc. Exptl. Biology and Medicine, Reticuloendothelial Soc., Chgo. Inst. Medicine, Transplantation Soc., Alpha Omega Alpha, Phi Lambda Upsilon. Asso. editor Jour. Immunochemistry, 1964—, Jour. Immunology, 1967—. Home: 222 E Pearson St Chicago IL 60611. Office: 835 S Wolcott St Chicago IL 60612

DRAZEK, STANLEY JOSEPH, coll. dean; b. Hagaman, N.Y., June 1, 1918; s. Joseph Walter and Magdalena (Lyczko) D.; B.S., State U. Coll., Oswego, N.Y., 1941; M.A., U. Md., 1947, Ph.D., 1950; m. Marjorie Elora Gifford, June 27, 1943; children—Judith Irene (Mrs. Laban Hodgson), Paul Alan, Janet Lynn, Jean Marie (dec.), David Lee, Richard Don. Instr., Liberty (N.Y.) High Sch., 1941-44; mem. faculty U. Md., 1946—, asst. dean Univ. Coll., 1950-55, asso. dean, 1955-70, dean, 1970—. Mem. ad hoc com. civil def. Dept. Def., 1962-67; chmn. state adv. council, adminstr. State of Md. Title I of HEA 1965, 1966—; cons. to univs. and govt. Bd. dirs. Center Study Liberal Edn. for Adults, Boston, 1963-65. Served with USAAF, World War 11. Recipient Distinguished Alumnus award State U. Coll., Oswego, 1963. Mem. Am. Assn. Sch. Adminstrs., Nat. U. Extension Assn. (bd. dirs. 1959-66; pres. 1964- 65), Nat. Assn. State Univs. and Land-Grant Colls. (sec. 1961-63; chmn. council extension 1966-67; mem. senate 1967-71), Phi Kappa Phi (pres. Md. chpt. 1960-61), Phi Delta Kappa (pres. Md. chpt. 1951-52), Epsilon Pi Tau, Iota Lambda Sigma. Contbr. profl. jours. Chmn. editorial bd. Expanding Horizons...Continuing Education, 1965; Social Unrest, Crime and Delinquency...What Can Adult Education Do?, 1968; The Agony of the Inner City...What Can Continuing Education Do?, 1967. Home: 3415 Metzerott Rd College Park MD 20740

DREBEN, BURTON SPENCER, educator, philosopher; b. Boston, Sept. 26, 1927; s. Robert and Florence (Levin) D.; B.A. summa cum laude, Harvard, 1949, Jr. fellow, 1952-55; student Oxford (Eng.) U., 1950-51; m. Raya Spiegel, Mar. 26, 1950; children—Elizabeth Karen, Jonathan Stephen. Instr., U. Chgo., 1955-56; mem. faculty Harvard, 1956—, prof. philosophy, 1965—. Fulbright fellow, 1950-51; Guggenheim fellow, 1957-58; fellow Am. Acad. Arts and Scis.; mem. Am. Math. Soc., Am. Philos. Assn., Assn. Symbolic Logic (editor jour. 1967—). Jewish religion. Contbr. profl. jours. Home: 65 Hillside Terrace Belmont MA 02178 Office: Emerson Hall Harvard Univ Cambridge MA 02138

DREES, THOMAS CLAYTON, hosp. supply co. exec.; b. Detroit, Feb. 2, 1929; s. Clayton Henry and Mildred (Stevenson) D.; B.A. with honors, Coll. Holy Cross, 1951; m. Elaine Hnath, Feb. 9, 1952; children—Danette, Clayton, Barry, Nancy. With Spaulding Fibre Co., Inc., 1953-70, sales engr., N.Y.C., 1953- 56, br. mgr., Toronto, Ont., Can., 1957-60, asst. to pres., Tonawanda N.Y., 1960-63, sec., 1961-70, v.p. internat., 1963-66, exec. v.p., 1966-70, also dir., mem. exec. com.; mng. dir. Spauldings, Ltd., London, Eng., 1964-70, dir., 1963-70, chmn. bd. dirs., 1964-70; gen. mgr. Spaulding Fibre of Can., Ltd., Toronto, 1957-60, v.p., dir., 1957-70; pres., dir. La Fibre Vulcanisee Spaulding, Paris, France, 1964-70; v.p., dir. Mycalex Corp. Am., Clifton, N.J., 1967-70, Spaulding Norton, Inc., North Westchester, Conn., 1968-70; group v.p. Ipco Hosp. Supply Corp., 1970—. Chmn., St. Thomas Sch. Bd.; mem. pres. council Holy Cross Coll. Served from ensign to lt. (j.g.), USNR, 1951-53. Fellow Inst. Dirs.; mem. I.E.E.E., Nat. Sales Execs. Assn., Am. C. of C. Republican. Roman Catholic (bd. advisers). Rotarian. Home: 61 Partridge Hill Upper Saddle River NJ Office: 161 6th Av New York City NY

DREGNE, HAROLD ERNEST, educator; b. Ladysmith, Wis., Sept. 25, 1916; s. Carl John and Clementine Ellen (Wagner) D.; B.S., Wis. State U., 1938; M.S., U. Wis., 1940; Ph.D., Ore. State U., 1942; m. Mary Johanna Mihevc, May 24, 1943; children—Sharon, Nancy, Diane, Arleen. Asst. prof. U. Ida., 1946-47; asst. soil scientist Wash. State U., 1947-49; prof. N.M. State U., 1949-69; prof. agronomy, chmn. dept. Tex. Tech. U., 1969—; tech. adviser FAO, 1960, UNESCO, 1967. Mem. U.S. Salinity Delegation to USSR, 1961. Served to lt. USNR, 1942-46. Recipient Distinguished Service award N.M. State U., 1967. Fellow A.A.A.S. (pres. Southwestern and Rocky Mountain div. 1966-67, chmn. com. arid lands 1970-72); mem. Western Soil Sci. Soc. (pres. 1958-59), Sigma Xi. Episcopalian. Kiwanian. Editor: Arid Lands in Transition, 1970. Home: 3424 54th St Lubbock TX 79413

DREIER, ALEX, TV and radio news commentator, ins. co. exec.; b. Honolulu, June 26, 1916; ed. Stanford; m. Geraldine Hogan. Commentator sta. KTTV, Los Angeles, ABC Radio, Los Angeles; adminstrv., v.p. United Ins. Co. Am., Chgo. Office: KTTV 5746 Sunset Blvd Los Angeles CA 90028

DREIER, JOHN C., educator; b. Bklyn., Dec. 27, 1906; s. H. Edward and Ethel E. (Valentine) D.; A.B., Harvard, 1928; m. Louisa C. Richardson, July 26, 1942; children—John, Susan, Alexander. With N.Y. Telephone Co., 1928-29; tchr. Cranbrook Sch., Bloomfield Hills, Mich., 1929-31; U.S. govt. conservation and land use programs Dept. of Agr., 1933-41; chief div. of spl. inter-Am. affairs Dept. of State, 1941-46; adviser to U.S. dels. Rio Conf., 1947; alternate del. 9th Internat. Conf. Am. States, Bogota, 1948; dir. Office of Regional Am. Affairs, Dept. of State, 1949; U.S. rep. Council of OAS with rank of ambassador, 1951, chmn. council, 1951-52; dir. Office Regional Polit. Affairs, Dept. of State, 1952-60; dir. Interam. Center, Sch. Advanced Internat. Studies, Johns Hopkins U., 1961—, prof. Latin Am. studies, 1970—. U.S. mem. Inter-Am. Peace Com. Adviser, U.S. delegation Gen. Assembly of UN, 1949-52, 54; del. 10th Inter-American Conf., Caracas, 1954. Clubs: Cosmos (Washington); Harvard (N.Y.). Home: 4717 Fulton St N W Washington DC 20007 Office: 1740 Massachusetts Av N W Washington DC 20036

DREIFKE, GERALD EDMOND, educator; b. St. Louis, June 21, 1918; s. Herman A. and Anna Margaret (Hollenbeck) D.; B.S., Washington U., 1948, M.S., 1948, D.Sc. (NSF fellow), 1961; m. Lorraine Ann Feldhaus, June 9, 1951; children—Mark A., Matthew G., Laura Maria, Anne Marie. Layout man Curtiss-Wright Co., St. Louis, 1936-39, design engr., 1939-44; layout man Douglas Aircraft Co., 1939; instr. engring. St. Louis U., 1948-50, asst. prof., 1950-54, asso. prof. elec. engring., dir. grad. program elec. engring., 1954-61, prof. elec. engring., 1961-71; mgr. research and devel. Union Electric Co., 1971—; cons. Emerson Electric Co., 1951-71, Monsanto Co., 1961-71; mem. tech. staff Bell Telephone Labs. N.J., summer 1963. Mem. St. Louis County Bd. Elec. Examiners, Gov.'s Sci. Adv. Com. Mo. Served with USNR, 1944-45. Recipient certificate of merit WPB, 1942; research grants NSF, 1964, NASA, 1965, Monsanto Co., 1965-69, Nancy McNair-Ring Outstanding Faculty award St. Louis U. chpt. Gamma Pi Epsilon, 1965-66. Registered profl. engr., Mo. Mem. Am. Soc. Engring. Edn. (past sec., com. chmn.), I.E.E.E. (past chmn. St. Louis sect.), Engrs. Club St. Louis (dir., com. chmn.), Mo. Soc. Profl. Engrs. (v.p. St. Louis chpt.), St. Louis Elec. Bd. Trade, Sigma Xi, Tau Beta Pi, Eta Kappa Nu, Pi Mu Epsilon, Phi Eta Sigma. Editor-in-chief ISA Transactions, 1966—. Contbr. articles profl. jours. Home: 4104 Oreon Dr Northwoods St Louis MO 63121

DREIKURS, RUDOLF, psychiatrist; b. Vienna; s. Sigmund and Fanny (Cohn) D.; M.D., U. of Vienna, 1923; m. Sadie Garland; children—Eric, Eva. Came to U.S., 1937, naturalized citizen. Began practice of psychiatry in Vienna, organizing mental hygiene and psychiat. social work; dir. clinics for child guidance, alcholics and psychopathics, asst. and collaborator Alfred Adler since 1923; prof. psychiatry Chgo. Med. Sch., 1942-66, now emeritus; with Tex. Tech. Coll., 1966-68; vis. prof. U. Vt., 1968—; dir. Alfred Adler Inst., Chgo.; cons. psychiatrist Hull House, 1940-43; vis. prof. U. of Rio de Janeiro, 1946, Northwestern U. Sch. Edn., 1947-51, U. Ore., 1957, Bar Ilan U., Ramat Gen., Israel, 1965-69; lectr. edn. Ind. U. at Gary 1951-54, Loyola U., 1959-61; lectr. psychology Roosevelt U., 1954-56. Med. dir. Community Child Guidance Centers of Chgo. Fellow Am. Psychiat. Assn., Am. Soc. Group Therapy and Psychodrama (pres. 1954-55); mem. Am. Soc. Adlerian Psychology (pres. 1954-56), Internat. Assn. Individual Psychology (vice chmn. 1954-67), American Humanist Assn. (v.p. 1950-56), Ill. Soc. for Personality Study (pres. 1954-56), Sociedade de Psychologia Individual of Rio de Janeiro (hon. pres.). Author books including: The Challenge of Marriage, 1946; The Challenge of Parenthood, 1947; Character Education and Spiritual Values in an Anxious Age, 1952; Fundamentals of Adlerian Psychology, 1950; Psychology in the Classroom, 1957;(with Dr. Donald Dinkmeyer) Encouraging Children to Learn, 1962; (with Vicki Soltz) Children: The Challenge; (with Loren Grey) Logical Consequences, a New Approach to Discipline, 1968, A Parents Guide to Child Discipline, 1970; Social Equality: The Challenge of Today, 1971. Home: 2608 N Lakeview Chicago IL 60614 Office: 6 N Michigan Av Chicago IL 60602

DREISKE, JOHN, polit. editor, columnist; b. Chgo., May 23, 1907; s. William D. and Rowena (Leach) D.; grad. Northwestern, 1929; m. Margaret Louise Hamilton, Sept. 1, 1930; children—John, Karin Hamilton. Editorial staff Chgo. Tribune, 1929, Detroit Mirror, 1930-32, Chgo. Herald-Examiner, 1932-33, Detroit Times, 1933-35, Chgo. Times, 1936-38, Chgo. Sun- Times, 1938—; instr. Medill Sch. Journalism, Northwestern, 1948- 50. Recipient Marshall Field award for most valuable contbn. to Sun-Times, 1967; Chgo. Newspaper Guild award, 1967. Mem. Ill. Legislative Corr. Assn. (former pres.). Home: 130 S Grove Oak Park IL 60302 Office: Sun Times Plaza Chicago IL 60611

DRENICK, RUDOLF, F., educator; b. Vienna, Austria, Aug. 20, 1914; s. Philip and Marie Drenick; Ph.D., U. Vienna, 1939; m. Joan Hanley, Sept. 28, 1946; childrenPhilip, Eileen, Andrew. Came to U.S., 1939, naturaliZed, 1945. Asst. prof. math. and physics Villanova U., 1939-49; engr. Gen. Electric Co., 1946-49; mgr. RCA, Camden, N.J., 1949-57; research mathematician Bell Telephone Labs., Murray Hill, N.J., 1957-61; mem. faculty Bklyn. Poly. Inst., 1961—, prof. elec. engring., 1961—; cons. to govt. and industry, 1961—. Served with AUS, 1945-46. Decorated Army Commendation ribbon; NSF faculty fellow, 1964. Fellow I.E.E.E. Author: Die Oplo, oerung linearer Regelsysteme, 1967. Home: R D 1 Long Hill Rd Millington, NJ 07946. Office: 333 Jay St Brooklyn NY 11201

DRENNAN, MERRILL WILLIAM, clergyman; b. Washington, Oct. 17, 1915; s. Milton William and Balbena (Altman) D.; B.C.S., Southeastern U., 1939; A.B., U. Md., 1950; S.T.B., Westminster Theol. Sem., 1953; D.D., Western Md. Coll., 1970; m. Frances Emily Dunn, Apr. 26, 1937; children—Marilyn (Mrs. Louis E. Brus), Kathleen. With banking dept. Am. Security and Trust Co., Washington, 1933-37; officer mgr. Brewood Engravers and Printers, Washington, 1937-42; spl. agt. FBI, 1942-48; ordained to ministry Methodist Ch., 1953; minister in Ashton, Md., 1950-54, Rockville, Md., 1954-65; supt. Balt. Southeast Dist., 1965-67; sr. minister Met. Meml. United Meth. Ch., Washington, 1967—. Del. Northeastern Jurisdictional Conf. Meth. Ch., 1964, 68, 72, Gen. Conf. United Meth. Ch., Dallas, 1968, Atlanta, 1972, Spl. Gen. Conf. United Meth. Ch., St. Louis, 1970. Mem. exec. bd. Nat. Capital area Boy Scouts Am. Bd. govs. Wesley Theol. Sem., Washington; bd. dirs. Meth. Corp., Met. Police Boys Clubs, Washington; trustee Am. U. Home: 3311 Nebraska Av N W Washington DC 20016 Office: Met Meml United Meth Ch Nebraska and New Mexico Avs NW Washington DC 20016

DRENNEN, WILLIAM MILLER, U.S. judge; b. Jenkins, Ky., Mar. 1, 1914; s. Everett and Louise Bright (Miller) D.; B.S., Ohio State U., 1936, J.D., 1938; m. Margaret Morton, Nov. 30, 1940; children—Margaret Penelope, William Miller, David Holmes, Dale Louise. Admitted to W.Va. bar, 1939; asst. to clk. Supreme Ct. of Ohio, 1937-38; law clk. to judge U.S. Dist. Ct., So. Dist. W.Va., 1938-40; with firm Jackson, Kelly, Holt & O'Farrell, and predecessor firms, 1940-58, partner, 1947-58; judge U.S. Tax Ct., Washington, 1958- -, chief judge, 1967—. Active worker Boy Scouts Am. Mem. Charleston City Council, 1955-58. Served as lt. comdr. USN, 1942-45. Mem. Am., W.Va., Charleston bar assns., West Va. Tax Inst. (past pres.), Family Service Charleston. Republican. Episcopalian. Club: Chevy Chase (Md.). Home: 8001 Aberdeen Rd Bethesda MD 20014 Office: Tax Ct Constitution at 12th St Washington DC 20044

DRESBACH, HOWARD, lawyer; b. Columbus, O., Mar. 3, 1902; s. Lyman H. and Grace (Dresbach) D.; A.B., U. Cin., 1924; LL.B., Harvard, 1927; m. Elizabeth Parker Sutherland, Aug. 29, 1936; children—Jonathan, Linda Ann. Admitted to Fla. bar, 1927, Ohio bar, 1933; asso. firm McCune, Hiaasen & Fleming, Ft. Lauderdale, Fla., 1927-32; asso., then partner firm Drewbach, Crabbe, Newlon, Collopy & Bilger, Columbus, 1933—; now counsel firm Crabbe, Newlon, Schmidt, Brown & Jones; commnr. uniform state laws Ohio, 1959—. Dir. White-Haines Optical Co., Columbus, 1957—, Van-Bolt Kreber Electrotype Co., Terry Engraving Co.; gen. counsel Farm Bur. Coop. Assn. and affiliates. Served to lt. col. AUS, 1941-45. Mem. Am., Ohio, Columbus bar assns., Fla. Bar, Nat. Conf. Commnrs. Uniform State Laws. Republican. Episcopalian. Home: 17 N Parkview Columbus OH 43209 Office: 42 E Gay St Columbus OH 43215

DRESCHER, CARL G., Oil corp. exec.; b. Washington, Oct. 10, 1910; s. Fred W. and Ann M. (Burke) D.; B.S., U.S. Naval Acad., 1933; M.B.A., Harvard, 1950; m. Mary E. Liddell, Aug. 7, 1935; children—Gerald C., Ann L. Commd. ensign USN, 1933, advanced through grades to rear adm.; ret. 1956; v.p. Sinclair Oil Corp., N.Y.C., 1956-64, now dir.; pres. Sinclair & BP Sales, Inc., 1959- 60, Sinclair Internat. Oil Co., 1961-64; pres. Sinclair Refining Co., 1964-68, former v.p., dir. Sinclair Oil Corp. Member Alumni Assn. U.S. Naval Acad., Alumni Assn. Harvard. Club: Army- Navy Country (Arlington, Va.). Home: 147 Churchill Rd Tenafly NJ 07670

DRESCHER, JOHN MUMMAU, clergyman, author; b. Manheim, Pa., Sept. 15, 1928; s. John L. and Anna (Mummau) D.; student Elizabethtown Coll., 1947-49; A.B., Eastern Mennonite Coll., 1951, Th.B., 1953; B.D., Goshen Bibl. Sem., 1954; m. Betty Keener, Aug. 30, 1952; children—John Ronald, Sandra Kay, Rose Marie, Joseph Dean, David Carl. Ordained to ministry Mennonite Ch., 1954; pastor Crown Hill Mennonite Ch., Rittman, O., 1954-62; bishop Ohio, Eastern Mennonite Conf., 1959-64; asst. moderator Mennonite Ch., 1967-69, moderator, 1969-71, bishop 1959—. Pres. Ohio Memmonite Mission Bd., 1956-62. Author: Meditations for the Newly Married, 1969; Heartbeats, 1970; Now Is The Time to Love, 1970; Follow Me, 1971. Editor Gospel Hearld, 1962—. Contbr. articles mags., jours. Home: Rt 1 Box 157 Scottdale PA 15683 Office: 616 Walnut Scottdale PA 15683

DRESDEN, MAX, educator; b. Amsterdam, Holland, Apr. 23, 1918; s. Abraham and Henriette (Smit) D.; student U. Amsterdam, 1935-38, U. Leyden, 1938-39; Ph.D., U. Mich., 1946; m. Bertha Evelena Cummins, Aug. 8, 1948; children—Janna, Danielle. Came to U.S., 1939, naturalized, 1949. Asst. prof. U. Kan., 1946-48, asso. prof., 1948-50, prof. theoretical physics, 1950-57; vis. prof. Northwestern U., summers 1950, 52, 53, 56, then prof., chmn. dept. physics; vis. prof. Johns Hopkins, 1957-58; prof. theoretical physics State U. Ia., 1961-64; prof. theoretical physics State U. of N.Y., Stony Brook, 1964—, also exec. dir. Inst. Theoretical Physics, Stony Brook; vis. scientist Am. Inst. Physics; vis. sr. scientist Brookhaven Nat. Lab; van der Waals vis. prof. U. Amsterdam, 1968. NSF sr. postdoctoral fellow, 1971-72. Fellow Am. Phys. Soc.; mem. Midwest Univs. Research Assn. (dir. 1956-61). Home: 15 Beacon Hill Dr Stony Brook NY 11790

DRESEL, CHARLES FRANCIS, banker; b. Napa. Cal., Dec. 29, 1930; s. Carl B. and Verona (Steere) D; B.S., U. Cal. at Berkeley, 1954; m. Mary Charlotte Aulwurm, June 28, 1958; children—Peter, Charles Francis, Mary Elizabeth, Anne. With Touche Ross, C.P.A.'s, San Francisco, 1956-65; auditor Bank of Cal. N.A., 1966-68, v.p., auditor, 1969—. Served to 1st lt. USAF, 1954- 56. C.P.A., Cal. Mem. Cal. Soc. C.P.A.'s. Home: 64 Wildwood Av Piedmont CA 94610 Office: 400 California St San Francisco CA 94120

DRESHER, RALPH F., utility exec.; b. 1901; married. with Ia. Electric Light & Power Co., Cedar Rapids, 1920—, sec., 1951-70, v.p., 1970—. Office: Security Bldg Cedar Rapids IA 52406*

DRESLER, EARL LOUIS, banker; b. Harrisonville, Ill., Sept. 23, 1918; s. Theo A. and Elizabeth (Illert) D.; student Seattle U., 1945-47; m. Jean Frances Karney, Aug. 28, 1946; children—Steven Michael, Peter, Teresa Ann. With Lindell Trust Co., St. Louis, 1938-41, Pacific Nat. Bank, Seattle, 1946-48; mem. comptroller of currency office, then nat. bank examiner Treasury Dept., 1948-59; with U.S. Nat. Bank Ore., Portland 1959—, cashier, 1964—, sr. v.p., 1966-68, exec. v.p., 1968-71, pres., 1971—, also dir. Bd. dirs. Portland Area council Campfire Girls. Served with USAAF, 1941-45. Mem. Bank Adminstrn. Inst., Financial Execs. Inst., Am. Mgmt. Assn., Portland C. of C., Assn. Res. City Bankers. Republican. Roman Catholic. Elk. Clubs: Multnomah Athletic (Portland); Waverly Country, Arlington. Home: 2540 S W 81st St Portland OR 97225 Office: 321 S W 6th Av Portland OR 97204

DRESSEL, PAUL LEROY, univ. adminstr.; b. Youngstown, O., Nov. 29, 1910; s. David Calvin and Aura Olive (Jacobs) D.; A.B., Wittenberg Coll., 1931, LL.D. (hon.), 1966; A.M., Mich. State Coll., 1934; Ph.D., U. Mich., 1939; m. Wilma Frances Sackett, Sept. 16, 1933; children—Carol Ann, Linda Kathleen, Jeana Lynn. From instr. to dir. counseling and chmn. bd. examiners Mich. State Coll., 1934-54; dir. coop. study evaluation gen. edn. Am. Council Edn., 1949-53; prof. univ. research Mich. State U., 1954—, dir. Office Evaluation Services, 1954-59, dir. instl. research, asst. provost, 1959- -. Mem. adv. com. Ednl. Records Bur.; mem. commn. scholars Ill. Bd. Higher Edn.; mem. exec. com. N. Central Assn. Commn. Colls. and Univs.; mem. exec. com. Am. Assn. Higher Edn., pres., 1970-71. Author: Comprehensive Examinations in a Program of General Education, 1949; Evaluation in the Basic College at Michigan State University, 1958; Evaluation in Higher Education, 1961; The Undergraduate Curriculum in Higher Education, 1963; College and University Curriculum, 1968; The Confidence Crisis, 1970. Home: 235 Maplewood Dr East Lansing, MI 48823.

DRESSELHAUS, MILDRED SPIEWAK, educator, engring.; b. Bklyn., Nov. 11, 1930; d. Meyer and Ethel (Teichtheil) Spiewak; A.B., Hunter Coll., 1951; Fulbright fellow Cambridge (Eng.) U., 1951-52; A.M., Radcliffe Coll., 1953; Ph.D. in Physics, U. Chgo., 1958; m. Gene F. Dresselhaus, May 25, 1958; children—Marianne, Carl Eric, Paul David, Eliot Michael. NSF postdoctoral fellow Cornell U., 1958-60; mem. staff Lincoln Lab., Mass. Inst. Tech., 1960-67, prof. elec. engring., 1968—. Abby Rockefeller Mauze vis. prof., Mass. Inst. Tech., 1967-68. Mem. Am. Phys. Soc., N.Y. Acad. Sci., Fedn. Am. Scientists. Home: 147 Jason St Arlington MA 02174 Office: Mass Inst Tech Cambridge MA 02139

DRESSER, DONALD MARKHAM, banker; b. Toledo, Oct. 3, 1905; s. Frank M. and Anna Marie (Werver) D.; grad. high sch.; m. Alberta Avaloo Boyd, Aug. 17, 1926; children—Avaloo Ann (Mrs. Jim L. Clinger), Donna Marie (Mrs. Bernard F. Claus), Marcia Jean (Mrs. Theodore V. Peykoff), John Clark. With Ernst & Ernst, C.P.A.'s 1924-34; with Toledo Trust Co., 1934—, pres., 1959-69, chmn. bd., 1969—, also dir.; dir. Jennison-Wright Corp., Champion Spark Plug Co. (both Toledo). Trustee Toledo Hosp. Active Greater Toledo Community Chest. C.P.A., Ohio. Mem. Ohio, Toledo chambers commerce. Mason (33, K.T.), Elk. Clubs: Toledo, Toledo Country; Belmont Country (Perrysburg, O.); Delray Dunes Golf and Country (Delray Beach, Fla.). Home: 3625 River Rd Toledo OH 43614 Office: Toledo OH 43603

DRESSER, JESSE DALE, real estate investment cons.; b. San Diego, May 5, 1906; s. Charlwood Fessenden and Ora (Evans) D.; ed. pub. schs.; m. Mary A. Goldsworthy, June 9, 1934; children—Dennis T., Brian D., Linda A. Trainee, Union Title Ins. Co., San Diego, 1926; sr. title examiner, chief title officer, v.p. So. Title & Trust Co., San Diego, 1927-51; v.p., chief title officer Security Title Ins. Co., San Diego, 1951-54; with San Diego Fed. Savs. & Loan Assn., 1954-69, v.p., sec., 1955-56, exec. v.p., dir. 1956-69; v.p., dir. Cal. Gen. Mortgage Service, Inc., 1967-69, San Diego Federated Ins. Agy., Inc., 1967-69; real estate investment cons., La Mesa, Cal., 1970—. Mem. San Diego County Savs. and Loan Clearing House, 1954—. Mem. U.S., Cal. savs. and loan leagues, San Diego C. of C. Club: Kona Kai, Cuyamaca Home: 3833 Acacia St Bonita CA 92002 Office: 4730 Palm Av La Mesa CA 92041

DRESSER, LAURENCE L., engr.; b. Litchfield, Mich., Aug. 4, 1895; s. Niles E. and Lou G. (Sherk) D.; B.S., Tri-State Coll., 1923, LL.D., 1951; m. La Vera L. McAllister, Dec. 29, 1915 (dec. Jan. 1946); children—Robert Mac, Doris L. (Mrs. Roehm A. West, Jr.), James M.; m. 2d, Mrs. Georgina McClain, Sept. 28, 1954. Founder, chmn. bd. Dresser Engring. Co., Tulsa. Registered Profl. engr., Okla., Tex., Kan., La., Ark., N.M. Mem. Nat. (past pres.), Okla. (past pres.) socs. profl. engrs., Tulsa C. of C., Sigma Tau (hon.), Tau Beta Pi.

Mason (Shriner, Jester), Rotarian. Clubs: Farm, Engineers. Headliners, Southern Hills Tulsa (Tulsa); Engineers of Dallas, Chapparal, Dallas Athletic (Dallas); Omaha Athletic. Home: 5808 S Evanston St Tulsa OK 74105 Office: 108 N Trenton St P O Box 2968 Tulsa OK 74101

DRESSER, LOUISA, museum curator; b. Worcester, Mass., Oct. 25, 1907; d. Frank Farnum and Josephine Rose (Lincoln) Dresser; A.B., Vassar Coll., 1929; student Harvard, 1932, U. London, 1934, Clark U., 1935-36. With Worcester Art Mus., 1932—, successively asso. in decorative arts, asso. curator decorative arts, curator decorative arts, acting dir., 1943-46, curator of collection, 1949—, also editor Annual; fellow John Simon Guggenheim Found., 1956-57. Adviser curatorial and exhibits com. Old Sturbridge Village, 1961—; Bd. dirs. Salisbury Mansion Assos.; corporator Craft Center, Worcester, John Woodman Higgins Armory, 1962—. Mem. Worcester Hist. Soc. (exec. bd.), Am. Assn. Museums, Archeol. Inst. Am., Am. Antiquarian Soc., Mass. Assn. Craftsmen, Soc. Arts and Crafts (sec.). Author: XVII Century Painting in New England, 1935; Early New England Printmakers, 1939; Likeness of America, 1949; (with others) Maine and its Role in American Art, 1963. Contbr. articles profl. jours. Home: 65 Wachusett St Worcester MA 01609 Office: 55 Salisbury St Worcester MA 01608

DRESSER, ROBERT BARTLETT, lawyer; b. Savannah, Ga., Dec. 28, 1880; s. Henery Bartlett and Mary Isadore (Griggs) D.; grad Phillips Exeter Acad., 1898; A.B., Yale, 1902; LL.B., cum laude (editorial bd. law rev. 1904-05), Harvard, 1906; m. Ruth Greene Nov. 29, 1919. Admitted to Mass. bar, 1906, R.I. bar, 1910; practiced in Providence, 1909—; mem. firm Edwards & Angell, 1915—. Trustee Estate Frank A. Sayles, 1927-71; dir. Sayles Finishing Plants, Inc., Spl. Fabrics, Inc. Mem. com. revise R.I. Corp. Laws, 1918-20; mem. nat. com. Taxpayers Com. to End Fgn. Aid, Washington; adv. bd. Com. Constl. Govt., N.Y.C. Del. Republican Nat. Conv., 1936, 44, 48. Fellow Am. Bar Found.; mem. Am. Bar Assn., N.A.M. (past bd. dirs.). Soc. Mayflower Descendants, S.A.R., Soc. Colonial Wars, Order Founders and Patriots Am. Episcopalian. Mason. Clubs: Yale (N.Y.C.); Hope, Agawam Hunt, Turks Head (Providence). Contbr. legal jours. Home: 525 Cole Av Providence RI 02906 Office: 15 Westminster St Providence RI 02903

DRESSNER, HOWARD ROY, found. exec., lawyer; b. N.Y.C., Feb. 14, 1919; s. Sol and Anna (Gross) D.; B.S., N.Y.U., 1940; LL.B., Columbia, 1948; m. Sonia Segoda, Apr. 6, 1942; 1 son, Robert. With N.Y.U., 1948-64, successively instr. pub. speaking, asst. prof. pub. speaking, asst. v.p. devel.; dir. Albert Gallatin Assos., 1956-65; asst. to v.p. domestic programs Ford Found., 1964-67, sec. found., 1967-71, sec., gen. counsel found., 1971—. Mem. exec. com. Commn. for Synagogue Relations. Candidate for N.Y. State Assembly, 1966. Served to maj. AUS, World War II. Decorated Bronze Star. Mem. Am. Bar Assn. (exempt orgns. com.), Assn. Bar City N.Y. (spl. com. on founds.). Club: Harmonie (N.Y.C.). Author: (with others) Business Writing. Home: 370 1st Av New York City NY 10010

DREVS, ROBERT M., pub. utility exec.; b. Chgo., Sept. 10, 1912; s. Robert M. and Kathryn (Minon) D.; B.S., DePaul U., 1935; M.B.A., U. Chgo., 1951; m. Beatrice Arado, Apr. 15, 1939; children—Donna (Mrs. Ralph Carlson, Jr.), Richard. With Peoples Gas Light & Coke Co., Chgo., 1933-69, sec., 1954-57, asst. v.p., sec., 1957-60, v.p., sec., 1960-61, v.p., 1961-66, exec. v.p., 1966-69, now dir.; pres. Peoples Gas Co., 1969—, also dir.; dir. North Shore Gas Co., Waukegan, Ill., Natural Gas Pipeline Co. Am., 1st Fed. Savs. & Loan Assn. of Chgo., Am. Nat. Bank & Trust Co. Chgo., Am. Nat. Corp. Mem. adv. bd. Citizenship Council Met. Chgo. Bd. dirs., v.p. Chgo. Crime Commn.; trustee, vice chmn. DePaul U.; bd. dirs. Oak Park YMCA. Mem. Am. Gas Assn., Blue Key, Phi Kappa Alpha. Roman Catholic. Clubs: Economic (dir.) University, Chicago, Commercial Executive Program of University of Chicago (Chgo.); Oak Park (Ill.) Country. Home: 921 Fair Oaks Av Oak Park IL 60302 Office: 122 S Michigan Av Chicago IL 60603

DREW, EDWIN HARRIS, judge; b. Fargo, Ga., Oct. 28, 1903; s. William T. and Idella (Edwards) D.; LL.B., John B. Stetson University, 1923, LL.D. (hon.), 1956; m. to Edith Turner, June 10, 1927; 1 dau., Melanie May. Admitted to Fla. bar, 1923, practiced West Palm Beach, Fla., 1923-52, as mem. Drew, Burns, Middleton & Rogers; atty. Town of Palm Beach, 1923-52; judge Fla. Supreme Ct., 1952-71, chief justice, 1955-57, 63-65. Former mem. bd. commrs. Port of Palm Beach. Vice pres. bd. overseers Stetson U. Coll. Law; chmn. bd. Law Center Found. St. Petersburg, Inc. Mem. awards jury Freedoms Found. at Valley Forge, 1956-64. Mem. Asso. Municipalities Palm Beach Co. (past pres.), Fla. Bar (past pres.), Am., Palm Beach County (past pres.) bar assns., Am. Law Inst., Stetson Alumni Assn. (past pres.), Delta Sigma Phi, Phi Alpha Delta. Mason. Contbr. articles profl. jours. Home: 2922 N Monroe St Tallahassee FL 32303

DREW, GARVIN ALDRICH, air controls co. exec.; b. Portsmouth, N.H., Sept. 18, 1903; s. William Garvin and Josephine (Aldrich) D.; S.B., Mass. Inst. Tech., 1925; M.B.A., N.Y.U., 1928; m. Lillian Jones, Aug. 19, 1933; children—William Garvin, Nancy Ballard, Robert Aldrich. With Scovill Mfg. Co., 1925-69, v.p., gen. mgr. A. Schraders Son. div., 1958-63, pres. A. Schrader's Son, Inc., 1959-63, v.p. internat. sales parent company, 1962-69; pres., dir. Schrader-Scoville Australia, 1964-69, ret.; v.p. sales Automation Systems, Inc., Nashua, N.H., 1970—; dir. Duncan Bros. (India), E. Bklyn. Savs. Bank. Lectr. marketing N.Y.U. Former mem. bd. dirs. Bklyn. USEUM, Bklyn. Vis. Nurses Assn. Mem. Bklyn. C. of C. (former dir.), N.Y. Sales Mgrs. Club (pres. 1939), Automotive Overseas Club (hon. life), Los Angeles Rubber Group (hon. life), Delta Tau Delta. Mem. Community Ch. (past chmn. bd. deacons, bd. trustees). Mason. Home: 31792 Isle Royal Dr Laguna Niguel CA 92677 Office: 360 Amherst St Nashua NH 03060

DREW, JANE, architect; b. Thornton Heath, Surrey, Eng., Mar. 24, 1911; d. Harry Guy Radcliffe and Emma Spering (Jones) Drew; diploma, Archtl. Assn., London, Eng., 1938; LL.D., Ibadan U.; m. J. T. Alliston, 1939; children—Sarah Jane Georgina (Mrs. Hugh O'Shaughnessy), Jennifer Ann Shirley (Mrs. James Madge); m. 2d, Edwin Maxwell Fry, Apr. 15, 1943. Partner archtl. firm with James Alliston, London, 1938-40; asst. town planning adviser to resident minister Brit. West African colonies, 1940-42; sr. architect on capital project Chandigarh, India, 1950-55; partner archtl. firm Fry, Drew, Drake and Lasdun, London, then firm Fry, Drew and Partners, London, 1961—; prin. works include Ibadan U., Nigeria, housing projects in Middle East, India, Britain, also Singapore and Ceylon, Open U., Eng., Torbey Hosp., Eng.; Bemis prof. architecture Mass. Inst. Tech., 1961; vis. prof. Harvard, 1970. Fellow Royal Inst. Brit. Architects (council); mem. Archtl. Assn. (past pres., council), Indian Inst. Architects, Inst. Contemporary Art. Author: (with Maxwell Fry) Architecture for Children, 1945, Tropical Architecture in the Humid Zone, 1956, Tropical Architecture; (with Maxwell Fry and Harry Ford) Village Housing in the Tropics, 1947. Founder, editor: Architects Yearbook, 1945—. Address: 63 Gloucester Pl London W1 England

DREW, JESSE MONROE, coll. dean; b. Bunceton, Mo., Jan. 20, 1905; s. Layton and Henrietta (Baylor) D.; B.S., Lincoln U., Jefferson City, Mo., 1929; M.Ed., U. Kan., 1939; Ed.D., Harvard, 1944; m. Alice A. Jones, Aug. 14, 1937. Tchr. math. Cobb High Sch., Cape Girardeau, Mo., 1929-36, prin., 1936- 42; prof. edn. Prairie View (Tex.) A. and M. Coll., 1943-44, dir. div. arts and scis., 1944-49, became dean instrn., 1949, former dean of coll., dean of grad. sch.

DREW, KATHERINE FISCHER, educator; b. Houston, Sept. 24, 1923; d. Herbert Herman and Martha (Holloway) Fischer; B.A., Rice Inst., 1944, M.A., 1945; Ph.D., Cornell U., 1950; m. Ronald Farinton Drew, July 27, 1951. Instr. history Rice U., 1946-48; asst. history Cornell U., 1948-50; mem. faculty Rice U., 1950—, prof. history, 1964—, chmn. dept. history, 1970—, editor Rice U. Studies, 1967—. Guggenheim fellow, 1959; Fulbright scholar, 1965. Mem. Am. Hist. Assn., Mediaeval Acad. Am., Internat. Soc. Study Rep. Instns., Phi Beta Kappa. Author: The Burgundian Code, 1949; Studies in Lombard Institutions, 1956. Editor: Perspectives in Medieval History, 1963; The Barbarian Invasions, 1970; also articles. Contbr. Life and Thought in The Middle Ages, 1967. Home: 509 Buckingham Houston TX 77024

DREW, ROBERT K., newspaper exec.. Gen. mgr., exec. v.p. Milw. Jour. Office: 333 W State St Milwaukee WI 53201*

DREW, THOMAS BRADFORD, educator, chemical engr.; b. Medford, Mass., Feb. 9, 1902; s. Henry Jay Washburn and Henrietta Cook (Cole) D.; S.B., Mass. Inst. Tech., 1923, S.M., 1924; m. Alice Wait, June 9, 1930; children—Mary, Emilie, Sarah. Instr. chem. engring. Drexel Inst., 1925-28, Mass. Inst. Tech., 1929-34; research and design chem. engr. E.I. du Pont de Nemours & Co., Wilmington, Del., 1934-40, cons., 1950-62; asso. prof. chem. engring. Columbia, 1940-45, prof., 1945-65, exec. officer, 1948-57; vis. prof. chem. engring. Mass. Inst. Tech., 1959-60, prof. chem. engring., 1965-67, prof. emeritus, 1967—; cons. Ford Found., New Delhi, 1963, Ford Found. program specialist Birla Inst. Tech. and Sci., New Delhi, India, 1964-65. With the Nat. Defense Research Com. (sect. XI) 1941-43, also Manhattan Dist. Projects: SAM Labs., 1943, TNX div., E.I. du Pont de Nemours & Co., 1943- 44; cons. Brookhaven Nat. Labs., Upton, L.I. N.Y., 1947—, mem. adv. com. on phys. sci., 1947-48, chmn. adv. com. on engring., 1947- 55. Mem. com. sr. reviewers AEC, 1952-57. Fellow N.Y. Acad. Sci., A.A.A.S.; mem. Mass. Soc. of Cin., Am. Inst. of Chem. Engrs. (William H. Walker award, 1937, Max Jakob Meml. award, 1967), Am. Soc. M.E. (honorary mem.; Max Jakob Meml. award 1967), Am. Chem. Soc., Sigma Xi, Phi Lambda Upsilon, Tau Beta Pi, Theta Tau. Democrat. Unitarian. Club: Chemists (N.Y.C.). Author: Vector and Polyadic Analysis; also author of papers on chemical engring. Editor: Advances in Chemical Engineering. Home: Revolutionary Rd Temple NH 03084 Office: Dept Chem Engring Mass Inst Tech Cambridge MA 02139

DREW, WILLIAM BROOKS, educator; b. Greenwich, Conn., Dec. 11, 1908; s. George A. and Rachel B. (Brooks) D.; B.S., Mass. State Coll., 1930; A.M. Harvard, 1931, Ph.D., 1934; student Marine Biol Sta., Woods Hole, Mass., summer 1930, U. Mich. Biol. Sta., summer 1936; m. Shirley Eaton Upton, Sept. 12, 1931; children—Cynthia, Marcia. Asst., Gray Herbarium, Harvard, 1931-35; botanist L.A. Boyd East Greenland Expdn., 1933; asst. prof. Am. Internat. Coll., Springfield, Mass., 1935-36, U. Tenn., 1936-37. U. Mo., 1937-38, 39-43; head dept. botany Carleton Coll., 1938-39; botanist U.S. Cinchona Mission to Ecuador, Colombia, S.A., 1943-45; forest ecologist U.S. Forest Service, Missoula, Mont., 1945; asso. prof. Mich. State U., 1945-48, prof., head dept. botany and plant pathology, 1948—. Fellow Am. Assn. for Advancement of Sci.; mem. Bot. Soc. Am., Am. Soc. Naturalists, N.Y. Acad. Scis., Bryological Soc. Am., Ecol. Soc. Am., Am. Assn. Plant Taxonomy, N.E. Bot. Club, Mich. Acad. Sci. Arts and Letters, Sigma Xi, Phi Kappa Phi. Home: 2900 Northwind Dr East Lansing MI 48823

DREW-BEAR, LOTTE, art dealer; b. Germany; student art history Munich and Berlin. Germany; Belles Lettres, Sorbonne, Paris; m. Robert G. Drew-Bear; children—Thomas Annette. Asst. to Julien Levy. Julien Levy Gallery, N.Y.C.; asst. to dir. Wadsworth Atheneum, Hartford, Conn.; now dir. Richard Feigen Gallery, Chgo.; tchr. art courses Trinity Coll., Hartford. Home: 910 N Lake Shore Dr Chicago IL 60611 Office: 226 E Ontario St Chicago IL 60611

DREWES, WERNER, painter, graphic artist; b. Canig, Germany, July 27, 1899; s. Georg and Martha (Schaefer) D.; student Bauhaus, Weimar, Germany, 1920-21, Dessau, Germany, 1927; m. Margaret Schrobsdorff, 1924 (dec. 1959); children—Harold, Wolfram, Bernard; m. 2d, Mary Lischer, 1960. Came to U.S., 1925, naturalized 1936. Traveled in Italy, Spain, S.Am., U.S., Japan, China, Russia, 1923-27; tchr. fine arts Columbia U., N.Y.C., 1936-40, Bklyn. Coll., 1944, Sch. of Design, Chgo., 1945, Washington U., St. Louis, 1947-65. Represented in collections in pub. libraries in Newark, N.Y.C., Boston, Honolulu Acad., Yale and Washington U.; art mus. in Chgo., Bklyn., Phila., San Francisco, Fogg Mus., Boston, St. Louis, Mus. Modern Art, N.Y.C., Library of Congress, Washington, Colls. of Victoria and Albert Mus., London, Nat. Collection Fine Arts, Smithsonian Instn., Guggenheim Mus., Met. Mus. Seattle, and others. Home: Old Ferry Rd Point Pleasant PA 18950

DREWRY, ELIZABETH BELLE, archivist; b. Washington June 13, 1907; d. George J. and Mary C. (Gaffney) Drewry; B.A., George Washington U., 1929, M.A., 1930; Ph.D. (Cornell fellow), Cornell U., 1933. Prof. history Penn Hall Jr. Coll., Chambersburg, Pa., 1932-36; archivist Nat. Archives, 1936-49; archivist and chief records retirement br., records mgmt. div. Nat. Archives and Records Service, Gen. Services Adminstrn., 1950-61; dir. Franklin D. Roosevelt Library, Hyde Park, N.Y., 1961-69; dir. Camp Robin Hood, Chambersburg, Pa., 1969—. Mem. President's Study Group on Careers for Women, 1966—. Recipient Distinguished Service award Gen. Services Adminstrn., 1964, Fed. Womans award Fed. Womans Award Bd., 1965. Fellow Soc. Am. Archivists. Address: Camp Robin Hood Chambersburg PA 17201

DREWRY, GUY CARLETON, author; b. Stevensburg, Va., May 21, 1901; s. Rev. Samuel Richard and Julia Harriett (Pinckard) D.; student pub. schs. Va.; m. Margaret Elizabeth McDonald, Apr. 2, 1942; children—Barbara Louise, Guy Carleton. Asso. editor The Lyric, 1929-49; vis. lectr. English, Am. poetry Hollins College, 1952-53; instr. in creative writing U. Va. Extension Div. Named Poet Laureate of Commonwealth of Va., 1970. Contbr. poetry to The Dial, later The Nation, The New Republic, Poetry; A Magazine of Verse also Voices. Work appears in N.Y. Times, N.Y. Herald Tribune, The Georgia Rev., Prairie Schooner, Sat. Review, Queen's Quarterly, Va. Quarterly Rev. and Yale Rev.; included in following anthologies: American Writing, Lyric Virginia Today, Moult's Best Poems, Virginia Reader, Poetry Awards (1949, 51), Proud Horns, 1933; The Sounding Summer, 1948; A Time of Turning, 1951; The Writhen Wood, 1953. Lyric Virginia Today, No. 2. The Best Poems of 1956; Cloud Above Clocktime, 1957. Winner The voices Award, 1940; Poetry Awards prize for best book of poetry pub. in 1951. Mem. Poetry Soc. Va. (pres. 1952- 55), Poetry Soc. of Am. (regional v.p.) Editor Southern Issue of Voices. Home: 2305 Maiden Lane S W Roanoke, VA 24015.

DREWRY, JOHN ELDRIDGE, educator; b. Griffin, Ga., June 4, 1902; s. Judson Ellis and Verdi May (Harrell) D.; A.B., U. Ga., 1921. B.J., 1922, A.M., 1925; postgrad. Columbia, summers, 1924, 25; m. Kathleen Merry, Dec. 24, 1925 (div. 1949) : 1 son, Milton Lee.; m. 2d, Miriam Thurmond, Mar. 16, 1950. Reporter, news editor Athens (Ga.) Banner-Herald, 1921-23, book reviewer, 1923—; corr. book reviewer Atlanta Jour., 1921-39; book reviewer Atlanta Constn., 1939—; corr. Christian Sci. Monitor, 1927-40. Instr. journalism Henry W. Grady Sch. Journalism, U. Ga., Athens, 1922-24, adj. prof., 1924-26 asso. prof., 1926- 30, prof., 1930—, dir., dean, dean 1940-69, dean emeritus, 1969—, organizer press bur., 1921, publicity dir., 1921-28, 1930-32, asso. editor Alumni Record, 1925-39; lectr. journalism Lucy Cobb Inst., 1925-26; state mail editor A.P., Atlanta, summer 1926; editor Univ. Items, summers, 1927-32; organizer, univ. dir. Ga. Scholastic Press Assn.; univ. adminstr. George Foster Peabody Radio and TV Awards, Ga. Radio and TV Inst., Ga. Press. Inst., So. Indsl. Editors Inst., Edn.-Industry Confs. Pub. Relations and Advt. Mem. Ga. Bicentennial Commn., 1933. Mem. Am. Assn. Tchrs. Journalism (pres. 1930), Am. Council Edn. Journalism, Ga. Edn. Assn., Newcomen Soc., Phi Beta Kappa (pres. U. Ga. chpt. 1948-49), Phi Kappa Phi, Sigma Delta Chi, Kappa Tau Alpha (nat. pres. 1958-60), Omicron Delta Kappa, Digamma Kappa, Kappa Alpha (So.), Phi Eta Sigma. Blue Key Council; first sec., nat. joint com. profl. edn. for journalism; mem. exec. com., formerly mem. Council on Research in Jour., AASDJ. Lt. col. staff Gov. Ellis Arnall. Named to Dixie Bus. Hall of Fame for Living, also recipient Distinguished Service award, 1954; recipient gold key award Columbia Sch. Press Assn., 1954; plaque Internat. Council Indsl. Editors, 1966; Distinguished Service awards U. Ga. Alumni Soc., 1969, Ga. Press Assn., 1969, Ga. Assn. Broadcasters, 1969. Democrat. Baptist. Rotarian. Club: Gridiron. Author, co- author, editor books, 1924—, including Concerning the Fourth Estate, 1938; Post Biographies of Famous Journalists, 1942; Book Reviewing, 1946; More Post Biographies, 1947; Journalism at Mid-Century, 1950; Journalism Enters a New Half Century, 1951; New Horizons in Journalism, 1952; Advancing Journalism. 1953; Journalism Is Communications, 1954; Dimensional Journalism, 1955; Communications: Key to So Much, 1957; The What, Why, and How of Communications, 1958: Are We Communicating?, 1959; Attaining Goals via Better Communications, 1960; Onward and Upward with Communications, 1961; Diagnosis and Prognosis in Journalism, 1962; Better Journalism for a Better Tomorrow, 1963; Communications Cartography, 1964; Higher Ground for Journalism, 1965; Writing Book Reviews, 1966; Greater Communications Effectiveness, 1966; A Forward Look for Communications, 1967; Journalistic Escalation, 1968. Editor: book column Publishers Auxiliary, syndicated book rev. column New Book News. Contbr. articles to mags. Home: 447 Highland Av Athens GA 30601 ☆

DREXLER, FRED, ins. co. exec.; b. Oakland. Cal., Nov. 17, 1915; s. Frederic I. and Jessie (Day) D.; A.B., U. Redlands, 1936; J.D., Golden Gate Coll., 1947; m. Martha Jane Cunningham, Dec. 26, 1936; children—Frederick Kenneth, Roger Cunningham, Martha Charlotte (Mrs. Joseph M. Lynn). Editor Mill Valley (Cal.) Record, 1936-42; employee relations Marinship Corp., 1942-45; office mgr. Bechtel Corp., 1945-46; asst. to pres. Indsl. Indemnity Co., San Francisco, 1946-48, asst. sec., 1948-51, sec., 1951-56, sr. v.p., sec., 1956-67, exec. v.p., sec., 1967, pres., 1968-70, chmn. bd., chief exec. officer, 1970—, also dir.; dir. Crum & Forster; admitted to Cal. bar. 1947. Mem. Cal. Workmen's Compensation Study Commn., 1963-65; sec.-treas. Cal. Workmen's Compensation Inst., 1968-70, pres., 1971—. Pres. Pacific Ins. and Surety Conf., 1967-68; chmn. Cal. Advisory Com. on Financial Supervision of Casualty Insurers, 1967. Pres. Marin (Cal.) United Fund, 1956; exec. bd. Marin Council Boy Scouts Am. 1948-68, adv. bd., 1968—, mem. region 12 com., 1960-68, hon. mem., 1968—, Silver Beaver, Silver Antelope awards; trustee Marin Country Day Sch., 1960-62; trustee Golden Gate Coll., 1957—, chmn. bd., 1968-70. Mem. Am., Cal. bar assns. Baptist. Clubs: Stock Exchange, Bankers (San Francisco); World Trade, Bohemian; California (Los Angeles). Home: 1 Myrtle Av Mill Valley CA 94941 Office: 255 California St San Francisco CA 94111

DREXLER, FREDERICK A., trust co. exec. Auditor, U.S. Trust Co. N.Y. Office: 45 Wall St New York City NY 10005*

DREXLER, MICHAEL DAVID, advt. exec.; b. Bklyn., Nov. 2, 1938; s. Benn and Evelyn (Goldfarb) D.; B.S., L.I. U., 1959; m. Nancy Koch, Sept. 12, 1959; children—Staci, Denise. Media buyer Franklin Spier, Inc., advt. agy., N.Y.C., 1959-60, media buyer, 1960-63, media supr., 1963-65, v.p., asso. media dir., 1965-69; sr. v.p., media dir. Ogilvy & Mather, N.Y.C., 1969—. Mem. Tau Delta Phi. Democrat. Jewish religion. Home: 240-27 67th Av Douglaston Queens NY 11363 Office: 2 E 48th St New York City NY 10017

DREYER, JOHN EDWARD, lawyer; b. Chgo., Feb. 22, 1929; s. Felix E. and Marie (Bungert) D.; B.S., Loyola U., Chgo., 1951; J.D., DePaul U., 1953; m. Shirley A. Fenhaus, May 29, 1954; children—Thomas, Laura, Gregory, Michael. Admitted to Ill. bar, 1953; practiced in Chgo., 1956-62, Aurora, 1956—; mem. firm Sears & Streit, 1956-61; jr. partner Sears, Streit, Tyler & Dreyer, 1961-63; sr. partner Dreyer, Foote & Streit, 1963—; dir. Valley Nat. Bank of Aurora. Served with Judge Adv. Gen.'s Corps, AUS, 1953-56. Mem. Am., Ill. (mem. exec. council jr. bar sect. 1961-64), Kane County, Aurora bar assns., Am. Judicature Soc., Ill. Soc. Trial Lawyers, Pi Gamma Mu, Phi Alpha Delta. Editorial bd. DePaul Law Rev., 1952-53. Home: Sugar Grove IL 60554 Office: 900 N Lake St Aurora IL 60506

DREYER, ROBERT A., corp. exec.; b. N.Y.C. 1916; grad. Lehigh U., 1936; ed. law, N.Y.U., 1939, Harvard, 1940. Vice pres., sec., gen. counsel Metromedia, Inc.; sec. Adamas Carbide Corp. Home: 6 Park Rd Short Hills NJ 07078 Office: Adamas Carbide Corp Market St Kenilworth NJ 07033*

DREYFOUS, FELIX JULIUS, architect; b. New Orleans, Oct. 21, 1896; s. Felix J. and Julia (Seeman) D.; student Tulane U., 1914-15; B.S. in Architecture, U. Pa., 1917; m. F. Vera Scherck, Nov 15, 1922 (dec. Aug. 1943); children—Carol (Mrs. Fred Eisenman, Jr., Felix John III; m. 2d, Ruth Simon, June 28, 1947 (dec. July 1961); m. 3d, Rosetta Hirsh, Apr. 24, 1964 (dec. July 1971). Practiced architecture, La., Georgia, Texas, Fla., Miss., Ala., 1919-20; partner Weiss, Dreyfous, 1920-23, Weiss, Dreyfous and Seiferth, 1924-42, Weiss, Dreyfous and Seiferth, 1945-52, Dreyfous and Seiferth, 1952-60, Dreyfous, Seiferth and Gibert (all New Orleans); now engaged in private practice, 1960—; architect for Louisiana Capitol, Baton Rouge, Charity Hosp., La. State U. Med. Sch., Touro Infirmary, Jung Hotel, Fed. Land Bank, Clairborne Elementary Sch. and L. B. Landry High Sch. (all New Orleans), bldgs. for La. State U., La. Creamery, Inc. (both Baton Rouge). Mem. New Orleans Bd. Park Commrs., 1920—. Mem. bd. adminstrs. Touro Infirmary, 1935—; mem. bd. adminstrs. Isaac Delgado Mus. Art, 1924—, pres., 1964. Served with U.S. Army, 1918; from capt. to lt. col., C.E., AUS, 1942-46. Mem. A.I.A. (pres. La. 1937). Home: 18 Audubon Pl New Orleans LA 70118 Office: Nat Bank Commerce Bldg New Orleans LA 70112

DREYFUS, ALFRED STANLEY, rabbi; b. Youngstown, O., Jan. 31, 1921; s. Marcel and Isabella (Mervis) D.; B.A.; U. Cin., 1942; B. Hebrew Letters, Hebrew Union Coll., Cin., 1942, M. Hebrew Letters, 1946, Ph.D., 1951, D.D., 1971; m. Marianne Cecilia Berlak, July 25, 1950; children—James Nathaniel, Richard Baeck. Ordained rabbi; rabbi in Terre Haute Ind., 1951-56, Galveston, Tex., 1956-65, Union Temple, Bklyn., 1965—; vis. lectr. liturgy and commentaries N.Y. Sch., Hebrew Union Coll. Jewish Inst. Religion 1966—. Pres. Assembly Tex. Rabbis, 1962-63, Bklyn. Assn. Reform Rabbis, 1967-68; pres. Bklyn. Bd. Rabbis, 1970—; mem. governing body World Union Progressive Judaism, 1967—. bd. govs. N.Y. Bd. Rabbis, 1967—; mem. Cath. Jewish Relations Com., Bklyn.- Queens Diocese, 1966—; bd. dirs. Synagogue Council Am., 1968—. Pres. Friends of Rosenberg Library, Galveston, 1961-62, bd. dirs., 1962-65; chmn. home service of Galveston chpt. A.R.C., 1956-65; hon. chmn. Bklyn. div. United Hosp. campaign, 1965—. Served as chaplain, lt. col. AUS, 1953-55. Mem. Central Conf. Am. Rabbis, Mil. Chaplains Assn., Res. Officers Assn. Rotarian, Mason (32 deg., Shriner), Elk; mem. B'nai B'rith. Club: Unity (Bklyn.). Home: 9 Prospect Park W Brooklyn NY 11215 Office: 17 Eastern Pky Brooklyn NY 11238

DREYFUS, JACK JONAS, Jr., found. exec.; b. Montgomery, Ala., Aug. 28, 1913; s. Jack Jonas and Ida (Lewis) D.; B.A., Lehigh U., 1934; m. Joan E. Personnette, Jan. 13, 1939; 1 son, John. With Merrill, Lynch, Pierce, Fenner & Beane, 1937-45; sr. partner Dreyfus & Co., N.Y.C., 1945—; chmn. bd. Dreyfus Fund, 1965—. Served with USCGR, 1943-44. Clubs: Cavendish Country, Stock Exchange, City Athletic (N.Y.C.); Metropolis Country, Century Country (White Plains, N.Y.). Home: Hobeau Farm Ocala FL

DREYFUS, LEE SHERMAN, univ. pres.; b. Milw., June 20, 1926; s. Woods Orlow and Clare (Bluett) D.; B.A., U. Wis., 1949, M.A., 1952, Ph.D., 1957; m. Joyce Mae Unke, Apr. 5, 1947; children—Susan Lynn Fosdick, Lee Sherman. Radio actor sta. WISN, Milw., 1933-49; instr. U. Wis., 1949-52; gen. mgr. radio sta. WDET, Detroit, 1952-56; asst. prof. speech Wayne State U., 1956-60, asso. prof. speech, asso. dir. mass communications, 1960-62; gen. mgr. sta. WHA-TV, Madison, Wis., 1962-65; dir. instructional resources U. Wis., 1965-67, prof. speech, chmn. radio-TV and films, 1962-67; pres. Wis. State U. at Stevens Point, 1967—; cons. in field, 1960—. Dir., Sentry Broadcasting Corp., Citizens Nat. Bank, Stevens Point, Radio Sta. WSPT. Mem. Nat. Army Adv. Panel on ROTC Affairs; chief of mission under Vietnam Contract for Higher Edn.-Wis. State U.-Stevens Point Found., Inc. Bd. dirs. Winnebago Children's Home, Sentry Ins. Found., Wis. Ballet Co. Wis. Fine Arts Found.; mem. adv. bd. St Michael's Hosp., Stevens Point. Served with USNR, 1944-46. Recipient citation for mental health Gov. Mich. Mem. Nat. Nat. Assn. Ednl. Broadcasters (bd. dirs.), Speech Assn. Am. (chmn. radio-TV-film com.), Broadcast Pioneers Am., N.O.R.A.D. (hon.), Phi Beta Kappa. Phi Eta Sigma, Phi Kappa Phi, Kappa Sigma. Episcopalian. Mason. Author: Televised Instruction, 1962; World's First Intercontinental Video Classroom Connection via Earlybird Satellite, 1965. Home: 408 W Maple Ridge Dr Stevens Point WI 54481

DREYFUS, LOUIS GOETHE, Jr., ret. fgn. service officer; b. Santa Barbara, Cal., Nov. 23 1889; s. Louis G. and Constance (Auerswald) D.; B.A., Yale, 1910, M.A., 1911; m. Grace Hawes, June 14, 1917. Apptd. consular asst., 1910; dep. consul gen., Berlin, Germany, 1911, v.p., dep. consul gen., 1914, vice consul, 1915; vice consul, Callao, Peru, 1912; consular agt., Quibdo, 1913; vice consul, Budapest, 1915; consul in charge, Sofia, 1916; consul assigned to Sivas, 1917, to Malaga, Spain, 1917, Paris, France, 1919, Palermo, Italy, 1920; consul, Dresden, Germany, 1921-24, consul gen., 1924; fgn. service insp. Dist. Western Europe, 1925-29; consul gen., Naples, Italy, 1929-31, Copenhagen, Denmark, 1931-33; counselor of Embassy, Lima, Peru, 1933-39; E.E. and M.P., Iran, 1939-44, Afghanistan, 1940-42, Iceland, 1944-46; spl. rep. of Pres. with rank of ambassador, ceremonies incident to inauguration 1st pres. Republic Iceland; E.E. and M.P. Sweden, 1946-47; acting chief Fgn. Service Inspection Corps, 1947-48; Am. ambassador to Afghanistan, 1949-50. Mem. Santa Barbara Com. on Fgn. Relations. Chmn. bd. Santa Barbara chpt. A.R.C., 1960, 61, now bd. dirs; bd. dirs. Iran-Am. Soc. of Washington, Santa Barbara Found. Mem. Union Interalliée (Paris), Montecito Protective Assn. Episcopalian. Clubs: Valley, Santa Barbara, Channel City (bd. dirs.). Home: 370 Hot Springs Rd Santa Barbara CA 93108

DREYFUS, PIERRE, French industrialist; b. Paris, Nov. 18, 1907; s. Emmanuel and Madeleine (Bernard) D.; LL.D., Coll. Law, Paris; m. Laure Ullmo, Mar. 9, 1936; 1 dau., Sylvie. Insp. gen. industry and commerce, head, gen. inspection corps, dir. cabinet minister industry and commerce, 1947-49; pres. Coal Mines Lorraine, 1950-55; mem. bd. dirs. Regie Nationale des Usines Renault, 1947, v.p., 1948-55, pres., gen. mgr., 1955—; dir. cabinet minister industry and commerce, 1954; dir., state rep. Coal mining France, 1954; pres. Energy Commn. to Plan; pres. Societe des Aciers Fins de l'Est, 1955—. Served as sgt. French Army, World War II; with French Underground. Decorated Legion of Honor, officier du Merite Agricole, officier de l'Ordre de Leopold, grand officier du Merite Italien, comdr. de l'Ordre Nat. Ivoirien, comdr. de l'Ordre Nat. Malgache. Address: Regie Nationale des Usines Renault 51 Avenue des Champs-Elysees Paris France Office: 8 Au Emile Zola 92 Boulogne Billancourt Paris France

DREYFUS-BARNEY, LAURA (Mme. L. Dreyfus-Barney), lectr., cons.; b. Cin., Nov. 3O, 1879; d. Albert Clifford and Laura Alice (Pike) Barney; ed. by pvt. tutors; m. Hippolyte Dreyfus (Cordozo), Apr. 1911. Served with Am. Ambulance at Lycée Pasteur as aux. night nurse, Paris, France, 1914-15; engaged in re-edn. of mentally and physically handicapped, Mil. Hosp., Marseilles, France, 1915-16; A.R.C., del. Refugee and Repatriate Service for 3 depts. of So. France, 1916-18; co-founder first children's hosp., L'Avenir des Enfants de Vaucluse, Avignon, France, 1918; formed under aegis League of Nations, liaison com. major internat. orgns. to promote better understanding between peoples and classes, 1925-47; apptd. by council of League Nations to consultative com. Orgn. of Intellectual Cooperation, 1926-39, active in establishment Nat. Agrl. Center, Salon, France (nr. Marseilles), 1928; organized for Internat. Council of Women, under auspices Internat. Inst. Ednl. Cinematography of League Nations, first internat. congress of women specializing in study of motion pictures and their effect upon human relations, Rome, Italy, 1931; expert of Internat. Inst. Edn. Cinematography of League Nations, 1931-37; elected mem. bd. of Congress, Rome, 1934; mem. com. experts League Nations, dealing with internat. radio broadcasting problems and relationships between peoples, 1937-38; vice chmn. Com. Women's Internat. Orgns. for Control and Reduction of Armaments Geneva, 1931-46; mem. U.S. delegation 2d Am. Conf. Nat. Coms. of Intellectual Cooperation, Havana, Cuba, 1941; sponsor, mem. Inst. on World Orgn., Washington, 1941- 61. Adv. chmn, and dir. tng. vol. information service War Hospitality Com., Washington, 1942-45; also rep. Nat. Council of Women on Coordinating Com. for Better Race Understanding, 1946; sr. liaison officer Internat. Council Women with UN and its specialized agys., UNESCO, FAO, ECOSOC, others; sometime accredited various internat. orgns. from non- govtl. orgns.; sometime chmn. study groups and orgns. of internat. assns. Founder Alice Pike Barney Meml. Trust Smithsonian Instn., 1951, for devel. of art in U.S.; donor (with sister) Studio House Cultural Center, Smithsonian Instn.; hon. pres. Barney Neighborhood Settlement, Washington. Mem. bd. Am. Soc. French Legion of Honor, N.Y.; officer French Legion of Honor; trustee Pres. James Monroe Found., Fredericksburg, Va. Author or co-author books, articles and monographs. Address: Am Security Trust Washington DC 20549

DREYFUSS, HENRY, Indsl. designer; b. N.Y.C., Mar. 2, 1904 s. Louis and Elsie (Gorge) D.; D.Sc., Occidental Coll., 1953; A.F.D., Pratt Inst., 1963; m. Doris Marks, 1930; children—John Alan, Gail (Mrs. George Campbell Wilson, Jr.), Ann. Opened indsl. design office, 1929; now corporate cons. Faculty Cal. Inst. Tech. Bd. dirs. Ford Found. Ednl. Facilities Labs.; trustee Cal. Inst. Tech.; mem. bd. govs. performing arts council Los Angeles Music Center; trustee People to People, Los Angeles County Art Mus. Decorated Order Orange-Nassau (Netherlands); recipient Archtl. League Gold medal, 1951; Benjamin Franklin fellow Royal Soc. Arts; Distinguished Contbn. award Am. Soc. Indsl. Designers, 1960; design award Phila. Mus. Coll. Art, 1962; design in steel award Am. Iron and Steel Inst., 1965, Ambassador award for achievement, Eng., 1965; Distinguished Contbns. award Nat. Assn. Schs. Art. Fellow Indsl. Designers Soc. Am. (bd. dirs.) Author: Designing for People, 1955, 2d edit., 1967; The Measure of Man, 1960, rev. edit., 1967. Home: South Pasadena CA 91030 Office: 500 Columbia St South Pasadena CA 91030

DREYFUSS, JOHN THORNTON, fgn. service officer; b. N.Y.C., Nov. 14, 1925; s. Travers H. and Nell (Liebmann) D.; B.A., Stanford, 1949; postgrad. Nat. War Coll., 1968-69; m. Janis Lucile Behr, Sept. 1, 1949; children—John R., Ricardo V., Lisa N., Amy G. Vice consul Am. Embassy, Naples, 1954-56; 2d sec. Am. Embassy, La Paz, Bolivia, 1956-58; officer-in-charge Ecuadorian affairs Dept. State, 1958-62; 1st sec., chief polit. sect. Am. Embassy, Guatemala, 1962-65, dep. chief of Mission, counselor of Embassy, 1970—; chief Argentine affairs Dept. State, 1965-68; counselor of Embassy and consul gen., Bridgetown, Barbados, 1968-69. Served with USMCR, 1942-46. Decorated Bronze Star medal. Mem. Kappa Alpha. Address: Am Embassy APO New York City NY 09891

DRICK, JOHN EDWARD, banker; b. Williamsport, Pa., Nov. 26, 1911; s. George R. and Charlotte (Quinn) D.; grad. Phillips Acad., Andover, Mass., 1930; B.S., Sheffield Sci. Sch., Yale, 1934; m. Caroline Whitehead, Mar. 14, 1936; children—Judith (Mrs. Toland), George Randall, Helen Whitehead. With First Nat. Bank, Chgo., 1935—, v.p. petroleum and term loan div., 1952- 64, sr. v.p. charge term loan div., 1964-65, exec. v.p., 1965-69, pres., 1969—, also dir.; dir. Stepan Chem. Co., Walter E. Heller & Co., MCA, Inc. Clubs: Chicago; Exmoor Country (Highland Park, Ill). Home: 1039 Miami Rd Wilmette Il 60091 Office: 38 S Dearborn St Chicago IL 60670

DRICKAMER, HARRY GEORGE, educator; b. Cleve., Nov. 19, 1918; s. George Henry and Louise (Strempel) D.; B.S., U. Mich., 1941, M.S., 1942, Ph.D., 1946; m. Mae Elizabeth McFillen, Oct. 28, 1942; childrenLee Charles, Lynn Louise, Lowell Kurt, Margaret Ann, Priscilla. Chem. engr. Pan Am. Refining Corp., 1942-46; asst. prof. U. Ill. at Urbana, 1946-49, asso. prof., 1949-53, prof. phys. chemistry and chem. engring., 1953—. Recipient, Bendix award, 1968. Guggenheim fellow, 1952. Fellow Am. Phys. Soc. (Buckley Solid State Physics award 1967), Am. Geophys. Union; mem. Am. Chem. (Ipatieff prize 1956), Am. Inst. Chem. Engrs. (Jr. award 1947, Alpha Chi Sigma award 1967), Faraday Soc., Nat. Acad. Scis., Center for Advanced Studies. Home: 405 W Washington Urbana IL 61801

DRIGGS, DON WALLACE, educator; b. Phoenix, Sept. 26, 1924; s. Golden Kenneth and Maude (Macdonald) D.; B.S., Brigham Young U., 1950; M.A., Harvard, 1955, Ph.D., 1956; Carnegie fellow, U. Mich., 1963-64; m. Marilyn Louise Fisher, Sept. 5, 1953 (div.); children—Deborah, Pamela, Christopher. Instr., then asst. prof. U. Nev., Reno, 1956-61, asso. prof. polit. sci., 1965-68, prof., chmn. dept. polit. sci., 1968—, chmn. Faculty Senate, 1968-69; asst. prof., asso. prof., chmn. div. social scis. Stanislaus State Coll., 1961-63, asst. to pres., 1964-65. Mem. platform com. Nev. State Democratic Conv., 1960, 68; mem. Nev. delegation Nat. Dem. Conv., 1968. Served with USAAF, 1943-46, USAF, 1951-52. Decorated Air medal. Mem. Am., No. Cal. (exec. council 1968-70), Western (sec.-treas. 1966-69) polit. sci. assns. Author: The Consitution of the State of Nevada: A Commentary, 1961. Contbr. Western Polit. Quar., 1957—, asso. editor, 1970—. Home: 945 Joshua Dr Reno NV 89502

DRIGGS, DOUGLAS HARMON, banker; b. Driggs, Ida., Apr. 8, 1901; s. Don C. and May (Robison) D.; m. Effie Killian, Aug. 31, 1926; children—John Douglas, Lois, Gary Harmon, Anne. Sec., Western Savs. & Loan Assn., Phoenix, 1929-33, pres., 1933-65, now chmn. bd., chief exec. officer. Past pres., now dir., nat. rep. Theodore Roosevelt council Boy Scouts Am. Bd. dirs., pres. Phoenix Symphony Assn. Mem. Ch. of Jesus Christ of Latter-day Saints. Rotarian (dist. gov. 1969-70). Home: 7610 Shadow Mountain Rd Phoenix AZ 85253 Office: 3443 N Central Av Phoenix AZ 85012

DRIGGS, JOHN DOUGLAS, mayor of Phoenix; b. Douglas, Ariz., June 16, 1927; s. Douglas H. and Effie (Killian) D.; A.B., Stanford, 1952; M.B.A., 1954; m. Patricia Gail Dorsey, Nov. 16, 1956; children—John Douglas, Andrew James, Thomas Dorsey, Adam Dorsey, Peter Dorsey. With Western Savs. & Loan Assn., Phoenix, 1956—, exec. v.p., 1967—; mayor of Phoenix, 1970—. Mem. President's Adv. Council Inter-govtl. Personnel Policy. Served with USNR, 1945-46. Mem. Savs. and Loan League Ariz. (pres. 1967-68), Am. Legion, Phi Gamma Delta. Republican. Mem. Ch. of Jesus Christ of Latter-day Saints. Home: 7301 N Central Av Phoenix AZ 85020 Office: 251 W Washington St Phoenix AZ 85003

DRIGGS, JUNIUS ELMARION, savs. and loan assn. exec.; b. Driggs, Ida., June 28, 1907; s. Don Carlos and May (Robison) D.; ed. pub. schs.; m. Bernice Crouse, May 18, 1933; children—Don C., Sharon (Mrs. Dave D. Hall), Deanna (Mrs. Clifford I. Franks), Stephen C., Michael R. With Western Savs. & Loan Assn., Phoenix, 1931—, exec. v.p., 1955-64, pres., 1964—. Mem. Phoenix Human Relations Commn., 1964-69; chmn. Ariz. Heart Assn., 1961; chmn. Phoenix chpt. Nat. Council Christians and Jews, 1965-67, mem. at large bd. trustees, bd. govs.; adv. bd. Phoenix Salvation Army, 1965—, Phoenix YMCA, 1959—, Roosevelt council Boy Scouts Am., 1956—. Mem. Ch. of Jesus Christ of Latter-day Saints (regional rep. Council of Twelve). Home: 5307 E Wonderview Rd Phoenix AZ 85018 Office: 3443 N Central Av Phoenix AZ 85012

DRINAN, ROBERT FREDERICK, congressman, clergyman; b. Boston, Nov. 15, 1920; s. James Joseph and Ann Mary (Flanagan) D.; A.B., Boston Coll., 1942, M.A., 1947; LL.B., Georgetown U., 1949, LL.M., 1950; Th.D., Gregorian U., Rome, 1954; study, Florence, Italy, 1954-55; LL.D., Worcester State Coll., 1970, L.I. U., 1970, R.I. Coll., 1971. Entered Soc. Jesus, 1942, ordained priest, Roman Cath. Ch., 1953. Admitted to D.C. bar, 1950, Mass. bar, 1956, U.S. Supreme Ct. bar, 1955; asst. dean Boston Coll. Law Sch., 1955-56, dean, 1956-70; vis. prof. U. Tex. Law Sch., 1966-67; mem. 92d Congress, 3d Dist. Mass., mem. jud. com., internal security com. Chmn. adv. com. Mass. U.S. Commn. Civil Rights, 1962-70. Member exec. com. Assn. Am. Law Schs. Fellow Am. Acad. Arts and Scis.; mem. Am., Mass. (v.p. 1961), Boston bar assns., Am. Law Inst. Corresponding editor America, nat. Cath. weekly. Author: Religion, the Courts and Public Policy, 1963; Democracy, Dissent and Disorder, 1969; Vietnam and Armageddon, 1970. Editor: The Right To Be Educated, 1968. Editor-in-chief Family Law Quarterly, 1967-70. Contbr. articles to jours. of opinion. Home: 140 Commonwealth Av Chestnut Hill MA 02167 Office: US Ho of Reps Washington DC 20515

DRINKARD, DONALD, dry goods co. exec.; b. Trenton, Mo., Mar. 29, 1919; s. Harry and Carrie (Kirk) D.; student Kansas City (Mo.) Jr. Coll.; m. Helen C. Polson, Sept. 29, 1939; children—Judith C. (Mrs. Eugene A. Pearsail), Donald Dwight. With Fitts Dry Goods Co., Kansas City, Mo., 1937-53, v.p., gen. mgr., 1949-53; v.p., gen. mgr. William R. Moore, Inc., Memphis, 1953-54, pres., 1954-58, pres., chmn. bd., 1958—; dir. Nat. Bank Commerce. Pres. Nat. Assn. Textile and Apparel Wholesalers, 1959-61. Past pres. Memphis Children's Bur.; pres. Memphis Cerebral Palsy Assn., Bd. dirs. Memphis and Shelby County Community Chest, William R. Moore Sch. Tech., Memphis U. Sch. Served to 1st lt. AUS, 1943-46. Mem. Memphis C. of C. (bd. dirs.) Mason. Clubs: Memphis Country, University (Memphis); Empire State (N.Y.C.). Home: 134 Grove Park Circle Memphis TN 38117 Office: 183 Monroe St Memphis TN 38101

DRINKER, HENRY SANDWITH, Jr., mfg. co. exec.; b. Phila., May 29, 1914; s. Henry S. and Sophie (Hutchinson) D.; B.S. in Engring., Haverford Coll., 1937; m. Ruth Brooks, June 28, 1942; children—Ann, Henry. Engr. SKF Industries, 1938- 41, Eclipse-Pioneer div. Bendix Aviation Corp., 1941-47, Graydon Smith & Co., Boston, 1947-50; with Foxboro Co. (Mass.), 1950—, sec., 1968- 70, now v.p., sec. Pres. Concord (Mass.) Community Chest, 1960-64. Mem. finance com., Concord, 1966—. Address: Foxboro Co 38 Neponset Av Foxboro MA 02035

DRINKO, JOHN DEAVER, lawyer; b. St. Mary's, W.Va., June 17, 1921; s. Emery J. and Hazel (White) D.; A.B., Marshall U., 1942; J.D., Ohio State U., 1944; postgrad. U. Tex., 1944; m. Elizabeth Webb Gibson, May 14, 1946; children—Elizabeth Lee, Diana Lynn, John Randall, Jay Deaver. Admitted to Ohio bar, 1945; partner firm Baker, Hosteller & Patterson, Cleve., 1955—, mng. partner, 1969—. Chmn. bd. Cleve. Inst. Electronics; dir. Preformed Line Products Co., Programmed Edn., Inc., Orvis Co., Inc., Ideal Builders Supply & Fuel Co., Sherwood Refractories, Inc.; sec., dir. Standard Products Co.; sec. Cloyes Gear & Products, Inc. Mem. nat. council Ohio State U. Law Sch., 1965—; exec. com. President's Club, Ohio State U., 1968—; chmn. parents and friends com. Mt. Holyoke Coll., 1970—. Trustee Thomas F. Peterson Found., Philip B. and Celia B. Arnold Found., Harry D. and Grace Myers Found. Recipient Distinguished Alumnus award Marshall U., 1968, Alumni Centennial award Ohio State U., 1970. Mem. Am., Ohio, Cleve. bar assns., Am. Judicature Soc., Order of Coif. Republican. Presbyn. (elder). Mason (Shriner, Jester). Clubs: Cleve. Athletic, Union (Cleve.); Mayfield Country; Detroit Athletic. Home: 4891 Middledale Rd Lyndhurst OH 44124 Office: Union Commerce Bldg Cleveland OH 44115

DRINKWATER, TERRELL CROFT, ret. air transportation exec.; b. Denver, July 15, 1908; s. Ray Lawrence and Geraldine (Croft) D.; A.B., Univ. of Colo., 1930; LL.B., 1932, LL.M., 1933; m. Helen Louise Kiddoo, Sept. 5, 1933; children—Terrell Thomas, Dorsey Ann. Practiced law in Denver, specializing aeronautical law, 1933-42; exec. vice pres., dir., gen. mgr. Continental Air Lines, Inc., 1942-44; vice pres., Am. Airlines, Inc., 1944-47; v.p., dir., Am. Overseas Airlines, Inc., 1945-47; pres., dir., Western Airlines, Inc., 1947-70; dir. Southern Cal. Edison Co., Union Bank, Los Angeles, Pacific Mut. Life Ins. Co., Los Angeles. Cons. to United States delegation in negotiation of internat. air pacts with United Kingdom at Bermuda, 1946. Mem. Colo. State Aeronautics com., 1938-42. Dir. Los Angeles chpt. A.R.C.; director YMCA. Mem. Air Transport Assn. Am. (mem. bd. dirs. 1942- 44, 47-48, 53-54, 59-60, 67-68), Los Angeles C. of C. (pres. 1952), Am. Bar Assn., Chi Psi, Phi Delta Phi. Republican, Presbyterian. Clubs: University (Colo.); Burning Tree (Washington); California, Los Angeles Country.

DRINNON, RICHARD, educator; b. Portland, Ore., Jan. 4, 1925; s. John Henry and Emma (Tweed) D.; B.A., Willamette U., 1950; M.A., U. Minn., 1951, Ph.D., 1957; m. Anna Maria Faulise, Oct. 20, 1945; children—Donna Elizabeth, Jon Tweed. Instr. humanities U. Minn., 1952-53, social sci., 1955-57; instr. Am. history U. Cal., 1957-58, asst. prof., 1958-61; Bruern fellow in Am. studies U. Leeds, 1961-63; faculty research fellow Social Sci. Research Council, 1963-64; asso. prof. history Hobart and William Smith Colls., 1964-66; prof., chmn. dept. history Bucknell U., 1966—. Mem. nat. exec. com. War Resister's League, 1968-69; active Resist. Served with USNR, 1942-46. Mem. Am. Hist. Assn. Anarchist. Atheist. Author: Rebel in Paradise: a Biography of Emma Goldman, 1961; The White Savage: John Donn Hunter, 1970. Contbr. articles profl. jours. Home: RD 1 Milton PA 17847 Office: Bucknell Univ Lewisburg PA 17837

DRIPPS, ROBERT DUNNING, physician; b. Phila., June 19, 1911; s. Robert Dunning and Madge (Heron) D.; A.B. Princeton, 1932; M.D., U. Pa., 1936 m. Diana Rogers, Feb, 11, 1939; children—Robert Dunning III, Susan Adair. Intern U. Pa. Hosp., 1938; instr. pharmacology U. Pa. Sch. Medicine, 1938-40, asso., 1942-45, asso. prof. surgery (anesthesia), 1943-49, prof., chmn. dept. anesthesia, 1949- -; dir. anesthesia Hosp. of U. Pa., 1943—, v.p. for med. affairs, 1971—. Commonwealth Fund fellow in anesthesiology U. Wis., 1941; mem. med. teaching mission to Greece and Italy, 1948; civilian cons. Army Med. Service Grad. Sch., 1949—; mem. surgery study sect. USPHS, 1951-56, mem. nat. adv. resources com., 1963—; sr. instr. internat. course anesthesiology WHO, Denmark, 1952; sr. civilian cons. anesthesia Surgeon Gen. of Army, 1953- -; chmn. com. anesthesia NRC, 1954-62; civilian cons. anesthesia U.S. Naval Hosp., Phila.; mem. subcom. trauma Office Surgeon Gen., U.S. Army; mem. med. bd. Project HOPE, 1968-; chmn. com. on anesthesia NIH, 1967- Pharmacology Research Tng. Grant Com., USPHS. Trustee The Agnes Irwin Sch., 1961-64, Princeton U., 1967-71, pres. U. Pa. Senate, 1965. Diplomate Am. Bd. Anesthesiology (bd. dirs. 1956-67). Mem. Am. Soc. Clin. Investigation, Am. Coll. Anesthesiologists, Am. Soc. Anesthesiologists, Am. Physiol. Soc., Am. Soc. Pharmacology, A.M.A., Am. Surg. Assn., Assn. Am. Physicians, Pa. Soc. Anesthesiology (pres. 1950), Assn. U. Anesthetists (founders group pres. 1957), Halsted Soc. (pres. 1957), Phi Beta Kappa, Sigma Xi, Alpha Omega Alpha. Republican. Presbyn. (elder 1971—). Clubs: Philadelphia; Merion Cricket (Haverford; Phila.). Author: Physiological Basis for Oxygen Therapy, 1950; Introduction to Anesthesia, 1967. Mem. revision com. U.S. Pharmacopeia, 1950-56; mem. editorial bd. Digest of Treatment. 1946-62, Jour. Pharmacology and Exptl. Therapeutics, 1953-57, Jour. Surg. Research, 1963-68, Rev. Surgery. 1964—; nat. editorial bd. Modern Medicine, 1954-56; cons. editor Survey of Anesthesiology. Home: 526 Avonwood Rd Haverford PA 19041 Office: University Hosp 3400 Spruce St Philadelphia PA 19104

DRISCOLL, ALFRED E., govt. ofcl.; b. Oct. 25, 1902; A.B., Williams Coll.; LL.B., Harvard; 19 honorary degrees; m. Antoinette Ware Tatem, 1932; 2 sons, 1 dau. Admitted N.J. bar 1929; mem., partner Starr, Summerill, Lloyd, 1929-47; state senator, N.J., 1938-41; gov. of N.J., 1947-54; dir., mem. exec. com. Warner-Lambert Co., Inc., 1954-71, pres., 1954-67, chmn. 1967, hon. chmn. bd., dir.,

1967-71; dir. Chem. Fund. Vice chmn. Pres.'s Commn. on Intergovtl. Relations, 1954-55; pres. Nat. Municipal League, 1963-67; chmn. N.J. Turnpike Authority, 1969—; mem. N.J. Tax Policy Commn., 1969—. Trustee Williams Coll., Samuel H. Kress Found.; bd. fellows Farleigh Dickinson U.; bd. dirs. N.J. Audubon Soc. Mem. S.A.R. Republican. Clubs: Taconic Country, Williams, Metropolitan, Lyford Cay. Home: Haddonfield NJ 08033 Office: 201 Tabor Rd Morris Plains NJ 07950

DRISCOLL, CLEMENT JOSEPH, lawyer; b. N.Y.C., Aug. 5, 1916; s. Clement Joseph and Elizabeth (Nolan) D.; B.A., St. John's U., 1937; LL.B., Columbia, 1940; m. Maria T. Matilla, Feb. 28, 1946; children—Elizabeth M. (Mrs. Boyle), Clement J., Anita M., David J., Jean M. Admitted to N.Y. bar, 1940, Ill. bar, 1946; spl. agt. FBI, 1941-46; atty. Armour & Co., Chgo., 1946-58; with Internat. Packers Ltd., 1958-69, corp. sec., 1962-69, v.p., gen. counsel, 1966-69, v.p., corp. sec. of successor firm Deltec Internat. Ltd., 1969—. Mem. Am. Soc. Corp. Secs., Soc. Former Agts. FBI. Home: 230 Heights Rd Ridgewood NJ 07450 Office: 1 Battery Park Plaza New York City NY 10004

DRISCOLL, DONALD GOTZIAN, bus. exec.; b. St. Paul, Minn., Feb. 20, 1897; s. Arthur Brown and Helen Evelyn (Gotzian) D.; Ph.B., Yale, 1920; m. Elizabeth Hotchkiss Aull, Dec. 29, 1920; childrenRobert Aull, David Aull. Purchasing dept. Sorg Paper Co., Middletown, O., 1920-33, sales dept. 1933-38, sec., 1927- 38, exec. v.p., 1938-44, pres. 1944-65, chmn., 1965—. Served as gunnery sgt. Marine Corps Aviation, U.S. Army, 1918. Mem. Book and Snake Soc. (Yale). Republican. Episcopalian. Home: 6685 Miralake Dr Cincinnati OH 45243 Office: Sorg Paper Co Middletown OH 45042

DRISCOLL, EDWARD JOSEPH, oral surgeon; b. New Orleans, Aug. 9, 1914; s. John Joseph and Feronie (Frederic) D.; D.D.S., Loyola U., New Orleans, 1936; postgrad. Grad. Sch. Medicine, U. Pa., 1954; m. Noelie Aviles, June 18, 1938; children—Mary (Mrs. Thomas Porter), Kathleen (Mrs. Edgar Girzone), Louise (Mrs. William Sevilla), Paul, Robert, Commd. USPHS, 1938, Col., 1956; dental intern USPHS Hosp., New Orleans, 1936-38: staff dental officer USPHS Hosp. Chgo., 1939, USPHS Dispensary, N.Y.C., 1939- 42; chief oral surgery USCG Manhattan Beach, N.Y., 1942-46; asst. chief dental service USPHS Hosp., New Orleans, 1946-50; chief dental service USCG Tng. Center, Cape May, N.J., 1950; asst. chief div. dental resources, USPHS, Washington, 1951-52; fellow anesthesiology Doctors Hosp., Washington, 1953; with Nat. Inst. Dental Research, NIH, 1954—, chief oral surgery sect., 1954-62, clin. investigations br., 1962-63, clin. dir., 1963-66, asso. dir. for extramural programs, 1966-67, chief anesthesiology sect., oral medicine br., 1967—. Diplomate Am. Bd. Oral Surgery. Mem. Am. Dental Assn. (cons. oral surgery and anesthesiology to council dental therapeutics), Am. Soc. Oral Surgeons (mem. com. on anesthesia), Greater Washington Soc. Oral Surgeons, Middle Atlantic Soc. Oral Surgeons, Am. Coll. Dentists, Am. Dental Soc. Anesthesiology, USPHS Clin. Soc. (pres. 1962-63), Delta Sigma Delta, Omicron Kappa Epsilon. Home: 9804 Culver Ct Kensington MD 20795 Office: Nat Inst Dental Research Nat Insts Health Bethesda MD 20014

DRISCOLL, FREDERICK JOSEPH, constrn. contractor; b. Bklyn., July 12, 1901; s. George Francis and Harriet (Hannigan) D.; grad. Fordham Prep. Sch., 1918; LL.D., Boston Coll., 1953, Fordham U., 1958; m. Dorothy Katherine Cornell, Apr. 23, 1924; children—Dorothy Anne (Mrs. Carlo D. Cella, Jr.), Frederick Joseph, John Henry. With George F. Driscoll Co., N.Y.C., 1919—, sec., 1922-28, v.p., 1928-31, treas., 1931—, pres., 1941—; pres. George F. Driscoll Co. of Venezuela, C.A., 1941-59; treas. pres. Moccia Constrn. Corp.; trustee Kings County Lafayette Trust Co., Bklyn., Greater N.Y. Savs. Bank. Chmn. bd. trustees Bricklayers Pension Fund, 1951—; trustee Mason Tenders Pension Fund, 1955-, Mary Immaculate Hosp., Jamaica, N.Y.C., 1955-58, Fordham U., 1958-67. Mem. Bldg. Contractors and Mason Builders Assn. (past pres.), Bldg. Traders Employers Assn. (past pres.) Clubs: Wheatley Hills Golf (East Williston, N.Y.); Lawrence Beach (Atlantic Beach, N.Y.); The Moles (N.Y.C.). Home: 8246 Kew Gardens Rd Kew Gardens NY 11415 Office: 529 Fifth Av New York City NY 10017

DRISCOLL, GLEN ROBERT, univ. chancellor; b. Sligo, Ohio, Apr. 29, 1920; s. William Arthur and Jennie (Smith) D.; student DePauw U., 1938-41; A.B., U. Louisville, 1947; M.A., U. Minn., 1949, Ph.D., 1952; m. Dorothy Little, Nov. 9, 1941; children-David Arthur, Robert Earl, Nancy Lee (Mrs. Russell Husted). From instr. to prof. history U. S.D., 1949-64; chmn. div. social scis., prof. history U. Mo. at St. Louis, 1964-65, dean arts and scis., dean Grad. Sch., 1965-68, dean faculties, 1968-69, chancellor, 1969—. Regional asso. Am. Council Learned Socs., 1957-61; mem. regional bd. for Woodrow Wilson Fellowship Found., 1968, 69, 70. Served with USAAF, 1942-46. Ford Found. fellow, Harvard, 1955. Mem. Am. Hist. Assn., History Sci. Soc., Soc. French Hist. Studies, Midwest Junto for The History of Sci., Am. Assn. U. Profs., Societe d'Histoire Moderne. Home: 42 Bellerive Acres St. Louis MO 63121

DRISCOLL, HUGH MACPHERSON, banker; b. St. Paul, July 27, 1898; s. Alfred E. and Isabelle (Scott) S.; B.A., Princeton, 1921; m. Margaret Burton, Oct. 17, 1936; children- -Hugh MacPherson, David Burton. Trainee, accountant Nat. City Bank of N.Y., 1921-23; mgr. credit dept., asst. cashier, asst. v.p. Blvd. Bridge Bank of Chgo., 1924-33, asst. v.p., v.p. successor Nat. Blvd. Bank of Chgo., 1933-49, exec. v.p., dir., 1949-65, vice chmn., 1962-65; v.p. Civic Center Bank & Trust Co., Chgo., 1966-70, now vice-chmn. bd.; pres., dir. 1st Nat. Bank Blue Island, 1970—; vice chmn., chief exec. officer, dir. Union Nat. Bank Chgo., 1971—; dir. Inland Newspapers, Market Centers, Inc., Smith-Bucklin & Assos., Tastee Freez Industries, Inc. Active Chgo. Community Fund, Boy Scouts: pres., dir. Off-the-Street Club of Chgo., 1936—. Trustee, v.p. Wesley Meml. Hosp., 1942—; trustee, pres. Chgo. M.E. Ch. Aid Soc.; pres. bd. trustees of Haris Schools. Served as 1st lt. inf., U.S. Army, World War 1. Mem. Robert Morris Assos. (past pres., dir.). Methodist (chmn. bd. trustees). Clubs: Chicago Yacht (dir.), University, Economic, Arts (treas., dir.), Bankers (Chgo.); Rotary. Home: 330 Diversey Pkwy Chicago IL 60614 Office: 13057 S Western Av Blue Island IL

DRISCOLL, JOHN FISKE, former ins. co. exec.; b. St. Paul, Oct. 15, 1903; A.B., Carleton Coll., Northfield, Minn., 1926. With St. Paul Fire and Marine Ins. Co., 1926-68, corp. sec., 1955-68. Treas. Greater St. Paul United Fund; v.p. Minn. Soc. Crippled Children and Adults. Trustee Children's Service Agy.; bd. dirs. St. Paul Rehab. Center, Family Service of St. Paul, Home Services Assn. Home: 9 Heather Pl St Paul MN 55102

DRISCOLL, JOHN GERALD, Jr., lawyer; b. Wadsworth, Nev., Sept. 5, 1897; s. John Gerald and Annie M. (Kearns) D.; A.B., Stanford, 1918, LL.B., 1920; m. Maybelle Branch, Jan. 6, 1917; children—Moyna, John Gerald, Harlan. Admitted to Cal. bar, 1920, Wash, bar, 1921, Wyo. bar, 1923; lectr. U. Wash., 1920-23; dean law sch. U. Wyo., 1923-26; private practice, San Diego, 1927—. U.S. Commr. Inter-Am. Tropical Tuna Commn. Mem. Internat. Assn. Ins. Counsel, Am. Soc. Internat. Law, Am. Bar Assn. Clubs: Uiversity, Yacht, Propellor (San Diego). Home: 3221 Russell St San Diego CA 92106 Office: 530 Broadway San Diego CA 92101

DRISCOLL, JOHN LYNN, ret. banker; b. Craig, Neb., May 3, 1891; s. John and Hannah Matilda (Hill) D.; B.A., U. Neb., 1914; m. Rachael Louise Kellogg, Sept. 16, 1916; children—John Lynn (dec.), Harriett Lenore. With Overland Nat. Bank, Boise, Ida., 1915-19, asst. to pres. Live Stock Exchange Nat. Bank Chgo. and its successor, Stock Yards Nat. Bank of Chgo., 1919-25; v.p. Boise Live Stock Loan Co. of Chgo., 1919-29; v.p. Chgo. Live Stock Loan Co., 1827-29; pres. First Security Bank of Boise, 1929-33; elected exec. v.p. and dir. First Security Bank Ida. (consolidation of 14 banks), 1933, pres. and dir. nat. assn., 1944-56, chmn. bd. dirs., nat. assn., 1956-68, chmn. exec. com., 1968-69. Dir. First Security Corp. of Ogden, Utah; pres. Ida. State Sheep Commn., 1925-37; pres. State Predatory Animal Bd., 1928- 37; pres. Boise C. of C., Mem. adv. com. Salt Lake City br. RFC, 1932-38; mem. com. Boise br. Regional Agrl. Credit Corp., 1932-38. Pres. bd. trustees Boise Ind. Sch. Dist. No. 1, 1931-38; pres. bd. dirs. Boise Jr. Coll., 1943-50; chmn. Ida. Permanent Bldg. Fund Adv. Council, 1961-64; bd. dirs., pres. Children's Home Soc. Ida.; v.p., dir. St. Luke's Hosp. and Nurses Tng. Sch. Ltd., Boise; mem. exec. council Am. Bankers Assn., 1944- 47. Mem. Ida. Bankers Assn. (pres. 1951-52), Phi Kappa Psi. Republican. Mason. Clubs: Arid, Hillcrest Country. Home: 1200 Happy Dr Boise ID 83704 Office: First Security Bank of Ida NA P O Box 7069 Boise ID 83707

DRISCOLL, JOSEPH PATRICK, law and gen. bus. co. exec.; b. Worcester, Mass., Dec. 11, 1918; s. Patrick Joseph and Delia Agnes (McInerney) D.; A.B., Harvard, 1941, LL.B., 1943; postgrad. George Washington U., 1946-49. Admitted to Mass. bar, 1943; counsel, bd. Contract Appeals, Navy Dept., 1946-49; legislative atty. Legislative Counsel's Office, Treasury Dept., 1949-55; asso. prof. law George Washington U., Washington, 1955-57; partner Southwest Prodn. Co., Dallas, 1958—; founder, chmn. bd. Tyler Corp., Dallas, 1966—, Mich. Gen. Corp., Dallas, Detroit, 1968—. Mgr. personal investments, 1963—. Bd. govs. Downtown YMCA, Dallas, 1968—. Served with USNR, 1945-47. Fellow Tex. Law Found.; mem. Am. Bar Assn. (tax sect.). Clubs: University (Washington); Harvard (Dallas). Home: 2625 Hudnall Dallas TX 75235 Office: 3108 Southland Center Dallas TX 75201

DRISCOLL, JUSTIN ALBERT, bishop; b. Bernard, Ia., Sept. 30, 1920; s. William J. and Agnes (Healey) D.; B.A., Loras Coll., Dubuque, Ia., 1942; postgrad. Cath. U. Am., 1945, Ph.D., 1952. Ordained priest Roman Cath. Ch., 1945; tchr. Loras Acad., Dubuque, 1945-48; sec. to Archbishop Rohlman, 1948-49, to Archbishop Binz, 1952-53; supt. schs., Dubuque, 1953-67; chaplain Mr. St. Francis Convent Motherhouse, Dubuque, 1954-67; pres. Loras Coll., 1967-70; bishop Diocese of Fargo (N.D.), 1970—; Dir. Confraternity Christian Doctrine, Dubuque, 1953-67; moderator Council Women, Dubuque, 1953-67. Chmn. U.S. Cath. Sch. Supts. Assn. of U.S. Cath. Conf., 1966-67; mem. Ia. N. Central Sch. Com., 1957- 67. Mem. Cath. Bus. Edn. Assn. (bd. dirs.), Alumni Assn. Theol. Coll. Cath. U. Am. (first v.p. 1965—), Nat. Cath. Edn. Assn. (exec. bd.). K.C. (4). Author: We Pray for Our Priests, 1965; The Pastor and the School, 1966; With Faith and Vision: Schools of the Archdiocese of Dubuque, 1936-1966, 1967. Contbr. articles to profl. jours. Mem. adv. bd. Cath. Sch. Jour. Address: 608 Broadway Fargo ND 58103

DRISCOLL, LEE FRANCIS, Jr., mdsg. co. exec.; b. Phila., July 27, 1926; s. Leon F. and Helen Carroll) D.; A.B., U. Pa., 1949, LL.B., 1953; m. Phoebe Albert, Dec. 30, 1959; children—Lee Francis III, Patrick McGill, Phoebe Poultney, Helen Louise. Admitted to Pa. bar, 1954; with firm White & Williams, Phila., 1954-56; asst. gen. counsel Slater System Inc., Phila., 1956-59, gen. counsel, 1959-63; gen. counsel, sec. Automatic Retailers Am., Inc., 1963-67; sr. v.p., gen. counsel ARA Services, Inc., 1967—. Chmn. Phila. Com. of 70, 1960-62; mem. nat. exec. com. Ams. for Dem. Action, 1964—. Dem. candidate for U.S. Congress, 1962. Served with inf. AUS, 1944-46, 50-51. Decorated Bronze Star. Mem. Am., Phila. bar assns., Sharswood Law Club, Zeta Psi. Roman Cath. Clubs: Racquet (Phila.); Penllyn (Pa.); Federal City (Washington). Home: Swedesford Rd Ambler PA 19002 Office: Independence Sq W Philadelphia PA 19146

DRISCOLL, MARGARET WEYERHAEUSER, (Mrs. Walter Bridges Driscoll), church and assn. exec.; b. Cloquet, Minn., Oct. 20, 1902; d. Rudolph M. and Louise B. (Lindeke) Weyerhaeuser; B.A., Vassar Coll., 1923; L.H.D., Macalester Coll., 1948, Westminster Coll. (Pa.), 1958; m. Walter Bridges Driscoll, Nov. 27, 1926 (dec. 1937); children—Walter John, Rudolph W. Bd. mgrs., chmn. finance com. United Ch. Women; trustee emeritus Macalester Coll., St. Paul; United Presbyn. Found.; bd. dirs., treas. Child Welfare League Am.; trustee Opera Assn. N.M., Santa Fe Prep. Sch., Presbyn. Hosp. Center, Albuquerque; past mem. bd. regents N.M. Highlands U., Las Vegas. Home: 196 Circle Dr Santa Fe NM 87501 Office: 1st Nat Bank Bldg St Paul MN 55101

DRISCOLL, PHILLIP, coll. adminstr.; b. Boston, June 4, 1922; s. Edgar Joseph and Katharine (Rooney) D.; B.A., Amherst Coll., 1943; M.A., Harvard, 1947; m. Eileen Rooney, Jan. 20, 1951; children—Katharine Eileen, Ellen, Philip John, Hope Elizabeth, Moira Julia. Instr. English, U. Notre Dame, 1947-48, Boston U., 1949-53; mem. faculty Brandeis U., 1952-69, instr. English, 1953-67, dir. admissions, 1957-59, dean, 1960-66, dean of students, 1966- 69; exec. dir. Twelve Coll. Exchange, 1969—. Mem. Mass. Bd. Edn., 1958-65, chmn., 1962-63; mem. Mass. Bd. Collegiate Authority, 1958-65, Mass. Coll. Bldg. Authority, 1958-65, Mass. High Ednl. Facilities Commn., 1964-66; vis. rep. Coll. Entrance Exam. Bd., 1961-63, vice-chmn. nominating com., 1968—. Mem. Mass. adv. com. on Racial Imbalance. Chmn. bd. trustees. Mass. State Colls., 1963- 65; bd. dirs. Internat. Student Assn. 1958-64, Boston Council for Internat. Visitors, 1969—; trustee Dedham Pub. Library, 1971—; commn. bd. trustees Beaver Country Day Sch., 1963—. Served with AUS, 1942-44. Club: St. Botolph (Boston). Home: 24 Spruce St Dedham MA 02026 Office: Twelve Coll Exchange 2 Hebe Ct Norton MA 02766

DRISCOLL, ROBERT EDWARD, Jr., lawyer; b. Lead, S.D., Feb. 8, 1916; s. Robert Edward and Louise (Fearon) D.; A.B., Stanford, 1937; LL.B., U. Colo., 1942; m. Elinor Ash, Dec. 29, 1937; 1 son, Mike E. Salesman, Am. Colloid Co., Chgo., 1937-39; admitted to S.D. bar, 1942, mem. Philip, Leedom & Driscoll, Rapid City, 1946-50, Kellar, Kellar & Driscoll, Lead, 1950—; asst. gen. counsel Homestake Mining Co., Lead, 1950—; dir. First Nat Bank Black Hills, Belle Fourche Bentonite Products Co., Am. Colloid Co., Chgo., Dakota Steel & Supply Co., Rapid City, Bentonit Internat. G.m.B.H., Duisburg, Germany, Volclay Ltd., Wallsley, Eng. Mem. nat. adv. council Practicing Law Inst.; mem. Spl. Pres.'s Com. Civil Rights Under Law Bd. dirs. S.D. State Hosp. Adv. Council, trustee Rocky Mountain Mineral Law Found., Am. Coll. Probate Council. Mem. Am. Bar Assn., Am. Bar Found., Am. Inst. Mining, Metall. and Petroleum Engrs., S.D. State Bar Commrs., State Bar S.D. (pres.). Republican. Home: 632 Ridge Rd Lead SD 57754 Office: Box 898 Lead SD 57754

DRISCOLL, ROBERT SWANTON, investment co. exec.; b. N.Y.C., Jan. 12, 1912; s. Clarence Uler and Elizabeth (Pinchbeck) D.; A.B. with honors, Columbia, 1933; m. Jane Word, Sept. 30, 1936; children—Robert Swanton IV, Steven Word, David Christopher. Investment counselor, 1934-40; with Research Mgmt. Council, Inc., subsidiary Lord, Abbett & Co., 1941-47, v.p., 1942, pres., 1944; v.p. Lord, Abbett & Co., Inc., 1948, partner, 1949, mng. partner, 1964—; v.p., dir. Am. Business Shares, Inc., N.Y.C., 1949-61, exec. v.p. 1961-64, pres., chief exec. officer, 1964—; v.p., dir. Affiliated Fund, Inc., N.Y.C, 1949-61, exec. v.p., 1961-64, pres., chief exec. officer, 1964—; pres., chief exec. officer, dir. Lord, Abbett Bond-Debenture Fund, Inc. Mem. bd. govs. statis. review com., guide to bus. standards com. Investment Co. Inst. Commr. Washington Irving council Boy Scouts, 1959- 61, pres., 1961-64, v.p., 1964—. Mem. Investment Bankers Assn., Am. (chmn. investment cos. com.), Nat. Assn. Securities Dealers, N.Y. Soc. Security Analysts, Fencers League (treas. 1947-52). Clubs: Fencers, Inc. (pres. 1949-58, v.p.,). Broad Street (N.Y.C.) Mount Kisco (N.Y.) Country. Mem. Olympic Fencing Com., 1947-52, nat. épée champion, 1943. Home: 345 Roaring Brook Rd Chappaqua NY 10514 Office: 63 Wall St New York City NY 10005

DRISCOLL, WILLIAM MICHAEL, assn. exec.; b. Boston, Feb. 15, 1929; s. Edgar J. and Katharine (Rooney) D.; student Yale Comml. Execs. Sch., 1952-53; m. Catherine Moore, Sept. 12, 1959; children—William Michael, Sean Moore, Geoffrey Moore, David Moore. Exec. trainee F.W. Woolworth Co., 1946-50; sec. Retail Bd. Trade, Lawrence, Mass., 1950-52, Greater Lawrence C. of C., 1952-54; with Sales & Marketing Execs. Internat., N.Y.C., 1954—, mng. dir., 1963—. Served with AUS, 1954-56. Mem. Am. Marketing Assn., Am. Soc. Assn. Execs., Pi Sigma Epsilon. Clubs: Larchmont (N.Y.); Yacht, Misquamicut (Watch Hill, R.I.); Canadian (N.Y.C.). Home: 3 Fairmont Av Hastings-on-Hudson NY 10706 Office: 630 3d Av New York City NY 10017

DRISCOLL, WILLIAM ROBERT, steel co. ofcl.; b. Chgo., Apr. 15, 1926; s. Arthur J. and Helen M. (O'Connell) D.; B.S., U. Ill., 1949, J.D., 1950; m. Norma Christine Podeschi, Aug. 23, 1952; children—Peter A., Mary K., James C., Michael W. Admitted to Ill. bar, 1950; gen counsel Libby, McNeill & Libby, Chgo., 1950-66, sec., 1966-67, v.p., 1967-69; gen. counsel Inland Steel Co., Chgo., 1969—, v.p., 1971—. Served with USAAF 1944-46. Mem. Am., Inter Am., N.Y., Ill., Chgo. bar assns., Nat. Canners Assn., Am. Arbitration Assn. Home: 325 N Elm St Hinsdale IL 60521 Office: 30 W Monroe Chicago IL 60603

DRISKELL, DAVID CLYDE, educator, artist; b. Eatonton, Ga., June 7, 1931; s. George W. and Mary L. (Clyde) D.; A.B., Howard U., 1955; M.F.A., Catholic U. Am., 1962; student Skowhegan Sch. Painting and Sculpture, 1953, Rijksbureau voor Kunsthistorisches Documentatie, The Hague, 1964; m. Thelma G. DeLoatch, Jan. 9, 1952; children—Daviryne Mari, Daphne Joyce. Asso. prof. art Talladega Coll., 1955-62; asso. prof., acting chmn. dept. art Howard U., 1963-64; prof. art. chmn. dept. Fisk U., Nashville, 1966—, dir. div. cultural research, 1968—; vis. prof. U. Ife (Nigeria), 1970; exhbns. include Rhodes Nat. Gallery, Salisbury, Rhodesia, 1957, Smithsonian Instn., 1962, The White House, 1966, U. Cal. at Los Angeles Galleries, 1967, Oakland (Cal.) Mus., 1967, N.A.D., 1968, Norfolk (Va.) Mus., 1969, Corcoran Gallery, 1965. Cons. Life mag. on Black History, 1968, Nat. Def. Edn. Act Insts. on Negro Culture and History, 1968. Bd. dirs. Tenn. Fine Arts Center; trustee Am. Fedn. Art, Mus. African Art and Frederick Douglass Inst., Tenn. Arts Commn. Visual Arts Panel. Danforth Found. fellow 1961; Rockefeller Found. fellow, 1964; Govt. of Netherlands fellow, 1964. Co-author: Black Dimensions in Contemporary American Art, 1971. Home: 1601 Phillips St N Nashville TN 37208 also 115 Johnson Rd Falmouth ME 04105

DRISLER, WILLIAM ARTHUR, Jr., textile co. exec.; b. Bklyn., Mar. 26, 1914; s. William Arthur and Jessie (Rathbun) D.; grad. Hackley Sch., Tarrytown, N.Y., 1933; student Cornell U., 1933-35; m. Jean Thomas, Oct. 21, 1938; childrenPamela Jean, Deborah Thomas, Holly Susan. Retail salesman Gen. Foods Corp., 1935-36; asst. advt. and promotion mgr. Bates Fabrics, Inc., 1936-39; with Cannon Mills, Inc., 1939-58, v.p., gen. mgr. charge womens hosiery div., 1950-58; v.p., asst. to pres., dir., mem. exec. com. James Lees & Sons Co., 1958-60; pres. Burlington-Balfour Mills div. Burlington Industries, 1960-61; v.p. consumer products marketing B.F. Goodrich Co., 1961-65; group v.p. Indian Head, Inc., 1965-66, Exec. v.p., 1966—. Mayor, trustee Village Hewlett Neck, N.Y., 1950-56. Bd. dirs. Lawrence Sch., Hewlett, L.I., 1958-63. Served to lt. USNR, World War II. Mem. Assn. Nat. Advertisers (past dir.), Met. Advt. Golf Assn. (pres. 1952), Sigma Phi. Clubs: Lawrence Beach (treas., gov.) (Atlantic Beach, L.I.); Rockaway Hunting (Cedarhurst, L. I.); Union League (N.Y.C.); Weavers. Home: 246 Causeway Lawrence NY 11559 Office: Indian Head Inc 1430 Broadway New York City NY 10018

DRISS, RACHID, former Tunisian diplomat; b. Tunis, Tunisia, Jan. 27, 1917; grad. Sadiki Coll., Tunis; m.; 1 child. Mem. Neo-Destour Party, 1934—, dir. party newspaper El Amal, 1955, mem. polit. bur., 1958—; civil servant dept. finance during French rule; exiled, 1946-55; a founder Office Arab Maghreb, Cairo, also engaged in missions to Arab States, Indonesia, India and Pakistan during exile; dep. Constl. Assembly Tunisia, 1956, participated drafting constn. and proclamation of republic, 1957; sec. of state for post office and communications, 1957; elected mem. Nat. Assembly Tunisia, 1958; tour Latin Am. as presdl. rep., 1961; rep. Tunisia Conf. African Ministers Fgn. Affairs, Dakar, 1963; former A.E. and P. of Tunisia to U.S., also ambassador to Mexico. Address: 5131 Broad Branch Rd NW Washington DC 20008

DRIVAS, ROBERT, actor; b. Chgo., Oct. 7; s. James and Harriet (CunninghamWright) D.; student U. Chgo. Theatrical appearances include Night Must Fall, 1957. Sweet Bird of Youth, 1957, Tea and Sympathy, 1957, The Lady's Not for Burning, 1957, Death of a Salesman, 1957, Thieves Carnival, 1957, A View From the Bridge, 1957, The First Born, 1958, One More River, 1960. The Wall, 1960, Diff'rent, 1961, Mrs. Dally Has a Lover, 1962, Lorenzo, 1963, The Irregular Verb to Love, 1963; numerous TV appearances. Recipient Theatre World award, 1963. Mem. Actors Equity Assn., Stage Actors Guild. A.F.T.R.A. Home: 16 Commerce St New York City NY 10014*

DRIVER, ALBERT WESTCOTT, chain store exec.; b. Bridgeport, Conn., Aug. 4, 1927; s. Albert W. and Bessie (Ferns) D.; B.A., Yale, 1949; LL.B., U. Va., 1952; m. Martha Lou Miller, Aug. 5, 1951; children—Martha, Sara. Admitted to N.Y. bar, 1952; asso. firm Cravath, Swaine & Moore, N.Y.C., 1952-60; with J.C. Penney Co., Inc., 1961—, sec., 1969—. Trustee, sec. Westfield (N.J.) Hosps. Assn. Served with USNR, 1946. Mem. Am., N.Y. State bar assns., Assn. Bar City N.Y., Nat. Retail Merchants Assn. (chmn. lawyers com.). Club: Echo Lake Country (Westfield). Home: 549 Tremont Av Westfield NJ 07090 Office: 1301 Av Americas New York City NY 10019

DRIVER, DONALD, author, director; b. Portland, Ore., Oct. 21, 1922; s. Herbert Leslie and Edna Mae (Luke) D.; student Pomona Coll., 1945-47; m. Doris Margaret Atkinson, Dec. 24, 1953; children—Shan Fleming, Dion Luke, Actor-dancer, 1950-57; dir., 1958-; dir. over 50 popular musicals, 1958-66, Princeton Repertory Co., 1964-65; artistic dir. Shakespeare Festival, Washington, 1963-66; Broadway dir. Marat de Sade, 1967, Mike Downstairs, 1968, Jimmy

Shine, 1969, Our Town, 1970; author, dir. Your Own Thing, 1968. Recipient Drama Critics Circle award, Vernon Rice award, Outer Circle Critics award, all for Your Own Thing, 1967-68. Address: Shandion Prodns 140 W 58th St New York City NY 10019

DRIVER, FRANK LUTHER, III, alloy mfg. co. exec.; b. Newark, May 6, 1930; B.S. in Engring., Princeton, 1951; m. Corinne Lovell Francis, Aug. 2, 1958; children— Jean, Frank, Timothy, Andrew. With Driver-Harris Co. Harrison, N.J. 1951—, successively engineer, asst. to works mgr., v. p., adminstrv. v.p., 1957-59, exec. v.p., 1959-62, pres., 1962—, also mem. bd. dirs. Trustee of N.J. Blue Cross. Served from ensign to lt. (j.g.), C.E., USNR, 1951-54. Mem. Am. Soc. Metals, Am. Inst. Mining and Metall. Engrs. Home: 98 Oldchester Rd Essex Falls NJ 07021 Office: 201 Middlesex St Harrison NJ 07029

DRIVER, LOTTIE ELIZABETH, librarian; b. Newport News, Va., Dec. 6, 1918; d. James W. and Lottie (Williams) Driver; student Averett Coll., 1936-37; B.S., Mary Washington Coll. of U. Va., 1939; A.B. in Library Sci., Coll. William and Mary, 1944. Band instr. Hampton (Va.) Sch. System, 1939-41; asst. librarian Newport News Pub. Library, 1941-47, librarian, 1947-70; asst. dir. Newport News Pub. Library System, 1970—; author book rev. column in Daily Press; library news reporter radio sta. WGH, 1959. Active United Fund. Mem. Am., Southeastern, Va. library assns., Am. Assn. U. Women, P.E.O., D.A.R., Phi Theta Kappa, Alpha Phi Sigma. Baptist. Author articles for library supply house. Home: 14 Westover Rd Warwick Newport News VA 23601 Office: 110 Main St Newport News VA 23601

DRIVER, RANDOLPH SCARBOROUGH, govt. ofcl.; b. Ridley Park, Pa., May 5, 1911; s. Philip B. and Alice C. (Davison) D.; A.B., U. Pa., 1932, M.A., 1933; m. Cynthia Milward-Oliver, Sept. 26, 1940; 1 dau., Susan (Mrs. Frederick S. Crysler). With Atlantic Richfield Co., Phila., 1931-67, mgr. indsl. relations, 1965-67; asst., instr. psychology U. Pa., 1933-37; asst. instr. psychology Swarthmore Coll., 1935-37; dep. under sec. navy for manpower Dept. Navy Washington, 1967-68, former asst. sec. navy manpower and res. affairs. Club: Union League (Phila.). Home: 211 Ladbroke Rd Bryn Mawr PA 19010

DRIVER, TOM FAW, educator, writer; b. Johnson City, Tenn., May 31, 1925; s. Leslie Rowles and Sarah (Broyles) D.; A.B., Duke, 1950; B.D., Union Theol. Sem., 1953; Ph.D., Columbia, 1957; m. Anne Barstow, June 7, 1952; children—Katharine Anne, Paul Barstow, Susannah Ambrose. Ordained to ministry Methodist Ch., 1951; dir. youth work Riverside Ch., N.Y.C., 1955-56; faculty Union Theol. Sem., N.Y.C., 1956—, prof. theology and lit., 1967—; drama critic Christian Century, 1956-62, reporter, 1963-64; vis. asso. prof. English, Columbia, 1964-65; vis. asso. prof. religion Barnard Coll., 1965-66, Fordham U., 1967; drama critic WBAI-FM, 1960-61. Bd. dirs. dept. worship and arts Nat. Council Chs., 1958- 63, Found. for Arts, Religion and Culture, 1963-67. Served with AUS, 1943-46. Kent fellow 1953—; Guggenheim fellow, 1962-63. Mem. Modern Lang. Assn., Soc. Religion in Higher Edn., Am. Assn. U. Profs., Am. Civil Liberties Union, Clergy and Laymen Concerned about Vietnam, Phi Beta Kappa, Omicron Delta Kappa. Author: (liberetto for oratorio) The Invisible Fire: The Sense of History in Greek and Shakespearean Drama, 1960; Jean Genet, 1966; Romantic Quest and Modern Query. A History of The Modern Theater, 1970. Editor: (with Robert Pack) Poems of Doubt and Belief, 1964; also articles. Home: 606 W 122d St New York City NY 10027

DRIVER, WILLIAM JOSEPH, assn. exec.; b. Rochester N.Y., May 9, 1918; s. John J. and Bridget Anna (Farrell) D.; B.B.A. cum laude, Niagara U., 1941; LL.B., George Washington U., 1952, M.A., 1965; m. Marian R. McKay, Aug. 18, 1947; children—William Joseph, Kellie McKay. Dir. compensation and pension service VA, Washington, 1956-59, chief benefits dir., 1959-61, dep. adminstr. vets. affairs, 1961-65, adminstr. vets. affairs, 1965-69; pres. Mfg. Chemists Assn., 1969—. Mem. Pres.'s Council Aging, 1965-69, Pres.'s Com. Employment Physically Handicapped, 1965-69, Pres.'s Com. on Health Manpower, 1967-69. Served to lt. col. AUS, 1941-45, U.S. Army, 1951-53. Decorated Legion of Merit, Bronze Star medal; Order Brit. Empire; Croix de Guerre (France); recipient Meritorious Service medal VA 1957, Exceptional Service medal, 1960, Career Service award Nat. Civil Service League, 1964, Achievement award Soc. Advancement Mgmt., 1965; Alumni Achievement award George Washington U., 1967. Mem. D.C. Bar Assn. Home: 215 W Columbia St Falls Church VA 22046

DRIVER, WILLIAM RAYMOND, Jr., banker; b. Germantown, Pa., Nov. 1907; s. William R. And Mary (Swift) D.; A.B. Harvard, 1929, M.B.A., 1933; m. Charlotte I. Noyes, Apr. 9, 1937; children—Sarah J., William R., Dorothy Q., Mary S., Emily N. With Colo. Nat. Bank, 1930-31, Central Hanover Bank & Trust Co., N.Y.C., 1933-34; sec-treas. 2 divs. Am. Pulp & Paper Assn., 1934-36; asst. cashier Bank of Manhattan Co., 1938-43, asst. v.p., 1943-46, v.p., 1946; v.p. Chase Manhattan Bank, 1946- 60; partner Brown Bros. Harriman & Co., 1961—; corporator, trustee Suffolk Franklin Savs. Bank; corporator Provident Instn. for Savs.; dir., Samson Cordage Works, Hoerner Waldorf Corp. Mem. Boston Stock Exchange. Bd. dirs. Boston chpt. A.R.C.; corporator Mass. Gen. Hosp.; treas., trustee Museum of Sci.; trustee, corporator Northeastern U. Mem. New Eng. Gas and Electric Assn. (trustee). Episcopalian. Clubs: Dedham Country and Polo; Harvard, Somerset, Commercial (Boston); The Country; Harvard (N.Y.C.). Home: 1184 South St Needham MA 02192 Office: 10 Post Office Sq Boston MA 02109

DROESSLER, EARL GEORGE, meterologist, ednl. adminstr.; b. Dubuque, Ia., Jan. 14, 1920; s. George Joseph and Mary Elizabeth (Steffes) D.; A.B., Loras Coll., 1942, D.Sc., 1958; Naval Aerological Engr., U.S. Naval Post Grad. Sch., 1944; postgrad. (Fulbright fellow meterology), U. Oslo, 1950-51; m. Virginia Kittridge Hastings, Sept. 17, 1944 (dec. Dec. 1947); 1 dau., Carol Joan; m. 2d, Carol Stoops, June 29, 1957; children—Maureen, Christopher, Mary Doran and Martha Gaylord (twins). Joined USN, 1942, commd. ensign, 1943, advanced through grades to lt. comdr., separated 1947; meterologist Office Naval Research, 1946-52; exec. dir., com. on geophysics and geography Office Asst. Sec. Def. (research and devel.), 1952-53, exec. sec. coordinating com. on gen. scis., 1954-58; program dir. atmospheric scis. program NSF 1958-66; prof. atmospheric scis., v.p. research State U. N.Y. at Albany, 1966-71; now adminstrv. dean for research N.C. State U. at Raleigh. Dept. Def. rep. U.S. adv. com. on weather control, 1953-57; mem. U.S. nat. com. IGY, 1955-64; vis. research fellow radio-physics div. CSIRO, Sydney, Australia, 1963-64. Trustee-at-large Univ. Corp. for Atmospheric Research; trustee Dudley Obs. Fellow Am. Geophys. Union; mem. Am. Meterol. Soc. (councilor 1960- 62), Sigma Xi, Delta Epsilon Sigma. Roman Catholic. Club: Cosmos (Washington). Asso. editor Jour. Geophys. Research 1966-68. Contbr. articles to profl. jours. Office: North Carolina State U 2205 Hillsboro Raleigh Raleigh NC 27607

DROGHEDA, EARL OF, (Moore Charles Garrett Ponsonby), newspaperman; b. London, Eng., Apr. 23, 1910; s. Earl of Drogheda and Kathleen (Pelham-Burn) M.; student Cambridge U., 1929-30; m. Joan Carr, May 17, 1935; 1 son, Dermot (Viscount Moore). With Financial News, 1933, dir., 1938, following merger with Financial Times, became mng. dir. Financial Times, Ltd., 1945, chmn., 1971—; dir. Economist Newspaper, Ltd., Pearson Longman, Ltd. Chmn. Royal Opera House, Covent Garden. Asst. sec. Brit. Ministry of Prodn., 1941. Served as capt. Brit. Army, 1939. Mem. Inst. Dirs. (council). Home: 8 Lord North St London S W 1 England Office: Bracken House 10 Cannon St London E C 4 England

DROPKIN, JOHN JOSEPH, physicist, educator; b. Russia, Feb. 22, 1910; s. Samuel and Celia (Levine) D.; came to U.S., 1912, naturalized, 1924; B.A., Columbia, 1930; M.S., Bklyn. Poly. Inst., 1947, Ph.D., 1948; m. Zelda Stern. Oct. 1, 1933 (dec. Sept. 1956); children—Frances, Vivian; m. 2d, Ruth Zeitlin, Dec. 1, 1957; stepchildren—Devorah, Jonathan. Asst. physics Columbia, 1930-35; tchr. high sch. physics and math, N.Y.C. Bd. Edn., 1936-48; faculty Bklyn. Poly. Inst., 1948—, Thomas Potts prof. physics, 1957- -, head dept., 1957-65. Fellow Am. Phys. Soc.; mem. Am. Assn. Physics Tchrs., Am. Assn. U. Profs., A.A.A.S., Phi Beta Kappa, Sigma Xi, Sigma Pi Sigma. Research on photoconductivity and luminescence in insulators and phosphors. Home: 473 E 18th St Brooklyn NY 11226

DROSDOFF, MATTHEW, educator; b. Chgo., Dec. 15, 1908; s. Nachman and Anna (Wolf) D.; B.S., U. Ill., 1930; M.S., U. Wis., 1932, Ph.D., 1934; m. Sarah Max, Oct. 27, 1935; children—Ruth Ann, Daniel Aaron. Soil scientist U.S. Dept. Agr., Washington, also Gainesville, Fla., 1935-55, adviser soils ICA, Peru, 1955-60, dep. chief agr. div. ICA, Vietnam, 1960-62; chief agr. div. U.S. AID, Vietnam, 1962-64; adminstr. Internat. Agrl. Devel. Service, U.S. Dept. Agr. Washington, 1964- 66; prof. soil sci. Cornell Univ., 1966—; cons. RCA, Abaca Mission to C.A., 1950; soils adviser Nat. Coffee Fedn., Columbia, 1951-53; cons. FOA Spl. Mission to Bolivia, 1954. Dir. Hillel Found., U. Fla., 1944-47. Mem. Am. Soc. Agronomy, Soil Sci. Soc. Am., Internat. Soc. Soil Sci., Am. Agrl. Econs. Assn., A.A.A.S., Am. Soc. Hort. Sci., Sigma XI. Mem. B'Nai B'rith (sec. Fla. Fedn. 1942- 48, pres. 1949-50). Contbr. articles sci. publs. Office: care Cornell U Ithaca NY 14850

DROSSIN, JULIUS, educator; b. Phila., May 17, 1918; s. Alexander and Rachel (Rosenberg) D.; B.Mus., U. Pa., 1938; M.A., Western Res. U., 1952, Ph.D., 1956; m. Esther Weinstock, May 17, 1941; children—Phyllis, Alexander, Beverly (Mrs. Nelson Siegel); m. 2d, Barbara Wolpaw Wallach, Feb. 4, 1967; stepchidren—Laurie, Penny. Cellist, Phila. Opera Co., 1938-43, Cleve. Symphony Orch., 1948-57; tchr. music Villa Maria Coll., Erie, Pa., 1951-59; asst. prof., then asso. prof. Fenn Coll., 1856-66, chmn. music dept., 1958; prof. music chmn. dept. Cleve. State U., 1966—. Mem. adv. bd. Cleve. Bd. Edn., 1966-. Trustee Koch Sch. Music; bd. dirs. Cleve. Philharmonic Orch. Served with AUS, 1943-45; ETO. Mem. Composers Guild Cleve. (pres. 1970—). Composer: 4 Symphonies, 1956, 60, 62, 65; Kaddish for Orchestra and Chorus, 1967; also 8 quartet, 5 sonatas, short works for instruments and/or voice. Home: 3141 Somerset Dr Shaker Heights OH 44120 Office: Cleve State Univ Cleveland OH 44115

DROSTE, EDWARD PHILIP, ret. educator; b. Godfrey, Ill., Apr. 27, 1902; s. August Carl and Lena (Lueking) D.; B.S., Shurtleff Coll., 1924, LL.D., 1954; Ed.M., Harvard, 1941; postgrad. U. Wis., Washington U., St. Louis; m. Roberta Elise Megowen, Dec. 25, 1929 (dec. 1969); children—Adele Louise (Mrs. James H. Cunningham), Carl Sanders; m. 2d, Katherine L. Holmgreen, Nov. 27, 1970. Tchr. math. and sci., head coach Saunemin (Ill.) High Sch., 1924-26, Western Mil. Acad., 1926-41; asst. mgr. Rancho Mesa Verde for Boys, Colo., summers 1926-28; headmaster Howe (Ind.) Mil. Sch., 1941-48, Elgin (Ill.) Acad., 1948-54; dir. studies Tex. Mil. Inst., San Antonio, 1954-64, headmaster, acting pres., 1964- 66, pres., 1966-70, pres. emeritus, 1970—. Treas. Ind. Schs. Assn. Central States, 1953-54, Ind. Schs. Assn. Southwest, 1965-66; pres. Tex. Prep. League, 1967-69, Pres. Elgin Civic Music Assn., 1950-53, San Antonio Rock and Lapidary Soc., 1964, 71. Mem. Shurtleff Coll. Alumni Assn. (pres. 1932), Assn. U.S. Army. Episcopalian (vestryman; past chmn. sch. bd.). Lion (pres. Howe club 1945-46), Rotarian (pres. Elgin club 1952-53), Kiwanian. Clubs: Argyle; Harvard of San Antonio; Men's Garden. Originator potential achievement rate system of guidance, 1941. Home: 124 Encino Av San Antonio TX 78209

DROTT, EDWARD, mfg. co. exec. Pres., Drott Mfg. Co. Office: PO Box 1087 Wausau WI 54401*

DROUGHT, JAMES WILLIAM, publisher, author; b. Aurora, Ill., Nov. 4, 1931; s. Earl Mervin and Sarah (Bagot) D.; B.A., Knox Coll., 1956; m. Lorna Beryle Carlson, Feb. 12, 1953; children—James Henry, Sara Bess, and William Alexander Drought. Started as state editor Galesburg (Ill.) Register-Mail, 1955- 56; editor Home and Highway mag., Skokie, Ill., 1957-60; articles editor This Week mag., N.Y.C., 1960-61; mng. editor Saga mag., N.Y.C., 1961-62; chmn. bd. pres. Skylight Press Inc., Norwalk, Conn., 1963—; pres. of Moon Light Movies Inc., 1967—; writer in residence Western Ill. U. Served with AUS, 1952-54. Recipient Janet Greig Post Fiction prize, 1956, Am. Mag. Pubs. award, 1961. Mem. Am. Book Sellers Assn., Internat. Platform Assn., also mem. Beta Theta Pi. Democratic party. Author: The Secret, 1963 (Wormwood award 1963); Mover, 1964; The Gypsy Moths, 1964; Memories of a Humble Man, 1964; Green, Brown and Red, 1964; Two ii: A Duo, 1964; The Enemy, 1964; Drugoth, 1965; The Enemy (movie), 1967; (play for voices): The Wedding, 1959; The Master, 1968; The Master (movie), 1969. James Drought Collection Letters. Boston U., 1965. Address: 1127 W Carroll Macomb IL

DROWN, GARY KIDD, life ins. co. exec.; b. Des Moines, Dec. 3, 1932; s. Hampton Kidd and Mary (Nichola) D.; B.S. in Bus. Administrn. with gen. honors, Drake U., 1955; postgrad. bus. mgmt. Ohio State U., 1962-63; m. Patricia Ann Walston, Nov. 30, 1968; children by previous marriage—Debra Sue, Catherine Louise, Paula Marie; stepdaus.—Bonnie Sue, Laura Jeanne. With Am. Asso. Ins. Cos., 1949-55; with Ohio Nat. Life Ins. Co., Cin., 1955—, actuary, 1965-69, v.p. 1969—. Vice-pres. bd. trustees Wesley Hall, Cin. Fellow Soc. Actuaries; mem. Am. Acad. Actuaries, Beta Gamma Sigma, Kappa Mu Epsilon, Omicron Delta Kappa, Delta Sigma Pi. Methodist. Author articles. Home: 8671 Empire Ct Cincinnati OH 45231 Office: PO Box 237 Cincinnati OH 45201

DRUCK, KALMAN BRESCHEL, pub. relations counselor; b. Scranton, Pa., Dec. 6, 1914; s. Jacob L. and Mabelle (Breschel) D.; B.S. in Journalism, magna cum laude, Syracuse U., 1936; m. Pearl Spiro, Nov. 26, 1936; children—Ellen (Mrs. Laurence M. Wassong), Nancy (Mrs. Jan W. Brassem). With Hearst Enterprises, 1936-39, Carl Bvoit & Assos., 1939-59; pres. Harshe-Rotman & Druck, Inc., N.Y.C., 1960—; supr. courses pub. relations Baruch Sch. Bus., Coll. City N.Y. 1939-55. Mem. adv. com. Syracuse U. Sch. Communications; bd. dirs. Union Am. Hebrew Congregations; bd. dirs. N.Y. Fedn. Jewish Philanthropies. Names Pub. Relations Profl. Man of Year, 1966. Mem. Pub. Relations Soc. Am. (pres. N.Y.C. 1953-55, nat. vice chmn. 1971). Club: Quaker Ridge Golf (Scarsdale, N.Y.). Home: 2 Winding Brook Dr Larchmont NY 10538 Office: 300 E 44th St New York City NY 10017

DRUCKER, BERTRAM MORRIS, educator; b. N.Y.C., Oct. 6, 1919; s. Max and Ray (Friedberg) D.; A.B., U. N.C., 1940, M.A., 1946, Ph.D., 1953. Instr., U. N.C., 1943-49; grad. fellow Oak Ridge Inst. Nuclear Studies, 1951-53; faculty Ga. Inst. Tech., 1953—, prof. math., 1962—, dir. Sch. Math., 1962-7O. Mem. Am. Math. Soc., Math. Assn. Am., Phi Kappa Phi, Omicron Delta Kappa. Home: 620 Peachtree St Atlanta GA 30308

DRUCKER, DANIEL CHARLES, civil engr., educator; b. N.Y.C., June 3, 1918; s. Moses Abraham and Henrietta (Weinstein) D.; B.S., Columbia, 1937, C.E., 1938, Ph.D., 1940; m. Ann Bodin, Aug. 19, 1939, children—R. David, Miriam. Instr. Cornell U., 194O-43; supr. Armour Research Found., Chgo., 1943-45; asst. prof. Ill. Tech., 1946-47; asso. prof. Brown U., Providence, 1947-50, prof., 1950-64, L. Herbert Ballou Univ. prof., 1964-68, chmn. div. engring., 1953-59, chmn. phys. scis. council, 1960-63; dean Coll. Engring., U. Ill., Urbana, 1968—; Marburg lectr. Am. Soc. Testing Materials, 1966. Mem. U. S. Nat. Com. on Theoretical and Applied Mechanics; del. Gen. Assembly Internat. Union Theoretical and Applied Mechanics; chmn. adv. com. for engring. NSF; mem. adv. com. for USSR and Europe, Nat. Acad. Scis.; hon. chmn. 3d SESA Internat. Congress on Exptl. Mechanics. Guggenheim fellow, 1960-61; NATO Sr. Sci. fellow, 1968; Fulbright travel grantee, 1968. Recipient. Lamme award Am. Soc. Engring. Edn. 1967. Fellow Am. Soc. M.E. (past v.p., mem. exec. com. Council chmn. applied mechanics div. 1963-64, v.p. policy bd. communications 1964-71), Am. Acad. Arts and Scis., Am. Inst. Aero. and Astronautical Scis. (asso.), Am. Soc. C.E.'s (von Karman medal, 1966; past pres. New Eng. Council, past pres. Providence sect., chmn. exec. com. engring. mechanics div.); mem. Nat., R.I. (dir.), Ill. socs. profl enqrs., Soc. Exptl. Stress Analysis (hon.; past pres., W. M. Murray lectr. 1967; M.M. Frocht award 1971), Am. Technion Soc. (past pres. So. N.E. chpt.), Soc. for Rheology, Am. Soc. Engring. Edn., Am. Acad. Mechanics, Providence Engring. Soc., Nat. Acad. Engring., Sigma Xi (past pres. Brown U. Chpt.), Phi Kappa Phi, Tau Beta Pi, Pi Tau Sigma, Sigma Tau. Author: Introduction to Mechanics of Deformable Solids, 1967. Contbr. chpts. in tech. books; also tech. papers to mech. and sci. jours. Office: Engring Hall U Ill Urbana IL 61801

DRUCKER, MIRIAM KOONTZ, psychologist, educator; b Mechanicsburg, Pa., Feb. 3, 1925; A.B., Dickinson Coll., 1947; M.A., Emory U., 1948; Ph.D. Peabody Coll., 1955; m. 1957. Counselor psychology Millsaps Coll., 1949-51; instr. Monticello Coll., 1951-52; asst. prof. psychology Agnes Scott Coll., Decatur, Ga., 1955-58, asso. prof., 1958, now prof., chmn dept. psychology. Mem. Am. Psychol. Assn. Address: Dept Psychology Agnes Scott Coll Decatur GA 30030

DRUCKER, PETER FERDINAND, mgmt. cons., educator; b. Vienna, Austria, Nov. 19, 1909; s. Adolph Bertram and Caroline D.; grad. Gymnasium, Vienna, 1927; LL.D., U. Frankfurt, 1931; D.C.S., Pace Coll., 1956; D. Econs., Nihon U., Tokyo, Japan, 1962; LL.D., U. Scranton, 1964. Wayne State U., 1964; Dr. Oec., St. Gallen, Switzerland, 1970; D.H.L., Temple U., 1971; Sc.D., U. Bradford, Eng., 1971; m. Doris Schmitz, Jan. 15, 1937; children—Kathleen Romola, J. Vincent, Cecily Ann, Joan Agatha. Came to U.S., 1937, naturalized, 1943. Economist, London Banking House, 1933-37; Am. adviser for Brit. banks, Am. corr. Brit. newspapers, 1937-42; cons. maj. bus. corps., U.S., 1940—; prof. philosophy, politics Bennington Coll., 1942-49; prof. mgmt. N.Y. U., 1950—, chmn. mgmt. area, 1957-62; Clarke prof. social sci. Claremont Grad. Sch. (Cal.), 1971—. Recipient Parlin Meml. medal Am. Marketing Assn., 1957; gold medal Internat. U. Social Studies, Rome, Italy, 1957; Wallace Clark Internat. Mgmt. medal, 1963; Hegemann medal (West Germany), 1966; Taylor Key, Soc. for Advancement Mgmt., 1967; Presdl. citation N.Y. U., 1968. Fellow A.A.A.S. (council), Internat., Am. acads. mgmt., Brit. Inst. Mgmt (hon.); mem. Soc. for History Tech. (pres. 1965-66). Author: The End of Economic Man, 1939; The Future of Industrial Man, 1941; Concept of the Corporation, 1944; The New Society, 1950; Practice of Management, 1954; America's Next Twenty Years, 1957; The Landmarks of Tomorrow, 1959; Managing for Results, 1962; The Effective Executive, 1967; The Age of Discontinuity, 1969; Technology; Management and Society; 1970; Men, Ideas and Politics, 1971. Producer (movie series) The Effective Executive, 1969, Managing Discontinuity, 1971. Address: 636 Wellesley Dr Claremont CA 91711

DRUEHL, WILLIAM CHARLES, packing co. exec.; b. Salt Lake City, May 18, 1918; s. William C. and Eva (Dix) D.; B.S., U. Cal. Berkeley, 1940; m. Dorothy A. Selley, Jan. 25, 1941; children—Lynn, Gregory. With Cal. Packing Corp., 1940—, mgr. Eastern operations, San Francisco, 1959-63, mgr. pineapple and seafood operations, 1963-64, pres., v.p. internat. operations Del Monte Corp.; pres., dir. Alaska Packers Assn., Inc., Del Monte P.R. Inc., Del Monte Internat., Inc.; chmn., pres. Del Monte del Ecuador, C.A.; dir. Utah Canners Assos., Salt Lake City, Bd. dirs. Atherton Civic Internat. League. Mem. Kappa Sigma. Clubs: Commonwealth, St. Francis Yacht (San Francisco). Home: 73 Ashfield Rd Atherton CA 94025 Office: 215 Fremont St San Francisco CA 94119

DRUIAN, RAFAEL, violinist; b. Vologda, Russia, Jan. 20, 1922; came to U.S., 1932, naturalized, 1940; grad. Curtis Inst. Music, Phila., 1943; m. Phyllis Prescott Rugg, June, 1943; children—Michael Gregory, Peter Rugg. Concert master Dallas Symphony Orch., 1947-49, Mpls. Orch., 1949-60; Cleve. Orch., 1960-71, N.Y. Philharmonic, 1971—; asst. prof. music U. Minn., 1949-60; artist in residence Cleve. Inst. Music, 1962-69; asso. dean Sch. Music Cal. Inst. Arts, 1969-71; music dir. Young Musicians Found., 1970-71; vis. lectr., condr. Chamber Orch. U. Cal. at San Diego, 1969-71. Served with AUS, 1943-46. Office: Philharmonic Hall New York City NY

DRUKKER, DOW HENRY, Jr., business exec.; b. Passaic, N.J., June 4, 1903; s. Dow Henry and Helena (Deunhower) D.; B.S., Mass. Inst. of Tech., 1925; m. Margaret Adams, Feb. 4, 1926; children—Joan, Dow Henry. Pres. Union Bldg. & Constrn. Corp., 1940—, now chmn.; pres., dir. Drukker & Co., 1955—; pres. Marion Co., Inc., 1956—, sec. Bleachery and Printing Co., Carlton Hill, N.J., 1932-60; v.p., pub. The Herald- News, Passaic-Clifton, N.J., 1942-56; v.p. Union Bldg. & Investment Co., 1936-56, N. J. Broadcasting Co., Paterson, N.J., 1942-56. Commr. Port N.Y. Authority, 1953-58. Trustee Stevens Inst. Tech. 1955- -; gov. Passaic Gen. Hosp. Mem. Phi Sigma Kappa. Clubs: Upper Montclair Country, Pennington (Passaic, N.J.). Office: 315 Howe Av Passaic NJ 07055

DRUKKER, RICHARD, newspaper exec.; b. Passaic, N.J., Mar. 30, 1906; s. Dow H. and Helena M. (Denhouwer) D.; A.B., Amherst Coll., 1929; LL.B., Rutgers U., 1943; m. Caroline Cleveland Crane, Sept. 16, 1930; childrenRichard, Austin. Messenger, Dominick & Dominick, N.Y.C., 1929; treas., dir. Union Bldg. & Investment Co., 1933; exec. v.p., 1953-63., ; pres., 1963—; dir. Herald- News, Passaic, 1934—, treas., 1943, v.p. treas., 1954-56, pres., 1956—, pub., 1963—; pub. Daily Advance. Dover, N.J., 1962—; dir. Bank of Passaic & Clifton, Passaic. Pres., Talking Newspapers for Blind, Herald-News-Drukker Found. Bd. dirs. Def. Orientation Conf. Assn.; trustee YMCA, Passaic, Passaic Gen. Hosp. Mem. Passaic Area C. of C. (dir.), N.J. Press Assn. (past pres.), Psi Upsilon, Delta Theta Pi. Episcopalian Kiwanian Clubs: Metropolitan (N.Y.C.); Seaview Golf (Absecon, N.J.); Pennington (Passaic); Upper Montclair Country (Clifton, N.J.); Montclair (N.J.) Golf; National Press (Washington). Home: 66 Virginia Av Clifton NJ 07012 Office: Herald-News 988 Main Av Passaic NJ 07055

DRUMHELLER, ALBERT E., educator; b. Pottstown, Pa., June 26, 1906; s. Clayton and Bessie (March) D.; B.S., Pa. State Tchrs. Coll., 1930; M.Ed., U. Pitts., 1935; student N.Y. U.; m. Margaret Louise Feather, June 9, 1934. Chmn. bus. edn. depts. West York (Pa.) High Sch., 1927-29, Latrobe (Pa.) High Sch., 1930-36, Indiana (Pa.) Jrs.-Sr. High Sch., 1936-38; tchr. bus. edn. dept. Indiana (Pa.) State Tchrs. Coll., 1938-56, chmn. bus. edn. dept., 1956-66, dean, prof., 1966—. Chmn. Pa. Commn. on Bus. Tchr. Certification. Mem. Omega Chi, Pi Omega Pi (treas.), Phi Sigma Pi, Kappa Delta Pi, Phi Delta Kappa, Delta Pi Epsilon. Presbyterian (sec. bd. trustees 1960-63). Kiwanian (sec. 1942—). Home: 119 S 11th St Indiana PA 15701

DRUMM, HOWARD VICTOR, publishing co. exec.; b. Columbia, Mo., July 14, 1924; s. Victor Howard and Lois Drumm; student U. Mo., 1940-42, 46-48; m. Phyllis Ann Streit, Nov. 13, 1948; children—Christopher, Lawrence. Sales mgr. Chem. and Engring. News mag., also Progressive Architecture mag. Reinhold Pub. Corp., 1948-61; pub. Electronic Design mag. Hayden Pub. Co., 1961-64; v.p. operations F.W. Dodge Co., div. McGraw-Hill, Inc., 1964-68, formerly v.p. Information Systems div. Mem. Assn. Indsl. Advertisers (co. chmn. 1949-64). Presbyn. Clubs: Chemists (chmn. 1953-64) N.Y.C.; Darien Country. Home: 2 Hickory Lane Darien CT 06830

DRUMM, STREUBY LLOYD, business cons.; b. New Orleans, Jan. 26, 1901; s. Ferdinand Streuby and Daisy Leonora (Degruy) D.; B.S., U.S. Naval Acad., 1922; m. Honor Vera Cone, Dec. 26, 1925; children—Streuby Lloyd, Hughes DeGruy. Asst. elec. engr. Phoenix Utility Co., 1923-25; with New Orleans Pub. Service Inc., 1925-54, successively comml. engr., div. sales mgr., gen. sales mgr., v.p., 1949-54; exec. v.p., dir. West Penn Power, 1954-58, pres., 1958-66; v.p. Gulf States Assets Mgmt., Inc., 1971—; bus. exec. in residence Tulane U., New Orleans, 1966-70. Dir. Fed. Res. Pitts., 1961-66. Mem., Pa. State Planning Bd., 1963-66, Regional Indsl. Devel. Corp., 1957-66; dir. Commerce and Industry Bd. La., 1952-54; v.p., mem. bd. Internat. House New Orleans, 1950-54, hon. dir., 1954—; past pres. Greater New Orleans, Inc., hon. dir., 1954—; pres. bd. dirs. Bur. Govtl. Research, 1966—, Met. Area Comm., 1968—. Served as capt. USNR, 1942-45. Mem. Navy League U.S. (v.p. 1953-56, mem. bd., 1953- 57, mem. adv. council 1956-57), N.A.M. (bd. 1951-54), Omicron Delta Kappa, Beta Gamma Sigma. Presbyn. Mason. Clubs: Boston, Stratford (New Orleans). Home: 410 Audubon St New Orleans LA 70118

DRUMMOND, DONALD FRANCIS, educator; b. Kalamazoo, Sept. 24, 1917; s. Merle Vaughan and Phyllis (DeWindt) D.; A.B., Western Mich. U., 1938; A.M., U. Mich, 1939, Ph.D., 1949; m. Elizabeth Ruth Biddle, Aug. 30, 1944; 1 son, Robert Ward. Instr., then asst. prof. history U. Mich., 1948-57; chmn. dept. social studies Coll. Edn., Geneseo (N.Y.) State U., 1957-58; prof. history Eastern Mich. U. 1958- -, head dept. history and social sci., 1958-65, dean Coll. Arts and Scis., 1965—; summer vis. prof. U. N.M., 1957, U. Mich., 1960. Served with AUS 1941-45. Mem. Am. Hist. Assn., Orgn. Am. Historians, Mich. Acad. Sci., Arts and Letters, Phi Beta Kappa, Phi Kappa Phi. Author: The Passing of American Neutrality, 1937-41, 1955; (with Dorothy M. Fraser and Frank Alweis) Five Centuries in America, 1963. Contbr. American Secretaries of State in the Twentieth Century, 1961. Home: 1813 Waltham Dr Ann Arbor MI 48103 Office: Eastern Mich U Ypsilanti MI 48197

DRUMMOND, EDWARD JOSEPH, educator; b. East St. Louis, Ill., Apr. 6, 1906; s. William Riley and Mary Elizabeth (Streuber) D.; A.B., St. Louis U., 1928, A.M. 1930, S.T.L., 1938; Ph.D., U. Of Ia., 1942. Ordained priest Roman Catholic Ch., 1937. Mem. Soc. Jesus, Instr. in English, Latin, Greek, Creighton Prep. Sch., 1931-34; grad. fellow in English, St. Louis U., 1935-37; lectr. in religion and ethics, U. of Ia., 1942; instr. in English. Marquette U., 1942-44, asso. prof., 1944-62, acting dir. dept. Eng., 1947-48, dean grad. sch. 1944-53, acting v.p., 1953-54, v.p. acad. affairs, 1954-62; v.p. Med. Center St. Louis U., also asso. prof. English, 1962-70, prof. edn., 1970—. Cons. task force orgnl. structure, bd. dirs. Nat. League Nursing; mem. long range planning com. Wis. State Coordinating Com. for Higher Edn., 1960-62; mem. bd. commrs. Nat. Commn. on Accrediting, 1967—. Catholic chaplain and dir. of Newman Club, U. of Ia., 1942. Editor: Mo. Province News-Letter, 1934- 36. Mem. North Central Assn. (commr. and mem. exec. bd. commn. on colls. and us. 1958-64, vice chmn. 1961-62, chmn. 1962-64; chmn. adv. com. ann. meeting program 1964; v.p. 1967-68, pres. 1968-69, dir. 1967—), Nat. Cath. Ednl. Assn. (mem. commn. on grad. studies, 1945-53, chmn. resolutions com. 1952 conv., chmn. plans and problems com. 1953-54; chmn. com. on faculty welfare coll. and univ. dept. 1958-62), Am. Assn. Med. Colls., Hosp. Assn. Met. St. Louis, Jesuit Edn. Assn. (chmn. commn. on grad. studies 1948-49), N.E.A., Fedn. Regional Accrediting Commns. Higher Edn. (vice chmn. exec. com. 1964-66, chmn. 1966-70), Am. Hosp. Assn. (mem. com. nursing edn. 1964, mem. council on manpower and edn. 1968—), Sigma Tau Delta, Phi Alpha Theta. Contbr. articles, revs. and books. Home: 221 N Grand Blvd St Louis MO 63103

DRUMMOND, FORREST STUART, law librarian; b. Chgo., Nov.5, 1910; s. Stuart Lamond and Naomi Laura (Hansen) D.; Ph.B., U. Chgo., 1932, J.D., 1934; m. Helen I. Prime, Nov. 20, 1943; 1 son, Forrest Stuart. Admitted to Ill. bar, 1934, practiced in Chgo., 1934-37; librarian, asst. prof. law, law sch., U. Chgo., 1937-46; asst. librarian Assn. Bar City of N.Y., 1946-50; librarian Los Angeles Co. Law Library 1950—. Served with USNR, active duty, 1942-45; now captain, ret. Decorated Bronze Star medal, Commendation Ribbon. Mem. Law Library Assn. Greater N.Y. (pres. 1948-49), Am. (pres. 1952-53), Internat. assns. law libraries (pres. 1952-53), Am., Internat. bar assns., Navy League, Comml. Law League Am., U.S. Naval Inst., Assn. of Bar of City N.Y. Chairman Index to Legal Periodicals, 1947-52, 54—. Home: 2930 San Pasqual St Pasadena, CA 91107. Office: Los Angeles County Law Library Los Angeles CA 90012

DRUMMOND, ROSCOE, columnist; b. Theresa, N.Y.; s. John Henry and Georgia Estella (Peppers) D.; B.S.J., Syracuse U., 1924; Litt.D., Dartmouth, 1947; D.H.L. (hon.), Principia Coll., Elsah, Ill.; LL.D., Syracuse U., 1955; Postgrad. Ricker College, 1962; m. Charlotte Bruner, Sept. 11, 1926; 1 son, Geoffrey. Reporter for Christian Sci. Monitor, Boston, 1924, continuing as asst. city editor, asst. to exec. editor, chief editorial writer, European editorial mgr., gen. news editor, mem. editorial board, exec. editor, 1934-40, chief Washington News Bur., 1940-53 and creator of State of the Nation: on leave as dir. information E.C.A. in Europe, Paris, 1949-51, chief Washington Bur. N.Y. Herald Tribune, 1953-55, and author syndicated column Washington; now Washington columnist for Los Angeles Times Syndicate. Trustee Freedom House, 1962-67. Recipient prize for best editorial pub. in an Am. newspaper on significance of Internat. Press Exhbn. at Cologne, 1928; George Arents award for proficiency in journalism, 1946. Mem. Am. Soc. Newspaper Editors, Alpha Kappa Psi, Sigma Phi Epsilon, Beta Gamma Sigma, Sigma Delta Chi. Clubs: Gridiron, Overseas Writers, National Press, Metropolitan (Washington, D.C.). Author: (with Gaston Coblentz) Duel at the Brink, 1960. Contbr. to Am. and Brit. mags. Mason. Home: 3029 Cambridge Pl N W Washington DC 20007 Office: Nat Press Bldg Washington DC 20004

DRUMMOND, SALLY HAZELET, artist; b. Evanston, Ill., June 4, 1924; d. Craig Potter and Frances (Gillam) Hazlet; student Rollins Coll., 1942-44; B.S., Coumbia, 1946; postgrad. Inst. Design, Chgo., 1949-50; M.A., U. Louisville, 1952; m. F. Weichel Drummond, Mar. 25, 1961; 1 son, Craig Potter. Exhibited in one man shows at Hadley Gallery, Louisville, 1952, Tanager Gallery, N.Y.C., 1955, 57, 60, Green Gallery, N.Y.C., 1962, Fishbach Gallery, N.Y.C., 1968; exhibited in group shows at Am. embassy, Rome, 1953, Fgn. Artists Invitational, Bordighiera, Italy, 1953, Am. Artists Ann., 1960, Whitney Mus., N.Y.C., 1958-59, 64 Green Gallery, 1961, Mus. Modern Art, N.Y.C., 1963; rep. permanent collections at Mus. Modern Art, Whitney Mus., Speed Mus., Louisville, U. Ia. Mus. Art, Iowa City, Joseph H. Hirshorn, Greenwich, Conn., Hudsons Dept. Store, Detroit, AVCO Corp. Recipient Fulbright grant to Venice, 1952- 53; Guggenheim fellow to France, 1967-68. Home: 371 Wilton Rd E Ridgefield CT 06877

DRUMMOND, THEODORE HAMILTON, govt. ofcl.; b. Salt Lake City, June 17, 1908; s. Elza H. and Grace J. (Surline) D.; B.S. in Civil Engring., U. Utah, 1931; part-time student, U. So. Cal., 1943-45; m. Mary V. Lafferty, September 12, 1947 (dec. Feb. 1965); 1 dau., Mary Karen; m. 2d, Harriet Thorstad, July 23, 1967. Engaged in practice as surveyor, 1931-37, engr. draftsman, 1937-42; topographic draftsman to chief photogrammetry sect. Corps. Engrs., Los Angeles, 1942-48; engr.-illustrator Bur. Land Mgmt., Dept. Interior, 1948-57, asst. mgr. records improvement project, 1957-58, adminstr. Dept. Interior Mus., 1958-; paintings, etchings, sculpture exhibited Los Angeles, San Francisco, Salt Lake City, N.Y.C., Lexington, Ky.; permanent exhbn. Dept. Interior Mus.; designer gold medal valor award, also deptl. service pins, Dept. Interior. Recipient Outstanding Performance award Bur. Land. Management, 1956. Mem. Am. Mus. Assn., Am. Mus. Natural History. Presbyn. (past nat. officer Nat. Presbyn. Mariners, past pres. Mariners Washington Presbytery). Compiler, composer, illustrator. A Syllabus of Measurement, 1954: The Public Land Records, 1959. Home: 1212 Tanley Rd Silver Spring, MD 20904. Office: Dept Interior Washington DC 20240

DRUMMOND, WILLIAM HIXON, lawyer; b. Kansas City, Mo., July 18, 1931; s. William Franklin and Letta (Searfoss) D.; B.S. in Chem. Engring., U. Mo., 1956, LL.B., 1961; children-Susan Leigh, William Hixon, Jamie Elaine, Robert Edward, Jack Steven. Admitted to Mo. bar, 1961; chem. engr. Monsanto Chem. Co., 1956- 59; patent lawyer Am. Oil Co., 1961, Gulf Oil Co., 1962-63; partner firm Drummond, Cahill & Phillips, Phoenix, 1964—. Served with USAF, 1952-53, AUS, 1953-54. Mem. Am., Mo., Ill., Ariz. bar assns., Am. Arbitration Assn., Am. Patent Law Assn., Am. Chem. Soc., Am. Inst. Chem. Engrs., Am. Inst. Mining, Metall. and Petroleum Engrs., Phi Alpha Delta, Alpha Chi Sigma. Democrat. Club: Arizona (Phoenix). Home: 512 W Gardenia St Phoenix AZ 85021 Office: 4502 N Central Av Phoenix AZ 85021

DRUMMOND, WINSLOW, lawyer; b. Phila., Jan. 29, 1933; s. Winslow Shaw and Dorothy (Moore) D.; A.B., Coll. of Wooster (O.), 1954; LL.B., Duke, 1957; m. Lou Ann Unzicker, June 13, 1953; children—Judith L., Kathryn W., Winslow Shaw II. Admitted to Ark. bar, 1957, since practiced in Little Rock; mem. firm Wright, Lindsey & Jennings, 1957—, partner, 1962—. Pres., bd. dirs. Urban League Greater Little Rock; bd. dirs. Little Rock Sch. Dist. Served with AUS, 1957-58. Mem. Am., Ark. (past chmn. exec. com.), Pulaski County bar assns., Fedn. Ins. Counsel, Am. Judicature Soc., Order of Coif, Phi Alpha Theta. Democrat. Presbyn. Co-author: Arkansas Model Jury Instructions-Civil, 1965. Home: 7314 F St Little Rock AR 72205 Office: Worthen Bank Bldg Little Rock AR 72201

DRURY, ALLEN STUART, author; b. Houston, Sept. 2, 1918; s. Alden Monteith and Flora (Allen) D.; B.A., Stanford, 1939; Lit.D. (hon.), Rollins Coll., 1961. Editor, Tulare (Cal.) Bee, 1940-41; county editor Bakersfield Californian, 1941- 42; mem. Senate staff U.P.I., Washington, 1943-45; free lance corr., 1946; nation editor Pathfinder mag., 1947-53; nat. staff Washington Evening Star, 1953-54; mem. congl. staff N.Y. Times, 1954-59; polit. contbr. Reader's Digest, 1959-62. Served with AUS, 1942-43. Recipient Pulitzer Prize for fiction Advise and Consent, 1960. Mem. Sigma Delta Chi (nat. award for editorial writing 1941), Alpha Kappa Lambda. Clubs: National Press, Cosmos, University (Washington); Players (N.Y.C.); Bohemian (San Francisco). Author: Advise and Consent, 1959; A Shade of Difference, 1962; A Senate Journal, 1963; That Summer, 1965; Three Kids in A Cart, 1965; Capable of Honor, 1966; "A Very Strange Society", 1967; Preserve and Protect, 1968; The Throne of Saturn, 1971. Address: care DruKill Co Box 927 Maitland FL 32751

DRURY, CHARLES EDWIN, indsl. exec.; b. Albany, Ill., Feb. 24, 1921; s. William B. and Mary E. (Ege) D.; B.S. Mech. Engring., U. Ill., 1949; m. Diana Amy Gardener, Apr. 13, 1946; children—Pamela (Mrs. Edward R. Godfrey), Charles E., Michael G., Deborah A. Trainee central foundry div. Gen. Motors Corp., Danville, Ill., 1949-50, factory mgr. Saginaw (Mich.) malleable iron plant, 1955-56, works mgr. central foundry div., Saginaw, 1963-69; pres., chief operating officer Hayes-Albion Corp., Jackson, Mich., 1969- -; dir. City Bank and Trust Co., Nat. Assn. Jackson. Served to capt., C.E., AUS, 1942-46. Mem. Am. Foundrymen's Soc. (nat. dir. 1956-59), Soc. Automotive Engrs. (past chmn. Mid-Mich. sect.), Malleable Foundrs Soc. Clubs: 300 of Republican Party, Country, Town (Jackson, Mich.). Home: 3775 Stonewall Rd Jackson MI 49203 Office: 437 Fern Av Jackson MI 49202

DRURY, CHARLES MILLS, Canadian govt. ofcl.; b. May 17, 1912; s. Victor Montague and Pansy Jessie (Mills) D.; student Bishops Coll. Sch., Lennoxville, Quebec, Royal Mil. Coll. of Can., Kingston, Ont.; B.C.L. McGill U.; student U. Paris (France); m. Jane Fenier Counsell, 1939; 2 sons, 2 daus. Practice of law, 1936-39; chief UNRRA Mission to Poland, 1945-46; mem. Dept. External Affairs Can., 1947-48; dep. minister nat. def., Can., 1949-55; Pres., mng. dir. Provincial Transport Co., Montreal, 1955-61; pres. Avis Transport Can. Ltd., 1961-63; minister def. production and minister of industry of Canada, 1963-68, pres. Treasury Bd., 1968—. Served to brig. with Canadian Army, 1939-45. Decorated Legion of Honor (France); Order Polonia Restituta (Poland); comdr. Order Brit. Empire, Distinguished Service Order. Clubs: Rideau (Ottawa); Royal St. Lawrence Yacht (Dorval, Que.) Home: 23 Mackay St Ottawa Ontario Canada Office: Confederation Bldg Ottawa Ontario Canada

DRURY, CHIPMAN HAZEN, leasing co. exec.; b. Montreal, Que., Can., July 15, 1917; s. Victor Montague and Pansy (Mills) D.; grad. Royal Mil. Coll., 1938; B.Chem. Engring., McGill U., 1939; M.B.A., Harvard, 1947; m. Dorothy Janet Dobell, Dec. 27, 1945; childrenSally, Chipman M., Penny, Pansy, Reid. With Canadian Car Co., Ltd., Montreal, 1947-54, v.p. purchasing, 1952-54; v.p., mgr. Canadian Gen. Transit Co., Ltd., 1954-56, pres., mng. dir., 1956-63; exec. v.p. Dominion Steel & Coal Corp., Montreal, 1963-64; pres. Dosco Steel Ltd., 1964-68; chmn. bd. Avis Transport of Can., Ltd., 1968- -, also dir.; dir. Guardian Royal Exchange, Caledonian-Can. Ins. Co., Quebec Industries, Ltd. Served to lt. col. Royal Canadian Arty., 1939-45. Mem. Newcomen Soc. N.Am., Montreal Bd. Trade, Engring. Inst. Can., Corp. Profl. Engrs. Que., Soc. Automotive Engrs. Clubs: University, Canadian, Canadian Ry., Mt. Royal, Mt. Bruno Country, Canadian of Montreal. Home: 56 St Sulpice Rd Westmount 217 Quebec Canada Office: 750 Laurentien Blvd Montreal 379 Quebec Canada

DRURY, CLIFFORD MERRILL, educator, author; b. Early, Ia., Nov. 7, 1897; s. William and Mae (Dell) D.; A.B., Buena Vista Coll., 1918, D.D., 1941; B.D., San Francisco Theol. Sem., 1922, S.T.M., 1928; Ph.D., U. Edinburgh 1932; Litt.D., Whitworth College, 1955; D.H.L., Whitman Coll., 1964; m. Miriam Mayhew Leyrer, Nov. 17, 1922; children—Robert Merrill, Patricia, Philip Edward (dec.). Ordained to ministry Presbyn. Ch., Mar. 19, 1922; asst. pastor First Ch., Berkeley, Calif., 1921-23; pastor Community Ch. (Am.), Shanghai, China, 1923-27; First Presbyn. C., Moscow, Ida., 1928-38; prof. ch. history, San Francisco Theol. Sem., 1938-63; lectr. Presbyn. history Fuller Theol. Sem., Pasadena, 1964-69. Served in Chem. Warfare Service, U.S. Army, at Yale U., 1918; A.R.C., Ft. Des Moines, Ia., 1919; Chaplain (capt.) USNR, 1933-58; active duty, 1941-46; historian Chaplain Corps., USN, 1944-56. Recipient award Presbyn. Hist. Soc., 1960, Capt. Robert Gray medal Wash. Hist. Soc., 1968. Mem. Phi Beta Kappa. Republican. Author: Henry Harmon Spalding, Pioneer of Old Oregon, 1936; Marcus Whitman, M.D., Pioneer and Martyr, 1937; Mary and Elkanah Walker, Pioneers Among the Spokanes, 1940; A Tepee in His Front Yard, 1949; Presbyterian Panorama, 1952; Diary of Titian Peale, 1956; History of Chaplains Corps., U.S. Navy, 2 vols., 1950-51; U.S. Navy Chaplains, 3 vols., 1949-57; The Diaries and Letters of Henry H. Spalding and Asa Brown Smith, 1958; The First White Woman Over the Rockies, 3 vols., 1963-66; San Francisco YMCA; One Hundred Years by the Golden Gate, 1963; William Anderson Scott, No Ordinary Man, 1967; Rudolph James Wig (Biography), California Imprints, 1846-1876, 1968. Contbr. to religious and hist. jours. Home: 2889 San Pasqual St Pasadena CA 91107

DRURY, NEWTON B., conservationist; b. San Francisco, Apr. 9, 1889; s. Wells and Ella Lorraine (Bishop) D.; B.L., U. Cal., 1912, LL.D. (hon.), 1947; m. Elizabeth Frances Schilling, June 29, 1918; children—Betty (Mrs. Austin L. Edwards), Newton Hugh Wells. Reporter on San Francisco and Oakland newspapers, 190611; instr. in English, asst. prof. in forensics, sec. to the pres., U. Cal., 1912-18; partner in Drury Co., advt. agency and pub. relations counsel, San Francisco. 1919-40; sec. Save-the-Redwoods League, 1919-40; exec. Calif. Park Commn., 1929-40; mem. adv. bd. Yosemite Nat. Park, 1938-40; dir. Nat. Park Service, 1940-51; chief Div. State Parks, Cal., 1951-59; sec. Save the Redwoods League. Served as 2d lt., Air Service, U.S. Army (aerial observer Balloon Corps). 1918-19; 1st lt. Air Service Res., 1919- 22. Recipient Conservation award Trustees of Public Reservations. Boston, 1940; Pugsley medal Am. Scenic and Historic Preservation Soc., N.Y., 1940; Hutchinson medal Garden Club of America, 1945; Conservation award U.S. Dept. Interior, 1968. Regional trustee Mills Coll., Oakland, Cal., 1941-43; research Asso. Carnegie Instn. of Washington, 1938-43. Hon. vice pres. Sierra Club; hon. mem. Am. Soc. Landscape Architects; hon. mem. Soc. Am. Foresters, 1949. Clubs: Faculty (U. Cal.); Commonwealth (San Francisco); Boone and Crockett (v.p.) (N.Y.C.). Home: 822 Mendocino Av Berkeley CA 94707 Office: 114 Sansome St San Francisco CA 94104

DRURY, ROBERT EDWARD, mfg. co. exec.; b. Detroit, May 19, 1916; s. John Francis and Theresa (Thomas) D.; student Highland Park Jr. Coll., 1933-35; LL.B., J.D., U. Detroit, 1938; m. Lois Lochridge, Oct. 16, 1944; children—Robert J., Diane L., Susan J. Admitted to Mich. bar, 1938; practiced in Detroit, 1938-42; investigator Air Force Intelligence, 1942-46; personnel dir. Chrysler Corp., 1946-52; v.p. mfg. Redmond Co., Owosso, Mich., 1952-61; group v.p. King-Seeley Thermos Co., Ann Arbor, Mich., 1961—, sec., 1969—, also dir. Pres., County United Found., 1960-61; dir. A.R.C., 1954-60. Mem. Am. Soc. for Personnel Adminstrs. (regional dir.). Rotarian. Home: 2920 Provincial Dr Ann Arbor MI 48104 Office: 3858 Research Park Dr Ann Arbor MI 48104

DRURY, ROBERT FINLEY, ret. govt. ofcl.; b. Washington, Sept. 11, 1918; s. Horace Bookwalter and Ruth (Williamson) D.; B.A., U. Chgo., 1939; m. Kathryn Jane Chetham, June 21, 1940; children—Kathryn Susan, Robert Finley, Julia Elizabeth, Richard Alexander, John Williamson. With U.S. Bur. of Census, 1940-71, asst. dir. operations 1966-67, dep. dir. of census, 1967-71. Active local Boy Scouts Am. Served to lt. USNR, 1943-45. Recipient Gold medal award for distinguished achievement Dept. Commerce, 1966. Mem. Am. Statis. Assn., Phi Beta Kappa, Delta Upsilon. Presbyn. Home: 2311 Connecticut Av Washington DC 20008

DRURY, ROBERT MERRILL, librarian; b. Shanghai, China, June 8, 1925 (parents Am. citizens); s. Clifford Merrill and Miriam (Leyrer) D.; A.B., U. Cal., Berkeley, 1949; B.D., McCormick Theol. Sem., 1953; M.S. in L.S., U. Ill., 1958; m. Gloria Josephine Wilson, May 30, 1953; children—Nancy Jean, Janet Anne. Ordained to ministry Presbyn. Ch., 1953; pastor Presbyn. Ch., Grand Ridge, Ill., 1953-54, Blairstown, Ia., 1954-56; asst. reference librarian Purdue U. Libraries, 1958-61; librarian Central Baptist Theol. Sem., Kansas City, Kan., 1961—. Served with AUS, 1943-45. Mem. Am. Theol. Library Assn. (chmn. periodical exchange com.), Am. Baptist Hist. Soc. (bd. mgrs.), Kansas City Posse, The Westerners, Alpha Gamma Omega. Baptist (deacon.). Home: 2521 Washington Av Kansas City KS 66102 Office: 2915 Minnesota Av Kansas City KS 66102

DRURY, THOMAS JOSEPH, bishop; b. County Sigo, Ireland, Jan. 4, 1908; s. Michael and Margaret (Lannon) D.; student St. Benedict's Coll., Atchison, Kan., 1926-29; A.B., Kenrich Sem., 1931. Ordained priest Roman Cath. Ch., 1935; asst. and pastor Sacred Heart Cathedral, 1935-45; pastor St. Elizabeth's and Christ the King Chs., Lubbock, Tex., 1956-61; bishop Diocese of San Angelo, 1961-65, consecrated, 1962; bishop Diocese of Corpus Christi, 1965—. Sec. of Matrimonial Ct., 1935, promotor of justice, 1938—. defender of the bond, 1939-; diocesan dir. Confraternity of Christian Doctrine, 1936, Soc. Propagation of the Faith, 1936-, Cath. Action, Holy Name Soc.; mem. bd. Diocesan Adminstrn., 1938—. Chmn. Amarillo council Boy Scouts Am.; v.p. Amarillo Cath. Welfare Bur. Served to maj., Chaplains Corps, USAAF, 1945-47, USAF, 1949-55. Editor, bus. mgr. Texas Panhandle Register, 1936-38, Home: 4109 Ocean Dr Corpus Christi, TX 78411. Office: 620 Lipan St Corpus Christi TX 78401

DRUSHAL, JOHN GARBER, coll. pres.; b. Lost Creek, Ky., July 1, 1912; s. George Emery and Ada (Garder) D.; A.B., Ashland Coll., 1935; M.A., Ohio State U., 1938, Ph.D., 1951; m. Dorothy Loree Whitted, June 12, 1938; childrenMichael, Jane (dec.), Richard, Douglas. Instr., Ashland Coll., 1936-37, U. Mo., 1938-39; asst. prof. Capital U., 1939-46; prof. Coll. of Wooster (O.), 1946-63, dean of coll., 1963-66, dean, v.p. acad. affairs, 1966-67, acting pres., 1967-68, pres., 1968—. Instr. summers Bowling Green State U., 1941, U. Mo., 1942, Queens Coll., 1948; dir. Citizens Nat. Bank. Pres., Wooster City Council, 1960-70. Trustee Ashland Coll.; v.p. trustee Ohio Retirement Homes at Wooster. Mem. Am. Assn. U. Profs. (past chpt. pres.), Speech Assn. Am., Acad. Polit. Sci., Central States Speech Assn. (past. sec.), Ohio Assn. Coll. Tchrs. Speech (past sec., pres.), Ohio Assn. Speech and Hearing Therapists (past pres.), Ohio Coll. Assn. (past exec. sec.), Wooster Auto Club (dir.), Delta Sigma Rho (past nat. v.p.). Mem. Brethren Ch. Rotarian (past pres. Wooster). Author: (with Bonthius, Davis) The Independent Study Program in the United States, 1957. Home: 433 E University St Wooster OH 44691

DRY, JOHN MARION, mfg. exec.; b. Mexico, Mo., Dec. 12, 1907; s. John Wesley and Margaret (Sappington) D.; A.B., U. Mo., 1929; LL.B., Harvard, 1932; m. Jean Arrowsmith, Sept. 6, 1935 (dec.); 1 dau., Sarah Bradford; m. 2d, Isabelle Heard Bland, Dec. 26, 1948; 1 dau., Marion Marshall. Admitted to Mass. bar, 1932; asso. Nutter McClennen & Fish, Boston, 1932-41, partner, 1941-43; asst. to pres. United-Carr Inc., Boston, 1943- 45, sec., 1945-70, v.p., 1946-70, dir., 1951-70; gen. counsel United-Carr Divs. TRW Inc., 1970—; asst. sec. TRW Inc., 1971—; dir. Cambridge Trust Co., Cambridge Savs. Bank, Cambridge. Chmn. library com. Harvard Law Sch. Fund.; past pres. Cambridge Council Churches. Bd. dir. YMCA, Cambridge Tb and Health Assn., New Eng. Deaconess Hosp. Corp., Buckingham Sch. Cambridge; trustee, pres. The Avon Home, Cambridge, Mass.; trustee Mt. Auburn Hosp., Cambridge; Member Am., Boston bar assns., Cambridge C. of C., Beta Theta Pi. Episcopalian. Clubs: Rotary, Cambridge, Union (Boston). Home: 68 Avon Hill St Cambridge MA 02140 Office: Prudential Center Boston MA 02199

DRYDEN, GORDON ROBERT, lawyer; b. Guelph, Ont., Can., May 3, 1926; s. George Beverley and Florence (Parkinson) D.; B.A., U. Toronto, 1947, Barrister-at-Law, Osgoode Hall Law Sch., Toronto, 1950; m. Mary Louise Lonergan, Sept. 23, 1967; 1 son, John George Lonergan. Called to Ont. bar, 1950; with firm Levinter, Dryden, Bliss, Maxwell & Hart, and predecessors, Toronto, 1950—, partner, 1963—. Mem. spl. com. on election expenses Canadian Govt., 1964—. Active Liberal Party, 1945—; sec. treas. Liberal Fedn. Can., 1964-68; treas. Liberal Party Can., 1968—. Home: 50 Alexander St Toronto Ontario Canada Office: 100 Adelaide St Toronto Ontario Canada

DRYDEN, JOHN RICHARD, banker; b. Berkeley, Cal., Apr. 17, 1912; s. Henry Francis and Mathilde (Richard) D.; B.S., U. Cal. at Berkeley, 1933; m. Loneta Yerington, July 23, 1943 (dec. Sept. 1963); children—John Yerington (dec. 1969). David James, Thomas Richard; m. 2d, Elizabeth Eisele, July 25, 1964. With Anglo & London Paris Nat. Bank, San Francisco, 1930-32; with Anglo- Cal. Nat. Bank, San Francisco, 1932-56, asst. cashier, 1948-50, asst. v.p., 1950-56; v.p. Crocker Anglo Nat. Bank San Francisco, 1956-63; v.p. Crocker Nat. Bank, San Francisco, 1963-68, sr. v.p., chmn. sr. loan com., 1968-69, exec. v.p., 1969—. Home: 75 Elrod Av Oakland CA 94618 Office: 1 Montgomery St San Francisco CA 94138

DRYE, JOHN WILSON, Jr., lawyer; b. Van Alstyne, Tex., May 28, 1900; s. John Wilson and Elizabeth (Cave) D.; student Valparaiso U., 1917-18, U. Mich., 1918; LL.B., Washington and Lee U., 1920, LL.D., 1956; m. Loraine Caldwell, Oct. 26, 1926, children—Robert Caldwell, Anne Elizabeth. Admitted to N.Y. bar, 1922; asso. Larkin, Rathbone & Perry, 1920-29, partner same and successor firms Rathbone, Perry, Kelley & Drye and Kelley, Drye, Newhall, Maginnes & Warren, 1930, now Kelley, Drye, Warren, Clark, Carr & Ellis; pres. Park 81st Corp.; dir. Franklin United Life Ins. Co., Security Reins. Corp., Ltd.; dir. mem. exec. com. Continental Corp., Continental Ins. Co. and various N.Y. subsidiary cos., Bklyn. Union Gas Co.; gen. counsel, dir., mem. exec. com. Union Carbide Corp. Pres. Juilliard Mus. Found.; bd. dirs. Juilliard Sch., Coe Found., Planting Fields Found. Lincoln Center for Performing Arts, Inc., Met. Opera, Continental Corp. Found. Mem. Am., N.Y. State, N.Y.C., N.Y. County bar assns., Sigma Chi. Methodist. Clubs: Knickerbocker, Nassau Country, Racquet and Tennis, Board Room (N.Y.C.); Burlington (Vt.) Country; Mid Ocean (Bermuda). Home: 940 Park Av New York City NY 10028 Office: 350 Park Av New York City NY 10022

DRYER, EARL DAVID, utilities exec.; b. Marsahll, Mo., July 16, 1913; s. Curtis E. and Anna (Erdwin) D.; student Central Meth. Coll., 1930-32; B.S. in Elec. Engring., U. Mo., 1935; m. Helen Willis, May 21, 1938; 1 son, David R. With Mo. Pub. Service Co., Kansas City, 1937—, v.p. operations, dir., 1964-66, exec. v.p., dir., 1966—. Dir. Kansas City Indsl. Found. Third v.p. Mid-Continent council Girl Scouts Am., 1967—. Mem. I.E.E.E., Electric Assn. Kansas City, Newcomen Soc., Mo., Kansas City, Raytown chambers commerce, Pi Mu Epsilon. Presbyn. Rotarian. Clubs: Engineers (Kansas City); Crackerneck Country (Independence, Mo.). Home: 8635 E 73rd Terrace Kansas City MO 64133 Office: Mo Pub Service Co 10700 E 50 Hwy Kansas City MO 64138

DRYNAN, WILLIAM INNES, food processor; b. Buckingham, Que., Sept. 13, 1900; s. William Rapley and Alice Marian (Innes) D.; grad. Royal Mil. Coll. of Can.; m. Mary Katharine Kirk, Sept. 1, 1928; children—William Innes Kirk, George Sydney, Alice Mary. With Canadian Canners, Ltd., Hamilton, Ont., 1923—, dir., 1943—, asst. gen. mgr., 1947-50, 28 v.p., 1950-51, v.p. charge prodn., 1951-53, pres., 1953-65, vice chmn. bd., 1965-68; Hamilton adv. bd. Royal Trust Co. Bd. dirs. Hamilton Found. Former comdg. officer Royal Hamilton Light Infantry. Mem. Canadian Manufacturers Assn. (exec. council), Inst. Internat. Affairs, Hamilton and District Officers Inst. Clubs: Hamilton (Ontario); Hamilton Golf and Country, Tamahaac (Ancaster, Ont.): Albany (Toronto). Home: 293 Park St S Hamilton Ontario Canada Office: 293 Park St S Hamilton Ontario Canada

DRYSDALE, DOUGLAS, lawyer; b. Phila., Aug. 9, 1924; B.A., U. Va., 1944, LL.B., 1953. Admitted to Va. bar, 1952, D.C. bar, 1964; now mem. firm Caplin & Drysdale, Washington. Lectr. taxation U. Va. Law Sch., Charlottesville, 1960—. Mem. Am., Va. bar assns., Order of Coif, Phi Beta Kappa, Phi Delta Phi. Office: 1101 17th St NW Washington DC 20036*

DUANE, HARKEY W., Jr., life ins. co. exec.; b. Petersburg, Va., Apr. 11, 1911; s. Harley W. and Mary (Feild) D.; B.S. in Chemistry, Va. Mil. Inst., 1932; student U. Richmond Sch. Bus. Adminstrn.; m. Jane Massey; children—Harley W. III, Mary Feild, Jane Townsend. With Life Ins. Co. Va., Richmond, 1932—, corp. sec., officer charge personal ins. service dept., 1968—. Home: 6318 Ridgeway Rd Richmond VA 23226 Office: 910 Capitol St Richmond VA 23209

DUANE, MORRIS, lawyer; b. Phila., March 2O, 1901; s. Russell and Mary (Burnside) M.; student Episcopal Acad., Phila., 1913-15, St. George's Sch., Newport, R.I., 1915-19; A.B., Harvard, 1923; Univ. Pa. Law Sch., 1923-25; LL.B., Stetson U., 1927, LL.D., 1965; LL.D., Bucknell U., 1967, LaSalle Coll., 1970; L.H.D., Women's Med. Coll. Pa., 1967; Litt.D., Beaver Coll., 1969; m. Maud S. Harrison, June 11, 1927; children—Margaretta Sergeant, Russell. Engaged in gen. practice of law, Phila., 1927—; mem. firm Duane, Morris & Heckscher, 1931—. Dir. Girard Trust Corn Exchange Bank, Penn. Mut. Life Ins. Co., Phila. Saving Fund Soc., The Phila. Contributionship and other corps., United Fund, Ednl. Facilities Labs., Inc. Co-chmn., dir. Greater Phila. Movement; mem. Com. on Tri State Regional Devel. (Pa., N.J., Del.). Bd. dirs. Univ. City Sci. Center, Phila. Orch. Corp., 1976 Bicentennial Corp., 1967-71, Phila. Urban Coalition; v.p., trustee Presser Found.; pres. bd. trustees Episcopal Acad., 1948-51; mem. Harvard Fund Council, 1949-55. Served as lt. to cmdr., USNR, 1943-45; head materials and resources group, bur. aeros., U.S. Navy, 1944-45; rep. naval aviation on War Prodn. Bd. requirements com., Army and Navy munitions bd. exec. com., 1944-45; mem. Naval Air Reserve Adv. Council (chmn. 1947). Awarded Commendation Ribbon, 1945. Mem. Am. Philos. Soc., Am. Lawn Tennis Assn. (chmn. inter-collegiate com. 1928-33), Am. Pa., Phila. bar assns., Juristic Soc., Com. of Seventy (1938-46), Salvation Army (mem. exec. bd., Phila.), Delta Psi. Republican. Episcopalian. Clubs: Philadelphia, Gulph Mills Golf, Legal (Phila.); Metropolitan (Washington); Fly (Cambridge); Sharswood Law (U. Pa.). Author: New Deal in Court, 1934. Contbr. articles to legal periodicals. Home: 439 Garden Lane Bryn Mawr PA 19010 Office: Land Title Bldg Philadelphia PA 19110

DUANE, THOMAS DAVID, physician; b. Peoria, Ill., Oct. 10, 1917; s. Joseph Francis and Alexa (Fischer) D.; B.S., Harvard, 1939; M.D., Northwestern U., 1943 M.S., 1944; Ph.D., State U., Ia., 1948; m. Julia Ann McElhinney, Mar. 22, 1944; children—Alexa (Mrs. Michael John Bresnan), Joseph McElhinney, Rachel, Andrew Thomas. Intern Evanston (Ill.) Hosp., 1943-44; resident ophthalmology U. Ia., 1944-47, instr. physiology, 1947-49; practice medicine, specializing in ophthalmology, Bethlehem, Pa., and Phila., 1949—; instr. physiology U. Pa., 1952-56, instr. ophthalmology, 1958-62; prof., chmn. ophthalmology Jefferson Med. Coll., 1962—; cons. USN, 1958—, NASA, 1966—. Served to lt. USNR, 1950-53. Diplomate Am. Bd. Ophthalmology, Am. Bd. Preventive Medicine. Mem. A.M.A., Am. Acad. Ophthalmology and Otolaryngology, Assn. Research Ophthalmology, Am. Ophthal. Soc. Author: Ophthalmic Research; USA. Contbr. articles to profl. jours. Home: Bedminster PA 18910 Office: 1025 Walnut St Philadelphia PA 19107

DUARTE, SERGIO DEQUEIROZ, Brazilian diplomat; b. Rio de Janeiro, Brazil, Nov. 17, 1934; s. Ary deQueiroz and Celuta (Cavalcante) D.; ed. U. Rio de Janeiro, 1954-59, Pub. Adminstrn. Sch., 1955-57, Rio Branco Inst., 1956-57; m. Lucia Maria Sobral, May 17, 1958; children—Carlos Sergio, Luciana Helena. 3d sec. Brazilian Embassy, Rome, 1961-62, 2d sec., Buenos Aires, 1963-66; 2d sec. Brazilian delegation to UN, Geneva, 1966-68; chief communications div. Ministry External Relations, Brazil, 1968-70; 1st sec. Brazilian Embassy, Washington, 1970—. Decorated Order Rio Branco (Brazil). Home: 5500 Ridgefield Rd Bethesda MD 20016 Office: 3007 Whitehaven St NW Washington DC 20008

DUBA, JOHN GORMAN, educator; b. Norfolk, Va., Dec. 17, 1921: s. John and Helen Agnes (Swann) D.; student R.I. State Coll., 1940-43; B.S. in Civil Engring. Washington U., 1947; M.S., U. Mo. Sch. Mines and Metallurgy, 1949; C.E. (hon.), U. Mo., 1967; m. Sunny Boyd, Dec. 11, 1945; children—Cynthia, John G., Phyllis, Laura, Douglas. Instr. civil engring. U. Mo. Sch. Mines and Metallurgy, 1947-49; instr. civil engring Ill. Inst. Tech., 1949-51, asst. prof., 1951-53; civil engr., asst. administrv. engr., adminstrv. engr. pub. works City Chgo., 1953-57, mayor's administrv. officer, 1957-61, chmn., commr. Chgo. Dept. Urban Renewal, 1962-65, commr. Chgo. Dept. Devel. and Planning, 1965-67; prof. environmental engring. Poly. Inst. Bklyn., 1967-70, head dept. civil engring., dir. Center for Urban Environmental Studies, 1967-70; adminstr. Municipal Service Adminstrn., N.Y.C., 1969; v.p. airport facilities Air Transport Assn., Washington, 1970—. Cons. various municipalities, research and indsl. firms, cons. engrs., architects, 1947—, part-time lectr. Northwestern U., 1955-70. Exec. dir. Chgo. Land Clearance Commn., 1961-62. Served with USAAF, 1943-45. Registered profl. engr. Ill., N.Y. Mem. Ill. Engring. Council (pres. 1958), Am. Soc. C.E., Nat. Soc. Profl. Engrs., Am. Pub. Works Assn. (chmn. edn. found. 1963-69), Sigma Alpha Epsilon, Chi Epsilon. Home: 2725 N Fillmore St Arlington VA 22207 Office: 100 Connecticut Av NW Washington DC 20036

DUBAIN, MYRON, ins. co. exec.; b. Cleve., June 3, 1923; s. Edward D. and Elaine (Byrne) DuB.; B.A., U. Cal., 1943, grad. exec. program Stanford Grad. Sch. Bus., 1967; m. Alice Elaine Hilliker, Sept. 30, 1944; children—Cynthia Lynn, Donald Aldous. With Fireman Fund Ins. Co., San Francisco, 1946—. sr. v.p., 1968—; dir. Am. Automobile Ins. Co., Nat. Surety Corp. Cal. Trustee Ins. Forum San Francisco, 1967-70. Served as officer USNR, 1943-46, 50-52. Mem. San Francisco Symphony Assn., San Francisco C. of C. Republican. Episcopalian. Clubs: University, Commonwealth, California Tennis (San Francisco); Belvedere (Cal.) Tennis. Contbg. author: Property and Casualty Handbook, 1960; The Practical Lawyer, 1962. Home: 36 Evergreen Dr Kentfield CA 94904 Office: 3333 California St San Francisco CA 94120

DUBAY, WILLIAM HENRY, author; b. Long Beach, Cal., Dec. 24, 1934; s. John Lewis and Viola (Gauger) DuB.; B.A., St. John's Sem., Camarillo, Cal., 1956; m. Mary Ellen Rochester Wall; children—Billy, Alison, Megan, Michael, Alfred. Ordained priest Roman Catholic Ch., 1960; asst. pastor Northridge, Cal., 1960-62, La Canada, Cal., 1962-63, Compton, Cal., 1963- 64, Anaheim, Cal., 1964-65; chaplain St. John's Hosp., Santa Monica, Cal., 1965-66, Synanon Found. Santa Monica, 1966—. Active Compton Welfare Planning Commn., 1963-64, Compton Human Relations Council, 1963- 64, also Synanon Found., Santa Monica, 1966-67. Active integration movement. Founder, Am. Fedn. Priests 1966-68. Author: The Human Church, 1966, also articles, lectures. Address: PO Box 26 Mountain Center CA 92361

DUBCEK, ALEXANDER, Czechoslovak politician; b. Uhrovec, Nov. 27, 1921; s. Stefan and Pavlina Dubcek; Ph.D. in Polit. Sci., Communist Party Coll., Moscow, 1958; ed. law faculty Comenius U., Bratislava; m. Anna Dubcek; children—Paul, Peter, Milan. Chief sec. regional com. Communist Party Slovakia, Banska Bystrica, 1953-55; chief sec. regional com. Communist Party Slovakia, Bratislava, 1958-60; mem. Presidium. also sec. Central Com. Communist Party Czechoslovaki, 1963—; 1st sec. central com. Communist Party Slovakia; 1962-68; 1st sec. central com. Communist Party Czechoslovakia, 1968—; chmn. central com. Slovak Nat. Front; dep. to Nat. Assembly, 1951-55, 60, 64—; to Slovak Nat. Council, 1964—; mem. exec. com. Presidium Central Com. Communist Party Czechoslovakia, 1968—; chmn. State Def. Council. 1969—, House of the People, 1969—. Decorated Order Feb. 25, 1948, 1949; recipient award for merits in constrn., 1958; Czechoslovak Peace prize, 1968. Address: care Central Com Communist Party Czechoslovakia Prague 1 nab Kyjevske brigady 12 Czechoslovakia*

DUBE, JEAN-EUDES, Canadian legislator; b. Matapedia, Que., Can., Nov. 6, 1926; s. J. Albert and Flore (Poirier) D.; student Gaspe (Que.) Coll., St. Joseph U., Memramcook, N.B., Ottawa U., Georgetown U.; B.C.L., U. N.B.; m. Noella Babin, June 25, 1956; children—Marie Flore Rachelle, Jean Francois. Alderman Campbellton City Council, 1959-63; mem. Canadian Ho. of Commons for Restigouche, N.B., 1962—; minister vets. affairs, 1968—. Pres. Canadian NATO Parliamentary Assn., N. Atlantic Assembly, 1967; Appointed Queen's Counsel, 1969. Home: 1694 Playfair Dr Ottawa Ontario Canada Office: Ho of Commons Ottawa Ontario Canada

DUBE, JOHN, lawyer; b. Montreal, Que., Can., July 14, 1899; s. Joseph Edmond and Marie Louise (Quintal) D.; B.L., B.S., Montreal U., 1920, B.C.L., 1923; licentiate in Civil Law, Paris U., 1924; postgrad. U. Oxford, 1925; m. Lucie Velutini, Nov. 22, 1950; 1 son, John Edmund. Came to U.S., 1926, naturalized, 1945. Admitted to Montreal bar, 1925, N.Y. bar, 1945; apptd. king's counsel, 1941, now Queen's counsel; Supreme Ct. U.S., U.S. Treasury Dept.; practiced in N.Y.C., 1926-32, 45- -, Paris, France, 1923-32, Nice, France, 1933-40; asso. Coudert Bros., 1926-32, Col. Cabot Ward, 1933-36. Past pres. Le Moulin Legumes Corp., Wilmington, Del.; past v.p. Bengue, Inc., Union City, N.J. Consul of Monaco, N.Y.C., 1949—, now consul gen.; dep. permanent observer for Monaco at UN, 1956-71, permanent observer, 1971—. Trustee Soc. Rehab. Facially Disfigured, Found. for Research in Medicine and Biology. Decorated officer Order of Grimaldi (Monaco). Mem. Union Interalliée (Paris), Assn. Bar City of N.Y., Am., Internat. bar assns., Am. Fgn. Law Assn., Am. Soc. Internat. Law, Soc. Fgn. Consuls, Société de Legislation Comparee, Confrerie des Chevaliers du Tastevin (comdr.). Clubs: Ardsley Country, Paris American. Home: 115 E 64th St New York City NY 10021 Office: 200 Park Av New York City NY 10017

DUBE, JOHN EDWARD, valve mfg. co. exec.; b. Vienna, Austria, Sept. 15, 1905; s. Otto S. and Stephanie (Shultham) D.; M.E., U. Cin., 1929; m. Leona A. Turner, June 15, 1939; children—John Ronald, Karen Linda. Exptl. engr. AC Spark Plug Co., 1929-33; devel. engr. Fulton Sylphon Co., 1933-38; with Alco Controls Corp., St. Louis, 1938—, v.p., gen. mgr., 1945-49, pres., 1949- 70, chmn. bd., 1970—, also dir.; v.p., dir. Quality Products Co., Clarksville, Tenn., 1959- 66, pres., 1966—; dir. Alco-Nobis Co., Cologne, W. Germany, Killebrew Engring. Co., St. Louis. Treas. Community Music Sch., St. Louis, 1958-60; pres., dir. John Burroughs Sch., St. Louis, 1950-59; bd. dirs. Met. YMCA, St. Louis, 1954- -, pres., 1962-63. Mem. Refrigeration Equipment Mfrs. Assn. (pres. 1952- 53), St. Louis C. of C. (bd. dirs. 1961-66), Air Conditioning and Refrigeration Inst. (adv. bd. 1953—), Am. Standards Assn. bd. dirs. 1959-62), Am. Soc. Heating, Refrigerating and Air Conditioning Engrs. (pres. 1964-65), Am. Soc. Automotive Engrs., Internat. Inst. Refrigeration (vice chmn. U.S. com. 1958-68), Newcomen Soc. Presbyn. Rotarian. Clubs: Bellerive Country, Clayton (St. Louis). Home: Route 2 Box 390 Chesterfield MO 63017 Office: PO Box 12700 St Louis MO 63141

DUBERMAN, MARTIN, historian; b. N.Y.C., Aug. 6, 1930; s. Joseph M. and Josephine (Baume) D.; B.A., Yale 1952; M.A. Harvard, 1953; Ph.D., 1957. Teaching fellow Harvard, 1955-57; instr. history Yale, 1957-61, Morse fellow, 1961-62; bicentennial preceptor (asst. prof.) Princeton, 1962-65, asso. prof., 1965-67, prof., 1967-71; Distinguished Service prof. Lehman Coll., City U. N.Y., 1971—. Mem. Am. Historical Assn., Phi Beta Kappa. Author: Charles Frances Adams, 1807-1886 (Bancroft prize 1962), 1961; In white America (Vernon Rice award, 1963- 64); James Russell Lowell (finalist Nat. Book award 1967), 1966; The Uncompleted Past, 1969. Editor, contbr. Antislavery Vanguard, 1965; contbr. Metaphors (play) to Collision Course, 1968; The Memory Bank (plays), 1970. Address: 112 W 13th St New York City NY 10011

DUBILIER, MARTIN HENRY, mfg. co. exec.; b. N.Y.C., Aug. 31, 1926; s. William Florence (Don) D.; B.S. in Elect. Engring., Princeton, 1950 M.B.A., Harvard, 1952; m. Mary Jane Jobson, Sept. 12, 1953; children—Michael, Patricia, William Frank. Partner, Radio Patents Co., 1955-60; pres., dir. Internat. Electric Corp., 1959-63; pres., chief exec. officer, dir. Kearney Nat. Inc., until 1971; exec. v.p. dir. Friden, Inc., 1964—; dir. Jobson Pub. Co., Decision Scis., Inc. Patentee metallurgy and mechanics. Home: 1 Ridgeway Rd Larchmont NY

DUBIN, ALVIN, chemist, educator; b. Russia, Jan. 23, 1914; s. Solomon and Fanny (Beilly) D.; came to U.S., 1923, naturalized, 1935; B.A. Bklyn. Coll., 1940, M.S., 1942; m. Gwennie Goldman, May 18, 1946 (dec. Oct. 1963). Chief chem endocrinology Beth-El Hosp., Bklyn., 1938-42, asst. dir. labs., 1942-47; chief biochemist Cook County Hosp. and Hektoen Inst., Chg., 1947-53, dir. biochemistry, 1953—; prof. clin. chemistry Cook County Grad. Sch. Medicine, Chgo., 1958—; asst. prof. dept. biochemistry U. Ill. Coll. Medicine, Chgo., 1960—; cons. clin chemistry Oak Forest (Ill.) Hosp., MacNeal Hosp., Berwyn, Ill.; cons. biol. div. Upjohn Pharm. Co., Kalamazoo. Chmn. Cook County Hosp. fund drive Combined Jewish Appeal. Diplomate Am. Bd. Bio Analysts, Mem. Am. Assn. Clin. Chemistry (pres. Chgo. 1955-57, chmn. 17th nat. meeting 1965), Soc. Exptl. Biology and Medicine, A.A.A.S., N.Y. Acad. Scis. Sigma Xi. Home: 6101 N Sheridan Rd Chicago IL 60626 Office: 707 S Wood St Chicago IL 60612

DUBIN, ROBERT, educator; b. Chgo., Mar. 19, 1916; s. Aaron Joseph and Gertrude (Rozett) D.; A.B., U. Chgo., 1936, A.M., 1940, Ph.D., 1947; m. Elisabeth Ruch, Jan. 16, 1937; children—Thomas Joseph (dec.), John Robert, Lucy Sarah, Amy Christina, George Ruch. Head labor relations and training sect. Chgo. Ordnance Dist., U. S. Army, 1940-43; research asso., asst. prof. indsl. relations, mgr. indsl. relations center U. Chgo., 1946-48; asso. prof. sociology U. Ill., 1948-52, prof. sociology and mgmt., 1952-54; prof. sociology, head dept., U. Ore., 1954- 58; research prof. sociology, 1958-69; prof. sociology and adminstrn. U. Cal., Irvine, 1969—; fellow Center for Advanced Study Behavioral Scis., 1956-57. Served from pvt. to capt. AUS., 1943-46, dept. chief labor br. Office Chief of Ordnance. Guggenheim fellow, 1963-64, Fulbright Research scholar, 1963-64, 68-69. Mem. Am. Sociol. Assn. (council 1964-66, exec. com. 1965-66), Indsl. Relations Research Assn. (dir. 1953-55), Soc. Gen. Systems Research, Sociol. Research Assn., Am. Assn. Univ. Profs. Author: (with F. H. Harbison) Patterns of Union-Management Relations, 1947; Human Relations in Administration, 1951, 3d edit., 1968; The World of Work, 1958; Working Union-Management Relations, 1958; (with others) Social Science Approaches to Business Behavior, 1962, Leadership and Productivity, 1965; Theory Building, 1969. Co-editor, contbr. Indsl. Conflict. 1954. Contbr. articles to profl. jours. Home: 2639 Bunya St Newport Beach CA 92660

DUBINSKY, DAVID, labor leader; b. Brest-Litovsk, Poland, Feb. 22, 1892; s. Zallel and Shaine (Wishingrad) D.; ed. Zionist and Konshtat schs., Poland and evening schs., N.Y.C.; LL.D. (hon.), Columbia, 1968; m. Emmal Goldberg, 1915; 1 dau., Jeannette. Came to U.S., 1911, naturalized, 1916. Baker's apprentice, Poland; active bakery worker's union and because of activities banished to Siberia at age of 16; returned to European Russia, then came to U.S.; learned cloak cutting trade; joined Local 10, Internat. Ladies Garment Workers Union, 1911, mgr.-sec., 1921-29; v.p. Internat. Ladies Garment Workers Union, 1922-29, gen. sec., treas., 1929-32, pres., 1932-65; v.p. AFL-CIO; v.p. and mem. exec. council A.F. of L., 1934-36, resigned, 1936, because of views on inds. unionism; rep. A.F. of L. to Governing Body Internat. Labor Office, Geneva, Switzerland, 1935; mem. Conf. on Workers Edn. called by Internat. Fed. Trade Unions, London, Eng., 1936, and Conf. Internat. Clothing Workers Fedn., 1936. Co-founder Am. Labor Party in State of N.Y., 1936, also presdl. elector for Am. Labor Party and Democratic Party, 1936; apptd. mem. Wage and Hour ladies' apparel industry coms., 1938-41, also mem. Spl. Wage and Hour P.R. Com., 1940; vice chmn. Am. Labor Conf. on Internat. Affairs; labor rep., Nat. Coat and Suit Indsl. Recovery Bd., 1942; founder, vice-chmn. Liberal Party, N.Y. State, 1944; mem. bd. dirs. Willkie Meml., 1945; A.F.L. rep. Mgmt. and Labor Conf., elected v.p. A.F.L. exec. council, 1945; A.F. L. cons., U.N. Econ. and Social Council, 1946; mem. Trade Union Adv. Com. on Internat. Labor Affairs of U.S. Dept. Labor; mem. bd. dirs. Am. Overseas Aid-U.N. Appeal for Children. Apptd. Apr. 1941, to War Dept. Bd. on claims for tax amortization of emergency defense facilities; bd. dirs. Nat. War Fund, Joint Distbn. Com., Greater N.Y.

Fund, F. D. Roosevelt Meml. Found.; mem. spl. com. on labor standards and social security apptd. by sec. of state. Founder Ams. for Democratic Action, 1947; mem. exec. com. of Citizens' Com. to Support the Marshall Plan, Workers Edn. Bur.; mem. 1948 Greater N.Y. for United Negro Coll. Fund, 1948; mem. Nat. Sponsors Com. of Am. Heart Assn., 1948. Home 201 W 16th St New York City NY 10011 Office: 1710 Broadway New York City NY 10019

DUBISCH, ROY, educator; b. Chgo., Feb. 5, 1917; s. Otto and Flora (Gossing) D.; B.S., U. Chgo., 1938, M.S., 1940, Ph.D., 1943; m. Joyce Marie Nielsen, Nov. 18, 1939; children—Jill Susanna, Russell, Ralph. Asst., Wilson Jr. Coll., Chgo., 1938-40; instr. Mont. State U., 1942-46; asst. prof., chmn. dept. Triple Cities Coll., Syracuse U., 1946-48; asso. prof. Fresno State Coll., 1948-55, prof., chmn. dept. math., 1955-61; prof. U. Wash., Seattle, 1961—; lectr. U. Cal. at Berkeley, 1959- 60. Faculty fellow Fund for Advancement Edn., 1951-52. Mem. Math. Assn. Am. (bd. govs.), Am. Math. Soc., Nat. Council Tchrs. Maths. (v.p.), Phi Beta Kappa, Sigma Xi. Author: Nature of Number, 1952; Trigonometry, 1955; Intermediate Algebra, 1960; The Teaching of Mathematics, 1963; Lattices to Logic, 1964; Introduction to Abstract Algebra, 1965. Editor: Mathematics Mag., 1964-69. Home: 19248 93d Pl W Edmonds WA 98020

DUBLIN, THOMAS DAVID, physician; b. N.Y. City, Jan. 18, 1912; s. Louis I. and Augusta (Salik) D.; A.B., Dartmouth Coll., 1932; M.D., Harvard, 1936; M. Pub. Health, Johns Hopkins, 1940, Dr. Pub. Health, 1941; m. Christina Macondald Carlyle, June 3, 1939; children—Sarah Carlyle, Barbara (Mrs. Clayton T. Koelb, Jr.). Intern Boston City Hosp., 2d Harvard Med. Service, 1936-38; instr. prev. medicine Johns Hopkins Med. Sch., 1940- 41; instr. preventive medicine and public health Albany Hosp., 1942; lectr. epidemiology DeLamar Inst. Pub. Health, Coll. Phys. and Surgs., Columbia, 1942-45; asso. prof., dept. preventive medicine and community health Long Island Coll. of Medicine, Brooklyn, 1942-43, prof. and exec. officer 1943-48; epidemiologist Kingston Ave. Hosp., Brooklyn, 1943-48; exec. dir. Nat. Health Council, 1948-53; med. cons. Nat. Found. for Infantile Paralysis, 1953-55; med. dir. USPHS, 1955—; med. dir. Community Services Programs, Office of Dir., Nat. Insts. Health, Bethesda, Md., 1955-60; chief epidemiology and biometry br. Nat. Inst. Arthritis and Metabolic Diseases, Bethesda, Md., 1960-66; research adviser, health service Office Tech. Cooperation and Research AID, 1966- 68; former dir. Office Health Manpower, U.S. Dept. Health, Edn. and Welfare. Member of expert advisory panel on Public health administration WHO, 1954—; mem. Nat. Adv. Com. Epidemiology and Biometry, 1956-60. Diplomate Nat Bd. Med. Examiners, Am. Bd. of Preventive Medicine (mem. bd. 1961—; vice. chmn. for gen. preventive medicine 1965—). F. Am. Public Health (mem. governing council, 1954-60; chmn. research policy committee, 1957-60), N.Y. Acad. of Med.; member A.M.A., A.A.A.S., Am. Epidemiol. Society, Assn. Tchrs. Preventive medicine (sec. 1944-48), Delta Omega. Home: 6907 Bradley Blvd Bethesda MD 20034

DUBOC, RAY B., ins. exec.; b. Brookings, S.D., Feb. 1889; s. Albert M. and Julia P. (Denison) D.; ed. pub. schs., Oskaloosa, Ia.; m. Fern Miller, Nov. 27, 1919. Pres. Western Ins. Securities Co. of Kansas City, 1925—, also chmn. bd.; chmn. bd. Western Fire Ins. Co., Western Casualty & Surety Co., Ft. Scott, Kan. Mason, Rotarian (pres. 1947-48). Clubs: Kansas City, Mission Hills Country, (Kansas City). Home: 1243 W 64th St Kansas City MO 64113 Office: 916 Walnut St Kansas City MO 64106

DUBOC, ROBERT MILLER, lawyer; b. Ft. Scott, Kan., Sept. 1, 1927; s. Ray Boardman and Fern (Miller) D.; A.B., U. Kan., 1950; LL.B., U. Mich., 1954; m. Nancy Woodruff, Mar. 30, 1951; children—Karen, Robert Miller, Susan, Ann, Carol. Admitted to Mo. Bar 1954, since practiced in Kansas City; former partner Swanson, Midgley, Jones, Blackmar & Eager; now pvt. practice; dir. Western Ins. Securities Co. Mem. Am. Bar Assn. Home: 601 W 55th St Kansas City MO 63113 Office: 828 Commerce Tower 922 Walnut St Kansas City MO 64105

DUBOFF, SAMUEL J., accountant; b. Bklyn., July 30, 1915; s. Jacob and Dora (Finkelstein) D.; B.B.A. cum laude, Coll. City N.Y., 1934; m. Elizabeth E. Epstein, July 20, 1941; children—Judith A., Robert S., David B. With Seidman & Seidman, C.P.A.'s, 1934-42; with S. D. Leidesdorf & Co., 1946—, partner, 1957—. Former mem. N.Y. State Bd. C.P.A. Examiners. Past Pres. Bd. Edn., Scarsdale. Trustee Am. Jewish Com., Westchester, Mem. Am. Inst. C.P.A.'s (council), N.Y. State Soc. C.P.A.'s (past v.p.; dir. and pres.) Beta Gamma Sigma. Clubs: Quaker Ridge Golf; Town (past pres.) (Scarsdale). Home: 20 Barry Rd Scarsdale NY 10583 Office: 125 Park Av New York City NY 10017

DUBOIS, ALLEN CORSON, investment banker; b. Clayton, N.J., May 6, 1903; s. Peter K. and Maria (Corson) DuB.; B.A., Lehigh U., 1925, LL.D., 1969; m. Roberta Bossard, Nov. 25, 1929 (dec. June 1953); children—Joan, Peter, Susan; m. 2d, Margaret Raymond, Feb. 6, 1960 (dec. 1968); m. 3d, Margaret M. Quayle, May 27, 1969. With Wertheim & Co., N.Y.C., 1938—, partner, 1945; pres. Peter and Maria DuBois Found. Trustee Lehigh U. Clubs: Gulfstream Golf; Country of Fla.; Ocean (Delray Beach, Fla.); Kirtland Gulf (Cleve.); Old Baldy (Saratoga, Wyo.). Home: 2665 N Ocean Blvd Delray Beach FL 33444 Office: 1 Chase Manhattan Plaza New York City NY 10005

DU BOIS, CORA, anthropologist, educator; b. N.Y.C., Oct. 26, 1903; d. Jean Jules Philip and Mattie (Schreiber) Du Bois; B.A., Barnard Coll., 1927; M.A., Columbia, 1928; Ph.D., U. Cal. at Berkeley, 1932; Sc.D., Wilson Coll., 1958; LL.D., Mills Coll., 1959; H.H.D. (hon.), Mt. Holyoke Coll., 1960; D.Sc. (hon.), Wheaton Coll., 1963. Research asso. anthropology U. Cal., 1932-35, NRC fellow, 1935-36; tchr. Hunter Coll., 1936-37; Social Sci. Research fellow Columbia, 1937-39; tchr. Sarah Lawrence Coll., 1939-42; br. chief OSS, also Dept. State, 1942-50; social sci. cons. WHO, UN, 1950-51; dir. research Inst. Internat. Edn., 1951-54; Zemurray-Stone prof. anthropology Harvard and Radcliffe Coll., 1954-69, prof. emeritus, 1969—: curator S. Asian Ethnology, Peabody Mus., Harvard, 1969—; vis. prof. U. Cal., 1948, Colo., 1954; Carnegie vis. prof. U. Hawaii, 1957. Fellow Center for Advanced Study Behavioral Scis., Palo Alto, Cal., 1958-59. Recipient exceptional civilian service award, U.S. Army 1946; Decorated Order of Crown of Thailand 3d class, 1949. Recipient Achievement award Am. Assn. U. Women, 1961. Mem. Assn. Asian Studies (pres. 1970-71), Am. Acad. Arts and Scis., Am. Anthropol. Assn. (pres. 1968-69), A.A.A.S. (sectional v.p. 1966-67), Phi Beta Kappa, Sigma Xi. Author: People of Alor, 1944; Social Forces in Southeast Asia, 1949; Foreign Students and Higher Education in the United States, 1956. Editor: Lowie's Selected Papers in Anthropology, 1960. Contbr. profl. jours. Field research in India, 1961—. Home: 20 Coolidge Hill Rd Cambridge MA 02138

DUBOIS, EDMUND LOUIS, army officer; b. Boston, Jan. 8, 1919; s. Bird Spencer and Pauline (Baldwin) DuB.; B.S. in Civil Engring., U. Ill., 1941; M.S. in Phys. Scis., U. Chgo., 1948; grad. Army War Coll., 1962; m. Ethel Raynor McDonald, Oct. 21, 1944; children—Edmund Louis, John William, Laurence McDonald, Diane Catherine, Geoffrey Baldwin. Commd. 2d lt. U.S. Army, 1941, advanced through grades to brig. gen., 1967; served in PTO, World War II; assigned Joint Chiefs Staff, 1945-46, 62-65, 68-70, Army Gen. Staff, 1955-58, armed forces spl. weapons project Sandia (N.M.) Base, 1952-55, SHAPE, 1958-61, Army Air Def., Seattle, 1965-67, Joint Task Force 2, Sandia Base, 1967-68; comdg. gen. 6th region ARADCOM, Ft. Baker, Cal., 1970—. Decorated Legion of Merit with 2 oak leaf clusters, Army Commendation medal with 2 oak leaf clusters. Mem. Delta Tau Delta. Club: Commonwealth (San Francisco). Address: Hdqrs 6th Region ARADCOM Fort Baker CA 94965

DUBOIS, JOSIAH ELLIS, Jr., lawyer; b. Camden, N.J., Oct. 21, 1912; s. Josiah Ellis and Amelia (Ayles) DuB.; A.B., U. Pa., 1931, LL.B., 1934; m. Dorothy Frances Clement, June 12, 1937; children—Robert Clement, Jeraldine Dale. Admitted to D.C. bar 1938, N.J. bar, 1940; law clk. gen. counsel's office U.S. Treasury Dept., Washington, 1936-38; gen. practice law, partner firm DuBois & DuBois, Camden, 1938-41; atty. gen. counsel's office Treasury Dept., 1940-43, chief counsel fgn. funds control div., 1943, asst. gen. counsel 1944, asst. to sec. treasury, 1944—; gen. counsel War Refugee Bd., 1944—; pvt. practice, Camden, 1946-59; partner firm DuBois, Maiale & Du Bois, 1959—; Mem. spl. mission Central Am., 1941, North Africa, 1942-43; accompanied sec. treasury to Eng., France on spl. mission for pres., 1944; mem. Allied Reparations Com., Moscow, 1945, U.S. delegation Berlin Conf., 1945; dep. chief counsel for War Crimes, charge I.G. Farben case, Nuremburg, Germany, 1947-48. Mem. Am., N.J. bar assns., Order of Coif. Club: Franklin Chess (Phila.). Author: The Devil's Chemists, 1952. Home: 58 Colonial Av Pitman NJ 08071 Office: 511 Cooper St Camden NJ 08108

DUBOIS, KENNETH PATRICK, pharmacologist, educator; b. Aberdeen, S.D., Aug. 9, 1917; s. Clarence C. and Mary (Cronin) DuB.; B.S., S.D. State Coll., 1939; M.S., Purdue U., 1940; Ph.D., U. Wis., 1943; m. Jere A. Deroin, Nov. 16, 1957; children—Elizabeth, Kenneth, Thomas. Mem. faculty U. Chgo., 1943—, prof. pharmacology, 1956—, dir. USAF Radiation and Toxicity Labs., 1953—. Cons. USPHS, 1956—, U.S. Army, 1960—; mem. NDRC, 1941-43, NRC-Nat. Acad. Sci. com. 1965—. Mem. A.M.A., Soc. Toxicology (past v.p.; Merit award 1971), Am. Soc. Pharmacology and Exptl. Therapeutics, Am. Chem. Soc., Soc. for Exptl. Biology and Medicine, Radiation Research Soc., A.A.A.S., Am. Indsl. Hygiene Assn., N.Y., Ill. acads. scis. Author: Textbook of Toxicology, 1959. Asso. editor Radiation Research, 1954-56; mng. editor Jour. Toxicology and Applied Pharmacology, 1960-64; field editor Toxicology, 1965-70, Drug Metabolism, 1970—; mem. editorial bd. Jour. Pharmacology and Exptl. Therapeutics, 1953-65. Contbr. articles profl. jours. Home: 1214 E 48th St Chicago IL 60615

DUBOIS, PHILIP HUNTER, psychologist; b. Newburgh, N.Y., July 8, 1903; s. Henry Reynolds and Hattie Aletha (Clough) DuB.; A.B., Union Coll., 1925; M.A., Columbia, 1929, Ph.D., 1932; m. Margaret Eloise Barcaly, Dec. 27, 1936; 1 dau., Margaret (Mrs. Richard W. Watson). Instr. English, Am. U., Beirut, Lebanon, 1925-28; instr. psychology Columbia, 1930-33; intern psychol. N.Y. State Psychiat. Inst. and Hosp., 1932-33; asst. prof. psychology Ida. State Coll., Pocatello, 1933-35; asst. prof., later asso. prof. and dir. bur. of tests and records, U. N.M., 1935-46; prof. Washington U., St. Louis, 1946—. Test technician, later supr., N.M. Merit System Council, 1940-42; psychol. cons. U.S. VA and dept. police, St. Louis, 1947—; cons. human resources research labs. Air Research and Devel. Command, 1951-54; mem. panel on personnel, com. on human resources Research and Devel. Bd., Dept. Def., 1952-54; expert Air Force Personnel and Tng. Center, 1954-57; mem. panel on personnel and tng. Office Asst. Sec. Def., research and devel., 1954-57; cons. Cross Cultural Research Project in Social Psychology, Cairo, Egypt, summer, 1954, USAF Sch. Aviation Medicine, 1955-58, U.S. Office Edn., 1963-67, University City (Mo.) Schs., 1963-66. Dir. Psychol. Assos., 1958—, Psychol. Corp., 1963—; chmn. ETS Invitational Conf. on Testing Problems, 1969. Aviation psychologist, USAAF, 1942-46, asst. dir. Psychol. Research Unit 2, 1943, chief psychol. sect. Med. and Psychol. Examining Unit 7, 1943-44, chief publs. unit, psychol. sect., Hdqrs. A.A.F. Training Command, 1944-46; lt. col., U.S. Air Force Reserve ret. Diplomate in counseling and guidance Am. Bd. of Examiners in Profl. Psychology, Mem. A.A.A.S., Am. (pres. mil. div. 1954-55, pres. div. evaluation and measurement 1968-69), Mo. (pres. 1954-55) psychol. assns., Psychometric Soc. (past sec., past pres.) Am. Assn. U. Profs., Soc. Multivariate Exptl. Psychology., Nat. Council Measurement in Edn., Phi Beta Kappa, Sigma Xi, Phi Kappa Phi, Psi Upsilon. Author: Multivariate Correlational Analysis, 1957; An Introduction to Psychological Statistics, 1965; A History of Psychological Testing, 1970. Editor, A.A.F. Aviation Psychology Report 2, The Classification Program, 1947. Co-editor: Research Strategies for Evaluating Training (monograph). Contbr. to profl. jours. Home: 94 Aberdeen Pl Clayton MO 63105 Office: Dept of Psychology Washington U St Louis MO 63110

DUBOIS, ROBERT LEE, educator; b. Omaha, Jan. 25, 1924; s. Lee and Lucille (Boyce) DuB.; B.S., U. Wash., 1949, M.S., 1950, Ph.D., 1954; m. Jeanette Gillespie, Sept. 2, 1947; 1 dau., Michelle J. Instr. geology U. Wash., 1952; prof. geology and geophysics U. Ariz., 1952-67; Kerr-McGee prof. geology and geophysics U. Okla., Norman, dir. earth scis. obs., 1967—. Cons. Jet Propulsion Lab., Nat. Park Service, industry; geologist U.S. Geol. Survey Sci. Collaboration; participant vis. scientist program Am. Geophys. Union, 1964—. Served with AUS, 1943-46. Registered profl. geologist, Ariz. Fellow Geol. Soc. Am.; mem. Am. Geophys. Union, Okla. Acad. Sci., A.A.A.S., Sigma Xi. Research paleo-archeomagnetism, archeomagnetic chrology. Home: 2313 Crestmont St Norman OK 73069

DUBOS, RENE JULES, bacteriologist; b. Saint Brice, France, Feb. 2O, 1901; s. Georges Alexandre and Adeline Madeleine (De Bloedt) D.; student Coll. Chaptal, Paris, 1915-19, Institut Nat. Agronomique, Paris, 1919-21; Ph.D., Rutgers U., 1927, Sc.D. (hon.), 1949; Sc.D. (hon.), Rochester U., 1941, Harvard, 1942, Paris U., 1950, New Sch. for Social Research (N.Y.C.), 1956, U. Rio de Janeiro, Dartmouth; M.D. (hon.), Liege U., 1947, Yeshiva U., 1961, U. Alta., 1963, U. Pa., 1965, U. Cal. 1965; hon. degree, Colby Coll., 1966, Carleton Coll., 1966, St. John's U., 1968, Queen's U., Can., 1969, U. Sherbrooke (Can.), 1969, Loyola U., 1970, Clark U., 1970, Kalamazoo Coll., 1971, Bard Coll., 1971, Marquette U., 1971; m. Marie Louise Bonnet, Mar. 23, 1934 (dec. 1942)); m. 2d, Letha Jean Porter, Oct. 16, 1946. Came to U.S., 1924, naturalized, 1938. Asst. editor staff Internat. Inst. Agr., Rome, Italy, 1922-24; research asst. soil microbiology, instr. bacteriology N.J. Exptl. Sta., Rutgers U., 1924-27; fellow Rockefeller Inst. Med. Research, 1927-28, asst., 1928-30, asso., 1930-38, asso. mem. 1938-41, mem., 1941-42, 1944-56; mem., prof. Rockefeller U., 1957—; George Fabyan prof. comparative pathology, prof. tropical medicine Harvard Med. Sch., 1942-44. Served in French Army, 1921-22. Recipient numerous awards, most recent being: Howard Taylor Ricketts award U. Chgo., 1958; Passano award A.M.A., 1960; Robert Kock Centennial award R. K. Inst., Berlin, Germany; Sci. Achievement award A.M.A., 1964; gold medal and prize Pacific Science Center, 1966; Pulitzer prize, 1969. Mem. Nat. Acad. Scis., Am. Philos. Soc., NRC. Club: Century Assn. Author books including: The Bacterial Cell, 1945; Bacterial and Mycotic Infections of Man, 1948; Louis Pasteur-Free Lance of Science, 1950; The White Plague-Tuberculosis, Man-Society, 1952; The Dreams of Reason, 1961; Pasteur and Modern Medicine, 1960. The Unseem World, 1962; The Torch of Life, 1962; Health and Disease, 1965; Man Adapting, 1965; So Human an Animal, 1968; Man, Medicine and Environment, 1968; Reason Awake: Science for Man, 1970. Home: Garrison NY 10524 Office: Rockefeller U 66th St and York Av New York City NY 10021

DUBOSE, CHARLES, architect; b. Savannah, Ga., Aug. 16, 1908; s. Charles S. and Augusta (Wood) DuB.; B.S. in Tech., 1929; M. Arch., U. Pa., 1930; diploma Fontainebleau (France), Sch. Fine Arts, summers 1928, 30; m. Ruth Bogaty, Mar. 26, 1937; 1 dau., Pamela Barry. Pvt. practice architecture, N.Y.C., 1936-48, Hartford, Conn., 1958—; instr. archtl. design U. Pa., 1931; partner Frank Grad & Sons, architects and engrs., Newark, 1948-56; pres. F. H. McGraw & Co. of Can., Montreal, Que., 1956-58; prin. works include Constitution Plaza, Hartford, Pratt and Whitney Aircraft, East Hartford, Conn., Monmouth Park Jockey Club, Oceanport, N.J., U.S. Air Force Bases in France. Trustee Fontainebleau Fine Arts and Music Schs., 1947—. Winner internat. competition for design nat. capitol, Ecuador, 1946; awards of Merit for design, A.I.A. and U.S. Urban Renewal Adminstrn., 1964; honor awards Conn. chpt. A.I.A. and Conn. Bldg. Congress. Fellow A.I.A.; mem. Archtl. League N.Y., Conn., Hartford socs. architects, Chi Phi, Tau Sigma Delta. Clubs: Hartford, Hartford Golf. Home: 134 Woodrow St West Hartford CT 06107 Office: 49 Woodland St Hartford CT 06105

DUBRIDGE, LEE ALVIN, physicist; b. Terre Haute, Ind., Sept. 21, 1901; s. Frederick Alvin and Elizebeth Rebecca (Browne) DuB.; A.B., Cornell Coll., Ia., 1922, Sc. D., 1940; A.M., U. Wis., 1924, Ph.D., 1926; Sc.D., Wesleyan U., 1946, Bklyn. Poly. 1946, Washington U., 1948, U.B.C. 1947, Occidental Coll., 1952, U. Md., 1955, Columbia, 1957, Ind. U., 1957, U. Wis., 1957, Pa. Mil. Coll., De Pauw U., 1962, Pomona Coll., Rockefeller Inst., Carnegie Inst. Tech., 1965, Syracuse U., 1969, Cath. U., 1969, Renssalaer Poly. Inst., 1970; LL.D., U. Cal., 1948, U. Rochester, 1953, U. So. Cal., 1957, Northwestern U., 1958, Loyola U. of Los Angeles, 1963, U. Notre Dame, 1967, Ill. Inst. Tech., 1967; L.H.D., Redlands U., 1958, U. Judaism, 1958; D.C.L., Union Coll., 1961; m. Doris May Koht, Sept. 1, 1925; children- -Barbara (Mrs. David MacLeod), Richard Alvin. Asst. in physics, U. Wis., 1922-25, instr., 1925-26; fellow NRC Cal. Inst. Tech., 1926-28; asst. prof. physics, Wash. U., St. Louis, 1928-33; asso. prof., 1933-34; prof. physics, chmn. dept. physics U. Rochester, 1934-46, dean faculty arts scis. 1938-41; investigator, Nat. Defense Research Com., dir. radiation lab., Mass. Inst. Tech., 1940-45; pres. Cal. Inst. Tech., 1946-69; sci. adviser to Pres. U.S., 1969-70. Trustee, Rand Corp., Santa Monica, Cal., 1948-61. Mem. gen. adv. com. A.E.C., 1946-52; Naval Research Adv. Com., 1945-51; Air Force Sci. Adv. Bd., 1945-49; mem. Pres.'s Communications Policy Bd., 1950-51; mem. Nat. Sci. Bd., 1950- 54, 58-64; chmn. sci. adv. com. Office Defense Moblzn., 1952-56; mem. Nat. Manpower Council, 1951-64; mem. Nat. Adv. Health Council, 1960-61; mem. distinguished civilan service awards bd. U.S. Civil Service Commn., 1963-65; chmn. Greater Los Angeles Urban Coalition, 1968—; mem. Pres.'s Air Quality Adv. Bd., 1968-69; bd. dirs. Nat. Merit Scholarship Corp., 1963-69, Nat. Ednl. TV, N.Y., 1962-69. Trustee Mellon Inst., 1958-67, Rockefeller Found., 1956-67, Nutrition Found., 1952-63, Carnegie Endowment Internat. Peace, 1951-57, Community TV So. Cal., Los Angeles, 1962-69, Henry E. Huntington Library and Art Gallery, 1962-69, Thomas Alva Edison Found., 1960-69. Recipient Research Corp. award, 1947; Medal for Merit (U.S.), 1948; King's Medal for Service (Gt. Britain), 1946; Benjamin Franklin fellow Royal Soc. Arts. Fellow Am. Phys. Soc. (pres. 1947); mem. Nat. Acad. Sci., Am. Philos. Soc., A.A.A.S., Phi Beta Kappa, Sigma Pi Sigma, Eta Kappa Nu, Sigma Xi, Tau Kappa Alpha, Tau Beta Pi. Presbyn. Author: Photoelectric Phenomena (with A.L. Hughes), 1932; New Theories of Photoelectric Effect, 1935; Introduction to Space, 1960. Contbr. numerous scientific and ednl. articles to mags. Home: 2355-3A Via Mariposa W Laguna Hills CA 92653

DUBRUL, ERNEST LLOYD, educator, biologist; b. N.Y.C., Apr. 5, 1909; s. Ernest Alfred and Berthe (Frechette) Du B.; student L.I.U., 1930-32, Columbia, 1933; D.D.S., N.Y.U., 1937; M.S., U. Ill., 1949, Ph.D., 1955; m. Florence Kirsch, July 9, 1956. Mem. staff N.Y. Hosp., 1939-42, Polyclinic Hosp., N.Y.C., 1940-42; mem. faculty U. Ill. Colls. Medicine and Dentistry, 1946—, prof. anatomy, 1959—, prof. oral anatomy, head dept., 1966—; vis. prof. summer inst. coll. tchrs. comparative anatomy Harvard, 1962, U. Wash., 1968. Served to maj. AUS, 1942-46. Fellow A.A.A.S.; mem. Chgo. Acad. Scis. (v.p.), N.Y. Acad. Scis., Am. Soc. Zoologists, Am. Assn. Phys. Anthropologists, Am. Assn. U. Profs., Sigma Xi. Author: (with H. Sicher) The Adaptive Chin, 1954; Evolution of the Speech Apparatus, 1958; (with H. Sicher) Oral Anatomy, 1970; also numerous articles. Home: 624 Fullerton Pky Chicago IL 60614

DUBRUL, STEPHEN MCKENZIE, Jr. investment banker; b. Detroit, Mar. 18, 1929; s. Stephen McKenzie and Nan (Corcoran) DuB.; B.A. in Econs.; U. Mich., 1950; M.B.A., Harvard, 1956; m. Antonia Paepcke, June 22, 1957; 1 son, Nicholas P. With CIA, Washington, 1950-52; asso. Lehman Bros., N.Y.C., 1956-60; partner, 1961- -; dir. RCA Corp., Continental Can Corp.; May Dept. Stores, St. Louis, Jewel Cos., Inc. Mem., pres. U.S. Consumer Adv. Council, 1962-64. Bd. dirs., treas. Vis. Nurse Service N.Y. Served with AUS, 1952-54. Clubs: Links, River (N.Y.C.): Union (Cleve.); Maidstone (East Hampton, N.Y.). Home: 171 73d St New York City NY 10021 Office: 1 William St New York City NY 10004

DUBS, ADOLPH, fgn. service officer; b. Ill., Aug. 4, 1920; B.A., Beloit Coll., 1942; student Georgetown U., 1946-48; m.; 1 daughter, Lindsay Jane. Asst. to dir. tng. Navy Sch., 1948- 49; assigned Dept. State, 1949-50; resident officer, Frankfurt, Germany, 1950-52; 2d sec., vice consul, Monrovia, Liberia, 1952-54; 2d sec., vice consul. Ottawa, Can., 1954-55, consul, 2d sec., 1955-57; Russian lang. area tng. Fgn. Service Inst., 1957-58, Harvard, 1958; internat. relations officer, Dept. State, 1959-61; 1st sec., consul Am. Embassy, Moscow, USSR, 1961; assigned Nat. War Coll., 1963-64; chief polit. sect. Am. embassy, Belgrade, Yugoslavia, 1964-65 counselor of embassy for polit. affairs, 1965-68; country dir. Soviet Union affairs State Dept., Washington, 1968—. Chmn. Internat. Sch. Bd. of Belgrade. Served to lt. (s.g.) USNR 1942-46. Home: 5221 Duvall Dr Bethesda MD 20034 Office: Dept State Washington DC 20525

DUBUFFET, JEAN, French painter; b. LeHavre, France, July 31, 1901; s. George S. and Jeanne (Paillette) D.; studies art Ecole des beaux-arts, Le Havre; m. Paulette Bret, Feb. 25, 1927; 1 dau.,; m. 2d, Lili Dubuffet. Wholesale wine mcht., Paris, 1930-39, 40-46; painter, 1931-34, 1942—; exhibited Galerie Rene Drouin, Paris, 1944, Pierre Matisse, Cordier-Warren galleries, Mus. Modern Art, N.Y.C.; executed murals Vue de Paris, Grand Paysage, 1945-46; exhibited statuettes Galerie Rive Gauche, 1954; retrospective exhbn. Musée des arts decoratits, Paris, 1961. Princ. paintings include: Mirobolus, Macadam et Cie, Sols et terrains, Hautes Ptes, Corps de dames, la Vie de famille, Paysages mentaux, Tables pay sagées, Pierres philosophiques, Texturologies. Address: 51 rue de Verheuil Paris 7e France*

DUBUISSON, ANDRE CELESTIN MARIE GHISLAIN, elec. machinery co. exec.; b. Dampremy, Belgium, Sept. 21, 1912; s. Georges and Elise (Gillion) D.; Ingénieur civil électricien, Université Catholique de Louvain, 1936, Ingénieur civil mécanicien, 1937; m.

Lucie Devuyst, Oct. 20, 1940; children—Etienne, Philippe, Jean, Francoise (Mrs. Marc Van Ossel). Engr., ACEC Charleroi, 1940-50; asst. to dir. Société Générale de Belgique and mng. dir. SABCA, 1950-62; counsellor S.G.B., 1962, dir., 1965; pres. Ateliers De Constructions Electriques de Charleroi, 1970—; chmn. Fabrique Nationale Herstal, SYBETRA, Brugeoise et Nivelles, air products; dir. Clark Equipment Cy. Chmn. Fonds Léon A. Bekaert; vice chmn. Assn. des Dirigeants et Cadres Chrétiens. Club: Royal Golf Tervueren. Home: 1 Clos du Taillis Brussels Belgium 1150 Office: 3 Montagne du Parc Brussels Belgium 1000

DUCAYET, EDWIN JOSEPH, helicopter mfr.; b. Newton Mass., May 18, 1908; s. Kirby S. and Alice (Sharpe) D.; B.S., Mass. Inst. Tech., 1931; m. Elsie Lobner, Aug. 20, 1938; children—Edwin Joseph, Alice. Contracts mgr. Curtiss-Wright Corp., 1931-50; v.p. Bell Helicopter Corp., Ft. Worth, 1950-60, pres., 1960—; adv. dir. First Nat. Bank of Ft. Worth. Mem. nat. citizens com. United Community Campaigns Am. Bd. dirs. Casa Manana Musicals, Ft. Worth, 1962—, Tex. Christian U. Research Found.; bd. govs. Ft. Worth Community Theatre, 1962—, Ft. Worth's Progress, 1962—. Mem. Am. Helicopter Soc., Assn. U.S. Army (adv. bd. dirs.); Nat. Aero. Assn., Army Aviation Assn. Am., Navy League U.S., Ft. Worth Airpower Council, Am. Ordnance Assn. Home: 3471 Sagecrest Fort Worth TX 76109 Office: P O Box 482 Fort Worth TX 76101

DUCE, LEONARD ARTHUR, educator; b. Princeton, Ont., Can., May 26, 1909; s. Richard Robinson and Mary Alice (Hey) D.; A.B., McMaster U., 1928, B.Th., 1930, B.D., 1931; S.T.M., Andover Newton Theol. Sem., 1937; Ph.D., Yale, 1946; m. Irma Harriet Gynn, Aug. 7, 1933; children—Robert Arthur, David Alan (dec.). Ordained to ministry Baptist Ch., 1931; pastor, Midlaand, Ont., Can., 1931-36; asst. pastor First Ch., Needham, Mass., 1936-37; pastor Montowese Ch., North Haven, Conn., 1938-42, Chandler, Mo., 1945- 47; prof. hist. theology Central Bapt. Theol. Sem., 1943-45; prof. philosophy William Jewell Coll., 1942-49, chmn. dept. philosophy, 1947- 49, dean coll., 1945-49; prof. philosophy and chmn. dept. Baylor U., Waco, Tex., 1949-60, asst. dean, 1949-55, asso. dean Grad. Sch., 1955- 56, dean, 1956-60; dean Grad. School, Trinity U., 1960—; vis. prof., administrv. cons. Hong Kong Bapt. Coll., 1958-59; vis. lectr. theology U. So. Cal.; summer 1946; instr. aerial navigation and naval history Naval Flight Sch., William Jewell Coll., 1942-44. Commr. San Antonio Housing Authority, 1961-68. Chmn. orgn. and extension com., Waco dist. Boy Scouts Am., 1950; chmn. Waco Social Welfare Council, 1957. Bd. dirs. Goodwill Industries of San Antonio, Ecumenical Center Religion and Health, Tex. Council Crime and Delinquency. Mem. A.A.A.S., Texas Assn. Grad. Schs. (pres. 1960-61), Vis. Tchrs. Assn. Tex. (chmn. adv. council), Am. Studies Assn. Tex. (pres. 1963-64), Am. Philos. Assn., Southwestern Philos. Conf. (pres. 1963), Tex. Social Welfare Assn. (pres. 1961-63), Nat. Assn. Housing and Redevel. Ofcls., N.E.A. (Dept. Higher Edn.), Am. Assn. U. Profs., Am. Conf. Acad. Deans, Beta Beta Beta. Rotarian. Contbr. articles to religious, social work, edn., hosp. administrn. and other jours. Home: 130 Oakmont Ct San Antonio TX 78212

DUCHIN, PETER OELRICHS, musician; b. N.Y.C. July 28, 1937; s. Edwin Frank and Marjorie (Oelrichs) D.; grad. Hotchkiss Sch., 1954; B.A., Yale, 1958; student polit. scis. and music conservatory, Paris, France, 1957; m. Cheray Zauderer, June 22, 1964; children—Jason Edwin, Courtnay Oelrichs; Colin Z., Malcolm. Pres. of Peter Duchin Orchs.; 1963—. Bd. dirs. Greater N.Y. councils Boy Scouts Am. Served with AUS, 1958-60. Clubs: Yale, Lambs (N.Y.C.); Racquet and Tennis. Office: 400 Madison Av New York City NY 10017

DUCK, FRANCES, librarian; b. Middletown, N.Y., July 14, 1903; d. Lester Philip and Florine (Horton) Duck; student Washington Square Coll., N.Y. U., 1925-29; certificate Grad. Library Sch., U. Wis., 1938. First asst. circulation dept. Free Pub. Library, East Orange, N.J., 1931-41; librarian Milburn (N.J.) Pub. Library, 1941-46, Stevens Inst. Tech., Hoboken, N.J., 1946-68; curator spl. collections; asso. librarian S.C. Williams Library, Stevens Inst. Tech., Hoboken, 1968—. Mem. A.L.A. Met., N.J. library assns. Home: Colonial House Castle Point Hoboken NJ 07030 Office: Stevens Inst of Technology Castle Point Hoboken NJ 07030

DUCKETT, JAMES WILLIAM, coll. pres.; b. Greenwood, S.C., July 8, 1911; s. James William and Eva (Hattaway) D.; B.S., The Citadel, 1932; M.S. in Chemistry, U. Ga., 1934; Ph.D., U. N.C., 1941; m. Gertrude Elizabeth Hass, Dec. 26, 1936; children—Elizabeth Eva (Mrs. Thomas J. Krilowicz), Gertrude Hass (Mrs. John E. Reeves), James William. Faculty The Citadel, 1934—, prof. organic chemistry, 1946-54, registrar, 1954-62, administrv. dean, 1962-63, dean of coll., 1963-68, v. p., 1968-70, pres., 1970. commn. on colls. So. Assn. of Colls. and Schs.; chem. biol. and radiol. adv. council Dept. of Def. Served with Chem. Corps, AUS, 1941-46. Decorated Legion of Merit; Commendation ribbon. Mem. Am. Chem. Soc., S.C. Acad. Sci., Greater Charleston C. of C., Sigma Xi, Pi Mu Epsilon. Lion. Spl. research syntheses N1-isocyclic sulfa ilamides, resene in pinus carrebae. Home: 1-A The Citadel Charleston SC 29409

DUCKETT, JOHN WARNER, surgeon, educator; b. Florence, Ala., Aug. 2, 1901; s. John Davis and Annie (Warner) D.; B.A., U. Tex., 1922; M.D., Johns Hopkins, 1926; m. Carolyn Knorr, Oct. 25, 1930; children—Ann (Mrs. Edward C. Reed), John Warner. Intern Johns Hopkins Hosp., 1926-28; with gen. surgery dept. Boston Children's Hosp., 1928-29; resident in surgery Dallas Med. and Surg. Clinic, 1930-31, staff, 1931-53; pvt. practice, Dallas, 1953—; mem. surg. staff Baylor U. Med. Center, 1930, Tex. Childrens Med. Center, 1945, Gaston Episcopal Hosp., 1950; instr. to asso. prof. clin. surgery Southwestern Med. Sch., 1930-49; asso. prof. clin. surgery U. Tex. Southwestern Med. Sch., 1949-60, prof. clin. surgery, 1960—; staff Presbyn. Hosp.; Morton Cancer and Research Hosp. Highland Park Ind. Sch. Dist., 1936-42. Diplomate Am. Bd. Surgery. Fellow A.C.S., Tex. Surg. Soc., So. Surg. Assn., Dallas Heart Assn.; mem. Tex., Dallas County med. socs., A.M.A., Dallas So. Clin. Soc., Phi Beta Kappa, Alpha Omega Alpha. Contbr. articles to sci. jours. Home: 3529 Caruth St Dallas TX 75225 Office: 1004 N Washington St Dallas TX 75204

DUCKETT, TORAL, utility co. exec.; b. 1906; married. With Central Telephone & Utilities Corp., 1928—, v.p., 1958-62, exec. v.p., gen. mgr., 1962—, also dir.; dir. subsidiaries. Address: 7410 Old Post Rd Lincoln NB 68520

DUCKLES, VINCENT HARRIS, librarian, musicologist; b. Boston, Sept. 21, 1913; s. Frederick Monroe and Harriet (Harris) D.; A.B., U. Cal. at Berkeley, 1936, Ph.D., 1953; M.A., Columbia, 1937, Ed.D., 1944; m. Madeline Taylor, June 10, 1937; children—Lawrence, Christopher, Lee, Peter, Jeremy. Pub. sch. music tchr., 1938-44; head music library U. Cal. at Berkeley, 1947—, mem. faculty, 1951—, prof. music, 1960—; spl. research 17th century English song. Fulbright Sr. Research fellow, U. Cambridge (Eng.), 1950-51, U. Göttingen (Germany) 1957-58; grantee Am. Council Learned Socs., 1964-65. Mem. Music Library Assn. (pres. 1961-62), Am. Musicol. Soc. (exec. com. 1963-66). Author: Music Reference and Research Materials, 1964; (with Minnie Elmer) Thematic Catalog of MS Collection of Italian Instrumental Music in the U. of Calif. Music Library, 1963. Home: 51 Eucalyptus Path Berkeley CA 94705

DUCKWORTH, FRANK AUSTIN, pharm. co. exec., lawyer; b. Quitman, Ga., Sept. 27, 1921; s. Frank and Cora (Phillips) D.; B.S. in Pharmacy, U. Fla., 1942, J.D., 1948; LL.M., N.Y.U., 1954; m. Katherine Alexander, Aug. 30, 1946; children—John Marvin, Katherine R. Admitted to Fla. bar, 1948, N.Y. bar, 1957; practice law, Jacksonville, Fla., 1948; asst. prof. U. Fla., 1949-53; with Pfizer Inc., N.Y.C., 1954—, sec., asso. gen. counsel, 1969—. Served with USAF, 1943-45. Mem. Am., Fla., N.Y. State bar assns. Home: 81 Salisbury Av Garden City NY 11530 Office: 235 E 42d St New York City NY 10017

DUCKWORTH, GEORGE ECKEL, educator; b. Little York, N.J., Feb. 13, 1903; s. Edwin James and Eva (Eckel) D.; A.B., Princeton, 1924, A.M., 1926, Ph.D., 1931; m. Dorothy Elwood Atkin, July 8, 1929; children—Dorothy Ann (Mrs. Donald L. Brown), Thomas Atkin. Instr. classics, Princeton, 1924- 25, U. Neb., 1926-28; faculty Princeton 1929—, acting chmn. classics dept., 1943-46, Giger prof. classics; 1946-71; dir. summer session, sch. classical studies Am. Acad. in Rome, 1952-55; vis. prof. classics Harvard, 1955-56. Trustee Am. Acad. in Rome, 1948-59. Guggenheim fellow, 1957-58. Mem. Archaeol. Inst. Am., Classical Assn. Atlantic States, Am. Philol. Assn. (pres. 1956), Phi Beta Kappa. Author books including: The Nature of Roman Comedy, 1952; Structural Patterns and Proportions in Vergil's Aeneid, 1962; Vergil and Classical Hexameter Poetry, 1969. Contbr. to ednl. jours. Home: 25 Haslet Av Princeton NJ 08540

DUCKWORTH, KENTON M., govt. ofcl.; b. Mt. Olive, Miss., July 2, 1917; s. Cooper E. and Heneritta (Barnes) D.; grad. Soule Bus. Coll., 1936; B.C.S., Benjamin Franklin U., 1940, M.C.S., 1942; m. Ruth L. Parrish (dec. Mar. 1958); children—Kenton M., Thomas C.; m. 2d, Maxine M. Manley, 1960; stepchildren—Leslie (Mrs. Richelsen), Susan Jane Manley. Cost auditor Gen. Accounting Office, 1936-46; administrv. analyst USPHS, 1946; auditor, accountant CAA, 1946-51, NPA, 1951-53; with Agy. Internat. Devel., Dept. State, 1953—, exec. officer, 1954-57, sr. mgmt. analyst, 1958-59, spl. asst. to sec. state for administrn., 1958, asst. chief personnel operations div., 1959-61, chief Overseas Employment br. Office Personnel, 1962-64, chief performance evaluation br., 1964-65, spl. asst. for mgmt. and adminstrn. Office Material Resource, 1965-67; dir. mgmt. staff Office War on Hunger, 1967-69, chief spl. operations br. Office of Personnel and Manpower, 1969—. Served with inf. AUS, 1944-46. Mason. Home: 3132 Holmes Run Rd Falls Church VA 22042 Office: 1601 N Kent St Arlington VA 22209

DUCKWORTH, T.A., ins. co. exec.; b. Albany, Mo., Mar. 26, 1912; s. Thomas Alexander and Sally (Edwards) D.; student Central Coll., Fayette, Mo., 1930-33; LL.B., U. Mo., 1936; m. Edwina Nelson, July 12, 1941; children—Sally (Mrs. David P. Hansen), Celeste Nelson (Mrs. James Natwick), Jane Chilton. With Employers Ins. of Wausau (Wis.); 1936—, sec., 1957-60, sr. v.p., sec., 1960—, Mem. Gov. Wis. Health Policy and Program Council; chmn. adv. council Wis. Comprehensive Health Planning; bd. dirs., exec. com. Wis. Tb and Respiratory Disease Assn.-Nat. Tb and Respiratory Disease Assn.; adv. com. Wis. Found. Ind. Colls.; pres. Wis. Regional Med. Program; trustee Lawrence Univ. Mem. Wis., Mo. bars, A.M.A. (adv. com. on health care Am. people), Delta Theta Phi, Phi Kappa Delta. Presbyn. (elder). Mason (Shriner), Rotarian. Home: 918 McIndoe St Wausau WI 54401 Office: 2000 Westwood Dr Wausau WI 54401

DUCKWORTH, WINSTON HOWARD, ceramic engr.; b. Greenfield, O., Oct. 15, 1918; s. Benton Raymond and Carrie Lois (Schrock) D.; B.Chem. Engring., Ohio State U., 1940, M.S., 1941; m. Clara Elizabeth Ayres, Dec. 15, 1941; children—Winston, Christopher. With Battelle Meml. Inst., Columbus, O., 1946—, research engr., 1946-48, asst. chief, ceramic research, 1948-52, chief, ceramic research, 1952-66, fellow, materials dept., 1966—, dir. Def. Ceramic Information Center, 1967—. Served with AUS, 1941-46. Fellow Am. Ceramic Soc. (trustee 1968—); mem. Nat. Inst. Ceramic Engrs. (pres. 1964), Canadian Ceramic Soc., A.A.A.S., Ohio Acad. Sci. Author: Engineering Properties of Ceramics, also numerous articles. Home: 63 Brevoort Rd Columbus OH 43214 Office: 505 King Av Columbus OH 43201

DUCLOS, ROBERT MARCEL, grain export co. exec.; b. Paris, France, Apt. 21, 1915; s. Marcel Henri and Julienne (Dossunet) D.; student Ecole de Physique et Chimie Industrielles, Paris, 1933; m. Maria Mercedes Mulvany, Feb. 22, 1964; children by prev. marriage—Jean-Claude, Patrice, Yves de Preville, Francois de Preville. Came to U.S., 1963. With Louis Dreyfus & Cie, Paris, 1938-58; pres. Canadian Louis Dreyfus, Montreal, 1958-66, Louis Dreyfus Corp., N.Y.C., 1963-69; treas. ATA ETS Walon SA, Paris, France, 1970—.

DUCOFF, HOWARD S., biologist, educator; b. N.Y.C., May 5, 1923; s. Dave and Tillie (Machinist) D.; B.S., City Coll. N.Y., 1942; Ph.D. in Physiology, U. Chgo., 1953; m. Rose Hirsch, Aug. 25, 1946; childrenSandra, Barbara, Paul J., Laura. With Argonne (Ill.) Nat. Lab., 1946-63, asso. scientist, 1951-57, cons., 1957-63; faculty U. Ill., Urbana, 1957—, prof. physiology and biophysics, 1965—. USPHS spl. fellow dept. zoology U. Cambridge (Eng.), 1964-65. Served with AUS, 1943-46. Mem. Am. Soc. Cell. Biology, Am. Soc. Zoologists, Radiation Research Soc., Soc. Gen Physiologists, Soc. Protozoologists, Sigma Xi. Editor: (with C. F. Ehret) Mitogenesis, 1959. Author articles. Home: 1516 W Charles St Champaign IL 61820 Office: Burrill Hall Urbana IL 61801

DUCOFFE, ARNOLD L., educator; b. Montreal, Que., Can., Mar. 22, 1921; s. Jack A. and Rose (Shapiro) D.; B.S., Ga. Inst. Tech., 1943, M.S., 1947; Ph.D., U. Mich., 1951; m. Polly Lou Rich, May 31, 1961; children—Michael, Peter, Patrice (Mrs. Lee B. Plant), Rich, Keith, Jack. Aero. engr. Chance Vought Aircraft Co., Stratford, Conn., 1943-44; instr. Ga. Inst. Tech., 1945-46, asst. prof., 1946-48, asso. prof., 1951-56, prof., 1957—, dir. aerospace engring., 1963—. Sr. v.p., dir. Unitron Internat. Systems, Inc., Hayward, Cal.; dir. Universal Co., Ltd., Montreal, Rich's, Inc., Atlanta; cons. Sandia Corp., Albuquerque. Chmn. Cub Scouts, 1953-54; adviser Atlanta High Schs., 1960—. Dist rep. Republican Party, 1964. Ga. Inst. Tech. Found. fellow, 1948-51. Mem. Am. Inst. Aeros. and Astronautics (past sect. chmn.), N.Y. Acad. Sci., A.A.A.S., A.A.S., Am. Soc. Engring. Edn., Ga. Inst. Tech. Nat. Alumni Assn. (trustee), Ga. Edn. Assn., Sigma Xi, Phi Kappa Phi, Sigma Gamma Tau. Contbr. articles profl. jours. Home: 3544 Paces Ferry Rd NW Atlanta GA 30327

DUCOMMUN, CHARLES EMIL, business exec.; b. Los Angeles, Apr. 27, 1913; s. Emil C. and Bescelia (Shemwell) D.; A.B., Stanford, 1935; M.B.A. with distinction, Harvard, 1942; m. Palmer Gross, June 15, 1949; children—Robert Constant, Electra Bradford. With Ducommun Inc. (formerly Ducommun Metals & Supply Co.), Los Angeles, 1936—, dir., 1938—, sec., 1938-46, treas., 1946, v.p., treas., 1946-50, pres., 1950—; dir. Ducommun Realty Co., 1938-70, v.p., 1947-70; dir. Farmers & Merchants Nat. Bank of Los Angeles until merger 1957 with Security Pacific Nat. Bank, now dir.; dir. Pacific Telephone and Telegraph Co., Dillingham Corp.; adv. dir. Investment Co. Am. mem. Central City Com.; trustee Com. for Econ. Devel. Mem. of Rep. Nat. Finance Com., 1953-54; chmn. Rep. Finance Com. of Cal., 1953-54; del. Rep. Nat. Conv., 1960, 68; mem. Rep. State Central Com., 1953-56, 64-69. Trustee Los Angeles County Mus. Arts., So. Cal. Area Bldg. Funds; chmn. Stanford Cabinet, 1965-71; chmn. Invest-in-Am., 1969, now dir.; past chmn.; now dir. Los Angeles Civic Light Opera Assn.; trustee Claremont Men's Coll.; trustee Stanford U., 1961-71, v.p. 1964-70. Served as lt., aide to chief staff U.S. Fleet, USNR, 1942-46. Mem. Los Angeles C. of C. (chmn. fed. affairs com., pres. 1957, treas. 1958, dir. 1952-61), Harvard Bus. Sch. Alumni (exec. council 1953-57), Navy League U.S. (chpt. dir. 1955-60), Stanford Asso., Harvard Bus. Sch. (mem. overseers vis. com. 1962-68, 70—), Delta Kappa Epsilon. Club: Lincoln (pres. 1969, bd. govs.) Office: 612 S Flower St Los Angeles CA 90017

DUCREST, WILLIS FRANCIS, musician, educator; b. St. Martinville, La., Dec. 13, 1910; s. Frank Martin and Anna (Mouton) D.; Mus.B., La. State U., 1932, Mus.M., 1933; postgrad. Ohio State U., 1944, Ind. U., 1950; m. Grace Simons, Dec. 23, 1948 children—Stephen, Frank, Ted. Instr. voice and opera, dir. women's chorus La. State U., 1933-37; asst. prof. voice, dir. women's glee club Okla. Coll. for Women, 1937-40; asso. prof. music U. Southwestern La., 1940-45, prof., head dept., 1945-; choral arranger numerous publs. G. Schirmer, Inc., N.Y.C., 1936-60; recitalist, opera and oratorio singer, choral condr. Mem. Gov.'s Adv. Bd. Culture and Performing Arts, 1964. Bd. dirs. La. Council for Music and Performing Arts. Served with USNR, 1943- 45. Mem. Nat. Assn. Tchrs. Singing (state chmn. 1952-54), Music Tchrs. Nat. Assn. (hon. life mem.; div. pres. 1959-61, nat. pres. 1965-69), La. Music Educators Assn. (state festival chmn. 1948—) La. Music Tchrs. Assn. (hon. life mem.; state pres. 1955-57, 57-59), Nat. Music Council, Phi Mu Alpha Sinfonia (hon life mem.) Phi Kappa Phi. Rotarian (bd. dirs. 1962-65). Contbr. articles to profl. jours. Home: 103 Tackaberry Rd Lafayette LA 70501

DUDA, KAREL, diplomat of Czechoslovakia; b. May 31, 1926; s. Karel and Marie Duda; ed. Charles U., Prague; m. Danuse Bares, Oct. 25, 1952; children—Jitka, Alena, Karel. With Ministry of Fgn. Affairs, 1954—; 1st sec. embassy, Washington 1956-59; A.E. and P. from Czechoslovakia to U.S., 1963-69; with Ministry of Finance, 1949-54. Address: Embassy of Czechoslovakia to US 3900 Linneau Av NW Washington DC 20008

DUDAN, PETER, banker; b. Paterson, N.J., Mar. 30, 1920; s. Michael and Mary (Tuchty) D.; grad. Phillips Acad., 1939; A.B., Amherst Coll., 1943; postgrad. Rutgers U., 1956-58; m. Jane Louise Fairchild, Apr. 10, 1948; children—Sandra (Mrs. Alfred T. Mahan IV), William Wade, Noel, Donald Michael. Asst. to div. sales mgr. U.S. Gypsum Co., Chgo., 1948-50; with Marine Midland Bank of Southeastern N.Y., Nyack, 1950—, chmn. bd., chief exec. officer, 1971—; dir. Marine Midland Municipals Co., Buffalo; exec. council Marine Midland Banks, Inc., Buffalo. Dir., v.p. Rockland County (N.Y.) Indsl. Devel. Com., 1962-67; mem. legislative com. Group VI, N.Y. State Bankers, 1968-71, nominating com., 1967—; dir., exec. com. Mid-Hudson Patterns for Progress, 1970—; chmn. Statewide Parks Adv. Com., 1971; mem. Palisades Interstate Park Commn., 1971; mem. Nyack Action Council, 1965-71. Trustee, Nyack Hosp.; mem. exec. com. Rockland County YMCA, bd. dirs. 1965-69. Served to lt. USNR, 1943-46. Mem. Rockland County Assn. (dir., v.p. 1967-71), Nyack C. of C., Psi Upsilon. Republican. Episcopalian. Rotarian (pres. Nyack 1969). Club: Rockland (N.Y.) Country. Home: 100 N Greenbush Rd West Nyack NY 10994 Office: Marine Midland Bank of Southeastern N Y 17 S Broadway Nyack NY 10960

DUDDEN, ARTHUR POWER, educator, historian; b. Cleve., Oct. 26, 1921; s. Arthur Clifford and Kathleen (Bray) D.; A.B., Wayne State U., 1942; A.M., U. Mich., 1947, Ph.D., 1950; m. Adrianne Churchill Onderdonk, June 5, 1965; 1 dau., Alexis B.; children by previous marriage—Kathleen (Mrs. James S. Andrasick), Candace L. (Mrs. Thomas Klocek). Faculty Bryn Mawr Coll., 1950—, prof. history, 1965—; instr. coll. City N.Y., summer 1950; vis. asst. prof. Am. civilization U. Pa., 1953-54, ednl. coordinator spl. program Am. civilization, 1956, faculty Inst. Humanistic Studies for Execs., 1953-59, vis. asso. prof. history, summers 1958, 62-65, vis. prof. history, 1965-68; vis. asso. prof. Princeton, 1958-59, Haverford Coll., 1962-63; vis. prof. Trinity Coll., summer 1965; cons. Peace Corps, 1962-66. Served with USNR, 1942- 45. Sr. Fulbright scholar, Denmark, 1959-60. Fellow Am. Studies Assn. (sec.-treas. 1957-59, pres., 1960-61, treas., 1968, Exec. sec. 1969; mem. Am. Hist. Assn., Orgn. Am. Historians (local arrangements chmn. Phila. 1969), Am. Studies Assn. Assn., Am. Assn. U. Profs. Author: Teachers Manual to the American Republic, vols. I and II, 1959, 60, 70; Understanding the American Republic, vols. I and II, 1961, 70; Objective Tests; The American Republic, 1962; The Assault of Laughter, 1962; The United States of America; A Syllabus of American Studies, 2 vols., 1962; The Instructor's Guide to the United States, 2d edit., 1967; The Student's Guide to the United States, 2d edit., 1967; Joseph Fels and the Single Tax Movement, 1971. Editor: Woodrow Wilson and the World of Today, 1957. Home: 829 Old Gulph Rd Bryn Mawr PA 19010

DUDDY, FRANK EDWARD, Jr., coll. pres.; b. Poughkeepsie, N.Y., Sept. 26, 1917; s. Frank Edward and Neva Inez (Warfel) D.; B.A. cum laude, DePauw U.; 1939, LL.D.; 1959; A.M., Harvard, 1940, Ph.D. (Buckley scholar), 1942; L.H.D., Westminster Coll., Utah, 1968; m. Eleanor Lorraine Ibach, Dec. 25, 1940; children—Elizabeth Jean (Mrs. P.M. Gibbons), Frank Edward III. Instr. English, history Northeastern U., 1940-41; instr. history DePauw U., 1942; instr. humanities Stephens Coll., 1942-43; instr. U.S. Naval Acad., 1946-48, asst. prof., 1948-51, asso. prof., 1951-56; pres. Westminster Coll., Salt Lake City, 1956-63, Marietta (O.) Coll., 1963—, also trustee ex-officio. Pres., exec. dir. Intermountain Colls. Assn., 1958-63; mem. exec. com., nominating com. Ind. Coll. Funds Am.; past chmn. East Central Coll. Consortium. Mem. adv. commn. on relations with pvt. instns. and fed. facility grants Ohio Bd. Regents; trustee, mem. exec. com., vice chmn. Ohio Found. Ind. Colls. Served with USNR, 1943-46. Mem. C. of C. (trustee), Newcomen Soc. N.Am., Assn. Ind. Colls. and Univs. Ohio (sec., mem. exec. com.), Fedn. state Assns. Ind. Colls. and Univs. (dir., mem. nominating com.), Assn. Am. Colls. (nominating com.), Ohio, Washington County hist. socs., Omicron Delta Kappa, Beta Theta Pi, Phi Mu Alpha, Alpha Phi Omega. Presbyn. (elder). Rotarian. Club: Marietta Country. Contbr. articles to profl. publs. Home: 301 5th St Marietta OH 45750

DUDEK, RICHARD ALBERT, educator; b. Clarkson, Neb., Sept. 3, 1926; s. Emil E. and Jennie (Indra) D.; B.S., in Mech. Engring., U. Neb., 1950; M.S. in Indsl. Engring., U. Ia., 1951, Ph.D., 1956; m. Helen M. Staver, Dec. 19, 1954; children—Richard Emil, Rustin Max. Plant indsl. engr. Fairmont Foods Co., Sioux City, Ia., 1951-52, div. indsl. engr., Omaha, 1952-53; research asst. U. Ia., 1953-54; asst. prof. mech. engring. U. Neb., 1954-56; research asso. Sch. of Health Professions, also asso. prof. indsl. engring. U. Pitts., 1956-58; prof., head dept. indsl. engring. Tex. Tech U., Lubbock, 1958—, dir. Center of Biotech. and Human Performance, 1969—, Horn Prof., 1970—. Tech. cons. industry, instns., religious orgns., hosps., 1951—; instr. TV courses. Dir. Found. Internat. Research and Devel., Lubbock, 1960-65. Bd. dirs. South Plains chpt. Muscular Dystrophy Assn. Am., 1966—, campaign chmn., 1968. Mem. Am. Inst. Indsl. Engrs. (pres.

Great Plains chpt. 1960-61; chmn. nat. student chpt. 1961-63, ECPD guidance rep. 1965-68, research com. 1967-69, regional v.p. 1969—), Am. Soc. M.E.'s, Am. Soc. Engring. Edn. (editor indsl. engring. div. 1965-66, sec. indsl. engring. div. 1966-67, vice chmn. 1967-68, chmn. 1968-69, chmn. planning com. of council of tech. divs. 1970-71), Inst. of Mgmt. Sci., Sigma Xi (pres. Tex. Tech. chpt. 1971—), Phi Kappa Phi (chpt. pres. 1967), Pi Mu Epsilon, Pi Tau Sigma, Alpha Pi Mu. Contbr. to profl. jours. in field. Home: 3707 46th St Lubbock TX 79413

DUDGEON, FARNHAM FRANCIS, editor; b. St. James, Minn., Feb. 16, 1912; s. Hugh G. and Mary Josephine (Nugent) D.; student St. John's Univ., 1928-29; B.S. U. N.D., 1934; m. Gould Crook, July 6, 1937; children—Michael, Patrick, Timothy, Colleen. Labor relations, investigative work N.D. state, fed. agencies, 1934-39; mem. editorial staff, Western Newspaper Union, 1939-42, editor-in-chief, 1942-52; editor and pub. Feature Publs., Inc., 1952—. City commr., mayor pro tem, Frankfort, 1965-68. Mem. Sigma Delta Chi, Theta Chi, Phi Delta Kappa. Roman Catholic. K.C. Contbr. weekly news analysis to 2,500 community newspapers 1940-43. Home: 105 Dakota Rd Frankfort KY 40601 Office: 100 E Main St Frankfort KY 40601

DUDICK, MICHAEL JOSEPH, bishop; b. St. Clair, Pa., Feb. 24, 1917; s. John and Mary (Jurick) D.; B.A., Ill. Benedictine Coll., Lisle, Ill., 1943; theol. studies St. Procopius Sem., Lisle, 1943-45. Ordained priest Roman Cath. Ch., 1945; vice chancellor Exarchate of Pitts., 1946-55; chancellor Diocese of Passaic (N.J.), 1963-68, bishop, 1968—. Mem. N.J. Coalition of Religious Leaders. Mem. N.J. Project Equality. Trustee Seton Hall U., 1968—. K.C. (4). Home: 56 Highland Av Montclair NJ 07042 Office: 101 Market St Passaic NJ 07055

DUDLEY, ALBERT HENRY, Jr., physician; b. Richmond, Va., Mar. 12, 1922; s. Albert Henry and Lillie (Gaines) D.; student Washington and Lee U., 1940-42, Johns Hopkins, 1942- 43; M.D., Med. Coll. Va., 1946; m. Emily Jane Belding, Dec. 27, 1943; children—Albert Henry III, Martha Miller, Jack Belding, Michael Gaines, Jeffrey Lee. Intern Union Meml. Hosp., Balt., 1946-47; resident obstetrics and gynecology Union Meml. Hosp., also Hosp. for Women Md., 1949-53; pvt. practice gynecology and obstetrics, Balt., 1953—; chief staff Union Meml. Hosp., 1965—; asst. gynecology and obstetrics Johns Hopkins Sch. Medicine, also gynecologist and obstetrician Johns Hopkins Hosp., 1953—. Trustee McDonogh Sch., 1955—; bd. dirs. Balt. City unit Am. Cancer Soc., 1965—, Florence Crittendon Home, 1964—. Served with USNR, 1947-49, 50-51. Diplomate Am. Bd. Obstetrics and Gynecology. Fellow Am. Coll. Obstetricians and Gynecologists; mem. A.M.A., Med. and Chirurgical Faculty Md., Balt. City Med. Soc., Delta Tau Delta, Phi Chi. Methodist (ofcl. bd.). Home: 6203 Blackburn Lane Baltimore MD 21212 Office: 1201 N Calvert St Baltimore MD 21202

DUDLEY, EASTHAM WALLER, lawyer; b. Alexandria, Va., Feb. 12, 1923; s. Luther H. and Katherine (Waller) D.; A.B., Washington and Lee U., 1943, LL.B., 1947; m. Letty Waugh, Sept. 24, 1946; children—Letty Carter, Waller T., Luther H. Admitted to Va. bar, 1947, since practiced in Alexandria; partner firm Boothe, Dudley, Koontz, Blankingship & Stump, 1952—. Dir. Alexandria Nat. Bank. Chmn. Indsl. Devel. Authority Alexandria; past chpt. chmn. A.R.C. Trustee Va. Coll. Fund; organizer, past trustee No. Va. Fine Arts Assn. Served to lt. (j.g.) USNR, 1943-46. Fellow Am. Coll. Trial Lawyers; mem. Va. Bar Assn. (pres.), Omicron Delta Kalpa. Episcopalian (past vestryman). Home: 512 W Braddock Rd Alexandria VA 22302 Office: 711 Princess St Alexandria VA 22313

DUDLEY, ELFORD SAMUEL, educator; b. Norfolk, Va., Oct. 17, 1923; s. Elford Samuel and Annabelle Lee (Warriner) D.; B.B.A., U. Mich., 1950, M.A., 1955, Ph.D., 1960; student Norfolk div. William and Mary Coll., also Va. Poly. Inst., 1941-43, 48, Hope Coll., 1943-44, Am. U., 1953; m. Eleanor Jeane Mulder, Aug. 9, 1947; children—David Michael, Sandra Lee. Tchr., Rufner Jr. High Sch., Norfolk, Va., 1951-52; exec. sec. United World Federalists, Ind., Mich., Ohio, 1952-54; speech instr. U. Mich., 1955-59; asst. prof. speech U. Ala., 1959-62; prof., head dept. speech Miss. State U., 1962—, dir. summer program academically talented students, 1965—. Served with AUS, World War II. Decorated Purple Heart medal, Bronze Star medal. Mem. Speech Communication Assn. (mem. legislative council 1970—), So. Speech Communication Assn. (pres. 1971), Miss. Speech Assn. (pres. 1964-66), Miss. TV Council for Higher Edn. (chmn. 1968—), Phi Kappa Phi, Phi Delta Kappa. Presbyn. (deacon 1968—). Home: Rt 3 Box 292 Starkville MS 39759 Office: Drawer NJ State College MS 39762

DUDLEY, FRANCIS MARION, lawyer; b. Welch, Okla., Feb. 2, 1893; s. James D. and May (Gwinn) D.; LL.B., U. Okla., 1916; m. Ruth Sullivan, Dec. 20, (dec. Mar. 1961); children—Ruth Eugenia (Mrs. William G. Schmidt), Charles D.; m. 2d, Jessie R. Webb, Nov. 21, 1969. Admitted to Okla. bar, 1916; practice in Coalgate, 1916-17, 19-22, Ardmore, 1922-25, Oklahoma City, 1942—; counsel firm Fowler, Rucks, Baker, Jopling, Gramlich & Mee, 1964—; County atty., Ardmore, Okla., 1925-29; asst. atty. gen. Okla., 1929-34, 36-39; asst. U.S. atty. Okla. City, 1934-36; chief counsel Okla. Tax Commn., 1939-42. Served to 2d lt. U.S. Army, 1917-19. Democrat. Baptist. Mason. Club: Men's Dinner (Oklahoma City). Home: 209 N W 34th St Oklahoma City OK 73118 Office: First Nat Bldg Oklahoma City OK 73102

DUDLEY, GEORGE AUSTIN, educator, architect; b. Pitts., Dec. 24, 1914; s. Samuel William and Mabel Eva (Allen) D.; B.A., Yale, 1936, B.F.A. in Arch., 1938, M.F.A. in City Planning, 1940; children—George Bergin, Sally Jean (Mrs. Michael Heneveld), John Phillips, Samuel William III. With Office Coordinator of Inter-Am. Affairs, 1941-45; dir. research Conn. Post War Planning Bd., 1944-45; with archtl. firm Harrison & Abramovitz, N.Y.C., 1945-48, 59-60; sec. internat. bd. design UN Hdqrs., 1945-46; pres. IBEC Housing Corp., 1948-59; cons. Internat. Devel. Adv. Bd., 1951; dir. N.Y. State Office Regional Devel., also sec. Planning Coordination Bd. of Gov. Rockefeller, 1960-62; planning coordinator N.Y. State New Capital, 1962; dean Sch. Architecture, Rensselaer Poly. Inst., 1962-65; dean Sch. Architecture and Urban Planning, U. Cal. at Los Angeles, 1965-68; pres. N.Y. State Environmental Facilities Corp., 1967—, N.Y. State Council on Architecture, 1967—. Trustee Inst. for Architecture and Urban Studies; mem. Yale Council; chmn. Yale Council Com. for Sch. Architecture and Art. Mem. A.I.A. Contbg. editor Archtl. Forum. Home: 121 W 15th St New York City NY 10011 Office: 1700 Broadway New York City NY 10022

DUDLEY, GUILFORD, Jr., U.S. ambassador; b. Nashville, June 23, 1907; s. Guilford and Anne (Dallas) D.; student Loomis Inst., Peabody Coll.; A.B., Vanderbilt U., 1929; LL.D., Cumberland U., children—Guilford, Robert Lusk; m. Jane Anderson; one dau., Trevania Dallas. Formerly pres., dir. Life & Casualty Ins. Co., of Tenn., Nashville, Nashville Mag., WLAC Radio, WLAC-TV Casualty Ins. Co. of Tenn.; chmn., dir. World-Wide Life Assurance Co., Ltd., London; dir. 3d Nat. Bank, Nashville; named amb. to Denmark by Pres. Nixon, 1969—. Bd. dirs. Cumberland Coll., Vanderbilt U., Ensworth Sch., Tenn. Bot. Gardens and Fine Arts Center, Jr. Achievement Nashville (pres. 1968-69), YMCA, United Givers Fund, So. States Industrial Council. Mem. Natl. Planning Assn., Nat. Steeplechasing and Hunt, Midwest Hunt Racing Assn., Phi Delta Theta. Episcopalian. Clubs: Turf and Field, River (N.Y.C.); Nashville City, Cumberland, Belle Meade Country (Nashville); Palm Bay (Miami, Fla.); Hillsboro Hounds Hunt; Lost Tree, Everglades, Bath and Tennis, Coral Beach, Seminole Golf (Palm Beach, Fla.); Turf (London). Author: The Skyline Is A Promise. Home: Harding Pl at Hillsgoro Rd Nashville TN 37215 also 1820 S Ocean Blvd Palm Beach FL 33480 Office: Am Embassy Copenhagen Denmark

DUDLEY, LAVINIA PRATT, editor; b. N.Y. City; d. Charles H. and Harriet (Hartman) Pratt; student N.Y.U.; Litt.D., (hon.), Mo. Valley Coll., 1947; m. Ivan Ross Dudley, Feb. 19, 1927 (dec. December 1961). Began career as assistant to dean sch. retailing N.Y.U., 1921-24; asst. to Am. editor, also mgr. editorial office Ency. Brit., 1925-29, mgr. book shops, 1930-33; ednl. dir. Brit. Jr., editor study units for rural schs., 1934-38; asst. editor Ency. Americana, 1939-47, exec. editor American publs., 1948-59, editor in chief, 1959-64; cons. editor Am. Peoples Encyclopedia, N.Y.C., 1964, consultant, 1965—. Named profl. women of year for State of N.Y., 1959. Fellow Am. Geog. Soc.; mem. Acad. Polit. Sci., Nat. Audubon Soc. Republican. Club: Women's U. (N.Y. City). Editor Americana Reading Guides in engring., chemistry, commerce, agr., Latin Am. Home: 314 E 41st St New York City NY 10017 Office: 575 Lexington Av New York City NY 10022

DUDLEY, TILFORD E., public affairs counsellor; b. Charleston, Ill., Apr. 21, 1907; s. Dr. Gerry Brown and Esther Wilhoit (Shoot) D.; Ph.B. cum laude, Wesleyan U., 1928; LL.B., Harvard, 1931; m. Martha Fairchild Ward, Aug. 28, 1937; children—Donica Ward, Gerric Ward, Martha Fairchild. Admitted to Ill. bar, 1931; gen. practice of law, Aurora, Illinois, 1931-34; chief legal sect. Land Program, Fed. Emergency Relief Adminstrn., 1934-35; chief land sec., Suburban Resettlement Adminstrn., 1935-37; chief, land acquisition, R.D.P., Nat. Parks Service, 1936-37; trial examiner, Nat. Labor Relations Bd., 1937-42; prin. mediation officer Nat. War Labor Bd., 1942-43, dir. of disputes, Region VI, 1943-44, prin. adminstrv. officer, 1944; asso. gen. counsel and Washington rep., United Packinghouse Workers Am., 1944-45. Asst. to Sidney Hillman, chmn. C.I.O. Political Action Com., 1945-46, asst. dir. CIO Polit. Action Com., 1946- 55; asst. dir. AFL-CIO AFL-CIO Com. on Polit. Edn., 1955-58; dir. AFL-CIO Speakers Bureau, 1958-69; dir. Washington office council for Christian Social Action, United Church of Christ, 1969—. Chmn. of Citizens Council for D.C., 1962-67. Member exec. bd. div. Christian life and work and mem. gen. bd. Nat. Council of Chs., 1954-57, 64, exec. bd. div. life and mission, 1965—; cons. 2d Assembly World Council Chs., 1954. Alt. mem. Dem. Nat. Com., 1948-68; del. Dem. Nat. Conv., 1948, 52, 60, 68; vice chmn. Dem. Central Com. for D.C., 1964-67, chmn., 1967-68. Mem. Nat. Assn. for Advancement Colored People, Ams. for Democratic Action, Sigma Chi, Delta Sigma Rho. Meth. and Conglist. Club: Harvard (Washington). Author: The Harvard Legal Bur., its History and Purposes, 1930; Harvard Legal Aid Bureau, 1931; Digest of Decisions of Nat. Labor Relations Bd., Vol. 8, 1939; The Washington Report, 1969—. Home: 895 7th St Charleston IL 61920 also 2942 Macomb St Washington DC 20008 Office: 110 Maryland Av NE Washington DC 20002

DUDMAN, RICHARD BEEBE, newspaperman; b. Centerville, Ia., May 3, 1918; s. Virgil Ernest and Wilma (Beebe) D.; A.B., Stanford, 1940; m. Helen Sloane, Mar. 14, 1948; children—Janet Sloane, Martha Tod. Reporter, photographer Oroville (Cal.) Mercury-Register, summer 1937; reporter Denver Post,1946-49; reporter St. Louis Post-Dispatch, 1949-53, mem. Washington bur., 1954—, chief bur., 1969—. Served with USNR, 1942- 45. Nieman fellow, Harvard, 1953-54. Clubs: Nat. Press, Gridiron (Washington). Author: Men of the Far Right, 1962; 40 Days with the Enemy, 1971; also articles. Home: 3409 Newark St N W Washington DC 20016 Office: 1701 Pennsylvania Av N W Washington DC 20006

DUDROW, LOUIS ALBERT, banker; b. New Windsor, Md., May 11, 1924; s. LeRoy Andrew and Mabel (Geiman) D.; A.B., Denison U., 1945; m. Nancy Leonie Dangoisse, July 24, 1948 (dec. Apr. 1958); children—Patricia, Richard, Caryn; m. 2d, Thelma Jean Allin, July 11, 1959; children—Elizabeth, Jennifer. With Union Trust Co. Md., Balt., 1948—, treas., 1958-69, sec., 1960—, v.p., 1969. Served to lt. USNR, 1946, 50-53. Mem. Am. Soc. Corp. Secs. Democrat. Presbyn. Home: 102 Park Lane Baltimore MD 21210 Office: Union Trust Co Baltimore and St Paul Sts Baltimore MD 21203

DUE, JOHN FITZGERALD, educator, economist; b. Hayward, Cal., July 11, 1915; s. Jackson Angelo and Emmarene (Hurd) D.; A.B., U. Cal. at Berkeley, 1935, Ph.D., 1939; A.M., George Washington U., 1936; m. Margaret Jean Mann, Aug. 18, 1950; children—Allan, Kevin. Instr., U. Utah, 1939-42, asst. prof., 1945-48; economist Treasury Dept., 1942; faculty U. Ill., 1948—, prof. econs., 1951—, chmn. dept., 1963-67, 71—. Served with USMCR, 1942-45. Mem. Am. Econ. Assn., Nat. Tax Assn., Internat. Inst. Pub. Finance, Phi Beta Kappa. Author: Government Finance, 4th edit., 1968; Taxation and Economic Development in Tropical Africa, 1963; Indirect Taxation in Developing Economics, 1970; State and Local Sales Taxation, 1971. Co- author: The Electric Interurban Railway in America, 1960; Rails to The Ochoco Country-The City of Prineville Railway, 1968. Home: 808 Dodds Dr Champaign IL 61820 Office: Com W Univ Ill Urbana IL 61801

DUECY, CHARLES MICHAEL, lawyer; b. Everett, Wash., Oct. 16, 1912; s. Patrick Rowan and Marie (Maecker) D.; student U. Wash., 1929-34, Stanford, 1954-55; J.D., U. Ariz., 1957; m. Gratia Sanborn Riesche, Oct. 16, 1940; children—Charles Michael, Gratia (Mrs. Jimmy R. Evans), Margaret Theresa, Robert Riesche. Sec.-treas. Coos Head Timber Co., Coos Bay, Ore., 1945-50; sec.-treas. Menasha Plywood Co., Coos Bay, 1948-54; pres. Menasha Sales Co., Chgo., 1952-54; sec.-treas. Builders Mortgage & Trust Co., 1954—; admitted to Ariz. bar, 1957, since practiced in Scottsdale; sr. partner Duecy, Moore, Petsch & Robinson, 1957—; dir. Columbia Riverlog Scaling & Grading Bur., 1948-52. Mem. Pulp, Paper, Lumber and Plywood Labor Relations Com., 1948-52; spl. counsel state atty. gen. on city annexation work, 1962-64; chmn. Gov.'s Com. on Alcoholism, 1966-68; counsel Legal Aid Soc. juvenile work, 1964—, Retarded Childrens Assn., 1960—. Bd. dirs. Scottsdale Bapt. Hosp. Served to lt. USNR, 1942- 46: ETO. Mem. Internat. Bar Conf., Am., Ariz. bar assns., Am. Judicature Soc., Phi Delta Phi, Phi Delta Theta. Democrat. Episcopalian. Author: Odd Adventures of the Electrical Pussy Cat, 1964. Contbr. articles profl. jours. Home: 4229 E Desert Crest Dr Scottsdale AZ 85253 Office: 7301 E 4th St Scottsdale AZ 85251

DUEMELAND, LORIN ERNEST, ranch co. exec.; b. St. Paul, May 6, 1916; s. George A. and Della (Hoffman) D.; student U. N.D., 1933-34, N.D. State U., 1937; m. Olga Christianson, May 6, 1939; children—George T., Judith A. With Patterson Land Co., Bismarck, N.D., 1935—, pres., 1960—. Pres. N.D. Winter Futurity Com., 1953; dir. N.D. Beef Council, 1955—, 1st Nat. Bank, Bismarck, 1969—. Named Outstanding Young Man, Bismarck Jr. C. of C., 1948; named Hon. State Farmer, Future Farmers Am., 1966; recipient Outstanding Service award N.D. Winter Show, 1966. Mem. Am. (bd. dirs. 1962-68, pres. 1965), N.D. (pres. 1950, bd. dirs. 1946-68) Hereford assns., N.D. Flying Farmers (pres. 1946), Beta Theta Pi. Republican. Presbyn. Clubs: Toastmasters (pres. Bismarck-Mandan 1952); Kiwanis (pres. Bismarck 1951, lt. gov. Minn.-Dakotas dist. 1954); Executive (pres. Bismarck-Mandan 1959-60). Home: 723 Williams St Bismarck ND 58501 Office: 601 Main Av Bismarck ND 58501

DUEMLER, ROBERT F., utility exec.; b. 1909; student U Pa.; married. Formerly with Koppers Phila. Coke Co. & Phila. Gas Works Inc., W.R. Grace & Co., W.Va. Coal & Coke Corp., Crown Cork & Seal Co. Inc.; founder Robert F. Duemler & Assos., mgmt. cons. firm, 1956-59; with Columbia Gas System Inc., N.Y.C., 1959—, sr. v.p. bus. employee and pub. relations, 1967—, also dir. Office: 120 E 41st St New York City NY 10017*

DUENSING, DAVID LOUIS, food co. exec.; b. Chgo., July 2, 1922; s. Oscar F. and Dorothy (Snyder) D.; student U. Fla., 1942-43; m. Evelyn M. DeGroot, July 1, 1944; children—David W., Gail E., Diane H. With Armour & Co., 1946—, exec. v.p., 1968—, also dir., mem. exec. com.; pres., chief exec. officer Armour-Dial, 1968—, also dir., mem. exec. com.; dir. DeSoto Inc., Greyhound Computer Corp., Gen. Fire & Casualty Co., Greyhound Corp. Served with USAAF, 1943-47. Mem. Chgo. Assn. Commerce (bd. dirs.), Grocery Mfrs. Assn. Clubs: Racquet, Mid-America (Chgo.); Glen Oak Country (Glen Ellyn). Home: 717 Kenilworth Av Glen Ellyn IL 60137 Office: 111 E Wacker Dr Chicago IL 60601

DUERBECK, EDWIN MARTIN, former govt. ofcl.; b. Chgo., Sept. 16, 1906; s. Adolph and Amanda (Reidland) D.; student Washington U., 1923-26, Columbia, 1944; A.B., U. Chgo., 1934, M.A., 1935; m. Louise McCutchan, Dec. 28, 1935. With Shell Petroleum Corp., 1926-33, P.W.A., 1935-37, Fed. Pub. Housing Authority, 1938-42, VA, 1946-49; with U.S. Dept. of State, 1949-55, chief accounting div., 1960, chief audit div., 1961-62, ret.; consul, 1st sec., chief budget and fiscal unit. Am. embassy, Bonn, Germany, 1955-59; regional adminstrv. officer N. Am. regional office FAO, Washington, 1962-68, ret. Comdr. USNR, ret. Mem. Am. Soc. Pub. Adminstrn., Fgn. Service Assn., Fgn. Policy Assn. Laguna Hills (sec.-treas.), Am. Legion. Club: International Town and Country. Home: 362A Laguna Hills CA 92653

DUERKSEN, WALTER JACOB, univ. dean; b. Enid, Okla., Feb. 21, 1907; s. Jacob and Helen (Friesen) D.; Mus.B., U. Wichita, 1931; Mus.M., Northwestern U., 1938; student Juilliard Conservatory, Columbia Tchrs. Coll., summer 1945; m. Virginia Kilbourn, June 5, 1938; children—Walter Kilbourn, Mary Virginia. Dir. instrumental music Wichita State U., 1931—, chmn. dept. music, 1944—, dean Sch. Music, 1949—, dean Coll. Fine Arts, 1961-70, Univ. prof., spl. asst. to pres., 1970—. Wichita Symphony Soc. Mem. Music Educators Nat. Conf., Music Tchrs. Nat. Assn., Am. Assn. U. Profs., Phi Mu Alpha, Kappa Kappa Psi. Conglist. Author pamphlet on coll. bands. Home: 1414 N Vassar St Wichita KS 67208

DUERRENMATT, FRIEDRICH, author; b. Konolfingen, Switzerland, Jan. 5, 1921; s. Reinhold and Hulda (Zimmermann) D.; grad. in lit., philosophy, natural scis., Univs. Zurich and Bern; m. Lotti Geissler, 1947; children—Peter, Barbara, Ruth. Author: (plays) Es steht geschrieben, 1947, Der Blinde, 1948, Romulus der Grosse, 1949, Die Ehe des Herrn Mississippi, 1952, Ein Engel kommt nach Babylon, 1953, Der Besuch der alten Dame (prod. N.Y.C. as The Visit), 1956, Frank U., 1959, The Physicists', 1962; Herkules Und der Stall Des Augias, 1963, Der Meteor, 1966, Die Wiedertaufer, 1967, König Johann, nach Shakespeare, 1970, Portat eines Planeten, 1970; (romane) Der Richter und Sein Henker, 1950, Der Verdacht, 1951, Grieche Sucht Griechin, 1955, Das Versprechen, 1957; Die Panne, 1956, Der Sturz, 1971; Der Doppelgänger, Der Prozess un des ESels Schatten, Nächtliches Gesprach, Stranitzky und der Nationalheld, others; (essay) Theaterprobleme, 1955. Recipient German War Blind radio-play award; Schiller award of City of Mannheim; Italian radio-play award Prix Italia; grand award Am. Critics. Address: 34 Pertuis du Sault Neuchatel Switzerland

DUESENBERRY, JAMES STEMBEL, economist; b. Princeton, W. Va., July 18, 1918; s. John Fisher and Rose (MacLellan) D.; B.A., U. Mich., 1939, M.A., 1941, Ph.D., 1948; m. Margaret Torbert, June 19, 1948; children—John Fisher II, Helen Rose, James Keith, Margaret Patricia. Teaching fellow econs. U. Mich., 1939- 41; instr. Mass. Inst. Tech., 1946; teaching fellow econs. Harvard, 1946- 48, asst. prof. econs., 1948-53, asso. prof., 1953-57, prof., 1957—, William Joseph Maier prof. money and banking, Ford Found. research prof., 1958-59; Fulbright research prof. Cambridge U., 1954-55. Former mem. Pres.'s Council Econ. Advisers. Cons. Com. Econ. Devel., 1956—. Served as capt., USAAF, 1942-45. Author: Income, Saving and the Theory of Consumer Behavior, 1949; Business Cycles and Economic Growth, 1958; (with Lee Preston) Cases and Problems in Economics, 1959; Money and Credit. Impact and Control, 1964. Home: 25 Fairmount St Belmont MA 02178 Office: Harvard U Littauer 230 Cambridge MA

DUFEK, GEORGE JOHN, museum dir., ret. naval officer; b. Rockford, Ill., Feb. 10, 1903; s. Frank and Mary (Wachuta) D.; B.S., U.S. Naval Acad., 1925; grad. Flight Tng. Sch., 1933; student Indsl. Coll. Armed Forces, 1947; LL.D., Carleton Coll.; L.H.D., LeMoyne Coll.; D.Sc., Rockford (Ill.) Coll., m. Murial Thomson Bones, 1947; children—Mary Ellen (Mrs. Bellit), Barbara Bones (Mrs. Phillips), George Cruzen, David Frank. Commd. ensign USN, 1925, advanced through grades to rear adm., 1955; assigned U.S.S. Maryland, 1925-27; asst. navigator, asst. communications officer U.S.S. Canopus, 1927-28; aviator U.S.S. Concord, 1933-36; navigator U.S.S. Saratoga, 1936-38; exec. officer U.S.S. Lexington, 1938-39; navigator U.S.S. Bear, flagship Antarctic Devel. Project, 1939; assisted constrn. devel. new naval air sta., Jacksonville, Fla., 1940; spl. U.S. Naval observer for aviation, London, 1942; sr. naval aviator, invasion North Africa, 1942; assisted devel. invasion plans for So. France; comdr. U.S.S. Bogue, 1944; comdg. officer naval air base, Ominato, Japan, also air transport service terminal nr. Tokyo, 1945; staff Naval Regulations Bd., Washington, 1946; chief staff officer on expdn. to establish weather bases northern Polar Regions, 1946; comdr. eastern group Task Force 68, to develop unknown coast line between Palmer Peninsula and Little Am. comdr. Task Force 80 to supply existing weather stas. and establish new stas. nr. North Pole, 1947; mem. logistics planning sect. Joint Chiefs Staff, Washington, 1949-50; comdr. U.S.S. Antietam, 1951; head spl. Antarctic Planning Group, Washington, 1954; comdr. logistic and operational task force Naval Operation Deepfreeze, 1955-59; 1st Am. at geographic South Pole, 1956; ret., 1959; dir. Mariners Mus., Newport News, Va., 1960—. Decorated Legion of Merit with 2 gold stars, Antarctic Expdn. medal; Distinguished Service medal with gold star (U.S.); Comdr. Order of Crown (Belgium); Hon. Companion Order of Bath (Eng.); Croix de Guerre, Legion of Honor (France); recipient Andre Medal, Swedish Geog. Soc., 1959 Mem. Am. Soc. Naval Engrs., Nat. Geog. Soc. (Hubbard medal. 1959) Am. Geophys. Union. Clubs: James River Country; Army-Navy, Explorers. Author: Operation Deep Freeze; Through the Frozen Frontiers, 1959. Home: 101 Museum Pkwy Newport News VA 23606 Office: Mariners Mus Newport News VA 23601

DUFF, FRATIS LEE, state ofcl., ret. air force officer; physician; b. Randlett, Okla., July 7, 1910; s. George E. and Mae E. (McNeill) D.; B.S. in Chemistry, U. Okla., 1933, M.D. with honors, 1939; M.P.H., Johns Hopkins, 1950, D.P.H., 1953; grad. various service schs.; m. Beryl Hilborne, Sept. 18, 1937; children—Dennis E., Randolph L. Intern Colo. Gen. Hosp., 1939-40; commd. 1st lt., M.C., USAAF, 1940, advanced through grades to brig. gen. USAF, 1963; various assignments, U.S., Egypt and Japan, 1940-48; chief profl. services br. Command Surgeon's Office FEAF, Japan, 1948-49; prof. mil. sci. and tactics Johns Hopkins, 1949-51; chief preventive medicine div. Surgeon's Gen. Office, USAF, 1951-53; comdr. Gunter br. Sch. Aviation Medicine, 1953-59; dep. surgeon USAF Europe, Weisbaden, Germany, 1959-62; command surgeon Air Force Systems Command, Andrews AFB, Md., 1962-63, Tactical Air Command, Langley AFB, Va., 1964-68, ret.; dir. planning Tex. Dept. Health, 1968-69, dep. commr. for program planning, 1969—. Decorated Legion of Merit with 2 oak leaf clusters, various unit and area ribbons; recipient Certificate Achievement, Surgeon Gen. USAF, 1962. Diplomate Am. Bd. Preventive Medicine. Author articles. Home: 4211 Lostridge Dr Austin TX 78731 Office: Tex Dept Health Austin TX 78756

DUFF, IVAN FRANCIS, educator, physician; b. Pendleton, Ore., July 20, 1915; s. Frank and Nina (Jack) D.; A.B., U. Ore., 1938; M.D., U. Mich., 1940; m. Betty Anne Macduff, Feb. 14, 1942; children—David B., Frank N. Intern Univ. Hosp., Ann Arbor, Mich., 1940-41, asst. resident, 1942, resident, 1946; mem. faculty U. Mich. Med. Sch., 1946—, charge Rackham Arthritis Research Unit, 1953-69, in charge arthritis div., 1960—, dir. regional arthritis control program in Mich., 1969-71, prof. internal medicine, 1960—. Mem. gen. med. study sect. Dept. Health, Edn. and Welfare, 1957-61, mem. arthritis tng. com., 1961-65; trainee Nat. Inst. Arthritis and Metabolic Diseases, Karolinska Sjukhuset, Stockholm, Sweden, 1957. Served to comdr., M.C., USNR, 1942-46. Fellow Commonwealth Fund, 1964-65, 67. Diplomate Am. Bd. Internal Medicine. Fellow A.C.P.; mem. Am. Fedn. Clin. Research, Central Soc. Clin. Research, Am. (exec. com. 1957-61, 2d v.p. 1971—), Mich. (pres. 1958-59) rheumatism assns., Nat. Soc. Rheumatologists. Home: 4 Ridgeway Ann Arbor MI 48104

DUFF, JOHN CARR, educator; b. Pittsburgh, July 23, 1901; s. Dr. Alexander McGill and Edna (Carr) D.; Ph.B. cum laude, Kenyon Coll., 1923, A.M., 1924; Ph.D., N.Y. U., 1934; m. Gladys Hays, July 1, 1922; children—Robert Russell, John Hays, Thomas. Teacher high sch., 1924-25; organized LaFayette Jr. High Sch. and Benjamin Franklin Jr. High Sch., Uniontown, Pa., 1925; prin. Benjamin Franklin Jr. High Sch., 1925-30; supervising prin. Dist. 6, Scarsdale, N.Y., 1935-37; successively teaching fellow, instr., asst. prof., asso. prof., prof., N.Y. Univ. School of Edn., asst. dean, 1946- 48, chmn., dept. adult edn., 1948-59, prof. of adminstrn. and supervision, 1959-67, mem. div. advanced studies, sch. edn.; sr. cons. Bur. Ednl. Studies and Services, also lecturer adminstrn. Sch. Edn., Hofstra U., 1967—; ednl. cons.; co-ordinator N.Y. U. Summer Sch., Chautauqua, 1950-52 (leave absence while serving with War Dept., 1943- 45); mem. summer faculty U. P.R., 1958, 59, U. Florida, 1958, State U. of N.Y. at Buffalo, 1963; mem. N.Y. State Dept. Edn. project on cost of edn., 1959-60; mem. staff Center for Field Services, N.Y. U. Consultant on tng. Girl Scouts of U.S. Served with U.S. Army 1918; tng. specialist and civilian dir. civilian training, Office of Q.M. Gen., World War II. Recipient study award Fund for Adult Edn., 1955-56. Mem. Adult Edn. Assn. U.S., Am. Assn. U. Profs., Am. Assn. Sch. Adminstrs., Collegiate Assn. Devel. Ednl. Adminstrn., St. Andrew's Soc. N.Y.C., Phi Delta Kappa; hon. mem. Kappa Delta Pi. Mason. Editor, The Clearing House, 1935- 36. Author of books including following: Basic Principles of Guidance (with Cox and McNamara), 1948. Co-ordinator, N.Y. Univ. summer school at Chautauqua, N.Y., 1950-52. Home: 152 Wellington Rd Garden City NY 11530

DUFFEY, FRANK MARION, coll. dean; b. South Charleston, O., Apr. 22, 1915; s. Arthur Garfield and Iva Bertha (Moon) D.; A.B cum laude, Miami U., 1938; M.A., U. N.C., 1940, Ph.D., 1950; m. Gwendolyn Jenkins, June 19, 1940. Dept. State exchange fellow to Colombia, 1942; asst. prof. Spanish, U. N.C., 1950- 54, asso. prof., 1954-59, prof., 1959—, asso. dean Coll. Arts and Scis., 1960—, acting dean Coll. of Arts and Sci., 1965-66. Served to lt. (s.g.) USNR, 1943-46. Decorated Bronze Star medal. Mem. Modern Lang. Assn., Am. Assn. Tchrs. Spanish (pres. N.C. chpt. 1954), Council Basic Edn., South Atlantic Modern Lang. Assn. (exec. com. 1950—), Phi Beta Kappa, Sigma Delta Pi, Beta Pi Theta, Delta Kappa Epsilon. Author: The Early Cuadro de Costumbres in Colombia, 1956. Editor South Atlantic Bull, 1950—. Home: 23 Mt Bolus Rd Chapel Hill NC 27514

DUFFEY, JOSEPH DANIEL, urban specialist; b. Huntington, W.Va., July 1, 1932; s. Joseph Ivan and Ruth (Wilson) D.; A.B., Marshall U., Huntington, W.Va., 1954; S.T.M., Yale, 1964; B.D., Andover Newton Theol. Found., 1957; Ph.D., Hartford Sem. Found., 1969; m. Patricia Fortney, Aug. 24, 1952; children—Michael Robert, David King. Ordained to ministry Conglist. Ch., 1956; pastor, Davers, Mass., 1957-60; asst. prof. Hartford (Conn.) Sem., 1960-63, dir. Center for Urban Studies, 1965-70; fellow Harvard U. Kennedy Sch. Govt., 1971—. Vice pres. Robert Littleton Corp.; dir. Conn. Housing Investment Fund. Nat. chmn. Americans for Democratic Action, 1969-70. Del. Nat. Dem. Conv., 1968; Dem. candidate for U.S. Senate, 1970; mem. Nat. Dem. Policy Council, 1970—. Rockefeller fellow, 1963-65. Address: 175 Ridgefield St Hartford CT 06112

DUFFEY, ROBERT V., educator; b. Lancaster, Pa., Jan. 31, 1915; s. James William and Ada (Miller) D.; B.S., Millersville (Pa.) State Coll., 1938; Ed.M., Temple U., 1948, Ed.D., 1954; m. M. Arline Charles, Aug. 24, 1940; children—David R., Barbara E. Elementary sch. tchr. and prin., also high sch. tchr. Lancaster and York Counties, Pa., 1938-43; instr. Millersville State Coll., 1946-50; asst. prof. U. Del., 1951-52; asst. prof., then prof. Temple U., 1952-63; prof. early childhood elementary edn., head dept. U. Md., 1963—. Served with USAAF, 1943-46. Recipient Phi Delta Kappa award for research Temple U., 1954. Mem. Nat. Council Social Studies, Internat. Reading Assn., Am. Ednl. Research Assn., N.E.A., Phi Delta Kappa. Author: (with R. C. Preston) Primary Social Studies Test, 1967. Contbr. articles to profl. jours. Home: 9225 Limestone Pl College Park MD 20740

DUFFIELD, EUGENE SCHULTE, pub. co. exec.; b. Denver, July 10, 1908; s. Carroll Hogue and Mary Josephine (Schulte) D.; A.B., U. Wis., 1929, A.M., 1931. Asst. to dean, U. Wis., 1929-30, instr. in history, 1930-31; reporter U.S. Daily, 1931-33; with Washington bur. Chgo. Tribune, 1933-35; with Washington bur. Wall Street Jour., 1935-38, 40-42, chief of bur., 1941-42; asst. to sec. of treasury, 1938-39; asst. to under sec. of Navy, 1942-44; asst. to sec. of Navy, 1944-46; officer and dir. McGraw-Hill Pub. Co., 1946-50; asst. pub. Cin. Enquirer, 1950-56; v.p. Federated Dept. Stores, Inc., 1956-59; pres. Popular Sci. Pub Co., 1959- -; dir. Select Mags., Inc. Mem. Advt. Council (dir.), Mag. Pubs. Assn. (chmn.), Phi Beta Kappa, Sigma Delta Chi, Chi Phi. Clubs: Pinnacle, University, Dutch Treat (N.Y.C.). Collaborated in editing The Forrestal Diaries. Office: 355 Lexington Av New York City NY 10017

DUFFIELD, RICHARD, lawyer; b. Elizabeth, N.J., May 17, 1930; s. Stuart and Mildred (Horning) D.; B.A., Williams Coll., 1952; LL.B., Yale, 1957; m. Mary Rose Carroll, June 18, 1955; children—Christopher, John, Jennifer, Marjorie. Admitted to Ariz. bar, 1957; asso. firm Lewis, Roca, Scoville & Beauchamp, Phoenix, 1957-58; practice in Tucson, 1958—; partner firm Spaid, Fish, Briney & Duffield, 1963—. Chmn. bd. Legal Aid Soc. Tucson, 1964-66, Nature Conservancy Ariz., 1970. Chmn. Pima County Democratic Central Com., 1964-65, Democratic Party Ariz., 1966-70. Served to 1st lt. USAAF, 1952-54. Episcopalian (jr. warden 1970). Home: 4125 N Camino Encerrado Tucson AZ 85718 Office: Transamerica Bldg Tucson AZ 85701

DUFFIELD, ROBERT B., lab. exec.; b. 1917. Asst., later asso. prof. physics and chemistry U. Ill., Urbana, 1946-56; with John J. Hopkins Lab. gen. atomic div. General Dynamics Corp., San Diego, 1956-67, asst. dir. lab., until 1967, supr. constr. Peach Bottom (Pa.) reactor; dir. Argonne Nat. Lab., Lemont, Ill., 1967—. Served as cons. to AEC labs., Brookhaven, N.Y., Los Alamos, also del. Internat. Conf. on Peaceful Uses Nuclear Energy, Geneva, Switzerland. Trustee Scripps Clinic and Research Found., La Jolla, Cal. Office: Argonne Nat Lab Lemont IL 60439

DUFFIN, RICHARD JAMES, educator, mathematician; b. Chgo., Oct. 13, 1909; s. Daniel and Mary (Curran) D.; B.S. in Engring., U. Ill., 1932, Ph.D. in Physics, 1935; m. Carolyn Jeanne Hartman, July 19, 1947; children—Virginia Mae, Martha Jane. Teaching asst. physics U. Ill., 1935, asso. math., 1941-42; instr. math. Purdue U., 1936- 41; physicist terrestrial magnetism Carnegie Instn. Wash., 1942-46; faculty Carnegie-Mellon U., 1946—, prof. math., 1948-70, Univ. prof. math. scis., 1970—; vis. prof. Purdue U., 1949, Inst. Advanced Studies, Dublin, Ireland, 1959; dir. spl. research applied math. Duke, 1958; distinguished vis. prof. engring. U. State N.Y. at Stony Brook, 1967; distinguished vis. prof. math. Tex. A. and M. U., 1968; cons. in field, 1956—. Mem. Am. Math. Soc., Soc. Indsl. and Applied Math. (nat. lectr. 1961, 64), Nat. Philosophy Soc., Sigma Xi, Tau Beta Pi, Triangle. Co- author: Geometric Programming, 1967. Mem. editorial bds. jours. in field. Home: 424 S Linden Av Pittsburgh PA 15208

DUFFY, ADRIAN DOMINICK, psychiatrist; b. Belfast, Ireland, Apr. 27, 1932; s. Francis O. and Eileen (MacDowall) D.; Terenure Coll., 1949; L.R.C.S. & P., Edinburgh, 1957; D.P.M., Trinity Coll., Dublin, 1966; m. Eileen J. Mulligan, June 28, 1958; children—Patricia, Niall, Sheila, Doreen, Michelle. Came to U.S., 1957, naturalized, 1964. Intern Niagara Falls (N.Y.) Hosp., 1957-58; resident psychiatry Kan. U. Med. Center, 1959-63; sect. chief Columbia State Hosp., Columbia, S.C., 1963-65; supt. Marshall (Mo.) State Hosp., 1967-69, St. Louis State Hosp., 1969—; clin. instr. Mo. Inst. Psychiatry (St. Louis); asst. prof. psychiatry U. Mo. Mem. Am. Psychiat. Assn., A.M.A., Brit., Irish med. assns. Home: 10695 Lewis and Clark St St Louis MO 63136 Office: 10695 Bellefontaine St St Louis MO 63137

DUFFY, BRIAN FRANCIS, clegyman, educator; b. N.Y.C., Apr. 23, 1917; s. Thomas Charles and Ellen (Sullivan) D.; B.A., St. Bonaventure U., 1942. M.A., 1947; M.A., Columbia, 1956, doctoral candidate, 1958. Ordained priest Roman Catholic Ch., 1946; asst. prin. Bishop Timon High Sch., Buffalo, 1947-53; head dept. theology St. Bonaventure U., 1953-54, dean, 1954-55; dean Siena Coll., Loudonville, N.Y., 1958-64, pres., 1964-70, prof. English, 1970—. Address: Siena Coll Loudonville NY 12211

DUFFY, CHARLES, educator; b. Dubuque, Ia., June 16, 1903; s. Thomas Henry and Mary Elizabeth (Murphy) D.; Ph.B., U. Wis., 1926; M.A., U. Mich., 1927; postgrad. U. Vienna (Austria), 1930; Ph.D., Cornell U., 1939; m. Martha Sabeva, June 23, 1935; children—Julia (Mrs. Roscoe Ward), Elizabeth (Mrs. John Woodford). Instr. English, U. Detroit, 1927-29, De Paul U., 1936-37, Cornell U., 1937-42; asst. prof. La. State U., 1942-44; distinguished prof. English Lit. U. Akron, 1945—; vis. prof. Fordham U., 1945, U. Colo., 1961; staff Am. legation, Sofia, Bulgaria, 1933-36. Fulbright lectr. U. Tubingen, 1954-56. Mem. Modern Humanities Research Assn., Northeastern Ohio Coll. English Assn. (past pres.), Am. Assn. U. Profs., Modern Lang. Assn., Nat. Council Tchrs. English, Omicron Delta Kappa. Roman Catholic. Club: Franklin (Akron). Author: Correspondence of Taylor and Hayne, 1945; Hayne's Letters to Julia Dorr, 1950; (with Henry J. Pettit) Dictionary of Literary Terms, 1950; also articles. Book revs. for N.Y. Times, Cleve. Plain Dealer. Contbr. to encys. Home: 2896 Oak Hill Rd Peninsula OH 44264 Office: U Akron Akron OH 44304

DUFFY, EARL GAVIN, hotel exec.; b. Boston, Oct. 11, 1926; s. William Emmett and Mary (Costello) D.; ed. pub. schs.; m. Bernice Rose MacMaster, Feb. 14, 1948; children—Earl Gavin, Joan I., Mark C., Neil W., Lynn A. Engaged in hotel bus., 1941—; sales mgr. Somerset Hotel, Boston, 1952-56; Eastern sales mgr. Hotel Corp. Am., 1956-59, asst. nat. sales mgr., 1959-61, nat. sales mgr., 1961-64, v.p., gen. mgr., 1961—; guest lectr. Cornell U., 1961, U. Houston, 1965, Wash. State U., 1966. Chmn. Bus.-industry div. Harris County March of Dimes, 1964—; chmn. Greater Hartford Convention and Visitors Bur. Served with USNR, World War II; PTO. Recipient Golden Host award Hotel Mgmt. mag., 1964; named Hotel Salesman of Year, Sigma Iota, 1966. Mem. Hotel Sales Mgmt. Assn. (pres. New Eng. 1958, internat. pres. 1962), Hotel Mgmt. Assn. Houston (pres. 1966), Am., Conn. (v.p.) hotel and motel assns., New Eng. Innkeepers Assn. (bd. dirs.), Hartford C. of C. (bd. dirs.). Rotarian. Club: Skal (Houston). Home: 423 Mountain Rd West Hartford CT 06107 Office: Hotel America Hartford CT 06103

DUFFY, EDWARD C., utilities exec.; b. Cambridge, N.Y., Mar. 5, 1909; s. Edward D. and Helen A. (McClallen) D.; B.S. in Mech. Engring., U. Notre Dame, 1930; m. Helene M. Playford, Oct. 23, 1931; children—Maureen Helene (Mrs. R.L. Forrester), Robert Francis, Linda Mary. Engring. and constrn. depts. Consol. Edison Co. N.Y., Inc., 1930-42; engr. Long Island Lighting Co., Mineola, N.Y., 1942-45, supt. generating stas. and substas., 1945-48, mgr. elec. products, 1948-50, asst. v.p., 1950-53, v.p., 1953-58, sr. v.p., 1958-65, exec. v.p., 1965-68, pres., 1968—, also dir.; dir. Empire State Atomic Devel. Assos., Inc., Atomic Power Devel. Assos., Inc., L.I. Trust Co., Utilities Mut. Ins. Co.; trustee Power Reactor Devel. Co., Green Point Savs. Bank. Trustee Inst. Gas Tech. Fellow Am. Soc. M.E. (Prime movers award 1955); mem. Am. Gas Assn. (dir. 1968-70), Soc. Gas Lighting, I.E.E.E., L.I. Assn. Commerce and Industry. Clubs: Garden City (N.Y.) Golf; Seaview (N.J.) Country; North Fork Country; Engineers' (N.Y.C); Notre Dame N.Y. Home: 133 Marshall Av Floral Park Mineola NY 11001 Office: 250 Old Country Rd Minneola NY 11501

DUFFY, EDWARD WILLIAM, bldg. materials co. exec.; b. LaSalle, Ill., Sept. 25, 1919; s. Edward J. and Margaret (Brunick) D.; grad. LaSalle-Peru Jr. Coll., 1938; student Loyola U., Chgo., also exec. devel. program, Cornell U.; m. Rosemary G. Dee, June 28, 1941; 1 dau., Jill Anne. Research chemist, 1941-45; engaged in sales, mdsg. and sales mgr., 1945—; v.p. U.S. Gypsum Co., 1963-69, exec. v.p., 1969-71, pres., 1971—. Home: 1815 W Ridgewood Lane Glenview IL 60025 Office: 101 S Wacker Dr Chicago IL 60606

DUFFY, FRANCIS RAMON, educator; b. Phila., Mar. 26, 1915; s. John J. and Anna (Rodgers) D.; B.A., Holy Ghost Coll., 1938; B.D., St. Mary's Coll., 1942; M.A., Cath. U., 1944; Ph.D., U. Pitts., 1955. Joined Congregation of Holy Ghost, 1933, ordained priest Roman Cath. Ch., 1941; asst. prof. sociology Duguesne U., 1943-50, prof., chmn. dept., from 1953; now dir. St. Joseph's House, Phila.; chaplain Juvenile Ct. Allegheny County, 1947-68; instr. Pitts. Police Acad., 1956-68; instr. Army Officer Career Course; vis. prof. St. Joseph's Coll.; cons. Pitts. Behavior Clinic, also med. dept. Gulf Oil Corp.; producer radio series. Served as maj., chaplain, AUS, 1950-52; now col. Res. Fellow Royal Anthrop. Assn. Gt. Britain and Ireland; mem. Am., Pa. sociol. Socs., Royal Medico- Psychol. Soc., Am. Cath. Sociol. Soc. Am. Soc. Clin. Hypnosis, Am. Population Assn., Pa. Chiefs Police Assn., Am. Assn. U. Profs.; corr. asso. Royal Coll. Psychiatry. Knights of Equity. K.C. Author: Title System in Nigeria, 1944; Study of Male White Delinquents in Pittsburgh, 1955; Exploring the Child's World; Social Psychology of Growing Up; Juvenile Delinquency; Personal and Social Adjustment. Address: St Joseph's House 16th and Allegheny Av Philadelphia PA 19140

DUFFY, FRANCIS RYAN, judge; b. Fond du Lac, Wis., June 23, 1888; s. Francis Fee and Hattie (Ryan) D.; A.B., U. Wis., 1910, LL.B., 1912, LL.D., 1952; LL.D., DePaul U. Chgo., 1955; m. Louise Haydon, Jan. 26, 1918; children—Ann Louise, Francis Ryan, Haydon Robertson, James Hamilton. Practiced law in Fond du Lac, 1912-33; mem. U.S. Senate, 1933-39; juge U.S. Dist. Ct. 1939-49, U. S. Ct. of Appeals, 7th Circuit, 1949—, chief judge, 1954-59, Sr. U. S. circuit judge, 1966—. Served to maj. Motor Transport Corps., U.S. Army, World War I. Recipient Alumni award U. Wis. Law Sch., 1968. Mem. Am. Legion, Phi Alpha Delta, Delta Sigma Rho. Democrat. Elk, K.C. Club: Milwaukee Athletic. Home: 3107 N Hackett Av Milwaukee WI 53211

DUFFY, JACQUES WAYNE, educator; b. Nimes, France, July 1, 1922; s. Edward F. and Eveline (Lagier) D.; A.B., Columbia Coll., 1947, B.S., 1948, M.S., 1949, Ph.D., 1957; m. Angeline Coultas, June 17, 1950; children—Jacqueline, Philip, Paul. Mem. research dept. Grumann Aircraft Engring. Corp., 1950-52; research asst. Columbia U., 1952-54; prof. engring. Brown U., 1954—; Guggenheim fellow Cambridge (Eng.) U., 1964-65; editorial adv. bd. Inst. Scientific Information, 1970—. Trustee St. Dunstan's Day Sch. Served with AUS, 1943-46. Mem. Am. Soc. Mech. Engrs., Soc. for Exptl. Stress Analysis, Soc. Rheology, A.A.A.S. Home: 71 Lorraine Av Providence RI 02906

DUFFY, JAMES EDWARD, educator; b. Elkton, Md., May 1, 1923; s. Edward H. and Sara (Whitlock) D.; A.B., U. N.C., 1944; A.M., U. San Carlos de Guatemala, 1947; Ph.D., Harvard, 1952; m. Lillian Chase Johnson, Oct. 26, 1944; children—David Livingstone, Amanda Chase, Priscilla Kingsley. Instr., U. N.C., 1945-46; dir. acad. course Guatamalan-Am. Inst., 1946, dir. inst., 1947-48; teaching fellow Harvard, 1948-51; faculty Brandeis U., 1951—, now prof. history and literature; cons. State Dept., Council Fgn. Relations, Brookings Inst. Ford fellow, 1955-56; Bollingen fellow, 1962- 63; Social Sci. Research Council fellow, 1962-63; NSF fellow, 1962-63; Rockefeller fellow, 1964; Guggenheim fellow, 1966. Mem. African Studies Assn. (pres. 1967-68, exec. sec. 1969—), Phi Beta Kappa. Author: Shipwreck and Empire, 1955; Portuguese Africa, 1959; (with Robert Manners) Africa Speaks, 1961; Portugal in Africa, 1962; The Portuguese African Territories, 1961; A Question of Slavery, 1967; also articles. Home: Indian Hill Rd Groton MA 04150 Office: Shiffman Humanities Center Brandeis Univ Waltham MA 02154

DUFFY, JAMES JOSEPH, Jr., lawyer; b. Mobile, Ala., Aug. 4,1931; s. James Joseph and Regina (Tobler) D.; grad. Marion Mil. Inst., 1951; A.B., U. Ala., 1953, LL.B., 1957; m. Anne Hunter Williams, Jan. 3, 1953; children-James Joseph III, Lucy Hunter. Admitted to Ala. bar, 1957; mem. firm Inge, Twitty, Duffy & Prince, Mobile, 1957. Trustee St. Paul's Episcopal Day Sch. Served to 1st lt. AUS, 1953-55. Mem. Am., Ala., Mobile bar Assns., Maritime Law Assn., Am. Judicature Soc., Internat. assn. Ins. Counsel, Internat. Soc. Barristers, Delta Kappa Epsilon, Phi Delta Phi. Episcopalian. Clubs: Athelstan (Mobile), Mobile Touchdown (dir.), Mobile Country; Lakewood Country (Point Clear, Ala.); Downtown (Birmingham, Ala.). Home: 109 Pinebrook Dr Spring Hill Mobile AL 36608 Office: Mchts Nat Bank Bldg Mobile AL 36601

DUFFY, JOSEPH ALEXANDER, book industry exec.; b. Jersey City, Nov. 9, 1903; s. Joseph Alexander and Mary (Hetherington) D.; grad. Newman Sch., Lakewood, N.J.; student Columbia, 1922-24; m. 2d, Marguerite Rooney O'Brien, Nov. 24, 1949; 1 son, Mark Joseph; 1 dau. by previous marriage, Diana (Mrs. James Thomson). With Harper & Bros., 1924-29; sales mgr. Jonathan Cape & Harrison Smith, 1929-30, Longmans, Green & Co., 1930-32, Columbia U. Press, 1932-45; dir. sales, advt., promotion Henry Holt & Co., 1945-48; research dir. Am. Book Pubs. Council, in charge Ohio Book Project, 1948-49; book pub. cons., gen. mgr. Christophers Lit. Prize Contests, 1949-50; pub. dir. P.J. Kenedy & Sons, 1950-53; instr. English, editing, pub. Columbia, 1950-54; exec. dir. Am. Booksellers Assn., Inc., N.Y.C., 1953—. Mem. White House Library Com.; mem. steering com. Nat. Book Awards, 1964 —, Nat. Library Week, 1964—. Del., White House Conf. on Internat. Cooperation, 1965. Mem. Psi Upsilon. Democrat. Roman Catholic. Clubs: Dutch Treat Columbia Univ. (N.Y.C.); Pelham Country. Contbr. poetry, articles to profl. jours., popular mags. contbr. to Americana Ann., 1954—. Home: 21 Elm Pl Pelham Manor NY 10803 Office: 175 Fifth Av New York City NY 10010

DUFFY, KEVIN THOMAS, govt. ofcl.; b. N.Y.C., Jan. 10, 1933; s. Patrick John and Mary (McGarrell) D.; A.B., Fordham Coll., 1954, J.D., 1958; m. Irene Krumeich, Nov. 9, 1957; children-Kevin Thomas, Irene Moira, Gavin Edward, Patrick Giles. Admitted to N.Y. bar, 1958; clerk to circuit judge, N.Y.C., 1955-58; asst. chief criminal div. U.S. Atty.'s Office, N.Y.C., 1958-61; asso. firm Whitman, Ransom & Coulson, N.Y.C., 1961-66; partner firm Gordon & Gordon, N.Y.C., 1966-69; regional adminstr. SEC, N.Y.C., 1969—. Mem. N.Y. State, Westchester County bar assns., Assn. Bar N.Y.C., Fed. Bar Council (trustee 1970—), Fordham Law Sch. Alumni Assn. (trustee 1969—). Clubs: Adventurers (N.Y.C.); Westchester Country. Home: 15 Hewitt Av Bronxville, NY 10708 Office: Securities and Exchange Commn 26 Federal Plaza New York NY 10007

DUFFY, PHILIP B., paper co. exec.; b. Pitts., Jan. 1, 1909; s. Philip B. and Helen (Crowley) D.; m. Marjorie Krons, June 2, 1951; children—Pebble, Shawn, Pamela. Formerly with F. J. Kress Box Co.; 1945—; sr. v.p. St. Regis Paper Co. Home: Fox Chapel Manor Pittsburgh PA 15238 Office: 150 E 42d St New York City NY 10017.

DU FLON, HENRY A., business exec.; b. New Rochelle, N.Y., Mar. 1, 1915; s. Thaddeus Avery Van Zandt and Edith Dorothy (Albert) Du F.; A.B., Princeton, 1937; m. Barbara Van Clief, July 14, 1945; children—Deborah, Alison, Jeffrey Carroll, Dirck. Asst. to mag. ed., 1937-41; asst. manpower mgr. mfg. co., 1946-48, asst. to pres., 1948-52; cons. mgmt. orgn., 1952-53; spl. asst. to Pres., adviser personnel mgmt., 1953-55; dep. asst. sec. def. Dept. Def., 1955-56; dir. foundation, 1957-60; fgn. service officer, 1960—; dep. dir. USOM to Guatemala, 1960-61; chief regional office Central Am.-Panama,

AID/Washington, 1962; dir. Regional Office Central Am./Panama, Central Am./Panama, Dept. State, 1962-68; Asso. Boyden Associates, Inc., N.Y.C., Latin Am, 1968—. Served to maj. AUS, 1941-46. Episcopalian. Clubs: Salmagundi, Princeton (N.Y.); Coral Beach and Tennis (Bermuda); Izabal Tarpon, Antiqueno (Guatemala). Home: Quinta Avenida Sur No 32 Antiqua Guatemala Guatemala

DUFOUR, MAURICE FRANCIS, chem. engr.; b. New Orleans, Feb. 13, 1910; B.S., Tulane U., 1930, Chem. E., 1933; m. Lydia Mortee Penn, July 12, 1937; 1 dau., Lydia Ann. With Freeport Sulphur Co., N.Y.C., and subsidiaries, 1933—, v.p., 1956—, pres. subsidiary Freeport Research and Devel. Co., 1969—. Mem. Am. Inst. Chem. Engrs., Am. Inst. Mining, Metall. and Petroleum Engrs. Clubs: University, Chemists, Cloud (N.Y.C.); New Orleans Coutry, Internat. House. Home: 636 Burdette St New Orleans LA 70118 Office: P O Box 61520 New Orleans LA 70160

DUFRESNE, ROBERT AUSTIN, coll. pres.; b. Brainerd, Minn., Oct. 29, 1921; s. Joseph Antone and Margaret Bertha (Gleason) D.; B.S., St. Cloud (Minn.) Coll., 1950; M.Ed., U. Colo., 1954; Ed.D., U. N.D., 1959; m. Betty Elaine Heinmiller, May 30, 1947; 1 son, Jeffrey Robert. Tchr., Austin, Minn., 1950-59; asso. prof. edn. Mankato (Minn.) State Coll., 1959-63; prof., adminstr. Kearney (Neb.) State Coll., 1963-67; pres. Winona (Minn.) State Coll., 1967—. Served with USNR, 1942-46. Mem. Phi Delta Kappa. Home: 502 W Broadway Winona MN 55987

DUFTON, CHARLES HENRY, educator; b. Andover, Mass., Aug. 7, 1911; s. George Charles Henry and Susannah (Mitchell) D.; grad. cum laude, Phillips Acad., Andover, Mass., 1930; B.A. with honors in econs., Yale, 1934; M.A., U. Mich., 1936; m. Phyllis Louise Clark, Feb. 1, 1941; 1 dau., Gayle Louise. Teaching fellow econs. U. Mich., 1935-37; instr. econs. Harvard, 1937-39; economist Bur. Budget, 1939-42; sales economist radio div. Bendix Aviation Corp., 1942-45, sales and advt. supr. Bendix internat. div., 1945-46; prof. marketing, chmn. dept. Northeastern U., 1946—. Dir. Andover Consumers Coop., Inc., New Eng. Coops. Inc., Fitchburg. Pub. mem. Mass. Minimum Wage Bd., 1956, 57; sponsors adv. com. Boston Conf. Distbn., 1960—; participant visitors case writing program Harvard Grad. Sch. Bus. Adminstrn., 1955. Mem. Am. Marketing Assn. (chmn. student marketing com. 1953-54, pres. Boston, 1957-58, dir. 1953-60), Nat. Sales Execs. Club (pres. Merrimack Valley 1959-60), Advt. Fedn. Am., Internat. Trade Assn. New Eng., Am. Assn. U. Profs., Goethe Soc. New Eng., Phi Beta Kappa, Phi Kappa Phi, Beta Gamma Sigma. Clubs: Yale (Boston); Harvard (Andover) Colonie Francaise de Nouvelle-Angleterre; Vet. Motor Car Am.; Rolls-Royce Owners Am. Author: Selected Case Studies in Executive Management of Marketing Operations, 1957. Home: 35 Canterbury St Andovver MA 01810 Office: 360 Huntington Av Boston MA 02115

DUGAN, ALAN, poet; b. Bklyn., Feb. 12, 1923; student Olivet (Mich.) Coll.; grad. Mexico City Coll. Served with USAAF, World War II. Recipient award for poetry, 1946, Nat. Book award for poetry, 1961, Pulitzer prize for poetry, 1962; Guggenheim fellow, 1963-64; Levinson poetry prize, 1967; Rockefeller Found. fellow, 1966-67. Author: Poems, 1961; Poems 2, 1963; Poems 3, 1967; Collected Poems, 1969; also numerous poems in Poetry mag. others. Address: 59 W 10th St New York City NY 10011

DUGAN, EDWARD ALBERT, Jr., coll. pres.; b. Phila., July 10, 1928; s. Edward Albert and Katherine (Werner) D.; B.S. in Bus. Adminstrn., Temple U., 1955; m. Joan Marie Stapleton, June 11, 1955; children—Patricia, Pamela, Mark Craig. Asst. to v.p. Temple U., 1955; staff dir. Phila. United Fund, 1956; campaign dir. Burrill, Inc., 1960; v.p. Upper Ia. U., 1962; v.p., Coll. Osteo. Medicine and Surgery, Des Moines, 1965; exec. v.p. W.L. Darling Corp., 1966, now dir.; pres. Ind. Inst. Tech., Ft. Wayne, 1967- -; Ednl. cons., 1962—. Past dir. East-Central Improvement Corp.; mem. exec. council Anthony Wayne council Boy Scouts Am. Mem. finance com. Allen County Democratic Com. Bd. dirs. Ft. Wayne Urban League, African Heritage House. Served with USNR, 1946. Mem. Am. Council Edn., Delta Sigma Pi. Home: 1041 Schick St Fort Wayne IN 46803

DUGAN, FRANCIS WILLIAM, newspaperman; b. Oshkosh, Wis., Oct. 5, 1907; s. Michael Martin and Catherine (McGinley) D.; student John Carroll U.; m. Angel Rose Hahn, June 27, 1936; 1 son, John George. With Cleve. Plain Dealer, 1925—, gen. mgr., 1962—, v.p., 1963—; dir. Forest City Pub. Co., Art Gravure Corp. Ohio Bd. dirs. Cleve. Real Property Inventory. Trustee John Carroll U., St. John's Hosp., Cath. Charities Corp., Soc. for Crippled Children, Cleve. Served with AUS, World War II. Home: 22800 Lake Rd Rocky River OH 44116 Office: 1801 Superior Av Cleveland OH 44114

DUGAN, GEORGE, newspaperman; b. Toledo, Feb. 9, 1909; s. George and Mary Eleanor (Blauvelt) D.; student Blair Acad., 1925-27, U. Mich., 1927-30; m. Josephine Rearick, Nov. 24, 1937; 1 son, Brian. Reporter Religious News Service, 1938-47; reporter N.Y. Times, 1947-49, religious news editor, 1949-65, reporter, 1965—. Served as Spl. Agt. CIC, AUS 1945-47. Awarded Asso. Ch. Press award of merit, 1952, Nat. Religious Publicity Council award, 1950, James O. Supple Meml. award Sigma Delta Chi, 1959. Mem. Religious Newswriters Assn. (pres. 1951-52) Alpha Delta Phi Home: Hillsdale NJ 07642 Office: 229 W 43d St New York City NY 10036

DUGAN, HUGH PATRICK, civil engr.; b. Louisville, Colo., Apr. 15, 1914; s. Walter Hugh and Christine (Zurick) D.; B.S. in Civil and Irrigation Engring., Colo. State U., 1936; m. Alice L. Pennock, May 19, 1938; 1 dau., Michele Diane Kennedy. With Bur. Reclamation, Dept. Interior, 1936—, asst. chief devel. engr., 1954-59, regional dir. region 2, 1959-62, region 7, 1962-67, chief project investigations, 1967-68, chmn., U.S. commr. Upper Colorado River Commn., 1968—; civil engr., adviser World Bank, 1969-71; cons. engr. water resource devel., 1971—. Mem. Federal Exec. Bd. Denver, Central Bd. Civil Service Examiners; mem. U.S. nat. com. Internat. Commn. Irrigation and Drainage. Served to lt. USNR, World War II. Registered profl. engr., Cal., Colo. Mem. Nat. Soc. Profl. Engrs., Internat. Commn. Large Dams, Chi Epsilon. Address: 2417 Lomond Lane Walnut Creek CA 94598

DUGAN, JAMES PATRICK, banker; b. Indpls., Oct. 8, 1936; s. James Leo and Lillian (Murphy) D.; Ph.B., U. Notre Dame, 1958; postgrad. N.Y. U., 1962-63; m. Carmen Irene Hisnberger, Sept. 9, 1967; children—Danielle Lillian, Nicole Elizabeth. Staff accountant Price Waterhouse & Co., N.Y.C., 1962-64, sr. accountant, 1964-67, mgr., 1967-69; treas., controller Export-Import Bank of U.S., Washington, 1969, sr. v.p., treas., controller, 1970—. Pres., Knickerbocker Republican Club 64th A.D., N.Y.C., 1967-68; mem. Rep. County Com., County of Manhattan, N.Y.C., 1967-68; controller Nixon for Pres. Com., 1968; asso. finance chmn. Nixon Agnew Campaign Com., 1968, treas. transition com., 1968-69. Served with USAF, 1961-62. Mem. Am. Inst. C.P.A.'s, N.Y. State, Ind. socs. C.P.A.'s, Fed. Govt. Accountants Assn., Internat. Platform Assn., Notre Dame Alumni Assn. Roman Catholic. Home: 5607 Gloster Rd Wood Acres Bethesda MD 20016 Office: 811 Vermont Av NW Washington DC 20571

DUGAN, JOSEPH HARRY, aircraft co. exec.; b. Osceola Mills, Pa., Mar. 1, 1925; s. Joseph L. and Oral Ruth (Williams) D.; B.S., Villanova U., 1950; M.B.A., L.I. U., N.Y.U., 1967; m. Florence Cecelia Ostermaier, Nov. 15, 1952; children—Joseph, Michael, Frances, Patricia, John. Accounting supr. Montgomery Ward & Co., Balt., 1950-52; comptroller, treas. Airpax Electronics, Ft. Lauderdale, Fla., 1952-62; treas. Sound Scriber Corp., New Haven, 1962-64; div. controller Fairchild Hiller Corp., Bay Shore, N.Y., 1964-65, group controller, 1965-69, treas., Germantown, Md., 1969—. Served with USNR, 1943-46. C.P.A., Md. Mem. Am. Inst. C.P.A.'s, Nat. Assn. Accountants. K.C., Elk. Home: 1229 Clearfield Circle Lutherville MD 21093 Office: Fairchild Dr Germantown MD 20767

DUGAN, RUTH ROBERTA, educator; b. Union City, N.J., Jan. 29, 1920; d. Christopher P. and Hazel L. (Stewart) Newman; B.A., N.Y.U., 1940, M.A., 1950, Ph.D., 1958; m. James P. Dugan, August 5, 1939; children—Dianne R. (Mrs. Donald Williams, James P., and J. Christopher. Lecturer at John Marshall Coll., 1946-48, prof. and chmn. dept. natural scis., 1948-50; instr. Sch. Edn., Seton Hall U., 1950-52, dean of women, asst. prof. edn., 1952- 59; asso. prof. sci. Jersey City (N.J.) State Coll., 1959-63, prof. sci. 1963-65; prof. edn. and sci. Glassboro State Coll., 1965-67, dir. behavioral sciences research center, 1966—, asst. dean of grad. studies, 1967-68; speaker. Mem. Citizens Advisory of Union City, N.J.; chmn. art exhibits N.J. artists. Recipient Founders Day award, N.Y.U.; Dist. Service award, Seton Hall U., 1960. Mem. Am. Ednl. Research Assn., Nat. Assn. Research Sci. Teaching, Am. Assn. for Advancement Sci. Nat. Assn. Sci. Tchrs., Nat. Assn. Deans Women, Phi Lambda Theta (2d place award 1950), Kappa Delta Pi, Iota Mu Pi (founder). Contbr. numerous articles profl. jours. Home: Box 1237 Browns Mills NJ 08015

DUGAN, WILLIAM EDWARD, investment banker; b. Rutland, Vt., Feb. 15, 1907; s. William E. and Elizabeth (Travers) D.; B.S. in Econs., Wharton Sch. of U. Pa., 1929; M.B.A., N.Y.U., 1933; chartered financial analyst, 1964; m. Virginia Marshall, June 10, 1930; children-Isabell (Mrs. John L. LaCrosse), Ellen (Mrs. Dennis Daut), Martha (Mrs. Eric M. Erksine). With Laidlaw & Co., N.Y.C., 1929—, mng. partner, 1960—, chmn. bd., 1969—, also dir.; dir. Les Placements Laid-Law Que. Limitee, Laidlaw Securities Ont. Ltd., Hawley Mfg. Co. Clubs: Scarsdale Golf (Hartsdale, N.Y.); Ekwanok Country (Manchester, Vt.); Sky, Broad Street (bd. govs.) N.Y.C.).‡

DUGGAN, ALFRED, author: Winter Quarters, Children of the Wolf, Conscience of the King, The Story of the Crusades, others. Address: care Pantheon Books 22 E 51st St New York City NY 10022*

DUGGAN, BEN O., Jr., lawyer ; b. Chattanooga, 1902; s. Benjamin Oscar and Barbara E. (Graves) D.; LL.B., U. Tenn., 1926; m. Marion E. Moses, Aug. 9, 1929; children—Marion (Mrs. Paul Emerson Andrews), Barbara (Mrs. James Arthur Posner). Admitted to Tenn. bar, 1926, Ala. bar, 1930; practice of law, Knoxville, Tenn., 1926-29, Birmingham, 1936-42, Chattanooga, 1942—; mem. Duggan & McDonald, 1961—. Mem. Am., Tenn., Chattanooga bar assns., Fedn. Ins. Counsel, Internat. Assn. Ins. Counsel. Democrat. Baptist. Mason (Shriner). Home: 1846 Crestwood Dr Chattanooga TN 37415 Office: Provident Bldg Chattanooga TN 37402

DUGGAN, DENNIS, newspaper editor; b. Detroit, Oct. 12, 1929; s. Michael and Anne (Judge) D.; B.A., Wayne U., 1952; 1 dau. by previous marriage, Nancy Ellen. Reporter, N.Y. Herald Tribune, 1957-60; asst. editor N.Y. Times, 1960-62; sr. editor Newsday, N.Y.C., 1969—. Mem. N.Y. Financial Writers Assn., Soc. Silurians. Contbr. articles popular mags., TV, radio. Home: 235 W 11th St New York City NY 10014 Office: 230 W 41st St New York City NY 10036

DUGGAN, HERBERT GARRISON, sci. researcher; b. Knoxville, Tenn., Jan. 25, 1919; s. Claude Vernon and Fannie Mae (Garrison) D.; B.S. in Mech. Engring., U. Tenn., 1943, postgrad., 1950-53; m. Lilian Kathryn Calafati, June 5, 1948. Mech. engr. Buick Motor Div., Flint, Mich., 1943-44; mech. engr. Union Carbide-Oak Ridge Nat. Lab., 1946-48, design group leader, 1948-55, head, nuclear equipment design dept., 1955—. Tech. adviser Information Center for Nuclear Standards, 1971—. Served to lt. (j.g.) USNR, 1944-46; PTO. Registered profl. engr., Tenn. Mem. Am. Nuclear Soc. (chmn. remote systems tech. div. 1964-65), Am. Soc. M.E. (v.p. 1969-71). Elk. Instrumental in devel. remote handling techniques for nuclear industry; contbr. articles to profl. lit. Home: 400 Virginia Rd Oak Ridge TN 37830 Office: Oak Ridge Nat Lab PO Box X Oak Ridge TN 37830

DUGGAN, JAMES GRAYSON, metall. co. exec.; b. Chgo., July 28, 1923; s. Frank E. and Jessie (Kaiser) D.; B.A. cum laude Beloit Coll., 1947; J.D., Northwestern U., 1950; M.B.A., U. Chgo., 1967; m. Lois Sarty, Aug. 30, 1947; children—David G., Anne, Carole. Admitted to Ill. bar, 1950; mem. firm Defrees Fiske O'Brien & Thompson, Chgo., 1952-56; asst. sec., atty. Crane Co., Chgo., 1956-61; sec.- treas. Fansteel Inc., North Chicago, Ill., 1961—. Served with USMCR, 1943-46. 50-52. Rotarian (pres. North Chgo. chpt. 1967-68). Club: Lake Forest (dir. 1969—). Home: 958 Waveland Rd Lake Forest IL 60045 Office: 1 Tantalum Pl North Chicago IL 60064

DUGGAN, JEROME TIMOTHY, utilities exec.; b. Kansas City, Mo., Oct. 30, 1914; s. Jerry F. and Claire (Aaron) D.; A.B., U. Mo., 1936, LL.B., 1938; m. Dorothy Blanche Castle, May 4, 1940; children—Jerome Castle, Dorothy Lucinda Kobusch. Admitted to Mo. bar, 1938; with Hook & Thomas, Kansas City, 1938-4O; asst. city counselor, Kansas City, 1940-42; regional rationing atty. OPA, 1942-43; mem. firm Gage, Hillix & Phelps, 1946-50; gen. counsel Gas Service Co. Kansas City, Mo., 1950-68, v.p., dir., 1956-64, exec. v.p., dir., gen. counsel, 1964-68, pres., dir., 1968—, dir. Commerce Bank, Kansas City. Mem. Gov's. Adv. Commn. on Indsl. Devel., 1961—; chmn. Kansas City Housing Authority, 1947-5O; dir. Indsl. Council Kansas City, 1951-55; mem. Indsl. Devel. Commn., Kansas City, 1959—, Municipal Service Commn., 1955-56. Bd. dirs. Citizens Regional Planning Council, Downtown Inc., Kansas City Indsl. Found.; pres. bd. dirs. Asso. Inustries of Mo., 1970—; Trustee, pres. Research Hosp. and Med. Center, 1970-71; trustee Mo. Pub. Expenditure Survey, Midwest Research Inst.; bd. regents Rockhurst Coll. Served as lt. USNR, World War II. Mem. Am., Mo. bar assns., Am. Gas Assn., Fed. Power Bar Assn., Am. Royal Assn. (bd. govs.), Sigma Nu, Phi Delta Phi. Clubs: Saddle and Sirloin, Kansas City, University (v.p., dir. 1956-57), Mission Hills Country. Home: 11215 Holly St Kansas City MO 64114 Office: Scarritt Bldg Kansas City MO 64106

DUGGAN, JOHN MICHAEL, educator; b. Bridgeport, Conn., June 8, 1928; s. John Hanley and Mary (Dixon) D.; A.B., Coll. of Holy Cross, 1950; M.A., Yale, 1955, Ph.D., 1957; m. Claire Keenan, June 2, 1951; children—Michael, Christopher, Paul, Timothy, John. Instr. Canterbury Sch., New Milford, Conn., 1950-51, U. Bridgeport, 1951-53; asst. dean of freshmen Yale, 1953-57; dir. guidance services Coll. Entrance Exam. Bd., 1957-60, dir. program development, 1960-63, v.p., 1963-68; v.p., prof. psychology Vassar, 1968—. Mem. Am. Psychol. Assn., Am. Personnel and Guidance Assn. Address: Box 234 Vassar Coll Poughkeepsie NY 12601

DUGGAN, JOSEPH CHARLES, lawyer, govt. ofcl.; b. New Bedford, Mass., Oct. 18, 1910; s. Hugh A. and Margaret E. (Murphy) D.; A.B. cum laude, Holy Cross Coll., 1932; LL.B. cum laude, Columbus U., 1939; LL.M., Catholic U., 1941, S.J.D., 1946; LL.D. (hon.) Stonehill Coll., 1953; L.H.D., Anna Maria Coll., 1967; m. Helen Louise Bartley, Nov. 30, 1935; children—Margaret Ann (Mrs. Jules Ryckebusch), Joseph C., Jr., Dermot B. Admitted to D.C. bar, 1939, Mass. bar, 1942; spl. atty. Dept. of Justice, Washington, 1939-41, prin. atty., 1942-43, spl. asst. to Atty. Gen., 1944-46; asst. U.S. atty.-gen. 1951-52; 1st asst. U.S. atty. for Mass., 1946-47; instr. law Boston Coll. Law Sch., 1946-47; lectr. Mass. Lawyers Post-War Inst., 1946-47; pvt. practice, New Bedford, 1947-51; spl counsel, platform and resolutions com. Dem. Nat. Conv., Chgo., 1952, gen. counsel, 1956; city solicitor, New Bedford, 1956-58, 59-61; asst. atty. gen. Commonwealth of Mass., 1958-59, spl. asst. atty. gen., 1962; spl. city solicitor, Taunton, Mass., 1961-62. Special counsel for the Nauset Regional Sch. Dist., 1962; also co-counsel for the Presidents' Temp. Com. on Employee Loyalty, 1947. Mem. adv. bd. St. Hyacinth's Coll. and Sem., St. Columba's Coll. ad Sem., Anna Maria Coll. for Women, Marist College and Seminary, Oblate Coll. and Sem.; mem. bd. Stonehill Coll.; Archbishop Cushing Coll.; v.p. Cachalot council Boy Scouts Am., 1954-55, pres., 1956-57, exec. bd. 1957—. Hearing officer conscientious objector cases, D.C., World War II, Mass., 1948-51. Recipient Silver Beaver award, Boy Scouts Am. 1958; Selective Service medal U.S. Congress. Mem. Fed., Mass., Bristol Co., New Bedford bar assns. Democrat. Roman Catholic. K.C. Club: Luncheon (New Bedford). Author: Legislative and Statutory Development of Federal Concept of Conscription, 1946. Contbr. articles. Office: 179 William St New Bedford MA 01730

DUGGAN, STEPHEN PIERCE, lawyer; b. White Plains, N.Y., Apr. 25, 1909; s. Stephen Pierce and Sarah (Elsessor) D.; grad. Phillips Exeter Acad., 1927; B.S., Harvard, 1931; M.A., Columbia, 1932, LL.B., 1936; m. Beatrice Vail Abbott, Sept. 19, 1936; children—Stephen Pierce III, Marianne (Mrs. Raymond E. Bell), Peter Matthiessen, Hayden Abbott. Admitted to N.Y. State bar, 1938, since practiced in N.Y.C.; partner firm Simpson Thacher & Bartlett, 1943- -. Mem. USAAF Air Evaluation Bd. for S.W. Pacific Area, 1944-45. Pres. bd. trustees Storm King Sch., Cornwall-on-Hudson, N.Y., 1953—, trustee Phillips Exeter Acad., 1950-55, New Sch. Social Research, 1939-58, Vassar Coll., 1958-70, Inst. Internat. Edn., N.Y.C., 1950—; chmn. bd. trustees Natural Resources Def. Council, 1970—. Fellow Am. Bar Found., Am. Coll. Trial Lawyers; mem. Am., N.Y. State bar assns., Assn. Bar City, N.Y., Columbia Law Sch. Alumni Assn. Clubs: Century Assn., Down Town Assn. (N.Y.C.). Home: 47 E 88th St New York City NY 10028 Office: 1 Battery Park Plaza New York City NY 10004

DUGGAN, TIMOTHY JOHN, educator, philosopher; b. Worcester, Mass., Feb. 20, 1928; s. Timothy John and Esther (McDermott) D.; A.B., Brown U., 1952, A.M., 1953, Ph.D., 1957; M.A., Harvard, 1954; M.A. (hon.), Dartmouth, 1969; m. Joan Lamoureux, Aug. 23, 1951; children—Theresa Elizabeth, Timothy John, Christine Frances. Faculty Dartmouth, 1957—, prof. Philosophy, 1968—, chmn. dept. 1963-67. Served with USAAF, 1946-48. Mem. Am. Philos. Assn. Editor: The Philosophical Works of Thomas Reid, 1969. Home: 2 Spencer Rd Hanover NH 03755

DUGGAN, WILLIAM REDMAN, fgn. service officer; b. Durango, Colo., Feb. 11, 1915; s. William Edward and Pansy (Redman) D.; student Western State Coll., Gunnison, Colo., 1933-35; A.B., U. Notre Dame, 1938, M.A., 1939; postgrad. Boston U., 1955-56; m. Florence Olive Jewell, Aug. 30, 1952; 1 son, David W. Field office mgr. Social Security Bd., 1940-44; joined U.S. Fgn. Service, 1944—; vice consul, Durban, South Africa, 1944-47, Vancouver, B.C., Can., 1948-50; 2d sec., consul, Copenhagen, Denmark, 1951-55; polit. liaison officer U.S. delegation UN Gen. Assembly, 1956- 57; officer-in-charge West African Affairs Dept. State, 1957-58; consul gen., Dar-es-Salaam, Tanzania, 1958-62; mem. Policy Planning Council Dept. State, 1962-67; consul gen., Durban, S. Africa, 1967-71. Recipient meritorious award Dept. State, 1963, Distinguished Service award, 1971. Mem. Explorers Club, African Studies Assn., Am. Polit. Sci. Assn., Am. Fgn. Service Assn. Roman Catholic. Contbr. articles profl. jours. Home: 550 Waldo Av S E Salem OR 97302 Office: Am Consulate Gen Durban South Africa

DUGGER, ROBERT WELLFORD, agrl. implement Corp. exec.; b. East St. Louis, Ill., Oct. 31, 1910; s. Wellford Eugene and Elva (Whitaker) D.; student U. Miami (Fla.), 1930- 31, Washington U., St. Louis, 1932-33; m. Eugenia Barklage, Feb. 1, 1938; 1 son, Walter Edward. Asso., Broderick & Smith, labor relations conss., St. Louis, 1938-42; dir. labor relations Caterpillar Tractor Co., 1942-43, Midland Steel Products Co., 1943-49, Wyandotte Chem. Co., 1949-50; dir. indsl. relations Motor Products Co., 1950-55, Motor Wheel Corp., 1955-62; v.p. corp. relations J.I. Case Co., 1962-7O; v.p. indsl. relations Tenneco, Inc., Houston, 1970—. Curative Workshop, Racine, Wis., Racine Vocational Sch.; adv. bd. Racine Salvation Army. Mem. Mfrs. Assn. Racine (bd. govs.). Mason (Shriner). Home: 4944 Woodway Houston TX 77027 Office: PO Box 2511 Houston TX 77001

DUGGER, RONNIE E., writer; b. Chgo., Apr. 16, 1930; s. W.L. and Mary (King) D.; B.A., U. Tex., 1950, student 1954; student Oxford U., 195152; m. Jean Williams, June 13, 1951; children—Gary McGregor, Celia Williams. Journalist, Tex. newspapers, 1947-52; asst. to exec. dir. Nat. Security Tng. Commn., Washington, 1952-54; editor, gen. mgr. Tex. Observer, 1954-61, 63-65, editor-at-large, publisher, 1965—. Rockefeller fellowship, 1969; Researchh fellow Inst. Indls. Relations, U. Cal. Los Angeles, 1969-70. Mem. Authors Guild, Am. Civil Liberties Union (nat. com.), New Democratic Coalition, Tex. Inst. Letters, Tex. Folklore Soc., Philos. Soc. Tex. Club: Town and Gown (Austin). Author: Dark Star; Hiroshima Reconsidered in the Life of Claude Eatherly of Lincoln Park, Texas, 1967; also articles. Editor: Three Men in Texas, Bedichek, Webb and Dobie, 1967. Home: 1017 W 31st St Austin, TX 78705. Office: 504 W 24th St Austin TX 78705

DUGGER, WILLIE MACK, Jr., coll. dean; b. Adel, Ga., July 28, 1919; s. Willie Mack and Kate (Hendry) D.; B.S., U. Ga., 1941; M.S., U. Wis., 1942; Ph.D., N.C. State Coll., 1950; m. Dot Towler, June 12, 1946; children—Thomas, Lucinda. Asst. prof. botany U. Ga., 1946; asst. prof. plant physiology U. Md., 1950-55; asso. prof. plant physiology U. Fla., 1955-60; faculty U. Cal. at Riverside, 1960—, prof. botany, chmn. dept. life sci., 1963-68, dean Coll. Biology and Agr., 1968—, asso. dir. Citrus Research Center and Expt. Sta., 1971—. Served to capt. AUS, 1942-46. Mem. Am. Soc. Plant Physiology, Am. Inst. Biol. Scis., A.A.A.S., Sigma Xi, Phi Kappa Phi, Alpha Zeta, Gamma Sigma Delta. Home: 780 N University Dr Riverside CA 92507

DUGUID, LORNE WALLACE, beverage co. exec.; b. Bolton, Ont., Can., Apr. 4, 1911; s. Robert and Mary Jane (McCauley) D.; ed. pub. schs., Montreal; m. Gurteen Ireland, Dec. 8, 1938 (dec.); children—Lorne Austin, Robert Ralph, Gurteen Ireland. Profl. hockey player, 1930-41; with Hiram Walker & Sons Ltd., 1941—, Eastern sales mgr. of Can., 1945-55, v.p., gen. sales mgr., Toronto, 1955-67, exec. v.p., gen. sales mgr., 1967—; v.p. Gooderham & Worts

Ltd., 1959—; pres. James Barclay & Co. Ltd.; dir. H. Corby Dist. Ltd. Mem. Toronto Bd. Toronto Bd. Trade, Toronto Advt. and Sales Club, Dominion Comml. Travellers Assn., Canadian, Toronto hotel assns., Nat. Sales Execs. Club, Assn. Canadian Advertisers, Nat. Hockey League Old Timers Assn., Ont. Sports Writers and Sports Casters Assn. (asso.). Clubs: Granite, St. George's Golf and Country (Toronto); Calabogie (Ont.) Hunting and Fishing; Harbour Island (Ont.). Home: 625 Avenne Rd Toronto 7 Ontario Canada Office: 15 Toronto St Toronto 210 Ontario Canada

DUHAMEL, PIERRE ALBERT, educator; b. Putnam, Conn., Feb. 6, 1920; s. Albert and Rose (Comeau) D.; A.B., Holy Cross, Coll., 1941; M.A., Boston Coll., 1942; Ph.D., U. Wis., 1945; m. Helen L. Stowell, Sept. 4, 1943; 1 dau., Mary Elizabeth Prof., U. Chgo., 1945-49; faculty Boston Coll., 1949—, prof. English, 1949—, Philomatheia prof., 1954—; vis. prof. U. Wis., 1947, 49; moderator TV program I've Been Reading, 1956-63; lit. editor Boston Herald and Traveler, 1965—. Mem. Pulitzer Prize Jury, 1967, 68, 70; mem. adv. bd. Assumption Coll., 1958—. Mem. Am. Assn. U. Profs. (chpt. pres. 1949-56), Shakespeare Soc., Nat. Conf. Tchrs. English. Author: Essays in American Catholic Tradition, 1960; Rhetoric, 1962; Persuasive Prose, 1963; Principles of Rhetoric, 1964; Literature: Form and Function, 1965; also weekly columns, essays, book revs. Home: Saddle Ridge Rd Dover MA 02030 Office: Boston Coll Chestnut Hill MA 02167

DUHL, LEONARD, psychiatrist, govt. ofcl.; b. N.Y.C., May 24, 1926 s. Louis and Rose (Josefsberg) D.; B.A., Columbia, 1945; M.D., Albany Med. Coll., 1948; postgrad. Washington Psychoanalytic Inst., 1956-64; m. Carola Meyer, May 24, 1951 (separated 1971); children—Pamela, Nina, David, Susan. Intern Jewish Hosp., Bklyn., 1948-49; fellow Menninger Sch. Psychiatry, resident psychiatry Winter VA Hosp., Topeka, 1949-51, 53-54; med. dir., asst. health officer Contra Costa County Health Dept., 1951-53; dir. study psychosocial and statis. aspects of Tb, USPHS, 1951-53, psychiatrist profl. services br. Nat. Inst. Mental Health, 1954-64, chief office planning, 1964-66, chmn. com. psychol. variables as related to mental health Nat. Inst. Mental Health, 1959—; spl. asst. to sec. Dept. Housing and Urban Devel., 1966- 68; cons. Peace Corps, 1961—; asso. psychiatry George Washington Med. Sch., 1961-63, asst. clin. prof., 1963-68, assoc. prof., 1966; prof. urban social policy and pub. health Coll. Environmental Design and Sch. Pub. Health, U. Cal., Berkeley, 1968—, clin. prof. U. Cal., San Francisco, 1969—; chmn. Mayor's Task Force on Health, Washington, 1969; chmn. bd. tech. advisers U.S. Health Corp., San Francisco, 1969—; com. on mental retardation Dept. Health Edn. and Welfare, 1955-58, com. on recreation, 1956-59; research adv. com. Office of Edn., 1956-57; mem. recreation bd., Topeka, 1950; mem. Kan. com. White House Conf. on Children and Youth, 1950, Am. Friends Service Com., 1951-53. Rosenberg Found. grantee, San Francisco, 1951-53. Diplomate Am. Bd. Psychiatry and Neurology. Fellow Am. Pub. Health Assn., Am. Psychiat. Assn. (chmn. com. on poverty, 1963, chmn. com. preventive psychiatry (1964), Am. Coll. Psychiatry, Am. Ortho-psychiat. Assn. bd. dirs. 1963-66); mem. Berkeley Mental Hygiene Soc. (bd. dirs. 1952-53), Washington Psychoanalytic Soc., East Bay Psychiat. Soc., No. Cal. Psychiat. Soc., Group Advancement Psychiatry (chmn. com. prev. psychiatry 1962-66), Internat. Assn. Child Psychiatry and Allied Professions (asst. sec.-gen. 1962-66), Am. Assn. Mental Deficiency (councillor). Author: Urban Condition, 1963; Mental Health and Urban Social Policy, 1969. Asso. editor medicine and psychiat. sects. Am. Jour. Mental Deficiency, 1957-61; bd. editors Transaction mag., 1963—. Contbr. articles tech. lit. Home: 2718 Russell St Berkeley CA 94705

DUIGNAN, PETER JAMES, historian, curator; b. San Francisco, Aug. 6, 1926; s. Peter James and Delia (Conway) D.; B.S. cum laude, U. San Francisco, 1951; Ph.D., Stanford, 1960; m. Frances Sharpe, Aug. 13, 1949; children—Kathleen, Patricia, Peter, Frances, Rose Marie, Sheila Marie. Instr., Western Civilization, Stanford, 1955-57, 59-60, curator African collections, 1966—; mem. staff Hoover Instn., Stanford, 1959—, exec. sec., 1963-65, dir. African program, 1965—, also Stella W. and Ira S. Lillick African curator. Served with AUS, 1944-46. Ford Found. fellow Africa, 1957-59; fellow Rockefeller Found., 1963-64; fellow Nat. Def. Edn. Act, 1963. Fellow African Studies Assn. (chmn. libraries com. 1960-63, bd. dirs. 1965-68); mem. Assn. Research Libraries (chmn. subcom. Africa 1965-67), Am. Hist. Assn., N.A.A.C.P., Am. Civil Liberties Union. Roman Catholic. Author: (with L. H. Gann) White Settlers in Tropical Africa, 1962; (with C. Clendenen and R. Collins) United States and Africa, 1865-1900, 1966; (with L. H. Gann) Burden of Empire: An Appraisal of Colonialism in Africa, 1967; Handbook of American Resources for African Studies, 1967; Colonialism in Africa, 5 vols., 1970-71. Editor: U.S. and Canadian Publs. on Africa, 1961—; African Studies Bull. of African Studies Assn., 1965-66. Home: 939 Casanueva Pl Stanford, CA 94305.

DUISBERG, CLAUS-JURGEN, German diplomat; b. Frankfurt, Germany, Sept. 29, 1934; s. Curt and Helene (Fritsch) D.; student U. Bonn (Germany), 1955-56, U. Geneva (Switzerland), 1956-57; Dr. iur., U. Bonn, 1962; m. Christiane Paslat, Aug. 4, 1961; children—Christian, Alexander, Catharina, Thomas. Asst., U. Bonn, 1959-60; research asst. German Soc. Fgn. Policy, Bonn, 1961-63; joined Fgn. Ser. Germany, 1964; 3d sec., Moscow, 1964-65; assigned to Bonn, 1965-67; 1st sec., Washington, 1967—. Mem. Carl Duisberg Soc., Inc. (bd. dirs.). Author: Internationales Gewohnheitsrecht, 1963; Probleme der internationalen Abrustung, 1964. Home: 7310 Meadow Lane Chevy Chase MD 20015 Office: 4645 Reservoir Rd NW Washington DC 20007

DUKAS, PETER, educator, mgmt. cons.; b. Lewiston, Me., Apr. 7, 1919; s. Peter and Katherine (Bezantakos) D.; B.S., U. Chgo., 1950, M.S.A., 1951; m. Aphrodite Dukas, Aug. 18, 1951; 1 son, Stephen Peter. Operations analyst Brass Rail, N.Y.C., 1951-52; mgr. Mid City Enterprises, N.Y.C., 1953-54, Prince of Wales Hotel, Can., 1958; mgmt. cons., pres. Manco Assoc., Inc., Tallahassee, 1958—; prof., dir. Sch. Hotel and Restaurant Mgmt., Fla. State U., 1954—. Bd. dirs. Nat. Council Hotel and Restaurant Edn. Dir. Greek Orthodox Community, Tallahassee, 1961, pres. Ahepa Patmos chpt., 1961. Mem. Ahepa Ednl. Found. Bd. Served with USMCR, 1942-46. Recipient numerous awards from motel and restaurant assns. Mem. Internat. Soc. Food Service Cons., Am. Assn. U. Profs., Am. Hellenic Ednl. Progressive Assn. (dir.), Beta Gamma Sigma. Author: Hotel Front Office Management, 1957, 2d rev. edition, 1960, 3d rev. edition, 1970; How to Operate a Restaurant, 1960; How to Organize and Operate a Restaurant, 1971. also articles. Home: 1802 Sunset Lane Tallahassee FL 32303

DUKAY, ALEXANDER PAUL, hosp. supt.; b. Szeged, Hungary, June 29, 1919; s. Adolf and Maria (Csanyi) D.; B.A., Intermediate Coll. Kalksburg, Vienna, Austria, 1937; student U. Belgrad (Yugoslavia), 1937-41; M.D., U. Szeged, 1944; M.S., U. Mich., 1956; m.Madeline Ethel Vincze, Jan. 4, 1945; children—Alexander T., Victor G.R., Laura Maria. Came to U.S., 1951, naturalized, 1956. Rotating intern Univ. Hosps., Szeged, 1943; med. officer Internat. Refugee Orgn., U.S. zone, Germany, 1945-51; psychiat. resident Mental Health Inst., Independence, Ia. and Ypsilanti State Hosp., 1951-55; rotating intern Grace Hosp., Detroit, 1952-53; dir. research Ypsilanti State Hosp., 1957-59; part-time pvt. practice, 1958- 61, 64-65; mem. staff Ypsilanti State Hosp., 1959-65, 65-, med. supt., 1965—; dir. psychiat. unit Wyandotte (Mich.) Gen. Hosp., 1965—; lectr. Eastern Mich. U., 1961—; clin. research asso. Mental Health Research Inst., U. Mich., 1964—, research psychiatry, 1958-64; clin. asso. prof. psychiatry U. Mich., 1967—; cons. Psycho-Dynamic Research Assos., Inc., Dearborn, Mich., 1964—, Monroe County Mental Health Center. Recipient Research Fellow award Smith, Kline and French to Mass. Mental Health Center, Boston, 1957. Diplomate Am. Bd. Psychiatry and Neurology. Fellow Am. Psychiat. Assn.; mem. Mich. Assn. Neuropsychiat. Hosp. and Clinic Physicians (pres. 1957), Mich. Soc. Psychiatry and Neurology (counselor 1966-68). A.M.A., Washtenaw County, Mich. med. socs., Mich. Soc. Mental Health (resolution of appreciation 1967), Mich. Soc. Psychiatry and Neurology. Contbr. articles profl. jours. Address: 3501 Willis Rd Ypsilanti, MI 48197.

DUKE, ANGIER BIDDLE, found. adminstr.; b. N.Y.C., Nov. 30, 1915; s. Angier Buchanan and Cordelia (Biddle) D.; grad. St. Paul's Sch., 1934; student Yale, 1934-37; LL.D. (hon.), Iona Coll., 1957; L.H.D., Long Island U., 1967; LL.D. (hon.), Duke U., 1969; m. Robin Chandler Lynn, May 12, 1962; 1 son, Angier Biddle; children (by previous marriage)—A. St. George B., Maria-Luisa B., and Dario B. Pres. of Duke Internat. Corp., N.Y.C., 1945- 48; apptd. 2d sec. U.S. Fgn. Service, 1949; with U.S. Embassy, Buenos Aires, Argentina, 1949, spl. asst. to ambassador, Madrid, Spain, 1951; U.S. ambassador, El Salvador, 1952-53; chmn. N.Y. State Dem. Conv. Com., 1954; vice chmn. mayor's Puerto Rican Affairs Commn., 1954; co-chmn. Zellerbach Commn. European Refugee Situation, 1957-58; v.p. CARE, 1958- 60; pres. Am. Immigration and Citizenship Com., 1959-64; chief of protocol White House and Dept. of State, 1961-65; U.S. ambassador to Spain, 1965-66, chief of protocol Dept. of State, 1968-; U.S. ambassador to Denmark, 1968-69. Chmn. Dem. State Com. Nationalities and Intergroup Relations, 1960. Trustee Westminster Coll., Inst. for Am. Univs. (Aix-en-Provence); chmn. Neuwirth Investment Fund; bd. dirs. Duke U. Devel. Bd. L.I. State Park commissioner, 1955-61. Served from pvt. to maj., AUS, 1940-45, officer in charge Paris, France sect. Air Transport Command, 1945. Decorated Grand Officier, Ordre d'Honneur et Merite (Haiti); Commandeur, Nat. Order Viet Nam; Grand Cross of Merit, Order of Malta; Comdr., Order of George I, Greece. Mem. Nat. Council Fgn. Relations, Fgn. Service Assn., The Pilgrims, S.A.R., Soc. Colonial Wars. Clubs: Brook, River, Racquet and Tennis (N.Y.C.); Travellers (Paris, France). Address: 47 Chester Sq London SWI England

DUKE, ANTHONY DREXEL, sociologist, corp. exec.; b. Long Beach, L.I., N.Y., July 28, 1918; s. Angier Buchanan and Cordelia (Biddle) D.; grad. St. Paul's Sch., Concord, N.H., 1937; student Princeton, 1937-39; L.H.D. (hon.), Adelphi Coll., 1959; m. Diane Douglas, Sept. 12, 1957; children—Anthony Drexel, Nicholas Rutgers, Cordelia Biddle, Josephine, Ellen December, John Ordway, Barclay Robertson, Douglas Drexel. V.p. A.B. Duke & Co. 1946-49; pres. Duke Internat. Corp., N.Y.C., 1946-49, Anthony Drexel Duke Realty, Inc., Ft. Lauderdale, Fla., 1957-61, Summerplace Homes, Inc., Vero Beach, Fla., 1960—; dir. Am. Nat. Bank, Ft. Lauderdale, 1960-65; exec. com. Fla. Growth Fund, 1960—. Mem. N.Y.C. Youth Bd., 1955-58; hon. commnr. borough projects N.Y.C., 1954-57. Trustee Big Brother Movement, 1951-63; bd. dirs. Speedwell Services for Children, 1966—; founder, 1937, since pres. Boys Harbor; founder, 1955, since pres. Duke Family Found.; mem. nat. sponsoring com. Duke, 1965—; mem. adv. com. child care service Duke Endowment, 1965—. Served to lt. comdr. USNR, 1941-46; ATO, PTO. Decorated Bronze Star with combat V. Mem. Nat. Inst. Social Sci. Republican. Clubs: Racquet and Tennis, River, Brook (N.Y.C.); Deepdale (Manhasset, L.I., N.Y.); Maidstone (bd. govs.) (E. Hampton, L.I., N.Y.). Home: 895 Park Av New York City NY 10021 Office: 9 E 94th St New York City NY 10028

DUKE, CHARLES BRYAN, educator, physicist; b. Richmond, Va., Mar. 13, 1938; s. Charles Joseph, Jr. and Virginia (Welton) D.; B.S. in Math., Duke, 1959; Ph.D. in Physics, Princeton, 1963; m. Ann Evans, July 1, 1961; children—Amy Dickerson, Emily Elizabeth. Staff mem. Gen. Electric Corporate Lab., Schenectady, 1963-69; vis. asso. prof. U. Ill., Urbana, 1967-68, prof. physics, research prof. coordinated sci. lab., 1969—; cons. in phys. chemistry and semiconductor physics Gen. Electric Co., 1969—; tech. rep. Gen. Motors Corp., 1971—. Chmn. steering com. Internat. Conf. on Solid Surfaces, 1971. Fellow Am. Phys. Soc.; mem. Am. Vacuum Soc. (vice chmn. surface sci. div. 1971, chmn. 1972), Sigma Xi. Mem. Reformed Ch. of Am. Author: Tunneling in Solids, 1969; also articles theoretical physics. Home: 1204 Eliot Dr Urbana IL 61801

DUKE, CHARLES MARSDEN, ret. army officer; b. Jacksonville, Tex., June 24, 1917; s. Charles Henry and Bess (Butler) D.; B.S., U.S. Mil. Acad., 1939; M.S., Cal. Inst. Tech., 1947; grad. Command and Gen. Staff Coll., 1951, Armed Forces Staff Coll., 1955, Indsl. Coll. Armed Forces, 1959; m. Vernice Lang Jones, June 27, 1942; children—Charles Marsden, Allyson Lang. Commd. 2d lt., C.E., U.S. Army, 1939, advanced through grades to maj. gen., 1967; chief U.S. Hydrographic Office, Managua, Nicaragua, 1942-44; with intelligence div. Gen. Headquarters, 1945-46; instr., then asst. prof., dept. mil. arts and engring. U.S. Mil. Acad., 1947-50; sr. staff adviser constrn. and maintenance of installations Army Hdqrs., Heidelberg, Germany, 1951- 54; spl. adviser to chief of engrs., 1956-58, dist. engr. U.S. Army Dist., N.Y., also supr. N.Y. Harbor, 1959-62; asst. chief staff G4 (Logistics) I Corps, Korea, 1962-63; engr. commr. D.C., 1963- 66; comdg. gen. 18th Engr. Brigade, Dong Ba Thin, RVN, 1967, U.S. Army Engr. Command U.S. Army Vietnam Engr., Long Binh, RVN, 1967-68; chief engr. U.S. Army, Vietnam, comdg. gen. Engr. Troops, Vietnam, 1968-71. Mem. D.C. Pub. Service Commn.; past chmn. Washington Met. Area Transit Commn.; past pres. Met. Washington Council Govts.; past gov. Washington Bldg. Congress. Mem. exec. bd. Nat. Capital Area council Boy Scouts Am., 1963-66; bd. dirs. Met. Police Boys' Club. Decorated D.S.M., Legion of Merit, Bronze Star, Air medal with bronze oak leaf cluster, Army Commendation medal. Registered profl. engr., D.C. Fellow Am. Soc. C.E.; mem. Soc. Am. Mil. Engrs., Nat. Soc. Profl. Engrs., Newcomen Soc., West Point Soc., Indsl. Coll. Armed Forces, Cal. Inst. Tech. alumni assns., Assn. U.S. Army, Hon. Order Ky. Cols., Assn. Grads. U.S. Mil. Acad. Methodist. Clubs: Army and Navy; Army and Navy Country. Home: 3178 Stonehurst Dr Fairfax VA 20030

DUKE, CHARLES MARTIN, Jr., civil engr.; b. Wellsville, N.Y., Oct. 25, 1917; s. Charles Martin and Delia Applebee (Kerr) D.; B.S., U. Cal. at Berkeley, 1939, M.S., 1941; m. Saga May Immonen, May 24, 1942; 1 dau., Jenny Maria. Instr. civil engring. U. Cal. at Berkeley, 1939-45; structural designer Austin Co., Oakland, Cal.,1945-46; testing engr. Pacific Islands Engrs., Guam, 1946- 47; mem. faculty U. Cal. at Los Angeles, 1947-, prof. engring., 1956-, chmn. dept., 1961-67, asso. dean Coll. Engring., 1957-67, exec. sec. U. Cal. engring. master plan study, 1964-65; Fulbright research prof. Tokyo (Japan) U., 1956-57; vis. prof. U. Chile, 1966-67. Registered profl. engr., Cal. Mem. Am. Soc. C.E. (pres. Los Angeles 1963), Am. Soc. Engring. Edn. (chmn. Pacific S.W. sect. 1953), Earthquake Engring. Research Inst. (pres. 1970—), Seismological Soc. Am., Soc. Exploration Geophysicists. Author articles in field; designer civil engring. works. Home: 1110 N Bundy Dr Los Angeles CA 90049.

DUKE, EMANUEL, lawyer; b. Buffalo, Sept. 4, 1916; s. Harry and Ida (Malek) D.; B.A., Cornell U., 1937, LL.B., 1939; m. Ruth Lebrecht, May 12, 1942; children—Cathy E., James L. Admitted to N.Y. bar, 1939, since practiced in Buffalo; partner firm Saperston, Wiltse, Duke, Day & Wilson and predecessors, 1949—. Bd. mem.-at-large Jewish Fedn. Buffalo, 1948- 61, 63—; mem. bd. Jewish Family Service, 1963—; mem. bd. govs. American Jewish Com., Buffalo, 1963—. Served to lt. USNR, 1941-45, Mem. N.Y. State, Erie County bar assns., Erie County Trial Lawyers Assn., Sigma Alpha Mu. Jewish religion. Mem. B'nai B'rith (pres. lodge 1953-54, chmn. Buffalo council 1955). Club: Westwood Country (Williamsville, N.Y.). Home: 17 George Lane Williamsville NY 14221 Office: Liberty Bank Bldg Buffalo NY 14202

DUKE, FREDERICK ROBERT, educator; b. Unityville, S.D., Mar. 17, 1917; s. Lee Robert and Sophia (Stark) D.; student Dakota Wesleyan U., 1933-36; A.B., U. S.D., 1937; Ph.D., U. Ill., 1940; m. June Marie Morgan, June 14, 1941; children—Margaret (Mrs. John Treadwell), William, Catherine (Mrs. Clark Edwards), Sarah, James, John. Chemist, E.I. du Pont de Nemours & Co., Buffalo, 1940-42; instr. Princeton, 1942-45; asst. prof. Mich. State U., 1945-48; asso. prof. Ia. State U., 1948-54, prof., 1954-63; Robert A. Welch prof. Texas A. & M. U., 1963-65; prof. head phys. chemistry, Purdue U., 1965-68; prof., chmn. dept. chemistry U. Ia., Iowa City, 1968—. Mem. Am. Chem. Soc., Electrochem. Soc., Sigma Xi, Phi Lambda Epsilon. Author research publs. on reaction mechanisms and fused salts. Home: 6 Fairview Knoll Iowa City IA 52240

DUKE, LYMAN P., banker. Auditor, United Banking Group, Miami, Fla. Office: 120 Andalusia Av Miami FL 33134*

DUKE, PATTY, actress; b. N.Y.C., Dec. 14, 1946; d. John and Frances (McMahon) Duke; graduate of Quintano's School for Young Profls.; m. Harry Falk, Jr., 1965. TV appearances include Armstrong Circle Theatre, The Prince and the Pauper, Wuthering Heights, U.S. Steel Hour, Meet Me in St. Louis, Swiss Family Robinson, The Power and the Glory, numerous others; theatrical appearances include The Miracle Worker, 1959-61, Isle of Children, 1962; motion picture appearance in The Miracle Worker (Acad. award as best supporting actress 1963), 1962, Valley of the Dolls, Me Natalie; appeared in Billie, 1965; TV series Patty Duke Show, 1963-64. Nat. youth chmn. Muscular Dystrophy Assns. Am. Address: 80 Park Av New York City NY 10016

DUKE, ROBERT DOMINICK, mineral co. exec.; b. Goshen, N.Y., Oct. 14, 1928; s. Robert Dewitt and Elma Christina (Dominick) D.; B.A., Va. Mil. Inst., 1947; LL.B., Yale, 1950; M.B.A., U. Pa., 1952; m. Jeannette Parham, Apr. 24, 1954; children—Katherine Campbell, Robert Dominick, Peter Benjamin Dewitt, Lois Christina. Admitted to N.Y. bar, 1950; with Cravath, Swaine & Morre, N.Y.C., 1951-52, 54-64; with Freeport Minerals Co. and predecessor firm Freeport Sulphur Co., N.Y.C., 1964—, sec., 1965-67, v.p., 1967—, gen. counsel, 1970—; dir. Freeport Indonesia, Inc. Mem. Grace Church Sch. Bd., N.Y.C., 1969—. Served as 1st lt., J.A.G.C., AUS, 1952-54. Mem. Assn. Bar City N.Y., Am., N.Y. State bar assns. Presbyn. (trustee). Clubs: Powelton (Newburgh, N.Y.); Yale (N.Y.C.). Home: 32 Washington Sq New York City NY 10011 Office: 161 E 42d St New York City NY 10017

DUKE, STEVEN BARRY, legal educator; b. Mesa, Ariz., July 31, 1934; s. Alton and Elaine (Altman) D.; B.S., Ariz. State U., 1956; J.D., U. Ariz., 1959; LL.M., Yale, 1961; m. Janet Truax, Aug. 29, 1956, children—Glenn, Warren, Alison, Sally. Admitted to Ariz. bar, 1959; law clk. to Supreme Ct. Justice Douglas, 1959; grad. fellow Yale Law Sch., 1960, mem. faculty, 1961—, prof. law, 1966—; vis. prof. U. Cal. at Berkeley, 1965. Bd. dirs. New Haven Legal Assistance Assn., 1968-70; cons. legal def. fund N.A.A.C.P. Mem. Woodbridge (Conn.) Bd. Edn.; mem. Woodbridge (Conn.) Democratic Town Com. Mem. Am. Civil Liberties Union, Phi Kappa Phi, Alpha Tau Omega. Contbr. profl. jours. Editor-in-chief Ariz. Law Rev. Home: Center Rd Woodbridge CT 06511 Office: 127 Wall St New Haven CT 06520

DUKE, THOMAS WALTER DANIEL, lawyer; b. Richmond, Va., Dec. 13, 1896; s. T. Wiley and Mary Florence (Smith) D.; J.D., U. Va., 1922; m. Dolores Carrillo de Albornoz, Jan. 8, 1925 (div. 1942); children—Renee (Mrs. Tener Eckelberry), Diane (Mrs. Robert Amussen); m. 2d, Penny Nichol, Jan. 29, 1946. Admitted to Va. bar, 1920; N.Y. State bar, 1923; D.C. bar, 1942; practiced in N.Y. City, 1923—; partner firm of Duke & Landis, predecessor firms, 1926-65; cons., 1965—; co-organizer S.W. Forest Industries, Inc., Ariz.; dir. Venezuelan Devel. Corp., Paramount Motors Corp., Monorailway Corp. Dir., mem. exec. com. original Com. for Econ. Recovery. Served as flight Lt. USAC, World War I. Mem. Am. Legion. Mason. Clubs: Metropolitan (Washington); Union. Author various revs. of books on legal and econ. subjects. Home: 77 Park Av New York City NY 10016 Office: 150 Broadway New York City NY 10038

DUKE, WAYNE, coll. athletic adminstr.; b. Burlington, Ia., Nov. 9, 1928; s. Herald M. and Mildred (Lavine) D.; B.A., State U. Ia., 1950; m. Martha Buesch, June 11, 1950; children—Dan Wayne, Sarah Jane. Sports information dir. State Coll. Ia., 1950-51, U. Colo., 1951-52; asst. to dir. Nat. Collegiate Athletic Assn., Kansas City, Mo., 1952-63; commr. Big Eight Conf., Kansas City, 1963—, Nat. Collegiate Athletic Assn.-NBC television pub. relations liaison officer, N.Y.C., 1957. Conglist. Clubs: Rotary, Byline (Kansas City, Mo.); Kansas City Press. Home: 8827 Newton Dr Overland Park KS 66212 Office: Hotel Muehlebach Kansas City MO 64105

DUKE, WILLIAM MENG, corporate exec.; b. N.Y.C., May 20, 1916; s. William Miller and Rose (Meng) D.; B.S. in Mech. Engring., N.Y. U., 1935, Sc.M., 1936; M.E., Coll. State N.Y., 1947; Ph.D. in Math and Applied Mechanics, U. Cal. at Los Angeles, 1958; D.Engring. (hon.), Clarkson Coll. Tech., 1963; Sc.D., U. of Tampa, 1967; m. Catherine Polizos, 1950; children—Pamela, Alison, William Meng, Jeffrey. With Cornell U. Aero. Lab., 1943-55, v.p. tech. operations, 1950-55; with Space Tech. Labs., Los Angeles, 1956-62, program dir. Titan weapon system, 1956-57, v.p., dir. div. responsible engring. and tech. direction Atlas, Thor, Titan and Minuteman programs, 1958-59, sr. v.p. research and engring, 1960-62; pres. ITT Fed. Labs., Nutley, N.J., 1962-64, also gen. mgr. mil. and space group, v.p. ITT; pres. Whittaker Corp., Los Angeles, 1964-70, pres., chmn. Scis. Mgmt. Corp. subsidiary, 1970—; chmn. bd., chief exec. officer DynaScis. Corp., Tasker Industries, KHD Scis., Inc. Mem. subcoms. War Prodn. Council, 1942-45; sub.-com. aircraft structures NACA, 1957-59; subcom. structural loads NASA, 1959; mem. engring. adv. council U. Cal.; mem. com. on accelerated utilization new materials Nat. Materials Adv. Bd. Recipient Naval Ordnance Devel. award, 1945; Centennial Citation N.Y. U., 1955. Asso. fellow Am. Inst. Aeros. and Astronautics (chmn. missiles and space vehicles com. 1961-63); mem. A.A.A.S., N.Y. Acad. Scis., League Women Voters (mem. Los Angeles bus. and industry council), Sigma Xi, Tau Beta Pi, Sigma Pi Sigma, Iota Alpha. Home: 4367 Clear Valley Dr Encino CA 91316 Office: 11661 San Vicente Blvd Los Angeles CA 90049

DUKEMINIER, JESSE J., Jr., educator; b. West Point, Miss., Aug. 12, 1925; s. Jesse J. and Lucile (Weems) D.; A.B., Harvard, 1948; LL.B., Yale, 1951. Admitted to N.Y. bar, 1952, Ky. bar, 1957; practice in N.Y.C., 1951-53; asst. prof. law U. Minn., 1954-55; prof. law U. Ky., 1955-63, U. Cal. at Los Angeles, 1963—; vis. prof. U. Chgo., 1959, U. Miss., 1958; cons. Ky. Dept. Revenue, 1960. Vice chmn. Ky. Commn. Human Rights, 1956-62; v.p. Lexington (Ky.) Citizens Assn. Planning, 1960-62; bd. dirs. Environmental Goals Com., Los Angeles, 1966-69. Served with inf. AUS, 1943-45. Recipient award Lexington Citizens Assn. Planning, 1959. Mem. Am. Bar Assn., Am. Inst. Planners, Am. Soc. Planning Ofcls., Phi Beta Kappa, Sigma Alpha Epsilon. Democrat. Author: Perpetuities Law in Action, 1962; also numerous articles. Home: 1337 Cordell Pl Los Angeles CA 90069.

DUKER, ABRAHAM GORDON, educator, historian; b. Rypin, Poland, Sept. 27, 1907; s. Asher Zelig and Feiga Haya (Gorodeñsky) D.; came to U.S., 1923, naturalized, 1926; B.A., Coll. City N.Y., 1930; Ph.D., Columbia, 1956; m. Lillian Miriam Sandrow, Dec. 1, 1940; children—Nahum Johanan, Sara Rivkah, Dvora Peninah. Research librarian Grad. Sch. Jewish Social Work, N.Y.C., 1934-38; founding mng. and contbg. editor Contemporary Jewish Record, 1938-41; editor Jewish Social Studies, 1952—; vis. prof. Wayne State U., 1955; pres. Coll. Jewish Studies, Chgo., 1956-62; dir. libraries, prof. history and social instrs. Yeshiva U., 1962—; vis. prof. history Columbia, 1966-67; cons. in field. Bd. dirs. YIVO Inst. Jewish Research 1948—; bd. dirs. Conf. Jewish Social Studies, 1952—, pres., 1971—; bd. dirs. Am. Jewish Hist. Soc., 1957-66, Nat. Conf. Jewish Communal Service, 1941-44, 59-62, Nat. Council Jewish Edn., 1967-70. Served with AUS, 1943-45. Fellow Miller Found., Columbia, 1933-34; research grantee Am. Council Learned Socs., 1962, Am. Philos. Soc., 1962, Wurzweiler Found., 1967, Littauer Found., 1956. Mem. Am. Acad. Jewish Research, Jewish Acad. Arts and Scis., Polish Inst. Arts and Scis. in Am., Am. Hist. Assn., Zionist Orgn. Am., Am. Sociol. Assn., A.L.A., Soc. Am. Archivists, Soc. Jewish Bibliophiles. Author: Jewish Survival in the World Today, 1939-41; The Polish Great Emigration and the Jews, 1956; Jewish Community Relations, 1952. Home: 90 Laurel Hill Terrace New York City NY 10033

DULACKI, LEO JOHN, marine corps officer; b. Omaha, Dec. 29, 1918; s. Stanley and Anna (Jurczak) D.; B.S., Creighton U., 1941; M.A. in Internat. Affairs, George Washington U., 1965. Commd. 2d lt. USMC, 1941, advanced through grades to maj. gen., 1967; assigned U.S.S. Hornet, 1942; comdg. officer U.S.S. Belleau Wood, 1942-44; officer recruiting, Kansas City, Mo., 1945-47; assigned Marine Corps Recruit Depot, Parris Island, S.C., 1947-48; operations officer 1st Marine Brigade, Guam, 1948; asst. naval attache Am. embassy, Helsinki, Finland, 1950-52; battalion comdr., Korea, 1952; mem. UN Negotiations Team, Korea, 1953; instr. Marine Corps Edn. Center, Quantico, Va., 1954-56; asst. naval attache, Am. embassy, Moscow, USSR, 1958-61; joint staff, Def. Intellience Agy., Washington, 1961-64; comdg. gen. 5th Marine Div., 1968-69; operations officer, chief staff III Marine Amphibious Force, Vietnam, 1969-70; comdg. gen. 4th Marine Div., 1970- -. Decorated D.S.M., Legion of Merit with combat V, Bronze Star, Joint Service Commendation medal, Navy Commendation medal, Purple Heart, Presdl. Unit Citation with bronze star; Order of Lion (Finland); Order Mil. Merit (Chung Mu); Vietnam Nat. Order, Cross Gallantry with palm. Address: 4th Marine Div Camp Pendleton CA 92055

DULAN, HAROLD ANDREW, educator, ins. co. exec.; b. Bridgeton, N.J., June 28, 1911; s. Thomas Francis and Mamie (Corson) D.; B.B.A., U. Tex., 1936, M.B.A., 1937, Ph.D., 1945; postgrad. Harvard, summer 1955, U. Chgo. (Beloit, Wis.), 1956, 63; m. Bess Gunn, May 31, 1946; children—Susan Matilda (Mrs. Orville J. Hall, Jr.), Kathleen (Mrs. Robert K. Gardner), Elizabeth Ann (Mrs. Ronald D. Dorsey). Mem. faculty Tex. A. and M. Coll., 1938-42; pub. accountant, Dallas, 1941-46; financial economist Fed. Res. Bank, Dallas, 1944-46; faculty Dallas Coll., So. Meth. U., 1945; pvt. investment counsellor, Dallas, 1946; prof., former head dept. finance U. Ark., Fayetteville, 1946—; co-founder Participating Annuity Life Ins. Co., Fayetteville, 1954, chmn. investment com., v.p., pres., chmn. bd., 1954-68; financial cons. Argentine bus. concern, Buenos Aires, summer 1953; lectr., moderator Southwestern Bell Telephone Co. Mgmt. Seminars, Galveston, Tex., 1956- 58, Hot Springs, Ark., 1958; conferee Conf. Savs. and Residential Financing Savs. and Loan League, Chgo., 1958; mem. Financial Analysts Fedn. European Econ. Conf. Tour, 1964; mem. bd. dirs. First Ark. Devel. Finance Corp. Commr. Tex. Centennial Statehood, 1946; commnr., vice chmn. Gov.'s Commn. Status of Women for Ark., 1964- 65; fellow N.Y. Financial Dist., 1950. C.P.A., Tex., Ark. Mem. Am. Inst. C.P.A.'s, Am. Inst. Chartered Financial Analysts, Nat. Assn. Bus. Economists, Financial Mgmt. Assn., N.Y. Soc. Security Analysts, Am. Finance Assn., Am. Econ. Assn., Southwestern Social Sci. Assn. (past pres. finance sect.), Ark. Soc. C.P.A.'s, Fayetteville C. of C., Beta Gamma Sigma, Beta Alpha Psi, Sigma Iota Epsilon. Methodist. Rotarian. Clubs: Country of Austin, Fayetteville Country. Contbr. articles profl. jours. Home: 414 Ila St Fayetteville AR 72701

DULANEY, EUGENE L., biologist; b. Garbor, Okla., June 2, 1919; s. Grover C. and Juanita (Curtis) D.; B.S., Tex. Tech. Coll., 1941; M.A., U. Tex., 1943; Ph.D., U. Wis., 1946; m. Dorothy A. Drescher, June 1, 1962; 1 son, Eugene Drescher. Asst. biology Tex. Tech. Coll., 1939-41; tutor biology U. Tex., 1941-43; fellow U. Wis., 1943-44, Office Prodn. Research and Devel., 1944-46; with Merck & Co., Inc., 1946—, research asso., 1957-65, sr. research fellow, 1965—. Post doctoral fellow Nat. Research Council Can., 1955-56. Fellow N.Y. Acad. Scis. (chmn. div. microbiology 1964- 66), Am. Acad. Microbiology, A.A.A.S.; men. Theobald Soc. (sec. 1954- 55), Soc. Indsl. Microbiology (pres. 1962-63), Am. Inst. Biol. Scis. (gov. bd. 1959-63). Author articles; patentee in field. Home: 17 Plymouth Rd Summit NJ 07901 Office: Merck & Co Inc Rahway NJ 07065

DULBECCO, RENATO, biologist; b. Catanzaro, Italy, Feb. 22, 1914; s. Leonardo and Maria (Virdia) D.; M.D., U. of Torino (Italy), 1936; D.Sc. (hon.), Yale, 1968; LL.D., U. Glasgow, Scotland, 1970; m. Gulseppina Salvo, June 1, 1940 (div. 1963); children—Peter Leonard, Maria Vittoria; m. 2 d, Maureen Muir, July 27, 1963; 1 dau., Fiona Linsey. Came to U.S., 1947, naturalized, 1953. Asst. U. Torino, 1942-47; research asso. Ind. U., 1947-49; sr. research fellow Cal. Inst. Tech., 1949-52, asso. prof., then prof. biology, 1952-63; sr. fellow Salk Inst. Biol. Studies, San Diego, 1963—; vis. prof. Royal Soc. Great Britain, 1963-64; Clowes Meml. lectr., Atlantic City, 1961. Mem. Cal. Cancer Adv. Council, 1963. Guggenheim and Fulbright fellow, 1957-58; recipient John Scott award City Phila., 1958; Kimball award Conf. Pub. Health Lab. Dirs., 1959; Albert and Mary Lasker Basic Med. Research award, 1965; Howard Taylor Ricketts award, 1965; Paul Ehrlich-Ludwig Darmstaedter prize, 1967. Member of Nat. Acad. Scis., A.A.A.S., Genetics Soc. Am., Assn. Cancer Research, Am. Soc. Biol. Chemists, Accademia Nazionale dei Lincei. Home: 7206 Rue de Roark La Jolla CA 92037 Office: Salk Inst Biol Studies P O Box 1809 San Diego CA 92112

DULLEA, KEIR, actor; b. Cleve., May 30, 1936; s. Robert and Margaret (Ruttain) D.; grad. Neighborhood Playhouse; appeared in motion pictures The Hoodlum Priest, David and Lisa (best male performance San Francisco Film Festival 1962), Thin Red Line, The Naked Hours, Mail Order Bride, Bunny Lake is Missing, Madame X, The Fox, 2001: A Space Odyssey; appeared on Broadway in Butterflies Are Free, 1969-70; acted in TV shows including Bonanza, Hallmark Hall of Fame, U.S. Steel Hour, Naked City, Alcoa Hour, DuPont Show of Week, Kraft Mystery Theatre.

DULLES, ELEANOR LANSING, ret. diplomat, educator; b. Watertown, N.Y., June 1, 1895; d. Allen Macy and Edith (Foster) Dulles; A.B., Bryn Mawr Coll., 1917 (New Eng. scholarship, 1914), A.M. (fellow labor and indsl. economics, 1919-20), 1920; student London Sch. Econ., 1921-22; A.M., Radcliffe Coll., 1924, Ph.D., 1926; Faculté de Droit, U. Paris, 1925-27; LL.D., Wilson Coll., 1950, Western Coll., 1957; Dr. honoris causa, Free U. Berlin, 1957; LL.D., Mt. Holyoke Coll., 1962; Dr. Litt., Duke U., Durham, N.C., 1965; m. David Blondheim, Dec. 9, 1932 (dec. 1934); children—David Dulles, Ann Dulles Joor. Relief and reconstrn., Shurtleff Meml. Relief at Paris, France, 1917; relief work, Am. Friends Service, 1917-19; asst. personnel mgr., Am. Tube & Stamping Co., Bridgeport, Conn., 1920-21; research asso., Harvard and Radcliffe Bur. Research, France, 1925-27, Switzerland, 1930-32; tchr. Simmons Coll., Boston, 1924-25, 1927-28; asst. prof., Bryn Mawr Coll., 1928-30, lectr., 1932- 36; research asso., U. Pa., 1932-36; chief finance div., Social Security Bd., Washington, 1936-42; economist Bd. Economic Warfare, 1942; economic officer, Dept. State, 1942-45, financial attaché, Vienna, Austria, 1945-49; Western European div. Dept. State, 1949-51; with Nat. Prodn. Authority, Dept. of Commerce, 1951-52; spl. asst. Office of German Affairs, Dept. of State, 1952-62, ret.; lectr., vis. prof. Duke U., 1962- 63; prof. Georgetown U., 1963-71; with Center for Strategic Studies, Washington, 1964-67; research fellow Hoover Inst., Stanford, 1967-68; cons. Dept. State, 1970—; cons. Youth for Understanding, Ann Arbor, Mich., 1969—. Member of Geneva Conf. on Investment Social Security Funds, 1938; rep. U.S. Govt. on Bretton Woods Conf. on Internat. Monetary Fund, 1944. Investigated unemployment ins., Pres. Hoovers Com., 1931. Decorated Grand Cross of Merit Fed. Republic Germany. Recipient Distinguished Achievement award Radcliffe Coll., 1955; Carl Schurz plaque, 1958; Ernst Reuter plaque City of West Berlin, Germany, 1959; citation for distinction Bryn Mawr Coll., 1960. Member P.E.N., Phi Beta Kappa. Clubs: Cosmopolitan Club (N.Y.C.); Henderson Harbor Yacht, International. Author: The French Franc, 1928; The Bank for International Settlements at Work, 1932; Depression and Reconstruction, 1934; The Dollar, The Franc and Inflation, 1933; The Evolution of Reparation Ideas, monograph 1936; John Foster Dulles, The Last Year; Détente, Cold War Strategies in Transition, 1965; Dominican Action, 1965; Intervention or Cooperation, 1966; Berlin: The Wall Is Not Forever, 1967; American Foreign Policy in the Making, 1968; One Germany or Two The Struggle at The Heart of Europe, 1970. Contbr. articles in field social security, monetary policy investment, etc. Home: 3900 Watson Pl Washington DC 20016

DULSKI, THADDEUS J., congressman; b. Buffalo, Sept. 27, 1915; student Canisius Coll. and U. Buffalo; married; 5 children. With Bur. Internal Revenue, Treasury Dept., 1940-47; entered pvt. practice as accountant and tax cons., 1947; spl. agt. Price Stablzn. Adminstrn., 1951-53. Mem. 86th to 92d Congresses, 41st N.Y. Dist. Councilman, Walden Dist., 2 terms; council-at-large Buffalo, 4 yrs. Democrat-Liberal. Home: Buffalo NY 14205 Office: Cannon House Office Bldg Washington DC 20515

DUMA, WILLIAM JOSEPH, banker; b. Milw., Aug. 11, 1938; s. William W. and Catherine K. (Bauer) D.; B.B.A., U. NotreDame, 1960; M.B.A., Marquette U., 1966; grad. banking sch. U. Wis., 1970; m. Sarah M. Coffey, Jan. 31, 1959; children—Mary, W. Jeffrey, Robert, Michael. Staff auditor Price Waterhouse & Co., Milw., 1960-62; asst. auditor First Wis. Nat. Bank, Milw., 1962-68; asst. auditor First Wis. Bankshares Corp., 1962-68; auditor First Nat. Bank St. Paul, 1968—; instr. U. Wis., 1967-68; lectr. U. Minn., 1968—. Vice pres., dir. North Shore Jr. C. of C., 1964-67. Bd. dirs. Continental Little League, Milw. Served with U.S. Army, 1960-64. C.P.A., Minn., Wis. Mem. Am. Inst. C.P.A.'s, Minn., Wis. socs. C.P.A.'s, Am. Accounting Assn., Marquette Alumni Assn. Clubs: St. Paul Athletic, Notre Dame (St. Paul). Home: 3363 Glen Oaks Av White Bear Lake MN 55110 Office: 332 Minnesota St St Paul MN 55101

DUMAINE, FREDERIC C., Jr., bus. exec.; m. Margaret Williams, Oct. 9, 1926; children—Frederic C. III, Dudley B., Ruth (Mrs. G. E. Brooking, Jr.). Pres., dir. Amoskeag Co. Home: 201 Newton St Weston MA 02193 Office: Prudential Center Boston MA 02199

DUMAN, MAXIMILIAN GEORGE, educator; b. Nicktown, Pa., Feb. 21, 1906; s. Henry and Mary (Parrish) D.; A.B., St. Vincent Coll., Latrobe, Pa., 1932; student St. Vincent Sem., 1932-36; M.S., Cath. U. Am., 1937, Ph.D., 1941. Joined Order St. Benedict, 1930, ordained priest Roman Cath. Ch., 1936; instr. biology St. Vincent Coll., 1932-39, asso. prof., 1941-46, prof. biology, 1961—; pres. coll., 1961-63, chmn. dept. biology, 1963-69, dir. Sci. Center, 1969—; vis. instr. biology Cath. U., summers 1944-56, asso. prof. biology, 1957-61; lectr. bacteriology Latrobe Hosp. Sch. Nursing, 1946-58, 63-69. Mem. bot. expdns. to Hudson Bay, 1938, 39, N.E. Can., 1950, 51, James Bay, 1952-56, Yukon Territory, 1970, N.W. Ters., 1971; arctic field trip IX Internat. Bot. Congress, 1959. Bd. dirs. Latrobe Civic Music Assn., 1962-63. Fellow A.A.A.S.; mem. Bot. Soc. Am., Internat. Assn. Plant Taxonomy, Soc. Plant Taxonomy, Arctic Inst. N. Am., Pa. Acad. Sci., Sigma Xi, Delta Epsilon Sigma. K.C. (4). Co-author: Contribution a la flore du bassin de la baie d'Ungava, 1953; Contribution a la flore du versant occidental de la baie James, 1954; Contribution a la flore des iles et du versant oriental de la baie James, 1958; co-translator: Sertum Anglicum, 1963. Contbr. profl. articles jours. Address: St Vincent Coll Latrobe PA 15650

DUMARESQ, JOHN EDWARD, lawyer; b. Guernsey Channel Islands, Eng., Aug. 16, 1913; s. James Edward and Helen (Gilfillan) D.; came to U.S., 1924, naturalized, 1942; B.A. Columbia, 1935, B.S., 1936, M.S. 1937; LL.B., N.Y.U., 1941; m. Eleanor Merrell Clark, Sept. 14, 1946; children—Peter John, Thomas Alan, Philip Clark. Admitted to N.Y. bar, 1942; mem. firm Brumbaugh, Graves, Donohue & Raymond, N.Y.C., 1937-48, partner 1948—. Mem. Columbia U. Engring. Council, 1966—, United Ministries in Higher Edn. Nat. Commn., 1968—. Served to capt. AUS, 1943-46. Mem. Am., City N.Y. bar assns., Am., N.Y. patent law assns., I.E.E.E., Sigma Xi, Theta Tau. Home: 214 Manor Rd Douglaston NY 11363 Office: 90 Broad St New York City NY 10004

DUMAS, HAL STEPHENS, former tel. exec.; b. Macon, Ga., Sept. 19, 1892; s. William Jefferson and Ida (Anderson) D.; B.S., Ala. Poly. Inst., 1911, L.H.D.; m. Genevieve Burt, Oct. 3, 1914; children—Hal Stephens, Anderson (Mrs. C.W. Wallace). Traffic mgr. So. Bell Tel. & Tel. Co., Atlanta, 1911- 34, asst. v.p., 1934-36, gen. plant mgr., 1936-38, v.p. operations, dir., 1938-43, pres., 1943-51; exec. v.p., dir. Am. Tel. & Tel. Co., 1951- 56. Served with U.S. Army, 1918. Mem. Am. Legion, U.S. C. of C., Tau Beta Pi. Episcopalian. Clubs: Capital City, Piedmont Driving (Atlanta); Peachtree Golf, Gulf Stream Golf, Sapphire Valley; Wildcat Cliffs Golf (Highlands, N.C.). Home: 945 Hibiscus Lane Delray Beach FL 33444

DUMAS, LAWRENCE, lawyer; b. Talladega, Ala., Oct. 12, 1908; s. William Lawrence and Mary (Hicks) D.; A.B., Davidson Coll., 1929; LL.B., Harvard, 1932; LL.M., George Washington U., 1933; J.D., Georgetown U., 1935; m. Donald Berry, Dec. 4, 1940; children-Aleta McDonald (Mrs. Robert V. Schanbacher), Lawrence III, William Berry, John Hicks II. Admitted to Ala. bar, 1932, D.C. bar, 1933; atty. Fed. Farm Bd. and Pub. Works Adminstrn., 1932-36; practice in Birmingham, Ala., 1936-43, 44—; atty. OPA, asst. U.S. atty., 1943-44; mem. firm Dumas, O'Neal and Hayes, and predecessors, 1944—. Dir. Trustees Life Ins. Co. Mem. Ala. Constn. Commn., 1970—; adv. com. Ala. Ethics Commn., 1970. Mem. Ala. Ho. of Reps., 1947-55, Ala. Senate, 1959-66; chmn. Ala. Legislative Council, 1955, 63. Adv. bd. local Salvation Army, Girl Scouts. Mem. Am. Judicature Soc., Ala. Bar Found., Am. (Ala. chmn. jr. bar conf. 1947), Ala., Birmingham bar assns. Methodist (ofcl. bd.). Mason (Shriner). Club: Birmingham Exchange (pres. 1958-59). Contbr. articles legal jours. Home: 3251 Dell Rd Birmingham AL 35213 Office: Brown Marx Bldg Birmingham AL 35203

DUMAS, WOODROW WILSON, mayor; b. Opelousas, Va., Dec. 9, 1916; s. Juble Earl and Margaret A. (Jernigan) D.; student Baton Rouge Bus. Coll., 1938, Pope Secretarial Sch., 1939, Diesel Engring. Sch., 1944; m. Carol Epperson, Jan. 18, 1940; children—Diane, Woodrow Huntley. Pipefitter, Humble Oil & Refinery Co., Baton Rouge, 1938, personnel, 1941-63; mayor Baton Rouge, 1965—. City-Parish councilman, 1953-64; v.p. Greater Baton Rouge Port Commn., 1956; chmn. constrn. com. Baker (La.) High Sch. Stadium, 1952—, also Greenwood Golf Course, nr. Baker, 1962—; chmn. steering com. for erection Lane Meml. Hosp., Zachary, La., 1959—; pres. Baton Rouge Kids' Baseball Clinic, 1965—; mem. Nat. Adv. Com. on Hwy. Beautification, Miss. Valley Flood Control Assn., 1965—, La. Air Control Commn., 1965—. Mem. La. Democratic Central Com., 1964—. Served with USN, 1934-38, 42-49. Recipient award for outstanding service La. Recreation and Park Assn., 1964. Mem. La. Police Jury Assn. (pres. 1963, Outstanding Police Juror 1963, dist. pres. 1953-61), Nat. Assn. Counties (pres. 1965—), Am. Legion, V.F.W. Methodist. Lion, Eagle, Moose. Home: Route 1 Baker LA 70714 Office: Municipal Bldg Baton Rouge LA 70821

DU MAURIER, DAPHNE, author; b. London, Eng., May 13, 1907; d. Sir. Gerald and Muriel (Beaumont) du Maurier; ed. Camposena, Meudon, Paris; m. Lt. Gen. Sir Frederick Arthur Montague Browning, July 19, 1932; children—Tessa, Flavia, Christian. Author: The Loving Spirit, 1931; I'll Never Be Young Again, 1932; The Progress of Julius, 1933; Gerald-A Portrait, 1935; Jamaica Inn, 1936; The Du Mauriers, 1937; Rebecca, 1938; Happy Christmas, 1940; Come Wind, Come Weather, 1941; Frenchman's Creek, 1941; Hungry Hill, 1943; The King's General, 1945; The Years Between, 1945; September Tide, 1948; Castle Dor, 1962; The Glass-blowers, 1963. Dramatic works include: The Parasites, 1949; My Cousin Rachel, 1952; Kiss Me Again, Stranger, 1953; Mary Anne, 1954; The Scapegoat, 1957; The Breaking Point, 1958; The Infernal World of Branwell Bronte, 1961; The Flight of the Falcon, 1965; Vanishing Cornwall, 1967; The House on The Strand, 1969. Fellow Royal Soc. Literature. Home: Kilmarth Par Cornwall Address: care Curtis Brown Limited London WC England

DUMBAULD, EDWARD, judge; b. Uniontown, Pa., Oct. 26, 1905; s. Horatio S. and Lissa Grace (MacBurney) D.; A.B., Princeton, 1926; LL.B., Harvard, 1929, LL.M., 1930; Dr. Law, U. of Leyden, The Netherlands, 1932; m. Mary Ellen Whelpley, Jan. 1, 1941. Mem. Pa., D.C. U.S. Supreme Ct. bars; practitioner before ICC, FCC, and other adminstrn. agencies; former spl. asst. to atty. gen. of U.S., Washington (charge of litigation under acts regulating transp. and communications); judge of Ct. of Common Pleas Fayette County, 1957-61; U.S. dist. judge Western Dist. Pa., 1961- -. Sec. Am. Soc. Internat. Law. Democratic county chmn., Fayette County, Pa., 1934-36; del., Dem. Nat. Conv., Phila., 1936. Mem. Pa. Bar Assn. (chmn. com. on lawyers referral service). Presbyn. Kiwanian (president Uniontown, 1955). Club: Cosmos (Washington). Author: Interim Measures of Protection in International Controversies, 1932; Thomas Jefferson, American Tourist, 1946; The Declaration of Independence and What It Means Today, 1950; The Political Writings of Thomas Jefferson, 1955; The Bill of Rights and What It Means Today, 1957; The Constitution of the United States, 1964; Sayings of Jesus, 1967; Life and Legal Writings of Hugo Grotius, 1969. Home: 44 S Mt Vernon Av Uniontown PA 15401 Office: U S Court House Pittsburgh PA 15219

DUMBRILLE, PHILIP NORTON, former, security broker; b. N.Y.C., Aug. 13, 1905; s. H. Hilton and Edith Geraldine (Norton) D.; student U. Va., 1928. With Lybrand Ross Bros. & Montgomery, 1928-29; with various stock exchange firms, 1929-42; account exec. Spencer Trask & Co., N.Y.C., 1946-68. Vice pres. bd. mgrs. Washinghouse Sq. Home, N.Y.C. Served to maj. USMCR, 1942-45. Named knight of Malta, 1964, Hon. citizen of Korea, 1966. Mem. New Eng. Soc., Phi Sigma Kappa. Mason (32). Clubs: Church, Metropolitan (sec., bd. govs.), Union League (N.Y.C.). Home: Hillcrest Park Old Greenwich CT 06870

DUMKE, GLENN S., coll. chancellor; b. Green Bay, Wis., May 5, 1917; s. William F. and Marjorie S. (Schroeder) D.; A.B., Occidental Coll., 1938, A.M., 1939, LL.D., 1960; Ph.D., U. Cal., 1942; H.L.D., U. Redlands, 1962, Hebrew Union Coll., 1968, Windham Coll., 1969; LL.D., U. Bridgeport, 1963, Transylvania Coll., 1968, Pepperdine Coll., 1969; m. Dorothy Deane Robison, Feb. 3, 1945. Teaching asst. U. Cal. at Los Angeles, 1940-41; instr. history, Occidental Coll., 1940-43, asst. prof., 1943-46, asso. prof., 1947-50, prof. history, 1950—, Norman Bridge prof. Hispanic Am. history, 1954, dean faculty, 1950-57; pres. San Francisco State Coll., 1957- 61; vice chancellor Cal. State Colls., Los Angeles, 1961-62, chancellor, 1962—. Research fellow, Huntington Library, 1943- 45, Haynes Found. grantee, 1943; instr., air cadet tng. Los Angeles Adult Edn. System, 1942-44, leader pub. forums, 1945. Former dir. San Francisco YMCA; former v.p., dir. Bay Area Ednl. TV Assn.; past directing bd. mem. San Francisco Social Hygiene and Health Assn.; former mem. bd. San Francisco World Affairs Council; edn. adv. com. Community Television of So. Cal.; bd. commrs. Nat. Commn. on Accrediting, 1959-65, 70—; former mem. Bay Area Com. Econ. Devel.; Trustee North Cal. Council on Econ. Edn., U. Redlands, 1970—. Mem. Los Angeles World Affairs Council, Am. Cal., Mississippi Valley hist. assns., So. Cal. History Guild, Am. (Pacific Coast com. on humanities), Cal. (1st chmn. 1970—) councils econ. edn., Nat. commn. Accrediting, Assn. Higher Edn., Joint Council Econ. Edn. (bd. mem.), Western Coll. Assn. (past chmn. membership and standards com.), Am. Mgmt. Assn. (dir. 1970—), Inst. Internat. Edn. (nat. council 1970—), Phi Beta Kappa, Pi Gamma Mu, Sigma Alpha Epsilon, Alpha Mu Gamma. Republican (alt. del. to nat. conv., 13th dist., Cal., 1948, 24th dist., 1952). Methodist. Clubs: California; Bohemian; One Hundred (Los Angeles); Commonwealth, Town Hall. Author: The Boom of the Eighties in Southern California, 1944; Mexican Gold Trail, 1945; A History of the Pacific Area in Modern Times, 1949 (with Dr. Osgood Hardy); (under name Glenn Pierce) The Tyrant of Bagdad, 1955. Co- author, editor From Wilderness to EmpireA History of California, 1959. Lectr.; contbr. articles to profl. and popular pubs. Home: 285 W California Blvd Pasadena CA 91105 Office: 5670 Wilshire Blvd Los Angeles CA 90036

DUMOND, DWIGHT LOWELL educator; b. Kingston, O., Aug. 27, 1895; s. James Francis and Laura (Bell) D.; A.B., Baldwin-Wallace Coll., 1920, L.H.D.; M.A., Washington U., 1928; Ph.D., U. Mich.,

1929; D.Litt., No. Mich. U., 1965; m. Irene Margaret Hettel, June 6, 1921; childrenJack Wesley, Caryl-Bell. Acting prof. history Ohio Wesleyan U., 1929-30; asst. prof. history U. Mich., 1930-35, asso. prof., 1935-39, prof., 1939—. Commonwealth Found. lectr. U. Coll., London, 1938-39; Distinguished vis. prof. No. Mich. U., summer 1965, Howard U., 1965-66; O'Connor prof. Am. instns. Colgate U., 1968-69. Served with A.E.F., 1917-19. Recipient Distinguished Achievement award U. Mich., 1963. Mem. Soc. Am. Historians, Am. (com. on teaching history in schs. and colls. 1943), Miss. Valley (exec. com. 1939-40, pres. 1948-49), So. (bd. editors, 1935) hist. assns., Mich. Acad. Arts, Scis. and Letters. Mason. Club: Research (U. of Mich.). Author books including: A History of the United States, 1942; America in Our Time, 1947; Antislavery: Crusade for Freedom in America, 1961 (recipient Anisfield-Wolf award); America's Shame and Redemption, 1965. Editor pubs. including: Letters of James Gillespie Birney, 1831-1857, 2 vols., 1938. Home: 1613 Morton Ann Arbor MI 48104

DUMONT, DONALD ALBERT, fgn. service officer; b. Boston, Dec. 6, 1911; s. Joseph and Emma (Hayward) D.; student Oberlin Coll., 1930-31; S.B., Trinity Coll., 1934, A.M., 1939; grad. student internat. relations, Yale, 1938-39; m. Marie Paris, 1945; children—Patrick, Philippe, Cedric E. Master history and sci. Brent Sch., Baguio, Philippines, 1935-37; instr. English, Trinity Coll., 1937-39; with U.S. fgn. service, 1940—; formerly vice consul, Dakar and Rabat, consul, Tunis, Istanbul and Stuttgart; assigned Dept. of State, 1954-57; adviser U.S. delegation to UN Gen. Assembly, 1955; consul gen., Dakar, Senegal, 1958-62; U.S. minister to Kingdom of Burundi, 1962, named U.S. ambassador to Burundi, 1963; as sr. fellow Dept. State, assigned diplomat-in-residence U. Tenn., 1966-67, supr. intelligence splty., 1967—. Recipient Superior Service award Dept. of State, 1959. Mem. Sigma Nu. Author articles. Home: DeLancey NY 13752 Office: care U Tenn Knoxville TN 37916

DUMONT, EARLE JOSEPH, Jr., savs. and loan exec.; b. Phila., Sept. 5, 1920; s. Earle Joseph and Elizabeth (Jacoby) D.; B.S., U. Cal., Los Angeles, 1946; postgrad. Southwestern U. Law Sch., 1955-57, U. So. Cal., 1963-65; m. Gerladine Smalley, July 26, 1944; children-Donna Lynn, Glenn Earle. Exec. asst. to pres. Walter McCreery, Inc. Advt. Agy., Beverly Hills, Cal., 1946-50; exec. v.p. Bracken Television Prodns., Hollywood, Cal., 1950-52; pres. Dumont Mortgage Co., Sherman Oaks, Cal., 1952-60; chief adminstrv. officer, sr. v.p. Gibraltar Savs & Loan Assn., Beverly Hills, Cal., 1960- -; v.p. Pioneer Escrow Co., Security Allied Services, Beverly Hills Investment Co.; treas. Gibraltar Financial Corp. of Cal.; dir. Inner City Housing Corp., Los Angeles; guest lectr. U. Cal., Los Angeles and Irvine, Cal. Savs. and Loan Com. Co-Sponsor Youth Housing Opportunity Program, Los Angeles, 1969-70. Served to capt. USAF, 1941-45. Decorated D.F.C., Air medal, Purple Heart. Mem. USAF Acad. Athletic Assn., Theta Chi. Presbyn. (elder, chmn. bd. trustees). Home: 4285 Jubilo Dr Tarzana CA 91356 Office: 9111 Wilshire Blvd Beverly Hills CA 90213

DUMOUCHEL, PAUL, archbishop; b. Winnipeg, Man., Can., Sept. 19, 1911; s. Joseph and Josephine D.; grad. St. Boniface (Man.) Coll., 1930; student U. Man., 1929-30; Sem. Lebret, Sask., Can., 1931-36. Ordained priest Roman Cath. Ch., 1936; missionary to Indians of Man., 1936-50; retreat master, 1940-50; sch. prin., 1950-55; bishop of Keewatin, Can., 1955-67; 1st archbishop Le Pas, 1967—. Author: Saulteux Grammar, 1942. Address: 108 1st St W The Pas Manitoba Canada

DUMOULIN, L. ST. M., lawyer; b. B.C., Can., May 20, 1902; ed. Vancouver Law Sch. Admitted to B.C. bar, 1924; now partner firm Russell & DuMoulin, Vancouver. Past pres. Cong. of Governing Bodies of Legal Profession in Can. Gov., Canadian Tax Found. Fellow Am. Coll. Trial Lawyers, Am. Coll. Probate Counsel (regent 1961-70, life bencher); mem. Canadian (chmn. ins. law sect. 1950-52, v.p. B.C. 1960-62), Vancouver bar assns., Law Soc. B.C. (treas. 1966), Internat. Assn. Ins. Counsel. Office: 1075 W Georgia St Vancouver 5 British Columbia Canada*

DUMPSON, JAMES RUSSELL, univ. dean; b. Phila., Apr. 5, 1909; s. James T. and Edythe F. (Smith) D.; B.S., Pa. State Tchrs. Coll., 1932; A.B., New Sch. Social Research 1947, M.A., 1950; student U. Pa. Sch. Social Work, 1937-38, 44, 47; student Fordham U. Sch. Social Work, 1942-44, LL.D., 1964; L.H.D. (hon.), Howard U., 1960, St. Peters Coll., 1962; LL.D., Tuskegee Inst., 1963. Tchr. pub. schs., Oxford, Pa., 1932-37; supr. Phila. Dept. Pub. Assistance, 1937- 40; caseworker, supr., dir. children's instns. Children's Aid Soc. N.Y., 1940-47; asst. child care cons., then cons. corrections and delinquency Welfare Council N.Y.C., 1947-51; child care cons., cons. child-care planning bd. Fedn. Protestant Welfare Agencies N.Y., 1951-54; exec. sec. N.Y.C. Commn. Foster Care Children, 1954-56; dir. bur. child welfare N.Y.C. Dept. Welfare, 1955-58; 1st dep. commnr. welfare N.Y.C., 1958-59, commnr., 1959-65; asso. dean, prof. Hunter Coll. Sch. Social Work, City U. N.Y., 1965-67; dean, prof. Sch. Social Work, Fordham U. N.Y.C., 1967—; lectr. New Sch. Social Research, 1966—; chief cons. Community Service Soc. N.Y., 1971—. Vice chmn. of Mayor N.Y.C. Antipoverty Council and Antipoverty Operations Bd., 1964- 67; part-time mem. faculty N.Y. U. Grad. Sch. Pub. Adminstrn. and Social Service, 1949-60; UN adviser, chief tng. social welfare Govt. Pakistan, 1953-54; mem. U.S. delegation to UN Conf. of Ministers of Social Welfare, 1968; cons. to Govt. Pakistan, 1956, 61; vis. asso. prof. Fordham U. Grad. Inst. Mission Studies summer 1957; cons. on Pakistan to Asia Found., 1962-64; participant, chief UN delegation ECAFE for Asia and Far East seminar, Bangkok, Thailand, 1962; mem. President's Commn. Narcotics and Drug Abuse, 1963-64; mem. ad hoc com. pub. welfare Dept. Health, Edn. and Welfare, 1961, adv. com. aging, 1962, mem. nat. commn. on alcoholism, 1966, spl. cons. to sec. dept., 1966. Pres. Northside Center Child Devel. Mem. Nat., Pakistan assns. social worker Acad. Certified Social Workers, World Fedn. Mental Health, Internat. Cons. Social Work, Am. Orthopsychiat. Assn., Nat. Conf. Social Welfare (pres. 1971-72). Author: (with Malamud and Crawford) Working with Teen-Age Gangs, 1950, in French, 1958; After-Care: The Third Phase of Treatment, 1951; also numerous articles. Home: 1270 Fifth Av New York City NY 10029 Office: Fordham U Lincoln Center Campus New York City NY 10023

DUMSER, RAYMOND C., banker. Adminstrv. v.p. Nat. Comml. Bank & Trust Co., Albany, N.Y. Office: 60 State St Albany NY 12207*

DUNAWAY, FAYE, actress; b. Fla., 1941; an original mem. Lincoln Center Repertory Co.; appeared in Hogan's Goat, off-Broadway; played Bonnie in motion picture Bonnie and Clyde, 1967; appeared in motion picture Thomas Crown Affair. Recipient Most Promising Newcomer Award Brit. Film Acad., 1968. Address: care Warner Bros 4000 Warner Blvd Hollywood CA 90028*

DUNBAR, CHARLES EDWARD III, lawyer; b. New Orleans, Apr. 19, 1926; s. Charles Edward and Ethelyn (Legendre) D.; B.A., Tulane U., 1949, LL.B., 1951; m. Marguerite Stephanie Dinkins, July 23, 1959; children—Ladd Dinkins, Charles Edward IV, Ethelyn Legendre, George Bauer II. Admitted to La. bar, 1951, since practiced in New Orleans; partner firm Phelps, Dunbar, Marks, Claverie & Sims, 1955—. Mem. citizens adv. com. Bur. Child Welfare, New Orleans, 1955-62, chmn., 1961; citizens adv. com. Juvenile Ct. New Orleans, 1960-65, chmn. 1964; charter mem. Information Council Americas, bd. dirs., 1964-68. Del. Republican Nat. Conv., 1968; finance chmn. New Orleans Rep. party, 1969. Bd. dirs. La. Civil Service League, 1960—. vice chmn., 1964-69 pres., 1970; bd. dirs. New Orleans Area Health Planning Council. Served with USNR, 1944-46. Mem. Am., La., New Orleans bar assns., Maritime Law Assn. U.S., Assn. Average Adjustors, Am. Legion, Phi Beta Kappa, Delta Kappa Epsilon, Phi Delta Phi. Roman Catholic. Clubs: Propeller, Boston, Louisiana, Stratford, Round Table, International House (New Orleans). Home: 411 Fairway Dr New Orleans LA 70124 Office: Hibernia Bldg New Orleans LA 70112

DUNBAR, DUKE WELLINGTON, lawyer; b. Mt. Sterling, Ill., Sept. 3, 1894; s. Homer J. and Mary (Tebo) D.; LL.B., U. Mich., 1920; m. Eva Hillyard, June 5, 1922. Admitted to Ill. bar, 1920, Colo. bar, 1922; began practice in Quincy, Ill.; practiced in Denver, 1922-41; first asst. atty. gen., State Colo., 1941-44, deputy atty. gen., 1944-48, atty. gen. since 1951; asst. city atty., Denver, 1948-50. Served with U.S. Navy, World War I. Mem. Gamma Eta Gamma. Mason (Shriner), Elk. Home: 210 S Clermont St Denver CO 80222 Office: Capitol Bldg Denver CO 80203

DUNBAR, JOHN BURTON, univ. exec.; b. Birmingham, Ala., June 24, 1929; s. Collis Burton and Unavay (Gandy) D.; student Birmingham-So. Coll., 1947-49, A.B., 1957; D.M.D., U. Ala., 1953; M.P.H., Tulane U., 1959, Dr.P.H., 1963; m. Ruby F. Berry, June 29, 1953; 1 dau., Inga. Pvt. practice dentistry, Birmingham, 1953-54; instr. clin. dentistry U. Ala. Sch. Dentistry, 1953-54, trainee in epidemiology div. oral medicine and oral surgery, 1956-58, co-dir. study oral health in Iceland, asso. dir. Grad. Program in Epidemiology, asst. prof. dentistry, 1961-64, asst. to v.p. for devel. Med. Center, 1964-65, asso. prof. epidemiology and biometry, asst. dean Med. Coll. Ala. and U. Ala. Sch. Dentistry, coordinator research grants for Med. Center, interim dir. MedLARS Search Center, 1965-67, prof. dentistry, coordinator research grants for newly established U. Ala. in Birmingham, 1965-67, dir. Center for Urban Studies, 1969-70, v.p. student and community affairs, 1970—; jr. cons. U. Ky. Med. Sch., 1958; asst. dir. Ariz. Med. Sch. Study, Phoenix, 1960-61; demographer Mountain States Med. Edn. Study, 1963-64; program dir. Health Scis. Advancement Award div., research facilities and resources NIH, 1967-68; chief program projects br. Nat. Heart Inst., 1968-69. Pres. Jefferson County Com. for Econ. Opportunity, 1967, exec. com., chmn. projects planning com., 1969; mem. Mayor's Council on Youth Opportunity, 1969. Bd. dirs. Met. YMCA, 1971—. Served with USAF, 1954-56. Fellow Am. Pub. Health Assn.; mem. Ala. Acad. Sci., Phi Beta Kappa, Sigma Xi, Omicron Kappa Upsilon. Author articles. Home: 3220 Dundale Rd Birmingham AL 35216 Office: 1919 7th Av S Birmingham AL 35233

DUNBAR, KENNETH ALBERT, govt. ofcl.; b. Meade, Kan., Jan. 4, 1910; s. Orval and Mary (Yauch) D.; B.S. in Elec. Engring., Purdue U., 1932; 1 dau. (by previous marriage), Kennita Joan (Mrs. McGeath); m. 2d, Rose Bocinsky, Feb. 19, 1945; 1 dau., Jean Marie. Gen. tng., maintenance and engring. of pub. utility, 1932-41; with AEC, 1946—, mgr. constrn. and operations conversion facilities, 1946, staff Mound Lab., Miamisburg, 1947-49, mgr. prodn., engr. constrn., Oak Ridge, 1949-50, mgr. plant, Paducah, Ky., 1951-52, Portsmouth, O., 1952-57, Chgo. Operations Office, 1957—. Served from 2d lt. to maj., C.E., AUS, 1941-46; Manhattan Project. Recipient Outstanding Service award AEC. Home: R R 1 Naperville IL 60540 Office: 9800 S Cass Av Argonne IL 60439

DUNBAR, LEMUEL COTTON, petroleum co. exec.; b. Hampton, N.H., June 2, 1904; s. Melzar W. and Mary (MacDonald) D.; student Balt. City Coll., 1919-23, U. Balt., 1924-26; m. Mayre Catherine White, June 23, 1929; 1 son, William Melzar. With Eastern Rolling Mill Co., 1923-28, Am. Oil Co., 1928-37; with Am. Trading & Prodn. Corp. since 1937, asst. to v.p., 1945- 49, now v.p., dir.; chmn. bd., dir. Calvert Tankers Corp., 1956—; pres., dir. Belvedere Petroleum Corp., 1964—; v.p.,, dir. Montgomery County Properties Corp., Hamlet West Corp.; dir. Crown Central Petroleum Corp., Blaustein Industries, Inc., also Wilshire Properties, Inc. Organizer, dir. speakers bur. civilian def., Balt., 1940-42, mem. speakers bur. community fund, 1942-48. Mem. Speakers Guild Balt. (pres. 1942). Contbr. short stories, articles nat. mags., 1929- 31. Home: 2 Mallow Hill Rd Baltimore MD 21229 Office: 1 N Charles The Blaustein Bldg Baltimore MD 21201

DUNBAR, MAXWELL JOHN, educator, oceanographer; b. Edinburgh, Scotland, Sept. 19, 1914; s. William and Elizabeth (Robertson) D.; B.A., Oxford (Eng.) U., 1937, M.A., 1939; Ph.D., McGill U., 1941; m. Joan Jackson, Aug. 1, 1945; children—Douglas, William; m. 2d, Nancy Wosstroff, Dec. 14, 1960; children—Elisabeth, Andrew, Christine. Mem. faculty McGill U., Montreal, 1946—, prof., 1959—, also chmn. dept. marine sci., dir. Marine Sci. Center; dir. Eastern Arctic Investigations, Can., 1947-55. Guggenheim fellow, Denmark, 1952-53; recipient Bruce medal Royal Soc. Edinburgh, 1950. Fellow Royal Soc. Can., Linnaean Soc. London Arctic Inst. N.Am. (gov., past chmn.). Author; Eastern Arctic Waters, 1951; Ecological Development in Polar Regions, 1968. Contbr. articles profl. jours. Home: 488 Strathcona Av Westmount Quebec Canada

DUNBAR, ROBERT STANDISH, Jr., coll. dean; b. Providence, Nov. 30, 1921; s. Robert Standish and Lucie (Lowell) D.; B.S., U. R.I., 1949; Ph.D., Cornell U., 1952; m. Mary Agnes O'Grady, Dec. 8, 1941; children—Robert Standish, Barbara Louise (Mrs. John R. McKay). Mem. faculty W.Va. U., 1952—, prof. statistics, expt. sta. statistician, 1957-63, chmn. dept. animal and vet. sci., 1963-64, dean Coll Agr. and Forestry, 1964—. Served with AUS, 1942-46. Mem. Gamma Sigma Delta, Alpha Zeta. Rotarian. Home: 313 Simpson St Morgantown WV 26505

DUNBAR, WILLIAM ADAMS, ins. co. exec.; b. Bristol, Conn., Apr. 30, 1907; s. William H. and Nellie (Adams) D.; B.A., Yale, 1929; m. Carolyn Drennan, May 11, 1935; 1 dau., Nancy. With Gen. Reinsurance Corp., N.Y.C., 1930—, asst. treas., 1949-56, comptroller, 1956-66, treas., 1966-69, ret. Served with USAAF, 1943. Home: 46 Maple Hill Dr Larchmont, NY 10538.

DUNCAN, A. BAKER, investment banker; b. Waco, Tex., Dec. 29, 1927; s. A. Baker and Frances (Higginbotham) D.; grad. Woodberry Forest (Va.) Sch., 1945; B.A., Yale, 1949; M.A., U. Tex., 1952; m. Sally P. Witt, Jan. 31, 1953; children—Adddison Baker III, Richard Witt, Andrew Prescott. Master, Hill Sch., Pottstown, Pa., 1949-51; partner Rotan Mosle & Co., investment bankers, Houston, 1953-61; headmaster Woodberry Forest Sch., 1962-70; mem. firm Rotan, Mosle-Dallas Union, Inc., 1970—. Trustee Asheville (N.C.) Sch., Hockaday Sch., Dallas; bd. dirs. Ednl. Cons. Mem. Chi Psi. Democrat. Episcopalian. Home: 336 Geneseo San Antonio TX 78209 Office: 2119 Nat Bank Commerce Bldg San Antonio TX 78205

DUNCAN, ALEXANDER EDWARD, ret. comml. banker; b. nr. Louisville, May 27, 1878; s. John Thomas and Ida (Smith) D.; ed. Louisville Male High Sch.; m. Flora Ross, Apr. 11, 1900 (died June 20, 1936); 1 dau. Elizabeth Duncan Yaggy; m. 2d Mrs. E. Everett Gibbs (Anne Ranson), Mar 16, 1940. Began as bank clk. at Louisville, 1896; clerk Jungbluth & Rauterberg, Louisville, 1897-99; mem. Ross & Duncan, Crestwood, Ky., 1900-02; spl. and gen. agt. Ocean Accident & Guaranty Corp., Cincinnati, 1903-06; gen. agent at Baltimore for Am. Credit-Indemnity Co., 1907-09; organized, 1909, and pres., dir. until 1912, Manufacturers' Finance Co., Balt., Md. Organized, 1912, and pres., dir. Comml. Credit Co., Balt., chmn. bd., 1916-54, founder chairman, 1954-64, ret. member. Robert Garrett & Sons, investments, 18 mos., 1916-17; reorganized Humpherys Mfg. Co., Mansfield, O., 1917, merged 1956 into and dir. Borg Warner Corp., Chicago; director Am. Credit Indemnity Co. N.Y., Mercantile Safe Deposit & Trust Co. (both Baltimore, Md.). Gen. chmn. YMCA War Work campaign (Baltimore), 1917, and for United War Work campaign, 1918; pres. Community Fund of Baltimore, 1929-31; gen. chmn. Balt. Red Cross War Fund, 1943. Adv. bd. Women's Hosp., Children's Hosp., Inc., Keswich- Home for Incurables. Republican. Episcopalian. Clubs: Bachelors Cotillon, Maryland. Eldridge. Merchants. Center (Balt.). Home: Cedarwood 4604 N Charles St Baltimore MD 21210

DUNCAN, ANGUS, union ofcl.; b. Oct. 1, 1912; s. Augustin and Margherita (Sargent) D.; student pvt. schs., N.Y.C.; m. Dorothy Borner, June 13, 1942; children—Douglas, Pamela. Actor, 1932-41; bus. rep. Actor's Equity Assn., AFL-CIO, 1941-43, 45-47, asst. exec. sec., 1947-52, exec. sec., 1952—; v.p. Theatre Authority, 1952-, Asso. Actors and Artists Am., 1953—; mem. bd. N.Y. Council on The Arts. Served as cpl. AUS, 1943-45. Club: Players (N.Y.C.). Address: 165 W 46th St New York City NY 10036

DUNCAN, BUELL G., utility exec.; b. 1905; married. With S. Atlantic Gas. Co., Orlando, Fla., 1925-52; pres., chief exec. officer Piedmont Natural Gas Co., Inc., Charlotte, N.C., 1952-60, chmn. bd., 1970—; dir. Wachovia Bank & Trust Co., Charlotte & 1st Provident Co. Inc., Sanford, N.C. Office: 4301 Yancey Rd Charlotte NC 28210*

DUNCAN, CHARLES HOWARD, educator; b. Tarentum, Pa., Jan. 11, 1924; s. James Boyd and A. Elizabeth (Wilson) d.; B.S., Indiana (Pa.) U., 1950; M.Ed., U. Pitts., 1954, Ed.D., 1959; m. Mary Jane Ferrier, Nov. 23, 1954; children—Betsy Ann, Laurel Ann. Asst. dir. Franklin Comml. Coll., Connellsville, Pa., 1950-52; tchr. Butler (Pa.) Sr. High Sch., 1952-54; instr. U. Pitts., 1954-59; prof. Indiana (Pa.) U., 1959-65; prof., head dept. bus. edn. Eastern Mich. U., Ypsilanti, 1965-. Vol. instr. Wayne County Econ. Opportunity Com. Served with USNR, 1943-47. Recipient certificate of appreciation Wayne County Econ. Opportunity Com., 1968. Mem. Nat., Eastern, Tri-State, Pa. (past treas.), Mich. (past publicity dir.) bus. edn. assns., Delta Pi Epsilon. Kiwanian. Author: (with Lessenberry and Wanous) College Typewriting, 1964, 69. Services editor typewriting Business Education Forum, 1968—. Home: 2245 Valley Dr Ypsilanti, MI 48197.

DUNCAN, CHARLES KENNEY, naval officer; b. Nicholasville, Ky., Dec. 7, 1911; s. Charles Wallace and May (Kenney) D.; student U. Ky., 1928; B.S., U.S. Naval Acad., 1933; m. Sheila Anne Taylor, July 30, 1941; children—Bruce Douglass, Anne Kenney. Commd. ensign U.S. Navy, 1933, advanced through grades to adm., 1970; comdr. destroyer, World War II, amphibious ship, 1956; operations officer Pacific Fleet, 1956-58; comdr. Amphibious Group I, 1958-59, Amphibious Tng. Command, Pacific, 1959-61, Naval Base, Subic Bay, 1961-62; asst. chief naval personnel for plans, 1961-63; comdr. Cruiser Destroyer Force 1964-65, Amphibious Force, 1965-67, Second Fleet, 1967-68; chief of naval personnel, 1968-70; Supreme Allied comdr. Atlantic, NATO, also comdr.-in-chief U.S. Atlantic Command and Atlantic Fleet, 1970—. Decorated D.S.M. Home: Virginia House Naval Sta Norfolk VA 23511

DUNCAN, CHARLES THOMAS, univ. dean; b. Marietta, Minn., May 20, 1914; s. Henry and Clara B. (Olson) D.; A.B., U. Minn., 1936, M.A., 1946; m. Gretchen L. Altermatt, Nov. 8, 1940; children—Thomas Scott, Diana Lynn, Jean Marie. Engaged in newspaper work, Minn., 1936-40; instr. journalism U. Nev., 1940-42; asst. prof. journalism U. Neb., 1946-47; asst. prof. journalism U. Minn., 1947-49, asso. prof., 1949-50; asso. prof. journalism U. Ore., 1950-52, prof., 1952-62, dean Sch. Journalism 1956- 62; asso. dean faculties, 1965-67, dean faculties, 1967-70, asso. dean faculty, prof. journalism, 1970—. dean, prof. Sch. Journalism U. Colo., 1962-65. Served as lt. USNR, 1942-45. Mem. Assn. for Edn. in Journalism (pres. 1961), Am. Assn. U. Profs., Kappa Tau Alpha. Author: (with Blaustein and Porter) The American Lawyer, 1954. Editor: Horace Greeley's Overland Journey, New York to San Francisco, 1859, 1964. Contbr. newspapers, mags., profl. jours. Home: 2154 McMillan Eugene OR 97405 Office: Johnson Hall U Ore Eugene OR 97403

DUNCAN, CHARLES WILLIAM, internat. bus. cons.; b. Patoka, Ind., Aug. 20, 1908; s. John Obed and Pansy W. (Knaub) D.; student Evansville Coll., 1928-32; m. Jane S. Smith, Dec. 29, 1932; children—John William, James Careleton, Jay Michael. With Libby, McNeill & Libby, 1938—, successively retail salesman, Evansville, Ind., domestic salesman, South Bend, staff export div., subsidiary sales co. mgr., internat. sales rep., Chgo., mgr. export div., 1938-58, v.p. charge internat. div., including exports and internat. mfg. and trading operations, 1958-62, v.p. charge all internat. operations, 1962-69, dir.; cons. internat. affairs. Clubs: South Shore Country, Illinois Athletic, Mid-America. Home: 1450 Glenmoor Rd Evansville IN 47715 Office: 200 S Michigan Av Chicago IL 60604

DUNCAN, CHARLES WILLIAM, Jr., bottling co. exec.; b. Houston, Sept. 9, 1926; s. Charles William and Mary Lillian (House) D.; B.S. in Chem. Engring., Rice U., 1947; postgrad. mgmt. U. Tex., 1948-49; m. Thetis Anne Smith, June 10, 1957; children—Charles William III, Mary Anne. Roustabout, chem. engr. Humble Oil & Refining Co., 1947; with Duncan Foods Co. div. of Coca-Cola Co., Houston, 1948-67, adminstrv. v.p., 1957-58, pres., 1958-67, chmn. adv. bd., 1964-67, chmn. Coca-Cola Europe, 1967-70; exec. v.p. Coca-Cola Co., Atlanta, 1970—; dir. Coca-Cola Co., Great So. Life Ins. Co. Gov. adviser Rice U. Served with USAAF, 1944- 46. Mem. Nat. Coffee Assn. (past chmn.), Young Pres. Orgn., Sigma Alpha Epsilon, Sigma Iota Epsilon. Methodist (ofcl. bd.). Home: 2167 Mt Paran Rd NW Atlanta GA 30327 Office: 310 North Av NW Atlanta GA 30313

DUNCAN, CLARENCE AVERY, Jr., savs. and loan assn. exec.; b. LaGrange, Ga., Jan. 28, 1917; s. Clarence Avery and Maude (Borders) D.; student San Angelo (Tex.) Jr. Coll., 1935- 37, U. Tex., 1937-39; m. Billie Marguerite Blanton, Sept. 4, 1940; children—John Davis, David Ray, Lea Ann. With Farm & Home Savs. Assn., Nevada, Mo., 1945—, successively appraiser, Dallas br., mgr. Forth Worth br., 1945-50, v.p. Nevada, Mo., 1950-56, pres., dir., 1956—; dir. Citizens State Bank, Gt. Am. Res. Ins. Co., Dallas, Mortgage Guaranty Ins. Corp., Milw., Am. Founders Life Ins. Co., Austin. Mem. U.S. Savs. and Loan League (pres. 1965). Episcopalian. Rotarian. Home: 102 Country Club Dr Nevada MO 64772 Office: care Farm & Home Savings Assn 221 W Cherry St PO Box 248 Nevada MO 64772

DUNCAN, DAVID BEATTIE, educator, statistician; b. Sydney, Australia, June 16, 1916; s. Watson Cranston and Frances (Calman) D.; B.Sc. Agr., U. Sydney, 1938, B.A., 1941; Ph.D. in Math. Statistics,

Ia. State Coll., 1947; m. Mary Ann Kohli, Feb. 27, 1948; children—Robert Ames, George Walter, Margaret Ann. Came to U.S., 1950, naturalized, 1953. Lectr. agrl. biometrics, then sr. lectr. statis. methods U. Sydney, 1938-50; asso. prof., then prof. statistics Va. Poly. Inst., 1950-54; prof. U. Fla., 1955-56; research asso. then vis. prof. U. N.C., 1956-60; prof. statistics and biostatistics Johns Hopkins, 1961- -; statis. cons. Air Force Eastern Test Range, 1957-69; spl. research multiple comparisons and in recursive estimation. Pawlett scholar U. Sydney, 1945-47; recipient Horseley award Va. Acad. Sci., 1951. Fellow Am. Statis. Assn., Inst. Math. Statistics; mem. Biometric Soc., Australian Statis. Assn. Home: 800 Wellington Rd Baltimore MD 21212.

DUNCAN, DAVID DOUGLAS, photojournalist, author; b. Kansas City, Mo., Jan. 23, 1916, s. Kenneth Stockwell and Florence (Watson) D.; student archaeology, U. Ariz., 1935; B.A. in Zoology and Spanish, U. Miami (Fla.), 1938; m. Leila Khanki, Sept. 20, 1947 (div. 1962); m.2d, Sheila Macauley, July 13, 1962. Free-lance photojournalist, 1938-39; photographer Am. Mus.-Michael Lerner expdns., 1940-41, Chile-Peru coordinator Interam. affairs Mexico/Central Am., 1941-42; Life mag. photographer 1946-56; self-employed as photojournalist in Europe, Mid-East, Africa, Asia and Africa, 1956-67, photo-corr. Life mag. and ABC-TV, Vietnam, 1967-68; Photographed Presdl. Convs. at Miami Beach and Chgo. for NBC-TV, 1968. Served with USMCR, 1943-46; PTO. Decorated Legion of Merit, D.F.C. (2), Air medal (4), Purple Heart; recipient U.S. Camera Gold award, 1950; Overseas Press Club award, 1951, 52, Robert Capa Gold medal, 1968. Author: This is War!, 1951; The Private World of Pablo Picasso, 1958; The Kremlin, 1960; Picasso's Picassos, 1961; Yankee Nomad, 1966; I Protest, 1968. Self-Portrait: U.S.A., 1969; War Without Heroes, 1970. Address: Castellaras 53 Mouans-Sartoux Alps Maritime France

DUNCAN, DONALD, educator; b. Marietta, Minn., Jan. 31, 1903; s. Henry and Clara (Olson) D.; B.A., Carleton Coll., Northfield, Minn., 1923; M.A., U. Minn., 1927, Ph.D., 1929; m. Margaret Aileen Eberts, Sept. 18, 1924; children-Mary Jeanne (Mrs. Ronald Arthur Welsh), Margaret Caroline (Mrs. Nester Paul Arceneaux), Kathleen Elizabeth (Mrs. William Mowat Edwards). Asst. prof. anatomy U. Utah, 1929-30; asst. prof. anatomy U. Buffalo, 1930-32, prof., head dept., 1942-43; asso. prof. anatomy U. Tex. Med. Br., 1932- 42, prof., chmn. dept., 1946-68, Ashbel Smith prof. anatomy, 1968—, asso. dean grad. studies, 1952-69; mem. NIH Adv. Com. Med. Studies Research, 1961-63, anat. tng., 1960-65; chmn. USPHS, expert adv. panel chiropractic and naturopathy, 1968. Mem. Tex. Acad. Sci. (pres. 1962), Am. Assn.Anatomy (pres. 1967), Phi Beta Kappa, Sigma Xi, Nu Sigma Nu. Episcopalian. Contbr. articles profl. jours. Home: 114 Tarpon Galveston TX 77550

DUNCAN, DONALD PENDLETON, educator; b. Joliet, Ill., Feb. 24, 1916; s. Kenneth Whitney and Nettie (Pendleton) D.; student North Park Coll., 1934-35, Mich. Coll. Mining and Tech., summer 1935; B.S.F., U. Mich., 1937, M.S., 1939; Ph.D., U. Minn., 1951; m. Dymer Mercein Benzie, July 6, 1956; children—Kenneth Houlton, Nancy Susan, Debra Mercein. Shelter-belt asst. U.S. Forest Service, Meade, Kan., 1939-40, jr. forester, Harrison, Ark. and Brooklyn, Miss., 1940-41; instr. Kan. State Coll., Manhattan, 1941-42, extension forester, 1946-47; instr., asst. prof., asso. prof. U. Minn., St. Paul, 1947-59, prof., 1959-65, asst. dir. Sch. Forestry, 1964-65; dir. Sch. Forestry, U. Mo., Columbia, 1965—. Cons. Minn. Natural Resources Council, 1961-63; cons. Coop. State Research Service, 1969, Fgn. Area Fellowship Program, 1969, 70, Council Grad. Schs., 1970; vis. scientist NSF, 1965, 68, 69; mem. Nat. Coop. Forestry Research Adv. Bd., 1967—; exec. bd. Assn. State Coll. and U. Forestry Research orgns., 1967-68; chmn. Council Forestry Sch. Exec. 1970-71; chmn. Com. on Forestry Accreditation, 1970—. Dist. chmn. Boy Scouts Am., 1969-71. Served with AUS, 1942-45. Decorated Bronze Star medal, Purple Heart. Fellow A.A.A.S.; mem. Soc. of Am. Foresters (past sect. sec.-treas., chmn. recreation and edn. div.), Am. Forestry Assn., Am. Assn. U. Profs., Higher Edn. Assn., Ecol. Soc. Am., Wilderness Soc., Forest Products Research Soc. (sec., exec. bd.), Forest History Soc., Nat. Parks Assn., Mo. Acad. Sci., Sigma Xi, Gamma Alpha, Xi Sigma Pi, Phi Sigma, Gamma Sigma Delta. Research in forest ecology, forest influences and outdoor recreation. Home: 209 W Brandon Rd Columbia MO 65201

DUNCAN, DONALD STUART, educator; b. Bklyn., Aug. 3, 1915; s. Alfred C. and Florence (Higley) D.; student Pratt Inst., 1933-36; B.S., Mass. Inst. Tech., 1937; student U. Mich., 1946; M.S., N.Y. U., 1948; m. Jean Paradis, Oct. 17, 1946; children—David, Christopher. Mem. faculty Pratt Inst., 1938, prof. physics, 1965—; research engr. SAM Labs. Columbia, 1945-46; partner McGuinnes & Duncan, engrs., 1952—. Mem. Assn. Am. Physics Tchrs., Am. Soc. M.E., Am. Soc. Engring. Edn. Home: 179 Steuben St Brooklyn NY 11205.

DUNCAN, EDWIN, banker; b. Sparta, N.C., June 25, 1905; s. David C. and Della L. (Woodruff) D.; A.B., U. N.C., 1925; m. Katherine R. Reeves, Aug. 31, 1926 (div. 1934); 1 son, Edwin; m. 2d, Bessie L. Wellborn, June 29, 1935; children—Jance C., David C. (dec.). Cashier, Bank of Sparta, 1926-37; exec. v.p. Northwestern Bank, North Wilkesboro, N.C., 1937-58, pres., 1958-; sec.-treas. Northwestern Finance Co., North Wilkesboro, 1940—; chmn. Board Lowe's Cos., Inc., 1963—; partner Wythe Finance Co., Wytheville, Va., 1949-60; pres. Alleghany Devel. Corp., Sparta, N.C., 1953—, Northwestern Financial Corp., North Wilkesboro; dir. Holly Farms Poultry Industries, Wilkesboro; mem. N.C. Senate, 1953-55. 58-59. Mem. N.C. Banking Commn.; chmn. Northwestern Devel. Corp., Indsl. Com. N.C.; mem. election com. 9th Dist. N.C.; chmn. finance com. Allegheny County Dist. N.C., Alleghany County Hosp. Trustee Greater U. N.C. Mem. Cattle and Dairy Assn. Am. Democrat. Club: Twin City (Winston-Salem, N.C.). Home: 1 Duncan St Sparta NC 28675 Office: Northwestern Bank North Wilkesboro NC 28697

DUNCAN, EDWIN, Jr., banker; b. High Point, N.C., July 14, 1927; s. Edwin and Katherine (Reeves) D.; B.S. in Banking and Finance, U. N.C., 1950; m. Cynthia Allen, Dec. 18, 1948; children—Katherine Reeves (Mrs. Walter P. Purcell), Edwin III; m. 2d, Rachel Rose, June 15, 1968. Sec.-treas. So. Discount Corp., Wythevelle, Va., 1950-56; v.p. Northwestern Bank, N. Wilkesboro, N.C., 1956-62, sr. v.p., 1962—; pres., dir. Northwestern Security Life Ins. Co., N. Wilkesboro, 1958—; pres., dir. Northwestern Financial Corp., 1969—; sec. Northwestern Capital Corp., N. Wilkesboro; pres. Carolina Tice & Speedway S.A., San Jose, Costa Rica, 1965—. Mem. N.C. Banking Commn., 1965-69. Pres. Northwest N.C. Devel. Assn., 1966, chmn., 1968. Trustee Ashevelle-Biltmore Coll., 1961-65; bd. visitors Appalachian State U., 1968—. Served with AUS, 1945-47. Clubs: Paradise Valley Country (Phoenix); Asheville (N.C.) Country; Roaring Gap (N.C.) Country. Home: Route 2 Sparta NC 28675 Office: Northwestern Bank North Wilkesboro NC 28659

DUNCAN, FREDERICK GELLER, ins. exec.; b. N.Y.C., Apr. 24, 1911; s. William A. and Grace W. (McWilliam) D.; B.A., Princeton, 1932; m. Janet St. Clair Mullan, Mar. 12, 1938 (div. 1963); 1 son, William Mullan; m. 2d, Grace Sager Rippin, Mar. 15, 1963. With Guaranty Trust Co., N.Y.C., 1933-50, asst. treas., 1947-50; with N.Y. Life Ins. Co., 1950—, asst. treas., 1952-57, asst. v.p., 1957-61, 2d v.p., 1961-70, treas., 1970—; mem. Midtown adv. bd. Mfrs. Hanover Trust Co. Trustee Russell Sage Found. Served from lt. (j.g.) to lt. comdr., USNR, 1942-45; Africa and S. Pacific. Home: 25 East End Av New York City NY 10028 Office: 51 Madison Av New York City NY 10010

DUNCAN, GARFIELD GEORGE, physician, educator; b. Gloucester, Ont., Can., Aug. 2, 1901; s. Samuel and Matilda (Mansfield) D.; M.D., C.M., McGill U., Montreal, 1923; post-grad. work Physiatric Ins., Morristown, N.J., 1924-26; m. Dorothea E. Waterman, Sept. 3, 1927; children—Theodore Garfield, Barbara Nancy, Peter Waterman. Intern. Hamilton (Ont.) Gen. Hosp., 1923; practiced in Phila. since 1926; demonstrator clin. medicine, Jefferson Med. Coll., Phila., 1927-34, asso. in medicine, 1934-37; asso. prof. medicine, 1939-42, clin. prof. medicine, 1942-56, prof. clin. medicine, 1956-57; prof. medicine U. Pa., 1957-70, emeritus, 1970—; mem. staff Pa. Hosp., 1926—, chief med. service, 1937-46, dir. med. div., 1946-65, head dept. of metabolism and nutrition, 1946-65, physician to hosp., 1965-68, cons., 1968—, pres. staff, 1947-49, 54, 56, pres. Benjamin Franklin Clinic, 1950-53; cons. in metabolism, Del. County Hosp., 1940—; cons. Phoenixville Hosp., 1953-70, hon. cons., 1970—; lectr. Royal Coll. Physicians Can., 1953. Served as lt. col. in charge of med. service of Evacuation Hosp. No. 52; served overseas, Jan. 1942- July 1944; now serving as expert cons. to Surgeon Gen. of Army; past cons. VA, Washington Br.; med. cons. to 6th Army, 1943-44; promoted to Col. Med. Corps, Army of U.S., Apr. 1944; chief of Med. Service, Eng. Gen. Hosp., Aug.-Dec. 1944, med. cons. Second Service Command, 1945; nat. cons. in internal medicine to USAF, 1958-62. Pres., Garfield G. Duncan Research Found., 1968—. Awarded Legion of Merit for research work on malaria in S.W. Pacific Area, Army Commendation Ribbon (1946) for work in control of hepatitis; recipient Distinguished Teaching award Lindback Found., 1963; Banting and Best Medal (Czechoslovakia), 1963; Banting medal Am. Diabetes Assn., 1963; Outstanding Civilian Service medal, U.S. Army, 1970. Diplomate Am. Bd. Internal Medicine. Hon. fellow N.Y. Diabetes Assn.; fellow A.C.P. (v.p. 1959-60); mem. Assn. Am. Physicians, American Clin. and Climatological Assn., American Diabetes Assn. (council 1954-57), Canadian Med. Association, A.M.A., A.A.A.S., Soc. Med. Cons. to the Armed Forces (pres. 1950-51), Phila. County Med. Soc., Internat. Soc. Internal Medicine, Pa. Acad. Fine Arts, Soc. Air Force Physicians, Internat. Diabetes Fedn., Alpha Omega Alpha. Episcopalian. Clubs: Peale, Regency. Author: Diabetes Mellitus and Obesity, 1935; Diabetes Mellitus-Principles and Treatment, 1951; Modern Pilgrim's Progres, 1956, rev., 1967. Editor, co-author: Diseases of Metabolism, 1942, rev., 1947, 52, 59, 64. Editor-in-chief: Metabolism, 1957-70, asso. editor, 1970—; chmn. editorial adv. bd. History of Internal Medicine in World War II, 1952—. Contbr. to med. publs. Home: Donachaidh Farm Malvern RD 1 PA 19355 Office: 330 S 9th St Philadelphia PA 19107

DUNCAN, GEORGE THIGPEN, ret. army officer; b. Thomasville, Ga., Dec. 15, 1909; s. Rom Hawkins and Mary (Thigpen) D; student Auburn U., 1927-28; B.S., U.S. Mil. Acad., 1932; grad. Inf. Sch., 1936; Armed Forces Staff Coll., 1947, Army War Coll., 1951, Advanced Mgmt. Program, Harvard, 1956; m. LaTrelle Robertson, Mar. 26, 1935; 1 son, David Glasgow. Commd. 2d lt., inf., U.S. Army, 1932, advanced through grades to maj. gen., 1961; assigned 22d Inf., 1932-35, 16th Inf., 1937-39, 27th Inf. Regt., 1939-41, 65th Inf. Div., 1942-45, U.S. Forces in Austria, 1945-47, Army Gen. Staff, 1948-50, 51-52, 224th Inf., 40th Div., Korea, 1953-54, Hdqrs. 3d Army, 1954-56; comdg. gen. Berlin Command, 1956-58: assigned Hdqrs. Joint Task Force Seven, 1958-59, Army Gen. Staff, 1959-61; comdg. gen. IV U.S. Army Corps, 1961-62; chief staff Hdqrs. U.S. Continental Army Command, 1963- 66; dep. comdg. gen. 3d U.S. Army, Ft. McPherson, Ga., 1966-67, ret., 1967; asst. dir. Of Yerkes Primate Research Center, Emory U., Atlanta, 1967—. Decorated D.S.M. with oak leaf cluster, Silver Star with oak leaf cluster, Legion of Merit with oak leaf cluster, Bronze Star, Combat Inf. badge; Croix de Guerre with etoile vermeil (France). Mem. Kappa Sigma Presbyn. (deacon, elder). Kiwanian. Home: 3360 Pine Meadow Rd N W Atlanta GA 30327

DUNCAN, HEARST RANDOLPH, lawyer; b. Center Junction, Ia., Aug. 28, 1905; s. John Edgar and Maude (Stingley) D.; student Lenox Coll., 1922-24; A.B., George Washington U., 1928, J.D., 1931; m. Louise Ezell, June 16, 1932; children—Barbara Jean, Hearst R. Admitted to Ia. Bar, 1931; partner Ducan, Jones, Hughes, Riley & Davis, Des Moines; state's atty. Mitchell County, Ia., 1932-34; spl. asst. atty. gen. State Ia., 1937; Ia. atty. C., M., St.P & Pacific R.R.; officer, dir. Des Moines Union Ry. Co.; dir. Ia. Transfer Ry. Co. Fellow Am. Coll. Trail Lawyers; mem. Nat. Assn. R.R. Trial Counsel (UN nat. legacies com.), Am., Ia. (past pres.) bar assns., Order of Coif, Delta Sigma Rho. Home: 726 54th St Des Moines IA 50312 Office: Equitable Bldg Des Moines IA 50309

DUNCAN, HOBERT EDWARD, newspaper exec.; b. Mason City, Ia., Dec. 9, 1927; s. Hobert E. and Donna (Hindal) D.; B.A., U. Ia., 1952; m. Arlene Mary King, June 28, 1953; 1 son, Christopher Edward. With Mason City Globe-Gazette, 1952-53, Des Moines Register, 1950; with Honolulu Star-Bull., 1954—, mng editor, 1964—. Bd. dirs. Honolulu Symphony Soc.; v.p. Hawaii Opera Theatre; past regent Chaminade Coll., Honolulu. Served with AUS, 1946-48. Mem. Am. Journalism Edn. Assn. (bd. dirs., Hawaii Newsman's Assn. (bd. dirs.), A.P. Mng. Editors Assn. Club: Honolulu Press (past pres.). Home: 5322 Oio Dr Honolulu HI 96821 Office: PO Box 3080 Honolulu HI 96802

DUNCAN, JAMES FRANCIS, ret. univ. ofcl.; b. Mears, Mich., Apr. 28, 1900; s. Samuel Walter and Edith Lillian (Anderson) D.; A.B., Kalamazoo Coll., 1923, A.M., 1924; student Yale, 1926-27; M.A., U. Mich., 1927, Ph.D., 1929; m. Gladys Irene Killam, Sept. 8, 1928; children—Nevin James, Pan. Instr. physics Kalamazoo Coll., 1924-25; asst. Yale, 1926-27; prof. physics Lombard Coll., Galesburg, Ill., 1928-29, Hastings (Neb.) Coll., 1929-30; prof. physics Wis. State Univ., Oshkosh, 1930-70, prof. physics emeritus, 1970—, dean instrn., 1945-55, dean coll., 1955-62, dean of business affairs, 1962-63, v.p. bus. affairs, 1963-70. Fellow A.A.A.S.; mem. Am. Phys. Soc., Am. Assn. Physics Tchrs., Nat., Wis. edn. assns. Methodist. Home: 1847 Shore Dr South Pasadena FL 33707

DUNCAN, JAMES HERBERT CAVANAUGH, banker; b. Madison, Wis., June 13, 1925; s. Dorman L. and Marie (Cavanaugh) D.; student Western Mich. U., 1950; grad. Sch. Financial Pub. Relations, Northwestern U., 1954; Grad. Sch. Banking, U. Wis., 1962; m. Colleen Patricia Cloney, Sept. 14, 1946; children—James H., John P., Gary T., Phillip K., Katherine M., Thomas M., Mark J. Duncan. Associated with the First Nat. Bank & Trust Co. Kalamazoo, 1950—, sr. v.p., 1964-65, exec. v.p., 1965-69, pres., 1969—; dir. I.K.D. Corp. Gen. campaign chmn. Kalamazoo Community Chest, 1958, pres., 1964; pres. Constance Brown Hearing Center, Kalamazoo, 1960; chmn. Kalamazoo chpt. A.R.C., 1967. Mem., chmn. pres.' council Nazareth Coll., Kalamazoo, 1966-71. Trustee, pres. operating bd. Lift Foundation, Kalamazoo, 1967- 70; trustee W.E. Upjohn Inst., 1971—. Served to 2d lt., inf., AUS. World War II. Decorated Bronze Star with oak leaf cluster, Purple Heart with oak leaf cluster, Combat Inf. badge. Mem. Mich. Bankers Assn. (exec. com. 1967—, 1st v.p. 1970-71), Charge Account Bankers Assn. (pres. 1957). Kiwanian (pres. Kalamazoo 1964). Clubs: Kalamazoo Country, Park (pres. 1970) (Kalamazoo). Author articles in field. Home: 1806 Greenbrier Dr Kalamazoo MI 49001 Office: 108 E Michigan Av Kalamazoo MI 49006

DUNCAN, JAMES LOUGHLIN, bishop; b. Greensboro, N.C., Sept. 11, 1913; s. Robert and Mary (Loughlin) D.; B.A., Emory U., 1935, M.A., 1936; B.D., U. South, 1939, D.D., 1962; m. Evelyn Burgess, July 25, 1943 (dec. Jan. 1967); children—Mary Anna (Mrs. Edward B. Waters), John Robert, James Loughlin; m. 2d, Mrs. Elaine B. Gaither, Oct. 7, 1967. Ordained to ministry Episcopal Ch., 1938; asst. rector in Atlanta, 1939-40; rector in Rome, Ga., 1940-45, Winter Park, Fla., 1945-50, St. Petersburg, Fla., 1950-61; suffragan bishop Episcopal Diocese So. Fla., 1961-69; bishop Diocese Southeast Fla., 1969—. Exchangee, U.S.-South African Program, 1961. Chmn. Dade County Community Relations Bd., 1965. Mem. Kappa Alpha (knight comdr. 1957-58). Home: 3800 Alhambra Ct Coral Gables FL 33134 Office: 525 NE 15th St Miami FL 33132

DUNCAN, JAMES RUSSELL, mfg. exec.; b. Tucson, Apr. 17, 1917; s. Bradford and Mattielee (Josey) D.; student U. Ariz., U. Wis.; m. Mimi Galloway; children—Joanne, James Russell, Robert, Lance. Vice pres., gen. mgr. Peerless Machine Co., Racine, Wis., 1940-45; gen. mgr. Moore Machinery Co., Los Angeles, 1945- 46; sec.-treas. McCulloch Motors Corp., Los Angeles, 1946-48; chief of capital goods ECA Mission to Italy, 1948-50; cons., 1950-52; indsl. cons., pres. Electric Sprayit Co. and subsidiary, Sheboygan, Wis., 1952-53; asst. to pres. Stewart-Warner Corp., Cons., Chgo., 1954-55; v.p. Misco Corp., also Consol., Founderies & Mfg., Chgo., 1955-57; chmn., pres., dir. Mpls.-Moline Co., Hopkins, Minn., 1957-60; chmn. bd., chief exec. officer Sterling Precision Corp.; chmn. bd. Resource Exploration, Inc., Shreveport, La., Milw. Western Corp., Milw.; pres. Russdun Corp. Clubs: Minneapolis; Racquet, Saddle & Cycle (Chgo.); Memphis Country, Memphis Hunt and Polo; Delray (Fla.) Beach Yacht. Home: 4 Riverview Terrace New York City NY 10022 Office: 1 Rockefeller Plaza New York City NY 10020

DUNCAN, JOHN BONNER, cons.; b. Springfield, Ky., Feb. 6, 1910; s. Samuel E. and Lena Bell (Jordan) D.; A.B., Howard U., 1934, scholarship student Grad. Sch. Philosophy, 1933-35, Grad. Sch. Law, 1935-38; LL.B., Terrell Law Sch., Washington, 1938; m. Edith L. West, July 2, 1938 (dec. Mar. 1O, 1966); children—John Bonner, Joan West; m. 2d, B. Dolores Berry, Aug. 14, 1969. With Dept. of Interior, 1934-41; admitted to Md. bar, 1941; atty. Bituminous Coal Commn., 1942-43; atty., then sr. atty. solid fuels br. OPA, 1943-46; sr. atty., atty.-adviser Office Housing Expediter, 1947-49; sr. atty. research sect., law div. HHFA, 1949-52; recorder deeds D.C., 1952-61; commr. D.C., 1961-67; asst. to sec. interior for urban relations, 1967- 69; gen. cons., pres. Housing Devel. Assos., Washington, 1969—. Vice pres. Nat. Capital area Nat. Council Chs.; sponsor Club of All Nations, Bd. dirs. Nat. Capital area United Givers Fund; bd. dirs., chmn. personnel com. Nat. Capital area Big Bros.; trustee Barney Neighborhood House. Recipient Afro-Am. Newspaper award, 1950; citation Pitts.-Courier, 1951, Chgo. Defender, 1955; ann. award D.C. Fedn. Civic Assns., 1952, 62; award Washington Urban League, 1959; Brotherhood award Nat. Conf. Christians and Jews, 1961; award for community service Am. Legion, 1962, Nat. Assn. Colored Womens Clubs, 1962, Nat. Capital area Council of Chs., 1962, others. Mem. A.M.E. Zion Ch. Author: New Dimension Bidding in Contract Bridge 1963. Home: Watergate East Apts 2500 Virginia Av NW Washington DC 20037

DUNCAN, JOHN C., corp. exec.; b. N.Y.C., Sept. 29, 1920; s. John C. and Doris (Bullard) D.; grad. Hotchkiss Sch., Lakeville, Conn., 1938; B.A., Yale, 1942; m. Barbara Doyle, Dec. 12, 1942; children—Lynn (Mrs. Edwin J. Singleton), Wendy (Mrs. Edgar V. Van Winkle III), Craig, Gale. With W.R. Grace & Co., 1946-70, exec. v.p. charge Latin Am. operations, 1960-64, exec. v.p. corp., 1964-70; sr. v.p., trustee St. Joe Minerals Corp., 1970-71, pres., trustee, 1971—; dir. Massasoit Mgmt. Co., Fernley Assos., Inc. Trustee Hampton Inst., Experiment in Internat. Living. Served to capt., F.A., AUS, 1942-46; CBI. Mem. Peruvian-Am. Assn. (dir.), Pan Am. Soc. (bd.), Bus. Group for Latin Am. Presbyn. Clubs: Economic, Yale (N.Y.C.); Belle Haven (Greenwich). Home: Field Point Park Greenwich CT 06830 Office: 250 Park Av New York City NY 10017

DUNCAN, JOHN HOUSE, corp. exec.; b. Houston, Jan. 22, 1928; s. Charles William and Lillian (House) D; B.B.A., U. Tex., 1949; m. Jeaneane Booth, Sept. 8, 1951; children—John House, Jeaneane. Salesman, Duncan Coffee Co., Houston, 1945-49, v.p., sales promotion mgr., 1953-58; v.p. Gulf and Western Industries Inc., Houston, 1958-59, pres., 1959-67, also dir., chmn. exec. com.; dir. Houston Natural Gas, Bank of S.W., Houston. Served to 1st lt. USAF, 1949-53. Mem. Young Presidents Orgn., Sigma Alpha Epsilon. Clubs: Houston Country, River Oaks Country, Houston (Houston). Home: 306 Shadywood Houston TX 77027 Office: 2020 Post Oak Tower Houston TX 77027

DUNCAN, JOHN JAMES, congressman; b. Scott County, Tenn., Mar. 24, 1919; married; four children. Asst. atty. gen., 1947-56; dir. law, Knoxville, Tenn., 1956- 59, mayor, 1959-64; mem. 89th to 92d Congresses, 2d dist. Tenn. Served with AUS, 1942-45. Mem. Am., Tenn., Knoxville bar assns., Am. Legion (comdr. Tenn. 1954), Knoxville C. of C., Knoxville Tourist Bur., V.F.W. Republican. Presbyn. Address: House Office Bldg Washington DC 20515

DUNCAN, JOHN PAUL, educator; b. Indpls., Aug 15, 1909; s. John David and Ethel (Thornberry) D.; A.B. cum laude, Butler U., 1932; A.M., Ind. U., 1938, Ph.D., 1941; postgrad. U. Chgo., 1939-40; m. Bernice G. Giltner, Feb. 16, 1935. Instr. Butler U., 1933-38, Ind. U., 1938-39, 40-41, U. Akron (O.), 1942-45; asst. prof. Okla. State U., 1945-46; faculty U. Okla, Norman, 1946—, prof. polit. sci., 1957—, David Ross Boyd prof., 1967—. Fulbright lectr. Ein. Shams U., Cairo, 1952-53; minister Omega (Ind.) Christian Ch., 1933-41, Wooster Av. Christian Ch., Akron, 1942-45, Sumner (Okla.) Christian Ch., 1946-47; minister at-large Christian and Presbyn. Ch., Norman, 1947—. Asst. to exec. dir. FHA, Ind., 1934-35; pres. Okla. Council Chs., 1951- 52; chmn. Norman Bd. Adjustment, 1963-66; pres. Okla. div. UN Assn., 1967—. Bd. dirs. Inst. Mediterranean Affairs, 1967—. Ford fellow, 1952- 53; recipient award for excellence in teaching U. Okla., 1952-53; Erett Newby award for excellence in teaching, 1967. Mem. Am. Polit. Sci. Assn., Blue Key, Phi Delta Theta, Phi Kappa Phi, Pi Sigma Alpha, Pi Epsilon Delta, Tau Kappa Alpha, Omicron Delta Kappa, Democrat. Presbyn. and mem. Disciples of Christ Ch. Author: Constitutional Governemt in U.S. and Britain, 1953; also articles. Home: 809 Elmwood Dr Norman OK 73069

DUNCAN, JOHN VERNON, lawyer; b. N.Y.C., Nov. 5, 1904; s. William A. and Grace W. (McWilliam) D.; B.S., Princeton, 1925; LL.B., Columbia, 1928; m. Ula H. Tenney, Feb. 23, 1945; children—Michael (dec.), Helene H., Peter S., Joan A. Admitted to N.Y. bar, 1929, since practiced in N.Y.C.; partner firm Patterson, Belknap & Webb, and predecessors, 1944—. Sec. Jackson Hole Preserve, Inc. Bd. dirs. N.Y.C. Mission Soc. Mem. Am., N.Y. State, Internat. bar assns., Bar Assn. City Union (N.Y.C.). Home: 201 E 77th St New York City NY 10021 Office: 1 Wall St New York City NY 10005

DUNCAN, KENT WHITNEY, banker; b. Quincy, Ill., Feb. 13, 1915; s. Laurance Morgan and Margaret (Kent) D.; B.A., Grinnell Coll., 1936; postgrad. U. Wis., 1947-49, U. Ind., 1954-55; m. Deuel Rowan, Jan. 13, 1946; children—Cole Rowan, Sarah Whitney. With Harris Trust & Savs. Bank, Chgo., 1936—, v.p., 1958-68, sr. v.p., 1968—. Mem. exec. bd. Chgo. council Boy Scouts Am., 1954—, treas., 1964-68, v.p., 1968, mem. nat. council, 1970; gov. Citizens Greater Chgo., 1962—; mem. trustees adv. council Grinnell Coll., 1963—. Served to lt. col., C.E., AUS, 1941-46, Recipient Silver Beaver award, 1964. Mem. Robert Morris Assos. (past chpt. pres.), Ill. C. of C. (dir.). Roman Catholic. Clubs: Bankers, University, Economic, Chicago (Chgo.); Westmoreland Country (Wilmette, Ill.). Home: 595 Elm St Winnetka IL 60093 Office: 111 W Monroe St Chicago IL 60690

DUNCAN, LAURENCE ILSLEY, judge; b. Concord, N.H., Oct. 5, 1906; s. Charles and Charlotte (Ilsley) D.; A.B., Dartmouth Coll., 1927; LL.B., Harvard, 1930; m. Doris M. Hackett, June 25, 1932; children—Stuart B., James H.S. Admitted to N.H. bar, 1930; engaged in law practice, 1930-45; asso. justice N.H. Superior Ct., 1945-46; asso. justice N.H. Supreme Ct. since 1946. Del. N.H. Constl. Conv., 1938, 41; mem. Bd. of Bar Examiners, N.H., 1941-44. Former mem. council League N.H. Craftsmen; trustee Concord Hospital, 1944-63, 67—. Member of Am., N.H. bar assns., Am. Judicature Soc., Phi Beta Kappa, Phi Alpha Delta (hon.), Sigma Nu. Republican. Conglist. Office: Supreme Ct Bldg Concord NH 03301

DUNCAN, LOUIS CHARLES, finance co. exec.; b. Kokomo, Ind., Feb. 20, 1913; s. John P. and Nellie C. (Stevens) D.; B.A., Ind. U., 1933; m. Marguerite Dewees, Sept. 3, 1934 (dec. Aug. 1968); children—Carole (Mrs. William Kuehn), Craig; m. 2d, Eileen Hastings, Apr. 26, 1969. With Household Finance Corp., Chgo., 1936—, corporate dir. personnel, 1953-54, v.p., 1954-67, sr. v.p., dir., 1967—; dir. City Products of Chgo.; owner Heathercrest Farm (Gown Point, Ind.). Trustee English Speaking Union; mem. Chgo. Council Fgn. Relations. Trustee, chmn. acad. affairs com. Buena Vista Coll. Served as field dir., A.R.C., World War II. Recipient distinguished service award, Nat. Consumer Finance Assn., 1970. Mem. Employers Assn. Chgo. (dir.), Am. Soc. Personnel Adminstrs., Ill. C. of C., Pres.'s and Gov.'s Com. Employment of Handicapped, Execs. Club Chgo. Presbyn. (elder). Clubs: Illinois Athletic (Chgo.); LaGrange (Ill.) Country. Home: 901 Cleveland Rd Hinsdale IL 60521 Office: Prudential Plaza Chicago IL 60601

DUNCAN, LYMAN CAMPBELL, chem. and pharmaceutical mfr.; b. Flat Rock, Ill., Jan. 29, 1910; s. Lowe C. and Ella (Hughes) D.; A.B., DePauw U., 1932; M.Sc. in Econs., London (Eng.) Sch. Econs., 1934; m. Ruth B. Arnold, June 27, 1936; children—Janet, Hugh, John, Thomas. With Ohio Oil Co., 1934-37; asso. editor Barron's, Dow-Jones, Inc., N.Y.C., 1937-41; with Am. Cyanamid Co., Wayne, N.J. 1945-71, gen. mgr. Lederle Labs. div., 1955-61, v.p. company, 1960-71. Served to lt. col., Chem. Corps, AUS, 1941-45. Mem. Pharm. Mfrs. Assn. (dir.). Home: 21 Calumet Av Hastings-on-Hudson NY 10706

DUNCAN, MARION MAHAN, Jr., educator; b. Bloomfield, Mo., June 24, 1927; s. Marion Mahan and Marjorie (Fink) D.; B.S., Auburn U., 1949, M.S., 1953; Ph.D., Duke, 1956; m. Dora Tisdale, Mar. 18, 1948; children—Richard Eric, Diana. Aerodynamicist, Bell Aircraft Co., Buffalo, 1950-51; vis. asst. prof. Duke, 1956-60; asst. prof. Tex. A. and M. U., 1960-61; asso. prof. U. Ga., Athens, 1961-66, prof. physics, 1966—, head dept. physics and astronomy, 1968—. Served with USNR, 1945-46. Mem. Am. Phys. Soc., A.A.A.S., Am. Assn. U. Profs., Sigma Xi. Office: Physics Dept U Ga Athens GA 30601

DUNCAN, MARION MONCURE, orgn. ofcl.; b. Alexandria, Va., Dec. 19, 1913; d. Robinson and Ida Virginia (Grigg) Moncure; student William and Mary Coll., George Washington U.; grad. Bus. and Secretarial Sch., Washington, 1935; m. Robert V.H. Duncan, Oct. 26, 1939; children—Robinson Morton, Moncure, Bruce Grigg. Sec. to pres. Am. Tel. & Tel. Co., 1941; sec. to dir. Eastern area A.R.C., 1945-47; ct. reporter, Alexandria, 1948- 52; ins. broker, 1950—; head ins. dept. Bob Duncan Real Estate-Ins., Alexandria, 1953—. Mem. D.A.R., 1932—, regent John Alexander chpt., 1937-39, successively recording sec., vice regent, regent, Va., 1950-53, nat. organizing sec. gen., 1953-56, nat. pres. gen., 1962-65. First v.p. Order First Families Va., 1965-69, 1960-69; pres. Aquia Ch. Assn., 1959- 61; co-chmn. area fund campaign Woodrow Wilson Meml. Com.; 4th v.p. Kenmore Assn., 1950-53; bd. trustees Jamestown Corp., Williamsburg, Va. (producer Common Glory), 1953—. Mem. bd. visitors William and Mary Coll., 1966—. Mem. Alexandria C. of C. (chmn. pub. relations womens div.), Va. Assn. Ins. Agts. (chmn. pub. relations No. Va. 1959-61), No. Va. Assn. Ins. Agts. (v.p. 1961; recipient Outstanding Service award). Episcopalian. Club: Zonta Internat. Co-author: House of Moncure Geneology, 2 supplements, 1967-69. Home: 218 S Fairfax St Alexandria VA 22314 Office: P O Box 986 Alexandria VA 22313

DUNCAN, OTIS DUDLEY, human ecologist; educator; b. Nocona, Tex., Dec. 2, 1921; s. Otis Durant and Ola (Johnson) D.; B.A., La. State U., 1941; M.A., U. Minn., 1942; Ph.D., U. Chgo., 1949; m. Beverly Davis, Jan. 16, 1954. Research asso. in human ecology, prof., asso. dir. population research and tng. center U. Chgo., 1951-62; prof. sociology U. Mich., 1962—. Mem. aux. research awards com. Social Sci. Research Council; human ecology study sect. NIH; mem. Census Adv. Com. on Population Statistics; adv. panel on research grants Social Security Adminstrn., Commn. on Population Growth and the American Future. Served with AUS, 1942-46. Mem. Population Assn. Am. (pres. 1968-69), also Am. Statis. Assn., Am. Sociol. Assn., Am. Acad. Arts and Scis. Author: (with others) Social Characteristics of Urban and Rural Communities 1950, 1956; The Negro Population of Chicago, 1957; Metropolis and Region, 1960; Statistical Geography, 1961; The American Occupational Structure, 1967; Toward Social Reporting: Next Steps, 1969.

DUNCAN, PHILLIP AARON, educator; b. Bedford, Ind., Mar. 27, 1927; s. Aaron Jefferson and Roma (Claxton) D.; A.B., Ind. U., 1948, M.A., 1953, Ph.D., 1958; postgrad. U. Grenoble (France), 1948-49, Ecole des Langues Orientales, Paris, France, 1949-50; m. Carol Virginia Cornelius, Aug. 29, 1953; children—Meredith Anne, Craig Cameron. From instr. to asso. prof. French, Okla. State U., 1955-60; faculty U. Ky., Lexington, 1960—, prof. French, 1965—, chmn. dept., 1966-69. Served with USNR, 1945-46. Mem. Phi Beta Kappa. Author: Emile Zola, Lettres de Paris, 1963. Home: 1574 Lakewood Ct Lexington KY 40502

DUNCAN, RICHARD EDWARD, univ. dean; b. Rochester, N.Y., Jan. 15, 1913; s. John Thomas and Hattye (Henderson) D.; B.Mus., Eastman Sch. Music, 1935, Ph.D., 1953; M.A., Ohio State U., 1937; m. Ludmilla Paulus, July 14, 1938; children—Lynne Richard, Molly Ann. Head string dept. Ohio State U., 1935-37, Hastings Coll., 1937-39; founder, mus. dir. Omaha Symphony Orch., 1939-58; dean, dir. Creative Arts Center, W.Va. U., 1958—; v.p. Morgantown Community Concerts, 1958—; producer ednl. radio and TV programs. Chmn. music com. W.Va. Centennial, 1958—; mem. Pres. U.S. Nat. Cultural Com., 1956; adviser cultural presentations program Dept. State. Mem. W.Va. Coll. Music Educators Assn. (pres.), W.Va. Music Educators Assn. (exec. bd.), Nat. Assn. Schs. Music (opera com.), Am. Musicological Soc., Music Educators Assn., Music Tchrs. Nat. Assn., W.Va. Arts and Humanities Council, Nat. Council Fine Arts Deans. Home: 773 Kermit Pl Morgantown WV 26505

DUNCAN, RICHARD GERVIN, business services and publs. co. exec.; b. Jacksonville, Fla., Nov. 9, 1909; s. Rufus Bertram and Lola Maude (Morgan) D.; grad. Advanced Mgmt. Program. Harvard Univ., 1965; m. Eleanor Lux, Feb. 10, 1934; children— Richard Gervin, Joseph Edward. With Dun & Bradstreet, Inc., 1927-71, v.p., 1954-63, exec. v.p., 1963-66, pres. agy. divs., 1966-71, also dir.; dir. Fed. Home Loan Bank N.Y., Home: 44 Northern Dr Short Hills NJ 07078

DUNCAN, ROBERT, poet. Author: Opening of the Field; Roots and Branches, 1964; (verse and prose play) Medea at Kolchis, 1965; Bending the Bow, 1968; Cao and the Blackbird. Address: 833 Ashbury St San Francisco CA 94117*

DUNCAN, ROBERT MERRILL, ins. co. exec.; b. Jamaica, N.Y., Aug. 9, 1911; s. Thomas J. and Edna (Merrill) D.; B.S., N.Y. U., 1932; M.A., Columbia, 1933; m. Mildred Bretz, Sept. 20, 1935; children—Robert Merrill, George Thomas. Actuarial Supr. Home Life Ins. Co., N.Y.C., 1934-48; with Tchrs. Ins. & Annuity Assn. Am., N.Y.C., 1948—, actuary, 1949—, v.p., 1955-66, adminstrv. v.p., 1966-67, exec. v.p., 1967—. Dir. Greater N.Y. Blue Shield. Fellow Soc. Actuaries, Am. Acad. Actuaries. Club: Garden City Golf. Home: 5 Deerfield Rd Port Washington NY 11050 Office: 730 3d Av New York City NY 10017

DUNCAN, SHELDON FORBES, mfr. bedding and furniture; b. Oakland, Cal., July 17, 1910; s. Robert F. and Ida M. (Sheldon) D.; B.A., Stanford, 1931; m. Dorla Powell, Dec. 16, 1936; children—Stanley F., Calvin P. With Simmons Co., N.Y.C., 1932—, chief engr., Kenosha, Wis., 1951-55, div. prodn. mgr., 1956, gen. prodn. mgr., N.Y.C., 1957-59, v.p., 1959—, also dir., mem. exec. com., 1950—. Club: Scarsdale Golf. Home: 6 Forest Lane Scarsdale NY 10583 Office: 280 Park Av New York City NY 10017

DUNCAN, THOMAS CLARK, utility exec.; b. Pitts., July 16, 1905; s. Thomas S. and Margaret N. (Clark) D.; E.E., Cornell U., 1927; m. Thelma M. Ashworth, Jan. 26, 1927; children—Thomas A., William C., Margaret E. (Mrs. Donald R. Woodley). With Consol. Edison Co. N.Y., Inc., and predecessors, 1927-70, asst. v.p., 1962-64, v.p., 1964-67, sr. v.p., 1968-69, exec. v.p., 1969-70; exec. dir. N.Y. Power Pool, 1971—. Fellow I.E.E.E. Club: Engineer's (N.Y.C.). Home: 32 Kennworth Rd Port Washington NY 11050

DUNCAN, THOMAS WILLIAM, author; b. Casey, Ia., Aug. 15, 1905; s. William Thomas and Irene Alderman (Valentine) D.; student Drake U., Des Moines, Ia., 1922-26, A.M., 1931; A.B., cum laude, Harvard, 1929; m. Actea Carolyn Young, July 11, 1942. Reporter and spl. writer Des Moines Register, 1926, book reviewer 1934-35, Des Moines Tribune 1929-30; prof. English, Des Moines Coll. Pharmacy, 1934-38; asst. prof. journalism and dir. radio. Grinnell Coll., Grinnell, Ia., 1942-44. Awarded Lloyd McKim Garrison prize in poetry, Harvard, 1929. Mem. Sigma Delta Chi, Delta Theta Phi, Sigma Tau Delta. Author books including: Gus The Great (Book- of-Month Club selection), 1947; Big River, Big Man, 1959; Virgo Descending, 1961; The Labyrinth, 1967. Contbr. to mags. Address: Box 308 Mesilla NM 88046

DUNCAN, WALTER, crude oil producer; b. La Salle, Ill., Jan 11, 1889; s. Nicholas W. and Mary Ann (Stuart) D.; Ph.B., U. Notre Dame, 1912, LL.D., 1956; m. Velma M. Twomey, Oct. 24, 1914; children—Edward J., J. Walter, Vincent J., Raymond J. Engaged in ins. bus., 1912—, in oil bus., 1937—; pres. Walter Duncan, Inc., La Salle, 1956—; dir. La Salle Nat. Bank, Chgo. mem. bd. lay trustees U. Notre Dame. Served to 2d lt., inf., U.S. Army, World War I. Decorated Knights of Malta. Roman Catholic. K.C. Address: Apple Valley CA 92307

DUNCAN, WILLIAM ADOLPHUS, Jr., electric utility exec.; b. Washington, Aug. 2, 1912; s. William Adolphus and Sue (Ellis) D.; B.S. in Mech. Engring., U. Ky., 1935; m. Dorothy Decker McElrath, Nov. 14, 1939; childrenDorothy, Sara Sue, Mary Patton. Pres., dir. Ky. Utilities Co., Old Dominion Power Co.; dir. Electric Energy, Inc., Commonwealth Life Ins. Co., also dir. Ohio Valley Electric Corp. Trustee High Temperature Reactor Devel. Assn. Pres. Central Ky. Music Soc., 1965, bd. dirs., 1962-; bd. dirs. Commn. Mem. I.E.E.E., Civil War Roundtable, Triangle Frat. Baptist. Clubs: Optimist, Pyramid (Lexington, Ky.)

DUNCANSON, THOMAS SHERRIFF, corp. exec.; b. Edinburgh, Scotland, Nov. 15, 1896; s. James and Alice (Ronaldson) D.; student Toronto Tech. Sch.; m. Jean McGill, Sept. 3, 1922; 1 dau., Dorothy Jean (Mrs. Charles L. Walker). With Moore Corp., Ltd. (and predecessor firm), Toronto, Can., 1913—, sec., 1929-48, dir., 1948—, exec. v.p., 1953-55, pres., 1955-62, chmn. bd. corp. and all subsidiaries, 1962-67, now dir., mem. policy com. corp. and all subsidiaries; gen. mgr. F. N. Burt Co., Inc., Buffalo, 1935, v.p., gen. mgr., 1946-55, pres., 1952-62, chmn. bd., 1962—; chmn. bd. Moore Bus. Forms, Inc., Niagara Falls; dir. of Can. Life Assurance Company, also Nat. Trust Co. Presbyn. Clubs: National, York, York Downs Golf (Toronto); Buffalo, Buffalo Country: Niagara (Niagara Falls, N.Y.). Home: 1088 Delaware Av Buffalo NY 14209 Office: 330 University Av Toronto Ontario Canada

DUNDAS, FRED N., glass co. exec.; b. Wallaceburg, Ont., Can., Mar. 6, 1906; s. Thompson Brock and Bessie Norah (Ayres) D.; B. Commerce, U. Toronto, 1928; m. Marian Jean MacMillen, Nov. 19, 1932; children—John Brock, Robert Gordon, Frederick Norman. Sales rep. Royal Securities Corp., 1928-33; with Hanson Bros., Inc., 1933-35; with Dominion Glass Co., Ltd., Montreal, 1935-69, v.p., sec., 1955-56, exec. v.p., 1956-59, pres., 1959-69, chmn., 1967-69, also chief exec. officer, dir. Pres. Glass Container Mfrs. Inst., Inc., N.Y.C., 1959-61. Mem. Phi Gamma Delta. Clubs: Rotary, University, Amatuer Athletic Assn., Kanawaki Golf, Mount Royal Curling (Montreal); Seigniory (Montebello, Que); Canadian (N.Y.C.). Home: 359 Kindersley Av Town Mount Royal Quebec Canada

DUNDAS, JOHN ARTHUR, corp. exec.; b. Portland, Ore., Aug. 10, 1905; s. Arthur Livingstone and Ida Mae (Sears) D.; student U. Ore., 1923-25; B.A., U. So. Cal., 1927, LL.B., 1930; grad. student Harvard Law Sch., 1927-29; m. Wanda C. Yoakum, Aug. 12, 1931; children—John II, Dennis Franklin. Admitted to Cal. bar, 1930; pvt. practice, Los Angeles, 1930-39: dep. city atty., Los Angeles, 1939-42; regional enforcement exec. OPA, 1942-44; atty. Douglas Aircraft Co., Santa Monica, Cal., 1944-53, gen. counsel, 1953-57, v.p. adminstrn., 1957, exec. v.p., dir., 1957-62; v.p. internat. Gen. Dynamics Corp., N.Y.C., 1962—; dir. Canadair Ltd., Montreal. Mem. State Bar Cal., Phi Kappa Tau, Phi Alpha Delta. Episcopalian. Mason. Clubs: University (N.Y.C.); Lake Placid, Sky, Los Angeles Country. Home: 860 UN Plaza New York City NY 10017 also 2515 Burr St Fairfield CT 06432 Office: 1 Rockefeller Plaza New York City NY 10020

DUNDES, JULES, educator; b. N.Y.C., Sept. 12, 1913; s. Leopold and Ida (August) D.; B.S., Columbia, 1933; m. Frances Becker, July 31, 1937; children—Leslie Weir (Mrs. Peter Salmon Cox), Suresa. Sports reporter with the N.Y. Post, 1929-34; copywriter The Hallee Co., 1934-36; promotion copywriter CBS, 1936-40, advt. and sales promotion mgr. WCBS, N.Y.C., 1940-49, dir. sales and advt. KCBS, San Francisco, 1949-55, mgr., 1955-56, gen. mgr., 1961-67; v.p. advt., sales promotion CBS Radio, 1956, v.p. charge sta. adminstrn., 1956-61; v.p., gen. mgr. KCBS, 1961-67; lectr. in communication Stanford Univ., 1967—. Chmn. communications com. San Francisco Human Rights Commn. Bd. dirs. Cerebral Palsy Assn. Mem. San Francisco Radio Broadcasters Assn. (pres.), Cal. Broadcasters Assn. (chmn. of bd.), Radio Pioneers, Sigma Delta Chi. Home: 38 Rossi Av San Francisco, CA 94118. Office: Stanford U Stanford CA 94305

DUNFEY, WILLIAM LEO, mem. Democratic Nat. Com.; b. Lowell, Mass., Oct. 10, 1925; s. Leroy William and Catherine (Manning) D.; student Miami U., Oxford, O., 1946- 48; B.A., U. N.H., 1950, M.A. in Political Sci., 1954; D.Sc., Lowell Tech. Inst. 1967; m. Ruth Elaine Thomas, June 14, 1956; 1 dau., Julie Ann. Engaged in hotel and motor inn bus., 1950—; with Dunfey Corp., Hampton, 1956—, v.p. mgmt. devel. Parker House Hotel, Boston, also 11 other Dunfey Family Hotels and Motor Inns, located in New Eng., Royal Coach Inns, Atlanta, Dallas, Houston, Anaheim and San Mateo, Cal. Dem. Nat. Conv., Chgo., 1952; chairman N.H. Stevenson for Pres. Com., 1956; regional rep. Dem. Nat. Com., New Eng., N.Y. State, N.J., Del., 1958-60; Kennedy campaign coordinator in Me., N.H. and Vt., 1960; mem. Dem. Nat. Com. for N.H., 1960—, site com. for 1964 Nat. Democratic Conv.; Johnson campaign coordinator N.Y. State and New Eng., 1964; Chmn. Dem. State Com., 1965-67. Commr. N.H. Library, 1954-59. Served with USMCR, 1943-46. Mem. Nat. Assn. Real Estate Bds., Am. Hotel and Restaurant Assn. Home: 10 Causeway Rd Rye Beach NH 03871 Office: 490 Lafayette Rd Hampton NH 03842

DUNFORD, RALPH EMERSON, coll. dean; b. Amanda, O., Dec. 17, 1896; s. William Michael and Alice Ardella (Rockey) D.; B.A. with Dist., Ohio State U., 1923, M.A., 1924, Ph.D., 1929; m. Mary Ann Dingess, June 5, 1926; children—William Dingess, James Scott. Grad. asst., part time instr. Ohio State U., 1923- 26; formerly with U. Tenn., successively asst. prof., asso. prof., prof., dean of students, 1945; head employment officer TVA, 1940-44. Pres. University Concerts, Inc., 1938—. Mem. com. on Air Force ROTC curriculum Air Univ. Mem. Nat. Assn. Personnel Adminstrs., Am. Psychol. Assn., Phi Kappa Phi, Phi Delta Kappa, Phi Eta Sigma, Omicron Delta Kappa. Home: Route 3 Knoxville TN 37920

DUNGAN, RALPH ANTHONY, state govt. ofcl.; born Phila., Apr. 22, 1923; s. Ralph Anthony and Elsie Louise (Callaway) D.; B.S., St. Joseph's Coll., Phila., 1950; M.S. in Pub. Affairs, Princeton, 1952; m. Mary Theresa Rowley, Dec. 27, 1950; children—Christopher F., Peter, Nancy, James, Moira, Paul, Jennifer. With internat. div. U.S. Bur. Budget Legislative reference, 1951-56; legislative asst. to Senator John F. Kennedy, 1956-57; staff com. labor and pub. welfare U.S. Senate, 1957-60; spl. asst. to Pres. Kennedy, 1961-63; spl. asst. to Pres. Johnson, 1963-64; U.S. ambassador to Chile, 1964-67; chancellor Higher Edn., State N.J., 1967—. Mem. Council on fgn. relations. Served to lt. (s.g.) USNR, 1942-45. Club: Nassau. Home: 142 Hodge Rd Princeton NJ 08540

DUNGWORTH, DONALD LAWRENCE, educator; b. Hathersage, Eng., July 16, 1931; s. Lawrence and Alice (Dearnaley) D.; B.V.Sc., Liverpool U., Eng., 1956, M.R.C. V.S., 1956; Ph.D., U. Cal. at Davis, 1961; m. Margaret Alice Begg, July 28, 1962; children— Dawn Lesley, Duncan Lawrence. Came to U.S., 1957, naturalized, 1968. Grad. asst. Ont. Vet. Coll., Can., 1956-57; lectr. pathology Sch. Vet. Medicine, U. Cal., Davis, 1957-61; asst. prof. to prof., chmn. dept. vet. pathology, 1962—; lectr. pathology Sch. Vet. Medicine, U. Bristol (Eng.), 1961-62. Cons., Air Pollution Research Center, U. Cal., Riverside, also Radiology Lab., U. Cal., Davis. Served to lt. Brit. Army, 1949-51. World Health Assn. fellow, 1968-69; NIH grantee in comparative pathology, 1969—; prin. investigator (Nat. Inst.) Environmental Health Scis. research grant on air pollution, 1971—. Diplomate Am. Coll. Vet. Pathologists. Mem. Internat. Acad. Pathology, Am. Assn. Pathologists and Bacteriologists, Royal Coll. Vet. Surgeons, Sigma Xi. Contbr. articles profl. jours. ‡

DUNHAM, ALLISON, educator; born Wessington Springs, S.D., June 19, 1914; s. Frederick Niles and Rachel Mary (Allison) D.; A.B., Yankton Coll., 1936; LL.B., Columbia, 1939; m. Anne Campbell Toll, June 28, 1941; children—Allison (dec.), Stephen, Andrew. Admitted to N.Y. bar, 1940, Ill. bar, 1956; law clk. to Chief Justice Harlan F. Stone, 1939-41; draftsman, reporter Uniform Comml. Code for Am. Law Inst. and Nat. Conf. Commrs. Uniform State Laws, 1947-50; asst. prof. law U. Ind., 1945-47, asso. prof. Columbia, 1947-51, prof. U. Chgo., 1951—; exec. dir. Nat. Conf. Commrs. Uniform State Laws, 1962-69; vis. lectr. law Victoria Coll., 1953. Candidate town supr., Westchester, N.Y., 1949. Served as asst. naval attache U.S. Embassy, Managua, Nicaragua, 1941-44. Mem. of Am. Law Inst., Am. Bar Assn., Chgo. Bar Assn. Democrat. Conglist. Author: Modern Real Estate Transactions, 1952; also articles legal jours. Co-author: Mr. Justice, 1956. Home: 5719 Kenwood Av Chicago, IL 60637

DUNHAM, CHARLES LITTLE, physician; b. Evanston, Ill., Dec. 28, 1906; s. William Huse and Margaret (Little) D.; B.A., Yale, 1929; M.D., U. Chgo. (Rush), 1934; m. Lucia Elizabeth Jordan, June 22, 1932; children—George Stuart, Carol Jordan, Sara Gale. Intern internal medicine U. Chgo. Clinics, 1933-34; asst. resident medicine New Haven Hosp., 1934-35; asst., sch. medicine, U. Chgo., 1936-42, instr., 1942-46, asst. prof. medicine, 1946-49; asst. chief med. br. AEC, 1949-50, chief med. br., div. biology and medicine, 1950-54, dep. dir. div., 1954, dir., 1955-67; chmn. div. med. scis. Nat. Acad. of Scis.-N.R.C., Washington, 1967—. Mem. exec. committee Nat. Com. on Radiation Protection; WHO expert Advisory Panel on Radiation. Served as capt., M.C., U.S. Army, 1943- 46. Recipient U.S. AEC Distinguished Service award, 1957. Mem. Soc. of Nuclear Medicine, A.M.A., N.Y. Acad. Science, Am. Nuclear Soc., Health Physics Soc., Radiol. Soc. N. Am., Am. Rheumatism Assn., A.A.A.S., Radiation Research Soc. (pres. 1969-70), Acad. Med. Wash. Inst. Med. Chgo., Sigma Xi, Nu Sigma Nu, Delta Kappa Epsilon. Clubs: Cosmos (Washington); Elizabethan (Yale U.); International (Washington). Home: 5302 Carvel Rd Washington DC 20016 Office: National Academy of Sciences 2101 Constitution Av Washington DC 20418

DUNHAM, CLIVE FLEEMING, educator; b. Minonk, Ill., Jan. 15, 1909; s. Arthur Scott and Julia Dempster (Snedden) D.; B.S., U. Ill., 1929, M.S., 1931, Ph.D., 1935; C.P.A., Ill., 1935, Miss., 1947; m. Florence Stoaks, Aug. 15, 1939. Asst., U. Ill., Urbana, 1929-34, prof. accountancy, 1965—. acting head dept. indsl. adminstrn., 1965-66; McKinley prof. econs. Huron Coll., 1934-36; asst. prof. bus. adminstrn. U. S.D., 1936-37; asso. prof., head dept. accountancy U. Miss., 1937-38, prof., chmn. dept., 1938-65, dean sch. Bus. and Govt., 1950-65; Mem. Am. Inst. C.P.A.'s Miss. Soc. C.P.A.'s, Am. Accounting Assn., Beta Gamma Sigma. Methodist. Address: 605 W Delaware Urbana IL 61801

DUNHAM, DONALD CARL, UN ofcl.; b. Columbus, O., Aug. 30, 1908; s. Ray Stanley and Agnes (Jordan) D.; Ph.B., Yale, 1930; Ph.D., U. Bucharest, 1948; postgrad. Harvard Grad. Sch., 1939-40; m. Florence Atkins Ross. Am. Fgn. Service officer, 1931-39; vice consul, Berlin, Germany, 1931- 32, Hong Kong, 1932-35, Athens, Greece, 1935-38, Aden, Arabia, 1939; N.Y. State WPA mus. supr., 1940; adminstrv. asst. Met. Mus. Art, N.Y.C., 1941-42; dir. East and West Assn., 1942; initiated and promoted repeal of Chinese Exclusion Act, 1942-43; editor financial research program Nat. Bur. Econ. Research, 1943-45; asst. cable editor Life mag., 1945-46; UNESCO relations officer Dept. State, 1946; pub. affairs officer, Bucharest, Rumania, 1947-50, Bern, SWitzerland, 1950-52; pub. affairs officer Office U.S. Polit. Adviser, also dir. pub. information office Allied Mil. Govt., Trieste, F.T.T., 1952-55; dir. planning Am. Com. for Liberation, 1955-61; adj. asso. prof. Fordham U., 1962; dir. pub. services U.S. Mission to UN, 1962-68, rep. UN Devel. Program, UNICEF and Office UN High Commr. for Refugees, Australia and New Zealand, 1968—. Mem. Delta Kappa Epsilon. Clubs: Dutch Treat, Coffee House. Author: Envoy Unextraordinary. 1944; Rumanian Profile, 1948; Kremlin Target: USA, 1961; Zone of Violence, 1962. Contbr. articles to various publs. Home: care of Robert Ross 8205 Beech Tree Rd Bethesda MD 20034 Office: UNDP Box 20 New York City NY 10017

DUNHAM, DOUGLAS, educator; b. Wessington Springs, S.D., July 25, 1916; s. Fred Niles and Rachel Mary (Allison) D.; A.B., Yankton Coll., 1938; M.A., U. Mich., 1941, Ph.D., 1950; m. Esther Spangler, Aug. 18, 1940; children—David Frederick, Mary Dell. Instr. Norfolk (Neb.) pub. schs., 1938-43, 46-47, Norfolk Jr. Coll., 1943, 46-47; faculty Mich. State U., 1947—. Prof. social sci., 1958—, chmn. dept., 1960—. Chmn. city planning commn., E. Lansing, Mich., 1968—; chmn. E. Lansing Community Council, 1955-56. Served with AUS, 1943-46. Decorated Legion of Merit. Mem. Mich. Acad. Arts. Scis. and Letters, Am. Hist. Assn., Nat. Assn. for Gen. and Liberal Studies (pres.-elect 1970), Pi Gamma Mu, Phi Alpha Theta, Phi Delta Kappa. Presbyn. (trustee). Contbg. author: Modern Society, 1954, General Education Social Science, 1960, Building a General Education Curriculum, 1960. Co-editor: Readings in Social Science, 1957. Home: 1031 Marigold Av East Lansing MI 48823

DUNHAM, ELLEN-ANN, home economist; b. Powhatan, Va., Mar. 8, 1911; d. Warren Benjew and Margene (Brown) Dunham; student Swarthmore Coll., 1929; B.S., Cornell U., 1932; D.Sc. in Commerce, Drexel Inst. Tech., Phila.; D.Sc., Hood Coll. Home economist consumer service dept. Gen. Foods Corp., White Plains, N.Y., 1932-35, mgr. consumer kitchens, 1935-50, dir. Gen. Foods Kitchens, 1950—, v.p. Gen. Foods Corp., 1958—. Mem. Am. Home Econs. in Bus., Am. Home Econs. Assn. Club: Zonta (Teaneck, N.J.). Home: 251 Frances St Teaneck NJ 07666 Office: 250 North St White Plains NY 10625

DUNHAM, JOANNA, actress; b. Luton, Eng., May 6, 1936: d. Peter and Constance (Young) Dunham; student Froebel Inst., 1943-49, Bedales Sch., 1949-52, Slade Sch. Fine Art, U. London, 1953-56; diploma Royal Acad. Dramatic Art, 1958; m. Henry Osborne, Dec. 3, 1961; 1 dau. and 1 son. Actress appearing in numerous stage productions, including: The Green Years also, A Visit to a Small Planet, Lady from the Sea, Romeo and Juliet (Old Vic Co., on tour U.S. and Europe 1961-62), Merchant of Venice (Old Vic Co.), The Formation Dancers, A Month in the Country. La Musica, Breakdown, Soldiers; actress appearing in various TV plays including: Arms and the Men, I Remember Mama, A Problem of Girl Friends, Moment of Milo, On the Boundary, Blythe Spirit, Sanctuary series, Dangerous Coma, Platonov; motion picture film. The Greatest Story Ever Told, 1962-63, A Day At The Beach. Painter murals, pvt. homes, offices, 1956-60. Home: care of London Mgmt 235 Regent St London W 1 England

DUNHAM, KATHERINE, dancer, choreographer; b. Chgo.; d. Albert Millard and Annette (Poindexter) Dunham; student Univ. of Chgo.; spl. field tng. for West Indies Research, Northwestern U., 1936; Julius Rosenwald Travel Fellowship to West Indies, 1936-37; m. John Thomas Pratt, July 10, 1941. 1st major dance performance Chgo. World's Fair, 1934, with Chgo. Opera Co., 1935-36; Ballet L'Ag'ya for Fed. Theatre, 1938; supr. City Theatre writer's project on cult studies, Chgo., 1939; dance dir. Labor Stage, N.Y.C., 1939-40; appeared in Cabin in the Sky, 1940, 41, Carnival of Rhythm (Warner Bros. technicolor short), 1941, Star Spangled Rhythm, Paramount, 1942, Stormy Weather, 20th Century Fox, 1943; choreographer for Pardon My Sarong, Universal, 1942; guest artist, San Francisco Symphony Orch., 1943; toured Tropical Revue (Hollywood Bowl appearance), 1943-44; appeared with Los Angeles Symphony Orch.; established Katherine Dunham Sch. Cultural Arts, Inc., N.Y.C., 1945 (pres.); organized Katherine Dunham Dance Co. (producer-dir.); co- staged, choreographed and appeared in Carib song, 1945; choreographer Richard Kollmar's Windy City, spring 1946; starred in own prodn. Bal Negre, 1946-47; Motion picture, Casbah, Universal-Internat.; with co. in Mexico, Apr.-Oct. 1947; appeared in Teatro Esparante Iris and Palacio de Bellas Artes, Mexico City; toured cross-country with Bal Negre and New Tropical Revue, Jan.-Apr. 1948; Prince of Wales Theatre, London, Eng., June-Nov. 1948, Paris, Nov. 1948-Jan. 1949; also theatres in Brussels, Antwerp and Liege; engagements in Nice, Monte Carlo, Italy, Switzerland, and other countries; choreographer Aida for Met. Opera, 1964, film The Bible, also musicals Deux Anges, Paris, Ciao Rudy, Rome, 1965; State Dept. adviser First World Festival Negro Art, Dakar, 1966; artistic and tech. adviser to pres. Senegal, 1966-67; artist-in- residence fine arts div. So. Ill. U., 1967, cultural counsellor, dir. tng. center for performing arts, asso. Dynamic Mus., 1967-68. Mem. Lincoln Acad., Am. Guild of Musical Artists (mem. bd. gov.), Am. Fedn. of Radio Artists, Actors' Equity, Negro Actors' Guild, Sigma Epsilon. Author: Goombay in Mademoiselle, Nov., 1945; (book) Journey to Accompong, 1946; Form and Function in Primitive Dance, in Educational Dance, 1941; Thesis Turned Broadway in Cal. Arts and Architecture; contbr. to Esquire Mag. under pseudonym K. Dunn: (book) Island Possessed-Haiti. Office: care Lee Mosell 608 Fifth Av New York City NY 10020

DUNHAM, LOWELL, educator; b. Wellston, Okla., Oct. 14, 1910; s. James and Lola (Neeley) D.; B.A., U. Okla, 1932, M.A., 1935; Ph.D., U. Cal. at Los Angeles, 1955; m. Frances C. Ranson, Nov. 5, 1943. Tchr. Spanish, Latin, Idabel (Okla.) High Sch., 1935-36; instr. Spanish, Latin, French. Central State Coll., Edmond, Okla., 1936-40, prin. Tchr. Tng. Sch., 1938-40; spl. agt. FBI, 1940-46, asst. spl. agt. charge FBI, San Juan, P.R., 1942-46; asst. prof. modern langs. U. Okla., 1946-60, chmn. dept., 1957—, prof. modern langs., 1960—. Dir. nat. tchr. placement bur. Am. Assn. Tchrs. Spanish and Portuguese. Recipient Andrés Bello Lit. Prize Acad. of Lang., Caracas, 1949; Juan de Castellanos Lit. prize Miles M. Sherover Found., Caracas, 1958. Mem. Am. Council Tchrs. Fgn. Langs. (v.p. 1970, pres. 1971), Modern Lang. Assn. Am., Am. Assn. Tchrs. Spanish and Portuguese, South Central Modern Lang. Assn. (exec. com. 1961-63, v.p. 1972) Phi Beta Kappa, Eta Sigma Phi, Sigma Delta Pi, Kappa Delta Pi, Sigma Tau Delta. Author: Manuel Diaz Rodriguez, Maestro del estilo, 1948; Romulo Gallegos; Vida y Obra, 1957; Manuel Diaz Rodriguez; Vida y Obra. 1959. Translator, editor, author forward: A. Caso's The Aztecs: The People of the Sun, 1958; co-editor, co-author foreward, co-translator L. Zea's A Survey of Latin American Thought. Editor: Dona Barbara, 1942. Home: 439 Chautaugua St Norman OK 73069

DUNHAM, PETER, advt. exec.; b. Cedarhurst, L.I., N.Y., May 3, 1921; s. Carroll III and Ruth Harper (Pilling) D.; grad. Milton Acad., 1939; B.A., Harvard, 1943; m. Patricia Hopkinson, Jan. 29, 1946; children—Pamela Lewis, Peter. Dir. operational research and planning Transportes Aereos Centro America, Miami, Fla., 1946-48; asso. Chas. A. Rheinstrom Aviation Cons., N.Y.C., 1948-49; treas. sales mgr. Fla. Chem. Research Co., Sarasota, 1949-50; account rep. J. Walter Thompson Co., N.Y.C., 1950-54, mgr. Mexico City office, 1955-58, Toronto office, 1958-60, sr. v.p. Latin Am., N.Y.C., 1960—; mem. steering com., chmn. communications com. Council of Americas. Bd. dirs. Dows Estates, Inc., N.Y.C. Served with USAAF, 1944-45. Decorated Air medal with 5 oak leaf clusters. Mem. Nat. Planning Assn. (mem. com. overseas devel.), Pan Am. Soc., Brazilian-Am. Soc. Clubs: Country, Harvard of Fairfield County (sec.) (New Canaan); Harvard (N.Y.C.); Ausable (St. Huberts, N.Y.) Home: Woods End Rd New Canaan CT 06840 Office: 420 Lexington Av New York City NY 10017

DUNHAM, ROBERT SECREST, lawyer; b. N.Y.C., Nov. 15, 1906; s. Sturges Sigler and Stella (Warren) Secrest D.; A.B., Wesleyan U., 1927; LL.B., Columbia, 1930; m. Elizabeth Walls Cooper, June 15, 1934; children—Christopher Cooper, Sally Secrest, Nancy Nicholas. Admitted to N.Y. bar, 1931, since practiced in N.Y.C.; asso. Cooper, Kerr & Dunham, 1930-42, partner, 1942-47, successor firms, 1947-68, Cooper, Dunham, Henninger & Clark, 1968—. Chmn. bd. edn., Westport, Conn., 1955-61. Served from lt. to lt. comdr. USNR, 1943-46. Mem. N.Y. County Lawyers Assn., Am. Patent Law Assn., Assn. Bar City of New York (chmn. patents com. 1965-68), Am. Bar Assn., N.Y. Patent Law Assn., History Sci. Soc., S.R., Phi Beta Kappa, Psi Upsilon, Phi Delta Phi. Republican. Conglist. Home: Murvon Ct Westport CT 06880 Office: 330 Madisn Av New York City NY 10017

DUNHAM, THEODORE CHADBOURNE, educator; b. Columbus, O., Oct. 1, 1906; s. John Dudley and Mabel (Holmes) D.; A.B., Ohio Wesleyan U., 1929, Litt.D., 1965; A.M. (Lafrentz, Zehnter fellow), U. Wis., 1930. Ph.D., 1935; postgrad. (Wis. travelling fellow), U. Munich, 1932-33; m. Margaret Bigelow, Aug. 4, 1932; children—Philip Bigelow, Janet Patricia. Instr. German, U. Wis., 1934-35; instr. German, Ohio Wesleyan U., 1930-32, asso. prof.,1935-39, prof., 1939-54, head dept., 1935-54; prof. German and humanities Wesleyan U., Middletown, Conn., 1954-70, Weeks vis. prof. German, 1951-52, Kenan Prof. humanities, 1970-71, prof. emeritus, 1971—. Dept. State cons. to U.S. Information Centers in Germany, 1950, 51. Chmn. Haddam (Conn.) Planning Commn., 1963-67; mem. Haddam Zoning Commn., 1967-70, Mem. U.S. Strategic Bombing Survey, Morale Div., Germany, 1945. Mem. Modern Lang. Assn. of Am., Am. Assn. Tchrs. German, Am. Assn. U. Profs., Nat. Council on Religion in Higher Edn., Phi Beta Kappa, Phi Delta Theta, Omicron Delta Kappa, Theta Alpha Phi. Democrat. Conglist. Co-editor; Siddhartha (H. Hesse), 1962. Contbr. articles to profl. jours. Home: Candlewood Hill Rd Higganum CT 06441 Office: Wesleyan Univ Middletown CT 06457

DUNHAM, WILLIAM BARRETT, coll. ofcl.; b. Mpls., Jan. 20, 1918; s. Arthur Barrett and Eleanor Louise (Mason) D.; B.A., Carleton Coll., 1942; M.A., Fletcher Sch. Law and Diplomacy, 1943; m. Charlotte Mary Dodds, Apr. 8, 1944; children—Nancy Eustice, Warren Barrett, James Fraser, Edward Willson. Clk., Northwestern Nat. Life Ins. Co., 1936-38; asst. econ. warfare div. Dept. State, 1943-45, staff asst. to asst. sec. state for econ. affairs, 1945, desk officer Portugal, asst. desk officer Spain, 1945-48, desk officer Spain and Portugal, 1948-51, asst. chief French-Iberian affairs, sr. desk officer Spain and Portugal, 1951-54, chief Swiss-Benelux affairs, 1954-56; 1st sec., chief polit. sect. Am. embassy, The Hague. Netherlands, 1956-61; detailed to Dept. Def., asst. to dir. plans, USAF, 1961, asst. dept. dir. plans for policy, 1961-63; v.p., sec. Carleton Coll., Northfield, Minn., 1963—, also fgn. student adviser; former pres. Minn. Coll. Fed. Council. Rep. Carleton Coll., 7th Japan-Am. Student Conf., Tokyo, 1940. Mem. Netherland-Am. Found. Recipient Exceptional Service award USAF, 1963; Meritorious Service award U.S. State Dept., 1952. Mem. Am. Alumni Council, Nat. Assn. Fgn. Students Affairs, Am. Acad. Polit. and Social Sci., Air Force Assn., Am. Fgn. Service Assn., St. Paul-Mpls. Council Fgn. Relations, Fgn. Policy Assn. Minn. Episcopalian. Clubs: University (N.Y.C.); Minnesota, Minneapolis, Minneapolis Athletic; St. Paul Athletic. Home: 100 Winona St Northfield MN 55057

DUNHAM, WILLIAM HENRY, power co. exec.; b. Alexander, Me., June 21, 1910; s. William Henry and Jennie (Davis) D.; A.B. cum laude, Bates Coll., 1932; LL.B., Cornell U., 1937; m. Mary Elizabeth Saunders, July 3, 1938; children—William Henry, Stella Blanche, Mary Ann, Thomas Benson. Admitted to Mass. bar, 1937, Me. bar, 1940; law clk. Powers & Hill, Boston, 1937-39; atty. New Eng. Pub. Service Co., Central Me. Power Co., 1952—, pres., 1962—, also dir.; v.p., dir. Me. Devel. Credit Corp., Me. Electric Power Co.; pres., dir. Kennebee Water Power Co. (Me.), 1962—, Union Water-Power Co., Me. Yankee Atomic Power Co.; dir. Conn. Yankee Atomic Power Co., WCBB Ednl. TV, Oxford Paper Co., First Nat. Granite Bank, Yankee Atomic Electric Co., Rowe, Mass., Vt. Yankee Nuclear Power Corp. Trustee Bates Coll., Higher Edn. Assistance Found.; bd. dirs. Kennebee Valey Community Chest, Augusta YMCA. Home: Manchester ME 04351 Office: 9 Green St Augusta ME 04330

DUNHAM, WILLIAM HUSE, Jr., educator; b. Evanston, Ill., Dec. 31, 1901; s. William Huse and Margaret (Little) D.; B.A., Yale, 1923, Ph.D. (Sterling fellow, 1927- 28), 1929; Social Sci. Research Council Fellow, Eng. 1930- 31; Huntington Library Research fellow, 1941-42; Guggenheim fellow, 1944- 46; Fulbright Research Scholar, U. London, 1952-53; m. Helen S. Garrison, June 25, 1935; children—Stephanie Southgate, William Lee Huse. Master Univ. Sch., Cleve., 1923-24; instr. history Yale, 1925- 27, 1928-30, asst. prof., 1930-40, asso. prof., 1940-46, prof., 1946- 48, George Burton Adams prof. history, 1948-70, emeritus prof., 1970—, chmn. dept., 1948-52; fellow Saybrook College (Yale), 1933-55, acting master, 1955-56; master Jonathan Edwards College, 1956-61, former master, 1961—; Social Sci. Research Council faculty research fellow, 1961-62. Fellow Royal Hist. Soc., Medieval Acad. Am.; mem. Am. Hist. Assn., Conn. Acad. Arts and Sci. (pres. 1959-61), Selden Soc. London (council 1965—), Conf. on Brit. Studies (pres. 1967- 69, mem. exec. com. 1969-71), Psi Upsilon. Methodist. Clubs: Elizabethan (pres. 1963-65), Lawn. Author books including: The English Government at Work, 1327-1336 (ed.), 1950; Casus Placitorum and Reports of Cases in the King's Courts, 1274- 78, 1952; Lord Hastings' Indentured Retainers, 1956; Magna Carta and the British Constitution, 1965. Mem. bd. advisers Jour. Brit. History, 1960- 68. Contbr. articles scholarly jours. Home: 200 Everit St New Haven CT 06511

DUNIPACE, WILLIAM SMITH, lawyer; b. Bowling Green, O., June 18, 1908; s. William and Edna (Smith) D.; student Bowling Green State U., 1926-27, 33, Northwestern U., summer 1941; J.D., U. Ariz., 1942; m. Esther Morvyth McGeorge, Dec. 27, 1933 (dec.); children-Ian Douglas, Elizabeth Morvyth, Kimberly Kaye; m. 2d Ruth Ellen Hanson, Oct. 21, 1963. Librarian, Pima County Law Library, 1935-39; admitted to Ariz. bar, 1942, since practiced in Tucson; asso. Misbaugh & Fickett, 1942-48; partner Fickett, Dunipace & Tullar, 1948- 49; pvt. practice, 1949-51; partner Fickett & Dunipace, 1951-67, Fickett, Dunipace & Stewart, 1967, Robertson & Fickett, 1967—. Pres., dir. Scottish Rite Holding Co.; dir. Pacific Homes Corp. Spl. counsel Pima County Planning and Zoning Commn., 1949-53; dep. county atty., 1953- 57; mem. Tucson Planning and Zoning Commn., 1937-41, Bd. Appeals, 1949- 51. Alternate Democratic Nat. Conv., 1956; mem. City, County, State central coms. Dem. Party, 1934-58. Bd. dirs. Pima County Legal Aid Soc., Tucson YMCA. Recipient Legion of Honor Order DeMolay, 1969, Merit award State YMCA Youth and Govt. Com., 1970. Mem. Am., Ariz., Pima County (pres. elect) bar assns., Blue Key, Phi Delta Phi, Delta Sigma Rho, Pi Kappa Alpha. Methodist. Mason (K.T., 33 Shriner): mem. Order Eastern Star, Lion, Odd Fellow. Club: Toastmasters (past internat. dir.). Home: 7321 Camino de Cima Tucson AZ 85715 Office: 32 N Stone Av Tucson AZ 85701

DUNIWAY, BENJAMIN CUSHING, U.S. judge; b. Stanford, Cal., Nov. 21, 1907; s. Clyde A. and Caroline M. (Cushing) D.; B.A., Carleton Coll., 1928; LL.B., Stanford, 1931; B.A. (Rhodes scholar), Oxford U., 1933, M.A., 1964; m. Ruth Mason, Oct. 28, 1933; children—Anne (Mrs. Ray Barker), Carolyn (Mrs. Edward P. Hoffman), John M. Admitted to Cal. bar, 1931; practice in San Francisco, 1933-42, 47-59; partner firm Cushing, Cullinan, Duniway & Gorrill, 1947-59; regional atty. OPA, San Francisco, 1942-45, regional adminstr., 1945-47, asst. to adminstr., Washington, 1945; justice Dist. Ct. Appeals, 1st Appellate Dist. Cal., San Francisco, 1959-61; U.S. circuit judge 9th Circuit Ct. Appeals, 1961—. Mem. com. on trial practice and techniques Jud. Conf. U.S., 1969—. Dir. Schlage Lock Co., 1951-59. Chmn. Gov. Cal. Commn. Met. Area Problems, 1958-59; pres. Community Chest San Francisco, 1956-57, Cal. Conf. Social Work, 1950, Family Service Agy. San Francisco, 1950-51, Urban League San Francisco, 1952. Trustee Carleton Coll., 1958-71, Stanford, 1962—; trustee James D. Phelan Found., 1957-71, pres. 1969-71; trustee Rosenberg Found., 1960—, pres., 1964, 68-70; bd. dirs. Legal Aid Soc. San Francisco, 1955-70, Family and Childrens Agy. San Francisco, 1948-51. Recipient of the Presdl. Certificate of Merit, 1947. Mem. Am. Bar Association, Am. Judicature Soc., Am. Law Inst., Conf. Cal. Judges, Bar Assn. San Francisco (treas. 1958, sec. 1959), Soc. Cal. Pioneers, World Affairs Council San Francisco, Order of Coif, Phi Beta Kappa, Delta Smiga Rho. Clubs: Chit Chat, Commercial (San Francisco). Author: (with C.J. Vernier) American Family Laws, Vol. II, 1932. Home: 333 Fletcher Dr Atherton CA 94025 Office: P O Box 547 San Francisco CA 94101

DUNKEL, WILBUR DWIGHT, educator, author; b. Elwood, Ind., Feb. 15, 1901; s. Joel Ambrose and Lulu Dell (Baker) D.; A.B., Ind. U., 1922; A.M., Harvard, 1923; Ph.D., U. Chgo., 1925; m. Georgia Osborn, Aug. 29, 1925; children—Patricia Ann, Robert Osborn. Fellow in English, U. Chgo., 1923-25; mem. faculty U. Rochester, 1925-66, prof. English, 1947-66, Roswell S. Burrows prof. English, 1934-66, prof. emeritus, 1966—, chmn. dept., 1958-60; vis. prof. English, U. Hull (Eng.), 1955-56. Fellow Folger Shakespeare Library, 1960-61. Mem. Modern Lang. Assn., Council Tchrs. English, Coll. English Assn., Am. Assn. U. Profs., Soc. Theatre Research (London), Beta Theta Phi. Republican. Presbyn. Clubs: Grolier (N.Y.C.); Mountain View Country (Greensboro, Vt.), Author: The Dramatic Technique of Thomas Middleton, 1926; Sir Arthur Pinero, 1941; William Lambarde Elizabethan Jurist, 1536-1601, 1965; also newspaper column Literature and Life, 1942- 45. Mem. editorial bd. Theology Today; reviewer U.S. Quar. Book List. Contbr. edn. and religious jours. Home: 125 Commonwealth Rd Rochester NY 14618

DUNKELBERGER, HAROLD ABERLY, educator; b. Bangalore, India, May 9, 1915 (parents U.S. citizens); s. Roy Martin and Amy (Aberly) D.; A.B., Gettysburg Coll., 1936; B.D., Lutheran Theol. Sem., Gettysburg, 1939; Ph.D., Columbia, 1950; sr. fellow Mansfield Coll., Oxford (Eng.) U., 1962; m. Elizabeth Virginia Rebert, Sept. 14, 1940; children—Harold R., Lida Joanne. Ordained to ministry Luth. Ch., 1939; asso. protestant counsellor Columbia, 1939-41; pastor Trinity Luth. Ch., Mechanicsburg, Pa., 1941-42, 46-50; mem. faculty Gettysburg (Pa.), Coll., 1950—, prof. Bib. lit. and religion, chmn. dept., 1960—. Chmn. Mechanicsburg chpt. A.R.C., 1948-49, Adams County Housing Authority, 1966—. Served as chaplain USAAF, 1942-46. Mem. Am. Assn. U. Profs., Phi Beta Kappa (pres. Iota chpt. Pa. 1965- 67). Mason. Editor, contbr.; Lecture Outlines on Chinese Culture, 1966; Lecture Outlines on Indian Culture, 1967. Home: 78 E Broadway St Gettysburg, PA 17325.

DUNKELBERGER , TOBIAS HENRY, educator; b. Paxinos, Pa., Nov. 4, 1909; s. George Atwood and Hannah (Sober) D.; Sc.B., Dickinson Coll., 1930; Ph.D., U. Pitts., 1937; m. Esther Simons, Aug. 31, 1941; children—Judith Mae (Mrs. Jonathan Wouk), Janet Lee. Asst. prof. chemistry North Tex. Agrl. Coll., 1936-37, U. Ida., 1937-38, Duquesne U., 1938-41; N.Y. State Coll. Ceramics, 1941-44; prof., head dept. chemistry Duquesne U., 1944-52, pre-med. adviser, 1946-52; prof. chemistry and adminstrv. officer chemistry dept. U. Pitts., 1952-63, prof. chemistry, mem. U. Pitts. AID faculty in Quito, Ecuador, 1963-67, chief-of-party Guatemala Project, 1967-69, asso. dean Coll. Arts and Scis., 1969—. Fellow A.A.A.S.; mem. Soc. for Internat. Devel., Am. Chem. Soc. (nat. councilor, 1945-63, chmn. Pitts. sect. 1954-55, dir. Pitts. 1969—, Pitts. award 1970), Am. Assn. U. Profs. (pres. U. Pitts. chpt. 1961-62), Pa. Acad. Scis., Keramos, Alpha Epsilon Delta, Phi Beta Kappa, Sigma Xi, Phi Lambda Upsilon, Phi Eta Sigma. Club: Pittsburgh Chemists (pres. 1958-59). Author: (with C.J. Engelder and W.J. Schiller) Semi-Micro Qualitative Analysis, 1936, 40. Abstractor for Chemical Abstracts, 1937-62, asso. sect. editor, 1961-62, sect. editor, 1962. Home: 5132 Beeler St Pittsburgh PA 15217

DUNKLE, DAVID HOSBROOK, curator; b. Winnipeg, Man., Can., Sept. 9, 1911 (parents U.S. citizens); s. Frank and Della (Hosbrook) D.; A.B., U. Kan., 1935; Ph.D., Harvard, 1939; m. Helena Heckart, Aug. 21, 1930; 1 dau. Ann (Mrs. George B. David). Teaching asst. biology Harvard, 1936-39; asso. curator in charge geology dept. Cleve. Mus. Natural History, 1930-46; asso. curator dept. paleobiology U.S. Nat. Mus. Smithsonian Inst., Washington, 1946- 60, 62-68; tech. adviser Geol. Survey of Pakistan, U.S. Geol. Survey, geologic div. Office Inter-agy. Programs and Supporting Activities br. Fgn. Geology Project Investigations, Quetta, West Pakistan, 1960-62; curator dept. paleontology Mus. Natural History, adj. prof. dept. geology Case Western Res. U., Cleve., 1968—. Cons. fed., state agys. Recipient Distinguished Service award Wash. Acad. Sci., 1951. Research asso. Am. Mus. Natural History. Mem. Paleontol. Soc. Washington, Biol. Soc. Washington, Soc. Vertebrate Paleontology, Am. Soc. Zoologists, Sigma Xi, Phi Sigma. Clubs: Cosmos, Explorer. Home: P O Box 141 Gates Mills OH 44040 Office: 10600 E Boulevard Cleveland OH 44106

DUNKLE, WILLIAM EARL, aviation exec.; b. Seattle, Aug. 30, 1917; s. Wesley Earl and Florence (Hull) D.; student Menlo Sch., 1932, 36, Boeing Sch. Aeros., 1937, 38, Advanced Mgmt. Program, Harvard, 1965; m. Joan M. Martinson, Aug. 1, 1949; children—Julie, William M. Pilot, Alaska Air Lines (Star Air Service), 1938, 39; co-pilot United Air Lines, 1940-42, capt., 1942-58, adminstrv. flight mgr., 1959, asst. to sr. v.p., 1960-63, regional mgr. flight operations,

1964-69, sr. v.p. flight operations, Chgo., 1969—. Mem. Am. Inst. Aeros. and Astronautics, Internat. Air Transp. Assn., Air Transp. Assn. Club: Inverness Golf (Palatine). Home: 393 Firth Rd Palatine IL 60067 Office: PO Box 66100 Chicago IL 60666

DUNKLE, WILLIAM FREDERICK, Jr., clergyman; b. McAlester, Okla., May 16, 1911; s. William F. and Nell (Munn) D.; A.B., U. Fla., 1934; B.D., Emory U., 1936; Th.M., Union Theol. Sem., 1948; D.D., Am. U., 1951; LL.D., McMurray Coll., 1968; m. Olga Carolyn Watson, June 12, 1936; children—Amelia Ann (Mrs. B.W. Libby), William Frederick III, Zillah Beth. Ordained to ministry Meth. Ch., 1937; pastor, Pinecastle and Conway, Fla., 1936, Fernandina, 1936-41, Jacksonville, Fla., 1941-44, Barton Heights Ch., Richmond, Va., 1944-48, Grace Meth. Ch., Wilmington, Del., 1948-66; sr. minister Wilmette (Ill.) Trinity Parish Ch., 1966—; prof. polity, vis. lectr. Crozer Theol. Sem., Chester, Pa., 1958-59; vis. prof. liturgical theology Garrett Theol. Sem., Evanston, Ill., 1969—. Chaplain Va. Senate, 1946; exchange minister, London, 1950; rep. Am. Methodism, World Meth. Conf., Oxford U., 1951, Oslo, Norway, 1961, London, 1966; speaker Chgo. Sunday Evening Club: mem. commn. on worship Gen. Conf. Meth. Ch., 1940-46, sec., 1964-68, v.p., 1968—; mem. bd. evangelism Fla. Conf. Meth. Ch., 1940-42, Peninsula Conf., 1950; pres. bd. Christian edn. Peninsula Conf., 1960-64, trustee, 1960-66; del. Meth. Gen. Conf., 1964; del. Northeastern Jurisdictional Conf., 1960, 64, sec. com. Episcopacy, 1964; sec. Nat. Commn. on Worship Meth. Ch., 1964—; mem. editorial council Meth. Story; mem. adv. com. Meth. Ch. Sch. Curriculum. Del., White House Conf. on Children and Youth, 1950; adv. bd. Del. Youth Services Commn., Del. Commn. on Aging; mem. clergy adv. council Wesley Theol. Sem., Washington; mem.-at-large Nat. council Boy Scouts Am., 1950-60, mem. bd. Del-Mar-Va. council, 1950-60, N.E. Ill. council, 1970—; mem. bd. Goodwill Industries, 1950-60; chmn. Wesley Found., U. Del., Washington Coll., 1956-60; mem. bd. Ministerial Tng., 1967—; mem. Meth. Student Center Northwestern U., 1967—, Bd. Edn. No. Ill. Meth. Conf., 1967—. Trustee Meth. Found. No. Ill., 1968—, Wesley Coll., Drew U., Madison, N.J., Am. U. Recipient Order of Merit, Nat. council Boy Scouts, 1956, Silver Beaver award, 1962. Mem. Nat., Del. (pres. 1959- 60), Wilmington (pres. 1956-58) councils chs., Phi Delta Theta. Mason (32; Del. grand chaplain 1955-56), Rotarian. Clubs: Lincoln of Delaware; University, Torch; Union League (Chgo.); Michigan Shores; Westmoreland Country Club. Author: Church Year Values for Evangelical Churches, 1959; The Office of a Methodist Steward, 1963. Editor: Companion to the Methodist Book of Worship, 1970. Contbr. articles to religious publs. Home: 500 Forest Av Wilmette IL 60091 Office: 1024 Lake Av Wilmette IL 60091

DUNKLEBERGER, ALVAND C., newspaper editor; b. Elida, N.M., April 20, 1907; s. Augustus C. and Addie (Foreman) D.; m. Pauline Sechrest, Aug. 22, 1934; children—Paul A., Sandra, Carolyn. Editor, Johnson City (Tenn.) Staff-News, 1933-35; Sunday editor, Knoxville (Tenn.) Journal, 1937-38; asso. editor, Nashville Banner, 1935, editor 1942—. Mem. Am. Soc. Newspaper Editors. Club: Nashville Execs. Mem. Church of Christ. Home: 1140 Pierce Av Madison TN 37115 Office: Nashville TN 37202

DUNLAP, CHARLES EDWARD, pathologist; b. N.Y.C., June 8, 1908; s. Charles Bates and Anna (Carret) D.; A.B., Harvard, 1930, M.D., 1934; m. Lorna M. Alfred, Sept. 29, 1937; children—Elizabeth N., William P., Charles D., John A. Intern, resident pathology U. Chgo. Clinics, 1934-37; Littauer fellow pathology Harvard Cancer Commn., 1937-39; asst., instr. pathology Harvard Med. Sch., 1939-43; Faculty Tulane U. Sch. Medicine, New Orleans, 1943—, asst., then asso. prof., 1944- 45, prof. pathology, chmn. dept., 1945—; sr. vis. pathologist Charity Hosp., New Orleans, 1946—; mem. subcom. radiobiology NRC, 1947-50, path. effects of radiation, 1955-63; cons. Armed Forces Inst. Pathology, 1952-66, hon. cons., 1966—; cons. USAF Primate Lab., Austin, Tex., 1952-54; mem. pathology study sect. NIH, 1954-57, mem. research tng. grants com., 1957- 58, pathology tng. grants com., 1958-62, cancer tng. grants com., 1962-64; mem. radiation bioeffects and epidemiology adv. com. USPHS; pathology test com. Nat. Bd. Med. Examiners, 1955- 59; dir. Oak Ridge Inst. Nuclear Studies, 1955-62, Urban Maes Research Found., 1957-63. Adv. com. etiology of cancer Am. Cancer Soc., 1961-64; bd. dirs. New Orleans Eye bank, 1961-63. Recipient Distinguished Service award U. Chgo. Alumni Assn., 1957. Diplomate Am. Bd. Pathology. Fellow Am. Coll. Pathology (founder mem.; assemblyman 1960-61); mem. A.M.A., Am. Assn. Cancer Research, Am. Soc. Exptl. Pathology (council 1960-62, v.p. 1962, pres. 1963), Am. Assn. Pathology and Bacteriology, Internat. Acad. Pathology (council 1956-60), Am. Soc. Clin. Pathologists, Radiation Research Soc., Assn. Am. Med. Colls., Soc. Exptl. Biology and Medicine, Sigma Xi, Alpha Omega Alpha (hon.). Bd. editors: Archives of Pathology, 1950-62. Author articles on exptl. and human cancer, biol. effects of ionizing radiation. Home: 7431 Hampson St New Orleans LA 70118 Office: 1430 Tulane Av New Orleans LA 70112

DUNLAP, FREDERICK ALBERT, chemist, educator; b. Chicago, 1928; B.S. in Physics, Yale, 1950; Ph.D. in Chemistry, Harvard, 1956; m. Sally Ann Jones, July 5, 1957; children--Kenneth J., Nancy A. Chemist, Acme Chem. Co., Blue Island, Ill., 1950-51; director of Research Lab., Indsl. Chemicals Corp., Cambridge, Mass., 1956-60; project coordinator environmental sect. Steinmetz Assos., Chgo., 1960-61; v.p. for research Bauer Bros. Chem. Co., Inc., Memphis, 1961-64; asst. prof. chemistry Washington U., St. Louis, 1964-66, asso. prof., 1966-70, prof., 1970--, head of chemistry dept., 1970-71. Vis. prof. So. Ill. U., summer 1967, U. of Ore., 1969. Scoutmaster, Boy Scouts America, University City, Mo., 1968-70. Bd. dirs. Rest Haven Home for Elderly, 1960-61; trustee of the Lutheran Hosp., 1965-71. Served from lt. to capt., AUS, 1951-53. Mem. Am. Chem. Soc., Sci. Research Soc. Am. (chpt. treas. 1967), Sigma Xi. Author: (with others) Basic Inorganic Chemistry, 1971. Home: Fairfax Apts 7291 Windermere Dr University City MO 63105 Office: Dept Chemistry Washington University St Louis MO 63130

DUNLAP, GEORGE WESLEY, elec. engr.; b. Gardnerville, Nev., Apr. 13, 1911; s. Fred Sherwin and Rhoda (Early) D.; A.B., Stanford, 1931, E.E., 1933. Ph.D., 1936; m. Alice Catherine Lloyd, Mar. 2, 1935 (dec. Nov. 1966); children—Barbara Rae, George Wesley, John Frederick, James Lloyd; m. 2d Maude Harnden Gray, Apr. 20, 1968; stepson, Christopher G. Gray, With Gen. Electric Co., Schenectady, sinoe 1935, student engr., 1935-36; elec. engr. high voltage and impulse sect., Gen. Engring. Lab., 1936-45; asst. div. engr. high voltage and nucleonics div., Gen. Engring. & Cons. Lab. 1945- 51, div. eng. 1951-53, mgr. instrument and nuclear radiation engring. services, 1953-55, mgr. engring. physics and analysis lab., 1955-61, sr. engr., 1961-66, cons. engr. Research and Devel. Center, 1966—; vis. Webster prof. elec. engring. Mass. Inst. Tech., 1955-56. Recipient Harris J. Ryan High Voltage Research fellowship, 1932-35; Alfred Noble prize, 1943. Registered profl. engr. Fellow Am. Inst. E.E.; mem. Am. Phys. Soc., Am. Nuclear Soc., N.Y. State Soc. Profl. Engrs., Sigma Xi, Tau Beta Pi. Contbr. tech. jours. Home: 1970 Village Road Schenectady NY 12309 Office: Research and Development Center PO Box 43 Schenectady NY 12305

DUNLAP, HUGH D.; investment banker; b. Dallas, 1906; grad. Norwich U., 1927; postgrad. Harvard Grad. Sch. Bus., 1928. Gen. partner Goodbody & Co., Dallas. Mem. Investment Bankers Am. (gov.). Home: 5546 Drane Dr Dallas TX 75209 Office: Mercantile Dallas Bldg PO Box 237 Dallas TX 75201

DUNLAP, JACK WILBUR, psychologist; b. White Eagle, Okla., Aug. 11, 1902; s. John William and Abigail (Smythe) D.; B.S., Kan. State U., 1924, M.S., 1926, LL.D., 1960; postgrad. Stanford, 1926-27; Ph.D., Columbia, 1931; m. Hilda H. Frost, Dec. 25, 1923; 1 son, Jack William. Dean of men Territorial Normal School, Honolulu, 1927-29, dir. teaching, 1929-30; asso. prof. Fordham U., 1931- 37, U. Rochester, 1937-46; dir. div. bio-mechanics, Psychol. Corp., 1946-48; pres. Dunlap and Assos., Inc., 1948-66, chmn., 1948-70, now dir.; dir. Witt Co., Inc., Pioneer Med. Systems, Inc., Hamer Lazer, Inc. Dir. Research Com. on Pilot Selection and Tng., NRC, 1941-42; mem. bd. edn., Greenwich, Conn., 1952-54. Served as capt., USNR, 1942-46; ret. Diplomate indsl. psychology, Am. Bd. of Examiners Profl. Psychology. Fellow A.A.A.S., N.Y. Acad. Scis. (v.p. 1936-37), Operations Research Soc. Am., N.Y. (past pres.), Am. (past pres. divs. 13 and 14) psychol. assns., Am. Assn. for Applied Psychology (past treas.); mem. Human Factors Soc. (past pres.), Inst. Mgmt. Scis., Am. Ednl. Research Assn., Am. Statis. Assn., N.Y. Vocational Assn., Soc. for Advancement Mgmt., Psychometric Soc. (pres. 1940-41), Sigma Xi, Tau Kappa Alpha, Phi Kappa Phi, Phi Delta Kappa, Kappa Delta Pi. Clubs: Cosmos (Washington); Innis Arden Golf. Author: Handbook of Statistical Nomographs, Tables and Formulas (with A. K. Kurtz), 1932: The Computation of Descriptive Statistics 1937; Workbook in Statistical Method, 1939; also monographs, articles in psychol. jours. Editor Jour. Ednl. Psychology; mem. editorial bd. Psychometrika. Home: 1 Strawberry Hill Ct Stamford CT 06902 Office: 1 Parkland Dr Darien CT 06820

DUNLAP, JAMES ANDERSON, lawyer, univ. regent; b. Gainesville, Ga., May 5, 1920; s. Edgar Brown and Katharine (Anderson) D.; student Davidson Coll.; LL.B. cum laude, U. Ga., 1946; m. Mary Eleanor Hosch, Sept. 10, 1947; children—Edgar Brown II, Mary Eleanor, Nancy Elizabeth, James Anderson. Admitted to Ga. bar, 1942, since practiced in Gainesville; partner firm Whelchel, Dunlap & Gignilliat, 1942—. Chmn. bd. regents Univ. System Ga., 1962-66; bd. visitors Davidson Coll. Mem. Am. Law Inst., Am., Ga. bar assns., Nat. Assn. R.R. Trial Counsel, Internat. Assn. Ins. Counsel, Fedn. Ins. Counsel, Phi Beta Kappa, Phi Delta Theta, Phi Delta Phi. Home: 950 Rudolph St N W Gainesville GA 30501 Office: 405 Washington St SW Gainesville GA 30501

DUNLAP, LESLIE WHITTAKER, univ. librarian; b. Portland, Ore., Aug. 3, 1911; s. Frederick Cephas and Alice Barbara (Taylor) D.; B.A. with honors, U. Ore., 1933; postgrad. U. Freiburg (Germany), 1933-34; A.M. (grad. residence scholar), Columbia, 1938, B.S. in L.S., 1939, Ph.D., (A.L.A. fellow), 1944; m. Marie Gladys Neese, Apr. 15, 1933; children—Lesley Eileen, Bruce Michael. Reference and gen. asst. N.Y.C. Pub. Library, 1936-41; head acquisition dept. U. Wis. Library, 1942-45; asst. chief gen. reference and bibliography div. Library Congress, 1945-48, asst. chief manuscript div., 1948-49; librarian U. B.C., 1949-51; asso. dir., prof. library sci. U. Ill. Library, 1951-58; dir. libraries, archivist U. Ia., Iowa City, 1958-70, dean library adminstrn., 1970—. Library cons. Northwestern Coll., Orange City, Ia., St. Ambrose Coll., Davenport, Mt. St. Bernard Sem., Aquinas Inst. Theology, Dubuque. Chief, Surplus Books for Vets., 1946; participant survey library Nat. U. Mexico, 1948; dir. orientation program for librarians from India, 1936; mem. library adv. bd. Collier's Ency., 1960- -; mem. Nat. Commn. on Libraries and Information Sci., 1971—. Vice chmn. bd. dirs. Center for Research Libraries, 1963-64, chmn., 1964-65; cons.-examiner North Central Assn. Commn. on Instrs. Higher Edn., 1965—. Recipient Distinguished Service citation Northwestern Coll., Orange City, 1964. Mem. Am. (chmn. bibliography com. 1947-49, sec. intellectual freedom com. 1956- 58, chmn. library edn. div. awards com. 1962-64), Ia. (v.p. 1968, pres. 1969) library assns., Assn. Coll. and Research Libraries, Assn. Research Libraries (chmn. com. microfilming dissertations 1962-64, rep. Library of Congress adv. com. cataloging and photocopying manuscripts 1964—), Manuscript Soc., Am. Assn. for State and Local History, Phi Beta Kappa. Club: Caxton (Chicago). Editor: The Letters of Willis Gaylord Clark and Lewis Gaylord Clark, 1940; American Historical Societies, 1780-1860, 1944; Readings in Library History, 1971; also articles. Home: 326 Hutchinson Av Iowa City IA 52240

DUNLAP, MARJORIE SNYDER, univ. dean; b. Kansas City, Mo., Dec. 7, 1917; d. Carl R. and Alice (Cleary) Snyder; B.A., U. Mo., 1949; diploma Washington U. Sch. Nursing, St. Louis, 1942; M. Personnel Service, U. Colo., 1947; student U. Chgo., spring 1951; Ed.D., U. So. Cal., 1959; divorced. Staff nurse Vis. Nurse Assn. Mo., 1942-43; instr. St. Luke's Hosp. Sch. Nursing, Kansas City, Mo., 1943-45; clin. instr. St. Luke's Hosp. Sch. Nursing, Denver, 1945- 46; ednl. dir. Presbyn. Hosp. Sch. Nursing, Denver, 1946-48; mem. faculty U. Colo. Sch. Nursing, 1948-55, asso. prof. nursing dir. nursing service adminstrn. project, 1951-55; nursing service cons. Hawthorne (Cal.) Community Hosp., 1955-56; vis. asst. prof. U. Cal. Sch. Nursing at Los Angeles, 1956-57, mem. faculty 1957-66, asso. prof., 1963- 66; prof., dean Sch. Nursing, U. Hawaii, 1966-69; mem. liaison com. Queen's Hosp., Honolulu, 1966-69; dean Sch. Nursing U. Cal. Med. Cent., San Francisco, 1969—; cons. in field. Rocky Mountain Soroptomist fellow, 1954-55. Mem. Am. (chmn. EACT sect. 1953-54), Hawaii (pres. 1967- 69) nurses assn., Nat. Hawaii leagues nursing, Nat. Honor Soc., Phi Kappa Phi. Club: Toast Mistress (Inglewood, Cal.). Author articles, monographs. Home: 329 Warren Dr San Francisco CA 94131

DUNLAP, ROBERT CRAIG, Jr., geophysical co. exec.; b. Dallas, Apr. 28, 1911; s. Robert Craig and Emma Virginia (Smith) D.; B.S. with honors, So. Meth. U., 1933, B.A. with honors, 1933; student Harvard Grad. Sch., 1933-34; m. Rachael Boyd, Aug. 16, 1935. With Geophysical Service, Inc., Dallas, 1934—, v.p. U.S. and Canadian operations, 1953-59, pres., dir. 1950—; v.p. geoscis. div. Tex. Instruments, Inc., Dallas, 1961-67, equipment group v.p., 1967, sr. v.p., 1968—; operator cattle ranch, Freestone County, Tex., 1959—. Mem. bd. devel. So. Meth. U.; recipient Distinguished Alumnus award 1959, mem. bd. publs., 1963—. Member of the Soc. Exploration Geophysicists (pres. 1955-56), Am. Assn. Petroleum Geologists, European Assn. Exploration Geophysicists, Dallas Geophys. Soc. (pres. 1955), Dallas Geol. Soc., Dallas Council Sci. Socs. (pres. 1959-60), Dallas Council World Affairs, Dallas Geol. and Geophys. Assn. Methodist (ofcl. bd., commn. finance and mgmt.). Club: Dallas Petroleum. Author articles in field. Home: 5405 Falls Rd Dallas, TX 75220. Office: PO Box 5621 Dallas TX 75222

DUNLAP, ROY JOHN, Jr., editor; b. St Paul, Minnesota, July 18, 1918; s. Roy John and Lulu Marie (Trunkee) D.; student U. Minn., 1937-39; m. Frances Lillico, June 4, 1942; children—Michele Ann (Mrs. Joseph Grantham), Roy John II, Patricia Lynn, William Pierce, Dana Kathryn, Elizabeth. Mem. staff St. Paul Pioneer Dispatch, 1938-68, author column, Paul Light, 1951-62, mng. editor, 1962-68; exec. editor publ. services Webb Pub. Co., St. Paul, 1968—; editor TWA Ambassador mags., 1968—; lectr., 1950—; cinematographer, 1947—. Mem. aviation com. St. Paul area C. of C., 1 1954—. Bd. dirs. St. Paul Rehab. Center, St. Paul Indianhead council Boy Scouts Am., St. Paul Winter Carnival Assn., 1970. Served with AUS, 1942-45; PTO. Named Outstanding Aviator 1962, Minn. Aviation Assn. Presbyn. Clubs: Kiwanis (pres. 1969, dir.), St. Paul Athletic (dir.). Home: 771 Ridge St St Paul MN 55116 Office: 1999 Shepard Rd St Paul MN 55116

DUNLAP, WILLIAM CRAWFORD, physicist; b. Denver, July 21, 1918, s. William Crawford and Helen (Kiester) D.; B.S., U. N.M., 1938; Ph.D., U. Cal. at Berkeley, 1943; m. Ellen Hebrew, Mar. 22, 1940; 1 dau., Nancy. Asst. physicist Dept. Agr., 1942-45; research asso., research lab. Gen. Electric Co., 1945-55, cons. physicist electronics lab., 1955-56; supr. solid state research, research lab. Bendix Corp., 1956-58; dir. solid state electronic research Raytheon Co., 1958-64; asst. dir. electronic components research Electronics Research Center, NASA, Cambridge, Mass., 1964-68, dir. research, 1968-70; sci. adviser to dir. U.S. Transp. Systems Center, Cambridge, 1970—; spl. research transistor prodn. techniques in alloying, diffusion, epitaxy. Fellow I.E.E.E. (dir. 1966-68, dir. region I, 1966-68), Am. Phys. Soc., Am. Inst. Aeros. and Astronautics (asso.); mem. Sigma Xi, Phi Kappa Phi. Author: An Introduction to Semiconductors, 1957. Editor-in-chief Solid State Electronics, 1959—, Patentee in field. Home: 126 Prince St West Newton MA 02165 Office: 55 Broadway Cambridge MA 02142

DUNLEAVY, GARETH WINTHROP, univ. adminstr.; b. Willimantic, Conn., Feb. 24, 1923; s. Henry J. and Mabel (Hobbs) D.; A.B., Clark U., 1947; M.A., Brown U., 1949; Ph.D., Northwestern U., 1952; m. Elizabeth Anne Lucas, May 31, 1947 (div.); children—Gweneth Anne, Stephen Arthur. Asst. prof. to prof. English, U. Wis., Milw., 1956-63, chmn. dept. English, 1964-67, asso. dean Grad. Sch., 1967-68, coordinator grad. stuudies in English, 1970—. Served with AUS, 1943-45; ETO. Decorated Purple Heart. Mem. Modern Lang. Assn., Mediaeval Acad., Am. Com. for Irish Studies, Am. Assn. U. Profs., Am. Civil Liberties Union, Phi Beta Kappa, Sigma Tau Delta. Author: Colum's Other Island: The Irish at Lindisfarne, 1960. Contbr. to Old Ireland, 1965; Art and Age of Geoffrey Chaucer, 1967. Home: 2723 E Bradford Av Milwaukee WI 53211

DUNLOP, DONALD DEAN, army officer; b. Orange City, Ia., Feb. 20, 1920; s. George and Florence (Mitchell) D.; B.A., Coe Coll., 1941; M.A., George Washington U., 1961; m. Jane Elizabeth Wilson, Mar. 9, 1943; children—Jane (Mrs. William J. Gorman III), Nancy (Mrs. Steven W. Caudrey), Thomas, Sarah, Elizabeth. Commd. 2d lt. U.S. Army, 1941, advanced through grades to brig. gen., 1968; faculty Army War Coll., 1962-65; div. chief of staff, Bad Kreuznach, Germany, 1965-66; operations officer Corps G3, 1966-67; asst. div. comdr., adviser Republic Vietnam, 1967-69; chief mil. mission to Saudi Arabia, 1969—. Decorated D.S.M. with oak leaf clusters, Legion of Merit, Air medal with 18 oak leaf clusters, Combat Inf. badge, Bronze Star with 12 oak leaf clusters, Army Commendation medal; Croix de Guerre (France); also Vietnamese decorations. Mem. Tau Kappa Epsilon. Home: Dhahran Air Base Dhahran Saudi Arabia Office: Hdqrs USMTMSA APO New York City NY 09616

DUNLOP, DOUGLAS MORTON, educator, Orientalist; b. Paisley, Renfrewshire, Gt. Britain, Feb. 25, 1909; s. Hugh Morton and Helen Oliver (Dunn) D.; B.A., Oxford U., 1939, M.A., 1960; D.Litt., Glasgow U., 1955; M.A., Cambridge U., 1950; m. Margaret Sinclair Munro, Dec. 18, 1948. Came to U.S., 1962. Asst. to prof. Hebrew, Glasgow U., 1939-46, research asso., 1946-47; asst. to prof. Oriental Langs. St. Andrews U., 1947-48, lectr. Semitic langs., 1948-50; lectr. Islamic history Cambridge U., 1950-62; vis. prof. history Columbia, N.Y.C., 1962-63; prof. history Middle East Inst., 1963- -. Fellow Royal Asiatic Soc., Inst. Arts and Letters; mem. Soc. Brit. Orientalists, Internat. Soc. for Oriental Research, Am. Hist. Assn., Am. Oriental Soc., History Sci. Soc. Presbyn. Author: The History of the Jewish Khazars, 1954; The Aphorisms of the Statesman of Al-Farabi, 1961; Arabic Science in the West, 1965; Arab Civilization to A.D. 1500, 1971. Contbr. numerous articles and reviews profl. jours. Address: 423 W 120th St New York City NY 10027

DUNLOP, DOUGLAS WAYNE, educator, botanist; b. Milw., Jan. 27, 1915; s. John W. and Nellie (Pfeiffer) D.; Ph.B., U. Wis., 1937, Ph.M., 1938, Ph.D., 1940. Instr. biology Bklyn. Coll., 1940-43; prof. botany U. Wis.-Milw., 1946—, chmn. dept., 1969—. Served with AUS, 1943-46. Mem. Bot. Soc. Am., Am. Fern Soc., Internat. Soc. Plant Morphologists, Soc. Econ. Botany, A.A.A.S., Sigma Xi, Phi Sigma. Author: (with others) Ferns and Fern Allies of Wisconsin, 1940; also chpt. in book. Contbr. articles on cytology and biomagnetics to profl. jours. Research biol. effects high gravity, effects of magnetic fields and high gravity on morphology and anatomy of plants, plant cytology. Home: Route 1 Box 363 Mukwonago WI 53149 Office: Lapham Hall Univ Wis Milwaukee WI 53201

DUNLOP, JOHN THOMAS, educator; b. Placerville, Cal., July 5, 1914; s. John W. and Antonia (Forni) D.; A.B., U. Cal., 1935; Ph.D., 1939; LL.D., U. Chgo., 1968; m. Dorothy Webb, July 6, 1937; children—John Barrett, Beverly Claire, Thomas Frederick. Acting instr. Stanford, 1936-37; instr. Harvard, 1938-45, asso. prof. econs., 1945-50, prof. econ., 1950—, dean Faculty Arts and Scis., 1970—. Served as vice chmn. Boston Regional War Labor Bd., 1944-45; chmn. Nat. Joint Bd. for Settlement of Jurisdictional Disputes in the bldg. and constrn. industry, 1948-57. Cons. Office Econ. Stabilization, 1945-47, N.L.R.B., 1948-52, Atomic Energy Labor Panel, 1948-53. Mem. bd. inquiry Bituminous Coal Industry, 1950; pub. mem. WSB, 1950-52; arbitrator Emergency Bd., 1954-55, 60, 66, Presdl. Railroad Commn., 1960-62, Missile Sites Labor Commn., 1961-67; mem. Pres.'s Com. Equal Employment Opportunity, 1964-65; impartial chmn. constrn. Industry Joint Conf., 1959-68. Mem. Am. Acad. Arts and Scis. Author: Collective Bargaining; Principles and Cases, 1953; The Theory of Wage Determination, 1956; Industrial Relations Systems, 1958; (with D. C. Bok) Labor and the American Community, 1970. Home: 509 Pleasant St Belmont MA 02178 Office: Littauer Center Harvard University Cambridge MA 02138 ☆

DUNLOP, RALPH GORDON, educator, clergyman; b. Mason City, Ia., Aug. 31, 1915; s. Edmund Robinson and Laura Maude (Decker) C.; student Carleton Coll., 1933-34; B.A., U. Ill., 1939; B.D., Yale, 1942; postgrad. Union Theol. Sem., N.Y.C., summer 1948; D.D., Ill. Wesleyan U., 1962; m. Mary Helen Moss, Aug. 27, 1941; children—Charles E.M., Ralph Gordon, Ann Elizabeth. Ordained deacon Meth. Ch. 1941, elder, 1943; dir. Christian edn. First Ch., Ann Arbor, Mich., 1942-45; minister First Ch., Belleville, Mich., 1945- 48; coll. chaplain, instr. dept. philosophy and religion Allegheny Coll., 1948-50; asso. dir. Wesley Found., U. Ill., 1950- 53; univ. chaplain, asso. prof. dept. history and lit. of religions Northwestern U., Evanston, Ill., 1955—; vis. asso. prof. religion in higher edn. Garrett Theol. Sem., Evanston, 1956-63, Mem. Citizens Adv. Commn. on Integration Pub. Schs., Evanston; mem. adv. Council Danforth Found., 1962-63. Trustee U. Ill. YMCA, Kendall Coll., Evanston. Mem. Am. Civil Liberties Union, Nat. Assn. Coll. and U. Chaplains (pres. 1962-63), Am. Acad. Religion, Nat. Assn. Bibl. Instrs., Ill. Conf. United Meth. Ch., Evanston Inst. Ecumenical Studies (founder, sec.-treas. 1957-61), Phi Gamma Delta. Club: Illini (Chgo.). Contbr.:

Student at Prayer, 1960; On the Work of the Ministry, 1962—; Renewal mag., 1970. Home: 2246 Orrington Av Evanston IL 60201 Office: Alice Millar Chapel 1870 Sheridan Rd Evanston IL 60201

DUNLOP, ROBERT GALBRAITH, petroleum exec.; b. Boston, July 2, 1909; s. James B. and Caroline (Cowan) D.; B.S., U. of Pa., 1931; m. Emma L. Brownback, Dec. 4, 1937; children—Barbara E., Richard G. Asso. with Barrow, Wade, Guthrie & Co., 1931-33; with Sun Oil Co., Phila., 1933—; pres., now chmn. bd., also dir. Trustee U. Pa. C.P.A., Pa. Mem. Sigma Phi Epsilon, Beta Gamma Sigma. Republican. Presbyn. Home: 1062 Rock Creed Rd Bryn Mawr PA 19010 Office: 1608 Walnut St Philadelphia PA 19103

DUNN, ALAN, writer, cartoonist; b. Belmar, N.J., Aug. 11, 1900; s. George Warren and Sarah Benton (Brown) D.; student Columbia, 1918-19, N.A.D., 1919-23, L. Fontainebleau (France) Ecole des Arts, summer 1923, L.C. Tiffany Found., Oyster Bay, L.I., summers 1921-28; hon. vis. fellow Am. Acad. in Rome, 1923-24; m. Mary Petty, Dec. 8, 1927. Staff contbr. New Yorker mag., 1926—; editorial cartoonist Archtl. Reocrd, 1936—; paintings, cartoons exhibited nat., internat. exhbns.; works in permanent collections at various museums; comprehensive collections in Library of Congress, Alan Dunn Manuscript collection Syracuse U. Mem. Authors Guild, Phi Gamma Delta. Club: Century Assn. Author: Rejections, 1931: Who's Paying for this Cab?, 1945; The Last Lath., 1947; East of Fifth, 1948; Should It Gurgle? 1956; Is There Intelligent Life on Earth?, 1960; A Portfolio of Social Cartoons-1957-1968 by Alan Dunn, 1968. Office: care New Yorker Mag 25 W 43d St New York City NY 10036

DUNN, BRYANT WINFIELD CULBERSON, gov. of Tenn.; b. Meridian, Miss., July 1, 1927; s. Aubert C. and Dorothy (Crum) D.; B.B.A., U. Miss., 1950; D.D.S., U. Tenn., 1955; m. Betty Jane Prichard, Dec. 30, 1950; children—Charles Winfield, Donna Gayle, Julie Claire. Formerly practice dentistry; gov. of Tenn., 1971—. Chmn., Republican party, Shelby County, Tenn., 1964-68; state Young Republican vice chmn., Tenn., 1964-65; del. Republican Nat. Conv., 1968. Served with armed forces, 1947. Named Tenn. Young Man of Year, 1971. Mem. Am., Tenn. dental assns., Farm Bur. Fedn., Kiwanian. Home: 822 Curtiswood Lane Nashville TN 37204 Office: State Capitol Nashville TN 37219

DUNN, BURTON, banker; b. Corpus Christi, Tex., Apr. 4, 1889; s. Pat F. and Clara J. (Brown) D.; grad. Alamo City Bus. Coll., San Antonio, 1907; m. Buena V. Hill, June 30, 1917; children—Frances (Mrs. Samuel Seltzer), Lura (Mrs. Blake Sweat), Juliana (Mrs. Hart Smith), Patsy Ruth (Mrs. Edwin Singer). Formerly with Corpus Christi State Nat. Bank, pres., 1950-56, chmn. exec. com.; rancher on Padre Island, Tex., 1937—; dir. First Savs. Assn., Corpus Christi. Trustee Ada Wilson Crippled Childrens Hosp., M.G. and Johnnye D. Perry Found. Rotarian (past pres. Corpus Christi). Home: 5526 Ocean Dr Corpus Christi TX 78412

DUNN, CARROLL HILTON, army officer; b. Lake Village, Ark., Aug. 11, 1916; s. William L. and Ruth (Dewey) D.; B.S., U. Ill., 1938; M.S., State U. Ia., 1947; m. Letha Estelle Jontz, Nov. 11, 1939; children—Carolyn Jontz (Mrs. Douglas Lee Caldwell), Carroll Hilton. Commd. 2d lt. U.S. Army, 1938, advanced through grades to lt. gen., 1971; instr. Army Engr. Sch., Ft. Belvoir, Va., 1947-49; with engring. sect. Gen. Hdqrs. Far East Command, 1949-52; dir. Waterways Expt. Sta., C.E., Vicksburg, Miss., 1952-55; exec. officer to chief U.S. Army Engrs., 1955-58; constrn. supr. Greenland and U.S. Ballistic Missile Facilities, 1959-62; div. engr. Engr. Div. Southwestern, Dallas, 1962-64; dep. chief staff 8th U.S. Army, Korea, 1964-66; dir. constrn. U.S. Mil. Assistance Command, Vietnam, 1966, asst. chief staff for logistics J-4, 1966-67; dir. mil. constrn. Office Chief Engrs., Washington, 1967-69, dep. chief U.S. Army Engrs., 1969-71; dir. Def. Nuclear Agy., Washington, 1971—. Mem. NASA Aerospace Safety Adv. Panel. Decorated D.S.M., Silver Star medal, Legion of Merit, Bronze Star medal with oak leaf cluster, Purple Heart; Croix de Guerre with palm (France). Fellow Am. Soc. C.E.; mem. Soc. Am. Mil. Engrs. Baptist (deacon). Home: Quarters 58 Fort Belvoir VA 22060 Office: Def Nuclear Agy Dept Def Washington DC 20315

DUNN, CHARLES T., banker; b. Phila., Apr. 9, 1930; s. Charles A. and Helen (Courts) D.; B.S., St. Joseph's Coll., Phila.; M.B.A., U. Pa.; m. Barbara Helen Long, Sept. 4, 1954; children—Kathleen, Patricia, Charles, Barbara Ann, Rosemary, Carolyn Marie. With Fed. Res. Tng. Program, Phila., 1953-55; with S.Jersey Nat. Bank, Camden, N.J., 1955—, now sr. v.p. Active Camden council Boy Scouts Am., Trustee United Fund. Served to capt. USMCR, 1951-53. Mem. Camden Jr. C. of C. (past pres.). Rotarian. Home: 127 Dumas Rd Cherry Hill NJ 08034 Office: Broadway and Cooper Sts Camden NJ 08101

DUNN, CHARLES WILLIAM, educator, author; b. Arbuthnott, Scotland, Nov. 30, 1915; s. Peter Alexander and Alberta Mary Margaret (Freeman) D.; came to U.S., 1928, naturalized, 1961; B.A. with honors, McMaster U., 1938; A.M., Harvard, 1939, Ph.D., 1948; m. Patricia Campbell, June 21, 1941; children—Deirdre, Peter Arthur. Asst. English, Harvard, 1939-40, tutor, 1940-41; instr. humanities Stephens Coll., 1941-42; instr. English, Cornell U., 1943-46; instr. then asso. prof. English, Univ. Coll., U. Toronto, 1946-56; prof. English, N.Y.U., 1956-63; prof. Celtic langs. and lits., chmn. dept. Harvard, 1963—, master of Quincy House, Harvard, 1966—, Margaret Brooks Robinson prof. Celtic langs. and lits., 1967—; Taft lectr. U. Cin., 1956. Dexter fellow, N.S., summer 1941; Rockefeller fellow, N.S., 1942-43; Nuffield fellow, Dublin, Edinburgh and Aberystwyth, 1954-55; Guggenheim fellow, Scotland, Wales and Brittany, 1962-63; recipient Canada award Fedn. Gaelic Societies, 1955. Fell. Am. Acad. of Arts and Sci.; mem. Am. Folklore Soc., Modern Language Assn., Irish Texts Society. The Mediaeval Acad. Am., Early English Text Society, Royal Scottish Country Dance Society. St. Andrews Society N.Y., Comunn Gaidhealach (Scotland), Celtic Union Edinburgh (hon. pres. 1963—). Episcopalian. Clubs: Odd Volumes (Boston); Harvard (N.Y.C.). Author: Highland Settler: A Portrait of the Scottish Gael in Nova Scotia, 1953; The Foundling and the Werewolf: A Study of Guillaume de Palerne (Chgo. Folklore prize 1960), 1960. Editor: A Chaucer Reader, 1952; History of the Kings of Britain (Geoffrey of Monmouth), 1958; Chronicles (Froissart), 1961; Romance of the Rose, 1962; Lays of Courtly Love, 1963. Home: Master's Residence Quincy House 3 De Wolfe St Cambridge MA 02138

DUNN, CLARK ALLAN, engr., educator; b. Stichney, S.D., Sept. 9, 1901; s. Wilfred E. and Elizabeth (Batcheldor) D.; B.S., U. Wis., 1923; M.S., Okla. A. and M. Coll., 1934, C.E., 1936; Ph.D. (McMullen fellow), Cornell U., 1941; m. Mary Eveland, Sept. 6, 1928; children—Kenneth A., Gerald L. Engr., bridge div. S.D. Hwy. Commn., 1923-27; asso. with J. E. Kirkham, cons. engr., Pierre, S.D. 1927; constrn. engr. bridge div. Ark. Hwy. Dept., 1927-29; staff mem. Coll. Engring. Okla. State U., Stillwater, 1929—, prof. civil engring., 1941—, dir. engring. research, 1945-66, asso. dean engring., 1966—. Cons. Observer Task Force Frigid Operations, Fairbanks, Alaska, 1947; mem adv. mem. Okla. Planning and Resources Bd., 1948; chmn. Master Planning Bd., Stillwater, 1950; observer Air Force Operation Cool Sch., Newfoundland. Greenland, Alaska, Can., 1959. Registered profl. engr., Okla. Fellow A.A.A.S., mem. Am. Soc., C.E. (past pres. Okla. sect.), Am. Soc. for Engring. Edn., Nat. (nat. dir. 1951-55, v.p., 1955-57, pres. 1958-59), Okla. (past pres.) socs. profl. engrs., Sigma Tau, Chi Epsilon, Phi Alpha Theta, Tau Beta Pi, Phi Kappa Phi. Methodist. Home: 317 N Husband St Stillwater 0K 74074

DUNN, COLON H., educator, elec. engr.; b. Galena, Kan., June 12, 1921; s. Perry Leo and Nellie (Derfeit) D.; B.S., John Brown U., 1942; M.S., Rensselaer Poly Inst., 1953; m. Sibyl Ruth Rife, May 22, 1943; children—James, Frank, David, Diane. Instr. elec. engring. U. N.H., 1942-44; elec. engr. Naval Ordnance Lab., 1944-46; from instr. to asst. and asso. head dept. elec. engring. Rensselaer Poly Inst., 1947-59; prof. elec. engring., chmn. dept. Wichita State U., 1959—. Dir. Toolcraft Corp., Wichita. Mgr. patterning project to develop devices to assist treatment brain injured children. Registered profl. engr., Kan. Mem. Am. Soc. Engring. Edn. (chmn. Kan.-Neb. sect. 1962-64), I.E.E.E. (1st v.p. Wichita sect. 1967- 68), Am. Nuclear Soc., Sigma Xi (pres. Rensselaer chpt. 1957-59), Eta Kappa Nu, Tau Beta Pi. Author: Electrical Measurements Manual. Home: 2522 Gentry St Wichita, KS 67220

DUNN, EDGAR HART, Jr., utility exec., lawyer; b. Hyden, Ky., May 10, 1919; s. Edgar Hart and Mary Fern (Rollins) D.; student U. Ky., 1939-41; J.D., U. Fla., 1947; m. Lura Mae Laughmiller, Apr. 5, 1942; children—Marcia Joan, Sharon Lee. Admitted to Fla. bar, 1947, also fed cts.; gen. practice, 1947-61; with Fla. Power Corp., 1955-68, v.p., 1961-67, sr. v.p., 1967-68, gen. counsel, 1962-68, mem. bd. dirs., 1965-68; partner firm Bennett and Dunn, St. Petersburg, 1968—. Vis. prof. U. South Fla. Served as bomber pilot USAAF, 1941-46; served to col. USAF, 1951-52. Mem. Am., Fla., Fed. Power bar assns., Phi Delta Phi. Home: 1326 Snell Isle Blvd., St Petersburg FL 33704. Office: First Fed Bldg St Petersburg FL 33701

DUNN, EDWARD CLARE, army officer; b. White Lake, S.D., Feb. 28, 1913; s. Peter George and Catherine (Hanten) D.; B.S., U.S. Mil. Acad., 1936; M.A., Harvard, 1950; grad. Army Command and Staff Coll., 1951, Army War Coll., 1955; m. Jane Ellen Grace, June 15, 1940; children—Peter, Michael, John, Patrick. Commd. 2d lt. U.S. Army, 1936, advanced through grades to maj. gen., 1965; troop officer, 1935-42; comdr. battalion and regt., ETO, 1943-45; instr. U.S. Mil. Acad., 1946-50; various staff and command assignments in U.S., Turkey, S. Vietnam, 1951-61; dep. comdt. Armed Forces Staff Coll., 1963-64; chief staff III Corps. 1964-65, 4th U.S. Army, 1965-68. Decorated Distinguished Service medal, also the Legion of Merit, Joint Services Commendation medal, Bronze Star, Army Commendation medal (2); Croix de Guerre with palm (France). Mem. United Services Automobile Assn. (bd. dirs. 1965-68; mem. exec. com. San Antonio 1967-68), Assn. U.S. Army (past chpt. v.p.). Club: Ft. Leavenworth Hunt (Kan.) (past pres.) Author: USAA: Life Story of a Business Cooperative, 1970. Co-author: Contemporary Foreign Governments, 1949; also articles. Home: 123 Brandon Dr E San Antonio TX 78209

DUNN, EDWARD D., architect, writer; s. John Henry and Mary Emma (Delaney) C.; ed. privately; spl. student Harvard, 1921-22; m. Gertrude Herbert, April 22, 1913 (dec. 1933); children—Anton (Mrs. Lloyd P. Griscom), Gertrude Herbert, Edward D., Jr., Eric Warne. Licensed architect, N.Y. State; practiced as architect, N.Y.C., 1910-20; free-lance writer 1920—. Aide to liaison office between builders and designers Sea Otter type vessel, 1942. Episcopalian. Clubs: Union, Players, Tuxedo, Piping Rock, Turf and Field (New York); Metropolitan (Washington, D.C.); Spouting Rock, Reading Room, Newport Country, Clambake (Newport, R.I.); Everglades, Bath and Tennis (Palm Beach, Fla.). Author: Caravans; Double Crossing America by Motor; plays: The Claw; The Red Robe; The Last Waltz; Caroline; Dew Drop Inn; Midnight; The End of the World. Home: Union Club 101 E 69th St New York City NY 10021 Office: 333 W 57th St New York City NY 10019

DUNN, EDWARD JOSEPH, Jr., chemist; b. Dover Plains, N.Y., Dec. 8, 1903; s. Edward Joseph and Eliza (Morris) D.; grad. Pratt Inst., 1923; m. Sarah Linton Wolf, Apr. 19, 1929. With Procter and Gamble Soap Co., 1923-25; cons. chemist with Prof. L. T. Work, Columbia, 1925-26; with research lab. Nat. Lead Co., Highstown, N.J., 1926—, head phys. measurements dept., 1938—; cons., spl. research procedures better design and evaluation of pigments, coated products, lead-acid storage batteries, and stabilizers for plastics. Recipient tech. achievement award I.E.E.E. and Nat. Elect. Mfrs. Assn., 1962. Mem. Am. Chem. Soc., Optical Soc. Am., Soc. Nondestructive Testing, Fed. Socs. Paint Tech. (pres. 1965; Presidents award 1966), N.Y. Soc. Applied Spectroscopy (pres. 1950), N.Y. Soc. Paint Tech. (pres. 1958; R.H. Kienle award 1960, PaVac award 1962), Am. Soc. Testing and Materials (chmn. N.Y. sec. 1964-65; award of merit 1966). Twelve patents and co-authored 45 papers Nat. Lead Co. products. Home: 90A Gloucester Way Jamesburg NJ 08831 Office: Box 420 Hightstown NJ 08520

DUNN, EDWARD K., investment banker; b. Balt., June 15, 1899; s. Charles Irwin and Emily Oliver (Shiff) D.; A.B., Princeton, 1922; m. Anne Butler, Nov. 24, 1931; children—Anne Butler, Edward K., Pierce Butler. Asst. cashier Mchts. Nat. Bank and First Nat. Bank, Balt., 1923-29; with Robert Garrett & Sons, Balt., 1929—, sr. partner, 1954—, vice chmn. bd., 1964-70; dir., exec. com. Colonial Stores, Inc., Comml. credit Co., Balt., dir. Carey Machinery & Supply Co., Greenmount Cemetery, Balt. Bd. trustees Evergreen House Found., Gilman Sch., Thomas Wilson Sanitorium, Anna Emory Warfield Found.; trustee Heller Fund and Union Meml. Hosp. Mem. Gunpowder River Valley Park Commn. Served with USN, 1918; lt. col. A.C., AUS, 1942-45. Decorated Legion of Merit. Mem. Investment Bankers Assn. Am. (past gov.). Clubs: Maryland, Elkridge (Balt.); Brook (N.Y.C.). Home: 7117 W Bellona Av Baltimore MD 21212 Office: Robert Garrett & Sons South and Redwood Sts Baltimore MD 21203

DUNN, ELLEN CATHERINE, educator; b. Balt., July 30, 1916; d. William M. and Mary (Kailer) Dunn; A.B., Coll. Notre Dame of Md., 1938; M.A., Catholic U. Am., Washington, 1940, Ph.D., 1947. Lectr., Chevy Chase Jr. Coll., Washington, 1940-42; instr. Cath. U. Am., 1947-52, asst. prof., 1952-57, asso. prof., 1957-62, prof., 1963—, chmn. English dept., 1969—. Mem. Modern Lang. Assn. Contbr. articles profl. jours. Home: 8419D Loch Raven Blvd Baltimore MD 21204 Office: Cath U Am Washington DC 20017

DUNN, ELWOOD, clergyman; b. Grant County, Ind., Jan. 8, 1906; s. Sylvester M. and Ida Belle (Ferrell) D.; B.S.L. cum laude, Butler U., 1929; B.D. cum laude, Christian Theol. Sem., 1941; grad student Wayne State U., Mich. State U. Ordained to ministry Christian Ch., 1926; minister in Palestine, Ind., 1926-30, Etna Green, Ind., 1926-36, Medaryville, Ind., 1936-39, N. Salem, Ind., 1939-43, Wabash, Ind., 1943-46, Pontiac, Mich., 1946-49; gen. sec. Mich. Christian Endeavor Union, Detroit, 1948—; v.p. Leadership Tng., Inc., 1952-55; minister Ferndale (Mich.) Christian Ch., 1962—; asst. dir. Neighborhood Youth Corps, Pontiac, 1967, dir., 1967- -. Mem. Ind. youth work com. Christian Ch., 1936-40; chmn. Mich. youth work com. Christian Ch., 1947-49; pres. Ministerial Assn., Wabash, 1943- 44; v.p. Great Lakes region Internat. Soc. Christian Endeavor, 1951-55, v.p., 1955-61, chmn. youth work com., 1955-67, mem. exec. com., 1955—, pres., 1967-71. Mem. Mayor Pontiac Com. Youth Opportunity, 1968—, Avondale Area Youth Guidance Com., 1968-71; chmn. Oakland County Youth Assistance Com., 1971—. Recipient scholastic honors award dept. Christian doctrine Butler U., 1929. Mem. Theta Phi. Co-author: Training for Service Senior High Department, 1966. Home: 640 3d St Pontiac MI 48056 Office: 1 Lafayette St Pontiac MI 48053

DUNN, FAYETTE SMITH, lawyer, elevator co. exec.; b. Maryville, Mo., Oct. 31, 1903; s. Samuel Orace and Carrie Eliza (Smith) D.; A.B., U. Mich., 1925; J.D., Northwestern U., 1928; m. Mildred Ingeborg Lidell, June 30, 1939. Admitted to Ill. bar. 1928, N.Y., 1936; practice law. Chgo., 1928-55, N.Y.C., 1936-60; sec. Otis Elevator Co., N.Y.C., 1951-64, gen. counsel, 1960-64, pres., dir., 1964-68, chmn. bd. 1968-70, chmn. finance com., 1970—; dir. Mut. Trust Life Ins. Co., Irving Trust Co. N.Y., Gen. Cable Corp., N.Y.C. Mem. Commerce and Industry Assn. N.Y. (dir.). Clubs: University. India House, Pinnacle (N.Y.C.); Ekwanok Country (Manchester, Vt.). Home: 14 W 10th St New York City NY 10011 also Dorset VT 05251 Office: 260 11th Av New York City NY 10001

DUNN, FLOYD, elec. engr., biophysicist, educator; b. Kansas City, Mo., Apr. 14, 1924; s. Louis and Ida (Leibtag) D.; student Kansas City Jr. Coll., 1941-42, Tex. A. and M. U., 1943; B.S., U. Ill., Urbana, 1949, M.S., 1949, Ph.D., 1956; m. Elsa Tanya Levine, June 11, 1950; children—Andrea Susan, Louis Brook. Research asso. elec. engring. U. Ill., Urbana, 1954-57, research asst. prof. elec. engring., 1957-61, asso. prof. elec. engring. and biophysics, 1961-65, prof., 1965—. Served with AUS, 1943-46. NIH Spl. Research fellow Univ. Coll. Cardiff, 1968-69. Fellow Acoustical Soc. Am. (asso. editor Jour.); mem. Am. Inst. Physics, Biophys. Soc., A.A.A.S. Contbr. articles on biophys. accoustics to profl. jours. Home: RR 3 Champaign IL 61820 Office: Elec Engring Dept U Ill Urbana IL 61801

DUNN, FRANCIS JOHN, bishop; b. Elkader, Ia., Mar. 22, 1922; s. Peter A. and Josephine (Feeney) D.; B.A., Loras Coll., Dubuque, Ia., 1944; degree in philosophy, Kenrick Sem., St. Louis, 1948; J.C.L., Angelicum U., Rome, Italy, 1960. Ordained priest Roman Cath. Ch., 1948; asst. pastor in Ia., 1948-56; asst. chancellor Archdiocese Dubuque, 1956-60, chancellor, 1960- -, aux. bishop, 1969—; vicar gen. Archdiocese Dubuque, pastor St. Joseph's Ch., 1969—; dir. Family Life Program Archdiocese Dubuque, 1956- 69, Cemetery Assn., 1960-69. Trustee United Fund Dubuque. Mem. Dubuque C. of C. Cath, Order Foresters. K.C. (4). Home: 90 S Algona St Dubuque IA 52001

DUNN, HARRY LIPPINCOTT, lawyer; b. Santa Barbara, Cal., Feb. 24, 1894; s. Ebenezer Pedrick and Margaret Ann (Robinson) D.; A.B., U. Cal., 1915; postgrad. Columbia Law Sch., 1915-16, Harvard, 1919-21; m. Louise Dodge Reding, Feb. 7, 1925 (dec. 1952); children—Peter Reding, Priscilla (Mrs. Edward J. Flynn); m. 2d, Katharine Tilt McCay, Feb. 3, 1955; Admitted to N.Y. State bar, 1922; Cal. bar, 1925; asso. firm Cravath, Henderson, Leffingwell & de Gersdorff, N.Y.C., 1921-24; Asso. firm O'Melveny & Myers, Los Angeles, 1924-27, partner firm, 1927-68, counsel, 1968—. Trustee Claremont U. Center. Served Commn. for Relief in Belgium, 1916-17; with Am. Field Service, France, 1917; 1st lt., 6th F.A., 1st Div.; AEF, 1917-19; with Am. Relief Adminstrn. in Poland, 1919. Mem. Am., Los Angeles bar assns., Am. Bar Found., Los Angeles C. of C., Harvard Law Sch. Assn. (past v.p.), Friends of Claremont Colls. (past pres.), Phi Delta Theta. Republican. Clubs: California, Stock Exchange (Los Angeles); Annandale Golf, Harvard, Zamorano, Valley Hunt (Pasadena, Cal.). Home: 1360 Hillcrest Av Pasadena CA 91106 Office: 611 W 6th St Los Angeles CA 90017

DUNN, HUGH E., religious orgn. exec.; b. Schenectady, June 12, 1913; s. Hugh E. and Mary T. (McDermott) D.; B.A., Loyola University, Chgo., 1940; M.A., St. Louis U., 1943, Ph.D., Cath. U. Am., 1956. Entered Soc. of Jesus, 1935; ordained priest Roman Cath. Ch., 1946; tchr. English, Xavier U., summer 1947; asst. prof. sociology U. Detroit, 1953-56, v.p., 1968-71; pres. John Carroll U., Cleve., 1956- 67; treas. Detroit Province Soc. Jesus, 1971—. Mem. Am. Cath., Am. Sociol. socs., Acad. Religion and Mental Health, Nat. Council Family Relations, Pi Gamma Mu.

DUNN, JAMES CLEMENT, ret. U.S. career ambassador; b. Newark, Dec. 27, 1890; s. John Henry and Mary Emma (Delaney) D.; ed. privately; m. Mary Augusta Armour, Dec. 8, 1914; children—Marianna Armour (Mrs. Marianna Dunn Gevers), Cynthia Louisa (Mrs. Charles W. Thayer). Was engaged to practice as architect, 1913-17; 3d sec. embassy, Madrid, Spain, 1920-22; charge d'affaires Port au Prince, Haiti, 1922-24; 1st sec. Am. embassy, Brussels, Belgium, 1924-27; dir. ceremonies at White House, Washington, 1927-30, chief Div. of Internat. Conf. and Protocol, 1928-30, 31-35; counselor to Commn. for Study of Haiti, 1930; 1st sec. Am. embassy, London, 1930; sec. delegation 4th Pan-Am. Comml. Conf., Washington, 1931; sec. gen. Am. delegation 1st stage Gen. Disarmament Conf., Geneva, 1932; also asst. 1st meeting expert's prep. com. Internat. Monetary and Econ. Conf., Geneva.; sec. gen. Am. delegation Internat. Monetary and Econ. Conf., London, 1933; sec. gen. Am. delegation 7th Internat. Conf. Am. States, Montevideo, 1933; spl. asst. to sec. of State, 1934, chief Div. Western European Affairs, 1935-37, advisor on polit. relations 1937-44, dir. Office of European Affairs, 1944, apptd. asst. sec. of State, 1944; mem. U.S. group, Dumbarton Oaks Conversations on Internat. Orgn., Washington, 1944; adviser U.S. delegation U.N. Conf., San Francisco, 1945; chief polit. adviser Berlin Conf., 1945; dep. to U.S. mem. meetings of Council of Fgn. Ministers, London, Paris, N.Y.C., 1945-46, Paris Peace Conf., 1946; ambassador to Italy, 1946-52, France, 1952-53, Spain, 1953-54, Brazil, 1955-56. Lt. asst. U.S. Naval attaché, Habana, 1917-19. Decorated Victory medal, Order Leopold II (Belgium); grand cross Order of Knights of Malta; grand cross Order Star of Italy; grand cross Order Isabell II of Spain; grand cross Order So. Cross Brazil. Recipient D.S.M., U.S. Dept. of State. Clubs: Metropolitan (gov.), Alibi, Burning Tree, Chevy Chase (Washington); Knickerbocker, Regency, River, Whist (N.Y.C.). Address: Palazzo Caetani 32 Via Delle Botteghe Oscure Rome Italy

DUNN, JAMES HAROLD, corp. exec.; b. Dallas County, Tex., Apr. 22, 1904; s. Charles A. and Lottie (Webb) D.; B.S. and M.E., Tex., A. & M. Coll.; m. Louise McCallum, July 7, 1928; 1 dau. Alta Louise. Chief prodn. engr. Lone Star Gas Co., Dallas, 1926-38; v.p. and gen. mgr. Shamrock Oil & Gas Corp., 1938-45, pres., 1945-60. chmn. bd., 1960-67; dir. Diamond Shamrock Corp., 1967—; dir. Southwestern Life Ins. Co., 1st Nat. Bank, Amarillo, Boys Ranch, Inc., Sells Petroleum, Inc. Bd. dirs. Edna Gladney Home; adv. bd. Amarillo YWCA; dir. Amarillo YMCA, pres., 1955. Bd. dirs. Tex. A. & M. Coll., 1953-59, W. Tex. State Univ. Found., Amarillo Area Found., Inc.; mem. bd. Tex. A. & M. Coll. Devel. Fund; trustee, councillor Tex. A. & M. Research Found., pres. 1956-57, chmn. bd., 1964-66; trustee Geoscis. and Petroleum Engr. Found. of Tex. A. & M. U.; statewide chmn. Coll. Loyalty Alumni Support Program, 1965. Mem. Natural Gasoline Assn. Am. (pres. 1945-47), Ind. Petroleum Assn. Am. (dir.), Ind. Natural Gas Assn. Am., Amarillo C. of C. (dir.), Nat. Indsl. Conf. Bd., Mid-Continent Oil and Gas Assn., Panhandle-Plains Hist. Soc. (past pres., dir.), Tex. Research League (dir.). Presbyn. Clubs: Dallas Petroleum; Amarillo Country (dir.). Amarillo (pres. dir. 1948-50); Union (Cleve.). Contbr. to trade jours. Home: 2400 Van Buren St Amarillo TX 79109 Office: First Nat Bank Bldg Amarillo TX 79101

DUNN, JAMES JOSEPH, mag. pub.; b. N.Y.C., July 22, 1920; s. James A. and Mary A. (Kelly) D.; B.B.A., Manhattan Coll., 1941; m. Elinor M. Hargesheimer, Aug. 30, 1943; children—Patricia Ann, Kevin James, Gregory John, Sean David, Christopher Kelly. With McCall Corp., 1946-50; with Time, Inc., 1950-67, advt. dir., N.Y.C., 1961-67; publisher Forbes, Inc., 1967—. Served to lt. comdr. USNR, 1941-46. Home: Glenville Rd Greenwich, CT 06830 Office: 60 Fifth Av New York City NY 10011

DUNN, JAMES ROBERT, educator; b. Sacramento, Oct. 18, 1921; s. Walter Ray and Frances (Latta) D.; A.B., U. Cal. at Berkeley, 1943, Ph.D., 1950; m. Marjorie Ralph, Nov. 17, 1946 (div. 1970); children—Marsha, Brian, David, Sheldon; m. 2d, Nancy Berry Smyth, Oct. 24, 1970. Asst. prof. Rensselaer Poly. Inst., 1950-55, asso. prof., 1955-65, prof., 1965—; pvt. practice as geologic cons. various state agys. and to firms including Hudson Cement, Atlantic Cement, Hondaille Industries, Peckham Industries, N.Y. State U. Constrn. Fund; pres. James R. Dunn & Assos., Inc., 1960-70, chmn. bd., 1971—; geologic cons., Averill Park, N.Y. Fellow Geol. Soc. Am.; mem. Am. Inst. Mining, Metall. and Petroleum Engrs., Am. Inst. Profl. Geologists (v.p. 1969), Assn. Engring. Geologists, Clay Mineral Soc., Geochem. Soc., Am. Concrete Inst., Nat. Assn. Geology Tchrs., Am. Soc. Testing and Materials, Am. Inst. Planners, Empire State Concrete and Aggregate Producers Assn. (asso.), Nat. (asso.), N.Y. State crushed stone assns., Pa. Sand and Gravel Assn. (asso.), Soc. Econ. Geologist, Nat. Sand and Gravel Assn. (asso.), Pa. Stone Producer Assn. (asso.), Sigma Xi, Phi Kappa Tau. Contbr. articles profl. jours. Home: Mountain View Dr Averill Park NY 12018

DUNN, JOHN FRANCIS, publisher; b. Paterson, N.J., Sept. 16, 1926; s. William P. and Regina C. (Foley) D.; student Rutgers U., 1946-49; m. Margaret A. Callahan, Dec. 4, 1948; children—Gregory W., Brian M., Deborah Marie, Jacalyn A. Buyer, Gt. Atlantic & Pacific Tea Co., 1946-51; dist. trainer Procter & Gamble, 1951-55; dir. merchandising ABC 1955-59; account mgr. Ladies Home Jour., 1959-63, N.Y. mgr., 1963-64, gen. sales mgr., 1964-65, advt. dir., 1965-66, v.p., advt. dir., 1966-68; pub. Am. Home mag., N.Y.C., 1968—. Pres. Wyckoff Sch. Bd., 1965, Wyckoff Parochial Sch. Bd., 1966. Served to lt. (j.g.), A.C., USNR, 1943-46. Decorated D.F.C., Air medal with two oak leaf clusters. Clubs: North Jersey Country (bd. govs., chmn. communications com. 1969-70, chmn. entertainment com. 1970) (Wayne, N.J.); Seaview Country (Absecon, N.J.); Ponte Vedra (Fla.) Golf. Home: 796 Albemarle St Wyckoff NJ 07481 Office: 641 Lexington Av New York City NY 10022

DUNN, JOHN WILLIAM, supt. schs.; b. Halfway, Ore., July 28, 1915; s. Earl W. and Flossie E. Dunn; B.S., U. Ore., 1941, M.S., 1942; Ed.D., U. So. Cal., 1956; m. Ora A. Shirley, June 19, 1938; children—William R., Shirley J., Stephen E. Vocational co-ordinator Pendleton (Ore.) pub. schs., 1946; vocational adviser VA, La Grande, Ore., 1946-47; dean instrn. Ore. Tech. Inst., 1947-49; dean students Portand State Coll., 1949-52; dean students Palomar Coll., 1952-56, pres., 1956-64; dist. supt. Peralta Jr. Coll. Dist., Oakland, 1964-. Chmn., dir. Andrew M. Schmidt Scholarship Found. Served with USNR, 1942-46; capt. Res. Decorated Bronze Star; recipient Admiral's Commendation. Mem. Cal. Junior Coll. Assn. (exec. bd.). Rotarian. (dir., pres. Vista). Home: 6273 Girvin Dr Oakland CA 94611 Office: Peralta Jr Coll Dist 300 Grand Av Oakland CA 94610

DUNN, JOSEPH WILLCOX, Jr., journalist; b. Richmond, Va., Mar. 9, 1937; s. Joseph Willcox and Lelia (Taylor) D.; student U. Va., 1957; m. Alice Smiley Hubard, Aug. 17, 1957; children—Joseph Willcox III, Pauline Taylor. News editor Princess Anne Free Press, Virginia Beach, Va., 1957- 62; copy editor Virginian-Pilot, Norfolk, Va., 1962-63, telegraph editor, pilot, 1963-64, acting news editor, 1964-65, Va. Beach city editor, 1965-68, mil. writer, 1968, mng. editor, 1968—. Recipient eight writing awards Va. Press Assn., 1957-62. Episcopalian. Home: 216 84th St Virginia Beach VA 23451 Office: 150 W Brambleton Av Norfolk VA 23451

DUNN, JUSTIN STEPHEN, investment co. exec.; b. New Haven, Nov. 30, 1904; s. John E. and Elizabeth (Welch) D.; B.S. cum laude, Yale, 1927; m. Ann H. Knudsen, July 22, 1942; stepchildren—Earl D. and Eugene R. Knudsen. With A. Iselin & Co., 1928-37, Domminick & Dominick, 1937-41; with E.W. Axe & Co., Inc., 1941—, sr. v.p., 1964-67, pres., 1967—; pres., dir. Axe-Houghton Fund B, Inc., v.p. Axe-Houghton Fund A, Inc., Axe-Houghton Stock Fund, Inc.; v.p., dir. Axe Sci. Corp.; dir. Axe Sci. Mgmt., Axe Securities & Planning Counsellors, Inc. Bd. govs. Investment Co. Inst. Roman Catholic. Club: Knollwood (White Plains). Home: 50 Mayfair Way White Plains NY 10603 Office: 400 Benedict Av Tarrytown NY 10591

DUNN, KEMPTON, co. exec.; b. Phila., Mar. 5, 1909; s. Frederick Martyn and Inez B. (Kempton) D.; student Kent Sch., 1924-27; B.S., Yale, 1931; m. Susan Barret Gill, Nov. 3, 1934; children—Helene (Bodman); Kempton. Joined Am. Brake Shoe Co., N.Y.C., 1932, successively clk., asst. treas., treas., asst. sec., sec., v.p., 1st v.p., 1932-54, pres., 1954-63, chief exec. officer, 1957-71, chairman board, 1963-71, also dir., 1952-71; vice chmn. Ill. Central Industries; dir. Bankers Trust Company, Bucyrus-Erie Co., Pitney-Bowes, Inc.; trustee Franklin Savs. Bank. Member Board trustees National Safety Council, Gen. Theological Seminary; mem. of the bd. dirs. Boys Clubs of Am. Mem. Delta Psi. Episcopalian (vestryman). Clubs: Yale, Links, Sky (New York City, N.Y.); Tokeneke (Darien, Conn.); country (New Canaan); Chicago (Chgo.). Home: Wahackme Road New Canaan CT 06840

DUNN, KENNETH, mining co. exec.; b. Manchester, Eng., Apr. 21, 1921; s. William Warwick and Elizabeth (Williams) D.; grad. Manchester schs.; m. Freda Tomkinson, Oct. 12, 1939; children—Patricia (Mrs. Michel Gharbonneau), Joyce (Mrs. Peter McGill). Corp. finance mgr., treas. Rio Arcom Mines Ltd., Toronto, 1962-65; v.p. finance Atlas Steel Co., Welland, Ont., 1965-68; controller Falconbridge Nickel Mines Ltd., Toronto, Ont., Can., 1968—; dir. Falconbridge Internat. Ltd. Indusmin Ltd., Kiena Gold Mines Ltd., Toronto Mines Services, Ltd., others. Served with British Army, 1939-46. Mem. Engrs. Club Toronto. Home: 40 Acre Heights Crescent Scarborough Ontario Canada Office: 7 King St E Toronto Ontario Canada

DUNN, LEON J., mfg. exec.; b. Cleve., July 22, 1914; s. Martin J. and Katherine (McElheney) D.; student Gen. Motors Inst. of Tech.; m. Ruth Slyh, May 13, 1939; children—Noel Lee, William M., Edward, May Jane. With steel and tubes div., Republic Steel Corp., Cleve., 1939-41; Westinghouse Elec. & Mfg. Co., Cleve., 1938-39, Cleve. Hobbing Machinery Co., 1937-38, Gen. Motors Corp., 1931-37, Ford, Bacon & Davis, mgmt. cons., 1941-42; with Veeder-Root, Inc., Hartford, Conn., 1942-62, became asst. to exec. v.p., 1949, v.p. charge operations; pres. Duncaster corp., Bloomfield, Conn., 1953-57; gen mgr. Stanley Power Tool div. Stanley Works, New Britain, Conn., 1963-69; v.p. Stanley Works; now group v p. Ill. Tool Works, Chgo.; dir. Hartford Home Savs. & Loan Assn. Mem. personnel bd., Hartford Hosp., Bloomfield Town Ins. Com. Instr. mgmt. subject, U. Conn., 1942-45. Mem. Soc. for Advancement of Mgmt. (pres. Hartford chpt., 1946-47; nat. dir. and mem. nat. exec. com., 1947-48; asst. nat. v.p. in charge of new chpt. devel., 1948-49; nat. sec., 1949-50; nat. exec. v.p., 1950-51, pres., 1951-52), Electric Tool Inst. (pres., dir.). Lion. Clubs: Hartford, Wampanoag Country. Home: 655 W Gate Rd Deerfield IL 60015 Office: 8501 W Higgins Rd Chicago IL 60631

DUNN, LESLIE CLARENCE, geneticist; b. Buffalo, Nov. 2, 1893; s. Clarence Leslie and Mary Eliza (Booth) D.; B.Sc., Dartmouth Coll., 1915, D.Sc. (honorary), 1952; M.Sc. in Zoology, Harvard, 1917, D.Sc., 1920; m. Louise Porter, May 2, 1918; children—Robert Leslie, Stephen Porter. Asst. in zoology, Harvard, 1915-17, 19; geneticist Conn. (Storrs) Agrl. Expt. Sta., 1920-28, cons. geneticist since 1930; prof. zoölogy, Columbia, 1928-62, emeritus prof., 1962—, research asso. Nevis Biol. Sta., 1962—; dir. Inst. Study Human Variation, 1952-58, exec. officer dept. zoology, 1940-46; vis. lectr. in biology Harvard, 1949-50; research asso. Galton Lab., Univ. Coll., London, 1960-61. Served as 1st lt. infantry, U.S. Army, 1917-19, World War; with A.E.F., 1918-19. Fellow Am. Acad. Arts and Scis.; mem. Am. Soc. Human Genetics (pres. 1961), Accademia Patavina, Fedn. Am. Scientists, Am. Soc. Zoologists (sec.-treas. genetics sect. 1925-28), Am. Soc. Naturalists (pres. 1960), Genetics Soc. Am. (pres. 1932), Norwegian Acad. Scis., Am. Philos. Soc., Nat. Acad. Sci., Phi Beta Kappa. Mem. editorial bd. Genetics 1935-62, also served as mng. editor. Editor: The Am. Naturalists, 1950-60, Genetics, 1936-41. Author: Principles of Genetics (with E. W. Sinnott), 1925, 32, 39, 51, 58; Heredity and Variation, 1932; Heredity, Race and Society (with T. Dobzhansky), 1946; Biology and Race, 1951; Genetics in the 20th Century, 1951; Heredity and Evolution in Human Populations, 1958; A Short History of Genetics, 1965. Home: 635 W 247th St New York City NY 10034

DUNN, LOUIS GERHARDUS, engr.; b. Ermelo, Trnasvaal, S. Africa, Nov. 4, 1908; s. James Peter and Marie (Swart) D.; B.S., Calif. Inst. Tech., 1936, M.S. in mech. engring., 1937, M.S. in aeronautical engring., 1938, Ph.D. cum laude, 1940; m. Ruth N. Freeman, Aug. 1, 1935; children—Patricia Ann, Sandra Jane, Michael Edwin, Gerald, Linda. Came to U.S., 1930, naturalized, 1943. Stress analyst, test engr. Lockheed Aircraft Co., Burbank, Calif., 1936-37; research asst. Calif. Inst. Tech., 1937-39, research fellow, 1939-40, instr., 1940-41, asst. prof. aeros., 1941-46, asso. prof., 1946-49, research asso. jet propulsion, 1949, asst. dir. Jet Propulsion Lab., 1945-46, acting dir., 1946-47, dir., 1947—; asso. dir. Guided Missile Research div. Ramo-Wooldridge Corp., Los Angeles, 1954-55, v.p., dir. Guided Missile Research Div., 1955-57; exec. v.p. and gen. mgr. Space Tech. Labs., Inc., 1957-58, pres., 1958-61, chmn., 1961-63; v.p., gen. mgr. Sacramento plants Aerojet-Gen. Corp., 1963-64, sr. tech. adviser to the pres., 1964—. Decorated Medal of Merit. Fellow Am. Inst. Aeros. and Astronautics, A.A.A.S.; mem. Am. Ordnance Assn., Am. Assn. U. Profs., Sigma Xi. Author: Airplane Structural Analysis and Design (with E. E. Sechler), 1942. Home: PO Box 133 Mountain Ranch CA 95246

DUNN, MARVIN IRVIN, educator, physician; b. Topeka, Dec. 21, 1927; s. Louis and Ida (Leibtag) D.; B.A., U. Kan., 1950, M.D., 1954; m. Maureen Cohen, Mar. 10, 1956; children—Jonathan Louis, Marilyn Paulette; Intern USPHS, San Francisco, 1954-55; resident U. Kan., 1955-58, fellow, 1958-59; instr. medicine U. Kan., 1958-60, asso. in medicine, 1960-62, asst. prof. medicine, 1962-65, asso. prof., 1965-70, prof., 1970—, dir. Cardiovascular Lab., head sect. Cardiovascular Disease Med. Center, 1963—; cons. USAF, 1971-73. Bd. dirs. Hebrew Acad. Jewish Geriatric and Convalescent Center, Beth Shalom Synagogue. Served with AUS, 1946-47. Fellow, A.C.P., Am. Coll. Cardiology, Am. Heart Assn.; mem. Alpha Omega Alpha, Phi Cho. Translator Deductive and Polyparametric Electrocardiography, 1970. Home: 3205 Tomahawk Rd Shawnee Mission KS 66208 Office: 39th and Rainbow St Kansas City KS 66103

DUNN, MIGNON, mezzo-soprano; studied in Memphis; pupil of Karin Branzell and Mrs. Hardesty Johnson, Debut at Town Hall with Little Orch. Soc., 1954; debut in New Oreleans as Carmen, 1955; debut at N.Y.C. Opera as Carmen, 1956; debut with Met. Opera as nurse in Boris Godunoff, 1958. Recipient Bethoven prize Memphis; Exptl. Opera Theatre Am. award, 1955. Address: care Metropolitan Opera 147 W 39th St New York City NY 10018‡

DUNN, OSCAR LEWIS, Jr., elec. co. exec.; b. Sandborn, Ind., June 21, 1914; s. Oscar Lewis and Myrtle (Anderson) D.; B.S. in Bus. Adminstrn., Ind. U., 1936; m. Deborah Lewis, June 19, 1936; 1 son, Richard L. With Gen. Electric Co., 1936—, gen. mgr. direct current motor and generator dept., 1953-58, gen. mgr. motor and generator div., 1958-60, v.p., gen. mgr. motor and generator div., 1960-66, v.p., gen. mgr. indsl. drives systems div. and transp. systems div., 1966-68, v.p. marketing and pub. relations services, now v.p., group exec. constrn. industries group; dir. Canadian Gen. Electric Co. Ltd., Simplex-Gen. Electric, Eng. Mem. Newcomen Soc. N.Am., Am. Iron and Steel Inst., Beta Gamma Sigma, Sigma Alpha Epsilon. Clubs: West Side Tennis (N.Y.C.); Mohawk (Schenectady); Kahkwa (Erie); River (N.Y.). Home: 860 United Nations Plaza New York City, NY 10017. Office: 570 Lexington Av New York City NY 10022

DUNN, PARKER SOUTHERLAND, chem. co. exec.; b. Portsmouth, O., Aug. 25, 1910; s. Joseph Sidney and Florence (Bowen) D.; B. Chem. Engring., Ohio State U., 1930; M.S., Mass. Inst. Tech., 1931; m. Mayde Smith, July 15, 1939; children—Joseph Smith, Dwight James. Tech. asst. Mead Corp., Chillicothe, O., 1930-32; foreman Columbia Southern Corp., Barberton, O., 1932-33, asst. plant supt., Corpus Christi, Tex., 1934-38, tech. dir., 1938-41; research dir. Potash Co. Am., Carlsbad, N.M., 1941-46, resident mgr., 1946-51; asst. v.p. Am. Potash & Chem. Corp., Trona, Cal., 1951-52, v.p., Trona, 1952-55 Los Angeles, 1955-63, dir., 1958—, pres., 1963-69, chmn. bd., 1969—; v.p. Kerr McGee Corp., 1968—; v.p., dir. Am. Lithium Chems. Co., 1959-64, San Antonio Chem. Co., 1957—. Recipient Benjamin Garver Lamme medal Ohio State U., 1966. Mem. Am. Inst. Chem. Engrs., Am. Inst. Mining Engrs., Electro Chem. Soc., N.M. Mining Assn., Am. Nuclear Soc. Episcopalian. Clubs: Petroleum, Quail Creek Country, Beacon (Oklahoma City); Flintridge Riding (Los Angeles). Home: 3332 Quail Creek Rd Oklahoma City OK 73120. Office: Kerr McGee Bldg Oklahoma City OK 73102

DUNN, PAUL MILLARD, ret. paper co. exec.; b. Lennox, S.D., Oct. 15, 1898 s. James W. and Belle A. (Howard) D.; B.S. in Forestry, Ia. State Coll., 1923, M.S., 1933; m. Neva Pauline Kissinger, Jan. 21, 1926; childrenRobert Paul, James Wesley. Dist. forester and asso. state forester Mo. Forestry Dept., 1926- 31; asst. prof. and extension forester, Utah State Agrl. V., 1931-32 asso. prof. and extension forester, 1932-35, prof. and extension forester, 1935, prof. in charge Sch. Forestry, 1935-38, dean Sch. Forestry, 1938-42; dean Sch. Forestry, Ore. State Coll., 1942; dir. forestry St. Regis Paper Co., 1955-61, v.p., dir. forestry and timberlands, 1962-68, ret., now cons. Enlisted in Co. K, 2d Ia. Inf., 1917; served on Mexican Border and in France, 1918-19. Fellow Utah Acad. Arts, Scis. and Letters, A.A.A.S., Soc. Am. Foresters (pres. 1962-63); mem. Am. Forest Products Industries, Am. Forestry Assn. (pres. 1968-70), Forest History Soc. (pres. 1967-68), Forest Products Research Soc., Conservation Edn. Assn., Alpha Zeta, Gamma Sigma Delta, Sigam Delta Chi, Xi Sigma Pi, Phi Kappa Phi, Lambda Chi Alpha. Republican. Presbyn. Mason, Elk. Home: 124 NW 7th St Corvallis OR 97330

DUNN, R. ROY, utility exec.; b. Cleve., 1901. Dir. Potomac Electric Power Co.; dir. Acacia Mut. Life Ins. Co., Riggs Nat. Bank of Washington. Home: 4100 Cathedral Av NW Washington DC 20016

DUNN, R. WALTER, airline co. exec.; b. 1925; B.S., U. Colo., 1950; married; children—Randall V., Debra A. With Harold C. Greagor, C.P.A., 1950-52, Haskins & Sells, C.P.A.'s 1952-54, Henry B. Hill & Co., C.P.A.'s, 1955-56; supr. audit Husky Oil Co., 1956-58; supr. tax dept. Denver div. Martin Co., 1958-60; asst. treas. Frontier Airlines, Inc., 1960-62; controller Nat. Airlines Inc., 1962—, treas., 1967—. Address: PO Box 2055 Airport Mail Facility Miami FL 33159

DUNN, RAYMOND MARTIN, airline exec.; b. N.Y.C., Mar. 2, 1914; s. Martin Peter and Rose (Donahue) D.; student N.Y.U., 1933-35; m. Ann May Anderson, Nov. 25, 1937; children—Thomas Martin, Martin Raymond, Patricia Ann. Formerly with Trans World Airlines, dir. engring. and maintenance domestic and internat. divs., 1948-56, v.p. maintenance, stores, 1956-59, v.p. tech. services, 1959-63, sr. v.p., system gen. mgr., dir.; dir. Nat. Bank of North Kansas City (Mo.) 1959—. Mem. adv. council Naval Affairs. Kansas City, Mo., 1958—, U.S. Civil Air Transport exchange delegation to USSR, 1960—. Clubs: Pinacle Wings (N.Y.C.); American Yacht, Rye, N.Y. Home: 29 Colonial Rd White Plains NY 10605 Office: 605 3d Av New York City NY 10016

DUNN, RICHARD BYAM, pub. utility exec.; b. Gardner, Mass., May 21, 1913; s. Frederick Julian and Alice (Eaton) D.; B.A., Williams Coll., 1935; LL.B., Harvard, 1939; m. Margaret Pauline Myers, Dec. 31, 1938; children—Ellen Augusta (Mrs. H. Russ Zimmerman), Richard Byam, Erica Huth, Philip Julian. Admitted to Mass. bar, 1940, also U.S. Supreme Ct.; with New Eng. Electric System and subsidiaries, Boston, 1939—, sec., 1964—, gen. counsel, 1967—, v.p., 1970—; also v.p., clk. New Eng. Power Service Co., 1963—. Trustee Cushing Acad., Ashburnham, Mass., 1954—, clk., 1954-64, pres., 1964—. Served with USNR, 1944-46. Mem. Am., Fed. Power, Boston bar assns. Republican. Mem. Unitarian-Universalist Ch. (tchr. 1960-67, chmn. religious edn. com. 1966-67, chmn. standing com. 1956-57). Home: 49 Elm St Wellesley, MA 02181. Office: 20 Turnpike Rd Westboro MA 01581

DUNN, RICHARD MCILWAINE, Jr., lawyer; b. Richmond, Va., June 26, 1928; s. Richard McIlwaine and Maria (Moncure) D.; B.S., U. Va., 1951, LL.B., 1956; m. Wilton Rice, Mar. 1, 1952; children—Richard McIlwaine III, Christie Wilton. Admitted to Va. bar, 1956, since practiced in Richmond; mem. firm White, Cabell, Paris & Lowenstein. Served to 1st lt. AUS, 1951-54. Mem. S.R., Richmond Jr. C. of C., Phi Alpha Delta, Beta Theta Pi. Home: 1 S Westham Pkwy Richmond VA 23229 Office: 721 E Main St Richmond VA 23219

DUNN, ROBERT EARL, chem. co. exec.; b. Grand Rapids, Mich., June 27, 1921; s. Ralph Orace and Luella (McKay) D.; B.S. in Chemistry, Mich. State U., 1942; LL.B., U. Mich., 1950; m. Nancy Marie Wonsetler, June 18, 1943; children—Juliana Irene, William Robert. With Hercules Powder Co., 1942-43, Phillips Petroleum Co., 1943-46, 52-55; admitted to Mich. bar, 1951; with FBI, 1951-52; with BASF Wyandotte Corp. (Mich.), 1955—, sec., legal dir., 1969—. Mem. Am. Bar Assn., Am., Mich. patent law assns., State Bar Mich. Home: 2081 Sheraton St Trenton MI 48183 Office: 1609 Biddle St Wyandotte MI 48192

DUNN, ROBERT THOMAS, electronics co. exec.; b. Lyons, N.Y., Oct. 5, 1918; s. Thomas D. and Marie (Robinson) D.; B.S. in Econs., U. Pa., 1940; m. Carolyn McMichael, Oct. 8, 1946; children—Nancy, Michael, Carolyn. With Philips Export Co., N.Y.C., 1941-42, 46-55, v.p., 1951-55; v.p., treas. Consol. Electronics Industries Corp., N.Y.C., 1955-69, N. Am. Philips Corp., N.Y.C., 1969—; treas. Philips Electronics & Pharm. Industries Corp., N.Y.C., 1960-69, PEPI, Inc., N.Y.C., 1969—; treas., dir. Sessions Clock Co., Forestville, Conn., 1958-69, pres., 1969; dir. Digitronics Corp. Served with USAAF, 1942-46. Home: 33 Abington Av Ardsley NY 10502 Office: 100 E 42d St New York City NY 10017

DUNN, ROSS JOSEPH, lawyer; b. Toronto, Ont., Can., July 10, 1913; s. Alfred Michael and Mary (Morrison) D.; B.A., U. Toronto, 1933, M.A., 1934; postgrad. Osgoode Hall Law Sch., 1934-37; m. Margaret Hynes, Nov. 4, 1939; children—Mary Estelle, Michael, Brian. Paul, David, Stephen. Called to Ont. bar, 1937; asso. McMillan, Binch, Toronto, 1937-48. partner, 1948—. Dir., mem. exec. com. Algoma Steel Corp., Ltd. Bramalea Consol. Devels., Ltd., v.p., dir. Butterworth & Co. (Can.), Ltd.; dir. Canadian Motorways, Ltd., Bearium Metals Can., Ltd., B.S.A. Tools (Can.), Ltd. Bd. dirs. Social Planning Council Met. Toronto, 1959-64, 65-70, vice chmn. bd., 1961-64, v.p., 1966-68. Bd. dirs. St. Bernard's Convalescent Home, Nightingale Sch. Nursing. Served to lt. Royal Canadian Navy, 1943-45. Mem. Motor Carriers Lawyers Assn., Canadian Bar Assn. (council 1969—), Canadian Tax Found., Bd. Trade Met. Toronto, Delta Chi. Clubs: National, Royal Canadian Yacht, Granite (Toronto), Beaumaris Yacht (Muskoka). Home: 206 Inglewood Dr Toronto 7 Ontario Canada Office: 20 King St W Toronto 1 Ontario Canada

DUNN, STANNARD, lawyer; b. N.Y.C., Nov. 17, 1904; s. George M. and Ella (Stannard) D.; A.B., Columbia, 1926; LL.B., Harvard, 1929; m. Dorothy Odlin, Aug. 31, 1931; children—Dorothy (Mrs. Howell A. Jones, Jr.), Barbara (Mrs. David M. Roby). Admitted to N.Y. bar, 1930; asso. Chadbourne, Parke, Whiteside & Wolff, N.Y.C., 1929-38, partner, 1938—; gen. counsel Sperry Rand Corp., N.Y.C., 1965—, dir., 1968—; dir. Torrington Co., 1964-70. Mem. Phi Beta Kappa. Club: University (N.Y.C.). Home: 45 Tudor City Pl New York City NY 10017 Office: 25 Broadway New York City NY 10004

DUNN, STEPHEN FRANCIS, lawyer, assn. exec.; b. Scranton, Pa., Nov. 24, 1908; s. Stephen Francis and Elizabeth Longstreet (Hand) D.; A.B., Cornell, 1930; LL.B., U. Mich., 1933; m. Margaret Elizabeth Seaman, Apr. 7, 1934 (dec.); children—Barbara D. Walker, Margaret Elizabeth; m. 2d, Eleanor Frances Oliver, Nov. 27, 1945. Admitted to Mich. bar, 1934; sr. partner firm of McCobb, Heaney & Dunn, Grand Rapids, Mich., 1946-57; counsel to Employers Assn. Furniture Mfrs. Assn. Grand Rapids; gen. counsel, U.S. Dept. of Commerce, 1953-54; v.p., govt. relations div. N.A.M., Washington, 1957-60; pres. Nat. Coal Assn., 1960—. Mem. Phi Delta Phi, Theta Delta Chi. Methodist. Clubs: Burning Tree, Congressional Country, Downtown, Metropolitan (Washington); Cornell (N.Y.C.). Home: 3552 Chiswick Ct Silver Springs MD 20906 Office: The Coal Bldg 1130 17th St NW Washington DC 20036

DUNN, THELMA BRUMFIELD, pathologist; b. Renan, Va., Feb. 6, 1900; d. William Andrew and Effie (Thornton) Brumfield; A.B., Cornell U., 1922; N.D., U. Va., 1926; D.Sc. (hon.), Woman's Med. Coll.; M.D. (hon.), U. Perugia, Italy, 1969; m. William LeRoy Dunn, Dec. 26, 1929; children—William, John, Mary Degges. Intern Bellevue Hosp., N.Y.C., 1926-27; instr. pathology U. Va., 1927-28, asst. prof. pathology, 1928-30; research asst. pathology George Washington U. Med. Sch., 1935-42; med. officer, pathologist Nat. Cancer Inst., Bethesda, Md., 1942-69, ret. Recipient Fed. Woman's award, 1962, Distinguished Service award Health, Edn. and Welfare,

1962. Diplomate Am. Bd. Pathology. Fellow A.C.P., Coll. Am. Pathologists; mem. Am. Assn. Cancer Research (pres. 1961), Phi Beta Kappa, Alpha Omega Alpha, Alpha Omicron Pi. Contbr. articles profl. jours. Home: 1604 Jamestown Dr Charlottesville VA 22903

DUNN, THOMAS T., corp. exec.; b. Baton Rouge, Feb. 5, 1904; s. T. A. and Mary Ann (O'Malley) D.; B.S. La. State U., 1925; m. Mary Louise Brewton, February 6, 1939; children—Mary Brewton, Thaddeus Leland. Foreman, Robert G. Lassiter Co., road contractors, Raleigh, N.C., 1925-27; civil engr. Great So. Lumber Co., Bogalusa, La., 1927-31; chief engr. Gaylord Container Corp., 1931-40; general supt. of Union Camp Corp., Savannah, Ga., 1940-43, mill mgr., 1943-45, resident mgr., 1945-55, v.p. and resident mgr., 1949-55, exec. v.p., 1955-69, ret., now dir., cons.; dir. Savannah Bank & Trust Co. Mem. of T.A.P.P.I., Newcomen Soc. Eng. Clubs: Savannah Yacht, Savannah Golf, Oglethorpe. Home: 1408 Bacon Park Dr Savannah GA 31406

DUNN, WILLIAM EDWARD, trade assn. exec.; b. Ohio, Ill., July 30, 1909; s. James Patrick and Anna (Manning) D.; LL.B., DePaul U., 1937; m. Margaret Lyons, Apr. 19, 1937; children—James Albert, Mary Virginia (Mrs. Robert T. Metz), William Frederick, Roger, Mary Susanne. Admitted to Ill. bar, 1937, U.S. Supreme Ct., 1947; practice in Chgo., 1937-44; regional atty. WLB, Chgo., 1945-46; mem. staff Asso. Gen. Contractors Am., Washington, 1946- -, exec. dir., 1961—. Mem. President's Missile Sites Labor Commn., 1962- -; mem. nat. coms. apprenticeship and tng. Labor Dept., 1961—; bd. dirs. Programs Safety in Constrn., 1960-; trustee Nat. Joint Bd. Settlement Jurisdictional Disputes Constrn. Industry, 1961-. Clubs: Nat. Lawyers (Washington); Moles (N.Y.C.). Home: 4828 Ft Sumner Dr Washington DC 20016 Office: 1957 E St NW Washington DC 20006

DUNN, WILLIAM LEWIS, coll. dean; b. Lake Village, Ark., Oct. 18, 1914; s. William Lewis and Ruth Sheldon (Dewey) D.; A.B., U. of Ill., 1936; Ph.D., U. of Wis., 1941; m. Eleanor Majorie Tisdel, June 8, 1940; children—Carol Ruth, Janet Marjorie (dec.). Instr. in chemistry, Cornell Coll., Mt. Vernon, Ia., 1941-43, asst. prof. of chemistry, 1943-45; prof. of chemistry, Colo. State Coll. of Edn., 1945-49; acting chmn., div. scis., 1947-48; dean of the coll., Lake Forest (Ill.) Coll., 1949-62, v.p., 1962, provost and dean of faculty, 1962—. Mem. Phi Beta Kappa, Alpha Chi Sigma. Home: 11 College Campus Lake Forest IL 60045

DUNN, WILLIS JAMES, educator; b. Three Rivers, Mich., July 30, 1910; s. Ernest James and Mildred Rebecca (Mensch) D.; student Moody Bible Inst., 1929-32; A.B., Asbury Coll., 1935; M.A., Mich. State U., 1937, Ph.D., 1955; m. Henrietta Visscher, Oct. 1, 1935; children—Willis James, Joan Eileen (Mrs. Donald Ewan). Pub. relations dir., chmn. sociology dept. Taylor U., 1945-51; ordained to ministry Meth. Ch.; pastor, Rosebush, Mich., 1948-52; prof. sociology Neb. Wesleyan U., 1952-54; pastor, Franklin, Neb., 1954-58; registrar, dir. admissions U. Tampa (Fla.), 1959-66, dir. guidance and placement, chmn. sociology dept., 1966—; instr. various sociology courses, 1958—; marriage, family and personal counsellor; appeared on weekly radio broadcast, Tampa, 1958-60, Lexington, Neb., 1954-58; weekly TV program The World Today, St. Petersburg, 1965—. Chmn. ministerial tng. Neb. Conf. Meth. Chs., 1954-57. Mem. bd. Family Service Assn., Tampa, 1966—, pres., 1968-70; bd. dirs. Youth for Christ, St. Petersburg. Fellow Am. Sociol. Assn.; mem. So. Sociol. Assn., N.Y. Acad. Scis., A.A.A.S. Home: 5085 Flamingo Dr N St Petersburg FL 33714

DUNNAHOO, GILBERT LEE, physician; b. Benton, Ark., Nov. 27 1899; s. John Newton and Hannah (Guest) D.; A.B., U. of Utah, 1924; M.D., U. of Louisville, 1927; m. Margery Neill Wolfgang, July 15, 1927; children—Margot Jean, Marilee. Commd. lt., F.A., U.S. Army, 1924; commd. USPHS, 1928; served in various marine hosps., quarantine stations, leprosy investigations; Chief, Div. Fgn. Quarantine, 1943-52; asst. chief Bur. of Med. Services, 1945-48; chmn. World Health Orgn. Internat. Quarantine and Epidemiology, 1951-53, mem. Yellow Fever Panel, 1951; formerly chief spl. health services Dept. of Health Edn. and Welfare, Cons. Tb and chronic diseases USPHS, FSA Region; health officer Santa Cruz County, Cal., ret. 1968. Chmn. joint com. on water contamination from human pathogens Cal. Conf. Local Health Affairs, also chmn. com. on communicable diseases, mem. adminstrv. practices com. Recipient of Carlos Finley medal, 1939; Army Commendation Ribbon. Mem. (hon.) Airlines Med. Dirs. Assn., A.M.A., Am. Pub. Health Assn., Am. Bd. Preventive Medicine and Pub. Health, Phi Chi. Home: 260 15th Av Santa Cruz CA 95060 Office: P O Box 962 1060 Emeline Av Santa Cruz, CA

DUNNAN, DONALD WOOD, supt. schs.; b. Everett, Mass., Mar. 24, 1910; s. William J. and Maude (Myers) D.; B.S., U. N.H., 1933; M.Ed., Boston U., 1940; Ed.D., Harvard, 1951; m. Miriam Gardner, Aug. 11, 1930; children—Bernard Leslie, Nancy (Mrs. George Hall), Gardner Perley, Dana Myers, Miriam. Tchr. pub. schs., Billerica and Tewksbury, Mass., 1933-38; supt. schs., Burlington, Mass., 1938-41, South Kingstown, R.I., 1941-45, Franklin, N.H. 1945-50, Malone, N.Y., 1950-54, Meadville, Pa., 1954-58, Springfield, Ill., 1958-64, City St. Paul, 1964-69, Peabody, Mass., 1969—. Chmn. spl. gifts div. Community Chest, Franklin, 1945-48; mem. Franklin Hosp. Assn.; mem. White House Conf. on Edn., 1966; mem. White House Conf. on Children in Trouble, 1970. Mem. R.I. Inst. Instrn. (v.p. 1943-45), R.I. Sch. Supts. Assn. (sec. 1943-45), Am. Assn. Sch. Adminstrs, N.E., N.H. sch. supts assns., Phi Delta Kappa. Unitarian. Mason, Lion, Rotarian. Contbr. articles profl. jours. Address: Supts Office Peabody Pub Schs Peabody MA 01960

DUNNE, ARTHUR BERGIN, lawyer; b. San Francisco, Apr. 21, 1899; s. Peter Francis and Annie C. (Haehnlen) D.; A.B., U. Calif., 1920; LL.B., Harvard, 1923; m. Elizabeth MacArthur, Sept. 7, 1922; children—Arthur Bergin, Elizabeth A., Peter Francis III, Robert MacArthur. Admitted to Calif. bar, 1923 and since practiced in San Francisco; mem. Dunne, Dunne & Phelps, 1926-62; member firm Dunne, Phelps & Mills, since 1963-. Member board of govs. State Bar of Cal., 1944-47, v.p. 1946-47. Fell. Am. Bar Foundation, Am. Coll. Trial Lawyers: mem. Am., San Francisco (pres. 1942) bar assns. Republican (chmn. state central com. 1942, San Francisco central com. 1936-42; del. nat. convs., 1936-1940). Clubs: Pacific Union, Burlingame Country, Cyprus Point, San Francisco Golf. Author article in legal jour. Home: 2090 Vallejo St San Francisco CA 94123 Office: 601 California St San Francisco CA 94108

DUNNE, IRENE, actress; b. Louisville, Dec. 20; Mus.D., Chgo. Musical Coll., 1945; m. Francis D. Griffin, July 16, 1928; 1 dau., Mary Frances. Began in musical comedy, irene; starred in Back Street, Roberta, Magnificent Obsession, Showboat, Theodora Goes Wild, The Awful Truth, Joy of Living, Love Affair, Invitation to Happiness, When Tomorrow Comes, Penny Serenade; Unfinished Business, 1941; Lady in 9 Jam, 1942; A Guy Named Joe; The White Cliffs of Dover, others. U.S. del. 12th Gen. Assembly UN. Awarded Laetare Medal, given annually by U. of Notre Dame to most outstanding Catholic layman, June 1949. Dir. Technicolor, Inc., 1965—. Address: 461 N Faring Rd Los Angeles CA 90024

DUNNE, PHILIP, writer, director; b. N.Y.C., Feb. 11, 1908; s. Finley Peter and Margaret (Abbott) D.; student Harvard, 1925-29; m. Amanda Duff, July 15, 1939; children—Miranda, Philippa, Jessica. Writer, dir., producer motion pictures, 1932-; writer Count of Monte Cristo, 1934, The Rains Came, 1939, Stanley and Livingstone, 1940, How Green Was My Valley, 1941, The Late George Apley, 1946, The Ghost and Mrs. Muir, 1947, Pinky, 1950, David and Bathsheba, 1951, The Robe, 1953, The Agony and the Ecstasy, 1965; producer, dir. Prince of Players, 1955; writer, producer, dir. The View From Pompey's Head, 1956; writer, dir. Ten North Frederick, 1958, Blue Denim, 1961, Blindfold, 1965; dir. Lisa, 1963. Pres. bd. trustees Verde Valley Sch., Sedona, Ariz. Chief prodn. bur. motion pictures OWI, overseas br., 1942-45; gov. Motion Picture Acad. Arts and Scis., 1946-48. Recipient Laurel award Writers Guild Am., 1962. Mem. Writers Guild Am., Screen Dirs. Guild, Screen Producer's Guild, Screen Writer's Guild (v.p. 1938-40). Author: Mr. Dooley Remembers, 1963. Contbr. short stories to New Yorker mag. Home: 24708 Pacific Coast Hwy Malibu CA 90265 Office: 259 S Beverly Dr Beverly Hills CA 90212

DUNNELL, MILT, sports editor Toronto Star. Address: 80 King St W Toronto 1 Ontario Canada*

DUNNER, JOSEPH, educator, author; b. Fuerth, Bavaria, Germany, May 10, 1908; s. Samuel and Ella (Laske) D.; student U. Berlin, 1927-30; A.M., U. Frankfurt-Main, 1932; Ph.D., U. Basel, 1934; research fellow Internat. Inst. Social Research, 1930-35, Brookings Instn., 1936-37; m. Ada Bier, Dec. 24, 1935. Fgn. corr. under names Germanicus, Alexander Roth, for Swiss Press and Deutsche Freiheit, Saarbruecken, 1933-35; nat. lectr., cons. refugee problems Am. Jewish Joint Distbn. Com., United Jewish Appeal, 1937-42; fellow, research asso. N.Y. U., 1942-43; lectr. Sch. Overseas Adminstrn., Harvard, 1943-44; chief, intelligence sect. OWI, London, Eng., 1944-45, head press control sect. information control, Munich, Germany, 1945-46; chmn. polit. sci. dept. Grinnell Coll., 1946-58, dir. Inst. Internat. Affairs, 1946-58; Fulbright vis. prof. U. Freiburg (Germany), 1963-64; David Petegorsky prof. polit. sci. and internat. relations Yeshiva U., N.Y.C., 1964—. Trustee Inst. Mediterranean Affairs; dir. Am. Friends Hebrew U. Decorated Order of Ouissam Alaouite Cherifien by Sultan of Morocco, 1954. Mem. Polit. Sci. Assn., Am. Soc. Internat. Law, Internat. Polit. Sci. Assn. Author books including: The Republicc of Israel, Its History and Its Promise, 1950; Democratic Bulwark in the Middle East, 1953; Baruch Spinoza and Western Democracy, 1955; co- author: Am. Experiences in Military Government in World War II, 1948; Internationalism and Democracy, 1949; Constitutions and Constitutional Trends since World War II, 1951; The Palestine Refugee Problem, 1959; editor, co-author: Major Aspects of International Politics, 1948, Dictionary of Political Science, 1964, Leftist and Rightist Radicalism in American Politics, 1964; Handbook of World History, 1967. Home: 156-08 Riverside Dr New York City NY 10032 ☆

DUNNIGAN, FRANK JOSEPH, pub. co. pres.; b. Westport, Conn., Dec. 15, 1914; s. Francis P. and Kathryn (Grossmann) D.; A.A., Jr. Coll. Conn., 1934; B.S., N.Y. U., 1940; m. Teresa L. Razete, Aug. 13, 1966. Jr. accountant, Consol. Edison Co., N.Y.C., 1934-37; with Prentice-Hall, Inc., Engelwood Cliffs, N.J., 1937—, exec. v.p., 1965-71, pres., 1971—; dir., chmn. bd. Princetice Hall Corps System, Inc., N.Y.C. Trustee Pren-Hall Found. Served to capt. AUS, 1941-46. Mem. Newcomen Soc., Phi Theta Kappa. Club: Manor (Mt. Pocono, Pa.). Home: 2200 Central Rd Fort Lee NJ 07024 Office: Prentice-Hall Sylvan Av Englewood Cliffs NJ 07631

DUNNIGAN, THOMAS JOHN, govt. ofcl.; b. Canton, O., May 22, 1921; s. John Michael and Josephine Leona (Beck) D.; A.B., John Carroll U., 1943; M.A., George Washington U., 1967; m. Rae Marie Fox; children—Michael, John, Ralph, Leo, Claudia. Fgn. service officer in Berlin, 1946-50, London, 1950-54, Manila, 1955-56, Hong Kong, 1956-57, assigned Dept. of State, 1957-61, 65-69, Nat. War Coll., 1961-62, Bonn, 1962-65; polit. counselor The Hague, 1969—. Served with AUS, 1943-46. Mem. Am. Fgn. Service assn. Home: 2253 Maplewood Rd Cleveland Heights OH 44118 also Oranjelaan 3 Wassenaar Netherlands Office: Am Embassy The Hague Netherlands

DUNNING, HARRISON F., former paper co. exec.; b. West Hartford, Conn., Aug. 12, 1908; s. Stewart Northrop and Hazel (Case) D.; A.B., Dartmouth, 1930, M.A. (hon.), 1969; m. Kathleen Mulligan, Oct. 10, 1933; children—Harrison Case, Stephen Northrop, Kathleen Byron. Real estate broker, West Hartford, 1930-34; salesman and dist. mgr. Fuller Brush Co., Camden, N.J., 1934-35; with Scott Paper Co., 1935-71, exec. v.p., 1960-62, pres., 1962-68, chief exec. officer, 1966-71, chmn., 1969-71, dir., 1955-71, also dir. various fgn. affiliates; dir. Nat. Biscuit Co., Bell Telephone Co. Pa. Mem. bd. trustees of Dartmouth Coll., 1968—. Mem. Phi Delta Theta. Home: 12 Shady Hill Rd Moylan PA 19065

DUNNING, JAMES DORR, ins. co. exec.; b. St. Paul, Nov. 20, 1910; s. Roy Jay and Mary Adelaide (Painter) D.; A.B., James Millikin U., 1931; student U. Ill. Coll. Law, 1931-32; m. Mary Margaret Bourne, Dec. 25, 1934; 1 son, James Dorr. With N.Y. Life Ins. Co., 1932—, dir. advanced underwriting, 1949-51, asst. v.p., 1951-53, N.E. regional v.p., 1954-59, v.p., 1959—. Served with USNR, World War II; lt. comdr. Res. Mem. Nat. Assn. Life Underwriters (pres. Waterloo, Ia. 1941), Newcomen Soc., Sigma Alpha Epsilon. Episcopalian (past warden). Author articles trade jours. Home: 1175 York Av New York City NY 10021 Office: 51 Madison Av New York City NY 10010

DUNNING, JAMES HENRY FITZGERALD, chem. co. exec.; b. Balt., Aug. 26, 1902; s. H. A. Brown and Beatrice Garelle (Fitzgerald) D.; student Balt. City Coll., 1916-20; A.B., Johns Hopkins, 1924, Ph.D., 1927; m. Mary Frances McPherson, Mar. 27, 1926; children—James Henry Fitzgerald, Betty Carey (Mrs. Dushane Patterson). With Hynson, Westcott & Dunning, Inc., Balt., 1925—, sec.-treas., 1932- 45, gen. mgr., 1941—, pres., 1945—; dir. Equitable Trust Co. Chmn. vis. com. Sch. Hygiene and Pub. Health, Johns Hopkins, 1962—, co-chmn. nat. resources committee, since 1966—, trustee univ., 1960-66, 67-, mem. campaign com., 1967-, fund bd., 1968-; chmn. Johns Hopkins U. Alumni Roll Call, 1950; bd. dirs. Am. Found. Pharm. Edn., 1961—. Bd. dirs. Keswick (home for incurables), Balt. Mem. of Am. Chem. Soc. (chmn. Md. 1934-35), A.A.A.S., Am. Pharm. Assn. (council 1958-61), Am. Drug Mfrs. Assn. (pres. 1955-56), Pharm. Mfg. Assn. (dir. 1958—), Johns Hopkins Chem. Alumni Assn. (pres. 1952-54), Johns Hopkins Alumni Assn. (pres. 1954-56), Sigma Xi, Phi Gamma Delta, Omicron Delta Kappa. Clubs: Baltimore Country, Elkridge, Johns Hopkins (Balt.). Author articles profl. jours. Home: 107 Churchwardens Rd Baltimore MD 21212 Office: 1030 N Charles St Baltimore MD 21201

DUNNING, JAMES MORSE, dentist; b. N.Y.C., Oct. 16, 1904; s. William Bailey and Rose (Morse) D.; student Allen-Stevenson Sch., N.Y.C.; A.B., Harvard, 1926, M.P.H., 1947; D.D.S., Columbia, 1930; m. Mae Myrick Bradford, Aug. 24, 1935; children—Cornelia M. (now Mrs. Robert M. Hollister), and Rose. Summer dentist Grenfell Labrador Mission, 1930, 1932; asso. with father in pvt. practice of dentistry, N.Y.C., 1930-42; part time asst. in operative dentistry Columbia Dental Sch., 1930-35; part time dental dir. Met. Life Ins. Co., N.Y.C., 1935-45; attending dentist Heckscher Found. for Children, N.Y.C., 1932; dean Harvard School of Dental Medicine, Boston, 1947-52, dir. univ. dental health service, 1955-65; clin. asst. prof. pub. health dentistry Harvard, clin. prof. ecol. dentistry, 1963-65, prof.; engaged in private dental practice, 1952-65; pres. Dental Health Service Inc., 1941-45. Pres. Cambridge Mental Health Assn., 1960-65. Served as dental officer USNR, 1942-45, discharged rank of lt. comdr. Fellow Am. Coll. Dentists, N.Y. Acad. Dentistry, Am. Pub. Health Assn.; mem. Am. Dental Assn. and local components, Omicron Kappa Upsilon. Unitarian. Author: Principles of Dental Public Health, 1962, 2d edit., 1970. Contbr. articles to dental periodical lit., various phases dental pub. health. Home: 23 Buckingham St Cambridge, MA 02138. Office: 188 Longwood Av Boston MA 02115

DUNNING, JOHN RAY, physicist; b. Shelby, Neb., Sept. 24, 1907; s. Albert Chester and Josephine (Thelen) D.; A.B., with highest honors, Neb. Wesleyan Univ., 1929, D.Sc., 1945; Ph.D., Columbia, 1934; LL.D., Adelphi Coll., 1951; D.Sc. in Edn., Coll. Puget Sound, 1957; Sc.D., Temple U., 1955; Sc.D., Whitman College, Trinity College, 1958, U. Jacksonville, 1965, also Marquette U. 1967; LL.D. (hon.), Phila. Coll. Osteopathy, 1961; m. Esther Laura Blevins, Aug. 28, 1930; children—John Ray, Ann Adele. Began as physicist-radio engr., 1927; with Columbia since 1929, asst. in physics, 1929-35, Univ. fellow, 1932-33, instr. physics, 1933-35, Cutting traveling fellow, 1936, asst. prof. physics, 1935-38, asso. prof., 1938-46, prof., 1946—, dean faculty engring. and applied sci., 1950-69, Lindsley prof. applied sci., 1969—; dir. div. I, SAM Labs., 1942-45, dir. research Div. War Research, 1945-46, sci. dir. atomic energy Office Naval Research, 1946—. Dir. Vitro Corp., Nuclear Energy Corp., Oak Ridge Inst. of Nuclear Studies. Pres. Inst. Applied Sci., 1969—. Ofcl. investigator, OSRD, 1941-46; sci. adv. panel Dept. of Army; chmn. adv. commn. on sci. manpower N.Y.C. Bd. Edn.; mem. congl. panel Impact of Peaceful Uses of Atomic Energy, 1955; mem. sci. adv. com. Dept. Defense, 1954—; adv. com. Nat. Urban League, 1958—; chmn. nuclear program Empire State Atomic Devel. Assos.; chmn. N.Y. State Sci. Adv. Council to Legislature. Pres. Museum of Sci. and Tech., 1965-67. Bd. visitors U.S. Mil. Acad., West Point, 1953—, chmn., 1954; dir. Fund for Peaceful Atomic Development, 1954—; chmn. N.Y.C. Adv. Council Sci. and Tech., 1965—; pres. Hall Sci., N.Y.C., 1965—; dir. City Investing Corp.; trustee Armstrong Meml. Research Found., Sci. Service. Mem. div. com. for math., phys. and engring scis. NSF, 1958—, adv. com., 1961—; chmn. council for advancement research and devel. N.Y. State, 1959—; chmn. Empire State; Atomic Devel. Assn. Energy Policy Bd.; adv. com. Thomas A. Edison Found.; adv. council Am. Student Found., 1962—. Recipient Presdl. Citation, Medal for Merit, 1946; Stevens award, Stevens Inst. Tech., 1958; Pupin Medal, 1959, Pegram Medal, 1964, Grad. Faculties Alumni award Columbia, 1967; Outstanding Alumnus award Phi Kappa Tau, 1967. Chmn. Mayor's Committee for Atomic Energy, N.Y. Golden Anniversary. Chmn. of Am. Soc. M.E. and Nat. Research Council Com. on Nuclear Energy Glossary. Fellow Am. Phys. Soc., N.Y. Acad. Sci., A.A.A.S., (dir.), Am. Soc. M.E., Am. Nuclear Soc.; mem. Soc. History of Tech., Am. Assn. Physics Tchrs., Am. Inst. of Mining and Metall. Engrs., Optical Soc. Am., Nat. Acad. Scis. (chmn. pres.'s com. super sonic transport), Am. Soc. for Engring. Edn., Mining and Metall. Soc. Am., Newcomen Soc., Sigma Xi (nat. lecturer, 1948), Sigma Pi Sigma, Phi Kappa Phi, Phi Kappa Tau, Tau Beta Pi. Clubs: Columbia University, Cosmos, Engineers, Men's Faculty, University. Author books including: Matter, Energy and Radiation (a text with H.C. Paxton), 1941. Contbr. to various publs. Pioneered (with colleagues) 1st neutron expts. in U.S., from 1932. Home: Spring Lake Rd Sherman CT 06784

DUNNINGTON, FRANK GLASS, educator, physicist; b. Colo., May 7, 1903; s. Frank Hobbs and Gertrude Inez (Flagler) D.; B.S., U. Calif., 1929, Ph.D., 1932; m. Georgia L. Melton, May 12, 1928 (dec. Apr. 1943); children—Frank Melton, Mary Louise; m. 2d Frances L. Tulin, May 12, 1944. Fellow Nat. Research Council, Cal. Inst. Tech., 1932-35, research fellow, 1935-37; asst. prof. Rutgers U., New Brunswick, N.J., 1937-45, asso. prof., 1945-46, prof. physics, 1946-66, prof. physics and radiation sci., 1966—, chmn. nuclear sci. adv. com., 1952-62, radiol. health program com., 1961-63, dir. Rutgers Radiol. Health Program, 1963-68, dir. Radiation Sci. Center, 1966-68, mem. staff and group leader, radiation lab. Mass. Inst. Tech., 1941-45; research atomic constants, 1929-54; research and devel. radar, 1941-45, dir. group research in nuclear and electronic paramagnetism and low temperature studies, 1946-52. Mem. Gov.'s adv. com. radiation protection, 1955-57; chmn. N.J. Commn. on Radiation Protection, 1958-69; mem. N.J. Atomic Energy Study Commn. 1957-59. Fellow Am. Phys. Soc.; mem. Am. Assn. U. Profs., Am. Assn. Physics Tchrs., Conf. Radiol. Health, Phi Beta Kappa, Sigma Xi, Tau Beta Pi, Mu Theta Epsilon. Author articles in sci. jours. Home: 445 Wedgewood Dr Port Richey FL 33568

DUNNINGTON, JOHN HUGHES, ophthalmologist; b. Farmville, Va., Jan. 12, 1894; s. Walter Grey and India Wycliffe (Knight) D.; A.B., Hampden-Sydney Coll., 1911; M.D., U. of Va., 1915; LL.D., Hampden Sydney Coll., 1952; m. Genevieve Richards Parker, Nov. 26, 1919; 1 dau., Jean Parker. (Mrs. Jean Cullen). Intern S. I. Hosp. 1915-17, Manhattan Eye, Ear and Throat Hosp., N.Y.C., 1917-18; asst. surgeon N.Y. Eye and Ear Infirmary, 1920-26, sr. asst. surgeon, 1927-28; adj. asst. vis. surgeon, eye service Bellevue Hosp., 1926-28; attending ophthalmologist Presbyn. Hosp. and Vanderbilt Clinic, 1929-32, asst. dir. and attending ophthalmologist, 1934-38, clin. dir. and attending ophthalmologist, acting dir., eye service and attending ophthalmologist, 1942-44, dir. Inst. ophthalmology, and attending ophthalmologist, now cons.; instr. ophthalmology U. and Bellevue Hosp. Med. Coll., 1922-28, lectr. 1928-29; asst. prof. ophthalmology, N.Y. Postgrad. Med. Sch. and Hosp., asso. in ophthalmology Coll. Phys. and Surg., Columbia, 1928-30, asst. prof. ophthalmology, 1930-35, asso. prof. ophthalmology, 1936-37, asso. clin. prof. ophthalmology, 1938-39, prof. ophthalmology, 1940-59, prof. emeritus, 1959—. Chmn. Am. Bd. Ophthalmology, 1950-52. Served as 1st lt. M.C., U.S. Army, 1918-19. Fellow A.C.S.; mem. A.M.A., Am. Ophthal. Soc., (pres. 1950-51), Am. Bd. Opthalmology, N.Y. Acad. Med. (chmn. 1936-37), N.Y. Opthal. Soc., N.Y. State Med. Soc., N.Y. Acad. Scis., A.A.A.S., Am. Acad. Opthalmology and Otolaryngology (pres. 1958-59), Med. Soc. County N.Y., Phi Beta Kappa, Chi Phi, Phi Rho Sigma. Democrat. Presbyn. Clubs: The Virginians, Union, River (N.Y.C.); Nantucket Yacht. Home: 1120 Fifth Av New York City NY 10028 Office: 1 E 71st St New York City NY 10021

DUNNOCK, MILDRED, actress; b. Balt.; A.B., Goucher Coll.; M.A., Columbia. Made profl. debut in Life Begins, N.Y.C., 1932; toured with Katharine Cornell in Herod and Marianne, 1938, with George M. Cohan in Madam, Will You Walk?, 1941, in The Corn is Green, 1942; appeared in Richard III, N.Y.C., 1943, Only the Heart, 1944, Foolish Notion, 1945, Another Part of the Forest, 1946, The Hallams, 1948, The Leading Lady, 1948, Death of a Salesman, 1949, Pride's Crossing, 1950, appeared in film version The Corn is Green, 1945, also Child of Fortune, Love Me Tender, Baby Doll; Nun's Story, 1959; Story on Page One, Farewell Eugene, Butterfield 8, Barefoot in The Park; N.Y. Stage play The Cantilevered Terrace,

1962, Traveller Without Luggage, 1964; appeared in 7 Women, 1965. Recipient TV award, 1955. Address: care of Peter Witt Assos Inc 321 S Beverly Dr Beverly Hills CA 90212

DUNOYER DE SEGONZAC, ANDRE, French painter; b. 1884; ed. Lycee Henri IV, also Ecole des Beaux Arts, Paris. Many paintings exhibited in museums. Served with French Army, 1914-18. Decorated chevalier Legion of Honor; recipient Carnegie prize, 1933, Grand Prix Biennale, Venice, 1934. Hon. mem. Am. Inst. Arts and Letters, royal acads. London and Belgium. Illus.; Georgics, Sonnets (Ronsard), La Trielle Muscate. Address: 13 Rue Bonaparte Paris 6e, France.*

DUNPHY, DONAL, pediatrician, educator; b. Northampton, Mass., Feb. 24, 1917; s. Michael and Catherine (Duggan) D.; B.A., Holy Cross Coll., Worcester, Mass., 1939; M.D., Yale, 1944; m. Helen Woods, Feb. 7, 1944; children—Karen, Christine, Michael. Intern New Haven Gen. Hosp., 1943-45, resident, 1945- 46; instr. pediatrics Yale Sch. Medicine, 1947-50; attending physician Bridgeport (Conn.) Gen. Hosp., 1950-53; pvt. practice medicine, specializing in pediatrics, Stratford, Conn., 1950-53; asso. pediatrics dept. U. Buffalo, 1955-56, asst. prof., 1956-59, asso. prof., 1959-61; prof., chmn. dept. pediatrics U. Ia., 1961—; dir. outpatient dept. Grace New Haven Hosp., 1947-50; dir. outpatient dept. Buffalo Childrens Hosp., 1955-61, dir., co-investigator Child Devel. Program NINDB Collaborative Project, 1958-61, cons. to project, 1960-61. Served to capt. U.S. Army, 1953-55; ETO. Diplomate Nat. Bd. Pediatrics, Am. Bd. Pediatrics, (examiner). Mem. Am. Acad. Pediatrics, Am. Pediatric Soc., Midwest Soc. for Pediatric Research, N.Y. Acad. Sci., Am. Assn. U. Profs. Home: 224 Richards St Iowa City IA 52240

DUNPHY, EDWIN BLAKESLEE, ophthalmologist; b. Newark, Dec. 26, 1895; s. Alphonse L. and Hortense K. (Blakeslee) D.; student Newark Acad., 1907-14; A.B., Princeton, 1918; M.D., Harvard, 1922; m. Virginia Delano, June 23, 1923; children—Joan Delano, Priscilla Alden. Resident in Ophthalmology, Mass. Eye and Ear Infirmary, 1923-24, chief ophthalmology 1940-62; pvt. practice ophthalmology, Boston, 1924—; mem. faculty Harvard Med. Sch. since 1925, asst. in ophthalmology, 1925-35, instr., 1935-40, clin. prof., 1940-48, Henry Willard Williams prof. ophthalmology 1948-62, prof. emeritus, 1962—; cons. ophalmology Harvard Health Service; also cons. staff Childrens, Mass. Gen., Baptist hosps., Boston. Hon. v.p. Nat. Society Prevention of Blindness, Pan Am. Opthalmol. Soc. Recipient Howe prize in Ophthalmology, U. Buffalo, 1957; Howe medal Am. Ophthalmol. Soc., 1965. Diplomate Am. Bd. Ophthalmology (sec.-treas. 1946-54). Fellow A.C.S., Royal Soc. Medicine (hon.); mem. Am. Acad. Ophthalmology and Oto- Laryngology (pres. 1965), A.M.A. (recipient prize ophthalmology 1962), Am. New Eng. ophthalmol. socs., Alpha Omega Alpha. Clubs: Longwood, Cricket, Harvard (Boston); Brookline (Mass.) Country. Author numerous articles in profl. jours. Home: 255 Woodland Rd Chestnut Hill MA 02167 Office: 75 Mount Auburn St Cambridge MA 02138

DUNPHY, JOHN ENGLEBERT, surgeon, educator; b. Northampton, Mass., Mar. 31, 1908; s. Michael M. and Katherine C. (Duggan) D.; A.B., Holy Cross Coll., 1929, B.S. (hon.), 1964; M.D., Harvard, 1933; L.H.D., Seton Hall, 1964; LL.D., U. Glasgow (Scotland), 1965; m. Nancy Stevenson, Sept. 8, 1936; children—Sara Catherine, Elizabeth Ann, Mary Jane, John Englebert. Surg. intern Peter Bent Brigham Hosp., Boston, 1933-34, asst. resident surgeon, 1934-35, intern pathology, 1935-36, resident surgeon, 1936-38, 39-40, asso. surgery, 1940-42, sr. asso. surgery, 1945-48, surgeon, 1949; fellow surgery Lahey Clinic, 1938; George Gorham Peters traveling fellow, 1938; Arthur Tracy Cabot fellow surgery Lab. Surg. Research Harvard, 1938-39, instr. surgery Med. Sch., 1937-40, asso. surgery, 1940- 47, asst. prof., 1947-50, asso. clin. prof. surgery, 1950-53, clin. prof. surgery, 1953-55, prof., 1955-59; dir. 5th surg. service and Sears Surg. Lab., Boston City Hosp., 1959; Kenneth A.J. MacKenzie prof. surgery, chmn. dept. U. Ore., 1959-64; prof. surgery, chmn. dept. U. Cal. Sch. Medicine, San Francisco, 1964—. Served from capt. to lt. col. M.C., AUS, 1942-45. Diplomate Am. Bd. Surgery. Fellow A.C.S. (chmn. bd. regents), Am. Surg. Assn., Royal Coll. Physicians and Surgeons Can. (hon.); mem. A.M.A., Royal Coll. Surgeons Eng. (hon.), Assn. Surgeons Gt. Britain and Ireland (hon.), Royal Coll. Surgeons Edinburgh (hon.), Soc. for Surgery Alimentary Tract, So., Western, New Eng., Pacific Coast surg. assns., Soc. U. Surgeons, Royal Soc. Medicine, Assn. Am. Med. Colls., Am. Acad. Arts and Scis., Soc. U.S. Med. Consultants World War II, A.A.A.S. Republican. Roman Catholic. Clubs: Aescupalian, Harvard; Bohemian, St. Francis Yacht, University. Author: Physical Examination of the Surgical Patient, 1953. Editor: Repair and Regeneration, 1969. Contbr. articles to profl. jours. Address: U Cal Med Center San Francisco CA 94122

DUNSIRE, CHARLES JOHN, journalist; b. Seattle, Sept. 17, 1931; s. Charles John Campbell and Helen (Revelle) D.; B.A., U. Wash., 1953; m. Joan Lois Pennington, June 14, 1952; children—Teresa Elena, Caroline Jane, Laura Elizabeth. Reporter Daily Olympian (Wash.), 1953-56, Seattle Post-Intelligencer, 1956-59, TV sta. KIRO, 1959-61; editor editorial page, columnist Seattle Post-Intelligencer, 1961—; lectr. journalist Seattle U., 1966- -; N.W. corr. Nat. Observer, 1965—. Recipient 1st pl. reporting Wash. State Press Assn., 1958, hon. mention column writing, 1965, 1st pl. editorial writing, 1967. Mem. Nat. Conf. Editorial Writers, Seattle C. of C., World Affairs Council Seattle, Phi Kappa Sigma, Sigma Delta Chi. Roman Catholic. Home: 2041 NE 177th St Seattle WA 98155 Office: 521 Wall St Seattle WA 98111

DUNST, LAURENCE DAVID, advt. exec.; b. N.Y.C., Feb. 21, 1941; s. Philip R. and Mae (Fruchtendler) D.; B.A., Syracuse U., 1961; m. Diane Gordon, Dec. 22, 1962; children—Lee Gordon, Melissa Susan. Advt. copywriter R.H. Macy & Co., 1961-63; with Daniel & Charles, N.Y.C., 1963—, pres., partner, 1969—. Club: Writers (bd. dirs.) (N.Y.C.). Home: 1 Captains Lane Rye NY 10580 Office: 261 Madison Av New York City NY 10016

DUNSTAN, FLORENE JOHNSON, educator; b. Baxley, Ga., Mar. 21, 1904; d. Joseph James and Emma Frances (Nash) Johnson; A.B., Tift Coll., 1924; M.A., So. Meth. U., 1932; Ph.D., U. Tex., 1936; postgrad. U. Madrid, 1951, Nat. U. Mexico, 1932-44, U. Paris, 1938; m. Edgar Mullins Dunstan, Aug. 26, 1926; 1 dau., Dorothy Florene (Mrs. Walter E. Brown). Instr. Romance langs. So. Meth. U., 1936-41; instr. Spanish, Agnes Scott Coll., Decatur, Ga., 1941- 43, asst. prof., 1943-51, asso. prof., 1951-66, prof., 1966—, chmn. dept. Spanish, 1965—. Mem. budget com. Met. Atlanta Community Services, 1956-57; exec. com. Atlanta Com. for Internat. Visitors; chmn. Ga. Adv. Com. Fgn. Langs., 1967—. Carnegie research grantee, Brazil, 1949, Spain, 1951; Agnes Scott Coll. grantee, 1965. Named Atlanta Woman of Year in Edn., 1963. Mem. Modern Lang. Assn., Am. Assn. Tchrs. Spanish and Portuguese (Ga. pres. 1965-67), S. Atlantic Modern Lang. Assn., Am. Assn. U. Profs. (pres. Agnes Scott Coll. chpt. 1968-69), UN Assn. U.S.A., Am. Assn. U. Women (past pres. Atlanta br., chmn. fellowships Ga. div.), English-Speaking Union, Cirulo Hispano-Americano, D.A.R., U.D.C. Baptist. Club: Pan American (past pres. Atlanta). Co-translator: History of Mexican Literature, 3d edit., 1968. Home: 710 Pinetree Dr Decatur GA 30030

DUNTLEY, SEIBERT QUIMBY, research physicist; b. Bushnell, Ill., Oct. 2, 1911; s. George Silas and Nola Blanche (Seibert) D.; B.S., Mass. Inst. Tech., 1933, Sc.D. in Physics (teaching fellow 1937-39), 1939; M.S., Cal. Inst. Tech., 1935; m. Mabel Austin, Sept. 12, 1937; children—Susan A. (Mrs. Dean B. McKenney), Nola S. (Mrs. Robert J. Pierce), Stephen Q. Asst. physics Cal. Inst. Tech., 1933-34; instr. then asst. prof. Mass. Inst. Tech., 1939-52; tech. aide Nat. Def. Research Com., Office Emergency Mgmt., 1942-46; asso. research physicist Scripps Instn. Oceanography, U. Cal. at San Diego, 1952-55, research physicist, 1955—, dir. visibility laboratory, 1948—, prof., since 1966—; special research optics, spectrophotometry, environmental optics, visibility. Cons. to industry and government, 1940—; member executive council Armed Forces- NRC Com. Vision, 1961-64; chmn. Optical Society Am. delegation U.S. nat. com. Internat. Commn. Illumination, 1947—; chmn. U.S. nat. com. Internat. Commn. Optics, 1967-69. Bd. dirs. San Diego Industry-Edn. Council, 1961-63. Recipient Army-Navy Certificate Appreciation, 1948. Fellow Optical Soc. Am. (dir.-at-large 1958-61, president 1965-66, Frederick E. Ives medal 1961), San Diego Soc. Natural History; mem. Inter-Soc. Color Council San Diego Optical Socs., Sigma Xi. Home: 1475 Virginia Way LaJolla CA 92037 Office: Visibility Lab Scripps Instn Oceanography San Diego CA 92152

DUNTON, A. DAVIDSON, univ. pres.; b. Montreal, Que., Can., July 4, 1912; s. Robert Andrew and Elizabeth (Davidson) D.; student Lower Can. Coll., 1922-26, U. Grenoble, 1928-29, McGill U., 1930-31, Cambridge U., 1931-32, U. Munich, 1932-33; D.Sc., Laval U.; LL.D., U. Sask., Queen's U. B.C., U. Toronto, McGill U.; m. Kathleen Bingay, June 30, 1944; children—Darcy, Deborah. With Montreal Star, 1935-37, asso. editor, 1937-38; editor Montreal Standard 1938; asst. gen. mgr. Wartime Information Bd., Ottawa, Ont., Can., 1943-44, gen. mgr. 1944; chmn. Canadian Broadcasting Corp., 1945-58; pres. Carleton U., Ottawa, 1958—. Co-chmn. Royal Commn. on Billingualism and Biculturalism. Home: 410 Maple Lane Ottawa Ontario Canada

DUNTON, EDWARD ALBERT, govt. ofcl.; b. Mason City, Ia., Oct. 9, 1917; s. Edward and Julia (Carman) D.; A.B., DePauw U., 1939; J.D., Georgetown U., 1959; m. Margaret Sue Jolly, Sept. 6, 1941; children—John Edward, Thomas Granville. With U.S. Civil Service Commn., 1940—, dir. bur. recruiting and examining, 1969-71, dep. exec. dir., 1971—. Admitted to Md. bar, 1960. Served with USNR, 1942-46. Mem. Am. Soc. Pub. Adminstrn., Pub. Personnel Assn., Fedn. Bar Assn., Phi Beta Kappa. Home: 6509 Wiscasset Rd Washington DC 20016 Office: 1900 E St NW Washington DC 20415

DUNWODY, WILLIAM ELLIOTT IV, architect; b. Macon, Ga., June 1, 1893; s. William Elliott and Elizabeth (Webster) D.; student Mercer U., 1909-10; B.S., Ga. Tech. Inst., 1914; m. Mary Bennet Cox, June 9, 1926; children—William Elliott, Eugene Cox. Architect, Nisbet & Dunwody, 1915-20, Dunwody & Oliphant, 1920-29; pvt. practice architecture, Macon, 1928—, spl. projects include Mercer U., Wesleyan Coll., Macon, bldgs. at Ga. Inst. Tech., Middle Ga. Coll., U. Ga., Ga. State Coll. for Women; architect (with others) P.O., Fed. Bldg., Macon, Augusta, Ga. Mem. Ga. Bd. Exam. and Registration Architects, 1931-49; mem. master planning com. Downtown Council, Macon. Dir. First Nat. Bank & Trust Co. Pres., Central Ga. council Boy Scouts Am., 1938-40; past chmn. Macon-Bibb County chpt. Nat. Found. Infantile Paralysis; dir. A.R.C., chmn. local campaign, 1950; pres. Ga. Citizens Council, 1947-49, Macon Little Theatre, 1948-50; regent Univ. System of Ga., 1932-35. Bd. dirs. Ga. chpt. Arthritis Found.; bd. dirs. Macon YMCA, 1953-68, pres., 1960-61; Recipient Silver Beaver award Boy Scouts Am. Fellow A.I.A.; mem. Macon Art Assn. (pres. 1937-38), Macon Community Concert Assn. (v.p. 1963-68), Macon Opera Assn. (dir.), Kappa Alpha (nat. pres. 1946-51). Presbyn. Rotarian (pres. Macon 1935-36, dist. gov. 1944-45). Home: 4811 Rivoli Dr Macon GA 31204 Office: Town Pavilion 205 Boradway Macon GA 31201

DUNWODY, WILLIAM ELLIOTT, Jr., lawyer; b. Jacksonville, Fla., Dec. 17, 1910; s. William Elliott and Reba (Williams) D.; LL.B., U. Fla., 1933; m. Sara Jane Evans, June 8, 1940; children—Carolyn Dale, William Elliott III. Admitted to Fla. bar, 1933; practice in Miami, 1935—; partner firm Mershon, Sawyer, Johnston, Dunwody & Cole, 1946—. Home: 1049 Malaga Av Coral Gables FL 33134 Office: First Nat Bank Bldg Miami FL 33131

DUNWOODY, HAROLD HALSEY army officer; b. Paris, France, Jan. 9, 1919 (parents Am. citizens); s. Halsey and Doris (Sleater) D.; B.S., U.S. Mil. Acad., 1943; m. Elizabeth A. Hausheer, May 4, 1946; children—Harold Halsey II, Susan Mills, Ann Elizabeth, Jacqueline Lee, William Lawrence. Commd. 2d lt. U.S. Army, 1943; advanced through grades to brig. gen., 1968—, battalion exec. 3d Battalion 17th Inf. Regtl., S-3, 1950-51, comdr., 1951; chief spl. projects br. Office Asst. Sec. Army, 1952-53, chief manpower control br., 1953-55; exec. officer, battalion comdr. 11th Armored Cav. Regt., U.S., also Germany, 1956-58, chief spl. projects br., tng. div. G3, 7gh Army, Stuttgart, Germany, 1958-59, chief plans div., 1960; comdg. officer 6th Armored Cav. Regt., Ft. Knox, Ky., 1961-62; Armor Sch. Troops, 1962; dep. chief combined arms div. Office Personnel Directorate, Dept. Army, 1962-64; assigned chmn. Joint Chiefs Staff spl. studies group, 1964-67; spl. asst. to chief staff SHAPE, Belgium, 1967; chief strategic plans and programs br. SHAPE, also SHAPE rep. to NATO Def. Rev. Com. 1968; exec. to Supreme Allied Comdr. Europe, also to Comdr.-in-chief U.S. European Command, 1968—; comdg. gen. 1st brigade 5th Inf. div. Vietnam, 1971; dep. chief of staff Plans, Operations Intelligence, Vietnam, 1971—. Decorated D.S.C., D.S.M., Silver Star, Legion of Merit with oak leaf cluster, Bronze Star with oak leaf cluster, Purple Heart with oak leaf cluster, Army Commendation ribbon. Mem. Soc. Legion Honor, West Point Alumni Assn., Army Athletic Assn., Assn., Assn. U.S. Army. Home: 168 Main St Randolph NY 14772 Office: Hdqrs USARU (DCSOPS) APO San Francisco CA 96375

DUPEE, FREDERICK WILCOX, educator, author; b. Chgo., June 25, 1904; s. Leroy Church and Frances (Wilcox) D.; student U. Chgo., 1922-23; Ph.B., Yale, 1927; postgrad. English, Columbia, 1940-43; Litt.D., Bard Coll., 1965; m. Barbara Hughes, June 24, 1946; children—Joanna, Anthony. Instr. English, Bowdoin Coll., 1927-29; editorial bd. Miscellany, 1929-32; lit. editor New Masses, 1936; editorial bd. Partisan Rev., 1937-41; instr. English, Columbia, 1940-44, asst. prof., 1948-51, asso. prof., 1951-57, prof., 1957—; asst. prof. Bard Coll., 1944-48. Vis. prof. U. Lille (France), 1952, Harvard, 1957; faculty Salzburg (Austria) Seminar Am. Studies, 1966. Guggenheim fellow, 1951-52. Mem. P.E.N., Delta Kappa Epsilon. Author: Henry James, 1951; The King of the Cats and other essays, 1965. Editor: The Question of Henry James, 1945; Selected Letters of Charles Dickens, 1960; (with George Stade) Selected Letters of E.E. Cummings, 1969. Home: Mill Rd Rhinebeck NY 12507 Office: Columbia Univ New York City NY 10027

DUPEN, EVERETT GEORGE, sculptor, educator; b. San Francisco, June 12, 1912; s. George E. and Novelle (Freeman) DuP.; student U. So. Cal., 1931-33, Chouinard Art Sch., Los Angeles, summer 1932, Harvard Sch. Architecture, summer 1933; B.F.A. (scholar), Yale, 1937, European traveling fellow, 1937-38; m. Charlotte Canada Nicks, July 1, 1939; children—Stuart, Destia, Novelle, William, Ninia, Marguerite. Teaching fellow Carnegie Inst. Tech. Sch. Art, 1939-39; teaching asst. sculpture Washington U. Sch. Art, St. Louis, 1939-42; marine draftsman and loftsman Sausalito Shipbuilding Corp., Cal., 1942-45; instr. sculpture U. Wash. Sch. Art, Seattle, 1945-47, asst. prof., 1947-54, asso. prof. sculpture, 1954-60, prof. art, 1960—, chmn. sculpture div.; exhibited Prix de Rome Exhbn., Grand Central Gallery, N.Y.C., 1935-37, 39, St. Louis Mus. Ann., 1939-42, N.A.D., N.Y.C. 1943,49,53-55, 57-58, Seattle Art Mus. Ann., 1945-59, Pa. Acad. Art, Phila., 1950-52,55-58, Ecclesiastical Sculpture competition, 1950, Sculpture Center, N.Y.C., 1951, 53, 54, Pa. Acad. Fine Arts, 1954-58, Detroit Mus. Art, 1958, N.W. Inst. Sculpture, San Francisco Art Assn., 1959. Important works include pvt. commns. garden figures and portrait heads, archtl. medallions, sculpture panels for comml. bldgs. and theatres, figures and wood carvings various chs., relief panels U. Wash. campus, 1946, bronze fountain Wash. State Library, Olympia, 1959; Du Pen Fountain, Coliseum Century 21, Seattle World's Fair; 2 walnut screens Municipal Bldg., Seattle. Mem. U. Wash. Senate, 1952-55, exec. com., 1954-55; v.p. Allied Arts Movement for Seattle; mem. Seattle Municipal Art Commn., 1958-63. U. Wash. research grantee for creative sculpture, 1953-54. Recipient Saltus gold medal N.A.D., 1954; 1st prize for sculpture Bellevue (Washington) Arts and Crafts Fair, 1957. Fellow Nat. Sculpture Soc. (hon. mention Henry Herring competition); Artists Equity Assn. (bd. Seattle chpt.), Puget Sound N.W. Painters Group (bd.), N.W. Inst. Sculpture (pres. 1957), Allied Artists Am., U. Wash. Research Soc. Home: 1231 20th Av E Seattle WA 98102

DUPONT, ALEXIS FELIX, Jr., ret. investment exec.; b. Wilmington, Del., Oct. 2, 1905; s. A. Felix and Mary (Chichester) duP.; grad. St. Paul's Sch., Concord, N.H., 1925; student Princeton, 1925-27, Army Advanced Flying Sch., Kelly Field, Tex., 1928; m. Eleanor Hoyt, 1931 (div. 1945); children—Katharine G., Eleaine L., Michael H.; m. 2d, Martha Truesdale, Aug. 2, 1947; 1 son, Christopher T. With E.I. DuPont de Nemours & Co., 1932-36, Fiduciary Council, Inc., 1937; self employed as investment exec., 1937—; v.p., dir. Christiana Securities, Inc. Trustee Episcopal Ch. Sch. Found. for St. Andrews Sch. Served as lt. col. USAAF, World War II. Mem. Welfare Council of Del. (dir.). Club: Wilmington Country. Office: DuPont Bldg Wilmington DE 19801

DU PONT, ALFRED RHETT, investment banker, broker; b. Wilmington, Del., Dec. 10, 1907; s. Francis Irenee and Marianna (Rhett) DuP.; grad. St. George's Sch., 1926, U. Pa., 1931; postgrad. Va. Law Sch., 1932-33; m. Gertrude Murrell, May 4, 1935 (div. 1962); children—Alfred Rhett, Thomas Murrell, Francis Irenee; m. 2d, Dea Johnston, June 1962; 1 adopted son, Peter James Kipp. Partner, Francis I. Du Pont & Co., 1934—. Mem. N.Y., Midwest stock exchanges, Chgo. Bd. Trade. Trustee U. Pa. Mem. Phi Kappa Sigma. Clubs: Luncheon, Union of N.Y. Home: 1013 Middle St Sullivan's Island SC 29482 Office: 1 Wall St New York City NY 10005

DUPONT, ALFRED VICTOR, former architect; b. Wilmington, Del., Mar. 17, 1900; s. Alfred Irénée and Bessie (Gardner) DuP.; student Lawrenceville Sch., 1914-18, Sheffield Sci. Sch., Yale, 1924; student Beaux Arts, 1928-30. With explosives dept. E.I. DuPont de Nemours & Co., Inc., 1922-28; mem. firm Masséna & DuPont, architects, 1930-70. Mem. Del. Bd. Archtl. Registration and Examiners, 1933-35. Served with USMC, 1918-19; to lt. USNR, 1942-44. Mem. A.I.A. (nat. com. on membership 1939-42, treas. Del. chpt. 1938, exec. com. 1938), Archtl. League N.Y., Soc. Beaux Arts Architects, C. of C. Del. Republican. Episcopalian. Clubs: Wilmington Country, Wilmington; Yale (N.Y.C.); Annapolis (Md.) Yacht; Corinthian Yacht (Phila.). Home: 2501 Lucille Dr Fort Lauderdale FL 33316 Office: 2816 NE 25th St Fort Lauderdale FL 33305 Died Mar. 24, 1970.

DUPONT, CLIFFORD WALTER, Rhodesian govt. ofcl.; b. London, Eng., Dec. 6, 1905; s. Alfred Walter and Winifred Mary Dupont; ed. Bishops Stortford Coll., Clare Coll., Cambridge U.; m. Armenell Mary Betty Bennet, 1963. Solicitor, London, 1929-39, 45-48; emigrated to Rhodesia, 1948; M.P., Fed. Assembly, 1958-62; mem. S. Rhodesian Parliament, 1962—; minister of justice, minister of law and order S. Rhodesia, 1962-64; minister without portfolio, 1964; dep. prime minister, minister external affairs, 1964-65; dep. prime minister and minister external affairs and def., 1965; apptd. head of state, officer administering the govt., 1965; apptd. acting pres. Rhodesia, 1970; pres. Republic of Rhodesia, 1970—. Recipient Independence decoration, 1970. Home: P O Box 2078 Salisbury Rhodesia Office: Government House Salisbury Rhodesia*

DUPONT, EDMOND, investment banker, broker; b. Wilmington, Del., Aug. 23, 1906; s. Francis Irenee and Marianna (Rhett) DuP.; student Princeton, 1925-28, Oxford U., 1928-30; m. Averell Adelaide Ross, Feb. 26, 1932; children—Anthony Averell, Edmond Rhett. Cadet engr. Panhandle Eastern Pipeline Co., 1930-32; partner Francis I. duPont & Co. since 1933; chmn. emeritus Du Pont, Glore Forgan; dir. Del. Fund. Inc., 1938-49; dir. United Funds, Inc., Kansas City, Mo., 1949-62; pres. Francis I, duPont & Co., S.A., 1937; dir. United Internat. Fund, Ltd., Bermuda, 1939-64, United Investors Life Ins. Co., 1962-64, Continental Am. Life Ins. Co., 1964, Winterthur Corp., 1950. Dir. Episcopal Ch. Found., 1950; trustee P.E. Diocese of Del., 1957, U. Del., 1964. Clubs: Connatquot River, Recess, Sky (N.Y.C.); Greenville Country (Wilmington); Wilmington Country; Chesapeake Bay Yacht (Easton, Md.); Brook. Home: 2106 Grant Avenue Wilmington DE 19806 Office: duPont Bldg Wilmington DE 19801 also 1 Wall St New York City NY 10005

DUPONT, ELEUTHERE IRENEE, financial mgmt. co. exec.; b. Phila., May 21, 1921; s. Francis V. and Katharine (Clark) duP.; grad. Hill Sch., 1939; B.A., Williams Coll., 1943; certificate Harvard Bus. Sch., 1947; m. Arminda R. Dunning, Aug. 9, 1947; children—Charles F., Eleuthera D., Sarah Kate. Asst. treas. Bank of Del., Wilmington, 1950-54; treas. Continental Am. Life Ins. Co., Wilmington, 1955-64; chmn. Deifi Am. Corp., Wilmington, 1964-67, chmn. bd., 1967—; pres. dir. Sigma Investment Shares Fund, 1967—, Sigma Capital Shares, Inc., 1967—; chmn. trustees Sigma Trust Shares, 1967—; sec., dir. Eleutherian Mills-Hagley Found., 1953—. Past pres. Del. Art Mus.; sec., trustee Stoneleigh-Burnham Sch., Mass., 1968—. Served with USAAF, 1943-45. Republican. Clubs: Wilmington, Wilmington Country (bd. dirs.), Vicmead Hunt (treas. 1956) (Wilmington); Union (N.Y.C.). Home: 1115 Brandon Lane Wilmington DE 19807 Office: 3801 Kennett Pike Wilmington DE 19807

DUPONT, FRANCIS IRENEE, II, mfg. co. exec.; b. Buffalo, July 23, 1926; s. Emile F. and Sarah (Townsend) duP.; grad. Kent Sch., 1944; B.A., Yale, 1950; m. Rosamond Saltonstal Lee, Oct. 7, 1950; children—Augustus I., Emile Francis II, Maria Sloan, Sophie Gay, Louis Rhett. With E. I. duPont de Nemours & Co., Inc., 1953-69; now with Delfi Am. Inc., Wilmington, Del.; dir. Sigma Investment Shares. Served with USNR, 1944-46, 1951-52. Home: RD 2 Hockessin DE Office: 3801 Kennett Pike Wilmington DE 19807

DUPONT, GERALD ERNEST, educator, clergyman; b. Providence, Jan. 25, 1913; s. Urgel Simeon and Marie Anne (Desailliers) D.; A.B. cum laude, St. Michael's Coll., 1935; M.A. in Philosophy, U. Toronto, 1943; Licentiate in Medieval Studies, Inst. Medieval Studies, Toronto,

1943; Ph.D. magna cum laude, U. Montreal, 1958; LL.D., U. Vt., 1969. Ordained priest Roman Cath. Ch., 1939; asst. prof. history, philosophy St. Michael's Coll., Winooski, Vt., 1943-46, acad. dean, 1946- 58, pres., 1958-69, prof. philosophy, 1969—. Mem. Nat. Cath. Ednl. Assn. (exec. com., sec. com. on membership 1959-68), Am., Cath. (past v.p.) hist. socs., N.E.A., Am. Cath. Philos. Assn., New Eng. Assn. Colls. and Secondary Schs., Delta Epsilon Sigma. Address: St Michael's Coll Winooski VT 05404

DUPONT, IRENEE, Jr., engr.; b. Wilmington, Del., Jan. 8, 1920; s. Iréneé and Irene Sophie (duPont) duP.; student Dartmouth, 1938-40; B.S. in Mech. Engring., Mass. Inst. Tech., 1943; m. Barbara Batchelder, Apr. 15, 1944; children—Irene, Iréneé 3d, Cynthia, Sally Carpenter, Grace. Engr., Ranger Aircraft Engines, div. Fairchild Engine & Airplane Corp., 1943-46; engr. E. I. duPont deNemours & Co., Arlington, N.J., 1946-48, supr., Parkersburg, W.Va., 1948-51, Charleston, W.Va., 1951-53, various office positions Wilmington, Del., 1953—, now v.p., mem. exec. com., dir.; dir. Wilmington Trust Co. Trustee Tower Hill Sch. Mem. Society Plastics Engrs., Soc. Automotive Engrs. Home: Box 38 Montchanin DE 19710 Office: E I duPont DeNemours & Co Wilmington DE 19801

DUPONT, PIERRE SAMUEL, former business exec.; b. Wilmington, Del., Jan. 1, 1911; s. Lammot and Natalie (Wilson) duP.; grad. Tower Hill Sch., 1928; student Phillips Exeter Acad., 1928-29; B.S., Mass. Inst. Tech., 1933; LL.D., Baker U., 1961; m. Jane Holcomb, June 24, 1933; children—Pierre Samuel, Jane de Doliete, Michele Wainwright. Engring. dept. E.I. du Pont de Nemours & Co., Inc., 1934-39, devel. dept., 1940- 41, indsl. sales mgr. sales dept. nylon div., 1942-45, asst. dir. trade analysis div., 1945-47, dir., 1948-51, asst. dir. sales, rubber chems. div., 1951-54, sec., 1954-63, mem. finance com., 1959-63, v.p., mem. exec. com., 1963-65; v.p., dir. Christiana Securities Co., 1952-65; dir. Wilmington Trust Co. Trustee Tower Hill Sch., 1944, pres., 1952—. Mem. Am. Chem. Soc. Clubs: Wilmington, Wilmington Country; University, N.Y. Yacht, Cruising of Am. (N.Y.C.). Home: Rockland DE 19732 Office: Wilmington DE 19801

DUPREE, ANDERSON HUNTER, historian, educator; b. Hillsboro, Tex., Jan. 29, 1921; s. George W. and Sarah (Hunter) D.; A.B. summa cum laude, Oberlin Coll., 1942; A.M., Harvard, 1947, Ph.D., 1952; m. Marguerite Louise Arnold, July 18, 1946; children—Marguerite Wright, Anderson Hunter. Asst. prof. Tex. Tech. Coll., 1950-52; research fellow Gray Herbarium, Harvard, 1952-54, 55-56; vis. asst. prof. U. Cal. at Berkeley, 1956-58, from asso. prof. to prof., 1958-68, asst. to chancellor, 1960-62; George L. Littlefield prof. Am. history Brown U., Providence, 1968—. Cons. com. sci. and pub. policy Nat. Acad. Sci., 1963-64; mem. history adv. com. NASA, 1963—, AEC, 1967—; mem. panel on sci. and tech. U.S. Ho. of Reps. Com. on Sci. and Astronautics; project dir. on grants NSF, 1953-55, 61-68. Served to lt. USNR, 1942-46. Fellow Center Advanced Study Behavioral Scis., 1967-68. Fellow A.A.A.S.; mem. Am. Acad. Arts and Scis., Am. Hist. Assn., History Sci. Soc., Soc. History Tech., Am. Studies Assn., Phi Beta Kappa. Conglist. Author: Science in the Federal Government, 1957; Asa Gray, 1959. Editor: Gray, Darwiniana, 1963; Science and the Emergence of Modern America, 1963. Home: 114 Morris Av Providence RI 02906

DUPREY, WILSON GILLILAND, librarian; b. Van Wert, O., June 21, 1924; s. Rei and Berneace (Gilliland) D.; student Ohio State U., 1942-44; B.A., George Washington U., 1946; M.S., Columbia, 1949. Reference asst. Stanford Library, 1949- 51, with rare book room, 1951-53; reference asst. prints div. N.Y. Pub. Library, 1953-66; curator map and print room N.Y. Hist. Soc., N.Y.C., 1966—. Mem. L.I., Van Wert County hist. socs., Met. Mus. Art, Walters Art Gallery (Balt.), Bklyn. Mus. Republican. Methodist. Picture researcher: Kunitz & Colby European Authors, 1300-1900, 1967; Ewen Great Composers, 1300-1900, 1966. Home: 48 Pierrepont St Brooklyn NY 11201 Office: 170 Central Park West New York City NY 10024

DUPUCH, ALFRED ETIENNE JEROME, newspaper editor, pub.; b. Nassau, Bahamas, Feb. 16, 1899; s. Leon Edward Hartman and Harriet (Saunders) D.; L.H.D., St. Johns U. (Minn.); LL.D., Coll Mt. St. Vincent, 1966; m. Marie Annie Plouse; children—Eileen (Mrs. Roger Carron), Etienne, Bernard, Joan, Bette (Mrs. James Hull), Pierre. Editor-pub. The Tribune daily newspaper, Nassau, 1919—; rep. for Bahamas A.P., 1919—. Rep. Bahamas Press, Coronation Elizabeth II, 1953. Mem. Fighter Plane Com., Price Control Com., both Bahamas; mem. council Bahamas Red Cross, mem. Bahamas council Boy Scouts; founder Santa Claus Com.; dep. chmn. Com. United World Colls.; founding chmn. Crippled Childrens Com. Mem. Bahamas Ho. of Assembly, 1925-42, 49-56, Legislative Council (name changed to Senate, 1964), 1960-68; hon. consul to Haiti; mem. Bahamas Constitution Drafting Delegation, London, 1963. Mem. public bd. dirs. for agr., marine products, electricity, water and sewerage, health, and others. Served with British Army, 1916-19. Created knight; decorated officer Order British Empire, knight comdr. Ancient Order St. Gregory the Great (Vatican); officer Order Touissaint L'Ouverture, chevalier Honor and Merit (both Haiti); recipient medal Royal Arts Soc. (London). Mem. Commonwealth Press Union, Inter-Am. Press Assn. (recipient anti-discrimination award), Am. Newspaper Pubs. Assn., Internat. Press Inst., Caribbean Press Assn. Roman Catholic. Rotarian. Clubs: East Hill (Nassau); East Indian, Sports (both London). Author: The Tribune Story. Home: Camperdown Heights POB N-207 Nassau Bahamas Office: POB N-207 Nassau Bahamas

DUPUIS, JOHN DEREMO, banker; b. Cin., Aug. 16, 1907; s. Charles William and Lillie (Deremo) D.; student Bowdoin Coll., 1925-29; M.B.A., Harvard, 1931; student Columbia, U. Pitts.; m. Eileen Nevin, Apr. 21, 1934; children—Jeanne Nevin, Charles Thomas. With credit dept. Irving Trust Co., N.Y.C., 1931- 36; with Benjamin D. Bartlett & Co., brokers, Cin., 1936-38; credit mgr. Peoples-Pitts. Trust Co. (now Pitts. Nat. Bank & Trust Co.), 1938-42, asst. v.p., 1942-43, v.p., 1944-52, v.p. charge loan div., 1952- 59; sr. v.p. Fifth-Third Union Trust Co., Cin., 1962—. Trustee Bethesda Hosp. and Deaconess Assn. Home: 309 Compton Hills Dr Cincinnati OH 45215. Office: Fifth-Third Bank Fifth Third Center Cincinnati OH 45202

DUPUIS, RAYMOND, lawyer, business exec.; b. Montreal, Can., Aug. 2, 1907; s. Albert (K.S.G.) and Henriette (Beullac) D.; student Mont-Saint-Louis Coll., Montreal, 1917-24; U. Montreal, 1927-30, LL.D., 1959; m. Helene Saint-Pierre, Apr. 24, 1937 (dec. 1961); children—Albert, Claire, Nicole; m. 2d, Francoise Deméziéres, 1962. Read law with Godin, Dussault & Cadotte, Montreal, 1927-30; called to Bar of Prov. of Que. 1930, created K.C., 1945; elected dir. Dupuis Freres, Ltd., department store mail order house, Montreal, 1933, asst. sec.-treas., 1937-42, sec., 1942, treas., 1943-45, 2d v.p., pres. president and managing dir., 1945-61; dir. The Royal Bank of Canada, Domtar Co. Ltd., Burns Foods, Ltd., The Canada Life Assurance Co., Globe Indemnity Co. of Canada, Hudson Bay Ins. Co., Cie d'Assurance du Quebec, Western Assurance Co., Brit. Am. Assurance Co., Canadian adv. bd. Royal Ins. Co., Ltd., Liverpool & London & Globe Ins. Co. Ltd. Mem. Sales Tax Com., 1955. Bd. of Research Traffic and Transportation Problem, City of Montreal. Past pres. District of Montreal C. of C. Canadian C. of C.; mem. Montreal Bd. of Trade, Dollar Steerling Trade Adv. Council (Canadian sect.), Centre d'Etudes du Commerce de Paris. Past pres., member exec. com. of Federation of Rench Catholic Charities; director Canadian Welfare Council; P.Q. Society for Crippled Children; gov. Soc. des Concerts Symphoniques de Montreal, The Canadian Mental Health Assn., Notre Dame and Ste Justine hosps. Mem. French C. of C. in Canada (past v.p.) Roman Catholic. Clubs: Laval-sur-le-Lac, St. Denis, Cercle Universitaire de Montreal, Montreal Badminton and Squash, also Mount Royal, Palestre Nationale, Mount Bruno Country, Montreal, Canadian. Home: 21 Messier St St Hilaire (Bouville) Quebec Canada Office: 612 St James St W Montreal Quebec Canada

DUPUIS, RENE, elec. engr.; b. Pike River, Que., Can., May 5, 1898; s. Philias and Ernestine (Poissant) D.; B.A., Laval U., 1919, D.Sc. (hon.), 1954; postgrad. McGill U., 1921; Elec. Engr., U. Nancy (France), 1924; m. Simone Giroux, Sept. 17, 1931; children—Marthe (Mrs. Pierre Durand), Yolande (Mrs. J.Y. Leblanc), Andree (Mrs. G. Bellefeuille), Suzanne, Jacques, Helene (Mrs. Martin Filion). Engr. Shawinigan Water & Power Co., Montreal Que., 1928-42; founder, lst dir., prof. Laval U., Sch. Elec. Engring., 1942-47; supt. engr. Beauharnois Light, Heat & Power Co., 1947-48, v.p., 1948-61; commr. Que. Hydro-Electric Commn., 1948-61; mem. Internat. Joint Commn., Ottawa- Washington, 1962-69, tech. adviser. Bd. dirs. Ste. Jeanne d'Arc Hosp., Montreal. Recipient Laval Alumni Assn. medal, 1956. Decorated Palmes Academiques (France). Registered profl. engr., Que. Fellow I.E.E.E. (v.p. 1959-61), McGill Grad. Soc., Engring. Inst. Can., Internat. Assn. Hydraulic Engineers. Author: De l'anglais au francais en electrotechnique, 4th edit., 1939. Contbr. articles to profl. jours. Home: 4043 av Vendome Montreal Quebec Canada

DUPUIS, ROBERT NEWELL, chemist, exec.; b. Indpls., June 4, 1910; s. Arthur J. and Veronica (Cox) DuP.; A.B., U. Ill., 1931; Ph.D. in Organic Chemistry, N.Y. U., 1934; m. Eleanor Thomsen, June 29, 1935; children—Robert Thomsen, Eleanor Joan. Research chemist Miner Labs., Chgo., 1935-45, asst. dir., 1945-47; research and devel. mgr. S.C. Johnson & Son, Inc., 1947- 52; dir. research and devel. Philip Morris, Inc., Richmond, Va., 1952-55, v.p. research, 1955-60, dir., 1957-63; v.p. tech. Gen. Foods Corp., 1960-67; mgmt. cons., 1968—. Mem. Am. Chem. Soc., Soc. Am. Archivists, T.A.P.P.I., Phi Beta Kappa, Sigma Xi, Alpha Chi Sigma. Clubs: Chemists' (Chgo., N.Y.C.). Editor: Research Management, 1967-70. Contbr. to patent lit., sci. publs. Home: 3902 Exeter Rd Richmond VA 23221 Office: Va Hist Soc Box 7311 Richmond VA 23221

DUPUY, FRANK RUSSELL, Jr., mag. pub.; b. San Antonio, Jan. 20, 1907; s. Frank Russell and Sarah (Tankersley) D.; student Washington and Lee U., 1924-25; m. Nancy Jane McGinley, Oct. 24, 1954; children—Sarah Anne, Frank Russell III. Advt. rep. Los Angeles Examiner, 1930-41; asst. to pub. Good Housekeeping mag., 1946-59; advt. dir. Popular Mechanics, 1960-62; v.p., pub. Cosmopolitan mag., N.Y.C., 1962—. Served with AUS, 1942-46. Home: 45 E 72d St New York City NY 10021 Office: 959 8th Av New York City NY 10019

DUPUY, HOWARD MOORE, Jr., lawyer; b. Portland, Ore., Mar. 15, 1929; s. Howard Moore and Lola (Dunham) D.; B.A., U. Portland, 1951; postgrad. Willamette U., Salem, Ore., 1951; LL.B., Lewis and Clark Coll., 1956; m. Anne Irene Hanna, Aug. 26, 1950; children-Loanne Kay, Brent Moore. Admitted to Ore. bar, 1956, since practiced in Portland; asso. Green, Richardson, Green & Griswold, 1956; partner Morton & Dupuy, 1957-67; partner Phillips, Coughlin, Buell, Stoloff & Black and predecessor firm, 1968—. Mem. finance com. Ore. Republican Central Com., 1962. Served with AUS, 1946-47. Mem. Am., Ore., Multnomah County bar assns., Am. Arbitration Assn. (nat. panel arbitrators), Portland C. of C. Clubs: Gyro, Aero of Oregon (Portland). Home: 16116 NE Stanton St Portland OR 97230 Office: 621 SW Alder St Portland OR 97205

DUPUY, RICHARD ERNEST, former army officer, author: b. N.Y.C., Mar. 24, 1887; s. Georges Marie and Katharine Pauline (Chute) D.; grad. Augustinian Acad., S.I., N.Y., 1905, Field Atty. Sch., 1924, Command and Gen. Staff Sch., 1933; m. Laura Elizabeth Nevitt, June 1, 1915; 1 son, Trevor Nevitt. Reporter, spl. writer Evening Telegram, N.Y. Herald, N.Y.C., 1909-17. Mem. N.Y. N.G., 1909-17; entered fed. service as lst lt. C.A., 1917; served with A.E.F. as capt. 57th Arty., C.A.C., U.S. Army, comdg. Hdqrs. Co., adj., operations officer; capt. C.A.C., 1920; maj. F.A., 1935; lt. col., 1940, col., 1941; U.S. Mil. Acad., 1938-41; chief, news div. War Dept., Bur. Pub. Relations, 1941- 43; pub. relations officer Supreme Hdqrs., Europe, 1943-45; acting dir. War Dept. Bur. Pub. Relations, 1945; ret., 1946; bd. govs. Hist. Evaluation and Research Orgn., 1962—; gen. editor Mil. History of U.S., Hawthorn Books, Inc., 1963—. Decorated Legion of Merit with oak leaf cluster; Order Brit. Empire (Britain); Croix de Guerre with palm, Commemoratif, Verdun (France). Mem. West Point Soc. N.Y., Acad. Polit. Sci., Am. Mil. History Found., Assn. AUS, Armed Forces Pub. Relations Assn., Fellowship U.S. Brit. Comrades, Soc. First Div., U.S. Naval Inst. (asso.) Roman Catholic. Clubs: Army and Navy, Cosmos, National Press (Washington); Military-Naval (N.Y.C.). Author: With the Fifty-Seventh in France, 1929; (with G.F. Eliot) If War Comes, 1937; World in Arms, 1939; Perish by the Sword, 1939; Where They Have Trod, 1940; (with Hodding Carter) Civilian Defense of the U.S., 1942; (with T.N. Dupuy), To the Colors 1942; Lion in the Way, 1948; Men of West Point, 1952; Compact History of the United States Army, 1956. Co-author: Contemporary World Politics (a symposium), 1939; Contemporary Europe, 1941; (with T.N. Dupuy) Military Heritage of America, 1954, Brave Men and Great Captains, 1959, Compact History of the Civil War (Fletcher Pratt Meml. award Civil War Round Table N.Y.), 1960, Compact History of the Revolutionary War, 1963; Compact History of World War II, 1965; (with T.N. Dupuy) Encyclopedia of Military History, 1970; Five Days to War, 1967; (with W.H. Baumer) Little Wars of the United States, 1968; Compact History of the National Guard, 1971. Compiled Govs. Island, 1637-1937. Asso. editor Army, Navy, Air Force Register, 1957-62. Contbr. articles to Am. periodicals, mil. jours., fiction to popular mags. Address: 2558 N Lexington St Arlington VA 22207

DUPUY, TREVOR NEVITT, historian, research exec.; b. S.I., N.Y., May 3, 1916; s. Richard Ernest and Laura (Nevitt) D.; student St. Peter's Coll., 1933-34; B.S., U.S. Mil. Acad., 1938; grad. Joint Services Staff Coll., Latimer, Eng., 1948-49; student Harvard Grad. Sch. Pub. Adminstrn., 1953- 54; m. Jonna Slók Bjerggaard, Oct. 16, 1968; children by previous marriage—Trevor Nevitt, Richard Ernest II, George McVicar, Laura Nevitt, Charles Geissbuhler, Mirande Elisabeth, Arnold Geissbuhler, Fielding Davis. Commn. 2d lt., U.S. Army, 1938, advanced through grades to col., 1953; prof. mil. sci. and tactics Harvard, 1952-56, mem. original faculty Def. Studies program, 1954-56; dir. mil. history program Ohio State U., 1956, 57; ret., 1958; vis. prof. internat. relations program Rangoon (Burma) U., 1959-60; mem. internat. studies div. Inst. Def. Analyses, 1960-62; pres., exec. dir., bd. dirs. Hist. Evaluation and Research Orgn., 1962—. Trustee Coll. Potomac. Decorated Legion of Merit, Bronze Star with combat V, Air medal; Brit. Distinguished Service Order; Chinese Nat. Govt. Cloud and Banner (2 grades). Mem. Am. Hist. Assn., Am. Mil. Inst. (pres. 1958-59), Assn. U.S. Army, Inst. Strategic Studies, U.S. Naval Inst. Clubs: Army-Navy, Cosmos (Washington). Author: (with R.E. Dupuy) To The Colors, 1942; Faithful and True, 1949; (with R.E. Dupuy) Military Heritage of America, 1956; Campaigns of the French Revolution and of Napoleon, 1956; (with R.E. Dupuy) Brave Men and Great Captains, 1960; (with R.E. Dupuy) Compact History of the Civil War (Fletcher Pratt award 1960), 1960; Civil War Land Battles, 1960; Civil War Naval Actions, 1961; Military History of World War II, 19 vols., 1962-65; (with R.E. Dupuy) Compact History of the Revolutionary War, 1963; Military History of World War I, 12 vols., 1967; The Battle of Austerlitz, 1968; Modern Libraries for Modern Colleges: Research Strategies for Design and Development, 1968; Ferment in College Libraries: The Impact of Information Technology, 1968; Military History of the Chinese Civil War, 1969: (with R.E. Dupuy) An Encyclopedia of Military History, 1970; Military Lives, 12, vols., 1969; (with Grace P. Hayes) Revolutionary War Naval Battles, 1970; (with Gay M. Hammerman) Revolutionary War Land Battles, 1970. Editor, contbr. Holidays, 1965; Almanac of World Military Power, 1970. Home: 8116 N Park St Dunn Loring VA 22027

DUPY, JOHN D., constrn. co. exec.; b. Tonkawa, Okla., June 24, 1926; s. John and Stella (Back) D.; B.S. in Gen. Engring., U. Okla., 1946; M.B.A., Harvard, 1955; m. Mary Ann Windell, Dec. 20, 1952; 1 dau., Mary Cynthia. Engr. Gulf Oil Corp., Port Arthur, Tex., 1948-49, profl. engr., 1952-53; engr. Venezuela Gulf Refining Co., Puerto La Cruz, 1949-50; prodn. engr. Continental Oil Co., Harvey, La., 1955-57; asst. mgr. Plastic Applicators, Inc., Harvey, 1957; div. adminstrv. engr. J. Ray McDermott & Co., Inc., Morgan City, La., 1957-60, corp. sec., New Orleans, 1960—. Served with USNR, 1944-47,50-52. Mem. New Orleans C. of C., Harvard Bus. Sch. Alumni Assn. (area chmn. 1968-71). Episcopalian (vestryman 1965-67). Rotarian. Clubs: New Orleans Petroleum, Metairie Country. Home: 5575 Belaire Dr New Orleans LA 70124 Office: PO Box 60035 New Orleans LA 70160

DUQUET, JOHN EDWARD LEWIS, lawyer; b. Richmond, Que., Can., June 22, 1904; s. William James and Mary Ellen (Hayes) D.; B.A. magna cum laude, U. Montreal, 1926, LL.L. magna cum laude, 1929; LL.D., U. Sherbrooke, 1960; m. Aileen Caron, June 20, 1936; children—Dawn, Joan. Admitted to Que. bar, 1929; practiced law, 1929—; apptd. King's counsel, 1947; sr. partner Duquet, MacKay, Weldon, Bronstetter, Willis & Johnston, Montreal, Can., 1941—; v.p., dir., gen. counsel Canadair, Ltd., Asbestos Corp., Ltd., Can. W.I. Molasses Co., Ltd.; dir. Chromium Mining & Smelting Corp., Ltd., Prudential Ins. Co. Am., Royal Bank of Can., Domtar, Limited, St. Lawrence Corp., Ltd., Fraser Cos., Ltd., MLW Worthington Ltd., Champlain Oil Products, Ltd., Gillette of Can., Ltd., Claude Neon Advertising, Ltd., Liquid Carbonic Canadian Corp., Ltd., Timmins Investments Ltd., Chromasco Corp. Ltd. Mem. Montreal Bd. Trade. Life gov. Montreal Children's, Montreal Gen., St. Mary's hosps. Decorated Order St. Gregory the Great. Clubs: Mt. Royal, St. James, Engineers, Canadian (Montreal); Laval-Sur-le-Lac (Que.); Laurentian Golf and Country (Ste. Agathe, Que.); Rideau (Ottawa); Mt. Bruno (Que.); Canadian (N.Y.C.). Home: 99 Gordon Crescent Westmount 217 Quebec Canada Office: Royal Bank of Can Bldg Place Ville Marie Montreal 113 Quebec Canada

DUR, PHILIP FRANCIS, educator; b. St. Louis, June 30, 1914; s. Alphonse and Sarah (Ralston) D.; A.B., Harvard, 1935, Ph.D., 1941; postgrad. Fgn. Service Inst., 1961; m. Elena Delgado, June 30, 1942; children—Elena (Mrs. Philip A. Morris), Philip, Stansbury, Carmen (Mrs. Norman B. Conley, Jr.), Jacqueline, John. Consul, pub. affairs officer, Lyon, France, 1948-51; chief Office Pub. Affairs, Office U. S. High Commr. for Germany, Bonn, 1951-52; consul, exec. officer, Bremen, Germany, 1952-53; comml. controls officer Mil. Security Bd., Coblenz, Germany, 1953-54; consul Colon, Panama, 1954-55, Yokohama, Japan, 1955-58; pub. affairs adviser Dept. State, 1958-61; consul, Negoya, Japan, 1961-65; Jefferson Caffery prof. polit. sci. U. Southwestern La., Lafayette, 1965—, faculty senate, 1969—. Adviser, Council for Devel. of French in La., 1968—; mem. U. Southwestern La. Found., 1969—; pres. France- Amerique de la Louisiane Acadienne, 1970—. Served to lt. comdr. USNR, 1942-46. Mem. Am. Fgn. Service Assn., Am. Polit. Sci. Assn., Internat. Studies Assn., Soc. for French Hist. Studies, Phi Beta Kappa. Home: 517 Woodvale Av Lafayette LA 70501

DURAM, ARTHUR E. advt. exec.; b. Chgo., Sept. 20, 1912; s. Arthur E. and Alice L. (Hunt) D.; B.S., U. Ill., 1933; m. Marjorie Barnett, Dec. 19, 1947; 1 son, Michael B. Dr. TV sales CBS-TV Network, 1946-52; with Fuller & Smith & Ross, Inc., 1952—, sr. v.p., mgr. N.Y. office, 1965-66, pres., chmn. exec. com., 1966—. Served to maj. USAAF, World War II. Home: Trinity Pass Pound Ridge NJ 10576 Office: 666 Fifth Av New York City NY 10019

DURAN, SERVET AHMET, engring, educator; b. Kutahya, Turkey, Jan. 2, 1920; s. H. Muammer and Asiye (Rifat) D.; came to U.S., 1939, naturalized, 1959; B.S., Mo. Sch. Mines and Metallurgy, 1943; A.M., Stanford, 1945, Engr. Phys. Metallurgy, 1946, Ph.D., 1963; m. Martha Tucker, May 4, 1946; children—Meliha Sue, Frederick Rifat, Michael Halis. Teaching asst. Stanford, 1946, vis. asso. prof. materials sci., 1956-58; instr. Wash. State U., Pullman, 1947-49, asst. prof. metallurgy, 1949-53, asso. prof., 1953-61, prof., 1961—, chmn. metallurgy dept., 1959-70, head metals research sect., 1960-66; research metallurgist Kaiser Aluminum & Chem. Corp., 1954; cons. Middle East Tech. U., Ankara, Turkey, 1969. Bd. dirs. Pullman Concert Assn. Mem. Metall. Soc. of Am. Inst. Mining, Metall. and Petroleum Engrs., Soc. for Metals (chmn. Inland Empire chpt. 1953), Am. Soc. Engring. Edn. (chmn. materials div. 1965-66), Sigma Xi, Sigma Tau, Alpha Sigma Mu. Contbr. articles profl. jours. Home: 314 Derby St Pullman WA 99163

DURAND, DAVID, educator, statistician; b. Ithaca, N.Y., Oct. 6, 1912; s. Albert Cyrus and Ruth (Sawyer) D.; A.B., Cornell U., 1934; A.M., Columbia, 1938, Ph.D., 1941; m. Edith Elbogen, Aug. 7, 1954; 1 dau., Marie. With Nat. Bur. Econ. Research, N.Y.C., 1939-40, 46-49, 50-56, mem. research staff, 1950-56; research asso. Mass. Inst. Tech., 1954-55, faculty, 1955- -, prof. mgmt., 1958—. Mem. Inst. Advanced Study, Princeton, 1941; cons. Twentieth Century Fund, 1947-50. Served with USNR, 1942-46. Mem. Am. Econ. Assn., Am. Finance Assn., Am. Soc. Quality Control, Am. Statis. Assn., Biometric Soc., Inst. Math. Statistics, Internat. Assn. Statistics Phys. Scis. Author: Risk Elements in Consumer Installment Financing, 1941; (with L.A. Jones) Mortage Lending Experience in Agriculture, 1954; Stable Chaos: An Introduction to Statistical Control, 1971. Home: 212 Follen Rd Lexington MA 02173 Office: Sloan Sch Mgmt Mass Inst Tech Cambridge MA 02139

DURAND, GEORGE FRANCIS, paper co. exec.; b. London, Ont., Can., 1904; grad. U. Mich., 1926. Dir. Port Huron Sulphite & Paper Co. (Mich.). Home: 2990 Military St Port Huron MI 48060 Office: Port Huron Sulphite & Paper Co P O Box 289 Port Huron MI 48060*

DURAND, HARRISON FISHER, lawyer; b. Yankton, S.D., Dec. 24, 1903; s. George Harrison and Lillian (Fisher) D.; B.A., Yankton Coll., 1926; LL.B., George Washington U., 1928; m. Anne Sawyer, Dec. 21, 1931; children—James Harrison, Murray Sawyer (dec. 1968). Admitted to N.Y. bar, 1929, N.J. bar, 1936; partner Durand, Twombly & Imbriaco, and predecessors, Newark, 1936—, Putney, Twombly, Hall & Hirson, N.Y.C., 1967—; occasional lectr. Practising Law Inst., N.Y.C., 1961—, Inst. Continuing Legal Edn., N.J., 1958-
Trustee Yankton Coll., 1958—. Mem. Am. (chmn. sect. real

property, probate and trust law 1964-65; mem. ho. of dels. 1966- 67), N.Y. State (chmn. com. coop, N.J. Bar Assn. 1960-64), N.J., Essex County (pres. 1969-70) bar assns., Assn. Bar City N.Y., Am. Law Inst. (adv. com. fed. estate and gift tax project), Order of Coif, Phi Delta Phi, Sigma Alpha Epsilon. Clubs: Short Hills (N.J.) Baltusrol (N.J.) Golf: University (N.Y.C.); Essex (Newark). Contbr. articles to profl. jours., chpts. books. Home: 60 Woodcrest Av Short Hills NJ 07078 Office: 250 Park Av New York City NY 10117 also 744 Broad St Newark NJ 07102

DURAND, JOHN DONALD, lawyer; b. Cin., Aug. 16, 1911; s. Otto Ralph and Elsie (Baschang) D.; A.B. cum Laude (War Meml. scholar), Princeton, 1933; LL.B., U. Cin., 1936; m. Mary Elizabeth Liggett, Aug. 26, 1936; children—Nancy Liggett, Julie Rogers. Asso. editor Cin. Law Rev.; staff legal dept. Union Central Life Ins. Co., Cin., 1936-37; spl. atty. Office Gen. Counsel, U.S. Treasury Dept., 1937-38; spl. atty., reorgn. sec. Office Chief Counsel, Bur. Internal Revenue, 1938, staff asst. to survey and decentralize bur. functions, 1938-39, spl. atty. interpretative div. Office Chief Counsel, 1938-42, trial atty. appeals div., 1942-44; atty. Air Transport Assn. Am., 1944-52, asst. gen. counsel, sec., 1952-61, also counsel Airline Finance and Accounting Conf., Airlines Clearing House, Inc.; exec. dir., Com. Am. S.S. Lines, 1961-63; asst. dir. procurement and finance Aerospace Industries Assn., 1963-64; gen. counsel Assn. Oil Pipelines, 1964—. Rep. air transport industry various internat. Confs., Mem. Order of Coif, Phi Delta Phi. Clubs: Pipe Liners, University (Washington); Kenwood Country (Bethesda, Md.); Princeton (N.Y.C.). Home: 5910 Harwick Rd Woodacres MD also PO Washington 20016 Office: 1725 K St NW Washington DC 20006

DURAND, LOYAL, III, educator, physicist; b. Madison, Wis., May 19, 1931; s. Loyal and Dorothy (Lee) D.; B.S., Yale, 1953, M.S., 1954, Ph.D., 1957; m. Wesley Ann Travis, Dec. 22, 1954 (div.); children—Travis Loyal, Timothy Bartlett, Christopher Alan; m. 2d, Bernice Black, Oct. 18, 1970. Mem. Inst. Advanced Study, Princeton, 1957- 59; research physicist Brookhaven Nat. Lab., 1959-61; asst. prof. physics Yale, 1961-65; prof. physics U. Wis., Madison, 1965—, chmn. dept., 1969-71. Vis. prof. U. Colo., summer 1960; mem. policy adv. com. Nat. Accelerator Lab., 1969-71; chmn. exec. com. Aspen Center for physics, 1968—. Trustee Aspen (Colo.) Center Physics. Mem. Am. Phys. Soc., A.A.A.S., Sigma Xi. Contbr. articles to profl. jours. Spl. research theory elementary particles, high energy physics. Home: 4817 Sheboygan Av Madison WI 53705

DURAND, LOYAL, Jr., former educator; b. Milw., July 12, 1902; s. Loyal and Lucia Relf (Kemper) D.; A.B., U. Wis., 1924, A.M., 1925, Ph.D., 1930; m. Dorothy Lillian Lee, Dec. 25, 1929; children-Loyal, Philip, Lee Mcv., Kemper B. Asst., Wis. Geol. Survey, summer 1926; instr. U. Wis., 1928-30, asst. prof., 1930-44; faculty U. Tenn., 1944—, prof. geography, 1946-70. Vis. summer prof. Mankato (Minn.) Tchrs. Coll., 1929, Pa. State Coll., 1938,40,53, U. Utah, 1943, U. Wis., 1945, U. Colo., 1946, U. Cal. at Los Angeles, 1947, U. Neb., 1948,52, Central Coll. Edn., Ellensburg, Wash., 1950,60, U. Wash., 1954, U. Ore., 1956, U. Mich., 1957,61,66, U. Hawaii, 1957-58, U. Mont., 1959, U. Minn., 1962; land planning cons. Nat. Resources Bd., 1934-35, spl. land planning cons., 1941; research and analysis div. O.S.S., Washington, 1944. Mem. Nat. Acad. Scis. (nat. research council com., adv. to Office Naval Research 1951-54), Am. Assn. U. Profs., Assn. Am. Geographers (v.p. 1951), Nat. Council Geography Tchrs. (exec. bd. 1947—, v.p. 1949, pres. 1950), Wis. Acad. Scis., Arts and Letters (sec.- treas., editor 1935-44), Tenn. Acad. Sci., Phi Beta Kappa Assos., Phi Beta Kappa, Sigma Xi, Sigma Chi. Episcopalian. Author books including: World Economic Geography (with George T. Renner, C. Langdon White), 1951; World Geography, 1954; World Geography Today, 1960; Economic Geography, 1961. Geography editor: Macmillan social studies series; contbg. editor Economic Geography, 1947—. Contbr. articles to geog. mags. Home: 3940 Wilani Rd Knoxville TN 37919 Died Oct. 14, 1970

DURANT, ARIEL, writer; b. Russia, May 10, 1898; d. Joseph and Ethel (Appel) Kaufman; came to U.S., 1900, naturalized, 1913; student Columbia; LL.D., L.I. (N.Y.) U., 1968, Litt.D., 1968; L.H.D., Akron U., 1969; Ripon Coll., 1970; m. Will Durant, Oct. 31, 1913; 1 dau., Ethel Benvenuta. Collaborator with husband on books, 1957—; publs. include The Age of Reason Begins, 1961; The Age of Louis XIV, 1963; The Age of Voltaire, 1965; Rosseau and Revolution, 1967 (Pulitzer prize 1968); The Lessons of History, 1968; Interpretations of Life, 1970. Recipient Huntington Hartford Found. award creative writing, 1963; named Woman of Year in Lit., Los Angeles Times, 1965. Address: 5608 Briarcliff Rd Los Angeles CA 90028

DURANT, FREDERICK CLARK, III, museum exec., b. Ardmore, Pa., Dec. 31, 1916; s. Frederick Clark, Jr. and Cornelia Allen (Howel) D.; B.S. in Chem. Engring., Lehigh U., 1939; postgrad. Phila. Mus. Sch. Indsl. Arts, 1946-47; m. Carolyn Griscom Jones, Oct. 4, 1947; children—Carolyn M., William C., Stephen H. Engr., E.I. duPont de Nemours & Co., Inc., 1939-41; rocket engr. Bell Aircraft Corp., 1947-48; dir. engring. Naval Air Rocket Test Sta., 1948-51; cons., Washington, 1952-53; mem. sr. staff Arthur D. Little, Inc., 1954- 57; dir. Maynard Ordnance Test Sta., 1954-55; exec. asst. to dir. Avco-Everett Research Lab., 1957-59; dir. pub. and govt. relations, research and advanced devel. div. Avco Corp., Wilmington, Mass., 1959- 61; sr. rep. Bell Aerosystems Co., Washington, 1961-64; asst. dir. astronautics Nat. Air and Space Mus., Smithsonian Instn., Wash., 1964- -. participant ann. congresses Internat. Astronautical Fedn., 1951—, pres., 1953-56; mem. organizing com. Project Orbiter, 1954. Served to comdr. AC, USNR, 1941-46,48-52. Registered profl. engr., D.C., Mass. Recipient spl. medal L'Assn. Pour l'Encouragement de l'Aeronautique et de l'Astronautique, 1963. Fellow Am. Astronautical Soc. (chmn. awards com. 1961), Am. Inst. Aeros. and Astronautics, Am. Rocket Soc. (pres. 1953); mem. Internat. Acad. Astronautics, Nat. Space Club (gov. 1961); hon. fellow or mem. numerous fgn. rocket and space flight socs. Contbg. editor Missiles and Rockets, 1956-58. Clubs: Cosmos; Sherwood Forest. Contbr. to Ency. Brit., Ency. Americana; contbr. (space terms) Am. Heritage Dictionary. Home: 109 Grafton St Chevy Chase MD 20015 Office: Nat Air and Space Mus Smithsonian Instn Washington DC 20560

DURANT, JOHN, writer; b. Waterbury, Conn., Jan. 10, 1902; s. Harold R. and Mary (Walker) D.; A.B., Yale, 1925; m. Alice Rand, Aug. 6, 1942. Reporter N.Y. Times, 1927-28; mem. N.Y. Stock Exchange, 1929-44; free lance writer, contbr. nat. mags., 1936—. Served as lt. USNR, 1942-44. Mem. Outdoor Writers Assn. Am., Soc. Am. Travel Writers, Salt Water Fly Rodders Am. Republican. Presbyn. Clubs: Racquet and Tennis (N.Y.C.); Yale (N.Y.); Naples (Fla.) Yacht. Author: Come Out Fighting, 1946; The Story of Baseball, 1947; The Dodgers, 1948; The Yankees, 1949; Predictions, 1956; (with Otto Bettman) Pictorial History of American Sports, 1952; (with Alice R. Durant) Pictorial History of American Ships, 1953; Pictorial History of American Presidents, 1955; Pictorial History of the American Circus, 1957; The Heavyweight Champions, 1960; Highlights of the Olympics, 1961; Highlights of the World Series, 1963; The Sports of Our Presidents, 1964; (with Les Etter) Highlights of College Football, 1970. Editor: Yesterday in Sports, 1956. Home: 1851 Gulf Shore Blvd N Naples FL 33940

DURANT, THOMAS MORTON, educator, physician; b. Evanston, Ill., Nov. 19, 1905; s. Harry S. and Ida Ridgway (Hair) D.; B.S., U. Mich., 1928, M.D., 1930; Sc.D., Franklin and Marshall Coll., 1964; m. Jean Margaret deVries, June 25, 1929; children—John Ridgway, Carol Christine, Catherine Elizabeth. Intern U. Mich. Hosp., 1930-32; instr. internal medicine U. Mich., 1932-35; asso. physician Desert Sanatorium So. Ariz., Tuscon, 1935-36; asst. prof. Med. Sch. Temple U., 1936-38, asso. prof., 1938-46, prof. clin. medicine, 1946-56, prof., head dept. medicine, 1956-66, prof., 1966—. Ventnor Found. lectr. Weisbaden, Germany, 1956; vis. physician Phila. Gen. Hosp., 1947—; cons. cardiology U.S. Vets. Hosp., Phila.; cons. U.S. Naval Hosp., Phila., USAF. Mem. bd. examiners Am. Bd. Internal Medicine, chmn. bd., 1957-59; chmn. drug research bd. NRC. Recipient Strittmater award, Phila., 1964; Distinguished Alumnus award U. Mich. Med. Sch., 1970. Fellow A.C.P. (master 1970; gen. chmn. ann. meeting 1955, pres. 1964-65), Am. Coll. Cardiology; mem. Assn. Am. Physicians, A.M.A., Am. Heart Assn. (dir.), Phila. County Med. Soc. (dir.), Coll. Physicians Phila. (pres.), Am. Fedn. Clin. Research (pres. 1945), Am. Clin. and Climatol. Assn., Sigma Xi, Alpha Omega Alpha, Alpha Kappa Kappa, Beta Theta Pi. Clubs: Merion Golf, Racquet, Interurban Clinical. Mem. editorial bd. Am. Heart Jour.; asso. editor Am. Jour. Med. Scis. Home: 1242 Lafayette Rd Gladwynne PA 19035 Office: Einstein Med Center York and Tabor Rds Philadelphia PA 19141

DURANT, WILLIAM JAMES, author; b. North Adams, Mass., Nov. 5, 1885; s. Joseph and Marie (Allors) D.; B.A., St. Peter's Coll., Jersey City, 1907, M.A., 1908; Ph.D., Columbia, 1917; m. Ariel Kaufman, Oct. 31, 1913; children—Ethel Benvenuta, Louis R. Prof. Latin and French, Seton Hall Coll., South Orange, N.J., 1907-11; dir. Labor Temple Sch., N.Y.C., 1914-27; instr. philosophy Columbia, 1917; prof. philosophy U. Cal., Los Angeles, 1935. Recipient Huntington Hartford Found. award creative writing. Mem. Nat. Inst. Arts and Letters. Author: Philosophy and the Social Problem, 1917; The Story of Philosophy, 1926; Transition, 1927; The Mansions of Philosophy, 1929; The Case for India, 1930; Adventures in Genius, 1931; A Program for America, 1931; On the Meaning of Life, 1932; The Tragedy of Russia, 1933; The Story of Civilization: Part I, Our Oriental Heritage, 1935; Part II, The Life of Greece, 1939; Part III, Caesar and Christ, 1944; Part IV, The Age of Faith, 1950; Part V, The Renaissance, 1953; Part VI, The Reformation, 1957; (with Ariel Durant) Part VII, The Age of Reason Begins, 1961; The Age of Louis XIV, 1963, The Age of Voltaire, 1965, Rousseau and Revolution, 1967 (Pulitzer prize 1968); The Lesson of History, 1968, Interpretations of Life, 1970. Address: 5608 Briarcliff Rd Los Angeles CA 90028

DURANTE, JIMMY, (James Francis), comedian; b. N.Y. City, Feb. 10, 1893; s. Barthelmeo and Rosa Durante; ed. schs. of N.Y. City; m. Jeanne Olsen, 1916 (dec. 1943); m. 2d, Marjorie Little, Dec. 1960; 1 dau., CeCe Alicia. First worked in father's barbershop; piano player, Coney Island, at age of 17 years; organized 5 piece band, 1916; opened Club Durante with Eddie Jackson and Lou Clayton as partners (Lou Clayton is credited with coining the famous nickname, Schnozzola); the partners later formed comedy team, Clayton, Jackson and Durante, playing in night clubs, 1930; made Broadway debut at Loew's State Theatre, 1927, in Show Girl (Ziegfeld), 1928, The New Yorkers (Cole Porter), 1930; appeared in Hollywood pictures: Get Rich Quick Wallingford; The Cuban; Her Cardboard Lover; The Passionate Plumber; and others; returned to N.Y. City and starred with Ethel Merman in Strike Me Pink, 1934; motion pictures also include: Student Tour; George White's Scandals; Land Without Music; Carnival; Start Cherring; Sally, Irene and Mary; Music For Millions; On an Island with You; appeared at Paladium, London, 1936; in Broadway musicals: Jumbo, 1936; Red, Hot and Blue, 1937; entertainer at Copacabana, N.Y. City night club, 1943; began on radio and had own show to 1950, when entered TV Nov. 1950; TV shows include: All Star Revue, 1951, Colgate Comedy Hour, Texaco Star Theater, Club Oasis, others; TV spl. Jimmy Durante Meets the Seven Lively Arts, 1965; alt. guest-host The Hollywood Palace. Received Peabody award for radio-television performance, 1951. Home: 511 N Beverly Dr Beverly Hills CA 90210

DURBIN, HOWARD BORDER, chem. mfg. co. exec.; b. Evansville, Ind., Dec. 25, 1916; s. William Howard and Dorothy (Bausch) D.; A.B., U. Chgo., 1938; M.B.A., Harvard, 1940; m. Hersilia Warren, Aug. 31, 1943; 1 dau., Nathalie (Mrs. Robert Pratley). With Comml. Solvents Corp., N.Y.C., 1940—, sec., 1962—, treas., 1967-70. Served to lt. USNR, 1942-46, 51-53, lt. comdr. Res. Home: 22 Widgeon Way Greenwich CT 06830 Office: 245 Park Av New York City NY 10017

DURBIN, JAMES HAROLD, corp. exec.; b. Sharon, Pa., Mar. 17, 1898; s. Alfred and Mary (Dougherty) D.; LL.B., Georgetown U., Washington, 1920; m. Helen Frances Cleveland, Oct. 28, 1922; children—James Harold, Hugh Cleveland. Stenographer, Petroleum Iron Works Co., Sharon, 1914-17; clk. to sec. of war, Washington, 1917-20; admitted to D.C. bar, 1920; sec.,treas. Petroleum Supply Co., N.Y.C., 1920-23; treas. Am. Republics Corp., producer crude petroleum, 1923-26, v.p., exec. v.p., dir., 1926- 55; v.p., dir. Barber Oil Corp., 1955-56, pres., 1956-66; pres., dir. Burmah Oil Inc., N.Y.C., 1968—; chmn., dir. Edwin Cooper Inc., 1969—. Served with U.S. Army, 1918. Mem. Am. Bar Assn., Phi Alpha Delta. Roman Catholic. Clubs: Houston Country, Tejas (Houston); Sleepy Hollow Country (Scarborough on Hudson, N.Y.); Brook (N.Y.C.). Home: 51 Cypress Lane Briarcliff Manor NY 10510 Office: 30 Rockefeller Plaza New York City NY 10020 also 1345 Av Americas New York City NY 10019

DURBIN, RICHARD LOUIS, educator, adminstr.; b. Millersport, O., Aug. 28, 1927; s. Clark Babe and Mabel (Bushee) D.; B.A., Ohio State U., 1949; M.B.A., U. Chgo., 1956; m. Carolyn Bohrer, Mar. 23, 1955; children—Richard Louis, Margot Jane, Melissa. Research chemist Battelle Meml. Inst., Columbus, O., 1949- 50; sales rep. Am. Cyanamid Co., N.Y.C., 1953-54; adminstrv. asst. Lancaster (O.)-Fairfield Hosp., 1954; adminstrv. resident Gary (Ind.) Meth. Hosp., 1955-56; asst. adminstr. City of Memphis hosps., 1956-58, asso. adminstr., 1958-60; dir. outpatient and profl. services Presbyn.-St. Luke's Hosp., Chgo., 1960-61; asso. dir. grad. program in hosp. adminstrn., faculty U. Chgo. Grad. Sch. Bus., 1961-62; asso. prof. bus. adminstrn. Temple U., 1967-69, prof. mgmt., 1969-70, founder, dir. grad. program in health care adminstrn., 1967-70, adminstr. Univ. Hosp., 1966-70; adminstr. Lubbock County Dist. Hosp., Lubbock, Tex., 1970-71, now cons.; v.p. Coll. Medicine and Dentistry N.J., 1971—. Pres., D & H Enterprises; cons. div. hosp. and med. facilities Dept. Health Edn. and Welfare, 1967, U.S. Bur. Prisons, 1968—; mem. Hosp. Devel., Inc.; mem. adv. bd. Comprenetics, Inc., 1967—. Mem. steering commn. Tucson Hosp. and Health Planning Commn., 1962—, Asso. Hosp. Services Ariz., 1963-64; treas. Ariz. League Nursing, 1963- 64; mem. Phila. Crime Commn., 1967—. Bd. dirs. Ariz. Blue Cross. Served to lt. USNR, 1945-46, 50-53. Recipient editorial award Hosp. Mgmt. mag., 1961, 63, 65; certificate of merit Gov. Ariz., 1968. Fellow Am. Coll. Hosp. Adminstrs.; mem. Am. Chem. Soc., Nat. Assn. Clinic Mgrs., Am., Pa. hosp. assns., So. Ariz. Hosp. Council (pres. 1963), Am. Criminology Soc., Am. Soc. Pub. Adminstrn., A.I.M., Internat. Hosp. Fedn., Am. Mgmt. Assn. (Excellence award 1968), Am. Assn. U. Profs., Sigma Xi, Sigma Alpha Epsilon. Rotarian. Presbyn. Clubs: Tucson Press (life); Quadrangle (U. Chgo.); Buckeye Lake Yacht Club; Columbian Yacht Club (Chgo.); Hillcrest Country. Author: A Statistical Methodology of Educating a Medical Staff, 1961; New Ideas and Concepts in Outpatient Management, 1963; (with others) Ivory Tower to Workshop, 1964; Ambulatory Care Development, 1966; (with W.H. Springall) Organization and Administration of Health Care, 1969; (with Springall, P. High) Manual for Hospital Program and Performance Budgeting at the Operating Level, 1968. Cons. editor Hosp. Mgmt., El. Hosp., Hosp. Topics. Editor: The Forum. Contbr. articles to profl. jours. Home: 148 Hunt Dr Princeton NJ 08540 Office: 100 Bergen St Newark NJ 07103 also Lubbock County Courthouse Lubbock TX 79401

DURBROW, ELBRIDGE, ret. fgn. service officer; b. San Francisco, Sept. 21, 1903; grad. Shattuck Sch.; Ph.B., Yale, 1926; student Stanford, 1927, U. of Dijon, 1927, Académie de Driot International de la Haye, Netherlands, summer 1928; diploma, Ecole Libre des Sciences Politiques, 1929; married Emily M. Moore, July 23, 1938 (dec. May 1964); children—Bruce C., Chandler W.; m. 2d, Benice Balcom Helm, Jan. 2, 1965. Began career as vice consul, Warsaw, 1930, Bucharest, 1932; vice consul, Moscow, 1934, 3d sec., 1935, consul, 1937, with additional duties as 3d sec.; consul, Naples, 1937; detailed for spl. study at U. of Chicago, 1939; 2d sec., Rome, 1940; consul, Lisbon, 1940, Leghorn (temporary), 1940; 2d sec., Rome, 1941; U.S. observer Permanent Com. of International Inst. of Agr., Rome, 1941; detailed to Dept. of State, 1942; became asst. chief Div. of Eastern European Affairs, 1944, chief Eastern European Division, 1944-46; counselor of embassy, Moscow, U.S.S.R., 1946-48; dep. for Fgn. Affairs, Nat. War College, 1948-50; chief Div. Fgn. Service Personnel, Dept. of State, 1950; minister counselor, Am. Embassy, Rome, Italy, 1952-54; career minister, dep. chief of mission, 1954-55; minister, consul gen. Singapore, Malaya, 1955-57; U.S. ambassador to Viet Nam, 1957- 61; alternate U.S. permanent rep. N. Atlantic Council, 1961-67; adviser to comdr. Air U., Maxwell AFB, Montgomery, Ala., 1967-68, ret., 1968. Dir. Freedom Studies Center, Boston, Va., 1971. Served as liaison sec. UN Monetary and Financial Conf., Bretton Woods, N.H., 1944. Club: Metropolitan (Washington). Home: 3505 Porter St NW Washington DC 20016

DURDIN, FRANK TILLMAN, journalist; b. Elkhart, Tex., Mar. 30, 1907; s. Moses Adrian and Sally (Parks) D.; student Tex. Christian U., 1935-38; Nieman fellow Harvard, 1948-49; m. Margaret Louise Armstrong, Nov. 12, 1938. Reporter San Antonio Express, 1928-29, Los Angeles Times, 1929-30, Shanghai Evening Post, 1930-32; mng. editor China Press, 1932-37; mem. staff N.Y. Times, 1937—, fgn. corr., Far East, Africa, Europe, S.W. Pacific, 1967—, mem. editorial bd., 1961- 63, now assigned Hong Kong. Mem. Columbia Far East Seminar, 1962—. Council Fgn. Relations. Clubs: Overseas Press. Harvard (N.Y.C.); Am. National (Sydney, Australia); Foreign Correspondents (Hong Kong). Author: Southeast Asia, 1965. Address: care NY Times 229 W 43d St New York City NY 10036

DUREN, TERENCE, artist; b. Shelby, Neb., July 9, 1906; s. Jean Henri and Bertha Romaine (Hartel) D.; grad. Art Inst., Chgo., 1929; student Fontainebleau, France, 1932, Kunstgewerbliche Schule, Vienna, 1936. Recent work, Portrait of Am. Competition, appeared at Met. Mus. of Art, 1944; one man show Grand Central Art Galleries, N.Y.C., 1945, 46, 50, 60, Cowie Gallery, Hotel Biltmore, Los Angeles, 1952, Miller & Paine Co., Lincoln, Neb., 1957, Brownville, Neb., 1958, Scottsbluff, Neb., Grand Island, Neb., 1958; Beverly Hills, 1960; exhibited Carnegie Inst., Painting in the U.S., 1945-46, Audubon Artists, 1946., Who's Who in American Art, 1946; Adam Mickiewicz exhibitions, Prague, Geneva, Venice, Paris, Madrid; Art of Today exhbn., 1957; rep. in permanent collection of museums in Cleve., Springfield, Mass., Omaha, Chgo., Los Angeles, IBM, Ford Motor Co.; exhibiting Galerie Internationale; interviews and revs. in Time, Newsweek, Art Digest, Art News, Am. Weekly; former instr. Cleve. Mus. of Art, Western Res. U. Recipient awards Cleveland Mus. of Art, 1939, Springfield (Mass.) Mus. of Art, 1944, Joslyn Meml. Mus., Omaha, 1944, Art Inst., Chgo., Los Angeles County Mus. $500 prize, Portrait of America, Rockefeller Center, 1945; 1st prize Lincoln Artists Guild, 1952. Contbr. illustrations: The American West (Lucius Beebe), 1956. Currently on restoration of Brownville, Neb. Subject of numerous mag. feature articles. Address: Shelby NB 68662

DUREN, WILLIAM LARKIN, Jr., educator; b. Macon, Miss., Nov. 10, 1905; s. William Larkin and Mary Ethel (Bennett) D.; A.B., Tulane U., 1926, LL.D., 1959; Ph.D., U. Chgo., 1930; m. Mary Hardesty, Apr. 8, 1931; children—Peter L., Sarah Ann, David M. Instr., Wayne U., 1930-31; asst. prof. math. Tulane U., 1931- 36, asso. prof., 1937-42, prof. math., 1942-55, chmn. dept. math., 1947-55; dean Coll. of Arts and Scis., U. Va., 1955-62, Univ. prof. math., 1962—. Mem. div. math. NRC; acting program dir. for math. NSF, 1952; dir.-trustee Analytic Services Inc., 1965—. Operations analyst USAAF, Washington, 1943-45. Mem. Am. Math. Soc., Math. Assn. Am. (chmn. com. on undergrad. program, 1953-55, 56- 58, 63-65, pres. 1955-56, distinguished service 1967, Soc. Indsl. and Applied Math., A.A.A.S. (chmn. sect. A 1960), Phi Beta Kappa, Sigma Xi. Democrat. Methodist. Home: 2116 Twyman Rd Charlottesville VA 22903

DURFEE, HAROLD ALLEN, educator; b. Bennington, Vt., May 21, 1920; s. Lynn Stanton and Ethel (Foster) D.; Ph.B., U. Vt., 1941; B.D., Yale, 1944; Ph.D., Columbia, 1951; postgrad. Harvard, 1954-55, U. Oxford, 1968-69; m. Doris Graver, Aug. 10, 1944; children—Peter Allen, Gary Robert. Ordained to ministry Presbyn. Ch., 1944; chmn. dept. philosophy Park Coll., Parkville, Mo., 1946-55; asso. prof. philosophy Am. U., Washington, 1955-57, prof., chmn. dept. philosophy and religion, 1957—. Dir. seminar contemporary European philosophy, 1963. Pres. Mo. Philos. Assn., 1953- 54. Fund for Advancement Edn. fellow, 1954-55. Mem. Am. Philos. Assn., Metaphys. Soc. Am., Am. Acad. Religion, Am. Assn. U. Profs., Washington Philosophy Club (pres. 1961-62), Kappa Sigma, Phi Kappa Phi. Author: (with Harold E. Davis) The Teaching oi Philosophy in Universities of the United States, 1965. Home: 12405 St James Rd Rockville MD 20850 Office: Am U Washington DC 20016

DURFEE, JAMES RANDALL, judge; b. Oshkosh, Wis., Nov. 3, 1897; s. Thomas H. and Mary (Rossiter) D.; student Huron (S.D.) Coll.; 1917, 20; LL.B., Marquette U., 1926; m. Mona Burns, July 17, 1933; children—Mary (Mrs. David Clarke), James Randall, John. Admitted to Wis. bar, 1926, practiced in Antigo, 1927-51; dist. atty. Langlade County, Wis., 1928-32; ct. commr. 10th Jud. Circuit, 1934-50; commr. Pub. Service Commn. Wis., 1951- 53, chmn., 1953-56; chmn. CAB, Washington, 1956-60; judge U.S. Ct. Claims, Washington, 1960—. Served with U.S. Army, AEF, 1917-19; maj. Wis. State Guard, 1941-45. Mem. Am., Wis., D.C. bar assns., Am. Legion, Delta Theta Phi. Home: 5124 Worthington Dr Washington DC 20016 Office: US Ct Claims 717 Madison Pl Washington DC 20005

DURGIN, DON, broadcasting exec.; b. Chgo., Sept. 24, 1924; s. William Ryerson and Ada Cleveland (Emmett) D.; grad. Hotchkiss Sch., 1941; A.B. summa cum laude, Princeton, 1947; LL.B., N.Y. U., 1954. Asst. research account supr. Foote, Cone & Belding, N.Y.C.,

1947, asst. account exec., 1948; features and filler editor Pageant mag., 1948-49; asst. to advt. and promotion mgr., spot sales div. NBC, 1949-51; presentation writer ABC, 1951-53, mgr., tv spot sales devel., 1953, mgr. tv sales devel. ABC- TV Network, 1954; dir. research and sales devel. ABC Radio and TV Networks, 1954, v.p. charge ABC Radio Network, 1955-57; v.p. sales planning, tv network sales NBC, 1957, v.p., nat. sales mgr., 1958-59, v.p. charge sales, 1959-65, pres. NBC-TV Network, N.Y.C., 1966—. Served as 1st lt. USAAF, 1943-45. Office: RCA Bldg Radio City New York City NY 10020

DURGIN, EUGENE J., corp. exec.; b. 1916; LL.B., Suffolk Law Sch., 1938; married. Practiced law, 1938-41; with Howard Johnson Co., 1941—, exec. v.p., legal sec., gen. counsel, now v.p. Address: 1 Howard Johnson Plaza Boston MA 02125*

DURHAM, CLARENCE RAY, banker; b. Pineville, Ky., Sept. 1, 1930; s. James M. and Mattie (Lefevers) D.; B.S., Eastern Ky. U., 1957; m. Shelby Frances Wilburn, Aug. 18, 1956; children—Linda Rae, James Shelby. Agt., Internal Revenue Service, Louisville, 1957-65, spl. agt., criminal investigator, 1965-67; with Liberty Nat. Bank & Trust Co., Louisville, 1967—, mgr. accounting dept., 1968, comptroller, 1969—. Served with USN, 1950-54. Mem. Nat. Assn. Accountants (past asso. dir.), Bank Adminstrn. Inst., Planning Execs. Inst. Home: 9512 Gateway Dr Jeffersontown KY 40299 Office: 416 W Jefferson St Louisville KY 40202

DURHAM, FRANK L., investment exec.; b. Shreveport, La., Oct. 26, 1914; s. M.J. and Carrie (Smith) D.; B.A., Centenary Coll., 1934; m. Fannie Anderson, Jan. 26, 1938. Accountant, Peat, Marwick, Mitchell Co., Dallas., 1939-40, Mattison & Davey, Shreveport, La., 1940-46, Henslee, Hopson & Green Houston, 1946-47, Barrow, Wade, Guthrie & Co., 1947-49; v.p., treas. Panhandle Oil Corp., Dallas, 1949-56, co. merged with Am. Petrofina, Inc., 1956; sr. v.p., treas. Am. Petrofina, Inc., 1956-70; sr. v.p. investments Annuity Bd., So. Bapt. Conv., 1970—. Served from ensign to lt. (s.g.) USNR, 1942-45. Baptist (deacon, treas). Home: 7156 Blairview Dr Dallas TX 75230 Office: 511 N Akard St Dallas TX 75201

DURHAM, FRED DEWEY, mfg. exec., engr.; b. Howerton, Va., May 9, 1899; s. William F. and Eva J. (Coleman) D.; M.S., Va. Poly. Inst., 1922. Pres., C. Lee Cook Mfg. Co., Inc., Louisville, 1928-55; chmn., pres. Dover Corp., Washington, 1955-64, chmn. bd., 1964—. Clubs: Louisville Country, Pendennis (Louisville); Congressional Country, Tides Inn Country (Washington). Address: 277 Park Av New York City, NY 10017.

DURHAM, GEORGE HOMER, ednl. exec.; b. Parowan, Utah, Feb. 4, 1911; s. George Henry and Mary Ellen (Marsden) D.; A.B., U. Utah, 1932; Ph.D., U. Cal. at Los Angeles, 1939; m. Eudora Widtsoe, June 20, 1936; children—Carolyn (Mrs. John M. Peters,) Doralee (Mrs. R.H. Madsen), George. Finance div. mgr. Zion's Coop. Merc. Inst., Salt Lake City, 1935-36; fellow, asst. U. Cal., Los Angeles, 1937-39, vis. prof., summer 1950; polit. sci. dept. Utah State Coll., 1939- 42, Swarthmore Coll., 1942-43, U. Utah, 1944-60; dir. Inst. Govt., U. Utah, 1946-53, head polit. sci. dept., 1948-53, v.p. univ., 1953-60; pres. Ariz. State U., 1960-69; Utah commr. higher edn., Salt Lake City, 1969—. Mem. exec. com. Western Interstate Commn. for Higher Edn., 1955-60; mem. Ariz. State Bd. Edn., 1960-66; mem. U.S. nat. commn. for UNESCO, 1955-57,59; cons., current affairs analyst KTVT, Intermountain TV Corp., Salt Lake City, 1956-58; mem. lang. adv. devel. bd. U.S. Office Edn., 1959-63; mem. Air Force R.O.T.C. adv. panel to sec. air force, 1961-64, Army R.O.T.C. Panel, 1968—; adviser Army Command and Gen. Staff Coll., 1970—; mem. Bd. Fgn. Scholarships, 1963- 66. Bd. dirs. Am. Council on Edn., 1967-70, Ariz. Acad., Thunderbird Grad. Sch. Internat. Mgmt. Mem. Am. (exec. council 1949-51), Western (pres. 1948) polit. sci. assns., Am. Soc. Pub. Adminstrn. (council 1949-51, v.p. 1952, pres. 1959-60), Pi Gamma Mu, Pi Sigma Alpha, Phi Kappa Phi. Mem. Ch. of Jesus Christ of Latter-day Saints (world-wide exec. com. Sunday schs. 1971—). Clubs: Timpanogos, Windsor. Author: The Adminstration of Higher Education in Montana, 1958; other monographs. Contbg. editor The Improvement Era, 1946-70. Home: 515 S 10th E Salt Lake City UT 84102 Office: University Club Bldg Salt Lake City UT 84111

DURHAM, GEORGE STONE, chemist, educator; b. Portland, Ore., Dec. 26, 1912; s. George Clarke and Mary Helen (Josephi) D.; B.A., Reed Coll., 1935; Ph.D., N.Y. U., 1939; m. Alice Ingram, 1935 (div. 1957); children—George I., Douglas C.; m. 2d, Mary Gorey, 1958. Chemist Weyerhauser Timber Co., Longview, Wash., 1939-40; instr. chemistry Ore. State U., 1940-41, U. Ill., 1941-43; from instr. to asso. prof. chemistry Smith Coll., Northampton, Mass., 1943-59, prof., 1959—, chmn. dept., 1958-66. Vis. asst. prof. U. Mass., 1944-45, vis. lectr., 1957-62, mem. grad. faculty, 1961—; vis. asst. prof. N.Y. U., summers 1945,46; dir., prin. investigator grants or basic research contracts in phys. chemistry Sigma Xi, Office Naval Research, Air Force Office Sci. Research, Army Research Office (Durham), NSF. Mem. Am. Chem. Soc., Sigma Xi, Phi Lambda Upsilon. Contbr. articles to sci. publs. Home: 160 South St Northampton MA 01060

DURHAM, JAMES EDWARD, hotel exec.; b. San Diego, Oct. 10, 1922; s. Clarence R. and Eugenie (Reeves) D.; student Wash. State U., 1948; m. Elizabete Bock, Aug. 19, 1965; 1 dau., Susan Christjane. Chief steward Olympic Hotel, Seattle, 1948-51; asst. mgr. Chinook Hotel, Yakima,Wash., 1951-54; asst. mgr. Benjamin Franklin Hotel, Portland, Ore., 1954-55; asst. to pres. Western Internat. Hotels, Seattle, 1955-56; mgr. Finlen Hotel, Mont., 1956-59; mgr. Hawaiian Village Hotel, Honolulu, 1959-62; mgr. Multnomah Hotel, Portland, 1962-64; v.p. marketing Western Internat. Hotels, Seattle, 1964-66; v.p., mng. dir. Ilikai Hotel, Honolulu; dir. Capitol Investment Co. Mem. Hawaii Visitors Bur., 1966—. Served with AUS, 1943-46. Decorated Combat Inf. badge. Mem. Hawaii Hotel Assn. (dir.), Honolulu C. of C. Rotarian. Home: 1151 Waiholo St Honolulu, HI 96821. Office: 1777 Ala Moana Blvd Honolulu HI 96815

DURHAM, JOHN WYATT, educator; b. Okanogan, Wash., Aug. 22, 1907; s. John Wyatt and Sarah Evelyn (Vandiver) D.; B.Sc. in Geology, U. Wash., 1933, grad. student, 1933-35; M.A., U. Cal., 1936. Ph.D., 1941; m. Jane Roberts, Aug. 6, 1935; 1 son, John Wyatt. Geologist, Nederlandsche Pacific Petroleum Mij., Java, Sumatra, 1936-39; geologist, paleontologist Tropical Oil Co., Bogota, Colombia, 1943-46; asso. prof. paleontology Cal. Inst. Tech., 1946-47; asso. prof. paleontology U. Cal. at Berkeley, 1947-53, prof., 1953—, chmn. dept., 1956-59. Mem. U.S. Nat. Com. on Geology, 1966-70; mem. 1964 Galapagos Internat. Sci. Project Expdn. Guggenheim fellow, 1954-55, 65-66. Fellow Geol. Soc. Am., Cal. Acad. Scis. (trustee, pres. 1966-68), Paleontological Soc. (pres. 1965-66); mem. Am. Assn. of Petroleum Geologists, Soc. of Systematic Zoologists, A.A.A.S., Soc. Econ. Paleontologists and Mineralogists, Paleontological Research Instn., Palaeontographical Soc. London, Japan Palaeontological Soc., El. Institut. Ecuatoriano de Ciencias Naturales (corr.). Address: Dept Paleontology U Cal Berkeley CA 94720

DURHAM, LOWELL M., educator; b. Boston, Mar. 4, 1917; s. George H. and Nellie (Marsden) D.; B.A., U. Utah, 1941; M.A., U. Ia., 1942, Ph.D., 1945; m. Betty Dee Divers, Apr. 26, 1941; children—Lowell M., Susan, Thomas. Grad. asst. U. Ia., 1944-45; asst. physicist div. war research U. Cal., Pt. Loma, Cal., 1945-46; lectr. U. Utah, Salt Lake City, 1946-48, asso. prof., sec. Coll. Fine Arts, 1948-51, prof., 1951—, acting dean Coll. Fine Arts, 1954-55, dean, 1955-64. Music critic Salt Lake Tribune, Salt Lake City, 1946-64; program annotator Utah Symphony Orch., 1946—; owner Deseret Music Pubs., Salt Lake City. Ford fellow, N.Y.C., 1952-53. Mem. Coll. Music Soc., Am. Musicological Soc., Nat. Music Critics Assn. (v.p.), A.S.C.A.P. Mem. Ch. of Jesus Christ of Latter-day Saints (Deseret Sunday sch. bd. 1947-57). Composer; Prelude, Scherzo and Fugue (performed by Utah Symphony Orch.), 1951; (arrangement) New England Pastorale (performed by Utah Symphony, others), 1956; Battle Cry of Freedom (recorded Columbia Records by Mormon Tabernacle Choir with Phila. Orch., N.Y. Philharmonic); Variations for Strings; Autumn Sketch for Strings; Mormon Folkscape (commd. and performed by Beloit Symphony, performed by Utah, Ariz. State U. symphonies); also various choral selections, arrangements. Home: 2517 Hillside Circle Salt Lake City UT 84109

DURHAM, MILTON WORTH, surgeon; b. Seattle, Mar. 12, 1914; s. William Worth and Abbie (McNett) D.; B.S., U. Ore., 1936; M.D., 1939; m. Louise G. Journey, Aug. 6, 1938 (dec. 1958); children—Barbara J. (Mrs. Overstreet), Ronald M.; m. 2d, Lynn M. Dalthorp, 1959; children—Heidi, Lynn, Dana Lee. Intern, Good Samaritan Hosp., 1939-40; fellow Mason Clinic, 1945-48; pvt. practice surgery, Spokane, Wash., 1948—; surgeon with partnership Durham- Harper-Robnett, Ahlquist; surg. staff Deaconess, Sacred Heart, St. Luke's, Holy Family hosps.; cons. surgery VA; cons. surgeon USAF Hosp., Fairchild, Wash. Pres., Mikron Corp., Spokane, 1955—, Argonne Corp., 1958—, Argonne Investment Co., Spokane; dir. R.A. Pearson Co. Adv. com. Am. Cancer Soc.; med. adv. com. Western Interstate Commn. Higher Edn.; adv. com. Ednl. Facility Lab. (Ford Found.); founder, chmn. Sch. for U. Regents and Trustees. Pres. regents Wash. State U., 1966-67, pres. trustees, 1957-58; trustee Whitworth Coll., Spokane, St. George's Sch. Served from 1st lt. to lt. col. USAAF, 1940-45. Recipient Outstanding Citizen award Wash. Med. Assn., 1968; Wisdom award Honor, 1970. Diplomate Am. Bd. Surgeons. Fellow A.C.S.; mem. A.M.A., A.I.M., Spokane Surg. Soc., Assn. Governing Bds. State Univs. (Outstanding Regent 1964, pres. 1959-60), Spokane C. of C., Alpha Kappa Kappa, Tau Kappa Epsilon, Pi Mu Chi. Republican. Episcopalian. Clubs: Spokane, Spokane Country. Author: (with Manuel De Busk) Handbook for University and College regents, 1964; also sci., surg. publs. Co-developer Ahlquist- Durham Vena Cava Clamp. Home: W 1522 Fairway Dr Country Club Highlands Spokane WA 99218 Office: Doctor's Bldg W 104th 5th Av Spokane WA 99204

DURHAM, ROBERT CROOK, advt. exec.; b. Phila., Jan. 25, 1915; s. Knowlton and Pauline (Crook) D.; grad. Choate Sch., 1933; B.S., Yale, 1937; m. Virginia G. Arnold, Jan. 10, 1943; children—Robert L., Bette, Cathy, Dangia. With Benton & Bowles Inc., 1937-42; gen. supr. advt. service Met. Life Ins. Co., 1946- 52; asst. chmn. bd. Kenyon & Eckhart, Inc., 1952-56; sr. v.p. Ruthrauff & Ryan, Inc., 1956-57; pres. Robert Durham Assos., Inc., 1957-64; chairman of the board Market Planning Corp. Inter-pub. Group of Cos., Inc., 1964-66, exec. v.p. Interpublic, Inc., 1966-67; pres. Durham, Reid & Durham, Inc., N.Y.C., 1968—. Served from aviation cadet to maj., USAAF, World War II. Decorated Dist. Flying Cross with 2 clusters; Cross of St. Olaf (Norway). Mem. Am. Legion, Air Force Assn. Clubs: University, Overseas Press, (N.Y.C.); Campfire (Chappaqua, N.Y.); Rolling Rock. Co-Author: Hitch Your Wagon, 1947. Home: 1009 Park Av New York City NY 10028

DURHAM, ROBERT GREGORY, music co. exec.; b. Winnetka, Ill., Nov. 24, 1912; s. Raymond Ewing and Eleanor (Gregory) D.; A.B., Harvard, 1935; LL.B., Yale, 1939; m. Carol Margaret Borchard, Jan. 4, 1936 (div.); children—Edwin B., Anthony G. Admitted to Ill. bar, 1939; asso. Bell, Boyd, Marshall & Lloyd, Chgo., 1939-49; adminstrv. asst. to pres. Lyon & Healy, Inc., Chgo., 1949-52, exec. v.p., 1952-53, pres., 1953—, dir., 1952—; dir. First Nat. Bank of Winnetka, Steinway & Sons. Mem. Sch. bd. Northfield Pub. Schs., 1945- 48, Dir. Lyric Opera Chgo. Home: 2 Kent Rd Winnetka IL 60093 Office: 243 S Wabash Av Chicago IL 60604

DURHAM, ROBERT LEWIS, architect; b. Seattle, Apr. 28, 1912; s. William Worth and Abbie May (McNett) D.; student Coll. Puget Sound, 1930-31; B.Arch. cum laude, U. Wash., 1936; m. Dorothy Evelyn Wyatt, May 14, 1935 (dec. Nov. 1935); m. 2d, Marjorie Ruth Moser, Sept. 19, 1936; children—David Robert, Gail Maureen, Catherine Louise, Jennifer Ann. Draftsman B. Dudley Stuart, Architect, Seattle, 1936-38; cost engr. FHA, 1938-41; partner Stuart & Durham, Architects, Seattle, 1941-51, Robert L. Durham & Assos., Seattle, 1951-54, Durham, Anderson & Freed, Architects, Seattle, 1954—; prin. works include Anchorage-Westward Hotel, Shorewood Apts., 800 unit Ft. Lewis housing project, internat. br. Seattle-First Nat. Bank, Smith Gandy Bldg., Kenney Presbyn. Home, Downtown YWCA, student union Seattle Pacific Coll., Fidelity Savs. & Loan Assn. Mem. Bldg. Code Adv. Commn. City Seattle, Seattle Planning Commn., 1969—; mem. Seattle Municipal Art Commn., 1955-65, chmn., 1957-59; com. worship and arts Nat. Council Chs.; chmn. cultural arts com. Century 21 Expn., Seattle, 1958-62; speaker art, architecture. Recipient honor award for various chs. Ch. Archtl. Guild Am., 1952, 55, 57, 59, 60, 64; honor awards Wash. chpt. A.I.A., 52, 59, 54, 56; award for S.W. Br. Library, Seattle, A.I.A.-A.L.A., 1964. Fellow A.I.A. (past pres. Washington, nat. pres. 1967-68); hon. fellow Royal Archtl. Inst. Can., Mexican, Peruvian socs. architects; mem. Ch. Archtl. Guild Am. (v.p. 1963-65, dir.), Seattle C. of C., Tau Sigma Delta. Conglist. Kiwanian. Clubs: Cosmos (Washington); Seattle Engineers. Home: 9310 California Av SW Seattle WA 98116 Office: 1100 Eastlake E Seattle WA 98109

DURHAM, RONALD OATIS, newspaper writer; b. Perryton, Tex., Dec. 19, 1931; s. Byron and Luella (Oatis) D.; B.A., Eastern N.M. U., 1953; postgrad. U. Western Australia, 1964; S.T.B., Abilene Christian Coll., 1968; postgrad. Rice U., 1970—; m. Faye Knox, Aug. 5, 1951; children—Don, David, Douglas, Dennis, Delayna. Tchr. elementary sch., Tucumcari, N.M., 1953-55, Lander, Wyo., 1955-57; newspaper reporter Wyo. State Jour., Lander, 1957-59; ordained to ministry Ch. of Christ, 1959; minister Ch. of Christ, Lander, 1959-61, Perth, Australia, 1961-65, Abilene, Tex., 1965-68; dir. Australian Bible Coll., Sydney, New S. Wales, 1968-69; religion writer Houston Post, 1969—. Mem. Religion Newswriters Assn. Home: 4805 Ivy St Pasadena TX 77505 Office: 4747 Southwest Freeway Houston TX 77001

DURICK, JOSEPH ALOYSIUS, clergyman; b. Dayton, Tenn., Oct. 13, 1914; s. Stephen and Bridget (Gallagher) D.; student St. Bernard Coll., Cullman, Ala., 1930-33; B.A., St. Mary's Sem., Balt., 1936; B.Th., Urban Coll. Propagation of Faith, Rome, Italy, 1940. Ordained priest Roman Cath. Ch., 1940, domestic prelate, 1952—, aux. bishop, 1955—; dir. North Ala. Missions, 1940-57; pastor St. Margaret's Ch., Birmingham, 1949-57, St. Francis Xavier Ch., Mountain Brook, Birmingham, 1957-64; aux. bishop Mobile-Birmingham, 1955-62, vicar gen. Mobile- Birmingham, 1962; coadjutor bishop Diocese of Nashville, 1964-65, vicar gen., 1965-66, apostolic adminstr., 1966—, bishop Nashville, 1969—. Recipient Ann. Distinguished Service award Tenn. Council on Human Relations, 1970; Nat. Amistad award, 1970. Office: 421 Charlotte Av Nashville TN 37219

DURKEE, WILLIAM CARL, beverage co. exec.; b. St. Louis, Mich., Oct. 2, 1921; s. Robert L. and Mary E. (Faunce) D.; m. Katherine J. Barber, Apr. 3, 1943; children—Susan, Stephen, William Carl. With soft drink bus., 1939- 63; with Pepsi-Cola Co., 1950-63, v.p., mgr. central div., Chgo., 1955- 58, v.p. marketing, N.Y.C., 1958-61, sr. v.p. marketing 1961-63; pres. Rival Pet Foods, Chgo., 1963-66; exec. v.p. Royal Crown Cola Co., Columbus, Ga., 1966-69, pres., 1969—, also dir.; dir. First Nat. Bank. Served to capt. AUS, 1942-46. Home: 2221 Hilton Av Columbus, GA 31906. Office: 100 10th Av PO Box 1440 Columbus GA 31902

DURKEE, WILLIAM PORTER, lawyer, govt. ofcl.; b. Chgo., Apr. 27, 1919; s. William Porter and Helen Chapman (Stookey) D.; A.B. cum laude, Dartmouth, 1941; LL.B., Yale, 1947; m. Dorcas Mary Dunklee, Nov. 12, 1946; children—William Porter, Mary Vaughan, Edward Chapman. Staff Am. embassy, London, Eng., 1943-44; admitted to Cal. bar, 1949, Colo. bar, 1949; partner Dunklee, Dunklee & Durkee, Denver, 1949—. Asso. dir., exec. dir. Am. Com. United Europe, 1950-52; cons. U.S. Govt., 1952; attaché Am. embassy, Paris, France, 1955-58, U.S. Dept. State, 1958-61; dir. fed. assistance Office Civil Def., Dept. Def., 1961-62, dep. asst. sec. def., 1962-64, dir. civil def., 1964-66; v.p. Europe, Free Europe, Inc., with responsibility for Radio Free Europe, 1967-68, pres., 1968—. Served with the King's Royal Rifle Corps, Brit. Army, 1941-44. Recipient Distinguished Civilian Service award Dept. Army, 1965, 66. Mem. State Bar Cal., Colo. Bar Assn., Council on Fgn. Relations, Celer et Audax (London, Eng.), Psi Upsilon, Phi Delta Phi. Episcopalian. Home: 43 Fifth Av New York City NY 10003 Office: Free Europe Inc 2 Park Av New York City NY 10016

DURLAND, JACK RAYMOND, coffee co. exec.; b. Taylor, Tex., Sept. 21, 1916; s. Den D. and Percy (Langrill) D.; LL.B., U. Okla., 1941; m. June Kathryn Cain, Feb. 5, 1937; children—Jack Raymond, Diane Elizabeth. Admitted to Okla. bar, 1941; spl. agt. FBI, 1942-46; pvt. practice law, Oklahoma City, 1946-50; asst. to pres. Cain's Coffee Co., Oklahoma City, 1950-52, pres., 1952—; chmn. bd. Manhattan Coffee Co., St. Louis, 1960—. Chmn. bd. Nat. Coffee Assn., 1961-62. Bd. dirs. Met. YMCA, Oklahoma City. Mem. Am., Okla. bar assns. Lion. Home: 1620 Queenstown Rd Oklahoma City, OK 73116. Office: 13131 Broadway Extension Oklahoma City OK 73125

DURLAND, LEWIS HUDSON, univ. ofcl.; b. Watkins Glen, N.Y., Jan. 5, 1908; s. Charles M. and Clara A. (Johnson) D.; A.B., Cornell U., 1930; m. Margaret J. Carry, Jan. 8, 1939; children—Anne, Katherine; m. 2d, Barbara Underhill, Jan. 1969. With adminstrv. offices Cornell U., Ithaca, N.Y., 1936—, treas., 1948—. Chmn., First Nat. Bank & Trust Co., Ithaca, 1958—; dir. Security N.Y. State Corp., SCM Corp., Raymond Internat. Corp., Con Agra, Raymond Corp. Trustee Duncan Hines Found., Griffis Found. Mem. Ithaca C. of C., Chi Phi. Clubs: Cornell of N.Y., Magnassippi Fish and Game; Beaverkill Trout, Union League. Home: 528 Cayuga Heights Rd Ithaca NY 14850

DURNIAK, JOHN, editor, photographer; b. Yonkers, N.Y., Nov. 23, 1928; s. Daniel and Julia (Kurillo) D.; student Mohawk Coll., 1946-47, Syracuse U., 1947; B.A., Bowling Green State U., 1950; M.A. in Journalism, U. Ia., 1951; m. Rita Marie Cummings, June 9, 1956; children—Todd, Holly. Photographer's asst. Life mag., 1951-52; sports editor Bronxville (N.Y.) Reporter, 1952; TV picture script writer-editor United Press Pictures, 1952; mem. staff Popular Photography mag., 1953—, exec. editor, 1960-64, editor in chief, 1964-68; v.p., managing dir. Internat. Acad. of Communicating Arts and Scis., 1968—; lectr. in field. Mem. Photog. Adminstrs. Club, Circle of Confusion. Club: Overseas Press (N.Y.C.). Author: 100 Camera Projects, 1959. Editor: Polaroid Land Photography, 1963; Photography Annual, 1966; Donnybrook Report: Photography. Picture editor Time Mag., 1970. Contbg. editor: Infinity Mag. Home: 113 Lime Kiln Rd Suffern NY 10902 Office: Time-Life Rockefeller Center New York City NY 10020

DUROCHER, LEON ERNEST, Leo, profl. baseball club mgr.; b. West Springfield, Mass., July 27, 1906; m. 3d, Laraine Day (div.). 2d baseman N.Y. Yankees, 1926-28; shortstop Cin. Reds, St. Louis Cardinals; joined Bklyn. Dodgers, became mgr.; team won Nat. League pennant, 1951, 54; radio, tv exec.; coach Los Angeles Dodgers; mgr. Chgo. Cubs, 1966—. Known as The Lip, statement, nice guys finish last. Home: 9160 Beverly Blvd Beverly Hills CA 90210 Office: Wrigley Field Clark and Addison Sts Chicago IL 60613

DUROST, HENRY BEECHER, hosp. adminstr.; b. Woodstock, N.B., Can., Feb. 15, 1925; s. Henry Beecher and Clarissa (Perkins) D.; B.A., U. N.B., 1946; M.D., McGill U., 1950, diploma psychiatry, 1955. Intern Montreal Gen. Hosp., 1950-51; resident Verdun (Que.) Protestant Hosp., 1951-52, Allan Meml. Inst., Montreal, 1952-54, Maudsley Inst. Psychiatry, London, Eng., 1954, Queen Sq. Inst. Neurology, London, 1955; staff psychiatrist Verdun Protestant Hosp., 1955-65, exec. dir., 1965-71; asso. prof. psychiatry McGill U., 1965-71, pvt. practice Montreal, 1955-71; med. dir. Queen St. Mental Health Centre, Toronto, 1971—, asso. prof. psychiatry U. Toronto, 1971—; hon. cons. Jewish Gen. Hosp., Queen Mary Vets. Hosp. Vice pres., bd. dirs. Inst. Philippe Pinel; pres. bd. dirs. Forward House. Fellow Am. Psychiat. Assn., Am. Pub. Health Assn.; mem. Canadian Med. Assn., Canadian, Que. psychiat. assns., Montreal Med.-Chirurgical Soc., Montreal Council Social Agencies, Canadian Mental Health Assn. Rotarian. Home: 7 Jackes Av Toronto Ontario Canada

DURR, CLIFFORD JUDKINS, former lawyer; b. Montgomery, Ala., Mar. 2, 1899; s. John Wesley and Lucy (Judkins) D.; A.B., U. Ala., 1919; B.A. in Jurisprudence, Oxford (Eng.) U., 1922, M.A., B.C.L., 1964; m. Virginia Heard Foster, Apr. 5, 1926; children—Ann Patterson (Mrs. Walter A. Lyon), Lucy Judkins (Mrs. F. Sheldon Hackney), Virginia Foster (Mrs. Frank R. Parker III), Lulah Johnston (Mrs. Richard V. Colan). Admitted to Ala. bar, 1923, Wis. bar, 1924, D.C. bar, 1948; mem. firm Rushton, Crenshaw & Rushton, Montgomery, 1922-23, Fawsett, Smart & Shea, Milw., 1923-24, Martin, Turner & McWhorter, Birmingham, Ala., 1925-33; asst. gen. counsel RFC, 1933-41; gen. counsel, dir. Def. Plant Corp., v.p., dir. Rubber Res. Corp., 1940-41; commr. FCC, 1941-48; pvt. practice law, Washington, 1948-50, Montgomery, 1952-64. Lectr., Am., Brit. univs.; Regents lectr. theatre arts U. Cal., Los Angeles, 1966. Served with U.S. Army, 1918. Rhodes scholar, 1918; recipient Variety award, 1946, Sch. Broadcasters award, 1947, Page One award Am. Newspaper Guild, 1948, Lasker Civil Liberties award N.Y. Civil Liberties Union, 1966. Life mem. Inst. Edn. by Radio; mem. Phi Beta Kappa, Sigma Alpha Epsilon. Democrat. Presbyn. Contbr. articles to profl. jours.; contbr. books. Address: Route 4 Box 300 G Wetumpka AL 36092

DURRANT, STEPHEN DAVID, educator; b. Salt Lake City, Oct. 11, 1902; s. Stephen Thomas and Martha (Harman) D.; student Weber Coll., 1925-26; A.B., U. Utah, 1929, M.A., 1931; student U. Minn., 1931-32, U. Cal. at Berkeley, 1933, 38-39; Ph.D., U. Kan., 1950; m. Sylvia Jane Burt, Dec. 21, 1933; children—Sue Marilynn, Stephen Carl. Asst. zoology U. Utah, 1929-31; ranger Zion Nat. Park, summer 1931; asst. zoology U. Minn., 1931-32; faculty U. Utah, 1932—, prof. zoology, 1952—; supr. mosquito abatement Salt Lake City, 1935-36;

field dir. U.S. Bur. Fisheries, 1934; instr. zoology U. Kan., 1945; field dir. Upper Colo. River Devel.-U. Utah Ecol. Researches in coop. with Bur. Reclamation on Glen Canyon project, 1958, Flaming Gorge project, 1959, Navajo project, 1960, Curacanti project, 1961. Mem. Wildlife Soc., Soc. Systemic Zoology (pres. Pacific sect. 1965), Biol. Soc. Washington, Am. Assn. U. Profs., Utah Acad. Arts, Sci. and Letters, Am. Soc. Mammalogists (dir. 1950-55, pres. 1961-62, hon. mem.), Sigma Xi, Phi Sigma, Phi Kappa Phi. Author: Mammals of Utah, Taxonomy and Distribution, 1952; also articles. Home: 1381 S 10th East St Salt Lake City UT 84105

DURRELL, CORDELL, geologist, educator; b. San Francisco, Aug. 7, 1908; s. Earnest I. and Elizabeth (Loosli) D.; A.B., U. Cal. at Berkeley, 1931, Ph.D., 1936; m. Helen Margaret Spinning, May 22, 1937. Instr. geology U. Cal., Berkeley, 1936-37; geologist Richfield Oil Corp., Los Angeles, 1937-38; faculty dept. geology U. Cal., Los Angeles, 1938-63, asso. prof., 1946- 51, prof., 1951-63; prof. geology U. Cal. Davis, 1963—. Geologist, U.S. Geol. Survey, 1943-46; prof. geology Petrobras Cenap, Salvador, Bahia, Brazil, 1958-60. Fellow Geol. Soc. Am.; mem. Am. Assn. Petroleum Geologists, Contbr. articles to profl. jours. Home: 759 Elmwood Dr Davis, CA 95616.

DURRELL, DONALD DEWITT, educator; b. Fergus Falls, Minn., Dec. 18, 1903; s. William Benmore and Fanny (Richardson) D.; A.B., U. Ia., 1926, A.M., 1927; Edn.M., Harvard, 1929, Ed.D., 1930; L.H.D., Boston U., 1969; m. Katharine Burgess Moore, Aug. 3 children—Diana (dec.), Suzanne Louise, Elizabeth Jeanne. Tchr., Ia. High Sch., 1922-23; dir. extra curricular activities U. Ia. High Sch., 1923-25; research asst. in clin. psychology Ia. Psychopathic Hosp., 1925-27; asst. in edn. Harvard, 1927-28, instr., 1928-30; asst. prof. edn. Boston U., 1930-33, asso. prof., 1933-35, prof., 1935-69, dean Sch. Edn., 1942-52. Vis. prof. summers, Columbia, 1936-37, Cal., 1950, U. Colo., 1953. Mem. research adv. council U.S. Office Edn., 1961-64. Chief, operations analysis sect. 3d Air Force, 1945. Fellow A.A.A.S. (v.p. 1953); mem. Am. Ednl. Research Assn., Internat. Reading Assn. (citation of Merit 1970), Nat. Soc. for Study Edn., Phi Delta Kappa. Republican. Unitarian. Author books, tests, monographs, articles on elementary edn. Home: 13 Cypress Rd Wellesley Hills MA 02181 also York Harbor ME 03911

DURRELL, GERALD MALCOLM, author, zoologist; b. Jamshedpur, India, Jan. 7, 1925; s. Lawrence George and Louisa Florence (Dixie) D.; ed. in Europe by pvt. tutors, including Dr. Theodore Stephanides in Greece; m. Jacqueline Sonia Rasen, Feb. 26, 1951. Student/keeper Whipsnade Park, Bedfordshire, Eng., 1945; financed, organized, led animal collecting expdns. to Brit. Cameroons, Brit. Guiana, Argentina, Paraguay, Australia, New Zealand, Malaya, Mexico, which supplied zoos, wildlife instns., also museums with specimens, 1946-59; founder Jersey (Channel Isles) Zoo, 1959, Jersey Wildlife Preservation Trust, 1963; scriptwriter BBC, 1951—; TV appearances on own series, also other wildlife programs, 1954—. Fellow Internat. Inst. Arts and Letters, Zool. Soc. London; mem. Am. Soc. Herpetologists, Am. Assn. Zoo Parks and Aquariums, Brit. Ornithol. Union, Fauna Preservation Soc., Australian Mammal Soc., Nigerian Field Soc., Bombay Natural History Soc., Malayan Nature Soc., South African Wild Life Protection Soc., Avicultural Soc., Univ. Soc., Fedn. Animal Welfare, Brit. Mamal Soc., Royal Geog. Soc., Inst. Biology. Author: Overloaded Ark, 1952; 3 Tickets to Adventure (Annual Book award Secondary Edn. Bd. 1956), 1953; Bafut Beagles, 1953; The Drunken Forest, 1954; The New Noah, 1955; My Family and Others Animals, 1956; Zoo in My Luggage, 1958; Encounters with Animals, 1959; Island Zoo, 1961; Look at Zoos, 1961; Whispering Land, 1962; My Favourite Animal Stories, 1963; Menagerie Manor, 1964; Two in the Bush, 1966; Rosy Is My Relative, 1968; The Donkey Rustlers, 1968; Birds, Beasts and Relatives, 1969; Fillets of Plaice, 1971. Home: Les Augres Manor Trinity Office: Jersey Wildlife Preservation Trust Trinity Jersey Channel Islands

DURRELL, LAWRENCE GEORGE, writer; b. Julundur, India, Feb. 27, 1912; s. Lawrence Samuel and Louise Florence (Dixie) D.; ed. Coll. St. Joseph, Darjiling, India, also St. Edmund's Coll., Canterbury, Eng.; 2 daughters. Formerly with British fgn. service; press attache, Belgrade, Yugoslavia; dir. British Inst., Cordoba, Argentina; dir. pub. relations, Dodecanese Islands; press attache, Alexandria, Egypt; sr. press officer British Embassy, Cairo; dir. British Inst., Kalamata, Greece; sr. press officer, Athens, Greece; dir. pub. relations Govt. of Cyprus, 1954-56; spl. corr. for Economist in Cyprus, 1953; lectr. lit. for British Council in Greece and Argentina. Fellow Royal Soc. Lit. Author: (novels) Panic Spring, 1937, The Black Book, 1938, Prospero's Cell, 1945, Cefalu, 1947, Reflections on a Marine Venus, 1953, Justine, 1956. Bitter Lemons, 1956, Balthazar, 1958, Mountolive, 1958, Clea, 1960; (humor) Stiff Upper Lip, 1958, Esprit de Corps, 1957; (verse) Private Country, 1943, Cities Plains and Peoples, 1946, On Seeming to Presume, 1948, Tree of Idleness, 1946 Selected Poems, 1956, Sappho (play), 1950, Acte (play), 1962, An Irish Faustus (play), 1964; Collected Poems, 1960; Selected Poems, 1953-1963, 1964; The Ikons and other poems, 1967; Sauve Qui Peut, 1967; (criticism) A Key to Modern Poetry, 1952; (translations) Pope Joan, 1948; a Private Correspondence, 1963; Dark Labyrinth, 1962; Poetry of Lawrence Durrell's Teens, 1968; (novel) Tunc, 1968; Spirit of Place: letters and essays on travel, 1969; (novel) Nunquam, 1970; also articles mags., newspapers. Editor: The Henry Miller Reader, 1959.†

DURRENBERGER, ROBERT WARREN, educator; b. Perham, Minn., Oct. 2, 1918; s. John George and Mary Angela (Weibeler) D.; B.S., Moorhead State Coll., 1940; B.S. in Meteorology, Cal. Inst. Tech., 1941; M.S. in Geography, U. Wis., 1949; Ph.D. in Geography, U. Cal. at Los Angeles, 1955; m. Bernadine Ann Stiegel, July 15, 1946; children—Daniel Joseph, Mary Ann. Jr. exec. R.S. Bacon Veneer Co., Chgo., 1945-47; instr. U. Ky., 1948-49; asst. prof., chmn. dept. geography Los Angeles State Coll., 1949-58; asso. prof., prof., chmn. dept. geography San Fernando Valley State Coll., 1958-61, coordinator grad. studies, 1961-63, prof. geography, 1964-65,66-70; asso. dean acad. planning Cal. State Coll., 1963-64; vis. prof. U. Cal., Los Angeles, 1965-66; prof. Ariz. state U., Phoenix, 1970—. Served to maj. USAAF, 1940-45. Mem. Am. Meteorol. Soc., Assn. Am. Geographers, Nat. Council Geog. Edn., Pacific Coast Geographers, Cal. Council Geography Tchrs., Am. Water Resources Assn., Blue Key, Sigma Xi. Republican. Roman Catholic. Author: Patterns on the Land, 1957; The Geography of California, 1959; Sources of Information About California, 1961; California and the Western States, 1963; (film) California's Natural Regions, 1963; California - the Last Frontier, 1969; California: Its People, Its Problems, Its Prospects, 1971; Geographical Research and Writing, 1971. Contbr. articles to profl. jours. Contbg. editor World Book Ency. Home: 3406 N Valencia Lane Phoenix AZ 85018

DURRENBERGER, WILLIAM JOHN, univ. adminstr.; b. Wadena, Minn., Mar. 15, 1917; s. John George and Mary Angela (Weibeler) D.; B.S., U. Md., 1951; M.B.A., Syracuse U., 1954; student U. Minn., 1935-40; m. Alma Mary Pagliai, Jan. 3, 1947; children—William John, Robert Scott, Philip Michael. Commd. 2d lt. U.S. Army, 1939, advanced through grades to maj. gen., 1968; comdg. gen. Army Tank Automotive Center, Warren, Mich., 1965-66, U.S. Army Weapons Command, Rock Island, Ill., 1966-68; dep. chief of staff Logistics Hdgrs., U.S. Army, Pacific, 1968-70; ret., 1970; asst. v.p. ednl. services Drake U., 1971—. Active Boy Scouts Am. Decorated D.S.M., Bronze Star Mem. Internat. City Mgmt. Assn., Am. Ordnance Assn. Roman Catholic. Home: 912 44th St West Des Moines IA 50265

DURSLAG, MELVIN, author, newspaper columnist; b. Chgo., Apr. 29, 1921; s. William and Frieda (Berliner) D.; B.A., U. So. Cal., 1943; m. Lorayne Jane Sweet, Nov. 21, 1948; children—Ivy, William, James. Reporter, feature writer Los Angeles Examiner, 1938-43, reporter, 1946-53; columnist Los Angeles Examiner and Herald-Examiner, 1953—; syndicated by King Features Syndicate, Hearst Headline Service, free-lance writer, 1950—. Bd. dirs. Sch. Journalism, U. So. Cal. Served with USAAF, 1943-46; CBI. Decorated Bronze Star (5); recipient Nat. Headliners award, 1960. Mem. Sigma Delta Chi, Kappa Tau Alpha. Home: 523 Dalehurst Av Los Angeles CA 90024 Office: 1111 S Broadway Los Angeles CA 90054

DURUFLE, MAURICE, organist, composer; b. 1903; ed. Paris Conservatory. Organist of Saint- Etienne-du-Mont; asst. prof. Paris Conservatory, 1942-43, prof. d'harmonie, 1943—. Recipient prize for organ Paris Conservatory, 1922, prize for harmony, 1924, prize for accompainiment, 1926, prizes for fugue and composition, 1928; prix des Amis de l'Orgue, 1930. Composer: (organ) Scherzo, 1929; Prélude Adagio et Choral Varié sum le Veni Creator, 1931; Suite, 1934; Prelude et Fugue, 1942; (chamber music) Trio pour Flute, Alto et Piano; (for choir a cappella) Quatre Motets sur des themes grégorius, 1960; (for orch.) Trois Danses, 1935, Andante et Scherzo, 1940, Requiem pour Soli, Choeurs, Orchestre et Orque, 1947; Messe Cum Jubilo for baritone solo, baritone choir, orch. and organ, 1967. Address: 6 Pl du Pantheon Paris 5e France

DURYEE, A. WILBUR, physician; b. North Hackensack, N.J., July 5, 1899; s. Abram and Margaret (Clarke) D.; B.Sc., Rutgers Coll., 1921; M.D., Columbia, 1925; m. Helen Deborah Moore; children—A. Wilbur, Deborah Jane, Mary Ellen. Intern N.Y. Postgrad. Hosp., 1925-28; attending physician Univ. Hosp., Bellevue Hosp., N.Y.C.; cons. Samaritan Bklyn., Prospect Heights, Englewood, St. Claire hosps.; now prof. clin. medicine N.Y.U. Served as pvt. U.S. Army, World War I. Mem. Am. (exec. com.; dir.; v.p. 1959), N.Y. (pres.) heart assns., Am. Therapeutic Soc. (pres. 1947), Am. Acad. Compensation Medicine (pres. 1955). Club: University (N.Y.C.). Home: 350 E 57th St New York City NY 10022 Office: 140 E 54th St New York City NY 10022

DURYEE, SACKET ROLAND, business exec.; b. Washington, Jan. 25, 1909; s. Sacket Leverich and Gertrude (Moling) D.; student George Washington U., 1927-28; B.C.S., Benjamin Franklin U., 1933, M.C.S., 1934; D.Bus. Adminstrn. (hon.), Assumption Coll.; m. Marian Gardner, Sept. 16, 1932; children—Dolores (Mrs. Larry Desautels), Diana (Mrs. Paul Birchak). Pub. accounting, Washington, 1928-29; accountant RFC, 1929-33; supr. accountant Washington Post, 1933-35, HOLC, 1935-36; auditor Worcester Telegram Pub. Co. (Mass.), 1936-41; asst. treas. Wyman-Gordon Co., Worcester, 1941, treas., clk., 1947, v.p., treas., clk., 1955-61, v.p., treas., dir., 1961—; dir. Worcester Fed. Savs. & Loan Assn., Wyman-Gordon India, Ltd., Bombay; chmn. bd. Reisner Metals, Inc., Los Angeles, Androform Industries, Inc., North Dighton, Mass., Rollmet, Inc., Santa Ana, Cal. Active YMCA. Bd. dirs., incorporator Home for Aged Men, Worcester; bd. dirs. Worcester chpt. A.R.C., Worcester Taxpayers Assn.; adv. bd. Worcester Poly. Inst.; trustee, chmn., treas. George F. and Sybil H. Fuller Found.; trustee, past pres., v.p., treas., chmn. Worcester Hahnemann Hosp.; trustee Assumption Coll. Mem. Worcester Natural History Mus., Worcester Hist. Soc., Worcester Mus., Worcester County Mechanics Assn., Worcester Orchestral Soc., Newcomen Soc. Eng., Atlantic Salmon Assn. Mason (32). Clubs: Worcester, Worcester Country. Home: 15 Westwood Dr Worcester MA 01609 Office: 105 Madison St Worcester MA 01601

DUSARD, LEO FRANCOIS, Jr. air force officer; b. Kirkwood, Mo., Nov. 2, 1915; s. Leo Francois and Eugenia (Lindsey) D.; B.S., Washington U., St. Louis, 1938; grad. Armed Forces Staff Coll., 1947, Air War Coll., 1951; m. Beatrice Ann Pepoon, Sept. 14, 1939; children—Leo Francois III, Joan Trenchard, Deborah Ann, Christopher Rime. Commd. 2d lt. USAAF, 1939, advanced through grades to maj. gen. USAF, 1965; fighter group comdr., S.W. Pacific, 1943-45; mem. Joint Chiefs Staff, 1948-51, NATO staff, Italy and Eng., 1951-55; comdr., officer mil. schs. in San Antonio, 1955-57; comdr. Craig AFB, Selma, Ala., 1957-60; dir. tech. tng. Command, San Antonio, 1960-64; comdr. Tech. Tng. Command, San Antonio, 1960-64; comdr. Tech. Tng. Center, Chanute AFB, Ill., 1964-66; dir. personnel tng. and edn. Hdqrs. USAF, 1966-68; vice comdr. USAF Tng. Commd, San Antonio, 1968-. Decorated Legion of Merit with 2 oak leaf clusters, D.F.C., Air medal with 3 oak leaf clusters. Mem. Sigma Alpha Epsilon. Home: 12 S Park Randolph AFB, TX 78148. Office: Hdqrs USAF (AFPTR) Washington DC 20330

DUSCHA, JULIUS CARL, journalist; b. St. Paul, Nov. 4, 1924; s. Julius William and Anna (Perlowski) D.; student U. Minn., 1943-47; A.B., Am. U., 1951; postgrad. (Nieman fellow), Harvard, 1955-56; m. Priscilla Ann McBride, Aug. 17, 1946; children—Fred C., Steve D., Suzanne, Sally Jean. Reporter St. Paul Pioneer Press, 1943-47; publicist Democratic Nat. Com., 1948,52; writer Labor's League for Polit. Edn., AFL, 1949-52, Internat. Assn. Machinist, 1952-53; editorial writer Lindsay-Schaub Newspapers, Ill., 1954-58; nat. affairs reporter Washington Post, 1958-66; asso. dir. Profl. Journalism Fellowships Program, Stanford, 1966-68; dir. Washington Journalism Center, 1968—. Recipient award for distinguished Washington corr. Sigma Delta Chi, 1961. Mem. Kappa Sigma, Club: National Press (Washington). Author: Taxpayers' Hayride; The Farm Problem From the New Deal to the Billie Sol Estes Case, 1964; Arms, Money and Politics, 1965. Contbr. articles to mags. including Harper's Reporter, New Republic, N.Y. Times mag. Home: 3421 Raymond St Chevy Chase MD 20015 Office: 2401 Virginia Av NW Washington DC 20037

DUSEL, WILLIAM JOHN, educator; b. Menlo Park, Cal., Feb. 9, 1917; s. William John and Nettie Magdalene (Kuhn) D.; A.A., Menlo Coll., 1936; A.B magna cum laude, Stanford, 1938, M.A., 1940, Ph.D., 1956; m. Pauline Lucille Stevens, July 21, 1940; children—Ann Stevens, William John III, Cynthia Jane. Tchr. English, Menlo Jr. Coll., 1938-39, Sonora High Sch., 1940-42, Los Gatos Union High Sch., 1946-47; asst. prof. English, San Jose State Coll., 1947, supr. student teaching in English, 1947-56, asst. to pres., 1956-57, v.p. coll., 1957-67, exec. v.p., prof. English, 1967-70, prof. English, 1970—. Bd. dirs. Ednl. Devel. Corp., 1961-67. Served to 1st lt. USAAF, 1942-46. Mem. Cal. Assn. English Councils (pres. 1956-58), Phi Beta Kappa, Phi Eta Sigma. Author: Determining an Efficient Teaching Load in English, 1955. Contbr. profl. jours. Home: 15177 Piedmont Rd Saratoga CA 95070 Office: San Jose State Coll San Jose CA 95114

DUSENBERRY, WILLIAM HOWARD, educator; b. Carmichaels, Pa., June 6, 1908; s. William Smith and Edith Agnes (Miller) D.; A.B., Waynesburg Coll., 1932; A.M., U. Mich., 1936, Ph.D., 1941. Tchr., Carmichaels area pub. schs., 1932-38; instr. history Fresno State Coll., 1942; instr. history U. Cal. at Los Angeles 1946-48; asso. prof. history U. Pitts., 1948-61; prof. history, chmn. history dept. Waynesburg Coll., 1962—, liaison officer between Waynesburg Coll. and Regional Council Internat. Edn. Served with USAAF, 1942-46. Mem. Am., Pa., Greene County hist. assns., Agrl. Hist. Soc., Conf. on Latin-Am. History, Warriors Trail Assn., S.A.R. Author: The Mexican Mesta: Adminstration of Ranching in Colonial Mexico, 1963. Home: 53 S Morris St Waynesburg PA 15370

DUSHANE, JAMES WILLIAM, educator, physician; b. Madison, Ind., Apr. 17, 1912; s. Donald and Harriette Graham (McLelland) DuS.; A.B., DePauw U., 1933; M.D., Yale, 1937; m. Mary Margaret Hill, May 7, 1939; children—Mary Margaret, James Anderson. Intern, Yale-New Haven Hosp., 1937-38, resident pediatrics, 1938-39; resident Children's Meml. Hosp., Chgo., 1939-42; pvt. practice pediatrics, Evanston, Ill., 1942-44; instr. Northwestern U. Med. Sch., 1942-44; mem. staff Mayo Clinic, 1946—, head sect. pediatrics, 1957-69, mem. bd. govs., 1961—; prof. pediatrics Mayo Found., U. Minn., 1960—. Trustee Mayo Found., 1967—. Served to lt. USNR, 1944-46. Diplomate Am. Bd. Pediatrics (chmn. sub-bd. cardiology 1961- 66). Mem. A.M.A., Am. Acad. Pediatrics (founding chmn. cardiology sect. 1958), Am. Coll. Chest Physicians, Am. Pediatric Soc., Am. Heart Assn. (chmn. council rheumatic fever and cardiology 1960-62), Alpha Omega Alpha, Phi Kappa Psi. Contbr. articles to med. jours. Home: 1210 6th SW Rochester MN 55901 Office: Mayo Clinic Rochester MN 55901

DUSON, CURLEY PHARR, investment banker; b. El Campo, Tex., May 24, 1921; s. Curley Pharr and Clarice (Koch) D.; B.B.A., U. Tex., 1942; m. Betty Jo Tomforde, Mar 18, 1944; children—Betty M., Molly C., Stephen P. With Rotan, Mosle & Co., Houston, 1947-65, partner, 1953-65; formerly pres., dir., mem. exec. com. Rotan, Mosle-Dallas Union, Inc., Houston; dir. Western Nat. Bank, Houston, Fairmont Foods Co., Omaha. Bd. dirs. Family Service Bur., Houston, 1957-60, Harris County Mental Health Assn., 1963—. Served to capt. AUS, 1942-46. Mem. Nat. Assn. Securities Dealers (bd. govs. 1964-66), Investment Bankers Assn. (chmn. Tex. 1967), Kappa Sigma. Republican. Presbyn. (ruling elder). Home: 61 Briar Hollow Lane Houston TX 77027

DUTCHER, CLINTON HARVEY, hosp. adminstr.; b. Colorado Springs, Colo., July 27, 1909; s. Oliver Harry and Elsie (Taylor) D.; ed. pub. schs.; m. Elizabeth Bryant, July 28, 1931; 1 son, Clinton Harvey. Enlisted in U.S. Navy, 1927, commd. warrent officer, 1942, advanced through grades to lt. comdr. Med. Service Corps, 1954; ret., 1957; bus. mgr. Central Fla. Tb Hosp., Orlando, 1957-60; bus. mgr. Sunland Hosp., Orlando, 1960-63, adminstr., 1963—. Decorated Purple Heart. Mem. Am. Assn. Mental Deficiency, Ret. Officers Assn., Sojourners, Heroes of 76, Legion of Honor, Navy League. Mason (Shriner), Lion. Address: PO Box 3513 Orlando, FL 32802.

DUTCHER, FRANCIS EDWARD, bldg. products co. exec.; b. Vancouver, B.C., Can., Oct. 24, 1909; s. Bert Elroy and Eva (McQuay) D.; student St. Petersburg Jr. Coll., 1929- 30; B.S. in Bus., Miami U., Oxford, O., 1932; m. Nancy Jane Callander, Mar. 6, 1937; children—Barbara Ann (Mrs. Justin Kimball), Nancy Odette (Mrs. Peter Strohmeier). Came to U.S., 1914, naturalized. With Johns-Manville Sales Corp., 1933- -, v.p., sales mgr. dealer bldg. products, N.Y.C., 1958-59, v.p., gen. mdse. mgr. bldg. products div., 1959-61, sr. operating v.p. bldg. materials divs. Johns Manville Corp., N.Y.C., 1961—, also dir.; mem. adv. com. Chem. Bank, N.Y.C. Bd. dirs. Producers Council. Served to lt. USNR, 1943-46. Mem. Nat. Mineral Wool Assn. (pres. 1961), Mineral Fibre Asbestos-Products Bur. (chmn. exec. com.), Asphalt Roofing Mfrs. Assn. (past chmn. exec. com.). Clubs: Union League (N.Y.C.); Tokeneke (Darien, Conn.). Home: 18 Crooked Mile Rd Darien CT 06820 Office: 22 E 40th St New York City NY 10016

DUTEMPLE, OCTAVE JOSEPH, chme. engr., assn. exec.; b. Hubbell, Mich., Dec. 10, 1920; s. Octave Joseph and Marguerite Odina (Gadoury) DuT.; B.S., Mich. Coll. Mining and Tech., 1948, M.S., 1949; N.B.A., Northwestern U., 1955; m. Susan Margaret Keach, June 9, 1951; children—Lesley Ann, Octave Joseph. Civilian flight instr., dir. ground sch. tng. Army, Navy and Fgn. Aviation Cadets, 1942-45; pilot, also aircraft sales South and Central Am., 1946-47; chem. engr. Argonne Nat. Lab., Lemont, Ill., 1949-58; exec. sec. Am. Nuclear Soc., 1958—; pres. Plainfield Investors, Inc. Aviation cadet USAAF, 1945. Mem. Am. Inst. Chem. Engrs., Ill. Engrng. Council, Am. Chem. Soc., Research Soc. Am., Western Soc. Engrs., Phi Lambda Upsilon, Delta Sigma Phi (past pres. Chgo. alumni chpt.). Episcopalian. Home: 15W306 Plainfield Rd Hinsdale IL 60521 Office: 244 E Ogden Av Hinsdale IL 60521

DUTHIE, WILLIAM DWIGHT, educator; b. Pullman, Wash., June 30, 1912; s. Ora Lee and Ellen Fredberg (Carlson) D.; A.B., U. Wash., 1935, M.S., 1937; Ph.D., Princeton, 1940; postgrad. U.S. Naval Acad., 1942-43. Teaching fellow math. U. Wash., 1935-38; J.S.K. fellow math. Princeton, 1938-40; instr. math. U. Mich., 1940-46; prof. aerology U.S. Naval Postgrad. Sch., 1946-47, chmn. dept. aerology, 1947-59, chmn. dept. meteorology, 1959-63, Distinguished prof., 1966-71, prof. emeritus, 1971—; faculty US Naval Postgrad. Sch., Monterey, Cal. Served to comdr. USNR, 1940-46. Mem. Am. Math. Soc., Am. Geophys. Union, Soc. Sigma Xi, Phi Mu Epsilon. Contbr. tech. articles to profl. jours;, pamphlets on math., meteorology. Home: Route 1 62 Mt Devon Rd Carmel CA 93921 Office: US Naval Postgrad Sch Monterey CA 93940

DUTMERS, RAYMOND M., food co. exec.; b. Grand Rapids, Mich., Jan. 2, 1914; s. Martin J. and Elizabeth (Vander-Laan) D.; student bus. adminstrn., Davenport Sch. Bus., 1932-36; m. Dorothy H. Fassett, Nov. 14, 1940; 1 dau., Barbara. With Spartan Stores, Inc., 1949—, exec. v.p., 1967—; pres. Grand Rapids Coffee Co.; dir. Southland D. & W. Market. Served with AUS, 1943 46. Decorated Bronze Star. Catholic. Home: 539 Carnoustic St Grand Rapids, MI 49506. Office: 1111 44th St Grand Rapids MI 49508

DUTOURD, JEAN, author; b. Paris, France, Jan. 14, 1920; s. Francois and Andree (Haas) D.; Ph.D., Sorbonne, 1940; m. Camille Lemercier, May 22, 1942; children—Frederic, Clara. With newspapers Liberation, Franc-Tireur, L'Aurore, Paris, 1944-47; program asst. BBC, London, 1947-50; editor Gallimard Pubs., Paris, 1950-66; columnist La Tribune de Geneve, 1955- 65; film critic Carrefour, 1954-62; TV critic Candide, 1962-63, columnist, 1966—; dramatic critic France-Soir, 1963—. Candidate for dep. from Paris, 1958. Served with French Resistance, 1942-44. Decorated Legion d'Honneur. Mem. French Writers Union (past chmn.). Author: Le dejeuner du Lundi, 1948; Une Tete de Chien; Au Bon Beurre, 1952; Doucin, 1954; Les Dupes, 1959; Les Horreurs de L'amour, 1962; La Fin Des Peaux Rouges, 1964; Le Demi-Solde, 1965; Pluche ou L'Amour de L'Art, 1967; L'école des Jocrisses, 1970. Home: 63 Avenue Kleber Paris, France.

DUTSCHMANN, KARL THEODORE, ret. telephone exec.; b. Dresden, Germany, June 4, 1901; s. Karl A. and Hulda M. (Hammer) D.; brought to U.S., 1906, naturalized, 1912; E.E., Syracuse U., 1921; m. Loretta G. Hazel, Jan. 8, 1926; children—Janet Marie (Mrs. Harry McGann), Karl Theodore. Engr. N.Y. Telephone Co., 1921-31, engr. plant extension, 1931-35, gen. plant supr. Manhattan, Upstate, L.I.

areas, 1935-48, chief engr. L.I. area, 1948-55, v.p., 1955-63; group gen. mgr. Telephone Latin Am. Internat. Tel. & Tel., 1963-66. Vice pres., dir. Greater N.Y. Safety Council. Fellow Am. Inst. E.E.; mem. Telephone Pioneers Am. (pres. Manhattan Empire chpt. 1959-60). Club: Engineers' (N.Y.C.). Home: 119 California St Ridgewood NJ 07450

DUTTON, CLARENCE BENJAMIN, lawyer; b. Pitts., May 31, 1917; s. Clarence Benjamin and Lillian (King) D.; B.S. with distinction, Ind. U., 1938, LL.B. with high distinction, 1940, LL.D., 1970; m. Marion Jane Stevens, June 21, 1941; children— Victoria Lynn, Barbara King. Admitted to Ind. bar, 1940; instr. bus. law Ind. U. Sch. Bus., 1940-41; atty. E.I. duPont de Nemours & Co., Inc., Wilmington, Del., 1941- 43; asst. prof. law Ind. U. Sch. Law, 1946-47; pvt. practice law, Indpls., 1947—. Dir. Sarkes Tarzian, Inc., Oaklawn Meml. Gardens, Inc., Huber Hunt & Nichols, Inc., Paul Harris Stores, Inc., Central Supply Co., J L Realty, Inc. Mem. Ind. Jud. Study Commn., 1965—; Mem. regional adv. group Ind. U. Sch. Medicine, 1966—; mem., sec. Ind. Civil Code Study Commn., 1967—; mem. Indian Commn. on Uniform State Laws, 1970—. Bd. dirs. Found. for Ind. U. Sch. Bus., Found. Econ. and Bus. Studies. Served to lt. comdr. USNR, 1943-45. Mem. Am. (ho. dels. 1960-62, state del. 1967—, chmn. gen. practice sect. 1971-72, gov. 1971—), Ind. (bd. mgrs. 1957—, pres. 1961-62), Indpls. (v.p. 1957) bar assns., Ind. Soc. Chgo. Republican. Presbyn. Clubs: Lawyers (pres. 1959-60), Indianapolis Country (pres. 1955), Athletic, Columbia (Indpls); Woodstock, Ponte Vedra (Fla.); Traders Point Hunt. Author bus. law sect. Chemical Business Handbook, 1954. Contbr. articles to profl. jours. Home: 1400 W 52d St Indianapolis IN 46208 Office: Guaranty Bldg Indianapolis IN 46204

DUTTON, DONNELL WAYNE, aero. engr., educator; b. St. Louis, Sept. 24, 1913; s. Carol Masson and Ethel Johanna (Moller) D.; B.S., Mo. Sch. Mines and Metallurgy, 1935, M.E., 1959; M.S., Ga. Inst. Tech., 1940; m. Ruth Mullenburg, Dec. 14, 1940; children—Robert Wayne, Diana Louise, Susan Gay. Draftsman engring. dept. Allis-Chalmers Mfg. Co., 1935-38; student asst. Daniel Guggenheim Sch. Aeros., Ga. Sch. Tech., Atlanta, 1938- 40, asst. prof., 1940-43, prof., dir. sch., 1943-63, prof., research asso., 1963—; chief engr. Monocoupe Aircraft Corp., summer 1939; stress analyst Curtiss Wright Corp., Robertson, Mo., 1940. Cons. research and devel. div. War Dept., 1946-47; cons. to asst. sec. def. (research and devel.), 1956-58; ex-men. subcom. helicopters NAC. Served as 1st lt. C.E. Res., A.U.S., 1935-42. Mem. Inst. Aero. Scis., Am. Soc. Engring. Edn. (chmn. aviation div. 1947- 48,59-60, pres. S.E. sect. 1956-57), Am. Helicopter Soc., Ga. Engring. Soc., Registered Engrs. Ga., C. of C. (past chmn. aviation com.), Tau Beta Pi, Phi Kappa Phi, Theta Tau, Sigma Gamma Tau. Home: 41 Burdett Rd NW Atlanta GA 30327

DUTTON, FREDERIC BOOTH, chemist, educator; b. Cleve., Dec. 24, 1906; s. Charles Frederic and Elma (Booth) D.; A.B., Oberlin Coll., 1928, A.M., 1932; Ph.D., Western Res. U., 1937; m. Faith Kedzie; children—James Kedzie, Diane Hope (Mrs. John B. Haney). Instr. chemistry Baldwin-Wallace Coll., 1931-34, asst. prof., 1934-39, asso. prof., 1941-47; instr. Yale, 1939-40; prof. Olivet Coll., 1941; instr. Cleve. Coll., Western Res. U., 1938-39, summer 1939; asso. prof. chemistry Mich. State U., East Lansing, 1947-50, prof., 1950—, head sci. and math. teaching center, 1957-66, dean Lyman Briggs Coll., 1966—. Program dir. NSF, 1964-65. Fellow A.A.A.S. (sect. sec. 1964-67, sect. chmn., v.p. 1970); mem. Am. Chem. Soc. (sec. Cleve. 1943-46, chmn. elect 1946-47, treas. div. chem. edn. 1952-54, chmn. Mich. U. sect. 1949—), Nat. Assn. Research Sci. Teaching (pres. 1964-65), Nat. Higher Edn. Assn., Northeastern Ohio Chemistry Tchrs. Orgn. (pres. 1939, 4O, 42), N.E.A., Mich. (pres. 1963-64), Nat. sci. tchrs. assns., Sigma Xi, Alpha Chi Sigma. Home: 931 Wick Ct East Lansing, MI 48823.

DUTTON, FREDERICK GARY, lawyer; b. Julesburg, Colo., June 16, 1923; s. F.G. and Lucy Elizabeth (Parker) Dutton; B.A. with honors, U. Cal. at Berkeley, 1946; LL.B. (bd. editors Law Rev.), Stanford, 1949. Admitted to Cal. bar, 1949; with firm Kirkbride, Wilson, Harzfeld & Wallace, San Mateo, Cal., 1949-50; 1st asst. counsel So. Counties Gas Co. Cal., 1952-56; chief asst. atty. gen. Cal., 1957-58; exec. Sec. to gov. Cal., 1959-60; spl. asst. to Pres. Kennedy, 1961; asst. sec. of state for congl. relations, 1962-64; mem. firm Dutton, Gwirtzman, Zumas & Wise, 1965—; exec. dir. Robert F. Kennedy Meml. Found., 1968-70. Editor, Los Angeles Bar mag., 1955; spl. counsel judiciary com. Cal. Senate, 1956-57. So. Cal. chmn. Stevenson presdl. campaign, 1956; Cal. campaign chmn. Brown for Gov., 1958; dep. nat. chmn. Citizens for Kennedy and Johnson campaign, 1960; exec. dir. platform com. Democratic Nat. Conv., 1964; dir. research and planning nat. Dem. presdl. campaign, 1964; organizing dir. John F. Kennedy Meml. Library Oral History Project, 1964-65. Bd. dirs. Center for Community Devel. and Citizens Adv. Com., 1969-70; bd. regents U. Cal., 1962—. Served with inf. AUS, World War II; prisoner of war Germany; served with Judge Adv. Gen. Corps, AUS, Korea. Decorated Bronze Star, Purple Heart, Combat Inf. Badge. Mem. Fed. Bar Assn., State Bar Cal., Delta Tau Delta. Contbr. legal jours., mags. Author: Changing Sources of Power: American Politics in the 1970's, 1970.

DUTTON, LELAND SUMMERS, librarian; b. Lorain, O., Mar. 9, 1905; s. Joseph and Evalena May (Summers) D.; B.A., Miami U., Oxford, O., 1929; B.S. in L.S., Columbia, 1932, postgrad. summer 1939; m. Ruth Genevieve Clitty, Dec. 24, 1937; chilren—Lee Summers, Lymore Evalena. Asst. loan dept. Miami U. Library, 1929-31; asst. genealogy and local history N.Y. Pub. Library, 1931-34; mem. staff Miami U. Library, 1934—, dir. libraries, chmn. dept. library sci., 1956-69, prof. 1961—, research resources librarian, 1970—. Mem. Am., Ohio (pres. 1941, exec. bd. 1942-45) library assns., Oxford Mus. Assn. (pres. 1954) Coll. and Research Libraries Assn. Presby (elder). Contbr. articles, revs. to profl. jours. Home: 350 Patterson Av Oxford, OH 45056.

DUTTON, REGINALD DAVID LEY, corp. exec.; b. Skegness, Eng., Aug. 20, 1916; s. Reginald J.G. and Dora (Hiley) D.; student Magdalen Coll. Sch., Oxford, Eng., 1928-31; m. Pamela Jean Harrison, June 23, 1952; children—Jacqueline, Timothy Paul, Clive Nicholas. With Oxford U. Press, 1931-37; with Lopex Ltd. (formerly London Press Exchange), 1937—, mng. dir., 1954-70, chmn., 1971—; chmn. LPE Ltd., 1966-71, Leo Burnett-LPE Internat., 1969-71; dir. Leo Burnett Inc., 1969—. Served with Brit. Navy, 1939-40. Fellow Inst. Practitioners Advt. (pres. 1969-71); mem. Council Advt. Assn., Inst. Marketing, Brit. Inst. Mgmt. Home: 48 St Martin's Lane London WC 2 England also 3 Bournemouth Dr Herne Bay Kent England Office: 110 St Martin's Lane London WC 2 England

DUTTON, RICHARD KING, mfg. co. exec.; b. Pitts., June 18, 1919; s. Clarence Benjamin and Lillian Mary (King) D.; B.S. in Bus. Adminstrn., Ind. U., 1941; J.D., Stanford, 1947; m. Juliann Hoover, Mar. 14, 1942; 1 dau., Kathy Elaine. Admitted to Cal. bar, 1947, Ohio bar, 1960; asso., partner firm of Breed, Robinson & Stewart, Oakland, Cal., 1947-55; staff atty., asst. sec., gen. atty. Glidden Co., Cleve., 1955-63, sec., gen. counsel, 1963- 67, dir., 1967—; v.p., gen. counsel Glidden-Durkee div. SCM Corp., 1967- -; asst. sec. SCM Corp., 1967—. Mem. Citizens League Cleve., Greater Cleve. Growth Bd., Lake Erie Girl Scout Council, Lakewood Little Theater. Served to maj. USMCR, 1941-46. Mem. Am., Cal., Ohio, Cleve. (corp. counsel com.) bar assns., Am. Judicature Soc., Def. Law Inst., Chgo. Bd. Trade, Am. Soc. Corp. Secs., Am. Legal Execs., Ill., Ohio chambers commerce, Am. Mgmt. Assn., Edible Oils Inst., Ohio Corp. Counsel Inst., Nat. Paint, Varnish and Lacquer Assn., Grocery Mfrs. Assn., Beta Gamma Sigma, Phi Alpha Delta. Conglist. Clubs: Ponte Vedre; Cleveland Athletic, Lakewood Country; Ambassador, Admiral, 100,000 Miler. Research Lakeview Country; Sharon Golf; Briarwood Country; asst., writer Sutherland Statutory Construction, 3d edit., 1943. Home: 2324 Valley View Dr Rocky River OH 44116 Office: Union Commerce Bldg Cleveland OH 44115

DUTTON, WILMER COFFMAN, Jr., city planner; b. Ridgewood, N.J., Aug. 28, 1920; s. Wilmer C. and Florence (Bardsley) D.; A.B., Dartmouth, 1942; postgrad. U. N.C., 1947,48; m. Ann Pickells, July 29, 1949 (div. 1954); 1 son, Christopher; m. 2d, Frances Wilson Zerbst, Nov. 22, 1957; children—Sharon, Janet, Karen. Asst. dir. planning Greensboro, N.C., 1949-50; sr. planner Chgo. Housing Authority, 1950-51; dir. planning Cook County Housing Authority, 1951-53; dir. planning Charleston County (S.C.) Planning Bd., 1954-57; exec. dir. Am. Inst. Planners, Washington, 1958-63; dir. Nat. Capital Planning Commn., Washington, 1963-65; chmn. Md.-Nat. Capital Park and Planning Commn., 1965-71, planning adviser, 1965-66, 71—. Chmn., Nat. Com. Urban Life, 1963-65; chmn. Prince George's dist. Boy Scouts Am., 1969—. Served to 1st lt. AUS, 1942-46. Mem. Am. Inst. Planners (treas. Chgo. region 1953-54, pres. S.E. 1955-56), Nat. Assn. Housing Ofcls., Am. Soc. Planning Ofcls., Piping and Marching Soc., Lower Chalmers St., Md. Assn. County Planning Ofcls. (pres. 1970), Lambda Alpha, Epsicopalian. Rotarian. Home: 6513 41st Av University Park MD 20840 Office: 6600 Kenilworth Av Riverdale MD 20840

DUVAL, ALBERT FRANK, paper co. exec.; b. Holyoke, Mass., Oct. 31, 1920; s. Albert Frank and Lena (Potvin) D.; grad. Williston Acad., 1939; B.A., Amherst Coll., 1943; m. Mary Tague, Apr. 12, 1947; children—Susan, Denise, Richard, Nanette, Robert, Carolyn, Michele, Kathleen. Mgr. Cal. div. U.S. Envelope Co., 1946-52, sales mgr., 1952-55, v.p. sales, 1955-60, pres. 1960; v.p. Hammermill Paper Co., Erie, Pa., 1960-69, sr. v.p., 1969, pres. 1970—, also dir.; dir. Milton Bradley Co., Springfield, Mass., Security-Peoples Trust Co., Erie, Pa. Chmn. adv. bd. Mercyhurst Coll., 1968—; trustee St. Vincent's Hosp. Served with USAAF 1944-46; ETO. Mem. Envelope Mfrs. Assn. (pres. 1963-65), Am. Paper Inst. (chmn. printing-writing paper div. 1971). Club: Kahkwa (pres. 1969—) (Erie, Pa.). Home: R D 2 Fairview PA 16415 Office: E Lake Rd Erie PA 16512

DUVAL, ANNA MARIE, educator; b. Denver, Nov. 1, 1913; d. Edward Rene and Augusta Bertha (Marunde) D.; A.B., U. Denver, 1934, M.A., 1936; Ph.D., U. Colo., 1942. Asst. prof. U. Colo., 1942-48; asso. prof. U. Denver, 1948-52; prof. dept. chemistry U. Minn., Duluth, 1952—. Research fellow Child Research Council, 1936-42; vis. scientist Columbia, 1959-60. Allied profl. mem. Nat. League Nursing, 1952—. Mem. Am. Chem. Soc., Sigma Xi. Contbr. articles profl. jours. Home: 1122 Chester Park Dr Duluth MN 55812

DUVAL, MERLIN KEARFOTT, coll. dean, govt. ofcl.; b. Montclair, N.J., Oct. 12, 1922; s. Merlin Kearfott and Margaret (Smith) D.; A.B., Dartmouth, 1943; M.D., Cornell U., 1946; m. Carol Nickerson, June 21. 1944; children—David K., Barbara L., Frederick P. Intern, N.Y. Hosp., N.Y.C., 1946-47, Roosevelt Hosp., N.Y.C., 1949-50; resident surgery VA Hosp., Bronx, N.Y., 1951-54; instr., asst. prof. surgery State U. N.Y. Coll. Medicine, Bklyn., 1954-56; asst. prof., prof. surgery U. Okla. Med. Center, 1956-63; dean U. Ariz. Coll. Medicine, Tucson, 1964—; dir. Ariz. Med. Center, 1969—; asst. sec. health and sci. affairs U.S. Dept. Health, Edn. and Welfare, 1971—. Cons. VA, USPHS. Served with USNR, 1943- 45,47-49. Home: 10 Calle Encanto Tucson AZ 85716

DUVAL, MILES P., Jr., ret. naval officer; b. Portsmouth, Va., Apr. 19, 1896; s. Miles P. and Minnie Lee (Chalkley) DuV.; B.S., U.S. Naval Acad., 1918, postgrad. U.S. Naval War Coll., 1925-26; U.S. Naval Post Grad. Sch., 1930-31; M.F.S., Fgn. Service Sch., Georgetown U., 1937. Commd. ensign USN, 1918, advanced through grades to capt., 1945; comdg. officer U.S.S. Dupont, 1933-35, participant naval demonstration off Cuban ports, 1933-34; sec. Shore Sta. Devel. Bd., Navy Dept., Washington, 1936-38; comdg. officer U.S.S. Antares, 1939-40; capt. port, Balboa, C.Z., in charge marine operations Pacific subdiv. Panama Canal, 1941-44; planned, coordinated enlargement Balboa Harbor, 1942-43; developer high level terminal lake plan for improvement Panama Canal, May 1943; comdg. officer U.S.S. Dade, 1944- 46, participant Okinawa campaign, 1945; designated Navy Dept. liaison officer, coordinator for modernization studies Panama Canal, 1946; ret., 1949. Bd. dirs. Gorgas Meml. Inst. Tropical and Preventive Medicine. Vice chmn., gen. cons. John F. Stevens Hall of Fame Com., 1969—. Awarded Legion of Merit (Army), 1945. Fellow A.A.A.S.; mem. Va. Hist. Soc., U.S. Naval Inst., Soc. Am. Mil. Engrs. Panama Hist. Soc. (corr.), Panama Canal Soc. (Washington), Panama Canal Natural History Soc. (past v.p.), Naval Hist. Found. Soc., Va., Washington (past v.p.), permanent internat. assns. nav. congresses (life), Jamestowne Soc., Baronial Order Magna Charta, Mil. Order Crusades, Phi Alpha Theta (hon.). Clubs: New York Yacht, Explorers (N.Y.C.); Propeller of U.S., Cosmos, Army and Navy (Washington). Author: Series on Panama Canal: Cadiz to Cathay, 1940, 47, 68; And the Mountains Will Move, 1947, 69; George Rogers Clark-Conqueror of the Old Northwest; Matthew Fountaine Maury: Benefactor of Mankind; Sam Houston: The Washington of the Vast Southwest. Author of Papers on interoceanic cana problems. Address: 2121 Massachusetts Av NW Washington DC 20008

DUVAL, PHILIP LIVINGSTON ROLLIN, advt. sales exec.; b. N.Y.C., Apr. 6, 1920; s. Clive Livingston and Augusta (Lynde) DuV.; grad. Groton Sch., 1939; B.A., Yale, 1943; m. Barbara V. Wheeler, Dec. 27, 1952 (div. Nov. 1968); children—Philip L.R. II, Alexandra Lynde; m. 2d, Janis Locke Lee, Feb. 2, 1969. Salesman, Bates Fabrics Co., N.Y.C., 1946-51; asst. sales mgr. William Skinner & Sons, N.Y.C., 1953-54; category mgr. The New Yorker mag., N.Y.C., 1955-57; exec. v.p., mgr. sales and advt. Gordon Ford Sales Co., N.Y.C., 1957-59; with Harper-Atlantic Sales Co., N.Y.C., 1959—, exec. v.p., 1965-68, pres., 1968—; chmn. bd. Yale Alumni Publs., Inc., New Haven; Mem. membership com. Nat. Inst. Social Scis., 1968—; bd. mgrs. St. Andrews Soc. N.Y., N.Y.C., 1969—; officer New Canaan Volunteer Fire Co. #1, 1958—; chmn. zoning bd. appeals Town New Canaan, 1960—; mem. nat. exec. com. Purnell Sch., Pottersville, N.J., 1970—; mem. sponsoring com. Am.-Scottish Found. Served to comdr. USNR, 1942-46, 51-52. Decorated Bronze Star with valor clasp. Mem. Elihu Soc. (Yale), Soc. Colonial Wars, Mil. Order Fgn. Wars. Republican. Presbyn. (elder). Clubs: Yale, Union, Pilgrims (N.Y.C.); New Canaan Country. Home: 388 Brushy Ridge New Canaan CT 06840 Office: 535 5th Av New York City NY 10017

DUVALL, EVELYN MILLIS, family life educator; b. Oswego, N.Y., July 28, 1906; d. Charles and Bertha (Palmer) Millis; B.S. summa cum laude, Syracuse U., 1927; M.S., Vanderbilt U., 1939; postgrad. Columbia, 1938; Ph.D., U. Chgo., 1946; L.H.D., Hood. Coll., 1970; m. Sylvanus Milne Duvall, Dec. 19, 1927; children—Jean Louise, Joy Millis. Profl. staff leader Chgo. Assn. Child Study and Parent Edn., 1934-40; organizing dir. Assn. Family Living, 1940-45; exec. sec. Nat. Council Family Relations, 1945-51, mem. exec. com., hon. life mem., 1951—, chmn. com. on internat. liaison, 1960—. Distinguished prof. family life So. Ill. U., 1962; Univ. faculty, New Zealand, 1967; summer teaching various univs.; dir. original workship on marriage and family research U. Chgo. 1950, cons. family life edn., 1952; participant tour Family Life Leaders through Asia and Middle East, 1945-55; dir. Adolescent Study Course, Nat. P.T.A.; originator Town Hall Marriage Course, N.Y.C., 1947,48; co-chmn. Com. Dynamics Family Interaction, 1948; chmn. com. on internat. dels. Internat. Conf. on the Family, 1960, chmn. sect. on family life edn. New Delhi, 1967; mem. gen. council Internat. Union Family Orgns., 1960—, mem. nat. U.S. Com., 1964—; co-chmn. N.Am. Conf. on Ch. and Family, 1961. Recipient George Arents medal Syracuse U., 1952. Fellow Am. Sociol. Assn.; mem. Am. Assn. Marriage and Family Counselors (exec. com. 1949-50), Nat. Council Family Relations, Nat. Conf. Family Life (orgn. sec. 1946- 48), Am. Inst. Family Relations (regional cons.), Nat. Com. Parent Edn., Child Study Assn. Am. (adv. bd.), Soc. Research Child Devel., Nat. Council Chs. Christ Am. (bd. mgrs., div. on family), Nat. Council Ch. Women (charter bd. mem.), Citizens Schs. Com. Chgo. (adv. bd. mem.), Sigma Xi, Phi Kappa Phi, Pi Delta Nu, Pi Lambda Theta. Democrat. Conglist. Author books including: Family Living, 1950, rev. 1955,61, Japanese edit., 1954; Facts of Life and Love, 1950; When You Marry, 1953, rev. 1967; In-Laws; Pro and Con, 1954; Facts of Life and Love for Teenagers, rev. 1956; Family Development, 1957, rev. 1967,71; The Art of Dating, 1958, rev. 1967; (with Reuben Hill) Being Married, 1960; (with S.M. Duvall) Sense and Nonsense about Sex, 1962; Love and the Facts of Life, 1963, rev. 1967; (with David Mace, Paul Popenoe) The Church Faces the Family, 1964; Why Wait Til Marriage?, 1965; Today's Teen-Agers, 1966; (book, filmstrip) About Sex and Growing Up, 1968, Faith in Families, 1970. Asso. editor Marriage and Family Living, 1945-51; co-editor: Sex Ways in Fact and Faith, 1961. Contbr. to books; writer with husband syndicated feature, Let's Explore Your Mind, 1957-71. Address: 700 John Ringling Blvd Sarasota FL 33577

DUVALL, GEORGE EVERED, physicist; b. Leesville, La., Feb. 6, 1920; s. George W. and Sadie G. (Moore) D.; B.S., Ore. State Coll., 1946; Ph.D., Mass. Inst. Tech., 1948; m. Betty J. Morgan, Sept. 14, 1941; children—Jeffrey M., William S. Research asst. div. war research U. Cal. at Point Loma, 1941-43, asst. physicist, 1943-44, asso. physicist, 1944-45; research asso. Research Lab. Electronics, Mass. Inst. Tech., 1946-48; physicist, Gen. Electric Co., Hanford, Wash., 1948-50, head theoretical physics, 1950- 53; sr. physicist Stanford Research Inst., 1953-55, asst. dir. Poulter Labs., 1955-57, sci. dir. labs., 1957-62, dir. labs., 1962-64; prof. physics Wash. State U., Pullman, 1964—; research underwater sound, phys. electronics, reactor physics, detonation phenomena, shock waves in solids. Fellow Am. Phys. Soc.; mem. A.A.A.S., Combustion Inst., Soc. for Natural Philosophy, Sigma Xi. Democrat. Unitarian. Home: 300 Sunset Dr Pullman, WA 99163.

DUVALL, SEVERN PARKER COSTIN, educator; b. Norfolk, Va., Mar. 25, 1924; s. Severn Parker Costin and Helen (Hobbs) C.; A.B., U. Va., 1948; student U. N.C., 1943-44; M.A., Princeton, 1951, Ph.D., 1955; m. Marian Elizabeth Smith, June 16, 1950; children—Ridgely H., Severn Parker Costin III, Mary Staunton. Instr., Princeton, 1950-51; mem. faculty Dartmouth, Instr., Princeton, 1950-51; mem. faculty Dartmouth, 1953-62, asso. prof. English, 1961-62; prof. English, chmn. dept. Washington and Lee U., 1962—; Fulbright vis. prof. A.D.I. Germersheim a.R., U. Mainz (Germany), 1957-58, English Inst., U. Warsaw (Poland), 1971. Served to capt. USMCR, 1943-46, 51-52. Mem. Phi Beta Kappa, Delta Phi, Omicron Delta Kappa, Raven Soc. Home: 106 Paxton St Lexington VA 24450

DUVALL, WALLACE ODELL, savs. and loan assn. exec.; b. Pearson, Ga., July 23, 1901; s. W.L. and Carolyn (Ware) Duv.; student Young Harris Coll., 1918-21; A.B., U. Fla., 1924, LL.D., 1968; LL.B., Atlanta Law Sch., 1926; hon. LL.D.; m. Harriet Turner, Oct. 25, 1923; children—Carolyn (Mrs. J.T. Brumby), Frances (Mrs. P.H. Nichols). Admitted to Ga. bar, 1926; with McElreath & Scott, Atlanta, later mem. firm McElreath, Scott, Duckworth & DuVall to 1940; sec., atty. Atlanta Bldg. & Loan Assn., (now Atlanta Fed. Savs. & Loan Assn.), 1930-40, exec. v.p., sec., 1940-51, pres., 1951—, now chmn. bd.; pres. Ga. Savs. & Loan, Inc., 1940; dir. So. Life Ins. Co. of Atlanta, Fed. Home Loan Bank of Greensboro, N.C. Mem. com. on trends and econ. policies U.S. Savs. and Loan League, 1944-47, com. res. credits and banking regulations, 1949, legislative com., 1950—, spl. com. to study Fed. Home Loan Bank System, dir. Southeastern Group Conf., dir. U.S. Savs. and Loan League, 1957, v.p., 1958, pres., 1959-60. Mem. Fulton County Bd. Pub. Welfare, mem. Fulton-DeKalb Hosp. Authority, now chmn. Mem. Fla. Legislature, 1925-26. Bd. dirs. Atlanta Boys Club; trustee, treas. Young Harris Coll.; trustee Bapt. Village for Aged. Mem. Ga., Atlanta bar assns., Atlanta C. of C. (dir.). Democrat. Baptist (chmn. finance com.). Mason, Kiwanian (chmn. finance com.) Clubs: Atlanta Lawyers, Commerce, Capital City (Atlanta). Home: 526 W Wesley Rd Atlanta GA 30305 Office: 20 Marietta St Atlanta GA 30303

DU VIGNEAUD, VINCENT, educator; b. Chgo., May 18, 1901; s. Alfred Joseph and Mary Theresa (O'Leary) duV.; B.S., U. Ill., 1923, M.S., 1924, Sc.D., 1960; Ph.D., U. Rochester, 1927, Sc.D., 1965; Sc.D., Yale, N.Y. U., 1955, St. Louis U., 1965, George Washington U., 1968; m. Zella Zon Ford, June 12, 1924; children—Vincent, Marilyn Renée Brown. Asst. biochemist Phila. Gen. Hosp., asst. biochemist U. Pa. Grad. Sch. Medicine, 1924-25; teaching asst. Sch. Medicine U. Rochester, 1925-27; NRC fellow Johns Hopkins Med. Sch., 1927-28, Kaiser Wilhelm Inst., Dresden, Germany, U. Edinburgh Med. Sch., UCH Med. Sch., London, 1928-29; asso. dept. chemistry U. Ill., 1929-30, asst. prof., 1930-32; prof., head dept. biochemistry George Washington U. Sch. Medicine, 1932-38; prof., head dept. biochemistry Cornell U. Med. Coll., N.Y.C., 1938-67, emeritus prof. biochemistry, 1967—; prof. chemistry Cornell U., Ithaca, N.Y., 1967—. Lectr. various univs. Mem. Health Research Adv. Council City N.Y., 1958-62; nat. adv. arthritis and metabolic diseases council NIH, 1960-64. Trustee Rockefeller U. Recipient Hillebrand prize Chem. Soc. Washington, 1936; Borden award for Research in Med. Scis., 1947; Lasker award Am. Pub. Health Assn., 1948; Merit award for War Research, 1948; John Scott award, 1954; Sci. award Am. Pharm. Mfrs. Assn., 1955; Passano Found. award, 1955; Nobel prize in Chemistry, 1955; Chandler medal, 1956; Nutrition Found. 20th Anniversary award, 1961; 7th Ann. Hon. Lecture award Albany Med. Coll., 1963; A.C.P. award, 1965; Eli Lilly award Endocrine Soc., 1967. Fellow Am. Acad. Arts and Sciences, Royal Soc. Edinburgh (hon.), Chem. Soc. London, Royal Soc. Scis. Upsala (hon.), Royal Inst. Chemistry (London); mem. Am. Inst. Nutrition (Mead Johson vitamin award 1943), Am. Soc. Biol. Chemistry (pres. 1951-52), Am. Chem. Soc. (council at large 1943, chmn. N.Y. sect. 1943, Nichols medal N.Y. sect. 1945, Willard Gibbs medal Chgo. sect. 1956), Soc. Exptl. Biology (past chmn. bd.), Harvey Soc., Am. Philos. Soc., Nat. Acad. Scis. (chmn. sect. biochem. 1958-60), N.Y. Acad. Sci., Washington Acad. Medicine, Xi, Alpha Chi Sigma, Phi Lambda Upsilon, Sigma Alpha Omega Alpha (hon.). Club: Chemists' (hon., N.Y.C.). Contbr. articles to sci. jours. Home: 200 White Park Rd Ithaca NY 14850

DUVIVIER, PAUL FULLER, fgn. service officer; b. N.Y.C., Feb. 4, 1915; s. Joseph and Eleanor (Keyes) DuV.; student Munich (Germany) U., 1933; A.B., Princeton, 1938; M.S. Georgetown U., 1940; m. Margaret Elisabeth de Ropp, Apr. 10, 1944; children—Paul Trimble, Ann Keyes. Joined U.S. Fgn. Service, 1941; vice consul, St. John's, Newfoundland, 1941-42; Marseille France, 1942; interned in Vichy, France, also Germany, 1942-44; assigned State Dept., 1944; vice consul, Accra, 1944-46; 3d sec., Ottawa, 1946-50; 2d sec., comml. attache, Stockholm, 1950-54; chief comml. sect. U.S. High Commn. Occupied Germany, Berlin, 1954; assigned Econ. Commn. Europe, Geneva, 1954-55; asst. chief div. econ. reporting State Dept., 1955-58; 2d sec., asst. comml. attache, Paris, 1958-61; consul, Bordeaux, 1961-62, Nice and Monaco, 1962-65; consul gen., Edinburgh, Scotland, 1965-68, Frankfurt, Germany, 1968-72. Chairman in France, Princeton $53 Million Fund Campaign, 1960-62. Mem. Pi Gamma Mu. Rotarian. Clubs: Quadrangle (Princeton) Metropolitan (Washington). Home: 3013 Cleveland Av Washington DC Office: Am Consulate Gen Frankfurt Main Germany

DUVOISIN, ROGER ANTOINE, artist, illustrator; b. Geneva, Switzerland, Aug. 28, 1904; s. Jacques Jonas and Judith E. (Moré) D.; student in Geneva, Ecole Professionalle, 1915-17, Ecole des Arts et Métiers, 1917-24; m. Louise Fatio, July 25, 1925; children—Roger Clair, Jacques Alfred. Came to U.S., 1927, naturalized, 1938. Mgr. decorative pottery, Ferney, France, 1924-26; illustrator books, designer scenery for Geneva Opera, other prodns.; textile designer, Lyons and Paris, France, 1927, Mallinson Silk Co., U.S., 1927- 31; mag., book illustrator, writer juvenile books, 1932—. Exhibited Am. Inst. of Graphic Art in 50 Best Books of Year, 1933, 38, 39, 45-50; A.L.A. in 9 Best Children's Books of Year, 1937; N.Y. Times ten best books, 1952, 54, 55, 61, 65, 66; Am. Inst. Graphic Art exhbn. best books, 1953-54, 55-57, 58-60, 61-62, 1965-66, 67-68. Recipient bronze medal Paris Exhbn. of Potteries of Ferney, 1925; Herald Tribune prize, 1945, 52; Caldecott medal, 1948, German West Republic 1st prize for Juvenile, 1956; award Soc. Illustrators, 1961; Bi-centennial award Rutgers U., 1966; runner-up Hans Anderson Biennial award, 1968; U. So. Miss. award, 1971. Mem. Am. Inst. Graphic Arts. Author many juvenile books including: the Petunia series, Veronica series, 1960—; The Happy Hunter, 1961; The Happy Lions Books (with wife), Red-Bantam (with wife); The Missing Milkman, 1966; Tulip, 1969. Contbr. to New Yorker, 1934—, other mags. Home: Gladstone NJ 07934

DUWE, GEORGE E, ret. food mfg. exec.; b. Chgo., May 1, 1897; s. August and Amelia (Schmidt) D.; student pub. sch.; m. Dora Risch, Mar. 15, 1919; children— Dorothy, Betty. With Scholl Mfg. Co., 1919-21, Calumet Baking Powder Co., 1921- 29; with Mickelberry's Food Products Co., 1929-70, pres., dir., 1935-56, chmn. bd., 1956-70, sec.-treas., 1965-70. Home: 138 E 6th St Hinsdale IL 60521

DUWEZ, POL EDGARD, educator; b. Mons, Belgium, Dec. 11, 1907; s. Arthur and Jeanne (Delcourt) D.; Metall.E., Sch. Mines, Mons, 1932; D.Sc., U. Brussels, 1933; D.Sc. (research fellow), Cal. Inst. Tech., 1935; m. Nera Faisse, Sept. 4, 1935; 1 dau., Nadine, Instr., prof. Sch. Mines, Mons, 1935-40; research engr. Cal. Inst. Tech., Pasadena, 1941-45, chief materials sect. jet propulsion lab., 1945-54, asso. prof. materials sci., 1947-52, prof., 1952—. Campbell Meml. lectr., 1967; mem. sci. adv. bd. to chief of staff USAF, 1945-55. Recipient Charles B. Dudley award Am. Soc. Testing Materials, 1951; Francis J. Clamer medal Franklin Inst., 1968. Fellow Am. Inst. M.E. (C.H. Mathewson Gold medal 1964), Am. Soc. Metals; mem. Am. Ceramic Soc., A.A.A.S., Brit. Inst. Metals, Société Francaise des Ingenieurs Civils, Sigma Xi. Contbr. articles to profl. jours. Home: 1535 Oakdale St Pasadena, CA 91106.

DUX, DIETER, educator; b. Bydgoszcz, Poland, Feb. 27, 1918; s. Carl and Gertrud (Wolff) D.; student U. Berlin (Germany), 1936-37, London (Eng.) Sch. Econs., 1938; B.A., U. Chgo., 1939, Ph.D., 1948; m. Marilyn Ann Lord, Sept. 3, 1948; children—Christopher, Lisa, Peter, Mathew. Came to U.S., 1937, naturalized, 1946. Research asso. U. Chgo., 1946-48; chmn. polit. sci. dept., asso. prof. Rockford (Ill.) Coll., 1948-51; Ford Faculty fellow U. Chgo., 1951-52; vis. prof. univs. Goettingen and Freiburg (Germany), 1954; mem. faculty U. Cin., 1955—, prof. polit. sci., 1961- -, head dept., 1963—, dir. Center Study U.S. Fgn. Policy, 1963—. Mem. Hamilton County (O.) Democratic Central Com., 1965—. Mem. Am. Polit. Sci. Assn., Am. Assn. Advancement Slavic Studies, Phi Beta Kappa. Author: Ideology in Conflict, 1963; also articles. Home: 3945 N Cliff Lane Cincinnati, OH 45220.

DUX, MICHAEL J., fgn. service officer; b. Jacksonville, Fla., Feb. 3, 1920; s. Michael Joseph and Susanna (Otterbein) D.; A.B., Miami U., Oxford, O., 1941; m. Viola Backes, Aug. 2, 1945; children—Virginia, Jacquelyn. Economist, Office Financial and Devel. Affairs, also Office German Affairs, State Dept., 1946-55; mem. U.S. delegation Far Eastern Commn., Japan, 1947-49; joined U.S. Fgn. Service, 1955; consul, Madras, India, 1955-57; econ. officer, New Delhi, India, 1957-59; with trade agreements div. State Dept., 1960-64, asst. chief div., 1964; 1st sec. embassy, Bonn, Germany, 1964-67; consul, Duesseldorf, Germany, 1967-70; dep. permanent rep. U.S. to ECAFE, Bangkok, Thailand, 1970—. Served with USAAF, 1942-45. Mem. Sigma Alpha Epsilon. Home: 5432 Della Robbia Way Jacksonville FL 32210 Office: American Embassy Bangkok Thailand

DVORAK, AUGUST, educator; b. Glencoe, Minn., May 3, 1894; s. Joseph and Maud (Pulkrabek) D.; A.B., U. Minn., 1920, Ph.D., 1923; m. Hermione Louise Dealey, Sept. 8, 1921; children—Hermione Elizabeth Rice, Andrey Louise Snow, Dealey Ann Legett. Tchr. elementary schs., 1911-15, high sch., 1920-23; faculty U. Wash., Seattle, 1923—, prof. edn., 1937-64, prof. emeritus, 1964—, also dir. ednl. research, 1938-42. Dir. Carnegie Found. Investigation Typewriting, 1933-42, dir. admissions research 1947-52, asst. dir. div. counseling and testing services, 1956-64; vis. lectr. Univs. Tex., 1925, Mich., 1928, Hawaii, 1955, Sydney, 1962; cons. Ford Found., Nigeria, 1965,66. Research NSF com. on artificial limbs, 1946-47. Served with 1st Minn. F.A., 1915-17, with USNRF, 1918-19; served as lt. comdr. USNR, 1942-45; capt. Res. Mem. Sigma Xi, Sigma Delta Psi, Phi Delta Kappa. Author books including: (with N.L. Merrick, W.L. Dealey, B.C. Ford) Scientific Typewriting, 1939; Synergistic Typing, 1970. Contbr. articles to ednl. mags. Specialist time and motion study, visual edn., tng. films. Home: 7028 55th Av NE Seattle WA 98115

DVORAK, RAYMOND FRANCIS, educator; b. Algonquin, Ill., Mar. 31, 1900; s. Frank and Katharin (Prybl) D.; B.S., U. Ill., 1922, B.Mus., 1926; D. Mus. (hon.), Ill. Wesleyan U., 1950; m. Florence Marie Hunt, Feb. 1, 1936; children—Robert Regis, Katharine Louise, Theresa Anne, Antol Karel. Tchr., Urbana (Ill.) High Sch., 1922-25; faculty U. Ill., 1925-34; prof. music U. Wis., Madison, 1934-70, emeritus prof., 1970—, dir. bands, 1934-68. Mem. summer sch. faculty Chgo. Mus. Coll., 1923, 28, Nat. Music Camp, Interlochen, Mich., 1930, 31, Juilliard Sch. Music, 1932, Emporia (Kan.) State Coll., 1937, U. Cal. at Los Angeles, 1947, Wash. State Coll., Ellensburg, 1954-55, pres. Wis. Rehab. Assn., 1956-58; mem. Wis. Gov.'s Com. on Employment Handicapped, 1959-69; chmn. for Wis., Christmas Seals campaign, 1964; mem. Mayor Madison Com. Employment Handicapped, 1961-69. Bd. dirs. Wis. Neurol. Found., 1959-62. Served with U.S. Army, world War I. Named Wis. Handicapped Man of Year, 1955; recipient citation of honor Nat. Cath. Music Educators Assn., 1963; named Wis. Catholic Layman of Year, 1963; recipient Honor award Duquesne U., 1965; Honors Service award Pacific U., 1965, also citations President's and Gov.'s coms. employment handicapped, 1952; plaque of recognition G. LeBlanc Corp., 1967, Service to Mankind Award Wis. dist. Sertoma Internat., 1970. Mem. Am. (pres. 1960), Wis. (pres. 1950) bandmasters assns., A.S.C.A.P., Coll. Band Dirs. Nat. Assn. (pres. 1948), Midwest Nat. Band and Orch. Clinic dir. 1947—, medal of honor 1970, Am. Legion; hon. life mem. Am. Fedn. Musicians; hon. mem. Ia., S.D. Bandmasters assns., Scabbard and Blade, Phi Beta Mu, Kappa Kappa Psi, Delta Sigma Omicron (hon. life), Phi Kappa Phi, Phi Eta Sigma, Phi Mu Alpha, Roman Catholic. Rotarian. Author: The Band on Parade, 1936; The Art of Flag Swinging, 1938; (films) On Wisconsin, 1953, Marching Along with Sousa, 1956. Home: 2001 Jefferson St Madison WI 53711

DVORAKOVA, LUDMILLA, soprano with Met. Opera Company. Address: care Met Opera Co Lincoln Center Performing Arts New York City NY 10023*

DVORNIK, FRANCIS, clergyman, educator; b. Chomyz, Czechoslovakia, Aug. 14, 1893; s. Francis and Frances (Tomeckova) D.; student Classical Gymnasium, Kromeriz, Moravia; D.D., Faculty of Theology, Olomouce, 1920; student Charles U., Prague; diploma Ecole des Sciences Polit., Paris, 1923; D.és Lettres, Sorbonne, Paris, 1926; D.Litt. (hon.), London, also St. Procopius College, Fairleigh Dickinson University. Came to United States, 1948, naturalized, 1954. Ordained priest, 1916; prof. church history Charles U., Prague, 1928; dean faculty of theology, 1935; Schlumberger lectr. Coll. of France, Paris, 1940; Birbeck lectr., Cambridge U., 1946; prof. Byzantine history, Dumbarton Oaks, Harvard U., 1949—. Decorated Knight, French Legion of Honor. Fellow British.Acad., Am. Acad. Arts and Scis. of Boston; mem. Royal Hist. Soc. of London, Am. Medieval Acad., Royal Belgian Acad. Author: Les Slaves, Byzance et Rome an IXs., 1926; St. Grgoire el Decap, et les Slaves, 1926; St. Wenceslas, Duke of Bohemia, 1929; Les Légendes de Constantine et de Méthode, 1933; National Churches, 1944; The Photian Schism, 1948, French edit., 1950, Italian edit., 1952; The Making of Central and Eastern Europe, 1949; The Slavs, Their Early History and Civilization, 1956; The Idea of Apostolicity in Byzantium, 1958; The Ecumenical Councils, 1961; The Slavs in European History and Civilization, 1962; Byzance et la Primunté Romaine, 1964, English, German edit., 1966; Early Christian and Byzantine Political Philosophy, 1966. Home: 1703 32d St Washington DC 20007

DWIGHT, EDWARD HAROLD, mus. dir.; b. Cin., Aug. 2, 1919; s. Harold S. and Rosalind (Vail) D.; student Yale, 1937-39, Art Acad. Cin., 1939-40; St. Louis Sch. Fine Arts, 1940-41, Cornell U., summer 1941; m. Ruth Roudebush, Jan. 20, 1944; children—Timothy, Allen . Art critic Cin. Post, 1945; asst. to dir. Cin. Art Mus., 1946-47; dir. Cin. Modern Art Soc., 1947-49, asst. curator painting and sculpture, 1949-54, curator Am. art, 1954-55; curator Layton Collection, dir. Milw. Art Center, 1955-62; dir. Mus. of Art, Munson-Williams-Proctor Inst., Utica, N.Y., 1962—. Guest instr. Xavier U., 1954-55; guest lectr. Am. art U. Wis., 1955-57. Ford Found. fellow, 1961. Mem. Assn. Art Mus. Directors. Club: Fort Schuyler (Utica). Contbr. articles to profl. publs. Home: 8 Dwight Av Clinton NY 13323 Office: 310 Genesee St Utica NY 13502

DWIGHT, WILLIAM, publisher; b. Holyoke, Mass., Aug. 10, 1903; s. William George and Minnie (Ryan) D.; student Princeton, 1921-24; Litt.B., Sch. Journalism Columbia, 1926; m. Dorothy E. Rathbun, June 25, 1928; children—William, Donald R., Mary Emily. Treas., Valley Photo Engraving Corp., 1934—; pres. Hampden-Hampshire Corp., 1941-71. Holyoke Transcript Telegram Pub. Co., 1951—; pub. Concord (N.H.) Monitor; co-pub. Greenfield (Mass.) Recorder-Gazette; dir. Franklin County Trust Co. of Greenfield, A.P., Phoenix Mut. Life Ins. Co., Raleigh News and Observer. Trustee Williston Acad., Mt. Holyoke Coll., Northwest Utilities; bd. dirs. Holyoke Hosp. Mem. Bd. Aldermen Holyoke, 1927-29; commr. Hampden County, 1946-48; del. Republican Nat. Conv., 1948,64, Chmn., New Eng. Textile Com., 1954; mem. Princeton Alumni Council, 1954. Mem. Am. (dir., pres. 1956-58, chmn. bur. advt. 1966-68), N.E. Daily (pres. 1940-42) newspaper pubs. assns., Fedn. Internat. des Editeurs de Journaux et Publications (Am. v.p.), Sigma Delta Chi. Episcopalian. Rotarian. Home: 60 Lindor Heights Holyoke MA 01040 Office: 180 High St Holyoke MA 01040

DWIGHT, WILLIAM, Jr., newspaper exec.; b. Holyoke, Mass., June 19, 1929; s. William and Dorothy (Rathbun) D.; grad. Deerfield Acad., 1947; A.B., Princeton, 1951; m. Maria M. Burgee, Sept. 25, 1954; children—William H., Leslie R., Valle E., Timothy N., Ryan H. With Hartford (Conn.) Courant, 1953-55; reporter Holyoke Transcript-Telegram, 1955-57, asst. to pub., 1957-58, 61-66, asso. pub., 1966—, editor, 1968—; pres., dir. Concord (N.H.) Monitor, 1961- -; dir. Greenfield (Mass.) Recorder-Gazette, Catskill (N.Y.) Daily Mail. Co-chmn. Total Community Devel., 1966-67. Vice pres., bd. dirs. Mt. Tom council Boy Scouts Am., 1955-60; bd. dirs. YMCA, Vis. Nurse Assn., Pioneer Valley Assn., Mental Health Clinic. Adminstrv. asst. to Rep. Silvio O. Sonte, 1959-61. Served to capt. USMCR, 1951-53. Named Young Man of Year, Holyoke Jr. C. of C., 1963. Mem. Am. Newspaper Pubs. Assn., C. of C. (pres. 1965-67), Sigma Delta Chi. Republican. Episcopalian. Home: 30 Cleveland St Holyoke MA 01040 Office: 3 N State St Concord NH 03301 also 180 High St Holyoke MA 01040

DWINELL, LANE, former gov. N.H.; b. Newport, Vt., Nov. 14, 1906; s. Dean N. and Ruth (Lane) D.; A.B., Dartmouth, 1928, A.M. (hon.), 1955; M.C.S., Amos Tuck Sch., Bus. Adminstrn., 1929; D.C.S. (hon.), Suffolk U., 1952; LL.D., U. N.H., 1955; D.C.L., New Eng. Coll., 1957; m. Elizabeth Cushman, Apr. 16, 1932. Financial analyst Gen. Motors Corp., 1929-35; chmn., dir. Nat. Bank of Lebannon (N.H.); dir. Lebanon Realty Co., Currier Co., Granite State Electric Co., trustees N.H. Savs. Bank; spl. justice Lebanon Municipal Ct., 1944-54; gov. N.H., 1955-59; asst. sec. state for admimstrn., 1959-61; asst. adminstr. AID, 1969—. Chmn., Fed-State Relations com. Nat. Gov.'s conf., 1956-57; mem. N.H. Constl. Conv., 1948; mem. N.H. Ho. of Reps. 1949-52, chmn. com. ways and means, interim fiscal com., 1949-50, speaker, 1951-52; pres. N.H. Senate, 1953-54. mem. N.H. State Bd. Edn., 1949-52. Del. Republican Nat. Conv., 1952, 56,68, vice chmn. Rep. State Com., 1952. Trustee Colby Jr. Coll., New London, N.H. Mem. N.H. Mfrs. Assn. (pres. 1946-47), S.A.R., Grange, Theta Delta Chi. Conglist. Moose, Rotarian. Home: 94 Bank St Lebanon NH 03766

DWINGER, PHILIP, educator; b. The Hague, The Netherlands, Sept. 25, 1914; s. Aron and Geline (van Dam) D.; Ph.D. in Math., U. Leiden (The Netherlands), 1938. Came to U.S., 1956. Tchr. Lyceum, The Netherlands, 1937-52; prof. math., head dept. U. Indonesia, 1952-56; prof. Purdue U., 1956-62; prof. Tech. U. Delft, The Netherlands, 1962-65; prof. U. Ill. at Chgo. Circle, 1965—. Vis. prof. U. Hamburg (W. Germany), 1960; vis. mathematician Math. Assn. Am., 1966—. Mem. Math. Assn. Am., Am. Math. Soc., Math. Assn. The Netherlands, Sigma Xi. Author: Introduction to Boolean Algebras, 1961; also research papers. Home: 505 N Lake Shore Dr Chicago IL 60611

DWORETZKY, MURRAY, physician, educator; b. N.Y.C., Aug. 18, 1917; s. Samuel and Frieda (Newhoff) D.; B.A., U. Pa., 1938; M.D., State U. N.Y., Coll. Medicine, N.Y.C., 1942; M.S. in medicine, U. Minn., 1950; m. Barbara Ratner, June 11, 1943; children-Thomas Alan, Joan Mara. Intern, City Hosp., N.Y.C., 1942-43, asst. resident pathology, 1943, fellow in pathology, 1946-47; resident pathology U. Chgo., 1947-48; felllow in medicine Mayo Found., Rochester, Minn., 1948-50; practice medicine, specializing in internal medicine and allergy, N.Y.C., 1951—; asst. physician, N.Y. Hosp., 1951, physician, 1951-56, asst. attending physician, 1956-61, asso. attending, 1961-66, attending physician, 1966—, physiaian-in-charge Allergy Clinic, 1961—; asst. in medicine Cornell U. Med. Coll., 1951-52, instr. medicine, 1952-56, clin. asst. prof., 1956-6, clin. asst. prof. pub. health, 1957-62, clin. asso. prof. medicine, 1961-66, clin. prof. medicine, 1966—; attending physician Manhattan Eye, Ear and Throat Hosp., 1953-62. Med. dir.-at-large Allergy Found. Am., 1963-64, now bd. dirs., mem. exec. com. Served to capt., M.C., AUS, 1943-46. Diplomate Am. Bd. Internal Medicine, Am. Bd. Allergy, Pan Am. Med. Assn. Fellow Am. Acad. Allergy (past pres.), Am. Coll. Allergists, N.Y. Acad. Medicine, A.C.P., A.A.A.S.; mem. N.Y. County Med. Soc., N.Y. Allergy Soc. (past pres.), Soc. Exptl. Biology and Medicine, Harvey Soc., Am. Fedn. Clin. Research, Am.. Assn. Immunologists Contbr. articles profl. jours. Home: 21 E 87th St New York Y 10028 Office: 115 E 61st New York NY 10021

DWORKIN, RONALD MYLES, educator; b. Worcester, Mass., Dec. 11, 1931; s. David and Madeline (Taber) D.; B.A., Harvard, 1953, LL.B., 1957; B.A., Oxford (Eng.) U., 1955, M.A.; LL.B. (hon.), Yale, 1965; m. Betsy Ross, July 18, 1958; children—Anthony Ross, Jennifer. Admitted to N.Y. bar, 1959; law clk. Judge Learned Hand, 1957-58; asso. firm Sullivan & Cromwell, 1958-62; faculty Yale Law Sch., 1962—, master Trumbull Coll., 1966—, Hohfeld prof. jurisprudence, 1968-69; prof. jurisprudence Oxford, Eng., 1969—. Vis. prof. philosophy Princeton, 1963, Gauss seminarian, 1966; vis. prof. law Stanford, 1967. Contbr. articles to profl. jours. Home: 8 St Ronan Terrace New Haven CT 06511

DWORSCHAK, BALDWIN, clergyman; b. Arcadia, Wis., Mar. 1, 1906; s. Matt and Catherine (Waters) D.; student St. John's U., Collegeville, Minn., 1920-33. First vows as Benedictine monk, 1927; instr. English, St. John's U., 1935-50, pres., 1951-58, chancellor, 1958-71; prior St. John's Abbey, 1947-51, abbot, 1951—. Home: St John's Abbey Collegeville MN 56321

DWORSCHAK, LEO FERDINAND, clergyman; b. Independence, Wis., Apr. 6, 1900; s. Matthew and Katherine (Theisen) D.; ed. St. John's Prep., Collegeville, Minn., A.B., St. John's U., 1922, S.T.B., St. John's Sem.; 1925; LL.D., Loras Coll. Ordained priest Roman Catholic Ch., 1926; asst. St. Anthony's Ch., Fargo, N.D., 1926-35; sec. to bishop Fargo, 1929-35; chancellor Diocese Fargo, 1935-39, vicar gen., 1939-46; apptd. coadjutor bishop Rapid City, S.D., 1946; consecrated bishop, 1946; aux. bishop Fargo, 1947- 60, bishop, 1960-70, ret., 1970. Apptd. hon. Papal Chamberlain to Pope Pius XII, 1939, domestic prelate by Pope Pius XII, 1941. K.C. Home: Cardinal Muench Sem Route 2 Fargo ND 58102

DWORSKY, DANIEL LEONARD, architect; b. Mpls., Oct. 4, 1927; s. Lewis and Ida (Fineberg) D.; B.Arch., U. Mich., 1950; m. Sylvia Ann Taylor, Aug. 10, 1957; children—Douglas, Laurie, Nancy. Practice architecture as Daniel L. Dworsky & Assos., Los Angeles, 1953—; design critic, instr. arch. U. So. Cal. at Los Angeles, 1968—. Recipient Design citation Progressive Arch. mag., 1967; Gov. Cal. award, 1966; Los Angeles Grand Prix award So. Cal. dept. A.I.A. and Los Angeles, 1967. Fellow A.I.A. (awards So. Cal. chpt., dir. 1968-69); mem. Guild Religious Arch. Prin. works include CBS Exec. Office Bldg., North Hollywood, Cal., 1970, U. Cal. at Los Angeles Stadium, 1969, Stephen S. Wise Temple, Los Angeles, 1968, Equitable Savs. and Loan Bldg., Long Beach, Cal., 1969, U. Mich. Basketball Arena at Ann Arbor, 1968. Home: 9225 Nightingale Dr Los Angeles CA 90069 Office: 1017 N La Cienega Blvd Los Angeles CA 90069

DWYER, EDWARD JAMES, mfg. co. exec.; b. South Norwalk, Conn., Sept. 21, 1906; s. John Augustus and Alura (Waters) D.; B.A., St. John's Coll., Annapolis, Md., 1930; M.E., Johns Hopkins, 1933; J.D., George Washington U., 1938; m. Elizabeth Maclachlan, Dec. 30, 1933; children—Nancy Elizabeth (Mrs. W. Roy Kolb, Jr.), John Adam. Admitted to D.C. bar, 1938; engr., patent trainee, patent atty. Gen. Electric Co., 1933-41; resident patent atty. Electric Storage Battery Co. (now ESB, Inc.), Phila., 1941-48, asst. sec., 1948-54, sec., 1954-55, sec., dir. 1955- 56, v.p., sec., dir., 1956-59, pres., dir., 1959-71, chmn. bd., 1971—; dir. Budd Co., Phila., Leeds & Northrup, Phila. Fidelity Mut. Life Ins. Co., Phila. Mfrs. Mut. Ins. Co. Dir., Fed. Res. Bd. Phila. Bd. Mgrs. Germantown Hosp.; trustee, officer United Fund Phila. and vicinity; bd. dirs. St. Johns Coll., Annapolis, Md., Greater Phila. Movement. Mem. N.A.M. (officer, dir.). Republican. Presbyn. Clubs: Union League (officer, dir.) (Phila.); Huntingdon Valley Country (Abington, Pa.). Home: 1257 Lenox Rd Jenkintown PA 19046 Office: 5 Penn Center Plaza Philadelphia PA 19102

DWYER, FLORENCE, congresswoman; b. Reading, Pa., July 4, 1902; m. M. Joseph Dwyer (dec. 1968); 1 son. Mem. N.J. legislature, 1950-56; mem. 85th-92d congresses from 12th N.J. Dist. Republican. Home: Elizabeth NJ 07207 Office: House Office Bldg Washington DC 20515

DWYER, GILBERT EDWARD, copper co. exec.; b. Scranton, Pa., July 12, 1927; s. Edward Payson and Leah Alice (Doyle) D.; B.A., St. Lawrence U., 1950; J.D., Fordham U., 1955; m. Marjorie Bernadette Krieger, July 14, 1951; children—Anthony, Amanda, Deborah. Admitted to N.Y. bar, 1955; practiced in N.Y.C., 1955-56; atty. Gen. Electric Co., Schenectady, 1956-57, dept. counsel, Lynn, Mass., 1957-60, cons. employee relations, N.Y.C., 1961-64, mgr. relations and utilities, Syracuse, N.Y., 1964- 68; indsl. relations course Raytheon Co., Lexington, Mass., 1960; v.p. Kennecott Copper Corp., N.Y.C., 1968—. Pres., Urban League of Syracuse and Onondaga County, 1966, chmn. bd., 1967; bd. dirs., v.p. Syracuse Met. Devel. Assn., 1967- 68; bd. dirs. Community Found., Syracuse, 1965-68. Served with USMCR, 1945-46, 50-52. Mem. Greater Syracuse C. of C. (v.p. 1967-68). Clubs: Calvary, Century (Syracuse); Pinnacle (N.Y.C.); Stanwich (Greenwich, Conn.). Home: 244 Shelter Rock Rd Stamford CT 06903 Office: 161 E 42d St New York City NY 10017

DWYER, MRS. JAMES F., (see Welch, Galbraith)

DWYER, JOHN DUNCAN, educator; b. Newark, Apr. 26, 1915; s. William Charles and Elizabeth (Macsaac) D.; A.B., St. Peters Coll., 1936; M.S., Fordham U., 1938, Ph.D., 1941; m. Marie Rita Rozelle, Sept. 8, 1942; children—John Duncan, Joseph, James, Jerome. Tchr. St. Francis Coll., Bklyn., 1941-42, Union U., 1942-48, Siena Coll., 1948-53; faculty St. Louis U., 1953—, prof. biology, 1959—, chmn. dept., 1953-63; research asso. Mo. Bot. Garden, 1954-64, curator S.Am. Phanerogams, 1964- -. Cons. floristics of Panama, U.S. AID, summers 1962-63, U.S. Army Tropic Test Center, Panama, 1965, Middle Am., OAS, Guatemala, 1970—. Active in Nat. Conf. Christians and Jews. Grantee Danforth Found., NSF, Nat. Acad. Scis.

Mem. Am. Inst. Biol. Scis., Am. Soc. Plant Taxonomists, Bot. Soc. Am., Torrey Bot. Club, A.A.A.S., Mo. Acad. Sci. (pres. 1964-65), Internat. Assn. Plant Taxonomy, Sigma Xi (Chpt. pres, 1968) Home: 526 Oakwood St Webster Groves MO 63119 Office: 1402 S Grand St Saint Louis MO 63104

DWYER, JOHN PHILIP, music editor; b. Rochester, N.Y., Nov. 4, 1913; s. Eugene J. and Clara C. (Connell) D.; student U. Rochester, 1931-35; B.A. in Music, Eastman Sch. Music, 1937. Music, drama critic Rochester Evening News, 1937-39; reporter N.Y. Sun, 1939-40, U.P. Radio, 1940-42; news editor ABC Broadcasting Co., 1945-49; writing projects, 1950-55; music editor Buffalo Evening News, 1956—; mem. staff Criteria, nat. music critics mag. Served with USAAF, 1943-45. Mem. Music Critics Assn. Author: Salvo, 1945. Home: 211 Summer St Buffalo NY 14222 Office: 214 Main St Buffalo NY 14240

DWYER, JOHN WILLIAM, mfg. co. exec.; b. Waterbury, Conn., June 29, 1925; s. John Patrick and Gladys (Whitehouse) D.; B.S. in Bus. Adminstrn. with distinction, U. Conn., 1948; M.B.A., Western Mich. U., 1966; C.P.A., 1960; m. Eleanor Patrick, Apr. 20, 1950; children—John, Patricia, Scott, Andrew. Accountant, Price Waterhouse & Co., C.P.A.'s, N.Y.C., 1948-49; sr. auditor Am. Radiator-Standard San. Co., 1949-50; chief accountant, asst. controller Oliver Corp., 1950-61; sec.-treas. Am. Seating Co., Grand Rapids, Mich., 1961-68, exec. v.p., dir., 1968- 69, pres., dir., 1969—. Mem. Gov. Mich. Policy Com. Trans., 1967; budget com. Grand Rapids Community Fund, 1965. Mem. borough council, Mt. Wolf, Pa., 1956-1958; vice chmn. adv. bd. Grand Rapids Salvation Army, 1966—. Served to 1st lt. USAAF, 1943-45. Decorated D.F.C., Air medal. Mem. Financial Execs. Inst. (pres. Western Mich. chpt. 1966), Nat. Assn. Accountants (dir. York, Pa. Chpt. 1954-59), Am. Inst. C.P.A.'s (Elijah Watt Sells award 1960), Ill. Soc. C.P.A.'s (Gold medal 1960), Tax Execs. Inst. Presbyn. (ruling elder 1971—). Home: 2510 Oakwood Dr SE Grand Rapids MI 49506 Office: 901 Broadway NW Grand Rapids MI 49502

DWYER, JOSEPH GERALD, educator; b. N.Y.C., Mar. 19, 1912; s. Joseph Paul and Agnes (Keogh) D.; B.A., Georgetown U., 1934, M.A., 1935; M.A., Fordham U., 1939, Ph.D., 1950; m. Rita O'Connor, June 24, 1941; children—David, Kathleen, Michael. Asst. prof. Fordham U., N.Y.C., 1937-39; asst. prof. Coll. Mt. St. Vincent, N.Y.C., 1939-41; asst. prof. Coll. New Rochelle (N.Y.), 1941-43; supr. chem. prodn. Burroughs- Wellcome Co., Tuckahoe, N.Y., 1942-45; mem. faculty Iona Coll., New Rochelle, 1946—, chmn. div. arts, 1950-66, prof. history and Classical langs., 1950—, chmn. Classics dept., 1969—. Recipient Pro Operis award Iona Coll., 1966. Mem. Am. Assn. U. Profs., Am. Assn. for Higher Edn., N.E.A., Am., Am. Cath. hist. assns., Renaissance Soc. K.C. (4). Club: N.Y. Classical (N.Y.C.). Author: Reginald Pole's Defense of the Unity of the Church, 1965. Contbr. articles profl. jours. and encys. Home: 60 Wilson St Hartsdale NY 10530 Office: Iona Coll New Rochelle NY 10801

DWYER, MARTIN, former mfg. exec.; b. Albany, N.Y., June 28, 1897; s. Martin J. and Elizabeth Magdalene (Johnson) D.; grad. Hamilton Inst., N.Y.C., 1917; student N.J. Law Sch., 1920-21; m. May Baker Tredwell, June 28, 1919; children—Evelyn (Mrs. E. Dwyer Van Sciver), Martin, Thomas Johnson. Founder, Aerial Products, Ind., pres., chmn., 1941-58; operator, owner Dwyer Devel. Co. Mem. Md. Commn. on Econ. Devel., 1959- -. Served as lt. (j.g.) AC, USN, 1917-20. Recipient Naval Ordance Devel. award. Mem. Am. Legion, Nat. Security Indsl. Assn., Naval Order U.S. (founder aviation commandery), Quiet Birdmen. Clubs: Rockaway Hunting (Cedarhurst, L.I.); Wings (N.Y.C.); Elk River Yacht; Bay Head (N.J.) Yacht. Patentee ordnance constrn. Breeder registered Polled Hereford cattle. Home: Hilltop Farms Elkton MD 21921 Office: Elkton MD 21921

DWYER, RAYMOND JOSEPH, lawyer; b. Chgo., Jan. 1, 1924; s. Thomas Joseph and Olga (Homolka) D.; LL.B., DePaul U., 1949; m. M. Virginia Curtin, Sept. 11, 1954; children—Debra Lee, Scott Raymond, Karen Virginia. Admitted to Fla. and Ill. bars, 1949; spl. agent FBI, 1950-51; atty. anti-trust, Orlando, Fla., 1951-54; asst. state's atty. Dade County (Fla.), 1954-57; mem. firm Carey, Dwyer, Austin, Cole & Selwood, Miami, Fla., 1957—. Served to 1st lt., USAAF, 1943-46. Mem. Internat. Assn. Ins. Counsel, Ill., Fla. bar assns. Home: 10500 S W 136th St Miami FL 33156 Office: Seybold Bldg Miami FL 33132

DWYER, ROBERT FRANCIS, lumber co. exec.; b. Portland, Ore., Sept. 22, 1911; s. Anthony Joseph and Katherine (McCarthy) D.; student U. Portland, 1931; m. Aileen Kelly, Jan. 10, 1935; children—Robert Francis, Susanne, Patricia. With Dwyer Lumber & Plywood Co., Portland, 1931-64, v.p., 1939-64; partner Clackamas Logging Co., Portland, 1938—; pres. Trask Lumber Co., Tillamook, Ore., 1951-55, Wood Tractor Co., Portland, 1960-63, Dwyer Lumber Distbrs., Inc., Coachella, Cal., 1957—; partner T.A.C. Corp., Albuquerque, 1960—; chmn. bd. Columbia S.S. Co., 1966-68; chmn. Dwyer Overseas Timber Products Co., Portland, 1969—; dir. Portland br. Fed. Res. Bank San Francisco, 1956—. chmn., 1966, 68; dir. Commonwealth, Inc., Portland, Rem Metals Corp., Albany, Ore., Adobe Investment Co., Midland, Tex. Co-chmn. Lumbermen's Econ. Survival Com., 1963; participant econ. study mission USSR, 1963; mem. sec. commerce trade promotion mission Central Am., 1964, spl. Small Bus. Adminstrn. mission with sec. agr. VietNam, 1966; head forest resources adv. mission South VietNam, 1966. Mem. V.I. Corp., 1963-70; vice chmn. Nat. Export Expansion Council, 1964-69; exec. com., chmn. pub. links com. U.S. Golf Assn., 1962—. Commr., City of Portland Arboretum Commn., 1962- 66; mem. Ore. Gov.'s Nuclear Devel. Coordinating Com., Gov.'s Econ. Devel. Adv. Com. Bd. regents U. Portland; bd. dirs. Western Forestry Center. Named Lumberman of Year, 1963. Mem. Pacific Logging Congress (treas. 1950-68, pres. 1949), Western Forestry and Conservation Assn. (past v.p.), Soc. Am. Foresters, Am. Forestry Assn., Asso. Forest Industries Ore., Western (dir.), Northwest (past dir.) golf assns., Portland C. of C., Air Traffic Controllers Assn. Democrat. Roman Catholic. K.C. Clubs: Eldorado Country, Thunderbird Country (Palm Springs, Cal.); Waverley Country, Arlington, University (Portland); Royal and Ancient Golf (St. Andrews, Scotland); Burning Tree (Bethesda, Md.). Home: 1500 SE Waverley Dr Portland OR 97222 Office: Exec Bldg Portland OR 97204

DWYER, ROBERT J., archbishop; b. Salt Lake City, Aug. 1, 1908; s. John C. and Mabel (Maynard) D.; M.A., St. Patrick's Sem., 1936; Ph.D., Cath. U. Am., 1941. Ordained priest Roman Cath. Ch., 1932; monsignor, 1951; rector Cathedral of the Madeleine, Salt Lake City, 1947-52; promoted to see of Reno, Nev., May 1952, consecrated Aug. 1952, installed in Reno Cathedral, Aug. 27, 1952; archbishop, Portland, Ore., 1967-; editor Intermountain Catholic Register, 1934-52; supt. schs. Diocese of Salt Lake City, Mem. Utah State Hist. Soc. (v.p.). Author: The Gentile Comes to Utah, 1941. Home: 2728 SW Greenway St Portland OR 97201 Office: 2838 E Burnside St Portland OR 97207

DWYER, VINCENT MICHAEL, editor; b. Denver, Jan. 16, 1912; s. Miles Peter and Edith (Steinke) D.; A.B., Regis Coll., Denver, 1934; m. Frances Cronin, Aug. 10, 1936; children—Vincent, Frank. Reporter, Rocky Mountain News, 1934-36, city editor, 1948-51, mng. editor, 1951-70, editor, 1971—; reporter Denver Post, 1936-43; information officer Nat. War Labor Bd., Washington, 1944-45; asst. editor United Mine Workers Jour., Washington, 1945-46; reporter Washington Evening Star, 1947. Home: 650 Birch St Denver CO 80220 Office: 400 W Colfax Av Denver CO 80204

DWYER, WILLIAM GEORGE, state ofcl.; b. Rockland, Me., July 15, 1913; s. George F. and Amelia (Spankroy) D.; grad. Phillips Andover Acad., 1933; A.B., Dartmouth, 1937; Ed. M., U. N.H., 1946; Ed.D., Columbia Tchrs. Coll., 1949; m. Edith H. Smith, Oct. 4, 1943; 1 dau., Judith A. Tchr. high sch., Randolph, Vt., 1937-40, Saranac Lake, N.Y., 1940-42; head English dept. Saranac Lake High Sch., 1946-47, Jr. High Sch., Valley Stream, N.Y., 1947-48; exec. asst. office field relations and placement Columbia Tchrs. Coll., 1948,49, summer 50; dean coll. Westbrook Jr. Coll., Portland, Me., 1949-52; pres. Gulf Park Coll., Gulfport, Miss., 1952-58; dir. Muskegon (Mich.) Community Coll., 1958-60; pres. Orange County Community Coll., Middletown, N.Y., 1960-64; pres. Mass. Bd. Regional Community Colls., Boston, 1964—. Pres., Nat. Commn. on Accrediting. Served from ensign to lt. comdr. USCGR, 1942- 46. Mem. Am. Assn. Jr. Colls., Phi Delta Kappa. Home: 42 Mount Vernon St Boston MA 02108 Office: 141 Milk St Boston MA 02109

DYAL, KENNETH WARREN, Post Office official; b. Bisbee, Ariz., July 9, 1910; s. Kossuth and Hermie (Warren) D.; student pub. schs., Cal.; m. Gladys Fulkerson, Jan. 10, 1934; children—Kynra (Mrs. Gordon Lyman), Karen, Timothy, Terance. Postmaster, San Bernardino, Cal. 1947-54; v.p. Pioneer Title Ins. & Trust Co., San Bernardino, 1954-58, Title Ins. and Trust Co., San Bernardino, 1958-61; pres., mgr. Nat. Orange Show, 1961-64; mem. 89th Congress 33d dist Cal.; now regional office dir. U.S. P.O. Dept. San Francisco. Mem. adv. bd. Feather River Project Assn. Bd. dirs. Goodwill Industries, San Bernardino, 1948-62; trustee Patton State Hosp., 1962- 64. Served to lt. comdr. USNR, World War II. Mem. Am. Legion. Democrat. Kiwanian. Address: 631 Howard St San Francisco CA 94106

DYAR, ELIZABETH, coll. dean; b. De Smet, S.D., Dec. 12, 1912; d. Burt Alvano and Jessie (Welch) Dyar; B.A., Carleton Coll., 1933; M.S., Ia. State Coll.; Ph.D., U. Mo., 1940; m. Perry F. Gifford, Aug. 19, 1959 (dec.). Instr. nutrition U. Ariz., 1937-38, 40; asso. prof. foods and nutrition Colo. State Univ., 1940-45, prof., 1945—, vice dean sch. home Econs., 1945-48, acting dean, 1948-50, dean, 1950—. Chmn. Home Econs. Research Adminstrs. of Western Region, 1951-54; exec. com. home econs. div. Assn. Land Grant Colls. and Univs., 1950-55, sec. div., 1951-52, chmn. research sect. div., 1952-53. Fellow A.A.A.S.; mem. Am. Home Econs. Assn. (chmn. food and nutrition div. 1951-53, vice chmn. div. 1947-49, v.p. 1956-59), Am., Colorado (pres. 1952-53) dietetic assns., Am. Chem. Soc., Phi Beta Kappa, Sigma Xi, Phi Kappa Phi, Omicron Nu (nat. sec. 1943-45), Iota Sigma Pi, Gamma Sigma Delta. Home: 1023 Summer St Fort Collins CO 80521

DYAR, ROBERT, physician; b. De Smet, S.D., Nov. 15, 1909; s. Burt Alvano and Jessie (Welch) D.; M.B., U. Minn., 1934, M.D., 1935; M.P.H., Johns Hopkins, 1937, D.P.H., 1938. Intern Cleve. City Hosp., 1934-35; pvt. practice medicine, Huron, S.D., 1935-36; asso. epidemiology Johns Hopkins Sch. Hygiene and Pub. Health, 1938-40; with San Joaquin Local Health Dist., Stockton, Cal., 1940-42; chief div. preventive med. services Cal. Dept. Pub. Health, 1945-59, chief div. research, 1959-68; dean Grad. Sch. Med. Scis., U. Pacific, also exec. dir. Inst. Med. Scis., San Francisco, 1968-71, ret. 1971; lectr. U. Cal. at Berkeley, 1950—. Mem. nat. com. vital and health statistics USPHS, 1960-67, chmn., 1963-67; mem. NIH, 1956-64, chmn. epidemiology and biometry research tng. adv. com., 1960-64. Served with USAAF, 1942-45. Fellow Am. Pub. Health Assn. (gov. council 1946-48, 59-62, 64-69, tech. devel. bd. 1960-62); mem. Am. Epidemiol. Soc. (pres. 1965-67), Assn. Tchrs. Preventive Medicine. Home: 614 Santa Barbara Rd Berkeley CA 94707

DYAS, JOHN ROBERT, air force officer; b. Mobile, Feb. 4, 1917; s. Edmund Covington, Jr. and Estelle (Schreiner) D.; student Auburn U., 1935-39, George Washington U., 1952, Armed Forces Staff Coll., 1950, Air War Coll., 1954-55; m. Henrietta Hazel Brewer, Oct. 8, 1941; children—Judith Ann (Mrs. William Allen Wells), Joanna Lynn (Mrs. E.C. Smith), John Robert. Commd. 2d lt. USAAF, 1940, advanced through grades to brig. gen. USAF, 1964; group comdr. Brooks Field, Tex. and Langley Field, Va., 1946-48; adviser Peruvian Air Force, Lima, Peru, 1948-50; wing comdr. Shaw AFB, S.C., 1951-54; dep. comdr. 19th Air Force, Victoria, Tex., 1955-57; dep. chief of staff operations 4th Allied Tactical Air Force, Ramstein Air Base, Germany, 1957-59; asst. dep. chief of staff operation Hdqrs. USAF Europe, Wiesbaden, Germany, 1959-61; dep. dir. USAF Mil. Personnel, Washington, 1961-63; comdr. USAF Mil. Personnel Center, Randolph AFB, Tex., 1963-65; dep. comdr. 17th Air Force, Ramstein Air Base, 1966-68; comdr. Task Force Alpha, Nakon Phanong, Thailand, 1968-69; chief of staff Air Tng. Command, Randolph AFB, 1969—. Chmn. bd. United Cement Co., 1956-60. Hon mayor, Sumter, S.C., 1954—. Decorated Silver Star, Legion of Merit with 3 oak leaf clusters, Air medal, Air Force Commendation medal; Peruvian Aviation Cross 1st Class. Mem. Beta Kappa (past pres.). Home: 11 North Park Randolph AFB TX 78148 Office: Hdqrs ATC/CS Randolph AFB TX 78148

DYATT, BETTY MARIE, mut. fund exec.; b. Denver, Mar. 3, 1924; d. Andrew and Olive (Burnap) Dyatt; B.S. in Commerce, U. Denver, 1945, LL.B. cum laude, 1947. Admitted to Colo. bar, 1947; law clk. Justice Mortimer Stone, Supreme Ct. Colo., Denver, 1946; pvt. practice, Colo., 1947—; exec. v.p., sec., dir., house counsel Bank Stock Fund, Inc., 1965-70, pres., 1970—; v.p., sec., dir. house counsel, registered prin. First Colo. Investments, Inc., Colorado Springs, 1966—; exec. v.p., sec., dir., house counsel Ramah, Ltd., Colorado Springs, 1966—; v.p., dir., house counsel Silver Prince Mines, 1969—, Napolean Mines, 1969—, Elements Refining Corp., 1969—. Mem. adv. council El Paso Community Coll., 1969—, Family Counseling Service, 1959—, Inst. Internat. Edn., 1960—, League Women Voters, 1957—. Mem. El Paso County, Colo., Am. bar assns., Am. Assn. U. Women. Home: 1520 Culebra Av Colorado Springs CO 80907 Office: 105 E Colorado Av Colorado Springs CO 80902

DYBCZAK, ZBIGNIEW WLADYSLAW, educator; b. Zaleszczyki, Poland, June 27, 1924; s. Franciszek and Sylwia (Rozborska) D.; came to U.S., 1960; B.Sc. in Engring., U. London (Eng.), 1950; Ph.D., U. Toronto (Can.), 1959; m. Karolina Czarnota, Apr. 27, 1957; children—Maria Karolina, Mark Zbigniew. Design engr., Lincoln, Eng., 1949-51; research asst., demonstrator U. Toronto, 1952-54, instr., lectr., 1954-59; asso. mech. engr. Argonne Nat. Lab., 1960, resident research asso., summers 1961-65; prof., dean engring. Tuskegee Inst., 1960—. Stress analyst, cons. govt., founds., industry. Dir. mixed voice choir, Toronto, 1953-59; chmn. House of Providence Fund, Toronto, 1958-59, Served with R.A.F., 1941-46. Registered profl. engr., Ala., Ont. Mem. Am. Soc. Engring. Edn., Am. Nuclear Soc., Am. Soc. M.E., War Vets. Assn. (Polish pres. 1949-51), Sigma Xi, Pi Tau Sigma, Tau Beta Pi. Contbr. articles to profl. jours., book reviewer. Home: 307 Gregory Pl Tuskegee Institute AL 36088

DYBDAL, VICTOR ASLE, navy officer; b. Elbow Lake, Minn, May 20, 1914; s. Ellend A. and Mary (Sand) D.; B.S., U.S. Naval Acad., 1938; grad. Naval War Coll., 1954; M.A. in Internat. Affairs, George Washington U., 1966; m. Betty Bertha Marion Dexter, Mar. 4, 1944; children—James R., Dexter E., Noelle M. Commd. ensign U.S. Navy, 1938, advanced through grades to rear adm.; gunnery officer U.S.S. Helm, 1941; comdg. officer U.S.S. Drayton, 1945, U.S.S. Damato, 1950-51; assigned Supreme Hdqrs. Allied Powers Europe, 1951-53; chief staff to comdr. 7th Fleet, 1964-66; dep. dir. plans Def. Communications Agy., 1966-69; comdr. Amphibious Group One, 1969-70; comdr. Naval Forces Korea, 1970—. Decorated Legion of Merit with 2 gold stars, Bronze Star with gold star, Nat. medal of Vietnam 5th class. Mem. U.S. Naval Inst., Armed Forces Communications and Electronics Assn. Home: 417 Cleveland Av Fergus Falls MN 56537 Office: Comdr Naval Forces Korea APO San Francisco CA 96301

DYBVIG, CHARLES CARLETON, sales exec.; b. Whitehall, Mich., June 18, 1910; s. Olaf Nelson and Agnes (Schiller) D.; B.S. in Aero. Engring., U. Mich., 1931; m. Dorothy E. Schumaker, Sept. 12, 1936; children—Alan James, Richard Charles, Ned Turner, Karen Gay. Trainee Firestone Tire & Rubber Co., Phila., 1933, salesman, truck tire sales mgr., devel. engr., 1933- 43, resident engr., Detroit, 1944-54; gen. sales mgr. Dana Corp., Toledo, 1954—, v.p., 1958—; pres. Dana Internat. Pres., Toledo Orch. Assn. Mem. Soc. Automotive Engrs. (Chmn. Detroit 1956-57). Home: 1173 N Lake Angelus Rd Pontiac MI 48055 Office: Box 200 Taylor MI 48180

DYBWAD, GUNNAR, social worker, educator; b. Leipzig, Germany, July 12, 1909; s. Peter and Susanne (Weisbach) D.; J.D., U. Halle, 1934; certificate N.Y. Sch. Social Work, 1939; m. Rosemary Ferguson, Jan. 21, 1934; children—Peter John, Susan Margaret. Research penal and correctional instns., 1933-36; case supr., adminstrv. asst. N.Y. Tng. Sch. for Boys, 1937-41; dir. clin. services Boys Vocational Sch., Lansing, Mich., 1941-42; dir. child welfare Mich. Dept. Social Welfare, 1942-51; exec. dir. Child Study Assn. Am., 1951- 57; exec. dir. Nat. Assn. Retarded Children, 1957-64; dir. mental retardation project Internat. Union Child Welfare, Geneva, Switzerland, 1964-67; prof. human devel. Florence Heller Grad. Sch., Brandeis U., Waltham, Mass., 1967—, acting dean, 1970-71. Cons. USPHS, 1946—, Pres's. Com. on Mental Retardation, 1967—; cons. child welfare in Occupied Germany, Sec. Army, 1949, White House Conf. on Children and Youth 1960; exec. com. Pres.'s. Com. on Employment of Handicapped. Trustee James Foster Found. Fellow Am. Sociol. Assn., Am. Pub. Health Assn., Am. Orthopsychiat. Assn., Am. Assn. Mental Deficiency; mem. Am. Sociol. Soc., Nat. Assn. Social Workers, Adult Edn. Assn. U.S. (exec. com.), Nat. Council Chs. (chmn. com. on child welfare), World Fedn. Mental Health (chmn. Am. mem. assns.). Contbr. articles to profl. jours. Home: 390 Linden St Wellesley Hills MA 02181 Office: Heller Sch Brandeis U Waltham MA 02154

DYCHE, DAVID BENNETT, former chem. and drug mfr.; b. Evanston, Ill., Dec. 19, 1902; s. William Andrew and May Louise (Bennett) D.; B.S., Dartmouth, 1924; postgrad. Northwestern U., 1927-28; m. Julia Hoyt, Sept. 22, 1928; 1 son, David Bennett. With Ill. Steel Co., 1924-27, Arthur Andersen & Co., C.P.A.'s, 1927-31, Nat. City Co., N.Y.C., 1931-34, Lazard Freres & Co., investment bankers, 1934- 42; financial adviser, treas., v.p. and treas. Gen. Aniline & Film Corp., 1942-47; with CIBA Corp., and predecessor, 1947-67, v.p. finance, 1962-64; pres., 1964-67, dir., 1947-70; treas. Toms River Chem. Corp., and predecessor, 1948-55, pres., 1949-64, chmn. bd., 1962-64, dir., 1948-67; pres., dir. CIBA States Export Corp., 1950-67; treas., dir. Supramar Chems., Inc., 1947-67. Vice pres., dir. Nat. Fund for Grad. Nursing Edn. hon. trustee United Hosp., Port Chester, N.Y. Republican. Clubs: University, Anglers, Wall Street (N.Y.C.); Apawamis, Manursing Island (Rye). Home: PO Box 342 Bradford VT 05033

DYCK, MARTIN, lit. theoretician, educator; b. Grünfeld, Russia, Jan. 16, 1927; s. Martin and Helene (Peters) D.; came to U.S., 1956; B.A. with double honours in German lit. and pure math., U. Man. (Can.), 1953, M.A. in German and Math., 1954; Ph.D. in German, U. Cin., 1956; m. Marie Wiens, June 12, 1949; children—Vernon George M., Victor Herbert M., Martin Christopher C. and Ingrid Rose Marie (twins). Asst. prof. German and Russian, Mass. Inst. Tech., 1956-58; from asst. prof. to prof. German, U. Mich., 1958-65; prof. German and humanities Mass. Inst. Tech., Cambridge, 1965—. Guggenheim fellow, 1961- 62; fellow Am. Council Learned Socs, 1961-62; Taft Meml. fellow, 1954- 56; Isbister, McLean scholar, U. Man. travelling fellow, 1952-55, Am. Philos. Soc. grantee, Germany, 1969. Mem. Modern Lang. Assn., Am. Assn. Tchrs. German, Modern Humanities Research Assn., Internat. Vereinigung für germanische Sprach und Literaturwissenschaft, History of Sci. Soc., Freies Deutsches Hochstift Goethehaus (Frankfurt am Main), Am. Council Teaching Fgn. Langs., Am. Assn. U. Profs. Mennonite. Author: Novalis and Mathematics, 1960; Die Gedichte Schillers, 1967; Relativity in Physics and in Fiction, 1970; also numerous articles. Home: 18 Red Coat Lane Lexington MA 02173 Office: Mass Inst Tech Cambridge MA 02139

DYCKMAN, JOHN WILLIAM, educator, city planner; b. Chgo., May 3, 1922; s. Roy Edward and Mercedes (Sullivan) D. B.Ed., Chgo. Tchrs. Coll., 1944; M.A., U. Chgo., 1951, Ph.D., 1956; m. Louise Ann Madden, June 29, 1944; children—John M., Susanne L., Christina Marie. Research dir. South Side Planning Bd., Chgo., 1949-50; instr. Inst. Design, Ill. Inst. Tech., 1949-50; planner Chgo. Housing Authority, 1950-52; from lectr. to prof. city planning U. Pa., 1952-61; cons. N.Y.C. City Planning Dept., 1958-59; vis. prof. U. Cal. at Berkeley, 1959-60, prof., chmn. Center Planning and Devel. Research, 1963—, also chairman dept. city and regional planning, 1968- -. Chief urban and regional econ. devel. sect. A. D. Little Co., San Francisco, 1961-62; vis. prof. Stanford, 1961. Cons. ACTION, 1957-58, urban policy conf. Brookings Instn., 1963—; mem. President's Com. Natural Beauty, 1965-66; mem. com. on water Nat. Acad., Scis., 1965—; com. urban devel. U.S. C. of C. Salzburg Seminar, 1967. Served to lt. (j.g.) USNR, 1944-46; PTO. Mem. Am. Statis. Assn., Regional Sci. Assn., Am. Assn. U. Profs., Sigma Psi, Lambda Alpha. Author: (with R. R. Isaacs) Capital Requirements for Urban Development and Renewal. 1961; also articles, parts of books. Home: 1119 Park Hills Rd Berkeley CA 94708

DYE, JAMES D., lawyer; b. Woodruff, Kan., Feb. 28, 1908; s. Homer and Ada (Coffey) D.; student Ft. Hays State Tchrs. Coll.; LL.B., U. Kan., 1930; m. Halbur Bartlett, Nov. 8, 1931; children—Sheila Daneen (Mrs. Wm. G. Ward), Sharron Rae (Mrs. C.B. Hoffmans). Admitted to Kan. bar, 1930, since practiced in Wichita; partner firm Bever, Dye, Mustard and Belin, tax attys., 1944—; county atty., Grant County, Kan., 1931-34; asst. atty., Kan. Commn. Revenue and Taxation, 1939-40, chief. Kan. Income Divs, 1940-42, gen. atty. Kan, Commn, Revenue and Taxation, 1942-44; mem. Kan. Supreme Ct. Nominating Commn., 1961-66; dir. Central State Bank, Wichita, 1967—. Trustee, dir. Kan. Area Meth. Found., Inc., 1965—. Mem.

Am., Kan., Wichita (pres. 1955) bar assns., Phi Delta Phi, Sigma Phi Epsilon. Methodist. Mason, Elk, Lion. Home: 631 Brookfield Rd Wichita KS 67206 Office: First Nat Bank Bldg Wichita KS 67201

DYE, JOSEPH W., business exec.; b. Anderson, Ind., May 21, 1904; s. J. Welsey and Bertha (Brookins) D.; student Wabash Coll., 1922-23; m. Aline Sobocinska; children—Mary Ann (Shambaugh), Jean B. (Jefferis). With Wolf & Dessauer dept. store, Ft. Wayne, Ind., 1923-25, controller, div. mdse. engr., 1927-37, asst. gen. mdse. mgr., gen. mdse. mgr., 1937-44, exec. v.p., gen. mdse. mgr., 1947-48, pres., 1948-57; pres., dir. Internat. Trade Devel., Inc., Lucey Export, Ltd., London, Eng.; past pres., dir. Bowser Internat. Inc., Lucey Export Corp., dir. Arbita De Finanzas S.A., Buenos Aires, Argentina, Thyssen Steel Corp. Mem. fgn. commerce com. C. of C. U.S. Past pres. United Fund Allen Co., Inc., chmn. 1954-55 campaign; adv. group Nat. Distbn. Council, U.S. Dept. Commerce, Past pres. Ft. Wayne YMCA. Recipient Merite Comml. award French Govt. Home: 50 Sutton Pl S New York City NY 10022 Office: 199 Piccadilly London W 1 England also 301 E 48th St New York City NY 10017

DYE, ROY ANDERSON, ret. banker; b. Urbana, Ohio, Aug. 27, 1904; s. Thomas Edward and Alice (Burke) D.; student U. of Dayton (O.) Prep Sch., 1918-22, Ohio State U., 1922-25; m. Lucile Johnson, Dec. 12, 1945. With Nat. Bank of Commerce, N.Y. City, 1925-27; with Bankers Trust Co., N.Y. City, 1927-71, vice pres., 1945-71; dir. Lincoln National Life Ins. Co. N.Y. N.Y. Served with U.S. Air Corps Intelligence, 1942-45; with 5th Bomber Command, PTO Received Air Medal for 100 hours combat flying. Mem. Phi Kappa Psi. Roman Catholic. Clubs: Chicago; Union League (N.Y.C.). Home: 220 MacFarlane Dr Delray Beach FL 33444

DYE, STUART FORD, lawyer; b. Greendale, Va., Sept. 18, 1906; s. William T. and Lula (Hagy) D.; student Bluefield Jr. Coll., 1926-28; J.D., U. Tenn., 1933; m. Mathel Dysart, June 18, 1935; children—Giles Stuart, Marilyn Sue. Admitted to Tenn. bar, 1934, since practiced in Knoxville; mem. firm Kramer, Dye, Greenwood, Johnson & Rayson and predecessor firms, 1951—. Fellow Am. Coll. Trial Lawyers; mem. Am., Tenn., Knoxville bar assns. Home: 1301 Snowdon Dr Knoxville TN 37912 Office: Valley Fidelity Bank Bldg Knoxville TN 37901

DYE, WILLIAM HENRY HARRISON, (Tippy), univ. ofcl.; b. Harrisonville, O., Apr. 1, 1915; s. Harry C. and Mayme (Gilmore) D.; B.E., Ohio State U., 1937; m. Mary Kennedy Russell, June 12, 1937; children—Stephanie Dawne, William Henry Harrison III. With State Mut. of Mass. Life Ins., 1937; coach, profl. football player Cin. Bengals, 1937-39; sports coach Grandview (O.) High Sch., 1939-40; asst. in football, varsity basketball coach Brown U., 1940-41; asst. football and baseball, asst. basketball coach, Ohio State U., 1942, basketball coach, 1946-50; basketball coach U. Wash., 1950-59; dir. athletics Wichita U., 1959-62, U. Neb., 1962-67, Northwestern U., Evanston, Ill., 1967—. Served to lt. USNR, 1943-46. Mem. Phi Delta Theta. Episcopalian. Elk, Rotarian. Address: 1620 Judson St Evanston IL 60201

DYEN, ISIDORE, educator, linguistic scientist; b. Phila., Aug. 16, 1913; s. Jacob and Dena (Bryzell) D.; B.A., U. Pa., 1933, M.A., 1934, Ph.D. in Indo-European Linguistics, 1939; postgrad. Slavic, Columbia 1938-39, Yale, 1939-40; m. Edith Brenner, June 11, 1939; children—Doris Jane, Mark Ross. Faculty, Yale, 1942- -, prof. Malayopolynesian and comparative linguistics, 1958—; dir. grad. studies Indic and Far Eastern langs. and lit., 1960-62, Indic and Southeast Asia, 1960-66, dir. grad. studies linguistics, 1966-68. Linguist, Coordinated Investigation Micronesian Anthropology, Truk, 1947, Sci. Investigation Micronesia, Yap, 1949; vis. prof. U. Padjadjaran, Bandung, 1960-61, U. Auckland, 1970; coordinator linguistics sect. 10th Pacific Sci. Congress, Honolulu, 1961; asso. prof. U. Chgo. Linguistic Soc.'s summer 1955; prof. U. Mich. Linguistic Soc.'s ummer Inst., 1957; dir. S.E. Asia Linguistics Program, 28th Internat. Congress Orientalists, Canberra, 1971. Research fellow Slavic, Am. Council Learned Socs., 1938-40; Guggenheim fellow, 1949, 64; Tri-Instl. Pacific Program grantee, 1956-57; NSF grantee, 1960-66, 67-73. Mem. Linguistic Soc. Am., Am. Oriental Soc. (v.p. 1965-66), Am. Anthrop. Assn., Current Anthropology, New Haven Oriental Club (pres. 1963-64). Author: Spoken Malay, 2 vols., 1945; The Proto-Malayo-Polynesian Laryngeals, 1953; A Lexicostatistical Classification of the Austronesian Languages, 1965; A Sketch of Trukese Grammar, 1965; A Descriptive Indonesian Grammar, 1967. Office: Hall Grad Studies Yale Univ New Haven CT 06520

DYER, ALBERT JOSEPH, educator; b. Amity, Mo., Mar. 23, 1910; s. Albert Henry and Cora (Dieter) D.; M.S., U. Mo., 1939, Ph.D., 1949; m. Annabel McCallister, Dec. 17, 1935; children—JoAnn (Mrs. Anthony J. Ramos), Larry Manning. Tchr., Mo. rural schs., 1927-29; county extension agt., Carrollton, Mo., 1935-38; asst. animal husbandry U. Mo. at Columbia, 1934-35, mem. faculty, 1938-43, 46—, prof. animal husbandry, 1954—, chmn. dept., 1957—; marketing and livestock cons., cons. ICA, Chile, 1961. Served to capt. AUS, 1943-46. Mem. Am. Soc. Animal Sci., Block and Bridle (nat. treas.), Sigma Xi, Gamma Sigma Delta. Baptist. Author research papers. Home: 1032 Queen Ann Dr Columbia MO 65201

DYER, BRAINERD, ret. educator; b. Wheaton, Ill., Nov. 9, 1901; s. Frank and Mabel (Puckey) D.; A.B., Pomona Coll., 1923; A.M., Harvard, 1925, Ph.D., 1932; m. Karin Elise Anderson, Aug. 14, 1936; children—Karin Elise, Martin Brainerd. Instr. history Dartmouth, 1926-27, 1929-30; Francis Parkman fellow Harvard, 1927-28, teaching fellow, 1928-29; asso. U. Cal. at Los Angeles, 1930-32, instr., 1932-35, asst. prof., 1935-41, asso. prof., 1941-47, became prof. and chmn. dept. history, 1947,now prof. history emeritus. Fulbright ectr. Am. history U. Helsinki, 1955-56. Mem. Am, Miss. Valley So. hist. assns., Phi Beta Kappa, Delta Chi. Club: Lincoln. Author: Public Career of William M. Evarts, 1933; Zachary Taylor, 1946. Home: 10745 Wellworth Av Los Angeles CA 90024

DYER, DAVID WILLIAM, U.S. judge; b. Columbus, O., June 28, 1910; s. Joseph H. and Nelle (Peters) C.; student Ohio State U., 1932; LL.B., John B. Stetson Coll. Law, 1933; m. Helen Hannah. June 28, 1932; children—David William, Hannah. Admitted to Fla bar., 1933; partner firm Batchelor & Dyer, 1934-42, Smathers, Thompson & Dyer, 1945-61; judge U.S. Dist. Ct., So. Dist. Fla., 1961-66, chief judge, 1962-66, judge U.S. Court of Appeals, Fifth Circuit, 1966—. Served to maj., judge adv. gen. dept., AUS, 1942-45. Mem. Fla. Bar (exec. com. 1957-59), Maritime Law Assn. U.S. (exec. com. 1957-59), Dade County Bar Assn. (pres. 1955-56). Home: 4920 E Sunset Dr Miami FL 33143 Office: US PO and Court House PO Box 2319 Miami FL 33101

DYER, ELDON, educator; b. Corpus Christi, Tex., June 19, 1929; s. S.E. and LeClare (Groce) D.; B.A., B.S., U. Tex., 1947, Ph.D., 1952; m. Joan G. Landman, Mar. 9, 1967; children—Clare, James. Prof. math. U. Chgo., 1963-64, Rice U., 1964-66; prof. math. grad. div. City U. N.Y., 1966—, also chmn. math. dept., 1967-70. Mem. NRC, 1963-66. NSF postdoctoral fellow, 1955-56; Sloan fellow, 1960-62. Asso. editor transactions Am. Math. Soc., 1960-65, editor proc., 1961-67; math. adviser Ency. Brit., 1958—. Spl. research dimension theory, algebraic topology. Home: 750 Kappock St New York City NY 10463

DYER, EVERETT DIXON, educator, sociologist; b. Bristol, Vt., Mar. 23, 1918; s. Everett Wallace and Winnifred May (Dixon) D.; B.A., U. Houston, 1941; M.A., U. Tex., 1947; Ph.D., U. Wis., 1955; m. Jacqueline Lesh, Jan. 12, 1945; 1 dau., Janette. Instr., asst. prof. sociology U. Houston, 1947-50; teaching asst. sociology U. Wis., 1952-54; faculty U. Houston, 1954- -, prof. sociology, chmn. dept. sociology and anthropology, 1961—. Dir. curriculum S. Am. Youth Leaders Program, Houston, 1961—. Dir. city bd. Neighborhood Centers Assn., Houston, 1958—. Served with AUS, 1941-45. U. Houston Fellowship grantee for travel, research in Europe, 1964, summer research grantee 1966-67. Fellow Am. Sociol. Assn.; mem. Southwestern Sociol. Assn., (v.p. 1967, pres. 1968), Nat. Council Family Relations, Am. Assn. U. Profs. (chpt. pres. 1963), Houston C. of C., Phi Kappa Phi, Alpha Kappa Delta. Mason (32). Sociology editor Southwestern Social Sci. Quar., 1962-65; asso. editor Forum Mag. (U. Houston), 1965—. Home: 5026 Creekbend St Houston TX 77035

DYER, FRANK REYNOLDS, Jr., banker; b. Phila., Mar. 6, 1920; s. Frank Reynolds and Viola (Foster) D.; certificate, U. Pa., 1941; student Stonier Grad. Sch. Banking, Rutgers U., 1955-57; m. Ethel E. Ross, Mar. 6, 1943; 1 dau., Carol (Mrs. Robert Heimerl). With Phila. Nat. Bank, 1937—, v.p., 1959-68, sr. v.p., 1968-70, exec. v.p., 1970—; dir. Congress Factors Corp. Chmn. Phila. Coll. Textile and Sci., 1970—. Bd. dirs. Jr. Achievement Delaware Valley. Served with AUS, 1943-46; ETO. Mem. Robert Morris Assos. (nat. dir.). Mason, Rotarian. Home: 14097 Kelvin Av Philadelphia PA 19116 Office: Phila Nat Bank Broad and Chestnut Sts Philadelphia PA 19101

DYER, GARVIN HENRY, civil engr., assn. ofcl.; b. Ash Grove, Mo., Feb. 10, 1905; s. Lafayette and Alice (Huff) D.; grad. Internat. Corr. Schs.; profl. civil engring. degree U. Mo., 1967; m. Ruth M. Welch, June 13, 1924. With Springfield City Water Co. (Mo.), 1923-47, sec., 1944-47; mgr., chief engr. Independence div. Mo. Water Co., 1947—, dir., 1956—, v.p., 1957—, also dir.; dir. First Nat. Bank of Independence; v.p. Independence Savs. & Loan Assn. Chmn., Mo. Water and Sewerage conf., 1948. Bd. dirs. Jackson County (Mo.) Community Chest. Recipient award of merit Mo. Water and Sewerage Conf., 1954. Mem. Nat. (pres. 1957-58), Mo. (pres. 1953), socs. profl. engrs., Am. Water Works Assn. (hon., chmn. Mo. 1952, Fuller award 1958), Am. Soc. C.E. (chmn. Mid-Mo. 1946), Independence, Jackson County, Kansas City. Chambers commerce, Chi Epsilon. Mem. Unity Sch. of Christianity. Mason (Shriner), Lion. Club: Kansas City (Mo.) Engineers. Home: 10011 E 36th St Independence MO 64052 Office: 11610 Truman Rd Independence MO 64051

DYER, GEORGE BELL, writer, b. Washington, Apr. 12, 1903; s. George Palmer and Dorothy (Bell) D; grad. Phillips Acad. (Andover, Mass); student Ph. B., Oahu Coll.; Yale, 1925; M.A., U. Pa., 1948, Ph.D., 1950; m. Charlotte Leavitt, June 26, 1930. Ins. salesman, 1926; reporter San Francisco Examiner, 1929-30; free lance writer, 1930—; faculty U. Pa., 1947-50, Army Gen. Sch., 1950-52; instr. U. Pa. Grad. Sch. Arts and Scis., 1955-67, Yale, 1957-58. Co-founder, Dyer Inst. Interdisciplinary Studies, New Hope, Pa., 1952. Served as 2d lt. AUS, 1940-47, 1t. Col., 1950-52. Decorated Bronze Star. Fellow Co. Mil. Historians; mem. Nat. Rifle Assn. (life), Soc. Am. Mil. Engrs. (life) Am. Mil. Inst. (trustee, life), Zeta Psi, numerous others. Club: Cosmos (Washington). Author books including: Teh The Three- Cornered Wound, 1931; The Five Fragments, 1932; A Storm Is Rising, 1934; The Catalyst Club, 1936; The Long Death, 1937; Adriana, 1939; XII Corps, Spearhead of Patton's Third Army, 1947; (with Charlotte Leavitt Dyer) The Beginnings of a U.S. Strategic Intelligence System in Latin America, 1950; A Century of Strategic Intelligence Reporting, 1954; A Strategic Intelligence Lesson, 1955; The World Analyst, 1958; Estimating National Power and Intentions, 1960; Exercises on an Assumption of Violence, 1962. Home: Diabase Farm Box 111 Route 2 New Hope PA 18938 ☆'2'7

DYER, GEORGE CARROLL, former naval officer; b. Mpls., Apr. 27, 1898; s. Harry Blair and Georgia (Mortimer) D.; A.B., U.S. Naval Acad., 1918; m. Mary Adaline Shick, Apr. 2, 1921; children—Mary Elizabeth (Corrin), Georgia Mortimer (Burnett), Virginia Ann (Smith). Commd. ensign USN, 1918, advanced through grades to vice adm., 1955; comdr. U.S. ships D-3, 1919-20, L-10, 1920-22, S-15, 1922-24, Wickford, 1931-33, Gamble, 1933- 34, Submarine Div. 8, 1939, U.S.S. Astoria, 1944-45; staff of Comdr. Battle Force, 1939, comdr. in chief, 1940; comdr. in chief, chief naval operations, 1942; chief gen. planning group, naval operations, 1946; comdr. Cruiser Div. 10, 1946-48, dep. comdt. Nat. War Coll., 1949-51; comdr. UN Blockade and Escort Force, 1951-52, Tng. Command, U.S. Pacific Fleet, 1952; comdt. 11 Naval Dist. 1953-55. Jr. vice comdr. in chief Mil. Order World Wars, 1969. Decorated D.S.M. Legion of Merit with 3 gold stars, Bronze Star, Purple Heart; comdr. Brit. Empire; French Legion of Honour; others. Mem. Soc. Philatelic Ams., Am. Philatelic Soc., Soc. of Cincinnati, U.S. Naval Acad. Alumni Assn. (pres. 1959-61), Mil. Order World Wars (comdr.-in-chief 1969-70). Clubs: Army and Navy (Washington); Bald Peak Colony. Author: On the Treadmill to Pearl Harbor, 1958; Naval Logistics, 1960; The Amphibians Came to Conquer, 1968. Home: Pendennis Mount 4 Chase Rd Annapolis MD 21401 Office: PO Box 549 Annapolis MD 21404

DYER, HARRY BUTTORFF, steel fabricating co. exec.; b. Nashville, Jan. 6, 1900; s. Arthur James and Elizabeth (Buttorff) D.; student Vanderbilt U., 1917-18; C. E., Lehigh U., 1921; m. Lellie Bell, June 3, 1926; 1 dau., Cathrine (Mrs. Lamar M. Wise, Jr.). With Nashville Bridge Co., 1921—, pres., 1940-57, chmn bd., 1957—; dir. 1st Am. Nat. Bank, Nashville. Pres. So. States Indsl. Council, 1965-66; trustee Ohio Valley Improvement Assn. Mem. Engring. Assn. of Nashville (past pres.), Nashville C. of C. (past pres.), Miss. Valley Assn. (hon. life), Civil Air Patrol (hon. life). Rotarian (past pres. Nashville). Home: 1307 Chickering Rd Nashville TN 37215 Office: Nashville Bridge Co Shelby Av Nashville TN 37202

DYER, IRBY LLOYD, lawyer; b. Pecos, Tex., Aug. 26, 1916; s. Freeman Irby and Katie (Lloyd) D.; student Schreiner Inst., 1934-36, U. Tex., 1936-40; m. Jon Isabel Bellomy, June 6, 1942; children—Irby III (dec.), Deborah Frances (Mrs. Paul Martin Garmon, Jr.). Admitted to Tex. bar, 1940; asso. firm Hubbard & Kerr, Pecos, 1940-42; partner firm Turpin, Smith, Dyer, Harman & Osborn, Midland, Tex., 1945—. Gen. counsel, mem. exec. com., dir. Central Air-line Inc., Ft. Worth, 1963-68; pres. DST Exploration Corp., Midland, 1957—, White Sands Oil & Gas Corp., Midland and Corpus Christi, 1960—; gen. counsel, dir. Petroleum exploration & Devel. Funds, Inc., Abilene, Tex., 1967—. Chmn. A.R.C., Midland County, 1948. Served with USAAF, 1942-45. Decorated Bronze Star, Air medal. Mem. Am., Tex., Midland County bar assns., Midland Jr. C. of C. (past pres.). Presbyn. Clubs: Midland Petroleum, Midland Country. Home: 1200 Bedford Dr Midland TX 79701 Office: First Nat Bank Bldg Midland TX 79701

DYER, NEWMAN HOUGHTON, physician; b. Bolair, W.Va., Aug. 17, 1894; s. Cyrus Newman and Sarah Ann (Dodrill) D.; B.S., W.Va., U., 1924; M.D., U. Md. 1926; postgrad. U. Mich. Sch. Pub. Health, 1945-46, M.P.H., 1951; D.Pub. Adminstrn. (hon.), Marshall U., 1962; Pub. Health, W.Va. Wesleyan Coll., m. Canary Lucile Hylton, July 23, 1917; children—Ruby Haynes, Clytie Elva, Newman Allen, Dorothy Lucile. Tchr. pub schs. McDowell County, W.Va., 1917-20; med. dir. and plant physician Pond Creek Pocohontas Co., Bartley, W.Va., 1926-46; state health commr. W.Va., Charleston, 1946—. Cons. Charleston Mem. Hosp., 1951-52; chief med. and health services div. W.Va. Civil Def. Program, 1950—; mem. W.Va. adv. com. on S.S.S. Doctors, Dentists and Allied Specialists. Chmn., Gov.'s Task Force Emergency Planning Com., State Air Pollution Control Commn.; mem. Ohio River Valley Sanitation Commn., 1947—; mem. Interstate Commn. on Potomac River Basin, 1946—; McDowell County (W.Va.) Bd. Edn., 1933-46; mem. Gov.'s Adv. Council to Legislative Interim Com., 1943-46; mem. vis. com. Sch. Medicine, W.Va. U, 1952. Com. med. dir. USPHS Res. Diplomate Am. Bd. Preventive Medicine and Pub. Health. Fellow Am. Coll. Preventive Medicine; mem. A.M.A., Kanawha County Med. Soc., W.Va. State (exec. council) So. (vice chmn. sect. pub. health) med. assns., State and Territorial Health Officers Assn., Am. (exec. council So. br.), W.Va. pub. health assns. Democrat. Methodist. Mason. Home: 101 50th St SE Charleston WV 22901 Office: Capitol Bldg Charleston WV 22902

DYER, ROSS WATKINS, state justice; b. Halls, Tenn., Mar. 10, 1911; s. Clarence W. and Zona (Smith) D.; student U. Tenn., 1929-30, Cumberland U., 1930-31; LL.B., YMCA Law Sch., Nashville, 1937; m. Agnes Rebecca Moss, Nov. 1, 1936; 1 son, Thomas Ross. Inspector, Tax Dept. Tenn., 1933-39; admitted to Tenn. bar, 1939; adjustor, various ins. cos., 1939-41; pvt. practice law, Halls, Tenn., 1941-61; asso. justice Supreme Ct. Tenn., 1961—. Mayor of Halls, 1947-49; mem. Tenn. Constl. Conv., 1953; mem. Tenn. Senate, 1957-59. Trustee Lauderdale County Hosp. Served from pvt. to 1st lt., AUS, 1943-46. Methodist. Mason. Home: Halls TN 38040 Office: Supreme Ct Tenn Nashville TN 37203

DYER, WILLIAM ALLAN, Jr., newspaper exec.; b. Providence, Oct. 23, 1902; s. William Allan and Clara (Spink) D.; grad. Lawrenceville Sch., 1920; B.Ph., Brown U., 1924; m. Marian Elizabeth Blumer, Aug. 9, 1934; children-Allan H., William E. Reporter, Syracuse (N.Y.) Jour., 1923; various advt. positions Syracuse (N.Y.) Post-Standard, 1925-41; v.p., gen. mgr. Star Publishing Co., Indpls., 1944-49; v.p., gen. mgr. Indpls. Newspapers, Inc., 1949-70; dir. Central Newspapers, Inc., Indpls., 1949—, exec. v.p. 1964—, NYC dir. Metropolitan Sunday Newspapers, 1951-70, pres., 1969-70; dir. Am. Newspaper Pub. Assn. bur. advt., 1963-69, Research Inst., 1955-62, pres., 1963-64; pres. Central Newspapers Found. Indpls., 1969-70. Mem. exec. com. United Fund Indpls., 1954-70, pres. 1970; v.p. Comm. Service Council, Indpls. 1967-68. Trustee Brown U., 1952-59. Served to lt. comdr., USNR, 1941-44. Mem. Better Bus. Bur. Indpls. (dir. 1950-65, pres. 1958, 65), Nat. Better Bus. Bur. (dir. 1950-70), Council Better Bus. Burs. (dir. 1970), Indpls. C. of C. (dir. 1967-70), Am. Newspaper Publishers Assn. (labor relations com. 1953-63), Indpls. Advt. Club (dir. 1952-54, pres. 1952-53), Indpls. Comm. Hosp. Assn. (dir. 1952-54, 66-69, v.p. 1954). Club: Brown U. Ind. (Brown Bear award, 1968, sec. 1946-52, pres. 1952-54). Home: 401 Buckingham Dr Indianapolis IN 46208 Office: 307 N Pennsylvania Av Indianapolis IN 46206

DYER, WILLIAM HUGH, Jr., chain store exec.; b. Newport, Ark., Mar. 16, 1918; s. William Hugh and Joan (Banks) D.; A.A., Long Beach (L.I.) City Coll., 1940; m. Margaret Annette Glover, Feb. 27, 1942; children—William Hugh III. John David. Gen. mgr. Dollar Markets, Long Beach, 1946-52; v.p., gen. mgr. Jim Dandy Markets, Los Angeles, 1952-56; with Lucky Stores, Inc., 1956—, exec. v.p., 1960-67, pres., from 1967, now chief exec. officer, also mem. exec. com. and dir. Served to 1t. comdr. USNR, 1941-46. Decorated Purple Heart. Mem. Western Assn. Food Chains (pres. 1957, dir., mem. adv. com. 1952—). Mason. Home: 3150 Oakwood Lane Alamo CA 94507 Office: 1701 Marina Blvd San Leandro CA 94577

DYER-BENNET, JOHN, educator; b. Leicester, Eng., Apr. 17, 1915; s. Richard Stewart and Miriam (Clapp) Dyer-B.; came to U.S., 1925, naturalized, 1942; A.B., U. Cal. at Berkeley, 1936, A.M., 1937; M.A., Harvard, 1939, Ph.D., 1940; m. Mary Abby Randall, June 14, 1951; children—David, Barbara. Instr. math. Vanderbilt U., 1940-41, 45-46; from instr. to asso. prof. Purdue U., 1946-51, 52-60; faculty Carleton Coll., Northfield, Minn., 1960—, prof. math., 1965—, chmn. dept. math. and astronomy, 1964-66, tennis coach, 1961—, soccer coach, 1964—. Served to 1st lt. AUS, 1941-45, as capt., 1951-52. NSF sci. faculty fellow, 1958-59. Mem. Am. Math. Soc., Math Assn. Am., Am. Assn. U. Profs. (nat. council 1967-70), Am. Civil Liberties Union, Phi Beta Kappa, Sigma Xi. Democrat. Home: 907 Winona St Northfield MN 55057

DYER-BENNET, RICHARD, musician; b. Leicester, Eng., Oct. 6, 1913; s. Richard Stewart and Miriam Wolcott (Clapp) D.; came to U.S., 1925, naturalized, 1935; student U. Cal., 1932-35; vocal studies with Gertrude O- Wheeler Beckman, 1934-41, with Cornelius L. Reid, 1968—; guitar instrn., Jose Rey De La Torre, 1943-46; m. Elizabeth Hoar Pepper, June 1936 (div.); children—Ellen, Eunice; m. 2d, Melvene Ipcar, June 1942; children—Bonnie, Brooke. Profl. engagements, Le Ruban Bleu, N.Y.C., 1941, Village Vanguard, 1942-43; composed and broadcast propaganda songs, OWI, 1942-43; concert debut, Town Hall, N.Y.C., 1944, Carnegie Hall, 1944; under Hurck mgmt., 1944—, now Tornay mgmt., U.S.O. tour in Philippines, 1945, Ann. concert tours, U.S., 1945—, also recordings, night club engagements; partner Dyer- Bennet Records, 1955—; albums include The Lovely Milleress, 1968; asso. prof. theatre arts dept. State U. of N.Y. at Stony Brook, 1970—. Home: Blue Hill Road Monterey MA 01245 Office: care Tornay Mgmt 250 W 57th St New York City NY 10019

DYETT, JAMES G., hosp. equipment mfg. exec.; b. Buffalo, Apr. 26, 1911; s. James H. and Edna (Granger) D.; m. Irene Soyka, Dec. 23, 1945; children—Joan, Michael, April, Peter, Thomas. Chmn. bd., pres., dir. Hard Mfg. Co., Buffalo. Exec. com. Community Welfare Council, 1959-65; exec. allocations com. United Fund. Trustee Park Sch., Buffalo Hist. Soc., Buffalo Acad. Fine Arts, Internat. Inst. Mem. Zeta Psi. Episcopalian. Saturn (Buffalo). Author: From Sea to Shining Sea; This Is Your Navy. Home: One Penhurst Park Buffalo NY 14222 Office: 2020 Elmwood Av Buffalo NY 14207

DYHRENFURTH, NORMAN GUNTER, motion picture producer—dir.; b. Breslau, Germany, May 7, 1918; s. Gühter Oskar and Hettie (Heymann) D.; student Kantonale Handelsschule and Gymnasium; Zurich Switzerland, 1929-36; m. Sally Sudler, Feb. 4, 1946 (div.); stepson, John Hamilton Westermann m. 2d, Maria Sernetz- Erlbacher, August 6, 1966. Came to U.S., 1938, naturalized, 1944. Asst. cameraman Winter Olympics, 1936; ski instr., dir. Willard Pictures, N.Y.C., 1939-44; asso. prof. head motion picture div. U. Cal. at Los Angeles, 1948-53; cameraman, dir. Swiss Mt. Everest Expdn., 1952; leader Internat. Himalayan Expdn. 1955; dep. leader Slick-Johnson Snowman Expdn., 1958; cameraman, dir. Swiss Himalayan Expdn. to Dhaulagiri, 1960; organizer, leader Am. Mt. Everest Expdn., 1963; founder, pres. Am. Mt. Everest Found., 1963;

host weelky TV series, Expdn., Los Angeles, 1959; producer, div. films U.S. Dept. Interior, U.S. Army; world wide lecturer tours U.S. Dept. of State, 1965. Asst. chief motion picture dept., Convair-Astronautics Co., 1957-60; producer, dir., v.p. Summit Films, Inc., Colo. Served with AUS, 1944-46, Fulbright Research grantee, 1953- 54; recipient 1st prizes Berlin and Trient film festivals for Swiss Mt. Everest film, 1952; 1st prize Trient Mountain Film Festival for Ascent of Dhaulagiri, 1961; Hubbard medal Nat. Geog. Soc., 1963, Franklin L. Burr award, 1965, Elisha Kent Kane medal, Geog. Soc. Phila., 1st prize for Ams. on Everest, 1965 Trient Film Festival, Cortina Sports Film Festival 1st prize, Am. Film Festival 1st prize Golden Eagle award, C.I. N.E. Mem. Industry Film Producers Assn. Clubs: Am. Alpine (hon.), Swiss Alpine, Appalachian Mountain (hon.), Korea Alpine (hon.), San Diego Sierra (hon.); Explorers (N.Y.C.); Climbers (hon.) (Bombay, India). Dir. Explorers Club N.Y.C., (film) Castaway, 1942; producer, photographer (film) Crucifixation (award Festival Contemporary Arts, U. Ill. 1953), 1951. Address: PO Box 1148 Aspen CO 81611

DYKE, DELBERT AMMON, univ. adminstr.; b. Eagle City, Okla., Apr. 26, 1914; s. Lemuel Delbert and Bertha (Kerr) D.; B.S., Okla. State U., 1936, M.S., 1941; Ed.D., George Peabody Coll. Tchrs., 1957; m. Gladys June Saxton, Feb. 9, 1939; children—Dee Anne, Dennis Kerr. Tchr. indsl. arts Okla. pub. schs., 1936-41; civilian instr. U.S. Navy Aviation Service Sch., Jacksonville, Fla., 1941-42; asst. prof. indsl. arts and trade, supr. student industries shop Okla. State U., 1945-47; asso. prof. indsl. arts Middle Tenn. State U., 1947-52; prof., head indsl. arts dept. Sul Ross State U., 1952-57, registrar, dir. admissions, 1957-59, dean of Coll., 1961-63, v.p. in charge academic affairs, 1967—; field dir., tech. edn. cons. Govt. Pakistan Okla. State U.-Pakistan Tech. Edn. Program, 1959-61, 1963-67. Pres. Brewster County chpt. Am. Cancer Soc., 1969-70, chmn. Fund Drive, 1971; scoutmaster, local coordinator Buffalo trail council Boy Scouts Am., 1954-56. Served with USNR, 1942-45. Mem. Nat. Edn. Assn., Tex. State Tchrs. Assn., Nat. Assn. Doctors U.S., Tex. Assn. Coll. Tchrs., Tex. Indsl. Arts Assn., Iota Lambda Sigma, Phi Delta Kappa. Presbyn. (elder 1970-74). Home: 604 E Av B Alpine TX 79830

DYKE, FRANK JEFF, retail grocery co. exec.; b. Beaumont, Tex., Feb. 23, 1935; s. Frank Jeff and Justine Elizabeth (Patillo) D.; B.A., U. Tex., 1957; m. June Eleanor Amerman, June 15, 1956; children—Laura June, Karen Sue, Frank Jeff III, Earl Amerman. Advt. mgr. U-Tote-M, Inc., Houston, 1957-60; mgr. franchise operations, v.p., gen. mgr., dir. U-Tote-M of Austin, Inc. (Tex.), 1958-60; pres., dir. Nat. Convenience Stores, Inc., Houston, 1960—; dir. Pine-O-Pine Co., Inc. Mem. Sigma Chi. Episcopalian. Home: 3620 Willowick Houston TX 77019 Office: 3200 Travis St Houston TX 77006

DYKE, JAMES PARVIN, librarian; b. Breckenridge, Tex., Sept. 10, 1920; s. James Elvy and Glenna (Butler) D.; A.B., Hardin-Simmons U., 1942; B.A. in L.S., U. Okla., 1946; M.S., U. Ill., 1950, Ph.D., 1957; m. Thelma Margaret Tiner, Sept. 14, 1941; children—Glenna Margaret (Mrs. Fox), Thelma Lane, James Tiner; m. 2d, Dorothy Singleton, Aug. 1, 1970. Asst. librarian Hardin-Simmons U., 1946-48; mgr. Tiner Drug Store, Munday, Tex., 1948-49; research asst. unit on evaluation U. Ill., 1949- 51; librarian Eastern N.M., U., 1951-66; library dir., prof. Tex. A. & M.U., 1966-69; dir. libraries, also prof. N.M. State U., Las Cruces, 1969—; vis. prof. U. Okla., summer 1959. Served to capt. USAAF, 1942-45. Decorated D.F.C., Air medal with 3 oak leaf clusters. Mem. A.L.A. (chmn. membership com. 1959-60), Assn. Coll. and reference Librarians, Southwestern, N.M. (sec. 1956-57, v.p., 1957-58, pres. 1958- 59), Tex., Border Regional library assns., N.M. Edn. Assn., N.M. Audio-Visual Assn. (dir. 1955-57), Am. Assn. U. Profs. Democrat. Baptist. Mason. Club: Lions (dist. cabinet sec. 1959-60, local pres. 1961-62) (Portales). Home: 645 College Place Las Cruces NM 88001

DYKE, KEN REED, pub. relations, advt. exec.; b. N.Y. City, March 12, 1897; s. James Henry and Laura (Reed) D.; grad. Speyer Sch., 1912; grad. Ethical Culture Sch., N.Y. City, 1912-16; m. Valerie Edmonds Young; 1 son, David Kimball Dyke. Advt. writer United States Rubber Co., N.Y. City, 1919-26, asst. advt. mgr., 1926-28; sales promotion and advt. dir. Johns- Manville Corp., N.Y. City, 1928-33; dir. advt., Colgate-Palmolive Peet Co., N.Y. City, 1933-36; eastern sales mgr. Nat. Broadcasting Co., N.Y. City, 1937-38, dir. sales promotion and research, 1938-41, administrative v.p. 1946-49; v.p. on charge pub. relations and publicity Young & Rubicam, N.Y.C., 1949-58, v. p. international div. 1960; sr. v.p. Smith, Dingwell Assos., N.Y.C., 1960—, treasurer, Dir. Children's Village, Chief bur. campaigns OWI, Wash., 1942. Served with U.S. Army, 1918-19; with A.E.F. in France and Germany; res. officer 107th Inf., 1922-28; major, 1943; lt. col., 1943-44; col., 1944-45; brig. gen. since 1945; chief civil information and edn. sect., GHQ Supreme Comdr. Allied Powers, Tokyo, Japan, 1945-46; now brig. gen. U.S. O.R.C.; mem. adv. com. First Army. Decorated World War I Victory Medal (2 battle clasps), German Occupation Medal, Am. Theatre, Pacific Theatre (5 battle stars), Philippine Liberation medal, Phillipe Distinguished Service Star, Distinguished Service Medal, Legion of Merit, 1945, Presidential unit citation, Conspicuous Service Cross (N.Y. State). Chmn. bd. Assn. Nat. Advertisers, 1936-37; dir. Mil. Govt. Assn. Mem. Am. Assn. for U.N. (dir.), Japan Soc. (bd. dirs.), Grand Jury Assn. (dir.), Mil and Naval Officers World Wars, Res. Officers Assn. U.S. Alpha Delta Sigma (nat. pres. 1937-38), Am. Assn. for UN (dir.). Clubs: Circumnavigators, Union (N.Y.C.). Home: 14 E 90th St New York City NY 10028 Office: 342 Madison Av New York City NY 10017

DYKE, WILLIAM DANIEL, city ofcl.; b. Princeton, Ill., Apr. 25, 1930; s. Alfred Daniel and Vinnie Pauline (Thompson) D.; B.A., DePauw U., 1952; LL.B., U. Wis., 1959; m. Joan Piper, Apr. 2, 1953; children—Wade, Sarah, Kathryn. Admitted to Wis. bar, 1960; mem. firm Smith, Miller & Ebenhardt, Jefferson, Wis., 1960-61; city atty., Jefferson, 1961-63; private practice, Madison, 1961-69; asst. to lt. gov. Wis., 1963-64; mayor of Madison, 1969—; instr. taxation Madison Tech. Coll., 1964-69. Mem. adv. com. human environment to sec. state. Bd. dirs. Madison YWCA, children's service Madison Gen. Hosp. Served with AUS, 1952-55. Named Man of Year, Res. Officers Assn. Wis., 1971. Mem. Am. Bar Assn., Am. Judicature Soc., Alpha Tau Omega. Home: 3826 Council Crest St Madison WI 53711 Office: 210 Monona Av Madison WI 53701

DYKEMA, JOHN RUSSEL, lawyer; b. Washington, June 1, 1918; s. Raymond Kryn and Margery (Russel) D.; A.B., Princeton, 1940; J.D., U. Mich., 1947; m. Rosemary McDonald, June 21, 1950; children—Mary McDonald, John Russel, Peter Kryn. Admitted to Mich. bar, 1947; asso. firm Dykema, Gossett, Spencer, Goodnow & Trigg, and predecessor, Detroit, 1947-48, 49-51, 53-58, mem. firm, 1958—; law clk. to Justice Murphy, U.S. Supreme Ct., 1948-49; corp. and securities commr. Mich., 1951-53. Trustee Western Mich. U., 1964—. Served with USNR, 1941-45. Mem. State Bar Mich., Am., Detroit bar Assns. Home: 286 Cloverly Rd Grosse Pointe Farms MI 48236 Office: Penobscot Bldg Detroit MI 48226

DYKEMA, RAYMOND K., lawyer; b. Grand Rapids, Mich., Feb. 17, 1889; s. Kryn and Mary (Openeer) D.; LL.B., U. Mich., 1911; m. Margery Russel, Aug. 1917; children—John Russel, Mary (Mrs. Laurie C. Dickson, Jr.) Raymond K., Jere Hutchins. Admitted to Mich. bar, 1911; with Bundy, Travis & Marrick, Grand Rapids, 1911-12, Aleind, Boynton, McMillan, Bodman & Turner, 1912-16, Mich. Central R.R., 1917; pvt. practice law, 1919-23; partner Dykema & Wheat, 1923—, now Dykema, Gossett, Spencer, Goodnow & Trigg. Mem. adv. bd. United Found. Served as capt. AUS, 1917-19. Mem. Am., Mich., Detroit bar assns., Psi Upsilon. Clubs: Detroit, Country (Detroit); Grosse Pointe; Huron Mountain. Home: 233 Lothrop Rd Grosse Pointe Farms MI 48236 Office: Penobscot Bldg Detroit MI 48226

DYKES, CHARLES EDWIN, corp. exec.; b. Springfield. O., July 23, 1912; s. Otis Edwin and Winifred Bertha (Hodge) D.; diploma Tenn. Mil. Inst., 1932; B.S., Cornell U., 1936, postgrad., 1936-37; postgrad. Harvard, 1955; m. Doris E. Smallridge, Aug. 20, 1938; 1 dau., Susan (Mrs. David V. Black). Accountant Gen. Electric Co., 1937-39; accountant, controller Coop. G.L.F. Exchange, Inc., Ithaca, N.Y., 1939-57; controller, v.p. and controller Avon Products, Inc., N.Y.C., 1958-67; v.p. finance U.S. Gypsum Co., Chgo., 1967—, also dir.; dir. A.P. Green Refractories Co., USG Europe, S.A. (Belgium), A.E. Moore Co., Yeso Panamericano, S.A. (Mexico), U.S.G. Export Co., Kinkead Industries, Inc., Sears Bank & Trust Co., USG de P.R., Inc., Yeso Mexicano, S.A., Alodex Corp., Roewack, Inc., U.S. Gypsum Urban Devel. Mem. council financial execs. Nat. Indsl. Conf. Bd., 1968—. Campaign chmn. Community Chest, Ithaca, 1954; past pres. Tompkins County Meml. Hosp. Bd. dirs. Chgo. Heart Assn., gen. campaign chmn., 1970; trustee Cornell U. Recipient Distinguished Service awards Ithaca Jr. C. of C., 1947, N.Y. Jr. C. of C., 1947. Mem. Financial Execs. Inst. (treas. 1965-67), Chgo. Council Fgn. Relations (dir.), Newcomen Soc. N.Am., Beta Theta Pi. Presbyn. Mason. Clubs: Economic, Chicago, Cornell (past pres.), Cornell University of Chicago (dir.); Barrington Hills Country. Home: Caesar Dr Barrington Hills IL 60010 Office: 101 S Wacker Dr Chicago IL 60606

DYKES, JEFFERSON CHENOWTH, author; b. Dallas, July 20, 1900; s. George Richard and Melrose (Chenowth) D.; B.S., Texas A. and M. Coll., 1921; postgrad. Colo. Agrl. Coll., 1924-29; m. Martha Lewin Read, Aug. 1, 1923; 1 dau., Martha Ann. Tchr. vocation agr., Stephenville and McAllen, Tex., 1921- 29; prof. agrl. edn. Texas A. and M. Coll., 1929-35; erosion specialist Soil Conservation Service, Dept. Agr., Lindale, Tex., 1935, chief erosion control practices div., asst. regional conservator, Ft. Worth, 1936-42, asst. chief, 1942-50, dept. chief, 1950-53, asst. adminstr. field services, 1953-63, dep. adminstr. field services, 1963-65; western Americana dealer, 1965—. Fellow Soil Conservation Soc. Am. (council); mem. Western Writers Am., Range Soc. Am., The Westerners, Antiquarian Booksellers Assn. Am. Author: Billy The Kid, Bibliography Of The Legend, 1952; American Guide Series-A Bibliographic Check List, 1966; (with O.C. Fisher) King Fisher, 1966; Rangers All!, 1969; Four Sheriffs of Lincoln County, 1969; also articles, book revs. in mags. and profl. jours. Editor: Great Western Indian Fights, 1960; On the Border with Mackenzie, 1962; The West of the Texas Kid, 1962; Trans- Missouri Stock Raising, 1962; Cow Dust and Saddle Leather, 1968; co-editor: Flat Top Ranch: A Grassland Venture, 1957; asso. editor Brand Book, 1950—. Cons., Cowboys and Cattle Country, 1962. Home: 4511 Guilford Rd College Park MD 20740 Office: Western Books Box 38 College Park MD 20740

DYKMAN, JACKSON ANNAN, lawyer; b. Brooklyn, N.Y., July 11, 1887; s. William Nelson and Isabel (Annan) D.; B.A., Yale, 1909; LL.B., Harvard Law School, 1912; D.C.L., Nashotah House, 1947; m. Susan Brewer Merrick, Feb. 3, 1915. Admitted to New York bar, 1913; clerk Dykman, Oeland & Kuhn, 1913-15; partner of the law firm Cullen & Dykman, Bklyn., 1915—. Trustee Estate Belonging to Diocese of L.I., 1922-62, chancellor, 1925-52, standing com. Diocese of L.I., 1922-62; trustee Gen. Theol. Sem., 1925-61. Mem. Nat. Council Protestant Episcopal Ch., 1943-49. Served as lt. col., judge adv., U.S. Army, 1917- 19, special asst. to atty. gen. U.S., 1942-46, 1950-52. Fellow Am. Bar Found.; mem. Soc. Colonial Wars, Am., N.Y. State (pres. 1944), Nassau County, Bklyn. bar assns., Assn. of Bar of City of N.Y., Alpha Delta Phi. Republican. Clubs: The Links, Recess, Yale (N.Y.C.); Piping Rock (L.I.). Author: White and Dykman, Annotated Constitution and Canons of the Protestant Episcopal Church, 1953. Joint master Meadow Brook Hounds, 1931-33. Home: Glen Cove NY 11542 Office: 177 Montague St Brooklyn NY 11201

DYKSTRA, DANIEL JAMES, lawyer, univ. dean; b. Fremont, Mich., Feb. 25, 1916; s. John D. and Elizabeth (Groeteamat) D.; B.S., Wis. State U., 1938; LL.B. (Rockefeller research fellow), U. Wis., 1948, S.J.D., 1950; m. Lily M. Salay, Aug. 1, 1942; children—Daniel James, Ann Marie. Asst. prof. law Drake U., 1948-49; admitted to Wis. bar, 1948, Utah bar, 1952; faculty U. Utah Coll. Law, 1949-52, 52-66, prof. law, 1952-66, dean coll., 1954-61, acad. v.p., 1961-63; prof. law U. Cal. at Davis, 1966—, dean Sch. Law, 1971—; atty. OPA, 1952. Vis. prof. U. Minn., summer 1950, U. Wis., summers 1957, 58; Fulbright prof. U. Melbourne (Australia), 1959; Frederick William Reynolds lectr. U. Utah, 1959; vis. prof. law U. 1963-64. Served with USNR, 1942-45. Recipient Distinguished Alumnus award Wis. State U., River Falls, 1970. Mem. Am., Salt Lake County bar assns., Nat. Acad. Arbitrators, Order of Coif. Author: (monograph) Right Most Valued by Civilized Man, 1959. Home: 3024 Country Club Dr El Macero CA 95616 Office: Sch Law U Cal Davis CA 95616

DYKSTRA, DUEKEL IVAN, educator, clergyman; b. Platte, S.D., Mar. 15, 1915; s. Bert Duekel and Nellie (Schippers) D.; A.B., Hope Coll., 1935; Th.B., Western Theol. Sem. (Mich.), 1938; Ph.D., Yale, 1945; m. Kathryn Wisse, June 25, 1941; children—Brian James, Darrell Ivan. Ordained to ministry Ref. Ch. in Am., 1940; pastor Marbletown Ref. Ch., Stone Ridge, N.Y., 1940- 43, Hawthorne, N.J., 1943-47; prof. Greek and philosophy Hope Coll., Holland, Mich., 1947—, head dept. philosophy 1950. Lectr., Ford Found. Liberal Edn. for Adults, 1959—; coordinator com. on liberal arts study North Central Assn., 1956—. Mem. com. on internat. justice and goodwill Ref. Ch. in Am., 1947—. Mem. Am. Philos. Assn., Mich. Acad. Arts and Scis. (philosophy sect.). Home: Cosmopolitan House Hope Coll Holland MI 49423

DYLAG, ROMAN, bass, composer; b. Krakow, Poland, Feb. 22, 1938; student Warsaw Acad., also bass with brother; m. Simone Dylag. Joined Hot Club of Melomani group, 1957; recorded with Stan Getz, Don Ellis in Poland, Bud Powell in Paris; now living in Sweden; numerous tours of U.S. and Europe; appeared with Polish group The Wreckers in festivals at Newport and Washington; numerous TV and film recordings; rec. artist for Metronome, Swedish Columbia, Prestige records. Composer (with Eje Thelin for film) Att Alska. Address: Klockarv 6''' 14147 Huddinge, Sweden.

DYLAN, BOB, singer, composer; b. Duluth, Minn., May 24, 1941; student U. Minn., 1960; self-taught on guitar, piano, autoharp, harmonica; Mus.D. (hon.), Princeton, 1970; married. Performer numerous tours and concerts, 1960-68; devised and popularized folk-rock, 1965—. Composer many songs including: Blowin' in the Wind; Don't Think Twice, It's All Right; A Hard Rain's A-Gonna Fall; She Belongs to Me; It's All Over Now; Baby Blue: The Times They are A-Changin'; Just Like a Woman; I'll Be Your Baby Tonight; I Shall Be Released; Lay, Lady, Lay; If Not for You; Mr. Tambourine Man. Numerous albums recorded. Author: Tarantula, 1966, 71. Office: PO Box 36 Prince Station New York City NY 10012

DYMALLY, MERVYN MALCOLM, state senator, educator; b. Trinidad, British West Indies, May 12, 1926; s. Hamid A. and Andreid S. (Richardson) D.; B.A., Cal. State Coll., Los Angeles, 1954; M.A., Sacramento State Coll., 1970; LL.D. (hon.), U. W. Los Angeles; m. Alice M. Gueno; children—Mark, Lynn. Lectr., Whittler and Claremont colls.; mem. Cal. Assembly, 1962-66; mem. Cal. Senate, 1967—, chmn. majority caucus. Chmn. bd. Consensus Pubs., Inc. Mem. Cal. adv. com. U.S. Civil Rights Commn., 1964. Mem. Am. Assn. U. Profs., Am. Acad. Polit. Sci. Author: Black Politician-His Struggle for Power. Editor Black Politician. Address: 2622 S Western Av Los Angeles CA 90018

DYMOND, LEWIS WANDELL, airline exec.; b. Lansing, Mich., June 28, 1920; s. Lewis Wandell and Irene (Parker) D.; LL.B. cum laude, U. Miami, 1956; m. Betty Louise Blood, Sept. 6, 1942; children—Lewis W., Jean Ann; m. 2d, Joann Surrey, Sept. 3, 1966. With Nat. Airlines, Inc., Miami, Fla., 1938-62, mechanic, agt., Sta. mgr., flight dispatcher, operations mgr., pilot, v.p. operations and maintenance engring., 1955-62; pres., chief exec. officer, dir., Frontier Airlines, 1962-69, now dir.; admitted to Fla. bar, 1957; dir. Central Bank & Trust Co. of Denver, Comml. Dynamics Corp. Bd. dirs. Central City Opera Assn. Mem. U. Miami Alumni Club, Phi Kappa Phi, Phi Alpha Delta. Mason (32, Shriner). Clubs: Union League (N.Y.C.); Cherry Hills Country, Denver; Petroleum; Garden of the Gods (Colorado Springs, Colo.); Surf (Miami, Fla.). Office: 1250 Humboldt Denver CO 80218

DYSART, HAROLD FRANCIS, gen. merchandising co. exec.; b. Clarksville, Tex., June 9, 1910; s. Jesse A. and Fannie (Henry) D.; student Tex. A. and M. Coll., Victoria Jr. Coll., also U. Tex.; m. Mary Gilkey, Sept. 12, 1959; children—Joel A., C. Gregory, Thomas G. With Montgomery Ward & Co., 1933—, v.p., gen. operating mgr., 1958-60, v.p., controller, 1961-65, v.p., gen. operating mgr., 1965—, dir., 1966—. Mem. Ill. C. of C. (pres. 1962; dir.), Phi Kappa Psi. Episcopalian. Club: Westmoreland Country (Wilmette, Ill.). Home: 1347 Hackberry Lane Winnetka IL 60093 Office: 619 W Chicago Av Chicago IL 60607

DYSINGER, DON WARREN, educator, psychologist; b. Logansport, Ind., Sept. 8, 1904; s. William Stuart and Laura (McColm) D.; student Wittenberg Coll., 1924-27; B.A., U. Cal. at Los Angeles, 1928; M.A., State U. Ia., 1929, Ph.D., 1931; m. Charlotte T. Newman, May 30, 1938; stepchildren—Thomas M. Newman, Ann Newman (Mrs. John F. Hardy). Faculty, U. Neb., Lincoln, 1932—, prof. psychology, 1948—, chmn. dept., 1948-68. Diplomate in clin. psychology Am. Bd. Examiners Profl. Psychology. Fellow Am. Psychol. Assn.; mem. Midwestern Pyschol. Assn., Sigma Xi, Gamma Alpha. Home: 2466 Lake St Lincoln NB

DYSINGER, PAUL WILLIAM, physician, educator; b. Burns, Tenn., May 24, 1927; s. Paul Clair and Mary Edith (Martin) D.; B.A., So. Missionary Coll., 1951; M.D., Coll. Med. Evangelists, 1955; M.P.H., Harvard, 1962; m. Yvonne Minchin, May 11, 1958; children—Edwin, Wayne, John, Janelle. Intern, Washington, 1955-56; sr. asst. surgeon USPHS, with Blackfeet Indians in Mont., Navajos of Ariz., 1956-58; physician, med. adviser Am. embassy, PhnomPenh, Cambodia, 1958-60; research asso. dept. preventive medicine Loma Linda (Cal.) U. (formerly Coll. Med. Evangelists), 1960—, adminstrv. asst. div. pub. health, asso. prof. preventive medicine Sch. Medicine, 1965-67, asst. to dean, chmn. dept. tropical health Sch. Pub. Health, 1967-69, asst. dean for acad. affairs and internat. health, 1969-71, prof. internat. health, also asso. dean for academic affairs, 1971—. WHO fellow, Somalia, Ethiopia, India, Nepal, Burma, 1969. Diplomate Nat. Bd. Med. Examiners, Am. Bd. Preventive Medicine. Fellow Royal Soc. Tropical Medicine and Hygiene, Am. Pub. Health Assn., Am. Soc. Tropical Medicine and Hygiene, Am. Geog. Soc.; mem. So. Cal. Pub. Health Assn., A.A.A.S., Soc. Internat. Devel., Cal. Acad. Preventative Medicine. Seventh-day Adventist. Contbr. articles to med. publs. Home: 11625 Anderson St Loma Linda CA 92354

DYSINGER, WENDELL STUART, coll. dean; b. Freeport, Ill., Mar. 13, 1897; s. William S. and Laura (McColm) D.; A.B., Wittenberg Coll., 1918; B.D., 1921; M.A., State U. Ia., 1929, Ph.D., 1933; m. A. Ruth Fraser, May 10, 1921; children—Robert Holmes, Dale Wendell. Ordained to ministry United Luth. ministry, 1921; pastor 1st Ch., Los Angeles, Oakland, Cal., Iowa City; research asst. U. Ia., 1933-37; dir. personnel Thiel Coll., Greenville, Pa., 1937-40; dean, dir. personnel MacMurray Coll., Jacksonville, Ill., 1940-61, v.p., dean coll., 1961-65, v.p., dean emeritus, 1965—; acting acad. dean McKendree Coll., Lebanon, Ill., 1965-68; now psychologist Dept. Mental Health, State of Ill. Mem. motion picture research com. Payne Found.; mem. adv. council Inst. for Juvenile Research State of Ill.; personnel cons. Am. Council on Edn.; dir. tri-coll. study (Hanover, Wittenburg, MacMurray colls.) for U.S. Office Edn. Diplomate Am. Bd. Examiners in Profl. Psychology. Fellow Am. Psychology Assn.; mem. Ill. Psychol. Assn. (pres. bd. examiners), Ill. Guidance and Personnel Assn., Midwest Assn. Coll. Deans. Am. Bd. Psychol. Services (sec., treas.), Am. Coll. Personnel Assn., North Central Assn. Acad. Deans (pres.), Nat. Vocational Guidance Assn., Sigma Xi, Phi Gamma Delta. Rotarian. Author: Emotional Response of Children to the Motion Picture Situation, 1933; Self-Measurement for College Students, 1935; College Know-How, 1957. Contbr. articles to jours. Home: 238 Caldwell St Jacksonville IL 62650

DYSON, CHARLES HENRY, exec.; b. N.Y.C., Aug. 2, 1909; s. Martin Lawrence and Lillian (Patterson) D.; B.B.A., Pace Coll., 1930, D.C.S., 1965; m. Margaret Macgregor, Aug. 8, 1941; children—John Stuart, Robert Richard, Anne Elizabeth, Peter L. With Price, Waterhouse & Co., C.P.A.'s, N.Y.C., 1932-41; exec. v.p. and dir. holding co., pres., dir. operating co., Textron, Inc., 1946-49; v.p., mem. exec. com., dir. Burlington Mills Corp., 1949-51; cons. to nat. compaines, 1951—; chmn. exec. com. Wallace-Murray Corp. subsidiary Dyson-Kissner Corp., N.Y.C., 1968—; chmn. bd. Dyson-Kissner Corp., N.Y.C., 1954—, Kearney-Nat., Inc., N.Y.C., 1965—; Spl. cons. to sec. of war, Washington, 1941; rep. U.S. Treasury Dept., IMF., Bretton Woods, N.H., 1944. Bd. dirs. Nat. Indsl. Conf. Bd., 1950. Trustee Briarcliff Jr. Coll., 1946-54, Village of Scarsdale, N.Y., 1966-70; chmn. bd. trustee Pace Coll.; pres. bd. dirs. Greers Children Community. Served as col. USAAF, World War II. Decorated D.S.M. C.P.A., Mem. Pace Alumni Assn. (pres.). Clubs: Burning Tree; Scarsdale; Brook, Union League. Home: 24 Tompkins Rd Scarsdale NY 10583 Office: 230 Park Av New York City NY 10017

DYSON, FREEMAN JOHN, physicist; b. Crowthorne, Eng., Dec. 15, 1923; s. George and Mildred Lucy (Atkey) D.; B.A., Cambridge U., 1945; m. Verena Haefeli-Huber, Aug. 11, 1950 (div. 1958); children—Esther, George; m. 2d, Imme Jung, Nov. 21, 1958; children—Dorothy, Emily, Miriam, Rebecca. Operations research R.A.F. Bomber Command, 1943-45; fellow Trinity Coll., Cambridge U., Eng., 1946-49; Commonwealth fellow Cornell U., Princeton, 1947-49; prof. physics Cornell U., 1951-53; prof. Inst. Advanced

Study, Princeton, 1953—. Fellow Royal Soc. London; mem. Am. Phys. Soc., Nat. Acad. Scis. Home: 105 Battle Road Circle Princeton NJ 08540

DYSTEL, OSCAR, publishing co. exec.; b. N.Y.C., Oct. 31, 1912; s. Jacob and Rose (Pintoff) D.; B.C.S., N.Y.U., 1935; M.B.A., Harvard, 1937. m. Marion Deitler, Oct. 2, 1938; children—Jane Dee, John Jay. Circulation mgr. Sports Illus. and Am. Golfer, 1937; circulation, Promotion mgr. Esquire and Coronet mags., Chgo., 1938-40; circulation mgr. Coronet mag., 1940, editor, 1940-42, 44-48; mng. editor Collier's. 1948-49 exec. staff Cowles Mags., Inc., 1949-51; editorial adviser Parents Inst., Inc., 1951- 54; pres. Bantam Books, Inc., N.Y.C., 1954—; v.p., dir. National General Corp., Los Angeles; dir. Grosset & Dunlap, Great Am. Life Ins. Co., Am. Nat. Fire Ins. Co., Constellation Reinsurance Co. Finance mag. Editor of U.S.A. Mag., pub. OWI, 1942-43; engaged in psychol. warfare operations Allied Force Hdqrs., MTO, 1943-44. Decorated Medal of Freedom, 1946. Mem. U.S. Alumni Assn. Clubs: Overseas Press, Harvard (N.Y.C.). Author: Analysis of Paid and Controlled Circulation Among Business Papers, 1938. Home: Pine Lane Rye NY 10580 Office: 271 Madison Av New York City NY 10016

DZIEWANOWSKI, MARIAN KAMIL educator; b. Zhytomir, Russia, June 27, 1913; s. Kamil Antoni and Zofia (Kamienska) D.; M. Law, Warsaw (Poland) U., 1937; diploma Warsaw French Inst., 1937; M.A., Harvard, 1948, Ph.D., 1951; m. Ada Karczewska, Oct. 4, 1946; children-Barbara, Jan. Came to U.S., 1947, naturalized, 1953. Commentator BBC, London, Eng., 1942-44; research fellow Russian Research Center, Harvard, 1949-52; research asso. Center for Internat. Studies, Mass. Inst. Tech., 1952-53; prof. history Boston Coll., 1954-65; Ford exchange prof. in Poland, , 1958; exchange scholar in USSR, 1960; vis. prof. Brown U., Provvidence, 1961-62, 68; prof. history Boston U., 1965- -. Asso., Russian Research Center, Harvard, 1960—. Mem. Boston Com. Fgn. Relations. Served to lt. Polish Army, 1939-40; Polish, French campaigns; mil. asst. attach83e, Washington, 1944. Decorated Polish Cross of Valor (two). Fellow Am. Philos. Soc.; mem. Am. Hist. Assn., Am. Assn. Advancement Slavic Studies, Polish Inst. Arts and Scis. in Am. Author: The Communist Party of Poland, 1959; A European Federalist, 1969; co-author eleven other books. Editor: The Russian Revolution, 1970. Contbr. articles to scholarly jours. Home: 41 Katherine Rd Watertown MA 02172 Office: 226 Bay State Rd Boston MA 02215

DZIUBA, HENRY FRANK, univ. dean; b. Detroit, Feb. 16, 1918; s. Frank and Anna (Jarzynka) D.; D.D.S., U. Detroit, 1942; m. Stella Madeline Walush, May 28, 1948; children—Kenneth John, Denise Susan. With U. Detroit Sch. Dentistry, 1945—, coordinator clinics, 1962-63, prof. prosthetics, 1962—, asst. dean, 1962-66, dean, 1967—. Recipient inter-prof. award, Advocates, 1967. Fellow Am., Internat. colls. dentists; mem. Am. Prosthodontic Soc., Detroit Dist. Dental Soc., Am., Mich. dental assns., Am. Assn. Dental Schs., Am. Pub. Health Assn., Omicron Kappa Upsilon, Psi Omega. Home 250 Claremont St Dearborn MI 48124 Office: 2985 E Jefferson St Detroit MI 48207

EADE, GEORGE JAMES, air force officer; b. Lockney, Tex., Oct. 27, 1921; s. George William and Isabel Theresa (Barnd) E.; student Woodrow Wilson Coll., Chgo., 1939-41, Ill. Inst. Tech., 1941-42; m. Colette Elaine Cachelin, May 18, 1946; children—George Walter, Helen Marie-Louise (Mrs. Jean Oesch), Anne Catherine (Mrs. Howard E. Pullen), Christine Colette, Dominique Frances. Commd. 2d lt. USAAF, 1942, advanced through grades to H-gen., USAF, 1971; chief current operations br. Hdqrs. SAC, 1952-56; dep. dir. operations Hdqrs. 7th Air Div., Eng., 1956-58; dir. operations 4238 Strategic Wing, Barksdale AFB, La., 1958-59, dep. comdr. for operations, 1959-60, vice comdr., 1960, comdr., 1961; comdr. 7th Bombardment Wing, Carswell AFB, Tex., 1961-63; chief safety div. Hdqrs. SAC, Offutt AFB, Neb., 1963-65, chief control div., 1965-66, dir. command control, 1966-67, dir. operations plans DCS/Operations, 1967-70; dir. plans, dep. chief of staff plans and operations Hdqrs. USAF, Washington, 1970-71, asst. dep. chief of staff, 1971—; chmn. U.S. sect. Mil. Coordinating Com. U.S.-Can.; USAF rep. Sec. Def. Blue Ribbon Action Com. Pres. Catholic Edn. Assn., Omaha, 1968-70. Decorated D.S.M., Legion of Merit, Air Force Commendation medal with two oak leaf clusters. Mem. Air Force Assn., Order of Daedalians. Home: 8410 Blakiston Lane Alexandria VA 22308 Office: Asst DCS/Plans and Operations The Pentagon (AF/XO) Washington DC 20330

EADES, HOWARD EUGENE, retail co. exec., b. Rome, N.Y. Nov. 2, 1907; s. Enos H. and Katherine (Wilson) E.; student Lafayette Coll., Pa., 1925-26, Syracuse U., 1926-27; m. Margaret Barrett, July 8, 1931 (dec. 1959); children—Gail Marguerite, Judith Elva; m. 2d, Grace Cylwik, June 11, 1960. With W.T. Grant Co., 1927—, floorman Eastern area U.S., asst. mgr., store mgr., dist. mgr., personnel dir., 1927-57, v.p., personnel dir., 1957-62, v.p., mdse. dir., 1962-64, research and personnel v.p., dir., 1964-67, v.p., asst. to pres., 1967-68, adminstrv. v.p., 1968—. Served from 1st lt. to capt. USAAF, 1942-45. Mem. Kappa Phi. Home: 22 Red Coat Lane Greenwich CT 06830 Office: 1441 Broadway New York City NY 10018

EADES, JAMES BEVERLY, Jr., aero. engr., b. Bluefield, W.Va., July 22, 1923; s. James Beverly and Harriet Beulah (Smith) E.; student Bluefield Coll., 1940-42; B.S. in Aero. Engring., Va. Poly. Inst., 1944, M.S. in Applied Mechanics, 1949, Ph.D., 1958; m. Sara M. Porterfield, Dec. 20, 1950; children—Sara Leslie, Beverly Anne, James Christian. Asst. prof. aero. engring. Va. Poly. Inst., 1947-50, asst. prof., research asso. aero. engring., 1953- 58, prof. aero. engring., 1958-60, 60-67, head aerospace engring., 1961-67; aero. research scientist NACA, Langley Research Center, Langley Field, Va., 1958, 59, Naval Ordnance Lab., Silver Spring, Md., 1960, 63-69; research asso. Nat. Acad. Scis., Goddard Space Flight Center, NASA, Greenbelt, Md., 1967-69; with Analytical Mechanics Assos., Inc., Seabrook, Md., 1969—. Dir. Conf. Lunar Explorations, 1962. Served to lt. USNR, World War II, 1951-53; comdr. Ret. Res. Registered profl. engr., Va., W.Va. Fellow Am. Inst. Aeros. and Astronautics (asso., chmn. Blue Ridge sect. 1964, profl. edn. com. 1969—); mem. Celestial Mechanics Inst. (v.p.), Am. Astronaut. Soc. Va. Acad. Sci. (sec. engring. sect. 1961, chmn. sect. 1962, mem. council, chmn. space sci. and tech. sect. 1968), Sigma Xi, Sigma Gamma Tau, Tau Beta Pi. Mason. Asst. exec. editor Celestial Mechanics Jour., Home: 1603 Peacock Lane Silver Spring MD 20904 Office: 9430 Lanham Severn Rd Seabrook MD 20801

EADIE, THOMAS W., business exec.; b. Ottawa, Can., 1898; grad. McGill U. Dir. Bell Telephone Co. Can.; hon. dir. Royal Trust Co. Home: 18 Forden Av Westmont Quebec Canada Office: 1050 Beaver Hall Hill Montreal Quebec Canada

EADIE, WILLIAM ROBERT, ret. zoologist, educator; b. Manchester, N.H., May 5, 1909; s. James and Maria (Bremner) E.; B.S., U. N.H., 1932, M.S., 1933; Ph.D., Cornell U., 1939; m. Eva S. Wentzell, Dec. 20, 1933 (dec. Nov. 1964); children—William James, Dennis Robert; m. 2d, Laura C. Keenahan, May 19, 1967. Asst. zoology U. N.H., 1933-35, instr., 1935- 39, asst. prof., 1939-42; asst. prof. zoology Cornell U., 1942-47, asso. prof., 1947-54, prof., 1954-69, prof. emeritus, 1969—; vis. prof. U. Ore., summer 1949, Mont. State U. Biol. Sta., summer 1964. Cons. to United Fruit Co., Guatemala, 1958. Served as lt. (j.g.) USNR, 1944-46. Fellow A.A.A.S.; mem. Am. Soc. Mammalogists (dir.), Am. Soc. Zoologists, Wildlife Soc., Ecol. Soc. Am., Sigma Xi, Phi Kappa Phi. Author: Animal Control in Field, Farm, and Forest, 1954. Contbr. to profl. publs. Editor of Jour. Mammalogy, 1952-57. Home: 390 Deer Meadow Lane Chatham MA 02633

EAGAN, EMMETT EDWARD, lawyer; b. Detroit, July 28, 1910; s. Mathew Joseph and Mary Ida (Heuser) E.; A.B. magna cum laude, U. Mich., 1932, J.D. magna cum laude, 1934; m. Virginia Mary Raymo, July 7, 1939; children—Kathleen Ellen (Mrs. C. Webster Wheelock), Emmett Edward. Admitted to Mich. bar, also Supreme Ct. U.S.; practiced in Detroit, 1934—; asso. Miller, Canfield, Paddock & Stone, 1934-42, jr. partner, 1942-52, sr. partner, 1952—; prof. Law Sch., Wayne State U., 1946—. Dir. Tecumseh Products Co., (Mich.) Consol. Packaging Corp., Chgo., Snyder Corp., Harlan Electric Co., Fuller Labs., Inc.; secretary and mem. bd. directors Harlan Elec. Constrn. Co., Murraywood Corp., Motor City Electric Co. Mem. com. visitors Law Sch., U. Mich., 1962—; nat. chmn. U. Mich. Law Sch. Fund, 1965-67; mem. Mich. Council for Arts, 1966-67; mem. membership com. Civic Searchlight, Inc., 1967—; mem. nat. com. U. Mich. Sesquicentennial Fund, 1967. Trustee Herrick Found., Sage Found., Harlan Found., Morrison Found., Wilson Coll., Chambersburg, Pa., Maryglade Coll., Detroit. Recipient Sesquicentennial award U. Mich., 1967. Fellow Am. Bar Found.; mem. Mich., Detroit (dir., past com. chmn.) bar assns., Am. Judicature Soc., Am. Law Inst., Am. Acad. Polit. and Social Sci., Order of Coif, Phi Beta Kappa. Phi Kappa Phi, Phi Eta Sigma, Phi Kappa. Clubs: Detroit; Grosse Pointe; Tennis House; Indian Village Tennis; The Players. Home: 99 Stephens Rd Grosse Pointe Farms MI 48236. Office: Detroit Bank and Trust Bldg Detroit MI 48226

EAGEN, MICHAEL JOHN, state justice; b. Jermyn, Pa., May 9, 1907; s. Michael Joseph and Sarah (Nallin) E.; B.A., St. Thomas Coll., Scranton, Pa., 1927; student Harvard Law Sch., 1927-28; LL.D. (hon.), U. Scranton, 1955; m. Helen Fitzsimmons, June 27, 1935; children—Helen Marie (Mrs. Thomas J. Foley), Michael John III, Jerry, James. Admitted to Pa. bar, 1931; pvt. practice, 1931-41; dist. atty. Lacke County, 1934-41; judge ct. common pleas Lacke County, 1942-59; justice Supreme Ct. Pa., 1960—. Pres. Lackewanna United Fund. 1955-59. Decorated knight Equestrian Order Holy Sepulchre. Mem. Pa., Lackawanna County bar assns. Elk (past local exalted ruler), Moose. Home: 711 Taylor Av Scranton PA 18510 Office: Court House Scranton PA 18503

EAGER, HENRY GOSSETT, lawyer; b. Kansas City, Mo., Oct. 14, 1923; s. Henry I. and Claudine (Gossett) E.; A.B., U. Mo., 1943; J.D., U. Mich., 1948; m. Ruth Jule Riche, Apr. 2, 1948; children—Julianne, Caroline Riche, Henry Gossett. Admitted to Mo. bar. 1948; practiced in Kansas City, 1948—; partner firm Swanson, Midgley, Eager, Gangwere, and Thurlo, and predecessors, 1948—. Active Kansas City Philharmonic Assn., Friends of Art, Civil War Roundtable, Jackson County Hist. Soc., Soc. Fellows Nelson Art Gallery. Served to capt. USMCR, 1943-46, 50- 52. Mem. Mo. Bar (bd. govs. 1955-56), Am., Kansas City bar assns., Lawyers Assn. Kansas City (pres. jr. sect. 1952-53), Bar Assn. St. Louis, Am. Judicature Soc., Phi Delta Phi, Phi Delta Theta. Democrat. Conglist. Mason, Rotarian. Clubs: Mission Hills (Kan.) Country; Kansas City (Kansas City, Mo.). Home: 615 W 67th Terrace Kansas City MO 64113 Office: Commerce Bank Bldg Kansas City MO 64106

EAGER, HENRY IDE, state judge; b. Hopkinsville, Ky., July 16, 1895; s. Ben F. and Carrie (Downer) E.; student U. Wash., 1913-14; LL.B., U. Mich., 1920; m. Claudine Gossett, Dec. 2, 1922; 1 son, Henry G. Admitted to Mo. bar, 1920; practiced in Kansas City. 1920-55; as mem. firm Blackmar, Eager. Swanson, Midgley & Jones; judge Supreme Ct. Mo., 1955-69, spl. commr., 1969—. Mem. Bd. Law Examiners. 1946-54; lectr. dental jurisprudence Sch. Dentistry U. Kansas City, 1943-55. Served from 2d to 1st lt. 34th Inf., 7th Div., U.S. Army, 1917-19. Mem. Am., Mo. (gov., chmn. appellate practice com.), Kansas City bar assns., Lawyers Assn. Kansas City, Delta Theta Phi. Baptist. Home: 2323 W Main St Jefferson City MO 65101 Office: Supreme Court of Missouri Jefferson City MO 65101

EAGER, ROBERT WILLIAM. mfg. co. exec.; b. Balt., July 5, 1917; s. George Sidney and Ada Elizabeth (Heinz) E.; B.S. in Econs., Johns Hopkins, 1941; student U. Pitts., 1942-44; m. Cecelia Ann Heintzelman, Dec. 9, 1949; children—Richard George, Judith Ann. Indsl. engr. Westinghouse Electric Corp., 1941-51; with Joy Mfg. Co., Pitts., 1951-66, plant mgr., 1957-59, became v.p. mfg., 1959, then gen. mgr. New Philadelphia (O.) operations; v.p. mfg. Oshkosh Motor Truck Co. (Wis.), 1966-71; v.p., gen. mgr. Helmich Corp., Fairmont, W.Va., 1971—. Mem. Soc. Advancement Mgmt., A.I.M. (pres.'s council). Western Pa. Engrs. Soc., Am. Mgmt. Assn., C. of C. Mason (Shriner), Elk, Rotarian. Home: 4 Sands Dr Fairmont WV 26554 Office: PO Box 71 Fairmont WV 26554

EAGLE, DEAN, newspaperman; b. Corbin, Ky., Mar. 16, 1920; s. James C. and Terrie (Masters) E.; A.B., Berea Coll., m. Mary Lucille Sewell, Sept. 14, 1940; children-Linda Joan, Cynthia Deane. Asst. sports editor Louisville Courier-Jour., 1945-53; sports editor Louisville Times, 1953-68, Louisville Courier-Jour., 1968—. Mem. Nat. Turfwriters Assn. (past pres.), Sigma Delta Chi (past pres.). Home: 2225 Valley Vista Rd Louisville, KY 40205 Office: 525 W Broadway Louisville KY 40202

EAGLE, HARRY, physician, coll. adminstr.; b. N.Y.C., July 13, 1905; s. Louis and Sadie (Kushnoy) E.; A.B., Johns Hopkins, 1923, M.D., 1927; M.S. (hon.), Yale, 1948; D.Sc., Wayne State U., 1965; m. Hope Whaley, Aug. 31, 1928; 1 dau., Kay Whaley (Mrs. Robert B. Kyle, Jr.). Intern, asst. and instr. medicine Johns Hopkins, 1927-32; asst. and asso. prof. bacteriology U. Pa., 1933-36; commd. officer USPHS, 1936-61; dir. Venereal Disease Research Lab., Johns Hopkins Hosp., 1936-46; dir. Lab. Exptl. Therapeutics, Johns Hopkins Sch. Hygiene and Pub. Health, 1946-48, adj. prof. bacteriology, 1946-47; sci. dir. research br. Nat. Cancer Inst., 1947-49; chief sect. exptl. therapeutics Nat. Inst. Allergy and Infectious Diseases, NIH, 1949-58, chief Lab. Cell Biology, 1959- 61; prof., dept. cell biology Albert Einstein Coll. Medicine, 1961-70, chmn. div. biol. scis., 1968-70, asso. dean sci. affairs, 1970—. Trustee Found. Microbiology, Rutgers U. Recipient Eli Lilly Co. bronze medal, 1936; Alvarenga prize Coll. Physicians Phila., 1936; Presdl. Certificate Merit, 1948; Borden award Assn. Am. Med. Colls., 1965; Bertner Found. award U. Tex., 1967; Albert Einstein Commemorative award, 1968. Mem. Nat. Acad. Scis., Am. Acad. Arts and Scis., Am. Soc. Biol. Chem., Soc. Am. Microbiologists (past pres.), Soc. Clin. Investigation, Assn. Am. Physicians, Am. Assn. Immunologists (pres. 1964-65), Soc. Exptl. Biology and Medicine (pres. 1963-65), Am. Soc. Cell Biology, Am. Assn. for Cancer Research. Author: Laboratory Diagnosis of Syphillis, 1937; papers relating to immunology, chemotherapy and tissue culture. Home: 370 Oriental Av Mamaroneck NY 10543 Office: Albert Einstein Coll Medicine East-Chester Rd and Morris Park Av New York City NY 10461

EAGLE, HERBERT DAVID, business exec.; b. Boston, Feb. 1, 1918; s. Leon and Sadie (Lewis) E.; student St. John's U., 1935-37; B.A. in Psychology, U. Cal. at Los Angeles, 1939; m. Mildred Tepper, May 25, 1940; 1 dau., Lynne Barbara. Advt. salesman Los Angeles Times, 1940-41; with Occidental Life Ins. Co. of Cal., 1941-69, group sales rep., 1941-42, successively tchrs. group supr., asst. regional group mgr., So. Cal. regional group mgr., 1946-53, v.p. charge group sales and service, 1953-68, sr. v.p. marketing, 1968-69; v.p. marketing Transam. Corp., Los Angeles, 1969—; dir. Transam. Research Corp., Cinecolor, Inc. Gen. chmn. fund campaign Jr. Achievement So. Cal., 1966- 67; finance vice chmn. Citizens Com. for Rapid Transit, 1968—. Served to capt. USAAF, 1942-46. Mem. Sales and Marketing Execs. Internat. (sec.-treas., bd. dirs.), Inst. Life Ins. (mem. steering com. trend analysis program), Am. Marketing Assn., Sales and Marketing Execs. Assn. Los Angeles (life mem., past pres.), Am. Legion, U. Cal. at Los Angeles Alumni Assn. Home: 13101 Nimrod Pl Los Angeles CA 90049 Office: 1150 S Olive St Los Angeles CA 90015

EAGLE, JOHN EDWIN, educator; b. St. Anthony, Ida., Aug. 14, 1909; s. Samuel Peter and Ida Christine (Carlson) E.; B.S. in Engring. (scholar), Mont. State U., 1930, postgrad., 1930-31; M.A. in Edn., Stanford, 1940, Ed.D., 1947; postgrad. U. Chgo., 1933, U. Mont., 1936, Ore. State U., 1942-43, Brit. Museum, Inst. Math. Pedagogy, Brussels, 1970; m. Marjorie Ione Foote, Aug. 25, 1937; 1 dau., Elizabeth Christine (Mrs. Thomas John Nemeth, Jr.). Tchr. various high schs., Mont., Cal., 1931-43; asst. prof. math. Ore. State U., 1943-44; lectr. math., edn. Stanford, part-time 1944-46; mem. faculty San Diego State Coll., 1946—, prof. math., 1952—. Asso. dir., dir. various NSF Insts., 1959-70. Mem. Pi Kappa Delta, Phi Delta Kappa, Phi Kappa Phi, Phi Eta Sigma, Sigma Alpha Epsilon. Methodist (ofcl. bd.). Home: 5039 Campanile Dr San Diego CA 92115

EAGLE, JOHN FREDERICK, coll. dean, physician; b. N.Y.C., July 16, 1917; s. J. Frederick and Margery (Brown) E.; B.A., Yale, 1940; M.D., Columbia, 1943; m. Elizabeth Babcock, Aug. 29, 1943; children—John Frederick III, Anne Stanton, J. Breckenridge, Sally King, Franklin Babcock, Elizabeth Winslow. Intern Babies Hosp., N.Y.C., 1947-49; resident, then chief resident Children's Hosp., Buffalo, 1949-51; asso. prof. pediatrics U. Buffalo Med. Sch., 1951-55; dir. pediatrics St. Luke's Hosp., N.Y.C., 1956-63; asso. prof. pediatrics Columbia Coll. Phys. and Surg., 1963-67, asst. dean, 1963-67; dean, prof. pediatrics N.Y. Med. Coll., 1967—. Mem. N.Y.C. Health Research Council, 1968—. Served to capt., M.C., AUS, 1944-47. Diplomate Am. Bd. Pediatrics. Mem. Am. Acad. Pediatrics, Soc. Pediatric Research, Med. Soc. County N.Y., A.M.A., N.Y. Acad. Medicine Home: 161 E 64th St New York City NY 10021. Office: NY Med Coll Fifth Av and 106th St New York City NY 10029

EAGLEBURGER, LAWRENCE SIDNEY, fgn. service officer; b. Milw., Aug. 1, 1930; s. Leon Sidney and Helen (Van Ornum) E.; student Central State Coll., Stevens Point, Wis., 1948-50; B.S., U. Wis., 1952, M.S., 1957; m. Marlene Ann Heinemann, Apr. 23, 1966; 1 son by previous marriage, Lawrence Scott; 1 son, Lawrence Andrew. Joined U.S. Fgn. Service, 1957; 3d sec., Tegucigalpa, Honduras, 1957-59; assigned State Dept., 1959-62, 65-66; 2d sec., Belgrade, Yugoslavia, 1962-65; mem. staff NSC, 1966-67; spl. asst. under sec. State Dept., 1967- 69; exec. asst. to asst. to Pres. for nat. security affairs, 1969; polit. adviser, counselor for polit. affairs U.S. Mission to NATO, Brussels, Belgium, 1969—; teaching asst. U. Wis., 1956-57. Vice chmn. 7th Dist. Young Republicans Wis., 1950-51; mem. Wis. Young Rep. Exec. Com., 1949-51; pres. Wis. Young Reps. for Warren for President, 1952. Served to 1st lt. AUS, 1952- 54. Mem. Alpha Sigma Phi. Home: 14 Av Lloyd George Brussels Belgium Office: US NATO APO NY 09667

EAGLESON, PETER STURGES, educator, hydrologist; b. Phila., Feb. 27, 1928; s. William Boal and Helen (Sturges) E.; B.S. in Civil Engring., Lehigh U., 1949, M.S., 1952; Sc.D., Mass. Inst. Tech., 1956; m. Marguerite Anne Partridge, May 28, 1949; children—Helen Marie, Peter Sturges, Jeffrey Partridge, Jr. engr. George B. Mebus, cons. engr., Glenside, Pa., 1950-51; teaching asst. Lehigh U., 1951-52; research asst. Mass. Inst. Tech., 1952-54, mem. faculty, 1954—, prof. civil engring., 1965—, head dept. civil engring., 1970—; Fulbright sr. research scholar Commonwealth Sci. and Indsl. Research Orgn., Canberra, Australia, 1966-67. Served to 2d lt. C.E., AUS, 1949-50. Recipient Desmond Fitzgerald medal 1959, Clemens Herschel prize, 1965 (both Boston Soc. Civil Engrs.); research prize Am. Soc. C.E., 1963. Author: (with others) Estuary and Coastline Hydrodynamics, 1966; Dynamic Hydrology, 1970. Home: 34 Lowell Rd Wellesley Hills MA 02181 Office: Mass Inst Tech Cambridge MA 02139

EAGLESON, WILLIAM BOAL, Jr., banker; b. Phila., Dec. 10, 1925; s. William Boal and Helen (Sturges) E.; B.S., Lehigh U., 1949; M.B.A., U. Pa., 1951; m. Catherine West McLean, May 28, 1960; children—Elizabeth West, John McLean. With Fed. Res. Bank Phila., 1949-51; investment officer Girard Trust Bank, Phila., 1951-61, v.p., 1961, exec. v.p., 1967, pres., dir. Girard Co., Girard Trust Bank, 1970—; trustee Penn Mut. Life Ins. Co., dir. Potomac Ins. Co., Camden Fire Ins. Assn., Pa. Gen. Ins. Co., Girard Internat. Bank; mem. exec. com. U.S. br., dir. Gen. Accident Fire & Life Assurance Corp. Ltd. Trustee Acad. Natural Scis. Phila., Lehigh U.; bd. dirs. Am. Found.; bd. corporators Med. Coll. Pa. Served with USNR, 1944-46. Episcopalian. Home: 43 Jaffrey Rd Malvern PA 19355 Office: Girard Trust Bank Broad and Chestnut Sts Philadelphia PA 19101

EAGLETON, RICHARD ERNEST, judge; b. Peoria, Ill., June 29, 1930; s. William Lester and Mary Louise (Chandler) E.; B.A., Yale, 1952; LL.B., U. Ill., 1958; m. Elizabeth Louise Waterman, Jan. 31, 1953; children—David Pierce, Margaret Waters. Admitted to Ill. bar, 1958; pvt. practice, Peoria, 1958- 61, 69-70; asst. U.S. atty. So. Dist. Ill., 1961-64, U.S. atty., 1965-69; 1st asst. state's atty., Peoria, 1964-65; circuit judge 10th Ill. Circuit, 1970—. Bd. dirs. Peoria Mental Health Clinic, 1959-65, treas., 1964. Democratic candidate Ill. circuit judge, 1963. Served with USN, 1952-55; comdr. Res. Mem. Am. (nat. dir. crime control project 1969-70), Ill. (chmn. criminal Law sect. 1969-70), Peoria County (sec. treas. 1962-65) bar assns., Phi Gamma Delta, Phi Delta Phi. Baptist. Mason. Club: Country (Peoria). Home: 1610 W Moss Av Peoria IL 61606 Office: Peoria County Courthouse Peoria IL 61602

EAGLETON, THOMAS FRANCIS, U.S. senator; b. St. Louis, Sept. 4, 1929; s. Mark David and Zitta Louise (Swanson) E.; A.B. cum laude, Amherst Coll., 1950, J.D., 1970; LL.B. cum laude, Harvard, 1953; J.D. (hon.), Suffolk U., 1958, Park Coll., 1969, Rockhurst Coll., 1970; m. Barbara Ann Smith, Feb. 12, 1956; children—Terence Francis, Christin. Admitted to Mo. bar. 1953; pvt. practice, St. Louis, 1953-56; circuit atty., St. Louis, 1957-60; atty. gen. State of Mo., 1961-65, lt. gov., 1965-68; U.S. senator from Mo., 1969—. Served with USNR, 1948-49. Mem. Bar Assn. St. Louis, Lawyers Assn. St. Louis, Delta Kappa Epsilon. Office: Senate Office Bldg Washington DC 20510

EAGLETON, WILLIAM LESTER, Jr., fgn. service officer; b. Peoria, Ill., Aug. 17, 1926; s. William Lester and Mary Louise (Chandler) E.; B.A., Yale, 1948; student Inst. d'Etudes Politiques, Paris, France, 1948-49; m. Francoise Bosworth, Oct. 12, 1948 (div. 1966); children—Diane, Marc, Richard, Robert, Philip; m. 2d,

Kathleen Flannigan, Mar. 18, 1967; 1 son, Anthony Brian. Joined U.S. Fgn. Service, 1949; 3d sec. embassy, Madrid, Spain, 1950-51, Damascus, Syria, 1951-53, Beirut, Lebanon, 1953-54; pub. affairs officer, Kirkuk, Iraq, 1954-55; assigned State Dept., 1956-59; consul, Tabriz, Iran, 1959-61; chargé d'affaires embassy, Nouakchott, Mauritania, 1962-64; 1st sec. embassy, London, Eng., 1964-66; with Woodrow Wilson Sch. Pub. and Internat. Affairs, 1966-67; consul gen., 1967, chargé d'affaires, Aden, 1967-69; chief U.S. interests sect. Swiss embassy, Algiers, 1969—. Served with USNR, 1944-46. Author; The Kurdish Republic of 1946, 1963. Home: 837 N Cooper St Peoria IL 61606

EAKER, IRA C. mfg. exec.; b. Liano County, Tex., Apr. 13, 1896; s. Y.Y. and Dona Lee (Graham) E.; A.B., South Eastern Normal Coll., Okla., 1917; student U. Philippines (eves.), 1920-21, Columbia U. Law Sch., 1923-24, George Washington U. Law Sch., 1924-26; A.B. in Journalism, U. So. Cal., 1933; m. Ruth Huff Apperson, Nov. 23, 1931. Commd. 2d lt. Inf., U.S. Army, 1917; trans. to Air Corps, Nov. 1917; rated pilot, Sept. 1918; commd. capt. 1920, advanced through grades to lt. gen., 1943; acting air officer Philippine Dept., 1921; adj. Mitchel Field, 1922-24; asst. exec. Office Chief of Air Corps, 1924-26, exec., 1939-40; comdg. officer 20th Pursuit Group, 1941; comdg. gen. 8th Bomber Command, 1942; comdg. gen. 8th Air Force, U.K., 1943; comdr.-in-chief, Mediterranean Allied Air Forces, 1944; dep. comdr. A.A.F., and Chief Air Staff, 1945-47; v.p. Hughes Tool Co., 1947-57, became v.p. Eastern office Douglas Aircraft Co., Inc., 1957; chmn. adv. bd. Hughes Aircraft Co., 1961—. Decorated D.S.M., Legion of Merit, D.F.C. with 2 oak leaf clusters, Silver Star (U.S.); knight Order Brit. Empire; Order of Katusov, 2d Degree (USSR); Order Southern Cross (Brazil); Order Partisan Star, 1st Class (Yugoslavia); Order of Sun (Peru); Order of Liberator (Venezuela); Order of Condor of Andes (Bolivia); Order of Merit (Chile). Mem. Christian Ch. Author: (with Gen. H.H. Arnold) This Flying Game, 1936; Winged Warfare, 1940; Army Flyer, 1942. Made goodwill flight around South America, 1926; world endurance flight record as chief pilot of "Question Mark," 1929; 1st transcontinental blind flight (with instruments), 1936; transcontinental flight refueling in air, 1929; 1st attack by U.S. heavy bombers in Europe, Aug. 1942; 1st shuttle bombing mission to Russia, June 1944; ret., 1947. Writer weekly syndicated column on nat. security, 1962—. Home: 2202 Decatur Pl NW Washington DC 20006 Office: 1612 K St NW Washington DC 20006

EAKIN, CARL TURNEY, univ. dean; b. Clayton, N.M., Sept. 7, 1930; s. Marvin Sledge and Lella (Palmer) E.; B.B.A., W.Tex. State U., 1954; M.B.A., Ind. U., 1955, D.B.A., 1959; m. Mathida Durning, Dec. 25, 1952; 1 son, Carlon Mark. Instr., Hanover (Ind.) Coll., 1955-56; lectr. Ind. U. 1956-58; asst. prof. U. Notre Dame, 1958-60; asso. prof. U. Ga., Athens, 1960-65, dept. head, 1962-68, prof., 1965-68; dean Sch. Bus., U. Louisville, 1968—; cons. marketing, bus. policy, marketing research. Mem. Am., So. (pres.) marketing assns., Am. Econ. Assn., Sales and Marketing Execs. Internat., Beta Gamma Sigma, Pi Sigma Epsilion, Phi Kappa Phi. Home: 510 McCready Av Louisville KY 40206

EAKIN, PAUL JAMES, investment banker; b. Du-Bois, Pa., Feb. 18, 1904; son Mertz Arthur and Martha (Weller) E.; A.B., Muskingum Coll., 1924; M.B.A., Harvard, 1927; m. Jean Fulmer Gibson, Sept. 13, 1930; children—Michael, Robert, John, Martha. With Union Trust Co., Cleve., 1927-29; statistician Hornblower & Weeks (co. name now Hornblower & Weeks, Hemphill, Noyes), 1929-42, gen. partner 1942-65, limited partner, 1965-. Hon. trustee Health Hill Hosp., Andrews Sch. for Girls, Cleve. Inst. Music; mem. board of trustees Children's Fresh Air Camp; trustee, past chmn. finance com. Case Inst. Tech. Clubs: Union, Country, Cleveland Skating. Home: 2709 Southington Rd Shaker Heights OH 44120 Office: Union Commerce Bldg Cleveland OH 44114

EAKIN, RICHARD MARSHALL, educator; b. Florence, Colo., May 5, 1910; s. Marshall and Mary Elizabeth (Jack) E.; student U. Tulsa, 1927-29; A.B., U. Cal. at Berkeley, 1931, Ph.D., 1935; NRC fellow, univs. Erlangen and Freiburg (Germany), 1935-36; m. Mary Mulford, Aug. 8, 1935; children—David Marshall, Dorothy Alice, Lawrence (dec.). Instr. zoology U. Cal. at Berkeley, 1936-39, asst. prof., 1939-42, asso. prof., 1942- 49, chmn. dept., 1942-48, 1952-57, prof., 1949-, asst. dean coll. letters and sci., 1939-42, research prof. Miller Inst., 1961, 69, chmn. Miller Inst. Basic Research in Sci., 1962-68; vis. prof. U. Wash., summer 1950; Guggenheim fellow Stanford, 1953. Recipient Commencement citation for Distinguished Teaching, 1962; Distinguished Teaching prize Asso. Students U. Cal., 1967. Fellow NSF to Berne, Switzerland, 1957. Fellow Cal. Acad. Sci., Institute Internationale d'Embryologie; mem. Western Soc. Naturalists, Am. Soc. Zoology, A.A.A.S., Electron Microscope Soc. Am., No. Cal. Soc. for Electron Microscopy, Am. Soc. Cell Biology, Soc. for Developmental Biology, Sigma Xi, Phi Beta Kappa. Author: Vertebrate Embryology, 1964. Asso. editor Jour. Exptl. Zoology. Contbr. articles profl. jours., chpts. on photoreceptors to 3 books. Home: 1627 Spruce St Berkeley CA 94709

EAKIN, ROBERT EDWARD, educator; b. LaGrande, Ore., Jan. 23, 1916; s. Robert S. and Netta (Kiddle) E.; B.S., Ore. State U., 1937, M.A. (Standard Brands fellow), 1939; Ph.D. (Standard Brands fellow), U. Tex., Austin, 1942; m. Esther Aline, Oct. 13, 1940; children—Timothy, Patrick, Michael, Kelly. Research biochemist Nutrition Clinic, Hillman Hosp., Birmingham, Ala., 1941-42; research asso. U. Cin. Med. Sch., 1941-43; asst. to full prof. chemistry U. Tex., Austin, 1946—; cons. Eli Lilly & Co., Clayton Biochemical Found. for Research. Served with USNR, 1943-46. Mem. Am. Assn. Biol. Chemists, Am. Chem. Soc., A.A.A.S., Phi Lambda Upsilon, Sigma Xi, Phi Kappa Phi, Phi Delta Theta. Presbyn. Author: (with others) Biochemistry of the B Vitamins, 1951. Home: 1603 Scenic Dr Austin TX 78703

EALY, LAWRENCE ORR, author, educator; b. Ocean City, N.J., Sept. 17, 1915; s. Vance Lawrie Orr and Nelle Gray (Rohm) E.; A.B., Temple U., 1934; LL.B., U. Pa., 1937, M.A., 1947, Ph.D., 1951; student Navy Supply Corps Sch., Grad. Sch. Bus. Adminstrn., Harvard, 1941. Admitted to Ohio bar, 1938, Pa. bar, 1941; pvt. practice of law, Steubenville, O. and Phila., 1938- 41; instr. history Temple U., 1947-51, asst. prof., 1951-54, asso. prof., 1954-58; lectr. Naval Res. Officers Sch., 1956-57, Rutgers U., 1954-55; Ernest J. King prof. history Naval War Coll., Newport, R.I., 1958-59; provost, dean of faculties, prof. history Hobart Coll., William Smith Coll., 1959-62; dean, prof. history and govt. Rider Coll., Trenton, N.J., 1962-66, v.p. coll., 1966-70. Mem. Pa. Citizens Com. for Eisenhower, 1952. Trustee Temple U. Alumni Fund Council, 1947- 51, Ednl. Found. of Alpha Chi Rho, 1956-57. Served from ensign to comdr., USNR, 1941-46. Mem. Ohio, Pa., Phila. bar assns., Ret. Officers Assn., Internat. Assn. Torch Clubs, Am. Legion, Phi Alpha Theta, Pi Gamma Mu, Delta Sigma Pi, Alpha Chi Rho, Pi Delta Epsilon. Republican. Episcopalian. Elk. Club: Torch (pres. 1966-67) (Trenton, N.J.). Author: Under the Puppet's Crown, 1939; Tacony Farm, 1942; Republic of Panama in World Affairs, 1951; Yanqui Politics and the Isthmian Canal, 1970. Mem. bd. Am. Jour. Legal History, 1957—. Home: 25 Vander Veer Dr University Park, Trenton, NJ 08638.

EAMES, ALFRED WARNER, Jr., food co. exec.; b. Honolulu, June 20, 1914; s. Alfred Warner and Carrie Godfrey (McLean) E.; student U. Ore., 1932-33, 35; m. Marion Antoinette Lucas, Feb. 17, 1938; children—Alfred Warner IV, Anthony L., Peter M., A. Christopher. With Del Monte Corp. (formerly Cal. Packing Corp.), 1935—, prodn. mgmt., 1946-56, prodn. v.p., 1957-68, pres., 1968-69, chmn. bd., 1969—, also dir.; dir. Bank of Cal. N.A., Pacific Gas & Electric Co. Trustee Com. for Econ. Devel., Council of Americas, Nutrition Found.; bd. dirs. Internat. Exec. Service Corps. Mem. Cal. C. of C. (dir.), Grocery Mfrs. Am. (dir.), Nat. Canners Assn. (administrv. council, finance com.), The Conf. Bd., Newcomen Soc., Chi Psi. Clubs: Menlo Country, St. Francis Yacht, Stock Exchange. Home: 85 Laburnum Rd Atherton CA 94025 Office: 215 Fremont St San Francisco CA 94119

EAMES, CHARLES designer; b. St. Louis, June 17, 1907; s. Charles O. and Celine (Lambert) E.; m. Ray Kaiser, June 20, 1941; 1 dau. (by 1st marriage), Lucia (Mrs. Aristides Demetrios). Pvt. practice architecture in midwest; now designer, with wife, of furniture, toys, architecture and motion pictures, Venice, Cal. Charles Eliot Norton prof. poetry Harvard; Lethaby lectures Royal Coll. Art; lectr. Royal Inst. Architects. Recipient Gold medal A.I.A. Mem. Am. Acad. Arts and Scis., Nat. Council Arts. Home: 203 Chautauqua Blvd Pacific Palisades CA 90272 Office: 901 Washington Blvd Venice CA 90291

EAMES, EARL WARD, Jr., mgmt. cons., business exec.; b. Morris, Minn., Oct. 22, 1923; s. Earl Ward and Camilla (Hendricks) E.; student U. Minn., 1941; S.B., Mass. Inst. Tech., 1949; m. Anyes de Horst, June 26, 1954; children—Elizabeth Anne, Earl Ward III, Erik Michael, Christopher Paul. Vice pres., then pres. dir. Consutants Inc., Boston and Amsterdam, The Netherlands, 1949-54; prodn. specialist Found. Productivity Research, Helsinki, Finland, 1955- 57; pres. Gen. Mgmt. Assos., Boston, 1957-63; sr. asso. Cresap, McCormick & Paget, N.Y.C., 1963-66, v.p. operations, 1966; pres., chief exec. officer, dir. Council Internat. Progress in Mgmt., N.Y.C., 1967-69; v.p., dir. Reed, Cuff & Becker, N.Y.C., 1970—; lectr. internat. econs. Fisher Coll., 1954-55, 60-63. Mem. Gov. Com. Refugees, 1961—; chmn. trustee Nat. Service Secretariat, 1966—; rep. Internat. Council for Sci. Mgmt. to ECOSOC, 1967-69; mem. internat. exec. programs Ind. U. Grad. Sch. Bus., 1967—; mem. Columbia U. Sem. on Orgn. and Mgmt., 1968—. Treas. New Eng. Opera Theatre, 1958-63; mem. com. Friends of N.Y. Philharmonic, 1967—; corporate mem. Vols. for Internat. Tech. Assistance, 1967—. Served with USNR, 1942-46. Mem. Am. Soc. Pub. Administrn., Nat. Planning Assn., Am. Soc. Tng. and Devel. Newcomen Soc. Republican. Lutheran. Rotarian. Clubs: Plandome (N.Y.) Field and Marine; Columbia University, Mass. Inst. Tech. Alumni (N.Y.C.). Author: Estimation of Managerial and Technical Personnel Requirements in the Pulp and Paper Industry, 1968. Home: 70 South Dr Plandome, NY 11030. Office: 114 E 55th St New York City NY 10022

EAMES, HERBERT HOWELL, Jr., corp. exec.; b. Keene, N.H., Aug. 2, 1934; s. Herbert Howell and Mary Caroline (Shaffer) E.; grad. Valley Forge Mil. Acad., 1953; B.A., Tufts U., 1961; M.B.A., St. John's U., 1971; m. Pamela Hodgdon, Aug. 16, 1958; children—Elisabeth Mary, Stephen David, Peter Howell. Budget analyst Nestle Co., Inc., White Plains, N.Y., 1960-64; financial analyst McCall Corp., 1964-65; controller McCall Information Service Co., Dayton, O., 1965-68; asst. controller Bristol-Myers Co., N.Y.C., 1968-70, controller, 1970—. Served with USMC, 1953-57. Mem. Financial Execs. Inst., Controllers Inst. Am., Nat. Assn. Accountants, Zeta Psi. Home: 143 Lockwood Rd Riverside CT 06878 Office: 345 Park Av New York City NY 10022

EAMES, JOHN HEAGAN, etcher; b. Lowell, Mass., July 19, 1900; s. Albert Melvin and Amanda Kneeland (Matthews) E.; A.B., Harvard, 1922; student Royal Coll. Art. London, Eng., 1933, 35, 37; pupil of Malcolm Osborne and Robert Austin; m. Muriel MacMicken, May 17, 1924; 1 dau., Consuelo. Engaged in archtl. work, N.Y.C., 1923-31; artist, Eng. and France, 1931-39, N.Y.C., 1939—. Exhibited drawings, etchings Royal Acad., London, 1935, 37, 40, N.Y. World's Fair, 1939, Internat. Print Exhbn., Art Inst. Chgo., 1939, Biennial Exhbn., Venice, Italy, 1940, Met. Mus., 1942, 52, Carnegie Inst., 1945, N.A.D. Exhbn. Contemporary Am. Drawings, 1945, 46, Bklyn. Mus., 1950, Albany (N.Y.) Inst. History and Art, 1949, Albright Art Gallery, Buffalo, 1950, Sweat Meml. Art Mus., Portland, Me., 1952, 53, 54, Am. Acad. Arts and Letters, 1953, Smithsonian Instn. Traveling Exhbn. Am. Drawings, 1954, Soc. Am. Graphic Artists Exchange Exhbn., Eng., 1954; ann. exhibitor N.A.D., Soc. Am. Graphic Artists; represented permanent collection Library of Congress, Met. Mus. Art; also pvt. collections. Recipient Kate W. Arms Meml. prize for best miniature etching Soc. Am. Graphic Artists, 1952, 54, 57, John Taylor Arms prize for etching, 1953; Henry B. Shope prize, etching, 1957; Purchase prize Albany Inst. Art, 1957, 69. Served with U.S. Army, 1918. Asso. N.A.D.; asso. mem. Royal Soc. Painters- Etchers; mem. Soc. Am. Graphic Artists. Address: Boothbay Harbor ME 04538

EAMES, S. MORRIS, educator; b. Silex, Mo., June 5, 1916; s. Jesse S. and Velma (Morris) E.; A.B., Culver-Stockton Coll., 1939; M.A. in Philosophy, U. Mo., 1941, M.A. in Sociology, 1952; Ph.D., U. Chgo., 1958; D.Litt., Bethany (W.Va.) Coll., 1968; m. Elizabeth Ramsden, Aug. 21, 1952; children—Ivan Lee, Anne. Mem. faculty Culver-Stockton Coll., 1942-44, U. Mo., 1944-50, Washington U., St. Louis, 1951-63; mem. faculty So. Ill. U., 1963—, prof. philosophy, 1968—; Oreon Scott lectr. Bethany Coll., 1965; mem. editorial bd. Coop. Research Project for Dewey Publns., 1963—. Pres. Mo. Philos. Assn., 1961-62. Mem. Am. Philos. Assn., John Dewey Soc., C.S. Peirce Soc., Metaphys. Soc., Mind Assn., Disciples of Christ Hist. Soc. Author: The Philosophy of Alexander Campbell, 1966; co-author: Logical Methods, rev. edit., 1971. Co-editor, contbr.: Guide to the Works of John Dewey, 1970; John Dewey: The Early Works, 1882-1898. Contbr. articles, poems, revs. to profl. jours., mags. Home: 205 Gray Dr Carbondale IL 62901

EAMES, WILMER BALLOU, dental educator; b. Kansas City, Mo., May 8, 1914; s. Prescott W. and Alice (Ballou) E.; D.D.S., Western Dental Coll., Kansas City, Mo., 1939; m. Elma Elaine Bitter, July 2, 1939; children—Douglas, Alice (Mrs. James Lillian). Practice dentistry, Grand Junction, Colo., 1939-41, Denver, 1945-47, Glenwood Springs, Colo., 1947-61; prof. operative dentistry Northwestern U. Dental Sch., 1961-67, asso. dean, 1964-67; prof. operative dentistry, dir. student projects Emory U. Sch. Dentistry, 1967—. Served to maj., Dental Corps, USAAF, 1941-45. Fellow Am., Internat. colls. dentists; mem. Internat. Assn. Dental Research, Am. Dental Assn., Am. Acad. Restorative Dentistry, Sigma Xi, Omicron Kappa Upsilon. Research and publs. in dental materials; developed technique for preparation of dental amalgam. Home: 3898 Sable Dr Stone Mountain, GA 30083. Office: Sch Dentistry Emory U Atlanta GA 30322

EARDLEY, DORAL BEDSON, electric co. exec.; b. Bountiful, Utah, Apr. 15, 1910; s. Frank Holding and Eva (Smith) E.; A.B., U. Utah, 1935; m. Marguerite Keller, Aug. 12, 1935; children—Diane (Mrs. Charles Kirkey), Dennis R. Estimator, Norton & Norton Electric Co., Los Angeles, 1936; salesman Graybar Electric Co., Inc., Salt Lake City, San Francisco, 1937-53, mgr. lamp sales, San Francisco, 1953-55, br. mgr., Fresno, Cal., 1955-56, br. mgr., Salt Lake City, 1956-60, dist. sales mgr., Seattle, 1960-61, dist. mgr., Seattle, 1961-63, dist. mgr., Los Angeles, 1963-64, dist. mgr., dir., mem. exec. com., N.Y.C., 1964-67, v.p. supply products and markets, officer, 1967—. Served to comdr. USN, World War II; PTO. Mem. Nat. Assn. Elec. Distbrs. (exec. com.), Sigma Pi. Rotarian. Clubs: Winged Foot Golf (Mamaroneck, N.Y.), Pinnacle (N.Y.C.). Home: Sterling Rd Harrison NY 10528 Office: 420 Lexington Av New York City NY 10017

EARL, CHARLES HINKLE, lawyer; b. Morriton, Ark., Jan. 10, 1908; s. Robert David and Carra (Hinkle) E.; student Hendrix Coll., 1926-27, U. Ark., 1927-30; LL.B., Ark. Law Sch., 1940; m. Wanda Fiurry, Nov. 14, 1939; children—John Charles, Norma Charlotte. Admitted to Ark. bar, 1932; mem. firm Earl, Cazort & Eldridge, Little Rock, 1931-37; asst. Ark. revenue atty., Little Rock, 1937-41; pvt. practice, asst. Ark. atty. gen., 1945-50; pres. Earl Cotton Co., Inc., 1947—, Am. Protective Life Ins. Co., 1952- -, Earl Warehouse Co., Inc., 1956-61, Saf-T-Boom Corp., 1958—; v.p. Am. Equitable Assurance Co., 1955-57 (all Little Rock); v.p. Ins. Investments, Inc., Conway, Ark., 1957—, Besco Internat. Corp., Little Rock, 1963—; regional dir. Nat. Western Life Ins. Co., Denver, 1963—; dir. Union Standard Oil & Gas Corp., Collie, Inc. Mem. Pres.'s Adv. Bd. Postal Affairs, 1962—. Trustee James H. Mc-Clellan Meml. Fund; bd. dirs. C. H. Earl Scholarship, U. Ark., R.D. Earl Scholarship, Hendrix Coll.; trustee Med. Dental Found. Served with Intelligence Corps., AUS, 1942-46. Mem. Am., Ark., Pulaski County bar assns., Nat. Safety Council, Equipment Distbrs. Assn., Soc. Am. Mil. Engrs., Little Rock C. of C. (chmn. congl. com.), Million Dollar Round Table, Kappa Beta Phi, Kappa Sigma. Methodist. Mason (32, Shriner), Elk, Lion. Home: 32 Edgehill Rd Little Rock AR 72207 Office: 1613 Main St Little Rock AR 72202

EARL, KENNETH, former educator; b. Doylestown, Pa., Sept. 10, 1901; s. Howard M. and Susan (Latch) E.; B.S., U.S. Naval Acad., 1924; M.S., Mass. Inst. Tech., 1930; m. Mary Anne Maguire, Jan. 3, 1945; 1 dau., Susan E. Commd. ensign USN, 1924, advanced through grades to capt., 1943; staff comdr. So. Pacific, 1943-45; ret., 1954; tchr. St. John's Ravencourt Sch., Winnipeg, Can., 1954-55; tchr. Chauncy Hall Sch., Boston, 1955-64, headmaster, 1964-68; tchr. Friends' Central Sch., Phila., 1968-70. Home: Merion Manor Merion, PA 19066.

EARL, LEWIS HAROLD, govt. ofcl.; b. Guthrie, Tex., Dec. 17, 1918; s. Henry W. and Ruth (O'Neal) E.; B.A., Tex. Technol. Coll., 1939; student U. Tex., 1939-40, Am. U., 1941-42; J.D., Georgetown U., 1950; m. Patricia Miler, Mar. 5, 1943; children—William Lee, Patricia Lewise (Mrs. Nelson), Robert Charles, James Michael. Admitted to D.C. bar, 1950; with Bur. Labor Statistics, Dept. Labor, 1940-42, 46-54; industry, commodity economist NPA, Dept. Commerce, 1951-53; productivity specialist, economist, program analyst, asst. program officer US Tech. Cooperation Program in Brazil, 1953-57, program officer, Argentina, 1957-59, El Salvador, 1959-61; internat. relations officer AID, Washington, 1961-63; chief internat. research Office Manpower Automation and Tng., U. S. Dept. Labor, Washington, 1963-65, chief Fgn. manpower program staff Office Manpower Policy, Evaluation and Research, Dept. Labor, 1965-70; tech. dir. Seminar for Ministry Labor Tng. Coordinators, OAS, Mexico City, Mexico, 1970; asst. dir. for program devel. for Human Resources, U. Houston, 1970—; manpower planning officer Gulf Coast CAMPS Secretariate, City of Houston, 1970—. Served as lt. USNR, 1942-46. Mem. Acad. Polit. Sci., Am. Acad. Polit. and Social Soc., Soc. for Internat. Devel., Nat. Planning Assn., Indsl. Research Assn., Alpha Chi. Pi Sigma Alpha. Home: Peacock TX 79542 Office: Center for Human Resources U Houston Houston TX 79004

EARL, LLOYD ROBERT, mfg. exec.; b. Athlons, Cal., May 19, 1898; s. Robert and Lulu (Thompson) E. m. Kathleen M. Hurt, July 16, 1924; 1 son, Wayne Earl. Began as machinist, 1919; foreman machine shop Consol. Steel Corp., 1928, plant supt., 1932, gen. supt. operations, 1935, prodn. mgr., 1937, v.p. operations, 1938, dir., 1940, mem. exec. com., bd. dirs., 1941-51, v.p., dir. Consol Steel Corp., Cal., Tex., Consol. Constructors, Inc., Calif.; v.p. Consol. Western Steel Corp., Del.; pres., chmn. exec. com., mem. bd. of dirs. United Concrete Pipe Corp., Baldwin Park, Cal., 1952; chmn. bd. Smith Scott Co., Inc., Riverside, Cal., 1958—, United Pacific Concrete Corp., Honolulu, 1960, Rockwin Prestressed Concrete, Los Angeles, 1962—; dir. Am. Liquid Gas Corp. (Los Angeles), U.S. Pipe & Foundfy Co., Pacific Airmotive Corp. Mem. Southwest Mus. Assn., Los Angeles. Mem. Assos. Cal. Inst. Tech., C. of C. Republican. Methodist, Mason. Clubs: California, Annandale. Home: 805 San Marino Av San Marino CA 91108 Office: 14041 E Arrow Hwy Baldwin Park CA 91706

EARLE, DAVID PRINCE, Jr., educator, physician; b. Englewood, N.J., May 23, 1910; s. David Prince and Paula (Benner) E.; A.B., Princeton, 1933; M.D., Columbia, 1937, Sc.D. in Medicine, 1942; m. Elizabeth Temple Ingraham, June 27, 1936; children—David Prince III, Paul Winthrop, Kevin Campbell, Charles Benner. Intern St. Luke's Hosp., N.Y.C., 1937-39; resident Columbia Univ. Research Service, Goldwater Meml. Hosp., N.Y.C., 1939-41; research asso. N.Y.U. Service, 1939-41, dir. N.Y.U. Research Service, 1947-48; asst. prof. medicine, then asso. prof. N.Y.U. Coll. Medicine, 1943-54; prof. medicine Northwestern U. Med. Sch., 1954—, chmn. dept., 1965—; chmn. dept. research Chgo. Wesley Meml. Hosp., 1960-69, attending physician, 1969—; attending physician Bellevue Hosp., N.Y.C., 1948-54, Passavant Meml. Hosp., Chgo., 1954—. Sec. clin. testing panel, bd. coordination antimalarial studies NRC, 1943-45; mem. medicine test com. Nat. Bd. Med. Examiners, 1956-60, chmn., 1960; mem. cardiovascular study sect. NIH, 1958-61, mem. diabetes and metabolism tng. com., 1964-67, chmn., 1966-67, chmn. urology tng. com., 1967-68, mem. nat. adv. arthritis and metabolic diseases council, 1970—; mem. pharmacology adv. com. Walter Reed Army Inst. Research, 1967-; mem. sci. adv. bd. Nat. Kidney Found., 1965-68, Ill Kidney Found., 1966—, chmn., 1969-70, chmn. nat. med. adv. council, 1969-70; mem. malaria commn. Armed Forces Epidemiological Bd., 1966—; chmn. Internat. Com. Nomenclature and Nosology of Renal Disease. Fellow A.A.A.S., A.C.P. (rep. residency rev. com. internal medicine 1961-65); mem. Am. (bd. dirs. 1962-65, chmn. council circulation 1963-65), Ill., Chgo. (bd. dirs. 1966-69) heart assns., Central Soc. Clin. Research (pres. 1964-65), Am. Soc. Clin. Investigation (editorial com. 1952-57), Assn. Am. Physicians, Am. Physiol. Soc., Am. Clin. and Climatological Assn., Soc. Exptl. Biology and Medicine, A.M.A., Chgo. Soc. Internal Medicine, Chgo. Inst. Medicine (pres. 1967-68), Alpha Omega Alpha. Clubs: Indian Hill (Winnetka, Ill.); University (Chgo.). Author articles, chpts. in books in field. Editor Jour. Chronic Diseases, 1966--; editorial bd. Clin. Pharmacology and Therapeutics. Home: 1034 Westmoor Rd Winnetka, IL 60093. Office: 303 E Chicago Av Chicago IL 60611

EARLE, HENRY, investment banker; b. Steelton, Pa., Feb. 10, 1901; s. Thomas and Sara (Boyer) E.; student U. Mich., 1923; m. Mary Agnes Hillimeyer, July 31, 1961; children—Emily Frances (Mrs. Donald Goostrey), Henry Earle III. With First of Mich. Corp., and predecessor, 1923—, exec. v.p., 1960—, also dir.; dir. Southeastern Mich. Gas Co., C.A.C. Inc., Vesely Co. Mem. Newcomen Soc., Sigma

Phi. Clubs: Hundred, Bond, Detroit, Detroit Athletic; Country of Detroit (Grosse Pointe Farms). Home: 166 Cloverly Rd Grosse Pointe Farms, MI 48236. Office: Buhl Bldg Detroit MI 48226

EARLE, KENNETH MARTIN, neuropathologist; b. Jacksonville, Tex., Dec. 29, 1919; s. Allen and Flora Lois (Martin) E.; B.A., Rice U., 1942; M.D., U. Tex., 1945; M.Sc., McGill U., 1951; m. Mary Ellen Sammons, Mar. 12, 1944; children—Mary, Katherine, Thomas Hugh. Med. technologist Jefferson Davis Hosp., Houston, nights 1938-42, John Sealy Hosp., Galveston, Tex., nights 1942- 43, also radiol. technician; rotating intern John Sealy Hosp., 1945-46; resident gen. surgery U.S. Naval Hosp., San Diego, 1947-48; fellow neuroanatomy and neuropathology Montreal Neurol. Inst., McGill U., 1949- 51, fellow pathology Pathol. Inst., 1951-52; instr. pathology U. Cal. Sch. Medicine, Los Angeles, also sr. resident tng. VA Hosp., Los Angeles and VA Hosp., Long Beach, Cal., 1952-53; mem. faculty U. Tex. Sch. Medicine, 1953-62, prof. pathology, 1960-62, dean medicine, 1959-62; chief neuropathology Armed Forces Inst. Pathology, Washington, 1962—; lectr. George Washington U., 1962—. Mem. spl. study sect., nat. adv. heart council NIH, 1961, heart program project com., 1961-63. Served to lt. (j.g.), M.C., USNR, 1943-45, 46-49. Recipient Meritorious Civilian Service award Dept. Army, 1967, also Exceptional Civilian Service award, 1968. Diplomate Am. Bd. Pathology. Mem. Am. Assn. Pathologists and Bacteriologists, Am., Washington socs. pathologists, Am. Assn. Neuropathologists (chmn. program com. 1966, pres. 1966-67), Internat. Soc. Neuropathology (project sec. 1970—), Am. Acad. Neurology (asso.), Internat. Acad. Pathologists, alumni assns. Rice Inst., U. Tex. Sch. Medicine, Sigma Xi, Alpha Omega Alpha, Theta Kappa Psi. Presbyn. Mason (32). Co-translator: (P. del Rio-Hortegas) The Microscopic Anatomy of Tumors of the Central and Peripheral Nervous System, 1962. Contbr. articles to profl. jours. Home: 11402 Charlton Dr Silver Spring MD 20902 Office: Armed Forces Inst Pathology Washington DC 20305

EARLE, THOMAS THERON educator; b. Greenville, S.C., July 23, 1905; s. Theron Thomas and Lily (Montgomery) E.; B.S., Furman U., 1928; Ph.D., U. Minn., 1937; m. Esther Helen Wilson, Sept. 7, 1938. Grad. asst. in botany U. Minn., 1933-37; instr. biology Newcomb Coll., Tulane U., New Orleans, 1938-40, asst. prof., 1940-43, asso. prof., 1943-46, prof., 1946-47, prof. botany Coll. Arts and Scis., Tulane U., 1947-49, Ida A. Richardson Prof. botany, 1949—, acting dir. Univ. Coll., 1947- 48, asso. dir. Tulane summer session, 1946-47, dir., 1947—. Mem. U. Minn. bot. expdn. to Australia and New Zealand, 1934-35; cons. U.S. Army Engrs., marine growth eradication expts., 1948-50. Fellow A.A.A.S.; mem. Am. Fern Soc., Am. Soc. Plant Taxonomists, Bot. Soc. Am. New Orleans Acad. Sci. (treas. 1940-47, v.p. 1947-48, pres. 1948), Bot. Soc. New Orleans (pres. 1940-41), Delta Sigma Phi, Sigma Xi. Democrat. Baptist. Clubs: Torrey Botanical, Round Table (New Orleans). Contbr. to bot. publs. Research in anatomy of plants. Home: 30 A Newcomb Blvd New Orleans LA 70118

EARLE, WILLIAM PITT STRYKER, Jr., stock broker; b. N.Y.C., Mar. 19, 1909; s. William Pitt Stryker and Valerie (de Blois) E.; student Peddie Sch.; m. Vera Lumley Kelly, Oct. 25, 1963; 1 child, Doorgn; children (by previous marriage)—William de Blois, Julia Ferguson, Valerie de Blois. Partner W.E. Hutton Co., mems. N.Y. Stock Exchange and Am. Stock Exchange, 1967—; mem. Am. Stock Exchange, 1935—, bd. govs., 1962—. Club: Sleepy Hollow Country (Scarborough). Home: Sleepy Hollow Station Rd Scarborough, NY 10582. Office: 14 Wall St New York City NY 10005

EARLEY, ERNEST BENTON, educator, plant physiologist; b. Orangesburg, S.C., Dec. 19, 1906; s. Thomas Edward and Gussie Hydrick (Bair) E.; B.S. in Agronomy, Clemson U., 19288; M.S., Va. Poly. Inst., 1929; Ph.D., U. Ill., 1941; m. Liberty Mundo, Aug. 17, 1931; children-Carol Ann (Mrs. Edward L. Hanson), Thomas David. Asst. agronomy U. Ill. at Urbana, 1929-37; asst. agronomist Regional Soybean Lab., Bur. Plant Industries, Soils and Agrl. Engring., Dept. Agr., 1937-44; mem. faculty U. Ill. at Urbana, 1944—, prof. agronomy, 1955—. Active local Boy Scouts Am. Mem. Am. Soc. Agronomy, Am. Soc. Plant Physiologists, Sigma Xi, Phi Sigma, Gamma Sigma Delta. Presbyn. Home: 1102 S Garfield St Urbana IL 61801

EARLEY, JAMES STAINFORTH, educator, economist; b. Valley City, N.D., Oct. 16, 1908; s. James Jerome and May (Macgowan) E.; A.B., Antioch Coll., 1932; M.A., U. Wis., 1934, Ph.D., 1939; student U. London (Eng.), 1936-37; m. Emily Hornblower, June 19, 1939; children—Dorothy, Susan and Jerome (twins); m. 2d, Elizabeth Blankinship Pohle, Apr. 22, 1961. Mem. faculty U. Wis., 1937-67, prof. econs., 1947-67, chmn. dept., 1962-65; prof., chmn. dept. econs. U. Cal. at Riverside, 1967-70, dean Coll. Social and Behavioral Scis., 1970—; vis. prof. Yale, 1953-54, U. Hawaii, 1963, Athens Grad. Sch. Econs., U. Manchester, 1966, U. Philippines, 1965. Economist, then sr. economist with Nat. Def. Adv. Commn., OPA, 1940-45; adviser British Commonwealth affairs State Dept., 1945; mem. Com. Internat. Exchange Persons, 1953-57, Univs.-Nat. Bur. Com. Econ. Research, 1951-67; dir. quality credit program Nat. Bur. Econ. Research, 1960—. Trustee Antioch Coll., 1949- 52. Ford Found. fellow, 1957-60. Mem. Am., Midwest (1st v.p. 1955-56), Western econ. assns., Am. Finance Assn., Royal Econ. Soc. Author: British Wartime Price Administration, 2d edit., 1944; Economic Theory in Review, 1950; Pricing for Profit and Growth, 2d edit., 1962; Home Mortgage Delinquency and Foreclosure, 1970; also articles. Home: 393 Two Trees Rd Riverside CA 92507

EARLS, RICHARD F., banker; b. Ruleville, Miss., June 10, 1925; s. William Whitney and Stella (Grimes) E.; grad. Draughon's Bus. Coll., Grenwood, Miss., 1948, Banking Sch., U. Wis., 1967; m. Eva Louise Hellmers, May 18, 1963; children—Eva Louise, Richard Forrest, Elisabeth Anne. Bookkeeper, Greenville, 1949-51; prodn. supr. Kaiser Aluminum Corp., Chalmette, La., 1952-54; with Hibernia Nat. Bank, New Orleans, 1954-, now auditor, Served with USCGR, 1943-46, AUS, 1946-47. Mem. Am. Inst. Banking, Nat. Assn. Accountants, Bank Adminstrn. Inst. Home: 2413 Metairie Ct Metairie, LA 70001. Office: 313 Carondelet St New Orleans LA 70160

EARLY, BERT HYLTON, lawyer; b. Kimball, W.Va., July 17, 1922; s. Robert Terry and Sue Keister (Hylton) E.; student Marshall U., 1940-42; A.B., Duke, 1946; J.D., Harvard, 1949; m. Elizabeth Louise Henry, Juen 24, 1950; children—Bert Hylton, Robert Christian, Mark Randolph, Philip Henry, Peter St. Clair. Admitted to W.Va. bar, 1949, Ill., 1963; asso. firm Fitzpatrick, Marshall, Huddleston & Bolen, Huntington, W.Va., 1949-57; instr. Marshall U., 1950-53; asst. counsel Island Creek Coal Co., 1957- 60, asso. gen. counsel, 1960-62; dep. exec. dir. Am. Bar Assn., 1962-64, exec. dir., 1964-. Mem. W.Va. Jud. Council, 1960-62. Mem. Huntington City Council, 1961-62. Bd. dirs. Huntington Pub. Library, 1951-60, Morris Meml. Hosp. Crippled Children, 1953-60, Huntington Galleries, 1961-62, W.Va. Tax Inst., 1961-62; trustee Davis and Elkins Coll., 1960- 63; sec. bd. dirs. Community Renewal Soc. Fellow Am. Bar Found.; mem. Am. Law Inst., Am. Judicature Soc., Internat. (asst. sec.-gen. 1967—), Inter-Am., American (ho. of dels. 1958-59, nat. chmn. Jr. Bar Conf. 1958), W.Va. bar assns., W.Va. State Bar (chmn. jr. sect. 1951). Democrat. Presbyn. Clubs: Economic (Chgo.); University (Washington and Chgo.); Hinsdale (Ill.) Golf. Home: 136 S Oak St Hinsdale, IL 60521. Office: Am Bar Center Chicago IL 60637

EARLY, JACK JONES, assn. exec.; b. Corbin, Ky., Apr. 12, 1925; s. Joseph M. and Lela (Jones) E.; A.B., Union Coll., Barbourville, Ky., 1948; M.A., U. Ky., 1953, Ed.D. (So. scholar 1955-56), 1956; B.D., Coll. of Bible, Lexington, Ky., 1956; D.D., Wesley Coll., Grand Forks, N.D., 1961; LL.D., Parsons Coll., 1962; Litt.D., Dakota Wesleyan U., 1969; m. Nancy Bruce Whaley, June 1, 1952; children—Lela Katherine, Judith Ann, Laura Hattie. Ordained to ministry Methodist Ch., 1954; pastor Rockhold Circuit (Ky.), 1943-44, Craig's Chapel and Laurel Circuit, London, Ky., 1944-47, Trinity Ch., Oak Ridge, summer 1945, Hindman Ch. (Ky.), 1947- 52; dean of men Hindman Settlement Sch., 1948-51; asso. pastor Park Ch., Lexington, Ky., 1952-54; asst. to pres., dean Athens (Ala.) Coll., 1954- 55; v.p., dean of coll. Ia. Wesleyan Coll., Mt. Pleasant, Ia., 1956-58; pres. Dakota Wesleyan U., 1958-69, Pfeiffer Coll., Misenheimer, N.C., 1969-71; exec. dir. Am. Bankers Assn., Washington, 1971—. Active Boy Scouts Am. Mem. Ky. Ho. of Reps., 1952-54. Dir. S.D. Found. Pvt. Colls., S.D. Meth. Found., YMCA. Recipient Spoke award Mitchell Jr. C. of C., 1959, Distinguished Service award, 1960; Distinguished Service award S.D. Jr. C. of C., 1960; named Outstanding Former Kentuckian, 1963. Hon. fellow Wroxton Coll., Oxfordshire, Eng. Mem. Jr. C. of C. (dir. 1959), C. of C., Young Republican Clubs of Ky. (v.p. 1949-50), Blue Key, Kappa Delta Pi, Phi Delta Kappa, Kappa Phi Kappa, Alpha Psi Omega, Theta Phi, Pi Tau Chi. Home: 4202 Mt Vernon Meml Hwy Alexandria VA 22309 Office: 1120 Connecticut Av NW Washington DC 20036

EARLY, JAMES, univ. dean; b. Worcester, Mass., Apr. 19, 1923; s. Edward and Rose Helena (Shea) E.; B.A., Bowloin Coll., 1947; M.A., Harvard, 1949, Ph.D., 1953; m. Ann Marie McKenny, Aug. 20, 1949; children—Mark, Edward, Joanne. Instr., Yale, New Haven, 1953-57; asst. prof. Vassar Coll., Poughkeepsie, N.Y., 1957-64; asso. prof. So. Methodist U., Dallas, 1964-67, prof., 1968—, chmn. English dept., 1968-71, asso. dean Faculties of Humanities and Scis., 1971—; vis. prof. Stanford, Cal., 1967. Served with USAAF, 1943, AUS, 1943-46. Mem. Modern Lang. Assn., Coll. Art Assn., Am. Assn. U. Profs., Am. Civil Liberties Union, Colophon. Democrat. Author: Romanticism and American Architecture, 1965; Adventures in American Literature, 1968. Home: 7015 Lake Shore Dr Dallas TX 75214

EARLY, ROBERT EMIL, ins. co. exec.; b. Chgo., dec. 15, 1917; s. U. S. Grant and Gertrude Ida (Minkley) E.; A.A., Pasadena (Cal.) Jr. Coll., 1937; B.S., U. So. Cal., 1939; LL.B., Drake U., 1941; m. Margaret Emily Jones, June 21, 1942. Sales supr. Curtis Pub. Co., 1936-40; admitted to Cal. and Ia. bars, 1941; adjusters Farmers Ins. Group, 1942 1st v.p., 1955, now pres., exec. dir.; mem. Early, Maslach, Foran & Williams, Los Angeles, 1946—. Trustee Thomas and Dorothy Leavey Found., Drake U.; bd. councilors U. S. Cal. Law Center. Served with USNR, 1943-46. Mem. Internat. Assn. Ins. Counsel, Phi Nu Delta, Delta Theta Phi. Elk. Club: Wilshire Country (Los Angeles). Home: 130 S San Rafael Pasadena CA 91105 Office: 4680 Wilshire Blvd Los Angeles CA 90005

EARLY, ROBERT PAUL, editor; b. Indpls., Oct. 3, 1905; s. Henry Patrick and Emma Florence (Niklaus) E.; grad. Cathedral High Sch., Indpls., 1923; m. Helen Schluttenhofer, Aug. 26, 1935; children—Robert Joseph, Sharon, Thomas Christian. Reporter Indpls. bur. United Press 1925; reporter Connersville News-Examiner, 1926; with Indpls. Star, 1927—, reporter, 1927-40, asst. city editor, 1940-44, city editor, 1944-46, mng. editor, 1946—. Mem. 500 Festival Assos. Bd. dirs. Indpls. chpt. A.R.C. Mem. Indpls. C. of C., Asso. Press Mng. Editors Assn., Am. Soc. Newspaper Editors. Recipient Pall Mall award, 1948; Man of Year award Fraternal Order Police, 1962; Newsman of Year award Indpls. Press Club, 1969; award Nat. Headliners Club, 1964. Mem. Sigma Delta Chi. Roman Catholic. dir., Heather Hills Country; Indianapolis Athletic. Home: 1021 N Sadlier Dr Indianapolis IN 46219 Office: 307 N Pennsylvania St Indianapolis IN 46206

EARLY, WILLIAM JAMES, supt. schs.; b. Holyoke, Mass., Mar. 22, 1921; s. John J. and Mary Leah (LaPointe) E.; B.S., U. Toledo, 1946; M.A., U. Mich., 1949; Ph.D., Mich. State U., 1963; m. Clare Patricia Milacki, June 8, 1946; children—Patricia, John, Kathleen, Marilyn. Tchr. social studies and English, Bedford High Sch., Temperance, Mich., 1946-54; supt. schs. Deerfield (Mich.) Pub. Schs., 1954-57, Fenton (Mich.) Area Pub. Schs., 1957-63, Rochester (Mich.) Community Schs., 1963-66, Flint (Mich.) Community Schs., 1966—. Bd. dirs. Mich. Ednl. Research Assn., Mich.- Ohio Regional Ednl. Lab. Active Musical Performing Arts Assn., Flint Inst. Arts. Bd. dirs. Tall Pine council Boy Scouts Am. Served with USMCR, 1942-45. Decorated Silver Star, Purple Heart. Mem. Assn. Childhood Edn., Flint C. of C. Kiwanian. Clubs: Flint City, Flint Golf. Home: 924 E 6th St Flint MI 38503. Office: 923 E Kearsley St Flint MI 48502

EARNEST, ROBERT C., educator; b. Kansas City, Mo., Nov. 23, 1923; s. Clarence and Margaret (Ingraham) E.; B.S., Denver U., 1948, M.B.A., 1949; Ph.D., Ohio State U., 1956; m. Grace Stewart, Dec. 26, 1946; children—Sharon, Joan, Michael, Karla. Asst. instr. Ohio State U., 1949-51; asst. prof. Kan. State Coll., 1951-53; asso. prof. Marquette U., 1953-57; prof., chmn. area finance and Quantitative methods Fla. State U., 1957—, coordinator grad. studies, 1967—. Dir. Investor Industries, Recon, Inc. Served with USAAF, 1942-46. Mem. Am., So. econs. assns., Am. Finance Assn., Financial Mgmt. Assn. Author: History of Savings and Loan Associations in Wisconsin, 1956. Home: 605 Lothian Dr Tallahassee FL 32303

EARNEST, SUE W., educator; b. Grand Forks, N.D., Sept. 19, 1907; B.A., San Diego State Coll., 1929; M.A., U. So. Cal., 1937, Ph.D., 1947; married; 3 children. Instr. English, U. Louisville, 1945-46; asst. prof. San Diego State Coll., 1947-48, asso. prof. speech, 1948-54, prof., 1954—, also chmn. dept. speech pathology and audiology. Mem. western regional edn. commn. United Cerebral Palsy Assns., 1963. Mem. Am. Speech and Hearing Assn., Internat. Soc. for Rehab. of Disabled. Office: Dept Speech Pathology and Audiology San Diego State Coll 5402 College Av San Diego CA 92115*

EARNGEY, WILLARD PHELPS, Jr., hosp. adminstr.; b. Chgo., July 21, 1915; s. Willard Phelps and Elizabeth (Gardner) E.; A.B., Duke, 1938, certificate hosp. adminstrn., 1939; LL.D. (hon.), Tex. Wesleyan U., 1967; m. Irma Lawson McCaleb, Dec. 19, 1953; children—Willard Phelps III, Lynne (Mrs. Ferdie R. Fisher III), Martha Ann. Supt., Cherokee County Hosp., Gaffney, S.C., 1939-41, Norfolk (Va.) Gen. Hosp., 1941-44, 46-51; adminstr. Harris Hosp., Ft. Worth, 1951—. Pres. Ft. Worth Soc. Crippled Children and Adults, 1963- 64, Va. Hosp. Assn., 1948-49, N.W. Tex. Hosp. Assn., 1961-62. Tex. Hosp. Assn., 1958-59, Tex. Assn. Hosp. Accountants, 1954-55; chmn. bd. Tarrant County (Tex.) Heart Assn., 1967-68. Served to lt. (j.g.) USNR, 1944-46. Recipient Med. Staff award merit Harris Hosp., 1966; Distinguished Meml. award Tex. Assn. Hosp. Accountants, 1968; Boss of Year award Nat. Secs. Assn., 1966. Fellow Am. Coll. Hosp. Administrs., Royal Soc. Health (Eng.). Home: 3101 Tanglewood Trail Fort Worth TX 76109. Office: 1300 W Cannon St Fort Worth TX 76104

EARNHART, DON BRADY, container mfg. co. exec.; b. Marion, Ind., Aug. 5, 1925; s. Don A. and Bernice (Brady) E.; B.S., Ind. U., 1949; m. Suzanne Kersting, Aug. 5, 1950; children—Elizabeth Ann, Susan, Stephen. With Ernst & Ernst, C.P.A.'s, Indpls., 1949-53; with Inland Container Corp., Indpls., 1953- -, asst. treas., 1957-60, sec., asst. treas., 1961-64, sec., treas., 1965-67, v.p., treas., 1968—; dir., sec., treas. Anderson Box Co., Indpls., 1957-68, v.p., treas., dir., 1969—. Sec., treas. Inland Container Corp. Found., Inc., Krannert Found., Krannert Charitable Trust; mem. Community Service Council Met. Indpls. Chmn. edn. study team Ind. Gov.'s Economy Program, 1969. Trustee Ind. Central Coll.; trustee, treas. Indpls. Mus. Art; bd. dirs., past treas. Indpls. Met. YMCA; bd. dirs. Ind. U. Found., Jr. Achievement, Indpls., Indpls. Symphony Orch. Greater Indpls. Progress Com. Designated Sagamore of Wabash by Gov. Ind., 1969. Served with U.S. Mcht. Marine, 1943-46. C.P.A., Ind. Mem. Ind. Assn. C.P.A.'s (past dir., sec.), Indpls. C. of C. (dir.), Ind. U. Sch. Bus. Alumni Assn. (past exec. council). Home: 4625 Boulevard Pl Indianapolis IN 46208 Office: 120 E Market St Indianapolis IN 46206

EARP, CRONJE BURNFORD, educator; b. Selma, N.C., Oct. 27, 1900; s. Wiley Sherrod and Willie (Creech) E.; A.B., Wake Forest U., 1926; M.A., Columbia, 1927, Ph.D., 1939; m. Gladys Hammond Beck, Aug. 22, 1932; children—Emory Beck (Mrs. George Willis Austin), Elizabeth Beck (Mrs. Sammy Ray Merrill). Instr. Latin, L.I.U., 1927-28; instr. classics N.Y.U., 1928-29; instr. Latin and Greek, St. Stephens Coll., Columbia, 1929-31; asso. prof. Greek, Wake Forest U., Winston-Salem, N.C., 1940-42, prof., 1942-56, prof. classical langs., 1956—, dept. chmn., 1940—. Spl. Univ. fellow Columbia, 1926-27. Mem. Phi Beta Kappa, Eta Sigma Phi, Pi Kappa Alpha, Omega Delta Kappa. Democrat. Baptist. Mason (32, Shriner). Author: A Study of the Fragments of Three Related Plays of Accius, 1939. Home: Box 7343 Reynolda St Winston-Salem NC 27109

EARTHMAN, WILLIAM FLETCHER, banker; b. Nashville, Jan. 21, 1926; s. William Fletcher and Georgia (Bell) E.; student Cornell U., 1944-45; B.S., U.S. Mil. Acad., 1949; m. Alice Warfield Tyne, June 24, 1950 (div. 1966); children—William Fletcher III, Thomas, Elizabeth, John Christopher Burch; m. 2d, Dorothy Ann Bartlett, Sept 7, 1968. Commd. 2d lt. U.S. Army, 1949, advanced through grades to capt., 1954; ret., 1954; capt. Res.; with Commerce Union Bank, Nashville, 1954—, pres., 1961—, also dir., mem. exec. com. Mem. Am. Bankers Assn., Assn. Res. City Bankers, Tenn. Bankers Assn. Home: 105 Belle Meade Blvd Nashville TN 37205 Office: 400 Union St Nashville TN 37219

EASBY, DUDLEY TATE, Jr., lawyer, mus. cons.; b. Lock Haven, Pa., Dec. 3, 1905; s. Dudley Tate and Gertrude R. (Kephart) E.; ed. Manlius Sch., 1919-23; B.S. magna cum laude, Princeton, 1928; LL.B. cum laude, U. Pa., 1931; m. Elizabeth M. Kennedy, Oct. 15, 1949. Admitted to Pa. bar, 1931, N.Y. bar, 1946; with Ballard, Spahr, Andrews & Ingersoll, Phila., 1931-38; legal div. U.S. Treas. Dept., Washington, 1939-40; asst. gen. counsel Office Inter-Am. Affairs, 1940-43; chief counsel Pan-Am. br. Fgn. Econ. Adminstrn., 1943-45; sec. Met. Mus. Art, 1945-69, chmn. dept. primitive art, 1969-71. Mem. Tech. Indsl. Disarmament Mission to U.S. Group Control Council (Germany), 1945. hon. fellow Archaeol. Inst. Am. Trustee Allen Tucker Meml., Louis Comfort Tiffany Found.; fellow U. Pa. Mus. Recipient research grant for metalworking studies in Mexico, Am. Philos. Soc., 1959; decorated comdr. Order of Merit, officer Order of the Sun (both Peru); Order of Aztec Eagle (Mexico). Mem. Am. Soc. Metals, Sociedad Mexicana de Antropologia, Inst. Andean Research (v.p. 1960-64, pres. 1965-67), Internat. Inst. Conservation Historic and Artistic Works, Soc. Am. Archaeology, Am., Pa., Phila. bar assns., Assn. Bar City N.Y., Juristic Soc. Phila., Loyal Legion, Order of Coif; corr. mem. Colegio de Abogados de Buenos Aires, Hispanic Soc. Am. Mason. Clubs: Century, Cannon (Princeton, N.J.); Explorers (N.Y.C.). Contbr. to Ency. Brit. Author articles on pre-Columbian metalwork; note editor, U. of Pa. Law Review, 1930-31. Home: 2221 Rittenhouse Sq Philadelphia PA 19103

EASLEY, EDDIE VEE, educator; b. Lynchburg, Va., Nov. 16, 1928; s. George E. and Berta (Carpenter) E.; B.S., Va. State Coll., 1948; M.S., Ia. State U., 1951, Ph.D., 1957; m. Ruth Burton, Sept. 1, 1956; children—Jacqueline, Michael, Todd. Asst. prof., then asso. prof. marketing Drake U., 1957-65; asst. prof. commerce U. Wis.-Milw., 1965-66; prof. marketing, chmn. dept. Drake U., 1966—, dir. master of bus. program, 1970—; marketing analyst Kimberly-Clark Corp., Neenah, Wis., summers 1969, 70. Mem. Des Moines Bd. Zoning Adjustments, 1968-71. Bd. dirs. United Community Services Des Moines, 1969-70, Settlement House Assn., Des Moines, 1966-69; bd. dirs. Willkie House, 1960-65, pres., 1964-65. Served with AUS, 1954-56. Recipient Outstanding Tchr. award Drake U., 1968, Ford Found. fellow, summers 1959, 61, 62. Mem. Am. Marketing Assn. (pres. Ia. 1964), Alpha Phi Alpha, Delta Sigma Pi, Omicron Delta Kappa, Beta Gamma Sigma. Author: Negro in Business in Milwaukee's Inner Core, 1966. Home: 1431 41st Pl Des Moines IA 50311

EASLEY, J. BERT, supermarket cons.; b. Rush Springs, Okla., 1901. Former v.p., treas. Alpha Beta Acme Markets, Inc. Bd. dirs. Presbyn. Intercommunity Hosp. Home: 45737 Club Dr Indian Wells CA 92260

EASLEY, JOHN ALLEN, Jr., educator; b. Manning, S.C., Jan. 15, 1922; s. John Allen and Eleanor Martin (Robertson) E.; B.S. in Physics, Wake Forest Coll., 1943; M.Ed. in Sci. Edn., U. Hawaii, 1952; Ph.D., Harvard, 1955; m. Elizabeth Fumiko Fujioka, Aug. 15, 1948; children—Allen Ken, Robert Fumio, David Fumitaka, John Makoto. Radio engr. dept. terrestrial magnetism Carnegie Inst., Washington, Baffin Island, Hawaii, 1942-46; prin. Marshall Islands Intermediate Sch., 1949-50; instr. sci. edn. U. Hawaii, 1950-52, asst. prof. sci., 1955-60, asso. prof., 1960-62, acad. chmn., 1960-61; asso. prof. edn. U. Ill., Urbana, 1962-67, prof. secondary edn., 1967-69, prof. tchr. edn., 1969—, sec. com. for cognitive studies, 1971—. Cons. Peace Corps, 1961-62, UNESCO, 1970. Chmn. strategy com. United Commn. Campus Christian Ministries Ill., 1969-70. Danforth asso., 1969—. Fellow A.A.A.S.; mem. Am. Assn. U. Profs., Am. Ednl. Research Assn., Nat. Assn. Research in Sci. Teaching, Phi Delta Kappa. Mem. United Ch. of Christ. Author: (with Maurice Tatsuoka) Scientific Thought: Cases from Classical Physics, 1968. Home: 1406 W Green St Champaign IL 61820 Office: Dept Elementary Edn U Ill Urbana IL 61801

EASLICK, DAVID KENNETH, telephone co. exec.; b. Jackson, Mich., Jan. 10, 1921; s. Kenneth Alexander and Mercie Marie (VanAken) E.; A.B., U. Mich., 1942, postgrad. 1945-46; postgrad. George Washington U., 1946-47, Am. U., 1947; Sloan fellow Mass. Inst. Tech., 1954-55; m. Lucy Thomas Barnwell, Dec. 16, 1943; children—David Kenneth, Susan Biair, Anne Barnwell. With Mich. Bell Telephone Co., 1948-63, exec. asst., 1958-59, asst. v.p. labor relations, 1959-60, v.p. personnel, 1960-63; asst. v.p. Am. Tel. & Tel. Co., 1963; v.p. operations Ind. Bell Telephone Co., 1963-70, pres., 1970—, also dir.; dir. Am. Fletcher Nat. Bank & Trust Co., Indpls. vice pres. Greater Indpls. Progress com.; chmn. U.S. Savs. Bond Campaign, Payroll Savs., Indpls.; bd. govs. Central Ind. council Boy Scouts Am. Bd. dirs. 500 Festival Assos., Inc., Indpls., Ind. State Symphony Soc., Indpls., Central YMCA, Indpls., trustee Marion Coll., Indpls. Served to maj. AUS, 1942-45. Decorated Silver Star,

Bronze Star with oak leaf cluster, Presidential Citation with Cluster; Croix de Guerre (France). Mem. Ind. Telephone Assn. (dir.), Ind. C. of C. (dir.), Newcomen Soc., Soc. Sloan Fellows, Phi Kappa Psi. Episcopalian (vestryman). Clubs: University, Meridian Hills Country, Crooked Stick Golf, The Hundred, Rotary, Indianapolis Athletics, Columbia (dir.) (Indpls.) Home: 4519 Radnor Rd Indianapolis IN 46226 Office: Ind Bell Telephone Co 240 N Meridian St Indianapolis IN 46209

EASON, JOHN WALTER, mfg. co. exec.; b. Folkestone, Kent, England, Sept. 22, 1916; s. John DeLorme and Gisela (Detring) E.; came to U.S., 1928; naturalized. 1930; B.S. in Mech. Engring., U. Ill., 1937; m. Elizabeth Sibley Knipp, Aug. 17, 1940; children—Stephanie Eason (Mrs. Charles C.G. Evans, Jr.), Stuart Kirkpatrick, Douglas Bruce. Engaged in business in aircraft industry, 1937-44; with Revere Copper & Brass, Inc., 1944—, mgr. aluminum industry sales, 1957-59, v.p. Balt. div., 1959-67. exec. v.p., sales mgr. Aluminum Products div., 1967—. Mem. indsl. div. United Appeal Balt. Trustee South Balt. Gen. Hosp. Home: New Canaan CT Office: PO Box 2075 Baltimore MD 21203

EASON, ROBERT GASTON, educator; b. Bells, Tenn., May 15, 1924; s. William Bryant and Noba (Proctor) E.; B.A., U. Mo., 1950, M.A., 1952, Ph.D., 1956; m. Dorothy Jean Goodner, Sept. 5, 1952; children—Robert Gregory, Linda Joan. Postdoctoral fellow physiology U. Cal. at Los Angeles, 1956-57; research psychologist Navy Electronics Lab., San Diego, 1957-67; asst. prof. San Diego State Coll., 1960-63, asso. prof., 1963-66, prof., 1966-67; Excellence Fund prof., head psychology dept. U. N.C.-Greensboro, 1967—. Served with USAAF, 1943-46. Mem. Am., Southeastern psychol. assns., A.A.A.S., Soc. Psychophysiol. Research, Sigma Xi. Cons. editor Perceptual and Motor Skills, 1964—, Neurosci. Abstracts, 1968—. Home: 115 Falkener Dr Greensboro NC 27410

EASON, THADDEUS WINSTON, oil co. exec.; b. Marlow, Okla., Sept. 7, 1904; s. T. T. and Anna (Lee) E.; student Prep. Sch. Kan., 1923, Notre Dame U., 1923-25, Okla. U., 1925-26, Babson Inst., 1927-28; m. Ada Sohlberg, Jan. 30, 1929; 1 dau., Virginia Lee (Mrs. John G. Weinmann). Pres. T. T. Eason & Co. (Del.), 1949—; pres. Eason Oil Co., Oklahoma City, 1955-70, chmn. bd., chief exec. officer, 1970—; partner Wave Drilling, Inc. Mem. Okla. Legislature, 1933, 37. Bd. dirs. Oklahoma City Mental Health Assn., Oklahoma Eye Found.; trustee Frontiers Sci. Found.; indsl. adv. bd. Okla. A. and M. Coll.; pres., treas., mem. bd. trustees Okla. Art Center. Mem. Okla. Ind. Petroleum Assn. (dir. 1965—), Phi Delta Theta. Democrat. K.C. Clubs: Tres Vidas (Acapulco, Mex.); Oklahoma Golf and Country, Men's Dinner, Economic (past treas., dir.), Beacon, Tower, Petroleum (Oklahoma City). Home: 7212 Waverly Av Oklahoma City OK 73120 Office: Eason Oil Co PO Box 18755 Oklahoma City OK 73118

EAST, GILBERT LEE, retired army officer; b. Smithville, Ind., May 29, 1920; s. Della Roma and Nellie Cleon (Adams) E.; premed. student, Ind. U., 1939-42, 46-47; grad. numerous service schs.; m. Martha Alice Day, Aug. 30, 1942; 1 dau., Susan Elaine. Enlisted U.S. Army, 1942, commd. 2d lt., 1942, advanced through grades to col., 1966; various assignments in U.S., 1942-50; exec. officer 24th Med. Battalion, 25th Inf. Div., Korea, 1950-51, Leadership Sch., Med. Tng. Center, Ft. Meade, 1951-52, comdg. officer 3d Med. Battalion, 1952, asst. exec. officer center, 1952; med. adviser Ark. N.G., 1952-55; exec. officer 60th Sta. Hosp., Chenon, Frances, 1956-58, Martin Army Hosp., Ft. Benning, Ga., 1959-61; chief personnel div. Surgeon's Office, 5th Army, also chief med. personnel procurement office, 1961-65; comdg. officer 627th Hosp. Center, Ft. Sam Houston, Tex., also Camp Zama, Japan, 1965-66; exec. officer 627th Hosp. Center, Camp Zama, 1966; U.S. Army Hosp., 1966-68, U.S. Gen. Leonard Wood (Mo.) Army Hosp., 1968-71; retired, 1971; cons. in field. Chmn. ann. Nat. Health and Internat. Service Agencies Fund campaing, Ft. Leonard Wood, 1970. Decorated Legion of Merit with oak leaf cluster, Bronze Star, Army Commendation medal; recipient award outstanding service Nat. Health and Internat. Service Agencies, 1971. Mem. U.S. Army-Baylor U. Program Health Care Adminstrn. Alumni Assn., Ind. U. Alumni Assn., Assn. Mil. Surgeons, Am. Hosp. Assn., Res. Officers Assn., Assn. U.S. Army. Elk. Address: 1844 S Oakland St Aurora CO 80010

EAST, RICHARD CLAYTON, savs. and loan exec.; b. Memphis, Dec. 19, 1921; s. Thomas Franklin and Bessie (Andrews) E.; B.S., Memphis State Coll., 1943; LL.B., So. Law U., Memphis, 1942; m. Mary Kathryn Wiggis, July 13, 1945; children—Richard Clayton, Robert A., Carol E. Mortgage loan rep. Gen. Am. Life Ins. Co., Memphis, 1946-48, Oklahoma City, 1948-51; real estate mgr. Safeway Stores, Inc., Oklahoma City, 1951-53; appraiser Oklahoma City Fed. Savs. & Loan Assn., 1953-66, pres., 1966—; dir. Village Bank; pres. 1st Service Corp., Comac, Inc. Served to lt. (j.g.), USNR, 1943-46. Mem. Oklahoma City C. of C. (dir. 1966), Oklahoma City Bd. Realtors (v.p. 1963), Soc. Real Estate Appraisers (internat. v.p. 1966), Am. Inst. Real Estate Appraisers, U.S. Savs. and Loan League. Methodist. Clubs: Oklahoma City Kiwanis (v.p. 1969), Oklahoma City Golf and Country. Home: 8025 Lakehurst Dr Oklahoma City OK 73120 Office: 300 Park Av Oklahoma City OK 73102

EAST, WILLIAM G., fed. judge; b. Le Compton, Kan., Apr. 25, 1908; s. William G. and Bertha Mary (Waterbury) E.; B.A., U. Ore., 1931, LL.B., 1932; m. Louise Frances Wilhelm, Feb. 21, 1933; 1 dau., Sara Elizabeth. Admitted to Ore. bar, 1932; pvt. practice law, Eugene, Ore, 1932-42, 46-49; partner firm Harris, Bryson & East, 1941-42; city atty. City of Eugene, 1946-47; gen. counsel Eugene Water Bd., 1946-49; circuit judge 2d Jud. Dist., 1949- 55; U.S. dist. judge Ore. Dist., 1955-67; U.S. sr. dist. judge for Ore. dist., 1967—. Served with inf. AUS, 1942- 46; ETO. Mem. Am., Ore. (past mem. bd. govs., bd. bar examiners) bar assns., Am. Judicature Soc. (dir. from Ore.), Am. Law Inst., Ore. Assn. Circuit Judges (past pres.), Eugene Round Table (past pres.), Delta Tau Delta, Phi Delta Phi. Conglist. Club: Multnomah Athletic (Portland, Ore.). Home: PO Box 747 Neskowin OR 97149

EASTBURN, DAVID PLUMB, banker, economist; b. Doylestown, Pa., Jan. 9, 1921; s. Arthur Moses and Marie (Plumb) E.; A.B., Amherst Coll., 1942; M.A., U. Pa., 1945, Ph.D., 1957; m. Phyllis Ann Groff, June 25, 1949; children—David Rodman, Stephen Frazier, Susan Barbara, Laurie Ann. With Fed. Res. Bank of Phila., 1942—, pres., 1970—; instr. U. Pa., summer 1945, spring 1947. Author: The Federal Reserve on Record, 1965. Editor: Men, Money and Policy, 1970. Contbr. articles profl. jours. Home: 75 Short Rd RD 3 Doylestown PA 18901 Office: 925 Chestnut St Philadelphia PA 19101

EASTERLIN, RICHARD AINLEY, educator, economist; b. Ridgefield Park, N.J., Jan. 12, 1926; s. John Daniel and Helen Maud (Booth) E.; M.E. with distinction, Stevens Inst. Tech., 1945; A.M., U. Pa., 1949, Ph.D., 1953; m. Jacqueline Mandaville Miller, Sept. 11, 1949; children—John Daniel, Nancy Lincoln, Susan Provost, Andrew M. Faculty, U. Pa., 1953—, prof. econs., 1960—, chmn. dept., 1958-60, 61-62, 68; research asso. Nat. Bur. Econ. Research, 1955-56, mem. research staff, 1956-66; vis. prof. econs. Stanford 1960-61; fellow Center for Advanced Study in Behavioral Scis., Stanford, Cal., 1970-71. Served with USNR, 1943-46. Mem. Am. Econ. Assn., Population Assn. Am. (bd. dirs. 1965, 69-72), Econ. History Assn. (v.p. 1971-72), Internat. Union for Sci. Study Population. Author: The American Baby Boom in Historical Perspective, 1962; Labor Force and Long Swings in Economic Growth. Co-author: Population Redistribution and Economic Growth, United States, 1870-1950, vol. 1, 1957, vol. 11, 1960; Population, The American Experience, 1968. Home: 246 Chester Rd Devon PA 19333 Office: Dept Econs U Pa Philadelphia PA 19104

EASTERLY, FREDERICK JOHN, educator; b. Easton, Pa., Jan. 16, 1910; s. William Sylvester and Mary (Boylan) E.; A.B., St. Joseph's Coll., 1931; Ordained, St. Vincent's Sem., 1936; M.A., Cath. U. Am., 1938, Ph.D., 1941. Ordained priest Roman Catholic Ch., 1936; instr. Latin and religion St. John's Prep. Sch., 1936-37; chmn. dept. history St. John's Coll., St. John's U., 1941- 47; dean sch. edn. St. John's U., 1947-57, dir. admissions, 1957- 58, v.p. student personnel services. 1958-65; prof. history, chmn. dept. social studies St. John Vianney Sem., Miami, Fla., 1965—. Mem. Nat. Cath. Ednl. Assn., Am., Fla. hist. socs., Nat. Council for Social Studies, Nat. Cath. Forensic League (v.p. 1970—), Cath. Forensic League S. Fla. (pres. 1968—). Address: 2900 SW 87th Av Miami, FL 33165.

EASTERWOOD, HENRY LEWIS, artist; b. Villa Rica, Ga., Oct. 29, 1934; s. Clyde Harris and Lois (Bently) E.; B.F.A., Memphis Acad. Arts, 1958; student Royal Tapestry Mfr., Madrid, Spain, 1965, Wverij de Uil, Amsterdam, Netherlands, 1965. Asso. prof. art Memphis Acad. Arts, 1959—; chmn. textile dept. Haystack Mountain Sch. Crafts, Deer Isle, Me., 1966; one-man exhbns. include Memphis Acad. Arts, 1964, Group Gallery, Jacksonville, Fla., 1967, Louisville Art Center, 1966, Brooks Meml. Gallery Art, Memphis, 1968, Fairweather Hardin Gallery, Chgo., 1970, Miss. Art Assn., 1971; group exhbns. include Mus. Contemporary Art, N.Y.C., 1964, 66, America House, N.Y.C., 1965-70, Ark. Arts Center, 1966-68, Tulane U., 1966-68, Norfolk (Va.) Mus. Arts and Scis., 1968, St. Paul Mus., 1969, 61, 63; rep. permanent collections Memphis Acad. Arts, Brooks Meml. Gallery, Tenn. Collection Crafts, also pvt. collections. Mem. adv. panel crafts Tenn Arts Commn., 1969-70. Named An Outstanding Young Man in Am., 1966; recipient Craftsmanship award A.I.A., 1969; tapestry commns. in. Gov. and Mrs. Winthrop Rockefeller, 1965, Virgin Gorda for Laurence Rockefeller, 1965, St. Anne's Ch., Bartlett, Tenn., 1969, First Am. Nat. Bank, also Worthen Bank and Trust Co., Little Rock, 1969, Mayo Clinic, 1970, Tupperware Internat. for Edward Durrell Stone, architect, 1971. Mem. Am. Craftsmen's Council (rep. of Tenn. 1963-65; Nat. Merist award 1966), World Craft Congress. Home: 643 McConnell St Memphis TN 38112

EASTHAM, JAMES SAVILLE, lawyer; b. Methuen, Mass., Aug. 7, 1897; s. William Wilson and Elizabeth (Saville) E.; A.B., Brown U., 1919; LL.D., 1969; LL.B., Harvard, 1922; m. Marcia Dana Hill, Aug. 21, 1924; children—William Eaton, John Perry, James Dana, Nancy Elizabeth. Admitted to Mass. bar, 1922; with Ropes, Gray, Boyden & Perkins, Boston, 1922-23; partner, Rowell, Clay & Eastham, Lawrence, Mass., 1924-29; gen. counsel Eastern Gas & Fuel Assos., Boston, 1930-64, sec., 1940-64, v.p., 1958-64, former sec., clerk, gen. counsel subsidiaries, former v.p., dir. Conn. Coke Co., New Haven; former pres., dir. Virginian Corp.; pvt. practice law, Andover, Mass.; asst. atty. gen. Commonwealth of Mass., 1927-30; chmn. Bd. of Appeals under Zoning Law, Andover, 1936-58. Trustee Brown U., 1945-52; trustee, past pres. Methuen Meml. Music Hall; dir. Silver Bay Assn. Mem. Andover Hist. Soc. Am. Law Inst., Mass. Audubon Soc., Boston Bar Assn., Am. Forestry Assn., Am. Legion, Phi Beta Kappa (past pres. R.I.), Phi Beta Kappa Assn. (life), Delta Sigma Rho, Delta Upsilon. Episcopalian. Mason. Clubs: Union, Brown (Boston); University, Harvard (N.Y.C.); Lawrence Monday Night, Appalachian Mountain, Adirondack Mountain. Address: 16 Alden Rd Andover MA 01810

EASTHAM, JEROME FIELDS, educator; b. Daytona, Fla., Sept. 22, 1924; s. Jerome Folger and Polly (Fields) E.; B.S., U. Ky., 1948; Ph.D., U. Cal. at Berkeley, 1951; m. Laura Telford Newton, Dec. 20, 1949; children—Jerome Fields, Edward D., Grace, Katherine, David G. Fellow U. London, 1952; fellow U. Wis., 1953; prof. U. Tenn., 1954—; cons. Chemetron Corp., Lithium Corp., Union Carbide Nuclear Corp. Served with AUS, 1942-45. Mem. Am. Chem. Soc. , Chem. Soc. (London), Am. Assn. U. Profs., A.A.A.S., Phi Beta Kappa, Sigma Xi. Research chemistry steroids, physical organic chemistry, organometallic chemistry. Home: 1960 N Parkway Memphis TN 38112

EASTHAM, THOMAS, newspaper editor; b. Attelboro, Mass., Aug. 21, 1923; s. John M. and Margaret (Marsden) E.; student English, Northwestern U., 1946-52; m. Berenice J. Hirsch, Oct. 12, 1946; children—Scott Thomas, Todd Robert. With Chgo. American, 1945-56, asst. Sunday editor, 1953-54, feature writer, 1954-56; news editor San Francisco Call Bull., 1956-62; exec. editor San Francisco News-Call Bull., 1962-65, San Francisco Examiner, 1965—. Served with USMCR, 1941-45. Mem. Am. Soc. Newspaper Editors, Am. Soc. Newspaper Editors, Sigma Delta Chi. Home: 10 Panorana Ct Hillsborough CA 94010 Office: 10 Mission St San Francisco CA 94119

EASTIN, MARK E., Jr., mining co. exec.; b. Sturgis, Ky., 1904; s. Mark E. and Katherene (Sprague) E.; A.B., Vanderbilt U., 1929; m. June 17, 1929; children—Mark E. III, Anne Baxter. With St. Bernard Coal Co. and West Ky. Coal Co., Madisonville, 1929—, now pres., dir.; pres., dir. Nashville Coal. Inc., River & Gulf Transfer Co., Balt. Insular Line, Inc.; v.p., dir. Rail to Water Transfer Corp., Chgo., Hopkins Co., 1st Fed. Savs. & Loan Assn., Madisonville, Ky. Mem. Ky. Econ. Devel. Commn. Dir., charter mem. bd. Ky. Spindletop Research Center, Lexington. Dir. Nat. Coal Policy Conf. Mem. Mid-West Coal Producers Inst. (dir.), Nat. Coal Assn. (dir.). Methodist. Home: 134 Union St Madisonville KY 42431 Office: 444 S Main St Madisonville KY 42431

EASTLAKE, WILLIAM DERRY, author; b. N.Y.C., July 14, 1917; s. Gordon and Charlotte (Bradley) E.; student Alliance Francaise, Paris, France, 1948-50; LL.D., 1970; m. Martha Simpson, Oct. 22, 1942. Writer in residence Knox Coll., Galesburg. Ill., 1967; lectr. U. N.M., 1967-68, U. So. Cal., 1968-69, U. Ariz., 1969-71. Served with inf. AUS, World War II: ETO. Decorated Bronze Star; Ford Found. grantee, 1963; Rockefeller Found. grantee, 1966, 67. Mem. Writers Guild, Author's Guild, P.E.N., Am. Assn. U. Profs. Author: (novels) Go in Beauty, 1955; The Bronc People, 1958; Portrait of an Artist with Twenty-Six Horses, 1963; Castle Keep, 1965; The Bamboo Bed, 1969; (poems and essays) A Child's Garden of Verses for the Revolution, 1970; also stories pub. in 16 anthologies, 1 screen play, 3 text books, 7 fgn. lang. editions. Contbr. stories to Harper's, Sat. Eve. Post, Colliers, Evergreen Rev., numerous others. Address: Route 2 Box 761A Tucson AZ 85715.

EASTLAND, JAMES O., U.S. senator; b. Doddsville, Miss., Nov. 28, 1904; s. Woods Caperton and Alma (Austin) E.; student U. of Miss., 1922-24, Vanderbilt U., 1925-26, U. of Ala., 1926-27; m. Elizabeth Coleman, July 6, 1932; children—Neil, Anne, Sue, Woods Eugene. Admitted to Miss. bar, 1927, practiced Forest, Miss.; moved to Sunflower County, 1934; Mem. Miss. House of Reps., 1928- 32. Apptd. to U.S. Senate to fill vacancy, June-Sept. 1941; elected U.S. senator, 1943—; chmn. Senate com. on Judiciary, 1956—; mem. Agr. and Forestry com. Democrat. Home: Doddsville MS 38736

EASTLICK, HERBERT LEONARD, zoologist; b. Platteville, Wis., Apr. 24, 1908; s. Dan and Nora Belle (Israel) E.; A.B., U. Mont., 1930; M.S., Washington U., St. Louis, 1932, Ph.D., 1936; m. Margaret Gardiner, Aug. 1, 1935. Teaching fellow, Washington U., 1930-33, 1935-36, zoology dept. scholar 1931, Phi Sigma scholar, 1932, Collecting Net scholar, 1933; study and research Marine Biol. Lab., Woods Hole, Mass., summers 1931-33; instr. zoology Stephen Coll., Columbia, Mo., 1936-37, U. Mo., 1937-39; NRC fellow U. Chgo., 1939-40; asst. prof. zoology Wash. State U., 1940-44, asso. prof., 1944-47, prof., 1947—, chmn. dept. zoology, 1947-64. Fellow A.A.A.S.; mem. Am. Soc. Zoologists, Am. Assn. Anatomists, Soc. for Growth and Devel., Am., Western socs. naturalists, Am. Micros. Soc., Am. Assn. U. Profs., Soc. Exptl. Biology and Medicine, Sigma Xi, Phi Sigma, Phi Kappa Phi, Theta Xi, Phi Eta Sigma. Contbr. to sci. jours. Home: 408 Garfield St Pullman WA 99163

EASTLICK, JOHN TAYLOR, librarian; b. Norris, Mont., Apr. 28, 1912; s. Jack T. and Stella Mae (Tate) E.; A.B., Ariz. State Tchrs. Coll., 1934; B.L.S., U. Denver, 1940; M.A., Colo. State Coll. Edn., 1939. Instr. English, speech dramatics Yuma (Ariz.) Union High Sch., 1934-38; librarian U. Wis., Wis. High Sch., Madison, 1940-42; instr. library sci. Mich. State Coll., East Lansing, summers 1940, 1941, Wash. State Coll., Pullman, summer 1942; chief library div. VA, Denver, 1946-48; instr. hosp. and med. library coll. librarianship U. Denver, 1946-50, prof. librarianship Grad. Sch. Librarianship, 1969—; cons. to Sec. of Army, instructing Japanese educators in reorgn. Japanese ednl. system, Japan, 1948-49; circulation dept. Denver Pub. Library, 1939-40, asst. to librarian, 1948-51, librarian, 1951-61, 62-69; asst. state supt. edn. for library services State Hawaii, 1962. Dir. Adult Edn. Council (Denver); chmn. finance com., asst. treas. Bibliog. Center for Research, Rocky Mountain Region, 1949-51, treas., 1951-. Mem. adv. com. U.S. Office of Edn., 1956-57. Served as capt. USAAF, 1942- 46. Mem. A.L.A. (pres. pub. libraries div. 1956-57; com. architecture and bldgs. 1949-51, 2d v.p. 1959-60), Colo. Library Assn. (exec. bd.), Denver Dist. (pres. 1950-51), Ariz. State (pres. 1937) library assns., Alpha Psi Omega, Phi Delta Kappa. Club: City (Denver). Home: 1010 S Adams St Denver CO 80209.

EASTLUNDT, GEOFFRY ARTHURchemist, educator; b. Chicago, 1928; B.S. in Physics, Yale, 1950; Ph.D. in Chemistry, Harvard, 1956; m. Sally Ann Jones, July 5, 1957; children--Kenneth J., Nancy A. Chemist, Acme Chem. Co., Blue Island, Ill., 1950-51; director of Research Lab., Indsl. Chemicals Corp., Cambrige, Mass., 1956-60; project coordinator environmental sect. Steinmetz Assos., Chgo., 1960-61; v.p. for research Bauer Bros. Chem. Co., Inc., Memphis, 1961-64; asst. prof. chemistry Washington U., St. Louis, 1964-66, asso. prof., 1966-70, prof., 1970--, head of chemistry dept., 1970-71. Vis. prof. So. Ill. U., summer 1967, U. of Ore., 1969. Bd. dirs. Rest Haven Home for Elderly, 1960-61; trustee of the Lutheran Hosp., 1965-71. Served from lt. to capt., AUS, 1951-53. Mem. Am. Chem. Soc., Sci. Research Soc. Am. (chpt. treas. 1967), Sigma Xi. Author: (with others) Basic Inorganic Chemistry, 1971. Home: Fairfax Apts 7291 Windermere Dr University City MO 63105

EASTMAN, RICHARD HALLENBECK, educator; b. Erie, Pa., Oct. 30, 1918; s. A. Ford and Lois (Hallenbeck) E.; A.B., Princeton, 1941; M.S., Harvard, 1943, Ph.D., 1944; m. Margaret Patricia Lund, Mar. 27, 1942; children—Jeffrey Ford, Richard Cyrus, Thomas Morgan. Postdoctorate with Robert B. Woodward, Harvard, 1944-46; instr. Stanford, 1946-48, asst. prof., 1948-51, asso. prof., 1951-58, prof. chemistry, 1959—; NSF fellow, 1958-59; lectr. NSF, Air Force Acad. Mem. Am. Chem. Soc., Am. Assn. U. Profs., U.S. Power Squadron, Phi Beta Kappa, Sigma Xi. Author: General Chemistry-Experiment and Theory, 1970. Contbr. chpt. to Organic Chemistry, An Advanced Treatise, 1953. Contbr. articles profl. jours. Home: 634 Alvarado Row Stanford CA 94305

EASTON, CHARLES CLEMENT, Jr., chem. co. exec.; B. Allentown, Pa., July 14, 1930; s. Charles Clemant and Harriet (Williamson) E.; B.S. in Econs., U. Pa., 1952; M.B.A., Harvard, 1956; m. Priscilla Emma Herbert, Dec. 26, 1954; children—Joanne, Charles, June, Jennifer. With Inmont Corp., 1956—, treas., 1967—. Served to 1st lt. USAF, 1952-54. Mem. Alpha Chi Rho. Conglist. Clubs: Harvard (N.Y.C.); Racquets (Short Hills). Home: 99 Wellington Av Short Hills, NJ 07078. Office: 1133 Av of Americas New York City NY 10036

EASTON, DAVID, educator; b. Toronto, Ont., Can., June 24, 1917; s. Albert and Mary (Nisker) E.; B.A., U. Toronto, 1939, M.A., 1943; Ph.D., Harvard, 1947; LL.D., McMaster U., 1970; m. Sylvia Isobel Victoria Johnstone; 1 son, Stephen Talbot. Came to U.S., 1943. Teaching fellow Harvard, 1944-47; asst. prof. U. Chgo., 1947-53, asso. prof., 1953-55, prof., 1955—, now Andrew MacLeish Distinguished Service prof.; chmn. com. information behavioral scis. div. Nat. Acad. Sci.-NRC, mem. com. on sci. and tech. communications, 1968-70; fellow Center for Advanced Study in Behavioral Scis., Stanford, 1957-58; cons. Brookings Instn., 1955, Mental Health Research Inst., U. Mich., 1955-56, Royal Commn. on Bilingualism and Biculturalism, Can., 1964-66. Ford prof., 1960-61. Fellow Am. Acad. Arts and Scis.; mem. Am. Polit. Sci. Assn. (mem. council 1964-66, pres. 1968-69); Internat. Com. Social Sci. Documentation (pres. 1969-71). Author: The Political System, 1953; A Framework for Political Analysis, 1965; A Systems Analysis of Political Life, 1965; co-author: Children in the Political System, 1969. Editor: Varieties of Political Theory, 1966. Bd. editors Behavioral Sci., 1956—, Youth and Society. Office: Dept Polit Sci Univ Chicago Chicago IL 60637

EASTON, ELMER CHARLES, univ. dean; b. Newark, Dec. 23, 1909; s. Frank and Helen (Hagny) E.; B.S. in Elec. Engring., Lehigh U., 1931, M.S., 1933, D. Eng., 1965; S.D., Harvard, 1942. Research fellow, Lehigh U., 1931-33; mem. faculty Newark Coll. Engring., 1935-42; faculty grad sch. engring. Harvard, 1942-48, asst. dean engring. faculty, 1946-48; dean Coll. Engring., Rutgers U., 1948—; part time cons. engr. Cons. U.S. Govt., Africa, 1954, Korea, 1960. Registered profl. engr., Mass., N.J. Fellow I.E.E.E., A.A.A.S.; mem. Am. Soc. Engring. Edn. (pres. 1964-65), Nat. Soc. Profl. Engrs., Rutgers Engring. Soc., Blake Soc., Phi Beta Kappa, Sigma Xi, Eta Kappa Nu, Tau Beta Pi, Nu Alpha Sigma. Club: Lesamis. Author: Elements of Electrical Engineering, 1944; Calculus Laboratory Manual, 1940. Contbr. articles to profl. periodicals. Home: 4 Orchard Rd Piscataway, NJ 08854. Office: Engineering Bldg Rutgers U New Brunswick NJ 08903

EASTON, H. H., librarian; b. Rotherham, Eng., Jan. 12, 1910; s. Frank and Ethel (Jarvis) E.; B.A., U. Man. (Can.), 1931, M.A., 1936; B.L.S., U. Toronto (Ont., Can.), 1931, M.A., 1936; B.L.S., U. Toronto (Ont., Can.), 1938; m. Dorothy Ambrose Hutchison, Sept. 21, 1937; children—Joan (Mrs. J. Goring), Rosemary (Mrs. J. Unrau), Janet. Reference librarian Winnipeg (Man.) Pub. Library, 1929-30, asst. librarian, 1940-59, city librarian, 1959—. Mem. Canadian Library Assn. (pres. elect 1971). Home: 3742 Henderson Hwy RR 3 Winnipeg Manitoba Canada Office: 380 William Av Winnipeg 2 Manitoba Canada

EASTON, LOYD DAVID, educator; b. Rockford, Ill., July 29, 1915; s. Boyd J. and Elda (Holden) E.; A.B., DePauw U., 1937; M.A., Boston U., 1939, Ph.D., 1942; postgrad. Harvard, 1941-42, Glasgow U., 1946; m. Millison K. Shedd, June 14, 1942 (dec.); children—David, Carol, Judith; m. 2d, Martha Hutchison, Nov. 28, 1963; stepchildren—Martha Hutchison (Mrs. Leibert), Anne Hutchison (Mrs. Lundin). Borden Bowne fellow Boston U., 1939-40; instr. to asso. prof. philosophy Ohio Wesleyan U., 1946-54, chmn. dept. philosophy, 1952—, found. prof. philosophy, 1955—; vis. prof. Ohio State U., summer 1957; vis. prof. philosophy religion Meth. Theol. Sch. in Ohio, 1960-61. Kent fellow Soc. for Religion in Higher Edn., 1940- -. Served with AUS, 1942-46. Recipient grant-in-aid Am. Council Learned Socs., 1961-62, Am. Assn. for State and Local History, 1963. Mem. Am. Assn. U. Profs. (chmn. exec. com. Ohio Conf. chpts. 1950- 52, nat. council 1960-63), Am., Ohio (pres. 1964-67) philos. assns., Am. Civil Liberties Union, Phi Beta Kappa, Omicron Delta Chi. Methodist. Author: Ethics, Policy and Social Ends, 1955; Hegel's First American Followers, The Ohio Hegelians, 1967. Co-editor, co- translator: Writings of the Young Marx on Philosophy and Society, 1967. Contbr. articles to jours. in field. Home: 998 Braumiller Rd Delaware, OH 43015.

EASTON, ROBERT, actor; b. Milw., Nov. 23, 1930; s. John Edward and Mary Easton (Kloes) Burke; student U. Tex., 1948-49, U. Cal. at Los Angeles, 1949, 60, 68, 70, 71, Univ. Coll., London U., 1963; m. June Bettine Grimstead, Mar. 18, 1961. Appeared as 1 of original Quiz Kids on radio, 1945; appeared in 44 motion pictures in U.S., Gt. Britain, including Red Badge of Courage, The War Lover, Comin' Round the Mountain, Belles on their Toes, The Loved One, Paint Your Wagon; starred on over 350 radio shows for NBC, CBS, ABC, BBC and over 300 television shows, including Hallmark Hall of Fame, Gunsmoke, Playhouse 90, The Lucy Show, The Jack Benny Show, The Andersonville Trial, The Burns and Allen Show, Johnny Carson Show; starred in West Coast stage premiere of Tall Story, 1959; dir. diction and dialect workshops Nosotros, also Actor's and Dir.'s Lab., Hollywood, Cal., 1964; lectr. on dialects and regional speech at many univs. Mem. Screen Actor's Guild (nat. bd. dirs.), A.F.T.R.A. (nat., local bd. dirs.), Acad. Motion Picture Arts and Scis., Acad. Television Arts and Scis., Pacific Pioneer Broadcasters (charter). Contbr. sect. to book The American Indian, 1970, also articles to Variety, Hollywood Reporter. Writer spl. features for BBC radio, 1963-64. Address: c/o Screen Actor's Guild 7750 Sunset Blvd Hollywood CA 90046

EASTON, WILLIAM HEYDEN, educator; b. Bedford, Ind., Jan. 14, 1916; s. Harry Thomas and Katharine (Gillen) E.; B.S., George Washington U., 1937, M.A., 1938; Ph.D., U. Chgo., 1940; m. Phoebe Jane Beall, Aug. 10, 1940; children—Phoebe Beall, Robert Bruce, Katharine Louise. With Nat. Park Service, summers 1936, 37, Ark. Geol. Survey, summer 1939, U. Hawaii, summer 1963; with Ill. Geol. Survey, 1940-44; mem. faculty U. So. Cal., 1946—, prof. geology, 1951—, chmn. dept., 1963-67; with U.S. Geol. Survey, 1952-53; cons. geologist, 1950—. Served with USNR, 1944-46. Guggenheim fellow, 1959- 60. Fellow Geol. Soc. Am. (chmn. Cordilleran sect. 1965), So. Cal. Acad. Sci.; mem. Am. Assn. Petroleum Geologists (Distinguished lectr. 1955), Paleontol. Soc. (pres. West Coast br. 1950, pres. 1969), Soc. Econ. Paleontologists and Mineralogists (pres. Pacific sect. 1955), Coconut Island Inst., Sigma Xi, Sigma Gamma Epsilon. Author: Invertebrate Paleontology, 1960; also articles. Home: 3818 Bowsprint Circle Westlake Village CA 91361 Office: Dept Geological Sciences Univ Southern Calif University Park Los Angeles CA 90007

EASTWOLD, EARL RUSSELL, ret. naval officer, aircraft exec.; b. Canova, S.D., Aug. 17, 1909; s. Rasmus Russell and Ellen M. (Carlson) E.; B.S., U.S. Naval Acad., 1932; grad. Armed Forces Staff Coll., 1950; m. Mary Emily Hayes, Dec. 29, 1939; children—Theresa Ann (Mrs. Fred Abood, Jr.), Elizabeth Susan (Mrs. Frank W. O'Brien), John Russell. Commd. ensign USN, 1932, advanced through grades to rear adm., 1960; served in ships and flying squadrons, 1932-41; designated aviator, 1936; exec. officer, comdg. officer Radio Controlled Target Squadron, 1941-43; comdr. Spl. Task Air Group 2, 1943- 44; exec. officer U.S.S. Lunga Point, 1944-46, Naval Air Missile Test Center, Point Mugu, Cal., 1946-49, U.S.S. Norton Sound, 1950-51; air' operations officer on staff comdr. in chief U.S. Pacific Fleet, 1951-53; comdg. officer Naval Aux. Air Sta., Cabaniss Field, Tex., 1953-55, U.S.S. Tripoli, 1955-56, U.S.S. Essex, 1956-57; chief of staff to comdr. Carrier Div. 2, 1957-59; assigned Office Chief Naval Operations, 1959-61, Carrier Div. 16, also Hunter Killer Force, U.S. Atlantic Fleet, 1961-62; asst. chief field support Bur. Naval Weapons, 1962-63, asst. chief plans and programs, 1963-64, dep. chief bur., 1964- 66; comdr. Middle East Force, 1966-67; with Office Chief Naval Operations, 1967; ret., 1967; mgr. advanced planning, aircraft div. Hughes Tool Co., Culver City, Cal., 1967—. Decorated Bronze Star medal with gold star and combat V, Presdl. Unit citation, Legion of Merit. Club: Army Navy Country (Arlington, Va.). Home: 1308 Via Gabriel Palos Verdes Estates, CA 90274. Office: Aircraft Division Hughes Tool Co Culver City CA 90230

EASTWOOD, CLINT, actor; b. San Francisco, May 31; ed. Oakland Tech. High Sch., Los Angeles City Coll. Worked as lumberjack in Ore. before being drafted into the Army; starred in TV series Rawhide for seven and a half years; owner Malpaso Prodns., 1969—; motion pictures include A Fistful of Dollars, For a Few Dollars More, The Witches, The Good The Bad and The Ugly, Paint Your Wagon, Hang 'Em High, Coogan's Bluff, Where Eagles Dare, Two Mules for Sister Sara, Kelly's Heroes, Beguiled, Play Misty For Me. Address: c/o William Morris Agy 151 El Camino Los Angeles CA 90212*

EASTWOOD, DOUGLAS WILLIAM, anesthesiologist; b. Ellsworth, Wis., Sept. 17, 1918; s. Frederick William and Maud (Holmes) E.; student Washington and Jefferson Coll., 1936-37; A.B., Coe Coll., 1940; M.D., U. Ia., 1943, M.S., 1949; m. Ruth E. Beitel, June 12, 1943; children—William Ashley, Mary Ruth, Robert Douglas, James Edward. Intern Receiving Hosp., Detroit, 1944, asst. resident internal medicine, 1944-45; asst. resident anesthesiology U. Ia. Coll. Medicine, 1947-48, resident anesthesiology, 1948-49, instr. anesthesiology, 1949-50, asso. anesthesiology, 1950, asso. prof. div. anesthesiology, 1954-55; instr. dept. internal medicine Wayne U., 1944- 45; asst. prof., chief div. anesthesiology Washington U. Sch. Medicine, 1950-54; chmn. dept. anesthesiology U. Va. Hosp., 1955-71; prof. anesthesiology, 1971—; scholar-in-residence Lister Hill Center, Nat. Library of Medicine. Served as capt. AUS, 1945-47. Diplomate Am. Bd. Anesthesiology. Fellow Am. Coll. of Anesthesiologists; mem. Am. Soc. Anesthesiologists, A.M.A., Internat. Anesthesia Research Soc., Assn. U. Anesthetists, Albemarle County Med. Soc., Med. Soc. Va., Am. Assn. U. Profs., Sigma Xi. Home: Bell Air Charlottesville VA 22902 Office: University of Virginia Hospital Charlottesville VA 22904

EASTWORCH, ARTHUR CURTIS chemist, educator; b. Chicago, 1928; B.S. in Physics, Yale, 1950; Ph.D. in Chemistry, Harvard, 1956; m. Sally Ann Jones, July 5, 1957; children--Kenneth J., Nancy A. Chemist, Acme Chem. Co., Blue Island, Ill., 1950-51; director of Research Lab., Indsl. Chemicals Corp., Cambridge, Mass., 1956-60; project coordinator environmental sect. Steinmetz Assos., Chgo., 1960-61; v.p. for research Bauer Bros. Chem. Co., Inc., Memphis, 1961-64; asst. prof. chemistry Washington U., St. Louis, 1964-66. Salesman, Brown Mfg. Co., Boston, 1932-33; jr. engr. Ball Metals Co., Carson City, Nev., 1933-36, engr., 1936-37, sr. engr., 1937-40; project engr. Kingston Engring. Co., Los Angeles, 1940-43; with dept. engring. City of Denver, 1946-50, dep. head, 1950-52; 2d v.p. Johnson Mfg. Co., Kansas City, Kansas, 1952-54, v.p. for engring., 1954-57; v.p. research Consol. Industries, Inc., South Bend, Ind., 1957-60, exec. v.p., 1960-65, pres., 1965-70, chmn. bd., chief exec. officer, 1970--, also dir.; dir. ABC Chem. Co., 2d Nat. Bank, Country Food Storage Co., Providence Indsl. Corp. (Ind.), Wilson Investment Co., Inc., Hammond Life Ins. Co., Inc. Pres., Dewey High Sch., Kansas City, Mo., 1953-54; fund chmn. local div. Salvation Army, 19560. Mem. South Bend Republican Com., 1964-68. Bd. dirs. Ind. council Boy Scouts Am., 1969-71; trustee Lovell Found. Served to lt., Corps Engrs., AUS, 1943-45. Decorated Bronze Star medal. Member N.A.M., South Bend C. of C. (v.p. 1963-65, dir. 1965-70), Am. Mgmt. Assn., Ind. Engrs. Soc. (program com. 1961-62), Princeton Alumni Assn. Episcopalian. Home: 6823 Broad Terrace Av South Bend IN 46505 Office: PO Box 1019 South Bend IN 46501

EATON, ALLEN OBER, lawyer; b. Waterford, N.Y., May 28, 1910; s. Arthur Chester and Ethel (Obear) E.; B.S., U. Vt., 1932; LL.B., Harvard, 1935; m. Marjorie Eisenwinter, Sept. 8, 1934; 1 dau., Barbara. Admitted to Mass. bar, 1935; practiced in Boston, 1935—; with Ropes & Gray and predecessor firm, 1935-, partner, 1944-. Dir. Flintkote Co., Quincy Market Cold Storage & Warehouse Co., Central Vt. Pub. Service Corp., Winchester Nat. Bank, Vt. Yankee Nuclear Power Corp.; trustee Winchester Savs. Bank. Trustee U. Vt. Mem. Am., Mass., Boston bar assns., Sigma Phi. Conglist. Clubs: Harvard (N.Y.C.); Union (Boston); Winchester (Mass.) Country. Home: 77 Arlington St Winchester MA 01890 Office: 225 Franklin St Boston MA 02110

EATON, ANDREW JACKSON, librarian; b. Holley, N.Y., July 5, 1914; s. Carl Simon and Grace McConnell) E.; A.B., Coll. Wooster, 1935; A.B. in L.S., U. Mich., 1936; Ph.D., U. Chgo., 1944; m. Mary Emeline Eaton, May 3, 1944; children—Carolyn Alice, Marjorie Susan. Sr. asst. history div. Rochester (N.Y.) Pub. Library, 1936-39; research asst. Grad. Library Sch., U. Chgo., 1942-43; reference librarian Lawrence Coll., 1944-45; instr. library sch. La. State U., spring 1949, chief reference librarian, 1945-46, asso. dir. libraries, 1946-53; dir. libraries Washington U., St. Louis, 1953—; library sch. instr. Columbia, summer 1947, Fla. State U., summer 1948, N.C., summer 1952. Fellow Council on Library Resources, 1969-70. Mem. A.L.A. (mem. bd. on resources of Am. libraries 1949-53, council 1952-53), Mo. (exec. bd. 1955-56, pres. 1965-66), La. (exec. bd. 1951) library assns., Assn. Coll. and Research Libraries (dir.-at-large 1962-63, chmn. univ. library sect. 1964-65, rep. on A.L.A. council 1968-71), Assn. Research Libraries (pres. 1968), Phi Beta Kappa. Contbr. to library jours. Home: 21 Dwyer Pl St Louis MO 63124 Office: Olin Library Washington U St Louis MO 63130

EATON, BEN HARRISON, investment co. exec.; b. Denver, Aug. 31, 1920; s. Rea Lincoln and Carol (Hillhouse) E.; B.A., Stanford, 1942; m. Germaine Beaulieu, Feb. 18, 1947; children—William H., Carol R. With Dean Witter & Co., San Marino, Cal., 1946, office mgr., 1953-58, partner in firm, Los Angeles, 1958—, sr. v.p., 1968, exec. v.p., 1968—. Mem. Recreation Commn. San Marino, 1950's; active campaigns local YMCA, A.R.C., Community Chest. Served to maj. AUS, 1942-46; CBI. Mem. Los Angeles C. of C., Stock Exchange Club Los Angeles, Pacific Coast Stock Exchange (bd. govs. 1966-67), Los Angeles Bond Club (bd. dirs. 1969-70), Phi Delta Theta. Rotarian. Clubs: San Gabriel (Cal.) County; Laguna Nigel (Cal.) Country; Dana Strand Beach and Tennis (Dana Point, Cal.); Valley Hunt (Pasadena, Cal.); California (Los Angeles). Home: 1466 Charlton Rd San Marino, CA 91108. Office: 632 S Spring St Los Angeles CA 90014

EATON, BERRIEN CLARK, Jr., lawyer; b. Chgo., Feb. 12, 1919; s. Berrien Clark and Gladys (Hambleton E.; student Williams Coll., 1936-38; B.S., U. Va., 1940, LL.B., 1948; m. Margaret Patricia Anne Redmond Wheeler, Dec. 27, 1969; children-Theodore Hambleton, Ann. Berrien. Admitted to Mich. bar, 1948, Ariz. bar, 1969; practiced in Detroit, 1948-69, Phoenix, 1969—; asso. Miller, Canfield, Paddock & Stone, 1948-58, partner, 1958-69; asso. Brown, Vlassis & Bain, 1969, partner, 1970—; instr. Wayne State U. Law Sch., 1954-69; lectr. at law Ariz. State U. Law Sch., 1970—; legal cons. Andrews Philanthropic Giving (Russell Sage Found.), 1970. Past dir. Pontchartrain Hotel Co., Panax Corp., Gen. Underwtiters, Inc. Served to capt., F.A., AUS, 1941-46. Decorated Bronze Star medal; hon. Ky. col. Mem. Am. (past com. chmn.), Mich. (past com. chmn.; past chmn. Internal Revenue Service Liaison group Central region), Detroit (past com. chmn.), Ariz., Maricopa County bar assns., Newcomen Soc. N.Am., Order of Coif, Kappa Alpha. Republican. Episcopalian. Club: Thomas M. Cooley (Detroit). Author: Professional Corporations and Associations, 1970. Contbr. articles profl. jours. Home: 4959 E Red Rock Dr Phoenix AZ 85018 Office: 222 N Central Av Phoenix AZ 85018

EATON, CHARLES EDWARD, educator, author; b. Winston-Salem, N.C., June 25, 1916; s. Oscar Benjamin and Mary Gaston (Hough) E.; student Duke, 1932-33; A.B., U. N.C., 1936; postgrad. Princeton, 1936-37; M.A., Harvard, 1940; m. Isabel Patterson, Aug. 16, 1950. Instr. English U. Mo., 1940-42; prof. creative writing U. N.C., 1946-51; Am. vice-consul, Rio de Janeiro, Brazil, 1942-46. Recipient Ridgely Torrence Meml. award, 1951; Gertrude Boatwright Harris award, 1954; Ariz. Quar. award, 1956; Roanoke-Chowan Poetry Cup, 1970. Fellow Bread Loaf Writers Conf., 1941; fellow Boulder Writers Conf., 1942. Mem. Poetry Soc. Am., New Eng. Poetry Club, N.C. Art Soc., Phi Beta Kappa, Sigma Nu. Author: The Bright Plain, 1942; The Shadow of the Swimmer, 1951; The Greenhouse in the Garden, 1956; Countermoves, 1963; On the Edge of the Knife, 1970; short stories Write Me from Rio, 1959. Contbr. anthologies Best American Short Stories, 1952; American Literature: Readings and Critiques, 1961; Epoch Anthology, 1968; Best Poems of the Year, 1965, 68, 69, 70. Address: Merlin Stone Woodbury CT 06798

EATON, CHARLES FREEDOM, Jr., investment co. exec.; b. Princeton, Me., Feb. 3, 1898; s. Charles Freedom and Alice Mabel (Murchie) E.; grad. Phillips Exeter Acad., 1919, Harvard, 1923; m. Clarissa Metcalf, July 12, 1923; children—Joseph Emersin, Wilhellmina Mixter, Sarah Metcalf (Mrs. Dixon B. White), Charles Freedom III; m. 2d, Elizabeth Y. Edwards, Apr. 29, 1967. Asst. treas. First Nat. Corp., Boston, 1922-24; partner Eaton & Howard, 1924-31; pres., dir. Eaton & Howard, Inc., 1931—; trustee Eaton & Howard Stock Fund, Eaton & Howard Balanced Fund, Eaton & Howard Income Fund; dir. Eaton & Howard Growth Fund, Eaton & Howard Spl. Fund; chmn. bd., dir. Investors Bank & Trust Co.; mem. corp. Suffolk Savs. Bank, Boston. Trustee Boys' and Girls' Camps, Inc., New Eng. Peabody Home for Crippled Children. Mem. Investment Co. Inst., Investment Bankers Assn. Am. Republican. Mason. Clubs: The Country (Brookline, Mass.); Harvard (N.Y.C.); Duxbury (Mass.) Yacht; Down Town, Harvard (Boston); St. Bernard Fish and Game (Quebec). Home: Duxbury MA 02332 also 40 Chestnut St Boston MA 02108 Office: 24 Federal St Boston MA 02110

EATON, CLEMENT, historian; b. Winston-Salem, N.C., Feb. 23, 1898; s. Oscar Benjamin and Mary Gaston (Hough) E.; A.B., U. N.C., 1919, A.M., 1920; Ph.D., Harvard, 1929; D. Litt. (hon.), Wake Forest U., 1967; A.M. (hon.), Cambridge U., 1968; LL.D., U. Ky., 1970; m. Mary Elizabeth Allis, June 12, 1933; children—Allis (Mrs. Henry R. Bennett), William Clement, Clifton Packer. Instr., Whitman Coll., 1923-24; tutor. instr. Harvard, 1926-27; asst. prof. Clark U. 1929-30; asso. prof. history, Lafayette Coll., 1930-33, prof. history, head dept., 1933-46; prof. U. Ky., 1946-68, Hallam prof., 1961 (distinguished prof. of year 1956-57); Pitt prof. Am. history and instns. Cambridge U., 1968-69; prof. Coll. City N.Y., summers 1940, 41, U. N.C., summer 1946, Princeton, summer 1948; vis. prof. U. Wis., 1949, Columbia, summer 1951, U.S.C., 1970; Fulbright vis. prof. U. Manchester, Eng., 1951-52, Fulbright lectr. U. Innsbruck, Austria, 1957-58; Fulbright vis. prof., Bologna, Italy, 1964-65. Recipient Duke U. Press prize, 1939, Soc. Sci. Research Council award, 1953; Sheldon traveling fellowship, Harvard, 1927-28, Huntington Library research grant, 1955-56; Guggenheim Fellow, 1945-46. Mem. Am. (council mem.), Miss. Valley, So. (pres.) Hist. assns., Phi Beta Kappa, Tau Kappa Alpha, Golden Fleece (U. N.C. 1919). Democrat. Author: Freedom of Thought in the Old South, 1940; A History of the Old South, 1949; A History of the Southern Confederacy, 1954; Henry Clay and the Art of American Politics. 1957; The Growth of Southern Civilization, 1790-1860, 1961; Green Mount: a Virginia Plantation Family during the Civil War, 1962; The Leaven of Democracy: The Growth of the Democratic Spirit in the Time of Jackson, 1963; The Mind of the Old South, 1964, rev. 1967; The Freedom-of-Thought Struggle in the Old South, 1964; The Waning of the old South Civilization, 1860-1880, 1969. Contbr. to hist. publs. Home: 2995 Tate's Creek Rd Lexington, KY 40502.

EATON, CYRUS STEPHEN, industrialist and banker; b. Nova Scotia, Dec. 27, 1883; s. Joseph Howe and Mary Adelle (McPherson) E.; student Amherst Acad., Woodstock Coll.; A.B., McMaster U., Toronto, Canada, 1905; D.C.L., Acadia U., N.S., 1946; LL.D., Mount Allison U., Sackville, N.B., 1957, Bard Coll., N.Y., 1958, Charles U., Czechoslovakia, 1960, U. Sophia, Bulgaria, in 1961; m. Dec. 29, 1907 (dec.); children—Margaret G. (dec.), Mary Adelle (Mrs. Fay A. Le Fevre), Elizabeth Ann (Mrs. Lyman H. Butterfield), Anna Bishop, Cyrus Stephen, Augusta Farlee (Mrs. Farlee E. Hume), MacPherson; m. 2d, Anne Kinder Jones, 1957; 1 step dau., Alice Ewing Jones. Came to U.S., 1900, naturalized citizen, 1913. Held earliest business position with John D. Rockefeller, Sr.; subsequently associated with East Ohio Gas Co.; later organized Canada Gas & Electric Corp.; in 1912 began extensive activity in Am. utility industry, and formed Continental Gas & Electric Co., which consolidated a number of electric and gas companies in the Am. west; joined Otis & Co., 1916; principal middlewestern business assn. has been with steel, rubber and paint industries; in 1925 reorganized and became chmn. Trumbull Steel Co.; in 1929, with W. G. Mather, formed Cliffs Corp. (now Cleveland-Cliffs Iron Co.); holder substantial interest in six important iron and steel cos.; organized Republic Steel Corp., 1930; led in formation and reorgn. many other middlewestern companies; past dir. Republic Steel, Inland Steel, Youngstown Sheet & Tube and other companies, including Cleveland Trust Co. and Nat. Acme Co. in Cleveland; mem. banking house Otis & Co.; chmn. bd., dir. Steep Rock Iron Mines, Ltd., C. & O. Ry.; dir., past chmn. Detroit Steel Corp.; dir. Cleveland-Cliffs Iron Co., Sherwin-Williams Co., Cleve. Electric Illuminating Co., Kansas City Power & Light Co., Baltimore and Ohio Railroad Co. Trustee Denison U., U. Chgo., Case Inst. Tech., Cleve. Mus. Natural History. Elector Hall of Fame, dir. Cleve. Met. Park Bd., 1930-39. Fellow Am. Acad. Arts and Scis.; mem. Am. Council Learned Socs., Am. Acad. of Political and Social Sci., Royal Norwegian Acad. Scis., Can. Shorthorn Assn., Am. Hist. Assn., Am. Philos. Assn., Am. Shorthorn Breeders Assn. Author: The Third Term "Tradition," 1940; Financial Democracy, 1941; The Professor Talks to Himself, 1942; Investment Banking Competition or Decadence?, 1944; A New Plan to Reopen the U.S. Capital Market, 1945; The Engineer as Philosopher, 1961; others; also numerous articles and speeches in field. Clubs: Union, Mayfield, Chagrin Valley Hunt, Summit Hunt; Royal Nova Scotia Yacht Squadron; Glenelg Fishing (N.S.), Chester Yacht: Liverpool Yacht; Metropolitan (N.Y.). Home: Acadia Farms Northfield OH 44067 Office: Terminal Tower Cleveland OH 44113

EATON, CYRUS STEPHEN, Jr., bus. exec.; b. Cleve., Feb. 2, 1918; s. Cyrus S. and Margaret (House) E.; grad. Kent Sch., 1937; student Colgate U., 1937-41; m. Mary Stephens, July 11, 1942; children—Cyrus S. III, John S., Catherine Lee, Elizabeth Farlee. Chmn. bd. Cleyton Internat. Industries Ltd., Tower Internat., Inc.; dir., mem. exec. com. C. & O./B. & O. Railroads; dir. Kansas City Power & Light Co., Western Pocahontas Co., White Sulphur Springs Co. Co-chmn. edn. task force Greater Cleve. Urban Coalition. Trustee Cleve. Natural Sci. Mus., Kent (Conn.) Sch., Cleve. Council World Affairs. Served from lt. to maj. USAAF, 1941-45. Clubs: Chagrin Valley Hunt, Union. Home: Arrow Cottage Houghton Rd Northfield, OH 44067. Office: Terminal Tower Cleveland OH 44113

EATON, EDWARD HOUGH, glass co. exec.; b. Bryan, O., Jan. 6, 1917; s. O. Seaburn and Helen (Hough) E.; student Antioch Coll., 1934-37; B.S., Ohio State U., 1939; m. Judith A. Kerr, May 8, 1943; children—O. Seaburn III, Albert E., Judith A. Pub. accountant Ernst & Ernst, Pitts., 1939-44; v.p., treas. Pitts. Forgings Co., 1944-58; treasurer Pittsburgh Plate Glass Co. (name changed to PPG Industries, Inc.), 1958—. Trustee, v.p. financial Execs. Research Found. C.P.A., Pa. Mem. Financial Execs. Inst. Am. Inst. C.P.A.'s Home: 345A Blackburn Rd Sewickley, PA 15143. Office: 1 Gateway Center Pittsburgh PA 15222

EATON, ELDEN HENRY, rubber co. exec.; b. Hot Springs, S.D., Mar. 25, 1907; s. Leslie E. and Ethel (Bowen) E.; student Kansas City (Mo.) Sch. Accounting, 1924-26; m. Dorothy M. Lockwood, June 21, 1927; 1 son, William W. With Firestone Tire & Rubber Co., Akron, O., 1926—, asst. treas., 1956-65, treas., 1966-69, v.p. investments, 1970—. Trustee Akron YMCA, Akron Childrens Hosp. Home: 2485 Falmouth Rd Akron OH 44313 Office: 1200 Firestone Pkwy Akron OH 44317

EATON, FRANK LEVI, material co. exec.; b. Northville, Mich., July 4, 1923; s. Levi Medbury and Alice Eloise (Comlossy) E.; B.S. E. (Bus. Adminstrn.), M.B.A., U. Mich., 1948; m. Margery Jean Merriam, June 17, 1946; children—Robyn Lee, Timothy Andrew, Charles James. Bldg. engr. Panama Canal, 1948-51; sec., ins. mgr., dir. Rinker Material Corp., W. Palm Beach, Fla., 1951—; dir., sec. Constructors Aviation, W. Palm Beach; sec. Southeastern Materials, Inc., W. Palm Beach. Bd. dirs. Gulfstream Goodwill Industries. Served to lt. (j.g.) USNR, 1944-46. Mem. Am. Soc. Ins. Mgmt. (charter mem., past dir.). Presbyn. (elder). Club: Optimist (West Palm Beach, pres. 1958). Home: 1408 Indian Rd West Palm Beach FL 33406 Office: Box 231 West Palm Beach FL 33402

EATON, FREDRICK M., lawyer; b. Akron, O., May 21, 1905; s. Hugh McCurdy and Jessie (Smith) E.; A.B., Harvard, 1927, LL.B., 1930; m. Justine Allen, May 21, 1932. Admitted to bar, 1930; partner Shearman & Sterling, N.Y.C. Dir. First Nat. City Bank, Monsanto Co., N.Y. Life Ins. Co., Consol. Edison Co. N.Y.; gen. counsel WPB. Mem. Combined Raw Material Bd. and Combined Prodn. and

Resources Bd., 1945. chmn. Am. delegation to Disarmament Com., 1960. Trustee Commonwealth Fund, N.Y.C. Presbyn. Hosp. Clubs: Links (N.Y.C.); Links Golf (L.I.); Metropolitan (Washington). Home: 791 Park Av New York City NY 10021 Office: 53 Wall St New York City NY 10005

EATON, HAMBLEN COWLEY, physician; b. Warren, Pa., Mar. 1, 1901; s. Frederick Charles and May Gwin (Hamblen) E.; B.S., Allegheny Coll., 1922; M.D., Western Res. U., 1926; m. Zelma Mae Bowman, Aug. 10, 1928; children—David Charles, Robert Hamblen. Intern Allegheny Gen. Hosp., Pitts., 1926-27; resident Warren (Pa.) State Hosp., 1927-31; practice medicine, specializing in psychiatry, Warren, 1927-36, Polk, Pa., 1936-37, Harrisburg, Pa., 1937- -; asst. physician, pathologist, clin. dir. Warren State Hosp., 1927-36; clin. dir. Polk State Sch., 1936-37; clin. dir. Harrisburg State Hosp., 1937-54, supt., 1954-69; mem. staff Harrisburg Hosp., Masonic Homes Hosp., Elizabethtown, Pa. Served from lt. comdr. to capt. M.C., USNR, 1941-46. Fellow A.C.P., Am. Psychiat. Assn.; mem. A.A.A.S., S.A.R., Res. Officers Assn., Med. Soc. Pa. (chmn. com. mental hygiene, 1947-65), Dauphin County Med. Soc. (past pres.). Methodist. Mason (33). Home: 2902 Parkside Lane Harrisburg, PA 17110.

EATON, HENRY FELIX, pub. relations exec.; b. Cleve., Nov. 30, 1925; s. Henry F. and Stella (Simon) E.; A.B., U. Chgo., 1947; m. Barbara Feder, Aug. 28, 1950; children—Deborah, Richard, David, Susan. Asst. advt. mgr. Kromex Corp., Cleve., 1947-48; editor Material Handling Engring. mag., Cleve., 1948-52; chmn. exec. com. Dix & Eaton, Inc., Cleve., 1952—. Served with AUS, 1944-46. Mem. Pub. Relations Soc. Am., Assn. Indsl. Advertisers, Cleve. Advt. Club. Clubs: Midday; Oakwood Country. Home: 23690 Letchworth Rd Beachwood OH 44122 Office: The 1010 Euclid Bldg Cleveland OH 44115

EATON, JAMES ROBERT, educator; b. Bluffton, Ind., Nov. 1, 1902; s. James B. and Aldula (Baumgartner) E.; B.S. in Elec. Engring., Purdue U., 1925, Ph.D., 1942; M.S. in Elec. Engring., U. Wis., 1938; m. A. Ruth Sergeant, Sept. 16, 1929; 1 son, James Robert. Engr., Consumers Power Co., Jackson, Mich., 1925-37; instr., U. Wis., 1938-40; mem. faculty Purdue U., 1940-71, now emeritus prof. elec. engring.; vis. prof. U. Alaska, spring 1967, 69-70; cons. in field, 1950—. Mem. I.E.E.E., Am. Soc. Engring Edn., Sigma Xi, Tau Beta Pi, Eta Kappa Nu, Kappa Eta Kappa, Acacia. Baptist. Mason. Author: Beginning Electricity, 1952; Electrons, Neutrons and Protons in Engineering, 1966; also articles. Home: 175 Drury Lane West Lafayette IN 47906

EATON, JOE O., judge; b. Monticello, Fla., Apr. 2, 1920; s. Robert Lewis and Mamie (Gireadeau) E.; A.B., Presbyn. Coll., 1941; LL.B., U. Fla., 1948; practiced in Miami, Fla., 1948-51, 55-59; asst. state atty. Dade County, Fla., 1953; circuit judge, Miami, 1954-55, 59-67; mem. Fla. Senate, 1956-59; mem. law firm Eaton & Achor, Miami, 1955-58, Sams, Anderson, Eaton & Alper, Miami, 1958-59. judge U.S. Dist. Ct. So. Dist. Fla., 1967—. Instr. law U. Miami Coll. Law, 1954-56. Served with USAAF, 1941-45, USAF, 1951-52. Decorated D.F.C., Air medal. Methodist. Kiwanian. Home: 4901 SW 59th Av Miami FL 33155. Office: 300 NE 1st Av Miami FL 33101

EATON, LEONARD KIMBALL, educator; b. Mpls., Feb. 3, 1922; s. Leo Kimball and Elizabeth (Barber) E.; B.A., Williams Coll., 1943; M.A., Harvard, 1948, Ph.D., 1951; m. Carrol Faith Kuehn, Aug. 15, 1947; children—Mark R., Elisabeth K. Mem. faculty U. Mich., 1950—, prof. architecture, 1963—. Democratic candidate for council, Ann Arbor, 1957. Served with inf. AUS, World War II; MTO. Decorated Bronze Star; Ford Found. faculty fellow, 1954-55; recipient Finlandia award Finlandia Soc. Met. N.Y., 1965. Mem. Soc. Archtl. Historians (bd. dirs. 1957-58), Phi Beta Kappa. Club: Racquet (Ann Arbor). Author: New England Hospitals, 1790-1833, 1956; Landscape Artist in America, 1964; Two Chicago Architects and Their Clients, 1969; also numerous articles, revs. Book rev. editor Jour. Soc. Archtl. Historians, 1967-69. Home: 2601 Heather Way Ann Arbor, MI 48104.

EATON, LEWIS SWIFT, savs. and loan exec.; b. San Francisco, Aug. 10, 1919; s. Edwin M. and Gertrude (Swift) E.; B.A., Stanford, 1942; m. Virginia Stammer, Apr. 21, 1950; children—William L., Joan E., John W. With Fresno Guarantee Savs. & Loan Assn. (Cal.), 1946—, v.p., 1950-56, pres., 1956—, also chmn. bd.; mem. bd. Fed. Home Loan Bank, San Francisco, 1964-70. Pres. Fresno Zool. Soc., 1967-68. Mem. Fresno City Bd. Edn., 1958-66; pres., 1959-62. Trustee Fresno Community Hosp., 1965—, Fresno State Coll. Found., 1969—, Jr. Achievement, 1951—, Cal. Mus. Found., 1970—; mem. adv. bd. Fresno State Coll. 1965—. Served to capt., 77th Inf. Div., AUS, 1942-46. Decorated Army Commendation ribbon. Mem. Cal. (pres. 1959-60), U.S. (pres. 1970-71) savs. and loan leagues, C. of C. Fresno City and County (pres. 1967), Beta Gamma Sigma, Lambda Alpha. Home: 4115 N Van Ness Blvd Fresno CA 93704 Office: 1177 Fulton Mall Fresno CA 93721

EATON, MONROE DAVIS, Jr., virologist; b. Stockton, Cal., Dec. 2, 1904; s. Monroe Davis and Ida Virginia (Petty) E.; A.B., Stanford, 1927, A.M., 1928; M.D., Harvard, 1930; m. Laura Mitchell, Aug. 9, 1933; children—John Monroe, Lydia, Emily, Katharine. Asst. bacteriology Harvard Med. Sch., 1930-33, also instr. tutor biochem. scis. at coll.; instr. bacteriology Yale Med. Sch., 1933-36; asst. prof. bacteriology Washington U. Sch. Medicine, St. Louis, 1936-37; mem. staff internat. health div. Rockefeller Found., 1937-47; virus lab. Cal. Dept. Pub. Health, 1939- 47; asso. prof. bacteriology and immunlogy Harvard Med. Sch., 1947-68, prof., 1968-71, emeritus, 1971—, acting head dept. bacteriology 1954-57; sr. scientist med. microbiology Sanford Med. Sch., 1971—. Mem. U.S. Army Commn. Influenza, 1941-46, asso. mem., 1946-59; cons. jaundice and yellow fever vaccination surgeon gen. U.S. Army, 1942-44. Fellow A.A.A.S.; mem. Am. Acad. Arts and Scis., Am. Soc. Microbiology, Soc. Exptl. Biology and Medicine, Am. Assn. Immunologists, Phi Beta Kappa, Sigma Xi. Contbr. articles to profl. jours., chpts. to books. Editorial bd. Annual Revs. Microbiology, 1946-56; asso. editor Am. Jour Epidemiology, 1960—. Home: 1965 Byron St Palo Alto CA 94301 Office: Dept Med Microbiology Stanford Med Sch Stanford CA 94305

EATON, ORVILLE LEE, librarian; b. Thayer, Kan., July 15, 1912; s. Arthur L. and Della (Peterson) E.; B.S., Kan. State Tchrs. Coll., 1938, M.S., 1940; Ph.D., U. Kan., 1946; B.L.S., U. Chgo., 1948; m. Alta Moynihan, Oct. 5, 1935. Tchr. elementary schs., Kan., 1930-36, tchr. English, Joplin, Mo., 1938- 40; instr. U. Kan., 1940-42; editor, writer Command and Gen. Staff Coll., Ft. Leavenworth, Kan., 1943-46; dir. libraries U. Kansas City (Mo.), 1946-50; librarian, head dept. library sci. Kan. State Coll., Emporia, 1950-58, dir. grad. div., 1953-58; prof., head dept. library Central Mich. U., 1958-70, prof., chmn. dept. library sci., 1970—. Mem. A.L.A., Mich. Library Assn. (chmn. coll. sect. 1965-66), Mich. Edn. Assn., North Central Assn. (coordinator 1957- 62), Sigma Tau Delta, Phi Delta Kappa, Alpha Beta Alpha. Contbr. articles to profl. jours. Home: 808 W Preston Mt Pleasant MI 49272

EATON, RAMONE STANLEY, assn. exec.; b. Alexandria, Va., Aug. 29, 1907; s. George H. and Irene M. (Beach) E.; student Southeastern U., Washington, 1925-26, George Washington U., 1928, U. Ga., 1931; m. June L. Clark, Jan. 16, 1933; children—June Elaine, Lyndle Stanley. Dir. pub. recreation, Alexandria, 1926, phys. edn., YMCA, Washington, 1927; field rep. 1st aid and life saving A.R.C., 1928-39, asst. nat. dir., 1st aid and life saving, 1937-40, dir. roll call, 1940-41, adminstrv. asst. mgr. N. Atlantic area, 1942-43, mgr. Eastern area and Pacific area, 1943-48, v.p., 1940-70, sr. v.p., 1970—. Mem. Pub. Relations Soc. Am., Am. Canoe Assn., Phi Pi Phi, Alpha Sigma Phi. Episcopalian. Rotarian. (gov.). Clubs: Nat. Press (Washington); Fairfax Hunt (Va.); Toe-H; Commonwealth of Cal. (San Francisco); Court House Country (Va.). Contbr. to recreation, camping and safety edn. publs. Home: 1400 S Joyce St Arlington VA 22202 Office: American National Red Cross 17th and E Sts Washington DC 20013

EATON, REGINALD CURREN, physician; b. Blomidon, N.S., Can., July 8, 1917; s. Victor Bigelow and Leta (Chisholm) E.; B.S., Acadia U., 1938; M.D., Dalhousie U., 1949; m. Isobel F. Carson, Aug. 12, 1944; children—Janice, Nancy, James. Came to U.S., 1955, naturalized, 1960. Intern, resident Victoria Gen. Hosp., Halifax, N.S., 1949-52; practice medicine, specializing in psychiatry, Dartmouth, N.S., 1952-53; supt. Provincial Hosp., Campbellton, N.B., 1953- 55; supt. S. Fla. State Hosp., Hollywood, 1960-65; dep. dir. Fla. Div. mental health also dir. Fla. Community Health, 1965-69; pvt. practice, Ft. Pierce; Fla., 1970—. Served with Canadian Navy, 1941-45. Certified in psychiatry Royal Coll. Physicians and Surgeons Can. Fellow Am. Psychiat. Assn.; mem. Fla. Med. Assn., Fla. Psychiat. Soc. Address: 1701 S 8th St Ft Pierce FL 33450

EATON, ROBERT EDWARD LEE, pub. relations and mgnt. cons.; b. Hattiesburg, Miss., Dec. 22, 1909; s. Malcolm Jasper and Sallie Lucinda (Huff) E.; student U. Miss., 1926-27, Mass. Inst. Tech., 1936-37, Command and Gen. Staff Sch., 1942; B.S., U.S. Mil. Acad., 1931; m. Jo Kathryn Rhein, Jan. 1, 1939; children—Robert Edward Lee, Sallie, Charles. Commd. 2d lt., inf., U.S. Army, 1931; transferred to Air Corps, 1933; advanced through grades to maj. gen., 1947; operations officer 5th Bomb Squadron, 1935; weather officer, 1937; comdg. officer 7th Air Base Group, 1941; regional control officer 2d Weather Region, 1941; chief weather central div. AAF hdqrs., 1942; comdg. officer 451st Bomb Group, Zone of Interior and Italy, 1943-44; dep. dir. operations U.S. Strategic Air Forces, Europe, 1944-45; officer asst. chief air staff, personnel AAF hdqrs., 1945; Office of Dir. of Information, 1946; dep. dir. Office of Legislative Liaison, Office of Sec. of Def., 1949; dir. Legislation and Liaison Office of Sec. Air Force, 1951-53; comdr. 6th Allied Tactical Air Force, Izmir, Turkey, 1953-55; comdr. 10th Air Force, Selfridge AFB, Mich., 1955-59; asst. chief staff res. forces, hdqrs., 1959-62, ret.; pres. Eaton Assos., Inc., pub. relations and mgmt. cons., 1962—. Decorated Silver Star with oak leaf cluster, Legion of Merit, D.F.C. with oak leaf cluster, Bronze Star, Air medal with 4 oak leaf clusters, D.S.M., Croix de Guerre (France). Mem. Miss. State Soc. of Washington, Am. Legion (nat. exec. committeeman 1966-70, nat. vice comdr. 1970-71), 40 and 8. Episcopalian. Mason. Clubs: Columbia Country, Army-Navy, Burning Tree (Washington); Pine Valley. Home: 4921 Essex Av Chevy Chase MD 20015. Office: 1750 K St NW Washington DC 20006

EATON, SAMUEL DICKINSON, fgn. service officer; b. Plymouth, N.Y., Feb. 13, 1923; s. Harry W. and Nellie L. (Bernhard) E.; A.B., Drew U., 1947; student Columbia, 1947, Fletcher Sch. Law and Diplomacy, 1952-53; m. Mercedes Herrera, Feb. 16, 1949. Third sec. Am. embassy, La Paz, Bolivia, 1948-50; 2d sec. Am. embassy, Rio de Janeiro, 1950-52, Bangkok, Thailand, 1953-55; chief financial stblzn. br., div. internat. finance Dept. State, 1955-59; chief econ. sect. Am. embassy, Bogota, Colombia, 1959-65, also dep. dir. AID mission, 1962-65; dep. dir. N. Coast Am. Republic Affairs Dept. State, 1966-67, Nat. War Coll., 1967-68; dir. AID Mission to Peru, 1968-69; dep. chief mission Am. embassy, Quito, Ecuador, 1969-70; now mem. planning and coordination Staff Dept. State. Served as 2d lt. USAAF, 1945-46. Home: 6134 Tompkins Dr McLean VA 22101 Office: Dept State Washington DC 20525

EATON, SAMUEL KNOX, ret. army officer; b. New Bern, N.C., Aug. 6, 1914; s. Samuel Harrison and Mary Emma (Street) E.; student Davidson Coll., 1931-34; B.S., U.S. Mil. Acad., 1938; grad. Command and Gen. Staff Coll., 1942, Armed Forces Staff Coll., 1949, Nat. War Coll., 1957-58; m. Elizabeth Patricia Wash, Oct. 14, 1938; children—Constance (Mrs. John J. Colony III), Samuel Knox. Commd. 2d lt. U.S. Army, 1938, advanced through grades to maj. gen., 1966; served ETO, World War II; mem. Marshall Mission to China, 1946-47; with Army of Occupation, Japan, 1947-48; assigned joint staff Joint Chiefs Staff, 1949-52, SHAPE, 1952-55; comdg. officer 40th F.A. Group Ft. Carson, Colo., 1955-57; assigned Office Sec. Def., 1959- 64, 1st Cav. Div., Korea, 1964-65; chief Joint U.S. Mil. Aid Group Greece, 1966-69; ret., 1969. Decorated D.S.M., Legion of Merit, Bronze Star (U.S.); Order Cloud and Banner (China). Bd. dirs. Transatlantic council Girl Scouts, 1966-69; Boy Scouts Am., 1966-69. Mem. Sigma Alpha Epsilon, Sigma Pi Sigma. Home: 2114 McNell Rd Ojai, CA 93203.

EATON, WILLIAM JAMES, newspaperman; b. Chgo., Dec. 9, 1930; s. Wlliam Millar and Rose (Ellenbast) E.; B.S., Northwestern U., 1951, M.S., 1952; m. Marilynn Myers, Sept. 6, 1952; children—Susan, Sally Ann. With City News Bur., Chgo., 1952-53; with U.P.I., Washington, 1955-66; corr. Washington Bur., Chgo. Daly News, 1966—. Served with U.S. Army, 1953-55. Recipient Sidney Hillman award, 1970, Pulitzer prize for nat. reporting, 1970. Nieman fellow Harvard, 1962-63. Author: (with Frank Cormier) Reuther, 1970. Home: 1106 Trinity Dr Alexandria VA 22314 Office: Nat Press Bldg Washington DC 20004

EAVES, HETTIE DAWES, corp. exec.; b. Throckmorton, Tex., 1920; ed. N. Tex. State Coll., 1940. Exec. v.p. finance and adminstrn. Avondale Shipyards, Inc. Home: 5501 Marcia Av New Orleans LA 70124 Office: PO Box 50280 New Orleans LA 70150

EAVES, JAMES CLIFTON, mathematician; b. Hillside, Ky., June 26, 1912; s. John Ridley (Whippoorwill) and Agnes (Williams) E.; A.B., U. Ky., 1935, M.A. (Haggen fellow), 1941; Ph.D., U. N.C., 1949; m. Maona Shinkle, Aug. 20, 1938; children—James Clifton, Mona Jane, Tchr., Hillside, 1932-35; math. tchr., asst. athletic coach, debate coach Pineville (Ky.) City High Sch., 1935-37; math. tchr. Morton Jr. High Sch., Henry Clay High Sch., Lexington, Ky., 1937-40; grad. asst. U. Ky., 1941-42, instr., 1942- 43, 46, prof., 1954—, head dept. math. and astronomy, 1954-63, prof. math., 1963-67, Centennial prof. math., chmn. dept. math., 1967—; research cons., dir. Inst. Consultants Math., Statistics and Patent Law, 1956—; part-time instr. U. N.C., 1947-49; asst. prof. U. Ala., 1949-50; asso. prof. Ala. Poly. Inst., 1950-51, research asso. prof., 1951-52, prof., research asso. Auburn Research Found., 1952-53, prof., adminstrv. asst. dept. math. 1953-54. Dir. Ky. Space Flight Program in Mathematics and Astronomy. NASA. Scoutmaster, Pineville, Ky. Served as lt. USNR, 1943-46. Fellow A.A.A.S.; mem. Ky. Assn. Colls. and Secondary Schools (pres. math sect. 1957, 64), Ky. Soc. for Promotion Useful Knowledge, Math. Assn. Am. (lectr. Ky. sect. 1955-57), Am. Math. Soc., Am. Assn. U. Profs., Ala. Assn. Coll. Tchrs. Maths. (pres. 1953-54), Newcomen Soc. N.Am., Sigma Xi, Phi Delta Kappa (sec.), Pi Mu Epsilon (nat. councilor gen. 1960-63, nat. pres. 1967—), Mu Alpha Theta (nat. pres. 1959-62). Clubs: Kiwanis, Bluegrass (Lexington). Author: (with W. V. Parker) Matrices, 1954; (with A. J. Robinson) An Introduction to Euclidean Geometry, 1955; (with T. J. Pignani) Digital Computer Programing, 1959; Mathematics of Finance and Business, 1960. Gen. editor College Algebra and Basic Set Theory, 1963. Contbr. research articles profl. math. jours., author feature articles on astronomy. Patentee dial setting mechinism, buckle protector, design for award Key. Home: Hermit's Holler Route 4 Box 423 Morgantown WV 26505

EAVES, JOEL HARRY, athletic dir.; b. Copperhill, Tenn., June 3, 1914; s. Rufus Harry and Mabel (Puckett) E.; B.S. in Edn., Auburn U., 1937, m. Wealthy Elizabeth Lindsay, Jan. 20, 1946; children—Wealthy Joanne, Joel Harry. Basketball coach, asst. in football, U. of South, 1937-41, Boys High Sch., Atlanta, 1946-47; bastkeball coach, head football, Murphy High Sch., Atlanta, 1947-49; basketball coach Audburn U., 1949-63, asst. in football, 1949- 60; athletic dir. U. Ga., 1963—. Served to lt. col., F.A., AUS, 1941- 45. Named basketball coach of year S.E. Conf., 1958,60,62. Presbyn. Author: Basketball's Shuffle Offense, 1960. Home: 550 Forest Rd Athens, GA 30601.

EAVES, ROBERT WENDELL, educator; b. Rutherford Co., N.C., Nov. 23, 1903; s. Robert Wells and Della (Biggerstoff) E.; A.B., U. N.C., 1928; A.M., George Washington U., 1933, Ed.D., 1940; summer schs., Tchrs. Coll., Columbia, 1933, 34, Johns Hopkins, 1929, U. Va., 1930; m. Ruth Anderson, June 24, 1931; 1 son, Robert Wendell. Instr. elementary edn. Tchrs. Coll. Columbia, summer 1937, 38, Appalachian State Tchrs. Coll., Boon, N.C., 1939, Syracuse U., 1945, George Washington U., 1949-50, U. Mich., summers, 1950, San Francisco State Coll., 1951, 1956; chmn. com. and editor How to Know and Use Your Community, Dept. Elementary Sch. Prins., N.E.A., 1941, mem. and chmn. editorial com., 1942-45, exec. sec., then exec. sec. emeritus, cons. Dept. Elem. Prins., from 1950; now prof. edn. George Mason Coll. of U. Va., Fairfax. Sec. edn. com. President's Hwy. Safety Conf., 1946-50; sec. Nat. Commn. on Safety Edn., N.E.A., 1944-50; exec. officer Nat. Conf. on Sch. Transp., Jackson's Mill, W.Va., 1948; exec. dir. Nat. Conf. on Driver Edn., 1949; mem. planning and adv. bd. Nat. Aviation Edn. Council, 1953—; mem. President's Citizens Com. on Fitness and Youth, 1957—; mem. President's Com. on Employment of Handicapped; faculty U. Hawaii, summers 1958, 60, 65, Ill. So. U., summer, 1961, U. So. Cal., summer 1962, U. P.R., summer 1963, U. N.C., 1964; edn. cons. AID, Dominican Republic, 1962; mem. edn. com. People to People Program. Mem. U.S. Civil Service Bd. Examiners. Recipient distinguished service award President's Hwy. Safety Conf., 1951. Trustee Joint Council Econ. Edn., 1956-59. Mem. N.E.A. (life), Dept. Elem. Sch. Prins., George Washington U. Alumni Assn. (gov. 1964—), Phi Delta Kappa. Contbr. articles to ednl. publs. Home: 3700 N Glebe Rd Arlington VA 22207 Office: George Mason Coll Univ of Va Fairfax VA 22030

EAZOR, THOMAS A., business exec. Chmn., Eazor Express, Inc., Pitts. Office: Eazor Sq Pittsburgh PA 15201*

EBAN, ABBA, fgn. minister of Israel; b. 1915; ed. Queens Coll., Cambridge (Eng.) U., research fellow in Arabic and Persian, Pembroke Coll.; Hon. Dr., N.Y.U., U. Boston, U. Md., U. Cin., Temple U., Lehigh U. Liaison officer Allied Hdqrs. with Jewish population in Jerusalem, 1940; chief instr. Middle East Arab Centre in Jerusalem; joined service of Jewish Agy., 1946; liaison officer with UN Spl. Com. on Palestine, 1947; rep. Provisional Govt. of Israel to UN, 1948, permanent rep., 1949-59; ambassador to U.S., 1950-59; minister without portfolio of Israel, 1959-60, minister of edn., 1960-63, dep. prime minister, 1963- 66, minister of fgn. affairs, 1966—. Pres. Weizmann Inst. Sch., 1958- 66. Fellow World Acad. Arts and Scis., Am. Acad. Arts and Scis. Author: The Modern Literary Movement in Egypt, 1944; Maze of Justice, 1946; Voice of Israel, 1957; Tide of Nationalism, 1959; My People, 1968. Address: Office of Minister of Foreign Affairs Jerusalem, Israel.

EBAUGH, BESSIE MONROE, educator; b. Houston, June 29, 1905; d. John Thomas and Bessie (Pruett) Monroe; A.B., Tulane U., 1925; A.M., Columbia, 1927; 1 dau., Bessie (Mrs. Thomas G. Vandivier). Teaching fellow classical langs. Newcomb Coll., Tulane U., 1925-26, instr. classical langs., 1927- 28; mem. faculty U. Houston. 1930—, asso. prof., 1941-46, prof. English, 1947—, dean of women, 1955-70, dean emeritus, 1970—. Recipient Matrix award Theta Sigma Phi. Mem. League Women Voters, Nat. Council Tchrs. English, Tex. Assn. Women Deans and Counselors (pres. 1965- 67), Am. Assn. U. Women, Modern Lang. Assn., S. Central Modern Lang. Assn. Motrar Board, Phi Kappa Phi, Alpha Lambda Delta, Phi Mu, Delta Kappa Gamma. Methodist. Clubs: The Axson, Downtown (Houston). Home: 400 Emerson Av Houston TX 77006.

EBAUGH, FRANKLIN GESSFORD, psychiatrist; b. Reistertown, Md., May 14, 1895; s. Zachariah Charles and Elizabeth Bell (Gessford) E.; A.B., Johns Hopkins, 1915; M.D., 1919; m. Dorothy Reese, Apr. 9, 1921; children—Franklin G., David C., Donald R., Nancy Haines. Resident med. officer, Henry Phipps Clinic, 1919-20; asst. physician, N. J. State Hosp., 1920-21; dir. neuro- psychiat. dept., Phila. Gen. Hosp., 1920-24; instr. in psychiatry, U. Pa., 1922-24; dir. Colo. Psychopathic Hosp., Denver, 1924—; clin. prof. psychiatry U. Colo., Denver, 1924- 53, prof. emeritus, 1953—; pvt. practice psychiatry, 1953—. Served as col. M.C., AUS, neuropsychiat. cons. Eighth Service Command, Dallas, 1942-45, served in Pacific area, Office of Chief Surgeon, 1945-46. Dir. Div. Psychiat. Edn., Nat. Com. for Mental Hygiene, 1933-42; mem. Am. Bd. Psychiat. Examiners, 1933-41; chmn. sect. nervous and mental diseases, A.M.A., 1931-32; pres. Colo. Soc. for Mental Hygiene; chmn. Gov's. Com. Mental Health, Colo., 1960-61; mem. Ft. Logan Mental Health Center Adv. Com., 1964-65; mem. Am. Bd. of Psychiatry and Neurology, 1934-42; cons.-at-large USPHS; cons. Office of Surgeon Gen.; mem. Advisory bd. Med. Specialties, 1934-42, Council on Mental Health, Colo., 1957—; mem. com. on neuropsychiatry NRC. Recipient Distinguished Service award Am. Psychiat. Assn., 1966. Fellow Am. Psychiat. Assn. (council 1931-34, pres. Colo. dist. 1959-61, chmn. com. on psychiatry in med. edn.); mem. A.M.A., Colo. Med. Soc. (past chmn. com. mental health), Am. Neurol. Assn., Canadian Neuropsychiat. Assn. (hon.), Assn. Research Nervous and Mental Disease (pres. 1944), Central Psych. Assn. (pres. 1930), Grad. Med. Edn. (mem. commn. 1936-41), Royal Medico-Psychol. Assn. (corr.), Alpha Kappa Kappa, Sigma Xi, Alpha Omega Alpha. Republican. Episcopalian. Mason. Clubs: Mile High, Cactus, Denver Country. Co-author: (with E.A. Strecher) Practical Clinical Psychiatry, 1925, 8th edit., 1946; Psychiatry in Medical Education (with Charles A. Rymer), 1942; also articles in profl. jours. Mem. editorial bd. Am. Jour. Psychiatry, Current Med. Digest, Post-Grad. Medicine, Am. Practitioner, Diseases of Nervous System; contbg. editor Am. Jour. Med. Scis. Home: 1788 Glencoe St Denver CO 80220 Office: 1801 High St Denver CO 80218

EBAUGH, FRANKLIN GESSFORD, Jr., med. sch. dean; b. Phila., Dec. 25, 1921; s. Franklin G. and Dorothy (Reese) E.; B.A. magna cum laude, Dartmouth, 1944; M.D., Cornell U., 1946; m. Dorothy C.

Potter, June 18, 1971; children by previous marriage—Sandra D., Patricia S., Jeanette H., Mark F.; stepchildren—Chris H., Alison R., Bruce R. Potter. Intern, then resident N.Y. Hosp., 1946- 50; research fellow physiology Cornell U. Med. Coll., 1948; research fellow Evans Meml. Hosp., Boston U. Med. Sch., 1950-53; surgeon USPHS, 1953-55; asso. prof. clin. pathology, also asso. dir. labs. Dartmouth Med. Sch. and Mary Hitchcock Meml. Hosp., 1955-64; dean Boston U. Sch. Medicine, 1964-69; prof. medicine U. Utah, 1969—, dean Sch. Medicine, 1969—; mem. staff Evans Meml. Hosp., 1964-69; vis. physician Boston City Hosp., 1965-69; chmn. Boston VA Hosp. deans com., 1965-69. Cons. council health professions constrn. facilities USPHS, 1965-70; mem. study sect. tng. grants USPHS-NIH, 1960-64; mem. study sect. program projects grants NIH-Nat. Inst. Neurol. Diseases and Blindness, 1965-69. Mem. Am. Soc. Clin. Investigation, Am. Acad. Arts and Scis., A.C.P., Am. Coll. Pathologists, Am. Soc. Hematology (exec. dir. 1965-69), Am. Assn. Med. Coll. (exec. council 1967-69), Phi Beta Kappa, Sigma Xi, Alpha Omega Alpha, Delta Tau Delta, Nu Sigma Nu. Author articles, contbr. to books in field. Home: 2696 St Mary's Way Salt Lake City UT 84108

EBBITT, KENNETH COOPER, investment banker; b. Yonkers, N.Y., June 23, 1908; s. Nicholas John and Dora (Cooper) E.; student Manhattan Coll., 1927-30; m. Margaret Ann Quinn, May 10, 1936; children—Kenneth Cooper, Nicholas John II, Douglas James, Gordon L. J. Asso. Lehman Bros., 1933-45; partner Campbell Phelps & Co., N.Y.C., 1946-47; with Shelby Cullom Davis & Co., N.Y.C., 1948- -, now partner. Mem. N.Y. Stock Exchange. Mem. Municipal Forum N.Y., Municipal Bond Club N.Y., Bond Club N.J., Bankers Club Am. Club: Westchester Country. Home: 97 Park Av Bronxville NY 10708 Office: 116 John St New York City NY 10038

EBE, E. RICHARD, corp. exec.; b. Pitts., 1899; student Marston U.; m. Helen I. Ebe; 1 dau., Virginia (Mrs. Harrison Van Aken). Chmn. finance com. Erie Forge & Steel Corp. (Pa.); v.p., dir. Nat. Outlook Corp.; dir. Roblin Industries, Inc. Served in World War I. Clubs: LaCoquille (Palm Beach); Metropolitan (N.Y.C.). Home: 150 E 69th Street New York City NY 10021 Office: 60 E 42d St New York City NY 10017

EBEL, ALICE LUCINDA, educator; b. Orangeville, Ill., Feb. 14, 1905; d. Alfred Carl and Maude M. (Moore) Ebel; A.B., Heidelberg (O.) Coll., 1927; A.M., U. Chgo., 1931; postgrad. George Peabody Coll., 1940-41; Ph.D., U. Ill., 1960. Tchr. pub. high schs., Orangeville and Latham, Ill., 1927-34; mem. faculty Ill. State U., Normal, 1946—, prof. polit. sci., 1962—, head dept. 1966—. Mem. social studies curriculum com. Ill. Dept. Pub. Instrn., 1963-66; mem. exec. com. Ill. Center Edn. in Politics, 1962-65; mem. research staff Ill. Bd. Econ. Devel., 1962-63. Mem. Normal Library Bd., 1960-64; mem. McLean (Ill.) County Bd. Suprs., 1961—; mem. Gov.'s Ill. Constn. Research Group, 1969; mem. McLean County Regional Adv. Com. on Urban Area Govt., 1969—, Ill. Local Govt. Adv. Council, 1970—. Served to lt. USNR, 1943-45. Named Woman of Year, Bloomington-Normal Bus. and Profl. Women's Club, 1962. Mem. League of Women Voters (1st v.p. McLean County 1952-54), Am. Polit. Sci. Assn., Nat. Council Social Studies, N.E.A., Nat. Municipal League, Am. Assn. U. Profs. Republican. Presbyn. Mem. Order Eastern Star. Home: 204 Kingsley Street Normal IL 61761

EBEL, EDWIN WEYERS, food co. cons.; b. Bklyn., Sept. 28, 1901; s. Martin and Amelia (Weyers) E.; student pub. schs.; m. Virginia Arnold, Sept. 28, 1923 (div. 1930); 1 son, Edwin Clifton; m. 2d, Marie Natalie Foote, Apr. 12, 1940; children—Edwina, Peter Martin; m. 3d, Anne Benke, June 30, 1963. With Calkins & Holden, N.Y.C. 1919-35, Am. Weekly, 1935-39, Tracy Locke Dawson, 1940-42, Pedlar & Ryan, 1946-47; with Gen. Foods Corp., 1948- 66, v.p., dir. corporate marketing, 1955-56, v.p. advt. and consumer relations, 1956-57, v.p. advt. services, 1957-66; cons., 1966—. Bd. dirs. Acad. Television Arts and Scis. Found. Served with AUS, 1942-46. Decorated Legion of Merit; recipient ann. gold medal Internat. Radio and TV Soc., 1966. Mem. Assn. Nat. Advertisers (chmn., dir.), Advt. Council (past chmn., life dir.), Am. Marketing Soc. (founder mem.), Advt. Fedn. Am. (past dir.), Internat. Radio and TV Soc. (hon. life). Club: Union League (N.Y.C.). Home: 37 Pinecliff Rd Chappaqua NY 10514

EBEL, MARVIN EMERSON, educator, physicist; b. Waterloo, Ia., Sept. 23, 1930; s. Louis August and Emily (Mussett) E.; student Ia. State Tchrs. Coll., 1946-47; B.S., Ia. State Coll., 1950, M.S., 1952, Ph.D., 1953; m. Barbara Ann Schuck, July 22, 1960; children—Frederick Louis, Charles August, Elizabeth Ann, Katherine Susan. NSF postdoctoral fellow Inst. Theoretical Physics, Copenhagen, Denmark, 1953-54; mem. faculty Yale, 1954-57; mem. faculty U. Wis., 1957—, prof. physics, 1965—; cons. Los Alamos Sci. Lab., 1959—. Sloan fellow, 1957- 61. Fellow Am. Phys. Soc.; mem. Sigma Xi. Home: 910 Hampshire Pl Madison WI 53711

EBENSTEIN, WILLIAM, educator; b. Austria, May 11, 1910; s. Samuel and Gittel (Goldapper) E.; LL.D., U. Vienna, 1934; student U. London, 1934-36; Ph.D., U. Wis., 1938; m. Ruth Barbara Jaburek, Dec. 17, 1938; children—Philip James, Robert, Andrew, Alan. Came to U.S., 1936, naturalized, 1942. Fellow in econs. U. Wis., 1936-37, research asso. in law, 1937-38, instr. polit. sci., 1938-40, asst. prof. polit. sci., 1940-43, asso. prof., 1943-46; asso. prof. politics Princeton, 1946-49, prof. politics 1949-62, Ford fellow, 1953-54; prof. polit. sci. U. Cal. at Santa Barbara, 1962—. In charge UNESCO project Methods in Polit. Sci., Paris, 1948. Mem. Am. Polit. Sci. Assn. Author: Fascist Italy, 1939; Great Political Thinkers, 1951; Introduction To Political Philosophy, 1952; Modern Political Thought, 1954; Today's Isms, 1954; Political Thought in Perspective, 1957; Two Ways of Life: The Communist Challenge to Democracy, 1962; Totalitarianism: New Perspectives, 1962. Co-author: American Democracy in World Perspective, 1967; American Government in the Twentieth Century, 1968. Home: 2685 Glendessary Lane Santa Barbara CA 93105

EBER, GEORGE FRANCIS, architect; b. Budapest, Hungary, July 12, 1923; s. John and Elizabeth (Bensch) E.; architecture degree, Tech. U. Budapest, 1948; m. Dorothy Margaret Harley, June 8, 1958. Immigrated to Canada, 1950. Asso. firm John B. Parkin Assos., architects, Toronto, Ont., Can., 1952-61; pvt. practice architecture, Montreal, Que., Can., 1961—; prin. works include Netherlands pavilion Expo '67 (Reynolds award in architecture, 1968), U.S. pavilion Expo '67 (Spl. award excellence Am. Inst. Steel Constrn. 1968), Montreal Aquarium, Expo '67 (finalist Massey medals architecture 1970), Crichley-Waring residence (finalist Massey medals architecture 1961). Mem. Order St. John. Mem. Royal Archtl. Inst. Can., Que. Assn. Architects, Ont. Assn. Architects, Architects Assn. N.B., Assn. Canadian Indsl. Designers, Assn. Que. Indsl. Designers. Patentee cast aluminum curtain wall bldg. system. Clubs: University (Montreal); Royal Canadian Yacht (Toronto). Home: 1400 Pine Av W Montreal 109 Quebec Canada Office: 1420 Sherbrooke St W Montreal 109 Quebec Canada

EBER, GERHARD RICHARD, aero. research engr.; b. Leipzig, Germany, Aug. 7, 1907; s. August and Helene (Jacobi) E.; B.S. in Mech. Engring., Inst. Tech., Hannover, Germany, 1930, Dr. Ing., 1942; M.S., Inst. Tech., Dresden, Germany, 1933; m. Hildegard Rautenberg, Dec. 14, 1937; children—Ines, Karin, Petra. Came to U.S., 1946, naturalized, 1954. Instr. Inst. Tech., Danzig, Germany, 1934-37; chief thermodynamics br. Aerodynamic Inst., Army Research, Peenemuende, Germany, 1937-39, chief devel. div., 1939-45, cons. aeroballistics Naval Ordnance Lab., White Oak, Silver Spring, Md., 1946-50, chief aeroballistic div., 1951-53; adviser aeroballistics Air Force Missile Devel. Center, Holloman AFB, N.M., 1953-55, tech. dir. ballistic missile test, 1955-57, tech. dir. research and devel., 1957-60, tech. dir. research and devel. Directorate of Research Analysis, Air Force Office Sci. Research, 1960- 62, Office Research Analyses, 1962-70; tech. dir., Office Asst. for Study Support, Air Force Systems Command, Kirtland AFB, N.M., 1970—; design, constrn. aero. research, devel. facilities, exptl. investigation aerodynamic heating and supersonic heat transfer for guided missiles, Air Force System synthesis and analysis. Recipient meritorious civilian service award Naval Ordnance Lab., 1951; Outstanding Achievement award Office Aerospace Research. Asso. fellow Am. Inst. Aeros. and Astronautics; mem. A.A.A.S., Am. Ordnance Assn., Deutsche Gesellschaft fuer Luft and Raumfahrt (Germany), Sci. Research Soc. Am. Contbr. tech. publs. Home: 1812 Embudo Dr NE Albuquerque NM 87112 Office: Office of Asst for Study Support Kirtland AFB NM 87117

EBERHARD, JOHN PAUL, univ. dean; b. Chgo., Jan. 29, 1927; s. Carl A. and Clara (Schwolert) E.; B.S., U. Ill., 1952; student U. Louisville, 1947-48, Harvard, 1957-58; M.S., Mass. Inst. Tech., 1959; m. Lois Saxenmeyer, June 16, 1950; children—Carol Ann, John David, Richard Alan, Barbara Ann. Pres., Creative Bldgs., Inc., Urbana, Ill., 1952-58; dir. research Sheraton Corp., Boston, 1959-63; dep. dir. Inst. for Applied Tech., Washington, 1964-66, dir., 1966-68; dean Sch. Archtl. and Environmental Design, State U. N.Y. at Buffalo, 1968—; partner Eberhard & Murphy, Urbana, 1952-58; vis. lectr. Sch. Mgmt., Mass. Inst. Tech., 1959-63. Mem. U.S. nat. com. C.I.B., mem. adv. com. Ryerson Poly. Inst. Served with USMCR, 1945-47, USNR, 1947-49. Sloan fellow Mass. Inst. Tech., 1958. Mem. A.I.A., Urban Am., The Common Cause. Office: 2299 Elmwood Av Buffalo NY 14217

EBERHARD, WOLFRAM, sociologist; b. Potsdam, Germany, Mar. 17, 1909; s. Gustav B. and Gertrud (Muller) E.; Ph.D., U. Berlin, 1927-31; student Sch. Oriental Langs., Berlin, 1927-29; m. Alide Roemer, May 19, 1934; children—Rainer, Anatol. Asst., Far East dept. Mus. Anthropology, Berlin, 1929-34; field work in folklore, S.E. China and asst. prof. U. Peping, asst. prof. Nat. U. Peking, 1934-35; chief Far East dept. Mus. Anthropology, Leipzig, 1935-36; travels in Japan, Sachalin, S. China, 1937; prof. Chinese, U. Ankara (Turkey), 1937-48; lectr. dept. sociology U. Cal. at Berkeley, 1948-49, asso. prof., 1949-52, prof., 1952—. Adviser The Asia Found. Sociology Research Pakistan, 1956-58, Burma, 1958, China, Korea and Afghanistan, 1960. Fellow Baessler Found., Berlin, Germany, 1934, Moses Mendelsohn Found., N.Y.C., 1937, Guggenheim fellow, 1950. Mem. German and Bavarian acads. scis. (corr.). Author: Chinese Folk-Tales and Fairy- Tales, 1937; A History of China, 1960; Conquerors and Rulers, 1952; Chinese Festivals, 1952; Social Mobility in Traditional China, 1962; Folktales of China, 1965; Guilt and Sin in Traditional China, 1967; Settlement and Social Change in Asia, 1967; The Local Cultures of South and East China, 1968; articles and books in German, French and Turkish lang. Home: 604 Panoramic Way Berkeley CA 94704

EBERHARDT, HOMER CHRISTIAN, state judge; b. Banks County, Ga., Oct. 31, 1904; s. Linton W. and Josephine (Wheeler) E.; B.S. U. Ga., 1925; LL.B. Mercer U., 1927; m. Ruby Jones, Oct. 14, 1931 (dec. July 1958); children—Gretchen (Mrs. Wilby C. Coleman) (dec.), Jan (Mrs. Edward Sporledger); m. 2d, LaForrest Smith, Aug. 1, 1959. Admitted to Ga. Bar, 1927; practiced law, Valdosta, 1928-61, sr. partner Eberhardt, Franklin, Barham & Coleman, 1958-61; judge Ga. Ct. Appeals, 1961—. Mem. Ga. Bd. Bar Examiners, 1958-61; mem. rules com. Supreme Ct. Ga., 1957-61. Mem. Valdosta Bd. Edn., 1948-61. Trustee Mercer U. Fellow Am. Coll. Probate Counsel; mem. Am. (appellate judges conf.), Ga. (pres. 1960-61), Valdosta bar assns., So., Ga. Atlanta hist. socs., High Mus. Art. Methodist. Elk, Mason. Home: R F D 2 Lake Park GA 31636 also Peachtree Towers Atlanta GA 30308 Office: Judicial Bldg Capitol Sq Atlanta GA 30334

EBERHARDT, JOHN FOWLER, lawyer; b. Salina, Kan., Oct. 14, 1910; s. John J. and Mary Grace (Fowler) E.; A.B., U. Kan., 1932; LL.B., Harvard, 1935; m. Rebecca Jane Butts, Nov. 11, 1939; 1 dau., Gail. Admitted to Kan. bar, 1935, since practiced in Wichita; asso. Foulston, Siefkin, Powers & Eberhardt, and predecessors, 1935-38, partner, 1938—; gen. counsel The Coleman Co., Inc. Vice pres., dir. Kan. Found. for Blind, Inc., 1955—; chmn. bd. trustees Inst. Logopedics, Inc., Endowment Trust, 1958-68; trustee Epworth Assembly, 1960-66, Kan. U. Endowment Assn., 1970—; mem. adv. council Kan. Community Jr. Colls., 1965-68, Mid-Am. All-Indian Center, 1970—; bd. regents State Kan., 1965-68 chmn., 1967-68; chmn athletic bd. U. Kan., 1970—. Served to lt. USNR, 1943-46; PTO. Mem. Am., Kan. bar assns., Kan. U. Alumni Assn. (trustee 1963-65), Beta Theta Pi. Methodist. Rotarian. Asso. editor Kan. Bar Jour., 1939-41, editor in chief, 1942-43. Contbr. articles to profl. jours. Home: 1500 Spring Dr Wichita KS 67208 Office: Fourth Nat Bank Bldg Wichita KS 67202

EBERHART, BRUCE MACLEAN, educator; b. San Jose, Cal., Oct. 14, 1927; s. Roland F. and Janet (MacLean) E.; A.B., San Jose State Coll., 1950; Ph.D., Stanford, 1957; m. Geraldine P. Hubbard, June 24, 1951; children—Frederick, Linda, Janis. Instr., Princeton, 1956-58, asst. prof., 1958-62; prof., head dept. biology U. N.C., Greensboro, 1962—. Served with USNR, 1945-46. Mem. Genetics Soc. Am. Research on thiamine metabolism and cellulose decomposition. Home: 700 Sussex Ct Greensboro NC 27410

EBERHART, CONSTANCE, Richmond, ret. mezzo-soprano; b. York, Neb.; d. Oscar and Ellen Loretta McCurdy (Nelle Richmond) Eberhart; ed. pub. and high schs., Pitts., studied piano with Charles Wakefield Cadman, harmony with T. Carl Whitmer at Pa. Coll. for Women; studied voice with Sylvie Derdeyn McDermott and Arturo Papalardo; operatic study under Isaac Van Grove at Chgo. Mus. Coll. Sang in concert from early girlhood, chiefly with Charles Wakefield Cadman; operatic début as Dame Quickly, in Falstaff, at Eighth Street Theatre, Chgo., 1927; sang four seasons with Chgo. Civic Opera Co., 1927-30; 6 summers with Cin. Zoo Opera Co.; sang with Chgo. Civic Light Opera Co., spring 1930; toured four seasons as Witch in Hansel and Gretel; mem. Charles Wakefield Cadman Quartette, 1933-37; with Chgo. Grand Opera Co., 1934. Prin. roles: Frieka in Die Walküre; Laura in La Gioconda; Nancy in Martha; Ulrica in The Masked Ball; Suzuki in Madame Butterfly; Carmela in Jewels of the Madonna; Lady Pamela in Fra Diavolo; and many others. Tchr. voice, opera Conservatory Music, Kansas City, Mo., 1941- 46, 50-51; dir. summer opera Workshop Inspiration Point Fine Arts Colony, Eureka Springs, Ark., 1951-58. Mem. Theol. Soc., Nat. Opera Assn., Nat. Assn. Tchrs. Singing, N.Y. Singing Tchrs. Assn., Sigma Alpha Iota, Unitarian. Address: Hotel Wellington 7th Av at 55th St New York City NY 10019

EBERHART, MIGNON GOOD, author; b. Lincoln, Neb.; d. William Thomas and Margaret Hill (Bruffey) Good; student Neb. Wesleyan U., 1917-20, D.Litt. (hon.), 1935; m. Alanson C. Eberhart, Dec. 29, 1923 (div.), remarried, 1948; m. 2d, John P. Hazen Perry, 1946 (div.). Author: The Patient in Roof 18, 1929; numerous others, including among the latest: Five Passengers from Lisbon, 1946; Another Woman's House, 1947; House of Storm, 1949; Hunt With the Hounds, 1950; Never Look Back, 1951; Dead Man's Plans, 1952; Unknown Quantity, 1953; Man Missing, 1954; Post Mark Murder, 1956; Another Man's Murder, 1958; Melora, 1959; Jury of One, 1960; The Cup, the Blade or the Gun, 1961; Enemy in the House, 1962; Run Scared, 1963; Call After Midnight, 1964; R.S.V.P. Murder, 1965; Witness at Large, 1966; Woman on the Roof, 1967; Message from Hong Kong, 1968; El Rancho Rio, 1970; also writer short stories. Adv. faculty Famous Writers Sch. Mem. Soc. Midland Authors, P.E.N., Art Club. Club: Fortnightly (Chgo.). Contbr. mags. Office: care Brandt & Brandt 101 Park Av New York City NY 10017 ☆

EBERHART, RICHARD, poet; b. Austin, Minn., Apr. 5, 1904; s. Alpha LaRue and Lena (Lowenstein) E.; student U. Minn., 1922-23; A.B., Dartmouth, 1926, Litt.D. (hon.), 1954; B.A., Cambridge U., 1929, M.A., 1933; student grad. sch. arts and sci. Harvard, 1932-33; Litt.D. (hon.), Skidmore Coll., 1966, Coll. Wooster, 1969; m. Helen Elizabeth Butcher, Aug. 29, 1941; children—Richard Butcher, Margaret Ghormley. Tutor, son of King Prajadhipok of Siam, 1930-31; master English, St. Mark's Sch., Southborough, Mass., 1933-41; tchr. English, Cambridge Sch., Kendal Green, Mass., 1941-42; vis. prof. English, poet in residence U. Wash., 1952-53; prof. English, U. Conn., 1953-54; Wheaton vis. prof. English, poet in residence Wheaton Coll., 1954-55; resident fellow (prof.) in creative writing and Christian Gauss lectr. Princeton, 1955-56; prof. English, poet in residence Dartmouth Coll., 1956—, Class of 1925 prof., 1968-71, emeritus, 1970—; with Butcher Polish Co., Boston, 1946—, v.p., 1952, hon., 1958, bd. dirs.; mem. Yaddo Corp., 1955—, dir., 1964—. Cons. in poetry Library of Congress, 1959-61, hon. cons. in Am. letters, 1963-69, Phi Beta Kappa poet Tufts U., 1941, Brown U., 1957, Swarthmore Coll., Trinity Coll., Coll. William and Mary, 1963, U. N.H., 1964, Harvard U., 1967. Founder, first pres. The Poets Theater, Inc., Cambridge, Mass., 1951. Mem. adv. com. on arts Nat. Cultural Center, 1959—. Served from lt. to lt. comdr. USNR, 1942-46. Recipient Guarantors prize Poetry mag., 1946, Harriet Monroe Meml. prize, 1950; The Golden Rose, N.E. Poetry Soc., 1950; Shelley Meml. prize Poetry Soc. Am., 1951, $1000 grant from Nat. Inst. of Arts and Letters, 1955, Harriet Monroe poetry award, 1955, Bollingen prize, 1962; Pulitzer prize, 1966; Acad. Am. Poets fellow, 1969. Mem. Nat. Inst. Arts and Letters, Nat. Acad. Arts and Scis., Phi Beta Kappa (hon.), Alpha Delta Phi. Episcopalian. Clubs: Century (N.Y.); Buck Harbor Yacht (Me.). Author: A Bravery of Earth, 1930; Reading the Spirit, 1936-37; Song and Idea, 1940, 42; Poems New and Selected, 1944; Burr Oaks, 1947; Brotherhood of Men, 1949; An Herb Basket, 1950; Selected Poems, 1951; Undercliff: Poems, 1946-53; Great Praises, 1957; Collected Poems, 1930-60, 1960; Collected Verse Plays, 1962; The Quarry, 1964; Selected Poems, 1965; Thirty One Sonnets, 1967; Shifts of Being, 1968; The Visionary Farms (verse drama) produced Fogg Art Mus., 1952, The Playhouse, U. Wash., 1953, Inst. Contemp. Arts, Washington, 1957. Editor: War and the Poet (with Selden Rodman), 1945. Recording: Richard Eberhart Reading his Poetry, 1968. Home: 5 Webster Terrace Hanover NH 03755

EBERHARTER, FRANK JEROME, lawyer; b. Pitts., Nov. 25, 1914; s. Frank Simon and Florence (Hoffman) E.; A.B., U. Wash., 1937, LL.B., 1939; m. Mary Barbarus, June 21, 1941; children—Denis J. (dec. Jan. 1967), David M. Admitted to Wash. bar, 1939, since practiced in Seattle; partner firm Eberharter & Freedman; municipal judge pro-tem, 1952-53. Arbitrator, Am. Arbitration Assn.; moderator Thursday Forum, KCTS TV, U. Wash. Mem. citizens adv. council Wash. Law Enforcement Assn. Trustee Municipal League, Seattle-King County. Served to 1st lt. AUS, 1943-46. Mem. Wash. State (bd. govs. 1965-67), Am. (ho. of dels.), Seattle-King County (trustee 1953-56, pres. 1959-60, chmn. jud. discipline com., jud. discipline com.) bar assns., Am. Judicature Soc., Internat. Platform Assn. Home: 5730 S Upland Road Seattle WA 98118 Office: Hoge Bldg Seattle WA 98104

EBERLE, AUGUST WILLIAM, educator; b. Emporia, Kan., June 8, 1916; s. Carl and Minnie Ernestine (Merker) E.; B.S., Kan. State Tchrs. Coll., 1936, M.S., 1940; Ph.D., U. Wis., 1953; m. Elizabeth Ann Bush, July 31, 1940. Tchr. high sch., Pleasanton, Kan., 1936-40; prin. high sch., Dwight, Kan., 1940-41; tchr. Pratt High Sch. and Jr. Coll., 1941-42, asst. dean Pratt Jr. Coll., 1945-50; instr. U. Wis., 1950-52; asst. prof. Ind. U., 1952-55, asso prof., 1955-57, prof., Ind. U., Bloomington 1966—, chmn. dept. higher edn.; provost U. Chattanooga, 1957-65; chief ednl. services Oak Ridge Asso. Univs., 1965-66; dir., moderator weekly pub. affairs TV program, 1961-65. First chmn. Chattanooga-Hamilton Co. Health Dept. Adv. Com., 1964; 1st pres. Chattanooga-Hamilton Co. Community Action Program for Econ. Opportunity, 1965. Served with USAAF, 1942-45. Mem. N.E.A., Nat. Soc. Study Edn., Assn. Higher Edn., Ind. Tchrs. Assn. (chmn. higher edn. dept. 1970), Blue Key, Kappa Delta Pi, Phi Delta Kappa (mem. internat. commn. on higher edn. 1968-70), Alpha Phi Omega, Alpha Soc. Home: 3925 Sugar Lane Bloomington IN 47401

EBERLE, EDWARD RADCLIFFE, utility exec.; b. Hartford, Conn., June 21, 1909; s. Edward and Mabel (Beers) E.; B.S. in Elec. Engring., Yale, 1931; M.B.A., Harvard, 1933; m. Jane Austin Fields, Oct. 15, 1937; children—Patricia J. (Mrs. Robert M. Crunden), William E. With Pub. Service Electric and Gas Co., Newark, 1933—, gen. mgr., 1956-61, v.p. charge services, 1962-66, exec. v.p., 1966-68, pres., 1968—, chief exec. officer, 1971—, also dir.; dir. Pub. Service Transport Co., 1st Jersey Nat. Bank, Jersey City, Fireman's Ins. Co., Newark. Chmn. comml. div. United Appeals-A.R.C., Newark, 1960-61; gen. chmn. Newark United Appeals, 1965. Commr., chmn. Newark Parking Authority. Trustee Hosp. Service Plan N.J., Robert Treat Council Boy Scouts Am., Hosp. Center, Orange, Newark Mus. Mem. N.J. Utilities Assn. (pres. 1964-66), Am. (nat. chmn. accounting sect. 1955-56, mem. mgmt. com. gen. mgmt. sect.; award Order Accounting Merit 1952, dir.), N.J. gas assns., Edison Electric Inst. (dir.), Greater Newark C. of C. (dir.), Am. Mgmt. Assn., N.J. C. of C., Nat. Conf. Christians and Jews (N.J. bd. dirs.). Episcopalian (vestry). Clubs: Rock Spring Country (West Orange, N.J.); Essex (Newark). Home: 195 Midland Av Montclair NJ Office: 80 Park Pl Newark 1 NJ

EBERLE, GERALD JOSEPH, educator; b. Milw., Dec. 6, 1912; s. Joseph Louis and Amanda (Hauser) E.; A.B., St. Norbert Coll., 1934; M.A., U. Wis., 1936, Ph.D., 1945; m. Marjorie Marie Forstall, Aug. 27, 1941; children—Kathryn (Mrs. John Kevin Wildgen), Thomas Forstall, Michael Gerald. Mem. faculty Loyola U., New Orleans, 1936-66, asso. prof. English, 1945-49, prof., 1949-66, also chmn. dept., 1959-66; prof., dir. library La. State U. at New Orleans, 1966—; research fellow Folger Shakespeare Library, Washington, 1946-47. Mem. Am. Library Assn., London Bibliographical Soc., Mod. Lang. Assn. Am., Va. Bibliographical Soc., Democrat. Roman Catholic. Editor: Loyola University Studies in the Humanities, 1962. Home: 714 Marguerite Rd Metairie LA 70003 Office: La State U New Orleans LA 70122

EBERLE, IRMENGARDE, author; b. San Antonio, Nov. 11, 1898; d. Marcellus and Louise (Perlitz) Eberle; grad. Tex. State Coll. for Women; art course; m. 2d, Arnold W. Koehler, Oct. 4, 1953; 1 son (by previous marriage). Began as designer drapery fabrics, N.Y.C., 1920; then went into editorial work; editor Excella Mag., Pictorial Rev. Co., 1924-26; editor N.Y. Theatre Programs, 1927-28; contbg. editor N.Y. Woman (weekly), 1937-38; reviewer for Herald Tribune's children's book dept., summer 1948. Mem. Authors' League Am., Authors Guild (past sec., mem. council, an originator children's book sect.). Author numerous books, 1937—, the latest: Modern Medical Discoveries, 1948; Listen to the Mocking Bird, 1949; The Right Dog for Joe, 1949; Lorie, 1950; Big Family of Peoples, 1952; Secrets and Surprises (2d grade reader); Lone Star Fight (Tex. Inst. Letters award 1954), 1954; Evie and the Wonderful Kangaroo, 1955; Come Be My Friend, 1956; Evie and Cookie, 1957; Favorite Place (Jr. Lit. Guild selection), 1957; Rosemary's Secret, 1958; Robins on the Window Sill, 1958; Grasses, 1960; Johnny's Island Ark, 1960; Fawn in the Woods, 1961; Benjamin Franklin, Man of Science, 1961; Apple Orchard, 1962; Edward Jenner and Smallpox Vaccination, 1962; The New World of Glass, 1963; The Raccoon's Young Ones, 1963; The New World of Fabrics, 1964; Pete and the Mouse, 1964; A Chipmunk Lives Here (Jr. Lit. Guild selection), 1966; Bears Live Here, 1966; Foxes Live Here, 1966; The New World of Rubber, 1966; Koalas Live Here, 1967; The Dog Who Came to Visit, 1968; Mustang of the Prairie, 1968; Night Rovers; 1969, New World of Paper, 1969; Elephants Live Here, 1970; Moose Live Here, 1971; Mountain Holiday, 1971. Guest columnist, F.P.A.'s Conning Tower. Editor: (booklet) The United Nations and Writing for the Future Generation. Contbr. to Child Life, Story Parade, Woman's Home Companion, This Week, Seventeen, others. Home: 400 E 58th Street New York City NY 10022

EBERLE, JOSEF, editor; b. Rottenburg, Germany, Sept. 8, 1901; s. Josef and Berta (Entress) E.; student Pro-Gymnasium, Rottenburg, 1911-17; Dr. Phil. honoris causa, U. Tubingen; m. Else Lemberger, 1929. Editor, author, dir. sec. Süddeutscher Rundfunk, Stuttgart, Germany, 1927-33; staff Consul Gen. U.S., Stuttgart, 1936-41; founder, editor Stuttgart Zeitung, 1945-71. Decorated Grand Cross Merit of German Republic. Mem. Soc. Schiller (v.p. 1954—), Galerieverein (pres. 1957-71). Author: (under pseudonym Sebastian Blau) Swabian Poetry; Stunden mit Ovid, 1959; Sal Niger, 1963; Lateinische Nächte, 1966; Echo perennis, 1970. Home: 9 Rosengartenstrasse Stuttgart-Frauenkopf Federal Republic of Germany Office: Stuttgarter Zeitung 61 Eberhardstrasse Stuttgart Federal Republic of Germany

EBERLE, ROBERT WILLIAM, restaurant exec.; b. Albuquerque, Aug. 18, 1931; s. James Herman and Belt Ann (Vencil) E.; B.A., U. So. Cal., 1957, also postgrad.; m. Eileen T. Samuelson, Sept. 8, 1957; children—Janine, Michelle. Vice pres. Dempsey-Tegeler & Co., Inc., Los Angeles, 1960-66; exec. v.p., treas., dir. Denny's Restaurants, Inc., La Mirada, Cal., 1966—. Served with USNR, 1952-54. Mem. U. So. Cal. Commerce Assos., Delta Tau Delta. Home: 1047 Oak Grove Pl San Marino CA 91108 Office: 14256 E Firestone Blvd La Mirada CA 90638

EBERLE, WILLIAM DENMAN, bldg. and indsl. products, security systems mfg. co. exec.; b. Boise, Ida., June 5, 1923; s. J. Louis and Clare (Holcomb) E.; B.A., Stanford, 1945; M.B.A., Harvard, 1947, LL.B., 1949; m. Jean Cilista Quick, Sept. 20, 1947; children—Jeffrey Louis, William David, Francis Quick, Cilista Clare. Admitted to Ida. bar, 1950; partner firm Richards, Haga & Eberle, Boise, 1950-60; Mem. Ida. Ho. of Reps. from Ada County, 1953-63, majority leader, 1957, minority leader, 1959, speaker, 1961; dir. Boise Cascade Corp., 1952-68, sec., 1960-65, v.p., 1961-66; chmn., dir. Am. Standard, Inc., N.Y.C.; dir. Atlantic Group of Ins. Cos., Hewlett- Packard Co., PPG Industries Inc., Fed. Res. Bank N.Y., U.S. Natural Resources. Chmn. Ida. Republican Finance Com., 1961-66; mem. Nat. Rep. Finance Com., 1961-66. Trustee Stanford U., African-Am. Inst., Com. for Econ. Devel.; bd. dirs. Nat. Indsl. Conf. Bd.; co-chmn. Nat. Urban Coalition, Common Cause; mem. adv. bd. Stanford Grad. Sch. Bus. Served to lt. USNR, 1944-46. Named Man of Year, Boise Jr. C. of C., 1959. Mem. Council Fgn. Relations, Am., Ida. bar assns. Episcopalian. Home: 85 Club Rd Riverside CT 06878 Office: 40 W 40th St New York City NY 10018

EBERLY, ROBERT EDWARD, natural gas co. exec.; b. Greensboro, Pa., July 14, 1918; s. Orville S. and Ruth (Moore) E.; B.A. in Chemistry, Pa. State U., 1939; m. Elizabeth Mitchell, Nov. 9, 1940; children—Robert E., Paul O. Chemist, Navy Dept., Pitts., 1940-45; pres. Eberly Natural Gas Co., Uniontown, Pa., 1945—; gen mgr. William E. Snee & Orville Eberly, Oil and Gas Producers, Uniontown, Pa., since 19—; dir., vice chmn. bd. Gallatin Nat. Bank, Uniontown; pres. GNB Corp., 1970—; dir. Laurel Rest Home, Inc., Uniontown, 1966—. Pres. United Fund Greater Uniontown, 1956-58; mem. zoning commn. City Uniontown, 1956—, treas., mem. adv. bd. Pa. State U. at Fayette, 1966—. Bd. dirs. Indsl Fund Greater Uniontown, Fayette Heritage, Inc., Uniontown, Fayette County Devel. Council, Pa. State U. Found., Isaac Walton League; pres. bd. trustees Uniontown Hosp. Assn., 1968-70. Recipient Rockwell Recognition award Rockwell Mfg. Co., 1970. Mem. C. of C. Uniontown (bd. dirs.; named Man of Year 1968), Pitts. Geol. Soc., Independent Petroleum Assn., Ohio Oil and Gas Assn., Okla. Independent Petroleum Assn. Mason, Rotarian. Home: 56 Charles St Uniontown PA 15401 Office: PO Box 2023 Uniontown PA 15401

EBERMAN, PAUL WILMOT, coll. dean; b. Centerville, Pa., July 5, 1917; s. Gregg Franklin and Alta Alma (Allison) E.; B.S., N.Y. State Coll. Tchrs., Buffalo, 1938; M.A., N.Y.U., 1942; Ph.D., U. Chgo., 1950; summer student Syracuse U., 1941, Cornell U., 1940; children—Paul Wilmot, Kirk Galliford, Margo Ann, Karen Marie; m. 2d, Nina Renee Nikolenko, Jan. 19, 1968. Tchr. math. Bergen (N.Y.) Consol. Sch., 1938-39, R.K. Toaz Jr. High Sch., Huntington, N.Y., 1939-43; instr. N.Y. State Coll. Tchrs., Buffalo, 1946- 48; instr., teaching fellow U. Chgo., 1948-49; mem. faculty U. Wis., 1949-63, prof. edn., 1956-63, asso. dean Sch. Edn., 1958-63, dir. elementary lab. sch., 1949-51; dean Coll. Edn., Temple U., Phila., 1963—; vis. summer prof. Emory U., 1956, U. Chgo., 1958, U. Hawaii, 1961. Team leader U. Wis. tchr. edn. project, N. Nigeria for AID, 1962-63. Served to lt. Air Corps, USNR, 1943-46. Mem. Nat., Pa. edn. assns., Higher Edn. Assn., Am. Ednl. Research Assn., Am. Assn. Sch. Adminstrs., Phi Delta Kappa, Kappa Delta Pi, Kappa Kappa Kappa. Contbr. articles to profl. jours., author reports. Co-author: The Elementary School, 1956. Home: 626 Pine St Philadelphia PA 19106

EBERS, EARLE STREET, mfg. chemist; b. Saskatchewan, Can., May 20, 1910; s. Herman and Maud (Street) E.; B.S., Dalhousie U., Halifax, N.S., 1931; M.S., Harvard, 1933, Ph.D., 1936; Royal Soc. fellow, Ohio State U., 1936-37; m. Eleanor MacKay, Mar. 7, 1932; children—James Robert, Jean. With U.S. Rubber Co., 1937-70, devel. mgr. Naugatuck Chem. div., 1953-55, gen. sales mgr., 1955, asst. gen. mgr., 1956-57, v.p., gen. mgr., 1957-60, group v.p. charge polymer, fibre. chem. operations, 1960-70; divisional pres. Uniroyal Devel. Co., 1970—; pres., dir. Monochem, Inc. Mem. Mfg. Chemists Assn. (past dir.), Am. Chem. Soc., Soc. Plastics Industry, Internat. Inst. Synthetic Rubber Producers (past pres., dir.), Conglist. (past chmn. exec. com.). Club: Lions. Home: Calhoun St Washington Depot CT 06794 Office: Middlebury CT 06749

EBERSOLD, CHARLES WALDEMAR, Jr., communications exec.; b. Columbus, O., Dec. 11, 1913; s. Charles Waldemar and Hazel (Hudson) E.; A.B., Ohio State U., 1935, J.D. summa cum laude, 1938; m. Florence Whitcomb, Mar. 14, 1941. Mgr., Ill. Bell Telephone Co., Chgo., 1938-43, 46-47, gen. comml. mgr., 1954-57, gen. mgr. marketing, 1960-63, asst. to pres., 1963-71, sec., 1966-71, v.p. market planning, 1971—; engr. Am. Tel. & Tel. Co., N.Y.C., 1947-51, asst. v.p., 1958-60; gen. comml. supr. Wis. Telephone Co., Milw., 1951-53. Ill. crusade chmn. Am. Cancer Soc., 1961, v.p. Ill. div., 1963-67, dir., mem. exec. com., 1962—, vice-chmn. bd., 1967-69, chmn. bd., 1969—, nat. dir., 1966—, recipient Nat.-Div. award, 1966; bd. dirs. Welfare Council Met. Chgo., 1966—, v.p., 1967- 69; dir., mem. exec. com., sec. Chgo. South Loop Improvement Project, 1968—; mem. Chgo. Commn. on Human Relations, 1953-54, Nat. Commn. on Community Health Services, 1965-66, U. Chgo. Council Med. and Biol. Research, 1964-68; mem. exec. bd. Chgo. Area council Boy Scouts Am., 1967-68. Bd. dirs. Hosp. Service Corp., 1969—. Served to capt. Signal Corps, AUS, 1943-46. Decorated Army Commendation medal. Mem. Navy League U.S. (dir. Chgo. council 1965-67), Ill. State C. of C., Chgo. Assn. Commerce and Industry, Am. Legion, Newcomen Soc. N.Am., Ohio State U. Alumni Assn. (Nat. bd. dirs. 1965-70), Order of Coif, Delta Tau Delta. Republican. Conglist. Clubs: President's (dir., mem. exec. com. 1964-65 Ohio State U.); Economic, Executive, Union League (bd. dirs. 1965-70, v.p. 1968-69; bd. dirs. Civic and Arts Found. 1964—; trustee Found. for Boys Clubs 1965—) (Chgo.); Skokie Country (pres. 1967) (Glencoe, Ill.); Sky-Line. Home: 610 5th St Wilmette IL 60091 Office: Ill Bell Telephone Co 225 W Randolph St Chicago IL 60606

EBERSOLE, MARK CHESTER, univ. dean; b. Hershey, Pa., Nov. 3, 1921; s. Benjamin W.S. and Mary (Patrick) E.; B.S., Elizabethtown (Pa.) Coll., 1943, LL.D., 1969; B.D., Crozer Theol. Sem., 1946; M.A., U. Pa., 1948; Ph.D., Columbia, 1952; m. Dorothy Baugher, June 26, 1943; children—Philip B., Stephen B. UNRRA relief adminstr., Europe, 1946-47; asst. prof. religion and philosophy Elmira Coll., 1952-53; faculty Bucknell U., 1953-69, prof. religion, chmn. dept., chaplain of univ., 1958-61, asst. dean univ., 1961, dean Coll. Arts and Scis., 1961-62, v.p. acad. affairs, 1961-68, univ. provost, 1968-69; project specialist, spl. projects in edn. Ford Found., 1967-69, program adviser, 1969-71; dean Grad. Sch., Temple U., 1971—. J.P. Crozer Found. fellow, 1949-51. Mem. Delta Upsilon, Omicron Delta Kappa, Phi Eta Sigma. Author: Christian Faith and Man's Religion, 1961; also articles. Home: 256 Shady Brook Lane Princeton NJ 08540

EBERSTADT, RUDOLPH, Jr., indsl. mfg. co. exec.; b. Orange, N.J., Dec. 8, 1923; s. Rudolph and Alberta Virginia (Webb) E.; grad. Newark Acad., 1941; student Princeton, 1941-42, 45-46; m. Theodora Andrews, July 13, 1946; children—Otis Webb Davey (foster son), Susan Page, Rudolph III. Sales trainee Fawick Airflex Co., Cleve., 1946-47; development engr. Geometric Stamping Co., Cleve., 1947-48; sales engr. Cuyahoga Spring Co., Cleve., 1948-50, Jones & Logan, Detroit, 1950-52; mfrs. rep. Jones & Eberstadt, Detroit, 1952-53, Esler-Eberstadt, 1953-57; with Republic Indsl. Corp., N.Y.C., 1957-67, pres., chief exec. officer, 1961-67, pres., chief exec. officer Vare Corp., 1968-69; pres., chief exec. officer, dir. Microdot Inc., 1969—; pres., dir. Adams Supply Co., Aircraft Threaded Products, Inc., Clyde Iron Works, Inc., Drawn Metal Products Co., Elicon Corbin Inc., Elicon Detroit Inc., Elicon Riverton Inc., Everlock Charlotte Inc., Everlock Chgo. Inc., Kaynar Mfg. Co., Inc., Microdot Mich., Meyers Trims, Inc., Prestole Everlock Can. Ltd., Richmond Steel Co., Selastomer Chgo. Inc., Selastomer Detroit Inc., Toledo Plastics Co., Uni-Grip Products Corp., Varec, Inc., Wiley Mfg. Co. Home: Deer Park Rd New Canaan CT 06840 Office: 633 3d Av New York City NY 10023

EBERT, CHARLES H.V., educator; b. Hamburg, Germany, June 23, 1924 (parents Am. citizens); s. Carl A. and Clara (Hasenclever) E.; B.A., U. N.C., 1951, M.A., 1953, Ph.D., 1957; m. Ilse E. Pohle, Mar. 1, 1949; 1 dau., Monica Doris. Grad. teaching asst. U. N.C., 1951-54; instr. geology and geography U. Buffalo, 1954-56; asst. prof. geography State U. N.Y. at Buffalo, 1956-59, asso. prof., 1959-63, prof., 1963—, chmn. dept., 1963-71, dean div. undergrad. studies, 1971—. Served with AUS, 1946-50. Mem. Assn. Am. Geographers, Am. Geog. Soc., Soil Sci. Soc. Am., Am. Soc. Agronomy, Internat. Soil Sci. Soc. Home: 78 Sunset Terrace Tonawanda NY 14150

EBERT, EDGAR FRAZIER, educator; b. Ft. Collins, Colo., July 6, 1908; s. Cornelius Joseph and May (Frazier) E.; D.V.M., Colo. A. and M. Coll., 1931; m. Hazel Christine Jenkins, May 22, 1933. Practice of vet. medicine, Kansas City, Mo., 1931-42, 46-50; prof. dept. vet. medicine and surgery U. Mo., 1950- -, past chmn. dept.; dir. Veterinary Clinics. Served as maj. Vet. Corps, U.S. Army, 1942-46. Named Veterinarian of Year Mo. Vet. Med. Assn., 1966. Mem. Alpha Psi, Gamma Sigma Delta, Phi Kappa Phi, Phi Zeta. Club: Columbia Cosmopolitan Internat. (pres. 1955-56, gov. Mo.-Kan. fedn. 1955- 56, named Cosmopolitan of Year 1965). Home: Rocheport MD 65279 Office: University of Mo Columbia MO 65201

EBERT, EDMUND FRANCIS, banker; b. N.Y.C., Aug. 11, 1911; s. Samuel Harvey and Emily Grace (Cash) E.; student N.Y. U., 1930-32, 41; m. Lathelia Marie Keesey, Oct. 22, 1938; children—Beth Lynn (dec.), Douglas Edmund, Joan Marie. Began as messenger Bankers Trust Co. of N.Y., 1928, dept. head, 1934-39, field rep., 1939-42, asst. treas., 1942-46, asst. v.p., 1946-48, v.p., 1948-61, sr. v.p., 1961-70, exec. v.p., 1970—; v.p., dir. Interstate Color Co., Inc., 1936-51. Councilman Town of New Castle, N.Y., 1959-63, chmn. bd. ethics, 1970—). Commd. lt. (j.g.) S.C., USN, 1944, apptd. dep. fiscal dir., 1945; disch. as lt., 1946; lt. res., 1945-52. Bd. dirs., treas. Ednl. Found. for Fashion Industries. Mem. Am. Bankers Assn. (chmn. credit policy com.), Acad. Polit. Sci., Downtown Lower Manhattan Assn. (dir.). Conglist. Clubs: Union League (N.Y.C.); Mt. Kisco Country (pres. 1956, 57), Bankers of N.Y. Inc.; Seaview Country; Economic; Board Room. Home: 15 Bradley Farms Chappaqua NY 10514 Office: 280 Park Av New York City NY 10017

EBERT, ELOISE QUEEN, state librarian; b. Scottsbluff, Neb., Aug. 17, 1911; d. Ernest William and Daisy (Gamble) Ebert; B.S., U. Minn., 1936; M.S., U. Ill., 1957. Asst. librarian, Council Bluffs, Ia., 1931-35; librarian, Sauk Centre, Minn., 1936-37, Falls City, Neb., 1937-42; post librarian, Ft. Warren, Wyo., 1942-45; army librarian European Command, 1945-47, chief librarian, 1947-49; adminstrv. asst. Ore. State Library, 1949-58, state librarian, 1959—. Sr. trustee Salem Art Assn.; bd. dirs. Pacific Northwest Bibliographic Center. Mem. Am., Ore. (exec. bd.), Pacific N.W. (pres. 1961-62) library assns., Am. Library Trustee Assn. (2d v.p. 1970-71), Ore. Hist. Soc. (dir.), Am. Assn. U. Women, League Women Voters, Am. Assn. State Libraries (pres. 1963-64), Beta Phi Mu, Theta Alpha Phi, Delta Kappa Gamma (hon.). Named Woman of Achievement Portland chpt. Theta Sigma Phi, 1965. Home: 1100 Chemeketa St Salem Or 97301 Office: Oregon State Library Salem Or 97301

EBERT, JAMES DAVID, research biologist; b. Bentleyville, Pa., Dec. 11, 1921; s. Alva Charles and Anna Frances (Brundege) E.; A.B., Washington and Jefferson Coll., 1942; Ph.D., Johns Hopkins, 1950; m. Alma Christine Goodwin, Apr. 19, 1946; children—Frances Diane, David Brian, Rebecca Susan. Jr. instr. biology Johns Hopkins, 1946-49, Adam T. Bruce fellow biology, 1949-50, hon. prof. biology, 1956—, hon. prof. embryology Sch. Medicine, 1956—; instr. biology Mass. Inst. Tech., 1950-51; asst. prof. zoology Ind. U., 1951-54, asso. prof., 1954-56, Patten vis. prof., 1963; dir. dept. embryology Carnegie Instn. of Washington, 1956—; vis. scientist med. dept. Brookhaven Nat. Lab., 1953-54; Philips vis. prof. Haverford Coll., 1961; instr. in charge embryology tng. program Marine Biol. Lab., summers 1962-66, trustee, 1964—, dir., 1970—; mem. Commn. on undergrad. Edn. in Biol. Scis., 1963-66; mem. vis. com. for biol. and phys. scis. Western Res. U., 1964-68. Mem. panels on morphogenesis and biology of neoplasia of com. on growth NRC, 1954-56; mem. adv. panel on genetic and developmental biology NSF, 1955-56, mem. divisional com. for biology and medicine, 1962-66, mem. univ. sci. devel. panel, 1965-70, adv. com. for instl. devel., 1970—; mem. panel basic biol. research in aging Am. Inst. Biol. Sci., 1957-60; mem. panel on cell biology NIH, USPHS, 1958-62, mem. child health and human devel. tng. com., 1963-66, mem. bd. sci. counselors Nat. Cancer Inst. Mem. vis. com. to dept. biology Mass. Inst. Tech., 1959-68, mem. vis. com. biology Harvard, 1969—, Princeton, 1970—. Served as lt. USNR, 1942-46. Decorated Purple Heart. Fellow A.A.A.S. (v.p. med. scis. 1964—), Am. Acad. Arts and Scis., Internat. Inst. Embryology; mem. Nat. Acad. Scis., Royal Soc. Medicine London (affiliate), Am. Inst. Biol. Scis. (pres. 1963), Am. Soc. Naturalists, Am. Soc. Zoologists (pres. 1970), N.Y. Acad. Scis., Soc. Study Growth and Devel. (pres. 1957-58), Am. Assn. Anatomists, Phi Beta Kappa, Sigma Xi, Phi Sigma. Author: (with others) The Chick Embryo in Biological Research, 1952; Molecular Events in Differentiation Related to Specificity of Cell Type, 1955; Aspects of Synthesis and Order in Growth, 1955; Interacting Systems in Development, 2d edit., 1970. Contbr. to profl. jours. Mem. editorial bd. Jour. Embryology and Exptl. Morphology, Abstracts of Human Developmental Biology; editor Devel. Biology, Biosci., Internat. Jour. Cancer, Quar. Rev. Biology. Home: 6728 Glenkirk Road Baltimore MD 21239 Office: 115 W University Pkwy Baltimore MD 21210

EBERT, LEONARD TODD, banker; b. Collingswood, N.J., Apr. 17, 1920; s. Raymond M. and Ethel (Todd) E.; diploma Gibson Inst., 1949; diploma Grad. Sch. Banking, Rutgers U., 1954; m. Shirley R. Pfeil, June 22, 1963; children—Douglas, Cynthia, Todd. With Phila. Sav. Fund Soc., 1937—, v.p., controller, 1955-67, sr. v.p., 1967-71; vice chmn. 19771—. Bd. dirs. Med. Coll. Pa. Served with AUS, 1942-45: CBI. Mem. Financial Execs. Inst. (bd. dirs.). Home: 313 Springhouse Lane Moorestown NJ 08057 Office: 1212 Market St Philadelphia PA 19107

EBERT, LYNN JOHN, educator; b. Sandusky, O., Apr. 17, 1920; s. Harry and Wilma (Yerges) E.; B.S. in Metall. Engring., Case Inst. Tech., 1941, M.S., 1943, Ph.D., 1954; m. Mary Kathryn Schmitt, May 22, 1943; children—Mary Lynne (Mrs. James Pesto), Patricia Marie, Richard John, Timothy Edward. From research asst. to sr. research asso. Case Inst. Tech., 1941-53, mem. faculty, 1953—, prof. metallurgy, 1964—, acting head dept., 1965-66; cons. in field, 1947—. Mem. Cleve. Tech. Socs. Council (bd. govs. 1958- 63), Am. Soc. Metals (pres. Cleve. 1947-68, mem. nat. com. 1963-68), Am. Inst. Mining and Metall. Engring. (pres. Cleve. 1965-66, mem. nat. com. 1961-64), Sigma Xi, Tau Beta Pi, Phi Kappa. Republican. Roman Catholic. Author: Aluminum Casting Alloys, 1948; Significant Properties of Cold Worked Steels, 1955; also articles. Home: 104 E 197th St Euclid OH 44119 Office: University Circle 10900 Euclid Av Cleveland OH 44106

EBERT, ROBERT ALVIN, airlines co. exec.; b. Mpls., Oct. 13, 1915; s. Alvin C. and Caroline (Reutelsterz) B.; student U. Minn., 1933-35; LL.B. cum laude, St. Paul Coll. Law, 1939; m. Gertrude M. O'Leary, Feb. 8, 1947; children—Kathryn Anne, Richard F. Admitted to Minn. bar, 1939, and practiced in Brainerd until 1942; with Immigration and Naturalization Service, Dept. Justice, 1942-43; with Northwest Airlines, Inc., 1943—, v.p. personnel, 1960—. Mem. Minn., Ramsey County bar assns. Home: 534 S Mississippi River Blvd Saint Paul MN 55116 Office: Mpls-Saint Paul Internat Airport Saint Paul MN 55111

EBERT, ROBERT HIGGINS, physician, educator; b. Mpls., Sept. 10, 1914; s. Michael and Lilian (Gilbertson) E.; B.S., U. Chgo., 1936, M.D., 1942; D.Phil., Oxford U., 1939; A.M. (hon.), Harvard, 1964; D.Sc. (hon.), Northeastern U., 1968, U. Md., 1970; LL.D., U. Toronto, 1970; m. Emily Hirsch, June 17, 1939; children—John, Elizabeth (Mrs. W. W. Schmidt-Nowara), Thomas. Intern, asst. resident medicine Boston City Hosp., 1942-44; successively asst., instr., asst. prof., asso. prof. dept. medicine U. Chgo., 1946-55, prof., 1955-56; Hanna Payne prof. medicine Western Res. U., 1956- 58, John H. Hord prof. medicine, 1958-64; dir. medicine Univ. Hosps., 1956-64; Jackson prof. clin. medicine Harvard, 1964-65, prof. medicine, 1965—, dean Med. Sch., 1965—, dean faculty of medicine, 1965—, head Harvard dept. medicine Mass. Gen. Hosp., 1964-65; pres. Harvard Med. Center, 1965—; pres. Harvard Community Health Plan, 1968—. Trustee Rockefeller Found., 1966—, Population Council, 1966—, Dermatology Found. 1966—; mem. tech. bd. Milbank Meml. Fund, 1966—; mem. exec. com. Radcliffe Inst., 1966—; mem. Nat. Adv. Commn. on Health Manpower, 1966-67; mem. vis. com. on coll. U. Chgo., 1967-70; bd. regents Nat. Library Medicine, 1967—, chmn., 1970—; mem. bd. visitors U. Pa. Sch. Medicine, 1968—; mem. adv. com. to dir. NIH, 1968—; trustee Meharry Med. Coll., 1969—. Served to lt., USNR, 1944-46. Recipient Alumni Achievement medal U. Chgo., 1968, also Distinguished Service award, 1962; Rhodes scholar, 1936-39, Markle scholar, 1948. Examiner Am. Bd. Internal Medicine, 1961-64. Fellow A.C.P., Am. Pub. Health Assn., Am. Acad. Arts and Scis., mem. Am. Soc. Clin. Investigation, Am. Thoracic Soc. (chmn. com. med. research 1955, pres. 1961-62), Am. Clin. and Climatol. Assn., Assn. Am. Physicians (recorder 1962-66, councillor 1966—), A.M.A., Mass. Med. Soc., Phi Beta Kappa, Sigma Xi, Alpha Omega Alpha, Omicron Kappa Upsilon (hon.), Kappa Pi Eta. Clubs: Aeseulapian, Medical Exchange, Interurban, St. Botolph (Boston); Cambridge (Mass.) Scientific; Century (N.Y.C.); Harvard (N.Y.C., Boston). Home: 150 Brattle St Cambridge MA 02138 Office: 25 Shattuck St Boston MA 02115

EBERT, ROGER JOSEPH, film critic; b. Urbana, Ill., June 18, 1942; s. Walter H. and Annabel (Stumm) E.; B.S., U. Ill., 1964; grad. student U. Cape Town (S. Africa), U. Ill., U. Chgo. Editor, Daily Illini, 1963-64; pres. U.S. Student Press Assn., 1963-64; staff writer News-Gazette, Champaign-Urbana, Ill., 1958-66; film critic Chgo. Sun-Times, 1967—; instr. English, Chgo. City Coll., 1967-68; instr. film criticism, fine arts program U. Chgo., 1969—. Recipient award Overseas Press Club, 1963, Chgo. Headline Club, 1963. Mem. Am. Newspaper Guild, Writers Guild Am. West, Phi Delta Theta. Author: An Illini Century, 1967. Home: 151 W Burton Pl Chicago IL 60614 Office: 401 N Wabash Av Chicago IL 60611

EBERT, WALTER GALE, hosp. adminstr.; b. Parkersburg, W.Va., Aug. 2, 1909; s. Johnson Gale and Cara (Little) E.; B.S., U.S. Naval Acad., 1930; m. Jo Ann Crise, Apr. 24, 1959; children— Wendy Virginia, Susan Gale (Mrs. Joseph Arbaczawski), Carol. Commd. ensign USN, 1930, advanced through grades to rear adm., 1950; submarine comdr., World War II; naval liaison officer CBI Theatre, 1944-45; dept. head U.S. Naval Acad., 1945-47; ret., 1950; dir. Meml. Hosp., Marietta, O., 1950-52; adminstr. Ball Meml. Hosp., Muncie, Ind., 1952—. Sec. Delaware County (Ind.) Health Planning, Inc.; bd. dirs. Youngstown (O.) Blue Cross Plan, 1952-53, Ind. Blue Cross,

1965-68, United Fund Delaware County; mem. adv. group, exec. com. Ind. Regional Med. Program. Decorated Navy Cross, Silver Star medal with gold star, Legion of Merit, Bronze Star. Mem. Muncie C. of C., U.S. Submarine Vets. World War II, U.S. Naval Acad. Alumni Assn., Ind. Hosp. Assn. (past pres., trustee). Rotarian. Author: (with others) Naval Leadership, 1947. Home: 3830 Riverside Av Muncie IN 47304 Office: 2401 University Av Muncie IN 47303

EBERTS, EDMOND HOWARD, aluminum co. exec.; b. Montreal, Can., Nov. 2, 1906; s. Edmond Melchoir and Beatrice Muriel (Howard) E.; B.A., McGill U., 1928, B.C.L., 1931; m. Elisabeth Evelyn MacDougall, Nov. 12, 1926. Called to Que. bar, 1931; practice in Montreal, 1931-41; joined Aluminum Co. Can., Ltd., 1941—, mgr. gen. property dept., 1956, v.p., 1964, sec., 1961; now ret.; became pres. Kitimat Terminals Ltd., 1964; dir. Saguenay Transmission Co. Ltd., Alma & Jonquieres Ry. Co., Chaguaramas Terminals Ltd. Home: 105 Cote St Antoine Rd Westmount Montreal 6 Quebec Canada Office: Box 6090 Montreal 3 Quebec Canada

EBERWINE, VERNON GASKINS, food prodn., and processing exec.; b. Suffolk, Va., Feb. 4, 1896; s. John George and Annah Mildred (Gaskins) E.; student Randolph-Macon Coll., 1913-15; B.S., Va. Poly Inst., 1917; m. Gladys Evelyn Windsor, Feb. 14, 1918; children—Evelyn E. (Mrs. Paul de Woodward), Vernon Gaskins. Assisted orgn. Eberwine Bros., Inc., 1935, since pres.; dir. Nat. Bank of Suffolk. Chmn. bd. suprs. Nansemond County, 1925—; dir. State Bd. Agr.; v.p., dir. Tidewater Va. Development Council; commissioner Va. Dept. of Highways. Chairman bd. Va. Truck Expt. Sta.; dir. Va. Poly. Inst., 1945—, mem. exec. com.; pres. Louise Obici Meml. Hosp., Victory Meml. Hosp., Norfolk, 1942-47; dir. Norfolk Symphony and Choral Assn., Tidewater Auto Assn., Norfolk; secretary Sr. Citizens Home, Suffolk, Virginia. Served with the U.S. Navy, 1917-18, Recipient of citation for OPA and civilian def. work, World War II. Mem. Va. C. of C. (dir.), Assn. Governing Bds. State Univs. (pres.). Methodist. Mason. Clubs: Portsmouth (Va.) Executive; Hampton (Va.) Yacht. Home: P O Box 925 Route 2 Suffolk VA 23434

EBETHSTONE, GERALD ARTHUR educator, biologist; b. Ames, Ia.; B.A., Ia. State U., 1936, M.A., 1937, Ph.D. with honors, 1940; m. Ann Ross, Mar. 23, 1946; children--Edward, Thomas A., Mark. Instr., Ia. State U., 1946-47; asst. prof. biology Johns Hopkins, 1947-50, asso. prof., 1950-62, prof., 1962--, chmn. dept., 1963-69; vis. lectr. Stanford, 1970-71. Active Boy Scouts Am., 4-H Club. Served with AUS, 1940-46. Mem. Am. Soc. Biologists, Md. Soc. Cell Biologists, Am. Soc. Exptl. Biology, Internat. Union Biologists, A.A.A.S., Am. Acad. Arts and Scis., Phi Beta Kappa. Home: 48936 W Hancock Blvd Baltimore MD 20206

EBINGER, ROBERT FREDERICK, lawyer; b. Columbus, O., May 13, 1913; s. David H. and Esther (Heer) E.; A.B., Williams Coll., 1934; LL.B., Harvard, 1937; student Geneva Sch. Internat. Studies, 1935; m. Virginia Kurtz, May 24, 1939; children-Robert Frederick, Charles Kurtz. Admitted to Ohio bar, 1937, since practiced in Columbus; partner firm Alexander, Ebinger, Holschuh, Fisher & McAlister, 1948—. Chmn. bd. grievances and discipline Supreme Ct. Ohio, 1969. Dir. Kokomo Gas & Fuel Co., Exact Weight Scale Corp. Mem. Bexley (O.) Bd. Edn., 1948-56; pres., moderator Columbus Town Meeting, 1955-65; Trustee, chmn. Ohio Conservation Found., 1970; trustee Columbus Symphony Orch., 1967-70; pres., trustee United Communty Council, 1955-60. Served with AUS, World War II. Clubs: Harvard, Williams, Anglers (N.Y.C.); Castalia (O.) Trout; University, Rocky Fork Hunt, Columbus Country (Columbus). Home: 9230 White Oak Lane Westerville OH 43081 Office: 17 S High St Columbus OH 43215

EBLE, KENNETH EUGENE, educator; b. Shelby, Ia., Dec. 6, 1923; s. George and Blanche (Hill) E.; B.A., State U. Ia., 1948, M.A., 1949; Ph.D., Columbia, 1956; m. Peggy Leach, June 12, 1949; children—Melissa, Geoffrey, James. Asst. prof. Upper Ia. U., Fayette, 1949-50, Drake U., Des Moines, Ia., 1954- 55; mem. faculty U. Utah, 1955—, prof. English, 1966—, chmn. dept. 1964-69; on leave with Am. Assn. U. Profs.-AAC, 1969—. Served with inf. AUS, World War II; ETO. Decorated Purple Heart Mem. Nat. Council Tchrs. English, Modern Lang. Assn., Am. Assn. U. Profs., Phi Beta Kappa, Omicron Delta Kappa. Editor: Howells: A Century of Criticism, 1962; The Profane Comedy, 1962; F. Scott Fitzgerald, 1963; A Perfect Education, 1966; The Intellectual Tradition of the West, 1968. Home: 1934 Garfield Av Salt Lake City UT 84105

EBLEN, AMOS HALL, lawyer; b. Alton, Mo., Apr. 26, 1906; s. Joseph L. and Meekee (Gum) E.; LL.B., U. Mo., 1931, A.B., 1932; S.J.D., Harvard, 1934; m. Marguerite George, Aug. 11, 1932; children—Larry H., Gary T. Admitted to Mo. bar, 1930, Ky. bar, 1938; prof. law U. Mo., 1931-33, U. Ky., 1934-42; vis. prof. Emory U., 1935, Ohio State U., 1940-41; asso. Smith & Leary, attys., Frankfort, Ky., 1942-43, 46-50; reporter Ct. of Appeals of Ky., Frankfort, 1950-56, judge, 1958-59; mem. firm Eblen, Howard & Milner, Lexington, Ky., 1959—. Sec. Jud. Council of Ky., 1950-58; sec. Ky. Bd. Bar Examiners, 1949-50; mem. Ky. Bd. Bar Commrs., 1963-69. Served to capt. AUS, 1943-46. Mem. Am., Ky. bar assns. Baptist. Home: 108 Beechwood St Frankfort KY 40601 Office: Citizens Bank Bldg Lexington KY 40507

EBRIGHT, JAMES NEWTON, indsl. co. exec.; b. Columbus, O., Apr. 5, 1927; s. Don Harold and Martha (Miller) E.; B.Sc., Ohio State U., 1950, J.D., 1952; certificate, Stanford Exec. Program, 1966; m. Peggy Linden Short, Mar. 17, 1951; children—Don Harold II, Douglas Justin. Admitted to Ohio bar, 1952, Cal. bar, 1962, U.S. Supreme Ct. bar, 1964; with firm Wise, Roetzel, Maxon, Kelly & Andress, Akron, O., 1952-60; with Aerojet-Gen. Corp., 1960-70, sec., gen. counsel, 1966-70; v.p. adminstrn., gen. counsel Norris Industries, Inc., 1970—. Bd. dirs., mem. exec. com. Los Angeles United Way, 1967—. Served with USNR, 1945-46. Mem. Am., Los Angeles County, Ohio bar assns., Cal. Mfrs. Assn., State Bar Cal., Beta Theta Pi, Phi Delta Phi. Club: San Gabriel Country. Home: 2990 Lombardy Rd Pasadena CA 91107 Office: 5215 S Boyle Av Los Angeles CA 90058

EBY, MARTIN K., constrn. co. exec.; b. Topeka, Kan., 1907; grad. Kan. State U., 1929. Chmn. bd. Martin K. Eby Constrn. Co., Wichita, Kan.; dir. Equipment Rental & Sales Co., 1st Nat. Bank Wichita, Kan. Gas & Electric Co. Mem. adv. bd. Kan. State U. Coll. Architecture and Design, Schilling Inst. Bd. dirs. YMCA, Kan. Found. for Blind. Home: 1469 Perry St Wichita KS 67203 Office: 610 N Main St Wichita KS 67203*

EBY, MARTIN K., Jr., constrn. co. exec.; b. Wichita Falls, Tex., 1934; grad. Kan. State U., 1956. Pres., dir. Martin K. Eby Constrn. Co., Wichita, Kan. Home: 1635 Woodrow Ct Wichita KS 67203 Office: 610 N Main St Wichita KS 67203*

ECCLES, GEORGE STODDARD, banker; b. Baker, Ore., Apr. 9, 1900; s. David and Ellen (Stoddard) E.; B.S., Columbia Sch. Bus., 1922; LL.D., Utah State U., 1963, U. Utah, 1963; m. Dolores Dore, Mar. 4, 1925. Asst. cashier First Security Bank Utah, Nat. Assn. (formerly 1st Nat. Bank of Ogden), 1922, v.p., 1923, pres., 1934-70, chmn. bd., 1970—; chmn. exec. com., dir. First Security Bank of Ida., Nat. Assn.; v.p., dir. First Security Corp., 1928-46, now pres., gen. mgr., dir.; mem. exec. com. Aubrey G. Lanston & Co., Inc., N.Y.C.; dir. Utah Constrn. & Mining Co., Anderson Lumber Co., Ogden Union Ry. & Depot Co., U.P. R.R., U.P. Corp., Am. Bankers Life Ins. Co. of Fla. (hon.), Am. Bankers Ins. Co. of Fla. (hon.), Farmers Ins. Group, Los Angeles, Husky Oil Co., Husky Oil Can., Ltd., Gulf Sulphur Co., N.Y.C.; exec. com., dir. Amalgamated Sugar Co., Ogden. Past pres., dir., mem. exec. com. Assn. of Registered Bank Holding Cos.; mem. Comptroller of Currency's Nat. Adv. Com. Banking Policies and Practices. Trustee Los Angeles Found. Otology; bd. dirs. Deafness Research Found. N.Y., Nat. Indsl. Conf.; treas. bd. trustees U. Utah. Served in inf. U.S. Army, World War I. Mem. Am. Bankers Assn., Assn. Res. City Bankers (past pres.), Internat. Banking Conf., C. of C., Alpha Kappa Psi, Sigma Chi. Clubs: Ogden Golf and Country, Alta, Salt Lake Country; Eldorado Country (Palm Desert, Cal.); Pauma Valley Country (Pauma, Cal.). Home: 1525 Penrose Dr Salt Lake City UT 84103 Office: 79 S Main St Salt Lake City UT 84110

ECCLES, JOHN CAREW, med. educator; b. Jan. 27, 1903; s. William James and Mary Eccles; M.B., B.S. with honors, Melbourne U., 1925; Rhodes scholar, Victoria, 1925, Christopher Welch scholar, 1927; M.A., D.Phil. (Oxon.), 1929; jr. research fellow Exeter Coll., 1927- 32, Staines med. fellow, 1932-34, hon. fellow, 1961; Sc.D., Cambridge U., 1960; m. Irene Frances Miller, 1928 (div. 1968); 4 sons, 5 daus.; m. Helena Táboriková, 1968. Fellow, tutor Magdalen Coll., U. lectr. physiology, 1934-37; dir. Kanematsu Meml. Inst. Pathology, Sydney, Australia, 1937-44; prof. physiology U. Otago, Dunedin, New Zealand, 1944-51; Waynflete lectr. Magdalen Coll., Oxford, 1952; Herter lectr. Johns Hopkins, 1955; Ferrier lectr. Royal Soc., 1959; prof. physiology Australian Nat. U., Canberra, 1951-66; staff Inst. for Biomed. Research, A.M.A. Edn. and Research Found., 1966-68; distinguished prof. State U. N.Y. Buffalo, 1968—; pres. Australian Acad. Sci., 1957-61. Recipient Gotch prize, 1927, Rolleston Meml. prize, 1932, Baly medal Royal Coll. Physicians, 1961; co-recipient Nobel prize for medicine, 1963. Created knight, 1958. Hon. fellow Magdalen Coll., Oxford. Fellow Royal Soc. (Royal medal 1962), A.C.P. (hon.), World Acad. Art and Sci.; fgn. asso. Indian Acad. Scis., Royal Belgian Acad., mem. Pontifical Acad. Sci., Am. Acad. Arts and Scis. (fgn. hon.), Am. Philos. Soc. (fgn. hon.), Nat. (fgn. asso.), N.Y. (hon. life) acads. of science, Am. Physiol. Soc., Am. Neurol. Soc., Academia Nazionale dei Lincei, Deutsche Akademie der Naturforscher Leopoldina (Cothenius medal 1963). Author: Neurophysiological Basis of Mind, 1953; Physiology of Nerve Cells, 1957; The Physiology of Synapses, 1964; The Cerebellum as a Neuronal Machine, 1967; The Inhibitory Pathways of the Central Nervous System, 1969; Facing Reality, 1970. Contbr. papers profl. jours. Home: 100 Lincoln Pkwy Buffalo NY 14222

ECCLES, LORD, former mem. British Parliament, govt. ofcl.; b. London, Eng., Sept. 18, 1904; s. William McAdam and Anna Coralie (Anstie) E.; student Winchester Coll., 1918-23, New Coll., Oxford U., 1923-26; m. Hon. Sybil Frances Dawson, Oct. 10, 1929; children—John, Simon, Selina Polly. London mgr. Central Mining & Investment Corp., 1926-39; econ. adviser to His Majesty's ambassadors in Madrid, Spain and Lisbon, Portugal, Ministry Econ. Warfare, 1939; asst. dir.-gen. programs and planning Ministry of Prodn., 1942-43; elected as Conservative mem. to Brit. Parliament for Chippenham, Wiltshire, 1943, 45, 50, 51, 55, 59; apptd. minister of works, 1951, privy councillor, 1951, minister of edn., 1954, 59-62. Pres. Bd. of Trade, 1957, Paymaster gen. with responsibility for arts, 1970—. Created knight, 1953, baron, 1962, viscount, 1964. Club: Brook's (London). Home: Dean Farm Upper Chute nr Andover Hants England also 6 Barton St Westminster London S W 1 England

ECCLES, MARK, educator; b. Oxford, O., July 13, 1905; s. William Alexander and Anna (Williams) E.; A.B. summa cum laude in English and Classics, Oberlin Coll., 1927; A.M., Harvard, 1928, Ph.D., 1932; student U. London (Eng.), 1929-30; m. Elisabeth Norris, Apr. 20, 1933; children—Ann (Mrs. David Rose), Cynthia (Mrs. Neil Allen), Margaret, Robert Norris. Instr. English, Harvard, 1930-33; mem. faculty U. Wis., 1934—, prof. English, 1947—, R.E. Neil Dodge prof. English, 1969—; Fulbright lectr., Stratford-on-Avon, 1955-56. Research fellow Am. Council Learned Socs., 1933-34; fellow Huntington Library, 1940-41; Guggenheim fellow, 1955. Mem. Shakespeare Assn. (adv. bd.), Malone Soc., Renaissance Soc., Modern Lang. Assn., Internat. Assn. U. Profs. English, Phi Beta Kappa. Author: Christopher Marlowe in London, 1934; Shakespeare in Warwickshire, 1961; King Lear, An Outline-Guide to the Play, 1965. Editor: Othello, 1946; Twelfth Night, 1948; Richard III, 1964. Editor: The Macro Plays, 1969. Contbr. Ency. Brit. Home: 2 Roby Rd Madison WI 53705

ECCLES, MARRINER STODDARD, financier, bus. exec.; b. Logan, Utah, Sept. 9, 1890; s. David and Ellen (Stoddard) E.; student Brigham Young Coll., 1905-09; LL.D., U. Utah, 1943, Utah State U., 1963; m. May Campbell Young, July 9, 1913; children—Marriner Campbell (dec.), Mrs. Eleanore May Steele, John David; m. 2d Sara Madison Glassie, Dec. 29, 1951. Organized Eccles Investment Co., a holding co. for interests in family estate, 1916, v.p., gen. mgr. until 1929, pres., 1929—; pres. First Nat. Bank of Ogden and Ogden Savs. Bank, and successor banks, 1920-34; organizer First Security Corp., owning and operating banks in Utah, Ida. and Wyo., pres., 1928-34, chmn., 1952—; chmn. First Security Bank of Utah, Nat. Assn., 1955-70, now sr. dir.; chmn. Amalgamated Sugar Co.; hon. chmn. Utah Constrn. & Mining Co.; pres. Eccles Investment Co.; dir. Marcona Corp. Asst. to Sec. Treasury, 1934; gov. Fed. Res. Bd., 1934-36; bd. govs. Fed. Res. System, 1936-51, chmn. bd. govs., 1936-48; mem. bd. Econ. Stblzn., 1942-46; U.S. del. to Bretton Woods Conf., 1944; mem. nat. adv. council on Internat. Monetary and Financial Problems, 1945-48; adv. bd. Export-Import Bank, 1945-48; mem. Nat. Commn. Money and Credit, 1958-61, World Population Emergency Campaign; trustee Am. Assembly, 1959—; sponsor Atlantic Council, 1962—; mem. Nat. Com. on U.S.-China Relations; mem. exec. com. Nat. Citizens Com. Concerned About Deployment of ABM. Elector Hall of Fame, 1940—. Pres. Utah Bankers Assn., 1924-25. Bd. dirs. Planned Parenthood World Population. Mem. Sigma Chi. Clubs: Pacific Union, World Trade, Commonwealth, Golf, Stock Exchange (San Francisco); Eldorado Country (Palm Springs, Cal.): The Country, Alta (Salt Lake City); Chevy Chase Country, Burning Tree (Washington); Pauma Valley Country (Pauma Valley, Cal.) Author: Beckoning Frontiers. Home: Hotel Utah Salt Lake City UT 84111 also 290 Lombard St San Francisco CA 94104 Office: Deseret Bldg Main at First South Salt Lake City UT 84111 also 550 California St San Francisco CA 94104

ECCLES, ROBERT SPENCER, educator; b. Tacoma, Nov. 12, 1911; s. James Spencer and Effie (Dougherty) E.; A.B., U. Puget Sound, 1934; M.A., Northwestern U., 1943; B.D., Garrett Theol. Sem., 1944; Ph.D., Yale, 1952; research U. Bonn (West Germany), 1961; m. Kathryn Octavia Wann, Aug. 14, 1952; children—Thomas Allen, Bruce Douglas. Tchr. high sch., Olympia, Wash., 1936-42; asst. prof. religion Am. U., 1948-49; asst. prof. N.T., Ind. Sch. Religion, Bloomington, 1949-53; prof. philosophy and religion DePauw U., 1953—; ordained to ministry Methodist Ch., 1948. Fulbright travel grantee, 1961. Mem. Soc. Bibl. Lit., Am. Acad. Religion (membership chmn. 1959-60, program chmn. Midwest sect. 1957-59, asso. editor bull. 1965—). Contbg. author: Religions in Antiquity, 1968. Home: 817 Stadium Dr Greencastle IN 46135

ECCLES, SPENCER FOX, banker; b. Ogden, Utah, Aug. 24, 1934; s. Spencer Stoddard and Hope (Fox) E.; B.S., U. Utah, 1956; M.S. in Banking, Columbia, 1959; m. Cleone E. Peterson, July 21, 1958; children—Clista Hope, Lisa Ellen, Katherine Ann, Spencer P. Trainee, First Nat. City Bank, N.Y.C., 1959- 60, First Security Bank Utah, 1960; from asst. v.p. to sr. v.p. First Security Bank Ida., Boise, 1961-70, now dir.; exec. v.p. First Security Co., Salt Lake City, 1970—; dir., mem. exec. and investment coms. First Security Corp.; v.p., dir. First Security Savs. & Loan Assn.; dir., mem. exec. com. First Security Life Ins. Co. Tex.; dir. First Security Bank Utah, First Security State Bank, Eccles Investment Co., Anderson Lumber Co., Sun Valley Co., Utah Mortgage & Loan Corp., First Security Ins. Agy., Inc., First Security Ins., Inc., Am. Bankers Life Assurance Co., Am. Bankers Ins. Co. Fla. Bd. dirs. Utah Ski Racers Found., Ballet West. Served to 1st lt., inf., AUS, 1958. Mem. Beta Theta Pi. Home: 4371 Adonis Dr Salt Lake City UT 84117 Office: 79 S Main St Salt Lake City UT 84110

ECCLES, WILLARD L., banker; b. Logan, Utah, Feb. 12, 1909; s. David and Ellen (Stoddard) E.; student U.S. Agrl. Coll., Ore. State Coll., Babson Inst.; m. Ruth Pierpont, Aug. 20, 1930; children—Barbara, Susan. With First Security Bank of Utah, N.A., 1932—, now sr. v.p., sec., also dir.; v.p., sec., dir. First Security Corp.; v.p., dir. First Security Bank of Rock Springs, Wyo.; dir. Eccles Investment Co., Anderson Lumber Co., Pioneer Wholesale Supply Co., Western Mfg. Co., Browning Arms Co., Willard Bay Devel. Corp. Bd. dirs. Pacific Coast Banking Sch. Mem. Bank Marketing Assn., C. of C., Sigma Chi. Mem. Ch. of Jesus Christ of Latter-day Saints. Clubs: Alta, Weber, Ogden Golf and Country. Home: 2745 Fillmore Av Ogden UT 84403 Office: P O Box 390 Salt Lake City UT 84110

ECHAVARRIA, HERNAN, former Colombian diplomat; b. Medellin, Colombia, Apr. 7, 1911; s. Gabriel and Helena (Olozaga) E.; B.Sc., U. Manchester (Eng.), 1930; postgrad. London (Eng.) Sch. Econs., 1932; m. Loli Obregon, Feb. 22, 1942; children—Gabriel, Jose Antonio, Loli. Minister of pub. works, 1943-44, of communications, 1958-59; chmn. bd. Nat. Assn. Industralists, Bogota, 1967; pres. Compania Colombiana de Ceramica, Porcelana Sanitaria, Distribuidora Corona, Ltda., Laminas del Cariba, Ltda., 1950-67; ambassador of Colombia, to U.S., 1967-70. Bd. dirs. U. de Los Andes, 1957- -, Sch. Adminstrn. and Finance, Medellin, 1960—, Colombian Inst. Sci. Adminstrn., 1960—; chmn. bd. Colombian Inst. Tech. Specialization Abroad, 1960—. Home: Carrere 11 No 86-75 Bogota Colombia Office: Diagonal 34 No 4-28 Apartado Aereo 8585 Bogota Colombia

ECHLIN, JOHN EDWARD, mfg. exec.; b. Oakland, Cal., Feb. 28, 1897; s. Charles Claire and Madeline (Arndt) E.; student Poly. Coll. Engring., Oakland Cal., Alexander Hamilton Inst., LaSalle Extension U.; m. Beryl Goldsworthy, Feb. 8, 1927; children—Margaret Jane (Mrs. Paul Kammerer), John Edward. With Safe-Lite Mfg. Co., San Francisco, 1918-24; v.p. J. J. Schnerr Co., San Francisco, 1924-26; pres. Echlin & Echlin, Inc., San Francisco, 1926- 36; president Echlin Mfg. Co., New Haven, 1936-59, Branford, Conn., 1959- 67, chmn. board, mem. bd. directors, 1967—; pres. Echlin United of Can., Ltd., Echlin Sales Co. Past mem. automotive replacement parts mfrs. industry adv. com. OPS and N.P.A., elec. contact industry adv. com; mem. industry adv. U.S. Sec. Commerce. Trustee New Haven (Conn.) College. Mem. Nat. Metal Trades Assn. (director, past pres. Conn. br.), New Haven County Mfrs. Assn. (past dir.), Nat. Automotive Parts Assn. (dir. mfrs. council), Soc. Automotive Engrs., New Haven C. of C. (past dir.). Mason (32, Shriner). Home: Falcon Road Guilford CT 06437 Office: Echlin Mfg Co Echlin Road and U S 1 Brantford CT 06405

ECHOLS, JOHN MINOR, linguist, educator; b. Portland, Ore., Mar. 25, 1913; s. John Minor and Florence Crawford (McGuffin) E.; B.A., U. Va., 1937, M.A., 1938, Ph.D., 1940; summer student, U. Mich., 1938-40; m. Nancy Worthington Doner, June 7, 1941; children—Jane McGuffin, John Minor III, Florence Doner. Instr. German and Swedish, U. Chgo., 1947; asso. prof. linguistics, dep. dir. Fgn. Service Inst., Dept. State, 1947-52; asso. prof. linguistics Cornell U., 1952-57, prof. linguistics, 1957—, chmn. dept. Far Eastern studies, 1956-61. Dir., cons. Ford Found. and Inst. Internat. Edn. English Lang. Teaching Project, Indonesia, 1952-55. Served as lt. comdr. USNR, 1942-47; asst. naval attaché Am. legation, Stockholm, 1944-47. Recipient honor award Dept. State, 1951. Fellov Am. Anthrop. Assn.; mem. Linguistic Soc. Am. (life), Assn. Asian Studies, Am. Oriental Soc., Phi Beta Kappa. Presbyn. Author: (with Hassan Shadily) An Indonesian-English Dictionary, 1963. Home: 711 Hanshaw Rd Ithaca NY 14850

ECHOLS, ROY C., business cons.; b. Hubbard City, Tex., Apr. 22, 1903; s. Oscar and Mary Belle (Hammond) E.; student So. Meth. U., 1922-25; m. Lois Skielvig, Jan. 20, 1925 (div. 1930); 1 dau., Margaret (Mrs. Charles C. Ladenberger); m. 2d, Leatrice Echols, Aug. 19, 1933. Office boy Southwestern Bell Telephone Co., Dallas, 1919-25, chief clk., dist. wire chief, Fort Worth, 1925-35, gen. installation supt., St. Louis, 1935- 38, dist. plant supt., Ft. Smith, Ark., 1938-41, Little Rock, 1941-44, St. Louis plant supr., 1944-45, div. plant supt. San Antonio 1945-48, Oklahoma City, 1948-49, asst. v.p. St. Louis, 1949-50, gen. mgr., Okla., 1950-54; v.p., gen. mgr., dir., exec. com. Ind. Bell Telephone Co., 1954- 58; asst. v.p. Am. Tel. & Tel. Co., 1958-59, v.p., 1959-60; pres., dir., mem. exec. com. Ind. Bell Telephone Co., Indpls., 1960- 68, dir.; chmn. bd., chmn. exec. com. Indpls. Water Co., 1968-71, now dir.; dir. Am. Fletcher Nat. Bank and Trust Co., Indpls., Am. Fletcher Corp., Indpls., Park Fletcher, Inc. Pres., Civic Center Donors, Inc., Indpls.; mem. devel. council Butler U. Bd. dirs. Consumer Credit Counseling Service Central Ind., Inc., Central council Boy Scouts Am., Greater Indpls. United Fund, Indpls. Hosp. Devel. Corp., Jr. Achievement, Indpls., Indpls. Conv. and Visitors Bur., Starlight Musicals, Inc. Mem. Ind. (dir.), Indpls. chambers commerce, Telephone Pioneers Am., Newcomen Soc. N.Am. Clubs: Meridan Hills Country, Columbia, Indianapolis Athletic (Indpls.). Home: 7979 Meridian Hills Lane Indianapolis IN 46240 Office: 1220 Waterway Blvd Indianapolis IN 46202

ECK, JOHN EDGAR, Jr., lawyer; b. Gastonia, N.C., Oct. 20, 1923; s. John Edgar and Elizabeth (McDermott) E.; B.S., U.S. Merchant Marine Acad., 1944; LL.B., U. S.C., 1950; m. Jeanne Rice, June 18, 1945; children—Vincent, Francis. Admitted to N.C. bar, 1950, S.C. bar, 1950; partner C.P.A. firm Eck & Eck, Gastonia, N.C., 1946-58; partner law firm Garland & Eck, Gastonia, N.C., 1958-62; gen. counsel Akers Motor Lines, Gastonia, N.C., 1962-66; gen. counsel Greenwood Mills, Greenwood, S.C., 1966—; dir. Greenwood Motor Lines, Alliance Warehouse, Ninety Six Mfg. Co., Central Trust Co. Trustee Southeastern Founds., Mathews Found., Self Found.; adv. bd. dirs. Belmont Abbey Coll. Served with USNR, 1944-46. Mem. Am. Bar Assn. Democrat. Roman Catholic. Home: Timberlake Rt 5 Greenwood SC 29646 Office: Greenwood Bldg Greenwood SC 29646

ECKARDT, ARTHUR ROY, educator; b. Bklyn., Aug. 8, 1918; s. Frederick William and Anna (Fitts) E.; B.A., Bklyn. Coll., 1942; B.D., Yale, 1944; Ph.D., Columbia, 1947; L.H.D., Hebrew Union Coll.-Jewish Inst. Religion, 1969; m. Alice Eliza Lyons, Sept. 2, 1944; children—Paula Jean, Stephen Robert. Ordained to ministry Methodist Ch., 1944; asst. prof. religion Lawrence Coll., 1947- 50; asst. prof. religion Duke, 1950-51; asso. prof., head dept. religion Lehigh U., Bethlehem, Pa., 1951-56, prof., head dept., 1956—. Vice pres. Christians Concerned for Israel. Recipient Distinguished Alumnus award Bklyn. Coll., 1963. Fellow Harvard U. Fund For Advancement Edn., 1955-56, Lilly fellow U. Cambridge, 1963-64; fellow Nat. Found. for Jewish Culture, 1968-69. Mem. Am. Acad. Religion (past pres.), Am. Assn. U. Profs., Am. Philos. Assn., Soc. Sci. Study Religion, Am. Soc. Christian Ethics, Pi Gamma Mu. Author: Christianity and the Children of Israel, 1948; The Surge of Piety in America, 1958; Elder and Younger Brothers, 1967; (with Alice L. Eckardt) Encounter with Israel, 1970. Editor: The Theologian at Work, 1968; Christianity in Israel, 1971; Jour. of Am. Acad. Religion, 1961-69. Contbr. articles profl. jours.; research in Middle East, Europe. Home: 520 Oxford St Coopersburg PA 18036 Office: Lehigh U Bethlehem PA 18015

ECKARDT, FELIX VON, German State ofcl.; b. Berlin, Germany, June 18, 1903; s. Felix and Eva Marianna Victoria (Geffcken) von E.; student Hamburg, Germany, Prussian Cadet Corps (German mil. acad.); m. Edith Peters, 1927; children—Peter Felix, Konstantin. Apprentice newspaperman; corr. Muenchener Neuste Nachrichten, 1927; diplomatic reporter Ullstein publs., Berlin; press attache German Embassy, Brussels, 1929-32; script writer operattas, dramas, mysteries, Berlin, 1933-37; editor, pub. Weser Kurier, German newspaper; head Fed. Press and Information Office, Germany, 1952-55, 56-62; permanent observer to UN from Germany, 1955-56; sec. state, 1958; plenipotentiary of Fed. Republic in Berlin, 1962-. Home: Pücklerstrasse 14 Berlin-Dahlem West Germany Office: Bundeshaus Bundesallee 216-218 Berlin 15 Germany

ECKART, CARL, physicist; b. St. Louis, May 4, 1902; s. William E. and Lilly (Hellwig) E.; B.S., Washington U., 1922, M.S., 1923; Ph.D., Princeton, 1925. NRC fellow, 1925-27, Guggenheim fellow 1927; faculty U. Chgo., 1928-46, asst. prof., 1928-36, asso. prof., 1936-46; prof. Scripps Inst. Oceanography, 1946- 70, emeritus, 1971—; vice chancellor U. Cal., San Diego, 1965-67. Mem. A.A.A.S., Am. Phys. Soc., Nat. Acad. Sci., Acoustical Soc. Am., Am. Acad. Arts and Scis., Sigma Xi. Home: 8160 La Jolla Shores Dr La Jolla CA 92037

ECKART, CLARK ARNOLD, railroad ofcl.; b. Akron, O., May 21, 1907; s. Claude Henry and Clara (Smith) E.; B.S., Whitman Coll., 1928; LL.B., U. Wash., 1931; m. Margaret Boyd Maxson, Aug. 3, 1934; children—Marlene Louise (Mrs. Marvin E. Gloege), Patricia Anne (Mrs. Robert Hodgson), Claire Elizabeth (Mrs. Julian Brouillard). Admitted to Wash. bar, 1931, and practiced in Seattle until 1942; with Great No. Ry. Co., 1942—, v.p., Western counsel, 1958—; pres., dir. Pacific Coast R.R. Co., 1958—; trustee S.P. & S. Ry. Co., Portland, Ore. Bd. overseers Whitman Coll. Mem. Am., Wash., Seattle-King County bar assns., Seattle C. of C. Club: Rainier (Seattle). Home: 1600 43d Av E Seattle WA 98102 Office: 404 Union St Seattle WA 98101

ECKART, E. ALBERT, ret. paint mfr.; b. New Rochelle, N.Y., Sept. 5, 1902; s. Edmund and Emily (Gietl) E.; grad. Yale, 1923; m. Ruth C. Brumley, Oct. 15, 1926; children—Judith B., E. Albert. With Sapolin Paints, Inc., N.Y.C., 1923- -, formerly chmn. bd., now dir. Mem. Berzelius Soc. Republican. Clubs: Yale, N.Y. Athletic (N.Y.C.). Home: Westport CT 06880 Office: 201 E 42d St New York City NY 10017

ECKAUS, RICHARD SAMUEL, educator; b. Kansas City, Mo., Apr. 30, 1926; s. Julius and Bessie (Finklestein) E.; B.S., Ia. State Coll., 1946; M.A., Washington U., St. Louis, 1948; Ph.D., Mass. Inst. Tech., 1954; m. Risha Claypool, Mar. 23, 1951; 1 dau., Susan L. Instr., asst. prof., asso. prof. Brandeis U., 1951- 62; research asso. Center For Internat. Studies, Mass. Inst. Tech., Cambridge, 1954—, asso. prof., prof., 1962—; mem. Bd. Econ. Advisers to Gov. Mass., 1963-65. Served with USNR, 1944-46. Guggenheim and Social Sci. Research Council fellow, 1962, Ford Found. Faculty fellow, 1965. Mem. Am. Econ. Assn., Econometric Soc. Author: (with K. Parikh) Planning for Growth, 1968. Home: 283 Highland Av West Newton MA 02165 Office: Mass Inst Tech Cambridge MA 02139

ECKBERG, HERBERT FREDERIC, coll. dean; b. Jamestown, N.Y., May 19, 1906; s. Arvid Waldo and Clara (Lundquist) E., B.Sc., U.S. Naval Acad., 1927; M.S., U. Cal. at Berkeley, 1937; student U.S. Naval War Coll., 1948-50, Army War Coll., 1954-56; m. Ellen Virginia Cable, Aug. 11, 1928; 1 dau., Elenita Cable. Commd. ensign U.S. Navy, 1927, advanced through grades to capt., 1945; chief U.S. Naval Mission to Venezuela, 1942-43; comdg. officer U.S.S. Anne Arundel, 1945-46, U.S.S. Cambria, 1952; comdr. Transport Div. 22, Norfolk, Va., 1953-54; ret., 1956; dir. engring. Bucknell U., 1957-61, dean Coll. Engring., 1961-71, emeritus, 1971—. Decorated Legion of Merit; Order of Liberator, Medal Naval Merit (Venezuela); named prof. honoris causa Cath. U. Cordoba (Argentina), 1965. Registered profl. engr., Md. Mem. Am. Soc. M.E., Naval Inst., Am. Soc. Engring. Edn. Club: Army and Navy (Washington). Home: 1927 Pendennis Dr Annapolis MD 21401

ECKE, MELVIN WILLARD, educator; b. Green Bay, Wis., July 12, 1920; s. Fred Reuben and Caroline (Beglinger) E.; A.B., U. Wis., 1942; M.A., Princeton, 1949, Ph.D., 1951; m. Elizabeth Frances Branch, Mar. 24, 1946; children—Carol Ann, Elizabeth Catherine (Mrs. Richard Denver Hogue), Susan Emilie, Melanie Candace. Lectr. Rutgers U., 1948-50; instr. Marietta Coll., 1950-52, asst. prof., 1952-55, dir. adult edn., 1952-55; asst. prof. history Ga. State Coll. (now Ga. State U.), Atlanta, 1955-57, asso. prof., 1957-63, prof., 1963—; lectr. Ga. Inst. Tech., 1955-58, 59-62. Pres. Clarkston High Sch. P.T.A., 1961-63. Served with AUS, 1942-46. Mem. Am., So. hist. assns., Southeastern Conf. on Latin Am. Studies, Phi Alpha Theta. Methodist. Home: 4455 Erskine Rd Clarkston GA 30021 Office: Dept History Ga State U 33 Gilmer St SE Atlanta GA 30303

ECKEL, EDWIN BUTT, geologist; b. Washington, Jan. 27, 1906; s. Edwin Clarence and Julia Egerton (Dibblee) E.; B.S., Lafayette Coll., 1928; M.S. (fellow), U. Ariz., 1930; m. LaCharles Quarles Goodman, Apr. 22, 1931; children—Edwin Goodman, Charles Richard, Robert Roman. Geologist, U.S. Geol. Survey, 1930-67, chief engring. geology br., 1945-61, chief spl. projects br., 1962-67, research geologist, part-time 1968—; editor bull. Geol. Soc. Am., Boulder, Colo., 1968-71, exec. sec., 1970—. Chmn. landslide com. Hwy. Research Bd., 1950-62; tech. adviser Paraguay, 1952; mem. com. Alaska earthquake Nat. Acad. Sci., 1964-71. Recipient medallion of merit U. Ariz., 1960; Distinguished Service award Dept. Interior, 1965. Fellow Geol. Soc. Am., Mineral. Soc. Am.; mem. Soc. Econ. Geologists, Assn. Engring. Geologists, Am. Inst. Profl. Geologists, Assn. Earth Sci. Editors, Sigma Xi, Phi Kappa Phi, Delta Upsilon. Contbr. articles to profl. jours. Home: 1109 S High St Denver CO 80210 Office: 3300 Penrose Pl Boulder CO 80301

ECKELBERRY, DON RICHARD, artist, naturalist; b. Sebring, O., July 6, 1921; s. Ira Richie and Pearl (Schreckengost) E.; student Cleve. Inst. Art; m. Virginia Ruth Nepodal, May 10, 1944. Staff artist Nat. Audubon Soc., 1943-45; free- lance artist, 1945—; one man shows, N.Y.C., 1943, 46, 56, Louisville, 1970; exhibited alumni show Cleve. Inst. Art, 1970; illustrator fourteen books, 1946-, also articles and papers; artist bird postage stamps for British Honduras, 1962, murals for Adirondack Mus., 1960; art dir. Frame House Gallery. Patron Asa Wright Nature Center, Trinidad. Fellow Am. Ornithologists Union; mem. Nat., Fla. (Conservation award 1968), Audubon socs., Cooper, Wilson ornithol. socs., Soc. Animal Artists. Spl. research neotropical ornithology; field work in Middle and S. Am., also W.I. Address: 180 Woodsome Rd Babylon NY 11702

ECKELMANN, FRANK DONALD, educator; b. Englewood, N.J., May 25, 1929; s. Herman J. and Rosa (Schwarz) E.; B.S., Wheaton Coll., 1951; M.S., Columbia, 1954, Ph.D., 1956; m. Beverly Jean Roberts, June 20, 1953; children—Frank Donald, Susan Diane. Postdoctoral appointment geochemistry Columbia, 1956-57; asst. prof. Brown U., 1957-60, asso. prof., 1960-64, prof., 1964—, chmn. dept. geol. scis., 1961-68, dean coll., 1968-71. Fellow Geol. Soc. Am., Mineral. Soc. Am.; mem. Geochem. Soc., Am. Geophys. Union, Nat. Assn. Geology Tchrs., Yellowstone-Bighorn Research Assn., Sigma Xi. Contbr. articles profl. publs. Home: 1485 Pawtucket Av Rumford RI 02916

ECKELS, ARTHUR RAYMOND, educator; b. New Haven, Nov. 16, 1919; s. Orlando Fulton and Emily Thorine (Rose) E.; B.S. in Elec. Engring., U. Conn., 1941; M.S., Harvard, 1942; D.Eng., Yale, 1950; m. Marjorie Mills Robinson, Jan. 1, 1944; children—Alan Matthew, Peter John, Marilyn Jane, Christine Ann. Elec. engr. U.S. Navy, 1942-43; from marine engr. to chief engr. U.S. Merchant Marine, 1943-46; grad. asst. Yale, 1946-47, instr. dept. elec. engring., 1947-49; asso. prof. N.C. State Coll., 1949-55, prof., 1955- 56; prof., chmn. dept. elec. engring. U. Vt., 1956-61; prof. electrical engring. N.C. State Univ. at Raleigh, 1961—; cons. engineer and operations analyst U. N.C. Operations Analysis Standby Unit for USAF; vis. prof. elec. engring. (Fulbright grant), Inst. Electronics, Nat. Chiao-Tung U., Hsinchu, Taiwan, 1960, Japan Nat. Def. Coll., 1964. Past corporate mem. Bd. World Ministries, United Church of Christ. Registered profl. engr., Vt. Mem. Operations Research Soc. Am., Am. Soc. Engring. Edn., Sigma Xi, Tau Beta Pi, Eta Kappa Nu. Home: 1417 Dellwood Dr Raleigh NC 27607

ECKENHOFF, JAMES EDWARD, physician, educator; b. Easton, Md., Apr. 2, 1915; s. George L. and Ada (Ferguson) E.; B.S., U. Ky., 1937; M.D., U. Pa., 1941; D.Sc., Transylvania U., 1970, m. Bonnie Lee Youngerman, June 4, 1938; children—Edward Alvin, James Benjamin, Walter Leroy, Roderic George. Intern, Good Samaritan Hosp., Lexington, Ky., 1941- 42; Harrison fellow anesthesia U. Pa., 1945-48, mem. faculty Med. Sch. and Grad. Sch., 1948-65, prof. anesthesiology, 1955-65; physician anesthetist Hosp. U. Pa., 1948-65; prof. anesthesia Northwestern U. Med. Sch., Chgo., 1966—, chmn. dept., 1966-70, dean Med. Sch., 1970—; chief anesthesia Passavant Meml. Hosp., Chgo., 1966-70; chmn. anesthesia Chgo. Wesley Hosp., 1966-70; cons. VA Research Hosp., Childrens Hosp., Chgo., 1966—; surgeon gen. U.S. Navy, 1964—. Mem. surgery study sect. NIH, 1962-66, anesthesia tng. com., 1966-70; vis. prof. Australian and New Zealand Soc. Anesthetists, 1968, S. African Soc. Anesthetists, 1970. Served to capt. M.C., AUS, 1942-45; ETO. Commonwealth Fund fellow Queen Victoria Hosp., East Grinstead, Eng., 1961- 62. Diplimate Am. Bd. Anesthesiology (bd. dirs. 1965—). Fellow faculty anesthesia, also Hunterian prof. Royal Coll. Surgeons. Fellow Inst. Medicine Chgo., A.C.P.; mem. Australian, New Zealand, South African socs. anesthesiologists, Soc. Acad. Anesthesia Chairmen (pres. 1967-68), Soc. Med. Consultants to Armed Forces, Am. Soc. Anesthesiologists, A.M.A., Assn. Univ. Anesthetists (pres. 1962), Am. Assn. U. Profs., Chgo., Ill. med. socs., Am. Physicians Art Assn., Am. Physiol. Soc. Author: (with others) Introduction to Anesthesia, 3d edit., 1967; Anesthesia from Colonial Times, 1966; also numerous articles. Editor: Science and Practice in Anesthesia, 1965; (with J. Beal) Intensive and Recovery Room Care, 1969. Editor Jour. Anesthesiology, 1958-62, Yearbook of Anesthesia, 1970—. Home: 1 Canterbury Ct Wilmette IL 60091 Office: 303 E Chicago Av Chicago IL 60611

ECKENRODE, JOHN WILLIAM, pub.; b. Westminster, Md., June 18, 1905; s. Charles Edward and Emma (Kelley) E.: A.B., Loyola Coll., Balt., 1927; student Pratt Library Tng. Sch., 1927. Tchr., St. Rita's High Sch., Cin., 1927-28; cataloguer St. Mary's Sem. Library, Balt., 1929-30; librarian Calvert Hall High Sch., Balt., 1930-31; founder, dir. Newman Bookshop, Balt., 1932-70; founder, 1948, then pres. Newman Press, Westminster, Md., ret. 1970; now with Christian Classics, Inc., Westminster. Club: Chambersburg (Pa.) Golf. Home: 205 Willis St Westminster MD 21157

ECKER, ALLAN BENJAMIN, lawyer, corp. exec.; b. N.Y.C., 1921; s. Samuel and Frances (Schuman) E.; B.A., Harvard, 1941, LL.B., 1953; m. Elizabeth Jane Rice, May 19, 1956; children—David Rice, Sarah Rice. Partner firm Paul, Weiss, Rifkind, Wharton & Garrison, N.Y.C. Sec., dir., mem. exec. com. Kinney Services, Inc.; counsel, sec., dir. Wiltwyck Sch. Boys. Home: 133 E 94th St New York City NY 10028 Office: 345 Park Av New York City NY 10022

ECKER, HARRY ALLEN, electronic researcher; b. Athens, Ga., Oct. 22, 1935; s. Joseph Thomas and Martha (Holliday) E.; B.E.E., Ga. Inst. Tech., 1957, M.E.E., 1959; Ph.D., Ohio State U., 1965; m. Sandra Key Taylor, May 2, 1959; children—Stephen Mark, Sharon Holliday, Michael Andrew. Aerospace engr. Systems Engring. Group Wright-Patterson AFB, Ohio, 1962-64, chief operations analysis group Synthesis and Analysis Directorate, 1965-66; head radar br., electronics div. Ga. Inst. Tech., 1966—; cons. Inst. of Defense Analysis, 1969, Riegel Textiles, 1970-71. Bd. dirs. Ga. Tech. Wesley Found.; bd. dirs. Churches Home for Business Girls. Served with USAF, 1959-62. Mem. I.E.E.E., Sigma Xi, Omicron Delta Kappa, Phi Kappa Phi, Eta Kappa Nu, Tau Beta Pi, Phi Eta Sigma, Sigma Chi. Methodist (chmn. finance commn. 1969-71). Contbr. numerous articles sci. jours. Home: 3267 Ivanhoe Dr NW Atlanta GA 30327

ECKERT, ALLAN W., author; b. Buffalo, Jan. 30, 1931; s. Edward Russell and Ruth Rose (Roth) E.; student U. Dayton, 1951-52, Ohio State U., 1953-54; m. Joan Dowling, May 14, 1955; children—Joseph Matthew, Julie Anne. Formerly reporter, columnist Dayton Jour. Herald, also asso. editor N.C.R. News, Dayton; free-lance writer, 1960—; writer numerous TV scripts for NBC's Wild Kingdom; created course article writing Writer's Digest; cons. LaSalle Extension U., Chgo. Trustee Dayton Museum Natural History, 1963-65; bd. dirs. W. Charlotte County Civic Assn., Englewood, Fla. Served with USAF, 1948-52. Recipient Ohioana Book award, 1968; Best Book award Friend of Am. Writers, 1968. Life mem. Dayton Soc. Natural History; mem. Outdoor Writers Assn. Am. (bd. dirs.), Soc. Mag. Writers. Author: The Great Auk, 1963; A Time of Terror, 1965; The Silent Sky, 1965; Wild Season, 1967; The Frontiersmen, 1967; Bayou Backwaters, 1967; The Crossbreed, 1968; Blue Jacket, 1968; The King Snake, 1968; The Dreaming Tree, 1968; Wilderness Empire, 1968; In Search of a Whale, 1969; The Conquerors, 1970; Incident at Hawk's Hill, 1971; The Court Martial of Daniel Boone, 1972; The Owls of North America, 1971; (outdoordrama) Tecumseh, 1971; (screenplay) Tale of the Cat, 1971; also numerous articles. Address: 185 Sabal Lane Englewood FL 33533

ECKERT, CHARLES, surgeon; b. Denver, Nov. 22, 1914; s. Martin and Anne (Walker) E.; student U. Wis., 1932-35; M.D., Washington U., St. Louis, 1939; m. Lauramae Pippin, Sept. 25, 1943; children—William Pippin, Charles Dru. Intern Barnes Hosp., St. Louis, 1939-41, resident, 1941-44; attending surgeon St. Louis City Hosp., 1956-66; asst. surgeon Barnes and St. Louis Childrens Hosp., 1944-56; surgeon-in-chief Albany (N.Y.) Med. Center Hosp., 1956—; cons. Albany VA Hosp., 1956—. Instr. surgery Washington U., 1944-48, asst. prof., 1948-53, asso. prof., 1953-56; prof., chmn. dept. surgery Albany Med. Coll., 1956—. Dir. City and County Savs. Bank, Albany. Vice pres. United Fund, 1968-72. Asso. trustee Siena Coll. Diplomate Am. Bd. Surgery (chmn. 1969-70). Mem. A.M.A., A.C.S., Soc. U. Surgeons, Am., Central surg. assns., Societe Internationale de Chirurgie, So. Surg. Assn., Sigma Xi, Alpha Omega Alpha. Clubs: Fort Orange (Albany); Schuyler Meadows Country (Loudonville, N.Y.). Editor: Emergency Room Care, 1967. Contbr. articles to surg. jours., chpts. to surg. texts. Home: 355 Loudon Rd Loudonville NY 12211 Office: Albany Med Coll New Scotland Av Albany NY 12208

ECKERT, ERNST R. G., scientist, educator; b. Prague, Czechoslovakia, Sept. 13, 1904; s. Georg and Margarete (Pfrogner) E.; Diploma Ing., German Inst. Tech., Prague, 1927, Dr. Ing., 1931; Dr. habil., Inst. Technology, Denzig, 1938; Dozent, Inst. of Technol., Braunschweig, Germany, 1940; hon. doctorates Inst. Tech., Munich, 1968, Purdue U., 1968, U. Manchester (Eng.), 1968; m. Josefine Binder, Jan. 30, 1931; children—Rosemarie Christa (Mrs. Koehler), Elke, Karin, Dieter. Came to U.S., 1945, naturalized, 1955. Chief engr., lectr. Inst. Technology, Danzig, 1935- 38; chief thermodynamics sect. Aero. Research Inst., Braunschweig, 1938- 45; prof., dir. Inst. Technology, Prague, 1943-45; cons. USAF, 1945-49; cons. Lewis Flight Propulsion Lab., NASA, 1949-51; prof. mech. engring. dept. U. Minn., 1951—, dir. thermodynamics and heat transfer and of heat transfer lab., 1955—, Regents' prof. mech. engring., 1966- -; vis. prof. Purdue U.; cons. USAF, Gen. Electric Co., Flui-Dyne Engring. Corp., RAND Corp., The Trane Co. U.S. rep. aerodynamics panel Internat. Com. Flame Radiation. Recipient Max Jacob Meml. award, 1961, Distinguished Teaching award U. Minn., 1965, Western Electric Fund award I.E.E.E., 1965, Gold medal French Inst. Energy and Fuel, 1967. Registered profl. engr., Minn. Fellow N.Y. Acad. Scis., Am. Inst. Aeros. and Astronautics; mem. Am. Soc. Engring. Edn., Wissenschaftliche Gesellschaft für Luft and Raumfahrt, Sigma Xi, Pi Tau Sigma, Tau Beta Pi. Author: Introduction to the Transfer of Heat and Mass, 1950, 2d edit., 1959; Heat and Mass Transfer (translated by J. F. Gross), 1963; others in German and Russian. Chmn. hon. editorial adv. bd. Internat. Jour. Heat and Mass Transfer. Editor: Thermal Sciences series, Wadsworth Pub. Co., Belmont, Cal.; editor Wärme-und Stoffübertragung; co-chmn. adv. editorial bd. Heat Transfer Soviet Research. Contbr. articles to sci. mags. Home: 60 W Wentworth Av St Paul MN 55118 Office: U Minn Minneapolis MN 55455

ECKERT, J. PRESPER, engr.; b. Phila., Apr. 9, 1919; s. J. Presper and Ethel M. (Hallowell) E.; student William Penn Charter Sch.; B.S., U. Pa., 1941, M.S., 1943, D.Sc., 1964; m. Hester Caldwell, Oct. 28, 1944 (dec.); children—J. Presper III, Christopher; m. 2d, Judith A. Rewalt, Oct. 13, 1962; children— Laura R., Gregory A. Research asso. Moore Sch. Elec. Engring., U. Pa., 1941-46, instr. engring. sci. mgmt. def. tng. courses; designer radar range systems, 1941-42; co-designer, co-inventor (with Dr. J.W. Mauchly) electronic numerical intergrater and calculator ENIAC, 1942-46; co- designer, co-inventor automatic computers BINAC, 1946-49 and UNIVAC, 1948-51; partner Electronic Control Co., 1946-47; v.p. Eckert-Mauchly Computer Corp., 1947-50; dir. engring. Eckert-Mauchly div. Remington Rand, Inc., 1950-54, v.p. in charge engring. Eckert-Mauchly div., 1954-55; now v.p., tech. adviser to pres. UNIVAC div. Sperry Rand Corp. Recipient (with John W. Mauchly) Howard N. Potts medal, Franklin Inst., 1949, co-recipient John Scott medal City of Phila., 1964; recipient Nat. Sci. medal, 1968. Fellow I.E.E.E.; mem. Nat. Acad. Engring., Sigma Xi. Patentee in electronic and computer field. Home: 612 Mill Creek Rd Gladwyne PA 19035 Office: P O Box 500 Blue Bell PA 19422

ECKERT, ROBERT RAY, newspaper exec.; b. Binghamton, N.Y., Mar. 15, 1920; s. Clarence Calvin and Agnes (Malseed) E.; student Trinity Coll., 1943; B.A., Yale, 1946; m. Geane Louise Martin, June 12, 1948; children—Kathleen Rae, John Martin, David Roy. Reporter, Endicott (N.Y.) Bulletin, 1937-38, sports editor, 1938-40, news editor, 1940-41; city editor Oneonta (N.Y.) Star, 1946-47; founder, editor, pub. Vestal (N.Y.) News, 1947-54; bur. chief Riverside (Cal.) Enterprise, 1954-55; reporter-columnist Binghamton (N.Y.) Press, 1955-58, asst. to gen. mgr., 1958-59, bus. mgr., 1959-61; gen. mgr. Elmira (N.Y.) Star-Gazette, 1961-65; dir. operations Rochester (N.Y.) Times-Union, Democrat & Chronicle, 1965-67; pres., pub. Hartford (Conn.) Times, 1968—; dir. Community Offset Corp., 1968—; trustee Soc. for Savings, 1969—. Bd. dirs. Hartford Symphony, 1968—; trustee New Eng. Colls. Fund, 1969—. Served with USNR, 1941-46. Named Young Man of Year, Vestal, N.Y., 1954. Mem. Greater Hartford C. of C. (bd. dirs. 1968—), Conn. (dir. 1971—), New Eng. daily newspapers assns., Am. Newspaper Publishers Assn. Home: 7 Dorset Lane Farmington CT 06032 Office: 10 Prospect St Hartford CT 06101

ECKERT, RUTH ELIZABETH, (Mrs. Eric E. Paulson), educator; b. Buffalo, Apr. 2, 1905; d. Edward Lee and Elizabeth Margaret (Fix) Eckert; A.B. cum laude, U. Buffalo; 1930, M.A., 1932; Ed.D., Harvard (Austin fellowship), 1937; Litt.D. (hon.), Houghton Coll., 1962; D.Hum., Drake U., 1964; m. Eric Edwin Paulson, Apr. 2, 1941 (dec. Dec. 1962). Research asso. U. Buffalo, 1932-36; research adviser Am. Council Edn., 1937- 38; asso. prof. edn. U. Minn., 1938-45, prof. higher edn., 1945—, coordinator ednl. research, 1940-50; staff mem. charge studies secondary sch. students N.Y. Regents Inquiry, 1936-38; staff mem. Joint Legislative Com. Survey N.Y. City Pub. Colls., 1943; chmn. work com. charge studies higher ednl. needs in Minn., Minn. Comn. Higher Edn., 1945-49; ednl. cons. to individual coll. staffs in N. Central area. Mem. Nat. Adv. Com. on Presbyn. Colls., 1952-56, adv. com. on research U.S. Office Edn., 1956-58; mem. com. on research Ednl. Testing Service. Mem. N.E.A. (ednl. policies commn. 1956-60), Am. Ednl. Research Assn., Nat. Soc. Study Edn., Nat. Soc. Coll. Tchrs. Edn. (exec. com. 1951-56, 63-65, pres. 1954-55), Assn. for Higher Edn. (exec. com. 1947-49, 63- 66), Am. Assn. U. Profs., Phi Beta Kappa. Lutheran. Author: (with T.O. Marshall) When Youth Leave School, 1938; Outcomes of General Education, 1943; (with R.J. Keller) A University Looks at its Program, 1954; (with John E. Stecklein) Job Motivations and Satisfactions of College Teachers, 1961; (with Robert T. Alciatore) Minnesota Ph.D.'s Evaluate Their Training, 1968; also chpts. in edn. books. Editor: Studies in Higher Education, 1941, 43; Higher Education in Minnesota, 1950. Contbr. articles to profl. jours. Home: 1624 E River Terrace Minneapolis MN 55414

ECKERT, WILLIAM HENRY, lawyer; b. Pitts., Mar. 27, 1900; s. William George and Matilda (Nickel) E.; B.S. in Econs., U. Pitts., 1921, LL.B., 1924; m. Josephine B. Gibson, July 13, 1934; children—Josephine (Mrs. John S. Diggs), Dorothy (Mrs. Paul D. Grannis). Admitted to Pa. bar, 1924, since practiced in Pitts.; partner firm Eckert, Seamans & Cherin, and predecessors, 1930—; part-time prof. law U. Pitts. Law Sch., 1924-48. Mem. Pa. Supreme Ct. Procedural Rules Com., 1945—; vice chmn. adv. com. law decedents estates and trusts Pa. Joint Govt. Commn., 1945—. Mem. Rosslyn Farms Borough Council, 1942-45, Crafton Sch. Bd., 1936-40. Served with U.S. Army, 1918. Mem. Am., Pa. (pres. 1969-70), Allegheny County (pres. 1945-46) bar assns., Am. Law Inst. Republican. Presbyn. Home: 410 King Hwy Rosslyn Farms Carnegie PA 15106 Office: Porter Bldg Pittsburgh PA 15219

ECKHARDT, GEORGE STAFFORD, army officer; b. Winfield, Kan., Apr. 18, 1912; student Kearney (Neb.) State Tchrs. Coll., 1929-30, U. Wis., 1930-31; B.S., U.S. Mil. Acad., 1935; grad. Indsl. Coll. Armed Forces, 1946-47; M.A., Am. U., 1962; m. Margaret Lucille Jay, Mar. 5, 1942; children—Jay (Mrs. J.W. Britton), George Stafford. Commd. 2d lt. U.S. Army, 1935, advanced through grades to maj. gen., 1962; assigned operations div. War Dept. Gen. Staff, 1942-43; staff comdr. Fifth Fleet, 1943-45; with Office Under Sec. War, 1946; assigned Munitions Bd., Office Sec. Def., 1947-49, U.S. Constabulary Germany, 1950-52; internat. security affairs officer Office Asst. Sec. Def., 1952-54; assigned Chief Staff, U.S. Army Pacific, 1954-57; comdr. Arty. Air Def. Group, 1957-59; mil. asst. to chmn. Joint Chiefs Staff, 1959-60; comdr. Army Air Defenses Washington, Balt. and Norfolk, also 2d Air Def. Region, 1960-62; chief Mil. Assistance Adv. Group to Iran, 1962-65; comdg. gen. 9th Inf. Div., Ft. Riley, Kan., 1965-67; dep. comdg. gen. II Field Force, Vietnam, 1967- 68; sr. adviser IV Corps, Vietnam, 1968-69; comdt. U.S. Army War Coll., comdg. gen. Carlisle Barracks, Pa., 1969-71, comdg. gen. U.S. Army Mil. Hist. Research Collection, U.S. Army Combat Devel. Command Inst. Land Combat (all Carlisle Barracks); spl. asst. to comdr. Mil. Assistance Command Vietnam, 1971—. Decorated Legion of Merit with 3 oak leaf clusters, Air medal with 14 oak leaf clusters, Navy Star and V, Bronze Star, Commendation medal with 2 oak leaf clusters, D.S.M. with oak leaf cluster. Mem. Assn. U.S. Army. Methodist. Mason (Shriner). Address: CMDGP (JOIR) APO San Francisco CA 96222

ECKHARDT, ROBERT CHRISTIAN, congressman; b. Austin, Tex., July 16, 1913; s. Joseph Carl Augustus and Norma (Wurzbach) E.; B.A., U. Tex., 1935, LL.B., 1939; m. Orissa Stevenson (dec.); children—Orissa (Mrs. Lawrence L. Arend), Rosalind; m. 2d, Nadine Ellen Cannon, Mar. 8, 1962; children—Sidney, Shelby, William, Sarah. Admitted to Tex. bar, 1939; practiced in Austin, 1939-42, 46-48; S.W. regional dir. Office Coordinator Inter-Am. Affairs, 1944-46; practiced in Dallas, 1948-50, in Houston, 1950-67; mem. Tex. Ho. of Reps., 1958-66; mem. 90th-92d congresses from 8th Dist. Tex., mem. com. interstate and fgn. commerce, subcom. on commerce and finance. Served with USAAF, 1942-44. Mem. State Bar of Tex. Democrat. Home: 3312 N St NW Washington DC 20007

ECKHARDT, WILLARD LELAND, educator; B.S., U. Ill., 1935, J.D., 1937. Prof., dean Sch. Law U. Mo., Columbia. Office: Sch Law U Mo 417 S 5th St Columbia MO 65201*

ECKIS, ROLLIN POLLARD, geologist, ret. oil co. exec.; b. Oakland, Cal., June 26, 1905; s. Rollin Garfield and Daisy (Pollard) E.; A.B., Pomona Coll., 1927; M.S., Cal. Inst. Tech., 1929; m. Caroline Comstock, 1937; children—Rollin Charles, Nancy May, Ellen Mott. Engr., geologist div. water resources, State Cal., 1930-34; geologist Texas Co., 1934-47; dist. geologist Richfield Oil Corp., Los Angeles, 1937-46, chief geologist, 1946-54, v.p., 1954-56, exec. v.p., 1956-62, pres., 1962-66; exec. v.p. Atlantic Richfield Co., 1966-70, vice chmn. bd., 1969—. Trustee Pomona Coll., 1958—. Fellow Geol. Soc. Am.; mem. Am. Assn. Petroleum Geologists, Am. Petroleum Inst. (dir.), Sigma Xi. Home: 800 W First St Los Angeles CA 90012 Office: 445 S Figueroa St Los Angeles CA 90071

ECKLER, A. ROSS, cons.; b. Van Hornesville, N.Y., May 22, 1901; s. Albert Henry and Mary Jane (Young) E.; A.B., Hamilton Coll., 1922, D.Sc., 1966; A.M., Harvard, 1928, Ph.D., 1934; m. Jennie Howe, Aug. 7, 1924; children—Albert Ross, Mary Lois (Mrs. David S. Dennison). Tchr. math. Tome Inst., Port Deposit, Md., 1922-24; statistician and dir. statis. lab. Harvard Econ. Soc., 1924-31; asst. librarian and instr. pub. utility econs. Harvard, 1931-35; chief spl. inquiries and asst. dir. research WPA, Washington, 1935-39; chief econ. statistics, population div. Bur. Census, 1939-42, asst. chief population div., 1942-43, chief spl. surveys div., 1943-45, chief social sci. analyst, 1945-47, asst. dir. U.S. Bur. Census, 1947-49, dep. dir., 1949-65, acting dir., 1965, dir., 1965-69. Adviser, 6th Internat. Conf. Labor Statisticians, ILO, 1947, alternate del. 8th, 9th Internat. Confs., Geneva, 1954, 57; U.S. del. 27th conf. Internat. Statis. Inst., New Delhi, India, 1951, 30th Conf. Stockholm, Sweden, 1957, 32d Conf., Tokyo, Japan, 1960, 33d Conf., Paris, 1961, 34th Conf., Ottawa, Can., 1963, 35th Conf., Belgrade, Yugoslavia, 1965, 36th Conf. Australia, 1967, 37th Conf., London, Eng., 1969; U.S. alternate dele. com. improvement nat. statistics Inter-Am. Statis. Inst., Beunos Aires, Argentina, 1958. Recipient Gold Medal award Dept. Commerce, 1961, Nat. Civil Service League award, 1962. Fellow Am. Statis. Assn. (v.p. 1967-69, pres. 1969), Royal Statist. Soc. (Eng.) (hon.); mem. Paris Statis. Soc., Internat., Inter Am. statist. insts., Am. Econ. Assn., Phi Beta Kappa. Conglist. Mason. Clubs: Kenwood Golf and Country, Cosmos (Washington). Contbr. articles to profl. jours. Home: 3643 Brandywine St Washington DC 20008 also Van Hornesville NY 13475

ECKLER, JOHN ALFRED, lawyer; b. Elyria, O., July 2, 1913; s. Frank Roy and Ida Jean (Phipps) E.; A.B., Ohio Wesleyan U., 1935; J.D., U. Chgo., 1939; m. Mary Emily Rickey, Dec. 21, 1936; children—Rickey, Ida Jane, Mary Moulton. With Gen. Electric Co., Schenectady, 1935-36; admitted to Ill. bar, 1939, Ohio bar, 1945; asso. Knapp, Allen & Cushing, Chgo., 1939-43; adminstrv. asst. to Senator John W. Bricker, Washington, 1947-49; practice of law, Columbus, O., 1949—; partner Bricker, Evatt, Barton and Eckler, 1954—. Chmn. Ohio Bd. Bar Examiners, 1954-59; v.p. Nat. Conf. Bar Examiners, 1958-59, chmn., 1960-61, chmn. standing com. on multi- state bar exam., 1968—. Pres. Upper Arlington Civic Assn., 1952; active in United Appeals; mem. bd. health City Upper Arlington, 1956-70. Mem. chmn. bd. trustees Ohio Wesleyan U., 1958—; trustee, gen. counsel World Neighbors, Inc., 1952- -. Served as lt. USNR, World War II. Mem. Am. (chmn. spl. com. court congestion 1958-60, mem. Ho. of Dels. 1960-69), Ohio, Columbus (pres., bd. govs.) bar assns., Am. Legion, Ohio Wesleyan U. Alumni Assn. (pres. 1958-60), Phi Beta Kappa, Omicron Delta Kappa, Delta Sigma Rho, Phi Delta Theta, Order of Coif. Methodist. Mason (33). Clubs: University, Scroto Torch, Rotary (bd.) (Columbus). Contbr. articles U. Chgo. Law Rev., others. Home: 2105 Lower Chelsea Rd Columbus OH 43212 Office: 100 E Broad St Columbus OH 43215

ECKLES, LUCIUS ELKANAH, physician; b. Eskridge, Kan., Jan. 15, 1905; s. William Thomas and Nellie (Kingman) E.; A.B., U. Kan., 1927; M.D., Harvard, 1931; m. Josephine E. Meier, Nov. 1, 1959; children—Lucius Elkanah, Peter N., Amey. Intern, then resident Childrens Med. Center, Boston, 1931-35; pvt. practice pediatrics, Topeka, 1935-42, 46-62; med. dir. Waimano Tng. Sch. and Hosp., Pearl City, Hawaii, 1962—; asso. clin. prof. pediatrics Med. Sch. U. Hawaii, 1966—. Pres. Kan. Bd. Health, 1950. Served to comdr., M.C., USNR, 1942-46. Diplomate Am. Bd. Pediatrics. Mem. Sigma Chi. Address: Waimano Tng Sch and Hosp Pearl City HI 96782

ECKLEY, FREDERICK RALPH, Jr., telephone co. exec.; b. Delaware, O., Aug. 22, 1914; s. Frederick Ralph and Mary Taylor (May) E.; B.S.C., Ohio State U., 1936; m. Helen Warren, June 21, 1941; children—Marcia E. Yearout, Deborah E. (Mrs. Briggs). With N.J. Bell Telephone Co., 1936-47; with Am. Tel.& Tel. Corp., 1947-52, 56-61, dir. personnel and pub. relations long lines, 1959-61; with Northwestern Bell Telephone Co., 1952-56, asst. v.p. sales and mdsg., 1955-56; with Mich. Bell Telephone Co., Detroit, 1961-62; v.p., gen. mgr., dir. mem. exec. com. Ohio Bell Telephone Co., Cleve., 1962-64, pres., dir. 1966—; exec. v.p. Am. Tel. & Tel. Co., N.Y.C., 1964-66; dir. Republic Steel Corp., Eaton Corp., Galbreath 1st Mortgage Investments, Central Nat. Bank Mem. Navy League U.S., Ohio Soc. N.Y., Ohio (dir.), Cleve. (dir.) chambers commerce, Telephone Pioneers Am., Newcomen Soc., Phi Gamma Delta. Clubs: Baltusrol Golf; Gulfstream Golf; Clevelander; Pepper Pike, Union, Country (Cleve.); University (Columbus, O.). Home: 2825 Lander Rd Cleveland OH 44124 Office: 100 Erieview Plaza Cleveland OH 44114

ECKLEY, ROBERT SPENCE, coll. pres.; b. Kankakee, Ill., Sept. 4, 1921; s. George Alva and Mary (Spence) E.; B.S., Bradley U., 1942; M.B.A., U. Minn., 1943; M.A., Harvard, 1948, Ph.D., 1949; m. Nell Mann, Mar. 28, 1947; children—Robert George, Jane Ann, Paul Nelson, Rebecca Helen. Asst. prof. econs. U. Kan., Lawrence, 1949-51; indsl. economist Fed. Res. Bank of Kansas City (Mo.), 1951-54; mgr. bus. econs. dept. Caterpillar Tractor Co., Peoria, Ill., 1954-68; pres. Ill. Wesleyan U., Bloomington, 1968—. First v.p. Ill. Council of Churches, 1968-70. Trustee Meth. Hosp. Central Ill. Served to lt. (j.g.) USCGR, 1943-46. Recipient Phi Kappa Phi Alumni award Bradley U., 1966. Mem. Am. Econ. Assn., Nat. Assn. Bus. Economists, Am. Statis. Assn. Methodist. Contbr. articles to profl. publs. Home: 1201 N Park St Bloomington IL 61701

ECKLEY, WILTON EARL, Jr., educator; b. Alliance, Ohio, June 25, 1929; s. Wilton Earl and Louise (Bert) E.; B.A., Mt. Union Coll., 1952; M.A., Pa. State U., 1955; Ph.D., Case Western Reserve U., 1965; John Hay fellow Yale U., 1961-62; m. Grace Ester Williamson, Sept. 12, 1954; children—Douglas, Stephen, Timothy. Chmn. English Euclid (O.) Sr. High Sch., 1955-63; dir. tchr. tng. Hollins Coll., 1963-65; prof. English, chmn. dept. Drake U., 1965—. Coe fellow Am. Studies, 1957—. Mem. Modern Lang. Assn., Circus Hist. Soc., Phi Kappa Tau. Author: A Guide to E.E. Cummings, 1970; A Checklist of E.E. Cummings, 1970. Home: 529 Waterbury Circle Des Moines IA 50312

ECKLUND, GLENN ALGOT, ins. co. exec.; b. Omaha, Aug. 10, 1913; s. Sixten Gustav and Nellie (Johnson) E.; student Van Sant Sch. Bus., 1932, LaSalle Extension U., 1933-34; m. June Margaret Martinson, Sept. 6, 1936; children—Gary Glenn, Don Stanley, Nancy June, Roger Thomas. Stock clk. Orchard & Wilhelm Co., 1931-35; with United Benefit Life Ins. Co., Omaha, 1935—, asst. v.p., 1954-56, v.p., 1956-65, exec. v.p. accounting, 1965—. Bd. dirs. Omaha City Mission, Midwest Conf. Convenant Chs. Recipient Key Man award Jr. C. of C., 1948. Mem. Life Office Mgmt. Assn. Home: 9468 Pauline St Omaha NB 68124 Office: 3316 Farnam St Omaha NB 68101

ECKMAN, FERN MARJA, journalist; b. N.Y.C., Aug. 27; d. Isidor Peter and Zara Nettie (Sloate) Friedman; B.A., N.Y.U., 1957; m. Irving Eckman, June 21, 1957. Reporter, N.Y. Post, 1944—, assigned to the UN, 1945-49, 60-65; feature writer for nat. publns. Recipient George Polk Meml. award for distinguished met. reporting, 1951, 55; Page One award for community service N.Y. Newspaper Guild, 1955, 61; citation for community service Council Puerto Rican and Spanish-Am. Orgns., 1955; Lasker award for med. journalism, 1959; Front Page award for distinguished feature writing, Newspaper Women's Club N.Y., 1949, 51, 56, 64; Cultural News award Newspaper Reporters Assn., N.Y.C., 1967; Empire State award for excellence in med. reporting, 1968. Mem. Newspaper Women's Club N.Y. (distinguished service award 1970). Author: The Furious Passage of James Baldwin, 1967. Home: 749 West End Av New York City NY 10025 Office: 210 South Street New York City NY 10002

ECKMAN, JAMES RUSSELL, med. editor, tech. historian; b. Sioux City, Ia., Apr. 25, 1908; s. James Abram and Katherine Russell (Letts) E.; B.A., U. Minn., 1932; M.A., Georgetown U., 1944, Ph.D., 1946; m. Frances Elizabeth Kaklec, June 12, 1937. Asst. editor Jour.-Lancet, med. jour., Mpls., 1934-38; mem. sect. publs. Mayo Clinic, Rochester, Minn., 1938—, press officer, 1948-65, sr. cons. sect. publns., 1965—; asst. prof. history medicine Mayo Found., U. Minn., 1960—; hist. editor Printing Impressions, 1960—; owner Doomsday Press, Rochester, 1939—; cons. Assn. Med. Illustrators, 1965—. Bd. dirs. Rochester (Minn.) Civic Theatre, 1967—. Served to capt. AUS, 1943-45. Mem. Mediaeval Acad. Am., Am. Inst. Graphic Arts, Soc. Typographic Arts Chgo., Gutenberg Gesellschaft, Soc. Hist. Tech., History Sci. Soc., Minn., Omlsted County (sec. 1955-65) hist. socs., Minn. Newspaper Assn., Printing Hist. Soc. (Eng.), Bibliog. Soc. U. Va., Nat. Assn. Sci. Writers (asso.), Sigma Xi, Sigma Delta Chi, Phi Alpha Theta, Chi Phi. Clubs: Grolier, Typophiles (N.Y.C.); Press (Mpls.); Ampersand (Mpls.-St. Paul). Author: Jerome Cardan, 1946; Sterling P. Rounds and His Printers Cabinet, 1962; The Heritage of the Printer, Vol 1, 1965; also articles on hist. research tech. aspects printing methods. Editor: Among the Craft: Notes by the Way (Sterling P. Rounds), 1968; Minn. Med. Found. editorial bd., 1970—. Home: 921 8th Av SW Rochester MN 55901 Office: 200 1st St SW Rochester MN 55901

ECKMAN, JOHN WHILEY, bus. exec.; b. Forest Hills, N.Y., July 20, 1919; s. Samuel Whiley and Anna (Wolffram) E.; student Yale, 1937-38; B.S., U. Pa., 1943; m. Barbara Harding, Mar. 23, 1946; children—Alison Elizabeth, Stephen Keyler. With Smith Kline & French Labs., Inc., Phila., 1946-52; v.p. Thomas Leeming & Co., Inc., N.Y.C., 1952-62; exec. v.p., dir. William H. Rorer, Inc., Ft. Washington, Pa., 1962-66, pres., 1966—; exec. v.p., bd. dirs. Rorer-Amchem, Inc., Fort Washington, 1968-70, pres., 1970—; dir. Staats-Herold Corp., N.Y.C., First Pa. Bank, Phila. Trustee U.Pa.; bd. mgrs. Wistar Inst. Anatomy and Biology; bd. dirs. Haverford Sch., Pa. Export Corps, Digestive Disease Found. Served from ensign to lt., USNR, 1943-46. Mem. Pharm. Advt. Club (pres. 1960), Nat. Planning Assn. (nat. council 1969—), Hist. Soc. Pa., N.Y. Acad. Sci., A.A.A.S., Pa. Soc., Wharton Sch. Alumni Assn (dir. 1966-68, pres. 1968-70), S.R., Sigma Chi, Beta Gamma Sigma. Presbyn. Clubs: Philadelphia. Country, Union League Sunday Breakfast (Phila.); Nantucket (Mass.) Yacht; Yale (N.Y.C.). Home: 511 Hillbrook Rd Bryn Mawr PA 19010 Office: 500 Virginia Dr Fort Washington PA 19034

ECKRICH, DONALD PETER, meat processing co. exec.; b. Ft. Wayne, Ind., Sept. 6, 1924; s. Clement P. and Beatrice A. (Ek) E.; student Washington and Jefferson Coll., 1942; B.B.S., U. Mich., 1948; m. Barbara Jean Burke, Dec. 27, 1947; children—Emily, George Milton, Joseph Clement, Ellen, James Benedict, Eleanor, Louise, Diane. With Peter Eckrich & Sons, Inc., Ft. Wayne, 1948—, dir. operations, 1965-66, exec. v.p., 1966-69, pres., 1969—; dir. Am. Fed. Savs. & Loan Assn. Mem lay bd. advisers St. Joseph's Hosp., Ft. Wayne, St. Anne's Home, Ft. Wayne, Nazareth Coll., Kalamazoo. Served with inf., AUS, 1943-45. Mem. Am. Meat Inst. (dir.), Chgo. C. of C. (dir.). Home: 1210 Korte Lane Fort Wayne IN 46807 Office: 3515 Hobson Rd Fort Wayne IN 46805

ECKSTEIN, HARRY, educator; b. Schotten, Germany, Jan. 26, 1924; s. Moritz and Bella (Bachenheimer) E.; A.B., Harvard, 1948, M.A., 1950, Ph.D., 1954; student London (Eng.) Sch. Econs. and Polit. Sci., 1950-51, 52-53; m. Joan J. Campbell, Apr. 1, 1953; 1 son, Jonathan. Teaching fellow Harvard, 1949- 50, 51-52, instr. polit. sci., 1954-56, asst. prof., 1956-58; fellow Center Advanced Study Behavioral Scis., Palo Alto, Cal., 1958-59; asso. prof. politics Princeton, 1959-61, prof., 1961—, IBM prof. internat. studies, 1968—, research Asso. Center Internat. Studies 1959—, dir. workshop comparative politics, 1966—. Fellow Am. Acad. Arts and Scis.; mem. Am. Polit. Sci. Assn. Co-author: Patterns of Government, 1958; The English Health Service, 1958; Pressure Group Politics, 1960; A Theory of Stable Democracy, 1961; Division and Cohesion in Democracy, 1966. Editor: World Politics, 1960—, Sage Professional Papers in Comparative Political Studies. Editor, contbr.: Comparative Politics, 1963; Internal War, 1964. Home: 94 Maclean Circle Princeton NJ 08540

ECKSTEIN, JEROME, educator, philosopher; b. N.Y.C., June 28, 1925; s. Marcus and Blanche (Wohlberg) E.; B.A., Bklyn. Coll., 1949; Ph.D., Columbia, 1961; student Grad. Faculty New Sch. Social Research, 1949-50, Yeshiva and Mesifta Torah Vodaath, 1930-43, Rabbi Isaac Elehanan Theol. Sem., 1943-45; m. Sally A. Lawrence, Sept. 1, 1969; children by previous marriage—Sandra (Mrs. Kenneth L. Cohen), Michael J., Esther. Buyer antique silverware Blanche Eckstein Silverware, Bklyn., 1944-53; dir. edn. and youth activities various Hebrew congregations, 1950-61; fellow logic, lectr. philosophy Coll. City N.Y., 1955-56; lectr. philosophy Bklyn. Coll., 1955-60; instr. contemporary civilization and philosophy Columbia, 1960- 62; asst. prof., then asso. prof. philosophy, coordinator humanities div. Adelphi Suffolk Coll., Adelphi U., 1963-66; prof. philosophy edn. State U. N.Y. at Albany, 1966—; participant Internat. Philosophy Year, Brockport, N.Y., 1967. Mem. Am. Philoso. Assn., Am. Assn. U. Profs., Am. Fedn. Tchrs., Phi Beta Kappa. Author: The Platonic Method: An Interpretation of the Dramatic-Philosophic Aspects of the Meno, 1968; also numerous articles.

ECKSTEIN, OTTO, educator, economist; b. Ulm, Germany, Aug. 1, 1927; s. Hugo and Hedwig (Pressburger) E.; came to U.S., 1939, naturalized, 1945; A.B., Princeton U., 1951, LL.D. (hon.), 1966; A.M., Harvard, 1952, Ph.D., 1955; m. Harriett Mirkin, June 27, 1954; children—Warren Matthew, Felicia, June. Mem. faculty Harvard, 1955—, prof. econs., 1963- -; pres. Data Resources, Inc., 1969—. Tech. dir. employment, growth and price levels study Joint Econ. Com., U.S. Congress, 1959-60; mem. President's Council of Econ. Advisers, 1964-66; mem. Nat. Adv. Council on Econ. Opportunity, 1967-69; mem. President's Commn. on Income Maintenance Programs, 1968-69; mem. research adv. bd. Com. for Econ. Devel., 1967-70. Served with AUS, 1946-48. Fellow Econometric Soc.; mem. Am. Econ. Assn. (exec. com. 1967-70) Author: Water Resource Development, 1958; (with J.V. Krutilla) Multiple Purpose River Development, 1958; (with others) Economic Policy in Our Time, 1963; Public Finance, 1963. Editor: Foundations of Modern Economics Series, 1962—; Rev. Economics and Statistics, 1962-71. Home: 24 Barberry Road Lexington MA 02173 Office: Dept Econs Harvard Univ Cambridge MA 02138

ECKSTINE, BILLY, (William Clarence Eckstein), singer; b. Pitts., July 8, 1914; student Howard U. Night club singer, emcee, Buffalo, Detroit, then Club de Lisa in Chgo.; vocalist Earl Hines Band, 1939; night club soloist, 1943; with Budd Johnson organized bank featuring bop music, 1944; orchestra leader, singer, trombone player; popular ballad singer, 1948—, also jazz music; recordings with band National Records. Address: care William Morris Agy 2020 N Canon Dr Beverly Hills CA 90210

ECO, UMBERTO, publisher, educator; b. Jan. 5, 1932; ed. Univ. degli Studi, Turin, Italy. With Italian TV, 1954-59; asst. lectr. aesthetics U. Turin, 1956- 63, lectr., 1963-64; lectr. Faculty Architecture, U. Milan (Italy), 1964- 65; dir. nonfiction dept. Casa Editrice Bompiani, 1959-65; columnist L'Espresso, 1965—; prof. faculty architecture U. of Florence. Author: Il Problema Estetico in San Tommaso, 1956; Sviluppo dell'Estetica Medievale, 1959; Opera Aperta, 1962; Diario Minimo, 1963; Apocalittici e Integrati, 1964; L'Oeuvre Ouverte, 1965; La Strutfura Assente, 1968. Address: Via Piascane 12 Milan Italy

ECONOMOS, GEORGE THEMISTOCLES, educator, physician; b. N. Epiros, Greece, Feb. 2, 1922; s. Themistocles G. and Fotini (Papinghi) E.; B.S., M.D., U. Athens, 1949; M.D., U. Vt., 1954; m. Stavroula Perdikis, Sept. 6, 1959; children—Demetra, Gregory, Themis. Came to U.S., 1950, naturalized, 1959. Intern medicine George Washington U. Hosp., 1954-55, fellow medicine, 1959-60; asst. resident medicine D.C. Gen. Hosp., 1955-56, sr. resident medicine, 1958- 59; med. dir. Children's Center D.C., 1960—; pvt. practice diagnostic medicine and consultations, 1960—; mem. faculty George Washington U. Med. Sch., 1960—, asst. clin. prof. medicine, 1964—; spl. research mental retardation. Served to capt., M.C., AUS, 1956-58. Mem. Am., So. med. assns., D.C. Med. Soc., Smithsonian Soc. Assos., Am. Assn. Med. Supts., Assn. Mil. Surgeons, Am. Rheumatism Assn., Am. Heart Assn., Am. Soc. Internal Medicine, Am. Geriatrics Soc., D.C. Internal Medicine Soc., Vt. State Soc., U. Vt. Med. Alumni Assn., Am. Hellenic Edn. Progressive Assn., Pan Epirotan Soc. U.S., Nu Sigma Nu. Home: 7513 Arrowwood Rd Bethesda MD 20034 Office: 2141 K St NW Washington DC 20037

EDDINGER, LUCILLE ANNE, news corr.; b. Allentown, Pa., Apr. 27, 1925; d. Joseph B. and Margaret (Ward) E.; B.A., Moravian Coll. for Women, Bethlehem, Pa. With U.P.I., Washington, 1950-52; staff Wall Street Jour., Washington, 1952-55; asst. editor Conover-Mast Publs., 1955-57; staff Cincinnati Times-Star, Washington, 1957-58; Washington corr. Copley Press, Inc., 1958—. Club: Women's Nat. Press (Washington). Home: 2120 16th St NW Washington DC 20009 Office: 3000 39th Av NW Washington DC 20006

EDDISON, JOHN CORBIN, economist; b. N.Y.C., Nov. 4, 1919; s. William Barton and Mary (Corbin) E.; grad. St. Paul's Sch., 1938; A.B., Cornell U., 1942; M.S., 1948; Ph.D., Mass. Inst. Tech., 1955; m. Elizabeth Owsley Bole, Feb. 10, 1951; children—Jonathan B., Elizabeth O., Martha C. Personnel asst. E. I. duPont de Nemours & Co., 1947-48; indsl. engr. Campbell Soup Co., 1949- 51; indsl. adviser EDA, San Juan, P.R., 1955-56; asst. to rep. in Burma, Ford Found., 1956-57; econ. adviser to Govt. W. Pakistan, Harvard Adv. Group, Lahore, 1958-61, to Pakistan Planning Commn., Karachi, 1961-63;

dep. dir. AID mission to Bolivia, La Paz, 1963-65; dep. dir. Central Am. affairs Dept. State, Washington, 1965-68; dir. Near East affairs AID, 1968-69; econ. adviser to planning dept. Govt. Colombia, Harvard U. Devel. Adv. Service, Bogata, 1969-71, adminstr., Cambridge, Mass., 1971—. Served to capt., C.E., AUS, 1942-46. Overseas fellow Ford Found., 1953-54. Mem. Soc. Internat. Devel., Am. Civil Liberties Union, Am. Econ. Assn., Alpha Delta Phi. Episcopalian. Author papers, reports. Home: 202 Primrose St Chevy Chase MD 20015 Office: 1737 Cambridge St Cambridge MA 02138

EDDISON, PETER CHRISTMANN diversified mfg. co. exec.; b. Cin., May 21, 1910; grad. Phillips Acad., Andover, Mass., 1927; B.S., Princeton, 1931; postgrad. Mass. Inst. Tech., 1931-33; m. Jean R. Holland, June 16, 1935; children--Lois A., Andrew M., James. Salesman, Brown Mfg. Co., Boston, 1932-33; jr. engr. Ball Metals Co., Carson City, Nev., 1933-36, engr., 1936-37, sr. engr., 1937-40; project engr. Kingston Engring. Co., Los Angeles, 1940-43; with dept. engring. City of Denver, 1946-50, dep. head, 1950-52; 2d v.p. Johnson Mfg. Co., Kansas City, Kansas, 1952-54, v.p. for engring., 1954-57; v.p. research Consol. Industries, Inc., South Bend, Ind., 1957-60, exec. v.p., 1960-65, pres. 1965-70, chmn. bd., chief exec. officer, 1970--, also dir.; dir. ABC Chem. Co., 2d Nat. Bank, Country Food Storage Co., Providence Indsl. Corp. (Ind.), Wilson Investment Co., Inc., Hammond Life Ins. Co., Inc. Pres., Dewey High Sch., Kansas City, Mo., 1953-54; fund chmn. local div. Salvation Army, 1959-60. Mem. South Bend Republican Com., 1964-68. Bd. dirs. Ind. council Boy Scouts Am., 1969-71; trustee Lovell Found. Served to lt., Corps Engrs., AUS, 1943-45. Decorated Bronze Star medal. Member N.A.M., South Bend C. of C. (v.p. 1963-65, dir. 1965-70), Am. Mgmt. Assn., Ind. Engrs. Soc. (program com. 1961-62), Princeton Alumni Assn. Episcopalian. Rotarian, Optimist. Clubs: South Bend Golf; Links (N.Y.C.). Home: 6823 Broad Terrace Av South Bend IL 46505 Office: PO Box 1019 South Bend IN 46501

EDDLEMAN, HENRY LEO, clergyman; b. Morgantown, Miss., Apr. 4, 1911; s. Richard Aaron and Lucille (Power) E.; A.B., Miss. Coll., 1932; Th.M., So. Bapt. Theol. Sem., Louisville, 1935, Ph.D., 1942; D.D., Georgetown Coll., 1949; m. Sarah Fox, Sept. 7, 1937; children—Sarah Enfield (Mrs. D.G. Duvall), Evelyn Lucille (Mrs. J.K. Gordinier). Ordained to ministry Bapt. Ch., 1930; ednl. and religious work, Palestine, 1935-41; tchr. O.T., Hebrew, New Orleans Bapt. Sem., 1941-42; pastor Parkland Ch., Louisville, 1942-52; part-time faculty O.T., Hebrew, So. Bapt. Sem., Louisville, 1950-52, full time faculty, 1952-54; pres. Georgetown Coll., 1954-59; pres. New Orleans Baptist Theol. Sem., 1959-70; doctrinal reader Baptist Sunday Sch. Bd., Nashville, 1970—. Asst. moderator Gen. Assn. Bapts. in Ky., also chmn. state bd., chmn. budget com., chmn. com. for nominations, 1954; bd. mgrs. Western Recorder (Bapt. state paper); mem. hosp. bd., state bd. missions Ky. Bapts., also adv. com. Home for Aged; mem. fgn. mission bd., chmn. com. on ministerial edn. for Negroes, So. Bapt. Conv. Mem. Nat. Assn. Profs. Hebrew of Am., Internat. Platform Assn., Trust Moral and Civic Found., Am. Assn. Ind. Colls. and Univs. Rotarian. Author: To Make Men Free, 1954; Teachings of Jesus in Matthew 5-7, 1955; Missionary Task of a Church, 1961; Mandelbaum Gate, 1963; The Second Coming, 1963; Trustees and Higher Education, 1967; Guidelines to Ecumenicalism, 1967; Federal Aid, Trustees and Higher Education, 1969; Last Things, 1969. Home: 901 Capitol Towers Nashville TN 37219

EDDLEMAN, WILLIAM ROSEMAN, lawyer; b. Shelby, N.C., May 21, 1913; s. William Peter and Nellie Holland (Roseman) E.; student U. N.C., 1930-34, Pace Inst., 1934-35, Washington Coll. Law, 1935-37; LL.B., Gonzaga U., 1939; m. Ruth Carolyn Phelps, Aug. 31, 1952 (dec. Aug. 1966); 1 son, William Lammers; m. 2d, Elizabeth Dorothy Carp, Nov. 1, 1966. Admitted to Wash. bar, 1939, U.S. Supreme Ct., 1945; Licenciado en Derecho, Mexico, 1968; mem. firm Eddleman & Wheeler, Seattle, 1946-64, Perez, Verdia, Eddleman, 1963-64; with Parker Sch., Columbia, 1964; law faculty Nat. U. of Mexico, 1964-67. Del. Internat. Bar Assn. meeting, Mexico, 1964—; del. Inter-Am. Bar Assn. meeting, Mexico, 1944. Exec. bd. Chief Seattle council Boy Scouts Am., 1959-61. Republican dist. leader, 1949-52, mem. exec. com., 1950- 52. Mem. Internat. (charter patron), Am. (nat. chmn. younger lawyers 1948- 49, ho. dels. 1949-50), Wash. (chmn. war readjustment and traffic court coms. 1944-46), Whitman County (pres. 1943-44) bar assns., Fedn. Ins. Counsel (v.p. 1960-61), Comml. Law League Am. (pres. 1961-62), Selden Soc. Odd Fellow (sovereign grand rep. 1954), Lion (dir. 1963-64). Clubs: Spokane; Arctic (Seattle). Author: Legal Aspects of LAFTA, 1967; Full Faith and Credit in Federal Systems, 1968; Conflicts—Private International Law, 1969. Home: 2439 NW 58th St Seattle WA 98107 Office: Dexter Horton Bldg Seattle WA 98104

EDDS, MAC VINCENT, Jr., biologist; b. Mar. 25, 1917; s. Mac Vincent and Elizabeth M. (Green) E.; B.A., Amherst Coll., 1938, M.A., 1940, D.Sc. (hon.), 1968; Ph.D., Yale, 1943; m. Elizabeth Louise Tiffany, Sept. 7, 1940 (div.); children—Nancy E., Kenneth T., Carol; m. 2d, Louise M. Luckenbill, June 6, 1971. Research asst. U. Chgo., 1943-45; instr., asst. prof. anatomy U. Pitts., 1945-47; asst., asso. prof. biology Brown U., 1947-56, prof., 1956-71, chmn. dept. biology, 1960-63, dir. medicine, 1963-68; prof. zoology, dean faculty natural scis. and math. U. Mass., Amherst, 1971—. Instr., Woods Hole embryology course, 1951-55, in charge, 1956-60; vis. asso. prof. biology Mass. Inst. Tech., 1954, research asso., 1956-57; vis. lectr. anatomy Harvard. 1955; vis. prof. neurosci. U. Cal. at San Diego, 1968-69. Mng. editor Developmental Biology, 1958-71; mem. cell biology study sect. USPHS, 1959-64, chmn., 1961-64. Trustee, mem. exec. com. Marine Biol. Lab., 1961-68. Mem. Am. Assn. Anatomists, Soc. Devel. Biology, Am. Soc. Zoologists, Soc. Gen. Physiologists, Am. Soc. Cell Biology, Internat. Soc. Cell Biology, Am. Acad. Arts and Scis., Internat. Soc. Devel. Biology, Sigma Xi, Phi Rho Sigma, Home: 36 Bedford Terrace Northampton MA 01060 Office: South College U Mass Amherst MA 01002

EDDY, BOB, editor; b. Lake Benton, Minn., Jan. 24, 1917; s. Charles W. and Nona (Kimball) E.; A.B. summa cum laude, U. Minn., 1940, M.A., 1948; student Japanese lang., U. Mich., 1944; Nieman fellow, Harvard, 1951; m. Corinne Brandon, May 13, 1939; children—Bob II, Kay, Brandon, Jane, David. Copyreader, St. Paul Pioneer Press, 1939-40, asst. city editor 1941-43, 46, telegraph editor, 1947-51; editorial writer Mpls. Star, 1940-41; copydesk editor St. Paul Dispatch, 1952-56, mng. editor, 1957-62; editorial writer Dispatch and Pioneer Press, 1957; asst. to pub. Hartford (Conn.) Courant, 1962-68, editor, 1966—, also pub., 1968—. Lectr., Northeastern Univ., Boston: former lectr. U. Minn. Sch. Journalism. Incorporator, Hartford, St. Francis hosps., Inst. of Living. Trustee, Hartford Coll. for Women, Soc. for Savs. Served with AUS, 1943-46. Ogden Reid fellow, Europe, 1956. Mem. Am. Soc. Newspaper Editors, Phi Beta Kappa, Sigma Delta Chi. Episcopalian. Club: Twentieth Century. Contbr. articles to popular and profl. mags. Home: 125 Cliffmore Road West Hartford CT 06107 Office: 285 Broad St Hartford CT 06105

EDDY, CHARLES RUSSELL, banker; b. Newtonville, Mass., May 15, 1912; s. D. Brewer and Josephine (Russell) E.; B.A., Yale, 1934; m. Jeanette Elsa Kent, Sept. 24, 1938; children—Charles Russell, Dana Lee, Sarah Frances (Mrs. John P. Tederstrom), David Brewer. With New Eng. Merchants Nat. Bank, and predecessor, Boston, 1934—, sr. v.p., 1966—. Treas. Boston Seaman's Friend Soc.; trustee Walker Missionary Homes, Inc. Pres. trustees Walnut Hill Sch.; chmn. trustees Duxbury Free Library; trustee Sailor's Snug Harbor, Duxbury, Fruitlands Museums, Harvard, Mass. Home: 523 Washington St Duxbury MA 02332 Office: 28 State St Boston MA 02106

EDDY, CORBIN THEODORE, metall. engr.; b. Lake Linden, Mich., Apr. 17, 1904; s. Samuel and Georgie (Duquette) E.; B.S., Mich. Coll. of Mining and Tech., E.M., 1926, M.S., 1927, Ph.D., 1934; student U. Cal., 1927; spl. investigations Inst. für Eisenhüttenkunde of Technische Hochschule, Aachen, Germany, 1932; m. Helen Marie Perreault, June 12, 1941; children—Corbin Theodore John, Anthony Thomas, Mary Magdalen. Lab. instr. metallurgy, Mich. Technol. U., Houghton, 1926, instr. metall. engring., 1927-30, asst. prof. metall. 1930-32, asso. prof., 1932-40, prof. metall. engring., 1940-70, emeritus prof., 1970—, head dept., 1940-59, dir. metall. engring. research, 1940. Cons. engineer in processing and prodn. metallurgy. Recipient McNair Award, 1930, Alfred Nobel Prize, 1932. Mem. Am. Inst. M.E., Am. Soc. Metals, Am. Foundrymen's Assn., A.A.A.S., Am. Soc. Engring. Edn., Lake Superior Mining Inst., Phi Kappa Phi, Theta Tau, Tau Beta Pi, Alpha Sigma Mu. Author: The Constitution Diagram in Physical Metallurgy, 1938; Fundamental Principles in Physical Metallurgy, 1940. Contbr. to tech. and sci. jours. Home: 1009 College Av Houghton MI 49931

EDDY, DAYTON WILLIS, army officer; b. Vineyard Haven, Mass., July 23, 1915; s. Frank Lester and Alice (Stevens) E.; B.S., U. Vt., 1937; postgrad. Indsl. Coll. of Armed Forces, 1958-59; M.S., George Washington U., 1964; m. Beverly Jane Johnston, Sept. 5, 1944; children—Dana C., Janet L., Jay C. Communications engr. Western Union Telegraph Co., San Francisco, 1937- 40; commd. 2d lt., inf., AUS, 1937, advanced through grades to maj. gen., U.S. Army, 1961; comdr. 52d Signal Bn., 1944-46; with Office of Chief, Signal Office, 1946-52; command signal officer U.S. Army Alaska, 1952-54; dir. enlisted dept. Signal Sch., Ft. Monmouth, N.J., 1954-58; exec. to chief signal officer Office Chief Signal Officer, 1958; dep. asst. chief of staff for logistics U.S. Army Communications Zone, Orleans, France, 1962-63; comdr. Tobyhanna (Pa.) Army Depot, 1963-66; dep. comdg. gen. U.S. Army Security Agy., 1966-68; dir. communications-electronics Joint Staff, Orgn. Joint Chiefs of Staff, Washington, 1968—. Decorated D.S.M., Legion of Merit, Bronze Star. Registered profl. engr., D.C. Mem. Armed Forces Communications/Electronics Assn. (dir.). Home: 6388 Dockser Terrace Falls Church VA 22041

EDDY, EDWARD DANFORTH, Jr., coll. pres.; b. Saratoga Springs, N.Y., May 10, 1921; s. Edward Danforth and Martha (Henning) E.; B.A., Cornell U., 1944, Ph.D., 1956; B.D., Yale, 1946; LL.D., Thiel Coll., 1962; Dr. of Lit., Duquesne U., 1966; Litt. D., St. Vincent Coll., 1967; LL.D., U. N.H., 1967; L.H.D., Keuka Coll., 1968; m. Mary Allerton Schurman, June 23, 1949; children—Edward Danforth III, Mary Isabel, Catherine Schurman, David Henning. Asso. dir. interfaith agy. Cornell U. 1946-49; asst. to pres., instr. English, U. N. H., 1949-54, acting pres., 1954-55, v.p., provost, 1955-60; dir. Nat. Study of Character Influence in Edn., 1957-58; pres. Chatham Coll., Pitts., 1960—. Chmn. Select Commn. on Pitts. Sch. Bd.; commr. Pa. Pub. TV Network; mem. Ill. Gov.'s Commn. to Study Non-Public Higher Edn.; mem. liaison com. Pa. State Bd. Edn., Com. to Study Pa. Ind. Colls.; chmn. Pitts. Council on Higher Edn.; mem. sponsoring com. Allegheny Conf. Community Devel.; cons. Pitts. Found. Bd. dirs. Pitts. Symphony Soc., Pitts. Chamber Music Soc., vice chmn. bd. WQED-TV; chmn. bd. trustees Ruud Found.; trustee Wheaton Coll., Ellis Sch.; sec. bd. trustees Frick Ednl. Commn. Named one of 10 outstanding young men U.S. Jr. C. of C., 1955; recipient distinguished Service awards U. Buffalo, Pitts. Pub. Schs. Mem. Assn. Am. Colls. (mem. joint com. with Am. Assn. U. Profs. for improvement undergrad. teaching), Pa. Soc., Newcomen Soc., Omicron Delta Kappa, Sigma Phi, Phi Delta Kappa. Clubs: Yale of Pittsburgh (gov.), Duquesne. Author: Colleges for Our Land and Time, 1957; The College Influence on Student Character, 1959; (with others) the Public Schools and the Public, 1969. Contbr. articles to nat., ednl. jours. Home: 129 Woodland Rd Pittsburgh, PA 15232.

EDDY, GEORGE AMOS, educator; b. Unity, Sask., Can., June 8, 1928; s. Wilbur Lorne and Myrl Ruth (Phillips) E.; B.A., U. B.C., 1950; M.A., U. Toronto, 1951; Ph.D., McGill U., 1963; m. Margaret Roberta Follis, Aug. 5, 1950; children—Michael, Kathleen, Terrance, Jacqueline, Daniel. With Canadian Meteorol. Service, Edmonton, Alta., 1951-57, Montreal, Que., 1957-63; asst. prof. U. Tex., Austin, 1963-67, asso. prof., 1967-68; prof. meteorology U. Okla., Norman, 1968—. Pres., Term, Inc.; dir. Team Research Inst. Mem.'s rep. on UCAR bd. dirs. Fellow Royal Meteorol. Soc.; mem. Am. Meteorol. Soc., N.Y. Acad. Scis. (life), Am. Soc. Engring. Edn., Sigma Xi. Contbr. articles to profl. jours. Home: 318 Royal Oak St Norman OK 73069

EDDY, GERALD ERNEST, state govt. ofcl.; b. Lansing, Mich., Sept. 20, 1907; s. George Raymond and Eva (Hill) E.; B.S., Mich. State U., 1930; M.S., U. Mich., 1932; D.Sc. (hon.), Wayne State U., 1961; m. Mary Louise Lipka, Sept. 14, 1932; children—Catherine Ann (Mrs. Edwin A. Puchis), Susan Elizabeth (Mrs. William Kelly). With State of Mich., 1933-71, dir. conservation, 1951-64, state geologist, 1964-71. Chmn., Mich. Water Resources Commn., 1965-66; mem. Great Lakes Commn., 1955-64; ofcl. rep. Gov. Mich. on Interstate Oil Compact Commn., 1946-66. Served to capt. ordnance dept. AUS and USAAF, 1942-45. Recipient Career Service award Am. Soc. Pub. Adminstrn., 1962; Gov. Mich. Service Appreciation certificate, 1964. Fellow Geol. Soc. Am.; mem. Am. Assn. Petroleum Geologists, Internat. Assn. Fish, Game and Conservation Commrs., Mich. Acad. Sci., Mich. Basin Geol. Soc., A.A.A.S. Home: 2404 S Logan St Lansing MI 48910 Office: Geol Survey Div Mich Dept Conservation Lansing MI 48926

EDDY, HARVEY WILLIAM, air force officer; b. Saratoga Springs, N.Y., Jan. 7, 1919; s. Leonard Earl and Emma (Weil) E.; B.S. Mech. Engring., Worcester Polytech. Inst., 1941; M.B.A., U. Chgo., 1955; m. Ida Jean Harkness, Aug. 22, 1942; children—Carol (Mrs. William P. Velican), Anita (Mrs. Dennis Cheney Levan), Patricia Lynn, John Earl, Susan Lee. Commd. 2d lt. USAAF, 1942, advanced through grades to brig. gen. USAF, 1968; served as engring. officer, PTO, 1943-45; with USAF research and devel., 1948—; comdr. Office Aerospace Research, Arlington, Va., 1969—. Decorated Legion of Merit, Commendation medal (2). Mem. Beta Gamma Sigma, Sigma Alpha Epsilon. Home: 6719 Edgemere Dr Camp Springs MD 20031 Office: 1400 Wilson Blvd Arlington VA 22209

EDDY, NATHAN BROWNE, pharmacologist; b. Glens Falls, N.Y., Aug. 4, 1890; s. Charles Appleton and Aletta Amelia (Norcross) E.; M.D., Cornell U., 1911; D.Sc., U. Mich., 1963; m. Wilhelmina Marie Ahrens, Sept. 7, 1913; 1 son, Charles Ernest. Began practice of medicine, N.Y.C., 1911; instr. physiology McGill U., 1916-20; asst. prof. physiology and pharmacology U. Alta., 1920-28, asso. prof., 1928- 30; research prof. pharmacology U. Mich., 1930-39; formerly cons. biologist in alkaloids, USPHS, prin. pharmacologist, 1939-48, med. officer, 1948-60, cons. on narcotics, 1960—. Co-recipient 1st annual award Am. Pharm. Mfrs. Assn., 1939. Profl. asso. NRC, 1960-67, chmn. com. on drug dependence, 1970-71; exec. sec. com. on drug addiction and narcotics, 1947-67; mem. Expert Com. on Narcotic Drugs, WHO, chmn., 1949- 51, 57, 63, 67, 68; chmn. adv. com. to Bur. Narcotics under Narcotics Mfg. Act. of 1960; cons. Bur. Narcotics and Dangerous Drugs, 1968—. Recipient citation Dept. Health and Welfare; Sixth Lister Meml. Lect., Edinburg, 1960; William Freeman Snow award Am. Social Health Assn., 1967; Hillebrand prize Chem. Soc. Washington, 1968; Meml. award WHO, 1968; gold medal Eastern Psychiat. Research Assn., 1970. Fellow A.A.A.S.; mem. Soc. Pharmacol. and Exptl. Therapeutics (mem. council 1944). Soc. Exptl. Biology and Medicine, Coll. Clin. Pharmacology, Coll. Neuro-psychopharmacology, Internat. Narcotics Enforcement Officers Assn., Sigma Xi. Republican. Methodist. Club: Cosmos. Co- author: Pharmacology of Opium Alkaloids; Synthetic Drugs with Morphine- Like Effect; Codeine and Its Alternates for Pain and Cough Relief. Contbr. to med., sci. jours. Address: 7055 Wilson Lane Bethesda MD 20034

EDDY, STEPHEN CHRISTOPHER chemist, educator; b. Chicago, 1928; B.S. in Physics, Yale, 1950; Ph.D. in Chemistry, Harvard, 1956; m. Sally Ann Jones, July 5, 1957; children--Kenneth J., Nancy A. Chemist, Acme Chem. Co., Blue Island, Ill., 1950-51; director of Research Lab., Indsl. Chemicals Corp., Cambrige, Mass., 1956-60; project coordinator environmental sect. Steinmetz Assos., Chgo., 1960-61; v.p. for research Bauer Bros. Chem. Co., Inc., Memphis, 1961-64; asst. prof. chemistry Washington U., St. Louis, 1964-66, asso. prof., 1966-70, prof., 1970--, head of chemistry dept., 1970-71. Vis. prof. So. Ill. U., summer 1967, U. of Ore., 1969. Bd. dirs. Rest Haven Home for Elderly, 1960-61; trustee of the Lutheran Hosp., 1965-71. Served from lt. to capt., AUS, 1951-53. Mem. Am. Chem. Soc., Sci. Research Soc. Am. (chpt. treas. 1967), Sigma Xi. Author: (with others) Basic Inorganic Chemistry, 1971. Home: Fairfax Apts 7291 Windermere Dr University City MO 63105 Office: Dept Chemistry Washington University St Louis MO 63130

EDDY, WILLARD OSCAR, educator; b. Hamilton, Ind., Aug. 1, 1908; s. Guy C. and Mamie B. (McClellan) E.; B.A., DePauw U., 1930, M.A., 1932; postgrad. Yale, 1935-36; M.A., U. Neb., 1937; postgrad. U. Chgo., 1948-50; m. Gladys Louise Shellabarger, Aug. 21, 1938; children—Sandra Carol, William Radford. Prof. English, Hokkaido Imperial U., Sapporo, Japan, 1932-35; faculty Colo. State U., 1937—, prof. English, 1957-60, prof. philosophy, 1960-70, dir. univ. honors program, 1961—, Centennial prof. philosophy, 1970—. Served with M.I., AUS, 1942-45. Recipient Oliver P. Pennock faculty distinguished service award, 1956. Mem. Am. Philos. Assn., Am. Acad. Polit. and Social Sci., Nat. Collegiate Honors Council, Sigma Xi, Omicron Delta Kappa. Contbr. articles to profl. jours. Home: 509 Remington St Fort Collins CO 80521

EDDY, WILLIAM CRAWFORD, TV engr.; b. Saratoga Springs, N.Y., Aug. 28, 1902; s. William Daniel and Ethel (Thomas) E.; student N.Y. Mil. Acad., 1917-21; B.S., U.S. Naval Acad., 1926; m. Christine Woolridge, July 11, 1927; children—Nancy Jane (Mrs. George McClure), William Crawford, Dianna Kay (Mrs. Lucas Schuyler Van Orden). Employed Farnsworth TV, Phila., 1934-36, NBC-TV, N.Y.C., 1936-49; dir. TV sta. WBKB, Chgo., 1940-48; former chmn. bd., pres. Television Assos. of Ind., Inc.; cartoonist Ann. Mpls.-Honeywell Calendar, 1935—; cons. TV sta. installation, microwave network planning, installation, design, devel. equipment for TV studios, design, devel. audio-visual equipment. Served with U.S. Navy, 1936-34; comdg. officer radar tng. USN Radio Chgo., 1942-45; ret. as capt. Decorated Legion of Merit (Navy). Recipient Ann. Achievement award Nat. Assn. Radio and TV Broadcasters, 1947. Registered profl. engr., Ind. Mem. Soc. Motion Picture and Television Engr., Soc. Mil. Engrs., U.S. Naval Acad. Alumni Assn., Soc. Tv Pioneers. Club: Army-Navy. Author: Television, the Eyes of Tomorrow, 1945; A Little Humor Now and Then, 1956; Back to the Drawing Board, 1962; co-author: Wartime Refresher in Mathematics, 1943. Home: 2711 E Michigan Blvd Michigan City IN 46360

EDEL, ABRAHAM, educator; b. Pitts., Dec. 6, 1908; s. Simon and Fannie (Malamud) E.; B.A., McGill U., 1927, M.A., 1928; B.A., Oxford, 1930; Ph.D., Columbia, 1934; m. May Mandelbaum, Jan. 30, 1934; children—Matthew, Deborah. Mem. dept. philosophy Coll. City N.Y., 1931—, Distinguished prof. philosophy City U. N.Y. Grad. Center, 1970—. Vis. prof. Columbia, U. Cal., Berkeley, Swarthmore Coll., U. Pa., Western Res. U., State U. N.Y., Downstate Med. Center, others. Recipient Butler Silver medal Columbia, 1959. Guggenheim fellow, 1944-45; Rockefeller Found. grantee, 1952-53, NSF grantee, 1959-60. Mem. Am. Philos. Assn., Metaphys. Soc. Am., Am. Soc. Polit. and Legal Philosophy, Internat. Assn. Philosophy Law and Social Philosophy, Philosophy Edn. Soc. Author: The Theory and Practice of Philosophy, 1946, Ethical Judgment, 1955, Science and the Structure of Ethics, 1961, Method in Ethical Theory, 1963, Aristotle, 1967; (with May Edel) Anthropology and Ethics, 1959. Home: 171-07 84th Rd Jamaica NY 11432 Office: 33 W 42d St New York City NY 10036

EDEL, JOSEPH LEON, author, educator; b. Pitts., Sept. 9, 1907; s. Simon and Fannie (Malamud) E.; M.A., McGill U., 1928, Litt.D., 1963, Litt.D., U. Paris. Sorbonne, 1932, Union Coll., 1963; m. Roberta Roberts, Dec. 19, 1950. Writer, journalist, 1932-43; vis. prof. N.Y. U. 1950-52, asso. prof. English, 1954-55, prof. English, 1955- 66, Henry James prof. English and Am. letters, 1966—; citizens prof. English, U. Hawaii, 1970—; Mem. faculty Harvard, summer 1952; Centenary vis. prof. U. Toronto, 1967; Gauss seminar lectr. Princeton, 1953; vis. prof. Ind. U., 1954-55, U. Hawaii summer 1955, 69,-70; Alexander lectr., U. Toronto, 1956, vis. prof. Harvard, 1959-60, Center Advanced Study, Wesleyan Univ., 1965; Bollingen Found. fellow, 1958- 61. Mem. adv. com. edn. Met. Mus. Centenary, 1969-70. Served as lt. AUS, World War II. Decorated Bronze Star; recipient grant Nat. Inst. Arts and Letters, 1959; Pulitzer prize in biography, 1963; Nat. Book award for non-fiction, 1963. Guggenheim fellow, 1936-38, 65-66. Fellow Am. Acad. Arts and Scis., Royal Soc. Lit. (Eng.); mem. Nat. Inst. Arts and Letters (sec. 1965-67), W.A. White Psychoanalytic Soc. (hon.), Soc. Authors (Eng.), Authors Guild (mem. council, pres. 1969-70), P.E.N. (pres. Am. Center 1957-59), Modern Humanitites Research Assn., Internat. Fedn. Modern Langs. and Lits. Clubs: Century (N.Y.C.); Athenaeum (London, Eng.); Outrigger Canoe (Honolulu). Author: James Joyce: The Last Journey, 1947; Henry James: The Untried Years, 1953; The Psychological Novel. 1955; Literary Biography, 1957; (with E. K. Brown) Willa Cather, 1953; (with Dan H. Laurence) Bibliography of Henry James, 1957; Henry James: The Conquest of London, 1962; Henry James: The Middle Years, 1962. Editor: The Ghostly Tales of Henry James, 1949; The Complete Plays of Henry James, 1949; Selected Fiction of Henry James, 1953; Selected Letters of Henry James, 1955; The Future of the Novel, 1956: The American Essays of Henry James, 1956; (with Gordon N. Ray) Henry James and H. G. Wells, 1958; The Complete Tales of Henry James, 12 Vols., 1963-65; The Diary of Alice James, 1964; Henry James: The Treacherous Years, 1969; Stories of Supernatural, 1970; H.D. Thoreau, 1970; Henry James: The Master, 1972. Adv. editor Nineteenth Century Fiction. Office: 19 University Pl NY U New York City NY 10003 also Dept English Univ Hawaii Honolulu HI 96822

EDELCUP, NORMAN SCOTT, aluminum bldg. mfg. co. exec.; b. Chgo., May 8, 1935; s. Irving L. and Pauline (Bolz) E.; B.S. in Bus. Adminstrn., Northwestern U., 1957. Sr. accountant Arthur Andersen & Co., Chgo., 1957-62; sec.-treas. Acme Printing Ink Co., Chgo., 1962-65; accountant, asst. to chmn. Commonwealth Edison Co., Chgo., 1965-68; sr. v.p., vice-chmn. bd. Keller Industries, Miami, Fla., 1968—. Served with AUS, 1958-60. C.P.A., Fla., Ill. Mem. Am., Fla., Ill. insts. C.P.A.'s, Am. Accounting Assn. Home: 244 Atlantic Isle North Miami Beach FL 33160 Office: 18000 State Rd 9 Miami FL 33162

EDELL, DAVID CHARLES, cosmetic co. exec.; b. Bklyn., Apr. 29, 1932; s. Morton and Joan (Gutterson) E.; B.A., Syracuse U., 1954; m. Sheila Swirsky, Sept. 22, 1954; children—Dunnan, Drew, Douglas. Dir. purchasing Halogene Inc., Newark, 1954-55; v.p. Diversified Druggist Co., Newark, 1955-58, Dunnan & Jeffrey, Advt., N.Y.C., 1958-62; pres. Satin Soft Cosmetics, Newark, 1962-68; exec. v.p. Hazel Bishop, Inc., Union, N.J., 1965; pres. Perfect Film & Chem. Co., 1968-69, Lexington Internat., 1969—. Co-chmn. Essex County chpt. United Jewish Appeal, 1960-62, Heart Fund, 1964. Chmn. drug industry fund raising U.S. Olympics. Home: 41 Seminole Way Short Hills NJ 07078 Office: 2345 Vauxhall Rd Union NJ 07083

EDELL, MORTON, cosmetic co. exec.; b. N.Y.C., 1922. Pres., dir. Lanolin Plus, Inc., Newark; pres., dir. Bishop Industries, Inc., N.Y.C. Address: 37 Empire St Newark NJ 07114

EDELMAN, ALBERT I., lawyer; b. New Haven, July 21, 1916; s. Selig and Selma (Pfeiffer) E.; A.B., Columbia, 1936, LL.B., 1938; m. Eleanor Louise Weisman, Mar. 13, 1949; children-Gwen, Thomas, Jennifer, Cornelia. Admitted to N.Y. bar, 1938, since practiced in N.Y.C.; mem. firm Javits, Trubin, Sillcocks & Edelman, 1958—; asst. atty. gen. State N.Y., 1938-41; with Office Gen. Counsel, Treasury Dept., 1941-42; chief indsl. investigations br. Am. Mil. Govt. Germany, 1945-46; cons. State Dept., 1946; U.S. judge Arbitral Commn. on Property, Rights and Interests in Germany, 1956-58. Bd. dirs. Am. Assn. for UN, 1948-58; trustee Cooper Hewitt Museum Charitable Trust, Benjamin Franklin Found. Served to lt. comdr. USNR, World War II. Mem. Am., N.Y. State bar assns., Council Fgn. Relations, Assn. Internat. des Etud ants en Scis. Economiques et Commercials (bd. dirs.). Home: 23 Warwick Rd Bronxville NY 10708 Office: 375 Park Av New York NY 10022

EDELMAN, ARTHUR JAY, leather co. exec.; b. N.Y.C., July 19, 1925; s. Samuel and Beatrice (Edelman) E.; B.A., Sarah Lawrence Coll., Bronxville, New York, 1950; m. Theodora Joffe, May 28, 1950; children—Samuel, Sally, Antonia, David, Mary Elizabeth, John George. Actor appearing in the Big People, 1947, Nativity, 1948; with Fleming-Joffe Ltd., N.Y.C., 1951—, pres., 1963—; dir. Johnston Tanning Corp. Served with USNR, 1942-45. Recipient Mercury award Nat. Shoe Retailers Assn., 1963, Coty award Am. Fashion Critics, 1963; Neiman Marcus award, 1965. Home: Spring Valley Rd Ridgefield CT 06877 Office: 71 Park Av New York City NY 10016

EDELMAN, DANIEL JOSEPH, pub. relations counsel; b. N.Y.C., July 3, 1920; s. Selig and Selma (Pfeiffer) E.; grad. Columbia Coll., 1940; postgrad. Columbia, 1941; m. Ruth Rozumoff, Sept. 3, 1953; children—Richard, Renee, John. Reporter, Poughkeepsie (N.Y.) newspapers, U.P.I., 1941-42; news writer CBS, 1946- 47; staff mem. Edward Gottlieb & Assos., 1947; pub. relations dir. Toni Co., Chgo., 1948-52; founder Daniel J. Edelman, Inc., Chgo., 1952. Mem. pub. relations com. Jewish Fedn., 1960—; chmn. Chgo. chpt. Young Presidents Orgn., 1963; trustee Young Pres.'s Found., Chief Execs. Forum; bd. dirs. Lake Forest Acad., Assn. Crippled Children and Adults, Starfish; mem. exec. com. Anti Defamation League Chgo. served to 2d lt. AUS, 1942-46; ETO. Mem. Pub. Relations Soc. Am. past chmn. counselor sect., Publicity Club Chgo., Chgo. Press Club, Phi Beta Kappa, Zeta Beta Tau. Jewish religions. Clubs: Standard, Harmonie. Home: 1301 N Astor St Chicago IL 60610 Office: 221 N La Salle St Chicago IL 60601

EDELMAN, GERALD MAURICE, educator, biochemist; b. N.Y.C., July 1, 1929; s. Edward and Anna (Freedman) E.; B.S., Ursinus Coll., 1950; M.D., U. Pa., 1954; Ph.D., Rockefeller U., 1960; m. Maxine Morrison, June 11, 1950; children—Eric, David, Judith. Med. house officer Mass. Gen. Hosp., 1954-55; asst. physician hosp. of Rockefeller U., 1957-60, mem. faculty, 1960—, asso. dean grad. studies, 1963-66, prof., 1966—. Asso., Neurosciences Research Program. Served to capt., M.C., AUS, 1955-57. Recipient Spencer Morris award U. Pa., 1954; Ann. Alumni award Ursinus Coll., 1969. Mem. adv. bd. Basel Inst. Immunology; Sci. Council Center for Theoretical studies. Bd. govs. Weizmann Inst. Sci. Mem. Am. Soc. Biol. Chemists, Am. Assn. Immunologists, Genetics Soc. Am., Harvey Soc., Am. Chem. Soc. (Eli Lilly award biol. chemistry 1965), A.A.A.S., Am. Acad. Arts and Scis., Nat., N.Y. acads. scis., Sigma Xi, Alpha Omega Alpha. Research structure antibodies. Home: 35 E 85th St New York City NY 10028

EDELMAN, HAROLD, architect; b. N.Y.C., Aug. 4, 1923; s. Joseph S. and Rose (Kaminsky) E.; B.Arch., Cornell U., 1943; certificate civil engring., Stanford; student Ecole des Beaux Arts, Paris, 1951; m. Judith Hochberg, Dec. 26, 1947; children—Marc, Joshua. Asso. Huson Jackson, 1951-58; pvt. practice architecture, 1958-60; partner Stanley Salzman and Judith Edelman as Edelman & Salzman, N.Y.C., 1960—; asso. prof. architecture Pratt Inst., 1952-62; lectr. design Columbia, 1952-53; vis. lectr. urban design and architecture New Sch., Pa. State U. Served with AUS, 1943-46. Recipient spl. Brunner award A.I.A., 1960, 61, citation in house alteration, 1961; Bard 1st honor award for excellence in civic architecture and urban design City Club N.Y., 1969; residential design award A.I.A., 1969; award for design excellence U.S. Dept. H.U.D., 1970. Mem. A.I.A. Home: 13 Bank St New York City NY 10014 Office: 434 6th Av New York City NY 10011

EDELMAN, HERBERT, actor; b. Bklyn., Nov. 5, 1933; s. Mayer and Jennie (Greenberg) E.; student Bklyn. Coll., 1955-58; m. Louise Cohen, Dec. 20, 1964. Actor appearing in Broadway plays Barefoot in the Park, Bajour; appeared with Luv on Nat. Tour; movies include Barefoot in the Park, Odd Couple (as Murray the cop), Alice B. Toklas; TV series Good Guys, also numerous appearances as guest star. Home: 24802 Malibu Rd Malibu CA 90265

EDELMAN, ISIDORE SAMUEL, educator, scientist; b. N.Y.C., July 24, 1920; s. Abraham and Fannie (Thaler) E.; B.A., Ind. U., 1941, M.D., 1944; m. Florence Jaffe, Aug. 30, 1942; children—Arthur, Susan, Joseph, Ann. Intern Greenpoint Hosp., Bklyn., 1944-45; resident, Montefiore Hosp., Bronx, N.Y., 1947-49; postdoctoral research fellow Harvard Med. Sch., 1949-52; prof. medicine and physiology U. Cal. at San Francisco, 1960-67, prof. biophysics, 1969—, Samuel Neider Research prof. medicine, 1967—; editorial bds. Jour. of Membrane Biology, Current Topics in Membranes and Transpost; cons. on regulatory biology NSF; mem. research career awards com. Nat. Inst. Gen. Med. Sci., NIH, 1969—; mem. U.S. nat. com. Internat. Union of Pure and Applied Biophysics, 1971—. Served to capt. AUS, 1945-47. Mem. Assn. Am. Physicians, Am. Physiol. Soc., Am. Soc. Clin. Investigation, Biophys. Soc., Endocrine Soc., Soc. Gen. Physiology, Am. Soc. Biol. Chemistry, Western Assn. Physicians. Research transport solutes and water across cell membranes; molecular mechanisms in actions of adrenal, posterior pituitary and thyroid hormones. Home: 40 Linares St San Francisco CA 94116

EDELMAN, JUDITH HOCHBERG, architect; b. Bklyn., Sept. 16, 1923; d. Abraham and Frances (Israel) Hochberg; student Conn. Coll., 1940-41, N.Y. U., 1941-42; B.Arch., Columbia, 1946; m. Harold Edelman, Dec. 26, 1947; children—Marc, Joshua. Designer, draftsman Huson Jackson, N.Y.C., 1948-58; pvt. practice architecture, 1958-60; partner Edelman & Salzman, N.Y.C., 1960—; vis. lectr. urban renewal New Sch., 1968. Schermerhorn traveling fellow, 1950; recipient Bard 1st honor award City Club N.Y., 1969; Residential Design award A.I.A., 1969; award for design excellence U.S. Dept. H.U.D., 1970. Mem. A.I.A. (dir. N.Y. chpt., chmn. commn. archtl. edn. 1971-73), Columbia Archtl. Alumni Assn. (dir. 1968-71). Home: 13 Bank St New York City NY 10014 Office: 434 6th Av New York City NY 10011

EDELMAN, MARIAN WRIGHT (Mrs. Peter B. Edelman), lawyer; b. Bennettsville, S.C., June 6, 1939; d. Arthur J. and Maggie (Bowen) Wright; B.A., Spelman Coll., 1960; LL.B., Yale, 1963; m. Peter B. Edelman, July 14, 1968; children—Joshua, Jonah. Mem. staff N.A.A.C.P. Legal Def. and Edn. Fund, Inc., N.Y.C., 1963-64, Jackson, Miss., 1964-68; dir. Washington Research Project, 1968—. Mem. exec. com. Student Non-Violent Coordinating Com., 1961-63; mem. adv. council Martin Luther King, Jr. Meml. Library. Bd. dirs. Child Devel. Group of Miss., Internat. Self-Help Housing Assn., Citizens Crusade Against Poverty, Indsl. Areas Found., Nat. Office for Rights of the Indigent, Inst. for Community Devel. Mem. Nat. Sharecroppers Assn., Ams. for Democratic Action (dir.), Black Am. Law Students Assn. (dir.), Nat. Capitol Area Civil Liberties Union (dir.), World Council Chs., Nat. Council Chs. (dir. div. Christian life and missions). Address: 538 1/2 N Farish St Jackson MS*

EDELMAN, MAURICE, mem. Brit. Parliament, author; b. Cardiff, Wales, Mar. 2, 1911; s. Joshua and Ester (Solomon) E.; B.A., Trinity Coll. Cambridge U., 1932, M.A., 1941; m. Matilda Yager, 1932; children—Sonia, Natasha. Supr. research devl. timer and plastics, 1932-41; war corr. Picture Post, 1943-45; elected Labour mem. Parliament representing Coventry West, 1945-50, Coventry North, 1950; del. Anglo-French Parliamentary Relations Com., 1948; House of Commons del. consultative assembly, Council of Europe, mem. econ. com., Strasbourg, France, 1949, Parliamentary del., 1950, U.K. del., 1951, 65, 70; vice chmn. Franco-Brit. Parliamentary Relations Com., 1950-53, chmn., 1953. Decorated Coronation medal, 1953; officier Legion of Honor (France). Jewish religion. Author: G.P.U. Justice, 1938; Production for Victory, Not Profit, 1941; How Russia Prepared, 1942; France: The Birth of the Fourth Republic, 1944; A Trial of Love, 1951; Who Goes Home, 1953; A Dream of Treason, 1955; The Happy Ones, 1957; A Call on Kuprin, 1959; The Minister, 1962; The Fratricides, 1963; The Prime Minister's Daughter, 1964; Ben Gurion: A Political Biography, 1964; The Mirrow: A Political History, 1966; Shark Island, 1967; All on a Summer's Night, 1969. Contbr. polit. jours. and mags. Office: care House of Commons London SW 1 England

EDELMAN, MURRAY JACOB, educator; b. Nanticoke, Pa., Nov. 5, 1919; s. Kalman and Sadie (Wiesenberg) E.; B.A., Bucknell U., 1941; M.A., U. Chgo., 1942; Ph.D., U. Ill., 1948; m. Bacia Stepner, June 15, 1952; children—Lauren Beatrice, Judith Sybil, Sarah Miriam. Mem. faculty U. Ill., 1948-66, prof. polit. sci., 1958-65, chmn. dept. polit. sci., 1965-66; prof. polit. sci. U. Wis., 1966—. Cons. Ill. Commn. Study State Govt., 1950, Ill. Legislative Commn. Workmen's Safety, 1954, Nat. Wage Stblzn. Bd., 1951. Served with USAAF, 1942-45. Guggenheim fellow, 1962-63; Fulbright grantee to Austria, 1952, to Italy, 1956. Mem. Am. Polit. Sci. Assn. Author: The Licensing of Radio Services in the United States, 1927-47, 1950; Channels of Employment, 1952; National Economic Planning by Collective Bargaining, 1954; (with R. W. Fleming) The Politics of Wage-Price Decisions: A Four Country Analysis, 1965; The Symbolic Uses of Politics, 1964; Politics as Symbolic Action: Mass Arousal and Quiescence, 1971. Home: 1824 Vilas Av Madison WI 53711

EDELMANN, OTTO, opera singer; b. Vienna, Austria, Feb. 5, 1917; s. Wenzel and Maria (Kristufek) E.; grad. State Acad. Music, Vienna, 1938; m. Ilse Maria Straub, Apr. 18, 1960; children—Elisabeth, Peter-Alexander. First profl. appearances opera at Gera, Nürnberg and Berlin, Germany, 1938-39; mem. Viennese State Opera, 1948—, Salzburg Festival, 1948-52, Met. Opera Co., 1959—; other appearances at Bayreuth Festival, 1951, Scala Milano, 1952, Edinburgh Festival, 1952. First Meistersinger after World War II; nominated Kammersänger by Pres. Republic Austria, 1960; named chevalier de Liere classe de Daneborg (Denmark), 1962. Address: Wien 23 Kalksburg Breitenfurterstrasse 547 Austria also care Metropolitan Opera Co New York City NY 10023

EDELSON, DAVID, hosp. adminstr.; b. N.Y.C., Jan. 28, 1919; s. Max and Freida (Epstein) E.; m. Miriam Osnovitz, Apr. 3, 1943; children—Richard, Jeff. Dir. social service Evansville (Ind.) State Hosp., 1954-56; psychiat. social work supr. Dixon (Ill.) State Sch., 1956-57, supt., 1962—; asst. supt. East Moline (Ill.) State Hosp., 1958-62; instr. Evansville Coll., Moline Jr. Coll. Mem. Gov.'s Adv. Council Retardation, 1963—. Served to 1st lt. USAAF, 1942-45. Recipient ann. award Ill. Assn. for the Mentally Recarded, 1968. Address: 2600 Brinton Av Dixon IL 61021

EDELSTEIN, DAVID NORTHON, judge; b. N.Y.C. Feb. 16, 1910; s. Benjamin and Dora (Mancher) E.; B.S., A.M., LL.B., Fordham U.; m. Florence Koch, Feb. 18, 1940; children—Jonathan H., Jeffrey M. Admitted to N.Y. State bar, practiced in N.Y.C.; atty. claims div. Dept. Justice, 1944; asst. U.S. atty., So. Dist. of N.Y., 1945-47, spl. asst. to atty. gen. in charge lands div., 1947; asst. atty. gen. in charge of customs div. Dept. Justice, 1948; U.S. dist. judge So. Dist. of N.Y., 1951—. Assisted Pres.'s Temporary Commn. on Employee Loyalty, chmn. in preparation of its report, 1946. Mem. legislative com. Attys. Gen. Conf. on Crime, 1950. Mem. Fed. (past pres. Empire chpt. past nat. del.), Am. (past alternate del. ho. of dels. for Fed. Bar Assn.) bar assns., Bar Assn. City N.Y. (jud. mem.), Bklyn.- Manhattan Trial Lawyers Assn., Maritime Lawyers Assn., Am. Trial Lawyers Assn., Nat. Lawyers Club (hon.). Clubs: Downtown Athletic, Manhattan. Author: The History and Scope of The Fair Labor Standards Act of 1938, 1941. Home: 1040 Park Av New York City NY 10028 Office: US Court House Foley Square New York City NY 10007

EDELSTEIN, RICHARD MALVIN, educator; b. Los Angeles, May 28, 1930; s. Maurice S. and Sally (Fronenberg) E.; B.A., Pomona Coll., 1951; Ph.D., Columbia, 1960; m. Ruth Gertrude Whiteman, Aug. 7, 1955; children—Daniel, Amy. Elizabeth. Research asso. Carnegie-Mellon U., 1960-62, mem. faculty, 1962—, prof. physics, 1969—. Weizmann Inst. fellow, 1970-71. Fellow Am. Phys. Soc. Home: 133 S Linden Av Pittsburgh PA 15208

EDEN, CHARLES HENRY, lawyer; b. Boston, Apr. 14, 1895; s. Charles H. and Evelyn (MacLellan) E.; student N.Y. Mil. Acad., 1907-10; Moses Brown Sch., Providence, 1917- 14, Brown U., 1914-17; LL.B., Harvard, 1922; m. Harriet E. Carpenter, 1924 (div. 1949); children—Harriet E. (Mrs. Thomas Powell), Charles H. Admitted to Rhode Island bar, 1923, Mass. bar, 1927; practice of law, Providence, 1923—; town solicitor, Coventry, R.I., 1928-30; asst. U.S. atty. Dist. of R.I., 1930-33; co-founder, dir., sec. Fram Corp., E. Providence, R.I., 1932-43. Alderman, City of Providence, 1939-40; mem. governor's commn. to revise election laws, 1939-40; chmn. Willkie for Pres. Com. of R.I., 1940; mem. Republican State Central Com. R.I., 1942- 52, 54-60, chmn., 1952-54; delegate Republican National Convention, 1960; Republican candidate U.S. Congress, 1942, for mayor of Providence, 1946; mem. Eisenhower for Pres. Club, 1952; mem. Rep. Nat. Com., 1952- 54; chairman R.I. Goldwater for Pres. Com., 1964; chmn. Conservative Com. of R.I., 1965. Served with R.I. N.G., Mexican Border, 1916; AEF, 1917-19, AUS, 1943-44. Recipient R.I. Conservative of Year award Young Americans for Freedom, 1965. Member Am., Rhode Island bar assns., also mem. Am. Judicature Soc. Clubs: Young Republican of Providence (pres. 1937-38); Republican of Rhode Island (pres. 1940-41). Home: 895 Gilbert Stuart Rd Saunderstown RI 02874 Office: 15 Westminster St Providence RI 02903

EDEN, MURRAY, educator, elec. engr.; b. Bklyn., Aug. 17, 1920; s. Emanuel and Rae (Taran) Edelstein; B.S., Coll. City N.Y., 1939; M.S., U. Md., 1944, Ph.D., 1951; m. Patricia Warnock, Sept. 16, 1962; stepchildren—Shirley (Mrs. Thomas A. Seawell), John W. Hartle; children by previous marriage—Abigail, Susanna, Mark D. Physic. chemist Nat. Bur. Standards, 1943-49; biophysicist Nat. Cancer Inst., 1949-53; spl. fellow math. USPHS, Princeton, 1953-55; biophysicist Nat. Heart Inst., 1955-59; prof. elec. engring. Mass. Inst. Tech., 1959—; lectr. preventive medicine Harvard Med. Sch., 1960—, Am. U., 1949-50; cons. for research to dir. gen. WHO, 1963—. Chmn. U.S. Nat. Com. Engring. in Medicine and Biology. Mem. Am. Physiol. Soc., I.E.E.E. (chmn. adminstrv. com. group engring. in medicine and biology 1964-66), Biophys. Soc. Author: (with David Rutstein) Engineering and Living Systems, 1970. Editor: (with Paul Kolers) Recognizing Patterns, 1968; editor-in-chief Information and Control, 1961—; editor Methods of Information in Medicine, 1961—; mem. editorial bd. Med. Research Engring., 1964—; adv. editorial bd. Linguistic Inquiry, 1970. Home: 4 Ames St Cambridge MA 02139

EDEN, SIR ROBERT ANTHONY, see Avon, Earl of.

EDEN, WILLIAM GIBBS, educator; b. Talladega, Ala., May 3, 1918; s. George Grover and Maude (Parnell) E.; B.S., Auburn U., 1940, M.S., 1946; Ph.D., U. Ill., 1950; m. Evelyn Smith, June 1, 1940; children—Brenda (Mrs. W.F. Powell, Jr.), Jane (Mrs. James M. Buttram). Asst. country agrl. agt. Auburn U., Geneva, Ala., 1940-43, asst. prof. entomology, Auburn, Ala., 1948-50, asso. prof., 1950-57, prof., 1957-64; chmn. dept. entomology and nematology U. Fla., Gainesville, 1965—. Mem. Auburn City Council, 1960-65. Served with USNR, 1943-45. Mem. Entomol. Soc. Am., Fla. Entomol. Soc. Baptist Mason, Rotarian. Contbr. articles to sci. publs. Home: 4411 NW 17th Pl Gainsville FL 32601

EDENFIELD, NEWELL, judge; b. Stillmore, Ga., Aug. 10, 1911; s. John and Elizabeth (McCord) E.; LL.B., U. Ga., 1938; m. Theresa Pope, Apr. 8, 1938; children—Nancy, Newell, Bruce, Stephen, James, David. Admitted to Ga. bar; legal editor Edward Thompson Co. (now West Pub. Co.), 1938-41; practice law, Atlanta, 1941-67; mem. law firm Edenfield, Heyman & Sizemore, 1963-67; instr. Atlanta Law Sch., 1946-63; now U.S. dist. judge. Served to lt. (j.g.), USNR, 1942-45. Recipient Nathan Burkan Meml. award U. Ga. Law Sch., 1938. Fellow Am. Coll. Trial Lawyers; mem. Am., Ga. (pres. 1959-60), Atlanta (pres. 1954-55) bar assns. Home: 119 The Prado NE Atlanta GA 30309 Office: Old Post Office Bldg Atlanta GA 30301

EDENS, HENRY HARMAN, lawyer; b. Clio, S.C., Mar. 31, 1909; s. Jefferson Davis and Anna (Walser) E.; grad. Blue Ridge Sch. for Boys, Hendersonville, N.C., 1927; A.B., U.S.C., 1931; m. Jane Mason Gibbes, Nov. 25, 1933; children—Jane Mason (Mrs. William C. Hawley), Henry Harman, Anne Walser (Mrs. Tom Evins). Admitted to S.C. bar, 1934, also U.S., S.C. supreme cts., U.S. Dist. Ct., U.S. Ct. Appeals, U.S. Ct. Claims; asst. U.S. atty. Eastern Dist. S.C., 1937-49; spl. circuit judge, 1955; counsel U.S. Senate Com. for Investigations Govt. Employee Security Program, 1955. Pres. Heart of Columbia Motel, Inc., Midlands Devel. Co.; pres. Edenwood Water Co., Inc., Cayce S.C. Permanent mem. Fed. Jud. Conf., 4th Circuit. Mem. Internat. Acad. Trial Lawyers, Am. Trial Lawyers Assn. (bd. govs.), S.C. Bar Assn. (pres. 1959-60), Kappa Alpha, Omicron Delta Kappa. Home: 700 Sweetbriar Columbia SC 29205 Office: PO Box 11580 Columbia SC 29211

EDENS, JAMES BENJAMIN, lumber exec.; b. Saron, Tex., Oct. 13, 1913; s. William Frederick and Cordelia (Hooks) E.; student Stephen Austin Coll., Nacogdoches, Tex., 1932; m. Etheldred Devereaux, May 26, 1931; children—James Benjamin II, William D.; m. 2d, Rosa Reiser, Jan. 16, 1955; 1 dau., Cathy. With Edens- Birch Lumber Co., Corrigan, Tex., 1933-52, beginning in sales office, successively sales mgr., gen. mgr., pres., 1946-52; pres. Southwest Lumber Mills, Inc., Phoenix, 1952—, corp. named Southwest Forest Industries, Inc., 1960, now chmn. bd., chief exec. officer; former dir. Gt. Western Corp., Tucson, adv. dir. Gt. Western Bank, Tucson; pres., dir. Apache Railway Co. Mem. Forest Industries Com. on Timber Valuation and Taxation. Bd. dirs. Phoenix Symphony Assn.; trustee Phoenix Country Day Sch. Mem. S.W. Pine Assn. (past pres., past dir.), Western Wood Products Assn. (dir., past pres.), Nat. Forest Products Assn. (past pres., chmn.), N.A.M. (past dir.), Econ. Council Forest Products Industry (past chmn.), Newcomen Soc. N. Am., Am. Paper Inst. Methodist, Mason (Shriner). Clubs: Executives, Phoenix Country, Cloud, White Mountain Country, Internat. of Houston; Pinetop Country; Plimsoll; Tres Vidas, Paradise Valley Country, Arizona Press. Home: 5221 E Arroyo Rd Scottsdale AZ 85253 Office: 3443 N Central St Phoenix AZ 85012

EDENS, JAMES DRAKE, Jr., mem. Republican Nat. Com; b. Blaney, S.C., May 13, 1925; s. J. Drake and May (Youmans) E.; B.S. in Bus. Adminstrn., U. S.C., 1949; m. Ferrell McCracken, May 28, 1946; children—Robert Manning, Jenny. Vice pres. Edens Food Stores, Inc., Columbia, S.C., 1946-55; pres. Edens-Turbeville Gen. Ins. Agy., Columbia, 1956-63; now engaged in gen. investments, farming and timber mgmt.; owner, developer comml. real estate; active Rep. Pary, 1960—; chmn. S.C. Rep. Party, 1963-65; mem. Rep. Nat. Com. for S.C., 1965—, vice-chmn., 1965—, mem. exec. com. Mem., chmn. Nat. Adv. Bd. for Sports Fisheries and Wildlife, Dept. Interior, 1970—; bd. dirs., past 1st v.p. Alston Wilkes Prisoner Aid Soc.; mem. com. of 100, Emory Theol. Sem. Trustee S.C. Arthritis Found.; mem. U.S.C. Acad. and Athletic Scholarship Found., U.S.C. Alumni Assn. Ednl. Found. Served with USMCR, 1943-46; PTO. Mem. S.C., Greater Columbia chambers commerce, Columbia Community Relations Council, Nat. Wildlife Fedn., S.C. Farm Bur. Methodist (lay preacher). Mason. Clubs: Palmento, Forest Lake Country (Columbia); Spring Valley Country; Wateree Gun. Home: 905 Arbutus Dr Columbia SC 29205

EDENS, ROBERT LUTHER, Jr., advt. exec.; b. Bartlesville, Okla., Mar. 22, 1924; s. Robert Luther and Mona (Bates) E.; grad. Woodberry Forest Sch., 1942; B.A. cum laude, Yale, 1948; m. Frances

J. Talbert, June 3, 1946; children—Stephanie Talbert, Robert Edens III. With Fuller & Smith & Ross, 1948-50, Hicks & Greist, 1951-54; copy chief, then v.p. Warwick & Legler, 1954-62; asso. creative dir. Leo Burnett Co., 1962, v.p., creative dir., 1962-66, corporate dir., 1963-66; v.p., creative dir. J. Walter Thompson Co., 1966-67, exec. v.p., dir., mgr. Chgo. office, 1967—, mem. exec. com., 1968—; dir. Nat. Blvd. Bank, Chgo.; pres. Domingo Reyes, Inc.; chmn. bd. Talbert-Todd, Inc. Sect. chmn. Chgo. Crusade of Mercy, 1969. Served with AUS, World War II. Mem. Am. Assn. Advt. Agys. (chmn. Chgo.), Chi Phi. Clubs: Curling, Racquet, Commonwealth, Yale (Chgo.); Indian Hill (Winnetka); Yale (N.Y.C.); Ardsley Country, Sleepy Hollow Country (Westchester, N.Y.); Shoreacres (Lake Bluff, Ill.); DeLand (Fla.) Country; Hillsboro (Fla.). Home: 480 East Oak St Winnetka IL 60093 Office: 875 North Michigan Av Chicago IL 60611

EDER, HOWARD ABRAM, physician, educator; b. Milw., Sept. 23, 1917; s. Samuel and Rebecca (Abram) E.; A.B., U. Wis., 1938; M.D., Harvard, 1942, M.P.H., 1945; m. Barbara Straus, July 15, 1954; children—Rebecca, Susan, Michael. Intern, Peter Bent Brigham Hosp., Boston, 1942-43, asst. resident, 1943-44; research fellow in medicine Harvard Med. Sch., 1943-44, research fellow in biochemistry, 1945-46; asst. in medicine, asst. physician Rockefeller U. Hosp., 1946-50; asst. prof. medicine Cornell U. Med. Coll., N.Y.C., 1950-53; mem. staff Nat. Heart Inst., Bethesda, Md., 1953-55, mem. adv. com. Coronary Drug Project, 1969—, mem. task force on arteriosclerosis, 1970—; asso. prof. medicine State U. N.Y., Downstate Med. Coll., Bklyn., 1955-57; asso. prof. medicine Albert Einstein Coll. Medicine, 1957-60, prof., 1960—. Vis. prof. St. Marys Hosp. Med. Sch., London, Eng., 1965-66; vis. prof. medicine U. Cal. at San Francisco, 1965; mem. gen. clin. research center com. USPHS, 1961-63, mem. metabolism study sect., 1967-70; mem. N.Y. State Bd. Med. Examiners, 1957- 59. Mem. Assn. Am. Physicians, Am. Soc. Clin. Investigation, Interurban Clin. Club, Am. Soc. Biol. Chemists, Am. Physiol. Soc., Royal Soc. Medicine, Biochem. Soc. London, Soc. for Exptl. Biology and Medicine, N.Y. Acad. Medicine. Editorial bd. Jour. Lipid Research, 1960-64, asso. editor, 1968—; editorial bd. Am. Jour. Physiology, 1968—. Home: 4683 Waldo Av New York City NY 10471 Office: Albert Einstein Coll Medicine 1300 Morris Park Av New York City NY 10461

EDER, RAY, lawyer; b. St. Louis, Mar. 5, 1925; A.B., Harvard, 1947, LL.B., 1950. Admitted to Mo. bar, 1950; now partner firm Stolar, Heitzmann & Eder, St. Louis. Mem. Mo. Bar. Office: 515 Olive St St Louis MO 63101*

EDGAR, ALVIN RANDALL, educator; b. Eldora, Ia., Jan. 11, 1903; s. Fred John and Blanche (Foster) E.; B.A., Upper Ia. U., 1924, Mus.D. (hon.), 1948; M.A., State U. Ia., 1935; m. Mildred Lane, Nov. 7, 1925; children—Joyce Elaine (Mrs. Alvin F. Bull), Margaret Ann (Mrs. Donald McWilliams). Tchr. instrumental music pub. schs., Ia., 1924-35; cond. symphony orch. Ia. State U., 1935—, band dir., 1935-48, prof. music, 1948—, head dept. music, 1948-61; frequent vis. prof. clinics and music festivals; adjudicator music contests. Recipient Faculty citation Ia. State U. Alumni Assn., 1962. Mem. Ia. Bandmasters Assn. (pres. 1938), Coll. Band Dirs. Nat. Assn. (pres. 1949), Music Educators Nat. Conf., Ia. Music Educators Assn., Ia. Music Tchrs. Assn. (pres. 1958-60), Phi Mu Alpha (province gov., exec. com. 1948-58). Rotarian (dist. gov. 1948). Home: 111 Lynn Av Ames IA 50010

EDGAR, EARL EUGENE, educator; b. Dwright, Ill., Feb. 12, 1914; s. Earl Edward and Hazel (Losee) E.; A.B., DePauw U., 1935; M.A., U. Neb., 1937; student U. Wis., 1937-38; Ph.D., U. Cin., 1940; m. Joan Louise Dodds, May 29, 1944; children—Eric Reed, Ellen Louise, Earl Edward. Asso. prof. philosophy Culver-Stockton Coll., 1940-42; with wage stblzn. div. VI Regional War Labor Bd., 1942-45; instr. social scis. U. Chgo., 1945-46; asso. prof. philosophy Kan. State Coll., 1946-48, prof., 1948-61, asso. dir. Inst. of Citizenship, 1948-51, acting dir., 1951-53, head dept. gen. studies, 1953-61; prof. edn. Pa. State U. at University Park, 1961-67; dean Grad. Sch., prof. philosophy Youngstown (Ohio) State U., 1967-70, v.p. acad. affairs, 1970—. U.S. specialist grant Internat. Ednl. Exchange Program, Dept. State; cons. gen. edn., India, 1958. Fellow Philosophy of Edn. Soc.; mem. Am. Philos. Assn., Am. Assn. U. Profs., Phi Kappa Phi, Phi Delta Kappa. Home: 231 N Cadillac Boardman OH 44512 Office: Youngstown State Univ Youngstown OH 44503

EDGAR, JAMES WINFRED, govt. ofcl.; b. Briggs, Tex., Sept. 15, 1904; s. James William and Sarah (Morris) E.; B.A., Howard Payne Coll., 1928; M.A., U. Tex., 1938, Ed.D., 1948; LL.D., Austin College, 1958; Litt. D. (hon.), Southwestern U.; m. Sue Oakley, Aug. 22, 1927; children—Frances Ruth, Sarah Elizabeth, Susan Elaine. Tchr., Burnet County, Tex., 1923- 27; prin., Heidenheimer, Tex., 1928-29; asst. supt. schs., Victoria, Tex., 1929-30; supt. schs., Mirando City, Tex., 1930-39, Orange, Tex., 1939-47, Austin, Tex., 1947-50; state commr. edn., Tex., 1950—. Pres., Tex. Assn. Sch. Adminstrs., 1942-44, chmn. edn. policies com., Tex. State Tchrs. Assn., 1947, mem. legislative com., 1947-49; mem. editorial bd. Sch. Execs. Mag., 1947-52. Mem. Boy Scouts Am. (mem. nat. com. scouting in schs.), Am. Assn. Sch. Adminstrs. (mem. 1950 Yearbook commn.), N.E.A., Phi Delta Kappa. Presbyn. (mem. adv. council higher edn. U.S.). Home: 1517 Parkway Austin TX 78703 Office: Texas Education Agency State Capitol Austin TX 78711

EDGAR, ROBERT THOMAS, r.r. exec.; b. Shreveport, La., Jan. 12, 1917; s. Howard F. and Alice (Trosper) E.; B.S., La. State U., 1938; m. Katherine Dement, June 21, 1940; children—Joanne, Kay, Susan. Chemist, Rodessa Refining Corp., Shreveport, 1938-40; lab. supr. E. I. du Pont de Nemours & Co., 1940-45; operations supr. and supt. Ethyl Corp., 1945-55; mgr. mfg. Ethyl Corp. Can., 1955-59; v.p. prodn. U.S. Borax & Chem. Corp., 1959-66, v.p. mfg., 1966-69; pres. Bersaner Corp., Los Angeles, 1969-71; western mgr. Amtrack, 1971—. Mem. Am. Inst. Chem. Engrs., Sigma Alpha Epsilon. Club: Glendora (Cal.) Country. Home: 650 Hampton Rd Arcadia CA 91006 Office: 3345 Wilshire Blvd Los Angeles CA 90005

EDGE, ARTHUR B., Jr., former mill exec.; b. Newnan, Ga., Apr. 19, 1905; s. Arthur Brannon and Marie Aline (Pascal) E.; B.S. in Textile Engring., Ga. Inst. Tech., 1926; m. Florence W. West, Apr. 23, 1930; children—Arthur B. III, Edward W., Emily W. (Mrs. E. Morton III). With Callaway Mills, Inc., La Grange, Ga., 1926—, formerly asst. sec., sec., v.p., dir. purchases, exec. v.p., v.p., also gen. mgr. HDV div., pres., dir.; dir. Citizens & So. Bank of LaGrange. Past pres. Textile Edn. Found., Atlanta; past pres., trustee Callaway Found., Inc., Callaway Ednl. Assn. (both LaGrange); past pres. LaGrange Bd. Edn., Textile Edn. Found., Atlanta; treas., trustee City-County Hosp., LaGrange. Mem. Am. Cotton Mfrs. Inst. (past dir.), Am. Textile Mfrs. Inst., Ga. Textile Mfrs. Assn. (past pres.). Episcopalian (past sr. Warden). Mason, Rotarian (past pres.) Clubs: Augusta (Ga.) Nat. Golf; Highland Country (gov., past chmn.); Augusta Nat. Golf. Home: 1106 Vernon Rd LaGrange GA 30240

EDGE, FINDLEY BARTOW, educator, clergyman; b. Albany, Ga., Sept. 6, 1916; s. John Andrew and Daisey (Findley) E.; A.B., Stetson U., 1938, D.D., 1958; Th.M., So. Bapt. Theol. Sem., 1942, Th.D., 1945; M.A., Yale, 1955; grad. study Columbia, Union Theol. Sem.; m. Louvenia Littleton, June 3, 1939; children—Larry Findley, Hoyt Littleton. Ordained to ministry Bapt. Ch., 1938; pastor in Apopka, Fla., 1938-39, Simpsonville, Ky., 1940-45, Campbellsburg, Ky., 1945-47; Basil Manley, Jr. prof. religious edn. So. Bapt. Theol. Sem., Louisville, 1947—. Mem. div. Christian edn. Nat. Council Chs., 1958—, exec. com. profs. and research sect., 1967—; bd. dirs. Opportunities Industrialization Center, Inc.; recipient scholarship Am. Assn. Theol. Schs., 1964-65. Mem. Religious Edn. Assn. (dir. 1967-69), So. Bapt. Religious Edn. Assn. (past pres.). Author: Teaching for Results, 1956; Helping the Teacher, 1959; A Quest for Vitality in Religion, 1963; The Greening of the Church, 1971. Editorial bd. Watchman Examiner, 1964-69. Address: 2825 Lexington Rd Louisville KY 40206

EDGE, PETER, lawyer; b. N.Y.C., Mar. 25, 1913; S.B., Harvard, 1934, J.D., 1937. Admitted to Ill. bar, 1946, N.Y. bar, 1938; practice in Chgo., 1946—; mem. firm Arnstein, Gluck, Weitzenfeld, Minow, 1963—. Sec., dir. Hawk Mountain Sanctuary Assn. Mem. Am., Chgo. bar assns. Home: 1189 Oakley Av Winnetka IL 60093 Office: 120 S LaSalle St Chicago IL 60603

EDGELL, WALTER FRANCIS, educator; b. Kokomo, Ind., July 26, 1916; s. Marshall Hall and Lucretia (Farnsworth) E.; B.Sc., U. Cal. at Berkeley, 1939; postgrad. U. Minn., 1939-40; M.Sc., U. Ia., 1941; Ph.D., Harvard, 1943; m. Rene DaValle, Feb. 14, 1937; children—Marshall Hall, Richard Garrett, Colleen Francis, Geraldine Ann. Austine teaching fellow Harvard, 1943; instr. U. Ia., 1944-47, asso. prof. chemistry, 1947-49; prof. Purdue U., 1949—; cons. Philips Petroleum Co., Oak Ridge Nat. Labs., U.S. Nav. Weapons Center. Trustee Serra Club, Lafayette Diocese. Recipient Research award Ia. Acad. Sci., 1947; Guggenheim fellow, 1957. Mem. Am. Chem. Soc., Soc. Applied Spectroscopy, Coblentz Soc., Am. Chem. Soc. (chmn. Ia. 1947, chmn. Purdue U. 1952), Alpha Chi Sigma. Contbr. profl. jours. Home: 2507 Oswego Lane Lafayette IN 47907

EDGERLY, WILLIAM SKELTON, chem. mfg. co. exec.; b. Lewiston, Me., Feb. 18, 1927; s. Stuart and Florence (Skelton) E.; grad. Mt. Hermon Sch., 1944; B.S. in Econs. and Engring., Mass. Inst. Tech., 1949; M.B.A., Harvard, 1955; m. Lois Stiles, June 12, 1948; children—Leonard Stuart, Stephanie Lois. With Eastman Kodak Co., 1949-50, with Cabot Corp., Boston, 1952—, treas., 1960-63, v.p., treas., 1963-66, financial v.p., 1966-67, v.p., gen. mgr. Oxides div., 1967-69, dir., financial v.p., 1969—; dir. State St. Bank and Trust Co. (Boston), Arkwright- Boston Mfrs. Mutual Ins. Co., Mut. Boiler and Machinery Ins. Co. (both Waltham, Mass.). Trustee Comm. Econ. Devel., Childrens Hosp. Med. Center, Boston; mem. corp. Mass. Inst. Tech. Served with USNR, 1945- 46, 50-52. Mem. Boston Econ. Club, Mass. Inst. Tech. Alumni Assn., Harvard Bus. School Assn., Tau Beta Pi, Sigma Chi. Home: 32 Highland St Cambridge MA 02138 Office: 125 High St Boston MA 02110

EDGERTON, HAROLD EUGENE, educator, elec. engr.; b. Fremont, Neb., Apr. 6, 1903; s. Frank Eugene and Mary Nettie (Coe) C.; B.S., U. Neb., 1925, Dr. Engring. (hon.), 1948; M. Sc., Mass. Inst. Tech., 1927, D.Sc., 1931; LL.D. (hon.), Doane Coll., 1969, U.S.C., 1969; m. Esther May Garrett, Feb. 28, 1928; children—Mary Louise, William Eugene, Robert Frank. Elect. engr. Neb. Light & Power Co., 1920-25, Gen. Electric Co., 1925-26; Inst. prof. emeritus Mass. Inst. Tech.; hon. chmn. bd. EG & G, Inc. Recipient medal Royal Photographic Soc.; Gold medal Nat. Geog. Soc.; Modern Pioneer Award, Potts medal, Franklin Inst., Albert A. Michelson medal, 1969. Fellow I.E.E.E., Am. Geophys. Union, Am. Inst. Elec. Engrs., Soc. Motion Pictures and TV Engrs., Royal Soc. Gt. Britain; mem. Am. Phys. Soc., Nat. Acad. Scis., Nat. Acad. Engrs., Marine Tech. Soc., Acad. Applied Sci., Internat. Sci. Film Assn., Woods Hole Oceanographic Instn., Acacia, Sigma Xi, Eta Kappa Nu (eminent mem.), Sigma Tau. Republican. Conglist. Mason. Author: Flash!, 1939; Electronic Flash, Strobe, 1970; also tech. articles. Inventor of stroboscopic high- speed motion and still photography apparatus; designer underwater camera and high-resolution sonar equipment. Home: 100 Memorial Dr Cambridge MA 02142

EDGERTON, HOWARD, savs. and loan assn. exec. Chmn. bd. Cal. Fed. Savs. and Loan Assn., Los Angeles. Office: 5670 Wilshire Blvd Los Angeles CA 90054*

EDGERTON, JAMES HOWARD, savs. and loan exec.; b. Sulphur Springs, Ark., Feb. 12, 1908; s. Llewellyn H. and Dora (White) E.; A.B., U. So. Cal., 1928, LL.B., 1930; m. Catherine Colwell, May 21, 1933; children—Beverly (Mrs. Joan Jay Corley), Russell. Admitted to Cal. bar, 1930; pres., chief exec. officer Cal. Fed. Savs. and Loan Assn., Los Angeles, 1936-67, chairman board, director, 1967—. Member Community Redevelopment Agency of Los Angeles, 1953—; pres. 6th Dist. Agrl. Assn. Cal., 1955-. Pres. Cal. Museum Sci. and Industry, 1955—; bd. dirs. Internat. Sci. Found., 1958—. Served with USAAF, 1943-44. Mem. U.S. Savs. and Loan League (past pres.), Los Angeles C. of C. (dir. 1956-58, v.p. 1959), Skull and Dagger, Lambda Alpha, Phi Kappa Tau, Phi Alpha Delta. Rotarian (hon.), Mason (Shriner). Home: 328 N Rockingham Av Los Angeles CA 90049 Office: 5680 Wilshire Blvd Los Angeles CA 90036

EDGERTON, MILLS FOX, Jr., educator; b. Hartford, Conn., June 11, 1931; s. Mills Fox and Miriam (Reynolds) E.; B.A., U. Conn., 1953; student Nat. U. Autónoma de México, Mexico City, 1951; A.M., Princeton, 1955, Ph.D., 1960; m. Marianne Simonson, Dec. 27, 1957; children—Michael, Nicholas. Instr. Romance langs. Princeton, 1957, Rutgers U., 1957-60; asso. prof., chmn. dept. Spanish, Bucknell U., Lewisburg, Pa., 1960-66, prof., 1966—, chmn. dept. modern langs., lit. and linguistics, 1968—. Chmn. Northeast Conf. on Teaching Fgn. Langs., 1972, Spanish Com for Grad. Record Exams, 1965-69. Alexander von Humboldt Found. grantee, 1961, Am. Philos. Soc. grantee, 1962. Mem. Modern Lang. Assn., Am. Council Teaching Fgn. Langs., Am. Assn. Tchrs. French, Am. Assn. Tchrs. Spanish and Portuguese. Roman Catholic. Contbr. profl. jours. Home: 111 S 16th St Lewisburg PA 17837

EDGERTON, MILTON THOMAS, Jr., physician; b. Atlanta, July 14, 1921; s. Milton Thomas and Elizabeth (Roddick) E.; B.A., Emory U., 1941; M.D., Johns Hopkins, 1944; m. Patricia Jane Jones, June 30, 1945; children—Bradford Wheatly, William Alton, Sandra Roddick, Diane Miller. Intern Barnes Hosp., St. Louis, 1944-45; instr. surgery Johns Hopkins Hosp., 1947-49, plastic surgeon-in- charge, 1951-70; mem. faculty surgery Johns Hopkins Sch. Medicine, 1947- 70, asso. prof. surgery, 1953-62, prof. plastic surgery, 1962-70; prof. plastic surgery, chmn. dept. plastic surgery U. Va., Charlottesville, 1970—; plastic surgeon in chief U. Va. Med. Center, 1970—; pvt. practice medicine, specializing reconstructive and hand surgery, 1945-; vis. prof. plastic and reconstructive surgery Christian Med. Coll., Vellore, India, 1962, Rochester (N.Y.) U., 1966, Washington U., St. Louis, 1968, U. Chgo., 1969; cons. VA Hosp., Balt., 1953—, VA Hosp., Salem, Va., 1970—, Nat. Clin. Center, NIH, 1954—, Balt. City Hosps., 1956-70, Children's Hosp., Balt., 1965-70, Walter Reed Army Hosp., 1965—, Good Samaritan Hosp., Balt., 1968-70. Adv. bd. Medico, 1963—; mem. surgery study sect. NIH, 1967—. Member bd. trustees Lake Placid Ednl. Found., W. Alton Jones Cell Sci. Center, N.Y., Found. Soc. Plastic and Reconstructive Surgery. Served to capt. M.C., AUS, 1945- 47. Decorated Certificate of Merit. Diplomate Am. Bd. Surgery, Am. Bd. Plastic Surgery (mem. tripartite residency review com. in plastic surgery 1963-70, mem. bd. examiners 1964-70, vice chmn. 1969-70). Fellow A.C.S. (bd. govs. 1952—, mem. cancer commn. 1966—); mem. Am. Soc. Plastic and Reconstructive Surgery, Am. Assn. Plastic Surgeons, Soc. Head and Neck Surgeons (founder), Soc. Univ. Surgeons, A.M.A., Am. Assn. Cleft Palate Rehab., Plastic Surgery Research Council (founder), Instn. Nuclear Engrs. (med. sect.), Am. Assn. U. Profs., Assn. for Advancement Med. Instrumentation, Transplantation Soc., Am. Soc. Surgery of the Hand, Am., So. surg. assns., Med. and Chirurgical Faculty State of Md., Balt. Med. Soc., Albemarle County Med. Soc., Am. Psychosomatic Soc., Nat. Acad. Scis., Nat. Soc. Med. Research, Internat. Soc. Plastic and Reconstructive Surgery, Am. Soc. Aesthetic Surgery, Internat. Soc. Aesthetic Surgeons, Internat. Soc. for Capillary and Blood Research, Phi Beta Kappa, Eta Sigma Psi. Clubs: Hamilton Street, Elkridge (Balt.); Lake Placid (N.Y.); Farmington Country (Charlottesville, Va.); Lyford Cay (New Providence Island). Asso. editor Jour. Plastic and Reconstructive Surgery, 1963—, Transplantation Jour., 1961-68. Editor: Mind and Medicine. Contbr. numerous articles med. publs. Home: 8 Dogwood Lane Charlottesville VA 22901 Office: Dept Plastic Surgery U Va Med Center Charlottesville VA 22903

EDGERTON, NORMAN EDWARD, bus. exec.; b. Raleigh, N.C., June 14, 1898; s. Noah Edward and Alma (Wynne) E.; student Duke U., 1917-19; m. Mishew Rogers, Feb. 9, 1929; 1 dau., Mishew Ellen (Mrs. Mishew Edgerton Smith). Founder Raleigh Bonded Warehouse, Inc., 1923, pres. 1923—; mem. N.C. Conf. Meth. Bd. Publ. Inc. Former chmn. com. on improvement state care of mental patients; 1st chmn. N.C. Hosps. Bd. Control. Trustee emeritus Duke U.; former trustee Eastern Carolina Sch. Boys. Mem. Raleigh C. of C. (past pres.), Raleigh Y.M.C.A. (past pres.), Duke U. General Alumni Assn. (past pres.), S.A.R., Am. Legion, Omicron Delta Kappa, Phi Kappa Alpha. Mason (Shriner, past potentate), Kiwanian (past pres.). Clubs: Carolina Country, Coral Bay. Home: Tatton Hall Oberlin Rd Raleigh, NC 27608. Office: Box 6158 Raleigh NC 27608

EDGERTON, SAMUEL YOUNGS, Jr., educator, art historian; b. Cleve., Sept. 30, 1926; s. Samuel Youngs and Mary (Martineau) E.; A.B., U. Pa., 1950, M.F.A., 1956, M.A., 1960, Ph.D., 1965; m. Dorothy W. Dugan, June 2, 1951; children—Perky, Peter, Samuel Youngs III, Mary. Prof., chmn. dept. art history Boston U., 1964—. Fulbright Exchange tchr. to Germany, 1957-58; mem. Inst. for Advanced Study, Princeton, N.J., 1967-68; Nat. Endowment for Humanities grantee, 1967, 70-71; fellow Villa I Tatti, Florence, Italy, 1971-72. Mem. Coll. Art Assn., Renaissance Soc. Am. Home: 41 Mason Terrace Brookline MA 02146 Office: Dept Fine Arts Boston U 725 Commonwealth Av Boston MA 02215

EDGETT, JAMES DEYO, moving co. exec.; b. Gladwin County, Mich., Apr. 10, 1903; s. James William and Cora (Nolan) E.; LL.D. (hon.), Ind. Inst. Tech.; m. J. Margaret Olmstead, Aug. 28, 1938; 1 son, James Deyo II. Pres. N. Am. Van Lines, Inc., Ft. Wayne, Ind., 1947—, also dir. Trustee Ft. Wayne YMCA, Ind. Inst. Tech. Presbyn. Mason (32, Shriner), Rotarian. Home: 5249 Eastwick Dr Fort Wayne IN 46805 Office: N Am Van Lines Inc New Haven Av Fort Wayne IN 46803

EDGINGTON, RALPH, oil co. exec.; b. Delaware, O., Aug. 3, 1905; s. Robert Clinton and Clara Isabelle (Rouse) E.; B.A., Mont. U., 1927; LL.B., J.D., U. So. Cal., 1931; m. Ethel Loretta Jones, Sept. 8, 1928; children—Arlis (Mrs. James Whiffen), Lyn (Mrs. Kenneth W. Kendrick). Admitted to Cal. bar, 1931; practiced in Los Angeles, 1931-42; pres. Edgington Oil Co., Long Beach, Cal., 1942—; dir. Kern County Refinery, Edgington Oxnard Refinery, Edoco Tech. Products, Sahuaro Petroleum & Asphalt Co. Mem. Sigma Chi, Phi Alpha Delta. Republican. Methodist. Clubs: Virginia Country (Long Beach); California, Jonathan (Los Angeles). Home: 422 Parkwood Dr Los Angeles, CA 90024. Office: 2400 E Artesia Blvd Long Beach CA 90805

EDGREN, CARL HOBART, coll. dean; b. Chgo., Mar. 18, 1921; s. C. Henry and Mildred (Johnson) E.; B.S., Northwestern U., 1941, Ph.D., 1951; M.A., U. Mich., 1942; m. Jane I. Hanson, Sept. 8, 1949; children—Alan, Roger, Paul, Sara. Instr. English, Ripon (Wis.) Coll., 1946, Albion (Mich.) Coll., 1950-51; teaching asst. Northwestern U., 1947-50; chmn. dept. English, Elmhurst (Ill.) Coll., 1951-58; chmn. div. lang. and lit. N. Park Coll., Chgo., 1958-64, dean coll., 1964—. Cons., examiner N. Central Assn., 1962—. Mem. Am. Assn. U. Profs. Author: Of Marble and Mud, 1960; also articles, revs. Home: 5400 N Bernard St Chicago, IL 60625.

EDICK, GLENN ELLIS, agrl. co. exec.; b. Columbia Center, N.Y., Feb. 8, 1918; s. Ellis and Mary (Salesman) E.; B.S. in Agr., Cornell U., 1940; m. Janet Palmer, Sept. 23, 1939; children-Dolores (Mrs. John Puit), Darleen (Mrs. Dale Statucki). With Grange League Fedn., 1940-64; with Agway, Inc., DeWitt, N.Y., 1964—, v.p. prodn., 1968—; pres. United Coops., Alliance, O., 1962-65, Allied Seed Co., 1962—; v.p. Select Seeds, Fort Wayne, Ind., 1963—. Pres. Dryden Central Sch. Bd., 1954-64. Mason (32). Home: 4672 Ridge Rd Cazenovia NY 13035 Office: 333 Butternut Dr DeWitt NY 13214

EDIDIN, SOL MARTIN, transp. co. exec.; b. Chgo., Oct. 25, 1920; s. Abraham and Frieda (Sager) E.; B.A., U. Ill., 1942; J.D., U. Chgo., 1949; m. Lore Bauer, Aug. 30, 1946; children—Stephen R., Peter D. Admitted to Ill. bar, 1949; atty. legal div. TVA, 1949-57; v.p., corp. counsel Hertz Corp., 1954-68, v.p., sec., gen. counsel, 1968—; instr. U. Tennessee Law Sch., 1950-51; lectr. Practicing Law Inst., 1964-65. Mem. Nat. Motor Vehicle Safety Advisory Council. Served with AUS, 1942-46. Home: 39 Olmsted Rd Scarsdale, NY 10583. Office: 660 Madison Av New York City NY 10021

EDIE, STUART artist; b. Wichita Falls, Tex., Nov. 10, 1908; s. Stuart Carson and Maude (White) E.; student Kan. City Art Inst., 1926-27; Art Students League, N.Y., 1928-29; m. Elizabeth Terrell, Sept. 26, 1934; 1 son, Stuart Carson III. One-man exhibitions, New York, 1931-33, 1944-45; rep. in permanent collections; Metropolitan Mus.; Brooklyn Mus.; Newark Mus.; Whitney Mus. of Am. Art; Syracuse Mus.; Arizona Collection; Bruce Memorial Collection; Toledo (Ohio) Museum, Joslyn Memorial Museum; exhibited: Museum of Modern Art; Metropolitan Mus.; Chicago Art Inst.; Pa. Acad.; Carnegie Inst.; Corcoran Gallery of Art. Instr., Am. Artists School, N.Y., 1936-37; priv. classes, Woodstock, N.Y., 1937-42; instr., State Univ. of Ia., 1944; resident prof. of art, State Univ. of Ia., 1945-47. Mem. An Am. Group, Sawkill Painters and Sculptors, Woodstock Artists Assn. Home: 111 S Summit St Iowa City IA 52240 Office: Department of Art U of Iowa Iowa City IA 52240

EDINBURGH, PRINCE PHILIP, THE DUKE OF Earl of Merioneth, Baron Greenwich; b. Corfu, Greece, June 10, 1921; s. Prince Andrew of Greece and Denmark and Princess Alice (d. Marquess of Milford Haven); ed. Germany, Scotland and England; hon. degrees: LL.D., Wales, 1949, U. London, 1951, U. Edinburgh, 1952, U. Cambridge, 1952; D.C.L., U. Durham, 1951, Oxford U.; LL.D., Karachi U., Royal U. Malta; D.Sc., Delhi U., Reading U.; hon. degree engring. U. of Lima (Peru); m. Princess Elizabeth Alexandra Mary (now Queen Elizabeth II), Nov. 20, 1947; children—Charles Philip Arthur George, Anne Elizabeth Alice Louise, Andrew Albert Christian Edward, Edward Antony Richard Louis. Became naturalized British subject, Feb. 1947, adopting surname Mountbatten; created Baron Greenwich, County of London, Earl of Merioneth, and Duke of Edinburgh, with title of His Royal Highness, 1947; created Knight Most Noble Order of the Garter, 1947, Knight Most Ancient and Most Noble Order of the Thistle, 1952; Grand Master and First or Principal Knight of the Order British Empire, 1953; Prince of the United Kingdom of Great Britain and Northern Ireland, 1957; decorated Order of Merit, 1968. Became personal a.d.c. to King George VI, 1948. Privy Counsellor, 1951, Privy Counsellor of Can., 1957. Chancellor, U. Wales, 1948—; life gov. King's Coll., London; vis. Churchill Coll., Cambridge. Recipient Order of the Redeemer, Order of St. George and St. Constantine, 4th Class, Order of George I, Order of Phoenix of Greece; Order of Elephant (Denmark); Order of St. Olaf (Norway); Order of Seraphim (Sweden); Grand Cross of Legion d'Honneur (France); Grand Cross Order Netherlands Lion; Grand Cord on, Supreme Order of Chrysanthenum (Japan); and others. Granted Freedoms London, Greenwich, Edinburgh, Belfast, Cardiff, Glasgow, Melbourne, and several others. Mem. and former officer or current officer numerous orgns., assns., also clubs, yachting assns. and learned socs. Officer in Brit. Navy; with Mediterranean Fleet and Brit. Pacific Fleet, 1939-45. Author: Birds from Britannia, 1952. Address: Buckingham Palace London SW 1 England

EDINGER, ALBERT P., trust co. exec. Sr. v.p. First Trust & Deposit Co., Syracuse, N.Y. Office: Warren St at Washington St Syracuse NY 13201*

EDINGER, LOIS VIRGINIA, educator; b. Thomasville, N.C., Apr. 17, 1925; d. William Paul and Essie (Byerly) Edinger; A.B., Meredith Coll., 1945; M.Ed., U. N.C., 1959, Ph.D., 1964. Tchr., Thomasville High Sch., 1945-46; tchr. history, North Wilkesboro, 1946-47; youth dir. St. John's Bapt. Ch., Charlotte, N.C., 1947-49; tchr. social studies, Whiteville, N.C., 1949-57; studio tchr. U.S. history N.C. In-Sch. TV project, Chapel Hill, 1957-60; instr. tchr. edn. U. N.C., Chapel Hill, 1960-62, asst. prof., Greensboro, 1962-65, asso. prof., 1965-71, prof., 1971—. Del. to World Confedn. Orgns. Teaching Profession, 1959-61, 64-65, chmn. U.S. delegation, 1965; mem. Gov.'s. Commn. Ednl. TV, 1962-64; tech. cons. edn. theory SEARCH. Recipient N.C. Prin. award, 1965; O. Max Gardner award U. N.C. Mem. N.E.A. (pres. 1964-65), N.C. Edn. Assn. (past pres., past pres. div. classroom tchrs., chmn. resolutions com.), Nat., N.C. councils social studies, Am. Assn. U. Women, N.C. Hist. and Lit. Soc., Am. Acad. Polit. and Social Sci., Delta Kappa Gamma. Editor: Teaching: Your Career, 1954-55. Contbr. articles to profl. jours. Home: 2409 Berkley Pl Greensboro NC 27403

EDINGER, OSCAR H., Jr., former coll. pres., cons.; b. Pomona, Cal., Jan. 1, 1904; s. Oscar H. and Irene (Eddy) E.; student Pomona Coll., Occidental Coll., Eagle Rock, Cal.; B.A., LaVerne Coll., 1931, LL.D., 1958; M.A., Claremont Grad. Sch., 1932; m. M. Zilpha Johnson, June 18, 1925; 1 son, Donald C. Tchr., Leuzinger High Sch., Inglewood, Cal., 1932-33, Pomona High Sch. and Jr. Coll., 1933-37, asst. dir., 1937-46; dir. Mt. San Antonio Coll., 1946- 56, pres., dist. supt., 1956-69; cons. community coll. edn., 1969—. Mem., past chmn. Cal. Adv. Com. on Adult Edn.; mem. Cal. Jr. Coll. Agrl. Edn. Com. Mem. Am. Assn. Jr. Colls. (dir., past pres.), So. Cal. Jr. Coll. Assn. (past pres. Eastern conf.), N.E.A., Higher Edn. Assn., Am. Council Edn. (dir., mem. commn. plans and objectives, mem. commn. internat. edn.), Cal. Tchrs. Assn., Am. Council Edn. (Com. adult and higher edn.), Pomona C. of C. (past dir.). Elk, Kiwanian (pres. Pomona). Address: 3727 N Equation Rd Pomona CA 91767

EDINGTON, ROBERT SHERARD, lawyer, state senator; b. Mobile, Ala., Nov. 18, 1929; s. David Henry and Cornelia (Owen) E.; B.A., Southwestern U. at Memphis, 1950; J.D., U. Ala., 1956; m. Patricia Gentry, June 2, 1962; children—Sherard Caffey, Virginia Ellen. Admitted to Ala. bar, 1956, since practiced in Mobile; asso. Caffey, Gallalee & Caffey, 1956-59; partner Gallalee, Denniston and Edington, 1959—; consul of Guatemala at Mobile, 1959—, chmn. Consular Corps of Mobile, 1965. Mem. Ala. Ho. of Reps., 1962-70; mem. Ala. Senate, 1970—. Apptd. to U.S.S. Ala. Battleship Commn., 1963. Del. Democratic Nat. Conv., 1968. Served with USNR, 1951-55. Recipient Distinguished Service award Ala. Hist. Commn., 1970; Ala. Commendation medal, 1970. Mem. Am., Inter-Am. bar assns., Mobile Jr. C. of C. (past v.p.), Am. Legion, V.F.W., Omicron Delta Kappa. Presbyn. (elder). Kiwanian. Home: 307 Conti St Mobile AL 36602 Office: 50 St Emanuel St Mobile AL 36602

EDISON, ALLEN RAY, educator; b. Plainview, Neb., Sept. 21, 1926; s. Arthur and Lela (Johnson) E.; B.S., U. Neb., 1950, M.S., 1957; D.Sc., U. N.M., 1962; m. Betty Jean Broer, Dec. 27, 1949; children—Karl Arthur, Kathryn Johannah. Engr., Silas Mason Co., Burlington, Ia., 1950-53; instr. U. Neb., Lincoln, 1953-57, prof. elec. engring., 1957—, chmn. dept. elec. engring., 1964-70. Served with USNR, 1944- 46. Mem. I.E.E.E. (past sect. chmn.), Sigma Xi, Sigma Tau, Eta Kappa Nu. Home: 511 S 54th St Lincoln NB 68510 Office: 1400 R St Lincoln NB 68508

EDISON, BERNARD, retail co. exec.; b. Atlanta, Mar. 23, 1928; s. Irving and Beatrice (Chanin) E.; B.A., Harvard, 1949, M.B.A., 1951; m. Marilyn Schmulbach, Mar. 4, 1965; children—Julie, Robin, Peter. With Edison Bros. Stores, Inc., St. Louis, 1951, pres., 1968—; dir. Mercantile Trust Co., St. Louis, Bd. dirs., exec. com. United Fund Greater St. Louis; bd. dirs. Jewish Hosp., St. Louis; trustee John Burroughs Sch. Served with USAF, 1951-53. Home: 30 Southmoor Dr St Louis, MO 63105. Office: 400 Washington Av St Louis MO 63102

EDISON, CHARLES B., dept. store exec.; b. 1921; married. With Edison Bros. Stores Inc., 1941—, exec. v.p., 1968—, vice chmn. bd., 1968—, also dir. Served as officer USAAF, 1943-45. Address: 400 Washington Av St Louis MO 63102*

EDISON, HARRY SWEETS, jazz Trumpeter; b. Columbus, O., Oct. 17, 1915. Played with Count Basie, 1937-50, with Nelson Riddle, Lionel Newman, Benny Carter, Axel Stordhal in Hollywood, Cal., 1952-58; organized quintet and accoompanied Joe Williams on tour, 1960-61; went to Europe, 1964; played with Frank Sinatra, Count Basie band, 1965-66; frequently leads quartet Memory Lane Club, Los Angeles. Address: 3754 Chesapeake Los Angeles CA 90016*

EDISON, IRVING, retail exec.; b. Adel, Ga., Dec. 22, 1899; s. Abraham and Sarah (Halle) E.; student pub. schs. of Boston; m. Beatrice Chanin, Nov. 25, 1926; children—Bernard, Ruth, Charles (dec.). A founder (with 4 bros.) Edison Bros. Stores, Inc., St. Louis, 1922, formerly exec. v.p., dir., pres., 1958-68, chmn. exec. com., 1968—; mem. bd. dirs. Union Electric Co., St. Louis, Boatmen's Nat. Bank, Gen. Am. Life Ins. Co. Mem. retail shoe industry adv. com. WPB, 1942-45. Police commnr. St. Louis County. Bd. dirs. St. Louis Symphony; treas. John Burroughs Sch. Pres., Nat. Jewish Welfare Bd.; bd. dirs. U.S.O.; chmn. corp. div. War Bond Drive, 1945; vice chmn. Community Chest campaigns, 1946, 48; pres. World Fedn. YMCAs and Community Centers. Bd. dirs. United Fund; trustee St. Louis University; trustee, vice chmn. Barnes Hosp. Awarded Treasury Dept. Gold star for war bond sales, 1946. Mem. World Fedn. YMHA and Jewish Community Centers (pres.), C. of C. Met. St. Louis (chmn. 1962-63). Clubs: St. Louis, Mo. Athletic, Westwood Country, Noonday. Home: 220 N Kingshighway St Louis MO 63108 Office: 400 Washington Av St Louis MO 63102

EDISON, JOHN GALBRAITH, lawyer; b. Port Hope, Ont., Can., Jan. 19, 1911; s. Herbert Edison and Georgia (Galbraith) E.; B.A., U. Toronto, 1932; LL.B., Osgoode Hall Sch. Law; m. Margaret Elixabeth Hill, June 7, 1940; one son, John Robert Churchill. Admitted to Ont. bar, 1936; now partner firm Edison, Aird & Berlis, Toronto. Sec., dir. Mindustrial Corp. Ltd.; dir. Rio Algom Mines Ltd., Ash Temple Ltd., Butler Metal Products Ltd., Keeprite Products Ltd., other. Served with RCAF, 1941-45. Decorated Croix de Guerre; mentioned in despatches. Mem. Canadian Bar Assn. Presbyn. Clubs: Toronto, Toronto Golf; University. Home: 133 Dunvegan Rd Toronto 7 Ontario Canada Office: 111 Richmond St W Toronto 110 Ontario Canada*

EDISON, SIMON, shoe chain store exec.; b. Adel, Ga., June 15, 1901; s. Abraham and Sarah (Halle) E.; ed. pub. schs., Atlanta; m. Helen Audrey Davidson, Feb. 2, 1926; children—William Morton, Robert Leonard (dec.), Stephen David. A founder Edison Brothers Stores Inc., St. Louis, 1922, exec. v.p., 1922- 66, chmn. bd., 1966—, also dir. Bd. dirs. Jewish Community Centers Assn., St. Louis, 1966—, Jewish Center for Aged, St. Louis, 1965—. Fellow Brandeis U., 1967. Mem. Volumn Footwear Retailers Assn. (bd. dirs., past pres.), Am. Retail Fedn. (past bd. dirs.). Clubs: Missouri Athletic, Westwood Country (St. Louis). Home: 4 Fordyce Lane St Louis, MO 63124. Office: 400 Washington Av St Louis MO 63102

EDITH, SISTER MARY, hosp. adminstr. Adminstr., St. John's Hosp. and Sch. Nursing, Tulsa. Office: 1923 S Utica Av Tulsa OK 74104*

EDLER, NOEL L., sugar co. exec.; b. New Orleans, 1913; grad. Loyola U., 1948. Vice pres., treas., dir. Godchaux-Henderson Sugar Co., Inc., Mobile, Ala.; dir. La. Sugar Exchange, Inc. Mem. U.S. Cane Sugar Refiners Assn. (dir.). Home: 108 Rhonda Dr N Mobile AL 36608 Office: PO Box 2043 Mobile AL 36601*

EDLUND, MILTON CARL, physicist; b. Jamestown, N.Y., Dec. 13, 1924; B.S., M.S., U. Mich., 1948, Ph.D., 1966; Physicist reactor physics, gaseous diffusion plant Princeton, 1948-49, Oak Ridge Nat. Lab., 1949-50, physicist, lectr. Sch. Reactor Tech., 1950-51, sr. physicist and sect. chief, 1953-55; mgr. devel. dept. Babcock & Wilcox Co., 1955-65, asst. mgr. atomic energy div., 1965-66; prof. U. Mich., 1966-67; planning cons. AEC, 1967-68; exec. v.p. Nuclear Assurance Corp., Atlanta, 1967- 70; chmn. nuclear ongring. Va. Poly. Inst., also Va. State U., Blacksburg, 1970—. Vis. lectr. Swedish Atomic Energy Com., 1953. Recipient Ernest Orlando Lawrence award, 1965. Fellow Am. Nuclear Soc. Author: (with S. Glasstone) Elements of Nuclear Reactor Theory, 1952; (with J. Fried) Desalting Technology, 1971. Spl. research neuron diffusion, nuclear reactor design. Address: 1103 Highland Circle Blacksburg VA 24060

EDMAN, SILAS WARD GOULD, business exec.; b. Pittsfield, Mass., Jan. 31, 1931; s. George William and Alice (Gould) E.; ed. Hotchkiss Sch.; B.A., Amherst Coll., 1953; m. Jettabee Ann Christenson, May 21, 1966; children—Lisa C., Austin B., David R., Silas Ward Gould. With 1st Nat. Bank N.Y. in Brazil, 1953-58; controller asst. sec. N.Y. Philharmonic, N.Y.C., 1958-62; adminstrv. dir. Place des Arts, Montreal, Que., Can., 1962-64; gen. mgr. Orchestral Assn., Chgo. Symphony and Orch. Hall, Chgo., 1964-67; exec. dir. John F. Kennedy Ednl. Civic and Cultural Center, 1967-70; pres. Nassau Coliseum, Inc., 1967-71; v.p. Mitchel Field Devel. Corp., 1967-71; exec. v.p. Sweeney/Edman Enterprises, Inc., 1971—. Cons., Nat. Centre for Performing Arts, Ottawa, Can., Wascana Centennial Centre, Regina, Can., Wilson Coll., Chgo., Thornton Coll., Chgo., N.Y. State Council of Arts. Bd. dirs. Berkshire Boy Choir Sch., Assn.; trustee, sec. Nassau County Reference Library; mem. Hofstra U. Council; mem. exec. council U.S. Inst. Theatre Tech. Mem. Performing Assn. (bd. dirs.). Clubs: Cliffdwellers (Chgo.); Bath (L.I.). Home: 140 Turkey Lane Cold Spring Harbor NY 11714

EDMISTON, HENRY HOUX, ins. exec.; b. Columbia, Mo., Sept. 7, 1907; s. Henry Hileman and Roberta (Houx) E.; A.B., U. Mo., 1928; A.M., Washington U., St. Louis, 1929; m. Helen Mary Duncan, June 6, 1935 (dec.); children—Henry D., Peter H., John Dana (dec.), James C.; m. 2d, Rosemary Long Reed, Sept. 1962. Inst., Yale, 1931-33; fellow Brookings Inst., 1933; staff bd. govs. Fed. Res. System, 1934-41; asst. v.p. Fed. Res. Bank, St. Louis, 1941-43, v.p., 1943-46; spl. asst. to adminstr. War Foods Adminstrn., 1943; tech. advisor Am. delegation Internat. Monetary Conf., Bretton Woods, 1944; asst. v.p. Nat. Life Ins. Co. of Montpelier, Vt., 1946-49; with Kansas City Life Ins. Co., 1949-70, v.p., dir., 1950- 70; dir. Peoples Nat. Bank Warrensburg, Mo., Fed. Home Loan Bank Des Moines, Broadway Nat. Bank of Kansas City. First chmn. subcom. Voluntary Home Mortgage Credit Program. Region XI. Member American Econ. Assn. Club: Mission Hills Country. Office: 3520 Broadway Kansas City MO 64141

EDMISTON, MARCUS MORTON, Jr., lawyer; b. Yonkers, N.Y., Jan. 22, 1916; s. M. Morton and Kate (Sutherland) E.; B.A., Wesleyan U., 1938; LL.B., Fordham U., 1941; m. Josephine Brown, Nov. 19, 1941; children—Mark, Patricia, Kathleen, James. Admitted to N.Y. bar, 1942; trial atty. legal dept. Lumbermen's Mut. Casualty Co., N.Y.C., 1946-47; asst. corp. counsel City of Yonkers (N.Y.), 1948-50; asst. dist. atty. Westchester County, White Plains, N.Y., 1951-58; partner firm Cerrato, Mayor & Edmiston, Yonkers, 1958—. Westchester County supr. 8th ward, Yonkers, 1963-64; mem. county bd. suprs. Washington Irving Council Boy Scouts Am., 1952—. Trustee Woman's Inst., Yonkers. Served to lt. comdr. USNR, 1942-45. Recipient Silver Beaver award Boy Scouts Am., 1960. Mem. N.Y. State, Westchester bar assns., Yonkers Lawyers Assn., Am. Legion (comdr. Yonkers 1954-55), Wesleyan U. Alumni Assn. (manpower com. 1961—). Rotarian. Home: 70 Undercliff St Yonkers NY Office: 20 S Broadway Yonkers NY 10701

EDMOND, LESTER ELLIOT, fgn. service officer; b. N.Y.C., Apr. 28, 1922; s. David and Ethel Ruth (Gardner) E.; B.B.A., Coll. City N.Y., 1943; M.P.A., Harvard, 1948, M.A., 1949, Ph.D., 1950; postgrad. Nat. War Coll., 1965; m. Shom Atkin, Apr. 9, 1946; children—Lester Elliot, Ellen Randi, John Andrew. Internat. economist Dept. State, 1950-55; 1st sec., econ. officer, Tokyo, Japan, 1956-60; counselor econ. affairs, Helsinki, Finland, 1961-64; exec. asst. to dir. USIA, 1964-65; counselor mission OECD, Paris, France, 1966-69; minister econ. affairs, Tokyo, 1970—; lectr. Am. U., 1952-54. Served with AUS, 1943-46. Recipient Presdl. citation improvement govt. operations, 1964. Mem. Am. Fgn. Service Assn. Author: Market Dominance in the Shoe Machinery Industry, 1949; contbg. author: Economic Nationalism Would Not Pay, 1970.‡

EDMONDS, ANNE CAREY, librarian; b. Penang, Malaysia, Dec. 19, 1924; d. William John and Nell (Carey) Edmonds; student U. Reading (Eng.), 1942-44; B.A., Barnard Coll., 1948; M.S. in L.S., Columbia, 1950; M.A., Johns Hopkins, 1959; postgrad. Western Res. U., 1960-61. With War Damage Commn., London, Eng., 1944-46; children's asst. Enoch Pratt Free Library, Balt., 1948-49; reference librarian Sch. Bus. Adminstrn., Coll. City N.Y., 1950-51; reference librarian, then asst. librarian readers' services Goucher Coll., Balt., 1951-60; exchange reference librarian European services library BBC, London, 1955; instr. Sch. L.S., Syracuse U., summer 1960; librarian Douglass Coll., Rutgers U., New Brunswick, N.J., 1961-64, instr. Grad. Sch. Library Service, summer 1962, fall 1963; librarian Mt. Holyoke Coll., 1964—. Mem. A.L.A., Am. Hist. Assn., Am. Assn. U. Profs. Home: 79 Cold Hill Granby MA 01033

EDMONDS, ARNOLD L., C. of C. exec.; b. McLouth, Kan., Aug. 22, 1913; s. L.E. and Mable (Lapham) E.; A.B., Kan.U., 1936; m. Eleanor Robinson, June 26, 1938; children—Jon M., Melissa, Melinda. Research asst. Kan. Legislative Council, 1936-41; with Kan. Civil Service Dept., 1941-42; research asso. New Orleans Bur. Govtl. Research, 1942-44; with Pub. Adminstrn. Service, Chgo., 1944-46; research asso., research dir. Pa. State C. of C., Harrisburg, 1946-57, exec. dir., 1957—. Home: 332 Wyatt Rd Harrisburg, PA 17104. Office: 222 N 3d St Harrisburg PA 17101

EDMONDS, DEAN STOCKETT, lawyer; b. Washington, Dec. 20, 1879; s. Howard and Mary Elizabeth (Owen) E.; LL.B., Georgetown U., 1899, M.L., 1900; LL.D., Middlebury Coll., 1952; m. Mary Watkins Arms, Dec. 11, 1911; 1 son, Dean Stockett; m. 2d, Marie C. Moore, Aug. 24, 1967. Admitted to D.C. bar, 1900, N.Y. bar, 1910; mem. firm Pennie, Edmonds, Morton, Taylor and Adams. Chmn. bd. U.S. Radium Corp.; dir. Machelett X-Ray Tubes (Gt. Britain), Farrand Optical Co., Mem. Am., N.Y. patent law assns., Am., N.Y. County bar assns., Bar City N.Y., Loyal Legion. Republican. Episcopalian. Clubs: Racquet and Tennis, University, Union League, Grolier, Church, Pilgrims Society, Newcomen Soc., Union (all N.Y.), Pequot Yacht, Fairfield County Hunt, Fairfield Country (Conn.); Royal Palm Yacht and Country. Home: Fairfield CT 06430 Office: 330 Madison Av New York City NY 10017

EDMONDS, FRANK NORMAN, Jr., educator, astronomer; b. Mpls., Sept. 2, 1919; s. Frank Norman and Irene (Radcliffe) E.; A.B., Princeton, 1941; Ph.D., U. Chgo., 1950; m. Joan Mary McKinney, Mar. 24, 1945; children—Cynthia Ann, Christopher Norman. Asst. prof. astronomy U. Mo.-Columbia, 1950-52; mem. faculty U. Tex., Austin, 1952—, asso. prof., 1958-65, prof., 1965—. Mem. naval adv. com. astronomy NRC, 1958-61, chmn., 1960-61. Served to capt. AUS, 1941-45, USAAF, 1945-46. Guggenheim fellow, 1962-63. Mem. Internat. Astronom. Union, Am., Royal (Eng.) astron. socs., Sigma Xi. Home: 3005 Wade Av Austin TX 78703

EDMONDS, GEORGE P., corp. exec.; b. Boston, Mass., 1905; ed. Mass. Inst. of Tech. Hon. chmn. bd., Wilmington Trust Co.; mem. exec. com. Continental Can Co.; dir., mem. finance com. E. I. duPont de Nemours & Co.; dir. Continental Am. Life Ins. Co. Home: 920 Westover Rd Westover Hills Wilmington DE 19807 Office: Wilmington Trust Co 10th and Market Sts Wilmington DE 19899

EDMONDS, HAROLD FREDERICK, painter; b. Oberlin, O., Nov. 24, 1939; s. George Harold and Elma (Griffin) E.; B.F.A., Cleve. Inst. Art, 1959-64; student Carnegie Inst. Tech., 1964-65. Exhbn. Nat. Acad. Design, 1970; tchr. Carnegie Inst. Tech., 1964-65, now tchr. drawing and painting Art Inst. Pitts. Recipient 1st Julius Hallgarten prize for artist under 35. N.A.D., 1970, 3 awards Jr. Art Show, N.Y. Armory, 1954. Served with AUS, 1965-67. Presbyn. Home: 12641 Pyle Rd N Oberlin OH 44074

EDMONDS, HELEN GREY, educator, historian; b. Lawrenceville, Va., Dec. 3, 1911; d. John Edward and Ann (Williams) Edmonds; A.B., Morgan State Coll., 1933, LL.D., 1958; M.A., Ohio State U., 1938, Ph.D., 1946; postdoctoral research, U. Heidelberg (Germany), 1954-55. Dean women, prof. Greek, Latin and history Va. Sem., Lynchburg, 1933-35; instr. history St. Paul Norman Sch., Lawrenceville, 1935-40; cons. social scis. Va. Dept. Edn., summer 1940; prof. history Grad. Sch., N.C. Central U., Durham, 1940—, dean Grad. Sch., 1964—, mem. interim com. charge operation coll., 1966. Leader- specialist State Dept. to Germany, 1955, to Sweden, Denmark, Germany, Austria and France, 1957; rep. President Eisenhower to dedication ceremonies Liberian Capitol Bldg., Monrovia, 1957; U.S. alternate del. to UN, 1970—; del. 8th nat. conf. U.S. commn. UNESCO, Boston, 1961; mem. adv. council U.S. Peace Corps. Trustee St. Paul's Coll., Va. Voohrees, S.C. Grantee Gen. Edn. Bd., 1943-44, Carnegie Found., 1949, Fund Advancement Edn., 1954-55, Bd. dirs. So. Fellowship Fund; recipient Woman of Year plaque Bachelors-Benedicts Civic Club, 1958; named Woman of Year in So. Area, Nat. Links, 1965; sr. fellow Nat. Found. for Humanities, 1970. Mem. Council Grad. Deans, Am. Hist. Assn., Assn. Social Sci. Tchrs., Am. Tchrs. Assn., Assn. Study Negro Life and History, Va. Soc. Research, Nat. Links (pres. 1970), Phi Alpha Theta, Alpha Kappa Delta, Pi Gamma Mu, Alpha Phi Gamma, Kappa Delta Pi, Delta Sigma Theta. Episcopalian. Author: The Negro and Fusion Politics in North Carolina, 1951; also monographs, articles and hist. pageants. Co-editor: Appropriate Directions for the Modern College in the Challenging New Educational Era, 1962; Black Faces in High Places, 1971. Home: 118 Nelson St Durham NC 27707

EDMONDS, THOMAS SECHLER, lawyer; b. Chgo., Oct. 21, 1899; s. Howard Owen and Mary Addison (Sechler) E.; student Phillips Exeter Acad., 1914-18, Northwestern U. Law Sch., 1922-23; A.B., Harvard, 1922; J.D., U. Chgo., 1925; m. Elizabeth Fenley, Feb. 1, 1930; 1 son, Howard Owen. Admitted to Ill. bar, 1925; law clk. McCulloch & McCulloch, Chgo., 1925-26; partner firm Gordon, Buckley & Edmonds, 1941-53, Edmonds & Linneman, 1953-56, Ashcraft, Ashcraft and predecessor, 1957—. Member Am., Ill. (pres. 1955-56), Chgo. bar assns., Delta Tau Delta. Republican. Episcopalian. Clubs: Indian Hill (Winnetka, Ill.); University, Attic, Law, Legal (Chgo.). Home: 1630 Sheridan Rd Wilmette IL 60091 Office: 1 First Nat Plaza Chicago IL 60670

EDMONDS, WALTER DUMAUX, author; b. Boonville, N.Y., July 15, 1903; s. Walter Dumaux and Sarah (May) E.; student St. Paul's Sch., Concord, N.H., 1916-19, Choate Sch., Wallingford, Conn., 1919-21; A.B., Harvard, 1926; Litt.D., Union Coll., 1936, Rutgers U., 1940, Colgate U., 1947, Harvard, 1952; m. Eleanor Livingston Stetson, 1930; children—Peter B., Eleanor D., Sarah M.; m. 2d, Katharine Baker-Carr, 1956. Mem. bd. overseers Harvard, 1945-50; Pres., pub. Harvard Alumni Bull., 1957-66, dir., 1966—. Mem. Am. Acad. Arts and Scis., Phi Beta Kappa. Club: Saint Botolph's (Boston). Author: (latest books) In the Hands of the Senecas, 1947; The Wedding Journey, 1947; Cadmus Henry, 1949; Mr. Benedict's Lion, 1950; They Fought with What They Had, 1951; Corporal Bess, 1952; The Boyds of Black River, 1953; Hound Dog Moses and the Promised Land, 1954; Uncle Ben's Whale, 1955; They Had A Horse, 1962; Three Stalwarts, 1962; The Musket and the Cross, 1968; Time To Go House, 1969; Seven American Stories, 1970; Wolf Hunt, 1970. Contbr. fiction to Atlantic, The Forum, Harper's, Sat. Eve. Post, others. Home: 27 River St Concord MA 01742

EDMONDS, WILLIAM SYLVESTER, educator; b. Newport News, Va., July 22, 1919; s. William Sylvester and Lottie M. (Randolph) E.; B.S., Hampton Inst., 1939, M.S., Va. State Coll., 1942; M.A., Columbia, 1949, Ed.D., 1953; m. Bernyce Barbara Scott, July 22, 1950. Tchr., supr. pub. schs., Newport News, 1939-48; dean students Jackson (Miss.) State Coll., 1949-51; chmn. div. edn. Ala. A. and M. Coll., 1953-60, dean grad. study, 1958-60, dean coll., 1962-66; prof. psychology Va. State Coll., Petersburg, 1960-62, dir. div. grad. studies, 1966—. Dist. chmn. Community Service Fund, 1945-48; commnr. Tidewater council Boy Scouts Am., 1945—. Served to 1st lt. AUS, World War II. Mem. Am., Southeastern, Ala. psychol. assns., Ala. Tchrs. Assn., Am. Assn. U. Profs., Phi Delta Kappa, Kappa Delta Pi, Alpha Phi Alpha. Lectr., author in field. Home: 941 E 225th St Bronx NY 10466 Office: Va State Coll Petersburg VA 23803

EDMONDSON, EDMOND, congressman; b. Muskogee, Okla., Apr. 7, 1919; s. Edmond Augustus and Esther (Pullen) E.; grad. Jr. Coll., Muskogee, 1938; A.B., U. Okla., 1940; LL.B., Georgetown U., 1947; m. June Maureen Pilley, Mar. 5, 1944; children—James Edmond, William, John, June, Brian. Newspaperman, Muskogee (Okla.) Daily, also United Press, 1936-40; spl. agt. F.B.I., 1941-43; Washington corr. Muskogee Phoenix, Sapulpa Herald, Holdenville News, Daily Ardmoreite, 1946-47; admitted to D.C. bar, 1947, Okla. bar, 1947; practiced in Muskogee 1947—; asso. J. Howard Edmondson, 1948; atty. Muskogee Co., 1949-52; mem. 83d to 92d U.S. Congresses, 2d Dist. Okla. Served to lt. USNR, World War II. Mem. Am. Legion, V.F.W., Am., Okla. bar assns., Phi Beta Kappa, Phi Delta Phi, Delta Sigma Rho, Phi Gamma Delta. Democrat. Mason, Elk, Kiwanian. Home: P O Box 11 Muskogee OK 74401 Office: House Office Bldg Washington DC 20515

EDMONDSON, FRANK K., astronomer; b. Milw., Aug. 1, 1912; s. Clarence Edward and Marie (Kelley) E.; A.B., Ind. U., 1933, A.M., 1934; Ph.D., Harvard, 1937; m. Margaret Russell, Nov. 24, 1934; children—Margaret Jean, Frank K. Lawrence Fellow Lowell Obs., 1933-34, research asst., 1934-35; Agassiz fellow Harvard Obs., 1935-36, asst., 1936-37; instr. astronomy Ind. U., Bloomington, 1937-40, asst. prof., 1940-45, asso. prof., also dir. Kirkwood Obs., 1945-48, prof., 1949—; dir. Goethe Link Obs., 1948—, chmn. astronomy dept., 1944—; research asso. McDonald Obs., 1944—. Observations of asteroids in cooperation with Internat. Astron. Union's Minor Plant Center; program dir. for astronomy NSF, 1956-57; lectr. before astron. socs. Decorated Order of Merit (Chile). Fellow A.A.A.S. (chmn. sect. D, v.p. 1962); mem. Assn. Univs. Research in Astronomy (pres. 1962-65, dir. 1957—), Am. Astron. Soc. (treas. 1954—), Astron. Soc. Pacific, Internat. Astron. Union (chmn. U.S. nat. com. 1963-64, v.p. commn. minor planets, comets and satellites 1967-70, pres. 1970—,), Ind. Acad. Science, Am. Mus. Natural History (corr. mem.), Phi Beta Kappa, Sigma Xi. Contbr. numerous papers to Am., Brit., German astron. jours. Home: 716 S Woodlawn Av Bloomington IN 47401

EDMONDSON, FRAZOR TITUS, bakery co. exec.; b. Ft. Worth, Aug. 24, 1904; s. James Howard and Florence (Larson) E.; student Va. Mil. Inst., 1923-26; LL.B., Vanderbilt U., 1928; m. Sally Ann Anderson, Jan. 26, 1929; children—James Howard, Sally Ann (Mrs. Ben Sparkman). Admitted to Kan. bar, Tex. bar, 1940; gen. practice, Topeka, 1928-33; asst. atty. gen. Kan., 1931-33; gen. counsel Campbell Taggart Asso. Bakeries, Dallas, 1933—, chmn. of the bd., 1965—, also dir.; dir. First Nat. Bank Dallas. Bd. dirs. Econs. Distbn. Found., Pvt. Truck Council. Served to maj. AUS, 1942-44. Mem. Am., Tex., Dallas bar assns., Vanderbilt U. Alumni Assn. (mem. bd.), Sigma Alpha Epsilon. Presbyn. Club: Northwood Country (Dallas). Home: 6230 Bandera St Dallas TX 75225 Office: P O Box 2640 Dallas TX 75221

EDMONDSON, HUGH ALLEN, physician; b. Maysville, Ark., Jan. 3, 1906; s. James Turner and Julia Ann (Phillips) E.; A.B., U. Okla., 1926; M.D., U. Chgo., 1931; m. Dorothy E. Mossman, July 14, 1930; children—Hugh Allen, James Paul, Marian Ann, Marjorie Jean. Instr. pathology U. So. Cal. Med. Sch., 1938- 41, asst. prof. pathology, 1941-43, asso. prof. 1943-48, prof., 1948—, head dept., 1951—; attending staff Los Angeles County Hosp., 1939—; cons. pathologist Santa Fe Hosp., Children's Hosp., Los Angeles. Fellow A.C.P.; mem. A.M.A. (chmn. sect. pathology and physiology 1963-64), Coll. Am. Pathologists, Gastroent. Assn. Cal. Med. Assn. (past chmn. sec. pathology sect.), Am. Assn. Pathologists and Bacteriologists, Am. Soc. Clin. Pathologists, Internat. Acad. Pathology (council 1960-63), Sigma Xi, Sigma Alpha Epsilon, Nu Sigma Nu. Club: Valley Hunt (Pasadena). Contbr. articles med. publs. Home: 1411 Circle Dr San Marino, CA 91108. Office: 1200 N State St Los Angeles CA 90033

EDMONDSON, JOHN PRESTON, lawyer, publisher; b. Radford, Va., Feb. 28, 1903; s. Reese Thompson and Elnora (Shumate) E.; A.B., Va. Mil. Inst., 1924; LL.B., U. Va., 1929; m. Mary Dickson Cooke, May 28, 1938; children—Mary Royster (Mrs. Richard M. Cherouny), Eleanor Reese (Mrs. Charles J. Currie), Frances Cooke. Admitted to N.Y. bar, 1929; atty., sec., mem. bd. 20th Century Fox Film Corp., 1929-42, mem. bd., exec. com., pension com., audit com., 1969—, now chmn. exec. com.; exec. v.p., mem. bd. E.P. Dutton & Co., Inc., N.Y.C., 1946-68; Past pres., mem. bd. edn., Scarsdale, N.Y. Chmn. bd. trustees Mary Baldwin Coll., Staunton, Va. Served from 1st lt. to col. USAAF, 1942-45. Decorated Legion of Merit, Croix de Guerre. Mem. Am. Book Pubs. Council (treas., mem. bd.). Clubs: Princess Anne Country (Virginia Beach, Va.); Scarsdale Golf; Shenrock Shore; Fox Meadow Tennis; University (N.Y.C.). Home: 127 Pinewood Rd Virginia Beach VA 23451 Office: 444 W 56th St New York City NY 10019

EDMONDSON, JOHN RICHARD, pharm. mfr.; b. N.Y.C., Mar. 1, 1927; s. Richard Emil and Josephine (Schroeter) E.; A.B., Georgetown U., 1950; LL.B., Columbia, 1953; m. Rozanne Hume, Oct. 30, 1954; children—Lisa M., Kate H., Timothy N., Nicholas D., Julia M. Admitted to N.Y. bar, 1953; asso. atty. Winthrop, Stimson, Putnam & Roberts, N.Y.C., 1953-59; with Bristol-Myers Co., N.Y.C., 1950—, asst. sec., 1960-69, sec., 1969—. Served with AUS, 1945-47. Mem. Assn. Bar City N.Y. Clubs: University (N.Y.C.); Lake Waramaug Country (New Preston, Conn.). Home: 60 E 96th St New York City NY 10028 Office: 345 Park Av New York City NY 10022

EDMONSON, DAN HUTCHESON, mfg. exec.; b. Baskerville, Va., Nov. 12, 1916; s. Haynie Stokes and Nell (Jones) E.; B.A., Coll. William and Mary, 1937; m. Johnnie Naron, Mar. 9, 1947; children—Robert Stokes, Joan. Store mgr. Firestone Tire & Rubber Co., Richmond, Va., 1938-42; sales v.p. Mass. Mohair Plush Co., N.Y.C., 1947-55; v.p., sales mgr. Kroeher Mfg. Co., Naperville, Ill., 1955-62, v.p., gen. sales mgr., 1962—, dir. sales, 1964-69, exec. v.p. marketing, 1969—. Served as lt. USNR, 1942-46. Recipient Sports Illustrated silver anniversary award, 1961. Mem. Coll. William and Mary Dupage Alumni Assn. (pres. 1961-62). Methodist: Club: Glen Oak Country (Glen Ellyn, Ill.). Home: 22 W 309 Elmwood Dr Glen Ellyn IL 60137 Office: 225 E 5th St Naperville IL 60540

EDMONSON, MUNRO STERLING, educator, anthropologist; b. Nogales, Ariz., May 18, 1924; s. Everett Sterling and Lillian (Munro) E.; B.A., Harvard, 1945, M.A., 1948, Ph.D., 1952; m. Barbara Bay Wedemeyer, Aug. 1, 1953; children—Evelyn Mila, Ann Munro, Sallie Ross. Instr., Washington U., St. Louis, 1951; mem. faculty Tulane U., New Orleans, 1951—, prof. anthropology, 1960—. Vis. prof. U. de San Carlos, Quezaltenango, Guatemala, 1960-61, Purdue U., 1964, Harvard, 1965-66. Served to lt. (j.g.) USNR, 1944-46. Fellow Am. Anthrop. Assn.; mem. A.A.A.S., Am. Assn. U. Profs., Am. Ethnol. Soc. (pres. 1965-66), So. Anthrop. Soc. Author: Los Manitos, 1957; Status Terminology and Social Structure of North American Indians, 1958; (with others) The Eighth Generation, 1959; Quiche-English Dictionary, 1965. Home: 901 Cherokee St New Orleans, LA 70118.

EDMUNDS, DESAUSSURE DAVIS, former ins. co. exec.; b. Sumter, S.C., Mar. 16, 1904; s. Samuel Henry and Eliza Champion (Davis) E.; A.B., Presbyn. Coll. of S.C., 1925; C.L.U., 1937; m. Mary E. Henry, Sept. 3, 1927. With Equitable Life Assurance Soc., 1925—, beqinning as trainee, Cin. and Rock Hill, S.C., then asst. cashier, Nashville, Mpls., Jacksonville, Fla., agt., Charleston, S.C., dist. mgr., Winston-Salem, N.C., agy. mgr., Birmingham, Ala., field v.p., St. Louis, 2d v.p., N.Y.C., 1925-59, v.p., 1959-69; vol. mem. Internat. Exec. Service Corps, 1969—. Trustee Presbyn. Coll. S.C. Served from lt. to comdr., USNR, 1942-45. Mem. Nat., Ala (past pres.), N.C. (past pres.), Winston-Salem (past pres.) assns. life underwriters Am. Soc. C.L.U. (past pres. Birmingham chpt.), Birmingham Gen. Agts. and Mgrs. Assn. (past pres.), Huguenot Soc., Soc. of Cincinnati. Episcopalian. Home: Stuart Towne Apts Beaufort SC 29902

EDMUNDS, JOHN, composer; b. San Francisco, June 10, 1913; s. Charles Ellerington and Sophia Mary (Sandison) E.; student Rosario Scalero, Curtis Inst. Music, 1939-41; B.A., U. Cal. at Berkeley, 1940; M.A. (student of Walter Piston), Harvard, 1941; M.S., Columbia, 1954; m. Beatrice Quickenden, Aug. 29, 1940 (dec. Nov. 1967). Composer: Shepherd's Maze (boys chorus narrator and misc. instruments), 1963; Urban Muse (mixed chorus, organ and percussion), 1965; Hymns Sacred and Profane (mixed chorus, organ and percussion), 1966; (ballet with Ernest Bacon) Jehovoh and the Ark, 1968; Choric Requium; also numerous songs to anonymous Middle English texts, and to texts by W. B. Yates, Herrick, Blake, other poets; San Francisco Hymnal, 1962; Adams Book of Carols, 1966; Songs in History, 1967; editor numerous works by John Dowland, Thomas Campion, Henry Purcell, Alessandro Scarlatti, Benedetto Marcello, Antonio Vivaldi; asst. prof. music Syracuse U., 1946-48; founder, dir. Campion Festivals of Unfamiliar Music, San Francisco, 1946-53; head Americana collection, music div. N.Y. Pub. Library, 1957-61. Treas. Am. com. Italian Traveling Exhbt. of Contemporary Music, 1959; mem. music adv. com. Inst. Internat. Edn., 1959-62; mem. planning com. Am. music history project Music Library Assn., 1959—; music cons. Colonial Williamsburg, 1963-64; lectr. U. Cal. at Berkeley, 1965-66. Bd. dirs. Am. Music Center, 1959-61, chmn. membership com., 1959-62; chmn. bd. dirs. Composers Forum, 1959—. Ditson grantee research English song, 1950; Fulbright fellow research songs of Purcell, 1951; grantee Italian Govt. research solo cantatas Scarlatti and Benedetto Marcello, 1954; recipient annual awards serious music A.S.C.A.P., 1961—; fellow Folger Shakespeare Library, 1967; Fellow Ossabau Islam Found., 1968; fellow MacDowell Colony, fellow Am. Council Learned Socs., Sr. Fulbright fellow, Eng., 1968-69; Guggenheim fellow in composition, 1969-70. Author: (with Gordon Boeizner) Some Twentieth Century American Composers: a Selective Biography, 2 vols., 1959, 60; Williamsburg Songbook, 1964; Carols of the Western World, 1966. Translator: (with Alfred Mann) Steps to Parnassus (J. J. Fux), 1942. Home: 333 Avila St San Francisco CA 94123

EDMUNDS, JOHN OLLIE, coll. chancellor; b. Higgston, Ga., Mar. 1, 1903; s. Plato D. and Lee S. (Ganey) E.; A.B., John B. Stetson Univ., 1925, A.M., 1927, LL.B., 1928, LL.D., 1943, LL.D., U. Richmond, 1970; Litt.D. (hon.), U. Miami, 1951, Jacksonville U., 1964; D.Hum. (hon.), Rollins Coll., 1963; m. Emily Bryant, July 17, 1934; children—John, Jane. Admitted to Fla. bar, 1927; practiced in DeLand, Fla., 1927-30; judge Duval County, Jacksonville, Fla., 1931-44; pvt. practice, Jacksonville, 1944-48; pres. John B. Stetson U., DeLand, 1948-67, chancellor, 1967—; dir. Fla. Nat. Bank, Jacksonville, Jacksonville br. Fed. Res. Bank of Atlanta. Mem. President's Com. Devel. Scis. and Engrs., 1959-60. Duval County chmn. War Svgs. Bond Com. U.S. Treas., 1942; mem. Fla. Land Use and Control Commn., 1957-58. Served as lt. (j.g.) USCGR, exec. officer, Jacksonville Bn. Port Security Force, 1943-44. Recipient Freedom's Found. Award, 1952, 55, 68. Mem. Assn. Am. Colls. (pres. 1959), Omicron Delta Kappa, Phi Alpha Delta, Theta Alpha Phi, Delta Sigma Phi. Democrat (candidate for U.S. Senate 1944). Baptist (pres. Conv. 1961). Mason (33, Shriner), Rotarian. Clubs: Seminole, Timuquana Country, River (Jacksonville); Lake Beresford Yacht (DeLand); University (N.Y.C.), Olympic (San Francisco). Home: 405 N Amelia Av DeLand FL 32720

EDMUNDS, PALMER DANIEL, lawyer, educator; b. W. Terre Haute, Ill., Oct. 29, 1890; s. Amos and Mary Ann (Campbell) E.; A.B., Knox Coll., 1912, LL.D., 1945; LL.B., Harvard, 1915; m. Margaret Burton, June 29, 1932 (dec. 1964); m. 2d, Sarah Shepard Brown, 1970. Admitted to Ill. Bar, 1915, since practiced in Chicago; dir., counsel Ill. Service Recognition Bd., 1922-25; mem. firm Dodd, Matheny & Edmunds, 1925-29; commr. Supreme Court Ill., 1929-32; mem. Dodd & Edmunds, Chgo., 1932-58; lectr. conflict of laws and Ill. practice, John Marshall Law Sch., Chgo., 1926- 58, prof. law, 1958—, lectr. fed. practice, 1938-58, dir. Lawyers Inst.; vis. prof. law, Knox Coll., 1944-57; compliance commr. WPB and Civilian Prodn. Adminstrn., 1944-47; hearing commr. NPA, 1951-53. Charter mem. World Peace Through Law Center. Bd. trustees John Marshall Law School. First lt. A.E.F., 1917-19; capt. O.R.C. Past comdr. Black Hawk Post, Am. Legion, Chgo., past historian Dept. of Ill. Mem. Am. Polit. Sci. Assn., Am. Acad. Polit. and Social Sci., Fgn. Policy Assn., Am., Ill., Chgo., Internat. bar assns., India Soc., Internat. Law, Ill. Hist. Soc., S.A.R., Nat. Sojourners, Am. Bantam Assn., Sebright Club Am., 40 and 8, Soc. of 28th Div., Com. for Continuation Congl. Christian Chs. U.S., Phi Gamma Delta, Delta Sigma Rho. Democrat. Conglist. Mason, Elk. Club: Harvard (Chgo.). Author: (with W. F. Dodd) Illinois Appellate Procedure, 1929; Edmunds Common Law Forms, 1931; Illinois Civil Practice Forms, 1923; Edmunds Federal Rules of Civil Procedure, 1938; Cyclopedia of Federal Procedure Forms, 1939; Law and Civilization, 1959. Co-author: Encyclopedia of Federal Procedure (2d edit.), 1944; Edmunds Conflict of Laws, 1948. Editor and compiler: Jones Illinois Statutes Annotated, vols. 18-22, 24. Home: La Hogue IL 60947 Office: 315 Plymouth Ct Chicago IL 60604

EDMUNDS, ROBERT LARRY, textile co. exec.; b. Pell City, Ala., Dec. 19, 1930; s. Jesse Thomas and Eunice (Bain) E.; B.S. in Bus. Adminstrn., Auburn U., 1952; m. Sara Ann Peters, June 8, 1952; children—Melanie Jane, Mary Catherine, Robert Larry. With Avondale Mills, Sylacauga, Ala., 1954—, gen. auditor, 1963- 64, sec., 1964—. Baptist. Home: 20 Lake Louise Dr Sylacauga, AL 35150. Office: Avondale Mills Avondale Av Sylacauga AL 35150

EDMUNDS, STAHRL WILLIAM, univ. dean; b. Cambridge, Minn., May 15, 1917; s. Adoniran W. and Axeline (Holmgren) E.; B.B.A. with distinction, U. Minn., 1939, M.A., 1941; m. Amy Margaret Klein, Aug. 17, 1940; children—Dewey Edmunds, Laura (Mrs. Robert Newman), Rolin. Exec. asst. to pres. Northwestern Nat. Life Ins. Co., 1945-53; economist McGraw-Hill Pub. Co., also Nat. City Bank, N.Y.C., 1953-55, Ford Motor Co., 1955-58; marketing dir. Hughes Aircraft Co., 1959-65; indsl. devel. adviser Govt. of Ecuador of State Dept., 1966-67; vice chancellor U. Cal. at Riverside, 1967-69, dean Grad. Sch. Adminstrn., 1969—. Mem. research com. U.S. C. of C., 1953-55; mem. Tech. Adv. Com. Econ. Devel. Cal., 1961-65; mem. sci. adv. com. to Cal. Assembly, 1970—. Bd. dirs. Riverside Community Hosp., 1968-70. Served to lt. (s.g.) USNR, 1941-45. Mem. Am. Econ. Assn., Am. Marketing Assn. Author articles in field. Home: 2442 Prince Albert Dr Riverside CA 92507

EDMUNDSON, JAMES VALENTINE, air force officer; b. Hollywood, Cal., June 18, 1915; s. James Albert and Nora Valentine (Wakefield) E.; A.A., Santa Monica (Cal.) Jr. Coll., 1935; grad. Air War Coll., 1949; student George Washington U., 1953; m. Maddie Lee Turner, Nov. 21, 1940; children—Edwin J., Celia Lee. Commd. 2d. lt. U.S. Army, 1938, advanced through grades to lt. gen. USAF, 1965; designated pilot, 1938; various assignments U.S., Hawaii and Solomon Islands, 1937-42; comdr. 431st bomb squadron 11th Bomb Group, S.W. Pacific, 1942; dep. group comdr. 11th Bomb Group, 1942-43; asst. operations officer, dir. bomb tactical air command and tech. Hdqrs. USAAF, 1943; asst. dir. operations 58th Bomb Wing, 1943; comdr. 792d bomb squadron 468th Bomb Group, Kan. and CBI, 1943-44; group comdr. 468th Bomb Group, 1944-46; liaison officer Hdqrs. Task Force 5, 1946; planning officer, policy div. asst. chief air staff for plans Hdqrs. USAF, 1948-48; comdr. 22d Bomb Wing, Cal. and Korea, 1942; dir. operations 15th Air Force, March AFB, Cal., 1952; comdr. 92d Bomb Wing, 1952-54, 57th Air Div., 1954-55, 36th Air Div., 1955-57; dep. dir. operations SAC, 1957-58, dir. operations, 1958-60; dep. dir. personnel procurement and tng. Office Dep. Chief Staff Personnel, 1960, dir. personnel procurement and tng., 1960-62; comdr. 17th Air Force, Ramstein Air Base, Germany, 1962-65; vice comdr. in chief Pacific Air Forces, 1967- 70; dep. comdr. in chief Strike Command MacDill AFB (Fla.), 1970—. Commr. Transatlantic dist. council Boy Scouts Am., 1963-64. Decorated D.S.M., Silver Star, Legion of Merit with 2 oak leaf clusters, D.F.C. with 6 oak leaf clusters, Bronze Star, Air medal with 7 oak leaf clusters, Purple Heart; recipient Presdl. citation (Republic Korea). Mem. Am. Legion, V. F.W. Lion (hon.), Rotarian, Kiwanian; Toastmaster. Home: 405 Staff Loop MacDill AFB FL 33621 Office: Hdqrs US Strike Command MacDill AFB FL 33608

EDNER, CLARENCE F., banker; b. San Francisco, 1913; grad. Rutgers U., 1950. Sr. v.p. First Western Bank and Trust Co., Los Angeles. Home: 408 Hermosa Pl S Pasadena, CA 91030. Office: 548 S Spring St Los Angeles CA 90013 *

EDNIE, J. ERNEST, business exec.; b. Forfar, Scotland, Oct. 24, 1907; s. Andrew and Jemima (Pullar) E.; student Morgan Acad., Scotland; m. Roann D. Preston, Aug. 14, 1936; children—George, Richard, Sandra, Betty Jo. Came to U.S., 1931, naturalized, 1937. With Am. Factors, Ltd. (now Amfac, Inc.), Honolulu, 1932—, successively auditor and C.P.A., asst. sec., asst. sec.-treas., sec., 1932-51, mgr. plantation div., 1951-59, v.p. finance and devel., 1959-71, sr. v.p., dir., 1961-67, v.p., sec., 1967-69, sr. v.p., sec., 1969-71; past v.p., past sec. dir. Amfac-Silverado Corp., Kauai Sugar Storage Corp.; past v.p., dir. Kauai Electric Co., Ltd., Pacific Hawaiian Line, Inc.; past sec., dir. Amfac Financial Corp., Central Oahu Land Corp. Mem. C. of C. Hawaii. Clubs: Oahu Country, Pacific (Honolulu); Silverado Country (Napa). Home: 5245 Oio Dr Honolulu HI 96816 Office: P O Box 3230 Honolulu HI 96801

EDSALL, GEOFFREY, physician; b. Phila., Jan. 28, 1908; s. David Linn and Margaret Harding (Tileston) E.; M.D., Harvard, 1934; m. Helen Fogle, Aug. 13, 1935; 1 son, Richard Anthony. Intern Mass. Gen. 1934-36; research fellow Harvard, 1936-39, instr. bacteriology and immunology, med. and pub. health schs., 1940-47, asst. prof. pub. health bacteriology, public health school, 1947-49, vis. lectr., 1949-60, prof. applied microbilogoy, 1960—; asst. dir., div. biologic labs. Mass. Dept. Pub. Health, 1939-42, dir., 1942-49, supt. State Laboratory Inst., 1960—; prof. microbiology and head dept. Boston U. Sch. Medicine, 1949-52; dir. immunology div. Walter Reed Army Inst. Research, 1951-56, tech. dir. of research of communicable and parasitic diseases, 1956-60; dir. commn. on immunization Armed Forces Epidemiol. Board, 1952- 63; special cons. World Health Orgn., 1953, 55, 59, 63, 65—; mem. expert panel immunology, 1963-; cons. Surgeon Gen., U.S. Army, 1960—, USPHS, 1963—; adv. com. immunization practices USPHS, 1963—. Subcom. on blood O.D.M., 1951-52. Del. U.S. Pharmacopeial Conv., 1950, mem. revision com. U.S. Pharmacopeia, 1960-65; mem. U.S. delegation 13th World Health Assembly, 1960; mem. bd. sci. counselors, div. biologies standards of NIH, U.S. Public Health Service, 1968—. Trustee Bergey Manual Trust, 1957-65. Diplomate Am. Bd. Preventive Med. (founder mem.). Fellow A.A.A.S., Am. Acad. Arts and Scis., Am. Public Health Assn. sec. laboratory section 1947-48, chmn. (1950), Am. Acad. Microbiology (bd. govs. 1956-58), Royal Soc. Tropica Medicine and Hygience; mem. Am. Soc. Tropical Med. and Hygiene, Infectious Disease Soc. Am., A.M.A., Am. Epidemiological Soc., Am. Soc. Microbiol. (pres. N.E. br. 1950), Am. Assn. Immunologists (councillor 1947-49, pres. 1950), Soc. Exptl. Biology and Medicine, Conf. State and Provincial Lab. Dirs., Delta Omega. Clubs: Cosmos (Wash.), Harvard (Boston). Contbr. articles in field to profl. publs. Editor-in-chief Jour. Immunology, 1948-54, mem. editorial bd., 1954-59; mem. Am. Bd. Microbiology, 1960-61. Home: 85 Gate House Road Chestnut Hill, MA 02167. Office: 375 South St Boston MA 02130

EDSALL, JOHN TILESTON, educator; b. Phila., Nov. 3, 1902; s. David Linn and Margaret Harding (Tileston) E.; A.B., Harvard, 1923, M.D., 1928; postgrad. Cambridge (Eng.) U., 1924-26; D.Sc., U. Chgo., Western Res. U., U. Mich., N.Y. Med. Coll.; m. Margaret Dunham, May 1, 1929; children—James Lawrence Dunham, David Tileston, Nicholas Cranford. With Harvard, 1928—, asst. prof. biol. cham., 1932-38, asso. prof., 1938- 51, prof., 1951—. John Simon Guggenheim Meml. Found. fellow Cal. Inst. Tech., 1940-41, Harvard, 1954-56; Fulbright lectr. U. Cambridge, 1952, U. Tokyo (Japan), 1964; vis. prof. Coll. de France, Paris, 1955; pres. 6th Internat. Congress Biochemistry, N.Y.C., 1964. Recipient Passano Found. award, 1966; vis. lectr. Australian Nat. U., Canberra, 1970; scholar Fogarty Internat. Center NIH, Bethesda, Md., 1970-71. Mem. Am. Philos. Soc., Biochem. Soc. Gt. Britain, Societé de Chimie Biologique. Nat. Acad. Scis., Am. Chem. Soc. (sec. div. biol. chem. 1946-48, chmn. 1948- 49), Am. Soc. Biol. Chemists (pres. 1957-58), Am. Acad. Arts and Scis. (rep. on U.S. Nat. Commn. for UNESCO 1950-56), A.A.A.S., Deutsche Akademie der Naturforscher, Royal Danish Acad. Scis. Author: (with E.J. Cohn) Proteins, Amino Acids and Peptides, 1943; (with J. Wyman) Biophysical Chemistry, 1958; also papers on chemistry of proteins and amino acids. Editor (with F.M. Richards and C.B. Anfinsen) Advances in Protein Chemistry, Vols. 1-24, 1944—; Jour. Biol. Chemistry, 1958-67; chmn. editorial bd. Procs. Nat. Acad. Scis., 1968—. Home: 3 Berkeley St Cambridge MA 02138

EDSBERG, MOGENS, Danish diplomat; b. Rudkoebing, Denmark, Sept. 11, 1918; s. Theodor Behrendt and Ingeborg (Hansen) E.; LL.M., U. Copenhagen (Denmark), 1945; m. Karen Martha Bastrup, Dec. 5, 1945; children—Torben, Inger, Flemming. Joined Danish Fgn. Service, 1946; vice consul, Chgo., 1951-55; acting head civil aviation and shipping sect. Ministry Fgn. Affairs, 1955-56, head sect., 1956-59, dep. chief protocol, 1964-67; 1st sec. embassy, Rio de Janeiro, Brazil, 1959-62, counsellor of embassy, 1962-64; consul gen. in Los Angeles, 1967—. Decorated knight 1st class Order Dannebrog (Denmark); knight 1st class Order White Rose (Finland); comdr.

Order Cruzeiro do Sul (Brazil); officer Order Leopold (Belgium); comdr. Order Merit (Italy); comdr. Order Rio Branco (Brazil); named hon. citizen Tucson, 1967. Mem. Am. Inst. Fine Arts. Club: Los Angeles. Home: 427 Fordyce Rd Los Angeles CA 90049. Office: 3440 Wilshire Blvd Los Angeles CA 90005

EDSON, CHARLES FARWELL, Jr., educator, historian; b. Los Angeles, Dec. 26, 1905; s. Charles Farwell and Katherine (Philips) E.; B.A., Stanford, 1929; M.A., Harvard, 1931, Ph.D., 1939; m. Lovina Schneider, Apr. 7, 1951. Mem. faculty U. Wis., Midison, 1938—, prof. history, 1947—, sr. vis. mem. Humanities Inst., 1966-67. Served with AUS, 1942-45. Sheldon fellow Harvard, 1935-36; Guggenheim fellow, 1936-38, 56-57, mem. Inst. Advanced Study, Princeton, 1952-53, 62-63; Mem. Am. Hist. Assn., Am. Philol. Assn., Alumni Assn. Am. Sch. Classical Studies (Athens), Am. Soc. Papyrologists, Archaeol. Inst. Am., Classical Assn. Midwest and South, Wis. Acad., Wis. Hist. Soc. Club: Madison Exchange. Research inscriptions, hist. geography and history of ancient Macedonia. Home: 3207 Stevens St Madison WI 53705

EDSON, PETER, former editor; b. Hartford City, Ind., Feb. 8, 1896; s. Charles Bloomfield and Mary (Drayer) E.; A.B., Wabash Coll., 1920; A.M., Harvard, 1925; m. Dorothy Ann Shulze, Oct. 13, 1936 (dec. Aug. 1957); m. 2d, Joyce Beatty, Nov. 8, 1958; children—Mary, Margaret, Michael Peter. Sunday editor Fort Wayne News Sentinel, 1921, asst. Sunday editor Boston Post, 1924-25, Sunday editor New Haven Register, 1926, Pitts. Press, 1927; editor Every Week mag., 1927- 31; editor-in-chief N.E.A. Service, Inc., Cleve., 1932-41; Washington columnist N.E.A. Service newspapers, 1941-63; cons. Sch. Internat. Studies, Johns Hopkins, 1964-70. Trustee, Wabash College, 1955—. Recipient Sigma Delta Chi award for Washington corr., 1946, Raymond Clapper award for newspaper writing, 1948, Headliners award for nat. reporting, 1953. Served as lt. inf., U.S.A., 1917-19. Mem. Phi Beta Kappa, Sigma Delta Chi (charter mem. Washington Journalism Hall of Fame 1971), Phi Gamma Delta. Presbyn. Clubs: Cosmos, National Press, Overseas Writers (Washington). Home: 3714 University Av NW Washington DC 20016

EDSON, WILLIAM ALDEN, elec. engr.; b. Burchard, Neb., Oct. 30, 1912; s. William Henry and Pearl (Montgomery) E.; B.S., (Summerfield scholar), U. Kan. 1934, M.S., 1935; D.Sc. (Gordon McKay scholar), Harvard, 1937; m. Saralou Peterson, Aug. 23, 1942; children—Judith Lynne, Margaret Jane, Carolyn Louise. Mem. tech. staff Bell Telephone Labs., Inc., N.Y.C., 1937-41, super., 1943-45; asst. prof. elec. engring. Ill. Inst. Tech., Chgo., 1941- 43; prof. physics Ga. Inst. Tech., Atlanta, 1945-46, prof. elec. engring., 1946- 51, dir. sch. elec. engring., 1951-52; vis. prof., research asso. Stanford, 1952-56, cons. prof., 1956; mgr. Klystron sub-sect. Gen. Electric Microwave Lab., Palo Alto, Cal., 1955-61; v.p., dir. research Electromagnetic Tech. Corp., Palo Alto, 1961-62, pres., 1962-70; sr. scientist Vidar Corp., Mountain View, Cal., 1970—71; sr. research engr. Stanford Research Inst., Menlo Park, Cal., 1971—. Cons. high frequency sect. Nat. Bur. Standards, 1951-64. Fellow I.E.E.E. (chmn. San Francisco sect. 1963-64, com. standards piezoelectricity, 1950—); mem. Am. Phys. Soc., Sigma Xi, Tau Beta Pi, Sigma Tau, Phi Kappa Phi, Eta Kappa Nu, Pi Mu Epsilon. Author: (with Robert I. Sarbacher) Hyper and Ultra-High Frequency Engineering, 1943; Vacuum-Tube Oscillators, 1953. Home: 25346 La Loma Dr Los Altos Hills CA 94022 Office: 77 Ortege Av Mountain View CA 94040

EDWARD, JOHN THOMAS, educator; b. London, Eng., Mar. 23, 1919; s. John William and Jessie Christina (Simpson) E.; B.Sc., McGill U., 1939, Ph.D., 1942; D.Phil., Oxford U., 1949; M.A. (hon.), Dublin U., 1955, Sc.D., 1971; m. Deirdre Mary Waldron, Mar. 21, 1953; children—John Valentine, Jeremy Bryan, Julian Kevin. Explosives research NRC, Ottawa, Ont., Can., 1943-45; lectr. U. Man., Can., 1945-46; I.C.I. research fellow Birmingham (Eng.) U., 1949-52; lectr. Trinity Coll., U. Dublin, 1952-56; prof. dept. chem. McGill U., Montreal, Que., Can., 1956—. Sci. scholar Royal Commn. for Exhbn., 1851, 1946-49. Fellow Royal Soc. Can., Chem. Inst. Can.; mem. Corp. Profl. Chemists Quebec (v.p. 1970-71), Chem. Soc. London, Am. Chem. Soc. Home: 51 Chesterfield Montreal 217 Quebec Canada

EDWARDS, ALFRED CONWAY, publisher; b. N.Y.C., Feb. 16, 1906; s. Andrew Godfrey and Mary Florence (McKnight) E.; B.S., U. Pa., 1929; Litt.D. (hon.), Middlebury Coll., 1968; m. Eleanor A. Turnbull, Oct. 8, 1932; children—Donald C., Gordon S., Gail J. With Nat. City Bank of N.Y., 1929-45, asst. mgr., 1938-40, mgr. 1940-45; with Holt, Rinehart and Winston, Inc. Sunsidiary CBS, Inc., (formerly Henry Holt & Co., Inc.), 1945—, treas., dir. 1946—, exec. v.p., 1947-60, pres., 1960-67, chmn., 1967-70, cons., 1970—, also past chief officer; v.p., dir., now cons. CBS, Inc.; pres. CBS Holt Group, 1967-70. Trustee, v.p. Lasell Jr. Coll., Auburndale, Mass. Clubs: University, Publishers Lunch (N.Y.C.); Woodway Country (Conn.). Home: Dogwood Lane New Canaan CT 06840 Office: 383 Madison Av New York City NY 10017

EDWARDS, BENJAMIN FRANKLIN III, investment banker; b. St. Louis, Oct. 26, 1931; s. Presley William and Virginia (Barker) E.; B.A., Princeton, 1953; m. Joan Moberly, June 13, 1953; children—Scott P., Benjamin Franklin IV, Pamela M., Susan B. With A.G. Edwards & Sons, St. Louis, 1956—, pres., 1967—; dir. Univ. Computing Co., 1965-67, Psychol. Assos., 1969—; chmn. bd. Gateway Fund, 1969—. Served with USNR, 1953-56. Mem. Investment Bankers Assn. (bd. govs. 1968—). Presbyn. Clubs: Noonday, Old Warson Country, Racquet (St. Louis). Home: 9846 Old Warson Rd St Louis MO 63124 Office: One N Jefferson St Louis MO 63103

EDWARDS, BILLY MATT, hosp. adminstr.; b. Mt. Pleasant, Tex., Dec. 3, 1920; s. William Hampton and Dovie E. (Johnson) E.; student Washington Sch. Art, 1945-46; diploma hosp. adminstrn. Nat. Naval Med. Center, Bethesda, Md., 1955; LL.B., LaSalle U., 1956; J.D., Blackstone Sch. Law, 1967; m. Martiel Evelyn Austin, Feb. 22, 1941; children—Sandra Augusta (Mrs. Parker Council), Billie Sharon (Mrs. Robert Shettlesworth), Barry Michael. Enlisted as seaman U.S. Navy, 1939, commd. ensign 1951, advanced through grades to lt. comdr., 1961; served with Marine Corps at Guadalcanal, Tulagi, Okinawa, other S. Pacific areas; ret., 1962; med. adviser to Republic China, 1960-62; pres., Edwards Enterprises, Inc., Keokuk, Ia., 1962-71; v.p. Tranquilaire Corp., 1971—; adminstr. Tenn. and Research Inst., Memphis, 1963-70; v.p. Tranquillaire Mental Health Facilities, Inc., Memphis, 1970—. exec. dir. Conacol (cons. in alcohol), Memphis, 1967—; dir. BEM Ednl. Enterprises. Mem. Tenn. Long Term Psychiat. Care Co.; Memphis dist. adviser to hosp. engrs.; mem. Gov.'s Commn. Mental Retardation. Bd. dirs. Memphis-Shelby County Blood Bank; vice chmn. mayor's drug council. Recipient. citation comdr.-in-chief Republic China Navy, 1962, commendation chief U.S. Mil. Adv. Group, Taiwan, 1962. Mem. Tenn. Hosp. Assn., Memphis-Shelby County Hosp. Council, Coast Guard Aux. Methodist. Club: Memphis Yacht. Author: Kandid Kartoon Kapers, 1965. Composer songs. Inventor cartop boat-camping device. Home: 2000 St Elmo Av Memphis TN 38127 Office: P O Box 27225 Memphis TN 38127

EDWARDS, BLAKE, film dir.; b. Tulsa, July 26, 1922; ed. high sch. Writer radio shows Johnny Dollar, Line-Up, writer-creator Richard Diamond; creator TV shows Dante's Inferno, Peter Gunn, Mr. Lucky; co-producer, writer film Panhandle; co-producer, writer Stampede; writer Sound Off, All Ashore, Crusin' Down the River, Drive a Crooked Road, My Sister Eileen (mus. version), Operation Mad Ball, Notorious Landlady; writer-dir. movies Bring Your Smile Along, He Laughed Last, Mr. Cory, This Happy Feeling; dir. films Operation Petticoat, High Time, Breakfast at Tiffany's, Days of Wine and Roses; producer, co-writer, dir. Shot in the Dark, What Did You Do in the War, Daddy, Gunn; co-writer, dir. The Great Race; producer, co-writer, dir. The Party, Darling Lili, The Pink Panther; producer; dir. Experiment in Terror. Served with USCGR, World War II. Office: care MGM Studios 10202 W Washington Blvd Culver City CA 90230

EDWARDS, CHARLES H., Lawyer; b. Laramie, Wyo., Dec. 11, 1897; s. Charles Henry and Grace Winifred (Hayford) E.; student U. Wyo., 1916-17; J.D., LL.M., Chgo.-Kent Coll. Law; m. Margaret Coster, Aug. 31, 1941; children-Warren Keith, Joan Louise (Mrs. Warner Surber). With Ill. Mchts. Trust Co., 1924-27, Mchts. Nat. Bank, 1927-29; admitted to Ill. bar; practice in Aurora, 1929—. Co-chmn. Aurora Vets. Affairs, Municipal Code Commn., N.W. Sesqui-Centennial Commn.; chmn. Aurora Civic Center Planning Commn., corp. counsel City of Aurora; asst. atty. gen. Ill. Candidate for county judge, Kane County. Trustee Fox Valley Pleasure Driveway and Park Dist.; chmn. adv. bd. Salvation Army. Served with U.S. Army, World War I, AUS, World War II. Decorated Bronze Star medal, Silver Star medal, Croix de Guerre with palm; recipient Cosmopolitan Civic medal. Mem. Am., Ill., Kane County (past pres.), Aurora bar assns., Aurora C. of C. (past pres.), 40 and 8 (grand adv. Ill.), Res. Officers Assn. (com. chmn.), Am. Legion, Sigma Nu, Phi Alpha Delta. Moose. Home: 500 S Smith Blvd Aurora IL 60505 Office: 47 W Galena Blvd Aurora IL 60504

EDWARDS, CHARLES HAYDEN, R.R. ofcl.; b. Louisville, June 24, 1924; s. James P. and Margaret (Wathen) E.; A.B., Harvard, 1948; LL.B., U. Va., 1951; m. Sara Hulette Cummins, June 7, 1958; children—Richard Wathen, Cecilia Barber. Admitted to Ky. bar, 1951; asst. city atty., Louisville, 1952-57; pvt. practice law, Louisville, 1957-58; with L.&N. R.R., 1958—, sec., gen. atty., 1965-66, sec., treas., 1967—; dir., sec.-treas. Ky. Central Ry. Co., L&N Investment Corp., Houston-McCord Realty Co.; sec. Carrollton R.R.; sec., dir. Central Transfer Ry. & Storage Co., Nashville & Decatur R.R. Co., Paducah & Ill. R.R. Co. Louisville, Henderson & St. Louis Ry. Co.; sec.-dir. Cybernetics & Systems, Inc. Trustee Aquinas Prep. Sch., 1965-67. Mem. Am., Ky., Louisville bar assns. Democrat. Roman Catholic. Clubs: Louisville Country, Tavern, Filson, River Valley (Louisville); Harmony Landing Country (Goshen, Ky.). Home: 465 Lighfoot Rd Louisville KY 40207 Office: 908 W Broadway Louisville KY 40201

EDWARDS, CHARLES MUNDY, Jr., former coll. dean; b. Richmond, Va., Nov. 2, 1903; s. Charles Mundy and Lelia Le Moyne (Gahagan) E.; B.A. in Bus. Adminstrn., U. Richmond, 1925, LL.D. (hon.), 1963; M.S. in Retailing, N.Y.U., 1930; D.C.S., 1936; m. Nancy Blow Rawls, Apr. 2, 1931 (dec. Nov. 1968); children—Charles M. III, Richard Franklin m. 2d, Marie Elizabeth Flannery, Oct. 10, 1969. Instr. English, head track coach Staunton Mil. Acad. (Va.), 1925-29; with mgmt. div. James McCreery & Co., N.Y.C., 1929-30; merchandising and sales promotion exec. Frederick Loeser & Co., Bklyn., 1930-31; with N.Y.U. Inst. Retail Mgmt., 1930—, successively lectr., instr., asst. prof., asso. prof., prof., 1943-63, Mchts. Council prof. retail mgmt., 1964-70, dean, 1946-70, sr. dean univ., 1959-70, dean emeritus, prof. emeritus, 1970—. Cons. Retailers and mfrs., 1936—; dir. Vornado, Inc., Russ Togs, Inc., Concord Fabrics, Inc., Old Deerfield Fabrics, Inc. Served from 2d lt. to capt., CAC, U.S. Army Res., 1924-37; organizer, dir. Army Exchange Service Sch., ETO, with assimilated rank col., 1945. Decorated chevalier Ordre Du Merité Commercial (France); recipient Gold medal Mchts., 1958; named One of All-Time greats in retail sales promotion Nat. Retail Mchts. Assn., 1969. Mem. Nat. Retail Mchts. Assn. (dir. 1951-53), Am. Marketing Assn., Am. Collegiate Retailing Assn. (pres. 1948-49), Kappa Alpha, Omicron Delta Kappa, Eta Mu Pi, Alpha Delta Sigma. Author: (with William H. Howard) Retail Advertising and Sales Promotion, rev. edit., 1943, 3d edit. (with Russell A. Brown), 1959; (with Howard M. Cowee) The Retail Advertising Budget, revised edit., 1952. Editor: The Retailing Series, 1946-63; chmn. editorial bd. Jour. of Retailing. Contbr. articles to trade jours. Methodist. Home: 65 Hobart Av Summit NJ 07901 Office: 100 Washington Sq New York City NY 10003

EDWARDS, CLAUDE WILLIAM, food merchandising exec.; b. Los Angeles, Oct. 15, 1903; s. Arthur William and Edith (Thomas) E.; ed. high sch., Pomona, Cal.; LL.D. (hon.), Biola Coll., 1964; m. Ruth Louise Norwalt, Feb. 14, 1923; 1 dau., Shirley Jane (Mrs. William Radcliffe Deeley). Wholesale food distbr., 1921-22; with Alpha Beta Food Markets, Inc., 1922, v.p. gen. mgr., 1944-52, pres., gen. mgr., 1952-61, chmn. bd.; pres. Alpha Beta Acme Markets, Inc., 1961-68, chmn. bd., 1961—; dir., vice chmn., chmn. exec. com. World Vision Internat.; chmn. bd. Value Fair, Inc.; pres. Sunrich Mercantile Co.; vice chmn., dir. Acme Markets, Inc., Phila.; dir. Hy-Lo Drug Co. Mem. adv. bd. Cal. Angels of Am. League; dir. Presbyn. Inter-Community Hosp., Whittier, Cal.; trustee Chapman Coll., Orange, Cal., 1956-70. Mem. Western States Chain Grocers Assn. (pres. 1944-47), Super Market Inst. Chgo. (pres. 1949-51, exec. com. 1945—), Food Employers Council Inc. Los Angeles (gov.), Nat. Assn. Food Chains (chmn. bd. 1959-61), Am. Mgmt. Assn. (pres. assn.), Cal. Retailers Assn. (bd. dirs.), Pi Sigma Epsilon. Office: 777 S Harbor Blvd La Habra CA 90631

EDWARDS, CLIFFORD DUANE, educator; b. Atwood, Kan., Jan. 20, 1934; s. Murray Frank and Maude (Ray) E.; A.B., Ft. Hays Kan. State Coll., 1958; A.M. (Woodrow Wilson fellow), U. Mich., 1959, Ed.D. in English Lang. and Lit., 1963; m. Neva LouAnn Morgan, Aug. 28, 1954; children—Mark Duane, Marilyn Morgan, Cecily Morgan. Asso. prof. English, Ft. Hays Kan. State Coll., Hays, 1963-69; prof. English, head dept. Wis. State U., Platteville, 1969—. Served with USAF, 1951-55. Danforth Asso., 1966—. Mem. Modern Lang. Assn., Midwest Modern Lang. Assn., Nat. Council Tchrs. English, Phi Kappa Phi. Author: Conrad Richter's Ohio Trilogy, 1970. Home: 360 W Cedar St Platteville WI 53818

EDWARDS, DANIEL KRAMER, lawyer; b. Durham, N.C., Feb. 17, 1914; s. Charles W. and Eva Marie (Kramer) E.; A.B., Duke, 1935; LL.B., Harvard, 1938; m. Mary B. Partin, Dec. 24, 1941 (dec. 1958); children—Katharine LeRoy, Daniel Kramer, Claire Egan, Jane Harrison, Marie Fulmer; m. 2d, Virginia D. Duncan, Dec. 30, 1968. Admitted to N.C. bar, 1938, practiced in Durham, 1938-40, 1945—; mem. firm Edwards & Manson; mem. N.C. Gen. Assembly, 1947- 50, spl. session, 1956, chmn. com. pub. welfare Ho. of Reps., 1949; mayor City of Durham, 1949-51; asst. sec. def., Washington, 1951- 52; vice dep. U.S. rep. N. Atlantic Council, 1951-52; dept. U.S. spl. rep. in Europe for def. affairs, 1952; practicing atty., 1952—; state solicitor 10th Solicitorial Dist., 1963-71; mem. N.C. Gen. Statutes Commn. Bd. govs. ARC, 1949-51, Durham (N.C.) chpt. pres., 1948-49; mem. Army Res. Forces. Policy com. Served from 2d lt. to lt. col. inf. AUS, 1940-45; PTO; maj. gen., comdr. 30th Inf. Div. N.C. N.G. Decorated D.S.C., Silver Star, Bronze star with oak leaf cluster, Air medal, Purple Heart. Mem. Am., N.C. bar assns., N.C. Jud. Council, V.F.W., Am. Legion, Phi Beta Kappa, Sigma Pi Sigma, Phi Delta Theta. Club: Civitan (past pres.). Contbr. articles to profl. publs. Home: 406 Buchanan Rd Durham NC 27701 Office: 111 Corcoran St Durham NC 27701

EDWARDS, DAVID F., lawyer; b. Jersey City, Mar. 17, 1908; A.B., Princeton, 1929; LL.B., Harvard, 1932. Admitted to N.J. bar, 1934, N.Y. bar, 1939; mem. firm Havens, Wandless, Stitt and Tighe, N.Y.C. Mem. Assn. Bar City N.Y., Am. Bar Assn. Office: 99 Park Av New York City NY 10016*

EDWARDS, DAVID OLAF, educator; b. Liverpool, Eng., Apr. 27, 1932; s. Robert and Margaret Edwina (Larsen) E.; B.A. (Open Scholar), Brasenose Coll., Oxford (Eng.) U., 1953, M.A., Ph.D. (Sr. Hulme scholar), 1957; m. Wendy Lou Townsend, June 24, 1967; 1 dau., Rosalind. Came to U.S., 1958. Pressed steel research fellow, Oxford U., 1957-58; vis. prof. Ohio State U., 1958-60, asst. prof., 1960-62, asso. prof., 1962-65, prof., 1965—. Fellow Am. Phys. Soc. Club: Rocky Fork Beagles (hon. whipper-in) (Gahanna, O.). Editor proc. 9th Internat. Conf. on Low Temperature Physics, 1965. Contbr. research papers to sci. jours. Home: 2345 Dorset Rd Columbus OH 43221

EDWARDS, DON, congressman; b. San Jose, Cal., Jan. 6, 1915; s. Leonard P. and Clara (Donlon) E.; A.B., Stanford, 1936, student Law Sch., 1936-38; m. Clyda Magee, Nov. 19, 1951; children—Leonard P., Samuel D., Bruce H., Thomas C., William D. Agt., FBI, 1940-41; pres. owner Valley Title Co., San Jose, 1950—; mem. 88th-92d Congresses 9th Dist. Cal. Nat. chmn. Americans for Democratic Action, 1965—. Served to lt. USNR, 1941-45. Unitarian. Democrat. Home: 38 N 1st St San Jose CA 95113 Office: House Office Bldg Washington DC 20515

EDWARDS, DOUGLAS, radio, television news reporter; b. Ada, Okla., July 14, 1917; s. Tony and Alice (Donaldson) E.; student U. Ala., 1934-35, Emory U., 1936, U. Ga., 1937-38; m. Sara Byrd, Aug. 29, 1939; children—Lynn Alice, Robert Anthony, Donna Claire. Jr. announcer radio sta. WHET, Troy, Ala., 1932- 35; mem. radio news staff radio sta. WSB, Atlanta and Atlanta Jour., 1935-38; news reporter radio sta. WXYZ, Detroit, 1938-42; features World Today, Report to the Nation C.B.S., N.Y. City, 1942-45, fgn. corr., Britain, France, Germany, Middle East, 1945-46, feature World News Round Up and TV news since 1946, Nat. Conv. reporter radio, TV. Recipient Peabody award for news, 1955. Mem. Radio Correspondents Assn., Washington, Sigma Delta Chi. Clubs: Field (Weston, Conn.); Overseas Press (N.Y. City). Home: RFD 57 Weston CT 06880 Office: 485 Madison Av New York City NY 10022

EDWARDS, EDGAR OWEN, economist; b. Foxborough, Mass., Dec. 20, 1919; s. John Owen and Winifred Beatrice (Roberts) E.; A.B., Washington and Jefferson Coll., 1947; M.A., Johns Hopkins, 1949, Ph.D., 1951; m. Jean Elizabeth Lotz, Apr. 27, 1946; children—Kathryn Louise, Carolyn Jean, Douglas John. Prodn. controller Telescope Folding Furniture Co., Granville, N.Y., 1939-41; faculty Princeton, 1950-59, Richard Stockton preceptor, 1953-56, asso. prof. econs., 1956-59; Reginald Henry Hargrove prof. econs. Rice U., Houston, 1959-69, chmn. dept. econs., 1959-65, chmn. acad. planning com., 1963-64; on leave as program specialist Ford Found., 1963-65, 66-68, econ. adviser to Kenya Govt.; on leave to Yale U. Growth Center, 1968-69; econ. adviser Asia program Ford Found., N.Y.C., 1970—. Dir., regional Faculty Research Seminar Econs., Region V-S.W., summer 1962. Served to capt. inf. AUS, 1942-46. Guggenheim fellow, Sweden, 1954-55. Mem. Am. (com. on econ. edn), So. econ. assns., Am. Accounting Assn., A.A.A.S., Southwestern Social Sci. Assn., Am. Assn. U. Profs. (pres. Rice chpt. 1961-62), Am. Acad. Polit. and Social Sci., Phi Beta Kappa (pres. Rice U. chpt. 1962-63), Beta Theta Pi. Author: (with P. W. Bell) The Theory and Measurement of Business Income, 1961; The Nation's Economic Objectives, 1964; also articles, chpts. in books. Editorial bd. So. Econ. Jour., 1962-63, Bus. Rev., 1961-63. Home: 109 Kingston Av Yonkers NY 10701 Office: 320 E 43d St New York City NY 10017

EDWARDS, EDWARD EVERETT, educator; b. Bloomfield, Ind., July 15, 1908; s. Lewis Baker and Alta Ethel (Terrell) E.; B.S., Ind. U., 1928, M.S., 1934; m. Louise Robinson, Sept. 2, 1933; children—Robert Alan, Margaret Louise. Methods investigator Western Electric Co., 1928-31; statistician Ind. Dept. Financial Instns., 1933-36; Ind. dir. Nat. Youth Adminstrn., 1935- 36; asst. prof. Ind. U., Bloomington, 1936-41, asso. prof., 1941-48, prof. finance, 1948-62, Fred T. Greene prof. finance, 1962—, asso. dir. Grad. Sch. Savs. and Loan, 1946—; v.p. Bus. and Real Estate Trends, Inc., 1949—; cons. to chmn. Fed. Home Loan Bank Bd., 1961-62; dir. Irwin Union Bank, Columbus, Ind., Brown Country Fed. Savs. and Loan Assn. Vis. prof. Ariz. State U., 1968-69; adv. com. 1960 Census of Housing; cons. White House, Sec. Def., Sec. Army, 1948-50, Fed. Deposit Ins. Corp., 1964—. Served from capt. to lt. col. finance dept., AUS, 1942-46. Mem. Am. Finance Assn. (sec.-treas. 1947-51, pres. 1952), Am. Econ. Assn., Am. Assn. U. Profs., Am. Savs. and Loan Inst., Beta Gamma Sigma, Delta Sigma Pi. Democrat. Methodist. Cons. editor MGIC newsletter, 1968—. Home: Town Hill Rd Nashville IN 47448 Office: Box 183 Bloomington IN 47401

EDWARDS, EDWIN WASHINGTON, congressman; b. Marksville, La., Aug. 7, 1927; s. Clarence W. and Agnes (Brouillette) E.; LL.B., La. State U., 1949; m. Elaine Schwartzenburg, Apr. 5, 1949; children—Anna Laure, Victoria Elaine, Stephen Randolph, David Edwin. Admitted to La. bar, 1949; gen. practice in Crowley, La., 1949-66; sr. founding partner firm Edwards & Edwards, 1954; mem. Crowley City Council, 1954-62, La. Senate from 35th dist., 1964-66; mem. 89th- 92d Congresses 7th dist. La. Served with USNR, World War II. Mem. Internat. Rice Festival, Crowley C. of C., Crowley Indsl. Found., Am. Legion. Democrat. Catholic. Lion. Home: 1226 N Av J Crowley LA 70526 Office: Cannon Office Bldg Washington DC 20515

EDWARDS, FRANCIS HENRY, clergyman; b. Birmingham, Eng., Aug. 4, 1897; s. Francis Henry and Ellen (Smith) E.; student Graceland Coll., 1921-22, U. Kan., 1925, 28, Kansas City U., 1934, William Jewell Coll., 1942; m. Alice Myrmida Smith, June 27, 1924; children—Lyman Francis, Ruth Ellen, Paul Madison. Came to U.S., 1921, naturalized, 1938. Ordained to ministry of the Reorganized Ch. Jesus Christ of Latter Day Saints, 1916; mem., sec. Council of Twelve, Reorganized Ch. Jesus Christ of Latter Day Saints, 1922-46, counsellor in first presidency, 1946-66; elder spl. ministries, 1966—; first counsellor of presiding council Gen. Ch., which edits Saints Herald, 1946—, now corr. editor; lectr. history Graceland Coll. Mem. Mo. Hist. Soc. Author: Fundamentals, 1930; Life and Ministry of Jesus, 1933; Commentary on Doctrine and Covenants, 1938; Missionary Sermon Studies, 1940; God Our Help, 1943; Authority and Spiritual Power, 1956; All Thy Mercies, 1961; For Such a Time, 1962; The Divine Purpose, 1964; Church History, 1968, vol. V1, 1970; others. Home: 1307 Randall Rd Independence MO 64055 Office: The Auditorium Independence MO 64055

EDWARDS, FRANK WILLIAM, profl. engr.; b. Williamsburg, Ia., Aug. 10, 1905 s. Walter Ernest and Bertha Ethel (Stover) E.; B.S., U. Ia., 1928, M.S., 1930, C.E., 1944; m. Harriet Margaret Williams, June 3, 1928; children—Doris Ann (Mrs. Rodger W. Davenport), Carolyn (Mrs. Charles W. Soderberg). Asst. engr., then engr. in charge dist. Mgmt. & Engring. Corp., 1928-32; research asst. U.S. Bur. Agrl. Engring., 1932- 33; gauge reader, later prin. engr. several dists. U.S. C.E. and Panama Canal, War Dept., 1933-43, 45-46; asst. prof. civil engring. Pa. State Coll., 1943-44, asso. prof., 1944-45; prof. civil engring. Carnegie Inst. Tech., 1946-48; dir. dept. civil engring. Ill. Inst. Tech., 1948- 53; mgr. Chgo. office Stanley Engring. Co., cons. engrs., 1953-64, v.p., dir., 1961-64; pres. Limbaugh Engring. & Aerial Surveys, Inc., Albuquerque, 1964-66; pres., dir. Limbaugh Engrs., Inc., 1965-70, cons., dir., 1970—; cons. Bovay Engrs., Inc., 1970—, St. Lawrence Seaway Devel. Corp. Gen. mgr. Centennial of Engring., 1952, Inc.; adv. bd. Coll. Engring., U. Ida. Recipient Ill. award Ill. Soc. Profl. Engrs. Fellow Am. Soc. C.E. (pres. Ill. sect. 1953); mem. Am. Soc. M.E., Am. Soc. Engring. Edn., Nat. (nat. dir. 1959-64), Ill. (pres. Chgo. chpt. 1952, state pres., 1958-59, named hon. mem. 1965), N.M. socs. profl. engrs., Sigma Xi, Theta Tau (exec. council 1948-52), Tau Beta Pi, Omicron Delta Kappa, Chi Epsilon. Elk. Club: Petroleum (Albuquerque). Author: articles engring. jours. Home: 7700 Gladden Av NE Albuquerque NM 87110 Office: 3125 Carlisle Blvd NE Albuquerque NM 87110 also P O Box 30068 Albuquerque NM 87110

EDWARDS, FRED EDWARD, savs. and loan assn. exec.; b. Steubenville, O., Sept. 4, 1904; s. William and Jennie (Gettings) E.; grad. Am. Inst. Banking, 1929; m. Marion Olive Cook, Mav 14, 1925; children—Maryann (Mrs. Hugh Darling), Dianne (Mrs. Clayton Jacobson). From messenger to br. mgr. Bank of Am. Nat. Trust & Savs. Assn., Los Angeles, 1922-45; pres. S.W. Savs. & Loan Assn., Inglewood, Cal., 1945—; pres., dir. Western Escrow Co., Fred. E. Edwards Co., Inc., Morningside Investment Co. (Cal.), Ingleside Investment Co. Trustee Centinela Valley Community Hosp., S.W. Community Hosp. Assn. Mem. Inqlewood C. of C. (past pres.), Mason, Lion. Home: 3107 W Arbor Vitae St Inglewood CA 90305 Office: 2700 W Manchester Blvd Inglewood CA 90305

EDWARDS, G. FESLER, retail trade exec.; b. Johnstown, Pa., 1911; grad. U. Pa., 1932. Pres. Penn Traffic Co., Johnstown. Home: 769 Viewmont Av Johnstown PA 15905 Office: 319 Washington St Johnstown PA 15901

EDWARDS, GARTH WILLIAMS, mfg. co. exec.; b. Idaho Falls, Ida., Aug. 25, 1915; s. John Thomas and Mary Ann (William) E.; student George Washington U., 1935-36; B.S., U. Ill., 1939; m. Ollie Richmond Nance, Sept. 30, 1939; children—Garth Nance, Nancy Sue. With Gen. Motors Corp., Detroit, 1939-42, Nat. Assn. Real Estate Boards, 1946-47; with AEC, Washington, 1948-50, asst. mgr. Savannah River operations, 1950-55; controller Sylvania Electric Products Co., 1955-60; v.p. finance Stanley Works, New Britain, Conn., 1960—, dir.; dir. New Britain Machine Co., Allied Thermal Corp., New Britain Bank & Trust. Served to lt. (s.g.) USNR, 1942-45. Mem. Nat. Accounting Assn., Financial Execs. Inst., Sigma Chi. Club: N.Y. Economic. Home: 75 Windsor Rd Kensington CT 06037 Office: 195 Lake St New Britain CT 06052

EDWARDS, GEORGE, judge; b. Dallas, Aug. 6, 1914; s. George Clifton and Octavia (Nichols) E.; B.A., So. Meth. U., 1933; M.A., Harvard, 1934; J.D., Detroit Coll. Law, 1949; m. Margaret McConnell, Apr. 10, 1939; children—George Clifton III, James McConnell. Coll. sec. League Indsl. Democracy, 1934-35; prodn. worker Kelsey Hayes Wheel Co., 1936; rep. UAW- CIO, 1937, dir. welfare dept., 1938-39; dir., sec. Detroit Housing Commn., 1940-41; mem. Detroit Common Council, 1941-49, pres., 1945-49; admitted to Mich. bar, 1944; with firm Edwards & Bohn, Detroit, 1946-50, Rothe, Marston, Edwards and Bohn, 1950-51; probate judge charge Wayne County Juvenile Ct., 1951-54; judge 3d Jud. Circuit, Wayne County, 1954-56; justice Supreme Ct. Mich., 1956-62; commr. of police City Detroit, 1962-63; judge U.S. Ct. Appeals, 6th circuit, 1963- -. Chmn. com. adminstrn. criminal laws Jud. Conf. U.S., 1966-70; mem. Nat. Com. Reform of Fed. Criminal Laws, 1967-71. Chmn. S.E. Mich. Cancer Crusade, 1950- 51. Chmn. 13th Cong. Dist. Democratic party Wayne County, 1950-51. Served from pvt. to lt., inf., AUS, 1943-46. Recipient award for community work for social progress Workmen's Circle, 1949; award for community work for civil rights St. Cyprian's Episcopal Ch., 1950; Americanism award Jewish War Vets, 1953; award for outstanding achievement juvenile rehab. V.F.W., 1953; St. Peter's medal for outstanding service to youth St. Peter's Episcopal Ch., Detroit, 1956. Mem. V.F.W., Am. Legion, Am., Mich., Detroit bar assns., Nat. Council Judges, Nat. Council on Crime and Delinquency, Inst. Jud. Adminstrn., Phi Beta Kappa, Kappa Sigma. Democrat. Episcopalian. Mason. Author: The Police on the Urban Frontier, 1968. (with others) The Law of Criminal Correction, 1968. also articles on crime and delinquency. Home: 19925 Briarcliffe Detroit MI 48221 Office: Federal Bldg Detroit MI 48226

EDWARDS, GEORGE ALVA, physician, educator; b. Killeen, Tex., Oct. 19, 1916; s. John Clem and Maude May (Lam) E.; B.A., Howard Payne Coll., 1939; postgrad. N. Tex. State Coll., 1946; M.D., U. Tex. Southwestern, 1950; m. Winnie Belle Landes, Jan. 23, 1946; children—Karen Leigh, David Glen. Intern, Johns Hopkins Hosp., Balt., 1950-51, resident, 1952-53; resident Duke Hosp., Durham, N.C., 1951-52, Firmin Desloge Hosp., St. Louis, 1953-54; asst. chief med. service VA, St. Louis, 1954-55; chief med. service VA Hosp., McKinney, Tex., 1955-59, Pitts., 1959-66; asst. chief med. service VA Hosp., Dallas, 1966-68; chief med. service VA Hosp., Cin., 1968—. Asst. prof. U. Tex. Southwestern Med. Sch., 1955-59, asso. prof., 1966-68; asso. prof. U. Pitts., 1959-66; prof. medicine U. Cin., 1968—. Served with USAAF, 1940-46. Decorated Air medal. Fellow A.C.P.; mem. A.M.A., Cin. Soc. Internal Medicine, Alpha Omega Alpha. Baptist. Home: 5 Alexander Circle Fort Thomas KY 41075 Office: U Cin Coll Medicine 3200 Vine St Cincinnati OH 45220

EDWARDS, GEORGE KENT, lawyer; b. Ogden, Utah, Oct. 3, 1939; s. George and S. Ruth (Engelke) E.; A.B., Occidental Coll., 1961; J.D., U. Cal. at Berkeley, 1964; m. Barbara Lee Day, June 9, 1964 (dec. 1970); children—Scott M., Stacey R. Admitted to Cal. bar, 1965, Alaska bar, 1966; legislative counsel Alaska Legislature, 1964-66; partner firm Stevens, Savage, Holland, Erwin & Edwards, Anchorage, 1966-67; dep. atty. gen., Alaska, 1967-68, atty. gen., 1968-70; U.S. atty. Dist. Alaska, 1971—. Commr., Nat. Conf. Commnrs. Uniform State Laws, 1968-70; chmn. Gov. Alaska Planning Council Adminstrn. Criminal Justice, 1968-70. Pres. Greater Anchorage Area Young Republicans, 1967; orgn. chmn. Southcentral Alaska Rep. Commn., 1966-67. Mem. Am., Cal., Alaska, Juneau bar assns., Nat. Assn. Attys. Gen., Phi Delta Phi, Sigma Alpha Epsilon (Outstanding Sr. award Cal. Epsilon chpt. 1961). Home: 2113 Duke Dr Anchorage AK 99504 Office: PO Box 680 Anchorage AK 99501

EDWARDS, GEORGE ROBERT, aircraft designer; b. July 9, 1908; B.Sc. in Engring., London U., 1935, D.Sc. (hon.); D.Sc., Southampton U., Cranfield Inst.; m. Marjorie Annie Thurgood, 1935; 1 dau., Angela Mary. Gen. engring., 1928-35; design staff Vickers Aviation, Ltd., Weybridge, Surrey, Eng., 1935-40, exptl. mgr. Vickers-Armstrongs, Ltd., 1940-45, chief designer, 1945-53; dir. Vickers, Ltd., 1955-68; chmn., mng. dir. Brit. Aircraft Corp. Pro-chancellor U. Surrey. Decorated Order of Merit; comdr., Order Brit. Empire, 1952; created knight, 1957; recipient George Taylor medal, 1948, Brit. gold medal for aero., 1952; hon. fellow Manchester Coll. Sci. and Tech.; Daniel Guggenheim Medal, Soc. Automotive Engrs., 1959; Founders medal Air League, 1969. Hon. fellow Royal Aero. Soc. (pres. 1957-58), Am. Inst. Aeros. and Astronautics; fellow Royal Soc., Inst. Dirs., Inst. Mgmt.; mem. Royal Inst. Gt. Britain. Home: Albury Heights White Lane Guilford Surrey England Office: Brit Aircraft Corp Weybridge Surrey England

EDWARDS, GILBERT FRANKLIN, educator, sociologist; b. Charleton, S.C., June 2, 1915; s. Gilbert Franklin and Bertha (Allen) E.; A.B., Fisk U., 1936; Ph.D., U. Chgo., 1952; m. Peggy Jarvis Park, Sept. 8, 1946; 1 dau., Donalee Marie. Tchr. social studies Fessenden (Fla.) Acad., 1937-39; mem. faculty Howard U., Washington, 1941—, prof. sociology, 1960—. Vis. tchr. Washington U., St. Louis, summer 1954, Harvard, summer 1967, 68; cons. in field, 1961—. Pub. mem. Nat. Capital Planning Commn., 1965—, now vice chmn. Mem. Am. Sociol. Assn., Eastern Social Soc., Population Assn. Am., Phi Beta Kappa (alumni mem.). Author: The Negro Professional Class, 1959. Editor: E. Franklin Frazier on Race Relations, 1968. Home: 4643 16th St NW Washington DC 20011

EDWARDS, GORDON, food products co. exec.; b. Franklin, Va., May 29, 1907; s. Claude Joseph and Marion Lee (Lawless) E.; student Va. Poly. Inst., 1925- 27; B.A., George Washington U., 1931; LL.D. (hon.), St. Lawrence U., 1967; m. Alida Beamon, Oct. 22, 1932; children—Gordon B., Patricia Ann (Mrs. Alexander B. Platt), Alida (Mrs. George A. Meyers). With Kraftco Corp. (formerly Nat. Dairy Products Corp.), Washington, 1927-35, N.Y.C., 1935- 36, zone controller, Chgo., 1936-49, with Kraft Foods div., Chgo., 1949- 65, pres., 1964-65, dir. corp., N.Y.C., 1962—, pres., 1965—, chief exec. officer, 1966—, chmn. bd., 1968—; dir. Cluett, Peabody & Co., Inc., B. F. Goodrich Co., Irving Trust Co., Pitney Bowes, Inc., Communications Satellite Corp. Bd. dirs. Econ. Devel. Council N.Y.C. Mem. Grocery Mfrs. Am. (dir., mem. exec. com.), Econ. Club N.Y., Conf. Bd., Council Better Bus. Burs. (dir.). Conglist. Home: 74 Winding Lane Greenwich CT 06833 Office: 260 Madison Av New York City NY 10016

EDWARDS, HAROLD HOOPER, motor carrier co. exec.; b. Oklahoma City, Dec. 25, 1920; s. James Turner and Anna (Hooper) E.; B.S., Oklahoma City U., 1948; m. Mary Alice Stahl, July 5, 1946; children—Nancy Gayle, Harold Hooper, James Hunt. With Yellow Freight System, Inc., 1946—, v.p., treas., 1965—, v.p. finance, 1971—. Past pres. Transp. Clearing, Kansas City, Mo. Served to capt. USAAF, 1940-45. Decorated D.F.C., Air medal with 3 oak leaf clusters. Mem. Am. Trucking Assn. (past pres. financial council), Financial Execs. Inst. (bd. dirs., treas. Kansas City). Home: 4509 W 82d St Prairie Village KS 66208 Office: Yellow Freight System Inc 92d and State Line Rd Kansas City MO 64114

EDWARDS, HARRISON GRIFFITH, architect; b. Columbia, S.C., Aug. 21, 1907; s. William Augustus and Pearl (Brown) E.; B.S. Ga. Inst. Tech., 1930; m. Betty Grace Fountain, Feb. 22, 1936; children—Margaret Fountain, Alice Landru. Draftsman, Edwards & Sayward, architects, Atlanta 1930-36, Henry J. Toombs, architect, Atlanta, 1937-40; partner Edwards & Goodwyne, pvt. practice, Atlanta, 1940-55, Edwards & Portman, architects, engrs., Atlanta, 1956- -; successively asst. prof., asso. prof., prof. Sch Architecture Ga. Inst. Tech., 1946—, mem. alumni adv. bd. 1956—. Mem. Men's Council Atlanta League Women Voters, 1942—; chmn. Atlanta Merchandise Mart Bldg., 1964; chmn. architects, engrs. div. United Appeal Fund Drive, 1965. Trustee, mem. exec. com. Theatre Atlanta, Inc. Fellow Constrn. Specifications Inst. (past v.p., pres. dir. Atlanta chpt.; President's award for service 1961), A.I.A. (past pres., dir. Ga. chpt., Service to Inst. award 1962); mem. Atlanta C. of C. Ga. Engring. Soc., Assn. Collegiate Schs. Architecture, Sigma Chi. Episcopalian. Club: Ansley Golf. Author: Specifications, rev. edit., 1961. Prin. works include Atlanta Merchandise Mart, Peachtree Center Office Bldg., Greenbriar Shopping Center, Atlanta Decorative Arts Center, Regency Hotel, Infirmary Bldg. Ga. Inst. Tech., Oglethorpe, C.W. Hill, Hendon Schs. (all Atlanta), Dana Fine Arts Bldg. Agnes Scott Coll. (Decatur), Midway, Sequoyah, Hawthorne, Carey Reynolds Schs. (DeKalb County), Spalding Dr. Sch. (Fulton County). Episcopalian (vestryman 1964-66, jr. warden 1966). Home: 1681 Lady Marion Lane NE Atlanta GA 30309 Office: 2107 Peachtree Center Atlanta GA 30303

EDWARDS, HOMER MERIDETH, lawyer; b. Ironton, O., June 9, 1921; s. Homer M. and Pansy (Winters) E.; B.S., Ohio State U., 1943, J.D., 1948; m. Barbara Winchester, May 5, 1961; children—Robert, Elizabeth Jane, Mari Lynn. Admitted to Ohio bar, 1948, since practiced in Ironton; sr. partner Edwards, Klein, Compton and Allen, 1958—; v.p., gen. counsel, dir. First Nat. Bank, Ironton, 1948—. Mem. Ohio Bd. Bar Examiners, 1967—; mem. nat. council Ohio State U. Coll. Law. Chmn. Republican party Lawr County (O.), 1950-66; sec. Electoral Colls. U.S., 1952-56, v.p., 1956-60, pres., 1968—. Trustee Ohio Soldiers and Sailors Orphans Home, Xenia, 1962-66, chmn. bd., 1965- 66. Served to 1st lt. AUS, 1942-46. Fellow Am. Bar Found.; mem. Am., Ky., Ohio, Lawrence County bar assns., Ohio State U. Coll. Law Alumni Assn. (pres. 1969-70), Phi Delta Theta, Phi Delta Phi. Mason, Elk, Rotarian. Home: 701 S 6th St Ironton OH 45638 Office: First Nat Bank Bldg Ironton OH 45638

EDWARDS, HOWARD DAWSON, educator, physicist; b. Athens, Ga., Dec. 11, 1923; s. Howard Thomas and Inez (Glenn) E.; B.S., U. Ga., 1944; Ph.D., Duke, 1950; m. Mary Lemon, Mar. 10, 1961; children—David, Jerry, David Bradley (stepson), Kathy. Chief atmospheric energy br. Air Force Cambridge Research Labs., Bedford, Mass., 1949-55; operations research scientist Lockheed Aircraft Corp., Marietta, Ga., 1956-58; faculty Ga. Inst. Tech., Atlanta, 1959—, prof. aerospace engring., 1965—, dir. Aerospace Environment Lab., 1963—. Pres. Systems Instruments Research, Inc., 1963—. Mem. Ga. Acad. Sci. (pres. 1966). Contbr. articles profl. jours. Home: 365 Amberidge Trail Atlanta GA 30328

EDWARDS, HOWARD LEE, mining co. exec.; b. Baker, Ore., June 10, 1931; s. Elmer L. and Bernice (Stringham) E.; B.S., Brigham Young U., 1955; postgrad. Stanford, 1955-56, U. Utah, 1956-57; J.D., George Washington U., 1959; m. Carolyn Bagley, Mar. 19, 1954; children— Bryant B., H. McKay, Mitchell L., Paul S. Admitted to Utah bar, 1959; legal asst., atty. Office of Dir., Bur. Land Mgmt., Washington, Office of Solicitor, U.S. Dept. Interior, Salt Lake City, 1957-61; partner Van Cott, Bagley, Cornwall & McCarthy, Salt Lake City, 1964-68; asst. gen. counsel Anaconda Co., N.Y.C., 1968, asst. to chmn. bd., 1969, v.p., sec., 1970—. Trustee Rocky Mountain Mineral Law Found. Mem. Am., Fed., Utah bar assns., N.A.M., Am. Mining Congress, N.Y. C. of C. Republican. Mem. Ch. of Jesus Christ of Latter-day Saints. Club: Mining (N.Y.C.). Home: 36 Tennyson Dr Short Hills NJ 07078 Office: 25 Broadway New York City NY 10004

EDWARDS, HUGH STEPHENSON, supt. sanitarium; b. Pendleton, N.C., Sept. 26, 1908; s. Robert Lee and Lillie (Stephenson) E.; B.S. in Medicine, Wake Forest Coll., 1932; M.D., Med. Coll. Va., 1935; m. Kathleen A. Williams, Dec. 9, 1939; children—Deborah, David. Staff physician Worcester Country (Mass.) Sanatorium, 1935-39, Battle Hill Sanatorium, Atlanta, 1939-42; staff physician Pinecrest Sanitarium, Beckley, W.Va., 1942-47, supt., 1947—. Life mem. bd. dirs. Raleigh County Tb Assn. Mem. Am., W.Va., Raleigh County (past pres.) thoracic socs., Nat. Rehab. Soc. Episcopalian mem. vestry). Rotarian, Elk, Moose. Home: Pinecrest Sanitarium Beckley WV 25801

EDWARDS, JACK, congressman; b. Birmingham, Ala., Sept. 20, 1928; s. William Jackson and Sue (Fuhrman) E.; B.S. in Commerce and Bus. Adminstrn., U. Ala., 1952; LL.B., U. Ala., 1954; m. Jolane Vander Sys, Jan. 30, 1954; children—Susan Lane, Richard Arnold. Admitted to Ala. bar, 1954; pvt. practice, Mobile, 1954-58; gen. atty. G., M. & O. R.R., 1958-64; legal adviser Emergency Port Operations Mobile, 1961-64; mem. 89th-92d Congresses, 1st Dist. Ala. Chmn. America's Jr. Miss Pageant, 1960; pres. Ala. Deep Sea Fishing Rodeo, 1956-57; div. chmn. Mobile United Fund, 1960; mem. transp. adv. com. Mobile City Planning Commn., 1960-64; an organizer Freedom over Communism Com., Mobile, 1962. Served with USMCR, 1946-48, 50-51. Named one of outstanding young men U.S. Jr. C. of C., 1964. Mem. Am., Ala., Mobile (sec. 1956) bar assns., Mobile Jr. Bar Assn. (pres. 1957), Mobile Jr. C. of C. (pres. 1961-62), Kappa Alpha (pres. 1951-53), Omicron Delta Kappa. Presbyn. (elder, Sunday Sch. tchr.). Home: 1910 Hunter Av Mobile AL 36606 Office: House Office Bldg Washington DC 20515

EDWARDS, JAMES COOK, investment counselor; b. N.Y.C., Aug. 4, 1923; s. James A. and Edith (Cook) E.; grad. Buckley Sch., 1937; B.A., Yale, 1945; LL.B., Columbia, 1949; m. Sally Matson, Apr. 21, 1951; children—James Cook, Anne Matson. Admitted to N.Y. bar, 1949; v.p., sec., dir. Douglas T. Johnston & Co., Inc., N.Y.C., 1949—; pres., dir. Millan House, Inc., 1965—; v.p., dir. Johnston Mut. Fund, Inc., 1956-66. Mem. E. Hampton (N.Y.) Zoning Bd. Appeal, 1962-64. Trustee Buckley Sch. Served with AUS, 1943-45. Decorated Air medal with 8 oak leaf clusters. Presbyn. Clubs: Maidstone (pres., bd. govs), Union, Yale (N.Y.C.); Mastigouche (Can.) Fish and Game. Home: 115 E 67th St New York City NY 10021 Office: 460 Park Av New York City NY 10022

EDWARDS, JAMES D., univ. dean; b. Eclectic, Ala., Nov. 5, 1914; s. James DeAra and Lula (Harris) E.; B.A., Bob Jones U., 1936; student Gregg Coll., summer 1937, La. State U., summers 1938-39; M.A., U. Mich., 1951; LL.D., Northwestern Schs., 1952; m. Carolyn Elizabeth Reynolds, May 31, 1939; children—James D., Carolyn DeAra. Dean of men Bob Jones U., Greenville, S.C., 1936-43, prof. Am. history 1943—, coll. dean, 1943-47, dean sch. commerce, 1947-48, dean students, 1947-53, dean of adminstrn., 1953—. Mem. N.E.A., So. Hist. Assn., U. Mich., Bob Jones U. (pres. 1952-54) alumni assns. Home: Bob Jones U Greenville SC 29614

EDWARDS, JAMES DONALD, educator; b. Ellisville, Miss., Nov. 12, 1926; s. Thomas Terrell and Reitha Mae (Cranford) E.; B.S., La. State U., 1949; M.B.A., U. Denver, 1950; Ph.D., U. Tex., 1953; m. Clara Florence Maestri, Aug. 16, 1947; 1 son, James Donald. Instr., grad. asst. U. Denver, 1949-50, U. Tex., 1950- 51; instr. accounting Mich. State U., 1951-53, asst. prof., 1953-55, asso. prof., 1955-57, prof., 1957-71, acting head dept., 1957-58, head dept. accounting and financial adminstrn., 1958-71, acting asso. dean Grad. Sch. Bus. Adminstrn., 1960; dean Sch. Bus. Adminstrn., dean Grad. Sch. Bus. Adminstrn., U. Minn., 1971—; formerly with Touche, Ross, Bailey & Smart, C.P.A.'s. Mem. nat. research com. U.S. Bus. Edn. Assn. and Research Found. Mem. Am. Accounting Assn. (v.p. 1964, pres. 1970—, chmn. C.P.A. exam. com.), Am. Inst. C.P.A.'s (chmn. members in edn. com. 1960-61), Mich. Assn. C.P.A.'s., Am. Finance Assn., Am. Mgmt. Assn., Am., Midwest (program chmn. 1959) econ. assns., Nat. Assn. Accountants (v.p., asso. dir. publns., chpt. pres., nat. dir. 1962-63, chmn. research planning com., chmn. research grants com.), Omicron Delta Kappa, Phi Kappa Phi, Beta Gamma Sigma, Beta Alpha Psi, Delta Sigma Pi. Mason. Author: History of Accounting in the United States; Controllo Aziendale; co-author: Elementary Accounting, 1956, Intermediate Accounting, 1958; Administrative Control and Executive Action, Contributions of Four Accounting Pioneers, Preparation for the Professional CPA Examination, 2 vols., Financial and Management Accounting-A Programmed Text, vol. 1-2, 1967; (with Hermanson and Salmonson) The Dun and Bradstreet Business Course in Accounting. Editor, Jour. Accountancy. Contbr. articles to profl. publs. Home: 1957 Ryan Av St Paul MN 55113 Office: Sch Bus Adminstrn U Minn Minneapolis MN 55455

EDWARDS, JEROME, film co. exec. Vice pres., gen. counsel Twentieth Century-Fox Film Corp., N.Y.C. Office: 444 W 56th St New York City NY 10019*

EDWARDS, JESSE EFREM, physician, educator; b. Hyde Park, Mass., July 14, 1911; s. Max and Nellie (Gordon) E.; B.S., Tufts Coll., 1932, M.D., 1935; m. Marjorie Helen Brooks, Nov. 12, 1952; children—Ellen Ann, Brooks Sayre. Resident, Mallory Inst. Pathology, Boston, 1935-36, asst., 1937-40; intern Albany (N.Y.) Hosp., 1936-37; instr. pathology Boston U., 1938; instr. pathology, bacteriology, surgery Tufts Med. Coll., 1939-40; research fellow Nat. Cancer Inst. USPHS, 1940-42; cons. sect. pathologic anatomy Mayo Clinic, 1946-60; asst. prof. grad. sch. U. Minn., Mpls., 1946-51, asso. prof., 1951-54, prof. pathologic anatomy, 1954-60, clin. prof. med. sch., prof. pathology grad. sch., 1960—; chief pathologist. Chas. T. Miller Hosp., St. Paul, 1960—; cons. pathologist Hennepin County Hosp., Mpls., 1964—; cons. dept. medicine Mpls. Vets. Hosp., 1966—; cons. pathologist St. Paul Ramsey Hosp., 1967—; prof. med. tech. Macalester Coll., St. Paul, 1960-67. Mem. pathology study sect. USPHS, 1957-62; civilian cons. surgeon gen. AUS, 1947-69. Served from capt. to lt. col. M.C., AUS, 1942-46. Diplomate Am. Bd. Med. Examiners, Am. Bd. Pathology. Asso. fellow Am. Acad. Pediatrics; mem. Soci. Explt. Biology and Medicine, Am. (pres. 1967-68), Minn. (pres. 1962-63) heart assns., Internat. Acad. Pathology (pres. 1955-56), Am. Assn. Pathologists and Bacteriologists, Coll. Am. Pathologists, Am. Soc. Exptl. Pathology, Am. Soc. Study Arteriosclerosis, Am., Minn. med. assns., Sigma Xi, Alpha Omega Alpha. Author: Atlas Acquired Diseases of Heart and Great Vessels, 1961; (with T.J. Dry and others), Congenital Anomalies of the Heart and Great Vessels 1948; An (with others) Atlas of Congenital Anomalies of the Heart and Great Vessels, 1954; (with R.S. Fontana) Congenital Cardiac Disease, 1962; (with J.R. Stewart, O. Kincaid) An Atlas of Vascular Rings and Related Malformations of the Aortic System, 1963, (with C.A. Wagenvoort, D. Heath) Pathology of Pulmonary Vasculature, 1963; (with others) Congenital Heart Disease. Correlation of Pathologic Anatomy and Angiocardiography, 1965. Editor: Am. Heart Jour., Am. Jour. Cardiology, Geriatrics, Circulation. Contbr. articles to profl. jours. Home: 1565 Edgcumbe Rd St Paul MN 55116 Office: Chas T Miller Hosp St Paul MN 55102

EDWARDS, JOHN ALLEN, mfg. co. exec.; b. Chgo., Dec. 22, 1917; s. Thomas Michael and Pearl E. (McCorkel) E.; student Northwestern U., 1948; m. Ruth S. Anderson, June 13, 1942; children—Michael K., Patricia L. With Continental Ill. Bank & Trust Co., Chgo., 1936-40; with Liquid Carbonic Corp., Chgo., 1940—, v.p., treas., comptroller, 1956-61, exec. v.p., 1961-63, pres., 1963—. Mem. Chgo. Council on Fgn. Relations. Served to maj. USAAF, 1941-45. Mem. Compressed Gas Assn. (mem. exec. bd. 1963, 2d v.p. 1967, 1st v.p. 1968, pres.

1969), Delta Mu Delta. Clubs: Economic, Executives (Chgo.); Flossmoor Country. Home: 809 Bruce St Flossmoor IL 60422 Office: 135 S LaSalle St Chicago IL 60603

EDWARDS, JOHN OELHAF, educator; b. Sewickley, Pa., July 21, 1922; s. Robert D. and Frances (Lomas) E.; B.A., Colgate U., 1947; postgrad. Inst. Paper Chemistry, 1947-48; Ph.D., U. Wis., 1950; m. Ruth D. Christofferson, Sept. 20, 1950; children—Kathleen, Joan. Research asso. Cornell U., 1950-51; research chemist du Pont Co., 1952; prof. chemistry Brown U., 1952—; cons. chemistry FMC Corp., 1964—, U.S. Army Chem. Center, 1954—. Served with USMCR, 1942-45. Guggenheim fellow, 1967-68. Fellow A.A.A.S.; mem. Am. Chem. Soc. Lutheran. Author: Inorganic Reaction Mechanisms, 1964; also numerous articles. Editor chem. monographs. Home: 59 Irving Av Providence RI 02906

EDWARDS, JOHN S., orch. mgr.; St. Louis 1912. Began as music reviewer St. Louis Globe- Democrat; staff St. Louis Symphony Orch., later mgr.; formerly bus. mgr. Los Angeles Philharmonic Orch., also Hollywood Bowl; asst. mgr. Pitts. Symphony Orch., 1945-48; mgr. Balt. Symphony Orch., Washington Nat. Symphony Orch., 1948-55, Pitts. Symphony Orch., 1955-67; mgr. Chgo. Symphony Orch., 1967—. Past mem. adv. com. Nat. Cultural Center, Washington, Commonwealth Pa. Council on Arts. Bd. dirs. Am. Symphony Orch. League, Vienna, Va., past pres., chmn. bd., 1968—. Office: Chgo Symphony Orch S Michigan Av Chicago IL 60603

EDWARDS, JOSEPH CASTRO, physician; b. Springfield, Mo., Dec. 24, 1909; s. Lyman Paul and Lela (Bedell) E.; A.B., U. Okla., 1930; M.D., Harvard, 1934; m. Virginia Moser, Jan. 8, 1942; children—Virginia Lee (Mrs. Mario Barraco Murmol), Joseph Byron, Jonathan Paul. Tutorial fellow cardiology, Dr. Paul D. White, Mass. Gen. Hosp., 1934; intern Springfield (Mass.) Hosp., 1935; house physician med. service Barnes Hosp., 1936-37; Stroud fellow, resident Pa. Hosp., Phila., 1937-38; Eli Lilly fellow Washington U. Med. Sch., St. Louis, 1939, Smith Kline and French fellow in hypertension, 1940, instr. clin. medicine, 1939-60, asst. prof. clin. medicine, 1960—, cons. clinics and div. gerontology; asst. physician Barnes Hosp.; vis. physician St. Louis City Hosp.; mem. staff Deaconess Hosp.; mem. cons. staff St. Joseph (Mo.) Hosp.; cardiologist, dir. high blood pressure clinic St. Luke's Hosp.; area med. cons. hearings and appeals div. U.S. Social Security Admstrn.; med. cons. R.R. Retirement Bd. Bd. dirs. Boys Town Mo.; former bd. dirs. Speech and Hearing Soc. St. Louis; pres. Doctors Med. Found., St. Louis, 1964. Served as lt. col., M.C., AUS. Decorated Legion of Merit. Diplomate Am. Bd. Internal Medicine (cardiovascular disease). Fellow A.C.P., Am. Coll. Cardiology (gov. Mo. 1962- 65), Royal Soc. Medicine London); mem. Miss. Valley (pres. 1958), St. Louis (pres. 1970) med. socs.; Am., Mo. (dir.), St. Louis heart assns., St. Louis Cardiac Club (dir.), Central Soc. Clin. Research, A.M.A. (cons. council on drugs), So. Med. Assn., Am. Diabetes Assn., Endocrine Soc., Am. Therapeutic Soc. (v.p. 1961, treas. 1962), Constantinian Soc., Paul Dudley White Soc., Soc. for Acad. Achievement (mem. adv. and editorial bd.), Phi Beta Kappa, Sigma Xi. Methodist (ofcl. bd.). Clubs: Skeet and Trap, Internists, University (St. Louis); Marshland Duck. Author: Hypertensive Disease and Clinical Management, 1959; Management of Hypertensive Disease, 1960; also chpt. in Drugs of Choice, 1959, others. Cons. bd. Folia Clinica Internacional. Contbr. articles to profl. Jours. Home: 610 W Polo Dr St Louis MO 63105 Office: Queeny Tower 4989 Barnes Hospital Plaza St Louis MO 63110

EDWARDS, JOSHUA LEROY, physician, educator; b. Jasper, Fla., Aug. 9, 1918; s. Harry L. and Julia B. (Miller) E.; B.S., U. Fla., 1939; M.D., Tulane U., 1943; m. Heane Perrin, July 7, 1953; children—Julia E., Jeane A., Joshua Leroy III. Intern, Bapt. Hosp., New Orleans, 1943-44; practice medicine Lake City, Fla., 1946-48; resident pathology Touro Infirmary, New Orleans, 1948-49; asst. resident lab. pathology N.E. Deaconess Hosp., Boston, 1949-50, chief resident pathology, 1950-51; teaching fellow pathology Harvard Med. Sch., 1950-51; instr. pathology Duke Sch. Medicine, 1951-52, asso. pathology, 1951-52; asst. pathology and microbiology Rockefeller Inst. Med. Research, 1953-55; prof. pathology, chmn. dept. U. Fla. Coll. Medicine, 1955-67; prof. pathology, dir. combined degree program in med. scis. Ind. U., Bloomington, 1967-69, prof., chmn. dept. pathology, Ind. U. Med. Center, Indpls., 1969—. Served with M.C., AUS, 1944- 46. Diplomate Am. Bd. Pathology. Mem. Internat. Acad. Pathology, A.A.A.S., N.Y., Fla. acads. sci., Tissue Culture Assn., Reticuloendothelial Soc., Am., Fla. med. assns., Am. Soc. Exptl. Pathology, Am. Soc. Cell Biology, Phi Beta Kappa, Sigma Xi, Alpha Omega Alpha. Contbr. articles profl. jours. Home: 7601 Morningside Dr Indianapolis IN 46240

EDWARDS, JULIA SPALDING, journalist; b. Louisville, Oct. 6, 1920; d. James P. and Margaret (Wathen) Edwards; B.A., Barnard Coll., 1940; M.S., Columbia, 1942, postgrad. internat. relations, 1966. Reporter, Balt. Sun, 1942-44; re-writeman Chgo. Daily News, 1944-45; corr. to Frankfurt bur. chief Stars and Stripes, Germany, 1946-48; Washington corr. Pulliam Newspapers, 1949-50; editor USIA, Washington, Tokyo, 1951-52; mng. editor Worldwide Press Ser., N.Y.C., 1953-54; pub. information dir. Research Inst. Am., 1955-56; ind. fgn. corr., writer, editor, N.Y.C., 1957-67; dir. World Affairs Bur., Washington, 1968—. Mem. bd. Reform Democrats, N.Y.C., 1953-67. Mem. Overseas Press Club (chmn. Washington com. 1970—), Am. Newspaper Women's Club, Author's Guild. Author: The Occupiers, 1967. Home: 2440 Virginia Av NW Washington DC 20037 Office: Nat Press Bldg Washington DC 20004

EDWARDS, JULIUS HOWARD, orgn. exec.; b. Petersburg, Tenn., Jan. 10, 1914; s. Claude Hardison and Ella (Sowell) E.; student David Lipscomb Coll., Nashville, 1934-36; m. Jean Paschall, June 21, 1939; children—Beverly Ann (adopted), Paula Jane, Jan Howard. With Nashville Pure Milk Co., 1936- 42, Consol. Vultee Aircraft Corp., 1942-45; purchasing agt. V-M Corp., Benton Harbor, Mich., 1945-46, mgr. cost accounting, 1946-47, asst. gen. mgr., 1947-62, 66-71, dir., 1962-71; exec. dir. Area Resources Improvement Council, Benton Harbor, Mich., 1971—. Dep. dir. USOM to Korea, 1962-64; dir. AID Indonesia, 1964-65, dep. dir. Vietnam, 1965-66; exec. dir. Area Resources Improvement Council, 1971—. Active Community Chest, Sch. Bd. Mem. Am. Mgmt. Assn., Financial Execs. Inst., Benton Harbor C. of C. (dir.). Mason. Home: Wildwood Estates Bridgman MI 49106 Office: 777 Riverview Dr Benton Harbor MI 49022

EDWARDS, LENA FRANCES, physician; b. Washington, Sept. 17, 1900; d. Thomas W. and Marie (Cookley) Edwards; B.S., Howard U., 1921, M.D., 1924; m. L. Keith Madison, June 7, 1924; children—Marie S. (Mrs. Victor Metoyer), Edward K., Genevieve A., Thomas A., John J., Paul F. Asst. attending obstetrician Margaret Hauge Maternity Hosp., 1931-54, 65-70; asst. attending gynecologist Jersey City Med. Center, 1949-54; asst. prof. obstetrics and gynecology Howard U. Coll. Medicine, 1954-60; operator St. Joseph's Maternity Clinic, Hereford, Tex., 1960-65; gynecologist Jersey City Women's Job Corps of the Poverty Program; attending obstetrician and gynecologist Freedman Hosp.; participated numerous panels on sex edn. for schs., chs. Bd. dirs. Lona Whippen Home for Unwed Mothers. Named Woman Doctor of the Year, N.J. br. Am. Med. Women's Assn., 1955; recipient Medal of Freedom, 1964. Diplomate Am. Bd. Obstetrics and Gynecology. Fellow Internat. Coll. Surgeons, Am. Coll. Obstetrics and Gynecology; mem. N.J. League Women Voters, Nat. Fedn. Colored Women's Clubs, Delta Sigma Theta. Home: 892 Meyersville Rd Gillette NJ 07933

EDWARDS, LEVERETT, lawyer; b. Cordell, Okla., Jan. 21, 1902; s. Thomas Allison and Rose Catherine (Leverett) E.; LL.B., Univ. Okla., 1926; m. Louise Replogle, Nov. 5, 1929; children—Jamie Louise, Katherine Allison. Admitted to Okla. State bar, 1926, and practiced as asst. atty. gen. Okla., 1926-27; pvt. practice law, Okla. City, 1927-49; mem. State Indsl. Commn., Okla., 1949-50; served as mem. or chmn. of Ry. Emergency Bds. under Ry. Labor Act, 1946-49; mem. Nat. Mediation Bd., chmn., 1952; mem. industry adv. com. on aviation moblzn. Civil Aeros. Bd. Mem. Am., Okla. State, Co. bar Assns., Am. Law Inst., Nat. Acad. Arbitrators, Phi Delta Phi, Phi Delta Theta. Home: 5300 Westbard Av Washington DC 20016 Office: Liberty Nat Bldg Oklahoma City OK 73102 also 1230 16th St NW Washington DC 20036

EDWARDS, LOUIS WARD, Jr., diversified mfg. co. exec.; b. Detroit, July 22, 1936; s. Louis Ward and Sally (Tryke) E.; B.A., Albion Coll., 1958; m. Juanita Krause, Dec. 28, 1963; children—Louis Ward III, Preston Stephen, Alisa Macall. Mgr., Price Waterhouse & Co., C.P.A.'s, Milw., 1958-67; treas. Fuqua Industries, Inc., Atlanta, 1967—. Bd. dirs. Druid Hills Civic Assn. C.P.A., Wis. Mem. Am. Inst. C.P.A.'s, Ga. Soc. C.P.A.'s, Tax Execs. Inst. (treas. 1971). Republican. Home: 1156 Lullwater Rd Atlanta GA 30307 Office: First National Bank Tower Atlanta GA 30303

EDWARDS, MARCIA, former asso. dean univ.; b. El Paso, Tex., Oct. 22, 1901; d. W. Lister and Ella (Pickett) Edwards; A.B., Coll. Puget Sound, 1925, D.Sc. (hon.), 1953; A.M. (fellow Am. Assn. Collegiate Registrars), U. Minn., 1931, Ph.D., 1935. Instr. Coll. of Puget Sound, 1926-27, asst. registrar, 1927-30; research fellow U. Minn., 1931-33, instr. ednl. psychology, 1933-36, asst. prof., 1936-40, asso. prof., 1940-46, prof., 1946—, asst. to dean Coll. Edn., 1938-42, asst. dean, 1942-53, asso. dean, 1953-70, ret., 1970. Mem. Mpls. Citizens' Com. on Pub. Edn., 1951-60. Mem. U. Minn. Alumni Assn. Am., Minn. psychol. assns., Am. Coll. Personnel Assn. (past treas.), Am. Personnel and Guidance Assn., Nat. Vocational Guidance Assn., N.E.A., Nat. Soc. Study Edn., Am. Assn. U. Women, Pi Lambda Theta, Psi Chi. Home: 2349 Valentine Av St Paul MN 55108

EDWARDS, MARION LEE, ins. co. exec.; b. Rogers, Ark., Dec. 13, 1924; s. William B. and Ruby (Baker) E.; B.B.A., Ohio State U., 1949; m. Betty Ann Spannagel, Aug. 20, 1949; children—Julie, Nancy, Bradley. Accountant Nationwide Mut. Ins. Co., Columbus, O., 1949-55; accountant Ohio Casualty Ins. Co., Hamilton, 1955-59, asst. treas., 1960-64, treas., 1964-70; treas., asst. sec. Ohio Casualty Corp., Hamilton, 1970—. Chmn. Civic Adv. Bd. Mercy Hosp.; trustee Hamilton United Community Services, Mercy Hosp.; bd. dirs. Jr. Achievement. Served with AUS, 1943-46. Mem. Ins. Inst. (asso.). Republican. Presbyn. (elder 1969—). Kiwanian (pres. 1965—), Elk. Home: 878 Elizabeth Dr Hamilton OH 45013 Office: 136 N 3d St Hamilton OH 45012

EDWARDS, MARK WILLIAM, educator; b. Dorset, Eng., Sept. 22, 1929; s. Stanley Harold and Carrie (Rose) E.; B.A. in Latin, U. Bristol, 1950, B.A. in Greek, 1953; postgrad. Univ. Coll., London, 1953-54; student Princeton, 1954-55; M.A. in Classics, Bristol (Eng.) U., 1956. Instr., asst. prof. Brown U., Providence, 1955-62; asso. prof., prof. Queens U., Kingston, Ont., Can., 1962-69; prof. Stanford, 1969—, chmn. classics dept., 1970—. Served with Brit. Army, 1950-52. Mem. Am. Philol. Assn., Am. Inst. Archaeology, Soc. for Promotion Hellenic Studies. Office: Classics Dept Stanford U Stanford CA 94305

EDWARDS, MARSHALL HENRY, lawyer; b. Delhi, Ill., June 27, 1902; s. Fred M. and Lora Frances (Terry) E.; L.L.B., U. Ill., 1923; m. Dorothy Johnston, Aug. 11, 1934 (dec. May 1962). Admitted to Fla. bar, 1923; asso. R.B. Huffaker, Bartow, Fla., 1924; mem. Huffaker & Edwards, 1925-40; pvt. practice Bartow, 1940—. Mem. Fed. Farm Credit Board, 1953-63, chmn., 1958; mem. Bartow City Commn., 1936-40, mayor, 1937-40; mem. local bd. SSS, 1948-53; mem. com. civil proc. Fla. bar, 1952-53; pres. Polk. County Nat. Farm Loan Assn.,1934-54, mem. adv. com. and exec. com. Nat. Farm Loan Assn. Mem. Negligence and Compensation Lawyers Assn. Fla. (pres. 1952-53), Am., Fla. bar assns., Am. Law Inst., Theta Chi, Pi Delta Epsilon, Phi Alpha Delta. Methodist. Mason (32, K.T., Shriner), Elk, Kiwanian. Home: 1855 Mariposa St. Bartow FL 33830 Office: PO Box 270 Bartow FL 33830

EDWARDS, MAX NIXON, lawyer; b. Wichita, Kan., Dec. 4, 1921; s. Walter Lee and Jane (Nixon) E.; A.B., Dartmouth, 1947; LL.B., U. Ariz., 1950; m. Pamela Soldwedel, Oct. 21, 1952 (div.); 1 dau., Karen Potter; m. Leona Timko, Dec., 1967. Admitted to N.M. bar, 1950; practiced in Hobbs, 1950, 54- 60; mem. firm Edwards & Reese, 1954-60; asst. dist. atty. 5th Jud. Dist. N.M., 1951-53; gen. counsel N.M. Senate, 1959; asst. to sec. and legislative counsel Dept. Interior, 1961-67, asst. sec. for water quality and research, 1967-69; partner law firm Collier, Shannon, Rill and Edwards, Washington, 1969—. Chmn. Pres.'s Water Pollution Control Adv. Bd., 1968. Adviser Dem. Nat. Com., 1960. Recipient Distinguished Service medal U.S. Dept. Interior, 1967. Mem. Am., Inter-Am., N.M., Ariz. bar assns., Bar Assn. D.C., Bar Assn. U.S. Supreme Ct., Vets Fgn. Wars. Club: National Golf Links of America (Southampton, L.I., N.Y.). Home: 4201 Cathedral Av NW Washington DC 20240

EDWARDS, NORMAN BASIL, army officer; b. Quincy, W.Va., Mar. 2, 1911; s. Norman Alamander and Grace (Phillips) E.; student W.Va. Inst. Tech., 1928-31; B.S., U.S. Mil. Acad., 1935; grad. Command and Gen. Staff Coll., 1942, Armed Forces Staff Coll., 1948, Nat. War Coll., 1954; m. Florence Arden Wigzell, July 5, 1935; children—Arden Dorothy (Mrs. Ray Romani), Norman Bruce, Sandra Ann. Commd 2d lt. U.S. Army, 1935, advanced through grades to maj. gen., 1962; troop assignments, 1935-41; assigned Hdqrs. ETO, London, Eng., 1942-43, Hdqrs. III Corps, Metz, Ardennes, Roer, Remagen Bridge, Ruhr, also Austria, 1944-45, Canadian Arctic, 1946, Hdqrs. Army Ground Forces and Dept. Army Gen. Staff, 1947-50; regtl. comdr. 25th Div. Korea, also mem. UN Armistice Team, 1951-52; assigned Allied Forces So. Europe, Naples, Italy, 1954-57; dir. instrn. Inf. Sch., 1958-59; chief staff Tng. Center, Ft. Ord, Cal., 1960; asst. comdr. 4th Inf. Div., Ft. Lewis, Wash., 1961-62; chief Mil. Assistance Adv. Group, Korea, 1963-64; dep. chief personnel operations Dept. Army, 1965-66; chief staff 6th U.S. Army, San Francisco, 1966-67, ret., 1968; v.p. Coast and So. Fed. Savs. & Loan Assn., Los Angeles, 1968—. Dist. commnr. for Korea, Boy Scouts Am., 1962-63. Decorated D.S.M., Silver Star, Legion of Merit, Bronze Star; Croix de Guerre with gold star (France); Croix de Guerre with palm (Belgium); Croix de Guerre (Luxembourg); Ulchi Distinguished Service medal with gold star (Korea). Baptist. Mason. Author articles. Home: 2275 N Oxford Av Claremont CA 91711 Office: Coast and So Federal Savs & Loan Assn 9th and Hill Sts Los Angeles CA 90014

EDWARDS, PRESLEY WILLIAM, investment banker; b. St. Louis, June 21, 1904; s. B.F. and Flora (Woods) E.; A.B., Westminster Coll., 1925; m. Virginia Barker, Sept. 16, 1926 (dec.); children—Elizabeth W. (Mrs. Raymond E. Collins), Ben F. III, Constance L. (Mrs. Timothy A. Feager) (dec.), Judith S. (Mrs. Jackson P. Bayer); m. 2d, Mary G. Avis, Dec. 22, 1958. Partner A.G. Edwards & Sons, mem. N.Y. Stock Exchange, St. Louis, 1926—, now chmn.; dir. St. Louis Steel Castings Co. Bd. dirs. Covenant Theol. Sem. Home: 3950 Gordon Dr Naples FL 33940 Office: 1 N Jefferson St St Louis MO 63103

EDWARDS, RALPH LIVINGSTONE, television and radio producer, entertainer; b. Merino, Colo.; s. Henry Livingstone and Minnie Mae (Browns) E.; A.B., U. Cal., 1935; m. Barbara Jean Sheldon, Sept. 19, 1939; children—Christine Allison, Gary Livingstone, Lauren Avery. Radio writer, actor, producer, announcer radio sta. KROW, Oakland, Cal., 1929-35, KSFO, Oakland and San Francisco, KFRC, San Francisco, 1935-36; announcer C.B.S., N.Y.C., 1936- 38; announcer 45 weekly radio shows CBS and NBC, N.Y.C., 1938-40; originator, producer, emcee Truth or Consequences, Mr. Hush and Walking Man charity contests radio, 1940-51, Am. Heart Assn. Nationally; emcee, TV and radio show This Is Your Life, 1948-50; producer, emcee, creator NBC-TV show, This is Your Life, 1952—; emcee TV show Truth or Consequences, 1951, TV and radio Ralph Edwards Show, NBC, 1952—; producer, creator Place the Face, CBS-TV; creator, producer NBC-TV show It Could Be You, 1956, ABC-TV show of About Faces, 1959, End of the Rainbow, 1960, Wide Country, 1961, Who in the World, 1962; also actor for the RKO Pictures, movies include: 7 Days Leave, 1945; Radio Stars on Parade, 1947; Bamboo Blonde, 1948; Beat the Band, 1949. Nat. crusade chmn. Am. Cancer Soc. Recipient Eisenhower award (highest E bond salesman award of Treasury Dept.), 1946; named Alumnus of Year, U. Cal., 1965. Bd. dirs. So. Cal. Symphony; chmn. devel. bd. U. Cal. Trustees; devel. bd. Wabash Coll. Mem. Berkeley Fellows U. Cal., Robert Gordon Sproul Assn. (chmn. 1965-66), U. Cal. Alumni Assn. (dir.). Presbyn. Office: 1717 N Highland St Hollywood CA 90028

EDWARDS, RICHARD, mfg. exec.; b. Chgo., May 14, 1909; s. Richard Elbert and Marie (Stuart) E.; A.B., Harvard, 1931; m. Eloise Peek, Jan. 11, 1936; children—Richard Stuart, Burton Peek. With Deere & Co., since 1946, gen. mgr. Yakima, Wash., 1947-52, asst. to v.p. purchasing; acting dir. purchases, Chgo., 1952, v.p., dir. purchases 1953-61, dir., 1953—, treas., 1961—, v.p., 1970—. Served from lt. to comdr. USN, 1941-46. Clubs: Chicago, University (Chgo.); Rock Island (Ill.) Arsenal Golf; Augusta (Ga.) Nat. Golf; Indian Hill (Winnetka, Ill.); Glen View (Golf, Ill.). Home: 20 Forest Rd Davenport IL 52803 Office: Deere & Co Moline IL 61265

EDWARDS, RICHARD AUGUSTUS, Jr., army officer; b. Smithfield, Va., July 26, 1918; s. Richard Augustus and Hattie (Travers) E.; B.A., Va. Mil. Inst., 1939; student Nat. War Coll., 1964-65; m. Nancy Lyle Brown, Mar. 7, 1942; 1 son, Richard Augustus III. Commd. 2d lt. U.S. Army, 1940, advanced through grades to brig. gen., 1968; comdg. officer 4th Missile Command U.S. Army, Pacific, 1965-66; exec. officer, dep. dir. enlisted personnel, Washington, 1966-68; dep. chief staff for personnel and adminstrn., Vietnam, 1968; comdg. gen. I Field Force, Vietnam, 1968-69; dep. chief personnel operations, Washington, 1969, dir. officer personnel, 1969—. Decorated D.S.M., Legion of Merit with 2 oak leaf clusters, Air medal, Bronze Star. Mem. Mil. Order Carabao, Va. Mil. Inst. Alumni Assn. Methodist. Office: Dept Army 2d and V Sts SW Washington DC 20315

EDWARDS, ROBERT COOK, univ. pres.; b. Fountain Inn, S.C., Mar. 25, 1914; s. John T. and Effie (Cook) E.; B.S. in Textile Engring., Clemson Agrl. Coll., 1933; LL.D., The Citadel, 1959, Wofford Coll., 1960; m. Louise Odom, May 30, 1935; children—Robert Cook, Nancy Louise. Supr. quality control lab. Dunean Mill of J.P. Stevens & Co., Inc., Greenville, S.C., 1933-34; designer, then supt. Charles B. Thomas Co., Inc., textile mfg. plant, Red Springs, N.C., 1934-37; supt. weaving Aberfoyle, Inc., Norfolk, Va., 1937-39, plant supt., 1939-42; plant mgr. Abbeville Mills Corp. (S.C.), 1946-48; treas., gen. mgr. Abbeville group Deering-Milliken Mills, 1948-56; v.p. for devel. Clemson U., 1956-58, acting pres., 1958-59, pres., 1959—. Dir., Duke Power Co., Dan River, Inc., Bankers Trust of S.C. Mem. So. Regional Edn. Bd. Served from 2d lt. to maj., AUS, 1942-46. Mem. Am. Legion, Phi Psi, Phi Kappa Phi. Methodist (trustee, steward). Mason (Shriner). Home: Parkway Clemson SC 29631

EDWARDS, ROBERT VAUGHAN, author; b. Rock Springs, Wyo., July 2, 1899; s. Robert A. and Elinor (Vaughan) E.; A.B., Pomona Coll., 1923; m. Dorothy A. Vance, Aug. 6, 1923 (dec. 1933); children—Elinor, Robert; m. 2d, Anne Lorraine Harms, Mar. 11, 1935; m. 3d, Helen Jeffery, June 22, 1963; m. 4th C. Virginia Roberts, September 14, 1967. With Western Concrete Pipe Co., 1924-29; sales mgr. Am. Pipe and Constrn. Co., 1929-41, v.p., 1941-52, exec. v.p., 1952-54, pres. 1954-65, chmn. bd., 1957-67, dir.; dir. Met. Savs. & Loan Assn. Trustee Pomona Coll., 1957—. Mem. Asso. Gen. Contractors, Pomona Coll. Alumni Assn. (past pres.), Beavers (pres. 1965), Am. Legion, Phi Beta Kappa. Mason. Author: Vested Interests and Rising Tide of Government, 1947; Truman's Inheritance, 1952; From a Decade of Stewardship, 1967; Imperium, 1970. Home: 1459 Waverly Rd San Marino CA 91108 Office: 2975 Huntington Dr San Marino CA 91108

EDWARDS, RODERICK YERKES, coast guard officer; b. Phila., Sept. 20, 1909; s. David William and Elizabeth (Yerkes) E.; student Rutgers U., U. N.Y., Am. U., U. San Francisco; m. Rita Thiele, July 10, 1937; children—Roderick Yerkes, David Thiele. With Am. Export Lines, 1927-40; maritime tchr. N.Y. Bd. Edn., 1940-41; insp. hulls Bur. Marine Insp. and Navigation, 1941- 42; commd. lt. USCG, 1942, advanced through grades to rear adm., 1967; chief pub. and internat. affairs, 1966—. U.S. del. Internat. Maritime Consultive Orgn., 1966, vice chmn. com. marine pollution, 1967; chmn. Merchant Marine Council, 1966; mem. Nat. Cargo Bur., 1966, Am. Boat and Yacht Council, 1963. Bd. dirs. Nat. Air and Space Museum. Decorated Legion of Merit, Navy Commendation medal; named hon. citizen Antwerp, Belgium. Clubs: Army-Navy, Nat. Aviation, Propellor (Washington); Commerical (San Francisco). Home: 1600 S Eads St Arlington VA 22202 Office: 400 7th St NW Washington DC 20004

EDWARDS, ROY VERNELL, meat packing co. exec.; b. Altus, Okla., May 19, 1922; s. Robert Flynn and Virgie Lee (Bradford) E.; B.S., Okla. State U., 1946, M.S., 1947; m. Betty Jean Taylor, Sept. 20, 1943; children—Verna, Roy Vernell, Jean, Mary. With Wilson & Co., Inc., Chgo., 1947—, gen. mgr. pork div., 1955- 59, v.p., 1959-65, exec. v.p. and pres. Wilson Meat & Food Products Co., 1965-67, pres., dir. Wilson & Co., 1967—, also chief exec. officer, 1968—. Served to capt., inf. AUS, World War II. Mem. Phi Kappa Phi. Mem. Ch. of Christ. Clubs: Economic, Chicago Athletic Assn., Mid Am. Executive (Chgo.); Olympia Fields (Ill.) Country. Home: 20335 Ithaca Rd Olympia Fields IL 60461 Office: Wilson & Co Inc Prudential Plaza Chicago IL 60601

EDWARDS, RUSSELL, newspaper editor; b. Bklyn., May 11, 1909; s. Cyrus George and Katherine (Donaldson) E.; student St. John's Coll., 1927-28; Bates Coll., 1928-29; m. Martha Joe Verrill, Apr. 5, 1934; children—Priscilla (Mrs. Robert E. Browning), Constance Alden (Mrs. Robert W. Ott); m. 2d, Willette Ockendon Brown, May 24, 1968. Mem. staff N.Y. Times, 1929—, asst. head desk, then head desk obituary, culture and society sect., 1939-54, society editor, 1954—; author numerous feature articles on old New York. Clubs: Silurians, Overseas Press (N.Y.C.). Home: 411 E 57th St New York City NY 10022 Office: 229 W 43d St New York City NY 10036

EDWARDS, SHERMAN, composer-lyricist; b. N.Y.C., Apr. 3, 1919; s. Nathan Harrison and Rae (Rosenblat) E.; B.A. in History, N.Y.U., 1939; postgrad. Cornell U., 1939; m. Ingrid Secretan, May 28, 1950; children—Valerie, Keith. Actor in Pins and Needles, My Sister Eileen; arranger, conductor, pianist for Lisa Kirk, Eddie Fisher, Mindy Carson; pianist jazz concerts, Benny Goodman, Tommy Dorsey, Louis Armstrong; composer, lyricist 1776, 1969. Served with USAAF, 1942-46. Recipient Drama Critics award, 1969, Out Circle award, 1969, Antoinette Perry award, 1969. Mem. A.S.C.A.P., Dramatists Guild, Am. Fedn. Musicians. Composer; Dungaree Doll, 1957; Broken Hearted Melody, 1959; See You in September, 1960; Wonderful! Wonderful!, 1960; Johnny, Get Angry, 1962; See You in September (2), 1963; Wonderful! Wonderful! (2), 1964; Flaming Star, 1965; See You in September (3), 1966; Wonderful! Wonderful! (3). Mem. N.J. Hist. Soc. Address: N Beverwyck Rd Boonton Manor NJ 07005

EDWARDS, THOMAS CUNNINGHAM, Jr., ins. co. exec.; b. N.Y.C., July 22, 1919; s. Thomas Cunningham and Ora (Brian) E.; A.B., U. N.C., 1941; m. Marjorie Clark Peele, Mar. 29, 1941; children—Barbara Creighton, Nancy Cunningham. Agy. asst. N.W. Mut. Co., N.Y.C., 1946-47; asst. sec. Tchrs. Ins. & Annuity Assn. Am., N.Y.C., 1948-50, asst. v.p., 1950-55, v.p., 1955-63, exec. v.p., 1963—; pres. TIAA-CREF, 1966—. Mem. gen. pension com. Nat. Council Chs.; trustee Annuity Fund Congl. Ministers, Stoneleigh-Burnham Sch., Greenfield, Mass. Served to capt. AUS, 1942-45; ETO. Decorated Verdun medal (France). C.L.U. Mem. Am. Soc. C.L.U.'s, Am. Risk and Ins. Assn., Am. Pension Conf., Am. Council Edn., Phi Beta Kappa, Contbr. numerous articles on pensions and ins. to profl. publs. Home: 137 Olmstead Hill Wilton CT 06897 Office: 730 3d Av New York City NY 10017

EDWARDS, THOMAS HARVEY, educator; b. Chilliwack, B.C., Can., Feb. 12, 1924; s. Thomas Maddock and Daisy (Harvey) E.; B.A. with 1st class honors in Physics and Math., U. B.C., 1947, M.A. in Physics, 1948; Ph.D., U. Mich., 1955; m. Ivy Roberta Pronger, June 13, 1946; children—Thomas Mark, Bruce Harvey, Roger Alan, Kenneth Robert. Came to U.S., 1948, naturalized, 1954. Mem. faculty dept. physics Mich. State U., 1954—, asso. prof., 1959-65, prof., 1965—. Served with RCAF, 1943-45. Mem. Am. Phys. Soc., Am. Inst. Physics, Am. Assn. Physics Tchrs., Optical Soc. Am., Sigma Xi. Contbr. profl. jours. Home: 4450 Cordon Dr Williamston MI 48895 Office: Dept Physics Mich State U East Lansing MI 48823

EDWARDS, THOMAS ROBERT, Jr., educator; b. Findlay, O., Oct. 12, 1928; s. Thomas Robert and Helen Louise (Havighurst) E.; B.A., Amherst, 1950; M.A. (Am. Council Learned Socs. fellow), Harvard, 1951, Ph.D., 1956; m. Nancy Mathis, Sept. 3, 1957; children—Sarah Louise, John Morgan. Instr. to asso. prof. English, U. Cal., Riverside, 1956-64; asso. prof. English, Rutgers U., New Brunswick, N.J., 1964-66, prof., 1966—; lit. critic; journalist. Rutgers research fellow, 1967-68. Mem. Modern Lang. Assn., Phi Beta Kappa, Phi Gamma Delta. Author: This Dark Estate: A Reading of Pope, 1963; Imagination and Power, 1971. Home: 735 Belvidere Av Plainfield NJ 07062

EDWARDS, VINCE, (Vincent Edward Zoino), actor; b. Bklyn., July 7, 1928; s. Vincent and Julia Zoino; student Ohio State U., 1946-48, U. Hawaii, 1948, Am. Acad. of Dramatic Arts; m. Kathy Kersh, June 13, 1965 (div. Oct. 1965); 1 dau.; m. 2d, Linda Ann Foster, 1967. Participated in the Honolulu Community Theater, and also the U. of Hawaii Players; debut as chorus boy in Broadway musical, High Button Shoes; toured with road company Come Back Little Sheba; appeared TV shows including Gen. Electric Theater, Studio One, Alfred Hitchcock Presents, The Untouchables; motion pictures include Mr. Universe, Sailor Beware, Hiawatha, Rogue Cop, Serenade, Three Faces of Eve, Hit and Run, Scavengers, Night Holds Terror, City of Fear, Murder by Contract, The Killing, Too Late Blues; actor TV series Ben Casey, ABC-TV, 1961-66. Address: care Diamond Artists 8400 Sunset Blvd Hollywood CA 90069*

EDWARDS, WALTER ALDEN, corp. exec.; b. Logansport, Ind., Mar. 15, 1913; s. Edwin Jathan and Edna Mae (DeWitt) E.; student Purdue U., 1931-32; B.S., Ind. U., 1937; m. Elizabeth Knowlson, July 17, 1943; children—DeWitt, Timothy. Asst. to exec. v.p. Pullman-Standard Car Mfg. Co., Chgo., 1937-42, sales exec., 1945-50; mgr. govt.-industry relations dept. Owens-Illinois Glass Co., Toledo, 1950-53, Washington rep., 1954-58; dep. dir. containers and packaging div., spl. asst. to dir. NPA, also asst. adminstr. Bus. and Def. Services Adminstrn., U.S. Dept. Commerce, 1953-54, dep. asst. sec. commerce for domestic affairs, 1958-61, asst. sec. of commerce, 1961; exec. Chrysler Corp., Washington 1961—. Served as lt. comdr. USNR, 1942-45. Clubs: University (Chgo.); Army and Navy, Congressional Country, Burning Tree (washington). Home: Millboro Springs VA 24460 Office: 1700 K St NW Washington DC 20006

EDWARDS, WALTER MEAYERS, editor, photographer; b. Leigh-on-Sea, Essex, Eng., July 21, 1908; s. Walter James and Lillian Emma (Meayers) E.; student Lindisfarne Coll., Westcliff, Essex, Eng., 1917-26; m. Mary Woodward Worrall, Feb. 11, 1937. Came to U.S., 1930, naturalized, 1936. Staff Paris bur. N.Y. Times- Wide World Photos, 1926-27; with Topical Press Agy., London, 1927-29, Harris & Ewing, photographers, Washington, 1930-31; sec.-treas. Pioneer Air Transport Operators Assn., N.Y.C., Washington, 1931-33; illustrations staff Nat. Geog. mag., 1933-54, illustrations editor, 1955-58, fgn. editorial staff, 1958-62, chief pictorial research div., 1963—. Recipient Americanism medal D.A.R., 1968; Picture of the Year in mag. sports N.P.P.A., 1969. Christian Scientist. Mason. Clubs: Nat. Press, Overseas Writers (Washington); Explorers (N.Y.C.); Sierra (San Francisco); Alpine of Canada. Author of articles. Home: 6901 Armat Dr Bethesda MD 20034 Office: Nat Geog Soc 17th and M Sts Washington DC 20036

EDWARDS, WILBUR SHIELDS, pub. co. exec.; b. Charlotte, N.C., July 25, 1916; s. William James and Amy (Shields) E.; B.A., Davidson Coll., 1937; postgrad Yale Div. Sch., 1938; m. Jane Holman, Mar. 16, 1940; children—Ashton S., William J., Alisa Carroll. With CBS, 1938-56; v.p. Ency. Brit. Films, Inc., 1956-62, mem. adv. bd., 1962—; pres., dir., mem. exec. com. F.E. Compton & Co., Chgo., 1962—; exec. v.p. Ency. Brit. Ednl. Corp., 1966—, 1967—. Trustee, Shimer Coll., Mt. Carroll, Ill.; dir. exec. com. Asso. Colls. Ill. Presbyn. (stated clk.). Home: W County Line Rd Barrington IL 60010 Office: 425 N Michigan Av Chicago IL 60611

EDWARDS, WILLARD, newspaperman; b. Chgo., Dec. 7, 1902; s. Evan William and Mary (Kilday) E.; student St. Ignatius Acad., 1918-21; m. Leila Sullivan, Jan. 17, 1931; 1 son, Lee Willard. Reporter, City News Bur., Chgo., 1921; with Chicago Tribune, 1925—, became N.Y. corr., 1934, mem. Washington bureau, 1935—. Republican. Columnist, Capital Views, 1967- -. Home: 101 4th St SE Washington DC 20003 Office: 1750 Pennsylvania Av NW Washington DC 20006

EDWARDS, WILLARD ELDRIDGE, originator The Perpetual Calendar; b. Chatham, Mass., Dec. 11, 1903; s. Arthur Robbins and Mabel Hallett (Eldridge) E.; student Mass. Inst. Tech., 1922-26; B.S., U. Okla., 1929; M.S., Litt. D., Jackson Coll., 1960, M.A., 1961; m. Dorothy L. Shiell, June 13, 1942; children—Willard Eldridge, Annabelle (dec.), Arthur, Geraldine. Originator The Perpetual Calendar, 1919, officially endorsed by Legislature, Hawaii, 1943, Commonweatlh Mass., 1952, introduced in each Congress, 1943—, in 350 cities in 100 fgn. countries, on 7 world tours 1928, 52, 56, 60, 62, 66, 68; proposed by Congl. resolution and bill as ofcl. calendar U.S., also for adoption by all nations; writer, lectr., 1922—; research engr. Radio Corp. Am., N.Y.C., 1926-28; elec. engr. Alexander Aircraft Co., Colorado Springs, 1929; radio engr. trans- Pacific radio-telephony Am. Tel. & Tel. Co., Denver, also Dixon, Cal., 1929-33; radio engr. radio stas., KFI-KECA, 1933-40; elec. engr. Lockheed Aircraft Co., Burbank, Cal., 1940-41; elec. engr. 9th region CAA, Honolulu, 1946-49, 14th Naval Dist., Pearl Harbor, 1949-65; ret., 1965; corrosion cons., 1953—. Served as lt. comdr. USN, 1942-46, electronics engr. Pacific Islands, USN, ret. Registered professional engr. Mem. Internat. Platform Assn., Soc. Am. Mil. Engrs., I.E.E.E., A.A.A.S., Nat. Assn. Corrosion Engrs., Hawaiian Astron. Soc., Honolulu Meml. Soc. (pres.), Sigma Chi, Tau Omega, Alpha Sigma Delta, Alpha Eta Rho. Mason (32). Clubs: Kokua, Toastmasters, Pearl Harbor Officers, Wollaston (Mass.) Yacht, Los Serranos (Cal.) Country. Author: The Perpetual Calendar, 1943; American Samoa, 1949; For Perpetual Generations, 1951; How to Count the Years, 1953; Origin of Christian Time, 1955; Underground Corrosion and Cathodic Protection, 1956; Time and the Calendar, 1961; Logic in a Sea of Unreason, 1964. Contbr. profl. publs. Licensed comml. airplane pilot. Home and Office: 1434 Punahou St Honolulu HI 96822

EDWARDS, WILLIAM DAVID, corp. exec.; b. Lancaster, Pa., 1926; ed. Franklin and Marshall Coll., 1950. Treas. Mohasco Industries, Inc. Home: 2 Eltinge Pl Scotia NY 12302 Office: 57 Lyon St Amsterdam NY 12010*

EDWARDS, WILLIAM F., food mfg. co. exec.; b. Tampa, Fla., Sept. 26, 1916; s. La Marcus Colquitt and Berta (Ferguson) E.; student Va. Mil. Inst., 1934-35; m. Louise Hinson, July 1, 1943; children—Louise Ferguson, Mary Lynn. With Lykes Pasco Packaging Co., and predecessor, 1937—, now pres.; pwner Biledco. Vice chmn. Fla. Citrus Commn.; v.p. Fla. Canners Assn.; past pres. Nat. Assn. Frozen Food Packers. Served to 1st lt. USAAF, 1942-45. Home: 312 E Southview Av Dade City FL 33525 Office: PO Box 97 Dade City FL 33525

EDWARDS, WILLIAM F., educator; b. Emery, Utah, Apr. 26, 1906; s. William Foster and Rodelia (Williams) E.; B.S., Brigham Young U., 1928; M.S., N. Y. U., 1930, D.C.S., 1937; m. Catherine Eyring, Sept. 9, 1929; children—Carolyn Clive, Weston, Robert, Mildred (Mrs. Evans), Catherine (Mrs. Poelman), William. Investment analyst Bank of Manhattan, N.Y.C., 1929-35, Goldman, Sacks & Co., N.Y.C., 1935-39; partner Naess & Thomas, N.Y.C., 1940-45; economist for investment trusts, N.Y.C., 1946-50; dean coll. commerce, v.p. finance and bus. adminstrn. Brigham Young U., 1951-57, Driggs prof. finance, 1970—; sec. finance to first presidencey Ch. of Jesus Christ of Latter-day Saints, 1957-60; prof. banking and finance U. Utah, 1960-69; exec. v.p., dir. 1st Security Investment Co., Salt Lake City, 1960-70; v.p. First Security Bank, Utah; dir. Bonneville Internat. Corp. Trustee Utah Found. Home: 84 Marrcrest S Provo UT 84601 Office: 11 E 1st South Salt Lake City UT 84102

EDWARDS, WILLIAM HENRY, lawyer; b. Providence, Dec. 5, 1898; s. Sceber and Sarah Estella (Gurney) E.; grad. Moses Brown Sch., 1915; A.B., Brown U., 1919, LL.D., 1965; J.D. cum laude, Harvard, 1921; D.H.S. (hon.), Providence Coll., 1967; LL.D., U. R.I., 1967; m. Mabel Potter, June 18, 1921 (dec. Jan. 1969); children—Knight, Louise (Mrs. Charles E. Saul); m. 2d, Mary Rita McGinn, Sept. 8, 1969. Admitted to R.I. bar, 1922, Mass. bar, 1943, also U.S. Supreme Ct., other U.S. cts.; practiced in Providence, 1922-68; asso. Edwards & Angell, 1922-29, mem., 1929-68, counsel, 1969—. Mem. R.I. Juvenile and Dist. Ct. Commn. 1939; chmn. bd. appeal R.I. SSS, 1940-42; mem. Family Ct. Commn., 1956-58; chmn. R.I. selection com. Rhodes Scholarship candidates, 1957-68; chmn. Commn. Revision R.I. Constn., 1961-63. Pres. United Fund R.I., 1955-56; nat. bd. dirs. Planned Parenthood-World Population, 1965-71, mem. bd. R.I. affiliate; R.I. co-chmn. Nat. Conf. Christians and Jews; hon. dir. Urban Coalition R.I., R.I. Philharmonic Orch.; sec. R.I. Sch. Design, 1931-68, trustee, 1933-68, life trustee emeritus, 1968—; trustee, past pres. Providence Lying-In Hosp.; trustee Vassar Coll., 1935-43, Brown U., 1938-44; chmn. bd. trustees Moses Brown Sch., 1953- 57. Served with U.S. Army, 1918; with USNR, 1942-45; ret. lt. comdr. Res. (Fellow Am. Bar Found.; mem. Am., R.I. (pres. 1958-59, exec. com. 1930-33, 1956-60), Mass. bar assns., Am. Law Inst., Am. Coll. Trial Lawyers, Assn. Bar City N.Y., Am. Judicature Soc., Council Fgn. Relations, Harvard Law Rev. Assn., Am. Civil Liberites Union, Selden Soc. Nat. Municipal Leaque (mem. council), Phi Beta Kappa (pres. R.I. 1955-57), Alpha Delta Phi. Democrat. Conglist. Clubs: University, Art, Agawam, Turk's Head, Hope (Providence); Century, Harvard (N.Y.C.); Army and Navy (Washington). Contbr. articles various publs. and book reviews. Home: 154 Arlington Av Providence RI 02906 Office: 15 Westminster St Providence RI 02903

EEKMAN, THOMAS ADAM, educator, Slavist; b. Middelharnis, Holland, May 20, 1923; s. Thomas Adam and Anna (de Kruyff) E.; M.A., U. Amsterdam (Holland), 1946, Ph.D., 1951; m. Tine de Jong, May 2, 1946; children—Menno, Roeland, Ivo, Milja. Came to U.S., 1966. Research asst. Russian Inst., Amsterdam U., 1948-55, lectr. Slavic langs. at univ., 1955-60, asst. prof., 1960-66; vis. prof. U. Cal. at Los Angeles, 1960-61, prof. Slavic langs., 1966—, chmn. dept., 1968—. Decorated Order Yugoslav Flag, 1954. Mem. Western Slavic Assn., philol. Assn. Pacific Coast (pres. 1971). Humanist. Contbr. profl. jours. Editor: Anton Cechov, 1860-1960, 1960. Office: U Cal Los Angeles CA 90024

EELLS, HOWARD PARMELEE, Jr., refractories exec.; b. Cleve., Aug. 25, 1892; s. Howard P. and Alice Maud (Stager) E.; student Milton (Mass.) Acad.; A.B., Williams, 1915; m. Adele Chisholm, June 7, 1919. With Central Nat. Bank and Superior Savs. & Trust Co., Cleve., 1915; in accounting dept. Dolomite Products Co., 1916; with Basic Inc., and predecessor cos. 1919—, as v.p. and gen. mgr., now chmn., also dir. co., chmn. various subsidiary cos. Mem. Troop A, N.G., Cav., Mexican Border Service, 1916-17, First Officers Training Camp, Ft. Benjamin Harrison, Ind., 1917; 2d lt. F.A. U.S. Army, 1917-19; served in Eng., France and Germany with 149th F.A., 67th F.A. Brigade, 42d (Rainbow) Div., 1918-19. Awarded three Gold Chevrons. Trustee Mus. Arts Assn., Lake View Cemetery Assn. Western Res. Hist. Assn., Home: 13901 Shaker Blvd Cleveland OH 44120 Office: Hanna Bldg Cleveland OH 44115

EELLS, JOHN SHEPPARD, Jr. educator; b. San Francisco, Mar. 31, 1906; s. John Shepard and Marion (Coffin) E.; grad. Thacher Sch., 1924; B.A., Yale, 1928; J.D., Stanford, 1931; M.A., U. Cal., 1939, Ph.D., 1943; m. Juliet Guion Oakes, July 30, 1938; children—Guion Oakes, Marion. Admitted to Cal. bar, 1932; asso. Orrick, Palmer & Dahlquist, San Francisco, 1931-35; faculty mem. Thacher Sch., 1935-38, Pomona Coll., 1943-44, U. Chgo., 1944-45; prof. English, Beloit Coll., 1945-55, Winthrop Coll., 1955—; Distinguished prof., 1967—, chmn. honors council, 1960—, faculty rep. on bd. trustees. Mem. Modern Lang. Assn., So. Atlantic Modern Lang. Assn., Am. Assn. U. Profs., Cal. State Bar, Am. Soc. for Psychial Research, Phi Beta Kappa, Phi Kappa Phi. Clubs: Elizabethan (Yale); Caxton (Chgo.); Rock Hill Country. Author: The Touchstones of Matthew Arnold. Contbr. Kenyon Rev., others. Home: 623 Meadowbrook Lane Rock Hill SC 29730

EFFERSON, JOHN NORMAN, coll. ofcl.; b. Holden, La., Nov. 18, 1912; s. Whitney H. and Gladys (Musselman) E.; B.S., La. State U., 1934; M.S., Cornell U., 1936, Ph.D., 1938; m. Ruth Mansinger, Dec. 22, 1939; children—John W., Elizabeth, Sarah A. Undergrad. instr. agronomy La. State U., Baton Rouge, 1932-33, prof. agrl. econs., research economist, 1938-54, dir. agr. expt. sta., 1954-56, dean Coll. Agr., 1956—, now vice chancellor; instr. vocational agr., Welsh, La., 1933-34; research asst. agrl. econs. Cornell U., 1935-38, vis. prof. agrl. econs., 1940-41; agr. tour, study in Europe, 1938; internat. commodity specialist rice and sugar Dept. Agr., 1948, 49; food studies 45 countries, Asia, Africa, Europe, Central Am., S.AM.; lectr. internat. problems, 1948-51; econs. cons. Govt. Venezuela. Mem. postwar planning com. Nat. Land Grant Colls.; mem. Pres. Kennedy's task force on agrl. policy, 1961; board cons. Rockefeller Found., mem. found.'s study of diversification in Malaya, 1962, agr., Venezuela, 1963; cons. AID, El Salvador, 1964, agrl. adviser in British Guiana, 1965; special cons. studies agrl. devel. in Colombia and Venezuela, Ford Found., 1964; AID study of N.E. Thailand, 1965; Ford Found. study edn. in Malaysia, 1966; Nat. Acad. Sci. Com. on P.R., 1966; Ford Found. study agr. edn., Philippines, 1967, study rice marketing, Pakistan, 1968-71; AID study agr., Nicaragua, 1967. Trustee Agrl. Devel. Council, Rockefeller Bros. panel on econs. and social policy. Mem. Am. Farm Econ. Assn., Internat. Assn. Agrl. Economists, Am. Sugar Technologist Assn., Phi Kappa Phi, Alpha Zeta, Alpha Tau Alpha. Author: Principles of Farm Accounting, 1942; Farm Management, 1942; Farm Records and Accounts, 1949; The Principles of Farm Management, 1952; The Production and Marketing of Rice, 1954; also expt. sta. bulls., research circulars; contbr. profl. jours. Home: 5804 Boone Dr Baton Rouge LA 70808

EFFINGER, CECIL, educator, composer; b. Colorado Springs, Colo., July 22, 1914; s. Stanley Smith and Lucy (Graves) E.; A.B. in Math., Colo. Coll., 1935, Mus.D. (hon.), 1959; m. Corinne Ann Lindberg, June 14, 1968; children by previous marriage—Elizabeth Effinger (Mrs. Thomas M. Jones), Gove Effinger. Instr. math. Colorado Springs High Sch., 1936; instr. music Colo. Coll., 1936-41, asst. prof., 1946-48; instr. music Colo. Sch. for Blind, 1939-41; 1st oboist Denver Symphony, 1937-41; music editor Denver Post, 1946-48; asso. prof. music U. Colo., Boulder, 1948-56, prof., 1956—, faculty research lectr., 1955, faculty fellow, 1969-70; pres. Music Print Corp. Served with USAAF, 1941-46. Presser scholar, 1931; Cooke Daniel lectr. Denver Art Mus., 1957; recipient Stoval prize in composition Am. Conservatory, Fontainbleau, France, 1939, Naumburg Recording award, 1959; Gov.'s award in arts and humanities, 1971. Mem. A.S.C.A.P., Am. Fedn. Musicians, Sigma Chi, Tau Beta Sigma, Phi Mu Alpha, Pi Kappa Lambda, Delta Omicron. Composer numerous compositions, 1937—, more important being: Little Symphony No. 1, 1945; Symphony No. 5, 1958; Cello Suite, 1945; Quartet No. 5, 1963; Symphony for Chorus and Orchestra, 1952; The Glorious Day is Here, 1955; Set of Three for Chorus and Brass, 1961; Four Pastorales for Oboe and Chorus, 1962; Cyrano de Bergerac (opera), 1965; The Invisible Fire, 1957; Paul of Tarsus, 1968; The St. Luke Christmas Story, 1953, Inventor Musicwriter; designer Tempowatch. Home: 2620 Lafayette Dr Boulder CO 80303

EFFINGER, ROBERT CRAIG, ret. banker; b. Staunton, Va., May 24, 1890; s. John Frederick and Fannie Strother (Smith) E.; B.S., U. Va., 1914; m. Anne Turley, July 30, 1923; 1 son, Robert Craig. Cons. economist and statistician, 1919- 26; with Irving Trust Co., N.Y.C., 1927-54, v.p., 1931-54, ret. Enlisted U.S. Army, 1917, served 1st lt. Gen. Staff and Am. Commn. to Negotiate Peace. A.E.F., 1918-19, disch. rank capt., 1919. Mem. Zeta Psi. Episcopalian. Author: ABC of Investing, 1947. Home: Staunton VA 24401

EFFLER, DONALD BRIAN, surgeon; b. N.Y.C., Aug. 15, 1915; s. Louis Robert and Marie (Kennelly) E.; student St. John's Prep. Sch.; A.B., U. Mich., 1937, M.D., 1941; m. Joanna Stemplinski, Oct. 25, 1943; children—Gretchen Marie, Donald Brian, Brian Louis. Postgrad. surg. tng. Walter Reed Gen. Hosp., Washington, George Washington U. Med. Sch., Hosp. Good Samaritan, Los Angeles, 1945-47; postgrad. surg. tng. Cleve. Clinic Found., 1947-48, chief dept. thoracic surgery, 1949—. Served as maj. M.C., AUS, 1942-47. Diplomate Am. Bd. Surgery, Am. Bd. Thoracic Surgery. Fellow A.C.S.; mem. Am. Assn. Thoracic Surgeons, Soc. Vascular Surgeons, Central Surg. Assn., Internat. Cardiovascular Soc., Innominatum Soc., Cleve. Surg. Soc., A.M.A., Am. Surg. Assn. Home: 20001 S Woodland St Cleveland OH 44120 Office: 2020 E 93d St Cleveland OH 44106

EFRON, SAMUEL, lawyer; b. Lansford, Pa., May 6, 1915; s. Abraham and Rose (Kaduchin) E.; B.A., Lehigh U., 1935; LL.B., Harvard, 1938; m. Hope Bachrach Newman, Apr. 5, 1941; childrenMarc Fred, Eric Michael. Admitted to Pa. bar, 1938, D.C. bar, 1949, N.Y. bar, 1967; atty. forms and regulations div., also registration div. SEC, 1939-40, Office Solicitor, Dept. Labor, 1940-42; asst. chief real and personal property sect. Office Alien Property Custodian, 1942-43; chief debt claims sect., also asst. chief claims br. Office Alien Property, Dept. Justice, 1946-51; asst. gen. counsel internat. affairs Dept. Def., 1951-53, cons., 1953-54; partner firm Surrey, Karasik, Gould & Efron, Washington, 1954-61; exec. v.p. Parsons & Whittemore, Inc., N.Y.C., 1961-68; now partner Arent, Fox, Kintner, Plotkin & Kahn, Washington. Served to lt. USNR, 1943-46. Mem. Am., Fed., Inter-Am. bar assns., Am. Soc. Internat. Law, Assn. Bar City N.Y., Bar Assn. D.C., Phi Beta Kappa. Clubs: Army-Navy, Capitol Hill, Harvard, Internat., Nat. Press, Nat. Aviation, Fed. Bar (Washington); Harvard, Lehigh, Lotos (N.Y.C.). Author: Creditors Claims Under the Trading with the Enemy Act, 1948; Foreign Taxes on United States Expenditures, 1954; Offshore Procurement and Industrial Mobilization, 1955. Home: 3537 Ordway St NW Washington, DC 20016. Office: Fed Bar Bldg Washington DC 20006

EFROYMSON, ROBERT ABRAHAM, business exec.; b. Indpls., Sept. 27, 1905; s. Gustave A. and M. (Wallenstein) E.; A.B., Harvard, 1926, LL.B., 1929; LL.D., Butler U., 1969; m. Dorothy Falneder, Jan. 3, 1936 (dec. 1957); children—Gustave A., Daniel R., Mary Ann; m. 2d, Anna Thomas Richardson, Sept. 25, 1965. Practice law, Indpls., 1929-42; exec. v.p., later pres., Real Silk Hosiery Mills, Inc., 1945; dir. Lincoln Nat. Life Ins. Co., Ind. Nat. Bank. Chmn. bd. trustees Indpls. Found.; pres. William E. English Found.; bd. dirs. United Fund Indpls., Jewish Welfare Fedn. Indpls.; chmn. Indpls. Housing Authority; Served with AUS, 1942-45. Home: 502 Buckingham Dr Indianapolis IN 46208 Office: 611 N Park Av Indianapolis IN 46204

EGAN, CHARLES ROBERT, art dealer; b. Phila., June 29, 1911; s. Christopher and Mary (Burke) E.; ed. pvt. studies; m. Gertrude Lennon, Jan., 1928. (dec. 1940); children—Robert Charles; m. 2d, Teresa McNamara, Mar., 1951; 1 son, Kevin. Work with N.Y.C. art dealers, 1935-45; owner Egan Gallery, N.Y.C., 1945—; exhibitor works of contemporary artists. Mem. Internat. Platform Assn. Club: Artists. Home: 179 E 79th St New York City, NY 10021. Office: 41 E 57th St New York City NY 10022

EGAN, DANIEL, clergyman; b. N.Y.C., June 18, 1915; s. Thomas Joseph and Mary (Bierne) E.; A.B., Cath. U. Am. 1941, M.A., 1945. Joined Graymoor Franciscans, 1936, ordained priest Roman Cath. Ch., 1945; assigned Negro mission So. U.S., 1947-48, preaching missions Eastern U.S., 1949-59; originated Teen-Age Missions for Am. youth, 1949; founder Village Haven, half-way house for female drug addicts, N.Y.C., 1963; founder, dir. New Hope Manor, live-in therapeutic community for female addicts, Graymoor, Garrison, N.Y., 1970—; known as Junkie priest. Mem. White House Conf. on Youth, 1950, White House Conf. on Drugs, 1962. Address: Graymoor Garrison NY 10524

EGAN, DOUGLAS SCHMELZEL, ship broker; b. Seattle, Oct. 21, 1899; s. Henry and Gertrude Douglas (Hakes) E.; student U. Wash., 1919-23; m. Dorothy Clementine Evans, Jan. 22, 1930; children—Douglas Schmelzel, David Evans Lockwood, Mary Josephine (Mrs. David L. Kilbourn). In lumber export bus., 1924; steamship agt., freight and chartering broker, 1925-30; marine survey, cargo inspection, 1930-32; freight agt., marine supt., operating mgr. Gen. Steamship Corp., Ltd., 1932-40; chief fgn. trade div. field service, U.S. Dept. Commerce, Los Angeles, Seattle, N.Y.C., 1945-57, 60- 63, regional coordinator Office Emergency Readiness Planning, 1960-62; comml. attache Am. embassy, Rio de Janeiro, Brazil, 1957-60; mng. owner Seawest Co., ship brokerage. Spl. trade cons. U.S. Dept. Commerce, to trade fairs in Utrecht, Milan, Paris. Commodore, Seattle area Sea Scouts council Boy Scouts Am., 1936-40. Served from lt. (s.g.) to comdr. USNR, 1940-45; CBI. Mem. Mil. Order World Wars, Edmonds C. of C. (pres., mem. bd. trustees), Pan Xenia. Episcopalian. Clubs: Rio de Janeiro Yacht; Propeller (Seattle); Driftwood Key; Edmonds Yacht. Home: 715 Hanna Park Rd Edmonds WA 98020 Office: Seawest Co PO Box 2 Edmonds WA 98020

EGAN, F.E., advt. agy. exec. Sr. v.p. Brother-D.P. and Co., Detroit. Office: Gen Motors Bldg Detroit MI 48202*

EGAN, JOHN F., investment banker; b. Oakland, Cal., 1909; ed. St. Mary's Coll., 1928. Pres., dir. First California Co.; dir. Berkeley Brass Foundry Co. Home: 115 Sandringham Rd Piedmont CA 94611 Office: 300 Montgomery St San Frncisco CA 94104*

EGAN, JOHN TAYLOR, architect, ex-govt. ofcl.; b. New York City, Nov. 27, 1890; s. John Joseph and Mary (Godley) E.; ed. Columbia Sch. of Architecture, 1910-14; m. Alma Murphy, June 1, 1927; children—Catherine, Adrian. Gen. practice of architecture with N.Y. architects, 1914-18, 19- 22; registered architect, N.Y. State, 1922; pvt. practice in architecture, 1922-35; sr. architect, Farm Security Adminstrn., 1935-38; prin. housing project planner, U.S. Housing Authority, 1938-39; regional dir. for New York, Fed. Pub. Housing Authority (formerly U.S. Housing Authority), 1939-44, asst. commr. for project management, 1944-47; asst. commr. for program operations, Pub. Housing Adminstrn. (formerly Fed. Pub. Housing Authority), 1947, commr., 1948-53; became member Holden, Egan, Wilson and Corser, architects and planners, 1954; now retired from architectural practice. Served USAAF, 1918. Mem. A.I.A., Nat. Assn. Housing and Redevelopment Ofcls., John Carroll Soc. Democrat. Roman Catholic. Home: 5142 Newport Av Glen Cove MD 20016

EGAN, RICHARD LEO, educator; b. Omaha, Dec. 27, 1917; s. George Leo and Mary V. (Shearer) E.; B.S. in Medicine, Creighton U., 1938, M.D., 1940; m. Alice Larsen, May 1, 1943; children—Katherine Ruth, Richard George. Mem. faculty Creighton U. Sch. Medicine, Omaha, 1941-71, asso. prof. medicine, 1953- 69, prof. medicine, 1969-71, dean, 1959-70, asst. to pres. for health scis., 1970-71; asst. dir. dept. undergrad. med. edn. A.M.A., Chgo., 1971—. Mem. exec. com. health council United Community Services Omaha, 1956-66, chmn., 1958-60. Mem. Am. (bd. dirs. 1962-68), Neb. (bd. dirs., exec. com. 1957-70, sec. 1958, pres. 1960-61) heart assns., Am., Neb. (ho. dels. 1954-71) med. assns., Assn. Am. Med. Colls., Omaha-Douglas County Med. Soc. (exec. bd. 1958-60), Am. Assn. History of Medicine, Health Planning Council of Midlands (mem. exec. com. adv. council 1969-71), U.S. Catholic Conf. (mem. com. health affairs 1968-71), Alpha Omega Alpha. Home: 323 Cottage Lane Glen Ellyn IL 60137

EGAN, VINCENT JOSEPH, journalist; b. Toronto, Ont., Can., July 23, 1921; s. James Aloysius and Margaret (Ahearn) E.; B.A., U. Toronto, 1951, M. Commerce, 1955; m. Margaret Mary Maley, Apr. 23, 1962. Asst. editor Financial Post, Toronto, 1952-61; asst. to pres. Toronto Stock Exchange, 1961-62; financial columnist Globe and Mail, Toronto, 1962-68; financial editor Toronto Telegram, 1968—. Served with Royal Can. Navy, 1942-46. Decorated War medal, Can. Vol. Service medal. Roman Catholic. Club: Ticker (Toronto). Author: Making Money In The Market, 1955. Home: 50 Rolph Rd Toronto Ontario Canada Office: 440 Front St W Toronto Ontario Canada

EGAN, WILLIAM ALLEN, gov. Alaska; b. Valdez, Alaska, Oct. 8, 1914; s. William Edward and Cora (Allen) E.; grad. high sch., Valdez; LL.D., Alaska Meth. U.; m. Neva McKittrick, Nov. 16, 1940; 1 son, Dennis William. Mem. Ho. of Reps., Alaska Ty., 1941, 43, 47, 49, 51, Senate, 1953, 55; del., pres. Alaska Constl. Conv., 1955-56; Tennessee Plan senator to Washington, to promote statehood for Alaska, 1956-58; gov. Alaska, 1959- 66, 70—; dist. mgr. Equitable Life Assurance, 1967-70. Mayor, Valdez, 1946, mem. City Council, 1937—; chmn. Western Governors' Conf., 1961-62. Mem. Pioneers of Alaska, V.F.W., Am. Legion. Address: Gov's Office Pouch A Juneau AK 99801

EGAN, WILLIAM JOHN, physician; b. Hurley, Wis., Oct. 30, 1892; s. Timothy Francis and Mary (Murray) E.; B.S., U. of Mich., 1914, M.D., 1916; m. Viola Forster, Sept. 25, 1919; children—William John, James Forster, Vi Egan (Mrs. Richard A. Candee). Practice of internal medicine, 1919—; intern, Milw. Hosp., 1916-17; fellow Mayo Clinic; staff mem. Milw. Hosp., Columbia Hosp., Milwaukee Co. Hosp.; asst. prof. internal medicine, Marquette U., 1919-66; asso. prof. internal medicine emeritus, 1966—; former mem. bd. control Nat. Wholesale Druggists Assn.; chmn. Crandon Drug Co., Miami, Fla.; pres. Yahr-Lange Wholesale Drugs, Milw., La Crosse, Wis., Rockford, Ill. Former chmn. Milw. chpt. A.R.C. (dir. blood bank, 1944; exec. com. 1934—); former mem. bd. govs., Am. Nat. Red Cross, 1946; vice chmn. Milw. Safety Commn. Served as capt. Med. Res. Corps Red Cross, U.S.A. Base Hosp. No. 22 A.E.F., France, 1918-19. Hon. member faculty U. Guatemala, 1937. Mem. A.C.P., Am. Bd. Internal Medicine, A.M.A., Am. Rheumatism Assn., Wis. (councilor), Milwaukee Co. med. Socs., Wis. Rheumatism Assn., Milw. Acad. Medicine, Milw. Soc. Internists, Phi Rho Sigma, Alpha Omega Alpha, Am. Legion, Mil. Order of Fgn. Wars, Mil. Order of World War Officers. Roman Catholic. K.C. Clubs: Milwaukee, City. Author med. publs. and papers personnel mgmt. Home: 2601 Wahl Av Milwaukee WI 53211 Office: 525 E Wells St Milwaukee WI 53202

EGBERT, DONALD DREW, educator, color photographer; b. Norwalk, Conn., May 12, 1902; s. George Drew and Kate Estelle (Powers) E.; A.B., Princeton 1924, M.F.A., 1927; m. Virginia Grace Wylie, Aug. 9, 1946. Mem. faculty Princeton 1929—, prof. art, archaeology, architecture, 1946-70, Butler prof. history architecture, 1968-70, prof. emeritus, 1970—, Am. Civilization Program, 1942-70, acting chmn., 1943-44; lectr. Bryn Mawr Coll., 1930; one-man shows Princeton Univ. Library, George Eastman House, Rochester, N.Y., 1958. Fellow (life) Met. Mus. Art. Recipient Haskins medal, Mediaeval. Acad., 1943. Fellow International Inst. Arts and Letters; mem. Soc. Am. Studies, Mediaeval Acad., Soc. Archtl. Historians, Société Française d'Archeologie, Am. Acad. Polit. and Social Sci., Am. Soc. for Aesthetics, Coll. Art Assn., Am. Hist. Assn., Acad. Polit. Sci., Renaissance Soc. Am., Phi Beta Kappa. Author: The Tickhill Psalter and Related MSS., 1940; Princeton Portraits, 1947; Socialism and American Art, 1968; Social Radicalism and the Arts, Western Europe, 1970. Contbr. to Symposia; Foreign Influences in American Life (D. Bowers, editor), 1944; The Modern Princeton, 1947; Evolutionary Thought in America (S. Persons, editor), 1950; Religion in American Life (Smith and Jamison), 1961. Editor (with S. Persons) and co-author: Socialism and American Life, 1952. Home: 164 Moore St Princeton NJ 08540

EGBERT, LAWRENCE DEEMS, lawyer; b. St. Paul, Feb. 1, 1897; s. John Paul and Anna Louise (Deems) E.; A.B., U. Mich., 1919; postgrad. Harvard, 1919-21, Acad. Internat. Law, The Hague, 1923; Dr. en Droit summa cum laude, Faculte de Droit, U. Paris, 1926; m. Evelyn Loretta Forsyth, July 18, 1922; children—Lawrence, John, Charles F. Acting asst. prof. Occidental Coll., 1926-27; asso. U. Ill., 1927-29; asst. prof. Northwestern U., 1929-34; asst. to Law Librarian of Congress, Washington, 1935-36; specialist on comml. treaties and fgn. comml. policies U.S. Tariff Commn., 1936-41; admitted to D.C. bar, 1941; asst. chief central information div. OSS, 1941-43; commd. maj. AUS, 1943, advanced through grades to lt. col., 1945; retired 1949; lectr. law faculty U. Paris, Paris Sch. Advanced Studies, Nat. Sch. Adminstrn., 1947; mem. exec. staff U.S. chief counsel Nuremberg trial Nazi War Criminals, 1945-46; research coordinator State Dept., 1950-60; Latin Am. specialist with office internat. confs. State Dept., 1960-61; disarmament researcher Atlantic Research Corp., Washington, 1962; research dir. World Peace through Law Center, 1963—; adj. prof. internat. law Am. U., 1949-65; asst. sec.-gen. Congress of Comparative Law, The Hague, Holland, 1937. Decorated Croix de Guerre (France); Order of Leopold II (Belgium). Mem. Inter-Am. (exec. sec. Havana conf. 1941), Am. Fed. (asso. editor 1936-43) bar assns., Am. Soc. Internat. Law, Pi Sigma Alpha, Phi Alpha Delta. Club: Cosmos (Washington). Author: Law Dictionary; English, Espanol, Francais, Deutsch; also numerous articles. Editor: World Peace Through Law-The Athens World Conference, 1964; Nuremberg Trial Record, 1946-47. Address: 75 rue de Lyon Geneva, Switzerland

EGBERT, RICHARD COOK, investment banker; b. N.Y.C., June 23, 1927; s. Lester D. and Beatrice (Cook) E.; grad. Hotchkiss Sch., 1945; B.A., Yale, 1950; m. Anne Merrill Becker, Sept. 11, 1954; children—Allison Huntting, Anne Merrill, Richard Cook. With Chase Nat. Bank, 1950-53; with Estabrook & Co., N.Y.C., 1954- 68, partner, 1963-68; v.p., dir. Spencer Trask & Co., Inc., N.Y.C., 1968- -. Mem. Blue Hill Troupe, Ltd., N.Y.C., 1951—, pres., 1961-62; v.p., dir. 1030 Fifth Av. Corp. Trustee, treas., chmn. finance com. W. Side Day Nursery, N.Y.C. Served with USNR, 1945-46. Mem. Investment Assn. N.Y. (past sec.), Soc. Colonial Wars, Downtown Assn. N.Y., Chi Phi. Presbyn. (past deacon). Club: Bond (N.Y.C.). Home: Old Church Rd Greenwich CT 06830 Office: 60 Broad St New York City NY 10004

EGEBERG, ROGER OLAF, physician, govt. ofcl.; b. Chgo., Nov. 13, 1903; s. Hans Olaf and Ulrikka Rostrup (Nielsen) E.; B.A., Cornell U., 1925; M.D., Northwestern U., 1929; m. Margaret McEchron Chahoon, Sept. 5, 1929; children—Dagny (Mrs. William Hancock), Sarah (Mrs. Robert Beauchamp), Roger Olaf, Karen (Mrs. Richard Warmer). Intern, Wesley Hosp., Chgo., 1928-29; resident Passavant Meml. Hosp., 1929-30, Univ. Hosp., Ann Arbor, Mich., 1930-32; practice medicine, specializing in internal medicine, Cleve., 1932-42; chief med. service VA Hosp., Los Angeles, 1946-56; med. dir. Los Angeles County Hosp., 1956-59, Los Angeles County Dept. Charities, 1958-64; mem. staff Los Angeles County Gen. Hosp., Rancho Los Amigos Hosp., Downey, Cal., Olive View (Cal.) Hosp.; clin. prof. medicine U. Cal. at Los Angeles, 1948-64, Coll. Med. Evangelists, 1956-64; prof. medicine U. So. Cal., 1956-69, dean sch. medicine, 1964- 69; asst. sec. for health and sci. affairs U.S. Dept. Health, Edn. and Welfare, 1969—. Mem. Cal. Bd. Pub. Health, 1961—, pres., 1964—; chmn. Gov. Cal. Com. Study Med. Care and Health in Cal., 1959-60, President's Panel Narcotics Addiction, 1962, President's Adv. Commn. Narcotic and Drug Abuse, 1963, Nat. Adv. Cancer Council, 1964-67; mem. spl. med. adv. group to VA, 1965—, chmn. Cal. regional planning programs, 1967—; chmn. med. adv. com. Los Angeles chpt. Planned Parenthood-World Population Assn., 1965—; mem. bd. Cal. div. Am. Cancer Soc., 1959—. Served to col., M.C., AUS, 1942-46. Decorated Bronze Star, Legion of Merit; St. Olaf's medal (Norway). Diplomate Am. Bd. Internal Medicine. Fellow A.C.P.; mem. A.M.A., Cal., Los Angeles County med. assns., Am. Clin. and Climatol. Assn., Cal. Soc. Internal Medicine, Western Assn. Physicians, Pacific Interurban Club, Alpha Omega Alpha. Spl. research ecology of coccidioides Immitis. Home: 6918 Oporto Dr Los Angeles, CA 90028. Office: 2025 Zonal Av Los Angeles CA 00033

EGER, JOSEPH, conductor, music director, arranger; b. Hartford, Conn., July 9, 1925; s. Abraham and Clara (Ellovich) E.; grad. Curtis Inst., Berkshire Music Center; studied with Monteux, Stokowski, Steinberg, Lert, Rudolf, Dixon, Kahne; m. Dixie Blackstone, Sept. 15, 1957 (d. June 1969). First horn N.Y., Los Angeles, Israel Philharmonics, other maj. orchs.; faculty Aspen (Colo.) Music Festival, 1952-57, Peabody Conservatory, 1962-65; solo recording artist RCA Victor, motion picture, TV, radio recordings; became French horn soloist, 1956, world concert tours, lectr.; music dir. Eger Players; founder, condr. Camera Concerti Chamber Orch., 1958, Westside Symphony Orch., 1961, N.Y. Orch. Soc., 1963; condr. Midland (Mich.) Symphony, 1962-64; guest condr. Royal Philharmonic, London Philharmonic, Sinfonia of London, Pitts., Cin., Balt., Am. Symphony, Symphony of Am., Vienna Radio Orch., Dessoff Choir, Haifa, and other; condr. Town Hall series, 1962-63, Carnegie Hall, 1964-67, Philharmonic Hall, 1965, Young People and Teenage Concerts; creator Harlem Music Project; asso., Schirmer's, Consol. Music Pubs.; asso. condr. to Leopold Stokowski, 1967-70; condr. recording for Life mag., 1966, Westminster Record Co., 1967; music dir. Indian Hill, 1967; N.Y. Symphony Premiere Performance, 1968; music dir. N.Y. Orchestral Soc., N.Y. Concertante, Athens; condr. Athens Festival; founder, music dir. Symphony of N.Y.; founder Crossover; dir. Aware, N.Y., 1971—; composer score for film Carolina, 1970; recorded albums Classical Heads, Five Bridges. Served to staff sgt. USAAF. Mem. Nat. Assn. Am. Condrs. and Composers (program chmn. 1965-67). Contbg. author: Musical America ann., Musical Courier ann., Mus. Digest. Home: 40 W 67th St New York City NY 10023

EGER, MILTON JEROME, optometrist; b. Pitts., June 14, 1919; s. Herman and Sarah (Levin) E.; O.D., Pa. Coll. Optometry, 1940; m. Fern Bernice Taksa, Aug. 2, 1942; children—Diane Jill (Mrs. Arnold M. Rosenthal), Arnold Robert, Carol Ellen. Practice optometry, Aliquippa, Pa., 1940—; editor Jour. Am. Optometric Assn., 1965—, Pa. Optometrist, 1958-63; pres. Vision Conservation Inst., 1965-67, Assn. Optometric Editors, 1962-63. Mem. adv. bd. Western Pa. Nat. Bank, Aliquippa, 1965—; dir., incorporator, sec.-treas. Citizens State Bank Aliquippa, 1962-65. Sec. Hopewell Twp. Sch. Bd., 1963-68, pres., 1960, v.p., 1959; pres. Hopewell- Independence-Raccoon Joint School Bd., 1961-63; regional dir. Pa. Sch. Bds. Assn., 1963-65. Mem. Aliquippa Area Brotherhood Com., 1948—, chmn., 1965-67; pres., founder Aliquippa Jewish Community Center, 1954- 59. Chmn. trustees Beaver County Community Coll., 1967—; trustee Pa. Coll. Optometry, 1966-68; bd. dirs. Hopewell Township Sch. Bd. Served with USAAF, 1942-45. Recipient award Nat. Optometric Editors, 1959, 60, 62, 25th Annual award United Jewish Appeal, 1962, award Vision Conservation Inst., 1962, life membership award P.T.A.; named Man of Year, Aliquippa, Pa., 1970. Mem. Am., Pa. (pres. 1966-68, Presdl. award 1962) optometric assns., Pa. Coll. Optometry Alumni Assn. (bd. dirs. 1960-64), Am. Acad. Optometry, Am. Optometric Found., Better Vision Inst., Am. Legion, Aliquippa Area C. of C., Beta Sigma Kappa. Lion, Odd Fellow; mem. B'nai B'rith. Home: 401 Baker Dr Aliquippa, PA 15001. Office: 902 22d St Aliquippa PA 15001

EGERT, MILLAN LUDMIL, govt. ofcl.; b. York Village, Me., Feb. 8, 1910; s. Joseph and Maud (Weeks) E.; A.B., Colby Coll., 1930; J.D., George Washington U., 1939; m. Lillian Hanscom, Aug. 28, 1937; 1 son, Timothy. Admitted to D.C. bar, 1938; govt. service, 1934—; atty. Dept. Labor, 1938-42; mem. staff U.S. Senate Spl. Com. to Investigate Problems Am. Small Bus., 1941; dist. price exec., Washington, 1943; dep. dir. UNRRA Camp, Germany, 1945-46; labor adviser Office Housing Expediter, 1946-47; asst. dir. UNESCO relations staff Dept. State, 1947-56; 1st sec., dep. adminstrv. officer Am. embassy, Rome, Italy, 1956-59, 1st sec., adminstrv. officer, Kabul, Afghanistan, 1959-61; spl. asst. to asst. sec. of state for adminstrn. State Dept., 1961-63, exec. dir. Bur. Near Eastern and South Asian Affairs, 1963-65; consul gen. Am. consulate gen., Genoa, Italy, 1965—. Pres., Buckingham (Va.) Civic Assn., 1940; dir. Internat. Overseas Sch. of Rome, 1956-59, Anglo- Am. Nursing Home, Rome, 1957-59, Kabul Internat. High Sch., 1959-61. Served to sgt. AUS, 1943-45. Decorated commendatore Order of Merit (Italy). Mem. Academia Italiana della Cucina, Lambda Chi Alpha, Pi Kappa Delta. Clubs: International (Washington); Propeller, Union, Genoa, Genoa Rotary. Home: Via Lavinia 36 Genoa Italy Office: Am Consulate Gen Piazza Portello 6 Genoa Italy

EGGAN, FRED RUSSELL, educator; b. Seattle, Sept. 12, 1906; s. Alfred Julius and Olive M. (Smith) E.; Ph.B., U. Chgo., 1927, A.M., 1928, Ph.D., 1933; M.A., Oxford, 1970; m. Dorothy Way, Aug. 9, 1938 (dec. 1965); m. 2d, Joan Rosenfels, June 29, 1969. Research asso. in Philippine ethnology U. Chgo., 1934-35, instr. anthropology, 1935-40, asst. prof., 1940-42, asso. prof., 1942-48, prof., 1948—, chmn. dept., 1948-52, 61-63, dir. Philippine studies program, 1953—, Harold H. Swift Distinguished Service prof., 1963—; Morgan lectr. U. Rochester, 1964; Frazer lectr. Cambridge, 1971; vis. fellow All Souls Coll., Oxford, 1970. Ofcl. U.S. del. 8th Pacific Sci. Congress, Manila, 1953, 9th, Bangkok, 1957, 10th, Honolulu, 1961, 11th, Tokyo, Japan, 1966; mem. Pres.'s Com. on Scientists and Engrs., 1956-57; chmn. bd. Human Relations Area Files, Inc., 1964-67; research asso. Lab. Anthropology, Santa Fe, 1964—; adv. com. social scis. NSF, 1961-62; hon. cons. Bernice P. Bishop Mus., Honolulu; mem. Commn. Coll. Geography, 1965-67; councillor Smithsonian Instn., 1966—; mem. adv. bd. Desert Research Inst., U. Nev.; bd. dirs. Founds. Fund for Research psychiatry, 1967-69; mem. Pacific Science Bd., 1968—. Served as captain, AUS, 1943, dir. Civil Affairs Tng. Sch. for Far East, U. Chgo., 1943-45. Fulbright research scholar, P.I., 1949-50; Guggenheim fellow, 1953; fellow Center for Advanced Study in Behavioral Scis., Stanford, 1958-59; recipient Viking Fund medal and award, 1956; hon. curator Chgo. Natural History Mus., 1962—. Fellow Royal Anthrop. Inst. (hon.), Nat. Acad. Scis. (mem. com. on scis. and pub. policy 1965-67, mem. council 1967-70), Assn. Asian Studies (dir. 1966-68), Am. Anthrop. Assn. (pres. 1953, Memoirs editor 1960-64), Am. Philos. Soc., Am. Acad. Arts and Scis., Am. Ethnol. Soc., NRC (chmn. com. Asian anthropology 1952-53), Social Sci. Research Council (chmn. bd. 1953-56), Phi Beta Kappa, Sigma Xi, Tau Kappa Epsilon. Clubs: Cosmos; Quadrangle. Author: Social Organization of the Western Pueblos, 1950; The American Indian, 1966. Editor: Social Anthropology of North American Tribes, 1937, enlarged edit., 1955. Supr. Handbook on the Philippines, 4 vols., 1956. Mem. sr. adv. com. Ency. Brit., 1953—. Editorial bd. Sci., 1968—. Home: 5752 S Harper Av Chicago IL 60637 Office: 1126 E 59th St Chicago IL 60637 ☆

EGGEN, JOHN ARCHER, librarian; b. Virginia, Minn., May 4, 1915; s. John J. and Anne Marie (Berg) E.; student Va. Jr. Coll., 1932-35; B.A., U. Minn.; m. Eleanor Gray, Mar. 11, 1948 (dec. Feb. 1959); m. 2d, Trueda Monson, Jan. 14, 1961. Design engr., co. librarian Continental Machines, Inc., Mpls., 1941-45; librarian Fergus Falls (Minn.) Pub. Library, also Ind. Sch. Dist. 21, 1945-49; head librarian Cedar Rapids (Ia.) Pub. Library, 1949-56; city librarian St. Paul Pub. Library, 1956—. Mem. Am., Minn., Ia. library assns. Mason. Clubs: Rotary, Southview Country. Contbr. articles to library periodicals. Home: 360 S Lexington Pkwy St Paul MN 55105 Office: 90 W 4th St St Paul MN 55102

EGGER, CHARLES EDWARD, newspaperman; b. Columbus, O., May 20, 1913; s. Frank J. and Eleanor (Trott) E.; B.S., Ohio State U., 1935; m. Vivian Freiburghouse, Nov. 26, 1936; children—Emily, Frank. With Scripps-Howard Ohio Bur., 1935-38, 42- 43; with Columbus Citizen, 1938-42, 43-47, city editor, 1943-45, polit. editor, 1945-47; Washington corr. Cleve. Press and Columbus Citizen, also Cin. Post, 1947-50; night editor Scripps-Howard Newspaper Alliance, 1950- 52, mng. editor, 1953-67; editor Columbus Citizen Jour., 1967—. Bd. dirs. Columbus Symphony Orch. Mem. Columbus C. of C. (mem. bd.), Sigma Delta Chi. Club: Nat. Press (Washington). Home: 3846 Overdale Dr Columbus, OH 43220. Office: 34 S 3d St Columbus OH 43215

EGGER, GEORGE EDWARD, corp. dir.; b. St. Louis, July 9, 1905; s. George Edward and Drussie Lee (Logan) E.; A.B., Wash. U., 1925; m. Helen Alexander, Nov. 30, 1933; 1 son, Douglas Alexander. Sales exec. Gen. Foods, Inc. and Best Foods, Inc., 1925-35; v.p. Jefferson Island Salt Co., 1935-41, Harold H. Clapp, Inc., 1941-44; v.p., dir. George Washington Coffee Co., 1941-44; v.p. Reynolds Metals Co., Richmond, Va., 1944-47; pres. Morton Frozen Foods, Inc., 1950-58; pres., dir. WLKY-TV, Louisville, 1961-68; chmn. bd. Loma Linda Corp., Orlando, Fla.; dir. Glenmore Distilleries; dir. Citizens Fidelity Bank & Trust Co., Kingsford Co., Inc., Louisville. Mem. U.S. Savs. Bond Adv. Com., Louisville and Jefferson County, 1955-57; chmn. guarantors fund com. Louisville Park Theatrical Assn., 1952- 54. Dir. Washington U., St. Louis, 1962-65; chmn. Ky. State Racing Commn.; bd. dirs., Norton Children's Hosp., Inc., Louisville. Mem. Ky. C. of C. (dir. 1955-56), Ky. Thoroughbred Breeders Assn. (pres.), Sigma Chi. Episcopalian. Clubs: Wynn-Stay, Pendennis, Beagle, Filson,

Louisville Country, River Valley (Louisville); Owl Creek Country (Anchorage, Ky). Home: Osage Rd Anchorage KY 40223 also Greenhaven Lane KY Office: Starks Bldg Louisville KY 40202

EGGER, ROWLAND ANDREWS, educator, research dir.; b. Denison, Tex., Apr. 12, 1908; s. Ernest Linwood and Martha Aldora (Harmon) E.; A.B. cum laude Southwestern U., 1926, LL.D., 1959; A.M., So. Meth. U., 1927; Ph.D., U. Mich., 1933; m. Gretchen Lee Savin MacIlwaine, Jan. 5, 1932 (dec. April 1952). Instr. govt. So. Methodist U., 1926-28; univ. fellow U. Mich., 1928-29; instr. in politics, Princeton, 1929-31; tech. cons. State of N.J., 1930-31; asso. prof. polit. sci., dir. bur. of pub. adminstrn., U. Va., 1931-36, prof., 1936-64, chmn. Woodrow Wilson dept. fgn. affairs, 1956-64, dept. polit. sci., 1957-64, Edward R. Stettinius prof. of fgn. affairs, 1962-64, acting dean faculty, 1962-63; prof. politics and pub. affairs Princeton, 1964—. Exec. officer. Joint Com. on Public Adminstrn., Brussels, Belgium, 1935-36; vis. prof. internat. orgn., adminstrn. Columbia, 1947-48; vis. prof. govt. Harvard, 1961; cons. White House, UN, U.S. Bur. Budget, U.S. Dept. Agr., UNESCO, Commn. on Orgn. Exec. Br. of Govt., dir. Budget, Commonwealth of Va., 1939-42; adminstv. and financial adviser Pres. Bolivia, 1942; gen. mgr., dir. Corporación Boliviana de Fomento, 1942-45, dir. and U.S. rep., 1945-47; spl. rep. President U.S. to Govt. Bolivia, 1961-62; asso. dir. Pub. Adminstrn. Clearing House, 1951-53; adminstrv. adviser Prime Minister Pakistan, 1953; Near East rep. Ford Found., 1954-56; mem. UN Adminstrv. Tribunal, 1949-51. Mem. bd. overseers vis. com. grad. sch. pub. adminstrn. Harvard, 1954-60; vice chmn., bd. trustees Inter-U. Case Program. Decorated Officer Order Leopold (Belgium), Knight Comdr. Order of Condor (Bolivia). Comdr. Order Cedars (Lebanon); recipient Haldane prize Royal Inst. Pub. Adminstrn., 1960. Sr. fellow Social Sci. Research Council, 1958-59; mem. Royal Inst. Pub. Adminstrn., Am. Soc. Pub. Adminstrn., Am., So. polit. sci. assns., Internat. Inst. Adminstrv. Scis. (mem. council adminstrn., exec. com.), Nat. Acad. Pub. Adminstrn. Acad. Polit. Sci., Nat. Inst. Pub. Affairs (trustee), S.A.R., Raven Society, Phi Beta Kappa, Pi Kappa Alpha. Clubs: Farmington Country; Nassau (Princeton); Princeton (N.Y.); Cosmos (Washington, D.C.). Author: (with J.E. Gates) Municipal Ownership of Electrical Undertakings, 1937; Organization of Peace at the Administrative Level, 1945; (with Weldon Cooper) Research, Education and Regionalism, 1949; Improvement of Public Administration in Pakistan, 1961; Social and Economic Development of Bolivia, 1962; President and Congress, 1963; The President of the United States, 1967; Le Métier de Président, 1970. Editor, Internat. Rev. Adminstrv. Scis., 1968—. Contbr. various revs. on govt. and adminstrn. Home: 97 Hartley Av Princeton NJ 08540

EGGERS, ALBERT HERMAN, mfr.; b. Cin., Mar. 23, 1892; s. Albert George and Helene (Hillman) E.; student Cin. Tech. Sch., 1906-09, Cin. U., 1910-12; m. Grace Garrett, Nov. 21, 1917; children—Albert Herman, Joan (Mrs. Edward Flint Seaton), Gordon G. Machinist. Steptoe Shaper Co., Cin., 1913; foreman Moderon Machine Tool Co., 1914; joined Greenlee Bros. & Co., Rockford, 1915, beginning as foreman, ret. as chmn. bd.; dir. Protection Mut. Fire Ins. Co. Mem. Sigma Alpha Epsilon. Republican. Presbyn. Mason. Clubs: Union League (Chgo.); Rockford Country. University, Mid-Day. Home: 2325 Clinton Pl Rockford IL 61103

EGGERS, ALFRED JOHN, Jr., govt. ofcl.; b. Omaha, June 24, 1922; s. Alfred John and Golden (Myers) E.; A.B., U. Omaha, 1944; M.S., Stanford, 1949, Ph.D., 1956; m. Elizabeth Ann Hills, Sept. 9, 1950; children—Alfred John III, Philip Norman. With NASA, and predecessor, 1944—, chief vehicle environment div. Ames Research Center, 1959-63, asst. dir. research and devel. analysis and planning, 1963-64, dep. asso. adminstr. advanced research and tech. NASA hdqrs., 1964-68, asst. adminstr. for policy, 1968-71; asst. dir. for research applications NSF, 1971; spl. research supersonic and hypersonic aerodynamics, aerodynamics heating, aerospace vehicles. Mem. sci. adv. bd. USAF, 1958—. Vice chmn. Los Altos (Cal.) Sch. Community Devel. Com., 1963-64. Served to lt. (j.g.) USNR, 1942-46. Recipient Arthur S. Fleming award, 1956; named One of Ten Outstanding Young Men of Year, U.S. C. of C., 1957; recipient Outstanding Alumni award U. Omaha, 1958; H. Julian Allen award Ames Research Center, 1969. Fellow Am. Inst. Aero. and Astronautics (founder dir.; Sylvanus Albert Reed award 1962; founder chmn. pres.'s forum com. on interactions aerospace tech. and soc. 1966-70); mem. A.A.A.S., Am. Ordnance Assn., Am. Acad. Polit. and Social Sci., Sigma Xi, Tau Beta Pi. Home: 4425 N 33d Rd Arlington VA 22207 Office: Code RA Nat Sci Found Washington DC 20550

EGGERS, HENRY LAWRENCE, former architect; b. Denver, May 12, 1911; s. Henry and Grace (Bills) E.; B.Arch., Cornell U., 1932; m. Florence McAllister, Dec. 14, 1940; children—Henry Vickers, Laurence Paxson, Ann Allister. With U.S. Bur. Reclamation, Denver, 1933-36; designer Gordon Kaufmann, architect, 1936- 45; mem. firm Kaufmann, Lippincott & Eggers, Los Angeles, 1945-48; partner Henry L. Eggers, Wilkman & Whittle, Architects, Los Angeles, 1948-70, now ret.; design critic U. So. Cal. Coll. Architecture, 1954-59. Trustee Chandler Sch., Pasadena, 1960-61. Fellow A.I.A.; mem. Founding Friends Harvey Mudd Coll. Club: Valley Hunt. Home: 704 Heatherside Rd Pasadena CA 91105

EGGERS, MELVIN ARNOLD, educator, economist; b. Ft. Wayne, Ind., Feb. 21, 1916; s. Frederick Carl and Minnie (Kiel) E.; A.B., Ind. U., 1940, A.M., 1941; Ph.D., Yale, 1950; m. Mildred Grace Chenoweth, Apr. 5, 1941; children—Nancy Louise, William David, Richard Melvin. Clk., Peoples Trust & Savs. Co., Ft. Wayne, 1934-38; instr. econs. Yale, 1947-50; mem. faculty Syracuse U., 1950—, prof. econs., 1963—, chmn. dept., 1960-70, vice chancellor for acad. affairs, also provost, 1970-71, chancellor, 1971—. Mem. faculty Pacific Coast Banking Sch., 1955-70; cons. financial instns. Served to lt. USNR, 1942-46. Mem. Am. Econ. Assn., Am. Finance Assn., Am. Assn. U. Profs., Phi Beta Kappa. Home: 701 Walnut Av Syracuse NY 13210

EGGERS, PAUL WALTER, lawyer; b. Seymour, Ind., Apr. 20, 1919; s. Ernest H. and Ottillie (Carre) E.; B.A., Valpariaso U., 1941; LL.B., U. Tex., 1948; m. Frances May Kramer, Dec. 29, 1946; 1 son, Steven Paul. Admitted to Tex. bar, 1948; pvt. practice Wichita Falls, Tex., 1948-52; mem. firm Eggers, Sherrill, Pace & Rogers, Wichita Falls, Tex., 1953-69; gen. counsel Treasury Dept., 1969-70. Dir. City Nat. Bank, Wichita Falls, 1967-69. Trustee, sec. Episcopal Funds Diocese Dallas, 1965-69. Chmn. Wichita County Republican Com., 1966-68; Rep. candidate for gov. Tex, 1968,70. Served to maj. USAAF, 1941-46. Named Outstanding Layman of Year Dallas, 1968; recipient Silver Anniversary All Am. award Sports Illus. mag., 1966. Mem. Am., Fed. bar assns., State Bar Tex. (chmn. tax sect. 1968-69). Home: 2513 Amherst PO Drawer 5008 Wichita Falls TX 76308

EGGERSTEDT, FRED CHARLES, Jr., pub. utility exec.; b. Bklyn., Apr. 18, 1910; s. Fred Charles and Christine (Reimals) E.; B.S., Purdue U., 1932; student accounting Pace Inst., 1932-35; m. Ethel Walther, Apr. 19, 1936; children—Susan, Katherine (Mrs. Donald Dimaio) and Mary (Mrs. Ralph E. Schuster). Utility analyst Atlas Corp., 1935-40; treas. Central States Power & Light Corp., 1940-45; cons. engr. W.C. Gilman & Co., 1945-50; with Long Island Lighting Co., 1950—, v.p. finance, 1960-62, v.p., treas., 1962-69, sr. v.p., treas., 1969—. Lectr. U. Mich. Sch. Bus., 1958—. Bd. dirs., treas. Long Island Assn., Nassau County Health & Welfare Council; bd. dirs. L.I. Hosp. Planning Bd., Hofstra Coll. Registered profl. engr., N.Y. Mem. Edison Electric Inst. (past chmn. finance com.), Am. Gas Assn. (past chmn. finance com.). Club: Magouin Landing Yacht (past commodore), South Bay Cruising (commodore) (West Islip). Home: 8 Davison Lane W West Islip, NY 11795. Office: 250 Old Country Rd Mineola NY 11501

EGGERT, FRANKLIN PAUL, educator; b. Buffalo, May 13, 1920; s. Paul A. and Florence (Graf) E.; B.S.A., Cornell, 1942, M.S.A., 1947, Ph.D., 1949; m. Barbara Eccles, July 20, 1945; children—Edward Paul, Michael, Geoffrey M., Peter J. Grad. asst. N.Y. Agrl. Expt. Sta., Geneva, N.Y., 1946-49; head horticulture dept. Agrl. Expt. Sta., Orono, Me., 1949—, horticulturist, 1951—; extension horticulturist U. Me., Orono, 1949-51, prof., 1951—, head dept. horticulture, Coll. Agr., 1951- 63, dean Grad. Sch., 1962—, dir. research, 1963-67. Served as capt. USMCR, World War II. Mem. Am. Soc. Hort. Sci. (exec. com. 1953-54, chmn. N.E. br. 1954), Bot. Soc. Am., Am. Pomol. Soc., New Eng. Conf. on Grad. Edn. (past sec.), Am. Inst. for Biol. Scis., A.A.A.S., Nat. Council Univ. Research Adminstrs., Sigma Xi, Phi Kappa Phi. Home: 190 Main St Orono ME 04473

EGGERTSEN, CLAUDE ANDREW, educator; b. Thistle, Utah, Feb. 25, 1909; s. Claude E. and Helen El Deva (Blackett) E.; A.B., Brigham Young U., 1930, M.A., 1933; postgrad. Stanford, 1931; Ph.D., U. Minn., 1939; m. Nita Wakefield, June 3, 1931; children—Sheary Jill (Mrs. Virgil F. Fairbanks), Claude Wakefield, John Hale. Tchr., Carbon County (Utah) Sch. Dist., 1931-34; mem. faculty U. Minn., 1934-39, instr. edn., 1935-39; mem. faculty U. Mich., Ann Arbor, 1939—, prof. edn., 1953—, dir. program comparative edn., 1959—, dir. internat. edn. projects, 1966—, chmn. social founds., 1952-62, 68—; vis. faculty mem. Brigham Young U., 1935, U. Colo., 1937, Ohio State U., 1948, San Jose Coll., 1955, U. Cal. at Los Angeles, 1951; hon. vis. prof. U. Sheffield (Eng.), 1958, 62; vis. prof. edn., India, 1962, 64; vis. prof. Utah State U. Served to lt. (s.g.) USNR, 1944-46. Decorated Bronze Star medal. Fellow Philosophy Edn. Soc., John Dewey Soc.; mem. Nat. Soc. Coll. Tchrs. (sec. 1948-60), Comparative Edn. Soc. (co-chmn. history edn. sect. 1948-50, exec. com. 1959-61, pres. 1963-64), History Edn. Soc., Am. Ednl. Research Assn., Am. Hist. Assn., UN Assn. of U.S.A. (pres. Mich. div. 1966-70), Phi Delta Kappa, Phi Kappa Phi, Tau Kappa Alpha, Theta Alpha Phi. Author articles, chpts. in books. Editor: Studies in the History of Higher Education in Michigan, 1950; Studies in the History of the School of Education, The University of Michigan, 1955; History of Education Jour., 1950-60; Notes and Abstracts in American and International Education, 1962. Home: 1044 Ferdon Rd Ann Arbor MI 48104

EGGERTSEN, PAUL, educator; b. Provo, Utah, July 11, 1901; s. Simon Peter and Henrietta (Nielson) E.; B.S., Brigham Young U., 1926; A.M., Columbia, 1929; Ed.D., Temple U., 1942; m. Mabel Larsen, Sept. 4, 1930; 1 son, Richard. Instr. econs. Temple U., 1929-43; indsl. relations analyst Lockheed Aircraft Co., 1943-45; asso. prof. econs. Loyola U., Los Angeles, 1945-51, prof. gen. bus. and chmn. dept., 1951—, sabbatical leave for study in Europe, 1957. Mem. Am., Western econs. assns., Am. Risk and Ins. Assn. Home: 8351 Colegio Dr Los Angeles CA 90045

EGGLESTON, ARTHUR FRANCOIS, business exec.; b. Meriden, Conn., Nov. 19, 1890; s. Jere Dewey and Elizabeth Christy (Duncan) E.; student Williston Sem. Prep. Sch., Easthampton, Mass.; B.A., Cornell U., 1913; m. Grace Louise Lane, Dec. 29, 1914 (dec. Aug. 1930); 1 dau., Gertrude Elaine (Mrs. Robert T. Turton); m. 2d, Frances Evelyn Nordaby, Jan. 25, 1933; 1 dau., Polly Jane (Mrs. Foster M. Johnson, Jr.). With The Lane Constrn. Corp., 1914- -, beginning as sales mgr. and paymaster, successively sec., v.p., pres. and gen. mgr., now chmn. bd., chief exec. officer, mem. bd. dirs.; sec., pres. John S. Lane & Son, Inc., now chmn. bd.; dir. Home Nat. Bank & Trust Co.; trustee City Savs. Bank (both Meriden). Formerly pres., dir. Meriden Hosp., Meriden YMCA; former chmn. bd. mgrs. Bradley Home. Served as 2d lt., Inf., U.S. Army, World War I. Conglist. Clubs: Home (Meriden); Shuttle Meadow Country (New Britain, Conn.); Pine Orchard (Conn.) Yacht; Quinnipiack (New Haven); Vero Beach (Fla.) Golf, Riomar Yacht, Riomar Golf (Vero Beach). Home: 106 Alexander Dr Meriden CT 06450 Office: The Lane Construction Corp Meriden CT 06450

EGGLESTON, JOHN WILLIAM, judge; b. Charlotte C.H., Va., June 18, 1886; s. David Quinn and Sue (Daniel) E.; student Hampden-Sydney Coll., Va., 1902-04; B.A., Washington and Lee U., 1906, M.A., 1907, LL.B., 1910, LL.D., 1949; m. Ella Carrington, Oct. 15, 1912; children—Mary (Mrs. W. Perry Moore, Jr.), Suzanne (Mrs. William W. Simpson), Eleanor Carrington (dec.). Tchr., Washington and Lee U., 1906-07, 1908-10, McGuire's Prep. Sch., Richmond, Va., 1907-08; admitted to Va. bar, 1909; practiced at Norfolk, Va., 1910-35; mem. firms Baker & Eggleston; Hughes, Vandeventer & Eggleston; Vandeventer, Eggleston & Black; mem. Va. State Senate, 1932-35, chmn. legislative com. which drafted Alcoholic Beverage Control Act; justice Supreme Ct. Appeals of Va., 1935-58, 1969—, chief justice, 1958-69. Mem. Va. State Bar Assns., Va. Hist. Soc., Order of Coif, Phi Beta Kappa, Omicron Delta Kappa, Phi Delta Phi, Kappa Sigma. Democrat. Presbyn. Clubs: Princess Anne Country (Virginia Beach); Harbor (Norfolk). Home: 1115 Langley Rd Norfolk VA 23507 Office: City Hall Bldg Norfolk VA 23510

EGHBAL, MANOUCHEHR, Iranian physician, politician; b. Khorassan, Iran, Oct. 13, 1909; ed. Persia, also univs. Montpellier and Paris (France); hon. degrees Lafayette Coll., 1956, Paris U., 1959, Bordeaux U., 1959, U. Punjab, 1959, Pahlavi U., Shiraz, Iran, 1970, U. Bucarest, 1970; Prof. infectious diseases Med. Faculty, U. Teheran, 1939-53; successively under sec. state pub. health, minister pub. health, minister posts, telegraph and telephones, minister of nat. edn., minister of roads and communications, minister of interior, then gov.-gen. Azerbaidjan, all No. region Iran, 1942-50; rector U. Tabriz; senator, 1953; dean Faculty Medicine, Teheran U., 1955- 57, also rector univ., 1955-57, prof., 1960-61; minister to imperial ct., 1956; prime minister, 1957-60; mem. Parliament, 1961—; permanent rep. Iran to UNESCO, 1960—; chmn. bd., gen. mng. dir. Nat. Iranian Oil Co., 1963—; chmn. bd. Nat. Petrochem. Co. Iran, Nat. Iranian Gas Co. Pres., Irano-Turkish Friendship and Cultural Relations Soc.; founder mem. Soc. Protection Guardianless Children; mem. nat. com. World Congress for Elimination Illiteracy; mem. Iran Edn. Found.; founder mem., 1st v.p. Soc. Protection Fire and Scalding Casualties; mem. high council Charity Found; head high council Food and Nutrition Inst.; high council Iranian Orgn. Internat. Assemblies; mem. Nat. Soc. Protection Country's Natural Resources. Bd. dirs. Poliomyelitis Soc., Iran Infectious and Tropical Diseases Group of U. Tehran; founder mem., vice chmn. bd. dirs. Nat. Soc. Anti-Cancer Campaign; trustee Shiraz Pahlavi U., Nat. U. Iran, Iran Girls Coll., Children's Library Orgn., Arya Mehr Inst. Tech., Her Majesty Queen Pahlavi's Found., Tehran U., Gondi Shapour U., U. Ispahan, Orgn. for Shiraz Festival Art; mem. high exec. com. 65th World Olympic Congress; chmn. bd. Iran Med. Council. chmn. bd. trustees Iran Clinicians Soc. Recipient numerous decorations. Mem. Med. Assn. Paris Hosps., Nat. Acad. Medicine France (corr.), Iran PEN Club (pres.). Address: Elahieh Av Teheran Iran

EGIL, HERBERT HENRY, financial exec.; b. Berkeley, Cal., May 10, 1930; s. August A. and Anna (Haderli) E.; B.S., U. Cal., Berkeley, 1952; m. Janice Ann Culver, July 17, 1955; children—Steven, Elizabeth. With SCM Corp., N.Y.C., 1956—, v.p., controller Smith-Corona Marchant div., 1968-69, v.p., controller Glidden-Duykee div., 1968-69, v.p., corporate controller, 1969—. Served with U.S. Army, 1953-55. Mem. Financial Execs. Inst. Home: 41 Dartmouth Rd Cos Cob CT 06807 Office: 299 Park Av New York City NY 10017

EGK, WERNER JOSEPH, composer; b. Auchsesheim, Bavaria, May 17, 1901; s. Joseph and Maria (Buck) E.; student Conservatory for Music, Augsburg, Germany, also U. Munich; m. Elisabeth Karl, Mar. 29, 1923; 1 son, Titus. Conductor, Staatsoper, Berlin, 1936-40; dir. High Sch. for Music, West Berlin, 1950- 53; permanent guest condr. Staatsoper Munich, 1950—. Composer: (operas) Die Zaubergeige, 1935; Peer Gynt, 1938; Columbus, 1941; Irische Legende, 1955; Der Revisor, 1956; Die Verlobung in San Domingo, 1963; Siebzehn Tage und vier Minuten, 1966; (ballets) Joan von Zarissa, 1940; Abraxas, 1948; Ein Sommertag, 1950; Die Chinesische Nachtigall, 1953; Casanova in London; also works for orch., solos for orch. Mem. League German Composers (pres.), Acad. der Künste Berlin West, Acad. der schönen Künste Munich, Deutsche Akademie der Künste Berlin. Rotarian. Home: Lindenstrasse 1 Lochham b Munich Germany

EGLE, WALTER PAUL, educator, economist; b. Freiburg, Germany, Jan. 30, 1904; s. Paul and Bertha (Mutterer) E.; Dr. rer pol., U. Freiburg, 1930; m. Mary Bauermeister, Aug. 24, 1931 (div.); m. 2d, Elise Hoster, Jan. 18, 1947. Came to U.S., 1933, naturalized, 1941. Research asst. Inst. World Econs., U. Kiel (Germany), 1930-33; research asso. econs. U. Va., 1934- 35; asso. prof. econs. Rockford Coll., 1935-36; asst. prof. Ohio State U., 1936-44; prin. economist Office Alien Property Custodian, 1944-45; Charles P. Taft prof. econs. U. Cin., 1946—, also dir. grad. studies in econs. Rockefeller fellow, 1933-34. Mem. Cin. Council World Affairs, Am., Internat. econ. assns. Author: Neutral Money, 1932; Economic Stabilization: Objectives, Rules and Mechanism, 1952; also articles. Home: 20 Far Hills Dr Cincinnati, OH 45208.

EGLEVSKY, ANDRE, ballet dancer; b. Moscow, Russia, Dec. 21, 1917; s. Eugene Petrovitch and Zoe Alexievna (Obraszoff) E.; studied ballet with Maria Nevelska, Nice, France, 1928, Volinine, Paris 1930, N. Legat, London, 1934, also Fokine, Egorova, Kchessinska; m. Leda Anchutin, Dec. 27, 1938; children—Andre, Paul, Marina. Came to U.S., 1937, naturalized, 1943. Mem. corps de ballet col. de Basil Ballet Russe, 1933, 1st dancer, 1934-35, partner Davilova, Toumanoua Baronova; with Leon Woitzekowsky Ballet, Rene Blum Ballet de Monte Carlo, 1935, under Fokine, 1936-37; joined Balanchine Am. Ballet, 1935; appeared Dwight Deere Wiman mus. The Great Lady, 1938; with Leonide Massine Ballet Russe De Monte Carlo, 1938-42, on tour Ballet Theater, U.S., S.A., 1942-44; with Marquis de Cuevas Ballet Internat., Massine Ballet Russe Highlights, 1944-46; with original Ballet Russe, 1946, Maruquis de Cuevas Grand Ballet, 1947; with N.Y.C. Ballet, until 1958; operator, owner sch. dancing, Massapequa, N.Y., 1958—; artistic dir. Eglevsky Ballet Co. L.I. Address: 126 Rumson Rd Massapequa NY 11758

EHINGER, CHARLES E., aircraft co. exec.; b. Huntington, Ind., Dec. 2, 1928; s. Norbert Aloysius and Ruth (Smith) E.; B.S. in Bus. Adminstrn., U. Ind., 1950; C.P.A., Ind.; m. Dorothy Mary Kender, Apr. 28, 1962; children—Suzanne Marie, Beverly Ann. Financial analyst Ford Motor Co., Dearborn, Mich., 1950-56; asst. div. controller Curtiss-Wright Corp., Caldwell, N.J., 1959-63, div. controller, 1963-64, asst. corporate controller, 1964-65, asst. gen. mgr., 1965-66, gen. mgr., 1966-68, exec. dir., 1968-69, v.p. corporate services staff, 1970; v.p., treas. Dorr-Oliver Inc., Stamford, Conn., 1969—. Mem. Ind. U. Alumni Assn., Alpha Kappa Psi, Beta Gamma Sigma. Club: National Aviation (Washington). Home: 35 Cider Hill Upper Saddle River NJ 07458 Office: Passaic Ct Wood-Ridge NJ 07075

EHLE, JOHN MARSDEN, Jr., author; b. Asheville, N.C., Dec. 13, 1925; s. John M. and Gladys (Starnes) E.; B.A., U. N.C., 1949, M.A., 1953; m. Gail Oliver, Aug. 30, 1952 (div. Apr. 1967); m. 2d, Rosemary Harris, Oct. 22, 1967; 1 dau., Jennifer Anne. Faculty, U. N.C., Chapel Hill, 1951-63, asst. prof., 1954-57, asso. prof., 1957-64; spl. asst. to Gov. Terry Sanford, Raleigh, N.C., 1963-64; adviser programs Ford Found., N.Y.C., 1964-65, cons., 1966-67; vis. asso. prof. N.Y. U., 1958-59; author novels: Move Over, Mountain, 1957; Kingstree Island, 1959; Lion on the Hearth, 1961; The Land Breakers, 1964 (Sir Walter Raleigh prize); The Road, 1967; Time of Drums, 1970; The Journey of August King, 1971; non-fiction books: The Free Men (Mayflower Soc. cup), 1965; The Survivor, 1968, Shepherd of the Streets, 1960; plays: American Adventure (broadcast) 1954-56; pub. also in several fgn. countries. Mem. U.S. Nat. Commn. for UNESCO, 1965-68, White House Group for Domestic Affairs, 1964-66, Nat. Council Humanities, 1966-70, bd. visitors Appalachian State U., Boone, N.C., 1969—. Bd. dirs. Inst. Outdoor Drama, U. N.C., Chapel Hill, N.C. Sch. Arts Found., Winston-Salem, Anne C. Stouffer Found., Winston-Salem. Mem. Authors League, P.E.N. Home: 1 Westview Dr N Winston-Salem NC 27104 Office: care Robert Lantz Candida Donadio 111 W 57th St New York City NY 10019

EHLERS, HENRY JAMES, educator; b. Council Bluffs, Ia., Mar. 4, 1907; s. Henry T. and Anne Rose (McKinley) E.; Ph.B., Creighton U., 1928; M.A., U. Wis., 1931; Ph.D., U. Pitts., 1941; m. Retta Wooden Johnson, Dec. 23, 1939; children—Mary Ann (Mrs. Neil E. Waldo), Julia May (Mrs. David M. Quick). Tchr. instrumental music, Council Bluffs, 1923-24, Holdredge, Neb., 1929- 30; music tchr. Conroy Jr. High Sch., Pitts., 1936-41; prof. music, lead dept. State Tchrs. Coll., Plattsburg, 1941-44; head dept. music Eastern Ore. Coll., La Grande, 1944-47; mem. faculty U. Minn., Duluth, 1947—, prof. philosophy, 1955—; summer vis. prof. U. Ind., 1958, U. Bridgeport (Conn.), 1965, U. Wash., 1966, 69, 71. Mem. Am. Civil Liberties Union (state officer), Philosophy Edn. Soc., Am. Assn. U. Profs., N.E.A., Am. Philos. Assn., John Dewey Soc., Phi Delta Kappa. Author: Logic by Way of Set Theory, 1968. Editor: Crucial Issues in Education, 4th edit., 1969; (with Gordon C. Lee) Crucial Issues in Education, 3d edit., 1964. Home: 1809 Woodland St Duluth MN 55803

EHLERS, JOSEPH HENRY, civil engr., lawyer; b. Hartford, Conn., Dec. 31, 1892; s. C. Julius and Caroline T. (Sauer) E.; B.S., Trinity Coll., 1914; M.S. in Civil Engring., U. Cal., 1915; M.C.E., Cornell U., 1916; m. Marcellite Edwards Hardy, Feb. 15, 1945 (dec. Apr. 1964). Chief insp. for Modjeski & Angier, Pitts., 1919; prof. structural engring. Pei Yang U., China, 1920-24; constrn. engr. Asia Devel. Co. on diversion of Yellow River, 1923; U.S. trade commr. on earthquake reconstrn. and tech. devel. of Japan, 1926-30; acting comml. attache Am. embassy, Tokyo, 1929; tech. dir. Nat. Conf. on Constrn., Wahsington , 1931-33; asst. to dep. adminstr. Fed. Emergency Adminstrn. Pub. Works, Washington, 1933- 38; chief cons. engring. div. Fed. Works Agy., War Pub. Works Program, 1942-46; cons. engr., atty., Washington, 1946—; exec. dir. Nat. Conf. on Pub. Works, 1955-56; san. engring. dir. USPHS Res. Corps, ret.; asst. commr. tech. services Urban Renewal Adminstrn., Washington, 1955-58; housing coordinator ICA, Yemen, 1960-61 cons. U.N., 1962- 63; tech. advisor Govt. of Iraq Ministry Works at Baghdad. Mem. organizing com., del. World Engring. Congress, Tokyo, 1929; chmn. adv. com. engrs. U.S. Civil Service Commn., 1950-57; pres. Jack H. Ehlers Found., Russellville, Ky., 1971—. Decorated Order Brilliant Star (China). Registered professional engr., D.C. Fellow Am. Soc. C.E. (field rep. 1949-55, sec. city planning division); mem. Am., D.C. (member com. internat. law) bar assns., D.C. Soc. Profl. Engrs. (dir.); hon. mem. A.I.A. Republican. Clubs: Explorers (N.Y.C.); University (Washington). Author: Letters of Travel, 1965; Far Horizons—The Travel Diary of An Engineer, 1966. Editor, Jour. Chinese and Am. Engrs. Assn., 1923-24. Contbr. articles to profl. mags. Home: The Westchester Washington DC 20016 also 296 S Main St Russellville KY 42276 Office: 4000 Cathedral Av Washington DC 20016 also So Bank Ky Bldg Russellville KY 42276

EHLERS, RUSSELL W., educator. Prof., head. plastics tech. dept. Lowell Tech. Inst. Office: Plastics Tech Dept Lowell Tech Inst Lowell MA 01854*

EHLERT, JACKSON KARL, coll. dean; b. Hartford, Wis., Oct. 29, 1905; s. Dr. Edwin Henry and Elizabeth (Pike) E.; B.S., U. Minn., 1929, M.A., 1935; Ed.D., U. Colo., 1949; m. Marjorie Gehl, May 10, 1930; 1 dau., Sally. Supr. music pub. schs., New Richmond, Wis., 1929-34; dir. music Duluth (Minn.) State Tchrs. Coll., 1934-41, dir. fine arts, 1941-47; dir. fine arts, Duluth br. U. Minn., 1947-48; dean Sch. Fine Arts, Ithaca (N.Y.) Coll., 1950-52; dean Jordan Coll. Music, Butler U. 1952—. Mem. Music Tchrs. Nat. Assn., Music. Educators Nat. Conf., Ind. Music Educators, Am. Assn. U. Profs., Phi Delta Kappa, Phi Mu Alpha. Mason. Rotarian. Home: 4420 N Meridian St Indianapolis IN 46208

EHRE, VICTOR TYNDALL, ins. co. exec.; b. Boston, July 25, 1913; s. Victor H. and Ethel (Woods) E.; B.S. cum laude, U. Pa. Wharton Sch., 1935; m. Allison DeWolfe, Aug. 20, 1938; children—Victor Tyndall, Donald DeWolfe. With Travelers Ins. Co., 1935-38, Kemper Orgn., 1938-55, Buffalo Ins. Co., 1955- 64, pres., 1956-64; pres. Utica Mut. Ins. Co. (N.Y.), 1964—, chmn. bd., 1970- -, also dir.; dir. Security Mut. Life Ins. Co. N.Y., Marine Midland Banks-Central; pres., chief exec. officer, dir. Graphic Arts Mut. Ins. Co.; chmn. bd. UNI-Service Credit Corp., Available Funds, Inc., UNI-Service Life Agy., Inc., Utica Mutual Assos., Inc.; dir. Am. Mut. Ins. Alliance, Nat. Assn. Automotive Mut. Ins. Companies, Ins. Information Inst., Asso. Industries N.Y. State; vice chmn. exec. com. Improved Risk Mutuals. Bd. dirs., dir., adv. bd. State Traffic Council N.Y.; dir., past 1st pres. Western N.Y. Traffic Safety Council; chmn. Oneida County Traffic Safety Adv. Bd.; v.p. Greater Utica C. of C.; pres. bd. Greater Utica Community Chest and Planning Council; bd. dirs. Oneida County Indsl. Devel. Corp.; adv. com. Nat. Alliance Businessmen; pres. Civic Mus. Soc. Utica, Utica Bus. Opportunities Corp.; chmn. Operation Sunshine, Comets Bus. Boosters; mem. Gov. N.Y. Statewide Com. Children and Youth; chmn. Region II Boy Scouts Am., also mem. exec. bd. Nat. council; mem. U. Pa. Alumni Clubs Adv. Council; adv. bd. Utica Salvation Army; trustee State Univ. Upper Div. Coll. Served to lt. (s.g.) USNR, 1943-46. Recipient award of merit from Gov. Rockefeller of N.Y., 1965; named Indsl. Man of Year, 1968; recipient Rotarian Citizen's award 1969. Mem. Am. Arbitration Assn. (dir.), U. Pa. Alumni Club Western N.Y. (past pres.). Episcopalian (vestryman). Mason. Clubs: Buffalo; Lake Placid (N.Y.); Fort Schuyler (Utica); Yahnundasis (New Hartford, N.Y.); India House (N.Y.C.). Home: 1730 Sherman Dr Utica NY 13501 Office: P O Box 530 Utica NY 13503.

EHRENBURG, ILYA, novelist; b. Kiev, Russia, Jan. 27, 1891. Traveled Europe, 1908, lived in Paris, 1909-13; tchr., assisted with children's theatre, Moscow; resided in Belgium to World War II; reporter Russian Front, early 1940's; on tour U.S., 1946. Author: The Extraordinary Adventures of Julio Jurenito, 1921; The Love of Jeanne, Ney, 1024 (prod. as motion picture); Out of Chaos, 1934; Fall of Paris, 1943; The Tempering of Russia, 1944; European Crossroad, 1947; The Storm (Stalin prize), 1949; The Thaw, 1955; Ninth Wave, 1955; Stormy Life of Lasik Roitschwantz, 1960; Change of Season, 1962; Checkhov, Stendahl, and Other Essays, 1963; Memoirs, 1964; People and Life, 1962; Curtain Half Lifted, 1964; Mirror on the Highway, 1964; Survival's Favorite, 1964; Men, Years, Life; Post War Years '45-54.

EHRENFELD, JOHN HENRY, candy co. exec.; b. Sharpsburg, Pa., July 25, 1917; s. Charles and Mary (Conlon) E.; B.A., U. Pitts., 1939; m. Florence Maxwell, Feb. 14, 1941; children—Barbara, Carol, Robert. With Libby, McNeill & Libby, 1940-69, v.p. co., 1961-69, gen. mgr. canned meat div., 1953-69, v.p. sales, Chgo., 1966-69, v.p., gen. mgr. Western div., mgr. corporated bd. dirs.; v.p. marketing Tootsie Roll Ind., Chgo., 1969—. Mem. Cling Peach Adv. Bd. Mem. Nat. Meat Canners Assn. (pres. 1959-61, dir. 1956-61), Canners League of Cal. (dir.), San Francisco C. of C. (dir.). Lion. Home: 3543 Willow St Flossmoor IL 60422 Office: 7401 S Michigan Av Chicago IL

EHRENFREUND, DAVID, educator; b. N.Y.C., May 24, 1917; s. Leo and Henrietta (Huppert) E.; B.A., State U. Ia., 1943, M.A., 1945, Ph.D., 1947; m. Eleanor Nancy Stern, Mar. 6, 1943; children—Mark Joseph (dec. July 1967), Cathy Ann. From instr. to asso. prof. psychology Wash. State U., 1947-56; prof. psychology, chmn. dept. Adelphi Coll., 1956-62, So. Ill. U., 1962—. Fellow Am. Psychol. Assn., A.A.A.S.; mem. Midwestern Psychol. Assn. (pres. elect 1970-71), Psychonomic Soc., Sigma Xi. Contbr. articles to profl. jours. Office: Dept Psychology Southern Ill Univ Carbondale IL 62901

EHRENHAFT, JOHANN LEO, surgeon; b. Vienna, Austria, Oct. 10, 1915; s. Felix and Olga (Steindler) E.; came to U.S., 1934, naturalized, 1939; student U. Vienna, 1933-34; M.D., U. Ia., 1938; m. Jean Lovett, Oct. 17, 1953; 1 son, John Bruce. Intern Johns Hopkins Hosp., 1938-39, Halsted fellow in surgery, 1939-40; resident surgery U. Ia., 1940-42, 45-47, instr., 1947-48, asso., 1948-49, asst. prof., 1949-51, asso. prof., 1951-53, prof. surgery, 1953—; fellow in thoracic surgery Barnes Hosp., St. Louis, 1948-49; chmn. div. thoracic surgery, U. Ia. Hosps., Iowa City, 1949—. Mem. Council on Cardiovascular Surgery, Am. Heart Assn., 1952—, Bd. Thoracic Surgery, Inc., 1966—; regent Am. Coll. Chest Physicians. Served to maj. AUS, 1942-46. Diplomate Am. Bd. Surgery. Fellow A.C.S.; mem. A.M.A., Am. Assn. Thoracic Surgery, Am. Heart Assn., Soc. U. Surgeons, Am., Pan-Am. surg. assns., Am. Coll. Chest Physicians, Internat. Cardiovascular Soc., Soc. Thoracic Surgeons, Central Surg. Assn., A.C.S., Soc. Vascular Surgery, Société Internationale de Chirugie, Sigma Xi, Alpha Omega Alpha. Editorial bd. Annals Thoracic Surgery, 1964—. Contbr. articles on thoracic and cardiovascular surgery to med. jours. Home: 329 Ellis St Iowa City IA 52240

EHRENREICH, HENRY, educator, physicist; b. Frankfurt, Germany, May 11, 1928; s. Nathan and Frieda (Rosenstein) E.; came to U.S., 1940, naturalized, 1946; A.B., Cornell U., 1950, Ph.D., 1955; student Columbia, 1950-51; M.A. (hon.), Harvard, 1963; m. Tema P. Hasnas, Feb. 1, 1953; children—Paul, Beth-Ida, Robert. Theoretical physicist Gen. Electric Research Lab., Schenectady, 1955-63; vis. lectr. Harvard, 1960-61, Gordon McKay prof. applied physics, 1963—; vis. prof. Brandeis, 1969, U. Paris, 1969. Mem. sci. adv. bd. Itek Corp., 1967—. Fellow Am. Phys. Soc. (chmn. div. solid state physics 1969), Am. Acad. Arts and Scis.; mem. Phi Beta Kappa, Sigma Xi. Contbr. to profl. jours. Bd. editors Phys. Rev., 1965-67; co-editor Solid State Physics, 1966—. Office: Pierce Hall Harvard Univ Cambridge MA 02138

EHRENREICH, JOSEPH, optical co. exec.; b. 1907; married. Founder, chmn. bd., pres., chief exec. officer Ehrenreich Photo-Optical Industries, Inc., Garden City, N.Y. Office: 623 Stewart Av Garden City NY 11530*

EHRENSBERGER, RAY, coll. ofcl.; b. Indpls., Dec. 7, 1907; s. Edward H. and Elizabeth (M. Peetz) E.; A.B., Wabash Coll., 1929; A.M., Butler U., 1930; fellow Syracuse U., 1935-36, Ph.D., 1937; grad. student Ind. U., U. Wis.; LL.D., Wabash Coll., 1966; m. Helen L. Myers, Sept. 21, 1939; children—Betty Ann, Ray. Instr. speech Doane Coll., 1930-32; head speech dept. Franklin Coll., 1932-35; asso. prof. speech U. Md., 1936- 39, prof., chmn. dept. speech and dramatic art, 1939-52, dir. European program, Heidelberg, Germany, 1949-50, dean Coll. Spl. and Continuation Studies, 1952-59, dean Univ. Coll., 1959-70, chancellor, 1970—; dir. Bi- nat. Center, Dept. of State, Ankara, Turkey, 1951-52. Recipient Exceptional Service award U.S. Air Force. Mem. Speech Assn. Am., Phi Delta Kappa, Phi Kappa Phi, Sigma Chi, Omicron Delta Kappa, Delta Sigma Rho, Tau Kappa Alpha, Blue Key. Rotarian. Author: (with Elaine Pagel), A Notebook for Public Speaking, 1946. Home: 4608 Harvard Rd College Park MD 20740

EHRENZWEIG, ALBERT ARMIN, educator; b. Herzogenburg, Austria, Apr. 1, 1906; s. Albert and Emma (Bachrachová) E.; Dr. Utr. Jur., U. Vienna (Austria), 1928; LL.B., U. Bristol (Eng.), 1939; J.D., U. Chgo., 1941; LL.M., Columbia, 1942, J.S.D., 1952; Dr. honoris causa, Stockholm, Sweden, 1969; m. Erica Witrofsky, Apr. 9, 1933; children—Elizabeth (Mrs. David T. Steffen), Joan (Mrs. Egon von Kaschnitz). Came to U.S., 1939, naturalized, 1945. Admitted to N.Y. bar, 1945; clk., asst. judge Austrian Cts., 1929-33, judge, 1933-38; research asst. N.Y. State Law Revision Com., 1942-44; asso. firm Cravath, Swaine & Moore, N.Y.C., 1944-48; Walter Perry Johnson prof. law U. Cal. at Berkeley Law Sch., 1948—; hon. prof. pvt. internat. law U. Vienna, 1960—. Guggenheim fellow, 1952; Fulbright prof. U. Tokyo (Japan), 1956, U. Pavia (Italy), 1960, U. Rome (Italy), 1966; NATO prof. U. Leyden (Netherlands), 1964; hon. senator U. Vienna, 1965—. Mem. Am., N.Y. State bar assns., Am. Law Inst., Internat. Assn. Ins. Law (hon. pres. 1966—), Internat. Acad. Comparative Law. Author: Schuldhaftung, 1936; Negligence Without Fault, 1952; Full-Aid Insurance, 1954; Treatise on Conflict of Laws, 1962; Conflicts in a Nutshell, 1970; Private International Law, 1967; Specific Principles of Private Transnational Law, 1969; Psychoanalytic Jurisprudence, 1971; also numerous articles. Home: 258 Colgate Av Berkeley CA 94708

EHRHARDT, LAURENCE COHANE, lawyer, corp. exec.; b. N.Y.C., July 12, 1912; s. George Louis and Ella Ramsey (Cohane) E.; A.B., Fordham U., 1933; LL.B., Harvard, 1936; m. Jeanne Frances White, Apr. 10, 1939; children—Laurence White, Mary Victoria, John White, Jeanne Frances. Admitted to N.Y. bar, 1937; research asst. N.Y. State Jud. Council, 1936-38; asso. George L. Ehrhardt, 1938-41; gen. counsel Reiss Mfg. Corp., 1941-43; asso. Donovan, Leisure, Newton & Lumbard, N.Y.C., 1943-46; legal staff U.S. Maritime Commn., 1946-47; v.p. law McKesson & Robbins, Inc., N.Y.C., 1947—, sec., counsel, 1957-65, secretary and general counsel, 1965—. Mem. Fed., Am., N.Y. State bar assns., Bar Assn. City N.Y., U.S. Trademark Assn. (board of directors 1953-58), Am. Soc. Corporate Secs. (sec. 1963-65, dir., 1965—). Clubs: Harvard (N.Y.C.); American Yacht, Shenorock Shore (Rye). Home: Glendale Rd Rye, NY 10580. Office: 155 E 44th St New York City NY 10017

EHRICH, ROBERT WILLIAM, educator, anthropologist; b. N.Y.C., Apr. 23, 1908; s. William Joseph and Adelaide (Price) E.; B.A., Harvard, 1931, M.A., 1933, Ph.D., 1946; m. Ann Marie Hoskin, Mar. 12, 1937; children—Judith, Holly Ann (Mrs. Gerald M. Henderson). Archaeol. excavations and anthropometry in Iraq, 1929-30, Czechoslovakia, 1929-31, 60-61, Yugoslavia, 1932-33, 69-70, Turkey, 1934- 39, Saratoga (N.Y.) Battlefield, 1940-42; mem. faculty Bklyn. Coll. of City U. N.Y., 1947—, prof. anthropology, 1963—, chmn. dept., 1965-71, exec. officer anthropology, City U., 1966-68. Mem. adv. panel anthropology NSF, 1962-64; fgn. currency program Smithsonian Instn., 1965-70. Served to capt. USMCR, 1943-45. Decorated Bronze Star; Rockefeller fellow, 1946-47. Fellow Am. Anthrop. Assn. (exec. bd. 1960- 62, ethics com. 1970—), A.A.A.S., Royal Anthrop. Inst. Gt. Britain and Ireland; mem. Am. Assn. Phys. Anthropologists, Internat. Union Prehistoric and Protohistoric Scis. (permanent council 1963—), Am. Ethnol. Soc., Archaeol. Inst. Am., Archaeol. Soc. Yugoslavia (hon.), Sigma Xi; corr. mem. German Archaeol. Inst. Author: (with E. Pleslova-Stikova) Homolka, a Late Neolithic Village in Bohemia, 1967; also articles. Editor, contbr.: Relative Chronologies in Old World Archaeology, 1954; Chronologies in Old World Archeology, 1965; area editor for Central Europe and Balkans, Council Old World Archaeology, 1956—. Home: 285 Garfield Pl Brooklyn NY 11215

EHRICKE, KRAFFT ARNOLD, space engr.; b. Berlin, Germany, Mar. 24, 1917; s. Arnold F. and Ruth (Konietzko) E.; Aero. Eng., Tech. U., Berlin, 1942, courses atomic physics and celestial mechanics, 1941-42; L.H.D., Nat. Tchrs. Coll., Evanston, Ill., 1961; m. Ingeborg Mettull, Jan. 16, 1945; children—Krista, Astrid, Doris. Came to U.S., 1947, naturalized, 1955. Devel. engr. V-2 propulsion system, Peenemuende, Germany, 1942-45; jet propulsion engr. Dept. Army, Ft. Bliss, Tex., 1947-50; chief gasdynamics sect. Army Ballistic Missile Center, Redstone Arsenal, Ala., 1950-52; preliminary design engr. Bell Aircraft Corp., 1952-54; with Convair, div. Gen. Dynamics Corp., 1954-65, design specialist, 1954-55, chief design and systems analysis, 1956-57, asst. to tech. dir. Convair- Astronautics, 1957-58, originator, also program dir. Centaur space vehicle, 1958-62, dir. advanced studies dept., 1962-65; asst. div. dir. astrionics div. N.Am. Aviation, Autonetics div., Anaheim, Cal., 1965-68; chief scientist space systems and applications space div. N.Am. Rockwell Corp., Downey, Cal., 1968—. Recipient 1st Guenther Loeser medal for best paper (The Satelloid) presented during 6th Internat. Astronautical Congress, Internat. Astronautical Fedn., 1956, G. Edward Pendray award Am. Rocket Soc., 1961, Astronautics award Am. Rocket Soc., 1957; named to Internat. Aerospace Hall of Fame, 1966. Fellow Am. Astron. Soc., Am. Inst. Aeros. and Astronautics, Brit. Interplanetary Soc.; mem. Deutsche Ges. f. Weltraumforschg. (pres. 1942-43), Internat. Acad. Astronautics. Author: Space Flight, Vol. I, Environment and Celestial Mechanics, 1959, Vol. II, Dynamics, 1961; (with B.A. Miller) Exploring the Planets, 1969; Beyond Earth, 1971; numerous articles. Home: 845 Lamplight Dr LaJolla CA 92037 Office: 12214 Lakewood Blvd Downey CA 90241

EHRINGER, FRANK JOSEPH, electronics co. exec.; b. Newark, Mar. 3, 1915; s. Hermann and Albertine (Krell) E.; B. Elec. Engring., N.Y.U., 1943; evening student Stevens Inst. Tech., 1943-45; m. Marjorie J. Ward, Feb. 5, 1944; children—Drew Franklin and Bruce George (twins). With Tung-Sol Electric, Inc. (co. name changed to Wagner Electric Corp.), Newark, 1939—, v.p. automotive products div., 1958-63, pres., 1963—; dir. Studebaker Worthington, Inc. Mem. Soc. Automotive Engrs., Motor Equipment Mfrs. Assn. Home: Cove Pl Mountain Lakes, NJ 07046. Office: 1 Summer Av Newark NJ 07104

EHRLICH, ALVIN Q., advt. exec.; b. Washington, Mar. 15, 1911; grad. Emerson Inst., Washington, 1928; m. Mildred Margaret McIntyre, Mar. 14, 1948; children—Alvin McIntyre, Melissa Jane. Advt. mgr. Raleigh Haberdasher, Washington, 1929-30; account exec. Kal Advt., Washington, 1931-34, partner, 1935; partner, exec. v.p. Kal, Ehrlich & Merrick, Washington, 1955-67, pres., 1967—; pres. Ehrlich- Linkins & Assos., 1968—; dir. PepCom Industries. Mem. exec. com. Washington Conv. and Visitors Bur., 1956—. Bd. dirs. Am. Cancer Soc., D.C. Soc. Crippled Children; chmn. bd. consultants Dunbarton Coll. Holy Cross. Served with AUS, World War II. Named Ad Man of Year Advt. Club Washington, 1962; Marketing Man of Year Am. Marketing Assn., Washington chpt., 1964. Mem. Washington Ad Club (pres. 1938-39), Washington Bd. Trade, Radio Pioneers, Am. Marketing Assn., Exec. Vice Pres. Club, Nat. Communications Club (bd. govs.). Clubs: Variety (chief barker 1954), Saints and Sinners (Washington). Home: 6540 Bradley Blvd Bethesda MD 20034 Office: 4926 Wisconsin Av NW Washington DC 20016

EHRLICH, JACOB W., lawyer; b. nr. Rockville, Md., Oct. 15, 1900; legal edn. Georgetown U., m. Marjorie Mercer; children—Jacob, Dora Jane (Mrs. Guy Cherney). Formerly employed as drayman for Wells Fargo; boxed professionally; sec. to v.p. Western Pacific R.R.; admitted to Cal bar, 1922; spectacular record of acquittals, defense murder trials, also civil practice; well known as The Master. Lectr. Am. Trial Lawyers Assn., Practicing Law Inst., also seminars. Mem. Scribes, Nat. Law Writers Assn., Lawyers Lit. Club (bd. editorial advisers), Author's League Am., Dramatists Guild, Am. Soc. Legal History. Author: Ehrlich's Blackstone; Ehrlich's Criminal Evidence; What is Wrong with the Jury System; The Lost Art of Cross-Examination; The Educated Lawyer; The Contested Divorce Case; Howl of the Censor; The Holy Bible and the Law; A Reasonable Doubt; A Life in my Hands. Contbg. author: U. Cal. Continuing Edn. of Bar Series, Am. Jurisprudence Trial Series. Office: 300 Montgomery St San Francisco CA 94104

EHRLICH, PAUL RALPH, biologist, educator; b. Phila., May 29, 1932; s. William and Ruth (Rosenberg) E.; A.B., U. Pa., 1953; A.M., U. Kan., 1955, Ph.D., 1957; m. Anne Fitzhugh Howland, Dec. 18, 1955; 1 dau., Lisa Marie. Research asso. U. Kan., Lawrence, 1958-59; asst. prof. biol. scis. Stanford, 1959-62, asso. prof., 1962-66, prof., 1966—, dir. grad. study dept. biol. scis., 1966-69. Cons., Behavioral Research Labs., 1963—; cons. biology, editor in population biology McGraw Hill Book Co., N.Y.C., 1964—. Fellow Cal. Acad. Scis.; mem. Soc. for Study Evolution, Soc. Systematic Zoology, Am. Soc. Naturalists, Lepidopterists Soc., Am. Mus. Natural History (hon. life mem.), Nat. Pilots Assn., Airplane Owners and Pilots Assn. Club: Royal Aero of New South Wales (Australia). Author: How to Know the Butterflies, 1961; Process of Evolution, 1963; Principles of Modern Biology, 1967; Population Bomb, 1968; Population, Resources, Environment: Issues In Human Ecology, 1970; How to be a Survivor, 1970. Contbr. articles profl. jours. Home: 936 Valdez Pl Stanford CA 94305

EHRLICH, ROBERT WALTER, telephone co. exec.; b. Newark, Sept. 22, 1922; s. Walter Max and Florence Dorothea (Bullinger) E.; B.S., U. Mich., 1943; m. Katherine Lathrop, July 8, 1944; 1 dau., Virginia. With Am. Tel. & Tel. Co., 1946-65, 66—, asst. chief engr., N.Y.C., 1963-65, asst. treas., 1966-68, asst. sec., 1968-69, sec., 1969—; v.p. Pacific Tel. & Tel. Co., San Francisco, 1965-66. Served to 1st lt. AUS, 1943-46. Mem. I.E.E.E. (sr. mem.). Home: 40 Sammis Lane White Plains NY 10605 Office: 195 Broadway New York City NY 10007

EHRLICH, THOMAS, educator; b. Cambridge, Mass., Mar. 4, 1934; s. William and Evelyn (Seltzer) E.; A.B., Harvard, 1956, LL.B., 1959; m. Ellen Rome, June 18, 1957; children—David, Elizabeth, Paul. Admitted to Wis. bar, 1959; law clk. Judge Learned Hand U.S. Ct. Appeals 2d Circuit, 1959-60; individual practice law, Milw., 1960-62; spl. asst. to legal adviser Dept. State, 1962-64, spl. asst. to under-sec., 1964-65; asso. prof. law Stanford, 1965-68, prof., 1968—, also dean, 1971—. Author: (with Abram Chayes and Andreas F. Lowenfeld) The International Legal Process, 3 vols., 1968. Office: Stanford Sch Law Stanford CA 94305

EHRLICHMAN, BEN B., investment banker; b. Mpls., Aug. 20, 1895; grad. pub. schs., Tacoma and Seattle; m. Genevieve Ament Grout, 1920; 1 dau., Mrs. Nancy Ehrlichman Sobek. Office boy, Carstens & Earles, Inc., 1912-15; asst. cashier, mgr. bond dept. Guardian Trust & Savs. Bank, Seattle, 1915-17; mgr. bond dept. Nat. City Bank, Seattle, 1919-20, Puget Sound Nat. Bank, Tacoma, 1920-21; organized Drumheller, Ehrlichman Co., Seattle, pres., 1921-45, name changed to Pacific N.W. Co., 1945; dir. emeritus United Pacific Ins. Co., VWR United Corp. Vice chmn. Seattle Civilian War Commn., 1942-46; chmn. King County Aviation Council, 1948-58; pres. Municipal League Seattle and King County, 1950-53, trustee; regional v.p. Nat. Municipal League, N.Y.; dir. emeritus Seattle Symphony; adv. com., past pres. Central Assn. Seattle; trustee U. Puget Sound, Principia Corp., St. Louis; adv. council Chief Seattle council Boy Scouts Am. Served as 2d lt. AS, U.S. Army, 1918-19. Recipient distinguished citizen award Nat. Municipal League, 1955; 1st Citizen of Seattle award, 1962; Silver Beaver, Boy Scouts of Am., 1968. Mem. Investment Bankers Assn. Am. (past gov.), Seattle C. of C. (sr. council). Christian Scientist. Mason (32, K.T.), Rotarian. Clubs: Harbor (1st pres.), Seattle Tennis, Rainier. Home: Del Mesa Carmel Carmel CA 93921 Office: Norton Bldg Seattle WA 98104

EHRLICHMAN, JOHN D., govt. ofcl.; b. Tacoma, Mar. 20, 1925; A.B., U. Cal. at Los Angeles, 1948; J.D., Stanford, 1951. Admitted to Wash. and Cal. bars; Formerly counsel to President Nixon; now asst. to Pres. for domestic affairs; dir. Domestic Council. Mem. Council on Internat. Econ. Policy; mem. Pres.' Property Rev. Bd. Recipient Distinguished Eagle award Boy Scouts Am. Mem. Am., Wash. bar assns., State Bar Cal., Phi Delta Phi, Kappa Sigma. Address: The White House Washington DC 20500

EHRLING, SIXTEN, orch. condr.; b. Malmö, Sweden, Apr. 3, 1918; s. Gunnar and Emilia (Lundgren) E.; student Royal High Sch. Music, Stockholm, Sweden, 1936- 40; m. Gunnel Lindgren, Sept. 19, 1947; children—Elisabeth, Ann- Charlotte. Came to U.S., 1963. Condr., Royal Opera House, Stockholm, 1940-53, prin. condr., music dir., 1953-60; condr., music dir. Detroit Symphony Orch., 1963—; guest condr. U.S. and Europe, also concert pianist, accompanist. Home: 741 Trombley Rd Grosse Pointe Park MI 48236 Office: Ford Auditorium E Jefferson Av Detroit MI 48226

EHRMAN, FREDERICK L., investment banker; b. San Francisco, Jan. 3, 1906; s. Albert L. and Mina Louise (Schwabacher) E.; B.A., U. Cal. at Berkeley, 1927; m. Edith Koshland, June 25, 1929; children—Edith, Anita (dec.). Partner, Lehman Bros., 1941—; chmn. exec. com., dir. Lehman Corp.; dir., mem. exec. com. Greyhound Corp.; dir. Lehman Bros. Internat., Medallion Ins. Co., Beckman Instruments, Inc., Travelers Express Co., Inc., 20th Century Fox Film

Corp., Gen. Fire & Casualty Co. Vice chmn. Presdl. Com. for Observance 25th Anniversary UN; U.S. nat. chmn. UN Day, 1970. Chmn., mem. bd. N.Y. U. Med. Center; trustee Inst. for Crippled and Disabled, Ernest Lawrence Hall of Sci., at U. Cal.; trustee, mem. exec. com. N.Y. U. Served as comdr. USNR, 1941-45. Clubs: Bond (N.Y.); Petroleum (Los Angeles) Duchess Valley; Nimrod Valley; Century Country; Sky; Sleepy Hollow Country, Board Room. Home: Woodheath Farm Armonk Village Westchester County NY 10504 Office: 1 William St New York City NY 10004

EHRMANN, HENRY WALTER, educator; b. Berlin, Germany, Mar. 10, 1908; s. Walter and Eva (Wolff) E.; LL.B., U. Berlin, 1929; Dr. jur., U. Freiburg (Germany), 1932; M.A. (hon.), Dartmouth, 1962; m. Claire Sachs, Mar. 1939; children—Michael M., Paul L. Came to U.S., 1940, naturalized, 1949. Asso. Internat. Inst. Social History, Amsterdam, Paris, 1935-40; asso. grad. faculty New Sch. Social Research, N.Y.C., 1940-43; edn. specialist U.S. Govt., 1943-47; asso. prof. polit. sci. U. Colo., 1947-50, prof., 1950-61; prof. govt. Dartmouth, Hanover, N.H., 1961-64, Joel Parker prof. law and polit. sci., 1964-71, chmn. dept. govt., 1963-66; prof. polit. sci. McGill U., Montreal, 1971—; vis. prof. U. Cal., 1955-56, Free U., Berlin, Germany, 1967, 71, univs. Paris, Bordeaux, Grenoble, 1958-59, 62; mem. Inst. Advanced Study, 1950; nat. selections com. Fulbright awards, 1953-56. Social Sci. Research Council area research fellow, 1952-53, 58-59; Fulbright teaching award, Nice, France, summers 1958, 62; ednl. cons. Ford Found., Berlin, 1964. Mem. Am. Polit. Sci. Assn., Am. Civil Liberties Union, Am. Assn. U. Profs., Soc. for French Hist. Studies. Democrat. Author: French Labor from Popular Front to Liberation, 1947; Organized Business in France, 1957; Interest Groups on Four Continents, 3d edit., 1965; La Politique du Patronat Francais, 1959; Politische Bildung, 1966; Politics in France, 1968, 2d edit., 1971. Bd. editors Am. Polit. Sci. Rev., 1952-56. Editor: Democracy in a Changing Society, 1965. Contbr. articles to jours., contbr. to various U.S. and fgn. encys. Home: 3 Webster Terrace Hanover NH 03755

EHRMANN, WALTER H., banker; b. Chgo., 1923; grad. U. Chgo., 1948. Vice chmn., dir. Pullman Bank & Trust Co., Chgo., Standard Bank & Trust Co., County Bank & Trust Co., First Nat. Bank Lockport. Vice pres., trustee Roseland Community Hosp. Home: 2708 Chariot Lane Olympia Fields IL 60461 Office: 400 E 111th St Chicago IL 60628*

EHRMANN, WINSTON WALLACE, sociologist, coll. dean; b. Reno, May 17, 1912; s. Emil Ernest and Imogene (Irwin) E.; student Mass. Inst. Tech., 1930-31; B.S., Yale, 1934, Ph.D., 1938; m. Sarah Margaret Berlin, Sept. 13, 1934; children—Gretchen (Mrs. Bruce Maclachlan), Sally (Mrs. Andrew Baggs). Indsl. engr. U.S. Rubber Co., 1935-36; asst. prof. U. Fla., 1938-40, asso. prof., 1940-46, prof. sociology, 1946-59; prof. sociology Colo. State U., 1959-62; asso. sec. Am. Assn. U. Profs., Washington, 1962-66; prof., chmn. sociology dept. Cornell Coll., Mt. Vernon, Ia., 1966—, dean of coll., 1969—, provost, 1970—; tech. cons. White House Conf. on Children and Youth, 1960; vis. lectr. Ind. U., 1951, Miss. State Coll. for Women, 1955, Goddard Coll., 1963, Sch. Medicine U. Cal., 1967, Okla. State U., 1968, Ind. State U., 1970. Served from 1st lt. to col., C.E., AUS, 1941-46. Decorated Bronze Star medal. Fellow Am. Sociol. Assn.; mem. Am. Assn. U. Prof. (mem. council 1960-63, asso. editor Bull., 1962-66), Ia. Sociol. Soc. (pres. 1968-69), Phi Beta Kappa. Author: Premarital Dating Behavior, 1959. Asso. editor: Am. Sociol. Rev., 1960-63. Contbr. articles profl. jours. Home: 812 Summit Av Mount Vernon IA 52314

EHRNROOTH, GORAN, banker; b. Helsinki, Finland, Apr. 1, 1905; s. George and Ella (af Nyborg) E.; B.L., U. Helsinki, 1931, M.L., 1934; m. Louise von Julin, June 30, 1930; children—Casimir, Göran, Robert, Else. With Nordiska Föreningsbanken Ab, Helsinki, 1945—, chmn. exec. com. supervisory bd., 1970—; chmn. bd. Finlands Steamship Co., 1953—; dir. Vuoksenniska, Lojo Kalkverk Ab, Oy Tampella Ab, Kaukas Ab, Serlachius Oy, Oy Strömberg Ab, Oy Koverhar Ab, Oy Teko Ab. Mem. Finnish Red Cross, Mannerheim League Child Welfare. Decorated grand cross Order Lion (Finland); 1st class commodore Order Vasa (Sweden); Order Orange Nassau (Netherlands); Order Merit (Italy). Mem. Finnish Bankers Assn. (chmn. 1956-70). Home: 6 Södra kajen Helsinki 13 Finland Office: 30 Alexandersgatan Helsinki 10 Finland

EIB, PAUL B., hosp. adminstr. Dir., VA Hosp., Cleve. Office: 10000 Brecksville Rd Cleveland OH 44144*

EIBLING, HAROLD HENRY, supt. schs.; b. Dola, O., Aug. 5, 1905; s. Henry W. and Sarah (Stanyer) E.; B.S., Ohio No. U., 1926, Pd.D. (hon.), 1959; M.A., Ohio State U., 1932, Ph.D., 1950; D.Sc. in Edn. (hon.), Mt. Union Coll., 1953; LL.D., Miami U., Oxford, O., 1963; m. Evelyn Agner, Aug. 14, 1929; children—Judith Anne, Stephen Harold, David Michael. Tchr., prin., supt. Liberty Twp. Sch., Findlay, O., 1926-36; supt. Maumee (O.) Pub. Schs., 1936-47, Elyria (O.) Pub. Schs., 1947-49; asst. supt., Akron, O., 1949- 50; supt. schs., Canton, O., 1950-56, Columbus, 1956-71; edn. cons., 1971—. Dir. Columbus Savs. & Loan, City Nat. Bank. Mem. bd. Franklin County chpt. A.R.C. Trustee Ohio No. U. Recipient Educator's medal Freedoms Found., 1963; Liberty Bell award Columbus Bar Assn., 1964; Boss of Year award Jr. C. of C., 1964; Supt. of Year award Ohio Edn. Assn., 1966; Distinguished Citizen awards Pub. Relations Soc. Am., 1968, Columbus Dental Soc., 1969; honor citation Ohio legislature, 1969. Mem. Assn. Sch. Adminstrs. (pres. 1970-71), Columbus C. of C. (bd. dirs.), Central Ohio Tchrs. Assn. (pres. 1959). Presbyn. Mason (33). Clubs: University (pres.), Rotary. Co-author history textbooks; World Background for American History, 1965; Our Country, 1965; Great Names in American History, 1965; The Story of America, 1965; History of Our United States, 1964. Contbr. articles to ednl. jours. Home: 255 Ceramic Dr Columbus OH 43214

EICHELBAUM, STANLEY, journalist; b. N.Y.C., Oct. 5, 1926; s. Sam and Rebecca (Rosen) E.; B.A. magna cum laude, Coll. City N.Y., 1947; M.A., Columbia, 1948; Certificat d'Etudes, Sorbonne, Paris, France, 1949. Editorial researcher, reporter New Yorker Mag., N.Y.C., 1949-58; with San Francisco Examiner, 1958—, drama editor, critic plays and movies, 1961—; painter, exhbt. in group show Forum Gallery, N.Y.C., 1955-56; lectr. on arts, various colls., univs., clubs, 1961—. Mem. selections com. San Francisco Internat. Film Festival, 1962-65; instr. workshop in critical writing U. Cal. Extension, San Francisco, 1968—; mem. program San Francisco Art Inst., 1968-70. Mem. Phi Beta Kappa. Contbr. articles to mags. Home: 333 Green St San Francisco CA 94133 Office: San Francisco Examiner 110 5th St San Francisco CA 94103

EICHELBERGER, CLARK MELL, assn. exec.; b. Freeport, Ill., July 29, 1896; s. Joseph Elmer and Olive (Clark) E.; student Northwestern U., 1914-17, U. Chgo., 1919-20; LL.D., Kalamazoo Coll., 1964, So. Ill. U., 1967, Haverford Coll., 1968; m. Rose Kohler, Oct. 6, 1924. Lectr. nat. and internat. affairs Radcliffe Chautauqua System, Washington, 1922-28; dir. Mid-West officer League of Nations Assn., 1929- 34; nat. dir. League Nations Assn., later Am. Assn. for UN, now called UN Assn. of the U.S. of Am., 1934-64, v.p., 1964-68; temp. appointment League Nations Secretariat, 1938. Dir. Commn. to Study Orgn. of Peace, 1939-64, chairman, 1964-68, exec. dir., 1968—. Dir. Comm. to Defend America by Aiding the Allies, 1940-41; cons. to State Dept. 1942-43; cons. Am. del., San Francisco Conf., 1945. Served with U.S. Army and A.E.F., 1917- 19. Decorated Chevalier Legion of Honor (France), 1934. Presbyn. Club: Cosmos (Washington). Author: The United Nations Charter; What Was Done at San Francisco; UN: The First Ten Years, 1955; UN: The First Fifteen Years, 1960; UN: The First Twenty Years, 1965; UN: The First Twenty-Five Years, 1970. Chmn. drafting com. New Dimensions for the UN, 1966. Lectr. Home: 139 E 33d St New York City NY 10016 Office: 866 UN Plaza New York City NY 10017

EICHELBERGER, HAROLD C., corp. exec.; b. Boise, Ida., June 21, 1911; s. Charles E. and Jean (Gribble) E., B.A., Stanford, 1933; m. Isabel E. Falch, June 21, 1935; children—Harold F., Elisabeth, Margaret. With Amfac, Inc., Honolulu, 1933—, successively office boy, asst. treas., treas., sec., 1933-55, v.p., 1955-60, sr. v.p., 1960-61, exec. v.p., 1961- 63, pres., 1964-67, chmn. bd., 1967—, also dir.; dir. Kekaha Sugar Co., Ltd., Lihue Plantation Co., Ltd., Puna Sugar Co., Ltd., Oahu Sugar Co., Ltd., Pioneer Mill Co., Ltd., Am. Factors Assos., Ltd., 745 Fort St Corp., Teloha Corp., Hawaiian Antilles N.V., Hawaiian Electric Co., Inc. Regent U. Hawaii; bd. dirs. Health and Community Services Council, Oahu Devel. Conf., Maunalani Hosp.; trustee Punahou Sch. Mem. Honolulu C. of C., Hawaiian Sugar Planters Assn. Clubs: Oahu Country, Pacific (Honolulu); Kaneohe Yacht. Home: 1556 Mokulua Dr Kailua HI 96734 Office: 700 Bishop St Honolulu HI 96813 also PO Box 3230 Honolulu HI 96801

EICHELBERGER, MARTIN DAVIS, Jr., profl. golfer; b. Waco, Tex., Sept. 3, 1943; s. Martin Davis and Mary Nell (Johnson) E.; B.B.A., Okla. State U., 1966; m. Alyce Faye McBride, Jan. 22, 1966; 1 son, Martin Davis III. Profl. golfer, 1966—; playing on tour, 1967—. Address: 5101 Hawthorne Waco TX 76710

EICHELBRENNER, ERNEST A., educator, physicist; b. Rüstringen, Germany, June 28, 1913; s. Ernst C. and Katharina (Koehn) E.; student univs. Hamburg, Germany, Rome, Italy, 1931-37; Staatsexamen, Hamburg, 1938, Dipl.-Math., 1943; Dr. es Sc., Paris, France, 1955, Lic. es Lettres, 1956; m. Emilie M. Martin, Aug. 16, 1939; children—Hans-Michael, Detlef, Ursula, Etienne. Research engr. Deschimag, Bremen, Germany, 1938-45; asst. U. Hamburg, 1946; research engr. Onera, Chatillon-sous- Bangneux, France, 1947-58, cons., 1958-65; maitre de conf. U. Poitiers (France), 1958-60, prof. without chair, 1961-62, titular prof. 1962-65; titular prof. mech. engring. Laval U., Quebec, Can., 1965—. Cons. BTZ, Brunoy, France, 1958-63. Recipient Henry Bazin prize and medal French Acad. Scis., 1965. Asso. fellow Am. Inst. Aeros. and Astronautics; founding mem. Am. Acad. Mechanics; mem. Am. Soc. Mech. Engrs., Math. Soc. France, other profl. socs. Reviewer Zentralblatt fur Mathematik, 1958—. Research in fluid mechanics particularly boundary layer theory; 3-dimensional (laminar and turbulent) boundary layers, characteristics and criteria of separation and reattachment of 3-dimensional boundary layers; problems of heat transfer in 3-dimensional flow. Home: 1586 Cote Ross Ste-Foy Quebec 10 Quebec Canada

EICHELMANN, J.F., utility exec.; b. 1908; married. With El Paso Natural Gas Co. (Tex.), 1931—, v.p., exec. engr., 1956-66, sr. v.p., 1966—. Office: El Paso Natural Gas Co PO Box 1492 El Paso TX 79999*

EICHENBAUM, HOWARD SAMUEL, architect; b. Little Rock, Apr. 25, 1905; s. Ephriam H. and Sadie (Cohn) E.; B. Arch., Washington U., 1924; m. Helen Levin, Mar. 17, 1929; children—Howard Samuel, Lee, Dan. With Mann & Stern, Little Rock, 1924- 29; partner Erhart & Eichenbaum, 1930-45, Erhart, Eichenbaum, Rauch & Blass, 1945—; dir. 1st Am. Nat. Bank, North Little Rock, Ark., projects include hosps. and sanatoria. Sec. Ark. Architects Registration Bd., 1938-40, vice chmn., 1958, v.p., 1959; pres. Ark. Bd. Architects, 1962-63; mem. city planning commn., Little Rock, 1948-55, chmn., 1952-55, vice chmn., 1958; mem. exec. com. Pulaski County Met. Area Planning Commn., 1958-59, chmn. commn., 1963; chmn. North Little Rock Planning Commn.; chmn. Lakewood Property Owners Assn., 1966-67. Pres. Quapaw area council Boy Scouts Am., 1950-52, Nat. council, 1952-55. Trustee Benjamin Franklin Stiftung, Berlin, Germany, 1963—; trustee, v.p. Leo N. Levi Hosp., Hot Springs. Recipient Silver Beaver award Boy Scouts Am., 1951. Fellow Internat. Inst. Arts and Letter, A.I.A. (pres. Ark. chpt. 1947-48, dir. Gulf States region 1950-53, 2d v.p. 1953-55, chmn. nat. com. fees and contracts, 1959); mem. North Little Rock C. of C. (dir.). Jewish religion. Home: 5101 Edgemere Dr North Little Rock AR 72116 Office: Continental Bldg Little Rock AR 72201

EICHENBERG, FRITZ, artist; b. Cologne, Germany, Oct. 24, 1901; s. Siegfried and Ida (Marcus) E.; student Sch. Applied Arts, Cologne, 1916-20, State Acad. Graphic Arts, Leipzig, 1922-24; m. Mary Altmann, 1926 (dec. 1937); 1 dau., Suzanne; m. 2d, Margaret Ladenburg, 1941 (div. 1965); 1 son, Timothy. Came to U.S., 1933, naturalized, 1941. Staff artist and illustrator for German mags. and newspapers, 1926-33; with art dept. New Sch. for Social Research, 1935-41; mem. Pennell Fund com. Library of Congress, 1962-68; prof. art Pratt Inst., chmn. dept. graphic art, 1956-63; prof. U. R.I., 1966—, chmn. dept. art, 1966-69; founder, dir. emeritus Pratt Graphic Art Center; also illustrator numerous books with wood engravings and lithographs; works in ann. print exhbns.; represented by prints and drawings in major collections, U.S., also abroad; one-man shows New Sch. for Social Research, 1938, 49, N.Y. Pub. Library Print Gallery, 1949, AAA Galleries, N.Y., 1967. Recipient purchase prizes Library of Congress Print Exhibit, 1943-54, Pennell medal Pa. Acad. Print Exhibit, 1944, 1st prize Print exhibit Nat. Acad., 1946, Silver medal Ltd. Editions Club, 1954; J.D.R. III Fund grantee, 1968. Fellow Royal Soc. Arts; mem. Soc. Am. Graphic Artists, N.A.D., Am. Inst. Graphic Arts (dir., v.p.). Mem. Soc. of Friends. Author: Art and Faith, 1952. Author-illustrator: Ape in a Cape, 1952; Dancing in the Moon, 1955. Editor, founder Artist's Proof Ann. Home: 142 Oakwood Dr Peace Dale RI 02879 Office: Dept Art U R I Kingston RI 02881

EICHER, GEORGE JOHN, aquatic biologist; b. Bremerton, Wash., Aug. 27, 1916; s. George John and Caroline Agnes (Wolfer) E.; student Wash. State U., 1938; B.S., Ore. State U., 1941; m. Patricia Jane Davies, Feb. 17, 1951; children—George C., Kenneth. Research party leader in Alaska, U.S. Bur. Fisheries, 1939- 41; free-lance writer, 1941-43; fish biologist Ariz. Game and Fish Commn., 1943-47; charge salmon research in Western Alaska, U.S. Fish and Wildlife Service, 1947-56; chief aquatic biologist Portland Gen. Electric Co., 1956—; cons. in field, 1958—. Mem. Gov. Ore. Outdoor Recreation Council, 1960-; sci. bd. cons. demonstration grants water quality and pollution control Dept. Health, Edn. and Welfare, 1963—; adviser fisheries Nat. Izaak Walton League Am., 1960-65. Mem. Am. Fisheries Soc. (pres. 1965), Assn. Power Biologists (pres. 1958-60), Am. Inst. Fishery Research Biologists, Wildlife Soc., Am. Soc. Limnology and Oceanography, Am. Inst. Biol. Scis., Pacific Fishery Biologists (sec. 1950), U.S. (nat. resources com.), Portland (chmn. recreational and natural resources com. 1962; chmn. water standards com. 1966-70) chambers of commerce, Sigma Chi. Home: 60 N W 87th Av Portland OR 97229 Office: 621 S W Alder St Portland OR 97205

EICHERT, JEROME H., mfg. co. exec.; b. Manoa, Pa., Feb. 17, 1928; s. Edwin S. and Mary (Troutman) E.; B.S. in Econs., 1951; C.P.A., Pa.; m. Jean M. Kay, Sept. 23, 1950; children—Jean Karen, Mary Lynn, William Stuart, David Brian, Margaret Elaine. Accountant, Peat, Marwick, Mitchell & Co., Phil., 1953 57; controller, treas. Carlisle Corp. (Pa.), 1957—. Bd. dirs. Carlisle Area Sch. Dist., Carlisle YMCA. Served to 1st lt. AUS, 195153. Mem. Am., Pa. insts. C.P.A.'s. Republican. Episcopalian (vestry). Home: 777 W South St Carlisle, PA 17013. Office: 1285 Ritner Hwy Carlisle PA 17013

EICHHOFF, DARRELL DEAN, life ins. exec.; b. El Reno, Okla., June 5, 1923; s. Hans H. and Goldie (Lyle) B.; B.S., U. Mo., 1943; m. Corinne Wade, Oct. 27, 1945; children—Gay Louise, Sue Anne, Kim Marie. Gen. field clk. Met. Life Ins. Co., Southwestern terr., 1946, field clk., Mound City, Mo., 1946, agt., Clayton, Mo., 1946, asst. mgr., Clayton, 1947-50, field tng. instr., N.Y.C., 1950-52, field tng. supr., 1952-54, div. supt. field tng., 1954, mgr. dist. office, Mound City, 1955-57, Meramec, Mo., 1957, exec. asst. field tng., N.Y.C., 1958-60, asst. supt. agys., Central terr., 1960, 3d v.p. marketing adv. services, N.Y.C., 1961, supt. agys., New Eng., 1962, So. terr., 1963, agy. v.p., So. terr., 1964, v.p. agy. terrs., N.Y.C., 1965-68, v.p. Pacific Coast terr., San Francisco, 1968-69, sr. v.p. marketing and field mgmt., N.Y.C., 1969—. Trustee Christian Coll., Life Underwriting Tng. Council. Served to 1st lt. USAAF, 1943-46. Decorated Air medal with 1 silver and 1 bronze oak leaf cluster, D.F.C. C.L.U. Mem. Southwestern Conn. Life Underwriters, Am. Soc. C.L.U.'s, Life Ins. Agy. Mgmt. Assn. (chmn. exec. devel. com.), Gen. Agts. and Mgrs. Conf. Presbyn. (trustee). Club: Stanwich (Greenwich). Home: 151 Clapboard Ridge Rd Greenwich CT 06830 Office: 1 Madison Av New York City NY 10010

EICHHOLZ, GERHARD CARL, broadcasting co. exec.; b. Rochester, N.Y., Aug. 7, 1930; s. Gerhard Walter and Martha (Hesselbein) E.; B.S., State U. N.Y., Brockport, 1952; M.S., Bowling Green State U., 1953; Ph.D., Ohio State U., 1961; m. Antoinette Constance Rotondo, Aug. 23, 1952; children—Gerhard Thomas III, Anita Corinne. Instr., Bowling Green State U., 1952-53; tchr. Maumee County Schs. (O.), 1953-54; research asso. Ohio State U., 1958-60; dir. ednl. resources U. S.Fla., Tampa, 1960—; gen. mgr. WUSF Television and FM Stereo, Tampa, Fla., 1966—. Editor-in-chief Systems Cons., Tampa, 1967—. Served with AC USNR, 1954-58. Mem. Fla. Audio-Visual Assn. (pres. 1966-67). Contbr. articles profl. jours. Home: 13129 N 19th St Tampa FL 33612 Office: 4202 Fowler Av Tampa FL 33620

EICHIN, EARL SONNER, banker; b. Olney, Ill., May 20, 1918; s. Raymond Earl and Grace (Sonner) E.; B.A., Wesleyan U., Middletown, Conn., 1939; grad. Stonier Sch. Banking, 1951; grad. Exec. Mgmt. Sch., U. N.C., 1954; m. Polly Lewis, Oct. 13, 1940; children—Earl Sonner, Kathleen M. With Chase Nat. Bank, N.Y.C., 1939-41, First Nat. Bank, Phila., 1948-53; v.p. Security Nat. Bank, Greensboro, N.C., 1953-55; with Worcester County Nat. Bank (Mass.), 1957—, officer charge all banking offices, 1964, sr. v.p., 1964—, also mem. exec. com.; v.p., dir., Hampshire Fixtures, Inc., Janover, N.H.; dir. Cross Cos., White River Junction, Vt.; trustee, corporator Fitchburg Savs. Bank (Mass.). Mem. senatorial dist. bus. climate com. No. Worcester County; v.p., dir. Sunset Lake Devel. Corp., Past pres., dir., chmn. fund dr. United Fund Greater Fitchburg; trustee Cushing Acad., Ashburnham, Mass., 1960—. Mem. Am. Inst. Banking, Mass. Bankers Assn. (past chmn. comml. credit com.), Robert Morris Assos. Club: Fay (Fitchburg). Home: Cushing St Ashburnham MA 01430 Office: 799 W Boylston St Worcester MA 01600

EICHMAN, PETER LIEBERT, univ. dean; b. Phila., Nov. 18, 1925; s. Edward A. and Frances (Liebert) E.; B.S., St. Joseph's Coll., Phila., 1945; M.D., Jefferson Med. Coll., Phila., 1949; m. Phyllis Kettelhon, Dec. 12, 1959; children—Mary Katherine, Elizabeth Louise, Susan Lynn, Erich Liebert, Philip John. Intern, Fitzgerald-Mercy Hosp., Lansdowne, Pa., 1949-50; fellow, resident hepatic and metabolic diseases Walter Reed Army Hosp., 1950-51, infectious diseases Jefferson Med. Coll., 1951-52, medicine and neurology Mayo Found., 1952-54, neuropsychiatry U. Wis. Hosp., Madison, 1954-55; mem. faculty U. Wis. Med. Sch. and Univs. Hosps., 1955-, asst. dean clin. affairs, 1965, prof. medicine and neurology, dean Med. Sch., also dir. Med. Center, 1965—. Diplomate Am. Bd. Psychiatry and Neurology, Am. Bd. Internal Medicine. Mem. A.C.P., A.M.A., Am. Acad. Neurology, Am. Soc. Clin. Neurologists, Dane County Med. Soc. Home: 3429 Crestwood Dr Madison WI 53705

EICHMAN, RUSSELL H., banker; b. Bucyrus, O., Dec. 20, 1911; s. Cuno and Florence (Pfleiderer) E.; student Western Res. U.; grad. Rugters U. Grad. Sch. Banking; m. Bertha West, Oct. 16, 1937; children—Russell H, Marilyn West. With Central Nat. Bank, Cleve., 1932—, sr. v.p., 1963—. Mem. City Planning Commn., Pepper Pike, O., 1956—. Mem. Cleve. Sales Execs. Marketing Club (pres. 1960). Mason. Clubs: Cleve. Athletic, Union (Cleve.); Acacia Country; Preston Trail Country (Dallas). Home: 33076 Woodleigh Rd Cleveland OH 44124 Office: 123 W Prospect Av Cleveland OH 44115

EICHWALD, ERNEST JULIUS, medical educator; b. Hannover, Germany, Dec. 13, 1913; s. Paul A. and Jenny (Grahn) E.; student U. Frankfurt, 1933; M.D., U. Freiburg, 1938, U. Utah, 1953; children—Jenny, Paul Ramsay, John Gary. Came to U.S., 1938, naturalized, 1942. Asst. in pathology Harvard, 1943, instr. pathology, 1946; asst. pathologist Children's Hosp., Boston, 1946; asst. prof. pathology U. Utah Med. Sch., 1948-50, asso. prof., 1950-54, prof. surgery and pathology, 1967-68, chmn. dept. pathology, 1968—; dir. lab. exptl. medicine Deaconess Hosp., Gt. Falls, Mont., 1954-65; dir. McLaughlin Research Inst., Gt. Falls, 1966-67; prof. microbiology Mont. State U., 1966. Chmn. tissue transplantation com. Nat. Acad. Scis., 1957-68. Served with M.C., AUS, 1944-46. Mem. Soc. Exptl. Biology and Medicine, Am. Assn. Pathologists and Bacteriologists, Coll. Am. Pathologists. Unitarian. Editor Transplantation Bull., 1953-62, Transplantation, 1963—. Home: 40 South 9 East Salt Lake City UT 84102

EICOFF, ALVIN MAUREY, advt. exec.; b. Lewistown, Mont., June 8, 1921; s. Sam Herman and Sadye (Schwartz) E.; student Stanford, 1939-40; B.B.A., U. Tex., 1942, M.B.A., 1943; m. Helen Eleanor Topas, Feb. 1, 1947; children—Larry Lee, Jeffrey Allan. Advt. mgr. Lewistown Daily, 1946; comml. mgr. radio sta. KXOL, Lewistown, 1947; v.p. Marfree Advt., N.Y.C. and Chgo., 1947-49; v.p. d-Con Co., Chgo., 1948-57; chmn. bd. Mohr & Eicoff, N.Y.C. and Chgo., 1957-62; pres. A. Eicoff & Co., Chgo., 1966—; v.p. Grant Co., Chgo., 1950-60; partner Doman Products div. Jelmar, Chgo., 1969—. Served with AUS, 1943-46; ETO. Mem. Am. Legion, V.F.W., Tau Delta Phi. Moose, Mason. Home: 3500 Lake Shore Dr Chicago IL 60657 Office: 520 N Michigan Av Chicago IL 60611

EIDAM, JOHN EDWARD, banker; b. Scribner, Neb., Apr. 27, 1904; s. William and Catherine (Hartman) E.; LL.B., U. Omaha, 1931, J.D., 1969; m. Marie Wislicen, June 16, 1926; children—Marilyn (Mrs. H.B. Graves), Nancy (Mrs. Jack Williams). Admitted to Neb. bar, 1929; gen. practice, Omaha, 1929-34; counsel Omaha Bank for

Coops., 1934-48, pres., 1955-69; dir. pub. relations, asst. gen. mgr. Westcentral Coop. Grain Co., Omaha, 1948-55; pres. Credit Union Nat. Assn., 1949-50, dir., mem. exec. com., 1943-51; dir. Farmers Elevator Mut. Ins. Co., 1948-55; cooperative cons., atty., 1969—. Head team to study agrl. credit in Argentina, 1962. Sect. leader United Community Services drive, Omaha, 1963. Mem. dean's adv. com. Coll. Agr., U. Neb., 1960-66. Mem. Omaha, Neb. bar assns. Lutheran (vice chmn. bd. deacons). Rotarian, Mason (32, Shriner). Author articles in field. Home: 1222 S 118th St Omaha NB 68144 Office: 1222 S 118th St Omaha NB 68144

EIDMAN, KRAFT WARNER, lawyer; b. Liberty Hill, Tex., Jan. 17, 1912; s. Kraft H. and Vera (Bates) E.; student Rice U., 1929-30; A.B., U. Tex., 1935, LL.B., 1935; m. Julia Mary Bell, Aug. 31, 1940; children—Kraft Gregory, Dan Kelly, John Bates. Admitted to Tex. bar, 1935, since practiced in Houston; partner firm Fulbright, Crooker, Freeman, Bates & Jaworski, and predecessors, 1947—, lectr. law sci. insts., medico-legal insts., state bar meetings. Vice pres., dir. Def. Research Inst.; mem. library assos. U. St. Thomas; mem. Com. of 75, U. Tex. Trustee U., Tex. Law Sch. Found. Served to lt. comdr. USNR, 1942-45. Fellow Am. Coll. Trial Lawyers, Am. Bar Found.; mem. Am. Counsel Assn., Am. (vice chmn. trial tactics coms.), Tex. (chmn. tort and compensation law), Houston (pres. 1960-61) bar assns., Internat. Assn. Ins. Counsel (exec. com. 1957-60, 51-66, pres.-elect 1963-64, pres. 1964-65), Houston C. of C., U. Tex. Law Sch. Alumni Assn. (pres.). Democrat. Catholic. K.C., Kiwanian (pres. S.W. Houston 1958). Clubs: Houston, Champions Golf, Houston Country, Briar (pres. 1952), Chaparral (Dallas). Author articles in field. Editor Ins. Counsel Jour., 1961-63. Home: 5559 Sugar Hill Houston TX 77027 Office: Bank of Southwest Bldg Houston TX 77002

EIDSON, JOHN OLIN, coll. pres.; b. Johnston, S.C., Dec. 10, 1908; s. Olin Marvin and Margaret (Rushton) E.; A.B., Wofford Coll., 1929, Litt.D. (hon.), 1954; M.A., Vanderbilt U., 1930; Ph.D., Duke, 1941; m. Perrin Cudd, Aug. 7, 1952. Faculty, U. Ga., Athens, 1936-68, beginning as instr. English, successively dean Coordinate Coll., dir. U. Center in Ga., dean Coll. Arts and scis., 1957-68; pres. Ga. So. Coll., Statesboro, 1968-71; vice chancellor Univ. System of Ga., 1971—; vis. prof. Am. lit. U. Freiberg, Germany, 1956. Vice pres. Coastal Empire council Boy Scouts Am., 1970—. Served from lt. to maj., inf., AUS, 1942-46; lt. col. Res. Recipient M. B. Michael award for research, 1950. Mem. Am. Studies Assn., Modern Lang. Assn. Am., S. Atlantic Modern Lang. Assn., Assn. State Univs. and Land-Grant Colls. (mem. senate 1963-66), Southeastern Am. Studies Assn. (pres. 1966- 68), Conf. Acad. Deans So. States (sec.-treas. 1965-66, v.p. 1966-67, pres. 1967-68), Nat. Council Coll. Arts and Sci., English Assn. London, Newcomen Soc. N. Am., Am. Assn. State Colls. and Univs., Statesboro C. of C., Tennyson Soc. Eng., Sphinx, Phi Beta Kappa (chmn. S. Atlantic dist. 1958-61, pres. Coastal Ga.-Carolina assn. 1970—), Pi Kappa Delta, Phi Kappa Phi, Delta Phi Alpha (nat. sec. 1929-34), Tau Kappa Alpha, Kappa Delta Pi, Kappa Phi Kappa. Mem. Methodist Ch. (mem. ofcl. bd.). Rotarian. Author: Tennyson in America, 1943; Charles Stearns Wheeler; Friend of Emerson, 1951; (with W. W. Davidson) Reading for Pleasure, 1948. Editor: Ga. Rev., 1950-57, mem. Editorial bd. 1957—. Contbr. articles and revs. to scholastic jours. Home: Box 8033 Ga So Coll Statesboro GA 30458

EIDSON, O. BAIN, lawyer; b. Reading, Kan., June 14, 1890; s. Ansel M. and Sarah F. (Bain) E.; J.D., Washburn Coll., 1915; m. E. Agnes Ray, Nov. 24, 1915; children—Betty M. (Mrs. Joseph P. Fallin), Julia B. (Mrs. Lyle E. Christenson), Robert A., Sarah A. (Mrs. William A. Walton). Admitted to Kan. bar, 1915, also fed., dist., circuit and supreme ct. bars; mem. firm Eidson, Lewis, Porter & Haynes, Topeka, 1923—; gen. atty. U.P.R.R. Co., 1933—. Fellow Am. Coll. Trial Lawyers, Am. Bar Found.; mem. Internat. Platform Assn., Am. (past mem. ho. of dels.), Kan. (pres. 1957-58), Topeka (pres. 1945) bar assns. Republican. Presbyn. Clubs: Topeka Rotary (past pres.), Topeka, Country, Home: 4110 Twilight Dr Topeka KS 66614 Office: Mchts Bank Bldg Topeka KS 66612 •

EIDSON, RICHARD IRWIN, savs. and loan assn. exec.; b. Columbus, O., Jan. 1, 1931; s. Willard Cole and Helen (Irwin) E.; student Miami U., Oxford, O., 1950-51, Ohio State U., 1952-53; m. Molly Stewart, Dec. 2, 1961; 1 dau., Ann S. With First Fed. Savs. and Loan Assns., Columbus, 1953—, dir., 1958—, pres., 1964—. Mem. adv. bd. St. Anthony Hosp., Columbus. Mem. Nat. League Insured Savs. Assns. (state govs. bd.; exec. com. 1970-71), Young Pres.'s Orgn. Club: Presidents Ohio State U. Home: 328 Fairway Circle Columbus OH 43213 Office: 2450 E Main St Columbus OH 43209

EIDSON, ROBERT W., govt. ofcl.; b. Chgo., Dec. 13, 1907; s. William A. and Jessie I. (Maeloy) E.; B.S. in Chem. Engring., Mich. State U., 1929; m. Mary A. Nelson, May 28, 1932; children—John C., James R., Susan Lynne. With Am. Can Co., 1929—, gen. mgr. indsl. engring. dept., 1961-64, v.p. indsl. engring., 1965-70; dir. for engring., research and engring. dept. U.S. Postal Service, Washington, 1970—. Served as res. officer Arty. Corps, U.S. Army, 1929-39. Sr. mem. Am. Inst. Indsl. Engrs.; mem. Council Indsl. Engring., Alpha Chi Sigma, Phi Lambda Tau. Baptist. Home: 8908 Bridgehaven Ct Alexandria VA 22308 Office: Post Office Dept 12th and Pennsylvania Washington DC 20260

EIDSON, WILLIAM WHELAN, educator, physicist; b. Indpls., July 22, 1935; s. Alonzo Duncan and Gertrude (Whelan) E.; B.A., Tulane U., 1957; M.S., Ind. U., 1959, Ph.D. (NSF fellow), 1961; m. Susan Edwards, June 11, 1960; children—William Benjamin, Duncan McBrayer. Mem. Faculty Ind. U., Bloomington, 1961-67, asso. prof. physics, 1966-67; prof., chmn. dept. physics U. Mo., St. Louis, 1967—. Mem. Am. Phys. Soc., Am. Assn. Physics Tchrs., A.A.A.S., I.E.E.E., Sigma Xi, Sigma Pi Sigma. Home: 66 Bellerive Acres St Louis MO 63121

EIERMAN, WARREN H., banker. Pres., Community Nat. Bank, Pontiac, Mich. Office: 30 N Saginaw St Pontiac MI 48056•

EIFLER, CHARLES WILLIAM, army officer; b. Altoona, Pa., Dec. 1, 1914; s. Charles William and Emily (Cornelius) E.; B.S., Pa. State U., 1936; M.S., Mass. Inst. Tech., 1948; postgrad. Indsl. Coll. Armed Forces, 1956; m. Julia Knight, July 10, 1937; children—Julia Ann (Mrs. William J. Roberts), Mary Elizabeth (Mrs. Robert L. Stiles), Charles William III. Commd. 2d lt. U.S. Army, 1936, advanced through grades to lt. gen., 1969; comdg. officer 57th Ordnance Group, Europe, 1956-59; comdt. U.S. Army Ordnance Guided Missile Sch., Redstone Arsenal, Ala., 1959-61; comdg. officer Frankford Arsenal, Phila., 1961- 63; dep. comdg. gen. U.S. Army Missile Command, Redstone Arsenal, 1963- 65, comdg. gen., 1967-69; comdg. gen. 1st Logistical Command, Vietnam, 1966-67; dep. comdr.-in-chief 7th Army, Germany, 1969—. Mem. exec. bd. Tenn. Valley council Boy Scouts Am. Decorated D.S.M. with oak leaf cluster, Legion of Merit with oak leaf cluster, Bronze Star medal with oak leaf cluster, Air medal with oak leaf cluster, Korean Order Mil. Merit, Chung Mu, Vietnamese Nat. Order medal Fifth Class; Distinguished Service medal State of Ala. Fellow Am. Inst. Aeros. and Astronautics; mem. (life) Am. Ordnance Assn., Sci. Research Soc. Am. (life), Assn. U.S. Army, Triangle, Sigma Xi, Chi Epsilon. Rotarian. Home: 120 Alzeyerstrasse Worms Germany Office: Hdqrs U S Theater Army Support Command Europe APO New York City NY 09058

EIGEL, EDWIN GEORGE, Jr., educator; b. St. Louis, June 4, 1932; s. Edwin George and Catherine (Rohan) E.; B.S., Mass. Inst. Tech., 1954; postgrad. U. Marburg (Germany), 1954-55; Ph.D., St. Louis U., 1961; m. Marcia Jeanne Duffy, May 30, 1959; children-Edwin George III, Mary Marcia. Lectr. math. George Washington U., 1961; asst. prof. math. St. Louis U., 1961-64, asso. prof., 1964-69, asst. to dean Grad. Sch., 1965-67, prof., 1969—, dean Grad. Sch., 1967—, Danforth asso., 1964—. Served to 1st lt. AUS, 1959-61. Mem. Am. Math. Soc., Math. Assn. Am., Assn. Computing Machinery, Mo. Acad. Sci., Phi Beta Kappa, Sigma Xi, Pi Mu Epsilon. Research in math. applications of computers. Home: 6423 January Av St Louis MO 63109

EIGEN, MANFRED, physicist; b. Bochum, Germany, May 9, 1927; s. Ernst E. and Hedwig (Feld) E.; ed. physics and chemistry, U. Göttingen (Germany); hon. degrees, Harvard, U. Chgo., Washington U., St. Louis, m. Elfriede Müller; two children. Sci. asst. Inst. Phys. Chemistry, U. Göttingen, 1951-53; mem. staff Max Planck Inst. of Phys. Chemistry, Göttingen, 1953- -, now chmn.; vis. lectr. Cornell U. Co-recipient Nobel prize in chemistry, 1967. Mem. Bunsen Soc. Phys. Chemistry (Bodenstein preis), Faraday Soc., Nat. Acad. Scis. Author tech. papers. Address: 14 Georg Dehio Weg Göttingen Germany

EIGER, NORMAN NATHAN, circuit ct. judge; b. Chgo., Aug. 6, 1903; s. Isaac and Rachel (Brender) E.; J.D., De Paul U., 1924; m. Leona Wolan, Dec. 31, 1935; children—Lawrence H., Rodney I. Admitted to Ill. bar, 1924; mem. exec. staff, capital stock tax assessor Ill. Tax Commn., 1932-36; asst. to corp. counsel City Chgo., 1936-47; chmn. Ill. Bd. Rev., Dept. of Labor, 1948-52; judge Municipal Ct., Chgo., 1952-64; judge Circuit Ct. Cook County, Ill., Chgo., 1964—. Past v.p. Coll. Jewish Studies, now trustee; arbitrator, mem. panel Am. Assn. Arbitrators; lectr. groups; mem. Sponsors of Washington, Morris and Solomon monuments, Chgo.; v.p. Adult Edn. Council Met. Chgo.; mem. adv. bd. Ill. Police Res. Past chmn. lawyers div. Chgo. Combined Jewish Appeal; co- chmn. Conciliation Commn., Chgo. Fedn., United Am. Hebrew Congregations; past v.p. Bd. Jewish Edn., now hon. life trustee. Served with USCGR, World War II. Mem. Am. (nat. conf. state trial judges), Chgo. bar assns., Decalogue Soc. Lawyers (financial sec.), Patriotic Found. Chgo. (pres.), Ill. Judges Assn. (pres.), Nu Beta Epsilon (past grand chancellor), Alpha Epsilon Pi (hon.). Jewish religion (hon. life trustee). Mem. B'nai B'rith (past v.p. Chgo. Council, past pres. Jackson Park Lodge, mem. awards com. Youth Orgn.). Home: 2970 N Lake Shore Dr Chicago IL 60657

EIGES, SYDNEY HIRSH, broadcast exec.; b. New Kensington, Pa., May 15, 1909; s. Julius and Anna (Brisker) E.; A.B. cum laude, U. Pitts., 1930; m. Beatrice Wechsler, Apr. 21, 1940; children—Marilyn Sue, Mark Robert. Reporter, editor Internat. News Service, 1930-41; writer press dept. NBC, 1941, mgr., 1945, v.p. press and publicity, 1947-60, v.p. pub. information, 1960—. Mem. Internat. Radio and TV Execs. Soc., Omicron Delta Kappa, Sigma Delta Chi, Pi Lambda Phi. Clubs: Nat. Press (Washington); Lake Isle Country (Eastchester, N.Y.); Rockefeller Center Luncheon (N.Y.C.). Home: 9 Knox Rd Eastchester NY 10709 Office: 30 Rockefeller Plaza New York City NY 10020

EIGHMY, ANN MARIE, bank exec.; b. Indiana, Pa., Oct. 30, 1907; d. John Peter and Elizabeth (Macro) Cinque; student Muskingum Coll., 1924-25, Wittenberg Coll., 1926-27, Bliss Bus. Coll., 1931-32; m. Clifford John, Nov. 25, 1937. Tchr. elementary sch., Bellaire, O., 1927-31; sec. office Atty. Gen. Ohio, 1932-37; adminstrv. asst. Dept. War, Cleve., 1941-45; exec. asst. to chief execs. Central Nat. Bank, Cleve., 1945—. Mem. Am. Inst. Banking (chmn. local women's com., mem. nat. women's com. 1958), Nat. Assn. Bank Women. Republican. Methodist. Mem. Order Eastern Star. Home: 20100 Lorain Rd Cleveland OH 44126 Office: 800 Superior Av Cleveland OH 44114

EIGHMY, HERBERT HENRY, naval med. officer; b. Meadville, Pa., June 25, 1907; s. Herbert Henry and Nellie (Flanigan) E.; student Allegheny Coll., 1926-29, D.Sc. in Medicine, 1969; M.D., Hahnemann Med. Coll., 1933; postgrad. student medicine Northwestern U., 1947, surgery, U. Pa., 1954; m. Maud Marie Leonard, Mar. 26, 1928; children—Barbara Ellen (Mrs. Thomas T. Wylie), Herbert H. Intern, Hahnemann Hosp., Phila., 1933-34, asst. chief resident, 1934-35, chief resident, 1935-36; commd. lt. (j.g.), M.C., U.S. Navy, 1936, advanced through grades to rear adm., 1964; assigned ships Russell, 1939-40, Rapidan, 1940-41, Curtiss, 1942- 43, Bunker Hill, 1944-46, Coral Sea, 1948, New Jersey, 1950-52; naval flight surgeon, 1941; chief surgery naval, Great Lakes, Ill., 1955-57, Camp Pendelton, 1957-59; exec. officer San Diego Naval Hosp., 1959-60; comdg. officer Pensacola (Fla.) Naval Hosp., 1960-63; sr. med. officer U.S. Naval Acad., 1963-64; asst. chief Bur. Medicine and Surgery, Washington, 1964-66; comdg. officer Aerospace Med. Center, Pensacola, 1966-69; adminstr. Splty. Care Center, Bapt. Hosp., Pensacola, 1969—. Decorated Bronze Star with Combat V, Legion of Merit. Mem. A.M.A., A.C.S., Ill. Surg. Soc., Aerospace Med. Assn., Phi Beta Phi, Omega Xi, Phi Gamma Delta. Odd Fellow, Rotarian. Club: Toastmasters Internat. Home: 70 Star Lake Dr Warrington FL 32507 Office: Splty Care Center Bapt Hosp Pensacola FL 32501

EIJKELENBOOM, WOUTER, architect; b. Holland, Dec. 27, 1924; s. Arie Paulus and Elisabeth (De Ligt) E.; grad. Acad. Architecture, Amsterdam, 1957. With Ir. J.W. C. Boks-W. Eijkelenboom-A. Middelhoek, architects, 1964—; prin. works include Enck-Vlaardingen officer bldgs., gen. hosp., Vlaardingen, Netherlands Pavillon, Expo 67, bldg. centre, Rotterdam, also pvt. houses. Home: 58 Cornelis Bloemaertsingel Rotterdam Holland Office: 69 Wynhaven Rotterdam Holland

EIKEL, CHARLES FREDERICK, Jr., ins. exec.; b. New Orleans, 1907; s. Charles Frederick and Delia (McGraw) E.; student night courses Tulane U., 1928-29, Loyola U., New Orleans, 1926-28; m. Eunice Cunningham, Sept. 20, 1930; children—Lynn (Mrs. Mitchell C. Davitt), Lucia (Mrs. G.L. Higgins), Charles Frederick III. With investment dept. Pan-Am. Life Ins. Co., New Orleans, 1931-38, cashier, Los Angeles, 1930-31; field rep. Credit Union Nat. Assn., 1938-47; asst. mng. dir. Credit Union Nat. Assn.-CUNA Mut. Ins. Soc., 1947-56; exec. v.p. CUNA Mut. Ins. Soc., Madison, Wis., 1956-64, pres., 1964—; pres. CUMIS Ins. Soc., Inc., 1960—; dir. First Wis. Nat. Bank of Madison, 1967—. Mem. Madison C. of C. (dir. 1962-65), Inst. Life Ins., Am. Inst. Mgmt. (mem. pres.'s council), Nat. Indsl. Conf. Bd. Club: Madison. Home: 3975 Plymouth Circle Madison WI 53705 Office: P O Box 391 Madison WI 53701

EIKENBERG, JOHN H., mfg. and indsl. relations exec.; b. Balt., Oct. 10, 1909; s. Frederick and Margaret (Hack) E.; m. Evelyn A. Weber, May 29, 1935; children—John M., Richard L. Factory employee Revere Copper & Brass, Inc., Balt., 1924- 30, methods work, 1930-34, asst. mill supt., 1934-36, indsl. engr., 1934- 41, gen. indsl. engr., 1941-43, dir. indsl. relations, 1943-45, v. p. indsl. relations, Rome, N.Y., 1943-58, v.p. indsl. relations, mfg., 1958-61, pres., 1961-65, chmn. bd., chief exec. officer, 1965- -, also dir. Elk. Club: Mt. Kisco Country. Home: 236 W Lake Dr Valhalla NY 10595 Office: 605 3d Av New York City NY

EIKLEBERRY, ROBERT WOODROW, soil scientist; b. Havanna, Ark., Aug. 7, 1912; s. John Arthur and Hanna (Burton) E.; student Ark. Poly. Coll., 1933; B.S., Okla. State U., 1935; postgrad. U. Neb., 1958; m. Kara Lee Coldiron, Jan. 18, 1936; children—Melvyn R., Lana K. (Mrs. Clark R. Bloom), Daniel J., Jane L. Soil scientist Soil Conservation Service, U.S. Dept. Agr., Nowata, Okla., 1935-37, Hiawatha, Kan., 1937-44, Lincoln, Neb., 1944—; spl. soil cons. to Minister Agr. in Iran, 1967. Recipient Outstanding Service award Soil Conservation Service, 1967, Gov. of Ark. award, 1970. Mem. Soil Conservation Soc. Am. (pres.), Soil Sci. Soc. Am., Range Soc. Am., Nat. Assn. Soil Conservation Dists., Gamma Sigma Delta. Contbr. articles profl. jours. Office: 134 S 12th St Lincoln NB 68508

EILBERG, JOSHUA, congressman; b. Phila., Feb. 12, 1921; s. David B. and Miriam (Jaspan) E.; B.S., Wharton Sch., U. Pa., 1941; J.D., Temple U., 1948; m. Gladys Greenberg, Jan. 2, 1944; children—William H., Amy B. Admitted to Pa. bar, 1948, since practiced in Phila.; partner Eiberg, Corson & Getson, 1968—; asst. dist. atty., 1952-54; mem. Pa. Ho. of Reps. from Phila., 1954-66, majority leader, 1965-66; mem. 90th-92d Congresses, 4th Dist. Pa. Leader Democratic 54th Ward, Phila., 1957—; v.p. Dem. 90th Congress Club, 1967—; del. Dem. Nat. Conv., 1960, 64, 68; vice chmn. Phila. Dem. City Com., 1970—. Chmn. Frontier dist. council Boy Scouts Am. pres. N.E. Mental Health Clinic, Phila. Trustee Phila. Coll. Podiatry; bd. dirs. Phila. Geriatric Center, Home for Jewish Aged, Phila. Served to lt. (s.g.) USNR, 1942-46; PTO. Mem. Am., Fed. (pres. Phila. chpt.), Pa., Phila. bar assns., Am. Judicature Soc., Am. Arbitration Assn. (panel arbitrators), Am. Legion, V.F.W., D.A.V., Jewish War Vets., World Affairs Council Phila., Cruiser Olympia Assn. (dir.). Jewish religion (trustee congregation.) Mason; mem. B'nai B'rith. Home: 1522 Longshore Av Philadelphia PA 19149 Office: Longworth House Office Bldg Washington DC 20515

EILENBERG, SAMUEL, educator; b. Warsaw, Poland, Sept. 30, 1913; M.A., U. Warsaw, 1934, Ph.D., 1936. Came to U.S., 1939, naturalized, 1948. Instr. math. U. Mich., 1940-41, asst. prof., 1941-45, asso. prof., 1945-46; prof. math. Ind. U., 1946- 47, Columbia, 1947—; vis. lectr. Princeton, 1945-46; vis. prof. U. Paris, 1950-51, 66-67, Tata Inst. Bombay, 1953-54, Hebrew U., Jerusalem, 1954. Fulbright fellow, Guggenheim fellow, Paris, 1950-51. Mem. Nat. Acad. Scis., Am. Math. Soc. (councillor 1947-59, v.p. 1966-67), Math. Assn. Am. Author: (with N. E. Steenrod) Foundations of Algebraic Topology, 1952; (with H. Cartan) Homological Algebra, 1956; (with C.C. Elgot) Recursiveness, 1970. Address: Columbia U New York City NY 10028

EILERS, LOUIS KENNETH, chem. co. exec.; b. Gillespie, Ill., Apr. 11, 1907; s. William H. and Minnie (Luken) E.; A.A., Blackburn Coll., 1927; B.S., U. Ill., 1929; M.S., U. Va., 1930; Ph.D., Northwestern U., 1932; D.Sc. (hon.), Blackburn Coll., 1957; m. C. Frances Wampler, Oct. 18, 1930; children—Carol (Mrs. Roland Baggott), Lois (Mrs. Philip Paris), Carl Richard, William. With Eastman Kodak Co., Kodak Park, Rochester, N.Y., 1934—, successively chemist, supt. roll coating dept., asst. mgr. film mfg., asst. to gen. mgr. Kodak Park, asst. gen. mgr. Kodak Park, 1934-56, v.p., asst. gen. mgr. Eastman Kodak Co., 1956-59, exec. v.p., 1963-67, pres., 1967-70, chmn., 1970—, also chief exec. officer, dir.; dir. Rochester Telephone Corp.; trustee Rochester Savs. Bank; pres. Eastman Chem. Products, Inc., 1959-60, vice chmn. bd. dirs., 1960-63, v.p., 1963—, also dir.; 1st v.p. Tenn. Eastman Co., also Tex. Eastman Co., 1959-61, pres., 1961-63; pres. Carolina Eastman Corp., 1961-63; dir. Holston Def. Corp., Westinghouse Electric Co., Lincoln Rochester Trust Co., First Nat. City Corp. Mem. Am. Chem. Soc., Soc. Photog. Scientists and Engrs., Photog. Soc. Am., Sigma Xi, Phi Lambda Upsilon, Alpha Chi Sigma. Clubs: Oak Hill Country (Rochester); Genesee Valley. Home: 57 Knollwood Dr Rochester NY 14618 Office: 343 State St Rochester NY 14650

EILTS, HERMANN FREDERICK, fgn. service officer; b. Weissenfels Saale, Germany, Mar. 23, 1922; s. Friedrich Alex and Meta Dorothea (Prüser) E.; brought to U.S., 1926, naturalized, 1930; B.A., Ursinus Coll., 1942, LL.D., 1960; M.A., Johns Hopkins, 1947; student Arabic, Near East area, Dept. State Fgn. Service Inst. and U. Pa., 1950-51; m. Helen Josephine Brew, June 12, 1948; children—Conrad Marshall, Frederick Lowell. Fgn. service officer, 1947—; 3d sec., vice consul, Tehran, Iran, 1947-48, Jidda, Saudi Arabia, 1948-50; consul, prin. officer, Aden, Arabia, 1951-53; also 2d sec., consul, Sana, Yemen, 1951-53; 2d sec., consul, chief polit. sect., Baghdad, Iraq, 1954-56; officer-in- charge Baghdad Pact affairs (CENTO) Dept. State, Washington, 1957-59, Arabian Peninsula Affairs, 1959-61; detailed Nat. War Coll., Ft. McNair, 1961-62; 1st sec. Am. embassy, London, Eng., 1962-64; counsellor, dep. chief of mission Am. embassy, Tripoli, Libya, 1964-65; U.S. ambassador to Saudi Arabia, 1965-70; diplomatic adviser U.S. Army War Coll., Carlisle Barracks, Pa., 1970—. Served as 1st lt. with Mil. Intelligence, AUS, 1942-45. Decorated Purple Heart, Bronze Star; recipient Arthur Flemming award for govt. service, 1958. Fellow Royal Geog. Soc., Royal Asiatic Soc.; mem. Am. Fgn. Service Assn., Middle East Inst., Royal Central Asian Soc. Mem. Evangelical and Reformed Ch. Address: US Army War Coll Carlisle Barrack PA 17013

EIMERS, HOWARD GORDON, ins. co. exec.; b. Milw., June 28, 1926; s. Edward and Hilda (Brushaber) E.; B.S. in Bus. Adminstrn. with distinction, Northwestern U., 1950; M.A. in Math., U. Mich., 1951; m. Joyce Elsie Taylor, Jan. 14, 1950; children—Dennis John, Paul Timothy, David James. Actuary, N.Am. Life & Accident Ins. Co. Ky., 1951-53; with Washington Nat. Ins. Co., Evanston, Ill., 1953—, actuary, 1958-62, chief actuary, 1962-63, v.p., actuary, 1963-69, sr. v.p., actuary, 1969—; v.p., dir. Washington Nat. Corp.; chmn. bd. Washington Nat. Equity Co.; dir. Washington Nat. Trust Co., Anchor Nat. Life Ins. Co., Phoenix. C.L.U. Fellow Soc. Actuaries, Life Mgmt. Inst.; mem. Beta Gamma Sigma. Home: 240 Avon St Northfield IL 60093 Office: 1630 Chicago Av Evanston IL 60201

EINARSON, BENEDICT, educator; b. Chgo., Apr. 29, 1906; s. Benedict and Johanna Marie (Peterson) E.; A.B., U. Chgo., 1926, A.M., 1928, Ph.D., 1932; Sterling fellow Yale, 1932; jr. fellow Harvard, 1934-37. Instr. Latin, U. Wis., 1930; instr. classics Harvard, 1938-39; instr., asst. prof., asso. prof., prof. Greek, U. Chgo., 1940—, now also Edward Olson prof. Greek; Fulbright lectr., Oxford, 1958-59. Mem. Am. Philol. Assn. Author: Translation, Longinus on the Sublime, 1945. Editorial bd. Classical Philology. Contbr. articles, translations to jours. Home: 1524 E 59th St Chicago IL 60637

EINARSSON, STEFAN, educator; b. Iceland, June 9, 1897; s. Einar Gunnlaugsson and Margret Jónsdóttir; came to U.S., 1927; B.A., Coll. Reykjavik; M.A., U. Iceland, 1923; grad. student U. Helsingfors, Finland, 1924-25; Ph.D., U. Oslo, (Norway), 1927; Ph.D., Univ. Iceland, 1961; m. Margarethe Schwarzenberg, Aug. 26, 1925 (dec.); m. 2d, Ingibjörg Arnadottir, Dec. 15, 1954. Research fellow Johns Hopkins, 1927, instr. English philology, 1928-32, asso., 1932-36, asso. prof., 1936, prof. Scandinavian philology, 1945, emeritus, 1962- -. Hon. vice consul of Iceland, Balt., 1942-52, hon. consul, 1952—. Decorated knight Order of Iceland Falcon, 1939; Guggenheim fellow

Iceland, 1962-63. Mem. Am. Philos. Soc., Modern Lang. Assn. Am., Linguistic Soc. Am., Icelandic Nat. League of Winnipeg, Icelandic Lit. Soc., Icelandic Soc. Scis., Am. Scandinavian Found. Club: Johns Hopkins (Balt.). Author: Beitrage zur Phonetik der isländischen Sprache, 1927; A Specimen of Southern Icelandic Speech, 1931; Saga Erks Magnússonar, 1933; Thórbergur Thórdarson fimmtugur, 1939; Icelandic; Grammar, Texts, Glossary, 1945 History of Icelandic Prose Writers (1800-1940), 1948; Skáldthing, 1948; Um kerfisbundnar hljódbreytingar i islenzku, 1949; Linguaphone Icelandic Course, 1955; Arbok Ferdafelags Islands, 1955, 57; Islensk bokmenntasaga 1874-1960, 1961; co-editor and co-author Breiddaela, 1948; co-editor: 20th Century Scandinavian Poetry, 1950; Kemp Malone, Studies in Heroic Legend and in Current Speech, 1959. Author, contbr. Am., Icelandic and European learned journals. Cooperating editor, Jour. English and Germanic Philology, 1939—, Scandinavian Studies, 1947—, Modern Language Notes, 1955-62. Editor-in- chief Old Icelandic Dictionary, sponsored by the Arnamagnaean Commission, Copanhagen, Denmark, 1939-41. Home: Kirkjuteig 25 Reykjavik Iceland

EINERMAN, JOHN OSCAR, telephone co. exec.; b. Paterson, N.J., Mar. 10, 1908; s. John E. and Alice J. (Hoffman) E.; A.B., Columbia, 1929; m. Margaret Glick, June 22, 1931. Supervising accountant N.Y. Telephone Co., 1929-46; asst. chief accountant Am. Tel. & Tel. Co., 1946-51, asst. comptroller, 1951-58; v.p., comptroller Pacific Tel. & Tel. Co., 1958—; v.p., comptroller, dir. Bell Telephone Co. Nev., 1958—. Trustee San Francisco Theol. Sem., also Grad. Theol. Union, Berkeley, Cal. Mem. San Francisco C. of C., Transp. Club San Francisco. Presbyn. Club: San Francisco Stock Exchange. Home: 76 Broadmoor Dr San Francisco CA 94132 Office: 140 New Montgomery St San Francisco CA 94105

EINHORN, HERBERT ARTHUR, lawyer; b. N.Y.C., Feb. 5, 1913; s. William and Sadie (Reich) E.; A.B. cum laude, Ohio U., 1933; LL.B., Columbia, 1935; m. Roslyn Appel, Feb. 11, 1940; children—Eric Stanley, Diane Margery. Admitted to N.Y. bar, 1935; pvt. practice, N.Y.C., 1935-38, 41-43; sr. counsel N.Y. State Ins. Fund, 1938-40, spl. counsel, 1940-41; asst. atty. gen., N.Y., 1943-46; partner Aranow, Brodsky, Bohlinger, Benetar, Einhorn & Dann, N.Y.C., 1946—; lectr. Practicing Law Inst. N.Y., Law Sch. N.Y.U. Chmn. bd. dirs. Camp Loyaltown; trustee of Acad. of Ohio Univ., Athens, 1966—. Served with arty., AUS, World War II; capt. N.Y.N.G. Mem. Am., N.Y. State bar assns., N.Y. County Lawyers Assn., Assn. of the Bar City of New York, Columbia Law Sch. Alumni Assn. (dir. 1968—). Clubs: Friars; Hampshire Country (Mamaroneck, N.Y.); N.Y. University (N.Y.C.). Author: (with Edward R. Aranow) Proxy Contests for Corporate Control, 1957, revised edition, 1968; also contributor of articles to professional journals. Home: 12 Glen Eagles Dr Larchmont NY 10538 Office: 469 Fifth Av New York City NY 10017

EINKAUF, OSCAR ERNEST, Jr., corp. exec.; b. San Antonio, Sept. 14, 1924; s. Oscar Ernest and Ruby (Crowell) E.; B.B.A. in Accounting, U. Tex., 1949; m. Eunice Mary Armstrong, June 9, 1952; children—Oscar Ernest III, Robert Benson. Accountant, Rodgers, Chorpening & Jungmann, San Antonio, 1949-57, Johnston Testers, Inc., Houston, 1957-59; controller Houston Oil Field Materials Co., Inc., 1959-63; staff asst. to v.p. finance Sinclair Oil & Gas Co., Tulsa, 1963-64; v.p. Internat. Systems & Controls Corp., Houston, 1964-66; controller Black, Sivalls & Bryson, Inc., Kansas City, Mo., 1964-66; controller, mgr. Bank of Southwest Nat. Assn., Houston, 1966—; asst. sec.-treas. Southwest Banc Shares, Inc., Houston, 1970—. Mem. Am. Inst. C.P.A.'s, Tex. Soc. C.P.A.'s, Am. Inst. Banking, Delta Chi. Baptist. Home: 13315 Westport Lane Houston TX 77024 Office: PO Box 2629 Bank of Southwest Nat Assn Houston TX 77002

EINSIDLER, FREDERICK R., consulting firm exec.; b. N.Y.C., 1925; B.S., U.S. Mil. Acad., 1945. Pres., dir. Consultants and Designers Inc., N.Y.C. Home: 25 Herrick Dr Lawrence NY 11559 Office: 55 Fifth Av New York City NY 10003*

EIRICH, FREDERICK ROLAND, educator, chemist; b. Vienna, Austria, May 23, 1905; s. Otto George and Hermine (Perlhefter) E.; Ph.D., U. Vienna, 1929, Dr. Phil. habil., 1938; M.A., U. Cambridge (Eng.), 1939; m. Maria Dorothea Dehne, Feb. 1, 1936; children-Ursula D., Richard S. Moeller, Susan H., George H. Cohen. Came to U.S., 1947, naturalized, 1953. Research asso., lectr. U. Vienna, 1934- 38, U. Cambridge, 1939-47; mem. faculty Poly. Inst., Bklyn. 1948—, prof., 1952—; distinguished prof., 1969—, dean research, 1967-70; vis. prof. U. Uppsala, 1950, U. Bristol, 1965; cons. Govt. Com. Chems., Plastics and Rubber Industry. Fellow N.Y. Acad. Schs. (chmn. chem. sect. 1952-53); mem. Am. Chem. Soc. (chmn. colloid div. 1960), A.A.A.S. (chmn., councillor Gordon Confs. 1959-65), Soc. Rheology (v.p. 1970), Am. Phys. Soc., Faraday Soc., Sigma Xi. Author numerous research papers. Home: 22 Deerfield Av Tuckahoe NY 10707 Office: 333 Jay St Brooklyn NY 11201

EISCH, JOHN JOSEPH, chemist; b. Milw., Nov. 5, 1930; s. Frank Joseph and Gladys (Riordan) E.; B.S summa cum laude, Marquette U., 1952; Ph.D. (Procter and Gambel fellow 1955, Union Carbide fellow 1956), Ia. State U., 1956; m. Joan Terese Scheuerell, Sept. 5, 1953; children—Margaret, Karia, Joseph, Paula, Amelia. Postdoctoral fellow Max Planck Inst. fur Kohlenforschung, Mulheim, Germany, 1956-57; research asso. European Research Assos., Brussels, Belgium, 1957; faculty St. Louis U., 1957-59, U. Mich., 1959- 63; faculty Catholic U. Am., Washington, 1963—, prof. chemistry, 1967—, head dept., 1966—; cons. to various bus., Ethyl Corp., 1964—. Mem. Am. Chem. Soc., Am. Inst. Chemists, Sigma Xi, Phi Lambda Upsilon, Phi Kappa Phi. Author: The Chemistry of Organometallic Compounds 1967; (with R. B. King) Organometallic Syntheses, 1965. Research and publs. on the synthesis and properties of organometallic compounds (those with carbon-metal bonds) and heterocycles, with emphasis on the kinetics and stereochemistry of carbon-metal bond and hydrogen-metal bond additions to olefins, acetylenes; radical-anion, halogenation, nonbenzenoid aromatic studies. Home: 317 Waterford Rd Silver Spring MD 20901 Office: Maloney Chem Lab Catholic U Am Washington DC 20017

EISELE, DONN FULTON, astronaut; b. Columbus, O., June 23, 1930; s. Herman E. and June (Davisson) E.; B.S., U.S. Naval Acad., 1952; M.S. in Astronautics, USAF Inst. Tech., 1960; m. Susan H. Hearn, Aug. 2, 1969; children—Melinda Sue, Donn Hamilton, Jon, Kristin. Commd. 2d lt. USAF, 1953, advanced through grades to col.; assigned Rapid City, S.D., 1953- 55, Wheelus AFB, Libya, 1955-58; missile systems engr. Wright-Patterson AFB, O., 1960-61; student test pilot Aerospace Research Pilot Sch., Edwards AFB, Cal., 1962; exptl. flight test officer Kirtland AFB, N.M., 1962-63; astronaut NASA Manned Spacecraft Center, Houston, 1964-70; tech. cons. Langley Research Center, Hampton, Va., 1970—. Mem. Air Force Hist. Found., Nat. Geog. Soc., Tau Beta Pi. Mason. Home: 149 Indian Springs Rd Williamsburg VA 23185 Office: NASA Langley Research Center Hampton VA 23365

EISELEY, LOREN COREY, anthropologist, educator; b. Lincoln, Neb., Sept. 3, 1907; s. Clyde and Daisy (Corey) E.; A.B., U. Neb., 1933, Litt.D., 1960; A.M., U. of Pa., 1935, Ph.D., 1937; Social Sci. Research Council postdoctoral fellow Columbia and Am. Mus. Natural History, 1940-41; L.H.D., Western Res. U., 1959, N.Y.U., 1960, Washington Coll., 1963, U. No. Mich., 1966, Pace Coll., 1964, Kalamazoo Coll., 1967, So. Meth. U., 1969, Hope Coll., 1970; D.Sc., Franklin and Marshall, 1960, Hahnemann Med. Coll., 1965; LL.D., Alfred U., 1963, U. Bridgeport, 1970; Sc.D., U. B.C., 1967, U. Puget Sound, 1968, St. Lawrence Coll., 1970; Litt.D., U. Chattanooga, 1968, Brown U., 1964; m. Mabel Langdon, Aug. 29, 1938. Mem. Morrill Paleontol. Expdns. U. Neb., 1931-33, U. Pa. and Carnegie Expdn. to Southwest, 1934, Smithsonian Expdn. No. Colo., 1935; asst. prof. sociology and anthropology U. Kan., 1937-42, asso. prof., 1942-44; prof. sociology and anthropology and head of dept., Oberlin (O.), Coll., 1944-47; vis. prof. anthropology Columbia, summers 1946, 50, U. Cal. at Berkeley, summer 1949, Harvard, summer 1952; prof. anthropology U. Pa., 1947-59, chmn. dept., 1947- 59, provost, 1959-61, prof. anthropology and history of sci., chmn. dept. history of sci., 1961-63, Benjamin Franklin prof. anthropology and the history of sci., 1961—, curator of Early Man U. Pa. Mus., 1948—. Host, narrator NBC-TV ednl. series, 1966-68; mem. com. interrelationships of pleistocene research NRC, 1947-50, vice chmn. Div. of Psychology and Anthropology, 1950-52; fellow Center for Advanced Study Behavioral Scis., Stanford, Cal., 1961-62; mem. Presidential Task Force Conservation Natural Beauty, 1965; adv. bd. nat. parks Dept. Interior, 1966—. Bd. dirs. Samuel S. Fels Found. Research grants Wenner-Gren Found. Anthropology, 1952-53; Guggenheim Found. fellow, 1963-64; recipient Page One award Newspaper Guild Phila., 1960, Phila. Arts Festival award, 1962, Phila. Art Alliance medal achievement, 1967. Fellow Am. Acad. Arts and Scis., A.A.A.S. (v.p., chmn. sect. L. 1969, mem. Westinghouse sci. awards com.); mem. Internat. Assn. Human Biologists, Am. Acad. Polit. and Social Sci., Am. Assn. Phys. Anthropologists, Am. Anthrop. Assn.(v.p. 1948), Soc. for Am. Archaeology, Phila. Anthrop. Soc. (v.p. 1947, pres. 1948), Am. Philos. Soc., Phi Beta Kappa, Sigma Xi. Author: The Immense Journey, 1957; Darwin's Century, 1958 (Nat. Phi Beta Kappa sci. award, Athenaeum of Phila. lit. award, 1958); The Firmament of Time, 1960 (John Burroughs Asso. medal 1960; Lecomte du Noüy award 1961); The Mind as Nature, 1962; Francis Bacon and the Modern Dilemma, 1962; The Unexpected Universe, 1969; The Invisible Pyramid, 1970; also articles and verse in popular mags. Co-editor: An Appraisal of Anthropology Today, 1953; mem. editorial bd. Expedition. Home: Wyndon Apts Wynnewood PA 19096 Office: Dept Anthropology Univ Mus 33d and Spruce Sts Philadelphia PA 19104

EISEMAN, BEN, educator, surgeon; b. St. Louis, Nov. 2, 1917; s. Frederick B. and Justine (Godchaux) E.; B.A., Yale, 1939; M.D., Harvard, 1943; m. Mary Harding, Dec. 22, 1945; children—Jane, John, Lucy, Andrew. Surg. intern Mass. Gen. Hosp., Boston, 1943; surg. resident Barnes Hosp., St. Louis, 1946-50; instr., then asst. prof. surgery Washington U. Med. Sch., St. Louis, 1950-53; asso. prof., then prof. surgery U. Colo. Med. Sch., 1953- 61; prof., chmn. dept. surgery U. Ky. Med. Sch., 1961-67; prof. surgery U. Colo., Denver, 1967—; vis. prof. surgery Thailand, 1950, 51, 53, Burma, 1951, Singapore, 1960. Mem. surg. com. Nat. Bd. Med. Examiners; mem. surg. study sect. com. on trauma USPHS-NRC; mem. exam. com. Am. Bd. Surgery, 1964-70; cons. surgeon gen. USN, Vietnam, 1966, 68. Served to lt. (s.g.), M.C., USNR, 1943-46; rear adm. Res. Recipient Certificate of Merit U.S. Navy, 1969. Diplomate Am. Bd. Thoracic Surgery. Mem. A.C.S. (com. internat. relations), Am. Bd. Surgery, Am., So. surg. assns., Soc. Univ. Surgeons, Am. Thoracic Assn., Soc. Clin. Surgery, Am. Gastroent. Assn., Soc. Vascular Surgery, Internat. Surg. Soc., Internat. Cardiovascular Soc. Editorial bd. Am. Surgery, Gastroenterology. Author articles in field. Home: 3 Village Rd Englewood CO 80110 Office: Dept Surgery U Colo Med Sch 4200 E 9th Av Denver CO 80220

EISEMAN, FLORENCE, fashion designer, clothing mfr.; b. Mpls., Sept. 27, 1899; ed. pub. schs., Mpls.; m. Laurence H. Eiseman, Nov. 24, 1927; children—Zaurence H., Robert D. Engaged in children's clothing business, 1945— v.p., pres. and chmn. Florence Eiseman, Inc., Milw., 1945—, Florence Elseman Knits, Inc., Milw., 1960—. Recipient Distinguished Contbn. to Fashion award Neiman Marcus Co., 1955; Swiss Fabrics award, 1956. Mem. Council Fashion Designers Am., Zonta Internat. Home: 1961 N Summit Av Milwaukee WI 53202 Office: 301 N Water St Milwaukee WI 53202

EISEMAN, MYRON JOSEPH, textile mfg. exec.; b. N.Y.C., Feb. 28, 1919; s. Aaron and Estelle Viola (Alexander) E.; studnet N.Y. U., Columbia Extension Sch.; m. Marjorie Koenig, on Dec. 8, 1953 (dec.); children—Patricia, Nancy; m. 2d., Adrienne Kaster Heller, Jan. 10, 1967; children—Richard, Robin. With United Mchts. & Mfrs., 1937—, beginning as sample clk. and registry clk. Cohn Hall Marx Co. div., successively adminstrn. and sales overseas orgn., establishment affiliates fgn. countries, asst. treas. United Internat. div., 1937-50, v.p., 1950—, pres. United Internat. Corp., 1954-69, chmn. of bd., 1969—, v.p. United Merchants & Mfrs., Inc., 1958—; dir. United Mchts. and Mfrs. (U.K.), Ltd., The Airevale Curtain Co., Ltd., Artat Leeds, Ltd., Britsildye Balloch, Ltd., Cohn Hall Marx U.K., Ltd., Comark (U.K.) & Co., Ltd., Flanlon London, Ltd., David Fulton & Co., Ltd., Kenneth Curtain Fabrics (U.K.) Ltd., Peel Bank Engravings Co. Ltd., Arthur Tate & Co., Ltd., Arthur Tate (Bradford), Ltd., Seneca Textiles (U.K.) Ltd., United Mchts. (U.K.) Ltd., (all in Eng.), Polimeros Colombianos, Providersos Colombianos (both Colombia), British Silk Dyers, Ltd., Balloch, Scotland, Pan America de Panama, Spunglass Ltd. of Eng., Compaigne General Du Vtments, France. Spl. govt. asst. of internat. finance corp. missions; adv. com. to U.S. sec. commerce. Mem. Mexican C. of C., Ecuadorean Assn., C. of C. of C.Am., Textile Exporters Assn., Pan Am. Soc. Clubs: Inter-Com (N.Y.C.); Beach Point. Home: Sunny Ridge Rd Harrison NY 10528 Office: United Merchants and Manufacturers Inc 1407 Broadway New York City NY 10018

EISEMAN, PHILIP, banker; b. Boston, Mar. 11, 1904; s. Ludwig and Selma (Weil) E.; grad. Philips Andover, 1921; B.S., Harvard, 1925, M.B.A., 1927; m. Marion B. Becker, June 14, 1930; 1 dau., Anne (Mrs. Thomas S. Walker). With Old Colony Trust Co., Boston, 1927-30; asst. treas. Old Colony Trust Assos. (name later changed to Baystate Corp.), Boston, 1931-40, treas., v.p., 1940-48, pres., 1948-66, dir., 1948—, chmn. bd., 1966-69; dir. Branch Motor Industries, Inc., Asso. Mortgage Investors, Ltd., Newsome & Co., Inc. Vice pres. New Eng. region Am. Jewish Com.; bd. dirs., exec. com. Mass. Bay United Fund; v.p. bd. dirs. Planned Parenthood League of Mass.; v.p., adviser Cambridge Civic Assn., hon. trustee Combined Jewish Philanthropies; bd. dirs. Cambridge Community Services; trustee Boston Hosp. for Women; trustee Mt. Auburn Hosp. Served to lt. col., Signal Corps., AUS, 1943-46. Hon. mem. Assn. Registered Bank Holding Cos. Clubs: Harvard, Union, (Boston); Cambridge; Belmont (Mass.) Country. Home: 142 Brattle St Cambridge MA 02138 Office: 77 Franklin St Boston MA 02110

EISEMANN, CARL, Jr., educator; b. Milw., Sept. 28, 1917; s. Carl and Anna (Reinhardt) E.; Ph.B., U. Wis., 1939, Ph.D., 1956; M.S., Marquette U., 1945; m. Amanda P. Kittelmann, Jan. 25, 1941; children—Carl, Christine (Mrs. James Copeland), Eric, Sharon, Steven, John. Tchr., Shawano (Wis.) pub. schs., 1941-43, Kendall (Wis.) pub. schs., 1946; adminstr. Grafton (Wis.) pub. schs., 1946-49, Slinger (Wis.) pub. schs., 1949-55, Lakeland pub. schs., Minocqua, Wis., 1957-62; prof. edn., chmn. dept. Knox Coll., Galesburg, Ill., 1962—. Cons. seminars coll. adminstrn. White House Conf. Edn., 1956; mem. Israel study team Am. Assn. Colls. Tchr. Edn., 1965; mem. Ill. adv. council on degree granting instns.; summer tchr. Monmouth Coll., U. Ore., Colo. Coll., Wis. State Coll. at Stevens Point. Pres. bd. trustees Carl Sandburg Community Coll., 1965- -; pres. Ill. Commn. Tchr. Edn. and Profl. Standards, 1968-69. Served with USAAF, 1943-45. Recipient Tchr. Excellence award Am. Assn. Colls. Tchr. Edn., 1968. Mem. N.E.A. (del. 1967, 68), Am. Assn. U. Profs. Research improvement tchr. edn., devel. use videotape techniques. Home: 948 N Cherry St Galesburg IL 61401.

EISEN, HENRY, educator; b. Bklyn., Dec. 18, 1921; s. Irving and Dorothy (Wilchins) E.; B.S., St. John's U., 1949; M.S., Rutgers U., 1951; Ph.D. (Am. Found. Pharm. Edn. fellow), U. Conn., 1954. Mem. faculty St. John's U., Jamaica, N.Y., 1954—, prof. pharmaceutics, chmn. dept., 1961—; cons. pharm. industry, 1958—. Served with AUS, 1942-46. Mem. Am. Pharm. Assn., Acad. Pharm. Scis., Sigma Xi, Rho Chi. Home: 10-11 162d St Whitestone NY 11357

EISEN, IRVING R., business exec.; b. 1915; B.S., N.Y. U., 1937; married. Controller, Bloomingdale's Dept. Store, 1946-55; v.p., treas. W. & J. Sloane Co., 1955-60; treas. Kerris, Inc., 1960-66, Caldor, Inc., 1967-69, M.H. Fishman Co., Inc., N.Y.C., 1969—. Served with AUS, World War II. Office: 300 Park Av New York City NY 10010*

EISENBERG, FILLMORE BERNARD, beverage mfr.; b. Chgo., Mar. 7, 1910; s. Benjamin and Esther (Halperin) E.; student U. Ill., 1927-28, Northwestern U., 1933-36; m. Josephine Weinstein, Jan. 28, 1933; children—Diane (Mrs. Ray Kabaker), Robert M. Dir. purchasing and stores Trans World Airline, Inc., 1943-47; budget dir. Coca-Cola Co., 1948-53, asst. treas., 1954-59, controller, 1959-65, v.p., 1965-71, sr. v.p. finance, 1971—, also dir. Mem. Financial Execs. Inst. Home: 2632 Peachtree Rd NW Atlanta GA 30305 Office: 310 North Av NW Atlanta GA 30313

EISENBERG, JEROME CECIL, lawyer; b. Newark, Dec. 31, 1905; s. Herman and Esther (Sheps) E.; student Columbia, 1925-27; LL.B., N.J. Law Sch., 1925; m. Isabelle R. Roemer, Mar. 8, 1942; children—Peter R., Mary. Admitted to N.J. bar, 1927, since practiced in Newark; partner Clapp & Eisenberg, 1959—. Hearing commr. OPA, 1943. Sec., Lawyers Non-Partisan Com. for Constl. Revision, 1943-44; pres. West Orange Citizens Charter Assn., 1961-62. Trustee Far Brook Sch., Short Hills, N.J., pres., 1954-58; v.p., trustee N.J. Automobile Club. Mem. Am., N.J., Essex County bar assns., Am. Judicature Soc. Home: Ridge Rd West Orange NJ 07052 Office: 744 Broad St Newark NJ 07102

EISENBERG, LEON, child psychiatrist; b. Phila., Aug. 8, 1922; s. Morris and Elizabeth (Sabreen) E.; A.B., U. Pa., 1944, M.D., 1946; M.A. (hon.), Harvard, 1967; m. Ruth Harriet Bleier, June 11, 1948 (div. 1967); children—Mark Philip, Kathy Bleier; m. 2d, Carola Blitzman Guttmacher, Aug. 31, 1967; children—Laurence, Alan. Intern Mt. Sinai Hosp., N.Y.C., 1946-47; instr. physiology U. Pa., 1947- 48; resident psychiatry Sheppard-Pratt Hosp., Towson, Md., 1950-52; with Johns Hopkins, 1952-67, prof. child psychiatry Med. Sch., 1961-67, psychiatrist-in-charge childrens psychiat. service Harriet Lane Home, 1958-67; prof. psychiatry Harvard Med. Sch., 1967-; psychiatrist-in- chief Mass. Gen. Hosp., 1967—; psychiat. cons. Crownsville (Md.) State Hosp., 1954-58, Rosewood State Tng. Sch., Owings Mills, Md., 1957- 60, Balt. City Hosp., 1959-62, Childrens Guild, Balt., 1954-61; cons. to Sinai Hosp. Balt., 1963-67. Mem. subcom. psychiat. nomenclature, com. vital statistics USPHS; chmn. WHO Conf. Developmental Regulation, 1964-67; mem. Joint Commn. Mental Health of Children. Served to capt., M.C., AUS, 1948-50. Diplomate in child psychiatry and psychiatry Am. Bd. Psychiatry and Neurology. Fellow Am. Psychiat. Assn., Am. Orthopsychiat. Assn., A.A.A.S., Soc. Research Child Devel., Am. Pub. Health Assn.; mem. Am. Acad. Child Psychiatrists, Am. Assn. U. Profs. (past pres. Johns Hopkins), Am. Acad. Pediatrics, Am. Pediatric Soc., Assn. Research Nervous and Mental Disease, Am. Psychopath. Assn., Maryland Psychiat. Soc. (past pres.), Am. Acad. Arts and Scis., Psychiat. Research Soc. (pres.), Soc. Neuroscience, Mass. Med. Soc., Fedn. Am. Scientists, Phi Beta Kappa (chpt. pres.), Alpha Omega Alpha. Editor: Am. Jour. Orthopsychiatry; editorial bd. communications in Behavioral Biology, Jour. Child Psychology and Psychiatry, Comprehensive Psychiatry, Jour. Pediatrics, Jour. Psychiat. Research. Home: 9 Clement Circle Cambridge MA 02138 Office: Mass Gen Hosp Fruit St Boston MA 02114

EISENBERG, M. MICHAEL, educator, physician; b. N.Y.C., Jan. 27, 1931; s. George Herman and Dorothy (Rosenfeld) E.; A.B. cum laude, N.Y. U., 1952; M.D. cum laude, Harvard, 1956; m. Carol Frances Kossin, June 21, 1953; children—Elyse Debra, Ellen Beth, Andrea Carla. Surg. intern Peter Bent Brigham Hosp., Boston, 1956; surg. resident New Haven Med. Center, 1960; asst. prof. surgery, then asso. prof. U. Fla. Med. Sch., 1962-68; prof. surgery U. Minn. Med. Sch., Mpls., 1968—; chief surgery Mt. Sinai Hosp., Mpls., 1968. Cons. U. Minn., VA hosps.; sr. investigator NIH, 1968—. Mem. budget panel United Fund Mpls. Served with M.C., AUS, 1958-60. Mem. Phi Beta Kappa, Alpha Omega Alpha. Contbr. articles to med. jours. Home: 4649 E Lake Harriet Rd Minneapolis MN 55409

EISENBERG, MARVIN, educator; b. Phila., Aug. 19, 1922; s. Frank and Rosalie (Julius) E.; B.A., U. Pa., 1943; M.F.A., Princeton, 1949, Ph.D., 1954. Mem. faculty U. Mich., Ann Arbor, 1949—, prof. art history, also chmn. dept., 1962-69; mem. Inst. for Advanced Study, Princeton, N.J., 1970. Served with AUS, 1944-46. Guggenheim fellow, 1959; recipient Star of Solidarity II (Italy), 1961. Mem. Coll. Art Assn. Am. (bd. dirs. 1965-70, v.p. 1966, pres. 1968-69), Renaissance Soc. Am., Mediaeval Acad. Am., Royal Soc. Arts, Phi Beta Kappa, Phi Kappa Phi. Contbr. profl. jours. Home: 2200 Fuller Rd Ann Arbor MI 48105

EISENBERG, MATTHEW EMANUEL, mfr. knit goods; b. Jersey City, Feb. 10, 1904; s. Joseph and Mary (Geller) E.; ed. pub. schs., alsp pvt. tutoring, m. Margaret McCormick, Aug. 28, 1927. Asst. to pres., dir. Snead & Co., Jersey City, 1926-42; joined Flagg-Utica Co., Florence, Ala., 1942—, exec. v.p., 1952- 62, pres., 1963-66, chmn., chief exec. officer, 1966, also dir., mem. exec. com.; pres. Forest Mills Co., Montezuma, Ga., 1963—; bd. govs. Genesco, Inc. Mem. Florence C. of C. Club: Turtle Point Yacht and Country. Home: 417 Palisade Dr Florence AL 35630 Office: Flagg-Utica Co Florence AL 35630

EISENBERG, MAURICE, concert cellist; b. Koenigsberg, Germany, Feb. 24, 1902; s. Samuel J. and Fannie (Berlin) E.; brought to U.S., 1903, naturalized, 1905; student Peabody Conservatory of Music, Balt., also with Julius Klengel, Leipzig, Hugh Becker, Berlin Diran Alexanian, Paris, and Pablo Casals in Spain; student harmony with Nadia Boulanger, Paris; m. Paula M. Halpert, June 6, 1921; children—Pablo, Maruta Nadia (Mrs. John P. Friedler). Soloist, Royal Philharmonic, London Symphony in London, Pasdeloup Orch., Paris; soloist, Boston, Phila., Los Angeles, San Antonio orchs.; recitalist, lectr. Assn. Am. Colls., also at Harvard, Princeton, Mass. Inst. Tech., Oxford and Cambridge univs., Royal Acad. Music, London, McGill U., Montreal, others; head cello dept. Longy Sch. Music, Cambridge, Mass.; yearly master classes Internat. Summer

Courses, Estoril, Portugal; prof. violoncello and chamber music Juilliard Sch. Music; dir. Internat. Cello Centre, London, Eng. U.S. rep. internat. juries Pablo Casals cello competition, Paris, Mexico, Israel and Budapest. Recipient award N.J. Symphony Arts, 1966. Mem. Bohemians, Violoncello Soc. N.Y. (v.p.). Jewish religion. Author: Violoncello Playing of Today, 1957, now in 2d edit. Contbr. articles profl. jours. Home: 119 Cypress St Millburn NJ 07041

EISENBERG, ROBERT, govt. ofcl.; b. Austria, Feb. 29, 1908; s. Isaac and Malvine (Goldreich) E.; student Prague (Czechoslovakia) Comml. Coll., 1921-26; LL.D., German U., Prague, 1931; m. Lilian Marguerite Tetaz, Sept. 21, 1946. Came to U.S., 1941, naturalized, 1943. Chief econ. research for banking co., Prague, 1936-39; with State Dept., 1945—, fgn. service officer, 1951; adviser U.S. Delegation to German Debts Commn., London, 1951-52; charge U.S. Mission to European Coal and Steel Community, Luxembourg, 1955-56; U.S. comml. attache, Mexico City, 1957-58; financial adviser Govt. Kingdom of Laos, 1959-60; counselor Am. embassy, dep. chief mission, Tananarive, Madagascar, 1963-64; counselor for econ. affairs Am. embassy, Pretoria, South Africa, 1965-66; IMF adviser to Nat. Bank of Vietnam, Saigon, 1966-68; advisor to Turkey, 1968. Address: 187 Istikhah Cadd Istanbul-Beyoghn Turkey

EISENBERG, WALTER LEO, educator; b. N.Y.C., Oct. 11, 1920; s. Morris and Minnie (Tannenhaus) E.; B.S. in Social Sci., City College N.Y., 1941; M.A., Columbia, 1946, Ph.D., 1959; m. Beatrice Kaufman, Apr. 7, 1946; children—David Michael, Deborah Ellen. Instr., Bklyn. Coll., 1946-47; exec. sec. trucking industry panel WLB, 1943-46; regional asso. dir. Wage Stblzn. Bd., 1951-53; dir. research Internat. Brotherhood Teamsters regional council, 1953-57; mem. faculty Hunter Coll., 1962—, Prof. econs., 1966—, chmn. dept., 1965—; lectr. Columbia, 1959-61; econ. cons., 1957-62. Dir. econ. research Labor and Mgmt. Hospilization Trust Fund, 1959—; vice chmn., bd. dirs. Group Health Ins., Inc., 1957—. Bd. dirs. Young Adult Inst. and Workshop, 1964—. Recipient certificate of merit U.S. Govt., 1946; Rockefeller grantee, 1953. Mem. Nat. Acad. Arbitrators, Am. Arbitration Assn. (panel arbitrators), N.J. Bd. Mediation (panel arbitrators), Office Collective Bargaining (panel mediators), N.Y. State Pub. Employment Relations (panel mediators,) Am. Econ. Assn., Indsl. Relations Research Assn. Author articles. Home: 939 E 24th St Brooklyn NY 11210 Office: 695 Park Av New York City NY 10021

EISENBERG, WARREN, retail chain co. exec.; b. New Bedford, Mass., Aug. 20, 1930; s. Morris and Sarah (Herman) E.; grad. high sch., 1947; m. Maxine Holland, Jan. 10, 1954; children—Martin, Shelly, Ronald, Randi. With Arlan's Dept. Stores, Inc., N.Y.C., 1947—, exec. v.p., 1964-66, pres., 1966—, also dir. Jewish religion (trustee temple). Mem. B'nai B'rith. Home: 1335 Grandview Av Westfield NJ 14787 Office: 393 7th Av New York City NY 10001

EISENBIES, RAY FRED, mfg. co. exec.; b. Marengo, Ill., Sept. 4, 1897; s. Charles Joseph and Grace Lee (Hale) E.; ed. pub. schs.; m. Nona Helen Tkach, May 20, 1947; children—Ray Paul, Nona Lee. With Roberts & Schaefer Co., Chgo., 1915- 35, chief estimator, 1935; with Sawhill Tubular Products, Inc., Wheatland, Pa., 1935—, became pres., 1955; chmn. bd. dirs. Dietrich Industries, Pitts. Past pres. United Fund Shenango Valley. Mem. Am. Iron and Steel Inst. Clubs: Duquesne (Pitts.); Sharon Country; Iroquois (Conneaut Lake, Pa.). Address: 7 Minnetonka Rd Sea Ranch Lakes Ft Lauderdale FL 33308 also: P O Box 176 Conneaut Lake PA 16316

EISENBRANDT, LESLIE LEE, educator, pharmacologist; b. Chanute, Kan., June 23, 1908; s. Elmer L. and Bertha (Surbeck) E.; A.B., Coll. of Emporia, 1932; M.S., Kan. State Coll., 1934; Ph.D., Rutgers U., 1936; m. Ferne Tannahill, June 23, 1936 (dec. 1950); children—James L., David L.; m. 2d, Fae Evans Patrick, Feb. 22, 1952; foster children—Edward, Robert Patrick. Instr. biology U. Mo. at Kansas City, 1936-40, asst. prof., 1940-44, asso. prof. physiology Sch. Denistry, 1944-47, asso. prof. pharmacology Sch. Pharmacy, 1947-49, prof., 1949-66, dean Sch. Pharmacy, 1953-66; prof. biology Parsons Coll., Fairfield, Ia., 1966-67; prof. pharmacology Sch. Medicine U. Mo. at Columbia, 1967—; research asso. pharmacology Sch. Medicine, U. Cal., 1948-49. Trustee U.S. Pharmacopeia, 1970—. Mem. Am. Soc. Pharmacological and Exptl. Therapeutics, Am. Soc. Clin. Pharmacology and Therapeutics, Am. Soc. History Medicine, Am. Soc. Tropical Medicine and Hygiene, Soc. Exptl. Biology and Medicine, A.A.A.S., Sigma Xi, Rho Chi. Contbr. articles to profl. jours. Home: 1104 Vegas Dr Columbia MO 65201

EISENBRAUN, ROBERT ALFRED, publishing co. exec.; b. Rochester, N.Y., Nov. 9, 1928; s. Alfred R. and Florence (Unterborn) E.; B.S. in Econs., Wharton Sch. U. Pa., 1951; m. Eunice M. Fischer, June 29, 1954; children—Jeffrey, Gayle, Eric, Gary. Auditor, Wilson, Shults & Co., C.P.A.'s, Rochester, 1952-60; supr. Peat, Marwick, Mitchell & Co., Rochester, 1961-66; auditor Gannett Co., Rochester, N.Y., 1966-68, controller, 1968—. C.P.A., N.Y. Mem. Am. Inst. C.P.A.'s, N.Y. Soc. C.P.A.'s, Tax Execs. Inst., Inst. Newspaper Controllers and Finance Officers. Club: Oak Hill Country (Rochester). Home: 148 Mendon Center Rd Pittsford NY 14534 Office: Gannett Co Inc 55 Exchange St Rochester NY 14614

EISENBUD, MERRIL, educator, environmentalist; b. N.Y.C., Mar. 18, 1915; s. Kalman and Leonora (Kopaloff) E.; B.S. in Elec. Engring., N.Y. U., 1936; Sc.D., Fairleigh Dickinson U. 1960; m. Irma Onish, Jan. 22, 1939; children—Elliott, Michael, Fredrick. Indsl. hygienist Liberty Mutual Ins. Co., 1936-47; asso. prof. indsl. medicine Postgrad. Sch. Medicine N.Y. U., 1945-55, adj. prof., 1956-59, prof. environmental medicine, dir. lab. environmental studies, 1959—; adminstr. N.Y.C. Environmental Protection Adminstrn., 1968-70; dir. health and safety lab. AEC, 1947-57, mgr. N.Y. Operations Office, 1954-59; cons. U.S. AEC, 1959—; chmn. bd. dirs. Environmental Analyst, Inc. Mem. Nat. Commn. on Radiation Protection and Measurements, 1965—; mem. toxicology com. NRC, 1952-62; mem. expert panel on radiation hazards WHO, 1956- -; cons. USPHS; chmn. N.Y. State Gen. Adv. Com. Atomic Energy, mem. N.Y. State Atomic and Space Devel. Authority; bd. dirs. Asso. Hosp. Services of N.Y. Fellow A.A.A.S., Am. Nuclear Soc., Health Physics Soc. (pres. 1965-66), Am. Pub. Health Assn.; mem. Am. Indsl. Hygiene Assn., Radiation Research Soc., Am. Bd. Health Physics, Sigma Xi, Eta Kappa Nu. Club: Cosmos (Washington). Author: Environmental Radioactivity, 1963. Home: W Lake Rd Sterling Forest Tuxedo NY 10987 Office: N Y U Med Center Tuxedo NY 10987

EISENDRATH, MAURICE NATHAN, rabbi; b. Chgo., July 10, 1902; s. Nathan Julius and Clara (Oesterreicher) E.; A.B., U. Cin., 1925, LL.D., 1957; rabbi, Hebrew Union Coll., Cinc., 1926, D.D., 1945; LL.D., Brown U., 1964; m. Rosa Brown, Nov. 24, 1926 (dec. July 1963); m. 2d. Rita Hands, June 1964; stepchildren—Linda, Charles. Rabbi, Charleston, W.Va., 1926-29, Holy Blossom Temple, Toronto, Cincinnati, O., 1943-46; pres. Union Am. Hebrew Congregations, 1946—, pres. for life, 1952—, rep. to Synagogue Council Am. Bd. govs. Hebrew Union Coll.-Jewish Inst. Religion; bd. dirs. Nat. Jewish Welfare Bd.; vice chmn. Am. bd. World Jewish Congress; mem. theologian's com. Am. Assn. for Internat. Office of Edn.; v.p. World Union for Progressive Judaism; nat. co-chmn. commns. on religious orgns. Nat. Conf. Christians and Jews; mem. nat. council Joint Distbn. Com. Campaign; mem. Nat. Community Relations Adv. Council; mem. exec. bd Central Conf. Am. Rabbis. Author: The Never Failing Stream, 1939; Can Faith Survive, 1958. Contbr. to Dimensions, American Judaism, Jewish Layman. Office: 838 Fifth Av New York City NY 10021

EISENHARDT, RAYMOND F., banker. Sr. v.p. Buffalo Savs. Bank. Office: 545 Main St Buffalo NY 14203*

EISENHART, CHARLES ROBERT, coll. pres.; b. Binghamton, N.Y., Mar. 12, 1912; s. John A. and Nellie (Van Patten) E.; Ph.B., Muhlenberg Coll., 1933; M.A., N.Y. State U. at Albany, 1940; Ed. D., Columbia, 1954; H.D., Defiance Coll., 1961; m. Judith Annabel Russell, Aug. 31, 1935; children-Charles Robert, Judith Annabel, John Brainard. Tchr. rural schs., 1934-35; tchr., Harpursville, N.Y., 1935-37, Johnson City, N.Y., 1937-43; asso. prof., dean men Hartwick Coll., 1946-54; dean Jacksonville (Fla.) U., 1954-56; dean Defiance Coll., 1956-61; pres. Adirondack Community Coll., Glens Falls, N.Y., 1961—. Ohio del. White House Conf. Aging, 1961; chmn. Defiance County Com. Problems of Aging, 1959-61, del. state conv. Bd. dirs. Hyde Art Collection; exec. bd. Mohican council Boy Scouts Am. Served with AUS, World War II; col. USAF Res. Mem. Am. Meteorol. Soc., Res. Officers Assn., Phi Sigma Kappa, Phi Sigma Iota, Kappa Phi Kappa, Phi Delta Kappa. Home: 238 Bay St Glens Falls NY 12801

EISENHAUER, ROBERT STOLL, mfg. co. exec.; b. Cleve., June 2, 1913; s. John Adam and Helen (Stoll) E.; A.B., Oberlin Coll., 1934; m. Frances Spelbrink, Jan. 18, 1941; children—Christine, Lawrence, Eric, Susan. Jr. accountant Johns Manville Corp., Cleve., 1934-37; city editor Lorain (O.) Jour., 1937-39; reporter, asst. city editor, picture editor Cleve. News, 1939-52; news editor C. & O. Ry., Cleve., 1952- 53; dir. pub. relations and advt. Chesapeake Industries, Inc., N.Y.C., 1953-56; dir. pub. relations and advt. N.Y. Central R.R., 1956-60; dir. pub. relations and advt. Textron Inc. 1960-61, v.p., 1962—. Mem. Pub. Relations Soc. Am., Investor Relations Assn. Presbyn. (elder). Clubs: Rhode Island Country (Barrington); Turk's Head, Art (Providence). Home: 2 Rumstick Circle Barrington RI 02806 Office: 10 Dorrance St Providence RI 02903

EISENHOWER, JOHN SHELDON DOUD, U.S. ambassador; b. Denver, Aug. 3, 1922; s. Dwight David and Mamie (Doud) E.; B.S., U.S. Mil. Acad., 1944; M.A. in English Lit., Columbia, 1950; m. Barbara Jean Thompson, June 17, 1947; children—Dwight David II, Barbara Anne (Seora de Echavarria), Susan Elaine, Mary Jean. Commd. 2d lt. U.S. Army, 1944, advanced through grades to lt. col., 1963; assigned Army of Occupation, Europe, 1945-47, Korean War, 1952-53; resigned, 1963; col. Res.; with Doubleday and Co., 1961-64; engaged in writing, 1965-69; U.S. Ambassador to Belgium, 1969—. Chmn. Pa. Citizens for Nixon, 1968. Trustee Eisenhower Coll., Eisenhower Fellowships. Decorated Legion of Merit, Bronze Star medal, Combat Inf. badge. Author: The Bitter Woods, 1969. Home: 111 White Horse Rd Phoenixville PA 19460 Office: American Embassy Brussels Belgium

EISENHOWER, MAMIE GENEVA DOUD; b. Boone, Ia.; Nov. 14, 1896; d. John Sheldon and Elivera M. (Carlson) Doud; ed. Miss Wolcott's Sch.; L.H.D. (hon.), Colo. Woman's Coll., 1946; LL.D. honoris causa St. Joseph Coll., 1959; m. Dwight David Eisenhower. Hon. pres. Girl Scouts of Am. Hon. mem. Woman's Med. Coll. of Pa. Decorated Order of Malta, Italy, 1952, Cavalier Order of So. Cross, Brazil, 1946, Grand Cross Order of Honor and Merit, Cuba, 1953. Mem. Daus. of Colo., Ia. Hist. Soc. (hon.), Distinguished Daus. Pa., D.A.R., Army and Navy Union Aux., Daus. Cin. (hon.). Republican. Presbyn. Home: Gettysburg PA 17325

EISENHOWER, MILTON STOVER, ret. univ. pres.; b. Abilene, Kan., Sept. 15, 1899; s. David Jacob and Ida (Stover) E.; B.S., Kan. State U., 1924; hon. degrees from thirty-six univs. and colls., m. Helen Elsie Eakin, Oct. 12, 1927 (dec.); children—Milton Stover, Ruth Eakin. Am. vice consul, Edinburgh, Scotland, 1924-26; asst. to sec. of agr., 1926-28; dir. information U.S. Dept. Agr., 1928-41; dir. War Relocation Authority, 1942; asso. dir. OWI, 1942-43; pres. Kan. State U., Manhattan, 1943- 50, Pa. State U., 1950-56, Johns Hopkins U., Balt., 1956-67, pres. emeritus, 1967-71, pres., 1971—. Dir. B. & O. R.R., C. & O. Ry., ISI Instnl. Funds A and B, ISI Trust Fund, ISI Growth and Income Funds, Comml. Credit Co., Chesapeake and Potomac Telephone Co., Merc. Safe Deposit & Trust Co. Public gov. for N.Y. Stock Exchange, 1962- 65. Mem. Famine Emergency Relief Com., 1946; exec. bd. UNESCO, 1946; mem. Pres.'s Com. on Govt. Orgn., 1953-60; spl. ambassador personal rep. Pres. U.S. Latin Am. Affairs, 1953, 56, 57-60, ambassador, cons. Latin Am. affairs, 1968-69; chmn. U.S. Nat. Commn. for UNESCO, 1946-48, del. UNESCO Confs. 1946, 47, 48, 49; mem. numerous govtl. commns. and coms., 1940—; chmn. Pres.'s Commn. on Causes and Prevention Violence, 1968-69; mem. Pres.'s Commn. Atlantic-Pacific Interoceanic Canal Study, 1965-70. Bd. dirs. Johns Hopkins Hosp., Greater Balt. Center, Balt. Mus. Art; bd. visitors and govs. Washington Coll.; trustee Nat. Com. for Econ. Devel. 1947-51. Dir. Freedoms Found. Inc., 1951—; chmn. gen. awards jury, 1950; dir. The Geisinger Meml. Hosp., 1952-67; chmn. Am.-Korean Found., 1952-53; mem. bd. visitors U.S. Naval Acad., 1958-61. Recipient several awards fgn. govts. Fellow Am. Acad. Arts and Scis.; mem. Acad. Polit. Sci. (hon.), Kan. Acad. Sci., Phi Kappa Phi, Sigma Alpha Epsilon, Alpha Zeta. Episcopalian. Author: The Wine Is Bitter, 1963; also numerous fed. bulls. and leaflets. Contbr. several mags. Office: 4545 N Charles St Baltimore MD 21210

EISENHUT, GREGORY mfg. exec.; b. Lima, O., Apr. 1, 1932; B.S., U. San Francisco, 1954; M.S., Stanford University, 1956; m. Rosemarie Lois Brown, May 15, 1955; 1 son, Anthony Robinson. Sales rep. Ames-Brockton Fabricated Products, Akron, O., 1956-58, sales mgr. Coshocton, Ohio, 1959-61, gen. manager plant, 1961-68, v.p. sales, 1968--. Instr. bus. Coshocton Jr. College, 1968-69. Secretary Coshocton YMCA, 1960-61; active Boy Scouts of America. Named Man of Year, Coshocton Junior Chamber of Commerce, 1968. Mem. Coshocton C. of C. (vice president 1967-68, pres. 1969-70), English Speaking Union, Coshocton Sertoma Club, Nat. Assn. Mfrs., Sales Executives Institute, Phi Beta Kappa, Sigma Chi, Phi Mu. Democrat. Mem. Christian Ch. (lay leader). Mason (32, Shriner). Clubs: Coshocton Country, Coshocton City, Running Deer Country. Home: 2d Av Coshocton OH Office: 3d Av Coshocton OH

EISENMAN, GEORGE, educator; b. N.Y.C., May 6, 1929; s. William and Nadia (Geffen) E.; A.B., Harvard, 1949, M.D., 1953; m. Nancy Crawford Dunn, Dec. 20, 1952; children—Richard Newton, Frederick Maxwell. Research fellow Harvard, 1950, 53-55, research asso., 1955-56; sr. scientist Eastern Pa. Psychiat. Inst., Phila., 1956-62; asso. prof. Coll. Medicine, U. Utah, 1962-65; prof. biophysics and physiology U. Chgo., 1965-69; prof. physiology U. Cal. Med. Sch. at Los Angeles, 1969—. Cons. Corning (N.Y.) Glass Works, 1962—; mem. BBCB study sect. NIH. Mem. Am. Physiol. Soc., Biophys. Soc. Editor: Glass Electrodes for Hydrogen and Other Cations: Principles and Practice, 1966. Inventor sation selective glass electrodes. Home: 10570 LeConte Av Los Angeles CA 90024

EISENMENGER, ROBERT WALTZ, banker; b. N.Y.C., June 30, 1926; s. Walter S. and Emily (Brenner) E.; B.A., Amherst Coll., 1949; M.F., Yale, 1951; M.P.A. (Conservation fellow), Harvard, 1955, Ph.D. in Econs. (Littauer fellow), 1964; m. Carolyn Lois Shaver, Oct. 11, 1952; children—Anne Waltz, Katherine Carol, Lisa Ellen. Asst. forester Dept. Interior, Eugene, Ore., 1951-52, forest economist, Portland, Ore., 1952-53, forester, Salem, Ore., 1953-54; economist Fed. Reserve Bank Boston, 1955-63, dir. research, 1963—, v.p., 1966-68, sr. v.p., 1968—; lectr. Wellesley Coll., 1969. Chmn. research com. New Eng. Council, 1968—; mem. Labor adv. com., Natick, Mass., 1970—, finance com., 1960-62, town meeting, 1964—; mem. New Eng. Bd. Higher Edn., 1970—. Served with USNR, 1944-46. Mem. Nat. Assn. Bus. Economists, Am. Econ. Assn. Club: Amherst (Boston). Author: The Dynamics of Growth in New England's Economy 1870-1964, 1967. Home: 92 Woodland St Natick MA 01760 Office: Fed Reserve Bank Boston 30 Pearl St Boston MA 02106

EISENPREIS, ALFRED, retail co. exec.; b. Vienna, Austria, June 16, 1924; s. Zygmunt and Claire (Silberman-Günsberg) E.; came to U.S., 1939, naturalized, 1942; A.B., U. Scranton, 1943; grad. N.Y. Sch. Social Research; m. Elizabeth Jane Long, June 18, 1958; 1 son, Steven. Exec., Pomeroy's Inc., dept. store, Wilkes-Barre, Pa., 1943-57; with Allied Stores Corp., N.Y.C., 1957—, v.p. planning and research, 1963-69, v.p. marketing, 1970—; dir. Allerton, Berman & Dean, advt., N.Y.C. Chmn., Retail Research Inst., 1963-68; mem. com. dept. store statistics Fed. Res. System, 1960- 65; chmn. adv. com. Center Econ. Projections, Nat. Planning Assn., 1965- 68; mem. dept. urban research Nat. Acad. Scis., 1964-69; cons. U.S. Dept. Commerce, 1965-69; dir. Greater Jamaica Adv. Com., 1965-68. Trustee Fed. Statis. Users Conf., 1965-67, N.Y. Met. Regional Statis. Center, 1965-67; mem. nat. marketing adv. com. U.S. Dept. Commerce, 1968—; cons. Office of Emergency Preparedness, 1966—; mem. Nat. Def. Exec. Res. Trustee Wilkes Coll., Wilkes Barre, Pa., Reece Sch., N. Y. C., Union Am. Hebrew Congregations. Mem. Advt. Club N.Y., Am. Statis. Assn., Am. Econ. Assn., Am. Marketing Assn., Nat. Retail Mchts. Assn. (dir. 1963, mem. exec. committee 1968—, v.p. 1970—), Am. Retail Fedn. (dir., mem. exec. com. 1968—), N.Y. Acad. Scis., Am. Mgmt. Assn., Retail Research Soc. (hon.), Newcomen Soc. Regional Plan Assn. N.Y.C. (com. 2d regional plan). Jewish religion. Club: Forecasters (N.Y.C.). Author: The Changing Consumer, 1961; Organization for Multi- Unit Stores, 1962; Evaluation of Retail Store Location Research, 1965. Home: 40 E 83d St New York City NY 10028 Office: 401 Fifth Av New York City NY 10016

EISENRING, MAX EDUARD, ins. co. exec.; b. St. Gall, Switzerland, Jan. 14, 1910; s. Otto and Anna (Hilty) E.; student St. Gall State Coll., 1924-28; M.Sc., Fed. Inst. Tech. (Switzerland), 1933, D.Sc., 1942; m. Rita Caspar, Apr. 17, 1937; children—Meinrad Eduard, Arnold Renzo. Asst. prof. Fed. Inst. Tech., Zurich, 1934-36; housemaster Lyceum Alpinum, Zuoz, Switzerland, 1936-44; with Swiss Reins. Co., Zurich, 1944—, actuary, until 1955, life mgr., 1955-58, gen. mgr., 1958-64, chmn. bd., 1964—; chmn. Swiss Ins. Tng. Center, 1960—. Active various internat. univ. orgns., Geneva, Switzerland, 1932-42; sec. Swiss Student Exchange with U.S., 1931-36. Mem. Ins. Hall of Fame, other actuarial, ins., comml. and profl. orgns. Contbr. articles profl. jours. Home: 7 Alpenstrasse Rueschlikon 8803 Switzerland Office: 60 Mythenquai Zurich Switzerland

EISENSON, JON, educator, author; b. N.Y.C., Dec. 17, 1907; s. Abraham Eli and Sarah (Eisenson) E.; B.S., Coll. City N.Y., 1928; M.A., Columbia, 1930, Ph.D., 1935; m. Freda Francke, June 28, 1931; children—Elinore Ruth, Arthur Michael. Instr., then asst. prof. speech Bklyn. Coll., 1935-42; asst. prof., prof. speech, dir. speech and hearing clinic Queens Coll., 1946-62; prof. speech pathology and audiology Stanford, 1962- -, prof. speech and hearing sci. Sch. Medicine, 1968—, dir. Inst. for Childhood Aphasia. Lectr. otolaryngology Coll. Physicians and Surgeons, 1948-62; cons. clin. psychology and speech pathology for VA; mem. adv. speech and hearing panel U.S. Office Health, Welfare and Edn., 1958-62; cons. VA Central Office, 1966, Nat. Inst. Neurol. Diseases and Blindness; com. communications research tng. Nat. Inst. Neurol. Diseases and Stroke, 1968—. Chmn. spl. edn. and adv. com., pres., mem. med. and sci. com. United Cerebral Palsy Assn., 1964-68; pres. Am. Speech and Hearing Found., 1964-68; mem. adv. council Cal. Assn. for Crippled Children. Served from 1st lt. to maj., AUS, 1942-46; chief clin. psychol. Halloran Gen. Hosp., also Ft. Belvoir Tng. Center. Diplomate Am. Bd. Examiners Profl. Psychology. Fellow Am. Speech and Hearing Assn. (mem. council 1953-56, pres. 1958-59), Am. Psychol. Assn. (clin. div.), A.A.A.S.; mem. World Fedn. Neurology (mem. com. dyslexia and illiteracy), Phi Beta Kappa (hon. mem.). Author: Psychology of Speech, 1938; Psychology of Physically Handicapped, 1940; Defective in Speech, 1942; Examining for Aphasia, 1946, 54; Basic Speech, 1950; Speech Disorders, 1956; Speech Correction in the Schools, 1957, rev., 1962; Improvement of Voice and Diction, 1958; Stuttering: A Symposium, 1958: Psychology of Communication, 1963. Contbr. books. Home: 853 Mayfield Av Stanford CA 94305 Office: Stanford U Med Sch Palo Alto CA 94305

EISENSTAEDT, ALFRED, photo journalist; b. Dirschau, Germany, Dec. 6, 1898; s. Joseph and Regina (Schoen) E.; grad. Hohenzollern Gymnasium, Berlin, Germany; m. Alma Kathy Kaye, 1949. Came to U.S., 1935. Spl. photo reporter Pacific and Atlantic Photos, Berlin office, 1929-35 (this firm taken over with unchanged activities by A.P., 1931); staff photographer Life mag., 1936—. Work has covered outstanding events and persons throughout the world. A pioneer in introduction of candid camera technique into news reporting. Named Photographer of The Year, Ency. Brit. and U. Mo., 1951; recipient Culture prize in photography German Soc. for Photography, Cologne, 1962, achievement award Photographic Soc. Am. Author: Witness To Our Time; The Eye of Eisenstaedt; Martha's Vineyard, 1970. Home: 72-15 37th Av Jackson Heights NY 11372 Office: Time and Life Bldg Rockefeller Center New York City NY 10020

EISENSTEIN, IRA, rabbi; b. N.Y.C., Nov. 26, 1906; s. Isaac and Sadie (Luxenberg) E.; A.B., Columbia, 1927, Ph.D., 1941; Rabbi, Jewish Theol. Seminary Am., 1931, D.D., 1958; m. Judith Kaplan, June 10, 1934; children—Miriam Rachel, Ann Nehamah. Exec. dir. Soc. for Advancement of Judaism, 1930-31, asst. leader, 1931-33, asso. leader, 1933-45, leader, 1945-54; rabbi Anshe Emet Synagogue, Chgo., 1954-59; asso. chmn. editorial bd. The Reconstructionist, 1935-59, editor, 1959- -; pres. Reconstructionist Rabbinical Coll., 1968—; vis. prof. homiletics Jewish Theol. Sem., 1951. Pres. Jewish Reconstructionist Found., mem. bd. Cejwin Camps. Mem. Rabbinical Assembly Am. (pres. 1952-54), B'nai B'rith Adult Edn. Commn. Author: Creative Judaism, 1936; Ethics of Tolerance, 1941; Judaism Under Freedom, 1956; What We Mean by Religion, 1958; (with Judith K. Eisenstein) What is Torah, Our Bialik, Seven Golden Buttons, Reborn, Thy Children Shall Return. Co-editor: The New Haggadah, High Holiday Prayerbook, Sabbath Prayerbook; Mordecai M. Kaplan, An Evaluation; Daily Prayerbook; Guide to Jewish Ritual. Co- editor The Daily Prayer Book, 1963; editor Varieties of Jewish Belief. Home: 845 West End Av New York City NY 10025 Office: 15 W 86th St New York City NY 10024

EISENSTEIN, JULIAN CALVERT, educator, physicist; b. Warrenton, Mo., Apr. 3, 1921; s. Otto and Nell (Calvert) E.; B.S., Harvard, 1941, M.A., 1942, Ph.D., 1948; m. Elizabeth Lewisohn, May 30, 1948; children—Margaret, John, Edward. Instr., U. Wis., 1948-52; Nat. Research fellow Oxford, 1952-53; asst. prof., asso. prof. Pa. State U., 1953-57; physicist Nat. Bur. Standards, Washington, 1957-66; prof. George Washington U., Washington, 1966—. Pres., trustee Washington Gallery Modern Art, 1961-65. Mem. Am. Phys. Soc., Phi Beta Kappa, Sigma Xi. Club: Cosmos (Washington). Contbr. articles profl. jours. Home: 82 Kalorama Circle NW Washington DC 20008

EISNER, DAVID GEORGE, surgeon, ret. army officer; b. N.Y.C., Sept. 22, 1912; s. Adolph and Regina (Freier) E.; A.B., Western Res. U., 1933, M.D., 1937. Intern, resident gen. surgery Cleve. City Hosp., 1937-40; commd. 1st lt. U.S. Army, 1940, advanced through grades to col., 1956; resident Army hosps., 1947-50; comdg. officer U.S. Army Hosp., Ft. Polk, La., 1957-58, 65th Med. Group, Korea, 1963-65, Womack Army Hosp., Ft. Bragg, N.C., 1964-66; surgeon Hdqrs. Mil. Assistance Command, Vietnam, 1966-67; comdg. officer Walsom Army Hosp., Ft. Dix, N.J., 1967-71; ret., 1971; clin. dir. dept. surgery R.E. Thomason Gen. Hosp., El Paso, Tex., 1971—. Decorated Legion of Merit with two oak leaf clusters (U.S.); Medal of Merit 1st Class, Army Distinguished Service Order 2d Class (Vietnam). Diplomate Am. Bd. Surgery. Fellow A.C.S.; mem. A.M.A., Phi Beta Kappa, Alpha Omega Alpha. Jewish religion. Mason (32). Address: C-8 252 Shadow Mountain Dr El Paso TX 79912

EISNER, MONROE, business exec.; b. Red Bank, N.J., Jan. 14, 1893; s. Sigmund and Bertha (Weis) E.; student Philips Exeter Acad., 1910; A.B., Harvard, 1914, M.B.A., 1915; m. Winone Jackson, Sept. 16, 1916 (dec. July 1964); 1 son, Robert; m. 2d, Frances Eisner, 1965. With Sigmund Eisner Co., 1915—, pres. 1948—; v.p. Sego Trading Co. 1935-55, pres., 1955- -. Mem. bd. Monmouth County chpt. A.R.C.; mem. bd. Monmouth County Orgn. Social Service; sec. Monmouth Med. Center, 1918-59, pres., 1960-70. Mem. Monmouth Co. Hist. Soc. (dir.). Clubs: Harvard (N.J.); Hollywood Golf; Palm Beach (Fla.) Country; Ocean Beach, Elberon (N.J.) Beach. Home: Prospect Av Red Bank NJ 07701 Office: Red Bank NJ 07701

EISNER, ROBERT, educator, economist; b. N.Y.C., Jan. 17, 1922; s. Harry and Mary (Goldberg) E.; B.S.S., Coll. City N.Y., 1940; M.A., Columbia, 1942; Ph.D., Johns Hopkins, 1951; postgrad. U. Paris, 1945-46; m. Edith Avery Chelimer, June 30, 1946; children—Mary, Emily. Economist, statistician U.S. Govt., 1941-42, 46-47; instr. to asst. prof. econs. U. Ill., 1950-52; from asst. prof. to prof. econs. Northwestern U., 1952—, also research asso. Nat. Bur. Econ. Research, 1969—; econ. cons. Chmn. exec. com. Conf. Research in Income and Wealth, 1967-68. Adv. bd. Mems. of Congress for Peace Through Law, 1969—. Trustee Roycemore Sch., 1969—. Served to capt., F.A., AUS, 1942-46. Guggenheim fellow, 1960; fellow Center Advanced Study in Behavior Scis., 1968. Fellow Econometric Soc.; mem. Am. Econ. Assn. (exec. com. 1971-73), Phi Beta Kappa. Author: Determinants of Capital Expenditures: An Interview Study, Some Factors in Growth Reconsidered. Bd. editors of Am. Econ. Review, 1966-68. Contbr. articles profl. jours. Home: 800 Lincoln St Evanston IL 60201

EISNER, WILL, cartoonist, publisher; b. N.Y.C., Mar. 6, 1917; s. Samuel and Fannie (Ingber) E.; student Art Student's League, N.Y.C., 1935; m. Ann Louise Weingarten, June 15, 1950; children—John David, Alice Carol (dec.). Author, cartoonist syndicated newspaper feature The Spirit, 1940-52; pub. Eisner- Arnold Comic Group, 1940-46; editor Firepower mag., U.S. Army Ordnance, 1942-45; pres. Am. Visuals Corp., 1949—, N.Am. Newspaper Alliance, 1962- 64, Ednl. Supplements Corp.; exec. v.p. Koster-Dana Corp., 1962-64. Bd. dirs. Westchester (N.Y.) Philharmonic. Recipient award as comic book artist of yr. Nat. Cartoonist Soc., N.Y., 1967, Best Artist award, 1968-69; ann. award for quality of art in comic books Soc. Comic Art Research, 1968. Mem. N.Y. Advt. Club. Clubs: Nat. Press (Washington); Overseas Press (N.Y.C.). Author: America's Combat Weapons, 1960; America's Space Vehicles, 1961. Home:' 8 Burling Av White Plains NY 10605 Office: 461 Park Av New York City NY 10016

EISSMAN, HAROLD F., educator, dentist. Chmn. dept. crown and bridge Sch. Dentistry U. Cal. Med. Center, San Francisco. Office: U Cal Med Center 619 Med Scis Bldg San Francisco CA 94122*

EISTER, ALLAN WARDELL, sociologist, educator; b. Upper Sandusky, O., Feb. 10, 1915; s. Allen Bertram and Helen Louise (Wardell) E.; A.B., DePauw U., 1936; M.A., Am. U., 1937; Ph.D., U. Wis., 1945; m. Dorothy M. Zulick, Jan. 2, 1948; children—Karen E., David A. Instr., asst. prof. Hood Coll., 1944-46; asst. prof., asso. prof. So. Meth. U., 1946-53; mem. faculty Wellesley Coll., 1953—, prof. sociology, 1962—, chmn. dept., 1960-65, Albert J. Beveridge fellow, 1936-38; Fulbright lectr. U. Karachi (Pakistan), 1959-60; vis. fellow All Souls Coll., Oxford, 1967. Faculty fellow Ford Found., 1952-53; grantee Am. Philos. Soc., 1959-60; grantee joint com. Near and Middle East studies Social Sci. Research Council and Am. Council Learned Socs., 1959-60; grantee Am. Assn. Middle East Studies, 1963, 65. Fellow Am. Sociol. Assn., (life mem.), life mem. Am. Acad. Polit. and Social Sci.; mem. Eastern Sociol. Soc., Soc. Sci. Study Religion (council, book rev. editor jour.), Phi Beta Kappa. Mem. Soc. of Friends. Author: The U.S. and the A.B.C. Powers, 1889-1906, 1950; Drawing Room Conversion: A Sociological Account of the Oxford Group Movement. Home: 8 Cottage St Wellesley, MA 02181.

EITEL, HUBERT MESSINGER, bus. exec.; b. Chgo., Feb. 14, 1915; s. Edumund H. and Helen (Messinger) E.; student U. Va., 1932-33, Northwestern U., 1933-37; m. Barbara Todd, Mar. 7, 1942; children—Nancy Messinger (Mrs. James W. Reeves), James Riley. With Chgo. Title & Trust Co., 1935-37, Price Waterhouse & Co., C.P.A.'s, Chgo., 1937-46; with Wilson & Co., Inc., Chgo., 1946-67, comptroller, 1965-67; v.p. Ling- Temco-Vought, Inc., Dallas, 1967-69, v.p., controller, 1969—; dir. Wilson & Co., Inc., LTV Aero-space Corp., LTV Electrosystems, Inc., LTV Ling-Altec, Inc. Served with AUS, 1943-46, C.P.A. Mem. Financial Execs. Inst., Am. Inst. C.P.A.'s. Home: 7118 Elmridge Dr Dallas TX 75240 Office: Ling-Temco-Vought Inc P O Box 5003 Dallas TX 75222

EITEL, KARL EMIL, hotel exec.; b. Chgo., Dec. 26, 1928; s. Karl F. and Suzanne (Schmidt) E.; grad. Lake Forest Acad., 1946; student Trinity Coll., 1946-48; B.S., Mich. State U., 1951; m. Mary Ann Lease, June 16, 1951; children—Richard, Susan, Janet. Room clk. St. Anthony Hotel, San Antonio, 1951-52; with Cosmopolitan Hotel, Denver, 1952-58, exec. asst. mgr., 1954-58; exec. asst. mgr. Sir Francis Drake Hotel, San Francisco, 1958-61; mgr. Broadmoor Hotel, Colorado Springs, Colo., 1961-66, v.p., gen. mgr., 1966—; pres. Grand Imperial Co., Silverton, Colo.; pres., dir. Broadmoor Mgmt. Co.; dir. Broadmoor Hotel, Inc., Broadmoor Hotel Water & Power Co., El Pomar Investment Co., Vail Asso. Dir. Colo. Visitors Bur. Mem. Am. (dir.), Rocky Mountain (pres.), Colo.-Wyo. hotel and motel assns., Hotel Greeters Am., Colorado Springs C. of C. (dir.), Hotel Sales Mgmt. Assn., Inter-Am. Hotel Assn., Nat. Assn. Travel Orgns. Clubs, U.S. Tennis Lawn Assn., Navy League U.S., Assn. U.S. Army, Colo.-Wyo. Restaurant Assn., Sigma Nu Mem. Community Ch. Clubs: Broadmoor Golf, Broadmoor Ski; Cheyenne Mountain Country. Home: 15 Thayer Rd Colorado Springs CO 80906 Office: The Broadmoor Hotel Colorado Springs CO 80906

EITEMAN, WILFORD J., educator, author; b. Rock Island, Ill., Feb. 13, 1902; s. Wilford Lee and Elida (Palmer) E.; B.M., Chicago Mus. Coll., 1922; A.B., Ohio Wesleyan U., 1926, M.A., 1928; Ph.D., Ohio State U., 1931; m. Sylvia F. Chmelik, June 15, 1927; children—David Kurt, Dean Spencer. Instr. econs. Ohio Wesleyan U., 1926- 28; prof. accounting Miami-Jacobs Coll., 1928-29; asst. instr. econs. Ohio State U., 1929-31; prof. econs. Albion Coll., 1931-37; Social Science Research Council fellow, 1932-33; asst. prof. econs. Duke U., 1937-44, asso. prof., 1945-46; asso. prof. finance Sch. of Business Adminstrn., Rutgers U., 1946-47; prof. finance U. Mich., 1947—; vis. prof. econs. U. Ceylon, 1954-55. Economist of Zinc, Tin, and Lead div. OPA, 1942, territorial price exec., Alaska, 1942-1943; instr. Army Univ. Center, Biarritz, France, 1945-46; ednl. adviser European Productive Agy., Paris, France, 1959-60; Carnegie vis. prof. finance U. Hawaii, 1964; vis. prof. finance U. Fla., 1968, Ariz. State U., 1970. staff mem. Twentieth Century Fund Inc., stock market investigation, 1933-34; chmn. economics sect. Mich. Acad. Arts. Scis. and Letters, 1937-38. Mem. Am. Econ. Assn., Delta Sigma Pi, Beta Gamma Sigma, Phi Mu Alpha, Delta Sigma Phi. Co-author: Stock Market Control, 1934; The Security Markets, 1935. Author: Corporation Finance, 1948; Price Determination, Theory and Practice, 1949; Graphic Budgets, 1949; (with C. N. Davisson) The Lease, 1950; Investment Advice for Professional Men, 1951; Essays in Finance, 1963; Personal Finance and Investment, 1952; Business Forecasting, 1954; Essentials of Accounting Theory, 1961; Price Determination by Monopolists, 1961; (with D.S.Eiteman) Common Stock Values and Yields, 1962; (with D.K. Eiteman) The Stock Market, 4th edit., 1966, World Leading Stock Exchanges, 1946; (with S.C. Eiteman) Nine Leading Stock Exchanges, 1968. Contbr. to profl. jours. Home: 226 Sumac Lane Ann Arbor MI 48105

EITNER, LORENZ EDWIN ALFRED, educator, art historian; b. Brunn, Czechoslovakia, Aug. 27, 1919; s. Wilhelm and Katherina (Thonet) E.; came to U.S., 1935, naturalized, 1943; A.B., Duke, 1940; M.F.A., Princeton, 1948, Ph.D., 1952; m. Trudi von Kathrein, Oct. 26, 1946; children—Christy, Kathy, Claudia. Research unit head Nuremberg War Crimes Trial, 1946-47; from instr. to prof. art U. Minn., 1949-63; chmn. dept. art, dir. mus. Stanford, 1963—; organized exbhn. 19th Century drawings for Guggenheim Mus. and Minn. U. Gallery, 1962. Mem. Regional Arts Council San Francisco Bay Area. Served as officer OSS, AUS, 1943-46. Fulbright grantee, Belgium, 1952-53; Guggenheim fellow, Munich, Germany, 1956-57. Mem. Coll. Art Assn. Am. (dir., past v.p.), Phi Beta Kappa. Author: The Flabellum of Tournus, 1944; Gericault Sketchbooks in the Chicago Art Institute, 1960; Introduction to Art, 1961; Neo-Classicism and Romanticism, 1969; co- author: The Arts in Higher Education, 1966; also articles. Home: 684 Mirada Stanford CA 94305 Office: Stanford Univ Stanford CA 94305

EKBERG, ANITA, actress; b. Malmo, Sweden, Sept. 29, 1931; m. Anthony Steele, 1956 div. 1959); m. 2d, Rick Van Nutter, 1963. Came to U.S., 1951. Began career as model; motion pictures include War and Peace, Back from Eternity, Zarak, Pickup Alley, Sheba and the Gladiator, Sign of the Gladiator, La Dolce Vita, Boccaccio 70, The Alphabet Murder, The Cobra. Address: care Paul Ross 9145 Sunset Blvd Los Angeles CA 90069*

EKBERG, CARL EDWIN, Jr., educator; b. Mpls., Oct. 28, 1920; s. Carl Edwin and Ruth Elizabeth (Olin) E.; B. Civil Engring., U. Minn., 1943, M.S., 1947, Ph.D., 1954; m. Dorothy Heley, May 25, 1944; children—Carl Edwin III, Gretchen Heley, Janet Heley, Thomas William. Instr. math. and mechanics U. Minn., 1946- 51; structural engr. M., St. P.&S.Ste.M. R.R., summers, 1948-51; asst. prof. civil engring. N.D. State U., 1951-53; asst. prof., asso. prof. civil engring. Lehigh U., 1953-59; prof. civil engring., head dept. Ia. State U., 1959—. Dir. Univ. Bank & Trust Co., Ames. Served as lt. (j.g.) USNR, 1943-46. Registered civil and strucural engr., Minn. Mem. Nat. Soc. Profl. Engrs., Internat. Assn. Bridge and Structural Engring., Am. Soc. C.E., Am. Concrete Inst., Am. Soc. Engring. Edn., Am. Ry. Engring. Assn., Sigma Xi, Tau Beta Pi, Chi Epsilon, Phi Kappa Phi. Rotarian. Author articles in field. Home: 420 E 20th St Ames IA 50010

EKEBERG, JOHN M., govt. ofcl.; b. Rockford, Ill., May 1, 1912; s. Albert T. and Hilda (Ekback) E.; B.A., Beloit Coll., 1933; student U. Chgo., 1934, 38; m. Margaret Dewey, Aug. 1, 1939 (dec.); children—Jan (Mrs. K. L. Ring), John Anders; m. 2d, Edna L. Osborn, Jan. 1, 1964. With Dept. Labor, 1942- -, dir. Bur. Employees Compensation, 1969—; dir. minimum wage bur., N.Y.C., 1962-63. Served with AUS, World War II. Mem. Disabled Am. Vets, Phi Kappa Psi. Home: 4400 East-West Hwy Bethesda MD 20014 Office: Dept of Labor Washington DC 20003

EKEBLAD, FREDERICK ALFRED, coll. dean; b. Providence, Sept. 6, 1917; s. Carl Alfred and Eva (MacCrea) E.; A.B., Brown U., 1938, M.A., 1941; Ph.D., Northwestern U., 1947; m. Dorothy L. Sebbens, June 9, 1942; children—Steven Frederick, Russell Alfred, Louise Elizabeth. Sales research L. Baumberger & Co., 1938-39; faculty Northwestern U., 1941-66, prof. bus. statistics, 1962-66, chmn. dept., 1958-66; dean Coll. Business Administration, Bridgeport (Conn.), 1966—. Mem. Full Employment Com. Chgo., 1963-65. Counselor Evanston YMCA, 1957-59; coach Evanston Little League, 1957-58. Mem. Am. Statis. Assn. (editorial collaborator 1956—, v.p. Chgo. chpt. 1961-65, pres. 1965-66), Am. Econ. Assn. (chmn. election com. 1964), Acad. Mgmt., Phi Beta Kappa, Beta Gamma Sigma. Club: Patterson. Author: The Statistical Method in Business, 1962. Home: 101 Spring Hill Rd Fairfield CT 06430 Office: Coll Bus Adminstrn U Bridgeport Bridgeport CT 06602

EKERN, HALVOR OLAF, fgn. service officer; b. Lewistown, Mont., Mar. 31, 1917; s. Halbor O. and Ruby Eleanor (Putnam) E.; student U. Mont., 1935-41; m. Margaret J. Tanner, Oct. 3, 1942; children—Margaret Kay, Brian Robertson, Holly Noel, Carol Lynn. Quadripartite dir. Allied Commn. Austria, 1945-55, chief polit. div., Am. embassy, Vienna, 1955-56; joined Fgn. Service State Dept., 1950—; dep. chief mission, chargé d'affaires Am. embassy, Freetown, Sierra Leone, 1961-63; Bur. Intelligence and Research, 1964-67; chief polit./mil. affairs embassy, Bonn, 1967-69; polit. adviser to comdr.-in-chief U.S. Army Europe, Heidelberg, Germany, 1969—. Served from 2d lt. to lt. col., inf. AUS, 1941-47. Decorated Bronze Star with oak leaf clusters. Mem. Acad. Polit. Sci., Scabbard and Blade, Phi Sigma, Sigma Phi Epsilon. Home: Polson MT 59860 Office: POLAD USAREUR APO NY 09403

EKIN, KENNETH HUNTLEY, railroad ofcl.; b. Takoma Park, Md., Aug. 2, 1909; s. John J. and Estelle (Huntley) E.; student Johns Hopkins, 1927-28; LL.B., U. Va., 1933; m. Margaret Roop, Sept. 6, 1934. Admitted to Md. bar, 1933; pvt. practice, Balt., 1933-45; partner firm Hershey, Donaldson, Williams & Stanley, 1941-45; with B. & O. R.R., 1946—, gen. atty., 1951-61, gen. counsel, 1961-66, v.p. law, 1966—; v.p. law C. & O. Ry. Co., 1966—; dir. Union Trust Co., Md., Reading R.R. Co., Crown Central Petroleum Corp., Western Md. Ry. Co. Trustee S. Baltimore Gen. Hosp. Served with AUS, 1942-45. Mem. Am., Md., Balt. bar assns.; Sigma Phi Epsilon. Republican. Presbyn. Clubs: University (Balt.); Hillendale Country (Phoenix, Md.). Home: 540 Valley View Rd Towson MD 21204 Office: 2 N Charles St Baltimore MD 21201

EKLUND, ARNE SIGVARD, internat. atomic energy ofcl.; b. Kiruna, Sweden, June 19, 1911; s. Severin and Vilhelmina (Pettersson) E.; Dr. Sci., U. Uppsala (Sweden), 1946; Ph.D. (hon.), U. Graz (Austria), 1968; m. Anna-Greta Johansson, June 25, 1941; children—Kerstin, Anders, Gudrun. Asst., later sr. scientist Nobel Inst. Physics, Stockholm, Sweden, 1937-45; sr. scientist Research Inst. Nat. Def., Stockholm, 1946-50; asso. prof. nuclear physics Royal Inst. Tech., Stockholm, 1946-56; dir. research AB Atomenergi, Stockholm, 1950-56, dir. reactor devel. div., 1957-61, dep. mng. dir., 1950-61; dir. gen. Internat. Atomic Energy Agy., Vienna, 1961—. Recipient Atoms for Peace award, 1968. Fellow Am. Nuclear Soc.; mem. Royal Swedish Acad. Engring. Scis., Swedish Physicists Assn., Brit. Nuclear Energy Soc. (hon.). Home: Krapfenwaldgasse 48 A-1190 Vienna Austria Office: Internat Atomic Energy Agy Kärntnerring 11 Vienna I Austria

EKLUND, COY GLENWOOD, life ins. co. exec.; b. Brookston, Minn., Sept. 6, 1915; s. Nels and Melba (Tester) E.; student U. Mich., 1933-34; B.S., Mich. State U., 1939; m. Nina Wolkoff, Sept. 20, 1940; children—Melanie, Glenwood, Ronald. With Equitable Life Assurance Soc., N.Y.C., 1939—, agy. mgr., Detroit, 1947-59, v.p., asst. to pres., 1959-61, agy. v.p., 1961—, sr. agy. v.p., 1964-69, exec. v.p., 1969—, also dir. Mem. Mich. for Eisenhower Com., 1951-52. Bd. dirs. Oakland Found., Oakland U., 1957-59; mem. governing com. David McCahan Found., 1960—; trustee Am. Coll. Life Underwriters, 1964—, Nat. Safety Council, Salk Inst. Biol. Studies, 1962—. Recipient Distinguished Alumnus award Mich. State U., 1965. Served as officer AUS, 1942-46; lt. col. ret. Decorated Croix de Guerre. C.L.U. Mem. Am. Soc. C.L.U.'s, Nat. Assn. Life Underwriters (nat. v.p. 1958-59), Mich. Res. Officers Assn. (pres. 1947-48), Life Ins. Agy. Mgmt. Assn. (trustee 1965-68). Home: 8 Riverwind Dr New Canaan CT 06840 Office: 1285 Av of the Americas New York City NY 10019

EKLUND, JOHN MANLEY, educator, labor exec.; b. Burlington, Ia., Sept. 14, 1909; s. Carl Petrus and Laura Alvira (Malnburg) E.; A.B., Bethany Coll., Lindsborg, Kan., 1931; A.M., U. Denver, 1936; Th. M. Iliff School Theology, Denver, 1936; Ed.D, Columbia, 1953; m. Zara Frances Zerbst, Sept. 9, 1934; children—Joan Sue, Carl Andrew, Gary Philip. Coach Burdick (Kan.) H.S., 1931-33; asst. pastor Trinity Methodist Ch., Denver, 1934-35; pastor Oak Creek(Colo.) Community Ch., 1934-35; Lakewood Community Ch., Denver, 1935-36; teacher Denver pub. schs., 1936- 46, became appraiser Denver schools Vets. Adminstrn. Guidance Center, 1946; mem. adv. com. U.S. Office of Edn. 1953; dir. adult edn. Nat. Farmers Union, 1954—, dir. orgn. and edn., 1957—, asst. to pres., 1964—; exec. v.p. Farmers Union Internat. Assistance Corp.; pres. Agrl. Co-Op Devel. Internat., 1968—. AFL delegate to UNESCO Conf., 1947, 49 (mem. A.F. of L. subcom. on vocational edn.; com. on ednl. reconstrn.); mem. labor adv. com. to UNESCO 1949; mem. U.S. Nat. Commn. for UNESCO since 1951; mem. U.S. del., 6th Gen. UNESCO Conf., Paris, 1951 10th Conf. Food and Agr. Orgn., Rome, Italy, 1959. Mem. steering com. of planning com., Mid- Century White House Conf., 1950. One of two Am. dels. to 15th Congress of the Peace, Paris, 1949; U.S. cons. to 5th Far East Conference on Agricultural Credit and Cooperatives, Korea, 1965; del. White House Conf. on Edn., 1955. Mem. Adult Edn. Assn. (exec. com.), Ams. for Dem. Action (mem. bd., 1949-54), Am. Fedn. Tchrs. (v.p., 1946-48, pres. 1948- 52), Am. Assn. for Adult Edn., Colo. Fedn. Tchrs. (mem. bd., 1946-53), Denver Fedn. Tchrs. of A.F. of L. (chmn. 1946-48); Pi Kappa Delta, Phi Delta Kappa. Meth. Clubs: Internat., Democratic (Washington). Author of Tools for Peace, published 1960. Guest editorialist for daily newspapers. Contbr. articles in ednl. and labor mags. Home: 1015 E Tufts St Englewood CO 80110 Office: 1012 14th St NW Washington DC 20005

EKLUND, LAURENCE CONRAD, former newspaperman; b. Tomahawk, Wis., May 16, 1905; s. John and Mary (Olson) E.; A.B., U. Wis., 1927; m. Ethel J. Chipman, Aug. 8, 1931; 1 son, John Conrad. Reporter Capital Times, Madison, Wis., 1927; with Milw. Journal, 1927—, successively as reporter local and state news, Wis. polit. campaigns, also nat. polit. convs. since 1932, Washington corr., 1947-70, now ret., covered Operation Deep Freeze on Antarctica. Mem. Antarctican Soc., Am. Polar Soc., Swedish Pioneer Hist. Soc., Theta Chi, Sigma Delta Chi. Conglist. Clubs: Milwaukee Press; Gridiron, Nat. Press (Washington). Home: 5602 York Lane Bethesda MD 20014

EKLUND, NILS OSSIAN, Jr., corp. exec.; b. Portland, Ore., June 4, 1911; s. Nils O. and Signe (Anderson) E.; student U. Ore., 1928-30, Behnke Walker Bus. Coll., Portland, 1930; m. Elizabeth Loukes Fairchild, July 12, 1930; children—Karin Anna, Jay Dee (dec.). Salesman, Standard Oil Co. of Cal., Portland, 1930-33, supr., 1933-38; sales mgr. Boyd Coffee Co., Portland, 1938-41; successively engr., asst. supt. and supt. assembly operations, Portland and Vancouver shipyards Kaiser Co., Inc., 1942- 45; successively supt., asst. gen. supt., gen. supt. Kaiser Frazer Corp., Willow Run, Mich., 1946-48; tech. cons. Motor House, Ltd., Bombay, India, 1948; successively asst. midwest sales mgr., Midwest sales mgr., gen. sales mgr. Kaiser Motors Corp., 1949- 52, asst. exec. v.p., 1952-54; gen. mgr. Detroit engine div. Willys Motors, Inc., 1954-56; asst. v.p. Henry J. Kaiser Co., Oakland, Cal., 1956-59; v.p. Kaiser Industries Co., Oakland, 1959—. Pres., dir. District Adminstrn. Bldg. Corp., 1966- -. Mem. Cal. Citizens Legislative Adv. Commn., 1957-61; gen. campaign chmn., pres. Alameda County United Fund, 1959-61, mem. exec. com., bd. govs., 1959-; v.p. United Bay Area Crusade, 1959-61, mem. exec. com., bd. govs., 1959-65, pres., chief exec. officer, 1963-64, 66, mem. bd. trustees 1966—; mem. nat. adv. council United Community Funds and Councils of Am., 1963-66; mem. adv. bd. Cal. State Coll., Hayward, 1962-68, chmn. adv. bd., 1966-68; mem. exec. com., panel chmn. Gov.'s Transp. Task Force, 1967—; chmn. citizens adv. com. to rules com. Cal. Senate; bd. dirs. Internat. House U. Cal.; mem. Bay Area Transp. Study Commn., 1963-69, chmn., 1965-69; chmn. Alameda County Health Care Services Adv. Commn., 1970—; participant global strategy discussion Naval War Coll.; pres. Oakland Econ. Devel. Found., adv. com. Children's Hosp., East Bay, 1966-67; chmn. Cal. State Affiliates, Inc.; bd. trustees San Francisco Bay Area Council. Mem. govs. San Francisco Bay Area Council, chmn. transp. com., 1969—. Mem. Oakland C. of C. (dir., pres. 1962-63; exec. com.), Navy League U.S. (v.p. Met. Oakland council 1966), Nat. Council Urban Am., Inc., Am. Ordnance Assn. (1st v.p. 1970—, bd. San Francisco chpt.), Harold Brunn Soc. Med. Research, Cal. State C. of C. (exec. com. Central Coast region), Sigma Phi Epsilon. Presbyn. Clubs: Bohemian, Commonwealth, Pacific Union (San Francisco); Sutter (Sacramento); 100 (dir. 1962-65, pres. 1964) (Oakland). Office: 300 Lakeside Dr Oakland CA 94604

EKMAN, ERNST, educator; b. Chgo., Oct. 28, 1926; s. Ernest W. and Nancy (Thompson) E.; B.A., Yale, 1948; postgrad. Goteborgs Universitet, 1948—; M.A., U. Minn., 1950; Ph.D., U. Cal. at Los Angeles, 1954; m. Iris Phedra Chamberlain, Sept. 23, 1948; children—Anders Filip, Jonathan Ivar. From instr. to prof. history U. Cal. at Riverside, 1954—, chmn. dept., 1968—. Fellow Am.

Scandinavian Found., 1953, Social Sci. Research Council, 1960, Soc. Religion in Higher Edn., 1964. Mem. Am. Hist. Assn., Phi Beta Kappa. Republican. Lutheran. Contbr. articles profl. jour. and encys. Home: 2059 Arroyo Dr Riverside CA 92506

EKMAN, WILLIAM ELVIN, educator; b. Wilmot, S.D., Mar. 15, 1907; s. Axel Frithiof and Karoline Marie (Rustand) E.; A.B., U. S.D., 1929, A.M., 1930; postgrad. Brown U. 1931-34, State U. Ia., 1938-39, summers 1940, 41; m. Louise Groen, Aug. 30, 1932: children—Mary Jean, William Lyle. Instr. math. U. S.D., Vermillion, 1929-31, Brown U., 1931- 34, and astronomy, U. S.D., 1934-38, instr. in math. and astronomy, acting head dept., 1939-43, prof. math. and astronomy, chmn. dept., 1943—; cons. Nat. Lexicographic Bd., Ltd. Mem. Vermillion Bd. Edn., 1952-58. Mem. Math. Assn. Am., A.A.A.S., Am. Assn. U. Profs., Am.-Scandinavian Found., World Calendar Assn., S.D. Acad. Sci. (sec. 1947, pres. 1950), S.D. Edn. Assn., Swedish Pioneer Hist. Soc., Phi Beta Kappa, Sigma Xi, Pi Mu Epsilon. Republican. Methodist. Mason (K.T.). Clubs: University of S.D. Research, Commercial, Lions. Contbr. math. articles in Proc. S.D. Acad. Sci. Home: 104 S Yale St Vermillion SD 57069

EKSTROM, WILLIAM FERDINAND, coll. ofcl.; b. Rockford, Ill., June 14, 1912; s. Anton Ivar and Mabel Elizabeth (Mattoon) E.; B.A., U. Ill., 1935, M.A., 1936, Ph.D., 1947; Indsl. Adminstr., Harvard, 1943. Instr. English, U. Ill., 1946-47; asst. prof. English, U. Louisville, 1947-51, asso. prof. English. 1951-56, head dept. 1955-67, prof. English, 1956—, v.p. academic affairs, 1967—. Mem. curriculum study com. Commonwealth of Ky. Pub. Edn. Comm., 1961. Served with USAAF, 1943-45; instr. Chinese Air Force. Bd. dirs. Louisville Presbyn. Sem. Mem. Am. Assn. U. Profs. (pres. Ky. conf. 1955-56), Ky. Council Tchrs. English, Arts in Louisville Assn., Modern Lang. Assn., Coll. English Assn., Nat. Council Tchrs. English, Am. Studies Assn. (pres. Ky.-Tenn. 1961- 62), Modern Humanities Research Assn., English-Speaking Union, Phi Beta Kappa, Phi Kappa Phi, Lambda Chi Alpha. Presbyn. (exec. council Presbytery of Louisville). Author: Toward Better English, 1940; Guide to Composition, 1953. Home: 2426 Newburg Rd Louisville KY 40205

EL-ABIAD, AHMED HANAFY, educator; b. Mersa Matruh, Egypt, May 24, 1926; s. Mohamed H. and Fatima (Abdel-Rahman) El-A.; B.Sc. in Elec. Engring., Cairo U., 1948; M.S. in Elec. Engring., Purdue U., 1953, Ph.D., 1956; m. Doha M. Gouda, Apr. 17, 1952; children—Amira, Omar A. Came to U.S., 1958, naturalized, 1963. Asst. engr. Egyptian State Tel. & Tel. Co., Cairo, 1948-49; teaching asst. elec. engring. Cairo U., 1949-52, lectr., 1956-58; Fulbright grad. exchange student Purdue U., 1952-53, asst. prof., 1958-62, asso. prof., 1962-65, prof. elec. engring., 1965—; vis. prof. Mass. Inst. Tech., 1961-62; co- founder, partner Tech. Engring. and Trading Office, Cairo, 1952-57; cons. to industry, 1956—. Sr. mem. I.E.E.E.; mem. Soc. Gen. Systems Research, Am. Soc. Engring. Edn., Research Assn. Applied Geometry (Japan), Tensor Soc. Gt. Britain, Sigma Xi, Eta Kappa Nu. Author: (with G.W. Stagg) Computer Methods in Power System Analysis, 1968; also articles. Home: 140 Drury Lane West Lafayette IN 47906 Office: Sch Elec Engring Purdue Univ Lafayette IN 47907

ELAM, JAMES O., physician; b. Austin, Tex., May 31, 1918; s. William Nile and Hallie Mae (Hedgpeth) E.; A.B., U. Tex., 1942; M.D., John Hopkins, 1945; postgrad. U. Minn., 1946-47, Washington U., St. Louis, 1947-48, State U. Ia., 1949-51; m. Elinor Mae Foster, Oct. 20, 1946; children—Michael, JoAnne, Peter, Susan, David. Intern, Bethesda (Md.) Naval Hosp., 1945-46, Barnes Hosp., St. Louis, 1947-48; resident anesthesiology State U. Ia. 1949-51; asst. prof. anesthesia Washington U. Sch. Medicine, 1951-53; dir. dept. anesthesia Roswell Park Meml. Inst., Buffalo, 1953-63; prof., chmn. dept. anesthesiology U. Mo., Kansas City, 1964-66; prof. anesthesiology, prof. obstetrics-gynecology, chief anesthesia Chgo. Lying In Hosp., U. Chgo., 1966—; contractor, cons. U.S. Army Office Surgeon Gen., 1954-70. Served to maj., M.C., AUS, 1953-55. Recipient Albion O. Berstein award N.Y. State Med. Soc., 1962. Diplomate Am. Bd. Anesthesiology. Fellow Am. Coll. Anesthesiologists, A.M.A., Ill. State Med. Soc., Ill. Soc. Anesthesiologists. Author: (with J.R. Jude) Fundamentals of Cardiopulmonary Resuscitation, 1965. Research in resuscitation and anesthesia. Home: 6723 S Euclid St Chicago IL 60649

ELAM, JOHN CARLTON, lawyer; b. Fort Wayne, Ind., Mar. 6, 1924; s. Bernard C. and Eunice (Gawthrop) E.; B.A., U. Mich., 1948, J.D., 1949; m. Virginia Mayberry, July 14, 1945; children—Nancy Lee, Patricia Scott, Mary Jane, John William. Admitted to Mich. bar, 1949, Ohio bar, 1950; with firm Vorys, Sater, Seymour & Pease, Columbus, O., 1949—, partner, 1954—. Adj. prof. Ohio State U. Law Sch. Govt. appeal agt. SSS, 1954—; pres. United Appeal Columbus and Franklin County, 1963-65; permanent del. 6th Circuit Jud. Conf.; chmn. region IV nat. com. U. Mich. Law Sch. Fund, 1965-66; mem. Upper Arlington Bd. Edn. Fellow Am. Coll. Trial Lawyers; mem. Am. (vice chmn. com. trial techniques, sect. ins., negligence and compensation law 1964—), Ohio (mem. ho. of dels.), Columbus (pres. 1964) bar assns., Columbus Area C. of C. (chmn. bd.), Assn. Ins. Attys. (exec. council, pres. 1967- 68), Phi Kappa Phi, Phi Delta Theta. Home: 4012 Lyon Dr Columbus OH 43221 Office: 52 E Gay St Columbus OH 43215

ELAM, THEODORE MARINUS, lawyer; b. Enid, Okla., Dec. 18, 1934; s. Roy J. and Sara (Godschalk) E.; student U., Colo., 1952-54; B.B.A. in Finance, U. Okla., 1957, LL.B., 1959; m. Lyn Pryse, Feb. 2, 1958; children-Pryse Roy, Elain, Elizabeth. Admitted to Okla. bar, 1959, since practiced in Oklahoma City; partner firm Andrews, Mosburg, Davis, Elam, Legg & Kornfeld, 1964- -; spl. lectr. securities law U. Okla. Dir. Carousel Fashions, Inc., Founders Bank and Trust Co. Chmn. Outstanding Citizen of Oklahoma City, 1963. Mem. Am., Okla., Oklahoma City bar assns., Oklahoma City Jr. C. of C., Order of Coif, Omicron Delta Kappa, Phi Delta Theta, Phi Alpha Delta. Republican. Episcopalian. Contbr. articles profl. jours. Home: 6638 Avondale St Oklahoma City OK 73116 Office: United Founders Tower Oklahoma City OK 73112

ELBAUM, CHARLES, educator; b. Lublin, Poland, May 15, 1926; s. Chil and Anna (Kaffe) E.; M.A.Sc., U. Toronto (Ont., Can.), 1952, Ph.D., 1954; m. Eleanor Dinaburg, Aug. 5, 1956; children—Michael, Daniel, David. Research fellow, spl. lectr. applied sci. U. Toronto, 1954-57; research fellow Harvard, 1957-59; mem. faculty Brown U., 1959—, asso. prof., 1961-63, prof., 1963—. Fellow Am. Phys. Soc.; mem. Am. Inst. Mining and Metallurgy, Sigma Xi. Contbr. profl. jours.‡

ELBERG, SANFORD SAMUEL, educator; b. San Francisco, Dec. 1, 1913; s. Solomon and Elizabeth (Levene) E.; A.B., U. Cal., 1934, Ph.D., 1938; L.H.D. (hon.), Hebrew Union Coll., 1967; m. Sylvia Marans, July 11, 1943; children—Cassandra, Graeme. Instr. Wash. State Coll., also San Francisco City Coll., 1940- 41; instr. U. Cal., 1941-46, asst. prof. bacteriology, 1946-47, asso. prof., 1947-52, prof., 1952—, prof. med. microbiology and immunology, 1966—, vice chmn. dept., 1949-52, chmn. dept. bacteriology, 1952-57, dean grad. div., 1961—, acting dir. Naval Biol. Lab., 1956-57; John Simon Guggenheim fellow, 1957-58; With WHO and Guggenheim Found., Spain, 1957; cons. chief Office Naval Research, 1950-55. Mem. adv. panel Naval Biol. Lab., 1952-69; cons. Naval Radiol. Def. Lab., 1951-57; mem. expert panel brucellosis, chmn. com. WHO-FAO, UN; mem. Armed Forces Epidemiology Bd., Commn. Radiation, Infection, 1965-70; F.G. Novy lectr. U. Mich., 1964. Served from 1st lt. to major AUS, 1942-46. Fellow A.A.A.S., Am. Acad. Microbiology; mem. USPHS (study sect.), Am. Assn. Immunologists, Soc. Am. Bacteriologists, Biochem. Soc. Gt. Britain, Soc. Exptl. Biology and Medicine, N.Y. Acad. Scis., Western Assn. Schs. and Colls. (commn. on accreditation), Assn. Grad. Schs. (pres. 1965-66), Sigma Xi, Phi Beta Kappa, Delta Omega, Phi Sigma. Author papers on immunology, infectious diseases, cellular immunity. Home: 1066 Park Hills Rd Berkeley CA 94708

ELBERT, SAMUEL HOYT, educator; b. Des Moines, Aug. 8, 1907; s. Hoyt Hugh and Ethelind Swire (Beer) E.; A.B., Grinnell Coll., 1928; B.Lit., Columbia, 1931; Ph.D., Ind. U., 1950. Mem. faculty U. Hawaii, 1949—, prof. Pacific langs. and linguistics, 1949—, hon. asso. linguistics B.P. Bishop Mus. 1952—; Polynesian cons. Merriam-Webster Co., 1952—; coordinator investigation Micronesian anthropology, 1947; Tri-Instl. Pacific Program grantee to Rennell Island, 1957-58. Mem. Com. Preservation Hawaiian Lang., Art and Culture, 1960—. Served to lt. comdr. USNR, 1942-45. Fulbright fellow, Denmark, 1964-65; NSF grantee linguistic study Puluwat, 1967. Fellow Am. Anthrop. Soc.; mem. Linguistic Soc. Am., Am. Folklore Soc., Polynesian Soc., Phi Beta Kappa. Author: Trukese-English and English-Trukese Dictionary, 1947: (with Samuel A. Keala) Conversational Hawaiian, 5th edit., 1964; (with Mary K. Pukui) English-Hawaiian Dictionary, 3d edit., 1965; (with Torben Monberg) From the Two Canoes, Oral Traditions of Rennell and Bellona Islands, 1965; (with Mary K. Pukui) Place Names of Hawaii, 1966, Spoken Hawaiian, 1970; Na Mele o Hawaii Nei, 101 Hawaiian Songs, 1970. Editor: Selections from Fornander's Hawaiian Antiquities and Folklore, 1959. Address: 3293 Huelani Dr Honolulu HI 96822

ELBERT, WILLIAM JOSEPH, distbn. co. exec.; b. Bklyn., Nov. 30, 1916; s. Jacob J. and Kathryn (Sheerin) E.; B.B.A., Coll. City N.Y., 1936; m. Anna H. Hoddersen, July 4, 1942; children—William J., Robert E. Accountant, Price, Waterhouse & Co., N.Y.C., 1936-47; treas. Swanee Paper Corp., N.Y.C., 1947-58; sec.-controller Stahl-Meyer, Inc., N.Y.C., 1959-61; financial cons., N.Y.C., 1961-63; dir. corporate accounting Foremost Dairies, Inc., San Francisco; v.p., controller Foremost-McKesson, Inc. (merger Foremost Dairies, Inc. and McKesson & Robbins, Inc.). Served to 1st lt. AUS, 1943-46. C.P.A., N.Y. Mem. Am. Inst. C.P.A.'s, N.Y., Cal. socs. C.P.A.'s. Mason (Shriner). Clubs: Olympic, World Trade, Merchants Exchange (San Francisco); New York Athletic. Home: 188 San Aleso Av San Francisco CA 94127 Office: 1 Post St San Francisco CA 94104

ELBIN, PAUL NOWELL, educator; b. Cameron, W.Va., Apr. 21, 1905; s. Harry and Nellie (Nowell) E.; student Fairmont (W.Va.) State Coll., 1923-25; A.B., Ohio State U., 1926; A.M., Teachers Coll., Columbia U., 1928, Ph.D., 1932; D.D., Davis and Elkins Coll., 1960; Litt.D., W. Va. U., 1965; m. Helen Elizabeth Pierce, Sept. 3, 1929. Tchr. Cameron High Sch., 1926-27; with West Liberty (W.Va.) State Coll., 1928—, head dept. English and speech, also chaplain, 1928-35, pres., 1935-70, dean interfaith chapel, prof. speech, 1970—; exec. dir. Oglebay Inst., 1944- 46; music editor Wheeling (W.Va.) News Register, 1947-61; staff writer Etude music mag., 1953-56. Mem. Am. Guild Organists dean Wheeling chpt.). Admitted to Wheeling Presbytery, 1956. Author: The Improvement of College Worship, 1932; The Bible Question Bee, 1943; Brotherhood Through Religion, 1944; The Enrichment of Life, 1945; Fifty Devotional Services, 1950; Worship for the Young in Spirit, 1956. Home: Colonial Heights West Liberty WV 26074

ELBRICK, CHARLES BURKE, ambassador; b. Louisville, Mar. 25, 1908; s. Charles J. and Lillian (Burke) E.; A.B., Williams Coll., 1929; m. Elvira Lindsay Johnson, July 27, 1932; children—Alfred Johnson, Valerie Burke. Vice consul, Panama, C.Z., 1931; student Fgn. Service Sch., 1932; vice consul Southampton, Eng., 1932-34; 3d sec. Port-au-Prince, 1934-37, Warsaw, Poland, 1937-38, 39, Praha, 1938-39, Bucharest, 1939, Warsaw (Angers, France), 1939-40, Madrid, Spain, 1940; vice consul Lisbon, Portugal, 1940-41; 3d sec. Lisbon, 1941, 2d sec., 1941- 43, Tangier, 1943-44; Div. of African Affairs, Dept. State, 1944-45; 1st sec., Warsaw, 1945; asst. chief Div. Eastern European Affairs, Dept. State, 1946-48; student Nat. War Coll., 1948-49; counselor of embassy, Habana, 1949-51; counselor N. Atlantic Council Delegation London, 1951, Paris, 1952-53; dep. asst. sec. of state, 1953-56, asst. sec. of state, 1957-58; Am. ambassador to Portugal, Lisbon, 1959-63, to Yugoslavia, Belgrade 1964-69, Brazil, 1969-70. Mem. Phi Delta Theta. Clubs: Metropolitan, Chevy Chase (Washington). Home: 2137 R St NW Washington DC 20520 Office: care Dept of State Washington DC 20520

ELCONIN, VICTOR A., educator; b. Cleve., Nov. 21, 1912; s. Henry and Yetta (Frankel) E.; B.S., Ohio State U., 1934, M.A., 1938, Ph.D., 1947; m. Janet Overbagh, June 12, children—William Douglas Handy (stepson), Joan. Grad. asst. English, Ohio State U., 1937-42, instr., 1946-47; faculty U. Okla., 1947- -, prof. English, 1957—, chmn. dept., 1955—, McCasland prof. of English, since 1963—. Served with AUS, 1942-46. Mem. Okla. Council Tchrs. English, S. Central Modern Lang. Assn., Modern Lang. Assn. Am. Assn. U. Profs. Home: 906 Elm Av Norman OK 73069

EL-DABH, HALIM, composer; b. Cairo, Egypt, Mar. 4, 1921; s. Abdel Messih and Balsam Benyamin (Fam) El-D.; came to U.S., 1953, naturalized, 1961; student Schulz Conservatory, Cairo, 1941-44, N.M. U., 1950, Berkshire Music Center, 1951, 52; B.Sc., Cairo U., 1945; Mus.M. in Music Composition and Theory, New Eng. Conservatory Music, 1953; M.F.A. in Creative Composition, Brandeis U., 1954; m. Mary Hyde, Aug. 6, 1952; children—Shadia, Amira. Chief music adviser, cons. Ministry Culture, Cairo, 1959-60; asso. prof. music Haile Selassie I U., Addis Ababa, Ethiopia, 1962-64; guest lectr. Egyptian music U. Cologne (Germany), Inst. Music and Seminar African Studies, Göttingen, Germany, State Inst. Folk Studies, Berlin, Germany, also Internat. Inst. Comparative Music Studies, Berlin, 1964-65; mem. Columbia-Princeton Electronic Music Center, 1958, 61; asso. prof. music African studies and research, resident composer Howard U., Washington; spl. research folk music Ethiopia and Coptic ch. music Ethiopia, Sudanese Nubia and Upper Egypt, also Greek, Byzantine and Macedonian music. Recipient 1st prize composition Cairo Opera House, 1942; Fulbright fellow, 1950; teaching fellow Brandeis U., 1954; Guggenheim fellow, 1959, 61. Mem. Broadcast Music Inc., Am. Music Center. Composer: Toree Dance Music Tableaus, 1954; Clytemnestra (music-dance drama), 1958; Concerto for Drum and String Orchestra, 1958; Tahmeela for Orchestra, 1959; House of Atreus, 1959; Symphony Number 3, 1959; The Ghost (Kabuki dance drama), 1960; Leiyla and the Poet, 1961; One More Gaudy Night, 1961; A Look at Lightening, 1962; Nomadic Waves, 1962; (with Otto Luening) Electronic Fanfare, 1963; Doxastico, 1965; The Eye of Horus, 1967; Black Epic, 1969; The Night Worshippers, 1969; also chamber music, piano music, music for percussion and drums. Author articles. Home: 3102 33d Pl N W Washington DC 20008

ELDEN, HENRY THEODORE, architect; b. Boswell, Pa., May 28, 1914; s. Frank C. and Grace Mertile (Morrison) E.; B.Arch., Carnegie-Mellon U., 1937; m. Evelyn Carskadon, Oct. 10, 1942; children—Barbara Ann (Mrs. Robert Scavullo), Henry Theodore. Pvt. practice architecture and engring., Charleston, W.Va., 1948—; owner Henry Elden & Assos., architects, engrs. and planners; chmn. bd. Elden Enterprises, Inc. Mem. Citizens Air Pollution Council, 1965-67, Gov. W.Va. Task Force Housing, 1966; mem. pub. adv. panel archtl. services Gen. Services Adminstrn., 1970—; mem. Nat. Council Archtl. Registration Bds., 1970—, W.Va. Bd. Architects, 1970—. Mem. Charleston City Council, 1958-62. Served to lt. USNR, 1943-46. Recipient award Bell System, 1967, archtl. award excellence Am. Inst. Steel Constrn., 1968, design in steel citation Am. Iron and Steel Inst., 1968. Mem. A.I.A., Nat. Soc. Profl. Engrs., W.Va., Charleston (bd. dirs.) chambers commerce, Phi Kappa Psi. Mason (K.T., Shriner), Kiwanian. Club: Berry Hills Country (Charleston). Home: 1 Ramu Rd Charleston WV 25332 Office: PO Box 3201 Charleston WV 25332

ELDER, FRED KINGSLEY, Jr., Physicist, educator; b. Coronado, Cal., Oct. 19, 1921; s. Fred Kingsley and Ethel S. (Tait) E.; B.S. in Physics, U. N.C., 1941, M.S. in Physics, Yale, 1943, Ph.D., 1947; m. Elinor Jean Goertz, July 5, 1947; children—Nancy Elisabeth, Jessie Custer, Jacqueline Lesesne, Elinor Tait, Lydia Jean, Robert Abraham, Mary Grace, John Philip. Instr. Yale, 1943-44, U. Pa., 1947-49; asst. prof. U. Wyo., 1949-50; sr. physicist applied physics lab. Johns Hopkins, 1950-53; asso. prof. physics Wabash Coll., Crawfordsville, Ind., 1953-55; prof., chmn. physics dept and div. natural scis. and math. Belhaven Coll., Jackson, Miss., 1955-59; research physicist U.S. Naval Ordnance Lab., White Ok, Md., summers 1957 59; head research br. antisubmarine warfare lab. U.S. Naval Air Devel. Center, Johnsville, Pa., 1959-65; prof., head physics dept. Rochester (N.Y.) Inst. Tech., 1965—. Scoutmaster Nat. Capital Area council Boy Scouts Am., 1950-53, Central Indiana council, 1953-55. Trustee Westminster Theol. Sem., Phila., 1960—, mem. exec. com., 1965—; trustee Presbyn. Guardian Pub. Corp., 1958—; mem. various denominational bds., coms. gen. assembly Orthodox Presbyn. Ch., 1952—. Served to lt. comdr. USNR, 194446; physicist U.S. Naval Research Lab., Washington. Mem. Am. Assn. Physics Tchrs., Netherlands, Am. phys. socs., Franklin Inst., U.S. Naval Inst., Phi Beta Kappa, Phi Kappa Phi, Sigma Pi Sigma, Sigma Xi. Orthodox Presbyn. (ruling elder 1952—). Research, publs. on physics of fluids. Home: 341 Barrington St Rochester NY 14607 Office: Rochester Inst Tech Rochester NY 14623

ELDER, JAMES LANPHERE, lawyer; b. Hanover, Ill., Mar. 21, 1914; s. Frank Ray and Frances (Lanphere) E.; B.A., Hampden-Sydney Coll., 1936; LL.B., Harvard, 1939; m. Frances Emily Wagner, Jan. 27, 1950; children—James Lanphere, William Paddack, Suzanne DuVal. Admitted to Pa. bar, 1940, Ohio bar, 1941; practice in Phila., 1940, Cin., 1941—; asso. firm Taft, Stettinius & Hollister, Cin., 1942-49; partner firm Nieman, Aug, Elder & Jacobs, and predecessor, Cin., 1949—; prof. Salmon P. Chase Coll Law, Cin., 1952-60. Mem. distbn. com. Greater Cin. Found., 1964—, chmn., 1970—. Served with AUS, 1942-44. Mem. Am., Ohio (chmn. real property sect. 1966-70), Cin. (pres. 1966-67) bar assns. Republican. Presbyn. (elder). Author: (Elder's revision) Stearns on Suretyship, 1951. Home: 815 Greenville Av Glendale OH 45246 Office: Atlas Bank Bldg Cincinnati OH 45202

ELDER, JOHN HOWARD, Jr., army officer; b. Richmond, Va., June 14, 1920; s. John Howard and Mildred (Stratton) E.; B.S. in Civil Engring., Va. Poly. Inst., 1941; grad. Command and Gen. Staff Coll., 1955, Army War Coll., 1960; m. Mary Jane Harrold, June 10, 1941; children—John Howard III, Douglas Alan, Bruce Harrold, Lizabeth Ann. Commd. 2d lt. U.S. Army, 1941, advanced through grades to maj. gen., 1970; various assignments in U.S., ETO and Korea, 1941-51; assigned 11th Airborne Div., Germany, 1955-57, 7th Army, Germany, 1957-59, Army Gen. Staff and Joint Staff, 1960-64, Office of Chmn., Joint Chiefs Staff, 1965-67; engr. command assignments, Vietnam, 1968-69; dep. dir. strategic arms and policy directorate, Orgn. Joint Chiefs Staff, 1969—. Decorated D.S.M., Legion of Merit, Bronze Star with V device and 4 oak leaf clusters, Air medal with 5 oak leaf clusters. Mem. Scabbard and Blade, Omicron Delta Kappa, Pi Delta Epsilon. Presbyn. Home: 4106 Sulgrave Dr Alexandria VA 22309 Office: The Pentagon Washington DC 20301

ELDER, JOHN PETERSEN, educator; b. Auburn, N.Y., Aug. 1, 1913; s. William Seward and Josephine Hill (Petersen) E.; A.B., Williams Coll., 1934; A.M., Harvard, 1935, Ph.D., 1940. Instr. Greek and Latin, Harvard, 1940-42, asst. prof., 1946-50, asso. prof., 1951-54, prof., 1955—, dean grad. sch. arts and scis., 1954—, asst. editor Speculum, co- editor Harvard Studies Classical Philology, also dir. Middle East Center; chief grad. fellowships Nat. Def. Edn. Act, 1958. Mem. vis. com. on classics Princeton, 1955; vice chmn. adminstrv. com. Hellenic Center, Washington, 1961—; trustee Mass. State Library; chmn. bd. trustees Marlboro Coll., 1967-69. Served with AUS, 1942-46, asst. mil. attaché to govts. exiled in Eng., 1945, asst. mil. attaché, The Hague, 1946. Mem. Am. Philol. Assn., Medieval Acad. Am., Am. Acad. Arts and Sci. (v. p. class IV 1960—), Am. Council of Learned Socs. (dir.), Classical Assn. N.E., Gesellschaft für Altere Deutshe Geschichtskunde. Presbyn. Clubs: Somerset (Boston); Harvard (N.Y.C.). Home: 145 Pinckney St Boston MA 02114

ELDER, LONNE, III, playright; b. Americus, Ga. A founder Negro Ensemble Company, N.Y.C., 1967. Author: Ceremonies in Dark Old Men. Address: 1545 N Broadway New York City NY *

ELDER, OMAR FRANKLIN, Jr., lawyer, broadcasting and film co. exec.; b. Atlanta, May 24, 1919; s. Omar Franklin and Marielen (Hargrove) E.; A.B. with honors, Emory U., 1940; LL.B., Harvard, 1943; m. Betty Anne Nyman, Nov. 16, 1946; children—Betty Anne, Omar Franklin III. Asso. O'Brien, Driscoll & Raferty, N.Y.C., 1946-47; admitted to N.Y. bar, 1947; with ABC, N.Y.C., 1947-64, beginning as atty., successively asst. sec. 1951-56, asst. gen. counsel, 1953-59, sec., 1956-59, v.p., 1959-64, gen. counsel TV network, 1959-61, gen. atty., 1961-64; asst. sec. Am. Broadcasting Paramount Theatres, Inc., ABC Radio Network, Inc., Blue Network Co., Inc.; sec., dir. ABC TV Center Co., Inc., Fine Arts Enterprises, Inc., ABC-TV Network Services of Mich., Inc.; sec. WXYZ, Inc., Detroit, Allegheny Broadcasting Corp., Pitts.; atty. Metro-Goldwyn-Mayer, Inc., 1964-69, CBS, Inc., 1970—. Served from ensign to lt. USNR, 1942-46. Mem. Am., Fed. Communications bar assns., Assn. Bar City N.Y., Radio and TV Execs. Soc. (dir., v.p., sec.), Acad. TV Arts and Scis., Internat. Radio and TV Soc., N.Y. Southern Soc., Chi Phi. Clubs: Harvard, Athletic (N.Y.C.); Piedmont Driving, Capital City (Atlanta). Home: Hawkwood Lane Greenwich CT 06830

ELDER, PAUL, newspaperman; b. Berkeley, Cal., Mar. 12, 1906; s. Paul and Emma (Moore) E.; student U. Cal. at Berkeley, 1928; m. Eloise Nichols, Oct. 10, 1930. With Paul Elder & Co., retail booksellers, San Francisco, 1931-68, pres., mgr., 1943-68; book editor San Francisco Examiner, 1970—. Bd. dirs. Retail Merchants Assn. San Francisco, 1941-68, San Francisco C. of C., 1959-61. Mem. Alpha Delta Phi. Rotarian. Club: Bohemian (San Francisco). Home: 216 Ricardo Rd Mill Valley CA 94941 Office: 110 5th St San Francisco CA 94119

ELDER, ROBERT MARTIN, banker; b. Albuquerque, Aug. 21, 1900; s. James Edward and Mabel (Kellog) E.; A.B., U. N.M., 1926; m. Dorothy Goelitz, July 10, 1928; children—Robert William, James Thomas, Mary Jane (Mrs. William C. Carlson). With Albuquerque Nat. Bank, 1926—, exec. v.p., dir., 1941-70, now cons. Vice pres. Albuquerque Sch. Bd., 1960-69. Mem. Newcomen Soc. N.M., Pi Kappa Alpha. Republican. Presbyn. Mason (Shriner). Clubs: Albuquerque Country, Albuquerque Petroleum. Home: 8901 Frontage Rd NE Albuquerque NM 87113 Office: P O Box 1344 Albuquerque MN 87103

ELDER, SAMUEL ADAMS, educator; b. Balt., July 13, 1929; s. Fred Kingsley and Ethel (Tait) E.; B.S., Hampden-Sydney Coll., 1950; Sc.M., Brown U., 1953, Ph.D., 1956; m. Sylvia Maynard, Jan. 1, 1955; children—Susan Spottiswoode, Sheila Jean, Sarah Maynard, Sandra Louise, Sharon Elisabeth. Sr. staff physicist Johns Hopkins Applied Physics Lab., Silver Spring, Md., 1956-64; asso. prof. physics U.S. Naval Acad., 1964-68, prof., 1968—. Mem. computer policy bd. USN, 1968—. Mem. Acoustical Soc. Am. (chmn. Washington chpt. 1969-70), Am. Assn. Physics Tchrs., Canadian Information Processing Soc., Catgut Acoustical Soc., Am. Sci. Affiliation, Phi Beta Kappa, Sigma Xi. Presbyn. (elder). Republican. Research and publs. in non-linear acoustics, musical acoustics, optical pyrometry, computer-aided education. Composer: Random Afternoon, 1969. Home: 308 Halsey Rd Annapolis MD 21401

ELDER, WILLIAM HANNA, educator; b. Oak Park, Ill., Dec. 24, 1913; s. Robert A. and Margaret (Hanna) E.; B.S., U. Wis., 1936, Ph.M., 1938, Ph.D., 1942; m. Nina Leopold, Sept. 20, 1941; children—Nina, Patricia. Game technician Ill. Natural History Survey, 1941-43; toxicologist NDRC, U. Chgo., 1943-45; asst. prof. zoology, U. Mo., Columbia, 1945-47, asso. prof., 1948-51, prof., 1952-54, chmn. dept. zoology, 1950-53, William Rucker Bucker prof., 1954—. Sabbatical year study in Europe, 1953; Guggenheim Found. fellow for research in Hawaii, 1956-57; Fulbright fellow for research, Rhodesia, 1965-66; NSF grantee for elephant research, Zambia, 1967-68. Mem. Nature Conservancy (pres. Mo. 1959, 68), Soc. Zoologists, Soc. Mammalogists, Wildlife Soc. (editorial bd. 1956—), Wilson Ornithol. Soc., Phi Beta Kappa, Sigma Xi, Gamma Alpha. Home: Quarry Rd Columbia MO 65201

ELDERFIELD, ROBERT COOLEY, educator; b. Niagara Falls, N.Y., May 30, 1904; s. Charles James and Nellie (Cooley) E.; A.B., Williams Coll., 1926, D.Sc., 1952; Ph.D., M.I.T., 1930; m. Mary Elizabeth Betts, Aug. 7, 1930; children—Margaret Helen, Anne Elizabeth. Instr. chemistry, Colby Coll., 1930; asst., Rockefeller Inst. Med. Research, 1930-32, asso., 1932-36; asst. prof. chemistry, Columbia, 1936-37, asso. prof. 1937-41, prof., 1941-52; prof. chemistry U. Michigan, 1952-70, emeritus, 1970—; instr. chemistry, U. of Ill., summer 1938; sect. mem. Nat. Defense Research Com., 1941-45; exec. sec. panel on synthesis Bd. for Coordination Anti-malarial Studies, 1943-46; mem. malaria study sect., Nat. Institutes of Health, U.S. Pub. Health Service, 1946-49, consultant, 1946-49; sci. cons. Sloan- Kettering Inst., 1952-55; chmn. panel on synthesis Cancer Chemotherapy Nat. Service Center, Nat. Cancer Inst., 1956-60; cons., mem. chemistry adv. com. Walter Reed Army Inst. Research, 1964-70; mem. malaria commn. Armed Forces Epidemiol. Bd., 1964—; cons. to surgeon gen. Dept. of Army, 1964—; Am. Inst. Biol. Scis. exobiology adv. panel NASA, 1964—; adv. bd. mil. personnel supples Nat. Acad. Scis.-NRC, 1964-67; vis. scientist Nat. Research Council, Ottawa, Can., 1959-60; Sigma Xi Nat. Lectr., 1959. Received Presidential Certificate of Merit, 1948; Distinguished Faculty Achievement award U. Mich., 1969; Outstanding Civilian Service medal Dept. of Army, 1970. Mem. Am. Chem. Soc. (chmn. organic chemistry div. 1952, dir. 1960-66), Am. Soc. Biol. Chemists, National Malaria Soc., Nat. Acad. Sci., Sigma Xi, Phi Lambda Upsilon, Alpha Chi Sigma, Delta Kappa Epsilon. Presbyterian. Republican (Independent). Author Editor (5 vols.), Treatise on Heterocyclics, 1950; editor, Jour. Organic Chemistry. Home: 1800 Hermitage Rd Ann Arbor MI 48104

ELDERING, GRACE, former microbiologist; b. Myers, Mont., Sept. 5, 1900; d. Herman Joseph and Mary (Grierson) Eldering; B.A., Mont. State U., 1927; Sc.D., Johns Hopkins, 1941. Tchr. rural and elementary schs., Mont., 1920-25; bacteriologist Mich. Dept. Health, 1928-51, chief br. lab., 1951-69, ret., 1969; spl. research pertussis immunization, antigenic analysis pertussis bacillus and related organisms, diagnostic procedures in whooping cough. Diplomate Am. Bd. Microbiology. Fellow Am. Pub. Health Assn., Am. Acad. Microbiology, A.A.A.S.; mem. Am. Soc. Microbiology, Sigma Xi, Delta Omega. Home: 3424 Bayberry N W Grand Rapids MI 49504

ELDERSVELD, SAMUEL JAMES, educator; b. Kalamazoo, Mar. 29, 1917; s. Samuel P. and Minnie (Kooiman) E.; A.B., Calvin Coll., Grand Rapids, 1938; Ph.D., U. Mich., 1946; children—Lucy Angeline, Samuel Keith. Mem. faculty U. Mich., Ann Arbor, 1946—, prof. polit. sci., 1957—, chmn. dept., 1964-70. Mayor of Ann Arbor, 1957- 59. Served to lt. USNR, 1942-46. Mem. Am. Polit. Sci. Assn. Democrat. Episcopalian. Author: Political Parties: A Behavioral Analysis (Woodrow Wilson Found. award 1965), 1964; also articles. Home: 602 Oswego St Ann Arbor MI 48104

ELDJARN, KRISTJAN, pres. of Iceland; b. Iceland, Dec. 6, 1916; s. Thorarinn and Sigrun Eldjarn; student U. Copenhagen, 1936-39; M.A., U. Iceland, 1944, Ph.D., 1957; m. Halldora Kristin Ingolfsdottir, Feb. 6, 1947; children—Olof (Mrs. Stefan O. Stefansson), Thorarinn, Sigrun, Ingolfur. Asst. curator Nat. Mus. Iceland, 1945-47, dir., 1947-68; pres. of Iceland, 1968- -. Decorated grand master Order Falcon, also fgn. decorations. Mem. Icelandic Sci. Soc. Research archaeology Iceland, Greenland and Newfoundland, 1937-67. Author archaeol. papers. Home: Bessastadir Iceland Office: The Presidential Office Reykjavik Iceland

ELDREDGE, HANFORD WENTWORTH, educator; b. Bklyn., Oct. 16, 1909; s. Hanford W. and Elizabeth (Taylor) E.; A.B., Dartmouth, 1931; Ph.D., Yale, 1935; m. Diana Younger, Apr. 21, 1947; children—James Wentworth, Alan Wentworth. Instr. sociology Dartmouth, 1935-39, asst. prof., 1939-49, prof., 1949—, chmn. dept. sociology, 1953-57, 65-68, chmn. internat. relations program, 1959-62, chmn. city planning and urban studies program, 1959-65; guest lectr. Royal Archtl. Assn. London, Yale U., U. Pa., U. N.C., Mass. Inst. Tech., Cornell U.; vis. lectr. on city planning Harvard, 1963; vis. prof. city planning U. Cal. at Berkeley, 1967; orgns. analyst Dept. Justice, 1942, intelligence officer Dept. State, 1942; cons. Exec. Office of The President, 1956; guest lectr. NATO Def. Coll., Paris, 1955- 60, Institut des Hautes Etudes Defense Nationale, Paris, 1960, Fuehrungs Akademie der Bundeswehr, Hamburg, 1960, USAF Acad., 1961, Ecole de Guerre, Brussels, 1962; faculty of Salzburg Seminar in Am. Studies, 1965. Trustee Outboard Bound, Inc. Served with USAAF, 1942-45. Decorated Bronze Star medal. Mem. Am. Sociol. Soc., Am. Soc. Planning Ofcls., Am. Inst. Planners, Am. Assn. U. Profs., Beta Theta Pi. Clubs: Wianno, The Brook; American (London). Author: (with F.E. Merrill), Culture and Society 1952. Editor The Second American Revolution, 1964; Taming Megalopolis, 1967. Contbr. to Studies in the Science of Society, 1937. Home: Tarn House Norwich VT 05055

ELDREDGE, LAURENCE HOWARD, lawyer, educator, author; b. Cold Spring, N.J., Mar. 18, 1902; s. Irvin H. and Marie Louise (Benton) E.; B.S., Lafayette Coll., 1924, Litt. D., 1970; LL.B., U. Pa., 1927; m. Helen Biddle Gans, Sept. 30,1926; children—Mary Harriet, Deborah (Mrs. duPont), and Helen Louise (Mrs. James W. Bradley). Reporter Pub. Ledger, Phila. 1924-25; writer syndicated news articles 1925-27; admitted to Pa. bar, 1927; asso. Montgomery & McCracken (formerly Roberts & Montgomery), 1927-38; mem. firm Norris, Lex, Hart & Eldredge, 1944-56; prof. law Temple U., 1928- 33, adj. prof., 1947-52; asso. in law U. Pa., 1933-34, 1937-38, prof. law, 1938-44, lectr. med. jurisprudence. Graduate School of Medicine, 1958-59, Med. Sch., 1940-68, vis. prof. law, Columbia, spring, 1941, summer, 1946; vis. prof. law Hastings Coll. Law, San Francisco, 1970-71, prof. law, 1971; spl. dep. atty. gen., Pa., 1948-49. Chmn. bd. Pa. Alcoholic Beverage Study, Inc.; past pres. Better Bus. Bur. of Phila., Inc. (dir. since 1940); Art Alliance, 1949-66. Pres. Phila. Served from lt. to comdr., USCGR: supt. Coast Guard Volunteer Port Security Force Tng. Sch., Phila., World War II. Chmn. bd. Mrs. John S. Sheppard Found.; sec.-treas. Magee Meml. Hosp., 1953-59, trustee, 1946-59; pres. Episcopal Hosp., 1946-53, Mus. Council, Phila., 1958-59; bd. dirs. Hosp. Council, 1952-60. Recipient citation Lafayette Coll., 1960; Phila. Art Alliance medal achievement, 1966. Fellow Royal Soc. Arts London; mem. Am. Law Inst. (life mem., adviser on torts and evidence), Phila. Medico-Legal Inst. (pres.), Am., Pa., Phila. (chmn. bd. govs. 1960-61) bar assns., Soc. Mayflower Descs. (past gov.), Soc. Colonial Wars Commonwealth Pa. (past sec.), Colonial Soc. Pa. (gov. 1962-64), Lafayette Coll. Alumni Assn. (pres. 1961-62), S.R., Phi Beta Kappa, Phi Beta Kappa Assos. (dir.), Delta Upsilon (meritorious service award 1961), Pi Delta Epsilon, Delta Theta Phi, Order of Coif (pres. U. Pa. chpt. 1959-61). Republican. Episcopalian. Mason. Clubs: Franklin Inn, Union League, Racquet, Penn, Lawyers of Phila. Author: Eldredge on Modern Tort Problems, 1941; Pennsylvania Annotations to Restatement, Torts, Vols. I and II, 1938, 1938; Trials of a Philadelphia Lawyer, 1968. Revising reporter, Restatement of the Law of Torts, 1946-47. Reporter decisions Supreme Ct. Pa., 1942-68. Editor Pa. Bar Assn. Quarterly, 1938-42. Author articles and book revs. in law publs. Home: 1021 Green Valley Rd Bryn Mawr PA 19010 Office: 1600 Three Penn Center Philadelphia PA 19102

ELDREDGE, WILLIAM AUGUSTUS, Jr., lawyer; b. Memphis, July 21, 1925; s. William Augustus and Lucile (Crews) E.; LL.B., U. Ark., 1949, J.D., 1969; m. Lee Campbell, Aug. 4, 1951; children-Michael Charles, Elizabeth Lee, William Augustus III. Admitted to Ark. bar, 1949, since practiced in Little Rock; partner Smith, Williams, Friday & Bowen and predecessor firm, 1953—; vol. instr. legal medicine U. Ark. Sch. Medicine, 1954—. Chmn. city and county campaign March of Dimes, 1959-61; chmn. Pulaski County chpt. Nat. Found., 1961-62. Served with USNR, 1944-46; to 1st lt., Judge Adv. Gen. Corps, U.S. Army, 1951-53. Recipient Kappa Sigma Distinguished Alumni award, 1965. Mem. Am., Ark., Pulaski County (past pres.) bar assns., Fedn. Ins. Counsel, Def. Research Inst., Blue Key, Kappa Sigma, Delta Theta Phi. Methodist. Home: 6608 Granada St Little Rock AR 72205 Office: Boyle Bldg Little Rock AR 72201

ELDRIDGE, CARL WALLACE, banker; b. Seattle, Aug. 24, 1923; s. Clark Henry and Eleanor (Niles) E.; student U. Wash., 1941; m. Grace Elizabeth Hall, June 4, 1943; children—Susan Carol (Mrs. Harry J. Repstad), George Earl. Purchasing agt. Met. Constrn. Co., Seattle, 1946-47; gen. mgr. mortgage loan and real estate investment dept. Prudential Ins. Co. of Am., Seattle, Portland, Ore., Newark, Los Angeles, 1947-64; sr. v.p., trustee Wash. Mut. Savs. Bank, Seattle, 1964—; dir. Security Title Ins. Co. Wash. Mem. Seattle Regional Adv. Council, Small Bus. Adminstrn. Served with USNR, 1943-45; PTO. Mem. Seattle Mortgage Bankers Assn. (past pres.), Mortgage Bankers Assn. Am., Wash. Bankers Assn., Fed. Nat. Mortgage Assn. (nat. adv. com.), Nat. Assn. Mut. Savs. Banks. Republican. Presbyn. Rotarian. Clubs: Rainier (Seattle); Mercerwood Shore (Mercer Island). Home: Lake House 2330 43d St E Seattle WA 98102 Office: 1101 2d Av Seattle WA 98101

ELDRIDGE, DONALD ATKINS, coll. pres.; b. New Haven, Dec. 8, 1909; s. William Atkins and Lottie (Latham) E.; B.A., Wesleyan U., 1931, M.A., 1932; postgrad. Yale, 1939-44; m. Emley Louise Clogston, Apr. 15, 1933; children—Muriel Elizabeth (Mrs. Paul D. Anderson), Richard Leete. Tchr., coach Hillhouse High Sch., New Haven, 1932-37; dir. audio-visual edn. pub. schs., New Haven, 1938-42; asst. to pres. Wesleyan U., 1942-44, dir. admissions, 1946-49, dean of students, 1949-57; pres. Bennett Coll., 1957—; dir. Am. Council Edn., 1965-68. Dir. Bank Millbrook. Chmn. com. on sch. and coll. relations Ednl. Records Bur., 1960-65; past chmn. sch. nursing council Conn. State Hosp., Middletown; mem. U.S. Nat. Commn. on UNESCO, 1970—; vice chmn. Com. on World Edn. for UNESCO, 1971—; mem. N.Y. State Asso. in Arts Com. Hon. trustee Kents Hill Sch., Me.; bd. govs. Lyall Meml. Federated Ch., Millbrook. Served to lt. USNR, 1944-46. Carnegie Corp. travel grantee for coll. adminstrs., 1955. Mem. Am. Assn. Jr. Colls. (chmn. com. on internat. edn., past pres., dir.), Asso. Colls. Mid-Hudson Area (past pres., dir.), Newcomen Soc., Middle States Assn. Colls. and Secondary Schs. Clubs: Millbrook Golf and Tennis, Arlington Rotary (past pres.). Contbr. articles jours. and mags. Address: Bennett Coll Millbrook NY 12545

ELDRIDGE, FLORENCE, (Mrs. Fredric March), actress; b. Bklyn., Sept. 5, 1901; d. James and Clara Eugenie McKechnie; ed. high sch., Bklyn.; m. Fredric March, May 30, 1927; adopted children—Penelope, Anthony. Acting debut in stock play Seven Days Love; first Broadway appearance in chorus of musical comedy Rock-a-Bye Baby, 1918; Theatre Guild appearance in Ambush, 1921; other plays include Cat and the Canary, 1922, The Great Gatsby, 1926; with husband on tour Theatre Guild repertory co., 1927-28; motion picture debut with husband in Studio Murder Case; other motion pictures include Les Miserables, 1935, Mary of Scotland, 1936, Another Part of Forest, Inherit the Wind; co-star with husband on stage in The American Way, 1939, Hope for a Harvest, 1941, The Skin of Our Teeth, 1943, Years Ago, 1946, Now I Lay Me Down to Sleep, 1950, An Enemy of the People, 1950, The Autumn Garden, 1951, Long Day's Journey Into Night, 1956. Office: care Roland Mader Inc Box 25940 Los Angeles CA 90025

ELDRIDGE, JOHN WILLIAM, chem. engr., educator; b. Nashua, N.H., Aug. 22, 1921; s. Clarence C. and Grace (Hamor) E.; B.S., U. Me., 1942; M.S., Syracuse U., 1946; Ph.D., U. Minn., 1949; m. Lucille Eleanor Patten, May 26, 1942; children—John William, Stephen Chapman, David Patten. Chem. engr. Carnegie-Ill. Steel Co., Clairton, Pa., 1942; chem. engr. Semet-Solvay Co., Syracuse, N.Y., 1942-46; chem. engr. Barrett div. Allied Chem. & Dye Corp., Phila., 1949- 50; cons. Albemarle Paper Mfg. Co., Richmond, Va., 1951-64; prof. U. Va., 1950-62; prof. U. Mass., Amherst, 1962—. Mem. Am. Inst. Chem. Engrs., Am. Chem. Soc., Am. Soc. Engring. Edn., Am. Assn. U. Profs., Sigma Xi, Alpha Chi Sigma, Phi Lambda Upsilon. Contbr. articles profl. jour. Patentee in field. Home: 39 Kendrick Pl Amherst MA 01002

ELDRIDGE, JOSIAH BAKER, trucking co. exec.; b. Oxford, N.C., Apr. 2, 1927; s. James and Mary (Cheek) E.; B.S. in Commerce, U. N.C., 1950; m. Roxie Ann Walters, June 30, 1951; children—Jo Ann, Jeffery, Mark. Resident auditor State of N.C., Raleigh, 1950-52; with McLean Trucking Co., Winston-Salem, N.C., 1952—, asst. comptroller, 1961-71, comptroller, 1971—. Served with USNR, 1944-46. Mem. Adminstrv. Mgmt. Soc. (Merit award 1966), Nat. Assn. Accountants, N.C. Motor Carriers Assn. (chmn. N.C. accounting council 1961-62), Am. Trucking Assn. (2d v.p. nat. accounting and finance council 1970-71), Delta Sigma Pi. Contbr. articles tech. jours. on accounting in motor carrier industry. Home: Rt 8 Green Meadows Winston-Salem NC 27106 Office: 617 Waughtown St Winston-Salem NC 27102

ELDRIDGE, PAUL, author, educator; b. Phila., May 5, 1888; s. Leon and Jeanette (Lefleur) E.; B.S., Temple U., 1909; M.A., U. Pa., 1911; Docteur de l'Université, Université de Paris, 1913; m. Sylvette De Lamar. Lectr. Am. Lit., Sorbonne, Paris, 1913; tchr. Romance langs., high sch., N.Y.C., 1914-46. Mem. Author's League Am., Dramatists' League. Author: books of verse, stories, plays and novels including: My First Two Thousand Years, 1928; Salome, 1930, Cobwebs and Cosmos (verse), 1930; The Invincible Adam, 1932; One Man Show (stories), 1933; If After Every Tempest (novel), 1941; I Bring A Sword (verse), 1945; Men. and Women, 1946; Two Lessons in Love, 1946; And Thou Shalt Teach Them, 1947; The Bed Remains (play), 1948; The Crown of Empire (The Story of New York State), 1957; Tales of the Fortunate Isles, 1959; The Second Life of John Stevens, 1959; Seven Against The Night (essays), 1960; The Tree of Ignorance (novel), 1962; Maxims for a Modern Man, 1965; The Homecoming (novell), 1966; Parables of Old Cathay (verse), 1969; The Story-Tellers (essays), 1970. Contbr. to mags. Home: 227 Riverside Dr New York City NY 10025

ELDRIDGE, ROY, jazz musician; b. Pitts., Jan. 39, 1911; s. Alexander and Blanche (Oakes) E.; student high sch., Pitts.; m. Viola Lee Fong, Jan. 24, 1936; 1 dau., Carole Elizabeth. Drummer, trumpeter; began profl. career with Greater Sheesley Shows, carnival, 1927; played with Chocolate Dandies, Teddy Hill, Mckinney's Cotton Pickers, Fletcher Henderson Band; organized own band, later joined Gene Krupa, 1941; with Jazz at the Philharmonic, 1945-51, on tour of Europe, 1949-51; recording artist for Mercury Records. Recipient Citation of Merit, Muscular Dystrophy Assn.; awards Down Beat mag., Westinghouse Trophy award, others. Presbyn. Home: 194-19 109th Av Hollis NY 11423

ELDRIDGE, WILLIAM CAMERON, mgmt. cons.; b. Omaha, Jan. 13, 1912; s. Oliver W. and Hazel Clee (Smith) E.; A.B., Dartmouth, 1934, student Amos Tuck Sch. Bus. and Finance, 1933-34; m. Helen Randolph, Oct. 27, 1939 (div. 1960); children—Joan, Lynn, Beth; m. 2d, Charlotte Rutledge, Dec. 17, 1964. Asst. merchandiser Montgomery Ward & Co., Chgo., 1934- 38; sales research mgr. Crane Co., Chgo., 1939-42; account research Lord & Thomas, Chgo., 1942; market research supr. RCA, Chgo., 1942-44; mgmt. cons. Booz, Allen & Hamilton, Los Angeles, 1944-59, partner, 1947-59; William Eldridge & Co., 1959—; v.p., dir. Western Travelers Life Ins. Co. Mem. Econ. Round Table. Rotarian. Club: California (Los Angeles). Home: 897 S Lucerne Blvd Los Angeles CA 90005 Office: 523 W 6th St Los Angeles CA 90014

ELDSMOE, RUSSELL MERLE, educator; b. Beresford, S.D., Oct. 4, 1905; s. Christopher A. and Olena (Nessa) E.; A.B., Yankton Coll., 1927, Ed. D., 1968; M.A., U. S.D., 1935; postgrad. univs. Minn. and Chgo.; m. Beulah Ann Hoffert, Nov. 25, 1926; children—Robert Russell, John Allen. Classroom tchr. history and speech, Hetland, S.D., 1927-28; mgr. real estate dept. Grandy-Pratt Co., Sioux City, Ia., 1928-30; supt. of schs., Hetland, 1930-32; supt. of schs., Volga, S.D., 1932-39; head dept. edn. and placement bur. Yankton (S.D.) Coll., 1939-47; head dept. edn. and placement bur. Morningside Coll., Sioux City, 1947—, chmn. div. social scis., dean men, 1950—, dir. seminar tour, 1960. Mem. N.E.A., Ia., S.D. ednl. assns., Am. Assn. Univ. Profs. Republican. Methodist. Clubs: Rotary, Sioux City Knife and Fork. Author: A History of the South Dakota Indian Reservation System, 1935; A Pupil's Rating Scale of an Instructor, 1946; A Student's Evaluation of an Instructor, 1961. Co-author: Teacher Education in Liberal Arts Colleges, 1962. Home: 4404 Morningside Av Sioux City IA 51106

ELEBASH, HUNLEY AGEE, bishop; b. Pensacola, Fla., July 27, 1923; s. Eugene Perrin and Ann (Agee) E.; B.S., U. of South, 1944, B.D., 1950, D.D., 1969; m. Maurine Ashton, Nov. 2, 1946; children—David Hunley, Brett Randolph. Ordained to ministry Episcopal Ch., 1950; rector in Jacksonville, Fla., 1950-57, Wilmington, N.C., 1957-65; exec. sec. Diocese E. Carolina, 1965-68, bishop coadjutor, 1968—. Sec. Diocese Fla., 1953-57, Diocese E. Carolina, 1965-68; del. Gen. Conv. Episcopal Ch., 1961, 64, 67. Trustee U. of South. Served to lst lt. USMCR, 1943-46. Fellow Coll. Preachers, Washington, 1958. Home: 1902 Essex St Kinston NC 28501 Office: Box 1318 Kinston NC 28501

ELEGANT, LAWRENCE, advt. exec.; b. Bklyn., Feb. 24, 1928; s. Nathan and Fanny (Friedienthal) E.; B.A. in Marketing, N.Y. U., 1951; m. Susan Grobstein, Feb. 20, 1954; children—Elizabeth, Peter, Amy. Formerly creative group head McCann Marschalk N.Y.C.; asso. creative dir. Fuller, Smith & Ross, N.Y.C.; creative dir. Erwin, Wasey, N.Y.C.; creative supr. Ogilvy & Mather, N.Y.C.; now v.p. Marschalk Co., N.Y.C. Served with AUS, 1946-47. Recipient Gold Key Awanny awards, Andy award, Internat. Film Festival awards. Mem. Advt. Writers Assn. N.Y. Home: 49-28 Annandale Lane NY 11362 Office: Time Life Bldg New York City NY 10036

ELEGANT, ROBERT SAMPSON, journalist, author; b. N.Y.C., Mar. 7, 1928; s. Louis and Lillie Rebecca (Sampson) E.; A.B., U. Pa., 1946; diploma proficiency, Inst. Far Eastern Langs. and Lit., Yale, 1948; M.A. in Chinese and Japanese, Columbia, 1950, M.S. in Journalism, 1951; m. Moira Clarissa Brady, Apr. 16, 1956; children—Victoria Ann, Simon David Brady. Far East corr. Overseas News Agy., 1951-52; war corr. Internat. News Service, Korea, 1953; corr. in Singapore for CBS, N.Am. Newspaper Alliance, also MCGraw-Hill News Service, 1954-55; S. Asian corr., chief New Delhi (India) bur. Newsweek mag., 1956-57, Southeast Asian corr., chief Hong Kong bur., 1958-61, chief Central European bur., Bonn (Germany) bur., 1962-64; chief Hong Kong bur. Los Angeles Times, 1965-69, fgn. affairs columnist, 1970—; lectr. in field, 1964—. Served with AUS, 1946-48. Pulitzer Travelling fellow, 1951-52; fellow Ford Found., 1954-55; citation best mag. reporting from abroad Overseas Press Club, 1962, award for best interpretation of foreign news, 1967, 69; Edgar Allan Poe award Mystery Writers Am., 1967; Sigma Delta Chi award, 1967. Mem. Asia Soc., Authors League, Phi Beta Kappa. Clubs: Hong Kong Foreign Correspondents' (pres. 1960), Royal Hong Kong Yacht. Author: China's Red Masters, 1951; The Dragon's Seed, 1959; The Center of the World, 1964, rev. 1968; (novels) A Kind of Treason, 1966, The Seeking, 1969; Mao's Great Revolution, 1971; also numerous articles. Address: care Los Angeles Times Times Mirror Sq Los Angeles CA 90053

EL EMARY, ABDEL GALEEL, internat. banker; b. Egypt, Mar. 30, 1907; s. Ibrahim and Fatma Abdelnabi; student Cairo U., Leeds (Eng.) U.; m. Azza Seif El Dine, June 18, 1942; children—May (Mrs. Moneim), Hany, Mona, Hisham. With Egyptian Ministeries Finance and Commerce and Supplies, 1932-47; under-sec. finance. 1947-50; minister finance, 1952-54; gov. Central Bank Egypt, 1957-60; dir.

devel. bank services Internat. Finance Corp., 1962-63, dir. investments for Africa, Asia and Middle East, 1963-65; dir. Africa dept. Internat. Bank Reconstrn. and Devel., 1965-69, spl. adviser to pres. for Africa and Arab states, 1970—. Home: 3117 38th St NW Washington DC 20016 Office: 1818 H St NW Washington DC 20433

ELETA, A. FERNANDO, former Panamanian govt. ofcl.; b. Panama City, Panama, Aug. 10, 1921; s. Carlos and Aurora (Almaran) E.; B.S. in Social Sci., Stanford, 1942; degree in structural engring. Mass. Inst. Tech., 1947; LL.D., Yankton Coll., 1961; m. Mercedes Casanovas (dec.); children—Maria de las Mercedes, Fernando, Aurora; m. 2d, Graciela Quelquejeu, Jan. 31, 1960; children—Graciela, Yolanda, Ximena, Diego. Minister finance and treasury, Republic of Panama, 1958-60, minister fgn. relations, 1964-68; pres. or dir. various Panamanian firms engaged in banking, radio, TV, real estate, tobacco, pharms., export-import, airlines, others. Founding gov. Inter-Am. Devel. Bank; signatory Act of Bogota (found. Alliance for Progress), Treaty over Panama Canal. Decorated Manuel Amador Guerrero, Grado de Gran Cruz, Vasco Nunez de Balboa, Grado de Gran Cruz (both Panama), 1958; Sol de Peru, Grado de Gran Cruz, 1960; Libertador San Martin, Grado ed Gran Cruz (Argentina), 1965; Jose Matias Delgado, Grado de Gran Cruz (El Salvador), 1964; Quetzal, Grado de Gran Cruz (Guatemala), 1966; Aguila Azteca, Grado de Banca de Primera Clase (Mexico), 1966; Isabel la Catolica, Grado de Gran Cruz, (Spain), 1966. Mem. Nat. Indsl. Conf. Bd. (internat. council), Bus. Execs. Assn. Panama (founding pres.), Panama C. of C., Panama Indsl. Assn. Home: P O Box 1795 Panama Republic of Panama

EL-FARRA, MUHAMMAD HUSSEIN, diplomat of Jordan; b. Khan-Yunis, Palestine, Apr. 20, 1923; s. Hussein and Muftiyya (Yusif) El-F.; LL.B., Suffolk U., Boston, 1950, LL.M., Boston U., 1951; J.S.D., U. Pa., 1958. Lectr. univs. in U.S., 1955-59; speaker for League Arab States in U.S., 1955-59; joined Jordan Fgn. Service, 1959; dir. Arab affairs Ministry Fgn. Affairs, 1959-60, dir. Palestine div., 1960-61; dep. permanent rep. Jordan to UN, 1962-64; minister plenipotentiary Jordan embassy, Cairo, 1964-; rep. Jordan 12th- 17th Gen. Assemblies UN, 31st-5th sessions ECOSOC, Conf. League Arab States on UN and Budgetary Questions, Shtura, Lebanon, 1961; member Jordan delegation Arab Foreign Ministers Conference, Cairo, Egypt, 1960; chairman Jordan delegation Arab League conferences on Palestine, 1961, 62; v.p. ECOSOC, 1962 63; chmn. Jordan del. preparatory com. UN Internat. Trade Conf., 1963; pres., Jordan rep. Arab Econ. Unity Council, Cairo, 1964-65, permanent rep., 1965-66; ambassador extraordinary and plenipotentiary, permanent rep. of Jordan to UN, 1966- -, rep. of Jordan on Security Council, 1965-66, pres., 1966—. Vice president of the Arab Students Orgn. U.S., 1954-55. Recipient Mathewson prize Boston U., 1951. Home: Khan-Yunis Gaza United Arab Republic Office: 866 UN Plaza New York City NY 10017

ELFENBEIN, JOSEF AARON, educator; b. Dillon, S.C., Sept. 16, 1920; s. Samuel Stanford and Frances (Fass) E.; B.A., Bklyn. Coll., 1941; M.A., La. State U., 1942; Ph.D., N.Y.U., 1951; m. Esther Klein, Sept. 3, 1950; children—Jill Libbie, Sara Louise, Seth Samuel, Adam Daniel and Lisa Katherine (twins). Instr. speech Bklyn. Coll., 1946-47; instr. communication skills and drama State U. Ia., 1947-48; instr. English, speech and theater State U. N.Y. at Oneonta, 1948-51, asso. prof., 1951-57, prof., 1957—, chmn. speech and theater dept., 1969—, dir. Coll. Community Summer Theater, 1965—, cons. ednl. theater programs and facilities. Mem. Upper Susquehanna Community Council Arts, 1970—. Served with AUS, 1942-45. Alvin Cohen Theater fellow, 1962-65. Mem. Am. Ednl. Theater Assn., Speech Communication Assn. Am., Childrens Theater Conf., Speech Assn. Eastern States, N.Y. State Speech Assn., State U. N.Y. Senate Profl. Assn., Speech Faculty Assn. N.Y., Alpha Psi Omega, Tau Delta Tau. Jewish religion. Author: American Drama 1782-1812 as an Index to Socio-Political Thought, 1951; Pirate Ship, 1953; Tall-Tale and the Fast Freight, 1954; The Tailor's Apprentice, 1956. musical plays: Lucinde, 1959; Song of Gammer Gurton, 1968. Contbr. to profl. jours. Home: 10 Bugbee Rd Oneonta NY 13820

ELFERS, HENRY C., accountant; b. N.Y.C., 1914; ed. U. Pa., 1935. Partner Lybrand, Ross Bros. & Montgomery, C.P.A.'s, N.Y.C. Home: 565 Gifford Av Oceanside NY Office: 60 Broad St New York City NY 10004*

ELFIN, MEL, magazine editor; b. Bklyn., July 18, 1929; s. Joseph and Bess (Margulies) E.; A.B., Syracuse U., 1951; M.A., Harvard, 1952; student New Sch. Social Research, 1955-58; m. Margery Lesser, June 21, 1953; children—David, Dana. Copywriter, Marvin and Leonard, advt., Boston, 1953-54; successively reporter, travel editor, asst. city editor L.I. Daily Press, Jamaica, N.Y., 1954-58; mem. staff Newsweek mag., 1958—, gen. editor, 1964-65, chief Washington bur., 1965—. Cons. Ednl. Facilities Lab., N.Y.C. Served as officer, SAC, USAF, 1952-53. Recipient George Polk Meml. award reporting, 1957, N.Y. Newspaper Guild Page One award, 1957; award Edn. Writers Assn., 1966. Mem. White House Corr. Assn., World Press Inst. (adv. bd.), Phi Beta Kappa, Clubs: International, Press, Federal City (Washington). Author: (with others) Bricks and Mortarboards, 1963; also articles. Home: 2804 29th St N W Washington DC 20008 Office: 1750 Pennsylvania Av N W Washington DC 20006

ELFSTROM, ROBERT LEWIS, business exec., state senator for Oregon; b. Concordia, Kan. Aug 30, 1904; s. Evar V. and Anna (Johnston) E.; student farmers short course, Kan. State Coll., 1923-24; m. Hulda Roth, Dec. 16, 1928; children—Robert Lewis, Patricia (Mrs. William Johnson). Mcht. and contractor under name R. L. Elfstrom Co., Salem, 1932-69; treas. Continental Enterprises, Inc.; chmn. bd., dir. Comml. Bank, Salem, Ore, Mayor of Salem, -Ore., 1947-50; state legislator, 1953-63, chmn. house hwy. com., vice chairman legislative highway interim committee, 1955-56, Fish and Game, Alcoholic Control Com., 1957-58; sec. legislative interim com. on hwys., 1965-66. Fish and Game Interim Com., 1957-58; member Oregon Senate, 1963—, chmn. financial affairs, minority leader, 1967. Chairman of the Oregon State Liquor Control Commn., 1951-52, Alcoholic Control Com., 1959-60; minority leader of House of Representatives of Oregon, 1959-60, Past pres. Cascade Area Boy Scouts Am. (Silver Beaver Award); dir. YMCA: trustee Willamette U.; past trustee San Anselmo Theol. Sem.; chmn. Marion County March of Dimes, 1952. Del. Republican Nat. Convention, 1956, 60, 64, Mem. C. of C. (past dir.), Ore. Motor Ct. Assn. (vice president), League of Oregon Cities (president 1948), Phi Delta Theta, Republican. Presbyterian, Mason (Shriner), Elk, Rotarian (past pres.). Home: 325 13th St N E P O Box 470 Salem OR 97303

ELFTMAN, HERBERT, anatomist; b. Mpls., Oct.31, 1902; s. Arthur H. and Ida C. (Magnusson) E.; B.A., U. Cal. at Berkeley, 1923, M.A., 1925; Ph.D., Columbia, 1929; m. Alice Gooding, Jan. 23, 1930; children—Barbara, Eric. Faculty, Columbia, N.Y.C., 1925—, prof. anatomy in charge gross anatomy, 1948—. Cons. to com. on artificial limbs NRC, 1946-57, mem. com. on prosthetics research and devel., 1957—, chmn., 1965-69. Mem. Am. Assn. Anatomists, Am. Physiol. Soc., Histochem. Soc., A.A.A.S., N.Y. Acad. Sci., Phi Beta Kappa, Sigma Xi. Contbr. articles to tech. jours. Research on biomechanics, human locomotion, muscular activity in movement and structure and function of foot, evolution upright posture, histochemistry endocrine glands and target organs. Home: 407 Park Av Leonia NJ 07605 Office: 630 W 168th St New York City NY 10032

ELGART, LARRY, orch. leader; b. New London, Conn., Mar. 20, 1922; s. Arthur M. and Bessie (Aisman) E.; m. Lynn Walzer, June 28, 1963; children by previous marriage—Brock, Brad. Altosaxophonist; formed Les and Larry Elgart Orch., 1947; recording artist for Decca, RCA Victor, MGM and Columbia records. Recipient Downbeat, Cashbox and Billboards awards in popularity polls; Billboard award for outstanding achievement in recorded music, 1959; Most Played Band award Disco Jockey poll, 1959; nomination Nat. Acad. Recording Arts and Scis., 1959. Address: 55 E 74th St New York City NY 10021

ELGIN, JOSEPH CLIFTON, educator; b. Nashville, Feb. 11, 1904; s. John C. and Elizabeth (Vogely) E.; Chem. E., U. Va., 1924, M.S., 1926; Ph.D., Princeton, 1929; m. Anne Marjorie Wilkins, Sept. 18, 1929 (dec. April 1959); children—Alice (Mrs. G.R. Bishop Jr.), Sarah (Mrs. Edward J. Timberlake, III), Joseph Clifton; m. 2d, Eleanor Hite Bradley, July 20, 1960; 1 stepson, William Bradley, Jr. Asst. prof. U. Va., 1926-27; mem. faculty Princeton 1929—, prof. chem. engring., 1939—, chmn. dept., 1936-54, asso. dean engring., 1951-54, dean of engring., 1954-71; cons. and offical investigator NDRC and OSRD, 1940-44; chief polymer devel. br., Rubber Dirs. Office, WPB, 1942-44; div. chief SAM Labs., Manhattan project, Columbia, 1944-45; dir. U.S. Rubber Reclaiming Co.; cons. AEC, 1946-55; mem. grants com. Research Corp., 1952-63, now dir.; dir. Neptune Meter Co., mem. spl. commn. on synthetic rubber research NSF, 1955; chmn. sect. indsl. and engring. chemistry XIIth Internat. Congress Pure and Applied Chemistry, 1951. Trustee Princeton U. Press, 1952-56, Princeton Country Day Sch., 1951-54, Procter Found., 1953-57, 62—; mem. bd. trustees Asso. Univs., Inc., 1950-62, 68-71, chmn. bd., 1957-58; dir. Textile Research Inst., 1965-71. Recipient William H. Walker award Am. Inst. Chem. Engrs., 1958, Lamme award Am. Soc. Engring. Edn., 1969. Mem. Am. Inst. Chem. Engrs. (dir.), Am. Chem. Soc., Am. Soc. Engring. Edn. (exec. bd. engring. coll. adminstrv. council), NRC (exec. com. div. chem. and tech. 1946-56), Sigma Xi, Tau Beta Pi, Sigma Phi Epsilon, Alpha Chi Sigma, Raven Soc. Contbr. articles to chem. and sci. jours. Home: 218 Prospect Av Princeton NJ 08540

ELGOOD, WILLIAM RICHARD, librarian; b. Que., Can., Oct. 26, 1922; s. Felix and Leslie (Ross) E.; came to U.S., 1923, naturalized, 1933; A.B., U. Vt., 1950; M.A., U. Mich., 1951, M.A. in Library Sci., 1964; m. Ann Drew, Aug. 30, 1952; children—Ross, Leslie, Frances. Mem. faculty, debate coach U. Mich., 1950-53; mem. faculty Gen. Motors Inst., Flint, Mich., 1953-58, dir. library, 1958—. Treas. Inter-Assn. Library Scholarship Fund, 1964—; mem. Mich. Adv. Council, 1968—, Flint Beautification Commn., 1970—, Flint Planning Commn., 1971—. Mem. adv. bd. Flint Community Coll., 1968—. Served with RCAF, 1941-45. Mem. Spl. Libraries Assn., Am. Soc. Engring. Edn. Home: 1615 East Ct Flint MI 48503 Office: 1700 W 3d Av Flint MI 48502

EL GOULLI, SLAHEDDINE, diplomat; b. Sousse, Tunisia, June 22, 1919; s. Abdesselam and Hannah Bent Hadj (M'Hamed Lahouel) El G.; Law Degree, U. Paris (France), 1944, Diplome Superieur d'Economie Politique, 1945, Diplome Superieur Drot Publique, 1946, Dr. in Law, 1947; m. Zineb Larre, Nov. 23, 1958; 1 dau., Nora. Admitted to Tunisian bar, 1947; engaged in business, 1946-56; joined Tunisian Fgn. Ministry, 1956; consul gen., Marseilles, France, 1956-58, counsellor, then minister plenipotentiary embassy, Washington, 1958-61; exec. dir. World Bank, 1961-62; ambassador to Brussels, Netherlands, Luxembourg, European Econ. Community, 1962-69; permanent rep. to UN, 1969; ambassador to U.S. and Mexico, 1969—. Decorated grand cordon de l'ordre de La Couronne de Belgique; grand cordon de Nassau, du Chene de Luxembourg; grand cordon de Leopold Ier, de la Republicque Tunisienne. Author articles. Home: 5131 Broad Branch Rd Washington DC 20008 Office: 2408 Massachusetts AV N W Washington DC 20008

ELIADE, MIRCEA, historian, author; b. Bucharest, Romania, Mar. 9, 1907; s. Gheorghe and Ioana (Stonenescu) E.; M.A., U. Bucharest, 1928, Ph.D., 1932; student U. Calcutta, 1928-31; m. Georgette C. Cottescu, Jan. 9, 1950. Asso. prof. faculty letters Bucharest U., 1933-39; vis. prof. Ecole des Hautes Etudes, Sorbonne, Paris, 1946-48; Haskell lectr. U. Chgo., 1956, vis. prof. history religion, 1956-57, prof., 1958—, Sewell L. Avery distinguished service prof., 1963—; lectr. univs. Rome, Lund, Marburg, München, Frankfort, Strasbourg, Padova; cultural attache Romanian legation, London, Eng., 1940-41; cultural conseiller Romanian legation, Lisbon, Portugal, 1941-44. Dir. Zalmoxis, Revue des études religieuses, Paris, Bucharet, 1938-42; pres. Centre Roumain de Recherches, Paris, 1950-55. Mem. Am. Soc. for Study of Religion (pres. 1963-67), Romanian Writers Soc. (Sec. 1937), Société Asiatique, Frobenius Institut. Author: Yoga, 1936; Techniques du Yoga, 1948; Traité d'Histoire des Religions, 1949; Le Chamanisme, 1951; Images et Symboles, 1952; The Myth of the Eternal Return, 1954; Fort Interdite, 1954; Forgerons et Alchimistes, 1956; Patterns in Comparative Religions, 1958; Birth and Rebirth, 1958; Myths, Dreams and Mysteries, 1959; Images and Symbols, 1960; The Forge and the Crucible, 1962; Myth and Reality, 1963; Shamanism, 1964; The One and the Two, 1965, From Primitives to Zen, 1967; The Quest, 1969. Address: Swift Hall U Chgo Chicago IL 60637

ELIAS, PETER, educator; b. New Brunswick, N.J., Nov. 26, 1923; s. Nathaniel Mandel and Ann (Wahrhaftig) E.; S.B., Mass. Inst. Tech., 1944; M.A., Harvard, 1948, M.Engring. Sci., 1949, Ph.D., 1950; m. Marjorie Forbes, July 8, 1950; children—Daniel, Paul, Ellen. Jr. fellow Harvard, Cambridge, Mass., 1950-53; asst. prof. elec. engring. Mass. Inst. Tech., 1953-56, asso. prof., 1956-60, prof. elec. engring., 1960—, head dept. elec. engring., 1960-66; vis. Mackay prof. elec. engring. U. Cal. at Berkeley, 1958; vis. prof. elec. engring. Harvard, 1968. Fellow A.A.A.S., I.E.E.E., Am. Acad. Arts and Scis.; mem. Inst. Math. Statistics, Sigma Xi, Eta Kappa Nu. Contbg. author: Handbook of Automation, Computation and Control, Vol. 1, 1958. Author tech. articles on information theory and coding problems. Home: 98 Raymond St Cambridge MA 02140

ELIAS, ROBERT HENRY, educator, writer; b. N.Y.C., Sept. 17, 1914; s. Henry Hart and Edna Weil (Bernhard) E.; A.B., Williams Coll., 1936; A.M., Columbia, 1937; Ph.D., U. Pa., 1948; m. Helen Beatrice Larson, June 13, 1947; children—Jonathan Hart, Abigail, Sara, Eben Lars. Instr. English, asst. history U. Pa., 1942-45; instr. English, Cornell U., Ithaca, N.Y., 1945-49, asst. prof., then asso. prof. English, 1949-59, prof., 1959-68, Ernest I. White prof. Am. studies, also chmn. com. Am. studies, 1959- 64, 66-67, sec. faculty, 1965-68, Goldwin Smith prof. English literature and Am. studies, 1968—. Fulbright-Hays lectr. U. Toulouse, France, 1963-64, Centre d'Etude Anglaises et Nord-americaines, Pau, France, 1968. Harrison fellow U. Pa., 1941-42; Ford Found. fellow, 1952-53. Mem. Am. Assn. U. Profs., Am. Studies Assn. (co-founder N.Y. State 1951), Mod. Lang. Assn. Author: Theodore Dreiser: Apostle of Nature, 1949, rev. edit., 1970. Editor: Chapters of Erie (Charles Francis Adams, Jr. and Henry Adams), 1956; Letters of Theodore Dreiser, 1959. Asso. editor Epoch, 1947-54. Contbr. numerous periodicals. Home: 101 Devon Rd Ithaca NY 14850

ELIAS, ROSALIND, mezzo-soprano; b. Lowell, Mass., Mar. 13, 1931; d. Salem and Shelahuy Rose (Namy) Elias; student N.E. Conservatory Music, also in Italy. Debut with Boris Goldowsky, Boston, 1948; appeared San Carlo Opera, Naples, Italy; debut Metropolitan Opera Co., 1954; originated role of Erika in Samuel Barber's opera, Vanessa; TV and concert artist; recordings for RCA, Columbia records. Mem. Sigma Alpha Iota. Home: 24 Park St Lowell MA 01852 Office: Metropolitan Opera Co Broadway and 39th St New York City NY 10023

ELIASON, NORMAN ELLSWORTH, educator; b. Glenwood, Minn., Mar. 12, 1907; s. Andrew and Marie (Sagvold) E.; A.B., Luther Coll., Decorah, Ia., 1927; A.M., U. Ia., 1931; Ph.D., Johns Hopkins, 1936; m. Dorothy Haskins, Aug. 23, 1930. Prin. high sch., Charter Oak, Ia., 1927-28; instr. English, Luther Coll., 1928-29, U. Neb., 1929-32; instr., asst. prof. Ind. U., 1932-37; prof. English, U. Fla., 1937-46; prof. English, U. N.C., Chapel Hill, 1946-66, Kenan prof., 1966—; research at the Linguistic Inst., Mich., 1936, U. Oslo, summer 1939; vis. prof. U. Ia., summer 1952, U. Innsbruck (Austria), 1956, King's Coll., U. London, 1962, Columbia, summer 1964, U. Wash., 1965, Harvard, 1966, Stanford, 1968. Served from lt. (j.g.) to lt. comdr. USNR, 1942-46. Guggenheim fellow, 1951-52; sr. fellow Southeastern Inst. Medieval and Renaissance Studies, 1969. Mem. Am. Dialect Soc. (exec. com. 1956-60), Linguistic Soc. Am. (exec. com. 1940), Modern Lang. Assn. (chmn. practical phonetics group 1937-39; sec. exptl. phonetics group 1942-44; sec. Old English group 1954, chmn. 1955; sec. English sect. 1960, chmn. 1961), Medieval Acad. Am., Internat. Assn. U. Profs. English (mem. cons. com. 1965—), N.C. Folklore Soc. Democrat. Episcopalian. Author: Tar Heel Talk: An Historical Study of the English Language in North Carolina to 1860, 1956. Co-author: The effect of Stress upon Vowel Quantity, 1939. Co-editor: Ideas and Models, 1935; Studies in Heroic Legend and Current Speech, 1959; Aelfric's First Series of Catholic Homilies, 1966. Asst. editor So. Folklore Quar., 1937-47; adv. editor Am. Speech, 1939-40, 60-61; co-editor Anglistica, 1964—. Contbr. articles and revs. to profl. jours. Home: Round Hill Rd Chapel Hill NC 27514

ELIASSEN, ROLF, environmental engr., educator; b. N.Y.C., Feb. 22, 1911; s. Olaf and Effie (Albrethsen) E.; B.S., Mass. Inst. Tech., 1932, M.S., 1933, Sc.D., 1935; m. Mary F. Hulick, Dec. 12, 1941; children—Thomas R., James H. Design engr. J.N. Chester Engrs., Pitts., 1935-36; san. engr. Dorr Co., Inc., Chgo., Los Angeles, 1936-39; asst. prof. civil engring. Ill. Inst. Tech., 1939-40; asso. prof. san. engring. N.Y. U., 1940-42, prof., 1946-49; design engr. Parsons, Klapp, Brinckerhoff & Douglas, N.Y.C., 1941; chmn. civil engring. dept. Biarritz Am. U., France, 1945; prof. san. engring., dir. Sedgwick Labs San. Sci., Mass. Inst. Tech., cons. engr., 1949-60, acting head dept. civil engring., 1960-61; prof. civil engring. Stanford, 1961—, now Silas H. Palmer prof. civil engring.; sr. v.p. Metcalf & Eddy, Inc., cons. engrs., Palo Alto, 1961—. Cons., IAEA, WHO, UN, Exec. Office Pres., Cal. Dept. Water Resources, Fed. Power Commn., U.S. Senate Com. on Pub. Works; mem. gen. adv. com. AEC, 1970—. Served to lt. col., C.E., AUS, 1942-46; France. Mem. Am. Acad. Arts and Sci., Am. Soc. C.E., Nat. Acad. Engring., Am. Water Works Assn., Am. Soc. Engring. Edn. (George Westinghouse award 1950), Tau Beta Pi, Sigma Xi. Conglist. Contbr. articles tech. jours. Home: 1910 Newell Rd Palo Alto CA 94303 Office: Coll Engring Stanford U Stanford CA 94305 also 1029 Corporation Way Palo Alto CA 94303

ELICKER, PAUL H., corp. exec.; b. N.Y.C., 1923; B.S., Yale, 1942; M.B.A., Harvard, 1948. With Ford Motor Co., 1942-51, Mckinsey & Co., 1952-56; with S C M Corp., 1956—. v.p. finance, 1968—, also dir. Home: 2704 Long Ridge Rd Stamford CT 06903 Office: 410 Park Av New York City NY 10022*

ELIEL, ERNEST LUDWIG, educator, chemist; b. Cologne, Germany, Dec. 28, 1921; s. Oskar and Luise (Tietz) E.; came to U.S., 1946, naturalized, 1951; student U. Edinburgh (Scotland), 1939-40; D.Phys.-chem. Sci., U. Havana (Cuba), 1946; Ph.D., U. Ill., 1948; m. Eva Schwarz, Dec. 23, 1949; children—Ruth Louise, Carol Susan. Mem. faculty U. Notre Dame, South Bend, Ind., 1948—, prof. chemistry, 1960—, head dept., 1964-66, mem. faculty affairs com. bd. trustees, 1970—; E.C. Franklin Meml. lectr. U. Kan., 1969; summer cons. Am. Oil Co., 1956. Pres. Internat. Relations Council St. Joseph Valley, 1961-63; chmn. United World Federalists St. Joseph County, 1956. NSF sr. research fellow Harvard, 1958, Cal. Inst. Tech., 1958-59, E.T.H., Zurich, Switzerland, 1967-68. Recipient Coll. Tchrs. award Mfg. Chemists Assn., 1965; Morley medal Cleve. sect. Am. Chem. Soc., 1965, Laurent Lavoisier medal French Chem. Soc., 1968. Mem. Am. Chem. Soc. (chmn. St. Joseph Valley sect., 1960, councillor 1965—, council publs. 1966—), A.A.A.S., Chem. Soc. London (Anniversary lectr. 1964), Am. Assn. U. Profs. (chpt. pres. 1971—), Sigma Xi, (chpt. Pres. 1968-69), Phi Lambda Upsilon, Phi Kappa Phi. Author: Stereochemistry of Carbon Compounds, 1962; Conformational Analysis, 1965; Elements of Stereochemistry, 1969. Co-editor: Topics in Stereochemistry, Vols. I-VI, 1967-71. Editorial bd. Jour. Organic Chemistry, 1962-66. Home: 17305 Parker Av South Bend IN 46635

ELION, GERTRUDE BELLE, research scientist; b. N.Y.C., Jan. 23, 1918; d. Robert and Bertha (Cohen) Elion: A.B., Hunter Coll., 1937; M.S., N.Y. U., 1941; D.Sc. (hon.), George Washington U., 1969; D.M.S. (hon.), Brown U., 1969. Lab. asst. biochemistry N.Y. Hosp. Sch. Nursing, 1937; research asst. in organic chemistry Denver Chem. Mfg. Co., N.Y.C., 1938-39; tchr. chemistry and physics N.Y.C. secondary schs., 1940-42; food analyst Quaker Maid Co., Bklyn., 1942-43; research asst. in organic synthesis Johnson & Johnson, New Brunswick, N.J., 1943- 44; biochemist Wellcome Research Labs., Tuckahoe, N.Y., 1944-50, sr. research chemist, 1950—; asst. to asso. research dir., 1955-62, asst. to the research dir., 1963-66, head exptl. therapy, 1966—; cons. USPHS, 1960-64. Chmn., Gordon Conf. on Coenzymes and Metabolic Pathways, 1966. Recipient Garvan medal, 1968. Fellow N.Y. Acad. Scis.; mem. Am. Chem. Soc., A.A.A.S., Chem. Soc. (London), Am. Soc. Biol. Chemists, Am. Assn. Cancer Research, Am. Soc. Hematology, Transplantation Soc. Contbr. articles profl. jours. Patentee in field. Home: 1 Banbury Lane Chapel Hill NC 27514 Office: 3030 Cornwallis Rd Research Triangle Park NC 27709

ELIOT, ALEXANDER, author, critic; b. Cambridge, Mass., Apr. 28, 1919 s. Samuel Atkins, Jr. and Ethel (Cook) E.; student Black Mountain Coll., 1936-38, Boston Mus. Sch., 1938-39; m. Jane Winslow Knapp, May 3, 1952; children—May Rose, Jefferson, Winslow. Dir. Pinkney St. Artists Alliance, Boston, 1940-41; asst. to producer March of Time newsreel, 1941-42; asst. dir. films OWI, 1942-43; editor films Coordinator Inter-Am. Affairs, 1943-45; art editor Time mag., 1945-60; contbg. editor Art in America, 1960-65; lectr., participant panel discussions; contbr. to various mags. Guggenheim fellow, 1960. Fellow Internat. Inst. Arts and Letters. Clubs: Century Assn., Dutch Treat (N.Y.C.). Author: Proud Youth (novel), 1953; Three Hundred Years of American Painting (art history), 1957; Sight and Insight (art philosophy), 1959; Earth, Air, Fire and Water, 1962; Greece, 1963; Love Play (novel entertainment), 1966; Creatures of Arcadia, 1967; Socrates, 1967; Every Man's Dream (film), 1968; also essays. Home: Oak Tree Cottage Forest Row Sussex, England Office: care William Morris Agy 1350 Av of the Americas New York City NY 10019

ELIOT, CHARLES WILLIAM II, planner; b. Cambridge, Mass., Nov. 5, 1899; s. Samuel Atkins and Frances Stone (Hopkinson) E.; grad. Browne & Nichols Sch., Cambridge, 1916; A.B., Harvard, 1920; M.L.A., Harvard Grad. Sch. of Landscape Architecture, 1923; m. Regina Phelps Dodge, Oct. 11, 1928; children—Charles William III, Carolyn (Mrs. John B. Ruckdeschel), John, Lawrence. Landscape architect, Boston, 1924-26; city planner for Arlington, Mass., and other towns; Nat. Capital Park & Planning Commn., Washington, 1926-30, dir. of planning, Washington and environs, 1930-33; exec. officer Nat. Planning Bd. PWA, 1933-34, Nat. Resources Bd., 1934-35, Nat. Resources Com., 1935-39; dir. Nat. Resources Planning Bd., 1939-43; dir. Haynes Found., 1944- 45; planning cons. pvt. practice 1945—; adviser on plans for Riverside, Redlands, Upland, Corona, La Jolla, Coachella Valley, Cal., Olympia, Wash., Boxford, Lincoln, Dover, Groton, Hamilton, Middleton, Harvard, Wilmington, Mass., York County, Me., Nat. Capital Region, Greater Burlington, Vt., others; dir. resources program Ford Found., 1952-53; Charles Eliot prof. landscape architecture and regional planning Grad. Sch. Design Harvard U., 1955- 59, prof. city and regional planning, 1959-66. Pres. emeritus Bunker Hill Monument Assn.; v.p. Hubbard Ednl. Trust; mem. Boston Met. Area Planning Council; mem. Cambridge Hist. Com. Served with A.R.C. Ambulance Corps, Italy, 1918; 2d lt. F.A., O.T.S., 1918-19. Decorated Croce di Guerra (Italy). Trustee Mass. Trustees of Reservations (sec. 1925-26), Hancock County Trustees of Pub. Reservations of Me. Fellow Am. Soc. Landscape Architects, Am. Acad. Arts and Scis., mem. Am. Inst. Planners (Distinguished Service award 1961), Am. Soc. Planning Ofcls., Boston Soc. Landscape Architects (past pres.), Regional Sci. Assn., Urban Am., Inc., Cambridge Hist. Soc. (pres.). Unitarian. Club: Cosmos. Contbr. profl. publs. and planning reports. Address: 25 Reservoir St Cambridge MA 02138

ELIOT, MILTON EARL, steel co. exec.; b. Dallas, Dec. 14, 1914; s. William Mack and Etta (Cundiff) E.; B.S. in Civil Engring., U. Tex., 1935; M.S., U. Ill., 1936; m. Agnes Field, Feb. 14, 1943; children—Emily Ann (Mrs. Charles Oren Hon III), William Eugene, Charles Scott. Draftsman, Mosher Steel Co., Houston, 1936-39, chief engr., Dallas, 1939-56, v.p. and works mgr., 1956-64, exec. v.p., Houston, 1964-66, pres., 1968—, also dir.; dir. Mosher Steel Co. of La., Comml. Iron Works. Trustee Mosher Found., United Fund of Houston and Harris County. Fellow Am. Soc. C.E.; mem. Tau Beta Pi, Chi Epsilon, Delta Kappa Epsilon. Home: 2220 Looscan Lane Houston TX 77019 Office: 3910 Washington Av Houston TX 77007

ELIOT, THEODORE LYMAN, ednl. adminstr.; b. Cambridge, Mass., Apr. 4, 1903; s. Samuel Atkins and Frances (Hopkinson) E.; A.B., Harvard, 1925; m. Martha Williams Bigelow, Sept. 19, 1925; children—Joan (Mrs. Eliot O'Bryan), Theodore Lyman, Gwladys (Mrs. Eugene Scott), Mary Williams (Mrs. Robert F. Winne, Jr.), With Internat. Merc. Marine Co., N.Y.C., 1925-28, William B. Nichols & Co., N.Y.C., 1928-30, Brown Bros. Harriman Co., Boston, 1930-32; travel agt., Boston, 1932-42; exec. Am. Pres. Lines, San Francisco, 1946-56, Matson Navigation Co., 1956-63; dir. devel. San Francisco Art Inst., 1963, exec. dir., 1964—. Served to capt. USNR, 1942-46. Clubs: Nuttall Ornithological (Cambridge); Harvard (past pres.), University (past pres.) (San Francisco). Home: 401 Golden Gate Av Belvedere CA 94920 Office: San Francisco Art Inst 800 Chestnut St San Francisco CA 94133

ELIOT, THEODORE LYMAN, Jr., govt. ofcl.; b. N.Y.C., Jan. 24, 1928; s. Theodore Lyman and Martha Williams (Bigelow) E.; B.A., Harvard, 1948, M.P.A., 1956; m. Patricia F. Peters, Apr. 14, 1951; children—Sarah Winslow, Theodore Lyman III, Wendy Peters, Peter Bigelow. Vice consul, 3d sec. Am. embassy, Colombo, Ceylon, 1950-52; U.S. information and cultural officer, Germany, 1953- 55; 2d sec. Am. embassy, Moscow, USSR, 1956-58; spl. asst. to under sec. of state, 1959-61. to sec. treasury, 1961-62; 1st. sec. Am. Embassy, Tehran, Iran, 1963-66; country dir. for Iran, Dept. of State, 1966-69; exec. sec. Dept. State, also special asst. to sec. of state, 1969—. Adviser U.S. delegation to meeting Inter-American Devel.- Bank, Rio de Janeiro, 1961, NATO meeting, Paris, 1961, others. Mem. Am. Fgn. Service Assn. (vice chairman board of directors 1967-69, pres. 1970—). Home: 6601 Virginia View Ct Washington DC 20016 Office: Dept State Washington DC 20520

ELIOT, THOMAS HOPKINSON, ednl. adminstr.; b. Cambridge, Mass., June 14, 1907; s. Samuel Atkins and Frances Stone (Hopkinson) E.; prep. edn. Browne and Nichols Sch., Cambridge, 1916-23; A.B., Harvard, 1928, LL.B., 1932; postgrad. Emmanuel Coll., Cambridge, Eng., 1928-29; LL.D., Drury Coll.; L.H.D., Hobart and William Smith Colls., St. Louis U., Rockhurst Coll.; D.Hum., Washington U., St. Louis; m. Lois A. Jameson, Oct. 10, 1936; children—Samuel Atkins, Nancy Freeman. Reporter, Boston Globe, 1923-24; admitted to N.Y. State, Mass., U.S. Supreme Ct. bars; asso. firm Kenefick, Cooke, Mitchell, Bass & Letchworth, Buffalo, 1932-33; asst. solicitor Dept. Labor, 1933-35, regional dir. Wage and Hour div., 1939-40; counsel Pres.'s Com. on Econ. Security, 1934-35; gen. counsel Social Security Bd., 1935-38; lectr. govt., Harvard, 1937-38, 48-51; New Eng. chmn. United Negro Coll. Fund, 1946-48; mem. 77th Congress from 9th Mass. Dist.; spl. asst. to ambassador and head Brit. div. London Office War Information, 1943; chmn. Appeals Com., Nat. War Labor Bd., 1943-44, OSS, 1944; chief counsel Div. Power, Dept. Interior, 1944-45; partner firm Foley, Hoag & Eliot 1945-52; prof., chmn. dept. polit. sci., Washington U., St. Louis, 1952-61, chancellor, 1962-71, prof. constl. law Law Sch., 1958-62, dean Liberal Arts 1961- 62; pres. Salzburg Seminar in Am. Studies, 1971—. Vis. prof. Princeton, 1958-59. Exec. dir. Spl. Commn. on Structure of State Govt., 1950- 52. Mem. nat. com. Am. Civil Liberties Union, 1942-67; vice chmn. U.S. Adv. Commn. Intergovtl. Relations, 1964-67. bd. overseers Harvard, 1964-70; trustee Monticello Coll. 1958-60. Mem. Am. Polit. Sci. Assn. (council 1956-58, book rev. editor 1960-62), Am. Acad. Arts and Scis. Democrat. Unitarian. Author: Basic Rules of Order, 1952; American Government Problems for Analysis, 1959; Governing America, 1960; Public and Personal, 1971; co- author State Politics and the Public Schools, 1963. Contbr. articles to profl. jours. Office: 17 Dunker St Cambridge MA

ELISCU, FRANK, sculptor; b. N.Y.C., July 13, 1912; s. Charles Henry and Florence (Kane) E.; student Beaux Arts Inst. Design, Pratt Inst., 1930-33; m. Mildred Norman, May 3, 1942; 1 dau., Norma (Mrs. Francis Banas, Jr.). One-man exhbn. sculpture, Mexico, 1955; works represented Bookgreen Gardens, S.C., portrait busts Aero. Hall of Fame, other works Stevens Inst., Cornell Med. Sch., Olin Hall, N.Y., Heismann Meml. Trophy, Naiad (fountain figure), N.Y.C., Heroii (Atoms for Peace figure) Ventura, Cal., Headley Mus. (The Astronauts), Lexington, Ky., Steuben Glass Co. (Noah), St. Christopher's Chapel (St. Christopher), N.Y.C., Soc. Medallists (Sea Treasures). Recipient Edith S. Moore prize for sculpture, 1948; Bennet prize Nat. Sculpture Soc.; Henry Hering award, 1960. Fellow Sculpture Soc. (pres. 1967-70); mem. Archtl. League N.Y. (v.p. sculpture, silver medal 1958), Sculpture Center N.Y., Nat. Academician. Author: Sculpture, Three Techniques, Clay, Wax, Slate; Slate Sculpture; Direct Wax Sculpture. Address: 440 Rock House Rd Easton CT 06612

ELISOFON, ELIOT, photographer, painter; b. N. Y.C., Apr. 17, 1911; s. Samuel and Sarah (Narazimski) E.; B.S., Fordham U., 1933; m. Mavis Lyons, July 1, 1941 (div. 1946); m. 2d, Joan Baker Spear, July 15, 1950 (div. 1965); children—Elin, Jill. Staff photographer Life mag., 1942, engaged on nat. and internat. assignments Mexico, C.A., S.Am., Africa, South Seas, Japan, Europe; research fellow primitive art Peabody Mus., Harvard; color cons. motion picture Moulin Rouge, 1952, Bell, Book and Candle, 1958, Warlord, 1964; dir. prologue film Khartoum, 1965; dir. Egypt portion Man Builds (Nat. Ednl. TV), 1965; still photographer Dr. Doolittle, 1966; creative dir. ABC-TV Africa Project, 1966-67; visual cons. stage prodn., Baylor U., Of Time and the River; exhibited one-man shows Durlacher Bors., 1958, 60, watercolors Gekkoso Gallery, Tokyo, 1969; rep. permanent collection Mus. Modern Art, N.Y.C., Phila. Mus. Art, Pa. Acad. Fine Arts, Colby Coll. of Me., Fogg Art Mus., Cambridge, Dallas Mus. Contemporary Art, Hononlulu Acad. Art, Nat. Mus. Western Art, Tokyo; lectr. Dallas Theater Center, Yale, Syracuse U., Radcliffe Coll., Wellesley Coll., Sarah Lawrence Coll., Mus. Modern Art, Chgo. Art Inst. Mem. Harvard Peabody Mus. New Guinea expdn., 1961. Mem. Royal Anthrop. Soc. Clubs: Overseas, Explorers (N.Y.C.). Author: Food is a Four Letter Word, 1948; Color Photography, 1961; The Nile, 1964; Java Diary, 1969. Illustrator: The Art of Indian Asia, 1955. Illustrator, editor; The Sculpture of Africa, 1958; Hollywood Style (Arthur Knight), 1969; Indian Cookbook, 1969. Collector Am. folk art, Pre-Columbian, Pacific, African sculpture in U.S. Address: 145 E 27th St New York City, NY 10016.

ELIZABETH, QUEEN, II, (Alexandra Mary), Queen of the United Kingdom of Great Britain and Northern Ireland, and her other realms and Territories, head of the Commonwealth; b. Apr. 21, 1926; d. King George VI and Queen Elizabeth; m. Prince Philip, Duke of Edinburgh, Nov. 20, 1947; children—Charles Philip Arthur George, Anne Elizabeth Alice Louise, Andrew Albert Christian Edward, Edward Antony Richard Louis. Succeeded to the throne following death of father, Feb. 6, 1952; crowned queen, June 1953. Address: Buckingham Palace London S.W. 1, England

ELKEN, JOHN HAYNES, ins. co. exec.; b. Mayville, N.D., Dec. 29, 1926; s. Guy L. and Gladys (Haynes) E.; B.S., Stanford, 1949; M.S., U. Mich., 1950; m. Colleen LaMae Bakke, July 6, 1947; children—Eric Mikkel, Ann Louise. With Bankers Life Co., 1950—, 2d v.p. underwriting, 1968-70, v.p., 1970—. Served with USNR, 1944-46. Asso. Soc. Actuaries; mem. Acad. Actuaries, Home Office Life Underwriters Assn. Conglist. (trustee 1963-67). Club: Des Moines Golf and Country (dir. 1969—). Home: 124 53d St Des Moines, IA 50312. Office: 711 High St Des Moines IA 50307

ELKES, JOEL, physician; b. Nov. 12, 1913; s. Elkanan and Miriam (Malbin) E.; M.B., Ch.B., U. Birmingham (Eng.), 1947, M.D. with honours, 1949; m. Charmian Bourne, Dec. 18, 1943; 1 dau., Anna Rosalind. Came to U.S., 1957. Lectr. pharmacology U. Birmingham, 1945-48, sr. lectr., acting dir. dept., 1948-50, prof., chmn. dept. exptl. psychiatry, 1951- 57; cons. psychiatrist Birmingham United Hosp., Birmingham Regional Hosp. Bd., 1953-57; sci. dir. Birmingham Regional Psychiat. Early Treatment Center, 1953-57; chief clin. neuropharmacology Research Center, Nat. Inst. Mental Health, Bethesda, Md., 1957-63, mem. psychopharmacology study sect. NIH, 1957-1964; dir. research St. Elizabeth's Hosp., Washington, 1957-63; clin. prof. psychiatry George Washington U. Med. Sch., 1957-63; Henry Phipps prof. psychiatry Johns Hopkins Sch. Medicine, Balt., 1963—; psychiatrist- in-chief Johns Hopkins Hosp., 1963—; formerly cons. WHO: mem. central com. Internat. Brain Research Orgn.; chmn. subcom. on edn. UNESCO. Bd. dirs. Found. Research Psychiatry. Fellow Am. Acad. Arts and Scis., Am. Psychiat. Assn.; mem. Am. Soc. Pharmacology and Exptl. Therapeutics, Group Advancement Psychiatry, Am. Psychopath. Assn. (pres. 1968), Soc. Biol. Psychiatry, Physiol. Soc. Gt. Britain, Pharmacol. Soc. Gt. Britain, Royal Medico Psychol. Assn., Royal Soc. Medicine, Brit. Electroencephalographic Soc., Soc. Study Drug Addiction, Brit. Psychol. Soc., Washington Acad. Medicine, Am. Coll. Neuropsychopharmacology (pres. 1962). Clubs: West Hamilton Street (Balt.); Cosmos (Washington). Editor: Psychopharmacologia, 1958; asso. editor Jour. Psychiat. Research. Home: 3925 Canterbury Rd Baltimore MD 21280 Office: Johns Hopkins Hosp Baltimore MD 21205

ELKES, TERRENCE ALLEN, corp. counsel; b. N.Y.C., Apr. 28, 1934; s. Sidney and Beatrice (Sachnin) E.; B.A. cum laude, Coll. City N.Y., 1955; J.D., U. Mich., 1958; m. Ruth Jerkowsky, June 14, 1959; children—Steven Andrew, David Adam, Daniel Arthur. Admitted to N.Y. bar, 1959; atty. Prentice Hall, Inc., 1958-59; counsel internat. div. Norwich Pharmacal Co., 1959-65; corp. counsel Parsons & Whittemore, Inc. 1965—, also v.p., sec.; corp. counsel Black Clawson Co., 1965—; treas. Prince Albert Pulp Co. Ltd. Mem. Am., N.Y. State bar assns. Home: 60 Stratford Lane Hastings-on-Hudson NY 10706. Office: 200 Park Av New York City NY 10017

ELKIN, ELEANOR SCOTT, civic worker; b. Phila., Oct. 23, 1917; d. Charles Marshall and Augusta (Manderson) Scott; student Albright Coll., Reading, Pa., 1958-60; m. Philip Elkin, Sept. 16, 1939; children—Richard Brooke, Margot deNise. Pres., Bucks County (Pa.) chpt. Assn. Retared Children. 1954, Pa. Assn. Retarded Children, 1957-59; bd. dirs. Nat. Assn. Retarded Children, 1965—, v.p., 1966-67, pres., 1967-69; mem. Gov. Pa. Com. Handicapped, 1958-60; mem. Pres.'s Task Force on The Mentally Handicapped, 1970; cons. Pres.'s Com. on Mental Retardation, 1970—; mem. adv. bd. Partners Rehab. and Edn. Program, Partners of the Americas, 1970—; mem. Gov.'s Task Force on Human Services, 1971—. Pres. River Crest Sch., 1962-64, bd. dirs. 1960-62; bd. trustees White Haven State Sch. and Hosp., 1964; mem. bd. Ken-Crest Centers. Mem. Tau Phi Gamma. Presbn. Home: School Lane House Apt Philadelphia PA 19144 Office: 420 Lexington Av New York City NY 10017

ELKIN, MILTON, educator, physician; b. Boston, Feb. 24, 1916; s. Philip and Rose (Dexter) E.; A.B., Harvard, 1937, M.D., 1941; m. Gloria King, Nov. 12, 1943; children—Philip, Karen, Laura. Asso. radiologist Peter Bent Brigham Hosp., Boston, 1951-52; dir. radiology Cambridge (Mass.) City Hosp., asst. radiologist New Eng. Med. Center, Boston, 1952-53; asso. radiologist Cedars of Lebanon Hosp., Los Angeles, 1953-54; prof., chmn. dept. radiology Albert Einstein Coll. Medicine, Yeshiva U., N.Y.C., 1954—; dir. radiology Bronx Municipal Hosp. Center, N.Y.C., 1954—. Spl. cons. radiology tng. com. Nat. Inst. Gen. Med. Scis., NIH, USPHS, 1966-70, cons. Gen. Med. Reseearch Program-Project Com., 1970—. Fellow Am. Coll. Radiology; mem. A.M.A., Harvard Med. Soc., Am. Roentgen Ray Soc., Radiol. Soc. N.Am., Assn. U. Radiologists, N.Y. Roentgen Soc. (pres.). Contbr. articles profl. jours. Home: 13 Kingston Rd Scarsdale NY 10583 Office: 1300 Morris Park Av New York City NY 10461

ELKIN, STANLEY LAWRENCE, author, educator; b. N.Y.C., May 11, 1930; s. Philip and Zelda (Feldman) E.; A.B., U. Ill., 1952, M.A., 1953, Ph.D., 1961; m. Joan Marion Jacobson, Feb. 1, 1953; children—Philip Aaron, Bernard Edward, Molly Ann. Faculty Washington U., St. Louis, 1959—, prof. Am. lit., 1969- -. Vis. lectr. Smith Coll., 1964-65; vis. prof. U. Cal. at Santa Barbara, 1967, U. Wis. at Milw., 1969. Served with AUS 1955-57. Recipient Longview Found. award, 1962. Guggenheim fellow, 1966-67; Rockefeller grantee, 1968-69. Author: Boswell, 1964; Criers and Kibitzers, Kibitzers and Criers, 1966; A Bad Man, 1967; The Dick Gibson Show, 1971. Home: 225 Westgate University City MO 63130 Office: Duncker Hall Washington Univ St Louis MO 63130

ELKIND, MORTIMER MURRAY, biophysicist; b. Bklyn., Oct. 25, 1922; s. Samuel and Yetta (Lubarsky) E.; B. Mech. Engring., Cooper Union, 1943; M.M.E., Poly. Inst. Bklyn., 1949; M.S. in Elec. Engring., Mass. Inst. Tech., 1951, Ph.D. in Physics, 1953, m. Karla Annikki Holst, Jan. 27, 1960; children—Sean Thomas, Samuel Scott, Jonathan Harald. Asst. project engr. Wyssmont Co., N.Y.C., 1943; project engr. Safe Flight Instrument Corp., White Plains, N.Y., 1946-47; head instrumentation sect. Sloan Kettering Inst. Cancer Research, 1947-49; physicist Nat. Cancer Inst. on assignment to Mass. Inst. Tech., 1949-53, on assignment to Donner Lab., U. Cal. at Berkeley, 1953-54; physicist Lab. Physiology, Nat. Cancer Inst., Bethesda, Md., 1954-67, sr. research physicist, 1967-69; sr. biophysicist biology dept. Brookhaven Nat. Lab., Upton, L.I., N.Y., 1969—. Mem. radiation study sect. NIH, 1962-66. Served with USNR, 1944-46. Recipient E.O. Lawrence award AEC, 1967; Superior Service award Dept. Health, Edn. and Welfare, 1969. Mem. A.A.A.S., Biophys. Soc., Radiation Research Soc. (council 1965-66, asso. editor jour. 1965-68), Tissue Culture Assn., Sigma Xi, Tau Beta Pi. Author monograph. Home: 42 Bellport Lane Bellport NY 11713 Office: Experimental Radiopathology Research Unit Med Research Council Hammersmith Hospital London W12 England

ELKINS, EARL COOK, physician; b. Spearfish, S.D., Sept. 19, 1904; s. William Scott and Harriet (Cook) E.; B.S., Buena Vista Coll., 1927, M.D., George Washington U., 1933; m. E. Elizabeth Williams, Jan. 25, 1935; children—Elizabeth Ann (Mrs. Ronald Rosanove), E. Robert, Thomas W., Joan G. Intern, Central Dispensary and Emergency Hosp., Washington, 1933- 34, asst. resident surgeon, 1934-35; fellow Mayo Found., Rochester, Minn., 1935-39, prof. phys. medicine and rehab., 1961-69; cons. sect. phys. medicine and rehab. Mayo Clinic, Rochester, 1939-69, head sect., 1958-65, sr. cons., 1965-69, emeritus, 1969—. Chmn., Am. Registry Phys. Therapists, 1953-68. Mem. Minn. Adv. council Hosp. Constrn., 1955—. Dir. Ability Bldg. Center, Inc., Rochester. Diplomate Am. Bd. Phys. Medicine and Rehab. (sec.-treas.). Fellow A.C.P.; mem. A.M.A., (sec. sect. phys. med. 1957-63), Am. Congress Phys. Medicine and Rehab. (pres. 1948-49; Distinguished Service Key award 1955), Am. Acad. Phys. Medicine and Rehab., Alumni Assn. Mayo Found., Sigma Xi. Author numerous articles in field. Home: 1131 7th St S W Rochester MN 55901 Office: First Nat Bank Bldg Rochester MN 55901

ELKINS, FRANCIS CLARK, educator; b. Scranton, Ark., Feb. 24, 1923; s. Frank and Auby (Moore) E.; B.A., State Coll. Ark., 1943; M.A., U. Ark., 1947; Ph.D., Syracuse U., 1953; m. Norma Trice, Aug. 18, 1946; 1 dau., Annette. From instr. to prof., chmn. div. social sci. Henderson State Coll., Arkadelphia, Ark., 1946-61; pres. Chadron (Neb.) State Coll., 1961-67, N.E. Mo. State Coll., Kirksville, 1967-69; coordinator Univ. Coll., Ark State U., 1969- 70, v.p. instr., 1970—. Mem. exec. com. Rocky Mountain Edn. Lab.; mem. Neb. Ednl. TV Council Higher Edn., 1966-67; adv. council Mo. 4-H Found. Served with USAAF, 1943-45. Decorated D.F.C., Air medal with four oak leaf clusters. Mem. Am. Assn. Colls. Tchr. Edn. (bd. dirs. 1968-71), Nat. Council Accreditation Tchr. Edn. (chmn. visitation and appraisal com. 1963-68), Asso. Orgns. Tchr. Edn. (adv. council), N.E.A. (life), Ark. Edn. Assn., Phi Delta Kappa, Kappa Delta Pi, Phi Alpha Theta, Alpha Chi, Sigma Tau Gamma, Sigma Nu. Methodist. Elk, Rotarian. Home: 1400 Linden Av Jonesboro AR 72401 Office: Arkansas State Univ State University AR 72467

ELKINS, JAMES ANDERSON, banker, lawyer b. Huntsville, Tex., Sept. 25, 1879; LL.B., U. Tex., 1901; m. Isabel Mitchell (dec.); children—W.S., James Anderson. Partner firm Vinson, Elkins, Searls & Connally, Houston; sr. chmn. bd. First City Nat. Bank, Houston. Mem. Am. Tex., Houston bar assns. Home: Warwick Hotel Houston TX 77001 Office: First City Nat Bank Bldg Houston TX 77001

ELKINS, JAMES ANDERSON, Jr., banker; b. Galveston, Tex., Mar. 24, 1919; s. James Anderson and Isabel (Mitchell) E.; grad. Hill Sch., 1937; B.A., Princeton, 1941; m. Margaret Wiess, Nov. 24, 1945; children—Elise, James Anderson III, Leslie K. With First City Nat. Bank, Houston, 1941—, v.p., 1946-50, pres., 1950, now chmn. bd.; dir. Cameron Iron Works, Inc., Rothschild Intercontinental Bank Eastern Airlines, Bank of Houston. Trustee Princeton, Tex. Children's Hosp., Baylor U. Coll. Medicine; bd. regents U. Houston. Episcopalian. Home: 101 Farish Circle Houston TX 77024 Office: First City Nat Bank Houston TX 77001

ELKINS, JAMES JAY, lawyer; b. N.Y.C., Nov. 10, 1930; s. Paul M. and Edith (Rose) E.; student Coll. City N.Y., 1948-50; LL.B., Bklyn. Law Sch., 1953; LL.M., N.Y. U., 1959; m. Harriet Bokowsky, Nov. 27, 1954; children—David Seth, Geri Lynn. Admitted to N.Y. bar, 1954; asso. atty. Mahoney, Spohr & Mahoney. N.Y.C., 1956-59; with Royal McBee Corp., 1959-65 (became Royal Typewriter Co., Inc. div. Litton Industries, Inc. 1965), sec., counsel, 1964-65; sec. Robotyper Corp., Henderson, N.C., 1964-65; div. counsel bus. equipment group Litton Industries Paramus, N.J., 1965-66, dir. adminstrn. Royfax div., 1966-67, mgr. operations, 1967-68; pres., dir. Internat. Tape Cartridge Corp., N.Y.C., 1968-69; asst. to pres. Zenith Labs, Inc., Northvale, N.J., 1970—. Vice chmn. Ramapo Com. Effective Town Planning, 1961-65; Republican committeeman, Ramapo, N.Y., 1962-69. Served with AUS, 1953-56. Mem. Am. Bar Assn., N.Y. County Lawyers Assn., Phi Epsilon Pi. Home: 12 Old Tappan Rd Old Tappan NJ 07675 Office: 850 3d Av New York City NY 10022

ELKINS, LLOYD EDWIN, petroleum engr.; b. Golden, Colo., Apr. 1, 1912; s. Edwin and Beulah M. (Feitch) E.; Petroleum Engr., Colo. Sch. Mines, 1934; Ph.D. in Sci., Coll. Ozarks; m. Virginia L. Crosby, May 27, 1934; children—Marylou, Barbara Lee, Lloyd Edwin. With Pan Am. Petroleum Corp., 1934—., successively field engr., petroleum engr. Tulsa gen. office, sr. petroleum engr., petroleum engring. supr., asst. chief prodn. engr., chief prodn. engr., chief engr. prodn. dept., prodn. research dir. oil and gas prodn., 1949-. Named to Engring. Hall of Fame, Okla. State U. 1961; recipient Distinguished Service medal Colo. Sch. Mines, 1961. Mem. Am. Assn. Petroleum Geologists, Am. Petroleum Inst. (chmn. mid-continent dist. div. prodn. 1948-49, chmn. adv. com fundamental research on occurrence and recovery petroleum 1951-52), Am. Inst. Mining, Metall, and Petroleum Engrs. (hon., v.p. 1953-59, pres. 1962; Anthony F. Lucas gold medal 1966), Tulsa Geol. Soc., Australian Inst. Mining and Metallurgy (hon.). Presbyn. Clubs: Engineers (pres. 1950-51), Petroleum, Tulsa Country (Tulsa). Contbr. articles to profl. jours. Home: 2806 E 27th St Tulsa OK 74114 Office: P O Box 591 Tulsa OK 74101

ELKINS, STANLEY MAURICE, historian, educator; b. Boston, Apr. 27, 1925; s. Frank and Frances (Reiner) E.; A.B., Harvard, 1949; M.A., Columbia, 1951, Ph.D., 1959; m. Dorothy Adele Lamken, June 22, 1947; children—Susan Roselyn, Robert Joel, Barbara Marion, Sara Ann. Tchr., Fieldston Sch., N.Y.C., 1951-54; asst. prof. history U. Chgo., 1955-60; faculty Smith Coll., Northampton, Mass., 1960—, prof. history 1964—. Served with AUS, 1943-46; Social Sci. Research Council fellow, 1963-64; Rockefeller fellow, 1954-55. Mem. New Eng. Am. Studies Assn. (pres. 1968-69). Author: Slavery: A Problem in American Institutional and Intellectual Life, 1959. Home: 17 Kensington Av Northampton MA 01060

ELKINS, WILSON HOMER, univ. pres; b. Medina, Tex., July 9, 1908; s. Will and Mae (Stevens) E.; B.A., A.M., U. Tex., 1932; Litt. B., Ph.D. (Rhodes Scholar), Oxford (Eng.) U., 1936; LL.D., Washington Coll. 1954, Johns Hopkins, 1955; m. Dorothy Blackburn, June 12, 1937 (dec. 1971); children—Carole Ann (Mrs. Edward G. Neal), Margaret Elise (Mrs. Charles T. Frost). Instr. history U. Tex., 1936-38; pres. San Angelo (Tex.) Jr. Coll., 1938-49; pres. Tex. Western Coll. (formerly Tex. Coll. Mines and Metallurgy), El Paso, 1949-54, U. Md., College Park, 1954—. Chmn. bd. dirs. Fed. Res. Bank of Richmond. Mem. steering com. Edn. Commn. of States; mem. So. Regional Edn. Bd, Washington Center Met. Studies. Mem. N.E.A., Md. Tchrs. Assn., Middle States Assn. Colls. and Secondaru Schs. (past pres.), Nat. Assn. State Univs. and Land-Grant Colls. (pres.), So. U. Conf. (pres.), Phi Beta Kappa, Sigma Nu, Omicron Delta Kappa, Alpha Phi Omega, Phi Alpha Theta, Tau Kappa Alpha. Episcopalian. Home: 3618 Campus Dr College Park MD 20740

ELKINTON, CHARLES MOORE, fgn. service Officer; b. Eau Claire, Wis., Aug. 13, 1909; s. Charles Holden and Alice Emma (Brown) E.; B.S., U. Wis., 1932, M.S., 1933, Ph.D., 1947; student U. Chgo., 1938-39; m. Cecelia Daniels, Aug. 19, 1933; children—Ann D. (Mrs. Stanley G. McClure), Charles Holden, Jane Wealthy. Prof. agrl. econs. Ia. State Coll., 1933-42; price exec. OPA, 1942-44; dep. chief Balkans mission UNRRA, 1944-45; econ. cons. Dept. Commerce. 1945-48; head dept. agrl. econs. Wash. State Coll., 1948-50, 51-52; chief program div. U.S. Regional Office, Paris, France, 1950-51, dir. food and agr. div., 1952-55; agrl. attache, Rio de Janeiro, Brazil and Tokyo, Japan, 1955-61; asst. adminstr. Fgn. Agrl. Service, Dept. Agr., 1962; food and agrl. Officer AID mission, Karachi, Pakistan, 1962-67, asso. dir. of mission, 1967. Mem. Pakistan Am. Cultural Center. Co-author: Financing Defense, 1942. Home: 530 S Orchard St Madison WI 53715 Office: US AID Karachi Pakistan

EL-KONY, MOHAMED AWAD, govt. ofcl. of UAR; b. Cairo, Egypt, Aug. 1, 1906; s. Awad and Xeinab (Tohdi) El-K.; grad. faculty law U. Cairo, 1928; m. Ateya Sobhi, 1941; children—Mona (Mrs. Mohamed Chadker), Hisham, Joined UAR Fgn. Service, 1929; sec. consulate, Rome, Italy, 1929-32; vice consul, Berlin, Germany, 1932-37; attache embassy, Washington, 1937-41; consul. Bombay, India, 1941-44; 2d sec. embassy, Moscow, USSR, 1944-47; chef de cabinet of under-sec. state fgn. affairs, Cairo, 1947-50; counsellor embassy, Washington, 1950-52; dir. polit. dept. Ministry Fgn. Affairs, Cairo, 1952-55; A.E. and P. to Moscow, 1955-61, to London, 1961-64, to UN, Washington, 1964; now minister of tourism. Office: UAR Mission to UN 900 Park Av New York City NY 10021

ELKS, HAZEL HULBERT, librarian; b. Franklin, N.J., June 16, 1916; d. Harry C. and Hazel (Ball) Hulbert; student Library Sch., Trenton State Coll., summer 1938; extension student Rutgers U.; m. David L. Elks, July 6, 1957. With Elizabeth (N.J.) Pub. Library, 1941—, librarian Monroe Av. br., 1946- 49, personnel dir., 1949-62, dir. library, 1962—. Trustee Elizabeth YWCA, 1960-62, Elizabeth League Women Voters, 1959-62, Mem. N.J. Library Assn. (chmn. fed. relations com. 1965—). Home: 1389 Vauxhall Rd Union, NJ 07083. Office: 11 S Broad St Elizabeth NJ 07202

ELKUS, RICHARD J., financial co. exec.; b. San Francisco, May 12, 1910; s. Eugene S. and Miriam (Meyerfeld) E.; m. Ruth Kahn, Mar. 23, 1933; children—Richard J., Peter K. Pres. Mangrum Holbrook & Elkus, San Francisco, 1939-48, First Nat. Bank San Mateo County, Redwood City, Cal., 1950-55; exec. v.p. Wells Fargo Bank, San Francisco, 1955-56, dir., 1955-60; pres. U.S. Leasing Corp., San Francisco, 1960-64, chmn. bd. dirs., 1964-69, now dir.; dir. Ampex Corp., Redwood City, Merc. Credit Co., London, Eng. Past mem. commn. legislation and taxation Cal. Bankers Assn. Chmn. San Francisco Bay Area council Sequia chpt. A.R.C., San Mateo County Charter Revision Commn.; bd. govs. Smaller War Plants Corp., World War II, also mem. Coordinating Council San Francisco, mem. Prodn. Urgency Com, Manpower Priorities Com. Bd. dirs. San Francisco Boy Scouts Am., Children's Health Council, Meml. Blood Bank, Vis. Nurses Assn., Coro Found., Golden Gate chpt. A.R.C.; pres. bd. dirs. Mental Research Inst.; bd. govs. United Crusade San Francisco. Mem. San Mateo County Hist. Soc. (dir.), Am. Horse Shows Assn. (dir.), Am. Hackney Horse Soc. Clubs: St. Francis Yacht, Family, Commonwealth (San Francisco); Sequoia (pres.) (Redwood City); Los Altos Hunt (Woodside, Cal.). Author: Alamos: A Philosophy in living, 1965. Office: P O Box 432 Redwood City CA 94064

ELLEDGE, SCOTT BOWEN, educator; b. Pitts., Jan. 7, 1914; s. Harvey Gerald and Eva (Bowen) E.; A.B., Oberlin Coll., 1935; A.M., Cornell U., 1936, Ph.D., 1941; m. Liane von Krolikiewicz, Feb. 15, 1950. Instr. English, Purdue U., 1936-38, 39-40, Cornell U., 1941-45, Harvard, 1945-47; asso. prof. English, Carleton Coll., Northfield, Minn., 1947-52, chmn. dept., 1951-62, prof., 1952-62; prof. English, Cornell U., Ithaca, N.Y., 1962—; co-founder Salzburg (Austria) Seminar in Am. Studies, 1947. Me. Am. Assn. U. Profs., Modern Lang. Assn., Phi Kappa Phi. Editor; Eighteenth Century Critical Essays, 1961; The Continental Model, 1960; Lycidas (Milton), 1966. Contbr. articles to ednl. jours. Home: 107 Overlook Rd Ithaca, NY

ELLEFSON, BENNETT STANLEY, engring. adminstr.; b. Canby, Minn., Jan. 10, 1911; s. Halvor S. and Sarah (Lewison) E.; A.B., St. Olaf Coll., 1932; M.S., U. Minn., 1933; student N.Y.U. 1933-34; Ph.D., Pa. State U., 1937; m. Dorothea Kinter, Nov. 25, 1948; children—Dana, Kristi Gayle. Teaching fellow N.Y.U., 1933- 34; research asst. Pa. State U., 1934-37; with Sylvania Electric Products, Inc., Bayside, N.Y., 1937-60, successively research chemist, asst. to v.p. engring., dir. central engring. labs., dir. research, 1937- 56, v.p. engring and research, 1956-59, v.p. tech. planning, 1959- 60; v.p. Gen. Telephone and Electronics Labs., Inc., 1960—. Fellow I.E.E.E., A.A.A.S.; mem. Am. Chem. Soc., Am. Ceramic Soc. Home: 214-04 33d Rd Bayside NY 11361 Office: 730 3d Av New York City NY 10017

ELLEMAN, JAMES DAVIS, comml. banker; b. Troy, O., Dec. 24, 1920; s. Ernest Zeller and Jane (Davis) E.; A.B., Dartmouth, 1943; m. Shirley Nelson, Sept. 20, 1952; children—Peter N., Gary D., Melinda Ann. Div. treas. Aluminum Co. Am., Pitts., Detroit, 1947-50; v.p. Cham. Bank N.Y., Trust Co., N.Y.C., 1951-64; pres. Trust Co. Nat. Bank, Morristown, N.J., 1964-69; chmn., chief exec. officer Am. Nat. Bank & Trust of N.J., Morristown, 1969—; mem. adv. bd. N.J. 2d Fed. Res. Dist.; dir. Suburban Propane Gas Co., Automatic Switch Corp. Bd. dirs. YMCA, United Fund Morris County, Boys Club Am., Jr. Achievement; trustee Morristown Meml. Hosp.; mem. alumni council* Dartmouth. Served with USNR, 1943-46. Mem. Sphinx, Am. (exec. council), N.J., (exec. com.), Morris County (pres.), bankers assns., Beta Theta Pi. Presbyn. Clubs: Morris County Golf (Convent Station, N.J.), Morristown, Roxciticus Golf (Mendham); Skytop (Pa.); Dartmouth of New York. Home: Colville Dr Medham NJ 07945 Office: 225 South St Morristown NJ 07960

ELLENBERGER, FREDERICK RAYMOND, machinery mfg. co. exec.; b. Buffalo, Jan. 18, 1916; s. Fred and Caroline (Oberli) I.; B.S. in Mech. Engring., Newark Coll. Engring., 1947; m. Anne Weidl, Nov. 30, 1951. With Worthington Corp., Harrison, N.J., 1938—, v.p., gen. mgr. Worthington (Can.) Ltd., 1956-60, v.p., group exec. internat. parent corp., 1961-64, v.p. of mfg., 1965-68, v.p. operations, 1969—. Registered profl. engr., Ont. Mem. Am. Soc. M.E., Assn. Profl. Engrs. Ont. (Can.), Am. Mgmt. Assn. Home: 41 Elm St Morristown NJ Office: 401 Worthington Av Harrison NJ 07029

ELLENBOGEN, BERT L., educator; b. N.Y.C., July 5, 1917; s. A. Eugene and Carrie (Spier) E.; B.A., U. Wis., 1948, M.A., 1950, Ph.D., 1957; m. Ruth Hill, Aug. 2, 1945; 1 dau., Barbara. Asst. prof., then asso. prof. rural sociology Cornell U., 1955-66; vis. prof. Inst. Internat. Studies, U. Cal. at Sao Paulo, Brazil, 1962-64; prof. sociology, chmn. Latin Am. Studies Program, U. Minn., 1966-68; prof. sociology and anthropology, chmn. dept. Colo. State U., 1968—; cons. in field. dir. Cornell health survey NIH, 1958-66, mem. adv. bd. Mid-Western Inst. Comparative Sociology, 1967-68. Bd. dirs. Empire State Health Council, 1959-66. Served with USAAF, 1942-45. Fellow Am. Sociol. Assn.; mem. Rural Sociol. Soc. (chmn. arrangements com. Denver 1970), Soc. Applied Anthropology, Am. Assn. U. Profs. Author: Social and Economic Problems of the Venezuelan Andes, Vol. 1, 1955, Vol. 11, 1956; also chpts. in books, articles. Editor: Perspectives of Change and Development: The Highland Areas of Latin America, 1970; mng. editor Jour. Rural Sociology, 1960-61; asso. dir. Sociologia, 1962-64. Home: 1113 Ellis St Fort Collins CO 80521

ELLENBOGEN, GLADYS B., educator, economist; b. N.Y.C., Feb. 4, 1925; d. Maxim and Beatrice Birnkrant; B.A., Hunter Coll., 1945; M.A., Yale, 1946; Ph.D., U. Wis., 1954; m. Jack Ellenbogen, May 5, 1950; 1 son, Benjamin G. Faculty, Montclair State Coll., Upper Montclair, N.J., 1965—, prof. econs., 1968—; cons. in pensions and health ins., 1960—. Mem. Am. Pub. Health Assn., Am. Econ. Assn., Gerontological Soc., Am. Assn. U. Women. Home: 2 Greenlea Ct Westport CT 06880 Office: Montclair State Coll Dept Econs Upper Montclair NJ 07043

ELLENDER, ALLEN JOSEPH, U.S. senator; b. Montegut, La., Sept. 24, 1890; s. Wallace Richard and Victoria (Javaux) E.; Tulane U., 1913; A.M. (hon.), St. Aloysius Coll., New Orleans; m. Helen Calhoun Donnelly, Mar. 19, 1917 (dec. 1949); 1 son, Allen Joseph. Admitted to La. bar, 1913; city atty., Houma, La., 1913-15; dist. atty. Terrebonne Parish, 1915-16, del. Constl. Conv. of La., 1921; mem. La State Ho. of Reps., 1924-36, floor leader, 1928-32, speaker 1932- 36; mem. U.S. Senate from La., 1937—, pres. protempore, 1971—, also chmn. appropriations com. Dem. nat. committeeman from La., 1939-40. Address: Senate Office Bldg Washington DC 20510

ELLENDER, RAPHAEL THEODORE, artist; b. N.Y.C., Feb. 22, 1906; s. Theodore and Ada (Miller) E.; B.A. (N.Y. State Regents Scholar), Columbia, 1926, student Tchrs. Coll., also Sch. Architecture, 1924-26; student Academie Colerossie, Paris, France, 1929, N.A.D., 1938, Art Students League (Saltus Scholar), 1926-27, 37-43. Advt. art dir. for N.Y.C. dept. stores, advt. agys., 1926-46; cons. art dir., 1947-57; instr. drawing and painting Workshop Sch. of Art, N.Y.C., 1947-49, Am. Art Sch., N.Y.C., 1950, Art Students League, 1950, 61, N.Y.U., 1958-64. Exhibited one-man show at Pietrantonio Galleries, N.Y.C., 1970; group exhbns. include Milch Gallery, 1941-47, Kraushaar Gallery, 1940- 42, Portraits, Inc., 1940-45, Asso. Am. Artists, 1938-40; jury shows include N.A.D., 1960, Met. Mus. Art, 1943, Bklyn. Mus. Art, 1943, Am. Water Color Soc., 1925, 39-44, Corcoran Gallery Art, 1939, Pa. Acad. Fine Arts, 1938, Chgo. Art Inst., 1939, Allied Artists, 1961, 63, 70; portrait commns. include Bernard F. Gimbel, Dr. John H. Garlock, Harold Rome, William Kamm. Recipient Benjamin Altman prize for landscape N.A.D., 1960. Life mem. Art Students League, Allied Artists Am. (Famous Artists Sch. prize 1964, honorable mention 1970). Clubs: Salmagundi, Manhattan Chess (N.Y.C.). Author: Basic Drawing, 1964. Address: 338 W 72d St New York City, NY 10023.

ELLENTUCK, ERIK, educator; b. N.Y.C., May 13, 1934; s. David and Lillian (Goldstein) E.; B.A., N.Y. U., 1956; Ph.D., U. Cal., Berkeley, 1962; m. Midori Ishii, Mar. 11, 1969. With Shell Devel. Co., 1962, IBM, 1963; NSF and Inst. fellows Inst. Advanced Study, Princeton, 1963, 64, 71; prof. math. Rutgers U., New Brunswick, N.J., 1965—; prof. math. Kyoto U., 1968. N.J. Research Council Faculty fellow, 1968, 71. Recipient Founders Day award N.Y. U., 1957. Mem. Assn. for Symbolic Logic, Am. Math. Soc., Phi Beta Kappa, Pi Mu Epsilon, Sigma Pi Sigma, Beta Lambda Sigma. Home: 21 Hardin Rd Princeton NJ 08540

ELLER, CHARLES HOWE, physician; b. Bloomington, Ind., June 5, 1904; s. Charles Asbury and Alice Belle (Howe) E.; A.B., Stanford, 1927; M.D., Colo. U., 1930; Dr. P.H., Johns Hopkins, 1934; m. Jacqueline Marie Rousseau, Dec. 1933; children—Patricia Ann, Mary Jacqueline. Health officer Valencia and Bernalillo countries, N.M., 1931-34; health officer, Charlottesville, Va., 1934-35; asso. prof. preventive medicine U. Va. Med. Sch., 1934-35; asst. dir., later dir. rural health Va. Health Dept., 1935-37; dir. Eastern health dist., Balt., 1937-46; asso. prof. pub. health adminstrn. Johns Hopkins Sch. Hygiene, 1937-46; dir. health, Richmond, Va., 1946- 49, Louisville, also Jefferson County, Ky., 1949-55; asso. prof. preventive medicine Med. Coll. Va., 1946-49; prof., chmn. dept. community health U. Louisville, 1949-59; commr. health, St. Louis County, Mo., 1959—; prof. pub. health Washington U. Sch. Medicine, 1959—. Bd. dirs. Louisville Rehab. Center. Cons. NIH, 1951-55, 57-59; spl. cons. commn. Research Assos., N.Y.C., 1955—; former asso. area med. dir. United Mine Workers's Welfare and Retirement Fund; cons. preventive medicine, Ft. Knox, 1958; mem. task force Nat. Commn. Community Health Services, 1963; mem. Mo. Adv. Council for Comprehensive Health Planning, 1968—. Diplomate American Bd. Preventive Medicine and Pub. Health. Fellow Am. Pub. Health Assn. (gov. 1962-65 67-70, exec. bd. 1970—), Am. Coll. Preventative Medicine: mem. Am., Mo. med. assns., St. Louis County Med. Soc. (past pres.), Mo. Pub. Health Assn. (past pres.). Address: 1408 Fawn Valley Rd St. Louis, MO 63131.

ELLER, ERNEST MCNEILL, ret. naval officer; b. Marion, Va., Jan. 23, 1903; s. Edward Everett and Elizabeth (McNeill) E.; B.S., U.S. Naval Acad., 1925; A.M., George Washington University, 1934; L.H.D., Moravian College, 1958; m. Agnes Fogle Pfohl, May 27, 1926; children—Peter McNeill, John Christian. Commd. ensign U.S. Navy, 1925, advanced through grades to rear adm., 1954; sea duty, 1925-32, submarine duty, 1927-29; tchr. English and history U.S. Naval Acad., 1932-35; headed tng. sch., U.S.S. Utah, 1935-38; tchr. history and gunnery U.S. Naval Acad., 1938-40; naval observer for anti-aircraft in British fleet, 1940-41; gunnery Officer U.S.S. Saratoga, 1941-42; duty in gunnery and tng. Admiral Nimitz staff, 1942-45; comdr. assault transport, 1945; pub. information duty Navy Dept., 1946-48; Nat. War Coll., 1948-49; staff Joint Chiefs of Staff, 1949-50; comdr. Middle East Force, 1950-51; service U.S.S. Albany, 1951-52; Office comdr. naval operations, 1952-54; ret., 1954; dir. engring, Bucknell (Pa.) U., 1955-56, also mem. engring. adv. com., returned to active duty as dir. naval history Navy Dept., 1956-70. Past mem. President's Disarmament Study Com., v.p. Naval Hist. Found. Decorated Legion of Merit (2) (U.S.); Merito Tamandari (Brazil); recipient Alfred Thayer Mahan award Navy League U.S., 1967. Mem. U.S. Naval Inst., Am. Ordnance Assn., Nat. (trustee), Am., Va. (exec. com), N.C., Md., Mass., hist. socs. Democrat. Baptist. Clubs: Army and Navy (Washington); New Yrok Yacht. Author: Houses of Peace; Comenius School of Infancy; Salem: Star and Dawn; Soviet Sea Challenge, 1971; also naval textbooks, tech. mans., various naval hist. works; co-author; The Soviet Navy, 1958. Contbr. to Nat. Geog., other pubs.; contbr. U.S. Naval Inst. Proc. (recipient 1st prize for essays, 1932, 42, 50). Home: 2 Kent Rd Wardour Annapolis MD 21401

ELLER, JAMES GERALD, univ. dean; b. Robbinsville, N.C., Jan. 30, 1921; s. John Wesley and Lillie (Rogers) E.; B.S., Western Carolina U., 1943; Ph.D., U.N.C., 1963; M. Juanita Ethel Fisher, Nov. 6, 1943; children-Jerri Lee (Mrs. Tyson Moore Cathey), Steven Fisher, Jeanne Marie. Mem. faculty Western Carolina U., Cullowhee, N.C., 1947—, prof. zoology, 1963—, dean sch. Arts and Scis., 1967—; tchr. zoology U.N.C. at Chapel Hill, summers 1960-63. Served with USNR, World War II. Mem. A.A.A.S., N.C. Acad. Sci., Am. Conf. Acad. Deans, Sigma Xi. Democrat. Methodist. Rotarian. Home: Rt 67 Box 5N Cullowhee NC 28723

ELLER, JOHN CLINTON, assn. exec.; b. Salem, Va., Sept. 25, 1916; s. Christian Emery and Rebecca Martha (Henry) E.; A.B., Bridgewater (Va.) Coll., 1941; B.D., Bethany Theol. Sem., 1948; M.S. in Hosp. Adminstrn., Northwestern U., 1952; m. Jessie Mae Conner, June 9, 1943; children—John Thomas, Michael Conner. Tchr., Fincastle, Va., 1939-40; prin. Cloverdale (Va.) Elementary Sch., 1941-42; ordained to ministry Ch. of Brethren, 1936; pastor in Crab Orchard, W.Va., 1942-44; with Bethany Brethren Hosp., Chgo., 1945-66, chaplain, 1945-50, asst. adminstr., 1950-52, adminstr., 1952-64, exec. dir., 1964-66; exec. dir. Am. Protestant Hosp. Assn., Chgo., 1966—. Bd. dirs. Chgo. Hosp. Council, 1954-66, pres., 1959-61; bd. dirs. Ill. Hosp. Assn., 1962-65, Sears, Roebuck YMCA, Chgo., 1958-66. Mem. Am. Protestant Hosp. Assn. (dir. 1958, pres. 1965), Am. Coll. Hosp. Adminstrs., Brethren Health and Welfare Assn. (pres. 1954-57, 68-69, sec. 1964-66), Assn. for Clin. Pastoral Edn., Am. Soc. Assn. Execs., Internat. Hosp. Fedn., Am. Pub. Health Assn., Am. Hosp. Assn., Nat. Geog. Soc., Am. Audubon Soc., Nat. Parks Assn., Nat. Wildlife Fedn. Club: Torch. Home: 742 S Lombard Av Lombard IL 60148 Office: 840 N Lake Shore Dr Chicago IL 60611

ELLER, ROBERT, business exec. Sec., Daring and Armstrong, Inc., Detroit. Office: 2041 Fenkell Av Detroit MI 48238*

ELLERT, FREDERICK CHARLES, educator; b. Holyoke, Mass., Aug. 7, 1905; s. Rudolf and Maria (Schwemberger) E.; B.A., U. Mass., 1930; postgrad. U. Heidelberg (Germany), summer 1930, Middlebury (Vt.) Coll., summer 1933, Columbia, summer 1935; M.A., Amherst Coll., 1943; Ph.D., Stanford, 1956; m. Isadora Hatch, July 18, 1936. Mem. faculty U. Mass., 1930—, prof. German, 1951-70, prof. emeritus, 1970—, chmn. dept., 1951-57, chmn. dept. German-Russian, 1957-66; founder, Mass. Rev., editor, 1959-61, co-editor, 1961-63, contbg. editor, 1963—, initiator co-organizer U. Mass. Atlantic Studies Center, Freiburg, Germany, lectr. German lit. at Center, 1966-67. Mem. adv. council Hampshire Coll., 1965-66. Mem. Am. Assn. U. Profs., Modern Lang. Assn., Am. Assn. Tchrs. German, Phi Kappa Phi. Author: (with Peter Heller) German One: For Laboratory and Classroom, 1962; Franz Werfel's Great Dilemma; also chpt. in book, articles. Editorial cons. Britannica World Language Dictionary, 1953-55. Home: 71 Blue Hills Rd Amherst MA 01002

ELLIKER, PAUL R., educator; b. LaCrosse, Wis., Feb. 12, 1911; s. Gottfried Daniel and Emilie (Muehlméier) E.; B.S., U. Wis., 1934, M.S., 1935; Ph.D., 1937; m. Anne Leone Roets. Aug. 27, 1938; children—David Karl, Donald Paul, Susan Elizabeth. Instr. bacteriology U. Wis., 1937-38, 39-40; indsl. fellow food microbiology U. Md., 1938-39; asst., then asso. prof. dairy microbiology Purdue U., 1940-43, 45-47; prof. microbiology Ore. State U., 1947—, chmn. dept. microbiology and microbiologist in charge Ore. Agrl. Expt. Sta., 1952—. Dairy ambassador Dairy Soc. Internat.; tech. dir. U.S.A. exhibit, Spain Internat. Trade Fair, Madrid, 1959; ofcl. U.S. del. Internat. Dairy Congress, 1962, 66. Served to capt., San. Corps AUS, 1943-45. Recipient ann. Ore. State U. All Campus research award Sigma Xi, 1952; Borden award for dairy mfg. research, 1954. Mem. Am. Dairy Sci. Assn. (dir.), Soc. Am. Microbiologists, Acad. Microbiology, Inst. Food Tech., Internat. Assn. Milk, Food and Environmental Sanitarians (pres. 1966-67), Sigma Xi, Phi Sigma, Alpha Zeta, Phi Tau Sigma. Conglist. Author: Practical Dairy Bacteriology, 1949. Asso. editor Jour. of Dairy Sci. Home: 1110 NW Fillmore Av Corvallis OR 97330

ELLIMAN, DONALD MACKAY, banker; b. N.Y.C., Mar. 2, 1912; s. Roland Franklin and Lois (Mackay) E.; grad. Choate Sch., 1930; student Yale, 1930-33; m. Grace W. Friberg, May 17, 1939; children—Dale, Donald. Trainee clk. Corn Exchange Bank Trust Co., 1933-37, asst. mgr. bus. development, 1937-39, asst. sec., 1939-45, asst. v.p., 1945-47, v.p., 1947-54; v.p. Chem. Corn Exchange Bank, 1954-55, County Trust Co., White Plains, N.Y., 1955-56; v.p. Bank of N.Y., 1956-57, exec. v.p., 1957, pres., 1957-61, also trustee; adminstrv. v.p. Marine Midland Trust Co. N.Y., 1962-64; exec. v.p. Marine Midland Bank Co. N.Y., 1964—; trustee Union Dime Savs. Bank N.Y.C.; dir. Great West Life Assurance Co. (Winnipeg, Can.). Trustee, Greenwood Cemetery, Bklyn.; treas. Village of Bronxville, 1956-57. trustee, 1957-60; mem. adv. bd. Salvation Army: v.p. Community Welfare Fund, Bronxville, 1954; chmn., dir. United Hosp. Fund. Served from lt. (j.g.) to lt. comdr., USNR, 1942-45, Mem. N.Y. C. of C. (v.p., exec. com.), Assn. Res. City Bankers, New Eng. Soc., Newcomen Soc. Clubs: St. Andrews Golf; New York Yacht; American Yacht, Wall Street, Bond, Downtown Assn. (N.Y.C.) Home: 51 Valley Rd Bronxville NY 10708 Office: 140 Broadway New York City NY 10015

ELLIMAN, DOUGLAS LUDLOW, former real estate broker; b. Flushing, N.Y., May 24, 1882; s. William and Mary Lawrence (Bogert) E.; student Berkeley (N.Y.) Sch., 1897-98, Cutler (N.Y.) Sch., 1898-99; m. Theodora Trowbridge, Oct. 20, 1900; children—Douglas Trowbridge, George Trowbridge, Ludlow; m. 2d, Katherine Scales Moon, Dec. 9, 1929; children—Mary Lawrence, Edward Scales. Clk., Vermilye & Co., bankers, 1899-1903; broker and officer Pease & Elliamn, 1903-11; organized Douglas L. Elliman & Co., Inc., 1911, hon. chmn. bd., dir., 1964—; dir. Underhill Soc., 58th and Park Av., Inc.; trustee emeritus Greenwich Savs. Bank. Served as ensign USNRF, 1918. Mem. St. Nicholas Soc., St. George Soc., Real Estate Bd. N.Y. (pres. 1935), N.Y. Bldg. Congress (life), Nat. Assn. Real Estate Bds., Pilgrims U.S., Mil. Order World Wars, USNR Officers Assn., Am. Legion, Navy Leagues U.S. (dir.). Clubs: Racquet and Tennis, Piping Rock, numerous others. Home: 485 Park Av New York City NY 10022

ELLIMAN, GEORGE TROWBRIDGE, mgmt. cons.; b. N.Y.C., Dec. 17, 1905; s. Douglas Ludlow and Theodora Polhemus (Trowbridge) E.; grad. St. Paul's Sch., 1923; A.B. magna cum laude, Princeton, 1928; grad. Nat. War Coll., 1958; m. Natica De Acosta, June 4, 1931; 1 son, Peter Bogert. With Doubleday, Doran & Co., 1928-33; advt. mgr. Sat. Rev. Lit., 1933-36; with Butler & Baldwin, real estate, N.Y.C., 1936-39; with U.S. Govt. agys. engaged in def. and war work, 1939-42; exec. dir. Office Fgn. Liquidation, State Dept., 1945-48; asst. dir. tech. assistance div. ECA, 1948-51; dir. fgn. div. NPA, 1951-52; adviser fgn. activities Dept. Commerce, 1952-59; joined U.S. fgn. service, 1959; comml. attache Am. embassy, Rome, Italy, 1959-64; dir. internat. activities staff Bus. and Def. Services Adminstrn. U.S. Dept. Commerce, 1964-69, dir. U.S. mission on trade and indsl. devel. to Ireland, Portugal, 1966-67, spl. asst. ILO affairs, also mem. U.S. delegation to ILO, 1967-69, mem. Fgn. Service selection bd., 1969; self-employed cons. mgmt., Middleburg, Va., 1969—. Served to lt. comdr. USNR, 1942-45. Address: Middleburg VA 22117

ELLINGHAUS, WILLIAM M., communications exec; b. Balt., Apr. 19, 1922; grad. high sch.; m. Erlaine Dietrich, May 30, 1942; children—Marcia A., Eric J., Douglas A., Barbara E., Raymond W., Mark D., Christopher C., Jonathan Paul. With Bell System, 1940—, comml. mgr. Chesapeake & Potomac Telephone Co. Md., Balt., 1950-51, pub. office mgr. Chesapeake & Potomac Telephone Co. Va., Norfolk, 1951-52, dist. comml. mgr., Culpeper, 1952-55, gen. comml. supr. Chesapeake & Potomac Telephone Co. W.Va., Charleston, 1955-57, div. comml. mgr., 1957, gen. accounting supr., 1957-58, comptroller, 1958-60, v.p., dir., 1960-62, v.p. accounts Chesapeake & Potomac Telephone Cos., Washington, 1962, v.p. personnel, 1962-65; v.p. planning Am. Tel. & Tel. Co., N.Y.C., 1965-66, asst. v.p. marketing and rate plans, 1967-70, exec. v.p., 1970—; pres., dir. N.Y. Telephone Co., 1970—; dir. Bankers Trust Co., J.C. Penney Co., Inc., Ball Corp. Mem. adv. council Coll. Bus. Adminstrn., U. Notre Dame; mem. Steering Com. Coalition Jobs, Mayor N.Y.C. Com. Enviroment. Bd. dirs. United Fund Greater N.Y., Econ. Devel. Council N.Y.C. Served with USNR, 1943- 45. Mem. Am. Soc. Corp. Execs., N.Y.C. of C. Club: Economic (N.Y.C.). Home: 55 Crows Nest Rd Bronxville NY 10708 Office: 140 West St New York City NY 10007

ELLINGSON, HAROLD VICTOR, physician, b. Parker, Ida., Feb. 26, 1913; s. Ole and Katherine (Friel) E.; B.S., U. Ida., 1935; M.S., U. Wis., 1936, Ph.D., 1939, M.D., 1941; M.P.H., Johns Hopkins, 1946; m. Frances J. Kadulski, Nov. 18, 1944. Intern Wis. Gen. Hosp., Madison, 1941-42; commd. 1st lt. U.S. Army, 1942; trans. to USAF, 1949; advanced through grades to col., 1956; comdr. USAF Med. Service Sch., 1959-62; comdr. Sch. Aerospace Medicine, 1963-66; ret., 1966; prof., chmn. dept. preventive medicine Ohio State U., Columbus, 1966—. Decorated Legion of Merit with oak leaf cluster, Air medal. Diplomate Am. Bd. Preventive Medicine, 1966—. Fellow Am. Coll. Physicians; mem. Am. Coll. Preventive Medicine (past pres.), Aerospace Med. Assn., A.M.A. (past sect. chmn.), Internat. Acad. Aviation and Space Medicine, Am. Inst. Aeros. and Astronautics, Am. Pub. Health Assn., Phi Beta Kappa, Sigma Xi, Sigma Chi. Contbr. to Cecil- Loeb Textbook of Medicine, 1970. Contbr. articles profl. jours. Home: 2288 Johnston Rd Columbus OH 43221 Office: 410 W 10th Av Columbus OH 43210

ELLINGSON, MARK, educator; b. Magrath, Alta., Can. (parents American citizens), June 5, 1904; s. Ole and Katherine (Friel) E.; Asso. in Edn., Ida. State Univ., 1924; A.B., Gooding Coll. (Ida.), 1926; M.A., U. Rochester, 1930, LL.D., 1951; Ph.D., Ohio State U., 1936; m. Marcia Cooke Randall, July 12, 1934; children—Laura (Mrs. Leslie V. Chapmen), Louise (Mrs. Roger H. Kuite), Karen (Mrs. Harry P. Trueheart Ill) Jon Eric. Instr. econs. Rochester Inst. Tech., 1926, supr., photographic tech., 1930-36, pres. 1936-70; chmn. bd. community Sav. Bank Rochester (N.Y.), 1954-64, 1969—, also trustee. Mem. N.Y. State Commn. Ind. Colls. and Univs. Trustee Rochester Bur. Municipal Research, now chmn. bd.; trustee George Eastman House. Recipient Rochester's Distinguished Salesman of Year award, 1964; Rochester Rotary award, 1965; Lester P. Slade Civic award Real Estate Board Rochester, 1968; fellow Rochester Mus., 1961. Mem. Printing Industry Assn. Rochester (hon.), Rochester C. of C. (pres. 1946, adv. bd.), Am. Craftmen's Council (trustee), Am. Ednl. Research Assn., Nat. Soc. for Study Edn., Rochester Mus. Assn. (acad. council), Rochester Engring Soc., Am. Ordnance Assn. (dir. Empire post, pres. 1960-62), Am. Soc. Engring. Edn., N.E.A., Printing Industries N.J. (Hon.), Newark Club Printing House Craftsmen (hon. mem.), Newcomen Soc. Republican. Rotarian (pres. 1940). Club: Genesee Valley (Rochester). Author chpts. and sects. books, articles, papers. Address: 50 Main St West Rochester NY 14614

ELLINGSON, STEVEN, newspaper exec.; b. Havana, N.D., Oct. 6, 1910; s. Stephen and Florence (Young) E.; B.S., U. Minn., 1932; m. Lois Lawson, Feb. 22, 1958. Credit mgr. Bullicks, Los Angeles, 1935-41; spl. investigator Western Def. Command, Fourth Army, 1941-42; syndicated newspaper columnist, 1942—; pres. U-B Newspaper Syndicate, Van Nuys, Cal., 1947—. Bd. dirs. Valley Youth Found. Mem. Los Angeles Press Club, Phi Sigma Kappa. Mason. Home: 15155 Saticoy St Van Nuys CA 91405 Office: 15241 Stagg St Van Nuys CA 91409

ELLINGTON, BUFORD, gov. Tenn.; b. Holmes County, Miss., June 27, 1907; s. Abner E. and Cora (Grantham) E.; m. Catherine Cheek, Dec. 20, 1929; children—John Earl, Ann. Mgr. Tenn. Farm Bur. Ins. Service, 1949-51; commr. agr., Tenn., 1953-58; gov. Tenn., 1959-63, 67—. Vice pres. L. & N. R.R., 1963-64; dir. Office Emergency Planning, 1965-66. Chmn. So. Regional Edn. Bd., 1961, So. Gov.'s Conf., 1961-62; mem. exec. com. Nat. Gov.'s Conf., 1961-62, now chmn.; pres. Council State Govts.; chmn. Cordell Hull Found.; mem. Nat. Adv. Council Econ. Planning. Mem. nat. council Boy Scouts Am. Bd. dirs. Bill Wilkerson Speech and Hearing Center. Trustee George Peabody Coll. for Tchrs., U. Tenn., Rust Coll. Mem. Millsaps Coll. Alumni Assn. (dir. Alpha Zeta, hon.), Alpha Gamma Rho, Lambda Chi Alpha, Delta Kappa. Methodist, Mason (Shriner). Home: Curtiswood Lane Nashville TN 37203 Office: State Capitol Nashville TN 37203

ELLINGTON, EDWARD KENNEDY, Duke, composer, arranger; b. Washington, Apr. 29, 1899; student pub. schs. Washington; studied music with Henry Grant; hon. degrees Wilberforce U., 1949, Milton Coll., 1964, Coll. Arts and Crafts, 1966, Morgan State, 1967, Yale, 1967; m. Edna Thompson, 1918. First profl. appearance as jazz player, 1916, N.Y.C., 1922; engaged Cotton Club, N.Y.C., 1927-32; toured Europe, 1933, 50, 58, 60, 62, 64, 65, 69, 70, Eng. and France, 1948, Japan, 1964, 1966, 70, also Latin America, 1968, Far East and Australia, 1970; appeared ann. concerts Carnegie Hall, 1943-50, Met. Opera House 1951; appeared motion picture Check and Double Check, 1930; compositions and recordings include Mood Indigo, Solitude, Sophisticated Lady, Caravan, I Let a Song Go Out of My Heart, Do Nothing Till You Hear From Me, Don't Get Around Much Any More, In a Sentimental Mood, Black and Tan Fantasy, Creole Love Call; composed motion picture scores for Anatomy of a Murder, Paris Blues, Assault on a Queen, Change of Mind; pioneered in wordless use of voice as mus. instrument in orchestration, also use of miniature concerto form in bldg. jazz arrangements around a soloist; pioneered in extended orchestral jazz compositions and suites including Reminiscing in Tempo, 1935, Black, Brown and Beige (a tone parallel to the history of the American Negro), 1943, New World A-Coming, 1945, Liberian Suite, 1948, Harlem, 1950, Suite Thursday, 1960, Latin American Suite, 1968, New Orleans Suite, 1970; conceived and wrote A Concert of Sacred Music, premiered Grace Cathedral San Francisco, 1965, Cathedral Ch. St. John the Divine, N.Y.C., 1968; ballet score The River for Am. Theater Ballet, 1970. Recipient numerous mag. poll awards including readers poll Down Beat, 1967, critics poll, 1968, 69, 70; Internat. Jazz Critics Poll, 1968, 69, 70; Grammy Nat. Acad. Rec. Arts and Scis., 1967. Spingarn medals N.A.A.C.P., 1959; Medal of Freedom presented by Pres. Nixon on 70th birthday, 1969. Address: 116 Central Park S New York City NY 10019

ELLINGTON, JESSE THOMPSON, Jr., advt. exec.; b. Phila., Sept. 21, 1931; s. Jesse Thompson and Elizabeth (Turner) E.; student U. Va., 1953; m. Nancy Cabell Meredith, Aug. 18, 1959; children—Elizabeth Cabell, Jesse Thompson III, Keren Meredith. With Ellington & Co., advt., N.Y.C., 1953-63, account exec., 1962-63; with Young & Rubicam, Inc., 1963—, sr. v.p., mgr. Western operations, 1970—. Mem. Alpha Tau Omega. Republican. Club: Jonathan (Los Angeles). Home: 1791 Virginia Rd San Marino CA 91108 Office: 3435 Wilshire Blvd Los Angeles CA 90005

ELLINGTON, THOMAS KENNETH, trade assn. exec.; b. Chgo., Nov. 3, 1909; s. William Kenneth and Catharine Agnes (Flannery) E.; grad. Am. Inst. Banking, 1931, Advanced Mgmt. Program, Harvard, 1951; m. Harriet Bradbury, July 23, 1937 (dec. 1969). 1 son, Richard V. Reporter, commentator Sta. WFBM, Indpls., 1934- 37; news, spl. events dir. CBS, Chgo., 1937-41; radio dir. Aero C. of C., Washington , 1941-43; sec. Aircraft War Prodn. Council East Coast, Inc., N.Y.C., 1943-45; pub. relations cons. Hill & Knowlton, N.Y.C., 1945; dir. pub. relations Republic Aviation Corp., Farmingdale, N.Y., 1945-64, v.p., 1955-64, ret., 1964; Western mgr. Aerospace Industries Assn. Am., Inc., Los Angeles, 1965-; cons. Office Sec. USAF, 1959-63. V.p. Long Island Fund; pres. L.I. Assn., 1963-65. Trustee, chmn. bus. adv. com., also honorary fellow Adelphi Coll. Recipient of Distingusidhed Service citation Adelphi Coll., 1953, Medal of Merit, Air Force Assn., 1958. Mem. Aerospace Industries Assn. (past chmn. nat. pub. relations adv. com. Am.), Nat. Aero. Assn. (nat. v.p. 1965—), Am. Australian Assn. (bd. dirs.), Los Angeles C. of C. (aerospace adv. bd.), Newcomen Soc., Air Force Assn. (nat. dir.). Clubs: Nat. Press (Washington); Bel-Air Country (Cal.); Abalone Shore (Cal.). Office: 6151 W Century Blvd Los Angeles CA 90045

ELLIOT, BEVERLEY VALLACK, lawyer; b. Norwich, Ont., Can., Feb. 11, 1900; s. Reginald and Jessie (Carling) E.; B.A., U. Toronto, 1922; LL.B., Osgoode Hall, 1925; m. Iris Elaine Lanskail, Sept. 27, 1930. Called to Ont. bar, 1925, created Queen's counsel, 1944; partner firm Borden, Elliot, Kelley & Palmer, Toronto, 1936—. Dir. James Howden & Parson of Can. Ltd., Can. Security Assurance Co. Mem. Phi Kappa Pi. Mason. Clubs: York, Rosedale Golf, National (Toronto); Le Club Shawinigan (Shawinigan Falls, Que.); Canadian Salmon (Gaspe, Que.). Home: 242 Cortleigh Blvd Toronto 310 Ont Can Office: 250 University Av Toronto 110 Ont Can

ELLIOT, JACK, musician, Recording artist for Prestige, Vanguard, Delmark records. Address: care Vanguard Records 154 W 14th St New York City NY 10011 *

ELLIOT, REED ARCHER, civil engr.; b. Somerville, Mass., Jan. 6, 1910; s. Reed L. and Helen B. (Quarelle) E.; B.S., Tufts U., 1933; m. Evelyn Byrom, Sept. 1938; children—Evelyn Archer, Nancy Oliver. Field survey Pub. Works Dept., Mass., 1931; field engr. J.R. Worcester & Co., cons. engrs., Boston, 1933; supr. E.R.A. program Medford (Mass.) Engr. Dept., 1934-35; with TVA, Knoxville, Tenn., 1935—, began as hydraulic engr.; power sect., asst. to sect. head, engring. asst. to chief water control planning engr., chief project planning br., asst. chief water control planning engr., 1935-55, chief water control planning, 1955-63, dir. water control planning, 1963—. Mem. Am. Soc. C.E.s (past pres. Knoxville br.), Tech. Soc. Knoxville (past pres.), Tau Beta Pi, Chi Epsilon, Alpha Tau Omega. Presbyn. Home: 5600 Marilyn Dr Knoxville TN 37914 Office: TVA Evans Bldg Knoxville TN 37901

ELLIOT, ROBERT SHERRARD, Jr., financial cons.; b. Ossining, N.Y., July 28, 1901; s. Robert Sherrard and Clara (McCord) E.; student Phillips Exeter Acad., 1917-19; A.B., Princeton, 1923; m. Jean Pirnie Robertson, Apr. 19, 1929. With Am. Exchange Nat. Bank, N.Y.C., 1923-26; joined Equity Corp., and predecessors, 1926, asst. treas., 1927-31, sec., 1931-36, v.p., 1936-50, exec. v.p., 1950-59; v.p. Financial Gen. Corp., 1946-53, exec. v.p., 1953-66, also dir.; now financial cons.; chmn. finance com., dir. Internat. Bank, Washington; dir. Bradford Speed Packaging and Devel., Inc., Clarendon Trust Co., Foster Wheeler Corp., Alexandria Nat. Bank (Va.), Am. Installment Credit Corp., Intermediate Credit Corp., Bankers Financial Life Co., Pierce Governor Co., Inc., Kliklok Co., Woodman Co., Inc., Bankers Security Life Ins. Soc., Avis Indsl. Corp., Marion Malleable Iron Works, Inc., H.G. Smithy Co. Clubs: Union League (N.Y.C.); Washington Golf and Country (Arlington, Virginia); Metropolitan (Washington); Belle Haven Country (Alexandria), Home: 323 S Fairfax St Alexandria VA 22314 Office: 1701 Pennsylvania Av NW Washington DC 20006

ELLIOTT, ALBERT RANDLE, coll. pres.; b. St. Louis County, Mo., Jan. 10, 1914; s. Thomas Barrett and Olinda (Hoevel) E.; A.B., Westminster Coll., 1935; LL.D., 1962; A.M., Harvard, 1938, Ph.D., 1949; m. Gwendolyn Stager Crawford, January 28, 1948; 1 dau., Dawn. Teaching asst., depts. govt. Harvard and Radcliffe Coll., 1936-39; research asso. Fgn. Policy Assn., 1939-41; adminstrv. asso. Inst. Internat. Edn., N.Y.C., 1941-43, adminstr. Washington bur., 1946-47; dir. Counsel and Guidance Center for Fgn. students in U.S., Washington, 1943-45; econ. analyst U.S. Strategic Bombing Survey, Eng. and Germany, 1945; chief reports officer Office Mil. Govt. for Germany, Berlin, 1945- 46; London corr. McGraw-Hill World News. London, Eng., 1947-48; exec. dir. Greer Sch., Hope Farm, Dutchess County, N.Y., 1949-61; pres. Hood Coll., 1961-71; pres. Bay Path Jr. Coll., Longmeadow, Mass., 1971—. Exec. Bd. Dutchess County council Boy Scouts Am., 1950-61, mem. nat. council, 1953-58; mem. Md. State Com. for Fulbright Scholarships, 1967-71. Rockefeller Foundation research fellow, 1939-41. Mem. Council World Affairs (vice chmn. Dutchess County 1955- 61), Council Fgn. Relations, Am. Polit. Sci. Assn., Acad. Polit. Sci., Assn. Ind. Colls in Md. (dir. 1961-71, pres. 1964-66), Am. Acad. Polit. and Social Sci., Am. Mus. Nat. History, Md. Ind. Coll. and Univ. Assn. (sec.-treas. 1970-71), Omicron Delta Kappa, Pi Kappa Delta, Beta Theta Pi. Republican. Mem. United Ch. of Christ. Rotarian. Clubs: Harvard (N.Y.C.); Millbrook (N.Y.) Golf and Tennis. Author: Spain After Civil War, 1940; The Resources and Trade of Central America, 1941; (with others) The United States at War, 1942; The Institute of International Education, 1919-44, 1944. Editor numerous govt. reports. Contbr. articles to periodicals, Address: Bay Path Junior College Longmeadow MA 01106

ELLIOTT, BYRON KAUFFMAN, lawyer, bus. exec.; b. Indpls., May 5, 1899; s. William Frederick and Effie (Marguardt) E.; A.B. cum laude, Ind. U., 1920, LL.D., 1955; LL.B., Harvard, 1923; m. Helen Alice Heissler, July 15, 1938; children—Barbara (Mrs. John D. Niles), Kent, David. Admitted to Ind. bar, 1921; began practice in Indpls.; asst. atty. gen. Ind., 1925; judge Superior Ct., Indpls., 1926-29; pres. Curtiss Flying Service of Ind., 1927-29; mgr. gen. counsel Am. Life Conv., 1929- 34; pres. Am. Service Bur., 1929-33, chmn. bd. 1933-34; with John Hancock Mut. Life Ins. Co., 1934-69, gen. counsel, 1936, v.p., gen. counsel, 1937-47, exec. v.p., 1947-57, pres., 1957-65, chmn. finance com. 1961-69, chmn., 1963-69, also dir.; dir. Tech. Projects, Ltd., Am. Research and Devel. Corp., Arthur D. Little, Inc., Boston Edison Co., Am. Fletcher Corp.; hon. dir. 1st Nat. Bank of Boston; trustee Provident Instn. Savs., 1950-70. Bd. dirs. Baystate Sci. Found., Nat. Commn. Coop. Edn.; trustee Wellesley Coll., 1951-69, Ind. Coll. Funds Am., Boston Mus. Sci., 1952-70, Fed. City Council, Washington, Tufts Civic Edn. Center, hosp. research and edn. trust Am. Hosp. Assn., 1960-69; bd. overseers Boston Symphony Orch.; chmn. bd. trustees, chmn. corp. Northeastern U.; bd. dirs. Ind. U. Found., World Wildlife Fund, Boston Opera Assn., World Affairs Council Boston, 1950-68; bd. advisers Nat. Fund for Med. Edn.; mem. corp. Peter Bent Brigham Hosp. Served as 2d lt. CAC, World War I. Fellow Am. Acad. Arts and Scis.; mem. Am. Bar Assn., Am. Law Inst., Am. Jud. Soc., Council Fgn. Relations, Assn. Life Insurance Counsel (pres. 1949-50), Mass. Charitable Fires Soc., Mass. Com. Catholics, Protestants and Jews (exec. com. 1957-60), Inst. of Life Ins. (dir., chmn. 1965-66), Mass. Space and Def. Assn. (dir.), Am. Legion, Mil. Order Loyal Legion, S.A.R., Bostonian Soc., U.S. C. of C. (mem. task force on econ. growth), Ind. Pioneers, Inst. for the Future (adv. council), Scribes, Beta Theta Pi, Sigma Delta Chi. Republican. Presbyn. Mason (33). Clubs: Commercial, Harvard, Brookline Country, Dedham Country and Polo, Algonquin, St. Botolph (Boston); Casino, Tavern, Chicago (Chgo.); Sky (N.Y.C.); Woodstock, Columbia (Indpls.), Author booklets, articles ins. law. Home: 1135 Webster St Needham MA 02192 Office: 200 Berkeley St Boston MA 02117 ☆

ELLIOTT, CAMPBELL WALTER, mfg. co. exec.; b. St. Louis, June 25, 1913; s. James C. and Gertrude C. (O'Brien) E.; LL.B., City Coll. Law, St. Louis, 1936; m. Dorothy C. Mueller, Jan. 30, 1937; children—Mary Francis, Carol Ann, George, Michael. Asst. to pres., asst. dir. indsl. relations Cramp Shipbuilding Co., 1942-45; v.p. indsl. relations Mpls.-Moline Co., 1945-56; v.p. Midland-Ross Corp., Cleve., 1956-70; pres., dir. Am. Shipbuilding Co., 1970—; dir. Freeway Washer & Stamping Co., Continental Bank. Past mem. bd. dirs. Jr. Achievement Greater Cleve., pres.; bd. dirs. Brentwood Hosp.; trustee John Carroll U., Cleveland YMCA. Mem. Pub. Relations Soc. Am., U.S. C. of C., N.A.M., Advt. Club Cleve. (trustee). Club: Cleveland Athletic (dir.; pres. 1966-67). Home: 22315 Canterbury Lane Shaker Heights OH 44122 Office: 55 Public Sq Cleveland OH 44113

ELLIOTT, CHALMERS WILLIAM, univ. athletic dir.; b. Detroit, Jan. 30, 1925; s. Joseph Norman and Alice (Marquis) E.; student Purdue U., 1943-44; A.B., U. Mich., 1948; m. Barbara Conard Apr. 30, 1949; children—William Conard, Robert J., Elizabeth A. Asst. football coach Ore. State U., 1949-51, U. Ia., 1952- 56; asst. football coach U. Mich., 1957-58, head football coach, 1959- 68, asso. athletics dir., 1969-70; dir. athletics U. Ia., 1970—. Served to 2d lt. USMCR, 1943-46. Home: 1127 Dill St Iowa City IA 52240

ELLIOTT, DANIEL WHITACRE, educator, surgeon; b. Greenville, O., Aug. 5, 1922; s. James Scott and LaVirge (Whitacre) E.; student Ohio State U., 1942-43, M.Med. Sci., 1956; M.D., Yale, 1949; m. Elizabeth Lucille Wolff, Aug. 11, 1961; children—James Calvin, Lisa Ann. Intern surgery Columbia Presbyn. Hosp., N.Y.C., 1949-50; surgery resident Ohio State U. Hosp., 1951, 53-57; mem. faculty Ohio State U. Sch. Medicine, 1957-64; prof. surgery U. Pitts. Sch. Medicine, 1965—; chief surgery Pitts. VA Hosp., Pitts., 1965—; staff Presbyn. Hosp., Western Pa. Hosp., Shadyside Hosp., Childrens Hosp., Pitts. Served with AUS, 1943-45, as capt., M.C. USAF, 1951-53. Diplomate Am. Bd. Surgery. Fellow A.C.S.; mem. Am., Central, Western, Internat. surg. assns., Am. Burn Assn., Soc. Univ. Surgeons, Am. Gastroenterology Assn., Soc. Surgery Alimentary Tract, Sigma Xi. Alpha Kappa Kappa, Alpha Omega Alpha. Contbr. numerous articles in field. Editorial bd. Am. Jour. Surgery, Am. Surgeon. Home: 657 Morewood Av Pittsburgh PA 15213 Office: VA Hosp University Dr Pittsburgh PA 15240

ELLIOTT, EDWARD PROCTER, architect; b. Warrington, Eng., Oct. 25, 1916; s. Arthur Spencer and Ethel Gertrude (Musket) E.; B.Arch., Liverpool U., Eng., 1939; fellow in City Planning, Cranbrook Acad. Art, Mich., 1939-40; m. Cynthia Jean Heideman, June 7, 1958; children by former marriage—Stewart, Edward, Lauren, Eleanor. Came to U.S., 1939, naturalized, 1951. Chief designer Eero Saarinen & Assos., architects, Bloomfield Hills, Mich., 1945-50; partner Elliott & Dworski, Birmingham, Mich., 1950-57; planning supr. Knoll Assos., Inc., 1951-57; partner Knorr-Elliott & Assos., San Francisco, 1957—. Mem. nat. council Archtl. Registration Bds. Asso. Mich. Acad. Sci. Arts and Letters, 1957. Served to lt. comdr. Royal Canadian Navy, 1940-45. Recipient A.I.A. awards, 1953, 56, 59, 63, Nat. Gold medal Exhbn., N.Y., 1962, award of excellence Am. Inst. Steel, 1963, Nat. award U. Alaska, 1967, Top Ten awards Comml. Indsl. Bldgs., 1968. Mem. Royal Inst. Brit. Architects, A.I.A., Archtl. Research Group of Ottawa, Can. Home: 12 Baywood Av Ross CA 94957 Office: 631 Clay St San Francisco CA 94111

ELLIOTT, FRANK NELSON, coll. pres.; b. Dunkirk, N.Y., Mar. 18, 1926; s. Warren D. and Ima M. (Wilson) E.; B.A. cum laude with dept. honors, Alfred U., 1949; M.A., Ohio U., 1950; Ph.D., U. Wis., 1956; m. Mary Elizabeth Neish, July 26, 1952; children—Robert Frank (dec.), Susan Marie, Ann Neish. Grad. asst. Ohio U., 1949-50; Draper fellow Wis. Hist. Soc., 1951-52, field rep., field supr., 1952-56; curator history, asst. prof. history Mich. State U., 1956-61; asso. dean Sch. Gen. Studies, Columbia, 1961-64, acting dean, 1964; dir. div. arts and scis. State U. N.Y., College at Cortland, 1964-65, acting dean, 1965-66; v.p. Hofstra U., Hempstead, N.Y., 1966- 69; pres. Rider Coll., Trenton, N.J., 1969—. Served with AUS, 1944-46: PTO. Trustee, Alfred U., 1964-69. Mem. Assn. State and Local History (council 1960-62), Miss. Valley hist. assns., Mich. Hist. Soc. (trustee 1959-61, award for TV lectures 1960), Am. Mus. Assn. Presbyn. Co-author; Michigan Civil War History: an Annotated Bibliography, 1961. Contbr. articles profl. jours. Home: 2064 Lawrenceville Rd Trenton NJ 08638

ELLIOTT, FREDERICK NAPIER, physician; b. Vancouver, B.C., Can., Feb. 2, 1911; s. Frederick Garrard and Hannah (Moore) E.; student U. B.C.; M.D., U. Man., 1946; M.H.A., Northwestern U., 1960; m. Mary Ellen Mitchell, Feb. 7, 1939; children—Frederick Mitchell, Kathryn Ruth. Came to U.S., 1958. Intern St. Boniface Hosp., 1945-46; pvt. practice medicine, 1946-58; surveyor Joint Com. Accreditation Hosps., 1959; dir. hosp. counseling program. Am. Hosp. Assn., 1960-64; asso. exec. dir. Cedars-Sinai Hosp., Los Angeles, 1964-67; asst. dir. Am. Hosp. Assn., 1967-70; gen. dir., v.p. Mt. Sinai Hosp., Chgo., also prof. community medicine Chgo. Med. Sch., 1969-71; prof. community medicine U. So. Cal., also asso. med.

dir. Rancho Los Amigos, 1971—; cons. to dir. Am. Hosp. Assn. Trustee Ednl. Council Fgn. Med. Grads. Address: PO Box 3818 Downey CA 90242

ELLIOTT, GEORGE BURGER, mfg. co. exec.; b. Columbus, O., July 13, 1906; s. Alva and A. and Edith H. (Burger) E.; B.S. in Bus., U. Ill., 1928, M.S. in Bus. Adminstrn., 1930; m. Ruth Helen Bell, June 27, 1931; children—Susanne (Mrs. Ralph J. Sogard), George C. With Inland Box. Co., 1929-30; with Inland Container Corp., Indpls., 1930—, pres., 1952-63, vice chmn., 1963-66, chmn. finance com., 1966—, also dir.; dir. Ga. Kraft Co., Ind. Nat. Bank of Indpls. Trustee Christian Theol. Sem.; bd. govs. James Whitcomb Riley Meml. Found.; bd. dirs. United Fund Greater Indpls., U. Ill. Found., Indpls. YMCA, Herman Charles and Ellnora D. Krannert Found., Inland Container Corp. Found.; trustee Franklin (Ind.) Coll. Mem. Ind. Mfrs. Assn. (dir.), Indpls. (dir.), Ind. chambers commerce, Fibre Box Assn., Phi Eta Sigma, Beta Gamma Sigma, Phi Kappa Tau, Beta Alpha Psi. Republican. Mem. Christian Ch. Rotarian. Clubs: Columbia, Meridian Hills Country (Indpls.). Home: 7410 n Illinois St Indianapolis IN 46260

ELLIOTT, GEORGE PAUL, author, educator; b. Knightstown, Ind., June 16, 1918; s. Paul R. and Nita (Gregory) E.; B.A., U. Cal. at Berkeley, 1939, M.A., 1941; D.H.L., St. Lawrence U., 1971; m. Mary Emma Jeffress, Jan. 18, 1941; 1 dau., Nora Catherine. Instr., then asst. prof. English, St. Mary's (Cal.) Coll., 1947-55, 62-63; asst. prof. Cornell U. Ithaca, N.Y., 1955-56; asst. prof. Barnard Coll., 1957- 60; lectr. U. Ia., 1960-61; prof. English Syracuse U., 1963—. Mem. corp. Yaddo Found., 1965—. Recipient Albert Bender grant-in-aid, 1951; fellow Fund Advancement Edn., 1953, Hudson Rev., 1956; Guggenheim fellow, 1961, 70; Ford fellow, 1965; award Nat. Inst. Arts and Letters, 1969. Mem. Am. Assn. U. Profs., P.E.N., Phi Beta Kappa. Author:(novels) Parktilden Village, 1958; David Knudsen, 1962; In the World, 1965; (short stories) Among the Dangs, 1961; An Hour of Last Things, 1968; (essays) A Piece of Lettuce, 1964; Conversions, 1971; (poems) Fever and Chills, 1951; From the Berkeley Hills, 1969. Editor: Fifteen Modern American Poets, 1956; Types of Prose Fiction, 1964. Office: English Dept Syracuse Univ Syracuse NY 13210

ELLIOTT, HOWARD, lawyer; b. St. Louis, June 29, 1904; s. Thomas John and Pauline (Peters) E.; student Columbia Law Sch., 1929-30; J.D., Washington U., 1931; m. Ruth Ann Thomas, Nov. 21, 1931; children—Howard Elliott, Mary Ann, David Thomas John. Admitted to Mo. bar, 1930; sr. mem. Elliott & Snow, 1931-37, Elliott, Coburn & Elliott, 1937-41, mem. law firm Boyle Priest, Elliott and Weakley, 1958—. Regional dir. code authorities NRA, 1933-35; mem. Gov.'s Commn. on Social Security, 1938, Interstate Cooperation and Reciprocity, 1939, Statutory Revision, 1939; mem. Supreme Cit. Commn. Civil Procedures, 1940; freeholder Transit, 1953-54; commr. State Reorgn. Commn. Mo., 1970—. Mem. Mo. Ho. of Reps., 1937-48, speaker, 1943-47, minority floor leader, 1939-42. Parliamentarian Rep. State Conv., 1938, 40, 42, 48, chmn., 1956; Rep. candidate for gov. Mo., 1952. Mem. Am., St. Louis (parliamentarian 1946-63) bar assns., Mo. Bar, Lawyers Assn. St. Louis, Am. Judicature Soc., Acad. Sci., State Hist. Soc. Mo., Mo. Hist. Soc., Phi Delta Theta, Phi Delta Phi. Kappa Phi Sigma, Clubs: Missouri Athletic, Bellerive Country, Noonday Clayton (St. Louis). Author: Taxation of Interests in Exempt Fee Estates, 1969. Home: 34 Rio Vista Dr Ladue MO Office: 705 Olive St St Louis MO 63101

ELLIOTT, HOWARD CLYDE, Jr., educator; b. Birmingham, Sept. 21, 1924; s. Howard Clyde and Charlotte Augusta (Smith) E.; B.S., Birmingham So. Coll., 1948; M.S., U. Ala., 1951, Ph.D., 1956; m. Mary Claire Baker, Apr. 24, 1958; children—Ann BeAyre, Catherine Claire and Ellen Clyde (twins). Asso. prof. chemistry U. Ala., Birmingham, 1959-64, prof. chemistry, also asst. prof. dept. medicine, 1965—, asso. chmn. natural sci. and math. Coll. Gen Studies, 1968-69, vol. research prof. chemistry, 1970—; asso. Casey, Lohmann & Elliott, Birmingham, 1969—; biochemistry cons. Bapt. Hosp. Labs., 1955-64. Served with M.C., AUS, 1943-46. Recipient Kimble Nat. Med. Tech. award, 1961. Mem. Am. Assn. Clin. Chemists (chmn. S.E. sect. 1968-69), Soc. Exptl. Biology and Medicine, Am. Diabetes Assn., Am. Chem. Soc., Sigma Xi. Presbyn. (elder). Clubs: Vestavia Country, The Club (Birmingham). Contbr. articles sci. jours. Home: 4260 Sharpsburg Dr Birmingham AL 35213

ELLIOTT, J. RANDOLPH, cement co. exec.; b. Los Angeles, July 22, 1923; s. Harry William and Ruth (Cass) E.; student Princeton, 1941-42; A.B., LL.B., Stanford; m. Evelyn Severance, May 14, 1949; children—Steven Severance, David Harrison, Linda, Robert Cass. Admitted to Cal. bar; gen. practice in Los Angeles, 1952-54; sec., asst. counsel, dir. natural gas co. 1954-63; sec. Pacific Lighting Corp., San Francisco, 1963-69; exec. v.p., Diversified div., gen. counsel, sec. Cal. Portland Cement Co., 1969—; dir. Landsdale Investment Co. Served with AUS, 1942-46 Mem. Am., Cal., Los Angeles, San Francisco bar assns., Fed. Power Bar Assn., Am. Legion (past post commander), Alpha Gamma Delta, also mem. Phi Alpha Delta. Author articles. Home: 435 S Curson Av W Los Angeles CA 90036 Office: 612 S Flower St Los Angeles CA 90017

ELLIOTT, JAMES, mus. dir.; b. Medford, Ore., Feb. 19, 1924; s. Bert R. and Marguerite (Heyer) E; B.A., Willamette U., 1947; A.M., Harvard, 1949; m. Judith Ann Algar, Apr. 23, 1966; children—Arabel Joan, Jakob Maxwell. Teaching fellow fine arts Harvard, 1950-51; art critic N.Y. Herald-Tribune, European edit., 1952- 53; curator, acting dir. Walker Art Center, Mpls., 1953-56; asst. chief curator, also curator modern art Los Angeles County Mus. 1956-63; chief curator Los Angeles County Mus. Art, 1963-66; dir. Wadsworth Atheneum, Hartford, Conn., 1966—. Mem. Conn. Commn. on Arts, 1971—. Trustee Bushnell Meml. Hall, Hartford, 1967—. Served with USNR, 1943-46. Mem. Coll. Art Assn., Am. Assn. Museums (pres. New Eng. Conf. 1971—), Internat. Council Museums, Assn. Art Mus. Dirs. Home: 262 Old Main St Rocky Hill CT 06067 Office: 600 Main St Hartford CT 06103

ELLIOTT, JAMES BARTON, corp. oflc.; b. Mt. Vernon, N.Y., Jan. 20, 1913; s. James and Irene Emma (Barton) E.; grad. Phillips Andover Acad., 1931; A.B., Yale, 1935; m. Sally Byron, June 5, 1935; children—Betsy, Sally, Wendy, Barton. With Amstar Corp., N.Y.C., 1935—, sec., 1955-65, v.p., 1957—; dir. Barton Mines Corp., North Creek, N.Y., Duff-Norton Co., Inc., Charlotte, N.C., The Hoffmaster Co., Inc., Oshkosh, Wis. Home: 1000 Esplanade Pelham Manor NY 10803 Office: 1251 Av of Americas New York City NY 10020

ELLIOTT, JAMES ROBERT, U.S. judge; b. Gainesville, Ga., Jan. 1, 1910; s. Thomas M. and Mamie Lucille (Glenn) E.; Ph.B., Emory U., 1930, LL.B., 1934; m. Brownie C. Buck, Aug. 3, 1949; children—Susan G., James Robert. Admitted to Ga. bar, 1934, engaged in corporate and trial practice; U.S. judge Middle Dist. Ga., 1962—. Mem. Ga. Ho. of Reps., 1937-49; mem. Democratic Nat. Com., 1948-56. Served as lt. USNR, World War II; PTO. Mem. Ga. Jr. C. of C. (pres. 1941-42), Ga. Bar Assn., Lambda Chi Alpha, Phi Delta Phi. Kiwanian. Home: 2612 Carson Dr Columbus GA 31906 Office: U S Dist Ct Columbus GA 31902

ELLIOTT, JOANNE, educator; b. Providence, Dec. 5, 1925; d. John Sanderson and Martha Hester (Robertson) Elliott; B.A., Brown U., 1947; M.A., Cornell U., 1949, Ph.D., 1950. Instr. math. Swarthmore Coll., 1950-52; asst. prof. Mt. Holyoke Coll., 1952-55; vis. asst. prof. Brown U., 1954-55; from asst. prof. to asso. prof. Barnard Coll., 1955-64, chmn. dept. math., 1963-64; prof. math. Rutgers U., New Brunswick, N.J., 1964—. Anne Crosby Emory fellow, 1947; recipient Alumni Convocation citation Brown U., 1959; NSF sr. postdoctoral fellow, 1961-62, summer research grantee, 1964-69, 71. Mem. Am. Math. Soc., Math. Assn. Am., Phi Beta Kappa, Sigma Xi. Contbr. articles to profl. jours. Home: 88 Prospect Av Edison NJ 08817 Office: Math Dept Rutgers U New Brunswick NJ 08903

ELLIOTT, JOHN, Jr., advt. exec.; b. N.Y.C., Jan. 25, 1921; s. John and Audrey Neilson (Osborn) E.; student Browning Sch., 1928-34; grad. St. Paul's Sch., 1938; A.B., Harvard, 1942; m. Eleanor Lansing Thomas, July 27, 1956. Copywriter, Batten, Barton, Durstine & Osborn, 1945-49, account exec., 1949-60, v.p., 1956-60, dir., 1958-60; sr. v.p., dir. Ogilvy, Benson & Mather, N.Y.C., 1960-65; chmn. Ogilvy & Mather, 1965—; dir. Fireman's Fund Am. Life Ins. Co. N.Y. Gen. chmn. Red Cross Campaign for Mems. and Funds in N.Y., 1970, 71. TV adviser Republican Party, 1950-53. Bd. dirs. Park Assn. N.Y.C., 1956-60; trustee Browning Sch., 1950-60, Mus. City N.Y., 1956-65, Internat. House, 1967—; bd. dirs. Advt. Research Found., 1968-69. Served from pfc. to capt., USMCR, 1942-45; maj. Res. Mem. Am. Assn. Advt. Agys. (dir., chmn. com. on govt. and pub. relations), Am. Advt. Fedn. (dir. 1969-70). Episcopalian. Clubs: Bedford Golf and Tennis; Racquet & Tennis, Harvard (N.Y.C.). Home: 1035 Fifth Av New York City NY 10028 Office: 2 E 48th St New York City NY 10017

ELLIOTT, JOHN ALFRED, corp. exec.; b. Earleton, Kan., Apr. 11, 1912; s. Alfred J. and Hazel (Miller) E.; B.S., U. Kan., 1935; m. Ruth Marie Nelson, Aug. 30, 1939; children—Karen, Nelson, Roger. Accountant, auditor Firestone Tire & Rubber Co., Akron, O., 1935-39; accountant White Motor Co., Cleve., 1939- 40, Thompson Products. Inc., 1941-42; accounting supr. Beech Aircraft Corp., Wichita, Kan., 1942-47, chief accountant, 1947-51, treas.-sec., 1951—, dir., 1958, dir., sec.-treas., various subsidiaries, 1959—; dir. Union Nat. Bank. Mem. exec. com. Quivera council Boy Scouts Am., 1964—. Bd. dirs. United Fund. Wichita. Mem. Nat. Assn. Accountants, Wichita C. of C. (treas. 1964-65). Presbyn. Clubs: Rotary, Crestview Country. Home: 8601 Shannon Way Wichita KS 67206 Office: Beech Aircraft Corp Wichita KS 67201

ELLIOTT, JOHN C., fgn. trade cons.; b. Washington Nov. 12, 1907; s. Wm. Smith and Martha (Boyd) E.; grad. Ga. Mil. Coll., 1925; student Ga. Sch. Tech., 1925-27, George Washington U., 1927-31; LL.B., Nat. U., 1939; m. Catherine Flagg, Dec. 8, 1934; 1 dau., Jane Lee. Various positions, including adminstrv. and legal positions Dept. State, 1929-42, munitions control officer, 1942-44, specialist UN Affairs, 1946-47, asst. chief and acting chief Div. Internat. Security Affairs UN, 1948-49; chief munitions div. and exec. sec. Nat. Munitions Control Bd. 1949.; dir. office Munitions Control, Dept. State, 1952; dir. Robert Schasseur, Inc., fgn. trade reps., N.Y.C., Washington Lee Savs. & Loan, Arlington, Va.; gen. partner Tysons Triangle; dir., adv. bd. Security Nat. Bank (Falls Church, Va.); advisor U.S. rep. UN Commns. on Atomic Energy and Conventional Armament; exec. sec. Interdepartmental. Com. on Armament Regulations, U.S., 1948-49; adviser Ivory Coast Govt., 1962—. Served with AUS, 1944-45. Decorated officer Nat. Order Ivory Coast. Mem. George Washington U. Alumni Assn., Am. Fgn. Service Assn. Am. Legion, Gamma Eta Gamma. Presbyn. Clubs: Wings, International of Washington (Washington): River Bend Country (Va.). Home: The Highlands Charlestown WV 25414 Office: 2424 Massachusetts Av N W Washington DC 20008

ELLIOTT, JOHN FRANK, educator; b. St. Paul, July 31, 1920; s. Stowe E. and Helen (Grube) E.; B.S., U. Minn., 1942; Sc.D., Mass. Inst. Tech., 1949; m. Frances Pendleton, May 4, 1946; children—William S., Dorothy P. Phys. chemist Fundamental Research Lab. U.S. Steel Corp., Kearny, N.J., 1949-51; research metallurgist Inland Steel Co., East Chicago, Ind., 1951-54, asst. supt. quality control, 1954-55; asso. prof. dept. metallurgy Mass. Inst. Tech., Cambridge, 1955-60, prof. dept. metallurgy, 1960—. Mem. at large engring. div. NRC. Served to lt. comdr. USNR, 1942-46. Howe Meml. lectr. Am. Inst. Mining, Metall. Engrs., 1963; John Simon Guggenheim fellow, 1965. Fellow Metall. Soc., Am. Inst. Mining and Metall. Engrs.; mem. Am. Acad. Arts and Scis., Am. Inst. Chem. Engrs. Am. Soc. Metals (White distinguished teaching award 1971), Brit. Iron and Steel Inst., A.A.A.S., Sigma Xi, Tau Beta Pi. Author: Thermochemistry for Steelmaking, vol. I, 1960, vol. II 1963; Steelmaking: The Chipman Conference, 1965. Editor: The Physical Chemistry of Steelmaking, 1958. Contbr. profl. jours. Home: 118 Arlington St Winchester MA 02139 Office: 77 Massachusetts Av Cambridge MA 02139

ELLIOTT, JOHN L., ins. co. exec.; b. Ft. Dodge, Ia., Oct. 30, 1912; s. John L. and Gertrude (Best) E.; student Drake U., 1931-33; m. Lyle Johnson, June 23, 1937; children—Judy Jo (Mrs. Marsh), Wendy Lee (Mrs. Harper). With Washington Nat. Ins. Co., Evanston, Ill., 1931—, regional dir., 1946-50, territorial mgr., 1950-60, v.p. in charge marketing and man power devel., 1960-65, v.p., dir. dist. agys., 1965-68, sr. v.p., 1969—. Exec. com. combination companies Life Ins. Agy. Mgmt. Assn. Served to capt. USMCR, 1943-46. Fellow Life Office Mgmt. Assn. Methodist. Mason. Home: 91 Sycamore Pl Highland Park IL 60035 Office: 1630 Chicago Av Evanston IL 60201

ELLIOTT, JOHN MONTGOMERY, labor union ofcl.; b. Phila., Aug. 10, 1913; s. William J. and Catherine (Montgomery) E.; m. Marie Lindtner, Sept. 19, 1934; children—John Montgomery, Catherine Marie. Internat. rep. Amalgamated Assn. of Street, Electric Ry. and Motor Coach Employees of Am. (name now Amalgamated Transit Union), AFL-CIO, 1945-48, v.p., 1948-57, mem. gen. exec. bd., asst. to pres. internat. hdqrs., 1955-57, exec. v.p., 1957- 59, internat. pres., 1959—; dir., exec. com. Union Labor Life Ins. Co.; trustee, mem. planning com. Venice (Fla.) Nacomas Bank, Exec. bd. Internat. Transport Workers Fedn. Home: 2714 Sheridan St Hollywood FL 33020 Office: 5025 Wisconsin Av N W Washington DC 20016

ELLIOTT, JOSEPH BLACK, business exec.; b. Williamston, S.C., July 6, 1904; s. Henry C. Elliott and Kate B. (Buhler) E.; ed. Mount Zion Inst.; student Ga. Sch. Tech., 1921-22, Columbia Univ., 1 yr.; m. Mary Harlan Dickey, Dec. 22, 1928; children—Mary Ann, Elzabeth Dickey, Joseph Black. Salesman, Coca- Cola Co., Atlanta, 1923; sales mgr. Coca-Cola Bottling Co., Cumberland, Md., 1924-26; salesman Brunswick Radio Corp., Baltimore, 1927, sales mgr. Boston branch, 1927-30, Baltimore branch, 1930-32; sec. Mavis Bottling Co. of America, N.Y. City, 1932-35; dist. mgr. Radio Corp. of Am., Boston, 1936-39, sales mgr., radio div., Camden, N.J., 1939-44; v.p. charge sales and advt. Schick Inc., Stamford, Conn., 1944-54, pres., 1954-60; v.p. Home Instrument Div., Radio Corp. of Am., 1945-49, v.p. charge consumer products. 1949-54, exec. v.p. charge consumer products div., 1954; pres. Tele-Dynamics Inc., 1958-60; pres. York div. Borg-Warner Corp., Chgo., 1960-63, chmn. bd. division, 1963—, also chmn. York Corp., subsidiary: chmn. bd. Omnitronics, Inc. Served with S.A.T.C., Ga. Sch. Tech., 1921-22. Mem. Kappa Sigma. Home: 1010 Red Rose Lane Villanova PA 19085 Office: York Div Borg-Warner Corp Villanova PA 19085

ELLIOTT, KATHLEEN OVERMYER, coll. dean; b. Lindsey, O., May 2, 1910; d. Martin V. and Catherine (Yeagle) Overmyer; B.A., B.S., Ohio State U., 1931; grad. student U. Chgo., 1934, 35; Ph.D., Radcliffe Coll., 1942; m. Van Courtlandt Elliott, 1938. Exec. sec. to com. on admissions Radcliffe Coll., 1943-45, chmn., 1945-53, dir. admissions, 1946-53, asso. dean instruction, 1953- 59, dean instruction, 1959-63, dean coll., 1963—, v.p., 1968—, lecturer classics Harvard, 1953—. Mem. adv. council Sch. Nursing, Mass. Gen. Hosp. Mem. Medieval Acad. Am., Am. Philol. Assn., New Eng. Classical Assn., Phi Beta Kappa. Home: 107 Walker St Cambridge MA 02138

ELLIOTT, LAWRENCE, writer; b. Bklyn., Jan. 18, 1924; s. Samuel and Gussie (Goldsmith) Edelstein; B.S.S., City Coll. N.Y., 1950; m. Gisèle Kayser, July 1969; children by previous marriage—Jain, Elizabeth, Barbara. Asso. editor Coronet mag., 1948-54; free-lance writer, 1954-62; staff writer Reader's Digest, 1962—, European corr., 1968-69, roving editor, 1971—. Served to 1st lt. AUS, 1942-46. Recipient Freedoms Found. award, 1950, Alaska Press Club Award, 1966, German Jugendbuch preis, 1970. Mem. Soc. Mag. Writers, Authors Guild. Club: Overseas Press (N.Y.C.). Author: A Little Girl's Gift, 1963; George Washington Carver: The Man Who Overcame, 1966; On the Edge of Nowhere (with James Huntington), 1966; Journey to Washington (with Senator Daniel K. Inouye), 1967; The Legacy of Tom Dooley, 1969. Address: 1385 York Av New York City NY 10021

ELLIOTT, LESTER MELVIN, cons.; b. Greentown, Dec. 23, 1906; s. Harry Hayes and Nora (Jones) E.; B.S., Northwestern U., 1929; m. Margaret Saunders, Nov. 21, 1936; children—Carolyn, Elizabeth (Mrs. James Bradner). Sr. accountant Arthur Andersen & Co., C.P.A.'s, 1932-39; controller's staff U.S. Steel Corp., 1939-43; sec.-treas. Agaloy Tubing Co., 1943-45; v.p. McCord Corp., 1945-59, dir., 1st v.p., 1959-63, v.p., mem. exec. com., 1963-67, also dir., officer several affiliated cos.; sec.-treas. Bryan Metals, Inc., 1955-67, past dir. pres. McCord-Garcia, S.A.; dir. financial cons. AID Program, Korea Prodn. Center, Seoul, Korea, 1970—. Northwestern U., 1937-39, Pa. State U., 1942-43. C.P.A., Ill. Mem. Am. Inst. C.P.A.'s, Financial Execs. Inst. (pres. Detroit 1952-53), Nat. Assn. Accountants (pres. Detroit 1960-61), Northwestern U. Alumni Assn. (pres. Detroit 1958-60, regent 1961—), Newcomen Soc. N. Am. Clubs: Economic (Detroit); Detroit Athletic. Contbr. to accounting periodicals: collaborator in revision Auditing, 1939. Home: 111 Touraine Rd Grosse Pointe MI 48236

ELLIOTT, LLOYD HARTMAN, univ. pres.; b. Clay County, W.Va., May 21, 1918; s. John and Belva (Stone) E.; A.B., Glenville State Coll., 1937; M.A., W.Va. U., 1939, LL.D., 1967; Ed.D., U. Colo., 1948; LL.D., U. N.H., 1963, Colby Coll., 1965, Concord Coll., 1966, U. Me., 1969, Husson Coll., 1970, Georgetown U., 1971; m. Evelyn Elder, Aug. 25, 1936; children—Lloyd Gene, Patricia Ann. Tchr. pub. sch., Wilden. W. Va., 1937-39, elementary, high sch. prin., 1939-42; instr. U. Colo., summer 1947; asst. supt. Boulder pub. sch., 1947-48; vis. prof. U. Tex., 1948; asst. prof. edn. Cornell U., 1948-50, asso. prof. edn., 1950-54, dir. summer session, 1953-58, prof. edn., 1954, exec. asst. to pres. 1956-58; pres. U. Me., 1958-65; pres. George Washington U., Washington, 1965—. Dir., Chesapeake & Potomac Telephone Co., Am. Security and Trust Company, Acacia Mut. Life Ins. Co. Bd. dirs. Consortium Washington Univs., Greater Washington Ednl. TV Assn. Mem. N.E.A., Assn. Urban Univs. (pres.), Am. Assn. Sch. Adminstrs., Nat. Geog. Soc. (trustee), Am. Council on Edn. (sec. 1967), Phi Kappa Phi, Phi Delta Kappa. Club: Cosmos. Contbr. articles profl. publs. Home: 2330 Tracy Pl N W Washington DC 20008

ELLIOTT, MABEL AGNES, educator, author; b. Liscomb. Ia., May 13, 1898; d. William Lee and Nora Belle (Bash) Elliott; A.B., Northwestern U., 1922, A.M., 1923, Ph.D., 1929. Instr. sociology U. Minn., 1926-27, vis. prof., 1936-37; instr. Stephens Coll., 1927- 28; part-time instr. sociology Northwestern U., 1928-29; asst. prof. sociology U. Kan., 1929-37, asso. prof., 1938-47; cons. sociologist A.R.C., 1946-47; lectr. Am. U., 1947, on leave U. of Kan.; chmn. dept., prof. sociology Chatham Colt Coll., Pitts., 1947-65, Irene Heinz Given prof. sociology (hon.), 1962—. Univ. prof. sociology Hunter Coll., U. City N.Y., 1966-67; adj. prof. sociology Bklyn. Coll., 1965-66; Phi Beta Kappa lectr., 1959-62; Distinguished vis. prof. E. Tex. State U., 1969. Mem. Kan. Temp. Pub. Welfare commn., 1931-33, Pa. Com. Penal Affairs, Mayor's Civic Com., Pitts. Mem. adv. bd. Pitts. Community Councils. Mem. com. Fulbright and Mundt awards in sociology Fgn. Exchange Program, Fulbright screening com., 1956-59, chmn., 1957-59; mem. adv. research com. Mayor's Com. on Human Relations, 1959—. Wieboldt research fellow sociology, 1924; Carola Woerischoffer Meml. fellow in social economy, 1924-26; Fulbright award, U. Bonn, Germany (lectr. criminology), 1955-56; named Pitts. Woman of Year, 1957. Fellow Am. Sociol. Assn. (nat. council 1955-58); mem. Internat. Platform Assn., Eastern Sociol. Soc., Kan. Conf. Social Work (dir. 1930-36, exec. sec. 1933-34, treas. 1936-37), Internat. Sociol. Assn., Soc. Study Social Problems (exec. com. 1953—, pres. 1956- 57), Am. Assn. U. Profs., Am. Assn. Social Workers, Phi Beta Kappa, Phi Beta Kappa Assoc., Alpha Kappa Delta, Alpha Pi Zeta. Democrat. Episcopalian. Clubs: Faculty, University Women. Author: several books in sociology. 1926-47, also Coercion in Penal Treatment: Past and Present, 1947; (with F.E. Merrill) Social Disorganization 1950, rev. 1961); Crime in Modern Society. 1952 (translated into Jugoslovenian 1962); (with others) Marriage and the Family, 1955. Asst. editor Am. Sociol. Rev. 1940-48, Dictionary of Sociology, 1944. Author articles and book revs. profl. jours. Contbr. Ency. Brit., 1961, 65. Home: 7524 Graymore Rd Pittsburgh PA 15221 ☆

ELLIOTT, MARTIN ANDERSON, corp. sci. adviser; b. Balt., Feb. 21, 1909; s. Walter and Lillian (Kesmodel) E.; B.E., Johns Hopkins, 1930. Ph.D., 1933; m. Mary Helen Parker, June 23, 1934; children—James Parker, Virginia Layfield. Instr. dept. gas engring. Johns Hopkins, 1933-34; asst. to supt. gas mfr. Balt. Gas & Electric Co., 1934-38; gas engr., prin. chem. engr., asst. chief explosives div. U.S. Bur. Mines, Pitts., 1938-46, asst. chief and chief synthetic liquid fuels research, 1946-52; research prof. mech. engring. Ill. Inst. Tech., Chgo., 1952-56, dir. inst. gas tech., research prof. chem. engring., 1956-61, acad. v.p., 1961-67; corporate sci. adviser Tex. Eastern Transmission Corp., Houston, 1967—. Dir. Utah Corp., 1962-70, also AutoResearch, Inc. (Chgo.), 1961-70. Sigma Xi. Distinguished Faculty lectr., 1965. Trustee Chgo. Planetarium Soc., 1961-67. Recipient Distinguished Service medal Dept. Interior, Bur. Mines, 1952; Percy Nicholls award Am. Soc. M.E. fuel div., 1968. Mem. Am. Inst. Chem. Engrs., Am. Soc. M.E., Am. Gas Assn., Soc. Automotive Engrs., Am. Soc. Engring. Edn., Inst. Fuel (U.K.), Sigma Xi, Tau Beta Pi, Pi Tau Sigma, Omicron Delta Kappa, Alpha Tau Omega. Clubs: University (Chgo.); Cosmos (Washington); Houston. Author tech. articles. Home: 13623 Alchester Rd Houston TX 77024 Office: Tex Eastern Transmission Corp P O Box 2521 Houston TX 77001

ELLIOTT, OSBORN, editor; b. N.Y.C., Oct. 25, 1924; s. John and Audrey N. (Osborn) E.; grad. St. Paul's Sch., 1942 A.B., Harvard, 1946; m. Deirdre M. Spencer, May 8, 1948; children—Diana, Cynthia, Dorinda. Reporter, N.Y. Jour. Commerce, 1946-49; contbg. editor Time mag., 1949-52, asso. editor, 1952- 55; sr. bus. editor Newsweek, 1955-59, mng. editor, 1959-61, 1961-69, editor-in-chief, vice chmn., 1970—; dir. Washington Post Co. Trustee Am. Mus. Natural History, N.Y. Public Library, St. Paul's Sch., U.S. Churchill Found. mem. bd. overseers Harvard, 1965—. Served with USNR, 1944-46. Mem. Council Fgn. Relations, Asia Soc. (trustee). The Century Assn. Clubs: Harvard, Coffee House, Racquet and Tennis (N.Y.C.). Author: Men At the Top, 1959. Editor: The Negro Revolution in America, 1964. Home: 206 E 72d St New York City NY 10021 Office: 444 Madison Av New York City NY 10036

ELLIOTT, OWEN N., lawyer; b. Marion, Ia., Mar. 13, 1886; s. Herbert I. and Martha (Owen) E.; A.B., Coe Coll., Cedar Rapids, Ia., 1907; LL.B., U. of Ia., 1910; m. Leone Lorimor, Nov. 12, 1929. Admitted to Ia. bar, 1910; city atty., Cedar Rapids, Ia., 1916-24. Pres. Owen and Leone Elliott Inc., charitable trust. Mem. Internat., Am., Ia. bar assns., Acacia, Phi Beta Kappa, Phi Delta Phi. Mason (32, Shriner), Elk. Clubs: Pickwick, Country, Embassy (Cedar Rapids). Home: Montrose Hotel Cedar Rapids IA 52406

ELLIOTT, PHILIP CLARKSON, educator, artist; b.Mpls., Dec. 5, 1903; s. Charles Burke and Edith (Winslow) E.; student U. Minn., 1921-23; B.F.A., Yale, 1926; Chaloner fellow for European study, 1929-33; m. Virginia Isobel Cuthbert, June 8, 1935. Asst. prof. fine art U. Pitts., 1934-41; dir. Albright Art Sch., U. Buffalo, 1941—; now prof., dir. dept. art State U. N.Y. at Buffalo. Exhibited paintings Mus. Modern Art, Phila. Acad., Carnegie Internat., Albright Art Gallery, Whtney Mus. Am. Art, Met. Mus., Albright-Knox Gallery, Butler Art Inst. Ann., Syracuse (N.Y.) State Expn., Three Rivers Art Festival, W. N.Y. Art Exhbins.; represented permanent collection Albright-Knox Gallery, also numerous pvt. collections. Recipient Distinguished Faculty fellowship U. State N.Y., 1967. Mem. Buffalo Fine Arts Acad. (hon. life). Coll. Art Assn., Nat. Schs. Art, Patteran Artists. Democrat. Episcopalian. Home: 147 Bryant St Buffalo, NY 14222.

ELLIOTT, RALPH EDWARD, banker; b. Ruckinge, Kent, England, May 7, 1908; s. Frederick Worsley and Minnie (Woods) E.; student schs. Ashford, Kent, Eng.; m. Phyllis Craig, Apr. 14, 1934; children—Jessica Mary, Charles Edward, Andrew Craig. Joint gen. mgr. Westminster Bank Ltd., London, 1958-65, dep. chief gen. mgr., 1965, chief gen. mgr., 1966-68; joint chief exec. Nat. Westminster Bank Ltd., London, 1968-70, dir. (also Westminster Fgn. Bank Ltd., 1969—), 1968—, dep. chmn., 1970—. Fellow Inst. Bankers. Home: Little Hendra Shire Lane Charleywood Hertfordshire England Office: Nat Westminster Bank Ltd 41 Lothbury London EC2 England

ELLIOTT, RAYMOND HENRY, savs. and loan assn. exec.; b. Milford, Mass., May 17, 1930; s. Henry Sanborn and Bessie Una (Marshall) E.; grad. Boston Inst., 1950, Exec. Devel. Sch. U. Ga., 1963, Grad. Sch. Savs. and Loan Ind. U., 1967, Advanced Mgmt. program Harvard, 1969; m. Marie DelCastello, Apr. 4, 1951; children—Steven G., Janet M. Gen. sales mgr. Martin Cerel, Realtor, Inc., Natick, Mass., 1954-59; with N.E. Fed. Savs. & Loan Assn., Watertown, Mass., 1959—, pres., 1969—, also dir. Founding chmn. Loan Officers Workshop of New Eng., 1964; spl. corr. on nat. mortgage outlook Christian Sci. Monitor, 1965; mem. adv. com. Mass. Housing Finance Agy., 1969—; vice chmn. mortgage finance com. Greater Boston Real Estate Bd., 1969, chmn., 1971-72; founding chmn. Mass. Council Service Corp., 1970; pres., bd. dirs. N.E. Resources Corp., 1970—; pres. Better Cities, Inc., 1971; mem. Mass. Real Estate Bd., 1960—. Served with USNR, 1950-54. Mem. Soc. Real Estate Appraisers, Nat. Assn. Home Builders, Harvard Bus. School Assn. Boston, Clubs: Harvard (Boston); Framingham Country. Home: 584 Water St Framingham MA 02172 Office: 75 Main St Watertown MA 02172

ELLIOTT, RICHARD HOSS, lawyer; b. Clarksburg, W.Va., Dec. 31, 1919; s. Donald Finley and Pauline (Hoss) E.; A.B., Depauw U., 1942; J.D., U. Ariz., 1951; m. Vonnie Maxine Yeatman, Oct. 19, 1946; children—Malinda, James Finley II, William Lewis. Copywriter, display advt. dept. Republic & Gazette, Phoenix, 1945-48; admitted to Ariz. bar, 1951; practiced in Phoenix, 1951—; mem. firm Carson, Messinger, Elliott, Laughlin & Ragan, 1956—; spl. asst. to U.S. atty. gen., 1954-67; Ariz. commr. uniform state laws, 1969—. Bd. dirs. Cook Christian Tng. Sch., 1959-68. Served to 1st lt. AUS. 1942-45. Mem. Am., Maricopa County (dir. 1956-61, pres. 1960) bar assns., State Bar Ariz. (bd. govs., treas. 1961-63), Phi Kappa Psi, Phi Delta Phi. Clubs: Lawyers (dir. 1967—), Cloud (dir. 1964-67), Wigwam Country. Home: 1523 W Myrtle Av Phoenix AZ 85021 Office: United Bank Bldg 3550 N Central Av Phoenix AZ 85012

ELLIOTT, ROBERT CARL, educator; b. Indpls., Nov. 23, 1914; s. Robert Carl and Lucy (Woodbridge) E.; A.B., Wabash (Ind.) Coll., 1936; M.A., Columbia, 1937; Ph.D., Brown U., 1946; m. Mary Curtin, May 19, 1945. Instr. English, U. Hawaii, 1937-39, 41; from instr. to prof. English, Ohio State U., 1946- 64; prof. English, U. Cal. at San Diego, 1964—, chmn. lit. dept., 1968- 71. Served to lt. USNR, 1942-46. Decorated Bronze Star. Mem. Modern Lang. Assn., Am. Assn. U. Profs. (pres. Ohio State U. 1963-64)., Internat. Assn. U. Profs. English, P.E.N., Phi Beta Kappa. Author: The Power of Satire: Magic, Ritual, Art, 1960; The Shape of Utopia, 1970; also articles. Home: 1381 Coast Walk La Jolla CA 92037

ELLIOTT, ROBERT GEORGE, communications exec.; b. Craigmont, Ida., Oct. 6, 1907; s. Oliver and Louise (Roberts) E.; B.S. U. Ida., 1928; m. Dorothy Louise Avery, Sept. 15, 1934 (dec. 1957); 1 dau., Marianne (Mrs. Robert Spencer Familton II); m. 2d, Erna Schnabel Thurston, Feb. 27, 1960. Various engring., plant dept. assignments Pacific Tel. & Tel. Co., Seattle, 1928-50, gen. program engr., San Francisco, 1950-51, plant extension engr., Los Angeles, 1951-53, chief engr., 1953-54; asst. chief engr. Am. Tel. & Tel. Co., N.Y.C., 1954-56; chief engr. So. Bell Tel. & Tel. Co., Atlanta, 1956-57, v.p. staff operations, 1957-61, v.p. marketing, 1961-66, v.p. planning, 1966—. Registered profl. engr., Ga. Fellow I.E.E.E.; mem. Ga. Engring. Soc., Sigma Tau. Clubs: Commerce, Capital City (Atlanta). Home: 4883 Roswell Rd NE Atlanta GA 30305 Office: Hurt Bldg Atlanta GA 30303

ELLIOTT, ROBERT HARE EGERTON, physician, educator; b. Flushing, N.Y., Sept. 9, 1906; s. Robert Hare Egerton and Fannie (Bogaert) E.; grad. Kent (Conn.) Sch., 1924; B.A., Princeton, 1928; M.D., Columbia, 1932, Med. Sc.D. in Surgery, 1938; spl. research fellow Cambridge (Eng.) U., 1933; m. Mary Amelia Turnbull, Nov. 20, 1935; children—Mary Stewart (Mrs. E. T. Fogarty), Robert Hare Egerton, Susan Anthony. Surgery intern Presbyn. Hosp., 1933-35, surg. resident, 1935-38, asst. surgery, 1941-46, clin. dir. NRC study contaminated wounds and burns, 1942-45, asst. attending surgeon, 1946-49, asso. attending surgeon, 1949-52, chief East surg. service, 1952-66, attending surgeon, 1952—, asst. v.p., 1966—; asst. surgery Vanderbilt Clinic, 1938-41, asst. chief clinic surgery, 1941-46, chief clinic surgery 1946-50; asso. attending surgeon Columbia div. Bellevue Hosp., 1949-52; civilian cons. surgery Sta. Hosp., U.S. Mil. Acad., 1949-66; cons. surgery Southhampton (N.Y.) Hosp., 1956—, Harlem Hosp., 1964-67; mem. faculty Columbia Coll. Physicians and Surgeons, 1938—, prof. clin. surgery, 1965—, asso. dean Faculty Medicine, 1966—; sec., 1970. Lewis Linn McArthur lectr. Frank Billings Found., Inst. Medicine, Chgo., 1947; mem. interdisciplinary com. on health manpower utilization and tng. N.Y. Met. Regional Med. Program, 1970—. Chmn. dept. Christian social relations Episcopal Diocese N.Y., 1961-62, mem. council, 1958-62, mem. standing com., 1962-66. Bd. dirs. Nat. Assn. Practical Nurse Edn. and Service, 1969—, mem. exec. com., 1971—; past trustee Fieldston Property Owners, Inc., Decorated comdr. Am. Soc. Most Venerable Order St. John Jerusalem, 1970. Diplomate Nat. Bd. Med. Examiners, Am. Bd. Surgery. Fellow A.C.S.; mem. A.M.A., N.Y. State, New York County med. socs., A.O. Whipple Surg. Soc. (past pres.), Soc. Univ. Surgeons, N.Y. Acad. Medicine, N.Y. Surg. Soc., Soc. Alumni Presbyn. Hosp. (past pres.), Am. Thyroid Assn., Assn. Schs. of Allied Health Professions, Phi Beta Kappa, Alpha Omega Alpha. Episcopalian (vestryman, former sr. warden). Clubs: Riverdale Yacht, Century Assn. (N.Y.C.). Contbr. to profl. jours. Home: 4961 Henry Hudson Pky Bronx NY 10471 Office: 630 W 168th St New York City NY 10032

ELLIOTT, THOMAS ANTHONY KEITH, diplomat; b. Burford, Eng., May 27, 1921; s. Ivo D'Oyly and Margery Helen (Carey) E.; grad. Eton Coll., 1939; B.A. in History with honors, Balliol Coll., Oxford U., 1947; m. Alethea Richardson, Oct. 6, 1951; children—Victoria, Catherine, Anne, Thomas. Joined Brit. Fgn. Service, 1947; 2d sec. brit. embassy, Belgrade, Yugoslavia, 1949-52; with Fgn. Office, London, 1952-53, 1st sec., 1953-57; head chancery, Peking, China., 1957-60, Athens, 1960-61; asst. head Western Orgns. Dept., Fgn. Office, London, 1961-64, counsellor, head tng. sect., 1964-65; polit. adviser Hong Kong Govt., 1965-68; head chancery, Washington, 1968—, minister, 1970—. Served as capt. King's Shropshire Light Inf., 1941-46; E. Africa, Somaliland. Decorated comdr. Order St. Michael and St. George, 1968. Home: 2825 McGill Terrace Washington DC 20008 Office: 3100 Massachusetts Av Washington DC 20008

ELLIOTT, WARREN G., lawyer, ins. co. exec.; b. Pueblo, Colo., Jan. 3, 1927; s. Wallace Ford and Hazel (Ellsworth) E.; student U. Neb., 1944-45, U. Colo., 1947-49; LL.B., U. Mich., 1952; m. M. Martha McCabe, June 20, 1953; children—Mark, Winthrop, Carolyn, Byron. Admitted to Colo. bar, 1952; asst. city mgr., city atty., Pueblo, 1952-55; adminstrv. asst., legislative counsel U.S. Senator Gordon Allott, 1956-61; asst. gen. counsel Life Ins. Assn. Am., Washington, 1961-68; gen. counsel Aetna Life & Casualty Co., Hartford, Conn., 1968—; dir. Aetna Financial Services, Inc., Aetna Investment Mgmt., Inc., Hartford brs. Conn. Bank & Trust Co. Pres. Civic Tobytown Devel. Corp., Potomac, Md., 1966-68; commr. Met. Dist., 1970—. Corporator Hartford Hosp. Served with USAAF, 1944-46. Mem. Am., Fed. bar assns., Greater Hartford C. of C., Congl. Club Greater Hartford, Phi Gamma Delta, Phi Alpha Delta. Club: Hartford . Home: 1414 Asylum Av Hartford CT 06105 Office: 151 Farmington Av Hartford CT 06115

ELLIOTT, WILLIAM MICHAEL, aluminum co. exec.; b. Leavenworth, Kan., Apr. 18, 1934; s. James Edward and Grace Margaret (Slack) E.; B.A., U. Mo. at Kansas City, 1959; J.D., 1962; m. Maria Esther Vega, Apr. 30, 1960; children—Carmen Marissa, Stephanie Lynn. Admitted to Mo. bar, 1962, Mich. bar, 1965, Cal. bar, 1965; asst. div. atty. Mobil Oil Corp., 1962-68; asst. gen. counsel Harvey Aluminum Inc., Torrance, Cal., 1968-69, sec., gen. counsel, 1969—. Served with USMC, 1953-56. Mem. Am., Mo., Mich., Los Angeles, Orange County bar assns., Phi Alpha Delta. Home: 15782 Clarendon St Westminster CA 92683 Office: 19200 S Western Av Torrance CA 90509

ELLIOTT, WILLIAM YANDELL, author; b. Murfreesboro, Tenn., May 13, 1896; s. William Yandell and Annie Mary (Bullock) E.; A.B., Vanderbilt U., 1917, A.M., 1920; certificate Sorbonne, Paris, France, 1919; D. Phil. (Rhodes scholar), Balliol Coll., Oxford (Eng.) U., 1923; LL.D.; m. Barbara Foster, June 28, 1923; children—William Yandell (dec.), Paul Pinkerton Foster, Charles James Fox Wharton; m. 2d, Mary Louise Ward, Aug. 26, 1936; children—Ward Edward Yandell, David William Penn. Instr., Vanderbilt U., 1919-20, U. Cal., 1923-24, asst. prof., 1924-25; lectr. and tutor govt. dept., asst. prof., Harvard, 1925-29, asso. prof., 1929-31, prof., 1931-63, prof. emeritus, 1963—, Williams prof. history and govt., 1942, dir. summer sch., 1950-60; Univ. prof. Am. U., Washington, 1963-69, prof. emeritus 1969—; Buell G. Gallagagher Distinguished vis. prof. Coll. City N.Y., 1968—. Cons. Pres.'s Com. on Adminst n. Mgmt., 1936, Nat. Adv. Def. Commn., 1940, Office Prodn. Mgmt., 1941, Ho. of Reps. Spl. Com. on Postwar Econ. Policy and Planning, 1945-46; cons. sec. state, 1958-63; mem. Senator Tydings mission to Philippines, 1945; dir. Stockpile and Transp. Div., WPB, 1942-44, vice chmn. Civilian Requirements, 1944-45; staff dir. House Select Com. Fgn. Aid, 1947-48, Ho. Com. Fgn. Affairs, 1947-49; asst. dir. O.D.M., 1951-53; mem. planning bd. Nat. Security Council 1953-57. Served to 1st lt., 114th Field Arty., 30th Div. A.E.F. World War I. Mem. Bus. Council (hon. mem., conf. nat. orgn.), Phi Beta Kappa, Sigma Chi. Mem. Disciples of Christ. Author books in field of polit. sci., including Pragmatic Revolt on Politics; New British Empire; Need for Constitutional Reform. Editor: The British Commonwealth at War, 1943; Western Political Heritage (with N. A. McDonald), 1949; American Foreign Policy; Organization and Control, 1952; Political Economy of the Foreign Policy of the United States, 1955; Television's Impact on American Culture, 1956; Education and Training in the Developing Countries: Foreign Aid, 1966. Co-author: The Idea of Colonialism, 1958; The Secretary of State, 1960; The U.S. and the UN, 1961. Home: Hidden Valley Farm Haywood VA 22722

ELLIS, AILEEN VIRGINIA, librarian; b. Cranberry, N.C.; d. Cale Donald and Josephine Juanita (Hyder) Ellis; A.B. summa cum laude, Milligan Coll., B.S., Peabody Coll., M.A., 1958; postgrad. Fla. State U., 1966-68. Librarian, Maxwell AFB, 1958-63; staff librarian Robins AFB, Ga., 1963-66; base librarian Eglin AFB, Fla., 1966-70, chief library br., 1970—. Historian, Montgomery Little Theatre, 1962-63. Recipient Outstanding award Dept. Air Force, 1970. Mem. Am., Southeastern, W.Fla. (v.p.), Fla., Spl. (sec. Fla. chpt.) library assns., Am. Assn. U. Women (v.p. Fla. div.), D.A.R., Hist. Soc. Okaloosa and Walton Counties. Republican. Presbyn. Club: Lake Lorraine Country (Shalimar, Fla.). Indexer: Ala. Librarian, 1963-70. Home: 30 12th St Shalimar FL 32579 Office: PO Box 1732 Eglin AFB FL 32542

ELLIS, ALBERT, clin. psychologist; b. Pitts., Sept. 27, 1913; s. Henry Oscar and Hettie (Hanigbaum), E.; B.B.A., Coll. City N.Y., 1934; M.A., Columbia, 1943, Ph.D., 1947; m. Rhoda Winter, May 26, 1956 (div.). Free-lance writer, 1934-38; personnel mgr. Distinctive Creations, 1938-48; sr. clin. psychologist N.J. State Hosp., Greystone Park, 1948-49; instr. psychology Rutgers U., 1948-49, N.Y.U., 1949; chief psychologist N.J. State Diagnostic Center, Menlo Park, 1949-50, N.J. Dept. Instns. and Agys., Trenton, 1950-52; pvt. practice psychotherapy and marriage counseling, N.Y.C., 1943-68; exec. dir. Inst. for Rational Living, Inc., N.Y.C., 1959—; dir. clin. services Inst. Advanced Study in Rational Psychotherapy, 1968—. Cons. clin. psychology VA, 1961-67. Diplomate Am. Bd. Profl. Psychology; in clin. hypnosis Am. Bd. Psychol. Hypnosis. Fellow Am. Psychol. Assn. (pres. div. cons. psychology 1961-62, exec. com. div. psychotherapy 1969-71), A.A.A.S., Am. Assn. Marriage Counselors (exec. com. 1957-59), Soc. Sci. Study Sex (exec. com. 1957-68, pres. 1960-62), Am. Orthopsychiat. Assn., Am. Sociol. Assn., Am. Assn. Applied Anthropology; mem. N.Y. Assn. Clin. Psychologists in Pvt. Practice (chmn. 1952-54), N.Y. Joint Council Psychologists on Legislation (exec. com. 1951-53), Am. Group Psychotherapy Assn., Am. Acad. Psychotherapists (mem. exec. com. 1954-64, v.p. 1962-64), Mensa, Am. Assn. Advancement Psychotherapy, N.Y. State Psychol. Assn., Soc. Exptl. and Clin. Hypnosis. Author: An Introduction to the Principles of Scientific Psychoanalysis, 1950; The Folklore of Sex, 1951; (with A.P. Pillay) Sex, Society and the Individual, 1953; The American Sexual Tragedy, 1954; Sex Life of the American Woman and the Kinsey Report, 1954; New Approaches to Psychotherapy Techniques, 1955; (with Ralph Brancale) The Psychology of Sex Offenders, 1956; How to Live With a Neurotic, 1957; Sex Without Guilt, 1958; What Is Psychotherapy, 1959; The Place of Values in the Practice of Psychotherapy, 1959; The Art and Science of Love, 1960; (with Robert A. Harper) Creative Marriage, 1960; A Guide to Rational Living, 1961; (with Albert Abrabanel) The Encyclopedia of Sexual Behavior, 1961; Reason and Emotion in Psychotherapy, 1962; The Intelligent Woman's Guide to Manhunting, 1963; If This Be Sexual Heresy, 1963; Sex and the Single Man, 1963; The Origins and the Development of the Incest Taboo, 1963; (with Edward Sagarin) Nymphomania, A Study of the Over-Sexed Woman, 1964; Homosexuality: Its Causes and Cure, 1965; Suppressed: Seven Key Essays Publishers Dared Not Print, 1965; The Case for Sexual Liberty, 1965; The Search for Sexual Enjoyment, 1966; (with others) How to Prevent Your Child From Becoming a Neurotic Adult, 1966; (with Roger O. Conway) The Art of Erotic Seduction, 1967; Is Objectivesm a Religion?, 1968; (with John M. Gullo) Murder and Assassinations, 1971, A Casebook of Rational Emotive Therapy, 1971; Growth Through Reason, 1971; Rational Sensitivity: Self-fulfillment for Executives, 1971. Office: 45 E 65th St New York City NY 10021

ELLIS, ANTHONY THORNTON, mining co. exec.; b. Eminence, Ky., Feb. 26, 1929; s. Anthony Thornton and Georgiana (Swinney) E.; B.S., U. Cal., Berkeley, 1951; M.B.A., Harvard, 1956; m. Jane Canning, Nov. 11, 1956; children—Susan, Winnifred, David. Asst. casher First Nat. City Bank, N.Y.C., 1958-60, asst. v.p., 1960-62, v.p., 1962-70; treas. Kennecott Copper Corp., N.Y.C., 1970—. Bd. dirs. Forest Neighborhood House, Bronx, N.Y. Served to lt. (j.g.) USNR, 1951-54. Mem. Beta Theta Pi. Republican. Clubs: Racquet and Tennis (N.Y.C.), Bronxville Field. Home: 15 Edgewood Lane Bronxville NY 10708 Office: 161 E 42d St New York City NY 10017

ELLIS, BROOKS FLEMING, geologist; b. Jonestown, W.Va., Aug. 2, 1897; s. Leander A. and Harriet E. (Fleming) E.; A.B., Marietta Coll. 1923, Sc.D. (hon.), 1953; M.S., N.Y.U., 1929, Ph.D., 1932; postgrad. Yale and Columbia; m. Nell L. Reed, Dec. 25, 1920 (dec. Apr. 1966); m. 2d, Alice Gilman, Aug. 2, 1966. Instr. Sci. W.Va. high schs., 1923- 26, N.Y., 1927-29; instr. geology, N.Y. U., 1930-36, asst. prof., 1936-43, asso. prof., dept. chmn., 1943-46, prof., dept. chmn. 1946-58, prof., dept. chmn., dept. head all-univ. dept., 1958-66, prof. emeritus, 1966—; adj. prof. geology Rutgers U. of N.J., 1966-70; curator micropaleontology Am. Mus. Natural History, 1941-44, curator and chmn. micropaleontology, 1944-67, curator emeritus, 1967—; instr. Bklyn. Coll. (evening) , 1933-39; dir. Am. Mus. Research Project on Foraminifers, 1930-41. Dir. Equitable Petroleum Corp. Served with U.S. Navy, 1917-19. Fellow A.A.A.S., Am. Geog. Soc., Geol. Soc. Am.; mem. Paleontol. Soc., Soc. Econ. Palentologists and Mineralogists, Am. Assn. Petroleum Geologists, Soc. Study Evolution, Schweizerischen Palaontolgischen Gesellschaft, Société Geologique Suisse, Deutschen Geologischen Gesellschaft, Deutschen Palaontologischen Gesellshaft, Société Geologique de France, Am. Geophys. Union, Am. Polar Soc., Phi Beta Kappa, Sigma Xi. Club: Explorers. Author: (with A.R. Messina) Catalogue of Foraminifera, 69 vols., Catalogue of Ostracoda, 29 vols., (with A.F. Messina) Catalogue of Index Larger Foraminifera, 3 vols.; (with A.R. Messina, Richard Charmatz, Lilly Ronai) Catalogue of Index Smaller Foraminifera, 3 vols. Co-editor Micropaleontology (quarterly). Home: 72 Clarendon Rd Scarsdale NY 10583

ELLIS, CALVERT N., former coll. pres.; b. Zion City, Ill., Apr. 16, 1904; s. Charles Calvert and Emma Read (Nyce) E.; A.B., Juniata Coll., Huntingdon, Pa., 1923, LL.D. , 1963; B. Th., M.A., Princeton, 1927; Ph.D., Yale, 1932; D.D., Bethany Bib. Sem., 1950; LL.D., Manchester Coll., 1956; m. Elizabeth Olier Wertz, June 18, 1929; children—Elizabeth Anne, David Wertz. Instr. Lewistown (Pa.) High Sch., 1923-24, Wilson Coll., Chambersburg, Pa., 1927-28; asst. prof., prof. bibl. studies and philosophy, Juniata Coll., Huntingdon, Pa., 1931-43, pres., 1943-68, pres. emeritus, 1968—; mgr. D.M. Wertz Orchards, Waynesboro, Pa., 1940-59. Dir. First Nat. Bank, Huntingdon. Mem. adv. com. to AID, 1966-69; cons. higher edn., 1968—. Trustee J.C. Blair Hosp., Huntingdon,; chmn. Gen. Brotherhood Bd., Elgin, Ill., 1948-54, 66-67; adv. com. higher edn. to Edn. Compact of the States, 1966—, adviser Ho. of Reps., 1944. chmn. commn. on legislation Assn. Am. Colls., 1961-64, chmn. bd., 1969. Mem. Nat. Assn. Bibl. Lit. and Exegesis, Middle States Assn. Colls. and Secondary Schs. (pres. 1965). Rotarian. Author: The Conception of Revelation in the Dielectic Theory, 1932; Church of the Brethren. Home: Taylor Highlands Huntingdon PA 16652

ELLIS, CHARLES CALVERT, banker; b. Balt., Feb. 2, 1919; s. Luke and Olivia (Kelley) E.; A.B., Juniata Coll., Huntingdon, Pa., 1940; M.B.A., Harvard, 1942; m. Jean Ella Good, Dec. 29, 1942; children—Charles Calvert III, Pauline Olivia, Nancy Ruth, Richard James. With Armstrong Cork Co., 1946-52, plant controller, Beaver Falls, Pa., 1949-52; with Ford Motor Co., 1952-59, regional finance exec., internat. div. Latin Am., 1958-59; controller Kordite Corp., 1959-62; with Philco Ford Corp., 1962-65, controller consumer products div., 1964-65; with Irving Trust Co., N.Y.C., 1965—, sr. v.p., comptroller, 1966-69, exec. v.p. 1969—; asst. treas. Charter N.Y. Corp., 1966-69, sr. v.p., treas., 1969—; dir. Ford of Portugal, 1958-59; tchr. extension U. Mich., 1956-59. Chmn. accounting and finance com. Nat. Flexible Packaging Assn., 1961-62; chmn. accounting and tax com. N.Y. Clearing House, 1968-69. Trustee Juniata Coll., 1966—. Served to lt. USNR, 1942-46. Home: 761 Red Oak Lane Kinnelon NJ 07405 Office: 1 Wall St New York City NY 10015

ELLIS, CLYDE TAYLOR, lawyer, cons.; b. nr. Garfield, Ark., Dec. 21, 1908; s. Cecil Oscar and Minerva Jane (Taylor) E.; B.S. in Bus. Adminstrn., U. Ark., 1958; m. Izella Baker, Dec. 20, 1931; children—Patricia Suzanne, Mary Lynn; m. 2d, Camille W. Fitzhugh, Sept. 23, 1966. Supt. schs., Garfield, Ark., 1920- 34; admitted to Ark. bar, 1933, practiced in Garfield and Bentonville; gen. mgr. Nat. Rural Electric Coop. Assn., Washington, 1943-67; mem. Nat. Water Commn., Washington, 1968-70; rural devel. asst. to Senator John L. McClellan, 1971—. Spl. cons. to Sec. of Agr. Mem. Ark. Gen. Assembly, 1933-34, Ark. Senate, 1935-36; mem. 76-77th congresses from 3d Ark. Dist. Mem. Nat. Capitol Democratic Club. Served with USNR, World War II. Mem. Ark., Washington bar assns. Democrat. Episcopalian. Mason. Clubs: Cosmos, Congressional Country (Washington). Author: Giant Step, 1967. Home: 5317 Kenwood Av Chevy Chase MD 20015 Office: 818 18th St NW Washington DC 20006

ELLIS, CONSTANCE DIMOCK, editor, coll. trustee; b. Flushing, N.Y., Aug. 2, 1915; d. Edward Jordan and Constance (Bullard) Dimock; B.A. (fellow 1938), Vassar Coll., 1938; postgrad. Columbia, 1938-39, Yale, 1939-41, 46; m. Frank Hale Ellis, Dec. 20, 1940; 1 dau., Gay. Instr. English, Vassar Coll., 1942-46; editor Vassar Alumnae mag., 1946-52; asso. editor, cons. John G. Holmes Assos., N.Y.C., 1958-61; dir. pub. relations Northampton (Mass.) Sch. Girls, 1961-68; editor Smith Coll. Pamphlets, 1961—. Trustee Vassar Coll., 1961—, Democrat. Editor: Sex and the College Student, 1965; The Magnificent Enterprise: A Chronicle of Vassar College, 1961. Address: 146 Elm St Smith Coll Northampton MA 01060

ELLIS, DAVID MALDWYN, educator; b. Utica, N.Y., Oct. 14, 1914; s. Samuel and Margaret Brymer (Jones) E.; B.A., Hamilton Coll., 1938; M.A., Cornell U., Ithaca, N.Y., 1939, Ph.D., 1942; m. Carolyn Crawford, June 20, 1953. Instr. history U. Vt., 1942- 44; asst. prof. history Cornell U., Ithaca, N.Y., 1944; faculty Hamilton Coll., 1946- -, V. Rogers prof. history, 1957—, also chmn. history dept., 1968—. Pres., N.Y. Assn. Am. Studies. Fellow N.Y. Hist. Assn.; mem. Am. Hist. Assn., Orgn. Am. Historians, Am. Studies Assn. (exec. bd.), Phi Beta Kappa. Presbyn. Author: Landlords and Farmers in the Hudson- Mohawk Region 1790-1850, 1946. Co-author: New York the Empire State, 1969; A History of New York State, 1967; also articles. Gen. editor The Frontier in American Development, 1969. Home: 250 College Hill Clinton NY 13323

ELLIS, DON A., bus. exec.; b. 1916; B.S., U. Cin., 1941. With Boeing Aircraft Co., 1944-46, Hyster Co., 1946-49, Iron Fireman Mfg. Co., 1950-51; with Tektronix, Inc., 1951—, treas., 1958—; chmn. bd. dirs., treas. Rodgers Organ Co.; dir. Richard Abel & Co., Omsi/Kit Inc. Address: PO Box 500 Beaverton OR 97005

ELLIS, DON EDWIN, educator; b. Ames, Ia., Apr. 8, 1908; s. Charles Elmer and Bertha Helen (Fraker) E.; A.B., Neb. Central Coll., 1928, B.S., 1929; M.S., La. State U., 1932; Ph.D., U. N.C., 1945; m. Helen Margaret Watkins, Dec. 29, 1928; 1 dau., Carol Don (Mrs. Winston Delane Montague). Sci. tchr. Juniata (Neb.) High Sch., 1929-31; research asst. La. State U., 1931-33; asst. pathologist div. forest pathology U.S. Dept. Agr., Ariz., N.M., 1934-40; asst. prof. N.C. State U., Raleigh, 1940-44, asso. prof., 1945-50, prof., 1950—, head, dept. plant pathology, 1954—. Visited agrl. areas and research installations in Mexico, Guatemala, 1962, Venezuela, 1966, Colombia, Panama, 1970; plant pathology cons. Peru, Servicio de Investigacion y Promocion Agraria, Universidad Agraria, N.C. State Agr. Mission to Peru, 1963, 66, 70. Mem. Am. Phytopath. Soc. (pres. So. div. 1962, mem. council 1957-59, chmn. com. on awards and honors 1960-63, v.p., 1967-68, pres. 1969-70), Am. Inst. Biol. Scis., Mycol. Soc. Am., Assn. Tropical Biology, N.C. Acad. Sci., Sigma Xi, Gamma Sigma Delta (Merit award 1970-71). Contbr. articles sci. publs. Home: 324 Shepherd Raleigh NC 27607

ELLIS, DONALD HOWARD, real estate investment co. exec.; b. Long Beach, Cal., Feb. 9, 1931; s. Carl O. and Reta (Cooper) E.; A.A., Pasadena City Coll., 1951; B.S., U. Cal., Los Angeles, 1953; m. Mary Elin Gomes, Aug. 12, 1953; children—Mark, Lisa. Account exec. Univac Div. Sperry Rand Co., Los Angeles, 1956-63; dir. research Financial Sec., Inc., Los Angeles, 1963- 65, dir., 1965-66; pres. Property Research Corp., Los Angeles, 1965—; exec. v.p., dir. Property Research Financial Corp.; tchr. computer programming Los Angeles Met. Coll., 1963-64. Mem. steering com. syndication div. Cal. Real Estate Assn. Served with USNR, 1953-55. Mem. Nat. Assn. Security Dealers. Presbyn. (deacon). Home: 17 Eastfield Dr Rolling Hills CA 90274 Office: 1880 Century Park East Los Angeles CA 90067

ELLIS, DONALD JOHNSON, trumpet player, composer: b. Los Angeles, July 25, 1934; s. Evert Ezra and Winston E. (Johnson) E.; Mus. B., Boston, U., 1956; postgrad. U. Cal. at Los Angeles, 1963-64; m. Constance Cynthia Coogan, July 28, 1961; children—Bray Johnson, Tran Robert. Trumpet player with numerous orchs., 1952-66, including Glenn Miller, 1956, Charlie Barnet, Maynard Ferguson, 1958-60; numerous recordings with own groups, 1960-66; leader Don Ellis Orch., 1965—; soloist Nat. Symphony Orch., Washington, 1962, N.Y. Philharmonic Orch., 1963-64; performed Los Angeles Music Center with Stan Kenton Neophonic Orch. in original composition, Synthesis, 1966; rec. artist for Candid, Prestige, Pacific Jazz, Columbia records. Recipient First Place award Internat. Jazz Critics Poll, 1962. Rockefeller grant Center Creative and Performing Arts State U. N.Y., Buffalo, 1964-65. Author: Future: Tense, 1970; composer works including Reach, a cantata, 1968; movie score Moon Zero Two, The French Connection. Home and Office: 5436 Auckland Av North Hollywood CA 91601

ELLIS, EDWARD EVAN, food co. exec.; b. Miami, Fla., Sept. 13, 1931; s. Thomas Jean and Lucile Ann (Hutson) E.; B.A., Washington and Lee U., 1952, LL.B. magna cum laude, 1956; postgrad. Academie de Droit Internat., The Hague, Netherlands, 1955; m. Hollis Titman, Dec. 23, 1963; children—John Christopher, Sara Dee, Steven Weeks, Martha Blair. Admitted to N.Y. bar, 1957, Ky. bar, 1971; asso. law firm Davis, Polk & Wardwell, N.Y.C., 1956-57, 59-63; corporate lawyer Interpub. Group of Cos., N.Y.C., 1963-69; gen. counsel, sec. Ky. Fried Chicken Corp., Louisville, 1969—. Served as 2d lt. USAF, 1953, as 1st lt., 1957-59. Mem. Assn. Bar City New York, Am. Bar Assn., Order of Coif, Phi Beta Kappa, Omicron Delta Kappa, Kappa Alpha, Phi Delta Phi. Club: Louisville Boat. Home: 2502 Longest Av Louisville KY 40204 Office: 1441 Gardiner Lane Louisville KY 40213

ELLIS, EFFIE O., pediatrician, govt. ofcl.; b. Ga., circa 1913; m., 1 dau. Formerly taught medicine Harvard; became child health specialist for Welfare Dept., Chgo., 1964; named commr. for Midwest region U.S. Social and Rehab. Service, Chgo., 1967; organized Compcare, child health program, Chgo., 1966; spl. asst. for health services A.M.A.; mem. Pres.'s Com. on Employment Handicapped, 1970—.*

ELLIS, ELMER, historian, educator; b. McHenry County, N.D., July 27, 1901; s. Thomas Clarkson and Lillie Jane (Butterfield) E.; A.B., U. N.D., 1924, A.M., 1925, LL.D., 1946; Ph.D., U. Ia., 1930; LL.D., Central Coll., 1955, Drury Coll., 1956, Washington U., St. Louis, 1960; L.H.D., Culver- Stockton Coll., 1961; Litt.D. (hon.), St. Louis U. 1965; m. Ruth Clapper, Aug. 14, 1925. Lectr. in history U. Ia., 1928-30; prof. history and govt. N.D. State Tchrs. Coll., 1925-28; asst. asso. and prof. of history U. Mo., 1930-71, acting dean Grad. Sch., summers 1936, 39, 41, v.p., 1945-46, dean Coll. Arts and Scis., 1946-55, acting pres. univ., 1954-55, pres., 1955-66, pres. emeritus, 1966—. Vis. Fulbright prof. Am. history U. Amsterdam, 1951-52; instr. in history U. N.D., summer 1925; vis. prof. history Ohio State U., summer 1937; faculty Salzburg Seminar Am. Studies, 1952; chmn. hist. adv. com. U.S. Army, 1957-59; mem. bd. Fgn. Scholarships State Dept., 1958-62; cons. higher edn. Edn. Commn. States, 1967—; cons. U. Del Valle, Cali, Colombia, 1968, Orissa U. Agr. and tech., India, 1970; mem. adv. bd. on civil rights Dept. Agr., 1966-69; bd. curators Stephens Coll., 1967—. Pres. bd. Harry S. Truman Library Inst. Nat. and Internat. Affairs. Provost Marshall Gen.'s Sch., Ft. Custer, 1943; Hist. br. G-2, War Dept. Gen. Staff AUS, 1943-45. Guggenheim fellow, 1939-40. Pres. Nat. Council for Social Studies, 1937; bd. dirs. Social Sci. Research Council, 1947-51; pres. Nat. Commn. on Accrediting, 1962-64. Mem. Am. Council Edn. (exec. bd. 1962- 64, sec. 1964), Assn. State Univs. and Land-Grant Colls. (exec. bd. 1962-64, pres. 1964-65), Phi Beta Kappa. Democrat. Editor: Education Against Propaganda, 1937; Mr. Dooley at His Best, 1938. Author: Henry Moore Teller, Defender of the West, 1941; Mr. Dooley's America, a Life of Finley Peter Dunne, 1941. Editor: Toward Better Teaching in College, 1954. Mem. editorial bd. Miss. Valley Hist. Rev., 1947-50. Home: 107 W Brandon Rd Columbia MO 65201

ELLIS, FRANK HALE, educator; b. Chgo., Jan. 18, 1916; s. Frank Hale and Gay (Shepherd) E.; B.S., Northwestern U., 1939; Ph.D., Yale, 1948; m. Constance Dimock, Dec. 20, 1940; 1 dau., Gay. Mem. faculty U. Buffalo, 1941-42; mem. faculty Yale, 1945-51, asst. prof. English lit., 1950-51; with Dept. State, Washington, 1951-54; mem. faculty Smith Coll., 1958—, prof. English lit., 1966—. Served with AUS, 1942-45; ETO and PTO. Decorated Bronze Star. Morse fellow, 1950-51. Mem. Cum Laude Soc., Conn. Acad. Arts and Scis., Modern Lang. Assn., Phi Beta Kappa. Clubs: Elizabethan, Lawn (New Haven). Author: Swift's Discourse, 1967; Twentieth Century Interpretations of Robinson Crusoe, 1969; Poems on Affairs of State, 1697-1704, 1970. Contbr. articles to profl. jours. Home: 146 Elm St Northampton MA 01060

ELLIS, FRANKLIN HENRY, Jr., educator, surgeon; b. Washington, Sept. 20, 1920; s. Franklin Henry and Katherine (McClintock) E.; A.B., Yale, 1941; M.D., Columbia, 1944; Ph.D. in Surgery, U. Minn., 1951; m. Elizabeth Dunston Watson, Nov. 17, 1945; children—Katherine de Saulles (Mrs. David M. Felsen), Elizabeth Dunston, Franklin Henry III, Margot McClintock, Laura Lawson, Marie-Armide Longer, Hedrick Watson. Intern, Bellevue Hosp., N.Y.C., 1944-45; fellow surgery Mayo Clinic, 1945-46, 48-51, fellow thoracic surgery, 1951-53; asst. to surg. staff Mayo Clinic, 1952-53, cons. surgery, 1953-70; mem. faculty Mayo Grad. Sch. Medicine, 1953-70, prof. surgery, 1964-70, chmn. thoracic surg. sect., 1966-70; chief cardiovascular surgery Lahey Clinic Found., 1970—. Lectr. surgery Harvard Med. Sch., 1970—. Served with USNR, 1946-48. Diplomate Am. Bd. Surgery, Am. Bd. Thoracic Surgery. Mem. Am. Assn. Thoracic Surgery, A.C.S., Am. Heart Assn., A.M.A. (Billings Gold medal 1955), Am. Surg. Assn., Central Surg. Assn., Internat. Cardiovascular Soc., Internat. Soc. Surgery, Boston Surg. Soc., Soc. Clin. Surgery, Soc. Univ. Surgeons, Soc. Vascular Surgery, Soc. Thoracic Surgeons, Phi Beta Kappa, Sigma Xi, Alpha Omega Alpha. Home: 75 Wilson Lane Needham MA 02192

ELLIS, FRED WILSON, educator; b. Heath Springs, S.C., Apr. 24, 1914; s. George Dixon and Mary Jane (Hammond) E.; B.S., U. S.C., 1936; postgrad. Yale, 1936-37; M.S., U. Fla., 1938; Ph.D., U. Md., 1941; certificate in medicine U. N.C., 1948; M.D., Duke, 1952; m. Elizabeth Ervin Landrum, Aug. 6, 1940; children—Barbara (Mrs. Glenn E. Minah), Marybeth (Mrs. Jacques Weltert), Frances, Frieda (Mrs. Thomas W. Bell). Asso. pharmacology Jefferson Med. Coll., 1942-44; asst. prof. pharmacology U. N.C. Sch. Medicine, 1944-47, asso. prof., 1947-64, prof., 1964—. Vis. prof. pharmacology U. Ky. Med. Center; cons. Research Triangle Inst., N.C. Vice-chmn. Chapel Hill Bd. Edn., 1961-63, mem., 1963-67. Postdoctoral fellow U. Md. Sch. Medicine, 1941-42; research grantee Nat. Inst. Mental Health, 1969—. Mem. A.M.A. (cons. council pharmacy, chemistry, drugs), A.A.A.S., Soc. Exptl. Biology and Medicine (sec. Southeastern sect. 1958-62), Psychopharmacology Study Sect. NIH, Am. Soc. Pharmacology and Exptl. Therapeutics, Sigma Xi. Research pharmacology alcohols. Contbr. articles to sci. jours. Home: 805 Old Mill Rd Chapel Hill NC 27514

ELLIS, GEORGE HATHAWAY, economist, banker; b. Orono, Me., Jan. 29, 1920; s. Milton and Carrie (White) E.; B.A., U. Me., 1941, LL.D., 1962; M.A., Harvard, 1948, Ph.D., 1950; LL.D., Nasson Coll., 1961, Bates Coll., 1968, U. Mass., 1968; D.C.S. (hon.) Western New Eng. Coll. 1968; m. Sylvia Poor, Aug. 18, 1946; children—Rebecca Anne, George Milton, Randall Poor, Deborah Josephine. Teaching fellow econs. Harvard, 1948-49; asst. prof. U. Me., 1949-51; indsl. economist Fed. Res. Bank Boston, 1951-53, dir. research, 1953-57, v.p., dir. research, 1957-61, pres., 1961-68; pres. Keystone Custodian Funds, Inc., 1968—, chief exec. officer, 1970—. Mem. com. on N.E. economy Pres.'s Council Econ. Advisers, 1950-51; dir. research com. N.E., NPA, 1951-55; econ. adviser N.E. Gov.'s Com. Pub. Transp., 1955-57; research com. chmn. Greater Boston Econ. Study Com., 1957-61; chmn. New Eng. Econ. Research Found., 1962-70; chmn. econs. study com. Investment Co. Inst. Bd. dirs. YMCA, Boston, United Fund., Boston, Bay United Fund, Inc., Internat. Center New Eng., Inc.; trustee New Eng. Econ. Edn. Council; mem. Mass. spl. study commn. budgetary powers U. Mass., 1962; devel. council U. Me., also edn. planning council; adv. council Sch. Bus. Adminstrn. U. Mass., Mass. Sci. and Tech. Found. Served from 2d lt. to maj. AUS, 1941-45. Mem. Am. Acad. Arts and Scis., Newcomen Soc. N.Am., Nat. Planning Assn., New Eng. Council, Mus. Fine Arts Boston, Am. Econ. Assn., Regional Sci. Assn., C. of C. Greater Boston (dir.), Phi Beta Kappa, Phi Kappa Phi, Beta Gamma Sigma (nat. honoree). Conglist. Clubs: Commercial Merchants, Economic (Boston); Wellesley; Harvard of Boston. Home: 177 Benevenue St Wellesley MA 02181 Office: 99 High St Boston MA 02110

ELLIS, GILBERT R., co. exec.; b. Mo., 1915. Exec. v.p., dir. Household Finance Corp. Home: 1188 Estate Lane Lake Forest IL 60045 Office: Household Finance Corp Prudential Plaza Chicago IL 60601

ELLIS, GORDON, food co. exec.; b. Black Rock, Ark., Feb. 6, 1915; s. Harry and Pauline (Creager) E.; student Alexander Hamilton Inst.; grad. Advanced Mgmt. Program, Harvard, 1960; m. Marion Louise Jacobs, Dec. 25, 1938; children—Richard Gordon, Emily Ann, Susan Lee, David Edward. With Kroger Co., 1932-37, Gen. Mills Co., 1938-40; with Pet, Inc. (formerly Pet Milk Co.), 1940-68, pres. food products div., 1961-66, exec. v.p. operations co., 1962-66, pres., chief operating officer, 1966-68, also dir.; pres., dir. Fairmont Foods Co., 1968—, also chief exec. officer, 1970—; dir. Alcon Labs. Omaha Nat. Bank, Wetterau Foods, Inc., Leonard Pit Barbecue. Trustee MacMurray Coll. Neb. Meth. Hosp., Mid-Am. council Boy Scouts Am.; bd. dirs. Omaha Jr. Achievement. Bd. govs. AK-SAR-BEN. Mem. Pres.'s Assn. of Am. Mgmt. Assn., Newcomen Soc.; Omaha C. of C. (dir.), N.A.M. (dir.), Grocery Mfrs. Am. (dir.). Methodist. Home: 1806 N 101st St Omaha NB 68114 Office: 3201 Farnam St Omaha NB 68101

ELLIS, GRAYDON HALLS, lawyer; b. Beloit, Wis., Nov. 3, 1907; s.Roy O. and Ethel (Halls) E.; B.A., Beloit Coll., 1929; LL.B., Harvard, 1932; m. Harriet L. Cook, Sept. 15, 1932; children—Margaret Ann (Mrs. Rüdiger Pflaumbaum), Graydon Halls. Admitted to Ill. bar, 1932, since practiced in Chgo.; partner firm Lord, Bissell & Brook, 1948—. Director W. W. Grainger, Inc. Mem. Am. Ill. (past chmn. probate and trust law council), Chgo. (past chmn. probate practice com.) bar assns., Law Club Chgo., Phi Beta Kappa, Beta Theta Pi. Author articles in field. Home: 1630 Ravine Terrace Highland Park IL 60035 Office: 135 S LaSalle St Chicago IL 60603*

ELLIS, HAROLD BERNARD, educator; b. Havre, Mont., Dec. 31, 1917; s. Arthur Thomas and Ammie Lillian (Smith) E.; B.S. in Elec. Engring., Wash. State U., 1941; M.S. in Civil Engring., Mass. Inst. Tech., 1947; Ph.D., Ia. State U., 1963; m. Virginia Joan Adams, May 18, 1944; children—Mary Virginia, Nancy Jeanne, Susan Catheleen, Stephen Randolph. Commd. 2d lt. C.E., U.S. Army, 1941, advanced through grades to lt. col., 1951; assigned PTO, World War II; staff officer Aviation Engr. Force, Wolters AFB, Tex., 1953-55; asso. prof. mil. sci. and tactics Army R.O.T.C., Ia. State U. Ames, 1955-59; dep. comdr. for depot operation U.S. Army Gen. Depot, Chinon, France, 1959-62; ret., 1962; prof. civil engring. and constrn. tech., head dept. engring. tech. Ia. State U., 1962—. Cons. AID Summer Sci. Inst., Chandigahr, India, 1966; year-in-industry prof. engring. dept. E.I. duPont de Nemours & Co., Wilmington, Del., 1969-70. Pres. Ames Zoning Adjustment Bd., 1969. Decorated Bronze Star, Purple Heart. Registered profl. engr., Tex. Mem. Am. Soc. C.E., Am. Soc. Engring. Edn., Nat. Soc. Profl. Engrs., Ia. Engring. Soc., Phi Delta Kappa, Alpha Tau Omega, Sigma Tau, Sigma Delta Psi, Phi Kappa Phi, Scabbard and Blade. Rotarian. Office: Iowa State Univ Ames IA

ELLIS, HARRY BEARSE, journalist; b. Springfield, Mass., Dec. 9, 1921; s. Harry Dutton and Helen (Bearse) E.; B.A., Wesleyan U., Middletown, Conn., 1947, L.H.D., 1959; m. Ann Sherman Michelson, June 25, 1949; 1 son, Andrew Bearse. With Christian Sci. Monitor, Boston, 1947—, Middle East corr., 1952-54, Mediterranean corr., 1958-60, chief Paris bur., 1961-64, staff corr. Germany, 1964—; tv, radio commentary NBC, Westinghouse Broadcasting Corp. CBS; lectr. fgn. affairs. Served as 2d lt. AUS, 1943-45. Decorated Bronze Star medal, Combat Inf. Badge. Mem. Authors Guild, Authors League, Phi Beta Kappa. Author: Heritage of the Desert, 1956; Israel and the Middle East, 1957; The Arabs, 1958; Challenge in the Middle East, 1960; The Common Market, 1965; Ideals and Ideologies, Communism, Socialism, and Capitalism, 1968; The Dilemma of Israel, 1970. Contbg. author The United States and the Middle East, 1964. Home: 285 Barcliff Av Chatham MA 02633 Office: 1 Norway St Boston MA 02115

ELLIS, HOWARD SYLVESTER, educator; b. Denver, July 2, 1898; s. Sylvester Eldon and Nellie Blanche (Young) E.; A.B., State U. Ia., 1920; A.M., U. Mich., 1922; A.M., Harvard, 1924, Ph.D., 1929; postgrad. Heidelberg U. (Germany), 1924-25, U. Vienna, 1933-35; LL.D., U. Mich., 1951, U. Cal., 1968; m. Lilah Priscilla Whetstine, Jan. 1925; 1 dau., Audrey Elinor; m. 2d, Hermine Johanna Hoerlesberger, July 1935; children—Dorothy Margeret, Martha Josephine. Instr. econs. U. Mich., 1920-22, 25-29, asst. prof., 1929-35, asso. prof., 1935-37, prof., 1937-38; prof. econs. U. Cal., 1938, then Flood prof. econs., now prof. econ. emeritus. On leave to Fed. Res. Bd., Washington, 1943-46, asst. dir. div. research and statistics, 1945-46; vis. prof. econs. Columbia, 1944-45, 49, U. Tokyo, 1951, U. Bombay, 1958-59, Claremont Coll., 1969; UNESCO Specialist, Latin Am., 1960; dir. Marshall aid project, Council on Fgn. Relations, N.Y.C., 1949- 50; econ. cons. U.S. Dept. State, 1952-53; research prof. Center Econ. Research, Athens, Ga., 1963; chief UCB-AID party, Rio de Janeiro, 1965-67. Fellow Social Sci. Research Council, Europe, 1933-35. Sheldon traveling fellow; Ricardo prize fellow; recipient Wells award Harvard. Mem. Internat. (pres. 1953-56, exec. com. 1956-62, hon. pres.), Am. (pres. 1949) econ. assns., Royal Econ. Soc. Phi Beta Kappa. Author books including: Exchange Control in Central Europe, 1941; (with others) Approaches to Economic Development, 1955; Private Enterprise and Socialism in the Middle East, 1970. Contbr. articles to econ. jours. Co-editor: Readings in Theory of International Trade, 1949; Kyklos. Editor: A Survey of Contemporary Economics, 1948; The Economics of Freedom, 1950; Economic Development for Latin America, 1961; The Teaching of Economics in Latin America, 1962; Industrial Capital in Greek Development, 1964; The Economy of Brazil, 1969. Home: 936 Cragmont Av Berkeley CA 94708

ELLIS, JAMES REED, lawyer; b. Oakland, Cal., Aug. 5, 1921; s. Floyd E. and Hazel (Reed) E.; B.S., Yale, 1942; J.D., U. Wash., 1948; m. Mary Lou Earling, Nov. 18, 1944; children—Robert Lee, Judith Ann, Lynn Earling, Steven Reed. Admitted to Wash. bar, 1949; partner firm Preston, Thorgrimson, Starin, Ellis & Holman, Seattle, 1969—; dep. pros. atty. King County, 1958—. Mem. Nat. Water Commn., 1970—; mem. urban transp. adv. council Dept. Transp., 1970—; mem. Wash. Planning Adv. Council, 1965—; pres. Forward Thrust Inc., 1966—. Trustee Ford Found.; bd. regents U. Wash., 1965—; mem. council Nat. Municipal League, 1968—. Served to 1st lt. USAAF, 1943-46. Mem. Am., Wash., Seattle bar assns., Municipal League Seattle and King County (past pres.), Seattle C. of C. (trustee), Order of Coif, Phi Delta Phi, Phi Gamma Delta, Order of Hosp. of St. John of Jerusalem. Club: Rainier (Seattle). Home: 903 SE Shoreland Dr Bellevue WA 98104 Office: IBM Bldg Seattle WA 98101

ELLIS, JAMES WATSON, univ. dean; b. Uruguaiana, Brazil, Aug. 16, 1927 (parents Am. citizens); s. James Elijah and Frances (Watson) E.; A.B., Wofford Coll., 1948; M.S., Tulane U., 1951, Ph.D. in Math., 1952; m. Betty Jane Brock, Aug. 4, 1951; children—Cynthia Ann, Wendy Sue, Marcia Lynn. Asst. prof., then asso. prof. math. Fla. State U., 1952-58; mem. faculty La. State U. in New Orleans, 1958—, prof. math., chmn. dept., 1961-64, prof. math., dean jr. div., 1964—. Chmn. colls. and univs. div. New Orleans United Fund drive, 1967-68. Served with AUS, 1953-55. AEC Postdoctoral fellow, 1948-52. Mem. Am. Math. Soc., Math. Assn. Am., Phi Beta Kappa, Sigma Xi. Methodist. Home: 2328 Lark St New Orleans LA 70122

ELLIS, JOHN TAYLOR, pathologist, educator; b. Lufkin, Tex., Dec. 27, 1920; s. John Taylor, Jr. and Rowena (McCurdy) E.; B.A., U. Tex., 1942; M.D., Northwestern U., 1945; m. Marian A. Caldwell, Dec. 26, 1942; children—Evelyn, George Taylor. Intern pathology St. Luke's Hosp., Chgo., 1945-46; resident N.Y. Hosp., N.Y.C., 1948-50; practice medicine, specializing in pathology, N.Y.C., 1950—; asst. in pathology Cornell U. Med. Coll., 1948-49, instr. pathology, 1949-50, asst. prof. pathology, asst. prof. pathology in surgery, 1950-56, asso. prof., 1956-62, prof., chmn. dept. pathology, 1968—; prof., chmn. dept. pathology Emory U. Sch. Medicine, 1962-67; pathologist-in-chief N.Y. Hosp., 1968—. Mem. pathology study sect. A, NIH, 1965-69, chmn., 1969—; mem. com. on blood Exec. Office of Pres., Office Emergency Planning, 1964—; pres. Am. Assn. Chairmen Med. Sch. Dept. Pathology, Inc., 1969-70; mem. sci. adv. bd. cons. Armed Forces Inst. Pathology, 1970—. Served with U.S. Army, 1946-48. Diplomate Nat. Bd. Med. Examiners, Am. Bd. Pathology. Mem. Am. Assn. Pathologists and Bacteriologists, Am. Soc. Exptl. Pathology, Soc. for Exptl. Biology and Medicine, Am. Soc. Clin. Pathologists, Internat. Acad. Pathology, Coll. Am. Pathologists, N.Y. Path Soc. (past pres.), Arthur Purdy Stout Soc., Harvey Soc., A.M.A. Bd. editors: Am. Jour. Pathology, 1966—. Home: 180 East End Av New York City NY 10028 Office: 1300 York Av New York City NY 10021

ELLIS, JOHN TRACY, clergyman, educator; b. Seneca, Ill., July 30, 1905; s. Elmer Lucian and Ida Cecilia (Murphy) E.; A.B., St. Viator Coll., 1927; A.M., Cath. U. Am., 1928, Ph.D., 1930; student Sulpician Sem., Washington, 1934- 38; D.H.L., Mt. Mary Coll., 1954; LL.D., U. Notre Dame, 1957, Belmont Abbey Coll., 1960; Litt.D. (hon.), Loyola Coll., Balt., 1960, U. Portland, 1969; L.H.D., St. Mary's Coll.,

Cal., 1962, Stonehill Coll., 1963; Prof. history St. Viator Coll., 1930-32, Coll. St. Teresa, 1932-34; ordained priest Roman Catholic Ch., 1938; instr. history Cath. U. Am., 1938-41, asst. prof., 1941-43, asso. prof., 1943-47, prof. ch. history 1947-64; prof. ch. history U. San Francisco, 1964—. Vis. prof. Brown U., 1967, U. Notre Dame, 1970; lectr. ch. history St. Patrick's Sem., Menlo, Cal., 1968, Grad. Theol. Union Berkeley, Cal., 1970—. Bd. govs. Center Research and Edn. in Am. Liberties Columbia U. Domestic prelate of Pope Pius XII, 1955; recipient John Gilmary Shea prize, 1956. Campion award, 1965. Mem. Fellow Am. Benedictine Acad., 1969. Mem. Am. Cath. Hist. Assn. (pres. 1969), Am. Hist. Assn., Am. Soc. Ch. History (pres. 1969), Orgn. Am. Historians. Author: Anti-Papal Legislation in Mediaeval England, 1066-1377, 1930; Cardinal Consalvi and Anglo-Papal Relations, 1814-1824, 1942; The Formative Years of the Catholic University of America, 1946; The Life of James Cardinal Gibbons, Archbishop of Baltimore, 1834-1921, 2 vols., 1952; American Catholicism, 1956, rev. edit., 1969; Documents of American Catholic History, 1956, rev. edits 1962, 67; American Catholics and the Intellectual Life, 1956; A Guide to American Catholic History, 1959; Perspectives in American Catholicism, 1964; Catholics in Colonial America, 1965; Essays in Seminary Education, 1967. Editor: The Catholic Priest in the United States: Historical Investigations; mng. editor Cath. Hist. Rev., 1941-63, adv. editor, 1964—. Address: U San Francisco San Francisco CA 94117

ELLIS, KENT, educator, radiologist; b. Grand Rapids, Mich., June 22, 1921; s. Luther Edward and Dorothy (Groman) E.; B.S., Yale, 1942, M.D., 1950; m. Barbara Janet Koehler, June 10, 1950; children—Stephen Mark, Karen, Kent Bradford. Intern, Walter Reed Army Hosp., Washington, 1950-51; resident radiology Columbia Presbyn. Med. Center, 1952-54, attending radiologist, 1955-69; prof. radiology Columbia Coll. Physicians and Surgeons, 1958—; cons. USPHS, Yale Med. Sch., Inter-Soc. Commn. for Heart Disease Resources, N.Y. Heart Assn. Served to lt. (s.g.) USNR, 1943-46. Diplomate Am. Bd. Radiology. Mem. Med. Soc. State N.Y. (chmn. sect. radiology 1968-69), Assn. U. Radiologists, Assn. U. Profs., St. Anthony Hall. Presbyn. Contbr. profl. jours. Home: 226 Chestnut St Englewood, NJ 07631 Office: 622 W 168th St New York City NY 10032

ELLIS, LESLIE LEE, Jr., educator, scientist; b. Norfolk, Va., Sept. 13, 1925; s. Leslie Lee and Mary Teresa (Stickley) E.; B.S., Tulane U., 1948, M.S., 1949; Ph.D., U. Okla., 1952; m. Dorothy Copes Diboll, Dec. 22, 1949; children—Leslie Lee, Chrsitian Hart, Robin Chamblin, Daniel Diboll. With USPHS, 1952; mem. faculty Miss. State U., 1952-68, prof. zoology, 1960-68, chmn. dept., 1962-68; prof. biol. scis. Fla. Tech. U., 1968-69, chmn. dept. biol. scis., 1968-69, dir. research and grad. studies, 1969-70, dean grad. studies and research, 1971—, spl. research aquatic biology, parasitology; cons. in field, 1962—; panelist NSF, 1959—. Asst. dist. commr. Boy Scouts Am., 1962-63. Served with USNR, 1944-46. Mem. Entomol. Soc. Am., Am. Inst. Biol. Scis., A.A.A.S., Assn. Southeastern Biologists. Presbyn. (deacon). Lion. Contbr. profl. jours. Editor Jour. Miss. Acad. Scis., 1967-68. Home: 250 Nottaway Trail Maitland FL 32751 Office: Box 25000 Office Research and Grad Studies Fla Tech U Orlando FL 32816

ELLIS, LEWIS ETHAN, educator; b. Otisco, N.Y., Sept. 9, 1898; s. Lewis Martin and Catherine Louise (Henderson) E.; A.B., Syracuse U., 1920; A.M., U. Chgo., 1924, Ph.D., 1927; m. Helen Elizabeth Breckenridge, Sept. 5, 1931; children—Ethan Breckenridge, Robert Walter. Instr. history Emory U., 1920-23, Purdue U., 1927-28; asst. prof. Rutgers U., 1928-40, asso. prof., 1940-47, prof., 1947-63, chmn. dept. history, 1951-53, 54- 57, Voorhees prof., 1954-63, prof. emeritus, 1963—. Author: A History of the Chicago Delegation in Congress, 1823-1925, 1931; Reciprocity, 1911; A Study in Canadian-American Relations, 1939; Print Paper Pendulum: Group Pressures and the Price of Newsprint, 1948; A Short History of American Diplomacy, 1951; Newsprint: Producers, Publishers, Political Pressures, 1960; Frank B. Kellogg and American Foreign Relations, 1925- 29, 1960; Republican Foreign Policy, 1921-33, 1968; also articles and revs. profl. jours. Home: 30 Logan Lane Piscataway NJ 08854

ELLIS, MICHAEL, theatrical producer; b. Phila., Oct. 25, 1917; s.Alexander and Mollie (Fein) Abrahamson; grad. Wyo. Sem., 1935; B.A., Dartmouth, 1939; student U. Grenoble, 1937, Sorbonne, 1937-38; m. Neva Patterson, Mar. 22, 1953 (div.); m. 2d, Mary Elizabeth Walker, May 10, 1958; children—Sandra, Gordon, Thomas. Actor, also stage mgr. Broadway shows; prodn. five Broadway shows with James Russo, 1948-53, Come Blow Your Horn, with William Hammerstein. 1961, The Advocate, with William Hammerstein, 1963, The Beauty Part, 1962, Absence of a Cello, with Jeff Britton, 1964, The Paisley Convertible, 1967, The Girl in the Freudian Slip, 1967; off Broadway Sweet Eros and Witness, 1968, Ceremonies in Dark Old Men, 1969; owner and operator Bucks County (Pa.) Playhouse (now State Theatre Pa. 1959), 1954-64; producer Angela with Elliot Martin, 1969, Who's Happy Now? with Samuel Broustein, 1969. Mem. adv. bd. Hopkins Center, Dartmouth; trustee Solebury Sch., 1967-70. Home: Lloyd Rd Bernardsville NJ 07924

ELLIS, PAUL NIEMEIER, clergyman; b. Birs, Ill., Sept. 30, 1912; s. Osmon Polson and Flora (Niemeier) E.; B.A. magna cum laude, U. Ill., 1945; D.D. (hon.), Greenville Coll., 1965; m. Delois Adeline Wells, Aug. 5, 1935; children—John Paul, Stanley Eugene, Charles Winston. Ordained to ministry Free Methodist Ch., 1936; pastor, Indpls., 1935-38, Olney, Ill., 1938-42, Urbana, Ill., 1942-48, Toronto, Can., 1942-54, Indpls., 1954-63; conf. supt. Wabash Conf. Free Meth. Ch., 1963-64; bishop Free Meth. Ch., Winona Lake, Ind., 1964—. Pres. World Fellowship Free Meth. Chs., 1969—; chmn. Commn. on Christian Edn., Free Meth. Ch., 1964—, chmn. Gen. Council Ch. in Mission, 1969—. Trustee Asbury Theol. Sem. Mem. Phi Beta Kappa, Psi Chi. Author: The Book We Believe, 1956; The Beginnings, 1956; God's People, 1957; God the Father, 1957; The Church in the New Testament, 1958; God the Son, 1958; To Keep Yourself Free, 1963; also articles. Home: 1008 W Canal Winona Lake IN 46590 Office: Board of Bishops Free Methodist Hdqrs Winona Lake IN 46590

ELLIS, PIERCE GEORGE, utility exec.; b. Chgo., Sept. 18, 1909; s. Walter George and Caroline Jenny (Hamilton) E.; B.S. in Chem. Engring., U. Wis., 1931, M.S., 1933; m. Margaret Elizabeth Trayser, Agu. 17, 1935; children—James, Marion (Mrs. Richard O. Trummer). Instr. chem. engring U. Wis., 1931-36; with Wis. Pub. Service Corp., 1936—, rate engr., Oshkosh, 1936-39, budget dir., asst. to pres., Milw., 1939-61, v.p. div. operations, Oshkosh, 1961-70, sr. v.p., Green Bay, 1970—. Bd. dirs. Trees for Tomorrow. Recipient Distinguished Service citation U. Wis., 1963. Registered profl. engr., Wis., Cal., Colo. Mem. Am. Soc. Engring. Edn., Am. Gas Assn., Nat. Council Engring. Examiners, Engrs. and Scientists Milw. (pres. 1951-52), Nat. (pres. 1969-70), Wis. (pres. 1953-54) socs. profl. engrs., Wis. Examining Bd. Architects and Profl. Engrs. (chmn. engrin. sect. 1965-71), Sigma Xi, Tau Beta Pi, Phi Lambda Upsilon. Rotarian. Club: Madison (Wis.). Home: 930 Hickory Av DePere WI 54115 Office: 700 N Adams St Green Bay WI 54305

ELLIS, RALPH EDGAR, drug co. exec.; b. Chgo., Feb. 3, 1915; s. Ralph Edgar and Delia Howard (Hazeltine) E.; grad. Asheville Sch., 1932; B.S., Yale, 1936; m. Dorothea Nicholson, June 3, 1939; children—Judith H. (Mrs. J. Austen Wood), Martha E., Anne Wistar. Asst. mdse. mgr. Dennison Mfg. Co., 1939-42; regional adminstrv. officer Office Def. Transp., Chgo., 1942-45; account exec. Grant Advt., Inc., Chgo., 1945-50; account exec. Leo Burnett Co., Chgo., 1950-53, v.p., 1953-56; pres., dir Hazeltine & Perkins Drug Co., Grand Rapids, Mich., 1956-64; exec. v.p. Midwester, Brunswig Drug Co., 1964-67, exec. v.p., 1967-69, also dir.; exec. v.p., dir. Bergen-Brunswig Corp., 1969—; pres. Marketing Promotions, Inc. Trustee Asheville Sch., 1964—. Mem. Nat. Wholesale Druggists Assn. (pres. 1965-66), Western (pres. 1957), Chgo. (pres. 1953-54) tennis assns., Chgo. Tennis Patrons (pres. 1955). Clubs: Saddle and Cycle (past pres.) (Chgo.); Kent Country (past pres.) (Grand Rapids); Chevy Chase (Washington); St. Elmo (New Haven); Chicago (Charlevoix, Mich.); Ojai (Cal.) Country. Home: 1301 Brinkley Av Los Angeles CA 90049 Office: 1900 Av of the Stars Los Angeles CA 90067

ELLIS, RICHARD ARCHIE, clergyman; b. nr. Barnwell, S.C., Mar. 1, 1916; s. Dr. Ephraim Washington . and Mabel Walker (Heathe) E.; A.B., Furman U., 1937, D.D. (hon.), 1953; student So. Bapt. Theol. Sem., 1940-41; m. Lois Slate Avant, Nov. 4, 1941; children—Richard Archie, John Avant. Ordained to ministry, Bapt. Ch., 1937; pastor Riverside Ch., Greenville, 1937-39, First Ch., Landrum, S.C., 1939-42, Wadesboro, N.C., 1942-44, Salisbury, N.C., 1944- 53, First Bapt. Ch. Columbia, S.C., 1953—. Vice pres. N.C. Bapt. Conv., 1945-46, pres., 1952-53, mem. exec. bd., 1946-50, pres., 1949-50; v.p. So. Bapt. Conv., 1958-59, mem. exec. com., vice. chmn. exec. com., 1959- 60; exec. bd. S.C. Bapt. Conv., 1962. Trustee Furman U., Wake Forest Coll., Benedict Coll.; chmn. A.R.C. fund drive Rowan County, N.C., 1946; chmn. S.C. Bd. of Public Welfare, 1965—. Recipient Freedoms Found. at Valley Forge award, George Washington Honor medal, 1961, 63. Mem. Pi Gamma Mu, Delta Chi Alpha. Rotarian. Home: 2830 Spann Rd Columbia SC 29204 Office: 1306 Hampton St Columbia SC 29201

ELLIS, RICHARD WINFIELD, investment banker; b. Chgo., July 25, 1901; s. William J. and Jenny (Appleyard) E.; A.B., U. Wis., 1923; m. Catharine Hastings, Sept. 13, 1924; 1 dau., Gwen (Mrs. Ronald M. Melvin). With analytical dept. Lee Higginson Corp., 1923-37, sales mgr., v.p., dir., 1937-48; pres. Blunt Ellis & Simmons, Inc., Chgo., 1948—; chmn. exec. com., dir. Nalco Chem. Co.; dir. Canadian Corp. Mgmt., Ltd., Toronto, Lawter Chems., Inc. (all Chgo.), Daniel Woodhead, Inc., Northbrook, Ill. Chmn. Met. Chgo. dist. 1st War Loan Dr., vice chmn. 2d dr. Bd. dirs. Chgo. council Boy Scouts Am., past v.p., mem. nat. war finance com. Ill. council. Decorated hon. comdr. Order Brit. Empire. Mem. Am. Stock Exchange (past gov.), British-Am. C. of C. of Midwest (past hon. chmn. and pres.). Clubs: Racquet, Mid-America, Attic, Chicago (Chgo.); Casino. Home: 70 E Cedar St Chicago IL 60611 Office: 111 W Monroe St Chicago IL 60603

ELLIS, ROBERT ARTHUR, educator; b. Hudson, N.Y., May 31, 1926; s. Lawrence Louis and Jean (Hudson) E.; B.A. in Psychology, Yale, 1952, M.A. in Sociology, 1953, Ph.D. (Ford Found. fellow), 1956; m. Dorothy Caryle Godin, Aug. 31, 1950; children—Roger Morgan, Robert A. Instr. to asst. prof. U. So. Cal., 1955-57; asst. prof. Stanford, 1957-60; vis. asst. prof. Mich. State U., summer 1959; asso. prof. U. Ore., Eugene, 1960-65, prof., dir. Center for Research in Occupational Planning, 1965-70; chmn. dept. sociology U. Md., College Park, 1970—. Served from pvt. to 2d lt. AUS, 1946-48. Recipient Social Sci. Research Council and Nat. Inst. Mental Health grant. Mem. Am. Sociol. Assn. (exec. council, sect. on sociology edn. 1963-66), Pacific Sociol. Assn. (sec.-treas. 1964-67), So. Sociol. Soc. Research on social mobility through higher edn.; book rev. editor Am. Sociol. Rev., 1960-62; asso. editor Estudios Sociologia, 1960-62; mem. adv. bd. Jour. Human Resources, 1965—. Home: 10500 Greenacres Dr Hillandale MD 20903

ELLIS, ROBERT LESLIE, bldg. products co. exec.; b. Johnstown, Pa., Aug. 17, 1921; s. Caradoc and Sarah H. (Davies) E.; B.A., Pa. State U., 1942; m. Margaret Elizabeth Middleton, June 17, 1944; children—Robert Leslie, Daniel Middleton. With Armstrong Cork Co., Lancaster, Pa., 1944—, controller, 1965-66, controller, dir. mgmt. information, 1966—, v.p., 1968—. bd. dirs., past pres. Lancaster County Mental Health Assn.; bd. dirs. Lancaster Symphony Orch., 1965-67. Served with AUS, 1942-44. Mem. Financial Execs. Inst., Nat. Assn. Accountants (pres. Lancaster 1961-62, nat. bd. dirs. 1964—, nat. v.p., 1967-68, exec. com. 1967—), Inst. of Mgmt. (bd. dirs. Lancaster 1964-67, pres. 1967-68), Phi Eta Sigma, Pi Gamma Mu, Beta Alpha Psi. Republican. Presbyn. (elder). Mason. Clubs: Optimist (past officer), Hamilton (Lancaster). Home: 1826 New Holland Pike Lancaster PA 17601 Office: Armstrong Cork Co Lancaster PA 17604

ELLIS, RONALD JESSI, lawyer; b. Trail, Okla., Oct. 17, 1907; s. Walter J. and Samantha (Shroyer) E.; A.B., U. Ariz., 1931, J.D., 1934; m. Pearl M. Simmons, Mar. 30, 1954; children—Ginger L. (Mrs. David Kingman), Virginia L. (Mrs. Reed Gardner). Admitted to Ariz. bar, 1934; asst. county atty. Pinal County, Ariz., 1935-43, county atty., 1943-47; gen. practice in Eloy, 1947-60; mem. firm. Rawlins, Ellis, Burrus & Kiewit, Phoenix, 1960—. Mem. bd. edn. Florence Union High Sch., 1936-43, Santa Cruz Union High Sch., 1948-60. Served with USNR, 1943-45. Mem. Pinal County Bar Assn. (pres. 1956), Phi Kappa Phi, Delta Chi. Mason. Home: 920 W Indian School Rd Phoenix AZ 85013 Office: Security Bldg Phoenix AZ 85004

ELLIS, ROY GILMORE, educator; b. Peterborough, South Australia, July 10, 1906; s. Hoard and Mary (Gilmore) E.; D.D.S., U. Toronto, 1929, B.Sc.D., 1930, M.Sc.D., 1942; LL.D., U. Western Ont. 1968; m. Constance Ferguson, July 29, 1935; children—Paul Gilmore, Brian Gilbert. Faculty, U. Toronto, 1931—, prof. operative dentistry, 1945-70, dean faculty dentistry, until 1970; chmn. Health Scis. Council, 1970—. Fellow dental surgery Royal Coll. Surgeons, Royal Coll. Dentists Can. (hon.); mem. Can., Ont. dental assns., Toronto Acad. Dentistry (hon. life). Author: Classification and Treatment of Injuries to the Teeth of Children, 1945. Home: 426 Glencairn Av Toronto 12 Ontario Canada

ELLIS, RUDOLPH LAWRENCE, ins. co. exec.; b. N.Y.C., Mar. 27, 1911; s.August and Alice (Lamoureaux) E.; m. Lois Dale Bankenship, Apr. 18, 1947; children—Rudolph Lawrence, Douglas Hassell. With Union Labor Life Ins. Co., N.Y.C., 1928—, v.p., group adminstr., 1950-56, exec. v.p., 1956- 68, pres. 1969-, exec. com., finance com., 1969-. Mem. Life Ins. Assn. Am., Health Ins. Assn. Am., Life Office Mgmt. Assn., Nat. Indsl. Conf. Bd. Home: 35 Kerry Lane Chappaqua NY 10514 Office: 850 3d Av New York City NY 10022

ELLIS, SYDNEY, educator; b. Boston, Apr. 20, 1917; s. George I. and Sarah (Gaull) E.; B.S., Boston U., 1938, M.A., 1939, Ph.D., 1941; m. Marion Gardener, Oct. 8, 1942; children—Jeanne (Mrs. Richard P. Jaffe), Richard Jay. Fellow, then asst. Harvard Med. Sch., 1941-44; asst. prof. Duke Sch. Medicine, 1946-49; asso. prof. Temple U. Sch. Medicine, 1949-57; prof. pharmacology, chmn. dept. Woman's Med. Coll. Pa., 1957-67, U. Tex. Med. Br., Galveston, 1967—; cons. in field. Mem. pet study sect. NIH, 1960- 64, med. chem. B study sect., 1964-68. Served to capt. AUS, 1944-46. Recipient Lindback Found. award distinguished teaching, 1964. Mem. Am. Soc. Pharmacology (councilor 1967-70), Am. Chem. Soc., Soc. Exptl. Biology and Medicine, A.A.A.S., N.Y. Acad. Sci., Am. Assn. U. Profs., Sigma Xi (pres. Temple U. chpt. 1957). Home: 1223 Marine Dr Galveston TX 77550

ELLIS, SYDNEY TREZVANT, chem. mfg. exec., engr.; b. Evington, Va., June 2, 1913; s. Edwin Sydney and Anne (Haden) E.; B.S. in Chem. Engring., Va. Poly Inst., 1934; m. Jane Hetrick, Dec. 10, 1949; children—Ruth Jordan, Thomas Haden, Andrew Callaway, Philip Gore, Stephen Jeffries. Devel. engr. E. I. duPont de Nemours, 1934-37; chief engr. Wortendyke Mfg. Co., 1938-41; engr., jr. officer W. R. Grace & Co., 1946-50; exec. v.p., dir. Comml. Solvents Corp., 1951-59; pres. Petro-Tex Chem. Corp., Houston, Tex., 1959-69; vice chmn. Tenneco, Inc., Houston, 1969-70, exec. v.p., 1970—. Served from lt. to lt. col. C.E., AUS, 1941-45. Decorated Bronze Star medal. Clubs: Houston; Chemists, Union League (N.Y.C.). Episcopalian. Home: 409 Baywood Dr Seabrook TX 77586 Office: 1010 Milam Houston TX 77002

ELLIS, T. FLETCHER, advt. agy. exec.; b. Chrisman, Ill., 1917; grad. U. Ill. 1939. Exec. v.p. Keller-Crescent Co., Evansville, Ind. Home: 555 S Ruston Av Evansville IN 47714 Office: PO Box 3 Evansville IN 47706*

ELLIS, TELLIS BURTHORNE, Jr., educator; b. Vicksburg, Miss., May 26, 1912; s. Tellis Burthorne and Sidney (Brown) E.; B.A., Morehouse Coll., 1935; M.Ed., Boston U., 1953; m. Lucinda Jenkins, June 15, 1931; children—Tellis Burthorne III, Sidney W., Maurice K., Agnes Y. Lab. technician Emory U. Med. Coll., 1935-39; area chmn. health and phys. edn. Jackson (Miss.) State Coll., 1940-46, dir. athletics, 1946—, dir. phys. edn. summer workshop, 1960-61, also now asso. prof., head dept. phys. edn.; doctorate teaching fellow Boston U., 1962-63. Chmn. phys. edn. com. Jackson YMCA, 1959-61; div. chmn. Andrew Jackson council Boy Scouts Am., 1965-66. Served with USAAF, World War II. Mem. Miss. Tchrs. Assn. (chmn. health and phys. edn. sect. 1951-57), Am. Assn. U. Profs., Am. Assn. Health, Phys. Edn. and Recreation, N.E.A., Miss. Assn. Intercollegiate Athletics (exec. sec. 1960-62), Kappa Alpha Psi. Elk. Home: 1053 Biloxi St Jackson MS 39203

ELLIS, VAN CALVIN, business exec.; b. Dallas, Dec. 22, 1926; s. Calvin Crosswaith and Ophir Roberta (Edwards) E.; ed. pub. schs., Dallas; m. Loumelia Jane Morton, Mar. 6, 1948; children—Monica Lane, Meredith Lou, G.C. Morton, Calvin Campbell. Pres., ME, Inc., Bomber Bait Co., Inc.; dir. Fair Park Nat. Bank, Dallas, Gandy Dairies, Inc. Trustee St. Marks Sch. for Boys. Mason (32,Shriner). Clubs: Dallas; Northwood Country. Home: 4814 Crooked Lane Dallas TX 75229 Office: 2833 Century St Dallas TX 75220

ELLIS, WADE, educator; b. Chandler, Okla., June 9, 1909; s. Whit and Maggie (Boldukes) E.; B.S., Wilberforce U., 1928; M.S., U. N.M., 1938; Ph.D., U. Mich., 1944; m. Agatha C. Hampton, Feb. 6, 1932; children—William W., Wade. Instr. math. Fisk U., 1938-40, U. Mich., 1943-45; lectr. math. Boston U., 1946-48; asst. prof. Oberlin (O.) Coll., 1948-50, asso. prof., 1950-54, prof., 1954-67; prof. math., asso. dean Horace H. Rockham Sch. Grad. Studies, U. Mich., Ann Arbor, 1967—. Treas., dir. B.L. Scott Constrn. Co., Oberlin, O., 1970—. Cons. Basic sci. edn. Ford Found., Mexico City, 1965-66. Adviser to Greek Ministry of Edn., Athens, 1960, Peruvian Ministry of Pub. Edn., Lima, 1961; NSF sci. faculty fellow, 1961-62; mem. Internat. Congress Math., Stockholm, 1962; exec. bd. commn., instns. higher edn. N. Central Assn. Colls. and Secondary Schs., 1970—. Mem. Oberlin City Charter Commn., 1953, Oberlin City Council, 1957-62, 64-66. Local fund chmn. A.R.C., 1952, Elyria br. dir., 1956—, mem. exec. com., 1956-66; trustee Marygrove Coll., Detroit, 1968- -, Inst. Man and Sci., Rensselaerville, N.Y., 1970—. Rosenwald Fund fellow, 1938, 42-43, Gen. Edn. Bd. fellow, 1940-42, Fund for Advancement Edn. fellow, 1954-55, Ford Found sci. faculty fellow, 1954-55. Decorated Comendador en la Orden de las Palmas Magisteriales del Peru (Peruvian govt.). Mem. Math. Assn. Am. (chmn. Ohio sect. 1961), Phi Beta Kappa, Sigma Xi. Home: 1141 Chestnut Rd Ann Arbor MI 48104

ELLIS, WILLIAM ALLAN, govt. ofcl.; b. Edmonton, Alta., Can., Oct. 27, 1929; s. Allan Spurdens and Evelyn (Strom) E.; came to U.S., 1935, naturalized, 1950; B.A., U. Wash., 1951; M.P.A., Harvard, 1968; m. Mildred Elizabeth Solhaug, Mar. 24, 1950; children—Jeannette, Eric. With U.S. Bur. Budget, 1957-59; with AID, 1959—, dir. mission to Brazil with rank of minister, 1968—. Served to lt. (j.g.) USNR, 1953- 57. Home: 2138 N 133d St Seattle WA 98133 Office: American Embassy Brasilia Brazil

ELLIS, WILLIAM EDWARD, naval officer; b. Burlington, N.C., Nov. 7, 1908; s. Charles Britt and Margaret (Cannady) E.; B.S., U.S. Naval Acad., 1930; m. Barbara Elizabeth Decker, Dec. 24, 1934; 1 son. William Edward. Commd. ensign U.S. Navy, 1930, advanced through grades to vice adm., 1964; designated naval aviator, 1932; various assignments in ships and ashore, U.S. and C.Z., 1932-42; comdr. Escort Fighting Squadron 26, 1942-43; comdg. officer Air Group 18, 1943-44; air officer U.S.S. Intrepid, 1944-45, exec. officer, 1945; chief staff officer to comdr. Naval Air Bases, 12th Naval Dist., 1945-48 comdg. officer Fleet All Weather Tng. Unit, Atlantic, 1948-50; assigned Naval War Coll., 1950-51, Joint Staff Office, Joint Chiefs Staff, 1951-53; comdr. U.S.S. Badoeng Strait 1953- 54; chief staff and aide to comdr. Operations Devel. Forces, 1954-56; comdr. aircraft carrier U.S.S. Forrestal, 1956-57; chief staff and aide to comdr. Carrier Div. 6, 1957-58; dir. air warfare div. Office Chief Naval Operations, 1958-59; asst. chief field support Bu. Naval Weapons, 1959-61; comdr. Carrier Div. 2, 1961-62; asst. chief naval operations air, Navy Dept., 1962-64; comdr. 6th Fleet, Mediterranean, 1964-66; chief staff to NATO's Supreme Allied Condr., Atlantic, Norfolk, Va., 1966—. Decorated Navy Cross, D.F.C., Air medal, Navy Commendation medal, D.S.M., numerous unit and area ribbons. Home: 50 W Brainard St Pensacola FL 32501 Office: Chief Staff Supreme Allied Comdr Atlantic US Naval Sta Norfolk VA 23511

ELLIS, WILLIAM LEIGH, govt. ofcl.; b. Petoskey, Mich., Jan. 26, 1908; s. William E. and Gertrude May (Webb) E.; A.B., Hillsdale (Mich.) Coll., 1929; LL.B., George Washington U., 1933, LL.M., 1936; m. Norma Foster, Nov. 16, 1935; children—William L., Amy Foster. In govt. service, 1930—, State Dept., TVA, 1930-35; admitted to Mich. bar, 1935; atty., Gen. Accounting Office, 1935-45, asst. to comptroller gen., 1945-49, chief of investigations, 1949-55; lectr. law George Washington U., 1942-52; trial atty. Fed. Power Commn. 1955-57, hearing examiner, 1960—; dep. dir. Adminstrv. Office U.S. Courts, 1957- 60. Mem. Fed. Bar Assn. (pres. 1952-53). Mason. Club: Cosmos. Home: 1307 New Hampshire Av Washington, DC 20036. Office: Fed Power Commn Washington DC 20426

ELLISON, DAVID ERNEST, banker; b. Tacoma, Aug. 15, 1921; s. Herbert Ray and Vena (Norris) E.; student Whitman Coll., 1940, U. Wash., 1945-46; J.D., U. Mont., 1948; m. Diane Morris, Dec. 23, 1947; children—Dava Rae, Darlene, Dayle Gwen, Drew Mitchell.

Admitted to Wash. bar, 1948; hearing examiner Wash. Dept. Pub. Utilities, 1948-49; with Seattle-1st Nat. Bank, 1949—, now v.p., mgr. trust and investment div.; tchr. Pacific Coast Banking Sch. Served to capt., USAAF, 1941-45. Mem. Am., Mont., Wash. bar assns., Am. Bankers Assn., Corporate Trustees Assn. Wash. (pres.), Seattle C. of C. Home: 3655 Evergreen Point Rd Bellevue WA 98004 Office: Seattle-1st National Bank PO Box 3586 Seattle WA 98124

ELLISON, DAVID MCQUOWN, Jr., lawyer; b. Baton Rouge, Apr. 4, 1933; s. David McQuown and Marth (Ellington) E.; B.A., La. State U., 1954, LL.B., 1956, J.D., 1969; m. Kathryn Gwin, Aug. 2, 1955; children—Diane, Kathryn Ann, David McQuown III, William C., John Bennett, Robert G., Oliver Scott. Admitted to La. bar, 1956, since practiced in Baton Rouge; partner firm Taylor, Porter, Brooks, Fuller & Phillips, 1962-69, Ellison & Gary, 1970—. Mem. mineral law adv. com. La. Law Inst., 1954-56. Served with AUS, 1957. Mem. Am., La., Baton Rouge bar assns., Kappa Alpha. Presbyn. Mason. Clubs: Baton Rouge Country, Camelot (Baton Rouge). Home: River Rd Sunshine LA 70780 Office: 451 Florida St Baton Rouge LA 70801

ELLISON, DEAN BRACKETT, steel co. exec.; b. Holyoke, Mass., Nov. 13, 1924; s. Norman Brackett and Elizabeth Dean (Wright) E.; B.S. in Indsl. Engring., Lehigh U., 1948; m. June Caldwell Ide, Feb. 22, 1951; children—Wendy Erb, Lucinda Dean, Lindsay Ide, Christopher Ide Brackett. Employed with Eastern Stainless Steel Corp. div. EASCO, Balt., 1948-50, 60—, former exec. v.p., now pres. mill div. also dir.; with Indsl. Stainless Steels, Inc. Cambridge, Mass., 1952-60. Served to capt. USMCR, 1942-45, 50-52; Korea. Mem. Am. Iron and Steel Inst., Am. Soc. Metals, Phi Gamma Delta. Home: Owings Mills MD 21117 Office: Caves Rd Baltimore MD 21203

ELLISON, FRED PITTMAN, educator; b. Denton, Tex., Jan. 11, 1922; s. Lee Monroe and Hixie (Pittman) E.; B.A., U. Tex., 1941; M.A., U. Cal. at Berkeley, 1948, Ph.D., 1952; m. Adeline Frances Story, June 20, 1947; children—Carol, Thomas, Jamie, Cynthia, John. Translator, spl. agt. FBI, 1941-44; asso. prof. Spanish and Portuguese, U. Ill., 1952-61; prof. Spanish and Portuguese, U. Tex., 1961—, dir. Lang. and Area Center Latin Am. Studies, 1962-64, asso. dean Grad. Sch., 1970—; cons. in field, 1952—. Mem. joint com. Latin Am. Studies, Social Sci. Research Council-Am. Council Learned Socs., 1960-65. Served to lt. (j.g.) USNR, 1944-46. Grantee Nat. Def. Edn. Act, 1960-62; OAS fellow to Brazil, 1962. Mem. Modern Lang. Assn., Instituto de Catedraticos de Literatura Ibero- american, Am. Assn. Tchrs. Spanish and Portuguese (chmn. Portuguese Lang. devel. group 1964-67). Author: Brazil's New Novel, 1954; (with others) Development and Evaluation of Methods and Materials to Facilitate Foreign Language Instruction in Elementary Schools, 1963; (coordinator) Modern Portuguese, rev. edit., 1971. Home: 2907 Townes Lane Austin TX 78703

ELLISON, HARLAN JAY, author; b. Cleve., May 27, 1934; s. Louis Laverne and Serita (Rosenthal) E.; student Ohio State U., 1953-55; m. Charlotte Stein, 1956 (div. 1959); m. 2d, Billie Joyce Sanders, 1961 (div. 1962); m. 3d, Lory Patrick, 1965 (div. 1965). Actor, Cleve. Play House, part time 1944-49; a founder Cleve. Sci.-Fiction Soc., 1950, pub. mag. Sci.-Fantasy Bull. (later retitled Dimensions); editor Rogue Mag., Chgo., 1959-60; pub. Regency Books, Chgo., 1960-61; script writer for television series Route 66, Ripcord, Alfred Hitchcock Hour, Cimarron Strip, Star Trek, Outer Limits, Young Lawyers, others, 1962-71; writer 7 scripts for Burke's Law; writer motion pictures The Oscar, The Dream Merchants (adaptation), Khadim, Nick the Greek, Better By Far, Swing Low, Sweet Harriet, Harlan Ellison's Movie, others; lectr. numerous colls. and univs. Served with AUS, 1957-59. Recipient 2 awards for Most Outstanding Scripts Writers Guild Am., 1965, 67, 4 Hugo awards World Sci.-Fiction Conv., 1966, 67, 68, 69, Spl. Achievement award, 1968; 2 Nebula awards Sci. Fiction Writers Am., 1965, 69. Mem. Writers Guild Am. (screen bd., mem. West council 1971—), Sci. Fiction Writers Am. (v.p. 1965-66). Author numerous books, including Rumble, 1958, The Man With Nine Lives, 1960, Gentleman Junkie, 1961, Memos from Purgatory, 1961, Paingod, 1965, I Have No Mouth and I Must Scream, 1967, Love Ain't Nothing But Sex Misspelled, 1968, Over the Edge, 1970, Alone Against Tomorrow, 1971, Partners in Wonder, 1971; editor, compiler Dangerous Visions, anthology, 1967; writer weekly television column The Glass Teat, Los Angeles Free Press, 1968-71. Address: 3484 Coy Dr Sherman Oaks CA 91403

ELLISON, JEROME, editor, author; b. Maywood, Ill., Oct. 28, 1907; s. Earl J. and Vera D. (Engmark) E.; student U. Wis., 1925-26; A.B., U. Mich., Ann Arbor, 1930; M.S., So. Conn. State Coll., 1966; children by previous marriage—Jerome III (dec.) and Judith Ann (twins); m. 2d, Miriam T. Neftel, 1950; 1 dau. Julie. Editor, Mich. Gargoyle, U. Mich., 1929, Circle of Zeta Psi, 1930-32; asst. editor Life mag., 1932-33; free-lance cartoonist, also writer monthly column for Life mag., 1933-34; asso. editor Readers Digest, 1935-42; editor-in-chief Liberty mag., 1942-43; mng. editor Collier's mag., 1943-44; editorial dir., bur. overseas publs. OWI 1944-45; instr. in mag. journalism N.Y. U., 1945; founder Asso. Mag. Contbr., Inc.; editor, pub. The Magazine of the Year, 1946-47; with journalism dept. Ind. U., 1955-60; founder, editor, pub. Best Articles & Stories mag., 1957-61; lectr. English and humanities New Haven Coll., 1964-66, prof. English and humanities, 1966—; lectr. continuing edn. div. U. Conn., 1964-66. Mem. Zeta Psi. Episcopalian. Author books including: John Brown's Soul, 1951; Report to the Creator, 1955; (pseudonym N. Emorey) A Serious Call to an American (R) Evolution, 1967, mass edit., 1971; God on Broadway, 1971; (with Arthur Ford) The Life Beyond Death, 1972. Contbr. essays to Nation, Christian Herald, Mich. Quar. Rev., Southwest Rev., New Eng. Quar., articles and stories in numerous periodicals. Address: Durham Rd Guilford CT 06437

ELLISON, LORIN BRUCE, appliance co. exec.; b. Chgo., Jan. 5, 1932; s. Edward L. and Bertha A. (Haverson) E.; B.S. in Bus. Adminstrn., Drake U., 1954; m. Beverley A. Burtar, July 24, 1953; children—Richard, Glen, Kirk, Kevin. Auditor, Arthur Andersen & Co., Chgo., 1957-62; mem. corporate staff, div. controller Interlake Steel Co., Chgo., 1962-65; v.p., controller Tappan Co., Mansfield, O., 1965—. C.P.A., Ill. Mem. Financial Execs. Inst. Home: 550 Beech Av Mansfield OH 44906 Office: Tappan Co 180 Park Av W Mansfield OH 44902

ELLISON, NEWELL WINDOM, lawyer; b. Parrottsville, Tenn., Oct. 4, 1894; s. John Ford and Laura Elizabeth (Ottinger) E.; A.B., George Washington U., 1917, LL.B., 1921, LL.D., 1957; J.D., Tenn. Wesleyan Coll., 1964; m. Anna Marie Kraus, Sept. 11, 1930 (dec.); children—Newell Windon (dec.), Jon Monroe (Mrs. Jon E. Brandt). Admitted to D.C. bar, 1921, since practiced in Washington; mem. Covington & Burling, 1925—; dir. Union Trust Co. Chmn. Com. on Adminstrn. Justice Bd. govs. St. Albans Sch.; bd. trustees George Washington U. Named Lawyer of Yr., Bar Assn. D.C., 1969. Fellow American Bar Found.; mem. Am. Judicature Soc., Am. Bar Assn., Bar Assn. D.C., Washington Foreign Law Soc. (past pres.), Washington Inst. Foreign Affairs, Sigma Alpha Epsilon, Phi Delta Phi, Order of Coif. Presbyn. Clubs: Chevy Chase, Burning Tree, Metropolitan, 1925 F Street (Washington). Author articles legal jours. Home: 2323 Wyoming Av NW Washington DC 20009 Office: 888 16th St NW Washington DC 20006

ELLISON, RALPH WALDO, writer; b. Oklahoma City, Mar. 1, 1914; s. Lewis Alfred and Ida (Millsap) E.; student Tuskegee Inst., 1933-36; Ph.D. in Humane Letters (hon.), 1963; Litt. D. (hon.), Rutgers U., 1966, U. Mich., 1967, Williams Coll., 1970, L.I. U., 1971; L.H.D., Grinnell Coll., 1967, L.H.D., Adelphi U., 1971; m. Fanny McConnell, July 1946. Participated N.Y.C. Writer's Project; lectr. Am. Negro culture, folklore, creative writing N.Y. U., Columbia, Fisk U., Antioch, Princeton, Bennington, others; tchr. Russian and Am. lit. Bard Coll., Annandale-on-Hudson, N.Y., 1958-61; Alexander White vis. prof. U. Chgo., 1961; vis. prof. writing Rutgers U., 1962-64; Albert Schweitzer prof. in the humanities N.Y. U., 1970—. Hon. cons. in Am. letters Library Congress, 1966—; mem. Carnegie Commn. Ednl. TV, 1966-67. Trustee John F. Kennedy Center Performing Arts. Served with Mcht. Marine, 1943-45. Recipient Rosenwald fellowship, 1945; Nat. Am. Acad. Arts and Letters fellowship in Rome, 1955-57; Medal of Freedom, 1969; decorated chevalier Ordre des Artes et Lettres (France); vis. fellow Am. studies at Yale, 1966. Mem. P.E.N. (v.p.; exec. bd.), Nat. Council Arts, Am. Acad. Arts and Scis., Inst. Jazz Studies, Inc. (bd. advisers), Nat. Inst. Arts and Letters (council; chmn. lit. grants com. 1964). Club: Century. Author: Invisible Man (Nat. Book award 1953, Russwurm award 1953, Nat. Newspaper Pubs. award 1954), 1952; Shadow and Act (essays), 1964. Editorial bd. Am. Scholar. Contbr. short stories, articles book revs., popular and profl. mags., 1939—. Home: 730 Riverside Dr New York City NY 10031

ELLISON, SAMUEL PORTER, Jr., geologist, coll. dean; b. Kansas City, Mo., July 1, 1914; s. Samuel Porter and Mary Frances (Edwards) E.; student Jr. Coll. Kansas City, 1930- 31; A.B. with honors, U. Kansas City, 1936; A.M. (Gregory fellow), U. Mo., 1938, Ph.D., 1940; m. Dorothy Mabel Cannady, June 9, 1949; children—Samuel David, John Robert, Stephen Paul. Instr. geology U. Md. Sch. Mines and Metallurgy, 1939-43, asst. prof., 1943-44; ranger, naturalist Yellowstone Nat. Parks, Wyo., summer, 1941; jr. geologist, asst. geologist U.S. Geol. Survey, Washington, summers 1941-44; geologist Stanolind Oil & Gas Co., Midland, Tex., 1944-47, dist. geologist, Wichita Falls, 1947-48; prof. geology U. Tex., 1948—, chmn. dept. geology, 1952-62, acting dean Coll. Arts and Scis., 1970-71, dean, 1971—. Geol. cons. Shell Oil Co., Casper, Wyo., summers 1953-56; cons. John A Jackson. Dallas, 1957, Humble Oil and Refining Co. Houston, 1959-64, Esso Prodn. Research Co., 1964—. Fulbright sr. research fellow Germany, 1970. Fellow Geol. Soc. Am. (councilor), Paleontol. Soc., A.A.A.S.; mem. Am. Assn. Petroleum Geologists, Soc. Econ. Paleontologists and Mineralogists (sec.-treas. 1954-58, pres. 1959), Am. Inst. Mining and Metall Engrs., Nat. Assn. Geology Tchrs. (v.p. 1964-64, pres. 1964-65), West Tex. Geol. Soc., Tex. Acad. Sci., Am. Inst. Profl. Geologists (pres. Tex. sect. 1969). Methodist. Contbr. profl. jours. Home: 5948 Highland Hills Dr Austin TX 78731

ELLISON, SPEARL ALBERT, hotel exec.; b. Arp, Tex., Feb. 26, 1913; s. James W. and Mandy (Moore) E.; student Abilene Christian Coll., Hardin Simmons U., 1929-30, 30-31, Daughn Bus. Coll., 193233; m. Alma A. McNutt, May 19, 1933; 1 dau., Earlyne (Mrs. James E. Murphy). Various positions Hilton Hotel, Abilene, Texas, 1929-35, El Paso, Tex., 1935-38; exec. asst. mgr. Sir Francis Drake Hotel, San Francisco, 1938-39; mgr. various Hilton Hotels, including Long Beach, Cal., Albuquerque, El Paso, Rooslyn Hotel, Los Angeles, 1940-46, v.p. Hilton Hotels, Chgo., 1946-64, sr. v.p., 1964-66, exec. v.p., 1966-68; chmn. pension com. Hilton Hotels Corp,; chief exec. officer Atlas Hotels, Town and Country Hotel, several Cal. restaurant corps. Dir. Conrad N. Hilton Found., 1946—. Bd. dirs. Providence Meml. Hosp., El Paso. Home: PO Box 308 Ramona CA 92065

ELLITHORN, HAROLD EDWARD, educator; b. Detroit, Oct. 11, 1911; s. Henry Edward and Elizabeth Mabel (Leitch) E.; B.S., Union Coll., Schenectady, 1934; M.S., Harvard, 1935; Ph.D., U. Notre Dame, 1945; m. Geraldine Marie Wiehl, Dec. 31, 1938; 1 dau., Carol Ann. Engr., Sylvia Electric Co., 1935-36, supr. engring. labs., 1936-38; instr. elec. engring. U. Notre Dame, 1940-43, asst. prof., 1943-46, asso. prof., 1946-54, prof., head dept., 1954-62; sr. staff engr. Hughes Aircraft Co., 1961-64; prof. elec. engring. Marquette U. Milw., 1964—, chmn. dept., 1964-68. Registered profl. engr., Ind., Wis. Mem. Am. Soc. Elec. Engrs., Am. Soc. Profl. Engrs., Am. Faculty Engring. Edn., I.E.E.E., Sigma Xi, Psi Upsilon. Roman Catholic. Contbr. tech. jours. Home: 13330 Bluemound Rd Elm Grove WI 53122 Office: Engineering Coll Marquette U Milwaukee WI 53233

ELLMAN, LAWRENCE, restaurant exec.; b. N.Y.C., July 12, 1926; s. Jacob William and Lillian (Barison) E.; student Sch. Commerce, N.Y. U., 1943-46; m. Elaine Wasserstrom, May 8, 1965; children—Kevin, Nikki, Sean, Eden. Pres., Freshway, Inc., N.Y.C., 1956-58; pres. Cattleman Restaurant, Inc., N.Y.C., 1959-67; pres., chmn. Longchamps, Inc., N.Y.C., 1967—; chmn. Steak n' Shake, Inc., St. Louis, 1969—; pres., dir. The Dakota, Inc., N.Y.C., 1971—. Served with U.S. Maritime Service, 1944-45. Clubs: Aspetuck Golf (Westport, Conn.); Palm Bay, Jockey (Miami, Fla.). Home: 1 W 72d St New York City NY 10023 Office: 230 Park Av New York City NY 10017

ELLMANN, RICHARD, educator; b. Highland Park, Mich., Mar. 15, 1918; s. James Isaac and Jeanette (Barsook) E.; B.A., Yale, 1939, M.A., 1941, Ph.D., 1947; B. Litt., Trinity Coll., Dublin, Ireland; M.A., Oxford U., 1970; m. Mary Donahue, Aug. 12, 1949; children—Stephen Jonathan, Maud Esther, Lucy Elizabeth. Instr., Harvard, 1942-43, 1947-48, Briggs-Copeland asst. prof. English composition, 1948-51; prof. English, Northwestern U., 1951-64, Franklin Bliss Snyder prof., 1964-67; prof. English, Yale, 1967-70; Goldsmiths' prof. English lit. Oxford (Eng.) U., 1970—; Frederick Ives Carpenter vis. prof. U. Chgo., 1959, 67. Mem. Nat. Inst. Arts and Letters, 1971—. Served with OSS, USNR, 1943-46. Rockefeller fellow in humanities, 1946-47; Guggenheim fellow, 1950, 57, 70; Kenyon rev. fellow criticism, 1955, Am. Philos. Soc. grantee; fellow Sch. Letters, Ind. U., 1956, 60, sr. fellow, 1966—; fellow New Coll., Oxford U., 1970—. Fellow Am. Acad. Arts and Scis.; mem. Am. Assn. U. Profs., English Inst. (chmn. 1961-62), Modern Lang. Assn. (exec. council 1961-65, mem. editorial com. publs. 1968—), Elizabethan Club, Phi Beta Kappa, Chi Delta Theta, Signet. Author: Yeats: The Man and the Masks, 1948; The Identity of Yeats, 1954; James Joyce, 1959 (Nat. Book Award 1960); Eminent Domain, 1967; Ulysses on the Liffey, 1972. Editor: Selected Writings of Henri Michaux, 1951; My Brother's Keeper (Stanislaus Joyce), 1958; (wtih others) English Masterpieces, 1958; The Symbolist Movement in Literature, 1958; (with Ellsworth Mason) The Critical Writings of James Joyce; Edwardians and Late Victorians, 1960; World Classics Oscar Wilde, 1961; (with Charles Feidelson) The Modern Tradition, 1965; Letters of James Joyce, Vols. II and III, 1966; Giacomo Joyce (James Joyce), 1968; The Artist as Critic (Oscar Wilde), 1969; Oscar Wilde (Twentieth Century Views), 1970; Selected Letters of James Joyce, 1971. Home: 39 St Giles Oxford England

ELLMANN, WILLIAM MARSHALL, lawyer; b. Highland Park, Mich., Mar. 23, 1921; s.James I and Jeannette (Barsook) E.; student Occidental Coll., 1939-40; A.B., U. Mich., 1946; LL.B., Wayne State U., 1951; m. Sheila Estelle Frenkel, Nov. 1, 1953; children—Douglas S., Carol E., Robert L. Admitted to Mich. bar, 1951, since practiced in Detroit; partner firm Ellmann and Ellmann, 1962—; spl. com. atty. gen. Mich. to study use of state troops in emergencies, 1964-65. Mem. exec. com. Inst. Continuing Legal Edn., 1964-68. Served with USAAF, 1942-46. Fellow Am. Bar Found.; mem. Am. Arbitration Assn. (adv. council 1964—), Am. (mem. ho. of dels. 1969—), Detroit (vice chmn. pub. relations com. 1959) bar assns., State Bar Mich. (commr. 1959-69, pres. 1966-67), Practicing Law Inst. (adv. council 1969—, spl. asst. atty. gen. 1970), Sigma Nu Phi. Home: 28000 Weymouth Farmington MI 48024. Office: Penobscot Bldg Detroit MI 48226

ELLS, JONATHAN FAIRBANKS, lawyer; b. Waterbury, Conn., Nov. 9, 1908; s. Arthur Fairbanks and Dorothea (Gross) E.; grad. Deerfield Acad., 1926; B.A., Amherst Coll., 1930; LL.B., Yale, 1933; m. Ruth Mercer Brown, July 8, 1939; children—Dorothea Gross, Janis Brown, Warren Fairbanks. Admitted to Conn. bar, 1933, since practiced in Winsted; mem. firm Ells, Quinlan, Eddy & Febbroriello and predecessor; 1949—; pros. Town Ct. of Winchester, 1935-43; coroner Litchfield County (Conn.), 1943-52, pros. atty. ct. common pleas Litchfield County, 1952-61. Mem. Jud. Council Conn., 1959—. Dir., v.p. Mechanics Savs. Bank, Winsted, Conn. Mem. adv. bd. Conn. Bank & Trust Co. Corporator, trustee, v.p. Gilbert Sch. Mem. Am. (former chmn. standing com. on unauthorized practice of law), Conn., Litchfield County bar assns., Bar. Assn. Conn. (pres. 1958-59, chmn. jud. com. 1969—), Phi Beta Kappa, Alpha Delta Phi. Mem. Church of Christ. Kiwanian (pres. 1937). Home: Coe St Winsted CT 06098 Office: 510 Main St Winsted CT 06098

ELLSBERG, EDWARD, engr., author; ret. naval officer; b. New Haven, Conn., Nov. 21, 1891; s. Joseph and Edna (Lavine) E.; student U. Colo. 1910, Eng. D., 1929; B.S., U.S. Naval Acad., 1914; grad. sch., 1916; M.D., Mass. Inst. Tech., 1920; Sc.D., Bowdoin Coll. 1952; L.H.D., U. Me. 1955; m. Lucy Knowlton Buck, June 1, 1918; 1 dau., Mary Phillips (Mrs. Goldwin Smith Pollard). Served with U.S. Navy until 1926, advancing through grades to lt. comdr., promoted to comdr. by Spl. Act of Congress, 1929 for work as Salvage officer raising U.S. Submarine S-51 from sea bottom, 1926, and initial operations on S-4, 1927; reappointed USN, World War II, advanced to rear adm., 1951; salvage officer Red Sea, Western Mediterranean Area; participated in Normandy Invasion, 1944, in connection with installation of artificial harbors along Normandy coast; supr. Shipbuilding USN, for Cleve. area, 1945. Chief engr. Tide Water Oil Co. 1926-35, cons. engr., 1935-41. Decorated D.S.M. Mem. N.J. Soc. Profl. Engrs., Am. Petroleum Inst., Naval Inst., Am. Polar Soc., Soc. Am. Historians, Soc. Am. Mil. Engrs., P.E.N., Am. Academy Polit. and Social Sci. Clubs: Army and Navy (Washington); Mil.-Naval (N.Y.); Explorer's; Causeway (Southwest Harbor,Me.); Northeast Harbor Fleet; Ends of the Earth; Pot and Kettle (Bar Harbor). Author numerous books, fiction and non-fiction, 1927—, including: On The Bottom, 1928; Under The Red Sea Sun, 1946; No Banners, No Bugles, 1949; The Far Shore, 1960; frequent mag. contbr. Inventor underwater torch for cutting steel; designer system for salvaging submarines; inventor in field of petroleum; designer low pressure desalinization systems in gen. use in naval vessels. Home: Southwest Harbor ME 04679

ELLSON, EDWIN OWEN mfg. exec.; b. Lima, O., Apr. 1, 1932; B.S., U. San Francisco, 1954; M.S., Stanford University, 1956; m. Rosemarie Lois Brown, May 15, 1955; 1 son, Anthony Robinson. Sales rep. Ames-Brockton Fabricated Products, Akron, O., 1956-58, sales mgr. Coshocton, Ohio, 1959-61, gen. manager plant, 1961-68, v.p. sales, 1968--. Instr. bus. Coshocton Jr. College, 1968-69. Secretary Coshocton YMCA, 1960-61; active Boy Scouts of America. Named Man of Year, Coshocton Junior Chamber of Commerce, 1968. Mem. Coshocton C. of C. (vice president 1967-68, pres. 1969-70), English Speaking Union, Coshocton Sertoma Club, Nat. Assn. Mfrs., Sales Executives Institute, Phi Beta Kappa, Sigma Chi, Phi Mu. Democrat. Mem. Christian Ch. (lay leader). Mason (32, Shriner). Clubs: Coshocton Country, Coshocton City, Running Deer Country. Home: 2d Av Coshocton OH Office: 3d Av Coshocton OH

ELLSWORTH, ARTHUR WHITNEY, publisher; b. N.Y.C., May 31, 1936; s. Duncan Steuart and Esther Bowes (Stevens) E.; grad. St. Paul's Sch., 1954; B.A., Harvard, 1958; m. Sarah Bingham, Oct. 11, 1958 (div. 1963); 1 son, Barry; m. 2d, Priscilla Wear, July 1, 1967. Editorial asso. The Atlantic, 1959-63; pub. N.Y. Rev. Books, 1963—. Trustee, Harvard Advocate. Bd. dirs. Ellsworth Meml. Clinic, Chester Vt. Served with AUS, 1958-59. Office: 250 W 57th St New York City NY 10019.

ELLSWORTH, CLAYTON SUMNER, educator; b. Forest City, Ia., Apr. 18, 1905; s. Wallace Henry and Helma (Goranson) E.; B.A. magna cum laude in History, Oberlin Coll., 1927; Ph.D., Cornell U., 1930; m. Frances L. Fuller, June 18, 1929; children—Clayton Sumner, Lucius F., Frank L., Christina G. Instr., Oberlin Coll., 1930-31; mem. faculty Coll. Wooster, 1931—, prof. history, 1945—, Michael O. Fisher prof., chmn. dept. history, 1965—; summer tchr. U. Okla., N.M. Highlands U., Western Res. U. Mem. Am. Hist. Assn., Orgn. Am. Historians, Ohio Hist. Soc., Ohio Acad. History (chmn. hist. socs. com. 1963-67, pres. 1968-69, Distinguished Service award 1971). Contbr. profl. jours. Adv. bd. America; History and Life, 1965-69. Home: 1107 E Wayne Av Wooster OH 44691

ELLSWORTH, DONALD WILLIAM, investment counselor; b. Meredith, N.H., June 3, 1895; s. Perry Alvin and Annie (Foss) E.; S.B., Harvard, 1918; m. Ruth Elizabeth Mesmer, Apr. 24, 1926; children—Donald Bruce, Nancy E. (Mrs. Edward J. Walsh). With Gen. Electric Co., 1918-22, Am. Tel. & Tel. Co., 1922-25; asst editor, then editor The Annalist, N.Y. Times Co., 1925-40 Wall St. corr. London (Eng.) Observer, 1928-40; with Nat. Indsl. Conf. Bd., 1940-42; v.p.; then sr. v.p., exec. v.p. E.W. Axe & Co., Inc., Tarrytown, N.Y., 1942- -, also dir.; pres., dir. Axe Sci. Corp., Axe Sci. Mgmt. Corp., Axe-Houghton Stock Fund; dir. Axe-Houghton Fund A, Axe- Houghton Fund B, Axe Securities Corp. Served with P.A., U.S. Army, World War I. Mem. N.Y. Soc. Security Analysists. Baptist. Mason. Clubs: Coveleigh (Rye, N.Y.); Harvard of Westchester. Home: 19 Coprock Rd Pocantico Hills North Tarrytown, NY 10591. Office: 400 Benedict Av Tarrytown NY 10591

ELLSWORTH, JAMES CLARIDGE, banker; b. Safford, Ariz., Apr. 8, 1908; s. James Clarence and Julia (Claridge) E.; student U. Utah, 1929-31, Kansas City (Mo.) Law Sch., 1931-33; m. Nell Larson, June 7, 1933; children—John William, Christine (Mrs. L. J. Cottam), Thomas James, David Larson, Mary Kathryn. With FBI, 1935-54, spl. agt. charge field divs., 1952-54; with United Cal. Bank, and predecessors, 1954—, v.p., 1959-61, sr. v.p., 1961-71. Pres., dir. Unemployment Insurance Assn., 1961-71; pres. West German Mission, Ch. of Jesus Christ of Latter Day Saints, Frankfurt, 1971—. Pres., Nat. Edn. Inst., Los Angeles, 1970—; mem. adv. council Coll Bus., Brigham Young U. Bd. dirs. Bishop Gooden Home, Pasadena, Cal. Mem. Soc. Former Agts. FBI (pres. 1969), Am. Soc. for Indsl. Security (dir. 1967—), Americanism Ednl. League (dir. 1966—), Los Angeles C. of C., Delta Phi. Republican. Mem. Church of Jesus Christ of Latter Day Saints (pres. Pasadena stake 1963-71). Clubs: Jonathan, Stock Exchange, Town Hall (Los Angeles). Home: 1459 Bradbury Rd San Marino CA 91108 Office: 600 S Spring St Los Angeles CA 90054

ELLSWORTH, JOHN EDWARDS, mfg. exec.; b. Simsbury, Conn., Sept. 15, 1904; s. Henry Edwards and Susan (Starr) E.; grad. Hotchkiss Sch., 1922; B.A., Yale, 1926; m. Grace Walker White, May 5, 1939; children—Elinor Walker (Mrs. Honeckman), Starr, Ann Toy (Mrs. Broughton), Timothy Edwards. With Ensign-Bickford Co., Simsbury, 1926—, exec. v.p., 1955-60, pres., 1960—, chmn. bd., 1970—; pres., dir. Village Water Co. of Simsbury, 1948—, Bickford Research Labs., 1962—; dir. Darworth, Inc., Cia. Mexicana de Mecha para Minas, Simsbury Bank & Trust Co., Hartford Spl. Machinery Co. Chmn., Simsbury Tercentenary Com. Bd. dirs. Hartford Festival of Music; bd. dirs., v.p. Conn. Opera Assn.; pres., bd. dirs. Ensign-Bickford Found., Inc., 1966—, Talcott Mountain Forest Protective Assn., 1970; dir., treas. Council for Internat. Progress in Mgmt.; bd. dirs. Symphony Soc. Greater Hartford, Conn. River Watershed Council, Farmington River Watershed Assn., Jr. Achievement of Hartford; trustee Inst. Trend Research; corporator Inst. for Living, Hartford, Hartford Hosp., Mt. Sinai Hosp., St. Francis Hosp., Health care Facilities Planning Council Greater Hartford, Inc.; mem. regional adv. com. Capitol Region. Mem. Pub. Relations Soc. Am., Simsbury Hist. Soc. (v.p., dir.), Nat. Planning Assn., Newcomen Soc. N.Am., Nat. Indsl. Conf. Bd., Antiquarian and Landmarks Soc. Conn. (trustee), Pilgrims of U.S. Clubs: Yale (N.Y.); Hartford Sportsman (Hartford); Wampanoag Country (West Hartford); Hopmeadow Country (Simsbury). Author: The History of Simsbury 1935; 100 YearsThe Ensign-Bickford Co., 1936. Home: Box 515 Simsbury CT 06070

ELLSWORTH, MELVIN ANDREW, engring. and constrn. co. exec.; b. Paducah, Tex., Apr. 30, 1910; s. Clyde Calvin and Myrtle Ann (Stone) E.; B.S. in Indsl. Engring., Okla. State U., Stillwater, 1934; m. Aladine Louise Ray, May 18, 1935; children—Richard R., Marcia L. With Fluor Corp., Ltd., Los Angeles, 1940- -, v.p., 1956—, exec. v.p. engring. and constrn., 1962- 68; pres., 1968—; v.p. Fluor Corp. Can., Ltd., 1962—, Fluor Internat., S.A., 1958—; dir. Fluor Engring & Constrn. Co., Ltd. (London), Fluor Nederland, N.V., Haarlem, Holland. Home: 625 Canterbury Rd San Marino CA 91108 Office: 2500 S Atlantic St Los Angeles CA 90022

ELLSWORTH, RALPH E. educator, librarian; b. Forest City, Ia., Sept. 22, 1907; s. Wallace Henry and Helma Christina (Gorenson) E.; A.B., Oberlin Coll., 1929; B.L.S., Western Res. U., 1931, LL.D. (hon.), 1956; Ph.D., U. Chgo., 1937; m. Theda Chapman, Aug. 25, 1931; children—Peter Chapman, John David. Librarian, Adams State Tchrs. Coll., 1931-35; library adviser to grad. students Colo State Coll. Edn., 1936; dir libraries prof bibliography U. Colo., 1937-43; dir. libraries, prof. library sci., 1958—. dir. librarians and prof. librarianship U. Ia., 1945-58. Mem. Am. Library Assn., Assn. Coll. and Research Libraries, Ia. Library Assn., Assn. Coll. and Reference Libraries (pres.-elect). Democrat. Episcopalian. Club: Cactus (Denver). Author: The State of the Library Art: Buildings, 1960; Planning of College and University Library, 1960; (with Sarah Harris) The American Right Wing, 1960; The School Library: Facilities for Independent Study, 1963; The School Library, 1964; The Economics of Book Storage, 1969. also articles library and ednl. jours. Home: 860 Willowbrook Rd Boulder CO 80302

ELLSWORTH, SAMUEL GEORGE, educator, historian; b. Safford, Ariz., June 19, 1916; s. James Clarence and Julia (Claridge) E.; B.S. Utah State Agrl. Coll., 1941; M.A. in History, U. Cal. at Berkeley, 1947, Ph.D., 1951; m. Maria Smith, Oct. 24, 1942; children—Stephen George, Mark Addison. Prin., Virgin Valley Latter-day Saints Sem., also tchr. Virgin Valley High Sch., Bunkerville, Nev., 1941-42; teaching asst. U. Cal. at Davis and Berkeley, 1948-50; faculty Utah State U. (formerly Utah State Agrl. Coll.), Logan, 1951—, asst. prof. history, 1951-54, asso. prof., 1954- 63, prof., 1963—, head dept., 1966-69. Vis. prof. W.Va. U., 1954, Brigham Young U., 1956. Served with AUS, 1942-46. Faculty Honor lectr. humanities Utah State U. Faculty Assn., 1951, named Prof. of Year and recipient Robins award, 1965. Mem. Am., Western, Mormon history assns., Orgn. Am. Historians, Utah, Cache Valley hist. socs. (officer 1951-56, pres. 1954-56, sec. 1962, archivist 1956—, award merit Am. Assn. State and Local History 1955-56), Utah Acad. Scis., Arts and Letters (exec. council, chmn. social scis. div.), Phi Kappa Phi, Phi Alpha Theta. Author articles Utah and Mormon history. Mng. editor Western Hist. Quar., 1969—. Home: 496 N 3d Av East Logan UT 84321

ELLUL, JACQUES, educator; b. Bordeaux, France, Jan. 6, 1912; s.Joseph and Marthe (Mendes) E.; Baccalauriat, Lycee Bordeaux, 1929; masters degree of letters, Faculty Letters, U. Bordeaux, 1933, master degree of law, 1932, doctorate of law, 1936, aggregation faculty law, 1943; LL.D. (hon.), U. Amsterdam (Holland); m. Yvette Lensvelt, July 31, 1937; children—Jean, Simon, Yves, Dominque. Charge courses faculty law U. Montpelier (France), 1937, U. Strasbourg (France), 1938-40; prof. law faculty U. Bordeaux, 1944-70, Inst. Polit. Sci., 1947-70, in charge courses sociology, 1949—, Mem. nat. synod and nat. council Reform Ch. in France. Dep. to mayor of Bordeaux, 1944-46. Decorated chevalier Legion of Honor. Author: The Technological Society, 1966; The Political Illusion, 1966; Presence of the Kingdom, 1967; Violence, 1968; the Prayer and Moder Man, 1969; the Meaning of the City, 1970. Home: La Marierre 33 Pessac France Office: Faculte de Droit Univ Bordeaux Bordeaux France

ELLWANGER, JAMES WARREN, food service co. exec.; b. Dubugue, Ia., Mar. 2, 1921; s. John C. and Marjorie (Dumbaugh) E.; B.S., N.Y.U., 1942; student grad. sch., 1945-48; m. Lorean Nicholson, June 10, 1947; children—Thomas J., James M., Nancy J., Betsy J. Mng. accountant Price Waterhouse & Co., C.P.A.'s, N.Y.C., 1945-61; v.p. finance, sec-treas. Servomation Corp., 1961—. Pres. Knollwood Civic Assn., Millburn, N.J., 1957. Served to 1st lt., inf., AUS, 1942-45. C.P.A., N.Y., N.J. Mem. Am. Inst. C.P.A.'s, N.Y., N.J. socs. C.P.A.'s Financial Execs. Inst. Presbyn. (elder, treas.). Mason (32). Home: 21 Hobart Av Short Hills NJ 07078 Office: 777 3d Av New York City NY 10017

ELLWOOD, WILLIAM PRESCOTT, lawyer; b. Cedar Rapids, Ia., Sept. 5, 1909; s. Floyd Edwin and Gertrude (Prescott) E.; B.A., U. Ia., 1931, J.D., 1933; postgrad. Harvard Law Sch., 1938-39; m. Doris Cook, Mar. 26, 1935; children—Scott, Sutherland, John. Admitted to Ia. bar, 1933, Mich. bar, 1939; spl. agt. FBI, 1934-38; asso. firm Clark, Klein, Brucker & Waples, Detroit, 1940- 45; partner law firm Simmons, Perrine, Albright & Ellwood, Cedar Rapids, 1945—; sec. Lefebure Corp., 1957—; partner Eisenhauer Mfg. Co., 1944- -; dir. Roosevelt Hotel Co., 1946—, Creswell, Munsell, Schubert & Zirbel, Inc., 1963—. Trustee Cornell Coll., Mt. Vernon, O., Cedar Rapids Art Center. Mem. Am., Ia., Linn County bar assns., Cedar Rapids C. of C. (dir. 1964-67), Beta Theta Pi Episcopalian. Home: 3845 Indiandale Circle SE Cedar Rapids IA 52403 Office: Merchants Nat Bank Bldg Cedar Rapids IA 52401

ELMAN, PHILIP, lawyer, educator; b. Paterson, N.J., Mar. 14, 1918; s. Jacob and Anne (Nirenberg) E.; A.B., Coll. City N.Y., 1936; LL.B., Harvard, 1939; m. Ella M. Shalit, Dec. 21, 1947; children—Joseph, Peter, Anthony. Admitted to N.Y. bar, 1940, D.C. bar, 1948; law clk. to Judge Magruder, U.S. Ct. Appeals, 1939-40; atty. FCC, 1940-41; law clk. to Supreme Ct. Justice Frankfurter, 1941-43; asst. chmn. Office Fgn. Econ. Coordination, State Dept., 1943-44; atty. Solicitor Gen.'s Office, Dept. Justice, 1944-45; legal adviser Mil. Govt. U.S., Berlin, Germany, 1945-46; asst. to solicitor gen. U.S., 1946-61; mem. FTC, 1961-70; prof. law Georgetown U. Law Center, Washington, 1970—. Recipient Rockefeller Pub. Service award 1967. Mem. Judicature Soc., Am. Law Inst., Am., Fed., D.C. bar assns., Harvard Law Sch. Assn., Phi Beta Kappa. Editor: Of Law and Men (papers of Felix Frankfurter), 1956. Home: 6719 Brigadoon Dr Bethesda MD 20034 Office: 1320 19th St NW Washington DC 20036

ELMENDORF, FRANCIS LITTLETON, bus. cons.; b. Indpls., July 16, 1902; s. William Horris and Ada May (Littleton) E.; student Ind. U., 1919-20, Butler U., 1921-22; m. Dorothy Amantha Fulton, Mar. 3, 1928; children—William Wood, Judith Ann (Mrs. Dennis T. Fratianne). Mgr. mail order sales, The Higbee Co., Cleve., 1923, 24, various exec. positions, 1926-30; self-employed, sales promotion and advt., 1925, ins., Cleveland, 1931-33; with Robert Heller & Assos., engrs. and consultants, 1933-62, pres., 1958-62; pres. Elmendorf & Co., 1962-68. Cons. to sec. of state, chmn. FTC, 1953-54; cons. to postmaster gen., 1953-59, gov. Ind., 1955-56; mem. Pres.'s Ann. Assay Commn., 1953. task force leader, Post Office Dept. Project, Hoover Commn., 1948; cons. Sec. Def., dir. mgmt. adv. group Dept. Defense, 1949-51. Bd. dirs. Am. Cancer Soc. Mem. Cleve. C. of C., Am. Numis. Assn., Holland Soc. of N.Y., Soc. Colonial Wars, S.A.R., Sigma Chi. Republican. Episcopalian. Mason. Clubs: Mayfield, Mid-Day, Union (Cleve.); Chicago. Home: 18975 Van Aken Blvd Shaker Heights OH 44122 Office: Investment Plaza Cleveland OH 44114

ELMENDORF, JOHN VAN GAASBEEK, coll. pres.; b. South Orange, N.J., Sept. 9, 1916; s. Arthur Raymond and Frances (Johnson) E.; grad. Choate Sch., 1933; A.B., U. N.C., 1937, M.A., 1947, Ph.D., 1951; A.M., Brown U., 1961; m. Mary Tillery Lindsay, Dec. 27, 1937; children—Calvin Lindsay, Susan Johnson. Prin., Pottsville (Ark.) High Sch., 1937-38; instr. French and German, Hopkins Grammer Sch., New Haven, 1939-41; instr. French and Spanish, Putney (Vt.) Sch., 1941-43; dep. commr. for Europe, Am. Friends Service Com., 1946; grad. instr. French and Spanish, U. N.C., 1946-49; exec. dir. Mexican-Am. Inst., Mexico City, 1950-52; v.p., dean faculty prof. linguistics Mexico City Coll., 1953-61; v.p. Brown U., Providence, 1961-65; pres. New Coll., Sarasota, Fla., 1965—. Exec. bd. Anglo-Am. Com. for UN, 1957- 61; mem. exec. com. R.I. Equal Opportunity Council. Bd. dirs. Providence Country Day Sch., Internat. House of R.I., Am. School Found., 1955-61; pres. trustees Mexico City Acad., 1959-61. Served with AUS, 1943-46; ETO. Decorated Bronze Star medal with 3 oak leaf clusters. Mem. Linguistic Soc. Am., Phi Beta Kappa (v.p. Mexico 1955-61). Democrat. Mem. Soc. of Friends. Clubs: Field, Bird Key Yacht (Sarasota, Fla.). Home: 535 Blvd Presidents Sarasota FL 33577 Office: New Coll Sarasota FL 33578

ELMENDORF, WILLIAM WELCOME, educator; b. Victoria, B.C., Can., Sept. 10, 1912 (parents Am. citizens); s. William Judson and Mary (Johnson) E.; B.A., U. Wash., 1934, M.A., 1935, Ph.D., U. Cal. at Berkeley, 1949; m. Eleanor Gerlough, Oct. 12, 1940; children—William John, Anthony Daniel. Teaching asst. U. Cal. at Berkeley, 1940-42; instr., then asst. prof. anthropology U. Wash., 1946-57; teaching asso. Northwestern U., 1950-51; lectr., then asso. prof. Wash. State U., 1957-65; mem. faculty U. Wis., 1963—, prof. anthropology, 1964—. Profl. cons. Skokomish Indian Claims Case, 1956. Served to capt. AUS, 1942-46, 51-52. Fellow Am. Anthrop. Assn., Am. Ethnol. Soc.; mem. Linguistic Soc. Am., Central States Anthrop. Soc., Northwest Anthrop. Conf. (pres. 1958), A.A.A.S., Sigma Xi. Author: The Structure of Twana Culture, 1960; Skokomish and Other Coast Salish Tales, 1961; Lexical and Cultural Change in Yukian, 1968.

ELMER, J. O., banker; b. New Orleans, Apr. 17 1908; s. J. O. and Marion Elizabeth (Lewis) E.; m. Florence Downs, June 15, 1929 (div. Nov. 1956); children—John P., Paul R.; m. 2d, Virginia D. Elmer, June 2, 1957. With Pacific Nat. Bank, San Francisco, 1925-27, E. Bay Nat. Bank, Oakland, Cal., 1927-28, Peoples Trust & Savs. Bank, Chgo., 1928-29; with Wells Fargo Bank (name changed Wells Fargo & Co. 1968), San Francisco, 1929—, sr. v.p., 1959—. Mem. Am. Bankers Assn. (chmn. state legislative com., chmn. adv. com. on state legislation), Western States Bankcard Assn. (chmn., dir.) Interbank Card Assn. (dir). Home: 2164 Hyde St San Francisco CA 94109 Office: 464 California St San Francisco CA 94120

ELMER, WILLIAM MORRIS, pipe line exec.; b. Rochelle, Ill., Apr. 25, 1915; s. Gertis Dresser and Josephine (Morris) E.; student Lyons Twp. (Ill.) Jr. Coll., 1934; B.A., U. Ill., 1936; m. Ruth Alexander, July 9, 1939; children—Ruth Ann, William A. Accounting mgr. Arthur Andersen & Co., 1936-46; sr. v.p. Tex. Gas Transmission Corp., 1946-57, exec. v.p. 1957, pres. 1957-68, chmn. bd., chief exec. officer, 1968—, also dir.; pres. Tex. Gas Exploration Corp., 1953-58, now chmn. Served as lt. comdr. USNR, 1942- 46. Mem. Ill. Soc. C.P.A.'s, Ind. Natural Gas Assn., Am. Gas Assn., Am. Petroleum Inst., Mid-Continent Oil and Gas Assn. Mason. Home: 2022 Winston Dr Owensboro KY 42301 Office: 3800 Frederica St Owensboro KY 42301

ELMEZZI, THOMAS, beverage co. chemist; b. N.Y.C., Dec. 9, 1914; s. Joseph and Mary (Battaglia) E.; student Coll. City N.Y., Pratt Inst.; m. Jeanne Mastronardo, Apr. 29, 1939. With PepsiCo, Inc. (formerly Pepsi- Cola Co.), N.Y.C. 1933—, beginning as asst. chief chemist, successively asst. v.p., v.p., 1945-58, sr. v.p., 1958-63, exec. v.p., 1963—, also dir.; adviser cons. Pepsico, Inc., 1968—. Mem. Am. Chem. Soc. Inst. Food Technologists, Am. Pub. Health Assn., Assn. Food and Drug Ofcls. of U.S., Flavoring Extract Mfrs. Assn., N.Y. Bd. Trade, Nutrition Found., Sugar Industry Technicians. Club: Sugar. Home: 90 Knightsbridge Rd Great Neck NY 11021 Office: PepsiCo Purchase New York City NY

ELMLARK, HARRY EUGENE, newspaper feature syndicate exec.; b. Hudson, N.Y., July 25, 1909; s. David and Anna (Finkelstein) E.; B.S., U. Va., 1931; m. Lillian Rosenthal, Sept. 17, 1933; 1 dau., Walli (Mrs. Jerome Kellert). Reporter, Washington Post, 1931-33; free-lance mag. and newspaper writer, 1933-36; with Washington Star Syndicate, and predecessor, 1936- -, gen. mgr., v.p., 1958-62, pres., 1962—, also editor. Home: 201 E 66th St New York City NY 10017 Office: Washington Star Syndicate 444 Madison Av New York City NY 10022

ELMORE, FRANKLIN HARPER, judge; b. Jacksonville, Fla., Mar. 22, 1903; s. F. H. and Anna Madeleine (Daniel) E.; ed. Sewanee (Tenn.) Mil. Acad.; LL.B., U. Fla., 1926; m. Vivian Gay, April 27, 1927; children—Elisabeth Gay (Mrs. G.W. Gilleland, Jr., Madeleine (Mrs. Elmore Ingram, Mary C. (Mrs. D.M. Harrell). Admitted to Fla. bar, 1926; practiced in Jacksonville, 1926-34; asst. counsel, NRA, Washington, 1934-36; spl. asst. atty. gen. Dept. Justice, Washington, 1936-37, 38-43; partner Latham & Elmore, attys., Jacksonville, 1937-38, 47-52; partner Wise, Corlett & Canfield, Washington, 1944-46; legal counsel for Arab States, Fgn. Operations Adminstrn., Am. embassy, Cairo, Egypt, 1953-55; partner Elmore & Clark, 1955-60, circuit judge 4th Jud. Circuit of Fla., 1960—. Pres. Council of Social Agys., Jacksonville, 1948-50. Mem. Am., Fla. (bd. govs. 1950- 52), Jackaonville (pres. 1950) bar assns., Jacksonville Hist. Soc. (past pres.), Fla. Hist. Soc., Kappa Alpha Order, Phi Delta Phi. Democrat. Episcopalian. Clubs: Florida Yacht. Home: 4274 Venetia Blvd Jacksonville FL 32210 Office: Duval County Court House Jacksonville FL 32202

ELMORE, MARJORIE JANE, nurse, univ. dean; b. Marshfield, Mo., Sept. 27, 1916; d. J. Stanley and Terrie (Childress) Elmore; A.B., Park Coll., 1937; B.S. in Nursing, U. Mo., 1943, M.A., 1945; D.Edn., Columbia, 1964. Instr. sci. Deaconesss Hosp. Sch. Nursing, St. Louis, 1943-46, Park Coll., Parkville, Mo., 1946-47; exec. sec. Mo. Nurses Assn., 1948-54, Ore. Nurses Assn., 1954-55; asst. dir. dept. diploma and asso. degree programs Nat. League for Nursing, N.Y.C., 1956-57; research asso. Am. Nurses Found., N.Y.C., 1960-62; dean U. Nev. Orvis Sch. Nursing, Reno, 1962—, prof., 1962—. Co-dir. study family adjustments to crisis of cardiac disease USPHS, 1960-62. Mem. Am. Nurses Assn., Nat. League for Nursing, Nat. Honor Soc., Pi Lambda Theta, Kappa Delta Pi, Phi Kappa Phi. Presbyn. Mem. order Eastern Star. Home: 1390 Alturas Av Reno NV 89503

ELMORE, NEWELL JOUETT, machine tool exec.; b. Richmond, Ky., July 7, 1911; s. N. Clarence and Hazel (Jouett) E.; student U. Ky., 1929, U. Cin., 1930-33; B.C.S., Chase Coll., 1941, LL.D., 1966; m. Hester Ellen Richardson, Dec. 10, 1939; children—Rodney, Donald, Joyce. Comptroller, Cin. Milacron, Inc., 1943—; sec.-treas., dir. Cin. Milacron Chems., Inc., 1949—; comptroller Cin. Milacron Co., 1950—; sec., dir. Advance Internat., Ltd., 1955—; sec.-treas., dir. Advance Solvents & Chem. Corp. Can., Ltd., 1955—; sec., dir. Milacron Internat. Finance Corp., 1966—; treas. dir. Factory Power Co., 1956—; v.p., dir. Cin. Milacron Comml. Corp., 1967- -; treas. Amertool Services, Inc. Trustee, treas. Chase Coll. C.P.A., Ohio. Mem. Am. Inst. C.P.A.'s, Ohio Soc. C.P.A.'s, Nat. Assn. Accountants, Financial Execs. Inst. Baptist (trustee). Home: 1387 Thomwood Dr Cincinnati OH 45224 Office: 4701 Marburg Av Cincinnati OH 45209

ELMORE, WILLIAM CRONK, physicist; b. Montour Falls, N.Y., Sept. 16, 1909; s. Thaddeus P. and Grace (Cronk) E.; B.S., Lehigh U., 1932; Ph.D., Yale, 1935; m. Barbara Page, June 6, 1936; children—Mary-Leigh, David, Elizabeth. Instr. Mass. Inst. Tech., 1935-38; prof. Swarthmore Coll., 1938—, chmn. dept. physics, 1948—, now Clothier prof. physics; engaged in research Bartol Research Found., 1942-43, Los Alamos Sci. Lab., 1944-46, 57-58. Fellow A.A.A.S., Am. Phys. Soc.; mem. Phi Beta Kappa, Sigma Xi. Author: (with M. Sands) Electronics, Experimental Techniques, 1949. Holder 12 patents. Home: 525 Walnut Lane Swarthmore PA 19081

ELMORE, WILLIAM SOLLIE, adj. gen. Alaska; b. Goldwaite, Tex., Apr. 26, 1915; s. Wheeler-Soloman and Viggina Bell (Russell) E.; grad. Civilian Pilot Tng. Sch., 1941, Air Force Command and Staff Sch., 1963; m. Kathryn Ellen Sisinger, Jan. 23, 1947; children—William John, Kathryn Elizabeth (Mrs. William E. Christy), Earlene Jennifer (Mrs. James R. Caress), Morgan Robert, Foster Sollie (Mrs. Thomas James Coco), Charles Wesley. Entered U.S. Army, 1942, commd. 2d lt. AC, 1943; B24 pilot in S. Pacific, 1946-48; propr. Elmore & Miller Aviation Enterprises, Casper, Wyo., 1947-49; homestead in Alaska, 1950-54; joined Alaska Air N.G., 1954; comdr. base detachment, Anchorage, 1956-64; adj. gen. Alaska, 1964-67, 71—; safety dir. check pilot FAA, Anchorage. Chief of staff, lt. col. Air N.G. Home: Elmore Rd Star Route A Box 479 Anchorage AK 99502 Office: MacKay Bldg Anchorage AK 99504

ELMS, JAMES CORNELIUS IV, govt. ofcl.; b. East Orange, N.J., May 16, 1916; s. James Cornelius, Jr. and Iva Marguerite (Corwin) E.; B.S. in Physics, Cal. Inst. Tech., 1948; M.A. in Physics, U. Cal. at Los Angeles, 1950; m. Patricia Marguerite Pafford, Jan. 4, 1942; children—Christopher Michael, Suzanne (Mrs. Michael F. Rogers), Francesca, Deborah. Mgr. armament control N. Am. Aviation Co., 1950-57; mgr. avionics Martin Co., 1957-59; exec. v.p. Crosley div. Avco Corp., 1959-60; dir. electronics aero. div. Ford Motor Co., 1961-62; dep. dir. Manned Spacecraft Center, NASA, 1963-64; v.p. Raytheon Co., 1964- 65; dep. asso. adminstr. for manned space flight NASA, 1965-66, dir. Electronics Research Center, 1966-70; dir. Transp. Systems Center, U.S. Dept. Transp., Cambridge, Mass., 1970—; faculty U. Cal. at Los Angeles, 1949-50. Served to capt. USAAF, 1942-46. Recipient spl. award NASA, 1964, Exceptional Service medal, 1969, Outstanding Leadership medal, 1970. Registered profl. engr., Cal. Fellow I.E.E.E.; asso. fellow Am. Inst. Aero. and Astronautics; mem. Am. Phys. Soc. Episcopalian. Home: 67 Maugus Av Wellesley Hills MA 02181 also 112 Kings Pl Newport Beach CA 92660 Office: Transp Systems Center US Dept Transp Cambridge MA 02114

ELONEN, ANNA SIVIA, educator, psychologist; b. Laihia, Finland, Feb. 25, 1904; d. Herman M. and Susanna (Lyyski) Elonen; came to U.S., 1910, derivative citizen; B.A., Lawrence Coll., 1925; M.A., U. Minn., 1927; Ph.D., U. Chgo., 1948. Psychologist, Minn. Bd. Control, 1927-37; instr., then asst. prof. U. Chgo., 1937-50; prof. psychology U. Mich., Ann Arbor, 1950—. Fulbright lectr., Finland, 1953-54; Fulbright research worker, Finland, 1958-59; program dir. Mott Found. and Lang. for Deaf Children thru Parent Edn., 1968—; cons. in field, 1950—. Grantee Founds. Fund Research Psychiatry, 1966. Mem. Am. Assn. Mental Deficiency, Am., Finnish, Mich. psychol. assns., Soc. Research Child Devel., Am. Orthopsychiat., Council Exceptional Children, Mich. Emotionally Disturbed Assn. Author articles in field. Home: 2460 Glacier Way Ann Arbor MI 48105

ELORRIAGA, JOHN AMBROSE, holding co. exec.; b. Jordan Valley, Ore., Oct. 20, 1923; s. Ambrose and Maria (Goicoechea) E.; A.A., Boise Jr. Coll., 1949; B.B.A., U. Ore., 1951; M.B.A., U. Pitts., 1953; grad. Pacific Coast Sch. Banking, 1959; m. Lois Corinne Newman, June 14, 1952; children—Dana W., John M., Sharon P., Steven M., Linda M., Lisa A. Vice pres. U.S. Nat. Bank, Portland, Ore., 1957-67; exec. v.p. Evans Products, Portland, Ore., 1967-70; pres., chief exec. officer Columbia Nyematic System Inc., Portland, Ore., 1970—; dir. Acme Trading Co.; cons., dir. Rader Pneumatic Inc.; instr. Portland State Coll., Am. Inst. Banking, Multnomah Coll. Chmn. bd. dirs. Jesuit High Sch. Mem. Portland C. of C. (ednl. com. 1963), Ore. Heart Assn., Ore. Bankers Assn., Am. Bankers Assn., Am. Inst. Banking, Phi Theta Kappa, Chi Psi. Republican. Roman Catholic. Clubs: Multnomah Athletic, Portland Golf. Home: 4841 SW 60th Pl Portland OR 97221 Office: 2300 SW 1st Av Portland OR 97201

ELSASSER, ROBERT WILLIAM, mgmt. and econ. analyst; b. N.Y.C., Mar. 10, 1900; s. William Carl and Clara Anna (Koppe) E.; A.B., Dartmouth, 1921, M.C.S., 1922; m. Minnie Helen Pelton, Apr. 10, 1922. Instr. econs. Dartmouth, 1921-22, 24-26; accountant, statistician Eastman Kodak Co., 1922-24; from asso. to prof. bus. statistics and mgmt. Tulane U., 1926-39, prof. econs. and mgmt., 1939-42; spl. asst. to adminstrs. Tulane Ednl. Fund., 1946-47; personnel dir., v.p. personnel Pendleton Shipyards Co., Inc., 1942, v.p., gen. mgr., 1942-46; profl. practice mgmt., econ. and statis. analysis, 1947- -; sect. leader Sch. Banking South, La. State U., 1950—; dir. Lake Lawn Park, Inc., I.L. Lyons & Co., Ltd. Chmn. Citizens Com. Revenues City New Orleans, 1955-56, Citizens Com. Economy and Revenues, 1961- 62, Citizens Com. Finances Orleans Parish Sch. Bd., 1958, New Orleans Indsl. Dispersion Com., New

Orleans Census Tract Com. Bd. dirs. New Orleans Hosp. Service Assn., Bur. Govtl. Research New Orleans; trustee Com. Econ. Devel. Chartered Financial Analyst. Fellow Acad. Mgmt.; mem. C. of C. (pres. 1956, dir.), Am. Econ. Assn., Am. Statis. Assn. Am. Accounting Assn., Am. Mgmt. Assn., Soc. Advancement Mgmt. (pres. New Orleans 1950), So. Econ. Assn., New Orleans Assessment Study Com. (vice chmn. 1963-65), Financial Analysts New Orleans (pres. 1965-66), Phi Beta Kappa, Beta Gamma Sigma, Omicron Delta Kappa, Chi Phi. Clubs: Internat. House (dir., exec. com. 1956-61, v.p. 1965), Round Table, Pickwick (New Orleans). Home: 8004 Freret St New Orleans LA 70118 Office: 833 Howard Av New Orleans LA 70113

ELSASSER, THEORDORE HERMAN, surgeon; b. Union City, N.J., Dec. 19, 1899; s. Adolph Otto and Mary (Klein) E.; student N.Y.U., 1919-20, M.D., 1924, postgrad. surg. course, 1927-30; m. Elise Valentine Zibetti, Mar. 17, 1924; children—Elise Theodora, Mary Ellen, Elaine Dores; m. 2d, Margaret Grogan, Apr. 1946; children—Elizabeth, Theodore. Intern North Hudson Hosp., Weehawken, N.J., 1924-25; instr. surgery N.Y. U. Coll. of Medicine, 1928—; asso. gynecologist, North Hudson Hosp., Weehawken; dir. cancer research, asso. surgeon Christ Hosp., Jersey City; asso. surgeon French Hosp., N.Y.C.; asso. with Prof. George B. Wallace, dept. of pharmacology, N.Y.U., in cancer research, 1930—; asst. prof. surgery Seton Hall U., Jersey City, 1959. Served in R.O.T.C., 1919. Diplomate Am. Bd. Abdominal Surgery, 1958. Fellow A.C.S.; mem. Clin. and Post Grad. Surg. Soc. N.Y.U., A.M.A., Hudson City and North Hudson Physicians Soc., Sigma Xi, Phi Alpha Sigma. Contbr. to med. jours. Address: 7206 Park Av North Bergen NJ 07047

ELSASSER, WALTER MAURICE, physicist; b. Mannheim, Germany, Mar. 20, 1904; s. Moritz and Johanna (Masius) E.; Ph.D., U. Goettingen (Germany), 1927; m. Margaret Trahey, July 17, 1937; children—Barbara, William; m. 2d, Suzanne Rosenfeld, June 24, 1964. Came to the U.S., 1936, naturalized 1940. Instr. U. Frankfurt (Germany), 1930-33; research fellow Sorbonne, Paris, 1933-36, Cal. Inst. Tech., 1936-41; war research on radar U.S. Signal Corps, also Columbia, 1941-47; prof. physics U. Pa., 1947-50, U. Utah, 1950-56, U. Cal. at La Jolla, 1956-62; chmn. dept. physics U. N.M., Alburquerque, 1960-61; prof. geophysics, dept. geology Princeton, 1962-68; research prof. Inst. Fluid Mechanics and Applied Math., U. Md., College Park, 1968—. Fellow Am. Phys. Soc., Am. Geophys. Union (Bowie medal 1959); mem. Nat. Acad. Sci. Author: (theory of earth's magnetic field) The Physical Foundation of Biology, 1958; Atom and Organism. 1966. Home: 3450 Toledo Terrace Hyattsville MD 20782 Office: Inst Fluid Mechanics and Applied Math U Md College Park MD 20740

EL-SAYED, MOSTAFA AMR, educator, chemist; b. Zifta, Egypt, May 8, 1933; s. Amr and Zakia (Ahmed) El-S.; B.Sc., Ein Shams U., Cairo, 1953; Ph.D., Fla. State U., 1959; m. Janice Jones, Mar. 15, 1957; children—Lyla, Tarric, James, Dorea Jehan, Ivan Homer. Came to U.S., 1954, naturalized, 1965. Research fellow Yale, 1957, Harvard, 1959-60, Cal. Inst. Tech., 1960-61; asst. prof. U. Cal. at Los Angeles, 1961-64, asso. prof. chemistry, 1964-67, prof., 1967—; cons. N.Am. Aviation Minute Man Program, 1965-66. Recipient Distinguished Teaching award U. Cal., Los Angeles, 1964, Fresenius Nat. award, 1967, McCoy Research award, 1969; Alfred P. Sloane, Guggenheim fellows, 1965. Mem. Am. Phys. Soc., Am. Chem. Soc., A.A.A.S., Am. Assn. U. Profs., Western Spectroscopy Assn. Contbr. articles profl. jours. Home: 3325 Colbert Av Los Angeles CA 90066

ELSBERG, MILTON LEONARD, drug co. exec.; b. Balt., Sept. 29, 1912; s. Simon and Ida (Levy) E.; Ph.G., U. Md., 1931; m. Rita Kahn, Sept. 13, 1936; 1 son, Stuart Michael. Disc jockey radio sta. WCBM, Balt., 1930; clk. Lober Bros., N.Y.C., 1932; pharmacist Nat. Press Pharmacy, Washington, 1933; mgr. So. Drug Co., Washington, 1935-37; partner Drug Fair, Washington, 1938—, pres., chief exec. officer, 1940—; dir., mem. exec. com. Riggs Nat. Bank, Washington. Bd. dirs. Better Bus. Bur. Met. Washington, Greater Nat. Capital com. Kauffman Camp for Boys and Girls, Fed. City Council, Brand Names Found.; trustee Boys Club Washington, United Jewish Appeal Greater Washington; nat. trustee, chmn. drive Eleanor Roosevelt Inst. Cancer Research; mem. pres.'s council Brandeis U. Recipient award of achievement Advt. Club, 1958, Brand Name Retailers of Year awards for chains in U.S. and Can., 1958, 64. Mem. Washington Bd. Trade, Nat. Assn. Real Estate Bds., Bd. Affiliated Drug Stores, Nat. Assn. Chain Drug Stores, Washington Bd. Realtors, D.C. C. of C. Clubs: Variety, Saints and Sinners, Advertising, Internat., Georgetown (Washington); Centre (Balt.); Woodmont Country (Rockville, Md.). Home: Shoreham Hotel Washington DC 20008 Office: 6315 Bren Mar Dr Alexandria VA 22314

ELSBREE, JOHN FRANCIS, banker; b. Methuen, Mass., Apr. 19, 1912; s. Leslie Francis and Beatrice (Roberts) E.; student Harvard, 1928-30, Am. Inst. Banking, 1933-45, Stonier Grad. Sch. Banking, 1955-57; m. Ida Letitia Brooks, Aug. 13, 1938; children—Janet Elaine (Mrs. Ronald Kent Amoling), John Francis, Marjorie Evelyn (Mrs. Walter Scott Evans), David Brooks, Ruth Elizabeth. With Webster & Atlas Nat. Bank, Boston, 1930-48, auditor, 1945-48; asst. auditor Rockland-Atlas Nat. Bank, Boston, 1948-51, auditor, 1951-57, asst. v.p., 1957-61; asst. v.p. State St. Bank & Trust Co., Boston, 1961-62, v.p., 1962-64, v.p., gen. auditor, 1964—; v.p., gen. auditor State St. Boston Financial Corp., 1970—. Lectr., Am. Inst. Banking, Northwestern U., No. New Eng. Sch. Banking, NABAC Sch. at U. Wis. Treas., Boston Latin Sch. Assn., 1955—. Semi-finalist Am. Inst. Banking Nat. Debate Contest, 1950, 53, 54. Mem. Bank Officers Assn. Boston (past dir.), Am. Inst. Banking (past asso. councilman, nat. debate chmn.), Inst. Internal Auditors (dir. New Eng. chpt. 1968—, v.p. New Eng. chpt.), Bank Administrn. Inst. (past pres. Boston chpt., state, dist. dir. 1970-71, chmn. bd. regents). Episcopalian. Author: A Study of Social, Economic and Political Causes and Effects of Commercial Bank Mergers, 1957. Contbr. articles to profl. publs. Home: 56 Brooks St Brighton Boston MA 02135 Office: 225 Franklin St Boston MA 02101

ELSE, GERALD FRANK, educator; b. Redfield, S.D., July 1, 1908; s. Frank Marston and Minnie Marylouise (Beckman) E.; student U. Neb., 1924-27; A.B. summa cum laude, Harvard, 1929, M.A., 1932, Ph.D., 1934; m. Martha Post Wight, June 15, 1939, (dec. 1961); children—Martha (Mrs. J.S. Wyman, Jr.), Stephen. Instr. in Greek and Latin, Harvard, 1935-38, faculty instr., 1938-42; prof., head dept. classics U. Ia., 1945-57; prof. Greek and Latin, U. Mich., 1957—, chmn. dept. classical studies, 1957-68, dir. Center for Coordination of Ancient and Modern Studies, 1969—. Mem. Nat. Council on the Humanities, 1966—, vice chmn., 1968-71. Served as capt., USMCR, 1943-45. Fellow Am. Acad. Arts and Scis.; mem. Am. Philol. Assn. (pres. 1964), Classical Assn. Middle West and S. (pres. 1955-56), Archaeol. Inst. Am., Phi Beta Kappa. Club: Cosmos (Washington). Author: Aristotle's Poetics: The Argument; The Origin and Early Form of Greek Tragedy. Translator: Poetics (Aristotle). Contbr. articles and revs. on classical subjects to periodicals. Office: Center for Coordination Ancient and Modern Studies U Mich Ann Arbor MI 48104

ELSENBAST, ARTHUR chemist; b. N.Y.C., July 16, 1890; s. George J. and Wilhelmina Nickle (Reinhardt) E.; B. Chem., Cornell U., 1912; m. Dorothy Evelyn Chisholm, Apr. 18, 1940. Analytical chemist Nichols Copper Co. (now Phelps Dodge), Long Island City, N.Y., 1912-15; works chemist Central Dyestuff & Chem. Co., Neward, 1915-16, Dr. A. Gessler, S.I., N.Y., 1916; plant chemist Seydel Chem. co., jersey City, 1917; joined Johns-Manville Corp., N.Y.C., 1917, gen. mgr. Celite div., 1946-56, v.p. 1951-56; v.p. Johns-Manville Sales Corp., 1937-56; now ret. Mem. Am. Chem. Soc., Am. Inst. Chemists. Clubs: Chemist, Cornell, New York Athletic (N.Y.C.); Greenwich (Conn.) Country. Home: Stanwich Lane Greenwich CT 06830

ELSEY, GEORGE MCKEE, assn. exec., b. Palo Alto, Cal., Feb. 5, 1918; s. Howard McKee and Ethel May (Daniels) E.; A.B., Princeton, 1939; A.M., Harvard, 1940; m. Sally Phelps Bradley, Dec. 15, 1951; children—Anne Bradley, Howard McKee. mem. staff White House, 1947-53; with A.R.C. 1953-61, v.p., 1958-61; with various divs. Pullman, Inc., 1961-65, asst. to chmn. and pres., 1966-70; pres. Am. Nat. Red Cross, 1970—; dir. Am. Security & Trust Co. Pres. Meridian House Found., Washington, 1961-66, vice chmn., 1967-68, trustee, 1968-71; trustee Landon Sch., 1969—, Brookings Instn., 1971—; trustee Nat. Trust Historic Preservation, 1967—, vice chmn., 1969—. Active duty, USNR, 1941-47; released to inactive duty as comdr. Decorated Legion of Merit, Order of Brit. Empire, recipient Distinguished Pub. Service medal Dept. Def. Mem. Washington Inst. Fgn. Affairs, A.A.A.S., The Conf. Bd., Phi Beta Kappa. Presbyn. (ruling elder). Clubs: Princeton (N.Y.); Chevy Chase, Metropolitan (Washington). Home: 2201 King Pl NW Washington DC 20007 Office: 17th and D Sts NW Washington DC 20006

EL-SHIBIB, TALIB, Iraqi diplomat; b. Baghdad, Iraq, Mar. 22, 1934; s. Hussain and Kaijiya El-Shibib; B.S., London U. (Eng.), 1956. Various positions in journalism and politics, 1956-62; minister fgn. affairs, 1963; Arab League ambassador to London, 1966-68; ambassador of Iraq, Turkey, 1968-70; Iraqi ambassador to UN, N.Y.C., 1970—. Home: 45 E 89th St New York City NY Office: 14 E 79th St New York City NY

ELSING, WILLIAM TADDES, lawyer; b. Bisbee, Ariz., May 8, 1910; s. Morris J. and Celestine (Marks) E.; student Stanford, 1928, U. Cal. at Berkeley, 1929; J.D., U. Ariz., 1933; m. Ferol Cox, May 29, 1941. Admitted to Ariz. bar, 1933, Cal. bar, 1946; practiced in Prescott, 1933-38, Phoenix, 1938—. Chmn. bd. govs. Ariz. Dept. Mineral Resources. Served with CIC, AUS, 1942-45. Mem. Am., Cal., Ariz., Maricopa County bar assns., Soc. Mining Engrs., Am. Inst. Mining, Metall. and Petroleum Engrs., A.A.A.S., Phi Delta Phi. Republican. Presbyn. Home: 6545 N 13th St Phoenix AZ 85014 Office: Ariz Bank Bldg 34 W Monroe St Phoenix AZ 85003

ELSNER, SIDNEY EDGAR, journalist; b. Cleve., May 30, 1919; s. Sidney Edgar and Charlotte (Sill) E.; B.S., Ohio State U., 1941; m. Jean Helen Leaf, June 8, 1947; children—David M., Lawrence B., Michael C. Sports editor Washington Court House (O.) Record-Herald, 1941-42; reporter Springfield (O.) Daily News, 1942; copy editor Columbus (O.) Citizen, 1942-43; reporter, copy editor, asst. city editor, state editor, day city editor, met. editor, asso. editor/editorial writer Plain Dealer, Cleve., 1943—. Attended City Editors Seminar, Am. Press Inst. at Columbia, 1960. Recipient Best News Reporting award Cleve. Newspaper Guild, 1950, 54. Mem. Workmens Circle, Sigma Delta Chi. Jewish religion. Club: City (chmn. forum com. Cleve. 1967-68). Home: 4222 Stilmore Rd South Euclid OH 44121 Office: 1801 Superior Av N E Cleveland OH 44114

ELSON, ALEX, lawyer; b. nr. Kiev, Russia, Apr. 17, 1905; s. Jacob and Rebecca (Brodsky) E.; brought to U.S., 1906, naturalized, 1913; Ph.B., U. Chgo., 1925, J.D., 1928; m. Mirian Almond, July 6, 1933; children—Jacova, Karen. Admitted to Ill. bar, 1928; bill drafter Legislative Reference Bur., Springfield, Ill., 1929; atty. Legal Aid Bur., Chgo., 1927-34; asso. atty. Tolman, Chandler & Dickinson, 1934- 38; regional atty. Wage-Hour Div., Chgo., 1938-41; regional atty. and asst. gen. counsel OPA, 1941-45; lectr. Yale Law Sch., 1946, U. Chgo., intermittently 1933—; seminar-labor relations Northwestern U. Sch. Law, 1961-65. Former pub. mem. Regional War Labor Bd. and chmn. Chgo. Rent Commn.; former dir., vice chmn. Ill. div. Am. Civil Liberties Union; former vice chmn. Ill. Commn. on Children; former chmn. Bd. Health Commrs. State Ill. Past dir. Hull House Assn. Bd. dirs. Law in Am. Soc. Found.; cons. Ford Found., 1963-68. Mem. Am., Ill., Chgo (bd. mgrs.) bar assns., Am. Law Inst., Nat. Acad. Arbitrators, Inst. Psychoanalysis (dir.). Author: Civil Practice Forms, 1934; co-author Civil Practice Forms, Illinois-Federal, 1952, rev. 1965. Contbr. articles to profl. jours., also to Ency. Brit. Home: 5642 Dorchester Av Chicago IL 60637 Office: 11 S La Salle St Chicago IL 60603

ELSON, CHARLES, educator, stage designer; b. Chgo., Sept. 5, 1909; s. Jacob and Rebecca (Brodsky) E.; student Hull House Little Theatre, Chgo., 1914-32, U. Ill., 1929- 30; Ph.B., U. Chgo., 1932; M.F.A., Yale, 1935; m. Diana Rivers, Aug. 12, 1938; 1 dau., Alexandra. Instr., U. Ia., art dir. Univ. Playhouse, 1935-36; asso. prof. U. Okla., art. dir. Univ. theatre, 1937-43; civilian design engr. tng. aid USNR, 1943-45; prof. Hunter Coll., dir. Theatre Workshop, 1948-69; vis. lectr. stage design, dept. drama Yale, 1950-51; vis. critic stage lighting Yale Sch. Drama, 1964-67, vis. prof. design, 1967—; art dir. and stage lighting dir. WPA Fed. Theatre Project, Los Angeles, 1936-37; art dir. Ogunquit (Me.) Summer Theatre, 1939-41, 45; design asst. Broadway plays, operas, 1945-47, stage designer, 1947—; first N.Y. prodn. Twelfth Night; designed or lighted settings for plays, operas and ballets including, Hidden Horizon, Virginia Sampler Duet for Two Hands, First Mrs. Fraser, Power Without Glory, Kathleen, Cup of Trembling, Private Lives, Regina, Nina, The Flying Dutchman, The Lady is Not For Burning, Out of This World, Enemy of the People, Rose Tattoo, Kiss Me Kate (London), Music In The Air, Deep Blue Sea, Lohengrin, His and Hers, Don Giovanni, Norma, Champagne Complex, The Lovers, Compulsion, Blue Denim, Troilus and Cressida Henry IV, Richard II, Wildcat, Photo Finish; Dialogues of the Carmelites; exhbns. City Center Gallery, U. Conn., 1955—; Fulbright lectr., India, 1959-60. Bd. dirs. North Castle Citizens Council; pres. bd. Northcastle Pub. Library. Fellow Internat. Inst. Arts and Letters; mem. Am. Edn. Theatre Assn., United Scenic Artists Am. chmn. exam. bd. India Council, Asia Soc. Am. editor: State Design Throughout the World (Brussels), Vol. 1, 1956, Vol. 2, 1964. Home: 1 Faraway Lane Armonk Village NY 10504 Office: 695 Park Av New York City NY 10021

ELSON, EDWARD LEE ROY, clergyman; b. Monongahela, Pa., Dec. 23, 1906; s.Lee Roy and Pearl (Edie) E.; B.A., Asbury Coll., 1928; M.Th., U. of Southern Cal., 1931, grad. study, 1932-33, L.H.D., 1954; D.D., Wheaton Coll., 1934, Occidental Coll., 1947; grad. study, Am. Seminar in Europe and Russia, 1936; Litt.D., Centre Coll., 1952, Lafayette Coll., 1958, Gettysburg Coll., 1960; LL.D. (hon.), Norwich U., 1953, Davis and Elkins Coll., 1955, Ashbury Coll., 1958. Hope Coll., 1961; S.T.D., Coll. Emporia, 1955, Ripon Coll., 1956; D.Hum., Parsons Coll. 1955; L.H.D., Washington and Jefferson Coll., 1960 Coll. Wooster, 1960; m. Frances B. Sandys, May 22, 1929 (dec., Dec., 1933); m. 2d, Helen Louise Chittick, Feb. 8, 1937; children—Eleanor F. (Mrs. Erland H. Heginbotham), Beverly L., Mary F. (Mrs. Duncan MacRae), David Edward. Ordained, Presbyterian minister, Santa Monica, California, April, 1930; assistant minister ad interim, 1st Church, Santa Monica, 1930-31; minister 1st Presbyn. Ch., La Jolla, San Diego, Calif., 1931-41; pastor, Nat. Presbyn. Ch., Wash., D.C., 1946—; chaplain, U.S. Senate, 1969—; moderator, Presbytery of Los Angeles, 1938; commr. Gen. Assembly Presbyn. Ch., U.S.A., 1933, 38, 51, 56, 67, Nat. Chaplain D.A.V., 1950-51; pres. Wash. Fedn. Chs., 1952-54; Western Region dir. Presbyn. post-war Restoration Fund., 1946; mem. Bd. Pensions, 1948-57, also com. chaplains and service personnel Presbyn. Ch., 1947-57, moderator Presbytery of Washington City, 1966. Mem. com. John F. Kennedy Center Performing Arts; bd. dirs. Maryville Coll.; pres. bd. trustees Wilson Coll., 1960—. apptd. chaplain U.S.A. Res. 1931, advanced through grades to Col., 1944, active duty, 1941-46; ret. 1961. Decorated, Legion of Merit, Bronze Star, Army Commendation medal; Croix de Guerre avec Palme (France); Am. Theatre Medal, European Theatre Medal, World War II Victory Medal, German Occupation Medal; gold medal Lebanese order of Merit; Silver Star (Jordan); comdr. Order Medal of Freedom (France); recipient of Freedoms Found. award, 1951, 54, 57, 58, 59, 60, 62-64; Clergy-Churchman of Year citation, Ch. Mgmt. and Wash. Pilgrimage of Am. Churchmen, 1954. Mem. St. Andrews Soc., Am. Friends of Middle East, Inc. (First annual lectureship), Disabled Am. Vets., Acad. Religion and Mental Health, Am. Acad. of Church History, Church Service Soc., World Alliance Ref. Chs., V.F.W., Am. Legion, Mil. Order of World Wars, Military Chaplains' Assn. (nat. pres. 1957-59), Res. Officers' Assn. (chaplain Calif. dept., 1937-38), Phi Chi Phi, Chi Alpha, Theta Sigma. Clubs: Cosmos, Army and Navy (Washington D.C.); Kiwanis (past pres.) (La Jolla, Cal.). Speaker at colls. and univs. Author: One Moment with God, 1951; America's Spiritual Recovery, 1954; And Still He Speaks, 1960; The Inevitable Encounter, 1962; sermons and other articles for ch. periodicals. Home: 4000 Cathedral Av NW Washington DC 20016 Office: 4123 Nebraska Av NW Washington DC 20016

ELSON, JOHN ALBERT, educator; b. Kiating, China, Mar. 2, 1923; s. Albert Joseph and Evelyn Amelia (Hockey) E.; B.Sc., U. Western Ont., 1945; M.Sc., McMaster U., 1947; Ph.D., Yale, 1956; m. Jeanne Bridgman Hickey, Jan. 4, 1957; children—Sarah Bridgman, Rebecca Ann Wood. Lectr., McMaster U., Hamilton, Ont., 1945-46; geologist Geol. Survey Can., Ottawa, Ont., 1946-56; asst. prof. McGill U., Montreal, Que., 1956-64, asso. prof., 1964-68, prof., 1968—. Cons. geologist, 1956-67. Fellow Geol. Soc. Am., Geol. Assn. Can.; mem. Am. Soc. Photogrammetry, NRC Can. (asso. com. for quaternary research 1971—). Home: 467 Clarke Av Montreal 217 Quebec Canada

ELSON, SAM, lawyer; b. N.Y.C., Dec. 25, 1908; s. Alex and Sarah (Reichick) E.; A.B., Washington U., St. Louis, 1927, LL.B., 1930; J.S.D., Yale, 1931; m. Gertrude Clems Palmer, June 28, 1934; children—Edward C., David L., Dorothy M., (Mrs. Donald Rosenthal). Admitted to Mo. bar. 1930; mem. faculty Washington U. Sch. Law, 1931-35; asso. firm Husch, Eppenberger, Donohue, Elson & Confeld, and predecessor, St. Louis, 1932—, partner, 1936—. Mem. St. Louis Council Human Relations, 1949; pres. Jewish Community Relations Council St. Louis, 1947-51. Bd. dirs. Jewish Fedn. St. Louis, 1952-55. Sterling fellow Yale Law Sch., 1930. Mem. Am., Mo. bar assns., Bar. Assn. St. Louis, Am. Law Inst., Am. Judicature Soc., Mo. Assn. Social Welfare, Nat. Conf. Christians and Jews, St. Louis Com. Fgn. Relations, Phi Beta Kappa, Order of Coif, Order of Artus. Contbr. articles legal jours. Mng. editor St. Louis Law Rev., 1930. Home: 6911 Cornell Av University City MO 63130 Office: 7 N 7th St St Louis MO 63101

ELSTAD, LEONARD M., coll. pres.; b. Ossee, Wis., Feb. 8, 1899; s. Ole Haagenstad and Mathilda (Jenson) E.; A.B., St. Olaf Coll., 1922; LL.D., 1946; A.M., Gallaudet Coll. 1923, LL.D., 1952; m. Margaret Wafter, June 16, 1924; children-Elizabeth Jane, Margaret Jean. Teacher in rural schs., Esmond, N.D., 1917-18; instr. Gallaudet Coll., Washington, D.C., 1923- 24; prin. Kendall Sch. Columbia Inst. for Deaf, Washington, D.C., 1924-25; asst. prin. Wright Oral Sch., N.Y. City, 1925-26, prin. and mgr., 1926-32; supt.. Minn. Sch. for Deaf, Faribault, Minn., 1932-45; pres. Gallaudet Coll. 1945—. Served as pvt., S.A.T.C., 1918. Past pres. Convention Am. Instrs. of Deaf. Awarded Silver Antelope, Boy Scouts Am. Mem. Washington Bd. of Trade. Clubs: Cosmos, Nat. Press, Fed. Schoolmen's (Washington); University. Past dist. gov. Rotary Internat. Home: Gallaudet Coll Washington DC 20002

ELSTON, LLOYD WARREN, confectionery co. exec.; b. Lewistown, Pa., May 5, 1926; s. Clair Mortimer and Irene (Brickwood) E.; B.A. in Indsl. Administrn., Yale, 1949; m. Dorothea Kazanjian, June 22, 1949; children—Calvin Warren, Lynn Butler, Richard Lloyd. Asst. engring. dept. Collins Co., Collinsville, Conn., 1949-50; with Peter Paul, Inc., 1950—, exec. v.p., 1962-65, pres., 1966—; dir. Colonial Bank & Trust Co., Waterbury, Conn. Trustee, Waterbury Hosp.; pres. trustees Gunnery Sch.; treas., trustee Calvin K. Kazanjian Econs. Found. Served with USNR, 1944-46. Mem. Naugatuck C. of C. Mason, Rotarian (v.p. Naugatuck 1966, pres. 1967). Home: Cleft Rock Lane Woodbridge CT 06525 Office: Peter Paul Inc New Haven Rd Naugatuck CT 06770

ELSTON, WILBUR EVANS, editor; b. Hastings, Minn., July 14, 1913; s. Harry Raymond and Dorothy Caroline (Anderson) E.; B.A., U. Minn., 1934; m. Gretchen E. Stege, Oct. 14, 1938; children—Cynthia Doty (Mrs. John Murray), Elizabeth Ann (Mrs. James Dealing), Sarah Grace. Reporter, Mpls. Star, 1934-35; editor St. Peter (Minn.) Herald, 1935-40, Worthington (Minn.) Daily Globe, 1940-43; with Mpls. Star and Tribune, 1943-63, successively news editor, spl. asst. to exec. editor, mem. Washington bur., asst. exec. editor, editor editorial pages, 1956-63; asso. editor Detroit News, 1963—, also editorial page dir. Mem. Minn. Civil Service Bd., 1939-44. Mem. Nat. Conf. Editorial Writers (pres. 1967), Am. Soc. Newspaper Editors, Sigma Delta Chi. Clubs: Country (Detroit); Nat. Press (Washington). Home: 15 Provencal Rd Grosse Pointe Farms MI 48236 Office: Detroit News Detroit MI 48231

ELTING, VICTOR, Jr., advt. exec.; b. Winnetka, Ill., Aug. 12, 1905; s. Victor and Marie (Winston) E.; grad. Hotchkiss Sch., 1924; B.S., Princeton, 1928; m. Helen Stanley, May 7, 1932; children—Helen (Mrs. Walter Love Stratton), Victor III, Sarah (Mrs. Lewis J. Finocchio, Jr.). With Quaker Oats Co., Chgo., 1931-71, mgr. new products, 1942-48, advt. brand mgr., 1948-52, advt. dir., 1952-53, v.p. charge advt., 1953-59, v.p. advt. and merchandising, 1959-63, v.p. advt., 1963-70, v.p. marketing services, 1970-71. Pres. Libertyville Countryside Assn. Trustee Condell Meml. Hosp., Libertyville, Ill., Village of Mettawa. Mem. Am. Advt. Fedn. (nat. chmn. 1970-71). Republican. Episcopalian (jr. warden). Clubs: Winter, Onwentsia (Lake Forest); Merchants and Manufacturers (Chgo.). Home: Box 102 Old School Rd Libertyville IL 60048 Office: Quaker Oats Co Merchandise Mart Plaza Chicago IL 60654

ELTON, ROGER DILWORTH, banker; b. Dorchester, Mass., Oct. 16, 1910; s. Frederic G. and Ella W. (Smith) E.; student Brown U., 1933, Harvard, 1954; m. Helen C. Stell, July 28, 1938; children—Douglas A., Nancy (Mrs. John J. Hartnett), David. With Mfrs. Trust Co., N.Y.C., 1934-61; sr. v.p. Franklin Nat. Bank, N.Y.C.,

1961, now exec. v.p.; dir. Nat. Industries, Inc., Louisville. Clubs: Marco Polo (dir.) (N.Y.C.); Nassau Country, Hempstead Harbor Yacht (Glen Cove). Home: 17 Eastland Dr Glen Cove NY 11542 Office: 410 Madison Av New York City NY 10017

ELTON, WALLACE WESLEY, internat. service co. exec.; b. Dorchester, Mass., Dec. 15, 1907; s. Frederic and Ella (Smith) E.; Ph.B., Brown U., 1929; m. Mary Helen Birchard, Aug. 15, 1934. With N.W. Ayer, 1929-40; staff J. Walter Thompson Co., N.Y.C., 1940-41, v.p. dir., 1945-61 exec. v.p., 1961-66, exec. com., 1960-66; v.p. U.S., operations, then v.p. devel. Internat. Exec. Service Corps, 1966—; with firm Lennen & Mitchell, 1941-42. Alumni dir. Brown U. Served to lt. comdr. USNR, 1942-45. Mem. Assn. Am. Advt. Agys. (chmn. Eastern region 1959), Brown Alumni (regional dir. 1967—), Nat. Soc. Art Dirs. (pres. 1953- 55), Art Dirs. Club (exec. bd. 1950-52), Soc. Illustrators. Clubs: Coveleigh, American Yacht (rear commodore 1968—) (Rye); Brown U. (pres. 1967) (N.Y.C.); Westchester Country; University of N.Y. Author: Navy in the Sky, 1943; Guide to Naval Aviation, 1944; Responsibilities of Advertising Men, 1967. Home: Pine Island Lane Rye NY 10580 Office: 545 Madison Av New York City NY 10022

EL-WAKIL, MOHAMED, educator; b. Alexandria, Egypt, Mar. 9, 1921; s. Mohamed and Tafida El-Wakil; came to U.S., 1946, naturalized, 1959; B.S., Cairo U., 1943; M.S., U. Wis., 1947, Ph.D., 1949; m. Tatiana Pronin, Oct. 29, 1950; children—Fred W., Leila J. Lectr. U. Alexandria, 1950-52; research asso. U. Wis.-Madison, 1954-55, asst. prof., 1955-57, asso. prof., 1957-61, prof. mech. and nuclear engring., 1961—; asst. prof. U. Minn., 1954-55. Recipient award for meritorious paper Am. Soc. M.E., 1952; award for excellence in instruction of engrs. Am. Soc. E.E., 1969; Benjamin Smith Reynolds award U. Wis., 1970; Distinguished Teaching award nuclear engring. div. Am. Soc. E.E., 1971; Fulbright scholar, 1966. Mem. Am. Soc. M.E., Am. Nuclear Soc., Am. Soc. for Engring. Edn., Combustion Inst., Sigma Xi, Tau Beta Pi, Pi Tau Sigma. Author: Nuclear Power Engineering, 1962; Nuclear Heat Transport, 1971; Nuclear Energy Conversion, 1971; also articles. Home: 31 Bagley Ct Madison WI 53705

ELWELL, CLARENCE EDWARD, bishop; b. Cleve., Feb. 4, 1904; s. George John and Josephine (Messer) E.; B.A., John Carroll U., 1925, LL.D., 1959; student theol. faculty U. Innsbruck (Austria), 1925-29; M.A., Western Res. U., 1934; Ph.D., Harvard, 1938. Ordained priest Roman Cath. Ch., 1929; dir. high schs. and academies Cleve. Diocese, 1938-46; prof. edn. grad. div. St. John Coll., 1938-48; asst. supt. schs., Diocese Cleve., 1933-38, supt. schs., 1946—; aux. bishop Cleve., 1962-68; bishop of Columbus (O.), 1968—. Author: Our Quest for Happiness, 4 vols., 1945; Our Holy Faith, 8 vols., 1959; New Catholic, Speller, 8 vols., 1963; Christian Child Reading Series, 1959-64; New Ways with Numbers, 8 vols., 1964. Address: 198 E Broad St Columbus OH 43215

ELWELL, HERBERT, musician, critic; b. Minneapolis, May 10, 1898; s. George Herbert and Belle (Horn) E.; student U. Minn., 1916-19; pvt. study in composition with Ernest Bloch, N.Y. City, 1919-21, Nadia Boulanger, Paris, France, 1922- 27; Doctorate (hon.), Western Res. U., 1946, U. Rochester, 1954; m. Maria Cecchini, July 27, 1927. Head composition dept. Cleve. Inst. Music, 1928-45; music critic Cleve. Plain Dealer 1932- 65; program note editor Cleve. Orchestra, 1930-36; tchr. composition Oberlin Conservatory Music 1945—. Eastman Summer Sch., Rochester, N.Y., 1940—. Performance of prin. compositions; Ballet Suite, Happy Hypocrite, Charles Weidman, Dance Repertory Theatre, N.Y.C., 1931; Introduction and Allegro, N.Y. Philharmonic, 1942; Quintet for strings and piano, Paris, 1925; String Quartet, N.Y.C., 1944; Blue Symphony, N.Y.C., 1946; Lincoln Requiem, Oberlin (internat, radio broadcast N.B.C.), 1946; Pastorale for voice and orchestra, Cleve. Orchestra, under Szell, 1948; Violin and Piano Sonata, Chgo, 1948; Ode for Orchestra, under Stokowski, Houston, 1953; The Forever Young for voice and orchestra, under Stokowski, St. Louis, under Szell, Cleveland, 1954; Suite for Violin and Orchestra, Louisville, 1957. chmn 1952 Yaddo Festival, mem. Yaddo Corp. Fellow Am. Acad. in Rome, 1923-26. Awarded Paderewski prize, 1945; Ohioana Library Assn. award, 1947. Mem. Phi Delta Theta, Pi Kappa Lambda. Home: 2371 Edgerton Rd Cleveland OH 44118 Office: Cleveland Plain Dealer Cleveland OH 44114

ELWELL, LEONARD, physiologist, educator; b. Climax, Mich., Dec. 20, 1913; s. Lester and Georgiana (Eyre) E.; A.B., Kalamazoo Coll., 1935; M.S. in Zoology, Kan. State Coll., 1937; postgrad. Columbia, 1938-39; M.S. in Physiology, U. Mich., 1942, Ph.D., 1951; m. Minnie A. Dewey, June 14, 1941; children—Martha, Stephen. Asst., Carnegie Inst. Washington, Cold Spring Harbor, N.Y., 1937-38, N.Y. Med. Coll., 1938-40; instr., asst. prof. U. Mich., 1951-58; asso. prof., prof. and chmn. physiology dept. U. Ore. Dental Sch., Portland, 1958—. Served with AUS, 1942-45. Mem. Am. Physiol. Soc., A.A.A.S., Am. Assn. Dental Schs., Sigma Xi. Presbyn. Home: 515 SW Bancroft St Portland OR 97201 Office: 611 SW Campus Dr Portland OR 97201

ELWIN, FITE, coll. dean; b. Willow Springs, Mo., Nov. 25, 1913; s. Austin Roe and Minnie (Hiestand) F.; B.S. in Edn., S.W. Mo. State Coll., 1934; M.M., Northwestern U., 1941; Ed.D., George Peabody Coll. Tchrs., 1953; m. Mildred Mae McKee, Dec. 23, 1936; children—Barbara (Mrs. William Scearce), James Elwin. Asst. prof. edn. Austin Peay State Coll., Clarksville, Tenn., 1948, S.W. Mo. Coll., Springfield, 1948-50; supr. student teaching George Peabody Coll. Tchrs., Nashville, Tenn., 1950-52; chmn. music dept. Amarillo (Tex.) Coll., 1952-53; chmn. div. edn. and psychology Northeastern State Coll., Tahlequah, Okla., 1960-62, dean of coll., 1962—. Served with USNR, 1944-46. Mem. C. of C. Tahlequah (past bd. dirs.). Baptist. Kiwanian. Author: (with V. Travis) Student Teaching Handbook, 1959. Home: Rt 3 Box 311 Tahlequah OK 74464

ELWOOD, HUGH MCJUNKIN, marine corps officer; b. Pitts., Nov. 14, 1915; s. Robert David, Jr. and Cornelia (McJunkin) E.; B.S., U.S. Naval Acad., 1938; m. Harriet Mildred Theobald, Feb. 8, 1947; children—Barbara, Hugh T., Nancy. Commd. 2d lt. USMC, 1938, advanced through grades to lt. gen., 1971; designated aviator; communications officer, also aide-de-camp to comdg. gen. Marine Aircraft Wings, PTO, later exec. officer, comdg. officer Marine Fighting Squadron 212, Solomon Islands area, operations officer Air Def. Command, Marianas, World War II; operations officer Naval Aviation Mission, Peru, chief of mission, 1945-46; insp.gen. Peruvian Air Force, 1945-46; comdr. marine air detachment Marine Air Reserve Tng. Command, St. Louis, 1946-49; instr. aviation U.S. Naval Acad., 1949-51; chief air sect. Marine Corps Ednl. Center, Quantico, Va., 1953-56; combat in Korea, 1951-52; asst. chief of staff operations 1st Marine Aircraft Wing, Iwakuni, Japan, 1959-60, asst. wing comdr., 1966-67; chief staff for amphibious troops in Eastern Atlantic and Mediterranean, then asst. chief of staff logistics 2d Marine Aircraft Wing, Cherry Point, N.C., 1956-57, then comdr., 1967 68, also comdr. Marine Aircraft Group 32, Beaufort, S.C., 1957-59; chief basic war plans br. Office Joint Chiefs Staff, 1960-62; officer Office Dep. Chief of Staff for Plans, USMC hdqrs., 1962-63; comdg. gen. Marine Air Res. Tng. Command, Glenview, Ill., 1963-66; asst. wing comdr. 1st Marine Aircraft Wing and chief of staff 3d Marine Amphibious Force, Vietnam, 1966-67; asst. chief of staff for operations, comdr.-in-chief Pacific Area Forces, Hawaii, 1968-71; dep. chief staff plans and programs Hdqrs. Marine Corps, Washington, 1971—. Decorated D.S.M., Legion of Merit, D.F.C. with 1 star, Bronze Star, Air medal with 1 star; Cross of Gallantry, Nat. Order (both Vietnam); Flying Cross (Peru). Episcopalian. Club: Army and Navy (Washington). Home: Marine Barracks Washington DC 20390 Office: Hdqrs US Marine Corps Washington DC 20380

ELWOOD, ROBERT B., fgn. service officer; b. Omaha, Nov. 30, 1912; s. William D. and Josephine B. (Bailey) E.; B.S., Ia. State Coll., 1935, M.S., 1940; m. Lora Lee McCook, September 19, 1947; childrenJean Carol, Robert B., John M., Christopher L. With Nat. Research Project, W.P.A., 1936-39; research asst., Ia. State Coll., 1939-40; agr. extension service, U. Tenn., 1941; Am. Field Service, Egypt and N. Africa, 1942-43; U.S. Fgn. Econ. Adminstrn., Cairo, Egypt, 1943-45; apptd. fgn. service officer, 1945; agr. officer, Cairo, 1945-48; 2d sec., Rio de Janeiro, Brazil, 1948-51, 1st sec., 1951; advanced tng. in economics. Harvard, 1951-52; 1st sec. and econ. officer, Taipei, Formosa, 1952-55, Beirut, Lebanon, 1955, Counselor for Economic Affairs Beirut, Lebanon, 1956-57; counselor of embassy and dep. chief of mission, Kabul, Afghanistan, 1957-59; detailed Fgn. Service Inst., Dept. State, Washington, 1959-60, dir. Office of research and analysis for Near East and S. Asia, Bur. Intelligence and Research, 1960-63; counselor for econ. affairs Am. embassy, Rio de Janeiro, Brazil, 1963-67; counselor of embassy, dep. chief mission, Port of Spain, Trinidad and Tobago, 1967—. Address: 32 Elizabeth St Port of Spain Trinidad and Tobago

ELY, ATWOOD COLLINS, banker; b. Hartford, Conn., Jan. 18, 1918; s. Matthew Griswold and Marion Atwood (Collins) E.; grad. Phillip's Acad., 1936; B.S., Yale, 1940; M.B.A., Harvard, 1948; grad. Rutgers U. Stonier Grad. Sch. Banking, 1955; m. Harriet Paine Woodman, Feb. 1, 1947; children—Jonathan, Eleanor, Marion, Richard. With Bethlehem Steel Co., N.Y.C., 1940-42; with Hartford Nat. Bank & Trust Co. (Conn.), 1948—, br. mgr., 1956-64, v.p., 1958-64, sr. v.p., area mgr., 1964-70, head br. adminstrn. dept. charge all branches, 1971—. Vice chmn. United Fund of S.E. Conn., 1968-70; asst. treas. Conn. Coll., New London; vice chmn. region I exec. com. Boy Scouts Am., 1967-71. Corporator Am. Sch. for Deaf, 1950—, Inst. Living, 1968—, Hartford Hosp., 1971—; trustee, bd. mgrs. Lawrence and Meml. Hosp., New London, Conn.; trustee MacCurdy-Salisbury Ednl. Found., Hartt Coll.; regent U. Hartford. Served from ensign to lt. USNR, 1941-46. Recipient Silver Beaver Boy Scouts Am., 1964, Silver Antelope award, 1971. Mem. Southeastern Conn. C. of C. (v.p. 1966-70), Marine Hist. Assn. (trustee 1965—, treas. 1966—). Clubs: Thames (New London); Hartford (Conn.); Ram Island Yacht (Noank, Conn.). Home: 4 W Mystic Av Mystic CT 06355 Office: 777 Main St Hartford CT 06115

ELY, CHARLES JARVIS, banker; b. Newark, Jan. 4, 1903; s. Charles Henry and Jane (Jarvis) E.; B.C.S., N.Y.U., 1923; m. Edith M. Schroeder, Feb. 3, 1926. Asst. statistician Western Union Telegraph Co., N.Y.C., 1923-24; partner Harrigan & Ely, 1925-28; statistician Sulzabacher, Granger & Co., N.Y.C., 1928-33; investment adviser Lehman Bros., N.Y.C., 1935-43; head investment dept. Kuhn Loeb & Co., 1943-56, gen. partner, 1956-68, ltd. partner, 1968—; dir. Seas Shipping Corp. Mem. Kappa Sigma. Republican. Clubs: Arcola Country, Wall Street; High Mountain Golf (dir., treas.); Yacht and Country of Stuart (Fla.). Home: 343 Algonquin Rd Franklin Lakes NJ 07417 also 2281 St Lucie Blvd Stuart FL 33494 Office: 40 Wall St New York City NY 10005

ELY, CLAIRE GERALD, ret. laundry equipment mfr.; b. Osage, Ia., July 30, 1905; s. Edwin George and Fern Luella (Alchon) E.; student U. Minn., 1923; m. Dorothy H. Moeller, Oct. 16, 1926; children—Jon Moeller, Mary Alice (Mrs. Oliver Slocum). With Maytag Co., Newton, Ia., 1924—, successively retail salesman, retail sales mgr., regional mgr. Mpls. br., asst. br. mgr. Kansas City, br. mgr., mgr., product and market planning, 1924-54, gen. sales mgr., Newton, 1954-57, v.p. marketing, 1957-70, dir., 1962-70; dir. Maytag Co., Ltd., Toronto, Can. Member N.A.M., Newton C. of C. Republican. Presbyn. Clubs: Des Moines; Newton Country (dir.). Home: 1100 S 6th Av W Newton IA 50208

ELY, JAMES WALLACE, banker; b. Summit, N.J., Nov. 13, 1909; s. James and E. Maud (Hopping) E.; A.B., Princeton, 1932; student night law sch., N.Y.U., 1934; m. Edythe M. Farnham, Aug. 20, 1932; children—James Wallace, William L., Suzanne F. With Nat. City Bank of N.Y., 1932-35; with Security Trust Co., Rochester, 1935—, exec. v.p., 1952-60, pres. 1960—, also bd. dirs.; dir. Sybron Corp., Neisner Brothers, Page Airways, Rochester Telephone Co., Goulds Pumps. Inc. Crosman Arms, Inc., Richardson Corp., Will Sci., Inc. Pres., Rochester Clearing House; mem. pub. adv. com. N.Y. State Joint Legislative Com. To Revise Banking Law. Pres., dir. Highland Hosp.; dir., pres. YMCA; treas. Rochester Hosp. Fund; trustee Univ. Rochester; chmn. exec. com., mem. finance com., past pres. Eastman Dental Dispensary; bd. dirs. Community Chest. Mem. Robert Morris Assos. (nat. dir., past pres.), Am. Inst. Banking, Rochester Assn. Credit Men, C. of C. (pres., trustee). Clubs: Country Rochester (past pres.), Genesee Valley, Rochester Yacht. Home: 255 Sandringham Rd Rochester NY 14610 Office: 1 East Av Rochester NY 14604

ELY, NORTHCUTT, lawyer; b. Phoenix, Ariz., Sept. 14, 1903; s. Sims and Elizabeth (Northcutt) E.; A.B., Stanford, 1924, J.D., 1926; m. Marica McCann, Dec. 2, 1931; children—Michael and Craig (twins), Parry Haines. Admitted to Cal. bar, 1926; N.Y. bar, 1927, D.C. bar, 1930, U.S. Supreme Ct. bar, 1930; practiced law in Cal. and N.Y.C., 1926-29; exec. asst. to sec. of interior, Washington, 1929-33, represented Sec. Ray Lyman Wilbur in negotiation of Hoover Dam power contracts, 1930, Boulder Canyon water contracts, 1930-33, "seven-party" agreement settling Colorado River priorities among Cal. claimants, 1931, Ariz. Colo. River negotiations, 1933, chmn. tech. and adv. com. Fed. Oil Conservation Bd., 1931-33; participated in Kettleman Hills Oil field unitization negotiations, 1931, pvt. practice, D.C. and Cal., 1933—; counsel gov. Okla. in negotiation of Interstate Oil Compact, 1934-35; counsel states, pub. agys. in fed. power, nat. gas litigations, 1940—, govts. Saudi Arabia, Turkey, Thailand, Ethiopia, Malagasy Republic, Republic of China, Ruler of Sharjah, in preparation mineral law, govts. Taiwan, Sharjah, Thailand in seabed boundary disputes; chief counsel (spl. asst. atty. gen.) for Cal. defendents in Ariz. versus Cal., U.S. Supreme Ct., 1954-71; gen. counsel Am. Pub. Power Assn., mem. legal adv. commn. Fed. Power Commn. Nat. Power Survey, 1963—; mem. Nat. Petroleum Council, 1970—, now bd. dirs. cons. Nat. Water Commn., 1970—. U.S. del. UN Conf. on Application of Sci. and Tech. for Benefit Less Developed Areas, Geneva, Switzerland, 1963, UN Conf. on Mineral Legislation, Manila, P.I., 1969. Mem. Hoover Inst., Stanford. Trustee Hoover Birthplace Found. Mem. Am. Law Inst., Am. Bar Assn. (chmn. elect sect. mineral and natural resources law), Mining and Metall. Soc. Am. Am. Judicature Soc., Internat. Law Assn. (chmn. Am. br. com. on deep sea mineral resources), Am. Soc. Internat. Law, Marine Tech. Soc., Stanford Assos., Phi Delta Phi, Sigma Delta Chi, Sigma Nu. Clubs: Chevy Chase, University, Metropolitan (Washington); Berkeley (Cal.) Tennis; Bohemian (San Francisco); California (Los Angeles). Author: Oil Conservation through Interstate Agreement; The Oil and Gas Conservation Statutes Annotated; The Hoover Dam Power & Water Contracts; (with Ray Lyman Wilbur) The Hoover Dam Documents; Summary of Mining and Petroleum Laws of the World, 1961-70; Policy Choices in Mineral Legislation, 1963. Co-author: Economics of the Mineral Industries; The Conservation of Oil; Administration of International River Basins, others. Home: Kenwood MD 20015 also Los Altos CA 94022 Office: Watergate Six Hundred Bldg Washington DC 20005

ELY, RICHARD HENDERSON, apparel exec.; b. Kennett, Mo., July 4, 1918; s. R. Wayne and Amy Nelle (Henderson) E.; A.B., Westminister Coll., 1940; LL.B., Washington U., St. Louis, 1943; m. Florence E. Chambers, Jan. 19, 1946; children—Thomas Chambers, Amy Nelle, Carolyn Sue. Admitted to Mo. bar, 1942; with firm Ely & Ely, St. Louis, 1946-52; with INTERCO Inc. (formerly Internat. Shoe Co), St. Louis, Mo., 1952—, gen. counsel, 1963-69, senior counsel, 1969—, Sec. 1966—, also dir., mem. exec. com. Bd. dirs., mem. exec. com. Asso. Industries Mo.; board mgrs. Downtown St. Louis YMCA. Served with AUS, 1942-46. Recipient Alumni Achievement award Westminister Coll., 1967. Mem. Am., Mo., St. Louis bar Assns., Am. Soc. Corp. Secretaries (pres. St. Louis regional group 1970-71, nat. dir. 1971—), Phi Delta Theta, Phi Delta Phi. Rotarian. Club: Missouri Athletic (St. Louis). Home: 21 Sylvester Av Webster Groves MO 63119 Office: 10 Broadway St Louis MO 63177

ELY, ROY ADDISON, banker; b. Rochester, N.Y., June 1, 1914; s. George Gaylord and Estelle (Rohr) E.; B.S., U. Pa., 1934; postgrad. Rutgers U., 1950-52; m. Martha Stonebraker, Aug. 11, 1951; children—Victoria, Mark R. With Lincoln Rochester Trust Co., 1934—, now exec. v.p. earning assets div.; dir. Carhart Photo, Inc. Club: Oak Hill Country (Pittsford, N.Y.). Home: 249 Dunrovin Lane Rochester NY 14618 Office: 183 E Main St Rochester NY 14603

ELY, WALTER RALEIGH, Jr., judge; b. Baird, Tex., June 24, 1913; s. Walter Raleigh and Lucy Ann (McCoy) E.; A.B., U. Tex., 1935, LL.B., 1935; LL.M., U. So. Cal., 1949; m. Billie Bernice Gambill, Oct. 27, 1937; 1 son, William Raleigh; m 2d, Ruby Ilene Walters, Sept. 18, 1945; m. 3d, Joan Jaffe Lawson, Mar. 22, 1967. Admitted to Tex. bar, 1935, Cal. bar, 1945; gen. practice, Abilene, Tex., 1935-39; asst. atty. gen. Tex., 1939-40; judge U.S. Ct. Appeals, 9th Circuit, 1964—. Mem. exec. com. Cal. Conf. State Bar Delegates, 1957-60; spl. counsel U.S. Senate, 1955. Served with USMCR, 1941-44. Decorated Silver Star medal. Fellow Am. Coll. Trial Lawyers; mem. Am. (ho. of dels. 1961-64), Los Angeles County (pres. 1962) bar assns., V.F.W., Phi Delta Phi, Delta Kappa Epsilon. Methodist. Mason (Shriner, K.T.). Clubs: Los Angeles Athletic, Chancery (Los Angeles); Pacific Coast Club (Long Beach, Cal.). Contbr. articles to profl. jours. Home: 169 N McCadden Pl Los Angeles CA 90004 Office: US Courthouse Los Angeles CA 90012

ELYTIS, ODYSSEUS, poet, art critic; b. Irahlion, Crete, Nov. 2, 1911; s. Danayotis and Maria (Vzana) E.; ed. law U. Athens, 1935, lit., Sorbonne, Paris, 1942. Poet influenced by surrealistic movement, pub. 1st poems 1935; founder with Georges Lefevre of AvantGarde group NEA Grammata; played prin. role in artistic rebirth of his country; theatre and painting have attracted him as a translator and art critic; dir. Greek Radio Broadcasting, 1953-54; counsellor to Nat. Theatre Athens. Served as under lt. in Res. war against Italian Fascist aggression. Decorated comdr. Royal Order Phoenix. Mem. Internat. Assn. Art Critics, European Culture Soc. Author: Orientations, 1940; First Sun, 1943; Heroic and Funeral Songs for an under-lieutenant fallen in Albania, 1946; Dignum Est, 1959; Six plus one Remorse for the Sky, 1960; Open cards, 1970. Address: 23 Rue Skoufa, Athens 136, Greece.

EL-ZAYYAT, MOHAMED HASSAN, diplomat; b. Damietta, Egypt, Feb. 14, 1915; s. Hassan Ibrahim and Badica (Abboud) El-Z.; B.A., Cairo U., 1939, M.A., 1941; D.Phil., Oxford U., 1947; m. Amina Taha-Hussein, June 12, 1948; children—Hassan, Sawsan, Mona. Asst. prof. Alexandria U., UAR, 1950; cultural attache, 1st sec. UAR Embassy, Washington, 1950-55; charge d'affaires ad interim, Teheran, Iran, 1955-57; rep. UN Adv. Council and Trusteeship Council, Somaliland, 1957-60; dir. Dept. Arab Affairs, Cairo, 1960; permanent rep. of UAR to Arab League, 1960-62; alternate rep. UN, N.Y.C., 1962-64; ambassador to India and Nepal, 1964-65; under sec. Ministry Fgn. Affairs, 1965; vice- minister charge information and ofcl. spokesman UAR, 1967-69; permanent rep. of UAR to UN, N.Y.C., 1969—. Recipient decorations from Somalia, Iran, Senegal, Mauritania, Poland, UAR. Home: 903 Park Av New York City NY 10021 Office: 36 E 67th St New York City NY 10021

EMANS, LESTER M., univ. dean; b. Peoria County, Ill., Nov. 13, 1902; s. C. H. and Mattie (Huff) E.; B.A., Lawrence Coll., 1925; M.A., U. Wis., 1929, Ph.D., 1947; m. Anita M. Jones, June 15, 1929; children—Ann Marie (Mrs. Robert Polzer), Robert L. Tchr. high sch., Menasha, Wis., 1925-27; prin. elementary and high sch., Sauk City, Wis., 1927-29; supt. elementary and high sch., Lancaster, Wis., 1929-35, Waupaca, Wis., 1935-40; prin. elementary sch., Madison, Wis., 1940-46; dir. tchr. edn. Wis. State Coll., Eau Claire, 1946-59, dean adminstrn., 1959-63, dean Sch. Edn. and Sch. Grad. Studies, 1963-69, dean emeritus, 1969—. Chief ednl. field party Tech. Asst. Program to Paraguay, 1953-55; chmn. Wis. Commn. Tchr. Edn. and Profl. Standards, 1959-65. Recipient Decoration of Honor, Republic Paraguay, 1955. Mem. Nat., Wis. (life; pres. 1950) edn. assns., Wis. Assn. Student Teaching (pres. 1956), Wis. Council for Regional Edn. Labs. (pres. 1966- 68), Council Deans Schs. Edn. Wis. State Univs. (chmn. 1966-67), Internat. Reading Assn. (Chmn. reading for aged com. 1970—). Contbr. to profl. jours. Home: 204 E Clairemont S Eau Claire WI 53701

EMANUELSON, KENNETH WILLIAM, former telephone co. exec.; b. Davenport, Ia., June 11, 1902; s. Henry G. and Josephine (Johnson) E.; B.S.C., State U. Ia., 1924; m. Miriam G. Hammond, July 10, 1931; 1 dau., Karen M. (Mrs. Robert C. Kenagy). With Northwestern Bell Telephone Co., Omaha, Neb., 1926, became sec.-treas., 1957, now ret. Mem. Neb. Investment Council. Trustee, Luth. Med. Center. Mem. Omaha C. of C. Republican. Club: Omaha Country; Omaha Athletic. Home: 14614 Boswell Blvd Sun City AZ 85351

EMBLETON, TONY FREDERICK WALLACE, govt. ofcl.; b. Hornchurch, Essex, Eng., Oct. 1, 1929; s. Frederick William Howard and Lucy Violet Muriel (Wallace) E.; B.Sc. with honours, U. London, 1950, Ph.D. in Physics, 1952, D.Sc., 1964; m. Eileen Loraine Blackall, Nov. 14, 1953; 1 dau., Sheila. Came to Can., 1952. With NRC, Ottawa, Ont., Can., 1952—, postdoctoral fellow, 1952-53, asst. research officer, 1954-57, asso. research officer, 1957-62, sr. research officer, 1962—; vis. lectr. U. Ottawa, 1959-69, Mass. Inst. Tech., 1964, 67. Mem. Rockcliffe Park Pub. Sch. Bd., 1966-69. Bd. dirs. Youth Sci. Found. Fellow Acoustical Soc. Am. (asso. editor Jour., mem. exec. council, recipient Biennial award 1964). Club: University (Ottawa). Patents, publs. in field. Home: 26 Birch Av Ottawa Ontario Canada K1K 3G6 Office: Montreal Rd Ottawa Ontario K1A OS1 Canada

EMBRY, LLOYD BOWERS, artist, portrait painter; b. Washington, Nov. 22, 1913; s. Ashton Fox and Harriet Grace (Frost) E.; B.F.A., Yale, 1936; m. Virginia J. Block, Feb. 8, 1941; children—Penelope

Lamm (Mrs. Robert J. McGoey), Lloyd Bowers, Dean Frost, Wendy Delahaye. Exhbns. include Audubon Soc., N.Y.C., 1947, Northon Mus., W. Palm Beach, Fla., 1948, D'Oley Gallery, Houston, 1949, Corcoran Biennial, 1951, Am. Scandinavian Found., N.Y.C., 1953; portraits and sculptures rep. permanent collections Rice Inst., Riksbank, Stockholm, Sweden, U.S. Senate Bldg. and Dist. Bldg., State Capitol Bldg., Nashville, Swedish embassy, Washington, Yale Gallery, Dept. Def., U.S. Ho. Reps., Georgetown U. Med. Sch., Phila. Hist. Mus., Grace Luth. Ch., Washington, Western Md. Coll., Westminister, U. Md., Rosewood Sch. Retarded Children, Harvard Club, N.Y.C. (sculpture John F. Kennedy), U.S. Post Office Dept., Washington, Internat. Am. Life Ins. Co., NSF, Washington, Ithaca (N.Y.) Coll., Miami U., Oxford, O., U. South, U. Ky.; painted arctic landscapes for USAF, 1958. Recipient 1st prize portraiture Soc. Washington Artists, 1946, New Haven Paint and Clay Soc., 1948. Mem. Provincetown (Mass.) Art Assn. (life). Address: 6123 30th St NW Washington DC 20015

EMCH, ARNOLD FREDERICK, mgmt. cons.; b. Manhattan, Kan., Nov. 3, 1899; s. Arnold and Hilda (Walters) E.; A.B., U. Ill., 1925, A.M., 1926; postgrad. U. Chgo., 1930; Ph.D., Harvard, 1934; m. Minna Libman, July 22, 1927 (dec. Sept. 1958); m. 2d, Eleanore Merckens, June 30, 1960; children—Arnold Devere, Frederick Bolebec. Pres. Emch Constrn. Co., Wichita, Kan., 1920-22; regional dir. Tambly & Brown Co., Chgo., 1926-29; exec. dir. Chgo. Hosp. Council, 1936-39; asso. dir. Am. Hosp. Assn., 1939-42, U. Chgo. Inst. for Hosp. Adminstrn., 1939-42; mgr. Booz, Allen & Hamilton, mgmt. consultants, Chicago, 1942-48, partner, 1948-60, ret.; cons. corp., 1960- -; pvt. and personal mgmt. cons.; pres. North End Water Co., Colo., 1964-67, sec.-treas., 1967—; dir. mgmt. cons. Cal.-Time Petroleum Corp., 1967-70; pres. Glory Ranch Arabian Stables, 1966—. Served in A.E.F., France, 1918-19; comdr. USNR and mgmt. cons. to Navy Surg. Gen., 1942-45, hon. cons. Navy Surg. Gen., 1945—. Trustee William Alanson White Psychiat. Found., Washington, 1945-46, v.p., 1947, pres. 1948-52; dir. Washington School Psychiatry, 1946-56, Mental Health Soc. Greater Chgo., 1958-59, Council on Hosp. Planning and Resources Devel. State Colo., 1961—. Mem. Am. Philos. Assn., A.A.A.S., Shakespearean Authorship Soc., English Cocker Spaniel Club of Am., Chi Psi. Clubs: Harvard, University (Chgo.); Colo. Arabian Horse. Author: Uncommon Letters to a Son, Field Guide to Life and Love; Crowded Years; also articles in field. Address: Glory Ranch Devil's Gulch Rd Estes Park CO 80517

EMELIN, ARTHUR CHARLES, former pharm. mfg. exec.; b. N.Y.C., May 14, 1904; s. Emanuel Joseph and Bertha (Wolf) E.; Ph.G., Columbia, 1923, Ph.C., 1924; m. Mildred Barnes, Aug. 1, 1927; children—Noel, John. Retail pharmacist, Mamaroneck, N.Y., 1924-34; sales dept. Parke, Davis & Co., N.Y. br., 1934-44; with Schenley Labs., Inc., Lawrenceburg, Ind., 1944-53, pres., 1951-53; dir. operations Pfizer Labs., Bklyn., 1953-56; gen. mgr. J. B. Roerig & Co. div. Chas. Pfizer, 1956-58; pres. Wallerstein Co. div. Baxter Labs., Inc., 1958-67, chmn., 1966-67; chmn. Wallerstein Co. div. Travenol Labs., 1967-68; v.p. Baxter Labs., Inc., 1958-67; dir. Glyco Chems., Inc.; trustee Union Savs. Bank Westchester County; ret. Bd. dirs. N.Y. Tb and Health Assn. Trustee Columbia U. Coll. Pharmacy, 1957-64, Richmondtown Restoration; asso. trustee Mamaroneck Free Library. Mem. Am. Pharm. Assn., Pharm. Advt. Club. N.Y. (pres 1958), S.I. C. of C. (pres. 1964), Newcomen Soc., Kappa Psi. Lion. Home: 1340 Flagler Dr Mamaroneck NY 10543

EMELYANOV, VASILY SIMONOVICH, physicist; b. 1901; ed. Moscow (USSR) Mining Acad. Dir. Standards Com., 1940-46; metallurgist in tank factory, Ural, World War II; designed gun turret for T-34 tank; dir. adminstrn. Peaceful Uses Atomic Energy, 1958-60, chmn. State Com. Atomic Energy, 1958-60, dep. chmn., 1962—. Decorated State prize, Order of Lenin. Mem. Soviet Acad. Scis. Address: care State Com for Atomic Energy Moscow USSR*

EMENEAU, MURRAY BARNSON, educator; b. Lunenburg, N.S., Can., Feb. 28, 1904; s. Archibald and Ada (Barnson) E.; B.A., Dalhousie U., Halifax, 1923, LL.D., 1970; B.A. (Rhodes scholar), Oxford U., 1926, M.A., 1935; Ph.D., Yale, 1931; L.H.D., U. Chgo., 1968; m. Katharine Fitch, Apr. 16, 1940. Came to U.S. 1926, naturalized, 1943. Instr. Latin, Yale, 1926-31, research fellow Sanskrit, linguistics, 1931-40, research in India, 1935-38; asst. prof. Sanskrit, gen. linguistics U. Cal. at Berkeley, 1940-43, asso. prof., 1943-46, prof., 1946-71, emeritus, 1971—, chmn. dept. linguistics, 1953-58, dept. classics, 1959-62, faculty research lectr., 1955-56. Recipient Wilbur Lucius Cross medal Yale Grad. Sch., 1969. Guggenheim fellow, 1949-50, 1956-57. Fellow Royal Asiatic Soc. (hon.); mem. Am. Philos. Soc., Linguistic Soc. Am. (pres. 1949), Am. Acad. Arts and Scis., Am. Oriental Soc. (asso. editor 1941-47, editor 1947-51, pres. 1954-55, pres. Western br. 1964-65), Assn. Am. Rhodes Scholars, Philol. Soc. Gt. Britain, Nat. Inst. Humanistic Scis. Vietnam, Linguistic Soc. India, Internat. Assn. Tamil Studies (v.p. 1966), Phi Beta Kappa, Sigma Xi. Author: Kota Texts, 1944- 46; Studies in Vietnamese (Annamese) Grammar, 1951; Sanskrit Sandhi and Exercises, 1952; Kolami, A Dravidian Language, 1955; A Dravidian Etymological Dictionary (With T. Burrow), 1961; Dravidian Borrowings from Indo-Arvan, 1962; Brahui and Dravidian Comparative Grammar, 1962; Kalidasa's Sakuntalā translated from the Bengali Recension, 1962; Dravidian Linguistics, Ethnology and Folktales; Collected Papers, 1967; (with T. Burrow) A Dravidian Etymological Dictionary; Supplement, 1968; Toda Songs, 1971. Contbr. to ednl. publs. Home: U Cal Berkeley CA 94720

EMENY, BROOKS, author, lectr., educator; b. Salem, O., July 29, 1901; s. Frederick James and Elizabeth Miller (Brooks) E.; student Gov. Dummer Acad., 1917-18; grad. Mercersburg (Pa.) Acad., 1920; A.B., Princeton, 1924; student Sorbonne, Paris, France, 1924-25, London (Eng.) Sch. Econs., 1925-26, Kohsular Akademie, Vienna, Austria, U, Madrid (Spain), 1926-27; Ph.D., Yale, 1934; m. Winifred Rockefeller, Dec. 15, 1928 (dec. 1951); children—Elizabeth Brooks (dec.), Faith R. (Mrs. Richard S. Conger), Winifred Theodate (dec.), Josephine Brooks (dec.); m. 2d, Barbara Cox, Nov. 27, 1954. Instr. govt. Yale, 1927-31, research govt., 1931-33; research and writing, Washington, 1933-35; asso. prof. internat. relations Cleve. Coll., 1935-47; dir. Fgn. Affairs Council, 1935-42; pres. Council World Affairs, 1943-47, mem. bd. dirs. Fgn. Policy Assn., 1947—, pres., 1947-53; adv. council Internat. Orgn. Research Program, Maxwell Grad. Sch. Citizenship and Pub. Affairs, 1965- -; cons. Dept. State, 1941—; chmn. fgn. affairs com. White House Conf. People-to-People Program, 1956-59; lectr. USIS, East Africa, 1956, Middle East, 1957, South East Asia, 1958, Africa, 1960. Bd. dirs. Avon Old Farms School, 1930—, Oberlin Coll., 1936- 50, The Atlantic Council of U. S., 1963—, Princeton in Asia, 1969—; mem. adv. councils Princeton, Woodrow Wilson Sch. of Pub. and Internat. Affairs 1957—, Dept. of Oriental Studies, 1958—, Dept. Modern Langs. and Lits., 1959—; adv. council Sch. of Internat. Service, Am. U., Washington, 1960—. Mem. Am. Acad. Political and Social Sci., Am. Geog. Soc., Am. Soc. Metals. Fgn. Policy Assn., Council Fgn. Relations, Inst. Pacific Relations (bd. dirs. 1940-53), Acad. Polit. Sci., Washington Inst. Fgn. Affairs. Clubs: Princeton (N.Y.C.); Metropolitan (Washington); Century, University (N.Y.C.); Nassau, Bedensbrook (Princeton, N.J.); Bras Coupe Hunting and Fishing (pres.). Author: Mainsprings of World Politics; Strategy of Raw Materials; Great Powers in World Politics. Contbr. articles jours. Home: 221 Elm Rd Princeton NJ 08540

EMERICH, DONALD WARREN, educator; b. Schuylkill Haven, Pa., July 12, 1920; s. Edward Robert and Minie (Beck) E.; B.S. in Chem. Engring., Pa. State U., 1942; Ph.D. in Chemistry, Ohio State U., 1951; m. Evelyn Freda Graulich, Sept. 24, 1943; children—Douglas William, Dwight Edward, David Graulich. Research and devel. Hercules, Inc., Parlin, N.J., 1942-43; prodn. supr. Badger Ordnance Works, Baraboo, Wis., 1943-45; research and devel. U.S. Vanadium Corp., Niagara Falls, N.Y., 1945-47; instr. Kan. State U., Manhattan, 1951-53, asst. prof., 1953-54; asso. prof. Centenary Coll., Shreveport, La., 1954-58, prof., 1958-60; asso. prof. Miss. State U., State College, 1960-62, acting head chemistry dept., 1964-66, prof. chemistry, 1962—, head dept., 1966—. Violinist, Miss. State Coll. Women-Community Orch., 1963-65; pres. Starkville Civic Orch., 1969-70, violinist, 1969—. Mem. Starkville C. of C., A.A.A.S., Sigma Xi, Tau Beta Pi, Sigma Tau, Phi Lambda Upsilon, Pi Mu Epsilon. Home: 2007 Pin Oak Dr Starkville MS 39759 Office: Box CH State College MS 39762

EMERICH, IRA, former newspaper exec.; b. Balt., Apr. 11, 1894; s. David and Adeline (Sulzbacher); E.; m. Cornelia Watts Van Siclen, Oct. 17, 1958. Sales dir. Esquire Features, Inc., 1934-41, Chgo. Sun Syndicate, 1941-42; sales dept. Hall Syndicate, 1946-55, sales dir., 1955-56, exec. v.p., 1956-67, dir., bd. 1958-67; dir. newspaper relations Pubs.-Hall Syndicate, 1967-68. Chief press distbn. sect. OWI, 1942-44; newspaper liaison officer War Finance Program, Treasury Dept. 1944-46. Master ceremonies Washington Stage Door Canteen, 1943-45. Served with F.A., U.S. Army, World War I. Recipient Distinguished Service citation Treasury Dept., 1945. Clubs: National Press (Washington); Forty Plus (dir.) (N.Y.C.); Gipsy Trail (Carmel, N.Y.). Home: 45 Sutton Pl S New York City NY 10022 Office: 30 E 42d St New York City NY 10017

EMERICK, HAROLD BURTON, steel co. exec., assn. ofcl.; b. New Brighton, Pa., July 6, 1913; s. Clyde Chalmers and Melissa Vivian (Freed) E.; student Carnegie-Mellon U., 1932-38; m. Elsie Prellwitz, Oct. 23, 1938; children—Richard Bruce, Martha Jean (Mrs. Paul C. Franklin). With Jones & Laughlin Steel Corp., 1935—, dir. tech. services, 1955-69, v.p. research and tech., 1969—. Fellow Metall. Soc. Am. Inst. Mining, Metall. and Petroleum Engrs. (pres. 1965-66). Fellow Am. Soc. Metals; mem. Am. Inst. Mining and Metall. and Petroleum Engrs. dir. 1962-68, v.p. 1966-67; McKune Meml. award, 1943), Am. Iron and Steel Inst. Presbyn. Co-editor: Basic Open Hearth Steelmaking, 1951. Home: 479 Salem Dr Pittsburgh PA 15243 Office: Jones & Laughlin Steel Corp Pittsburgh PA 15230

EMERLING, ERNEST, travel writer; b. Dayton, O., Dec. 22, 1904; s. Gustav Frederick and Nora (White) E.; ed. Art Students League, N.Y.C., advt. course, Columbia; m. Helen Louise Schneble, Apr. 25, 1926; children—Anne (Mrs. Al Brown), Carol (Mrs. Larry Boudreau), Ernest, Mary (Mrs. Larry Purcell). With Loew's Theatres, Inc., 1921-71, city mgr., Birmingham, Ala., Dallas and Memphis, 1926-30, asst. to advt. dir., N.Y.C., 1930-46, advt. dir., 1946-71, v.p. 1959-71; advt. dir. Loew's Hotels, Inc., 1960-70, corp. v.p. pub. relations, 1970-71; free lance travel writer, 1971—. Mem. fund raising com. Will Rogers Meml. Hosp. Mem. Met. Motion Picture Theatres Assn. N.Y.C. Address: 29 Deepdale Dr Great Neck NY 10019

EMERMAN, DAVID, mfg. co. exec.; b. Akron, O., Sept. 18, 1896; s. Solomon and Deborah (Rudd) E.; student Case Sch. Applied Sci., 1916-17, U. Mich., 1918-19; m. Edith Bergman, Dec. 17, 1939; children—Denise (Mrs. Donald Schmerin), Nancy, Laurie Ann. Chmn. bd., dir. Unit Crane and Shovel Corp., Milw., 1948—, Davis & Thompson, Milw., 1948—, Allied Products Corp., Detroit, 1962—, chmn., 1963—. Active fund raising drives United Founds., Brandies U., United Jewish Appeal. Served with USNR, 1917. Home: 26575 Willowgreen St Franklin MI 48025 Office: 24209 Northwestern Hwy Southfield MI 48075

EMERSON, ALFRED EDWARDS, zoologist; b. Ithaca, N.Y., Dec. 31, 1896; s. Alfred and Alice Louisa (Edwards) E.; B.S., Cornell U., 1918, A.M., 1920, Ph.D., 1925; Sc.D., Mich. U. 1961; m. Winifred Jelliffe, May 3, 1920 (dec. 1949); children—Helena Leeming (Mrs. Eugene Wilkening), William Jelliffe; m. 2d Eleanor Fish, Sept. 3, 1950. Asst., Tropical Research Sta., N.Y. Zool. Soc., 1919, asso., 1920, asst. dir., 1924; instr., U. Pitts., 1921-23, asst. prof., 1923-25, asso. prof., 1925-29; asso. prof. U. Chgo., 1929-34, prof., 1934-62, emeritus; asst. Am. Mus. Natural History, 1920, research asso., 1940—; research asso. Chgo. Natural History Mus., 1942—. Guggenheim Meml. Found. fellow, 1926-27; Belgian Am. Edn. Found. fellow, 1948; instr., biology lab., Cold Spring Harbor, N.Y., 1922; distinguished prof. natural sci. Mich. State U., 1960. Fellow N.Y. Zool. Soc.; mem. Ecol. Soc. Am. (sec.-treas. 1931, pres. 1941, Eminent Ecologist citation 1967), Am. Entomol. Soc., Soc. Systematic Zoologists (pres. 1958), Soc. Study Evolution (v.p. 1946, 48, pres. 1960), A.A.A.S. (sect. v.p. 1946), Ill. Acad. Sci. (pres. 1946), Nat. Acad. Sci. Author numerous publns. including: (with W. C. Allee, O. Park, T. Park, K. P. Schmidt) Principles of Animal Ecology, 1949; The Supraorganismic Aspects of the Society, 1952; The Biological Foundations of Ethics and Social Progress, 1952; Biogeography of Termites, 1952; Biological Species, 1954; Social Homeostasis, 1954; Distribution of Termites, 1955; Evolution of Behavior, 1958; Evolution of Adaptation in Population Systems, 1960; Impact of Evolution on Religion, 1960; Vestigial Characters and Processes of Regressive Evolution, 1961; Impact of Darwin on Biology, 1962; Human Cultural Evolution, 1965. Home: Huletts Landing NY 12841

EMERSON, DANIEL EVERETT, telephone co. exec.; b. Passaic, N.J., Oct. 22, 1924; s. Daniel T. and Jennie (VanBeveren) E.; B.E.E., Cornell U., 1949; student George Washington U., Boston U., also N.Y.U., 1951-56, Dartmouth, 1956, U. Pa., 1959-60; m. Patricia Thorston, June 14, 1947; children—Patricia Sue, Nancy Ellen, Pamela Thorston. With Am. Tel. & Tel. Co., 1949—, v.p. fed. relations, 1968—. Trustee Montclair (N.J.) Acad., 1965—. Served to 1st lt. USAAF, 1943-45. Decorated Air medal. Mem. Newcomen Soc., Pewter Collectors Club Am., Tau Beta Pi, Eta Kappa Nu, Theta Xi. Clubs: Lackawanna Cornell; Canoe Brook Country (Summit, N.J.); Internat. (Washington). Home: 18 Chaucer Rd Short Hills NJ 07078 Office: 195 Broadway New York City NY 10007

EMERSON, DONALD CONGER, educator; b. Toronto, Ont., Can., Sept. 17, 1913; s. Henry Conger and Isabel (Rife) E.; came to U.S., 1926, naturalized, 1940; B.A., U. Wis., 1938, M.A., 1946, Ph.D., 1950; m. Glenys Belle Truax, June 19, 1943; children—Margaret Anne, John Andrew. Instr., U. Wis., Milw., 1948-54, asso. prof., 1955-59, prof. English, 1960—, asst. dean Coll. Letters and Sci., 1958-62. Served with inf., AUS, 1942-45. Decorated Bronze Star medal. Mem. Authors League Am., Modern Lang. Assn., Midwest Modern Lang. Assn. (v.p. 1962-63), Am. Assn. U. Profs. (chpt. pres. 1966-67), Am. Studies Assn., Nat. Council Tchrs. English. Author: Span Across a River, 1967; Court Decision, 1968. Contbr. to Ency. of World Literature in the 20th Century, 1967. Home: 3233 N Hackett Av Milwaukee WI 53211

EMERSON, EDWARD EVERETT, investment co. exec., former educator; b. Danvers, Mass., Sept. 2, 1905; s. George Waldo and Susan Mabel (Hood) E.; A.B., Dartmouth, 1926; postgrad. Harvard; m. Margaret Swann Lees, Aug. 6, 1938; children—Edward Everett, Thomas Lees. Bus. mgr. Howard Sch., West Bridgewater, Mass., 1926-27; traffic mgr. New Eng. Tel. & Tel. Co., 1927-31; headmaster Emerson Sch. Boys, Exeter, N.H., 1931-50; asso. prin. Stoneleigh-Burnham Sch., Greenfield, Mass., 1950-56, headmaster, 1956-70; dir. Burnham-by-the-Sea, girls summer sch., Newport, R.I., 1950—; pres. Meadowbrook Investment Corp., 1969—. Mem. corp. Boston Athenaeum. Trustees, Stoneleigh-Burnham Sch., 1950-68, Emerson Sch. for Boys, Exeter, N.H. Mem. Ind. Schs. Assn. No. New Eng. (past sec.-treas.), New Eng. Hist. Geneal. Soc., Nat. Assn. Prins. Schs. Girls, Gamma Delta Chi, Alpha Chi Rho. Republican. Conglist. Home: RD Proctorsville VT 05153

EMERSON, FRED CLARENDON, state govt. ofcl.; b. Billings, Mont., Oct. 17, 1913; s. Paul S. and Bessie (Bump) E.; student Bay Path Sch., 1931-32; grad. Meriden (Conn.) Trade Sch., 1935; m. Joan E. Marsh; children—Bruce L., Betsy L. Sports editor Cheshire (Conn.) Chronicle, 1935; office clk. Spartan Saw Works, Inc., Springfield, Mass., 1936-39, asst. sales mgr., advt. mgr. and export mgr., 1939-42, sales mgr., 1942-69, v.p. dir., 1946-69; asso. commnr. Mass. Dept. Labor and Industry, 1969—; v.p. Eastern Snowbile Races, Inc.; pres. Camper-Chef Co.; corporator Springfield Credit Union; trustee Springfield Inst. Savs. Cons., All States Asphalt Co. Chmn. met. affairs com. Springfield Citizens Action Commn., 1961-64; past chmn. Agawam Planning Bd.; pres. Met. Planning Council, 1960-62; adviser, examiner Boy Scouts Am.; chmn. regional planning com. Joint Civic Agys., 1964-66, v.p., 1963-65; past chmn. Springfield Fgn. Trade Council; past pres. Indsl. Advt. and Marketing Council; pres. Conn. Valley Water Control Assn., 1950-60, Agawam Lions Park, Inc., 1962-65; internat. adv. com. Hall Free Enterprise; mem. Gov. Mass. Adv. Com. Blue Laws; exec. com. Agawam Betterment Commn., 1962-64. Selectman, Town of Agawam, 1950-56, chmn. bd., 1951-55; finance com. Town Worthington, Mass., 1966-68; dep. sheriff, Hampshire County, 1966—. Trustee, mem. bus. adv. com. U. Mass.; Trustee Eastern States Expn.; pres. Agawam YMCA, 1962-64; trustee Grad. Sch. Sales Mgmt. and Marketing, Syracuse U., 1962-65. Mem. Am. Supply and Machinery Assn. (pres. 1959-60), Western New Eng. Advt. Assn. (pres. 1946-47), Assn. Indsl. Advertisers (past dir.), Springfield Export Mgrs. (pres. 1943-44), Mass. (past pres.), Hampden City (past pres.) selectmen's assns., Hampden County Republican Club (pres. 1961-62), Pioneer Valley Assn. (dir.), Salesmasters (dir. Phoenix), Nat. Indsl. Advt. Assn. (past dir.), Sales and Marketing Execs. Internat. (pres. 1960-61), Springfield Sales Execs. (pres. 1947- 48), Nat. Travel Club, Ancient and Hon. Arty. Co. Mass., Izaak Walton League (dir. Springfield), Pi Sigma Epsilon (dir.), Beta Gamma Sigma (hon.). Mason (K.T., Shriner). Clubs: Springfield Exchange (past officer); Worthington Rod and Gun; Drummers (pres., treas.); Lions (pres. Agawam 1957-58, v.p. Huntington); Trestle Board (pres. 1957-58); Mawaga Sporting (pres. 1942-43); Agawam Sportsmen's (dir. 1956—); Nat. Rifle. Home: Old Main Rd Worthington MA 01098 Office: 100 Fisk Av Boston MA

EMERSON, GLADYS ANDERSON, biochemist, nutritionist; b. Caldwell, Kan., July 1, 1903; d. Otis Anderson and Louise (Williams) Anderson; A.B., B.S., Okla. Coll. Liberal Arts, 1925; M.A., Stanford, 1926; Ph.D., U. Cal. (Univ. fellow), 1932; postgrad. U. Gottingen, 1932-33. Teaching asst. Okla. Coll. for Women, 1923-25; asst. Stanford, 1925-26; research asso. Inst. Exptl. Biology, U. Cal., 1933-42, vis. lectr. pharmacology med. sch., 1945; research asso. Sloan-Kettering Inst. Cancer Research, 1950-53; head dept., animal nutrition Merck Inst. Therapeutic Research, Rahway, N.J., 1942-56, dir. nutrition Merck, Sharpe & Dohme Research Labs., 1956-57; Marie Curie lectr. Pa. State Coll., 1951; research lectr. Ia. State Coll., 1952; prof., chmn. dept. home econs., U. Cal. at Los Angeles, 1957-61, prof. nutrition, 1961—, head div. Sch. Pub. Health, 1961-69; vis. lectr. biochemistry and nutrition, U. Neb., 1958; lectr. univs., sci. and profl. socs., Japan, 1964; engaged in research OSRD, 1943-45; mem. liaison and sci. adv. bd. Q.M. Food and Container Inst., 1949-50; food and nutrition research com. NRC, 1952, mem. Food and Nutrition Bd., 1959-64, mem. com. dietary allowances, 1960-64; exec. council Am. Bd. Nutrition, 1959-68; panelist Rensselaer Poly. Inst. indsl. council, 1955; organizing com. 5th International Congress Nutrition, co-chmn. S. Cal. sect. WHO, 1969—; vice chmn. panel on new foods White House Conf. on Food, Nutrition and Health, 1969—; del. confs. in field; instr. trainees Peace Corps., 1962, 63, 64; mem. State Nutrition Com., 1966—; sponsor Cal. Freedom from Hunger Campaign, 1966—. Mem. Sci. bd. Meals for Millions. Recipient Garvan medal, 1952; named to Okla. Hall Fame, 1943. Fellow Am. Inst. Chemists, A.A.A.S., N.Y. Acad. Scis.; mem. Am. Chem. Soc. (chmn. women's service com., 1953-58), Am. Inst. Nutrition, (councillor 1952- 55, chmn. membership com. 1964), Soc. Exptl. Biology and Medicine, Gordon Research Conf. (chmn. vitamins and metabolism 1952, vice chmn. 1951), Pan Am. Med. Assn. (council 1959-60), Internat. Union Nutrition Scientists (del.; nat. com. 1959-62), Sigma Xi. Delta Omega, Sigma Delta Epsilon, Iota Sigma Pi (nat. v. p. 1945-51, nat. pres. 1951-57, nat. hon. mem.). Author articles sci. jours. Asso. editor Jour. Nutrition, 1952-56. Home: 319 Amalfi Dr Santa Monica CA

EMERSON, PAUL CARLTON, assn. exec.; b. Biddeford, Me., July 21, 1923; s. James E. and Clara (Macomber) E.; student Grove City Coll., 1942-43; m.; 1 dau., Beverly Ann. Exec. dir. Portland (Me.) Vets. Service Center, 1945-46, field mgr. Me. State C. of C., Portland, 1946-47, exec. mgr., 1947-68, exec. v.p., 1968—. Mem. Me. Com. Youth Opportunities, 1960—, Me. Com. Aging, 1960- -, Me. Com. Vocational Edn., 1958—, Me. Adv. Council Higher Edn., 1966, Can.-U.S. Commn. U.S. C. of C., 1967—; founder (with others) Me. World Trade Council; mem. regional export expansion council U.S. Dept. Commerce, 1969—; gov.'s task force on Me. environment, 1969—. Bd. dirs. Vacation Travel Council Me.; trustee Osteopathic Hosp. Me., 1969—, Me. Council Econ. Edn. Served to 1st lt. USAAF, 1943-45; lt. col. Res. Mem. Am., New Eng., Me. (founder, treas.) assns. C. of C. Execs. Club: Cumberland (Portland). Home: Spurwink Av Cape Elizabeth ME 04107 Office: 477 Congress St Portland ME 04111

EMERSON, RALPH, botanist, educator, assn. exec.; b. N.Y.C., Apr. 19, 1912; s. Haven and Grace (Parrish) E.; B.S., Harvard, 1933, M.A., 1934, Ph.D., 1937; student (NRC Council fellow), Cambridge U., 1937-39; m. Enid Merle Budelman, July 17, 1942; children—Peter Dietrich, Grace. Prof. botany U. Cal. at Berkeley, 1953—, acting Chmn. dept. botany, 1964- 65, chmn., 1967-71; special lectr. botany London U., 1950. Guggenheim fellow, 1948-49, 56-57. Fellow A.A.A.S., Am. Acad. Arts and Scis.; mem. Nat. Acad. Scis., Mycol. Soc. Am. (pres. 1955-56). Cal. Acad. Scis. (v.p. 1967—), Bot. Soc. Am. (pres. 1967), Brit. Mycol. Soc. (v.p. 1971), Am. Inst. Biol. Scis. (governing bd. 1965-70), Sigma Xi. Author: (with Donald G. Cooney) Thermophilic Fungi. Photographer; Game Fish of the Pacific (L. A. Walford), 1937. Home: 454 Beloit Av Berkeley CA 94708

EMERSON, RICHARD MARC, educator, sociologist; b. Salt Lake City, Jan. 12, 1925; m. Patricia Emerson; children—Leslie, Marc. Prof. sociology U. Cin. until 1964; now prof. sociology U. Wash.,

Seattle; spl. research social psychology. Mem. Am. Everest Expdn., 1963. Mem. Am. Sociol. Assn. Club: Sierra. Home: 4919 NE Princeton Way Seattle WA 98115

EMERSON, ROY C., union ofcl. Sec.-treas. Barbers, Hairdressers, Cosmetologists and Proprietors' Internat. Union Am., AFL-CIO. Office: 4755 Kingsway Dr Indianapolis IN 46205

EMERSON, RUPERT, educator; b. Rye, N.Y., Aug. 20, 1899; s. William Key Bond and Maria Holmes (Furman) E.; A.B., Harvard, 1921; Ph.D., London Sch. Econs., 1927; m. Alla Julievna Grosjean, Sept. 14, 1925; children— William Key Bond, Nina Ule, Natasha Maria, Rupert Allan. Reporter N.Y. Sun, 1921- 22; instr. Harvard, 1927, prof. internat. relations, 1946-70, prof. govt. emeritus, 1970—. vis. prof. U. Cal. Berkeley, 1953-54, at Los Angeles, 1965-71; lectr. Yale, 1937-38; dir. div. territories and island possessions U.S. Dept. Interior, Washington, 1940-41; apptd. Office of Coordinator of Inter-Am. Affairs, 1941, regional adminstr. for territories and possessions OPA, 1942; asst. adminstr. Lend-Lease, 1943; dir. Liberated Areas Br. FSA, 1944- 45. Trustee, Inst. Pacific Relations; pres. Far Eastern Assn., 1952-53. Served as 2d class seaman U.S. Navy, 1917-18. Mem. Am. Acad. Arts and Scis., Am. Politi. Sci. Assn., Assn. for Asian Studies, African Studies Assn. (pres. 1965-66), Council on Fgn. Relations, Inst. of 1770, Spee (Harvard). Author: State and Sovereignty in Modern Germany, 1928; Malaysia, 1937; The Netherlands Indies and the U.S., 1942; Representative Government in Southeast Asia, 1955; From Empire to Nation, 1960; Self-Determination Revisited in the Era of Decolonization, 1964; Africa and United States Policy, 1967. Contbr. articles to jours. Home: 5 Buckingham Pl Cambridge MA 02138

EMERSON, STERLING, biologist; b. Lincoln, Neb., Oct. 29, 1900; s. Rollins Adams and Harriet Theresa (Hardin) E.; B.Sc., Cornell U., 1922; A.M., U. Mich., 1924, Ph.D., 1928; m. Mary Foote Randall, May 29, 1924; children—Ann Katherine (Mrs. J. R. S. Fincham), Sterling Jonathan. Instr. botany U. Mich., 1924- 28; Internat. Edn. Bd. fellow to Scandinavia, 1925-26; with Cal. Inst. Tech., 1928—, prof. genetics emeritus, 1971—; vis. prof. (Fulbright fellow) Cambridge U., 1951-52; geneticist AEC, 1955-57; vis. prof. U. Wash., 1964, Cornell U., 1965, U. Copenhagen, 1966-67. John Simon Guggenheim Meml. Found. fellow for study in Eng., France. Fellow A.A.A.S.; mem. Nat. Acad. Sci., Genetics Soc. Am. (pres. 1964), Sigma Xi, Phi Kappa Phi, Gamma Alpha, Alpha Gamma Rho. Home: 1207 Morada Pl Altadena CA 91001 Office: California Inst Tech Pasadena CA 91109

EMERSON, THOMAS IRWIN, lawyer; b. Passaic, N.J., July 12, 1907; s. Luther Lee and Wilhelmina (Runft) E.; A.B., Yale, 1928, LL.B., 1931, M.A., 1946; m. Bertha R. Paret, Oct. 9, 1934 (dec. 1958); children—Joan Paret, Robert Madden, Luther Lee; m. 2d, Ruth B. Calvin, May 27, 1960. Admitted to N.Y. bar, 1932; asso. with law firm Engelhard, Pollak, Pitcher & Stern, N.Y.C., 1931-33; asst. counsel Nat. Recovery Adminstrn., 1933-34; prin. atty. NLRB, 1934-36, asst. gen. counsel, then asso. gen. counsel, 1937-40; prin. atty. Social Security Bd., 1936- 37; spl. asst. to atty. gen. U.S. Dept. Justice, 1940-41; asso. gen. counsel OPA, 1941-43, dep. adminstr. for enforcement, 1943-45; gen. counsel Office of Economic Stabilization, 1945; gen. counsel Office War Mobilization and Reconversion, 1945-46; prof. law Yale, 1946—, Lines prof. law, 1955. Guggenheim fellow, 1953; vis. prof. London Sch. Econs. Polit. Sci., 1953-54; vis. prof. Brookings Instn., 1960-61. Mem. Nat. Lawyers Guild (pres. 1950-51). Author: Political and Civil Rights in the United States (with David Haber and Norman Dorsen), 1952, 3d edit., 1967; Toward a General Theory of the First Amendment, 1966; The System of Freedom of Expression, 1970. Contbr. to profl. periodicals. Home: 2271 Ridge Rd North Haven CT 06520 Office: Yale Law Sch New Haven CT 06520

EMERSON, WILLIAM KEITH, zoologist; b. San Diego, May 1, 1925; s. Horace P. and Vera (Vaught) E.; A.B., San Diego State Coll., 1948; M.S., U. So. Cal., 1950; Ph.D., U. Cal. at Berkeley, 1956. Paleontologist, U. Cal. Mus. Paleontology, Berkeley, 1951-55; asst. curator invertebrates Am. Mus. Natural History, 1955-61, asso. curator, 1961-66, curator, 1966—, chmn. dept. living invertebrates, 1960—; research asso. San Diego Natural History Mus., 1962—. Leader Puritan expdn. to Western Mexico, Am. Mus. Natural History, 1957, mem. Belvedere Expdn. to Gulf of Cal., 1962. Fellow A.A.A.S.; mem. Cal. Acad. Scis., Am. Malacological Union (pres. 1961-62, mem. council 1963—), Western Soc. Malacologists (pres. 1968-69, mem. council 1970—), Paleontology Soc., Soc. Systematic Zoology (mem. council 1960-63), Paleontol. Research Instn., San Diego Soc. Nat. History, Cal. Malacozool. Soc. Blue Key, Sigma Xi, Sigma Phi Epsilon. Author: (with M.K. Jacobson) Shells of the New York City Area, 1961, Wonders of the World of Shells: Sea, Land and Fresh Water, 1971. Contbr. papers to profl. jours. Home: 10 E End Av New York City NY 10021 Office: Am Mus Natural History Central Park W at 79th St New York City NY 10024

EMERY, ALBERT WALDRON, Jr., advt. agy. exec.; b. Denver, Jan. 15, 1923; s. Albert Waldron and Margaret (Grimson) E.; student DePauw U., 1943-44; B.S., U. Va., 1948; m. Lucille E. Eye, Oct. 22, 1948; children—Linden, Lisa, Thomas Alan, Courtney. Sales promotion asst. Westinghouse Electric Corp., 1948-50, advt. account rep., 1950-53; div. mgr. Gen. Products Advt., 1953-54, Indsl. Products Advt., 1954-55; account exec. Harris D. McKinney, Inc., Phila., 1955-56, v.p., account supr., 1956-59, exec. v.p., 1960-62, pres., 1962- , chmn. bd., 1964—. Served with USNR, 1940-46. Mem. Assn. Indsl. Advertisers, Franklin Inst., Sigma Chi. Clubs: Poor Richard, St. David's Golf and Country, Virginia, Union League (Phila.). Home: S Forge Mountain Dr Valley Forge PA 19481 Office: 12 S 12th St Philadelphia PA 19107

EMERY, ALDEN HAYES, Jr., educator; b. Pitts., May 2, 1925; s. Alden Hayes and Dorothy (Radde) E.; B.S., Pa. State U., 1947; M.S., Mass. Inst. Tech., 1949; Ph.D., U. Ill., 1955; m. Verna Elizabeth Murphy, Mar. 1, 1952; children-Janice Elaine, Gregg Alden. Chem. engr. E.I. duPont de Nemours & Co., Willmington, Del., 1949-52; asst. prof. Sch. Chem. Engring., Purdue U., Lafayette, Ind., 1954-58, asso. prof., 1958-64, prof., 1964—. Served with USNR, 1944-45. Fulbright scholar, 1967. Mem. Soc. Rheology, Am. Inst. Chem. Engrs., Am. Chem. Soc., A.A.A.S., Am. Assn. U. Profs. Home: 815 Vine St West Lafayette IN 47906

EMERY, ALFRED CHARLES, univ. pres.; b. Salt Lake City, Jan. 24, 1919; s. Frank S. and Retta (Callister) E.; B.S., U. Utah, 1940, J.D., 1947; m. Belva White, June 17, 1942; children—Alfred Charles, James Frank, Gary W., Michael Neil. Mem. faculty U. Utah, 1947—, provost, 1967-71, pres., 1971—; 35th annual Reynolds lectr., 1971. Bd. dirs. Asso. Western Univs., 1971—; mem. Nat. Assn. State Univs. and Land Grant Colls., 1971—; mem. presidents' council Western Athletic Conf., 1971—. Bd. dirs. Richards Meml. Found., Children's Center, Salt Lake City. Served to lt. USNR, 1942-47. Sterling fellow Yale, 1953-54. Mem. Am. Council Edn., Salt Lake City C. of C., Order of Coif, Phi Kappa Phi. Mem. Ch. of Jesus Christ of Latter-day Saints (elder). Clubs: Alta, Fort Douglas; Timpanogos (Salt Lake City). Home: 1765 Kenwood Circle Salt Lake City UT 84106

EMERY, CLIFTON WOODFORD, Jr., coll. pres.; b. Somerville, Mass., June 4, 1919; s. Clifton Woodford and Marion Georgie (Somes) E.; B.S., Tufts U., 1940; Ed.M., Harvard, 1943; postgrad. Mass. Inst. Tech., 1943-44; Ed.D., Columbia, 1950; children—Nancy M., Clifton Woodford III, Peter; m. Florence M. Emery, Jan. 28, 1962. Instr. psychology Nichols Jr. Coll., Dudley, Mass., 1940-42; teaching fellow, tutor psychology Harvard, 1942-43, counselor Vets. Guidance Center, 1945-48; employment mgr. Dewey & Almy Chem. Co., 1943-45; asst. in guidance Columbia, 1948-49; asso. prof. edn. Tufts U., 1949-62, acting dir. counselling, 1951-52, asst. dean Coll. Liberal Arts, 1952-54, dean men, 1953-62, mil. coordinator, 1957- 62; pres. Worcester (Mass.) Jr. Coll., 1962—. Corporator Worcester Five Cents Savs. Bank; pres. Mass. Assn. Mental Health, 1957- 59, dir., mem. exec. com., 1965-69; dir. Worcester Housing Devel. Corp. (Model Cities). Pres., New Eng. Jr. Coll. Council; mem. state adv. council guidance and counseling Mass. Dept. Edn., 1958-69. Bd. govs. Huntington Sch., 1957—; mem. Ednl. Research Corp., Cambridge, Mass.; bd. dirs. Worcester Consortium for Higher Edn., 1968—, vice chmn., 1971—. Fellow Mass. Psychol. Assn.; mem. Nat. Assn. Mental Health (dir.), Am. Assn. Jr. Colls. (commn. student personnel), Worcester C. of C. (v.p. 1965-69), N.E. Assn. Coll. Deans (past sec.), Am. Coll. Personnel Assn., Eastern Assn. Deans and Advisers, N.E. Assn. Coll. and Secondary Schs. Rotarian. Club: Harvard (Boston). Home: 173 Winter St Framingham Centre MA 01701 Office: 768 Main St Worcester MA

EMERY, GUY TRASK, educator, physicist; b. Manchester, N.H., May 22, 1931; s. Henry Alfred and Ruth Madlyn (Trask) E.; A.B., Bowdoin Coll., 1953; A.M., Harvard, 1954, Ph.D., 1959; m. Marilyn Judkins, June 18, 1955; children—Karen Lee, Kimberly Lynn. Research asso., asso. physicist Brookhaven Nat. Lab., Upton, N.Y., 1959-66, cons., 1967—; vis. asso. prof. State U. N.Y., Stony Brook, 1965-66; asso. prof. Ind. U., Bloomington, 1966-69, prof., 1969—. Served to 1st lt. AUS, 1958-59. Fellow Am. Phys. Soc.; mem. Am. Assn. Physics Tchrs., A.A.A.S., Ind. Acad. Sci., Sigma Xi. Research in nuclear spectroscopy, chem. effects on nuclear processes, neutron capture, nuclear structure theory. Home: 700 S Highland Bloomington IN 47401

EMERY, HARLAN JULIEN, govt. ofc.; b. Bar Harbor, Me., Nov. 16, 1903; s. Julien and Addie (Higgins) E.; B.S. in Agr., U. Me., 1926; M.S. in Agrl. Econs., Ore. State Coll., 1930; student U. Cal. at Berkeley, 1930-33; m. Gwenydd K. Lewis, July 22, 1932; children—Stephen J., Rockwell L., Donald H. With Dept. Agr., 1934—, dir. livestock and dairy policy staff Agrl. Stblzn. and Conservation Service, 1964—. Recipient Superior Service Honor award Dept. Agr., 1959, Certificate of Merit, 1964. Mem. Sigma Nu, Alpha Zeta. Conglist. Home: 4900 27th St N Arlington VA 22207 Office: Dept of Agriculture Washington DC 20250

EMERY, JOHN COLVIN, Jr., air freight co. exec.; b. Madison, Wis., July 14, 1924; s. John Colvin and Janet (Millar) E.; student Dartmouth, 1942-43; m. Frances Toomy, May 28, 1960; children—John Colvin III, Susan Farlow, Ann Louise, Michael William, Patricia Millar. With United Airlines, 1944-45, Nat. Airlines, 1945-46; with Emery Air Freight Corp., Wilton, Conn., 1946—, v.p. sales, 1956-62, exec. v.p., 1963-68, pres. 1968—, also dir.; dir. Robbins Co., Attelboro, Mass., Investors Funding Corp. N.Y., Intermodal Transp. Systems, Inc.; mem. adv. bd. Chem. Bank, N.Y.C. Trustee Manhattan Coll., N.Y.C. Rep. town meeting. Greenwich, Conn. 1960-62, Darien, Conn., 1964-66. Served with A.C., USNR, 1943-44. Mem. Sales Execs. Club N.Y. (pres. 1967-68, dir. 1963—), Nat. Def. Transp. Assn. (life). Episcopalian (vestry). Clubs: Wee Burn Country (Darien, Conn.); Wings, Union League, (N.Y.C.). Office: Emery Air Freight Corp Wilton CT 06897

EMERY, MYRON DELEUW, lawyer, educator; b. Chgo., Aug. 12, 1927; s. Charles Eugene and Dora (Guettel) E.; A.B., Stanford, 1952; LL.B., U. Denver, 1956; m. Robin Wein, Oct. 22, 1954; children-Meg Erin, Jason Deleuw. Admitted to Cal. bar, 1957, also U.S. Customs Ct., Tax Ct. U.S.; practice in Beverly Hills, 1960—; mem. faculty U. Cal., at Los Angeles, U. So. Cal., U. Cal. at Riverside, U. Cal. at Irvine, U. Cal. at Santa Barbara; asso. prof. San Fernando Valley State Coll.; lectr. U. So. Cal. Sch. Bus. Adminstrn.; legal counsel Am. Advt. Fedn., Western Region, Hollywood Radio and Television Soc.; gen. counsel Pub. Relations Soc. Am., Los Angeles; conducted seminars Motorola Co., U. Cal., Bakersfield Coll.; adviser U. Cal., Los Angeles Extension for Pub. Relatins and Advt. and Profl. Assn. Program Designers. Served with USNR, 1945-46. Mem. Am., Cal. bar Assns., Am. Arbitration Assn., Am. Advt. Fedn. (regional dir.), Western States Advt. Agy. Assn. (mem. edn. bd.). Author: Legal Aspects of Public Relations and Advertising, 1966. Contbr. chpt. to Profl. Pub. Relations, 1968. Contbr. articles profl. jours. Office: 300 S Beverly Dr Beverly Hills CA 90212

EMERY, RICHARD WILDER, educator; b. Malden, Mass., July 23, 1912; s. George Webster and Pearl (Grose) E.; A.B., Columbia, 1934, A.M., 1935, Ph.D., 1941; m. Muriel A. Brassler, Sept. 4, 1941; children—David, Margaret. Tchr., Coll. City N.Y., 1940-42; faculty Queens Coll. of City N.Y., 1942-43, 46—, prof. history, 1960-71, emeritus, 1971—, dean faculty, 1960-62, 65-66. Vis. prof. Columbia, 1958- 59. Served USAAF, 1942-45. Am. Field Service Fellow, 1938-39; Guggenheim fellow, 1952-53, 59-60. Author: Heresy and Inquisition in Narbonne, 1941; The Jews of Perpignan in the 13th Century, 1959; The Friars in Medieval France, 1962. Home: Hemlock Farms Burning Tree Dr Hawley PA 18428 Office: Queens Coll Flushing NY 11367

EMERY, STEPHEN ALBERT, author; b. Chgo., Aug. 14, 1902; s. Stephen and Nellie Babbitt (Thaiheimer) E.; A.B., Cornell U., 1923, Ph.D., 1928; student Edinburgh (Scotland) U., 1926-27; m. Sarah Martha Watson, Sept. 11, 1948; children—Stephen, John Loring. Grad. asst. philosophy Cornell, 1923- 25, Susan Linn Sage fellow philosophy, 1925-26, 27-28; asst. prof. philosophy U. N.C., 1928-32, asso. prof., 1932-43, prof., 1943-63; instr. Cooke County Jr. Coll., Gainesville, Tex., 1963-64; prof. philosophy Bishop Coll., Dallas, 1964-68. Mem. Am. Philos. Assn., Am. Soc. Aesthetics, Phi Beta Kappa, Phi Kappa Phi. Republican. Translator: (with William T. Emery) The Essence of Philosophy (by Wilhelm Dilthey), 1954; Aesthetics and Theory of Art (by Max Dessoir), 1970. Home: 2301 N Akard St Dallas TX 75201

EMIL, ALLAN D., lawyer; b. N.Y.C., Mar. 25, 1898 s. Morris and Rose (Dlugasch) E.; student Erasmus Hall High Sch., N.Y.C., 1911-15; student Columbia U. Extension, 1915-16, N.Y. Law Sch., 1916-18; LL.B., Bklyn. Law Sch., 1919; m. Kate Silverman, June 26, 1921; children—Arthur D., Judy Anne. Admitted to N.Y. bar, 1920, since practiced in N.Y.C.; partner law firm Roseman, Colin, Kaye, Petschek, Freund & Emil; dir. Square D. Co., Phillips-VanHeuson Co., Walter Reade Orgn., Midland Glass Co., Guardian Mut. Fund. Asso. chmn. Fedn. Jewish Philanthropies, N.Y.C., 1965-66, fund raising campaign chmn., 1966-68. Trustee Albert Einstein Coll. Medicine, Austin Riggs Center, Inc. Bennington Coll.; v.p., dir. Psychoanalytic Found.; exec. v.p. Montfiore Hosp. and Med. Centre: Served with U.S. Navy, 1917-18. Spl. hon. mem. Am. Inst. Aeros. and Astronautics. Dir. George Jr. Republic. Mem. Assn. Bar N.Y.C., N.Y. County Lawyers Assn., Am. Fedn. Arts (trustee). Clubs: Sands Point (L.I.) Golf (hon., trustee); Glen Oaks Golf (Great Neck, N.Y.) (hon., trustee); Harmonie, Grolier. Home: 60 Sutton Pl S New York City NY 10022 Office: 575 Madison Av New York City NY 10022

EMIL, SISTER MARY, ednl. adminstr.; b. Detroit, Aug. 8, 1916; d. Emil Louis and Nellie (Houben) Penet; A.B., Marygrove Coll., Detroit, 1936; student U. Detroit Law Sch., 1936-37; Ph.D., St. Louis U., 1951; LL.D., Marquette U., 1957, St. Mary Coll., Notre Dame, Ind., 1959, U. Notre Dame, 1959, Seattle U., 1960; D.Ped., St. John's U., 1959; D.Litt. (hon.), DePaul U. 1964. Joined Sisters of Immaculate Heart of Mary, 1937; tchr. Monroe, Mich., Detroit, Akron, O., 1939-47; instr., then asst. prof. philosophy Marygrove Coll., Detroit, 1951-56, asso. prof., 1957, pres., 1961-68, dir. Edn. Research Center, 1968-69: Mem. staff Nat. Cath. Ednl. Assn., Washington, 1957-61; nat. chmn. Sister Formation Conf., 1953-57, exec. sec., 1957-60, community cons., dir. spl. projects, 1960-61; dir. Everett (Wash.) Curriculum Workshop, 1956; mem. tchr. edn. com. New Horizons Project, Nat. Commn. Tchr. Edn. and Profl. Standards, 1960-61; curriculum cons. Seattle U., spring 1960; staff Marquette U. Curriculum Workshop, 1958-61; mem. Nat. Commn. on Presdl. Scholars, 1969—. mem. adv. bd. com. on Cath. edn., Archdiocese of N.Y., 1968—; mem. higher edn. adv. com. Commn. on States, 1968-69. Trustee, Marywood Coll., Scranton, Pa., 1968-69. Mem. nat. bd. dirs. Citizens for Ednl. Freedom, 1968. Fund Advancement Edn. grantee, 1956; recipient St. John Baptist de la Salle medal Manhattan Coll., 1957; Alumni Merit award St. Louis U., 1957; Ursula Laurus media Ursuline Coll., Cleve., 1960; Centennial Medallion award Wayne State U., 1967; Elizabeth Seton medal Marillac Coll., 1968; Merit award Nat. Cath. Edu. Assn., 1970. Mem. Assn. Am. Colls. (mem. commn. on coll. and soc. 1965-66, chmn. com. on profl. accreditation 1965-68), Am. assn. Colls. for Tchr. Edn. (exec. com. 1965-68), Nat. Cath. Ednl. Assn. (chmn. survey dept. tchr. edn. sect., coll. and univ. dept. 1952, sec. Midwest coll. and univ. dept. 1955, v.p. coll. and univ. dept. 1966-67), Religious Edn. Assn. (dir. 1957—), Nat. Council for Accreditation Tchr. Edn. (visitation and appraisal com. 1964-66, exec. com. 1965-68), Council Coop. Tchr. Edn. (exec. com. 1958-60). Author: Property and Right in Representative Catholic Moralists of the 13th to 17th Centuries, 1950; also numerous articles. Editorial bd. Cath. Youth Ency., 1960—; adv. bd. Sponsa Regis, 1959-65; chmn. editorial bd. Jour. Tchr. Edn., 1968-69; editorial bd. Cath. Sch. Jour., 1968-70. Address: Marygrove Coll Detroit MI 48221

EMILIANI, CESARE, educator; b. Bologna, Italy, Dec. 8, 1922; s. Luigi and Maria (Manfredini) E.; D.Geology, U. Bologna, 1945; Ph.D. in Geology, U. Chgo., 1950; m. Rosita Manzanares, June 26, 1951; children—Sandra, Mario. Came to U.S., 1948. Geologist, Soc. Idrocarbori Nazionali, Florence, Italy, 1946-48; research asso. U. Chgo., 1950-56; mem. faculty U. Miami (Fla.), 1957—, prof. geology, 1963—, chmn. dept. geology and div. marine geology and geophysics, 1967—. Mem. A.A.A.S., Am. Geophys. Union, Soc. Econ. Paleontologists and Mineralogists, Sigma Xi. Research applied oxygen isotopic analysis to pelagic microfossils from deep-sea sediment cores; reconstrn. in detail climatic history Pleistocene Epoch. Home: 151 Edgewater Dr Coral Gables FL 33133 Office: Sch Marine Atmospheric Scis Univ Miami Virginia Key Miami FL 33149

EMISON, JOHN CLINTON, Jr., copper and brass co. exec.; b. N.Y.C., May 6, 1922; s. John Clinton and Faye Ruth (Miller) E.; A.B., DePauw U., 1943; M.B.A., Harvard, 1948; m. Barbara Jane Evans, Feb. 1, 1947; children—Lucy Adair, Nancy Jane, Patricia Anne. With Revere Copper and Brass Inc., 1948—, asst. treas., 1952-61, asst. sec., 1953—, treas., 1961—, also v.p., 1967- -. Served to lt. (j.g.) USNR, 1942-46. Mem. Phi Kappa Psi. Presbyn. (past trustee, life elder). Clubs: Rome; Lake Delta Yacht. Home: 1200 N George St Rome NY 13440 Office: Revere Copper and Brass Inc Rome NY 13440

EMISON, SAM SHANNON, former chem. mfg. co. exec.; b. Higginsville, Mo., Sept. 15, 1903; s. Samuel Grant and Sallie Forrest (Smith) E.; B.S., Rice Inst., 1925; m. Frances Mary Loock, Sept. 1, 1926; 1 son, Sam Shannon. Plant supt. Tex. Chem. Co. (merged to become Consol. Chem. Industries, Inc., 1929), Houston, 1925-29, plant mgr., Ft. Worth, 1929-41, sales mgr., 1942- 54, v.p. sales, 1954-56, (co. merged to become Stauffer Chem. Co., N.Y.C., 1956), v.p. indsl. chem. sales div., 1956-59, sr. v.p., 1965-68, dir., ret., 1968. Gov. alumni Rice U.; past pres., bd. dirs. Chlorine Inst. Mem. Am. Chem. Soc. (chmn. S.E. Tex. sect. 1952), Houston Engring. and Sci. Soc., Am. Philatello Soc., Soc. Chem. Industry, Tau Beta Pi. Rotarian. Clubs: Houston, Houston Chemical (pres. 1955-56); Sky (N.Y.C.). Home: 5025 Riverway Dr Houston TX 77027 Office: 6910 Fannin St Houston TX 77025

EMKEN, ROBERT ALLAN, diversified co. exec.; b. Portland, Ore., June 13, 1929; s. Cecil Wheeler and Grace (Hill) E.; B.S., U. Md., 1951; M.A., George Washington U., 1957; m. Constance Cook, May 1, 1954; children—Judith, Janice, Robert A. Staff accountant Stoy, Malone & Co., Washington, 1956-58; comptroller R. J. Reynolds Tobacco Co., Winston-Salem, N.C., 1958-70, R. J. Reynolds Industries, Winston-Salem, N.C., 1970—. Served with USCGR, 1951-54. Mem. Am. Inst. C.P.A.'s, Financial Execs. Inst., Nat. Assn. Accountants. Home: 681 Lichfield Rd Winston-Salem NC 27104 Office: RJ Reynolds Industries Winston-Salem NC 27102

EMLEN, JOHN THOMPSON, Jr., biologist, educator; b. Phila., Dec. 28, 1908; s. John Thompson and Mary Carpenter (Jones) E.; B.S., Haverford Coll., 1931, D. Sc., 1970; Ph.D., Cornell U., 1934; m. Virginia S. Merritt, June 25, 1934; children—John Merritt, Stephen Thompson, James Woodruff. Instr. zoology U. Cal. at Davis, 1935- 41, asst. prof., 1941-43; research on rodent ecology and rat control OSRD, Johns Hopkins, 1943-45; asso. prof. zoology U. Wis., 1945-50, prof., 1950—, chmn. dept., 1951-53. Fullbright fellow Guggenheim fellow for biol. research in Central Africa, 1953-54; NSF fellow for research on primates, Congo, 1959, research on penguins, Antarctica, 1962, 64. Fellow Am. Ornithologists Union, Am. Soc. Zoologists, A.A.A.S.; mem. Phi Beta Kappa, Sigma Xi, Phi Kappa Phi. Author articles in sci. jours. on distbn., ecology, populations and behavior of birds and mammals. Home: 2122 Van Hise Av Madison WI 53705

EMLER, PAUL WIGGINS, utility exec.; b. Plainfield, O., Feb. 2, 1911; s. Michael G. and Mahala E. (Wiggins) E.; B.S. in Elec. Engring., Purdue U., 1931; postgrad. U. Mich., 1956; m. Mary E. Miskimen, July 8, 1933; children—Paul W., John M., Sarah E. Various comml. positions, then div. comml. indsl. mgr. Ohio Power Co., 1931-48; dir. indsl. sales Am. Gas & Electric Service Corp. (now Am. Electric Power Service Corp.), N.Y.C., 1948-57, asst. v.p., 1957-58, v.p., 1958—, also dir.; dir. Appalachian Power Co., Ky. Power Co., Kingsport Power Co., Ohio Power Co., Twin Br. R.R. Co., Wheeling Elec. Co. Mem. Edison Electric Inst., Ohio Soc. N.Y. Methodist (trustee). Clubs: Chatham Fish and Game, Harbor View (N.Y.C.); Purdue of Northern N.J. Home: 66 Rolling Hill Dr Chatham NJ 07928 Office: 2 Broadway New York City NY 10004

EMMA, ARTHUR JEROME, retailer; b. Bklyn., Feb. 1, 1921; s. Sidney and Gertrude (Lambert) C.; B.S., Cornell U., 1941; m. Ruth Wolf, Dec. 25, 1941; children—Jeanne, William, Edward, Daniel. Buyer, Jordan Marsh, Boston, 1951-54; div. mdse. mgr. Gimbel's, Milw., 1954-66; gen. mdse. mgr. Thalhimer's, Richmond, Va.,

1966-69; pres. M. O'Neil Co., Akron, O., 1969—. Served to capt. USAAF, 1942-46; ETO. Mem. Nat. Retail Mchts. Assn., Phi Kappa Phi. Clubs: City, Silver Lake Country (Akron). Home: 1953 Stockbridge Rd Akron OH 44313 Office: 226 S Main St Akron OH 44308

EMMANUEL, MICHEL GEORGE, lawyer; b. Clearwater, Fla., May 16, 1918; s. George M. and Alexandra (Damianakes) E.; B.S., U. Fla., 1940, LL.B., 1948; LL.M., N.Y.U., 1949; m. Betty Boring, Dec. 19, 1942; children—George Michel II, Martha Alexandra. Admitted to Fla. bar, 1948; partner Mabry, Reaves, Carlton, Fields & Ward, Tampa, 1951-63; mem. firm Carlton, Fields, Ward, Emmanuel, Smith & Cutler, 1963—, now head tax dept. Mem. adv. com., lectr. N.Y.U. Tax Inst. Bd. dirs., past pres. Hillsborough County Crime Commn., bd. dirs. The Anclote Found., United Fund Tampa, U. of S. Fla. Found.; bd. counsellors U. Tampa. Served to comdr. USNR, World War II. Decorated D.F.C., Air medal with 2 stars, Purple Heart. Mem. Am., Hillsborough County, Tampa bar assns., Fla. Bar (past chmn. tax sect.), Tampa C. of C. (past pres.); U.S. C. of C. (taxation com.). Episcopalian. Rotarian. Clubs: Ye Mystic Krewe of Gasparilla, University (past pres.), Tampa Executives, Yacht and Country, Rotary (pres.) (Tampa). Author publs. in field. Home: 1201 Bayshore Blvd Tampa FL 33606 Office: Exchange Nat Bank Bldg Tampa FL 33601

EMMENEGGER, FREDERICK J., banker; b. 1911; B.S., Northwestern U., 1933. With Nat. Bank N. Am., 1963—, now v.p., controller. Office: 44 Wall St New York City NY 10005*

EMMERSON, JOHN KENNETH, ret. fgn. service officer; b. Canon City, Colo., Mar. 17, 1908; s. John Woods and Margaretta (Hitchcock) E.; diploma U. Paris, Sorbonne, 1928; A.B., Colo. Coll., 1929, LL.D., 1968; M.A., N.Y.U., 1930; postgrad. Georgetown U., 1931-33; m. Dorothy McLaughlin, Aug. 18, 1934; children—Dorothy Louise, Donald Kenneth. Fgn. service officer in Taiwan, Washington, Peru, China, Russia; counselor, dep. chief mission Am. embassy, Karachi, Pakistan, 1952, Beirut, Lebanon, 1955; polit. counselor, Paris, 1957; consul gen. Lagos, Nigeria, 1958; then consul gen. Salisbury, Fedn. Rhodesia and Nyasaland; then counselor minister, Tokyo, Japan; diplomat in residence Stanford U., 1967, now Sr. research fellow at univ. Sr. adviser U.S. delegation UN Gen. Assembly, 1956-57. Recipient Meritorious Service award Dept. State, 1954. Mem. Phi Beta Kappa. Home: 24899 Olive Tree Lane Los Altos Hills CA 94022 Office: Hoover Instn Stanford U Stanford CA 94305

EMMERT, JOHN J., ins. co. exec.; b. Detroit, June 7, 1911; ed. Wayne State U. With Standard Accident Ins. Co., 1934-62, controller, 1954-62; became controller Reliance Ins. Co., 1962, treas., 1964—. Mem. Soc. Ins. Accountants, Financial Execs. Inst. Mason (K.T.). Home: 1149 King of Prussia Rd Radnor PA 19088 Office: 4 Penn Center Plaza Philadelphia PA 19088 *

EMMERT, THEODORE JONATHAN, mfg. co. exec.; b. Smithboro, Ill., Sept. 9, 1915; s. William Theodore and Annie Marie (Meyer) E.; student Huron (S.D.) Coll., U. Wash.; m. Dorothy Mildred Klingberg, Sept. 26, 1936; children—Theodore James, Judith Ann. With Boeing Aircraft Co., 1935-47, asst. to exec. v.p., 1943- 47; with Canadair Ltd., Montreal, 1947-50, v.p., 1947-50, dir., 1948-50; with Ford Motor Co. Can., 1950-59, exec. v.p., dir., 1950-59; v.p. N. Am. operations Massey-Ferguson Ltd., Toronto, 1959-61; pres., chief exec. officer Hawker Siddeley Can. Ltd., 1961-69; pres., chmn. Dominion Steel and Coal Corp. Ltd., 1964—; chmn. bd. Dominion Coal Co. Ltd., 1963—; dir. Orenda Inc., Chgo., Canadian Gen. Transit Co.; chmn. De Havilland Aircraft Can. Ltd. Mem. exec. and council Bd. Trade Met. Toronto. Clubs: Toronto Golf National, York (Toronto); Mount Royal (Montreal); Rideau (Ottawa); MidOcean (Bermuda). Home: 500 Avenue Rd Toronto Ontario Canada Office: 7 King St E Toronto Ontario Canada

EMMET, THOMAS ADDIS, Jr., educator, mgmt. cons.; b. Detroit, July 26, 1930; s. Thomas Addis and Leona Margaret (Schneider) E.; Ph.B., U. Detroit, 1952, M.Ed., 1954; M.A., U. Mich., 1955, Ed.S., 1963. Tchr., St. Joseph's High Sch., Detroit, 1952; housing dir., asst. to dean men U. Detroit, 1952-53, asst. dir. evening div., instr. gen. studies, 1954- 57, asst. dean men, 1954-57, dean men, 1957-64, asst. prof. edn., 1957-67, adj. prof. higher edn., 1970—, dean McNichols Evening Div., 1964-66, spl. asst. to acad. v.p., 1966-67; asst. exec. v.p. Marquette U., Milw., 1967-68; pres. Higher Edn. Exec. Assos., 1968—. Fellow Nat. Council Geography Tchrs.; mem. Nat. Assn. Student Personnel Adminstrs., Nat., Mich., Jesuit (sec. conf. student personnel adminstrs. 1958-68) edn. assns., Assn. Am. Geographers, Am. Ednl. Research Asssn., Assn. Counselor Edn. Suprs., Am. Coll. Personnel Assn., Adult Student Personnel Assn. (v.p. 1961- 66), Assn. U. Eve. Colls., Council Student Personnel Assns. in Higher Edn. (sec. 1966-69, chmn. joint commn. profl. devel. council 1962-65), Blue Key, Phi Kappa Phi, Phi Delta Kappa, Alpha Sigma Nu. Roman Catholic. Editor Jour. Nat. Assn. Student Personnel Adminstrs., 1963-64. Author, editor numerous articles, surveys, studies on higher edn. and student personnel work. Address: 3420 N Lake Shore Dr Chicago IL 60657

EMMETT, JOHN LESTER, physician; b. Ogden, Utah, Aug. 3, 1903; s. Walter R. and Joan (Woodmansee) E.; A.B., U. Utah, 1926; M.D., Northwestern U., 1930; M.S., U. Minn., 1934; m. Erma Blood, June 4, 1932; children—Susan, Sally, John L., Stephen Blood. Intern Passavant Meml. Hosp., Chgo., 1930-31; fellow 1st asst. Mayo Found., 1931-35; cons. urology Mayo Clinic, Rochester, Minn., 1935—; prof. urology U. Minn. Diplomate Am. Bd. Urology. Mem. A.M.A., Am. Urol. Assn., Am. Assn. Genito-Urinary Surgeons, Brit. Assn. Urol. Surgeons (corr. mem.), Sigma Xi, Phi Kappa Phi, Phi Chi. Author: Clinical Urography, 2d edit., 1963, 3d edit. (with David M. Witten), 3 vol., 1971; sect. in Urology (by Meredith Campbell), 1963. Contbr. profl. jours. Home: 617 9th Av SW Rochester MN 55901 Office: 200 1st St SW Rochester MN 55901

EMMETT, PAUL HUGH, ret. chemist; b. Portland, Ore., Sept. 22, 1900; s. John Hugh and Vina (Hutchens) E.; B.S. in Chem. Engring., Ore. State Coll., 1922, D.Sc. (hon.), 1939; Ph.D., Cal. Inst. Tech., 1925; Docteur honoris causa, U. Lyon (France), 1964; m. Lela Jones, July 24, 1930. Instr. chemistry Ore. State Coll., 1925-26; research in catalysis Fixed Nitrogen Research Lab., U.S. Dept. Agr., Washington, with final rank of sr. chemist, 1926-37; lectr. on catalysis George Washington U., alternate years, 1927-36; prof. chem. and gas engring. Johns Hopkins, 1937-44, W.R. Grace prof. chemistry, 1955-70; cons. U.S. Dept. Agr., 1937-44; research for Manhattan Project, Columbia, 1943-44; with Mellon Inst. Indsl. Research, 1944-55. Recipient Phila. Catalyst Soc. award, 1970; hon. councilor Consejo Superior, Spain. Mem. Nat. Acad. Sci., Am. Chem. Soc. (Pittsburgh award 1953, Kendall Co. award in Colloid Chemistry 1958, Md. sect. award 1970), Sigma Xi, Sigma Tau, Delta Sigma Rho, Phi Kappa Phi, Phi Kappa Tau. Contbr. articles on results of research in catalysis, adsorption, nitrogen fixation to sci. jours. Asso. editor Jour. Am. Chem. Soc., 1942-52. Home: 600 Waverly Ct Milwaukie OR 97222

EMMINGER, OTMAR, German banker, govt. ofcl.; b. Augsburg, Germany, Mar. 2, 1911; s. Erich and Annamaria (Scharff) E.; Dr. oec. publ., U. Munich, 1934; children—Haimo, Arno. Asst. lectr. U. Berlin (Germany), 1934-35; mem. Inst. Bus. Research, Berlin, 1935-45; law assessor, 1938; with Ministry Econs., Munich, 1947-49; mem. German delegation to Orgn. European Econ. Coop., Paris, 1949-50; with Deutsche Bundesbank, Frankfurt am Main, 1950—, mem. directorium, 1953-69, dep. gov., 1970—, mem. central bank council, 1958-69, vice chmn., 1970—; exec. dir. for Germany of Internat. Monetary Fund, Washington, 1953-59; vice chmn. monetary com. Eurpean Econ. Community, 1959—; chmn. Deps. of Group of Ten, 1964-67; chmn. working party OECD, Paris, 1969—. Home: 36 Hasselhorstweg Frankfurt am Main West Germany Office: Deutsche Bundesbank Frankfurt am Main West Germany

EMMONS, ALTON THOMAS, utility co. exec.; b. What Cheer, Ia., Nov. 23, 1911; s. Wilson Thomas and Amy (Penrose) E.; A.B., William Penn Coll., 1934; M.B.A., Harvard, 1936; m. Mary Louise Else, July 6, 1937; children—David, John, James. Mgr., Price Waterhouse & Co., N.Y.C., 1936-53; asst. comptroller W. Penn Power Co., Greensburg, Pa., 1953-60, comptroller, 1960-71, v.p., 1964—; comptroller, dir. Allegheny Pitts. Coal Co., West Penn W.Va. Water Power Co., W. Penn Rys. Co.; comptroller Allegheny Power Service Corp. C.P.A., N.Y. Mem. Am., Pa. insts. C.P.A.'s, Financial Execs. Inst., N.A.M., Edison Electric Inst. (chmn. accounting div. 1968-69). Presbyn. Clubs: Greensburg Country; Harvard-Yale- Princeton (Pitts.). Home: R R2 Beech Hills Jeannette PA 15644 Office: Cabin Hill Greensburg PA 15601

EMMONS, C.S., lawyer; b. 1908; A.B., LL.B., Willamette U., Salem, Ore. Admitted to Ore. bar, 1931; now mem. firm Emmons, Kyle & Kropp, Albany. Mem. Am., Ore, (past pres.) bar assns. Address: 507 S Washington Albany OR 97321*

EMMONS, DONN, architect; b. Olean, N.Y., Oct. 4, 1910; s. Frederick E. and Mary (Fogarty) E.; student Cornell U., 1928-33, U. So. Cal., 1934; m. Nancy Pierson, Apr. 4, 1942; children—Zette, Luli, Andrew; m. 2d, Audrey Durland, Oct. 29, 1960. With office William W. Wurster, architect, San Francisco, 1938-42; partner Wurster, Bernardi & Emmons, San Francisco, 1945-63; prin. Wurster, Bernardi, & Emmons, Inc., 1963—, pres., 1969; cons. architect U. Cal. at Berkeley, 1968—; prin. works include Golden Gateway Redevel. Project, San Francisco, Ghirardelli Sq., San Francisco, Capitol Towers Redevel. Project, Sacramento, Bank of Am. World hdqrs. in San Francisco and offices in Sacramento and San Mateo, Cal., Merritt Coll., Oakland, Woodlake and Oakcreek Apt. Projects, Operation Breakthru for Dept. Housing and Urban Devel., Sacramento, San Francisco Civic Center, U. Victoria (B.C., Can.), Oakland Coll. Mem. Potomac River Task Force for rehab. river. Served to lt. comdr. USNR, 1942-45. Recipient over 80 awards for excellence in design. Fellow A.I.A. (pres. No. Cal. chpt. 1953-54, dir. Cal. council 1953-54). Home: 654 Sausalito Blvd Sausalito CA 94965 Office: 1620 Montgomery St San Francisco CA 94111

EMMONS, GLENN LEONIDAS, banker; b. Atmore, Ala., Aug. 15, 1895; s. John Davidson and Martha Jane (Huggins) E.; student U. of N.M.; m. Dorothy Frances Hockaday, June 11, 1924. Locomotive fireman (when 15 yrs. old), Am. Lumber Co., Zuni Mountains, N.M.; entered banking, Gallup, N.M., 1919; chmn. bd. and pres. First State Bank, Gallup, 1935-1964; U.S. comm. Indian Affairs, 1953-61. Mem. of nat. adv. bd. Girl Scouts Am.; chmn. Greater U. N.M. Devel. Fund. Bd. mgrs. Sch. Am. Research, Santa Fe, N.M. Served as 1st lt., U.S. Air Service, 1917-19. Candidate for Rep. nomination for gov. of N.M., 1944. Mem. bd. regents U. of N.M., 1930-32. Mem. Am. Bankers Commn. on country bank operations 1945-46. Recipient award of Merit, D.A.R. of N.M.; Distinguished Service Award, Dept. Interior. Mem. Am. Bankers Assn. (treas., 1949-51; mem. adminstrv. com.; mem. exec. council; mem. finance com.; mem. pub. relations council, 1946-47); pres. N.M. Bankers Assn., 1940- 41; mem. Newcomen Soc. of England, Pi Kappa Alpha. Republican. Episcopalian. Mason. Club: Albuquerque Country. Home: 1512 Los Alamos Av SW Albuquerque NM 87104

EMMONS, HOWARD WILSON, educator, mech. engr.; b. Morristown, N.J. Aug. 30, 1912; s. Pete Wilson and Margaret (Lang) E.; M.E., Stevens Inst. Tech., 1933, M.S., 1935; S.D., Harvard, 1938; m. Dorothy Gertrude Allen, July 9, 1938; children—Beverly Ann, Scott, Keith. Research engr. Westinghouse Electric, 1937-39; asst. prof. mech. engring. U. Pa., 1939-40; instr. to asso. prof. Grad. Sch. Engring. Harvard, 1940- 46, Gordon McKay prof. engring. sci., 1946-52, Gordon McKay prof. mech. engring., 1952—; on leave as Hunsaker prof. aero. engring., Mass. Inst. Tech., 1957-58; Guggenheim and Fulbright fellow Cambridge U., Eng., 1952-53; cons. aerodynamics and thermodynamics Pratt and Whitney Aircraft, 1940-60; cons. on supersonic aerodynamics Army Ordance, Aberdeen Proving Ground, Md., 1942-56; mem. sci. adv. bd. Navy Ordnance Lab., White Oaks, Md., 1947-52; mem. Naval Ordnance Test Sta. Adv. Bd., Inyokern, Cal., 1948-56. Mem. supersonic aerodynamics subcom. NASA 1946-47, mem. compressor subcom., 1943-56, mem. internal flow subcom. 1947-50; chmn. Citizens Sch. Survey of Sudbury, Mass.; mem. Naval Tech. Mission to Europe, 1945, Am. Gas Turbine Mission to Britain, 1947; mem. fire research com. Nat. Acad. Scis., 1956—, chmn., 1968-70; mem. Gov.'s Adv. Com. for Sci. and Tech., 1965-71; mem. space tech. panel Office Sci. and Tech. Selectman, Sudbury, 1969—, chmn., Mass. Sci. and Tech. Found., 1970—. Fellow Am. Soc. M.E. (sec. applied mechanics div. 1946, chmn. 1947, sec. fluids engring. div. 1960, chmn. 1961; v.p. for basic engring. 1965-70); mem. Phys. Soc. (sec., treas. fluid dynamics 1946-48), Am. Acad. Arts and Scis., Math. Assn. Am., Nat. Acad. Engring., Nat. Acad. Scis., Sigma Xi (sec. Harvard chpt. 1945-46), Tau Beta Pi. Author: Gas Dynamics Tables for Air, 1947. Collaborating editor: Quar. Applied Math., Fundamentals of Gas Dynamics. Home: Concord Rd Sudbury MA 01776 Office: Pierce Hall Harvard U Cambridge MA 02138

EMMONS, RICHARD CONRAD, educator, geologist; b. Winnipeg, Man., Can., Aug. 28, 1898; s. W.E. and Ellen (McCrossan) E.; B.A., U. B.C., 1919, M.A., 1920; Ph.D., U. Wis., 1924; m. Pearl Elizabeth Hocking, June 8, 1926; 1 dau., Nancy Jean (Mrs. R.A. Smith). Came to U.S., 1920, naturalized, 1926. Faculty U. Wis., 1926—, prof. geology, 1936—. Fellow Geol. Soc. Am. (v.p. 1945); mem. Mineral. Soc. Am. (pres. 1944). Rotarian (pres. Madison 1951-52). Author: Universal Stage, 1943; Petrogenic Aspects of Plagioclase, 1953. Home: 801 Huron Hill Madison WI 53711

EMONT, MILTON DAVID, educator; b. Paterson, N.J., Apr. 11, 1923; s. George and Rose (Hoffspiegel) E.; B.A., Montclair State Coll., 1943; postgrad. U. Cin., 1944, Sorbonne, Paris, France, 1945, U. Grenoble (France), 1951-52; A.M., Middlebury Coll., 1948; Ph.D., U. Wis., 1958; m. Marietta Gruenbaum, Jan. 29, 1950; children—Carl Denis, George Daniel. Telegraph operator airline communications Trans World Airline Co., Orly Field, Paris, France, 1946-47; tchr. Vets. Evening High Sch., Jersey City, 1948-49; teaching asst. U. Wis. Madison, 1949-51, 52-54; mem. faculty Denison U., Granville, O., 1954—, prof. French, 1965—, chmn. dept. modern langs., 1970—. Served with AUS, 1943-46. Fulbright scholar, 1951-52; Markham traveling fellow, 1960-61. Mem. Modern Lang. Assn., Am. Assn. Tchrs. French, Ohio Coll. Assn. (pres. modern lang. sect.). Home: 3 Mount Parnassus Dr Granville OH 43023

EMOREY, HOWARD OMER, hwy. trailer exec.; b. Royal Oak, Mich., Mar. 22, 1928; s. Edward O. and Grace (Crissman) E.; B.A., Mich. State U., 1951; m. Elmer B. Bell, June 9, 1951; children—Kathryn, Martha, Lee. Jr. accountant to audit mgr. Price Waterhouse & Co., Detroit, 1951-66; with Fruehauf Corp., Detroit, 1966—, mgr. financial planning, 1966-69, treas., 1969—. Mem. Mich. State U. Annual Detroit Mgmt. Conf. Com., 1967-71. Served as p.f.c., AUS, 1946-48. C.P.A., Mich. Mem. Am. Inst. C.P.A.'s, Mich. Assn. C.P.A.'s, Nat. Assn. Accountants (dir. Detroit chpt. 1961-66). Methodist (chmn. adminstrv. bd.). Clubs: Red Run Golf (dir.) (Royal Oak, Mich.); Golf Assn. Michigan (Detroit). Home: 2321 Hunt Club Dr Bloomfield Hills MI 48013 Office: 10900 Harper Av Detroit MI 48232

EMPEY, LESTER H., banker; b. Oakland, Cal., July 14, 1908; s. Lester H. and Anna W. (Thies) E.; student San Mateo Jr. Coll.; m. Helen M. Hughes, Jan. 27, 1934; children—Peter Hughes, Michael R. With Am. Trust Co. (now Wells Fargo Bank), San Francisco, 1928—, beginning as messenger, successively asst. cashier, asst. v.p., 1928-49, v.p., 1949-59, sr. v.p., 1959—. Mem. Am. Bankers Assn., Investment Bankers Assn. Am. (nat. gov.). Home: 734 Parrott Dr San Mateo CA 94402 Office: 464 California St San Francisco CA 94104

EMPIE, PAUL CHAUNCEY, clergyman; b. St. Johnsville, N.Y., Feb. 10, 1909; s. Charles Gideon and Grace Louise (Diefendorf) E.; grad. Muhlenberg Coll., 1929, D.D. (hon.), 1944; postgrad Lutheran Theol. Sem., Phila., 1929-32; LL.D., Capital U., 1950; L.H.D., Hartwick Coll., 1951; Th.D., U. Goettingen (Germany), 1952; D.D., Gustavus Adolphus Coll., 1960, Augustana Coll., Sioux Falls, S.D., 1962; m. Katharine Goodwin Smith, Dec. 27, 1930; children—Barbara, Charlotte, Susan. Ordained to ministry United Lutheran Ch., 1932; established mission church, Phila., organized as Luth. Ch. of Prince of Peace, served as pastor until 1937; supt. Luth. Home for Orphans and Aged, Germantown, Phila., 1937-41; sec. Benevolence of Pa. Ministerium of United Luth. Ch. in Am., 1941-44; asst. exec. dir. Nat. Luth. Council, 1944-48, exec. dir., 1948-66; gen. sec. U.S.A. nat. com. World Luth. Fedn., 1967. Dir. Luth. World Action, 1944—; chmn. Luth. Ch. Prodns., Inc., 1951-65; pres. Luth. Film Assos., 1955-66; chmn. Dept. Commn. Religious Liberty Nat. Council Chs. U.S., 1965-67; chmn. world service Luth. World Fedn., 1952-70; pres. Luth. World Relief, 1968—; periodic visits to Europe, Asia, Africa and S.Am. in interests of relief, reconstrn. and service to refugees. Trustee Muhlenberg Coll., 1965—. Recipient Mannerheim medal; Orders of Finlandia, White Rose and Finland's Lion, 1949; Comdr.'s Cross of Order of Merit (Fed. Republic Germany), 1961; Wichern medal Evangelical Ch. in Germany, 1967. Author numerous pamphlets. Home: 72 Norwood Av Upper Montclair NJ 07043 Office: 315 Park Av S New York City NY 10010 ☆

EMPSON, WILLIAM, poet, critic; b. Yorkshire, Eng., Sept. 27, 1906; s. Arthur Reginald and Laura (Micklethwait) E.; B.A., Magdalene Coll., Cambridge (Eng.) U., 1929, M.A., 1935; m. Hester Henrietta Crouse, Dec. 1941; children—William Hendrick Mogador, Jacobus Arthur Calais. Prof. English lit. Bunrika Daigaku, Tokyo, Japan, 1931-34, Peking (China) Nat. U., 1937- 39, 46-52, Sheffield (Eng.) U., 1953—; Chinese editor BBC, 1941-46. Fellow Royal Soc. Lit. Author: Seven Types of Ambiguity, 1930; Poems, 1935; Some Versions of Pastoral, 1935; (verse) The Gathering Storm, 1940; The Structure of Complex Words, 1951; Collected Poems, 1955; Milton's God, 1961. Home: Studio House 1 Hampstead Hill Gardens London NW 3 England

EMRICH, DUNCAN BLACK MACDONALD, educator, diplomat, author; b. Mardin, Turkey, Apr. 11, 1908; s. Richard Stanley Merrill and Jeannette (Wallace) E.; student Phillips Andover Acad., 1922-26; A.B., Brown U., 1932; A.M., Columbia, 1933; Doctor en Letras, U. Madrid, 1934; Ph.D., Harvard (Shattuck scholar 1935-36, Austin fellow, 1936-37), 1937; student U. Aix en Provence, Sorbonne, U. Cologne, Escuela de Estudios Arabes; grad. Command and Gen. Staff Sch., Ft. Leavenworth, 1943; m. Sally R. Selden, Nov. 20, 1955. Asst. prof. English, U. Denver, 1940-42; chief Archives Am. Folksong, Library Congress, 1945-46, chief folklore sect., 1946-55; cultural relations attache Am. embassy, Greece, 1956-58; consul and cultural affairs officer Am. Consulate Gen. of Calcutta, India, 1959-62; Near East analyst USIA, 1962- 64; pub. affairs officer Am. embassy, Lome, Togo, 1964-66; desk officer, former French West African colonies USIA, Washington, 1966-69; prof. Am. folklore Am. U., 1969—. Weekly NBC radio broadcasts on folklore, 1953-55. Served as maj. U.S. Army 1942- 45; ofcl. Am. hist. SHAEF, 1943-45. Guggenheim fellow, 1949-50; Fulbright lectr. U. Rome, 1952-53. Fellow Nat. Council Religion Higher Edn.; mem. Parnassus Soc. (hon., Athens, Greece). Author: Who Shot Maggie in the Freckle and other ballads of Virginia City, Nevada, 1940; Casey Jones and other Ballads of the Mining West, 1941; It's an Old Wild West Custom, 1949; Comstock Bonanza, 1950; The Cowboy's Own Brand Book, 1954; The Folklore of Love and Courtship, 1970; The Folklore of Weddings and Marriage, 1970; The Nonsense Book, 1970; The Book of Wishes and Wishmaking, 1971; Folklore on the American Land, 1972; also articles. Co-editor: The Lucius Beebe Reader, 1967. Home: 2141 Wyoming Av NW Washington DC 20016 also Virginia City NV 89440 Office: English Dept American U Washington DC 20008

EMRICH, RAYMOND JAY, physicist, educator; b. Denver, Nov. 30, 1917; s. Jay Leroy and Lola Mary (Baker) E.; A.B., Princeton, 1938, A.M., Ph.D., 1946; Henry fellow Cambridge (Eng.) U., 1938-39; student Cornell U., 1939-40; m. Carolyn Sarah Schleicher, Sept. 4, 1942; children—Fredrica Lucile Smith, Lynn Margaret Roller. Physicist, Nat. Def. Research Com., Princeton, 1941-46; mem. faculty Lehigh U., 1946—, prof. physics, 1955—, head dept., 1958-66, chmn. dept. physics, 1966-68, principal investigator shock tube research program, 1948—. Cons. Sandia Corp., 1954-55, Los Alamos Sci. Lab., 1961-62; vis. scientist Ernst Mach Inst., Germany, 1968; Nat. Acad. Scis. exchange visitor, Novosibirsk, Siberia, 1970-71. Fellow Am. Phys. Soc. (chmn. div. fluid dynamics 1967, div. councilor 1967-71); mem. Am. Assn. Physics Tchrs., Am. Soc. Engring. Edn. (chmn. physics div. 1963-65), Am. Assn. U. Profs., Franklin Inst. (com. on sci. and arts 1960—), Sigma Xi, Tau Beta Pi. Episcopalian. Contbr. articles profl. jours. Editorial bd. Physics of Fluids, 1958-60. Home: 517 7th Av Bethlehem PA 18018

EMRICH, RICHARD STANLEY MERRILL, bishop; b. Mardin, Turkey, Mar. 11, 1910 (parents Am. citizens); s. Richard Stanley Merrill and Jeannette (Wallace) E.; student Phillips Andover Acad., 1923-27; A.B., Brown U., 1932; LL.D., 1949; postgrad. Episcopal Theol. Sch., 1932-33; B.D., Union Theol. Sem., 1935; Ph.D., U. Marburg, 1937; S.T.D., Kenyon Coll., 1948; D.D., Huron Coll., Ontario, Can., 1950; LL.D., Rensselaer Poly. Inst., 1955, Wayne U., 1961; L.H.D., Hillsdale Coll., 1960, U. Mich., 1962, U. Detroit, 1966; m. Beatrice Anne Littlehales, Nov. 24, 1937; children—Richard Stanley Merrill, Frederick Ernest. Ordained minister Episcopal Ch., 1936; asst. St. John's Ch., Waterbury, Conn., 1936-37; instr. to prof. Episcopal Theol. Sch., Cambridge, Mass., 1937-46; rector St. Anne's Ch., South Lincoln, Mass., 1944-46, St. Gabriel's Ch., Marion, Mass., 1944-46; suffragan bishop of Mich., 1946- 48, bishop, 1948—. Former mem. Nat. Council Episcopal Chs. Decorated Comdr. Order Brit. Empire. Mem. Zeta Psi, Phi Beta Kappa (hon.). Clubs: Detroit, Economic (dir). Author: The Conception of the Church in the

Writings of Baron von Hugel, 1938; Earth Might be Fair, the Presiding Bishop's Book for Lent, 1945. Contbr. numerous articles to mags. and pamphlets. Columnist Detroit News. Home: 368 Washington Rd Grosse Pointe MI 48230 Office: 4800 Woodward Av Detroit MI 48201

EMRICK, EDWARD, Jr., petroleum exec.; b. Aledo, Ill., Feb. 17, 1909; s. Edward Everett and Nannie May (Love) E.; B.S., U. Ill., 1931; m. Mary Bentley Woods, Mar. 17, 1934; children—Robert E., Ann Bentley, Katherine W., William P. Asst. treas. Ashland Oil, 1932, chief accounting officer and asst. sec., 1939, purchasing agent, 1942, dir., 1947, exec. asst., 1949; with Ashland (Ky.) Oil & Refining Co. and affiliated cos. 1931-70, exec. asst., 1949-51, dir. purchases, 1952-70, treas., 1959-70; dir. 3d Nat. Bank; treas., dir. Ashland Overseas Corp., 1968-70; dir. Rosenblooms, Inc., Gablers, Inc., Ironton, O., Palais Royal, Richmond, Ind. Active Boyd County Community Chest, 1942. Mem. Nat. Assn. Purchasing Agts., Am. Petroleum Inst. Presbyn. (elder). Club: Lion (past dir.). Home: 1725 The Oaks Dr Ashland KY 41101 Office: 1409 Winchester Av Ashland KY 41101

EMSHWILLER, ED, motion picture producer, dir.; b. Lansing, Mich., Feb. 16, 1925; s. Errol E. and Susie (MacLellan) E.; B.Design, U. Mich., 1949; student Ecole des Beaux Arts, Paris, France, 1949-50; m. Carol Fries, Aug. 30, 1949; children—Eve, Sue, Peter. Engaged as painter, 1951-64, as illustrator sci. fiction, 1951-64, as motion pictures producer, dir. 1959-; films shown at festivals in N.Y.C., London, Eng., Oberhaussen, Germany, Tours, France, Montreal, Can., Edinburg, Scotland, Bergamo, Italy, Brussels, Belgium; producer-dir. Mixed Media Presentations, 1965- -; short exptl. films include Dance Chromatic, 1959, Life Lines, 1960, Thanatopsis, 1962, Totem, 1963, George Dumpson's Place, 1964, Relativity, 1966, Art Scene USA, 1966, Fusion, 1967, Project Apollo, 1968, Film with Three Dancers, 1970, Carol, 1970; (mixed media) Body Works, 1966; feature films include Image, Flesh and Voice, 1969, Branches, 1970. Trustee Am. Film Inst. Served to 2d lt., inf., AUS, 1943-46. Grantee Ford Found., 1964. Mem. Filmmakers Coop. N.Y.C. (bd. dirs.). Address: 43 Red Maple Dr N Wantagh NY 11793

ENARSON, HAROLD L., univ. pres.; b. Villisca, Ia., May 24, 1919; s. John and Hulda (Thorson) E.; A.B., U. N.M., 1940; M.A., Stanford, 1946; Ph.D., Am. U., 1951; m. Audrey Pitt, June 7, 1942; children—Merlyn Pitt, Elaine Pitt, Lisa Pitt. Teaching asst., research asst. Stanford, 1940-41, asst. prof., 1949-50; examiner Bur. Budget, Washington, 1942-49; asst. prof. Whittier Coll., 1949; exec. sec. Steel Industry Bd., summer 1949; cons. Nat. Security Resources Bd., summer 1950; spl. asst. The White House, Washington, 1950-52; pub. mem. WSB, 1952-53; asst. dir. commerce City of Phila., 1953; exec. sec. mayor of Phila., 1953-54; exec. dir. Western Interstate Commn. Higher Edn., 1954-60; cons. on utilization of coll. teaching resources project Fund for Advancement of Edn., 1957; Carnegie Corp. adminstrs. fellowship, 1958; mem. surgeon gen.'s cons. group on med. manpower, 1960; cons. Ford Found. in UAR, 1960; adminstrv. v.p. U. N.M., 1960-61, acad. v.p., 1961-65, past project dir. U. N.M. Internships in Latin Am.; pres. Cleve. State U., 1966—. Cons. AID, 1965, dir. edn. services Offices Human Resources and Social Devel., 1963-64; mem. nat. adv. heath council USPHS, 1964-68, mem. com. to evaluate health relationships; cons. Ford Found., C. Am., summers 1961-63; mem. commn. internat. edn. Am. Council on Edn., 1965-67; mem. com. internat. edn. Am. Assn. Colls. for Tchr. Edn., 1967-69; com. on internat. edn. Coll. Entrance Exam. Bd., 1967-70. Mem. bd. visitors Air U., 1968-70; mem. Nat. Dental Research Council, 1958-62; former bd. dirs. mem. Nat. League Nursing; mem. gen. bd. Cleve. chpt. A.R.C.; trustee Cleve. Council World Affairs; bd. dirs. Am. Council on Edn., 1970—. Served with inf. AUS, 1943-46. Mem. Am., Western polit. sci. assns., Am. Soc. Pub. Adminstrn., Indsl. Relations Research Assn. Rotarian. Home: 14706 Larchmere Shaker Heights OH 44120

END, HENRY, interior and indsl. designer; b. Salford, Eng., Nov. 3, 1915; s. Maximillian and Adela (Blain) E.; student architecture and art St. Martins Sch. Art London, 1930; A.R.C.A., Royal Coll. Art, London, 1934; m. Jessica Marion Claas, July 5, 1947; 1 dau., Lindsay. Came to U.S., 1946. Founder, 1950, since pres. Henry End Assos., Miami, Fla.; founder Internat. Design Center of Los Angeles and Miami, 1960; designer sets 20th Century Fox, Warner Bros., Universal, Selznick; interior designer hotels and restaurants, condominiums, office bldgs., including Cocoanut Grove, Los Angeles, Carlton Tower, London, Mayflower, Washington, Hotel Quito, Ecuador, El Conquistador, P.R., Carlton Beach, Bermuda, Lucayan Beach Hotel, Grand Bahama Island, Nassau Beach Hotel, Ritz Carlton, Montreal, Seacoast Towers West, Seacost Towers V, 733 Park Av. Bldg., N.Y.C., Marriott Chain motor hotels, tourist hotels for Govt. Tunisia, Hilton, Sheraton (Rio de Janeiro and Buenos Aires), Sonesta Internat. (Brussels and Munich), Hyatt Internat., Trust Houses/Fortes Hotels, Esso Hotel, Antwerp. Belgium; designed feature exhibits Room of Tomorrow, Designs for Dining, Internat. Hotel Expn., N.Y.C., Chgo., Los Angeles, Internat. Restaurant Expn., Chgo., U.S. Rubber Pavilion, Coliseum, N.Y.C. Served with RAF, 1940-46. Recipient spl. citation A.I.A.; awards Art Dirs. Club, Design Derby; citation Societe Culinaire Philanthropique; citation of merit also 2 design awards Am. Inst. Interior Designers, 13 design awards Institutions mag. Fellow Inc. Inst. Brit. Decorators and Interior Designers, Am. Hotel Assn.; mem. Am. Inst. Interior Designers, Indsl. Designers Soc. Am., Nat. Soc. Interior Designers. Author: Interiors Book of Hotels and Motor Hotels, 1963. Home: 1201 NE 94th St Miami FL 33147 Office: 4100 N Miami Av Miami FL 33127 also 204 E 58th St New York City NY 10022 also 4 Williams St London SW1 England

ENDE, JOSEPH, motion picture co. exec.; b. N.Y.C., 1913; B.S. in Accounting, N.Y.U., 1933; m. Controller, Film Classics, Inc., 1933-50; asst. treas. United Artists Corp., 1950-55, controller, 1955-60, v.p., asst. treas., controller, mem. exec. com., 1960-67, v.p., treas., dir., 1967—. Home: 65 Walker St Malverne NY 11565 Office: 729 7th Av New York City NY 10019*

ENDERS, JOHN FRANKLIN, univ. prof.; b. West Hartford, Conn., Feb. 10, 1897; s. John Ostrom and Harriet Goulden (Whitmore) E.; A.B., Yale, 1920, Sc.D. (hon.), 1953; M.A., Harvard, 1922, Ph.D., 1930; Sc.D., 1956; Sc.D., Trinity, 1955, Northwestern, 1956; Sc.D., Western Res. U., 1958, Tufts U., 1960; LL.D., Tulane U., 1958; L.H.D., Hartford U., 1960; m. Sarah Frances Bennett, Sept. 17, 1927 (dec.); children—John Ostrom II, Sarah; m. 2d, Mrs. Carolyn Keane, May 12, 1951; 1 stepson, William Edmund Keane. Asst. dept. bacteriology and immunology, Harvard, 1929-30, instr., 1930-32, faculty instr., 1932-35, asst. prof., 1935-42, asso. prof., 1942-56; prof. Children's Hosp., Harvard Med. Sch., 1956—. Served from ensign to lt. (j.g.), Naval Res. Flying Corps., 1917-20. Civilian cons. to sec. to war on epidemic diseases, 1942-46; mem. Commn. on Viral Infections, Armed Forces Epidemiological Board; sci. adv. bd. Armed Forces Inst. Pathology; chief of research dept. of infectious diseases. Children's Hosp., Boston; Recipient Passano Found. award for culturing poliomyelitis viruses in living tissues, 1953; Lasker Award, 1954; Nobel Prize in Medicine and Physiology, 1954; Cameron prize U. Edinburgh, 1960, Howard Taylor Ricketts Meml. award U. Chgo., 1962, Diesel Gold medal, 1962, Robert Koch medal, 1962 (Germany), Sci. achievement award A.M.A., 1963, Presdl. Medal of Freedom, 1963. Fellow Am. Acad. Arts and Scis.; mem. Nat. Acad. Scis., Harvey Soc., Am. Philos. Soc., Soc. Gen. Microbiology (hon.), Soc. Am. Bacteriologists, Am. Assn. Immunologists (pres.), Soc. Exptl. Biology and Medicine, Am. Pub. Health Assn., A.A.A.S., Sigma Xi, Alpha Omega Alpha (hon.); asso. mem. Mass. Med. Soc. Clubs: Harvard (Boston); Brookline (Mass.) Country. Author: (with Hans Zinsser and Leroy D. Fothergill) Immunity: Principles and Application in Medicine and Pub. Health, 1939. Contbr. to Virus and Rickettsial Diseases, 1958, 64. Editor: Jour. of Immunology, 1942-58, Jour. Bacteriology, 1964—. Home: 64 Colburne Crescent Brookline MA 02146 Office: 300 Longwood Boston MA 02115

ENDERS, RICHARD WARREN, retail co. exec.; b. Harrisburg, Pa., July 11, 1915; s. Warren Winfield and Carrie Kinter (Charles) E.; A.B., Catawba Coll., Salisbury, N.C., 1937; postgrad. Pa. State U., 1938; m. Jean Elizabeth Swomley, Nov. 8, 1941; children—Michael, Peter, Carol. Collection mgr. Palais Royal, Washington, 1941-43; with Julius Garfinckel & Co., Inc., Washington, 1943—, asst. sec., 1963-65; v.p. research and planning Garfinckel div. Garfinckel, Brooks Bros., Miller & Rhodes, Inc., 1966—, corp. sec., 1965—, corp. v.p., 1969—. Mem. Health and Welfare Council Nat. Capital Area, 1965—. Home: 9319 Bells Mill Rd Rockville MD 20854 Office: 1401 F St NW Washington DC 20004

ENDERS, ROBERT KENDALL, biologist, educator; b. Essex, Ia., Sept. 22, 1899; s. S.E. Allen and Frances Marie (Seibert) E.; A.B., U. Mich., 1925, Ph.D., 1927; m. Abbie Gertrude Crandell, Aug. 29, 1923; children—Abbie Gertrude, Allen Coffin. Asst. prof. biology Union Coll., 1927-28; prof. Mo. Valley Coll., 1928- 30; mammalogist Ohio Conservation Commn., 1930; asst. prof. zoology Swarthmore (Pa.) Coll., 1932-38, asso. prof., 1938-44, prof., 1944-70, chmn. dept., 1946-67; agt. Dept. Agr., 1945—; collaborator Dept. Interior, 1949-60; Fulbright lectr., Pakistan, 1952-53. Trustee Biol. Abstracts, 1958—, pres., 1961-63; dir. Rocky Mountain Biol. Lab., 1958- 69, pres., 1969—, cons. Joint Rabies Control Bd., 1961-64, Pacific Sci. Bd., 1950-60, various panels NSF, 1957—. Fellow NRC, 1930-32; research fellow Acad. Natural Scis., 1937—. Contbr. articles to profl. and trade jours. Home: 311 Elm St Swarthmore PA 19081

ENDERS, THOMAS OSTROM, fgn. service officer; b. Hartford, Conn., Nov. 28, 1931; s. Ostrom and Alice Dudley (Talcott) E.; grad. Phillips Exeter Acad., 1949; B.A., Yale, 1953; Docteur de l'Universite, U. Paris, 1955; M.A., Harvard, 1957; m. Gaetana Elena Mathilde Costanza Marchegiano, June 6, 1955; children—Domitilla Elena, Alice Talcott, Claire Whitmore, Ostrom. Joined U.S. Fgn. Service, 1958; assigned Washington, 1958-60, 63-69, Stockholm, 1961-63; spl. asst. to under sec. state for polit. affairs, 1966-68; dep. asst. sec. state internat. monetary affairs, 1968-69; dep. chief mission, Belgrade, 1969-70, Phnom Penh, 1971—. Recipient Arthur S. Flemming award, 1969. Home: 1320 29th St N W Washington DC 20007 Office: American Embassy Phnom Penh Cambodia Box P APO San Francisco CA 96346

ENDICOTT, FRANK SIMPSON, educator; b. Mankato, Minn., June 25, 1904; s. Ira L. and Lillie M. (Simpson) E.; A.B., Cornell Coll., 1927; M.A., Northwestern U., 1929, Ph.D., 1938; m. Edith J. Franks, July 25, 1931; children—Robert Frank, Judith Louise (Mrs. Peter Calderaro). Tchr. high sch., Winnetka, Ill., 1929-30; dir. guidance, Eveleth, Minn., 1930-35; mem. faculty Northwestern U., 1935—, dir. placement, 1942—, prof. edn., 1960—. Mem. Nat. Inst. Tchr. Placement Assn. (pres. 1937), N. Central Assn. Colls. and Secondary Schs. (pres. 1970), Ill. Assn. Sch., Coll. and Univ. Staffing (pres. 1966), Midwest Coll. Placement Assn. (pres. 1957), Phi Delta Kappa. Presbyn. Author: Guiding Superior and Talented High School Students, 1961; How 300 Companies Hire College Graduates, 1962; How to Plan for College, 1967; A College Student's Guide to Career Planning, 1967; Parents Guide to College Planning, 1967; How to Get The Right Job and Keep It, 1969. Home: 2724 Lincolnwood Dr Evanston IL 60201

ENDICOTT, KENNETH MILO, physician; b. Canon City, Colo., June 6, 1916; s. James Milo and Florence Violet (Doran) E.; B.A., U. Colo., 1936, M.D., 1939; m. Anne Virginia Bingham, June 12, 1939; 1 dau., Judith Anne; m. 2d, Frances Ann Clarke, Jan. 21, 1950; children—James Milo, Linda Gail. Intern U.S. Marine Hosp., 1939-40; commd. asst. surgeon USPHS, 1939, advanced through grades to med. dir., 1951; assigned Relief Sta., Portland, Ore., 1940, U.S. Quarantine Sta., San Francisco, 1941-42, Med. Center Fed. Prisoners, Springfield, Mo., 1942; exptl. pathology NIH, 1942-51, sci. dir. div. research grants, 1951-55, chief cancer chemotherapy Nat. Service Center, 1955-58, asso. dir. NIH, 1958-60, dir. Nat. Cancer Inst., 1960—, dir. bur. health manpower edn., 1968-71. Diplomate Am. Bd. of Pathology. Mem. A.M.A., Am. Assn. Pathologists and Bacteriologists, Am. Soc. Exptl. Pathology, A.A.A.S., Soc. Exptl. Biology and Medicine, Washington Acad. Sci., Farm Bur., Alpha Omega Alpha, Phi Rho Sigma, Theta Xi. Home: Beall Mt River Rd Potomac MD 20854 Office: Nat Insts Health Bethesda MD 20014

ENDICOTT, ROBERT RANTOUL, editor, pub. cons.; b. Detroit, Feb. 14, 1905; s. John and Mary Elizabeth (Booth) E.; B.A., Phillips Exeter Acad., 1922; B.A., Harvard, 1926; m. Harriet Hastings, Mar. 14, 1945; children—John, Eve. Instnl. advt., sales depts. Gen. Motors Corp., 1926-29; advt., publicity dir. Internat. Merc. Marine Co., 1930-31; mng. editor Family Circle mag., 1932-35, editor, 1936-54; editor New Homes Guide and Home Modernizing, 1955-56, Today's Living, mag. of N.Y. Herald Tribune, 1956-61, The Am. Heritage New Illus. History of U.S., 1962-63; now pub. cons. Clubs: University, Dutch Treat, Overseas Press, Harvard (N.Y.C.). Home: Lower Church Hill Rd Washington Depot CT 06794

ENDLEMAN, ROBERT, educator, sociologist; b. Sudbury, Ont., Can., Oct. 2, 1923; s. Harry Max and Rose (Cherin) E.; came to U.S., 1946, naturalized, 1957; B.A., U. Toronto, 1946; M.A., U. Wis., 1947; Ph.D., Harvard, 1955; psychoanalytic tng., Nat. Psychol. Assn. Psychoanalysis; m. Moselle Galbraith, 1961 (div. 1964); 1 dau., Julie. Instr. social scis. U. Minn., 1949-51; asst. prof. sociology State U. N.Y., 1951-52; research sociologist U. Chgo., 1952-54; instr. to asst. prof. sociology U. Ill. at Chgo., 1953-57; asst. prof. sociology Hofstra Coll., 1957-58; asso. prof. social sci. State U. N.Y. at Oyster Bay, 1958-61; asso. prof. sociology Adelphi U., 1961-64, prof., 1964—, chmn. dept. sociology, 1963-69; vis. prof. sociology McGill U., 1970; pvt. practice psychotherapy, N.Y.C. Active Nassau County Health and Welfare Council, League Indsl. Democracy. Recipient Clement Staff award, Psychoanalytic Review, 1966. Mem. Internat., Am. sociol. assns., Eastern Sociol. Soc., Am. Anthropol. Assn., Soc. Study Social Problems, Soc. Psychol. Study Social Issues, Nat. Psychol. Assn. for Psychoanalysis. Co-author: Human Reactions to Disaster, 1954; author: Personality and Social Life, 1967; Culture and Personality Dynamics, 1971. Home: 150 W 82d St New York City NY 10024 Office: Adelphi Univ Garden City NY 11530

ENDRES, C. ELMORE, banker; b. Closter, N.J., Dec. 20, 1902; s. William C. and Lavina, (Van Sciver) E.; grad. Am. Inst. Banking, Columbia, N.Y.U.; m. Dorothy M. Van Wirt, Apr. 21, 1928; children-Mrs. Peter S. Pell, William Earl, Mrs. Robert H. Tolle. With Closter Nat. Bank (N.J.), 1927-63, pres., 1940-63; pres. Citizens Nat. Bank, Englewood, N.J., 1963, chmn. bd., 1964—. Pres. Closter Bd. Edn., 1949. Lion. Clubs: Englewood; White Beeches Golf and Country (Haworth). Home: 322 Chestnut St Haworth NJ 07641 Office: 1 Engle St Englewood NJ 07631

ENELL, JOHN WARREN, educator, assn. exec.; b. N.Y.C., June 24, 1919; s. William Howard and Cristabel (Baumann) E.; B.S., U. Pa., 1940, M.E., 1948; M. Adminstrv. Engring., N.Y.U., 1947, D. Engring. Sci., 1949; m. Anna Louise Lefferts, June 4, 1949; children—Margaret Ann, Janet Ellen, Kathryn Laurel, Mark William. Test engr., asst. project engr., sr. exptl. engr. Wright Aero. Corp. div. Curtiss-Wright Corp., Paterson, N.J., 1940-45; research asst. N.Y.U., 1946-47, instr., 1947-49, asst. prof., 1949-55, asso. prof., 1955-58, prof., 1958-59; mem. U.S. Mut. Security Adminstrn. mission to Italy, 1952-53; dir. information service and surveys Am. Mgmt. Assn., 1954-61, dir. research, 1961-66, v.p. for research, 1967—; dir. research Am. Found. Mgmt. Research, 1961-62, v.p., 1970—; mem. AID mission to Vietnam, 1972. Mem. Am. Soc. M.E., Am. Inst. Indsl. Engrs. (chmn. bd. govs. Met. N.J. chpt., nat. v.p. 1966-68, nat. pres. 1968-69), Acad. Mgmt., Am. Mgmt. Assn., Am. Soc. Quality Control, Am. Statis. Assn., Engrs. Council Profl. Devel. (bd. dirs. 1970—), Adminstrv. Mgmt. Soc., Inst. Mgmt. Scis., Sigma Xi, Alpha Pi Mu. Author: Are Your Findings Trustworthy?, 1950; (with others) Quality Control Handbook, 1951, Production Handbook, 1958; (with G.H. Haas) Setting Standards for Executive Performance, 1960. Editorial bd. Jour. Indsl. Engring. Home: 165 Lake Dr W Packanack Lake Wayne NJ 07470 Office: 135 W 50th St New York City NY 10020

ENELOW, ALLEN JAY, educator; b. Pitts., Jan. 15, 1922; s. Isadore M. and Rose (Kasdan) E.; A.B., W. Va., U., 1942; M.D., U. Louisville, 1944; m. Mary Cleveland, July 21, 1946 (div. Sept. 1965); children—David, James, Susan, Margaret, Patience, Abigail; m. 2d, Sheila Kearns, Oct. 1, 1966; stepchildren—Lauren, Lisa. Intern Michael Reese Hosp., Chgo., 1944-45; resident psychiatry Winter VA Hosp., Topeka, 1947-49; mem. staff Menninger Found. and Asso. Hosps., 1947-52; practice medicine specializing in psychiatry, Beverly Hills, Cal., 1952-58, Pacific Palisades, Cal., 1956-64; mem. faculty U. So. Cal. at Los Angeles, 1960-67; prof., chmn. dept. psychiatry Mich. State U. at East Lansing, 1967—. Cons. Nat. Inst. Mental Health, VA others. Served with M.C., AUS, 1945-47. Fellow Am. Psychiat. Assn., A.C.P.; mem. A.M.A. (chmn. sect. nervous and mental disease 1967-68). Author: Psychiatry in the Practice of Medicine, 1966. Contbr. numerous articles profl. jours. Home: 936 Southlawn St East Lansing MI 48823

ENEMARK, WILLIAM ANDREW, army officer; b. San Francisco, Aug. 23, 1913; s. Leon H. and Bertha (Fischer) E.; A.B., Stanford, 1935; grad. Command and Gen. Staff Coll., 1942, 48, Army War Coll., 1954, Nat. War Coll., 1959; m. Gertrude Day, Feb. 8, 1941; 1 son, Peter. Commd. 2d lt. U.S. Army, 1937, advanced through grades to maj. gen., 1965; various arty. assignments, U.S., ETO and Aleutian Islands, 1936-47; staff officer plans and operations div. Dept. Army, 1948-50; battalion comdr. 20th F.A. Bn., 1950-51; comdr. 35th F.A. Europe, 1951-52; chief staff 1st Inf. Div., Europe, 1952-53; comdt. Officer Candidate Sch., Ft. Sill, Okla., 1954-56; asst. chief staff, G-4, Arty. and Guided Missile Center, 1956-57; dep. chief U.S. Mil. Tng. Mission, Saudi Arabia, 1957-58; adviser Nat. Def. Coll., Burma, 1959; chief manpower and tng. tng. div. ODMA, OASD, 1960-61; dir. Western hemisphere region OASD, 1961-63; asst. div. comdr. 24th Inf. Div., Europe, 1963-65; chief staff Hdqrs. Central Army Group, Germany, 1965-66; sr. army mem. Weapons Systems Evaluation Group, Washington, 1966-67; comdr. 7th Inf. Div., Korea, 1967-68; insp. gen. U.S. Army, 1968—. Decorated Legion of Merit, Bronze Star with oak leaf cluster, Air medal, Purple Heart (U.S.); Order de la Couronne with palm, grand officer, Croix de Guerre with palm (Belgium), Order Nat. Security Merit (Korea). Mem. Phi Gamma Delta. Home: Quarters 2 Ft Lesley J McNair Washington DC 20024 Office: Office of Inspector General Dept Army Washington DC 20314

ENERSEN, BURNHAM, lawyer; b. Lamberton, Minn., Nov. 17, 1905; s. Albert H. And Ethel (Rice) E.; A.B., Carleton Coll., 1927; LL.B., Harvard, 1930; m. Nina H. Wallace, July 21, 1935; children—Richard W., Elizabeth. Admitted to Cal. bar, 1931; asso. McCutchen, Doyle, Brown & Enersen, San Francisco, 1930- 43, partner, 1943—. Dir. Cal. Pellet Mill Co., TI Corp., Pomfret Estates, Inc., Prentice Electronics Co. Chmn. Gov.'s Com. Water Lawyers, 1957; mem. Cal. Jud. Council, 1960-64; vice chmn. Cal. Constn. Revision Commn., 1964—. Pres. United Bay Area Crusade 1962; pres. United Crusades of Cal., 1969—. Fellow Am. Bar Found.; mem. Am. Judicature Soc., Am. Bar. Assn. (mem. ho. of dels. 1970—), State Bar Cal. (pres. 1960), Bar Assn. San Francisco (pres. 1955), Bar Assn. City N.Y., Am. Law Inst., Cal. C. of C. (dir. 1962—, v.p. 1966—). Clubs: Bohemian, Pacific- Union, Commercial (pres. 1966), Commonwealth Cal. (dir. 1965-67), San Francisco Golf (San Francisco); Pauma Valley Country. Home: 40 Arguello Blvd San Francisco CA 94118 Office: 601 California St San Francisco CA 94108

ENEY, HARRY VERNON, lawyer; b. Balt., Aug. 16, 1908; s. William I. and Minnie F. (Hush) E.; student McCoy Coll., Johns Hopkins, 1929-30; LL.B., U. Balt. 1929; LL.D., Goucher Coll., Towson, Md., 1968; m. Margaret F. Davis. Apr. 24, 1931; children—Joan Frances (Mrs. William F. Kuehn), Margaret Ann (Mrs. John E. Richmond). Admitted to Md. bar, 1929, since practiced in Balt.; partner firm Venable, Baetjer & Howard, 1951—; asst. atty. gen. Md., 1938-40. Dir. U.S. Fidelity & Guaranty Co., Central Savs. Bank, Merc.-Safe Deposit & Trust Co., Merc. Bankshares Corp. Mem. rules com. Md. Ct. Appeals, 1946-59; mem. Md. Tax Survey Commn., 1949; Md. del. Nat. Conf. Commrs. Uniform State Laws, 1947-50; pres. Constl. Conv. Md., 1967-68. Trustee Goucher Coll. Served with USNR, 1943-45. Fellow Am. Coll. Trial Lawyers, Am., Md. bar founds.; mem. Am. (ho. dels.), Md. (pres. 1963-64), Balt. City bar assns., Am. Law Inst. (mem. council 1967—), Am. Judicature Soc. (dir.), Jud. Conf. 4th Circuit, Order Coif, Sigma Delta Kappa. Home: Belfast Rd Sparks MD 21152 Office: Mercantile Bank & Trust Bldg Baltimore MD 21201

ENEY, WILLIAM JOSEPH, engr.; b. Baltimore, Jan. 27, 1906; s. William Irvin and Minnie F. (Hush) E.; B.E., Johns Hopkins, 1927; M.S., Lehigh U., Bethlehem, Pa., 1938; m. Florence Davis, Sept. 17, 1928; 1 dau., Florence Lois. Jr. engr. and designer on bldg. plans and constrn., Loyola Constn. Co. and F. W. Casselbaum, Balt., 1923-27; successively engring, inspector, engr. on surveys and constrn., bridge designer, B. & O. R.R., in Md., Pa., N.Y., etc., 1927-36; instr. Lehigh U., 1936-38, asst. prof., 1938- 39, asso. prof., 1939-44, Stuart prof. civil engring., 1945—, head dept. civil engring. and Fritz Engring. Lab., also dir. of curriculum in civil engineering, 1947-66; consultant Bethlehem Steel co., Tenn. Valley Authority, 1939-41; cons. David Taylor Model Basin. U.S. Navy, and in pvt. practice, 1941—. Recipient of the Hillman award in 1955. Registered profl. engr., Pa. Mem. Am. Concrete Inst., Am. Railway Engr. Assn., Am. Soc. C.E., Am. Soc. for Engring. Edn., also Sigma Xi. Tau Beta Pi. Author: (with Hessemer) Problems in Engineer Drawing, 1940: Structural Drafting and Detailing, 1941; also tech. papers on structural model analysis, structural research. Inventor of instruments for structural model analysis. Home: 62 Wall St Bethlehem PA 18018

ENFIELD, CLIFTON WILLIS, lawyer; b. Watertown, N.Y., Nov. 26, 1918; s. George Hyson and Anna Murel (Humerick) E.; B.S. in Textiles, N.C. State Coll., 1938; LL.B., U. Va., 1948; m. Mary Verone Sullivan, Feb. 14, 1948; children—Douglas George, Brian Michael. Sales rep. Textiles Distbrs., Inc., Thomasville, N.C., 1938-39; cloth prodn. mgr. E.M. Holt Plaid Mills div. Burlington Mills, Inc., N.C., 1939-40; admitted to Ore. bar, 1948, Md. bar, 1959; asst. atty. gen. State of Ore., 1948-56; asst. counsel Ore. Hwy. Commn., 1948-51, chief counsel, 1951-56; gen. counsel Bur. Pub. Rds., Dept. Commerce, 1956-61; minority counsel Com. Pub. Works of U.S. Ho. of Reps., Washington, 1961—. Served from 2d lt. to lt. col. inf. AUS, 1940-46. Mem. Fed., Am., Ore. bar assns., Am. Rd. Builders Assn., Nat. Acad. Sci., Am. Right of Way Assn., Delta Theta Phi, Sigma Tau Sigma, Order Coif. Presbyn. Contbr. articles hwy. and legal publs. Home: 1706 Tilton Dr Silver Spring MD 20902 Office: Rayburn House Office Bldg Washington DC 20515

ENG, BJARNE REIDAR, corp. exec.; b. Mpls., Feb. 13, 1914; s. Hans and Borghild (Sorensen) E.; B.B.A., U. Minn., 1935; J.D., De Paul U., 1947; m. Katherine E. Lehman, July 25, 1936; children—Janet (Mrs. Arthur Gollberg), Richard Alan, Julie Katherine (Mrs. Richard Wylie). With Fairbanks, Morse & Co., Chgo., 1936-61, controller, 1958-61, v.p., 1959-61; controller Control Data Corp., Mpls., 1961-69, v.p. accounting mgmt., 1969—; dir. Valley Nat. Bank, St. Paul. C.P.A., Ill.; admitted to Ill. bar, 1947. Mem. Ill. Bar Assn., Financial Execs. Inst., Am. Inst. C.P.A.'s. Presbyn. Home: 5701 Code Av Edina MN 55436 Office: 8100 34th Av S Minneapolis MN 55440

ENGAR, KEITH MAURICE, educator; b. Preston, Ida., Apr. 2, 1923; s. Charles J. and Alveretta (Staples) E.; B.A., U. Utah, 1947, M.A., 1948; Ph.D., U. Minn., 1951; m. Amy Kathryn Lyman, Nov. 23, 1946; children—Elizabeth, Richard Charles, Kristin, William Keith. Announcer, writer, producer KSL radio, 1939-42, KDYL radio, 1942-47 (both Salt Lake City); mgr. prodn. KDYL-TV, 1948; instr. speech U. Minn., 1948-51; mem. faculty U. Utah, Salt Lake City, 1951—, exec. dir. Pioneer Meml. Theatre, 1964—; chief ednl. broadcasting br. FCC, 1962; cons. Peace Corps, 1962-64; exec. dir. Promised Valley, outdoor drama, Salt Lake City, 1968—. Bd. dirs. Utah Inst. Fine Arts, Salt Lake City, Utah Symphony Orch. Served to 1st lt. USAAF, 1943-46. Decorated Air medal with oak leaf cluster; Fulbright Research grantee, Paris, France, 1956-57. Mem. Am. Ednl. Theater Assn. (bd. dirs., exec. com.), Univ. Resident Theater Assn. (chmn. exec. com.), Nat. Assn. Ednl. Broadcasters. Author plays: Montrose Crossing, 1954; All in Favor, 1968; Arthur and the Magic Sword, 1951. Home: 2231 Blaine Av Salt Lake City UT 84108

ENGBRETSON, WILLIAM EARL, educator; b. Milw., Oct. 9, 1926; s. Earl Wilfred and Frances Cecelia (Sears) E.; A.B., Western Mich. U., 1947; M.A., Mich. State U., 1950; Ph.D., Northwestern U., 1955; m. Catherine Ann Sampe, Aug. 23, 1947; children—Kristine Marie, Jan Earl, Gregg William. Tchr. social studies Portage Township High Sch., Portage Center, Mich., 1948; grad. asst. basic coll. Mich. State U., 1948-49; county welfare agt., juvenile ct. referee Ingham County, Mich., 1949-50; elementary sch. tchr., Glencoe, Ill., 1950-53; lectr. edn. Roosevelt U., Chgo., 1952-53, asso. prof., 1953-54; asst. prof., asso. prof. edn. Western Mich. U., Kalamazoo, 1954-57; vis. asso. prof. U. Fla., 1957; asso. sec. Am. Assn. Colls. Tchr. Edn., 1957-59; prof. edn., asst. to pres. Kan. State Tchrs. Coll., Emporia, 1959-60; prof. edn., dean Sch. Edn., Ind. State U., Terre Haute, 1960-66; prof. higher edn. U. Denver, 1966-68; prof. Temple U., Phila., 1968-69; prof. higher edn., pres. Governors State U., Park Forest South, Ill., 1969- ; cons. colls., univs., pub. schs., founds., govt. agys. Served with USNR, 1944-46. Fellow A.A.A.S.; mem. N.E.A. (life), Am. Edn. Research Assn., Am., Ill. assns. sch. adminstrs., Am. Assn. Higher Edn. (life), Ill. Edn. Assn., Am. Assn. Coll. Tchr. Edn. (pres. 1968-69), N.A.A.C.P., Urban League, Am. Civil Liberties Union, Am. Assn. U. Profs., World Future Soc., Phi Delta Kappa, Kappa Delta Pi. Contbr. profl. jours. Home: 101 Monee Rd Park Forest IL 60466

ENGDAHL, JAMES CAMERER, lawyer; b. Geneseo, Ill., Mar. 11, 1918; s. Victor E. and Edith (Young) E.; A.B., Stanford, 1940, J.D., 1943; m. Joyce R. Stringer, Aug. 3, 1947; children-Victor, James, David. Admitted to Cal. and Ariz. bars, 1946; practice in Phoenix, 1946—; partner firm Engdahl, Jerman, Butler & Estep, 1958—. Dir. Pacific Homes Corp. Mem. Phoenix Planning Commn., 1960-63, vice chmn. 1963; mem. Phoenix Streets Adv. Com., 1960—. Bd. dirs. First Methodist Found., Phoenix, 1954—, pres., 1965—. Trustee Sch. Theology, Claremont, Cal. Served with AUS, 1943-46. Mem. state bars Ariz., Cal., Am. Bar Assn. Home: 6135 N 38th St Paradise Valley AZ 85253 Office: 222 N Central Av Phoenix AZ 85004

ENGEBRETSEN, ED, business exec. Pres., Consol. Badger Coop. Office: 116 N Main St Shawano WI 54166*

ENGEBRETSON, OSCAR EDWIN, clergyman; b. Whalan, Minn., June 3, 1905; s. Halvor and Caroline (Hjelle) E.; student Luther Acad., 1920-23; B.A., Luther Coll., 1927; C.T., B.Th., Luther Sem., 1930; m. Irene Octavia Lembke, July 2, 1930; children—Conrad, Henrik, Mark. Ordained to ministry Evang. Luth. Ch., 1930; pastor Rolette, Overly, N.D., 1930-37, Walcott, N.D., 1937-41, Washington Prairie Luth. Ch. (one of Twelve Great Churches in Am. 1950), Decorah, Ia., 1941-52, Trinity Ch., Spring Grove, Minn., 1952-57, Faith Ch., Madison, Minn., 1960-70, Estherville (Ia.) Luth. Ch., 1970—; evangelist Evang. Ch., Mpls., 1957- 60; mem. commn. research and social action Am. Luth. Ch., 1959—, mem. dept. town and country ch., 1960-64; rural life commn. Evang. Luth. Ch., bd. parish edn., 1944-50; mem. bd. edn., 1950-54; councillor Nat. Luth. Council, 1956-67. Recipient certificate of service King Haakon, Norway, 1949; Distinguished Service award Luther Coll., 1967. Author: Chosen Witnesses, 1952; Faith and Service, 1958; Exile and Restoration, 1967. Contbr. to religious publs. Home: 908 12th St N Estherville IA 51334

ENGEL, ARTHUR BRIGHT, ednl. adminstr.; b. Grand Rapids, Mich., May 1, 1914; s. George and Helen (Bright) E.; B.S., U.S. Coast Guard Acad., 1938; M.S., Mass. Inst. Tech., 1945; m. Edna K. Janzen, Oct. 6, 1940; children—Douglas B., Bruce J., Elizabeth J. Commd. ensign USC., 1938, advanced through grades to rear adm., 1967, ret., 1970; chief machinery sect. naval engring. div. Coast Guard Hdqrs., 1947-51; design supt. Coast Guard Yard, 1953-57, comdg. officer, 1965-67; chief naval engring, 13th Coast Guard Dist., comdg. officer Coast Guard Cutter Klamath, 1959-61; head dept. applied sci. and engring. Coast Guard Acad., New London, Conn., 1961-65, supt., 1967-70; supt. U.S. Mcht. Marine Acad., Kings Point, N.Y., 1970—. Mem. Marine Hist. Assn., Nathan Hale Com. Conn., Am. Soc. Naval Engrs., Coast Guard Acad. Alumni Assn., Newcomen Soc. (dir.), U.S. Power Squadrons, Propeller Club U.S., Am. Soc. Engring. Educators. Address: Quarters A US Merchant Marine Acad Kings Point NY 11024

ENGEL, CARL HENRY, metal products co. exec.; b. Detroit, Mar. 31, 1924; s. Karl and Augusta Mildred (Sarns) E.; B.S. in Engring., U. Mich., 1947; M.B.A., Harvard, 1949; m. Helen Elaine Masson, July 13, 1946; children—Carolyn (Mrs. Richard W. Comfort, Jr.), Richard Masson, Margaret Jane. Indsl. engr. Harris-Intertype Co., Cleve., 1949-53, budget mgr., 1953-56; div. budget dir. W.R. Grace, Cambridge, Mass., 1956-59; asst. treas. Raymond Internat., Inc., N.Y.C., 1959-65; v.p. finance Hunter-Douglas Ltd., N.Y.C., 1965-67; v.p., treas., dir. Ranco, Inc., Columbus, O., 1967—; dir. Knowledge Communication Fund, Inc., Columbus. Served with USNR, 1943-46. Mem. Financial Execs. Inst. Presbyn. Office: Ranco Inc 601 W 5th Av Columbus OH 43201

ENGEL, CHARLES ROBERT, educator; b. Vienna, Austria, Jan. 28, 1922; s. Jean and Lucie (Fuchs) E.; B.A., U. Grenoble, 1941; M.Sc., Swiss Fed. Inst. Tech., Zurich, 1947, D.Sc., 1951; D.Sc., U. Paris, 1970; m. Edith H. Braillard, Aug. 6, 1951; children—Lucie Tatiana, Christiane Simonne, Francis Pierre, Marc Robert. Research fellow, asst. Swiss Fed. Inst. Tech., Zurich, 1948-51; asst. prof. med. research Collip Med. Research Lab., U. Western Ont., London, 1951-55, asso. prof. med. research, 1955-58, hon. spl. lectr. chemist, dept. chemistry, 1958—; prof. chemistry Laval U., Quebec, Que., 1958—; vis. prof. Inst. de Chimie des Substances Naturelles CNRS, Gif-sur-Yvette, France, 1966-67. Sec. Lieutenancy of Can., Equestrian Order of Holy Sepulcre of Jerusalem, 1964-70, lt., 1970—. Bd. dirs. Catholic Culture Center, London, Ont. Decorated comdr. Equestrian Order of Holy Sepulcre of Jerusalem, 1964, comdr. with star, 1970; medal Austrian Ministry of Edn. Fellow Chem. Inst. Can. (chmn. organic div. 1960-65), Chem. Soc. London; mem. Am. Chem. Soc., Swiss, French chem. socs., Canadian Biochem. Soc., Que. Assn. Profl. Chemists. Editorial bd. Steroids, 1964—; hon. editorial bd. Current Abstracts of Chemistry, 1971—, Index Chemicus, 1971—. Office: Laval U Quebec 10 Quebec Canada

ENGEL, ELWOOD PAUL, automobile co. exec.; b. Newark, Feb. 10, 1917; s. Paul and Christina (Freienschner) E.; grad. in indsl. design, Pratt Inst., 1939; children—Paul, Lloyd, Charles Edward, Ross John, Victoria. Stylist, Gen. Motors Corp., 1939-42; staff stylist George Walker Co., 1946-51; chief stylist Ford Motor Co., 1951-61; v.p., dir. styling Chrysler Corp., 1961- . Served with C.E., AUS, 1942-46. Mem. Indsl. Designers Inst. (award 1958, 61). Engring. Soc. Detroit. Office: Chrysler Corp 341 Massachusetts Av Detroit MI 48203

ENGEL, EVA JOHANNA, educator; b. Dortmund, Germany, Aug. 18, 1919; d. Stefan and Margarete (Litten) Engel; came to U.S., 1952; B.A. with honours, U. London (Eng.), 1941; M.A., Cambridge (Eng.) U., 1955; Ph.D., Cornell U., 1954; m. Albert E. Holland, June 12, 1970. Teaching fellow Cornell U., 1952-54; research fellow, asst. lectr. Girton Coll., Cambridge U., 1955; lectr. Keele (Eng.) U., 1960; vis. prof. Boston U., 1967-68; prof. German lit. Wellesley Coll., 1968—; vis. prof. Harvard, summer 1970. Mem. Am. Assn. Tchrs. German (pres. Mass. 1970-72), Philol. Soc., Modern Lang. Assn., Modern Humanities Research Assn., Internat. Germanisten Verein. Author: C.P. Moritz, 1954; Schulme sterlein-Wutz, 1961; German Narrative Prose, 1965. Home: 83 Leighton Av Wellesley MA 02181

ENGEL, GILSON COLBY, surgeon; b. Balt. Aug. 25, 1898; s. William Henry and Anna May (Metcalfe) E.; student Balt. City Coll., 1913-17; A.B., Johns Hopkins, 1922; M.D., Harvard, 1926; m. Doris Gherky, Dec. 22, 1923. Resident physician Lankenau Hosp., Phila., 1926-28; asst. surgeon Germantown Hosp., 1929-32; demonstrator in anatomy Jefferson Med. Coll., 1928-29, asso. prof. surgery, 1949-63; with Grad. Sch. Medicine, U. of Pa., 1929—, asst. instr. surgery, 1929-31, instr. 1931-35, asso., 1935-37, asst. prof. 1937-46, asso. prof., 1946, prof. clin. surgery, 1946-67, emeritus prof. clin. surgery, 1967—; surgeon Lankenau Hosp., 1931-42, chief surgeon, Service B, 1942- 64, sr. surg. cons., 1964—; chief surgeon, Service B, Children's Hosp. of Mary J. Drexel Home, 1942-53; dist. med. officer, Med. Service Assn. of Pa., 1946. Chmn. Middle Atlantic States Com. Emergency Med. Service for Atomic Def., 1948; mem. men's adv. com. Emergency Aid Pa; mem. gov's. adv. health bd., Commonwealth Pa., 1952-56. Trustee (hon.) Student Am. Med. Found., 1957—. Served with USN, 1917-19, Q.M., 1st class, World War I. Diplomate Am. Bd. of Surgery. Fellow A.C.S., Phila. Coll. Physicians, Phila. Acad. Surgery, A.M.A. (mem. house dels., 1950-68, vice chmn. council on postgrad. programs, chmn. 1965-67; mem. Pa. Med. Soc. (chmn. bd. trustees 1951-54, pres. 1948-49, speaker ho. of dels., 1958-62), Pa. Health Council (pres. 1949-53), Asso. Hosp. Service of Pa. (dir.), Phila. County Med. Soc. (dir. postgrad. inst. 1946-5O), Phila. Pathol. Soc., Phila. pediatrics Soc., Eastern Surg. Assn., World (chmn. for Pa. 1956- 58), Am. (gen. chmn. clinical session, 1957) med. assns. Kappa Alpha (So.), Omicron Delta Kappa, Nu Sigma Nu. Republican. Episcopalian. Clubs: Union League, Racquet (Phila.); Aesculapian (Boston). Author numerous articles on surgery. Creator of Engel gastric pouch following total gastrectomy; co-inventor Engel-May 2-plane direction finder for nailing fractures of the femur. Home: The Kenilworth Apts Alden Park Philadelphia PA 19144 Office: Lankenau Med Bldg Philadelphia PA 19151

ENGEL, IRVING M., lawyer, author, lectr.; b. Birmingham, Ala., Oct. 19, 1891; s. Michael P. and Sophie (Kronenberg) E.; LL.B. cum laude, Yale 1913; D.Litt., Dropsie Coll. Hebrew Learning, 1958; L.H.D., Hebrew Union Coll.-Jewish Inst. Religion, 1958; LL.D., L.I. U., 1964; m. Katharine I. Asher, Jan. 14, 1926 (dec.) 1 dau., Susan E. Levy. Admitted to Ala. bar, 1910, N.Y. bar, 1925; practiced Birmingham, 1913-24; N.Y.C., 1924- -, sr. partner Engel, Judge & Miller, Title ins. adv. com. Title Guarantee Co. 1948-71; mem. bd. govs. Real Estate Bd. N.Y., 1948- 51, arbitration bd. and legislation com.; lectr. on real estate and taxation Practicing Law Inst., Am. Bar Assn., N.Y. U. Mem. Nat. Com. on Segregation in Nation's Capital, 1949; pres. Ednl. Found. for Jewish Girls, 1945-50; now hon. chmn. bd. Co-chmn. gov. bd. consultative council Jewish Orgns., 1954-59; mem. Citizens Com. on Displaced Persons (chmn. policy com. 1947-50); Am. Com. for Israel's Tenth Anniversary Celebration (vice chmn. policy com. 1958); pres. Am. Jewish Com., 1954-59, now hon. pres.; mem. Pres.'s Com. on Govt. Contract Compliance, 1951-53. Candidate for Congress, Dem. and Liberal Parties, 17th dist., N.Y., 1950; alternate del. to Dem. Nat. Conv., 1952, alternat-at-large. 1956, mem. fgn. policy sub-com. nat. adv. council Nat. Dem. Com., 1959-61; chmn. exec. com. N.Y. Com. for Dem. Voters, 1959-60; chmn., 1961, chmn. adv. council, 1962-63; chmn. civil rights com. Dem. State Adv. Com.; chmn. polit. and planning com. N.Y. Citizens for Kennedy and Johnson, 1960. Mem. Mayors Com. on Judiciary, 1962-65; mem. state com. Pub. Employee Security, 1954. Del. German-Am. Confs. East-West Tensions, 1959, 61, 62, 67. Served to 1st lt. 319 F.A., U.S. Army, A.E.F., 1917-19. Decorated Grand Officer Order Micham Iftikhar (Tunisian Legion Honor), 1954; chevalier French Legion of Honor, 1958. First pres. Alabama Jr. C. of C., 1920-21. Mem. Council Fgn. Relations Mem. bd. dir. Nat. Com. against Discrimination in Housing, 1960—. Mem. Yale Law Sch. Assn. (v.p., dir.), Nat. Citizens Com. on Community Relations, Clubs: University, City (N.Y.C.), Yale. Author: Income Taxes and Real Estate. Mem. the Pres.' Spl. Mission, inauguration. Pres. Remon, Panama, 1952. Home: 24 Central Park S New York City NY 10019 also Miller Pl Long Island NY 10019 Office: 52 Vanderbilt Av New York City NY 10017

ENGEL, JOSEPH HENRY, mathematician, educator; b. N.Y.C., May 15, 1922; s. Arthur and Jennie (Gotthilf) E.; B.S. (Tremaine gift 1940), Coll. City N.Y., 1942; postgrad. Yale, 1946; M.A., U. Wis., 1947; Ph.D., 1949; m. Beverly Roseblum, May 2, 1943; children—Wendy, Eric, David. With Operations Evaluation Group, Center Naval Analyses, 1949-67, dir., 1962- 65; asst. chief scientist Center Naval Analyses, 1965- 67; dir. planning research and services Communications Satellite Corp., 1967-71; prof., head systems engring. dept. U. Ill., Chgo. Circle, 1971—. Chmn. NATO Adv. Panel on Operational Research, 1970—. Bd. dirs. Columbia Computer Corp.; trustee Cybernetics Research Inst. Served to 1st lt. USAAF, 1942-46. Decorated D.F.C. Fellow A.A.A.S.; mem. Washington Operations Research Council (trustee 1965-68), Am. Math. Soc., Mil. Operations Research Soc. (dir. 1966-68), Operations Research Soc. Am. (sec. 1964-66, v.p. 1967, Pres. 1968), Sigma Xi, Pi Mu Epsilon. Club: Cosmos (Washington). Contbr. articles on Lanchester's Law, math. models, mil. operations research. Asso. editor Operations Research 1963—. Home: 1213 Forest Av Highland Park IL 60035 Office: Systems Engineering Dept U Ill at Chicago Circle Chicago IL 60680

ENGEL, LEHMAN, composer, condr., author; b. Jackson, Miss., Sept. 14, 1910; s. Ellis and Juliette (Lehman) E.; student Cin. Conservatory, Cin. Coll. Music, Cin. U.; fellow Juilliard Grad. Sch., 1930, grad., 1934; pvt. student with Roger Sessions, 1935; Mus.D., Boguslawski Coll. Music, 1944 L.H.D., Millsaps Coll., 1971; Condr., Lewisohn Stadium, 1951, New Friends of Music, Town Hall, N.Y.C., 1952; mus. dir. State Fair Musicals, Dallas, 1949-52; condr., lyric theatre; Wonderful Town, The Consul, Call Me Mister, Shadow Play, Johnny Johnson, Fanny, Li'l Abner, Do Re Mi, others; composer incidental music for St. Joan, Anne of the Thousand Days, A Streetcar Named Desire, Yellow Jack, A Kiss for Cinderella, John Gabriel Borkman, The Trojan Women, Time of Your Life, others; composer, condr. incidental music The Birds, Macbeth, Hamlet, Murder in the Cathedral, others, many documentary and instructional films for U.S. Navy; composer concert works for various solo instruments, orch., voices, also Pierrot of the Minute (opera), 1928, The Soldier (opera), 1956; works for TV, films, radio, condr. What Makes Sammy Run, Bajour; mus. theatre cons. to Columbia Pictures; recordings RCA-Victor, Columbia, Decca, Brunswick, Atlantic; pres. Arrow Music Press, Inc.; dir. Mus. Theatre Workshop, Broadcast Music, Inc., N.Y.C., Los Angeles, Nashville and Toronto; exec. dir. mus. theatre devel. Columbia Pictures-Screen Gems; guest condr. St. Louis Municipal Opera, 1968, Porgy and Bess with Turkish State Opera, The Consul at Temple U. Festival, world premiere Scarlett, Tokyo, 197O; guest condr. Boston Symphony Orch.; lectr. Cin. Coll. Conservatory Music, Wagner Coll., S.I. Adv. bd. Sch. Performing Arts, Music Sch. Henry St. Settlement, N.Y.C. Served to lt. (s.g.) USNR, 1942-45. Recipient Bellamann award, 1964; Scroll from Consular Law Soc., 1968; Decoration from Republic Austria. Mem. League Composers (composers com.), Composers and Lyricists Guild Am. (v.p.). Author: Planning and Producing a Musical Show, 1956, rev. edit., 1966; This Bright Day (autobiography), 1956; The American Musical Theatre, 1967; Words with Music, 1971; Renaissance to Baroque, 7 vols. Home: 350 E 54th St New York City NY 10022

ENGEL, LEONARD, scientist, journalist; author Operation, 1958; Sea, 1968; New Genetics; editor (Darwyn) Voyage of the Beagle; regular contbr. to Sci. Am., Harpers, N.Y. Times.*

ENGEL, LEWIS LIBMAN, biochemist; b. N.Y.C., Sept. 2, 1909; s. Adolph and Esther (Libman) E.; B.S., Harvard, 1930; Ph.D., Columbia, 1936; LL.D., U. Glasgow, 1969; m. Margaret Fisher Knox, Nov. 21, 1938. Asst. biol. chemistry Columbia, 1931-33; guest investigator Royal Cancer Hosp., London, Eng., 1936-37; instr. biochemistry Mayo Found. Med. Edn. and Research, 1942-43; asso. prof. biol. chemistry Mass. Gen. Hosp. and Harvard, 1958-66, Am. Cancer Soc. prof. biol. chemistry, 1966—; acting chmn. bd. tutors biochem. sci. Harvard, 1963-65; Macfarlane prof. Glasgow (Scotland) U., 1967-68; Fachhoerer Fed. Poly. Inst., Zurich, Switzerland, 1935-36. Bd. dirs. Mass. div. Am. Cancer Soc., 1968—. Served to capt. San. Corps, AUS, 1943-46. Recipient Bronze medal Am. Cancer Soc., 1967. Mem. Am. Soc. Biol. Chemists, Am. Acad. Arts and Scis., Endocrine Soc. (Eli Lilly award 1970, past v.p.). Editor: (with C.A. Villee) Mechanism of Action of Steroid Hormones, 1961; Physical Properties of Steroid Hormones, 1963. Mem. editorial bd. Endocrinology, 1957-65, Jour. Biol. Chemistry, 1959- 64, 65—. Home: 2 Hawthorne Pl Boston MA 02114 Office: Huntington Labs Mass General Hosp Boston MA 02114

ENGEL, LOUIS HENRY, Jr., writer, ret. broker; b. Jacksonville, Ill., Nov. 27, 1909; s. Louis H. and Maud Letitia (Salyers) E.; Ph.B., U. Chgo., 1930; m. Viola De Berrienne, July 29, 1932 (div.); m. 2d, Mary Montgomery, June 19, 1943 (div.); children—James Montgomery, Thomas Edward, Jonathan Clark; m. 3d, Nina Phillips Washburn, Aug. 8, 1954. Staff, U. Chgo. Press, 1930-32; staff Advt. and Selling Mag., 1932, mng. editor, 1933- 34; news editor Business Week, 1934-35, marketing editor, 1935-36, mng. editor, 1937-46; advt. mgr. Merrill Lynch, Pierce, Fenner & Smith, Inc., N.Y.C., 1946-69, v.p., 1954-69, ret.; writer advertisement included in Watkins' 100 Greatest Advertisements. Trustee, Village of Ossining, N.Y., 1970—. Mem. Phi Beta Kappa. Author: How to Buy Stocks, 1953, 5th edit., 1971. Home: Revolutionary Rd Scarborough NY 10510

ENGEL, RUBEN WILLIAM, educator; b. Shawano, Wis., July 10, 1912; s. Earnest E. and Emma (Erdman) E.; Ph.B., U. Wis., 1937, Ph.D., 1939; m. Frances Holiday, June 27, 1939; children—Nancy (now Mrs. Matthew J. Barlow), Bonnie, (now Mrs. James R. Hupton), and William Frederick. Member Faculty Auburn U., 1939- 43, 46-52, prof. animal nutrition, 1946-52; prof. animal nutrition, head dept. biochemistry and nutrition Va. Poly, Inst., 1952-66, asso. dean research Coll. Agriculture, 1966—. Del. Internat. Union Nutritional Sci., 1960, alternate del., 1963; mem. U.S. nat. com. nutrition Nat. Acad. Scis.-NRC, 1957-62, 64-65, exec. com. food and nutrition bd., 1960—; cons. nutrition NIH, Dept. Def.; mem. expert com. calcium FAO-WHO, 1961. Served as officer AUS, 1943-46; lt. col. Res. Mem. Am. Inst. Nutrition (sec. 1954-57, gov. bd. 1954-57, councilor 1960-63, pres. 1964-65, mem. editorial bd. jour, 1952-54, 58-60), A.A.A.S., Am. Chem. Soc., Sigma Xi (pres. Va. Poly. Inst. chpt. 1960-61) Phi Sigma, Phi Lambda Upsilon. Home: 108 Southgate Dr Blacksburg, VA 24060.

ENGEL, SAMUEL GAMLIEL, motion picture producer; b. Woodridge, N.Y., Dec. 29, 1904; s. Morris Hyman and Mary (Berman) E.; Ph.G., Union U., 1924; m. Ruth Franklin, Dec. 4, 1936; children—Charles Franklin, Mark Ethridge. Former 2d asst. dir., then 1st asst. dir. Warner Bros.; dir. Imperator Prodns., Inc.; pictures include My Darling Clementine, Come to the Stable, Jackpot, Rawhide, Follow the Sun, The Frogman, Belles on Their Toes, A Man Called Peter, Daddy Long Legs, Good Morning Miss Dove, Boy on a Dolphin, Bernardine, The Story of Ruth, The Lion, My Darling Clementine, Sitting Pretty, Mr. Belvedere Goes to College, Come to the Stable, The Street with No Name. Vice chmn. bd. Brandeis Inst.; mem. pres.'s council Loyola U., Los Angeles, Cal. Served as lt. USNR, 1942-45; now comdr. Res. Mem. Screen Producers Guild (pres.), Acad. Arts and Scis. (v.p.), Screen Writers Guild, Rho Pi Phi. Mason. Office: 20th Century-Fox Beverly Hills CA 90213

ENGEL, WILLIAM KING, neurologist; b. St. Louis, Nov. 19, 1930; s. William Ernst and Opal (King) E.; B.A., Johns Hopkins, 1951; M.D., C.M., McGill U., 1955; m. Jane Wagner, Dec. 30, 1954; children—W. Keith, Peter J., Bradford C. Intern U. Mich. Hosp., 1955-56; clin. asso. Nat. Inst. Neurol. Diseases and Blindness, 1956-59; clin. clk. Nat. Hosp., London, 1959-60; with Nat. Inst. Neurol. Diseases and Blindness, 1960—, chief med. neurology br., 1963—. Mem. med. bd. NIH, 1968-69; asso. examiner Am. Bd. Neurology and Psychiatry. Pres. Locust Hill Citizens Assn., Bethesda, Md., 1967-68; Longhouse chief YMCA Indian Guides, 1965-66. Recipient Meritorious Service medal USPHS, 1971. Diplomate Am. Bd. Neurology and Psychiatry. Fellow Am. Acad. Neurology (S. Weir Mitchell award 1962); mem. A.M.A., Histochem. Soc., Am. Soc. Cell Biology, Am. Assn. Neuropathologists, World Commn. Neuromuscular Disease, Am. Neurol. Assn.; hon. mem. Societe Francaise de Neurologie. Author numerous papers in field. Home: 4702 Broad Brook Dr Bethesda MD 20014 Office: Nat Insts Health Bethesda MD 20014

ENGELBERG, EDWARD, educator; b. Germany, Jan. 21, 1929; s. Jakob and Paula (Weber) E.; came to U.S., 1939, naturalized, 1944; A.B., Bklyn. Coll., 1951; M.A., U. Ore., 1952; Ph.D., U. Wis., 1957; m. Elaine A. Rosen, July 27, 1950; children—Stephen Paul, Michael Joseph, Elizabeth Joyce. From instr. to asso. prof. English, U. Mich., 1957-65; mem. faculty Brandeis U., 1965- -, prof. comparative and English lit., chmn. comparative lit. program, 1965—, chmn. dept. Romance langs. and comparative lit., chmn. joint program lit. studies, 1971—; cons. in field, 1951. Recipient Am. Civilization award Bklyn. Coll., 1951; Fulbright scholar Cambridge (Eng.) U., 1955-56. Mem. Am. Assn. U. Profs., Modern Lang. Assn., Am. Comparative Lit. Assn., Phi Beta Kappa. Author: The Vast Design; Patterns in W.B. Yeats's Aesthetic, 1964. Editor: The Symbolist Poem, The Development of the English Tradition, 1967. Home: 58 Turning Mill Rd Lexington MA 02173 Office: Brandeis Univ Waltham MA 02154

ENGELBERT, ARTHUR FERDINAND, univ. dean; b. St. Johnsburg, N.Y., Dec. 18, 1903; s. Ferdinand and Anna (Fetzer) E.; student Concordia Coll., 1922-24, Concordia Theol. Sem., 1924-27; M.A., U. Pitts., 1929, Ph.D., 1935; postgrad. Duke, 1941, U. Chgo., 1949; m. Ruth B. Bunt, Aug. 14, 1930; 1 dau., Carol (Mrs. Ervin S. Palmer). Asst. pastorate Immanuel Lutheran Ch., Braddock, Pa., 1927- 31; grad. asst. U. Pitts, 1929-30, instr. modern langs. 1930-31; prof., head dept. modern langs. Mt. Union Coll., Alliance O., 1931-59; dean Coll. Liberal Arts, Washburn U., Topeka, 1959—, acting pres., 1961, also v.p. for acad. affairs. Coordinator liberal arts com. N. Central Assn. Colls. and Secondary Schs., 1951-56. U.S. rep. of Danish Internat. Student Com. Chmn. Alliance chpt., A.R.C., 1956-58; mem. planning council for Shawnee County Health Facilities Commn. Mem Am. Assn. Acad. Deans, Acad. Deans Kan. Colls. and Univs. (pres. 1968-69), Tau Delta Pi, Psi Kappa Omega. Rotarian. Clubs: Sagamore, Fortnightly. Contbr. articles to edn. jours. Editorial bd. Soc. for Acad. Achievement. Home: 1166 Collins St Topeka KS 66604

ENGELBRECHT, ROBERT MARTIN, architect; b. Jefferson City, Mo., Aug. 16, 1923; s. Otto A. and Jessella P. (Gibler) E.; student Central Mo. State Coll., 1941-42, U. Notre Dame, 1942-44; B.Arch., Cornell U., 1948; postgrad. Ill. Inst. Tech., 1949; m. Vivian Jeanette Foltz, Aug. 16, 1947; children—Martin Steward, George Marshal. Apprentice, Holabird-Root, architects, Chgo., 1948-50; asso. William B. Tabler Architect, N.Y.C., 1950-55; prin. Robert Martin Engelbrecht & Assos., architects and planners, Princeton, N.J., 1955—; dir. Bronzewood Corp., Vacation Plans & Properties Unlimited. Chmn. various confs. Nat. Acad. Sci.-Bldg. Research Inst.; dir. bldg. research adv. bd. Bldg. Research Inst.-Nat. Acad. Sci., 1969—. Pres. Rocky Hill (N.J.) Sch. Bd., 1956-60; mem. Zoning Bd. Adjustment, Rocky Hill, 1960-65, Environmental Bd., Princeton, 1967—. Exec. dir. Basic Materials Research Program, 1958-62; bd. dirs. Bldg. Research Inst., 1966-69. Served with USMCR, 1942-45. Mem. A.I.A., Nat. Council Archtl. Registration Bds., Nat. Assn. Bldg. Mfrs. Cons., archtl. editor Living for Young Homemakers Mag., 1955-62; This Week Mag., 1962-64; New Homes Guide Mag., 1964-68. Important works include Century 21 World's Fair Modular Research House, 1962, U.S. Pavilion: Sydney Australia's World Trade Fair, 1963; designs exhbt. museums. Home: 145 Mansgrove Rd Princeton NJ 08540 Office: 925 Highway One at College Rd Princeton NJ 08540

ENGELDINGER, HARVEY YOUNG, publishing co. exec.; b. Alburnett, Ia., May 10, 1912; s. E.J. and Lusena (Huntley) E.; B.S. in Indsl. Sci., Ia. State U., 1934; m. Marjorie Davis, Sept. 3, 1937; children—Harvey Young, Mary. With Onthank Co., Des Moines, 1947-52; with Meredith Corp., Des Moines, 1952—, treas., 1960—, v.p. finance, 1966—, dir., 196—; dir., mem. exec. com. Apache Corp., Mpls.; dir. West Des Moines State Bank. Asst. sec., treas. Edwin T. Meredith Found. Mem. Kappa Sigma. Presbyn. Mason (Shriner). Home: 2830 Gilmore St Des Moines, IA 50312. Office: 1716 Locust St Des Moines IA 50303

ENGELER, ERWIN, educator; b. Schaffhausen, Switzerland, Feb. 13, 1930; s. Erwin and Frieda (Brauchli) E.; diploma Swiss Fed. Inst. Tech., Zurich, 1955, Dr. Sc. math., 1958, Privatdozent, 1964; m. Margaret Knecht, Apr. 14, 1957; children—Christopher, Suzanne. Faculty, U. Minn., Mpls., 1958—, now prof. math. Vis. asst. prof. U. Cal., Berkeley, 1962-63; research mathematician IBM Research Lab., Zurich, 1963-64; docent Swiss Fed. Inst. Tech., 1968-69, 71. Mem. Am. Math. Soc., Assn. for Symbolic Logic, Assn. for Computing Machinery. Author: Formal Languages and Automata, 1968. Editor: Symposium on the Semantics of Algor, Languages, 1971. Home: 1563 E River Terrace Minneapolis MN 55414

ENGELHARDT, ALLEN HILTY, mining engr.; b. Sioux Falls, S.D., Feb. 15, 1903; s. Frederick Conrad and Ida Mabel (Hilty) E.; student Ala. Poly. Inst., 1920-22; B.S., Montana Sch. Mines, Butte, Montana, 1931, E.M., 1954; m. Beryl Moore, June 21, 1934; 1 son, Terry Moore. With United Verde Copper Corp., Jerome, Ariz., 1925-27, Anaconda Copper Co., Butte, Mont., 1927- 31; various positions S.A. Devel. Co., Ecuador, 1931-38, gen. supt., resident mgr., v.p., 1938-50; cons. engr. Cotopaxi Exploration Co., 1940-49; v.p., resident mgr. Calera Exploration Co., 1945-50; asst. mgr. operations Cerro Corp., 1950-51, mgr. operations 1951-57, v.p. 1953- 57, v.p. mining operations, 1957-68. Decorated rank of Comendador (Ecuador), Mem. Mining and Metall. Soc. Am., Am. Inst. Mining Metall. and Petroleum Engrs., Mining Club, Sigma Rho, Kappa Sigma. Mason. Clubs: Canadian (N.Y.C.); Greenwich Country. Home: Port Royal Plantation Hilton Head Island SC 29928 Retired

ENGELHARDT, FRED EDWARD, diversified mfg. co. exec.; b. Naugatuck, Conn., Apr. 15, 1932; s. George J. and Dorothea (Fitzpatrick) E.; A.B., Yale U., 1953; M.B.A., N.Y. U., 1959; m. Janet Ruth de Faria, May 19, 1962. Audit mgr. Arthur Andersen & Co., N.Y.C., 1955-64; asst. treas. Callahan Mining Corp., N.Y.C., 1964-67; v.p., treas. Athlone Industries, Inc., Parsippany, N.J., 1967—. Served with AUS, 1953-55. Mem. N.Y. State Soc. C.P.A.'s, Am. Inst. C.P.A.'s. Home: 170 Park Row New York City NY 10038 Office: 200 Webro Rd Parsippany NJ 07054

ENGELHARDT, LEROY A., paper co. exec.; b. Saginaw, Mich., Mar. 15, 1924; s. Herman J. and Alma (Engelhard) E.; B.B.A., U. Mich., 1949, M.B.A., 1950; m. Arlene L. Papineau, July 12, 1947; children—Richard C., Kay C., Douglas R. Plant, div. or subsidiary controller Chrysler Corp., 1950-60; mgmt. controls cons. Diehl K.G., Nuremberg, Germany, 1960-63; sec. Genesee Brewing Co., Rochester, N.Y., 1963-67; controller Consol. Papers, Inc., Wisconsin Rapids, Wis., 1967—. Served with AUS, 1943-46. Mem. Nat. Assn. Accountants. Home: 444 2 Mile Av Wisconsin Rapids WI 54494 Office: PO Box 50 Wisconsin Rapids WI 54494

ENGELHARDT, NICKOLAUS LOUIS, Jr., ednl. cons.; b. Auburn, N.Y., July 8, 1907; s. Nickolaus Louis and Bessie (Gardner) E.; B.S., Yale, 1929; A.M., Columbia, 1938, Ph.D., 1939; m. Florida Beatrice Kramer, Nov. 30, 1933; children—David, John (dec.). Asso. devel. air transp. in Pitts. Aviation Industries Corp. and as asst. to v.p. Transcontinental and Western Air, Inc., 1929-36; mem. staff Harrison & Fouilhoux, architects, N.Y.C., 1936-38; research asso. div. field studies Tchrs. Coll., Columbia, 1938- 40; prof. edn. U. Fla., 1939-40; dir. research Newark Pub. Sch. System, 1940-43, vis. lectr. U. Wis., 1941; ednl. cons. CAA, 1942; dir. Air-Age edn. research Am. Airlines, N.Y.C., 1943-47; prof. N.Y. U., summer 1949; cons. to bds. edn. and architects in planning sch. bldgs. and orgn. sch. systems as mem. firm Engelhardt & Engelhardt, Inc., N.Y.C., 1947—, now pres., chmn. bd. Cons. to Fla. Work Conf. on Sch. Problems and So. States Work Conf., 1941. Mem. Newark (N.J.) Def. Council, 1942; mem. bd. edn. Edgemont Dist., Scarsdale, 1948-51; cons. N.Y. State Citizens Com. for Pub. Schs.; dir. Denver Congress on Air Edn., 1945, World Congress of Air Edn., 1946. Recipient Frank B. Brewer trophy for outstanding contbn. aviation edn. by Nat. Aeros. Assn., 1947. Fellow A.A.A.S.; mem. Am. Assn. Sch. Adminstrs., N.E.A., Am. Ednl. Research Assn., Phi Delta Kappa, Theta Xi. Author: School Building Costs, 1939; Planning Community Schools (with N.L. Engelhardt and S. Leggett), 1940; Social Trends and the Schools, 1941; Education for the Air Age, 1942; New Frontiers of Our Global World, 1942; (with N.L. Engelhardt and S. Leggett) Planning Secondary School Buildings, 1950, Planning Elementary School Buildings, 1952; School Building and Planning Handbook, 1956; Complete Guide for Planning New Schools, 1970. Contbr. to profl. periodicals. Address: Purdy Station Westchester County NY 10461

ENGELHARDT, THOMAS ALEXANDER, editorial cartoonist; b. St. Louis, Dec. 29, 1930; s. Alexander Frederick and Gertrude Dolores (Derby) E.; student Denver U., 1950-51, Ruskin Sch. Fine Arts, Oxford (Eng.) U., 1954-56, Sch. Visual Arts, N.Y.C., 1957; m. Katherine Agnes McCue, June 25, 1960; children—Marybeth, Carol Marie, Christine Leigh, Mark Thomas. Free-lance cartoonist, comml. artist, N.Y.C., 1957-60, Cleve., 1961-62; asst. editorial cartoonist Newspaper Enterprise Assn., Cleve., 1960-61; editorial cartoonist St. Louis Post- Dispatch, 1962—. Served with USAF, 1951-53. Office: 1133 Franklin Av St Louis MO 63101

ENGELHARDT, WILLIAM R., lawyer; b. Chgo., June 24, 1909; s. William M. and Louise (Steinke) E.; Ph.B., U. Chgo., 1930, J.D., 1932; m. Doris R. Rickard, Jan. 18, 1936; children—Robert Rickard, Margo Louise. Admitted to Ill. bar, 1932, since practiced in Chgo.; partner law firm Norman & Billick, and predecessors, 1938—. Dir. Cook County (Ill.) Sch. Dist. 17, 1942-45; treas. Tri-County Schs. Bd. of Ill. Assn. Sch. Bds., 1943-45; pres. Inverness (Ill.) Assn., 1953. Trustee Village Inverness, 1962-65, mayor, 1965-69. Mem. Am., Ill., Chgo. bar assns., Phi Beta Kappa, Order of Coif, Phi Alpha Delta (pres. Marshall chpt. 1931-32). Clubs: University, Executives, Legal (Chgo.); Inverness Golf (bd. dirs. 1947-55). Home: 416 N Inverway Rd Inverness PO Palatine IL 60067 Office: 69 W Washington St Chicago IL 60602

ENGELKING, DELMER FRANK, ednl. adminstr.; b. Albion, Ida., Nov. 14, 1911; s. Frank E. and Clara (Satchwell) E.; B.S. in Edn., U. Ida., 1941, M.S., 1951; m. Thelma Bott, Nov. 29, 1939; children—Sandra Jo (Mrs. David Prichard), Jeri Lee. Tchr., Ida. pub. schs., 1933-39; supt. schs. Ida., 1940-50, supt. pub. instru., 1958—; sch. supt. Idaho County, 1950-54; supt. schs., Blackfoot, Ida., 1954-58. Mem. C. of C., Phi Delta Kappa. Democrat. Methodist. Mason (Shriner), Lion, Rotarian. Home: 3807 Sycamore D Boise ID 83703 Office: Statehouse, Boise, ID 83702.

ENGELMAN, HUGO OTTO, educator; b. Vienna, Austria, Sept. 11, 1917; s. Otto Hugo and Karolina (Skrceny) E.; came to U.S., 1939, naturalized, 1944; student U. Vienna Law Sch., 1935-38; B.A. in Polit. Sci., U. Wis., 1941, Ph.D. in Sociology, 1953; m. Ruth Marie Gould, Oct. 4, 1941; 1 son, John Hugh. Instr. social sci. Mich. State U., 1945-48; from instr. to prof. sociology U. Wis.-Milw., 1948-69, chmn. dept., 1964-67; prof. sociology No. Ill. U., 1969—; founder, 1965, since editor Clearinghouse for Sociol. Lit. Fellow Am. Sociol. Assn., Am. Anthrop. Assn.; mem. A.A.A.S., Wis. Sociol. Assn. (pres. 1962-63). Author: Essays in Social Theory and Social Organization, 1966; Theoretical Sociology: Its Bases and Place in Modern Science, 1966; Sociology: A Guided Study Text, 1969; also articles book revs. Asso. editor Sociol. Quar., 1963-66; editor Wis. Sociologist, 1960-69. Home: 421 Hillcrest Dr DeKalb IL 60115

ENGELMAN, ROBERT S., merchandising exec.; b. Rahway, N.J., Sept. 25, 1912; s. Bernard and Lena (Pachman) E.; A.B., Dartmouth, 1934; m. Mary Straus, Jan. 6, 1938; children—Tilden S., Robert S., John S. and Stephen B. (twins), Mary Margaret. Re-buyer Spiegel, Inc., 1934-37, buyer, 1937-40, div. mdse. mgr., 1940-51, v.p., 1949-54, gen. mdse. mgr., 1951-54, pres., gen. mgr., 1954-60, exec. v.p., 1960-69, pres., 1970—, dir., 1951—; partner K. S. Engelman Assos., Bus. Consultant, 1971—; pres. K. S. Engelman Investment Co., 1971—. Past pres., bd. dirs. Chgo. A.D.L.; bd. dirs. Community Fund, Chgo.; chmn. commerce div. Crusade of Mercy, Chgo., 1955, 56, 63, 70, 71; treas., bd. dirs. Jewish Fedn. Met. Chgo. Clubs: Fox River, Valley Hunt, Lake Shore Country, Tavern. Home: 61 Hazel St Highland Park IL 60035 Office: 1061 W 35th St Chicago IL 60609

ENGELMANN, LOTHAR KLAUS, coll. dean; b. Rudolstadt, Germany, Jan. 30, 1926; s. Karl and Frida (Zange) E.; Dr. phil. nat., J.W. Goethe U., Frankfurt, Germany, 1955; m. Gudrun Drewello, Jan. 10, 1948; children—Bettina, Randolph.. Cambe to U.S., 1957, naturalized, 1969. Mgr. photo- paper dept. Adox Fotowerke, Frankfurt, 1952-57; sr. photog. chemist Polaroid Corp., Cambridge, Mass., 1959-60; supr. silver halide research 3M Co., St. Paul, 1962-65, mgr. prodn. tech. dept., Rochester, N.Y., 1966-69; dean Coll. Graphic Arts and Photography, prof. photog. sci. Rochester Inst. Tech., 1969—. Mem. Am. Chem. Soc., Soc. Photog. Scientists and Engrs., Royal Photog. Soc. G.B., Ges. Deutscher Chemiker, Tech. Assn. Graphic Arts, Profl. Photographers Am., Phi Kappa Phi. Patentee tanning chemistry and photo sci. Home: 128 Thatcher Rd Rochester NY 14617

ENGELMORE, IRWIN B., ret. advt. exec.; b. N.Y.C., Mar. 22, 1910; s. Abraham Paul and Minnie (Esserman) E.; student Cooper Union, 1927-28, Grant Central Sch. Art, 1929-30, U. So. Cal., 1936-37, N.Y.U., 1944-45; m. Clair Ornstein, June 15, 1933; children—Robert Searl, Anthony Richard. Advt. mgr. Broadway Dept. Stores, Los Angeles, 1935-41; exec. v.p. Sterling Advt. Agy., N.Y.C., 1941-54; chmn. bd. Engelmore Advt. Inc., and prececessor, N.Y.C., 1954—. Active fund raising advt. div. B'nai B'rith. Served to 1st lt. Civil Air Patrol, 1942-45. Mem. N.Y.C. Advt. Club, Aircraft Owners and Pilots Assn., Nat. Aero. Club. Republican. Clubs: Nat. Republican (N.Y.C.); Shinnecock (L.I., N.Y.) Anglers. Home: 35 Library Av Westhampton Beach NY 11978 also 1501 S Ocean Dr Hollywood FL 33020

ENGELS, NORBERT ANTHONY, writer, educator; b. Green Bay, Wis., Sept. 4, 1903; s. William Peter and Euphrasia (Dave) E.; B.Mus., U. Notre Dame, 1926, A.M., 1928; m. Eleanore Lucille Perry, June 19, 1929 (dec. 1966); children—John, David, Julie Anne; m. 2d, Laone Gagnon Brown, 1968. Profl. musician, 1917-29, appearing with concert bands, symphonies, dance ensembles, played trans-Atlantic liners, toured Europe, 1925-26; instr. English, U. Notre Dame, 1927-31, asso. prof., 1931-34, asst. prof., 1934- 39, prof., 1939-69, prof. emeritus, 1969—. Served in USNR, 1919. Mem. Am. Assn. U. Profs., Internat. Mark Twain Lit. Soc. (hon. life). Roman Catholic. Author: Thou Art My Strength (poems), 1947; Man Around the House (essays and drawings), 1949; (with John Engels) Writing Techniques, 1962, Experience and Imagination, 1965. Contbg. editor Sci. and Mechanics Mag., 1951-60. Contbr. poems, essays and stories to periodicals and anthologies. Home: Half Moon Lake Pound WI 54161

ENGELS, ROBERT HENRY, utility exec.; b. Galena, Ill., Apr. 2, 1910; s. John H. and Elizabeth (O'Holleran) E.; ed. pub. schs., Galena; m. Marjorie Mailand, Feb. 26, 1938; children—Jane Engels (Mrs. Paul J. Tschida), Peter J., Stephen E., Robert M. With No. States Power Co., Mpls., 1926—, v.p., 1957-63, sr. v.p., 1963-64, exec. v.p., 1964-68, pres., 1968—, chmn. bd., chief exec. officer, 1972—, also dir.; dir. No. States Power Co. Wis., No. States Power Co. Minn., Northwestern Nat. Bank Mpls. Mem. indsl. adv. com. to Def. Electric Power Adminstrn. Chmn., 1st Sioux Empire Farm Show, Sioux Falls, S.D., 1953; mem. lay adv. bd. Cath. Welfare Service Mpls. Trustee Coll. of St. Benedict, Dunwoody Indsl. Inst.; bd. govs. St. Mary's Hosp.; bd. dirs. Marian Med. Research Found., North Star Research and Devel. Inst., Greater Mpls. Met. Housing Corp. Mem. Nat. Assn. Electric Cos. (dir.), Minn. Assn. Commerce and Industry (dir.), N. Central Electric Assn. (past pres.) Edison Electric Inst. (mem. rural electrification com.). K.C. Clubs: Minneapolis, Minneapolis Athletic, Minikahda, Sierra (Mpls.); Home: 1921 Humboldt Av S Minneapolis MN 55403 Office: 414 Nicollet Mall Minneapolis MN 55401

ENGEN, TRYGG, educator; b. Oslo, Norway, Feb. 18, 1926; s. Johan and Agnes (Rognsaa) E.; came to U.S., 1948, naturalized, 1958; B.A., Central Mich. Coll., 1950; M.A., U. Detroit, 1952; Ph.D., U. Neb., 1954; D.Sc., Central Mich. U., 1965; m. Elizabeth Ann Barclay, June 16, 1951; children—Anders Johan, Ivar Holm. Mem. faculty Brown U., Providence, 1954—, prof. psychology, 1965—; cons. food scientists and perfumers, 1956—. Served with Royal Norwegian Air Force, 1946-47. NATO fellow U. Stockholm, 1961-62; Spl. fellow USPHS, 1968-69. Mem. Psychonomic Soc., Eastern Psychol. Assn., A.A.A.S. Research on application psychophys. methods to taste and odor. Home: 297 Doyle Av Providence RI 02906

ENGER, WALTER MELVIN, navy officer; b. Urbana, Ill., May 11, 1914; s. Melvin Lorenius and Mary (Crawford) E.; B.S. in Civil Engring., U. Ill., 1935; m. Charlotte Hope Tuttle, Dec. 25, 1935; children—Susan Hope (Mrs. William A. Riley), Thomas Arthur. Jr. engr., asst. engr. Bur. Reclamation, Denver, Parker Dam, also Shasta Dam, Cal., 1935-41; commd. lt. (j.g.), Civil Engrs. Corps, U.S. Navy, 1941, advanced through grades to rear adm., 1965; officer charge constrn. civil works contracts on West Coast, 1941-44; exec. officer 59th and 72d Naval Constrn. Bn., Guam and Japan, 1944-45; officer charge 72d and 31st Naval Constrn. Bn., Japan, 1945-46; dep. dist. pub. works officer 8th Naval Dist., New Orleans, 1946-48; instr. marine engring. U.S. Naval Acad., 1948-51; pub. works officer Marine Corps Base, Camp Pendleton and Twenty-nine Palms, Cal., 1951-53; detail officer Civil Engr. Corps, Bur. Naval Personnel, 1953-56; dep. chief staff Naval Constrn. Forces Pacific, Pearl Harbor, 1956-59; pub. works officer Naval Air Sta., Point Mugu, Cal., 1959-61; asst. chief mil. readiness Bur. Yards and Docks, 1961-64; dir. Chesapeake Div. Bur. Yards and Docks, 1964-65; vice comdr. Naval Facilities Engring. Command, Washington, 1965- 69; comdr. Naval Facilities Engring. Command, chief of civil engrs. of Navy, 1969—. Decorated Navy Commendation medal, Legion of Merit. Registered profl. engr., D.C. Fellow Am. Soc. C.E.; mem. Soc. Am. Mil. Engrs., Kappa Sigma. Home: 1200 N Nash St Arlington, VA 22209. Office: Naval Facilities Engring Command Washington DC 23090

ENGERT, CORNELIUS VAN H., ret. U.S. ambassador; b. Vienna, Austria, Dec. 31, 1887 (mother Am. citizen); s. John Cornelius and Mary (Babbitt) E.; brought to U.S. as child; B.Litt., U. Cal., 1909, M.Litt., 1910, student Law Sch., 1908-11; Le Conte Meml. fellow Harvard, 1911-12; m. Sara Cunningham, Dec. 16, 1922; children—Roderick, Sheila (Mrs. F. Gillen). Teaching fellow history U. Cal., 1909-11; attaché Am. embassy, Constantinople, Turkey, 1912-16, represented embassy at Chanak during Dardanelles campaign, 1914-15; spl. mission to Syria and Palestine, 1916-17, interned by Turks for several weeks upon rupture diplomatic relations with U.S., 1917; attached to Viscount Ishii's Japanese mission to U.S., 1917; 3d sec. Am. legation, The Hague, 1917-19; asst. to U.S. High Commr., Constantinople, 1919-20; 2d sec. legation, Tehran, Iran, 1920-22; first U.S. Diplomatic officer to visit Kabul, Afghanistan, 1922; Dept. State, 1922-23; 1st sec. Am. embassy, Havana, Cuba, 1923-25, San Salvador, C.Am., 1925-26, negotiated and signed Treaty Friendship between U.S. and Republic El Salvador, 1926; 1st sec. Santiago Chile, 1926-27, Caracas, Venezuela, 1927-30, Peking, China, 1930-33, Cairo, Egypt, 1933-35; minister resident and consul gen., Addis Ababa, Ethiopia, 1935-37; chargé d'affaires, Tehran, 1937-40; consul gen. Beirut and Damascus, 1940-42; in charge Brit. interests, Syrian campaign, 1941; 1st U.S. minister to reside in Kabul, Afghanistan, 1942- 45; traveled overland, Kabul to Moscow, via Bokhara and Samarkand, 1945, visited Katmandu, Nepal, 1945; asst. and acting diplomatic adviser UNRRA, 1946-47; spl. mission to Middle East, 1946; rep. Internat. Bank for Reconstrn. and Devel., Middle East, India, Pakistan and Ceylon, 1948- 51; founder (with others) Am. Friends of Middle East, Inc., 1951, mem. bd. dirs., until 1970; founder (with others) Anglo-Am. Coll., Oxfordshire, Eng., 1966, lectr. at coll., 1968, now mem. bd. govs. Awarded lectureship for 1954 in Turkey, Iran, Afghanistan, Pakistan and India; hon. comdr. Order Brit. Empire; asso. knight Order of Saint John of Jerusalem. Fellow Am. Geog. Soc., Royal Geo. Soc., Royal Central Asian Soc.; mem. English-Speaking Union (pres. Washington br. 1951-58, now v.p., mem. bd.) Presbyn. Clubs: Sierra (San Francisco); Royal Societies (London). Home: Berkeley CA 94701 Address: 2022 Columbia Rd NW Washington DC 20009

ENGGAS, CARL E., lawyer; b. Kansas City, Mo., June 3, 1900; s. Main C. and Eva M. (Killip) E.; A.B., U. Mich., 1923, J.D., 1925; m. Jane M. Greene, Feb. 4, 1925; 1 dau., Marion Jane (Mrs. John H. Kreamer). Admitted to Mo. bar, 1925, since practiced in Kansas City; asso. Inghram Hook, 1925-31, Watson, Gage, Ess, Groner & Barnett, 1931-36; mem. firm Watson, Ess, Marshall & Enggas and predecessors, 1936—. Member, sec. Kansas City Bd. Election Commrs., 1961-65; mem. Jackson County Charter Commn., 1957-58. Served with U.S. Army, World War I. Fellow Am. Coll. Trial Lawyers;

mem. Am., Bar Assn., Mo. Bar, Lawyers Assn. Kansas City, Lawyers Club Ann Arbor (Mich.), Am. Judicature Soc., C. of C., Order of Coif, Alpha Tau Omega. Clubs: River; University (past pres.) (Kansas City). Home: 1200 W 60th Terrace Kansas City, MO 64113. Office: Home Savings Bldg Kansas City MO 64106

ENGI, JURG GADIENT, chem. co. exec.; b. Basel, Switzerland, Oct. 13, 1910; s. Gadient and Alice (Hollenweger) E.; Dr. jur., U. Basel, 1934; Dr. ès sc. h.c., U. Neuchtel, 1970; m. Margrit Meyerhans, Aug. 27, 1942; children—Corina, Gabrielle (Mrs. Schultz-Grunow), Christian, Dorette. Mgr. CIBA Ltd., Basel, 1935-64; chmn. bd. LONZA Ltd., Basel, subsidiaries and affiliated cos., 1964—; dir. Brown, Boveri & Co. Ltd., Baloise Ins. Cos., Ciba-Geigy Ltd., Swiss Bank Corp. Consul, Austria, 1968. Mem. Internat. (mem. conf. bd. 1970—), Basel chambers commerce, Internat. Law Assn. Lion. Home: 31 Rebgasse Arlesheim 4144 Switzerland Office: 38 Münchensteinerstrasse Basel 4002 Switzerland

ENGLAND, ANTHONY W., astronaut; b. Indpls., May 15, 1942; s. Herman U. and Betty (Steel) E.; S.B. S.M. (NSF grantee), Mass. Inst. Tech., 1965, Ph.D., 1970; m. Kathleen Ann Kreutz, Aug. 31, 1962. With Texaco Co., 1962; field geology Ind. U., 1963; NSF grantee, 1965-67, scientist-astronaut NASA, 1967—; qualified jet pilot, 1968. Mem. Am. Geophys. Union, Am. Geol. Inst., Soc. Exploration Geophysicists, Sigma Xi. Home: 1503 Mirror Lake Dr Seabrook TX 77586 Office: NASA MSC CB Houston TX 77058

ENGLAND, EDMUND B., corp. exec.; b. Birmingham, Ala., 1910. Vice pres., sec. Vulcan Materials Co., Birmingham. Home: 14 Montcrest Dr Birmingham AL 35213 Office: PO Box 7497 Birmingham AL 35223*

ENGLAND, WILBUR BIRCH, ret. educator; b. Cleve., Dec. 4, 1903; s. John H. and Hilda M. (Burch) E.; A.B., Adelbert Coll., Western Res. U., 1926; M.B.A., Harvard, 1930; m. Ruth E. Reynolds, Jan. 27, 1939; children—Elizabeth M., Jane M. Instr. econs. Ala. Poly., 1927-28; research asst. Harvard, 1930-32; exec. R.K.O. Corp., 1932-48; v.p. operations ABC Vending Corp., 1948-52, treas., 1951-52; lectr. Harvard, 1952-54, prof. bus. adminstrn., 1954—, chmn. marketing area faculty, 1965-68, Sebastian S. Kresge prof. marketing, 1967-70, emeritus, 1970—; vis. prof. mgmt. Ariz. State U., 1971. Dir. Cal. Products Co. Selectman, Town of Harvard, Mass., 1960-63. Pres., Nat. Assn. Purchasing Agts. Purchasing Ednl. Found., 1965-68. Recipient J. Shipman Gold medal Nat. Assn. Purchasing Mgmt., 1969; Harry Graham award New Eng. Purchasing Assn., 1968. Mem. Nat. Assn. Purchasing Agts. (chmn. univs. and colls. com.), Am. Marketing Assn. Club: Harvard (N.Y.C.). Author: (with Lewis) Industrial Procurement, 1962; Modern Procurement Management, 1970; (with others) Problems in Marketing, 1957, 61; Operating Results of Food Chains in 1955, 56, 57, 58, 59, 60; The Purchasing System, 1967; Modern Procurement Management, 1970. Asso. editor: Jour. Purchasing, 1965—. Home: South Bristol ME 04568 Office: Baker Library Soldiers Field Boston MA 02163

ENGLANDER, ROGER, producer, dir.; b. Cleve., Nov. 23, 1926; s. Will Cedric and Frieda (Osteryoung) E.; Ph.B., U. Chgo., 1946, postgrad., 1947-49; postgrad. Chgo. Mus. Coll., 1948, Goodman Theater, Art Inst. Chgo., 1948. Asst., Cain Park Theatre, Cleve., 1945, Berkshire Music Center, Tanglewood, Mass., 1946; asst. to gen. mgr. Chgo. Opera Co., 1946-47; asst. to Gian Carlo Menotti, producing 1st network TV operas, 1947-49; producer NBC-TV, 1949-50; asso. dir. ABC-TV, 1950-53; producer, dir. CBS-TV, 1953-58; free lance producer, dir., N.Y.C., 1958—; prod. Children's Concerts, Little Orch. Soc. N.Y., 1957-60; producer, dir. with Leonard Bernstein, Young People's Concerts, N.Y. Philharmonic, 1958—; prod. Promenade Concerts, 1963-65, also program series Bell Telephone Hour, Concert of the Week, S. Hurok Presents, Candid Camera, Vladimir Horowitz at Carnegie Hall; stage dir. N.Y. City Opera Co., 1959-63, also Am. Opera Co.; instr. Sch. Arts N.Y. Univ., 1966—, Inst. Film and Television, 1970—; producer, co-founder Am. Dance Theater, 1964, pres. bd. trustees; co-chmn. Adv. Panel on Dance; mem. Adv. Panel Pub. Media; mem. dance panel Nat. Endowment Arts; dir. Omnibus, Odyssey, Let's Take a Trip, Twentieth Century, Great American Dream Machine, 60 Minutes, The Performing Arts; stager entertainments for state Dinners at the White House for President's Kennedy and Johnson. Vis. prof. Parsons Coll., Fairfield, Ia., summers 1963-66, U. S.C., 1969, State U. N.Y. at Brockport, 1970; guest lectr. schs. including N.Y. U., Ind. U., Ohio State U., U. Chgo.; cons. N.Y. State Council on Arts, Pub. Relations Bd. Chgo. Trustee Mannes Coll. Music, N.Y.C.; bd. dirs. Profl. Children's Sch., N.Y.C., Dance Notation Bur., N.Y.C., Nat. Choral Council, N.Y.C., In Concerts for Peace, Washington. Recipient Emmy award Nat. Acad. TV Art and Scis., 1961, 62, 65; Producer's awards Ohio State U., 1960, 61, Saturday Rev., 1960, 62, 63, 64; Edison award, 1966; Broadcast Preceptor San Francisco State Coll., 1968; Prix Jeunesse (Munich), 1968; Christopher award, 1970. Mem. Acad. TV Arts and Scis. (gov. N.Y. chpt. 1959-71, nat. trustee 1961-69, internat. dir. 1964-69), Dirs. Guild Am., Am. Guild Mus. Artists, Writers Guild Am., ANTA, Internationales Institut fur Musik, Tanz und Theater in den Audio-visuellen Media (Vienna), Conseil International de la Musique (Paris), Renaissance Soc. U. Chgo. Club: University (mem. cabinet) (Chgo.). Author: (works for narrator and orch. with Mary Rodgers) Three to Make Music, 1960; (with Lee Sutton) Mark Twain, 1964; also ballet scenarios, TV scripts, articles. Home: 15 St Lukes Pl New York City NY 10014 Office: CBS Television 524 W 57th St New York City NY 10019

ENGLE, HAROLD MARTIN, med. adminstr.; b. Chgo., Nov. 29, 1914; s. Nathan Hale and Sarah (Wolson) E.; student Northwestern U., 1931-32, Central Coll., 1932-35; B.S., U. Ill., 1937, M.D., 1939; m. Marilyn Roe Detweiler, Aug. 22, 1942; children—Maurine Sara (Mrs. William George Flesner), Paige Renee. Intern Michael Reese Hosp., Chgo., 1939-40; resident 1940-42; med. officer Ft. Harrison VA Hosp., Helena, Mont., 1946-47; asst. chief med. service VA Hosp., Portland, Ore., 1947-48; chief profl. service VA Hosp., Vancouver, Wash., 1948-50; chief med. service VA Hosp., Spokane, 1950-52; chief profl. service VA Hosp., Seattle, 1952-53, also asso. instr. med. U. Wash. Med. Sch.; dir. VA hosps., Salt Lake City, 1953-55, Denver, 1955-60; clin. asst. prof. medicine U. Colo., Med. Sch., Denver, 1953-55, clin. asso. medicine, 1955-60; dep. chief med. dir. VA Central Office, Washington, 1960-64; chief med. dir. VA, 1966-70; clin. prof. med. U. Cal. at Los Angeles, Med. Sch., 1964-66; vice-chancellor, hosp. med. dir. U. Ill., Med-Sch., Chgo., 1970—. Mem. nat. adv. health council Office of Surgeon Gen., USPHS, 1966-70, Pres.'s Nat. Adv. Commn. Health Manpower, 1966-70, Fed. Task Force Health, 1966-70. Bd. regents Nat. Library Medicine. Served to maj., M.C., AUS, 1942-46. Recipient Distinguished Service award Fed. Hosp. Inst. Alumni Assn., 1969. Fellow A.C.P.; mem. A.M.A. (ho. dels. 1960-64, 66-70), Assn. Mil. Surgeons (exec. council, 1966-70), Home: 505 N Lake Shore Dr Chicago IL 60611 Office: 840 S Wood St Chicago IL 60612

ENGLE, PAUL HAMILTON, writer, educator; b. Cedar Rapids, Ia., Oct. 12, 1908; s. Hamilton Allen and Evelyn (Reinheimer) E.; A.B., Coe Coll., 1931; A.M., State U. Ia., 1932; postgrad. Columbia, 1932-33; A.B., Merton Coll., Oxford (Eng.) U. (Rhodes Scholar), 1936, A.M., 1939; Litt.D., Coe Coll., Monmouth Coll., Ia. Wesleyan; m. Mary Nomine Nissen, July 3, 1936; children—Mary, Sara. Writer, Prof. English, dir. program in creative writing U. Ia., Iowa City, 1966—; librettist opera Golden Child, produced TV, 1960; pub. lectr. lit. at colls., Town Hall, N.Y.C., CBS-TV, others. Mem. adv. com. John F. Kennedy Cultural Center, Washington; mem. nat. council on arts White House; judge Nat. Book Award, 1955, 70, Lamont award Acad. Am. Poets, 1958-61. Recipient award for West of Midnight, Friends Am. Writers, Chgo., 1941. Fellow Found. for Advancement Edn., 1952- 53, Guggenheim Found., 1953-54. Mem. Phi Kappa Phi, Phi Gamma Delta. Author books poetry including: American Child, 1945; The Word of Love, 1951; Poems in Praise, 1959; A Prairie Christmas, 1960; A Woman Unashamed; Golden Child (opera libretto), 1960; Golden Child (prose fiction), 1962. Editor: Midland (anthology), 1961; (with Joseph Langland) Poet's Choice (anthology). Past editor: O. Henry Prize Stories; On Creative Writing, 1964; An Old Fashioned Christmas, 1964; co-editor: Reading Modern Poetry. Contbr. to popular mags., N.Y. Times. Home: 221 Magowan Iowa City IA 52240

ENGLE, RALPH LANDIS, Jr., physician, educator; b. Phila., June 11, 1920; s. Ralph Landis and Ruth (Enck) E.; B.S., U. Fla., 1942; M.D., Johns Hopkins, 1945; m. Mary Allen English, June 7, 1945; children-Ralph Landis III, Marilyn Elizabeth. Intern pathology N.Y. Hosp., 1945-46, intern medicine, 1948-49, asst. resident medicine, 1949-51, asst. attending physician, 1952-57, asso. attending physician, 1957-69, attending physician, 1969—; Am. Cancer Soc. research fellow anatomy Washington U. Med. Sch., St. Louis, 1951- 52; practice medicine, specializing in internal medicine, N.Y.C., 1952- -; chief div. med. systems and computer sci., dept. medicine N.Y. Hosp.-Cornell U. Med. Center, 1969—; asst. prof. medicine Cornell U. Med. Coll., 1952-57, asso. prof., 1957-69, prof., 1969—. Mem. com. on sci. and tech. communications Nat. Acad. Scis.-Nat. Acad. Engring., 1967-70, chmn. Ad Hoc Task Group on Toxological Information 1969-70; mem. toxicological information program com., div. med. scis., 1968—; mem. cancer clin. investigation rev. com. Nat. Cancer Inst., 1968—. Served from 1st lt. to capt., M.C., AUS, 1946-48. Markle scholar in med. sci., 1952-57. Fellow A.C.P., N.Y. Acad. Medicine, N.Y. Acad. Scis.; mem. Internat., Am. socs. hematology, N.Y. Soc. for Study Blood (past pres.), Am. Fedn. Clin. Research, Am. Physiol. Soc., Soc. Exptl. Biology and Medicine, A.A.A.S., Harvey Soc. (past sec.), Assn. Computing Machinery, Am. Soc. Information Sci., Sigma Xi, Chi Phi, Nu Sigma Nu Presbyn. Club: Pelham Counntry. Author: (with L.A. Wallis) Immunoglobulins, Immune Deficiency Syndromes, Multiple Myeloma and Related Disorders, 1969; also numerous articles. Home: 1 Country Club Lane Pelham Manor NY 10803 Office: 525 E 68th St New York NY 10021

ENGLE, SHIRLEY H., educator; b. Bloomingdale, Ind., Apr. 16, 1907; s. Washington Joshua and Eudora Harriet (Morrison) E.; B.S., U. Ill., 1928, M.S., 1933, Ed.D., 1953; m. Ora May Edgar, June 23, 1930; children—Robert Bruce, Patricia Jo (Mrs. Jon Annis Stewart), Richard Francis. Tchr. social studies Bement (Ill.) Twp. High Sch., 1928-36, West Chicago (Ill.) Community High Sch., 1936-41, Lyons Twp. High Sch. and Jr. Coll., LaGrange, Ill., 1941-42; instr. Sch. Edn., U. Ill., 1942-45; instr., critic tchr. social studies Sch. Edn., Ind. U., 1945-52, asst. prof., tchr. social studies, 1952-55, asso. prof. edn., 1955-58, prof. edn., 1958—, asso. dean grad. devel., 1959-64, asso. dean advanced studies, 1965-68, tech. adviser Univ. with U.S. mission to Thailand, 1961-62; vis. prof. edn. U. Fla., summer 1961. Mem. adv. com. edn. ECA, 1950; conferee FCDA, 1952; mem. sch. and univ. adv. bd. Citizens Com. for Hoover Report, 1954; dir. Monroe County Fair Assn., 1957—, pres., 1963-65; bd. advisers Council Study Mankind, 1963—; bd. mem. Council Civic Edn., 1965—; mem. U.S. Nat. Commn. for UNESCO, 1968- -. Recipient Frederic Bachman Lieber meml. award for distinguished teaching Ind. U., 1959. Mem. N.E.A., Nat. Higher Edn. Assn., Nat. Soc. Coll. Tchrs. Edn., Am. Assn. U. Profs., Nat. (dir. 1957-62, pres. 1970), Ind. (pres. 1947-48) councils social studies, Assn. Supervision and Curriculum Devel. (commn. on social studies 1969—), Nat. Soc. for Study Edn., Am. Acad. Polit. and Social Sci., Am. Ednl. Research Assn., Phi Delta Kappa, Kappa Delta Pi. Mem. Christian Ch. (elder, past chmn. ch. bd.). Co-author: New Challenges in the Social Studies, 1965. Editor: New Perspectives in World History. Author articles, bulls., contbr. yearbooks. Home: 451 Blue Ridge Dr Bloomington IN 47401

ENGLEKIRK, JOHN EUGENE, educator; b. N.Y.C., Sept. 24, 1905; s. John and Lena (Didion) E.; B.A., St. Stephen's Coll., Bard, N.Y., 1926; M.A. (teaching fellow), Northwestern U., 1928; diploma (travel fellow Instituto de las Espaas, Columbia, also Residencia de Estudiantes, Madrid), Centro de Estudios Históricos, Madrid, Spain, 1930; Ph.D., Columbia, 1934; diploma (Chilean travel and study scholar Inst. Internat. Edn.), U. Chile, 1938; m. Fern Carolyn Houp, Feb. 14, 1931; children—Robert E., June Carolyn (Mrs. Frederick T. Grade), John Allan. From instr. to asso. prof. Romance langs. U. N.M., 1928-39; asst., then instr. Spanish, Columbia, 1931-33; asso. prof., prof. and chmn. dept. Spanish and Portuguese, Tulane U., 1939-58; prof. Spanish and Portuguese, U. Cal. at Los Angeles, 1958—, chmn. dept., 1959-62; vis. prof. various univs. Dir. European office Inst. Internat Edn., Paris, 1950-51. Tulane U. research grantee, Mexico, 1940, Venezuela and Colombia, 1947, Caribbean, 1954; Am. Council Learned Socs. grantee Mexico, 1942, Uruguay and Brazil, 1959; Middle Am. Research Inst. grantee, Mexico, Central Am., Venezuela, 1957; Smith- Mundt fellow and lectr., Spain and Portugal, 1955-56; U. Cal. at Los Angeles research grantee, Uruguay and Brazil, 1959-60; Del Amo Found. fellow, Spain, 1962, 70; Fulbright-Hays award for study in Latin Am., 1965; Am. Philos. Soc. grant for study in Latin Am., 1966; Fulbright grant for study in Spain, 1967. Mem. Instituto Internacional de Literatura Ibero- americana (founder mem., pres. 1940-42, v.p. 1961-63), Am. Assn. Tchrs. Spanish and Portuguese (pres. 1949), Modern Lang. Assn. (pres. S. Central sect. 1952), La. Fgn. Lang. Tchrs. Assn. (pres. 1953-55), Modern Lang. Assn. So. Cal. (pres. 1961-62), Am. Assn. U. Profs., Internat. Comparative Lit. Assn., Ateneo Americano de Washington (corr. mem.), Academia de la lengua Espaola en U.S.A., Phi Kappa Phi, Theta Alpha Phi, Sigma Alpha Epsilon, Phi Sigma Iota, Sigma Delta Pi. Author: Poe in Hispanic Literature, 1934; Bibliografía de obras norteamericanas en traducción espaola, 1944; A literatura norteamericano no Brasil, 1952; (with Gerald E. Wade) La novela colombiana, 1952; El epistolario Pombo-Longfellow, 1956; El teatro folklórico hispanoamericano, 1957; De lo nuestro y lo ajeno, 1966; (with M. M. Ramos) La narrativa uruguaya, 1967; editor, co-author An Outline History of Spanish American Literature, 1965; An Anthology of Spanish American Literature, 1968; also texts, numerous articles. Co-editor Revista Ibero-americana, 1940-53, 57-59, editor, 1959-61; co-editor Hispanofila, 1958—. Home: 11164 Ophir Dr Los Angeles CA 90024

ENGLER, ARNOLD, educator; b. Czernovitz, Rumania, July 19, 1927; s. Norbert and Blanka (Korn) E.; student Hebrew U., Jerusalem, 1946-47, 48-49; Ph.D., U. Berne (Switzerland), 1953; m. Eva Marie Fischer, Mar. 26, 1961; children—Jonathan Jacob. Came to U.S., 1956, naturalized, 1966. Research asso. U. Berne, 1953-54, U. Bristol (Eng.), 1954-56; research asso., asst. prof. U. Rochester, 1956-58; sr. research officer U. Oxford, Eng., 1958-60; asso. prof. Duke, 1960-61, Northwestern U., 1961-62; asso. prof. physics Carnegie-Mellon U., Pitts., 1962-66, prof., 1966—; guest scientist Brookhaven Nat. Lab., 1962—. Served with Israeli Army, 1948-49. Fellow St. Cross Coll., Oxford, Eng., 1966-67. Fellow Am. Phys. Soc. Research elementary particle physics, 1960—, cosmic rays, 1954-60. Home: 5521 Woodmont Pittsburgh PA 15217

ENGLER, HENRY JULIUS, Jr., coll. dean; b. New Orleans, Sept. 26, 1916; s. Henry Julius and Ruby Melanie (Patureau) E.; Ph.B., Loyola U., New Orleans, 1938, B.B.A., 1949; M.B.A., Harvard, 1949; student Columbia, Detroit U., Princeton, Tulane U.; m. Rita Myrtle Talen, Aug. 25, 1937; children—Carolyn Rita, Elaine Valerie. Engr., accountant, 1938-42; labor cons., 1944-46; indsl. engr. 8th Naval Dist., 1944-46; prof. Loyola U., 1949-54, dean Coll. Bus. Adminstrn., 1954—; partner Ringstrom Engler Market Analysts, 1954- -; sec.-treas., dir. Precon Process & Equipment Corp.; dir. Caltronics, Inc. Ednl. adminstr. Am. Inst. Banking, New Orleans; ednl. cons. So. Inst. Mgmt.; exec. bd. La. Coll. Conf. Mem. nat. bd. Boy Scouts Am.; budget com. New Orleans Community Chest; mem. voting bd., La., 1955—. Chmn, Orleans Parish Dem. Exec. Com. Pres. Frey Found. Served as ensign Supply Corps, USNR, 1942- 44. Recipient Blue Key Beta Gamma Sigma, Silver Beaver award Boy Scouts Am. Mem. Soc. Advancement Mgmt., Acad. Mgmt., Am. Soc. Safety Engrs., New Orleans C. of C., Delta Safety Soc. (v.p.), Blue Key (nat. exec. officer). Club: Ionia (New Orleans). Author: Management Policies and the Older Worker, 1954; A Guide to Managerial Self-Analysis, 1970. Editor: Public Relations for Your Bank. Home: 120 14th St New Orleans LA 70124 Office: 6363 St Charles Av New Orleans LA 70124

ENGLER, JEAN EVANS, assn. exec., ret. army officer; b. Aug. 3, 1909; B.S., U.S. Mil. Acad., 1933; m. Lessie B. Helms; children—Jean H., Mrs. Edwin Bryan Connerat Jr., Michael Evans. Commd. 2d lt., 1933, advanced through grades to lt. gen., ordnance, now ret.; dep. comdg. gen. U.S. Army Material Command, later dep. chief of staff for logistics; dir. tech. Am. Ordnance Assn. Decorated D.S.M. with 3 oak leaf clusters, Legion of Merit with oak leaf cluster, Bronze Star medal, Air Medal with oak leaf cluster; Order Mil. Merit Ulchi (Korea); Nat. Order of Vietnam. Mem. Am. Ordnance Assn., Res. Officers Assn., Assn. U.S. Army. Home: 4471 N 33d St Arlington VA 22207

ENGLER, LESLIE WINFRED, educator; b. Boston, Feb. 18, 1909; s. Samuel and Gertrude (Carlson) E.; B.S. in Civil Engring., Mass. Inst. Tech., 1930, M.S., 1933; m. Doris Marie Howard, June 18, 1938; children—John Howard, Robert Edward, Ellen Marie. Tchr., dept. civil engring. Coll. City N.Y., 1934—, dean adminstrn., 1949—, prof. civil engring., 1950—, developed course in Soil Mechanics and Foundations in civl engring. curriculum, 1936. Pres. Tenafly Civic and Welfare Assn. Trustee Engelwood Cliffs (N.J.) Coll. Mem. Am. Soc. C.E., Am. Soc. Engring. Edn., Tau Beta Pi, Chi Epsilon, Phi Kappa Theta. Licensed profl. engr., N.Y. Home: 9 Hillcrest Rd Tenafly NJ 07670 Office: Coll City NY 139th St and Convent Av New York City NY 10031

ENGLER, MARTIN RUSSELL, Jr., utilities exec.; b. San Diego, July 30, 1924; s. Martin Russell and Lura (Griffin) E.; B.S. in Mech. Engring., Cal. State Poly. Coll., 1950; m. Mary Russell Belford, June 7, 1948; children—William Erickson, Mary Elizabeth, Kathryn Louise. Coordinator student activities Cal. State Poly. Coll., 1949-50; engr. San Diego Gas & Electric Co., 1950-60, supt. gas supply, 1960-65, mgr. gas div., 1965-66, v.p. gas, 1966-69, v.p. operations services, 1969-70, sr. v.p., 1971—. Lectr. liquefied natural gas tech. Bd. dirs. San Diego Aerospace Mus., Internat. Aerospace Hall of Fame, San Diego. Served to capt. USAAF, 1943-45. Decorated D.F.C., Air medal with 11 oak leaf clusters, Fourragere (Belgium). Mem. Nat. Fire Protection Assn. (subcom. utility gas plants 1967, chmn. tech. com. liquefied natural gas 1968), Am. Soc. M.E., Am., Pacific Coast gas assns., Order Daedalians, Cross and Cockade. Developer liquefied natural gas utilization techniques. Home: 1419 Vue du Bay Ct San Diego CA 92109 Office: 101 Ash St San Diego CA 92101

ENGLER, ROBERT, educator, author; b. N.Y.C., July 12, 1922; s. Isidore and Esther (Haber) E.; B.S.S., Coll. City N.Y., 1942; M.A., U. Wis., 1943, Ph.D.,1947; m. Rosalind Elowitz, May 16, 1946 (div. June 1960); children—Richard J., Elise P.; m. 2d, Inea Bushnag, Sept. 5, 1968. Mem. faculty U. Wis., 1946-47, Syracuse U., 1947-50, Columbia, 1959-63; prof. polit. sci. Queens Coll. City U. N.Y., 1964-69, Bklyn. Coll. City U. N.Y., 1969—, Sarah Lawrence Coll., 1951—; mem. faculty New Sch. Social Research, 1961-64; vis. prof. U. P.R., 1961. Asst. to pres. Nat. Farmers Union, Washington, 1950-51; dir. Encampment for Citizenship, N.Y.C., 1961, 64. Served with AUS, 1943-46; ETO. Recipient Sidney Hillman Found. prize award polit. writing, 1955. Mem. A.A.A.S., Am. Civil Liberties Union. Author: The Politics of Oil: A Study of Private Power and Democratic Directions, 1961; also articles. Contbg. author: The Dissenting Academy, 1968. Home: 28 Bank St New York City NY 10014 Office: Graduate Center City Univ of NY 33 W 42d St New York City NY 10036

ENGLERT, ROY THEODORE, govt. ofcl., lawyer; b. Nashville, Sept. 11, 1922; s. Roy T. and Ruth Rowe (Tindall) E.; B.A., Vanderbilt U., 1943; LL.B., Columbia, 1951; LL.M., George Washington U., 1953; m. Helen Frances Wiggs, Sept. 25, 1948; children—Lee Ann, Roy Theodore. Asst. supr. Nat. Life & Accident Ins. Co., Nashville; admitted to Tenn. bar, 1951, D.C. bar, 1952, also Supreme Ct. bar; asst. counsel Office Comptroller of Currency, U.S. Treasury Dept., 1951-58, chief counsel, 1958-62, asst. gen. counsel of dept., 1962-66, dep. gen. counsel, 1966—. Mem. Sr. Seminar in Fgn. Policy, Dept. State, 1963—; lectr., writer on banking law. Served from apprentice seaman to lt. USNR, 1943-46. Mem. Fed., Am., Tenn. bar assns. Presbyn. Clubs: Nat. Lawyers (Washington); Springfield Golf and Country. Home: 6720 Bellamy Av Springfield VA 22152 Office: Main Treasury Bldg Washington DC 20224

ENGLES, WILLIAM NORBERT, banker; b. Macon, Ga., Mar. 5, 1905; s. Ira B. and Katherine (McKay) E.; student Mercer U., Am. Inst. Banking, Columbus U. Formerly with First Nat. Bank and Trust Co. of Macon (formerly Macon Nat. Bank), Luther Williams Bank and Trust Co., Macon; with RFC, 1934- 53, successively charge adminstrn. loans to bus. engaged in essential civilian and def. prodn. work, also asst. to exec. dir. Def. Plants Corp.; dep. adminstrs. financial assistance Small Bus. Adminstrn., 1954- 58; pres. Chgo. City Bank and Trust Co., 1958-69, chmn. bd., chief exec. officer, 1969-71; pres., chief exec. officer Merc. Nat. Bank of Miami Beach (Fla.), 1971—. Member Chgo. Housing Authority, Chgo. Dwelling Assn. Served from 1st lt. to maj. USAAF, 1942-44; lt. col. Res. Mem. Big Bros. Am., Englewood Bus. Men's Assn. (pres. 1958-60), Am. Inst. Banking. Clubs: South Shore Country Executives, Chicago Athletic; Bankers. Home: 286 Bal Bay Dr Bal Harbour FL 33154 Office: 420 Lincoln Rd Mall Miami Beach FL 33139

ENGLEY, DONALD BROWN, librarian; b. Stafford Springs, Conn., July 19, 1917; s. Frank Ballantine and Annie (Brown) E.; B.A., Amherst Coll., 1939, M.A. (hon.), 1959; B.S. in L.S., Columbia, 1941; M.A., U. Chgo., 1947; m. Hope I. Lummis, Oct. 31, 1942. Library asst. Amherst Coll., 1936-40, Columbia, 1940-41, N.Y. Pub. Library, 1941; librarian Norwich U., Northfield, Vt., 1947-49; asso. librarian Trinity Coll., Hartford, Conn., 1949-51, librarian, 1951—; librarian, trustee

Watkinson Library, Hartford, 1959- -. Sec. Trinity Coll. Library Assos., 1951-; adv. com. Mark Twain Meml. and Library Commn., Hartford, 1954—; chmn. Conn. Gov.'s Com. Libraries, 1961-63; mem. Conn. State Library Com., 1964—; mem. univ. council library com. Yale, 1966-70. Trustee Noah Webster Found., 1966—. Served to capt. AUS, 1941-46. Decorated Bronze Star. Mem. Conn. Library Assn. (past pres.), Conn. Hist. Soc., Amherst Assn. Conn., Bibliog. Soc. Am. Conglist. Clubs: Grolier (N.Y.C.); Acorn of Conn.; Columbiad. Editor, contbr. Trinity Coll. Library Gazette. Home: 123 Vernon St Hartford CT 06106

ENGLEY, FRANK B., Jr., educator, microbiologist; b. Wallingford, Conn., Oct. 26, 1919; s. Frank B. and Anne (Brown) E.; B.S., U. Conn., 1941; M.S., U. Pa., 1944, Ph.D., 1949; postgrad. Johns Hopkins, 1946-47; m. Beatrice Winslow Doak, July 26, 1948; children—Karen Winslow, Elizabeth Anne, Heather Cooke, Frank B. III. Research technician Atwater Animal Disease Labs., Storrs, Conn., 1938-41; asst. instr. microbiology U. Pa. Sch. Medicine, 1941-44; research microbiologist U.S. Govt., 1946-50; asso. prof. bacteriology and parasitology, cons. microbiologist Univ. Hosps., U. Tex. Med. Br., 1950-55; prof. microbiology, chmn. dept. U. Mo. Sch. Medicine, 1955-, asst. dean, 1956-60, prof., acting chmn. dept. pub. health and preventive medicine, 1960-61. Cons. in field, 1954—; mem. Am. Inst. Biol. Scis. adv. com. to NASA on spacecraft sterilization, 1966-67. Served with AUS, 1944-46. Recipient Civil Service award, 1948; Osteon Faculty award U. Tex. Med. Br., 1954; Commonwealth Fund research and travel award, Switzerland, 1965-66; SAMA Faculty Teaching award, 1970. Diplomate Am. Bd. Microbiology. Fellow A.A.A.S., Am. Pub. Health Assn. (pres. Mo. br. 1964), Am. Acad. Microbiology; mem. Am. Soc. Microbiology (pres. Mo. br. 1959), Research Soc. Am., A.M.A. (affiliate mem.), Royal Acad. Health, Soc. Exptl. Biology and Medicine, N.Y. Acad. Scis., Am. Assn. Med. Colls., Sigma Xi. Author: Pocket Reference Guide to Medical Microbiology, 1963; Persistence of Microorganisms, 1963; Advanced and Elementary Laboratory Manuals for Medical Microbiology, 1965; also numerous articles. Mem. editorial bd. Jour. Bacteriology, Health Lab. Sci., Cytobios and Microbios. Home: 609 Westmount Av Columbia MO 65201

ENGLISH, CHARLES BRAND, lawyer; b. Urbana, O., June 10, 1924; s. Edwin L. and Margaret (Brand) E.; student Dartmouth, 1941-42, Denison U., 1942-43; A.B., U. Mich., 1944, LL.B., 1947; m. Constance Coulter, 1946 (dec. 1953); 1 son, Thomas C.; m. 2d, Eva Uber, Oct. 3, 1954; children—Gwendolyn, Carolyn (dec.). Admitted to Ohio bar, 1947, since practiced privately in Urbana. Farm mgr., 1950—; adv. bd. dirs. Citizens Holding Co., Columbus, O., 1965—; dir. W.H. Marvin Co., 1965-69. Bd. dirs. Milk Producers Union, Cin., 1957-62, Nat. Milk Producers Fedn., 1966—; v.p. Cin. Milk Sales Assn., 1966—, dir., 1962—. Mem. bd. edn. Triad Sch. Dist., 1951-59, Glen Helen Adv. Bd., 1959—; open sapec legal adviser for Com. for Country Common, 1963—. Trustee Urbana Coll., 1966—, vice chmn., 1969—. Named one of hon. 100 alumni Ohio State U. Sch. Natural Resources, 1970. Mem. Am., Ohio, Campaign County (pres. 1958) bar assns., Ohio Conservation Found. (sec.-treas. 1969—), Am. Humanist Assn. (bd. dirs. 1957-66, sec. 1959- 66), Community Water Resources Com. Champaign County (co-chmn. 1970—), S.W. Ohio Water Devel. Study. (adv. bd. 1969). Unitarian. Author articles. Home: R R Cable OH 43009 Office: Citizens Nat Bank Bldg Urbana OH 43078

ENGLISH, EARL FRANKLIN, educator; b. Lapeer, Mich., Jan. 29, 1905; s. Robert W. and Esther (Bell) E.; A.B., Western Mich. Coll., 1928, B.S., 1932; A.M., Ia. U., 1937, Ph.D., 1944; m. Ceola Bartlett, June 14, 1930; children—Esther Dawn, Barbara Lu. Newspaperman, Imlay City, Mich., 1920; reporter Kalamazoo Gazette, 1926-28; pub. sch. tchr., 1928-36; instr. journalism Ia. U., 1937-44; prof. U. Mo., 1945-70, dean, 1951-70, emeritus, 1970—; cons. to Allen Kander & Co.; Am. specialist Dept. State, Europe, 1963. Dir. Lee Enterprises, Inc. Mem. steering com. Hearst Found., 1960-70, chmn., 1968- 70. Recipient Pacemaker award, 1936, Sigma Delta Chi award for research in journalism, 1944; award of Merit, Nat. Editorial Assn., 1958; Fourth Estate award Freedom Found., 1960, Golden 50 award Alpha Delta Sigma, 1963; Mo. Distinguished Service award Journalism, 1970, Mo. Faculty-Alumni award, 1970. Mem. N.W. Mo. Press (pres. 1964-65), Am. Council Edn. Journalism (exec. sec. accrediting com. 1946-48, chmn. nat. com. research 1942, chmn. appeals com. 1971), Assn. Edn. in Journalism (pres. 1958-59), Am. Assn. Schs. and Depts. Journalism (pres. 1953-54), Am. Soc. Newspaper Editors (distinguished service), Assn. Edn. Journalism, Sigma Xi, Sigma Delta Chi, Kappa Tau Alpha (U. Ia. Hall of Fame 1964) Alpha Delta Sigma, Kappa Alpha Mu. Rotarian. Author: Exercises in Journalism; (with others) Introduction Journalism Research; co-author: Scholastic Journalism. Editor: Ia. Pub., 1940-42, Mo. Journalism Bull. Series, 1945—. Home: 2205 Bluff Blvd Columbia MO 65201

ENGLISH, ELLIS D., milling exec.; b. Campbell, Mo., Feb. 24, 1904; s. William Bedford and Mildred (Davis) E.; student Ark. A. and M. Coll., 1923, LL.D., 1959; m. Nell Zachry, May 31, 1925; 1 dau., Jane (Mrs. Carl H. Brust, Jr.). Salesman Commander-Larabee Milling Co., Kansas City, Mo., 1931, v.p., dir., 1937, exec. v.p. charge Southwestern operations, 1947, pres., 1949—; v.p. Archer-Daniels-Mildand Co., 1950-. Mem. Food for Peace Council, 1961-62. Mem. Nat. Assn. Grain Producers, Handlers and Processors (exec. dir. 1965-66), Am. Assn. Chemists (hon. life mem.), Millers' Nat. Fedn. (hon. mem.; dir., pres., mem. exec. com.). Clubs: River (Kansas City); Minneapolis, Minikahda. Home: Smithtown Bay Excelsior MN 55331 Office: Investors Bldg Minneapolis MN 55402

ENGLISH, EUGENE SCHUYLER, editor, author; b. N.Y.C., Oct. 12, 1899; s. Eugene Montgomery and Clara (Stoiber) E.; grad. Phillips Acad., Andover, Mass., 1918; student Princeton, 1918-20; Litt.D., Wheaton (Ill.) Coll., 1939; m. Eva Linde Schultz, March 2, 1937 (dec. August 1956); m. 2d Ruth Hill Kephart, July 4, 1959. Sec. Sterling Pure Food Co., Phila., 1920-21; asst. purchasing agt. Curtis Pub. Co., 1922-31; pres. Am. Bible Conf. Assn., Inc., 1930-47; mng. editor Revelation mag. 1931-39; mem. faculty Phila. Sch. Bible, 1935-47, pres., 1936-39; asso. editor Our Hope mag., 1939-45, editor, 1946-58; editor The Pilgrim (missionary publ.), 1944—; v.p. Arno C. Gaebelein, Inc., So. Bible Book House; radio broadcaster Phila. Stas. on Bible Study themes, 1935-46. Served as pvt. U.S. Army, Sept.-Dec. 1918. Author: Studies in the Gospel According to Matthew, 1935; By Life and By Death, 1938; The Life and Letters of St. Peter, 1941; Studies in the Gospel of Mark, 1943; Studies in the Epistle to Colossians, 1944; The Shifting of the Scenes, 1945; H. A. Ironside, Ordained of the Lord, 1946; Things Surely to Be Believed, 1946; Studies in I and II Thessalonians, 1947; Robert G. Lee, A Chosen Vessel, 1949; Re-Thinking the Rapture, 1951; Studies in the Epistle to the Hebrews, 1954. Editor-in-chief Pilgrim Edition of The Holy Bible, 1948. Contbr. to Revelation, Our Hope, etc. Chmn. editorial com., New Scofield Reference Bible, 1967. Editor: Revised N.T. Berkley Bible, 1969. Home: Skytop PA 18357 also 47 E Wynnewood Rd Merion PA 19066 Office: 1211 Arch St Philadelphia PA 19107

ENGLISH, GEORGE WASHINGTON, lawyer, banker; b. Vienna, Ill., Feb. 19, 1898; s. George W. and Lillie May (Farris) E.; B.S., U. Ill., 1921; LL.B., Harvard, 1924; m. Alma R. Witt, Sept. 11, 1935; 1 son by previous marriage, George Washington III. Admitted to Ill. bar, 1924, Fla. bar, 1925; city atty., Ft. Lauderdale, Fla., 1928-39; sr. mem. English, McCaughan & O'Bryan, Ft. Lauderdale, 1946. Chmn. bd., dir. First Nat. Bank Ft. Lauderdale, Plantation 1st Nat. Bank, Ft. Lauderdale, Guaranty First Nat. Bank, Consol. Bankshares of Fla., Inc.; dir. First Nat. Bank, Pompano Beach, Fla., Fla. Power & Light Co., Wright & Putnam, Inc., Caulley Steel and Aluminum Co., Harbor Beach Cos., Utilities Operating Co. Mem. bd. control Fla. Instns. Higher Learning, 1952-55; trustee U. Fla. Found., Nova U. Advanced Tech., Pine Crest Prep. Sch. (hon.). Served as lt. inf. U.S. Army, 1918-19, lt. col. Judge Adv. Gen. Dept., USAF, 1942-45. Fellow Am. Coll. Probate Counsel; mem. Am. Judicature Soc., Am., Fla., Broward County bar assns., S. Fla. Econ. Soc. Miami (dir.), Ft. Lauderdale Hist. Soc. (trustee), Newcomen Soc., Am. Legion, Fla. Council 100, Sigma Chi, Beta Gamma Sigma. Presbyn. Mason (Shriner), Elk. Clubs: Harvard, Hundred (Broward County, Fla.); Lauderdale Yacht (Ft. Lauderdale, Fla.); University (N.Y.C.). Home: 1636 SW 15th Av Fort Lauderdale FL 33312 Office: First Fed Bldg Fort Lauderdale FL 33301

ENGLISH, HAROLD MEDVIN, psychiatrist, hosp. adminstr.; b. Martinsburg, W.Va., May 20, 1923; s. Harold C. and Sara Kathryn (Bowers) E.; student Washington Coll., 1941-44; M.D., George Washington U., 1949; m. Patricia Maud Dougherty, Dec. 4, 1948; children—Eric Harold, Dorilyn, Evan Allen, Daylanne Kathryn. Intern St. Elizabeth's Hosp., Washington, 1949-51; resident in psychiatry U.S. Naval Hosp., Bethesda, Md., 1952-56; dir. hosp. inspection and licensure Md. Dept. Mental Hygiene, 1961-62; supt. Eastern Shore State Hosp., Cambridge, Md., 1962—; regional mental health dir. State of Md., 1965—; instr. psychiatry Johns Hopkins Sch. Medicine, Balt., 1961—. Served with USNR, 1944-45; to lt. comdr., M.C., USNR, 1950-60. Recipient Gov. Md. citation for service to handicapped, 1965. Fellow Am. Psychiat. Assn. Home: Teal Point Easton MD 21601 Office: Eastern Shore State Hospital Cambridge MD 21613

ENGLISH, JAMES ANDREW, ret. dental educator; b. Harrison Valley, Pa., May 14, 1910, s. Andrew and Ethel Lela (Ross) E.; B.S., Pa. State U., 1932; D.D.S., U. Pa., 1936, M.S., 1948; Ph.D., Johns Hopkins, 1955; m. Marjorie Elizabeth Lyons, June 2, 1934; children—James Andrew II, Beverly Anne (Mrs. Robert Koch); m. 2d, H. Delphine Patton, June 20, 1960. Commd. lt. (j.g.) U.S. Navy, 1936, advanced through grades to capt., 1952, various assignments in ships and hosps., 1936-44; assigned med. supply depots in Bklyn. and Hawaii, 1944- 47; research Naval Med. Research Inst., 1948-55, head dental dept., 1950- 52; mem. dental study sect. NIH, 1952-55; head dental br. Office Naval Research, also head dental br., research div. Bur. Medicine and Surgery, 1952-53, sci. liaison officer Office Naval Research, London, Eng., 1956-57; head medicine and dentistry br. Office Naval Research, Bur. Medicine and Surgery, also U.S. Naval Dental Sch., 1958- 60; ret., 1960; dean Sch. Dentistry State U. N.Y. at Buffalo, 1960-70. Fellow Am., Internat. colls. dentists, A.A.A.S., mem. Internat. Assn. Dental Research (pres. 1961), Am. Dental Assn., Federation Dentaire Internationale (chmn. commn. on research), N.Y. Acad. Scis., Royal Soc. Medicine, Am. Acad. Oral Pathology, Sigma Xi, Eta Sigma Sigma, Omicron Kappa Upsilon, Alpha Chi Rho. Contbr. numerous articles in field. Home: 180 S Cayuga Rd Buffalo NY 14225

ENGLISH, JAMES FAIRFIELD, Jr., banker; b. Putnam, Conn., Feb. 15, 1927; s. James Fairfield and Alice Bradford (Welles) E.; grad. Loomis Sch., 1944; B.A., Yale, 1949; M.A., Cambridge (Eng.) U., 1951; LL.B., U. Conn., 1956; m. Isabelle Spotswood Cox, July 9, 1955; children—Alice, James Fairfield III, Margaret, William. With Conn. Bank and Trust Co., Hartford, 1951—, sr. v.p., 1961-63, exec. v.p., 1963-66, pres., 1966-70, chmn. bd., chief exec. officer, 1970—, also dir.; chmn. bd. CBT Corp.; dir. Conn. Gen. Ins. Co., Emhart Corp., Terry Corp., Am. Thread Co., Loctite Corp., Conn. Natural Gas Co. Mem. univ. council Yale, 1969—. Trustee Conn. Coll., Conn. Atheneum, Hartford Sem. Found.; chmn. bd. trustees Loomis Sch.; bd. dirs. Inst. for Living, Hartford Hosp. Served with AUS, 1944-46. Mem. United Ch. of Christ. Home: 33 Fernwood Rd West Hartford CT 06119 Office: 1 Constitution Plaza Hartford CT 06115

ENGLISH, JOHN EARLE, banker; b. New Haven, May 4, 1918; s. James and Leila (Earle) E.; B.A., Yale U., 1940; grad. Sch. Banking Rutgers U., 1953; m. Janice Beckwith, June 25, 1938; children—Sarah E. (Mrs. Robert N. Waite), John Earle II, Olivia S., Timothy H., Gail B. Rate specialist United Illuminating Co., New Haven, 1940-48; sec.-treas. Stratford Machine Co. (Conn.), 1939-46; with First New Haven Nat. Bank, 1948—, sr. v.p., head trust dept., 1967—, treas., dir. Yale Co-Operative Corp., New Haven; dir. Wyatt, Inc., New Haven. Pres. United Fund Greater New Haven, 1966-68. Pres., bd. dirs. Albie Boothe Found.; treas., trustee Hamden Hall Country Day Sch. 1948-57, Hopkins Com. of Trustees Hopkins Grammar Sch. Served to lt. comdr. USNR, 1942-46. Episcopalian (sr. warden 1958-65). Clubs: Sachen's Head Yacht (commodore 1962-63); Off Soundings (commodore 1968-70); Cruising Am. (rear commodore 1967-68); Mory's New Haven Lawn (bd. govs. 1965—); Quinniplack (bd. govs. 1958-60), Dauntless; Yale Corinthian Yacht; Royal Ocean Racing (London); Royal Swedish Yacht. Home: 10 Old Farm Rd North Haven CT 06517 Office: 1 Church St New Haven CT 06502

ENGLISH, JOSEPH T., physician, med. adminstr.; b. Phila., May 21, 1933; A.B., St. Joseph's Coll., 1954 M.D., Jefferson Med. Coll., 1958; m. Ann Carr Sanger, Dec. 20, 1969. Intern Jefferson Med. Coll. Hosp., Phila, 1958-59; resident in psychiatry Inst. of Pa. Hosp., Phila., 1959-61, Nat. Inst. Mental Health, Bethesda, Md., 1961-62; practice psychiatry, 1962—; psychiatrist Office of Dir., Nat. Inst. Mental Health, 1964-65, asst. chief policy and program co-ordination, 1965-66, dept. chief office interagy. liaison, 1966, chief psychiatrist med. program div. Peace Corps, Washington, 1962-66; dep. asst. dir. health affairs Office Econ. Opportunity, Washington, 1966, acting asst. dir., 1966-68, asst. dir., 1969; pres. N.Y. City Health and Hosps. Corp., 1970—. Mem. sr. seminar asso. faculties program in community psychiatry Washington Sch. Psychiatry; chmn. interagy. task force emergency food and med. program for U.S., Office Econ. Opportunity-U.S. Dept. Health Edn. Welfare-U.S. Dept. Agr., 1968-69, adminstr. Health Services and Mental Health Adminstrn., Health, Edn., Welfare, 1969-70; chmn. Alaska Subcom. Fed. Health Programs Pres.'s Rev. Commn. Alaska, 1968—. Served to capt. USAF Res., 1958- 63; sr. surgeon USPHS, 1963-66. Named One of Outstanding Young Men of Year, U.S. Jr. C. of C., 1964; recipient John XXIII medal Coll. New Rochelle, N.Y., 1966; Meritorious award For exemplary achievement pub. adminstrn. William A. Jump Meml. Found., 1966; Flemming award, also personal commendation from President of U.S., 1968. Fellow Am. Psychiat. Assn. (mem. nat com. mental health programs Americans 1968—; council nat. and internat. affairs 1967—; ad hoc com. U.S. Poverty Program 1966- -); mem. A.M.A. (com. mental health services to poor 1965-66), Acad. Religion and Mental Health (profl. adv. bd. 1966—), Am. Coll. Health Assn., Am. Pub. Health Assn., Am. Orthopsychiat. Assn., Group Advancement Psychiatry, Pa., Phila. County, D.C. med. socs., Washington Psychiat. Soc., Soc. of Jefferson for Research (charter), Arnold Air Soc., Alpha Omega Alpha, Kappa Beta Phi, Alpha Sigma Nu. Author spl. reports on Peace Corps, other govtl. programs; contbr. articles in psychiat. and mental health fields profl. jours. Home: 40 E 62d St New York City NY 10021 Office: 125 Worth St New York City NY 10013

ENGLISH, LOWELL EDWARD, ret. marine corps officer, mgmt. cons. b. Fairbury, Neb., July 8, 1915; s. George William and Hazel (Browning) E.; B.A., U. Neb., 1938; m. Eleanor R. McCallum, Feb. 24, 1941; children—Loellen Kay (Mrs. Weaver H. Gaines, Jr.), Bruce Browning, Becky Lynne. Commd. 2d lt. USMC, 1938, advanced through grades to maj. gen., 1967; various assignments prior to World War II; mem. 3d Marine Div., World War II; mem. acad. staff U.S. Naval Acad., 1946-49; instr. mil. psychology and leadership U.S. Mil. Acad., 1949-52; comdg. officer 3d Battalion, also regtl. exec. officer 1st Marines, Korea; mem. staff U.S. 8th Army, 1953; chief staff Recruit Tng. Command, San Diego, 1954; comdr. tng. and test regt., 1957, also Basic Sch., Marine Corps Schs., Quantico, Va., 1958-60; grad. Army War Coll., 1961; assigned Office Asst. Sec. Def., 1961-63; chief staff for comdr. in chief U.S. Naval Forces, Eastern Atlantic and Mediterranean, 1963-64; dep. chief plans directorate, J-5, U.S. Strike Command, MacDill AFB, Fla., 1964-65; asst. div. comdr. 3d Marine Div., Vietnam, 1965-67; comdr. Marine Corps Recruit Depot, San Diego, 1967-69; mgmt. cons., 1969—. Vice chmn. San Diego chpt. A.R.C. Bd. dirs. San Diego 200th Anniversary, San Diego United Community Services, Childrens' Health Center, San Diego U.S.O. Decorated D.S.M. (2), Legion of Merit (2), Bronze Star (2), Purple Heart. Mem. Navy League (dir. San Diego Council). Kiwanian. Home: 5865 Madra San Diego CA 92120

ENGLISH, MARION C., banker; b. 1915; M.B.A., U. Chgo., 1948; married. With First Nat. Bank Chgo., 1931—, v.p., comptroller, 1966-69, v.p., gen. auditor, 1969—. Office: One First Nat Plaza Chicago IL 60670*

ENGLISH, MAURICE, author, pub.; b. Chgo., Oct. 21, 1909; s. Michael and Agnes (Sexton) E.; A.B. magna cum laude, Harvard, 1933; m. Fanita Blumberg, Apr. 25, 1945; children—Jonathan Brian, Deirdre Elena. Journalist, U.S. and Europe, 1933-53; editor, pub. Chicago mag., 1953- 57; free-lance writer, 1957-61; mng. editor, sr. editor U. Chgo. Press, 1961-69; dir. Temple U. Press, Phila., 1969—. Fulbright fellow, France, 1966-67. Mem. Phi Beta Kappa. Author: (anthology writings Louis Sullivan) The Testament of Stone, 1963; (poems) Midnight in the Century, 1964; (translations) Selected Poems of Eugenio Montale, 1966; (play) The Saints in Illinois, 1969. Home: 1530 Locust St Philadelphia PA 19102 Office: Temple U Press Philadelphia PA 19122

ENGLISH, NICHOLAS CONOVER, lawyer, YMCA ofcl.; b. Elizabeth, N.J., Apr. 12, 1912; s. Conover and Sara Elizabeth (Jones) E.; grad. Pingry Sch., 1929; A.B., Princeton, 1934; LL.B., Harvard, 1937; m. Agnes N. Perry, Mar. 18, 1939 (div. 1947); children—Henry H. P., Anne Whitall (Mrs. Edward J. Wardwell); m. 2d, Eleanor Morss, May 1, 1948; children—Priscilla, Sara (dec.), Sherman, Eleanor. Admitted to N.J. bar, 1937, since practiced in Newark; partner firm McCarter & English, 1947—. Bd. dirs. Summit (N.J.) YMCA, 1950-57; chmn. exec. com. Central Atlantic Area YMCA, 1957-63; mem. Nat. council YMCA, 1954, 58—, v.p., 1959-60; mem. Nat. bd. YMCA, 1960—, vice chmn., 1969—. Mem. trustees Pingry Sch.; pres. bd. trustees Kent Pl. Sch.; bd. dirs. Nat. Legal Aid Assn., 1953-56. Served to lt. USNR, 1943-46. Mem. Am. (ho. of dels. 1957-58), N.J., Essex County bar assns., Am. Bible Soc. (bd. mgrs. 1964—), Am. Law Inst. Republican. Presbyn. Clubs: Essex (Newark); Princeton (N.Y.C.). Home: 149 Kent pl Blvd Summit NJ 07901 Office: 577 Broad St Newark NJ 07102

ENGLISH, O. SPURGEON, physician; b. Presque Isle, Me., Sept. 27, 1901; s. G. Wesley and Annie L. (Hemphill) E.; student U. Me., 1918-20; M.D., Jefferson Med. Coll., 1924; m. Ellen Mary Brown, Feb. 28, 1933; children—Wesley, O. Spurgeon (dec.), Carroll, Cheryl Ann. Intern Jefferson Med. Coll. Hosp., 1924-27, Boston Psychol. Hosp., 1927-28; resident physician Montefiore Hosp., N.Y.C., 1928-29; Commonwealth fellow in psychiatry, 1929-32; student Berlin Psychoanalytic Inst., 1931-33; clin. prof. psychiatry Temple U. Med. Sch., 1933-38, prof. psychiatry, 1938—, head dept. psychiatry, 1938-64; pvt. practice psychiatry and psychoanalysis, Phila., 1938—. Fellow A.C.P., Am. Psychiat. Assn., A.M.A.; mem. Am. Psychoanalytical Assn., Phila. Psychiat. Soc. (past pres.), Phila. Psychoanalytic Soc. (past pres.). Author: numerous books including: The Emotional Problems of Living (with G.H.J. Pearson), 1945; Psychosomatic Medicine (with Edward Weiss); Fathers are Parents, Too (with Constance Foster), 1951; Introduction to Psychiatry (with Stuart H. Finch), 1954; Direct Analysis and Schizophrenia (with others), 1961. Home and office: 449 Righters Mill Rd Narberth PA 19072

ENGLISH, RONALD WILLIAMS, clergyman; b. Atlanta, Feb. 20, 1944; s. Jethro and Auretha (Jolly) E.; B.A., Morehouse Coll., 1967; postgrad. Andover Newton Theol. Sch., 1968- 69, Interdenominational Theol. Center, 1966—; m. Myrtolyn Jones, Jan. 15, 1967; 1 dau., Rondalyn Kristia. Ordained to ministry Bapt. Ch.; asst. minister, youth adviser Ebenezer Bapt. Ch., Atlanta, 1966—; dir. pub. relations and alumni affairs Interdenominational Theol. Center, Atlanta, 1969—. Mem. commn. theology Nat. Com. Black Churchmen. Mem. Soc. Bib. Lit., Alpha Phi Alpha. Home: 1881 Bayberry Dr SW Atlanta GA 30311 Office: 671 Beckwith St SW Atlanta GA 30314

ENGLISH, SPOFFORD GRADY, chemist, govt. ofcl.; b. Mt. Pleasant, Tenn., Nov. 16, 1915; s. Spofford G. and Ruby May (Warnock) E.; student U. Chattanooga, 1933-34; B.S., U. Okla., 1938, M.S., 1940; Ph.D., U. Cal. at Berkeley, 1943; m. Muriel K. Frodin, Sept. 18, 1942; children—Susan P., Elizabeth H., Helen W. Chemist, Okla. Geol. Survey, 1936-40; teaching asst. chemistry U. Cal. at Berkeley, 1940-42; group leader Manhattan Project, U. Chgo., 1942-43; sect. chief chemistry div. Clinton Lab., Oak Ridge, 1943-46; asst. prof. chemistry U. Cal. at Berkeley, 1946-47; mem. staff AEC, 1947—, dep. dir. research, 1960-61, asst. gen. mgr. research and devel., 1961—, chmn. plowshare adv. com., 1960—. Tech. adviser U.S. delegation UN Disarmament Conf., London, Eng., 1955, U.S. delegation Conf. Cessation Nuclear Weapons Test, Geneva, Switzerland, 1959; mem. U.S. delegation Internat. Atomic Energy Agy., 1956. Mem. Phi Beta Kappa, Sigma Xi. Home: 8204 Thoreau Dr Bethesda MD 20034 Office: Atomic Energy Commn Washington DC 20545

ENGLISH, VAN HARVEY, educator; b. Miami, Fla., July 18, 1914; s. Elbert G. and Ethel (Watkins) E.; B.A., Colo. State Coll. Edn., 1936; Ph.D., Clark U., 1942; m. Natalie Plummer (dec. 1952); 1 dau., Gwendolyn Warner; m. 2d, Francis Ryder Lake, Sept. 25, 1954; stepchildren—Martha Lake, Peter Lake, Ann Lake. Cartographer OSS, Washington, 1942-45; geographer Dept. State, Washington, 1945-46; prof. geography Dartmouth, 1946—, chmn. dept. geography, 1952-56, 62-68; vis. prof. Colo. State Coll. Edn., summers 1941-47, U. Ore., summer 1966; cartographic editor and producer. Mem. Allied Reparations Commn. to Moscow, 1945. Mem. Am. Geog. Soc., Am. Assn. Geography, Latin Am. Stuies Assn., Nat. Council Geography Tchrs. Home: Norwich VT 05055 Office: Dartmouth U Hanover NH 03755

ENGLISH, WOODRUFF JONES, lawyer; b. Elizabeth. N.J., Apr. 28, 1909; s. Conover and Sara Elizabeth (Jones) E.; grad. Pingry Sch., Elizabeth, N.J., 1927; A.B., Princeton, 1931; LL.B., Harvard, 1934; m. Carolyn Barton, Dec. 19, 1942; children-Woodruff Jones II, Virginia Pierpont, Barton Conover, Elizabeth Cooper, Carolyn Whitaker. Admitted to N.J. bar, 1935, since practiced in Newark; partner firm McCarter & English, 1947—; lectr. on trusts and estates. Dir. Jersey Mortgage Co. Trustee Presbyn. Hosp., Newark, 1947- 58; trustee United Hosps. Newark, 1959—, chmn. bd., 1967-70; trustee Overlook Hosp., Summit, N.J., 1949-55, pres., 1953-55; trustee United Community Fund Newark, 1957—, pres., 1961-65; trustee Frost Valley YMCA, 1959—, pres., 1967—; trustee Overseas Ministries Study Center, 1958—, sec., 1958—; bd. dirs. Newark YM-YWCA, 1951—, pres., 1957-61; mem. internat. com. Nat. Bd. YMCA, 1953—, exec. com., 1953—, sec. exec. com., 1960-64; trustee Colonial Symphony Soc., 1951-61, vp., 1959- 61. Served to lt. comdr. USNR, 1941-45. Fellow Am. Coll. Probate Counsel; mem. Am. Law Inst., Am. Judicature Soc., Am., N.J., Essex County bar assns., Assn. Bar City N.Y., Soc. Hosp. Attys. of Am. Hosp. Assn. Republican. Presbyn. Clubs: Essex (Newark); Nassau (Princeton, N.J.); Princeton (N.Y.C.). Home: 90 Whittredge Rd Summit NJ 07901 Office: 550 Broad St Newark NJ 07102

ENGLUND, CARL RUDGERD, agriculturist; b. Kerman, Cal., Sept. 30, 1914; s. Daniel Isadore and Othella Borghild (Wickstrom) E.; student U. Cal. at Berkeley, 1933-36, 38; B.S., U. Cal. at Davis, 1939, postgrad., 1939-40; postgrad. Cal. State Poly. Coll., 1941-47; m. Harriet Jarmain, Nov. 2, 1936; children—Michael Rudgerd, Anne Elizabeth. Dir. agr. Parlier (Cal.) Union High Sch., 1940-41; agrl. instr. Reedley (Cal.) Union High Sch. and Jr. Coll., 1940-42, dir. agr., 1942-48; deciduous fruit dealer, Reedley, 1944-47; head crops dept. Cal. State Poly. Coll., San Dimas, 1948-51, asst. dean, 1951-52, dean agr., Kellogg- Voorhis campus, Sam Dimas and Pomona, 1952-69; on leave for internat. devel. work with FMC Corp. Internat., Iran, Yugoslavia, Turkey, 1968-69, now sr. agriculturist FMC Corp., San Jose, Cal. Mem. Cal. Agr. Liaison Com., 1960—. Mem. Alpha Zeta. Club: Commonwealth. Home: 20812 4th St Saratoga CA 95070 Office: FMC International San Jose CA 95110

ENGLUND, FREDERICK W., dept. store exec.; b. 1906; m. Dist. mgr., asst. gen. sales mgr., corp. personnel dir., v.p. personnel Carson, Pirie, Scott & Co., 1955-69, v.p. adminstrn., 1969—. Address: 1 S State St Chicago IL 60603*

ENGLUND, JOHN EMIL, educator, mech. engr.; b. Canton, O., July 5, 1909; s. John. A.A. and Isabelle M. G. (McLaughlin) E.; Sc.B., Brown U., 1934; m. Jessie M. Romer, Mar. 28, 1942; children—Christina (Mrs. Paul A. Bogrow), John H., William A. Employed as machinist, toolmaker, 1926-30; constrn. designer machine tools Brown and Sharpe Mfg. Co., 1934-40; design machine tools Landis Tool Co., 1940-41; asso. mech. engring. Columbia, 1942-46, asst. prof. mech. engring., 1946-47, asso. prof., 1947-56, prof., 1956—, exec. officer, chmn. mech. engring., 1955-58. Mem. Am. Soc. M.E., Am. Assn. U. Profs., Am. Soc. Engring. Edn., Am. Gear Mfrs. Assn., Soc. for History Tech., A.A.A.S. Patentee power transmission mechanism. Author articles on machine design and metal working processes. Home: 326 Redford Rd Pleasantville NY 10570 Office: Dept Mech Engring Columbia U New York City NY 10027

ENGRAM, WILLIAM CARL, psychologist, educator; b. Frankfort Heights, Ill., Aug. 12, 1921; s. William and Joyce B. (Horrell) E.; A.B., Washington U., 1949; M.A., U. Mo., 1951; Ph.D., Cornell U., 1966; m. Barbara J. Knapp, Aug. 7, 1954; children—Pamela Sue, Melanie Jane, William Marc. Instr. psychology U. Mo., 1951-52, counselor, 1952; counselor, instr. psychology Stephens Coll., 1953; asso. prof. to prof. psychology, chmn. dept. Lindenwood Coll., St. Charles, Mo., 1953-64; counselor Univ. Counseling Service, Cornell U., 1964-65; spl. instr. Elmira Coll., 1965-66; asso. prof. psychology State U. N.Y. at Albany, 1966-67; dir. counseling services Alfred U., 1967-69, prof., chmn. dept. psychology, 1967—. N.Y. state committeeman Liberal Party, 1967—, co-chmn. Steuben County com., 1968-70. Served with AUS, 1942-46. Mem. Am., Eastern, N.Y. State psychol. assns., Am. Psychology-Law Soc., A.A.A.S., Am. Assn. Univ. Profs., N.Y. Acad. Scis., Council Chmn. Grad. Study Psychology, Psi Chi, Alpha Pi Zeta. Home: 80 Genesee St Hornell NY 14843 Office: Alfred Univ Alfred NY 14802

ENGSTROM, ELMER WILLIAM, business exec.; b. Mpls., Aug. 25, 1901; s. Emil and Anna (Nilssen) E.; B.S., U. Minn., 1923; Sc.D. (hon.), N.Y. U., 1949, Rutgers U., Franklin and Marshall U., 1963, Monmouth Coll., 1966; LL.D., Findlay Coll., 1960, Rider Coll., 1961, W.Va. U., 1962, Thiel Coll., 1963, North Park Coll. and Theol. Sem., 1964, Lycoming Coll., 1966, Houghton Coll., 1967; Eng.D., Drexel Inst. Tech., 1963, Lafayette Coll., Poly. Inst. Bklyn., 1966, Worcester Poly. Inst., 1970; D.F.A., Bethany Coll., 1966; L.H.D., Taylor U., 1968; D.Tech., Chalmers Inst. Tech. (Sweden), 1970; m. Phoebe Leander, July 28, 1926; 1 son, William Leander. From devel. engr. to div. engr. Gen. Electric Co., Schenectady, 1923-30; div. engr. RCA Mfg. Co., 1930-31, dir. gen. research, 1932-39, dir. research, 1939-42, dir. gen. research RCA Labs div. RCA, 1942-43, research dir., 1944-45, v.p. in charge research, 1945-51, v.p. charge RCA Labs., 1951-54, exec. v.p. research and engring. RCA, 1954-55, sr. exec. v.p., 1955-61, pres., 1961-66, chmn. exec. com., 1966-71, chief exec. officer, 1966-67, dir. 1966-71, now cons.; dir. Prudential Ins. Co. Am. Mem. adv. com. research div. Coll. Engring., N.Y. U., 1949—; mem. exec. tech. devels. bd. Poly. Inst. Bklyn.; vis. com. Nat. Bur. Standards. Bd. dirs. Christianity Today; trustee Westmont Coll., A.m. Scandinavian Found., U. Minn. Found.; bd. govs. Am. Swedish Hist. Found.; mem. bd. Overseers Found. for Advancement Grad. Study in Engring. Recipient Outstanding Achievement award U. Minn. 1950; John Ericsson medal Am. Soc. Swedish Engrs., 1956; Christopher Columbus Internat. prize in Communications, 1959; Medal of Honor, Electronic Industries Assn., 1962; medal for advancement research Am. Soc. for Metals, 1962; Swedish-Am. of Year award Vasa Order, 1963; award of merit Aerospace Elec. Soc., 1963; William Proctor prize Sci. Research Soc. Am., 1966; decorated comdr. Order Merit Italian Republic, Royal Order Vasa (Sweden). Registered profl. engr. N.Y. State. Fellow I.E.E.E. (Founders award 1966); mem. Nat. Acad. Engring. (charter, Steinmetz Centennial medal 1965, mem. council), Soc. Motion Picture and Television Engrs. (hon., Progress medal 1955), Sigma Xi (past pres. local chapter). Rotarian. Contbr. numerous articles to profl. jours. Home: 75 B Amherst Lane Rossmoor Jamesburg NJ 08831 Office: 30 Rockefeller Plaza New York City NY 10020

ENGSTROM, WILLIAM WEBORG, educator, physician; b. Milaca, Minn., June 29, 1915; s. Otto and M. Caroline (Weborg) E.; B.S. with distinction, U. Minn., 1935, M.D., 1940, M.S. in Biochemistry and Medicine, 1944; m. Elizabeth G. Wulf, July 12, 1943; children—Ann Rigby, Frederick William, Sara Elizabeth. Intern Johns Hopkins Hosp., 1939-40; fellow Mayo Found., 1941-44; instr., then asst. prof. medicine Yale Sch. Medicine, 1946-50; mem. faculty Marquette U. Sch. Medicine, 1950—, prof., chmn. dept. medicine, 1958—; med. dir. Milw. County Hosp., 1958—. Mem. Am. Field Service Com., Elm Grove, Wis., 1960—. Served to capt., M.C., AUS, 1944-46. Recipient Teaching award Phi Chi, 1957; Distinguished Achievement award U. Minn., 1964; Tri-State Teaching award, 1971. Mem. Assn. Am. Physicians, Am. Soc. for Clin. Investigation, Central Soc. Clin. Research, A.A.A.S., A.C.S., Endocrine Soc., Am. Thyroid Soc. Author articles on metabolis diseases, internal medicine, med. philosophy. Home: 735 Brinsmere Dr Elm Grove WI 53122 Office: Milwaukee County Hosp Milwaukee WI 53226

ENLUND, E. STANLEY, savs. and loan. assn. exec.; b. Chgo., July 5, 1917; s. John R. and Alice (Schoenian) E.; J.D., DePaul U., 1942; m. Calista E. Olson, Mar. 36, 1943; 1 son, John Delos. With Continental Ill. Nat. Bank & Trust Co., Chgo., 1934-57, asst. sec., 1951-57; admitted to Ill. bar, 1942, with Sears Bank & Trust Co., Chgo., 1957-63, v.p., trust officer, sec. bd. dirs., 1958-63; exec. v.p. First Fed. Savs. and Loan Assn., Chgo., 1963, pres., 1963—, also dir.; dir. Allstate Enterprises. Bd. dirs. Better Bus. Bur. Met. Chgo., 1965—. Pres. Ill. Arthritis Found., 1967-70; mem. Leadership Council Met. Open Communities, 1964—, Chgo. Urban Renewal Com., 1964—; mem. zoning com., also bd. appeals, Hinsdale, Ill., 1965—; mem. adv. bd. Citizenship Council Met. Chgo., 1966—; treas. Chgo. YMCA, 1963-67, pres., 1968-70; mem. bd. Nat. Council YMCA's; lay bd. trustees De Paul U. Served to lt. USNR, 1941-45. Mem. Am. Inst. Banking (pres. 1957-58; life mem.), Fed. Savs. and Loan Council Ill. (bd. dirs.), U.S. Savs. and Loan League, Cook County Council Insured Savs. Assns., Ill., Chgo. bar assns., Chgo. Assn. Commerce and Industry (bd. dirs.), Ill. C. of C. (pres. 1966-68), DePaul U. Alumni Assn. (pres. 1966-67). Mem. Evangel. Lutheran Ch. Clubs: Chicago Sunday Evening (trustee 1969-70), Legal, Union League (Chgo.). Home: 822 S Lincoln St Hinsdale IL 60521 Office: 1 S Dearborn St Chicago IL 60603

ENNIS, BILLY MACK, food co. exec.; b. Shoffner, Ark., Apr. 10, 1938; s. Rex Dale and Geraldine N. (McCoy) E.; B.S., Ark. State U., 1965; m. Paula Joy Morgan, Nov. 27, 1960; 1 dau., Sherry. Accountant Touche, Ross & Co., Memphis, 1965-68; v.p., sec., treas., dir. United Foods, Inc., Memphis, 1968—. Mem. Am. Inst. C.P.A.'s, Tenn. Soc. C.P.A.'s. Home: 3045 Inverness St Memphis TN 38118 Office: 5050 Poplar St Memphis TN 38117

ENNIS, THOMAS ALLEN, lawyer; b. N.Y.C., Aug. 21, 1920; s. Thomas Leland and Madeleine Clark (Smith) E.; grad. St. Mark's Sch., 1938; B.A., Yale, 1942, LLB., Columbia, 1949; m. Alfreda Learoyd Wallace, Sept. 13, 1947; children—Madeleine Elizabeth, Thomas Wallace. Admitted to N.Y. State bar, 1949; asso. Shearman & Sterling, N.Y.C., 1949-54; counsel Combustion Engring., Inc., N.Y.C., 1954-59, v.p., counsel, 1959—, also dir.; dir. Miss. Glass Co., Combustion Engring.-Superheater Ltd., Montreal, Can., Combustion Engring. Overseas, Inc., Windsor, Conn., Lummus Co. (N.J.), Lummus Co Can., Ltd., Combustion Pub. Co., N.Y.C. Served to 1st lt. USAAF, 1943-46. Mem. Am. Bar Assn., Assn. Bar City N.Y., New Eng. Soc. in N.Y., Chi Psi. Episcopalian. Clubs: University, Cloud, Pinnacle, Links. Home: 863 Park Av New York City NY 10021 Office: 277 Park Av New York City NY 10017

ENNIS, THOMAS ELMER, Jr., educator; b. Salisbury, N.C., Jan. 1, 1930; s. Thomas Elmer and Annie (Williams) E.; B.S. in Bus. Adminstrn., U. N.C., 1952, M.B.A., 1955; Ph.D., U. Mich., 1964; m. Loraine May Van Dam, Aug. 21, 1959. Mem. faculty Washington and Lee U., 1955—, instr., 1955-57, asst. prof. accounting, 1957-64, asso. prof., 1964-68, prof., 1968—. Served with AUS, 1952-54. Mem. Am. Accounting Assn., Nat. Assn. Accountants, Phi Beta Kappa, Beta Gamma Sigma, Omicron Delta Epsilon. Home: Maury Heights Route 5 Box 93 Lexington VA 24450 Office: 31 Newcomb Hall Washington and Lee U Lexington VA 24450

ENNIS, THOMAS GATES, marine corps officer; b. Norwalk, Conn., Aug. 1, 1904; s. Edward Clarkson and Emma Louise (McNaughton) E.; B.S., U.S. Naval Acad., 1928; m. Helen Leila Smith, Oct. 1, 1930. Commd. 2d lt. USMC, 1928, advanced through grades to maj. gen., 1957; designated naval aviator, 1930; exec. officer Marine Aircraft Group 14 and Bomber Command, Marine Aircraft Wing, Guadalcanal, 1942; G-1, Marine Aircraft Wings, South Pacific, 1943; G-4 Div. of Aviation USMC, 1944; comdr. Marine Aircraft Group 32, P.I., 1945-46, also China; chief staff Marine Air Res. Tng. Command, 1946-48; comdr. Marine Aircraft Group 12, 1948-49; student, then instr. Indsl. Coll. Armed Forces, 1949-52; comdr. Marine Corps Air Sta., Miami, Fla., 1952-54; asst. comdg. gen. 1st Marine Air Wing, Korea, 1954-56; dir. Reserve, hdqrs. USMC, 1956-57; comdr. gen. 3d Marine Aircraft Wing, 1957-59, insp. gen. U.S.M.C., 1959-60, comdg. gen. Parris Island, 1960- 62. Legion of Merit with cluster, Presdl. Unit Citation, Navy Unit Citation (U.S.); Collar Order Cloud and Banner (Nat. Chinese); Order Brit. Empire. Mason (32, Shriner). Address: Hdqrs US Marine Corps Washington DC 20380

ENNIS, THOMAS MICHAEL, found. exec.; b. Morgantown, W.Va., Mar. 7, 1931; s. Thomas Edson and Violet Ruth (Nugent) E.; student W.Va. U., 1949-52; A.B., George Washington U., 1954; J.D.,Georgetown U., 1960; m. Julia Marie Dorety, June 30, 1956; children—Thomas John, Robert Griswold. Subrogation-arbitration examiner Govt. Employees Ins. Co., Washington, 1956-59; asst., legislative analyst to v.p. pub. affairs Air Transport Assn. Am., Washington, 1959-60; dir. ann. support program George Washington U., 1960-63; nat. dir. devel. Project HOPE, People to People Health Found., Inc., Washington, 1963-66; nat. exec. dir. Epilepsy Found. Am., Washington, 1966—. Clin. instr. dept. community medicine and internat. health Georgetown U. Sch. Medicine, 1967—. Cons. health and med. founds., related orgns.; cons. Am. Health Found., 1967-69, Reston, Va.-Georgetown U. Health Planning Project, 1967-69; mem. Pres.'s Com. on Employment Handicapped, Internat. Bur. Epilepsy, Nat. Com. for Research in Neurol. Disorders. Nat. del. trustee, v.p. Nat. Capitol Area chpt., bd. dirs., exec. com. Nat. Kidney Found., 1969—. Mem. Am. Soc. Internat. Law, Soc. Internat. Devel., Nat. Rehab. Assn., Am. Pub. Health Assn., Assn. Schs. Allied Health Professions, Phi Alpha Theta, Phi Kappa Psi. Republican. Roman Catholic. Home: 14209 Greenspan Lane Rockville MD 20853 Office: 733 15th St N W Washington DC 20005

ENOCHS, RODNEY LEE, ins. co. exec.; b. Midway, O., Feb. 8, 1926; s. Edgar Ernest and Mary (Halliday) E.; B.S. in Bus., Miami U., Oxford, O., 1949; LL.B., Fordham U., 1958, J.D., 1968; m. Elizabeth M. Gunderson, Feb. 11, 1961; children—Karen Elizabeth, Ross Alexander. Admitted to N.Y. bar, 1959; with Equitable Life Assurance Soc. U.S., 1950—, sec., 1966—. Served with USAAF, World War II. Mem. Am. Soc. Corporate Secs., Am., N.Y. State bar assns., N.Y. County Lawyers Assn., Newcomen Soc. N. Am., Pi Kappa Alpha, Delta Sigma Pi. Home: 41 Carla Lane Irvington-on-Hudson NY 19533 Office: 1285 Av of Americas New York City NY 10019

ENOS, GEORGE ELDRIDGE, coal and steel co. exec.; b. Cleve., Feb. 12, 1916; s. George Albert and Ethel (Drake) E.; A.B., Harvard, 1937; m. Nancy Jane Crawford, Aug. 29, 1938; children—George Eldridge, Marguerite, Lucy. With Enos Coal Mining Co., Cleve., 1937-63, pres., 1956-63; exec. v.p. Interlake Iron Corp., 1963, chmn. bd., 1964, dir., pres. Enos Coal Mining div., 1963-64; pres. Enoco Collieries, Inc. 1948-62; v.p., treas. Algers, Winslow & Western Ry. Co., 1946-64, chmn. exec. com. Interlake Inc., 1965—, also dir.; dir., mem. exec. com. Bucyrus-Erie Co.; dir. Gould Inc., Youngstown Steel Door Co., Arthur G. McKee & Co. Cleve. Trust Co., Hoover Co., North Canton, O. Bd. dirs., mem. exec. com. Cleve. Clinic Found.; pres. bd. trustees U. Sch., Cleve. Mem. Nat. Coal Assn. (hon. dir., chmn. 1961-62). Clubs: Union, Hermit, Mayfield Country (Cleve.); Pepper Pike Country; Chagrin Valley Hunt. Home: SOM Center Rd Hunting Valley Chagrin Falls OH 44022 Office: Union Commerce Bldg Cleveland OH 44114

ENOUEN, WILLIAM ALBERT, paper corp. exec.; b. Columbus, O., Nov. 7, 1928; s. John J. and Bertha (Thiry) E.; B.S., U. Dayton, 1952; m. Joan Claire Batsche, June 20, 1953; children—William A., Robert, Kathryn, James, Patricia. Various accounting positions Touche, Ross & Co., Dayton, O., 1952-59; asst. to controller, asst. to group v.p. and financial cons. affiliated cos. The Mead Corp., Dayton, 1959-68, controller, 1969—; v.p. Brunswick Pulp & Paper Co., 1968-69. Served with AUS, 1946-47. Mem. Ohio Soc. C.P.A.'s (v.p. Dayton chpt. 1959-60). Home: 4617 Ackerman Blvd Dayton OH 45429 Office: 118 W 1st St Dayton OH 45402

ENRIGHT, JOHN JOSEPH, lawyer; b. Chgo., June 16, 1927; s. John Joseph and Maxine (Davis) E.; Ph.B., U. Chgo., 1947, J.D., 1951; m. Marilyn L. Wright, Nov. 3, 1951; children—John J., Kathleen N., Rosemary A., Michael R., Mark E., William R., Ruth V., Paul J., Edward H. Admitted to Ill. bar, 1951, since practiced in Chgo.; mem. firm Enright & Enright, 1951-54; chief enforcement atty. U.S. Securities and Exchange Commn. Chgo. Regional Office, 1954-64; partner Arvey, Hodes & Mantynband, 1964—. Served with USNR, 1945-46. Recipient William A. Jump Meml. Found. award for exemplary achievement in pub. adminstrn., 1960. Mem. Fed., Ill., Chgo. bar assns. Home: 9372 S Longwood Dr Chicago IL 60620 Office: 1 N La Salle St Chicago IL 60602

ENRIGHT, WILLIAM FAIRLEIGH, banker; b. St. Joseph, Mo., Feb. 23, 1894; s. Charles Frederick and Jennie (Fairleigh) E.; A.B., Harvard, 1916, postgrad. Sch. Business Adminstrn., 1916-17; m. Lucie Graham Howell, Feb. 5, 1918 (div. 1933); children—Jane Fairleigh (Mrs. Jane Enright Minton), William Fairleigh; m. 2d., Maurine O'Malley, Aug. 16, 1944. With Empire Trust Co., St. Joseph, Mo., 1919—, bookkeeper, teller, sec., treas. and v.p. to 1935, pres., 1935-60, consol. with Tootle Nat. Bank, 1960, chmn. bd. Tootle-Enright Nat. Bank (consol. with Am. Nat. Bank 1963), St. Joseph, now co- chmn. exec. com.; v.p., dir., Mo. Water and Stream Supply Co. Col. on staff of Gov. of Mo., 1937-41, 49-53, 57-65; mem. adv. bd. Mo. State Conservation Commn.; del. from Mo. to 1st Inter-Am. Travel Congress, San Francisco, 1939; del. from Mo. to Nat. Rivers and Harbors Congress, Washington, D.C., 1939; chmn. Selective Service Board No. 1 Buchanan County, Mo. mem. City Planning Commn. St. Joseph. Bd. dirs. Northwest Mo. Assn. for the Blind; mem. bd. edn. Mo. Sch. Dist.; mem. Mo. State Commn. Resources and Devel. Chmn. Bd. trustees, Employees Retirement Fund St. Joseph Sch. System. Active in Dem. Pary in Mo.; organized Dem. Boosters Club, St. Joseph, 1930, pres. 1930-34. Entered 1st O.T.C., Ft. Riley, Kan., May 10, 1917; commd. 2d lt. Coast Arty. Corps, U.S. Army, Fortress Monroe, Va.; served with 75th Arty., 1919. Elk. Clubs: Benton, St. Joseph, St. Joseph Country; Harvard (N.Y.C.); Garden of the Gods, Cheyenne Mountain Country, Broadmoor Golf (Colorado Springs, Colo.) River (Kansas City, Mo.). Home: 2901 Douglas St Joseph MO 64506 Office: American Nat. Bank 6th and Francis Sts St Joseph MO 64502

ENRIQUEZ, ALFREDO BORUND, govt. ofcl.; b. La Union, N.M., Oct. 29, 1915; s. Jose Carvajal and Felipa (Borunda) E.; B.S., N.M. State U., 1942; m. Beatriz Siquerros Provencio, Oct. 29, 1944; children—Alfred Thomas, Suzanne P. With N.M. Extension Service, 1946-47, Vets-on-Farm Tng., N.M. Vocational Agr. Dept., 1947-50; with AID (and predecessor agencies), various locations, 1953—, West Pakistan, 1964-70, Izmir, Turkey, 1970—. Served with AUS, 1942-45. Fulbright tchrs. exchange grant, Portugal, 1951-52. Mem. Fgn. Service Assn. Democrat. Roman Catholic. Home and Office: PO Box 2565 APO New York City NY 09224

ENSIGN, CHESTER OSCAR, Jr., geologist; b. Statesville, N.C., Oct. 23, 1924; s. Chester Oscar and Ruth (Dillon) E.; B.S. in Bus. Adminstrn., U. N.C., 1948; B.S. in Geology, 1950, M.S. in Econ. Geology, 1951; m. Elizabeth Dunlop, Mar. 18, 1950; children—Stephen Willard, Chester Oscar. Instr. geology U. N.C., 1949-51; supr. exploration, mines planning engr. Davison Chem. Corp., Bartow, Fla., 1951-55; sr. exploration geologist Am. Metal Climax, Inc., 1955-61; chief geologist Copper Range Co., N.Y.C., 1961-68, v.p. exploration, 1968-69, exec. v.p., chief operating officer, 1969-70, pres., chief exec. officer, 1970—. Served with USNR, 1943-46. Mem. Am. Inst. Mining, Metall. and Petroleum Engrs., Geol. Soc. Am., Soc. Econ. Geologists, Am. Inst. Profl. Geologists, Mining and Metall. Soc., Canadian Inst. Mining and Metallurgy, Soc. Exploration Geophysists. Methodist. Rotarian. Clubs: Ontonagon (Mich.) Golf (v.p.); Toastmasters (past pres.) (White Pine, Mich.); Saugatuck Harbor Yacht (Westport); Westchester Country (Rye N.Y.). Contbr. articles profl. jours. Home: 226 North Av Westport CT 06880 Office: 630 Fifth Av New York City NY 10020

ENSIGN, WILLIAM JAMES, state ofcl.; b. Cleve., June 21, 1924; s. Harmon Oliver and Isabelle T. (McKay) E.; student Eastern Ill. State Coll., 1946-48; A.B., U. Notre Dame, 1950, A.M., 1951; m. Joan Marie Kennedy, Nov. 18, 1950; children—Maria Therese, Kimberly Anne, Christopher William, Joel Francis, Madonna Maureen, Thomas Shannon. Purchasing agt. Brodhead-Garrett Co., Cleve., 1941-42; caseworker, juvenile parole officer, South Bend, Ind., 1950-51; probation officer Lucas County, O., 1951-60; exec. sec. Ohio Pardon and Parole Commn., 1960-63; welfare dir. Lucas County, 1963-67; mayor of Toledo, 1967-71; dir. Ohio Youth Commn., 1971—; part time instr. sociology Mary Manse Coll., 1953-60, 63-67. Served with USMCR, 1942-46; PTO. Mem. U.S. Conf. Mayors, Nat. Leagues Cities, Am. Legion, Disabled Am. Vets, Old Newsboys Goodfellow Assn., Sigma Tau Gamma. Democrat. Roman Catholic. Address: 1707 Potomac Dr Toledo OH 43607

ENSIGN, WILLIS LEE, lawyer; b. Binghamton, N.Y., Apr. 5, 1922; s. Willis Lee and Willnita (Strider) E.; A.B., Southwestern U., 1942; LL.B., Harvard, 1948; m. Jule K. Donald, June 13, 1953; children—Donald W., John S. Admitted to N.Y. bar, 1948, Ala. bar, 1953; atty. Western Union Telegraph Co., 1948-50; atty. Ford Motor Co., 1950-52; asso. firm Carter, Ledyard & Milburn, 1953-59, partner, 1959—. Mem. N.Y. State Bar Assn., Assn. Bar City N.Y., Am. Bar Assn. Office: 2 Wall St New York City NY 10005

ENSLEY, FRANCIS GERALD, clergyman; b. Morrow County, O., Aug. 12, 1907; s. Louis Alfred and Nellie Jane (McConnell) E.; A.B., Ohio Wesleyan U., 1927, S.T.B. magna cum laude, Boston U., 1931, Ph.D., 1938; D.D., 1957; postgrad. (Jacob Sleeper fellow) U. Berlin (Germany), 1931-32; D.D., Ohio Wesleyan U., 1946, Westmar Coll., 1963; LL.D., Baker U., 1964, Ia. Wesleyan Coll., 1953; L.H.D., Simpson Coll., 1953, Mount Union Coll., 1969; Litt.D., Morningside Coll., 1960, Am. U., 1961, Rio Grande Coll., 1966; Ecum.D., Ohio No. U, 1965; Pd.D., Baldwin- Wallace Coll., 1966; m. Eunice Irene LeBourveau, July 6, 1935; children—Frederick Louis, Philip Chalfant,

Elizabeth, Charlotte Ensley Linville. Ordained to ministry Meth. Ch., 1936; asso. minister Islington (Mass.) Community Ch., 1932-33; minister North Hampton (N.H.) Congl. Ch., 1933-35, United Church of Norwood (Mass.), 1935-44; instr. homiletics Boston U. Sch. Theology, 1938-44, prof. systematic theology, 1944; minister North Broadway Met. Ch., Columbus, O., 1944-52; consecrated bishop Meth. Ch., 1952, assigned to Ia. area, 1952-64, Ohio West area, Columbus, 1964—. Chmn. div. higher edn. Meth. Ch., 1960-64, pres. gen. bd. social concerns, 1960-64, chmn. commn. on ecumenical affairs, 1964-68; pres. Am. sect. World Meth. Council, 1966—; v.p. Council on World Service and Finance, 1969—, chmn. com. on evangelism world Meth. Council, 1970—; Willson lectr., 1966, Loud Meml. lectr., 1949; Mendenhall lectr. DePauw U., 1959; mem. Gen. Conf. Meth. Ch., 1948, 52, Ecumenical Conf., 1951-56, 61-66. Trustee Scarritt, Mt. Union, Baldwin-Wallace colls., Ohio Wesleyan U., Ohio No. U. Mem. Delta Sigma Rho, Omicron Delta Kappa, Torch. Mason (33). Contbr. to Ency. Religion, Personalism in Theology, A Symphony of Prayer. Author: John Wesley, Evangelist; Paul's Letters to Local Churches; The Marks of Christian Education; Persons Can Change. Home: 31 Meadow Park Av Columbus OH 43209 Office: 395 E Broad St Columbus OH 43215

ENSLEY, GROVER WILLIAM, assn. exec.; b. Colfax, Wash., Apr. 13, 1915; s. Dwight and Mary (Ummel) E.; B.A., U. Wash., 1937, M.B.A., 1938; M.S., U. Denver, 1940; Ph.D., N.Y.U., 1947; postgrad. Harvard, George Washington U.; m. Creta Mabie, Aug. 24, 1940; children—Diane Catherine, Philip Keith, Clifford James, David Richard. Research economist Tax Found., N.Y.C., 1940-41; fiscal analyst U.S. Bur. Budget, 1941-47; tech. adviser Sen. Ralph Flanders, 1947-49; exec. dir. Joint Econ. Com., Washington, 1949-57; exec. v.p. Nat. Assn. Mut. Savs. Banks, N.Y.C., 1957—. Lectr. econs. George Washington U., U. Denver, Wis. Grad. Sch. Banking, Am. Bankers Assn. Grad. Sch. Banking Rutgers U., Brown U. Grad. Sch. Savs. Banking; U.S. del. to GATT, Geneva, Switzerland, 1953; chmn. Spl. Com. on 20th Anniversary of Employment Act 1946, 1965-66; chmn. nat. assns. com. Internat. Savs. Bank Inst., Geneva. Served to lt. (j.g.) USNR, 1944-45. Mem. Am. Econ. Assn., Am. Soc. Pub. Adminstrn. (pres. Washington 1952-53), Am. Finance Assn. (chmn. real estate finance com.), Am. Statis. Assn., Nat. Acad. Econs. and Polit. Sci. (dir.), Conf. Bus. Economists, Am. Soc. Assn. Execs., Met. Econ. Assn., Royal Soc. Arts of Eng., Beta Gamma Sigma. Club: Economic (N.Y.C.). Contbr. articles profl. jours. Home: 19 Woodland Pl Scarsdale NY 10583 Office: 200 Park Av New York City NY 10017

ENSLIN, MORTON SCOTT, educator; b. Somerville, Mass., Mar. 8, 1897; s. Theodore Vernon and Ada Eudora (Scott) E.; A.B., Harvard, 1919, Th.D., 1924; B.D., Newton Theol. Instn. 1922; D.D., Colby Coll., 1945; D.H.L. (hon.), Hebrew Union Coll., 1964; m. Ruth May Tuttle, June 21, 1922; children—Theodore Vernon, II, Priscilla. Prof. N.T. lit. and exegesis, head dept. Crozer Theol. Sem., Chester, Pa., 1924-54; lectr. textual criticism Phila. Div. Sch., 1924-25; lectr. patristics Grad. Sch., U. Pa., 1926-54; Craig prof. Bibl. langs. and lit. Theol. Sch., St. Lawrence U., 1955-65; vis. lectr. history of religion Bryn Mawr Coll., 1965-68; prof. Dropsie Coll., 1968—; vis. prof. Chgo. Theol. Sem., summer 1929, Drew Theol. Sem., 1953-54, Iliff Sch. Theology, summer 1956. Ensign U.S.N.R.F., 1918-22; active duty, 1918-19. Mem. mng. com. Am. Sch. Classical Studies, Athens. Mem. Am. Theol. Soc. (treas. 1927- 55, pres. 1952), Soc. Bibl. Lit. (pres. 1945), Am. Oriental Soc., Phila. Oriental Club (pres. 1938-39), Phi Beta Kappa, Pi Gamma Mu. Republican. Baptist. Mason (K.T., Shriner). Author several books, including; The Ethics of Paul, 1930, rev. 1962; Christian Beginnings, 1938; The Prophet from Nazareth, 1961; Letters to the Churches, 1963, From Jesus to Christianity, 1946. Editor, Crozer Quar., 1941-52, Jour. Bibl. Lit., 1960- 69. Home: 708 Argyle Rd Wynnewood PA 19096

ENSMINGER, MARION EUGENE, agrl. educator, cons.; b. Stover, Mo., May 28, 1908; s. Jacob and Ella (Belt) E.; B.S., U. Mo., 1931, M.S., 1932; Ph.D., U. Minn., 1942; m. Audrey Helen Watts, June 11, 1941; children—John Jacob, Janet Aileen (dec.). Field agt. U. Mo., summers 1929-30; instr. Mo. State U., Marysville, summers 1931-32; asst. to supt. U.S. Soil Erosion Sta., Bethany, Mo., 1933; soil erosion specialist U.S. Dept. Interior, U.S. Dept. Agr., Ill., 1934; mgr. Dixon Springs (Ill.) project U.S. Dept. Agr., 1934-37; asst. prof. U. Mass., 1937-40; teaching asst. U. Minn., 1940-41; prof., chmn. dept. animal sci. Wash. State U., 1941-62; owner, pres. Consultants-Agriservices, Clovis, Cal., 1962—; Distinguished prof. Wis. State U., 1963—; collaborator U.S. Dept. Agr., 1965—; v.p., dir. Mems. Ins. Co., 1965-68; mem. adv. bd. Nat. Bank Agr., 1970—; dir. Horse Sci. Schs., Stockmen's Sch. Cons. nucleonics dept. Gen. Electric Co., AEC, 1947-66; mem. nat. bd. field advisers Small Bus. Adminstrn., 1959-60. Mem. adv. bd. People-to-People Found.; pres. Agriservices Found., Pegus Co., Inc. Named Hon. state farmer Future Farmers Am. Fellow A.A.A.S.; mem. Am. Genetic Assn., Soil Conservation Soc. Am., Am. Soc. Range Mgmt., Am. Soc. Animal Sci. (sec.-treas., v.p., pres. Western sect., Distinguished Tchr. award, plaque), Am. Soc. Agrl. Consultants (1st pres.), CATEC France, (hon. v.p.), Sigma Xi, Alpha Zeta, Lambda Gamma Delta. Author: Animal Science; Beef Cattle Science; Sheep and Wool Science; Swine Science; Horses and Horsemanship; Dairy Cattle Science; Poultry Science; The Stockmen's Handbook; Dairy Cattle Science; Poultry Science. Syndicated columnist The Stockman's Guide, 1956—, Horses, Horses, Horses, 1962—. Address: 3699 E Sierra Av Clovis CA 93612

ENSOR, LOWELL SKINNER, clergyman, coll. pres.; b. Balt., May 15, 1907; s. John T. and Birdie (Skinner) E.; A.B., Johns Hopkins, 1928; B.D., Drew U., 1931; D.D. (hon.), Western Md. Coll., 1944; L.H.D. (hon.), U. Md., 1950; LL.D., Am. U., 1963, Coll. Notre Dame of Md., 1968; m. Eloise Bittner, May 28, 1931; 1 dau., Caryl Jeanne (Mrs. James Lewis). Ordained to ministry Meth. Ch., 1931; pastor Calvert M.E. Ch., Prince Frederick, Md., 1931-34, Ames Ch., Pikesville, Md., 1934-40, Westminster Ch., 1940-47; pres. Western Md. Coll., 1947—; dir. Carroll Co. Bank and Trust Co., Balt. Fed. Savs. and Loan Assn. Pres. Assn. Ind. Colls. of Md., 1953-55, mem. Gov's. Commn. to Study Needs of Higher Edn. in Md., 1953-55; mem. So. Regional Edn. Bd., 1967—. Trustee Asbury Meth. Home, Gaithersburg, Md., Balt. Cont. Pensions Fund, Inc., v.p., 1958—; bd. mgrs. Md. Gen. Hosp., mem. univ. senate Meth. Ch. 1952—; mem. Jurisdictional Conf., 1952-64. Kiwanian. Clubs: Johns Hopkins, Center (Balt.). Home: College Hill Westminster MD 21157

ENTENZA, JOHN DYMOCK, former found. exec., author; b. Calumet, Mich., Dec. 4, 1905; s. Antonio P. and Ellen S. (Dymock) E.; student Stanford, Tulane U., U. Va.; LL.D., Ill. Inst. Tech., 1968; 1 son, Kenneth Keating. Editor-pub. Arts and Architecture mag., 1940-60; dir. Graham Found. Advanced Studies Fine Arts, Chgo., 1960-71. Cons. Bur. Reclamation, Dept. Interior. Mem. steering com. Master Plan for Humanities and Arts, Ill. Bd. Higher Edn.; v.p., dir. Internat. Design Conf., Aspen, Colo.; v.p., trustee Mus. Contemporary Art, Chgo., Tamarind Found., Los Angeles, Nat. Citizens Com. for Broadcasting; mem. Commn. on Chgo. Hist. and Archtl. Landmarks; mem. Yale council com. Sch. Architecture; bd. visitors Carnegie-Mellon U. Hon. mem. A.I.A., also Los Angeles and Chgo. chpts. A.I.A.; recipient Distinguished Service citation A.I.A.; medalist Yale Sch. Art and Architecture, 1966. Home: 900 Lake Shore Dr Chicago IL 60611

ENTERS, ANGNA, dancer, playwright, artist, lectr.; b. N.Y.C., Apr. 28, 1907; d. Edward and Henriette (Gasseur-Styleau) Enters; self-educated in U.S., Europe, Near East; m. Louis Kalonyme. Creator 161 Episodes and Compositions in Dance Form in Theatre of Angna Enters, 1926—, shown in many large cities, colls. of U.S., Can., London, Paris, Cuba, Hawaii, White House, Ringling Mus. Art, Sarasota, Fla., 1952; presented Greek Mime Pagan Greece (performing 12 characters with costumes and music of own creation), Met. Mus. Art, N.Y.C., 1943. Originator phrase dance mime. Guggenheim fellow, 1934, 35. Exhibited paintings Newhouse Galleries, N.Y.C. (12th exhbn. marked debut as sculptor, 18th exhbn. included 1st work in ceramics), other leading cities U.S., London, Eng., many museums; also exhibited drawings of Greek Archaic forms Met. Mus., 1943; 2 weeks repertory, Mercury Theater, London (Arts Council of Gt. Britain) for 10 seasons, including engagement at Cambridge U. Arts Theatre, 1952; mural painting Penthouse Theater, U. Wash., Seattle, 1950; represented Am. Theatre with week's solo performances Berlin Internat. Arts Festival, 1951; spoke on arts Cambridge U., 1951; created Commedia dell'Arte sequence for film Scaramouche, 1952; dir., designer settings, costumes of Yerma, Denver U. Theatre Festival, Ithaca (N.Y.) Coll. Theatre, 1958. Represented in Met. Mus., Honolulu Mus. Art. Author: First Person Plural, 1937; Love Possessed Juana (play), 1939; Silly Girl (book personal remembrance self-illustrated), 1944 (bought by M.G.M.); Mama's Angel (screen play produced as Lost Angel by M-G-M), 1943; A Thing of Beauty (novel), 1949; You Belong to Me (screen play), 1949; Among the Daughters, 1955; Artist's Life, 1957; The Loved and the Unloved, 1961; screen Tenth Avenue Angel; contract as writer, actress, M- G-M, 1945—; artist in residence Baylor U., 1961-62; play dir. Dallas Theatre Center; fellow Center for Advanced Studies, Wesleyan U. (Conn.), 1962. Contbr. articles Mime in Pulpit to Mag. of Art, 1943; essay in Nat. Theatre Conf. Bull., 1944; Pantomime, Ency. Brit. Author: Angna Enters on Mime, 1965. Home: 35 W 57th St New York City NY 10019

ENTREMONT, PHILIPPE, pianist; b. Rheims, France, June 7, 1934; s. Jean and Renée (Monchamps) E.; student Rose Aye Lejour, Marguerite Long, Jean Doyen, George Chavchavadze, Paris Conservatory; m. Andrée Ragot, 1955; 1 dau. First recital, 1951; U.S. debut Carnegie Hall, 1953; appeared with Phila. Orch., 1956, numerous others. Winner prize competitions Paris Conservatory; recipient Grand Prix, Marguerite Long-Jacques Thibaud Competition, 1953; Harriet Cohn piano medal, 1953. Address: Care Ingpen & William Ltd 14 Kensington Ct London W 8 England

ENTWISLE, GEORGE, educator, physician; b. Bolton, Eng., May 27, 1922; s. Nathan and Edith (Wilkinson) E.; came to U.S., 1923, naturalized, 1926; B.S., U. Mass., 1944; M.D., Boston U., 1948; m. Doris Helen Roberts, Aug. 31, 1946; children—Barbara, Beverly, George. Intern, Evans Meml. Hosp., 1948-49, fellow physiology, 1949-51, asst. resident medicine, 1951-52, resident medicine, 1952; lectr. physiology, then instr. medicine Boston U. Sch. Medicine, 1952-56; faculty U. Md. Sch. Medicine, 1956—, prof. preventive medicine, chmn. dept., 1958—. Served with AUS, 1943-44, 52-54. Diplomate Nat. Bd. Med. Examiners, Am. Bd. Internal Medicine; Fellow A.C.P., Am. Coll. Preventive Medicine, Am. Pub. Health Assn.; mem. Md. Rehab. Assn. (pres. 1963-64), Assn. Tchr. Preventive Medicine (pres. 1967-68), Mass., Balt. med. socs., Med and Chirurg. Faculty Md., Am. Fedn. Clin. Research, Sigma Xi. Home: 905 East Wind Rd Baltimore MD 21204

ENTWISTLE, CLIVE ERNEST, architect, city planner; b. London, Eng., May 3, 1916; s. Ernest George and Florence Vivienne (Mellish) E.; student Philol. Sch., London, 1933, Royal Inst. Architects, 1948; m. Helen Piers Groom, May 3, 1944 (div. 1952); children—David Lancelot, Aladine Maria; m. 2d, Angelika H. Federer, Feb. 14, 1963. Came to U.S., 1960. Pvt. own. archtl. and design practice, London, 1945—, Paris, France, 1953-60; practice in N.Y.C., 1960-68; prin. works include Trans. and Travel Bldg., N.Y. World's Fair, New Madison Sq. Garden; house in London in assn. with Le Corbusier, 1939; projects for Nat. Cultural Center, also Liverpool Cathedral; exhbt. Mus. Modern Art, 1960. Served with Royal Engrs., 1941-45. Mem. Soc. Gen. Systems Research, Soc. Cybercultural Research (sci. adv. bd.), Royal San. Inst. Author: Holopolis: Toward a Civilisation, 1969; also articles, reviews. Translator: (Le Corbusier) The Home of Man, Concerning Town Planning. Patentee demountable Chair, 1962, tensile bldg. system, 1966.‡

ENVELA-MAKONGO, GUSTAVO BODJEDI, diplomat of Equatorial Guinea; b. Bolondo, Rio Muni, Equatorial Guinea, June 6, 1926; s. Samuel Envela Pua and Catalina Udendo Makongo; diploma in theology, Dager Theol. Sem., Cameroon, W. Africa, 1949; B.D., Lincoln (Pa.) Theol. Sem., 1957; m. Maravilla Malata Buanga, Mar. 29, 1953 (dec. 1957); 1 son, Teodoro; m. 2d, Victoria Mahua, Mar. 29, 1960; children—Envela, Manuel, Eleuterio, Gustavo. Ordained to ministry Presbyn. Ch., 1953; pastor, Bata, Rio Muni, 1953-69; ambassador of Equatorial Guinea to UN, 1969—. Translated Gospel of Mark in Kombe, 1956-57. Address: 440 E 62d St New York City, NY 10021.

ENVER, EHSAN UL HAQ, Pakistani diplomat; b. Jullunder City, India, July 27, 1926; s. Mohammed and Barkat (Baksh) E.; B.A. in English with honours, Punjab U., 1944; m. Mary Alice Powell, Aug. 5, 1958; children—Shireen, Tariq. Joined Pakistan Fgn. Service, 1948; assigend Karachi, 1949, 1956-57, 1961-63, Ottawa, Can., 1949- 53, Washington, 1953-54, Colombo, Ceylon, 1954-56, London, 1957-58, Calcutta, 1958-60, 61, Shillong, 1960-61, Rawalpindi, 1961, N.Y.C., 1964-65, Madrid, 1965-67; consul gen., San Francisco, 1968—. Adviser various Pakistan delegations. Home: care Ministry Fgn Affairs Karachi Pakistan Office: 2606 Pacific Av San Francisco CA 94115

ENYART, CHARLES WATSON, corp. exec.; b. Agency Ia., 1899. Chmn. bd. C. L. Gougler Machine Co., Kent, O., Equity Corp., United Bd. and Carton Co., dir. Mohawk Rubber Co., Wheelabrator Corp., Bell Intercontinental Corp., Gen. United Group, Inc.; pres., dir. Bonnot Co. Home: 2193 Ridgewood Rd Akron OH 44313 Office: 705 Lake St Kent OH 44312*

ENYEDY, GUSTAV, Jr., chem. engr.; b. Cleve., Aug. 23, 1924; s. Gustav and Mary (Silay) E.; B.S. in Chem. Engring., Case Inst. Tech., 1950, M.S., 1955; m. Zoe Agnes Zachlin, Agu. 25, 1956; children—Louise Elaine, Roseann Marie, Arthur Gustav, Lillian Alice, Edward Anthony. Engr., Rayon Tech. div. E.I. duPont, Richmond, Va., 1950-51; project engr. Grasselli Chem. Div., Cleve., 1951-54; devel. engr. Diamond Alkali, Soda Products, Painesville, O., 1954-60; process engr. Central Engring., Cleve., 1960-61, staff engr. research dept., Painesville, 1961-65, supr. computer services, 1965-68; mgr. Diamond Shamrock Corp., Painesville, 1968—. Lectr. chem. engring. Fenn Coll., Cleve., 1957-61. Treas., cubmaster Gates Mills Cub Scout Pack, 1970-71. Served with AUS, 1943-46. Decorated Bronze Star medal, Combat Inf. badge. Registered profl. engr., Ohio. Mem. Am. Assn. Cost Engrs. (tech. v.p. 1966-68, pres. 1969-70), Am. Inst. Chem. Engrs. (speakers' bur. program 1971—), Nat., Am. mgmt. assns., Inst. Mgmt. Scis., Cleve. Engring. Soc. (chmn. course on capital cost estimating), Tau Beta Pi, Pi Delta Epsilon. Assisted in nuclear fuels plant design, start-up and prodn. Contbr. articles to tech. jours., textbooks. Home: Sugarbush Lane Gates Mills OH 44040 Office: PO Box 348 Painesville OH 44077

ENZMANN, ROBERT DUNCAN, elec. engr., geologist; b. Peking, China, Nov. 5, 1930 (parents Am. citizens); s. E. von Enzmann and Florence Kelly (Goodman) von E.; A.B., Harvard, 1949; B.S. with honors, M.S., U. Witwatersrand (Transvaal, Republic S. Africa), 1953; research Uppsala U., 1954-56; Ph.D. (NSF scholar), Mass Inst. Tech., 1956; m. Joanna Margaret Muckenhoupt, 1958; children—Cassandra-Boell, Alexander, Pendragon, Heidi-Pandora, and Edirland Enzmann. Engaged as consulting geologist, geophysics, mining cos. in Africa, Mediterranean Basin and Greenland, 1950-57; lectr. dept. physics U. Witwatersrand, 1950-54; cons. weapon systems RCA, 1958-59, systems engr., 1958-62; asst. prof. geology and geophysics Boston U., 1958-63; design specialist Convair Astronautics, Atlas Intercontinental Ballistic Missiles, 1958-59; sr. engr., Alaska and Greenland, 1960-62; co. plans and projects Avco Corp., 1962-67; employed with Raytheon Corp., 1967—; research asst., prof. radiation lab. U. Mich., 1962, sr. elec. engr., 1963; lectr. space scis. and aerospace weapons systems Northeastern U., 1963—; organizer, gen. chmn. New Eng. acad. community for space application conf. on planetology and Space mission planning with astronautical society; gen. chmn. confs. on planetology and space mission planning with N.Y. Acad. Scis. Served with USNR, 1943- 46. Mem. New Eng. Cyronics Soc. (pres.), Am. Geophysical Union, Am. Inst. Aero and Astronautics, Geol. Soc. Am., Assn. Am. Physics Tchrs., Am. Phys. Soc., Geol. Soc. S. Africa. Swedish Geol. Soc., German Geol. Soc. Author: Aspects of War and Aerospace Weapons Systems; Systematic Planetology. Contbr. numerous articles profl. publs. Home: 29 Adams St Lexington MA 02173

EPANGUE, MICHEL KOSS, Cameroonian diplomat; b. Bouene-Wouri, Cameroon, Dec. 17, 1939; s. Jacques and Walles (Kottin) E.; Licence en Droit, U. Sorbonne, Paris, 1964; degree polit. sci. U. Grenoble, France, 1962; diploma Inst. Overseas Higher Studies, U. Paris, 1964; student Acad. Internat. Law, The Hague, 1964. Mem. Am. div. Ministry of Fgn. Affairs, Yaounde, 1965, dir. internat. orgns., 1965-68; counselor Cameroon Embassy, Washington, 1963—; mem. legal div. Cameroonian Bank for Devel.; tng. with W.H.O., I.L.O., Geneva, 1966-68; lectr. Carnegie Center Internat. Relations at Yaounde, 1966-68; mem. Cameroon delegation to UN, 21st through 26th sessions. Home: 1255 New Hampshire St NW Washington DC 20036 Office: 1705 New Hampshire Av NW Washington DC 20009

EPES, HORACE HARDWAY, Jr., naval officer; b. Washington, Aug. 10, 1917; s. Horace Hardaway and Virginia (Millan) E.; student N.Y. U., 1934-37; grad. Naval War Coll., 1959; B.A., George Washington U., 1966; m. Katherine Read, Aug. 9, 1941. Commd. ensign U.S. Navy, 1941, advanced through grades to rear adm., 1966; carrier fighter pilot, World War II; comdr. Fighter Squadron 33, Korean War, Air Devel. Squadron 5, 1953, Carrier Air Group 15, 1954- 55, U.S.S. Thetis Bay, 1961-62, U.S.S. Kitty Hawk, 1963-64; comdr. Carrier Div. 1, 1967-68; assigned Bur. Aero., 1945-47, Office Chief Naval Operations 1953, naval test pilot, 1955-57, operations officer 6th Fleet, 1959-61; asst. chief naval personnel, 1965-67; chief Far East Div. (J-5), Joint Chiefs Staff, from 1968. Decorated Legion of Merit, D.F.C., Air medal; Vietnamese Cross Gallantry. Mem. U.S. Naval Inst. Clubs: Nat. Aviation (Washington); N.Y. Yacht; Army Navy Country (Arlington, Va.); Ponte Vedra (Fla.). Home: 1600 S Eads St Arlington VA 22202

EPHRUSSI, BORIS, educator; b. Moscow, USSR, May 9, 1901; s. Samuel and Liuba (Foukelman) E.; M.A., U. Paris (France), 1922, Sc.D., 1932; D.Sc., LL.D., U. Glasgow, 1954; U. Brussels, 1960; m. Harriett Taylor, Oct. 5, 1949; 1 dau., Ann. Asso. prof. biology Johns Hopkins, 1941-44; prof. genetics U. Paris, 1946—; dir. lab. physiol. genetics Centre National de la Recherche Scientifique, 1946—. Exchange prof. Harvard, 1954, Cal. Inst. Tech., 1959; F.H. Herrick distinguished prof. biology Western Res. U., 1961—; spl. research cell differentiation, genetic mechanisms somatic cell variation, cells cultured in vitro. Decorated Legion of Honour. Mem. Royal Danish Acad.; fgn. asso. Nat. Acad. Scis. Author: La Culture des Tissues, 1932; Nucleocytoplasmic relations in micro-organisms, 1953; Contbr. articles to profl. jours. Address: Centre de Génétique Moléculaire du Centre National de la Recherche Scientifique 91 Gif-sur-Yvette France

EPLEY, LEWIS EVERETT, Jr., lawyer; b. Ft. Smith, Ark., Apr. 28, 1936; s. Lewis Everett and Evelyn (Wood) E.; B.S., J.D., U. Ark., 1961; m. Donna Louise Swopes, Feb. 24, 1962. Admitted to Ark. bar, 1961, since practiced in Eureka Springs; city atty., 1969—. Dir. Bank of Eureka Springs. Del. Ark. Constl. Conv., 1969-70. Mem. Carroll County Central Democratic Com., 1964-68. Bd. dirs. Eureka Springs Ozark Folk Festival 1964-69; chmn. adv. bd. Eureka Springs Municipal Hosp. Mem. Ark., Carroll County (pres.) bar assns., Eureka Springs C. of C. (past pres.), Phi Alpha Delta, Kappa Kappa Psi. Baptist. Rotarian. Home: 99 Wall St Eureka Springs AR 72632 Office: 104 Spring St Eureka Springs AR 72632

EPLEY, MALCOLM, newspaperman; b. Broken Bow, Neb., July 13, 1904; s. Lloyd L. and Mina (Hall) E.; A.B., U. Ore., 1929; m. Jane Dudley, Jan. 8, 1927; children—Malcolm, John MacNaughton, Alexandra (Mrs. Richard Traver). Reporter, Riverside (Cal.) Enterprise, 1923-25; news editor Eugene (Ore.) Register, 1928-30; mng. editor Klamath Falls (Ore.) Herald & News, 1931-49; now columnist Long Beach Ind. and Press-Telegram. Mem. Southland Water Com., Cal. Fire Prevention Com. Chmn. bd. Long Beach Heart Assn.; mem. chpt. bd. Nat. Conf. Christians and Jews. Mem. Internat. Press Inst., Sigma Alpha Epsilon, Alpha Phi Gamma, Sigma Delta Chi. Republican. Mem. United Methodist Ch. Elk (dist. dep. Ore. South 1946), Kiwanian. Club: Pacific Coast; International City. Author: Highlights and Anecdotes-An Illustrated History of Long Beach. Home: Box 132 Fort Bidwell CA Office: 6th and Pine Sts Long Beach CA 90812

EPLEY, MARION JAY, Jr., oil co. exec.; b. Hattiesburg, Miss., June 17, 1907; s. Marion Jay and Eva (Quin) E.; LL.B., Tulane U., 1930; m. Dorris Glenn Ervin, Feb. 12, 1934; children—Marion Jay III, Sara Perry (Mrs. Richard H. Davis). Admitted to La. bar, 1930; practiced in New Orleans, 1930-42, 45-47; gen. atty. legal dept. Texaco, Inc., New Orleans, 1947-50, gen. atty., N.Y.C., 1950-58, v.p., asst. to chmn. bd., N.Y.C., 1958- 60, sr. v.p., 1960-61, exec. v.p., 1961-64, pres., 1964-70, chmn. bd., 1970-71, also dir.; pres., dir. Oceanic Devel. Co. Inc., 1971—. Served as lt. USNR, 1942-45. Mem. Am., La. bar assns., Am. Petroleum Inst. Clubs: River (N.Y.C.); Boston (New Orleans); Everglades, Bath and Tennis (Palm Beach, Fla.); Roaring Gap (N.C.). Address: 810 S Ocean Blvd Palm Beach FL 33480

EPP, EDWARD RUDOLPH, med. researcher; b. Saskatoon, Sask., Can., July 21, 1929; s. Abram David and Catherine (Janzen) E.; B.A., U. Sask., 1950, M.A. (Canadian Cancer Soc. scholar), 1952; Ph.D. (Nat. Cancer Inst. Can. fellow), McGill U., 1955; m. Shirley Mae Bishop, May 25, 1957. Came to U.S., 1957. Mem. sci. staff Nat. Research Council Can., 1952-53; radiation physicist Montreal Gen. Hosp., 1955-57; asst. Sloan-Kettering Inst. for Cancer Research,

N.Y.C., 1957-60, asso., 1960-64, asso. mem., 1964-69, mem., 1969—, chief, div. phys. biology, 1968—. Asso. attending physicist Meml. Hosp. for Cancer and Allied Diseases, 1967—; asst., dept. biophysics Sloan-Kettering div. Grad. Sch. Med. Scis., Cornell U., 1957-58, asso., 1958-60, asst. prof. biophysics, 1960-66, asso. prof., 1966-70, prof., 1970—, chmn. biophysics unit, 1966—; mem. radiation study sect. NIH, 1971—. Pres., chmn. bd. 12 W. 96th St. Corp., N.Y.C., 1971—. NIH grantee, 1964—, Damon Runyon Meml. Fund grantee, 1971—. Mem. Am. Assn. Physicists in Medicine (dir. 1971—), Radiation Research Soc., Am. Phys. Soc. (task group for internat. commn. on radiol. units and measurements), Health Physics Soc. Club: Manhattan Chess (N.Y.C.). Contbr. articles sci. publs. Home: 12 W 96th St New York City NY 10021 Office: 410 E 68th St New York City NY 10021

EPPENBERGER, FRED ARNOLD, lawyer; b. Chgo., Oct. 30, 1906; s. Arnold A. and Laura (Doerr) E.; student St. Louis U., 1923; LL.B., Washington U., 1928; m. Emily V. Hurd, Nov. 26, 1937; children—Katherine C., Frederick H. Admitted to Mo. bar, 1928; asso. firm Husch, Eppenberger, Donohue, Elson & Cornfeld and predecessors, St. Louis, 1928—, partner, 1936—. Active drafting of adoption law, juvenile court code; chmn. St. Louis County Commn. on Human Relations. Bd. dirs. Mid-County YMCA, St. Louis; bd. dirs. Family and Children's Service of Greater St. Louis, v.p. 1955-58; mem. citizens advisory bd. Juvenile Court of St. Louis, Chmn., 1963; advisory bd. St. Louis County Children's Treatment Center. Recipient Alumni citation Washington U., 1962, Order of Coif, 1967. Fellow Am. Bar Found., Am. Coll. Probate Counsel; mem. Am. Bar Assn. (ho. dels. 1961-68), Am. Judicature Soc. (dir. 1962-65), Bar Assn. St. Louis (chmn. juvenile laws com.; exec. com. 1944-50), Mo. Bar (chmn. juvenile laws com.; bd. govs. 1955—; pres. 1960, pres. Found. 1962-65), Phi Delta Phi. Conglist. Club: Missouri Athletic (St. Louis). Home: 7141 Washington St University City MO 63130 Office: 7 N 7th St St Louis MO 63101

EPPERT, RAY R., business exec.; b. Carbon, Ind., July 5, 1902; s. Russell and Effie (Webster) E.; L.H.D., Hillsdale Coll., 1956; LL.D., Western Mich. U., 1961, Mich. State U., 1962; D.Sc., B.A., Detroit Inst. of Tech., 1961; D.Sc., U. Detroit, 1967; m. Helen Marie Chaffee, Dec. 30, 1923. With Burroughs Corp., 1921-67, beginning as shipping clk. and advancing to v.p. in charge marketing, 1946-51, exec. v.p., 1951-58, pres., 1958-66, chmn. bd., chief exec. officer, 1966-67, dir., 1948- 67; dir. Mich. Bell Telephone Co., Mich. Consol. Gas Co., Cunningham Drug Stores, Inc. Vice chmn. Internat. Exec. Service Corps. Mem. adv. com. on hosp. effectiveness Dept. Health, Edn. and Welfare; adv. com. on internat. bus. problems Dept. State. Mem. bd., mem. exec. com. United Found. of Met. Detroit; dir., mem. exec. com. Mich. United Fund; dir. Mich. Soc. Mental Health; mem. exec. com. Met. Detroit Bldg. Fund; pres. Detroit Medical Center Devel. Corp.; adv. com. Internat. Marketing Inst., Harvard Grad. Sch., Mich. State U. Sch. Bus. Adminstrn.; chmn. bd. trustees Harper Hosp.; trustee Hillsdale Coll.; lay trustee U. Detroit; dir. Cranbrook Sch. Decorated chevalier Legion of Honor (France); comdr. Order Brit. Empire. Mem. U.S. C. of C., N.A.M., Nat. Planning Assn. Clubs: Detroit, Detroit Athletic, Economic (Detroit); Bloomfield Hills Country; Pine Lake Country; Capitol Hill (Washington); Harbor View (N.Y.). Home: 295 Lone Pine Rd Bloomfield Hills MI 48013 Office: Penobscot Bldg Detroit MI 48226

EPPINGER, EUGENE, physician; b. Pendleton, Ore., Sept. 30, 1902; s. Charles A. and Catherine (Vaughan) E.; A.B., Williams Coll., 1926; M.D., Harvard, 1930; m. Catherine Codman, July 13, 1935; children—Catherine Codman, Margaret Vaughan. Successively jr., sr., asso. and physician Peter Bent Brigham Hosp., Boston, 1937—, acting physician-in-chief, 1951-52; asst. in medicine, instr. med. sch. Harvard, 1937-42, asst. dean, 1945-66, asst. clin. prof., 1945-58, asso. clin. prof., 1958-64, clin. prof. medicine, 1964-69, clin. prof. emeritus, 1969; indsl. relations div. Proctor & Gamble Co., Cin., 1936-37; asso. physician Boston Lying In Hosp.; cons. Free Hosp. for Women; cons. in medicine to Surgeon Gen., U.S. Army. Served as col. M.C., AUS, 1942-45. Fellow A.C.P.; mem. Am. Soc. Clin. Investigation, Am. Clin. Climatol. Assn., Am. Heart Assn., Soc. Med. Consultants World War II, Assn. Am. Physicians. Home: 27 Kingsbury Rd Chestnut Hill MA 02167 Office: Harvard 75 Mt Auburn St Cambridge MA 02138

EPPINGER, JOSUA, Jr., editor; b. San Francisco, Oct. 7, 1902; s. Josua and Hilda (Levy) E.; B.S., U. Cal., 1924; m. Helen Kahn, Jan. 8, 1933 (dec. 1956); children—Wendy Claire (Mrs. J.A. Shulman), Josua, Frederick Dwight; m. 2d, Consuelo B. Hofmann, Aug. 20, 1957; children—Robert, Paul, David, Judith (Mrs. Peter Coy), Michael Hofmann. Reporter San Francisco Examiner, 1924-38, city editor, 1938-46, exec. city editor 1946, now asso. mng. editor. Served at lt. col. AUS, 1941-45. Mem. Alpha Kappa Psi, Delta Sigma Lambda, Sigma Delta Chi. Club: Press (San Francisco). Home: 1010 Francisco St San Francisco CA 94109 Office: San Francisco Examiner San Francisco CA 94103

EPPLER, JEROME CANNON, investment exec.; born Englewood, N.J., Mar. 16, 1924; s. William E. and Aileen (Vaughan) E.; B.S. in Mech. Engring., Tex. A. and M. Coll., 1946; M.B.A., U. Pa., 1949; m. Debora E. Nye, Feb. 17, 1951; children—Stephan Vaughan, William Durand, Margaret Nye, Elizabeth Scott, Edward Curtis. With Gen. Electric Supply Corp., Newark, 1949-50; investment banker Equitable Securities Corp., Nashville, mgr. Houston office, 1950-53; gen. partner Cyrus J. Lawrence & Sons, N.Y.C., 1953-61 (mem. N.Y. Stock Exchange), Eppler & Co., 1961 —; chmn. bd., dir. ISI, Inc., San Francisco; dir. Allegheny Airlines, Washington, Recognition Equipment, Inc., Dallas, Swift & Co., Chgo.; dir., mem. exec. com. Westmount Life Ins. Co., Montreal. Served to lt. (j.g.), USNR, 1942-46. Mem. N.Y. Soc. Security Analysts. Episcopalian. Clubs: Union League, Downtown Assn. (N.Y.C.); The Morristown; Morris County Golf; Stock Exchange (San Francisco). Home: 2 Dellwood Dr Madison NJ 07940 Office: 20 Community Pl Morristown NJ 07960

EPPLER, WILLIAM BURGESS, investment banker; b. Scranton, Pa., July 13, 1921; s. H. Rufus and Phoebe (Burgess) E.; m. Jeannette Smith, June 17, 1950; children—Richard Beall, John Rufus, Jennifer, Margaret. Exec. vice pres., dir. Eppler, Guerin & Turner, Inc., Dallas, 1951—; dir. Southwestern Investors, Inc., Dallas, 1953—, Southwestern Investors Growth Fund, Inc., Dallas, 1960—, Fund of the S.W., Inc., Dallas, Keystone Valve Corp., Miller Bros. Hat. Co., Inc. Served to capt., F.A., AUS, 1942-46; N. Africa, Italy. Episcopalian. Clubs: Dallas Country, Bankers Am. Home: 4411 Belfort Place Dallas TX 75205 Office: First Nat Bank Bldg Dallas TX 75202

EPPS, AUGUSTUS CHARLES, lawyer; b. Richmond, Va., Feb. 2, 1916; s. John Lindsey and Lily Madeline (Becker) E.; B.S., U. Va., 1936, LL.B., 1938; m. Rosalie Suzanne Garrett, Aug. 17, 1946; children—Augustus Charles, George Garrett, John Daniel. Admitted to Va. bar, 1937; practice in Richmond, 1938-42, 46—; asso. atty. Christian, Barton & Parker, 1938-42; partner Christian, Barton, Parker, Epps & Brent, 1946—. Dir., gen. counsel Richmond Life Ins. Co., 1952-69; dir. Universal Acceptance Corp., Universal Finance Co., United Paper Co., Newsome Air Conditioning Co., Va. Suppliers Inc., Community Heating & Air Conditioning Co., Inc. Mem. Richmond Sch. Bd., 1963- 70. Past pres., bd. dirs. Friends Richmond Pub. Library; past vice chmn., bd. dirs. Richmond YMCA; bd. dirs., exec. com. Legal Aid Soc. Met. Richmond; bd. dirs. Richmond Offender Aid and Restoration; trustee Roslyn Diocesan Center, Episcopal Diocese Va. Served Served to maj. AUS, 1942-46. Fellow Am. Bar Found., Am. Coll. Trial Lawyers; mem. Am. (past chmn. com. legal edn., admission to bar), Va. (pres. 1966-67, past chmn. joint com. legislation, law reform, past mem. exec. com.), Richmond (past chmn. legal aid com., past pres.) bar assns., Am. Judicature Soc., Internat. Assn. Ins. Counsel, Assn. Life Ins. Counsel, Fed. Jud. Conf., U. Va. Law Sch. Assn. (mem. council, chmn. Law Day 1972, past chmn. com. scholarships), Phi Beta Kappa, Order of Coif, Phi Delta Phi, Alpha Tau Omega. Episcopalian. Bd. editors, bd. mng. editors Va. Law Rev., 1937-38. Contbr. articles to profl. jours. Home: 6323 Ridgeway Rd Richmond VA 23226 Office: Mutual Bldg Richmond VA 23219

EPPS, WILLIAM MONROE, educator, plant pathologist; b. Latta, S.C., Oct. 31, 1916; s. Silas Wightman and Caroline (Monroe) E.; B.S., Clemson U., 1937; Ph.D., Cornell U., 1942; m. Evelyn Luella Baker, June 27, 1942; children—James William, Philip Olin. Asso. plant pathologist S.C. Agrl. Expt. Sta., Charleston, 1945-56; mem. faculty Clemson U., 1945—, prof. botany and bacteriology, 1956-69, chmn. dept., 1956-69, prof. plant pathology and physiology, 1969—; chmn. dept., 1969—. Served to maj. AUS, 1942-46. Mem. Am. Phytopath. Soc., Am. Soc. Hort. Sci., Soc. Nematologists, Sigma Xi, Alpha Zeta, Phi Kappa Phi, Gamma Sigma Delta. Methodist (chmn. ofcl. bd., 1952, 59, 69, charge lay leader 1963-66). Developed, released 2 disease resistant tomato varieties (Marion and Culiacan I). Home: 211 Wyatt Av Clemson, SC 29631.

EPSTEEN, CASPER MORLEY, medical educator; b. East Chicago, Ind., May 6, 1902; s. Hyman and Sarah Ida (Goodman) E.; B.Sc., U. Ill., 1923, M.D., 1925; D.D.S., Loyola U., Chgo., 1930; m. Aline Gertrude Grossman, Sept. 26, 1934; children—Lynn, Robert. Intern Michael Reese Hosp. and Med. Center, Chgo., 1925-26, now sr. attending surgeon; preceptorship with Dr. Truman W. Brophy, 1926-29; practice medicine specializing maxillofacial and plastic surgery, Chgo., 1926—; cons. Weiss Meml. Hosp., Jackson Park Community Hosp. and Med. Center, Central Community Hosp.; clin. prof. maxillofacial surgery Chgo. Med. Sch., 1960—. Guest of honor 1st Internat. Congress Maxillofacial Surgeons, Venice, Italy, 1971; recipient hon. mention for research salivary glands Am. Soc. Plastic and Reconstructive Surgeons, 1953. Diplomate Internat. Bd. Surgery. Mem. Am. Soc. Maxillofacial Surgeons (pres. 1960, leadership award 1960, distinguished award 1966), Chgo. (pres. 1962-63, award merit 1963), Ill. (1st v.p. 1968) med. socs., A.M.A., Am., Internat. colls. surgeons, World Med. Assn., Chgo. Natural History Museum (life). Clubs: Quadrangle, Executive (Chgo.). Author: Tice's Practice of Medicine, 1948. Guest editor Am. Jour. Surgery, Dec. 1952. Home: 5750 S Kenwood Av Chicago IL 60637 Office: 25 E Washington St Chicago IL 60602

EPSTEIN, ALFRED, brewery exec.; b. Austria, Sept. 6, 1894; s. Samuel and Sophia (Friedman) E.; student pub. schs., Detroit; 1 son, Herbert. Pres. Pfeifer Brewing Co., Detroit, 1935; now vice chmn. Asso. Brewing Co., dir. City Bank Detroit. Dir. Detroit Symphony Orchestra, Inc. Mason (Shriner). Home: 15444 Windmill Pointe Dr Grosse Pointe Park MI 48236 Office: 3740 Bellevue Av Detroit MI 48207

EPSTEIN, ALVIN, actor; b. Bronx, N.Y., May 14, 1925; s. Harry and Goldie (Budnick) E.; student Queens Coll., N.Y.C., 1942-43, Martha Graham Sch. Dance, N.Y.C., 1946-47, Ecole de Mime Etienne Decroux, Paris, 1947-51, Sanford Meisner Profl. Class, N.Y.C., 1951-52. Actor, Thétre de Mime Etienne Decroux, Paris, 1947-51, Habima Theatre, Israel, 1952-55; made Am. profl. debut with Marcel Marceau, Phoenix Theatre, N.Y., 1955; has appeared in many Broadway, off-Broadway touring and regional prodns. including The Fool (with Orson Welles) in King Lear, N.Y., 1956, Lucky in original Broadway prodn. Waiting for Godot, 1956, Puck in A Midsummer Night's Dream, Empire State Music Festival, N.Y., 1956, O'Killigain in Purple Dust, N.Y.C., Octave in Clerambard, N.Y.C., Clov in Endgame, N.Y.C., Luc Delbert in No Strings, N.Y.C., title role in Enrico IV, Milw., Chgo., Beranger in The Pedestrian in the Air, Chgo., Theseus and Oberon in A Midsummer Night's Dream, N.Y.C.; various roles in Postmark Zero, N.Y.C., Landau in The Latent Heterosexual, Los Angeles, Sgt. in Dynamite Tonite, N.Y.C.; appeared in Whores, Wars and Tin Pan Alley, Chgo., New Haven, N.Y.C., Los Angeles, Washington; mem. Yale Repertory Theatre, New Haven, 1968—, directing, appearing in various prodns. including dir. Caligula, 1971-72; appeared in many television shows on all networks; tchr. Chamber Theatre, Israel and Neighborhood Playhouse, N.Y.C., Circle in Sq. Theatre Sch., N.Y.C.; acting tchr. Yale Drama Sch., 1968—. Served with AUS, 1943-46; ETO. Recipient Obie award for Dynamite Tonite, 1968, Brandeis U. Creative Arts award in theatre, 1966. Ford Found. grantee, 1959-60. Fellow Trumbull Coll., Yale. Co-founder, actor Berkshire Theatre Festival, Stockbridge, Mass., 1966. Home: Bethany Wood Bethany CT 06525 Office: Yale Repertory Theatre 222 York St New Haven CT 06520

EPSTEIN, BARBARA, (Mrs. Jason Epstein), editor; b. Boston, Aug. 30, 1928; d. H.W. and Helen (Diamond) Zimmerman; A.B., Radcliffe Coll., 1949; m. Jason Epstein, Dec. 30, 1953; children—Jacob, Helen. Editor, New York Rev., N.Y.C. Home: 33 W 67th St New York City NY 10023 Office: 250 W 57th St New York City NY 10019

EPSTEIN, BENJAMIN ROBERT, assn. exec.; b. N.Y.C., June 11, 1912; s. Hyman and Sadie (Ziess) E.; Ph.B. cum laude, Dickinson Coll., 1933, L.H.D., 1963; exchange fellow Inst. Internat. Edn., U. Berlin, 1934-35; traveling fellow U. Pa., 1934, 38, M.A., 1936; LL.D., Talladega Coll., 1957; m. Ethel Schwartz, Oct. 21, 1935; children—Ellen, David. Instr. German, U. Pa., 1935-36; faculty Coatesville (Pa.) High Sch., 1936-38; staff N.Y. Fedn. Jewish Charities, 1938; staff Anti-Defamation League of B'nai B'rith, 1939-44, dir. Eastern region, 1944-47, nat. dir., 1947—, nat. commr., 1956—; translator. Mem. Bur. Intercultural Edn. (dir.), Nat. Assn. Intergroup Relations Officers, Assn. Jewish Community Relations Workers, Phi Epsilon Pi. Mem. B'nai B'rith. Author: The Troublemakers (with Arnold Forster), 1952; Germany-Nine Years Later (with Jacob Alson and Nathan C. Belth); Crosscurrents (with Arnold Forster), 1956; (with Arnold Forster) Some of My Best Friends ..., 1962, Danger on the Right, 1964, The Radical Right: Report on the John Birch Society and Its Allies, 1967. Home: 411 E 53d St New York City NY 10022 Office: 315 Lexington Av New York City NY 10016

EPSTEIN, BERNARD, educator; b. Harrison, N.J., Aug. 10, 1920; s. Isaac and Sophie (Goldenberg) E.; B.A., N.Y. U., 1940, M.S., 1942; Ph.D., Brown U., 1947; m. Florence Goldstein, Nov. 23, 1947; children—David, Deborah, Ruth, Jeremy, Jonathan, Rebecca. Physicist, Nat. Bur. Standards, 1941-43, Manhattan Project, 1943-45; research asso. in aero. engring. Harvard, 1946-47; mem. faculty dept. math U. Pa., 1947-60; prof. Yeshiva U., 1960-63; prof. math. and statistics U. N.M., 1963-64, 66—; liaison scientist Office Naval Research, London, Eng., 1964-66. Mem. Am. Math. Soc., Math. Assn. Am., London Math. Soc. (Eng.), Edinburgh Math. Soc. (Scotland), Phi Beta Kappa, Sigma Xi. Author: Partial Differential Equations, 1962; Orthogonal Families of Analytic Functions, 1965; Linear Functional Analysis, 1970. Contbr. math. jours. Home: 3704 Utah St NE Albuquerque NM 87110

EPSTEIN, ELENI SAKES, (Mrs. Sidney Epstein), editor; b. Washington, May 17, 1925; d. Constantine and Aspasia (Economon) Sakes; student George Washington U., 1943-45, Columbia, 1947; m. Sidney Epstein, Mar. 30, 1957. Copygirl, women's staff writer Washington Evening Star, 1945-46, fashion editor, 1946—. Recipient J.C. Penney Fashion Writing award U. Mo., 1961, citation Nat. Women's Party, 1966. Mem. Washington Fashion Group, Advt. Club Washington, Women's Nat. Press Club (sec. 1949-50), Am. Newspaper Women's Club (v.p. 1952-54). Greek Orthodox. Home: 2807 Cathedral Av NW Washington DC 20008 Office: 225 Virginia Av SE Washington DC 20003

EPSTEIN, FRANKLIN HAROLD, educator, physician; b. Bklyn., May 5, 1924; s. Max and Fannie (Geduld) E.; B.A., Bklyn. Coll., 1944; M.D., Yale, 1947; m. Sherrie Spivack, Aug. 12, 1951; children—Mark, Ann, Sara, Jonathan. Asst. prof. medicine Yale, 1954-59, asso. prof., 1959-66, prof. medicine, 1966—, chief, div. metabolism, 1965—. Cons. U.S. Army Surgeon Gen., 1964—. Served to capt., M.C., AUS, 1950-53. Diplomate Am. Bd. Internal Medicine. Mem. USPHS (metabolism study sect. 1962-66, research career award 1964), Am. Soc. Clin. Investigation, Assn. Am. Physicians, Interurban Clin. Club, Sigma Xi, Alpha Omega Alpha. Asso. editor Jour. Clin. Investigation, 1957-62. Contbr. papers, book chpts. on renal physiology, disease of kidneys. Jewish religion. Home: Wepawaug Rd Woodbridge CT 06525 Office: 333 Cedar St New Haven CT 06510

EPSTEIN, HERBERT S., brewing co. exec.; b. Detroit, Oct. 6, 1926; s. Alfred and Edna (Feldstein) E.; A.B., U. Mich., 1950; m. Babe Vader, Aug. 21, 1950; children—Herbert Alfred, Robert Neil, Beth Suzanne. With Asso. Brewing Co., Detroit, 1951—, exec. v.p., 1958-59, pres., 1959—, also dir. Active fund raising Nat. Conf. Christians and Jews, Jewish Welfare Fedn. Mem. Young Pres. Orgn., Detroit Sales Execs. Club, Phi Sigma Delta. Mason (Shriner), Lion. Club: Standard City (Detroit). Home: 15660 Windmill Pointe Dr Grosse Pointe Park MI 48236 Office: 3740 Bellevue Av Detroit MI 48207

EPSTEIN, JOSEPH, educator; b. N.Y.C., Jan. 19, 1917; s. Isador and Ida (Snofsky) E.; B.S., Coll. City N.Y., 1939; Ph.D., Columbia, 1951; M.A. (hon.). Amherst Coll., 1961; m. Lucille Goldberger, June 22, 1940; children—Joshua Morris, Samuel David. Physicist, research and devel. U.S. Army Signal Corps. Labs., 1942-44, Fed. Telephone & Radio Corp., Newark, 1944-46; from lectr. to asst. prof. Columbia, 1946-51; faculty Amherst (Mass.) Coll., 1952-71, prof. philosophy, 1961-71; grad. faculty dept. philosophy U. Mass., 1971—. Vis. prof. philosophy Yale, 1966-67. Grantee Rockefeller Found., 1958. Mem. Am. Philos. Assn., Symbolic Logic Assn., Am. Assn. Physics Tchrs., A.A.A.S., Am. Assn. U. Profs., Mind Assn., Sigma Xi. Editor: Alexandrian Editions, 1960; Rene Descartes: A Discourse on Method and Other Works, 1965; (with Gail Kennedy) The Process of Philosophy, 1967. Contbr. articles to profl. jours. Patentee in field. Home: 249 S Pleasant St Amherst MA 01002

EPSTEIN, LEON DAVID, educator; b. Milw., May 29, 1919; s. Harry Aaron and Anna (LeKachman) E.; B.A., U. Wis., 1940, M.A., 1941; Ph.D., U. Chgo., 1948; m. Shirley Galewitz, Jan. 12, 1947. Jr., also asst. economist Nat. Resources Planning Bd., 1941-42; asst. prof. polit. sci. U. Ore., 1947-48; mem. faculty U. Wis., 1948—, prof. polit. sci., 1954—, chmn. dept., 1960- 63, dean Coll. Letters and Sci., 1965-69; fellow Center for Advanced Study in Behavioral Scis., 1970-71. Served to capt. AUS, 1942-46. Mem. Am. Polit. Sci. Assn., Am. Assn. U. Profs., Midwest Polit. Sci. Assn. (pres. 1970-71). Author: Britain-Uneasy Ally, 1954; Politics in Wisconsin, 1958; British Politics in the Suez Crisis, 1964; Political Parties in Western Democracies, 1967; also articles. Home: 2806 Ridge Rd Madison WI 53705

EPSTEIN, NATHAN BERNARD, dept. store exec.; b. Boston, Sept. 30, 1910; s. Louis H. and Martha (Basch) E.; A.B., Harvard, 1931; M.S., N.Y.U., 1931; m. Beatrice L. Stern, July 3, 1946; children-Barbara L., Susan R. With Lerner Stores Corp., 1933—, sec., 1967—, sr. v.p., 1961—, also dir. Mem. Tarrytown (N.Y.) Planning Bd., 1961-64; pres. Tarrytown Bd. Edn., 1968-69. Served to maj. AUS, 1942-46; ETO. Decorated Bronze Star; Order of Crown (Italy). Jewish religion (pres. temple 1957-58). Club: Tarry Crest Swin (pres. 1956-64) (Tarrytown). Home: 153 Crest Dr Tarrytown NY 10591 Office: 460 W 33d St New York NY 10001

EPSTEIN, RALPH JEROME, engring. and archtl. co. exec.; b. Milw., Sept. 18, 1913; s. Louis G. and Helen (Furth) E.; B.S. in Civil Engring., U. Ill., 1934; postgrad. Cal. Inst. Tech., 1940; m. Berenice Bachrach, Nov. 3, 1935; children—Barbara (Mrs. Charles A. Stevens), Irene (Mrs. Samuel Shanes). Structural engr., A. Epstein & Sons, Chgo., 1934-40, 50-59, v.p., 1959-63, exec. v.p., 1963-70, pres., 1970—; designer Lockheed Aircraft Corp., Burbank, Cal., 1940-46; designer Craftex Products Corp., Los Angeles, 1946-50. Chmn. bldg. trades div. Combined Jewish Appeal, 1964; chmn. bldg. trades div. United Settlement Appeal, 1964-65; co-chmn. trades, industries and professions Jewish United Fund, 1967—; mem. campaign cabinet Nat. Jewish Hosp., Denver, 1967—; chmn. Youth Services of B'nai B'rith Yough Found., 1970. Bd. dirs. Union of Am. Hewbrew Congregations, 1961-64, Chgo. Fedn. Settlement Centers and Neighborhood Houses, 1966-67, Jewish Vocational Service, 1969—, Jewish Fedn. Met. Chgo. trustee Central Mfg. Club, 1963-66, U. Ill. President's Club, U. Ill. Found.; mem. Chgo. exec. com. Anti-Defamation League, 1964-69. Recipient Big Ten medal for proficiency in athletics and scholarship, 1934. Mem. Tribe of Ill., Phi Epsilon Pi. Jewish religion (dir., past pres. temple). Club: Standard (Chgo.). Home: 4950 Chicago Beach Dr Chicago IL 60615 Office: 2011 W Pershing Rd Chicago IL 60609

EPSTEIN, RAYMOND, engring. and archtl. exec.; b. Chgo., Jan. 12, 1918; s. Abraham and Janet (Rabinowitz) E.; student Mass. Inst. Tech., 1934-36; B.S., U. Ill., 1938; m. Betty Jadwin, Apr. 7, 1940; children—Gail, David, Norman, Harriet. With A. Epstein & Sons, Inc., Chgo., 1938—, beginning as jr. designer, successively sr. designer, project engr., v.p., pres., 1959-61, chmn. bd. dirs., 1961—. Past pres. Young Men's Jewish Council; dir. United Israel Appeal; mem. housing com. Mayor's Commn. Sr. Citizens; v.p. Council Jewish Fedn. and Welfare Funds, Inc.; chmn. bd. dirs. Jewish United Fund; pres. Jewish Welfare Fund Met. Chgo.; mem. exec. com. United Jewish Appeal. Trustee Chgo. Med. Sch.; mem. citizens bd. Loyola U.; life dir. Mt. Sinai Med. Research Found. Registered architect, profl. engr. Mem. Am. Soc. C.E., Soc. Am. Registered Architects, Am. Concrete Inst., Western Soc. Engrs., Nat., Ill. socs. profl. engrs., Structural Engrs. Assn. Ill., Constrn. Specifications Inst., Assn. Engrs. and Architects in Israel, French Engrs. in the U.S., Inc., Pi Lambda Phi. Clubs: Standard (past trustee), Illini, M.I.T., Museum Shores Yacht, Caxton (Chgo.). Home: 4950 S Chicago Beach Dr Chicago IL 60615 Office: 2011 W Pershing Rd Chicago IL 60609

EPSTEIN, SAUL LEON, paper co. exec.; b. Bklyn., May 8, 1905; s. Louis and Sarah (Broadman) E.; L.H.D., Hofstra U., 1970; m. Evelyn Segal, Jan. 5, 1930; children—Howard, Raymond. Vice pres. Atlantic Containers Corp., 1934-39; with Interstate Container Corp., N.Y.C., 1939—, now pres.; dir. Nat. Bank N.Am., N.Y.C. Pres. The Epstein Found. Inc. Trustee Hofstra U.; pres. Jewish Med. Center, N.Y.C., 1950-56, hon. pres., 1956, also trustee. Mason (Shriner). Home: 980 Fifth Av New York City NY 10021 Office: 300 E 42d St New York City NY 10017

EPSTEIN, SAUL THEODORE, educator, physicist; b. Southampton, N.Y., June 14, 1924; s. Joseph Samuel and Jeannette (Friedman) E.; S.B., Mass. Inst. Tech., 1944, Ph.D., 1948; m. Jean Elizabeth Hoopes, Jan. 30, 1948; children—Joanne, Peter, David. Mem. Inst. Advanced Study, Princeton, 1947-48; instr. Columbia, 1948-51; lectr. Stevens Inst. Tech., 1951-52, Boston U., 1952- 53; from asst. prof. to prof. U. Neb., 1954-63; prof. physics U. Wis., Madison, 1963—, mem. Theoretical Chemistry Inst., 1963—. Guggenheim fellow, 1971-72. Mem. Am. Phys. Soc., Am. Assn. Physics Tchrs. Home: 2325 Kendall Av Madison WI 53705

EPSTEIN, SEYMOUR, author; b. N.Y.C., Dec. 2, 1917; s. Joseph and Jenny (Pomerantz) E.; student Coll. City N.Y., 1937-38, N.Y.U., 1938-39; m. Miriam Kligman, May 5, 1956; children—Alan, Paul. Worked at various jobs to 1960; tchr. creative writing New Sch. Social Research, N.Y.C., 1963—; now lectr. U. Denver. Served with USAAF, 1942-45; ETO. Author: Pillar of Salt, 1960; The Successor, 1961; Best Short Stories of 1962; Leah, 1964; Short Story 1; Caught in That Music, 1967; The Dream Museum, 1971. Contbr. short stories popular mags. Home: 2924 S Monroe St Denver CO 80210

EPSTEIN, SIDNEY, corp. exec.; b. Chgo., 1923; ed. U. Ill., 1943. Pres., dir. The A. Epstein Cos., Inc., Chgo.; dir. Met. Bank & Trust Co., Amalgamated Trust & Savs. Bank. Co-chmn. Chgo Youth Centers. Bd. dirs. Chgo. Assn. Commerce and Industry. Vice pres. Lyric Opera Chgo.; governing mem. Chgo. Symphony Orch. Club: Standard (pres., dir.) (Chgo.). Home: 4950 Chicago Beach Dr Chicago IL 60615 Office: 2011 W Pershing Rd Chicago IL 60609

EPSTEIN, SIDNEY, editor; b. Wilmington, Del., Oct. 11, 1920; s. Abraham and Ida (Kelrick) E.; student George Washington U., 1937-41; m. Eleni Sakes, Mar. 30, 1957; 1 dau., Diane. With Washington Herald, 1937-54; city editor Washington Times-Herald, 1952-54; city editor Washington Evening Star, 1958-68, asst. mng. editor, 1968—. Served to capt. USMCR, 1942-46. Home: 2807 Cathedral Av NW Washington DC 20008 Office: 2d and Virginia Av SE Washington DC 20003

EPSTEIN, STEPHAN, educator, physician; b. Nuremberg, Germany, Mar. 14, 1900; s. Ernst and Margaret (Scherbel) E.; M.D., U. Erlangen (Germany), 1925; m. Elsbeth Lauinger, May 27, 1926; children—Ernst, Wolfgang. Came to U.S., 1936, naturalized, 1941. Intern City Hosp., Nuremberg, Germany, 1925; resident U. Breslau (Germany) Skin Clinic, 1926-30, chief radiotherapy dept., 1930-35; dermatologist Marshfield (Wis.) Clinic, 1936-65; pres. Marshfield Clinic Found. Med. Research and Edn., 1960-65; clin. asso. prof. dermatology U. Minn. Med. Sch., 1946-68; clin. prof. dermatology U. Wis. Med. Sch., Madison, 1965—. Mem. A.M.A., Am. Dermatol. Soc., Am. Acad. Dermatology, Am. Coll. Allergists, Wis. Med. Soc. Author numerous articles on photosensitivity, contact allergy. Editor, translator: Atlas and Manual of Dermatology and Venerology (Burckhardt), 2d edit., 1965. Home: 2921 Harvard Dr Madison WI 53705 Office: 2705 Marshall St Madison WI 53705

EPSTEIN, WILLIAM LOUIS, educator, physician; b. Cleve., Sept. 6, 1925; s. Norman N. and Gertrude (Hirsch) E.; A.B., U. Cal., Berkeley, 1949, M.D., 1952; m. Joan Goldman, Jan. 29, 1954; children—Wendy, Steven. Mem. faculty U. Cal. at San Francisco, 1957—, asso. prof. div. dermatology, 1963-69, dir. dermatol. research, 1957—, acting chmn. div. dermatology, 1966-69, chmn. dept. dermatology, 1970—, cons. dermatology Outpatient Dept.; cons. various hosps., Cal. Dept. Pub. Health; dir. div. research Nat. Program Dermatology, 1970—. Mem. A.A.A.S., A.M.A., Am. Acad. Dermatology and Syph., Pacific Dermatologic Assn., Am. Fedn. Clin. Research, Soc. Investigative Dermatology (bd. dirs.), Am. Dermatol. Assn., Phi Beta Kappa, Sigma Xi. Home: 135 San Benito Way San Francisco CA 94127

EPSTINE, HARRY M., bus. exec.; b. Chillicothe, O., Apr. 2, 1899; s. Benjamin and Bella (Adolph) E.; student engring. U. Mich.; LL.D. (hon.), St. Vincent Coll.; m. Jane B. Metzger, Apr. 6, 1936; children—Beatrice, Marianna. Asst. gen. mgr. Summerfield & Hecht, Detroit, 1919-30; with May Stern & Co., Pitts., 1931—, pres., 1948—; pres. Epley Land Co., Millard Realty Co., Porter-Gratiot Realty Co.; v.p. Riverview Homes; dir. Comml. Bank & Trust Co. Trustee Falk Med. Fund, Allegheny Gen. Hosp.; bd. dirs. Am. Cancer Soc., Better Bus. Bur.; treas., trustee Montifiore Hosp.; bd. dirs. St. Vincent's Coll.; nat. exec. com. Conf. Fedns. and Welfare Funds, Am. Jewish Com.; hon. pres. United Vocational and Employment Service; bd. dirs. United Jewish Fund, Fedn. Philanthropies, YM and YWHA, Atlantic Union Com.; co-chmn. Nat. Conf. Christians and Jews. Served with U.S. Army, 1917-18. Clubs: Furniture, Standard (Chgo.); Westmoreland, One Hundred, Concordia (Pitts.). Home: 5023 Frew Av Pittsburgh PA 15213 Office: 914 Penn Av Pittsburgh PA 15222

EPTON, BERNARD EDWARD, lawyer; b. Chgo., Aug. 25, 1921; s. Arthur I. and Rose (Goldstein) E.; student U. Chgo., 1938-39, Northwestern U., 1939-40; LL.B., DePaul U., 1947; m. Audrey Issett, June 8, 1945; children—Teri Lynn, Jeffrey David, Mark Richard, Dale Susan. Admitted to Ill. bar, 1947, since practiced in Chgo.; partner firm A.I. Epton & Sons, 1941-47, Epton, Scott, McCarthy & Epton, 1947-63, Epton, McCarthy, Bohling & Druth, 1963—; v.p., dir. Potter-Englewood Co., Eliel & Loeb Co. Mem. South Shore O'Keefe Conservation Community Council, 1960-66; mem. Jewish Bd. Edn., 1965-70. Mem. Ill. Gen. Assembly 24th Dist.; chmn. financial instns. Bd. dirs., v.p. Jane Dent Home Aged Negro, 1961—; bd. dirs. Jewish Community Centers Chgo.; trustee Coll. Jewish Studies; mem. president's council St. Xavier Coll.; mem. estate planning council DePaul U. Served to capt. USAAF, 1942-45; ETO. Decorated D.F.C. with oak leaf cluster, Air medal with three oak leaf clusters. Mem. Am., Ill., Chgo. bar assns., Decalogue Soc. Lawyers (bd. dirs. 1949, pres. 1961-62), Trial Lawyers Club, Am. Legion, Air Force Assn. (bd. dirs. 1947-50), South Shore C. of C. (bd. dirs., counsel 1953—, pres. 1959-61), Mil. Order World Wars (vice comdr.), Chgo. Hist. Soc. (life), U. Chgo. Alumni Assn. (life). Clubs: Standard (Chgo.); Idlewild Country (bd. dirs. 1964-67) (Flossmoor, Ill.). Home: 5555 S Everett St Chicago IL 60637 Office: 69 W Washington St Chicago IL 60602

EPTON, SAUL ARTHUR, judge; b. Chgo., July 17, 1910; s. Arthur I. and Rose (Goldstein) E.; student U. Mich., 1930; LL.B., John Marshall Law Sch., 1932; m. Ena Bollaert, June 2, 1935; 1 dau., Nancy Ann. Admitted to Ill. bar, 1932, since practiced in Chgo.; sr. partner firm Epton, Scott, McCarthy & Bohling, 1940—; judge circuit court Cook County, 1959—. Special asst. atty. gen. ins. matters, Ill., 1942-46; mem. Ill. Civil Service Commn., 1953-59. Trustee, pres. Mt. Sinai Medical Research Found., Chgo.; trustee Morgan Park (Ill.) Mil. Acad. Mem. Am., Ill., Chgo. bar assns., Decalogue Soc. Lawyers (trustee), Fedn. Ins. Council (past v.p.), S. Shore C. of C. (past pres.). Home: 7414 S Constance St Chicago IL 60649 Office: 141 W Jackson Blvd Chicago IL 60604

ERALP, ORHAN, Turkish diplomat; b. Izmir, Turkey, Jan. 28, 1915; s. Emin Fikri and Rabia Eralp; B.A., Robert Coll., Istanbul, 1933; LL.B., Univ. Coll., London, Eng., 1936; Ph.D., London Sch. Econs., 1939; m. Jale Mizanoglu, July 18, 1956; children—Emin, Osman. Joined Turkish Ministry Fgn. Affairs, 1939; from 3d to 1st sec. embassy, Washington, 1942-48; del. UN Conciliation Commn. for Palestine, 1949-50; permanent rep. of Turkey to European office UN, Geneva, Switzerland, 1951; counsellor embassy, London, 1952; dir. gen. polit. affairs Ministry Fgn. Affairs, 1952-56; ambassador to Sweden, Stockholm, 1952-56, to Yugoslavia, Belgrade, 1959-64; ambassador, permanent rep. Turkey to UN, 1964-71; sec. gen. ministry Fgn. Affairs, Ankara, Turkey, 1971—. Served with Turkish Air Force, 1940-42. Clubs: River (N.Y.C.); Piping Rock (L.I.). Author: Turkey and State Succession, 1939. Office: Ministry Fgn Affairs Ankara Turkey

ERASMUS, P.J., brewery exec.; b. Senekal, S. Africa, Feb. 16, 1932; s. Paul Jacobus and Sairey (Botha) E.; B.Commerce, Rhodes U., S. Africa, 1952; chartered accountant, S. Africa, 1956, Ont., 1961. With Rothmans World Group of Companies, 1957—; pres. Canadian Breweries Ltd., 1969—, also dir.; dir. Carling Brewing Co., Inc., Rothmans of Pall Mall Can. Ltd. Mem. Inst. Chartered Accountants Ont. Clubs: Bayview Country; Granite, Lawn Tennis (Toronto); Queen's. Home: 21 Rosedale Rd Toronto Ontario Canada Office: 79 St Clair Av E Toronto 7 Ontario Canada

ERB, CARL LEE, Jr., civil engr.; b. Lincoln, Neb., Sept. 11, 1913; s. Carl Lee and Clarence Lillian (Larson) E.; B.Sc. in Civil Engring., U. Neb., 1935; m. Phyllis Lenore Richey, Dec. 6, 1936; children—Julann (Mrs. Lauren E. Meyers), Philip Michael. Constrn. engr. C., B. & O. R.R., 1935-37; office engr. Kingsley Dam Western Neb., designer hydropower and irrigation structures Central Neb. Power & Irrigation Dist., 1938-41; with Howard, Needles, Tammen & Bergendoff, cons. engrs., Kansas City, Mo., Cleve., N.Y., 1941—, partner, 1957—; dir. Grand Av. Bank, Kansas City, Mo. Recipient Thomas Arkle Clark award Alpha Tau Omega, 1935, Man of Year award, 1971. Registered profl. engr., Conn., Ida., Ind., Ky., La., Mo., Mont., Neb., N.Y., Ohio, Okla., Pa., W.Va., Wis. Mem. Am. Inst. Cons. Engrs. (nat. pres. 1971), Am. Soc. C.E., Nat. Soc. Profl. Engrs., Kansas City Engrs. Club, Engring. Inst. Can., Am. Rd. Builders Assn., Cons. Engrs. Council, Sigma Xi, Alpha Tau Omega, Sigma Tau, Pi Mu Epsilon. Methodist. Rotarian. Clubs: Mission Hills (Kan.) Country; Kansas City (Mo.); Mid-Ocean (Bermuda). Prin. designer, adminstr. maj. bridges and expressways including Del. Meml. Bridge, Pres. Truman Bridge, Kansas City, Me. Turnpike, Denver-Boulder Turnpike, urban expressways systems in Cleve., Akron (O.), Toledo, other large cities. Home: 6543 Overhill Rd Mission Hills KS 66208 Office: 1805 Grand Av Kansas City MO 64108

ERB, DONALD, composer; b. Youngstown, O., Jan. 17, 1927; s. Tod and Janet (Griffith) E.; B.S., Kent State U., 1950; Mus.M., Cleve. Inst. Music; Mus.D., Ind. U., 1964; m. Lucille Hyman, June 10, 1952; children—Christine, Matthew, Stephanie, Janet. Tchr., Cleve. Inst. Music, 1953-61, composer-in- residence, 1966; grad. asst. Ind. U., 1961-62, 63-64; asst. prof. composition Bowling Green State U., 1964-65; vis. asst. prof. research electronic music Case Inst. Tech., 1965-67; composer-in-residence Dallas Symphony, 1968-69; featured composer, lectr. conductors festivals at U. Minn., Ashland Coll., Albany State Coll., Tex. Tech. Coll., Oberlin Coll., U. Hartford, Wis. State U., Augustana Coll., Whitman Coll.; co-dir. Portfolio, contemporary music series, Cleve., 1966 —; staff composer Bennington Composers Conf., 1969-70. Ford Found. composer-in-residence, Bakersfield, Cal., 1962-63; Rockefeller Found. grantee for performance of Symphony of Overtures, 1965; Guggenheim fellow, 1965-66; grantee Nat. Council on Art, 1967-68; recipient Cleve. Arts prize; Distinguished Alumnus award Ind. U. Sch. Music. Served with USNR, 1945-46. Mem. Am. Music Center, Broadcast Music, Inc., Cleve. Composers Guild. Composer: Dialogue for Violin and Piano, 1958; Correlations for Piano, 1959; Music for Violin and Piano, 1959; String Quartet No. 1, 1960; Music for Brass Choir, 1960; Sonata for Harpsichord and String Quartet, 1962; Chamber Concerto, 1961; Sonneries for Brass Choir, 1961; Four for Percussion, 1962; Bakersfield Pieces, 1962; Compendium, 1962; Dance Pieces, 1963; Cumming's Cycle, 1963; Hexagon, 1963; Concertant for Harpsichord and Strings, 1963; Antipodes, 1963; Symphony of Overtures, 1964; VII Misc., 1964; Fallout?, 1964; N, 1965; Reticulation, 1965; Phantasma, 1965; Concert Piece 1, 1966; Diversion for Two, 1966; Stargazing, 1966; Concerto for Solo Percussion and Orchestra, 1966; Andante for Piccolo, Flute and Alto Flute, 1966; String Trio, 1966; Summermusic, 1966; Kyrie, 1967; Reconnaissance, 1967; In No Strange Land, 1968; the Seventh Trumpet, 1969; Basspiece, 1969; Klangfarbenfunk I, 1970. Home: 1681 Cumberland Rd Cleveland Heights OH 44118

ERB, PAUL, editor, clergyman; b. Newton, Kan., Apr. 26, 1894; s. Tillman M. and Lizzie (Hess) E.; student Hesston (Kan.) Coll., 1915-16; B.A., Bethel Coll., 1918; M.A., State U. Ia., 1923; student U. Chgo., 1939-42; m. Alta M. Eby, May 27, 1917; children—Winifred (Mrs. Milford Paul), J. Delbert. Instr. English, Hesston Coll., 1917-40, acting dean, 1924-29, registrar, 1929-33, dean, 1933-40; prof. English, Goshen Coll., 1940-45; ordained to ministry Mennonite Ch., 1919; exec. sec. Mennonite Gen. Conf., 1954-61; editor Gospel Herald, Scottdale, Pa., 1944-62; book editor Herald Press, Scottdale, 1960-64; chmn. pub. com. Mennonite Ency., 1946-59; field worker Allegheny Mennonite Conf., 1966-69; vis. prof. Eastern Mennonite Coll., 1969-71. Pres. Mennonite Community Assn.; field rep. Mennonite Bd. Missions and Charities, Elkhart, Ind., 1962-64; pres. Mennonite Bd. Edn., 1963-65. Author: Old Testament Poetry and Prophecy, 2d edit., 1956; The Alpha and the Omega, 1955; Don't Park Here, 1962; Our Neighbors South and North, 1965; We Believe, 1968; Orie O. Miller, 1969. Home: Mennonite Apts Scottdale PA 15683 Office: Mennonite Pub House Scottdale PA 15683

ERBE, NORMAN ARTHUR, govt. ofcl.; b. Boone, Ia., Oct. 25, 1919; s. Otto L. and Louise (Festner) E.; B.A., U. Ia., 1946, J.D., 1947; m. Jacqueline D. Doran, Sept. 27, 1942; children—DeElda, Jennifer, Kevin. Admitted to Ia. bar, 1947; partner Doran & Erbe, Boone, 1947-57; spl. asst. atty. gen. Ia. Hwy. Commn., 1955-57; atty. gen., Ia., 1957-61; gov. Ia., 1961-63; asst. to pres. Diamond Labs.; later exec. dir. Nat. Paraplegia Found.; now regional rep. of sec. U.S. Dept. Transp., Chgo.; Chmn. East Boone Co. chpt. A.R.C., 1949-50. Chmn. Boone County Republican Central Com., 1952-57. Served as co. comdr. inf. AUS, 1941-42; as pilot 8th Air Force, USAAF, 1943-45. Decorated D.F.C., Air medal with clusters; recipient Community Distinguished Service award, 1952. Mem. Boone C. of C. (pres. 1951-52), Am., Ia., Boone County bar assns., Am. Judicature Soc., Luth. Laymens League. Lutheran. Lion. Club: Boone Golf and Country (pres. 1952- 53). Author: Iowa Highway Road and Street Laws, 1956; Iowa Drainage Laws, 1957. Home: 450 E Park St Arlington Heights IL 60005 Office: 3158 Des Plaines Av Des Plaines IL 60018

ERBER, THOMAS, educator; b. Vienna, Austria, Dec. 6, 1930; B.Sc., Mass. Inst. Tech., 1951; M.S., U. Chgo., 1953, Ph.D. in Physics, 1957; married. Naturalized Am. citizen. Asst. prof. physics Ill. Inst. Tech., Chgo., 1957-62, asso. prof., 1962-70, prof., 1970—. Research fellow, Brussels, Belgium, 1963-64. Mem. Am. Phys. Soc., Am. Math. Soc. Office: Dept Physics Ill Inst Tech Chicago IL 60616*

ERBURU, ROBERT F., newspaper pub. co. exec.; b. Ventura, Cal., 1930; grad. U. So. Cal., 1952, Harvard Law Sch., 1955. Sr. v.p., dir. Times Mirror Co., Los Angeles. Home: 1518 Blue Jay Way Los Angeles CA 90069 Office: Times Mirror Sq Los Angeles CA 90053*

ERDLE, PHILIP JOHN, air force officer; b. Bethlehem, Pa., Sept. 17, 1930; s. Louis Jacob and Elizabeth (Costigan) E.; B.S., U.S. Mil. Acad., 1952; M.S., U. Mich., 1960; Ph.D., U. Colo., 1964; m. Carolyn M. Knies, June 14, 1952; children—Patricia M., Michael P., Anne E., Terry J., Margaret E. Commd. 2d lt. USAF, 1952. advanced through grades to col., 1966; asst. dean research USAF Acad., 1963-64, asst. dean engring., 1964-65, prof. engring. mechanics, head dept., 1965—; cons. to industry, 1965—. Co-founder, pres. Internat. Mechanics Symposium, Inc., 1969—. Decorated Army Commendation ribbon, Air Force Commendation medal, D.F.C., Air medal, Meritorious Service medal. Mem. Am. Soc. Engring. Edn. (chmn. mechanics div. 1968-69), Soc. Exptl. Stress Analysis. Co- author mechanics textbook. Editor: (textbook) Engineering Fundamentals and Design. Home: 720 Northfield Rd Colorado Springs CO 80907

ERDMAN, CARL L. N., banker; b. Reading, Pa. , Aug. 3, 1915; s. Lee Marcus and Ella (Nolde) E.; B.A., Dartmouth, 1937; m. Carolyn M. Wilson, Sept. 10, 1938; children—Lee W., Christine N. (Mrs. Robert D. Keeler). With Am. Bank and Trust Co. Pa., Reading, 1953—, exec. v.p., 1966—. Pres. borough council Wyomissing, Pa., 1964—. Bd. regents Mercersburg Acad., 1966—. Served with USNR, 1943-46, 50-52. Recipient Silver Beaver award Boy Scouts Am., 1961. Mem. Beta Theta Pi. Rotarian. Home: 1415 Parkside Dr N Wyomissing PA 19610 Office: 35 N 6th St Reading PA 19603

ERDMAN, RICHARD, motion picture and theater dir., actor; b. Enid, Okla., June 1, 1925; s. Otto and Allie June Erdman; grad. Hollywood (Cal.) High Sch., 1943; m. Sharon Randall, Jan. 29, 1953; 1 dau., Erica. Actor films The Men, 1948, Janie, The Time of Your Life, The Happy Time, 1951, Stalag 17, 1953, and others; dir. TV: The Dick Van Dyke Show, 1966, Mooch, 1970; films: Bleep, 1970, The Caves of Sacromonte, 1971; dir. over 40 plays including Under the Yum Yum Tree, 1962, The Girl from Utah, 1971; pres. Screen Projects Internat., 1962, Baerdman Prodns., 1968—; gen. partner Bleep, Ltd., 1969—. Recipient award Funniest Performance of 1948, Life mag., 1948. Address: 16160 Anoka Dr Pacific Palisades CA 92072

ERDMAN, WILLIAM JAMES, II, physician; b. Phila., Apr. 8, 1921; s. Frederick and Mary (Hickok) E.; B.A. in Econs., Swarthmore Coll., 1943; M.D., U. Pa., 1950, M.S., 1954; m. Betty Jane Frick, June 30, 1956; children—Mary Belle, Jane Elizabeth. Intern Presbyn. Hosp., Phila., 1950-51; asst. instr. phys. medicine and rehab. U. Pa. Sch. Medicine, 1951-53, instr., 1953-54, asst. prof., chmn. dept., 1954-56, asso. prof., chmn. dept., 1956-60, prof., chmn. 1960—, also with Grad. Sch. Medicine, 1951—, asst. instr., 1951-53, instr., 1953-54, asso., 1954-55, asst. prof., 1955-56, asso. prof., 1956-60, prof., 1960—, chmn. dept., 1955—, asst. dean, 1968—, dir. dept. phys. medicine and rehab. Hosp. U. Pa., chmn. med. staff, 1965-67, med. dir., 1968—; mem. spl. med. adv. group VA, Washington; cons. Lebanon, Wilmington VA hosps.; chmn. dept. phys. medicine and rehabilitation Phila. Gen. Hosp.; cons. Presbyn. Hosp., Phila., VA Hosp., U.S. Army Hosp., Valley Forge. Med. dir. Presbyn. Ministers Fund. Served with AUS, 1943-46. Decorated Bronze Star, Purple Heart. Diplomate Am. Bd. Phys. Medicine and Rehab. Fellow A.C.P.; mem. A.M.A. (chmn. sect. phys. medicine and rehab. 1967-68), Am. Congress Phys. Medicine and Rehab. (pres. 1964-65, treas. 1970—), Internat. Rehab. Medicine Assn. (treas. 1969—), Am., Pa. (pres. 1958-59) acads. phys. medicine and rehab., Coll. Physicians Phila., Gold Key. Presbyn. (elder) Home: 3803 The Oak Rd Philadelphia PA 19129 Office: 3400 Spruce St Philadelphia PA 19104

ERDMANN, CHARLES ALBERT, accountant; b. Manitowoc, Wis., Sept. 20 1917; s. Herbert F. and Lily (Englebrecht) E.; B.A., U. Wis., Madison, 1940; m. Aileen Souder, Oct. 12, 1940 (div. April 1965); children—Lawrence, Nancy, John, Robert, David. With Fonteine, McCurdy & Co., 1938-42, Nordberg Mfg. Co., 1942-43, Fred V. Gardner & Assos., 1946; sec.-treas. Lakeside Labs., 1946-51; controller Parke, Davis & Co., Detroit, 1951-56, v.p. and controller, 1961—. Served to lt. comdr. USNR, 1943-46, C.P.A., Wis. Mem. Nat. Assn. Accountants (nat. dir., past pres. Detroit), Greater Detroit Bd. Commerce, Financial Execs. Inst. (dir. Detroit), Am. Pharm. Mfrs. Assn., Wis. Soc. C.P.A.'s A.I.M., Am. Mgmt. Assn. Clubs: Detroit Athletic, Detroit Yacht, Detroit Golf. Home: Lafayette Towers W Detroit MI 48207 Office: Jos Campau at the River Detroit MI 48232

ERDOS, ERVIN GEORGE, educator; b. Budapest, Hungary, Oct. 16, 1922; s. Andor and Aranka (Breuer) E.; grad. U. Budapest Sch. Medicine, 1950, M.D., U. Munich (Germany), 1950; m. Irene Meyerhof, Dec. 11, 1952; children—Martin, Peter, Philip. Came to U.S., 1954, naturalized, 1959. With hosp., Munich, 1951; research asso. biochem. research lab. U. Munich, 1952-54; research asso. anesthesia Mercy Hosp., Pitts., 1955-58; fellow biochemistry, ind. research Mellon Inst., Pitts., asso. prof. pharmacology U. Pitts. Med. Sch., 1958-63; faculty U. Okla. Sch. Medicine, Oklahoma City, 1963—, George Lynn Cross research prof., 1970—. Vis. prof. Tulane U., 1963; vis. scientist U.S.-Japan Coop. Sci. Program, NSF, 1966, cons. in field. Mem. coms. Nat. Heart and Lung Inst. Fellow Deutsche Forschungsgemeinschaft, 1954; Wellcome Research travel grantee, 1964. Mem. Am. Soc. Pharmacology and Exptl. Therapeutics, European Soc. Biochem. Pharmacology, A.A.A.S., Soc. Exptl. Biology and Medicine. Editor books in field, also mem. editorial bd. jours. Home: 5109 N Everest St Oklahoma City OK 73111

ERFFT, KENNETH REYNDERS, univ. adminstr.; b. Chgo., Nov. 14, 1908; s. Victor Athen and Ethel (Reynders) E.; A.B., No. Mich. U., 1932; M.A., U. Richmond, 1936, D.S.C., 1967; Litt.D., Maclean Coll., 1947; LL.D., No. Mich. U., 1961; m. Nancy Fontaine Creath, June 8, 1940. Tchr., Ironwood (Mich.) High Sch., 1932-34; clk. Bd. Edn. Petersburg (Va.) Pub. Schs., 1936-42; bus. mgr. Furman U., Greenville, S.C., 1946-54; comptroller Pa. State U., 1954-57; v.p., treas. Rutgers U., 1957-62, Jefferson Med. Coll. and Med. Center, 1962-64; pres. Kenneth R. Erfft Assos., Inc., ednl. consultants, Phila., 1964-66; v.p. Duquesne U., Pitts., 1966—. Chmn. bd. dirs. A Future Fund, A Fortress Fund, Carlisle-Asher Asher Mngmt. Co., Kenbar Corp. Mem. adminstrv. com. Cal. and Western Conf. Cost and Statis. Study, 1955-57. Chmn. bd. dirs. Nationwide Conf. Edn. Centers, College Housing and Dev. Corp. Served from lt. (j.g.) to comdr., USNR, 1942-46. Mem. Eastern Assn. Coll. and Univ. Bus. Officers (pres.), Am. Assn. U. Profs., Middle States Assn., Delta Sigma Phi, Phi Epsilon, Tau Kappa Alpha, Omicron Delta Kappa, Theta Omicron. Clubs: Internat. Torch, University (Pitts.). Co-author: Administrators in Higher Education, 1962. Editorial com. College and University Business Administration, rev. edits. Home: Chatham Center Pittsburgh PA 15219

ERHARD, LUDWIG, former West German ofcl.; b. 1897; student Handelschochschule, Nuremberg U. Frankfurt; Dr. hon. causa., U. Berlin, 1952, U. Nürnberg, 1954, U. Santiago de Chile, 1954, U. Aligarh, India, 1958, U. Tokyo, 1958, Wabash Coll. (Crawfordsville, Ind.) 1959, U. Wash., 1959. U. Tehran, 1960, U. Madrid, 1961, U. Coimbra Portugal, 1961, U. St. Gallen, 1961, U. Milwaukee, 1958, Harvard, 1964, U. Maryland, 1956, U. Colombia, 1965. U. Michigan, 1967. Wartburg Coll., 1967, Weizmann Inst., 1967. U. Guatemala, 1968, U. Bogota, Head Institut für Wirtschaftsbeobachtung, Handelschochschule, Nüremberg, 1928-42. Institut für Industrieforschung, Nuremberg, 1943-45; minister trade and industry, Bavaria, 1945; chmn. spl. agy. preparation plan for currency reform, Bizonal Council, 1947, head bizonal econ. council, 1948; dir. dept. econs. United Econ. Territory, Frankfurt-Höchst, 1948-49; federal minister econ., 1949-63; vice chancellor of West Germany from 1957-63, chancellor, 1963-66. Hon. prof. U. Munich, 1947, U. Bonn, 1949, Christian Dem. Union mem. 1st, 2d, 3d, 4th, 5th, German Bundestag, 1949, 53, 57, 61, 65, German gov. World Bank, 1952-63.. Home: Johanniterstr 8 Bonn Germany

ERHART, CHARLES HUNTINGTON Jr., mfg. co. exec.; b. New York City, July 31, 1925; s. Charles Hungtington and Katherine (Kent) E.; grad. Groton Sch., 1944; B.A., Yale, 1949; m. Sylvia Montgomery, June 24, 1948; children—Victoria, Margaret, David, Stephen, Julia. With W.R. Grace & Co., 1950—, asst. treas., 1955-63, v.p. charge adminstrv. controls, 1963-68, exec. v.p., chief financial officer, mem. appropriations com., 1968—, also dir.; dir. Chemed Corp., Cin.; mem. adv. bd. Bankers Trust Co. Bd. dirs. Leake and Watts Childrens Home, N.Y.C., Evergreens Cemetry, N.Y.C., trustee Episcopal Sch., N.Y.C. Mem. Newcomen Soc., Beta Theta Pi. Clubs: Racquet and Tennis, Lunch, Church. (N.Y.C.); Somerset Hills Country (Far Hills, N.J.); Northeast Harbor Fleet. Home: 149 E 73d St New York City NY 10021 Office: 7 Hanover Sq New York City NY 10005

ERICH, JOHN BERNHARDT, plastic surgeon; b. Chgo., Jan. 14, 1907; s. John F. and Alma (Dow) E.; B.S., U. Ill., 1929, M.D., 1932, D.D.S., 1933, M.S., 1935; m. Edith Gebhardt, Mar. 26, 1932. Fellow plastic surgery Mayo Clinic, 1933-36, cons. plastic surgery, 1937—, head sect. plastic surgery, 1955-67, sr. cons. plastic surgery, 1967—; prof. plastic surgery, grad. sch. U. Minn., 1949—. Served as lt. M.C., USNR, 1942-48. Diplomate Am. Bd. Plastic Surgery (bd.), Am. Bd. Otolaryngology. Fellow A.C.S., Am. Acad. Ophthalmology and Otolaryngology; mem. Am. Laryngol. Assn., Triological Soc., Am. Soc. Head and Neck Surgeons, A.M.A., Am. Assn. Plastic Surgeons, Am. Soc. Plastic and Reconstructive Surgeons, Am. Soc. Maxillofacial Surgeons (past pres.), Am. Fracture Soc. (v.p.) Minn. Acad. Ophthalmology and Otolaryngology, Minn. Med. Soc., So. Minn. Med. Assn., Sigma Xi. Home: 716 10th St SW Rochester MN 55901 Office: Mayo Clinic Rochester MN 55901

ERICKSEN, EPHRAIM GORDON, educator, sociologist; b. Salt Lake City, Sept. 7, 1917; s. Ephraim Edward and Edna (Clark) E.; B.S., Utah U., 1938, M.S., 1939; Ph.D., U. Chgo., 1947; m. Darlene Anderson, Apr. 24, 1944; children-Craig, Heidi, Dana. Mem. faculty U. Ind., 1946-47, U. Cal. at Los Angeles, 1947-49, U. Kan., 1949-65, U. Tenn., 1965-68; mem. faculty Va. Poly. Inst. and State U., 1968—, prof. sociology, chmn. dept., 1968—; cons. in field. Fellow Am. Sociol. Assn.; mem. Midwest Sociol. Soc., Population Assn. Am., Phi Delta Kappa, Pi Kappa Alpha. Author: Urban Behavior, 1954; The West Indies Population Problem, 1962; Africa Company Town, 1964; also articles. Home: 610 Country Club Dr Blacksburg VA 24060

ERICKSEN, JERALD LAVERNE, educator; b. Portland, Ore., Dec. 20, 1924; s. Adolph and Ethel Rebecca (Correy) E.; B.S., U. Wash., 1947; M.A., Ore. State Coll., 1949; Ph.D., Ind. U., 1951; m. Marion Ella Pook, Feb. 24, 1946; children—Lynn Christine, Randolph Peder. Mathematician, solid state physicist U.S. Naval Research Lab., 1951-57; faculty Johns Hopkins, 1957—, prof. theoretical mechanics, 1960—; editorial bd. Archive for Rational Mechanics and Analysis, 1958—. Served with USNR, 1943-46. Mem. Math. Assn. Am., Soc. Rheology, Soc. Natural Philosophy. Co-editor: Springer Tracts in Natural Philosophy. Editorial adv. bd. Internat. Jour. Solids and Structures. Home: 509 E Seminary Av Towson MD 21204 Office: Mechanics Dept Johns Hopkins Baltimore MD 21218

ERICKSON, ALBIN HAROLD, ins. co. exec.; b. Hawick, Minn., Sept. 25, 1904; s. Erick Gustaf and Signe (Holmgren) E.; student North Park Coll., 1929-31; B.S., U. Minn., 1933, M.S., 1934; postgrad. Northwestern U., 1940; m. Alpha Lungren, Aug. 14, 1935; children—Ruth JoAnne, James Edward, Paul Harold. Instr. chemistry North Park Coll., 1934-46, dir. summer and evening sessions, 1945-46, dean students, 1946-63, dean coll., 1949-57; v.p. North Park Coll. and Theol. Sem., 1963-70; v.p., treas. Nat. Mut. Ch. Ins. Co., Willmar, Minn., 1969—. Mem. Ill. Assn. Jr. Colls. (pres. 1954- 55), Central Council Jr. Colls. (v.p. 1955-56), Chgo. Tract Soc., Am. Assn. Sch. Adminstrs., Assn. Higher Edn., Phi Theta Kappa, Alpha Sigma Pi, Phi Delta Kappa, Phi Lambda Upsilon. Home: 1112 15th St W Willmar MN 56201

ERICKSON, ALFRED A., banker; b. Barber, Mont., 1914; student U. Mont.; married. Accountant, Ernst & Ernst, 1943-46; with Nat. Bank of Commerce, Seattle, 1946—, sr. v.p. bank property adminstrn., 1967—. Served with USNR, 1941-43. Office: 2d Av at Spring St Seattle WA 98124*

ERICKSON, ALLAN C., coll. dean; B.S., No. Ill. U.; M.S., Ed.D., Mich. State U. Dean grad. studies Central Conn. State Coll., New Britain. Office: Central Conn State Coll New Britain CT 06050*

ERICKSON, ARTHUR ERIC, meat co. exec.; b. Chicago, Dec. 22, 1911; student Northwestern U., 1930- 34; C.P.A., Ill. Staff Accountant Price Waterhouse & Co., Chicago, 1930- 40; with Oscar Mayer & Co., Madison, Wis., 1940—. successively controller, 1945-53, treasurer, 1953—, v.p., 1955-66, exec. v.p., 1966—, also dir. Madison Family Service Assn., 1959-64, Oscar Mayer Found., 1956—. Mem. Financial Execs. Inst., Am. Inst. C.P.A.'s Wis. Soc. C.P.A.'s Nat. Assn. Accountants. Home: Office: 910 Mayer Av Madison WI 53701

ERICKSON, ARVEL BENJAMIN, educator; b. Eveleth, Minn., Sept. 15, 1905; s. Gust and Anna (Mallom) E.; B.A. U. Minn., 1929; M.A., U. Wash., 1933; Ph.D., Western Res. U., 1939; m. Alva C. Roslund, June 9, 1931; 1 dau., Lynn G. (Mrs. Thomas Burnett). Instr., Case Inst. Tech., 1937-40; instr. history Western Res. U., 1940-42, mem. faculty, 1944—, prof. history, 1952—, Carl Frederick Wittke Found. prof., 1964—; regional economist OPA, 1942-44; vis. summer prof. U. Man., 1962, U. Victoria, 1963. Recipient Distinguished Tchr. award Western Res. U., 1964; research grantee Social Sci. Research Council, 1953, Am. Philos. Soc., 1853, 61. Mem. Am. Hist. Assn., Ohio Acad. History, Midwest Conf. Brit. Historians, Phi Alpha Theta, Omicron Delta Kappa. Author: The Public Career of Sir James Graham, 1952; Edward Cardwell: Peelite, 1959; also numerous articles. Co- author: Readings in English History, 1967; England: Prehistory to the Present, 1968. Asso. editor: Jour. Social History. Home: 3432 Clarendon Rd Cleveland Heights OH 44118 Office: 11125 Bellflower Rd Cleveland OH 44106

ERICKSON, CHARLES BURTON, II, retail trade exec.; b. Monett, Mo., Oct. 17, 1932; s. Albion Burton and Ruth Louise (Harris) E.; A.B., U. Mo., 1958, LL.B., 1960; m. Marjorie Lay, Jan. 1, 1953; children—Catherine Elaine, Charles Burton III. Admitted to Ill. bar, 1960; atty. First Nat. Bank of Chgo., 1960-63, United Air Lines, 1963-64; sec., asst. gen. counsel Jewel Cos., Inc., Chgo., 1964—. Served with USMCR. Mem. Chgo. Bar Assn., Am. Soc. Corporate Secs., Order of Coif, Phi Beta Kappa. Club: Economic (Chgo.). Home: 26 W 248 Blackhawk Dr Wheaton IL 60187 Office: 5725 E River Rd Chicago IL 60631

ERICKSON, DONALD JOSEPH, accountant; b. Madison, Wis., Oct. 11, 1914; s. Eric W. and Gertrude (Fuss) E.;B.A., U. Wis., 1936; m. Irma Ann Osterman, Aug. 9, 1939; children—Richard James, Donald Joseph, Emily Jane, Cynthia Ann. With Arthur Anderson & Co., C.P.A.'s, 1936—, partner, Chgo., 1947— Commnr. park dist., Winnetka, Ill. Chmn. bd. Chicago Heart Assn.; trustee ednl. TV channel 11; bd. dirs. Nat. Conf. Christians and Jews, Jr. Achievement, Chgo., Mem. Chgo. Assn. Commerce and Industry (bd. dirs.). Clubs: Chicago, Attic, Mid-Am. (Chicago); Glenview (Ill.) Home: 137 Sheridan Rd Winnetka IL 60093 Office: 69 W Washington Blvd Chicago IL 60602

ERICKSON, ELLWORTH VINCENT corp. exec.; b. Muskegon, Mich., Jan. 5, 1906; s. John and Ida Marie (Nelson) E.; M.E., Rensselaer Poly. Inst., 1928; m. Alyce Rudeen, Mar. 28, 1940; children—Martha Ann, John Vincent, Instr. mech. engring. dept. Rensselaer Poly. Inst., 1929; engr. Carrier Corp., N.Y.C., 1929- 39; v.p., gen. mgr. Keller Tool Co., Grand Haven, Mich., 1939-52, pres., 1952-55; exec. v.p. Gardner-Denver Co., 1956-61, sr. v. pres., 1961-68, also dir.; chmn. bd., dir. Security First Bank & Trust Co., Grand Haven, Mich.; dir. AGM Industries, Inc., Grand Rapids, Mich., J-S-J Corp., Grand Haven. Commr., Mich. Hwy. Commn., 1971—. Trustee Alma Coll., Loutit Found. Mem. Delta Tau Delta. Clubs: University (Chgo.); Detroit Athletic; Peninsular (Grand Rapids, Mich.). Home: 8345 Woodlawn St Grand Haven MI 49417 Office: 300 Franklin St Grand Haven MI 49417

ERICKSON, ERNST WALFRED librarian; b. Superior, Wis., Nov. 21, 1911; s. John and Caroline (Pearson) E. B.Ed., Superior State Tchrs. Coll., 1935; M.A., U. Ia., 1936; B.S. in L.S., U. Minn., 1946; Ph.D., U. Ill., 1958; m. Marion J. Ihrig, July 2, 1938; children—Karen, Susan, David. Tchr. English, pub. schs., Superior, 1936-45; searcher catalog dept. U. Minn., 1945- 46; asst. librarian Moorhead State Tchrs. Coll., 1946-47; head librarian Eastern Ore. Coll., La Grande, 1947-50; research asst. U. Ill. Library Sch., 1950-51, circulation asst. library, 1951-52; head librarian Eastern Mich. U., 1952-69; library cons. Coll. of Edn., Somali Democratic Republic, 1969-70; vis. prof. U. Mich. Sch. Library Sci., 1970—. Smith-Mundt grantee to Nepal to organize central library for govt., 1958-59. Mem. Ypsilanti Human Relations Commn., 1960-64. Mem. Am. (council 1963-67), Mich. (2d v.p. 1963-64), library assns., Assn. Coll. and Research Libraries (dir. 1963-67), Am. Assn. U. Profs., Beta Phi Mu. Democrat. Author: College and University Library Surveys, 1938-1952, 1961; (with LeMoyne W. Anderson) Report of a Survey of the Western Washington State College Library, 1962; (with A.F. Kuhlman and A.R. Rogers) Report of a Survey of Murray State University Libraries, 1969; also articles. Home: 1209 Whittier Rd Ypsilanti MI 48197

ERICKSON, EUGENE ROBERT, hosp. adminstr; b. Mpls., Sept. 13, 1918; s. Carl Robert and Bertha (Nelson) E.; B.S. in Indsl. Mgmt., U. Cal., Los Angeles, 1941; M.S. in Pub. Adminstrn., U. So. Cal., 1950; m. Gertrude Arthur, July 16, 1955; children—Diane, Kathleen. Adminstrv. asst. Los Angeles County Supt. Charities, 1948-50; gen. services mgr. Olive View Tb Sanatorium, Los Angeles County, 1951; asst. dir. Rancho Los Amigos Hosp., Downey, Cal., 1952-55, adminstr., 1956—; dir. John Wesley County Hosp., 1955. Mem. Gov.'s Com. Rehab. Physically Handicapped, 1957-60; mem. Cal. Joint Council to Improve Health Care Aged, Cal. Commn. for Accreditation Nursing Homes and Related Facilities, 1960-67; mem. Cal. Bd. Examiners Nursing Home Adminstrs. Served to lt. USNR, 1942- 46. Fellow Am. Coll. Nursing Home Adminstrs., Am. Coll. Hosp. Adminstrs.; mem. Hosp. Council So. Cal., Am., Western, Cal. hosp. assns., Am. Legion. Home: 3908 Cerritos Av Long Beach CA 90807 Office: Rancho Los Amigos Hosp Downey CA 90242

ERICKSON, EVERETT RUSSELL, educator; b. Eeverett, Wash., May 9, 1904; s. Richard and Clara Georgine (Baardson) E.; A.B., U. Ida., 1926, M.S., 1933; Far East Civil Affairs diploma, Stanford, 1945; m. Merion Thomson Smith, Sept. 24, 1960. Tchr. elementary and high schs., Ida. Alaska, 1926-37; asst. prof. later prof., head dept. edn. U. Alaska, 1937-42, 46-48; dep. commr. edn. Alaska, 1949-51, commr. edn., 1951-53; treas., dir. Hal H. Moor, Inc. dispensing opticians, Portland, 1953-55; dir. Alaska Tchrs. Retirement System 1951-53; exec. officer vocational edn., Alaska, 1951-53; supt. of schs., Navy 230, Seattle, Wash., 1956-57; asso. field rep. Office Edn., Dept. Health, Edn. and Welfare, Chgo., 1957-59, field rep. Seattle, 1959—. Served with Q.M.C., AUS, 1942-46; mil. head dept. edn. Kyunggi Province, Korea, 1945-46; lt. col., USAF Res., now retired Mem. N.E.A. (life mem., state dir., 1936-42, 47-48, v.p., 1939-40, 46-47) Am. Assn. Sch. Adminstrs. (dept. elementary sch. prins.) Pioneers of Alaska, Mil. Order World Wars, Ret. Officers Assn., Alpha Tau Omega, Delta Sigma Rho, Kappa Delta Pi. Episcopalian, Elk, Mason (K.T., Shriner); mem. Order Eastern Star, Nat. Sojourner. Clubs: Ft. Lawton Officers, Swedish; Marine Memorial (San Francisco). Home: 4800 Fremont Av N Seattle WA 98103 Office: Republic Bldg Seattle WA 98101

ERICKSON, FLORENCE HENRIETTA, nurse, educator; b. McKeesport, Pa., Feb. 22, 1914; d. Harry and Esther (Johnson) Erickson; grad. McKeesport Hosp. Sch. Nursing, 1935; B.S. in Nursing Edn., U. Pitts., 1947, Ph.D., 1957; M.S., Yale, 1954. Orthopedic staff nursing N.Y. Orthopedic Hosp., N.Y.C., 1935-36; indsl. nursing Jones & Laughlin Steel Co., McKeesport Tin Plate, 1936- 44; instr. pediatric nursing, asst. prof., then prof. and chmn. dept. U. Pitts., 1945—. Chmn. interdivisional council maternal and child health nursing Pa. League for Nursing, 1953; mem. nursing research study sect. NIH, 1965-67. Mem. Am. Nurses Assn., Nat. League for Nursing (steering com. inter-div. council on maternal and child health, 1957-61, vice chmn. and chmn. elect 1963-67), Alpha Tau Delta (past nat. treas., nat. pres. 1947). Baptist. Author monograph. Home: 4425 Schenley Farms Terrace Pittsburgh PA 15213

ERICKSON, FRANKLIN CARL, educator; b. Worcester, Mass., Dec. 16, 1903; s. Sven August and Hilda (Hendrickson) E.: A.B., Clark U., 1928, A.M., 1930, Ph.D., 1935; Swiss- Am. exchange student, Zurich, 1932-33; m. Albertha May Naas, Sept. 6, 1936; children—Betty Mae, Sally Hilda. Cartographer Macmillan Pub. Co., 1928-29; asso. prof. U.S.C., 1935; prof. geography U. N.C., 1936-43, 44- 47; prof. geography Boston U. 1947—, chmn. dept. 1949—, asso. dean coll. liberal arts, 1959—. Chief cartographic sect. Bur. Econ. Warfare, Washington, 1942-44. Mem. Am. Assn. Geographers, Am. Soc. Profl. Geographers, Sigma Xi, Pi Gamma Mu, Lambda Chi Alpha. Mason. Author articles on land use. Home: 355 Cabot St Newtonville MA 02160 Office: Boston U Boston MA 02215

ERICKSON, GEORGE ABRAHAM, advt. exec; b. Chicago, Mar. 23, 1904; s. Erick and Juliana (Helsing) E.; student Knox Coll., 1924-25; m. Nellie Knight, June 24, 1930; children—Pamela June (Mrs. Edward F. Hudson III), George Knight. Salesman, Met. Newspaper Feature Syndicate, 1926-29. Stone, Webster & Blodget, investment bankers, 1930-33; with Doremus & Co., advt. and pub. relations, N.Y.C., 1934—, account exec., v.p., exec. v.p., 1953-62, vice chmn., 1962-67, chmn. bd., 1967—. mem. fiannce com., 1962-68, chmn., chief exec. officer, 1968—, dir. 1953—. County committeeman Republican Party, 1950-51. Trustee Knox Coll. Mem. Pelham Sch. Bd. 1953-59, pres. sch. bd., 1958-59. Mem. Tau Kappa Epsilon. Clubs: Bankers (N.Y.C.); Huguenot Yacht (New Rochelle, N.Y.); Pelham Country, Pelham Men (pres. 1946-47). Home: 18 Clifford Av Pelham NY 10803 Office: 120 Broadway New York City NY 10005

ERICKSON, HAROLD LEWIS, banker; b. Rockford, Ill., June 16, 1924; s. Harold Lewis and Mina M. (Kliver) E.; B.A., U. Cin., 1949; postgrad. Rutgers U., 1959; m. Frances E. Carnell, July 16, 1949; children—Harold Lewis III, William C., David C., Dorothy Mina Anne, James T. Asst. v.p. Fifth Third Union Trust Co., Cin., 1940-61; v.p. Am. City Bank & Trust Co., Milw., 1961-66, pres., 1966—; dir. Hampton State Bank, Commerce Capital Corp., Assn. Life Ins. Co. Mem. Glendale Water Comm., 1965-68. Served with AUS, 1943-45. Decorated Bronze Star; French de Guerre with silver star. Mem. Wis. Bankers Assn. (dir.), Beta Gamma Sigma. Republican. Mason. Club: Tripoli Country (Milw.) Home: 7685 N Berwyn Av Milwaukee WI 53209 Office: 740 N Plankinton Av Milwaukee WI 53203

ERICKSON, HAROLD MARTIN, physician, surgeon, health officer; b. Missoula, Mont. June 25, 1908; s. Knute Edwin and Victoria (Pederson) E.; student U. Wash., 1925-27; A.B., U. Ore., 1930, M.D., 1933; M.P.H., Johns Hopkins, 1940; m. Marjorie Shirley Porter, June 25, 1935; children—Harold Martin, Robert Porter, Donald Knute, Richard Howard. Pvt. practice, The Dalles, 1937; health officer Wasco County, 1937-40; maternal and child health dir. Ore. Bd. Health, Portland, 1940-42, asst. state health officer, 1942-45, state health officer, 1945-60; chief dep. dir. health State of Cal., 1960- 66; spl. cons. family planning Ford Found., India, 1966-68; dir. health and mental health Riverside County (Cal.), 1968—. Del., World Health Assembly, held at Geneva, Switzerland, 1954; mem. Pres.'s Adv. Com. on Water Pollution Control, 1957-59; former exec. sec. Ore. Bd. Health, Ore Chiropodists Exam. Bd., Ore. Bd. Eugenics, State Sanitary Authority; co-chmn. Cal. Inter-Agy. Council Tb Control; mem. Cal. Gov's Emergency Med. Adv. Com.; cons. Salt Lake City and County study, also mem. task force on environmental health Nat. Commn. on Community Health Services; mem. Cal. Regional Bd. Mental Retardation; med. adv. bd. Pacific State Hosp.; exec. bd. Riverside County Comprehensive Health Planning Assn.; mem. bd. So. Cal. Comprehensive Health Planning Assn. Served from 1st lt. to capt., M.C., U.S. Army (Res.), 1933-42; passed asst. surgeon USPHS(R), 1943-47, now med. dir. Diplomate Am. Bd. Preventive Medicine and Pub. Health. Fellow Am. Pub. Health Assn.; mem. Am. Assn. Pub. Health Physicians (past pres.), Assn. State and Territorial Health Officers (past pres.), Am. Assn. Preventive Medicine. Mason (Shriner). Clubs: City Commons (Berkeley, Cal.). Contbr. to The Child, Northwest Medicine, assn. jours. Mem. bd. editors Pub. Health Reports, 1954-57. Home: 5509 Glenhaven Av Riverside CA 92506 Office: 3575 11th St Mall Riverside CA 92501

ERICKSON, HOMER THEODORE, educator; b. Pulaski, Wis., Mar. 8, 1925; s. Elmer and Luella (Thorson) E.; B.S., U. Wis., 1951, M.S., 1953, Ph.D., 1954; Prof. Honorus Causa, Fed. U., Vicosa, Minas Gerais, Brazil, 1963; m. Carolyn J. Cochran, Sept. 10, 1955; children—Ann, Jean, Charles, Neal. Asst. prof. U. Me., 1954-56; mem. faculty Purdue U., 1956—, prof. horticulture, 1964—, head dept., 1967—. Served with AUS, 1946-47. Mem. Am. Genetics Assn., A.A.A.S., Am. Soc. Hort. Sci., Wilsons Ornithol. Soc., Delta Theta Sigma; hon. mem. Brazil Hort. Soc. Lutheran. Club: Optimist Internat. Home: 1409 N Salisbury St West Lafayette IN 47906

ERICKSON, JAMES HARRISON MILLER, univ. dean; b. Mankato, Minn., Oct. 25, 1923; s. Arvid S. and Johanna (Miller) E.; B.S. cum laude, U. Minn., 1949; M.Ed., U. Colo., 1949; Ed.D., U. Wyo., 1954; m. Mittie M. Berry, June 3, 1956; children—Karen, Mark. English tchr. pub. schs. to 1954; asst.. prof. English, Ball State U., 1954-55; asst. prof. edn., chmn. secondary edn. dept. Ariz. State U., 1955-58; prof. edn. Wis. State U., La Crosse, 1958—, dean Grad. Coll., 1963—. Bd. dirs. United Campus Ministry, La Crosse. Served with AUS, 1943-46, U.S. Army, 1953-54. Mem. N.E.A., Kappa Delta Pi, Phi Delta Kappa, Phi Kappa Phi. Presbyn. (elder). Home: 2161 Wedgewood Dr La Crosse WI 54601

ERICKSON, LEIF, mem. Democratic Nat. Com; b. Cashton, Wis., July 29, 1906; s. Oluf and Dora B. (Swanson) E.; student U.N.D., 1925-26; Ph.B. J.D., U. Chicago; m. Huberta B. Brown, Dec. 29, 1932; children—Katherine (Mrs. David Mitchell), Leif Barton, Elizabeth Ruth. Admitted to Mont. bar; practice in Helena; county atty. Richland County, 1926-37; asso. justice Mont. Supreme Ct., 1938-46. Dem. nominee for gov. Mont., 1944, for U.S. Senator, 1946; del., mem. platford drafting com. Dem. Nat. Conv., 1952, 56. 60; chmn. Mont. Dem. Party, 1956-57; Dem. Nat. Committeeman, 1962—. Pres., chmn. bd. First State Bank Mineral County, Superior, Mont. Mem. presdl. emergency bd. Ry. Labor Bd., 1945-52. Chmn. Helena Community Chest, 1958. Mem. Am., Mont., Lewis and Clark bar assns. Club: Montana (pres. 1955). Home: Blackstone Apts Helena MT 59601 Office: 347 N Last Chance Gulch Helena MT 59601

ERICKSON, LEROY ALEXANDER, electronic mfg. co. exec.; b. Valley City, N.D., June 22, 1921; s. Henry Oscar and Myrtle Eleanor (Jacobson) E.; B.S., U. Ore., 1947; m. Mary Dixon, Dec. 22, 1946; children—Carol, David. Pres., Luminator, Inc., 1963-70; pres., chief exec. officer, dir. Varo, Inc., Garland, Tex., 1971—; chmn. bd. Varo-Semiconductor, Inc., 1971—; dir. Coastal Plains, Inc., Dallas, First Bank & Trust Co. Bd. dirs. So. Meth. Inst. Tech. Mem. Dallas Area Mfrs. and Wholesalers Assn. (pres. 1970), Phi Delta Theta. Clubs: Northwood, Preston Trail Golf, City (Dallas); Washington Athletic (Seattle). Home: 7227 Birchwood Dr Dallas TX 75240 Office: 111 S Garland Rd Garland TX 75040

ERICKSON, LUTHER EUGENE, educator, chemist; b. Pulaski, Wis., June 30, 1933; s. Elmer and Luella (Thorson) E.; B.A., St. Olaf Coll., 1955; Ph.D., U. Wis., 1959; m. Jenny Sue Payne, June 22, 1957; children—Louise Elizabeth, Hans Luther. Asst. prof. chemistry Dickinson Coll., Carlisle, Pa., 1959-62; mem. faculty Grinnel (Ia.) Coll., 1962—, prof. chemistry, 1968—. NSF sci. faculty fellow, 1968-69. Mem. Am. Chem. Soc., Ia. Acad. Scis., A.A.A.S. Contbr. articles profl. jours. Home: 1415 Summer St Grinnell IA 50112

ERICKSON, MALCOLM JOEL, banker; b. Denver, June 23, 1907; s. William G. and Hilda (Gustafson) E.; B.A. in Commerce U. Denver. With Colo. Nat. Bank, Denver, 1925-42, 46-69, v.p., cashier Lakewood Nat. Bank (Colo.), 1969—. Served with AUS, 1942-46. Home: 520 Oneida St Denver CO 80220 Office: Lakewood Nat Bank Lakewood CO 80215

ERICKSON, RALPH O., educator; b. Duluth, Minn., Oct. 27, 1914; s. Charles W. and Stella (Sjostrom) E.; B.A., Gustavus Adolphus Coll., 1935; M.S., Washington U., St. Louis, 1941, Ph.D., 1944; m. Elinor M. Borgstedt, June 17, 1945; children—Diane Ruth, Elizabeth Jane. Instr., Gustavus Adolphus Coll., 1935-39; asst. chemist Western Cartridge Co., East Alton, Ill., 1942-44; instr., then asst. prof. botany U. Rochester, 1944-47; mem. faculty U. Pa., 1947—, prof. botany, 1954—, chmn. grad. group botany, 1957- 58, chmn. grad. group biology, 1968—, acting dir. div. biology, 1961-63. Guggenheim fellow Cal. Inst. Tech., 1954-55. Mem. Bot. Soc. Am., Soc. Developmental Biology (pres. 1959), Am. Soc. Naturalists, Sigma Xi. Author articles in field. Home: 1920 Dog Kennel Rd Media PA 19063 Office: Dept of Biology U Pennsylvania Philadelphia PA 19104

ERICKSON, RAYMOND LEROY, educator, psychologist; b. Jamestown, N.Y., Feb. 11, 1925; s. Raymond J. and Grace (Myers) E.; B.A. magna cum laude, State U. N.Y. at Buffalo, 1951; M.A., U. Cal. at Los Angeles, 1954, Ph.D., 1962; m. Barbara Joan Golden, Apr. 29, 1956; children—Leslie Ann, Laurel Meredith, Douglas Alan. Psychol. intern Cal. Dept. Corrections, 1954; lectr. U. Md. Overseas Program, 1956-58; instr., then asst. prof. Whittier Coll., 1958-63; mem. faculty U. N.H., 1963—, prof. psychology, 1967—, chmn. dept., 1965-71. Served with AUS, 1943-46. Mem. Am., N.H. (pres. 1967-68) psychol. assns., Phi Beta Kappa. Home: Emerson Rd Durham NH 03824

ERICKSON, ROBERT LEWIS, electronics exec.; b. Edgeley, N.D., Nov. 14, 1929; s. Lewis and Katherine (Henricksen) E.; B.A., St. Olaf Coll.; LL.B., S.D. U.; m. Margaret Ann Giere, Apr. 29, 1961. Admitted to S.D. bar, 1957; clk. to U.S. dist. judge, 1957-59; atty. N.W. Bell Telephone Co., 1959-62; asst. gen. atty. Collins Radio Co., Dallas, 1962-67, gen. atty., 1967-69, v.p., counsel, 1969—. Served with AUS, 1951-53. Mem. Minn., Tex. bar assns. Lutheran (mem. council). Home: 15731 Mapleview Circle Dallas TX 75240 Office: Collins Radio Co Dallas TX 75207

ERICKSON, ROLAND AXEL, cons.; b. Worcester, Mass., Sept. 8, 1913; s. Axel and Anna (Erickson) E.; A.B., Clark U., 1935; A.M., Tufts U., 1937; LL.B., Susquehanna U., 1970; m. Roxie Erickson, Apr. 6, 1940; children—Brent, Lorna. Instr. econs. Tufts U., 1935-37; economist Norton Co., 1937-41; v.p. Guaranty Bank & Trust Co., 1941-45, v.p., treas., dir., 1945-47, pres., 1947-64; sr. v.p., dir. Gen. Foods Corp., 1964-66, exec. v.p., dir., 1966-70; chmn., dir. New Eng. High Carbon Wire Corp.; now cons.; dir. Norton Co., State Mut. Life Assurance Co. Am. Past mem. bankers com. New Eng. Council. Past pres. and chmn. exec. com. Worcester Community Chest. Trustee Clark U.; Bankers Trust adv. com. Decorated Knight Royal Order Vasa First Class (Sweden). Mem. Newcomen Soc., Nat. Assn. Bus. Economists, Am-Swedish Hist. Found. (gov.). Am. Econ. Assn., Am. Acad. Polit. and Social Sci., Phi Beta Kappa, Baptist. Mason (32) Clubs: Worchester, Stanwich, Worcester Country, Odin. Contbr. articles on corporate finance, money and banking, fiscal policy to profl. publs. Home: 11 Skyridge Rd Greenwich CT 06830 Office: 1 Greenwich Plaza Greenwich CT 06830

ERICKSON, ROY LYDEEN, agribusiness exec.; b. Kelliher, Minn., Apr. 20, 1923; s. Albert E. and Victoria (Lydeen) E.; B.B.A., U. Minn., 1948; J.D., Wm. Mitchell Coll. Law, 1961; m. Beverly E. Hurrle, July 12, 1957. With treas. dept. financial and computer areas Archer-Daniels-Midland Co., Decatur, Ill., 1948-60, atty., asst. sec., 1961-68, sec., gen. counsel, 1969—, v.p., 1970—; admitted to Minn. bar, 1961; practice law, Mpls., 1961-69, Decatur, Ill., 1969—. Chmn. Planning and Zoning Com., Columbia Heights, Minn., 1962; spl. Municipal Ct. judge, Columbia Heights, 1964-68. Served with USNR, 1940-45. Named Ky. col. Mem. Am., Minn., Hennepin County bar assns. Home: 494 Shoreline Dr Decatur IL 62521 Office: 4666 Faries Pkwy Decatur IL 62525

ERICKSON, RUSSELL F., mfg. exec; b. Mpls., June 11, 1910; s. Hjalmar Franz and Edna Natalia (Tack) E.; B. in Mech. Engring., U. Minn., 1932; postgrad. Columbia, Pratt Inst., 1937, 38; m. Dorothy Lucille Hovend, May 28, 1938; children—Franz, Virginia, Kristin Natalie, Holly Karen. Engr. Minn. and Ont. Paper Co., Internat. Falls, Minn., 1933-37; design engr. George F. Hardy, cons. engrs., N.Y.C., 1937- 39; plant engr. Hollingsworth & Whitney Co., Mobile, Ala., 1939-45; with Rayonier Inc., Fernandina, Fla., 1946—, mill mgr., 1947-49, v.p. engring. and mfg., N.Y.C., 1950-57, exec. v.p., 1957-58, pres., 1958-68, dir., 1956—, pres., chief officer, 1968—; dir. Rayonier Can., Ltd., Grays Harbor Paper Co., Internat. Tel. & Tel. Corp. Mem. Am. Paper Inst. (gov.), T.A.P.P.I., Pi Tau Sigma. Clubs: Pinnacle, Winged Foot Golf (pres.) (N.Y.C.). Home: 16 Eastwoods Lane Scarsdale NY 10583 Office: 161 E 42d St New York City NY 10017

ERICKSON, VICTOR HUGO, business exec.; b. Palo Alto, Cal., 1916; ed. San Jose State Coll. Vice pres., treas. Fibreboard Corp. Home: 11520 Arroyo Oaks Los Altos CA 94022 Office: 55 Francisco St San Francisco CA 94119*

ERICKSON, WILLIAM CLARENCE, educator; b. Chgo., Nov. 21, 1930; s. Clarence Adolph and Alberta Petty Louise (Johnson) E.; B.A. in Math., U. Minn., 1951, M.A. in Physics, 1955, Ph.D., 1956; m. Donna Joan Ottensmeyer, Dec. 27, 1952; children—William P., Steven D., Timothy H. Carnegie fellow Radio Astronomy Research, Carnegie Inst. Washington, 1956-57; sr. staff scientist radio astronomy research, head, physics sect. Convair Sci. Research Lab., San Diego, 1959-61; sr. sci. staff Benelux Cross Antenna Project, also project leader U. Leiden, 1962-63; prof. astronomy U. Md., College Park, 1963—. Cons. in field. Alworth scholar, 1948-53; NSF fellow, 1953-55; Carnegie fellow, 1956-57. Mem. A.A.A.S., Am. Phys. Soc., Astron. Soc. Pacific, Am. Geophys. Union, Am., Royal astron. socs., Internat. Sci. Radio Union (chmn. com.), Phi Beta Kappa, Sigma Xi. Contbr. numerous articles to profl. jours. Home: 10925 Bond Rd Aldelphi MD 20783 Office: Astronomy Program U Md College Park MD 20742

ERICKSON, WILLIAM HURT, judge; b. Denver, May 11, 1924; s. Arthur Xavier and Virginia (Hurt) E.; Petroleum Engr., Colo. Sch. Mines. 1947; postgrad. U. Mich., 1949—; LL.B., U. Va., 1950; m. Doris Rogers, Dec. 24, 1953; children—Barbara Ann, Virginia Lee, Stephen Arthur, William Taylor. Admitted to Colo. bar, 1951; practiced law, Denver; now justice Colo. Supreme Ct. Served with USAAF, 1943. Recipient award of merit Colo. Com. Continuing Legal Edn., 1968. Fellow Internat. Acad. Trial Lawyers (sec.), Am. Coll. Trial Lawyers, Am. Bar Found., Internat. Soc. Barristers (past pres.); mem. Nat. Legal Aid and Defender Assn., Am. Law Inst., Practising Law Inst. (nat. adv. council), Colo. (bd. govs.), Denver (past pres., trustee), Am. (chmn. council criminal law sect., mem. fed. rules com., dep. chmn. com. to implement standards criminal justice 10th circuit) bar assns., Scribes. Home: 10 Martin Lane Englewood CO 80110 Office: State Capitol Bldg Denver CO 80203

ERICKSON, WILLIAM J., corp. exec., lawyer; b. Northfield, Minn., July 25, 1930; s. Edwin O. and Minnie (Johnson) E.; student Carleton Coll., 1948-50; B.S. summa cum laude, Ohio State U., 1952; LL.B., Harvard, 1955; m. Miriam Christine Thrall, Mar. 18, 1951; children—Susan, Kristin, Karen, Richard. Admitted to Minn. bar, 1955; staff atty. Dorsey, Owen, Barker, Scott & Barber, Mpls., 1955-57; counsel select com. small bus. U.S. Senate, 1957-58; partner firm Erickson, Popham, Haik & Schnobrich, Mpls., 1958-65; sec., treas., gen. counsel, dir. Fire Engrs., Inc., 1961—; chief exec. Officer Consumers Financial Corp., Mpls., 1965-69; chmn. bd. Asso. Fund, Inc., St. Louis, 1965-68; chief exec. officer, chmn. bd., dir. N. Am. Equitable Life Assurance Co., Brookings Internat. Life Ins. Co.; pres., chief exec. officer Colonial Services Co., 1970—; Mem. Am. Fed., Minn., Hennepin County bar assns. Conglist. Clubs: Athletic (Mpls.), Home: 5912 Bernard Pl Edina MN 55436 Office: 2835 Nicollet Av Minneapolis MN 55408

ERICKSTAD, RALPH JOHN judge; b. Starkweather, N.D., Aug. 15, 1922; s. John T. and Anna Louisa (Myklebust) E.; student U. N.D., 1940-43; B.Sc. in Law, U. Minn., 1947, LL.B., 1949; m. Lois Katherine Jacobson, July 30, 1949; children—John Albert, Mark Anders. Admitted to N.D. bar, 1949; practiced in Devils Lake, 1949-62; State's atty. Ramsey County, 1953-57; mem. N.D. Senate from Ramsey County, 1957-62, asst. majority floor leader, 1959, 61; asso. justice Supreme Ct. N.D., 1963—. Treas. N.D. States Attys. Assn., 1955, v.p., 1956; mem. N.D. Legislative Research Com., 1957-59; mem. N.D. Budget Bd., 1961-63; mem. Gov. N.D. Spl. Com. Labor, 1960. Mem. exec. com. Mo. Valley council Boy Scouts Am. Chmn. bd. trustees Mo. Valley Family YMCA. Served with USAAF, 1943-45; ETO. Mem. Am., N.D. bar assns., Am. Legion, V.F.W. Lutheran (del. 1st biennial conv., mem. nominating com.). Kiwanian. Home: 1266 W Highland Acres Rd Bismarck ND 58501 Office: State Capitol Bismarck ND 58501

ERICSSON, WILLIAM G. banker; b. Evanston, Ill. Nov. 4, 1927; s. Eric G. and Alice (Johnson) E.; B.S. in Bus. Adminstrn., Northwestern U., 1950; J.D., Loyola U., Chgo., 1955; m. Marjorie Hyams, June 4; children—Lisa, Kristin, Tod. Admitted to Ill. bar; with No. Trust Co., Chgo., 1950-58, 2d v.p., 1958; with Am. Nat. Bank & Trust Co., Chgo., 1958—, now pres.; dir. Bear Mfg. Co., Rock Island, Ill. Trustee, mem. exec. com. Ravinia (Ill.) Festival Soc. Mem. Am., Chgo. bar assns., Phi Kappa Psi, Phi Alpha Delta, Beta Gamma Sigma. Club: Northwestern Univ. (pres. Chgo.) Home: 1020 Forest Av Evanston IL 60202 Office: 33 N LaSalle St Chicago IL 60690

ERIKSEN, CHARLES WALTER, psychologist, educator; b. Omaha, Feb. 4, 1923; s. Charles Hans and Louella (Carlson) E.; B.A., U. Omaha, 1943; Ph.D., Stanford, 1950; m. Garnita Tharp, July 22, 1945 (div. Jan. 1971); children—Michael John, Kathy Ann; m. 2d, Barbara Becker, Apr. 1971. Asst. prof. Johns Hopkins, 1949-53, research scientist, 1954-55; lectr. Harvard, 1953-54; mem. faculty U. Ill. at Urbana, 1956—, prof., 1959—. Research cons. VA, 1960—; mem. psycho-biology panel NSF, 1963; mem. expt. psychology study sect. NIH, 1958-62, 66—. Recipient Stratton award Am. Path. Assn., 1964, Nat. Inst. Mental Health Research Career award, 1964. Mem. Psychonomic Soc., Soc. Exptl. Psychologists, Midwestern Psychol. Assn., A.A.A.S., Sigma Xi. Author: Behavior and Awareness, 1962. Editor Am. Jour. Psychology, 1968; prin. editor Perception and Psycho Physics, 1971; cons. editor Jour. Exptl. Psychology, 1965—. Contbr. articles profl. jours. Home: RRI White Heath IL 61884 Office: Psychol Bldg Champaign IL 61820

ERIKSEN, JOHN GEORGE, coll. dean; b. Mpls., Aug. 14, 1918; s. N. Henry and Caroline (Hagen) E.; B.S., U. Mnn., 1942, M.A., 1950, Ph.D., 1957; certificate U. Ia., 1944, U. Marburg (Germany), 1948; m. Anne Laurette Duenbostle, May 1, 1948; 1 son, Mark John. Teaching asst., then instr. polit. sci. U. Minn., 1947-48, 49-50, 50-51; mem. faculty U. Okla., 1951-66, prof. polit. sci., 1965-68, asso. dean Coll. Arts and Sci., 1954-66, dir. honors, 1963-64, dir. U. Munich (Germany) Center, 1963-68, dir. internat. programs, 1967-68; dean Coll. Arts and Scis., prof. polit. sci. Bowling Green State U., 1968—. Served with AUS, 1943-46. Mem. Am. Polit. Sci. Assn., Am. Assn. Advancement Slavic Studies. Author articles. Editor: The Development of Soviet Society: Plan and Performance, 1970. Home: 427 N Prospect Av Bowling Green OH 43402

ERIKSEN, STEIN, profl. skier. Formerly Olympic and World ski champion; now promoter ski fairs and movies, also author books on skiing. Owner Ski Rental Shop, Sport Shops, Aspen; dir. Aspen Skiing Corp. Recipient 4 Gold medals, Silver medal, Bronze medal. Address: Box 1245 Aspen CO 81611

ERIKSON, ERIK HOMBURGER, psychoanalyst; b. Frankfurt-am-Main, Germany, June 15, 1902; grad. Vienna Psychoanalytic Inst., 1933; M.A. (hon.), Harvard, 1960; LL.D., U. Cal., 1968; D.Sc. (hon.), Loyala U., 1969; Sc.D., Yale, 1971; m. Joan Mowat Serson, Apr. 1, 1930; children—Kai T., Jon M., Sue (Mrs. Harland G. Bloland). Came to U.S., 1933, naturalized, 1939. Psychoanalyst, 1933—; tng. psychoanalyst, 1942—; teaching, research Harvard Med. Sch., 1934-35, Yale Sch. Medicine, 1936-39, U. Cal. at Berkeley and San Francisco, 1939-51; sr. staff mem. Austen Riggs Center, Stockbridge, Mass., 1951-60; vis. prof. U. Pitts. Sch. Medicine, 1951-60; prof. human devel., lectr. psychiatry Harvard, 1960-70, prof. emeritus, 1970—. Recipient Aldrich award Am. Acad. Pediatrics, 1971. Fellow Am. Acad. Arts and Scis.; mem. Nat. Acad. Edn., Am. Psychoanalytic Assn. (life), Cambridge Sci. Club, Signet Soc., Phi Beta Kappa (hon.). Author: Childhood and Society, 1950; Young Man Luther, 1958; Insight and Responsibility, 1964; Identity; Youth and Crisis, 1968; Gandhi's Truth, 1969 (Nat. Book award, 1970, Pulitzer prize, 1970). Editor: Youth: Change and Challenge, 1963; Home: Stockbridge MA 01262

ERIKSON, GEORGE EMIL, anatomist; b. Palmer, Mass., May 3, 1920; s. Emil and Sofia (Gustafson) E.; B.S., Mass. State Coll., 1941; M.A., Harvard, 1946, Ph.D., 1948; m. Suzanne J. Henderson, Apr. 23, 1950; children—Ann, David, John, Thomas. Mem. faculty Harvard Med. Sch., 1945-65, asst. prof. anatomy, 1955-65, asso. curator Warren Anatomical Mus., 1961-65; prof. med. sci. Brown U., 1965—; cons. dept. surgery, anatomist R.I. Hosp; spl. research new world primates, history medicine and biology, Rockefeller Found. cons. medicine and pub. health, S.Am., 1959; specialist State Dept., Brazil, 1962. Sheldon traveling fellow, C.Am., 1946; Guggenheim fellow S.Am., 1949. Mem. A.A.A.S., Am. Assn. Phys. Anthropologists. Am. Soc. Mammalogists, History Sci. Soc., Am. Soc. Zoologists, Am. Assn. Anatomists, Am. Assn. History Medicine, Sigma Xi. Home: 153 Bay Rd Norton MA 02766 Office: Div of Biol and Med Sci Brown U Providence RI 02912

ERIKSON, KAI THEODOR, sociologist; b. Vienna, Autria, Feb. 12, 1931; s. Erik H. and Joan (Serson) E.; B.A., Reed Coll., 1953; M.A., U. Chgo., 1955, Ph.D., 1962; m. Joanna M. Slivka, Jan. 21, 1961; children—Keith S., Christopher J. Came to U.S., 1933, naturalized, 1937. Instr. psychiatry U. Pitts., 1959- 63; asso. prof. psychiatry Emory U., 1963-66; prof. sociology Yale, master Trumbull Coll. Yale, 1969—. Served with AUS, 1955-57. Fellow Am. Sociol. Assn. (MacIver award 1967); mem. Soc. Social Social Problems (pres. 1970-71). Author: Wayward Puritans: A Study in the Sociology of Deviance, 1966. Home: 100 High St New Haven CT 06517

ERIM, KENAN TEVFIK, educator; b. Istanbul, Turkey, Feb. 13, 1929 s. Kerim Tevfik and Fahime (Osan) E.; came to U.S., 1947; student Coll. de Geneve, 1941-46, B.A., N.Y.U., 1953; M.A., Princeton, 1955, Ph.D., 1958. Vis. instr. Ind. U., 1957-58; asst. prof. N.Y.U., New York City, 1958-62, asso. prof. classics, 1962—, field dir. research project, 1961, now dir. excavation archeol. discovery Aphrodisias in Turkey. Guggenheim fellow, 1961-62. Mem. Archaeol. Inst. Am., Royal Numis. Soc., Türk Tarih Kurumu (corr.). Research in field. Home: 16 Boudinot St Princeton, NJ 08540.

ERINGEN AHMED CEMAL aerospace scientist; b. Kayseri, Turkey, Feb. 15, 1921; s. Sukru and Meva Eringen; M.S. in Mech. and Aero. Engring., Tech. U., Istanbul, 1943; Ph.D. in Applied Mechanics, Poly. Inst. Bklyn., 1948; m. Jean Dennis, Sept. 8, 1949; children—Meva, Peri, Lisa, Leyla. Head Structures dept. aircraft factory Turkish Air League, Ankara, 1946; asst. prof., asso. prof. mechanics Ill. Inst. Tech., Chgo., 1948-53; asso. prof., prof. engring. sci. Purdue U., Lafayette, Ind., 1953-66; prof. aerospace and mech. scis., chmn. solid mechanics program, dir. solid mechanics labs. Princeton (N.J.), 1966—. Cons., Gen. Tech. Corp., Lawrenceville, N.J., 1958—, Recipient certificate of achievement Poly. Inst. Bklyn., 1957, award as outstanding researcher of year Sigma Xi, 1962. Mem. Soc. Engring. Sci. (founder, pres.) Soc. Natural Philosophy, Am. Phys. Soc. Author: Nonlinear Theory of Continuous Media, 1962; Mechanics of Continua, 1967. Editor: Proc. of Engring. Sci., 4 vols. Research and numerous publs. on deformable bodies, interaction of electromagnetic waves with deformable media, mech. properties of solid and fluid composites and mixtures, mechanics, thermodynamics and electromagnetic properties of deformable media with microstructure, viscoelastic materials, wave propagations. Home: 129 Broadmead St Princeton, NJ 08540.

ERK, FRANK CHRIS, educator, biologist; b. Evansville, Ind. Dec. 17, 1924; s. Carl Benjamin and Matilda (Schumacher) E.; A.B. magna cum laude, Evansville Coll., 1948; Ph.D. in Genetics, Johns Hopkins, 1952; m. Ruth Parker Hobgood, June 12, 1948; children—Susan Patricia, Elisabeth Carlene, Stephanie Diane. Jr. instr. Johns Hopkins, 1948-51, Adam T. Bruce fellow, 1951- 52, Lalor faculty fellow, 1956; asso. prof. biology, chmn. dept. Washington Coll., Chestertown, Md., 1952-57, dir. coll. choir, 1952-57; prof. biology State U. NN.Y., Long Island Center, Oyster Bay, 1957-61, chmn. div. sci. and math., 1958-59, chmn. dept. biology, 1958-61, dir. univ. choir, 1957-61; prof. biol. scis. State U. N.Y. at Stony Brook, 1962—; chmn. dept. 1962-67. Vis. asso. prof. biology, Carnegie intern. gen. edn. U. Chgo., 1954-55; research collaborator Masonic Med. Research Lab., Utica, 1968—; vis. investigator Poultry Research Centre, Agrl. Research Council, U. Edinburgh (Scotland), 1964-65, Inst. di Genetica, U. di Milan (Italy), 1965, U. Sussex, Eng., 1971-72; cons. writer Biol. Scis. Curriculum Study, Boulder, Colo., 1960-70; dir. Madrigal Singers, Stony Brook, 1963—; mem. examining com. Advanced Placement Biology College Entrance Exam. Bd., 1967-71. Served to 1st lt. USAAF, 1943-46; PTO. Mem. A.A.A.S., Am. Assn. U. Profs., genetics socs. Am., Can., Am. Genetics Assn., Nat. Assn. Biology Tchrs., Sigma Xi, Phi Beta Chi, Omicron Delta Kappa. Author: (with others) Biological Science-Molecules to Man, 1963, 68; (with others) Biological Science: Interaction of Experiments and Ideas, 1965, 70. Exec. editor Quar. Rev. Biology, 1966-69, editor, 1969—. Home: 33 Yorktown Rd Setauket NY 11733 Office: Div Biol Scis State U NY Stony Brook NY 11790

ERLANDER, TAGE, former prime minister Sweden; b. Ransäter, Värmland, Sweden, June 13, 1901; s. Erik and Alma (Nilsson) E.; M.A., U. Lund, 1928; m. Aina Andersson, 1930; children—Sven, Bo. Began in journalism, then entered polit. career; mem. city council Lund, 1931-38; mem. second chamber Swedish Riksdag, 1933-44, 1949—, 1st chamber, 1945-48; apptd. sec. Ministry Social Affairs, 1938-44; minister without portfolio Coalition Cabinet, 1944-45; minister edn. and ch. affairs Social Democrat Cabinet, 1945-46; premier Sweden 1946-69. Mem. Social Democrat party (chmn. 1946—). Swedish Lutheran. Co-editor Svensk Uppslagbok (ency.), 1932-38. Home: Fryrverkarbacken 21 Stockholm Sweden

ERLANDSON, RAY SANFORD, educator; b. Wausau, Wis., May 3, 1893; s. Paul and Torgine (Olson) E.; A.B., U. Wis., 1918; M.A., George Washington U., 1921; m. Margery McKillop, Aug. 22, 1919; children—Dr. Paul McKillop, Ray Sanford, William. Sch. adminstr. Chippewa Falls, Wis., 1913-16; asst. sec., bus. mgr. N.E.A., 1919-24; bus. mgr. Internat. Council Religious Edn., 1924- 27; sales exec. John Rudin & Co., 1927-29, Grigsby Grunow Co., 1929- 32, Zenith Radio Corp., 1932-35; v.p. Rudolph Wurlizer Co., 1935-45; v.p. San Antonio Music Co., 1945-50, pres., 1950-53; pres. Bledsoe Furniture Co. 1950-53; chmn. dept. bus. adminstrn. Trinity U. 1950-53; chmn. dept. bus. adminstrn. Trinity U., 1953-64; pres., chief exec. officer The Children's Fund, San Antonio, 1964-70; pres., chmn. bd. Am. Inst. Character Edn., 1970—; dir. S.W. Research Center. Dir. First Federal Saving & Loan Assn. Founder Am. School of the Air, 1929; pres. Am. Music War Council, 1942-44; chmn. nat. trade practice code com., music industry, 1944-53. Nat. vice chmn. A.R.C., 1959-60; past dir. San Antonio Symphony Soc., San Antonio chpt. Am. Red Cross, Taxpayers League, Community Welfare Council. Dir., exec. com. Southwest Research Inst., chmn. bd. of control, 1961-64. Served as lt. F.A., U.S. Army World War I; cons. joint Army-Navy com. on welfare, recreation, World War II. Named father of year, San Antonio, 1951; Distinguished Alumnus award Wis. State U., 1969. Mem. N.E.A., San Antonio Chamber Music Soc. (pres. 1950-56), Research and Planning Council (pres. 1957), Am. Assn. U. Profs., Nat. Municipal League, San Antonio Council Presidents (pres. 1951), Nat. Assn. Music Mchts. (pres. 1950-52; hon. life mem.), Am. Marketing Assn. Republican. Presbyterian. Mason. Clubs: San Antonio Rotary (gov. dist. 584 internat. 1958-59), Knife and Fork, Breakfast, San Antonio. Author: (with others) Principle of Retailing, 1955, Marketing 1958; Principles of Advertising. Home: 401 Shook Av San Antonio TX 78212 Office: Three America's Bldg 118 Broadway San Antonio TX 78205

ERLANDSON, THEODORE ROY, univ. dean; b. Detroit, Feb. 3, 1918; s. Roy G. and Agnes (Moriarty) E.; B.A., Loyola U., Los Angeles, 1940; M.A., Harvard, 1947; Ph.D., U. So. Cal., 1964; m. Mary Casilda Krug, Dec. 27, 1952; children—Gregory, Anthony, Patrick, Mary Agnes, Karen, Martha, Eric, Paul. Instr. English dept. Loyola U., Los Angeles, 1946-49, asst. prof., asso. prof., 1949-68, prof. English and communication arts, 1968, chmn. dept. English, 1953-69, dean Coll. Arts and Scis., 1970—. Served with USAAF, 1942-46. Mem. Coll. English Assn. So. Cal. (pres. 1966-67), Modern Lang. Assn. Am., Philol. Assn. Pacific Coast, Alpha Sigma Nu (v.p., nat. dir.). Home: 1990 Avenida Feliciano San Pedro CA 90732 Office: 7101 W 80th St Los Angeles CA 90045

ERLANGER, BERNARD FERDINAND, biochemist, educator; b. N.Y.C., July 13, 1923; s. Leo and Frieda (David) E.; B.S., Coll. City N.Y., 1943; M.A., N.Y.U., 1949; Ph.D., Columbia, 1951; m. Rachel Fenichel, June 23, 1946; children—Laura, Louis, Leon. Chemist, U.S. Indsl. Chems. Co., Inc., Newark, 1943-44; tech. adviser Manhattan Project, U.S. Army, Los Alamos, 1944-46; prodn. mgr. Hexagon Labs., Inc., N.Y.C., 1946-48; faculty Columbia, 1951- -, prof. microbiology, 1966—. Vis. scientist Instituto Superiore di Sanita, Rome, Italy, 1961-62; cons. to industry; mem. Fulbright-Hays Award Com., 1966—. Fulbright scholar U. Republic Uruguay, 1967; Guggenheim fellow Inst. Biologie Physico-Chimique, Paris, 1969. Mem. Am. Chem. Soc., Am. Soc. Biol. Chemists, Biochem. Soc., Harvey Soc. Research on mode of action of antibiotics; investigation of mechanisms of enzyme catalysis, immunochemistry of macromolecules concerned with genetics. Home: 163-16 15th Dr Beechhurst NY 11357 Office: 630 W 168th St New York City NY 10032

ERLENBORN, JOHN NEAL, congressman; b. Chgo., Feb. 8, 1927; s. John H. and Veronica M. (Moran) E.; student U. Notre Dame, 1944, U. Ill., 1945-46; J.D., Loyola U., Chgo., 1949; m. Dorothy C. Fisher, May 10, 1952; children—Debra Lynn, Paul Nelson, David John. Admitted to Ill. bar, 1949; practiced law office Joseph S. Perry, Wheaton, 1949-50; partner firm Erlenborn, Bauer & Hotte, and predecessor, Elmhurst, 1952—; mem. 89th-92d Congresses, 14th Dist. Ill. Asst. states atty. DuPage Co., Ill., 1950-52; mem. Ill. Ho. of Reps from DuPage Co., 1956-64. Served with USNR, 1944-46. Mem. Elmhurst C. of C., Am. Legion. Republican. Lion. Home: 445 Emery Lane Elmhurst IL 60126 Office: House Office Bldg Washington DC 20515

ERLEWINE, JOHN ALBERT, govt. ofcl.; b. Houston, Jan. 6, 1923; s. Clarence Daniel and Edith (Feighner) E.; A.B., U. Mich., 1943; LL.B., Columbia, 1948; m. Millicent Virginia Watson, Nov. 15, 1946; children—Christopher, Mark, John Raymond. Admitted to Ill. bar, 1948; asso. firm Nicholson & Nisen, Chgo., 1948-50; with AEC, 1952—, asst. gen. mgr. operations, 1964—; dep. for Euratom affairs U.S. mission to European communities, Brussels, Belgium, 1961-64. Served to 1st lt., inf. AUS, 1943-45; to capt., mil. govt. and judge adv. gen. dept., AUS, 1950-52. Decorated Bronze Star. Home: 609 Hyde Rd Silver Spring MD 20902 Office: US Atomic Energy Commn Washington DC 20545

ERLICH, VICTOR, educator; b. Petrograd, Russia, Nov. 22, 1914; s. Henryk and Sophie (Dubnov) E. M.A., Free Polish U., Warsaw, 1937; Ph.D., Columbia, 1951; M.A. (hon.), Yale, 1963; m. Iza Sznejerson, Feb. 27, 1940; children—Henry Anthony, Mark Leo. Came to U.S., 1942, naturalized, 1943. Asst. lit. editor New Life mag., Warsaw, 1937-39; research writer Yiddish Ency., 1942-43; from asst. prof. to prof. Slavic lit. and langs. U. Wash., 1949-63; Bensinger prof. Russian lit. Yale, 1963—, chmn. dept. Slavic langs., 1963-68. Served with AUS, 1943-45; ETO. Decorated Purple Heart. Ford Fellow, 1953-54; Fulbright lectr. 1957-58; Guggenheim fellow, 1958, 64; Nat. Endowment for Humanities fellow, 1968-69. Mem. Am. Assn. Advancement Slavic Studies (dir.) Modern Lang. Assn. (exec. council), Internat. Assn. Slavic Langs. and Lits. (exec. council), Am. Assn. U. Profs., Am. Comparative Lit. Assn., Am. Soc. Aesthetics. Author: Russian Formalism: History, Doctrine, 1955; The Double Image: Concepts of the Poet in Slavic Literatures, 1964; Gogol, 1969. Home: 25 Glen Parkway Hamden CT 06517. Office: Yale Univ New Haven CT 06520

ERLICK, EVERETT HOWARD, broadcasting co. exec.; b. Birmingham, Ala., Sept. 12, 1921; s. Julian H. and Bertha Lorraine (Engel) E.; A.B., Vanderbilt U., 1942; LL.B., Yale, 1948; m. Nancy Ruth Jacobs, July 11, 1953; children—James M., Lorre Bert. Admitted to N.Y. bar, 1948; asso. atty. Engel, Judge & Miller, N.Y.C., 1948-51; asst. gen. counsel Young & Rubicam, N.Y.C., 1951-55, v.p. asso. dir. media relations dept., 1955-58, v.p. radio-TV dept., 1959-61; v.p. gen. counsel Am. Broadcasting-Paramount Theatres, Inc. (now Am. Broadcasting Cos., Inc.), 1961—, dir., 1962—, now group v.p.; dir. AB-PT, Inc., WLS, Inc. Mem. Pres.'s Bus. Adv. Com. on Desegregation, 1963, Pres.'s Nat. Citizens Com. for Community Relations, 1964, Nat. Com. for Immigration Reform, 1965; mem. campaign Am. Cancer Soc., 1965—. Mem. Phi Beta Kappa. Home: 22 Chester Dr Rye NY 10580 Office: 1330 Av Americas New York City NY 10019

ERLY, ROBERT BROUSSARD, naval officer; b. Washington, June 12, 1914; s. Alfred Angus and Estelle (Harice) E.; B.S., U.S. Naval Acad., 1937; postgrad. internat. relations, George Washington U., 1962-63; m. Lois Richards, Apr. 14, 1944. Commd. ensign USN, 1937, advanced through grades to rear adm., 1965; various assignments in battleships and destroyers, 1937-43; mem. U.S. Naval Mission to Cuba, 1943-44; comdr. destroyer U.S.S. Phelps, 1944-46; mem. U.S. Naval Mission to Venezuela, 1946-48; exec. officer U.S.S. Yosemite, 1948-49; instr. Gen. Line Sch., Newport, R.I., 1949-50; comdr. U.S.S. James C. Owens, 1950-52; student Armed Forces Staff Coll., 1952-53; asst. operations and tactical officer for Amphibious Group 2, 1953-55; assigned Office Chief Naval Operations, 1955-58; comdr. U.S.S. Paul Revere, 1958-59; asst. chief of staff, operations for Amphibious Force, Pacific Fleet, 1959-61; comdr. Amphibious Squad 5, 1961-62; assigned Nat. War Coll., 1962-63; chief of staff for Amphibious Force, Pacific Fleet, 1963-65; comdr. Amphibious Group 3, 1965-66; dir. Pan Am. affairs and naval del. to Inter-Am. Def. Bd., 1966-68; insp. gen. Atlantic Fleet, 1968-69, dep. chief staff, 1969-71; comdr. Iberian Forces, Atlantic, also chief Mil. Assistance Adv. Group, Portugal, 1972—. Decorated Legion of Merit with gold star, Bronze star with combat V, Joint Service Commendation medal, Navy Commendation medal with two gold stars and combat V. Home: 612 E Beach St Gulfport MS 39501 Office: Comdr Iberian Forces Atlantic Portugal

ERMENC, JOSEPH JOHN, educator; b. Milw., Nov. 11, 1912; s. John and Mary (Jeray) E.; B.S., U. Wis., 1934; M.S., U. Mich., 1940; M.A. (hon.), Dartmouth, 1945; m. Mary Wilkinson Steele, June 30, 1952; children—Christine, Elsie, Joseph Steele. Instr. Purdue U., 1936-37, Rensselaer Poly. Inst., 1937-42; asst. prof. mech. engring. Thayer Sch. Engring., Dartmouth, 1942-45, prof., 1945—; hon. research asso. U. Coll., London, Eng., 1962-63. Mem. N.H. SSS adv. com. on sci., engring. specialized personnel. NSF Science Faculty fellow, 1962-63. Mem. Am. Soc. M.E. (history and heritage com. 1971—), Am. Soc. Engring. Edn. Author articles on history of tech. Home: 77 E Wheelock St Hanover NH 03755

ERNEMANN, ANDRE, Belgian diplomat; b. Antwerp, Belgium, Aug. 31, 1923; s. JosephJean and Marthe Ernemann; degrees in bus. adminstrn. and philosophy, U. Leuven; m. Ginette Matthys, Dec. 20, 1949. Joined Belgium Fgn. Service, 1947; attache, Rome, 1950-52; sec. Teheran, 1953-56; counsellor, Paris, 1959- 66; econ. counsellor for Eastern European nations, Brussels, 1966-69; minister plenipotentiary, 1967; consul gen. in N.Y.C., 1969—. Decorated knight Order Crown, officer Order Crown, comdr. Order Crown (Belgium), comdr. Order Tadj (Iran); officer, Legion of Honor (France). Address: Belgian Consulate Gen 50 Rockefeller Plaza New York City NY 10020

ERNEST, JOHN HENRY, univ. adminstr.; b. Swanwick, Ill., Sept. 11, 1905; s. John Albert and Susan Ellen (Kelly) E.; B.S. in Bus. Adminstrn., Washington U., St. Louis, 1930. M.S., 1932; m. Flossie Anna Logan, May 1, 1932. Mem. staff Washington U., 1932—, treas., 1956-64, vice chancellor bus. and finance, 1961-64, sec. to bd. dirs. 1961-64, prof. accounting, 1964—, financial adviser to chancellor, 1964—. Mem. Am. Accounting Assn. Baptist. Mason. Home: 940 Campus Av Redlands CA 92373

ERNEST, JOSEPH MCDONALD, Jr., coll. adminstr.; b. Chattanooga, Aug. 27, 1915; s. Joseph McDonald and Ethel (Wright) E.; B.A., Maryville Coll., 1937; M.A., U. Tenn., 1942, Ph.D., 1952; m. Juanita Shinlever, June 28, 1946; children—Joseph McDonald III, Bernie Herschell. Tchr., English, Oliver Springs (Tenn.) High Sch., 1937-42; instr. Ga. Sch. Tech., U. Tenn., 1946-52; asst. prof., then asso. prof. English, Miss. So. Coll., 1952-56; prof. English, dean instrn. William Carey Coll., 1956-62, acad. vice pres. 1967—; dean Carson-Newman Coll., Jefferson City, Tenn., 1962- 67; state chmn. high sch. writing competition Nat. Council Tchrs. English, 1969. Pres. Forrest County chpt. A.R.C., 1961. Served from ensign to lt. (s.g.) USNR, 1942-46; lt. comdr. Res. Mem. Am. Studies Assn. Lower Miss. (v.p. 1959). Baptist (deacon). Rotarian (pres. 1960). Home: 816 Velma St Hattiesburg MS 39401

ERNI, HANS, painter; b. Lucerne, Switzerland, Feb. 21, 1909; s. Gotthard and Maria (Schär) E.; student Sch. Art and Craft, Lucerne, 1927-28. Acad. Julian (1st prize competition), Paris, 1928-29. Berlin Acad., 1929-30; m. Doris Kessler; children—Simone, Sibylle, Felix. Executed fresco for Triennale, Milan, Italy, 1936, large mural for Swiss Nat. Exhbn., 1939, mural Creative Energy for Switzerland Planning and Bldg Exhbn., London, 1946, 8 large panels for internat. exhbn. L'Habitation et l'Urbanisme, Paris, 1947, mural for WHO, Zurich, 1950, large mural Les Conquêtes de l'Homme, Musee d'Ethnographie in Neuchatel, 1954, 3 large murals La Conquête du Temps for Swiss Pavillion, Brussels Exhbn., 1958, mural In Health There is Freedom for UN Pavillion Brussels, 1958; mural Le Cafe for r Nestlē adminstrn. building in Vevey, 1959; floor-mosaique for Abbaye at St. Maurice, Valais, Switzerland, 1961; 2 mosaics for Swiss Radio and TV Bldg., 1964; exhbs. throughout US., Europe, Japan, Australia; works permanently rep. museums in Switzerland, Eng., Sweden, France, U.S. Recipient Gold medal Cannes Internat. Exhbn., 1955. Mem. Schweizerischer Werkbund, Alliance Graphique Internat., Societe Europeanne de Culture. Illustrator luxury editions: Le Banquet de Platon, 1941, Das Lied des Friedens, 1942, Olympiques, 1944. Oedipus Rex, 1949, Antigone, 1950, Daphnis and Chloe. 1950. Historeis Naturelles, 1953. Esquisses pour Doris, 1953, La Cantate de Narcisse, 1955, Lafontaine Fables, 1955, Ovide, 1957, Odyssee, 1957-59, Message de Paix, 1958. Address: 6045 Meggen Lucerne Switzerland

ERNST, ALBERT EDWARD, oil cons.; b. Cin., July 24, 1901; s. Arthur Augustus and Louise Kathryn (Tuerck) E.; B.S., U. Cin., 1923, postgrad 1924; m. Anita Rose Dolle, Nov. 2, 1933; children—John DeBolt, Edward Selton, Frederick Vincent. Internat. oil bus. in various countries of Asia, Europe, Africa and South Am., beginning in 1925; chief petroleum div. Lend Lease Adminstrn. and Fgn. Econ. Adminstrn., Washington, 1943-45; v.p., asst. to chmn. bd. dirs. Cal. Tex. Oil Co., Ltd., N.Y.C., 1946-59; v.p. Continental Oil Co., 1959-66; internat. oil cons., 1966- -. Mem. Council on Fgn. Relations, Beta Gamma Sigma, Beta Theta Pi. Clubs: Metropolitan (N.Y.C.); Graduate (New Haven); Sunningdale Golf (Berks. Eng.); Silver Spring Country (Ridgefield, Conn.). Address: Florida Hill Rd Ridgefield CT 06877

ERNST, EARLE, educator; b. Miffintown, Pa., Dec. 15, 1911; s. David Kuhns and Esther (Smith) E.; A.B., Gettysburg (Pa.) Coll., 1933; M.A., Cornell U., 1939, Ph.D., 1940. Mem. faculty U. Hawaii, 1940—, sr. prof. drama and theatre, 1960—, chmn. dept., 1963—, dir. grad. study, 1950—; dir. first prodns. in English of Oriental plays; lectr. Waseda U., Tokyo, Japan, 1952, Ind. U., 1962; adminstr. Rockefeller grant for translation Oriental plays, 1950-52; cons. in field. Served with AUS, 1944-47; Japan. Rockefeller fellow, 1937-38, grantee, 1951-53. Mem. Phi Kappa Phi. Author: The Kabuki Theatre, 1956; Three Japanese Plays from the Traditional Theatre, 1959; also articles. Contbr. Ency. Britannica. Home: 3368 Huelani Dr Honolulu HI 96822

ERNST, EDWARD WILLIS, educator; b. Great Falls, Mont., Aug. 28, 1924; s. Paul Wilson and Grace Vio (Woodmore) E.; B.S., U. Ill., 1949, M.S., 1950, Ph.D. in Elec. Engring., 1955; m. Helen Kitty Todd, Jan. 29, 1950; children—Deborah Kitty, Thomas Edward. Research engr. Gen. Electric Co., Syracuse, N.Y., 1955; research engr. Stewart Warner Electronics, Chgo., 1955-58; asso. prof. dept. elec. engring. U. Ill., Urbana, 1958-68, prof., 1968—, asso. head dept., 1970—. Bd. dirs. McKinley Found., Champaign, Ill., 1962—, pres., 1968—. Mem. Nat. Electronics Conf. (dir. 1959-70, pres. 1964, chmn. bd. 1966), I.E.E.E. (sr. mem.), Am. Soc. E.E., Am. Assn. U. Profs., A.A.A.S., Sigma Xi, Eta Kappa Nu, Tau Beta Pi, Sigma Tau, Phi Kappa Phi. Presbyn. Home: 2104 Cureton Dr Urbana IL 61801

ERNST, FREDERIC, educator, editor; b. Belgium, July 13, 1888; s. Charles and Selma (Milcamps) E.; Licence es Sciences, U. Liege (Belgium), 1909; M.A., U. Wis., 1911; m. Jeanne Romiflat, Aug. 4, 1920; 1 son, Maurice. Came to U.S., 1910, naturalized, 1919. Instr. U. Wis., 1910-17, asst. prof., 1919-23; asst. prof. N.Y.U., 1925-27, asso. prof., 1928-30, prof., 1930—, chmn. depts. French, Italian, Russian, 1946-53; dir. Inst. French Edn., Pa. State Coll., 1929-43; gen. editor modern lang. texts Dryden Press, 1930-53, asso. editor The Dryden Press, 1953- 58; cons. editor Henry Holt & Co., N.Y.C., 1950—. Interpreter in France, U.S. Army, A.E.F., 1914-19. Decorated Legion of Honor (France). Mem. Modern Lang. Assn., Am. Assn. Tchrs. French, Phi Beta Kappa. Author: (with Dondo), Principes de Grammaire et de Style 1935; (with Levy) Le Français, 1952; La France et les Français, 1961; Gens de France, 1967. Home: 17 E 89th St New York City NY 10028

ERNST, JIMMY, artist; b. Cologne, Germany, June 24, 1920; s. Max and Louise Amalia (Straus) E.; student Lindenthal Real-Gymnasium, Cologne, 1932-36, Sch. Arts and Crafts, Altona, Germany, 1938, Naturalized, 1951. Prof. dept. art Bklyn. Coll. 1951—; one-man shows Walker Art Center, Mpls., Grace Brogenicht Gallery, N.Y.C., Venice Biennial, Brussels World Fair, Kunstverin Cologne (Germany) Mus. 1963, other nat. internat. shows; work represented permanent collections Mus. Modern Art, Metropolitan Mus. Corcoran Gallery, Washington, Guggenheim Mus. Whitney Mus. Chgo. Art Inst., Albright Art Gallery, Buffalo, others; mural commns. include exec. dining room Gen. Motors Tech. Center, Am. President Lines, S.S. Adams, Continental Nat. Bank, Lincoln. Neb.; lectr. various mus. in U.S. Am. specialist Dept. State's Cultural Exchange Program to Russia and Poland, 1961; vis. artist Norton Galleries, Palm Beach, Fla.; exhbns. in Cologne, Germany, Bielefeld Mus., Germany, 1963-64. Recipient Brandeis creative arts award, 1957; Guggenheim grant for creative painting, 1961. Home: Ponus Ridge New Canaan CT 06840 Office: Brooklyn Coll New York City NY 11210

ERNST, KEVIN MELVIN, Jr. educator, biologist; b. Ames, Ia.; B.A., Ia. State U., 1936, M.A., 1937, Ph.D. with honors, 1940; m. Ann Ross, Mar. 23, 1946; children--Edward, Thomas A., Mark. Instr., Ia. State U., 1946-47; asst. prof. biology Johns Hopkins, 1947-50, asso. prof., 1950-62, prof., 1962--, chmn. dept., 1963-69; vis. lectr. Stanford, 1970-71. Active Boy Scouts Am., 4-H Club. Served with AUS, 1940-46. Mem. Am. Soc. Biologists, Md. Soc. Cell Biologists, Am. Soc. Exptl. Biology, Internat. Union Biologists, A.A.A.S., Am. Acad. Arts and Scis., Phi Beta Kappa. Home: 48936 W Hancock Blvd Baltimore MD 20206

ERNST, MORRIS LEOPOLD, lawyer; b. Uniontown, Ala., Aug. 23, 1888; s. Carl and Sarah (Bernheim) E.; A.B., Williams Coll., 1909; LL.B., N.Y. Law Sch., 1912; J.D., Nasson Coll., 1963; D.H.L., Lincoln U., 1964; m. Susan Leerburger (dec. 1922); m. 2d, Margaret Samuels, Mar. 1, 1923; children—Constance, Roger, Joan. Mfr. shirts, 1909-11, retail furniture, 1911-15; mem. law firm Greenbaum, Wolff & Ernest, N.Y., 1915—; spl. counsel Am. Newspaper Guild; served as arbiter for Mayor La Guardia in taxicab strike, 1934; drafted legislation for Gov. Lehman on ins. and banking matters; mem. Pa. Anthracite Coal Commission. Mem. N.Y. State Banking Bd. since inception, by apptmt. Gov. Roosevelt and Gov. Lehman, 1933-45. Counsel Dramatists Guild and Authors League of Am.; spl. asst. atty.-gen. in election fraud matters; counsel to N.Y. State Legislative Commn. for Hard of Hearing; spl. cons. War Prodn. Bd.; personal rep. to Pres. Roosevelt during war on various missions to England; governmental mission, Germany, 1946; mission Virgin Islands, 1935. Apptd. by Pres. Truman to Pres. Truman's Civil Rights Com.; apptd. by Pres. to adv. bd. for the Post Office. Mem. chancellor's council U. Tex., 1969. Decorated Order French Legion Honor. Mem. Bar Assn. City N.Y. (Lawyer of Year 1960), N.Y. County Lawyers Assn., P.E.N., Am. Polit. Sci. Assn., Phi Beta Kappa, Phi Gamma Delta, Alpha Kappa Delta (hon.), Gargoyle Society. Clubs: City (past trustee), Williams, New York University Faculty (N.Y.); University (Washington); Savile (Eng.). Author: (with William Seagle) To the Pure, 1928; (with Pare Lorentz) Censored, 1930; America's Primer, 1931; Hold Your Tongue (with A. Lindey), 1932; (with others) Sex Life of the Unmarried Adult, 1934; Ultimate Power, 1937; (with A Lindey) The Censor Marches On, 1939; Too Big, 1940; The Best Is Yet, 1945; The First Freedom, 1946; So Far So Good, 1948; author with D. Loth: American Sexual Behavior and the Kinsey Report, 1948; The People Know Best, 1949; For Better or Worse, 1952; Report on the American Communist, 1952; Utopia, 1976, (1955); Touch wood (diary), pub. 1960; Untitled, A Diary of the 72d year, 1962; (with Alan U. Schwartz) Privacy: The Right to be Let Alone, 1962; (with Alan U. Schwartz) Lawyers and What They Do, 1964, Censorship: The Search for the Obscene, 1964; (with David Loth) How High Is Up, 1964; The Teacher, 1967; (with Judith Posner) Comparative Internat. Almanac, 1968; A Love Affair With The Law, 1968; Triple Crosstricks, 1968; (with Mary Batten) Discovery By Chance, 1968; (with Malcolm A. Hoffmann) Back and Forth, 1969. Contbr. to mags. and encys. Lectr. clubs and colls. Home: 2 Fifth Av New York City NY 10011 Office: 437 Madison Av New York City NY 10022

ERNST, ROBERT CRAIG, former dean, chem. engr.; b. Cin., Sept. 27, 1900; s. Arthur Henry and Mary (Talbott) E.; B.S. in Chem. Engring., N.C. State Coll., 1921; M.S., U. Minn., 1923, Ph.D., 1930; m. Sarah Warren Carter, Jan. 3, 1924; children—Robert Craig, Richard Thomas. Grad. asst., instr. chem. engring. U. Minn., 1921-26; asst. prof. chem. engring., U. Louisville, 1926-31, asso. prof., 1931-33, prof., head dept., 1933-47, dir. Div. of Indsl. Research. 1940-44, dean Speed Sci. Sch., 1947-69, dir., exec. v.p. U. Louisville Inst. Indsl. Research, 1945-47, pres., dir., 1947-69. Cons. numerous corps., govtl. agys. Registered Profl. engr., Ky. Chmn., Ky. Adv. Com. on Nuclear Energy, 1957-61; past mem. Ky. Bd. Registration Licensing Profl. Engrs. and Land Surveyors, Ky. Atomic Energy and Space Authority; mem. econ. atlas com. agrl. and Indsl. Devel. Bd. Ky.; mem. NRC Com. on Design, Constrn. and Equipment of Labs. Mem. Royal Soc. Arts. Am. Inst. Chem. Engrs. Am. Soc. Engring. Edn., Am. Chem. Soc., Oak Ridge Inst. Nuclear Studies (councillor 1943-68), Ky. Soc. Profl. Engrs. (past pres.), Ky. Acad. Sci., A.A.A.S., Nat. Mgmt. Council, Am. Acad. Polit. and Social Sci., Soc. Chem. Industry (London), Louisville Engring. and Sci. Socs. Council, Newcomb Soc., Sigma Xi, Sigma Tau, Phi Kappa Phi, Phi Lambda Upsilon, Gamma Sigma Epsilon, Theta Chi Delta, Gamma Alpha, Sigma Phi Sigma, Omicron Delta Kappa. Methodist. Rotarian. Clubs: Audubon Country Chemists (N.Y.); Filson of Ky.; Pendennis. Contbr. articles to jours. Holder 6 patents. Home: 3315 Oriole Dr Louisville KY 40213 ☆

ERNST, ROGER, govt. ofcl.; b. N.Y.C., June 2, 1924; s. Morris L. and Marguerite (Samuels) E.; B.A. cum laude, Williams Coll., 1948; fgn. area and lang. study, U. Md., 1944; grad. Nat. War Coll., 1956; m. Jean O'Mara, Mar. 15, 1952; children—Deborah, David. Joined U.S. Fgn. Service, 1948; Austria desk officer Marshall Plan, State Dept., 1948-50; asst. dir NATO, Dept. Def., 1950-55; asst. dir. planning Dept. Def., 1956-59; mem. staff President's Com. Study Fgn. Aid Program, 1958-59; asst. to dir. AID mission to India, 1959-62; rep. Peace Corps in India, 1961-62; dep. dir. AID mission to China, 1962-64, to Korea, 1964-68; dir. AID mission to Ethiopia, 1968—. Served as officer AUS, 1943-47. Decorated Bronze Star. Mem. Nantucket Hist. Assn. Home: Monomoy Nantucket MA also 5400 Duvall Dr Washington DC 20016 Office: USAID Ethiopia APO New York City NY 09319

ERNSTENE, ARTHUR CARLTON, physician; b. Parker, S.D., Aug. 4, 1901; s. Edwin Carl and Alice (Goddard) E.; A.B., State U. Ia., 1922, M.D., 1925; D.Sc. (hon.), John Carroll U., 1959, Baldwin-Wallace Coll., 1964; m. Beatrice McGarvey, June 25, 1925 (dec. 1925); 1 son, Marshall Paul; m. 2d, Audra N. Miller, Nov. 20, 1954. Intern Henry Ford Hosp., Detroit, 1925-26; asst. resident Thorndike Meml. Lab., Boston City Hosp., 1926-27, resident, 1927-28; research asso. Beth Israel Hosp., Boston, 1928-32; asst. in medicine Harvard, 1927-30, instr., 1930-32; head dept. cardiovascular disease Cleve. Clinic, 1932-48, chmn. div. medicine, 1948-66. Served as lt. comdr. M.C., USNR, 1942- 44; chief of medicine, hosps. at Auckland, New Zealand, Espiritu Santo, New Hebrides. Bd. lay trustees John Carroll U. Recipient Golf Heart award Am. Heart Assn., 1964. Diplomate Am. Bd. Internal Medicine (mem. sub-specialty bd. on vardiovascular disease 1956-61). Fellow A.C.P. (gov. Ohio 1957-63, regent 1963-69, pres. 1965-66), A.A.A.S.; mem. A.M.A. (sec. sect. internal medicine 1953-56, chmn. 1956-57), Am. Clin. and Climatol. Assn. (v.p. 1950), Am. Soc. for Clin. Investigation, Central Soc. Clin. Research, Assn. Am. Physicians, Am. (dir. 1953-63; chmn. sect. clin. cardiology 1952-54, pres. 1959-60), Ohio State (founders group, 1st pres. 1950-52) heart assns., Cleve. Area Heart Soc. (founders group, 1st pres. 1949-51), Acad. of Medicine of Cleve. (sec.-treas. 1940-42, dir. 1946-49), Ohio State Med. Assn. (chmn. com. on sci. work 1951-59), Interurban Clin. Club Cleve. Med. Library Assn. (trustee), Phi Beta Kappa, Sigma Xi, Alpha Omega Alpha, Phi Kappa Psi, Nu Sigma Nu. Author: Coronary Heart Disease, 1948; also articles and papers in field. Home: 13400 Shaker Blvd Cleveland OH 44120 Office: Cleveland Clinic Cleveland OH 44106

ERNSTROM, CARL ANTHON, educator; b. Draper, Utah, Mar. 28, 1922; s. Carl Ludvig and Jennie Charlotte (Nielsen) E.; student U. Colo., 1943-44; B.S., Utah State U., 1949, M.S., 1951; Ph.D., U. Wis., 1956; m. Maurine A. Lawrence, Aug. 24, 1949; children—Brian, Carl R., Jean, Maren. With Wis. Extension Service, 1953-54; researcher Hansen Lab., Milw., 1955-56; asst. then asso. prof. dept. dairy and food industries U. Wis., 1956-65; prof., head dept. food sci. and industries Utah State U., Logan, 1967—; cons. to industry. Served with USMCR, 1943-46, 51-52. Recipient Pfizer award Am. Dairy Sci. Assn., 1968. Mem. Am. Dairy Sci. Assn., Inst. Food Technologists, Sigma Xi, Phi Kappa Phi. Home: 730 Mountain View Dr Logan UT 84321

ERNZEN, WILLIAM NICHOLAS, railroad ofcl.; b. Downers Grove, Ill., Aug. 17, 1911; s. Frank and Mary (Hargarten) E.; m. Helen Morton, July 4, 1940; children—Paul, Philip. With C.,B.&Q. R.R., 1928-70, v.p., comptroller, 1962-70; v.p. finance Burlington No.

Inc., 1970-71, v.p., controller, 1971—; v.p., comptroller Colo. & So. Ry. Co., Ft. Worth & Denver Ry. Co.; v.p., gen. auditor, dir. Burlington Truck Lines, Inc.; pres., dir. Burlington Equipment Co., St. Louis & Kansas City Land Co.; v.p., dir. Gt. Midwest Corp. & affiliates; controller, dir. Glacier Park Co.; v.p., trustee S.P. & S.Ry.; dir. Packers Carline, Merc. Nat. Bank, Chgo. Controller Burlington No. Found. C.P.A., Ill. Mem. Assn. Am. R.R.'s, Western Ry. Club, Financial Execs. Inst., Newcomen Soc. Republican. Roman Catholic. Clubs: Union League, Executives (Chgo.); St. Paul Athletic; Minnesota; Pool and Yacht. Home: 2023 Upper St Dennis Rd St Paul MN 55116 Office: 176 E 5th St St Paul MN 55101

ERPF, ARMAND GROVER, investment banker; b. N.Y.C., Dec 8, 1897; s. Bartholomew and Cornelia (von Greiner) E.; B.A., Columbia, 1917; L.H.D., Catholic U. Am.; LL.D., Manhattan Coll.; m. Sue Stuart Mortimore, Apr. 7, 1965; children—Cornelia, Armand. Asst. sec. Suffern Co. of N.Y., also asst. mgr. Suffern Co. of Brazil, 1917-19; officer, part owner C.E. Erpf & Co., brokers, 1919-23; made survey of textile enterprise in Saxony, Germany, 1923-24; statistician, later officer, dir. and part owner Cornell, Linder & Co., Inc., N.Y.C., 1924-33; dir. statis. and research depts., later investments adv. dept. Loeb, Rhoades & Co., 1933-36, gen. partner, 1936-71; chmn. exec. com., dir. Crowell Collier & Macmillan, Inc.; chmn. Aneid Equities; dir. Adela Investment Co., S.A., Gen. Instrument Corp., Macmillan Co., Jefferson Ins. Co., Chris-Craft Industries, Inc., Dorr-Oliver, Inc., Jersey External Trust, Stein, Roe & Farnham Internat. Fund. Chmn. council Grad. Sch. Bus., Columbia; chmn. Arkville Erpf Fund. Trustee Whitney Mus. Am. Art; bd. govs. N.Y. Cultural Center. Commd. lt. col., U.S. Army, 1942, promoted col., 1944; apptd. to Gen. Staff Corps., 1944; assigned Office of Comdg. Gen., Hdqrs. A.S.F., Washington, 1942-45; duty with Hdqrs. U.S. Army Forces, Western Pacific, and with comdg. gen. USAF, China Theater, 1945-46. Decorated Legion of Merit. Mem. Am. Assn. Museums (chmn. trustees com.), Chamber Music Soc. at Lincoln Center (trustee), Victorian Soc., Pierpont Morgan Library, Council on Fgn. Relations, Inc., Affiliated Bus. Fellows of Columbia, Delta Sigma Phi. Knight of Malta (grand prior). Clubs: Athenaeum (Phila.); Art Collectors, Economic, Wall Street. Died 2/2/71. Home: 820 Fifth Av New York City NY 10021 also Arkville NY 12406 Office: 42 Wall St New York City NY 10005

ERPF, CARL K., investment banker; b. Woodmere, N.Y., 1925. Partner Ladenburg, Thalmann & Co., N.Y.C.; dir. Atlantic Industries, Broad Alliance Corp., Petro-Lewis Corp.; pres., dir. 960 Park Corp. Sec.-treas. Walter and Lucie Rosen Found., Inc.; pres. bd. trustees Columbia Grammar Sch.; trustee Arkville ERPF Fund, Inc. Home: 960 Park Av New York City NY 10028 Office: 25 Broad St New York City NY 10004

ERRION, ARTHUR ROBBINS, naval officer; b. Woodhaven, N.Y., Feb. 29, 1916; s. Harry Christian and Jennie (Robbins) E.; B.A., U. Pa., 1938, M.D., 1942; m. Jessie Ann Pszenny, Oct. 2, 1948; children—Ann Elizabeth, Jennifer Genvieve. Commd. lt. (j.g.) U.S. Navy, 1942, advanced through grades to capt., 1956; intern U.S. Naval Hosp., Phila., 1942-43; service in U.S.S. McGowen, PTO, 1943-45; resident U.S. Naval Hosp., Chelsea, Mass., 1947-49, St. Francis Hosp., Trenton, N.J., 1949-50; chief medicine Naval Hosp., Key West, Fla., 1957-60, Naval Hosp., St. Albans, N.Y., 1962-65; chief medicine, exec. officer Naval Hosp., Yokosuka, Japan, 1965-67, comdg. officer, 1967-69; comdg. officer Naval Hosp., Chelsea, Mass., 1969—; mem. staff comdr. naval forces, Japan, 1967-69; dist. med. officer 1st Naval Dist., 1970. Fellow Peabody Museum. Deocrated Legion of Merit (Navy). Diplomate Am. Bd. Internal Medicine. Fellow A.C.P., N.Y. Acad. Medicine, Am. Coll. Chest Physicians; mem. Coll. Physicians Phila., Am. Thoracic Soc., Indsl. Med. Soc., A.M.A. Home: 359 Essex St Salem MA Office: US Naval Hosp Boston Chelsea MA 02150

ERSKINE, ALBERT RUSSEL, Jr., editor, b. Memphis, Apr. 18 1911; s. Albert Russel and Nell (Craig) E.; B.A., Southwestern Coll., 1932; M.A., Vanderbilt U., 1939; student La. State U., 1934-39; m. Katherine Anne Porter, 1938 (div. 1942); m. 2d Peggy Griffin Anthony, 1942 (div. 1954); m. 3d, Maria Luisa Bisi, 1959; 1 dau., Silvia. Bus. mgr. So. Rev., 1935-40; asso. editor La. State U. Press, 1936-40, New Directions, 1940-41; advt. mgr. Sat. Rev. of Lit., 1941-42; asso. editor Doubleday, Doran & Co., Inc., 1942-43; editor, head mfg. dept. Reynal & Hitchcock, Inc., 1943-47, sec., dir., 1946-47; editor Random House, Inc., N.Y.C., 1947-55; mng. editor, 1955-59, now v.p., editorial dir. Club: Century Assn. (N.Y.C.). Editor: (with Robert Penn Warren) Short Story Masterpieces, 1954; Six Centuries of Great Poetry, 1953—. Home: 36 Cavalry Rd Westport CT 06880 Office: 201 E 50th St New York City NY 10022

ERSKINE, DONALD EDWARD, corp. exec.; b. Oak Park, Ill., May 14, 1924; s. Robert N. and Florence (Matthes) E.; B.S., U. Ill., 1949; LL.B., 1951; m. Ann Harrison, June 17, 1950; children—Donald E., James A., Bruce H., John T. Admitted to Ill. and Ohio Bars, with Arthur Anderson & Co., C.P.A.'s Chgo., 1951-52, Glidden Co., Cleve., 1952-67; v.p., controller, SCM Corp., N.Y.C., 1969—; dir. SELF, Inc., New York City. Served with AUS, 1942-45. Mem. Financial Execs. Inst. (pres. Cleve. 1966-67). Home: Cedarbrook Terrace RD2 Princeton NJ 08540 Office: 299 Park Av New York City NY 10017

ERSKINE, GEORGE BERNARD, electronic mfg. co. exec.; b. St. Marys, Pa., Apr. 17, 1908; s. Bernard Garfield and Jane (Evans) E.; student Canisuis Coll., Buffalo, 1927-29; m. Marie M. Montgomery, June 17, 1930; children—William M., Jacquelyn Marie (Mrs. Paul Petigrew); m. 2d, Helen M. Housler, Jan. 18, 1950. Plant mgr. Sylvania Electric Products, Inc., 1929-46; pres. Emporium Specialties Co. (Pa.), 1946—. Meteor Mfg. Co., Emporium, 1959—; chmn. bd., chief exec. officer Art Metal Co., Inc., Jamestown, N.Y., 1961- 63, mem. exec. com., dir., 1963-65; chmn. bd. M.W. Mfg. Corp.; Driftwood, Pa., 1961—, Personalized Leasing Corp., Nivel Corp., Metco. Corp. (all Danville, Pa.); v.p., sec. Emporium Trust Co.; dir. Gateway Steel Co., Pitts., Motor Coils Mfg. Co., Braddock, Pa., Home Tel. Co., Ridgeway, Pa. Bd. dirs. Emporium Found. Home: RD 1 Emporium PA 15834 Office: Box 231 Emporium PA 15834

ERSKINE, HELEN WORDEN, see Worden, Helen.

ERSKINE, RALPH, architect; b. London, Eng., Feb. 24, 1914; s. George and Mildred (Gough) E.; A.R.I.B.A., Regent St. Polytechnic, London, 1937, A.M.I/P.I., 1939; student Konstskademin i Stockholm, 1944-45; m. Ruth Monica Francis, Aug. 29, 1939; children—Jane Kristine, Karin Elizabeth, Patrick Jon. Pvt. practice architecture, Drottningholm, Sweden, 1946—; exhibitor, lectr. various parts of world; guest prof., Zurich, Switzerland, 1965; works include housing estates, shopping center, indsl. bldgs., mountain hotel schs., Clare Hall (Cambridge, Eng.), slum clearance and housing estates in Eng. Mem. A.I.A. (hon.), Swedish Archtl. Soc. Home: No 2 Gustav III's vag Rottningholm 170 11 Sweden Office: No 4 Gustav III's vag Drottningholm 170 11 Sweden

ERSLEV, ALLAN JACOB, educator, physician; b. Copenhagen, Denmark, Apr. 20, 1919; s. Aage Holger and Anina (Henriques) E.; M.D., U. Copenhagen, 1945; m. Elisabeth Curtis Lewis, Dec. 21, 1947; children—Wendy, Carole Elisa, Eric Allan, Barbara Kim. Came to U.S., 1946, naturalized, 1949. Intern Copenhagen County Hosp., 1945-46; research fellow Meml. Hosp., also Sloan Kettering Found., N.Y.C., 1946-48; intern, resident, research fellow Yale Sch. Medicine, 1948-53; asso., asst. prof. med. Thorndike Lab., Harvard Med. Sch., 1955-59; asso. prof. medicine Jefferson Med. Coll., 1959-63, Cardeza research prof. medicine, dir. Cardeza Found., 1963—. Served as lt. Danish Army, 1943-45, as capt. AUS, 1953-55. Damon Runyon fellow, 1951-52; Guggenheim fellow, 1967-68. Mem. A.M.A., Am., Internat. socs. hematology, Assn. Am. Physicians; Am. Soc. Clin. Investigation, Interurban Clin. Club. Spl. research control red cell prodn. Home: 436 Conestoga Rd Wayne PA 19087 Office: 1015 Sansom St Philadelphia PA 19107

ERSTEIN, RICHARD, govt. ofcl.; b. N.Y.C., May 30, 1913; s. Benedict and Florence (Rosenthal) E.; grad. Phillips Acad., Andover, Mass., 1931; B.A., Brown U., 1935; grad. Nat. War Coll., 1959; m. Katherine Rahilly, Nov. 28, 1946; 1 dau., Lynn Katherine. Engaged in comml. banking, 1935- 38; producer CBS, 1938-41, 46-47; sr. producer Lowell Inst., Coop. Broadcasting Council, Boston, 1947-51; information officer embassy, Athens, Greece, 1951-55; asst. mgr. programs Voice of Am., 1956-58; pub. affairs officer embassy, Accra, Ghana, 1959-61, consulate gen., Salisbury, Rhodesia, 1961-64; program coordinator for Africa, USIA, 1964- 65, deputy asst. dir. Africa, 1965-66; dep. asst. dir. adminstrn. USIA, Washington, 1966-69; pub. affairs Officer and first sec. Am. Embassy, Nairobi, Kenya, 1969-71; dep. chief research service USIA. Washington, 1971—. Served to lt. comdr. USNR 1942-46. Mem. Beta Theta Pi. Club: Ft. McNair (D.C.) Officers. Address: 2905 Cathedral Av NW Washington DC 20008

ERTELL, MERTON WILLIAM, univ. adminstr.; b. Buffalo, Jan. 31, 1918; s. William F. and Caroline D. (Meurer) E.; B.S., U. Buffalo, 1938, M.B.A., 1949; Ph.D., U. Chgo., 1955; m. Agnes A. Black, Nov. 20, 1940; children—Carolyn Anne, Richard M. Accountant Chevrolet div. Gen. Motors Corp., 1938-41; sr. bus. specialist OPA, 1941-43; exec. officer Statis. Control Office, Hdqrs. 4th Air Force, USAAF, 1943-46; asst. dean Sch. Bus. Adminstrn., State U. N.Y. at Buffalo (formerly U. Buffalo), 1946-55, asst. vice chancellor for ednl. affairs, 1955-58, asso. prof. econs and indsl. relations, dean Univ. Coll., 1958-60, Melvin H. Baker prof. Am. enterprise, 1961-69, asst. v.p. ednl. affairs, dir. instnl. studies, 1961-65; vice chancellor for univ. wide activities State U. N.Y., 1969-70, dep. vice chancellor, 1970—; co-ordinator inter-instnl. coop. research project N.Y. State Edn. Dept., 1957; staff dir. Ill. Gov.'s Commn. to Study Non-Public Higher Edn., 1968-69. Mem. exec. bd. Buffalo area council Boy Scouts Am. Mem. Buffalo Area C. of C. (chmn. econ. affairs com.), Am. Econ. Assn., Econometric Soc., Assn. Higher Edn., Indsl. Relations Research Assn., Am. Assn. U. Profs., Buffalo Council Chs., Beta Gamma Sigma, Alpha Phi Omega, Alpha Kappa Psi. Presbyn. (pres. bd. trustees, mem. gen. council; moderator Presbytery Western N.Y. 1967). Home: 2 Monroe Ct Guilderland NY 12084 Office: State U NY Albany NY 12201

ERTZ, SUSAN, author; b. Walton-on-Thames, Surrey, Eng.; d. Charles Edward and Mary (Le Viness) Ertz; privately ed.; m. Maj. J. Ronald McCrindle, August 6, 1939; Fellow the Royal Soc. Authors. Author: Madame Claire, pub. 1923; Nina, 1925; Now East, Now West, 1927; The Story of Julian, 1930; The Galaxy, 1931; The Proselyte, 1933; Now We Set Out, 1934; Woman Alive, 1935; No Hearts to Break, 1937; Big Frogs and Little Frogs, 1938; Black White and Caroline, 1938; One Flight More, 1940; Anger in the Sky, 1943; Mary Hallam, 1947; The Prodigal Heart, 1950; Invitation to Folly, 1953; Charmed Circle, 1956; In the Cool of the Day, 1960. Home: 17 Sloane Ct W London SW3 England Office: care Harper & Bros 49 E 33d St New York City NY 10016

ERVIN, FRANK, educator, physician; b. Little Rock, Nov. 3 1926; s. Frank Raymond and Ailee (Prothro) E.; B.A., U. Tex., 1955; M.D., Tulane U., 1951; m. Patricia Dean McTee, Oct. 18, 1948; children—Stuart, Stephen, Sean, Scott, Erin.; Intern, Brackenridge Hosp., Austin, Tex., 1951-52; resident Charity Hosp., New Orleans, 1952-55; engaged in research and teaching neurophysiology of behavior, 1955—; asst. prof. psychiatry, then asso. clinic prof. of psychiatry Harvard Med. Sch., 1961—; dir. Stanley Cobb Labs., Mass. Gen. Hosp., 1961—; adj. prof. human devel. Hampshire Coll., 1970—. With Cyber, Inc.; spl. research on brain; pres. Neuro-Research Found., Boston, 1968-69. Served with USNR, 1946-48. Co-author: Violence and the Brain, 1969. Editor: The Fallen Sky, 1961. Home: 46 Kendal Common Rd Weston MA 02193 Office: Box 70 Mass Gen Hosp Boston MA 02114

ERVIN, JOHN Jr., pub.; b. Mt. Vernon, N.Y., Jan. 8, 1927; s. John and Edith Gertrude (Atkinson) E.; B.S. with honors, Yale, 1949; m. Jean Adams, June 17, 1950; children—Keith, Andrew, Bruce, Alec, John A. Editorial staff Princeton U. Press, 1952-57; dir. U. Minn. Press, 1957—. Served with USNR, 1945-46. Mem. Assn. Am. U. Presses (dir. 1964-65, v.p. 1970-71), Am. U. Press Services (dir. 1964-65, v.p. 1970-71), Phi Beta Kappa. Home: 59 Seymour Av SE Minneapolis MN 55414 Office: U Minn Press 2037 University Av SE Minneapolis MN 55455

ERVIN, JOHN WESLEY, lawyer, educator; b. Los Angeles, June 22, 1917; s. Frank Earl and Lillian Pearl (Gray) E.; student U. Cal. at Los Angeles, 1935-39, LL.B., 1944; LL.M. (research fellow 1945-47), Harvard, 1945, S.J.D., 1955; m. Patricia Connelly, May 24, 1958; children (by previous marriage)—Nancy Gray, Shelley Hutchinson, John Chipman Gray. Admitted to Cal. bar, 1944; research asst. justice Cal. Supreme Ct., 1943-44; prof. law, dir. and editor ann. Insts. on Fed. Taxation, U. So. Cal., 1947-70; sr. mem. firm Ervin, Cohen & Jessup, Beverly Hills, Cal., 1953—; spl. adviser to sec. treasury on fed. tax legislation, 1955. Sec., dir. Philos. Research Soc., Internat. Communications Found.; dir. UN Assn. Mem. Am. (chmn. publs. com. taxation sect. 1954-55), Cal., Beverly Hills bar assns., Am. Law Inst., Am. Judicature Soc., Order of Coif, Phi Delta Phi. Author: Federal Taxation and the Family, 1955. Office: 9171 Wilshire Blvd Beverly Hills CA 90210

ERVIN, RALPH WILLIAM Jr., banker; b. Wyncote, Pa., July 10, 1921; s. Ralph William and Marion (Lachot) E.; B.A., Pa. State Coll., 1942; m. Ann Kindig. Apr. 19, 1947; children—Ralph William III, Peter M., Suzanne L. With Buckley Bros., investment bankers, Phila., 1945-49; with Fidelity Mut. Life Ins. Co., Phila., 1949-69, exec. v.p., 1960-69; exec. v.p. 1st Pa. Bank, Phila., 1969—; chmn. Vestaur Corp.; trustee 1st Pa. Mortgage Trust; mem. investment com. Gen. Accident Group. Vice chmn. bd. dirs. S.E. Pa. chpt. A.R.C., Trustee Abington Meml. Hosp., bd. dirs. Pa. Plan To Develop Scientists in Med. Research. Mem. Phi Kappa Psi. Club: Huntingdon Valley (Pa.) Country (bd. govs.); Racquet of Philadelphia; Seaview Country (Absecon, N.J.). Home: 1323 Washington Lane Rydal PA 19046 Office: 1st Pa Bank 15th and Chestnut Sts Philadelphia PA 19101

ERVIN, RICHARD WILLIAM, justice; b. Carabelle, Fla., Jan. 26, 1905; s. Richard William and Carrie Marvin (Phillips) E.; LL.B., U. Fla., 1928; m. Frances Blois Baker, Nov. 23, 1933; children—Richard William, Sara Eve. Admitted to Fla. bar, 1929; practiced in Clearwater, Fla., 1929, Palatka, Fla., 1930- 36; right-of-way atty. Fla. Rd. Dept., Jacksonville, 1936-37, resident atty., Tallahassee, 1937-43; atty. Overseas Rd. Toll Bridge Dist., Marathon, Fla., 1937-43; asst. atty. gen. Fla., 1943- 45; sec. Fla. R.R. and Pub. Utilities Commn., 1945; sec. Fla. resident atty. Fla. Rd. Dept., 1945-48; atty. gen. Fla., 1949-64; justice Fla. Supreme Ct., 1964—, chief justice, 1969-70. Chmn. bd. trustees Woodmen of World Life Ins. Co. Recipient Good Govt. award, Fla. State Jr. C. of C., 1950. Mem. Woodmen of World, Phi Kappa Tau, Omicron Delta Kappa, Phi Alpha Delta. Democrat. Baptist. Mason. Elk; Club: Exchange. Home: 601 Ingleside Av Tallahassee FL 32303 Office: Supreme Court Tallahassee FL 32303

ERVIN, ROBERT MARVIN, lawyer; b. nr. Ocala, Fla., Jan. 19, 1917; s. Richard William and Carrie (Phillips) E.; B.S. in Bus. Adminstrn., U. Fla., 1941, LL.B., 1947; m. Frances Anne Cushing, Dec. 25, 1941; children—Anne Cushing (Mrs. Henry Lamar Rowe), Robert Marvin. Admitted to Fla. bar, 1947; practice in Tallahassee, 1947—; partner firm Ervin, Pennington, Varn & Jacobs, 1954—. U.S. referee in bankruptcy No. Dist. Fla., part time 1952—; mem. Fla. Constn. Revision Commn., 1965—; dir. Wilson Nat. Life Ins. Co.; sec., dir. Interstate Groves Corp., M & L Devel. Corp.; dir. Leon Abstract Co.; pres. REFG, Inc., Tallahassee, 1961—; gen. counsel Fla. Home Builders Assn., 1955—. Trustee U. Fla. Law Center Assn. Served with USMCR, 1941-45; PTO; col. Res. Recipient Distinguished Service award for legal edn. John B. Stetson U., 1966; Distinguished Service award Armed Forces League, 1966. Fellow Am. Bar Found., Internat. Acad. Trial Lawyers; mem. Fla. Bar (pres. 1965-66, Distinguished Service award 1966), Am. Bar Assn. (ho. of dels.), Nat. Conf. Referees in Bankruptcy (pres. 1963-64), Res. Officers Assn., Marine Corps Res. Officers Assn., Fla. Blue Key, Phi Alpha Delta, Alpha Kappa Psi. Democrat, Baptist. Elk. Home: 1434 Crestview Av Tallahassee FL 32303 Office: 305 S Gadsden St PO Box 1170 Tallahassee FL 32302

ERVIN, SAMUEL JAMES, Jr., U. S. senator; b. Morganton, N. C., Sept. 27, 1896; s. Samuel J. and Laura Theresa (Powe) E.; A.B., U. N.C., 1917, LL.D., 1951; LL.B., Harvard, 1922; LL.D., Western Carolina Coll., 1955; Dr. Pub. Adminstrn., Suffolk U., Boston, 1957; m. Margaret Bruce Bell, June 18, 1924; children—Samuel James III, Margaret Leslie (Mrs. Gerald Hansler), Laura Powe (Mrs. William E. Smith). Admitted to N.C. bar, 1919; engaged in gen. practice, Morganton, 1922—; rep. from Burke County, N.C. Gen. Assembly, 1923, 25, 31; judge Burke County Criminal Ct., 1935-37, N.C. Superior Ct., 1937-43; resigned to resume practice of law; representative in Congress from 10th N.C. Dist., 1946-47; asso. justice N.C. Supreme Ct., 1948-54; U.S. senator from N.C., 1954—, mem. Senate coms. on armed services, equal ednl. opportunity judiciary (chmn. subcom. constnl. rights, subcom. revision and codification of laws govt. operations. Mem. N.C. Bd. Law Examiners, 1944-46; N.C. Democratic Exec. com., 1930-37. Trustee Morganton Graded Schools, 1927-30, U. N.C., 1932-35, 1945-46, Davidson Coll., 1948—. Served with Co. I, 28th Inf., 1st div., U.S. Army; AEF in France 18 mos. (twice wounded in action, twice cited for gallantry in action), World War I. Decorated French Fourragere, Purple Heart with oak leaf cluster, Silver Star, D.F.C.; U.D.C. cross mil. service. Mem. Am., N.C. bar assns., N.C. State Bar, Jr. Order Knights Pythias, Am. Legion, V.F.W., Disabled Am. Vets., Soc. 1st Div., Army and Navy Legion Valor, Morganton C. of C., Am. Judicature Soc., N.C. Lit. and Hist. Assn., So. Hist. Assn., Soc. Mayflower Descendants N.C. (gov. 1950-52), Gen. Alumni Assn. U.N.C. (pres. 1947-48), Soc. Cincinnati, S.A.R., Sigma Upsilon, Phi Delta Phi. Democrat, Presbyn. Mason (33, K.T.), Moose, Kiwanian. Home: Morganton NC 28655 Office: Senate Office Bldg Washington DC 20510

ERVIN, THOMAS EDGAR, lawyer; b. Middleport, O., Nov. 28, 1911; s. Edgar and Margretta (Davis) E.; A.B., Ohio State U., 1932; LL.B., Columbia, 1935; m. Norma Murray, Feb. 7, 1943; 1 son, William Edgar. Admitted to N.Y. bar, 1936, pvt. practice, N.Y.C. 1936-41; legal dept. NBC, 1948—, v.p., gen. atty., 1953-68, exec. v.p., 1968—, dir., 1962—. Served as lt. Col. AUS, 1941-46; dept. U.S. chief of counsel for War Crimes, Nuremberg, 1946-48. Awarded Legion of Merit. Mem. Am. Bar Assn., Phi Beta Kappa. Home: 530 E 72d St New York City NY 10021 Office: 30 Rockefeller Plaza New York City NY 10020

ERWIN, ALBERT RICH, educator, physicist; b. Charlotte, N.C., May 1, 1931; s. Albert Rich and Lois (Lee) E.; B.S., Duke, 1953; Ph.D., Harvard, 1958; m. Mary Jane Murray, June 12, 1954; 1 dau., Christy Lee. Research asso. Brookhaven Nat. Lab., 1956-58; mem. faculty U. Wis., 1959, prof. physics, 1965—. Spl. research on high energy particles physics. Home: 5437 Esther Beach Rd Madison WI 53713

ERWIN, CLAUDE MAYO, lawyer; b. Newport, Ark., Aug. 31, 1906; s. Claude Mayo and Elizabeth (Watson) E.; student Hendrix Coll., 1924-25, U. Ark., 1925-27; grad. Ark. Law Sch., 1931; m. Mildred Sloan, June 24, 1936; children—Claude Mayo III, Harold Sloan. Admitted to Ark. bar, 1930; practice in Newport, 1932—; pros. atty. 3d Jud. Circuit Ark., 1937-40; county and juvenile judge Jackson County, 1944; city atty., Newport, 1961-63. Pres. Erwin, Inc., Ozark Corp.; dir. Zenith Seed Co., Inc. Pres. Newport Pub. Library Assn.; trustee Remmel Playground Park Assn. Mem. Am., Ark., Newport (past pres.), 8th Chancery (past pres.) bar assns., Am. Trial Lawyers Assn., Sigma Nu. Democrat. Methodist. Mason (K.T.). Home: 706 Newport Av Newport AR 72112 Office: 110 Main St Newport AR 72112

ERWIN, CYRAL PHILPOTT, engr., bus. exec.; b. Dallas, July 14, 1910; s. Martin Cyral and Lillian Paxton (Philpott) E.; student So. Coll., 1928-29, Tex. Christian U., 1931-32; spl. student Tex. A. and M. Coll., 1935-38; m. Margaret Garrett Walker, May 5, 1934 (div. Mar. 1958). Design engr. Denison Dam, 1938; chief engr. Star Mfg. Co., Oklahoma City, 1929- 41; partner Erwin-Newman Co., designers-constructors airplane hangars, Houston, 1941—, now chmn. Erwin-Newman Co., Inc.; pres. Tex. Airline, Houston, 1941-42, Am. Infra-Red Radiant Co., Inc., Houston, 1920—, Fireless Gas Heater Corp., Houston, 1958—, Universal Oxygen Control Corp., Houston, 1960—, Rinnai Internat., Inc., Japan; v.p. Senoc Devel. Corp., Houston, 1961—. Recipient spl. award in bldg. off-shore drilling founds. Magnolia Petroleum Co., 1949. Mem. S.A.R., Soc. Am. Mil. Engrs., Am. Rifle Assn. Lion. Designer, builder largest cantilever aircraft hangar in world, Marietta, Ga. Home: PO Box 1308 Houston TX 77001 Office: 2400 Old Spanish Trail Houston TX 77025

ERWIN, FRANK CRAIG Jr., lawyer, univ. regent; b. Waxahachie, Tex., Jan. 25, 1920; s. Frank Craig and Margaret (Edwards) E.; LL.B., U. Tex., 1948; m. June Carr (dec.); 1 son, Frank Craig. Admitted to Tex. bar, 1948; now partner Brown, Erwin, Maroney & Barber, Austin. Mem. bd. regents, chmn. U. Tex.; chmn. Commn. Governing Bds. State-Supported Colls. and Univs. Mem. exec.. com., past pres. Austin Symphony Orch. Soc.; bd. dirs., past treas. Tex. Kappa Sigma Ednl. Found.; vice chmn. citizens commn. to draft new city charter for Austin, 1952. Mem. Democratic Nat. Com. for Tex.; vice chmn. Tex. delegation Dem. Nat. Conv., 1964; past chmn., past sec. Tex. Dem. Exec. Com.; chmn. Travis County Dem. Conv., 1962. Served with USNR, 1941-46; PTO. Mem. Am., Travis County (past pres., chmn. bd. dirs.) bar assns., State Bar Tex., Internat. Assn. Ins. Attys., Def. Research Inst., Tex. Assn. Def. Counsel, U. Tex. Ex- Students

Assn. (past pres. Travis County; life mem.), T Assn. (hon.), Phi Beta Kappa, Phi Eta Sigma, Phi Sigma Alpha, Phi Delta Phi, Kappa Sigma. Episcopalian. Club: Longhorn (founder). Home: 2307 Woodlawn Blvd Austin TX 78703 Office Brown Bldg Austin TX 78701

ERWIN, FRANK WILLIAM, Mgmt. cons., pub. co. exec.; b. Elizabeth, N.J., Nov. 22, 1931; s. Frank J. and Jessie (Rugero) E.; B.A. cum laude, N.Y.U., 1957; m. Bridget E. Taddeo, June 26, 1965. With MBS, 1957-62, asst. to pres., asst. sec. to bd. dirs., 1960- 62; dep. dir. div. selection, dir. recruiting operations Peace Corps, 1962-65; exec. asst. to sec. labor, 1965-68; pres. Richardson, Bellows, Henry & Co., Inc., 1968—; chmn. Norvec Pub. Co., 1969—. Served with AUS, 1949-52. Mem. Internat. Radio and TV Execs. Soc., Am. Psychol. Assn,, Am. Soc. Personnel Adminstrn., Am. Numis. Assn., Am. Soc. Pub. Adminstrn. Home: 1400 S Joyce St Arlington VA 22202 Office: 1140 Connecticut Av NW Washington DC 20236

ERWIN, JAMES OTIS, coll. pres., clergyman; b. Marion, N.C., Apr. 28, 1922; s. John Adam and Idella (Cannon) E.; B.A., Johnson C. Smith U., 1943; B.D., Garrett Theol. Sem., 1946; M.R.E., Iliff Sch. Theology, 1953, S.T.M., 1964; LL.D., Rust Coll., 1971; m. Adeline Comer, Aug. 13, 1947; children—JoNina Marie, Janel Ann, Judith Kathryn. Ordained to ministry United Methodist Ch., 1946; chaplain, instr. Morristown (Tenn.) Coll., 1946-48, pres., 1970—; chaplain, chmn. dept. religion, philosophy Wiley Coll., Marshall, Tex., 1948-53; asst. prof. philosophy Lincoln U., Jefferson City, Mo., 1953-66, founder Wesley Found., 1953, minister, dir., 1953-66; asso. minister Wesley Found., U. Ia. 1966-67; dean students, chaplain Philander Smith Coll., Little Rock, 1967-70. Mem. citizens participation com. Douglas-Cherokee Office Econ. Opportunity, 1970—; active Cherokee Guidance Center, Morristown, 1970—; vice chmn. Boy Scouts Am., Little Rock, 1968-70; recording sec. Council Presidents United Meth. Colls., 1971—. Mem. Am., Mo. philosophy assns., Assn. Pvt. Minority Jr. Colls. (founder with others 1970, nat. pres. 1970—). Contbr. articles profl. jours. Home: 215 E 6th St N Morristown TN 37814

ERWIN, JAMES SHREWSBURY, atty. gen. Me.; b. N.Y.C., Nov. 27, 1920; s. James Robinson and Elizabeth M. (Davidson) E.; A.B., Dartmouth, 1942; LL.B., Columbia, 1949; m. Anne Ruprecht, May 31, 1947; children—Charlotte Elizabeth, Sarah Anne, James Robinson, Martha Jane, Admitted to Me. bar, 1949; practice with Ralph Hawkes, York, Me., 1949-53; partner firm Sewall, Strater, Erwin and Winton and predecessor, York, 1953-67; pvt. practice, York, 1967—; atty. gen. Me., 1967—. Mem. Me. Senate from York, 1961- 62, Ho. of Reps. from York, 1965-67; chmn. York County Republican Com., 1954-58; mem. Me. Rep. Com., 1958-64. Trustee York Sch. Dist., 1951-63, York Hosp., 1952—; bd. dirs. Pine Tree Soc. Crippled Children and Adults, 1962-65. Served to 2d lt. AUS, 1942-46. Mem. Am., Me. (pres. 1967-68), York County bar assns., Am. Judicature Soc. Mason (Shriner). Conglist. Home: RFD 4 Gardiner ME 04345 Office: Atty Gen State House Augusta ME 04330

ERWIN, WILLIAM JAMES, textile co. exec.; b. Pineville, N.C., Nov. 18, 1900; s. Robert Monroe and Dovie Juanita (Potts) E.; B.S., Clemson U., 1921; Dr. Textile Engring., 1960; Dr. Textiles, Phila. Coll. Textiles and Sci., 1966; m. Mary Elizabeth Suttle, January 18, 1930; 1 son, William J. Textile engr. Consol. Textile Co., Lynchburg, Va. 1921; mgr. Ella Mills div., 1927; asst. to pres. Republic Cotton Mills, Great Falls, S.C., 1929, v.p., dir., 1939; v.p. J.P. Stevens & Co., Inc. N.Y.C., 1946-49; v.p., dir. Riegel Textile Corp., Ware Shoals, S.C., 1949-53; pres., dir. Dan River Mills, Inc., 1953-66, chmn. bd., dir., 1966-70; dir., chmn. bd. Schoolfield Finishers, Inc., Dan River Internat. Corp; dir. Isolin-Jefferson Co., Inc., Am. Nat. Bank & Trust Co., Isolin-Jefferson Financial Co., Inc., Caroline & Northwestern Ry. Co., Webco Mills, Inc., Webco Dyers, Inc., Webco Realty Company, Inc., Dan River Cotton Co., John Preston Warehouse Co. Mem. regional exec. com. Boy Scouts Am. Pres., dir. Dan River Mills Found.; trustee Stratford Coll., Clemson U. Found., Hampden-Sydney Col., Woman's Coll.; sponsor trustee U. Va. Grad. Sch. Bus. Adminstrn.; bd. dirs. N.C. Textile Found., Danville Meml. Hosp., Va. Found. Ind. Colleges; v.p., dir. Va. Indsl. Development Corp. Recipient Silver Antelope award Boy Scouts Am., 1964, ann. award textile sect. N.Y. Bd. Trade, 1966, Distinguished Alumni award Clemson U., 1966. Mem. Am. Textile Mfrs. Inst. (dir., past pres.), Danville C. of C. (dir.), Nat. Council Am. Newcomen Soc. N.Am., N.Y. So. Soc., Omicron Delta Kappa. Presbyn. (elder). Clubs: University, Weavers (N.Y.C.); Danville Golf. Address: Dan River Mills Inc Danville, VA 24541

ESAU, KATHERINE, educator; b. Ekaterinoslav, Russia, Apr. 3, 1898; d. John J. and Margarethe (Toews) Esau; student Coll. Agr., Moscow, 1916-17, Coll. Agr. Berlin, 1919-22; Ph.D., U. Cal., 1931, LL.D., 1966; D.Sc., Mills Coll., Oakland, Cal., 1962. Came to U.S., 1923, naturalized, 1928. Plant breeder Spreckels Sugar Co., (Cal.), 1924-28; asst. U. Cal., 1928-31, instr., 1931-37, asst. prof., 1937-43, asso. prof., 1943-49, prof., 1949-65, prof. emeritus, 1965, jr. botanist agrl. exptl. sta., 1931-37, asst. botanist, 1937-43, asso. botanist, 1943-49, botanist 1949—; John Simon Guggenheim Found. fellow, 1940; John M. Prather lectr. Harvard, 1960, Mem. Nat. Acad. Sci., Royal Swedish Acad. Sci., A.A.A.S., Am. Acad. Arts and Sci., Bot. Soc. (pres. 1951). Am. Philos. Soc., Phi Beta Kappa, Sigma Xi. Author books on plant anatomy. Contbr. articles bot. jours. Home: 8 W Constance Santa Barbara CA 93105

ESCH, I. LYND, ret. coll. pres., clergyman; b. Flinton, Pa., Nov. 17, 1905; s. Joseph I. and Mary Catherine (Gates) E.; M. in Indsl. Engring., Goodyear Indsl. U., Akron, O., 1927; ministerial trg. United Brethren Ch., 1931-33; student Williams Jr. Coll., Berkely, Cal., 1934-36; A.B., Chapman Coll., Los Angeles, 1940, D.D., 1961; Th.M., U. So. Cal., 1941, Ph.D., 1942; D.D., York Coll., 1950; LL.D., Butler U., 1955; L.H.D., Lebanon Valley Coll., 1957, Ind. U., 1971; Litt. D., Rose Poly. Inst., 1970, Ind. Central Coll., 1970; m. Alverda Ruth Weston, Aug. 30, 1924 (dec); 1 son, Lynd. Prof. Goodyear Indsl. U., 1927-33; ordained to ministry United Brethren Ch., 1933; pastor Rockbridge Ch., Oakland, Cal., 1933-36, San Diego. 1936-38, Los Angeles, 1938-45; pres. Ind. Central Coll., 1945-70, now pres. emeritus; pres. Bankers Life Ins. Co. of Indpls., 1964-67. Dir. Christian edn. United Brethren Ch., Akron. 1929-33; pres. bd. of Christian edn. Cal. Conf. United Brethren Ch., 1942-45; chmn. dept. of evangelism Church Fedn., Los Angeles, 1941-45; exec. sec.- treas. Home for Ret. Ministers, Puenta, Cal., 1941-45; mem. bd. govs. Norway Found., 1949—, St. Francis Hosp.; pres. Ind. Central U. Found., 1970—; pres. Asso. Colls. of Indiana, 1958-65, pres. Indpls. YMCA, 1950-58, chmn. met. program com., 1954-56; bd. dirs. A.R.C., Indpls., 1960—; mem. nat. council adminstrn. Evang. United Brethren Ch., 1942-54,58-68; mem. judicial council United Methodist Ch. Mem. Indiana State Bd. of Public Instrn., 1957-61; mem. Ind. Scholarship Comm., 1969-71, chmn. coordinating com. on higher edn. state of Ind., 1969-71; mem. Ind. Employment Security Bd., 1960-70, v.p., 1964-68, pres., 1968-70; mem. adv. bd. Indpls. Community Hosp., 1960-64, bd. dirs., 1964—; pres. ch. Fedn. Greater Indpls., 1963-65; pres. bd. dirs. Univ. Heights Hosp., 1965-69. Mem. Am. Guild Organists (hon.) Assn. Am. Colls. chmn. commn. on Christian edn. 1956-58, C. of C., (bd. dirs. 1962-69), Nat. Soc. Arts and Letters, Internat. Platform Assn., Newcomen Soc. Am. Phi. Beta Kappa, Theta Phi, Alpha Kappa Delta, Phi Kappa Phi. Republican. Mason (33) Clubs: Kiwanis (pres. 1959), Torch, Columbia (Indpls). Contbr. articles to religious and ednl jours. Home: 4305 B Declaration Dr Indianapolis IN 46227

ESCH, MARVIN L., congressman; b. Flinton, Pa., Aug. 4, 1927; A.B. in Polit. Sci., U. Mich., 1950, M.A. 1951, Ph.D. in Speech and Edn., 1957; m. Olga Jurich; children—Emily, Leo, Thomas. Asso. prof. speech Wayne State U., also instr. U. Mich.-Wayne State U. Inst. Labor and Indsl. Relations, 1952- 66; mem. Mich. Ho. of Reps., 1965-66; mem. 90th to 92d Congresses, 2d Dist. Mich. Served with U.S. Maritime Service, World War II. Named Outstanding New Legislator, Lansing Newsmens Assn., 1965. Republican. Home: Ann Arbor MI 48103 Office: House Office Bldg Washington DC 20515

ESCH, ROBIN ERNEST, educator, mathematician; b. Chevy Chase, Md., Feb. 25, 1930; s. Fred Henry and Harriette (Fish) E.; B.A., Harvard, 1951, M.A., 1953, Ph.D., 1957; m. Joan L. Brockway, June 25, 1965; children—Elizabeth Francesca, David Nathaniel, Thomas Benjamin. Asst. prof. Harvard, 1957-62; head applied mechanics dept. Sperry Rand Research Center, Sudbury, Mass., 1962-66; prof. math. Boston U., 1966—, chmn. dept., 1968—. Co-chmn. Boston Numerical Math. Seminar, 1967—. Mem. Am. Math. Soc., Math. Assn. Am., Soc. Indsl. and Applied Math., Amateur Chamber Music Soc. Home: 371 Plainfield Rd Concord MA 01742 Office: 270 Bay State Rd Boston MA 02215

ESCHBACH, JESSE ERNEST, Federal judge; b. Warsaw, Ind., Oct. 26, 1920; S. Jesse Ernest and Mary W. (Stout) E.; B.S., Ind. U., 1943, J.D. with distinction, 1949; m. Sara Ann Walker, Mar. 15, 1947; children—Jesse Ernest III, Virginia. Admitted to Ind. bar, 1949; partner firm Graham, Rasor, Eschbach & Harris, Warsaw, 1949-62; city atty., War&aw, 1952-53; dep. pros. atty. 64th Jud. Circuit Ct. Ind., 1952-1954; judge U.S. Dist. Ct. Ind., 1962—. Pres. Endicott Church Furniture, Inc., 1960-62; sec., gen. counsel Dalton Foundries, Inc., 1957-62. Mem. bd. trustees Ind. U., 1965-70. Served with USNR, 1943-46. Hastings scholar, 1949. Recipient U.S. Law Week award, 1949. Mem. U.S. (labor relations com. 1960-62), Warsaw (pres. 1955-56) chambers commerce, Nat. Assn. Furniture Mfrs. (dir. 1962), Ind. Mfrs. Assn. (dir. 1962), Am., Ind. (bd. mgrs. 1953-54, ho. dels. 1950-60, 7th Circuit Fed. bar assns., Am. Judicature Soc., Order of Coif. Presbyn. Rotarian (pres. Warsaw 1956-57). Editorial staff Ind. Law Jour., 1947-49. Home: 2000 N Bay Dr Warsaw IN 46580 Office: US Post Office and Court House Fort Wayne IN 46802

ESCHENBACH, CHRISTOPH, concert pianist; b. Breslau, Germany, 1940; ed. Musikhochschulen, Cologne and Hamburg undeı Prof. E. Hansen. Concert pianist in all countries, also plays violin and conducts. Address: Magdalenstrasse 64' Hamburg 13 Federal Republic of Germany *

ESCHENBURG, EMIL PAUL, army officer; b. nr. Mt. Clemens, Mich., Dec. 26, 1915; s. Paul F. and Ella (Wiese) E.; B.S., Mich. State U., 1939; grad. Nat. War Coll., 1957, advanced mgmt. course Harvard, 1960; m. Betty Gunn, June 5, 1943; children—Paula (Mrs. Terry Scott), Emil P., Erich Gunn, Lise Ann. Commd. 2d. lt. U.S.Army, 1940, advanced through grades to brig. gen., 1963; spl. asst. to chief staff SHAPE, 1960-63; asst. div. comdr. 101st Airborne Div., 1963-65; chief joint mil. assistance adv. group, Ethiopia, 1965-67; asst. div. comdr. 1st Inf. Div., 1967-68, acting comdg. gen., Tet offensive, 1968; dep. and acting comdg. gen. Capital Mil. Assistance Command, Vietnam, 1968-69; acting comdg. gen., dep. U.S.Army Tng. Center, Ft. Polk, La., 1969-70; assigned George Washington U., 1970—. Decorated D.S.M., Silver Star with 3 oak leaf clusters, Legion of Merit with 4 oak leaf clusters, D.F.C. with 3 oak leaf cluster, Soldier's medal with oak leaf cluster, Bronze Star, Air medal with 4 oak leaf clusters, Joint Service Commendation medal, Army Commendation medal with oak leaf cluster, Purple Heart U.S.); Cross of Valor (Italy); Nat. Order 4th Class, Nat. Order 5th Class, Distinguished Service Order 1st Class, Cross of Gallantry with palm (Vietnam). Home: 7205 Normandy Lane Falls Church VA 22042

ESCHENMOSER, ALBERT JAKOB, educator, chemist; b. Ersfeld, Switzerland, Aug. 5, 1925; s. Alfons Josef and Johanna (Oesch) E.; Dr. Sc. nat., Swiss Fed. Inst. Tech., Zurich, 1951; Dr. h.c. rer. nat., U. Fribourg (Switzerland), 1966; Sc.D. (hon.), U. Chgo., 1971; m. Elizabeth Baschnoga, Oct. 11, 1954; children—Juerg, Esther, Philippe. Mem. faculty Swiss Fed. Inst. Tech., 1960—. prof. organic chemistry, 1965—; A.D. Little vis. prof. Mass. Inst. Tech., 1961; Brittingham vis. prof. U. Wis., 1965; M. Kharasch vis. prof. U. Chgo., 1970. Recipient Ruzicka award in chemistry Swiss Fed. Inst. Tech., 1958; Fritzche award Am. Chem. Soc., 1966. Mem. A.A.A.S., Am. Acad. Arts and Scis. (fgn. hon.), Swiss, Am. (Fritzsche award 1966), English, German chem. socs. Home: 9 Bergstrasse Kuesnacht Switzerland Office: Swiss Fed Inst Tech Zurich Switzerland

ESCHMAN, DONALD FRAZIER, educator, geologist; b. Granville, O., Oct. 22, 1923; s. Karl Henry and Agnes (Frazier) E.; A.B., Denison U., 1947; M.A., Harvard, 1950, Ph.D., 1953; m. Dorothy Ruth Nelson, Dec. 21, 1946; children—Peter, Christine, James, Laura. Geologist U.S. Geol. Survey, Boston, 1948—, instr. geology Tufts U., 1951-53; instr. geology U. Mich., 1953-56, asst. prof., 1956-59, asso. prof., 1959-64, chmn. dept. geology and mineralogy, 1961-66, prof., 1964—. Served to lt. USNR, 1943-46. Fellow Geol. Soc. Am. (v.p. N. Central sect. 1966-67); mem. Nat. Assn. Geology Tchrs. Arctic Inst. N. Am., A.A.A.S., Sigma Xi, Phi Gamma Delta, Phi Mu Omicron Delta Kappa. Episcopalian. Home: 3035 Fairlane Ann Arbor MI 48104

ESCOBAR CERDA, LUIS, economist; b. 1927; ed. U. Chile, also Harvard. Dir. Sch. Econs., U. Chile 1951-55, dean faculty econs., 1955-64, financial adviser 1954-60; minister econs., devel. and reconstrn., Chile, 1961-63; mem. Inter-Am. Com. on Alliance for Progress, 1964-66; exec. dir. Internat. Monetery Fund, 1964-66, 68—; exec. dir. Internat. Bank for Reconstrn. and Devel. 1966-68. Mem. Council Soc. Internat. Devel., 1969-. Author: The Stock Market, 1959; Organization for Economic Development, 1961; A Stage of the National Econimic Development, 1962; Considerations on the Tasks of the University, 1963; Organizational Requirements for Growth and Stability, 1964; The Role of the Social Sciences in Latin America, 1965; The Organization of Latin America Governments, 1968. Home: Los Tulipanes 2979 Santiago Chile.*

ESCOBEDO, MANUAL GREGORIO, lawyer; b. Zacatecas, Zacatecas, Mexico, May 9, 1896; s. Enrique and Ana Maria Dia de Leon Escobedo; Ph.B., Licentiate in Law, Instito Cientificio de Mexico, 1907-14; Nat. U., 1914-15, Law Sch. Mexico City, 1916-20, U. Paris, 1921-22, London U., 1922-25; m. Elsie Fulda, Aug. 22, 1931; children—Elena, Miguel. Prof. comml. law Escuela Libre de Derecho, 1927-37; asso. Basham & Ringe, 1927-34; sr. partner Noriega y Escobedo, Mexico City, 1934—; Pro. civil law Nat. U.,1947-62; prof. civil law Escuela Libre de Derecho, 1965—. bd. dirs. Asbestos de Mexico, S.A., Banco del Atlantico, S.A., Cinzano de Mexico, S.A., Ciba de Mexico, S.A., Devoe de Mexico, S.A., Gen. Motors Acceptance Corp. de Mexico, S.A., Johnson & Johnson de Mexico, S.A., Olivetti Mexicana, S.A. Productos de Maiz, S.A., Reaseguradora Patria, S.A., Sanborn Hermanos, S.A., Sanborn Monterrey, S.A., Cia de Equipo Industrial Acme de Mexico, S.A., Cia Mercantil Internacional, S.A., Steeinbock de Mexico, S.A., Garlock de Mexico, S.A., Cia Mexicana Impresora de Valores, S.A., Pre-Concreto del Pacifico, S.A., Ascensores Schindler Mexicana, S.A., Sulzer Hermanos, S.A. Becton Dickenson de Mexico and also Vitos de Mexico, S.A., Underwood Mexicana, S.A., Norton de Mexico, S.A. de C.V., Preconcreto, S.A., Quimica Niagara de Mexico, S.A., Electronquimica Mexicana, S.A., Mem. International (co-pres.), Am. Inter-Am. bar assns., Asso. Bar City N.Y., Union Iberoamericana de Colegios y Agrupaciones de Abogados (v.p. 1957-), Nat. Coll. Lawyers, Mexico City Bar, Nat. Acad. Law and Jurisprudence. Home: 23 Historiadores Mexico City 20 Mexico Office: 14 Av Juarez Mexico City 1 Mexico

ESCOTO-GOENAGA, GUSTAVO ADOLFO, diplomat of Nicaragua; b. Leon, Nicarague, May 6, 1932; s. Gonzalo Escoto-Munoz and Margarita Goenaga; licenciado en ciencias economicas Universidad Nacional Autonoma de Mexico, 1956; M.A., Georgetown, 1971; m. Guadalupe Abaunza Portocarrero, Sept. 9, 1965; children—Margarita Mercedes, Dora Francis, Gonzalo Ignacio. Jr. economist Econ. Commn. for Latin Am. UN, Mexico City, 1952-53, Nacional Financiera, Mexico City, 1954-59; gen. mgr. Banco del Pequeno Comercio, Tampico Temaulipas Mexico, 1959-62; br. mgr. Banco de Industria y Comercio, Mexico City, 1962-63; head dept. econ. studies, dept. Central Am. integration Ministry Econs. Nicaragua, Managua, 1963-65; minister counselor for econ. affairs Nicaraguan embassy, Washington, 1966—; prof. econs. Universidad Nacional Autonoma de Nicaragua, 1963-64. Mem. Liberal Nationalist Party. Roman Catholic. Author: Influencia del Credito Oficial en las Provincias, 1964. Home: 3522 Yuma St Washington DC 20008 Office: 1627 New Hampshire Av Washington DC 20009

ESELMAN, J. CLIFTON, ednl. adminstr. Prof., head dept radiology, asso. dean U. Pitts. Office: Sch Dental Medicine U Pitts Pittsburgh PA 15213*

ESENBEL, MELIH, Turkish diplomat; b. Istanbul, Turkey, Mar. 19, 1915; s. Ziya and Ismet (Orfi) E.; Law Degree, U. Istanbul, 1936; m. Emine Dengiz, Oct. 2, 1937; children—Selcuk, Ahmet. Joined Turkish Fgn. Office, 1936; assigned France, 1939-43; counsellor embassy, Washington, 1945-52; successively dir. gen., asst. sec. gen., sec. gen. Turkish Fgn. Office, 1952-60; ambassador to U.S., 1960-61, 67—, to Japan, 1963-66. Address: 1606 23d St NW Washington DC 20008

ESHBACH, WILLIAM WALLACE, architect; b. Allentown, Pa., Mar. 12, 1917; s. William W. and Anna (Krum) E.; B.Arch., U. Pa., 1941; m. Hilda Kern Campbell, Nov. 5, 1943; 1 son, William Wallace, Designer, draftsman engring. dept. DuPont Co., Wilmington, 1941-43; with George Daub, architect, Phila., 1946-47; asso. and project mgr. Vincent G. Kling, Phila., 1947-52; partner William W. Eshbach, architect and assos., Phila., 1952-54, Eshbach, Pullinger, Stevens & Bruder, architects and engrs., 1954—; chmn. bd. dirs. TEI Cons. Engrs., Inc., 1970—. Mem. panel Am. Arbitration Assn., 1958—; mem. pub. adv. panel on archtl. services Gen. Services Adminstrn., 1969—; mem. adv. panel on new sch. arch. Temple U., Phila., 1970—. Served from ensign to lt., USNR, 1943-46; PTO. Fellow A.I.A. (v.p. 1964-65, regional dir. nat. bd., 1960-62; Edward C. Kemper award 1966), Pa. Soc. Architects (pres., 1959-60, dir. 1956-60. Prin. archtl. works include: State Office Bldg., Harrisburg; Arts and Humanities Bldg., Pa. State U.; housing complex U. Pa.; Kent & Queen Anne's Hosp., Chestertown, Md.; Class and Adminstrn. Bldg., Rutgers U., Camden, N.J.; Law School and Social Sci., Temple U. Home: 1023 West Av Springfield PA 19064 Office 1510 Chestnut St Philadelphia PA 19102

ESHELMAN, WILLIAM ROBERT, librarian, editor b. Oklahoma City, Aug. 23, 1921; s. Cyrus Lenhert and Fern (Reed) E.; A.B., Chapman Coll., Los Angeles, 1943; M.A. (Shirle Robbins Poetry prize 1949), U. Cal. at Los Angeles, 1950; B.L.S., U. Cal. at Berkeley, 1951; m. Mimi Blau, July 3, 1952 (div. Aug. 1956); m. 2d, Eve Kendall, June 21, 1957; children—Ann, Benjamin, Zachary. Conscripted in civilian pub. service, Waldport, Ore., 1943-46, asst. dir., 1944-45; teaching asst. U. Cal. at Los Angeles, 1949-50, library asst., 1950; faculty Los Angeles State Coll., 1951-65, asst. librarian, 1954-59, librarian, 1959-65; librarian, prof. bibliography Bucknell U., 1965-68; editor Wilson library Bell. 1968—; editor Cal. Librarian, 1960-63; partner Untide Press, Pasadena 1946-. Mem. adv. council edn. for librarianship U. Cal., 1961-64; mem. acad. senate Cal. State Colls., 1964-65. Mem. Am. Assn. U. Profs., (v.p. Los Angeles State Coll. 1958-59, pres. 1964-65), Am. (1st prize Library Periodicals award, 1960, editorial com. 1964-66), Cal. (chmn. intellectual freedom com., pres. so. dist. 1965) library assns., Assn. Coll. and Research Libraries (publs. com.), Assn. Cal. State Coll. Profs., Am. Civil Liberties Union, Friends Com. Legislation, Pa. Library Assn. Clubs: Book of Cal.; Rounce and Coffin (sec.-treas, 1953-56) (Los Angeles); Typophiles. Editorial bd. Choice. Home: 592 Gail Ct Teaneck NJ 07666. Office: 950 University Av Bronx NY 10452

ESHENAUR, WOODROW RALPH, brick co. exec.; b. Sinking Springs, Pa., Jan. 16, 1920; s. Russel G. and Eva A. (Bohn) E.; B.S.C., Grove City (Pa.) Coll., 1942; m. Renee Lou Bryson, Mar. 28, 1945; children—Nancy Kay, Patricia Fay, Ronald Russel. With Glen Gery Corp., Reading, Pa., 1945—, exec. v.p., 1957- 59, pres., 1959-68, now chmn., pres., chief exec. officer, also dir.; v.p., dir. Alwine Brick Corp., New Oxford, Pa., 1958—; dir. mem. exec. com. Bank of Pa., Reading; dir. Kurtz-Gery Corp., Denver, Pa. Bd. dirs. Structural Clay Products Inst., 1958-71, v.p., 1962-63, pres., 1968-70. Pres. Hawk Mountain council Boy Scouts Am. Mem. C. of C., Mgrs. Assn. Home: 1432 Delaware Av Wyomissing PA 19610 Office: 227 N 5th St Reading PA 19601

ESHERICK, JOSEPH, architect, educator; b. Phila., Dec. 28, 1914; s. Joseph and Helen (Gangwisch) E.; B.Arch., U. Pa., 1937; m. Ann Rowe, Feb. 14, 1953; children—Maria, Julia; children by previous marriage—Lisa, Joseph, Peter. Propr. own archtl. office, San Francisco, 1946-53; pres. Joseph Esherick & Assos., San Francisco, 1953—; mem. faculty U. Cal. at Berkeley, 1952—, prof. architecture, 1958—; art commnr. City of San Francisco, 1959—. Prin. works include Coll. Union Bldg. at Cal. State Poly. Coll., 1967, Sea Ranch, Sonoma County, Cal., 1965, Adlai Stevenson Coll. at U. Cal. at Santa Cruz, 1966, The Nunnery, San Francisco, 1967, William Wurster Hall at U. Cal. at Berkeley, 1964, Child Study Center, Berkeley, 1960, Langley Porter Neurophychiatric Inst., U. Cal. Med. Center, San Francisco, 1966, seven stas. for San Francisco Bay Area Rapid Transit, 1965. Served with USNR, 1943-46. Recipient award No. Cal. chpt. A.I.A., 1953, No. Cal. and East Bay award, 1963, Nat. Merit award, 1963, Homes for Better Living award, 1966, hon. mention Homes for Better Living, 1966, spl. citation, 1967; Wester Home award A.I.A. and Sunset mag., 1965-66; certificate of excellence Governor's Design Awards, 1966; Merit award William Wurster Hall, U. Cal. at Berkeley, 1967; A.I.A. hon award, hon. fellow Adlai Stevenson Coll., U. Cal., Santa Cruz, 1968. Fellow A.I.A. (sec. No. Cal. 1959-60), Graham Found. Advanced Studies Fine Art. Home: 2707 Larkin St San Francisco CA 94109 Office: 120 Green St San Francisco CA 94111

ESHLEMAN, EDWIN D., congressman; b. Lancaster County, Pa., Dec. 4, 1920; s. Reeder L. and Mary (Barbara) E.; B.S. in Polit. Sci., Franklin and Marshall Coll., 1942; postgrad. Temple U., 1948; m. Kathryn E. Dambach, Dec. 26, 1942; children—E. Bruce, R. Lee. Tchr. pub. schs., 1946-49; mem. Pa. Ho. of Reps. from Lancaster County, 1954-66, majority and minority whip; mem. 90th-92d congresses 16th Dist. Pa. Vice chmn. Pa. Higher Assistance Agy., 1963-67. Served with USCGR, 1942-45. Recipient Distinguished Service award Pa. Jr. C. of C., 1956; named to Pa. Young Rep. Hall of Fame, 1966. Mem. Am. Legion, V.F.W., Amvets, Pa. Soc. Mason, Elk. Home: 2173 West Ridge Dr Lancaster PA 17603 Office: Cannon House Office Bldg Washington DC 20515

ESHLEMAN, VON RUSSEL, educator, radar astronomer; b. Darke County, O., Sept. 17, 1924; s. Earl Ellsworth and Lydia Mae (Kneisly) E.; student Ohio State U., 1946-47; B.Elec. Engring., George Washington U., 1949; M.S., Stanford, 1950, Ph.D., 1952; m. Patricia May Middleton, Mar. 6, 1947; children—Mary Angela, Kathleen Carol, Eric Earl, David Middleton. Research asso. electronics labs. Stanford, 1952-57, mem. faculty, 1957—, prof. elec. engring., 1961—, co-dir. center radar astronomy, 1961—. Cons. NASA, Nat. Acad. Scis., Stanford Research Inst., N. Am. Aviation, Inc., Nat. Oceanographic and Atmospheric Adminstrn. Served with USNR, 1943-46. Fellow I.E.E.E., A.A.A.S., Royal Astron. Soc. (Britain); mem. Internat. Sci. Radio Union, Am. Astron. Soc., Am. Inst. Aeros. and Astronautics, Internat. Astron. Union, Internat. Aero. Congress, Am. Geophys. Union, Sigma Xi, Sigma Tau. Author numerous articles in field. Pioneer radar astronomy as technique for studying moon, sun, planets, meteors, astron. space, man-made satellites; obtained 1st radar echoes from sun, 1959. Home: 576 Gerona Rd Stanford CA 94305

ESKEW, CLETIS THEODORE, educator; b. Cloud Chief, Okla., July 10, 1904; s. Edward and Ruth (Macom) E.; B.S., Southwestern State Coll., 1931; student U. of Wyo., 1935; M.S., U. of Okla., 1937; Doctor of Edn., North Texas State, 1960; m. Annie Laurie Smith, Mar. 13, 1935; 1 son, Mark Franklin. Prin. grade schs. Caddo Co., Okla., 1924-30; supt. Retrop (Okla.) Pub. Schs., 1931-37; prin. sr. high sch., Mangum, Okla., 1937-39; dean Mangum Jr. Coll., 1937-39; prof. botany Southwestern State Coll., 1939-42; prof. biology Hardin Coll., 1942-48; dean adminstrn. Midwestern Univ., Wichita Falls, Texas, 1948-56, dean instrn., 1956-59, dean arts and scis., 1959-63, asso. dean instrn., dir. div. scis. and mathematics, 1963-68, prof. biology, also dean grad. studies, 1968—. President Southwestern Okla. Athletic Conf., 1937-38. Fellow Tex. and Okla. acads. Sci.; mem. Texas Assn. Colls. (mem. com. on standards and classification, 1951-63), Phi Delta Kappa, Beta Beta Beta, Alpha Phi Omega, Pi Gamma Mu, Phi Beta Sigma. Phi Sigma. Baptist. Mason, Rotarian. Author books including: The Vegetation of Oklahoma, 1941. Home: 2718 Chase Dr Wichita Falls TX 76308 ☆

ESKEW, RHEA TALLAFERRO, press assn. exec.; b. Lebanon, Tenn., Nov. 16, 1923; s. Robert Edward and Sammie (Taylor) E.; student U. Tenn., 1941-42; B.A., Emory U., 1948; m. Nancy Portlock Hall, June 13, 1953; children—Rhea Taliaferro, Elizabeth Vaughan, Tucker Alexander, Hall Edward. With U.P., 1948-55, bus. rep. N. C., S.C. and Va., 1951-55; pub. relations with So. Bell Telephone Co., 1955-56; with U.P.I., and predecessor, 1956—, gen. mgr. communications, N.Y.C., 1963-64, So. div. mgr., Atlanta, 1964—, also cons. communications. Served with AUS, 1942-45; ETO. Mem. Sigma Delta Chi(regional dir.). Republican. Methodist. Club: Atlanta Commerce. Home: 339 Camden Rd Atlanta GA 30309 Office: 1211 William St Atlanta GA 30309

ESKILDSON, MUCO NATHANIEL, Jr., govt. ofcl.; b. Denver, Aug. 24, 1918; s. Hugo Nathaniel and Lillie F. (Anderson) E.; B.S. in Commerce, U. Denver, 1940; LL.D., Capitol U., 1958; m. Anita C. Knemeyer, Sept. 4, 1941 (div.); children—Loyd, Howard; m. 2d, Elizabeth S. King, Feb. 3, 1968; step-children— Diane Bodek, Gerald King. Research asst. Bur. Bus. and Social Research, U. Denver, 1940-41; with Coordinator Information, Washington, 1941-42; asso. econ. analyst Office Def. Transp., 1942-43; with Airlines Negotiating Conf., N.Y.C., 1946-49; with AEC, Oak Ridge, Idaho Falls, Ida. and Washington, 1949-67, spl. asst. to asst. sec. for adminstrn. Dept. Housing & Urban Devel., 1968-69; with Bur. of Budget, 1969-70; exec. sec. Commn. on Govt. Procurement, Washington, 1970—. Nat. v.p. Am. Lutheran Ch., 1956-60, recipient Distinguished Citizen award, 1956. Served with Air Transp. Command, USAF, 1943-46. Home: 1793 Reading St Crofton MD 21113 Office: 1717 H St NW Washington DC 20006

ESKOW, SEYMOUR, coll. pres.; b. N.Y.C., Apr. 19, 1924; s. Joseph and Bluma (Kravitz) E.; student Coll. City N.Y., 1940-42; A.B., U. Cal. at Berkeley, 1943; M.A., Columbia Tchrs. Coll., 1946; Ph.D., Syracuse U., 1965; m. Lynette Alice Temple, Dec. 27, 1946; children—John, Gary, Richard. Tchr. English, Coll. City N.Y., 1945, Fairleigh Dickinson U., 1945-46; instr. English, Mohawk Valley Community Coll., 1946-53, head dept. gen. studies, 1953- 56, dean, 1956-63; pres. Rockland Community Coll., Suffern, N.Y., 1963- ; tchr. Grad. Sch. Edn., N.Y.U., 1965—; writer, lectr., cons. in field. Mem. commnr.'s com. two year coll. N.Y. State Edn. Dept., 1965—; mem. commn. instrn. Am. Assn. Jr. Colls., 1965—. Trustee Rockland Country Day Sch.; bd. dirs. United Fund Rockland County. Mem. Phi Delta Kappa. Author: Guide to the Two-Year Colleges, rev. edit., 1965. Home: 7 Kevin Dr Suffern NY 10901

ESLICK, LEONARD JAMES, educator, philosopher; b. Denver, Nov. 8, 1914; s. Theodore Parker and Leila (Van Natta) E.; A.B., U. Chgo., 1934; M.A., Tulane U., 1936; Ph.D., U. Va., 1939; m. Florence Elizabeth Weber, May 3, 1935. Instr. philosophy Drake U., Des Moines, 1939-42; tutor St. John's Coll., Annapolis, Md., 1943-48; asso. prof. St. Louis U., 1948-57, prof., 1957—; vis. prof. U. Va. at Charlottesville, 1961, U. Ill. at Urbana, 1965, U. Notre Dame, 1968. Served with AUS, 1942. Mem. Am., Mo. (pres. 1958-59) Philos. assns., Metaphys. Soc. Am., Cath. Commn. Intellectual and Cultural Affairs. Asso. editor Modern Schoolman, 1950—, editorial Bd. Process Studies, 1970—. Contbr. articles on metaphysics, Plato, A.N. Whitehead to philos. jours., books. Home: 4253 Flora Pl St Louis MO 63110

ESMAN, MILTON JACOB, educator; b. Pitts., Sept. 15, 1918; s. Mayer and Hermoine (Bernstein) E.; B.A., Cornell U., 1939; Ph.D., Princeton, 1942; m. Janice Newman, Oct. 23, 1949; children—Michael, Oliver, Judith. Program planning officer U.S. Civil Service Commn., 1947-51; intelligence research officer State Dept., 1951-54; fgn. aid adminstr., Washington and Saigon, Vietnam, 1954-59; prof., head dept. econ. and social devel. Grad. Sch. Pub. and Internat. Affairs, U. Pitts., 1959-66, research dir. Interuniv. Research Program Instn. Bldg., 1963-66 sr. adviser devel. adminstrn. Prime Minister's Dept., Govt. Malaysia, 1966; dir. Center for Internat. Studies, also John S. Knight prof. Cornell U., 1969—. Served with AUS, 1942-46. Home: 903 Triphammer Rd Ithaca NY 14250

ESPELAGE, BERNARD THEODORE, bishop; b. Cincinnati, O., Feb. 16, 1892; s. Bernard J. and Clara (Schottelkotte) E.; student St. Francis Coll., 1905-10, Franciscan Sem., 1911-18, Catholic U. of Am., 1925-26 (J.C.L.). Entered Franciscan Order, 1910. Ordained priest Roman Catholic Ch., 1918; nominated Bishop of Gallup, N.M., July 23, 1940, consecrated, Oct. 9, 1940; installed as first bishop, Gallup, Oct. 30, Titiel Bishop, Gallup. Home: 406 W Aztec St Gallup NM 87301

ESPELIE, ERNEST MARVIN, librarian; b. Stoughton, Wis., June 22, 1908; s. Even and Mamie (Oftelie) E.; A.B., Luther Coll., 1931; A.B. in L.S., U. Mich., 1932, A.M., 1935; m. Mary Belle Whitten, Sept. 11, 1933; children—Solveig, Mary, Karl. Asst., U. Mich. Libraries, 1932-37; librarian, asst. prof. Concordia Coll., Moorhead, Minn., 1937-38; librarian, prof. with grades from lt. to comdr. U.S. Coast Guard Acad., 1938-58, ret., 1958; librarian, prof. Augustana Coll., 1959—. Pres. New London (Conn.) P.T.A. council, 1952- 53, High Sch. P.T.A., 1958, 63. Letterstedska Foreningen Study grantee Scandinavia, 1967. Mem. A.L.A., Assn. Coll. and Research Libraries, Am. Scandinavian Found. (pres. Augustana chpt. 1961- 63), Norwegian-Am. Hist. Assn. (dir. 1965—), Augustana Hist. Soc., Am. Assn. U. Profs. Lutheran. Kiwanian. Editor: (with J. I. Dowie) The Swedish Immigrant Community in Transition, 1963. Editor: Augustana Library Publs., 1959—. Contbr. articles to profl. jours. Home: 3407 30th St Rock Island IL 61201

ESPENSHADE, EDWARD BOWMAN, Jr., geographer, educator; b. Chgo., Oct. 23, 1910; s. Edward B. and Mary E. (Jones) E.; B.S., U. Chgo., 1931, Ph.D., 1944; m. Dorothy Elizabeth Barrows, June 17, 1939; children—Jean Ellen, Nancy Elizabeth. Asso. prof. geography Northwestern U., 1948-55, prof., chmn. dept., 1958—; geog. cons., geog. editor Rand McNally & Co. Chmn. div. earth scis. Nat. Acad. Sci.-NRC, 1960-62. Mem. Assn. Am. Geographers (pres. 1964-65, chmn. commn. on coll. geography 1967-69), Geog. Soc. Chgo. (past sec., pres. 1969-71). Editor: Goode's World Atlas, 1947—. Home: 2811 Garrison Av Evanston IL 60201

ESPIE, ROBERT GRANT, actuary; b. Toronto, Can., Dec. 15, 1913; s. Robert James and Carrie Anderson (Benson) E.; B. Comm., U. Toronto, 1934; m. Jeanne Struthers, May 14, 1938; children—Heather, Elizabeth. Came to U.S., 1938, naturalized, 1943. With Aetna Life & Casualty Cos., 1938—, chief accounting officer, 1953-59, asst. comptroller, v.p., 1959-65, v.p., comptroller, 1965-71, v.p., corporate comptroller, 1971—. Fellow Soc. Actuaries, Casualty Actuarial Soc.; mem. Inst. Actuaries, Phi Kappa Sigma. Home: 188 Westmont West Hartford CT 06117 Office: 151 Farmington Av Hartford CT 06115

ESPINOSA-YGLESIAS, MANUEL, banker; b. Puebla, Mexico, May 9, 1909; s. Ernesto Espinosa and Guadalupe Yglesias; ed. Colegio Católico, Colegio del Estado, Academia de Comercio León Pararán (all Puebla); Dr. honoris causa Universidad de. las Americas; m. Amparo Rugarcía, June 27, 1940; children—Amparo (Sra. Julio Serrano), Angeles (Sr. Josè Antonio Alonso). Manuel, Guadalupe (Sra. Jorge Larrea, Jr.) Mgr. Compaia Operadora de Teatros, 1944-45, Ingenio de Astencingo Puebla, 1945-50; with Banco de Comercio, Mexico City, Mexico, 1950—, pres., gen. dir., now chmn., mng. dir., dir., 1955- -; mem. bd. various banks Bancos de Comercio System. Pres. Mary Street Jenkins Found. Created comdr. Order San Gregorio Magno; decorated cross of honor Asociación del H. Colegio Militar; great cross Civil Merit (Spain). Mem. Bankers Nat. Assn. (pres. 1965-66) Clubs: Banqueros, Golf Mexico, Americano, University, Industriales (Mexico); Campestre (Mexico City); Libanès; Espaa; Jockey. Author papers; lectr. profl. orgns. Address: Via Carranza 44-8 Mexico City Mexico

ESPOSITO, ANTHONY JAMES, profl. hockey player; b. Sault Ste. Marie, Ont., Can., Apr. 23, 1943; s. Patrick O. and Francis (DiPietro) E.; B.Sc., Mich. Tech. U., 1967; m. Marilyn R. Mezzomo, Sept. 3, 1966; children—Mark Anthony, Jason Patrick. Goal tender Nat. Hockey League team Chgo. Blackhawks, 1968—. Recipient Veniza Calder Meml. trophy, 1968. Home: 233 Walnut St Elmhurst IL 60126 Office: Chgo Blackhawks 1800 W Madison St Chicago IL 60612

ESPY, ROBERT HAMILTON EDWIN, church exec.; b. Portland, Ore., Dec. 30, 1908; s. Harry Albert and Helen Medora (Richardson) E.; B.A., U. Redlands, 1930, D.D., 1944; B.D., Union Theol. Sem., N.Y.C., 1933; student Tuebingen, Heidelberg U., Germany, 1933-35; Ph.D., Yale. 1950; L.H.D. (hon.), Oberlin Coll., 1965; Litt. D., Keuka Coll., 1969; m. Cleo Lovace Mitchell, Sept. 21, 1944. Student pastor various schs., 1930-33; youth sec. World Alliance Internat. Friendship Through the Churches, provisional com. World Council Chs., Geneva, Switzerland, 1936-39; exec. sec. First World Conf. Christian Youth, Amsterdam, 1939; general sec. Student Volunteer Movement N.Y., 1940-43; exec. sec. Nat. Student Council YMCA, N.Y.C., 1943-55; asso. exec. sec., div. Christian life and work Nat. Council Chs. Christ in U.S. 1955-57, asso. gen. sec., 1958-63, gen. sec. 1963—; lecturer religion in higher edn. various div. schs. Leader, Second World Conf. Christian Youth, Oslo, 1947, Third World Conf. Christian Youth, Travancore, India, 1952, First Assembly World Council Chs., Amsterdam, 1948, Second Assembly, Evanston, 1954, Third Assembly, New Delhi, 1961, Cent. Com., Nigeria, 1965, Enugu, 1965, Geneva, 1966, Crete, 1967, Canterbury, 1969; mem. joint working group World Council of Chs. and Roman Cath. Ch., 1965—; Centennial Conf. World's Alliance of YMCA's, Paris, 1955. Dir. Nat. Planning Assn., World U. Service (U.S. dir. 1953-57). Dir. Union Theol. Sem. 1959—; chmn. Nat. Interreligious Com. U.S., 1968-69. Fellow Nat. Council Religion in Higher Edn.; mem. World's Student Christian Fedn. (gen. com. 1933-55), Fed. Council Chs. (commn. on bases of just and durable peace), N.Y. Bapt. City Soc. (bd. mgrs. 1951-57), Sigma Tau Delta, Alpha Phi Gamma, Theta Alpha Phi, Pi Kappa Delta. Mem. Am. Baptist Ch. Clubs: University, Columbia University Faculty, Quill (N.Y.C.). Author: The Religion of College Teachers, 1951. Contbr. articles profl. publs. Home: 375 Riverside Dr New York City NY 10025 Office: 475 Riverside Dr New York City NY 10027

ESSELBURNE, GEORGE H., journalist. Book editor Buffalo News. Office: 318 Main St Buffalo NY 14240*

ESSELEN, WILLIAM BRIGHAM, educator; b. Boston, July 31, 1912; s. William B. and Thirza (Ballard) E.; B. S., U. Mass., 1934, M.S. (Research fellow), 1935, Ph.D., 1938; m. Katherine Louise O'Brien, Aug. 3, 1938; 1 son, Richard William. Research asst. nutrition U. Mass. at Amherst, 1936-38, asst. research prof. food tech., 1941-47, asso. research prof., 1947-51, research prof. food sci. and tech., 1951—, chmn. dept., 1957—; food technologist Owens-Ill. Glass Co., 1939-41; cons. War Price Adminstrn., U.S. Dept. Agr., 1942-45; food technician Q.M.C., U.S. Army, Germany, 1945—; exchange prof. Hokkaido U., Sapporo, Japan, 1960-61; vis. lectr. food tech. P.R. Agr. Expt. Sta., 1964-65; cons . food sci. and tech., 1942—. Mem. Amherst Town Meeting, 1957—. Bd. dirs. Hokkaido Internat. Sch., Inc. Fellow Am. Pub. Health Assn.; mem. Inst. Food Technologists (councilor-at-large 1952-53; chmn. com. sci. lectrs. 1964—; nat. councilor N.E. sect. 1964-66, chmn., 1964-65), Am. Chem. Soc., Soc. Am. Bacteriologists, Sigma Xi, Phi Kappa Phi, Phi Tau Sigma (past nat. pres.). Contbr. numerous articles profl. jours. Research in nutritive value of fruits, effect of processing on nutritive value and quality of foods, thermal destruction of bacterial spores, processing canned foods, thermal destruction of enzymes, fruit juices, apple and cranberry products and pickles. Home: 55 Hills Rd Amherst MA 01002

ESSENBURG, FRANKLIN, educator, mechanician; b. Holland, Mich., Aug. 2, 1924; s. Frank and Katherine (Bakker) E.; B.S. in Mech. Engring., U. Mich., 1945, LL.B., 1948, M.S. in Physics, 1949, M.S. in Engring. Mechanics, 1950, Ph.D. in Engring. Mechanics, 1956; m. Doloris May Gerhardt, Sept. 18, 1946; children—Sally Kay, Sandra Karen. Admitted to Mich. bar, 1948; patent atty. Bell Telephone Labs., Murray Hill, N.J., 1950-51; engaged in pvt. constrn. bus., Holland, Mich., 1951-53; instr., then asst. prof. mechanics U. Mich., 1953-58; asso. prof., then prof. mechanics Ill. Inst. Tech., 1958-62; prof. mechanics, chmn. dept. mech. engring. U. Colo., 1962—. Served with USNR, 1943-45. Mem. Am. Soc. Mech. Engring., Mich. Bar. Assn., Sigma Xi. Pi Tau Sigma, Phi Kappa Phi, Tau Beta Pi. Home: 2165 Vassar Dr Boulder Co 80302

ESSENE, FRANK J., educator, anthropologist; b. Glendive, Mont., Jan. 23, 1908; s. Frank J. and Edna Irene (Conrad) E.; A.B., U. Cal. at Berkeley, 1934, Ph.D., 1947; m. Rieva Molly Blazek, Aug. 9, 1935; children—Eric John, Karen Ann. Teaching asst. U. Cal. at Berkeley, 1937-40 45-46, asso. prof., summer 1954; prof., summers 1961, 64; instr. U. Tex., Austin, 1946-47; asst. prof. Washington U., St. Louis, summers 1947, 48; asst. prof. U. Ky., 1947-48, asso. prof., 1948-57, prof., 1957—, head dept. anthropology, 1957-66; asst. prof. U. Minn., summer 1948; research asso. U. Ore., summer 1959; prof. Ind. U., summer 1968; research Am. Indians and Baganda of Africa. Served from 2d lt. to capt. Ordnance Dept., AUS, 1941-46. Fellow Am. Anthrop. Assn., Central States Anthrop. Soc., Am. Ethnol. Soc. (treas. 1965—), So. Anthrop. Soc. (pres. 1967-68), Soc. Am. Archaeology; mem. Sigma Xi, Phi Delta Kappa, Alpha Kappa Delta. Democrat. Unitarian. Home: 405 Cochran Rd Lexington KY 40502

ESSEX, MARTIN WALKER, sch. adminstr.; b. Ray, O., Mar. 25, 1908; s. John S. and Cora (McCormick) E.; B.S., Ohio State U., 1930, M.A., 1934; D. Pd. (hon.), Baldwin-Wallace Coll., 1950; LL.D., U. Akron, 1958; m. Blanche Davis, Aug. 12, 1933. Tchr., Middleport, O., 1930-32, high sch. prin., 1932-35, supt. schs., 1935-41; prin., East Liverpool, O., 1941-43, supt. schs., 1943-45; prin., Ferndale, Mich., 1945-46, supt. schs., 1946-47; supt. schs., Lakewood, O., 1947-55, Akron, 1955-66; supt. pub. instrn. State of Ohio, 1966—; guest lectr. Cornell U., Harvard, U. Mo., Northwestern U., U. Ore., A. and M. Coll. of Tex., U. Toledo, U. Wis., 1958, and others, Mem. exec. com. Joint Council on Econ. Edn.; chmn. adv. council on vocational edn. U.S. Dept. Health, Edn. and Welfare, 1966-67; nat. chmn. sch. savs. program U.S. Treasury Dept., 1966-68. Chmn. adv. council Nat. Merit Scholarship Corp. Trustee Council of Chief State Sch. Officers. Named Man of Year, Am. Vocational Assn., 1968. Mem. N.E.A., Am. Assn. Sch. Adminstrs. (pres. 1959-60), Phi Alpha Theta, Phi Delta Kappa. Rotarian. Editorial bd. The Nation's Schs. Study tour Russia, 1959, 64. Home: 3117 Carisbrook Rd Columbus OH 43221 Office: State Office Bldg 65 S Front St Columbus OH 43215

ESSIGMANN, MARTIN WHITE, univ. dean; b. Bethel, Vt., Jan. 14, 1917; s. John Martin and Sybil Gertrude (White) E.; B.S. in Elec. Engring., Tufts U., 1938; S.M. in Elec. Engring., Mass. Inst. Tech., 1947; m. Rita Lorraine Nolan, June 6, 1943; children—Nancy, John, Joyce. Mem. faculty Northeastern U., 1938- 44, 48—, prof. elec. engring., chmn. dept., 1959-61, dean research, Mass. Inst. Tech., 1944-48. Vice pres. Mt. Washington Obs., 1968—. Chmn. Gov.'s adv. Com. Sci. and Tech. Sr. mem. I.E.E.E.; mem. Am. Soc. Engring. Edn., A.A.A.S., Sigma Xi, Tau Beta Pi, Eta Kappa Nu, Phi Kappa Phi. Home: 10 Roland St Medford MA 02155 Office: 360 Huntington Av Boston MA 02115

ESSLER, WARREN ORVEL, coll. dean; b. Davenport, Ia., Apr. 22, 1924; s. Orvel E. and Elsie (Moormann) E.; B.S. in Elec. Engring., U. Ia., 1953, M.S., 1955, Ph.D. in Elec. Engring. and Physiology (NIH fellow 1959-60), 1960; NSF faculty fellow Ia. State U. Sci. and Tech., 1958-59; m. Gloria Helen Meeker Finch, Jan. 17, 1944; children—Stephen Robert, Nancy Lee, Elizabeth Ann. Research asso., teaching asst. U. Ia., 1953-54; mem. elec. engring. staff Collins Radio Co., 1954-55; instr. S.D. State Coll., 1955-57, asst. prof., 1957-58, asso. prof., 1960-61; prof. elec. engring., chmn. Served with AUS, 1942-45. Mem. A.A.A.S., I.E.E.E., Am. Soc. Engring. Edn., Nat. Soc. Profl. Engrs., Sigma Xi, Tau Beta Pi, Eta Kappa Nu, Sigma Tau frats. Methodist. Mason. Author articles in field. Home: Birch Rd Shelburne VT 05482 Office: Univ Vermont Coll Technology Burlington VT 05401

ESSLINGER, ARTHUR ALBERT, univ. dean; b. Cin., Jan. 14, 1905; s. George and Mary (Link) E.; B.S. in Phys. Edn., U. Ill., 1931, M.S. in Edn., 1932; Ph.D., U. Ia., 1938; m. Mary Agnes Jeffries, June 19, 1931; 1 dau., Nancy (Mrs. Richard Ross). Asst. prof. Bradley U., 1931-38; asso. prof. Stanford, 1938-43; prof., dir. phys. edn. Springfield Coll., 1946-53; dean Sch. Health and Phys. Edn., U. Ore., 1953—. Dir. Eugene YMCA, Little League Baseball, Inc. Served as maj. AUS, 1943-46; chief phys. tng. Sch. Spl. Services, 1943-44, chief phys. reconditioning Office Surg. Gen., 1944-45, chief phys. tng. ASF, 1945-46. Recipient honor award A.A.H.P.E.R., 1952, also Luther Gulick award in 1967. Mem. A.A.H.P.E.R. (pres. 1959-60, chmn. Nat. Found. 1968-70), Am. Acad. Phys. Edn. (pres. 1967-68), Am. Coll. Sports Medicine, Coll. Phys. Edn. Assn. Rotarian. Author: (with Dr. E. F. Voltmer) The Organization and Administration of Physical Education, 4th edit., 1967. Home: 2075 Hubbard Lane Eugene OR 97403

ESTABROOK, HUBERT ARTHUR, lawyer; b. Dayton, O., Dec. 15, 1890; s. Arthur S. and Willie (Hubert) E.; certificate in law Ohio State U., 1913; m. Gladys Collins, Aug. 18, 1920; 1 son, Hubert Arthur. Admitted to Ohio bar, 1913, since practiced in Dayton; partner Estabrook, Finn & McKee, 1915—. Dir. State Fidelity Fed. Savs. and Loan Assn., The 1st Nat. Bank of Dayton. Served as 1st lt. Ordnance, AEF, 1917-18. Mem. Am. Ohio, Dayton bar assns., Phi Delta Phi, Sigma Nu. Clubs: Dayton Racquet, Dayton Country; Queen City (Cin.). Home: 318 Southview Rd Dayton OH 45419 Office: Hulman Bldg Dayton OH 45402

ESTABROOK, ROBERT HARLEY, editor; b. Dayton, O., Oct. 16, 1918; s. Charles and Christianne M. (Harley) E.; A.B., Northwestern U., 1939; postgrad. extension Coe Coll., 1941, Am. Press Inst., Columbia, 1947; m. Mary Lou Stewart, Dec. 22, 1942; children—John Stewart, James Ross, David Morse, Margaret Harley. City editor Emmet County Graphic, Harbor Springs, Mich., 1936; editor Daily Northwestern, Northwestern U., 1938-39; reporter Cedar Rapids (Ia.) Gazette, 1939-40, editorial writer, 1940-42; editorial writer Washington Post, 1946-53, editor editorial page, 1953-62, chief fgn. corr., London, Eng., 1962-65, asso. editor, 1965-66, UN and Can. corr., 1966-71; editor, pub. Lakeville (Conn.) Jour., 1971—; lectr. journalism U. Md., 1948-49. Served from pvt. to capt. AUS, 1942-46, in charge Army newspaper and radio sta., Brazil, 1945. Recipient award for best editorial Sigma Delta Chi. 1954; Deadline Club award for UN corr. Sigma Delta Chi, 1969. Mem. Nat. Conf. Editorial Writers (founder; life mem.; pres. 1951), Council Fgn. Relations, Overseas Writers, UN Corr. Assn., Phi Beta Kappa, Sigma Delta Chi, Delta Tau Delta. Unitarian. Clubs: National Press, Metropolitan

(Washington). Editor: A Manual for Correspondents, 1966. Contbr. mags. Home: Box 73 Lakeville CT 06039 Office: Lakeville Jour Lakeville CT 06039

ESTEN, LEROY WHITELAW, utility exec.; b. Glendale, R.I., Aug. 22, 1902; s. Fred L. and Eliza Frances (Johnston) E.; student Vannais Accounting Sch., Nat. Elec. Lighting Assn., also spl. courses Columbia and Irving Trust Co.; m. Jaunita Dudley, Nov. 1, 1930; 1 dau., Lauray Dudley, With Tarklin Woolen Mfg. Co., 1922-23, Producers Nat. Bank, 1923-24, Blackstone Valley Gas and Elec. Co., 1924-25, 27-33, Key West Elec. Co., 1925-27; with Central Ill. Electric and Gas Co., Rockford, 1933—, v.p., treas., 1954- 63, pres., 1963—, also dir.; Am. Nat. Bank and Trust Co., Rockford; operator real estate holding, Old Saybrook, Conn. Pres. Rockford Community Chest, 1961, bd. dirs., 1948-52; pres. Rockford Civic Syphony Assn., 1948; co-chmn. St. Anthony Hosp. capital funds drive, 1959, mem. adv. bd., 1959—; chmn. Christmas Seal campaign Winnebago County Tb Assn., 1963; mem. Blackhawk area council Boy Scouts Am., 1960—. Mem. adv. council Mgmt. Devel. Program, U. Ill., 1957—; bd. dirs. Rockford Jr. Achievement, 1958—; adv. council Rockford Girl Scouts, 1935-50, Rockford YWCA, 1955—. Mem. Am. Gas Assn., Edison Electric Inst., Rockford C. of C. (pres. 1955-56). Republican. Conglist (deacon, past chmn. fund raising). Lion (pres. 1948), Elk. Club: Mauh Nah Tee See Country (treas. 1936), Medelssohn (adv. council), University, Midday, Forest Hills Country (Rockford); Union League (Chgo.). Home: 2234 Harlem Blvd Rockford IL 61103 Office: 303 N Main St Rockford IL 61101

ESTEP, SAMUEL D., lawyer, educator; b. Kans., Mar. 13, 1919; s. Alvernon D. and Mary E. (Paul) E.; A.B., Kan. State Tchrs. Coll., Emporia, 1940; J.D., U. Mich., 1946; div.; children—Michael D., Julia L., David F. Admitted to Mich. bar, 1946; asso. firm Cook, Smith, Jacobs & Beake, Detroit, 1946-48; mem. faculty U. Mich. Law Sch., 1948—, prof. law, 1954—; cons. to govt., 1956—. Vice pres. Ann Arbor United Fund, 1957-58. Served with USNR, 1942-45. Mem. Am., Mich. bar assns., Order of Coif. Prin. author: Atoms and the Law, 1959; co-author: Atomic Energy Technology for Lawyers, 1956; State Regulation of Atomic Energy, 1956; also articles. Home: 3390 Andover Rd Ann Arbor MI 48105

ESTERHAI, JOHN LOUIS, lawyer; b. Phoenixville, Pa., Jan. 26, 1920; s. Louis and Mary (Wolarik) E.; B.S.C., Temple U., 1940; LL.B., U. Pa., 1946; m. I. Louise Moyer, Nov. 13, 1943; children—John L., Louise Clayton. Admitted to Pa. bar, 1947; law clk. to Hon. Herbert F. Goodrich, 1946-47; asso. legal dept. Philco Corp., Phila., 1947-58; v.p., sec., dir. Philco Finance Corp., 1958-62; asst. counsel The Penn Mut. Life Ins. Co., 1962-65, asso. counsel, 1965-69, asso. gen. counsel, 1970—. Bd. mgrs. Meml. Hosp., Roxborough (pres. 1969—). Served to lt. USNR, 1942-45. Mem. Am., Pa., Phila. bar assns., U.S. Trade Mark Assn. (pres. 1958-60), Internat. Assn. Protection Indsl. Property (treas. 1954-58), Assn. Life Ins. Counsel, Pa. Soc. Republican. Baptist. Mason. Club: Union League (Phila.). Author: (with others) Trademark Management, 1955. Home: 8423 Pembrook Rd Philadelphia PA 19128 Office: 530 Walnut St Philadelphia PA 19106

ESTERLY, BRUCE EVERETT, rubber co. exec.; b. Tiffin, O., May 23, 1920; s. Fred B. and Hazel (Holtz) E.; B.S. in Bus. Adminstrn., Bowling Green State U., 1942; m. Marie Decker, July 28, 1942; children—Marsha Lynne, Lee Ann. With Cooper Tire & Rubber Co., Findlay, O., 1946—, v.p. finance, 1960-70. exec. v.p., 1970—, also dir.; dir. Hancock Savs. & Loan Co., Findlay, Gen. Ohio S & L Corp., Findlay. Pres. United Community Fund Hancock County, 1963, No-We-Oh council Camp Fire Girls, 1965; treas. Asso. Charities Findlay, 1960-69. Trustee Blanchard Valley Hosp., Findlay, 1965-68. Served to capt. AUS, 1942-46, 50-52. Decorated Bronze Star with cluster. Mem. Financial Execs. Inst. (pres. Toledo 1965), Pi Kappa Alpha, Beta Alpha Psi. Mason, Elk, Rotarian. Home: 135 Church Hill Dr Findlay OH 45840 Office: Cooper Tire & Rubber Co Lima at Western Av Findlay OH 45740

ESTERN, NEIL, sculptor; b. N.Y.C., Apr. 18, 1926; s. Marc J. and Molly (Sylbert) E.; B.F.A., B.S. in Edn., Temple U., 1947; m. Anne Graham, May 27, 1947; children—Peter Alan, Evan Andrew, Victoria. Exhibited in numerous one man and group shows in Conn., N.Y.C., Phila., N.J., Italy; rep. permanent collection Bklyn. Mus.; have done portraits of LaGuardia, J. Robert Taft, Danny Kaye, John F. Kennedy, J. Edgar Hoover; did portrait bust of John F. Kennedy for J.F. Kennedy Meml. erected in Grand Army Plaza, Bklyn., 1965; sculptor for doll industry. Recipient John Gregory award, 1966, Samuel F.B. Morse Gold medal, 1970. Address: 82 Remsen St Brooklyn NY 11201

ESTES, BAY EDWARD, Jr., steel co. marketing exec.; b. Boston, July 11, 1910; s. Bay Edward and Mellie Grover (Timberlake) E.; A.B., Harvard, 1932, M.B.A., 1934; m. Ruth E. Stubbs, Apr. 25, 1936; children—Bay Edward III, Barbara Ellen, Karen Jean, David Allan. Asst. dean Harvard Grad. Sch. Bus. Adminstrn., 1934-35; asst. buying dept. Goldman, Sachs & Co., 1935-39; analyst comml. research div. U.S. Steel Corp., 1939-43, asst. mgr., 1943-47, dir. comml. research div., 1947-57, dir. Mem. adv. bd. Mgmt. Sci. Center, U. Pennsylvania. staff adminstrn., 1957-58, v.p. marketing, 1958-67, asst. to exec. v.p. comml., 1967—, Mem. Am. Marketing Assn. (dir. 1956, 57, nat. v.p. 1957, 58), Am. Iron and Steel Inst. Home: 525 William Penn Pl Pittsburgh PA 15240 Office: 5 Gate way Center Pittsburgh PA 15230

ESTES, ELEANOR, author; b. West Haven, Conn., May 9, 1906; d. Louis and Caroline (Gewecke) Rosenfeld; grad. Pratt Inst. Sch. Library Sci. (Caroline M. Hewins scholarship 1931), 1932; m. Rice Estes, Dec. 8, 1932; 1 dau., Helena. Children's librarian Free Pub. Library, New Haven, 1924-31, N.Y. Pub. Library, 1932-40. Recipient Newberry medal for distinguished contbn. to Am. lit. for children, 1951; ann. Alumni award Pratt Inst., 1967. Mem. P.E.N. Episcopalian. Author: The Moffats, 1941; The Middle Moffat, 1942; The Sun and the Wind and Mr. Todd, 1943; Rufus M., 1943; The Hundred Dresses, 1944; The Echoing Green, 1947; The Sleeping Giant, 1948; Ginger Pye (winner Herald Tribune Spring Book Festival award), 1951; A Little Oven, 1955; Pinky Pye, 1958; The Witch Family, 1960; The Alley, 1964; Miranda The Great, 1967; The Lollipop Princess, 1967. Home: 175 Steuben St Brooklyn NY 11205

ESTES, ELLIOTT M., automobile mfg. Co. exec.; chief engr. Pontiac motor div. Gen. Motors Corp., 1956-61, gen mgr., corp. v.p., 1961—, v.p., gen. mgr. Chevrolet, 1965-67, v.p. Chevrolet, 1967—, v.p., gen. mgr. Car and Truck div., 1969—. Address: 196 Oakland Av Pontiac MI 48053

ESTES, HOWELL MARION, Jr., ret. air force officer, airline exec.; b. Ft. Oglethorpe, Ga., Sept. 18, 1914; s. Col. Howell Marion and Juanita (Dickson) E.; B.S., U.S. Mil. Acad. 1936; grad. Flying Schs., 1940, Air War Coll., 1949; m. Annah Verbeck, Mar. 8, 1941; children—Howell Marion III, Michael Summer, Charles Dickson. Commd. 2d lt. Cav., U.S. Army, 1936, USAF, 1940—, advanced through grades to gen. USAF, 1964; assigned 7th Cav., Ft. Bliss, Tex., 1936-37; acting aide-de-camp to comdr. 1st Cav. Div., 1937-39; flight instr., Brooks Field, 1940, comdt. cadets Advanced Flying Sch., 1940-42, dir. flying, 1942-43, dir. tng., 1943-44; comdg. officer Blackland Air Base, Waco Tex., 1944; comdr. Lubbock Army Air Field, 1944-45; chief plan and policy br., operations div. USAF Europe, Wiesbaden, Germany, 1946, chief staff for operations, 1946-47, asst. chief staff for plans, 1947; assigned 22d Bomb Wing, March Air Base, Cal., 1949, comdr. 1st Air Base Group, 1949; with 22d Bomb Group, U.K., 1949-50, dep. comdr., chief staff 22d Bomb Wing, 1950-51; comdr. 44th Bomb Wing, March Air Base, 1951; vice comdr. Far East Air Forces Bomber Command, 1951; comdr. 320th Bomb Wing, March Air Base, 1951-52, 12th Air Div., 1952-53, Air Task Group 7, 4, 1952-54; dir. weapon systems operations Wright Air Devel. Center, Air Research and Devel. Command, Wright-Patterson AFB, O., 1954-55, asst. dep. comdr. for weapon systems, comdr. detachment no. 1, Hdqrs. Air Research and Devel. Command, dir. systems mgmt., 1955-57; asst. chief staff for air def. systems Hdqrs. USAF, Washington, 1957-58, asst. dep. chief of staff, operations, 1958-61; dep. comdr. aerospace systems Air Force Systems Command, Los Angeles, 1961-62; vice comdr. Air Force Systems Command, Andrews AFB, 1962-64; comdr. Mil. Airlift Command, 1964-69; ret., 1969; sr. v.p. World Airways, Inc., Oakland, Cal., 1969-71, exec. v.p., 1971—, also dir.; dir. Worldam. Investors Corp. Bd. dirs., Bay Area U.S.O., Boy Scouts Am. Decorated Legion of Merit with two clusters, D.F.C., Air Medal with 2 clusters, D.S.M. (Army), D.S.M. (USAF); War Cross (Czechoslovakia). Recipient Gen. H. H. Arnold trophy. Mem. Nat. Def. Transp. Assn. (def. adv. council), Bay Area Council, Am. Ordnance Assn. (dir. San Francisco chpt.), Newcomen Soc. Address: care World Airways Inc Oakland Internat Airport Oakland CA 94614

ESTES, JOE EWING, judge; b. Commerce, Tex., Oct. 24, 1903; s. Joe Guinn and della Marshall (Loy) E.; student E. Tex. State Tchrs. Coll., 1923-24; LL.B., U. Tex., 1927; m. Carroll Virginia Cox, Dec. 1, 1931; children—Carl Lewis II, Carol Lynn. Admitted to Tex. bar, 1927; partner Crosby & Estes at Commerce. Tex., 1928-30. Phillips. Trammell, Estes. Edwards & Orn. Ft, Worth, 1930-45. Sanford, King. Estes & Cantwell at Dallas, 1946-52, Estes & Cantwell, 1952-55; U.S. dist. judge, Dallas, 1955-60; chief judge U.S. Dist. Ct. No. Dist. Texas. Trustee, mem. exec. com. S.W. Legal Foundation, Chmn. exec. com. bd. trustees St. Marks Sch. of Tex., Dallas, 1951-55; v.p. The Law-Science Found. of Am. Research fellow, member med.-legal com., chmn. Oil and Gas Institute of S.W. Legal Found. Served as lt. comdr. USNR, 1942-45; mem. Res. Fellow Am. Bar Found.; mem. Nat. Conf. Commrs. on Uniform State Laws, Am. Law Inst., Inter-Am., Fed., Am. (chmn. sect. jud. administrn. 1961-62, mem. ho. dels.), Dallas (past v.p.), Fort Worth (past mem. bd. dirs.) bar assns. State Bar Tex., Am. Judicature Soc., Nat. Lawyers Club, Philos. Soc., Texas, Newcomen Soc., Am. Legion. Chancellors, Phi Delta Phi, Kappa Sigma, Order of Coif. Methodist. Mason (33, Shriner, hon. inspector gen., Tester). Contbr. profl. jours.; also to Handbook of Recommended Procedures for the Trial of Protracted Cases; co-author Handbook for Effective Pretrial Procedure, Handbook for Newly Appointed U.S. District Judges. Editorial bd. Manual for Complex and Multidistrict Litigation. Home: 5846 Desco Dr Dallas TX 75225 Office: US Court House Dallas TX 75201

ESTES, JOHN ADAMS, (Sleepy), pioneer blues singer; b. Lauderdale County, Tenn., Jan. 25, 1900; s. Daniel and Millie (Bell) E.; m. Lutelia Gause, Aug. 15, 1919; m. Ola Ball, Dec.1, 1948; children—Virginia, Willie, Albert, Lucille, Charles, Mary. Performances in colls., radio, TV, night clubs, coffeehouses; mem. 4th Am. Folk-Blues Festival Tour of Europe, 1964, 68, Newport Folk Festival, 1964, Ann Arbor Blues Festival, 1969; recs. include the Girl I Love Has Long Hair, Take That Right Hand Road, Diving Duck, Some Day Baby, You Won't Worry My Mind Anymore, Everybody Ought to Change Sometimes, Sooner or Later You Are Going to that Lonesome Ground, Need More Has Harmed Many Man, That's My Reason for Making a Change, Black Mattie Blues, Floating Bridge, Drop Down Mama, Rats in My Kitchen, Legend of Sleepy John Estes, Broke and Hungry. Address: care Delmark Records 7 W Grand Av Chicago IL 60610*

ESTES, PETER G., lawyer; b. Marble Hill, Mo., Feb. 8, 1916; s. Willis Gay and Myrtle (Hughes) E.; student U. Okla., 1935-36; LL.B., J.D., U. Ark., 1942; m. Frances Louise Hannah, May 21, 1938; children—Nancy Louise (Mrs. Huland Nations), Peter Gay, Janey Hannah. Admitted to Ark. bar, 1942, since practiced in Fayetteville; partner firm Estes & Storey, 1946—. Vice pres., dir. Home Mut. Fire Ins. Co., Midwest Underwriters, Inc.; dir. Northwest Ark. Paper Co.; partner Estes Devel. Co. Served to lt. comdr. USNR, 1942-46. Mem. Am., Ark. bar assns., Am. Trial Lawyers Assn., Phi Alpha Delta. Mason (Shriner). Home: 1626 W Ridgeway St Fayetteville AR 72701 Office: 64 E Mountain St Fayetteville AR 72701

ESTES, RICE, librarian; b. Spartanburg, S.C., Apr. 27, 1907; s. Elliott, and Sara Jane (Smith) E.; A.B., U. S.C., 1928; B.L.S., Pratt Inst., 1932; A.M., U. So. Cal., 1941; postgrad. Columbia, 1943-45; m. Eleanor Rosenfeldt, Dec. 8, 1932; 1 dau., Helena. Librarian, U.S.C. Sch. Edn., 1931, Housing Study Guild, 1933; library asst. Bklyn. Coll., 1933-35, reference librarian, 1938-43; library asst. Stuyvesant High Sch., N.Y., 1936-38; alumni sec. Pratt Inst., 1944, asst. prof. library sci., 1944- 48, acting dean Library Sch., 1955-56, librarian, 1955—, asso. prof., 1955-59, prof. bibliography, 1959, sec. Pratt Inst., 1956-71; asst. librarian U. So. Cal., 1948-52; librarian Fairfield (Conn.) Pub. Library, 1952-53; chief asst. librarian George Washington U., 1953-55. Dir. Bklyn. coll. libraries research project Council for Higher Ednl. Instns. N.Y., 1962-63. Mem. Eastern Coll. Librarians Conf. (chmn. 1965), A.L.A. (chmn. Grolier award com. 1965-66, chmn. Clarence Day award com. 1968-69), N.Y., Conn. (sec. 1953) library assns., Spl. Libraries Assn., Assn. Colls. and Research Libraries, Acad. Libraries of Bklyn. (pres. 1969-70), Bibliog. Soc. Am., Am. Assn. U. Profs., Met. Coll. Inter-Library Assn. (pres. 1962-63), Phi Beta Kappa, Beta Phi Mu (hon. mem.; exec. council 1968-71). Episcopalian. Clubs: Archons of Colophon, New York Library (pres. 1961-62). Author: A Study of Seven College Libraries and Their Cooperative Potential. Contbr. articles profl. jours. Book reviewer Library Jour. Home: 175 Steuben St Brooklyn NY 11205

ESTES, ROBERT MASON, electric co. exec., lawyer; b. Meredith, N.H., Jan. 25, 1912; s. James French and Margaret (Sullivan) E.; B.A., Dartmouth, 1933; LL.B., Harvard, 1936; m. Priscilla Alden Nelson, Mar. 2, 1947; children—Mark, Peter, Carolyn. Admitted to N.Y. bar, 1938, Ky. bar. 1957, Ill. bar. 1959; asso. Donovan, Leisure, Newton & Lumbard, N.Y.C., 1936-46; counsel electronics div. Gen. Electric Co., 1947-58, Hotpoint div., 1959-60, maj. appliance div., 1961-64, v.p., gen. counsel, sec., 1964-70, sr. v.p., gen. counsel, sec., 1970—. Served from 2d lt. to lt. col., C.W.S., AUS. 1941-45. Mem. Am., FCC bar assns., Am. Judicature Soc., Nat. Lawyers Club, Bar Assn. City N.Y., N.Y. State Bar Assn., Assn. Gen. Counsel, Am. Soc. Corporate Secs., Phi Beta Kappa. Clubs: Manursing Island; Apawamis (Rye). Home: North Island Dr Rye NY 10580 Office: 570 Lexington Av New York City NY 10022

ESTES, THOMAS STUART, constrn. co. exec.; b. Rumford, Me., Jan. 23, 1913; s. Richard Henry and Helena May (Coombs) E.; student Am. U., 1949-50, Harvard U. Grad. Sch. Bus. Administrn., 1952; m. Dorothy Astrid Milner, Dec. 4, 1939; children—Elisabeth, Stuart; m. 2d, Ruth Elaine Fullerton, Jan. 1957; 1 dau., Jane. Interior decorator, Worcester, 1932-34; fgn. service officer 1937—; v. consul, Bangkok, Siam, 1938-41; v. consul Office U.S. Polit. Adv., Algiers, 1941-43, Italy, 1943-45; 2d sec., Vienna, 1945-46; consul, Que., Can., 1946-49; with Dept. of State, 1949, 52; 1st sec., Athens, Greece, 1952-55; dep. asst. sec. of state, 1955-60; sr. seminar in fgn. policy, 1960-61; U.S. ambassador to Republic of Upper Volta, 1961-66; State Dept. adviser Naval War Coll. Newport, R.I., 1966-70; v.p. fgn. affairs Charles A. Maguire & Assos., Inc., 1970—. Served as pvt., U.S.M.C., 1934- 37. Decorated: Bronze Star for service as civilian, Allied Force Hdqrs., Mediterranean Theatre World War II (Army); Meritorious Award for services during World War II (Dept. of State, meritorious award, 1956). Mason. Home: 6710 Melrose Dr McLean VA 22101

ESTES, WILLIAM KAYE, educator, psychologist; b. Mpls., June 17, 1919; s. George D. and Mona m. Katherine Walker, Sept. 26, 1942; children—George E., Gregory W. Mem. faculty Ind. U., 1946-62, prof. psychology, 1955-60, research prof. psychology, 1960-62; faculty research fellow Social Sci. Research Council, 1952-55; lectr. psychology U. Wis., summer 1949; vis. prof. Northwestern U., spring 1959; fellow Center Advanced Study Behavioral Scis., 1955-56; spl. univ. lectr. U. London (Eng.), 1961; prof. psychology, mem. Inst. Math. Studies Social Scis., Stanford, 1962-68; prof. Rockefeller U., 1968—. Served with AUS. 1944-46. Fellow Am. Psychol. Assn. (pres. div. exptl. psychology 1958-59; Distinguished Sci. Contbn. award 1962); mem. Nat. Acad. Scis., A. A. A. S., Soc. Exptl. PsychologistS (Warren medal), 1963), Inst. Math. Statistics, Psychometric Soc., Midwestern Psychol. Assn. (pres. 1956-57). Author: An Experimental Study of Punishment, 1944; Learning Theory and Mental Development, 1970; co-author: Modern Learning Theory, 1954; also numerous articles. Co-editor: Studies in Mathematical Learning Theory, 1959; editor Jour. Comparative and Physiol. Psychology, 1962-68; asso. editor Jour. Exptl. Psychology, 1958-62. Home: Killingworth CT 06417

ESTEVE, MAURICE, artist; b. Culon, 1904; typographer, funiture designer, Barcelona, Spain, 1923; painter, 1923—; work based upon search for synthesis of form, space and light; collaborator decorations Aviation and Railroad pavilions Paris World's Fair, 1937; one-man exhbns. include Galerie Carre, 1948, Galerie Galanis, Paris, 1955-56' also retrospectives in museums of Copenhagen and Hanover, Address: care Realites Nouvelles Ste 18 Rue Quatre Vents Paris 5e, France.*

ESTEVES, VERNON RAFAEL, educator; b. Mayaguez, P.R., Oct. 24, 1920; s. Luis Rawl and Lupe (Navarro) E.; B.A., U. P.R., 1942; M.Econ., Harvard, 1945, Ph.D., 1948; m. Isabel Loyd, June 4, 1948; children—Vernon Xavier, María Cristina, María Isabel. Mem. faculty U. P.R., Río Piedras, 1947, 65-69, 71—, dean Coll. Bus. Adminstrn., 1965-69, prof. finance, 1971—; sr. economist Internat. Monetary Fund, Washington, 1948; econ. adviser to Gov. P.R., 1949-51, exec. sec. Finance Council, 1958-65; fgn. payments specialist Econ. Cooperation Adminstrn. U.S. (Marshall Plan), Paris, France, 1951-53; pvt. practice econ. consulting Miami, Fla., 1953-58; v.p. Govt. Devel. Bank P.R., 1958-65. Exec. dir. Gov.'s Adv. Council for Devel. Govt. Programs, 1969-71; mem. adv. bd. Ins. Commr. P.R., 1966-69; bd. dirs. Housing Bank P.R., Commonwealth Job. Devel. Center, Phillips P.R. Core, Inc. Mem. Am. Econ. Assn., Soc. Internat. Devel., Assn. Puertorriquena de Economía y Estadísticas. Contbr. profl. jours. Home: Laguna Terr 12A 6 Joffre St Condado PR 00907 Office: Dept Finance Coll Bus Adminstrn U PR Río Piedras PR 00931

ESTRICH, ROBERT MARK, educator; b. Mt. Pleasant, Mich., Apr. 10, 1906; s. Charles Henry and Florence Adele (Moore) E.; B.A., Ohio U., 1928; M.A., Ohio State U., 1929, Ph.D., 1935; m. Helen Elizabeth Watts, Aug. 9, 1932 (dec. Sept. 1944); m. 2d, Alice Elizabeth Heyes Olliffe, Dec. 24, 1947. Instr. English, Ohio State U., 1929-37, asst. prof., 1937-45, asso. prof., 1945- 47, prof., 1947—69, prof. emeritus, 1969, chmn. dept., 1952-64. Mem. Linguistic Soc. Am., Modern Lang. Assn., Phi Beta Kappa. Author: (with Hans Sperben) Three Keys to Language, 1952. Contbr. articles in field profl. jours. Home: 3440 Olentangy River Rd Columbus OH 43202

ESTRUP, PEDER JAN ZWERGIUS, educator; b. Copenhagen, Denmark, July 15, 1931; s. Lauritz A. and Alice (Horneman) E.; M.Sc., Poly. Inst. Denmark, Copenhagen, 1954; Ph.D. (Fulbright fellow, Sheffield Sci. fellow), Yale, 1959; m. Faiza Fawaz, Sept. 15, 1960. Came to U.S., 1956. Postdoctoral fellow European Center Nuclear Research, Geneva, Switzerland, 1959-61; mem. tech. staff Bell Tel. Labs., Murray Hill, N.J., 1961-64; research scientist Bartol Research Found., Swarthmore, Pa., 1964-67; prof. physics, chemistry Brown U., Providence, 1967—. Served to lt. Danish Army, 1954-56. Mem. Am. Phys. Soc., Am. Chem. Soc., Am. Vacuum Soc. (exec. com. surface sci. div.). Editor: Surface Phenomena, 1970. Contbr. numerous articles profl. jours. Research in physics and chemistry of surfaces. Home: 15 Adelphi Av Providence RI 02906

ESTY, FRED RUSSELL, bank note co. exec.; b. Chgo., Aug. 22, 1915; s. Fred Russell and Rae E. (Groetzinger) E.; m. Lucille A. Bailey, Oct. 22, 1938; 1 son, Fred Russell III. With Central Banknote Co., Chgo., N.Y.C., 1934-41; with Security-Columbian Banknote Co. (now U.S. Banknote Corp.), N.Y.C., 1941—, pres., dir., 1957-66, chmn. bd., chief exec. officer, dir., 1966—. Bd. dirs. McAuley Water Street Mission, N.Y.C.; chmn. bd. trustees Barrington Coll.; bd. mgrs. N.Y. Bible Soc. Mem. Far East- Am. Council Commerce and Industry (pres.), Gideons. Presbyn. Clubs: Canoe Brook Country (Summit, N.J.); Metropolitan, Sky, Downtown Athletic, Wall Street (N.Y.C.). Home: 51 Silver Lake Dr Summit NJ 07901 Office: 200 Park Av New York City NY 10017

ESTY, JOHN CUSHING, Jr., educator; b. White Plains, N.Y., Aug. 9, 1928; s. John Cushing and Virginia Bellaurie (Place) E.; B.A., Amherst Coll., 1950, L.H.D., 1970; M.A., Yale, 1951; postgrad. U. Cal. at Berkeley, 1959-60; m. Katharine Woolsey Cole, Dec. 21, 1955; children—Daniel Cushing, Paul Cameron, Benjamin Cole, Joshua Dwight. Asst. dean, asst. dir. admission Amherst Coll., 1953-58, asso. dean, 1958-63, lectr. math., 1958-63; headmaster Taft Sch., Watertown, Conn., 1963—. Served to 1st lt. USAF, 1951-53; capt. Res. Mem. Math. Assn. Am., History Sci. Soc., Phi Beta Kappa, Sigma Xi, Psi Upsilon. Conglist. Address: Taft School Watertown CT 06795

ETCHEN, FREDERICK RUDOLPH, Jr., advt. exec.; b. Chgo., Aug. 4, 1923; s. Frederick Rudolph and Ethyle (Park) E.; student So. Meth. U., 1941-42; m. Harriett McCormick, July 9, 1948; children—James Randolph, John Hugh, Joel Frederick. Sales mgr. explosive dept. Western Hercules Power Co., 1946-50; dist. mgr. Remington div. E. I. DuPont de Nemours & Co., Inc., Seattle, 1950- 52; v.p. sales Jarvis Mfg. Co., Wichita, Kan., 1953-66; sr. v.p. gen. mgr.; Pitts., 1959-61, exec. v.p. Pitts., 1961-66, now dir.; vice chmn. bd. Communications Counselors, Inc., Pitts., 1967; v.p. Inter-Public, Inc., 1967-69; chmn. bd., pres. Sovereign Industries, Inc., Phoenix, 1969—; dir. Erwin Wasey of Can., Ltd. Served with USNR, World War II. Mem. Am. Petroleum Inst., Ducks Unltd. (Pa. chmn., nat. trustee). Clubs: Duquesne (Pitts.): Rolling Rock (Ligonier, Pa.); Tavern (Chgo.); Marco Polo (N.Y.C.). Author articles, books on shooting. Home: Burnt Chimney Farm RD 4 Ligonier PA 15658 Office: 3018 E Weldon St Phoenix AZ 85016

ETCHESON, AUDREY THOMAS, banker; b. Webb City, Mo., July 1, 1911; s. Elijah Thomas and Bessie Edith (Holforty) E.; B.S., U. Ill., 1934; m. Genevieve Eileen Mott, June 26, 1937; 1 dau., Patricia Jean. Exec. v.p. Ill. Bankers Assn., 1954-60, dir., 1961—; exec. v.p. Lake Shore Nat. Bank, Chgo., 1960-61, pres., 1962—, dir., 1959—. Pres. Central States Banking Conf., 1959-60; mem. Ill. Banking Adv. Bd., 1958-67; mem. U. S. Treasury Savs. Bond Adv. Com. for Ill., 1955—. Trustee Ill. Council on Econ. Edn.; bd. dirs. Lawson YMCA. Mem. Am. Soc. Assn. Execs., Mil. Order World Wars, Am. Legion, Am. (adv. com. on state legislation 1962-66, state chmn. com. on econ. edn. 1966-67, mem. exec. council 1966—, savs. bond coordinator for Ill. 1967—), Ill. (chmn. state com. on legislation 1960-65, 70—, vice chmn., 1965-70, mem. council of adminstrn. 1961-68, 70—, treas. 1963-64, dir. 1961—; hon. life mem.) bankers assns., Asso. Employers Ill. (treas. 1966—, dir.), Chgo., Ill. chambers commerce, Greater N. Michigan Av. Assn. (dir., treas. 1960-62), 40 and 8, Assn. U.S. Army (dir.), Newcomen Soc., Chgo. Assn. Commerce and Industry, Chgo. Council Fgn. Relations. Clubs: Economic, Bankers, University, Chicago Press, Executives (exec. dir. 1947- 54, bd. dirs. 1954-58, hon. life mem.) (Chgo.); Hinsdale (Ill.) Golf. Home: 24 E 9th St Hinsdale IL 60521 Office 605 N Michigan Av Chicago IL 60611

ETEMADI, NOUR AHMAD, Afghanistanian govt. ofcl.; b. 1920; ed. Istiqlal Lyceum, Kabul U. Formerly in diplomatic posts in London and Washington; with econ. sect. Ministry Fgn. Affairs, 1953-64, dep. minister fgn. affairs, 1963, minister fgn. affairs, 1965—, ambassador to Pakistan, 1964; now also prime minister. Address: Office of Prime Minister Kabul Afghanistan*

ETHER, JOHN ALFRED, educator; b. N.Y.C., Aug. 11, 1927; s. Nicholas J. and Elizabeth (Chapman) E.; B.S., City Coll. N.Y., 1942-47; M.A., Columbia Tchrs. Coll., 1948, Ed.D., 1956; m. Mildred Berwind, July 7, 1946; children—Candice, Diane, Margo. Tchr. English Bronx Vocational High Sch., 1948, William E. Grady Vocational High Sch., Bklyn., 1949, pub. sch. 98, N.Y.C., 1949-52; adminstrv. asst. to supt. Guilderland (N.Y.) Central Sch. Dist., 1952-53; prin. Westmere Elementary Sch., Guilderland, 1953-59; supt. schs., Mineville, N.Y., 1959-62; prof. edn. State U. N.Y. at Albany, 1962—. Bd. dirs. Albany chpt. A.R.C., 1962—. Served with USAF 1946-47. Kellog intern, 1952. Mem. N.Y. State Assn. Elementary Sch. Prins., Am. Assn. Sch. Adminstrs., N.Y. State Assn. Supervision and Curriculum Devel. Author: Current Curricula Issues, 1965. Editor: (with Ellen Regan) The Disaffected Child, 1965. Home: Brandle Rd Altamont NY 12009 Office: State Univ NY at Albany 1400 Washington Av Albany NY 12003

ETHEREDGE, ROBERT FOSTER, lawyer; b. Birmingham, Ala., July 14, 1920; s. Joel H. and Nell (Cain) E.; A.B., U. Ala., 1946, LL.B., 1949; m. Joanna Carson, Aug. 28, 1948; children—Robert Foster, Carson, Nancy. Admitted to Ala. bar, 1949, since practiced in Birmingham; partner firm Spain, Gillon, Riley, Tate & Ansley, and predecessor, 1949—. Mem. Ala. Ho. of Reps. from Jefferson County, 1963—. Mem. adv. com. Family Ct. Bd. dirs. Ala., Jefferson County socs. crippled children and adults, No. Ala. Rehab. Facility. Served to 1st lt. AUS, 1943- 46. Mem. Am., Birmingham bar assns., Ala. State Bar, Internat. Assn. Ins. Counsel, Ala. Law Inst., Ala. Def. Lawyers Assn., Farrah Law Soc., Am. Legion, V.F.W., Omicron Delta Kappa, Pi Kappa Alpha. Democrat. Methodist. Elk, Eagle, Rotarian. Clubs: Birmingham Country, Relay House (Birmingham). Home: 3748 Locksley Dr Birmingham AL 35223 Office: First Nat Bldg Birmingham AL 35203

ETHERIDGE, JACK PAUL, judge; b. Atlanta, Mar. 16, 1927; s. Anton Lee and Jessie Shephard (Brown) E.; grad. Darlington Sch., Rome, Ga., 1945; B.S., Davidson Coll., 1949; LL.B., Emory U., 1955; m. Ursula Schlatter, Feb. 2, 1952; children—Jack Paul, Margaret Ann, Mary Elizabeth. Admitted to Ga. bar, 1955, since practiced in Atlanta; mem. firm Huie, Etheridge & Harland, 1959-66; mem. Ga. Gen. Assembly from Fulton County, 1963-66; judge Fulton Superior Ct., 1966—. Mem. adv. bd. Juvenile Ct. Atlanta, 1961-64; mem. Ga. Crime Commn., 1971—. Bd. dirs. Atlanta Legal Aid Soc., 1960-70; trustee Davidson Coll., 1966—, Arts Festival of Atlanta, 1971—, Wesley Homes, Inc., 1971—. Served with USNR, 1945-46; with AUS, 1949-52. Named Young Man of Year in Professions, Atlanta Jr. C. of C., 1962. Mem. Atlanta Bar Assn. (pres. 1962-63), Atlanta Hist. Soc. (trustee 1969—), Beta Theta Pi. Presbyn. Home: 4715 Harris Trail NW Atlanta GA 30327 Office: Courthouse Atlanta GA 30303

ETHERIDGE, RICHARD EMMET, educator, zoologist; b. Houston, Sept. 16, 1929; s. Jerry Haller and Ethel (Hans) E.; B.S., Tulane U., 1951; M.S., U. Mich., 1952, Ph.D., 1959. NSF fellow U. So. Cal., 1959-60, lectr., 1960-61; mem. faculty zoology San Diego State Coll., 1961—, prof., 1968—, chmn. dept., 1969—. Research asso. Los Angeles County Mus., 1961—, Ohio State U., 1961-62; curator herpetology San Diego Natural History Mus., 1962—; interim curator herpetology U. Fla., 1963-64. Served with USNR, 1952-56. Mem. Am. Soc. Ichthyologists and Herpetologists (gov. 1967-69), So. Cal. Acad. Scis. (dir. 1967—), Herpetologists League (exec. council 1967—). Editorial bd. Herpetologica, 1966—. Contbr. articles profl. jours. Home: 4865 Lucille Pl San Diego CA 92115

ETHERINGTON, EDWIN DEACON, univ. pres.; b. Bayonne, N.J., Dec. 25, 1924; s. Charles K. and Ethel (Bennett) E.; grad. Lawrenceville Sch., 1943; B.A. with honors and distinction, Wesleyan U., 1948; LL.B., Yale, 1952; m. Katherine Colean, Sept. 11, 1953; children—Edwin D., Kenneth C., Marion, Robert. Asst. dean, instr. English, Wesleyan U., 1948-49; asst. instr. Yale Law Sch., 1951-52; admitted to D.C. bar, 1953, N.Y. bar, 1955; law clk. Judge Ct. of Appeals, Washington, 1952-53; asso. Wilmer & Broun, Washington, 1953- 54, Milbank, Tweed, Hope & Hadley, N.Y.C., 1954-56; sec. N.Y. Stock Exchange, 1956-58, v.p., 1958-61; partner Pershing & Co., 1961-62; pres. Am. Stock Exchange, 1962-66; pres. Wesleyan U., Middletown, Conn., 1966-70; pres. Nat. Center for Voluntary Action, Washington, 1971—. Dir. Am. Express Co., N.Y.C., Conn. Gen. Life Ins. Group, Hartford, U.S. Trust Co. of N.Y., So. New Eng. Telephone Co., New Haven. Chmn. Conn. Gov.'s Commn. on Services and Expenditures, 1971; mem. hon. com. sponsors, 50th Anniversary, League Woman Voters; Incprporator Nat. Housing Partnership. Hon. trustee Neighborhood Council, Montclair, N.J.; trustee Alfred P. Sloan Found., N.Y.C., Schumann Found., Montclair, Martin Luther King, Jr. Meml. Center, Atlanta. Served with AUS 1943-44. Mem. Socratic Lit. Soc. (dir.), Internat. Platform Assn., Nat. Planning Assn. (nat. council), Pilgrims of U.S., Phi Beta Kappa, Kappa Beta Phi, Phi Delta Phi, Order of Coif. Conglist. Clubs: Down Town Assn. (N.Y.C.); Black Hall Golf, Old Lyme Country (Old Lyme Conn.), Hartford, (Conn.); Jupiter Island, Hobe Sound (Fla.); Montclair Golf; Metropolitan. Home: Sill Lane Old Lyme CT 06371

ETHERINGTON, ROGER BENNETT, banker; b. Bayonne, N.J., Nov. 18, 1923; s. Charles K. and Ethel (Bennett) E.; student Wesleyan U., Middletown, Conn., 1941-43, 47-48; A.B., Columbia, 1950; m. Barbara H. Dean, Nov. 22, 1946; children-Sandra, Kim Anne, Caryn, R. Barrie. With Am. Nat. Bank & Trust, Montclair, N.J., 1950—, pres. 1969—. Treas. United Fund W. Essex, Montclair Ambulance Assn; v.p. Montclair Art Mus. Trustee Montclair State Coll. Devel. Fund, Montclair Urban Coalition, Mt. Hebron Cemetery Assn., Montclair YMCA. Served as officer AUS, 1943-46, 51-52. Mem. Montclair C. of C. (trustee), Montclair Bus. Assn. (trustee), Morgan Horse Club, NJ. Morgan Horse Assn. (pres. 1967). Conglist. (trustee, treas. 1964-67). Club: Montclair Golf. Home: 465 Park St Upper Monclair NJ 07043 Office: 475 Bloomfield Av Montclair NJ 07042

ETHINGTON, JAMES W., aerospace mfg. co. exec.; b. Terre Haute, Ind., Aug. 8, 1917; s. Joseph L. and Emma (Lundgren) E.; student Dickinson Sch. Bus., 1939, Sch. Credit and Financial Mgmt., Dartmouth Coll., 1954; m. Marian Ostrom, May 9, 1942; children—Julie M., James E., Janice M., John William, Joseph A. With Sundstrand Corp., Rockford, Ill., 1939—, controller, 1955-57, treas., 1957-64, financial v.p., sec. 1964-68, pres., now vice chmn.; dir. RFD Screw Products Co., Modern Metal Products Co., Standard Am. Life Ins., Colonial Nat. Bank. Bd. dirs. Goodwill Industries. Mem. Ill., Rockford chambers commerce, Financial Execs. Inst., M.A.P.I. Lutheran. Clubs: Forest Hills Country; Union League (Chgo.). Home: 2902 Springcreek Rd Rockford IL Office: 2531 11th St Rockford IL 61101

ETHRIDGE, MARK FOSTER, ret. pub. exec.; b. Meridian, Miss., Apr. 22, 1896; s. William Nathaniel and Mary (Howell) E.; student U. Miss., 1914-15, Mercer U., 1916-17; m. Willie Snow, Oct. 12, 1921; children—Mary Snow, Mark Foster, Goergia Cubbedge and William Davidson. Began as reporter for Meridian Star, 1913, later reporter with Columbus (Ga.) Enquirer Sun; city editor, Macon (Ga.) Telegraph 1919-22, mng. editor, 1925-33; with N.Y. Sun and Consol. Rress. 1923-24, A.P., 1933; asst. gen. mgr. Washington Post, 1933-34; pres. and pub. Richmond (Va.) Times Dispatch, 1934- 36; v.p. and gen. mgr. Courier Jour. and Louisville Times, 1936-42, pub., 1942-62, chmn. bd., 1962-63; v.p., editor Newsday, Garden City, L.I., N.Y., 1963-65. Visited Balkans for State Dept., 1945; Am. del. to U.N. Commn. to Study Greek Border Disputes, 1947; chmn. U.S. adv. commn. on information, 1948-50; lectr. journalism U. N.C., 1965-66. Trustee Ford Found., 1954-67. Served from yeoman to ensign USN, 1917- 19. Mem. Sigma Alpha Epsilon, Sigma Delta Chi. Democrat. Baptist. Club: Century Assn. Home: Route 1 Moncure NC 27559

ETHRIDGE, MARK FOSTER, Jr., newspaperman; b. N.Y.C., July 29, 1924; s. Mark Foster and Willie (Snow) E.; grad. Phillips Exeter Acad., 1942; A.B., Princeton, 1946; m. Margaret Burns Furbee, Apr. 24, 1948; children—Mark Foster III, Russell F., Margaret B., Mary D. Reporter, Winston-Salem (N.C.). Jour., 1947-50, London (Eng.) Daily Mail, 1950-51; asst. city editor Washington Post, 1951-52; editor editorial page Newsday, L.I., 1952-55; editor Raleigh (N.C.) Times, 1955-57. Ravenswood (Va.) News, 1957-60, Detroit Free Press, 1967—; v.p. Star Printing & Pub. Co., Ravenswood, W.Va.; dir. Ravenswood News. Trustee Merrill Inst., Detroit, U. Mich. Dearborn Campus. Served with Am. Field Service, 1943-45. Mem. Am. Soc. Newspaper Editors, Internat. Press Inst., Detroit Hist. Soc., Sigma Delta Chi. Clubs: Detroit; St. Clair River Country. Home: 686 Washington Rd Grosse Pointe MI 48230 Office: 321 Lafayette Blvd Detroit MI 48226

ETHRIDGE, SAMUEL BROUGHTON, assn. exec.; b. Brewton, Ala., Dec. 22, 1923; s. Frank and Lillie (Foster) E.; student Stillman Jr. Coll., 1940-42; A.B., Howard U., 1948; M.Ed., U. Cin., 1957; m. Cordia Elizabeth Baylor, Nov. 11, 1946; children—Samuel David, Sherman George, Camille LaVerne, Steven Edsel. Tchr., Central High Sch., Mobile, Ala., 1948-54; prin. Chickasaw Terrace Sch., Mobile County, 1954-56; supr. secondary schs., Mobile, 1956-58; asst. dir. intergroup relations Nat. Found.-March of Dimes, N.Y.C., 1958-60; free lance fund raising, pub. relations, N.Y.C., 1960-62; dir. So. region United Negro Coll. Fund, Atlanta, 1962-64; asst. sec. Commn. on Profl. Rights and Responsibilities, N.E.A., Washington, 1964-65, asso. sec., 1965-67, dir. Center for Human Relations, 1967—, asst. sec. tchr. rights, 1969—; asso. Nat. Tng. Labs. Camping chmn. Mobile Area, Boy Scouts Am., 1951-58; chmn. alumni fund dr. Stillman Coll., 1966-68. Bd. dirs. Nat. Comm. Against Discrimination in Housing. Served with USAAF, 1943-46. Mem. Am. Bridge Assn. (pub. relations dir. 1965-67). Home: 1602 Allison St NW Washington DC 20011 Office: 1201 16th St NW Washington DC 20036

ETHRIDGE, WILLIE SNOW, author; b. Savannah, Ga., Dec. 10, 1900; d. William Aaron and Georgia (Cubbedge) Snow; A.B., Wesleyan Coll., Macon Ga., 1920; Litt.D., U. Ky., 1942; Litt.D., Ohio Wesleyan U., 1962; m. Mark Foster Ethridge, Oct. 12, 1921; children—Mary Snow, Mark, Georgia, David. Reporter Macon (Ga.) Telegraph, 1920; writer newspaper and mag. articles, 1920—, contbg. to well known publs. Recipient Minerva Award for merit U. Louisville, 1963. Carl Schurz Found. fellowship, 1933. Democrat. Author books including; As I Live and Breathe, 1937; Mingled Yarn, 1937; I'll Sing One Song, 1941; This LIttle Pig Stayed Home, 1944; It's Greek To Me, 1948; Going to Jerusalem, 1950; Let's Talk Turkey, 1952; Nila, 1956; Summer Thunder, 1959; Russian Duet, 1959; There's Yeast in the Middle East, 1963; I Just Happen to Have Some Pictures, 1964; You Can't Hardly Get There from Here, 1965; Strange Fires, 1971. Home: Route 1 Moncure NC 27559

ETKIN, BERNARD, educator; b. Toronto, Ont., Can., May 7, 1918; s. Harry and Mary (Goldberg) E.; B.A.Sc., U. Toronto, 1941, M.A. Sc., 1947; D.Eng. (hon.), Carleton U., 1971; m. Maya Kesselman, May 17, 1942; children—Carol Elizabeth (Mrs. Mario Mandarino), David Alexander. Mem. faculty U. Toronto, 1941—, lectr., 1942-48, asst. prof., 1948-53, asso. prof., 1953-57, prof., 1957—, chmn. engring. sci. div., 1967—. Cons. aerospace engring. and indsl. aerodynamics; v.p. Aercol, Toronto, 1967—. Recipient Centennial medal Govt. Can., 1967. Fellow Royal Soc. Can., Am. Inst. Aeros. and Astronautics, (Canadian Aero. and Space Inst.) (councillor 1970—; McCurdy award 1969); mem. Assn. Profl. Engrs. Ont., Am. Soc. Engring. Edn. Jewish religion. Author: Dynamics of Flight, 1959, also articles. Patentee in field. Home: 8 Bitteroot Rd Downsview 475 Ontario Canada Office: Galbraith Bldg U Toronto Toronto Ontario Canada

ETLER, ALVIN DERALD, composer, educator; b. Battle Creek, Ia., Feb. 19, 1913; s. Henry Peter and Mary (Smith) E.; student U. Ill., 1930-31, Western Res. U., 1931-33; Mus.B., Yale, 1944; m. Nancy Jean Cochran, May 28, 1967; children by previous marriage—Margo Turner (Mrs. Thomas D. Doyle), David Christian, Margaret Mary (Mrs. James A. Homola); one dau., Susan Lee, Began career as free-lance oboist, 1933-38; oboist Indpls. Symphony Orch., 1938-40; instr. Yale, 1942-46; asst. prof. Cornell U., 1946-47; asso. prof. U. Ill., 1947-49; prof. music Smith Coll., 1949—, Henry Dike Sleeper prof. music. 1968—; vi.s prof. Mt. Holyoke Coll., 1952-53, 59-60, Yale, 1965-66; artist in residence U. Wis. at Milw., summer 1960; tour Latin Am. with N. Am. Woodwind Quintet, 1941; an inaugurater, planner Festival Contemporary Music, U. Ill., 1948, Yaddo Festival Contemporary Music, 1952; judge student composer awards Broadcast Music, Inc., 1963, 67, young composer awards Am. Fedn. Music Clubs, 1954, 55; com. Mary Duke Biddle scholarship awards, 1966. Recipient 4th award Concours Mus. Internat. Reine Elisabeth de Belgique, 1953; Guggenheim fellow, 1940-41, 63. Mem. Phi Mu Alpha. Composer: Woodwind Quintet I, 1955, II, 1957; Concerto in One Movement for Orchestra, 1957; Sonata for Viola and Harpsichord, 1959; Ode to Pothos for Mixed Chorus, 1960; Concerto for Woodwind Quintet and Orchestra; Triptych for Orchestra, 1961; Concerto for Clarinet and Chamber Group, 1962; Quintet for Bass Instruments, 1963; Quartet I for Strings, 1963, II, 1965; Onomatopoesis for Male Chorus, Winds, Brass and Percussion, 1965; Concerto for Brass Quintet, String Orchestra and Percussion, 1967; Concerto for String Quartet and Orchestra, 1967; Convivialities for Orchestra, 1967. Home: 130 Leverett Rd Amherst MA 01002 Office: Sage Hall Smith Coll Northampton MA 01060

ETNIER, STPHEN MORGAN, artist; b. York, Pa., Sept. 11, 1903; s. Carey and Susan Ellen (Smith) E.; student Yale, Class of 1926, Haverford, Class of 1928, Pa. Acad. Fine Arts, 1925-29; A.F.D., Bates Coll., 1969, Bowdoin Coll., 1969; m. Mathilde Gray, June 1926 (div. 1932); m. 2d, Elizabeth Jay, June 1933 (div. 1948); m. 3d, Jane Pearce, Sept. 1948 (dec. June 1949); m. 4th, Samuella Rose, Apr. 5, 1950; children—Suzanne (Mrs. Bruce Hughes), Penelope (Mrs. David Dinsmore), Stephanie (Mrs. John Doane), Victoria (Mrs. Rafael Villamil), John, David. Paintings represented permanent collections Met. Mus., N.Y.C., Boston Mus., Avery Meml., Hartford, Conn., Toledo (O.) Mus., New Britain Mus., Phillips Meml. Mus., Washington, Farnsworth Mus., Rockland, Me., Vassar Coll., Pa. Acad. Fine Arts, Bowdoin Coll., Brunswick, Me., Fairleigh Dickinson Coll., Rutherford, N.J., Buck Hill Art Assn., Buck Hill Falls, Pa., IBM, Dallas, Los Angeles, Springfield (Mass.) museums, Marine Mus., Searsport, Me., Brooks Meml. Mus., Memphis, Parrish Art Mus., Southampton, L.I., several others; murals Everett (Mass.), Spring Valley (N.Y.) post offices, Served as lt. USNRF World War II. Recipient Hon. mention Chgo. Art Inst., 1932; Saltus gold medal N.A.D., 1955, 2d Altman prize, 1956, Samuel F.B. Morse medal, 1964, purchase prize Butler Art Inst., Youngstown, O. Academinician N.A.D. Home: Old Cove South Harpswell ME 04079 Address: Midtown Galleries 11 E 57th St New York City NY 10022

ETRA, MAX JACOB, lawyer; b. Galicia, Austria, Apr. 24, 1903; s. Aaron and Sarah (Goldman) E.; brought to U.S., 1907, naturalized, 1915; B.S., Coll. City N.Y., 1924; J.D., Fordham U., 1928; LL.D., Yeshiva U., 1958. Admitted to N.Y. bar, 1929, since practiced in N.Y.C. Chmn. bd. trustees Yeshiva U.; trustee Ramaz Sch.; v.p. Beth Israel Hosp.; hon. pres. Union Orthodox Jewish Congregations Am., Congregation Kehilath Jeshurun; mem. nat. council Boy Scouts Am. Founder, mem. bd. overseers Albert Einstein Coll. Medicine; chmn. Am. Jewish Tercentenary. Mem. Assn. Bar City N.Y., N.Y. County Lawyers Assn., Am. Jewish Hist. Soc., Am. Assn. Jewish Edn. (gov.), Grand St. Boys Assn., Friars. Elk. Home: 21 E 87th St New York City NY 10028 Office: 745 Fifth Av New York City NY 10022

ETS, MARIE HALL, (Mrs. Harold Ets), author, illustrator; b. Milw.; d. Walter Augustus and Mathilda (Carhart) Hall; student N.Y. Sch. Fine and Applied Art, 1916-17; Ph.B., U. Chgo., 1924; student art Art Inst. Chgo.; student Chgo. Sch. Civics and Philanthropy, U. Chgo., Columbia; m. Milton T. Rodig, Nov. 30, 1917 (dec. Jan. 1918); m. 2d, Harold N. Ets, June 6, 1930 (dec. June 1943). Author, illustrator children's books: Mister Penny, 1935, The Story of a Baby, 1939, In the Forest, 1944; (with Ellen Tary and A.A. Alland) My Dog Rinty, 1946; Oley: The Sea Monster, 1947; Little Old Automobile, 1948; Mr. T.W. Anthont Woo, 1951; Beasts and Nonsense, 1952; Another Day, 1953; Play With Me, 1955; Mister Penny's Race Horse, 1956; Cow's Party, 1958; (with Aurora Labestida) Nine Days to Christmas: A Story of Mexico, 1959; Mister Penny's Circus, 1961; Gilberto and the Wind, 1963 (honor book N.Y. Herald Tribune Children's Spring Book Festival 1963); Automobiles for Mice, 1964; Just Me, 1965; Bad Boy, Good Boy, 1967; Talking Without Words, 1968; Rosa: The Life of an Italian Immigrant, 1970; Elephant in a Well, 1971. Vol. resident Chgo. Commons, 1919- 29; orgn. for Child Health in Czechoslovakia, A.R.C., 1923-24; investigator U.S. Coal Commn., W.Va. and So. Ill. mining camps, 1926—. Recipient prize N.Y. Herald Tribune Spring Book Festival, 1947; honor book Internat. Jury for H.C. Hendersen medal, Stockholm, 1956; recipient Caldecott medal, 1960. Address: 501 W 123d St New York City NY 10027

ETS-HOKIN, JEREMY MOSES, corp. exec.; b. San Francisco, July 3, 1926; s. Abraham Louis and Rose (Hartman) Ets-H.; B.A., Stanford; m. Judith Bregman, Apr. 23, 1961; children—Celeste, Emily, Joshua, Rebecca, Solomon, Gabriel. Job supt. Ets-Hokin & Galvan, 1949-55, mgr. San Francisco br., 1955-59; v.p. sales Ets-Hokin Corp., San Francisco, 1959- 60, pres., 1960-68; pres. Applied Urbanology, Inc., 1969—; dir. Murphy-Pacific Corp., Judson- Pacific-Murphy, Hidrocivil Corp., S.Am., Madrid, Tech. Constrn. Co., Cal. Union Bank, Murphy Pacific Salvage Co. Chmn. Cal. Ship Bddg. Commn. Mem. San Francisco Art Commn.; chmn. Western States Conf. Municipal Art Authorities. Chmn. trustees Conf. Municipal Art Authorities, Spanish Speaking Citizens Found. Served with USCGR, World War II. Mem. Nat. Assn. Corrosion Engrs., Assn. Illumination Engrs., Air Force Assn., UN Assn. (nat. committeeman). Democrat. Jewish religion. Clubs: Commonwealth; World Trade; Press. Exhbns. of paintings in one-man and group shows, San Francisco, N.Y.C., Boston and Maine. Author: Transfiguration of a Fat Slob, 1968. Contbr. San Francisco mag. Home: 3421 Pacific Av San Francisco CA 94123 Office: 1208 Market St San Francisco CA 94105

ETS-HOKIN, LOUIS, engring. co. exec.; b. Chgo., July 28, 1893; s. Samuel and Esther (Simon) Ets-H.; A.B., Cornell U., 1915, M.E., 1917; m. Rose Hartman, June 19, 1921; children—Jeremy M., Esther Naomi (Mrs. Robert S. Leuter). Pres. Ets-Hokin Corp., and predecessor, San Francisco, 1920-59, chmn. bd. Murphy-Pacific Marine Slavage Co. Pres. Assn. Boat Industries, 1946-49, San Francisco Marine Exchange, 1954-56, Western Ship-bldg. Assn., 1959-61; environmental engineer Civil Defense, 1968—; chmn. Gov. Cal. Com. Ship-bldg., 1953-58; mem. San Francisco Bay Conservation and Development Commn., 1965—. bd. dirs. San Francisco Fedn. Jewish Charities, 1950-54; pres. San Francisco Maritime Mus. 1955-57; adv. bd. San Francisco Bay Transp. Study. Served with U.S. Navy, 1917-19. Registered profl. engr., Cal. Home: 999 Green St San Francisco CA 94133 Office: 551 Mission St San Francisco CA 94105

ETSTEN, BENJAMIN, physician; b. Lawrence, Mass., May 24, 1908; s. Louis and Bertha (DuFine) E.; B.S., Tufts U., 1932; M.D., St. Andrew's Med. Sch., 1936; m. Jessica Drooz, Feb. 18, 1938; children—Pamela Susan, Edward Louis, Thomas Paige. Resident anesthesia Albany Hosp., 1938-40, dir. dept. anesthesia, 1942-48; instr. anesthesia Albany Med. Sch., 1940-41, asst. prof., 1942-48, asso. prof. pharmacology and physiology, 1943-48; asst. prof. anesthesia Tufts U. Sch. Medicine, 1949-50, asso. prof., 1950-52, asso. pharmacology, 1950—, prof. anesthesia, 1952—; dir. dept. anesthesia New Eng. Center Hosp. and Med. Center, 1948—; cons. anesthesia VA Hosp., Lemuel Shattuck, New Eng., St. Margaret's hosps., Boston, Cape Cod Hosp., Hyannis, Mass. Diplomate Am. Bd. Anesthesiology. Mem. Am., Mass. (pres. 1957-58) socs. anesthesiologists, Am. Coll. Anesthesiology (gov. 1945-51), Mass. Med. Soc. (chmn. sect. Anesthesiology 1953-54, pres. Assn. U. Anesthetists (charter mem., pres 1965—), New Eng., Mass. (sec.-treas. 1955- 56) socs. anesthesiology, Am. Soc. Pharmacology and Exptl. Therapeutics. Editorial Cons. Oral Surgery, Oral Medicine, Oral Pathology. Home: 37 Gordon Rd Milton MA 02187 Office: New England Center Hospital Harrison Av and Bennet St Boston MA 02111

ETTELDORF, RAYMOND PHILIP, archbishop; b. Ossian, Ia., Aug. 12, 1911; s. Andrew and Regina (Wagner) E.; student Conception (Mo.) Coll., 1929-30; B.A., Loras Coll., Dubuque, Ia., 1934; student Gregorian U., Rome, Italy, 1934-38; J.C.L., Lateran U., Rome, 1956. Ordained priest Roman Catholic Ch., 1937; mng. editor The Witness, Dubuque, 1939-46, editor-in-chief, 1945-51; apptd. ofcl. of Sacred Congregation for Oriental Chs., Vatican, 1951-64; sec. gen. Superior Council of Papal Soc. for Propagation of the Faith, Rome, 1964-68; sec. Prefecture for Econ. Affairs, Vatican, 1968; apostolic del. to New Zealand and Islands of Pacific, 1968—; named titular archbishop of Tindari, 1968; ordained to episcopal dignity by Pope Paul VI, 1969. Author: The Catholic Church in the Middle East, 1959; The Soul of Greece, 1963. Address: 112 Queen's Dr Wellington 3 New Zealand

ETTELSON, GEORGE W., mfg. co. exec.; b. 1925; grad. Yale, 1945; M.B.A., Harvard, 1949; married. With R.H. Macy Co., 1949-60; asst. to pres. Dymo Industries Inc., Emeryville, Cal., 1963-64, v.p., 1964-67, exec. v.p., dir., 1967—. Served with USNR, 1943-46. Office: 6701 Bay St Emeryville CA 94608*

ETTELSON, LEONARD BERT, lawyer; b. Chgo., Mar. 6, 1905; s. Benjamin J. and Julia (Sanditz) E.; A.B., U. Mich., 1924; J.D., U. Chgo., 1947; LL.D., Ill. Wesleyan U., 1955; m. Lueka Bone, Aug. 6, 1934; 1 dau., Leanne. Admitted to Ill. bar, 1927; law clk. Schuyler, Ettelson & Weinfeld, Chgo., 1927; Now partner firm Ettelson, O'Hagan, Ehrlich & Frankel, Chgo. Chmn. bd. First Drovers Corp.; dir. Allied Structural Steel Co., Drovers Nat. Bank, Chgo., Lytton's, Henry C. Lytton & Co., Chgo. Mem.-at-large Boy Scouts Am. Chmn. trustees Barat Coll.; bd. dirs. Henrotin Hosp., Chgo. Mem. Am. Ill., Chgo. bar assns., Chgo., Mich. alumni assns. Clubs: Mich. Union (Ann Arbor); Tower, MidAmerica (Chgo.); Bankers, Lawyers (N.Y.C.); Racquet (Palm Springs, Cal.); LaQuinta Country (Cal.). Home: 1040 Lake Shore Dr Chicago IL 60611 Office: 209 S LaSalle St Chicago IL 60604

ETTER, BETTY, editor; b. Sigourney, Ia., Aug. 3, 1911; d. William Luther and Flora Alice (Cotton) Etter; student Wilson Coll., 1927-29; B.J., U. Mo., 1931; m. Everett Meyers, Jan. 19, 1959. Reporter, Ponca City (Okla.) Daily News, 1931-32; society editor Cedar Rapids (Ia.) Gazette, 1932-34; asso. editor Bankers mag., 1935-37, Am. Home, 1938-40; editor Ideal Pub. Co., 1941-51, Lady's Circle, N.Y.C., 1967—; tchr. mag. editing Coll. City N.Y. Club: Overseas Press of N.Y.C. (gov.). Home: 78 State St Brooklyn NY 11201 Office: 21 W 26th St New York City NY 10010

ETTER, DAVID PEARSON, poet; b. Huntington Park, Cal., Mar. 18, 1928; s. Harold Pearson and Judith (Goodenow) E.; B.A., U. Ia., 1953; m. Margaret Ann Cochran, Aug. 8, 1959; children—Emily Louise, George Goodenow. Editor Northwestern U. Press, Evanston, Ill., 1961-63; asst. editor Ency. Brit., Chgo., 1964- 66, staff writer, 1966—. Served with USA, 1953-55. Mem. Midland Authors, Ill. Hist. Soc. Democrat. Author: (poems) Go Read the River, 1966, The Last Train to Prophetstown, 1968, Strawberries, 1970. Contbr. poems lit. mags. Home: 416 S 1st St Geneva IL 60134 Office: 425 N Michigan Av Chicago IL 60611

ETTER, HARRY STOUGH, naval officer; b. Shippensburg, Pa., Oct. 15, 1915; s. Harry Blaine and Helen Augusta (Stough) E.; M.D., Duke, 1940; m. Frances Goodhart July 14, 1936; children—Barbara (Mrs. Ross Berkowitz), Rachel (Mrs. James Anderton), Betty (Mrs. Gary Speicher), Patricia Jean, Harry Stough, Robert Goodhart, Nancy Jo. Commd. lt. (j.g.), M.C., USN, 1940, advanced through grades to rear adm., 1967; dir. planning div. Bur-Medicine and Surgery, 1962-65; exec. officer Naval Hosp., Portsmouth, Va., 1965-66; comdg. officer Naval Hosp., Bethesda, Md., 1966-67; asst. chief planning and logistics Bur. Medicine and Surgery, Washington, 1967—; Mem. A.M.A., Phi Delta Theta. Republican. Lutheran. Home: 105 Primrose St Chevy Chase MD 20015 Office: Bur Medicine and Surgery 23d and E Sts NW Washington DC 20390

ETTER, LEWIS ELMER, radiologist, educator; b. Pitts., Jan. 17, 1901; s. Charles E. and Elsie M. (Gnann) E.; student U. Cal., 1920-21; B.S., U. Pitts., 1924. M.D., 1927; m. Grace D. Ripple, June 4, 1927. children—Robert L., Charles W. Instr. radiology U. Pitts. Med. Center. 1946-52, asst. prof., 1952-55, clin. asso. prof., 1955-57, prof., 1957—; also prof. radiology, chief radiol. service Western Psychiat. Inst. and Falk Clinic; staff Presbyn.- Univ. Hosp., Pitts.; cons. radiology Pitts. State Tb Hosp., Leech Farm, Pitts.; research X-ray anatomy of skull supported by grants Sarah Mellon Scaife found., 1947-53, NIH, 1960-61, Health Research and Services Found., 1962-65. Served with M.C., AUS, 1941-46. Recipient Bronze medal Am. Roentgen Ray Soc., 1964. Diplomate Am. Bd. Radiology. Fellow Am. Coll. Radiology; mem. A.M.A., Am. (certificate of merit 1946, 51, 66), Pitts. (pres. 1959-60), Ind. State, Phila. (hon. mem.) Roentgen Ray Socs., Radiol. Soc. N.A., Pa. Radiol. Soc. (pres. 1957-58), Am. Soc. Neuroradiology, Am. Assn. U. Profs., A.A.A.S., Inter Am. Coll. of Radiology, Sigma Xi. Mason. Clubs: University, Faculty (Pitts.). Author: Atlas of Roentgen Anatomy of the Skull, 1955; Glossary of Words an Phrases Used in Radiology and Nuclear Medicine 1960, 2d edit., 1970; Roentgenography and Roentgenology of the Middle Ear and Mastoid Process, 1964. Contbr. manuals, also articles to med. publs. Editor: American Lectures in Roentgen Diagnosis, 13 vols., 1958-; Modern Concepts in Radiology, Nuclear Medicine and Ultra Sound, 1967—, 16 vols. Author, editor, compiler: The Science of Ionizing Radiation, 1965. Home: Pinewood Farm Warrendale PA 15086 Office: 3601 5th Av Pittsburgh PA 15213

ETTING, EMLEN, artist; b. Phila., Aug. 24, 1905; s. Emlen Pope and Florence (Lucas) E.; student Ecole Nouvelle, Lausanne, Switzerland, 1914-17; grad. St. George's Sch., Newport, R.I., 1924; B.S., Harvard, 1928; student Academie Andre Lhote, Paris, 1929-32; m. Gloria Braggiotti, June 20, 1938. One man shows, Paris, Phila., N.Y.C., Cleve., Boston; murals include Market Street Nat. Bank, Italian Consulate, Phila.; instr. drawing, paintings Tyler Sch. Fine Arts, 1949-52, Fla. So. Coll., 1952- 54, Phila. Mus. and Sch. Art, 1953—; works represented in Whitney Mus., Addison Gallery, Pa., Acad. Fine Arts, also pvt. collections. Served as assimilated capt. French radio div. OWI, 1944-45. Decorated Italian Star of Solidarity; chevalier Legion d'Honneur (France). Member of Phila. Art Alliance, Artists Equity Assn. (hon. pres.), Alliance Francaise (hon. pres.). Society of the Cincinnati, Nat. Soc. Mural Painters, Philadelphia Athenaeum. Club: Century Assn. Home: 1927 Panama St Philadelphia PA 19103 Office: care Midtown Galleries 11 E 57th St E 56th St New York City NY 10022

ETTINGER, AUSTEN ARNOLD, advt. exec.; b. N.Y.C., Feb. 23, 1923; s. Bertrand and Lucy E. (Costabile) E.; m. Shirley Riche, June 5, 1944; 1 son, John R. With McCall Corp., N.Y.C., 1956-62, advt. promotion mgr., 1956-58, asst. pub. Redbook mag., 1958-62; with Crowell-Collier Pub. Co., 1962-63, asst. gen. mgr. Collier Books, N.Y.C.; pres. Jameson Advt., Inc., N.Y.C., 1963—. Home: 345 E 56th St New York City NY 10022 Office: 10 E 44th St New York City NY 10017

ETTINGER, GEORGE HAROLD, ret. educator; b. Kingston, Ont., Can., May 9, 1896; s. John George and Elizabeth Jane (Watts) E.; B.A., Queen's U., 1916, M.D., 1920; student U. Chgo., 1923, U. Edinburgh, 1928-29; D.Sc., U. Western Ont., 1958; M.D. (hon.), U. Ottawa, 1963; LL.D., Queen's U., 1967; m. Pearl Elizabeth Blyth, Dec. 21, 1920 (dec. 1958); 1 dau., Barbara Joan (Mrs. John Edward Hinton); m. 2d, Margaret McKay Sawyer, Apr. 19, 1969. Lectr. physiology Queen's U., 1920-29, asst. prof., 1923-33, asso. prof., 1933-37, prof., 1937-62, head dept., 1949-62, dean faculty medicine, 1949-62, research adv., 1962-64; dir. med. planning Alcoholism and Drug Addiction Research Found., Ont., 1962- 70; research asso. dept. med. research U. Toronto, 1931-35; mem. asso. com. med. research Nat. Research Council, Ottawa, 1939-46, asst. dir. div. med. research, 1946-58. Decorated Order Brit. Empire, 1946. Fellow Royal Soc. Can., A.A.A.S.; mem. Am. Assn. Anatomists, Am., Canadian physiol. socs., Physiol. Soc. Gt. Britain, Canadian Med. Assn. Home: Cartwright's Point Kingston Ontario Canada

ETTINGHAUSEN, RICHARD, educator; b. Frankfurt-on-Main, Germany, Feb. 5, 1906; s. Edmund S. and Selma (Stern) E.; Ph.D., U. Frankfurt, 1931; student Munich U., Cambridge U. (Eng.); m. Basia Gruliow, 1934 (dec. 1935); m. 2d, Elizabeth Sgalitzer, Sept. 22, 1945; children—Stephen Edmund, Thomas Andrew David. Came to U.S., 1934, naturalized, 1938. Research asso. Am. Inst. Persian Art and Archaeology, 1934- 37; mem. Inst. Advanced Study, Princeton, 1937-38; asso. prof. Islamic art U. Mich., 1938-44, research prof. Islamic art, 1949—; asso. Near Eastern art Freer Gal. of Art, Smithsonian Instn., 1944-58, curator, 1958-61, head curator, 1961-67; adj. curator Los Angeles County Mus. Art, 1967-69; adj. prof. Inst. Fine Arts, N.Y.U., 1961-67, prof., 1967—; consultive chmn. Islamic dept. Met. Mus. Art, N.Y.C., 1969—. Trustee Phillips Gallery, Washington; trustee, exec. com., chmn. accessions com. Textile Mus., Washington. Mem. Coll. Art. Assn. Am., Am. Oriental Soc., Asia House, Am. Research Center in Egypt, Internat. Soc. Oriental Research, Wash. Soc. Archeol. Inst. Am. (pres. 1960-61, 63-64), Institut d'Egypte (asso.), German Archeol. Inst. (hon.), French Academie des Inscriptions et Belles Lettres (corr.), Brit. Acad. (hon.). Author: Studies in Muslim Iconography: The Unicorn, 1950; Paintings of the Sultans and Emperors of India in American Collections, 1961; Persian Paintings in the Bernard Berenson Collection, 1961; Arab Painting, 1962. Co-author: Turkey-Ancient Miniatures, 1961; Treasures of Turkey, 1966. Editor: Annotated Bibliography of Books and Articles of the Near and Middle East, 1952; Aus der Welt der Islamichen Kunst, 1959. Editor of Ars Islamica, 1938-50; Near Eastern editor Arts Orientalis, 1954-57, mem. editorial bd., 1957-61; editorial bd. Artibus Asiae, 1971—, Art Bull.; co-editor Kunst des Orients, 1968—. Home: 24 Armour Rd Princeton NJ 08540 Office: 1 E 78th St New York City NY 10021

ETTINGTON, RICHARD M., mfg. co. exec.; b. Tulsa, July 2, 1925; s. Martin and Mildred (Westner) E.; B.S., Rensselaer Poly. Inst., 1947; m. Elizabeth Ann Kirkpatrick, Dec. 22, 1951; children—Martin Kirkpatrick, Cathryn Lynn. Mfg. engr., corporate dir. labor relations Ingersoll Rand, N.Y.C., 1947-66, gen. mgr., Painted Post, N.Y., 1966-67; v.p. mfg., pres. Alco Products, Inc., Schenectady, 1967-68; group v.p. Studebaker-Worthington, Schenectady, 1970—; chmn., chief exec. officer MLW-Worthington of Can., Montreal, Que., 1970—. Served to lt. (j.g.) USNR, World War II. Mem. Am. Soc. Mech. Engrs. Clubs: Mohawk Golf, Mohawk (Schenectady). Home: 1513 Dorwaldt Blvd Schenectady NY 12309 Office: Dorchester Towers 555 Dorchester Blvd W Montreal 128 Quebec Canada

ETZELL, GEORGE FERDINAND, mem. Republican Nat. Com.; b. Clarissa, Minn., Feb. 1, 1909; s. George A. and Ida (Hammer) E.; student pub. schs., Clarissa; m. Ione Margaret Koch, Oct. 4, 1934; children—Peter, Gretchen, Paul, Mary, Martha. Pub. Clarissa Independent, 1940—; state printer, Minn., 1939-43; spl. adviser Gov. C. Anderson, 1951-52; pres. Etzell Publs., Inc.; mem. Rep. Nat. Com. from Minn., 1952—. Dist. chmn. Young Rep. League, 1937-38; chmn. Rep. com. 6th Congl. Dist., 1945-52; chmn. rules com. Rep. nat. conv., 1960, 64. Mem. Nat., Minn. newspaper assns., Sigma Delta Chi. Roman Catholic. K.C. Clubs: Minneapolis Athletic, Minn. Press. Home: Clarissa MN 56440

ETZIONI, AMITAI WERNER, sociologist; b. Cologne, Germany, Jan. 4, 1929; s. Willi Falk and Gertrude Hannauer (Falk) E.; B.A., Hebrew U., Jerusalem, 1954, M.A., 1956; Ph.D., U. Cal. at Berkeley, 1958; m. Minerva Morales, Sept. 14, 1965; children—Ethan, Oren, Michael, David. Mem. faculty Columbia, 1958—. research asso. Inst. War and Peace Studies, 1961—, prof. sociology, 1967—, chmn. dept., 1969—, dir. Center for Policy Research, 1968—. Social Sci. Research Council faculty fellow, 1960-61, 67-68. Fellow Center for Advanced Study in Behavioral Scis., 1965-66; Guggenheim fellow, 1968. Mem. Am. Sociol. Assn. Author: A Comparative Analysis of Complex Organizations, 1961; Modern Organizations, 1964; Political Unification; A Comparative Study of Leaders and Forces, 1965; Studies in Social Change, 1966; The Active Society, 1968; also numerous articles. Mem. editorial bd. Science, 1969—. Developed organizational analysis, a typology based on means used to control mems. macrosociol. theory to study socs. able to solve their problems. Home: 450 Riverside Dr New York City NY 10027

ETZKORN, KLAUS PETER, educator; b. Karlsruhe, Germany, Apr. 18, 1932; s. Johnannes and Luisa (Schlick) E.; A.B., Ohio State U., 1955; student Ind. U., 1955-56; A.M., Princeton, 1958, Ph.D., 1959; m. Hildegard Elizabeth Garve, Sept. 3, 1953; children—Kyle Peter, Lars Peter. Came to U.S., 1952, naturalized, 1958. Asst. prof. U. Cal. at Santa Barbara, 1959-63; asso. prof. Am. U. Beirut (Lebanon), 1963-64; dir. Office Instl. Research, chmn. dept. sociology and anthropology U. Nev., 1964-67; prof., chmn. faculty sociology and anthropology U. W.Fla., 1967-68; prof. sociology San Fernando Valley State Coll., 1968-69, U. Mo.-St. Louis, 1969—; cons. in field. Mem. Gov. Nev. Com. on Dept. Correction, 1966; mem. Escambia County (Fla.) Juvenile Ct. Adv. Com., 1967; mem. Mo. Adv. Com. on Humanities. Fellow Am. Sociol. Assn., Am. Anthrop. Assn.; mem. Soc. Ethnomusicology (council 1963-71, editor spl. publs.), Inst. Internat. Sociologie, Internat. Polit. Sci. Assn. Author: The Conflict in Modern Culture, 1968; Methodology in Higher Education, 1967; Leisure and Higher Education, 1969; also articles. Home: 8042 Gannon Av St Louis MO 63130

EUBANK, SEVER LANDON, educator; b. Winona, Miss., Oct. 7, 1921; s. Ernest Wright and Betty (Grantham) E.; B.A., Colo. Coll., 1947, M.A., 1950; Ph.D., George Peabody Coll. Tchrs., 1954; m. Clara Ruth Pointer Reed, Aug. 16, 1962; children—Sever Landon, Rebecca Jan, William Rex. Instr. history Central High Sch., Jackson, Miss., 1947-51, Sebring (Fla.) pub. schs., 1953-54; prof. Howard Payne Coll., 1953-56; asst. prof. history Southeastern Okla. State Coll., 1956-62; prof. Black Hills State Coll., Spearfish, S.D., 1962—, chmn. social sci. div., 1964—. Chmn. Lawrence County (S.D.) Democratic Central Com., 1967-70; committeeman S.D. Dem. Central Com., 1970—; chmn. Brown County (Tex.) Dem. campaign, 1956; candidate for mayor of Spearfish, 1967. Mem. Rocky Mountain, S.D. (pres. 1971-72) social sci. assns., Assn. Am. Historians, Am. Legion, Spearfish C. of C. (dir. 1968, pres. 1969). Baptist. Lion (v.p. Spearfish 1968-69, pres. 1970-71). Home: 1430 W Jackson St Spearfish SD 57783

EUBANK, WAYNE CARTER, educator; b. Claude, Tex., May 23, 1909; s. John C. and Buena (Cobb) E.; B.A.W. Tex. State U., 1931; M.A., Northwestern U., 1935; Ph.D., La. State U., 1943; m. Martha Twitty, Sept. 1, 1949. Tchr., prin. Friona (Tex.) High Sch., 1931-35; grad. teaching asst. La. State U., 1939-42; chmn. dept. speech Amarillo Coll., 1935-39; asso. prof. speech, debate dir. U. Fla., 1946-49; chmn. dept. speech, prof. speech U. N.M., Albuquerque, 1949—. Served with AUS. 1942-46. Mem. Am., So. (v.p., 1948-49), Western (pres. 1955) speech assns., Am. Forensic Assn. (v.p. 1950). Tau Kappa Alpha (nat. pres. 1951-55 1963-66). Delta Sigma Rho. Kiwanian. Contbr. articles profl. jours. Home: 1113 Florida St NE Albuquerque NM 87110

EUBANK, WEAVER KEITH, educator; b. Princeton, N.J., Dec. 8, 1920; s. Weaver Keith and Grace (Holden) E.; B.A. magna cum laude, Hampden-Sydney Coll., 1942; M.A., Harvard, 1947; Ph.D., U. Pa., 1951; m. Marilyn Jean Climenson, Sept. 8, 1951; children—David Keith, Ellen Jane. Instr. history Bloomfield Coll., 1950-53; asst. prof. N. Tex. State U., 1954-56, asso. prof., 1956-59; prof., 1959-64; prof. Queens Coll. of City U. N.Y., 1964—, chmn. dept. history, 1967—. Editor Berkshire Studies in History; cons. editor Holt, Rinehart & Winston. Served with AUS, 1942-46. Mem. Am., So. hist. assns. Author: Paul Cambon, Master Diplomatist, 1960; Munich, 1963; The Summit Conferences, 1919-60, 1966; The Origins of World War II, 1969. Home: 5 Apex Rd Melville NY 11746 Office: Queens Coll Flushing NY 11367

EUBANKS, ERNEST MORRIS, chem. co. exec.; b. Effingham, Ill., July 16, 1915; s. Louis Lafayette and Amelia (Thoms) E.; B.S., U. Ill., 1937; m. Dorotha Aline Hickman, Oct. 5, 1947; children—Judith Ann, Michael Charles. Operator, Hiram Walker & Sons, Inc., Peoria, Ill., 1937-41; equipment engr. U.S. Ordnance Dept., Joliet, Ill., 1941-43; with Grain Processing Corp., Muscatine, Ia., 1943—, v.p., 1951-66, exec. v.p., 1966—. Mem. Am. Chem. Soc., Ia. Engring. Soc., Alpha Chi Sigma. Home: 1110 Halstead St Muscatine IA 52761 Office: 1600 Oregon St Muscatine IA 52761

EUBANKS, LUTHER BOYD, U.S. judge; b. Caprock, N.M., July 31, 1917; s. J.P. and Evelyn (Downs) E.; B.A., U. Okla., 1940; m. Lois Stevens, Sept. 5, 1942; children—Nancy (Mrs. Rutledge McClaran), Carolyn, Stephen. Admitted to Oklahoma bar, 1944; county atty. Cotton County, Oklahoma, 1946-49; mem. Oklahoma House Reps. from Cotton County, 1949-53; district judge, Lawton, Okla., 1956-65; U.S. district judge Western Dist. Okla., 1965—. Served with AUS, World War II; ETO. Rotarian.‡

EUBANKS, RALPH, banker; b. Elko, Ga., Oct. 18, 1908; s. C. E. and Maye (Smith) E.; A.B., B.S.C., Mercer U., 1928; m. Dorothy Slappey, Feb. 21, 1945; children—Donald Charles, David Ralph, John Smith. With Citizens & So. Nat. Bank, Macon, Ga., 1928—, v.p., 1949-57, exec. v.p., 1957—, also mem. adv. bd.; dir. Bank of Warner Robins (Ga.). Pres. Macon United Givers Fund, 1965; mem. Macon Housing Authority, 1961—, chmn., 1969-70; mem. Bibb County Bd. Edn., 1959—, treas., 1967-70, v.p., 1971. Served with AUS, 1942-44. Mem. Nat. Assn. Bank Auditors and Controllers, Am., Ga. bankers assns., Macon C. of C. (treas. 1966-67, dir. 1969-70), Delta Sigma Pi (past pres. Macon). Baptist. Elk, Lion. Clubs: Idle Hour Country (Macon, Ga.); Houston Lake Country (Perry, Ga.); Milledgeville (Ga.) Country. Home: 1414 Twin Pines Dr Macon GA 31201 Office: PO Box 4007 Macon GA 31208

EUBANKS, ROBERT ALONZO, educator; b. Chgo., June 3, 1926; s. Alonzo and Mary (Jones) E.; B.S., Ill. Inst. Tech., 1950, M.S., 1951, Ph.D., 1953; m. Helaine Lois Moody, Apr. 5, 1969. Instr., then asst. prof. mechanics Ill. Inst. Tech., 1950- 54; sr. engr. Bulova Research Lab., 1954-55; research engr. Am. Machine & Foundry Co., 1955-56; scientist Borg Warner Research Center, 1956-60; sr. scientist Armour Research Found., 1960-63; sci. adviser mech. and structrual engring. IIT Research Inst., 1963-65; prof. civil engring sd and theoretical and applied mechanics U. Ill. at Urbana, 1965—, George A. Miller vis. prof., 1964-65, exec. dir. Afro-Am. Studies Commn., 1970- -; adj. prof. Ill. Inst. Tech., 1961-64. Adviser Midwest Program Equal Ednl. Opportunity, 1969-70; pres. Council Community Integration, 1964—. Served with AUS, 1942-46. Mem. Am. Soc. M.E. (adviser 1966-69), Am. Assn. U. Profs. (chpt. pres. 1966-69), Soc. Indsl. and Applied Math., Am. Math. Soc., Acoustical Soc. Am., Am. Acad. Mechanics, Sigma Xi, Sigma Pi Sigma. Home: 2005 Vawter St Urbana IL 61801

EUGERE, EDWARD JOSEPH, educator; b. New Orleans, May 26, 1930; s. Edward and Lena (Darensbourg) E.; B.S. in Pharmacy (scholar 1949), Xavier U., New Orleans, 1951; M.S., Wayne State U., 1953; Ph.D. in Pharmacology (Fesler fellow 1954-56), U. Conn., 1956; m. Yolande Rousseve, Aug. 28, 1954; children—Edward, Jan, Gail, Lisa. Grad. teaching asst. Wayne State U., 1951-53, U. Conn., 1953-54; lectr. chemistry Detroit Inst. Tech., 1957, asst. prof. pharmacology, 1956-57; lectr. chemistry Highland Park Jr. Coll., Detroit, 1956-57; prof. pharmacology Tex. So. U., 1957—, dean Sch. Pharmacy, 1958-70. Active Mainfield (Conn.) State Sch. and Hosp.; mem. constrn. of schs. pharmacy rev. com. NIH, 1968, pharmacy rev. com., 1969—. Co-chmn. Catholic Interracial Council Houston, 1963-66. Mem. Am., Tex., Lone Star State (exec. sec. 1957-60), Houston (pres. 1958-61) pharm. assns., Am. Assn. Colls. Pharmacy, Tex. Assn. Coll. Tchrs., Harris County Pharm. Assn. (bd. dirs. 1968-69), Grand Jury Assn. Houston-Harris County (pres. 1969—, v.p. 1968-69, dir. 1967—), Houston Assn. Laymen (treas. 1970—), Chi Delta Mu (pres. Tex. 1958-61), Rho Chi, Alpha Phi Alpha. Democrat. Roman Catholic. Contbr. articles profl. jours. Home: 3306 Calumet Houston TX 77004

EULAU, HEINZ, educator, polit. scientist; b. Offenbach, Germany, Oct. 14, 1915; s. Arthur and Martha (Spier) E.; A.B., U. Cal. at Berkeley, 1937, M.A., 1938, Ph.D., 1941; m. Cleo Mishkin, June 8, 1946; children-Lauren, Peter. Research asso. Library of Congress, 1941-42; sr. analyst Spl. War Policies Unit, Dept. Justice, 1942-44; asst. editor New Republic, 1944- 47; from asst. prof. to prof. Antioch Coll., 1947-57; prof. polit. sci. Stanford, 1958—; vis. legislative research prof. U. Cal. at Berkeley, 1961-62; vis. prof. Inst. Advanced Studies, Vienna, Austria, 1964-65. Mem. behavioral sci. div. NRC, 1969-71. Fellow Fund Advancement Edn., 1951-52, Center Advanced Study Behavioral Scis., 1957-58. Fellow A.A.A.S.; mem. Am. Polit. Sci. Assn. (pres. elect 1970-71). Author: Class and Party in the Eisenhower Years, 1962; The Legislative System, 1962; Journeys in Politics, 1963; The Behavioral Persuasion in Politics, 1963; Micro-Macro Political Analysis, 1969. Home: 753 Frenchmans Rd Stanford CA 94305

EUMONT, JACK VICTOR, petroleum co. exec.; b. New Orleans, Dec. 6, 1928; s. Clarence Y. and Lena (Scariano) E.; B.B.A., Loyola of the South, 1949; m. Joyce Raphael, Mar. 3, 1951; children—Janelle Ann, Jack Victor, Judy Lynn, Jill Marie, Jeffrey Raphael, Jerry C. Chief accountant Nat. Tax and Record Service, New Orleans, 1949-52; sr. accountant Peat, Marwick, Mitchell & Co., New Orleans, 1953-57; with The La. Land and Exploration Co., New Orleans, 1957—, asst. sec., 1961-62, treas., asst. sec., 1962-69, v.p., treas., 1969—. Served with USAF, 1951-52. C.P.A., La. Mem. New Orleans Petroleum Accountants Soc. (pres. 1966-67), Independent Petroleum Assn. Am. (mem. tax com.), Soc. La. C.P.A.'s, C. of C. New Orleans,

Am. Inst. C.P.A.'s. Club: Timberlane Country (Gretna). Home: 733 Fairfield Av Gretna LA 70053 Office: 225 Baronne St New Orleans LA 70112

EUNSON, ROBERT CHARLES ROMAINE, newspaperman, writer; b. Billings, Mont., July 23, 1912; s. Robert Strong and Jessie (Romaine) E.; student Va. Mil. Inst., 1931-32; B.A. in Edn., Ariz. State Coll., Flagstaff, 1936, LL.D., 1961; m. Katherine Rabogliatti, Feb. 22, 1935; children—Eve Anne (Mrs. Jackson R. Rannells), Dale Ellen (Mrs. Richardson Morse), Lisa Kei. Editor, Holbrook (Ariz.) Tribune-News, 1936-41; with AP, 1941—, chief bur. Japan, Korea and Okinawa, 1950-56, chief bur. San Francisco, 1956-63, gen. exec. for Asia, 1963-65, asst. gen. mgr., N.Y.C., 1965-69, asst. sec. in charge broadcasting div., 1965—; dir. AP of Can. Vice pres. Press Assn., 1965—; pres. Fgn. Corr. Club Japan, 1956, San Francisco Press and Union League Club, 1962. Mem. Radio Television News Dirs. Assn., Nat. Assn. Broadcasters. Clubs: Overseas Press (N.Y.C.); National Broadcasters (Washington); Apawomis (Rye, N.Y.). Author: The Pearl King, 1954; Mig Alley, 1958; Trial at Odawara, 1964. Home: 4 Meredith Pl Bronxville NY 10708 Office: 50 Rockefeller Plaza New York City NY 10020

EURE, THAD, state ofcl.; b. Gates County, N.C., Nov. 15, 1899; s. Tazewell A. and Armecia (Langstun) E.; student U. N.C., 1917-19, Law Sch., 1921-22; LL.D. Elon Coll., 1958; m. Minta Banks, Nov. 15, 1924; children—Armecia (Mrs. J. Norman Black, Jr.), Thad. Lawyer; mayor City of Winton, N.C., 1923-28; atty. Hertford County, N.C., 1923-31; prin. clk. N.C. Ho. of Reps., 1931, 33, 35, 36; sec. state State of N.C., Raleigh, 1936—. Mem. N.C. Ho. of Reps., 1929; keynote speaker N.C. Democratic Conv., 1950, permanent chmn., 1962. Chmn. bd. trustees Elon Coll. Mem. Nat. Assn. Secs. of State (pres. 1942; dean 1961), Am. Legion, 40 and 8, Theta Chi. Mem. United Ch. of Christ. Elk. Home: 2345 New Bern Av Raleigh NC 27610 Office: State Capitol Bldg Raleigh NC 27602

EURICH, ALVIN CHRISTIAN, educator; b. Bay City, Mich., June 14, 1902; s. Christian H. and Hulda (Steinke) E.; B.A., N. Central Coll., 1924, Litt.D., 1949; M.A., U. Me., 1926; Ph.D., U. Minn., 1929; LL.D., Hamline U., 1944, Alfred U., 1949, Clark U., 1950, Miami U., 1951, Yeshiva U., 1954, Redlands U., 1960, U. Me., 1965; Litt.D., New Sch. Social L.H.D., U. Fla., 1953, U. Miami (Fla.), 1968, Albion Coll., 1965; Sc.D., Akron U., 1960; m. Nell P. Hutchinson, Mar. 15, 1953; children—Juliet Ann, Donald Alan. Instr. U. Me., 1924; served from asst. in ednl. psychology to prof. U. Minn. 1926-37; prof. edn. Northwestern U., 1937-38; prof. edn. Stanford, 1938-48, v.p., 1944-48, acting pres., 1948; 1st pres. State U. N.Y., 1949-51; v.p. Ford Fund Advancement Edn., 1951-64, mem. bd. dirs., 1952-67; exec. dir. edn. div. Ford Found. 1958-64; pres. Aspen Inst. Humanistic Studies, 1963-67; pres. Acad. Ednl. Devel., 1963—; vice chmn. bd. Ednl. Facilities Labs., Inc. Trustee Penn Mutual Life Ins. Co. Cons. U.S. govt. agencies during and following war yrs.; supr. various ednl. surveys; served as mem. or cons. various commns. on ednl. research, including Hoover Commn.; mem. Pres. Truman's Commn. Higher Edn., Pres. Kennedy's Task Force Edn.; chmn. Surgeon Gen.'s Commn. Nurses; cons. NASA; chmn. U.S. nat. commn. UNESCO, vice chmn. U.S. delegation to gen. conf. 1968; pres. Found. Human Resources Devel; chmn. adv. com. Haile Selassie U.; mem. Pres.'s Commn. Libraries; vis. prof. various univs.; vis. fellow Clare Coll., U. Cambridge (Eng.), 1967. Bd. dirs. FAS, Internat., Am. Lovelace Found., Belgian Am. Found. Served from lt. comdr. to comdr., USNR, 1942-44; dir. standards and curriculum div. Naval Personnel. Fellow A.A.A.S. (council 1941-45), Am. Psychol. Assn., Aspen Inst.; mem. Sigma Xi, Phi Delta Kappa. Clubs: University, Century (N.Y.C.); Cosmos (Washington); Athenaeum (London); Bohemian (San Francisco). Author or co-author books and studies in education; also psychol. and achievement tests. Contbr. ednl. jours. gen. periodicals. Recipient Outstanding Achievement award U. Minn., 1951; Times Sq. Club's 4th Ann. award, 1953; Ann. award N.Y. Acad. Pub. Edn., 1963. Author: Reforming American Education, 1969. Editor: Campus 1980, 1968; High School 1980, 1970. Home: Sherman CT Office: 437 Madison Av New York City NY 10022

EURICH, NELL, coll. dean; b. Norwood, O., July 18, 1919; d. Clayton W. and Adah (Palmer) Plopper; A.A., Stephens Coll., 1939; B.A., Stanford, 1941, M.A., 1943; Ph.D., Columbia, 1959; m. Alvin C. Eurich, Mar. 15, 1953; children—Juliet Ann, Donald Alan. Dir. student union U. Tex., 1942-43; resident counselor Barnard Coll., 1944-46; asst. to pres. Woman's Found., 1947-49; officer charge pub. relations State U. N.Y., 1949- 52; acting pres. Stephens Coll., 1953-54; asst. prof. English, N.Y.U., 1959- 64; acad. dean New Coll., Sarasota, Fla., 1965; dean faculty, prof. English, Vassar Coll., 1967-70; provost, dean faculty, prof. English, Manhattanville Coll., Purchase, N.Y., 1971—. Dir. project reorganize curriculum Aspen (Colo.) pub. high sch., 1966; mem. nat. selection com., chmn. Rocky Mountain regional com. Nat. Endowment Humanities, 1966-67; mem. Middle States commn. Marshall Scholarships, 1967-69, chmn. Northeastern region, 1970—; mem. U.S. Commn. on Ednl. Tech., Dept. Health, Edn. and Welfare, 1968-69; mem. overseer's com. on summer sch. and univ. extension vis. com. Harvard, 1969—; mem. panel of judge's Fed. Woman's award, 1969. Past trustee Bark St. Coll. trustee Hudson Guild Settlement House, 1948-54, 71—; past trustee Colo. Rocky Mountain Sch.; trustee New Coll., 1962—. Mem. Modern Lang. Assn., World Soc. of Ekistics, Nat. Council Women (hon.). Author: Science in Utopia, 1967; (with B. Schwenkmeyer): Great Britain's Open University, 1971. also articles. Home: 24 W 55th St New York City NY 10019

EUSDEN, JOHN DYKSTRA, educator, clergyman; b. Holland, Mich., July 20, 1922; s. Ray Anderson and Marie (Dykstra) E.; A.B., Harvard, 1943, student Law Sch., 1946; B.D. cum laude, Yale, 1949, Ph.D. in Religion, 1954; m. Joanne Reiman, June 14, 1950; children—Andrea Bonner, Alan Tolles, John Dykstra, Sarah Jewell. Ordained to ministry United Ch. of Christ, 1949; instr., then asst. prof. religion Yale, 1953-60; research fellow Kyoto (Japan) U., 1963-64; mem. faculty Williams Coll., 1960—, prof. religion, chaplain, 1965—; research fellow U. Utrecht (The Netherlands), 1968. Mem. adv. council campus ministry program Danforth Found., 1966—. Trustee Lingnan U., Hong Kong, 1964—. Served to 1st lt., aviator USMCR, 1943-45. Scholar, Harvard, 1940-41; Kent fellow, 1949-53; Sterling fellow, 1952- 53; Faculty fellow Am. Assn. Theol. Schs., 1958-59; Folger Shakespeare Library fellow, 1958-59; Lilly postdoctoral fellow, Danforth campus ministry grant, 1963-64; Am. Council Learned Socs. fellow, Fulbright research travel grantee, 1968. Mem. Am. Acad. Religion, Am. Assn. U. Profs., Am. Soc. Ch. History, Am. Soc. Christian Ethics, Nat. Assn. Coll. and Univ. Chaplains, Soc. Religion in Higher Edn. Author: Puritans, Lawyers and Politics in Early 17th Century England, reprint, 1968; also articles. Translator, editor, introduction William Ames (Puritan theologian) The Marrow of Theology, 1968. Home: College Pl Williamstown MA 01267

EUSTIS, ALLAN CHOTARD, Jr., investment banker; b. New Orleans, Aug. 28, 1904; s. Allan Chotard and Adele (Brittin) E.; B.S., Sheffield Sci. Sch., Yale, 1925; m. Ann Hyde, Nov. 6, 1947; children—Annette C. (Mrs. Rufus E. Jarman, Jr.), Allan Chotard, III, Brittin Cartwright II, Adele Brittin. With Spencer Trask & Co., N.Y.C., 1925—, partner, 1947—. Served to lt. col. USAAF, 1942-46. Mem. Nat. Assn. Securities Dealers (bd. govs. 1964-66, chmn. 1966). Home: 110 Belden Hill Rd Wilton CT 06897 Office: 60 Broad St New York City NY 10004

EUSTIS, ALVIN ALLEN, Jr., educator; b. Coeur D'Alene, Ida., June 17, 1917; s. Alvin Allen and Blanche (Kruse) E.; A.B., U. Cal. at Berkeley, 1938, M.A., 1939, Ph. D., 1947; m. Helen Sarah Lathrop, May 16, 1942; 1 dau., Anne Dorothy. Mem. faculty U. Cal. at Berkeley, 1948—, prof. French, 1962—. Mem. French exam. com. Coll. Entrance Bd., 1964-69; mem. grad. record exam. French com. Ednl. Testing Service, 1963-69. Served with USNR, 1941-45. Mem. Am. Assn. U. Profs., Modern Lang. Assn., Am. Assn. Tchrs. French, Philol. Assn. Pacific Coast, Phi Beta Kappa, Sigma Chi, Pi Delta Phi. Author: Racine Devant La Critique Francaise, 1838- 1939, 1949; Hippolyte Taine and The Classical Genius, 1951; Trois Critiques de la Nouvelle Revue Francaise, 1961. Home: 945 Euclid Av Berkeley CA 94708

EUSTIS, BRITTIN CARTWRIGHT, investment banker; b. New Orleans, Nov. 30, 1905; s. Allan Chotard and Adele (Brittin) E.; B.S., Sheffield Sch., Yale, 1926; m. Peggy Fox, Oct. 1, 1930; children—Peggy Brittin, Miriam Cartwright (Mrs. Theodore H. Irwin II). With Spencer Trask & Co., N.Y.C., 1927-68, gen. partner, 1944-68; pres., dir. Spencer Trask & Co., Inc., 1968-69, chmn. bd., 1969—; dir. Coastal States Gas Producing Co., Kal/Graphic, Inc. Bd. govs. Assn. Stock Exchange Firms, 1956-63, pres., 1961-62. Episcopalian. Clubs: Essex Fells (N.J.) Country; Recess, Yale (N.Y.C.); Boston (New Orleans). Home: 32 Old Chester Rd Essex Fells NJ 07021 Office: 60 Broad St New York City NY 10004

EUSTIS, JOHN NORMAN, investment banker; b. N.Y.C., May 26, 1912; s. John Rutty and Cecil (Weil) E.; B.S. in Econs., U. Pa., 1933; m. Doris Chase Hills, Apr. 5, 1939; children—Gretchen Hills Flock, Thomas E. John C., Cecily Eustis. Partner Granberry & Co., 1937-41; dept. head Riter & Co., 1943, 45-50; dir. procurement Piasecki Helicopter Corp., 1951-55; pres., dir. Strong Cobb & Co., Cleve., 1955-59; pres., dir. Strong Cobb Arner Inc., Cleve., 1959- 63, vice chmn., chief financial officer, 1963-65, exec. v.p., dir., 1965-69; v.p. Nat. City Bank of Cleve., 1969—. Served to maj. USAAF, 1942-45. Mem. Phi Gamma Delta. Clubs: Cleveland Skating; Country (Hudson, O.). Home: Hudson OH 44236 Office: 623 Euclid Av Cleveland OH 44114

EUWEMA, BEN, retired educator; b. Chgo., May 3, 1904; s. Ralph and Anna (Helmholt) E.; A.B., Calvin Coll., 1925; A.M., U. Mich., 1926; Ph.D., U. Chgo., 1934; m. Catherine Michmerhuizen, July 4, 1928; children—Robert Noel, Carol Joyce. Instr. English, Westminster (Pa.) Coll., 1928-29, asst. prof., 1929-31, prof., head English dept., 1931- 36; asso. prof. English, Kent State U., 1936-37; asst. prof. Mich. State Coll., E. Lansing, 1937-39, asso. prof., 1939-42, prof., head dept. lit. and fine arts, 1944-46, prof., head English dept., 1942-46, dir., div. lang. and lit., 1944-46; dean Coll. Liberal Arts, Pa. State U., 1946-64, prof. English, 1964-69, emeritus, 1969—. Mem. Phi Kappa Phi. Author books and articles. Asso. editor Jour. Gen. Edn. Home: 509 Westview State College PA 16801 ☆

EUWER, ROBERT F., banker; b. Jeannette, Pa., 1907; grad. Princeton, 1930. Sr. v.p. Bank of Commerce, N.Y.C.; dir. Euwer & Co. Home: 15 Hawthrone Rd Short Hills NJ 07078 Office: 56 E 42d St New York City NY 10017*

EVANG, KARL, Norwegian govt. ofcl.; b. Oslo, Norway, Oct. 19, 1902; s. Jens Ingolf and Beate (Wexelsen) E.; M.D., U. Oslo, 1929; internat. course in indsl. hygiene, U. Berlin, 1937; studies in Eng., France, Germany, 1938; m. Gerda Sophie Landmark Moe, Dec. 4, 1929; children—Anders, Turid Sofie, Kari Bente, Anne Cecilie. Pvt. practice medicine, 1929—; mem. staff Oslo Municipal Hosp., 1932-34; med. officer State Factory Inspection Office, 1937-39; dir. gen. Health Services Norway, 1939- -. Vice chmn. bd. dirs. Norwegian Found. for Assistance to Underdeveloped Countries, 1952—. Rep., League of Nations Conf. Nat. Nutrition Council, Geneva, 1937, UN Conf. FAO, Hot Springs, Va., 1943; Norwegian del. UNRRA, Montreal, Can., 1944; adviser Norwegian delegation San Francisco Conf., 1945; mem. standing adv. com. on nutrition FAO, 1945-47; mem. tech. prep. commn. for WHO, 1946; chmn. Norwegian delegation Internat. Health Conf., N.Y.C., 1946; mem. Interim Commn. WHO, 1946-48; chmn. Norwegian Nutritional Council and FAO Com., 1946—; mem. Norwegian delegation 2d FAO Conf., Copenhagen, 1947; chmn. Norwegian delegation WHO Health Assembly, Geneva, 1948, and subsequent assemblies; pres. 2d WHO Assembly, Rome, 1949; mem. WHO exec. bd., 1964-66, chmn., 1965-66; chmn. joint ILO-WHO Commn. on Hygiene of Seafarers, 1949, mem., 1954; chmn. WHO expert com. Pub. Health Adminstn., 1952; vice chmn. expert Mission to Israel, 1950, India, 1952 (sponsored by WHO- Unitarian Service Com.). Decorated comdr. with star Royal Order St. Olav (Norway); chevalier Legion d'Honneur. Hon. fellow Royal Soc. Medicine, London, Am. Pub. Health Assn.; mem. Norwegian Med. Soc., Norwegian Soc. Hygiene. Author: Birth Control, 1930; Norwegian Medical Dictionary, 1933; Race Policy and Reaction, 1934; Education to Peace, 1947; The Rehabilitation of Public Health in Norway, 1947; The Public Health Services, 1948; Sexual Education, 1951; Health Service, Society and Medicine, 1958; Health Service, Society and Medicine. 1958; Health Services in Norway, 1960. Home: 24 Holmenveien Vinderen Oslo Norway Office: Helsedircktoratet Oslo Norway

EVANGELISTI, FRANCO, composer Proporzioni, for solo flute. Address: Time Records Inc 2 W 45th St New York City NY 10036.*

EVANS, ABBIE HUSTON, poet; b. Lee, N.H., Dec. 20, 1881; d. Lewis Darenydd and Hester Annette (Huston) Evans; B.A., Radcliffe Coll., 1913, M.A. 1918; LL.D. Bowdoin Coll., 1961. Mem. Advisory Bd. Contemporary Poetry, 1940—; mem. jury Shelley Meml. award, 1940; mem. jury United States Award (poetry), 1967; staff mem. Settlement Music Sch., Phila., 1923-53, Coll. Settlement Farm-Camp, 1953-57. Recipient Guarantors' prize Poetry Chgo., 1931; Loines award for poetry Nat. Inst. Arts and Letters, 1960; Golden Rose award New Eng. Poetry Club, 1965; citation Me. Commn. on Arts and Humanities, 1970, Pa. Council on Arts and Internat. Poetry Forum, 1970. Mem. Americans for Dem. Action, Civil Liberties Union, Phi Beta Kappa. Author: Outcrop, 1928; The Bright North, 1938; Fact of Crystal 1961; Collected Poems, 1970; also verse in anthologies and collections. Home: 404 N Walnut St West Chester PA 19380

EVANS, ALFRED SPRING, physician, educator; b. Buffalo, Aug. 21, 1917; s. John H. and Ellen (Spring) E.; A.B., U. Mich., 1939, M.P.H., 1960; M.D., U. Buffalo, 1943; M.A. (hon.) Yale, 1966; m. Brigitte Kluge, July 26, 1952; children—John Kluge, Barbara Spring, Christopher Paul. Intern U. Pitts. Hosps., 1943-44; resident Goldwater Hosp., N.Y.C., 1944; USPHS postdoctoral research fellow Yale Med. Sch., 1947-48, from instr. to asst. prof. medicine, 1949-50, prof. epidemiology, dir. WHO serum reference bank, dept. epidemiology and pub. health, New Haven, 1966—; resident Buffalo Gen. Hosp., 1948-49; asso. prof. preventive medicine and med. microbiology U. Wis. Sch. Medicine, 1952-59, prof., chmn. dept. preventive medicine, also dir. Wis. State Lab. Hygiene, 1959-66. Mem. microbiology fellowship panel NIH, 1960-64; mem. microbiol. panel space flight NRC/NASA; cons. Philippine Health Dept., WHO, 1962, 1964; cons. in epidemiology Surgeon Gen. U.S. Army, 1969—. Served to capt. M.C., AUS, 1944-46, 50-52; col. Res. ret. Diplomate Am. Bd. Internal Medicine. Fellow Am. Pub. Health Assn.; mem. Assn. Tchrs. of Preventive Medicine, Am. Epidemiological Soc. (sec.-treas. 1968—), Internat. Epidemiological Assn., Soc. Exptl. Biology and Medicine, Central Soc. Clin. Research, Delta Omega. Contbr. articles on infectious diseases and epidemiology. Home: 38 Dogwood Circle Woodbridge CT 06525 Office: 333 Cedar St New Haven CT 06510

EVANS, ALONA ELIZABETH, educator; b. Providence, Feb. 27, 1917; d. Robert R. and Florence (Weatherhead) Evans; A.B., Duke, 1940, Ph.D., 1945. Intern personnel adminstrn. War Dept., 1942; jr. divisional asst. State Dept., 1942-43; instr. Duke, 1944-45, Westminster Coll., Pa., 1945; mem. faculty Wellesley Coll., 1945—, prof. polit. sci., 1958—, chmn. dept., 1959-70, Elizabeth Kimball Kendall prof., 1966—. Fellow Social Sci. Research Council, 1948-49; Fulbright grantee, India, 1961; fellow Harvard Law Sch., 1961-62, 71-72; recipient Harbison Fund award Wellesley Coll., 1954-55; grantee Am. Philos. Soc., 1971-72. Mem. Am. Soc. Internat. Law (exec. council 1956-59, 65- 68), Internat. Law Assn. (chmn. Am. br. com. legal problems asylum 1963- -, exec. com. 1971—), Indian Soc. Internat. Law, Am., New Eng. (pres. 1966-67) polit. sci. assns., Am. Assn. U. Women (bd. dirs. 1963-67, cons. 1968-70; Achievement award 1971), Am. Judicature Soc., Am. Assn. U. Profs., Phi Beta Kappa. Contbr. articles law jours. Bd. editors Am. Jour. Internat. Law. Home: Fiske House Wellesley MA 02181

EVANS, ANDREW JULIUS, Jr., air force officer; b. Charleston, S.C., Nov. 11, 1918; s. Andrew Julius and Lillian (Laurey) E.; student The Citadel, 1935-36; B.S., U.S. Mil. Acad., 1941; m. Claire B. Bickerton, Nov. 2, 1941; children—Andrew Jay, Richard G., Susan C., Cathy A. Commd. 2d lt. USAAF, 1941, advanced through grades to maj. gen., 1966; secretariat Air U., 1946-47; student Air Command Staff Sch., 1947-48; secretariat Joint Chiefs of Staff, 1948- 50, exec. asst. Chief of Staff USAF, 1950-51; student Air War Coll., 1951-52, instr., 1953-56; dep. comdr. 49th Fighter Bomber Wing, Korea, 1952-53; comdr. 414th Interceptor Group, Oxnard, Cal., 1956; vice comdr. N.Y. Air Def. Sector, McGuire AFB, N.J., 1957-59; comdr. 65th Air Div., Torrejon Air Base, Spain, 1960-63; dep. dir. devel. planning Hdqrs. USAF, 1963-64; dir. devel., spl. asst. to dep. chief of staff research and devel. for counterinsurgency Hdqrs. USAF, 1964-68; comdr. Tactical Air Warfare Center, Eglin AFB, Fla., 1968-70; comdr. 7th and 13th Air Forces, APO San Francisco, 1970—. Decorated D.S.M., Silver Star, Legion of Merit, D.F.C. with two oak leaf clusters, Air medal with 11 oak leaf clusters, Purple Heart (U.S.); French Croix de Guerre; Korean Ulichi with silver star. Home: 17 Country Club Rd Shalimar FL 32579 Office: Box 1 Hdqrs 7/13th Air Force APO San Francisco CA 96237

EVANS, ARTHUR THOMPSON, physician; b. Huron, S.D., Nov. 26, 1919; s. Arthur Thompson and Anna Matilda (Hansen) E.; A.B. in Zoology, Miami U., Oxford, O., 1941; M.D., U. Chgo., 1944; m. Jean Porter Evans, Sept. 12, 1942; children—Christine, Arthur T., William, Charles. Intern Cin. Gen. Hosp. 1944-45, resident gen. surgery, 1945-46, urology, 1950; individual practice medicine, specializing in urology, Cin., 1950—; dir. div. urology U. Cin. Med. Center, 1961—, also dir. Urologic Assos. tng. program. Served to capt. USAAF, 1946-48. Diplomate Am. Bd. Urology. Fellow A.C.S.; mem. Am. Urol. Assn. (exec. com. 1968—, film library, 1967—, chmn. paraurologic edn. com. 1969—), A.A.A.S., Am. Med. Writers Assn., Internat. Coll. Surgeons, Soc. Pediatric Urology, Soc. Univ. Urologists, Am. Assn. Genito-Urinary Surgeons, Am. Assn. Clin. Urologists, Phi Beta Kappa (hon.). Editorial bd. Urol. Survey, 1969—. Home: 2200 Victory Pkwy Cincinnati OH 45206 Office: 234 Goodman St Cincinnati OH 45229

EVANS, AUSTIN JAMES, hosp. adminstr.; b. Mt. Pleasant, Ia., Feb. 26, 1920; s. WIlliam Henry and Estelle (Lamb) E.; B.S., Ia. Wesleyan Coll., 1941; M.S., Yale, 1950; m. Wilma Mildred Stephens, Mar. 26, 1944; children—Mary Beth, Susan Louise. Adminstrv. resident State U. Ia. Hosps., 1949-51; bus. adminstr. Mental Health Inst., Independence, Ia., 1951-54; adminstr. Hadley Meml. Hosp. and Rehab. Center, Hays, Kan., 1954-63; dir. Cleve. Met. Gen. Hosp., 1963-65; adminstr. Lake View Meml. Hosp., Danville, Ill., 1965—; hosp. cons. Methodist Bd. Hosps. and Homes, Evanston, Ill., 1965—. Chmn. Independence chpt. A.R.C. fund drive, 1951-53, Hays service unit Salvation Army, 1954-63; pres. Cerebral Palsy Vermilion County. Chmn., Citizens' Referendum Com., Danville. Bd. dirs. Danville C. of C., Danville United Fund, YMCA. Served to lt. USNR, 1942-46. Named Man of Year in Independence, 1953. Fellow Am. Coll. Hosp. Adminstrs.; mem. Kan. Hosp. Assn. (pres. 1958), Danville Musical Cycle (pres.). Methodist. Rotarian (pres. Danville). Contbr. profl. jours. Home: 1128 Walnut St Danville IL 61832 Office: 812 Logan St Danville IL 61832

EVANS, BARTON, electronics co. exec.; b. Danvers, Mass., June 26, 1909; s. Clarence Augustus and Dorothy Ashwood (Barton) E.; grad. Phillips Exeter Acad., 1927; A.B. cum laude, Williams Coll., 1931; m. Viola May Gompf, June 7, 1945; children—Barton, Bruce Marshall, Barbara Ashwood. With Goodbody & Co., N.Y.C., 1931-40, Trans-World Airlines, Kansas City, 1946; with CIA, Washington and Los Angeles, 1947-51; with Hughes Aircraft Co., Culver City, Cal., 1952—, corporate dir. services, 1961-64, corporate dir. pub. affairs, 1964—. Served to comdr. USNR, 1942-45. Mem. Chi Psi. Episcopalian. Clubs: Los Angeles; Bel-Air Bay (Pacific Palisades). Home: 955 Bienveneda Av Pacific Palisades CA 90272 Office: Hughes Aircraft Co Centenela and Teale Sts Culver City CA 90230

EVANS, BENJAMIN FRANKLIN, Jr., army officer; b. Wilkes-Barre, Pa., Sept. 3, 1912; s. Benjamin Franklin and Minnie (Guyler) E.; B.S., U.S. Mil. Acad., 1936; grad. Inf. Sch., 1939, Armed Forces Staff Coll., 1950, Nat. June Coll., 1955, Advanced Mgmt. Program, Harvard, 1957; m. Marjorie Hughes, June 13, 1936; children—Benjamin Franklin III, David Walter, Sandra Guyler, Robert Lloyd, James Allen. Commd. 2d lt. U.S. Army, 1936, advanced through grades to maj. gen., 1959; various assignments in U.S., 1936-40; assigned 27th Inf. Regt., Hawaii and S.W. Pacific, 1940-44, 25th Inf. Div., S.W. Pacific, 1944; mem. theater group operations div. War Dept. Gen. Staff, 1944-46; brig. adj., dept. tactics U.S. Mil. Acad., 1946-49; with personnel and adminstrv. div. Hdqrs. EUCUM, Heidelberg, Germany, 1950-52; regtl. comdr. 18th Inf. Regt., 1st Inf. Div., USAREUR, Aschaffenberg, Germany, 1952-53; sec. to gen. staff Hdqrs. 1st Army, N.Y., 1953-54; with inf. sect. Hdqrs. U.S. Continental Army Command, 1955-59; comdr. Army Forces Iceland, 1959-60; assigned Office Strategic Plans and Policy Directorate, Office Dep. Chief Staff Mil. Operations, 1960-61; asst. dep. chief staff operations, plans and tng. Hdqrs. U.S. Continental Army, 1961-62; asst. dep. chief staff individual tng. USCONARC, 1962-63; comdg. gen. XIII U.S. Army Corps. 1963-65; chief JUSMMAT, Ankara, Turkey, 1965-67; spl. asst. to Joint Chiefs of Staff for Arms Control, Washington, 1967-69; dep. comdg. gen. Hdqrs. 3d U.S. Army, Ft. McPherson, Ga., 1969—. Decorated Silver Star, Legion of Merit, Bronze Star with V device and oak leaf cluster, D.S.M. Episcopalian. Address: Hdqrs 3d US Army Fort McPherson GA 30330

EVANS, BERGEN, author, educator; b. Franklin, O., Sept. 19, 1904; s. Rice Kemper and Louise (Cass) E.; A.B., Miami U., Oxford, O., 1924, L.H.D., 1959; A.M., Harvard, 1925, Ph.D., 1932; B. Litt., U. Coll., Oxford, Eng., 1931; D.Litt., Franklin and Marshall Coll., 1959; m. Jean Whinery, Aug. 5, 1939; children—Derek, Scott. Prof. English, Northwestern U., Evanston, Ill., mem. guiding faculty Famous Writers Sch., Westport Conn. Author: (with George Mohr) The Psychiatry of Robert Burton, 1944; Natural History of Nonsense, 1946; The Spoor of Spooks, 1954; Comfortable Words, 1962. Editor: Fifty Essays, 1936; Essays by Samuel Johnson, 1940; Boswell's Life of Johnson, 1952; The World, The Flesh, and H. Allen Smith, 1954; (with Cornelia Evans) Dictionary of Contemporary American Usage, 1957; Comfortable Words, 1962; Word-A-Day, 1963; Dictionary of Quotations, 1968; Dictionary of Mythology, 1970. Contbr. essays and sketches to Atlantic, New Republic, other nat. mags. Author: The Skeptic's Corner dept. American Mercury mag., 1946-50. Lectr.; master of ceremonies TV Quiz shows Down You Go, The Last Word, English for Americans, Words in the News, Inquiry, Of Many Things. Writer daily syndicated newspaper feature The Last Word. Recipient George Foster Peabody award for excellence in radio and TV broadcasting, 1959. Home: 2313 Bur Oak Road Northfield IL 60093 Office: Northwestern University Evanston IL 60201

EVANS, BILL WILLIAM J., pianist, composer; b. Plainfield, N.J., Aug. 16, 1929; studied piano, violin, flute; degree Southeastern La. Coll.; student Mannes Sch. Music, N.Y.C. With brother, organized own group; played with Mundell Lowe, Red Mithell, with Herbie Fields, 1950, with Jerry Wald, Tony Scott, 1954-58, with combo of Miles Davis, 1958; free-lance, leader trio; performed at Village Vanguard, N.Y.C., Manne Hole, Los Angeles; faculty Sch. Jazz, Lenox, Mass., summer 1959; recordings include Ivory Hunters, Odds Against Tomorrow, Modern Jazz Concert, Conversations with Myself. Recipient awards Downbeat Critics' Poll, New Star of 1958; Grammy award. Address: 77 W 104th St New York City NY 10025*

EVANS, BOB OVERTON, electronics co. exec.; b. Grand Island, Neb., Aug. 19, 1927; s. Walter Bernard and Lillian (Overton) E.; B.S. in Elec. Engring., Ia. State U., 1949; m. Maria Bowman, Nov. 19, 1949; children—Cathleen L., Robert W., David D., Douglas B. Electric operating engr. No. Ind. Pub. Service Co., Hammond, 1949-51; with IBM Corp., 1951—, designed and developed large digital electric computers, v.p. devel. Data Systems div., 1962-64, pres. Fed. Systems Div., 1965-69, pres. Systems Devel. div., 1970—; cons. govt. agys.; area bd. mem. Md. Nat. Bank. Exec. bd. mem. Nat. Capital Area council Boy Scouts Am. Served with USNR, 1945-46. Recipient Distinguished Pub. Service award NASA. Fellow I.E.E.E. (chmn. computer group conf. 1970); mem. Nat. Acad. Engring., Profl. Group Electronic Computers, Nat. Security Indsl. Assn. (trustee), Armed Forces Communications and Electronics Assn. (trustee), Aerospace Industries Assn. (exec. bd.). Presbyn. (elder). Home: Ivanhoe Lane Greenwich CT 06830 Office: 1000 Westchester Av White Plains NY 10604

EVANS, CARLYLE WALTER, chain drug store exec.; b. Delphos, O., Apr. 7, 1906; s. Albert D. and Eda (Archer) E.; B.S., Ohio State U., 1928; m. Ellen Margaret Gee, June 15, 1929; children—Sarah Anne (Mrs. William Jeffers), William C. With Gray Drug Stores, Inc., Cleve., 1931—, accounting clk., sec., v.p., exec. v.p., 1931- 55, pres., 1955-66, chmn. bd., 1966—; past pres. Affiliated Drug Stores, Inc. Mem. Ohio Council Retail Mchts. (past pres.), Nat. Assn. Chain Drug Stores (past pres.). Presbyn. Home: 19901 Van Aken Blvd Shaker Heights OH 44122 Office: 666 Euclid Av Cleveland OH 44114

EVANS, CHARLES ALBERT, microbiologist; b. Mpls., Feb. 18, 1912; s. Albert Grant and Susan Briery (Thompson) E.; B.S., U. Minn., 1935, B.M., 1936, M.D., 1937, Ph.D., 1943; m. Allie Ann Christman, Dec. 22, 1939; children—Nicholas John (dec.), Susan Ethel, Thomas Charles, Carol Ann. Research asst. to R.G. Green, U. Minn., 1934-41; NRC fellow U. Rochester (with G.P. Berry), 1941-42; asst. prof., later asso. prof. bacteriology U. Minn., 1942-46; prof. microbiology U. Wash., Seattle, 1946—, chmn. dept., 1946-70, spl. asst. to pres., dir. office of spl. student programs, 1968-70. Cons. Office Naval Research, 1948-51; microbiology study sect. USPHS, 1951-56, 57-58. Mem. Nat. Adv. Cancer Council, 1958-60, 63-67; mem. research adv. council Am. Cancer Soc., 1965-70, chmn. council, 1967-70. Mem. Soc. Am. Bacteriologists (pres. 1959-60), Am. Acad. Microbiology (gov. 1959-65, chmn. bd. 1960-61), Am. Soc. Microbiology, A.A.A.S., Soc. Exptl. Biology and Medicine, Sigma Xi, Alpha Omega Alpha. Editorial com. Annual Rev. Microbiology 1957-61. Research viruses, bacteria. Home: 4774 NE 180th St Seattle WA 98155

EVANS, CLIFFORD, mus. curator; b. Dallas, June 13, 1920; s. Clifford and Pearl (Weiss) E.; A.A., San Bernardino Jr. Coll., 1939; A.B., U. So. Cal., 1941; Ph.D., Columbia, 1947; m. Betty J. Meggers, Sept. 13, 1946. Asst. archeology, dept. anthropology Columbia, 1946-48; instr. anthropology U. Va., 1949-51; asso. curator div. archeology U.S. Nat. Mus., Smithsonian Instn., Washington, 1951-62, curator div. archeology, 1962-69, chmn. dept. anthropology, 1969—; archeol. field work, Brazil, Ecuador, Peru, Venezuela, Brit. Guiana, Ponape, Caroline Islands, Dominica in Lesser Antilles. Served to 2d lt. USAAF, 1943-45. Decorated Air medal with cluster; Merit Ofcl. Order (Ecuador); recipient outstanding achievement award in sci. Washington Acad. Scis., 1954; Gold medal 37th Internat. Congress Americanists, 1966. Fellow Am. Anthrop. Assn.; mem. Anthrop. Soc. Washington (treas.), Inst. Andean Research (pres. 1960-65), Soc. Am. Archeology, Sigma Xi. Author: (with W.D. Strong) Cultural Stratigraphy in Viru Valley, Northern Peru, 1952; (with B.J. Meggers) Archeological Investigations at the Mouth of the Amazon, 1957; (with Meggers) Archeology of British Guiana, South America, 1960; (with Meggers) The Early Formative Culture of Ecuador, 1965; (with Meggers) Archeological Investigations on the Rio Napo, Eastern Ecuador, 1968; also articles. Home: 1227 30th St NW Washington DC 20007 Office: Dept Anthropology US Nat Mus Smithsonian Inst Washington DC 20560

EVANS, DANIEL FRALEY, retailer; b. Crawfordsville, Ind., Feb. 24, 1922; s. Benjamin C. and Ruth (Fraley) E.; A.B., Wabash Coll., 1944; M.B.A., Harvard, 1948; LL.D., Ind. Central Coll., 1969; m. Julia Delo Sloan, Oct. 15, 1945; children—Daniel Fraley, David S., Julia Anne. With L. S. Ayres Co., Indpls., 1948—, successively acting tng. dir., staff asst. to exec. v.p., div. operating supt., asst. store mgr., 1949-58, treas., asst. sec., 1958-64, exec. v.p., 1964-65, pres., 1965—; dir. Ind. Nat. Bank, Stokely-Van Camp, Inc. Chmn. Ind. Tax and Financing Policy Commn., 1967-69. Mem. Ind. Ann. Conf.; mem. commn. on structure United Meth. Ch. Trustee Meth. Hosp. Ind. (pres. 1965-68), Wabash Coll. Served as lt. (j.g.) USNR, World War II; PTO. Decorated Bronze Star with four clusters; recipient medal of honor U. Evansville, 1970, Alumni award merit Wabash Coll., 1968. Mem. Ind. Retail. Council (pres. 1961-64), Indpls. C. of C. (dir.), Indpls. Urban League (dir.). Home: 6463 N Illinois St Indianapolis IN 46260 Office: 1 W Washington St Indianapolis IN 46204

EVANS, DANIEL JACKSON, gov. Wash.; b. Seattle, Oct. 16, 1925; s. Daniel Lester and Irma (Ide) E.; B.S. in Civil Engring., U. Wash., 1948, M.S., 1949; LL.D., Whitworth Coll., Seattle Pacific Coll., Linfield Coll., St. Martin's Coll., Whitman Coll.; D.Engring., Worcester Poly. Inst., 1969; m. Nancy Ann Bell, June 6, 1959; children—Daniel Jackson, Mark L., Bruce M. Asst. mgr. Mountain-Pacific chpt. Asso. Gen. Contractors, Seattle, 1953-59; cons. civil engr., Seattle, 1949-51; partner Gray & Evans, structural and civil engrs., Seattle, 1959-65; mem. Wash. Ho. of Reps. from King County, 1956-64; gov. of Wash., 1965—. Chmn. constl. revision com. Nat. Govs. Conf., 1966-68, chmn. com. on exec. mgmt. and fiscal affairs, 1969, chmn. transp., commerce and tech. com., 1969—. Mem. steering com. Edn. Commn. States, 1967-68, Urban Coalition, 1969—; mem. Commn. of Cities in 70's, 1971—. Chmn. campaign com. Republican Govs. Assn., 1965-66, mem. policy com., 1967-68, chmn., 1970, mem. exec. com., 1969; mem. Nat. Rep. Coordinating Com., 1967-68; Keynote Speaker Rep. Nat. Conv., 1968; mem. Rep. Gov.'s Adv. Com. to Pres., 1969. Served to lt. USNR, 1943-46, 51-53. Named Outstanding Freshman Legislator, 1957; recipient Key Man award Seattle Jr. C. of C., 1955; Human Rights award Pacific N.W. chpt. Nat. Assn. Intergroup Relations Ofcls., 1967; Service to the Profession award Cons. Engrs. Council, 1969; Scales of Justice award Nat. Council Crime and Delinquency, 1968; Pub. Ofcl. of Year award Wash. Environmental Council, 1970; Silver Beaver, Silver Antelope awards Boy Scouts Am. Registered profl. engr., Wash. Mem. Western Govs. Conf. (chmn. 1968-69). Conglist. Home: Executive Mansion Olympia WA 98501 Office: Legislative Bldg Olympia WA 98501

EVANS, DAVID A., constrn. co. exec.; b. Texas City, Tex., Feb. 4, 1925; s. Adolph Roemer and Augusta (Henderson) E.; student U. Ark., 1943-44; diploma in Bldg. Contracting, Internat. Corr. Schs., 1949; LL.B., Lasalle U., 1965; children—David Joseph, Tanya Rene. Foreman, W.S. Bellows Constrn. Co., Texas City, 1946-48; supt. E.N. Williams Constrn. Co., Texas City, 1948-49; gen. foreman Rust Engring. Co., Texas City, 1949, LeBlanc, Inc., Texas City, 1949-50; owner, operator Evans Constrn. Co., Texas City, 1949—; dir. Texas City Hotel Corp., Provident Security Ins. Co., Houston. Chmn. tax equalization bd. Texas City Schs., 1959; dir. Texas City Civil Def.; pilot commr. Galveston-Texas City, 1963—. Bd. dirs. Tex. Lions Camp for Crippled Children, Kerrville. Served with AUS, 1943-45; ETO. Recipient Good Neighbor award Continental Oil Co., 1960. Mem. Nat., Tex. (dir.) assns. home builders, Texas City C. of C. (dir.). Methodist (steward, lay del. Ann. Conf. Meth. Chs.). Lion (dist. gov. Texas City 1959-60, dir. Internat. Presidents award 1960; internat. dir. 1962-64, internat. pres. 1968). Address: Box 2727 Texas City TX 77591

EVANS, DAVID WOOLLEY, advt., pub. relations exec.; b. Salt Lake City, Mar. 5, 1894; s. John Alldridge and Florence (Neslen) E.; A.B., U. Utah, 1915; m. Beatrice Cannon, Sept. 9, 1920; children—David C., Robert C., Edmund C., Wayne C., Carleton O. Copywriter, account exec., v.p., agr. mgr. Stevens & Wallis, Inc., Salt Lake City, 1919-43; editor, gen. mgr. Utah Farmer, 1931-33; pres., gen. mgr. David W. Evans & Assos., advt. and pub. relations, Salt Lake City, 1943-65, chmn. bd., chief exec. officer, 1965-68, chmn. bd., 1968— (both Salt Lake City); dir. Evans-Williams and Assos., Inc., San Francisco; chmn. bd., pres. Evans Supply, Inc., Evans Supply & Mfg. Co., Ltd., Calgary, Alta., Can.; pres., dir. Bamberger Right-of-Way, Inc.; v.p., dir. Syndicated Investors Co.; chmn. bd. Withers- Evans, Ltd.; dir. David W. Evans & Assos. San Francisco, Inc., Utah Resources Internat., Inc., Great Western Pipeline Corp., 1st Thrift & Loan, Key Credit Corp., Key Finance Co., Utah Woolen Mills. Vis. lectr. Brigham Young U., 1969-70; coordinator exhibits N.Y. World's Fair Pavilion, 1962-65; mem. information service com. Ch. of Jesus Christ of Latter-day Saints, 1959—; mem. Gov. Utah Operations and Expenditures Com., 1964-69; mem. exec. com. Region 12 Boy Scouts Am., exec. council Great Salt Lake council, mem.-at-large Nat. council. Mem. Republican pub. relations adv. panel 90th congress; active pub. relations, publicity for numerous candidates Rep. Party, 1948-70. Bd. dirs. Center Study Causes of War and Conditions for Peace; trustee Park City Inst. for Arts and Scis., 1970—. Served with Signal Corps, U.S. Army, 1918. Recipient spl. citations for information campaign and legislative liaison for Upper Colorado River Project, 1956; Silver medal Advt. Fedn. Am.-Printer's Ink mag., 1966; Distinguished Service award dept. communications Brigham Young U., 1966; Distinguished Alumni award U. Utah, 1971. Mem. Advt. Fedn. Am., Utah Mfrs. Assn., Counselors Pub. Relations Soc. Am., Newcomen Soc. in N. Am. Mem. Ch. of Jesus Christ of Latter-day Saints. Rotarian. Clubs: Timpanogos; Ambassador. Contbr. articles various publs. Home: 1038 S 12th St E Salt Lake City UT 84105 Office: 110 Social Hall Av Salt Lake City UT 84111

EVANS, DONALD F., life ins. co. exec.; b. Marcus, Ia., Dec. 7, 1920; s. Julian P. and Ellen (Souhan) E.; LL.B., Creighton U., 1947; m. Betty J. Ring. May 22, 1948; children—Jeanne P., Ann M., Mark D., David M., John J. Admitted to Neb. bar, practice in Omaha atty. Mut. of Omaha Ins. Co., 1947-51; v.p.; gen. counsel United Benefit Life Ins. Co., 1951—. Served with USAAF, World War II. Mem. Neb., Ia., Omaha bar assns., Assn. Life Ins. Counsel, Omaha C. of C., Delta Theta Phi. Republican. Roman Catholic. Home: 1322 S 95th St Omaha NB 68124 Office: 3316 Farnam St Omaha NB 68131

EVANS, DONALD KIRK, former textile co. exec.; b. White Plains, N.Y., June 19, 1904; s. Myron Edward and Mary Elizabeth (Kirk) E.; grad. Lawrenceville Sch., 1922; B.A., Princeton, 1926; m. Janet Hinchman, June 24, 1929; children—Julia (Mrs. Rogers. M. Doering), Kirk. Treas. Riegel Textile Corp., 1946-69, financial v.p., 1963-69, also dir. Home: Cantitoe St Bedford NY 10506

EVANS, EARL ALLSON, Jr., biochemist; b. Balt., Mar. 11, 1910; s. Earl Alison and Florence (Lewis) E.; student Balt. Poly. Inst., 1924-28; B.Sc.; Johns Hopkins, 1931; Ph.D., Columbia, 1936. Research asst. pharmacology Johns Hopkins Med. Sch., 1931-32, asst. lab. endocrine research, 1932-34; univ. fellow biochemistry Columbia, 1934-36; instr. biochemistry U. Chgo., 1937-39, asst. prof., 1939- 41, asso. prof. biochemistry, chmn. dept. 1941-42 (on leave, 1947- 48), prof., chmn. dept. biochemistry 1942—; fellow Rockefeller Found., U. of Sheffield (Eng.), 1939-40; chief sci. officer Am. embassy, London, 1947- 48; cons. to sec. state, 1951-53. Mem. bd. sci. counselors Nat. Inst. Arthritis and Metabolic Diseases, NIH, 1960-63; mem. div. med. scis. NRC, 1962-65; chmn. com. postdoctoral fellowships Nat. Acad. Sci. NRC, 1963-65; mem. divisional com. biol. and med. scis. NSF, 1963-66. Adv. bd. Am. Found. Continuing Edn. Recipient Eli Lilly Prize $1000 in biol. chemistry Am. Chem. Soc., 1942; fellow All Souls Coll., Oxford U., 1969. Fellow A.A.A.S.; mem. Am. Chem. Soc., Am. Soc. Biol. Chemists, Biochem. Soc. (Brit., Am. Soc. Bacteriologists, Asociacion Quimica Argentina, Sigma Xi, Tau Beta Pi. Episcopalian. Clubs: Cosmos (Washington); Quadrangle, University (Chgo.); R.A.C., Travellers (London). Author: Biochemistry of Bacterial Viruses, 1952; (with others) Biological Smyposia V., 1941; Somposium on Respiratory Enzymes, 1942. Editor: Biological Action of the Vitamins, 1942. Contbr. various sci. periodicals. Home: 12 E Scott St Chicago IL 60610

EVANS, EDWARD GORDON, Jr., educator; b. Youngstown, O., Nov. 4, 1916; s. Edward Gordon and Helen Marie (Harris) E.; student Youngstown U., 1934-35; B.Mus., Cin. Conservatory Music, 1939; M.Mus., Northwestern U., 1940; Ph.D., Western Res. U., 1950; m. Jeanne Elise Goodman, Mar. 7, 1942 (dec. Jan. 1963); children—Natasha, Vyki, Edward G. III; m. 2d, Helen S. Greene, Oct. 8, 1964. Teaching fellow, instr. Northwestern U., 1939-41; vocational counsellor and psychologist VA, Youngstown, 1946-47; asst. prof. Southeastern La. Coll., 1947-48; teaching fellow Western Res. U., 1948- 50. successively asst., then asso. prof., 1950-57, prof. music, 1957-68, chmn. dept., 1957-68, chmn. dept. humanities, 1958-68; prof., chmn. music lit. dept. Eastman Sch. Music, U. Rochester (N.Y.), 1968-70, chmn. musicology and music history dept., 1970—; chmn. music history, lit. and musicology Cleve. Inst. Music, 1965-68. Trustee Cleve. Mus. Sch. Settlement, Mus. Arts Assn., Cleve. Chamber Music Soc., Cleve. Friends of Music; adv. bd. Cleve. Philharmonic Orch. Served to maj. USAAF, 1941-46; CBI. Mem. Am. Soc. Aesthetics, Am. Musicol. Soc., Am. Assn. U. Profs. Author TV syllabus, also articles. Adv. bd. Fine Arts mag. Office: Eastman Sch Music U Rochester Rochester NY 14604

EVANS, EDWARD STEPTOE, Jr., business exec.; b. Richmond, Va., Mar. 19, 1906; s. Edward Steptoe and Virginia (McCormick) E.; ed. Va. Episcopal Sch., U. Mich., U. Lausanne (Switzerland); H.H.D., Hillsdale (Mich.) Coll., 1960; m. Florence Allington, Apr. 5, 1934; children—Virginia Beverley, E. S. Evans III, John Derby. Vice pres. Evans Appliance Co., 1929-41; exec. v.p. Evans Products Co., 1935-45, dir., 1935—, pres., 1945-62, chmn. bd., 1962-64, now dir., pres., dir. Evans Products Co., Ltd., Vancouver, B.C., 1945-62; chmn. bd. Lockhart Mfg. Corp., 1964-70, Evarie Corp., 1964—, Alsteel, Inc., Battle Creek, 1965-67, pres. Evans Communications Systems Inc., Charlottesville, Va., 1968-70, chmn. bd., 1970—; dir. Bloomfield Inc., Ivy, Va., 1968—, Capital Trinity Fund, Inc., Charlottesville, Va., 1969—. Pres. Detroit Aviation Com., 1963-67. Mem. adv. council Grad. Sch. Bus., U. Va., 1968—; bd. dirs. English Speaking Union, Charlottesville, 1968—. Mem. Nat. Def. Trans. Assn., Mich. Mfrs. Assn. (dir. 1962-67), Greater Detroit Bd. Commerce (chmn. bd. 1965-66), Newcomen Soc. N.Am., Psi Upsilon. Clubs: Grosse Pointe, Country, Yondotega (Detroit); Farmington Country, Boar's Head (Charlottesville); Mill Reef (Antigua, B.W.I.). Home: Ragged Mountain Farm Route 3 Charlottesville VA 22901 Office: 32840 W Eight Mile Rd Farmington MI 48024

EVANS, EDWIN CHARLES, cons., former mfg. exec.; b. Waterford, N.Y., May 23, 1910; s. Edwin Bernard and Sarah (Slavin) E.; student Rensselaer Poly. Inst., 1930-31, Siena Coll., 1939- 40, Harvard Grad. Sch. Bus. Adminstrn., 1949; m. Renette Wendell, July 22, 1944. Civil engr. N.Y. State Engring. Dept., 1928-34; with Behr- Manning div. (now Abrasive and Tape divs.) Norton Co., Troy, N.Y., 1934-68, beginning as mem. sales analysis dept., successively staff purchasing dept., asst. purchasing agt., purchasing agt., asst. to v.p. charge engring. and mfg. asst. gen. mgr., 1955-59, gen. mgr., 1959-70, pres., 1961-70; cons. N.Y. State Dept. Commerce, 1970—; v.p. Norton Co., Worcester, Mass., 1961-68; dir. Marine Midland Nat. Bank of Troy. Dir. United Community Services of Mohawk- Hudson Area, Vanderheyden Hall, Inc.; trustee Russell Sage Coll., Albany Med. Coll. of Union U. Mem. Harvard Advanced Mgmt. Assn. Clubs: Troy, Troy Country. Home: East Acres Route 53 Troy, NY 12180 Office: NY State Dept Commerce 112 State St Albany NY 12207

EVANS, ELINOR LUCILE, artist, educator; b. Mount Ida, Kan., Aug. 4, 1914; d. Robert Yantis and Edith (Krone) Evans; B.A., Okla. State U., 1938; M.F.A., Yale, 1954. Instr., Asst. prof., asso. prof. Okla. State U. 1946-60, 62-64; lectr. art U. Ill., 1960-62; prof. architecture Rice U., 1964—; exhibited Guggenheim Mus., Mus. Contemporary Crafts, Bklyn. Mus., Chgo. Art Inst., Los Angeles County Mus., Pasadena (Cal.) Art Mus., Nelson Gallery, Kansas City, Dallas Mus. Fine Arts. Recipient Nat. Merit award for tapestry Craftsmen U.S.A., 1966. Home: 1305 Vassar Pl Houston, TX 77006.

EVANS, ELIZABETH CORNELIA, educator; b. Little Boar's Head, N.H., Mar. 19, 1905; d. David H. and Cornelia (Draper) Evans; A.B., Radcliffe Coll., 1926, A.M., 1927, Ph.D., 1930; fellow Am. Acad. in Rome, 1930-32. From instr. to asso. prof. Greek and Latin, Wheaton (Mass.) Coll., 1932-42; faculty Vassar Coll., 1942-53, asso. prof., 1942-53; prof. classics, chmn. dept. Conn. Coll., 1953-70, Henry B. Plant prof., 1963-70. Shirley Farr fellow, 1960-61; grantee Am. Philos. Soc., 1960-61. Mem. Am. Assn. U. Women, Am. Philol. Assn., Mediaeval Acad. Am., Archaeol. Inst. Am., Classical Assn. New Eng., Phi Beta Kappa. Author: The Cults of the Sabine Territory, 1939; Physiognomics in the Ancient World, 1969. Contbr. articles to profl. jours. Home: 4 Winchester Rd New London CT 06320

EVANS, ELLIOTT WILLARD, lawyer; b. Minden, Neb., July 28, 1907; s. Willard Vine and Clara (Anderson) E.; LL.B., U. Utah, 1930; m. Aline Johnson, Oct. 6, 1933; children—Claudia Ann (Mrs. Richard M. Hunsaker), Susan Jane (Mrs. Leo J. Walz), Elliott W. Admitted to Utah bar, 1930; practice of law, Binghan Canyon, Utah, 1930-47, Salt Lake City, 1947—; asso. Evans, Neslen & Elggren, 1954-59; partner Parsons, Behle, Evans & Latimer, 1959-68. Mem. Utah (pres. 1952-53), Am., Salt Lake County bar assns., Am. Judicature Soc., Phi Kappa Phi. Mason (grand master 1954-55). Home: 955 Fairview Av Salt Lake City UT 84105

EVANS, ELLSWORTH E., lawyer; b. Cedar Rapids, Ia., 1903; LL.B., John Marshall Law School, 1928; m.; 2 children. Admitted to S.D. bar, 1928; since practiced in Sioux Falls; mem. firm Davenport, Evans, Hurwitz & Smith; former state's atty. and asst. atty. gen. Fellow Internat. Acad. Trial Lawyers; mem. Am., Minnehaha County bar assns., State Bar S.D. (pres. 1958-59), Am. Coll. Trial Lawyers, Delta Theta Phi. Address: Nat Res Bldg Sioux Falls SD 57102

EVANS, ELWYN, cardiologist; b. Dodgeville, Wis., Dec. 15, 1901; s. George B. and Kathryn (Jones) E.; student U. Wis., 1920-23; B.S., Lewis Inst., Chgo., 1927; M.D., U. Chgo., 1934; postgrad. student Harvard, 1940-41, 46, U. Mich., 1947; m. Leone Hendrickson, Sept. 6, 1935; children—Sara Jane, Elwyn Kim. Student asst. histology U. Chgo., 1929-30; intern Ill. Central Hosp., Chgo., 1934; resident No. Pacific Hosp., St. Paul, 1936- 37; grad. asst. Mass. Gen. Hosp., 1942-43, clin. fellow, 1946; cons. staff Fla. Sanitarium and Hosp., Orlando, 1942-52, electrocardiographer, 1942—, chief med. service, 1953-55, v.p. med. staff, 1954, pres. med. staff, 1955; asst. cardiac clinic Boston Lying-In Hosp., 1946; attending physician Orange Meml. Hosp., Orlando, v.p. med. staff, 1949; practice of cardiology, Orlando and Winter Park, Fla., 1946—; cons. Fla. Tb Sanitorium, Orlando, 1947-55, Brevard Hosp., Melbourne, Fla., 1954-67, South Lake Meml. Hosp., Clermont, Fla., 1956-67; cardiologist Fla. Children's Home Soc., 1947; cons. West Orange Meml. Hosp., Winter Garden, Fla.—1957—, Leesburg (Fla.) Gen. Hosp. Walker Meml. Hosp., Avon Park, Fla., St. Cloud (Fla.) Gen. Hosp. Mem. med. adv. bd. SSS, Mass., 1942-47, Fla., 1951—. Recipient D.S.M., Am. Heart Assn., 1956, 57. Diplomate Am. Bd. Internal Medicine in cardiovascular disease, Pan Am. Soc. Internal Medicine, Fellow Am. Med. Authors, Am. Geriatric Soc. (indsl. adv. com. 1950-60), Am. Gerontologic Soc., Internat. Heart Assn., Am. Coll. Cardiology (trustee Florida gov.), Am. Med. Writers Assn.; mem. A.M.A., Am. Therapeutic Soc., Am. (dir. 1956-59), Fla. (dir. 1949—, pres. 1951-52), Orange County (pres. 1953) heart assns., Orange County Med. Soc. (v.p. 1954), Phi Chi. Episcopalian. Contbr. med. articles profl. publs., encys. Home: 105 Glenridge Way Winter Park FL 32789 Office: 500 E Colonial Av Orlando FL 32803

EVANS, EMORY GIBBONS, educator, historian; b. Richmond Va., Jan. 21, 1928; s. Wallace R. and Margaret (Strickland) E.; B.A., Randolph-Macon Coll., 1950; M.A., U. Va., 1954; Ph.D., 1957; m. Winifred Burton, Dec. 19, 1953; children—Jeffrey, Christopher, Philip. Instr. Darlington Sch., Rome, Ga., 1950-52, U. Md., College Park, 1956-58, U. Pitts., 1958-60, asst. prof., 1960-64; asso. prof. No. Ill. U., DeKalb, 1964-68, prof., 1968—, chmn. history dept., 1964—; vis. prof. U. Va., Charlottesville, 1969- 70. Served with AUS, 1946. Recipient grants-in-aid (summers) Am. Philos. Soc., 1959, 64, Colonial Williamsburg, Inc., 1959, 60, 61, 62, 64. Mem. Am. Hist. Soc., Am. Assn. U. Profs., Orgn. of Am. Historians, So. Hist. Assn., Am. Civil Liberties Union. Contbr. essays to books, periodicals, mags. Home: 211 Ridge Dr DeKalb IL 60115

EVANS, ERNEST EDWARD, educator; microbiologist, immunologist; b. Parkersburg, W.Va., Dec. 14, 1922; s. Ernest Edward and Vivian F. (Enoch) E.; A.B., Ohio U., 1945; M.S., Ohio State U., 1947; Ph.D., U. So. Cal., 1950; m. Marjorie Lydia McConville, Sept. 2, 1947. Teaching asst. bacteriology Ohio State U., 1945-47; lectr. bacteriology, teaching asst. med. microbiology U. So. Cal., 1947-50; instr. bacteriology U. Mich., 1950-51, Horace H. Rackham faculty fellow, 1951, asst. prof., 1951-55; asso. prof. microbiology Sch. Medicine and Dentistry, U. Ala., Birmingham, 1955-61; Chmn. dept., 1961-69, prof., 1961—; vis. investigator Lerner Marine Lab., Am. Mus. Natural History, Bimini, Bahamas, 1966—; vis. research biologist U. Cal. at Santa Barbara, 1970; sr. research microbiologist Mote Marine Lab., Sarasota, Fla., 1970—; Mem. com. bacteriologic technique Am. Thoracic Soc., 1954-58, com. fungus entigens, 1962-66. Fellow Am. Acad. Microbiology, A.A.A.S.; mem. Am. Soc. Microbiology, Am. Assn. Immunologists, Ala. Acad. Sci., Am. Assn. U. Profs., Soc. Exptl. Biology and Medicine, Internat. Soc. Human and Animal Mycology, Soc. Invertebrate Pathology, Soc. Am. Bacteriologists, Phi Beta Kappa, Sigma Xi. Editorial bd. Jour. Bacteriology, 1961-66. Contbr. articles profl. jours. Home: 3525 Crestbrook Rd Mountain Brook AL 35223 Office: 1919 7th Av S Birmingham AL 35233

EVANS, FRANK EDWARD, congressman; b. Pueblo, Colo., Sept. 6, 1923; s. Frank Edward and Mildred Louise (Hoag) E.; student Pomona (Cal.) Coll., 1941-43; B.A., U. Denver, 1947, LL.B., 1949; m. Eleanor Trefz, Apr. 5, 1952; children—Peter, Frances, Susan, Charles. Admitted to Colo. bar, 1950, since practiced in Pueblo; mem. Colo. Legislature from Pueblo County, 1960-64, Democratic whip, 1962-64; mem. 89th-92d congresses from 3d Dist. Colo. Mem. Pueblo Indsl. Devel. Corp., 1958-62, Pueblo Community Welfare Council, 1954-64; pres. Jr. Achievement, Pueblo, 1956; mem. bd. Family Service Soc., Pueblo, 1958-64, Colo. Hist. Soc., 1960-64; active Single Fund Pueblo, 1950. Served as patrol pilot USNR, World War II. Named Outstanding Freshman Rep., Denver Press Assn., 1961. Presbyn. Kiwanian (past pres. Pueblo). Home: 4935 Quebec St N W Washington DC 20016 Office: House Office Bldg Washington DC 20515

EVANS, FRANK OWEN, lawyer; b. Gordon, Ga., Dec. 15, 1910; s. Robert Earl and Anna R. (Owen) E.; B.S., Washington and Lee U., 1930; LL.B., Mercer U., 1933; m. E. Anne Bone; children-Frank Owen, Robert Earl. Engaged in gen. practice law, Milledgeville, Ga., 1933—; former U.S. dist. atty., Macon, Ga. Chmn. Ga. div. Am. Cancer Crusade, 1958. Mem. Ga. Republican Central Com., 1932-38; vice-chmn. 6th Dist. Exec. Com., 1936-40; gen. counsel Ga. Central Com., 1944-52; alternate del. Rep. Nat. Conv., 1944, del. from 6th Congl. Dist., vice-chmn. Ga. Delegation, 1948; presdl. elector, 1948, 52. Chmn. exec. com., bd. govs. Woodward Acad.; chmn. found. bd., Ga. Coll., Milledgeville. Mem. Hon. Order Ky. Colonels, Pi Kappa Phi, Phi Alpha Delta. Methodist. Mason (Shriner), Elk. Clubs: Idle Country (Macon); Milledgeville Country. Kiwanis. Home: Milledgeville GA 31061 Office: 201 S Wayne St Milledgeville GA 31061

EVANS, FRANKLIN BACHELDRR, educator; b. Chgo., Feb. 9, 1922; s. Franklin B. and Arline (Brown) E.; A.A., U. Chgo., 1941, A.B., 1943, M.B.A., 1954, Ph.D., 1959; m. Barbara B. Both, Sept. 16, 1943; children—Mary A., Amy B. (Mrs. David C. Farmer), Geoffrey B., Christopher G. Asst. prof. marketing U. Chgo., 1957-64; prof. marketing U. Hawaii, 1964-69; prof. advt. Northwestern U., 1969—; cons. to bus. and industry. Served with AUS, 1943-45; CBI. Decorated Bronze Star. Mem. Am. Statis. Assn., Am. Sociol. Assn., Am. Marketing Assn., Am. Acad. Adut., A.A.A.S., Am. Assn. Univ. Profs., Psi Upsilon. Contbr. articles profl. jours. Home: 2025 Sherman Av Evanston IL 60201

EVANS, FREDERICK HARRIS, otolaryngologist; b. Terre Haute, Ind., Feb. 1, 1916; s. Frederick H. and Grace (Wilson) E.; A.B., Fisk U., 1941; M.D., Meharry Med. Coll., 1944; m. Shirley Richardson, Jan. 10, 1939; children—Frederick Harris III, Noel G. Intern Freedmens Hosp., Washington, 1944-46; gen. practice, Indpls., 1946-52; resident otolaryngology Ind. U. Hosp., 1955-58; pvt. practice otolaryngology, Indpls., 1958—; chmn. otolaryngology sect. Methodist Hosp., 1966-70; asso. otalaryngloy staff Ind. U. Med. Center, 1958—. Martin Center, Out Lady of Fatima Retreat House. Bd. dirs. Indpls. Found., Catholic Youth Orgn., Indpls. Speech and Hearing Center; trustee Vincennes U. Served with AUS, 1952-54. Decorated Bronze Star. Diplomate Am. Bd. Ophthalmology and Otolaryngology. Fellow Am. Acad. Ophthalmology and Otolaryngology; mem. Am., Nat. med. assns., Hooiser State (pres. 1965-66), Ind., Marion County, Aesculapian med. socs., Ind. Acad. Ophthalmology, Pan Pacific Surg. Assn., Pan- Am. Assn. Oto-Rhino-Laryngology and Broncho-Esophagology, N.A.A.C.P. (life), Nat. Urban League, Cath. Physicians Guild, Nat. Council Cath. Men, Wisdon Hall of Fame, Kappa Alpha Psi. K.C. Club: Serra Internat. Home: 1705 Kessler Blvd W Dr Indianapolis, IN 46208. Office: 2140 N Capitol Av Indianapolis IN 46202

EVANS, GEORGE A., mfg. co. exec.; b. Baraboo, Wis., 1912; ed. U. Wis., 1933. Sec., gen. atty. Rex Chainbelt Inc. Home: 968 E Circle Dr Milwaukee WI 53217 Office: 4700 W Greenfield Av Milwaukee WI 53214*

EVANS, GEORGE GRAY, plywood and paper co. exec.; b. Leonia, N.J., Feb. 11, 1912; s. George A. and Grace Edith (Tucker) E.; student San Jose (Cal.) State Coll., 1929-30; B.S. in Forestry, U. Cal. at Berkeley, 1933; m. Elinor Jean Flaherty, Sept. 5, 1937; children-Donald Gray, Susan Alice. With U.S. Forest Service, 1933; with Hammond Lumber Co., Eureka, Cal., 1934-44, 46- 58, logging mgr., 1950-58; gen. mgr. timber and logging Ga.-Pacific Corp., Portland, Ore., 1958-63, v.p., 1964—. Bd. dirs., pres. Cal. Forest Protective Assn. Served to lt. (s.g.) USNR, 1944-46. Mem. Soc. Am. Foresters. Mason (Shriner). Home: 2865 S W 99th Av Portland OR 97225 Office: Equitable Bldg Portland OR 97204

EVANS, GEORGE HEBERTON, Jr., educator; b. Balt., Jan. 20, 1900; s. George Heberton and Mary Virginia Crawford (Sherlock) E.; A.B., Johns Hopkins U., 1920, Ph.D., 1925, LL.D., 1970; m. Elinor Virdin, Nov. 26, 1924; children—George Herberton III, Richard Virdin, Ellen (dec.). Instr. polit. economy Johns Hopkins U., 1924-27, asso., 1927-35, asso. prof., 1935-42, prof., 1942-70, prof. emeritus, 1970—, chmn. dept. 1942-60, charge Army's fgn. area and lang. tng. program, 1943-44, dean faculty of philosophy, 1959-66, dean emeritus, 1970—; seminar asso. Columbia U., 1969—. Corporator Savs. Bank of Balt. Served in S.A.T.C., 1918. Trustee Roland Park Country Sch., 1941- 53, Commn. Govt. Efficiency and Economy, 1943-46, 49-51, 54-56. Mem. Md. State Bd. Pub. Accountancy, 1953-67, Nat. Bur. of Econ. Research (research asso., 1939-40). Mem. Am. Econ. Assn., Am. Statis. Assn., Am. Assn. U. Profs., Econ. Hist. Assn. (past v.p.), Phi Beta Kappa, Beta Theta Pi. Episcopalian. Club: Johns Hopkins (Baltimore). Author: British Corporation Finance, 1775- 1850; A Study of Preference Shares, 1936; Principles of Investment (with George E. Barnett), 1940, Spanish edit., 1947; Business Incorporations in the U.S., 1800-1943, 1948; Basic Economics, 1950. Editor: Reprint of Economic Tracts. Contbr. articles in econ. jours. Home: 6134 Barroll Rd Baltimore MD 21209 Office: Johns Hopkins U Baltimore MD 21218

EVANS, GEORGE ROBERT, Jr., graphic arts exec.; b. San Antonio, June 24, 1931; s. George Robert and Maude Ellen (Davis) E.; B.S., Wagner Coll., 1953; postgrad. Northwestern U., 1960-61, U. Cal. at Los Angeles, 1967-69; m. Alma Emma Behling, Feb. 23, 1952; children—Sandra, Robert, Teri, John, James, Patrick, Michelle. Works mgr., dir. marketing, v.p., gen. mgr. U.S. Gypsum Co., 1953-69; pres. U.S. Gypsum Export Co., 1966-68; pres., chief exec. officer Kingsport Press, Inc. (Tenn.), 1969-71; group v.p. Arcata Nat. Corp., N.Y.C., 1971—. Mem. Nat. UN Com., 1971—. Bd. dirs. U. Tenn. Devel. Council. Mem. Book Mfg. Inst. (dir.), Newcomen Soc. N.Am. Lutheran. Rotarian. Home: 18 Surrey Glen Wilton CT 06897 Office: 30 Rockefeller Center New York City NY 10020

EVANS, GERAINT, opera singer; b. Cilfynydd, nr. Pontypridd, S. Wales, Feb. 16, 1922; s. William John and Gladys May (Thomas) E.; student Guildhall Sch. Music; Mus.D. (hon.), U. Wales, 1965; m. Brenda Evans Davies, Mar. 27, 1948; children—Alun Grant, Huw Grant. Appearances include Royal Opera House, Govent Garden, London, England, 1948—, Glyndebournse Festival Opera, 1950- -, also Vienna (Austria) State Opera, La Scala, Milan, Italy, San Francisco Opera, Chgo. Lyric Opera, Salzburg (Austria) Festival, Teatro Colon, Buenos Aires, Argentina, Met. Opera House, N.Y.C.; promenade concerts, also appearances on TV and radio. Fellow Guildhall Sch. Music; decorated comdr. British Empire, 1959. Home: Lone Pool 34 Birchwood Rd Petts Wood Kent England Office: care Colbert Artists Mgmt 850 7th Av New York City NY 10019

EVANS, GIL, (Ian Ernest Gilmore Green), composer, pianist; b. Toronto, Ont., Can., May 13, 1912 (parents Australian citizens). Leader own band, Stockton, Cal., 1933-38; arranger Skinny Ennis, 1938-41; arranger Claude Thornhill Orch., 1941-48; orchestrator recordings, Moondreams, Boplicity; free lance as arranger, N.Y.C., 1952-57; with Miles Davis and 19 piece band, recorded Miles Ahead, 1957; recording bandleader, 1958; leader own band, appearing Birdland, 1959; recordings include: New Bottle, Old Wine, Great Jazz Standards, Big Stuff; (arranger for Miles Davis) Miles Ahead, Porgy and Bess, Birth of the Cool. Address: Whitby Apts 325 W 45th St New York City NY 10036

EVANS, GLENN, laundry products mfg. exec.; b. Indpls., May 19, 1915; s. Robert Benjamin and Norma (Kelso) E.; student Miami U., Wittenburg Coll. Extension, 1934-37, Ind. U., 1937-39; m. Ruth Hunt, Oct. 20, 1940; children—Lynn, Richard. Asst. dir. quality control, then factory mgr. Omaha plant, dir. mfg. engring. Martin Co., 1939-55; with Whirlpool Corp., St. Joseph, Mich., 1955—, gen. mgr. Marion, O., 1955- 57, gen. mgr., St. Joseph, 1957-59, now dir.; dir. Warwich Electronics. Mem. evaluation team for offshore procurement aircraft in Europe, USAF, 1951. Exec. bd. Boy Scouts Am. Bd. dirs. Mich. Children's Aid Soc., Twin Cities Community Chest. Mem. Am. Soc. Tool Engrs., Soc. Automotive Engrs., C. of C. (exec. bd.). Christian Scientist. Rotarian. Home: 1105 St Joseph Dr Joseph MI 49085 Office: Whirlpool Corp St Joseph MI 49085

EVANS, GORDON GOODWIN, educator; b. Bklyn., Feb. 13, 1921; s. William Fuller and Beatrice Annie (Briley) E.; A.B., Princeton, 1942; Ph.D., Harvard, 1950; m. Doletha Soorn Watt, Oct. 14, 1944; children—Doletha Marian, William Soorn, Jocelyn Briley, Lawrence Watt, Ruth Christina, Charlotte Deirdre, Chemist, E.I. du Pont de Nemours & Co., Inc., Buffalo, 1942-43; instr. chemistry Tufts U., 1949-52, asst. prof., 1952-65, asso. prof., 1965—. Served with AUS, 1943-46. Mem. Am. Chem. Soc., A.A.A.S., New Eng. Assn. Chemistry Tchrs., Am. Assn. U. Profs. Unitarian-Universalist. Home: 51 South Rd Bedford MA 01730 Office: Dept Chemistry Tufts University Medford MA 02155

EVANS, GORDON WRIGHT, utility exec.; b. Deport, Tex., Sept. 21, 1904; s. William P. and Alice (Wright) E.; student Trinity U., 1920-22; U. Tex., 1922-23, U. So. Cal., 1923, Okla. Sch. Accounting and Law, 1926-29; m. Mabel Marian Leigh, Apr. 21, 1926; 1 son, Dennis Leigh. With Pub. Service Co. of Okla., 1925- 28; sec.-treas., v.p. Okla. Power & Water Co., 1928-37; v.p. Mo. Pub. Service Corp., 1937-41; pres. Mo. Edison Co., 1941-47; asst. to pres. Kan. Gas & Electric Co., 1947-48, v.p., gen. mgr., 1948-53, pres., 1953-69, chmn., chief exec. officer, 1969—; dir. First Nat. Bank, Wichita, Kan. Bd. dirs. Wichita Symphony Soc. Mem. Kan. C. of C. Clubs: Wichita, Wichita Country, Petroleum, Rotary (Wichita, Kan.); Wichita Home: 108 S Pinecrest St Wichita KS 67218 Office: 215 N Market St Wichita KS 67202

EVANS, GRIFFITH CONRAD, mathematician; b. Boston, May 11, 1887; s. George William and Mary (Taylor) E.; A.B., Harvard, 1907, A.M., 1908, Ph.D., 1910; postgrad. U. Rome, 1910-12; LL.D., U.Cal., 1956; m. Isabel Mary John, June 20, 1917; children—Griffith Conrad, George William, Robert John. Instr. math. Harvard, 1906-07, 09-10; Sheldon fellow in Italy, 1910-12; asst. prof. math. Rice Inst., 1912-16, prof., 1916-34; vis. prof. U. Cal., summers 1921, 28, prof. math., 1934-55, chmn. dept., 1934-49, now emeritus; vis. prof. U. Chgo., summer 1925, U. Minn., summer 1941, Rice U., 1959; faculty research lectr. U. Cal., 1962; spl. lectr. colls., univs. Mem. NRC, 1927-31, 40-43, 50-53. Tech. cons., sci. expert ordnance War Dept., 1943-47. Served as capt. Signal Corps., U.S. Army, 1918-19. Recipient Distinguished Assistance award U.S. Army, 1946; Presdl. certificate of merit, 1948. Fellow Econometric Soc.; mem. Am. Acad. Arts. and Scis., Nat. Acad. Scis., Am. Philos. Society, Am. Math. Soc. (v. p. 1924-26, pres. 1938-40), Math. Assn. Am. (v.p. 1932), A.A.A.S. Author: Mathematical Introduction to Economics, 1930; Stabiliteé et Dynamique de la Production dans l'Economie Politique (Memorial des Sciences Math.), 1932; Functionals and Their Applications, Cambridge Colloquium, Part I, 1918, rev., 1964; The Logarithmic Potential, Vol. 6, 1927 rev., 1928, rev., 1930; also tech. papers and lit. publs. Home: 319 North Gate Rd Walnut Creek CA 94598

EVANS, GRIFFITH CONRAD, Jr., state govt. ofcl.; b. Lynn, Mass., May 17, 1918; s. Griffith Conrad and Isabel (John) E.; A.B. in Anthropology, U. Cal. at Berkeley, 1940; m. Arlene Westbo Callahan, Jan. 1, 1939; children—Judith, Nancy Lea, Griffith Conrad III, Carol Susan. Clk., State Farm Mut. Automobile Ins. Co., 1940-41; chief clk. Matson Navigation Co., 1946-50; exec. sec. Oceanographic Commn. Wash., 1967—; exec. dir. Oceanographic Inst. Wash., 1968—. Dir. Sea Use Program, 1968—; mem. Seattle Aquarium Com., 1968—. Chmn. steering com. for task force occupational edn. Seattle Sch. Bd., 1968-71; mem. pollution control tech. adv. com. Shoreline Community Coll., 1970—. Enlisted U.S. Navy, 1941, commd. ensign USNR, 1942, served to lt., 1942-46, returned to active duty, 1950, advanced through grades to capt., 1963; comdr. U.S.S. Everett, 1951-53, U.S.S. Burton Island, 1960-61, U.S S. Edisto, 1961-62; Thailand rep., comdr. in chief U.S. Pacific Fleet, Bangkok, 1966-67; ret., 1967. Decorated Legion of Merit, Navy Commendation medal. Mem. Marine Tech. Soc., Am. Soc. Oceangraphy. Peninsula in Belingshausen Sea in Antarctic named for him. Home: 4005 SW Massachusetts St Seattle WA 98116 Office 312 1st Av N Seattle WA 98109

EVANS, GROSE, curator; b. Columbus, O., Dec. 15, 1916; s. Marshall Blakemore and Elizabeth Theodora (Grose) E.; B.F.A., Ohio State U., 1941, A.M., 1942; Ph.D., John Hopkins, 1953i m. Grace Elizabeth Orvis, Jan. 4, 1946; 1 dau., Grace Elizabeth Grose. Lectr. Nat. Gallery of Art, 1946-54, asst. curator ednl. work, 1954-58, asso. curator, 1958-60, curator decorative arts Index Am. Design and Extension Service, 1960-70, curator exhbns. and loans, 1970—; guest lectr. baroque and modern art Cath. U. Am., 1948-49; guest lectr. modern art Am. U., 1952-53; lectr. modern art George Washington U., 1953-56, professorial lectr. theories of art, 1956-61; curriculum dir. Research in Tchr. Tng. Program U.S. Office Edn., 1966, Arts and Humanities Inst., 1967. Author: Subtle Satire of Magnasco, Gazette des Beaux Arts, 1948; Benjamin West and the Taste of His Times, 1959. Home: 2308 Glasgow Rd Hollin Hills Alexandria VA 22307 Office: Nat Gallery of Art Constitution Av at 6th St NW Washington DC 20565

EVANS, GWYNNE BLAKEMORE, educator; b. Columbus, O., Mar. 31, 1912; s. Marshall Blakemore and Theodora (Grose) E.; A.B., Ohio State U., 1934; M.A., U. Cin., 1936; Ph.D., Harvard, 1940; m. Florenoe Elizabeth Richey, June 1, 1943; children—Michael Blakemore, Pamela Grose. Asst. tutor Bklyn. Coll., 1940- 41; instr. U. Wis., 1941-42, 45-46, asst. prof., 1946-47; asst. prof. U. Ill., 1947-51, asso. prof., 1951-56, prof., 1956-67; prof. English and lit. Harvard, Cambridge, Mass., 1967—. Served with Signal Corps Intelligence, AUS, 1942-45. Dexter Traveling fellow, 1940, Guggenheim fellow, 1948-49. Mem. Renaissance English Text Soc. (past pres.). Author: Plays and Poems of William Cartwright, 1951; Supplement Vol. to Variorum I Henry IV, 1857; Shakespearean Prompt-Books of the 17th Century, 5 vols., 1960-70. Editor: Jour. of English and Germanic Philology, 1955-62. Mem. editorial bd. Publs. of Modern Lang. Assn., 1963-69. Home: 16 Lincoln St Belmont MA 02178 Office: Warren House Harvard Cambridge MA 02138

EVANS, HAROLD, lawyer; b. Phila., Pa., Oct. 26, 1886; s. Jonathan Evans and Rachel R. (Cope) E.; A.B., Haverford Coll., 1907, LL.D., 1968; LL.B., U. Pa., 1910; LL.D., Wilmington Coll., 1964, Haverford Coll., 1968; m. Sylvia Hathaway, May 1, 1914; children—Sylvia (Mrs. Joseph H. Taylor), Margaret (Mrs. John T. Carson, Jr.), Nathaniel H., Faith (Mrs. H. Garth Blakely), Thomas, Anna (Mrs. Arnold R. Post), Admitted to Pa. bar, 1910; mem. firm MacCoy, Evans, Hutchinson & Lewis, Phila., 1911-34, MacCoy, Britain, Evans & Lewis, 1934-49, MacCoy, Evans & Lewis, 1949—. Municipal commr. for Jerusalem for UN, 1948. Mem. Pa. Pub. Service Commn., 1925-26; chmn. Phila. Co. Relief Bd., 1936-37; trustee Community Fund of Phila., 1937- 43; chmn. Phila. Emergency Com. on Pub. Edn., 1938-39; hon. mem. bd. mgrs. Haverford Coll., trustee Penn Community Services, 1921-61, emeritus, 1969—; dir. emeritus Am. Friends Service Com., chmn., 1960-63. Mem. Am., Pa., Phila. bar assns., Am. Law Inst., Phi Beta Kappa. Club: Founders Home Awbury Philadelphia PA 19138 Office: Two Penn Center Plaza Philadelphia PA 19102

EVANS, HAROLD EDWARD, banker; b. Detroit, Apr. 23, 1927; s. Harold J. and Mary Esther (Keenoy) E.; B.B.A., U. Mich., 1950; certificate Nat. Assn. Bank Auditors and Controllers Sch., U. Wis., 1968; children—D'lorah Ann, M'liss Lorraine, David Keenoy, Craig Edward. Auditor, Second Nat. Bank Saginaw, Mich., 1952-61, controller, 1961—. Mem. Greater Saginaw Area Health Facilities Planning Council, Saginaw Citizens Council for Central Bus. Dist., 1970—; mem. adv. bd. Urban Renewal, chmn. econ. base study com., 1954- 55; chmn. Downtown Saginaw Beautification Commn., 1968—; chmn. Greater Saginaw Beautification Residental Com., 1965-68. Sec., trustee Saginaw Osteo. Hosp.; treas., trustee Saginaw Symphony Orch.; trustee Saginaw Hist. Mus.; treas., dir. United Rehab. Services, 1951-64. Served with USNR, 1945-46. Mem. Saginaw C. of C., Bank Adminstrn. Inst. (pres. Eastern Mich. conf. 1955-56, v.p. Mich. 1958-59., life mem.), Econ. Club Detroit. Republican. Mem. Unity Ch. Elk. Clubs: Breakfast Optimist (dir. 1960—, treas. 1961-63, pres. 1970—). Univ. Mich. Alumni (Saginaw). Home: 17 Riverside Blvd Saginaw MI 48602 Office: 111 N Washington St Saginaw MI 48607

EVANS, HARRY LEE, electronics exec.; b. Bedford, Ia., Nov. 22, 1919; s. Harry L. and Clara Edna (Fowler) E.; B.S., U. Okla., 1948; M.S., U. Mich., 1952; m. Dixie Maxine Sandmire, Jan. 1, 1941. Commd. 2d lt. USAAF, advanced through grades to maj. gen., 1966; squadron comdr. Randolph AFB, Tex., 1940-44; assigned Guam, 1944-45, B-29 Service Group, Tucson, 1945-46; squadron comdr., 1948-50; assigned Sandia Base, N.M., 1952-56, Air War Coll., 1956-57; dep. comdr. for space Air Force Ballistic Missile Div., Cal., 1957-60; vice dir., satellite systems Space Systems Div., Los Angeles, 1960-62, asst. vice comdr., 1962; chief research and devel. Joint Chiefs Staff, 1962-65; vice dir. Manned Orbiting Lab. Program, also dep. comdr. for space Air Force Systems Command, 1965-67. ret., 1967; v.p., gen. mgr. Space & Information Systems div. Raytheon Co., Sudbury, Mass., 1967-69 v.p. corporate devel., Lexington, Mass., 1969—. Decorated Purple Heart, D.F.C., Air medal with oak leaf cluster, Legion of Merit with oak leaf cluster. Mem. Order Daedalians. Home: 41 Suffolk Rd Wellesley Hills MA 02181 Office: Raytheon Co Lexington MA 02173

EVANS, HELEN WARD, educator; B.A., Walla Walla Coll., 1949; M.A., Stanford, 1955, Ph.D., 1965. Prof., chmn. dept. English, Walla Walla Coll., College Place, Wash. Office: Dept English Walla Walla Coll College Place WA 99324*

EVANS, HENRY COTHEAL, investment banker; b. Balt., Sept. 17, 1895; A.B., Johns Hopkins, 1918; m. Eleanor O'Donovan, 1921; 6 children. Chmn. bd., then hon. chmn. Stein Bros. & Boyce, Inc. (now merged into Bache & Co.), mems. N.Y., other stock exchanges, Balt.; dir. Eutlaw Savs. Bank, William E. Hooper & Son Co. Pres. Balt. Stock Exchange, 1939-41. Md. state chmn. U.S.O. Chmn. bd. Enoch Pratt Free Library, Served with Am. Field Service 1917, to capt. F.A., U.S. Army, 1917-19; AEF in France; mem. Md. N.G., 1921-57, advancing to maj. gen.; served from col. to maj. gen., AUS, 1941-57; overseas, 1944; ret., 1957. Decorated D.S.C., Silver Star, Legion of Merit, Bronze Star with oak leaf cluster (U.S.): Fourragére, Legion of Honor, Croix de Guerre (France); Croix de Guerre (Belgium, Luxembourg), Knight of St. Gregory (Pope Paul VI); recipient Andrew White medal Loyola Coll., Balt., 1964; Distinguished Alumnus award Johns Hopkins, 1967; Distinguished Service medal State of Md., 1970; Silver Beaver award Balt. Area council Boy Scouts Am. mem. Balt. Assn. Commerce (pres. 1962-63). Home; 200 Longwood Rd Baltimore MD 21210 ☆

EVANS, HERBERT EMLYN, broadcasting co. exec.; b. Colwyn Bay, Wales, U.K., Sept. 1, 1901; s. Elias and Anna (Hughes) E.; came to U.S., 1905, naturalized, 1920; student Springfield (Mass.) Coll., 1921; D.Bus. Adminstrn. (hon.), Yankton (S.D.) Coll., 1958; Litt. D. (hon.), Kirksville (Mo.) Coll., 1957; L.H.D. (hon.), Morningside Coll., Sioux City, Ia., 1959, Coll. Osteopathic Medicine and Surgery, Des Moines, Ia., 1960, Chgo. Coll. Osteopathy, 1963; LL.D., from Lincoln Memorial U., 1964; m. Ella Weed, April 11, 1925; children—Jane Carolyn (Mrs. George R. Shappo), Richard McCastline. Counsellor to Protestant students Columbia, 1920-36; v.p. Consumer Distbn. Corp., N.Y.C., 1936-42; v.p. personnel Nationwide Ins. Cos., Columbus, O., 1942-52; v.p. gen. mgr. Peoples Broadcasting Corp., Columbus, 1952-59, pres., 1959—; v.p., dir. Cleve. Browns Profl. Football Team, 1954-61, Peoples Travel Service, Columbus, 1958—. Bd. govs. Franklin U., Columbus; trustee Springfield Coll.; bd. dirs. Doctors Hosp., Columbus; pres. Nat. Council YMCA's, N.Y.C., 1961-62, now mem.; exec. com. nat. bd. YMCA; exec. com. U.S. and Can., Internat. Com. YMCA; exec. com. World Alliance YMCA; chmn. trustees National Osteo. Found., Chgo., Yankton Coll.; trustee Lincoln Meml. U., Harrogate, Tenn. Mem. Nat. Assn. Broadcasters (representative to U.S. nat. commn. for UNESCO: V.P.), Inter-Am Assn. Broadcasters (directive bd.), Honourable Soc. Cymmrodorion (London, Eng.), Handel Opera Soc. (London). Clubs; Friars (N.Y.C.); Broadcasters (Washington); Columbus Athletic. Home: 113 W Hudson St Columbus OH 43202 Office: 246 N High St Columbus OH 43215

EVANS, HOWARD ENSIGN, educator; b. East Hartford, Conn., Feb. 23, 1919; s. Archie J. and Adella (Ensign) E.; B.A., U. Conn., 1940; M.S., Cornell U., 1941, Ph.D., 1949; m. Mary Alice Dietrich, June 6, 1954; children—Barbara, Dorothy, Timothy. Asst. prof. Kan. State Coll., Manhattan, 1949-52; asst. prof. entomology Cornell U., 1954-59; asso. curator Mus. Comparative Zoology, Harvard, 1959-63, curator, 1963-69, Alexander Agassiz prof. zoology, 1969—. Served to 2d lt. AUS, 1942-45. Mem. Soc. Study Evolution, Entomol. Soc. Am. Author: Song I Sing, 1950; Studies on the Comparative Ethology of Digger Wasps of the Genus Bembix, 1957; Wasp Farm (nominated for Nat. Book award 1964), 1963; The Comparative Ethology and Evolution of the Sand Wasps, 1966; Life on a Little Known Planet, 1968; (with M.J.W. Eberhard) The Wasps, 1970; (with M.A. Evans) William Morton Wheeler, Biologist, 1970. Contbr. articles profl. jours. Home: 17 Frances Rd Lexington MA 02173 Office: Mus Comparative Zoology Harvard Cambridge MA 02138

EVANS, HOWARD VERNON, educator; b. Red Granite, Wis., Sept. 29, 1922; s. Robert L. and Ethel (Newbold) E.; Ph.B., U. Wis., 1948, M.S., 1950, Ph.D., 1955; m. Charlotte Buff, July 4, 1947; children—Robert Thomas, Janice Elizabeth. Asst. dir. edn. U.S. Armed Forces Inst., 1952-56; prof. history, dean of coll. Muskingum Coll., 1956-67, v.p. acad. affairs, dean of coll., 1967-69; asso. prof. history Central Mich. U., 1969—. Served to lt. col., inf. AUS, 1942-46. Mem. Mich. Acad. Sci., Arts and Letters, Am. Soc. Eighteenth-Century Studies, Soc. French Hist. Studies, Am. Hist. Assn., Higher Edn. Assn., Phi Eta Sigma, Phi Alpha Theta. Presbyn. Rotarian. Author: William Pitt, William Miles and The French Revolution; The Liberal Arts College in an Age of Increasing Nihilism; Current Trends in American and European Historiography. Home: 30 Cedar Dr Mount Pleasant MI 48858

EVANS, HUGH HINTON, savs. and loan assn. exec.; b. Arkadelphia, Ark., Oct. 25, 1898; s. Benjamin H. and Tennessee (Dawdy) E.; B.A., U. Ark., 1920; m. Gladys Crail, Nov. 1, 1928; children—Mary Crail, Hugh Hinton. Frank A. Vanderlip scholar Nat. City Bank, N.Y.C., 1919, with fgn. exchange dept., 1919-22; br. mgr. Security First Nat'l. Bank, 1923-35; founder Coast Fed. Savs. & Loan Assn., 1935, pres., 1935- -; dir., mgr. Western Fed. Savs. & Loan Assn., Los Angeles, 1937—, pres., 1955—; dir., founder Pioneer Savs. & Loan Assn., 1937, chmn. bd. dirs., 1937—; pres. S.W. Title & Tax Co., Park-Hill Ins. Co.; dir. Am. Savs. & Loan Assn. Mem. Cal. Commn. Jud. Qualifications. Founder, chmn., trustee Democratic Assos., Los Angeles; del. Dem. Nat. Conv., 1960. Served to 2d lt., inf. U.S. Army, World War I. Clubs: Optimist (past pres.); California; Los Angeles Country. Home: 419 S Lorraine Blvd Los Angeles CA 90005 Office: 600 S Hill St Los Angeles CA 90014

EVANS, HUGH MCCLOSKEY, dept. store exec.; b. New Orleans, Mar. 17, 1907; s. Frederick Watkins and Hughetta Virginia (McCloskey) E.; student Tulane U., 1927-32; m. Sidonie de la Houssaye, Oct. 14, 1933; children—Sally Watkins (Mrs. Richard Hodges), Sidonie de la Houssaye (Mrs. Frank Schmidt), Hugh McCloskey. Pres., D.H. Holmes Co., Ltd., also chief exec. officer; dir. Frederick Atkins, Inc., Central Gulf S.S. Corp., Flambeaux Printing Co. Bd. dirs. Adult Edn. Center, Assn. Retarded Children. Mem. Nat. Retail Mchts. Assn., Nat. Retail Dry Goods Assn. (dir.), C. of C., Phi Delta Theta. Home: 1520 Toledano St New Orleans LA 70115 Office: 819 Canal St New Orleans LA 70112

EVANS, IDRIS WILLIAM, educator, sociologist; b. Bonham, Tex., July 6, 1930; s. Kenneth and Helen (Ford) E.; B.A., East Tex. State U., Commerce, 1951; M.A., U. Tex., 1952, Ph.D., 1959; m. Jane Garland Monteith, Feb. 27, 1954; children—Kenneth Ford, Diane Alise. Instr. sociology U. Tex., 1956-57; instr., then asso. prof. U. Mont., 1957-66; postdoctoral fellow U. Mich., 1966-67; prof., chmn. dept. sociology and social welfare U. Mont., 1967—, chmn. dept. anthropology, 1967-69. Served with AUS, 1952- 54. Fellow Am. Sociol. Assn.; mem. Pacific Sociol. Assn., Am. Inst. Urban and Regional Affairs, Center Study Democratic Instns., Planning Assn. Washington. Home: 3808 Bellecrest Dr Missoula MT 59801

EVANS, JACK EARL, lawyer; b. Cape Girardeau, Mo., Jan. 21, 1933; s. Dorcey R. and Emma (Yount) E.; B.S. in Bus. Adminstrn., U. Mo., 1958, LL.B., 1961; m. Elizabeth Jean Schwaner, Mar. 23, 1952; children-Constance Suzanne, Jack Earl. Admitted to Mo. bar, 1960, Ariz. bar, 1962; accountant Price Waterhouse & Co., C.P.A.'s, St. Louis, 1958-59; tchr. U. Mo., 1958-60; with Firm Kuraner, Freeman, Kuraner, Kansas City, Mo., 1960-61; pres. Evans & Kunz, Ltd., Phoenix, 1961—. Pres. Golden Gate Settlement, Phoenix, 1967—. Mem. Ariz. Acad., Phoenix, 1967—. Bd. dirs. Phoenix Met. YMCA, 1967—, Phoenix United Fund, 1965-69. Served with USAF, 1951- 55. Named Man of Year, Phi Delta Phi, 1960. Mem. Am., Mo., Ariz. bar assns., Phi Delta Phi. Republican. Episcopalian, Kiwanian, (pres. Valley of Sun Club 1969—). Club: Thunderbirds, Phoenix Country (Phoenix). Editor, contbr. Mo. Law Rev., 1959-60. Home: 73 N Country Club Dr Phoenix AZ 85014 Office: 3800 N Central Av Phoenix AZ 85012

EVANS, JAMES CARMICHAEL, govt. offcl.; b. Gallatin, Tenn., July 1, 1900; s. James Royal and Lillie (Charmichael) E.; A.B., Roger Williams U., 1921; B.S., Mass. Inst. Tech., 1925, M.S., 1926; LL.D., Va. State Coll., 1955, Central State Coll., 1956; L.H.D., Agrl. and Tech. Coll. N.C., 1961; m. Rosalline McGoodwin, Aug 28, 1928; children—James Carmichael, Rose Evangeline Wells. Engaged in elec. engring, constrn., Miami, Fla., 1926-28; tchr. Booker T. Washington High Sch., Miami, 1927; prof. tech. industries, dir. trade and tech. div. W.Va. State Coll. 1928-37, adminstrv. asst. to pres., 1937-42; asst. civilian aide to sec. war. 1943-47, civilian aide, 1947-48; adviser to sec. def., 1947-49, asst. 1947—, counsellor civil affairs, 1964—. Adj. prof. elec. engring. Howard U. 1946—; v.p. Afro-Am. Life Ins. Co., 1954. Vocational tng. dir. asso. Council Nat. Def., War Manpower Comm., Washington, 1941-43; mil. instr., World War I; coordinator tng. programs for civilian, mil. pilots, 1939-43. Recipient Harmon award in sci. research in electronics, 1926; Dorie Miller Meml. Found. award, 1953; Career Service award Nat. Civil Service League, 1959: Sec. Def. Meritorius Civilian Service medal, 1970. Mem. Nat. Tech. Assn. (exec. sec. 1932-57), Nat. Inst. Sci., Am. Inst. E.E., I.R.E., Am. Assn. U. Profs., N.E.A. Tau Beta Pi, Epsilon Pi Tau, Alpha Kappa Mu, Alpha Phi Alpha, Sigma Pi Phi. Baptist. Clubs: Adelphian (Miami); Musolit, Cosmos (Washington). Writer monographs tng. and placement in tech. fields. Patentee utilization of exhaust gases to prevent icing on aircraft. Home: 3533 Warder St NW Washington DC 20010 Office: Pentagon Washington DC 20301

EVANS, JAMES HURLBURT, bus. exec., b. Lansing, Mich., June 26, 1920; s. James L. and Marie (Hurlburt) E.; A.B., Centre Coll. Ky., 1943; J.D., U. Chgo., 1948; m. LoRaine Bertram, Sept. 30, 1944; children—Eric Bertram, Carol Ruth, Joan McLeod. Admitted to Ill. bar, 1949; atty., loan officer Harris Trust & Savs. Bank, Chgo., 1948-56; sec.-treas. Reuben H. Donnelley Corp., Chgo., 1956-57, v.p., N.Y.C., 1957-62, also dir.; co. merged in Dun & Brad street, Inc., 1961, financial v.p., 1962-65, dir., 1962—; pres., Seamen's Bank for Savs., N.Y.C., 1965- 68, chmn. bd., 1968-69, trustee, 1965—; pres., dir. Union Pacific Corp., 1969—; dir. U.P. R.R., 1965—, vice chmn. bd., 1969—; dir. Bristol-Myers Co. Pres., Nat. Recreation Found. Bd. govs. A.R.C.; trustee Union Pacific Found., Centre Coll. Ky.; bd. dirs. Josiah Macy Jr. Found.; trustee, mem. exec. com. Nat. Recreation and Park Assn.; bd. overseers Sweet Briar Coll.; bd. mgrs. N.Y. Bot. Garden. Served to lt. USNR, 1943-46. Mem. Am., Chgo. bar assns., Omicron Delta Kappa, Delta Kappa Epsilon. Presbyn. Clubs: Union League, Economic, Downtown Assn., River, Links (N.Y.C.); Bronxville Field, Siwanoy Country (Bronxville); Shenorock Shore (Rye, N.Y.) Home: 376 New Rochelle Rd Bronxville NY 10708 Office: 345 Park Av New York City NY 10022

EVANS, JAMES WILLIAM, food co. exec., b. Chilhowee, Mo., Sept. 21, 1908; s. George Walter and Lucy Elizabeth (Webb) E.; B.S., Central Mo. State Coll., 1928; postgrad. U. Mo., 1929; Ph.D., U. Minn., 1940; grad. Advanced Mgmt. Program, Harvard, 1957; m. Helen Hughes, Aug. 31, 1930; 1 son, James William. Research chemist Union Starch & Refining Co., Granite City, Ill., 1930- 37, 40-43; research asst. U. Minn., 1938-39, instr., 1939-40; head food and carbohydrate sect., research dept. Gen. Mills, Inc., 1943-50; with Am. Maize Products Co., N.Y.C., 1950—, v.p. research and devel., 1958- 64, pres., chief exec. officer, 1964—, also dir. Mem. Am. Chem. Soc., Am. Assn. Cereal Chemists (pres. 1961-62), Inst. Food Technologists. Home: 301 E 47th St New York City NY 10017 Office: 250 Park Av New York City NY 10017

EVANS, JANE, religious worker, editor, lectr., writer; b. N.Y.C.; grad. Xavier U., Cin. With Nat. Fedn. Temple Sisterhoods of Union Am. Hebrew Congregations (Reform Judaism), 1933—, now exec. dir.; mem. polit. sci. faculty New Sch. Social Research, N.Y.C. Cons. to U.S. delegation at drafting of UN charter, San Francisco, 1945; past chmn. com. displaced persons Am. Jewish Conf., World War II; head of delegations to UNRRA (now UNRWA) sessions, U.S., Can., Europe; pioneer woman sec., also mem. governing body, exec. com. World Union Progressive Judaism; past pres. Nat. Peace Conf.; past vice-chmn., conf. group, past exec. com. U.S. Nat. Orgns. on UN; mem. nat. panel judges ann. high sch. contest UN; sponsor UN Assn. U.S.A. Named Woman of Achievement, Fedn. Jewish Women's Orgns.; Jane Evans Wood planted by Nat. Fedn. Temple Sisterhoods, Bar Kochba Forest, Israel; recipient numerous citations. Mem. Jewish Braille Inst. Am. (treas., exec. bd.), Commn. Social Action Am. Reform Judaism (chmn. com. world peace), Joint Distbn. Com. (nat. council). Editorial bd. Dimensions mag. Address: 838 Fifth Av New York City NY 10021

EVANS, JOHN ARTHUR, physician; b. N.Y.C., Mar. 13, 1909; s. John and Edythe (Wilkie) E.; B.S., N.Y.U., 1931; M.D., Cornell U., 1935; m. Dorothy Reilly, Aug. 27, 1937; children—Linda, Jane, John, Susan. Intern French Hosp., N.Y.C., 1935-37, N.Y. Hosp., 1937-40; faculty Cornell U. Med. Coll., 1946—, prof., chmn. dept. radiology, 1952—; staff N.Y. Hosp., 1945—. radiologist-in-chief, 1952—. Served as Col., M.C., AUS, 1941-45. Decorated Legion of Merit. Diplomate Am. Bd. Radiology (pres.). Fellow Am. Coll. Radiology; mem. N.Y. State Med. Soc., Am. Roentgen Ray Soc., Am. Gastroenterol. Assn., Radiol. Soc. N.Am., N.Y. Roentgen Soc. Asso. editor Radiology. Home: 435 E 70th St New York City NY 10021 also Shelter Island NY 11964 Office: 525 E 68th St New York City NY 10021

EVANS, JOHN HARVEY, educator, naval architect; b. Rochester, N.Y., May 1, 1914; s. John and Mabel (Harvey) E.; B.Engring., U. Liverpool (Eng.), 1937; m. Edith Miriam Price, July 3, 1943; children—Harvey David, Gail Edith. Engr. and supr. Bethlehem Steel Co., 1937-47; mem. faculty Mass. Inst. Tech., 1947- -, prof. naval architecture, 1961—; cons. to industry, 1947—. Mem. maritime transp. research bd. Nat. Acad. Sci., 1965-68; del. Internat. Ship Structures Congress, 1960—. Mem. Soc. Naval Architects and Marine Engrs. (council 1966—, mem. exec. com. 1969—), Sigma Xi. Author papers in field. Home; 33 Robinson Rd Lexington MA 02173 Office: Mass Inst Tech Cambridge MA 02139

EVANS, JOHN JAMES, mgmt. cons.; b. N.Y.C., Aug. 12, 1923; s. James J. and Mary (Galan) E.; student U. Neb., 1943; B.B.A. cum laude, Coll. City N.Y., 1948, M.B.A., 1950; postgrad. N.Y.U., 1951; m. Sophie Soviczki, July 25, 1951. Mgr., Roman Silversmiths, 1946-49; systems Addressograph-Multigraph Corp., 1949-53; mgmt. cons., v.p. Fairbanks Assos., Greenwich, Conn., N.Y.C. and Washington, 1953-59, pres., 1959—. Served with AUS, 1943-46; ETO. Mem. Inst. Mgmt. Consultants, Am. Soc. Assn. Execs., Am. Mgmt. Assn., Beta Gamma Sigma. Club: University (Washington). Contbr. articles profl. publs. Home: 30 Browning Rd Short Hills NJ 07078 Office: 509 Madison Av New York City NY 10022

EVANS, JOHN KRYDER, ret. mfr.; b. Elk Lick, Pa., July 9, 1890; s. John Miles and Ellelia (Bott) E.; Ph.B., Franklin and Marshall Coll., 1911; m. Marion Lloyd Hallowell, Oct. 21, 1916; 1 dau., Janet (Mrs. Alexander McBride 3d). Salesman, asst. sales mgr. Arbuckle Bros., N.Y.C., 1911-18; asst. to pres. Franklin Baker Co., Hoboken, N.J., 1918-27; v.p. Gen. Foods Corp., ret. 1955, gen. mgr. Maxwell House div., Hoboken, 1927-55; cons., exec. com. Pan-Am. Coffee Bur., 1956-65. Trustee, exec. com. Franklin and Marshall Coll., 1940—; adv. bd. Pace Coll., N.Y.C., 1935-56. Del. 1st World Coffee Conf., Rio de Janeiro, 1958. Recipient Order of So. Cross, Brazil, 1960. Mem. Nat. Coffee Assn. (hon. life; dir. 1939-51, 53-54, exec. com. of bd. 1945-50), Am. Brazilian Soc., Phi Kappa Sigma. Mem. Soc. of Friends. Clubs: Union League (Phila.); Bankers of Am. (N.Y.C.); Granite (Toronto, Ont., Can.). Home: 510 Grove Terrace South Orange NJ 07079 summer Champlain Point Atherley Ontario Canada Office: 120 Wall St New York City NY 10005

EVANS, JOHN MONROE, communication co. exec.; b. El Paso, Tex., Feb. 14, 1914; s. George and Louise (Rumsey) E.; B.A., Columbia, 1936, LL.B., 1938; m. Arline Walker, May 16, 1952; children—John Morgan, Louise Elliott, Peter Owain. Admitted to N.Y. bar, 1938, since practiced in N.Y.C.; asso. firm Rogers & Condon, 1938-53; sec., asso. gen. counsel El Paso Natural Gas Co., 1954-66; v.p., gen. counsel Western Union Telegraph Co., N.Y.C., 1966-70, now dir., v.p., gen. counsel, sec. Western Union Corp., N.Y.C., 1970—. Served to lt. USNR, 1942-46. Mem. Am. Bar Assn., Am. Soc Corporate Secs. Home: 25 Chestnut Ridge Rd Saddle River NJ 07459 Office: 85 McKee Dr Mahwah NJ 07430

EVANS, JOHN MORRIS, univ. adminstr.; b. W. Pittston, Pa., June 7, 1918; s. Thomas Owen and Elizabeth Alice (Simonson) E.; evening student U. Pa., 1937-41, 47; B.S., Ind. U., 1948, M.B.A., 1949; children—Gail Arlene, Paula Jean. Asst. prof. mgmt. U. Okla., 1949-51; head internal audit div. Ind. U., 1951-55, budget officer, 1957-58, asst. bus. mgr., 1958-60; mem. Cal.-Western conf. cost study Ford Found., 1955- 57; v.p. financial affairs U. Conn., Storrs, 1960—. Chmn. bd. dirs. Conn. Bank & Trust Co., Willimatic. Bd. dirs. Windham Hosp., Willimantic. Served as officer AUS, 1942-45. Mem. Eastern Assn. U. Bus. Officers Assn., Nat. Fedn. U. Bus. Officers Assn., Beta Gamma Sigma, Alpha Phi Omega, Phi Delta Kappa, Delta Sigma Pi. Home: 11 Westwood Rd Storrs CT 06268

EVANS, JOHN STEPHENSON, banker; b. Montgomery, Ala., Jan. 7, 1913; s. Henry Green and Ethel (Hatcher) E.; A.B., Princeton 1934, student Duke Law Sch., 1935, Vanderbilt U. Law Sch., 1936; m. Mary S. Collier, June 28, 1938; children—Elizabeth Collier (Mrs. H.W. Pearson III), Ethel Hatcher (Mrs. Barry Wildman). With Robinson-Humphrey Co., Atlanta, 1936-38, Indsl. Arts Co., Atlanta, 1938-42; pres. Evans-Glenn Co., Marietta, Ga., 1946- 51; sr. v.p. Trust Co. Ga., Atlanta, 1951—. Served to maj. AUS, 1942- 45. Decorated Bronze Star. Clubs: Peachtree Golf, Commerce (Atlanta); Princeton (N.Y.C.). Home: 3603 Dumbarton Rd NW Atlanta GA 30327 Office: Trust Co of Ga Bldg Atlanta GA 30302

EVANS, JOHN WAINWRIGHT, Jr., astrophysicist, geophysicist; b. N.Y.C., May 14, 1909; s. John Wainwright and Edith (Claggett) E.; A.B., Swarthmore Coll., 1932, Sc.D., 1970; student U. Pa., 1932-34; A.M., Harvard, 1936, Ph.D., 1938; D.Sc., U. N.M., 1967; m. Elizabeth F. Harlan, Aug. 23, 1932; children—Wainwright, Nancy Jane, Jeanne Harlan. Tchr. astronomy U. Minn., 1937-38, Mills Coll., 1938-42; research, devel. optical instruments Inst. Optics, U. Rochester, 1942-46; research solar activity and terrestrial effects, devel. telescopes, coronagraphs, spectropgraphs High Altitude Obs., Boulder, Colo., 1946-52, leader obs. Eclipse Expdn. to Sudan, 1952, to Puka Puka Cook Islands, 1958; dir. Sacramento Peak Obs., Air Force Cambridge Research Labs., Sunspot, N.M., 1952—. Recipient Newcomb Cleveland prize A.A.A.S. (with Schwarzschild and Rogerson), 1957; Distinguished Civilian Service award Dept. Def., 1965, Rockefeller Pub. Service award, 1969. Mem. Internat. Astron. Union, A.A.A.S. (past v.p. for astronomy), Astron. Soc. Pacific, Am. Astron. Soc. (past rep. NRC, mem. council 1967-70) Am. Acad. Arts and Scis. Constructed and developed optical theory of birefringent filters, 1940—. Home: Sunspot NM 88349 Office: Sacramento Peak Observatory Sunspot NM 88349

EVANS, JOSEPH CEDRIC, elec. mfg. co. exec.; b. St. Louis, June 18, 1915; s. Gomer Louis and Sybilia (Burgess) E.; B.S. in Elec. Engring., Washington U., St. Louis, 1935; m. Dorothy Marie Fairbanks, July 27, 1941; children—John Fairbanks, Joseph Cedric. With Wagner Electric Corp., St. Louis, 1935—, controller, 1956-61, v.p., controller, 1961-66, v.p., 1966-68, controller Wagner div., 1968—; sec., treas. Wagner Brake Co. Ltd., Toronto. Mem. Financial Execs. Inst., Adminstrv. Mgmt. Soc. (pres. St. Louis 1953-54), Nat. Assn. Accountants (dir. St. Louis 1950- 52), Sigma Xi, Tau Beta Pi. Mem. Reorganized Ch. of Jesus Christ of Latter Day Saints. Home: 1448 Dougherty Ferry Rd Kirkwood MO 63122 Office: 6400 Plymouth Av St Louis MO 63133

EVANS, JOSEPH EARLY, journalist; b. Dubuque, Ia., Feb. 5, 1919; s. John D. and Ellen (Early) E.; student Loras Coll., 1935-37, U. So. Cal., 1937-38; A.B., State U. Ia., 1939, M.A., 1941; m. Marie Petrackova, Mar. 11, 1948; children-Christopher, Catherine, Elisabeth. Grad. teaching asst. in English lit. State U. Ia., 1940-42; fgn. corr. Wall Street Jour., Berlin and Europe, 1946-49, editorial writer 1949-50, fgn. editor, 1950-51, chief Washington bur., 1952-53, asso. editor, 1953-65, sr. asso. ediotr, 1965-70, editor editorial page, 1970—. Served as tech. sgt. U.S. Army, 1942-45. Recipient Irving Babbitt Meml. prize, 1941; Silurian Soc. editorial writing award, 1956, 58, 65, 66, 67; Am. Artists Profl. League award, 1965; Freedoms Found. award, 1953, 65, 66, 69. Mem. Nat. Conf. Editorial Writers. Am. Soc. Newspaper Editors. Clubs: Overseas Press, Nat. Press (Washington). Author Chpt. in This Is Germany (Arthur Settel), 1950; Through Soviet Windows, 1957. Home; 450 Highbrook Av Pelham Manor NY 10803 Office: 30 Broad St New York City Ny 10004

EVANS, JOSEPH PATRICK, neurological surgeon; b. La Crosse, Wis., Nov. 29, 1904; s. Edward and Sarah (Thompson) E.; student U. Notre Dame, 1921-23; A.B., Harvard, 1925, M.D., 1929; M.Sc., McGill U., 1930, Ph.D., 1937; postgrad U. Chgo. U. Minn., Yale, Cambridge U., London U., Nat. Hosp., Queen Sq., London; Breslau; D.Sc. (hon.), Loyola U., Chgo., 1964; m. Hermene Eisenman, June 24, 1929; children—Mary Frances Bapst, Edward, Frederick Nicholas, Caroline de Villa, Anne W. Lanctt, Hermene W., John F., Thomas More. Asso. prof. surgery charge neurol. surgery U. Cin., 1937-54; prof. emeritus neurol. surgery U. Chgo.; dir. div. neurol. surgery U. Chgo. Clinics, 1954-67; fellow Adlai Stevenson Inst. Internat. Affairs, 1967-69, hon fellow, 1969—; Rockefeller fellow, 1935-36; research asso. physiology Yale, 1948; med. mission, Austria, 1947. Dir. N.Am. Liturgical Conf., 1960-66; mem. investigating commn. Dissent and Disorder, 1968-69. Diplomate Am. Bd. Neurol. Surgery (bd. mem. 1944-50), Am. Bd. Psychiatry and Neurology. Fellow A.C.S.; mem. Am. Acad. Neurol. Surgery (pres. 1940-41), A.M.A., Assn. Research Nervous and Mental Diseases, Am. Assn. Neurol. Surgeons (v.p. 1961-62), Soc. Neurol. Surgeons (v.p. 1963-64), Am. Neurol. Assn. (v.p. 1966-67); hon. fgn. socs. in field Contbr. articles med. jours. Home: 1160 E 56th St Chicago IL 60637 Office: U Chgo Hosps Chicago IL 60637

EVANS, LEWIS ADOLPH, R.R exec.; b. Brownsville, Pa., June 22, 1907; s. William Charles and Hertha Vera (Kuchneisen) E.; B.S., Carnegie Inst. Tech., 1928; m. Anne Marie Weber, June 22, 1929; children—Daniel Richard, David Lewis. Asst. on engr. corps Pa. R.R., 1928, advanced various positions, 1928-48, supt. Indpls. div., 1948-51; v.p., gen. mgr. C. & W.I. R.R., also Belt Ry. Co. Chgo., 1951-53, Pres., gen. mgr., 1953- 62; pres., gen. mgr. Belt Ry. Co. of Chgo., 1962—. Mem. Am. Soc. Traffic and Transp., Nat. Freight Traffic Assn., Am. Ry. Engring. Assn., Tau Beta Pi. Republican. Mason. Clubs: Chicago; Traffic (Chgo. and N.Y.C.). Home: 7415 S Crandon Av Chicago IL 60649 Office: 6900 S Central Av Chicago IL 60638

EVANS, LLEWELLYN JOHNSON, aircraft co exec.; b. Usankinko, Korea, Aug. 2, 1920 (parents Am. citizens); s. Harry J. and Margaret (Johnson) E.; A.B., U. Cal. at Berkeley, 1942; LL.B., Harvard, 1947; m. Georgene Alice Hubbard, Dec. 25, 1945; 1 son, Llewellyn Johnson. Admitted to D.C. bar, 1947, N.Y. bar, 1952; with Grumman Corp., Bethpage, N.Y., 1951—, v.p., 1960-63, sr. v.p., 1963-66, Pres., dir., 1966- -; pres., dir. Grumman Aerospace Corp., v.p., dir. Montauk Aero Corp., dir. Grumman Allied Industries, Inc., Grumman Data Systems Corp., Grumman Pacific (Pte) Ltd., Travelers Corp., Grumman Internat., Inc. Served to 1st lt. USAAF, 1943-45. Decorated D.F.C., Air medal with 5 oak leaf clusters. Mem. Am., Fed. bar assns., Harvard Law Sch. Assn., Sigma Alpha Epsilon. Home: Tappan Town Lane Brookville NY 10983 Office: Grumman Corp Bethpage NY 11714

EVANS, LUTHER HARRIS, former univ. ofcl.; b. nr. Sayersville, Tex., Oct. 13, 1902; s. George Washington and Lillie (Johnson) E.; A.B., U. Tex., 1923, M.A., 1924; Ph.D., Stanford, 1927; D.H.L., Yale, 1946; D.Litt., Brown U., 1953, L.L.D., Pa. Mil. Coll., 1948, U. B.C., 1948, Loyola Coll., 1950, Columbia, 1953, Dartmouth, 1956, Denison U., 1961; hon. degrees Washington U., 1959, Adelphi Coll., 1960, Marietta Coll., 1962; m. Helen Murphy, Sept. 12, 1925; 1 son, Gill Cofer. Instr. freshmen orientation course Stanford, 1924-27; instr. govt. N.Y. U., 1927-28; instr. polit. sci. Dartmouth, 1928-30; asst. prof. politics Princeton, 1930-35; dir. hist. records survey WPA, 1935-39; dir. legislative ref. service Library Congress, 1939-40, chief asst. librarian, acting libarian, 1940-45, librarian, 1945-53; mem. U.S. Nat. Commn. UNESCO, 1946-52, 59-63, chmn., 1952, mem. exec. bd. UNESCO, 1949- 53 dir.-gen. 1953-58, U.S. del. or adviser Gen. Conf., 1947-53; cons. internat. studies programs U. Tex., 1959; dir. survey fed. deptl. libraries Brookings Instn., 1959-61; dir. project on ednl. implications of automation N.E.A., 1961-62; dir. internat. collections Columbia U. 1962-internat. and legal collection Columbia, 1962-67, dir. internat. collections, 1967-71. Mem. bd. Popular Printing Inc. Mem. organizing com. World Conf. on Role of Univs. in Quest for Peace, 1963-69; chmn. exec. com. Commn. to Study Orgn. of Peace. Chmn. U.S. delegation Inter-Am. Copyright Conf., Washington, 1946, Universal Copyright Conv., Geneva, 1952; chmn. U.S. Com. for Refugees, 1961-70, mem., 1970—; vice chmn. Nat. Book awards Adv. Com., 1964-71; Mem. bd. Lisle Fellowship; bd. dirs. Ednl. Products Information Exchange Inst.; mem. corp. Franklin Book Programs. Decorated by govts. Brazil, France, Japan, Lebanon, Peru. Mem. Am. Polit. Sci. Assn., Am. Civil Liberties Union, A.L.A. (life), N.E.A. (life), Am. Soc. on Information Sci., Goudy Soc. (bd.) Am. Antiquarian Soc., World Acad. Art and Sci., Soc. for Internat. Devel., Mexican Soc. for Internat. Law, Manuscript Soc. Author: The Virgin Islands from Naval Base to New Deal, 1945. Editor: (with George E. Arnstein) Automation and the Challenge to Education, 1962; (with others) Federal Department Libraries, 1963, 66. Editor Am. Documentation quar., 1961. Contbr. numerous articles to profl. jours. Home: 25 Claremont Av New York City NY 10027

EVANS, MARSHALL KENNETH, elec. mfg. co. exec.; b. Scranton, Pa., July 27, 1917; s. Thomas Lewis and Jesse Maude (Butler) E.; A.B. in Econs., Pa. State U., 1938; M.B.A., Harvard, 1940; m. Josephine Mary Bingham, Oct. 27, 1940; children—Marcia Elizabeth, Jonathan Lynn. Accountant, Am. Smelting & Refining Co., 1940- 41; instr. econs. Pa. State U., 1941-43; with Westinghouse Elec. Corp., 1943—, dir. mgmt. services, 1958-60, v.p. mgmt. services, 1960- 63, v.p. operations services, 1963-70, now vice chmn., also dir. Served with USAAF, 1945-46. Mem. Phi Beta Kappa, Phi Kappa Phi. Presbyn. (elder, tchr.). Mason. Contbr. articles to Harvard Bus. Rev.; controller Bull. Nat. Assn. Accountants. Home: 821 White Oak Circle Pittsburgh PA 15228 Office: Gateway 3 Pittsburgh PA 15222

EVANS, MATTHEW B., Jr., educator; B.A., Stanford, 1934, Ph.D.; M.A., U. Cal. at Berkeley, 1937. Prof. humanities and English, chmn. dept. humanities San Francisco State Coll. Office: San Francisco State Coll San Francisco CA 94132*

EVANS, MAURICE, actor-mgr.; b. Dorchester, Dorset, Eng., June 3, 1901; s. Alfred Herbert and Laura (Turner) E.; student Grocer's Co. Sch., London, Eng., 1912-18. Naturalized U.S. citizen, 1941. Brought to U.S. by Katharine Cornell to play Romeo to her Juliet, 1936; later played the Dauphin in St. Joan and Napoleon in St. Helena; produced Richard II, which ran 171 consecutive performances on Broadway, 1937, Hamlet, 1938-39, Henry IV, 1939; appeared in Twelfth Night with Helen Hayes, 1940-41; produced and appeared in Macbeth, which ran 131 consecutive performances on Broadway, 1941-42, Hamlet (131 performances), 1945-47, also Man and Superman, 1947-49 (293 performances), The Browning Version, 1949, The Devil's Disciple, 1950, Dial M for Murder, 1952-54, The Apple Cart, 1956- 57, Heartbreak House, 1959-60, Tenderloin, 1960-61, The Aspern Papers, 1961-62; with Helen Hayes in Shakespeare Revisited, A Program for Two Players, 1962-63; produced Teahouse of the August Moon, 1953, No Time for Sergeants, 1955; produced and starred in TV prodns. Hamlet, 1953, Richard II, Macbeth, 1954, Devil's Disciple, 1955, Taming of the Shrew, Man and Superman, 1956, Twelfth Night, 1957, Dial M for Murder, 1958, The Tempest, 1960; motion pictures Kind Lady, 1950, Androcles and the Lion, 1951, Gilbert and Sullivan, 1952, Macbeth, 1960, Warlord, 1965, Jack of Diamonds, Planet of the Apes, 1967, Rosemary's Baby, Thin Air, 1968, Planet of The Apes Revisited, 1969; as Richard II, N.Y. C. Center, 1951; artistic supervisor N.Y.C. Center Theatre Co. 1949-50. Served to maj. AUS, 1942-45. Recipient Drama League medal, 1937. Address: care L V Almirall 1 Chase Manhattan Plaza New York City NY 10005

EVANS, MAURICE HENRY, ins. co. exec.; b. Tupper Lake, N.Y., July 8, 1917; s. Jesse H. and Anna (Buhler) E.; A.A., San Bernardino Valley Coll., 1939; student U. Redlands, 1939-40; LL.B., McGeorge Coll. Law, 1951; m. Kaethe Poppe, 1963; 1 son, Stephen M. With Cal.-Western States Life Ins. Co., Sacramento, 1948—, group sales rep., 1948-49, mortgage loan rep., 1949-53, asst. sec., 1954-56, asst. treas., asst. sec., 1956-58, 2d v.p., 1958-61, v.p., treas., 1961—; lectr. investment subjects U. Cal. Extension, Sacramento, 1960—, Sacramento City Coll. Adult Edn. Program, 1955—. Bd dirs. Indsl. Sites Found. Sacra mento County, Sacramento chpt. A.R.C. Served from ensign to lt. comdr., USNR, 1940-46. Mem. Am. Bar Assn., State Bar Cal., Cal. Mortgage Bankers Assn. (dir.), Sacramento C. of C. (dir.). Clubs: Sutter (Sacramento), North Ridge Country. Home: 4341 College View Way Carmichael CA 95608 Office: Northern Life Ins Co PO Box 12530 Seattle WA 98111

EVANS, MEDFORD STANTON, newspaper editor; b. Kingsville, Tex., July 20, 1934; s. Medford Bryan and Alice Josephine (Stanton) E.; B.A., Yale, 1955; postgrad. N.Y. U., 1955; m. Sue Ellen Moore, Apr. 14, 1962. Asst. editor Freeman, 1955; editorial staff Nat. Rev., 1955-56, asso. editor, 1960- 68; mng. editor Human Events, 1956-59, contbg. editor, 1968—; publs. dir. Intercollegiate Soc. Individualists, 1956-59, trustee, 1960—; chief editorial writer Indpls. News, 1959-60, editor, 1960—. Broadcaster, Spectrum series CBS Radio, 1971—. Recipient Freedoms Found. awards for editorial writing, 1959, 60, 65, 66; award for outstanding editorial pages Nat. Headliners Club, 1960. Mem. Am. Soc. Newspaper Editors, Nat. Headliners Club, Am. Conservative Union (chmn.), Indpls. C. of C. Phi Beta Kappa, Sigma Delta Chi. Republican. Methodist. Clubs: Capitol Hill (Washington); Elizabethan (Yale); Indianapolis Press, Indianapolis Athletic; Yale of Indiana. Author: Revolt on the Campus, 1961; The Fringe on Top, 1962; The Liberal Establishment, 1965; The Politics of Surrenders, 1966; The Lawbreakers, 1968; The Future of Conservatism, 1968. Home: 6020 Winnepeny Lane Indianapolis IN 46220 Office: 307 N Pennsylvania St Indianapolis IN 46204

EVANS, MELBOURNE GRIFFITH, educator; b. Portland, Ore., Jan. 23, 1912; s. Griffith Edward and Agnes (Brown) E.; B.A., Reed Coll., 1937; M.A., U. Cal., Berkeley, 1940, Ph.D., 1948; m. Pauline Davidson, Sept. 6, 1950; children-Lynn Janet, Brian Griffith. Instr. philosophy Syracuse U., 1948-51; Am. Council Learned Socs. scholar, 1951-53; vis. asso. prof. philosophy U. Ala., 1955; lectr. philosophy and math. U. N.M., Albuquerque, 1955-60, asso. prof. philosophy, 1960-67, prof., 1967—, acting chmn. dept. philosophy, 1968-69. Served with Signal Intelligence Service, AUS, 1942-45; CBI. Mem. Am. Philos. Assn. Author: The Physical Philosophy of Aristotle, 1964, Contbr. articles profl. jours. Home: 5801 Coors Blvd Sv Albuquerque NM 87105

EVANS, MELVIN HERBERT, gov. Virgin Islands; b. Christiansted, St. Croix, V.I., Aug 7, 1917; s. Charles Herbert and Maude (Rogiers) E.; B.S., Howard U., 1940, M.D., 1944; M.P.H., U. Cal. at Berkeley, 1967; m. Mary Phyllis Anderson, Aug. 26, 1945; children— Melvin Herbert, Robert Rogiers, William Charles, Cornelius Duncan. Intern, Harlem Hosp., N.Y.C., 1944-45; physician-in-charge Frederiksted, Govt. V.I., 1945-58, 50-51; sr. asst. surgeon USPHS, Washington, 1948-50; chief municipal physician, St. Croix, 1951-56, 57-59; fellow cardiology Johns Hopkins Hosp., 1956-57; commr. health for V.I., 1959-67; pvt. practice medicine, specializing in internal medicine, St. Croix, 1967-69; gov. V.I., 1969—. Chmn. Bd. Med. Examiners, 1959-67. Mem. Gov.'s Commn. on Civil Def. 1961-66; chmn. Gov.'s Commn. on Human Services, 1962-66; mem. U.S. Selective Service Bd. Appeals, 1967-69. Chmn. bd. trustees Coll. V.I.; bd. dirs. Good Hope Sch., St. Croix; bd. advice St. Dunstan Sch., St. Croix, Island Center St. Croix; trustee New St. Croix Sav. Bank. Fellow A.C.P.; mem. A.M.A., Nat., Pan Am. med. assns., V.I. Med. Soc. (past pres.), Am. Assn. Pub. Health Physicians, Am. Pub. Health Assn., St. Croix C. of C., Phi Beta Sigma, Kappa Pi. Methodist. Mason, Rotarian. Club: St. Croix Yacht. Home: La Grande Princesse Christiansted St Croix VI 00820 Office: Govt House Charlotte Amalie St Thomas VI 00801

EVANS, NICHOLAS MONSARRAT, specialty household products mfg. co. exec.; b. Columbus, O., May 22, 1930; s. James Baxter and Laura (Monsarrat) E.; B.A. magna cum laude, Amherst Coll., 1952; M.B.A., Harvard, 1954; m. Christine Cornelius Thomas, June 13, 1955; children—Christine E., Nicholas M. Brand mgr. Procter & Gamble Co., Cin., 1954-57; account mgr. Doherty, Clifford, Steers & Schenfield, Inc., N.Y.C., 1957-59; brand mgr., v.p. products div. Bristol-Myers Co., N.Y.C., 1959-66; v.p. new products, v.p. marketing, pres. Bristol-Myers Drackett Co., Cin., 1966—; dir. U.S. Shoe Corp. Mem. Phi Beta Kappa. Republican. Episcopalian. Clubs: New Canaan (Conn.) Field; Camargo, Queen City (Cin.); Harvard (N.Y.C.). Home: 4950 Councilrock Lane Cincinnati OH 45243 Office: 5020 Spring Grove Av Cincinnati OH 45232

EVANS, NORMAN ALLEN, scientist, educator; b. Spearfish, S.D., Dec. 3, 1922; s. Allen C. and Claire (Doscher) E.; B.S., S.D. State U., 1944; M.S., Utah State U., 1947; Ph.D., Colo. State U., 1963; m. Jean Cole, Dec. 26, 1943; children—Douglas Robert, Elizabeth Ann, Garth William, Mathew. Asst. prof. N.D. State U., 1947-51; from asst. prof. to prof. civil engring. Colo. State U., Ft. Collins, 1951-59, prof., head dept. agrl. engring., 1956-69, dir. Environmental Resources Center, 1966—, dir. Office Gen. U. Research, 1970—; cons. in field. Dir. Engrs. Council for Profl. Devel., 1970-72. Mem. Colo. Water Pollution Control Commn., 1966—, vice chmn., 1970—; mem. Ft. Collins City Water Bd., 1963—, vice chmn., 1968—. Served to 1st lt. AUS, 1944-46. Registered profl. engr., Colo. Fellow A.A.A.S.; mem. Am. Soc. C.E., Am. Soc. Agrl. Engrs. (v.p. 1968-70), Sigma Xi, Phi Kappa Phi, Chi Epsilon, Alpha Epsilon, Gamma Sigma Delta. Home: 1847 Michael Lane Fort Collins CO 80521

EVANS, ORMOND KEISTER, Jr., assn. exec.; b. Ringgold, Va., May 10, 1939; s. Ormond Keister and Catherine (Booth) E.; B.Sc. in Agrl. Edn., Virginia Poly. Inst., 1961, M.S. in Ornamental Horticulture, 1968; postgrad. student ornamental horticulture, 1963; m. Judith May Carson, Nov. 21, 1962; one daughter, Emily Catherine. Asst. agricultural extension agt., Virginia Beach, Va., 1961-62; agrl. extension agt., Newport News, Va., 1963-64; exec. sec., editor Am. Rose Soc., Columbus, O., 1964-69; exec. dir. Am. Hort. Soc., 1970—; sec. Am. Rose Found., 1964—, Columbus Rose Commn., 1964—; registrar Internat. Rose Registration Authority, 1964-69. Mem. No. Bus. and Profl. Assn. (v.p. 1965-69), Soc. Nat. Assn. Publs., Am. Hort. Soc., Garden Writers Assn. Am., Royal Hort. Soc., Mass. Hort. Soc., Royal Nat. Rose Soc. Great Britain, Am. Soc. Assn. Execs., No. Columbus Jr. C. of C. Editor: Am. Rose Annual, 1965-68, Am. Rose mag., 1964-69; contbr. Ency. Gardening, 1966; also to nat. and internat. publs. Home: 800 S Lee St Alexandria VA 22314 Office: 901 N Washington St Alexandria VA 22314

EVANS, ORRIN BRYAN, educator; b. Baraboo, Wis., Oct. 6, 1910; s. Evan Alfred and Mary (Rountree) E.; A.B., U. Wis., 1931, LL.B., 1935; J.S.D., Yale, 1940; m. Margaret Louise Searle, Feb. 18, 1933; children—Margaret Aspinwall, Evan George, David Rountree. Asst. prof. law U. Ida., 1937-38; from asst. prof. to prof. U. Mo., 1938-47, atty. for univ., 1940-47; prof. U. So. Cal., 1947- 52, Henry W. Bruce law prof., 1952—, asso. dean Law Sch., 1952- 63, dean, 1963-67; vis. prof. law Yale, U. Wis., Northwestern U., U. Cal., others. Commr. Los Angeles Civil Service, 1961-65; state inheritance tax referee, 1967—. Mem. Am., Mo., Wis. Los Angeles County bar assns. Assn. Am. Law Schs. (exec. com. 1955), Order of Coif, Selden Soc. Phi Kappa Sigma, Phi Alpha Delta, Phi Kappa Phi. Episcopalian. Home: 5947 W Colgate Av Los Angeles CA 90036

EVANS, ORRON DRAYTON, ins. exec.; b. Rome, Ga., Sept. 13, 1886; s. Walter McCarthy and Lena A. (Godwin) E.; student Benton Coll., 1908; m. Bessie G. Healey, July 2, 1911 (dec. Nov. 1961); children—Margaret Lee, Jean; m. 2d, Elizabeth W. Robertson, July 1962. Freight car builder So. Car & Foundry, Anniston, Ala., 1902-04, Am. Car & Foundry, Co., Memphis, 1904-07; ins. agt. Orron D. Evans Underwriters Agy., Inc., St. Louis, 1908-26, dir., 1926—; chmn. bd. Standard Underwriters, 1957-70. Hon. life mem. St. Louis Ins. Bd. Bd. dirs. Christian Civic Found.; hon. life trustee Hannibal LaGrange Coll.; hon. trustee Mo. Sch. Religion; life trustee New Orleans Bapt., Central Bapt. theol. sems. Mem. Nat. Assn. Businessman (sec.-treas.), Mo. Archeol. Soc. (chmn. bd.), Friends of Land in Mo. (life), Rocks and Minerals Assn., State Hist. Soc. (life), Nat. Tax Equality (dir.), Rockwoods Assn. (life), Historic Hermann (hon. life), Baptist (hon. life trustee). Mason (32, Shriner). Clubs: Ambassadors; Amateur Archeological; Lehigh Acres Country, St. Louis Gem and Mineral. Home: 1040 Pinegate Kirkwood MO 63122 Office: 7730 Carondelet Av Clayton MO 63105

EVANS, P. G. sugar co. exec.; b. Orange, N.J., Dec. 19, 1923; s. Paul G. and Sarah (Nevins) E.; grad. Lawrenceville Sch., 1940; A.B., Princeton, 1943; LL.B., Fordham U., 1950; m. Katharine Redmond, June 6, 1944; children—Katharine, Johnston, Alice, Robert, Paul. Admitted to N.Y. bar, 1950; with firm Cravath, Swaine & Moore, N.Y.C., 1950-55; head legal dept. IBM Corp., 1958-60; sec. Nat. Sugar Co., 1965—. Served with USMCR, 1943-45. Home: 141 E 72d St New York City, NY 10021. Office: 100 Wall St New York City NY 10005

EVANS, PAUL LEWIS, journalist; b. Alpena, S.D., Oct. 31, 1914; s. John David and Margaret Vida (Smith) E.; B.S.. Dakota Wesleyan U., 1937; Nieman fellow Harvard, 1940-47; m. Lelah Everly Hayes, Jan. 8, 1938; children—Lance Darrel, Thomas John, Mary Paula, Marcia Lee. Reporter, sports editor Mitchell (S.D.) Daily Republic, 1937-40, exec. editor, 1943-50; information specialist A.A.A., Dept. Agr., 1941-42; editor Redfield (S.D.) Jour.- Observer, 1943; prof. journalism Ohio Wesleyan U., 1950-51; asst. dir. information TVA, 1951-52, dir. information, 1952—. Municipal judge, Norris, Tenn., 1970—. Mem. S.D. Asso. Press Mng. Editors' Assn. (press. 1949), So. Assn. of Nieman Fellows (v.p. 1958-61) Nieman Alumni Council, Norris Religious Fellowship. Home: 29 E Norris Rd Norris TN 37828 Office: New Sprankle Bldg Knoxville TN 37901

EVANS, PAUL RICHER, educator; b. Dunmore, Pa., Aug. 31, 1925; s. Clarence Frederick and Marguerite (Richer) E.; B.A. magna cum laude, Oberlin Coll., 1949; M.A., Yale, 1951; M.F.A., Princeton, 1957, Ph.D., 1964; m. Sally Hibbard Romer, June 30, 1949; children—Andrew Wilson, Jane Romer. Instr. Conservatory Music, Oberlin Coll., 1960-62, asst. prof. music history, 1962-64; asst. prof. U. Pa., 1964-69; prof. music history Smith Coll., 1969—. Served with AUS, 1943-46. Mem. Am. Musicological Soc., Internat. Musicol. Soc., Mediaeval Acad. Am. Author: The Early Trope Repertory of Saint Martial de Limoges, 1970. Home: 210 Elm St Northampton MA 01060

EVANS, PHILIP MAURICE MOODIE, ednl. adminstr., public relations; b. Seattle, Feb. 2, 1919; s. Albert and Priscilla Eggleston (White) E.; B.A., U. Wash., 1946, M.A., 1948; m. Georgann Street, June 19, 1948; children—Philip S. Sidney. Tchr., U. Wash., 1946; spl. corr. Europe, Seattle Post Intelligencer, also columnist Milw. Jour., 1948-50; dir. World Affairs Council of Seattle, 1950-56; fgn. and pub. affairs producer, commentator KOMO radio, TV, 1953-56; dep. mgr. Office Internat. Trade Fairs, Dept. Commerce, 1957, spl. asst. sec. commerce, 1958-60, also exec. dir. Cabinet com. on trade policy; U.S. comr. U.S. exhibit Century 21 Expn., 1960-61; adminstr. Grad. Sch., U. Wash., Seattle, 1961; pres. Philip M. Evans Assos., promotion, devel. and cons. services and pub. relations, also partner Projectophone Co., Seattle, 1962-66; dir. Western regional office Inst. Internat. Edn. San Francisco, 1966—. Mem. nat. commn. for UNESCO, 1959-60; chmn. bd. Citizens Planning Council Seattle. Republican candidate for congressman-at-large, Wash., 1956. Served to ensign USNR, 1941-46. Recipient Robert E. Sherwood hon. mention award for documentary TV film Fund for Republic, 1956, Ohio State award, 1954, English Speaking award, 1954. Mem. Delta Kappa Epsilon. Home: 1404 Greenwood Terrace Berkeley CA 94708 Office: 291 Geary St San Francisco CA 94102

EVANS, RALPH FRANCIS, educator; b. Grayville, Ill., Feb. 16, 1911; s. Chester William and Lizzie Lucretia (Arnold) E.; B.Ed., Eastern Ill. U., 1932; A.M., State U. Ia., 1937, Ph.D., 1941; m. Margaret Dorothy Schock, Sept. 9, 1939; children—Harold Anderson, Frances Kathleen. Tchr. Twp. High Sch., Neoga, Ill., 1932-35, Roosevelt Jr. High Sch., Decatur, 1935- 37; prin. Niantic High Sch., 1937-39; grad. asst. State U. Ia., 1939-41; vice prin. Mason City (Ia.) High Sch., 1941-43; prof. edn., head dept. Washburn Municipal U., 1946-47; prof. edn. Fresno State Coll. 1947—, head div. edn., 1947-57; vis. prof. U. Me., summer 1953, U. Md., summer 1961. Chief Fresno State Coll. contract team (AID) in Sudan, 1963-64; chief Cal. State Coll. contract team (AID) in Jamaica, 1968-69. Served as lt., naval air navigator USNR, 1943-46. Mem. N.E.A., Nat. Soc. Study Edn., Phi Delta Kappa, Kappa Delta Pi, Pi Gamma Mu, Kappa Mu Epsilon, Lambda Chi Alpha. Conglist. Home: 2963 Cornell Av Fresno CA 93705

EVANS, RAY MARSHALL, bus. exec; b. Montclair, N.J., June 9, 1900; s. Samuel Marshall and Bertha (Steig) E.; B.S., Princeton, 1922; m. Nelle Carmichael Dickinson, Feb. 29, 1928; children—Mary Dickinson (Mrs. Pierro Sella), Elizabeth Marshall (wife of Count Agenor Goluchowski), Nelle Quincy, Ray Marshall. With Evans Lead Corp., 1922-62, pres., 1924-62; pres. Dickinson Co.; dir. Thompson Weinman & Co., 1924—, chmn. bd., 1938—; dir. Kanawha Valley Bank, 1929—, chmn. bd., 1963—; dir. United Fuel Gas Co., Daniel Boone Hotel, White Pigment Co., Paga Mining Co., Quincy Coal Co., Columbia Gas System, Inc., Columbia Gas W.Va., Carbon Fuel Co. Bd. dirs. Meml. Hosp.; trustee Morris Harvey Coll., 1947—, chmn. bd., 1961—. Clubs: Rolling Rock, Porcupine, Brook, Berry Hills Country, Edgewood Country, Press, St. Bernard Fish and Game. Home: 1268 Louden Heights Rd Charleston WV 25314 Office: Kanawha Valley Bldg Charleston WV 25301

EVANS, RAYMOND F., indsl. exec.; b. Pitts., Dec. 23, 1908; s. T. Raymond and Ida Gray (Flaccus) E.; student Shady Side Acad., Princeton; m. Elizabeth Rutgers Whitney, Sept. 21, 1934; children—T. Raymond III, Whitney, Nona Whitney, Michael Jessup, Andrew William. Chem. engr. Diamond Alkali Co., 1931-38, mgr. research, 1938-40, v.p. in charge research, 1941, exec. v.p., 1943-46, pres., dir., 1947-64, chmn. bd., 1954—; pres. Diamond Magnesium Co., 1941-43; chmn., Diamond Shamrock Co.; dir. Mellon Nat. Bank & Trust Co., Eaton Yale & Towne, Inc. Mem. Am. Chem. Soc., A.A.A.S. Clubs: Kirtland Country, Pittsburgh Golf, Rolling Rock (Pittsburgh). Home: Little Mountain Rd Mentor OH 44060 Office: Diamond Alkali Co Cleveland OH 44115

EVANS, RICHARD LOUIS, radio exec., ch. ofcl.; b. Salt Lake City, Mar. 23, 1906; s. John Alldridge and Florence (Neslen) E.; B.A. in English, U. Utah, 1931, M.A. in Econs., 1932, LL.D., 1956; D.H.L., Cal. Coll. Medicine, 1957; Litt.D., Eastern Ky. State Coll., 1964; m. Alice Ruth Thornley, Aug. 9, 1933; children—Richard Louis, John T., Stephen T., William T. Missionary to Gt. Britain, Ch. of Jesus Christ Latter-day Saints, 1926-29, sec. European Mission, Liverpool, 1928-29; staff announcer radio sta. KSL, Salt Lake City, 1929, script writer, dir. publicity, prodn. mgr., 1929-36; radio producer, commentator writer, composer nationwide Tabernacle choir and organ broadcast Temple Square, Salt Lake City, 1930—, broadcast NBC, 1930-32, CBS, 1932—, dir. spl. features, 1936—; mng. editor Improvement Era, 1936-49, editor, 1950-70; feature writer King Features Syndicate, 1946-52; partner Evans Investment Co.; dir. David W. Evans Advt. Agy., Radio Sta. KSL, Inc., 1st Security Corp., Bonneville Internat. Corp. Mem. 1st Council of Seventy, Ch. of Jesus Christ Latter-day Saints, 1938-53, mem. Council of Twelve, 1953—; regents U. Utah, 1950-69, pres. alumni assn., 1950-53; trustee Brigham Young U., 1953—; mem. gen. bd. Young Men's Mut. Improvement Assn., 1935-48; mem. State Bd. Higher Edn., Utah, 1969—; mem. nat. council Boy Scouts Am. Recipient David O. McKay Humanities award Brigham Young U., 1967. Mem. Salt Lake C. of C., Utah Acad. Scis., Arts and Letters, Newcomen Soc., Pi Kappa Alpha. Rotarian (dist. gov. 1956-57, counselor 1957-58, internat. pres. 1966-67). Clubs: Fort Douglas, Athletic, Bonneville Knife and Fork (press 1953-54). Author: At This Same Hour, 1949; Tonic for Our Times, 1952; From the Crossroads, 1955; The Everlasting Things, 1957; May Peace Be with You, 1961; Faith in the Future, 1963; An Open Road, 1968; other books, compilation. Contbr. numerous articles to newspapers, mags., Ency. Brit. Home: PO Box 30 Salt Lake City UT 84110 Office: Radio Sta KSL Salt Lake City UT 84127

EVANS, RICHARD VIRDIN, educator; b. Balt., Mar. 29, 1930; s. George Heberton and Elinor (Virdin) E.; A.B., Princeton, 1951; D.Engring., Johns Hopkins, 1959; m. Elizabeth Morgan Eaton, June 28, 1958; children—Dorothy Eaton, Sally Morgan, Margaret Canby, Richard Virdin. Instr., U. Mich., 1958-59, asst. prof., 1959-62; asst. prof. U. Cal., Los Angeles, 1962-65; asso. prof. Case Western Res. U., 1965-69; prof. bus. adminstrn. U. Ill., Urbana, 1969—, acting head dept., 1969-70. Served to 2d lt. AUS, 1951-54. Lord Baltimore Press fellow, 1956-58. Mem. Operations Research Soc. Am. (asso. editor jour. 1965—), Inst. Mgmt. Sci., Inst. Math. Statistics, Royal Statis. Soc., Assn. Computing Machinery, Soc. Indsl and Applied Math. Contbr. articles to profl. jours. Home: 2507 Melrose Dr Champaign IL 61820 Office: Commerce West U Ill Urbana IL 61801

EVANS, ROBERT CURTIS, food co. exec.; b. Milw., Apr. 6, 1910; s. Curtis A. and Nellie (Schwartzburg) E.; student U. Mich., 1930-31, Ripon Coll., 1932-33; student advanced mgmt. program, Harvard, 1951; m. Nancy Noble, Sept. 15, 1934; children—Emily (Mrs. John King), Edward, Robert. With Carnation Co., Los Angeles, 1933—, successively student trainee, plant supt., asst. gen. supt., asst. to v.p., asst. v.p., 1933-55, v.p., 1955—, dir., 1957—. Bd. dirs. Am. Dry Milk Inst., Nat. Dairy Council. Mem. Psi Upsilon. Club: Beach (Los Angeles). Home: 156 Ashdale Av Los Angeles CA 90049 Office: 5045 Wilshire Blvd Los Angeles CA 90036

EVANS, ROBERT LEWIS, laundry equipment mfr.; b. Indpls., Aug. 20, 1911; s. Robert B. and Norma E. (Kelso) E.; graduate U. Cin., 1935; m. Alice C. Groner, Sept. 15, 1935. Purchasing dept. Delco Products, Dayton, O., 1930-42; prodn. supr. Glenn L. Martin, Balt., 1942, plant mgr., indsl. relations and planning mgr., 1943-51; plant mgr. Allied Aviation, Winston-Salem, N.C., 1942-43; gen. mgr. Clyd div. Whirlpool-Seeger Corp., Clyde, O., 1951-56, v.p. personnel Whirlpool Corp., 1957—, became v.p. Tectrol div., 1962, now group v.p. Tectrol div. Mason. Clubs: Rotary, Point o' Woods Golf. Home: 1850 Willow Rd Palo Alto CA 94304 Office: Whirpool Corp Tectrol Div 686 W Maude Av Sunnyvale CA 94086

EVANS, ROBERT VAN ORMAN, broadcasting co. exec.; b. Cleve., Jan. 15, 1920; s. Miles Erland and Edna (Koncana) E.; B.A., Dartmouth, 1941; LL.B., U. Mich., 1948; m. Virginia Michael, June 15, 1945; children—Amanda, Miles, David, Alison. With CBS, 1950—, gen. counsel, v.p., 1968—. Served with USNR, 1942-45. Mem. Am. Bar Assn., Assn. Bar City N.Y. Republican. Home: 19 Garden Av Bronxville NY 10708 also Les Marmottes CH-1961 Arolla Valais Switzerland Office: 51 W 52d St New York City NY 10019

EVANS, ROBLEY DUNGLISON, physicist; b. University Place, Neb., May 18, 1907; s. Manley Jefferson and Alice (Turner) E.; B.S., Cal. Inst. Tech., 1924-28, M.S., 1929, Ph.D., 1932; m. Gwendolyn Elizabeth Aldrich, Mar. 10, 1928; children—Richard Owen, Nadia Ann, Ronald Aldrich. With research lab. C.F. Braun and Co., Alhambra, Cal., 1929-31; instr. Polytech. Sch., Pasadena, Cal., 1931-32; nat. research fellow U. Cal. at Berkeley, 1932- 34; asst. prof. Mass. Inst. Tech., Cambridge, 1934-38, asso. prof., 1938-45, prof., 1945—; vis. prof. Ariz. State U., 1966-67; staff cons. Peter Bent Brigham Hosp., Boston, 1945—; cons. surgeon gen. Dept. Army, 1962-69, USN Radiol. Def. Lab., 1952-69; cons. div. biology and medicine AEC, 1950—; cons. physics Mass. Gen. Hosp., 1948—, USPHS, 1961—, Fed. Radiation Council, 1965-69, Roger Williams Hosp., Providence, 1965—. Chmn. Internat. Conf. Applied Nuclear Physics, Cambridge, 1940; vice chmn. com. on nuclear sci. NRC, 1946—; mem. Nat. Acad. Scis.-NRC panel 231 advisory to NBS on radiation physics, 1963-66, chmn., 1964; chmn. standing com. for radiation biology aspects of supersonic transport FAA, 1967; mem. com. on radioactive waste mgmt. Nat. Acad. Scis., 1968—; adviser U. Chgo., 1964-69; sci. adv. bd. New Eng. Deaconess Hosp., 1963-69; sr. U.S. del. Internat. Assn. Radiation Research, Cortina, 1966; mem. organizing com. U.S. Nat. Com. Med. Physics, 1966-69; vis. com. med. dept. Brookhaven Nat. Lab., 1965-68; cons. Blood Research Inst., 1967—; vice chmn. adv. com. to U.S. Transuranium Registry, 1968—; mem. tech. adv. com. Ariz. Atomic Energy Commn., 1971—. Vice pres. Found. for Study and Aid of Emotionally Unstable, 1948—. Recipient Theobald Smith medal in Med. Scis., 1937; Presdl. Certificate of Merit, 1948; Hull award and Gold medal A.M.A., 1963; Silvanus Thompson medal Brit. Inst. Radiology, 1966. Fellow Am. Phys. Soc., Am. Acad. Arts and Scis., N.Y. Acad. Scis.; mem. Am. Assn. Physicists in Biology and Medicine, Radiation Research Soc. (v.p., Pres.-elect 1965-66, pres. 1966-67), Am. Roentgen Ray Soc. (asso.), Am. Indsl. Hygiene Assn., Am. Assn. Physics Tchrs., A.A.A.S., Am. Nuclear Soc., Health Physics Soc. (pres. elect 1971), Nat. Com. on Radiation Protection and Measurements (council 1965—), Royal Sci. and Lit. Soc. (hon.), Kungliga Vetenshapoch Vitterhets-Samhallet, Goteborg, Sweden, Sigma Xi, Kappa Gamma, Tau Beta Pi, Pi Kappa Delta. Republican. Author: The Atomic Nucleus, 1956. Editorial bd. Mt. Washington Obs. Bull., 1962—, Health Physics, 1962-70, Physics in Medicine and Biology, 1963-66; editor physics Radiation Research, 1959-62. Contbr. sci. research papers various publs. Home: 4621 E Crystal Lane Scottsdale AZ 85253 Office: Mass Inst Tech Cambridge MA 02139 ☆

EVANS, ROWLAND, Jr., newspaper columnist; b. White Marsh, Pa., Apr. 28, 1921; s. Rowland and Elizabeth Wharton (Downs) E.; grad. Kent Sch., 1939; student Yale, 1940- 41; A.A., George Washington U., 1950; m. Katherine Winton, June 18, 1949; children—Rowland Winton, Sarah Warren. With A.P., 1945-55; mem. staff N.Y. Herald Tribune, 1955-63, syndicated columnist, 1963—; contbr. Sat. Eve. Post, Harpers, Reporter, New Republic; TV panelist and commentator. Served with USMCR, 1941-44. Author: (with Robert Novak) Lyndon B. Johnson: The Exercise of Power, 1966, Nixon in The White House: The Frustration of Power, 1971. Home: 3125 O St NW Washington DC 20007 Office: 1750 Pennsylvania Av Washington DC 20006

EVANS, ROWLAND CADWALADER, Jr., lawyer; b. Phila., Jan. 27, 1897; s. Rowland Cadwallader and May (Gimber) E.; A.B., Amherst Coll., 1919; LL.B., U. Pa., 1922; m. Elizabeth L. Suddards, Oct. 7, 1924; children—Rowland Cadwallader (dec.), Suzanne W. (Mrs. William T. Andrews), Charles S., Frederick L. Admitted to Pa. bar, 1922, since practiced in Phila.; mem. firm Krusen, Evans & Byrne, 1930—; ofcl. examiner Orphans Ct. Phila. County, 1935- 45. Commnr., Lower Marion Township, 1952-64. Served with U.S. Navy, 1917- 19. Mem. Am., Pa., Phila. bar assns., Internat. Acad. Trial Lawyers. Clubs: Lawyers, Racquet, Sharswood Law (Phila.); Merion (Pa.) Cricket. Home: Hampton House Penn Valley Narberth, PA 19072. Office: 21 S 12th St Philadelphia PA 19107

EVANS, ROY TRIPP, Jr., former army officer, can co. exec.; b. Pawtucket, R.I., Feb. 7, 1911; s. Roy Tripp and Lillian (Gradwell) E.; B.S., U.S. Mil. Acad., 1933; grad. Indsl. Coll. Armed Forces, 1948, Advanced Mgmt. Program, Harvard, 1954; m. Virginia Hamilton, Nov. 22, 1934; children—Roy Tripp III, John Gradwell, Alexander Hamilton. Commd. 2d lt. U.S. Army, 1933, advanced through grades to maj. gen., 1959; served in Europe, World War II, in Korea, 1953-54; comdt. Q.M. Sch., 1951-53; dep. chief Army and Air Force Exchange Service, 1957-58; dep. Q.M. gen., 1958-61; with Def. Supply Agy., 1961-63; ret. 1963; gen. mgr. purchases Continental Can Co., Inc., 1963-69, v.p. environmental control, 1969—. Decorated D.S.M., Legion of Merit with 1 oak leaf cluster, Bronze Star; comdr. Order Orange Nassau; Ulchi Distinguished Mil. Service medal with silver star (Republic Korea). Mason. Home: 51 Mallard Dr Greenwich CT 06830 Office: 633 3d Av New York City NY 10017

EVANS, RUPERT NELSON, educator; b. Terre Haute, Ind., Apr. 6, 1921; s. Loran Nelson and Hazel Mae (Rupert) E.; student Butler U., 1938-39; B.S., Ind. State Tchrs. Coll., 1946; M.S., Purdue U., 1949, Ph.D., 1950, D. Vocational Edn. (hon.), 1970; m. Barbara Jean Barbre, June 29, 1941; children—Ellen Anne (Mrs. Roger Collins), Catherine Nell (Mrs. Ronald Westman), Nancy Jean. Foreman, Allison div. Gen. Motors Co., 1940- 44; instr. Elkhart (Ind.) High Sch., 1946-48; grad. asst. Purdue U.,1948- 50; mem. faculty U. Ill., 1950—, prof. vocational and tech. edn., 1956- -, dean Coll. Edn., 1964-69; Fulbright lectr., Japan, 1957-58. Chmn. North Central States Manpower Adv. Com.; mem., past chmn. I11. Vocational Edn. Adv. Council; mem. Edn. Professions Devel. Council. Mem. sch. bd., Champaign, Ill., 1960-64. Mem. Am. Vocational Assn., Am. Indsl. Arts Assn., Mississippi Valley Indsl. Arts Conf. (life chmn.), Nat. Assn. Indsl. Tchr. Educators (past pres.), Am. Ednl. Research Assn., I11. Indsl. Edn. Assn. (pres.), Sigma Xi, Phi Delta Kappa, Kappa Delta Pi, Iota Lambda Sigma. Home: 1842 Maynard Dr Champaign IL 61820 Office: Education Bldg U Ill Urbana IL 61801

EVANS, RUSSELL WILMOT, corp. co. exec.; b. Birmingham, Eng., Nov. 4, 1922; s. William Henry and Ethel (Wilmot) E.; student King Edwards Sch., Birmingham, 1933-39; LL.B., U. Birmingham, 1942; m. Pamela Muriel Hayward, Sept. 1, 1956; children—Mark, Neil, Penelope. Admitted as solicitor, Eng., 1949; solicitor with Shakespeare & Vernon, Birmingham, 1949-51; asst. sec. Harry Ferguson, Ltd., Coventry, 1951-54; sec. Massey Ferguson Holdings, Ltd., London, 1954-62; dir. Wood Pritchett Holdings, Ltd., 1962-67; sec. The Rank Orgn., London, 1968—, dir. subsidiaries. Trustee Lisle Fellowship. Served with Brit. Army, 1942-46. Decorated Mil. Cross. Fellow Inst. of Dirs.; mem. Law Soc. Home: 13 Roehampton Gate London SW 15 England Office: 38 South St London W1A 4QU England

EVANS, THOMAS HAYHURST, engr., educator; b. Los Angeles, Apr. 8, 1906; s. Thomas C. and June (Hayhurst) E.; B.S., Cal. Inst. Tech., 1929, M.S., 1930; grad. work Carnegie Inst. Tech., U. Mich.; m. Eva K. Peterson, Apr. 10, 1945; children—Sally (Mrs. Rolland Moore), Thomas P., Kathryn. Instr. Engring. Sch., Yale, 1930-35; asst. prof., later asso. prof. civil engring. U. Va., 1935-42; prof., dir., Sch. Civil Engring., Ga. Inst. Tech., 1945-49; dean of engring. Colo. State U., 1949-63 (on leave 1959-61, to help organize and adminstr. SEATO Grad. Sch. Engring., Bangkok, Thailand as its 1st dean); dean of engring. Fresno State Coll., 1963—. Chmn. bd. trustees Colo. State U. Research Found. Served as lt. col. U.S. Army, 1942-45; col. C.E. Res. Registered profl. engr., Va., Ga., Colo. Mem. Am. Soc. C.E., Am. Soc. Engring. Edn., Am. Soc. M.E., Am. Inst. E.E., Assn. State Univs. and Land Grant Colls. (chmn. engring. div. 1963), Sigma Xi, Tau Beta Pi, Phi Gamma Delta. Rotarian. Contbr. articles to engring. jours. Home: Fresno CA 93707

EVANS, TITUS CARR, educator, radiobiologist, b. Lorena, Tex., Dec. 9, 1907; s. Charles William and Virginia (Whitsett) E.; B.A., Baylor U., 1929; M.S., State U. Ia., 1931, Ph.D., 1934; m. Mertie Ellen Jahnke, June 1, 1935 (div. Nov. 1968); children—Titus Carr, Susan Ellen, Lucy Virginia; m. 2d, Phyllis Allison, Aug. 9, 1971. Asst. prof. Tex. A. and M. U., 1936-38; research asst. prof. U. Ia., Iowa City, 1938-42, research prof. radiology and radiobiology, 1948—, head Radiation Research Lab., 1948—; asst. prof. Columbia Coll. Phys. and Surg., 1942-48; cons., mem. policy adv. bd. Argonne (Ill.) Nat. Lab., 1964-68. Mem. Nat. Council Radiation Protection, Soc. Nuclear Medicine (past pres.), Radiation Research Soc., Soc. Nuclear Medicine, Biophysics Soc., Am. Physiol. Soc., Am. Roentgen Ray Soc., Radiol. Soc. N.Am., Cancer Research Soc., Soc. for Exptl. Biology and Medicine, Am. Soc. Zoology, Am. Cancer Soc. (pres. Ia. 1965, mem. ho. dels., bd. dirs., 1971—; award distinguished service cancer control 1966), Health Physics Soc., Sigma Xi. Mng. editor Radiation Research, 1952-72; asso. editor Nuclear Medicine, 1960-69. Research, numerous publs. on effects X-ray on cell div. and embryonic devel. in invertebrates, radio-protective effect anoxia in mammals, relative effectiveness fast neutrons, devel. techniques for radiosotopes in biol. and med. research, effects X-rays on ascites tumor cells. Home: 19 Arbury Dr Iowa City IA 52240

EVANS, T.M., bus. exec.; b. Pitts., Sept. 8, 1910; s. Thomas M. and Martha (Jarnagin) E.; B.S., Yale, 1931; m. Elizabeth Parker, June 26, 1935 (div.); children—Thomas M., Edward Parker, Robert Sheldon; m. 2d, Josephine Schlotman Mitchell, Aug. 7, 1953. Pres., H.K. Porter Co., Inc., Pitts., subsidiary cos. until 1956, chmn., 1956-64; chmn., chief exec. officer Crane Co., N.Y., 1959—; pres. Evans & Co., Inc., N.Y.C. Mem. bd. visitors and govs. St. John's Coll., Annapolis, Md.; bd. dirs. Children's Village, Dobbs Ferry, N.Y., Boys Club of Pitts., Pitts. Opera. Republican. Presbyn. Home: Round Hill Rd Greenwich CT 06830 Office: Porter Bldg Pittsburgh PA 15219

EVANS, WALKER, photographer, educator; b. St. Louis, Nov. 3, 1903; s. Walker, Jr. and Jessie (Crane) E.; student Phillips Acad., Andover, Mass., 1922, Williams Coll., 1923, Sorbonne, Paris, France, 1926; Litt.D., Williams Coll., 1968; m. Isabelle Boeschenstein, Oct. 29, 1960. Contbg. editor Time mag., 1943-45; asso. editor Fortune mag., 1945-65; prof. graphic arts Sch. Art and Arch., Yale; exhbns. include Mus. Modern Art, 1938, 71, Art Inst. Chgo., 1942; represented permanent collections Met. Mus., Mus. Modern Art, Art Inst. Chgo. Guggenheim fellow, 1941; recipient award Carnegie Corp., N.Y.C., 1962. Fellow Am. Acad. Arts and Scis. Club: Century Assn. (N.Y.C.). Author: American Photographs, 1962; (with James Agee) Let Us Now Praise Famous Men, 1941; Message from the Interior, 1966; Many are Called, 1966; Walker Evans. 1971. Home: Old Lyme CT 06371 Office: 36 E 73d St New York City NY 10021

EVANS, WALTER FONTAINE, govt. ofcl.; b. Ft. Benning, Ga., Dec. 8, 1929; s. John Humphrey III and Sara Virginia (Pick) E.; diploma, Sorbonne, Paris, 1948; A.A., Madison (Wis.) USAF Inst., 1950; certificate U.S. Mil. Acad., 1953; C.E., George Washington U., 1959; postgrad. U. Md., 1960-61; D.Langs., Yongsei U., Seoul, Korea, 1961-62; m. Renate Runge, Oct. 8, 1963; children—John Humphrey, Stacey Woodings, Sara Frances. Civil engr. B.&O. R.R., Balt., 1955-56; dir. overseas mission, investment guaranty program AID, State Dept., 1956-66, 70—, served in Guinea, 1970—; asso. partner Cons. Internat., Washington, 1966-68; exec. v.p. ADC, Inc., Internat. Sales, Bremen, Washington, 1968-70, also dir. Guest lectr. engring. and constrn. mgmt. Lycee Nat., Bamako, Mali, Conakry, Guinea. Mem. Montgomery County Bd. Edn., Rockville (Md.), City Planning Commn., 1960-62, D.C. Commr.'s Traffic Adv. Bd., 1956-58. Vice regional chmn. Republican party, 1968, precinct chmn., 1966-68. Served with AUS, 1953-55. Named Outstanding Young Man in Md., Jr. C. of C., 1961. Mem. Am. Soc. C.E. (Meade award 1957), Soc. Am. Mil. Engrs., Am. R.R. Engring. Assn., Jr. Chamber Internat. (Outstanding Young Man in Asia 1962, nat. v.p., dep. world officer 1960-62), West Point Alumni Assn. (life). Author pamphlets: Housing in Ghana, 1963, Building in Liberia, 1964, Sewage Lagoons in Developing Countries, 1965. Home: 110 Woodford Potomac MD 20854 Office: Evans/PCD care Dept State Mail Room Guinea Washington DC 20521

EVANS, WAYNE C., advt. agy. exec. Exec. v.p., account supr. Evans-David W. and Assos., Phoenix. Office: 3003 N Central Av Phoenix AZ 85012*

EVANS, WILLIAM AUGUSTUS, lawyer; b. Cananea, Sonora, Mexico, Mar. 5, 1907; (parents Am. citizens); s. Tindall and Helen M. (Robinson) E.; student N.M. Mil. Inst., 1922-25; A.B., Stanford, 1927, LL.B., 1930; m. Margurete O'Malley, Feb. 18, 1933; children—Patricia, William A., Michael O. Admitted to Ariz. bar, 1930; asso. Ellinwood & Ross, Bisbee, Ariz., 1930- 35, Phoenix, 1935—, successor firm Evans, Kitchel & Jenckes, 1947—. Mem. Am. Bar Assn. (chmn. hard minerals com. 1959-60), Ariz. State Bar. Home: 506 E Catalina Av Phoenix AZ 85012 Office: 363 N First Av Phoenix AZ 85003

EVANS, WILLIAM M., lawyer; b. Indpls., Dec. 6, 1923; A.A., Princeton, 1943; LL.B., Harvard, 1948; LL.M., George Washington U., 1952. Admitted to Ind. bar, 1948, Ill. bar, 1949; mem. firm Bose, Buchanan, McKinney & Evans, Indpls. Mem. Ind. Judicial Study Commn., 1965—, Ind. Civil Code Study Commn., 1967—. Mem. Ind. Ho. of Reps., 1957-59. Mem. Am., Ind. (sec. 1968—), Indpls. bar assns., Am. Judicature Soc. (dir. 1963-69), Bar Assn. 7th Fed. Circuit (bd. govs. 1968—). Office: 1100 First Fed Bldg Indianapolis IN 46204*

EVANS, WILLIAM NEY, former commr. U.S. Ct. Claims; b. West Plains, Mo., June 18, 1898; s. William Nelson and Sarah Annis (Smith) E.; A.B., Duke, 1920; LL.B., Harvard, 1923; m. May Alcott Thompson, July 26, 1930. Admitted to Mo. bar, 1923; practiced in West Plains and Houston, Mo., 1923-25; prof. law U. Ark., 1925-27, U. N.C., 1927-28; admitted to N.C. bar. 1928; practiced in Greensboro and High Point, N.C. 1923-34; asst. gen. counsel Textile Labor Relations Bd., 1935; atty. Dept. Labor, 1936; atty. U.S. Maritime Commn., 1936-40, legislative counsel, 1940-42; asst. gen. counsel War Shipping Adminstrn., 1943-45; commr. U.S. Ct. Claims, 1942, 45-69, chmn. com. rules, 1960-69. Served with U.S. Army, 1918; to lt. comdr. USNR, 1942-45. Mem. Am., Fed., N.C. bar assns., Order of Coif, Sigma Chi. Democrat. Methodist. Mason. Club: Cosmos. Contbr. articles to profl. jours. Home: 4651 Kenmore Dr NW Washington DC 20007

EVANS, WILMOTH DUANE, economist; b. Watertown, N.Y., June 10, 1909; s. Albert Leslie and Leah Frances (Craig) E.; B.S., Clarkson Coll. Tech., 1930; m. Edna Blanchard, Oct. 19, 1939; children—Patricia, Craig. Engr., statistician, economist various govt. agys., 1930-40; chief productivity and tech. devel. div. U.S. Bur. Labor Statistics, 1941-47, chief div. interindustry econs., 1948-53, chief statistician, 1954-55, asst. commr., 1955-62, asso. commr., 1962-64; prof. econs. and statistics Cornell U., Ithaca, N.Y., 1964—; cons. Anglo-Am. Council Productivity, 1948- 52; faculty econs. and polit. sci. Cambridge U., 1953-54. Recipient Rockefeller Pub. Service award, 1953, Distinguished Service award, Dept. of Labor, 1953. Fellow Am. Statis. Assn., A.A.A.S., Washington Acad. Scis.; mem. Am. Econ. Assn., Econometric Soc., Conf. on Research in Income and Wealth. Home: 103 Highgate Rd Ithaca, NY 14850.

EVANS, DAME EDITH MARY, Brit. actress; b. London, Eng., Feb. 8, 1888; d. Edward and Caroline Ellen (Foster) E.; student St. Michael's Sch., Pemlico; D.Litt., London U., 1950, Cambridge, 1951, Oxford, 1954; m. Georgia Booth, 1927 (dec. Jan. 1935). Milliner's apprentice; appeared amateur drama group Streatham Shakespeare Players, as Beatrice in Much Ado About Nothing, 1912; on London stage, 1914-17, on tour Merry Wives of Windsor, Merchant of Venice; created roles of the Serpent, Oracle, She-Ancient in Back to Methuselah, Birmingham Repertory Theatre, 1923; played role of Helena, Midsummer Night's Dream, Drury Lane, 1925; 1st N.Y. stage appearance as Florence Nightingale in Lady with a Lamp. 1931; Broadway performance Katharine Cornell's prodn. Romeo and Juliet, 1934, Daphne Laureola, 1950; motion picture include Brit. film Queen of Hearts, Dolwyn, The Nuns Story, 1959, Look Back in Anger, 1959; most recent films include Fitzwilly, The Whisperers; Angel recordings Importance of Being Earnest, other Shakespeare roles: London prodns. The Dark is Light Enough, 1954- 55, The Chalk Garden, 1956; appeared in Young Cassidy, 1965. Entertained troops World War II. Decorated Dame Commander Order of the British Empire, 1946. Home: Albany Picadilly London W1 England. Office: care Angel Records 38 W 48th St New York City NY 10030*

EVANSON, PALMER HENRY, ret. sulphur co. exec.; b. Bellingham, Wash., May 2, 1910; s. Palmer Henry and Agatha (Moen) E.; A.B., U. Wash., 1935; student Harvard Bus. Sch., 1935-36; m. Marion Margaret Crawford, Sept. 5, 1936. Auditor, Lybrand, Ross Bros. and Montgomery, C.P.A.'s, N.Y.C., 1936-37; with Freeport Sulphur Co., N.Y.C., 1937-69, asst. v.p., 1961-62, controller, 1962-69, v.p., 1968-69. Mem. Nat. Assn. Accountants, Financial Execs. Inst. Home: Cross River Rd Katonah NY 10536

EVANSON, ROBERT VERNE, educator; b. Hammond, Ind., Nov. 3, 1920; s. Evan and Dorothy (Gordon) E.; B.S. in Pharmacy, Purdue U., 1947, M.S. in Indsl. Pharmacy, 1949, Ph.D. in Pharmacy Adminstrn., 1953; m. Helen Louise Wolber, June 29, 1947; children—Yvonne Louise (Mrs. Paul V. Nash, Jr.), Karen Denice. Apprentice pharmacist Physician's Supply Co., Hammond, 1946; grad. asst. pharmacy Sch. Pharmacy, Purdue U., 1947-48, mem. faculty, 1948—, prof. pharm. adminstrn., 1963—, head dept., 1966-; cons. in field. Served with AUS, 1943-46. Recipient Lederle Faculty award, 1964. Fellow Am. Found. Pharm. Edn. Conf. Tchrs.; mem. Am., Ind. pharm. assns., Am. Assn. Coll. Pharmacy. Mem. Fed. Ch. W. Lafayette. Author articles in field. Contbg. author Central Pharm. Jour., 1964—. Home: 400 Lindberg Av West Lafayette IN 47906

EVARTS, HARRY FRANKLIN, coll. pres.; b. Troy, N.Y., July 20, 1928; s. Leslie Herbert and Lenora Marie (Chapman) E.; student Sampson (N.Y.) Coll., 1948-49; B.S.C., Ohio U., 1951, M.S., 1952; D.B.A., Harvard, 1959; m. Drusilla Ann Riley, Sept. 9, 1951 (div. Aug. 1969); children—Dale Irene, Leslie Alan, Valerie Dru, Jill Ann. Work standards and methods engr. Gen. Motors Corp., 1952-55; indsl. engr. Gardner Bd. and Carton Co., 1955-57; asst. prof. prodn. mgmt. Northwestern U., 1958-63; asso. prof. Ohio U., 1963-65, prof. bus. adminstrn., dean Coll. Bus. Adminstrn., 1965-70; pres. Bryant Coll., Providence, R.I., 1970—; cons. in field, 1960—; cons. ICA and Japan Productivity Center, 1960. Bd. dirs. Ohio Council Econ. Edn., 1966-70, R.I. Council Econ. Edn., 1971—. Served with AUS, 1946-48; PTO. Ford Found. fellow, 1956-58. Mem. Am. Inst. Indsl. Engrs., Acad. Mgmt., Beta Gamma Sigma. Unitarian. Club: University. Author: (with others) Operations Management, 1961; Instruction to PERT, 1964; also articles, chpts. in books. Home: 3595 Post Rd Warwick RI 02886 Office: Bryant Coll Smithfield RI 02917

EVARTS, RICHARD CONOVER, lawyer; b. N.Y.C., Mar. 11, 1890; s. Prescott and Emily (Conover) E.; 1916; A.B., Harvard, 1913, LL.B., 1916; m. Mary Lillian Bragan, June 18, 1921 (dec. Sept. 1965); children—Nancy (Mrs. Joseph N. Guelich), Emily (Mrs. Richard S.

Gordon), Mary (Mrs. David L. Smith), Sarah (Mrs. Paul G. Haskell). Admitted to Mass. bar, 1916, since practiced in Boston; mem. firm Lyne, Woodworth & Evarts, 1923—; city solicitor, Cambridge, Mass., 1930, 38-42. Chmn. Cambridge Bd. Appeals, 1960—. Served with inf. U.S. Army, 1917-19. Mem. Am., Mass., Middlesex County, Boston (past mem. council), Cambridge (past pres.) bar assns., Cambridge Hist. Soc. (pres. 1965-70). Home: 120 Lake View Av Cambridge MA 02138 Office: 75 Federal St Boston MA 02110

EVE, HENRY PRONTAUT, lawyer; b. Augusta, Ga., Oct. 17, 1917; s. William Raiford and Helen (Davies) E.; B.S., Davidson Coll., 1936; LL.B., Emory U., 1939; m. Caroline Hull, Jan. 21, 1942; 1 dau., Mary Hull. Admitted to Ga. bar, 1939; practiced in Augusta, 1939-41, 45—; partner firm Cumming, Nixon, Eve, Waller & Capers, and predecessor, 1945—. Dir. 1st R.R. & Banking Co. of Ga., Richmond County Bank, 1st Ga. Devel. Corp. Mem. Ga. Ho. of Reps., 1947-49; mem. Ga. Senate, 1949-50. Served to lt. comdr. USNR, 1941-45. Decorated Bronze Star medal. Mem. Am., Augusta (pres. 1967) bar assns., State Bar Ga. (pres. 1965-66), Com. 1OO, Augusta C. of C. (past dir.), Phi Delta Phi, Sigma Alpha Epsilon. Elk. Clubs: Augusta Country (pres. 1963), Pinnacle (bd. dirs.) (Augusta). Home: 602 Bourne Pl Augusta GA 30904 Office: Ga RR Bank Bldg Augusta GA 30902

EVELAND, HARMON EDWIN, educator, geologist; b. Urbana, Ill., Feb. 9, 1924; s. Harmon Edwin and Bernicelyn (Jones) E.; B.S. in Geology, U. Ill., 1947, M.S. in Geology, 1948, Ph.D., 1950; m. Doris Jean Metzler, July 6, 1944; children—Kenneth Ward, Thomas Edwin, Richard Eugene, John Everett. Geologist, party chief Ind. Geol. Survey, summer 1950; asst. prof. geology U. Tenn., 1950-51; prof. geology, head dept. Lamar U., Beaumont, Tex., 1951- -. Served to 2d lt. AUS and USAAF, 1943-45; ETO, MTO. Fellow Geol. Soc. Am., Tex. Acad. Sci.; mem. Soc. Econ. Paleontologists and Mineralogists, Nat. Assn. Geology Tchrs., Tex. Assn. Coll. Tchrs., Sigma Xi, Phi Kappa Phi. Author: Pleistocene Geology of Danville Region, 1952; Physical Geology Laboratory Manual, rev. edit., 1966; Teachers Handbook, 1960; Outline of Elementary Geology, 1966, rev., 1969. Home: 4650 Baywood Lane Beaumont TX 77706

EVEN, FRANCIS ALPHONSE, lawyer; b. Chgo., Sept. 8, 1920; s. George Martin and Cecilia (Neuman) E.; B.S. in Mech. Engring., U. Ill., 1942; J.D., George Washington U., 1949; m. Margaret Hope Herrick, Oct. 16, 1945; children—Janet Beth, Dorothy Elizabeth. Engr., Gen. Electric Co., 1945-49; admitted to D.C. bar, 1949, Ill. bar, 1950; partner firm Fitch, Even, Tabin & Luedeka, patent and trademark law, Chgo., 1952—. Mem. bd. edn., River Forest, Ill., 1963-69. Served with combat engrs., AUS, 1942-45. Mem. Am. Patent Law Assn. (bd. mgrs. 1963-66), Am., Ill., Chgo. bar assns., Patent Law Assn. Chgo. Republican. Clubs: Union League (Chgo.); Oak Park (Ill.) Country; River Forest Tennis. Home: 1018 Park Av River Forest IL 60305 Office: 135 S LaSalle St Chicago IL 60603

EVENDEN, FREDERICK GEORGE, assn. exec.; b. Woodburn, Ore., Apr. 11, 1921; s. Fred and Carolyn (Waterhouse) E.; B.S., Ore. State U., 1943, Ph.D., 1949; m. Mildred J. Martin, Oct. 2, 1949; children—Angela, Jeanne. Wildlife research biologist U.S. Fish and Wildlife Service, 1949-53; exec. dir. Cal. Jr. Mus., Sacramento, 1953-56; investment and sales counselor, Sacramento, 1956-63; exec. sec. Wildlife Soc., Washington, 1963-68, exec. dir., 1968—. Treas. Rachel Carsons Trust for Living Environment, 1970—; mem. adv. bd. to Md. Dept. Natural Resources, 1971—; sec., treas. Am. Council Internat. Wild Life Protection; mem. exec. com. Natural Resources Council Am., 1963-65, Citizens Com. Outdoor Recreation, 1963-65; mem. adv. council Cal. Outdoor Recreation Com., 1957-63. Treas., dist. chmn. Golden Empire council Boy Scouts Am., 1962-64, mem. nat. conservation com., 1963-71, exec. bd. Nat. Capitol area council, 1966-69. Served with USAAF, 1943-46; CBI. Fellow A.A.A.S.; mem. Wildlife Disease Assn., Agr. Research Inst., Outdoor Writers Assn. Am., Canadian Soc. Wildlife and Fisheries Biologists, Internat. Assn. Game, Fish and Conservation Commrs., Am. Ornithologists Union, Am. Fisheries Soc., Nat. Audubon Soc., Am. Forestry Assn., Wildlife Soc., Nat. Wildlife Fedn., Izaak Walton League, Nat. Parks and Conservation Assn., Wilderness Soc., Conservation Edn. Assn., Cooper, Wilson ornithol. clubs, Soil Conservation Soc. Am., Washington Biologists Field Club, Am. Inst. Biol. Sci. Presbyn. (clk. session). Home: 7805 English Way Bethesda MD 20034 Office: 3900 Wisconsin Av NW Washington DC 20016

EVEREST, FRANK KENDALL, Jr., Air Force officer; b. Fairmont, W.Va., Aug. 10, 1920; s. Frank K. and Phyllis (Walker) E.; student Fairmont State Tchrs. Coll., 1939, W.Va. U., 1940; m. Avis G. Mason, July 8, 1942; children—Victoria A., Cynthia L., Frank Kendall III. Commd. aviation cadet USAAF, 1941, advanced through grades to brig. gen. USAF, 1965; fighter pilot during World War II; test pilot, 1946-56; dir. aerospace safety, 1966—. Decorated Legion of Merit with oak leaf cluster, D.F.C. with 2 oak leaf clusters, Air Force Commendation medal with oak leaf cluster, Air medal with 6 oak leaf clusters. Rotarian. Author: Fastest Man Alive, 1958. Set ofcl. world's speed record in F-100 of 755 miles per hour, 1953, unofcl. speed record in X-2 rocket airplane of 1957 miles- per-hour, 1956. Address: Quarters 84 Norton AFB San Bernardino CA 92409

EVEREST, HARVEY PETTIT, banker; b. Hutchinson, Kan., Apr. 10, 1895; s. Claude Harrison and Martie (Pettit) E.; student U. Okla., 1914-17; m. Ruth Whetstone, 1915; children—Jean I., Howard H. With Mid-Continent News Co., Pubs. News Co., Oklahoma City, mag. distbrs., 1912—, now chmn.; v.p., treas. Darby-Everest Cadillac, Inc., 1955—; dir. Liberty Nat. Bank & Trust Co., Oklahoma City, 1946—, exec. com., 1947—, pres., 1955- 70, hon. chmn. bd., 1970—. Past pres. Community Chest, Oklahoma City. Chmn. trustees Phillips U.; bd. dirs. United Community Funds and Councils Am., YMCA, A.R.C., Goodwill Industries, Family and Children's Service, Okla. Med. Research Found. Served as lt. USNR, World War II. Mem. Am. Bankers Assn., Oklahoma City C. of C. Mem. Christian Ch. (mem. bd., exec. com.). Home: 7414 North Country Club Dr Oklahoma City OK 73116 Office: PO Box 25848 Oklahoma City OK 73125

EVERETT, BELLE SMITH, Democratic nat. committeewoman; b. Marydel, Md., Oct. 15, 1898; d. Frank S. and Mary E. (Bickling) Smith; ed. pub. schs.; m. Levi L. Everett, Nov. 4, 1916; children—Franklin L., T. Marvel. Democratic committeewoman 3d dist., Del.; vice chmn. County Dem. Orgn.; vice chmn. Del. Dem. Orgn.; Dem. nat. committeewoman for Del., 1956—. mem. Del. Bd. Welfare, 1949-58.‡

EVERETT, BOYD NIXON, financial cons.; b. Pasadena, Cal., Dec. 19, 1904; s. Torrey and Mary Reeves (Nixon) E.; grad. Phillips Exeter Acad., 1922; B.S., Harvard, 1926, M.B.A., 1929; m. Margaret Bruce Carter, Feb. 4, 1933; children—Boyd N. (dec.), William Carter, Torrey, Bruce. Asso., Bond & Goodwin, N.Y.C., 1929-30, City Bank Farmers Trust Co., 1930-37; mgr. investment dept. Delafield & Delafield, 1937-38; financial sec. Continental Casualty Co. and Continental Assurance Co., Chgo., 1938-40, treas. 1940-64, sr. financial v.p., 1964-69; sr. financial v.p. CNA Financial Corp., 1968-69, financial cons., 1969—; dir. Whiting Corp., Rennzoil United, Inc., Duval Corp., Morlan Pacific Corp. Mem. Nat. council Boy Scouts Am.; treas. dir. Lake Forest Day Sch., 1940-43; dir., past pres. N. Shore Country Day Sch. Republican. Author: Term Loans (with Herbert V. Prochnow). Home: 61 Indian Hill Rd Winnetka IL 60093 Office: 310 Michigan Av Chicago IL 60604

EVERETT, CHAD, (Raymon Lee Cramton), actor; b. South Bend, Ind., June 11, 1937; s. Harry Clyde and Virdeen Ruth (Hopper) C.; student Henry Ford Community Coll., 1955-56, Mich. State U., 1956-57, Wayne State U., 1957-60; m. Brenda Lee Thompson, May 22, 1966; children—Katherine Kerrie, Shannon Kimberly. Actor, Warner Bros., 1960-63, M.G.M., 1963-67; dir. films Medical Center, The Nowhere Child; album All Strung Out. Served with USNR, 1955-63. Recipient Golden Globe, 1971, Don Quixote award, 1971. Mem. Screen Actors' Guild, A.F.T.R.A. Author: A Toast to Shelby, 1971. Office: care Algra Prodns MGM Culver City CA 90230

EVERETT, DONALD EDWARD, educator; b. Auburn, Ala., Dec. 10, 1920; s. Edward and Mary Rebecca (Hopkins) E.; B.A., U. Fla., 1941; M.A., Tulane U., 1950, Ph.D. (Ford Found. fellow), 1952; m. Mary Lou Melancon, Sept. 4, 1949; children—John Lauchlin, Mary Melancon. Instr. history Tulane U., also editorial asst. Mississippi Valley Hist. Rev. 1952-53; faculty Trinity U., San Antonio, 1953—, prof. history, 1964—, chmn. dept., 1967—. Mem. Bexar County Hist. Survey Com., 1961—; sec. Tex. Historic Theater Found. San Jose Mission, 1968-70. Bd. dirs. Inman Christian Center. Served with USAAF, 1942-45. Piper prof., 1970. Mem. Orgn. Am. Historians, So., Tex., San Antonio (pres. 1962) hist. assns., Yanaguana Soc., Phi Alpha Theta, Pi Sigma Alpha. Democrat. Presbyn. (elder). Editor: Chaplain Davis and Heed's Texas Brigade, 1962. Author: Trinity University: A Record of One Hundred Years, 1968. Contbr. articles to hist. jours. Home: 142 Laurel Heights Pl San Antonio TX 78212

EVERETT, FRANCIS DEWEY, investment banker; b. Worcester, Mass., Feb. 13, 1889; s. Oliver H. and Sarah Frances (Dewey) E.; student St. Marks Sch.; A.B., Harvard, 1911, M.E.E., 1913; m. Marion Alice Lesher, Oct. 1O, 1914; m. 2d, Mildred W. Ordway, July 17, 1954; m. 3d, Hertha Jordan, Dec. 1, 1962. With Westinghouse, Church, Kerr, engrs., N.Y.C., 1913-14; asst. Harvard Grad. Sch. Engring., 1914; at Saranac Lake and Ariz. (for health), 1914-18; asst. to Dr. Kennelly, Mass. Inst. Tech., 1918; with Hornblower & Weeks, N.Y.C., 1919—, head statis. dept., 1924, head buying dept., 1927, partner, 1929—. Gov. N.Y. Stock Exchange, 1937-38; gov. Investment Bankers Assn., 1938-41; gov. Assn. of Stock Exchange Firms, 1945-51. Served in USNRF, World War I. Home: 179 E 70th St New York City NY 10021 Office: 8 Hanover St New York City NY 10004

EVERETT, GEORGE DUDLEY, banker; b. Ft. Fairfield, Me., Sept. 6, 1892; s. Elden J. and Annie M. (Clark) E.; grad. Aroostook (Me.) Central Inst., 1912, Shaw Bus. Coll., Bangor, Me., 1913; LL.D. (hon.), U. Me., 1962; m. Gladys Collins, Feb. 20, 1915. With Merrill Trust Co., Bangor, Me., 1914—, v.p., treas., 1942-44, pres., 1944-59, chmn. bd., 1959—, also dir.; dir. Hannaford Bros. Co. Home: 88 Poplar St Bangor ME 04401 Office: 2 Hammond St Bangor ME 04401

EVERETT, GEORGE EDWARD, ret. transp. co. exec.; b. Bradford, Pa., Mar. 1O, 1900; s. George W. and Maude (Whiteman) E.; B.S. in Econs., Ohio State U., 1924; m. Maude L. Mathews; 1 son, Allen E. With Kansas City (Mo.) Jour. Post, 1924- 31; dir. pub. relations and advt. Transcontinental and Western Air Lines, 1930-36; pub. relations and sales work Western Petroleum Refiners Assn., 1936-39, Am. Petroleum Inst., 1939-41; dir. tank car sect., petroleum div. Office Def. Transp., World War II; with Gen. Am. Transp. Corp., Chgo., 1944-71, v.p., 1960-65, also dir. Mem. Beta Gamma Sigma, Delta Sigma Pi. Clubs: Chicago Athletic Assn.; Evanston (Ill.) Golf. Home: 6 Leeward Lane Gulf Harbors New Port Richey FL 33552

EVERETT, JAMES LEGRAND, III, utility exec.; b. Charlotte, N.C., July 24, 1926; s. James LeGrand and Charlotte (Keesler) E.; B.S. in Mech. Engring., Pa. State U., 1948, M.S., 1949; M.S. in Indsl. Mgmt., Mass. Inst. Tech., 1959; m. Marjorie Miriam Scherf, Sept. 3, 1947; children—James LeGrand IV, Christopher Glenn, John Keesler. Instr. mech. engring. Pa. State U., 1948-50; instr. civil and mech. engring. Drexel Evening Coll., 1950-52; head fuel sect. Atomic Power Devel. Assos., 1953-55, now dir., mem. exec. com.; with Phila. Electric Co., 1950—, exec. v.p., 1968-71, pres., 1971—, also dir., mem. exec. com. parent co., dir. subsidiaries; chmn., dir. Radiation Mgmt. Corp., 1971—; dir., mem. exec. com. Power Reactor Devel. Co.; dir. Phila. Nat. Bank, Tasty Baking Co., Fidelity Mut. Life Ins. Co. Bd. dirs. Chester County council Boy Scouts Am.; pres., bd. dirs. Met. YMCA Phila. Mem. vis. com. Drexel U.; mem. sci. and arts com. Franklin Inst. Served to ensign USNR, 1944-46. Sloan fellow 1958-59. Recipient Outstanding Young Man of Year award Phila. Jr. C. of C., 1961; Ann. engring. tech. award Temple U., 1963. Registered profl. engr., Pa. Mem. Am. Nuclear Soc. (bd. dirs., Pa. Charter mem., chmn. finance com.) Edison Electric Inst. (exec. com. engring. and operating div.), Am. Soc. M.E., Franklin Inst., I.E.E.E., Soc. Am. Mil. Engrs., Engrs. Club Phila., Nat., Pa. socs. profl. engrs. Tau Beta Pi, Pi Tau Sigma, Pi Mu Epsilon. Clubs: Union League (Phila.); Merion Golf (Ardmore, Pa.). Office: 1000 Chestnut St Philadelphia PA 19105

EVERETT, JOHN RUTHERFORD, educator; b. Portland, Ore., Dec. 27, 1918; s. Monroe Green and Margaret (Johnson) E.; A.B., Park Coll., 1942, LL.D., 1961; B.D., Union Theol. Sem., 1944; A.M., Columbia, 1943, Ph.D., 1945; LL.D., Roanoke Coll., 1960; m. Elizabeth Sloan, June 13, 1942 (div. June 1963); 1 dau., Margaret Elizabeth; m. 2d, Elsie Livesly, Jan. 21, 1964. Dir. YMCA, USO McBurney br., N.Y.C., 1943-44; instr. philosophy Columbia, 1943-45; asst. prof. philosophy, 1948-50, chmn. dept. philosophy, sch. gen. studies, 1948-50; asst. prof. philosophy Wesleyan U., Middletown, Conn., 1945-48; pres. Hollins Coll., 1950-60; chancellor City U.N.Y., N.Y.C., 1960-62; sr. v.p. Ency. Brit., Inc., also pres. Ency. Brit. Press, mem. bd. editors, 1962-64; pres. New Sch. Social Research, N.Y.C., 1964—. Dir. Shenandoah Life Ins. Co. Mem. Spl. Senate Investigating Com. on Edn. (Conn.). 1945-46; cons. Council For Financial Aid to Edn., 1956; adviser to Gov. Conn., 1948-50; del. chmn. 3d Ann. UNESCO Conf., Paris. 1952. Bd. dirs. Roanoke Guidance Center, 1951-56, Roanoke Fine Arts Center, 1951-55, Union Theol. Sem., 1961—; chmn. trustees New Lincoln Sch., N.Y.C., 1971—. Recipient U.S. Jr. C. of C. award as 1 of 10 Outstanding Young Men of Year, 1950. Fellow Nat. Council Religion Higher Edn.; mem. Am. Philos. Assn., Assn. Am. Colls. (commn. liberal edn. 1953-55, commn. finance 1959—), Am. Council Edn. (com. measurement and evaluation 1959—), Va. Edn. Assn. (ednl. policies com. 1959—), Va. Found. for Ind. (trustee 1952—, sec.-treas. 1952-53), Conn. Research Council (chmn. 1946-49), Council Higher Instns. N.Y.C. (pres. 1967-69). Democrat. Presbyn. Author: Religion in Economics, 1946; Religion in Human Experience, 1950. Book editor Jour. Philosophy, 1945-52. Contbr. article religion Ency. Americana, 1951, 56; articles, revs. in numerous learned jours. Office: 66 W 12th St New York City NY 10011

EVERETT, MARK REUBEN, med. educator; b. Slatington, Pa., Nov. 2, 1899; s. Alexander David and Mary Margaret (Scheidy) E.; B.S. in Chem. Engring., Bucknell U., 1920, Ph.D. in Med. Sci., Harvard, 1924, D.Sc. (hon.), 1948; m. Alice Gertrude Allen, June 21, 1924; children—Mark Allen, Kathleen Elizabeth. Teaching fellow Harvard Med. Sch., 1921-24; prof. biochemistry and pharmacology U. Okla. Sch. Medicine, chmn. dept., 1924-35, prof. biol. chemistry, chmn. dept., 1936—, dean Sch. Medicine and supt. Univ. Hosps., 1947-56, dir. Med. Center, dean Sch. Medicine, 1956-64, now dean emeritus and Regents Prof. Med. Scis. Mem. exec. council Assn. Am. Med. Colls; bd. dirs. Okla. Med. Research Found., Okla. Meml. Assn; adminstr. John A. Hatchett Meml. Fund; mem. Okla. Commn. for Crippled Children, Okla. Bd. Unexplained Deaths; chmn. Okla. Med. Research Commn. Served as pvt. U.S. Army, 1918. Named to Okla. Hall of Fame, 1946; Pa. Ambassador 1948. Mem. Am. Soc. Biol. Chemists, Am. Chem. Soc., Soc. Exptl. Biology and Medicine, Okla. Acad. Sci., Oklahoma City Acad. Medicine, Okla. Co. Med. Soc., Am. Assn. Cancer Research, A.A.A.S., Blue Cord, Am. Assn. U. Profs., Oklahoma City Clin. Soc., Assn. Am. Med. Colls. (mem. exec. council), Sigma Xi, Phi Beta Pi, Alpha Omega Alpha (dir.), Alpha Epsilon Delta. Democrat. Mem. Reformed Ch. Author: Medical Biochemistry, 1942: Pioneering for Research, 1966. Home: 1302 NW 21st St Oklahoma City OK 73106 Office: U of Okla Sch of Medicine 800 NE 13th St Oklahoma City OK 73104

EVERETT, NEWTON BENNIE, educator; b. Dundee, Tex., May 12, 1916; s. Henry B. and Lula Mae (Williams) E.; B.S., N. Tex. State Coll., 1937, M.S., 1938; Ph.D. (teaching fellow 1940-42), U. Mich., 1942; m. Naomi Doris Briggs, Sept. 11, 1940; children—Peter Ben, James Briggs. Instr. anatomy U. Mich., 1942-46; asst. prof. U. Wash., 1946-48, asso. prof., 1948-57, adminstrv. officer, 1955—, prof., 1957—, chmn. dept. anatomy, now prof., chmn. dept. biol. stucture. Mem. Am. Assn. Anatomists, Am. Physiol. Soc., Am. Internat. socs. cell biology. Internat. Am. socs. hematology. Royal Soc. Medicine (affiliate), Reticuloendothelial Soc., Sigma Xi. Home: 4315 53d Av NE Seattle WA 98105

EVERETT, ROBERT GEORGE, corp. exec.; b. Binghamton, N.Y., Mar. 15, 1931; s. Robert L. and Madaline Everett; B.S. in Accounting, Harpur Coll., 1953; M.B.A., Cornell U., 1955; m. Betty J. Whitten, Sept. 9, 1950; children—Elizabeth, Karen, Robert, Thomas. Various financial positions up to div. controller, corporate dir. financial planning IBM, 1955-69; exec. v.p. Great Western United Corp., Denver, 1969—. Served with USNR, 1949-54. Mem. C. of C. Clubs: Denver Athletic, City (Denver); Larchmont Shore. Home: Box 516 Upper Bear Creek Evergreen CO 80439 Office: Equitable Bldg Denver CO 80202

EVERETT, ROBERT RIVERS, corp. exec.; b. Yonkers, N.Y., June 26, 1921; s. Chester McKenzie and Ruth (Melius) E.; B.S., Duke, 1942; M.S., Mass. Inst. Tech., 1943; m. Helen Burns, Oct. 21, 1944; children—Robert F., Bruce M., Douglas F., Theodore J., Michael B. with Servomechanisms Lab. of Mass. Inst. Tech., 1942-51, asso. dir. Digital Computer Lab., 1951; asso. div. head Lincoln Lab., 1951-56, div. head, 1956-58; tech. dir. The Mitre Corp., Bedford, Mass., 1958-59, v.p. tech. operations, 1959-69, exec. v.p., 1969, pres., 1969—. Fellow I.E.E.E.; mem. Assn. Computing Machinery, A.A.A.S., Phi Beta Kappa, Sigma Xi, Tau Beta Pi. Contbr. articles tech. jours. Patentee digital computers. Home: 140 Cherry Brook Rd Weston MA 02193 Office: PO Box 208 Bedford MA 01730

EVERETT, ROBERTS, agrl. writer; b. Merrill, Mich., Mar. 17, 1894; s. John Edward and Helen (Glazier) E; student Oberlin Coll., 1911-12; B. Litt., Columbia Sch. Journalism, 1915; m. Evelyn Virginia Clay, May 31, 1917 (div. Aug. 1937): 1 dau., Mrs. Helen Everett Seaman; m. 2d, Frieda Wyandt, Apr. 2, 1938. Mem. staff N.Y. Tribune, 1915, N.Y. World, 1915-17; editor Air Travel, 1917; chief staff officer Dairy Industries Supply Assn., 1919- 60; mng. dir. Dairy Soc. Internat., 1946-60, now writer in agrl. field. Served as flying cadet, 1917-19, commd. 2d lt. Air Service, 1918. Recipient Distinguished Service award Am. Dairy Sci. Assn., 1961. Mem. Nat. Assn. Expn. Mgrs. (hon.). Club: Nat. Press (Washington). Author indsl. commentaries; contbr. numerous articles to mags. Home: 12602 Eldrid Ct Silver Spring MD 20904

EVERETT, SARA MANN, club woman; b. Atlanta; d. John Robert and Della (Rainey) Mann; tchrs. diploma Cocke Sch. Expression, Dallas, 1931; student So. Methodist U., Interamerican U., Saltillo, Mexico; m. Luther McKinley Everett, Aug. 25, 1913 (dec. 1956); children—John Robert, Thomas Hill, Luther McKinley. Mem. Nat. League Am. Pen Women, 1941—, nat. recording sec., 1960-62, nat. pres., 1962-64, nat. chmn. youth activities, 1964-66, mem. nat. pres., adv. council, 1970—, treas. Dallas br., 1964-70. Partner, dir. Better Monkey Grip Co., Dallas, 1937—. Chmn., Nat. Owlets, nat. pres., 1966—. Past dir. Dallas Pan Am. Round Table No. 2; mem. Dallas Mus. Fine Art, Dallas Symphony League, Nat. Audubon Soc., Cocke Sch. Expression Alumni Assn. (pres. 1965-66), Oak Cliff Soc. Fine Arts (life), Internat. Platform Assn. Clubs: Cherokee Village Country; Lakewood Country, Oak Cliff Browning (Dallas); Tanglewood-on-the-Lake Country (Lake Texoma, Tex.); Rolling Oaks Country; Avion Travelcade. Home: Terrace House 3131 Maple Av Dallas TX 75201 Office: 5320 Harry Hines Blvd Dallas TX 75235

EVERETT, WALTER, educator; grad. Sch. Journalism, Columbia, 1933; m. Betty Ruth Lindsey. Various newspaper positions, 1933-49, ending as city editor Providence Evening Bull.; with Am. Press Inst., Columbia U., N.Y.C., 1949—, now exec. dir. Mem. staff Pres. Truman's Internat. Devel. Adv. Bd., 1950. Home: Dobbs Ferry NY 10522 Office: American Press Institute Columbia Univ New York City NY 10027

EVERETT, WARREN SYLVESTER, govt. ofcl.; b. Wichita, Kan., Oct. 19, 1919; s. Carl S. and Effie (Barton) E.; B.S., U. Wichita, 1932, U.S. Mil. Acad., 1935; M.S., Cornell, 1939; student Army Engr. Sch., 1939-40, Army Command and Gen. Staff Coll., 1942, Princeton, 1945, Armed Forces Staff Coll., 1949, Army War Coll., 1956-57; m. Ruthmary Francis, June 13, 1935; children—Mary Margaret (Mrs. R.L. Graham), Judith Ann (Mrs. D.L. McKee), Warren Douglas. Commd. 2d lt. U.S. Army, 1935, advanced through grades to col., 1951; dir. U.S. Army Constrn. Agy., France, 1950-61; dist. engr., Vicksburg, Mis., 1961-63; retired, 1963; chief pub. works div. USOM to Vietnam, 1963-65; chief engr. U.S. AID mission to Nigeria, 1965-66; chief engr. AID, Vietnam, 1966-67; dir. excess property program AID, 1967-68; cons. Office Emergency Preparedness, Exec. Office of President, 1968—. Organized nat. fallout shelter survey and marking program, 1961. Pres. P.T.A., Am. Sch., Tokyo, 1953-54. Decorated Legion of Merit with oak leaf cluster, Commendation ribbon; Ulchi medal with silver star, Distinguished Service medal, Presdl. citation (Korea). Registered profl. engr., Wash. Fellow Am. Soc. C.E.; mem. Soc. Am. Mil. Engrs. (past pres. Vicksburg and Saigon), Nat. Soc. Profl. Engrs. Contbr. articles profl. jours. Home: 1401 Gower Ct McLean VA 22101 Office: Office Emergency Preparedness, 17th and F Sts N W Washington, DC 20504.

EVERETT, CURTIS, lawyer; b. Omaha, Aug. 9, 1930; s. Charles Edgar and Rosalie (Cook) E.; B.A. cum laude, Beloit Coll., 1952; J.D., U. Chgo., 1957; m. Joan Rose Bader, Sept. 7, 1951; children-Jeffrey, Ellen, Amy, Jennifer. Admitted to Ill. bar, 1957, since practiced in Chgo.; partner firm Bell, Boyd, Lloyd, Haddad and Burns, 1965—. Vice pres., sec., dir. Elcon, Inc., Frankfort, Ill., sec. Integraphics, Inc., Chgo., Country & Home Shopping Center, Inc., Arlington Heights, Ill. Chmn. So. suburban area Beloit Coll. Ford Found. challange program, 1964-65; pres. The Players, Flossmoor, 1970-71. Served with AUS, 1952-54. Mem. Am., Ill., Chgo. bar Assns., Order of Coif, Sigma Chi, Phi Alpha Delta. Clubs: Law, University (Chgo.). Editorial bd. U. Chgo. Law Rev., 1956-57. Home: 2302 MacDonald Lane Flossmoore IL 60422 Office: 135 S LaSalle St 1Chicago IL 60603

EVERGOOD, PHILIP (Howard Francis Dixon), artist; b. N.Y.C., Oct. 26, 1901; s. Miles and Flora Jane (Perry) E.; student Eton Coll., Eng., 1915-19, Trinity Hall Coll., Cambridge U., Eng., 1919-20, Slade Sch. Arts, London, 1921-23, Art Students League N.Y.C., 1923-25, Julien's Acad., Paris, 1925; m. Julia Vincent Cross, Aug. 15, 1931. Painter, lectr., tchr., draftsman 1921—. Exhibited in group shows Art Students League 1967-68, Gallery Modern Art at Huntington Hartford Mus., 1967, Whitney Mus. Am. Art, 1967, Smithsonian Instn., 1968, represented in maj. U.S. and fgn. collections including: Met. Mus., Mus. Modern Art, Library Congress, Widener Library, Los Angeles Mus., Whitney Mus. Am. Art, Bklyn. Mus., Boston Mus. Fine Arts, Carnegie Inst. Art, Nat. Gallery (Melbourne, Australia), Geelong Gallery Art (Victoria, Australia), Balt. Mus. Coll., Wadsworth Athenaeum, Hartford, Conn., Tel Aviv (Israel) Mus. Art, Fogg Mus., Cambridge, Mass., Mus. Contemporary Art Dallas, Syracuse U., Cornell U., others; murals Richmond Hill (L.I.) Pub. Library, Kalamazoo Coll. Instr. painting, summer sessions U. Minn., 1955, Ia. State Tchrs. Coll., 1957-58, Skowhegan (Me.) Sch. Art, 1963; retrospective exhbn. 1927-60 Whitney Mus. Am. Art, 1960. Recipient several prizes 1935—, including Carol H. Beck Gold medal, Pa. Acad., Phila., 1949; 2d prize Carnegie Inst. Art. Pitts., 1949; 2d prize, W.A. Clark silver medal Corcoran Gallery Art, 1951; 1st prizes 1st L.I. Art Festival, 1951, Terry Art Inst., Miami, 1952, Balt. Mus., 1955; Joseph E. Temple gold medal Pa. Acad., 1958, spl. drawing prize, 1961; Purchase award Ford Found., 1962; Knight of Mark Twain, Mark Twain Jour., 1967-68; others. Participant U.S. internat. exhbns., Art of the U.S.A., Venice, London, Brussels, Paris, C.Am., S.Am., Fellow Internat. Inst. Arts and Letters; mem. Artists Equity Assn., Nat. Inst. Arts and Letters (grantee 1956), Kappa Pi (hon.). Author: Evergood-Twenty Years of His Work, 1946; illustrations for Short Stories of Gogol, 1951; Evergood Graphics, 1966. Contbr. to art mags. Home: Route 67A RFD 1 Bridgewater CT 06752 Office: Kennedy Galleries 20 E 56th St New York City NY 10022 ☆

EVERHARD, EDWARD MELVILLE, former glass mfg. exec.; b. Massilon, O., June 29, 1905; s. Melville McCullough and May Dunlap (White) E.; student U. Cin., 1923-24, Ohio State U., 1924-26; m. Leila Bush Harvey, Mar. 17, 1938. With Libbey-Owens Ford Co. 1926-70, successively sales rep. N.Y.C. office, dist. sales mgr. Buffalo ty., New Eng. ty., Southwestern ty., charge Western sales, gen. offices, Toledo, gen. mgr. distbr. sales dept., charge distbr. sales throughout U.S., gen. sales mgr., 1952-53, v.p., 1953-70; pres. Libbey-Owens-Ford Export Co.; v.p. Libbey-Owens- Ford Glass Co., 1959-70. Clubs: Sales Executives, Toledo, Inverness, Rotary (Toledo). Home: 326 E Broadway Maumee OH 43537

EVERHARD, LLOYD RUSSELL, mfg. co. exec.; b. Cin., Dec. 2, 1909; s. John Harbaugh and Eliza Jane (Fenstermacher) E.; Comml. Engr., U. Cin., 1933; LL.B., Salmon P. Chase Coll. Law, 1951; m. Jean May Brown, Jan 1, 1941; children—Thomas Charles, Joseph Ellsworth. Accountant, Globe-Wernicke Co., Cin., 1933- 39; payroll auditor State Ohio, 1939-41; with Pullman Inc., and subsidiaries, 1941—, sec. Trailmobile Inc., 1941-65, sec. Pullman Inc., 1966—. Mem. adv. com. Pullman Inc. Found. Mem. Am. Soc. Ins. Mgmt. (pres. dir. Cin. 1960), Am. Soc. Corp. Secretaries. Episcopalian (past vestryman). Mason (32). Home: 911 S Grant St Hinsdale IL 60521 Office: 200 S Michigan Av Chicago IL 60604

EVERHART, DAVID LESLIE, hosp. administr.; b. Newark, O., May 24, 1928; s. William Alfred and Mary Elder (Lough) E.; B.A., Denison U., 1950; M.S., Columbia, 1953; m. Margaret Weber, June 23, 1951; children—John David, Barbara Weber, Margaret Leslie. Adminstrv. intern Ohio State U. Hosp., 1950-51; adminstrv. resident Henry Ford Hosp., Detroit, 1952-53, adminstrv. asst., 1953-55, asst. dir., 1955-61, asso. dir., 1961-63; adminstr. Johns Hopkins Hosp., Balt., 1963-70; exec. dir. New Eng. Med. Center Hosps., Boston, 1970—; cons. to surgeon gen. USAF. Mem. Am. Hosp. Assn., Am. Coll. Hosp. Adminstrs., Internat. Hosp. Fed., Soc. Hosp. Adminstrv. Assn., Assn. Am. Med. Colls., Mass. Hosp. Assn., Phi Gamma Delta, Phi Mu Alpha, Blue Key. Presbyn. Home: 26 Spywood Rd Sherborn MA 01770 Office: 171 Harrison Av Boston MA 02111

EVERHART, JOHN OTIS, educator;b. Mechanicsburg, O., Oct. 23, 1905; s. Warren Edgar and Rebecca Mabel (Myers) E.; student Wittenberg Coll., 1923-25; B. Ceramic Engring., Ohio State U., 1928, M.Sc., 1935, Ph.D., 1937; m. Gladys Marie Hayden, Aug. 30, 1929; children—John David, Nancy Jane (Mrs. Carl E. Rossi) Faculty Ohio State U., 1928-37, 44—, prof. ceramic engring., 1956—, chmn. dept., 1958—, dir. ceramic research, engring. expt. sta., 1957—; from ceramic engr. to v.p. Ky. Fire Brick Co., 1938-44. Trustee Edward Orton Jr. Ceramic Found. Registered profl. engr., Ohio. Fellow Am. Ceramic Soc.; mem. Nat. Inst. Ceramic Engrs., Ceramic Ednl. Council, Am. Soc. Engring. Edn., Am. Soc. Testing Materials, Ohio Ceramic Industries Assn. (gen. sec.), Ohioana Library Assn., Sigma Xi, Tau Beta Pi, Keramos. Republican. Methodist. Author articles in field. Home: 1160 Kingsdale Terrace Columbus OH 43220 Office: 2041 N College Rd Columbus OH 43210

EVERITT, GEORGE BAIN, banker; b. Forest Hills, L.I., N.Y., Apr. 21, 1914; s. George B. and Lois E. (Richter) E.; B.A., Duke, 1936; m. Barbara Taylor, Mar. 25, 1944; children—Lois V., Margaret M., Emily A., Elizabeth S. With Sears, Roebuck & Co., 1936; with Merchandise Nat. Bank of Chgo., 1936—, asst. v.p., 1941-49, dir., 1946—, v.p., 1949-60, pres., 1960-65, chmn. bd., 1965—. Secretary Hadley Sch. for the Blind, Winnetka, Ill., 1950-64, v.p., 1964—. Served with USNR, 1942-46. Mem. N. Side Bankers Club (past pres.). Home: 1190 Westmoor Rd Winnetka IL 60093 Office: Merchandise Nat Bank of Chicago Merchandise Mart Chicago IL 60654

EVERITT, WILLIAM LITTELL, cons. engr., former coll. dean; b. Balt. Apr. 14, 1900; s. William Littell and Margaret (Pownall) E.; E.E., Cornell U., 1922; M.S., U. Mich., 1926; Ph.D., Ohio State U., 1933; D. Eng., Bradley U., 1959, Tri-State Coll., 1964, U. Andes, Bogota, Colombia, 1966, Mich. Tech. U., 1967, U. Mich., 1964; D.Sc., Monmouth Coll. 1964. Ohio State U., 1966, U. Ill., 1969; LL.D., U. Denver, 1968; m. Dorothy Irwin Wallace, Aug. 30, 1923; children—Barbara Alice (Mrs. John H. Bryant), Bruce Wallace, Pamela Ann. Instr. elec. engring. Cornell U., 1920-22; engr. N. Electric Mfg. Co., 1922-24; instr. U. Mich., 1924-26; asst. prof. elec. engring. Ohio State U., 1926-29, asso. prof., 1929-34, prof., 1934-44; prof., head dept. elec. engring. U. Ill., 1944-49, dean engring., 1949-68, dean emeritus, 1968—; mem. tech. rev. bd. Univ. Patents, Inc. Dir. Champaign Nat. Bank, Astronautics Corp. Am. Mem. communication sect. Nat. Def. Research Com., 1940-42; electronics com. Joint Research and Devel. Bd., 1946-53; research and devel. tech. adv. panel electronics Dept. Def., 1954-57, mem. tech. adv. panel gen. scis., 1957-63; mem. adv. com. Pacific Missile Range, 1958-62, mem. sci. adv. panel U.S. Army, 1959-70, mem. electronics adv. group Electronics Command, 1963-65, mem. weapons command adv. group, 1965—, mem. computer command adv. group, 1971—, mem. tactical communications com., 1963-65; mem. Commn. Engring. Edn., 1961-67, chmn., 1964-66; tech. adv. bd. TV Electronics Fund, Inc. , 1948-66; mem. Ill. Sci. Adv. Council 1967—; mem. adv. com. emergency planning Nat. Acad. Scis., 1968—; mem. adv. bd. Tech. Fund, 1968—; trustee Electronics Compatability Analysis Center, 1968-70; chmn. internat. meeting Marine Radio Aids to Navigation, 1947; mem. Nat. Com. Devel. Scientists and Engrs., 1956-57; chmn. accreditation and edn. com. Engrs. Council Profl. Devel., 1956-58, pres., 1958- 61, also mem. council, 1958-64. Chmn. bd. visitors U.S. Signal Sch., 1957-60; mem. nat. council YMCA, 1961-70. Served with USMC, 1918-19; 2d lt., then maj. Signal Corps Res., 1922-41; dir. operational research staff Office Chief Signal Officer, U.S. Army, 1942-46. Recipient Exceptionally Meritorious Civilian award U.S. Army, 1946; Lamme medal Am. Soc. Engring. Edn., 1957; medal elec. engring. edn. Am. Inst. E.E., 1957; Washington medal Western Soc. Engrs., 1971. Registered profl. engr., Ohio, Ill. Fellow A.A.A.S., Am. Inst. E.E. (bd. dirs. 1947-51), I.R.E. (pres. 1945, bd. dirs. 1942-47, 49-51; Medal of Honor 1954), I.E.E.E. (Kelly medal for telecommunications 1963); mem. Nat. Acad. Engring. (charter; mem. telecommunication sci. panel commerce Tech. Adv. Bd. 1966-67, chmn. com. telecommunications 1968—), Hall of Fame Engring. Educators, Asso. Midwest Univs. (dir. 1958-65, v.p. 1953-55, pres., 1956-57), Engring. Coll. Administrv. Council (sec. 1951-53, chmn. 1953-55), Nat. (award 1969), Ill. socs. profl. engrs., Acoustical Soc. Am., Sigma Xi, Theta Chi, Tau Beta Pi (nat. councillor 1935-36), Phi Kappa Phi, Eta Kappa Nu, Pi Mu Epsilon, Gamma Alpha, Pi Tau Pi Sigma, Eta Kappa Nu (eminent mem.), Triangle (hon.), Omicron Delta Kappa (hon.). Presbyn. Rotarian. Clubs: University, Champaign Country. Author books including: Communication Engineering, 1932. Editor: Electrical Engineering Series, 1945-69. Home: 607 W Pennsylvania Av Urbana IL 61801 ☆

EVERLY, HUBERT VICTOR, coll. dean; b. Los Angeles, Mar. 27, 1915; s. Hubert V. and Nest (Jackson) E.; B.E., U. Hawaii, 1937, M.Ed., 1939; Ph.D., Ohio State U., 1946; m. Zoe A. Wist, Sept. 4, 1937; children—Jan, Gail, Ben. High sch. tchr., Hawaii, 1937-40, vice prin. jr. high sch., 1940-41; prin. Univ. High Sch., U. Hawaii, 1946-50; dir. secondary edn. U. Hawaii, 1950-55, chmn. dept. edn., 1955-56, dean Coll. Edn., 1956—. Chmn. bd. trustees Hawaii Retirement System, 1956—. Mem. Nat. Commn. for UNESCO, 1963-65. Mem. Hawaii Edn. Assn. (pres. 1950-51, 62-63), N.E.A. (dir. for Hawaii), Phi Kappa Phi, Phi Delta Kappa, Pi Gamma Mu. Lion. Home: 999 Wilder Av Honolulu HI 96822

EVERLY, ROBERT EDWARD, engr., landscape architect; b. Dubuque, Ia., Dec. 29, 1905; s. George R. and Bertha (Belden) E.; m. Beatrice Vance, July 2, 1930; children—Robert Vance, Bruce Belden Noel. Landscape engr., parks, estates, golf courses, 1925-30; supt. Glencoe (Ill.) Parks, 1930-60; pres. McFadzean, Everly, Ltd. (Can.), 1955-71, Deanee Groves, Inc., Everly Citrus Groves, Inc., McFadzean & Everly Ltd., landscape architects, engrs., community planners, Winnetka, Ill., 1935—, also chmn .; participant nat. workshops pertaining to parks and recreation, Jackson's Mill, W.Va., 1948, Columbia, 1952, Mich. State Coll., 1952-54; designer park systems, parks and sch. sites, U.S., Can., also zool. parks in U.S., Can., Peru, S. Africa; co-originator park-sch. concept. of planning; lectr. in field in India, 1970. Mem. Canadian Commn. to Visit and Study Zool. Parks, Am. and European continents, 1954-55; U.S. rep. 1st Internat. Congress on Park Adminstrn., London. Served with AUS, 1942-45. Registered profl. engr., Ill.; licensed landscape architect, Cal. Distinguished fellow Am. Park and Recreation Soc.; hon. fellow Am. Inst. Park Execs. (pres. 1948- 49): mem. Nat. Recreation and Parks Assn. (trustee 1965-66), Midwest Inst. Park Execs. (pres. 1936-37), Chgo. Hort. Soc. (v.p. 1946-50), Res. Officers Corps. Engrs., Am. Mil. Engring. Soc., U.S. Park and Recreation Council (pres. 1950-51), Nat., Ill. socs. profl. engrs. Mason (Shriner). Club: Engineers (Chgo.). Contbr. articles tech. lit. Home: 350 Jackson Av Glencoe IL Office: 874 Green Bay Winnetka IL 60093

EVERNHAM, CLARK C., museum dir.; b. Los Angeles, Nov. 26, 1918; s. Clarence Charles and Mary Evelyn (Smith) E.; B.A., U. Cal. at Los Angeles, 1941; m. Jocelyn Moore, Aug. 28, 1948; children—Lorraine, Charles Stewart. With San Diego Mus. off Man. 1949—, mng. dir., 1952—. Served with AUS, World War II. Mem. Am. Assn. Museums, Assn. Sci. Mus. Dirs. Rotarian (dir.). Home: 4425 Topa Topa Dr La Mesa CA 92041 Office: Balboa Park San Diego CA 92109

EVEROTE, WARREN PETER, film and pub. co. exec.; b. Farmington, Minn., Oct. 12, 1913; s. Peter William and Gladys (Ritter) E.; B.A., U. Cal. at Los Angeles, 1935, M.A., 1936; Ph.D., Columbia, 1943; m. June Meriam, Mar. 18, 1940; children—Jan Deneige, Linda Ann, Instr. pub. schs., Los Angeles, 1938- 42; research asso. Bur. Ednl. Research in Sci., Columbia, 1942-43; instr. sci. Lincoln Sch., N.Y.C., 1942-43; with Ency. Brit. Films, 1945-65, v.p. research and prodn., 1955-62, pres., 1962-64, dir., 1962- 66; pres. Ency. Brit. Press. 1964-65, Ency. Brit., Ltd.,1965—, Ency. Brit. Devel. Corp., 1966-67, Ency. Brit. Ednl. Corp., 1967-70; v.p. Ency. Brit. Ednl. Corp., 1970—; dir. Ency. Brit., 1962-70. Mem. phys. sci. study sect. Nat. Studies Ednl. Improvement, 1957-58, chemistry study sect., 1960-62. Served to lt. comdr. USNR, World War II. Recipient Scholastic Tchr. mag. award, 1949, 54, Inter-Agrl. Congress award, 1953. Fellow A.A.A.S., Ill. Acad. Sci.; mem. Nat. Assn. Research Sci. Teaching, N.Y. Acad. Sci., L'Ordre des Anysetiers du Roy (Paris), Phi Delta Kappa. Mem. Christian Ch. Author: Agricultural Science to Serve Youth, 1943; also articles film prodn. Home: 4265 Cresta Av Santa Barbara CA 93105 Office: 425 N Michigan Av Chicago IL 60611

EVERROAD, JOHN E., lt. governor Neb.; b. Columbus, Ind., Jan 13, 1913; ed. Franklin Coll., m. Ruby Baker, Nov. 6, 1936; 1 son, John E. Pres. Cummins Mid-West Co., Inc., Cummins S.D., Inc.; chmn. bd. dirs. Everroad Supply Co., Inc., E. & R., Inc.; lt. gov. Neb., 1966—. Past pres. Neb. Safety Council. Mem. Neb. (dir.), Omaha (past chmn. subcom. of pub. hwys. and inter-city coms.), Am. Trucking Assn. (v.p. Neb.); Neb. Motor Carriers Assn. (past pres.); allied mem. Assn. Gen. Contractors Am. Mem. Christian Ch. Rotarian. Home: 5555 Centre St Omaha NB 68105 Office: State Capitol Bldg Lincoln NB 68509

EVERS, EVLYN, banker; b. Oakland, Cal., Oct. 15, 1907; s. Carl Henry and Elva (Johnson) E.; student pub. schs., Oakland, Cal.; grad. Am. Inst. Banking, 1932; m. Rosalie Scott, July 20, 1929; 1 son, Charles Scott. Crocker-Citizens Nat. Bank, 1926—, v.p., mgr., 1949-68, sr. v.p., 1968— . Pres., Nat. Safety Council, 1951-52, Oakland police and Fire Retirement System, 1951—; treas. Salvation Army, 1955—, Community Chest, 1950—, Berkeley Concert Assn., 1948—. Trustee Oakland Renewal Found. Mason, Elk (past exalted ruler). Home: 59 Westminster Dr Oakland CA 94518 Office: 1 Montgomery St San Francisco, CA 94120.

EVERS, JAMES CHARLES, mem. Democratic Nat. Com.; b. Decatur, Miss., Sept. 11, 1922; s. Jim and Jessie (Wright) E.; B.A., Alcorn A. and M. Coll., Lorman, Miss., 1951; m. Nanie Magee, June 2, 1947; children—Patricia, Carolyn, Sheila, Yvonne. Dem. candidate for Congress, 1968; mem. Dem. Nat. Com. for Miss., 1968—; mayor Fayette, Miss., 1969—. Home: care Gen Delivery Fayette MS 39069 Office: 1072 W Lynch St Jackson MS 39203

EVERS, JASON, actor; b. N.Y.C., Jan. 2, 1927; s. William Evers; student Maria Ouspenskaya; m. Shirley Ballard, Dec. 24, 1953. Toured with Ethel Barrymore in repertory co., 1943; Broadway appearances include Janie, 1944, Fair Game, 1959; mem. Chgo. co. Dear Ruth, pre- Broadway prodn. Palm Tree in a Rose Garden; on tour in My Three Angels, I Am a Camera; motion picture appearances include Pretty Boy Floyd, House of Women; TV appearances include Studio One, Armstrong Theatre, Playhouse 90, Omnibus, Wrangler series. Bonanza, The Rebel, Cheyenne, Laramie, Wells Fargo, Gunsmoke, Frontier Circus, Adventures in Paradise, Hong Kong, Surf Side 6, Perry Mason, The Defenders, Bus Stop, Alcoa Premiere; now star TV series Channing. Served with AUS, 1944- 45. c/o CMA 8899 Beverly Blvd Los Angeles CA 90048*

EVERS, MYRLE, (Mrs. Medgar Evers), civil rights leader, author; m. Medgar Evers (dec. 1965). Asst. dir. center ednl. opportunity colls. Claremont, Cal., 1967—. Active N.A.A.C.P. Author: For Us, the Living, 1967. Address: care N.A.A.C.P., 1072 W Lynch St Jackson, MS.*

EVERS, NATHANIEL H., univ. dean; b. Chgo., Oct. 25, 1910; s. Albert and Emma L. (Horning) E.; B.S., U. Wis., 1939, M.S., 1947; Ph.D., Northwestern U., 1952; m. Lynn Miller, Aug. 18, 1945 (dec. 1960). Tchr., Wis. high schs., 1939-42, 46-47; asst. prof. Knox Coll., Galesburg, Ill., 1947-50, 51-52; prof. edn., chmn. dept. Washburn U., 1952-60; asst. dir. Nat. Council Accreditation Tchrs. Edn., 1961-62; dir. tchr. edn. Okla. State U., 1961-62; dir. Sch. Edn., U. Denver, 1962-68, dean Grad. Sch. Arts and Scis., 1968—. Assn. dir. Kan. Comprehensive Survey Edn., 1959-60; examiner, cons. N. Central Assn., Nat. Council Accreditation Tchrs. Edn. Served with AUS, 1942-45. Mem. Am. Assn. Coll. Tchrs. Edn. (pres. 1971-72). Home: 2401 E Warren St Denver CO 80210

EVERS, WALTER, mgmt. cons.; b. Englewood, N.J., May 9, 1914; s. Fritz Otto and Liesel Clara (Micho) E.; A.B., St. John's Coll., 1935; grad. student Georgetown U. Sch. Fgn. Service, also Maxwell Sch. of Syracuse U.; m. Emlen Davies Grosjean, Sept. 19, 1970; children by previous marriage—Alison Dorothy (Mrs. William Cornelius Daley, Jr.). Ridgely Clyde. Pres. Walter Evers & Co., mgmt. cons., Cleve., 1960—, Walter Evers, Inc., 1962—. Dir. exec. recruitment WPB, 1941-42; exec. sec. def. mgmt. com. Office Sec. Def., 1949-50. Past chmn. bd. visitors and govs. St. John's Coll., Annapolis, Md.; trustee St. John's Coll., Santa Fe, 1958—; adv. council Robert A. Taft Inst. Govt. Served to lt. USNR, 1943-45. Mem. Newcomen Soc., Cleve. C. of C., Cleve. Engring. Soc. Republican. Episcopalian. Clubs: Skating, Mid Day (Cleve.); University (N.Y.C.). Home: 13715 Shaker Blvd Shaker Heights OH 44120 Office: Union Commerce Bldg Cleveland OH 44115

EVERS, WILLIAM DOHRMANN, lawyer; b. San Francisco, May, 6, 1927; s. Albert John and Sepha (Pischel) E.; B.A., Yale, 1949; LL.B., J.D., U. Cal. at Berkeley, 1952; m. Edwina Bigelow Benington, Aug. 26, 1950; children—Elliot B., Anne B., Albert John II, William Dohrmann. Admitted to Cal. bar, 1952; asso. firm Chickering & Gregory, San Francisco, 1953-56; legal asst. to commr. SEC, 1956-57; asso. atty. Allen, Miller, Groezinger, Keesling & Martin, San Francisco, 1957-60; partner Miller, Groezinger, Pettit & Evers, San Francisco, 1960—; dir. Allied Equities Corp., 1965-69, Alpine Meadows of Tahoe, Inc., 1962—. Vice chmn. San Francisco Bay Conservation and Devel. Commn., 1967—; pres. Cal. Roadside Council, 1964-65, Vols. for Better Govt., 1959, Planning and Conservation League, 1965—; mem. air quality adv. bd. Dept. Health, Edn. and Welfare, 1970—. Vice chmn. San Francisco Republican County Central Com., 1959-63. Trustee Marin County Day Sch., 1967-70. Served with USNR, 1944-45. Mem. Am., San Francisco bar assns., State Bar Cal. Clubs: Bohemian, Pacific Union, Commonwealth, Merchants Exchange (San Francisco). Home: 3451 Jackson St San Francisco CA 94118 Office: 650 California St San Francisco CA 94108

EVERSON, LEONARD CHARLES, lawyer, econ. co. exec.; b. Schenectady, July 5, 1923; s. Leonard L. and Clara M. (Tierney) E.; student Duke, 1940-43; LL.B., Harvard, 1948; m. Marjory Whitty, Oct. 18, 1952; children—Mark W., Margaret, Charles. Admitted to N.Y. bar, 1948; staff atty. Ford Motor Co., 1950-57; sec. AOFC, Inc., 1957-62; sec. Internat. Basic Economy Corp., N.Y.C., 1962-66, v.p., gen. counsel, 1966—. Served with AUS, 1943-45. Home: 99 White Plains Rd Bronxville NY 10708 Office: 1271 Av Americas New York City NY 10020

EVERSON, WILLIAM K., film curator; b. Yeovil, Eng., Apr. 8, 1929. Publicity dir. Renoun Pictures Corp., Ltd., London, 1944, Allied Artists Internat. Corp., 1951; film critic; theatrical mgr., publicist, booking cons. Monseigneur News Theatres, London, 1949; producer, writer Paul Killiam Orgn., 1956; writer, editor, researcher TV series Movie Museum, Silents Please, also TV and theatrical releases The Legend of Valentino, Hollywood the Golden Years, The Great Director, The Love Goddesses; lectr., writer, tchr. on various aspects of film; film curator Sch. of Visual Arts, New Sch. for Social Research; rep. Am. Film Inst.; instr. film history N.Y.U. Author: The Western; The American Movie, 1963; The Bad Guys; The Films of Laurel and Hardy; The Art of W.C. Fields; Hal Roach. Office: care New School for Social Research 66 W 12th St New York City NY 10011*

EVERT, RAY FRANKLIN, educator; b. Mt. Carmel, Pa., Feb. 20, 1931; s. Milner Ray and Elsie (Hoffa) E.; B.S., Pa. State U., 1952, M.S., 1954; Ph.D., U. Cal. at Davis, 1958; m. Mary Margaret Maloney, Jan 2, 1960; children—Patricia Ann, Paul Franklin. Mem. faculty Mont. State U., 1958-60; mem. faculty U. Wis.-Madison, 1960—, prof. botany, 1966—; vis. prof. U. Nafal, Pietesmaritzburg, S. Africa, winter and spring, 1971, U. Göttingen, (W. Germany), summer 1971. Mem. gen. biology and genetics fellowship rev. panel NIH, 1964-68. Guggenheim fellow, 1965-66. Mem. Bot. Soc. Am., Am. Inst. Biol. Scis., A.A.A.S., Wis. Acad. Scis., Sigma Xi, Phi Kappa Phi, Phi Sigma, Phi Epsilon Phi. Contbr. articles on food conducting tissue in higher plants. Home: 810 Woodward Dr Madison WI 53704

EVERTON, JOHN SCOTT, coll. pres.; b. Rochester, N.Y., Mar. 7, 1908; s. Samuel and Bertha Ethel Mabel (Scott) E.; B.A., U. Redlands, 1931, LL.D., 1963; B.D., Colgate-Rochester Div. Sch., 1834; Ph.D., Yale, 1938; student Cambridge U., Eng., 1935-37; D.D. (hon.), Grinnell Coll., 1949; LL.D., U. Redlands, 1963: L.H.D., U. Chattanooga, 1964; m. Margaret Isabel Meader, June 11, 1935; children—Nancy (Mrs. Howard Fairweather), Barbara (Mrs. Jordon Getz), John Scott. Minister, Central Baptist Ch., Pa., 1937-41; dean of chapel, prof. philosophy and religion Grinnell Coll., 1941-49, chmn. dept. philosophy and religion, 1941-45, chmn. div. social studies, 1946-48, mem. exec. council, 1936-48; pres. Kalamazoo Coll., 1949-53; rep. Ford Found. in Burma, 1953-56, exec. asso. Ford Found., N.Y.C., 1956-59, asso. dir. internat. tng. and research program, 1959-61; U.S. ambassador to Burma, 1961-63; v.p. edn. and world affairs, exec. dir. Overseas Ednl. Service, 1963-68; pres. Robert Coll., Instanbul, Turkey, 1968—; bd. of studies, lectr. and external examiner in philosophy U. Rangoon. Sr. rep. Am. Friends Service Com., India, 1944-45, spl. rep., Finland, 1947 (on leave from Grinnell Coll.). Exec. vice chmn. Am. Med. Center for Burma. Trustee

Lingnan U., United Bd. for Christian Higher Edn., Asia; trustee, v.p. bd. Grinnell Community Hosp., 1946-49. Mem. Council Fgn. Relations, Nat. Council on Religion in Higher Edn., Am. Philos. Assn., Burma Research Soc., Wider Quaker Fellowship, Pi Kappa Delta. Presbyn. Contbr. articles on fgn. policy and edn. to profl. jours. Address: Robert Coll PK8 Bekek Istanbul Turkey.

EVERTS, HERBERT JAMES food co. exec.; b. Mpls., Oct. 18, 1905; s. George Washington and Christina J. (Edmond) E.; student Eastern U., 1940-42; m. Mary Elizabeth Goodman, June 2, 1945 (dec. Feb. 1958), m. 2d, Mary Agnes Commons, May 13, 1961. With A.P., Memphis 1923-24, A.S. Barboro, produce dealers, Memphis, 1924-25; accountant Fargason Co., wholesale grocers, Memphis, 1925-37; pub. accountant, Memphis, 1937-40; accountant C. D. Kenny Co., Balt., 1940- 42; v.p. Western Grocery div. Consol. Foods Corp., 1945-51; v.p., treas. Consol. Food Processors, 1951-54; v.p., treas. Consol. Foods Corp., Chgo., 1954—, now exec. v.p., vice chmn. bd. Served as warrant officer USAAF, 1942-45; C.P.A., Tenn., Ia. Mem. Am. Inst. Accountants. Home: P O Box 643 Barrington IL 60010 Office: 135 S LaSalle St Chicago IL 60603

EVES, JESSE PARVIN, retired publishing co. exec.; b. Springdale, Ia., June 27, 1894; s. Joseph Walter and Amanda (Worthington) E.; B.S. in Animal Husbandry, Ia. State U., 1916, M.Agr. (hon.), 1923; m. Edna M. Johnson, Apr. 12, 1918; children—Wayne Parvin, Nevlyn (Mrs. Paul A. Mongerson), Sec., Ia. Dairy Assn., Waterloo, 1916-23; with Meredith Corp., Des Moines, 1923-70, sales mgr., 1931-59, dir., 1959—. Pres., dir. Dairy Shrine Club, 1949—; chmn. type com. Brown Swiss Cattle Breeders Assn. Am., 1948-60; judge all breeds dairy cattle, N. and S. Am., also Can. Trustee Iowa 4-H Club Found.; life mem. bd. govs. Ia. State U. Found. Recipient Centennial award Ia. State U., 1958; Guest of Honor, Dairy Shrine Club, 1954. Mem. Alpha Zeta, Theta Delta Chi. Presbyn. Mason. Clubs: Tavern, Saddle and Sirloin (Chgo.); Detroit Athletic. Home: 10859 Cheryl Dr Sun City AZ 85351

EVETT, ROBERT, composer, critic; b. Loveland, Colo., Nov. 30, 1922; s. Charles Emery and Sarah (Warnock) E.; student Colo. Coll., 1941-46, Juilliard Sch. Music, 1951-52. Chmn. music dept. Washington Inst. Contemporary Arts, 1947-51; music editor New Republic, Washington, 1952-68, asst. lit. editor, 1952-54, books and arts editor, 1954-68; asso. editor Atlantic Monthly, 1968-69; contbg. critic Washington Star, 1964-65, 69— . Mem. Am. Composers Alliance, Nat. Assn. Am. Composers and Condrs., Music Critics Assn., Composer: Cello Concerto, No. I, 1954; Piano Concerto, 1957; Harpsicord Concerto, 1961; Symphony 1, 1963; Anniversary Concerto, 1964; Lauds, 1964; Symphonies 2 and 3, 1965; The Greater Trumps, 1966; Vespers, 1967; Prime, 1968; Mary Dyer, 1968; Bassoon Concerto, 1970; Cello Concerto No. 2, 1971. Home: 6515 Brookville Rd Chevy Chase MD 20015

EVINRUDE, RALPH, outboard motors mfg. exec.; b. Milw., Sept. 27, 1907; s. Ole and Bessie (Cary) E.; ed. U. Wis.; m. Marion Armitage, Jan. 3, 1931 (dec.); m. 2d, Frances Langford, Oct. 6, 1955. Testing mgr. Elto Outboard Motor Co., 1927-30; export sales mgr. Outboard Motor Corp., 1930-32, prodn. mgr., 1932-34, pres. 1934-36; Outboard Motors Corp. consol. with Johnson Motor Co. to form Outboard Marine & Mfg. Co., now named Outboard Marine Corp., of which became pres. and dir., now chmn. bd., chmn. exec. com. Mem. Phi Gamma Delta. Clubs: University, Yacht, Milw. Athletic (Milw.); Eldorado Country; Yacht and Country (Stuart, Fla.); Crown Colony (Bahamas). Home: Stuart FL 33494 Office: 4143 N 27th St Milwaukee WI 53216

EVINS, JOSEPH LANDON, congressman; b. DeKalb County, Tenn., Oct. 24, 1910; s. James Edgar and Myrtie (Goodson) E.; A.B., Vanderbilt U., 1933; LL.B., Cumberland U., 1934, LL.D., 1958; postgrad. George Washington U., 1938-40; m. Ann Smartt, June 7, 1935; children—Joanna Evins Carnahan, Jane, Mary. Admitted to Tenn. bar, 1934; gen. law practice, Smithville, Tenn., 1934-41; atty. FTC, Washington, 1935-38, asst. sec., 1938-40; v.p. First Nat. Bank, Smithville, Tenn., 1944-54, pres., 1954- 63, chmn. bd., 1963—; mem. 80th-82d Congresses, 5th Tenn. Dist., 82d-92d Congresses, 4th Congl. Dist., mem. com. on appropriations, chmn. select com. small bus., chmn. subcom. on pub. works appropriations, chmn. ind. offices subcom. Del., Democratic Nat. Convs., 1952, 56, 60, 64; Tenn. campaign mgr. Johnson-Humphrey, 1964. Trustee David Lipscomb Coll., Nashville, Cumberland Coll. Served to maj. AUS, 1942-46; ETO. Received Dem. nomination as state senator, 12th Tenn. senatorial dist. (declined nomination for pub. office during war), 1944. Mem. Am. Legion, V.F.W., Army Res. Corps, 40 and 8, Amvets. Phi Kappa Sigma, Alpha Kappa Psi, Phi Delta Phi. Mason (32, Shriner) Elk, Lion. Club: Commodore. Author: Understanding Congress, 1963. Home: 300 E Main St Smithville TN 37166 also 5044 Klingle St NW Washington DC 20016 Office: Rayburn Bldg Washington DC 20515

EVINS, LUCIUS SELWYN, Jr., ins. co. exec.; b. Birmingham, Ala., Nov. 22, 1915; s. Lucius Selwyn and Bertha (Cowan) E.; A.B., Birmingham So. Coll., 1937; m. Frances Hawkins, June 29, 1938; children—Selwyn (Mrs. Dan Arnold), Lucius Selwyn III; m. 2d, Betty Smith, Mar. 7, 1964; 1 stepson, Jack Christian; 1 dau., Alan. With Liberty Nat. Life Ins. Co., Birmingham, 1938—, asst. v.p., 1959- 60, v.p., 1960-64, agy. v.p., 1964-69, sr. agy. v.p., 1969—. Served to lt. USNR, 1943-46. Methodist. Clubs: Birmingham Country, Relay House, The Club (Birmingham). Home: 4020 Old Leeds Ridge Birmingham AL 35213 Office: 301 S 20th St Birmingham AL 35233

EVITT, WILLIAM ROBERT, paleontologist; b. Balt., Dec. 9, 1923; s. Raymond W. and Elsa (Schwarz) E.; A.B., Johns Hopkins, 1942; Ph.D., 1950; m. Gisela Cloos, July 29, 1950; children-Eric R., Steven D., Glenn M. Instr. U. Rochester, 1948- 51, asst. prof. geology, 1951-55, asso. prof. 1955-56, acting chmn. dept. geology, 1955-56; sr. research geologist Jersey Prodn. Research Co., Tulsa, 1956-59, research asso., 1959-62; vis. prof. Stanford, 1961, prof. geology, 1962—. Served to capt. USAF, 1943-46. Decorated Bronze Star. Fellow Cal. Acad. Scis., Geol. Soc. Am.; mem. Am. Assn. Stratigraphic Palynologists, Paleontol. Soc. (editor 1953-56, v.p. 1957), Bot. Soc. Am., Internat. Assn. Plant Taxonomists, Am. Inst. Biol. Scis. Home: 2074 Sandalwood Ct Palo Alto CA 94303 Office: Dept Geology Stanford U Stanford CA 94305

EVONS, HARRY, mercantile and entertainment co. exec.; b. N.Y.C., Dec. 25, 1914; s. Saul and Aususta (White) E.; student N.Y.U., 1934; m. Laura Marie Anderson, July 16, 1937 (div.); children—Richard, Thomas. Mgr., Photo Reflex Studios, Boston and Rochester, N.Y., 1936-40; U.S. regional and nat. dir. Arthur Murray Studios, 1940-56; pres., dir. Forsyth Oil Co., San Antonio, 1959—; v.p., dir. Signal Pictures Corp., 1959—; pres., treas., dir. Arthur Murray, Inc., N.Y.C., 1964—; pres., chmn. bd., dir., Kargl Instruments, Inc., San Antonio, 1961—; v.p., dir. mem. exec. com. Fed-Mart Corp., San Diego, 1957—; chmn. Fed-Mart World Tours, Inc., 1967—; pres., dir. Nat. Fiberglass Co., 1957—. Pres. San Antonio Safety Council, 1950-51; sec. Bexar County chpt. Am. Cancer Soc., 1953-54; commnr. Nat. Milk Bowl, 1955—. Vice pres., bd. dirs. Boys Homes Am., 1955, Philanthropic Inst., Dallas, 1960: vol. bd. Tex. Hosps., 1952. Served with USNR, 1942-45. Recipient George Washington medal of honor Freedom Found. at Valley Forge, 1957. Mason (Shriner), Lion (pres. San Antonio 1958). Club: Friars (N.Y.C.). Office: The Fed Mart Corp 8001 Othello San Diego CA 92111

EVOY, JOHN JOSEPH, educator; b. Seattle, Apr. 14, 1911; s. Martin and May (Harpur) E.; A.B., Gonzaga U., Spokane, 1936, M.A., 1937; S.T.L., St. Louis U., 1944; Ph.D., Loyola U., Chgo., 1953. Joined Soc. of Jesus, 1930, ordained priest Roman Cath. Ch., 1943; mem. faculty Gonzaga U., 1951—, prof. psychology, 1957—, chmn. dept. psychology, 1971—; asso. editor America mag., 1966-67; counselor, lectr. in field. Mem. Am. Psychol. Assn., Brit. Psychol. Soc. Co-author 4 books. Home: Gonzaga Univ Spokane WA 99202

EVRAIFF, WILLIAM, educator; b. St. Louis, Jan. 30, 1924; s. Morris and Fannie (Dinkin) E.; B.S., Washington U., 1948, B.S. in edn., 1949; M.A., Stanford U., 1950, Ed.D., 1954; m. Lois Ann Klehamer, Apr. 3, 1961; children—David. Tchr., counselor, asst. prin. pub. schs., 1951-56; asso. prof. edn. Wayne State U., 1956-63; prof. edn., chmn. dept. counseling, coordinator rehab. counselor edn. program San Francisco State Coll., 1963—; officer Ednl. and Community Consultants and Planners, Inc. Vice chmn. bd. govs. Frederic Burk Found. of San Francisco State Coll., 1969-72. Served with AUS, 1943-46; ETO. Life mem. Am., Cal. personnel and guidance assns. Author: (with others) The Role of the Teacher in Guidance, 1959; Helping Counselors Grow Professionally, 1963. Home: 104 Crespi Dr San Francisco CA 94132

EVTUSHENKO, EVGENY, see Yevtushenko, Yevgeny.

EWALD, ARNO W(ILFORD), educator, physicist; b. Fond du Lac, Wis., May 14, 1918; s. Herman Amiel and Martha (Sigrist) E.; B.S., Wis. State U., Oshkosh, 1941; M.S., U. Mich., 1942, Ph.D., 1948; m. Sara Jeanne Hauke, Dec. 24, 1943; children-Douglas Arno, Steven Kelsey, Norman Charles, Paul William. Research asso. U. Mich., 1944-48; mem. faculty Northwestern U., 1948—, prof. physics, 1961—. Fellow Am. mem. faculty Northwestern U., 1948—, prof. physics, 1961—. Fellow Am. Phys. Soc.; mem. Sigma Xi. First synthesized single crystals of gray tin, 1958. Home: 2311 Lake Av Wilmette IL 60091 Office: Northwestern Univ Evanston IL 60201

EWALD, EARL, utility exec.; b. St. Paul, July 2, 1908; s. Martin P. and Minna L. (Neumann) E.; B.S., U. Minn., 1930, postgrad., 1938-40; m. Marian Borglum, June 9, 1930; children—Carol (Mrs. Clark Johnson), Clark, Paula Wagner. With No. States Power Co., Mpls., 1930—, v.p. charge operations, 1954-62, exec. v.p., 1962-64, pres., 1964-65, pres., 1965-68, chmn. bd., 1968—, chief exec. officer, 1965-71; dir. St. Paul Cos., Inc., First Bank System. Chmn. West Central regional adv. com. Fed. Power Commn. Chmn. bd. Minn. Safety Council. Bd. dirs., pres. Upper Midwest Research and Devel. Council; bd. dirs. Minn. Orchestral Assn. Mem. I.E.E.E., Nat. Soc. Profl. Engrs., Minn. Fedn. Engring. Socs., Edison Electric Inst. (dir., exec. com. research div.), Electric Research Council, Assn. Edison Illuminating Cos., Triangle, Mason. Home: 11615 Timberline Rd Minnetonka MN 55343 Office: 414 Nicollet Mall Minneapolis MN 55401

EWALD, JOHN A., cosmetic mfr.; b. Maspeth, L.I., N.Y., Dec. 22, 1901; s. Adolph R. and Catherine C. (Fitting) E.; student N.Y.U.; m. Oliver Schumacher, Dec. 31, 1924 (dec. Jan. 1950); 1 son, John A.; m. 2d, Emma Lepotsky, Mar. 10, 1954. With Avon Products, Inc., N.Y.C., 1920—, chmn. bd., chief exec. officer, 1962-67, chmn. exec. com., dir., 1967—; dir. Marine Midland Trust Co. of N.Y. Bd. dirs., Nassau Hosp., Mineola, N.Y.; adv. bd., mem. fund raising com. Salvation Army. Mem. Toilet Goods Assn., Inc. (dir.). Presbyn. Mason. Clubs: Union League (N.Y.C.), Garden City (N.Y.) Golf, Thunderbird Country (Palm Springs, Cal.), U.S. Seniors Golf Assn. Home: 85 3d St Garden City NY 11530 Office: 30 Rockefeller Plaza New York City NY 10020

EWALD, PAUL P., ret. physicist; b. Berlin, Germany, 1888; Ph.D., U. Munich, 1912; D.Sc., Stuttgart U., 1954; Dr., U. Paris, 1958; D.Sc., Adelphi U., 1966; M.A., U. Belfast, 1946; Dr. h.c., U. Munich, 1968. Prof. theoretical physics Poly. Sch., Stuttgart, 1921-37; prof. math. physics, The Queen's U., Belfast, North Ireland, 1939-49; head physics dept. Poly. Inst. Bklyn., 1949-57, prof. physics, 1949-59. Fellow Royal Soc. (Gt. Britain), Phys. Soc. Britain, Am. Phys. Soc. (chmn. solid state div. 1961-62), Am. Acad. Arts and Scis. Deutsche Akademie der Naturforscher (Leopoldina); hon. mem. Deutsche Mineralog. Ges., Société Francaise de Mineralogie et de Cristallographie, Cambridge Philos. Soc.; corr. mem. Acad. Scis. Göttingen and Munich; mem. Internat. Union Crystallography (pres. 1960-63, exec. com. 1948-66), Am. Crystallographic Assn. (pres. 1952). Author: Fifty Years of X-ray Diffraction, 1962; other books and articles in field. Address: 108 Sheldon Rd Ithaca NY 14850

EWALT, JACK RICHARD, physician; b. Medicine Lodge, Kan., Jan. 27, 1910; s. Simeon and Edith (Crummack) E.; M.D., U. Colo., 1933; m. Beatrice Earl, Mar. 28, 1931; children—Ann, Jean; m. 2d, Patricia Littlefield. Asst. prof. psychiatry U. Colo., 1937-41; prof. psychiatry U. Tex., 1941-51, adminstr. hosps., 1948-50, dean Postgrad. Sch. Medicine, 1950-51; commr. mental health Commonwealth Mass., 1951-58; clin. prof. psychiatry Harvard, 1952-58, prof. psychiatry, 1958-62, Bullard prof. psychiatry, 1962—; supt. Mass. Mental Health Center, 1958—; cons. to surgeon gen. USAF, 1951-54. Mem. spl. med. adv. council VA, 1961-65; mem. Joint Commn. Mental Illness and Health, dir. Am. Bd. Psychiatry and Neurology, 1960-62, pres. 1963-64; mem. Nat. Adv. Mental Health Council, 1960-64. Fellow Am. Psychiat. Assn. (treas. 1954, pres. 1963-64); mem. Group Advancement Psychiatry (pres. 1951- 53), A.M.A., Sigma Xi, Alpha Omega Alpha (pres. Mass. dist. br. 1955). Author: Mental Health Administration, 1956; (with others) Practical Clinical Psychiatry, 1956; (with others) Textbook of Psychiatry. Home: 770 Boylston Boston MA 02199 Office: 74 Fenwood Rd Boston MA 02167

EWART, DONALD LINSLEY, coal co. exec.; b. Pitts., Dec. 7, 1929; s. John A. and Grace (McConnell) E.; A.B., U. Pitts., 1951, J.D., 1956; m. Martha J. McMichael, June 7, 1952; children—Ann, Donald Linsley, Ellen. Admitted to Pa. bar 1957; practice in Pitts., 1956-62; asso., then partner Rose, Houston, Cooper & Schmidt, 1956-62; asst. sec. Consol. Coal Co., Pitts., 1963-65, asst. v.p., 1965-66, gen. counsel, sec., 1966-70, v.p., 1968-71, pres. Midwestern div., 1971—. Served with USAF, 1951-53. Mem. Am., Pa., Allegheny County bar assns., Order of Coif, Omicron Delta Kappa, Sigma Alpha Epsilon. Club: Duquesne (Pitts.). Home: Butternut Hill Rd Box 25-3 Route 1 Carbondale IL 62901 Office: Box 218 Pinckneyville IL 62274

EWBANK, JOHN NELSON, Jr., air force officer; b. St. Paul, Minn., Sept. 5, 1912; s. John Nelson and Anna Belle (Fisher) E.; student U. Minn., 1931-34, Air U., 1946-47, Nat. War Coll., 1952-53; m. Hazel Virginia Eppard, Oct. 17, 1941; children—Johnie Anne (Mrs. Dean Carr), Susan Lee, Commd. 2d lt. USAAF, 1940, advanced through grades to maj. gen., 1964; comdr. 2d Bomb Squadron, 22d Bomb Group, New Guinea, 1942-43, dep. comdr. 19th Bomb Wing, Okinawa/Korea, 1950-52; staff Hdqrs. USAF, The Pentagon, 1953-57; comdr. 38th Tactical Bomb Wing, Laon, France, 1957; dep. chief staff operations Hdqrs. 3d Air Force, 1958; comdr. Nellis AFB, Las Vegas, Nev., 1959; chief operations Hdqrs. Tactical Air Command, Langley AFB, 1961-65; J-5 Plans, U.S. Mil. Assistance Command, Viet Nam, 1965- 67; chief staff Aerospace Def. Command, Colorado Springs, Colo., 1967- 69; assigned to Hdqrs. U.S. Strike Command, MacDill AFB, Fla., 1969—. Decorated D.S.M., Legion of Merit with 3 clusters, D.F.C., Presdl. Unit citation. Mem. Mil. Order Daedalians, Air Force Assn., Am. Ordnance Assn. Rotarian. Home: 795 Bayshore Dr MacDill AFB FL 33621

EWBANK, WEEB (Wilbur Charles), profl. football coach; b. Richmond, Ind., May 6, 1907; s. Charles C. and Stella Mae (Dickerson) E.; B.S., Miami U., Oxford, O., 1928, D.Athletic Arts (hon.), 1960; M.A., Columbia, 1932; m. Lucy Keller Massey, June 23, 1926; children—Luanne (Mrs. Robert Spenceley), Nancy Jane (Mrs. Charles Winner), Jan Lynn (Mrs. Jack Hudson). Head coach, athletic dir. Van Wert (O.) High Sch., 1928-29; coach McGuffey schs., Miami U., 1930-43, asst. prof. phys. edn., 1930-43, coach univ. basketball, 1939-40; asst. football coach, head basketball coach Brown U., 1946-47; head football coach, asst. basketball coach Washington U., St. Louis, 1947-48; asst. coach Cleve. Brown Profl. Football Team, 1949-53; head coach Balt. Colts Profl. Football Team, 1954-62 (world champions, 1958-59); gen. mgr., head coach N.Y. Jets Profl. Football Club (world champions 1968), 1963—. Treas. Ewbank-Walsh Oil Co., Balt., 1962—. Nat. chmn. Arthritis Found., 1971. Served to lt. USNR, 1943-46. Mem. Am. Football Coaches Assn., Am. Football Hall of Fame Found., Phi Delta Theta. Presbyn. Mason (Shriner). Home: 89 Ardell St Bronxville NY 10708 Office: 595 Madison Av New York City NY 10022

EWE, RALPH H., leather co. exec.; b. Dortmund, Germany, 1903; student U. Cologne, also Tanner's Sch., Freiberg, Germany. Vice chmn., dir. Ohio Leather Co.; dir. First Nat. Bank, Girard, O., Ozite Corp. Mem. Tanners' Council of Am. (dir.). Home: 4728 Logan Av Ext Hubbard OH 44425 Office: 1052 N State St Girard OH 44420

EWELL, ALBERT HUNTER, Jr., educator; b. Phila., Nov. 30, 1925; s. Albert Hunter and Emma (Kind) E.; B.A., Haverford Coll., 1946; postgrad. Princeton, 1946-49; Ph.D., N.Y. U., 1954. Instr. Middlebury (Vt.) Coll., 1952-55, asst. prof., 1955-61, chmn. dept. psychology, 1956—, asso. prof., 1961-67, prof. psychology, 1967—; cons. Vt. Rehab. Center, Burlington, 1959-67; research analyst Vt. Div. Vocational Rehab. Spl. Project, 1964-66. Mem. Am. Psychol. Assn., Optical Soc. Am., Acoustical Soc. Am., Phi Beta Kappa. Home: 28 Weybridge St Middlebury VT 05753

EWELL, JAMES MARVIN, mfg. co. exec.; b. Chgo., June 28, 1915; s. James Marvin Cady and Hazel (Crow) E.; student U. Ariz., 1932-34; B.S. in Chem. Engring., Mass. Inst. Tech., 1937; m. Marjorie A. Watson, Sept. 20, 1938; children—Dana, Bernard, Deborah, Jonathan. With Procter & Gamble Co., Cin., 1937—, Successively mfg. dept. of Port Ivory (N.Y.) plant, factory supt., div. supt., gen. prodn. supt., dir. mfg. English subsidiary Thomas Hedley & Co., Ltd., Newcatle-on-Tyne, Eng., mgr. mfg. Procter & Gamble, 1937-55, v.p. mfg., 1955-58, v.p. mfg. and employee relations, 1958-, dir., 1961-. Clubs: Camargo, Commonwealth, Commercial, Queen City. Home: 8700 Camargo Rd Cincinnati OH 45343 Office: ITC Bldg Cincinnati OH 45217

EWELL, JULIAN JOHNSON, army officer; b. Stillwater, Okla., Nov. 5, 1915; s. George Watkins and Jamie (Offutt) E.; student Duke, 1932-34; B.S., U.S. Mil Acad., 1939; grad. Army War Coll., 1953, Nat. War Coll., 1959; m. Beverly McCammon, June 4, 1955; children—Gillem J., Dale S. Moses, Stephen L. Moses. Commd. 2d lt. U.S. Army, 1939, advanced through grades to lt. gen., 1969; regtl. comdr. 101st Airborne Div., World War II, 2d Inf. Div., Korean War; comdr. 9th Inf. Div. and II Field Force, Viet Nam, 1969-70; mil. adviser Paris Peace Talks on Vietnam, 1970; chief staff Allied Forces So. Europe, 1971—. Decorated D.S.C., D.S.M. with 2 oak leaf clusters. Mem. Phi Delta Theta, Phi Eta Sigma, Beta Omega Sigma. Address: Chief Staff Allied Forces So Europe Box 130 FPO New York City NY 05924

EWELL, RAYMOND HENRY, chemist, economist, research administr.; b. Brockton, Mass., June 18, 1908; s. Robert Garfield and Arvilla Haynes (Thompson) E.; B.S., U. Toledo, 1928; M.S., Purdue U., 1930; M.A., George Washington U., 1935; Ph.D., Princeton, 1937; m. Libuse Sallerova, Dec. 22, 1945; children—Jeffrey, Randolph. Research chemist Nat. Bur. Standards, 1930- 35; instr., asst. prof. chemistry Purdue U., 1937-41; tech. aide NDRC, 1941-45; sr. economist Shell Chem. Corp., 1945-48; chmn. dept. chem. and chem. engring. Stanford Research Inst., 1948-50; mgr. Chem. Econs. Service, 1950-53; asst. dir. NSF, 1953-56; v.p. for research, prof. chem. engring. State U. of N.Y. at Buffalo, 1957—. Cons. on research Govt. Philippines, 1955-56; cons. on indsl. devel. Govt. India, 1956-57; cons. fertilizer industry, 1960-61, 63, 66, 69; cons. fertilizer industry UN Indsl. Devel. Orgn., 1963—. Decorated Medal for Merit, U.S., 1948. Mem. Am. Inst. Chem. Engrs., Am. Chem. Soc., Am. Econ. Assn., Soc. Internat. Devel., World Future Soc., Am. Inst. Chemists, Population Assn. Am., Inst. Strategic Studies, Sigma Xi, Phi Lambda Upsilon, Sigma Pi Sigma. Clubs: Saturn (Buffalo); Cosmos (Washington); Chemists (N.Y.C.). Author: Dining Out in San Francisco, 1948; Dining Out in America's Cities, 1954. Founder, 1st editor: Chemical Economics Handbook, 1950-53. Author numerous sci., econ. articles. Home: 56 Highgate Av Buffalo NY 14214

EWELL, TOM, actor; b. Owensboro, Ky., Apr. 29, 1909; s. Samuel W. and Martine (Yewell) Tompkins; student U. Wis., 1927-31; m. Marjorie Sanborn, Apr. 29, 1948; 1 son, Taylor Allen. Broadway actor, appearing in They Shall Not Die, 1934, Tobacco Road, 1936, Brother Rat, 1937, Family Portrait, 1939; John Loves Mary, 1947, Small Wonder, 1948, Seven Year Itch, 1952, Tunnel of Love, 1957; (movies) Adam's Rib, 1949, American Guerilla in Philippines, 1950, Up Front, 1950, Seven Year Itch 1954, The Lieutenant Wore Skirts, 1955, The Girl Can't Help It, 1956. Tender Is the Night, 1962; (Broadway production) A Thurber Carnival, 1959; Xmas in Las Vegas, 1965. On TV The Tom Ewell Show, weekly, 1960—. Served as lt. USNR, 1942-45. Mem. Phi Eta Sigma, Sigma Phi Epsilon, Rho Epsilon Delta. Club: The Players. Office: care Four Star Films Van Nuys CA 91412

EWEN, DAVID, musician, author; b. Lemberg, Austria, Nov. 26, 1907; s. Isaac and Helen (Kramer) E.; student Coll. City of N.Y., 3 years; mus. edn. with pvt. tutors, also spl. courses Columbia; m. Hannah Weinstein, Sept. 11, 1936; 1 son, Robert. Music editor Cue, 1937- 38; serious music record critic Stage, 1938-39; editor Musical Facts, 1940-41; dir. Allen, Towne & Heath, Inc., 1946-49; adj. prof. music U. Miami, (Fla.), 1965—. Mem. bd. Greater Miami Philharmonic Orch., Friends Chamber Music Miami. Served with AUS, 1944-45; authorized to write history of Am. paratroopers. Hon. life mem. Miami Beach Music and Arts League. Author many books on music and musicians, 1933-46, including: Haydn: A Good Life, 1946; Songs of America, 1947; American Composers Today, 1949; The Story of Irving Berlin, 1950; The Story of Arturo Toscanini, 1951; The Complete Book of Twentieth Century Composers, 1952; The Story of Jerome Kern, 1953; European Composers Today, 1953; (with Milton Cross), The Milton Cross Encyclopedia of Great Composers, rev. edit., 1969; The Home Book of Musical Knowledge, 1954;

Encyclopedia of the Opera, completely rewritten, 1969; A Journey to Greatness: The Life and Music of George Gershwin, completely rev., 1970; Panorama of American Popular Music, 1957; Richard Rodgers, 1957; The Complete Book of the American Musical Theatre, 1958; Ency. of Concert Music, 1959; The World of Jerome Kern, 1960; Leonard Bernstein: A Biography for Young People, 1960; The Story of the American Musical Theater, 1961; David Ewen Introduces Modern Music, 1962; The Book of European Light Opera, 1962; With A Song in His Heart (a young people's biography of Richard Rodgers), 1963; The Life and Death of Tin Pan Alley, 1964; The Complete Book of Classical Music, 1965; The Cole Porter Story, 1965: Great Composers: 1300-1900, 1966; American Popular Songs: From The Revolutionary War to the Present, 1966; Famous Modern Conductors, 1967; The World of Twentieth Century Music, 1968; Composers for the American Musical Theatre, 1968; Composers Since 1900, 1969; Great Men of American Popular Songs, 1970; New Complete Book of the American Musical Theater, 1970; Composers of Tomorrow's Music, 1971. Contbr. periodicals. Address: 2301 Collins Av Miami Beach FL 33139

EWEN, FREDERIC, educator; b. Lemberg, Austria, Oct. 11, 1899; s. Isaac and Helen (Kramer) E.; brought to U.S., 1912, naturalized, 1912; B.A., Coll. City N.Y., 1921; M.A., Columbia U., 1925, Ph.D., 1932; m. Miriam Gideon, Dec. 16, 1949; 1 son, Joel. Instr. Coll. City N.Y., 1923-30; asst. prof. Bklyn. Coll., 1930-52; lectr. Grad. Sch. Yeshiva U., Master Inst. N.Y.C., Bklyn. Acad., The Juilliard Sch., N.Y.C. Mem. Modern Lang. Assn., Am. Assn. U. Profs. Author: The Prestige of Schiller in England, 1932; Bibliography of 18 Century English Literature, 1935; The Poetry and Prose of Heinrich Heine, 1948; The Poetry of Heinrich Heine, 1969; Bertolt Brecht; His Life, His Art, and His Times, 1967; co-author: Musical Vienna, 1939; dramatic adaptations of James Joyce's A Portrait of the Artist, 1962-63; Thomas Mann's The Magic Mountain, dramatic adaptation of The Unknown Chekhov, CBS, Camera 3, 1968. Home: 410 Central Park West New York City NY 10025

EWEN, WILLIAM HOPKINS, food and chem. co. exec.; b. Yonkers, N.Y., May 2, 1913; s. William Carnegie and Marjorie (Wilde) E.; B.S., N.Y.U., 1935; m. Cathleen Ellen Ryan, Nov. 4, 1937; children—William Hopkins, Barbara Ellen. With Borden Co., 1936—, asst. v.p. foods co. div., 1960-61, corp. dir., advt. services, 1962—, dir. govt. relations, 1969—71. Chmn. bd. Audit Bur. Circulations, 1965-67; bd. dirs. Nat. Better Bus. Bur., Advt. Research Found. Unit dir. Greater N.Y. Fund, 1963-64, 66; chmn. Citizens Com. Hudson Valley, 1965-66; dir. Hudson River Conservation Soc. Mem. Steamship Hist. Soc. Am. (pres. 1946-50, mem. pres. adv. bd. 1960), N.Y. Hist. Soc., Newcomen Soc. N. Am., Assn. Nat. Advertiser (chmn. bd. dirs. 1968-69). Author, lectr. Am. steamboat history; guest lectr. Munson Inst. Maritime History; recorded steamboat sounds for hist. purposes; pvt. library and collection steamboat history. Home: 132 Edgars Lane Hastings-on-Hudson NY 10706 Office: 277 Park Av New York City NY 10017

EWERS, JOHN CANFIELD, museum adminstr.; b. Cleve., July 21, 1909; s. John Ray and Mary Alice (Canfield) E.; A.B., Dartmouth, 1931, D.Sc, 1968; M.A., Yale, 1934; LL.D., U. Mont., 1966; m. Margaret Elizabeth Dumville, Sept. 6, 1934; children—Jane (Mrs. Robinson), Diane (Mrs. Peterson). Field curator Nat. Park Service, Washington, Morristown, N.J., Berkeley, Cal., Macon, Ga., 1935-40; curator Mus. Plains Indian, Browning, Mont., 1941-44; asso. curator ethnology U.S. Nat. Mus., Smithsonian Instn., Washington, 1945-56, planning officer, 1956-59, asst. dir. Mus. History and Technology,1959-64, dir., 1964-65, sr. scientist Office Anthropology, 1965—, now sr. enthnologist Office Anthropology. Museum planning cons. Bur. Indian Affairs, 1948-49, Mont. Hist. Soc., 1950-54; cons. Am. Heritage, 1959. Served with USNR, 1944-46. Recipient 1st Exceptional Service award Smithsonian Instn., 1965. Fellow Am. Anthrop. Assn.; mem. Am. Indian Ethnologist Conf. (pres. 1960-61), Am. Assn. Museums, Anthrop. Soc. Washington. Author: Plains Indian Painting, 1940; The Horse in Blackfoot Indian Culture, 1955; The Blackfoot: Raiders on the Northwestern Plains, 1958; Artists of the Old West, 1965; Indian Life on Upper Missouri, 1968. Editor: Adventures of Zenas Leonard, Fur Trader, 1959; Crow Indian Medicine Bundles, 1960; Five Indian Tribes of the Upper Missouri, 1961; O-Kee-pa, A Religious Ceremony and Other Customs of the Mandans (George Catlin), 1967. Editor Jour. Washington Acad. Scis., 1955-56. Mem. editorial bd. The American West, 1965—. Contbr. articles profl. publs. Home: 4432 26th Rd N Arlington VA 22207 Office: Smithsonian Instn Washington DC 20560

EWERT, MARVIN HENRY, hosp. adminstr.; b. Dolton, S.D., Mar. 16, 1925; s. Henry J. and Lena (Tiahrt) E.; A.A., Freeman Jr. Coll., 1948; B.A., Bethel Coll., 1950; B.D., Bethany Bibl. Sem., 1953; postgrad. U. Chgo., 1953-55, U. Wichita, 1958, Cornell U., summer 1963; m. Eleanor B. Thiessen, June 12, 1953; children—Warren M., Brian H. Instr. Mennonite Bibl. Sem., Chgo., part time 1954-55; chaplain Bethel Deaconess Hosp. and Bethel Home for Aged, Newton, Kan., 1955-56; hosp. adminstr. Bethel Deaconess Hosp. and Bethel Home for Aged, Newton, 1957—; dir. Kan. Blue Cross, 1962-68. Bd. dirs. Prairie View Mental Health Center, Newton. Mem. Kan. (past pres., trustee), Am. (ho. dels.) hosp. assns., Kan. Assn. Homes for Aging (pres. 1964), Am. Protestant Hosp. Assn. (pres., past trustee), Newton C. of C., Am. Coll. Hosp. Adminstrs., Acad. Religion and Mental Health. Mem. Mennonite Ch. Kiwanian. Home: 305 SE 11th St Newton KS 67114 Office: 411 SE 2d St Newton KS 67114

EWING, BAYARD, lawyer; b. Sorrento, Me., Aug. 19, 1916; s. Thomas and Anna (Cochran) E.; grad. St. Paul's Sch., Concord, N.H., 1934; A.B., Yale, 1938; LL.B., Harvard, 1941; m. Harriet M. Kelley, Sept. 2, 1939; children—Linda L. (Mrs. R. T. Leeson), Gillian C. (Mrs. M. W. Ehrich), Bayard C., Gifford P., Harriet K. Admitted to R.I. bar, 1941; partner firm Tillinghast, Collins & Graham, Providence, 1949—. Dir. Boston & Providence R.R. Co., Wingate Co., Inc., Watering Inc., Hilliard Oil & Gas, Inc., Providence Instn. Savs. Del. Republican Nat. Conv., 1948, 52, 56, 60, 64, 68; rep. R.I. Gen. Assembly, 1950-52; candidate U.S. Senate from R.I., 1952, 58; mem. R.I. Public Expenditures Council; mem. Rep. Nat. Com., 1955-68. Campaign chmn. United Fund R.I., 1961, pres., 1961-65. Trustee Providence Boys' Club, R.I. Sch. Design (chmn.); chmn. United Way Am.; bd. dirs. Nature Conservancy, Center Vol. Action, Mem. Am., R.I. bar assns. Episcopalian. Mason (32). Home: 41 Waterman St Providence RI 02906 Office: 15 Westminster St Providence RI 02903

EWING, C. RALPH, corp. exec.; b. Phila., 1904; ed. Ga. Inst. Tech., 1925. Pres., dir. Dixie Yarns, Inc.; v.p., dir. Bebon Corp.; v.p., dir. Dixie Yarn & Thread Co. Mason Home: 205 Windmere Dr Chattanooga TN 37411 Office: 1100 Watkins St Chattanooga, TN 37404.*

EWING, DONALD EDGAR, farm supply co. exec; b. Parsons, Kan., Feb. 21, 1914; s. Oscar Ray and Nellie Oretta (Trammell) E.; grad. Parsons Jr. Coll., 1935; m. Maxine Fern Christy, Nov. 24, 1935; 1 dau., Linda Jane. With Farmland Industries, Inc., 1933—, financial v.p., treas., 1954—, also dir. subsidiaries. Pres. bd. N. Kansas City Sch. Dist., 1965—. Mem. Christian Ch. Home: 5315 N Cypress St Kansas City MO 64119 Office: 3315 N Oak Trafficway Kansas City MO 64116

EWING, ETHEL ELIZABETH, educator; b. Corry, Pa., June 2, 1906; d. Thomas Ralph and Grace Jane (Mason) Ewing; B.A. cum laude, Muskingum Coll., 1928; M.A., Radcliffe Coll., 1936; Ph.D., Cornell U., 1944. Engaged in study in Far East in Tokyo, 1937-38; vis. research fellow history Radcliffe Coll., 1949-50; doctor in residence Cornell U., 1951-52; mem. faculty Boardman (O.) High Sch., 1928-36, Lakewood (O.) High Sch., 1936-42; asst. prof. N.Y. State Coll., Albany, 1944-45; asst. prof. Far East dept. U. Wash., 1947-49; mem. faculty Cal. State Coll., Long Beach, 1952—, prof. anthropology, 1959—, chmn. dept., 1961-63. Mem. Am. Anthrop. Assn.; mem. Southwestern Anthrop. Assn., Assn. Cal. State Coll. Profs., Am. Assn. U. Profs., Phi Beta Kappa, Delta Kappa Gamma. Author: Our Widening World: A History of the World's Peoples, 3d edit. 1967. Address: Cal State Coll Long Beach CA 90801

EWING, FRANK MARION, lumber co. exec., indsl. land developer; b. Albany, Ga., Apr. 24, 1915; s. Frank Marion and Alpharetta (Tucker) E.; B.A. (Sereno Gaylord scholarship 1932-36), Yale, 1936; m. Hanna Anderson, June 15, 1935; children—Grace Marit (Mrs. George P. Lamb, Jr.), Linda Tucker (Mrs. Richard R. Mace), Frances Marion (Mrs. John Falconer); m. 2d, Jo Anne Bacon Hilley, Mar. 12, 1964; children (adopted—Kathleen Melinda, Wayne Edgar. Pres., chmn. bd. Frank M. Ewing Co., Inc., Washington, 1937—, Lumber Distbn. Co., Petersburg, Va., 1942-57, Ewing Lumber & Millwork Corp., Beltsville, Md., 1958—; developer Beltsville Indsl. Center, 1950- -; dir. Acacia Mut. Life Ins. Co., Citizens Bank Md., Md. State Savs. and Loan Assn., Washington Gas Light Co. Mem. industry adv. com. WPB, 1942-46; industry adv. com. to sec. commerce, 1947-50; dept. asst. sec. def., 1955-56; mem. bd. Met. Washington Bd. Trade, 1957-61. Gen. campaign chmn. Prince Georges Community Chest, 1955. Bd. dirs. Childrens Hosp., Washington; mem. cathedral thousand Washington Nat. Cathedral. Mem . Prince Georges C. of C. (pres. 1956-57). Kiwanian (bd. dirs. Prince Georges 1948-52), Mason. Clubs: Chevy Chase, Metropolitan, Burning Tree (Washington). Home: 10812 Pleasant Hill Dr Potomac MD 20854 Office: 10500 Ewing Rd Beltsville MD 20705

EWING, GALEN WOOD, educator; b. Boston, Mar. 14, 1914,; s. William Clinton and Florence A. (Wood) E.; B.S., Coll. William and Mary, 1936; Ph.D., U. Chgo., 1939; m. Alice C. Sipple, Nov. 26, 1942; children—Martin S., William G., Thomas E. Instr., Blackburn Coll., Carlinville, Ill., 1937-42; research chemist Sterling-Winthrop Research Inst., Rensselaer, N.Y., 1942-46; asst. prof., asso. prof. Union Coll., Schenectady, 1946-57; prof. N.M. Highlands U., Las Vegas, 1957-65; prof. Seton Hall U., South Orange, N.J., 1964—, chmn. dept. chemistry, 1969—. Cons. A.R.F. Products, Inc., Raton, N.M. Mem. Am. Chem. Soc. (chmn. Central N.M. sect. 1962), A.A.A.S., Soc. for Applied Spectroscopy, Phi Beta Kappa, Sigma Xi. Author: Instrumental Methods of Chemical Analysis, 1956. Instrumentation editor: Jour. of Chem. Edn., 1967—. Home: 301 Beechwood Terrace Orange NJ 07050

EWING, GEORGE MCNAUGHT, educator; b. Lexington, Mo., Sept. 30, 1907; s. Joel Harvey and Christie (Vaughan) E.; A.B., U. Mo., 1929, A.M., 1930, Ph.D., 1935; m. Mary Alice Jones, Aug. 6, 1937; children—Alicia M. (Mrs. Edwin M. Towster), Catharine V., Joel C. Part time instr. to full prof. U. Mo., Columbia, 1930-57; prof. math. U. Okla., Norman, 1960-63, research prof., 1963—. Instr., Princeton, mem. Inst. for Advanced Study, 1940-41; with magnetic subdiv. research div. Naval Ordnance Lab., Washington, 1944-45; with systems evaluation dept. Sandia Corp., Albuquerque, 1951-52, summer 1953; engaged in space tech. Ramo Wooldridge Corp., Los Angeles, 1954. Cons. to combat devel. dept. U.S. Army Arty. and Missile Sch., Ft. Sill, Okla., 1957-60. OSRD grantee, 1954, 1961-65. Mem. Am. Math. Soc., Math. Assn. Am., Soc. Indsl. and Applied Math., A.A.A.S., Am. Assn. U. Profs., Phi Beta Kappa, Sigma Xi. Democrat. Presbyn. (past deacon, trustee, elder). Author: Calculus of Variations with Applications, 1969; (with H. Betz, P.B. Burcham) Differential Equations with Applications, 1954, 2d edit., 1964. Contbr. articles to sci. jours. Home: 816 College Av Norman OK 73069

EWING, GIFFORD COCHRAN, oceanographer; b. Yonkers, N.Y., Nov. 1, 1904; s.Thomas and Anna (Cochran) E.; A.B., Yale, 1926; M.S., U. Cal. at Los Angeles, 1948, Ph.D., 1950; m. Frances L. Riker, 1926 (div. 1934); children—Alexandra (Mrs. Alexandre E. Whitney), Frances (Mrs. Fulton Rockwell); m. 2d, Alice R. Jones, 1934 (dec. 1964); children—Benton N. (stepson), Jane (Mrs. Ralph N. Philbrick), Eva; m. 3d, Winifred A. Forgit, 1965; stepchildren—Laurence, Richard, Deborah, Sabra, and Ely. Laboratory instr. Yale, 1927-28; oceanographer Bingham Oceanographic Lab., Yale, 1929-32; mem. Yale Oceanographic Expdn., 1931-32; oceanographic observer Operations Crossroads, Bikini, 1946; mem. staff Scripps Instn. Oceanography, 1948-63, chmn. oceanic research div., 1962- 64, research oceanographer, 1963-66; asso. phys. oceanography Woods Hole (Mass.) Oceanographic Instn., 1964-66, sr. scientist, 1967—; vis. lectr. mem. corp., 1960—; Am. Geophys. Union, U. Ariz., U. N.M., U. Wyo., 1962. Cons. Office Naval Research, 1951; project officer operation wigwam U.S. Navy, 1955, chmn. antisubmarine warfare infrared com., 1961- 65; mem. exhbt. com. San Diego Zoo. 1960-64; vis. scientist Mass. Inst. Tech., 1964-65; chmn. oceanographic team Apollo expt. support NASA, 1965, mem. NAVOCEANO ad hoc spacecraft adv. group, 1966—. Pres., dir. La Valenica Hotel, La Jolla, Cal., 1948—; dir. Oceanographic Fund, Inc. IUGG representative COSPAR, 1968—. Bd. dirs. San Diego Soc. Nat. History, 1950-64; mem. chancellor's adv. com. humanities and social sci. U. Cal. at San Diego, 1963-64. Served to capt. USNR, 1940-45. Recipient Medaille Albert 1er, Paris, France, 1964; Prix Manley Bemdall, Prince de Monaco, 1964. Fellow Cal. Acad. Sci.; mem. A.A.A.S., Am. Geophys. Union, Am. Meterorol. Soc., Sigma Xi. Episcopalian. Clubs: Cosmos (Washington); Yale (N.Y.C.); Quissett Harbor Yacht, Woods Hole Yacht (Woods Hole); New York Yacht. Author numerous papers in field. Home: Gansett Woods Hole MA 02543 Office: Woods Hole Oceanographic Instn Woods Hole MA 02543

EWING, GORDON A., govt. ofcl.; b. Newfane, N.Y., Nov. 1, 1912; s. Roy G. and Dorothy (Green) E.; student Stanford, 1930-31, Kiel (Germany) U., 1931-32; B.A., Wayne State U., 1935, M.A., 1936; m. Marjorie Edwards, June 29, 1946; 1 son, John Peter. Dept. dir., then dir. radio sta. RIAS, Berlin, Germany, 1949-57; dep. dir. Voice of Am., USIA, 1957-59; counselor of embassy for pub. affairs, Bonn, Germany, 1967—. Served to maj. AUS, 1941-45. Decorated Croix de Guerre; recipient Meritorious Service award Dept. State, 1952, USIA, 1959. Home: 40 Martin Luther King Strasse Bonn Bad Godesberg Germany Office: Am Embassy Bonn Germany

EWING, GORDON RICHARDSON, printing co. exec.; b. Kansas City, Mo., June 22, 1913; s. Albert and Estelle (Richardson) E.; B.S., Cal. Inst. Tech., 1936; M.B.A., Harvard, 1937; m. Miriam Cornish, Jan. 30, 1943; children—Ellen Stuart, Gordon Richardson. Engr.-analyst Chicago Corp., 1937-41; engr. Chgo. Ordnance Dist., War Dept., 1941-45; prodn. mgr. Clark Waterheater div. McGraw Electric Co., Chgo., 1945-48; staff asst. expenditures com. U.S. Senate, 1948-49; internal cons. R.R. Donnelley & Sons Co., Chgo., 1949-50, mgr. indsl. engring., Crawfordsville, Ind., 1950-55, dir. engring., Chgo., 1955-61, v.p., Chgo. , 1966-69, sr. v.p., 1969—; v.p., gen. mgr., dir. Meredith Printing, Inc., Des Moines, pres., 1962—; v.p. Meredith Pub. Co., 1962-66, pres., 1965-66, dir. corporate planning, mem. exec. com., dir. Mem. Phi Delta Theta. Republican. Clubs: University, Chicago Yacht. Home: 1448 Lake Shore Dr Chicago IL 60610. Office: 22235 South Park Way Chicago IL 00616

EWING, JOHN ARTHUR, research adminstr.; b. Euchee, Tenn., June 24, 1912; s. James Anderson and Harriette Mahala (Moulton) E.; B.S.A., U. Tenn., 1933, M.S., 1946; D.P.A., Harvard, 1956; m. Frances Mowry Burleson, Dec. 26, 1936; children—John Arthur, Ward Burleson, Jack Dunn. Vocational agr. tchr., Erwin, Tenn., 1934-35; asst. county agt., Carter County, Tenn., 1935-44; asst. supt. Middle Tenn. Expt. Sta., Columbia, 1944-46, supt., 1946-49; asst. dir. Agrl. Expt. Sta., U. Tenn., Knoxville, 1949-55, vice dir., 1955-59, dir., then dean Agrl. Expt. Sta., 1957—, sr. vice dean Coll. Agr. and Home Econs., sr. vice dir. Agrl. Extension Service, 1955-59; project leader AEC Agrl. Lab., U. Tenn., 1955—. Bd. dirs. Tenn. Research Corp., Knoxville; adminstrv. adviser So. region for grain marketing research, soybean research, water resources; mem. Nat. Cotton Seed policy com.; mem. nat. tobacco adv. com. sec. agr.; dir.'s rep. So. Land Econ. Research Com.; mem. Tenn. Air Pollution Control Bd.; mem. Cotton Breeding Policy Com. Mem. Expt. Sta. Dirs. in South, Agronomy Soc., So. Agrl. Workers Assn. (pres.), Am. Assn. Land Grant Colls. (chmn. expt. sta. sect.), Sigma Xi, Omicron Delta Kappa. Epsilon Sigma Phi. Phi Kappa Phi, Pi Kappa Alpha, Alpha Zeta, Delta Sigma Phi, Gamma Sigma Delta. Episcopalian (vestry). Mason. Clubs: Rotary, Dean Hill Country, Block and Bridle (Knoxville). Home: 2110 Terrace Av Knoxville TN 37916

EWING, MAURICE, geophysicist; b. Lockney, Tex., May 12, 1906; s. Floyd Ford and Hope (Hamilton) E.; B.A., Rice Inst., 1925, M.A., 1927, Ph.D., 1931, Hohenthal scholar, 1923-26, fellow in physics, 1926-29; D.Sc. (hon.), Washington and Lee U., 1949, U. Denver, 1953, Utrecht, 1957, Lehigh U., 1957, U. R.I., 1960, U. Durham, 1963, U. Del., 1968, L.I.U., 1969, U. Nacional de Colombia, 1969, Centre Coll. Ky., 1971; LL.D., Dalhousie U., 1960; m. Avarilla Hildenbrand, Oct. 31, 1928 (div. 1941); 1 son, William M. (dec.); m. 2d, Margaret Sloan Kidder, Feb. 19, 1944 (div. 1965); children—Jerome, Hope, Peter Duryee, Margaret; m. 3d, Harriett Greene Bassett, May 6, 1965. Instr. physics Pitts. U., 1929-30; mem. faculty Lehigh U., Bethlehem, Pa., 1930-44, successively instr. in physics, asst. prof., asso. prof.; asso. prof. geology Columbia, 1944-47, prof., 1947—, Higgins prof. geology, 1959—; on leave, 1940-44, from Lehigh U., and Columbia, 1944-45, to act as research asso. on Nat. Def. Research Com. projects, Woods Hole (Mass.) Oceanographic Inst., 1940-44, dir. research in physics, 1940-45; dir. Lamont Doherty Geol. Obs., Columbia, 1949—. Leader Nat. Geog. Soc.-Columbia Woods Hole Oceanographic Inst. Expdns., 1947, 48; leader Columbia Expdns., 1953—, IGY Expdn., 1957-58; mem. U.S. com. IGY, 1955-59. Decorated comdr. Order Naval Merit (Argentina); recipient service award U.S. Navy 1955; Agassiz medal Nat. Acad. Sci., 1955; William Bowie medal Am. Geophys. Union, 1957; Vetlesen prize, 1960; John Fleming medal Am. Inst. Geonomy and Natural Resources, 1960; medal of honor Rice U., 1962; Joseph Priestley award Dickinson Coll., 1961; Cullum Geog. medal Am. Geog. Soc., 1961, John J. Carty medal, 1963; Vega medal Swedish Soc. Anthropology and Geography, 1965; gold medal Royal Astron. Soc., 1964; Sidney Powers Meml. medal, 1968; Sesquicentennial medal St. Louis U., 1969; Wollaston medal Geol. Soc. London, 1969. Fellow Indian Geophys. Union (hon.); mem. Academia Nacional de Ciences Exactas Fisicas y Naturales (corr.), A.A.A.S., Geol. Soc. London (fgn. mem.), Am. Assn. Petroleum Geologists (hon.), Am. Geophys. Union (v.p. 1953-56, pres. 1956- 59), Soc. Exploration Geophysicists (hon.), Seismol. Soc. Am. (v.p. 1952 -54, pres. 1955-57), Royal Netherlands Acad. (fgn. mem.), Royal Soc. New Zealand (hon.), Nat. Acad. Sci., Geol. Soc. Am. (A.L. Day medalist 1949), Am. Acad. Arts and Scis., Am. Philos. Soc. Clubs: Century Assn., Explorers (N.Y.C.); Cosmos (Washington). Author: Propagation of Sound in the Ocean; (with W. Jardetzky and F. Press) Elastic Waves in Layered Media, 1957; also numerous papers in field. Editorial bd. several publs. Home: Torrey Cliff Palisades NY 10964 Office: Lamont Doherty Geol Observatory Palisades NY 10964 ☆

EWING, OSCAR ROSS, lawyer; b. Greensburg, Ind., Mar. 8, 1889; s. George McClellan and Nettie Moore (Ross) E.; A.B., Indiana U., 1910; J.D., Harvard, 1913; LL.D., U. N.C., 1967, Ind. U., 1970; m. Helen E. Dennis, Nov. 4, 1915 (dec. June 1953); children—James Dennis, George McClellan; m. 2d, Mary Whiting Mackay Thomas, Oct. 12, 1955. Instr. U. Ia. Law Sch., 1913-14; mem. Weyl, Jewett & Ewing, Indpls., 1915-16; asst. counsel Vandalia R.R. Co., St. Louis, 1916; asst. to gen. counsel Pa. Lines West of Pitts., 1917; mem. Hughes, Schurman & Dwight, N.Y., and predecessor firms 1920-37; mem. firm Hughes, Hubbard & Ewing, 1937-47. Asst. chmn. Dem. Nat. Com, 1940-42, spl. asst. to U.S. atty. gen. 1942-47, vice chmn. Dem. Nat. Com. 1942; Fed. Security Agy. adminstr. 1947-52. Am. mfrs. del. Conf. for Limitation Mfr. Narcotics, Geneva, 1931. Chmn. Research Triangle Found., 1963-67. Served from 1st lt. to capt., U.S. Army, 1918. Mem. N.Y. County Bar Assn., Assn. Bar City N.Y., Beta Theta Pi. Democrat. Episcopalian. Clubs: University, Down Town (N.Y.C.). Contbr. legal articles to mags. Home: 300 Tenney Circle Chapel Hill NC 27514

EWING, PARMER LELAND, state edn. ofcl.; b. Casey, Ill., Mar. 12, 1903; s. N.A. and (Frissel) E.; student James Millkin U., 1921-23; B.S., U. Ill., 1930, M.S., 1934; Ed.D., N.Y. U., 1950; m. Lalah Augustus, July 16, 1926; children—Carol Elizabeth (Mrs. John Sutton), Marilyn Louise (Mrs. John Kaneski). Instr. indsl. arts, coach athletics Shelbyville (Ill.) High Sch., 1923-30, prin., 1930-31; supt. schs., Highland, Ill., 1947-50, White Plains, N.Y., 1950-53, Buffalo, 1953-57; chmn. dept. adminstrn. and supervision, sch. edn. N.Y.U., 1957-65; prof. ednl. adminstrn., dir. ednl. cons. service So. Ill. U., Carbondale, 1965-68; dir. dept. higher edn. Office Supt. Pub. Instrn. Ill., 1968—. Active Buffalo Mus. Sci., Buffalo Philharmonic Soc., Albright Gallery, YMCA, Boy Scouts Am. Recipient Silver Beaver award Boy Scouts Am.; Alumni Merit award Millikin U., 1968; Sch. Edn. Merit award N.Y. U., 1968. Mem. N.E.A. (chem. internat. relation com. of regents com.), Am. Assn. Sch. Administrs., N.Y. State Tchrs. Assn., Buffalo Tchrs. Fedn., N.Y. State Council of Supts., Buffalo Hist. Soc., Phi Delta Kappa, Alpha Mu Sigma, Sigma Delta Sigma. Methodist. Mason (Shriner), Elk, K.P. Clubs: Rotary, Equality, Buffalo. Address: Supt of Pub Instrn Springfield IL 62708

EWING, RICHARD TUCKER, diplomat, educator; b. Albany, Ga., Sept. 25, 1918; s. Francis Marion and Alpharetta (Tucker) E.; B.A., Yale, 1940, M.A., 1942, postgrad., 1946-47, 49-51; m. Jacquelyn Randolph Knapp, Apr. 26, 1947; children—Maitland Marshall, Sara Almand, Richard Tucker, Elizabeth Harrison, Alpharetta Tucker, John Randolph. With Dept. State Fgn. Service, 1946-70, attache U.S. Legation, Bern, Switzerland, 1947-49, 2d sec. U.S. Embassy, Taipei, Taiwan, China; 1951-56, 1st sec. U.S. Embassy, Rangoon, 1959-62, dept. dir. div. research and analysis for Asia, Dept. State, 1963-65, dept. dir. Office S.E. Asian Affairs, 1965-66, country dirs., Burma and Cambodia, 1966-67; faculty Nat. War Coll., Washington, 1967-70, dir. dept. internat. relations and area studies; with Congl. Information Service, Bethesda, Md., 1970—. Pres. local sch. chpt. P.T.A., Rockville, Md., 1967-68. Trustee P.T.A., 1968-69. Served to capt. AUS, 1942-46. Decorated Bronze Star medal, Order Yun Huei. Mem. Kingsley Trust Assn., Assn. Asian Studies, Polit. Sci. Assn., Am. Hist. Assn., Inst. Strategic Studies, Fgn. Service Assn., Phi Beta Kappa. Home: Chance Farm Box 1285 Rockville MD 20850 Office: 4720 Montgomery Lane Bethesda MD 20014

EWING, ROBERT PAUL, ins. co. exec.; b. Kirksville, Mo., Feb. 8, 1925; s. Leo M. and Eva (Dodson) E.; B.S., N.E. Mo. State Coll., 1948; m. Ann D. Ewing, Aug. 22, 1945 (div. 1971); children—Robert I., Michael J., Patricia. With Bankers Life and Casualty Co., Chgo., 1948—, exec. v.p., 1965—; pres. Gotham Life Ins. Co. of N.Y., exec. v.p. Bankers Multiple Line Ins. Co., Des Moines, 1970—; dir. Constitution Life Ins. Co., Chgo., State Life Ins. Co. of Colo., Denver, Union Bankers Ins. Co. Dallas. Served to sgt. USAAF, 1943-45. Mem. Internat. Assn. Health Underwriters, Nat. Assn. Life Underwriters. Club: Park Ridge (Ill.) Country. Home: 2600 Windsor Mall Park Ridge IL 60068 Office: 4444 Lawrence Av Chicago IL 60630

EWING, RUSSELL CHARLES, educator; b. Manhattan, Kan., Feb. 16, 1906; s. Charles Edward and Blanche (Russell) E.; B.A., U. Cal. at Berkeley, 1929, M.A., 1931, Ph.D., 1934; m. Susan Sawyer, Nov. 14, 1929; children—David Russell, John Meredith, Russell Charles II. Regional historian region IV Nat. Park Service, 1935-37; mem. faculty U. Ariz., 1937—, prof. history, 1948—, head dept., 1959-69, Liberal Arts Faculty lectr., 1959; vis. lectr. San Francisco State Coll., summer 1948; participant Am. Assembly, 1959. Mem. Fed. Regional Archives Adv. Council region 9, 1971—. Mem. Tucson Sch. Bd., 1955-56, 64-66. Dir. Ariz. Palsy Found., 1955-56. Served to lt. comdr. USNR, 1942-46. Recipient Outstanding Male Faculty award U. Ariz., 1952, Faculty Recognition award Tucson Trade Bur., 1967; Smith-Mundt fellow U. Andes, Bogota, Colombia, 1956-57. Mem. Am. Hist. Assn., Western History Assn., Rocky Mountain Council Latin Am. Studies (pres. 1955-56), Com. Fgn. Relations, Phi Kappa Phi, Sigma Phi. Episcopalian. Editor, co- author: Six Faces of Mexico. Home: 822 Camino de Los Padres Tucson AZ 85718

EWING, SAMUEL EVANS, mfg. co. exec., lawyer; b. Bryn Mawr, Pa., July 27, 1906; s. Samuel E. and Fanny Badger (Neff) E.; student Haverford Sch., 1914-23; A.B., Princeton, 1927; LL.B., U. Pa., 1930; m. Mrs. Harriet Corning Sinkler, Mar. 22, 1947 (dec. Feb. 1966); children—Samuel Evans, Steven; stepsons—Wharton III, Edwin, Peter; m. 2d, Mary Alice Markell, July 23, 1966. Admitted to Pa. bar, 1931, D.C. bar, 1970; associate firm Saul, Ewing, Remick & Saul, Esquires, Phila., 1930-41, partner, 1946-47; counsel engring. products dept. RCA Victor div. RCA, 1947-48, gen. atty. div., 1948-53, mfg. and service divs., 1954-60, staff v.p., gen. atty. mfg. and service divs., 1960-67, v.p., Washington, 1967—. Bd. commrs. Lower Merion Twp., Pa., 1939-42, 48-60, v.p., 1952-56, pres., 1956-60. Bd. trustees Temple U., 1963—; trustee, exec. com. Fed. City Council. Served from pvt. to maj., AUS, 1941-45; overseas, 1944-45. Mem. Am., Pa., Fed., Phila., FCC bar assns., Juristic Soc. Phila., Electronic Industries Assn. (law com. 1949-67, bus.-govt. relations council 1968), Assn. Gen. Counsel. Club: Lawyers (Phila.). Home: 4125 52d St NW Washington DC 20016 Office: RCA 1800 K St NW Washington DC 20006

EWING, SHERMAN, lawyer, author, theatrical producer; b. Yonkers, N.Y., May 26, 1901; s. Thomas and Anna Phillips (Cochran) E.; ed. St. Paul's Sch., 1912-19; Peter House, Cambridge, Eng., 1919-20; A.B., Yale, 1924; LL.B., Harvard, 1927; m. Mary Peavey Heffelfinger (div. 1934); children—Sherman, Lucia (Mrs. John Steidl), Anna (Mrs. David Bull), Frank Heffelfinger; m. 2d, Marjorie Wallace Hughes Walsh, Apr. 18, 1938. Author: (plays) Wild Swans; Voltaire. Producer (with Marjorie H. Ewing) Angel in the Wings, 1947-48; The Rape of Lucretia (opera by Benjamin Britten), 1948-49. Dir. Mohasco Industries, Inc. Trustee Manhattan Sch. Music, bd. dirs., N.Y. Hort. Soc., Repertory Theater of Lincoln Center. Home: 160 E 72d St New York City NY 10021 Office: 14 E 55th St New York City NY 10022

EXLEY, CHARLES ERROL, Jr., mfg. co. exec.; b. Detroit, Dec. 14, 1929; s. Charles Errol and Helen Margaret (Greenizen) E.; B.A., Wesleyan U., Middletown, Conn., 1952; M.B.A., Columbia, 1954; m. Sara Elizabeth Yates, Feb. 1, 1952. With Burroughs Corp., Detroit, 1954—, controller Todd div., 1960-63, corp. controller, 1963-66, v.p., group exec., 1967-70, v.p. finance, 1970—. Mem. Financial Execs. Inst. Clubs: Detroit Athletic; Grosse Pointe (Grosse Pointe Farms, Mich.); Genesee Valley (Rochester, N.Y.). Home: 278 Rivard Blvd Grosse Point MI 48230 Office: 1 Burroughs Pl Detroit MI 48232

EXMAN, EUGENE, book publisher; b. Blanchester, O., July 1, 1900; s. Emmet and Mary Etta (Smith) E.; Ph.B., Denison U., 1922; M.A., U. Chgo., 1925; D.R.E., Middlebury Coll., 1952; m. Gladys Miller, June 6, 1929; 1 adopted son, Frank Walker; children—Wallace Miller, Judith. With U. Chgo. Press, 1925-28, mgr. religious book dept. Harper & Bros., N.Y.C., 1928, dir., 1944, v.p., 1955, now retired, continuing as archivist and historian (merger 1962), Harper & Row Pubs., Inc. Bd. trustees Wainwright House Inc., chmn., 1960-65; trustee Denison U., 1944—; trustee Sturgis Library, pres., 1968—. Club: Century Assn. (N.Y.C.). Author: The World of Albert Schweitzer, 1955; The Brothers Harper, 1965; The House of Harper, 1967. Contbr. articles periodicals, also parts of books. Home: Barnstable MA 02630 Office: 49 E 33d St New York City NY 10016

EXNER, VIRGIL MAX, industrial designer; b. Ann Arbor, Mich., Sept. 24, 1909; s. George W. and Iva (Shook) E.; student U. Notre Dame, 1926-28; m. Mildred M. Eshleman Mar. 7, 1931; children—Virgil M., Brian L. (dec.), Bronwen M., June Marie. With Advt. Artists, Inc., South Bend, Ind., 1928-34; chief stylist Pontiac div. Gen. Motors Corp., 1934-38; chief styling engr. Studebaker Corp., 1938-49; chief stylist advance styling studio Chrysler Corp., 1949-52, dir. of styling, 1953, now styling cons.; pres. Virgil M. Exner Inc., indsl. designers. Mem. Soc. Automotive Engrs. (v.p. body activities 1951-52), Soc. Illustrators. Club: Sports Car of America. Contbr. tech. articles profl. jours. Home: 1036 Westwood Dr Birmingham MI 48010 Office: Office: Virgil M Exner Inc 954 N Hunter Blvd Birmingham MI 48011

EXON, JOHN JAMES, gov. of Neb.; b. Geddes, S.D., Aug. 9, 1921; s. John James and Luella (Johns) E.; student U. Omaha, 1939-41; m. Patricia Ann Pros, Sept. 18, 1943; children—Stephen James, Pamela Ann, Candace Lee. Mgr., Universal Finance Corp., Neb., 1946-53; pres. Exon's, Inc., Lincoln, Neb., 1954-71; gov. Neb., 1971—. Active state, local, nat. Democratic coms., 1952—; del. Dem. Nat. Conv., 1964; Dem. nat. committeeman, 1968—. Served with Signal Corps, AUS, 1942-45. Mem. Am. Legion, Lincoln C. of C., Nat. Office Products Dealers. Mason (32, Shriner), Elk. Club: Optimists Internat. (past lt. gov. Neb. dist.). Home: 1615 Brent Blvd Lincoln NB 68520

EXTER, JOHN, banker; b. Chgo., Sept. 17, 1910; s. Joseph and Edith (Gray) E.; B.A., Coll. Wooster, 1932; M.A., Fletcher Sch. Law and Diplomacy, 1934; student Harvard, 1939-40; m. Marion Fitch. Dec. 18, 1937; children—John Kempton, Nancy (Mrs. Barry Jackson Downs), Janet (Mrs. Paul Butler), George. Tchr. history and econs. Western Res. Acad., Tufts Coll., Harvard, 1934-43; with radiation lab. Mass. Inst. Tech., 1943-45; economist, acting chief Far East bd. govs. Fed. Res. System, 1945-50; gov. Central Bank of Ceylon, 1950-53; chief Middle East div. Internat. Bank Reconstruction and Devel., 1953-54; v.p. Fed. Res. Bank N.Y., 1954-59; v.p. First Nat. City Bank of N.Y., 1959-60, sr. v.p., 1960—; v.p. Internat. Banking Corp., 1959—; dir., Am.-S. African Investment Co., Ltd. Mem. Joint Philippine-Am. Finance Commn., 1947; adviser central banking Philippine and Ceylon govts., 1948-50. Trustee Internat. Found. Mem. Am. Econ. Assn. , Acad. Polit. Sci., Council Fgn. Relations, Phi Beta Kappa. Conglist. Club: University. Home: 290 Boulevard Mountain Lakes NJ 07046 Office: 399 Park Av New York City NY 10022

EXTERMANN, RICHARD CHARLES, educator, physicist; b. Menton, France, Jan. 24, 1911; s. Paul Ernest and Lydia (Schneider) E.; licence es sciences, Geneva U., 1933, Ph.D., 1938, hon. prof., 1963; Dr. Honoris Causa, Dijon U., 1957; m. Antoinette Rosslaud, Dec. 22, 1938; children—Charles Ed, Laurent M., Philippe H. Faculty, U. Geneva, 1938-39, 46-63; research physicist Swiss Fed. Sch. Tech., Zurich, 1940-45; head dept. physics Cooper Union, N.Y.C., 1963—. Head sci. secretariat, also editor proc. UNESCO 1st Internat. Radio Isotopes Conf., Paris, 1957; cons. Sci. Directorate OECD, Paris, 1960-63. Mem. Am., French, Swiss phys. socs., Am. Assn. Physics Tchrs. Author: (with P. Grivet et al) La Resonance Paramagnetique Nucleaire, 1955. Contbr. articles profl. jours. Home: 270 Jay St Brooklyn NY 11215 Office: Cooper Union Dept Physics Cooper Sq New York City NY 10003

EXTON, HUGH MCCLELLAN, army officer; b. Salt Lake City, Oct. 31, 1913; s. Charles Wesley and Rose (McClellan) E.; B.S., U.S. Mil. Acad., 1935; grad. Nat. War Coll., 1955; m. Marjorie Louise Grant. Mar. 21, 1939; children—Leslie Grant, Hugh McClellan, Christopher Schuyler, Peter Walker, Thomas Michael. Commd. 2d lt. U.S. Army, 1935, advanced through grades to lt. gen., 1968; troop duty, 1935-41; battalion comdr., 1942-44; aide to sec. of war, 1945-46; instr. Command and Gen. Staff Coll., 1946-49; staff officer Hdqrs. European Command, 1949-51; regtl. comdr., 1951-52; dir. mil. physchology and leadership U.S. Mil. Acad., 1952-54; mem. staff Army Gen. Staff, 1955-57; asst. to chmn. Joint Chiefs Staff, 1957-59; dep. arty. comdr. 25th Inf. Div., 1961-62; dept. chief staff Continental Army Command, 1962-64; comdg. gen. 1st Cav. Div., Korea, 1964-65; dept. chief staff U.S. Army Europe, 1965-67; dir. ins. services Office Asst. Sec. Def. (Adminstrn.), Washington, 1967-70; dir. mil. support Office Chief Staff, U.S. Army, 1970—. Decorated Silver Star with 2 oak leaf clusters, D.S.M., Legion of Merit with oak leaf cluster, Bronze Star, Air medal, Purple Heart. Home: Fort Myer VA 22211 office: Dir Mil Support Office Chief Staff US Army Washington DC 20305

EXTON, WILLIAM, Jr., mgmt. cons. communications, business exec.; b. N.Y.C., Mar. 15, 1907; s. Dr. W.G. and Florence Nightingale Augusta (Phillips) E.; student Horace Mann Sch. Boys, N.Y.C., 1917-22; A.B., Harvard, 1926; M.A. in Ednl. Psychology, Tchrs. Coll., Columbia, 1951; m. Katherine Malandraki, Mar. 4, 1966; 1 son, William III. Propr., Exton-Aids, Millbrook, N.Y.; pres. Growth of Democracy, Inc., Inst. Human Communications, Inc.; sr. cons. Wm. Exton, Jr. and Assos.; pres., treas. Pay-Plus, Inc.; owner, operator Exton Plantations; lectr. N.Y. U. Grad. Sch. Pub. Adminstrn., 1955-59; mem. faculty univ. seminar on orgn. and mgmt. Columbia, co-chmn., 1967, chmn., 1967—; asso. dir. engring. mgmt. workshops Columbia; mem. faculty grad. sch. marketing and sales mgmt. Nat. Sales Execs. Internat., Syracuse U.; cons. univ., govts., industry on gen. mgmt., orgnl. effectiveness, marketing and sales, reduction of clerical error, human communication, tng. Program chmn. Gilbreth Meml., 1968. Vice chmn. trustees Inst. Gen. Semantics. Served from lt. (j.g.) to capt., USNR, 1941-47. Mem. Soc. Profl. Mgmt. Cons. (co-founder, dir., v.p.), Inst. Mgmt. Cons., Council for Internat. Progress in Mgmt. (dir.), Soc. for Advancement Mgmt., Nat. Soc. Study Communication, Am. Soc. Tng. Dirs., Brit. Assn. Comml. and Indsl. Edn., Mensa, Speech Assn. Am., N.Y. Film Council, Am. Legion. Clubs: Men's Faculty (Columbia U.); Harvard, Explorers, City (trustee), Daedalus (hon.) (N.Y.C.); Army and Navy Country (Washington); Millbrook Rod and Gun; Sandonona Beagles; Chestnut Ridge Rod and Gun. Author: Audiovisual Aids to Instruction; He's with the Destroyers Now; Employee Benefits- Asset or Liability, 1960; Dynamics of Management, 1960; The Effective Utilization of Banking Services, 1964; Improving Efficiency of Asian Crews, 1966; The Age of Systems, 1972; Clerical Errors: Their Cost and Cure, 1970; The Art of Motivating, 1972; also articles. Inventor Parts-Imparter and other teaching aids. Address: RD Dover Plains NY 12522 also 101 W 57th St New York City NY 10019 also 2 Amalias Av Athens Greece ☆

EXUM, GLENN, musician, mountaineer; b. Topaz, Ida., June 24, 1911; s. Oliver Kinch and Allie Vaughn (Tolman) E.; B.S. in Edn., U. Ida., 1934; mus. tng. St. Georges Boys Choir, Windsor Castle, Eng., 1935, 38; m. Beth Pauline Noben, Nov. 28, 1939; children—Edward Sherman, Glenda Lynne. Mountaineer in Grand Teton Nat. Park, Jenny Lake, Wyo., 1930—; operator Exum Sch. Am. Mountaineering and Guide Service, Grand Teton Nat. Park; supr. music Sch. Dist. 391, Kellogg, Ida., 1934-71. Adjudicator, dir. Massed Bands and Choruses in Alaska and Ida.; judge solo and ensemble music festivals in Wash., Alaska and Ida. Pres. Shoshone County Community Concerts Assn., 1942-57; chmn. Kellogg Planning Commn., 1957-58; bd. dirs. Jackass Ski Bowl, 1965-67, pres., 1967. Named Man of Year, Jr. C. of C., 1940; recipient Outstanding Citizenship award C. of C., 1959; Certificate of Recognition, Gov. State of Ida., 1971; Exum Glacier in Antarctic named in his honor, also Exum Cup given at Jackass Ski Bowl Races. Mem. Gyro Internat., Nat. Ski Patrol (charter mem.), Am. Alpine Club, Sigma Nu. Methodist. Club: Kellogg Country (chmn. 1970). Pioneered Exum Route on Grand Teton, 1931; first Am. to make solo ascent of Swiss Matterhorn, 1935. Home: XM Chalet 95 Ranch Moose WY 83012

EXUM, JAMES POWERS, cons. engr.; b. Mobeetie, Tex., Oct. 11, 1900; s. Frank and Nancy Magdeline (Powers) E.; B.S. in C.E., U. Tex., 1922; m. Louise Ramsay, Sept. 6, 1924; 1 son, James Powers. Draftsman, Harrington, Howard & Ash, cons. engrs., Kansas City, Mo., 1922-24, designer bridge div. Tex. Hwy. Dept., 1924-25; designer, chief draftsman Harrington, Howard and Ash, 1925-28; chief draftsman, prin. asst. engr., Ash, Howard, Needles & Tammen, Kansas City, Mo., 1928-32; asst. engr. bridge div. Tex. Hwy. Dept., 1932-38, sr. designing engr., 1938-43, bridge engr., 1943-48; asso. engr., Howard, Needles, Tammen & Bergendoff, N.Y.C., 1948-50, partner, 1950-65, mem. adv. bd.; cons., 1965—; prin. works: Del. Meml. Bridge, Woodrow Wilson Meml. Bridge, Cooper River Bridge, N.J., Me. and Del. turnpikes, Newark Bay Bridge and Jersey City Expressway, also Route 24 Expressway, N.J. Registered Distinguished Engring. Grad. award U. Tex., 1964. Registered profl. engr., Conn., Del., Me., N.J., N.Y., S.C., Tex., Va. Mem. Nat., Tex. (pres. 1947) socs. profl. engrs., Am. Soc. C.E. (pres. Tex. 1948), Am. Inst. Cons. Engrs. (pres. 1963), Am. Concrete Inst. Tau Beta Pi, Chi Epsilon, Theta Xi. Clubs: Canoe Brook Country (Summit); Royal Palm Yacht and Country (Boca Raton, Fla.). Home: 1314 Sabal Palm Dr Boca Raton FL 33432 Office: 99 Church St New York City NY 10007

EY, LAWRENCE H., trust co. exec. Auditor, Mercantile Safe Deposit & Trust Co., Balt. Office: Calvert and Redwood Sts Baltimore MD 21203*

EYADEMA, ETIENNA GNASSINGBE, pres. of Togo; b. Pya, Lama-Kara, 1935. Served with French Army in Indo-China, Dahomey, Niger and Algeria, 1953-61; commd., 1963; army chief staff, Togo, 1965; seized power, 1967; pres. Togo, minister def., 1967—. Decorated Croix de la Valeur Militaire, chevalier Legion of Honor (France); grand officer Ordre Nat. du Mono. Address: Office of President Lome Togo

EYE, GLEN GORDON, educator; b. Miltonvale, Kan., Oct. 19, 1904; s. Christopher J. and Dillie G. (Park) E.; B.A., Kan. Wesleyan U., 1925, L.H.D., 1957; Ph.M., U. Wis., 1930, Ph.D., 1942; m. Lucile Terry, June 21, 1927; children—Miriam Gale (Mrs. Fred G. Blum, Jr.), Kathryn Elaine (Mrs. Clarence W. Bading). Tchr. math. Sweetgrass County High Sch., Big Timber, Mont., 1925-27; prin. pub. schs., Park City, Mont., 1927-28; asst. prin. Custer County High Sch., Miles City, Mont., 1928-29; supt. schs., Miles City, 1929-37; asst. prin. Sr. High Sch., Ogden, Utah, 1937-39, prin., 1939-41; prin. Wis. High Sch., asst. prof., then asso. prof. U. Wis.- Madison, 1941-48, dir. student teaching, asso. prof., then prof., 1948-56, acting dean Sch. Edn., Milw., 1956-57, prof. edn., Madison, 1957-59, prof., chmn. dept. edn., 1959-62, chmn. dept. ednl. adminstrn., 1962-65, prof. ednl. adminstrn., 1962—, research dir. U.S. Office Edn. project, 1963-66; vis. prof. U. Ore., summer 1951. Mem. Mont. Textbook Commn., 1932-37; mem. Wis. Joint Com. Edn., 1944; mem. Ingraham Com. Function Univ., 1944; mem. U. Wis. Athletic Bd., 1951-56; chmn. all univ. adv. com. Program Pub. Policies and Adminstrn., 1968-69. Chmn. Wis. Post War Planning Com., 1943; chmn. Wis. Surplus Commodity Com., 1945. Mem. Wis. Edn. Assn. (commn. chmn., editor handbook), Secondary Sch. Prins. Assn., Wis. Secondary Sch. Prins. Assn. (past pres.), Am. Assn. Sch. Adminstrs., Wis. Assn. Sch. Dist. Adminstrs. (Outstanding Educator of Year 1969), Nat. (dir.), Wis. assns. supervision and curriculum devel., Am., Wis. edn. research assns., Phi Delta Kappa. Author: (with Milton O. Pella) Elementary Arithmetic Workbook 1946, Basic Arithmetic Book I, 1947, Basic Arithmetic Book II, 1947; (with Kurt R. Schoenoff) Objectives of Education, 1951; (with Willard R. Lane) The New Teacher Comes to School, 1956; (with Lanore A. Netzer) Supervision of Instruction: A Phase of Administration, 1965, 71, School Administrators and Instruction, 1969; (with others) Interdisciplinary Foundations of Supervision, 1969; (with others) Education, Administration and Change, 1970; (with others) Instructional Technology and the School Adminstrator, 1970; also articles. Home: 950 Mohican Pass Madison WI 53711

EYERLY, FRANK RINEHART, editorial cons.; b. Newton, Ia., June 3, 1903; s. Josiah Bartlett and Celia (Grandrath) E.; student U. Ia., 1923-27; m. Jeannette Hyde, Dec. 7, 1932; children—Jane, Susan. With Des Moines Register and Tribune 1927-69, successively reporter, copy reader, telegraph editor, news editor, asst. mng. editor, mng. editor, 1946-69; editorial cons., 1969—; past dir. Des Moines Register and Tribune Co.; v.p. Register and Tribune, Syndicate, Inc.; dir. Comml. Printing, Inc.; journalism lectr. U. Mich., U. Neb., U. Ia., Am. Press Inst. Bd. trustees Wilkie Community House. Mem. Internat. Press Inst., Am. Soc. Newspaper Editors, A.P. Mng. Editors Assn. (dir., sec., chmn. continuing studies 1954—, pres. 1957), Phi Gamma Delta, Sigma Delta Chi. Clubs: Nat. Press (Washington); Des Moines; Century Assn. (N.Y.C.) Author articles profl. bulls. Home: 231 42d St Des Moines IA

EYERLY, JEANNETTE HYDE, author; b. Topeka, June 7, 1908; d. Robert and Mabel (Young) Hyde; B.A., State U. Ia., 1930; m. Frank Eyerly, Dec. 6, 1932; children—Jane (Mrs. Lawrence Kozuszek), Susan (Mrs. Joseph A. Pichler). Contbr. mags. Am. Home, Am. Girl, Better Homes and Gardens, Ladies Home Jour., Woman's Home Companion, Coronet, Pageant, Canadian Home Jour., Canadian Star Weekly, McCalls, 1941-57; book reviewer Des Moines Sunday Register; author: Dearest Kate (with Valeria Winkler Griffith), 1961; More Than a Summer Love, 1962; Drop-Out, 1963; The World of Ellen March, 1964; Gretchen's Hill (Susan Glaspell award 1965), 1965; A Girl Like Me, 1966; The Girl Inside, 1968; Escape from Nowhere (Christopher award), 1970. Tchr. creative writing Des Moines adult edn. classes, 1955-57; lectr. A.P. Mng. Editors Assn., Seattle, 1959, Clarke Coll., 1953, State U. Ia., 1963, Am. Soc. Newspaper Editors Conv., Washington, 1963, State U. Ia., 1966. Bd. dirs. Polk County Mental Health Center; dir. Des Moines Child Guidance Center, 1949-54, St. Joseph Acad. Guild, 1954-57; mem. acquisition com. Des Moines Art Center, 1960-63. Mem. Authors League Am., Am. Assn. U. Women, League Women Voters, Nat. Audubon Soc., Ia. Ornithol. Union, Theta Sigma Phi. Roman Catholic. Home: 231 42d St Des Moines IA 50312

EYERMAN, ROBERT ALEXANDER, architect; b. Wilkes-Barre, Pa., May 25, 1908; s. Edward and Josephine E. (Firstenfeldt) E.; B.Arch., Cornell U., 1933; m. Alice Gardner Hopkins, Aug. 31, 1932; 1 dau., Jean G. (Mrs. Albert A. Prushinski). Sr. partner Eyerman-Csala & Assos., Wilkes-Barre, 1935—; pres., treas. Bear Creek Realty, Inc., Wilkes-Barre, 1952—; prin. works include indsl. and office bldgs. Wise Potato Chip Co., Berwick, Pa., 1950-61, Eberhard Faber Pencil Co., Wilkes-Barre, 1957-63, chapel VA Hosp., Wilkes-Barre, 1958, terminal bldg. Wilkes-Barre-Scranton Airport, Avoca, Pa., 1959, YWCA Bldg., Wilkes-Barre, 1961, office and studio WNEP-TV, Avoca, Pa., 1963. Pres. Pa. Bd. Examiners Architects 1957—; sec. Wilkes-Barre City Bldg. Code Com., 1950—; mem. Wilkes-Barre City Art Jury, 1936—. Trustee Wilkes-Barre YWCA; bd. dirs. Wilkes-Barre Children's Service Bur. Fellow A.I.A.; mem. Pa. Soc. Architects (past pres.), Jr. Chamber Internat. (Life; senator), Delta Tau Delta. Lutheran. Home: Bear Creek PA 18602 Office: 54 Public Sq Wilkes-Barre PA 18602

EYES, RAYMOND, magazine publisher; b. New Bedford, Mass.; s. Joseph Chester and Florence (Morgan) E.; B.A., U. Conn.; m. Anne Coleman, Dec. 27, 1947; children—Peter, Virginia, David, Edward. Engaged Advt. sales N.Y. News, 1950-53, Advt. Agy. mag., 1953-54; with McCall Corp., 1954—, now pub. McCall's mag. Bd. dirs. Day Care and Child Devel. Council Am. Served with AUS, 1944-46. Mem. New Eng. Soc. Club: Cedar Point Yacht (Westport). Home: 4 Orchard Lane Westport CT 06880 Office: 230 Park Av New York City NY 10017

EYESTONE, SHIRLEY FREDERICK, mfg. co. exec.; b. Newton, Kan., Nov. 23, 1919; s. Shirley Deming and Ruth Mildred (Guinty) E.; B.S. in Elec. Engring., Kan. State U., Manhattan, 1941; student U. Cal. at Los Angeles, 1946-55; m. Mona Marie Jones, May 29, 1941; 1 dau., Sheri Lynne (Mrs. Warren Emley III). With Gen. Electric Co., 1941; with N. Am. Aviation, Inc. (now N. Am. Rockwell Inc.), 1946-70, pres. autonetics div., 1967-70; v.p. internat. group Varian Assos., Palo Alto, Cal., 1970—. Served to 1st lt. USAAF, 1941-46. Recipient Meritorious Pub. Service citation USN, 1961; Distinguished Service award in engring. Kan. State U., 1961. Mem. Am. Inst. Aero. and Astronautics, Air Force Assn., Armed Forces Communication and Electronics Assn., Assn. U.S. Army, Inst. Navigation. Am. Ordnance Assn., I.E.E.E., Blue Key, Scabbard and

Blade, Steel Ring, Kappa Sigma, Sigma Tau, Pi Mu Epsilon, Eta Kappa Nu, Phi Kappa Phi. Home: 14930 Mar Vista St Whittier CA 90605 Office: 611 Hansen Way Palo Alto CA 94303

EYLER, WILLIAM ROSS, physician; b. Van Wert, O., Apr. 13, 1918; s. William H. and Florence (Ross) E.; A.B., Harvard, 1939, M.D., 1943; m. Freda Warner, June 13, 1942; children—Lee, Ross, Steven, James, Ann. Successively intern, resident physician, staff radiologist Mass. Gen. Hosp., Boston, 1943-52; asst. clin. prof. radiology U. Ill. Med. Sch., 1952-53; radiologist Henry Ford Hosp., Detroit, 1953—, chmn. dept., 1955—. Served to capt., M.C., AUS, 1944-46; ETO. Fellow Am. Coll. Radiology; mem. Detroit (pres. 1961-62), Am. Roentgen ray socs., Radiol. Soc. N. Am., Detroit Med. Club, A.M.A. Editor: Radiology, 1966-. Office: 2799 W Grand Blvd Detroit MI 48202

EYNON, DAVID LLOYD, Jr., mfg. co. exec.; b. Paterson, N.J., May 31, 1909; s. David Lloyd and Elizabeth (Sidebotham) E.; grad. Hotchkiss Sch., Lakeville, Conn., 1927; A.B., Williams Coll., 1931; M.S., Mass Inst. Tech., 1933; m. Grace Thomas Voyle, Sept. 15, 1934 (dec. Sept. 1970); children—Jane (Mrs. William S. Boesch), David Lloyd III, Lucy Voyle; m. 2d, Anneli U. Simpson, May 31, 1971. With Monsanto Chem. Co., 1933-54, prodn. mgr., asst. to gen. mgr., St. Louis, 1947-54; pres. Mobay Chem. Co., St. Louis, 1954-58; with Koppers Co., Inc., 1958—, gen. mgr. plastics div., 1958-62, v.p. corp. growth planning, 1962-70, v.p. environmental resources, 1970—. Chmn. High Explosives Industry Integration Com., 1944. Mem. Am. Inst. Chem. Engrs., Theta Delta Chi. Clubs: Duquesne (Pitts.); Allegheny Country (Sewickley). Home: 306 Sycamore Rd Edgeworth Sewickley PA 15143 Office: Koppers Bldg Pittsburgh PA 15219

EYRE, JOHN DOUGLAS, educator; b. Silverside, Del., Jan. 19, 1922; s. James K. and Clara (Wallace) E.; A.B., U. Mich., 1945, M.A., 1947, Ph.D., 1951; m. Olga Yobs, May 10, 1945; children—Eric D., Alex J., Katherine I. Mem. faculty U. Wash., 1951-57; mem. faculty U. N.C., Chapel Hill, 1957—, prof., chmn. dept. geography, 1962-67, coodinator for internat. studies, 1970—; mem. faculty U. Mich., summer 1952, Mich. State U., summer 1957. Served with AUS, 1942-46. Recipient grants Ford Found., 1953, Social Sci. Research Council, 1950; Fulbright research fellow Kyoto (Japan) U., 1965-66. Mem. Am. Geog. Soc., Assn. Am. Geographers, Assn. for Asian Studies. Field research, Japan, 1950- 51, 53-54, 58, 61, Contbr. articles profl. jours. Home: 619 E Franklin St Chapel Hill NC 27514

EYRING, ANTHONY IVINS, banker; b. Colonia Juarez, Chihuahua, Mexico, Oct. 30, 1905 (parents Am. citizens); s. Edward C. and Emma (Romney) E.; B.S., Brigham Young U., 1930; M.B.A., N.Y. U., 1931; m. Lois Rockhill, Mar. 16, 1927; 1 dau., Suzanne (Mrs. James R. Dixon); m. 2d, Janet Wornham Obee, Mar. 13, 1954; adopted childrenJohn Gary, Dennis Rodney, Thomas Ralph, Deborah Ann. With Chase Manhattan Bank, N.Y., 1930-63, v.p., 1959-63; pres. Wash. Mut. Savs. Bank, Seattle, 1963—, also trustee; dir., chmn. exec. com. KIRO, Inc., Seattle, 1963—; dir., mem. exec. com., investment com. Pacific Nat. Bank Wash.; dir. Thrift Pubs., Inc. Northwestern Mut. Ins. Co., Unigard Ins. Co., United Community Antenna System, Inc.; corporator Mt. McKinley Mut. Savs. Bank, Treas. Citizens Com. Wash. Cts., 1967—; chmn. Seattle Parking Commn., 1969—. Trustee Virginia Mason Hosp., 1966—, Seattle Symphony Orch., 1964—, Seattle World Trade Center, 1965—, Wash. Internat. Trade Fair, 1965—, Pacific Sci. Center, 1970—; treas. Seattle Found., 1970—; dir. Mut. Savs. Found. Am. 1969—; trustee, mem. exec. com. Central Assn. Seattle, 1963—, pres., 1966-67; mem. exec. bd., chmn. long range finance com. Chief Seattle council Boy Scouts Am., 1963—. Mem. Mut. Savs. Bank Assn. Wash. (pres. 1968-70), Nat. Assn. Mut. Savs. Banks (dir., mem. exec. com.), Wash. Bankers Assn., Seattle C. of C. (trustee), Indsl. Conf. Bd. (trustee). Republican. Mem. Ch. of Jesus Christ of Latter Day Saints. Clubs: Rainier, Metropolitan Diners (Seattle). Home: 5230 E Mercer Way Mercer Island WA 98040 Office: 1101 2d Av Seattle WA 98101

EYRING, HENRY, retired educator; b. Colonia Juarez, Mexico, Feb. 20, 1901; s. Edward Christian and Caroline (Romney) E.; came to U.S., 1912, naturalized, 1935; B.S., U. Ariz., 1923, M.S., 1924; Ph.D., U. Cal., 1927; postgrad. U. Berlin, 1929-30; D.Sc., U.. Utah, 1952, Northwestern U., 1953, Princeton, 1956, Seoul (Korea) Nat. U., 1963, Brigham Young U., 1965, Western Res. U., 1966, Denison U., 1967, Marquette U., 1969, Notre Dame U., 1969; LL.D., Ind. Central Coll., 1964; m. Mildred Bennion, Aug. 25, 1928; children—Edward Marcus, Henry Bennion, Harden Romney. Instr. U. Ariz. 1924-25; teaching fellow, U. Cal., 1925-27; instr. U. Wis., 1927-28, research asso., 1928-29; lectr. U. Cal., 1930-31; research asso. Princeton, 1931-36, asso. prof., 1935-38, prof. 1938-46; dean Grad. Sch., U. Utah, 1946-67; dir. fundamental research Textile Found., Textile Research Inst., 1944-46. Recipient scholarship NRC, 1929- 30; 9th annual prize A.A.A.S., 1932; plaque and honorarium Research Corp., 1949; Gibbs medal Chgo. sect. Am. Chem. Soc., 1968; Irving Langmuir award chem. physics Gen. Electric Found., 1968; Nat. Medal Sci., 1966; Madison Marshall award, 1968. Mem. Am. Acad. Arts and Scis., Nat. Acad. Scis., Am. Philos. Soc., Am. Chem. Soc. (dir. 6th dist., 1949-51, pres., 1962, Peter Debye award 1964), Nat. Sci. Bd., A.A.A.S. (dir., past pres.). Republican. Mem. Church of Jesus Christ of Latter-Day Saints. Author: Theory of Rate Processes (with Glasstone and K. J. Laidler), 1941; Quantum Chemistry (with J. Walter and G. E. Kimball), 1944; (with Frank H. Johnson and Milton J. Polissar) Kinetic Basis of Molecular Biology, 1954; (with Edward M. Eyring) Modern Chemical Kinetics, 1963; (with others) Statistical Mechanics and Dynamics; also articles. Editor Ann. Rev. Phys. Chemistry. Home: 2037 Herbert Av Salt Lake City UT 84105

EYRING, LEROY, chemist, educator; b. Pima, Ariz. Dec. 26, 1919; s. Edward Christian and Emma (Romney) E.; B.S., U. Ariz., 1943; Ph.D., U. Cal. at Berkeley, 1949; m. Ruth LaReal Patton, July 21, 1941; children—Michelle, Patricia, Cynthia, Gregory. Asst. prof., then asso. prof. State U. Ia., 1949-61; prof. chemistry Ariz. State U., 1961—, chmn. dept., 1961-69; spl. 7 postdoctoral Gottingen, Imperial Coll., and U. Stockholm, 1958-59; Guggenheim fellow, also Fulbright Hays Program awardee, U. Melbourne (Australia), 1959-60. Served with USNR, 1944-46. Mem. Am. Chem. Soc., A.A.A.S., Ariz. Acad. Sci., Phi Beta Kappa, Sigma Xi, Phi Kappa Phi, Phi Lambda Upsilon, Pi Mu Epsilon. Mem. Ch. Jesus Christ of Latter Day Saints (missionary 1939- 41). Editor: Progress in the Science and Technology of the Rare Earths, vol. I, 1964, vol. II, 1966, vol. III, 1967; Advances in High Temperature Chemistry, vol. I, 1967, vol. II, 1969; Rare Earth Research III, 1965; The Chemistry of Extended Defects In Non-Metallic Solids (with M. O'Keefe), 1970. Mem. editorial adv. bds. Jour. Solid State Chemistry, Progress In Solid State Chemistry, Jour High Temperature Sci. Contbr. articles sci. publs. Home: 6995 E Jackrabbit Rd Scottsdale AZ 85253

EYSENCK, HANS JURGEN, educator, psychologist; b. 1916; ed. univs. Dijon, Exeter and London. Research psychologist Mill Hill Emergency Hosp., 1942-45; psychologist Maudsley Hosp., 1945; reader, dir. psychol. dept. Inst. Psychiatry, U. London, 1950-55, prof. psychology, 1955—. Author: Dimensions of Personality, 1947; The Scientific Study of Personality, 1952; The Structure of Human Personality, 1953; The Psychology of Politics, 1954; The Dynamics of Anxiety and Hysteria, 1957; Perpetual Processes and Mental Illness, 1957; Manual for the Maudsley Personality Inventory, 1959; Handbook of Abnormal Psychology, 1960; Experiments in Personality, 1960; Manual for the Eysenck Personality Inventory, 1963; Crime and Personality, 1964; Experiments in Motivation, 1964; Causes and Cures of Neurosis, 1965; Experiments in Behavior Therapy, 1965; Fact and Fiction in Psychology, 1965; Smoking, Health and Personality, 1965; Check Your Own I.Q., 1966; The Structure and Measurement of Personality, 1969, many others. Address: Inst Psychiatry Maudsley Hosp Denmark Hill London SE England*

EYSKENS, GASTON, prime minister of Belgium; b. Lierre, Apr. 1, 1905; s. Antoine and Marie (Vaeten) E.; M.S., Columbia, 1927, LL.D.; D.C.S., U. Louvain, 1930, D.Polit. and Social Sci., 1931, Licencie en sciences economiques, 1930; Dr. Econs. (hon.), U. Cologne; m. Gilberte de Petter, Aug. 1931; children—Marc, Eric. Charge de cours U. Louvain, 1931, prof. polit. economy and pub. finance, 1934; chief of cabinet Minister of Labor, Belgian Govt., 1934-35, mem. Superior Council of Finance, 1936; counsellor Ministry Econ. Affairs, 1937; mem. Parliament, 1939—, minister of finance, 1945, 72—; gov. Internat. Bank for Reconstruction and devel., 1947; prime minister of Belgium, 1949-50, 58- 63; minister econ. affairs, 1950; v.p. ECOSOC, 1951; minister of state Belgium, 1963—, minister of finance 1965-66, now prime minister; former dean faculty econ. and social sci. U. Louvain. Mem. Royal Acad. of Belgium, Royal Flemish Acad. of Sci. Author. Le Port de New York dans son role economique, 1929; De Arbeider en de Bedrijfsleiding in Amerika, 1931; Beschouwingen van de Oorzaken van de Crisis in de Wereld economie, 1932; Les indices de la Conjoncture economique due Congo Belge depuise la Guerre, 1933; Vlaamsche Volkskracht van heden, 1939; Les Finances Publiques Belges dupuis la LibNeration, 1955; also articles in Belgian, Dutch or French sci. revs. on subjects of economics and sociology. Home: rue de Namur 60 Louvain Belgium

EYSSELL, GUSTAV S., real estate cons.; b. Kansas City, Mo., Nov. 6, 1901; s. William and Louise (Sauer) E.; student pub. schs. Kansas City; LL.D., Tusculum Coll. Greenville, Tenn.,1959; m. Mercedes Bergmann, Jan. 30, 1954. Treas. mgr. various local theatres, Kansas City, 1918-25; mgr. Paramount's Million Dollar Theatre, Los Angeles, 1925-27; Los Angeles mgr. Paramount Pulbix, 1927-30; Paramount dist. mgr. theatres San Antonio, Dallas and Houston, 1930-31; city mgr. charge Paramount, Rialto, Rivoli and Bklyn. Paramount theatres, 1931-33; joined exec. staff Radio City Music Hall, 1933, sec. Radio City Music Hall Corp., 1934-42; pres., mng. dir. Radio City Music Hall, mng. dir. Center Theatre, dir. Rockefeller Center, Inc., 1942; exec. mgr. Rockefeller Center, Inc., 1948, exec. v.p., 1949, pres. 1951-71; chmn. bd. Radio City Music Hall, 1951-70; former pres., dir. Rock- Time, Inc.; now real estate cons. Trustee Colonial Williamsburg Found. (Va.), Roosevelt Hosp., N.Y.C.; pres. Av. Ams. Assn.; exec. com. N.Y. Conv. and Visitors Bur.; bd. dirs. Rockefeller Center, Inc., 1942-70. Mem. Real Estate Bd. of N.Y. Trustee Ednl. Broadcasting Corp.; mem. bd. Inter-Racial Council for Bus. Opportunities. Mem. UN Assn. U.S.A. (dir.). Presbyn. (elder, pres. bd. trustees). Mason. Clubs: The Links, The Pilgrims (N.Y.C.); Metropolitan; Westchester Country (past pres.) (Rye, N.Y.) Home: 935 Park Av New York City NY 10028 Office: 630 Fifth Av New York City NY 10020

EYSTER, ELVIN S., bus. educator; b. nr. Angola, Ind., June 20, 1902; s. Arlow and Cora Mae (Shaffer) E.; B.C.S., Tri-State Coll., Angola, Ind., 1921; B.S., Ind. U., 1926, M.S. 1931, Ed.D., 1945; student intermittently, U. Chgo., 1932-34; m. Artista Beryl Diffendorfer, June 25, 1927. Teacher and head of bus. dept., Fort Wayne (Ind.) City Schs., 1923-40, dir. guidance, 1937-40; lecturer in accounting, extension div., Ind. Univ., 1927-40, visiting instr., sch. edn., summers, 1939-40, prof. bus. adminstrn. Grad. Sch. Bus., 1941—, prof. bus. edn. Grad. Sch. and Sch. Edn., 1941—, chmn. dept. bus. edn. and officer adminstrn., 1941-67, dir. Center for Edn. for Office Administrn., Lembaga Administrasi, Negara-Ford Found., Djakarta, 1963-67. Dir. U.S.N.T.S. for yeoman and storekeepers, 1942-44; spl. agt., research in bus. edn., U.S. Office of Edn., Washington, 1941. Chmn. joint publication commn. of Eastern Bus. Teachers Assn. and Nat. Bus. Teachers Assn., 1941-48; chmn. Associated Orgn. for Tchr. Edn. 1959-61. Recipient Distinguished Alumni award Tri- State Coll., 1959; John Robert Gregg Award, 1956. Mem. Internat. Soc. Bus. Edn., Nat. Bus. Teachers Assn. (pres. 1941), Nat. Assn. Bus. Teacher Training Instns. (pres. 1947), Nat. Assn. for Bus. Tchr. Edn. (chmn. com. on guidelines for bus. tchr. edn. 1968-69), Northeaster Ind. Teachers Assn. (pres. 1927), Nat. Office Management Assn., Phi Delta Kappa, Beta Gamma Sigma, Delta Pi Epsilon (nat. pres., 1948-50). Independent, Methodist. Mason (Scottish rite). Club: Rotary. Author: (with W. Harmon Wilson) Consumer Economic Problems, 3d-7th edits., (with W. Harmon Wilson, Roman Warmke, Eugene D. Wyllie) 8th edit., 1971. Editorial adv. bd. Jour. Bus. Edn., 1952—. Home: 310 Pleasant Ridge Rd Route 12 Box 3 Bloomington IN 47401

EYZAGUIRRE, CARLOS EDWARDS, educator, neurophysiologist; b. Santiago, Chile, Apr. 28, 1923; s. Carlos Gormaz and Ines (Edwards) E.; B.A., U. Chile, 1940, M.D., 1947; m. Elena Fontaine, Aug. 31, 1947; children—Carlos A., Elena M., Rodrigo J. Came to U.S., 1957. Mem. faculty Cath. U. Chile, Santiago, 1942-47, 50-52, asso. prof. neurophysiology, 1952-57; fellow Johns Hopkins, 1947-48, Emanuel Libman fellow, 1948-50, fellow Wilmer Inst., John S. Guggenheim Meml. Found. fellow, 1953-55; lectr. physiology Tchrs.'s Coll., U. Chile, 1951-53; asst. research prof. physiology U. Utah Coll. Medicine, Salt Lake City, 1957-59, asso. prof., 1959-62, prof., 1962—, chmn. dept., 1964—. Spl. cons. USPHS neurol. scis. research tng. Com., 1966-69. Recipient USPHS Research Career Devel. award, 1964. USPHS Sr. Research fellow, 1959-64. Mem. Am. Physiol. Soc., Biol. Soc. Santiago, Biol. Soc. Montavideo (hon.). Research, publs. in physiology of nervous system, physiology receptors and chemoreceptors, initiation of impulses in these areas. Home: 2217 Laird Way Salt Lake City UT 84108

EZEKIEL, WALTER NAPHTALI, research microbiologist; b. Richmond, Va., Apr. 26, 1901; s. Jacob Levy and Rachel (Brill) E.; B.S., U. Md., 1920, M.S., 1921, Ph.D., 1924; postgrad U.S. Dept. Agr. Grad. Sch., 1922-24; NRC fellow, U. Minn., 1925-27; m. Sarah Ritzen, Feb. 15, 1926; children—Herbert M., David H., Joseph L., Raphael S., Miriam (Mrs. Joseph E. Bernhardt). Asst. plant pathologist Md. Agrl. Expt. Sta., 1920-25; agt. Bur. Plant Industry, 1927-28; plant pathologist Tex. Agrl. Expt. Sta., also mem. grad. faculty Tex. A. and M. U., 1928-44; Prin. mycologist Naval Ordnance Lab., Silver Springs, Md., head mycologist in charge fungus and moisture proofing program Bur. Ordnance, Navy Dept., 1946-53, Bur. Yards and Docks, 1953-54; tech. reports officer Bur. Mines, 1955-56, technologist (microbiology), 1956-64; microbiologist Bur. Mines Research Center, College Park, Md., 1964-69, research microbiologist health div., coal mine health and safety, 1969-71. Mem. Va. Capital Bicentennial Commn., 1938; Trustee United Jewish Appeal of Greater Washington, chmn. Brazos County, Tex., 1940-44, vice chmn. Navy Dept., 1946-54, chmn. Interior Dept., 1957-64, exec. com. bd. dirs., vice chmn. govt. div., 1968—. Recipient Meritorious Civilian Service award with citation Bur. Ordnance, 1946. Fellow A.A.A.S., Tex. Acad. Sci.; mem. Am. Technion Soc. (chmn. Washington chpt. 1947-49), Zionist Orgn. Am., Friends of Hebrew U., Am. Phytopath. Soc., Mycol. Soc. Am., Am. Soc. Microbiology, Am. Inst. Biol. Scis., Cos. Indsl. Microbiology (organizer 1949, bd. dirs. 1952-54, hon. 1963—), Phi Sigma Delta, Sigma Xi. Jewish religion. Research and publs. in field. Editor: Coal Chronicle, 1962-64. Home: 3105 34th St NW Washington DC 20008

EZELL, JOHN SAMUEL, historian; b. Louisville, Mar. 9, 1917; s. Samuel Jones and Grace (Hicks) E.; B.A., Wake Forest Coll., 1938; M.A., Harvard, 1941, Ph.D., 1947; m. Martha Jean McLean, Feb. 17, 1945; childrenJohn McLean, Margaret Jean. Mem. faculty Carnegie Inst. Tech., 1947-48; mem. faculty U. Okla., 1948—, prof. history, 1959-65, chmn. dept., 1962- 65, David Ross Boyd prof. history, 1965—, dean Coll. Arts and Scis., 1965—; summer sch. tchr. Howard Coll., 1947, Wake Forest Coll., 1961. Cons. Pan Am. Petroleum Co., Service Pipe Line Co. Mem. U. adv. council for Inst. Life Ins., 1967—. Mem. Am., So. hist. assns., Orgn. Am. Historians, Phi Beta Kappa, Omicron Delta Kappa. Co-editor: Readings in American History, 2 vols., 3d edit., 1963; Fortune's Merry Wheel: The Lottery in America, 1960; The South Since 1865, 1963. Editor: The New Democracy in America: Travels of Francisco de Miranda in the United States, 1783-84, 1963. Contbr. articles hist. jours., Dictionary Am. Biography. Home: 801 Hoover St Norman OK 73069

EZELL, PAUL HOWARD, educator; b. Wyo., Aug. 12, 1913; B.A., U. Ariz., 1937, M.A., 1939, Ph.D. (Holliday fellow), 1956; married; 2 children. Field supr. archeol. project Works Progress Adminstrn., Ariz., 1939; research anthropologist Pima and Maricopa Indians, 1952—; asst. prof. anthropology San Diego State Coll., 1956-59, asso. prof., 1959-64, prof., 1964—, chmn. dept., 1968—. Research asso. State Mus., Ariz., 1951—; mem. Inter-Am. Inst. Indian Affairs. Served with USNR, 1943-46. Fellow Am. Anthrop. Assn.; mem. Am. Ethnol. Soc., Am. Soc. Archaeology. Author: The Maricopas, Anthropological Papers, 1963; The Aguiar Collection in the Arizona Pioneers Historical Society, 1964; Contbr. articles to profl. jours. Office: Dept Anthropology San Diego State Coll 5402 College Av San Diego CA 92115*

EZELLE, SAM III, labor union exec.; b. Evansville, Ind., July 16, 1920; s. Samuel Wahl and Augusta (Culley) E.; LL.B., Jefferson Law Sch., Louisville, 1948; LL.B., U. Louisville, 1951, J.D., 1969; m. Ruby Layman, Sept. 16, 1939; 1 son, Sam IV; m. 2d, Dorothy Wheatley, Dec. 16, 1967; children—Kent, Dale. Structural ironworker, 1941-46; dir. dept. research and edn. Ky. Fedn. Labor, 1946-52, exec. sec., 1952-58; exec. sec. Ky. AFL-CIO, 1958—; sec.-treas. Ky. Labor News, Inc., 1952—. Labor edn. specialist Mut. Security Agy., 1952; mem. Ky. Atomic Energy Commn., 1961—, U.S. Labor-Mgmt. Manpower Com., 1956—. Bd. regents Western State Coll., Bowling Green, Ky., 1957-59; trustee U. Ky., 1960-68. Served with USAAF, 1942-43. Democrat. Home: 2422 Dundee Rd Louisville KY 40205 Office: 706 E Broadway Louisville KY 40202

FAAS, HORST, photographer; b. Berlin, Germany, Apr. 28, 1933; s. Adalbert and Gerda (Schulze) F.; student Munich U.; m. Ursula Gerienne, May 22, 1964. Photographer, Keystone Photo Agy., Frankfurt, Berlin, Duesseldorf, 1951-55; photographer A.P., Bonn, Germany, 1955-60, Congo, 1960-62, Algeria, 1962, S.E. Asia, 1962, Vietnam, 1962—. Recipient citations Overseas Press Club, 1963, 64, Robert Capa award Overseas Press Club, 1965, Pulitzer prize, 1965, Asso. Press Mng. Editors award, 1965; Spl. Recognition award Nat. Press Photographers Assn., 1964, 65; George Polk Meml. award, 1967; Nat. Headliners award for photography, 1967; Sigma Delta Chi award for photography, 1970; Silver Medal award World Photo Contest Newspotography, 1970. Home: 31 Oxley Garden Singapore 9 Singapore Office: A P Rockefeller Plaza New York City NY 10020

FABENS, HENRY BRUCE, mfg. co. exec.; b. Wooster, O., Jan. 12, 1924; s. Andrew Lawrie and Rae (Wyse) F.; B.S., Mass. Inst. Tech., 1944; M.B.A., Harvard, 1948; m. Ann Caldwell, July 17, 1948; children—Bruce C., Elizabeth L., Rachel W., Frank B. With Lamson & Sessions Co., Cleve., 1948—, corporate sec., 1962-68, v.p., controller, 1968, v.p. finance, treas., 1968—; dir. Truline Bearing Co., Truline Casting Co. Served with USNR, 1944-46. Mem. Chi Phi, Tau Beta Pi. Episcopalian. Clubs: Union, Mayfield Country (Cleve.); Mentor (O.) Harbor Yachting; Huron (O.) Yacht. Home: 16600 S Woodland Rd Shaker Heights OH 44120 Office: 5000 Tiedemon Rd Cleveland OH 44144

FABER, JOHN EDGAR, Jr., educator; b. Highspine, Pa., Jan. 13, 1903; s. John E. and Anna (Parker) F.; B.S., U. Md., 1926, M.S., 1927, Ph.D., 1937; m. Olyure Hammack, 1929. Instr., U. Md., 1927-37, asst. prof., 1937-45, asso. prof., 1945- 46, prof. and head dept. microbiology, now prof. emeritus, lectr. Named to Lacrosse Hall of Fame. Fellow can Am. Pub. Health Assn.; mem. A.A.A.S., Washington Acad. Scis., Soc. Am. Bacteriologists, Sigma Xi, Alpha Zeta, Omicron Delta Kappa, Delta Sigma Phi. Author sci. articles. Home: 6900 Wake Forest Dr Calvert Hills MD 20740

FABER, JULIA TAYLOR, former mfg. co. exec.; b. Plainfield, N.J., Mar. 4, 1900; d. Duncan Warren and Alice (Cady) Taylor; B.A., Smith Coll., 1922; student Columbia, 2 yrs.; m. Eberhard Lothar Faber, June 24, 1922; children—Theo (Mrs. S. Albert Lumia), Eberhard Lothar IV. Vice pres. pub. relations Eberhard Faber Inc., 1953-65, chmn. bd., 1965-71, also dir. Chmn. Anthracite br. Cystic Fibrosis Soc., 1965; mem. area com. of Pocono Art Center. Trustee Wilkes Coll.; bd. dirs. Wilkes-Barre Philharmonic Soc. Named Woman of Year, Misericordia Coll., 1962. Mem. Greater Wilkes-Barre C. of C. Home: Bear Creek PA 18602

FABER, PAUL LOUIS, internat. civil servant; b. Farecariah, Guinea, Dec. 18, 1924; s. Michel and Jeanne (Katty) F.; Degree in Law with honors, Faculté de Droit et de Sciences Économiques de Lyon (France), 1947, Dr.'s Degree in Polit. Economy cum laude, 1948, Dr.'s Degree in Pvt. Law cum laude, 1949; Dr.'s Degree in Econs. cum laude, 1954; post-doctoral study Faculté de Sciences Economiques de Paris, 1967; m. Dienabou Diallo; children—Eva Janine, Hortense Isabelle, Lydie Solange, Michel Yves, Maria Eliza. Admitted to bar, 1948, practiced until 1958; atty. gen. Republic of Guinea, 1958-61; minister of justice Republic of Guinea, 1961-63; resident minister for Guinea in Ghana, 1963-64; alternate exec. dir., later exec. dir. IMF, 1964-68; dir. div. pub. finance and financial instns. UN, 1968—. 1st arbitrator for Republic Guinea for Internat. Center for Settlement Investment Disputes, 1969—. Created companion Independence of Guinea. Mem. Assn. Democratic Jurists (v.p. 1960), Organization Afro-Asian Jurists (acting sec.-gen., joint pres. 1962). Contbr. articles, reports in field. Home: 250 E 87th St New York City NY 10028 Office: UN Plaza New York City NY 10017

FABER, WALTER O., paper products mfg. exec. Pres., Dairypak, Cleve. Office: PO Box 9245 Cleveland OH 44138*

FABIAN, FRANCIS GORDON, Jr., corp. exec.; b. Evanston, Ill., Jan. 25, 1915; s. Francis G. and Dorothy (Gardner) F.; grad. cum laude, Choate Sch., 1933; B.S. in Indsl. Engring., Yale, 1937; m. Gretchen Hauschild, Oct. 1, 1938; children—Richard G., Jennifer C. Asst. to v.p. engring. and mfg., chief design engr. Lindsay Corp.,

Chgo., 1946-48, v.p., 1949-50; asso. and bus. planning mgr. Booz Allen Hamilton, 1950-53, asst. to gen. mgr. Dresser Mfg. div. Dresser Industries, 1953-55, gen. mgr., 1955-58, pres., 1958-60, exec. v.p. parent co., Dallas, 1960-62, pres., dir., mem. exec. com., 1962-65; pres., dir. finance com. Hunt Food Industries, Inc., Fullerton, Cal., 1965-66; chmn. pres. For Better Living Inc., Laguna Niguel, 1966—. Home: 43 Monarch Bay South Laguna CA Office: 27665 Forbes Rd Laguna Niguel CA 92677

FABIAN, HAROLD PEGRAM, lawyer; b. Salt Lake City, Mar. 1, 1885; s. Ferinand John and Minnie (Pegram) F.; student Mercersburg (Pa.) Acad.; A.B., Yale, 1907; LL.B., Harvard, 1910; LL.D., U. Utah, 1969; m. Ruth Chapman, Oct. 19, 1910; children—Ruth P., Ferdinand J. II.; m. 2d, Josephine Cunningham, Feb. 14, 1938. Admitted to Utah bar, 1910, and began practice at Salt Lake City; mem. firm Dey, Hoppaugh & Fabian, 1910- 17, Bagley, Fabian, Clendenin & Judd, 1919-23, now Fabian & Clendenin; pres. Rocky Mountain Packing Corp., 1934-45; exec. v.p., treas., trustee Jackson Hole Preserve, Inc., to 1954, now trustee; pres. and dir. Grant Teton Lodge & Transp. Co., 1946-52, exec. v.p., gen. mgr. dir., 1952-54; treas., trustee Jackson Hole Wild Life Park, 1946-52. Pres. Travelers Aid Soc., Salt Lake City, 1957-58; mem. Utah Pony Express Commn., 1959-60; v.p. trustee Nauvoo Restoration, Inc. Trustee St. Johns Hosp., Jackson, Wyo., 1963- 66; mem. trustee Utah Heritage Found. Chmn. Nat. Parks adv. bd., 1962-64; mem. of the bd. and pres. Sugarhouse Park Authority, Salt Lake City. Capt., maj. inf. U.S. Army, World War I. Del. Republican Nat. Conv., 1920; mem. Rep. Nat. Com., 1928-32; del.-at-large Rep. Nat. Conv. at Phila., 1940. Vice-pres. Bd. of Edn., Salt Lake City, 1920-26; mem. nat. adv. com. N.Y. World's Fair, 1939; organizer Citizens Def. Corps, Salt Lake City, comdr., 1941-42; mem. Utah Park and Recreation Commn. (pres. 1957-66). Recipient Forestry Conservation award Utah Foresters, 1958; Outstanding Service award Utah Recreation and Parks Assn., 1958; Pugsley medal Am. Scenic and Historic and Preservation Soc., 1964; Outstanding Conservation Service award plaque from Gov. Utah, on Harold P. Fabian Day in Utah, 1967; Service award U.S. Dept. of Interior, 1969. Mem. Am., Utah, Wyo. bar assns., C. of C. (pres. 1930-31 bd. govs.), S.A.R. (pres. 1947-48), Utah Soc. Mayflower Descendants, (gov. 1960-61), Conquistadores del Cielo (hon.), Psi Upsilon. Mason (32). Clubs: Alta, Bonneville (Salt Lake City); Elihu (Yale). Home: 29 S State St Salt Lake City UT 84111 Office: Continental Bank Bldg Salt Lake City UT 84111

FABIANI, ALBERTO, fashion designer; b. Rome, Italy, Nov. 18, 1912; s. Pietro and Vittoria (Tafani) F.; ed. San Giuseppe Sch.; m. Liliana Sambo, Sept. 10, 1941; 1 dau., Maria Cristina; m. 2d, Simonetta Colonna di Cesaro, Dec. 22, 1951; 1 son, Bardo. With Fabianl Fashion House, Rome, 1920—, dir., 1930—; dir. Fabiani Fashion House, Paris, France, 1962-. Home: 5 Via Gregoriana Rome, Italy. Office: Via Condotti II Rome Italy also Rue François 1 40 Paris France

FABIANI, AURELIO, mgr. Phila. Lyric Opera. Address: 1704 Walnut Philadelphia PA 19103*

FABIANI, DANTE CARL, industrialist; b. Waterbury, Conn., Aug. 13, 1917; s. Rosato Francis and Barbara (Poscente) F.; B.S., Tri-State Coll., 1938; student Purdue U., 1942; m. Virginia Parnham, July 15, 1944; childrenBarbara Camille (Mrs. Douglas Hart), James Parnham, Kathryn Louise. Employed with Auburn Rubber Corp. (Ind.), 1938-42, Gen. Electric Co., Ft. Wayne, Ind., 1942-45, Continental Can Co., Van Wert, O., 1945-47; controller, asst. mgr. Standard Products Co., Toledo, 1948-51; dir., sec.-treas. Townsend Co., New Brighton, Pa., 1951-59; v.p. finance H. K. Porter Co., Inc., Pitts., 1959-60; dir., v.p. finance McDonnell Aircraft Corp., St. Louis, 1960; exec. v.p. Crane Co., 1960-61, pres., dir., 1961- -; chmn. bd., dir. C.F.I. Steel Corp., Pueblo, Colo., 1970—; dir. Huttig Sash & Door Co., St. Louis. Republican. Clubs: Burning Tree (Bethesda, Md.); Patterson (Westport, Conn.); Union League (Chgo.). Hemisphere (N.Y.C.). Home: 15 North Av Westport CT 06880 Office: 300 Park Av New York City NY 10022

FABIK, THEODORE JOSEPH, ret. coast guard officer; b. E. St. Louis, Ill., Mar. 13, 1910; s. Anthony James and Theresa (Verzal) F.; B.S., U.S. Coast Guard Acad., 1932; student U.S. Naval Acad. Postgrad. Sch., 1938-40; M.S. in Marine Engring. Design, Mass. Inst. Tech., 1941; m. Jeanette Edna Dunning, June 20, 1934 (dec. Aug. 1963); children—Theresa Jeanette (Mrs. Edward R. Stearns), Elizabeth Lois, (Mrs. B. W. Richardson), David Dunning, Deborah Ellen (Mrs. J. Watts); m. 2d, Margaret W. Mellen, Feb. 4, 1970. Commd. ensign USCG, 1932, advanced through grades to rear adm., 1961; various assignments in cutters, 1932- 38; engring. officer cutter U.S.S. Campbell, 1941-42; assigned Office Navy Supr. and Resident Inspr. Shipbldg., N.Y.C., 1942-44; engring. officer, then exec. officer troop transp. U.S.S. Gen. Meigs, 1944-46; chief naval engring. sect. 1st Coast Guard Dist., Boston, 1946-47; mem. faculty U.S. Coast Guard Acad., 1947-52; exec. officer, then comdg. officer cutter U.S.S. Campbell, 1952-54; chief engring. div. 9th Coast Guard Dist., Cleve., 1954-55, 14th Coast Guard Dist., Honolulu, 1955-58; asst. engr.-in-chief Coast Guard Hdqrs., 1958-61; chief staff 5th Coast Guard Dist., Portsmouth, Va., 1961; comdr. 7th Coast Guard Dist., Miami, Fla., 1961-62; chief Office Engring., Coast Guard Hdqrs., 1962-66; comdr. Western Area, USCG, 1966-67; ret., 1967; now cons. engr. Chmn. Ship Structure Com., 1962—; v.p. Am. council Internat. Inst. Welding, 1962; mem. Merchant Marine Council, 1958—. Mem. Soc. Naval Architects and Marine Engrs., Soc. Am. Mil. Engrs. (bd. dirs.), Am. Soc. Naval Engrs. (council), Newcomen Soc. N. Am., Navy League U.S., Washington Soc. Engrs. , Nat. Sojourners (past chpt. comdr.). Mason. Clubs: Hawaii Yacht, Bohemian. Home: 4709 Moa St Honolulu HI 96816

FABLE, ROBERT COOPER, Jr., lawyer; b. Sellersville, Pa., Dec. 7, 1910; s. Robert C. and Janet E. (Grayson) F.; B.S., Temple U., 1931, LL.B., 1935; m. Ethel Smith Nock, Sept. 4, 1935 (dec. Oct. 1968); 1 dau., Janet Ann, (dec. Mar. 1968); m. 2d, Margaret Siebert Jansky, Feb. 28, 1969. Admitted to Pa. state bar, also U.S. cts., 1935; practiced in Phila., 1935-43; with VA, Washington, 1946-70, legislative atty., asst. dep. adminstr. vets. affairs, 1946-58, dep. gen. counsel, 1958-63, gen. counsel, 1963-70. Served to capt., AUS, 1943-46. Decorated Legion of Merit; recipient Meritorious Service award VA, 1957, Distinguished Career award VA, 1970. Mem. Am., Fed. bar assns., Sigma Phi Epsilon. Conglist. Mason (32). Club: Nat. Lawyers. Home: 2871 N Ocean Blvd Boca Raton FL 33432

FABRAY, NANETTE, actress; b. San Diego, Cal., Oct. 27; d. Racul Bernard and Lillian (McGovern) Fabares; student Los Angeles City Coll.; m. David Tebet, October 26, 1947 (div. July 1951); m. 2d, Ranald MacDougall, 1957; 1 son, Jamie. Appeared as actress in Broadway shows Let's Face It, Meet the People, By Jupiter, Bloomer Girl, High Button Shoes, Arms and the Girls, Love Life, Make A Wish, Mr. President; co-star with Sid Caesar on Caesar's Hour. CBS-TV, 1954-56; motion pictures include Elizabeth and Essex, The Bandwagon, The Happy Ending. Trustee Eugene O'Neill Meml. Found., Nat. Theatre of Deaf; mem. bd., v.p. Nat. Assn. Hearing and Speech Agys.; mem. bd. Pres.'s Nat. Adv. Com. on Edn. Deaf, Pres.'s Com. on Employment Handicapped, Muses of Cal. Mus. Found. Recipient two Donaldson awards for High Button Shoes, 1947; Tony award for Love Life, 1949; Emmy award as best comedienne, 1955, 56, best supporting performer Caesar's Hour, 1955; Eleanor Roosevelt Humanitarian award, 1964; Human Relations award Anti-Defamation League, 1969; 1st ann. Cogswell award Gallaudet Coll., 1970; Pres.'s Distinguished Service award, 1970; named Woman of Year, Radio and TV Editors, 1963, Jewish War Vets. Am., 1969. Home: 14360 Sunset Blvd Pacific Palisades CA 90272

FABRI, RALPH, artist; b. Budapest, Hungary, Apr. 23, 1894; s. Henrik L. and Helen (Fischer) F.; A.B., Royal State Gymnasium, Budapest, 1912; student Royal Inst. Tech., Budapest, 2 years; prof.'s degree. Royal Acad. Fine Arts, Budapest, 1918. Came to U.S. 1921, naturalized, 1927. Asso. prof. Coll. City N.Y., until 1967; rec. sec. Nat. Acad., 1950-53; instr. Nat. Acad. Sch. of Fine Arts. Paintings and etchings exhibited at Nat. Acad., N.Y.C.; Pa. Acad. Fine Arts, Phila.; Art Inst., Chgo. , etc.; one-man shows in N.Y.C., and many other U.S. cities; Budapest, 1946; participated in many internat. exhbns. Works owned by Library of Congress, Met. Mus. Art, N.Y.C., Smithsonian Inst., Honolulu Acad., others. Hon. life pres. of Audubon Artists. Recipient numerous prizes including: Ringius Prize, Hartford, Conn., 1945. Fellow Royal Soc. of Arts, London; mem. Soc. Am. Graphic Artists, Am. Assn. U. Profs., Knickerbocker Artists, Painters and Sculptors Soc. N.J., Am. Watercolor Soc., Nat. Acad. Design (treas. 1962-68), Contemporary Soc. Am. Artists, Nat. Soc. Painters in Casein (hon. life pres.), Allied Artists Am. (v.p.), Authors Guild. Author: Learn to Draw, 1945; Oil Painting, 1966; Color, a Complete Guide for Artists, 1967; Flower Painting, a History of the American Watercolor Society, 1968; Outdoor Painting; Painting Cityscapes, 1969; Artist's Guide to Composition, 1971. Editor Today's Art. Contbr. articles to art mags. Address: 54 W 74th St New York City NY 10023 ☆

FABRICAND, BURTON PAUL, educator, physicist; b. N.Y.C., Nov. 22, 1923; s. Irving Kermit and Frances (Sobler) F.; A.B., Columbia, 1947, A.M., 1949, Ph.D., 1953; m. Prudence Diane Montgomery, Sept. 5, 1952; children—Nicole Diane, Lorraine Stewart. Project engr. Philco Corp., Phila., 1952-54; lectr., research asso. U. Pa., 1954-56; sr. research scientist Columbia Hudson Labs., Dobbs Ferry, N.Y., 1957-69; prof. physics Pratt Inst., Bklyn., 1969—; cons. Moore Sch. Elec. Engring., U. Pa., 1954-60, Indsl. Electronic Hardware Corp., N.Y.C., 1960-64. Mem. Am. Phys. Soc., Sigma Xi. Author: Horse Sense: A New and Rigorous Application of Mathematical Methods to Successful Betting at the Track, 1965; Beating the Street, 1969. Home: 115 Judson Av Dobbs Ferry NY 10522 Office: 215 Ryerson St Brooklyn NY 11205

FABRICANT, SOLOMON, educator, economist; b. Bklyn., Aug. 15, 1906; s. Samuel and Sarah (Plotkin) F.; B.C.S., N.Y.U., 1926; B.S., Coll. City N.Y., 1929; M.A., Columbia, 1930, Ph.D., 1938; m. Bessie Blacksin, Feb. 7, 1934; children—Ruth, Peter, Sarah. Pub. accountant, 1925-29; research staff Nat. Bur. Econ. Research, 1930-53, 65—, dir. reseach, 1953-65; acting dir. requirements coordination div., European regional office UNRRA, 1944-45; lectr. econs. N.Y.U., 1946-47, asso. prof. econs., 1947-48, prof., 1948—; vis. prof. econs. Columbia, 1952. Cons. U.S. Bur. Census, 1945-50, Bur. Budget, 1946-52, NSRB, 1948-49, N.Y. State Tax Commn., 1951-52, U.S. Gen. Accounting Office, 1970—; mem. econ. forum Nat. Indsl. Conf. Bd., 1946- -; research adv. bd. Com. Econ. Development; dep. dir. nonmil. div. program bur. WPB, 1942-44; mem. President's Task Force Sci. Policy, 1969-70, President's Commn. Fed. Statistics, 1970—. Fellow Am. Statis. Assn.; mem. Am. Econ. Assn. (exec. com.), Joint Council Econ. Edn. (trustee), Am. Finance Assn., Am. Philos. Soc., Royal Econ. Soc., Econometric Soc., Econ. History Assn. (trustee), Internat. Assn. Research Income and Wealth (council), Am. Acad. Arts and Scis. Author: Capital Consumption and Adjustment, 1938; Output of Manufacturing Industries, 1940; Employment in Manufacturing, 1942; Trend of Government Activitiy, 1952; Investing in Economic Knowledge 1958; (with Spahr, others) Economic Principles and Problems, 1936; (with Backman, others) War and Defense Economics, 1952; (with others) Studies in Income and Wealth, 1958; The Study of Economic Growth, 1959; (with others) Economic Consequences of the Size of Nations, 1960; (with others) Labor An Economists View of Philantrophy, 1961; (with others) Labor Productivity, 1965; Primer on Productivity, 1969. Home: PO Box 59 South Salem NY 10593 Office: 261 Madison Av New York City NY 10016

FABRIKANT, BENJAMIN, educator; b. N.Y.C., Jan. 4, 1924; s. Samuel and Marcia (Fabryk) F.; student Va. Mil. Inst., 1944-45, Shriveham Am. U., 1945; B.A., Bklyn. Coll., 1948; M.A., Temple U., 1950; Ph.D., U. Buffalo, 1953; postdoctoral Am. U., 1958, L.I.U., 1962; m. Laurine Merriam Zucker, Aug. 28, 1949; children—Craig S., Gary K., Gail L. Psychologist, Topeka State Hosp., 1952-53; psychologist, asst. chief, chief psychol. research VA Hosp., Buffalo, 1953-59; chief psychologist Psychol. Service Center, Teaneck, N.J., 1959-62; mem. faculty Fairleigh Dickinson U., Teaneck, 1962—, prof., dir. clin. programs, 1971—, lectr. Grad. Sch. Orthodontics, 1964—; cons. in field. Bd. trustees North Bergen City YMCA, 1969-70; pres. Fabrikant Family Found. Served with AUS, 1942-45. Diplomate Am. Bd. Profl. Psychology, Am. Bd. Profl. Hypnosis. Fellow Soc. Projective Techniques, Am. Psychol. Assn.; mem. Bergen City (past pres.), N.J. psychol. assns., N.J. Group Psychotherapy Assn. (past pres.), Am. Acad. Psychotherapists, Soc. Clin. Exptl. Hypnosis, Sigma Xi. Author: (with J. Barron, J. Krasner) Psychotherapy, 1971. Asso. editor: New Jersey Psychologist. Contbr. articles profl. jours. Home: 18 Chimney Ridge Ct Westwood NJ 07675

FACCI, DOMENICO, sculptor; b. Hooversville, Pa., Feb., 2, 1916; s. Anthony and Grace (Polimeni) F.; student Roerich Acad., 1933-36; m. Penelope Facci; 1 son, Robert C. Teacher Coll. of City N.Y., 1934, 53-54, Sch. Art League, 1934-35, Nat. City Bank Art Group, 1947, A.T. & T. Art Group, 1948; pvt. classes own studio; instr. carving Craft Students League N.Y., 1966—; one man shows Village Art Center, N.Y.C., 1953, 56, D'Alessio Gallery, 1962-63, also Silvermine Guild, 1958-60; exhibited in group shows with Allied Artists of Am., 1954, Audubon Artists, 1955- -, Am. Graphic Artists Soc., 1955, Silvermine Guild, Norwalk, Conn., 1953—, Nat. Acad. 1936-53, 54, Arthur Brown Shows, 1949-50, Lighthouse Show, also Whitney Mus., 1951, Serigraph Gallery, 1951, A.C.A. Gallery, 1952, John Myers Found. Gallery, 1952-53, Bklyn. Mus., 1953, Pitts. Arts and Crafts Center, 1954-55, Am. Soc. Contemporary Artists yearly; represented in permanent collections Norfolk Mus., 1963; vis. prof. Fla. So. Coll., 1952, 53, 54, 69; instr. sculpture, Ridgewood Art Sch., N.J., 1961-63; tchr. Fair Lawn, N.J., 1967—; commission Am. Eagle, U.S. Pavilion at World's Fair N.Y. Bd. dirs. Artists Equity, Audubon Artists, Inc. Recipient 1st prize ceramic sculpture, 1953, Louisa Robins award, 1954, William Zell award Silvermine Guild of Artists, 1956, Sculpture House award Bklyn. Soc. Artists, 1955, Albert Dorne prize Audubon Artists, 1956, 61, award Am. Soc. Contemporary Artists, 1968, medal Audubon Artists, 1971, numerous other prizes, citations. Mem. Audubon Artists, Am. Soc. Contemporary Artists (pres. Knickerbocker Artsts, Am. Soc. Contemporary Artists (pres. 1961-63), Nat. Sculpture Soc., Silvermine Guild Artists, Painters and Sculptors Soc., Audubon Artists (exec. v.p. 1963-64, 72, pres. 1967-71), N.J., League Present Day Artists, Kappa Pi, Artists Equity (dir. N.Y. chpt.), Sigma Phi Epsilon. Club: Collectors (N.Y.C.). Address: 248 W 14th St New York City NY 10011

FACH, ALBERT W., banker. Vice pres., trust officer Nat. Bank of N.Am., N.Y.C. Office: 44 Wall St New York City NY 10005*

FACIUS, FREDERICK BAUMANN, mfg. co. exec.; b. Middletown, Conn., Dec. 7, 1901; s. Anton R. and Sophie (Grimm) F.; student pub. schs., corr. schs.; m. Theresa C. Krauth, June 15, 1927; children—Joan Ann (Mrs. Joseph Murphy), Mary Ellen (Mrs. Carlos B. Ellis, Jr.), Frederick Baumann, Elizabeth. Pres., treas. F.M. Caulkins Auto Co., Middletown, Conn., 1941—; former chmn. bd. Farmers & Mechanics Savs. Bank; mem. adv. bd., exec. bd. Hartford Nat. Bank, Middletown. Mem. sch. bd., Middletown, 1950-61, Middletown Water Commn., 1951—, charter revision commn., 1962—. Elk, Mason, K.P. Club: Automobile of Hartford (gov.). Home: 27 Berlin St Middletown CT 06457 Office: 493 Main St Middletown CT 06457

FACK, ROBBERT, Netherlands diplomat; b. Amsterdam, The Netherlands, Jan. 1, 1917; s. F.W. and A.C. (Hagendooren) F.; student U. Amsterdam, 1935-37; m. Patricia Henshaw Hawkins, Oct. 6, 1943; children—Julian, James, Jeremy, John. Joined Netherlands Fgn. Service, 1945; attached to Ministry Fgn. Affairs, The Hague, 1945-46, 48-50, 63-70; mem. Permanent Mission to UN, N.Y.C., 1946-48; served in Rome, 1950-54, Canberra, 1954-58, Bonn, 1958-63; ambassador-at-large, 1968-70; permanent rep. to UN, N.Y.C., 1970—. Served with arty., Netherlands Army, Res., 1937-45. Home: 1 Sutton Pl N New York City NY 10022 Office: 711 3d Av New York City NY 10017

FACKLER, BENJAMINE LLOYD, utility co. exec.; b. Meansville, Ga., Oct. 20, 1926; s. Ferris L. and Sallie (Storey) F.; student N. Ga. Coll. at Dahlonega, 1942-44; B.B.A. in Accounting, U. Ga., 1947; m. Patricia Cheney, Oct. 20, 1951; children—Gena Patricia, Carole Lloyd. With Atlanta Gas Light Co. (Ga.), 1947—, asst. treas., asst. sec., 1967-68, treas., 1968—. Served with USNR, 1944-46. Mem. Diabetes Assn. Atlanta (bd.), Systems and Procedures Assn. (bd. dirs. 1963-67), Phi Kappa Phi. Republican. Baptist (deacon, Sun. sch. supt., chmn. coms.). Club: Civitan. Home: 2381 Sagamore Hills Dr Decatur GA 30033 Office: PO Box 4569 235 Peachtree St NE Atlanta GA 30302

FACKLER, JOHN PAUL, Jr., educator, scientist; b. Toledo, July 31, 1934; s. John P. and Ruth (Moehring) F.; student Mass., Inst. Tech., 1952; B.A., Valpraiso U., 1956; Ph.D., Mass. Inst. Tech., 1960; m. Naomi Paula Steege, Sept. 2, 1960; children—Katherine G., Cheryl R., Karla S., John M. Jr. chemist Sun Oil Co., 1953-56; teaching asst. Mass. Inst. Tech., 1956-59, research asso., 1960; asst. prof. U. Cal., 1960-62; asst. prof. Case Inst. Tech., 1962-64; asso. prof. chemistry Case Western Res. U., 1964-69, prof., 1970; vis. prof. U. Cal. at Santa Barbara, 1969; Fulbright lectr., Colombia, 1969; cons. in chemistry Central State U., 1967-69. Dir. Luth. Met. Ministry, 1969—, Recipient Tech. Achievement award Cleve. Tech. Soc., 1971. Mem. Am. Chem. Soc. (councilor), Chem. Soc. London, A.A.A.S., Am. Crystolag. Assn., Sigma Xi, Phi Lambda Upsilon, Phi Delta Theta. Lutheran. Author: Symmetry in Coordination Chemistry, 1971. Contbr. articles profl. jours. Home: 4374 W Anderson Rd South Euclid OH 44121 Office: Case Western Reserve Univ Cleveland OH 44106

FACKLER, WALTER DAVID, economist, educator; b. Aitkin, Minn., Aug. 27, 1921; s. Leonard D. and Ruth (Wanous) F.; A.B. with distinction and spl. honors, George Washington U., 1950; postgrad. Johns Hopkins, 1951-54; m. Hazel Shepardson, May 24, 1951; children—Mark Duval, Neil Evan, Paul Leonard. Accountant, Pub. Service Co. of Ind., 1939-42; asst. prof. econs. George Washington U., Washington, 1950-56, asst. to dean faculties, 1953-56, dir. fgn. service rev. program, 1950-54; instr. polit. economy Johns Hopkins, 1952-54; asst. dir. econ. research dept. U.S. C. of C., Washington, 1956-59; sr. economist Cabinet Com. on Price Stability for Econ. Growth, Washington, 1959-60; asso. prof. bus. econs. U. Chgo. Grad. Sch. Bus., 1960-62, prof., 1962—, asso. dean, 1962-69, acting dean, 1968-69, dir. mgmt. programs, 1970—. Bus. and govt. cons., 1950—; lectr., 1950—. Served to capt. AUS, 1942-46. Decorated Bronze Star. Mem. A.A.A.S., Am. Econ. Assn., Am. Statis. Assn., Phi Beta Kappa. Club: University (Chgo.). Contbr. articles profl. publs. Home: 5811 S Dorchester Av Chicago IL 60637

FACTOR, DAVIS, cosmetic mfr.; b. N.Y., 1902; s. Max, Sr., and Jenny (Cook) F.; m. Anna Spector; 2 daus., 1 son. Chmn. bd. Max Factor & Co. Home: 550 S Beverly Glen Blvd West Los Angeles CA 90024 Office: 1655 N McCadden St Hollywood CA 90028

FACTOR, MAX, Jr., cosmetic chemist; b. St. Louis, Aug. 18, 1904; s. Max and Jenny (Cook) F.; student pub. schs., L.A.; m. Mildred Cohen, Mar. 26, 1933; children—Donald Lee, Mark Barry. Collaborated with Max Factor, Sr., in creation motion picture and soc. make-up 1921-38; joint creator color harmony prin. for cosmetics; dir. make-up studios, mfg. Max Factor, Hollywood, 1938—, also vice chmn. bd. Max Factor & Co., 1968—. Received special award perfecting Panchromatic make-up, Motion Picture Acad. Arts and Sci. Holder patents on TV Make-up, Pan-Cake Make-up. Home: 850 S Beverly Glen Beverly Hills CA 90024 Office: 1655 N McCadden Pl Hollywood CA 90028

FACTOR, TED H., advt. exec.; b. St. Louis, June 15, 1914; s. Nathan and Rose (Heiman) F.; student U. Cal., 1931-33, U. So. Cal., 1933-34; m. Margot Kadel, Oct. 19, 1946; m. 2d, Barbara Currey Wood, July 11, 1965. Fgn. publicity dir. Max Factor & Co., 1934-36; pres. Ted. H. Factor Agy., 1936-54, named changed to Factor-Breyer, Inc., 1951, merged with Doyle Dane Bernbach, Inc., 1954, sr. v.p. charge West Coast operations, 1954, now exec. v.p. West Coast operations, also dir., mem. exec. com.; dir. Econ. Resources Corp. Bd. dirs. So. Cal. Choral Music Assn., founding mem. Center Study Democratic Instns. Named Man of Yr., western states Advt. Agy., 1970. Mem. Am. Assn. Advt. Agys., Tau Delta Phi. Clubs: Beverly Hills Tennis (v.p.), Palm Springs Racquet, World Trade, Cave des Roys. Home: 1374 Laurel Way Beverly Hills CA 90210 Office: 6399 Wilshire Blvd Los Angeles CA 90048

FADELEY, HERBERT JOHN, Jr., banker, lawyer; b. Ambler, Pa., Feb. 14, 1922; s. Herbert John and Jennie Miller (Lewis) F.; B.S. in Commerce, Drexel U., 1946; J.D., Temple U., 1953; postgrad. Stonier Sch. Banking, Rutgers U., 1957; m. Eleanor A. Battafarano, Feb. 8, 1947; children—Herbert John, Brett Duane, Theresa Jane, Scott Lewis. Admitted to U.S. Supreme Ct. bar, 1957; asst. cashier First Nat. Bank, Media, Pa., 1951; v.p. Boardwalk Nat. Bank, Atlantic City, 1957-60, Indsl. Trust Co., Phila., 1960-62; v.p., trust officer County Trust Co., White Plains, N.Y., 1963-68; pres. Troy Savs. Bank (N.Y.), 1969—, also trustee. Lectr. banking and law Drexel U., 1962, Rockland Community Coll., Suffern, N.Y., 1964-68, Westchester County chpt. Am. Inst. Banking, 1965-68, Hudson Valley Community Coll., Troy 1970; vice chmn. Capital Dist. Post Vietnam Planning Com. Vice-chmn. dist. council Boy Scouts Am., 1969—; chmn. Rensselaer County Am. Cancer Fund Crusade, 1970-71, also treas., dir. Cancer Soc., 1970; commn. Troy Housing Authority; mem. Troy Zoning Bd. Appeals. mem. Troy Downtown Devel. Council, Tri-county Fifty Group. Bd. dirs. Russell Sage Coll., now treas.; bd. dirs. United Community Services, Soc. Friendly Sons St. Patrick, Mary Warren Free Inst., also v.p.; bd. dirs. Leonard Hosp., Uncle Sam Mall,

Inc., also v.p. Served to lt. (j.g.), USNR, 1942-43, 48-49. Named Outstanding Alumnus, Drexel U., 1961; recipient trust div. sch. awards N.Y. State Banker's Assn., 1967, 68. Mem. Am. Bar Assn., Am. Inst. Mgmt. (mem. pres.'s council Am. Judicature Soc., Assn. U.S. Army, Lambda Chi Alpha, Phi Alpha Delta (named outstanding alumnus 1957, chief justice Dr. Elden S. Magaw Alumni chpt. 1955-56), Greater Troy C. of C. (dir. 1969—, v.p.). Episcopalian. Mason (Shriner), Jester. Clubs: Troy, Country (Troy). Home: 37 Brunswick Rd Troy NY 12180 Office: 32 2d St Troy NY 12180

FADELL, EDWARD RICHARD, educator, mathematician; b. Niagara Falls, N.Y., Mar. 8, 1926; s. Shickery N. and Olga (Sorour) F.; B.A., U. Buffalo, 1948; M.A., Ohio State U., 1950, Ph.D., 1952; m. Patricia Lou Eiselt, June 15, 1953; children—Elizabeth, Richard. Instr., Harvard, 1952-55; mem. faculty U. Wis., 1955—, prof. math., 1962—; mem. Inst. Advanced Study, Princeton, 1964-65. Mem. Math. Assn. Am., Am. Math. Soc. Research papers topology and algebraic topology especially fiber spaces and fixed point theory. Home: 3813 Hillcrest Dr Madison WI 53705

FADENRECHT, JOHN H., educator; b. Windom, Minn., July 14, 1906; s. Ben B. and Helen (Hiebert) F.; A.B., Mayville Tchrs. Coll., 1933; A.M., U. N.D., 1938; Ed.D., U. Colo., 1946; m. Rose L. Loewen, July 26, 1931; 1 son, Robert John (adopted). Tchr., adminstr. pub. schs., N.D., 1929-38; dir. tchr. tng. Tabor Coll., Hillsboro, Kan., 1938-45; grad. asst., coll. edn. U. Colo., 1945-46; dir. tchr. tng. Wheaton (Ill.) Coll., 1946-50, acting dean, 1950-51, dean, 1951-66, chmn. dept. edn., 1966—. Mem. N.E.A., Phi Delta Kappa, Kappa Delta Pi. Mem. Wheaton Bible Ch. Author articles profl. jours. Home: 1002 Howard St Wheaton IL 60187

FADER, JACK, publisher; b. N.Y.C., Apr. 18, 1925; s. Louis and Rachel (Rotenberg) F.; m. Elsie Charnes, Apr. 2, 1949; children—Ann Sherrye, Robin Donna, Lee Hilton. Gen. mgr. Arts mag., N.Y.C., 1955-60, co-owner, 1960-65; publisher Art News, N.Y.C., 1965—. Home: 131-07 225th St Laurelton Queens NY 11413 Office: 444 Madison Av New York City NY 10022

FADIMAN, CLIFTON writer, editor, radio and television entertainer; A.B., Columbia, 1925; m. Annalee Whitmore Fadiman; children—Jonathan, Kim, Anne. Contbr. to numerous magazines, 1924—; editor Simon and Schuster, book pubs., 1929-35; book editor The New Yorker, 1933-43; master of ceremonies on "Information Please" radio program, 1938-48; also Conversation, radio program 1954-57; mem. selecting com. Book-of-the- Month Club; formerly regular essayist Holiday Mag.; cons., mem. guiding faculty Famous Writers Sch.; bd. editors Ency. Brit., 1959—, cons. Ency. Brit. Ednl. Corp., 1963—; Regents lectr. U. Cal. at Los Angeles, 1967. Bd. dirs. Council Basic Edn. Author: Party of One, 1955; Any Number Can Play, 1957; The Lifetime Reading Plan, 1959; Enter Conversing, 1962; Wally the Wordworm, 1964. Editor: The American Treasury, 1955; The Mathematical Magpie, 1962; Dionysus, 1962; Fifty Years, 1965. Asso. editor: Gateway to the Great Books. Address: 345 St Pierre Rd Los Angeles CA 90024

FADNER, FRANK LESLIE, univ. regent; b. Neenah, Wis., Jan. 11, 1910; s. Frank L. and Elizabeth Theresa (Regenfusz) F.; A.B., M.A., Georgetown Coll., 1940; Licenciate in Philosophy, Woodstock Coll., 1939, Th.L., 1943; Ph.D., U. London, 1949. Ordained priest Soc. of Jesus, Roman Cath. Ch., 1943; exec. asst. regent Sch. Fgn. Service, Georgetown U., 1949-55, regent, 1955-61, asso. prof. Russian history, 1949-62, prof. of Russian history, 1962—; regent Inst. Langs. and Linguistics, 1961—. Decorated Fundación Internacional Eloy Alfaro, knight comdr. Orden de Isabel la Catolica; Gran Oficial Al Merito, Peru, 1961. Mem. Am. Cath. Hist. Assn., Am. Hist. Assn., Nat. Fedn. Modern Lang. Tchrs. Assn., U.S. Naval Inst., Jesuit Ednl. Assn. Delta Phi Epsilon, Pi Gamma Mu, Gamma Rho Sigma, Delta Sigma Pi. Author: Seventy Years of Pan-Slavist Thought in Russia, 1800-1870, Karazin to Danilevskii, 1962. Home: Georgetown U 37 and O Sts NW Washington DC 20007

FADUM, HANS RATUS, electric co. exec.; b. Wilkinsburg, Pa., Mar. 27, 1915; s. Torgeir Bleken and Mimmi (Knudsen) F.; B.S., U. Ill., 1938; M.A., Yale, 1945; Ph.D., 1948. Asst. prof. econs. Yale, 1938-42, 45-51; with United Illuminating Co., New Haven, 1950—, sec.-treas., 1965—; dir., mem. exec. com. Conn. Devel. Credit Corp. Vice chmn. City Employees Retirement Bd. Served with USNR, 1942-45. Asso. fellow Saybrook Coll., Yale, 1965. Kiwanian. Clubs: Branford (Conn.) Yacht; Mory's, Graduates (New Haven). Home: 111 Park St New Haven CT 06511 Office: 80 Temple St New Haven CT 06506

FADUM, RALPH EIGIL, univ. dean; Pitts., July 19, 1912; s. Torgeir Bleken and Mimi (Knudsen) F.; B.S. in Civil Engring., U. Ill., 1935; M.S., Harvard, 1937, S.D., 1941; D.Eng., Purdue U., 1963; m. Nancy Isabelle Fields, July 19, 1939; 1 dau., Jane Fields, Parttime asst. civil engring. Harvard, 1935-37, instr., 1937-41, faculty instr., 1941- 43; asst. prof. soil mechanics Purdue U., 1943-45, asso. prof., 1945-47, prof., 1947-49; head of civil engring. dept. and prof. of civil engring. N.C. State U., Raleigh, 1949-62, dean of engring., 1962—; cons. Dept. Def., U.S. Corps Engrs. Mem. sci. adv. panel Dept. Army, 1959—; mem. research adv. com. Fed. Hwy. Adminstrn., 1963—; adv. bd. Ford Found.; vice chmn. Army Sci. Adv. Panel, Dept. Army, 1966-70, chmn. adv. group to comdr. gen., 1967-70. Mem. N.C. Water Control Adv. Council; commr. Raleigh Housing Authority. Chmn. bd. dirs. N.C. Water Resources Research Inst., U. N.C. Registered profl. engr., N.C. Mem. Am. Soc. C.E., U.S. Nat. Council Soil Mechanics and Found. Engring., Nat. Soc. Profl. Engrs., N.C. Soc. Engrs., Raleigh Engrs. Club, Am. Soc. Engring. Edn., Sigma Xi, Tau Beta Pi, Chi Epsilon, Phi Kappa Phi, Delta Upsilon. Clubs: Rotary (Raleigh); Carolina Country. Contbr. articles to profl. jours. Address: 3056 Granville Dr Country Club Hills Raleigh NC

FAEGRE, JOHN BARTHELL, lawyer; b. Flandreau, S.C., Oct. 3, 1889; s. Albert and Sarah Jane (Barthell) F.; A.B., U. Minn., 1911, LL.B., 1913; m. Mary Bohn, Oct. 20, 1910; children—John Barthell, Robert. Admitted to Minn. bar, 1913, and since practiced in Minneapolis; mem. firm Faegre & Benson 1923—; dir. C., R.I. & P. Ry. Co. Mem. bd. dirs., mem. exec. com. Mpls. Found. Mem. Phi Delta Phi, Beta Theta Pi. Republican. Episcopalian. Clubs: Minneapolis, Minikahda (Mpls.); Woodhill Country (Wayzata, Minn.); Chgo. Home: RFD 3 Wayzata MN 55391 Office: Northwestern Bank Bldg Minneapolis MN 55402

FAERBER, LOUIS JOSEPH, educator; b. Pitts., Apr. 6, 1909; s. Louis Joseph and Magdelena (Sturm) F.; B.A., U. Dayton, 1930; M.A. in English, Cath. U. Am., 1938, Ph.D., 1949. Joined Soc. of Mary, Roman Cath. Ch., 1927; head English dept. Cathedral Latin Sch., Cleve., 1933-35; head English dept. Chaminade High Sch., Mineola, N.Y., 1935-37, vice prin. 1938-39, prin., 1939-45; lectr., workshop mem. Cath. U. Am., 1947-48; prof. edn. U. Dayton, 1948-68, asso. dean Coll. Arts and Scis., 1951-60, head div. edn., 1951-60, mem. acad. and adminstrv. councils, 1951-65, dean Sch. Edn., 1960-65; asst. to dean Sch. Edn. charge of office evaluation and research U. Dayton (O.), 1968—; provincial dir. edn. N.Y. Province, Soc. of Mary, 1965-67. Del. gen. chpt. Soc. Mary, Fribourg, Switzerland, 1946, 51, 56, 66, 67, mem. provincial chpt., Province of Cin., 1942, 47, 52, 57, Province of N.Y., 1965-68; mem. Council of Provincial Superiors of North Am., 1965-68; mem. sch. bd. Archdiocese Cin., 1959-65; group chmn., analyst nat. conf. Nat. Commn. Tchr. Edn. and Profl. Standards, 1954, 58. Mem. citizens adv. com. Dayton Pub. Schs., 1961-65. Mem. Nat., Ohio edn. assns., Nat. Cath. Edn. Assn. (chmn. tchr. edn. sect., dept. higher edn. 1963-64, chmn. problems and plans com. 1963), Ohio Coll. Assn. (com. on teacher edn. 1963-66), Nat. Soc. Study Edn., Marianist Writers Guild (exec. sec. Dayton), Phi Delta Kappa. Author: Provisions for Low-Ability Pupils in Catholic High Schools, 1949. Editor: Our Lady in Education, 1958; Emerging Objectives of Catholic Education, 1970; New Issues and Trends in Catholic Education, 1971. Contbr. articles profl. jours. Address: 300 College Park Av Dayton OH 45409

FAGAN, FRANK, retail co. exec.; b. N.Y.C., July 31, 1905; s. James and Antoinette (Holahan) F.; student pub. schs., lit. and lang. studies Columbia; m. Valeska Hubbard, Dec. 29, 1934; children—Andrea, Peter, Dona Amy. Asst. advt. mgr. wholesale div. W. & J. Sloane, 1924-26, advt. mgr. reatil stores, 1926-28; mdse. mgr. John Wanamaker, Phila., 1928-31; pres. mdsg. and promotion div. Felix Lillenthal, 1931-34; with Young & Rubicam, Inc., 1934-64, mdsg. exec., 1934-38, account exec., 1938-41, v.p., account supr., 1943, mem. exec. com. and plans bd. 1946, sr. v.p., 1953-58, exec. v.p., 1958-64; pres. S. T. Preston & Son, Inc., Greenport, N.Y., 1959—. Clubs: New York Yacht; Manhasset Bay Yacht. Home: Young's Lane Orient NY 11957 Office: 102 Main St Greenport NY 11944

FAGAN, GEORGE VINCENT, librarian-historian; b. Phila., Oct. 4, 1917; s. William J. and Mary A. (Carrigan) F.; B.S., Temple U., 1940, M.A., 1941; M.A. in Library Sci., U. Denver, 1957; Ph.D., U. Pa., 1954; m. Ernestine M. Hudak, Nov. 21, 1942; children—George Vincent, William J., John E., Ernestine A.T., Terence P. Instr. history Temple U., 1940-41, 46-51; commd. 2d lt. AUS, 1942, advanced through grades to col. USAF, 1963; instr. U.S. Naval Acad., 1951-54; asso. editor Air U. Press, 1954-55; asso. prof. USAF Acad., 1955-56, prof. history and dir. library, 1956-69; lectr. Regis Coll., Denver, 1957-59, U. Colo., 1960-68; prof. library sci., head librarian Tutt Library, Colo. Coll., 1969—; exec. dir. Colo. Com. for Nat. Library Week, 1959-63. Trustee Colorado Springs Fine Arts Center, 1961-66. Mem. Am., Miss. Valley hist. assns., Air Hist. Found., A.L.A. Author: Alexander Dallas Rache, Educator, 1941; Study Guide for American History, 1948-57; Self-Evaluation, United States Air Force Academy, 1958; (with W. W. Jeffries) Geography and National Power, 1953; Pikes Peak Region and USAF Academy, 1962. Contbr. articles to periodicals. Home: 1408 N Cascade Av Colorado Springs CO 80907

FAGAN, JOHN PAUL, financial exec.; b. Yonkers, N.Y., Apr. 28, 1930; s. John J. and Winifred R. (Murray) F.; B.B.A., Pace Coll., 1962; m. Theresa A. Kivlon, Aug. 20, 1955; children—Robert, Nancy, Thomas. Sr. asst. treas. N.Y.C. R.R., N.Y.C., 1953-68; asst. v.p. I.C. R.R., Chgo., 1968-69; treas. Ill. Central Industries, Chgo., 1969—; dir. Philipsborn Equities, Inc., Chgo., 1971—. Mem. adv. bd. Cath. Charities, Chgo., 1971—. Served with USMCR, 1951-53. Home: 1319 Southwind Dr Northbrook IL 60062 Office: 135 E 11th Pl Chicago IL 60605

FAGAN, JOSEPH CHURCH, govt. ofcl.; b. Madison, Wis., Feb. 7, 1925; s. Joseph A. and Helen (Church) F.; B.S., U. Wis., 1949, J.D., 1952; m. Mary Ellen Purchner, June 25, 1949; children—Deborah Louise, Katherine Mary, Elizabeth Ann. Admitted to Wis. bar, 1952; practiced in Madison, 1952-53; legislative counsel Wis. C. of C., 1953-58; exec. dir. Wis. Assn. Gen. Contractors, 1958-60; legal and labor relations U.S. C. of C., 1960-63; exec. dir. Mil. Gen. Contractors, Milw., 1963-65; chmn. Wis. Dept. Industry Labor and Human Relations, 1965-70; exec. dir. U.S. Equal Employment Opportunity Commn., Washington, 1970—. Mem. Adv. Com. on Unemployment Compensation, adv. com. Wis. Employment Relations Bd., Wis. Adv. Com. on Workmens Compensation; mem. Milw. Constrn. Equal Employment Opportunity Com., Wis. Gov.'s Com. on Services to Minorities. Served with USNR, 1942- 46. Recipient Page One award Madison Newspaper Guild, 1968; named B'nai B'rith Man of Year, 1969; Human Rights award B'nai B'rith of Wis., 1970. Mem. Wis. Bar Assn., Am. Judicature Soc., Phi Alpha Delta, Delta Kappa Epsilon. Republican. Presbyn. Author: Employers Guide to Unemployment Compensation in Wisconsin, 1955—. Home: 629 Aster Blvd Rockville MD 20850 Office: 1800 G St NW Washington DC 20004

FAGAN, ROBERT MICHAEL, ins. co. exec.; b. Cin., June 1, 1919; s. Robert Michael and Anna (Fassbinder) F.; student U. Cin., 1937-41, Duke, 1942-44; m. Marian A. Hegner, July 9, 1941; 1 son, Dennis. Various positions with subsidiary cos. Dresser Industries, 1946-50; mgr. Union Iron & Steel Co., Cin., 1950-55; controller Ry. Supply & Mfg. Co., Cin., 1956-58; mgr. accounting and tax depts. Western & So. Life Ins. Co., Cin., 1956-67, comptroller, 1968—. Served to capt. AUS, 1941-46. Home: 841 Asbury Rd Cincinnati OH 45230 Office: 400 Broadway Cincinnati OH 45202

FAGAN, THOMAS E., savs. bank exec. Vice pres., controller L.I. Savs. Bank, Long Island City, N.Y. Office: Bridge Plaza N Long Island City NY 11101*

FAGAN, THOMAS GEORGE, mobile homes mfg. co. exec.; b. Pueblo, Colo., Sept. 2, 1914; s. Thomas James and Catherine Dorothy (Nogle) F.; B. Journalism U. Mo., 1940; m. Margaret Ruth West, Jan. 30, 1943; children—Margaret Ann, Catherine Jean, Thomas Duke. Regional sales mgr. Braniff Internat. Airways, 1940- 43; sales mgr. San. Refrigerator Co., 1946-50; v.p., dir. sales Kit Mfg. Co., Inc., Long Beach, Cal., 1950-71, v.p., dir. marketing, 1971—; dir. J.B.D. Corp., 1953- 62. Bd. dirs. Mobile Home Research Found. Served as officer USNR, World War II. Mem. Mobile Homes Mfrs. Assn. (pres. 1964-65), Trailer Coach Assn. (v.p. 1959-60; Distinguished Service award 1953), Kappa Tau Alpha, Sigma Delta Chi. Elk. Home: 1002 Cartagena Dr Long Beach CA 90807 Office: 1401 W 17th St Long Beach CA 90813

FAGERBERG, DIXON, Jr., accountant; b. Prescott, Ariz., Mar. 20, 1909; s. Dixon and Amy (Nelson) F.; A.B. with great distinction, Stanford, 1931; m. Mary Jergens, June 20, 1933; children—Dixon III, Mary, Nelson. Pvt. practice as C.P.A., Prescott, Ariz., 1934-37, Phoenix, 1937-57; partner Peat, Marwick, Mitchell & Co., Phoenix, 1957-71; 1st editor Practitioners Forum, jour. accountancy, 1954-57. Served with USNR, 1944-46. Mem. Am. Inst. C.P.A.'s (v.p. 1955-56), Phi Beta Kappa. Author articles, booklets on accounting and economics. Home: Oak Creek Cliffs Star Route 1 Sedona AZ 86336

FAGERHAUGH, KENNETH HAROLD, librarian; b. Opheim, Mont., Dec. 14, 1914; s. Ole and Bertha Jorgena (Shaw) F.; A.B., Luther Coll., Decorah, Ia., 1936; B.L.S., U. Mich., 1942. Instr. chemistry dept. Luther Coll., 1936-40; chemist E. I. duPont, 1942-43; librarian, supr. classified files Clinton Nat. Lab., Oak Ridge, 1943-45; research librarian Rohm & Haas Co., Phila., 1945-46; acting dir. tech. information sect. gen. labs., research and devel. br. Office Q.M. Gen., Phila. Q.M. Depot, 1946- 48; research librarian John Crerar Library, Chgo., 1948-50, asst. librarian, 1950-52; librarian, asso. prof. library sci. Carnegie Mellon U., 1952—. Fellow A.A.A.S., Phi Kappa Phi; mem. Pa. Library Assn. (pres. 1967-68), Spl. Libraries Assn., A.L.A., Am. Soc. for Information Sci. Home: Box 430-A RD 1 Coraopolis PA 15108

FAGG, JOHN EDWIN, educator; b. San Saba, Tex., Nov. 21, 1916; s. Edwin Earl and Bessie (Sanderson) F.; B.A., U. Tex., 1938; M.A., U. Chgo., 1939, Ph.D., 1942. Mem. faculty N.Y.U., 1946—, prof. history, 1962—, chmn. dept. Washington Sq. Coll., 1961-69, dir. Portuguese-Brazilian Center, 1961-65; expert cons. USAF, 1946-51, 56-57. Served with USAAF, 1942-46. Mem. Am. Hist. Assn., Phi Beta Kappa (hon.), Kappa Sigma. Episcopalian. Author: (essays) Rafael Altamira, 1942, Sir Charles Webster, 1961; Latin America: A General History, rev. edit., 1969; Cuba, Haiti, The Dominican Republic, 1965; also sects. ofcl. history USAF. Home: 6040 Kennedy Blvd E West New York NJ 07093 Office: New York Univ New York City NY 10003

FAGIN, HENRY, educator; b. N.Y.C., Apr. 9, 1913; s. Philip A. and Ester (Brody) F.; B.Arch., Columbia, 1937, M.S. in Planning, 1938; m. Eleanor Fine. Aug. 3, 1940; children—David Henry, Mara Eleanor. Editor, Fed. Writers Project, N.Y.C., 1938; architect, draftsman Mayer & Whittlesey, N.Y.C., 1939-42; planning dir. Churchill-Fulmer Assos., N.Y.C., 1946-49, N. Westchester (N.Y.) Joint Planning Program, 1949-51; planning dir. Regional Plan Assn., N.Y.C., 1952-58, exec. dir., 1959; research prof. U. Cal. at Berkeley, 1958; exec. dir. Pa.-Jersey Transp. Study, Phila., 1959-62; prof. planning U. Wis. at Madison, 1962-67; prof. adminstrn. Grad. Sch. Adminstrn., research dir. pub. policy research orgn. U. Cal. at Irvine, 1967—; chmn. U. Cal. Coordinating Council on the West Side San Joaquin Valley Project. cons., 1950—; prof. seminar Am. studies Salzburg, 1965. Chmn. panel I, spl. com. urban transp. research Hwy. Research Bd., Nat. Acad. Sci., 1961-62. Mem. Mayor Madison Civic Adv. Com., 1963-67, chmn., 1967; bd. dirs. Channing Murray Student Center, 1963-67, pres., 1966-67. Served with USNR, 1944-46. Registered profl. architect, N.Y. Mem. Wis. Civil Liberties Union (v.p. 1965-67), Regional Sci. Assn. (v.p. 1963-64), Am. Inst. Planners (pres. N.Y.-Pa. chpt. 1954-55), Am. Soc. Public Adminstrn. (pres. Wis. Capitol chpt. 1967, v.p. vis. Wis. 1966-67). Unitarian. Author: (with R. C. Weinberg) Planning and Community Appearance, 1958; The Policies Plan; Instrumentality for a Community Dialogue, 1965; (with Leo F. Schnore) Urban Research and Policy Planning, 1967. Bd. contbrs. Archtl. Forum, 1965—; contbr. Colliers Ency. Home: 1649 Sunset Ridge Dr Laguna Beach CA 92651 Office: Univ of Cal Irvine CA 92664

FAGIN, N. BRYLLION, author, univ. prof.; b. Russia, June 15, 1892; s. Nathan Bryllion and Matilda (Nelstadt) F.; brought to U.S., 1900, naturalized, 1913; student Mich. State Coll., 1912; A.B., George Washington U., 1923, A.M., 1924; student Columbia, summer 1924, Harvard, summer 1925; Ph.D., Johns Hopkins, 1931; m. Mary Berke, June 4, 1916 (dec. 1964); m. Clarissa Pearlman, Apr. 29, 1965. Clk., Bureau of Chemistry, Washington, 1916-21; instr. English, Nat. U., Washington, 1919-23; asst. prof. English, U. of Md., 1924-25; prof. English, U. of Baltimore, 1925-31; asst. prof. English, Johns Hopkins, 1931-47, asso. prof. English and drama, 1947-58, lectr., 1959—; Whitney vis. prof. English, LeMoyne Coll., Memphis, 1958-59, New Coll., Sarasota, Florida, 1967—; dir. Johns Hopkins Playhouse, 1931-58; vis. lectr. U. S.D., summer 1930; U. of Tenn., summer 1934; vis. asso. prof. English N.Y.U., summer 1951; vis. prof. English U. Rochester, 1953-55; with Salzburg Seminar in Am. Studies, summers, 1951, 1958. Member Modern Lang. Assn., Am. Assn. Univ. Profs., Am. Ednl. Theatre Assn., Am. Nat. Theatre and Acad., Authors League of Am. Edgar Allan Poe Soc. of Baltimore (former pres.). Clubs: Johns Hopkins; Tudor and Stuart. Author books including; The Histrionic Mr. Poe, 1949. Editor: Poe as a Literary Critic, 1946. Co-editor: O'Neill and his Plays, 1961. Contbr. to publs. Address: 518 El Vernona Av Sarasota FL 33577 ☆

FAGLEY, THOMAS FISHER, educator; b. Mt. Carmel, Pa., Sept. 7, 1913; B.S., Bucknell U., 1935, M.S., 1937; Ph.D. (Lindsay Light Co. fellow), U. Chgo., 1949. Instr. chemistry Bucknell U., 1938-40, 42-46; instr. Univ. Coll., Chgo., 1947, teaching fellow, 1948-49; asst. prof. chemistry Tulane U., 1946-54, asso. prof., 1954-61, prof., 1961—, also chmn. dept. Mem. A.A.A.S., Am. Chem. Soc. Office: Dept Chemistry Tulane U New Orleans LA 70118*

FAGOT, JOSEPH BURDELL, corp. cons.; b. Forest River, N.D., Apr. 23, 1917; s. Peter J. and Minnie (Eldredge) F.; B.B.A. with distinction, U. Minn., 1940; m. Joyce Bodwell Cawley, Aug. 31, 1940; children—JoAnn, Joel, Don, Larry, Lynne. Sales corr. Montgomery Ward & Co., St. Paul, 1940-41; exec. trainee, asst. dept. mgr. Sears-Roebuck & Co., Mpls., 1941-43; profl., adminstrv. and exec. placement Walker Employement Service, Mpls., 1943-44; placement mgr. Marathon Corp., Menasha, Wis., 1944-52; v.p. personnel and indsl. relations Omar, Inc., Omaha, 1952-58; v.p. orgn. and personnel Fibreboard Corp., 1958-62; v.p. operations Gold Bond Stamp Co., Mpls., 1962-66; pres., dir. Fed. Mart Stores, Inc., San Deigo, 1966-69; pres., owner J B Mgmt., Inc., San Diego, 1969—. Mem. San Diego C. of C. Republican. Roman Catholic. Author articles in field. Address: 804 La Jolia Rd La Jolia CA 92037

FAGOT, ROBERT FREDERICK, educator; b. Nicaragua, C.A., July 4, 1921 (parents Am. citizens); s. Fred Clark and Ruby (Howorka) F.; B.S. Mass. Inst. Tech., 1946; Ph.D., Stanford, 1956; m. Beverly I. Fields, Apr. 1, 1961; children—Brian Kevin, Clark Albert. Asst. prof. psychology U. Ore., Eugene, 1956-62, asso. prof., 1962-66, prof. 1966—, acting head dept., 1968—. Served to lt. USNR, 1942-46, 53-55. USPHS Sr. fellow U. Cal. at Berkeley, 1962-63. Mem. Am. Psychol. Assn., Am. Statis. Assn., Psychonomic Soc., Biometric Soc., A.A.A.S., Am. Assn. U. Profs., Am. Civil Liberties Union, Sigma Xi. Contbr. articles profl. jours. Home: 680 W. 35th Pl Eugene, OR 97405.

FAGOTHEY, AUSTIN JOSEPH, educator, clergyman; b. San Francisco, June 23, 1901; s. Joseph A. and Katherine (McDade) F.; A.B., Gonzaga U., 1923, M.A., 1924; S.T.L. Weston (Mass.) Coll., 1932; Ph.D., Gregorian U., Rome, Italy, 1949. Instr. philosophy U. Santa Clara (Cal.), 1932-34, 35-36; instr. theology Alma Coll., Los Gatos, Cal., 1936-38; prof. philosophy U. Santa Clara, 1938- , chmn. dept., 1938-67, also trustee univ. Mem. Am., Am. Cath., Jesuit philos. assns. Author: Right and Reason, Ethics in Theory and Practice, 4th edit., 1967. Address: Univ Santa Clara Santa Clara, CA 95053.

FAHERTY, CLARENCE JOSEPH, ins. co. exec.; b. Girardville, Pa., Aug. 21, 1907; s. Joseph and Ellen (Long) F.; B.S. in Econs., U. Pa., 1928; LL.B., Rutgers U., 1931; m. Helen Zabriskie, Dec. 28, 1929; childrenDavid, Roger, Peter, Dennis. Admitted to Ill. bar, 1933; with Prudential Ins. Co. Am., 1930-, 2d v.p. comml. and indsl. loan dept., 1957-61, v.p. charge dept., now sr. v.p. Mem. Community Builders Council, Newark Econ. Devel. Council, N.J. Gov.'s Com. Housing; pres. Summit (N.J.) Schs. Assn., Citizens Com. Trustee Urban Land Inst. Served to comdr. USNR, World War II; PTO. Mem. Phi Delta Theta, Delta Theta Phi, Lambda Alpha. Club: University of (pres. Suburban N.J. 1953, trustee 1954—). Home: 70 Portland Rd Summit NJ 07901 Office: Prudential Plaza Newark NJ 07102

FAHEY, GEORGE L(ITCHFIELD), educator; b. nr. Mpls., Oct. 8, 1907; s. John Hunt and Emma Katherine (Litchfield) F.; B.A., State U. Ia., 1935; Ph.D., U. Wis., 1939; m. Dallas Cynthia Darrow, June 16, 1930. Instr., U. Pitts., 1939-42, asst. prof., asso. prof., prof., 1949—, pres. Univ. Senate, 1966-68; also chmn. dept. ednl., developmental and sch. psychology, chmn. dept. higher edn.; asso. prof. U. Miami, Fla., 1948-49; cons. Fry Cons. Bd. dirs. Psychol. Services Pitts. Served from 1st lt. to maj., Adj. Gen. Dept., AUS, 1942-47. Diplomate Am. Bd. Examiners Profl. Psychology. Mem. Am. Psychol. Assn., Am. Assn. Higher Edn., Sigma Xi, Phi Delta Kappa. Contbr. articles profl. jours. Home: 201 Delafield Rd Pittsburgh PA 15215

FAHEY, JOHN LESLIE, physician; b. Cleve., Sept. 8, 1924; s. Leslie J. and Marguerite (Schardt) F.; student John Carroll U., 1942-43. Ohio State U., 1943-44; M.S. in Physiology, Wayne State U., 1949; M.D., Harvard, 1951; m. Jane A. Bishop, June 12, 1954; children—Marguerite Anne, James L., Catharine D. Teaching fellow physiology Wayne State U. Coll. Medicine, 1947-49; mem. staff Presbyn. Hosp., N.Y.C., 1951-53; mem. staff Nat. Cancer Inst., 1953-71, chief immunology br., 1964-71; prof., chmn. dept. med. microbiology and immunology U. Cal. at Los Angeles Sch. Medicine, 1971—. Home: 845 Toyopa Dr Pacific Palisades CA 90272 Office: Univ of Cal School of Medicine Los Angeles CA 90272

FAHEY, LESLIE J., investment banker; b. Cleve., Jan. 20, 1897; s. Peter R. and Sarah I. (Toole) F.; student Cleve. Coll., Western Res. U.; m. Marguerite Schardt, Jan. 27, 1923 (dec. Dec. 1932); childrenJohn Leslie, Thomas J., Robert J.; m. 2d, Alyse Evans, June 23, 1936. Sales dept. Gillette Safety Razor Co., 1917-22; with Mitchell, Herrick & Co., 1922-39, sales mgr., 1934-39; exec. v.p. Fahey, Clark & Co., 1939-42, pres., 1942-. Mem. bd. govs. Midwest Stock Exchange, 1951-54. Trustee Family Service Assn. of Cleve., 1946—, chmn. finance com., 1952-55, pres., 1955-57; mem. advisory bd. Catholic Child Guidance Clinic, 1961—. Mem. Investment Bankers Assn. Am. (chmn. No. Ohio group 1940-41, bd. govs. 1951-54). Clubs: Bond (pres. 1938), Union (Cleve.). Home: 2672 Derbyshire Rd Cleveland Heights, OH 44106. Office: Union Commerce Bldg Cleveland OH 44114

FAHEY, WALTER JOHN, elec. engr., educator; b. Winnipeg, Man., Can., Apr. 10, 1927; s. Gordon Joseph and Agnes (Larsen) F.; came to U.S., 1928, naturalized, 1956; B.S., Case Inst. Tech., 1957, M.S., 1959, Ph.D., 1963. Instr. elec. engring. Case Inst. Tech., 1959-62; asst. prof. Ohio U., 1963-65, asso. prof., chmn. dept. elec. engring., 1965-67, prof., dean Coll. Engring., 1967-68; prof., dean Coll. Engring., U. Ariz., Tucson, 1969—. Mem. Ohio Crime Commn., 1967-68; mem. Ariz. Bd. Tech. Registration, 1969—; mem. Tucson adv. com. Nat. Alliance Businessmen. Bd. dirs. Aviation Research and Edn. Found. Served with USNR, 1945-48, 1950-52. Recipient Outstanding Grad. award Case Inst. Tech., 1957. Am. Council on Edn. fellow, 1967-68. Mem. I.E.E.E., Am. Soc. Engring. Edn., Sigma Xi, Tau Beta Pi, Eta Kappa Nu, Tau Kappa Alpha, Theta Tau, Phi Kappa Phi. Office: Coll Engring U Ariz Tucson AZ 85721

FAHIEN, RAYMOND WILLIAM, educator; b. St Louis, Dec. 26, 1923; s. John H. and Alice K. (Schubkegel) F.; B.S., Washington U., St. Louis, 1947: M.S., Mo. Sch. Mines, 1950; Ph.D., Purdue U., 1954. Instr., Mo. Sch. Mines, 1947-50; process design engr. Ethyl Corp., Baton Rouge, 1953-54; asst. prof. Ia. State U., 1954-57, asso. prof., 1957-59; engr. Ames Lab. U.S. AEC, 1954-64; vis. prof. U. Wis., 1959-60; Fulbright lectr. div. chem. engring. U. Brazil, Rio de Janeiro, 1964; prof. chem. engring. dept. U. Fla., Gainesville, 1964—, chmn. dept., 1964-69. Mem. Am. Inst. Chem. Engrs. (tech. program chmn. 1968, research comm. 1962—), Am. Chem. Soc., Am. Assn. U. Profs. (chpt. pres. 1963-64, 68-70), Am. Soc. Engring. Edn., A.A.A.S., Sigma Xi, Phi Kappa Phi, Alpha Chi Sigma. Editor: Jour. Chem. Engring. Edn., 1967—. Contbr. articles profl. jours. Home: Rt 1 Box 46 Micanopy FL 32667

FAHLGREN, H. SMOOT, advt. exec.; b. Parkersburg, W.Va., Aug. 17, 1930; s. C. Herbert and Julia (Smoot) F.; B.S., R.A., U. Va. and Marietta (O.) Coll., 1952; m. Judith Ann Henninger, Dec. 7, 1953; children—Steven Smoot, Rebecca Ann, John David. With Smoot Outdoor Advt. Co., 1956-62; founder, 1962, since pres. Fahlgren & Assos., Inc., advt., Parkersburg and Pitts. Named Young Man of Year, W.Va. Jr. C. of C., 1958. Presbyn. Home: 12 Meadowcrest St Parkersburg WV 26101 Office: 220 8th St Parkersburg WV 26101

FAHLSTROM, ORVIND, painter; b. Saõ Paulo, Brazil, 1928. Came to U.S., 1961. Organizer, dir., participant various intermedia events, including The Ingrid Thulin Story. Ur Mellanöl. Fahlströms Hörna. Moderna Museet, Stockholm, 1964, Kisses Sweeter than Wine, in Theater and Engring., N.Y., 1966; exhibited one man shows Galleria Numero, Florence, 1952, Galerie Daniel Cordier, Paris, 1959, 62, Galerie Blanche, Stockholm, 1959, Cordier & Ekstrom, N.Y., 1964, XXXIII Biennale, Venice, 1966, Sidney Janis Gallery, N.Y., 1967; exhibited group shows including Galerie Aesthetica, Stockholm, 1955, Galerie Creuze, Paris, 1955, 65, V Saõ Paulo Beinal, 1959, II Bienale de Paris, 1961, Sidney Janis Gallery, 1962, Museo Nacional de Belles Artes, Buenos Aires, 1963, Musee d'Art Moderne de la Ville de Paris, 1964, L'Aquila, 1965, Guggenheim Mus., N.Y.C., 1966, Galleria Schwarz, Millan, 1967, Chgo. Mus. Contemporary Art, 1967. Recipient Guggenheim Internat. award, 1964. Home: New York City NY 10017 Office: care Janis Gallery 15 E 57th St New York City NY 10022*

FAHRER, GEORGE WILLIAM, Jr., assn. exec.; b. Cin., Feb. 5, 1923; s. George William and Lillian (Shropshire) F.; A.S., Ohio Coll. Applied Sci., 1943; m. Jean Lo Piccolo, Oct. 2, 1943 (div.); 1 dau., Kimberly; m. 2d, Alison Demarest. Sales rep. Diebold, Inc., 1946-47; advt. lithography div. Gibson and Perin Co., 1947-51; asst. advt. mgr. Baldwin Piano and Organ Co., 1951-56, advt. and sales promotion mgr., 1956-63; exec. sec. Music Tchrs. Nat. Assn., Inc., Cin., 1963—. Past area and div. chmn. Cin. United Appeal; past area chmn. Cin. United Fine Arts Fund. Served with AUS, 1943-45. Mem. Ohio Coll. Applied Sci. Alumni Assn. (past exec. com.), Phi Mu Alpha. Mason. Club: Cincinnati. Home: Lytle Towers Cincinnati OH 45202 Office: Carew Tower Cincinnati OH 45202

FAHRINGER, HERALD PRICE, Jr., lawyer; b. Lewisberg, Pa., Nov. 6, 1928; s. Herald Price and Adelaide Pauline (Dyer) F.; B.A., Pa. State U., 1950, M.A., 1951; LL.B., U. Buffalo, 1956, LL.D., 1968. Admitted to N.Y. bar, 1957, also U.S. Supreme Ct.; partner firm Lipsitz, Green, Fahringer, Roll, Schuller & Jmaes, Buffalo, 1965—. Served with AUS, 1946-48. Recipient Profl. Achievement award U. Buffalo Law Sch., 1966. Mem. Am., N.Y. State bar assns., Am. Trial Lawyers Assn. Home: 140 North St Buffalo NY 14201 Office: 1 Niagara Sq Buffalo NY 14202

FAHRNEY, DELMER STATER, ret. naval officer, aero. engr.; b. Grove, Okla., Oct. 23, 1898; s. Albert Franklin and Lillian (Pugh) F.; B.S., U.S. Naval Acad., 1919, postgrad., 1927; M.S., Mass. Inst. Tech., 1930; m. Agnes Whiting Kelly, June 2, 1925 (dec. Nov. 1949); children—Dawn (Mrs. Sanford Knotts, U.S.N.), Delmer Stater, Carol, Paula (Mrs. André F. Yon); m. 2d, Helen Sheehan Arthur, Nov. 27, 1970. Commd. ensign USN, 1919, advanced through grades to rear adm., 1950; served on following ships and stas.; U.S.S. Utah, U.S.S. Wadsworth, U.S.S. Stewart, U.S.S. Wright, U.S.S. W.Va., U.S.S. Lexington, Naval Air Station, Pensacola, Fla., also Pearl Harbor; insp. naval aircraft Wright Aeroplane Corp., Naval Aircraft Factory, Phila., also Bur. of Aeros.; served as first comdr. of Naval Air Missile Test Center, Point Mugu, Cal., 1948-50; cons. guided missiles since 1936; pioneered radio controlled aircraft, and guided missiles; cons. Eastern rep. Coleman Engring. Co., Culver City, Cal., 1951-52; cons., Eastern rep. White-Rodgers Electric Co., St. Louis, 1951-52, dir. aero. dept., Wilmington, 1952-54, naval historian on guided missiles, Bur. Aero., Navy Dept., 1954-58; sec. to com. on sci. and arts Franklin Inst., 1957—. Decorated Legion of Merit; awarded commendation for work on guided missiles Bur. Aero., commendation for radio control achievements, USN, 1938, 41; Gold star in lieu 2d Legion of Merit, 1957, for devel. of assault drone guided missile. Fellow Am. Inst. Aeros. and Astronautics; (asso.); mem. of The Franklin Inst., Nat. Geog. Soc., S.A.R. Holder patents on aircraft, guided missile developments. Home: Roundelay Chadds Ford PA 19317 Office: Franklin Inst Philadelphia PA 19139

FAHS, CHARLES BURTON, educator; b. Brooklyn, Sept. 22, 1908; s. Charles Harvey and Sophia Blanche (Lyon) F.; B.S., Northwestern U., 1929, M.A., 1931, Ph.D., 1933; student U. Berlin, 1929-30, Ecole Nationale des Langues Orientales Vivantes, 1933-34, Kyoto Imperial U., 1934-35, Tokyo Imperial U., 1935- 36; m. Jamie L. Ross, June 27, 1932; children—James Harvey, Barbara Ruth. Instr. Oriental affairs Pomona Coll., Claremont Coll., 1936-39, asst. prof., 1939-45; vis. prof. Coll. Chinese Studies, Peiping, 1940- 41; research analyst Office Coordinator Information, 1941-42, OSS, 1942- 45, chief Far East div., 1944-45; acting chief, div. research for Far East, Dept. State, 1945-46; asst. dir. humanities Rockefeller Found., 1946-48, asso. dir., 1949, dir., 1950-62; minister counselor for cultural and pub. affairs Am. embassy, Tokyo, 1962-65, minister for cultural affairs, 1965-67; Harry C. Trexler vis. prof., Muhlenberg Coll., Allentown, Pa., 1967-68; dir. internat. programs, prof. govt. Miami U., Oxford, O., 1968—. Mem. Am. Polit. Sci. Assn., Council on Fgn. Relations, Assn. Asian Studies, Japan Soc., The Asia Soc., Chindan Society Korea (hon.), Phi Beta Kappa. Club: Tokyo. Author: Government in Japan, Recent Trends in its Scope and Operation, 1940. Home: 4 Iveswood Dr Oxford OH 45056

FAIGENBAUM, HAROLD MORRIS, educator; b. Watervliet, N.Y., Sept. 4, 1902; s. Morris and Minnie (Smith) F.; Ch.E., Rensselaer Poly. Inst., 1923, Ph.D. in Inorganic Chemistry, 1926; m. Edith M. Sanders, Dec. 19, 1937; 1 son, Mark Alan. Russel Sage fellow Rensselaer Poly. Inst., 1923-26, mem. faculty, 1926- -, prof. inorganic chemistry, 1940-67, prof. emeritus, 1967—, asso. chmn. dept., 1949-67; chief chemist N.Y. State Biol. Survey, 1929-40; cons. in field, 1940—. Bd. dirs. Rensselaer County chpt. A.R.C., 1953—; mem. exec. com. United Community Services Mohawk- Hudson area, 1959—, pres., 1971—. Trustee, Union of Am. Hebrew Congregations, 1950—, vice chmn., 1967—, chmn. joint commn. synagogue adminstrn., 1962—. Mem. Am. Chem. Soc., Sigma Xi, Phi Lambda Upsilon, Phi Sigma Delta. Author: (with others) Laboratory Manual for General Chemistry, 1963; also articles. Home: 1912 Burdett Av Troy NY 12180

FAILEY, GEORGE LEO, Jr., pub. utility exec.; b. Binghamton, N.Y., Aug. 7, 1928; s. George Leo and Marion (Corliss) F.; B.S., Notre Dame U., 1952. With Arthur Andersen & Co., C.P.A.'s, 1952-59; with North Penn Gas. Co., Port Allegany, Pa., 1960—, exec. v.p., 1962—, also dir. Bd. dirs. Port Allegany Indsl. Devel. Corp., Tri-Area Devel. Corp. Served with AUS, 1946-48. Mem. Port Allegany C. of C., Pa. Soc., McKean County Indsl. Relations Assn., Am., Pa. (past dir., pres.) gas assns. Rotarian. Home: 101 Main St Port Allegany PA 16743 Office: 76-80 Mill St Port Allegany PA 16743

FAILING, GEORGE EDGAR, chancellor, clergyman; b. Kingston, Ont., Can., Nov. 25, 1912 (parents Am. citizens); s. Roy Augustus and Nellie (Richardson) F.; B.A. magna cum laude, Houghton Coll., 1940, Litt.D., 1960; M.A., Duke, 1947; m. Phyllis Ogden, Apr. 12, 1939; children—Bunnie Jean, Alice Joy, Lynn Ogden. Ordained to ministry Wesleyan Meth. Ch., 1938; pastor in Fillmore, N.Y., 1935-41, Louisville, 1941-44, Marion, Ind., 1953-56; prof. Central S.C. Wesleyan Coll., 1944-47; prof. Houghton (N.Y.) Coll., 1947-53, dir. pub. relations, 1947-53; editor Sunday Sch. Lit. Wesleyan Meth. Ch., Marion, Ind., 1956-59, editor Wesleyan Methodist, 1959-68; chancellor Satellite Christian Inst., San Diego, 1968—. Mem. gen. bd. trustees Wesleyan Meth. Ch. Am., 1959-68. Mem. Soc. Bibl. Lit. and Exegesis, Evang. Press Assn. (pres. 1965-67), Am. Schs. Oriental Research. Author: 1 Corinthians, 1963. Home: PO Box 1298 La Mesa CA 92041 Office: PO Box 047 San Diego CA 92115

FAILKA, LADISLAV ALOIS JAN, mime; b. Prague, Czechoslovakia, Sept. 22, 1931; s. Ladislav Alois and Bozena (Vondrousova) F.; grad. Prague Acad. Dance, 1956; m. Ludmila Kovarova, Oct. 10, 1959. Founder Pantomime group, Prague, 1953; co- founder Theatre Na Zabradli in On The Balustrades, Prague, 1958; choreographer Trnka Puppet Film Studio, 1956—, also dir., mime several film and theatrical prodns.; prof. Acad. Arts, Prague, 1961—; appearances in U.S., S. Am., C.A., Europe. Recipient 1st award World Festival Pantomime, West Berlin, Germany, 1962, prize City Praque, 1962, State prize Czechoslovakia, 1962. Home: Husova 23 Praha 1 Stare mesto Czechoslovakia Office: Divaldo Na zabradli Prague 1 Czechoslovakia

FAIMAN, ROBERT NEIL, ednl. adminstr.; b. Excelsior, Minn., June 25, 1923; s. Clarence C. and Henrietta (Baker) F.; B.S. in Elec. Engring., N.D. State Coll., 1947; M.S. in Elec. Engring., U. Wash., 1948; Ph.D., Purdue U., 1956; m. Eunice A. Kessler, Mar. 12, 1944; children—Robert Neil, John Charles. Asso. elec. engring. U. Wash., 1947-48; from asst. prof. to prof. N.D. State Coll., 1948-58, chmn. dept., 1951-58; engr., engring. scis. program NSF, 1957-59; dean Coll. Tech., dir. Engring. Expt. Sta., U. N.H., 1959-67, v.p. research, 1967—. Mem. N.H. Bd. Registration for Profl. Engrs. Served with USAAF, 1943-46; maj. Res. Recipient Alumni Achievement award N.D. Staate U., 1966. Registered profl. engr., N.H. Mem. I.E.E.E. (sr.), Am. Soc. Engring. Edn., Am. Assn. Land Grant Colls. and State Univs., N.H. Soc. Prof. Engrs., Sigma Xi, Tau Beta Pi, Eta Kappa Nu, Phi Kappa Phi, Rotarian. Home: 10 Newmarket Rd Durham NH 03824

FAIN, HASKELL, educator; b. N.Y.C., July 1, 1926; s. Max and Ethel (Frankenstein) F.; B.S., U. Ill., 1948, M.A., 1949, U. Cal. at Berkeley, 1951, Ph.D., 1956; m. Elaine Folk, Sept. 14, 1949; children—Jonathan Simon, Madeline Alessandra. Mem. faculty U. Wis., Madison, 1956—, prof. philosophy, 1966—, chmn. dept., 1968-70. Sr. Fulbright prof. U. Bergen (Norway), 1961-62; vis. asso. prof. U. B.C., 1963-64; vis. fellow Linacre Coll., Oxford U., 1966- 67; lectr. Oxford U., 1967; vis. prof. Fla. State U., 1970-71; cons., World Book Ency., 1961-65. Served with AUS, 1944-46. Mem. Am. Philos. Assn. Author: Between Philosophy and History, 1970. Home: 2306 Van Hise Av Madison WI 53705

FAIN, JIM, newspaper editor; b. Norman Park, Ga., Sept. 12, 1920; s. James Edward and Mary (McCalman) F.; A.B., Emory U., 1941; m. Laura Turner, Nov. 22, 1945 (dec. 1966); 1 son, Mike; m. 2d, Jill Carpenter, June 30, 1967; 1 stepdau., Melissa Moorhead. Mng. editor Columbus (Ga.) Ledger, 1946-47; news editor Atlanta Jour., 1947-53; editor Dayton (O.) Daily News, 1953—. Served to maj. USAAF, World War II. Home: 616 Evans Lane Dayton OH 45459 Office: Dayton Daily News Dayton OH 45401

FAIN, SAMMY, composer; b. N.Y.C., June 17, 1902. Composer music for sound pictures; writer scores for Hellzapoppin', Sons o' Fun, Boys and Girls Together; motion pictures include Calamity Jane, Three Sailors and a Girl, Lucky Me, Love is a Many-Splendored Thing; songs include When I Take My Sugar to Tea, You Brought a New Kind of Love to Me, That Old Feelin', I'll Be Seeing You, Dear Hearts and Gentle People, Dickey Bird Song. Recipient Acad. award, 1953, co-winner for song Love is a Many-Splendored Thing, 1955.

FAINSOD, MERIE, educator; b. McKees Rocks, Pa., May 2, 1907; s. Louis and Frieda (Marcus) F.; A.B., Washington U., 1928, M.A., 1930, LL.D., 1956; M.A., Harvard, 1931, Ph.D., 1932; m. Elizabeth Stix, Apr. 27, 1933; children—Elizabeth Stix, Mary Lewis. Instr. govt. Harvard, 1933-38, asst. prof., 1938-44, asso. prof., 1944-46, prof., 1946-64, Leroy B. Williams prof. history and polit. sci., 1964, dir. Harvard Library, librarian coll., 1964—; Carl H. Pforzheimer prof., 1965—, chmn. govt. dept., 1946-49; vis. lectr. Yale, 1940; mem. staff Pres.'s Com. on Adminstrv. Mgmt., 1936; cons. Temporary Nat. Econs. Com., 1940; price exec. Consumers Durable Goods, Office Price Adminstrn., 1941-42, dir. Retail Trade and Services div., 1942-43. Served as capt. AUS, 1943-45. Sheldon traveling fellow Harvard, 1932-33. Trustee East European Fund; bd. dirs. Russian Research Center. Mem. Am. Philos. Soc., Am. Council Learned Socs. (dir.), Am. Polit. Sci. Assn. (pres. 1966-67, exec. council 1948-50), Am. Acad. Arts and Scis. Author: American People and Their Government (with A.J. Lien), 1933; International Socialism and the World War, 1935; Government and the American Economy (with A.L. Gordon), 1941, 48; How Russia is Ruled, 1953, rev. 1963; Smolensk Under Soviet Rule, 1958. Contbr. to Pub. Adminstrn. Rev., Am. Econ. Rev., Yale Law Jour., Jour. Politics, Am. Polit. Sci. Rev. (asso. editor 1951). Home: 19 Follen St Cambridge MA 02138 Office: M18 Littauer Center Harvard Cambridge MA 02138

FAIR, HARRY GRANT, corp. exec.; b. Okmulgee, Okla., June 3, 1916; s. Charles Augustus and Florence Matilda (Cain) F.; B.S., U. Okla., 1939; m. Margaret Jane Swift, Mar. 3, 1940; children—Harry Grant, Martha Swift, William Charles, Robert Ervine. With Phillips Petroleum Co., Bartlesville, Okla., 1939-66, beginning as student chem. engr., resigning as v.p.; exec. v.p. The M.W. Kellogg Co., N.Y.C., 1966-68; exec. v.p. Pullman, Inc., Chgo., 1968—, also dir., mem. operating policy com. Mem. Am. Chem. Soc., Am. Inst. Chem. Engrs., U. Okla. Alumni Assn., Phi Kappa Sigma, Alpha Chi Sigma. Episcopalian. Clubs: Chicago; Duquesne (Pitts.). Home: 308 Woodley Rd Winnetka IL 60093 Office: 200 S Michigan Av Chicago IL 60604

FAIR, RONALD L., author; b. Chgo., Oct. 27, 1932; s. Herbert and Beulah (Hunt) F.; student Stenotype Sch. Chgo., 1953-55; m. Lucy Margaret Jones, Nov. 10, 1952; children—Rodney D., Glen A.; m. 2d, Neva June Keres, June 19, 1968. Ct. reporter, Chgo., 1955-67; full time writer, 1967—; now tchr. lit. Columbia Coll., Chgo.; tchr. lit. and fiction Northwestern U., fall 1968; vis. fellow Center for Advanced Studies, Wesleyan U., Conn., 1969, asso. prof., 1969—. Served with USNR, 1950-53. Author: (novels) Many Thousand Gone, 1965; Hog Butcher, 1966; Vincent. Address: 201 W 92d St Chicago IL 60620

FAIRBAIRN, DONALD, biologist, educator; b. Ottawa, Ont., Can., Feb. 4, 1916; s. Arthur Edwin and Maria (Spratt) F.; B.A., Queen's U., 1938; Ph.D., U. Rochester, 1942; m. Mary Woodhouse Crawford, June 24, 1944; children—Ian George, Stephanie Ann, Eleanor Mary (Mrs. Paul Parsons). Postdoctoral fellow U. Pitts., 1942; instr. Queens U., 1945-46; asst., asso. prof. McGill U., 1946-62; Commonwealth prof. zoology U. Mass., Amherst, 1962- -, head dept. zoology, 1962-70; vis. prof. Johns Hopkins, 1959-60, U. Sydney 1969; cons. NIH, chmn. tropical medicine and parasitol. study sect., 1961-66. Served to capt. Canadian Army, 1943-45. Mem. Am. Soc. Parasitologists (mem. council), A.A.A.S., Am. Chem. Soc., Am. Soc. Biol. Chemists, Biochemical Soc. Gt. Britain. Mem. editorial bd. Hygiene and Tropical Medicine, 1960-62, Am. Jour. Epidemiology, 1962-67, Exptl. Parasitology, 1963-70, Jour. Parasitology, 1964-69. Contbr. articles profl. jours. Home: 301 E Pleasant St Amherst MA 01002

FAIRBAIRN, HAROLD WILLIAMS, geologist; b. Ottawa, Ont., Can., July 10, 1906; s. Arthur E. and Maria (Spratt) F.; came to U.S., 1937, naturalized, 1949; B.Sc., Queen's U., Kingston, Ont., 1929; A. M., Harvard, 1931, Ph.D., 1932; student U. Wis., 1929-30, U. Innsbruck, Göttingen, 1932-34; m. Sheila May Sargent, Apr. 18, 1939; children—Ann, Patrick, Elspeth, Neil. Instr. mineralogy Queen's U., 1934-37; asst. prof. geology Mass. Inst. Tech., 1937-43, asso. prof. 1943-55, prof., 1955—. Fellow Geol. Assn. Can., Geol. Soc. Am., Mineral Soc. Am.; mem. Am. Geophys. Union, Geochem. Soc., Am. Acad. Arts and Sci. Author: Structural Petrology of Deformed Rocks, 1949. Home: 27 Marcia Rd Watertown MA 02172 Office: Mass Inst Technology Cambridge MA 02139

FAIRBAIRN, NATHAN LUTTED, ins. exec.; b. Kansas City, Mo., June 1, 1901; s. Thomas and Louise H. (Pries) F.; student pub. schs., Cal.; m. Ruth Binet. Began ins. career, 1924; organized Cal. Compensation Ins. Co., 1932, Gt. Western Fire & Marine Ins. Co., 1946 (merged 1955), pres. Cal. Compensation & Fire Ins. Co., San Francisco, 1932—. Home: 1940 Broadway San Francisco CA 94109 Office: 28 Geary St San Francisco CA 94108

FAIRBANK, HENRY ALAN, physicist, educator; b. Lewistown, Mont., Nov. 9, 1918; s. Samuel B. and Helen (Martin) F.; B.A., Whitman Coll., 1940, D.Sc., 1971; Ph.D., Yale, 1944; M.A., Oxford (Eng.) U., 1954; m. Martha E. Edmonds, June 17, 1943; children—Mary, Alan, Elizabeth. Mem. faculty Yale, 1942-44, 45-62, asso. prof. physics, 1954-62; physicist Manhattan Project, Los Alamos Lab., 1944-45; prof. physics, chmn. dept. Duke, 1962—; cons. Los Alamos Sci. Lab., 1957-67; adv. panel Nat. Bur. Standards, 1956-64; spl. research low temperature physics. Guggenheim fellow, 1953-54. Fellow Am. Phys. Soc.; mem. Phi Beta Kappa, Sigma Xi. Contbr. profl. jours. Home: 1515 Pinecrest Rd Durham NC 27705

FAIRBANK, JOHN KING, historian; b. Huron, S.D., May 24, 1907; s. Arthur Boyce and Lorena C. V. (King) F.; A.B. summa cum laude, Harvard, 1929; Ph.D., Oxford (Eng.), 1936; LL.D. Korea U., 1964, U. Toronto, 1967, Swarthmore Coll., 1968, Harvard, 1970, Oberlin Coll., 1971; L.H.D., U. Wis., 1969; m. Wilma Cannon, June 29, 1932; children—Laura, Holly. Mem. faculty dept. history Harvard, since 1936, Higginson prof. history, dir. East Asian Research Center, 1959—; with co-ordinator of information and O.S.S., Washington, 1941-42; spl. asst. to Am. ambassador in Chungking, China, 1942-43; with OWI, Washington, 1944-45; dir. U.S. Information Service in China, 1945-46. Mem. Nat. Com. U.S.-China Relations, 1966—. Mem. Far Eastern Assn. (v.p. 1950-51), Am. Inst. Pacific Relations (trustee 1947-51), Council on Fgn. Relations, Am. Hist. Assn. (pres. 1968), Assn. for Asian Studies (pres. 1959), Am. Acad. Arts and Scis., Am. Philos. Assn., Mass. Hist. Soc., Am. Council of Learned Socs. (Far Eastern studies com.). Author several books including: The

United States and China, 1948, latest rev. edit., 1971; Modern China; A Bibliographical Guide to Chinese Works, 1898-1937 (with K. C. Liu), 1950; A Documentary History of Chinese Communism, 1921-50 (with Conrad Brandt and Benjamin Schwartz), 1951; Trade and Diplomacy on the China Coast, 1954; China's Response to the West (with S. Y. Teng), 1954; East Asia; The Great Tradition (with E. O. Reischauer), 1960; East Asia; The Modern Transformation (with others), 1965. Contbr. articles to nat. periodicals. Home: 41 Winthrop St Cambridge MA 02129 Office: 1737 Cambridge St Cambridge MA 02138 ☆

FAIRBANK, ROBERT L., indsl. truck mfg. co. exec.; b. Cleve., Jan. 7, 1912; s. Lewis George and Elsie (Tegtmeir) F.; student Dartmouth, 1933; m. Dorothy Tomkinson, Apr. 18, 1936; children—Robert L., Jonathan T., Marianne. Dist. sales mgr. Cleve., Firestone Tire & Rubber Co., 1933-51; v.p. sales Towmotor Corp., 1951-62, exec. v.p., 1962-65, pres., 1965—, also dir.; dir. Lamson & Sessions Co., Morrison Products, Inc. (both Cleve.), Central Nat. Bank Cleve. Trustee St. Luke's Hosp., Univ. Sch., YMCA (all Cleve.). Mem. Indsl. Truck Assn., Material Handling Inst., Psi Upsilon. Home: 3300 Willowbrook Dr Pepper Pike OH 44124 Office: 16100 Euclid Av Cleveland OH 44112

FAIRBANK, WILLIAM MARTIN, educator, physicist; b. Mpls., Feb. 24, 1917; s. Samuel Ballantine and Helen Leslie (Martin) F.; A.B., Whitman Coll., Walla Walla, Wash., 1939, D.Sc. (hon.), 1965; postgrad. fellow, U. Wash., 1940-42; M.S., Yale, 1947, Ph.D. (Sheffield fellow), 1948; D.Sc., Duke, 1969; m. Jane Davenport, Aug. 16, 1941; children—William Martin, Robert Harold, Richard Dana. Mem. staff radiation lab. Mass. Inst. Tech., 1942-45; asst. prof. physics Amherst Coll., 1947-52; asso. prof. Duke, 1952-58, prof., 1958-59; prof. physics Stanford, 1959—; spl. research microwave radar systems, microwave propagation, cryogenics, quantized flux in superconductors, properties liquid helium II, He3, liquid helium bubble chambers, superconducting electron accelerators. Bd. overseers Whitman Coll. Named Cal. Scientist of Year, Cal. Museum Sci. and Industry, 1961; recipient Fritz London award, 1968; Wilbur Lucius Cross medal Yale U., 1968. Fellow Am. Phys. Soc. (Oliver E. Buckley Solid State Physics prize 1963, Research Corp. award 1965); mem. Nat. Acad. Scis., Am. Acad. Arts and Scis. Home: 141 E Floresta Way Menlo Park CA 94025 Office: Physics Dept Stanford Univ Stanford CA 94305

FAIRBANKS, AVARD, (Tennyson), sculptor; b. Provo, Utah, Mar. 2, 1897; s. John B. and Lily Annetta (Huish) F.; student Art Students League, N.Y.C., 1910-12, in Paris, 1913- 14; student Ecole Nationale des Beaux Arts, La Grande Chaumiere Academie Colarossi; student under J. B. and J. Leo Fairbanks, James E. Fraser, Charles R. Knight, Jean Antoine Ingalbert, G. Rossi, A. E. Zardo, Dante Sodini; B.F.A., Yale, 1925; M.F.A., U. Wash., 1929; M.A., U. Mich., 1933, Ph.D., 1936; D.F.A. (hon.), Lincoln Coll.; m. Beatrice Maude Fox, June 25, 1918; children—Avard Fox, Eugene Fox, Elliott Aldron, Justin Fox, Virgil Fox, Jonathan Leo, David Nathaniel, Grant Ruthven. Asst. prof. art U. Ore., 1920-27; asso. prof. sculpture U. Mich. 1927-47; prof. sculpture, dean Coll. Fine Arts. U. Utah 1947—, now cons. fine arts; sculptor in residence, spl. cons. fine arts U. N.D., 1965—; prof. sculpture, painting U. Hawaii, 1939. With personnel dept. Ford Bomber plant, 1943, pub. relations dept., 1944, 1945. Works include: The Doughboy of Idaho (state meml. , Trail marker), 91st Div. Meml., Ft. Lewis, Wash.,. Washington A. Roebling medal Am. Mineral Soc.; also many portrait busts and relief portraits; Pony Express (for Utah Centennial); Marcus Whitman, Statuary Hall, Washington; bust Lincoln, New Salem, Ill.; series of portrait busts for Western Hall of Fame. Guggenheim Meml. Found. fellow, 1927-28. The Genius of Man, His Mind and His Work. Clifton Award given to Pioneers Auto Industry at Automotive Golden Jubilee. Recipient medal of Knights of Themopylae, King of Greece; medal of Lycurgus, mayor of Sparta, Greece; Lincoln Diploma honor Lincoln Meml. U. Mem. Archtl. League N.Y., Nat. Sculpture Soc., S.A.B. (past pres. Washtenaw chpt.), Mich. Acad. (chmn. fine arts sect.), Phi Kappa Phi. Home: 1489 Michigan Av Salt Lake City UT 84105 ☆

FAIRBANKS, CHARLES HERRON, educator, anthropologist; b. Bainbridge, N.Y., June 3, 1913; s. Louis Byron and Henrietta Fox (Herron) F.; student Swarthmore Coll., 1931-32; A.B., U. Chgo., 1939; M.A., U. Mich., 1949, Ph.D., 1954; m. Evelyn Adams Timmerman, Feb. 8, 1941; children—Charles Herron, Marie Timmerman. Archeologist, U. Tenn.-TVA, 1937-38, Ocmulgee Nat. Monument, Nat. Park Service, Macon, Ga., 1938-43; supt. Fort Frederica Nat. Monument. St. Simons Is., Ga., 1946-48; with Nat. Park Service, 1950-54; mem. faculty Fla. State U., 1954-63; prof. anthropology U. Fla., 1963—, chmn. dept., 1963-70. Collaborator Indian claims div. Dept. Justice, 1958—. Chmn. Fla. Marine Salvage Com., 1964-65; mem. hwy. salvage com. Fla. Road Dept., 1958—. Served with AUS, 1943-46. Fellow Am. Anthrop. Soc.; mem. Soc. Am. Archaeology, Fla. Anthrop. Soc. (sec. 1955, pres. 1956, editor 1957-59, 61-66), Assn. Current Anthropology, N.C. Archaeol. Soc., Soc. Hist. Archaeology (dir. 1968; pres. 1971), Sigma Xi. Author numerous articles, revs., monographs in field. Asst. editor Am. Antiquity, 1958-60. Home: 621 NE 5th Terrace Gainesville FL 32601

FAIRBANKS, DOUGLAS ELTON, Jr., actor, producer, corp. exec.; b. N.Y.C., Dec. 9, 1909; s. Douglas Elton and Anna Beth (Sully) F.; ed. Boveé and Collegiate Schs. (N.Y.); attended Knickerbocker Greys (N.Y.), Pasadena Poly., Harvard Mil. Sch. (Los Angeles); pvt. tutors, London and Paris; D.F.A. (hon.), Westminster Coll., 1966; Sr. Churchill fellow Westminster Coll.; vis. fellow St. Cross Coll., Oxford U.; M.A., Oxon; m. Mary Lee Epling, Apr. 22, 1939; children—Daphne (Mrs. David Weston), Victoria (Mrs. Barend Van Gerbig), Melissa (Mrs. Richard Morant). Began film career, 1923, stage career, 1927; acted in 75 films (produced or co-produced 15); prod. 160 1 act TV plays; organized own prodn. co. Criterion Films Corp. (Eng.), 1934, The Fairbanks Co. (Cal.), 1946, Fairtel Corp. (N.Y.), 1969; chmn. Dougfair Corp.; producer TV films for Douglas Fairbanks Ltd. (Eng.), 1952-58, chmn.; pres. Boltons Trading Co., Inc.; dep. chmn. Roberts Realty Co. Ltd. (Bahamas); dir. Scripto Pens, Ltd., London, Scripto, Inc., Atlanta, Cavalcade Films, Ltd., Louis Marx Toy Mfg., Ltd., (Hong Kong), Fairbanks Internat., Inc. (U.S.), Thos. Holmes Corp. (U.S.), Westridge Films, Ltd., London, Rambagh Palace Hc el, Jaipur, India. Gov. Am. Mus. in Britain, Ditchley Found., Oxford, Eng.; trustee Edwina Mountbatten Trust; bd. govs. Music Theatre, Lincoln Center, N.Y.C., Royal Shakespeare Theatre, Stratford on Avon, Eng. Author of screen plays, short stories, polit. essays. Exhibitor drawings, illustrations and sculpture. Nat. vice-chmn., Com. Defend America by Aiding Allies, 1940-41; mem. Fight for Freedom Com., 1941, Franco-British War Relief Assn., 1939-41. Presdl. envoy for spl. S. Am. mission, 1941. Served as lt. (j.g.) USNR, 1941. Decorated Silver Star, Combat (V clasp) Legion of Merit, Cross of Mil. Valor (Italy), Order of Merit (Chile); Nat. medal of Korea, Hon. Citizen of Korea; City of Vienna medal (Austria), Knight Brit. Empire, D.S.C., Knight St. John of Jerusalem (Gt. Britain), Legion of Honor, Croix de Guerre with palm (France), Order So. Cross (Brazil), Order of the Crown (Belgium), K.C. Order of George I (Greece), Order Orange-Nassau (Netherlands), Order of Star of Italian Solidarity (Italy); recipient Gold medal of Honor, V.F.W., 1966. Apptd. spl. post-war missions; State Dept. Nat. v.p. Am. Assn. for UN, 1946-52; nat. chmn. CARE Com., 1946-50; trustee Pacific War Meml. sponsor War Meml. Chapel, Washington Cathedral; chmn. Am. Relief for Korea, 1950-53. Mem. English Speaking Union, Council Fgn. Relations. Brit-Am. Alumni Assn. (pres. 1950—), Pilgrim's Soc. Clubs: Century, Knickerbocker (N.Y.C.); Metropolitan (Washington); White's Buck's, Naval and Military (London); Traveller's (Paris); Puffins (Edinburgh). Address: 50 E 58th St New York City NY also 10 Park Pl St James's London SW 1 England and 28 The Boltons London SW 10 England and 6922 Hollywood Blvd Los Angeles CA 90028 ☆

FAIRBANKS, MADGE HOLBROOK, mem. Republic Nat. Com.; b. Washington, June 5, 1925; d. Hilliard Baxter and Madge (Lyon) Holbrook; R.N., Margaret Pillsbury Sch. Nursing, Concord, N.H., 1947; m. Bryce J. Fairbanks, Nov. 21, 1947; children—Bryce J. II, Jeffrey Michael, Jerald Ronald, Jan Leslie, James Andrew. Nurse Harper Hosp., Detroit, 1947-48; del. Rep. Nat. Conv., 1960, alternate 1964; vice chmn. Salt Lake County and Utah Young Reps., 1964-65; chmn. voting and legislative dist. V, 1964; dir. Salt Lake County, Utah Fedn. Rep. Women's Clubs, 1964; vice chmn. Salt Lake County Rep. Central Com., 1965-67; mem. Rep. Nat. Com. for Utah, 1967—. Vol. chmn. North Salt Lake Opportunity Center; mem. bd. UN Assn. Utah; past chmn. Salt Lake City Mental Health Com. Mem. Salt Lake County Med. Aux. Home: 1215 Catherine Salt Lake City UT 84116 Office: Crandall Bldg Salt Lake City UT 84101

FAIRBANKS, ROLLIN JONATHAN, educator, clergyman; b. Watertown, N.Y., Oct. 29, 1908; s. George A. and Ida (Heintzelmann) F.; A.B., U. Mich., 1933; B.D., Episcopal Theol. sch., 1936; D.D. (hon.), Ch. Div. Sch. Pacific, 1957; student U. Pa., 1964-65; m. Phyllis Maynard, Aug. 25, 1936; children—Rollin Jonathan, Jennifer Bliss (Mrs. G.C. Davenport), Peter Maynard, Pamela Wiley. Ordained to ministry Episcopal Ch., 1936; rector in St. Johns, Mich., 1936-39, Grosse Ile, Mich., 1939-43; chaplain Mass. Gen. Hosp., 1943-50; lectr. Harvard, 1944-54; instr. Boston U. Sch. Theology, 1947-48; lectr. Episcopal Theol. Sem., 1944-50, prof., 1950—; vis. prof. Harvard, 1961- 62. Fellow Nat. Inst. Mental Health. Mem. Nat. Assn. Mental Health. Editor Jour. Pastoral Care, 1947- 49, asso. editor, 1949-65, book rev. editor, 1965-70. Author articles. Home: 15 St John's Rd Cambridge MA 02138

FAIRBANKS, RUSSELL NORMAN, univ. adminstr.; b. N.Y.C., Oct. 4, 1919; s. Carleton Forrest and Norna (Johnson) F.; A.B., Harvard, 1941; LL.B., Columbia, 1952; m. Rachel France Fain, Apr. 28, 1942; children—Russell Norman, Jonathan, Norna. Admitted to D.C. bar, 1953; commd. 2d lt. U.S. Army, 1941, advanced through grades to lt. col., 1962; chief legal officer U.S.-Japan Procurement Agy., 1955-57; dir. acad. dept. Judge Adv. Gen.'s Sch., Charlottesville, Va., 1960-62; ret. 1962; asso. dean Columbia Law Sch., 1964-67; prof. law, dean Sch. Law, Rutgers U., 1967—. Mem. policy com., legal services unit Mlbzn. for Youth. Trustee Camden County Legal Services, Inc., N.J. Inst. for Continuing Legal Edn. Decorated Bronze Star. Mem. Am., Camden County bar assns., Assn. Bar City N.Y. Clubs: Harvard (Boston); Englewood Field; Riverton Country; Camden City. Democrat. Home: 729 Signal Light Rd Moorestown NJ 08057 Office: 406 Penn St Camden NJ 08102

FAIRBANKS, WILLIAM FRANCIS, advt. exec.; b. Bklyn., Feb. 27, 1912; s. John Waldo and Mary (Arnold) F.; student Bklyn. Polytech. Inst., also Coll. City N.Y.; m. Dulcie Gummersall, May 17, 1942; children—Gary, Lynn, Richard. Sales presentation dir. NBC, 1931-42; chief network allocation plan Office War Information, 1942-44; account exec. Compton Advt., Inc., 1944-45, MBC, 1946-50; nat. sales mgr. ABC, 1950-55; nat. sales mgr. NBC, 1955-59, v.p. charge sales radio network, 1960; now pres. Chairlift Advt. Bur., Fairbanks Laundry Service. Cons. Off the Wing Tip Radio, Advt. Council. Mem. Radio and Television Execs. Soc. Home: 15 W Way Old Greenwich CT 06870

FAIRBRIDGE, RHODES WHITMORE, educator; geologist; b. Pinjarra, Australia, May 21, 1914; s. Kingsley O. and Ruby E. (Whitmore) F.; B.A., Queens U. (Can.)., 1936; B.S., Oxford U. (Eng.), 1940; D.Sc., U. Western Australia, 1944; m. Dolores G. Carrington, June 19, 1943; 1 son, Kingsley. Field geologist Iraq Petroleum Co., 1938-41; asst. prof. geology U. Western Australia, 1946-53; asso. prof. U. Ill., 1953-54; prof. geology Columbia, N.Y.C., 1955—; leader Nubian Expdn., Sudan, 1961-62. Mem. expdn. Capricorn, Scripps Inst. Oceanography, 1953; founder Internat. Geology Rev., Am. Geol. Inst., 1958; vis. prof. Sorbonne U., Paris, 1962. Mem. Am., London, Swiss, Australian geol. socs., N.Y. Acad. Sci. (past pres. geology sect.), Am. Assn. Petroleum Geologists (past pres. Eastern sect.), Geologische Verein (Bonn), Soc. Geologique France. Author: Australian Stratigraphy, 1953; Encyclopedia of Oceanography, 1966; Encyclopedia of Atmospheric Sciences and Astrogeology, 1967; Encyclopedia of Geomorphology, 1968; (with Chilingar and Bissell) Carbonate Rocks, 2 vols., 1967. Contbr. articles profl. jours. Home: 420 Riverside Dr New York City NY 10025

FAIRBURN, ROBERT GORDON, fibre co. exec.; b. Cleve., July 2, 1911; s. William Armstrong and Louise (Ramsay) F.; grad. Groton Sch., 1928; A.B., Princeton, 1932; m. Mary Whitwell, July 15, 1933; children—Anne, Louise (Mrs. Leslie R. Lumley); m. 2d, Margaret Taylor Watson, July 2, 1951; 1 son, Robert Gardner. With Berst-Forster-Dixfield Co., N.Y.C., 1932-47, pres., gen. mgr., 1942-47; dir. Diamond Match Co., 1941-57, pres., 1947-57 (Diamond Match Co. merged with Gardner Board & Carton Co. to become Diamond Gardner Corp. 1957; Diamond Gardner Corp. merged with U.S. Printing & Lithograph Corp. to become Diamond Nat. Corp. 1959); chmn. bd., dir. Diamond Nat. Corp. to 1961; chmn. bd., dir. Keyes Fibre Co., N.Y.C., 1961—; dir. Canadian Keyes Fibre Co., Ltd., First Nat. Iron Bank, Morristown, N.J. Mem. Masters of Fox Hounds Assn. Am. Presbyn. Clubs: Princeton Quadrangle; Spring Valley Hounds (New Vernon, N.J.); Somerset Hills (N.J.) Country; Morristown; Fifth Avenue, Cloud (N.Y.C.); Cumberland (Portland, Me.); Mill Reef (Antigua); Mid Ocean (Bermuda). Home: PO Box 597 Cherry Lane Mendham NJ 07945 Office: Municipal Airport Morristown NJ 07960

FAIRBURN, ROBERT RANDELL, marine corps officer; b. Chgo., May 9, 1917; s. Robert W. and Clara L. (Randell) F.; B.A. in Bus. Adminstrn., U. Cal. at Berkeley, 1939; M.B.A., George Washington U., 1963; m. Ruth Imogene Grinager, Apr. 5, 1942; children—Kathleen (Mrs. Robert N. Armstrong), James R., Sarah A. Commd. 2d lt. USMC, 1941, advanced through grades to maj. gen., 1969; served with 3d Marine Div., World War II, 1st Marine Air Craft Wing, Vietnam; comdg. gen. Marine Corps Supply Activity, Phila., 1970—. Bd. dirs. Phila. U.S.O. Decorated Bronze Star. Home: Quarters M-1 US Naval Base Philadelphia PA 19112 Office: 1100 S Broad St Philadelphia PA 19146

FAIRCHILD, CLEM WILLIAM, lawyer; b. Valley Falls, Kan., Oct. 11, 1919; s. Charles Clement and Ada (Baker) F.; B.S. in Bus. Adminstrn., U. Kan., 1939; LL.B., U. Mo. at Kansas City, 1947; m. Winifred A. Kipp, Apr. 20, 1945; children—Roberta A., Judith W., Kipp C., Charles W. Admitted to Mo. bar, 1947, since practiced in Kansas City; partner firm Linde, Thomson, Van Dyke, Fairchild & Langworthy, and predecessors, 1946—; instr. U. Mo. Law Sch. at Kansas City, 1948. Dir. Stuart Hall Co., Inc. Mem. 16th Jud. Commn., 1963-70. Chmn. Kansas City Citizens Assn., 1955-58; co-chmn. Jackson County (Mo.) Charter Commn., 1970. Served with USMCR, 1941-45, 51-52. Mem. Mo., Kansas City (pres. 1965) bar assns., Mil. Order World Wars, Sigma Nu. Republican. Conglist. Club: Carriage (pres. 1969-70) (Kansas City, Mo.). Home: 453 W 68th Terrace Kansas City MO 64113 Office: Columbia Union Bank Bldg 900 Walnut St Kansas City MO 64106

FAIRCHILD, GEORGE E., union exec.; b. Maywood, Ill., Aug. 19, 1908; s. George H. and Florence (Sprague) F.; grad. high sch.; m. Lorraine Rose (dec. 1954); children-Betty Joanne (Mrs. Pauley), John Phillip, Patricia L.; m. 2d, Elaine E. Fairchild, Feb. 14, 1957. With Service Employees Internat. Union, 1934—, internat. rep., 1936—, gen. sec.-treas., Washington, 1955—. Mem. nat. operating com. COPE, sec. Police and Fire Commn., Forest Park, Ill.; mem. exec. bd. Nat. Conf. Christians and Jews; mem. conf. Sec.-treasurers, Conf. Internat. and Nat. Sec.-Treasurers (exec. bd.). Founder Proviso Twp. (Ill.) Young Democrats, Mason (Shriner). Office: Service Employees Internat Union Washington DC 20201

FAIRCHILD, HOXIE N., educator; b. N.Y.C., Sept. 7, 1894; s. Jarvis Rose and Sarah Lenita (Plumb) F.; grad., Hackley Sch., 1912; A.B., Columbia, 1917, Ph.D., 1928; m. Mary Creusa Tanner, July 28, 1919; children—Hoxie Mary (died 1930), Anne. Instr. in English, Columbia, 1919-28, asst. prof., 1928-34, asso. prof., 1934-40; prof. English, Hunter Coll., 1940-60, prof. emeritus; vis. lectr. Faculty of English, Cambridge, 1958; guest speaker at meetings and convs., 1935—. Past pres. mem. exec. com., English Grad. Union of Columbia U.; founding mem., past pres. Guild of Scholars of Episcopal Church; trustee Church of St. Mary the Virgin; founding mem. Conf. on Science, Philosophy, and Religion. Decorated Croix de Guerre (with palm), 1918; Chevalier de l'Ordre de la Couronne, 1st class, Belgium, 1920. Mem. Modern Language Assn. of Am. (group sec., chmn. com.). Clubs: Hunter College Humanities (past pres.), Faculty of Columbia University. Author: Religious Trends in English Poetry, 1939, Vol. IV, 1957, Vol. V, 1962, Vol. VI, 1968. Editor, co- author: Religious Perspectives in College Teaching, 1952. Contbr. articles to publs. Home: 464 Riverside Dr New York City NY 10027 ☆

FAIRCHILD, JOHN BURR, publisher; b. Newark, Mar. 6, 1927; s. Louis W. and Margaret (Day) F.; grad. Kent Sch., 1946; B.A., Princeton, 1949; m. Jill Lipsky, June 8, 1950; children—John Longin, James Burr, Jill and Stephen (twins). Mem. research dept. J. L. Hudson Co., Detroit, 1950-51; with Fairchild Publs., Inc., N.Y.C., 1951—, pub. Women's Wear Daily, also Daily News Record, 1960—, editor-in-chief publs., 1964—, pres. corp., 1966-70, chmn., 1970—; exec. v.p., dir. Capital Cities Broadcasting Co., 1968—. Served with AUS, 1947-48. Clubs: University (N.Y.C.); Travellers, Tur aix Pigeons (Paris, France); The Royal Bermuda Yacht Club. Author: Moonflower Couple, 1967. Home: RR 1 Cross Ridge Rd New Canaan CT 06840 Office: 7 E 12th St New York City NY 10003

FAIRCHILD, JOHNSON EDDY, geographer, educator; b. N.Y.C., Jan. 28, 1910; s. Eddy and Alma (Johnson) F.; student U. Hawaii, 1931-32, U. Alaska, 1932-33; B.A., Am. U. Beirut, 1934; M.A., Clark U., 1935; m. Magdoff, 1961; 1 dau., Susan Hopkins. Tutor, instr. Hunter Coll., Bronx, N.Y., 1937-41, asst. dean in charge vets. sessions, 1945-49; chief research analyst N.Y. Office M.I., Gen. Staff, War Dept., Aug. 1941; dir. adult edn., prof. social philosophy Cooper Union Advancement Sci. and Art, N.Y. City, 1949—; chmn. Cooper Union Forum, 1949—; former asst. to pres. the Cooper Union; conductor of geog. class Backgrounds for World Peace, radio sta. WMCA. Served as capt., squad intelligence officer, Group Intelligence, Combat and Photographic Intelligence, U.S. A.A.F., China-Burma-India Theatre, 1942-45. Decorated Air Medal. Fellow N.Y. Adult Edn. Council; mem. Nat. Council Geography Tchrs., Am. Assn. Geographers. Author: Geography for Adults; geog. articles. Editor: Women, Society and Sex; geog. editor of Crowell-Collier Encyclopedia; Basic Beliefs; The Religious Philosophies of Mankind, 1959; Personal Problems and Psychological Frontiers, 1960; America Faces the Nuclear Age, 1961. Home: 11 E 66th St New York City NY 10021 Office: Cooper Union for the Advancement of Science and Art 8th St and Astor Pl New York City NY 10003

FAIRCHILD, MAHLON LOWELL, educator, entomologist; b. Spencer, Ia., Oct. 13, 1930; s. Herbert Elmer and Faye (Eaton) F.; B.S., Ia. State U., 1952, M.S., 1953, Ph.D., 1959; m. Shirley Jean Natrig, Aug. 16, 1954; children—Bruce Charles, Jeanette Marie, Julie Ann. Grad. research asst. Ia. State U., 1952-53, 55-56; entomologist European Corn Borer Lab., Ankeny, Ia., 1957-59; mem. faculty U. Mo. at Columbia, 1959—, prof. entomology, 1967—, chmn. dept., 1969—. Served with AUS, 1953-55. Mem. Entomol. Soc. Am. (exec. com. N. Central br. 1966-69, chmn. plant protection div. 1968-69), Cosmopolitan Internat. (gov. Mo.-Kan. fedn. 1968-69, mem. internat. gov. bd. 1969-71), Sigma Xi, Gamma Sigma Delta (pres. Mo. chpt. 1968-69; award of merit 1965). Author articles in field. Home: 1209 Sunset Dr Columbia MO 65201

FAIRCHILD, PAUL WARNER, investment banker; b. Anderson, Ind., Aug. 14, 1906; s. Walter Henry and May (Mosher) F.; B.S., Northwestern U., 1928; m. Anne Petersen, June 29, 1934; children—Joan E. (Mrs. Lawrence D. Witherbee), Paul Warner. With First Boston Corp., 1929—, v.p., 1956—, head Chgo. office, 1960—, dir., 1964—. Pres. Hinsdale (Ill.) Bd. Edn., 1958-60. Mem. Investment Bankers Assn. Am. (bd. govs. 1959-62). Sigma Chi. Clubs: Bond (pres. 1963), Chicago, Chicago Golf, Attic (Chgo.). Home: 529 N Lincoln St Hinsdale IL 60521 Office: 231 S LaSalle St Chicago IL 60604

FAIRCHILD, THOMAS E., U.S. judge; b. Milw., Dec. 25, 1912; s. Edward Thomas and Helen (Edwards) F.; student Princeton, 1931-33; A.B., Cornell U., 1934; LL.B., U. Wis., 1938; m. Eleanor E. Dahl, July 24, 1937; children—Edward, Susan, Jennifer, Andrew. Admitted to Wis. bar, 1938, practiced Portage, Wis., 1938-41, Milw., 1945-48, 53-56; atty. O.P.A., Chgo., Milw., 1941- 45, hearing commr., Chgo. Region, 1945; atty. gen., Wis., 1948-51; U.S. atty. for Western Dist. Wis., 1951-52; justice Supreme Ct. Wis., 1957- 66, U.S. Ct. Appeals for 7th circuit, 1966—. Dem. candidate Senator from Wis., 1950, 52. Mem. Am., Wis., Fed., Milw. bar assns., Am. Judicature Soc., Am. Law Inst., Phi Delta Phi. Democrat. Mem. United Ch. of Christ. K.P. Office: Fed Bldg Milwaukee WI 53202 also Ct Appeals 219 S Dearborn Chicago IL 60604

FAIRCLOTH, EARL, atty. gen. Fla.; b. Chiefland, Fla., Sept. 24, 1920; s. Joseph William and Emma (Hogan) F.; B.A., LL.B., U. Fla.; m. Wilma Smith, June 5, 1945; children—Amy Lynn, David Earl. Admitted to Fla. bar; practiced in St. Petersburg and Tallahassee to 1953; mem. firm Hector, Faircloth & Davis, and predecessor, Miami. Organized Fla. Com. for Fair Apportionment, 1959; candidate Fla. Senate, 1960; mem. Fla. Ho. of Reps., 1963-64; atty. gen. Fla., 1965—. Served with C.E., AUS, 1944-45. Named Outstanding Young Man, Jr. C. of C., 1964. Mem. Am., Fla. bar assns., Am. Legion, V.F.W., C. of C., Blue Key, Delta Theta Phi, Tau Kappa Alpha. Baptist. Woodmen of the World. Home: 1103 Kenilworth Rd Tallahassee FL 32303 Office: Office Atty Gen Capitol Bldg Tallahassee FL 32302

FAIRES, VIRGIL MORING, educator; b. Gainesville, Fla., Dec. 8, 1897; s. Carl Franklin and Nevada (Moring) F.; student Ga. Sch. Tech., 1916-17, U.S. Naval Acad., 1917-20; B.S., U. Colo., 1922, M.E., 1926, M.S., 1927; 1 dau., Virginia Lee (Mrs. James Ashton Clay, Jr.); m. 2d, Lucile Haley Orr, Oct. 5, 1951. Instr., U. Colo., 1922-25; asst. prof. mech. engring. U. Vt., 1925- 26; asst. prof. mech. engring. Tex. A. and M. Coll., 1926-29, asso. prof., 1929-30, prof., 1930-51, head mgmt. engring, dept., 1941-50, dir. A.S.T.P., 1943-46, head dept. postgrad. studies, 1948-51; chief engring. sect. Am. U., Biarritz, France, 1945-46; prof. mech. engring. N.C. State Coll., 1952-58, U.S. Naval Postgrad. Sch., Monterey, Cal., 1958—. Mem. Am. Soc. M.E. (chmn. S. Tex. sect. 1944-45; Worcester Reed Warner Medal 1962), Am. Soc. Engring. Edn. (chmn. machine design div. 1940, past mem. council), Tau Beta Pi, Phi Kappa Phi, Pi Tau Sigma. Author: (with Grinter, et al), Engineering Preview, 1945; (with Chambers) Analytic Mechanics, rev. edit., 1952; Design of Machine Elements, rev. edit., 1965; Elementary Thermodynamics, rev. edit., 1957; Thermodynamics of Heat Power, rev. edit., 1958; Kinematics, 1959; (with Keown) Mechanism, rev. edit., 1960; Thermodynamics, 1962; (with Simmang Brewer) Problems on Thermodynamics, 1962; (with Wingren) Problems on Design Machine Elements, 1965. Home: Route 3 Box 525 Carmel CA 93921 Office: US Naval Postgraduate Sch Monterey CA 93940

FAIRFAX, EUGENE GEORGE, naval officer; b. Vernal, Utah, Nov. 6, 1916; s. Harry Eugene and Emily (Hollingshead) F.; B.S., U.S. Naval Acad., 1939; m. Juliana Daniels, Nov. 8, 1941; children—Michele (Mrs. J.R. Pettyjohn), Charlotte (Mrs. R.W. Chambliss), Jean Marie (Mrs. L. J. Canavan), Eugene George, Michael. Commd. ensign USN, 1939, advanced through grade to rear adm., 1966; duty on ships U.S.S. Mississippi, USS Tennessee, 1939-41; comdg. officer Fighter Squadron VF- 11, VF-98, then Fleet Airborne Electronics Tng. Unit, 1941-49; command and staff dept. Naval War Coll., 1951-53; navigator U.S.S. Mindoro, 1949- 51; navigator, operations officer U.S.S. Forrestal, 1955-57; operations officer head air programs br. Office Chief Naval Operations, Dept. of Navy, 1957-60; comdr. U.S. Passumpsic, 1960, U.S.S. Ticonderoga, 1961; chief of staff, aide to comdr. carrier div. 1, 1962-63; with weapons systems evaluation group Office of Sec. of Def., Washington, 1963-65; with Office Asst. Chief Naval Operations, 1965-66; dep. comdr. Joint Task Force 2 (Navy), 1966- 68, Antisubmarine Warfare Group 5, 1968-69, Alaskan Sea Frontier, 1969- -. Vice-pres. St. John's P.T.A., 1958-59. Decorated Legion of Merit with star, D.F.C. with 3 stars, Air medal (Navy) with 5 stars, Joint Service Commendation medal; Nat. Order medal Vietnam. Gallantry Cross (Vietnam). Address: Box 14 FPO Seattle WA 98790

FAIRGRAVE, D.J., lawyer; b. Des Moines, Sept. 10, 1906; LL.B., U. Ia., 1927. Admitted to Ia. bar, 1927; mem. firm Bradshaw, Fowler, Proctor & Fairgrave, Des Moines. Mem. Am., Ia., Polk County bar assns., Internat. Assn. Ins. Counsel. Office: Des Moines Bldg Des Moines IA 50309*

FAIRGRIEVE, WILLIAM ROBERTSON, accountant; b. Cleve., Oct. 30, 1916; s. William Ward and Nellie (Robertson) F.; B.B.S., Miami U., Oxford, O., 1941; m. Ruth L. Nielsen, Dec. 5, 1947; children—Margaret L., Anne R., William N. With Ernst & Ernst, C.P.A.'s, 1941—, partner, Buffalo 1954—. Mem. exec. bd. Greater Niagara Frontier council Boy Scouts Am.; bd. dirs. Community Action Orgn.; pres. bd. trustees Niagara Frontier Methodist Home; mem. council accountancy Canisius Coll. Served to capt., inf., AUS, 1942-46. C.P.A., N.Y.; chartered accountant, Ont., Can. Mem. Am. Inst. C.P.A.'s (pres. Buffalo 1964), Buffalo C. of C. (dir.), Phi Beta Kappa, Omicron Delta Kappa. Clubs: Buffalo Country of Buffalo. Methodist (ofcl. bd.). Home: 55 Knollwood Lane Buffalo NY 14221 Office: Western Bldg 15 Court St Buffalo NY 14202

FAIRHURST, CHARLES, educator; b. Widnes, Lancashire, Eng., Aug. 5, 1929; s. Richard Lowe and Josephine (Starkey) F.; B.Eng., U. Sheffield (Eng.), 1952, Ph.D., 1955; m. Margaret Ann Lloyd, Sept. 7, 1957; children—Anne Elizabeth, David Lloyd, Charles Edward, Catherine Mary, Hugh Richard, John Peter, Margaret Mary. Came to U.S., 1956, naturalized, 1967. Mining engr. trainee Nat. Coal Bd., St. Helens, Eng., 1949-56; research asso. U. Minn., Mpls., 1956-67, prof., 1967-70, head Sch. Mineral and Metall. Engring., 1969—, prof. dept. civil and mineral engring., 1970—; cons. U.S. Army C.E. Mem. Am. Inst. Mining, Metal. Engrs., S. African Inst. Mining and Metallurgy, Soc. Exptl. Stress Analysis, Am. Soc. Testing Materials, Internat. Soc. Rock Mechanics (past dir.), Sigma Xi. Roman Catholic. Home: 417 5th Av N South St Paul MN 55075 Office: Dept Civil and Mineral Engring U Minn Minneapolis MN 55455

FAIRLEY, ALBERT LANGLEY, Jr., mining co. exec.; b. Jackson, Miss., Dec. 28, 1913; s. Albert Langley and Alethe (Vardaman) F.; B.Sc., Birmingham-So. Coll., 1934; grad. student geology and mining engring., Johns Hopkins, 1935; m. Claire Elizabeth Haines, Aug. 20, 1949. Geologist, found. engr. TVA, 1935-37; asst. geologist Tenn. Coal, Iron and R.R. div. U.S. Steel Corp., 1937-41; asst. dep. dir. steel div. WPB, 1941-43; various operating and exec. positions Shenango Furnace Co., and subsidiaries, Pitts., 1946-58; pres., dir. Dominion Steel and Coal Corp., Ltd., Montreal, 1959-64, Hollinger Mines, Ltd., Labrador Mining & Exploration Co., Hollinger North Shore Exploration Co., Ltd., 1964—; dir., chmn. exec. com. Domtar Ltd.; dir. Sun Life Assurance Co. of Can. Canadian Imperial Bank of Commerce, Argus Corp.; adv. com. Crown Trust Co. Served to capt. USAAF, World War II. Mem. Can. Inst. Mining and Metallurgy, Am. Iron and Steel Inst., Am. Inst. Mining and Metall. Engrs., Soc. Econ. Geologists, Eastern States Blast Furnace and Coke Ovens Assn. Clubs: St. James's, Mount Royal, Forest and Stream (Montreal); Allegheny Country (Sewickley, Pa.); Duquesne (Pitts.); Kitchi Gammi (Duluth, Minn.); Birmingham (Ala.) Country; Toronto. Home: 3940 Cote des Neiges Rd Montreal 109 Quebec Canada Office: 1155 Dorchester Blvd W Montreal 2 Quebec Canada

FAIRLEY, FRANCIS HILLIARD, lawyer; b. Monroe, N.C., Oct. 3, 1915; s. Frank Hilliard and Janie (Phifer) F.; B.A. with honors, U. N.C., 1935, student and teaching- fellow, Grad. Sch., 1935-36, LL.B., 1939; student Columbia U. Sch. Law, 1936-38; m. Ella Doris McGuinn, Aug. 24, 1951; children—Mary Jane, Ella Frances. Admitted to N.C. bar, 1939, also U.S. Dist. Ct., Circuit Ct. Appeals, U.S. Supreme Ct., Court Claims, ICC, FCC, Tax Ct., Treasury Dept., U.S. Customs Ct.; law clk. to chief judge U.S. Ct. Appeals, 4th Circuit, 1939-40; sr. partner firm Fairley, Hamrick, Monteith & Cobb, Charlotte, N.C., 1939—; pros. atty. City of Charlotte, 1941; sr. asst. U.S. atty. Western Dist. N.C., 1948-53. Dir. So. Nat. Bank, Catawba Loan & Finance Co., Daniels Constrn. Co., Lenoir Finance Co., J. V. Griffith Co.; instr. negotiable instruments and comml. law Am. Inst. Banking, 1946-49, 51-52. Mem. Charlotte Estate Planning Council. Mem. N.C. Democratic Exec. Com., 1960—. Bd. dirs. N.C. Law Found. Served to lt. comdr. USNR, 1941-45. Fellow Am. Bar Found., Am. Coll. Probate Counsel, Comml. Law Found.; mem. Am. Acad. Polit. and Social Scis., Acad. Polit. Sci., Am. Law Inst., Am. Judicature Soc., Assn. Bar City N.Y., Internat., Inter-Am., Fed., Am. (life; ho. dels. 1962—), 26th Jud. Dist. (exec. com. 1950-54, past chmn. programs com. 1949-55) bar assns., N.C. State Bar (pres. 1962-63, past v.p., chmn. exec. com., mem. council), Am. Legion (post comdr.), 40 and 8, Comml. Law League Am. (bd. govs. 1963-69, v.p. 1966-67, pres. 1967-68), S.A.R., S.C.V., Fedn. Ins. Counsel, Nat. Assn. Probate and Bank Attys., U. N.C. Law Alumni Assn. (dir. 1953-64, pres. 1959-60), V.F.W., U.N.C. Gen. Alumni Assn. (life; dir. 1948- 51), Charlotte Opera Assn., Charlotte C. of C., Scribes, Phi Beta Kappa Assos., Phi Beta Kappa, Phi Delta Phi (province pres., 1947-64, nat. pres. 1967-69, chief justice 1969—). Episcopalian (sr. warden, lay leader). Clubs: Executives, Cotillion; Charlotte Country, Carmel Country (pres. 1957) (Charlotte). Contbr. articles profl. jours. Home: 424 Eastover Rd Charlotte NC 28207 Office: Law Bldg East Trade St Charlotte NC 28202

FAIRMAN, CHARLES, educator; b. Alton, Ill., July 27, 1897; s. Willis L. and Helen (Stelle) F.; A.B., U. Ill., 1918, A.M., 1920; Ph.D., Harvard, 1926, S.J.D., 1938; grad. work U. Paris, 1925-26; LL.B., U. London, 1934; m. Elizabeth Armstrong, Nov. 23, 1918. Tchr. pvt. sch., 1920-23; asst. prof. govt. Pomona Coll., 1926-28; lectr. govt. Harvard, 1928- 30; asst. prof. polit. sci. Williams Coll., 1930-36; asso. prof. polit. sci. Stanford, 1938-41, prof., 1941-53, prof. law, 1947-53; Nagel prof. of constl. law and polit. sci. Washington U., St. Louis, 1953-55; prof. law Harvard Law Sch., 1955-62, emeritus; Guggenheim Fellowship, 1960-61. Studies in history, the U.S. Supreme Ct. Cons., Commn. Orgn. Exec. Br. Govt., 1948. Served as cpl. 1st F.A., Ill. Nat. Gd., 1916-17; 1st lt. F.A., U.S. Army, 1918-19; maj., later lt. col., then col., U.S. Army, 1942-46; in judge advocate gen.'s office, Washington, as legal adv. G-5 Sect. A.F.H.Q., and chief, Internat. Law div. Office Theater Judge Advocate, E.T.O. Awarded Penfield travelling fellowship U. Pa., 1925. Brandeis research fellowship Harvard Law Sch., 1936-38. Fellow Am. Acad. Arts and Scis.; mem. Am. Polit. Sci. Assn. (3d v.p., 1946-47), Social Sci. Research Council, 1950-53, Theta Chi, Ma Wan Da. Awarded Legion of Merit. Democrat. Order of Coif. Author: The Law of Martial Rule, 1930, 2d edit., 1943; Justice Miller and the Supreme Court, 1862-1890, 1939; The History of the Supreme Court: Reconstruction and Reunion, 1864-1888, vol. 1, 1971. Contbr. numerous papers to law publs. Admitted to D.C., Mo., Mass., Supreme Ct. bars. Home: 5334 Calumet Av La Jolla CA 92037

FAIRMAN, MILTON, pub. relations counsel; b. Chgo., Dec. 8, 1904; s. George Simpson and Anna A. (Macauley) F.; student St. Ignatius Acad., Chgo., 1918-22. Loyola U., 1922-23, U. Chgo., 1923-24; m. Kathryn M. McSweeney, Aug. 5, 1929; 1 son, Roger Milton. Asso. librarian Loyola U., 1923; newspaper writer City News Bur. of Chgo. Chgo. Am., Chgo. Eve. Post, Chgo., Herald-Examiner, 1925-34; asst. to dir., press sect. U.S. Dept. of Interior and Pub. Works Adminstrn., 1935- 36; dir. pub. relations Borden's Dairy & Ice Cream Co., Columbus, O., 1937-43, The Borden Co., N.Y.C., 1943-57, asst. v.p., 1957- 63, v.p., 1963-68. Pres. Found. for Pub. Relations Edn. and Research, 1961-65. Recipient Golden Plate award from the Am. Acad. of Achievement, 1968. Mem. Pubic Relations Soc. Am. (founding mem., pres. 1951), Public Relations Soc. N.Y. (past chmn.). Internat. Public Relations Assn. Clubs: Canadian, Overseas Press (N.Y.C.); Nat. Press (Washington). Writer and speaker on pub. relations. Author: Managing the External Function, Top Mgmt. Handbook, 1960. Editor Public Relations Jour., 1954-55, 68—. Home: 80 East Hunting Ridge Rd Stamford CT 06903 Office: 845 3d Av New York City NY 10022

FAIRWEATHER, OWEN, lawyer; b. Chgo., Aug. 18, 1913; s. George O. and Nellie (Dieter) F.; A.B., Dartmouth, 1935; J.D., U. Chgo., 1938; m. Sally Hallberg, May 4, 1940; children—Ellen Vail, Peter Gustav. Admitted to Ill. bar, 1938, since practiced in Chgo.; partner firm Seyfarth, Shaw, Fairweather & Geraldson, 1945—. Dir. Microdot, Inc., N.Y., Danly Machine Corp., Self- Insurers Services, Inc., Chgo. Mem. Gov. Personnel Com. Med. adv. com. tech. and soc. Harvard; visitation com. U. Chgo. Law Sch. Mem. Am., Ill., Chgo. bar assns. Author comparative labor law texts. Contbr. legal jours. Home: 59 Hawthorne Rd Barrington IL 60010 Office: 111 W Jackson Blvd Chicago IL 60604

FAISAL IBN ABDUL AZIZ AL SAUD, KING, King of Saudi Arabia; b. Riyadh, Nejd, Arabia, 1905; 2d s. of Ibn Saud (Abdul Aziz al Saud), King of Saudi Arabia; 1 son (by previous marriage) Abdullah; m. 2d, Iffat; children—Mohammed, Khalid, Saud, Abd-al-Rahman, Sa'd, Bandar, Turki. As officer in army participated in battles that established kingdom, an absolute monarchy formed of Kingdom of Hejaz and Sultanate of Nejd, under reign of Ibn Saud, 1920-25; apptd. viceroy of Nejd, 1926; became sec. of state, Saudi Arabia, 1932; signed treaty confirming ofcl. relations between U.S. and Saudi Arabia, 1933; became minister fgn. affairs, 1934; upon death of father and elder brother's accession to throne was declared Crown Prince, 1953; prime minister and fgn. minister, 1953-64, minister def., 1958-64; in 1958 King Saud transferred to Faisal a large part of his absolute powers, including control of interior, fgn. and financial affairs; king of Saudi Arabia, 1964—. Del. San Francisco Conf. on International Orgn., 1945; chmn. Saudi Arabia delegation to UN Gen. Assembly. Recipient Hon. Knight Comdr. St. Michael and St. George (Gt. Britain). Address: The Royal Palace Riyadh Saudi Arabia*

FAISON, SAMSON LANE, Jr., educator, art critic; b. Washington, Nov. 16, 1907; s. Samson Lane and Zleanor Kerfoot (Sowers) F.; A.B., Williams Coll., 1929, Litt.D., 1971; M.A., Harvard, 1930; M.F.A., Princeton, 1932; m. Virginia Gordon Weed, June 1, 1935; children—Gordon Lane, George Weston, Christopher Maury, Samson Lane III. Instr., later asst. prof. history art Yale, 1932-36; asst. prof. Williams Coll., 1936-39, asso. prof., 1940-42, chmn. dept., 1940-69, prof. history art, 1946—; dir. Williams Coll. Museum of Art; Guggenheim Fellow, 1960-61; exec. sec. com. on visual arts Harvard, 1954-55; vis. prof. U. Pa., summers 1939, 40, Columbia, summer 1948, U. Cal. at Berkeley, summers 1949, 52, N.Y. U., summers 1950, 53; vis. research prof. U. Ga., 1968. Dir. Central Collecting Point, Munich (State Dept.), 1950-51. Served with art looting investigation unit OSS and USNR, 1942-46. Decorated chevalier Legion d'Honneur 1947. Mem. Coll. Art Assn. (pres. 1951-53), N.E. Council Museums, Internat. Assn. Art Critics, Am. Assn. Museums, Mass. Council Arts and Humanities. Clubs: Century Assn., Williams (N.Y.C.). Author: Daumier's Third Class R.R. Carriage, 1946; Manet, 1953; Guide to the Art Museums of New England, 1958; Art Tours and Detours in New York State, 1964; also articles art jours. Art critic The Nation, 1952-55. Home: Scott Hill Rd Williamstown MA 01267

FAISON, SETH SHEPARD, ins. broker; b. N.Y.C., Jan. 18, 1924; s. John Williams and Caroline Goree (Shepard) F.; B.A. with honors, Wesleyan U., 1947; m. Susan Tyler, Apr. 14, 1956; children—Katharine Tyler, Seth Shepard, Sarah, Ann Badger. Personnel mgr. NBC, N.Y.C., 1948-53; div. mgr. Am. Mgmt. Assn., N.Y.C., 1953-58; asst. v.p. Johnson & Higgins, Inc., N.Y.C., 1958-68, v.p., 1968—; trustee Kings Hwy. Savs. Bank, Bklyn., 1969-71. Chmn. Bklyn. Acad. Music, 1966-71; trustee Bklyn. Inst. Arts and Scis., 1963—, v.p., 1965-71, exec. v.p., 1971—; trustee Bklyn. Hosp., Poly Prep.; bd. dirs. Police Athletic League N.Y. Served to lt. (j.g.), USNR, 1943-46. Recipient N.Y. State award for Acad. Music (rehab. of 1 of state's most venerable theaters), 1969. Mem. Citizens Union, Ins. Brokers Assn. State N.Y. Unitarian (deacon). Clubs: Down Town Assn. (N.Y.C.); Heights Casino, Rembrandt (Bklyn.); Old Inlet, Bellport Bay Yacht (Bellport, N.Y.). Home: 1 Pierrepont St Brooklyn NY 11201 Office: 95 Wall St New York City NY 10005

FAITH, EDWARD LEROY, life ins. co. exec.; b. St. Louis, Mar. 24, 1908; s. Emil J. and Helen M. (Riedel) F.; m. Clara Baker, May 29, 1928; 1 dau., Nancy L. (Mrs. Stephen J. Sturm). With Gen. Am. Life Ins. Co., St. Louis, 1923—, v.p., actuary, 1959—. Fellow Soc. Actuaries. Club: Civitan (sec.-treas. Downtown club St. Louis). Home: 30 Willmore Rd St Louis MO 63109 Office: 1501 Locust St St Louis MO 63103

FAITH, PERCY, musician, condr.; b. Toronto, Can., Apr. 7, 1908; s. Abraham and Minnie (Ruthenberg) F.; ed. Lansdowne Grammar Sch. and Jarvis Coll. Sch., Toronto; m. Mary Palange, July 17, 1929; children—Marilyn, David Peter. Began as pianist in theatre and hotel work; arranger and condr. for Canadian Broadcasting Corp., 1933-40; condr. Carnation radio program, Chgo., 1940—; eastern musical dir. Columbia Records Inc., 1957-60, western music dir. popular div., 1960—. Recipient 1953 Record of Year with gold award for song from Moulin Rouge, Gold award for recording Summer Place, 1960; gold awards for albums Viva and Bouquet, 1964. Jewish religion. Club: Arts and Letters (Toronto). Composer and arranger of songs and other works, and known for musical backgrounds and arrangements for radio.‡

FAKHREDDINE, MOHAMED, diplomat of Sudan; b. Duiem, Sudan, Oct. 12, 1924; s. Mohamed Abdelbagi; ed. Gordon Coll., Khartoum, Sudan, also Durham (Eng.) U.; m. Suad Abdelrahman, Oct. 12, 1948; 1 dau., Reem Fakhreddine Mohamed. Controller, Pubs. Bur. Sudan, 1954-58; minister, counsellor Sudan embassy, London, Eng., 1958-60; ambassador to Pakistan, Afghanistan and China, 1960-64; rep. of Sudan to UN, 1964—. Home: 1155 Park Av New York City NY 10028 Office: 757 3d Av New York City NY 10017

FALBERG, WEAVER EMMANUEL, constrn. products co. exec.; b. Chgo., Jan. 23, 1916; s. Weaver D. and Emma (Kreiner) F.; student U. Cin., 1938-40; M.B.A., U. Chgo., 1956; m. Virginia Knodel, Apr. 5, 1941; children—Terry, Karen. With Joseph T. Ryerson & Son, Inc., Chgo., 1936—, v.p., central region and gen. mgr. Chgo. plant, 1963-68, dir., 1960—; pres. Inland-Ryerson Constrn. Products Co., 1968—, also dir. Bd. dirs. Inland-Ryerson Found., Mt. Sinai Hosp., Chgo., Couvracier, Paris, France, Soc. Industria Profilati Somaglia S.P.A., Milan, Italy, U. Chgo. Exec. Program Club. Mem. Steel Service Center Inst. (pres. central states chpt. 1968), Am. Soc. Metals, Ill. C. of C., Chgo. Assn. Commerce and Industry. Mason. Clubs: Union League (Chgo.); North Shore Country (Glenview, Ill.); Park Ridge Country. Home: 394 Edgemont Lane Park Ridge IL 60068 Office: 2621 S 15th Pl Chgo. IL 60680

FALBO, ERNEST SALVATORE, educator; b. Spokane, Feb. 14, 1923; s. Pasquale and Lucia (Pittarelli) F.; A.B., Reed Coll., 1949; Ph.D., U. Florence (Italy), 1954; m. Ruth Eilean Lear, July 16, 1956; children—Paula, Carla, Christopher, Francesca. Instr., Portland (Ore.) State Coll., 1955-56; asso. prof. modern langs. Lake Erie Coll., 1956-64; vis. asst. prof. Italian, U. Va., summers 1960, 61; prof. Italian, Gonzaga U., 1964-68, chmn. dept. modern langs., 1965-67; prof., chmn. fgn. lang. dept. State U. Coll. at Buffalo, 1968—. Dir. Edn. Professions Devel. Act. Inst. in Italian, Florence, summer 1969; dir. Nat. Def. Ednl. Act Inst. Advanced Study Italian, Florence, summer 1967. Served with USAAF, 1943-45. Decorated D.F.C., Air medal with 3 oak leaf clusters; Fulbright fellow, 1949-50. Mem. Pacific Northwest Conf. Fgn. Langs (pres. 1967), Am. Assn. Tchrs. Italian (sec.-treas. 1964-67), Am. Council Teaching Fgn. Langs. (nat. del. 1967—), Am.-Italian Hist. Assn. (bd. dirs. 1966—). Editor, translator: (Count Leonetto Cipriani) California and Overland Diaries, 1962; (Charles Olliffe) American Scenes, 1964. Compilor: Dictionary of Am. Assn. Tchrs. Italian, 1965. Home: 29 Washington Hwy Snyder NY 14226 Office: State University College of NY Buffalo NY 14222

FALCK, EDWARD, indsl. engr.; b. N.Y.C., June 22, 1911; s. Albert and Edna (Davis) F.; A.B., Columbia, 1930, B.S., 1931, M.S., 1932, univ. fellow, 1932-33; m. Ruth McGee, Dec. 12, 1936; children—Jon Edward, Edward Albert. Dir. rates and research TVA, 1933- 37; spl. asst. to v.p. Consol. Edison Co., N.Y.C., 1937-43; cons. to power br. WPB, 1941-42, asst. dep. dir. gen. for distbn., 1942-43; dep. dir. Office of War Utilities, 1943-44, dir., 1944-45; dir. Office Emergency Controls, Civilian Prodn. Adminstrn., 1946; cons. on electric power r Comisión Federal de Electricidad, Mexican Govt., 1946; cons. on electric power Select Com. for Fgn. Aid, U.S. Ho. of Reps., 1947; dir. office energy and utilities Nat. Security Resources Bd., 1948-50; cons. to President's Materials Policy Commn., 1951-52; cons. engr., 1945—. Mem. U.S. Tech. Mission on German Reparation, 1948. Mem. Am. Econ. Assn., Am. Statis. Assn., I.E.E.E., Nat., D.C. socs. profl. engrs., Am. Gas Assn., S.A.R., Sigma Xi, Presbyn. Clubs: Nat. Press, Congressional Country, George Town (Washington). Home: 9 Grafton St Chevy Chase MD 20015 Office: 1625 I St NW Washington DC 20006

FALCON, JACK NATHAN, food chain exec.; b. Cleve., May 21, 1912; s. Nathan and Rose (Golick) F.; B.A., Western Res. U., 1933; LL.B., Cleve. Marshall Law Sch., 1954; m. Natalie Gittelsohn, June, 24, 1937; children—Theodore G., Barbara J. Engaged as C.P.A., Cleve., 1946-64; admitted to Ohio bar, 1954; sec., treas. Fisher Foods Inc., Cleve., 1965-71. C.P.A., Ohio. Mem. Ohio Soc. C.P.A.'s, Am. Inst. Accountants, Ohio, Cleve. bar assns., Cleve. Treasurers Club. Home: 26621 Hendon Rd Beachwood OH 44124

FALCON, JOSEPH V., corp. exec.; b. Evanston, Ill., 1902; grad. Dartmouth, 1924. Pres., Savage Arms div. Emhart Corp. Home: Overbrook Rd Longmeadow MA 01106 Office: 86 Broadway Chicopee Falls MA 01020

FALCONER, DONALD PEARSON, sugar co. exec.; b. Oakland, Cal., May 21, 1920; s. Eric A. and Janet (Pearson) F.; A.B., U. Cal. at Berkeley, 1940, LL.B., 1947; m. Lavina Kelly, Jan. 3, 1945; children—John, Ethan, Julia. Admitted to Cal. bar, 1947; with Cal. and Hawaiian Sugar Co., 1947—, v.p., gen. counsel, sec., 1964—. Mem. exec. com. U.S. Cane Sugar Refiners Assn., 1964—. Served to capt. AUS, 1942-46. Mem. Cal., San Francisco bar assns., Order of Coif. Rotarian. Home: 1226 King Dr El Cerrito CA 94530 Office: 215 Market St San Francisco CA 94106

FALCONER, WILBERT LAWRENCE, geol. engr.; b. Stewart, B.C., Can., July 18, 1912; s. Thomas Wilbert and Olah Juantia (Salkirk) F.; student U. B.C., 1929-32; Geol. Engr., Colo. Sch. Mines, 1941; m. Regena Peterson, Dec. 18, 1941; 1 son, James Selkirk. With Abasand Oil Co., 1941-43, Imperial Oil, Ltd., 1943-48; operations mgr. Pacific Petroleums, Ltd., 1948-51; pres., mng. dir. Ponder Oils, Ltd., Calgary, Alta., Can., 1951—; pres. Discovery, Inc., 1960—, also Universal Printers, Ltd., 1960—; exec. v.p. Amurex Oil Co., 1955-57, pres., 1957-58; pres. Jet Lube of Can., Ltd., Calgary Holdings & Royalties, Ltd.; pres. Canadian Nat. div., 1957-58; dir. prairie div. Horsemen's Benevolent and Protective Assn. Fellow Geol. Assn. Can.; mem. Assn. Profl. Engrs. Alta., Am. Inst. Mining, Metall. and Petroleum Engrs., Am. Assn. Petroleum Geologists, Alta. Soc. Petroleum Geologists, Canadian Inst. Mining and Metallurgy. Home: 1141 9th St NW Calgary Alberta Canada Office: Lancaster Bldg Calgary Alberta Canada

FALES, DEAN ABNER Jr., museum cons.; b. Boston, Oct. 10, 1925; s. Dean Abner and Lenabel (Clark) Fales; A.B., Harvard 1950; A.M., Boston U., 1952; m. Martha Lou Gandy, Mar. 3, 1956. Teaching fellow English, Boston U., 1952-53; museum asst. Henry Francis du Pont Winterthur Mus., 1953-54, registrar, 1954-56, sec., 1956-59; dir. Essex Inst., Salem, Mass. 1959-67, editor Hist. Collections, 1960-67; museum cons., 1967—. Trustee Old Sturbridge (Mass.) Village, Brick Store Mus., Kennebunk, Maine; overseer Strawbery Banke, Inc., Portsmouth, N.H. Mem. Conn. Hist. Soc., Soc. Preservation New Eng. Antiquities, Essex Inst., Colonial Soc. Mass., Pewter Collectors Club Am. (past officer, editor bull. 1953- 55), Am. Assn. State and Local History, Nat. Trust Hist. Preservation, Walpole Soc. Republican. Conglist. Clubs: Polar Bear (Hammerfest, Norway); Odd Volumes (Boston). Author articles in field. Address: Kennebunkport ME 04046

FALICOV, LEOPOLDO MAXIMO, physicist, educator; b. Buenos Aires, Argentina, June 24, 1933; s. Isaias Felix and Dora (Samoilovich) F.; licenciado in chemistry Buenos Aires U., 1957; Ph.D., Cuyo U. Instituto J. Balseiro, Argentina, 1958; Ph.D. in Physics, Cambridge U., 1960; m. Marta Alicia Puebla, Aug. 13, 1959; children—Alexis, Ian. Came to U.S., 1960, naturalized, 1967. Research asso. dept. physics Inst. Study Metals, U. Chgo., 1960-61, instr. physics, 1961-62, asst. prof. physics, 1962-65, asso. prof., 1965-68, prof., 1968-69; prof. physics U. Cal. at Berkeley, 1969—; cons. in field. Alfred P. Sloan Found. fellow, 1964-68; vis. fellow Fitzwilliam Coll., Cambridge, Eng.; Fulbright fellow, 1969. Author: Group Theory and Its Physical Applications, 1966; La Estructura Electronica de los Solidos, 1967. Contbr. articles profl. jours. Home: 90 Avenida Dr Berkeley CA 94708

FALISE, ROBERT ALPHONSE, lawyer, corp. exec.; b. N.Y.C., Oct. 28, 1932; s. Alphonse and Anne (Tiedemann) F.; A.B., Columbia, 1954, J.D., 1956; m. Katharine Keith Stephenson, Apr. 21, 1967; children—Katherine Prentice, Elizabeth Stephenson, Christina Sumner. Admitted to N.Y. bar, 1956, to practice before Supreme Ct. U.S., U.S. Mil. Ct. Appeals; asso. Donovan Leisure Newton & Irvine, N.Y.C., 1956-57; asst. dir. U.S. Commn. Civil Rights, Washington, 1960-61; asso. Olwine, Connelly, Chase, O'Donnell & Weyher, N.Y.C., 1961-66; gen. counsel Dictaphone Corp., Rye, N.Y., 1966—, v.p., 1969—, sec., 1967—; dir. Dictaphone Internat. Corp., Jens Risom Design, Inc., Bryant & Stratton Bus. Inst., Inc., Grayarc Co., Inc., Echo Sci. Corp. U.S. del. legal com. Internat. Civil Aviation Orgn., Montreal, 1958. Served to capt., AUS, 1957-60. Mem. Fed., Am., N.Y. State bar assns., Bar City N.Y., Columbia Alumni Assn. (dir. 1963-66). Clubs: Metropolitan (N.Y.C.); Am. Yacht (Rye, N.Y.). Home: Quarry Pound Ridge Rd Bedford NY 10506 Office: 120 Old Post Rd Rye NY 10580

FALK, CARL ANTON, investment banker; b. Omaha, Dec. 12, 1907; s. Charles E. and Amanda C. (Quarnstrom) F.; student pub. schs. and bus. coll., Omaha; L.H.D., Midland Coll.; m. Gladys M. Gustafson, June 30, 1928; children—Carolyn (Mrs. Scott), Robert, Virginia (Mrs. Olson), Suzanne (Mrs. Ahlstrand). Dir., chmn. exec. com. Kirkpatrick, Pettis, Smith, Polian, Inc., investment bankers, Omaha; treas., dir. Immanuel, Inc.; mem. Midwest Stock Exchange, Chgo.; sec., treas., dir. Agrl. Warehouses, Inc.; chmn. bd. Neb. Blue Cross. Mem. Neb. Investment Bankers Assn. (past pres.), Omaha C. of C., Omaha Council Chs. (past pres.), Aksarben. Rotarian, Mason (Shriner, 33). Clubs: Omaha, Omaha Country, Noon Day (past pres.), Plaza (Omaha); De Anza Desert Country (Borrego Springs, Cal.); Garden of Gods (Colorado Springs, Colo.). Home: 3018 Paddock Rd Omaha NB 68124 Office: Omaha Bldg Omaha NB 68102

FALK, ELMER M., former fgn. service officer; b. New Bedford, Mass., May 6, 1911; s. Elmer H. and Selma P. (Larsen) F.; B.S. in Econs., Wharton Sch. U. Pa., 1931, M.S. in Edn., 1933; m. Margaret Fulton, Nov. 9, 1940; children—Christine M., Martin E. With Pa. Dept. Pub. Assistance, 1934-43, 46; dir. assembly center UNRRA, Salzburg, Austria, 1945-46; with Vocational Rehab. and Edn. Office, VA, Phila., 1946-48; dep. dept. chief, then dept. chief Internat. Refugee Orgn., Germany, 1948-51; dep. European coordinator, then coordinator U.S. Displaced Persons Commn., Frankfurt, Germany, 1951- 52; chief U.S. escapee program for Germany, Dept. of State, FOA/ICA, 1952-54; dep. chief intergovtl. refugee program div. ICA, Washington, 1954-56; with Office Internat. Adminstrn., Dept. of State, Washington, 1956-62; dir. office of refugee and migration affairs, 1962-68. Recipient Superior Honor award Dept. State, 1966. Home: 7828 Lee Av Wellington Alexandria VA 22308

FALK, EUGENE HANNES, educator; b. Czechoslovakia, Aug. 10, 1913; s. Herman and Helen (Kircova) F.; Ph.D. in French, Victoria U., Manchester, Eng., 1942; M.A. (hon.), Dartmouth, 1966; m. Ellen Wien, 1938 (div.); children—Ingrid Helen, Ronald Jonathan. Came to U.S., 1946, naturalized, 1953. Asst., then asst. lectr. German, U. Manchester (Eng.), 1939-42; master French, Alcester (Eng.) Sch., 1943-46; mem. faculty U. Bridgeport (Conn.), 1946-53, prof. fgn. langs., 1948-53, chmn. dept. fgn. langs., 1947-53; vis. prof. French, U. Minn., 1953-54; mem. faculty U. Minn., 1954-63, prof. French, 1957-63, chmn. dept. comparative lit., 1956-63, chmn. dept. Romance langs., 1960-63; mem. faculty Dartmouth, 1963-67, chmn. dept. Romance langs., 1964-67, Edward Tuck prof. French, 1964-67; prof. French and comparative lit. U. N.C., 1967—. Fellow Fund Advancement Edn., 1952-53. Mem. Modern Lang. Assn., Am. Assn. Tchrs. French, Am. Assn. U. Profs., Assn. Internat. d'Etude, Francaises Internat. Assn. Comparative Lit. Author: Renunciation as a Tragic Focus, 1954; Types of Thematic Structure, 1967. Home: 410 Wesley Dr Chapel Hill NC 27514

FALK, HAROLD FRANK, corp. exec.; b. Milw., Mar. 12, 1909; s. Harold Sands and Eugenia (Bechtner) F.; B.S. in Metall. Engring., U. Wis., 1933; m. Suzanne Douglas, June 28, 1934; children—Cynthia Jane (Mrs. Nelson A. Hyde, Jr.), Susan Gretchen (Mrs. Timothy E. Thompson). With Falk Corp., Milw., 1933—, exec. v.p., 1953-57, pres., 1957—, chmn. bd., chief exec. officer, 1962—, also dir.; pres. Falk Corp. Can., Ltd., 1960—; dir., mem. exec. com. Marshall & Ilsley Bank., Wis. Electric Power Co.; dir. Arnold Dyer Co., Employers Mut. Liability Ins. Co., Employers Mut. Fire Ins. Co., Marshall & Ilsley Bank Stock Corp., Oilgear Co., Silver Spring Bank, Wis. Telephone Co.; trustee Northwestern Mut. Life Ins. Co. Mem. exec. com. Pub. Expenditure Survey Wis.; treas. met. bd. Milw. YMCA. Mem. Carroll Coll. Council Met. Milw.; bd. dirs. Layton Sch. Art, Milw., St. Luke's Hosp. Research Found., Milw.; bd. regents Milw. Sch. Engring. Mem. Am. Ordnance Assn. (dir. Milw.), Wis. Mfrs. Assn. (dir.), Wis. Soc. Profl. Engrs., Soc. Naval Architects and Marine Engrs., Navy League U.S. Clubs: Milwaukee, Milwaukee Athletic, Wisconsin (Milw.). Home: 3069 E Newport Ct Milwaukee WI 53211 Office: Box 492 Milwaukee WI 53201

FALK, ISIDORE SYDNEY, bacteriologist, pub. health med. economist, social security expert; b. Bklyn., Sept. 30, 1899; s. Samsin and Rose (Stolzberg) F.; spl. student Sheffield Sci. Sch. Yale, 1915-17, Ph.B., 1920, Ph.D., 1923; m. Ruth Hill, Mar. 18, 1925; children—Sydney Westervelt, Stephen Ackley. Asst. dept. pub. health, Yale, 1915-20, instr., 1920-23; asst. prof. bacteriology, U. Chgo., 1923-26, asso. prof., 1926-29, prof. 1929; asst. dir. Bur. of Child Welfare, Chgo. Dept. Health, 1926-27; asso. dir. Com. on Costs of Med. Care, 1929-33; research asso. Milbank Meml. Fund, 1933-36; Div. Research and Statistics, Social Security Adminstrn., Washington, 1936-54, dir., 1940-54; cons. on health services, United Steelworkers of Am., 1958—; prof. pub. health (med. care) Yale Sch. Medicine, 1961-68, prof. emeritus, adj. lectr., 1968- -; pvt. cons. on pub. health and social security. Vice chmn. bd. dirs. Community Health Care Center Plan, New Haven. Served with AUS, 1918. Mem. govt. adv. coms. World War II. Decorated Congl. Selective Service medal, officer, Ordre de Honneur et Merite (Haiti), 1953; Cabalero, Orden de Vasco Nunez de Balboa (Panama) 1956. Fellow Am. Pub. Health Assn., A.A.A.S.; mem. several profl. assns. Author numerous books since 1923, primarily in field med. care. Conducted several health surveys and compiled reports thereon. Contbr. numerous tech. papers to jours. Research in eugenics of infant welfare, theory of microbic virulence, microbic cause of influenza, econs. of med. care and pub. health, social ins. Home: 472 Whitney Av New Haven CT 06511 ☆

FALK, KARL L., savs. and loan exec.; b. Berkeley, Cal., Sept. 12, 1911; s. Henry and Helen S. (Ruecker) F.; A.B., Stanford, 1932; Ph.D., U. Berlin, 1936; m. Doris Finger, June 21, 1936. Faculty dept. fgn. lang. Fresno State Coll., 1938-42, faculty div. soc. sci., 1946-68, head div. social sci., 1950-63, prof. econs., now prof. econs. emeritus, 1968—; acting pres. Fresno State Coll., 1969-70; chem. economist Dept. Commerce Washington, 1942; dean Sierra Summer Sch., 1948; Fulbright lectr. Technische Hochschule Stuttgart, Germany, 1954-55; pres. First Fed. Savings & Loan Assn., 1957—; dir. Cal. State Internat. Programs, Germany and Sweden, 1963-64; dir. internat. affairs Cal. State Colls., 1965-66. Mem. U.S. Nat. Commn., UNESCO, 1957-59. Chmn. Fresno City Housing Authority, 1951-69; pres. Nat. Assn. Housing and Redevel. Ofcls., 1960-61. Mem. Cal. Commn. for Housing and Community Devel., 1966-67. Bd. dirs. Found. for Coop. Housing, 1970—. Served with AUS, 1943-46. Mem. Am., Pacific Coast econ. assns., Phi Beta Kappa, Pi Gamma Mu. Author articles on chem. developments, European problems, housing and urban renewal problems, others; lectr. U.S. Dept. State in Germany, Austria, 1955, 56, 60, 64. Office: 1444 Fulton St Fresno CA 93721

FALK, LEON, Jr., corp. exec.; b. Pitts., Sept. 23, 1901; s. Leon and Fanny (Edel) F.; student Phillips Exter Acad., 1918-20; B.S., Yale U., 1924; LL.D. (hon.), U. Pitts., 1952; m. Katharine Sonneborn, June 24, 1926; children—Ellen, Sara, Sigo, David, Susannah; m. 2d, Josephine S. Ross, Dec. 23, 1948 (died Feb. 1962); m. 3d, Loti G. Gerard, Jan. 27, 1963. With Federated Metals Corp., charge of copper refining, then in charge of purchases; with Falk & Co., 1926, treas., 1926, chmn. bd., 1948-52; pres., dir. Chatham Center, Inc.; dir., exec. com. Nat. Steel Corp.; pres., dir. Webster Hall Hotel Corp.; dir. Duquesne Light Co., Pa. Indsl. Chem. Corp. Dir. Fgn. Commodities Div.; v.p. Commodity Credit Corp., Washington, 1943. Chief fats and oils bur. War Food Adminstrn., 1943-44; Am. rep. and chmn. sub-com. on fats and oils. Combined Food Bd., 1943-44. Mem. exec. com. Allegheny Conf. on Community Devel.; trustee, vice chmn. U. Pitts.; trustee, mem. exec. com. Presbyn. U. Hosp., Pitts.; chmn. bd. Maurice Falk Med. Fund. Decorated Order Juan Pablo Duarte (Dominican Republic); French Legion of Honor. Mem. Pi Lambda Phi. Republican. Mem. Reformed Jewish Ch. Clubs: Westmoreland Country (Pitts.): Concordia, Harvard-Yale-Princeton; Chemists (N.Y.C.); Cat Cay (Bahamas). Home: Chatham Center Pittsburgh PA 15219 Office: Grant Bldg Pittsburgh PA 15219

FALK, LOUIS WAHL, mfg. co. exec.; b. Milw., May 13, 1910; s. Harold Sands and Eugenia (Bechtner) F.; student Cornell U., 1933; m. Lovisa Margaret Fox, Aug. 5, 1933; children—Louis W., Lovisa (Mrs. B.J. Shrydeh), Martha (Mrs. Donald Moehrke), Mary C.; m. 2d, Pearl Gaudette, Nov. 27, 1952. With Claybourn Corp., 1936-37; with Falk Corp., Milw., 1937—, successively asst. to chief engr., exec. engr., v.p. engring., v.p. mfg., 1937-57, exec. v.p., 1957-70, vice chmn., 1970—, chmn. exec. com., 1962—, dir.; chmn. bd. Inland Press, 1961—; exec. com., dir. Protection Mut. Ins. Co.; dir. Park P.M. Corp., 1st Wis. Bank- shares Corp., 1st Wis. Trust Co. Bd. dirs. Herman W. Falk Found. Mem. Milw. Assn. Commerce, Am. Gear Mfg. Assn., Soc. Iron and Steel Engrs., Engrs. Soc. Milw., Chi Psi. Clubs: Town, University (Milw.). Patentee power transmissions. Home: 4723 N Cumberland Blvd Milwaukee WI 53211 Office: 3001 W Canal St Milwaukee WI 53201

FALK, PETER, actor; b. N.Y.C., Sept. 16, 1927; s. Michael and Madeline (Hauser) F.; B.A., New Sch. Social Research, 1951; M.P.A., Maxwell Sch., Syracuse U., 1953; pupil of Eva Le Gallienne, 1955, Sanford Meisner, 1957; m. Alyce Mayo, Apr. 17, 1960. Theatrical appearances include Don Juan, 1956, The Changeling, 1956, The Iceman Cometh, 1956, St. Joan, 1956, Diary of a Scoundrel, 1956, The Lady's Not for Burning, 1957, Purple Dust, 1957, Bonds of Interest, 1956, Comic Strip, 1958, The Passion of Josef D., 1964; motion picture appearances include Murder, Inc., 1960, Pocketful of Miracles, 1961, The Balcony, 1962, It's a Mad, Mad, Mad, Mad World, 1963, Italiano Bravo-Gente, 1963, Robin and the 7 Hoods, 1964; numerous TV appearances, 1960—, including Columbo in NBC Mystery Theater, 1971—. Recipient Emmy award for TV prodn. The Price of Tomatoes. Address: care Creative Mgmt Assn Ltd 9255 Sunset Blvd Los Angeles CA 90025*

FALK, RALPH II, business exec.; b. Boise, Ida., Apr. 14, 1922; s. Ralph and Marian Lucille (Citron) F.; B.A., Dartmouth, 1942; M.B.A., U. Mich., 1948; m. Suzanne Borden Clarke, January 4, 1959; children—Victoria, Melanie. With Baxter Labs., Inc. and subsidiaries, Morton Grove, Ill., 1948—, dir. 1951—, v.p., 1954-60, sr. v.p., 1960, chmn., 1960—, chmn. exec. com., 1971—; dir. Benner Tea Co., Burlington, Ia., Instructional Dynamics Inc., Chgo., Brougham Industries, Ft. Worth, R.S. Hershey Fund, Inc., Chgo. Trustee Ferry Hall Sch., Lake Forest. Served from ensign to lt. USNR, 1942-46. Mem. Delta Sigma Pi. Republican. Presbyn. Clubs: Onwentsia (Lake Forest, Ill.); Economic, Racquet (Chgo.). Home: 33 Stonegate Lane Lake Forest IL 60045 Office: 6301 Lincoln Av Morton Grove IL 60053

FALK, RICHARD ANDERSON, educator; b. N.Y.C., Nov. 13, 1930; s. Edwin Albert and Helene (Pollak) F.; grad. Fieldston Sch., 1948; B.S. in Econs., U. Pa., 1952; LL.B., Yale, 1955; J.S.D., Harvard, 1962; m. 2d, Florence Gross Goldstein, Dec. 15, 1967; children—Christopher, and Dimitri. Asst., then asso. prof. Coll. Law, Ohio State U., 1955-61; admitted to N.Y. bar, 1956; asso. prof. Princeton, 1961-65, Albert G. Milbank prof. internat. law and practice, 1965—. Cons. World Law Fund, U.S. Arms Control and Disarmament Agy., 1962-63, U.S. Senate Fgn. Relations Com. 1967; counsel before Internat. Ct. Justice, 1965. Mem. editorial policy bd. Pub. Broadcast Lab., 1967- 68; adv. bd. Amnesty Internat. Trustee Procedural Inst. Internat. Law and Fund for Peace; bd. dirs. Fgn. Policy Assn. Ford Found. fellow, 1958-59; McCosh Faculty fellow, 1965-69; fellow Center for Advanced Study in Behavioral Scis., 1968-69. Mem. Bar Assn. City N.Y., Am. Soc. Internat. Law (v.p. 1970—, exec. com., bd. rev. 1964-67, and devel. 1965-69), Council on Fgn. Relations, Internat. Law Assn., Am. Polit. Sci. Assn. Author: Law, War and Morality in the Contemporary World, 1963; The Role of Domestic Courts in the International Legal Order, 1964; Legal Order in a Violent World, 1968; Neutralization and World Politics, 1968; The Status of Law in International Society, 1970; This Endangered Planet, 1971. Editor: (with S.H. Mendlovitz) The Strategy of World Order, 4 vols., 1966; (with R. J. Barnet) Security Through Disarmament, 1965; (with C. E. Black, K. Knorr, O. R. Young) The Vietnam War and International Law, Vol. I, 1968, Vol. II, 1969; (with Wolfram Hamieden) International Law and Organization, 1968; (with C.E. Black) The Future of the International Legal Order, Vol. I, 1970, Vol. II, 1971. Mem. editorial bd. World Politics, 1962-68, Am. Jour. Internat. Law, 1964—, Fgn. Policy, 1970. Home: 168 Prospect Av Princeton NJ 08540

FALK, RICHARD LAWRENCE, bus. exec.; b. Cleve., Feb. 25, 1929; s. Lawrence T. and Hildegarde (Pfanholzer) F.; B.A. with distinction, U. Mich., 1951; m. Carol Ann McKenna, May 4, 1957; children—Sue Ann, Lynn Ann, Richard Lawrence. Mgr., Arthur Andersen & Co., N.Y.C., 1953-63; v.p., controller Norman, Craig & Kummel Inc., N.Y.C., 1963-65; controller The Hertz Corp., N.Y.C., 1965—. Served with AUS, 1951-53. Mem. Beta Gamma Sigma. Beta Alpha Psi. Clubs: Wykagyl (New Rochelle, N.Y.); N.Y. Athletic. Home: 15 Manhattan Av Crestwood, NY 10707. Office: 660 Madison Av New York City NY 10021

FALK, STANLEY G., lawyer; b. Buffalo, N.Y., Sept. 25, 1897; s. Isidor H. and Carrie (Geismer) F.; student Columbia, 1914-16; A.B., Harvard, 1919, LL.B., 1922; m. Hannah Brock, June 18, 1926; children—Doris, Virginia. Admitted to N.Y. State bar, 1922, and since practiced in Buffalo; mem. firm Falk, Siemer, Glick, Tuppen & Maloney; mem. N.Y. State Bd. Law Examiners, 1949- 69; Instr. law U. Buffalo Law Sch., 1925-30; chief rent enforcement atty. Buffalo Office OPA, 1942-43; chmn. Nat. Conf. Bar Examiners, 1962. Dir. Roblin Industries, Inc., J. & A. Keller Machine Co., Inc., Jerome H. Cargill Producing Orgn., Inc., Eagle Securities Co. Pres., Community Welfare Council Buffalo and Erie County, 1946-47, dir., 1946-53; pres. United Jewish Fedn. Buffalo, 1950-51, dir., 1946-53; chmn. United Jewish Fund Campaign, 1938, 54; Chmn. Buffalo USO Com., 1954-55; pres., dir. Eli D. Hofeller Found.; v.p., dir. William J. Conners Found.; dir. Buffalo and Erie County Pub. Library (chmn. 1964-66, vice chmn. 1968-69), dir. Children's Aid Soc. (pres. 1966-68); pres. Found. Jewish Philanthropies, 1945-65. Bd. dirs. Goodwill Industries Buffalo. Mem. Am., N.Y., Erie County bar assns., Internat. Inst. Buffalo (pres. 1961-63, dir.), Archaeol. Inst. Am., Republican. Jewish religion (pres. temple 1960-61). Clubs: Buffalo Athletic; Montefiore. Home: 33 Gates Circle Buffalo NY 14209 Office: Erie County Savs Bank Bldg Buffalo NY 14202

FALK, WERNER DAVID, educator; b. Berlin, Germany, Apr. 25, 1906; s. Fritz and Betty (Cassirer) F.; Ph.D. summa cum laude, U. Heidelberg, 1931; M.A., U. Oxon, 1938; M.A., U. Melbourne, 1955; m. Ruth Loeve. Lectr. philosophy New Coll., Oxford U., 1938-46; research fellow Nuffield Coll., 1947-50; acting head dept. moral philosophy U. Aberdeen (Scotland), 1946-47; reader U. Melbourne (Australia), 1950-58; vis. prof. U. Mich., 1957-58; vis. prof. Brown U., 1958; vis. prof. U. Ill., 1959; prof. Wayne State U., 1959-62; prof. Syracuse U., 1962-63; prof. U. N.C., Chapel Hill, 1963—, chmn. dept. philosophy, 1965—. Mem. Am. Philos. Assn., So. Soc. Philosophy and Psychology, Am. Soc. Polit. and Legal Philosophy. Contbr. articles profl. jours. Home: Buttons Rd Chapel Hill NC 27514

FALKE, LEE CHARLES, lawyer; b. Dayton, O., June 21, 1930; s. Lee J. and Elizabeth (Schwieterman) F.; student U. Dayton, 1948-51; B.S., Ohio State U., 1952, LL.B., 1955; m. Margaret Greenwood, Sept. 3, 1955; children—Joseph, Mary Elizabeth, Lee Charles. Admitted to Ohio bar, 1955, since practiced in Dayton; mem. firm Young, Pryor, Lynn, Strickland and Falke, 1958—; prosecuting atty. Montgomery County, 1965—. Pres. Young Democratic Club Montgomery County, 1964; mem. Montgomery County Dem. Exec. Com.; asst. treas. Gem City Dem. Club, 1970—. Mem. Am., Ohio, Dayton bar assns., Montgomery County Law Enforcement officers assn. (pres. 1966-68), Ohio Prosecuting Att.'s Assn. (pres.), Phi Delta Theta, Phi Delta Phi (pres. 1954). K.C. (dir. 500 council 1961—). Home: 2230 Patterson Blvd Dayton OH 45419 Office: Third Nat Bldg Dayton OH 45402

FALKENBERG, PAUL VICTOR, documentary film dir., editor; b. Berlin, Germany, Oct. 26, 1903; s. Herman and Bertha F. (Ginsberg) F.; ed. univs. Heidelberg. Berlin and Cologne (Germany), 1922-28; m. Alice H. Hirsekorn, Mar. 26, 1931 (dec. 1964); m. 2d, Lotte Hanemann, 1966. Came to U.S., 1938, naturalized, 1944. Asst. dir. with G.W. Pabst, Germany, 1928-30; film editor with Fritz Lang, Carl T. Dreyer, Alexis Granovsky, Gabriel Pascal, O. L. Preminger and Fedor Ozep in Berlin, Paris, London, Vienna and Rome, 1930- 38; tech. and dialogue dir. 20th Century Fox Film Co., Hollywood, Cal., 1940-41; writer-editor for coordinator Inter-Am. affairs Mus. Modern Art film library, 1941-45; producer-dir. for UN, Viking Fund, United Jewish Appeal, others, 1945—; asso. producer Guy Lombardo series, 1956; editor, adviser community edn. P.R. Govt., 1955-56; lectr. Columbia, Einstein Coll., New Sch. Social Research, Phila. Mus. Coll. Art, Film Inst. of Coll. City N.Y., Inst. for Advanced Study in Aesthetic Edn., Ill. State U. Mem. Dirs. Guild Am., Cinematologists (charter; 1st v.p.). Producer-dir.: A Time For Bach, 1949; (with Lewis Jacobs) Lincoln Speaks at Gettysburg (Freedom Found. award 1950), 1950; (with Hans Namuth) Jackson Pollock, 1951; (with Hans Namuth) Image from the Sea, 1956; producer, author: Duerer and Renaissance, 1961; Caravaggio and Baroque, 1961; editor: Rebelion de Modesta (1st prize Venice Biennale 1957), 1955; (TV series) Valiant Years, 1960-61; F.D.R., 1962; producer, designer: Truman series, 1963-64; Leukemia Soc. film, Gold Medal winner, N.Y. Internat. Film and TV Festival, 1965; 3 films on humanities, McGraw-Hill, 1967-68; producer (with Hans Namuth) Willow de Kooning, 1965; MosaicsJeanne Reynal., 1968. Home: 15 W 67th St New York City NY 10023. Office: 1600 Broadway New York City NY 10019

FALL, CHEIKH IBRAHIMA, Senegalese diplomat; b. Dakar, Senegal, Feb. 4, 1930; s. Abdoulaye Yarè and Fatou (Diouf) F.; diploma Bachelier Serie Phil., licencié en droit (lauret) des facultes de droit Econ. Scis., U. Rennes (France), 1955; m. Soukeyna (Fall), Aug. 6, 1956; children—Lamine, Yare, Issa, Abdoulaye, Ameth, Gusseynou. Chief-adj. prodn. service High Commissariat Afrique Occidental Francaise, 1956-57; tech. counselor Ministry Gen. Economy and Planning, Senegal, 1957-59; dir. Ministry of Commerce, Senegal, Mali Fedn., 1959-60; dir. econ. services Ministry Commerce, Industry, Artisanry, 1960-64; named ambassador, 1964, assigned to Senegalese embassies Germany and Netherlands, 1964-66, Moscow, USSR, Var- sovia, Poland, 1966-68, Washington, Ottawa, Ont., Can., Mexico City, Mexico, Port-of-Spain, W.I., 1968—. Created comdr. Italian order, 1962; decorated Order St. Sylvester (Vatican), 1962, grand cross of German Order, 1967. Home: 3036 Woodland Dr Washington DC 20008 Office: Senegalese Embassy 2112 Wyoming Av Washington DC 20008

FALLAW, WESNER, educator; b. Woodruff, S.C., Jan. 4, 1907; s. Henry Melton and Helen Hortense (McCarrell) F.; A.B., Furman U., 1927; student Union Theol. Sem., 1934-37; M.A., Columbia, 1936, Ed.D., 1944; m. Elinora Harrill, 1942; children—Thomas Lee, Nancy Elinora. Sec. YMCA, Charleston, S.C., 1927-33; mem. staff Furman U., 1933-34, asst. prof., 1937-39; fgn. travel, lectr., teaching, 1939-40; dir. religious edn., Winnetka, Ill., 1940-46; Howard prof. religious edn. Andover Newton Theol. Sch., 1946—; Wilson Lectr. Nashville Tenn.,

1959; summer teaching Union Sem., Columbia, Garrett Theol. Sem., Syracuse U.; Ward lectr. Greensboro Coll. 1965. Mem. corp. Emerson Coll.; founder, exec. dir. Newton Inst. Religious Studies. Mem. Religious Edn. Assn. (dir.). Author: The Modern Parent and the Teaching Church, 1946; Toward Spiritual Security, 1952; Church Education for Tomorrow, 1960; The Case Method in Pastoral and Lay Education, 1963. Contbr. chpts. books, articles ednl., religious periodicals. Home: 111 Herrick Circle Newton Centre MA 02159

FALLER, THEODORE SYLVESTER, business exec.; b. N.Y.C., Dec. 31, 1901; s. Theodore L. and Helen (McCabe) F.; B.B.A., Coll. City N.Y., 1923; m. Edith M. Jacoby, Feb. 19, 1944. Exec. v.p., corporate controller R.H. Macy & Co., Inc., 1921- 51; pres., trustee S.I. Savs. Bank, 1951—; dir. Savs. Banks Retirement System Instl. Securities Corp. Bd. dirs. Vis. Nurse Assn. S.I., S.I. chpt. A.R.C.; pres. St. Vincents Med. Center; trustee Notre Dame Coll., S.I. Served as col. AUS, 1942-45. Financial Execs. Inst., S.I. C. of C. (dir.). Roman Catholic. Knights of Malta. Clubs: Downtown Athletic (N.Y.C.); Richmond County (N.Y.); Port Jervis Country. Home: 8 Circle Rd Staten Island NY 10304 also Colesville NJ Office: 81 Water St Staten Island NY 10304

FALLERS, LLOYD ASHTON, Jr., educator; b. Nebraska City, Neb., Aug. 29, 1925; s. Lloyd A. and Fannie (Lincoln) F.; Ph.B., U. Chgo., 1946, M.A., 1949, Ph.D., 1953; student London (Eng.) Sch. Econs., 1949-50; m. Margaret Elinor Chave, June 18, 1949; children—Winnifred Mary, Beth Laura. Lectr. anthropology Princeton, 1953-54; fellow E. African Inst. Social Research, 1950-52, 54- 56, dir. inst., 1956-57; asst., then asso. prof. anthropology U. Cal. at Berkeley, 1957-60; mem. faculty U. Chgo., 1960—, prof. anthropology, 1963-70, prof. anthropology and sociology, 1970—. Fellow Center Advanced Study Behavioral Scis., 1958-59. Mem. Am. Anthrop. Assn., African Studies Assn., Assn. Social Anthropologists (Great Britain), Internat. African Inst., Royal Anthrop. Inst. (Great Britain). Democrat. Episcopalian. Author: Bantu Bureaucracy, 1956; Law Without Precedent, 1969. Editor, joint author: The King's Men, 1964. Asso. editor anthropology Internat. Ency. Social Scis., 1962—. Home: 5834 Stony Island Av Chicago IL 60637

FALLIS, LAURENCE SIDNEY, ret. surgeon; b. Millbrook, Ont., Can., Jan. 29, 1894; s. Albert James and Mary Jane (Larmer) F.; M.D., C.M., Queen's U., Kingston, Ont., 1919; M.R.C.S., L.R.C.P, St. Bartholomew's Hosp., London, Eng., 1922; postgrad. univs. London, Edinburg (Scotland), Vienna (Austria); m. Dorothy Marie Moloney, Aug. 16, 1930; children—Laurence Sidney, Richard James. Came to U.S., 1925, naturalized, 1943. Resident Ministry of Pensions Hosp., Toronto, 1919-21; house surgeon Royal Hosp., Portsmouth, Eng., 1921-24; med. dir. Campanhia Ford Indsl. do Brasil, Para, 1928-29; mem. staff Henry Ford Hosp., Detroit, 1925-28, 30-71, surgeon-in-chief, 1952-66, cons. surgeon, 1966—; chief surgeon Detroit, Toledo & Ironton R.R., 1951. Served with Canadian Army Med. Corps, 1915-18. Recipient plaque Davis & Geck, Inc., 1956. Diplomate Am. Bd. Surgery (a founder). Fellow Am., Royal colls. surgeons; mem. Am., World, Pan. Am. med. assns., Wayne County, Mich. med. socs., Am., Central (councillor 1960-63), Detroit (pres. 1951-52), Pan Pacific (v.p. 1963-66) surg. assns., Internat. Soc. Surgery, Assn. Francais de Chirugia de Cuba, Surg. Soc. Guadalajara (Mexico), Soc. Surgery Alimentary Tract, Detroit Acad. Surgery (pres. 1945-46), Detroit Acad. Medicine, Detroit Surg. Soc., Detroit Inst. Cancer Research (trustee 1945—, sec. 1956-58, pres. 1959- 61), Mich. Assn. Professions, Assn. Am. Railroads, Internat. Congress Gastroenterology, Internat. Congress Nutrition; hon. mem. Flint Acad. Surgery, Cin., Surg. Soc., Spokane Acad. Gen. Practice, Soc. Chilena de Gastro-Enterologia, Soc. Argentina de Proctologia, Detroit Econ. Club. Clubs: Detroit; Los Buenos Vecinos (Detroit); Nat. Travel (N.Y.C.). Home: 2742 NE 31st St Light House Point Pompano Beach FL 33064

FALLIS, WILLIAM DAVID, utility exec.; b. Neepawa, Man., Can., Mar. 14, 1909; s. Allan Benjamin and Minnie (Sutherland) F.; m. Donalda Christine Fallis, Sept. 26, 1936; 1 dau., Roberta (Mrs. Jacob Popoff). With Man. Power Commn. (merged with Man. Hydro-Electric Co. 1961), Winnipeg, Can., 1930—, comptroller, 1944-46, gen. mgr., 1946—; dir. Atomic Energy Can. Ltd., Ottawa. Mem. Civil Service Superannuation Bd., 1948—. Mem. Canadian (bd. dirs.), Man. elec. assns. Rotarian. Clubs: Griffons, Canadian, Manitoba, Winter (Winnipeg). Home: 117 Chataway Blvd Winnipeg 29 Manitoba Canada Office: PO Box 815 Winnipeg 1 Manitoba Canada also 820 Taylor Av Winnipeg 9 Manitoba Canada

FALLON, FRANCIS EDWARD, mfg. co. exec.; b. N.Y.C., Jan. 19, 1926; s. Francis Patrick and Nora (Curry) F.; B.A., St. John's U., 1950; LL.B., Columbia, 1953; m. Adelaide M. Haley, Dec. 26, 1953; children—Joseph, Stephen, Francis P., Donna Marie, Louise, James. Admitted to N.Y. bar, 1953, also Fed. bar; asst. counsel N.Y., N.H. & H.R.R., 1954-57; mem. legal staff Gen. Aniline & Film Corp., 1957-58; mem. legal staff, sec. Curtiss-Wright Corp., 1958—; dir. Curtiss-Wright Europa, N.V. Served with USNR, 1944- 46. Mem. Am. Bar Assn., Am. Soc. Corp. Secs. Home: 26 Concord Dr New City NY 10956 Office: One Passaic St Wood-Ridge NJ 07075

FALLON, GEORGE H., former congressman; b. Balt., July 24, 1902; s. Lawrence, Sr., and Mary (Dempsey) F.; ed. public schools, Calvert Bus. Coll., Johns Hopkins U.; m. Willa Virginia Thomas, 1929; 1 dau., Mary Joyce. Engaged in advt. sign bus.; partner Lawrence Fallon Co.; elected mem. Dem. State Central Com. Balt., 1938, chmn.; elected to Balt. City Council, 1939, 1943; mem. 79th-91st Congresses 4th District, Md. Democrat. Home: 911 E 37th St Baltimore MD 21218 Office: House Office Bldg Washington DC 20515

FALLS, ARTHUR GRAND PRE, physician; b. Chgo., Dec. 25, 1901; s. William Arthur and Santalia Angelica (Grand Pre) F.; student Crane Jr. Coll., 1920; B.S. in Medicine, Northwestern U., 1924, M.D., 1925; U. Chgo. Med. Sch., 1926, postgrad. U. Ill. Med. Sch., 1928, Cook County Grad. Sch. Medicine, 1940- 50; m. Lillian Steele Proctor, Dec. 6, 1928; 1 son, Arthur Grand Pre. Intern Kansas City (Kan.) Gen. Hosp., 1924-25; practice surgery, Chgo., 1925—; mem. staff Municipal Tb Sanitarium, 1939-44; sr. attending surgeon Provident Hosp., Chgo., 1926—, pres. med. staff, 1956-59; attending surgeon Michigan Av. Hosp., Chgo., 1963—. Chmn. bd. Progress Devel. Corp., Chgo., 1959—; organizer numerous consumer corps., 1935- 45; mem. Hyde Park Coop. Soc., Chgo. A founder South Central Med. Bldg., Inc., 1962, v.p., 1963-64, pres., 1969—. A founder Council for Biomed. Careers, 1962, pres., 1966—; founder Com. to End Discrimination in Chgo. Med. Instns., 1951, chmn., 1955—; mem. Founders and Friends Roosevelt U., Chgo., 1945- -; founder Chgo. Cath. Workers, 1936; mem. Cath. Interracial Council, Japanese-Am. Citizens League, Assn. on Am. Indian Affairs, Nat. Conf. Christians and Jews. Recipient numerous awards for civic activities, most recent being awards from Internat. Travelers Assn., 1961, Am. Freedom of Residence Fund, 1961, Chgo. Com. of 100, 1963. Fellow Am. Coll. Chest Physicians, Am. Geriatric Soc.; mem. A.M.A., Ill., Chgo. med. socs., Prairie State Med. Assn., Cook County Physicians Assn., Am. Cath. Sociol. Soc., Kappa Alpha Psi. Club: City of Chicago. Home: 4812 Fair Elms Av Western Springs IL 60558 Office: 5050 S State St Chicago IL 60609

FALLS, HAROLD FRANCIS, ophthalmologist; b. Winchester, Ind., Nov. 26, 1909; s. Thomas and Mary (Schmitt) F.; A.B., U. Mich., 1932, M.D., 1936, M. Ophthalmology, 1939; m. Emeline N. Duckwitz, Sept. 12, 1942; children—Thomas, Hariette (Mrs. James B. Gray, Jr.), Timothy. Intern U. Mich. Med. Center, 1936-37, resident, 1937-41; practice medicine, specializing in ophthalmology, Ann Arbor, Mich., 1941—; asst. prof. ophthalmology U. Mich., 1942-47; asso. prof., 1947-59, prof., 1959—, research asso. dept. human genetics, 1946- -; cons. Vets. Facility Wayne Gen. Hosp., Nat. Soc. Prevention Blindness. Mem. numerous coms. NIH. Recipient Billings Gold medal A.M.A. exhibit, 1962. Mem. A.M.A. (del.). Contbr. articles profl. jours. Home: 1525 Harding Rd Ann Arbor MI 48104 Office: U Mich Med Center Ann Arbor MI 48104

FALLS, MOTHER THERESA, coll. pres.; b. N.Y.C., Oct. 16, 1911; d. Henry P. and Elizabeth (Christy) Falls; A.B., Coll. New Rochelle (N.Y.), 1938; A.M., Cath. U. Am., 1944, Ph.D., 1950. Joined Order Ursuline Nuns, 1932; instr. English, then asst. prof. Coll. New Rochelle, 1939-46, asso. prof., 1950- 53; prioress Ursuline House Studies, New Rochelle, 1953-56, Ursuline House Grad. Studies, Washington, 1956-62; asso. prof. English, Coll. New Rochelle, 1962-63, pres., 1963-70; asst. for coordinating higher edn. for Africa and Madagascar, 1970—. Mem. com. Eastern region Sister Formation Conf., 1953—. Mem. Mayor New Rochelle Youth Conf., 1964. Trustee Ursuline Coll. Women, Cleve. Mem. Modern Lang. Assn., Am. Renaissance Soc., Am. Assn. U. Women, Nat. Council Tchrs. English. Address: Ursuline Convent PO Box 67019 Bryanston Transvaal South Africa

FALSGRAF, WENDELL ALBERT, lawyer; b. Cleveland, June 18, 1904; s. Albert E. and Daisy V. (McDonald) F.; A.B., Western Res. U., 1926, J.D., 1928; m. S. Catherine Johnson, Sept. 22, 1928; children—William Wendell, Sherwood Nourse. Admitted to Ohio bar, 1928; partner Falsgraf, Reidy, Shoup and Ault, Cleve., 1931-69, counsel, 1970-71; counsel Baker, Hostetler & Patterson, Cleve., 1971—. Dir. Wm. Tanksley & Assos., Inc., Cecil C. Peck Co., Quality Brands, Inc., Huron Realty Co., Bearings, Inc. Pres. Citizens League Cleve., 1946-47, Nationalities Service Center, 1965-67. Mem. U.S. 6th Region Loyalty Bd., 1949-52. Trustee Cleve. YMCA, 1954-57, Western Res. U., 1946-50, Hiram (O.) Coll., 1965—. Recipient of the Jr. C. of C. Award, 1938. Fellow Am. Bar Found., Am. Coll. Probate Counsel (gov. Ohio), Ohio State Bar Found. (trustee 1965-68); mem. Am. (ho. dels., 1960-64, chmn. citizenship com. 1962-68, mem. council section on individual rights and responsibilities 1965- 68), Ohio, Cleve. (pres. 1957-58) bar assns., Western Res. U. Law Sch. Alumni Assn. (pres. 1959-60), Delta Upsilon, Phi Delta Phi, Sigma Delta Chi. Clubs: Union, City (pres. 1946), Rotary (pres. Cleve. East 1938-39), Canterbury Golf (pres. 1952) (Cleve.). Home: 612 North St Chagrin Falls OH 44022 Office: Union Commerce Bldg Cleveland OH 44115

FALSTEIN, EUGENE I., psychoanalyst, psychiatrist; b. Chgo., Oct. 29, 1908; s. Samuel and Pearl (Levin) F.; B.S., U. Ill., 1928, M.D., 1930; Rockefeller fellow psychoanalytic tng. Chgo. Inst. Psychoanalysis, 1936-42; m. Charlotte Rosenfield. Dec. 25, 1932. Intern psychiatry Elgin State Hosp., 1930-31, psychiatrist, 1933-37; intern Michael Reese Hosp. and Med. Center, Chgo., 1931-33, psychiat. clinic staff, 1933-40, now senior attending psychiatrist dept. of psychiatry, chief adolescent care Inst. Psychosomatic and Psychiat. Research and Tng.; faculty Northwestern U. Med. Sch., 1933-37; child psychiatrist Inst. Juvenile Research, 1937-42; asst. prof. dept. criminology U. Ill., 1937-51; attending psychiatrist children's div. Ill. Neuropsychiat. Inst., 1940-51; now clin. prof. psychiatry Chgo. Med. Sch.; pvt. practice psychoanalysis and psychiatry, 1946—; psychiat. cons., adv. bd. Jewish Children's Bur.; hon. cons. Nicholas Pritzker Children's Center. Bd. dirs. Am. Friends of Hebrew U., Jewish Welfare Fund, Am. Jewish Physicians Com. Served as lt. comdr. USNR, 1942-46. Recipient Israel Scroll, 1957. Diplomate Am. Bd. Psychiatry and Neurology. Fellow Am. Psychiat. Assn. (life), Am. Orthopsychiat. Assn. (life), Am. Acad. Psychoanalysis, Am. Acad. Child Psychiatry, A.M.A.; mem. Ill. Med. Soc., Chgo. Psychoanalytic Soc., Chgo. Neurol. Soc., Am., Internat. psychoanalytic assns., A.A.A.S., Pan Am. Med. Assn., Chgo. Council Child Psychiatry (past pres.), Ill. Psychiat. Soc. (past sec.), Alpha Omega Alpha, Phi Delta Epsilon. Club: Ravisloe Country. Author sci. articles, chpts. in books. Home: 1300 N Lake Shore Dr Chicago IL 60610. Office: 25 E Washington St Chicago IL 60602

FALSTEIN, LOUIS, author; b. Ukraine, May 1, 1909; s. Joseph and Bessie (Kammerman) F.; came to U.S., 1925, naturalized, 1936; student Lewis Inst., Chgo., 1930- 32, N.Y.U., 1946-48; m. Shirley Gesser, Apr. 9, 1949; children—Jessica, Joshua. Tchr. novel workshops N.Y.U., 1949-50; tchr. short story writing Coll. City N.Y., 1956. Served with USAAF, 1943-45. Decorated Purple Heart, Air medal with three clusters. Mem. Authors League Am. Author: Face of A Hero, 1950; Slaughter Street, 1953; Sole Survivor, 1954; Spring of Desire, 1958; Laughter On A Weekday, 1965; The Man Who Loved Laughter: The Story of Sholom Aleichem (biography), 1968. Editor: The Martyrdom of Polish-Jewish Physicians, 1963. Address: 368 Eastern Pkwy Brooklyn NY 11225

FALVEY, MARY GERTRUDE, mfg. co. exec.; b. East Hartford, Conn., Nov. 2, 1904; d. John Joseph and Ellen (Scully) Falvey; student New Britain (Conn.) State Normal Coll., 1922; diploma Hartford (Conn.) Bus. Inst., 1923. With Heublein, Inc., Hartford, 1924—, asst. sec., corp. sec., 1951-70, now adv. dir.; corp. sec., dir. St. Pierre Smirnoff Fils, Inc., 1952—; sec., dir. Timely Brands (Can.), Ltd., 1962—. Sec., bd. dirs Jane and John Martin Found., 1958—. Mem. Am. Soc. Corporate Secs., Met. Opera Guild, Nat. Cath. Music Educators Assn. Roman Catholic. Home: 30 Outlook Av West Hartford CT 06119 Office: 330 New Park Av Hartford CT 06101

FAMA, SEBASTIAN, govt. ofcl.; b. N.Y.C., Oct. 29, 1918; s. Joseph and Iona (Scarcella) F.; student Coll. City N.Y., 1935-38; B.C.S., Benjamin Franklin U., 1951, M.C.S., 1952; m. Santa Ann Amatulli, Apr. 3, 1948; children—Joseph T., Rosemary A., James P., Ellen M. With Treasury Dept., Washington, 1952- -, chief deposits br., 1960-62, asst. dep. commr., 1962-65, dep. commr. bur. accounts 1965-69, dir. govt. financial operations, 1969—. Served to warrant officer C.E., AUS, 1941-46; ETO. Home: 5202 Augusta St Washington DC 20016 Office: Treasury Annex 1 Washington DC 20025

FAME, GEORGIE, (Clive Powell), organist, singer, bandleader; b. Leigh, Lancashire, Eng., June 26, 1943. Rock and roll pianist, 1959; switched to organ and formed own Blue Flames, 1961; toured Britain with Tamla-Motown shows, 1961; numerous appearances at concerts and festivals, as solo singer, also TV and radio shows; TV and concerts, Paris, 1965, Scandinavia, 1966; recording artist for Brit. Columbia Records. Recipient Melody Maker award, 1966. Address: care Rik Gunnell 47 Gerrard St London W 1 England*

FAN, KY, educator, mathematician; b. Hangchow, China, Sept. 19, 1914; s. Chi-Han and Wu- Shien (Fang) F.; B.S., Nat. Peking U., 1936; D.Sc. in Math., U. Paris, 1941; m. Yu-Fen Yen, Apr. 26, 1936. Came to U.S., 1945, naturalized, 1954. French Nat. Sci. fellow, charge de recherches Centre Nat. de la Recherche Scientifique, 1942-45; mem. Inst. for Advanced Study, 1945-47; faculty math. U. Notre Dame, 1947-60, prof., 1952-60; prof. math. Wayne State U., Detroit, 1960-61, Northwestern U., 1961-65; vis. prof. math. U. Tex., spring 1965; prof. math. U. Cal. at Santa Barbara, 1965—, chmn. math. dept., 1968-69. Mem. Academia Sinica, 1964—. Asso. editor Jour. Math. Analysis and Applications, 1960—; editorial bd. Linear Algebra and Its Applications, 1968—. Contbr. articles math. jours. Home: 1402 Santa Teresita Dr Santa Barbara CA 93105

FAN, LIANG-TSENG, educator; b. Taiwan, Formosa, Aug. 7, 1929; s. Chung-Chan and Chien-mai (Huang) F.; B.S., Nat. Taiwan U., 1951; M.S., Kan. State U., 1954; Ph.D. in Chem. Engring., W.Va. U., 1957, M.S. in Math., 1958; m. Eva Cheung, June 2, 1958; children—Tso Yee, Judith Tse-ling. Came to U.S., 1952, naturalized, 1970. Jr. chem. engr. Taiwan Agrl. Chem. Works, 1951-52; asst. chem. engr. Kan. State U., 1952-54, W.Va. U., 1954-58; phys. chemist Bur. Mines, Morgantown, W.Va., 1956-58, chem. engr., 1958-59; instr. chem. engring. Kan. State U., Manhattan, 1958-59, asst. prof., 1959-61, asso. prof., 1961-63, prof., 1963—, head dept., 1968—, faculty adviser Formosan Student Assn., 1970—, Kan. Power & Light Co. professorship, 1967—. Dir. Inst. Systems Design and Operation; cons. Air Quality Office Environmental Protection Agy., 1969—. Mem. Am. Chem. Soc., Am. Inst. Chem. Engrs., Am. Soc. for Engring. Edn., Internat. Water Pollution Control Assn., Chinese Inst. Chem. Engring., Soc. Chem. Engrs. Japan, Profl. Engrs. Formosa, Soc. Engring. Sci., A.A.A.S., Sigma Xi, Phi Kappa Phi, Phi Lambda Upsilon. Author: The Discrete Maximum Principle, 1964; The Continuous Maximum Principle, 1966. Contbr. articles to profl. jours. Home: 830 Lee St Manhattan KS 66502

FANCHER, GEORGE HOMER, petroleum engr., cons.; b. San Francisco, Sept. 3, 1901; s. William Woodruff and Gertrude (Frisbie) F.; B.S., U. So. Cal., 1923; Chem. Engr., U. Md., 1926, U. Mich., 1928; D.Sc., Colo. Sch. Mines, 1930; m. Mattie Stanfield, Sept. 10, 1931; children—Charles Cornell, George Homer, Carol Sue. Chem. engr., Universal Oil Products Co., 1923-24; gas engr. C.C.M. Oil Co., 1924-25; instr. U. Md., 1925-26; research fellow U. Mich., 1926-28; instr. Colo. Sch. Mines, 1928-29, asst. prof., 1920-30, asso. prof., 1930-31; asst. prof. Pa. State U., 1931-34; petroleum engr. York State Oil Co., 1934-35; prof. petroleum engring. U. Tex., Austin, 1935-39, grad. prof. petroleum engring., 1939-60, chmn. dept., 1956-60; v.p. gen. mgr., dir. Sinclair Research, Inc., Tulsa, 1960-65; v. p., dir. Sinclair Oil & Gas Co., 1965-66; petroleum cons., Austin, Tex., 1966—. Cons. Ministry Mines and Petroleum, Alberta, Can., 1948-49, Nat. Petroleum Council, Colombia, S.Am., 1948-49, Ministry Mines and Petroleum, Venezuela, S.Am., 1952-53, Empressa Colombiana de Petroleus, 1954-59, to pres. U. Americas, Mexico, 1969, 70, 71. Mem. of Internat. Exec. Service Corps, 1966—; dir. Tex. Petroleum Research Com., 1949-60; adviser land commr. of Tex.; mem. gov.'s com. Interstate Oil Compact Comm.; adviser formulation nat. policy of conservation Colombia. Adv. bd. Internat. Oil and Gas Center, S.W. Legal Found.; bd. dirs. Colo. Sch. of Mines Research Found.; adv. bd. to trustees Colo. Sch. of Mines; dir. Internat. Petroleum Expn., 1963—. Recipient Citation Venezuelan Govt., Distinguished Achievement medal Colo. Sch. Mines, 1963. Fellow Am. Inst. of Chemists, Inst. of Petroleum, Tex. Acad. of Sci.; mem. Am. Inst. Mining Engrs. (John Franklin Garll award Soc. Petroleum Engrs. 1968), Am. Petroleum Inst., Am. Arbitration Assn. (nat. bd. arbitrators), Am. Chem. Soc., S.A.R. (pres. Patrick Henry chapter Tex. 1969), Okla. Soc. Mayflower Descs., Sigma Xi, Tau Beta Pi, Phi Lambda Upsilon, Sigma Gamma Epsilon, Alpha Chi Sigma, Sigma Nu (past pres. alumni. Legion of Honor 1956), Pi Epsilon Tau (hon.). Episcopalian (vestry). Clubs: Westwood Country, Headliners, Rotary, The Citadel (Austin, Tex.); Tulsa, Tulsa University, American Club (Mexico City, Mexico). Author: Secondary Recovery of Petroleum in Arkansas, 1946; Oil Resources of Texas, 1954; Calculation of Flowing and Static Bottom Hole Pressures of Natural Gas Wells, 1959. Contbr. articles to various publs. Home: 600 E 32d St Austin, TX 78705.

FANCY, HENRY FRANKLIN, physician, ret. army officer; b. Gorham, N.H., Dec. 1, 1920; s. William S. and Gladys (Page) F.; B.S., U. N.H., 1942; M.D., C.M., McGill U., Montreal, Que., Can., 1945; m. Olive Marjorie Pidduck, Oct. 24, 1947; children—Jacqueline Yvette, Deborah Ann, Cindy Lou. Intern Montreal Gen. Hosp., 1945-46; resident gen. practice Madigan Gen. Hosp., Tacoma, 1950-53; resident internal medicine Brooke Gen. Hosp., Ft. Sam Houston, Tex., 1956-59; commd. 1st lt., U.S. Army, 1946, advanced through grades to col., 1964; chief outpatient dept. Murphy Gen. Hosp., Waltham, Mass., 1946-50; chief dept. medicine Ft. Leavenworth, Kan., 1959-62, 34th Gen. Hosp., Orleans, France, 1962-65, Ft. Dix, N.J., 1965-66; comdr. U.S. Army Hosp., Ft. Jackson, S.C., 1966-68; dep. surgeon U.S. Army Caribbean, 1955-56; med. cons. U.S. Army Europe, 1968-70; retired, 1970. Decorated Army Commendation medal. Diplomate Am. Bd. Internal Medicine, Nat. Bd. Med. Examiners. Fellow A.C.P.; mem. A.M.A. Episcopalian. Home: 1932 Golfview Av Fort Myers FL 33901 Office: Lee County Health Dept P O Box 1226 Fort Myers FL 33902

FANE, IRVIN, lawyer; b. Dallas, Nov. 17, 1904; s. Benjamin and Hanna (Weil) F.; A.B., LL.B., U. Mo., 1928; L.H.D., Hebrew Union Coll.-Jewish Inst. Religion, 1969; m. Bernice L. Smith, May 7, 1929; children—Lawrence S., Bruce E. Admitted to Mo. bar, 1928, since practiced in Kansas City; partner firm Spencer, Fane, Britt & Browne, and predecessors, 1928—; chief counsel Kansas City Power & Light Co. Mem. Kansas City Bd. Police Commrs., 1953- 57; mem. Adminstrv. Conf. U.S., 1961-62; mem. legal adv. com. Nat. Power Survey, 1963-64. Chmn. bd. Union Am. Hebrew Congregations, 1963-67; mem. am. bd. World Union Progressive Judaism, 1958-; pres. Congregation B'nai Jehudah, Kansas City, 1940-45., trustee, 1937—; a founder Jewish Welfare Fedn. Kansas City, 1933, mem. bd., 1933-38, 50-55; a founder Jewish Community Center Kansas City, 1935, v.p., 1943-45. Bd. dirs. Starlight Theatre Assn.; bd. counsellors Menorah Med. Center, Kansas City; hon. dir. Rockhurst Coll.; bd. govs. Hebrew Union Coll.-Jewish Inst. Religion, Cin.; mem. Greater Kansas City Sports Commn., 1966—; pres. U. Mo. Law School Found., 1970-71; bd. curators U. Mo., 1971—. Recipient Night of Sports award, 1960; U. Mo. Alumni Assn. citation of merit, 1966; Brotherhood award Nat. Conf. Christians and Jews, 1967. Mem. Am., Fed. Power, Kansas City bar assns., Mo. Bar, Lawyers Assn. Kansas City, Am. Judicature Soc., Kansas City C. of C., U. Mo. Alumni Assn., Edison Electric Inst. (legal com.), QEBH Hon. Soc., Zeta Beta Tau, Phi Delta Phi (hon.). Republican. Clubs: Oakwood Country, Kansas City (Kansas City, Mo.). Home: 4545 Wornall Rd Kansas City MO 64111 Office: 106 W 14th St Kansas City MO 64105

FANG, BERTRAND TIEN-CHUEH, educator; b. Nanking, China, Feb. 2, 1932; s. Thome H. and Lillian (Kao) F.; B.S., Nat. Taiwan U., 1952; M.S., Ia. State U., 1957; Ph.D., U. Minn., 1962; m. Bernice B. Feng, June 25, 1961; children—Elaine, Daniel, Harry, Roger, Constance. Came to U.S., 1955, naturalized, 1971. Research fellow U. Minn., 1957-61; mech. engr. Advanced Tech. Lab., Gen. Elec. Co., 1962-63; asst. prof. The Catholic U. Am., 1963-65, asso. prof., 1965-69, prof., 1969—. Mem. Am. Inst. Aero. and Astronautics, Am. Acad. Mechancis. Home: 2809 Farris Lane Bowie MD 20715 Office: 620 Michigan Av Washington DC 20017

FANG, JOONG, educator; b. Piongyang, Korea, Mar. 30, 1923; s. Gabiong and Igab (Kim) F.; student Chuo U., Tokyo, Japan, 1939-41; B.S., Coll. Tech. Seoul, Korea, 1941; M.A., Yale, 1950; Dr.Phil., U. Mainz (Germany), 1957; m. Helga Leist, May 15, 1957; children—Eva Maria, Guido Andreas. Came to U.S., 1957, naturalized, 1962. Asst. prof. math. Jinhae Coll., also U. Pusan (Korea), 1945-48, Valparaiso (Ind.) U., 1958-59, St. John's U., 1959-61, U. Alaska, 1961-62; asso. prof. No. Ill. U., 1963-67; prof. math. and philosophy Memphis State U., 1967—. Vis. prof. U. Munster (Germany), 1971. Mem. Am. Math. Soc., Am. Philos. Assn., Math. Assn. Am., Assn. for Symbolic Logic, Philosophy of Sci. Assn. Author: Das Antinomienproblem, 1957; Numbers Racket, 1958; Kant-Interpretationen, I, 1957; Abstract Algebra, 1963; Towards a Philosophy of Modern Mathematics, I, 1970, II, 1970. Editor, Philosophia Mathematica, 1964—. Home: 7543 Calmbach West Germany Office: Memphis State U Memphis TN 38111

FANGBONER, JOHN S., banker; b. Fremont, O., Apr. 21, 1908; s. James Raymond and Maude (Stokes) F.; student Kenyon Coll., Ohio State U.; m. Frances Taber, Jan. 13, 1934; 1 dau., Frances T. Chmn., Nat. City Bank, Cleve.; dir. Youngstown Sheet & Tube Co., Midland Ross Corp., Weatherhead Co., Anchor Hocking Glass Co., Addressograph-Multigraph Corp., Cleve. & Pitts. Ry. Co. Episcopalian. Clubs: Union, Chagrin Valley Hunt, Tavern Pepper Pike (Cleve). Home: 21306 Brantley Rd Shaker Heights OH 44122 Office: Cleveland OH 44101

FANGER, DONALD LEE, educator; b. Cleve., Dec. 6, 1929; s. Max Leon and Rae (Bercu) F.; B.A., U. Cal. at Berkeley, 1951, M.A., 1954; Ph.D., Harvard, 1962; m. Margot Taylor, June 18, 1955; children—Steffen, Ross, Katharine. Mem. faculty Brown U., 1960-66, asso. prof. Slavic langs. and lit., 1964-66; asso. prof. Slavic, dir. div. Stanford, 1966-68; prof. Slavic and comparative lit. Harvard, 1968—; mem. bd. syndics Harvard U. Press, 1968-73. Mem. program com. Internat. Research and Exchanges Bd. 1968-69, 70—. Served with AUS, 1953-55. Mem. Modern Lang. Assn., Internat. Comparative Lit. Assn. Author: Dostoevsky and Romantic Realism, 1965. Editor Brown U. Slavic Reprint Series, 1962-66. Home: 74 Putnam St West Newton MA 02165 Office: Boylston Hall Harvard Univ Cambridge MA 02138

FANKHAUSER, GERHARD, educator; b. Burgdorf, Switzerland, Mar. 11, 1901; s. Max and Anna (Hermann) F.; student U. Geneva, U. Zurich; Ph.D., U. Berne, 1924; m. Erna Koestler, Aug. 28, 1931; children—David Andreas, Anne and Marguerite (twins). Instr. zoology U. Berne, Switzerland, 1925-29; Rockefeller Found. fellow U. Chgo., Yale, 1929-31; asst. prof. biology Princeton, 1931-39, asso. prof., 1939-46, prof., 1946—, Edwin Grant Conklin prof. biology, 1956-69, emeritus, 1969—. Mem. A.A.A.S., Am. Soc. Zoologists, Am. Assn. Anatomists, Am. Genetics Soc., Am. Soc. Naturalists, Soc. Study Growth, Internat. Inst. Embryology, Internat. Soc. Cell Biology, Sigma Xi. Contbr. articles in field. Home: 177 Moore St Princeton NJ 08540

FANNIN, PAUL JONES, U.S. senator; b. Ashland, Ky., Jan. 29, 1907; s. Thomas Newton and Katherine (Davis) F.; student U. Ariz.; B.A., Stanford, 1930; m. Elma Addington, May 6, 1934; children—Thomas, Robert Paul, William, Linda. Vice pres. Fannin's Gas & Equipment Co., 1932-56; pres. Fannin's Gas Supply Co., 1956-58; pres. Fannin's Service & Supply Co., Safford, Ariz., 1945—; gov. of Ariz., 1959-64; U.S. senator from Ariz., 1965—, mem. Interior and Insular Affairs Com., P.O. and Civil Service Com., Labor and Pub. Welfare Com. Del. Mexico-U.S. Interparliamentary Conf., 1965, 66, 67, ILO, Geneva, Switzerland, 1966. Mem. Southwestern Golf Assn., Kappa Sigma, Thunderbirds. Republican. Methodist. Elk, Moose, Rotarian. Home: 5990 Orange Blossom Lane Phoenix AZ 85018 Office: Senate Office Bldg Washington DC 20510

FANNING, JOHN HAROLD, lawyer, govt. ofcl.; b. Putnam, Conn., Sept. 19, 1916; s. John J. and Eva M. (Dumas) F.; A.B., Providence Coll., 1938; LL.B., Cath. U. Am., 1941; m. Eloise M. Cooney, Dec. 5, 1942; children—Mary Ellen, John Michael, Ann Eloise, Gaele Therese, Stephen Thomas. Admitted to R.I. bar, 1942; solicitors office Dept. of Labor, 1942-43; dir. indsl. relations Dept. Def., 1951-57, also chmn. army contract adjustment bd. Chief labor standards br., indsl. personnel div., Hdqrs. A.S.F., 1943-45; chief indsl. relations br. Office JAG Army, spl. asst. to JAG, 1945-51; also chmn. Army Renegotiation Relief Adv. Com., gen. counsel Army War Contract Hardship Claims Bd. and Army Contract Adjustment Bd., labor adviser to Sec. of Army, chmn. indsl. labor relations com. Munitions Bd.; dir. Office Domestic Programs Dept. Def., 1956-57, mem. NLRB, 1957- -. Mem. R.I. Bar Assn., Providence Coll. Alumni Assn. Club: Providence College (pres. 1948-49, Washington). Home: 5905 Welborn Dr Woodacres MD 20016 Office: Office Asst Sec Def Pentagon Washington DC 20301

FANNING, WILLIAM HENRY, Jr., data systems analyst; b. N.Y.C., Feb. 12, 1917; s. William Henry and Terese Genevieve (Moloney) F.; B.S., Fordham U. Sch. Edn., 1940; postgrad. Cath. U. Am. Grad. Sch. Arts and Scis., 1940-41; m. Mary Major Winter, Sept. 5, 1940; children—Hugh M. (dec.), Helen A. (Mrs. Andrew Koppel), Mary M., William Henry III, Gerard. Instr. Greek and German, Gonzaga High Sch., Washington, 1940-41; reporter, copyreader Nat. Cath. Welfare Conf. News Service, 1941-42, 45- 47, news editor, 1947-55; chief Rome news bur. Radio Free Europe, 1955- 57, dir. news and information services, Munich, 1957-59, chief Paris news bur., 1959-60; asso. editor Cath. News, weekly, 1960-61, editor, 1961-66; v.p. promotion and advt. Diamond Prodns., Ltd., N.Y.C., 1967-69; programmer, analyst CGA Computer Assos., East Orange, N.J., 1969—; head Fanning Pub. Relations, 1966—. Lectr. journalism Good Counsel Coll., White Plains, N.Y., 1967-69; writer documentary scripts for TV, also instrnl. TV scripts for pubs. Mem. Pres.'s Com. on Employment Handicapped, 1947—; mem. Archdiocesan Edn. Com., 1961—. Bd. dirs. Westchester Cath. Edn. Council, 1963-69. Served to lt. comdr. USNR, 1942- 45. Mem. Writers Guild Am. East, Phi Kappa Theta (hon.). Home: 15 Summit St Hastings-on-Hudson NY 10706 Office: 415 Park Av East Orange NJ 07017

FANO, ROBERT MARIO, educator; b. Torino, Italy, Nov. 11, 1917; s. Gino and Rosetta (Cassin) F.; came to U.S., 1939, naturalized, 1947; B.S. in Elec. Engring., Mass. Inst. Tech., 1941, Sc.D. in Elec. Engring., 1947; m. Jacqueline M. Crandall, Mar. 26, 1949. children—Paola C., Linda, Carl. Teaching asst. elec. engring. dept. Mass. Inst. Tech., 1941-43, instr., 1943-44, staff mem. Radiation Lab., 1944-46, research asso. elec. engring. dept. and research lab. electronics, 1946-47, asst. prof., elec. engring dept., 1947-51, group leader Lincoln Lab., 1950-53, asso. prof. elec. engring. dept., 1951-56, prof., 1956-62, Ford prof., 1962—, dir. Project MAC, 1963-68, asso. head for computer sci. and engring., elec. engring. dept., 1971—; cons. to indsl. labs. Fellow I.E.E.E., Am. Acad. Arts and Scis.; mem. Assn. Computing Machinery, Sigma Xi, Eta Kappa Nu. Author: (with R. B. Adler and L. J. Chu) Electromagnetic Fields, Energy and Forces; Electromagnetic Energy Transmission and Radiation, 1960; Transmission of Information, 1961. Home: 17 Somerset Rd Lexington MA 02173 Office: Mass Inst Tech Cambridge MA 02139

FANSEEN, JAMES FOSTER, govt. ofcl.; b. Balt., Feb. 3, 1928; s. Foster Hooker and Lillian (Seguine) F.; A.B., U. N.C., 1950; LL.B., U. Md., 1954; grad. Inst. Police Community Relations, Mich. State U., 1958. Admitted to Md. bar, 1954, D.C. bar, 1968; magistrate Balt. City Police Ct., 1955-59; partner Fanseen & Chlan, Balt., 1959—; commr. Fed. Maritime Commn., 1967—, acting chmn., 1969, vice chmn., 1969-71; prof. polit. sci. Community Coll. Balt., 1963-70. Mem. Nat. Conf. Christians and Jews, 1965—; mem. Criminal Justice Commn., 1965—, pres., 1966-68. Served to maj. USAF Res., 1950-69. Mem. Am., Md., Balt. bar assns., Trial Judges Assn., Md. Law Enforcement Officers, Edgar Allan Poe Soc., Gamma Eta Gamma (past pres.), Phi Delta Theta. Republican. Methodist. Mason (Shriner). Clubs: Metropolitan, University (Washington); Baltimore Country; Yacht, Power Squadron (Annapolis, Md.). Home: 29 Blythewood Rd Baltimore MD 21210 Office: 1405 I St NW Washington DC 20573

FANT, CLYDE, E., City ofcl. Mayor of Shreveport. Address: 340 Ockley Dr Shreveport LA 71105*

FANTA, PAUL EDWARD, educator, chemist; b. Chgo., July 24, 1921; s. Joseph and Marie (Zitnik) F.; B.S., U. Ill., 1942; Ph.D., U. Rochester, 1946; m. LaVergne Danek, Sept. 3, 1949; children—David, John. Postdoctoral research fellow U. Rochester, 1946-47; instr. Harvard, 1947-48; mem. faculty Ill. Inst. Tech., 1948—, prof. chemistry, 1961—; exchange scholar Czechoslovak Acad. Sci., Prague, 1963-64, Soviet Acad. Sci., Moscow, 1970-71. NSF fellow Imperial Coll., London, Eng., 1956-57. Mem. Am. Chem. Soc., Chem. Soc. (London), Am. Assn. U. Profs., SANE, Am. Civil Liberties Union, Sigma Xi, Phi Lambda Upsilon. Contbr. profl. jours. Home: 947 S Clinton Av Oak Park IL 60304 Office: Ill Inst Tech Tech Center Chicago IL 60616

FANTE, JOHN THOMAS, writer; b. Denver, Apr. 8, 1909; s. Nicholas Peter and Mary (Capolungo) F.; student U. Colo., Regis Coll., Denver; m. Joyce H. Smart, July 31, 1937; children—Nicholas, Daniel, Victoria, James. Writer numerous screenplays including Full of Life, 1957 (nominated Acad. award best screenplay 1957), Walk on the Wild Side, Reluctant Saint, My Six Loves, 1962. Author: Wait Until Spring Bandini, 1938; Ask The Dust, 1939; Full of Life, 1952; (collection short stories) Dago Red, 1940; Bravo Burro, 1969. Contbr. nat. mags. Recipient Nat. Cath. Theatre Drama award, 1964. Home: 28981 W Cliffside Dr Malibu CA 90265

FANUCCI, JEROME BENEDICT, educator; b. Glen Lyon, Pa., Oct. 7, 1924; s. Benjamin and Celia (Lanuti) F.; B.S. in Aero. Engring., Pa. State U., 1944, M.S., 1952, Ph.D., 1956; m. Janice C. Bavitz, Jan. 26, 1952; children—Jerome Paul, Karen Marie. Aero. engr. Eastern Aircraft Corp., Trenton, N.J., 1944-45, Republic Aviation Corp., Farmingdale, N.Y., 1947-49; asst. prof. aerospace engring. Pa. State U., 1956-57; research engr. Gen. Electric Aerospace Sci. Lab., Phila., 1957-59; sr. research scientist Plasma and Space Applied Physics Lab., RCA, Princeton, N.J., 1959-64; chmn. dept. aerospace engring., prof. W.Va. U., Morgantown, 1964—; indsl. cons. Served with USAAF, 1946-47. Fellow Am. Inst. Aeros. and Astronautics (asso.); mem. Amateur Radio Relay League, Sigma Xi, Sigma Gamma Tau, Pi Tau Sigma. Contbr. articles profl. jours. Home: 1313 Anderson Av Morgantow.. WV 26505

FARAGHER, DONALD QUALTROUGH, architect; b. Rochester, N.Y., Apr. 11, 1906; s. William Henry and Ella (Qualtrough) F.; B.Arch., Syracuse U., 1930; m. Harriet Miller Thistlethwaite, June 20, 1931; children—Anthony Thistlethwaite, Rachel Qualtrough. Draughtsman, F.R. Scherer, Architect, Rochester, 1926-33; architect engrs. office City of Rochester, 1933-34; pvt. practice, Rochester, 1934-42, 45—; partner Faragher & Macomber, 1951—; supervising architect Rochester-Monroe County Civic Center, 1954—, master plan Rochester Civic Center, 1954—. Mem. Bd. Examiners Architects N.Y. State, 1950-59, pres., 1954-57; chmn. finance com. Nat. Council Architects Registration Bds., 1959—; adv. com. facilities and planning N.Y. Dept. Edn.; adviser Rochester Bldg. Bd. on N.Y. State Code, 1951—; mem. Bldg. Research Inst. representing A.I.A. on Nat. Acad. Sci., 1959; mem. sr. thesis juries Syracuse U. Sch. Architecture, 1949-59, coop. com., 1952—; bd. appeals N.Y. State Bldg. Constrn., 1960- -. Recipient Lillian Fairchild award U. Rochester, 1952; Arents medal Syracuse U., 1960; citation for Ellison Park Apts., Central N.Y. chpt. A.I.A. and N.Y. State Assn. Architects, 1950; certificate of merit for outstanding design of Rochester E. High Sch., N.Y. State Assn. Architects, 1958. Fellow A.I.A. (mem. commn. on edn. and research, dir. N.Y., trustee Found.); mem. N.Y. State (pres. 1951-52, dir. 1959-61, chmn. edn. com. 1953-60), Assn. Architects, Rochester (pres. 1948-50, chmn. legislative com. 1959-63) Soc. Architects, Rochester Engring. Soc. (pres. 1957-58, dir. 1958-61), Am. Soc. Testing Materials, Rochester C. of C., Rochester Music Assn., Syracuse U. Archtl. Alumni Assn. (pres. 1958), Sigma Alpha Epsilon, Sigma Upsilon Alpha. Republican. Presbyn. Clubs: Lake Placid (N.Y.); Rochester Country, Torch (dir. 1957-59), University (Rochester). Home: 22 Buckingham St Rochester NY 14607 Office: Powers Bldg Rochester NY 14614

FARAGHER, THOMAS ROBERT, banker; b. Seattle, July 5, 1912; s. Arthur Wesley and Pearl (Klenck) F.; B.B.A., U. Wash., 1934; postgrad. N.Y. U., 1934-35; m. Mary Jane Mueller, Sept. 2, 1939; children—Thomas James, Ann L. (Mrs. Fred L. Stoneback). With Guaranty Trust Co. of N.Y., N.Y.C., 1934-35; with Peoples Nat Bank of Washington, 1936- 51, v.p., 1947-51; v.p., mgr. Bank of Cal., N.A., Tacoma, 1951-62, sr. v.p., San Francisco, 1962-65; exec. v.p. Nat. Bank Commerce, Seattle, 1965-71, pres., chief exec. officer, 1971—, also dir.; dir. Marine Bancorp., Nat. Bank Americard, Inc., King County Bldg. Co., Nat. Bank of Commerce. Regional chmn. Nat. Alliance Businessmen. Bd. dirs. Automobile Club Wash. Mem. Seattle C. of C. (dir.), Assn. Res. City Bankers, Am. Bankers Assn. (exec. council), Beta Theta Pi, Beta Gamma Sigma, Alpha Kappa Psi. Republican. Episcopalian. Clubs: Seattle Golf, Rainier, Rotary (dir.), Harbor, Broadmoor Golf (Seattle); Tacoma. Home: 3425 St Andrews Way E Seattle WA 98102 Office: Box 3966 Seattle WA 98124

FARAGO, LADISLAS, author; b. Csurgo, Hungary, Sept. 21, 1906; s. Arthur and Irma (Lang) F.; grad. Acad. Commerce and Consular Affairs, Budapest, Hungary, 1926; m. Liesel Mroz, Mar. 22, 1934; 1 son, John Michael Arthur. Journalist in Hungary; with N.Y. Times-Wide World Bur., Berlin, Germany; spl. corr. A.P., Ethiopia: fgn. editor Sunday Chronicle, London, Eng., 1935; dir. research Com. Nat. Morale, N.Y.C., 1940-42; staff U.S. Office Naval Intelligence, 1942-46; editor Corps Diplomatique, 1946; sr. editor UN World, 1947-50; chief desk X, Radio Free Europe, 1950-52. Author: Abyssinia on the Eve, 1935; Abyssinian Stop Press, 1936; Palestine at the Crossroads, 1937; The Riddle of Arabia, 1937; German Psychological Warfare, 1940; Axis Grand Strategy, 1942; Behind Closed Doors, 1950; War of Wits, 1954; Burn After Reading, 1961: Strictly from Hungary, 1962: The Tenth Fleet, 1962; It's Your Money, 1964; Patton: Ordeal and Triumph, 1964; The Broken Seal, 1967. The Game of the Foxes, 1971, others. Home: 1225 Park Av New York City NY 10028

FARAGO, MARCEL, musician; b. Timisoara, Roumania, Apr. 17, 1924; s. Ludovic and Frida (Spitzer) F.; diploma of grad. Conservatory of Music, Timisoara; diploma grad. Royal Acad. Music in Bucharest, Accademia Chigiana in Siena (Italy); student Conservatoire de Paris; m. Adel Pauline Schima, Feb. 11, 1950. Mem. Bucharest Symphony, 1945, Budapest Municipal Orch., 1947-48, Cape Town (South Africa) Municipal Orch., 1952-53; prin. cellist Porto-Alegre Sympohony, 1954-55; mem. Phila. Orch., 1955—; concerts in Europe, South Africa, S.Am., U.S.; composer. Mem. Musicians' Union, A.S.C.A.P. Home: 707 Bradford Alley Philadelphia PA 19147 Office: Acad Music Broad and Locust Sts Philadelphia PA 19102

FARAH, ABDULRAHIM, diplomat. Ambassador of Somalia to UN. Address: 236 E 46th St New York City NY 10017*

FARB, PETER, author; b. N.Y.C., July 25, 1929; s. Solomon and Cecelia (Peters) F.; A.B. magna cum laude, Vanderbilt U., 1950; postgrad. Columbia, 1950-51; m. Oriole Horch, Feb. 27, 1953; children—Mark Daniel, Thomas Forest. Feature editor Argosy mag., 1950- 52; editor-in-chief Panorama, 1960-61; contbr., cons. to nat. mags., 1953—; curator Am. Indian Cultures, Riverside Mus., N.Y.C., 1964-71; cons. Smithsonian Instn., 1966-71; vis. lectr. in English, Yale, 1971-72. Judge, Nat. Book Awards Com., 1971. Bd. dirs. Allergy and Asthma Found. Am., 1970—. Fellow A.A.A.S.; mem. N.Y. Entomol. Soc. (past sec., mem. editorial bd. jour.), Ecol. Soc., Soc. Am. Historians, Soc. for Applied Anthropology, Anthrop. Soc. Washington, Am. Anthrop. Assn., P.E.N. Club, Phi Beta Kappa, Omicron Delta Kappa. Author: Living Earth, 1959; The Story of Butterflies and Other Insects, 1959; The Story of Dams, 1961; The Forest, 1961; The Story of Life: Plants and Animals through the Ages, 1962: The Insects, 1962; Ecology, 1963, rev. edit., 1970; Face of North America: The Natural History of a Continent (Book-of-Month Club selection, Outdoor Life Book Club selection, A.L.A. Notable Book selection, President Kennedy Internat. White House Library selection), 1963: The Forest Reader, 1964; Young Reader's Edition of Face of North America, 1964; The Land and Wildlife of North America, 1965; The Land, Wildlife, and Peoples of the Bible, 1967; Man's Rise to Civilization as Shown by the Indians of North America from Primeval Times to the Coming of the Industrial State (Book-of-Month Club selection, Book Find Club selection, Library of Sci. selection History Book of London selection), 1968; Yankee Doodle, 1970. Co-author: The Atlantic Shore, 1966. Co-editor: Prose by Professionals, 1961. Address: 39 Pokeberry Ridge Amherst MA 01002

FARBACH, CARL FREDERICK, lawyer; b. Cin., June 26, 1901; s. Elmer Jacob and Selma (Harmon) F.; A.B., Harvard, 1923, LL.B., 1926, S.J.D., 1930; m. Florence Allaire Whitehead, May 2, 1935; children—Peter Allaire, Karen Harmon (Mrs. James D. M. McComas). Asst. in govt. Harvard, 1924-26; admitted to N.Y. bar, 1927, Cal. bar, 1946, D.C. bar, 1967; asso. firm of Hawkins, Delafield & Longfellow, N.Y.C., 1926-29, Cotton, Franklin, Wright & Gordon, N.Y., 1930-32; counsel RFC, Washington, 1932-33; counsel Pub. Works Adminstrn., Washington, 1933-35, asst. gen. counsel, 1935-37, gen. counsel, 1937-39; gen. counsel U.S. Maritime Commn., 1939-42; spl. counsel and asst. to U.S. Maritime Comm., and spl. counsel to War Shipping Administrn., 1942-43; asso. with Cravath, Swaine & Moore, 1943-48; legal cons. Internat. Bank for Reconstrn. and Devel., 1947; with Hoover Commn. on Govt. Reorgn., 1948; in pvt. practice N.Y.C., 1948- 54; mem. firm Hecht, Hadfield, Farbach & McAlpin, N.Y.C., 1954-64; counsel Internat. Finance Corp., 1964-67; counsel von Baur, Coburn, Simmons & Turtle, Washington, 1969—. Mem. Assn. Bar City of N.Y., Internat., Am., Inter- Am., N.Y. State bar assns., Bar Assn. D.C., Am. Law Inst., Fgn. Law Assn., Am. Soc. Internat. Law, Phi Kappa Sigma. Presbyn. Clubs: Down Town Assn., Knickerbocker, Harvard (N.Y.C.); Chevy Chase, Internat. (Washington). Author articles on legal topics. Home: 4000 Massachusetts Av NW Washington DC 20016 Office: 1700 K St NW Washington DC 20006

FARBER, BERNARD, educator, sociologist; b. Chgo., Feb. 11, 1922; s. Benjamin and Esther (Axelrod) F.; A.B., Roosevelt U., Chgo., 1943; A.M., U. Chgo., 1949, Ph.D., 1953; m. Annette Ruth Shugan, Dec. 21, 1947 (div. 1970); children—Daniel, Michael, Lisa, Jacqueline. Research asso. U. Chgo., 1951-53; asst. prof. Henderson State Tchr. Coll., Arkadelphia, Ark., 1953-54; mem. faculty, U. I.., 1954-71, prof. sociology, 1964-71, asso. dir. Inst. Research Exceptional Children, 1967-69; prof., chmn. dept. sociology Ariz. State U., 1971—; cons. in field, 1957—. Mem. spl. edn. adv. com. Cerebral Palsy Research and Ednl. Found., 1961-64. Mem. Am. (council mem. family sect. 1966-69), Ill. (founding pres. 1965-66) sociol. assns., Internat. Sci. Commn. on Family, Soc. Study Social Problems, Am. Anthrop. Assn. Served with AUS, 1943-46. Jewish religion. Author: Family; Organization and Interaction, 1964; Mental Retardation: Its Social Context and Social Consequences, 1968; Kinship and Class, 1971. Address: Dept Sociology Ariz State U Tempe AZ 85281

FARBER, EMMANUEL, pathologist, biochemist; b. Toronto, Can., Oct. 19, 1918; s. Morris and Mary (Madorsky) F.; M.D., U. Toronto, 1942; Ph.D. in Biochemistry (Am. Cancer Soc. fellow 1947-49), U. Cal. at Berkeley, 1949; m. Ruth Wilma Diamond, Apr. 16, 1942; 1 dau., Naomi Beth. Came to U.S., 1946, naturalized, 1956. Intern, resident pathology Hamilton (Can.) Gen. Hosp., 1942-43, 44-46; Am. Cancer Soc. fellow Hektoen Inst. Med. Research, Cook County Hosp., Chgo., 1949-50; instr., asst. prof. pathology and biochemistry Tulane U. Sch. Medicine, 1950-55, asso. prof., 1955-59, Am. Cancer Soc. research prof., 1959-61; prof., chmn. pathology U. Pitts., 1961-70; Am. Cancer Soc. research prof. pathology and biochemistry Fels Research Inst., Temple U., Phila., 1970—. Mem. Surgeon Gen.'s Adv. Com. Smoking and Health; chmn. study sect. Nat. Insts. Health; mem. Nat. Adv. Cancer Council, 1966- 70; cons. div. chronic diseases Dept. Health, Edn. and Welfare: mem. sci. adv. bd. cons. Armed Forces Inst. Pathology, 1966-70. Recipient Am. Cancer Soc. scholarship, 1951-55, Parke-Davis award exptl. pathology, 1958, Bertha Goldblatt Teplitz Meml. award, 1961. Served from lt. to capt., M.C., Royal Canadian Army, 1942-46. Diplomate Am. Bd. Pathology. Fellow A.A.A.S.; mem. Am. Assn. Pathologists and Bacteriologists, Am. Soc. Exptl. Pathology (council), Am. Chem. Soc., Am. Soc. Biol. Chemists, Am. Assn. Cancer Research (dir., v.p. 1971-72), N.Y. Acad. Scis., Biochem. Soc., Histochem. Soc. (pres. 1967), Internat. Acad. Pathology, N.Y. Acad. Scis., Pa. Assn. Clin. Pathologists, Sigma Xi. Asso. editor Cancer Research; editorial bd. Jour. Histochemistry and Cytochemistry. Lab. Investigation. Cancer Research, Chemico-Biol. Interactions. Contbr. articles sci. jours. Office: Fels Research Inst Temple U Sch Medicine Philadelphia PA 19140

FARBER, EUGENE MARK, physician, educator; b. Buffalo, July 24, 1917; s. Simon and Matilda (Goldstein) F.; A.B., Oberlin Coll., 1939; M.D., U. Buffalo, 1943; M.S., U. Minn., 1946; m. Ruth Seiffert, Mar. 4, 1944; children—Charlotte, Nancy, Eugene, Donald. Intern Buffalo Gen. Hosp., 1943-44; fellow dermatology and syphilology Mayo Clinic, 1944-48, 1st asst., 1947-48; mem. faculty Stanford Med. Sch., 1948—, dir. div. dermatology, 1950—, prof. dermatology, 1959—, exec. head dept., 1961—; physician in chief Palo Alto Stanford Hosp.; cons. physician Presbyn. Med. Center Palo Alto VA Hosp.; cons. Parks AFB, Travis AFB, 1954-58; attending dermatology Stanford

Convalescent Home, 1957—; cons. surgeon gen. USAF, 1957-64; cons. Cal. Bd. Health, 1960-; chmn. sec. cutaneous system NRC, 1962—; chmn. psoriasis symposium Internat. Congress Dermatology, 1962; gen. clin. research center com. NIH, 1965—. Diplomate Am. Bd. Dermatology. Mem. A.M.A., Assn. Profs. Dermatology (sec. 1967), Am. Acad. Dermatology (dir. 1957- 60, chmn. edn. com., 1967-68), Soc. Investigative Dermatology (past dir., pres. 1966), Soc. Clin. Investigation, Am. Fedn. Clin. Research, Cal. Med. Assn., Pacific Dermatol. Assn., Santa Clara County Med. Soc., Soc. Exptl. Biology and Medicine, Am. Dermatol. Assn., Microcirculatory Conf., Am. Assn. U. Profs., A.A.A.S., Sigma Xi; hon. mem. Soc. Dermatology Austria, Dermatol. Soc. India, Soc. Dermatology Yugoslavia, Societe Francaise de Dermatologie, Venezuelan Soc. Dermatology. Club: Commonwealth (San Francisco). Author numerous research papers. Editorial bd. World Wide Abstracts of Gen. Medicine. Home: 167 Ramoso Rd Portola Valley CA 94025 Office: 300 Pasteur Dr Palo Alto CA 94304

FARBER, HAROLD D., life ins. co. exec.; b. Buffalo, June 3, 1907; s. Simon and Matilda (Goldstein) F.; student U. Buffalo, 1924-27; m. Grace Weber, 1929; 1 dau., Lois Carol (Mrs. Leonard A. Dopkins); m. 2d, Lillian Robertson, 1947; children—Eric A., Michael H., Paul C. Engaged in ins. bus., 1927- -; 1st pres., chmn. bd. Internat. Life Ins. Co., Buffalo, 1960—; dir. Protective Closures Co., Inc., Buffalo; founder, dir. Lake Ledge Park, Inc., Williamsville. Life Mem. Million Dollar Round Table. Mem. C. of C. Home: 50 Lake Ledge Dr Williamsville NY 14221 Office: 120 Delaware Av Buffalo NY 14202

FARBER, HERBERT OTIS, ednl. exec.; b. Geneseo, Ill., Feb. 4, 1912; s. Charles W. and Hulda E. (Ogden) F.; B.S., Northwestern U., 1933, postgrad., 1941-42; M.A., U. Ia., 1938; postgrad. U. Ill., 1939-40; m. Evelyn Irene McCully, Nov. 27, 1937 (dec. July 1969); children—Judith, Jane, Herbert Glenn; m. 2d, Mary K. Flora, Mar. 20, 1971. Tchr. Geneseo Twp. High Sch., 1936-40, J. Sterling Morton High Sch. and Jr. Coll., Cicero, Ill., 1940- 42; accountant U. Ill., 1942-46, asst. comptroller, 1946-53, comptroller, 1953—, v.p., 1956—; comptroller Univ. Retirement System Ill., 1953—. Treas. U. Ill. Found. C.P.A., Ill. Mem. Am. Inst. Accountants, Ill. Soc. C.P.A.'s Delta Sigma Pi, Delta Chi. Rotarian. Home: 2115 Bristol Rd Champaign IL

FARBER, ISADORE E., psychologist, educator; b. St. Joseph, Mo., May 21, 1917; s. Jacob and Rose (Malkin) F.; student St. Joseph Jr. Coll., 1934-36; B.A., U. Mo., 1939, M.A., 1940; Ph.D., U. Ia., 1946; m. Billie Frances Gulko, May 5, 1942; children—Ronna Ellen, Deborah. Instr. psychology U. Rochester, 1946-47; asst. prof. to prof. psychology U. Ia., 1947-64; vis. prof. U. Wis., 1955, Stanford, 1960; research cons. Med. Sch., U. of Okla., 1956-57; prof. psychology U. Ill., Chgo. Circle, 1964—, head dept. psychology, 1964-68; vis. prof. Hebrew U., Jerusalem, 1971-72. Served with Q.M.C., AUS, 1941-42; to 2d lt. USAAF, 1942-45. Fulbright fellow, 1971-72. Mem. Am., Midwestern (past pres.) psychol. assns., Psychonomic Soc., Am. Assn. U. Profs., Phi Beta Kappa, Sigma Xi. Jewish religion. Editor Jour. Exptl. Research in Personality, 1965-71, Psychology series Dodd, Mead & Co., 1965—. Cons. editor Jour. Abnormal and Social Psychology, 1955-61, Jour. of Personality, 1955-61. Contbr. profl. jours. Home: 7912 Church St Morton Grove IL 60053 Office: Dept Psychology U Ill Chgo Circle Harrison and Morgan Sts Chicago IL 60680

FARBER, JAY JOEL, educator; b. Phila., Nov. 6, 1932; s. Albert and Sarah (Efter) F.; B.A., U. Chgo., 1952, M.A., 1954; Ph.D. (Kellogg fellow), Yale, 1959; m. Ada Sachs, Apr. 5, 1952; children—Jonathan, Jeremy. Instr. in classics U. Chgo., 1957-60; asst. prof. classics Rutgers U., 1960-63; asso. prof. classics, chmn. dept. Franklin and Marshall Coll., Lancaster, Pa., 1963-70, John W. Wetzel prof. classics, 1970—. Vis. research asso. Center for Internat. Studies, Princeton, 1962-63; mem. com. examiners Coll. Entrance Exam. Bd., 1971—. Mem. Am. Philol. Assn., Archaeol. Inst. Am., Soc. for Promotion Hellenic Studies, Classical Assn. Atlantic States, Pa. Classical Assn. (pres. 1968-70, editor Bull. 1971—). Home: 871 Grandview Blvd Lancaster PA 17601

FARBER, LESLIE H., Author. Author The Ways of the Will. Address: 4915 30th Pl Washington DC 20008*

FARBER, MARVIN, educator; b. Buffalo, Dec. 14, 1901; s. Simon and Matilda (Goldstein) F.; B.S. summa cum laude, Harvard, 1922, Ph.D., 1925; postgrad. Berlin, Freiburg, Heidelberg Univs., 1922-24, 26- 27; Docteur h.c., l'Université de Lille, 1955; m. Lorraine F. Walle, Dec. 26, 1930; children—Lawrence Alan, Roger Evan, Carol Louise. Instr. philosophy, Ohio State U., 1925-26; instr. philosophy, U. Buffalo, 1927-28, asst. prof., 1928- 30, prof., 1930-61, chmn. dept., 1937-61, acting dean grad. sch. Arts and Scis., 1948, distinguished prof., 1954; prof., chmn. philosophy, U. Pa., 1961-64; Distinguished prof. State U. N.Y., Buffalo, 1964- -. Sheldon fellowship, 1922-23, Parker fellowship, 1923-24 (Harvard), Guggenheim Found. fellowship, 1944-45, grant-in-aid from Rockefeller Found., 1947; DeLaGuna Meml. Lecture, Bryn Mawr Coll., 1950; mem. Inst. Internat. de Philosophie, Paris. Pres. Internat. Phenomenological Soc., 1940—; mem. Am. Philos. Assn. (mem. exec. com. 1951-54; pres. Eastern div. 1963-64), C.S. Peirce Soc., Symbolic Logic Assn. (mem. exec. com., 1946-49), Am. Assn. U. Profs., Phi Beta Kappa. Author: Phenomenology as a Method and as a Philosophical Discipline, 1928; The Foundation of Phenomenology (Harvard), 1943; Husserl, 1956; Naturalism and Subjectivism, 1959; The Aims of Phenomenology, 1966; Phenomenology and Existence, 1967; Basic Issues of Philosophy, 1968. Co-author, editor: Philosophical Essays in Memory of Edmund Husserl, 1940; Philosophic Thought in France and the United States, 1950; L'activité philosophique contemporaine en France et aux Etats-Unis. 1950. Editor (with R. W. Sellars and V. J. McGill) and co-author: Philosophy for the Future, 1949. Editor of Philosophy and Phenomenological Research, 1940- -, American Lectures in Philosophy, 1951—, Modern Concepts in Philosophy, 1968—. Contbr. Twentieth Century Philosophy, 1943; Philosophie, 1950, 51; also to philos. jours. Home: 80 Lake Ledge Dr Williamsville NY 14221 Office: Dept Philosophy State U N Y at Buffalo Buffalo NY 14214

FARBER, ROBERT HOLTON, univ. dean; b. Geneseo, Ill., Jan. 12, 1914; s. Charles William and Hulda E. (Ogden) F.; A.B., DePauw U., 1935; M.A., U. Chgo., 1940; Ed.D., Ind. U., 1951; m. Edna Earle Klutts, Jan. 6, 1946; children—Betty Jean, Charles Robert. Field rep. DePauw U., 1935-36, sec. admissions, 1937-41, asst. dean students, dir. Edward Rector Scholarship Found., 1946-1952, dean of univ. 1952—, also chief adminstrv. officer, 1962-63; tchr. speech Bloomington (Indiana) High Sch., 1936-37. Chmn. Stillwater Nat. Deans Conf., 1972; mem. nat. coordinating commn. Nat. Council Accreditation for Colls. for Tchr. Edn.; dir. Study Tour, Europe and Russia, People to People Orgn., 1970, Japan, 1972. Served as maj. AUS, 1941-46. Decorated Bronze Star award, meritorious service plaque. Mem. of Am. Assn. Colls. for Tchr. Edn., North Central (pres.), Nat., Ind. past chmn. assns. academic deans, Ind. Assn. Independent and Ch. Related Colls., Phi Delta Kappa, Blue Key. Republican. Methodist. Mason (32), Kiwanian. Home: 712 Highridge Av Greencastle IN 46135

FARBER, SAUL JOSEPH, physician, educator; b. N.Y.C., Feb. 11, 1918; s. Isidor and Mary (Bunim) F.; A.B., N.Y.U., 1938, M.D., 1943; m. Doris Marcia Balmuth, Mar. 13, 1949; children—Joshua M., Beth Mina. Intern Sinai Hosp., Balt., 1943; research resident Goldwater Hosp., resident Bellevue Hosp., N.Y.U., 1946-48; fellow dept. medicine N.Y.U., 1948-49, asst. in medicine, 1949-50, instr., 1950-53, asst. prof. medicine, 1953-57, asso. prof., 1957-62, prof. medicine, 1962, acting chmn. dept., 1962-63, acting dean, dep. dir., 1963-66, Nathan Friedman prof. medicine, 1965—, chmn. dept. medicine, 1966—; dir. 3d and 4th med. divs. Bellevue Hosp., 1966-68, dir. medicine, 1968—; attending physician Univ. Hosp., 1962—, dir. medicine, 1966—; cons. VA Hosp., N.Y.C. Mem. nat. adv. research resources council and program planning com. USPHS, 1967-71; basic sci. adv. com. Nat. Cystic Fibrosis Found., 1967-71; adv. com. Inter-Soc. Commn. for Heart Disease Resources, 1968—; mem. hypertension- renal subcom. N.Y. Met. Regional Med. Program for Heart Disease, Cancer and Stroke, 1968—; med. adv. com. N.Y.C. Hosp. Corp. Task Force, 1969-71; adv. council Med Bds. Municipal Hosps., N.Y.C., 1970—. Bd. dirs. Russell Sage Inst. Pathology, numerous adv. bds. Served from lt. (j.g.) to lt., USNR, 1943-46. Diplomate Am. Bd. Internal Medicine (mem. bd. 1968—). Fellow A.C.P., N.Y. Acad. Medicine; mem. Am. Soc. Clin. Investigation (councilor 1960-63), Assn. Am. Physicians, Am. Physiol. Soc., Assn. Profs. Medicine (councillor 1970—), Soc. Urban Physicians (pres. 1970—), Am. (fellow council on circulation), N.Y. (pres.-elect) heart assns., N.Y. Soc. Nephrology, Interurban Clin. Club, Harvey Soc. (pres. 1968- 69, councillor 1969—), Soc. Exptl. Biology and Medicine, Am. Fedn. Clin. Research, Sigma Xi, Alpha Omega Alpha. Editor: Am. Jour. Med. Scis., 1970. Home: 25 Plaza St Brooklyn NY 11217 Office: 550 1st Av New York City NY 10016

FARBER, SEYMOUR MORGAN, physician, univ. dean; b. Buffalo, June 3, 1912; s. Simon and Matilda (Goldstein) F.; B.A., U. Buffalo, 1931; M.D., Harvard, 1939; D.H.L., St. Mary's Coll. (Moraga), 1964; m. Lynette True, Dec. 17, 1940; children—Burt, Margaret, Roy. Intern Newton (Mass.) Hosp., 1939-40; resident Gaylord Hosp., Wallingford, Conn., 1940-42; practice medicine, specializing chest diseases, San Francisco, 1946—; instr. dept. medicine U. Cal. at San Francisco, 1942-47, asst. prof., 1947-53, asso. prof., 1953-61, prof. clin. medicine, 1961—, asst. dean for continuing edn. medicine and health scis., 1956-63, dir. instrn. in extension, 1960- 61, dir. continuing edn. medicine and health scis., 1963-70, dean ednl. services, 1963-70, dean continuing edn. in health scis., 1970—, spl. asst. to pres., 1964—; lectr. U. Cal. Sch. Pub. Health, Berkeley, 1948—; chief U. Cal. Tb and chest service San Francisco Gen. Hosp., 1945-65, sr. cons., 1965—. Spl. cons. Nat. Cancer Inst., 1958-60; nat. cons. continuing edn. and chest diseases to surg. gen. USAF, 1962; mem. Pres.'s Commn. on Status of Women, 1962-63. Mem. Council Med. TV, Bary Area Council on Alcoholism, Bay Area Adv. Bd. on Air Pollution. Fellow Am. Coll. Chest Physicians (past pres.), Am. Coll Cardiology; mem. A.M.A. (chmn. chest diseases sect. 1959-60), Cal. Med. Assn., San Francisco County Med. Soc., Cal. Soc. Internal Medicine, Am. Fedn. Clin. Research, N.Y. Acad. Scis., Am. Trudeau Soc., Internat. Acad. Pathology, A.A.A.S., Pan Am. Med. Assn. (pres. sect. chest diseases), Assn. Am. Med. Colls., Am. Geriatrics Soc. Author: Cytological Diagnosis of Lung Cancer, 1950; Lung Cancer, 1954. Editor: The Air We Breathe, 1961; Control of the Mind, 1961; Man and Civilization: Conflict and Creativity, 1963; The Potential of Woman, 1963; Man Under Stress, 1964; The Challenge to Women, 1966; Food and Civilization, 1966; Teen-Age Marriage and Divorce, 1967; Sex Education and the Teen-Ager, 1967. Editorial board Diseases of Chest, 1948-61, General Practice, 1958- 61; bd. cons. Pre-Med. Jour., 1965—. Contbr. profl. publs. Office: 1255 Post St San Francisco CA 94109

FARBER, SIDNEY, physician; b. Buffalo, Sept. 30, 1903; s. Simon and Matilda (Goldstein) F.; B.S., U. Buffalo, 1923; M.D., Harvard, 1927; post- grad. research, Germany, 1928-29, Belgium, 1935-36; D.Sc., (hon.), Suffolk U., 1960, Boston U., 1961, Providence Coll., 1961, Albert Einstein Coll. Medicine, 1966, N.Y. Med. Coll., 1970; M.D. (hon.), U. Ghent (Belgium), 1962, Cath. U. Louvain (Belgium), 1965, Karolinska Instituet, Stockholm, Sweden, 1969; L.H.D. (hon.), Brandeis U., 1963; m. Norma C. Holzman, July 3, 1928; children—Ellen, Stephen Burt, Thomas David, Miriam. Faculty, Harvard Med. Sch. 1927-70, S. Burt Wolbach prof. pathology, 1967-70, prof. emeritus, 1970—; prof. pathology, Harvard Med. Sch. at Children's Hosp., 1948-67; pathologist-in- chief, chmn. div. labs. and research, Children's Med. Center 1946-70; chmn. staff Children's Hosp. Med. Center, 1964-70, cons. in pathology and oncology, 1970—. Founder, sci. dir. Children's Cancer Research Found. 1948—; cons. Armed Forces Inst. Pathology, U.S. Pub. Health Services, Nat. Cancer Inst. Trustee Worcester Found. Exptl. Biology, Southwest Found. Research and Edn., San Antonio; founding trustee United Cerebral Palsy Research and Ednl. Found.; mem. Nat. Adv. Cancer Council; chmn. panel on cancer Pres.'s Commn. Heart Disease, Cancer and Stroke, 1964. Pres., Am. Assn. Pathologists and Bacteriologists, 1957-58, Soc. Pediatric Research, 1947-48; pres. New Eng. Pathol. Soc., Boston Pathol. Soc.; bd. dirs. Belgian Am. Ednl. Found.; trustee Brandeis U., sec. bd. trustees, 1967; mem. sci. adv. bds. Roswell Park Research Inst., New Eng. Deaconess Hosp. Recipient Gt. medal U. Ghent, 1959; Modern Medicine award, 1962; Albert Lasker award for clinical research, 1966; Boston medal for distinguished achievement, 1967; Jurzykowski award in med. sci., 1970; Papnicolou award, 1971. Diplomate Am. Bd. Pathology. Fellow N.Y. Acad. Scis., Am. Acad. Arts and Scis.; mem. A.M.A., Am. Pediatric Soc., Asso. Cancer Inst. Dirs. (pres. 1963-65), Am. Assn. Cancer Research (hon.), James Ewing Soc. (hon.), Sigma Xi, Phi Beta Kappa, Alpha Omega Alpha. Club: Harvard. Editorial bd. Cancer, Biochem. Pharmacology. Home: 1010 Memorial Dr Cambridge MA 02138 Office: 35 Binney St Boston MA 12115

FARBER, WILLIAM OGDEN, educator; b. Geneseo, Ill., July 4, 1910; s. Charles William and Hulda Ella (Ogden) F.; A.B., Northwestern U. 1932, A.M., 1933; Ph.D., U. of Wis., 1935; law sch., U. of Colo., summer 1938. Harris scholar, Northwestern U., 1932-33; Univ. fellow U. Wis., 1933-35; prof. polit. and social sci. and head dept. N.D. Agrl. Coll., 1937-38; asst. prof. govt. U.S.D., 1935-37, prof. and head dept. govt. , 1938—, dir. govtl. research bur., 1939— (on leave 1942-46, 56-57, 58-59); lectr. U. Wis., summer, 1947; vis. prof. polit. sci. Northwestern U., 1956-57. State price officer O.P.A., 1942-43, cons., 1946; mem. regional loyalty bd. U.S. Civil Service Commn., 1948-53; dir. legislative research S.D. Legislative Council, 1951-55; ICA-U. Minn. pub. adminstrn. adviser, Seoul Nat. U., Korea, 1958-59; minority counsel U.S. Senate sub-com. Nat. Policy Machinery, 1960-61, cons. subcom. Nat. Security and Internat. Operations, 1966-71. Served as warrant officer USAAF , 1943-46. Mem. Am. Polit. Sci. Assn., Nat. Municipal League, Am. Acad. Polit. and Social Sci., Am. Soc. for Public Adminstrn., Governmental Research Assn., Am. Assn. U. Profs., Midwest Conf. Polit. Scientists (pres. 1963-64), Phi Beta Kappa. Presbyn. Author: City Manager Government in South Dakota, 1948; state corr. for Nat. Municipal Rev., Nat. Municipal Yearbook. Co-author: Indians, Law Enforcement and Local Government, 1957; Government of South Dakota, 1962, 68. Home: 413 E Clark St Vermillion SD 57069

FARBERMAN, HAROLD, condr., composer; b. N.Y.C., Nov. 2, 1930; s. Louis and Lena (Kramer) F.; diploma (scholarship 1947-51), Juilliard Sch. Music, 1951; B.S., New Eng. Conservatory Music, 1956, M.S., 1957; m. Corinne Curry, June 22, 1958; children—Thea, Lewis. Percussionist, Boston Symphony Orch., 1951- 63; condr. New Arts Orch., Boston, 1955-63; guest condr. Royal Philharmonic Orch., London, Eng., Denver Symphony Orch., BBC Symphony, Victoria (Can.) Philharmonic, Miami (Fla.) Philharmonic, N.Y. Philharmonic, New Philharmonia Orch., London, Eng.; condr. Colorado Springs (Colo.) Philharmonic, 1967-68; music dir., condr. Oakland Symphony Orch., 1971—; rec. artist (condr. or composer) for Columbia, Capitol, Mercury, Vanguard, Cambridge, Serenus, Boston records; rep. U.S. in Paris (France) Internat. Composition Competition, 1959. Mem. A.S.C.A.P., Nat. Assn. Composers and Conductors. Composer symphonies, string quartet, chamber music, operas, jazz. Pioneered recorded works of Charles E. Ives. Author in field. Address: 1726 Oakland Av Piedmont CA 94611

FARBMAN, AARON ABRAHAM, surgeon; b. Odessa, Russia, Apr. 24, 1902; s. Samuel and Bertha (Rubin) F.; brought to U.S., 1904; A.B., Columbia, 1923, M.A., 1924, M.D., 1928; m. Marie Arlene Prager, July 23, 1944; children—Leslie, Robin. Began practice of surgery, 1930; research with Drs. David J. Sandweiss, Harry C. Saltzstein on relationship of sex hormones to peptic ulcer, 1936. Company surgeon Continental Motors Corp. 1941-47; attending surgeon in gen. surgery North End Clinic; sec., staff Cottage Hosp., Grosse Pointe, Mich.; asso. attending surg. Sinai Hosp., Detroit; attending in gen. surgery Detroit Meml. Hosp. Pres. Chamber Music Players of Grosse Pointe. Trustee Detroit Music Settlement Sch. Awarded certificate of merit, for class I Scientific Exhibit by A.M.A., 1938. Diplomate Am. Bd. Abdominal Surgery. Fellow A.C.S., Internat. Coll. Surgeons, Am. Geriatric Soc., A.M.A., Amateur Chamber Music Players (nat. exec. com.), Phi Delta Epsilon. Jewish religion. Clubs: Economic, Clef. Contributed articles on endocrine and surg. to med. jours. Home: 809 Berkshire Rd Grosse Pointe Park MI 48236 Office: 14515 Kercheval Av Detroit MI 48215

FARBSTEIN, LEONARD, former congressman, lawyer; b. N.Y.C.; LL.B., N.Y.U., 1924; m. Blossom Langer, Sept. 19, 1947; 1 son, Louis J. Admitted to N.Y. bar, 1925; since practiced in N.Y.C.; mem. N.Y. legislature from 4th Assembly Dist. Manhattan, 1932-56; mem. 85th-91st Congresses, 19th N.Y. Dist. Served with USCG Res., World War II. Mem. Am. Judicature Soc., N.Y. County Lawyers Assn., Am., N.Y. State bar assns., Assn. Bar City of N.Y. Democrat. Home: 276 Fifth Av New York City NY 10001 Office: Rayburn Bldg Washington DC 20525

FARENTINO, JAMES, actor; b. Bklyn., Feb. 24, 1938; s. Anthony and Helen (Enrico) F.; grad. high sch.; m. Michele Lee Dusick, Feb. 20, 1966; 1 son, David Michael. Broadway appearance in Night of the Iguana, 1961; off-Broadway appearances in Days and Nights of BeeBee Fenstermaker, 1963, In the Summer House, 1964; film appearances include The War Lord, 1964, Rosie, 1966, Me Natalie, 1964, Banning, 1965, Rode to Hangman's Tree, 1965; starring TV appearances in Death of a Salesman, 1966, Vanished, 1971, (series) The Bold Ones, 1970—, John Dos Possos: U.S.A., 1971. Recipient Press award for most promising newcomer, 1966. Office: Universal Studios Universal City CA 91608

FARIBAULT, MARCEL, trust co. exec.; b. Montreal, Que., Can., Oct. 8, 1908; s. Rene and Annette (Pauze) F.; B.A., U. Montreal, 1927, Legum Licentiatus, 1930, D.C.L., 1936, LL.D., 1963; LL.D., Laval U., 1952; hon. degree, Royal Mil. Coll. Can., 1965; m. Marguerite Masson, Jan. 20, 1938; children—Bernard, Louise, Rene, Suzanne, Francoise, Jacques, Dominique. Called to Canadian bar, 1930; practiced in Montreal, 1930-50; sec. gen. U. Montreal, 1950-55; pres. Trust Gen. du Can., Montreal, 1955—, also dir.; dir. Bell Telephone Co. Can., Confedn. Devel. Corp., Cie d'Assurance Canadienne Mercantile, Cie d'Assurance Canadienne Nationale, Cie d'Assurance Generale de Commerce, La Prevoyance, Cie d'Assurance, Rougier Freres Inc., Canadian Arena Co., Compagnie Miron Ltée, Dominion Textile Co., Ltd., Internat. Bus. Machine Co., Ltd., L'Economie, Mutuelle d'Assurance, Roy Nat. Ltd.; pres. Sherbrooke Trust Co.; dir. Crédit Foncier Franco- Canadien. Mem. Royal Soc. Can. Roman Catholic. Clubs: Cercle Universitaire de Montreal, Saint James's, St. Denis, Laval-dur-le-lac, Montreal, Mount Royal (Montreal). Author: Traite de la Fiducie dans la Province de Quebec, 1936; (with Robert M. Fowler) Ten to One or the Confederation Wager, 1965. Home: 640 Dunlop Av Outremont Montreal 8, Quebec Canada. Office: 909 Dorchester Blvd W Montreal 2 Quebec Canada

FARICY, WILLIAM THOMAS, r.r. exec.; b. St. Paul, Mar. 7, 1893; s. John I. and Thecla (Brown) F.; student Coll. of St. Thomas, St. Paul, 1906-08; LL.B. magna cum laude, St. Paul Coll. of Law, 1914; m. Norma Hauser, Apr. 6, 1918; children—Norma H. (Mrs. Ralph W. Condee), Jean (Mrs. John B. Lord) (dec.). Atty. C., St. P. M. & O. Ry. Co., 1914; gen. practice, St. Paul, 1916-17, 1919-20; gen. atty., C., St. P., M. & O. Rd. Co., St. Paul, 1920-24; commerce atty. C.& N.W. Ry. Co., Chgo., 1924-25; v.p. Hauser Securities Co., and asst. to pres. Hauser Constrn. Co., Portland, Ore., and Long Beach, Cal., 1925-27; Minn. atty. C. & N.W. Ry. Co., St. Paul, 1927-29; gen. solicitor C., St. P. M.&O. Ry. Co., St. Paul, 1929-33; gen. solicitor C. & N.W. Ry. System, Chgo., 1933-42; gen. counsel, C. & N.W. Ry. Co., 1942-44; v.p. and gen. counsel C. St. P. M. & O. Ry. Co., 1942-47, v.p. and gen. counsel C. & N.W. Ry. Co., 1944-47; chmn. Western Conf. of Ry. Counsel, 1944-46; chief counsel, Carriers Conf. Com., rep. Class I Railroads of America. 1945- 56 Wage and Rules movement, and 1946 railroad strike; pres., treas., dir. of Grant Smith & Co. & McDonnell, Ltd.; adv. dir. Riggs Nat. Bank; chmn. Civilian Components Policy bd., Dept. Def., 1949-50; chmn. U.S. Nat. Commn. Pan-Am. Ry. Congress Assn., 1949-58, mem. 1959-67; pres. Def. Orientation Conf. Assn., 1955-56. Life trustee Northwestern U. Pres. Assn. Am. R.R.'s, 1947- 57, chmn. bd. 1957-58. Served as lt., capt. 350th Inf., France, AUS, 1917-19. Decorated officer French Legion of Honor; recipient Nat. Def. Transp. Award for individual def.-supporting achievement, 1958. Fellow Am. Bar Found.; mem. Am., Cal., Ill., Minn. bar assns., Chgo. Bar Assn. (bd. Am. Legion (chmn. nat. transp. com. 1950-52). Clubs: Law, Commercial (Chgo.); Bohemian (San Francisco); Metropolitan, Burning Tree, Alfalfa (Washington); Spokane (Wash.); Eldorado Country (Palm Desert, Cal.). Home: 4914 Glenbrook Rd Washington DC 20016 Office: care AAR 1920 L St NW Transp Bldg Washington DC 20036

FARIES, BELMONT, newspaper editor; b. Wilmington, Del., June 3, 1913; s. Clarence D. and Elva (Eddingfield) F.; B.A., U. Pa., 1935; m. Bette Jane Bonine, Sept. 5, 1945; children—Jain, Nancy, Jennifer. Reporter, Jour. Every Evening, Wilmington, Del., 1935-38; copy editor Evening Star, Washington, 1938- 55, news editor, 1955—, stamp editor, 1956—. Editor Soc. Philatelic Ams. Jour., 1962—, Minkus Stamp Jour., 1966—. Mem. Postmaster Gen.'s Stamp Adv. Com., 1967-69. Served to 2d lt. AUS, 1942-46. Mem. Am. Philatelic Congress (mem. council 1966—), Phi Beta Kappa. Home: 11713 Chapel Rd Clifton VA 22024 Office: 225 Virginia Av SE Washington DC 20003

FARINHOLT, LARKIN HUNDLEY, found. exec.; b. Balt. Sept. 24, 1905; s. Leroy Whiting and Elizabeth (Gwin) F.; B.S. in Chemistry, Johns Hopkins, 1927, grad. study, 1927-28; D. Phil. (Rhodes scholar), Oxford U., 1931; D.Sc. (hon.), Clarkson Coll. of Technol., 1967; m. Mary Kathryn Snyder, Dec. 26, 1947; children-Larkin, Kathryn, Mary Victoria. Asst. prof. chemistry Washington and Lee U., 1933-37, asso. prof., 1937-41; asso. prof. chemistry Columbia, 1947-54, prof., 1954-60, dir. Chem. Labs., 1953-60; adminstr. program for basic research in physical scis., Alfred P. Sloan Found., N.Y.C., 1960—, v. p. 1962-70, trustee, 1962-69; dept. sci. adviser State Dept., 1958-60; sci. attaché Am. Embassy, London, 1951-52. Exec. officer Explosives Research Lab., NDRC, OSRD, 1941-45, spl. asst. to chmn. NDRC, 1945-46, mem. Com. Internat. Exchange of Persons, 1953-56. Recipient Presdl. Certificate of Merit. Mem. Am. Chem. Soc., A.A.A.S. Phi Gamma Delta, Omicron Delta Kappa, Tau Beta Pi. Clubs: Century (N.Y.C.); Cosmos (Washington). Home: 149 Glenwood Av Leonia NJ 07605 Office: 630 Fifth Av New York City NY 10020

FARIS, ESRON MCGRUDER, Jr., educator; b. Norfolk, Va., May 24, 1925; s. Esron McGruder and Highland (Stevens) F.; B.S. in Bus. Adminstrn., Washington and Lee U., 1949, J.D., 1951; LL.M., Duke, 1954; m. Helen Davis, Feb. 18, 1950; children—Anne Martin, Douglas McGruder. Admitted to Va. bar, 1952, N.C. bar, 1960; asst. prof. law Washington and Lee U., 1951-57; asso. prof. law Wake Forest U., 1957-62, prof. law, 1962-65, 67—; lectr., prof. law, organizer-dir. overseas law program in Exeter, Eng., Coll. William and Mary, 1965-67; legal practice, Williamburg, 1965-68; legal cons. Security Life and Trust Co., summers 1960, 61, 65; vis. prof. summers Washington and Lee U., Christopher Newport Coll., Emory U., William and Mary in Eng. Legal adviser Revision Va. Income Tax Laws, 1956-57, N.C. Uniform Comml. Code, 1964-65, N.C. Corp. Law, 1967-71. Pres. Lexington-Rockbridge Jr. C. of C., 1957. Served with USAAF, 1943-46. Mem. Va., N.C. bar assns., Order of Coif, Phi Gamma Delta, Alpha Kappa Psi, Phi Delta Phi. Presbyn. (elder). Mason. Author: Accounting for Lawyers, rev. edit., 1964; also articles. Address: 200 Prince George St Williamsburg VA 23185

FARIS, JESSE EDWIN, Jr., educator; b. Wenatchee, Wash., Jan. 6, 1928; s. Jesse Edwin and Lois (Poe) F.; student Wenatchee Jr. Coll., 1944-45; B.S., Wash. State U., 1948, M.A., 1951; Ph.D., N.C. State U., 1955; NSF post doctoral fellow, U. Ill., 1962-63; m. Zorita Chloe Jackson, Sept. 8, 1951; children—Jeffrey Edwin, Kimberly Ann, Jill Marie, Margaret Sue. Soil conservationist Dept. Agr., Klamath Falls, Ore., 1948-49; research asso. Wash. State U., Pullman, 1951-52; research asst. N.C. State U., Raleigh, 1953-55; asst. prof. U. Cal. at Davis, 1955-61, asso. prof., 1961-67, prof., 1967-69; prof., head dept. agrl. econs. Va. Poly. Inst. and State U., Blacksburg, 1969—; adviser Chilean Govt., Santiago, 1966-67; cons. to AID, U.S. Dept. Agr., State of Cal. Served with USNR, 1945-46. Mem. Am., So. agrl. assns., Phi Kappa Phi, Gamma Sigma Delta, Alpha Zeta, Alpha Gamma Rho. Mem. Ch. of Christ. Contbr. articles in field to profl. jours., books. Home: 406 Apperson Dr Blacksburg VA 24060

FARIS, ROBERT E. LEE, educator; b. Waco, Tex., Feb. 2, 1907; s. Ellsworth and Elizabeth (Homan) F.; Ph.B., U. Chgo., 1928, M.A., 1930, Ph.D., 1931; m. Claire Guignard, Aug. 18, 1931; children—William Guignard, John Homan, Roger Stuart. instr., then asst. prof. sociology Brown U., 1931-38; asst. prof. McGill U., 1938-40; asso. prof. Bryn Mawr Coll., 1940-43; asso. prof., then prof. Syracuse U., 1943-48 prof. U. Wash., 1948—, exec. officer dept. sociology, 1953-66. Mem. Social Sci. Research Council (dir. 1953-60), Am. (pres. 1961), Pacific (pres. 1954) sociol. socs., Social Research Assn. (pres. 1959). Club: Seattle Yacht. Author: Social Disorganization 1948; Social Psychology, 1952; (with H. W. Dunham) Mental Disorders in Urban Areas, 1939; Chicago Sociology, 1920-32, 1967. Editor Am. Sociol. Review, 1952-54. Editor Handbook of Modern Sociology, 1964. Contbr. articles sociol, jours. Home: 4318 NE 41st St Seattle WA 98105.

FARKAS, NICHOLAS, cons. engr.; b. Oradea, Hungary, Oct. 26, 1900; s. Ignatz and Maria (Lindenfeld) F.; came to U.S., 1921, naturalized, 1927; student U. Tech. Sci., Budapest, Hungary, 1918-19; B.S. in Gen. Sci., Cooper Union Coll., 1926; B.S. in Civil Engring., N.Y.U., 1938; m. Martha Levine, June 4, 1927; children—Norma Suzanne (Mrs. David Fund), Edith Marion (Mrs. Arnold M. Gaines), Judith Ann. Partner, Davidson & Farkas, civil engrs., 1928- 30; jr. engr. Bd. Transp. N.Y.C., 1930-33; resident engr. PWA, 1933-37; asst. engr. Bd. Water Supply N.Y.C., 1937-42; sr. engr. F.R. Harris, Inc., N.Y.C., 1942-44; sr. designer Clark & Rapauno, N.Y.C., 1944-46; partner Farkas, Barron & Partners, N.Y.C., 1946—, also dir.; dir. Farkas, Barron, Jablonsky, Ltd., Toronto, Ont., Bldg. Planning Services, Ltd., Toronto. Mem. Housing and Planning Council, 1958—, N.Y. State Civil Def. Com., 1966—. Registered profl. engr., N.Y., Mass., R.I., Conn., Tenn., D.C. Mem. Am. Arbitration Assn. (panel 1966—), Technion Soc., N.Y. Assn. Cons. Engrs., Cons. Engrs. Council, N.Y. State Assn. Profl. Engrs., Am. Concrete Inst., Concrete Industry Bd., N.Y. State Assn. Professions. Democrat. Jewish religion. Co-author books. Contbr. articles profl. publs. Office: 309 W 23d St New York City NY 10011 also 2 St Clair Av W Toronto Ontario Canada

FARKAS, PHILIP FRANCIS, musician; b. Chgo., Mar. 5, 1914; s. Emil Nelson and Anna (Cassady) F.; studied with Louis Dufrasne, Chgo. Civic Orchestra; m. Margaret Groves, May 11, 1939; children—Carol, Lynn, Jean Ann, Margaret. Solo hornist Kansas City Philharmonic, 1934-36. Chgo. Symphony Orch., 1936-41, 47- 60, Cleve. Orch., 1941-45, 46-47, Boston Symphony Orch., 1945- 46; prof. music Ind. U., 1960—; French horn player symphony orch., radio, other orchestras. Author: The Art of French Horn Playing, 1956: The Art of Brass Playing, 1962. Editor of French Horn Excerpts from the Modern French Repertoire. Home: Rural Route 12 Box 323 Bloomington IN 47401

FARKAS, ROBIN LEWIS, retail co. exec.; b. N.Y.C., Oct. 13, 1933; s. George and Ruth (Lewis) F.; B.A., Harvard, 1954, M.B.A., 1961; m. Suzanne Ellen Gold, July 5, 1959; children—Andrew Lawrence, Bradford Lewis. From jr. exec. trainee to asst. store mgr. Alexander's Dept. Stores, N.Y.C., 1955- 59; staff cons. Arthur D. Little Inc., Cambridge, Mass., 1961-63; pres. Alexander's Rent-A-Car, 1963-69; sr. v.p., dir., treas. Alexander's Dept. Stores, 1963—. Bd. dirs. Bronx Bd. Trade and C. of C., 1964—. Mem. pres.'s council N.Y. U. Sch. Social Work; vis. com. on adminstrn. Harvard U. Trustee Beth Israel Hosp., N.Y.C.; bd. dirs. Nat. Conf. Christians and Jews, 1964—, Asso. YMHAs N.Y.C., 1965- -. Served with AUS, 1955-57. Recipient award service to youth Westchester-Bronx YMCA, 1966. Mem. Aircraft Owners and Pilots Assn. Clubs: Harvard (Boston and N.Y.C.); Harvard Business School (N.Y.C.); Beach Point Yacht. Home: 730 Park Av New York City NY 10021 Office: 500 7th Av New York City NY 10016

FARLAND, JOSEPH SIMPSON, U.S. ambassador; b. Clarksburg, W. Va., Aug. 11, 1914; s. Richard Ashville and Grace Ione (Simpson) F.; B.A., W. Va. U., 1936, LL.B., 1938, LL.D., 1963, Fairleigh Dickinson U., 1962, W.Va. Wesleyan U., 1965; student Princeton, 1944, Stanford, 1945; m. Virginia Maye Christopher, Nov. 25, 1939; children—Brooke Randolph, Page Christorpher (Mrs. John T. Ross), Richard Ashville, Christopher Simpson. Admitted to W. Va. bar, 1938, D.C. bar, 1966; practice law, W.Va., 1938-42; counsel Surrey, Karasik, Greene & Hill, Washington; agt. FBI, 1942-44; pres. Farland Fuel Corp., other coal cos. W.Va. and Pa.; cons. mutual security program Dept. State, 1956; U.S. ambassador Dominican Republic, 1957-60, Republic Panama, 1960-63, Republic Pakistan, 1969—. Chmn. exec. com., bd. trustees People-to-People, Inc., 1965-66, dir. health found. HOPE. Dir. Shering Corp., 1964-69. Cons. Reader's Digest, 1964-65; mem. research council and exec. com. Center for Strategic and Internat. Studies Georgetown U., Washington, also bd. dirs. univ., 1969—. Bd. dirs. W.Va. U. Found.; trustee Shenandoah Coll., Shenandoah Conservatory Music, Winchester, Va. Mem. nat. finance com. Republican party, 1966-69. Served with USNR, 1944-46; navel liaison Mil. Govt. Forces Korea, 1945- 46. Decorated Order Vasco Nunez de Balboa (Panama); Order Duarte, Sanchez y Mella (Dominican Republic); recipient W.Va. Bishop's Distinguished Service Cross, 1964. Mem. Beta Theta Pi, Phi Alpha Delta. Delta Sigma Rho. Episcopalian (chairman churchmen W.Va. 1954-56). Clubs: Chevy Chase (Md.); International (Washington); Lakeview Country (Morgantown, W.Va.); University (N.Y.C.); Union (Panama). Address: American Embassy, Rawalpindi, Republic Pakistan.

FARLEY, CLARE FRANCIS, govt. ofcl.; b. Belvidere, Ill., Aug. 21, 1920; s. Frank A. and Margaret (Cunningham) F.; B.S., U.S. Mil. Acad., 1943; M.S., U. Ia., 1946; m. Jane F. Noonan, Sept. 21, 1943; children—Patrick, Brian, Ellen, Kieran. Commd. 2d lt. C.E., U.S. Army, 1943, advanced through grades to ret., 1968; exec. officer NASA, 1968-71, dep. asst. adminstr. tech. utilization, Washington, 1971—. Registered profl. engr., N.Y. Home: 1432 Hard Ct McLean VA 22101 Office: NASA 400 Maryland Av Washington DC 20234

FARLEY, EDWARD INDERRIEDEN, finance exec.; b. Chgo., July 31, 1915; s. Edward Philip and Elise Marie (Inderrieden) F.; grad. Middlesex Sch., 1934; B.S., Harvard, 1938, grad. Advanced Mgmt. Program, 1952; m. Jane Thomson, Jan. 27, 1945; children—Jane Graham, Edward I., Alexander T. Asso., Rollins Burdick Hunter Co., 1939-52; v.p. Marsh & McLennan, N.Y.C., 1952-61; v.p. Field Enterprises, Inc., Chgo., 1961-64, sr. v.p., 1964-66, dir. financial and investment services, N.Y.C., also dir., mem. exec. com.; gen. partner Farley Assos.; v.p., dir. Edward I. Farley & Co., Inc. Cons. to Sec. Def. James Forrestal, 1947. Trustee Middlesex Sch. Served with USNR, 1940-45. Decorated Legion of Merit, Silver Star. Author: P.T. Patrol, 1957. Home: Horseshoe Rd Mill Neck NY 11765 Office: 100 E 50th St New York City NY 10022

FARLEY, EDWARD RAYMOND, Jr., mining and mfg. co. exec.; b. S.I., N.Y., Sept. 30, 1918; s. Edward Raymond and Ruth Veronica (Joyce) F.; grad. Lawrenceville (N.J.) Sch., 1936; A.B., Princeton, 1940; LL.B., Harvard, 1943; m. Irene Daly, Feb. 19, 1948; children—Thomas Joyce, Nancy Seaver, Jane Campbell, Edward Raymond III. Admitted to N.Y. bar 1944; with firm Simpson, Thacher & Bartlett, N.Y.C., 1944-55; v.p. Atlas Corp., N.Y.C., 1956-64, chmn. bd. dirs., 1964—, pres. 1966—; chmn. bd. Western Sky Industries, Inc., 1962—. Active local United Fund, also bldg. campaign N.J. Hosp., Princeton, fund raising for Princeton U. Trustee Lawrenceville Sch., 1970—. Mem. Atomic Indsl. Forum, Dial Lodge (trustee). Clubs: Princeton (N.Y.C.); Nassau (Princeton). Home: 188 Parkside Dr Princeton, NJ 08540. Office: 485 Madison Av New York City NY 10022

FARLEY, EUGENE SHEDDEN, educator; b. Phoenixville, Pa., Sept. 29, 1899; s. Robert and Sarah (Shoemaker) F.; B.S., Penn State, 1921; A.M. U. Pa., 1927, Ph.D., 1932; D.H.L., Alliance Coll.; Litt.D., Lafayette Coll.; D.Sc., Wilkes Coll.; LL.D., Seton Hill Coll., Bucknell U.; m. Eleanor Coates, Aug. 24, 1921 (dec.); children—Ethel (Mrs. Walter L. Douglass), Robert Coates, Eugene Shedden. Tchr. Germantown (Pa.) Acad., 1922-25; instr. Univ. of Pa., 1927-29; dir. research Bd. of Edn., Newark, 1929- 36; dir. Bucknell Univ. Jr. Coll., Wilkes-Barre, Pa., 1936-47; pres. Wilkes Coll., 1947-70, chancellor, 1970—. Dir. Pa. Power & Light Co.; dir. Pa. Millers Mutual Ins. Co. Mem. Govs. Com. 100 for State Constl. Revision; past pres. Pa. Commn. Ind. Coll.; bd. dirs. Osterhout Library, Greater Wilkes-Barre Indsl. Fund, Wyo. Valley Hosp., former mem. Found. Ind. Colls., Kosciuszko Found. Pa. State Council Edn. Mem. Am. Assn. Jr. Colls. (pres. 1947), Pa. Assn. Jr. Colls. (pres. 1945), Jr. Coll. Council of Middle States and Md. (pres. 1940), Middle States Commn. on Secondary Schs., Phi Delta Theta, Phi Delta Kappa. Republican. Mem. Soc. of Friends. Clubs: Torch, Kiwanis, Westmoreland. Home: 146 River St Wilkes-Barre PA 18702

FARLEY, JAMES A., bus. exec., former postmaster gen.; b. Grassy Point, N.Y., May 30, 1888; s. James and Ellen (Goldrick) F.; grad. Packard Comml. Sch., N.Y.C., 1906; D.C.L., U. of South, 1933, Lincoln Meml. U., 1935, St. Ambrose Coll., 1941, Villanova Coll., 1942; LL.D., Canisius Coll., Manhattan Coll., John Marshall Coll. Law, 1934, Niagara U., 1935, Hendrix Coll., 1939, Oglethorpe U., 1940, Seattle U., 1950, Ithaca Coll., Loras Coll., St. Anselm's Coll., 1951, St. Joseph's Coll., Collegeville, Ind., 1955, L.I. U., 1957, St. Joseph's Coll., Phila., 1960, St. Mary's Coll., San Antonio, 1961, St. Bonaventure U., 1961, Tuskegee Inst., 1963; D.C.S., N.Y.U., 1950, Suffolk U., 1956; Citation, U. Fla., 1950; D.S.S., Duquesne U., 1953; hon. degree Seton Hall U., 1967; m. Elizabeth A. Finnegan, Apr. 28, 1920 (dec. Jan. 1955); children—Elizabeth (Mrs. Glenn D. Montgomery), Ann (Mrs. Edward J. Hickey III), James A. Began as bookkeeper Merlin Heiholtz Paper Co., N.Y.C., 1906; sales mgr. Universal Gypsum Co., to 1926; organized James A. Farley & Co., 1926, firm merged with five other building material firms, organized as Gen. Builders Supply Corp., 1929, pres., dir. 1929-33, 49-58; chmn. bd. Coca-Cola Export Corp., 1940—; chmn. bd. Coca-Cola Interamerican Corp.; pres., dir. Coca-Cola Internat. Corp.; dir. Coca-Cola Co. Coca-Cola Co. Can., Ltd. Trustee Com. Econ. Devel., Cordell Hull Found., Alfred E. Smith Found., Little League Found.; bd. dirs. Nat. Fgn. Trade Council, Boys' Clubs Am., Far East-Am. Council Industry and Commerce, Catholic Youth Orgn. N.Y., N.Y. Conv. and Visitors Bur., Freedoms Found. at Valley Forge, Am. Heritage Found., Am.-Australian Assn., Cath. Med. Mission Bd. Town clk., Stony Point, N.Y., 1912-19; supr. Rockland Co., 1920-23; port warden Port N.Y., 1918-19; mem. N.Y. State Athletic Commn., 1923-33, chmn., 1925-33; mem. Commn. on Orgn. Exec. Br. Govt., 1953; mem. N.Y. State Banking Bd., 1955-60, N.Y. State Harness Racing Commn., 1959—. Mem. N.Y. State Assembly, 1923; chmn. Rockland Co. Dem. Com., 1919-29; sec. N.Y. State Dem. Com., 1928-30, chmn., 1930-44; chmn. Dem. Nat. Com., 1932-40; del. Dem. nat. convs., 1924, 28, 32, 36, 40, 44, 48; postmaster gen. U.S., 1933-40; mem. Electoral Coll., 1932, 36, 64, 68. Recipient Order Francisco de Miranda (Venezuela), Capt. Robert Dollar Meml. award for distinguished contbn. to advancement of Am. fgn. trade; Freedoms Found. award, 1953; Cardinal Newman award, 1956; Am. Irish Hist. Soc. award, 1956; Cross of Isabel la Católica (Spain); Living History award Research Inst. Am., 1960; Gold medal Hundred Year Assn. N.Y., 1962; award of Champions, Cath. Youth Orgn. N.Y., 1963; Gold medal Internat. Benjamin Franklin Soc., 1965; John F. Kennedy Meml. award Ancient Order Hibernians, 1966. Mem. Pan-Am. Soc., Inc., N.Y. State Hist. Assn., Am. Acad. Polit. and Social Sci., Albany Soc. N.Y., N.Y. Bd. Trade (Latin Am. sect.), Mexican C. of C. in U.S. Friendly Sons of St. Patrick, Ancient Order Hibernians, Newcomen Soc. N.Am., Delta Sigma Phi (hon.). Eagle, Elk. Red Man, K.C. Clubs: Sales Executives, Circumnavigators, Catholic, Economic, N.Y. Athletic, Nat. Democratic of N.Y. (v.p. 1930—), Lotos (N.Y.C.); Nat. Press (Washington). Author: Behind the Ballots, 1938; Jim Farley's Story, 1948. Home: 301 Park Av New York City NY 10022 Office: 515 Madison Av New York City NY 10022

FARLEY, JAMES DUNCAN, banker; b. Chgo., June 24, 1926; s. Donald Stephen and Alice (Duncan) F.; B.S., Georgetown U., 1949; m. Mary Kay Tracy, Feb. 27, 1960; children—Frances, James Duncan, Kathryn, Andrew. Trainee, mgr. First Nat. City Bank, Buenos Aires, Argentina, 1950-64, v.p. overseas div., N.Y.C., 1964-67; exec. v.p., gen. mgr. Merc. Bank of Can., 1967-68; sr. v.p. personal banking group First Nat. City Bank, N.Y.C., 1968, exec. v.p., 1969—; dir. Anaconda Co.; gen. partner Farley Assos. Co-chmn. March of Dimes fund raising campaign, 1970. Mem. adv. com. Georgetown U. Served to ensign USNR, 1945-46, lt., 1951-52. Clubs: Belle Haven, Round Hill (Greenwich, Conn.); Coral Beach (Bermuda); Lyford Cay (Nassau, Bahamas); University (N.Y.C.). Home: 1 Pheasant Lane Greenwich CT 06830 Office: 399 Park Av New York City NY 10022

FARLEY, JOHN JOSEPH, univ. dean; b. N.Y.C., Mar. 19, 1920; s. John Anthony and Margaret (Green) F.; B.A., Cath. U., 1940; M.A., Columbia, 1950, M.S., 1953; Ph.D., N.Y. U., 1964; m. Rita Johnston, Feb. 26, 1944; children—Janet, Eugene, Marian, Joseph, Veronica. Tchr., N.Y.C. schs., 1940-50; high sch. librarian, Cranford, N.J., 1952-53, W. Hempstead, N.Y., 1953-58; curriculum dir. Sewanhaka Central High Sch. Dist., N.Y., 1958-60; successively asst. prof., asso. prof., chmn. dept. library scis. Queens Coll. of City U.N.Y., 1960-67; vis. prof. library sci. San Jose (Cal.) State Coll., 1967; prof. library sci., dean Sch. Library Sci., State U. N.Y. at Albany, 1967-; cons. in field, 1958-. Served with USAAF, 1943- 46. Recipient Founders Day award N.Y. U., 1964; Pius X medal for distinguished service to confraternity Christian doctrine, 1966. Mem. A.L.A., Am. Assn. U. Profs., Nat. Council Tchrs. English, Am. Soc. Information Sci. Democrat. Roman Cath. Author: Introduction to Library Science, 1969; also articles. Home: 12 Granada Dr Elnora, NY 12065. Office: State U N Y at Albany Albany NY 12203

FARLEY, JOSEPH MCCONNELL, electric utility exec.; b. Birmingham, Ala., Oct. 6, 1927; s. John G. and Lynne (McConnell) F.; student Birmingham-So. Coll., 1944-45; B.S. in Mech. Engring., Princeton, 1948; student Grad. Sch. Commerce and Bus. Adminstrn., U. Ala., 1948-49; LL.B., Harvard, 1952; m. Sheila Shirley, Oct. 1, 1958; children—Joseph McConnell, Thomas, Mary. Admitted to Ala. bar, 1952; asso. firm Martin, Turner, Blakey & Bouldin, Birmingham, 1952- 57; partner successor firm Martin, Balch, Bingham & Hawthorne, 1957-65; exec. v.p., dir. Ala. Power Co., 1965-69, pres., 1969—; v.p. So. Electric Generating Co., 1970—, also dir.; dir. Ala. Property Co., Knox Devel. Corp., 1st Nat. Bank Birmingham, The So. Co., So. Services, Inc., Ala. Gt. So. R.R. Co., Liberty Nat. Life Ins. Co., Asso. Industries Ala. Mem. Local Govt. Commn. Jefferson County, Birmingham Mus. Bd.; pres. Birmingham Centennial Corp.; mem. exec. com. Ala. Sesquicentennial Commn. Mem. Jefferson County Republican Exec. Com., 1953-65; counsel, mem. Ala. Rep. Com., 1962-65; permanent chmn. Ala. Rep. Conv., 1962; alternate del. Rep. Nat. Conv., 1956. Bd. dirs. Southeastern Electric Exchange, Edison Electric Inst., Ala. Safety Council, Inc., Birmingham Festival of Arts Assn., Inc., Ala. Hall of Fame, Ia. State U. Conf. on Pub. Utility Valuation and Ratemaking Process, YMCA Birmingham Area, 1965-70, Operation New Birmingham, Warrior-Tombigbee Devel. Assn., Jefferson County Community Chest; trustee So. Research Inst., Thomas Alva Edison Found., Highlands Day Sch., Tuskegee Inst.; trustee, exec. v.p. Birmingham Symphony Assn., 1965-69, pres., 1970-71; trustee Childrens Hosp. Birmingham, 1966-70. Mem. Naval Res., 1948; now lt. ret. Mem. Am., Ala., Birmingham, Fed. bar assns., Nat. Assn. Electric Cos. (dir.), Ala. Assn. Ind. Colls. (dir.), Am. Ordnance Assn., Birmingham Area C. of C. (dir. 1967-68), Newcomen Soc. N.Am., Phi Beta Kappa, Kappa Alpha. Episcopalian (sr. warden). Clubs: Birmingham Country, Relay House, Downtown (gov. 1965-70), Princeton of Ala. (pres. 1968-69), Rotary of Birmingham, Mountain Brook, The Club, Inc. Home: 2831 Southwood Rd Birmingham AL 35223 Office: 600 N 18th St Birmingham AL 35203

FARLEY, PHILIP JUDSON, govt. ofcl.; b. Berkeley, Cal., Aug. 6, 1916; s. Guy E. and Ernestine (Kennedy) F.; B.A., U. Cal. at Berkeley, 1937, M.A., 1938, Ph.D., 1941; m. Mildred Bowling, 1938; children—Paul, Katherine, Kenneth. Teaching fellow U. Cal., 1938-41; faculty Corpus Christi Jr. Coll., 1941-42; staff AEC, 1947-54; with Dept. State, 1954-, spl. asst. sec. state for disarmament and atomic energy, 1957-61; spl. asst. sec. of state for atomic energy and outer space, 1961-62; chief polit. sect. U.S. Mission to NATO, Paris, 1962; dep. U.S. rep. to NATO, 1965-67; dep. asst. sec. state for polit.-mil. affairs, 1967-69; dep. dir. U.S. Arms Control and Disarmament Agy., 1969—; alternate U.S. rep. for U.S.-Soviet strategic arms talks, with personal rank of ambassador, 1969. Home: 2110 White Oaks Dr Alexandria VA 22306 Office: Dept of State Washington DC 20525

FARLEY, ROBERT JOSEPH, ret. educator; b. Hernando, Miss., Dec. 7, 1898; s. Leonard Jerome and Lilian (Lauderdale) F.; A.B., U. Miss., 1919, LL.B., 1924; J.S.D., Yale, 1932; m. Alice Lockard, Sept. 7, 1928. Prin. high sch., Canton, Miss., 1919-20, Natchez, Miss., 1920-21; mayor Oxford, Miss., 1923- 25; admitted to Miss. bar, 1924; mem. firm, Somerville and Farley, Oxford, Miss., 1924-29, pvt. practice, 1929-31, city atty., 1926-31; asst. prof. law U. Miss. part time, 1926-30, prof., 1932-35, dean., prof., 1946-63; prof. law, Tulane U., 1935-46, dean pro tem, Coll. Law, 1942-45; prof. law U. Fla., Gainesville, 1963-70. Served as pvt., Inf., U.S. Army, 1918. Compliance commr., War Production Board, New Orleans area, 1943-46; commr. on uniform state laws; hearing commr., Nat. Prodn. Authority. Mem. Am. Law Inst., Miss. Econ. Council (dir.), Miss. (pres. 1954-55), La. (hon.), New Orleans bar assns., La. Law Inst., Order of Coif, Phi Delta Phi, Sigma Upsilon, Sigma Chi. Compiler, Miss. Annotations, Restatement of the Law of Trusts, 1937. Louisiana Annotations, Restatement of the Law of Torts, 1941. Home: 111 Phillip Rd Oxford MS 38655

FARLEY, WALTER LORIMER, author; b. N.Y.C., June 26, 1920; s. Walter Patrick and Isabelle (Vermilyea) F.; grad. Mercersburg (Pa.) Acad., 1936; also ed. at Columbia, 1941; m. Rosemary Lutz, May 26, 1945; children—Pamela, Alice, Walter Steven, Timothy. Served with AUS, 1941-46. Author: The Black Stallion, 1941; Black Stallion and Flame, 1960; Black Stallion and Satan, 1949; Black Stallion Challenged, 1964; Black Stallion Mystery, 1957; Black Stallion Returns, 1945; Black Stallion Revolts, 1953; Black Stallion's Courage, 1956; Black Stallion's Filly, 1952; Black Stallion's Sulky Colt, 1954; Blood Bay Colt, 1950; Great Dane Thor, 1968; Horse Tamer, 1958; Horse that Swam Away, 1965; Island Stallion, 1948; Island Stallion Races, 1955; Island Stallion's Fury, 1951; Little Black, a Pony; Little Black Goes to the Circus, 1963; Little Black Pony Races, 1968; Man O'War, 1962; Son of the Black Stallion, 1947; Big Black Horse, 1953; Black Stallion's Ghost, 1969; Black Stallion and the Girl, 1971. Address: care of Random House 201 E 50th St New York City NY 10022

FARLEY, WILLIAM F., banker. Vice pres. trusts Ida. First Nat. Bank, Boise. Office: 10th and Idaho Sts PO Box 7009 Boise ID 83707*

FARLOW, ROBERT EUGENE, publisher; b. New Rochelle, N.Y., Dec. 4, 1907; s. Edwin Castle and Jessie (Clark) F.; A.B., Columbia Coll., 1929; m. Josephine Walker, Aug. 25, 1945. Editor, W.W. Norton & Co., Inc., N.Y.C., 1929—, dir. 1934—, sec., 1938-42, v.p., 1958—. Bd. dirs. Bucks County Conservancy; mem. editorial adv. bd. Marine Hist. Assn., Am. Neptune. Served with USMCR, 1942-45. Mem. Am. Inst. Graphic Arts, Marine Assos. of Peabody Mus., Marine Hist. Assn. Mystic, Conn., The Players, Delta Upsilon. Home: RD 2 Eagle Rd New Hope PA 18938 Office: 55 Fifth Av New York City NY 10003

FARMER, ARTHUR STEWART, trumpet player; b. Council Bluffs, Ia., Aug. 21, 1928. Appeared with Horace Henderson, Floyd Ray, Los Angeles, 1945, later with Johnny Otis; free-lance musician, N.Y.C., 1947-48, later with Maurice Grupp; with Benny Carter on West Coast, 1948, Wardell Gray, 1951, Lionel Hampton, 1952-53 (on tour Europe, 1953), Gigi Gryce, 1953-56 (formed quintet 1954), with Horace Silver, 1956, Gerry Mulligan, 1958; formed Jazztet with Benny Golson, 1959; recordings with Jay McShann, Gerald Wilson, 1949; with Gerry Mulligan in motion picture films, I Want to Live, The Subterranians. Recipient Down Beat Critics Poll award 1958.*

FARMER, FRANCES, librarian; b. Keysville, Va., Dec. 5, 1909; d. Horatio Weldon and Florence (Womack) Farmer; A.B., U. Richmond, 1931, LL.B., 1933. Sec. to dean, law sch. U. Richmond, 1931-38, law librarian, 1938-42; law librarian U. Va. since 1942. Mem. Am. Assn. Law Libraries (pres. 1959-60), Virginia State Bar Assn., Va. State Bar, Westhampton Coll. Alumnae Assn., U. of Richmond Alumni Assn. (former pres.), Order of the Coif, Phi Beta Kappa. Author: Manual of Legal Bibliography (with M. Ray Doubles), 1947. Editor: The Woodrow Wilson Reader, 1956. Home: 2031 Hessian Rd Charlottesville VA 22903 Office: U Va Law Library Clark Hall Charlottesville VA 22901

FARMER, GENE, mag. editor, journalist; b. Dora, Okla., Aug. 20, 1919; s. Hiram C. and Grace E. (Scott) F.; student Ark. Polytech. Coll., 1935-37; B.A., U. Ark., 1939; M.S. in Journalism, Northwestern U., 1940; m. Kay Doering, Sept. 30, 1949 (div.); children—Jeffrey K., Michele M.; m. 2d, Enid P. Colfer, Oct. 21, 1958; children—Thomas Ian, Terence Scott, Trist ram Evan. Reporter, state editor, city editor Cedar Rapids (Ia.) Gazette, 1940-45; nat. affairs corr. Life Mag., 1945-46, sports editor, 1947- 49, asst. editor nat. affairs, 1949-50, chief London corr., 1950-53, fgn. editor, 1953—, also sr. editor. Recipient Distinguished Alumnus citation U. Ark., 1954; decorated chevalier Legion of Honor. Mem. Phi Beta Kappa. Club: Overseas Press (N.Y.C.). Republican. Author: Massachusetts: The Anatomy of Quality. Editor: (with Armstrong, Collins, Aldrin) First on the Moon; (with Walter J. Hickel) Who Owns America? Home: 110 Bedford St Lexington MA 02173 Office: care Life Mag Prudential Center Boston MA 02199

FARMER, GUY, lawyer; b. Foster Falls, Va., Sept. 13, 1912; s. Harbert and Kate (Bell) F.; B.A., W.Va. U., 1934, LL.B., 1936; Rhodes Scholar, Oxford (Eng.) U., 1936-37; m. Helen Joura; children—Mary, Mark, Jane. Admitted to W.Va. and D.C. bars; atty. Nat. Labor Relations Bd., 1945, asso. gen. counsel, 1943-45, chmn., 1953-55; asso. Steptoe & Johnson, 1945-49, partner, 1949- 60; partner firm Patterson, Belknap, Farmer & Shibley, 1960—; lectr. labor law W.Va. U., 1948-49, Georgetown U., 1957-59. Dir. Bartlett Tree Co., Stamford, Conn. Mem. Am., D.C., W.Va. bar assns., Phi Beta Kappa, Phi Alpha Delta, Order of Coif. Club: Cosmos. Author articles labor topics. Home: 3600 Macomb St Washington DC 20016 Office: Bender Bldg Washington DC 20036

FARMER, JAMES, civil rights ofcl.; b. Marshall, Tex., Jan. 12, 1920; s. James Leonard and Pearl Marion (Houston) F.; B.S., Wiley Coll., Marshall, 1938; B.D., Howard U., 1941; HH.D., Morgan State Coll., Balt., 1964; m. Lula A. Peterson, May 21, 1949; children—Tami, Abbey. Founder, Congress of Racial Equality (CORE), 1942, nat. chmn., 1942-44, 50, nat. dir., 1961- 66; race relations sec. Fellowship of Reconciliation, 1941-45; organizer Upholsterer's Internat. Union N. Am., 1945-47; lectr. race and labor problems, 1948-50; student field sec. League Indsl. Democracy, 1950-54; internat. rep. State, County and Municipal Employees Union, 1954-59; program dir. N.A.A.C.P., 1959-61; leader CORE Freedom Ride, 1961; pres. Center for Community Action Edn., 1965—; asst. sec. for adminstrn. U.S. Dept. Health, Edn. and Welfare, 1969-70; adj. prof. N.Y. U., 1968; prof. social welfare Lincoln U., Lincoln U., Pa., 1966-67. Nat. exec. bd. Am. Com. on Africa, 1959-64; chmn. Council United Civil Rights Leadership, 1963—; sponsor Am. Negro Leadership Conf. on Africa, 1962- -. Vice chmn. Liberal Party N.Y. County, 1954-61. Bd. dirs. League Indsl. Democracy, Am. Civil Liberties Union, Americans for Democratic Action. Recipient Am. Friendship Club award, 1961, Am. Vets. Com. award, 1962, John Dewey award League Indsl. Democracy, 1962, Distinguished Postgrad. Achievement Alumni award Howard U., 1964, Omega Psi Phi award, 1961, 63. Author: FreedomWhen? 1965; also author essay, also numerous articles. Home: 5129 Chevy Chase Pkwy NW Washington DC 20008

FARMER, JOHN NEVILLE, educator; b. Simla, India, June 19, 1929; A.B., Coll. of Wooster, 1953; M.S., Ia. State U., 1958, Ph.D. in Parasitology, 1960; married; 3 children. Naturalized Am. citizen. Asst., Ia. State U., 1953-54, 56-59, instr. zoology, 1959-60; asst.prof. U. Mo., Columbia, 1960-65, asso. prof., 1965-69, now prof., chmn. dept. zoology. Served with AUS, 1954-56. Mem. Am. Soc. Parasitology. Office: Dept Zoology U Mo 417 S 5th St Columbia MO 65201*

FARMER, RICHARD NEIL, educator; b. Alameda, Cal., Aug. 19, 1928; s. George Albert and Alice (Mellin) F.; B.A., U. Cal. at Berkeley, 1950, M.A., 1951, Ph.D., 1957; m. Barbara Jean Flaherty, Sept. 18, 1951; children-Christine, Geoffrey, Sarah, Daniel. Asst. prof. Am. U. of Beirut, 1957-59; gen. mgr. Gen. Contracting Co., Al Khobar, Saudi Arabia, 1959-61; lectr. U. Cal., Davis, 1961-62; asst. prof. U. Cal. Los Angeles, 1962-64; prof. bus. Ind. U., Bloomington, 1964—, also adviser Black Entrepreneurial Program. Served with AUS, 1951-53. Fellow Acad. Mgmt.; mem. Am. Econ. Assn., Soc. Internat. Devel., Assn. for Edn. in Internat. Bus. Author: (with B. Richman) Comparative Management and Economic Progress, 1964, International Business, 1965; Management in the Future, 1967; International Management 1968; New Directions in Management Information Transfer, 1968. Home: 1115 E Wylie St Bloomington IN 47401

FARMER, THOMAS LAURENCE, lawyer; b. Berlin, Germany, July 26, 1923 (parents Am. citizens); s. Laurence and Else (Dienemann) F.; A.B., Harvard, 1943, LL.B., 1950; B.A. Brasenose Coll., Oxford (Eng.) U., 1948, M.A., 1953; m. Elizabeth Fairchild Becker, Sept. 1951 (div. Aug. 1970); children-Daniel Fairchild, Sarah Bennett, Elizabeth Lanham. Admitted to D.C. bar, 1951, N.Y. bar, 1956; law clk. to Judge M.O. Hudson, mem. Internat. Law Commn. of UN, Geneva, Switzerland, 1950; asso. firm Simpson, Thacher & Bartlett, N.Y.C., 1954-57, Washington, 1958-64; gen. counsel AID, Washington, 1964-68; partner Kominers, Fort, Schlefer, Farmer & Boyer, Washington, 1968-70; counsel Prather, Levenberg, Seeger & Doolittle, Washington, 1970—. Chmn. bd. Nat. Capital Transp. Agy., 1961-64. Mem. vis. com. Harvard, 1959-65; trustee Lincoln U.; dir. Overseas Devel. Council, Washington. Served with AUS, 1943-46. Mem. Am., Fed. bar assns., Am. Soc. Internat. Law, Grey's Inn Soc. Democrat. Clubs: Federal City, Metropolitan (Washington). Home: 3456 Macomb St NW Washington DC 20016. Office: 1101 16th St NW Washington DC 20036

FARMER, WELFORD STUART, banker, lawyer; b. Richmond, Va., Oct. 19, 1925; s. Joseph L. and Cora (Chamberlain) F.; B.S.B., U. Richmond, 1948, J.D., 1950; m. Ellen Azalee Harpe, Sept. 10, 1949; children—Welford Stuart, Jr., Joseph A., Neil P., Alison H. Admitted to Va. bar, 1951; with Fed. Res. Bank Richmond, 1950—, gen. counsel, 1961-63, v.p., gen. counsel, 1964-68, sr. v.p., gen. counsel, 1969-71, sr. v.p., spl. legal adviser, 1971—. Served with USNR, 1944-46. Mem. Va., Richmond bar assns., Sigma Alpha Epsilon, Phi Alpha Delta. Methodist. Clubs: Country of Va., Westwood Racquet (Richmond). Office: Fed Res Bank 9th and Franklin Sts Richmond VA 23261

FARNELL, GERALD WILLIAM educator; b. Toronto, Ont., Can., Aug. 31, 1925; s. Jack and Alice (Turner) F.; B.A. Sc., U. Toronto, 1948; M.S., Mass. Inst. Tech., 1950; Ph.D., McGill U., 1957; m. Norma Catherine McRae, Sept. 14, 1948; children—Sandra Rae, Gerald Douglas. Research asst. Mass. Inst. Tech., 1948-50; asst. prof. McGill U., Montreal, Que., 1950-57, asso. prof., 1957-61, prof. engrng. physics, 1962—, chmn. dept. elec. engrng., 1967—; Nuffield fellow Clarendon Lab., Oxford, 1960-61. Served with Canadian Army, 1943-45. Fellow I.E.E.E.; mem. Corp. Engrs. Que., Am. Soc. Engring. Edn., Canadian Assn. Physicists, Sigma Xi. Home: 1509 Sherbrooke St Montreal 109 Quebec Canada

FARNER, DONALD SANKEY, biologist; b. Waumandee, Wis., May 2, 1915; s. John and Lillian O. (Sankey) F.; B.A., Hamline U., 1937, D.Sc. (hon.), 1962; M.A., U. Wis., 1939, Ph.D., 1941; m. Dorothy S. Copps, Dec. 24, 1940; children—Carla M., Donald C. Instr. zoology U. Wis., 1941-43; asst. prof. zoology U. Kan., 1946-47, U. Colo., faculty Wash. State U., 1947-65, prof. zoophysiology, 1952-65, dean Grad. Sch., 1960-64; prof. zoophysiology, chmn. dept. zoology U. Wash., 1966-. Fulbright research scholar, hon. lectr. zoology U. Otago, New Zealand, 1953-54; Guggenheim fellow U. Western Australia, 1958-59; chmn. div. biology and agr. Nat. Acad. Scis.-NRC, 1969—. Served to lt. USNR, 1943-46; captain Res. Fellow A.A.A.S., Am. Ornithologists Union; mem. Am. Physiol. Soc., Am. Soc. Zoologists, Am. Chem. Soc., Soc. Exptl. Biology and Medicine, Internat. Union Biol. Scis. (pres. 1967—), Soc. Systematic Zoology, Am. Soc. Naturalists, Cooper Ornithol. Soc., Phi Beta Kappa, Sigma Xi, Phi Kappa Phi, Phi Sigma, Gamma Alpha, Omicron Delta Kappa. Home: 4533 W Laurel Dr Seattle WA 98105.

FARNHAM, WILLARD EDWARD, educator; b. Wichita, Kan., Sept. 29, 1891; s. Edward Willard and Josephine (Reynolds) F.; A.B., U. Wis., 1912, A.M., 1914; Ph.D., Harvard, 1917; LL.D., U. Cal. at Berkeley, 1961; m. Corinne Cassard, June 28, 1921 (dec. 1926); 1 dau., Diana Reynolds; m. 2d, Frances Fern Hicks, May 9, 1929; children—Anthony Edward, Nicholas Holt. Instr. English, U. Wis., 1917-18; Sheldon traveling fellow, Harvard, in Eng., France and Italy, 1919-20; asso. prof. English, Washington and Lee U., 1920-23; asso. prof. English, U. Cal. at Berkeley, 1923-35, prof., 1935-59, prof. emeritus, 1959—, chmn. dept., 1949-50, 52-55; research fellow Henry E. Huntington Library in U.S. and Eng., 1938-39; vis. lectr. Harvard, summer 1947, 1950-51; nat. rep. Woodrow Wilson Nat. Fellowship Found., 1960-61. Served as ensign, Aviation Corps, US NRF, 1918-19. Mem. Modern Lang. Assn. (chmn. Shakespeare group 1946), Philol. Assn. Pacific Coast, Am. Assn. U. Profs., Shakespeare Assn. Am. (adv. bd.), Phi Beta Kappa. Episcopalian. Club: Faculty (Berkeley). Author: The Medieval Heritage of Elizabethan Tragedy, 1936; Shakespeare's Tragic Frontier: The World of His Final Tragedies, 1950; The Shakespeare Grotesque: Its Genesis and Transformations, 1971. Editor: Shakespeare's Hamlet, 1957; Shakespeare's Troilus and Cressida, 1966; Twentieth Century Interpretations of Doctor Faustus, 1969. Contbr. periodicals. Home: 3 Greenwood Common Berkeley, CA 94708.

FARNSLEY, CHARLES, Rowland Peaslee, pub.; b. Mar. 28, 1907; s. Burrel Hopson and Anna May (Peaslee) F.; LL.B., U. Louisville, 1930, A.B., 1942, LL.D., 1950; grad. student U. Ky., 1943-44; LL.D., Wesleyan U., Middletown, Conn., 1959; m. Nancy Hall Carter, Feb. 27, 1937; children—Sally (Mrs. Robert S. Bird, Jr.), Ann (Mrs. Ronald Gascoyne), Alexander, Burrel Charles Peaslee, Douglass Charles Ellerbe. Practiced law, 1930-48, 54-64; mem. Ky. Ho. of Reps., 1936-40; mayor Louisville, 1948-54; mem. 89th Congress, 3d dist. of Ky.; pres. Lost Cause Press. Mem. bd. trustees U. Louisville, 1946-48, sec. bd. trustees, 1947-48, mem. bd. overseers, 1948-64; curator Transylvania U., Lexington, Ky., 1947-58; bd. trustees, Louisville Free Pub. Library, 1945- 48; dir. Louisville Philharmonic Soc., 1947-48, 54-. Mem. Soc. Colonial Wars, Delta Upsilon, Omicron Delta Kappa. Democrat. Episcopalian. Mason. Clubs: Harmony Landing, Pendennis, Wynn Stay, Filson (Louisville); Nat. Democratic, Century, Grolier (N.Y.C.); Federal (Washington). Home: Dartmouth Apts Louisville KY 40204. Office: Starks Bldg Louisville KY 40202

FARNSWORTH, ALAN COYLE, constrn. co. exec.; b. New Orleans, June 4, 1926; s. Richard A. and Dorothy (Coyle) F.; student Tulane U., 1943, Va. Poly. Inst., 1944; B.S., U. Tex., Austin, 1948; m. Mary Osborn, Oct. 19, 1951; children—Alan Kent, Randal Lee. Vice pres. Farnsworth & Chambers o., Inc., Houston, 1949-57; dir. H.A. Lott, Inc., Houston, 1957—, pres., 1959—; pres. Arrow, Inc., Arrow Precast, Inc., Halico, Inc., Houston; dir. Klean Kote, Inc., La Porte, Tex. Served with AUS, 1944-46. Mem. Phi Delta Theta, Tau Beta Pi, Chi Epsilon. Republican. Presbyn. Home: 13319 Conifer St Houston TX 77024 Office: 6315 Gulfton St Houston TX 77036

FARNSWORTH, CLYDE HENRY, journalist; b. Cleve., May 6, 1931; s. Clyde Addison and Marthe (Herailh) F.; B.A., Yale, 1952; m. Barbara Blaha, Sept. 8, 1956; children—Andrew Clyde, Alexander William. Reporter, U.P., 1953-59, N.Y. Herald Tribune, 1959-62; mem. staff N.Y. Times, 1962—, fgn. corr., Brussels, 1966-69, Paris, 1969—. Served with AUS, 1952-54; Korea. Decorated Bronze Star. Author: No Money Down, 1962. Home: 10 rue Eugène Labiche Paris 16e France Office: 39 rue Caumartin Paris 9e France

FARNSWORTH, DANA LYDA, physician; b. Troy, W.Va., Apr. 7, 1905; s. Henry Lyda and Isabell (Waggoner) F.; A.B., B.S., W.Va. U.; M.D., Harvard, 1933; D.Sc., Salem Coll., W. Va., 1959, Williams Coll., 1961, W.Va. U., 1965, Fairfield U., 1969; L.H.D., Lesley Coll., 1962, Roosevelt U., 1970; LL.D., U. Notre Dame, 1964, Harvard, 1971; m. Elma Morris, Mar. 18, 1931. Instr. chemistry and physics, Barrachville (W.Va.) High Sch., 1927-29; intern Mass. Gen. Hosp., Boston, 1933-35; asst. resident Boston City Hosp., 1935; asst. dir. health Williams Coll., 1935-41, dir. health, 1945-46; prof., med. dir. Mass. Inst. Tech. 1946-54, acting dean of students, 1950-51; lectr. in medicine Harvard Med. Sch., 1952-54, Henry K. Oliver prof. hygiene and dir. Univ. Health Services, 1954-71, Henry K. Oliver prof. hygiene emeritus, cons. on psychiatry Sch. Pub. Health, 1971—, mem. faculty pub. health, 1954—; Salmon lectr. psychiatry N.Y. Acad. Medicine, 1964; cons. neuropsychiatry U.S. Naval Hosp., Chelsea, Mass., 1947-54; asso. physician Childrens Med. Center, 1954—; asst. physician, later physician Mass. Gen. Hosp., 1946-66, bd. consultation, 1966—; cons. in medicine Peter Bent Brigham Hosp.; Phi Beta Kappa vis. scholar, 1970-71; vice chmn. Nat. Commn. on Marihuana and Drug Abuse, 1971—. Served with USN M.C., World War II, at naval hosps. in Phila., Oakland, Cal., Bethesda, Md., and on U.S.S. Solace in South Pacific; comdr. M.C. USNR, ret. Recipient Menninger award A.C.P., 1970; Pax Christi award St. John's U., 1971; Wm. A. Schonfeld Distinguished Service award Am. Soc. for Adolescent Psychiatry, 1971. John and Mary R. Markle fellow Austen Riggs Found., 1936-37. Diplomate Am. Bd. Psychiatry and Neurology. Fellow Am. Acad. Arts and Scis., Am. Psychiat. Assn., (mem. council, 1958-61, chmn. com. on ethics 1965-67, mem. council med. edn. and career devel. 1967-69, distinguished service award 1971); mem. A.M.A., (mem. council on mental health 1963—, chmn. 1967-70, mem. council health manpower 1968-70), Group for Advancement Psychiatry (pres. 1957-59), Am. Pub. Health Assn., Am. Coll. Health Assn. (pres. 1953-54, Edward Hitchcock award 1968), Boston Soc. Psychiatry and Neurology, No. New Eng. Br. Am. Psychiat. Assn., Mass. Med. Soc., Brit. Student Health Assn. (hon.). Clubs: Commercial, Harvard (Boston); St. Botolph, Tavern. Author: Mental Health in College and University, 1957; Living (with Fred V. Hein), 4th edit. 1965, 5th edit. (with Fred Hein and Charles B. Richardson), 1970; (with Jack R. Ewalt) Textbook of Psychiatry, 1963; Psychiatry, Education and the Young Adult, 1966 (Family Life book award Child Study Assn. 1967); (with others) Dimensions in Health, 1967. Editor and contbr. College Health Administration, 1964, (with Francis J. Braceland) Psychiatry, The Clergy and Pastoral Counseling, 1969, (with Graham B. Blaine, Jr.) Counseling and the College Student, 1970; asso. editor Am. Jour. Psychiatry, 1965—; editorial dir. Med. Insight, 1969—, Psychiatric Annals, 1971—; editorial bd. New Eng. Jour. Medicine, 1970—. Home: 52 Old Concord Rd Belmont MA 02178 Office: Harvard Sch Pub Health 55 Shattuck St Boston MA 02115

FARNSWORTH, DAVID NELSON, educator; b. Cullison, Kan., Feb. 11, 1929; s. Frank Lister and Laura (Axline) F.; B.S., Wichita State U., 1953; M.A. (Woodrow Wilson fellow), U. Ill., 1955, Ph.D. (Univ. fellow), 1959; m. Rita Eileen Lowe, Sept. 2, 1950; children—Diane Denise, Bradley Dale, Pamela Sue. Asst. prof. Wichita State U., 1956-61, asso. prof., 1961-66, prof., 1966—, chmn. polit. sci. dept., 1966-70; vis. asso. prof. U. So. Cal., summer 1962; vis. lectr. U. Ill., summer 1967. Sec. Wichita Com. on Fgn. Relations, 1962. Served with USAF, 1949. Mem. Am., Midwest, Kan. polit. sci. assns., Internat. Studies Assn., Pi Sigma Alpha. Unitarian (trustee, pres. congregation). Author: Senate Committee on Foreign Relations. 1961. Home: 3928 E Elm St Wichita, KS 67208.

FARNSWORTH, EDWARD ALLAN, educator, lawyer; b. Providence, June 30, 1928; s. Harrison Edward and Gertrude (Romig) F.; B.S., U. Mich., 1948; M.A., Yale, 1949; LL.B. (Ordronaux prize 1952), Columbia, 1952; m. Patricia Ann Nordstrom, May 30, 1952; children—Jeanne Scott, Karen Ladd, Edward Allan, Pamela Ann. Admitted to D.C. 1952, N.Y. bar, 1956; mem. faculty Columbia,1954-, prof. law, 1959—, Alfred McCormack prof. law, 1970—; vis. prof. U. Instanbul, 1960, U. Dakar, 1964, Harvard Law Sch., 1970-71; mem. faculty Salzburg Seminar Am. Law, 1963; mem. faculty Columbia-Leyden- Amsterdam program Am. law, 1964, 69; dir. orientation program Am. law Assn. Am. Law Schs., 1965-68; U.S. rep. UN Commn. Internat. Trade Law, 1970—; reporter Restatement of Contracts 2d, 1971—; cons. N.Y. State Law Revision Commn., 1956, 58, 59, 61; mem. com. validity internat. sales contracts Internat. Inst. Unification Pvt. Law, Rome, 1966—; spl. counsel city reorgn. N.Y.C. Council, 1966-68. Served to capt. USAAF, 1952-54. Mem. Am. Bar Assn., Am. Law Inst., Assn. Bar City N.Y. (chmn. com. fgn. and comparative law 1967-70), Phi Beta Kappa, Phi Delta Phi. Unitarian. Author: An Introduction to the Legal System of the United States, 1963; (with J. Honnold) Cases and Materials on Commercial Law, 2d edit., 1968; (with H.W. Jones and W.F. Young, Jr.) Cases and Materials on Contracts, 1965; Cases and Materials on Commercial Paper, 1968. Home: 201 Lincoln St Englewood NJ 07631 Office: 435 W 116th St New York City NY 10027

FARNSWORTH, FRANK ALBERT, educator; b. Manchester, N.H., June 4, 1919; s. Frank Adelbert and Lancing Claudine (Miller) F.; B.A. with honors, Colgate U., 1939; M.A., Harvard, 1946, Ph.D., 1952; m. Ruth Coburn, June 16, 1943 (dec. Dec. 1970); children—Nancy E. (dec.), Frank Adelbert, Ruth Ann, John Coburn. Vis. research fellow human relations Harvard, 1947-48; Fulbright research fellow Norwegian Sch. Econs., Bergen, 1954-55; dir. econs. study group Colgate U., 1949-51, faculty dept. econs., 1941-, prof., 1955-, chmn. dept., 1957-62, 70—, acting chmn. dept. econs., 1967-68; cons. Canadian economy Fed. Res. Bank Boston, 1951-55. Vice chmn. bd. Madison County Indsl. Devel. Agy. Mem. Am. Econ. Assn., Am. Assn. U. Profs., English Speaking Union, Alpha Chi Epsilon, Mu Pi Delta, Alpha Delta Phi. Republican. Baptist (past trustee). Mason. Home: 17 E Kendrick Av Hamilton, NY

FARNSWORTH, HARRISON EDWARD, ret. educator; b. Green Lake, Wis., Mar. 24, 1896; s. Edward H. and Marion (Fortnum) F.; A.B., Ripon Coll., 1918; A.M., U. Wis., 1921, Ph.D., 1922; D.Sc., Fairfield U., 1971; m. Gertrude Roming, 1925 (dec.); children—Edward Allan, James Alden (dec.); m. 2d, Alice Schultze, 1960. Physicist Western Electric Research Lab., N.Y., 1918; instr. U. Pitts., 1918-19; Nat. Research fellow U. Wis., 1922-24; asso. prof. physics U. Me., 1924-26; asst. prof. physics Brown U., 1926-29, asso. prof., 1929-46, prof., 1946-60, research prof., 1960-70, emeritus, 1970—, dir. Barus lab. surface physics, 1946-70, Annette L.R. Barstow U. prof., 1963-70; exec. sec. panel on electron tubes Research and Devel. Bd., dir. coordinating group on electron tube reliability, N.Y.C., 1952-53 (on leave from Brown U.); mem. Planning div. Office Naval Research, summer 1946; cons., 1946-47; cons. Philips Labs., Inc., 1947- 49; research physicist on war project Radiation Lab., Mass. Inst. Tech. (leave of absence from Brown U.), 1941; official investigator N.D.R.C., on war project, Brown U., 1942-43; chmn. dept. physics Brown U., 1942-43, mem. exec. com. dept. physics, 1954-55, mem. Phys. Scis. Council, 1953-63; cons. Lawrence Radiation Lab., Livermore, Cal., 1962-68, Ultek div. Perkin-Elmer corp., 1965-69, Yale, 1966-67, Nat. Phys. Research Lab., Pretoria, S. Africa, 1970-71; co-operating expert for Internat. Critical Tables; vis. research prof. Wash. State U., summer 1970. Recipient Alumni citation Ripon Coll., 1947; named to Wisdom Hall Fame, 1970. Fellow A.A.A.S., Am. Phys. Soc., Am. Acad. Arts and Scis.; mem Am. Chem. Soc., Internat. Platform Assn., Phi Beta Kappa, Sigma Xi, Gamma Alpha, Club: Faculty of Brown U. Contbr. numerous sci. articles on electron and single crystal physics. Home: 205 El Valle Green Valley AZ 85614

FARNSWORTH, HELEN ELLIOTT CHERINGTON, educator; b. Columbus, O., Jan. 23, 1903; d. Lemuel Bundy and Mae Florence (Elliott) Cherington; B.S., M.A., Ohio State U., 1924; Ph.D., Stanford, 1930; m. Paul Randolph Farnsworth, Aug. 31, 1926; children—Elliott Cherington, Susan March Cherington. Teaching asst., Ohio State U., 1924-26, Stanford, 1927-28; research asst., Food Research Inst., Stanford, 1929-32, jr. research asso., 1932-36, asso. economist,

1936-45, econ. and asso. prof., 1945-50, prof., 1950-68, emeritus prof., 1968—, asso. dir., 1960-62. Mem. Am. Econ. Assn., Am. Farm Econ. Assn., Alpha Phi, Mortar Board, Pi Lambda Theta, Beta Gamma Sigma. Author: Wartime Food Developments in Germany, 1941; Livestock in Continental Europe During World War II, 1944; World Grain Review and Outlook (with V.P. Timoshenko), 1945; Wheat Growers and the Tariff, 1946; Grain Savings for United States Export, 1947; Internat. Wheat Agreements and Problems, 1949-56; Multiple Pricing of American Wheat, 1958; American Wheat Exports, Policies and Prospects, 1960; Determinants of French Grain Production, Past and Prospective, 1964; (with K. Friedmann) The West German Grain Economy and The Common Market, 1966; French and EEC Grain Policies and Their Price Effects, 1920-70, 1967. Home: 715 Salvatierra St Stanford CA 94305

FARNSWORTH, HERBERT, cold storage co. exec.; b. Newton, Mass., Mar. 9, 1906; s. Jerome C. and Ethel (Simonds) F.; B.A., Harvard, 1928, M.B.A., 1930; m. Nathalie Bartlett, Dec. 31, 1936; children—Jerome, Noel, Martha. With Quincy Market Cold Storage & Warehouse Co., Boston, 1930-, treas., 1936-, pres., 1949-62, chmn. bd., 1962—, also dir.; dir. Union Freight R.R., Shenango Ceramics, Inc., Larchfield Corp., Tampa Cold Storage & Warehouse Corp. Pres. Refrigerated Research Found., 1951-53. Trustee Pike Sch., Andover, Mass., Addison Gilbert Hosp., Gloucester, Mass. Home: Porter Rd Andover, MA 01810. Office: 178 Atlantic Av Boston MA 02110

FARNSWORTH, JERRY, artist; b. Dalton, Ga., Dec. 31, 1895; s. Samuel and Lavinia (Pou) F.; studied at the Corcoran Sch., Washington, with Charles W. Hawthorne, Provincetown, Mass.; m. Helen Alton Sawyer, Aug. 26, 1924. Exhibited in N.Y.C., Chgo., Washington, Phila., Toledo, St. Louis, Cleve., others; Carnegie vis. prof. art, artist in residence U. Ill., 1942-43; dir., instr. Farnsworth Sch. of Art, Sarasota, Fla.; represented in Met. Mus., N.Y. C. by "Annabella". bought 1940; Whitney Mus. Am. Art by "My Neighbor Miss Williams", bought 1942; represented in permanent collection Syracuse U. Awards include: honorable mention Chgo. Art Inst. 1940; Portrait prize Nat. Arts Club, N.Y.C., 1941; purchase prize Los Angeles Mus., 1945; First purchase prize High Mus., Atlanta, for Loraine of Truro, 1946; Maynard Portrait prize Nat. Acad., 1952; purchase prizes Chrysler Mus. Art, Provincetown, Mass. Asso. Nat. Academician, 1933, Nat. Academician, 1935. Mem. Provincetown Art Assn. Club: Nat. Arts (N.Y.C.). Author: Painting with Jerry Farnsworth; Learning to Paint in Oil; Portrait and Figure Painting. Home: 3482 Flamingo Sarasota FL 33581 also North Truro Cape Code MA 02652

FARNSWORTH, MALCOLM MALLORY, mfg. co. exec.; b. Erie, Pa., Dec. 9, 1912; s. George A. and Elizabeth (Mallory) F.; B.S. in Mech. Engring., U. Mich., 1934, LL.B., 1937; m. Virginia R. Sleppy, Jan. 3, 1942; children—Ann Elizabeth, Malcolm Mallory, Virginia Louise. Admitted to Pa. bar, 1948; patent atty. Union Switch & Signal Co., Pitts., 1937-51; asst. gen. counsel Westinghouse Air Brake Co., Pitts., 1951-66. sec., 1966—. Councilman, Borough of Edgewood, Pa., 1964—. Pres. trustees C. C. Mellor Meml. Library, Edgewood, 1966—. Mem. Am., Allegheny County bar assns., Am., Pitts. patent law assns., Am. Soc. Corp. Secretaries, Theta Xi. Republican. Presbyn. Mason. Clubs: Duquesne, Press (Pitts.). Home: 521 Locust St Edgewood PA 15218 Office: 3 Gateway Center Pittsburgh PA 15222

FARNSWORTH, NORMAN ROBERT, pharmacognosist, educator; b. Lynn, Mass., Mar. 23, 1930; s. Lee M. and Zelma R. (Furbush) F.; B.S., Mass. Coll. Pharmacy, 1953, M.S., 1955; Ph.D., U. Pitts., 1959; m. Priscilla A. Marston, Sept. 5, 1953. Instr. biol. scis. U. Pitts., 1955-59, asst. prof. pharmacognosy, 1959-62, asso. prof., 1962-64, prof., chmn. dept. pharmacognosy, 1964-70; prof., head dept. pharmacognosy and pharmacology U. Ill., Chgo., 1970—; Alexander von Humboldt guest prof. U. Munich, 1967; cons. Amazon Natural Drug Co., Schering AG. Served with M.C., U.S. Army, 1948-49, inf., 1950- 51. Decorated Bronze Star medal with V device and oak leaf cluster, Combat Med. badge. Mem. Am. Soc. Pharmacognosy (past pres.), Am. Chem. Soc., Soc. for Econ. Botany, Am. Pharm. Assn., A.A.A.S., Nat. Geog. Soc., Marine Tech. Soc., Sigma Xi, Phi Sigma, Phi Delta Chi, Rho Chi. Methodist. Author The Lynn Index, Mono, 1969, also chpts. in books. Contbr. articles profl. jours. Home: 2800 Lake Shore Dr Chicago IL 60657 Office: Coll Pharmacy U Ill 833 S Wood St Chicago IL 60680

FARNSWORTH, RAYMOND BARTLETT, educator; b. Enterprise, Utah, May 21, 1915; s. Bartlett Canfield and Lillie Parthena (Holt) F.; B.S., Brigham Young U., 1937; M.S. (research fellow). Mass. State Coll., 1937; Ph.D. (research fellow), Ohio State U., 1941; postgrad. U. Ariz., Harvard, U. Cal. at Berkeley; m. Maurine Winsor, Dec. 31, 1943; childrenDennis Ray, Diane, Kevin, Karalie. Agronomist, Paulding Sugar Co. (O.), 1941; asst. agronomist Ohio Agrl. Expt. Sta., 1941-43; faculty Brigham Young U., 1946—. prof. agronomy, 1950—. chmn. dept., 1950-55, 61-67, chmn. dept. agronomy and horticulture 1967—, acting dean Coll. Applied Sci., 1952, Coll. Biol. and Agrl. Scis., 1955-59; soil scientist Ore. State Coll., 1958-59; soil sci. adviser Coll. Agr., U. Teheran (Iran), 1959-61; asso. dir. advanced sci. edn. program, dir. grad. fellowship program NSF, 1965-66. Bishop, Provo 8th ward Ch. of Jesus Christ of Latter-Day Saints, 1956-58. Served with USNR, 1943- 46. Mem. Western Soc. Soil Sci. (chmn. soil fertility sect. 1957), Utah Acad. Sci., Arts and Letters (chmn. biol. sect., 1949), Soil Sci. Soc. Am., Sigma Xi. Contbr. articles to profl. jours. Home: 1230 N Locust Lane Provo UT 84601

FARNSWORTH, RICHARD ARMSTRONG, contractor; b. Henderson, Ky., June 17, 1898; s. Richard Prentiss and Ada (Sisk) F.; student Washington U., 1917-19, Tulane U., 1919-20; m. Dorothy Coyle, Aug. 24, 1921; children—Patricia (Mrs. Elliot W. Jones), Richard Armstrong, Alan Coyle. Vice pres. R. P. Farnsworth & Co., Inc., 1920-49; chmn. bd. Farnsworth & Chambers Co., Inc., 1949-63; chmn. F. & C. Engring. Co., F. & C. Equipment Co., F. & C. Realty Co., So. Indsl. Piping Co., Farnsworth & Chambers, Ltd. Bd. dirs. Stillman Coll., Tuscaloosa, Ala., Houston Symphony Soc., 1947-57, Nat. Recreation Assn. Mem. internat. com. YMCA, 1943-53, vice chmn. World Service Com., 1944-55, bd. New Orleans, 1937-44, v.p. bd. Houston-Harris Co. 1945-57, pres. S.W. Area, 1954. Vice pres. Nat. Council Churches of Christ in U.S.A., 1954-57, bd. dirs, 1951-63; pres. Tex. Council Chs., 1956; mem. Com. Inter-Ch. Relations, Presbyn. Ch. U.S., 1945-53; trustee Tex. Presbyn. Found. Former mem. numerous ch. affiliated coms. and orgns. Visitor World Council Chs., Evanston, Ill., 1954. Mem. Council Christian Relations. Presbyn. Home: 3126 Newcastle Dr Houston TX 77027 Office: PO Box 74 Houston TX 77001

FARNSWORTH, SIDNEY WOODS, former mfg. exec.; b. Lancaster, Mass., Oct. 23, 1886; s. John Edward and Alice Peck (Woods) F.; B.S., Worcester Poly. Inst., 1906, E.E., 1908. D.Eng., 1967; m. Louise Stevenson, 1916; children—Emillie (Mrs. William Frick), Anne (Mrs. Arthur Huggler), Sidney Woods. Elec. engr. Westinghouse Electric Co., 1908-14; chief engr. U.S. Post Office Dept., Washington, 1922-25; v.p. Case Pomeroy & Co., N.Y.C., 1925-35; with Torrington Mfg. Co. (co. name changed to Torin Co.), 1945-65, pres., 1946-52, chmn. bd., 1952-65. Trustee and mem. exec. com. Worcester Poly. Inst., 1953-63. Asso. sci. attaché Am. Embassy, London, World War I; mem. Navy Price Adjustment Bd., World War II. Awarded Civilian Merit (USN). Mem. Sigma Xi, Alpha Tau Omega. Republican. Conglist. Clubs: Upper Montclair (N.J.) Country: Rockefeller Center Lunch (N.Y.C.). Home: 141 Lorraine Av Upper Montclair NJ 07043

FARNUM, CHARLES WADSWORTH, banker; b. Kansas City, Mo., Jan. 27, 1910; s. Arthur W. and Ellen M. (Pendergast) F.; grad. Kent (Conn.) Sch., 1926; A.B., Princeton 1931; m. Dorothy E. Whitney, Sept. 24, 1935 (dec. July 1965); children—Gail Elizabeth (Mrs. Timothy W. McGuire), Cornelia Ellen (Mrs. Peter M. (Whelan), Peter; m. 2d, Charlotte G. Rappolt, July 16, 1966. With Bankers Trust Co., N.Y.C., 1931—, sr. v.p. charge fiduciary and investment, 1967-70, exec. v.p., 1970—, dir., 1969—; dir., mem. finance com. Phoenix Assurance Co., N.Y.; dir. N. Am. Reins. Corp., N. Am. Reassurance Co.; tchr. Am. Inst. Banking, 1946-53. Trustee Tenafly Community Chest, 1966-68. Bd. dirs. Boyce Thompson Inst. Plant Research, Yonkers, N.Y., 1967—; mem. endowment fund com. Englewood (N.J.) Hosp. Assn., 1950—, chmn. 1953-68; mem. council and finance com. Assn. Aid Crippled Children, 1968—. Served as lt. USNR, 1943-46. Mem. Pilgrims of U.S., Phi Beta Kappa. Episcopalian (past treas., supt. ch. sch.; now warden lay reader). Clubs: Princeton (N.J.) Campus; Princeton (N.Y.C.): Knickerbocker Country (Tenafly). Home: 22 Leslie Pl Tenafly NJ 07670 Office: 280 Park Av New York City NY 10017

FARON, LOUIS CHARLES, educator; b. Bklyn., July 16, 1923; s. Louis C. and Erna (Rost) F.; A.B., Columbia, 1949, Ph.D., 1954; m. Amy Brewster, Nov. 16, 1945 (div. 1968); children—Amy, Kenneth; m. 2d, Barbara Ann Betus, Aug. 21, 1968; 1 son, John. Research asso. dept. anthropology U. Ill., Champaign-Urbana, 1955- 59; asst. prof. dept. anthropology Cal. State Coll. at Los Angeles, 1959- 62; asso. prof. dept. anthropology U. Pitts., 1962-64; prof., chmn. dept. anthropology State U. N.Y., Stony Brook, 1964—; engaged in fieldwork Chile, 1952-54, Peru, 1957-59, Panama, 1960, Mexico, 1963. Served with AUS, 1943-46. Guggenheim Found. fellow, 1970—. Fellow Am. Anthrop. Assn., Royal Anthrop. Inst. of Great Britain and Ireland; mem. A.A.A.S., Am. Acad. Polit. and Social Sci., N.Y. Acad. Sci., Internat. Congress of Americanists. Home: Main St Stony Brook NY 11790

FARQUHARSON, ANDREW GRAY, oil co. exec.; b. Dundas, Ont., Can., Oct. 4, 1907; s. Alexander Lockhart and Jessie Elizabeth (Middleton) F.; B.S., Queen's U., Kingston, Ont., 1930; m. Dora Kathleen Bogart, Dec. 20, 1932; children—Douglas Alexander, Jane Elizabeth (Mrs. David Burland). Mem. staff Queen's U., 1930-31; with Texaco Can. Ltd., and predecessor, 1931- -, v.p. refining, 1952-68, pres., 1969—, dir., 1957—; pres., dir. Regent Refining (Can.) Ltd. Bd. dirs. Que. Fedn. Fish and Game, Que. Forestry Assn. Registered profl. engr., Que. Mem. Corp. Profl. Engrs. Que., Engring. Inst. Can., Am. Petroleum Inst., Canadian Mfrs. Assn., Am. Soc. Metals, Canadian Standards Assn., Am. Soc. Testing Materials. Mason (32, Shriner), Kiwanian (pres. St. George, Montreal club 1960). Clubs: Mount Stephen (past pres.), Anglers and Hunters (past pres.) (Montreal); Lac Du Cap Fish and Game (past pres.); Ettezag Fish and Game (dir.); Still River Hunt. Home: 3033 Sherbrooke St W Montreal 215 Quebec Canada

FARQUHARSON, GORDON MACKAY, lawyer; b. Charlottetown, P.E.I., Can., July 12, 1927; s. Percy Alfred and Rachael Lillian (MacKay) F.; B.A., U. Toronto, 1950; LL.B., Osgoode Hall Law Sch., 1954; m. June Vivienne Malabar, Sept. 8, 1950; children—Douglas, Tanyss, Robbie, Karen. Called to Ont. bar, 1954, since practiced in Toronto; partner Lang, Michener, Cranston, Farquharson & Wright, 1964—. Instr. bar admission course Osgoode Hall Law Sch., 1959-66; sec., dir. GSW Ltd., Alfa Securities Corp. Ltd., Easy Washing Machine Co. Ltd., Guildwood Village Ltd. Pres., Eglinton Provincial Liberal Assn. and Eglinton Fed. Liberal Assn., 1963-66, Don Valley Liberal Assn., 1967-69; conv. chmn. for Mitchell Sharp in Fed. Leadership campaign, 1968. Bd. dirs. N. Toronto Youth Project, Lawrence Park Ratepayers Assn., Soc. Study Urban Shelters. Mem. Canadian Bar Assn., Phi Gamma Delta (pres. 1954). Club: University (Toronto). Home: 228 Stibbard Av Toronto Ontario Canada Office: 50 King St W Toronto Ontario Canada

FARR, GRANT NOEL, educator; b. Ogden, Utah, Dec. 25, 1919; s. Walter Nelson and Elizabeth (Parry) F.; B.S., U. Cal. at Berkeley, 1942, M.B.A. (Flood fellow), 1947, Ph.D., 1955; m. Carmen Marie Mendiola, May 21, 1945; children—Grant J., Barbara E. Teaching fellow U. Cal. at Berkeley, 1946-49; regional price economist OPA, Seattle, 1951-52; mem. faculty U. Colo., 1949-63, prof. econs., 1961-63, chmn. dept., 1957-60; prof. econs., head dept. Pa. State U., 1963—; cons. pub. assistance and services Colo., 1958. Served with AUS, 1942-46. Mem. Am., Western (editorial bd. 1961-63) econ. assns., Econ. History Assn., Beta Gamma Sigma, Omicron Delta Epsilon. Co-author: The Development and Utilization of Human Resources: A Guide for Research, 1967; Origins of Recent Labor Policy, 1959; (with P.T. Therkildsen) Public Assistance and Services in Colorado, 1958. Home: 340 Waring Av State College PA 16801 Office: Dept Economics Pennsylvania State Univ University Park PA 16802

FARR, JOHN E., business exec.; b. Pilchuck, Wash., Oct. 15, 1904; s. Pliny E. and Mabel (Murgatroyd) F.; student U. Wash., 1921-24; m. Josephine Grieves, June 5, 1934; childrenWynne (Mrs. Gordon Grimes), John E., Nancy Sue. Bond salesman Townsend & Co., 1925-28, sales supr., 1931-34; mgr. Dean Witter & Co., 1928-31; investigator 18th Regional Code Authority, Fed. Alcohol Control Adminstrn., 1934-35; liquor salesman McKesson & Robbins, Inc., 1935-36, sales supr., 1936-37, br. mgr., San Bernardino, Cal., 1937-38, Fresno, Cal., 1938-39; brand supr. for Lord Calvert, Calvert Distillers Corp., 1939-40; sales supr. Seagram Distillers Corp., 1940-42, dist. mgr., Los Angeles, 1942-43; regional mgr., Schenley Distillers Corp., Los Angeles, 1943-44, asst. Western div. mgr., 1944-45, asst. gen. sales mgr., 1945-46, asst. to pres., 1947-48, coordinator sales Western div., 1949-50, v.p., gen. sales mgr. Shenley Distbrs., Inc., 1950-52, exec. v.p., dir., 1952—, v.p. dir. sales Western div., San Francisco, 1954—; gen. sales mgr. Jos S. Finch Co., 1946-47; asst. gen. sales mgr. Melrose Distillers, Inc., 1948-49; exec. v.p., dir. Schenley Affiliated Brands Corp., 1962—. Mem. Theta Delta Chi. Clubs: Press, Union League, Transportation (San Francisco). Home: 1755 Jackson St San Francisco CA 94109 Office: 40 Park Lane Brisbane CA 94005

FARR, LEE EDWARD, physician; b. Albuquerque, Oct. 13, 1907; s. Edward and Mabel (Heyn) F.; B.S., Yale, 1929, M.D., 1933; m. Anne Ritter, Dec. 28, 1936; children—Charles E., Susan A., Frances A. Asst. pediatrics, sch. medicine Yale, 1933-34; asst. medicine Hosp. of Rockefeller Inst. Med. Research, 1934-37, asso. medicine, 1937-40; dir. research Alfred I. duPont Inst. of Nemours Found., Wilmington, Del., 1940-49; vis. asso. prof. pediatrics, sch. medicine U. Pa., 1940-49; med. dir., physician-in-chief hosp. Brookhaven Nat. Lab., 1948-62; prof. nuclear and environmental medicine U. Tex., Houston, 1962-68; chief sect. nuclear medicine, U. Tex.-M.D. Anderson Hosp. and Tumor Inst., 1962-67; prof. environmental health U. Tex. School Pub. Health, Houston, 1967-68; head disaster health services Cal. Dept. Health, 1968, chief emergency health services unit Berkeley, 1968-70, chief bur. emergency med. services, Berkeley, 1970—. Meml. lectr. U. Ore. Sch. Med., Portland, 1960. Mem. com. on naval med. research NRC, 1953-68, com. on atomic bomb, 1953-68, com. on medicine and surgery, 1955-59, exec. com., 1962-65; Naval Research Mission to Formosa, 1953; tech. adviser U.S. delegation to Geneva Internat. Conf. for Peaceful Uses Atomic Energy, 1955; mem. N.Y. Adv. Com. Atomic Energy, 1956-59; mem. com. med. isotopes NASA Manned Spacecraft Center, 1966-68; mem. expert adv. panel radiation World Health Orgn., 1957—; mem. sci. adv. bd. Gorgas Meml. Inst., 1967—, mem. Naval Research Adv. Com., 1970—. Mem. alumni bd. Yale U., 1962-65, mem. alumni fund, 1966—. Served as lt. comdr. M.C., USNR, 1942-46; capt. M.C. USNR. Recipient Mead Johnson award for pediatric research, 1940; decorated Gold Cross Order of Phoenix (Greece). Diplomate Nat. Bd. Med. Examiners, Am. Bd. Pediatrics. Fellow A.A.A.S., Am. Acad. Pediatrics, N.Y. Acad. Scis.; mem. Soc. Clin. Medicine, Royal Soc. Arts, Am. Soc. Clin. Investigation, Soc. Pediatric Research, Soc. Exptl. Biology and Medicine, Harvey Soc., Am. Pediatric Soc., Soc. Exptl. Pathology, Am. Acad. Pediatrics, Radiation Research Soc., A.M.A. (council postgrad. programs), Houston C. of C. (chmn. subcom. on quality in living), Med. Soc. Athens (hon.), Sigma Xi (nat. lectr. 1952-53), Alpha Omega Alpha, Phi Sigma Kappa, Nu Sigma Nu, Alpha Chi Sigma. Clubs: Commonwealth; Cosmos (Washington). Author articles on nuclear medicine, nuclear reactors, protein metabolism. Home: 26315 Scenic Rd Carmel CA 93921 Office: 2151 Berkeley Way Berkeley CA 94704

FARR, NEWTON CAMP, real estate; b. Chgo., Dec. 25, 1887; s. Marvin Andrus and Charlotte (Camp) F.; prep. edn. Harvard Sch., Chgo., Lawrenceville (N.J.) Sch., C.E., Cornell U., 1909; LL.D., Lincoln Meml. U., 1950. Civil engr. Raymond Concrete Pile Co., 1909-12; in real estate bus. since 1912; former pres. Rys. Co.; dir. Chgo. Title & Trust Co.; pres., dir. George Washington Carver Gardens, Inc.; former trustee Edith Rockefeller McCormick Trust. Regents prof. U. Cal. at Berkeley, spring 1959. Served as 2d lt. A.S., U.S.Army, asst. resident engr., Winchester, Eng., 1917-19. Trustee Ill. Inst. Tech., Research Inst., Faulkner Sch., Lincoln Meml. U. (past pres. bd.), Urban Land Inst. (past pres.). Sunday Evening Club; chmn. Ill. Lincoln Centennial Com.; vice chmn. Civil War Centennial Com. Ill.; past pres. Friends Chgo. Pub. Library. Mem. Ill. Hist. Library (trustee), Chgo. Geographic Soc. (past pres.), Real Estate Bd. (pres. 1930), Nat. Assn. Real Estate Bds. (v.p. 1938-39; pres. 1940), Am. Inst. Real Estate Appraisers (pres. Ill. chpt. 1936), Am. Soc. Real Estate Counsellors (past pres.), Chicago Assn. Commerce (past dir.), Chgo. Better Bus. Bur. (pres. 1932), Chgo. YMCA (pres. 1938-39, pres. bd. trustees 1961-66), Civic Fedn. (pres. 1941-44), Nat. Inst. Real Estate Brokers (pres. 1932), Chgo. Met. Home Bldrs. (life dir.), Greater N. Michigan Av. Assn. (past pres.), Ill Hist. Soc. (past pres.), Internat. Real Estate Fedn. (pres. Am. chpt.), S. E. Chgo. Commn. (dir.), United Service Orgns. (past chmn. Ill.), Cornell U. Council, Civil War Round Table (past pres.), Cornell Alumni Assn., Soc. Colonial Wars (gov. 1939), Delta Phi. Hon. asso. Chgo. chpt. Am. Inst. Architects. Clubs: Chicago, University, Tavern, Commercial, Indian Hill Country (Chgo.); Cornell (N.Y.). Contbr. articles to real estate jours. Home: 1120 Lake Shore Dr Chicago IL 60615 Office: 111 W Washington St Chicago IL 60602

FARR, URIAH JERRY, electric utility exec.; b. Morgan County, Ind., Mar. 12, 1911; s. Roscoe Conklin and Grace (Wampler) F.; student Ind. State U., 1928-28, extension, 1942-47, Internat. Accountants Soc., 1940, Alexander Hamilton Inst., 1942; m. Laura Evelyn Bloomenstock, Dec. 30, 1948; children—Nancy Kay (Mrs. Ralph M. Maquire), Sue Ann (Mrs. Ralph C. Kuhnert, Jr.). With Indpls. Power & Light Co., 1929—, controller, 1967—. Company rep. exec. mgmt. div. Indpls. United Fund. Mem. Tax Execs. Inst. (bd. dirs., past pres. Ind.), Nat. Assn. Accountants (bd. dirs., past pres. Indpls.), Econ. Forum, Edison Electric Inst. (chmn. gen. accounting com. 1968-69). Presbyn. (deacon). Clubs: Columbia, Press (Indpls.). Home: 4837 E 72d St Indianapolis IN 46250 Office: 25 Monument Circle Indianapolis IN 46204

FARR, WALTER GREENE, Jr., educator; b. Wenonah, N.J., Feb. 24, 1925; s. Walter Greene and Florence (Miner) F.; grad. St. Mark's Sch., 1942; B.S., Yale, 1948, LL.B., 1951; m. Louise Evans, June 24, 1950; children—Judith Evans, Catherine Austin, Elizabeth Lawton, Stephen Nicholas. Admitted to N.Y. bar, 1951; asso. firm Paul, Weiss, Rifkind, Wharton & Garrison. N.Y.C., 1951-54; asso. firm Gumbart, Corbin, Tyler & Cooper, New Haven, 1955-58, partner, 1958-62; with AID, 1962-67, dep. regional adminstr. Bur. Near East and S. Asian Affairs, 1964-67; dir. model cities adminstrn. Dept. Housing and Urban Devel. 1967-69; prof. law N.Y.U. Law Sch., 1969—; vis. lectr. Yale Law Sch., 1958-62. Served with AUS, 1943-45. Home: Bayard Lane Princeton NJ 08540

FARR, WILLIAM D., assn. exec. Pres., Am. Nat. Cattlemen Assn. Address: care Am Nat Cattlemen Assn 801 E 17th Av Denver CO*

FARRALL, ARTHUR W., educator, engr.; b. Harvard, Neb., Feb. 23, 1899; s. John W. and Olive A. (Frazell) F.; B.S., U. Neb., 1921, M.S., 1922, D. Eng. (hon.), 1955; grad. student U. Cal., 1926; m. E. Luella Buck, June 20, 1923; children—Margaret Longnecker, Robert Arthur. Tchr., U. Ca., 1922-29; research engr. Douthitt Engring. Co., Chgo., 1929-33; research engr., dir. research Creamery Package Mfg. Co., 1933-45; prof. agrl. engring., chmn. dept. Mich. State U., 1945-68, prof., chmn. emeritus, 1968—, chmn. dept., 1945-64, chmn. food tech., 1959-60; U.S. del. Internat. Dairy Congress, Stockholm, 1949; cons. U.S. Dept. Agr., 1964-65, Ford Found., Punjab Agr. U., India, 1968-69; cons. to industry in dairy and agrl. engring.; cons. food engring., Brazil, 1970. Mem. research adv. com. Food Industry Research Center, Nat. Restaurant Assn., 1958-61; gen. chmn. Centennial Farm Mechanization. Fellow Am. Soc. Agrl. Engring. (pres. 1962-63. chmn. food engring. com. 1965-66, editor Food Engring. newsletter 1967-68, Massey Ferguson award 1971); mem. Am. Soc. Engring. Edn. (chmn. agr. engring. div. 1960), Am. Assn. U. Profs., Am. Dairy Sci. Assn., Inst. Food Tech., A.A.A.S., Am. Legion, Phi Kappa Phi (exec. sec. Mich. State U. chpt. 1968—), Sigma Xi, Alpha Gamma Rho, Alpha Zeta, Tau Beta Pi, Pi Tau Sigma. Conglist. Club: State College. Author: Dairy Engineering, 1952; Engineering for Dairy and Food Products, 1963; History of the Farrall and Frazell Families, 1970; also bulls., tech. papers; co-author Ency. of Food Engineering, 1971. Editor dairy engring. sect. Am. Jour. Dairy Science (1945-52); asso. editor, co-author Dairy Handbook and Dictionary, 1958; editor-in-chief, co-author Agriculture Engineering-A Dictionary and Handbook; contbr. Refrigeration Handbook, 1937. Inventor inertial propulsion system; dir. research on frost prevention, continuous ice cream freezer, fruit feeder, butter machine. Home: 1858 Cahill Dr East Lansing MI 48823

FARRANFELDT, KEVIN MAX, diversified mfg. co. exec.; b. Cin., May 21, 1910; grad. Phillips Acad., Andover, Mass., 1927; B.S., Princeton, 1931; postgrad. Mass. Inst. Tech., 1931-33; m. Jean R. Holland, June 16, 1935; children--Lois A., Andrew M., James. Salesman, Brown Mfg. Co., Boston, 1932-33; jr. engr. Ball Metals Co., Carson City, Nev., 1933-36, engr., 1936-37, sr. engr., 1937-40; project engr. Kingston Engring. Co., Los Angeles, 1940-43; with dept. engring. City of Denver, 1946-50, dep. head, 1950-52; 2d v.p. Johnson Mfg. Co., Kansas City, Kansas, 1952-54, v.p. for engring., 1954-57; v.p. research Consol. Industries, Inc., South Bend, Ind., 1957-60, exec.

v.p., 1960-65, pres., 1965-70, chmn. bd., chief exec. officer, 1970--, also dir.; dir. ABC Chem. Co., 2d Nat. Bank, Country Food Storage Co., Providence Indsl. Corp. (Ind.), Wilson Investment Co., Inc., Hammond Life Ins. Co., Inc. Pres., Dewey High Sch., Kansas City, Mo., 1953-54; fund chmn. local div. Salvation Army, 19560. Mem. South Bend Republican Com., 1964-68. Bd. dirs. Ind. council Boy Scouts Am., 1969-71; trustee Lovell Found. Served to lt., Corps Engrs., AUS, 1943-45. Decorated Bronze Star medal. Member N.A.M., South Bend C. of C. (v.p. 1963-65, dir. 1965-70), Am. Mgmt. Assn., Ind. Engrs. Soc. (program com. 1961-62), Princeton Alumni Assn. Episcopalian. Home: 6823 Broad Terrace Av South Bend IN 46505

FARRAR, FRANK LEROY, former gov. of S.D.; b. Britton, S.D., Apr. 2, 1929; s. Virgil William and Venetia Soule (Taylor) F.; B.S., U. S.D., 1951, LL.B., 1953; LL.D. (hon.), Huron Coll.; m. Patricia Jean Henley, June 5, 1953; children—Jeanne Marie, Sally Ann, Robert John, Mary Susan, Ann M. Admitted to S.D. bar, 1953; and practiced in Britton, 1957- 63; agt. Internal Revenue Service, 1955-57; judge Marshall County, 1958; states atty. Marshall County, 1959-62; atty. gen. S.D., 1963-69; gov. S.D., 1969-70. Mem. Retarded Children's Sch. Bd., 1961; active local Boy Scouts Am.; fund raising chmn. S.D. Mental Health Assn.; chmn. S.D. March Dimes. Chmn. Marshall County Republican Party, 1959; asst. sgt. at arms Rep. Nat. Conv., 1960. Bd. dirs. Rural Coalition Am. Served to capt. AUS, Korean Conflict; mem. Res. Mem. S.D., Ind., Wash. bar assns., S.D. States Atty. Assn. (asst. pres.), Nat. Dist. Attys. Assn., Jr. C. of C. Alpha Tau Omega, Phi Delta Phi. Mason (Shriner, Jester), Lion, Elk, Odd Fellow. Club: Sportsmen (Britton). Home: Britton SD 57430

FARRAR, JOHN CHIPMAN, publisher, author; b. Burlington, Vt., Feb. 25, 1896; s. Edward Donaldson and Sally (Wright) F.; A.B., Yale, 1918; m. Margaret Petherbridge, 1926; children—John Curtis, Alison, Janice. Reporter, N.Y. Sunday World, 1919- 21; editor The Bookman, 1921-27; became editor George H. Doran Co., 1925; dir. Doubleday, Doran and Co., 1927; editor, v.p., then chmn. bd., Farrar & Rinehart, Inc., 1929-44; lectr., Columbia, 1945-47; chmn. bd., Farrar, Straus & Giroux, 1946—. Served as 1st lt., U.S. Air Service, 1917-19; with Overseas Publs., O.W.I., 1943-45. Mem. Nat. Conf. Christians and Jews (chmn. mag. com. 1948-49), Fed. Grand Jury Assn. (exec. com. 1949); v.p. Am. Center of P.E.N., 1952—; exec. bd., Poetry Soc. Am., 1959—. Clubs: Century, Elizabethan (New Haven, Conn.). Author: Forgotten Shrines, 1919; Songs for Parents, 1921; The Magic Sea Shell, 1923; The Middle Twenties, 1924; Songs for Johnny Jump-Up, 1930; Indoor and Outdoor Plays for Children, 1933; For the Record, 1943. Home: 16 E 96th St New York City NY 10028 Office: 19 Union Sq West New York City NY 10003

FARRAR, WILLIAM EDWIN, oil co. exec.; b. Marvell, Ark., Mar. 2, 1920; s. James Madison and Frances N. (McLure) F.; ed. pub. schs.; m. June Pike, Dec. 29, 1954; children—John, Mark, Michael. Engaged in cotton business, 1937-42; landman Mid-states Oil Corp., 1945-48; mgr. lands Union Oil Co. Cal., 1948-61; pres. Union Oil Co. Can. Ltd., 1961—; member board of directors Union Oil Co., also dir. Peace River Oil Pipe Line Company, Ltd. Served with AUS, 1942-45. Mem. Am. Assn. Petroleum Landmen, Calgary C. of C. (pres.), Canadian Petroleum Assn. (dir. Alta. div.). Home: 1316 Prospect Calgary Alberta Canada Office: 709 8th Av SW Calgary Alberta Canada

FARREL, FRANKLIN III, heavy machinery exec.; b. Ansonia, Conn., Mar. 23, 1908; s. Franklin and Marian V. (Brown) F.; B.A., Yale, 1931; m. Sallie L. Gibson, Sept. 9, 1933; children—Sallie G., Franklin IV, Lisa. With Farrel Corp. (became div. USM Corp. 1968), Ansonia, 1933—, beginning as foundry learner, successively foundry mgr., asst. mgr. mfg., plant mgr., sec.-asst. treas., 1933-55, pres., 1955—; exec. v.p. USM Corp., 1968—; dir. Union & New Haven Trust Co. Bd. dirs., Yale New Haven Hosp. Home: Northrup Rd Woodbridge CT 06525 Office: 25 Main St Ansonia CT 06401

FARRELL, ALEXANDER, business exec.; b. 1922; married. With P.S. Ross & Sons, Chartered Accountants, Toronto, Ont., Can., 1942-52; asst. sec., chief accountant, comptroller Cabot Carbon of Can. Ltd., 1952-65; asst. comptroller Cabot Corp., Boston, 1965-66, comptroller, 1966—. Office: 125 High St Boston MA 02110*

FARRELL, ALLAN PETER, educator; b. Grand Rapids, Mich., Feb. 14, 1896; s. Peter Daniel and Elfrida May (Allan) F.; student U. Detroit, 1914-16; A.B., St. Louis U., 1922, M.A., 1923; S.T.D., Pontifical Regional Sem. of Campania, Italy, 1930; Ph.D., Nat. U. of Ireland, 1933. Tchr. classical lit. Marquette U., 1923-26; entered Soc. Jesus, 1916; ordained priest Roman Cath. Ch., 1929; tchr. edn. Xavier U., Cin., 1932-34, 40-42, Loyola U., Chgo., 1934- 40; prof. edn. U. Detroit, 1948—, dean Grad. Sch. 1949-62; dir. reorgn. Sophia U., Tokyo, Japan, 1949-50. Dir. higher edn. Chgo. Province S.J., 1934-40. Mem. Jesuit Edn. Assn. U.S. (nat. dir. 1942-44; chmn. commn. grad. schs. 1954—), Nat. Conf. Christians and Jews (Cath. co-chmn. religious commn. 1943-49; commn. edn. orgns. 1950—), Nat. Cath. Ednl. Assn. (editor publs. on acceleration), Religious Edn. Assn. of U.S. and Can., Midwest Conference of Graduate Deans, Phi Delta Kappa. Author: Jesuit Code of Liberal Education, 1938; Missions and Cultural Life, 1945; The Jesuit Ratio Studiorum of 1599 Translated into English, 1970. Editor: Whither American Education? 1948; Pius XI's Encyclical on Christian Education of Youth, rev. edit. 1954. Editor Jesuit Ednl. Quar., 1938-44; mem. editorial bd. America, 1944-48, contbg. editor, 1948—. Address: U of Detroit Detroit MI 48221

FARRELL, AUSTIN JAMES, publishing co. exec.; b. Rockville, Centre, N.Y., June 10, 1932; s. James Hyslop and Grace (Moseley) F.; B.A., Haverford Coll., 1954; LL.B., Columbia, 1957; m. Margaret Root Auch, Sept. 8, 1955; children— Emily, Benjamin. Admitted to N.Y. bar, 1959; asso. firm Thacher, Proffitt, Prizer, Crawley & Wood, 1957-65; with Crowell Collier and Macmillan, Inc., 1965—, sr. counsel, sec., 1967—, v.p., sec., 1971—. Mem. Am. Soc. Corp. Secs., Am., N.Y. State bar assns., Assn. Bar City N.Y. Home: 85 Seven Bridges Rd Chappaqua NY 10514 Office: 866 3d Av New York City NY 10022

FARRELL, DAVID JOSEPH, newspaper editor; b. E. Rutherford, N.J., July 15, 1926; s. Thomas Arthur and Annie Elizabeth (Fitzsimmons) F.; B.S. in Polit. Sci., Boston Coll., 1948; m. Dorothy Ann Ahearn, Nov. 5, 1949; children—Colleen Ann, David Ahearn, Joanne Eleanor, Gregory Gerard, John William, Mary E., Mark X, Bridget F. Mem. staff Boston Traveler, 1948-60, asst. to pub., 1956-60; mem. staff Boston Herald, 1960—, mng. editor, 1963—, now assistant publisher Boston Herald Traveler, 1964—. Served with USNR, 1944-45. Mem. Charitable Irish Soc. Roman Cath. Club: Clover (Boston). Home: 36 Belcher Circle Milton MA 02186 Office: 300 Harrison Av Boston MA 02106

FARRELL, EDWARD JOSEPH, educator; b. San Francisco, Mar. 28, 1917; s. Christopher Patrick and Ethel Ann (Chesterman) F.; B.Sc., U. San Francisco, 1939; M.A., Stanford, 1942; m. Pearl Philomena Rongone, Aug. 21, 1954; children—Paul, Paula. Faculty, U. San Francisco, 1941—, prof. math., 1968—. Guest lectr. regional and nat. meetings Nat. Council Tchrs. Math., 1966, 67, 69; cons. Cal. Dept. Edn., 1971—; cons. math. text pubs. Mem. adv. panels NSF, 1966—, dir. summer and in-service insts., 1960—, dir. confs. geometry, 1967, 68, 70; mem. rev. panel Sci. Books. Served with AUS, 1944-46. NSF faculty fellow, 1956-57. Mem. A.A.A.S., Am. Assn. Physics Tchrs., Nat. Council Tchrs. Math., Sch. Sci. and Math. Assn. Republican. Roman Cath. Home: 2524 Gough St San Francisco CA 94123

FARRELL, EILEEN, singer, soprano; b. Williamantic, Conn., Feb. 13, 1920; d. Michael John and Catherine (Kennedy) Farrell; m. Robert V. Reagan, Apr. 4, 1946; children—Robert V., Kathleen. Made debut as singer Columbia Broadcasting Co., 1941; singer, own program, CBS, 6 yrs.; made opera debut in Il Trovatore with San Francisco Opera; singer with major symphony orchs. in U.S., toured throughout U.S. and in S.Am.

FARRELL, EUGENE GEORGE, editor; b. Bklyn., Feb. 12, 1905; s. Stephen Andrew and Anna Louise (Kronholm) F.; grad. St. Brigid's, 1919, Bklyn. Tech. High Sch., 1923; A.B. cum laude, U. Notre Dame, 1928; m. Margaret Frances Reidy, 1928 (dec. 1951); children—Stephen John, Francis Xavier, Peter Michael; m. 2d, Lois Jane Fegan. With L.I. Daily Press, Jamaica, N.Y., 1928-38, sports editor, 1937, city editor, 1938; editor L.I. Star, L.I. Star- Jour., 1938-41; city editor, mng. editor Newark Star-Ledger, 1942-48, editorial asst. to pub. Harrisburg (Pa.) Patriot (morning), News (eve.), 1948-51, founding editor Sunday Patriot-News; editor Jersey Jour., 1951- 70, exec. editor, 1970—. Mem. N.J. Pub. Market Commn., 1960-63, chmn., 1963. Bd. mgr. Jersey City Med. Center, chmn., 1966-70. Mem. Am., Newark Bay power squadrons, Aviation/Space Writers Assn., N.J. Press Assn., Am. Soc. Newspaper Editors, Sigma Delta Chi. Roman Catholic, K.C. Clubs: Marshall Chess (N.Y.C.); North Hudson Yacht, Little Ship (London); Bergen-Carteret (Jersey City); Richmond County Yacht. Home: 644 Jersey Av Jersey City NJ 07302 Office: 30 Journal Sq Jersey City NJ 07306

FARRELL, FRANK SAMUEL, r.r. exec., lawyer; b. Duluth, Minn., Nov. 29, 1920; s. Frank Hogan and Ora Jane (Crumpton) F.; B.S.L., U. Minn., 1947, LL.B., 1948; m. Floria Margaret Azzo, Sept. 7, 1946; children—Frank Samuel, Mary Jane, Alfred C. Admitted to Minn. bar, 1949; asst. atty. No. Pacific R.R., 1949-53, asst. commerce counsel, 1953-57, commerce counsel, 1957-60, asst. gen. solicitor, 1960-61, gen. solicitor, 1961-68, v.p., gen. counsel, 1968-70; v.p., gen. counsel Burlington No., Inc., St. Paul, 1970—. Dir. St. Paul Civic Center Authority, 1969—, Minn. Assn. Mental Health, Inc., 1964—, St. Paul Jr. Achievement, 1965—. Mem. Minn. Gov.'s Crime Commn., 1967-68, Minn. Gov.'s Reapportionment Com., 1964-66. Served to 1st lt., USAAF, 1943-46, PTO, 1951-52, Korea. Mem. Am., Minn., Ramsey County (pres.) bar assns. Recipient regents' outstanding achievement award, U. Minn., 1968. Clubs: Town and Country, St. Paul Athletic, Minnesota (St. Paul). Home: 56 N Mississippi River Blvd St Paul MN 55104 Office: 176 E 5th St St Paul MN 55101

FARRELL, GORDON, corp. exec. Dir. B.C. Packers, Ltd., Can. Trust Co., Ltd., MacMilan Bloedel Ltd.; chmn. Ocean Cement & Supplies Ltd. Home: 1890 SW Marine Dr Vancouver British Columbia Canada Office: 901 Pender St W Vancouver British Columbia Canada

FARRELL, JAMES AUGUSTINE, Jr., shipping exec.; b. Bklyn., Jan. 13, 1901; s. James Augustine and Catherine (McDermott) F.; B.S., Yale, 1924; D.C.S., Duquesne U., 1961; m. Emilie Hill, Jan. 27, 1934. Ship operator and owner, 1924—; chmn. bd. dirs. Farrell Lines, Inc.; dir. Maritime Exchange; trustee Emigrant Indsl. Savs. Bank. Bd. mgrs. Am. Bur. Shipping. Trustee Canterbury Sch. Served to comdr. USNR, 1941-44. Fellow Royal Acad. of Arts (Brit.); mem. Newcomen Soc., Am. Soc. M.E., Soc. Naval Architects, Delta Phi. Clubs: Yale, Leash, India House, Union (N.Y.C.); St. Elmo (New Haven); Edgartown Yacht, N.Y. Yacht, Indian Harbour Yacht, Royal Thames Yacht. Home: Old Farm Rd Darien CT 06820 Office: 1 Whitehall St New York City NY 10004

FARRELL, JAMES THOMAS, author; b. Chgo., Feb. 27, 1904; s. James Francis and Mary (Daly) F.; student U. Chgo. 1927-29; m. Dorothy Patricia Butler, 1931 (div.); m. 2d, Hortense Alden (div. Sept. 1955); 1 son, Kevin; m. 3d, Dorothy Butler, Sept. 1955. Served as clk. Am. Ry. Express Co. and cigar store, filling sta. attendant, campus newspaper reporter. Mem. Inst. Arts and Letters. Clubs: Nat. Press, Overseas Press. Recipient Guggenheim fellowship in creative writing, 1936-37; Book of the Month Club award for "Studs Lonigan", 1937. Author: Young Lonigan-A Boyhood in Chicago Streets, 1932; Gas House McGinty, 1933; The Young Manhood of Studs Lonigan, 1934; Calico Shoes, 1934; Judgment Day, 1935; Guillotine Party and Other Stories, 1935; A Note on Literary Criticism, 1936; A World I Never Made, 1936; Can All This Grandeur Perish, 1937; The Collected Short Stories of James T. Farrell, 1937; No Star Is Lost, 1938; Tommy Gallagher's Crusade, 1939; Father and Son, 1940; Ellen Rogers, 1941; $1,000 a Week and other stories, 1942; My Days of Anger, 1943; To Whom It May Concern, 1944; The League of Frightened Philistines, 1945; Bernard Clare, 1946; When Boyhood Dreams Come True, 1946; Literature and Morality, 1947; The Life Adventurous, 1947; The Road Between, 1949; A Misunderstanding, 1949; An American Dream Girl, 1950; This Man and This Woman, 1951; Yet Other Waters, 1952; The Face of Time, 1953; Reflections at Fifty and Other Essays, 1954; French Girls are Vicious, 1955; An Omnibus of Short Stories, 1956; A Dangerous Woman and Other Short Stories, 1957; My Baseball Diary, 1957; It Has Come to Pass, 1958; Boarding House Blues, a novel, 1961; Side Street and Other Stories, 1961; Sound of the City and Other Stories, 1962; The Silence of History, 1963; What Time Collects, 1964; Lonely for the Future, 1966; Childhood Is Not Forever, 1969. Contbr. to mags., to Asian press; poet. Co-author: (with Jeanette Nolan and Horace Gregory) The Frontier and James Whitcomb Riley, 1952; (with others) Dialogue with John Dewey. Editor: A Selected Book of Prejudices (H.L. Meneken), 1956; A Dreiser Reader, 1962; What Time Collects, 1964.

FARRELL, JAMES VINCENT, educator; b. Superior, Wis., Aug. 23, 1917; s. Hugh Vincent and Martha Adelaide (McGarry) F.; B.Ed., Superior State Tchrs. Coll., 1938; M.A., State U. Ia., 1947, Ph.D., 1949; m. Mary Louise Hamilton, May 1, 1943; children—Michael Katherine A., Scott J., Mark H., Mary Jo. Sci. tchr. McCaskill Sch., Superior State Tchrs. Coll., 1938; tchr. pub. schs., Superior, 1938-39, Mo. Mil. Acad., 1939-41; chmn. sci. dept. teaching Ia. State Tchrs. Coll., 1948-51; civilian educator Hdqrs. Air U., 1952-58; dean Sch. of Gen. Edn., Ferris State Coll., Big Rapids, Mich., from 1958, now v.p. for acad. affairs. Chmn. sci. teaching sect. Ia. Acad. Sci., 1949-50; chmn. edn. com. Ia. Conf. Children and Youth, 1950. Served to maj. USAAF, 1941-46, USAF, 51-52; lt. col. Res. Recipient Meritorious Civilian award Dept. Air Force, 1956. Mem. A.A.A.S., Phi Delta Kappa. Roman Cath. Elk. Contbr. articles profl. jours. Home: 218 Woodward Av Big Rapids MI 49307

FARRELL, JOHN A., lawyer; b. N.Y.C., Dec. 14, 1914; B.S., St. Francis Coll., Bklyn., 1938; LL.B., N.Y. U., 1941. Admitted to N.Y. State bar, 1942; partner Naylon Huber, Magill, Lawrence and Farrell, N.Y.C. Mem. N.Y. State Bar Assn., N.Y. County Lawyers Assn. Office: 61 Broadway New York City NY 10006*

FARRELL, JOHN EDWARD, lawyer; b. South Orange, N.J., Apr. 29, 1907; s. John and Johanna (Hefferman) F.; student Fordham U., 1927-28; LL.B., Georgetown U., 1932; m. Margaret Spellane, June 31, 1942; children—Margot, Ellen, John, Paul, Jane. Admitted to N.J. bar, 1933; pvt. practice, Newark, 1933-41; with P. Ballantine & Sons, Newark, 1941-67, sec.-counsel, 1951-54, v.p., 1954- 64, pres., 1964-67, chmn. bd., 1967; now engaged in practice of law, Newark. Bd. mgrs. Howard Savs. Instn., Newark; dir. Fidelity Union Trust Co., Fireman's Ins. Co. Newark. Mem. Newark Indsl. Devel. Corp. Trustee Essex County Blood Bank, Welfare Fedn. Newark, Irvington and W. Hudson, Seton Hall U. Served to maj. USAAF, 1942-45. Mem. N.J., Essex County bar assns., Greater Newark C. of C. (dir.), N.J. C. of C. (dir.). Catholic. Home: 328 Grove Rd South Orange NJ 07079 Office: 570 Broad St Newark NJ 07102

FARRELL, JOHN JOSEPH, surgeon, educator; b. Seneca, Wis., Sept. 6, 1917; s. Thomas Emmett and Caroline Mae (Nugent) F.; A.B., Loras Coll. , 1938; M.D., Harvard, 1942; m. Charlotte Rommel, Oct. 23, 1943; children—Mary Eileen, John Joseph, Patricia Ann. Intern, St. Joseph's Hosp., Lexington, Ky., 1942-43; resident surgery Albany (N.Y.) Hosp. and Albany Med. Coll., 1946-50, instr., then asst. prof. surgery Albany Med. Coll., 1950-54: prof. surgery, chmn. dept. U. Miami (Fla.) Sch. Medicine, 1954-61, clin. prof. surgery, 1962—; surgeon-in-chief Jackson Meml. Hosp., Miami, 1954- 61; dir. surgery Coral Gables (Fla.) VA Hosp., 1956-61, Kendall Hosp., Miami, 1958-63. Bd. dirs. John Elliott Blood Bank, Dade County, 1956-65, Dade County chpt. Am. Cancer Soc., 1958-65, Palm Beach County chpt. Am. Cancer Soc., 1966-. Served to capt., M.C., AUS, 1943-46; ETO. Fellow exptl. surgery Daxian Found., 1948-49. Diplomate Am. Bd. Surgery. Fellow A.C.S. (bd. govs. 1960-63); mem. Pan Am. Med. Assn., A.M.A., Southeastern Surg. Congress, Soc. Surgery Alimentary Tract, A.A.A.S., N.Y. Acad. Scis, Alpha Omega Alpha. Home: 260 N Country Club Dr Atlantis FL Office: 508 N Federal Hwy Lake Worth FL 33460

FARRELL, JOHN RHEA, former govt. ofcl.; b. Washington, Jan. 25, 1907; s. James Rollins and Annie (Ritchey) F.; A.B., George Washington U., 1943; m. Mildred Cole, July 14, 1931. Bd. govs. Fed. Res. System, 1927-43, 46-71, asst. dir. div. bank operations, 1955-58, dir. div. bank operations, 1959-71. Served from lt. (j.g.) to lt. USNR, 1943-45. Mem. Phi Beta Kappa. Home: 9500 Byeforde Rd Kensington MD 20795

FARRELL, JOSEPH D., banker. Sr. v.p. Fidelity Union Trust Co., Newark. Office: 765 Broad St Newark NJ 07101*

FARRELL, LYLE HARLAN, educator; b. Johnson, Vt., Jan. 4, 1905; s. James Donald and Nettie Josephine (Leach) F.; student Westbrook Sem., 1925; A.B., U. N.H., 1929, L.H.D., 1969; LL.D., New Eng. Coll., 1960; m. Avis Henning, Mar. 10, 1930 (dec. 1935); children—Ann, Judith, David; m. 2d, Alice Gardner, 1939. Tchr., coach Proctor Acad., 1929—, dir. dramatics, debating, asst. headmaster, 1934-52, headmaster, 1952—; dep. forest fire warden N.H. Forestry Dept. Exec. bd. N.H. Social Welfare Com. Trustee Squam Lake Sci. Center, Golden Rule Farm. Pres. No. New Eng. Assn. Ind. Schs. Mem. Nat. Assn. Remedial Teaching (founder, mem. exec. com.), New Eng. Reading Assn. (exec. com. 1950, pres. 1952), New Eng. Assn. Schs. and Colls., N.H. Unitarian Assn. (exec. com.). Eastern Amateur Ski Assn., Am. Malacol. Union, Kappa Sigma. Office: Proctor Academy Andover NH 03216

FARRELL, MALCOLM J., hosp. adminstr.; b. Woburn, Mass., May 7, 1906; s. Joseph and Elizabeth (Thompson) F.; B.S., Tufts U., 1928, M.D., 1931; m. Virginia Corbin, July 2, 1932; children—Malcolm J., Dudley C., Virginia A. (Mrs. Juan J. Blau). Intern, Long Island Hosp., Boston, 1931-32; asst. physician Met. State Hosp., Waltham, Mass., 1931-33, sr. physician, 1933-38; asst. supt. Fernald State Sch., Waverley, Mass., 1938-41, supt., 1945—. Sec.-treas. Group Advancement Psychiatry, 1950-69; instr. phsychiatry Boston U. Med. Sch. Past pres. New Eng. Soc. Psychiatry, Mass. Soc. Research in Psychiatry, 1954. Bd. dirs. Waltham chpt. A.R.C., 1958, Waltham Boys Club, 1959-61. Served to col., M.C., AUS, 1941-45. Decorated Legion of Merit. Fellow Mass. Med. Soc.; mem. A.M.A., Am. Psychiat. Assn. (past speaker assembly dist. brs.), Am. Assn. Mental Deficiency, Am. Coll. Psychiatry, Am. Acad. Mental Retardation. Rotarian (pres. Waltham 1955-56). Author articles in field. Address: Box C Waverley MA 02178

FARRELL, RAYMOND FRANCIS, govt. ofcl.; b. Pawtucket, R.I., Feb. 6, 1907; s. James E. and Jennie (Moran) F.; LL.D., Georgetown U., 1931; m. Charlotte M. Griedel, Nov. 11, 1961. Spl. asst. to gen. counsel U.S. Senate and House Joint Com. investigating TVA, 1938-39; with FBI, 1931-33, Dept. Interior, also Pub. Works Adminstrn., 1934-41; asst. commr. U.S. Immigration and Naturalization Service, 1952-58, asso. commr., 1958-62, commr., 1962- -. Chmn. fed. govt. div. United Givers Fund, Washington, 1960; del. White-House Conf. Children and Youth, 1950; adv. council Nat. Council Nationality and Citizenship, 1949—; mem. Pres's Council on Organized Crime, 1970; mem. Select Commn. on Western Hemisphere Immigration. Served to lt. col. AUS, 1942-46. Decorated Bronze Star medal; Grande Ufficiale, Order of Merit (Italy); recipient Alumni Achievement award Georgetown Univ., 1961; Founders award Assn. of Nationality and Immigtation Lawyers, 1968. Mem. Soc. of Former Agents the FBI, Am. Legion. Club: Nat. Press (Washington). Home: 2500 Q St NW Washington DC 20007 Office: 119 D St NE Washington DC 20002

FARRELL, RICHARD JAMES, lawyer; b. Uniontown, Pa., Nov. 7, 1916; s. John and Nora (Moran) F.; B.S., Washington and Jefferson Coll., 1938; LL.B., U. Pa., 1941; grad. Advanced Mgmt. Program, Harvard, 1954; m. Mary Hope Hudson, Feb. 20, 1942; children—Patricia Morris, Thomas Hudson, Richard James, Jane Elizabeth. Admitted to Pa. bar, 1942, N.Y. bar, 1947, Ill. bar. 1955, also Fed. Cts. and ICC; practice gen. and corp. law Cadwalader, Wickerham & Taft, N.Y.C., 1941-42; atty. Standard Oil Co. (Ind.) (formerly Pan Am. Petroleum & Transport Co.), 1942-55, gen. counsel, dir., 1961-62; atty. Standard Oil Co. (Ind.), 1955, asst. gen. counsel, 1957, asso. gen. counsel, 1959-60, gen. counsel, dir., 1963—, v.p. 1965—; dir. Midwest Oil Corp. Nat. adv. counsel for corporate law depts. Practicing Law Inst.; mem. adv. bd. Internat. Oil & Gas Ednl. Center, Southwestern Legal Found., 1967—. Trustee Am. Enterprise Inst., Ravinia Festival Assn; bd. dirs. Milestone Found., North Shore Mental Health Assn. Served to 1st lt AUS. World War II; legal officer Joint Army-Navy Petroleum Purchasing Agy. Mem. Am., Ill. bar assns., Assn. Bar City N.Y., Am. Judicature Soc., Assn. Gen. Counsel, Am. Petroleum Inst., Northwestern U. Assos., Pi Sigma Alpha, Delta Sigma Rho, Lambda Chi Alpha. Clubs: University, Law, Commonwealth, Economic (Chgo.); Westmoreland Country (Wilmette). Home: 1299 Hackberry Lane Winnetka IL 60093 Office: 910 S Michigan Av Chicago IL 60680

FARRELL, ROGER HAMLIN, educator; b. Greensboro, N.C., July 23, 1929; s. Charles A. and Anne (McKaughan) F.; Ph.B., U. Chgo., 1947, M.S., 1951; Ph.D., U. Ill., 1959; m. LeMoyne Goodman, Dec. 29, 1967. Faculty, Cornell U., Ithaca, N.Y., 1959—, now prof. math.; cons. Dept. Health Edn. and Welfare. Served with U.S. Army, 1954-56. Mem. Am. Math. Soc., Inst. Math. Statistics, Am. Statis. Assn. Contbr. articles profl. jours. Home: 120 Eastwood Terrace Ithaca NY 14850

FARRELL, SALLIE JOHNSON, librarian; b. Brookhaven, Miss., Dec. 29, 1909; d. William Henry and Ora Lee (Johnson) Farrell; B.A., Miss. State Coll. Women, 1931; B.S. in L.S. cum laude, U. Ill., 1932. Tchr.-librarian Picayune (Miss.) High Sch., 1932-33; asst. Queens Borough Pub. Library, Jamaica, N.Y., 1934-36, Tulane U. Library, 1936; reference librarian La. State Library, Baton Rouge, 1936-38; parish librarian Shreve Meml. Library, Shreveport, 1939, Winn, Rapides and Calcasieu parishes, La., 1940-46; field rep. La. State Library, 1946-54, dir. field services, 1954-62, state librarian, 1962—. Trustee Public Affairs Research Council. Mem. U.S.-USSR Libraries Exchange Mission, 1961; mem. La. Commn. on Status of Women, La. Commn. on Ednl. TV. Mem. Am. (v.p. 1954-55, council 1963- 67), La. (pres. 1943-44), Southwestern library assns., Nat. Fedn. Bus and Profl. Women's Clubs, Alpha Delta Kappa, Delta Kappa Gamma. Methodist. Contbr. to profl. jours. Home: 1922 Ramsey Dr Baton Rouge LA 70808 Office: Louisiana State Library Baton Rouge LA 70801

FARRELL, SUZANNE, (Roberta Sue Ficker), ballerina; b. Cin.; began study ballet Cin. Conservatory Music; became Ford Found. scholar Sch. Am. Ballet, 1960; m. Paul Mejia, Feb. 1969. With N.Y. City Ballet, 1961-69, became featured dancer, 1962, prin. dancer, 1965-69, roles include Arcade, Movements for Piano and Orchestra, Apollo, Bugaku, Clarinade, Episodes, Stars and Stripes, Glinkaiana, Xanakis, Western Symphony, Symphony in C, Concerto Barocco, Midsummer Night's Dream, Agon, Ballet Imperial, Irish Fantasy, Nutcracker, Don Quixote, La Sonnambula, Raymonda Variations, Brahms-Schoenberg Quartet, Variations, Swan Lake, The Jewels, Prodigal Son, Divertimento 15, Slaughter on 10th Av.; with Bejart Ballet of 20th Century, Brussels, Belgium, 1971—; created role in Bach Sonate #5; other ballets include Messe pour le temps present, Blakti Erotica pas de deux, Juliet in Romeo and Juliet; performed in film version A Midsummer Night's Dream, 1967; created The Young Girl in Rose in Nijinsky... Clown of God, 1971. Hon. lectr. dance U. Cin. Recipient Spl. award of merit in creative and performing arts, U. Cin., 1965; Merit award Mademoiselle mag., 1965. Address: P O Box 804 New York City NY 10023

FARRER, WILLIAM CAMERON, lawyer; b. Cleve., Apr. 27, 1922; s. William M. and Jean (Cameron) F.; A.B., U. Cal. at Los Angeles, 1943; LL.B., Duke, 1949; m. Constance Webb, July 25, 1953; children—William W., Cameron W., Jonathan S., Webb M. Admitted to Cal. bar, 1950, since practiced in Los Angeles; atty. Hill, Farrer & Burrill, 1950—, partner, 1958—; del. Cal. Bar Conf., 1952—. Dir. Dana Labs., Inc., First Fed. Savs. & Loan Assn. San Gabriel Valley, Pierce Nat. Life Ins. Co. Mem. Cal. Coordinating Council on Higher Edn., 1970. Bd. dirs. Greater Los Angeles Zoo Assn.; regent U. Cal. Served to capt., inf., AUS, 1943-46. Decorated Bronze Star medal. Fellow Am. Bar Found.; mem. Am. Bar Assn. (ho. of dels. 1957—, mem. council sect. internat. law 1964—), U. Cal. at Los Angeles Alumni Assn. (pres. 1969-71); Am . Law Inst., Phi Gamma Delta, Phi Alpha Delta. Home: 510 S Lucerne Blvd Los Angeles CA 90005 Office: 445 S Figueroa St Los Angeles CA 90017

FARRER, WILLIAM MELBOURNE, lawyer; b. Dorchester, Can., Jan. 8, 1894; s. Isaac Sowerby and Amelia Jane (Cochran) F.; B.A., Mt. Allison U., 1914; student Dalhousie Law Sch., 1915; LL.B., Kings Law Coll., 1916; m. Jean Frances Cameron, Dec. 24, 1919; children—William C., John F., Geoffrey M. Admitted to bar Sask., 1919, Alta., 1925, Cal., 1927; pvt. practice law, Sask., 1919-27, Los Angeles, 1927—; partner Hill, Farrer & Burrill, 1938-71. Mem. Combined Brit. Charitable Fund Los Angeles. Mem. Am. Judicature Soc. Los Angeles C. of C., Am., Cal., Inter Am., Internat., Los Angeles bar assns., Am. Soc Internat. Law, Fgn. Law Assn. So. Cal., Nat. Council Juvenile Ct. Judges. Mason (Shriner). Club: California (Los Angeles). Home: 5911 W Colgate Av Los Angeles CA 90036 Office: 445 S Figueroa St Los Angeles CA 90017

FARRETTA, ALVIN JOSEPH, mining co. exec.; b. San Francisco, Feb. 6, 1915; s. Michael and Elizabeth (Ferrari) F.; B.S. in Mining Engring., U. Cal. at Berkeley, 1937; m. Barbara A. Maloney, Dec. 27, 1946; children—Susan, Patricia, Mary K., Lee James. Laborer, jr. engr. various mines, Cal., Mexico, 1937-38; shift boss S.Am. Devel. Co., Ecuador, 1939-40, Itogon Mining Co., P.I., 1941; exploration engr. Panaminas, Inc., 1946-47; with Benquet Consol., Inc., Makati, Philippines, 1948—, gen. mgr., 1969—, v.p., 1966—, exec. v.p., 1969—. Served to capt. AUS, 1944-46. Decorated D.S.C., Bronze Star. Registered profl. engr., P.I. Mem. Am. Inst. Mining, Metall. and Petroleum Engrs., Philippine Soc. Mining, Metall. and Geol. Engrs. Home: 1952 Kasoy St Dasmarinas Village Makati Rizal Philippines Office: PO Box 611 Makati Comml Center Makati Rizal Philippines

FARRIN, JAMES MOORE, naval architect, marine engr.; b. Plain Dealing, La., July 16, 1908; s. James Moore and Fanne (Mosby) F.; B.S., U. S. Naval Acad., 1929; M.S., Mass. Inst. Tech., 1934; m. Marjorie Atkins Smith, June 15, 1931; 1 son, James Smith. Commd. Ensign USN, 1929, advanced through grades to rear adm., 1957; engring. duty officer, duties in ship design, constrn. and maintenance; comdr. Phila. Naval Ship Yard, 1955-58; asst. chief Bur. Ships, 1958-61; comdr. Pearl Harbor Naval Ship Yard, 1961-63, Norfolk, 1963-65; ret., 1965; shipyard cons. Aerojet-Gen. Corp., Jacksonville, Fla., 1965-68, asst. div. mgr. surface effect ships div., El Monte, Cal., 1968—. Decorated Legion of Merit, Bronze Star medal with Gold Star. Mem. Soc. Naval Architects and Marine Engrs. (hon. life v.p.), Am. Soc. Naval Engrs., Sigma Psi. Home: 630 W Huntington Dr Arcadia CA 91006 Office: 9200 E Flair Dr El Monte CA 91734

FARRINGTON, ELIZABETH PRUETT, govt. ofcl.; b. Tokyo, Japan, May 30, 1898; d. Robert Lee and Josephine (Baugh) Pruett; A.B., U. Wis., 1918; m. Joseph Rider Farrington (dec. June 19, 1954); children—Beverly (Mrs. Hugh F. Richardson), John. Pres. Dist. League Republican Women, Washington, 1947-49; nat. chmn. pub. relations Nat. Fedn. Women's Rep. Clubs, 1947-49, nat. pres., 1949-53; elected del. to Congress from Hawaii to succeed husband who died, 1954, reelected, 1954-57; pres., dir., Honolulu Star Bull., 1957-61, Hilo Tribune-Herald, 1957-61; pres. Hawaiian Broadcasting System, 1960- 61; pres., dir. Star-Bull. Printing Co., 1957-61; chmn. bd. dirs. Honolulu Lithograph Co., 1958-61; dir. Office Territories, Dept. Interior, 1969—. Mem. Am. Assn. U. Women, Nat. Council Chs., Theta Sigma Phi, Alpha Omicron Pi. Christian. Clubs: Pan Pacific Union, Congressional, Capitol Hill, 1925 F St (Washington). Home: 3180 Pacific Heights Rd Honolulu HI 96813 also 2445 Wyoming Av NW Washington DC 20008

FARRINGTON, SELWYN KIP, Jr., sportsman, writer; b. Orange, N.J., May 7, 1904; s. Selwyn Kip and Josephine (Taylor) F.; ed. Lawrenceville (N.J.) Sch., 1920; m. Sara Houston Chisholm. Aug. 6, 1934. Writer on outdoor sports especially salt water fishing, 1937—; salt water editor Field and Stream, 1937—. Mem. com. that designed emergency fishing kits to be placed in all life boats and rafts of U.S. Army, Navy and Coast Guard; sent to Western Pacific area by U.S. Army to show fishing and shooting pictures to armed forces, also to inspect railways, 1945; lectr. throughout U.S.; appeared 11 motion pictures on salt water fishing. Considered an authority on U.S. Mcht. Marine and shipping, also on Am. railroads, waterfowl, ice hockey. Decorated Order of Al Merito by Republic of Chile, 1943; Order of Merit by Republic of Peru, 1956. Mem. AM. Soc. Ichthyolgists, Am. Ornithologists Union. Republican. Episcopalian. Clubs: Chicago (Chgo.); St. Nicholas Hockey (past pres.), Racquet and Tennis (N.Y.C.); Chesapeake Duck (Brigham, Utah); Maidstone, Devon Yacht (East Hampton. L.I.); Beaver Dam Winter Sports (Locust Valley, N.Y.); Racquet (St. Louis); Southside Sportsmen L.I.; Anglers of N.Y.; Minnesota (St. Paul); hon. mem. many shooting fishing clubs throughout world. Author 23 books including: Ships of the U.S. Merchant Marine, 1947; Railroads of Today, 1949; Sport Fishing Boats, 1949; Fishing the Atlantic, 1949; Railroading the Modern Way, 1950; Fishing the Pacific, 1953; Railroading Around the World, 1954; Railroads of the Hour, 1958; Fishing with Hemingway and Glassell, 1971; Skates, Sticks and Men, 1971; The Santa Fe's Big Three, 1971. Contbr. chpts. and articles to various publs. Capt. of U.S. team in Internat. Fishing Matches, Eng. and Cuba. 1937. Held 6 world fishing records. Home: East Hampton NY 11937

FARRIOR, JEWEL REX, lawyer; b. Chipley, Fla., Oct. 5, 1896 s. Joseph R. and Gussie (Brown) F.; A.B., U. Fla., 1916, J.D., 1924; m. Lera Spotswood Finley, Nov. 24, 1925; children—Jewel Rex, Anne Preston (Mrs. Mitchell C. King, Jr.), Jennie Finley (Mrs. Joseph F. Cornelius, Jr.). Asst. football coach, asst. instr. algebra and history U. Fla., 1917-18; tchr. history, algebra, Latin, coach high schs. in Chipley, Pensacola, Gainesville, Fla., 1919-23; freshman football and basketball coach, varsity baseball coach, U. Fla., 1923-24; admitted to Fla. bar, 1924, since practiced in Tampa as mem. firm Shackleford, Farrior, Stallings & Evans; state attorney 13th Jud. Circuit Fla., 1933-53. Served with F.A., U.S. Army, 1918-19. Mem. Am., Fla., Tampa bar assns., Kappa Alpha, Phi Kappa Phi. Phi Delta Phi, Blue Key. Mason (Shriner, Jester), Kiwanian, Elk, K.P. Clubs: Palma Ceia Golf and Country; Tampa Yacht and Country, (Tampa). Home: 2413 Sunset Dr Tampa FL 33609 Office: Marine Bank Bldg Tampa FL 33601

FARRIS, CHARLES LOWELL, corporate ofcl.; b. Washington, Ind., Dec. 18, 1910; s. Bain and Pauline Frnaces (Love) F.; A.B., U. Notre Dame, 1933; student Army Indsl. Coll., Washington, 1944; m. Ruby Alberta Buzan, July 2, 1935; children—Charles M., William P., John T. Govt. ofcl., Washington and Dallas, 1935-49; chief field operations div. slum clearance and urban redevel. Housing and Home Finance Ag., 1949-51, dep. dir., 1951-53; exec. dir. Land Clearance for Redevel. Authority, St. Louis, 1953-66, exec. dir. St. Louis Housing Authority, 1955- 66; pres. Urban Programming Corp., 1966-69, St. Louis Land Clearance for Redevel. Authority, 1969—. Vice chmn. City Plan Commn. Served as lt. USNR, 1943-45. Mem. Nat. Assn. Housing and Redevel. Ofcls. (pres. 1959-60), Nat. Housing Conf., Inc. Democrat. Roman Catholic K.C. Club: Notre Dame (St. Louis). Home: 6515 Nottingham Av Saint Louis MO 63109 Office: 1300 Delmar Blvd St Louis MO 63103

FARRIS, JOHN LAUCHLAN, lawyer; b. Vancouver, B.C., Can., Sept. 5, 1911; s. John Wallace de Beque and Evelyn Fenwick (Keirstead) F.; B.A., U. B.C., 1931; LL.B., Harvard, 1934; m. Dorothy Beatrice Colledge, Sept. 13, 1933; children—Ann, John Haig de Beque, Katherine Colledge. Admitted to B.C. bar, 1935; now partner firm Farris, Farris, Vaughan, Wills & Murphy, Vancouver. Lectr. comml. law U. B.C., 1945-50; dir. Kelly, Douglas Co. Ltd., Sun Pub. Co. Ltd., Loomis Armored Car Service Ltd. Bd. govs. Crofton House Sch., 1959-63. Mem. Canadian (council 1955-58, vice chmn. 1960-61, v.p. for B.C. 1962-64, exec. com. 1966—), Vancouver (exec. council 1954-62, pres. 1959-60) bar assns., Law Soc. B.C. Mem. Liberal party. Clubs: Vancouver, Vancouver Lawn Tennis and Badminton; West Vancouver Yacht; Union (Victoria, B.C.). Office: 510 W Hastings St Vancouver 2 British Columbia Canada*

FARRIS, MILTON GLENN, oil co. exec., lawyer; b. Rockwood, Tenn., Oct. 13, 1906; s. Oscar Alexander and Myrtle Amy (Derrick) F.; LL.B., Atlanta Law Sch., 1935; m. Elizabeth Herzberg, Nov. 15, 1934; children—Sandra Glyn, Janet Gail, Milton Carl, William, Stuart. Admitted to Ga. Bar, 1935; practiced in Atlanta 1935—; asso. Atlanta div. Gulf Oil Corp., 1927—, mgr. bus analysis, market research, 1954-59, mgr. marketing services, 1960-62, mgr. Atlanta div., 1962-65, v.p. 1965—. Alderman, City Council, Atlanta, 1952-69; county commr. Fulton County, 1971—. Pres. bd. trustees Atlanta Pub. Library, 1940-52, awarded Trustee Citation at ALA Chgo. Conf. 1951. Mem. Am. Bar Assn., Ga. Bar Assn., West En Business Men's Assn. (dir.). Methodist. Mason (past master). Clubs: Lions (past pres.), Commerce, Capital City, Kiwanis (Atlanta). Home: 580 River Valley Rd NW Atlanta GA 30328 Office: Fulton County Ct House Annex Atlanta GA 30303

FARROW, JOSEPH HELMS, surgeon; b. Rocky Mount, Va., June 10, 1904; s. John Montgomery and Maggie (Shumate) F.; B.S., U. Va., 1926, M.D., 1930; m. Florence S. Skinner, Apr. 28, 1939. Intern St. Elizabeth's Hosp., Richmond, Va., 1930-31; resident surgery Watt's Hosp., Durham, N.C., 1931-33; fellow surgery and pathology Presbyn. Hosp., N.Y.C., 1933-34; mem. staff Meml. Hosp., N.Y.C., 1934—, asso. attending surgeon, 1947-60, attending surgeon, chief breast service, 1960-69, emeritus, 1969—; asso. vis. surgeon James Ewing Hosp., N.Y.C., 1959-60, vis. surgeon, 1960-69; asst. dir. tumor clinic, attending radiologist St. Agnes Hosp., White Plains, N.Y., 1938-42; cons. surgeon in oncology Nyack (N.Y.) Gen. Hosp., 1939—, Vassar Bros. Hosp., Poughkeepsie, 1939—. Harlem Valley State Hosp., Wingdale, N.Y., 1939-42, U.S. Naval Hosp., St. Albans, N.Y., 1946—, Yonkers (N.Y.) Gen. Hosp., 1953—, Stamford (Conn.) Hosp., 1963—, Fitkin Meml. Hosp., Neptune, N.J., 1963—, Strang Cancer Prevention Clinic, 1953-62; mem. faculty Cornell U. Coll. Medicine, 1950—, asso. prof. clin. surgery, 1960—; asso. clinician Sloan-Kettering Inst. Cancer Research, N.Y.C., 1954-60, clinician, 1960—. Served to comdr., M.C., USNR, 1942-46. Diplomate Am. Bd. Radiology; fellow A.C.S., A.M.A., N.Y. Acad. Medicine; mem. N.Y. State, N.Y. County med. socs., Am. Radium Soc. (treas. 1961- 63, pres. 1964-65), N.Y. Surg. Soc., James Ewing Soc. (pres. 1957), N.Y. Cancer Soc. (treas. 1963-64, pres. 1966-67), Pan-Pacific Surg. Assn., Am. Assn. Cancer Research, Am. Coll. Radiology, A.A.A.S.; hon. mem. Va. Surg. Soc., Honolulu Gen. Surg. Soc., Peruvian Acad. Surgery. Club: University (N.Y.C.). Contbr. profl. jours. Home: 333 E 68th St New York City NY 10021 Office: 112 E 74th St New York City NY 10021

FARROW, MIA VILLIERS, actress; b. Los Angeles, Feb. 9, 1946; d. John Villiers and Maureen Paula (O'Sullivan) Farrow; student pub. schs.; m. Andre Previn, Sept. 10, 1970; children—Matthew Phineas, and Sascha Villiers (twins). Actress appearing in TV and films; debut The Importance of Being Earnest, N.Y.C., 1964; starred in TV series Peyton Place; film include Guns at Batasi, Rosemary's Baby, Secret Ceremony, John and Mary, Peter Yates. Recipient best actress award French Acad., 1969, Golden Globe award, 1967, Rio Dijanero Film Festival award, 1969, Italian Acad. award, 1970. Home: The Haven Leigh nr Roigate Surrey England Office: 6399 Wilshire Blvd Los Angeles CA 90048

FARRUG, EUGENE JOSEPH, lawyer; b. Detroit, May 22, 1928; s. Michael Rosarius and Bridget (Foley) F.; B.B.A., U. Mich., 1950, J.D., 1958; m. Dolores Marie Augustine, Apr. 14, 1951; children—Elizabeth Marie, Eugene Joseph, Matthew Augustine, Pamela Ann, Bridget, Donna M. With Ford Motor Co., 1950-51; admitted to Ill. bar, 1958, since practiced in Chgo.; partner firm McKenna, Storer, Rowe, White & Haskell, 1962—. Served with USNR, 1951-55. Mem. Am., Dupage County, Ill., Chgo. bar assns., Trial Lawyers Club, Theta Chi, Phi Alpha Delta. Catholic. Kiwanian. Home: 206 N Lincoln St Hinsdale IL 60521 Office: 135 S LaSalle St Chicago IL 60603

FARSON, WILLIAM J., former labor union ofcl.; b. Phila., Dec. 9, 1904; student Swarthmore Coll. Advt. salesman Phila. Pub. Ledger, Phila. Inquirer; organized Phila. Camden Advt. Guild, AFL, 1936; mem. internat. exec. bd. Am. Newspaper Guild, 1937-40, 43-47, dir. orgn. of Guild, 1947-51, sec.- treas., 1951-55, exec. v.p., 1955-69; v.p. for N. Am. of Internat. Fedn. Journalists, Brussels, Belgium, until 1970. Mem. U.S. Nat. Commn. for UNESCO. Home: 4100 W St NW Washington DC 20007

FARTHING, BARTON ROBY, educator; b. Watauga County, N.C., Feb. 20, 1916; s. Herbert and Stella Doris (Farthing) F.; B.S., Wade Forest Coll., 1938; B.S., N.C. State U., 1952, M.S., 1954, Ph.D., 1958; m. Selma Hazel Thomas, May 24, 1938; children—Selma (Mrs. William Shinder), Barton, Teddi (Mrs. Dennis Stewart). Instr., asst. prof. N.C. State U., 1954-59; prof., statistician La. State U., 1959-64, prof., head dept. exptl. statistics, 1964—. Served with AUS, 1943-46. Mem. Biometric Soc., Am. Dairy Sci. Assn., Am. Soc. Animal Sci., A.A.A.S., Sigma Xi, Kappa Phi Kappa, Phi Kappa Phi, Gamma Sigma Delta. Baptist (chmn. bd. deacons). Home: 261 E Parkland Baton Rouge LA 70806

FARUKI, MAHMUD TAJI, psychiatrist, hosp. adminstr.; b. Jerusalem, Palestine, Dec. 18, 1919; s. Yousef Taji and Suad R. (Husseini) F.; M.D., Am. U., Beirut, Lebanon, 1945; m. Rita T. Trownsell, June 19, 1948; children—Charles Yousef, Rita Jane. Came to U.S., 1946, naturalized, 1952. Rotating intern Charity Hosp., New Orleans, 1946-47; rotating resident Mercy Hosp., Hamilton, O., 1947-48; resident in neuropsychiatry Pilgrim State Hosp., Brentwood, L.I., N.Y., 1948-51; practiced in Tinley Park, Ill., 1952-53; staff psychiatrist Dayton (O.) State and Receiving Hosp., 1955-58, dir. adult receiving hosp., 1959-61, dir., supt., 1961—; cons. in psychiatry USAF Hosp., Wright-Patterson AFB, O., 1961—, Old Sailors and Soldiers Home, Xenia, O., 1961—, Vis. Nurses Assn., Dayton, 1964—. Sec. research com. div. mental hygiene State of Ohio. Mem. Hosp. Planning Council Greater Miami Valley, Pastoral Counseling Service, Ch. Fedn. Greater Dayton; pres. Dayton Met. Hosp. Fedn., 1962. Bd. dirs. Adult Psychiat. Clinic, Dayton, Sr. Citizens' Center, Dayton, Social Health Assn. Dayton and Montgomery and Greene Counties, Montgomery County Mental Health Assn., Dayton Area Council Alcholism; bd. dirs. Health and Welfare Planning Council. Served to maj. M.C., U.S. Army, 1953-55. Diplomate Am. Bd. Psychiatry and Neurology. Fellow Am. Psychiat. Assn.; mem. A.M.A., Ohio Med. Assn., Montgomery County Med. Soc. (sr.), Ohio Psychiat. Assn., Assn. Supts. Mental Hosps. in Ohio (pres. 1965), Ohio Hosps. Assn. (dir. S.W. dist.). Home: 603 Allenwood Ct Dayton OH 45420 Office: 2335 Wayne Av Dayton OH 45420

FARVER, ALVIN D., dentist; b. Topeka, Ind., Oct. 25, 1893; s. Moses A. and Mary Elizabeth (Hostetler) F.; D.D.S., Ind. U., 1914; m. Marie Ellen Troyer, June 20, 1918; children—Charlene (Mrs. Jack E. Farley), Gloria Jean (Mrs. Richard L. Payton), Patricia Ann (Mrs. R. Jerry Lusk). Practice of dentistry, Miami Beach, Fla., 1927- -; instr. Dade County Dental Research Clinic, 1948—, pres., 1952-53; cons. restorative dentistry VA. Served as 1st lt., Dental Corps, U.S. Army, 1917-19. Fellow Internat. Coll. Dentists, Am. Coll. Dentists, Fla. Dental Soc. (pres. 1959-60); mem. Am. Dental Assn. (1st v.p.), East Coast Dist. (pres. 1942-43), Chgo., Miami Beach, Miami (pres. 1940) dental socs., Am. Acad. Restorative Dentistry, Fedn. Dentaire Internationale, Fla. Acad. Dental Practice Adminstrn., Am. Legion, 40 and 8, Xi Psi Phi. Mason (Shriner). Home: 4291 Nautilus Dr Miami Beach FL 33140 Office: 333 Arthur Godfrey Rd Miami Beach FL 33140

FARWELL, ALBERT EDMOND, govt. ofcl.; b. Providence, June 7, 1915; s. Albert Potter and Elizabeth (Shelmerdine) F.; A.B., Brown U., 1935; M.A., U. Ariz., 1937; m. Elizabeth Fuller Thurlow, May 18, 1940; children—Bruce Albert, Christopher James. Various non govtl. positions, 1939-45; exec. dir. Fgn. Trade Found., 1945-46; sr. editor Bur. Nat. Affairs, Washington, 1946-48; chief procedures and publ. br., Dept. Commerce, 1948-49; econ. analyst ELA, Greece, 1949-51; dep. dir. strategic controls div. Dept. Commerce, 1951-52; program analyst MSA, FOA, 1952-54; chief Near East div. FOA, ICA, 1955; program officer Near East and So. Asia, ICA, 1956-59; spl. asst. to undersec. mut. security Dept. State, 1959-60; dep. dir. AID, Nepal, 1960-65, dir., Costa Rica, 1965-67, dep. dir., Laos, 1967, dir., 1968, asso. dir., Vietnam, 1969—. Recipient Meritorious Service award ICA, 1953, 55, Dept. State, 1960. Mem. Am. Acad. Polit. and Social Sci., Am. Fgn. Service Assn. Address: USAID/ADLD APO San Francisco CA 96243

FARWELL, ELWIN D., coll. pres.; b. Branch County, Mich., May 1, 1919; s. Don J. and Dessa (Clingan) F.; B.S., Mich. State U., 1943, M.S., 1947; Ed.D., U. Cal. at Berkeley, 1959; B.D., Pacific Lutheran Theol. Sem., Berkeley, 1959; LL.D., Loras Coll.; m. Helen Irene Hill, Aug. 23, 1942; children—Don Lucian, Helen Kay, James Lyman, Judith Anne. Instr. animal husbandry Mich. State U., 1947-49, asst. prof., 1949-55; cons. point 4 program State Dept. U. Nacional, Colombia, S.A., 1952; adminstrv. asst. to chmn. Center Study Higher Edn., U. Cal. at Berkeley, 1956-59; ordained to ministry Luth. Ch., 1958; pastor in Andrew, Ia., 1959-61; academic dean Cal. Luth. Coll., Thousand Oaks, Cal., 1961- 63; pres. Luther Coll., Decorah, Ia., 1963—. Mem. Ia. Gov.'s Com. Conservation Natural Resources, 1964—, Ia. Gov's Commn. Coop. State and Local govt., 1964-66; mem. Ia. Coordinating Council Higher Edn., 1967—, pres. 1968-69; chmn. Com. Intergovtl. Coop. and Communication, 1964-65, Gov.'s Com. on Govt. Reorgn., 1966, State Adv. Com. on Community and Jr. Coll., 1965-69; mem. exec. com. Ia. Assn. Ind. Colls. and Univs., 1964—; mem. Decorah Human Relations Council, 1968—; mem. exec. com. Norwegian-Am. Mus. Assn., 1965—. Chmn. World Brotherhood Found., 1962—; mem. Am. Scandinavian Found.; bd. govs. Cal. Luth. Ednl. Found., 1957-59; bd. Nat. Luth. Campus Ministry, 1966—. Served to capt. AUS, 1943-46; PTO. Mem. Symra Soc., World League Norsemen, Central States Coll. Assn. (dir. 1964—, chmn. 1967), Norwegian-Am. Hist. Assn., Phi Delta Kappa, Alpha Gamma Rho, Alpha Zeta. Rotarian. Author: Livestock Development and Selection, 1951; Stability of Change. 1964; also articles profl. jours., encys. Home: 501 High St Decorah IA 52101

FARWELL, F. EVANS, steamship co. exec.; b. New Orleans, 1906; grad. U. Va., 1929. Pres. Milliken & Farwell, Inc., New Orleans, also dir; chmn. bd. and exec. com. Delta Steamship Lines, Inc.; pres., dir.

Westover Planting Co., Ltd.; dir. mem. exec. com. TCO Industries, Inc. Mem. Fed. Res. Bd., 6th dist., Atlanta. Mem. New Orleans Pub. Belt R.R. Commn.; mem. exec. com. Am. Sugar Cane League. Home: 5824 St Charles Av New Orleans LA 70115 Office: Whitney Bldg New Orleans LA 70130

FARWELL, FRANK LESTER, ins. co. exec.; b. Worcester, Mass., May 28, 1914; s. Frank Lester and Flora Louise (Arrington) F.; B.B.A., Boston U., 1937; grad. Advanced Mgmt. Program, Harvard, 1957; L.H.D., Boston U. 1969; m. Mary Lincoln Chambers, Sept. 24, 1938; children—Louise A. (Mrs. Charles W. Domina), Linda (Mrs. William Lange), With Liberty Mut. Ins. Co., Boston, 1934—, successively clk., asst. treas., treas., 1934-58, v.p., 1959-61, exec. v.p., 1961-62, pres., 1962—, dir.; pres. Liberty Mut. Fire Ins. Co., Liberty Life Assurance Co.; dir. First Nat. Bank Boston, First Nat. Boston Corp., USM Corp., Boston Edison Co., Dennison Mfg. Corp.; bd. trustees Newton Savs. Bank. Corporator Boston Mus. Sci., Northeastern U.; bd. dirs. Mass. Bay United Fund. Served as officer USNR, World War II. Clubs: Union, Wellesley Country, Algonquin, Commercial. Home: 60 Redington Rd Needham MA 02192 Office: 175 Berkeley St Boston MA 02117

FARWELL, JOHN VILLIERS, III, business exec.; b. Chgo. Nov. 22, 1895; s. Arthur L. and Katherine (Isham) F.; A.B., Yale, 1918; m. Margaret Willing, May 12, 1926; children—Joan, John. Pres., treas. dir. Sanitary Scale Co., Chgo. dir. LaSalle Nat. Bank, Nat. Tea Co., Served as naval aviator U.S. Navy, World War I. Republican. Presbyn. Clubs: Racquet, Saddle and Cycle (Chgo.). Home: 1260 Astor St Chicago IL 60610 Office: 664 N Michigan Av Chicago IL 60611

FARWELL, LORING CHAPMAN, educator; b. Chgo., June 29, 1915; s. Edward Parris and Elizabeth (Farwell) F.; B.S., Mass. Inst. Tech., 1937; M.B.A., Northwestern U., 1940, Ph.D., 1955; m. Martha Jane Campbell, Jan. 31, 1942; children—Edward Parris III, David Loring. With Sheridan, Farwell and Morrison, Chgo., 1937-39; mem. faculty Northwestern U., 1946—, prof. econs., 1955—. Served with AUS, 1941-46. Mem. Am. Econ. Assn., Am. Finance Assn., Econometric Soc., Financial Analysts Assn., Inst. Mgmt. Scis., Am. Assn. Univ. Profs. Club: University (Chgo.). Author: (with G. Leffler) The Stock Market, 3d edit., 1963; (with J.T. O'Neil and V. Boyd) Quantitative Controls for Business, 1965; (with others) Financial Institutions, 5th edit., 1971. Home: 735 Happ Rd Northfield IL 60093 Office: Northwestern Univ Evanston IL 60201

FASANO, CLARA, sculptor; b. Castellaneta, Italy, Dec. 14, 1900; d. Pasquale and Julia (de Feudis) Fasano; student Cooper Union Art Inst., Art Students League, 1917-21, Julien Academie, Colarossi, 1924-26; scholarship, Rome, Italy, 1922-24; m. Jean de Marco, July 8, 1936. Came to U.S., 1907, naturalized, 1939. Exhibited at Salon d'Automne, Paris, 1925; worked in own studio, exhibited in Rome, 1926-32; tchr. sculpture, adult edn. Bd. Edn. N.Y., 1948-58; exhibited works Worlds Fair, N.Y.C., 1939, Whitney Mus., Nat Acad. Design, Pa. Acad., Art Inst. Chgo., Met. Mus. Art, Am.-Brit. Center, N.Y.C., Ferragil, Buckholz galleries. others; works represented in permanent collections Met. Museum Art, N.Y.C., Manhattanville Coll. Sacred Heart, Purchase, N.Y., Norfolk Mus. Arts and Scis., Smithsonian Instn., Washington, Syracuse U., also pvt. collections U.S., abroad; tchr. Manhattanville Coll., Purchase, N.Y. Recipient Anonymous prize Nat. Assn. Women Artists, 1945, Marcia Brady Tucker prize, 1950, medal of Honor for sculpture, 63d ann. exhbn., 1955; grant and citation Nat. Inst. Arts and Letters, 1952; M. Grumbacher prize, Audubon Artists, 1954; medal of Honor, Nat. Assn. Women Artists, 1955; medal of Honor with citation, Am. Artists Mag., Audubon Annual Exhbn., 1956; hon. mention, Nat. Sculptor Soc., 1955. Archtl. League, N.Y., Gold Medals Exhbn., 1956; French medal N.A.D., 1965; Peter Caesar Alberti award Italian Execs. Am., Inc., 1967; Dessie Greer award (sculpture) N.A.D., 1968. N.A. Fellow Nat. Sculpture Soc.; mem. Audubon Artists, Sculptors Guild, Nat. Assn. Women Artists. Home: Cervaro-Prov Frosinone Italy Office: 1083 Fifth Av New York City NY 10028

FASANO, RENATO, conductor. Conductor Virtuosi de Roma. Address: (A) 174 Via Arcimede Rome Italy *

FASCELL, DANTE BRUNO, congressman; b. Bridgehampton, N.Y., Mar. 9, 1917; s. Charles A. and Mary (Gullotti) F.; LL.B., U. Miami, Coral Gables, Fla., 1938; m. Jeanne-Marie Pelot, Sept. 19, 1941; children—Sandra J., Toni F., Dante J. Admitted to Fla. bar, 1938, practiced in Miami, 1938-41, 46—, mem. Turner, Hendrick, Fascell, Giulford, Goldstein & McDonald, and predecessor firms, 1950—; legal attaché state legislative delegation Dade County, Fla., 1947-50; mem. Fla. Legislature, 1950-54; mem. 84th- 92d Congresses from 12th Dist. Fla. Pres. Dade County Young Democratic Club, 1947-48. Served as officer AUS, 1942-46. Named one of ten outstanding legislators Fla. Legislature, 1951, 53; one of five outstanding men in Fla., Fla. Jr. C. of C., 1951. Mem. Miami Jr. C. of C. (pres. 1947-48), Am., Dade County, Coral Gables bar assns., Fla. Bar, Am. Legion, Mil. Order World Wars, Kappa Sigma. Democrat. Clubs: Lions, Italian-American (pres. 1947-48). Home: 6300 SW 99th Terrace Miami FL 33156 Office: 740 Ponce de Leon Blvd Coral Gables FL 33134 also House Office Bldg Washington DC 20515

FASI, FRANK FRANCIS, mayor; b. East Hartford, Conn., Aug. 27, 1920; s. Carmelo and Josephine (Lupo) F.; B.S., Trinity Coll., 1924; m. Florence Omaha, Mar. 10, 1946; children—Toni Anne, Kathleen Helen, Carl Frederick, Francesa, Paul F. Pres. Frank F. Pasi Supply Co., 1946—; candidate Ho. Reps., Hawaii, 1950, candidate for mayor, 1952, 54; mem. Dem. Nat. Com. for Hawaii, 1952-56. Mem. Hawaii Senate, 1958-59; councilman at large, Honolulu, 1965-69, mayor, 1969—. Served as capt. USMC, 1942-46. Home: Alexander St Office: 2054 Makiki St Honolulu HI 96822

FASMAN, GERALD DAVID, educator; b. Drumheller, Alta., Can., May 28, 1925; s. Morris and Sarah (Stauffer) F.; B.S., U. Alta., 1948; Ph.D., Cal. Inst. Tech., 1952; postgrad. Cambridge (Eng.) U., 1951-53, Eidg. Technische Hochschule, Zurich, Switzerland, 1953-54, Weizmann Inst. Sci., Rehovoth, Israel, 1954-55; m. Jean Schalit, Dec. 27, 1953; children—Michael, Daniel, Johathan. Came to U.S., 1955, naturalized, 1964. Research asst. Children's Cancer Research Found., Childrens Med. Center, Boston, 1955-56; research asso. pathology Childrens Med. Center and Children's Cancer Research Found., Boston, 1957-61; asst. in pathology Harvard Med. Sch., 1957-58, research asso. pathology, 1958-60, research asso. biol. chemistry, 1960-61; lectr. protein chemistry Boston U., 1958-59; asst. head biophys. chemistry lab. Childrens Cancer Research Found., Boston, 1959-61; tutor in biochem. sci. Harvard, 1960-62; established investigator Am. Heart Assn., 1961-66; asst. prof. biochemistry Brandeis U., Waltham, Mass., 1961-63, asso. prof., 1963-67, prof., 1967—, Rosenfield prof. biochemistry, 1971—. Cons. African Primary Sci. Program, Ednl. Services, Inc., Dar es Salam, Tanzania, 1966, mem. program steering com., Accra, Ghana, 1967, mem. adv. group, 1968-69. NSF sr. postdoctoral fellow Protein Inst., Osaka (Japan) U. and Weizmann Inst. Sci., 1967-68. Fellow A.A.A.S., Am. Inst. Chemists; mem. Am. Chem. Soc., Biophys. Soc., Am. Soc. Biol. Chemists, Chem. Soc. (London), N.Y. Acad. Sci., Sigma Xi. Editor: Biological Macromolecules series. Home: 69 Kingswood Rd Newton MA 02166 Office: Brandeis U Waltham MA 02154

FASMAN, MICHAEL JACOB, lawyer; b. Chgo., July 17, 1909; s. Samuel and Beatrice (Horwitz) F.; LL.B., DePaul U., 1931; m. Betty Spector, Dec. 6, 1931 (dec. Aug. 1959); children—Barbara Ellen (Mrs. Kenneth Colgrove), Beryl Sheila (Mrs. Serge Zimberoff); m. 2d, Marjorie Lesser, Mar. 30, 1961. Admitted to Ill. bar, 1931, Cal. bar, 1947; practice in Chgo., 1931-46, Beverly Hills, Cal., 1947—; partner firm Allen, Fasman & Janger, 1947—. Sec. Fasallen Investments, Beverly Hills, 1951—; dir. Allied Auto Parks, Inc., Los Angeles, Royal Parking Service, Los Angeles. Sect. chmn. United Crusade, 1968, vice chmn. spl. gifts, 1970. Bd. dirs. Com. to Combat Huntington's Disease, Plays for Living, Reiss Davis Child Study Center. Mem. Ill., Los Angeles County, Beverly Hills, Chgo. bar assns., State Bar Cal., Am. Arbitration Assn. (panel). Club: Beverly Hills Tennis (pres. 1967-68). Home: 701 N Rexford Dr Beverly Hills CA 90210 Office: 9601 Wilshire Blvd Beverly Hills CA 90210

FASSEL, VELMER ARTHUR, educator, phys. chemist; b. Frohna, Mo., Apr. 26, 1919; s. Arthur Edward and Alma (Poppitz) F.; B.A., S.E. Mo. State Coll., 1941; Ph.D., Ia. State Coll., 1947; m. Mary Alice Katschke, July 25, 1943. Chemist, Manhattan Project, Ia. State U., Ames, 1942-47, mem. faculty, 1947—, prof. chemistry, sr. scientist, 1956—, sect. chief Ames Lab., AEC, 1966-69, dep. dir. Inst. Atomic Research and Ames Lab., AEC, 1969—. Tech. adviser Atoms for Peace Conf., Geneva, Switzerland, 1958; chmn. panel on analytic methods Nat. Acad. Sci., 1958-61. Recipient Distinguished Alumni award S.E. Mo. State Coll., 1965, award Spectroscopy Soc. Pitts., 1969, Maurice F. Hasler award, 1971, Anachem award, 1971. Fellow A.A.A.S., Optical Soc. Am.; mem. Soc. for Applied Spectroscopy (Ann. medal 1964), Am. Chem. Soc., Am. Inst. Physics, Coblentz Soc., Sigma Xi. Research, publs. on analytical atomic emission and absorption spectroscopy, spectroscopic instrumentation, analytical chemistry. Home: Route 4 Timberlane Heights Ames IA 50010

FASSNACHT, PAUL WILLIAM, corp. exec.; b. Phila., Nov. 29, 1905; s. Frank Eugene and Flora (Fries) F.; m. Maxine Wooldridge, Nov. 26, 1958; children—Frank E., Joan (Mrs. Stopher). With Technicolor, Inc., 1929—, pres., chief exec. officer, 1966-71, also dir., active cons., mem. exec. and finance coms.; former mng. dir., dir. Technicolor S.p.A., Rome; former chmn. bd. Technicolor Ltd., London; former pres., dir. Technicolor Fotografica, S.A., Barcelona, Spain; dir. Schick Electric Inc. Recipient Sci. award Acad. Motion Picture Arts and Scis.; spl. citation Am. TV Commls. Festival, 1967. Fellow Soc. Motion Picture and TV Engrs.; mem. Acad. Motion Picture Arts and Scis., Nat. Acad. TV Arts and Scis. Home: 2222 Av of Stars Los Angeles CA 90067 also 1195 E 1st St Tustin CA 92680 Office: 6311 Romaine St Hollywood CA 90038

FAST, HOWARD, author; b. N.Y.C., Nov. 11, 1914; s. Barney and Ida (Miller) F.; ed. George Washington High Sch., N.Y. C., Nat. Acad. Design; m. Betty Cohen, June 6, 1937; children—Rachel Ann, Jonathan. Began writing, 1932; European corr. for Esquire and Coronet mags., 1945; mem. overseas staff OWI, 1942-43; Army film project, 1944. Mem. World Peace Council, 1950-55. Am. Labor Party Congl. candidate 23d Dist., N.Y., 1952. Recipient Bread Loaf scholarship, 1935, Stalin Internat. Peace prize, 1953; Annual Book award, Secondary Edn. Bd., 1962. Jewish religion. Author: (novels) Two Valleys, 1932; Strange Yesterday, 1933; The Children, 1936; Place in the City, 1937; Conceived in Liberty, 1939; Haym Salomon (biography), 1941; The Last Frontier, 1941; Baden Powell (biography), 1941; The Unvanquished, 1942; Citizen Tom Paine, 1943; Freedom Road, 1944; Peekskill, U.S.A., 1951; Spartacus, 1952, The Naked God, 1957; Moses, Prince of Egypt, 1958. Editor: Selected Works of Paine, 1945; Collection of Short Stories: Patrick Henry and the Frigate's Keel, 1945; The American (biography of Peter Altgeld, former gov. of Ill.), 1946; Carkton, 1947; My Glorious Brothers, 1948; Departure, 1949; Literature and Reality, 1949; The Proud and the Free, 1950; The Passion of Sacco and Vanzetti, 1953; Silas Timberman, 1954; The Story of Lola Gregg: The Winston Affair, 1959, April Morning, 1961; Power, 1962; The Crossing (play), 1962; Agrippa's Daughter, 1964; The Hill (drama), 1963; Torquemada, 1966; The Hunter and the Trap, 1967; The Jews, 1968. Contbr. Saturday Evening Post, Ladies Home Jour., Saturday Rev., Midstream, Esquire. Office: care Paul Reynolds 599 Fifth Av New York City NY 10017

FATELEY, WILLIAM GENE, scientist, educator, adminstr.; b. Franklin, Ind., May 17, 1929; s. Nolan William and Georgia (Scott) F.; A.B., Franklin Coll., 1951, D.Sc. (hon.), 1965; postgrad. Northwestern U., 1951-53, U. Minn., 1956-57; Ph.D., Kan. State U., 1956; m. Wanda Lee Glover, Sept. 1, 1953; children—Leslie Kaye, W. Scott, Kevin L., Jonathan H., Robin L. Head phys. measurement Dow Chem. Co., Williamsburg, Va., 1958-60; fellow Mellon Inst., Pitts., 1960-62, head sci. relations, 1962-64, asst. to pres., 1964-67, sr. fellow in ind. research, 1965—, asst. to v.p. for research, 1967—; prof. chemistry Carnegie-Mellon U., 1970—. Dir. Pitts. Conf. on Analytical Chemistry and Applied Spectroscopy, 1964-65, pres., 1970-71; asso. editor Jour. Applied Spectroscopy. Recipient Coblentz award for outstanding contbn. to molecular spectroscopy, 1965; named 1st outstanding grad. chemistry Kan. State U., 1964. Mem. Am. Chem. Soc. (pres. phys.-inorganic sect. Pitts. 1969-70), Sigma Xi, Sigma Alpha Epsilon, Phi Lambda Epsilon, Pi Mu Epsilon. Contbr. articles profl. jours. Home: 3 Alma Dr Pittsburgh PA 15238

FATEMI, NASROLLAH SAIFPOUR, educator; b. Nain, Iran, June 15, 1917; s. Saifulolma and Tuba (Tabe Tabai) F.; came to U.S., 1946; naturalized, 1960; B.A. with honors, Stuart Meml. Coll., Isfahan, Iran, 1932; M.A., Columbia, 1949; Ph.D., New Sch. Social Research, 1954; m. Shayestech Ostowar, May 10, 1932; children—Faramarz, Fariborz, Farivar. Mem., v.p. legislative council Province Isfahan, Iran, 1936-39; mayor Shiraz, Iran, 1939-41; gov.-gen. Province Fars, Iran, 1941-43; mem. Iranian Parliament, 1943-47; rep. Iran UNESCO Conf., 1948, Internat. Congress Americanists, 1949; del. Iran to UN, 1952-53; mem. Iranian Mission presenting case of Iran to UN Security Council, 1951; econ., polit. adviser Permanent Delegation Iran to UN, 1952-53; lectr. Asia Inst., 1949; tchr. Oriental culture and civilization Princeton, 1950-55; prof. social scis. Fairleigh Dickinson U., 1955—, chmn. dept., 1960—, dean Grad. Sch., 1965- -, dir. Grad. Inst. for Internat. Studies. Mem. Am. Assn. Middle Eastern Studies (exec. bd.), Acad. Polit. Sci., Inst. Mediterranean Affairs (vice chmn.), Am. Assn. U. Profs. Author: Diplomatic History of Persia, 1951; Oil Diplomacy, 1954; The Dollar Crisis, 1964; also 5 books in Persian. Co-author: Humanities in the Age of Science, 1967. Home: 47 Chestnut Ridge Rd Saddle River NJ 07458 Office: 1000 River Rd Teaneck NJ 07666

FATES, JOSEPH GILBERT, TV producer; b. Newark, Sept. 29, 1914; s. Joseph and Dora (Racicot) Faatz; B.S., U. Va., 1937; m. Faye Appleberry Smith, Sept. 29, 1946; children—Decia, Amy, Dailey Gilbert. Actor, stage mgr. Broadway legitimate theatre, 1937-40; writer, producer, perfomer CBS-TV, 1941- 50; free-lance TV producer, 1950-53; exec. producer Goodson-Todman Prodns., v.p. Goodson-Todman Enterprises, Ltd., 1953—; exec. producer What's My Line, To Tell the Truth, I've Got a Secret. Served to lt. USCGR, 1942-46. Mem. Sigma Nu. Home: Boulder Brook Rd Greenwich CT 06830 Office: 375 Park Av New York City NY 10022

FATT, ARTHUR CORNELL, advt. exec.; b. N.Y.C., July 7, 1904; s. William and Josephine (Lesser) F.; student N.Y.U., 1921-23; m. Virginia Agnes Finder, Sept. 5, 1926 (dec.); children—Barbara Ann Heine, Marjorie Jean Chester; m. 2d, Barbara Cappeau, Feb. 17, 1948. Founder chmn. Grey Advt., Inc.; chmn. Grey Advt. Ltd., Montreal, P.Q., Can.; dir. Charles Hobson and Grey Ltd., London, Dorland & Greys, S.A., Paris, Brussels; dir. Rasgo-Grey Madrid, Grey Advt. Agy., Sydney, Australia, Grey-Daiko, Tokyo, Kittay-Grey, Caracas. Mem. exec. com. Nat. Marketing Adv. Com., Dept. Commerce. Vice pres., trustee Hillside Hosp.; trustee Fedn. Jewish Philanthropies of N.Y. Fellow Brandeis U. Jewish Religion. Clubs: Pinnacle, N.Y. Unviersity, Harmonie (N.Y.C.); Metropolis Country (White Plains, N.Y.); Palma Yacht (Palma de Mallorea, Spain). Author: How To Increase Your Business Thru Department Stores, 1941. Contbr. advt. publs. Home: 941 Park Av New York City NY 10028 also Cala Vicky Illetas Palma de Mallorea Spain Office: 777 3d Av New York City NY 10022

FATZER, HAROLD RALPH, judge Supreme Ct. Kan.; b. Fellsburg, Kan., Aug. 3, 1910; s. John R. and Rella (Shannon) F.; student Kan. State U., 1928-30; J.D., Washburn Coll., 1933; m. Frances Josephine Schwaup, Mar. 21, 1936; 1 son, John Richard. Admitted to Kan. bar, 1933, and practiced in Kinsley, 1933-41; admitted to bar of U.S. Supreme Ct., 1950; county atty. Edwards County, 1934-41; chief counsel State Dept. Social Welfare, 1941-43; asst. atty. gen. for Kan., 1943, 45-49, atty. gen., 1949-56; justice Supreme Ct. Kan., 1956—. Mem. Appellate Judges Seminar, N.Y.U. Sch. Law, 1959. Trustee Kan. Masonic Found., Washburn Coll. Recipient Distinguished Service award Washburn Law Sch. Assn., 1967; named hon. asst. atty. gen. Ga., 1954; admiral Navy State of Neb. Mem. Nat. Assn. Attys. Gen. (pres. 1952-53), Kan. Bar Assn., Am. Bar Assn., Kansas County Attys. Assn. (pres. 1939- 40), Am. Legion, 40 and 8, Am. Vets., Am. Judicature Soc., Washburn U. Alumni Assn. (pres. 1966, Distinguished Service award 1964), D.A.V., Inst. of Judicial Adminstrn., Kan. Hist. Soc. (dir.), Washburn Law Sch. Assn. (dir.), Kappa Sigma, Delta Theta Phi, Tau Delta Pi. Republican. Conglist. Mason (Shriner). Home: Kinsley KS also 1415 Ward Pkwy Topeka KS 66604 Office: Statehouse Topeka KS 66612

FAUBER, JOSEPH EVERETTE, Jr., architect, historian; b. Charlottesville, Va., Aug. 15, 1908; s. Joseph Everette and Alma (Carter) F.; B.S., U. Va., 1929; m. Ella Whitmore Williams, Sept. 5, 1936; children—Joseph Everette III, Rodger Williams, Stuart Carter. Archtl. draftsman Perry, Shaw & Hepburn, Boston, 1930-32; partner Fauber & Poston, Lynchburg, Va., 1933-41; chief architect Wiley & Wilson, Camp Ritchie, Md., 1941-43; prin. J. Everette Fauber, Jr., F.A.I.A., Lynchburg, 1945—; instr. U. Va., 1929-30; restoration architect for Old Appomattox Courthouse, The Octagon (Washington), John Marshall House (Richmond), St. Patrick's Ch., Newcastle, Me.; Mem. Va. Bd. Examiners Architects, Engrs. and Land Surveyors, 1949-59; Va. State Preservation Coordinator, 1968-71; mem. adv. bd. Historic Lexington, Inc., 1969—. Pres. Citizens Com. Greater Lynchburg, 1968; mem. Lynchburg Planning Commn., 1950-52. Recipient William C. Noland award, Va. chpt. A.I.A., 1967. Fellow A.I.A. Home: 3921 Royal Blvd Lynchburg VA 24503 Office: 2309 Atherholt Rd Lynchburg VA 24501

FAUBUS, ORVAL EUGENE, former gov. Ark.; b. Combs, Ark., Jan. 7, 1910; s. John Samuel and Addie (Joslen) F.; student pub. schs.; m. Alta Haskins, Nov. 21, 1931; 1 son, Farrell Eugene; m 2d, Elizabeth Thompson-Westmoreland, Mar. 21, 1969; adopted children—Kim, Ricci. Rural sch. tchr., 1928-38; circuit clk., county recorder, Huntsville, Ark., 1939-42; acting postmaster, Huntsville, 1946-47, postmaster, 1953-54; editor, owner, pub. Madison County Record, Huntsville, 1947-69; owner Ark. Statesman, Little Rock, 1960-69; hwy. commr., adminstrv. asst. to gov., dir. hwys. for Ark., 1949-53; gov. Ark., 1955-67; pres. Recreational Enterprises, Inc., operating theme park Dogpatch U.S.A., in the Ozarks. Chmn., So. Gov.'s Conf., 1963. Rural scout commr. N.W. Ark., 1924-38. Served as maj. inf., AUS, 1942-46. Decorated Bronze Star. Mem. Madison County C. of C. (pres. 1953-54). Am. Legion, V.F.W., D.A.V., Sons Confederate Vets. Baptist. Mason (32), Elk. Club: Huntsville Lions (sec.-treas. 1939). Home: Skyline Terrace Harrison, AR 72601.

FAUCETT, PHILIP MATSON, Jr., govt. ofcl.; b. Chgo., Mar. 28, 1917; s. Philip Matson and Beulah Woodward (Bach) F.; B.S., U. Ill., 1940, postgrad. in Econs., 1947-50; M.B.A., Harvard, 1942; postgrad. in Econs., U. Chgo., 1950-52; m. Elizabeth Pusey Lohmann, Sept. 7, 1946; children—Philip Matson III, Melissa Jane, Carolyn Woodward. Economist, Fed. Res. Bank of Chgo., 1950-52; lectr. Grad. Sch. Bus. Adminstrn., Northwestern U., 1952-58; sr. economist, dir. research Wolf Mgmt. Engring. Co., Chgo., 1958-63; with AID, State Dept., 1963—; banking adviser, Bolivia, 1963-65, capital assistance officer, 1965-66; asst. dir. operations Regional Office, Guatemala; 1966-67, dep. mission dir., Bolivia, 1967-69; asst. dir. industry, Vietnam, 1969, asst. dir. commodity mgmt. and indsl. devel., 1970, dep. asso. dir. comml. and capital assistance, 1970-71; dep. dir. mission, Ecuador, 1971—; adviser to Agrl. Bank of Bolivia, Mining Bank of Bolivia, Indsl. Devel. Bank of Bolivia, Central Am. Bank for Econ. Integration, Bolivia Ministry Economy, Artisan's Bank, Israel, Israel Productivity Center, Indsl. Devel. Center, Vietnam. Chmn. bd. Am. Embassy Commissary, Bolivia; bd. dirs. Coop. Sch., La Paz, Bolivia, 1968-69. Served with USAAF, 1943-44. Mem. Am. Econ. Assn., Econometric Soc., Am. Assn. Mgmt. Scis. (treas. Chgo. chpt. 1953-54), Order of Artus, Beta Theta Pi, Beta Gamma Sigma. Rotarian. Club: University (Chgo.). Home: 910 Lincolnshire Dr Champaign IL 61820 Office: USAID ADCCA APO San Francisco CA 96243

FAUCETT, RALPH EUGENE, naval med. officer; b. Milton, Ind., July 28, 1916; s. Clark E. and Iva Mabel (Bertsch) F.; B.S., Ind. U., 1938, M.D., 1942; A.B., Earlham Coll., 1939; postgrad. Sch. Medicine U. Pa., 1948; m. Elizabeth C. Carpenter, June 1, 1941. Intern U.S. Naval Hosp., Great Lakes, Ill., 1942-43; resident U.S. Naval Hosp., San Diego, 1946-48, 49-70; commd. ensign USNR, 1941, advanced through grades to rear adm. M.C., USN, 1968; with occupational forces, Mariana Islands, 1945, Submarine Medicine Research Lab., 1950-51; med. officer Submarine Force, Atlantic, 1959-62; dir. residency tng. program Naval Hosp., San Diego, 1955-59; chief medicine, dir. intern tng. Naval Hosp. Yokosuka, Japan, 1962-65; exec. officer, chief profl. services, chief outpatient service Naval Hosp., St. Albans, N.Y., 1965-67, comdg. officer, 1967-69; dist. med. officer 3d Naval Dist., 1967-69. Decorated Presdl. Unit citation. Mem. A.C.P., A.M.A., Mil. Surgeons U.S., N.Y. Acad. Medicine, Ind., Aerospace med. assns., Undersea Med. Soc., Royal Soc. Medicine, Phi Chi, Theta Chi. Home: 3542 Hamlet Pl Chevy Chase MD 20015 Office: Bur Medicine and Surgery Code 7 Dept Navy Washington DC 20390

FAUCETT, THOMAS RICHARD, educator, mech. engr.; b. Hatton, Mo., Aug. 22, 1920; s. Thomas A. and Nora (Craghead) F.; B.S. in Mech. Engring., U. Mo., 1942; M.S., Purdue U., 1949, Ph.D., 1952; m. Ruth G. Phelps, May 23, 1942; children—Thomas W., John P., Lucia A., Dennis R. Design analyst Cleve. diesel engine div. Gen. Motors Corp., 1942-46; instr. mech. engring. Purdue U., 1946- 52; asso. prof. U. Rochester, 1952-60; prof. Mo. Sch. Mines and Metallurgy, 1960-62, prof. mech. engring., head dept. State U. Ia., 1962- 65; prof., chmn. mech. and aero. engring. dept. U. Mo. Rolla,

1965—; cons. mech. engr., 1946—; dir. KDI Inc., Rochester, N.Y., 1958-60. Mem. Am. Soc. M.E., Am. Soc. Engring. Edn., Sigma Xi, Tau Beta Pi, Pi Tau Sigma. Presbyn. (elder, trustee). Author articles design analysis, vibrations stress analysis. Home: 25 McFarland Dr Rolla, MO 65401.

FAUDE, CORVIN WILLIAM, advt. exec.; b. Chgo., Jan. 28, 1903; s. William and Mathilda (Schmall) F.; B.S., U. Ill., 1925; m. Alma Davison, June 22, 1927; 1 son, William Davison. With Cramer-Krasselt Co., Milw., 1925—, treas., 1946-68, exec. v.p., 1955-62, pres., 1962-68, chmn. bd., chief exec. officer, 1968—, also dir. Mem. Wis. Devel. Authority. Bd. dirs. Jr. Achievement S.E. Wis., Luth. Men Am. Mem. N.A.M. (employee health and benefits com.), Am. Assn. Advt. Agys. (com. of bd. agy. mgmt.), U. Ill. Alumni Assn., Sigma Pi, Alpha Delta Sigma. Lutheran (council). Mason Elk. Clubs: Wisconsin, North Shore Country, Press (Milw.). Home: 6140 N Dent Av Milwaukee WI 53217. Office: 733 N Van Buren St Milwaukee WI 53202

FAUGHT, COURTNEY LAMAR, air force officer; b. Jackson, O., Feb. 11, 1918; s. Courtney Cary and Hazel (Radcliffe) F.; student Ohio Wesleyan U., 1936-38, 40-41; grad. Flying Schs., 1942, Command & Gen. Staff Coll., 1945, Air Command and Staff Sch., 1951, Nat. War Coll., 1960; m. Mary Anne Young, May 20, 1942; children—Courtney Stewart, Catherine Lamar. Commd. 2d lt. USAAF, 1942, advanced through grades to maj. gen., 1968; assigned S.W. Pacific, World War II; dir. operations 315th Air Div., Far East Air Forces, 1953; various command and staff positions Mil. Air Transp. Service, 1957-59; served in key assignments Hdqrs. USAF, 1960-65; dep. chief of staff operations Mil. Airlift Command 1966, chief of staff, 1969; NDTA co-chmn. operations panel NDTA/MAC Airlift Com., 1966-69; dep. dir. Dept. Army, Washington, 1969—. Decorated D.S.M., Legion of Merit, D.F.C., Bronze Star, Air medal with oak leaf cluster, Army Commendation medal. Mem. Nat. War Coll. Alumni Assn., Daedalians, Douglas MacArthur Meml. Group, Alpha Sigma Phi. Kiwanian. Home: 465 E Church St Urbana OH 43078

FAUGHT, HAROLD FRANKLIN, govt. ofcl.; b. Washington, Oct. 16, 1924; s. Robert A.N. and Bessie I. (Townes) F.; B.S. in Mech. Engring., Cornell U., 1945; M.S. in Mech. Engring., U. Pa., 1951; certificate in Advanced Mgmt., Harvard, 1961; m. Kathleen Quinn, June 21, 1947; 1 son Richard Harold, Jr. design engr. Westinghouse Electric Co., 1964-68, gen. mgr. Astronuclear Lab., 1968- 69; asst. postmaster gen. for research and engring., Washington, 1969—. Bd. mgrs. South Suburban br. YMCA, Pitts., Johnson County (Kan.) YMCA. Served to lt. (j.g.) USNR, 1943-46. Mem. Am. Nuclear Soc., Nat. Indsl. Security Assn., Atomic Indsl. Forum, Am. Inst. Aeros. and Astronautics. Patentee in field. Home: 8817 Harness Trial Potomas MD 20854 Office: US Post Office Dept Washington DC 20269

FAUL, HENRY, educator, nuclear geophysicist; b. Prague, Czechoslovakia, July 17, 1920; B.S., Mass. Inst. Tech., 1941, Ph.D., 1949; M.S., Mich. State U., 1942. Prof., chmn. dept. geology U. Pa., Phila., 1966—. Author: Ages of Rocks, Planets and Stars, 1966; Nuclear Clocks, 2d edit., 1968. Editor: Nuclear Ecology, 1954. Research geochemistry and geophysics. Office: Dept Geology U Pa Philadelphia PA 19104

FAULCONER, ALBERT, Jr., physician; b. Arkansas City, Kan., Oct. 24, 1911; s. Albert and Grace (McMillen) F.; grad. Kemper Mil. Sch., Boonville, Mo., 1928; B.S., U. Kan., 1932, M.D., 1936; M.S., U. Minn., 1947; m. Mary Jean Whie, June 18, 1938; children—Albert III, David White, Barbara. Intern Harper Hosp., Detroit, 1936-37; practice of medicine, Rochester, Mich., 1938- 41; fellow anesthesiology Mayo Found., now prof. of anesthesiology; consulting anesthesiologist Mayo Clinic, 1947; chmn. dept. anesthesia, 1953—, bd. govs., 1964-70; cons. anesthesia, surgeon gen. U.S. Army, 1957—. Mem. Am. Bd. Med. Spcialities; asso. anesthesia NRC, 1950-61. Served as maj. M.C., AUS, 1941-45; chief anesthesiologist Ft. Custer Sta. Hosp., also Finney Gen. Hosp. Diplomate Am. Board Anesthesiology (dir. 1955-69, pres. 1964). Fellow Am. Coll. Anesthesiology (gov. 1948-55); mem. Assn. U. Anesthetists (pres. 1955), Soc. Pharm. and Exptl. Therapy, Am. Soc. Anesthesiologists, A.M.A., Sigma Xi, Beta Theta Pi, Nu Sigma Nu. Home: 1040 Mayowood Rd SW Rochester MN 55901 Office: 200 1st St SW Rochester MN 55901

FAULHABER, ROBERT WILLIAM, educator, economist; b. Cleve., July 28, 1920; s. Frank F. and Agnes J. (Youkel) F.; certificate Am. Inst. Banking, 1942; A.B., Cath. U. Am., 1948; M.A., U. Chgo., 1950; Doctorat d'Universite de Paris, (France), 1952; m. Martha L. Finke, June 17, 1950; children—Roberta, Peter, Christina, Elizabeth. Messenger-teller Cleve. Trust Co., 1939-42; instr. econs. Loyola U., Chgo., 1949-50; mem. faculty DePaul U., Chgo., 1952—, prof. econs., 1964—. Mem. long-range planning com. Cath. Interracial Council Chgo., 1959; treas. Greater Ill. Faculty Com. on Vietnam, 1965. Chmn. legislative com. Ind. Voters Ill., 1954. Served with USAAF, 1942-45; PTO. Mem. Am. Assn. U. Profs., Am., Cath. econ. assns., Econ. et Humanisme, Phi Beta Kappa, Pi Gamma Mu. Catholic. Asso. editor Rev. Social Economy. Home: 5653 S Harper St Chicago, IL 60637.

FAULK, E. WARD, banker. With Merchants Nat. Bank, Mobile, 1925—, sr. v.p., 1952-63, pres., 1963—, also dir. Campaign chmn. United Fund Mobile County, 1955, now pres. Mem. U.S. C. of C. (dir., past chmn. fgn. commerce com.). Home: Riviere du Chien Rd Route 4 Box 50 Mobile AL 36609 Office: 110 St Francis St Mobile AL 36613*

FAULK, JOHN HENRY, author, lectr.; b. Austin, Tex., Aug. 21, 1913; s. John Henry and Martha Cynthia (Miner) F.; B.A. in English, U. Tex., 1936, M.A., 1940; m. Elizabeth Peake, May 29, 1965; 1 son, John Henry III; children by previous marriage—Tannehill, Johanna, Evelyn, Frank Dobie. Faculty English dept. U. Tex., 1942; fellow Julius Rosenwald Found., 1941-42; field dir. A.R.C., Cairo, Egypt, 1942-44; star radio programs CBS, N.Y.C., 1946-48; star John Henry Faulk Show, sta. WCBS, 1951-57, It's News to Me, Leave It to the Girls, Walk a Mile for a Camel, CBS-TV, 1953-55; lectr. on humor and Am. heritage, 1949-65; appeared in movies All the Way Home, 1963, The Best Man, 1964. Precinct chmn. Austin Democratic Com.; mem. Travis County Dem. Exec. Com. Served with AUS, 1944-46. Mem. A.F.T.R.A. (past v.p.), Screen Actors Guild, Internat. Platform Assn. (bd. govs. 1967-). Author: Fear on Trial, 1964. Home: 1420 Red Bud Trail Austin, TX 78746.

FAULK, LLOYD BUFORD, banker; b. Hawkins, Tex., Aug. 28, 1915; s. John William and Libbie (Crow) F.; grad. Sch. Bank Audit, Control and Operations, U. Wis., 1956; m. Marion Louise Jones, Dec. 27, 1939; 1 dau., Barbara Louise. With First Nat. Bank, Ft. Worth, 1935—, auditor, 1954—. Served with USAAF, 1942-45; to capt. USAF, 1950-52. Decorated D.F.C., Air medal with two oak leaf clusters. Mem. Tex. Bankers Assn. (past sect. chmn.), Nat. Assn. Bank Auditors and Controllers (past chpt. pres., dir., past state, dist. dir.), Inst. Internal Auditors. Mason (Shriner). Home: Route 1 Box 77 N Azle, TX 76020. Office: 1 Burnett Plaza Fort Worth TX 76102

FAULKNER, ARTHUR, life ins. co. exec.; b. Springfield, Mass., May 9, 1907; s. John T. and Sarah (Coen) F.; ed. pub. schs., Springfield; m. Esther Pond, June 15, 1935; children—Quentin P., Karen (Mrs. Robert Olson), Lynne S. (Mrs. William Holton). With Mass. Mut. Life Ins. Co., Springfield, 1925—, v.p. new bus. adminstrn., 1963—. Mem. Home Office Life Underwriters Assn. (past pres., sec. editor). Home: 12 Twin Brook Circle Longmeadow MA 01106 Office: 1295 State St Springfield MA 01109

FAULKNER, AVERY COONLEY, architect; b. Bronxville, N.Y., Jan. 23, 1929; s. Waldron and Elizabeth Ferry (Coonley) F.; A.B., Yale, 1951, B.Arch., 1954, M.Arch., 1955; m. Alice Brown Watson, June 7, 1951; children—Sara Coonley, Waldron Mason, Lydia Avery. Designer Faulkner, Kingsbury & Stenhouse, Washington, 1958-64; partner Faulkner, Stenhouse, Fryer & Faulkner, Washington, 1964-68; sr. partner Faulkner, Fryer & Vanderpool, Washington, 1968—; cons. Surgeon Gen. U.S. Army. Chmn. com. preservation hist. bldgs. A.I.A. Mem. McLean (Va.) Planning Com. Mem. Yale Alumni Bd.; alumni trustee St. Alban's Sch., 1966-69; dir. Coonley Found., Hillsboro Assn., Washington Area Tennis Patrons Found. Served as 1st lt., USAF 1955-58. Recipient honor award A.I.A., 1970, award of excellence Archtl. Record, 1966, honor award Washington Bd. Trade, 1964; Alice Kimball English traveling fellow, Yale, 1954; Magnus T. Hopper Hosp. Planning fellow, Yale, 1955. Mem. A.I.A. Episcopalian. Clubs: Yale (pres. 1967-69), Hillsboro, Gibson Island, Chevy Chase, Metropolitan (Washington). Home: 1161 Crest Lane McLean VA 22101 Office: 2000 L St NW Washington DC 20036

FAULKNER, CLAUDE WINSTON, educator; b. Barbourville, Ky., Apr. 24, 1916; s. James Edward and Eulah (Swearingen) F.; A.B., Union Coll., Ky., 1936, Litt.D., 1962; M.A., University of Kentucky, 1938; Ph.D., U. Ill., 1947; m. Nancy Isabel McCallum, Dec. 9, 1944; children—Linda Jo, Keith Edward, Sally Ann, Charles Douglas. Instr. English, U. Ill., 1947; faculty U. Ark., 1947—, prof. English, 1953—, chmn. dept., 1953—. Served to capt. USAAF, 1942-46; lt. col. Res. Named Distinguished Alumnus, Union Coll., 1954. Mem. Modern Lang. Assn., Phi Beta Kappa, Phi Kappa Phi. Author: Writing Good Sentences, 1950. Co-author: Writing Good Prose, 1961, 3d edit., 1971. Home: 306 W Prospect St Fayetteville AR 72701

FAULKNER, EDWIN JEROME, ins. co. exec.; b. Lincoln, Neb., July 5, 1911; s. Edwin Jerome and Leah (Meyer) F.; B.A., U. Neb., 1932; M.B.A., U. Pa., 1934; m. Jean Rathburn, Sept. 27, 1933. With Woodmen Accident & Life Co., Lincoln, Neb., 1934—, successively claim auditor, v.p., 1934-38, pres., dir., 1938—; pres., dir. Comml. Mut. Surety Co., 1938—; dir. First Nat. Bank, Lincoln Tel. & Tel. Co., Universal Surety Co., Inland Ins. Company. Chmn. Health Ins. Council, 1959-60. Chmn. Lincoln- Lancaster County Plan Commn., 1948-67; mem. medicare adv. com. Dept. Def., 1957-70. Neb. Republican State Finance chmn., 1968—. Pres., trustee Bryan Meml. Hosp.; mem. bd. trustees Doane Coll., Lincoln Found.; trustee Am. Coll. Life Underwriters, Phila. Served from 2d lt. to lt. col., USAAF, 1942-45. Decorated Legion of Merit; recipient Distinguished Service award U. Neb., 1957; Harold R. Gordon Meml. award Internat. Assn. Health Ins. Underwriters, 1955, Ins. Man of Year award Ins. Field, 1958; Exec. of Yr. award Am. Coll. Hosp. Adminstrs., 1971. Mem. Health Ins. Assn. Am. (1st pres. 1956), Am. Legion, Am. Life Conv. (exec. com. 1961-70, pres. 1966-67), Phi Beta Kappa, Phi Kappa Psi, Alpha Kappa Psi (hon.). Republican. Presbyn. Mason, Elk. Author: Accident and Health Insurance, 1940; Health Insurance, 1960. Editor: Man's Quest for Security, 1966. Home: 4100 South St Lincoln NB 68506 Office: 1526 K St Lincoln NB 68508

FAULKNER, ELIZABETH COONLEY, civic worker; b. Chgo., Dec. 3, 1902; d. Avery and Queene (Ferry) Coonley; grad. Madeira Sch., Greenway, Va., 1920; A.B., Vassar Coll., 1924; m. Waldron Faulkner, Nov. 18, 1926; children—Avery Coonley, Winthrop Waldron, Celia Ferry (Mrs. Raymond C. Cleveger III). Tchr., Madeira Sch., 1925-26. Pres. Madeira Sch. Alumnae Assn., 1929-31, bd. dirs., 1943-68; pres. Vassar Coll. Alumnae Assn., 1933-36; pres. Vassar Club D.C., 1942-44; pres. class 1924, Vassar Coll., 1949-60; trustee Vassar Coll., 1958-66; pres. John Eaton Sch. P.T.A., Washington, 1936- 38; trustee Potomac Sch., 1948-51; pres. bd. D.C. YWCA, 1951-53, chmn. D.C. com. interpretations and support Nat. Bd., 1952-62, mem. Area Council, 1952-63, mem. Nat. Capital Area, 1964—; chmn. com. curriculums D.C. subcom. White House Conf. Edn., 1956; chmn. women's activities, centennial conv. A.I.A., 1957; pres. women St. Margaret's Episcopal Ch., 1953-55, mem. vestry, 1958-62; pres. Wilmer Conf. Center Corp. Episcopal Diocese D.C., 1960—; mem. bd. Episcopal Center Children, 1962-68. Mem. Am. Assn. U. Women. Clubs: Cosmopolitan (N.Y.C.); Sulgrave, Zonta (hon.) (Washington). Address: 3415 36th St NW Washington DC 20016.

FAULKNER, ERIC ODIN, banker; b. St. Albans, Hertfordshire, Eng., Apr. 21, 1914; s. Alfred E. and Florence Edith (Nicoll) F.; student Corpus Christi Coll. Cambridge (Eng.) U., 1933-36; m. Joan Mary Webster, Sept. 7, 1939; children—Tristina Anne (Mrs. John Wheelwright), Nicholas Odin. With Glyn, Mills & Co., London, Eng., 1936-68, mng. dir., 1950-63, chmn., 1963-68; dep. chmn. LLoyds Bank Ltd., London, 1968-69, chmn., 1969—; dir. Hudson's Bay Co., Vickers Ltd., Nat. & Comml. Banking Group Ltd., Lloyds & Bolsa Internat. Bank Served to lt. col. Royal Arty., 1939-45. Decorated Order Brit. Empire. Home: Chart Cottage Seal Chart Sevenoaks Kent England Office: 71 Lombard St London EC 3 England

FAULKNER, HAROLD CLIFFORD, lawyer; b. nr. Boise, Ida., Nov. 21, 1895; s. Herbert F. and Margaret A. (Dolan) F.; LL.B., San Francisco Law Sch., 1917; m. Carrie B. Meighan, June 25, 1924 (dec.); 1 son, Harold C.; m. 2d, Nome D. Vilas, Mar. 26, 1960. Admitted to Cal. bar, 1917, U.S. Supreme Ct., 1926; pvt. practice, San Francisco, 1917-27, with firm Faulkner & O'Connor, 1927-42, mem. firm Faulkner, Sheehan & Wiseman and predecessor firms, 1942—. Mem. Am. Bar Assn., Am. Judicature Soc., Am. Coll. Trial Lawyers, Bar Assn. San Francisco. Republican. Mason (Shriner). Clubs: Bohemian, Family, Olympic, Commonwealth. Home: 1940 Vallejo St San Francisco CA 94123 Office: Balfour Bldg San Francisco CA 94104

FAULKNER, HERBERT WINTHROP WALDRON, architect; b. Paris, France, Jan. 21, 1898 (parents Am. citizens); s. Herbert Waldron and Mary (John) F.; Ph.B., Yale, 1919, B.F.A., 1924; m. Elizabeth Coonley, Nov. 18, 1926; children—Avery Coonley, Winthrop Waldron, Celia Ferry (Mrs. Raymond C. Clevenger III). Practice of architecture, N.Y.C., 1927-34, Washington since 1934, specializing instnl. bldg.; with A.B. Trowbridge, 1934-39; partner Faulkner, Kingsbury, Washington, 1939-46, sr. partner firm Faulkner, Stenhouse, Fryer & Faulkner and predecessor firms, 1946- -; pres. Inter-Soc. Color Council, 1956-57; mem. Commn. on Ch. Architecture and Allied Arts, 1948-54. Bd. examiners and registrars architects, D.C., 1946-51. Fellow A.I.A. (pres. Washington 1942-43); mem. Washington Housing Assn. (pres. 1947-51), Nat. Acad. of Design (asso. mem.), Washington Urban League (pres. 1938-41). Episcopalian. Clubs: Century Assn. (N.Y.C.); Cosmos (pres. 1953), Yale (Washington). Home: 3415 36th St Washington DC 20016 Office: 2000 L St NW Washington DC 20036

FAULKNER, JAMES MORISON, physician; b. Keene, N.H., Dec. 16, 1898; s. Herbert K. and Emily (Morisoon) F.; student Phillips Exeter Acad., 1913-16; A.B., Harvard, 1920, M.D., 1924; D.Sc., Boston U. 1959; married Mary B. du Pont, Sept. 1, 1928; chilren—H. Kimball, Elise (Mrs. J. Parry Jones), Emily M. (Mrs. Richard C. Stevens), Charles S., Rosemary (Mrs.Radoslav Bachvarov), Henry B., Andrew G. Interne Mass. Gen. Hosp., 1924-25, asst. to outpatients, 1927-38; asst. resident physician Hosp. of Rockefeller Inst., 1926, John Hopkins Hosp., 1926-27; mem. vis. staff Boston City Hosp., 1928-47, dir. 1st and 3rd Med. Services, 1945-47; physician Mass. Meml. Hosps., 1940-43; asst. and instr. Harvard Med. Sch., 1928-40; asst. prof. medicine Boston U. Sch. Medicine, 1940-43, prof. clin. medicine, 1947-58, dean, 1947-55; dir. Boston U.-Mass. Meml. Hosps. Med. Center, 1961; med. dir. Mass. Inst. Tech., 1955-60, cons. in medicine, 1960—; prof. medicine Tufts Coll. Med. Sch., 1943-47. Trustee Phillips Exeter Acad. 1954-60; mem. New Eng. Bd. of Higher Edn., 1955-58, Nat. Bd. Med. Examiners, 1956-68. bd. overseers Harvard Coll., 1958-64; pres. Nat. Fund for Med. Edn., 1964-66; pres. Med. Found., Inc., 1957-60; mem. bd. United Health Found. Served from pvt. to sgt., 101st Engrs., 1917-19; lt. comdr. M.C. USNR, 1935-42, promoted comdr., 1942-44, capt., 1944. Decorated Croix de Guerre, 1918, Navy Commedation Ribbon, 1944. Diplomate Am. Bd. Internal Medicine. Fellow A.C.P., Royal Soc. Medicine; mem. Am. Acad. Arts and Scis., Mass. Med. Soc., Am. Med. Assn., Am. Heart Assn., Am. Soc. Clin. Investigation, Am. Clin. and Climatol. Soc. Republican. Clubs: St. Botolph (Boston); Century Assn. (N.Y.C.). Home: 255 Goddard Av Brookline MA 02146 Office: 535 Boylston St Boston MA 02116

FAULKNER, RAFFORD LOCHEAD, govt. ofcl.; b. Somerville, Mass., Jan. 24, 1909; s. Charles H. and Helen Elizabeth (Taylor) F.; S.B., Mass. Inst. Tech., 1933; m. Concetta Damian, Mar. 31, 1943; children—Carol Ann, Helen Frances. Geologist, Cerro Corp., Peru, 1933-40; engr.-examiner RFC, 1940-49; engr. Export- Import Bank, 1949-50; with div. raw materials AEC, 1950—, dep. dir., 1957-63, dir., 1963—. Dep. 3d Internat. Conf. Peaceful Uses Atomic Energy, 1964, Internat. Nuclear Industries Fair, 1966. Served with USNR, 1943-46. Registered profl. engr., D.C. Mem. Am. Inst. Mining, Metall. and Petroleum Engrs., Am. Nuclear Soc. Home: 8624 Beech Tree Rd Bethesda, MD 20034. Office: Div Raw Materials Atomic Energy Commn Washington DC 20545

FAULKNER, RAY N., art educator; b. Charlevoix, Mich., June 3, 1906; s. Ray Whitcomb and Sadie Rose (O'Neill) F.; A.B., U. Mich., 1927; M.L.A., Harvard, 1929; Ph.D., U. Minn., 1937; m. Sarah Key, Sept. 12, 1945; children—James, John, William, Patrick. Instr. fine arts Ohio State U. 1932; instr. art edn. and gen. arts, U. Minn., 1933-38, asst. prof. art edn., 1938-39; head dept. fine and indsl. arts, Tchrs. Coll., Columbia, 1939-46; exec. head dept. art, Stanford, 1946-61, prof. art, 1946-71, emeritus, 1971—; dir. test and research div. Bur. Naval Personnel, Washington. Served as lt. comd. USNR. Mem. N.E.A., Research Assn., Psychol. Assn., Coll. Art Assn., Phi Delta Kappa, Psi Chi, Delta Phi Delta. Author: (with E. Ziegfeld) Art Today 1941, 5th edit., 1969; (with H. Davis), Teachers Enjoy the Arts, 1943; (with Sarah Faulkner). Inside Today's Home, 1954, 3d edit., 1968. Home: 765 Frenchman's Rd Stanford CA 94305

FAULSTICH, ALBERT JOSEPH, govt. ofcl.; b. New Orleans, May 28, 1910; s. Albert and Mary (Balser) F.; B.S. in Accounting and Econs., Columbus U., Washington, 1938, M.S. in Accounting and Finance, 1948; m. Anna Emily Collingnon, June 30, 1940; chilren—Albert Joseph, Richard Charles. With Treasury Dept., 1939-64, dir. Office Security, 1961, spl. asst. Office Sec., 1961-64, asst. to comptroller currency, 1962-64; dir. FDIC, 1965- 66, dep. adminstr. of nat. banks, 1965—, mem. bd. rev., spl. com., com. liquidations, loans and purchases assets, 1966—. Chmn. comptroller currency orgn. for nation-wide campaign for Kennedy Library Fund, 1964. Served to lt. USNR, 1943-46. Decorated Commendation medal; recipient commendation Treasury Dept., 1962. Democrat. Roman Cath. Home: 505 Elderwood Rd Silver Spring MD 20904 Office: 550 17th St NW Washington DC 20429

FAUNCE, ANTHONY, fgn. service officer; b. Boston, May 23, 1916; s. Kenneth W. and Grace (Tufts) F.; A.B. in Internat. Law and Relations, Harvard, 1937; m. Mary Gill; children—Eunice Amanda, Jeannette, Jessena, Sandra. Trainee, then asst. underwriter Ins. Co. N.Am., 1937-42; salesman, account handler Obrion, Russell & Co., 1946-48; salesman, account handler John C. Paige & Co., 1948-52. gen. partner, head internat. div., 1952-68; dep. asst. gen. fgn. assistance State Dept., 1969—; corporator Suffolk Franklin Savs. Bank, 1960. Bd. dirs. Internat. Center New Eng., 1966-69; trustee Lowell Tech. Inst., 1966-69, Nashoba Country Day Sch., 1967-69. Served to lt. USNR, 1942-46. Clubs: Harvard (Boston, N.Y.C.); Downtown (Boston); Camden (Me.) Yacht; Capitol Hill, International (Washington). Address: State Dept Washington DC 20515*

FAUNCE, GEORGE, III, credit card club exec.; b. Pitts., Jan. 23, 1926; s. George and Helen (Colwell) F.; grad. Phillips Exeter Acad., 1943; A.B., Princeton, 1948; LL.B., N.Y. U., 1954; m. Sally Van Kleeck Swift, June 18, 1949; children—Theodore Swift, Rebecca Winslow. Asst. sec. Hanover Bank, N.Y.C., 1948-55; with firm Nixon, Hargrave, Devans & Dey, Rochester, 1955-58; with AFCO Credit Corp., 1956—, chmn. bd., 1969—; pres. Diners Club, Inc., N.Y.C., 1969—, also dir. Pres. Princeton Class 1947, 1967—. Served to ensign USNR, 1943-46, to lt., 1952-53. Mem. Drugg and Chem. Club N.Y.C. Episcopalian. Clubs: Mansruing Island, Apawamis (Rye, N.Y.). Home: Hidden Spring Lane Rye NY 10580 Office: 10 Colmbus Circle New York City NY 10019

FAUNCE, WILLIAM ALDEN, sociologist, educator; b.. Petoskey, Mich., May 2, 1928; s. Roland Cleo and Mae (Upendkelder) F.; B.A., Mich. State U., 1950; M.A., Wayne State U., 1952, Ph.D., 1958; m. Margaret Sheila Maule, June 19, 1954; children-Nancy, Eric. Instr. to prof. Mich. State U., East Lansing, 1957- -, chmn. dept. sociology, 1968—; research cons. U.S. Dept. Labor, summers 1961-62. Served with M.C., U.S. Army, 1951-53. Mem. Am., Mich. sociol. assns., Ohio Valley Sociol. Soc. Author: Readings in Industrial Sociology, 1967; Problems of an Industrial Society, 1968; (with W.H. Form) Comparative Perspectives on Industrial Society, 1969. Contbr. articles profl. jours. Home: 916 Wick Ct East Lansing MI 48823

FAUNTROY, WALTER, congressman; b. Washington, Feb. 6, 1933; s. William T. and Ethel (Vine) F.; A.B., Va. Union U., 1955; B.D., Yale U. Divinity Sch., 1958; m. Dorothy Simms, Aug. 3, 1957; son, Marvin Keith. Ordained to ministry Baptist Ch., 1958; pastor New Bethel Baptist Ch., Washington, 1958-71; pres., chmn. bd. Model Inner City Community Orgn. Inc., Washington, 1965—; mem. 92d Congress. Vice-chmn. D.C. City Council, 1967-69. Home: 4105 17th St NW Washington DC 20011 Office: Longworth Bldg Washington DC 20515

FAURE, GUNTER, educator; b. Tallinn, Estonia, May 11, 1934; s. Arnulf and Stella (von Harpe) F.; B.Sc., U. Western Ont., 1957; Ph.D., Mass. Inst. Tech., 1961, fellow Sch. Advanced Studies, 1961-62; m. Barbara L.L. Goodell, Sept. 5, 1959; children—Mary Jennifer, John Eric, Pamela Anne, David Christopher. Asst. prof. geology Ohio State

U., 1962-65, asso. prof., 1965-68, prof., 1968—. Recipient univ. gold medal in honours geology, U. Western Ont., 1957, distinguished teaching award, Ohio State U., 1970. Fellow Geol. Soc. Am.; mem. Am. Geophys. Union, Geochem. Soc., Geol. Soc. Am., A.A.A.S., Ohio Acad. Scis., Geologische Vereinigung, Sigma Xi. Author: (with J.L. Powell) Strontium Isotope Geology, 1972. Contbr. articles profl. jours. Home: 2047 Fairfax Rd Columbus OH 43221

FAURI, FEDELE FREDERICK, univ. dean; b. Crystal Falls. Mich., Apr. 28, 1909; s. Joseph and Angela (Chesky) F.; A.B., U. Mich., 1930, J.D., 1933; m. Iris M. Peterson, June 11, 1938; children—David Peter, Eric Joseph, Paul Frederick, Greta Susan. Supr., Mich. State Bur. Social Security, 1941-43; dir. Mich. State Dept. Social Welfare, 1943-47; cons. on pub. assistance, ways and means com. Ho. Reps., 1945-46. social security adviser, 1949; sr. specialist legislative reference service Library Congress, 1947-51; pub. assistance research dir., adv. council social security Senate Com. Finance, 1948, social security adviser, 1950-56; mem. Gov. Commn. to Study Problems of Aging; dean, prof. pub. welfare adminstrn. Sch Social Work U. Mich., 1951—; v.p., dir. Mich. Welfare League; chmn. council on employment security U.S. Dept. Labor, 1954-60; chmn. Adv. Council Pub. Welfare, U.S. Dept. Health, Edn. and Welfare, 1964—; mem. nat. com. Citizens Crusade Against Poverty; trustee Nat. Council Crime and Delinquency, 1963-65; pres. Council on Social Work Edn., 1954-56; adv. com. on pub. and pvt. pensions Nat. Bur. Econ. Security; bd. Mich. United Fund. Recipient award National Conf. Social Work, 1955, W. S. Terry, Jr. Meml. Merit award, Am. Public Welfare Assn., 1957; Distinguished Service award Council on Social Work Edn., 1968. Mem. Internat., Nat. confs. social work, Mich. Bar Assn., Am. Pub Welfare Assn. (dir, pres. 1967—), Mich. Welfare League (pres. 1967—), Council on Social Work Edn. (dir. 1967—). Nat. Conf. on Social Welfare (pres. 1961-62), Phi Kappa Phi. Author: Study of Employment Security Administrative Costs (with J. Borus), 1953; Significant Findings on the Impact of The 1957-58 Recession (with Harber & Cohen), 1959. Chmn. editorial bd. Ency. Social Work, 1963. Contbr. articles profl. jours. Home: 1025 Spruce Dr Ann Arbor MI 48104

FAUS, WARREN WILSON, educator, artist; b. Ismay, Mont., Feb. 12, 1919; s. Walter Josiah and Anna (Steen) F.; student Mpls. Sch. Art, 1938-39; B.A., Mont. State Coll., 1942; M.A., Stanford, 1954; m. Frances Mist Korb, July 24, 1956; stepchildren—Marion Mist Korb, Frances Louise Korb. Mem. art faculty San Jose (Cal.) State Coll., 1946—, prof., 1961—; chmn. dept., 1960-67; watercolorist and Asian art historian. Bd. dirs. Montalvo Assn. Served to maj. AUS, 1942-46. Decorated Bronze Star. Mem. Western Assn. Art Museums (pres. 1960-61), Soc. Asian Art (dir. 1968—), Phi Kappa Phi, Delta Phi Delta. Home: 15561 Toyon Dr Los Gatos CA 95030 Office: San Jose State Coll San Jose CA 95114

FAUSOLD, MARTIN LUTHER, educator; b. Irwin, Pa., Nov. 11, 1921; s. Samuel and Edna (Breegle) F.; B.A., Gettysburg Coll., 1945; Ph.D., Syracuse U., 1953; m. Daryl Ethel Clement, June 18, 1949; children—Sharon Anne, Cynthia Lynn, Marti Clement, Martin Samuel. Partner, Fausold Dairy Co., Blairsville, Pa., 1946-49; grad. teaching asst. Syracuse U., 1952; from asst. prof. to prof. history and govt. State U. N.Y. at Cortland, 1952-58, prof. history and govt., chmn. social studies dept., 1959-65; chmn. div. social scis. State U. N.Y. at Geneseo, 1965-69, prof. Am. history, 1969—. Chmn. social sci. subcom., awards com. State U. N.Y. Research Found., 1965-69; chmn. univ. awards com. State U. N.Y., 1970—, joint awards council, 1970—. Chmn. Cortland Bd. Pub. Works, 1956; mem. Cortland County Civil Service Commn., 1956. Mem. Faculty Assn. State U. N.Y. (pres. 1964- 67), Orgn. Am. Historians, Am. Hist. Assn., Am. Assn. U. Profs. Presbyn. (elder 1968-70) Author: Gifford Pinchot: Bull Moore Progressive, 1961; (with others) Annotated Bibliography of American History, 1969; also articles, book revs. profl. jours. Cons. editor Kennikut Press, 1969—. Home: 29 Oak St Geneseo NY 14454

FAUST, JAMES E., lawyer; b. Delta, Utah, July 31, 1920; s. George A. and Amy (Finlinson) F.; B.A., LL.B., U. Utah, 1948; m. Ruth Wright, Apr. 21, 1943; children—James H., Janna, Marcus, Lisa, Robert. Admitted to Utah bar, 1948, since practiced in Salt Lake City; mem. firm Rice & Faust. Mem. Utah Bar Commn., 1960—. Pres. Green Ditch Water Co., Salt Lake City, 1952- -; chmn. bd. Wright Pontiac-Cadillac, 1961—; dir. Deseret News Pub. Co.; adviser Cottonwood Holladay office Zions 1st Nat. Bank. Vice pres. Citizens for A Better Utah. Mem. Utah Legislature from Salt Lake County, 1949. Active Boy Scouts Am. Trustee, sec. Health Services Corp.; bd. dirs. United Fund. Served to 1st lt. USAAF, 1942- 45. Mem. Utah Bar Assn. (pres. 1962-63). Mem. Ch. of Jesus Christ of Latter Day Saints (region rep. council of twelve). Home: 5093 S 2100 East St Salt Lake City UT 84117 Office: Kearns Bldg Salt Lake City UT 84101

FAUST, LEO HARRY, lawyer; b. Ansonia, O., Oct. 25, 1899; s. Charles F. and Susan (Sentman) F.; A.B., Miami U., Oxford, O., 1923; J.D., Ohio State U., 1926; m. Persis Martha Johnson, Aug. 13, 1927; 1 dau., Jeannine (Mrs. Kenneth J. Kennedy). Admitted to Ohio bar 1926, also U.S. Supreme Ct.; practice in Troy, 1926—; sr. partner firm Faust, Harrelson and Thornburgh, 1952—. Mem. Troy Bd. Edn., 1940-63, v.p., 1942-62, pres., 1962-63. Mem. Am., Ohio, Maimi County bar assns. Republican. Baptist. Rotarian (pres. Troy 1961). Home: 222 Ridge Av Troy OH 45373 Office: 12 S Cherry St Troy OH 45373

FAUST, RAYMOND JOHNS, former assn. exec.; b. Millersburg, Pa., Sept. 16, 1901; s. Francis Martin and Emma Rebecca (Johns) F.; B.S. in San. Engrng., Pa. State U., 1923, C.E. in San. Engrng., 1935; m. Margaret Caroline Arthur, Apr. 26, 1935; 1 son, James Arthur. San. engr. Mich. Dept. Health, 1923-51; exec. asst. sec. Am. Water Works Assn., N.Y.C., 1951-59, sec., 1959-67. Registered profl. engr., Mich., N.Y. Mem. Am. Water Works Assn., Am. Pub. Health Assn., Water Pollution Control Fedn., Am. Soc C.E., Am. San. Engring. Intersoc. Bd. (dir., chmn. specialty com.). Home: 108 Wyatt Rd Garden City NY 11530

FAUSTINO, CARLOS A., Philippine diplomat; b. Manila, P.O., Oct. 8, 1913; s. Timotes Magno and Aqueda (Amphil) F.; LL.B., U. Philippines, 1938; m. Purificacion de la Curz, Oct. 20, 1960. Admitted to Philippine bar; asst., later jr. partner Cavanna Law Offices, 1940-46; vice consul, 1948-58; consul, 1958-62; career minister, 1962; career ambassador, 1969—; now consul gen. of Philippines in Los Angeles. Home: 972 Aurora Blvd Quezon City Philippines Office: 3075 Wilshire Blvd Los Angeles, CA 90005.

FAUVER, ROBERT NEWCOMB, lawyer; b. Elyria, O., Aug. 10, 1910; s. Louis B. and Inez (Farmer) F.; B.A., Amherst Coll., 1932; J.D., U. Mich., 1935; m. Jane Herig, July 22, 1939; children—Stuart L., Lynn (Mrs. John Brandt), Barbara, Robert Newcomb. Admitted to Ohio bar, 1935; practiced in Elyria, 1935-37, Oberlin, 1937—; mem. firm Fauver & Fauver, Elyria, 1935-37, Oberlin, 1937—; dir. Lorain County Savs. & Trust Co., Oberlin Off-Street Parking Co., Oberlin Canteen Co. Mem. Am., Ohio, Lorain County (pres.) bar assns., Oberlin C. of C. Club: Oberlin Exchange. Home: 294 Forest St Oberlin OH 44074 Office: 5 W College St Oberlin OH 44074

FAUX, DONALD EUGENE, banker; b. Ft. Wayne, Ind., Dec. 14, 1919; s. Ralph Burke and Nina (Wolf) F.; B.S., Ind. U., 1947; m. Lillian Maxine Walsh, Apr. 4, 1942; children—Marian Grace, Rebecca Ann, Donald Eugene II. Date processing mgr. Nat. Homes Corp., Lafayette, Ind., 1955-60; v.p. operations Merchants Nat. Bank, Indpls., 1960-66; gen. v.p., cashier City Nat. Bank, Detroit, 1966—. Served with USNR, 1942-45, 51-52. Decorated Purple Heart, Bronze Star medal. Mem. Financial Execs. Inst., Bank Adminstrn. Inst. Home: 31161 Tiverton St Farmington MI 48024 Office: Penobscot Bldg Detroit MI 48231

FAVELL, THOMAS ROYDEN, fgn. service officer; b. Rice Lake, Wis., Jan. 23, 1919; s. Dr. Ernest John and Inga Maria (Olsen) F.; B.A., U. Wis., 1941; M.A., Fletcher Sch. Law and Diplomacy, Tufts U., 1946; M.A.L.D., 1947, Ph.D., 1950; m. Barbara M. Branham, Feb. 6, 1943; children—Christine Anne, Judith Elaine. Fgn. service officer, 1947—; 3d sec., vice consul Am. embassy, Bogota, Colombia, 1947-50; 2d sec., vice consul, Madrid, Spain, 1950-53; 2d sec., consul, Havana, Cuba, 1953-56; internat. economist Dept. State, 1956-59, chief pvt. investment br. Bur. Econ. Affairs, 1958-60; econ. counselor Am. embassy, Santiago, Chile, 1960-65; dep. chief mission, consul gen., Wellington, New Zealand, 1965-68; diplomat in residence U. Mo., 1968-69; econ. counselor AID coordinator Am. embassy, Mexico City, 1969—. Served from ensign to lt. comdr., USNR, 1941-45. Mem. Am. Soc. Internat. Law. Home: Monte Carpatos 635 Mexico City Mexico Office: American Embassy Mexico City Mexico

FAVERTY, FREDERIC EVERETT, educator; b. Sparta, Ill., Sept. 29, 1902; s. Clarence Walter and Amelia (Riemer) F.; A.B., Washington U., 1924; M.A., Harvard, 1929, Ph.D., 1930; m. Margaret Ellen Beckett, June 20, 1934; childrenKathleen Margaret, Richard Beckett. Instr. English, Western Res. U., 1925-28; instr. English, Northwestern U., 1930-33, asst. prof., 1933-39, asso. prof., 1939-45, prof. and chmn. dept. of English, 1945-58, Morrison prof. English, 1958—. Book reviewer Mag. of Books, Chgo. Tribune; cons. on Victorian lit. to publs. Modern Lang. Assn., 1960—; cons. div. research and humanities Nat. Found. Arts and Humanities, 1966. Mem. bd. overseers vis. com. to dept. English, Harvard, 1954- 58. Mem. Am. Assn. U. Profs., Modern Lang. Assn. Am., Phi Beta Kappa. Presbyn. Editor: Northwestern Univ. Press, 1945-50. Author: Mathew Arnold the Ethnologist, 1951; Your Literary Heritage, 1958. Editor, contbr. The Victorian Poets; a Guide to Research, 1956; editorial jour. Victorian Studies, 1958-60; adv. bd.. Victorian Poetry, 1964—. Contbr. to Harvard Studies in Philology and Literature; Modern Philology, Studies in Philology, others. Club: University (Evanston). Home: 1423 Judson Av Evanston IL 60201

FAVOUR, CUTTING BROAD, physician, educator; b. Tereva, Ariz., July 19, 1913; s. Dr. Richmond and Dorothy (Chapman) F.; A.B., Hendrix Coll., 1936; M.D., Johns Hopkins, 1940; m. Barbara Hope Griffin, Sept. 6, 1941; children—Joanne Barbara, Emily Howe, Paul Cutting. Intern medicine Osler Wards, Johns Hopkins, 1940-41; asst. resident medicine Peter Bent Brigham Hosp., 1941- 42, successively med. resident, jr. asso. medicine, asso., sr. asso. and cons. bacteriology and immunology, 1942-54; also with Harvard Med. Sch. 1941-54, research fellow, asst., instr. asso. medicine; cons. bacteriology Channing Home for Tb, 1948-54; lectr. medicine Simmons Coll., 1947-54; attending medicine Rutland Vets. Hosp., 1949-54; cons. Tb, infectious diseases Boston Lying-In-Hosp., 1952-54; cons. medicine VA Hosp., West Roxbury, Mass., 1953-54; pvt. practice, Boston, 1943-54, Palo Alto, Cal., 1954-60; asst. vis. physician Stanford Service, Dept. Pub. Health City and County Hosp. of San Francisco, 1955-60; asst. clin. prof. Stanford, 1955-60; staff Palo Alto Hosp., 1955-60, Palo Alto Med. Clinic, 1955-60; cons.-lectr. internal medicine USN Hosp., Oak Knoll, Cal., 1956-60; dir. dept. immunology Palo Alto Med. Research Found., 1955-60; prof. preventive medicine, chmn. dept., also asso. prof. medicine Georgetown U. Sch. Medicine, 1960-62; chief Georgetown Med. Service, D.C. Gen. Hosp., 1960-62; chief dept. epidemiology Nat. Jewish Hosp., Denver; dir. med. edn. St. Mary's Hosp., San Francisco, 1966-70; med. dir. Kaiser Center, Kaiser Industries Corp., Oakland, 1970—; lectr. medicine, dept. medicine U. Cal., San Francisco; vis. investigator Rockefeller Inst. Med. Research, 1946-47. Diplomate Am. Bd. Internal Medicine. Mem. Soc. Exptl. Biology and Medicine, Am. Fedn. Clin. Research, Tissue Culture Assn., A.M.A., A.A.A.S., Soc. Am. Bacteriologists, Am. Rheumatism Assn., Am. Thoracic Soc., Am. Heart Assn., N.Y. Acad. Scis., Am. Acad. Allergy, Soc. Nuclear Medicine, Western Soc. Clin. Research. Contbr. articles med. jours. Address: 300 Lakeside Dr Oakland CA 94604

FAVOUR, JOHN MCLEAN, lawyer; b. Prescott, Ariz., Sept. 9, 1921; s. Alpheus Hoyt and Eva (McLean) F.; student Amherst Coll., 1940-42; B.S., U. Ariz., 1946, LL.B., 1949; m. Betty Ogg, Jan. 22, 1943; children—Mollie Zimmerman, Jock McLean, Charles Temple. Admitted to Ariz. bar, 1949, since practiced in Prescott; partner firm Favour and Ouail, 1949—. Trustee Prescott Coll., 1961-65. Served with USAAF, World War II. Mem. Am., Ariz. (pres. 1964-65), Yavapai County bar assns., Chi Phi, Phi Delta Phi. Conglist. Home: 1415 Linden Rd Prescott AZ 86301 Office: PO Box 1391 Prescott AZ

FAVROT, CLIFFORD F., realty exec.; b. New Orleans, July 18, 1898; s. Charles A. and Beatrice M. (Freret) F.; B.E. in Chem. Engrng., Tulane U., 1919; m. Agnes M. Guthrie, Oct. 2, 1920; children—Clifford F., Thomas B., C. Allen, D. Blair, Propr., Favrot Roofing and Supply Co., 1922-39; pres. R.J. Dorn Co. (later Asbestone Corp.) 1939-52; chmn. bd. Carondelet Realty Corp., 1953—; dir. Nat. Gypsum Co. South Central Telephone Co., Whitney Nat. Bank. Royal St. Louis. Inc. Pub. Affairs Research Council, La. Civil Service League. Mem. Nat. Indsl. Cont. Bd., Bur. Govt. Research, Met. Crime Commn., Met. Safety Council. Mayor's Adv. Commn. on Housing Improvement; mem. coordinating com. NASA; nat. trustee Federal City Council. Bd. dirs. New Orleans A.R.C., 1937—, fund chmn. 1937. chpt. chmn., 1950. mem. nat. bd. govs., 1952-53; bd. govs. New Orleans Community Chest, 1946-49, fund chmn., 1946, chest chmn., 1949; a founder, dir. United Fund, 1952-59. pres. 1956 mem. 1952—; bd. dirs. Internat. House, ACTION, Inc.; 1st v.p. bd. adminstrs., past chmn. devel. council Tulane U. Mem. Recipient Times Picayune 1956 Loving Cup, 1957; was Rex of New Orleans Mardi Gras, 1957; recipient 1960 Ann. award New Orleans chpt. Nat. Conf. Christians and Jews; Salvation Army Man of Year award, 1962. Mem. N.A.M., New Orleans Area C. of C. (chmn. finance com.), Delta Kappa Epislon (nat. hon. pres. 1955-56), Tau Beta Pi, Omicron Delta Kappa. Home: 1801 Palmer Av New Orleans LA Office: Carondelet Bldg., New Orleans, LA 70130.

FAW, DUANE LESLIE, lawyer, marine corps officer; b. Loraine, Tex., July 7, 1920; s. Alfred Leslie and Noma Leigh (Elliott) F.; student Tex. State Coll., 1937-41; J.D., Columbia, 1947; m. Lucile Elizabeth Craps, Feb. 20, 1943; children—Cheryl Leigh, Bruce Duane, Debra Leoma, Melanie Loraine. Admitted to Tex. bar, 1948, D.C. bar, 1969, also U.S. Supreme Ct.; individual practice law, Denton and Van Horn, Tex., 1948-52; with USMC, 1942-45, 52—; atty., Cal., 1952-53, Korea/Japan, 1954, Parris Island, S.C., 1955-58; Amphibious Warfare Sr. Sch., 1958-59; battalion comdr., 1959-61; staff judge adv. marine div., 1961-62; policy analyst Marine Hdqrs., 1964-67; dep. chief of staff III Marine Amphibious Force, 1967-68; judge Navy Ct. Mil. Review, 1968-69; dir. Judge Adv. Div. Marine Hdqrs., 1969—; one of original 12 judges Navy Ct. Mil. Review; lectr. mil. law. Decorated Air medal (2), Navy Commendation medal, Legion of Merit with combat V; UN Cross of Gallantry with gold star; UN Honor medal 1st class. Mem. Am. Bar Assn. (adv. com. mil. justice 1969—, adv. com. lawyers in Armed Forces 1969—), Fed. Bar Assn. (council), Judge Advs. Assn. Mason (32). Home: 666 29th Rd S Arlington VA 22202 Office: Hdqrs USMC Washington DC 20380

FAW, HILARY ATKINS Jr., mfg. co. exec.; b. North Wilkesboro, N.C., May 14, 1920; s. Hilary Atkins and Rachel Elizabeth (Decker) F.; student Blue Ridge Coll., 1938-41, Randolph-Macon Coll., 1942; certificate, Pace Coll., 1951; m. Margot McElwain, Jan. 26, 1946; children—Michele, John, Meredith, Mark, David, Andrew. With IBM Corp., 1946—, div. controller data systems div., 1959- 63, corp. controller, 1963-65, asst. treas., dir. bus. practices, 1965—. Mem. Mt. Kisco Planning Bd., 1967-69. Mem. adv. council Pace Coll. Served with USAAF, 1942-45. Mem. Nat. Assn. Accountants, Nat. Maritime Soc. (charter), U.S. Naval Inst. Rotarian. Home: 213 Rowayton Av Rowayton CT 06853 Office: Old Orchard Rd Armonk NY 10509

FAWCETT, DON WAYNE, anatomist; b. Springdale, Ia., Mar. 14, 1917; s. Carlos J. and Mabel (Kennedy) F.; A.B. cum laude, Harvard, 1938, M.D., 1942; m. Dorothy Marie Secrest, 1941; children—Robert S., Mary Elaine, Donna, Joseph. Intern surgery Mass. Gen Hosp., Boston, 1942-43; instr. anatomy Harvard Med. Sch., 1946-48, asso. anatomy, 1948-51, asst. prof. anatomy, 1951-55, Hersey prof. anatomy, 1958—, James Stillman prof. comparative anatomy, 1962—; prof. anatomy Cornell Med. Coll., 1955-58. Served as capt. M.C., AUS, 1943-46, bn. surgeon A.A.A. John and Mary Markle scholar med. sci., 1949-54; recipient Lederle Med. Faculty award, 1954. Fellow Am. Acad. Arts and Sci., Royal Microscopical Soc. (hon.); mem. A.A.A.S., N.Y. Acad. Sci., Am. Assn. Anatomists (pres. 1964-65), N.Y. Soc. Electron Microscopists (pres. 1957-58), Histochem. Soc., Tissue Culture Assn. (v.p. 1954-55), Soc. Exptl. Biology and Medicine, Am. Soc. Zoologists, Am. Soc. Mammalogists, Electron Microscope Soc. Am., Soc. Study Devel. and Growth, Harvey Soc., Am. Soc. Cell Biology (pres. 1961-62), Mexican (hon.), Canadian (hon.) assns. anatomists, Sigma Xi. Author: Atlas of Fine Structure: The Cell, 1966; Textbook of Histology, 1968. Home: 15 Wamesit Rd Waban MA 02168 Office: 25 Shattuck St Boston MA 02115

FAWCETT, HENRY MITCHELL, rubber co. exec.; b. Canton, O., Nov. 30, 1919; s. John Andrew and Pauline (Heingartner) F.; B.A., Colgate U., 1941; indsl. adminstrn. degree, Harvard, 1943; m. Mary Ellen Bloch, Mar. 27, 1943; children—Mary Ellen, Jane M., Julie Ann. Various sales positions Mohawk Rubber Co., Akron, O., 1946-51, asst. pres., 1951-56, pres. 1956—, dir.; dir. Twin Coach Co., Buffalo, 1st Nat. Bank Akron, Pfleuger Corp., Akron. Trustee Boy Scouts Am., YMCA, Salvation Army, Children's Hosp. Akron, Akron City Hosp. Served as lt. USNR, 1942-45. Mem. Akron C. of C. (trustee), Harvard Bus. Sch. Alumni Assn., Newcomen Soc., Sigma Nu. Clubs: Portage Country, University. Home: 470 Delaware Av Akron OH 44303 Office: 1235 2d Av Akron OH 44305

FAWCETT, NOVICE G., univ. pres.; b. Gambier, O., Mar. 29, 1909; s. John Henry and Mary Allie Lampson) F.; B.S. magna cum laude, Kenyon Coll., 1931, LL.D., 1952; student Ashland (O.) Coll., summers 1929, 30; A.M., Ohio State U., 1937, postgrad., 1943-47; LL.D., Kent State U., 1956, Miami U., 1957, Heidelberg Coll., 1960, U. Cin., 1960, Hanover Coll., 1961, Millikin U., 1962, Central State Coll., 1964; L.H.D., Wittenberg U., 1957; Litt.D., Akron U., 1958; D.P.S., Ohio Wesleyan U., 1959, Rio Grande Coll., 1964; H.H.D., U. Americas, 1967; Ped.D., Morris Harvey Coll., 1970; m. Maude E. Yarman, June 17, 1931 (dec. 1948); children—Mary Joan, Jane Elizabeth; m. 2d, Marjorie E. Keener, Aug. 19, 1949. Tchr., Gambier High Sch., 1931-34, supt. schs., 1934-38; supt. schs., Defiance, O., 1938-43, Bexley, O., 1943-48; 1st asst. supt. schs., Akron, O., 1948-49; supt. schs., Columbus, O., 1949-56; instr. grad. sch. Ohio State U., summer 1947; pres. Ohio State U., Columbus, 1956—. Dir. Ohio State Life Insurance Co., Buckeye Fed. Savs. & Loan Assn., Ohio Bell Telephone Co. Past pres. Nat. Assn. State Univs. and Land Grant Colls.; past bd. dirs. Ohio Council on Econ. Edn.; mem. Small Bus. Adv. Council for Ohio, Center for Sci. and Industry Operating Com., Am. Council Edn.; trustee Galbreath First Mortgage Investments, Mut. Investing Found. Mem. Ohio Coll. Assn. (pres. 1966-67), Assn. Am. Univs. (chmn. membership com.), N.E.A., Ohio C. of C. (dir.), Columbus C. of C. (dir.), Pres.'s Profl. Assn., Newcomen Soc. N.Am., A.I.M. (pres.'s council), Phi Beta Kappa, Kappa Phi Kappa. Methodist. Mason (33). Clubs: Columbus Country, Faculty, Kit Kat, University, Rotary, Athletic. Address: Ohio State U Columbus OH 43210

FAWCETT, ROGER KNOWLTON, pub. co. exec.; b. St. Paul, Dec. 3, 1909; s. W.H. and Viva Claire (Meyer) F.; student U. Minn., 1928-29; m. Helen Aline Bergquist, Oct. 17, 1934; children—John R., Thomas Knowlton. Editor, Fawcett Publs., Inc., N.Y.C., 1933-35, sec.-treas., 1935-40, v.p., gen. mgr., 1940-69, pres., 1969—; pres. Fawcett World Library, Crest Books, Gold Medal Books, Premier Books, Fawcett Printing Corp. Mem. Phi Kappa Psi. Republican. Episcopalian. Club: N.Y. Athletic. Home: 998 Fifth Av New York City NY 10028 Office: 1 Astor Plaza New York City NY 10036

FAWCETT, SHERWOOD LUTHER, research lab. exec.; b. Youngstown, O., Dec. 25, 1919; s. Luther T. and Clara (Sherwood) F.; B.S., Ohio State U., 1941; M.S., Case Inst. Tech., 1948, Ph.D., 1950; m. Martha L. Simcox, Feb. 28, 1953; children—Paul, Judith, Tom. Mem. staff Columbus Labs. Battelle Meml. Inst., 1950-64, mgr. physics dept., 1959-64, dir. Pacific Northwest Labs., Richland, Wash., 1964-67; exec. v.p. Battelle Memorial Inst., Columbus, O., 1967- 68, pres., 1968—. Served with the USNR, 1941-46. Decorated Bronze Star. Registered profl. engr., Ohio. Mem. Am. Phys. Soc., Am. Nuclear Soc., Nat. Soc. Profl. Engrs., Sigma Xi, Delta Chi, Sigma Pi Sigma, Tau Beta Pi. Home: 2820 Margate Rd Columbus OH 43221 Office: 505 King Av Columbus OH 42201

FAWLEY, JOHN JONES, banker; b. Phila., Oct. 1, 1921, s. James L. and Edna (Jones) F.; B.S. in Econs., Wharton Sch., U. Pa., 1948; grad. Rutgers U. Grad. Sch. Banking, 1957; m. Ann Kemp, Jan. 8, 1944; children—Jo Ann (Mrs. Richard High), Christine, James K. With First Pa. Bank, Phila., 1948-69, sr. v.p., 1968- 69; pres., dir. United Va. Bank/First & Citizens Nat. Bank, Alexandria, Va., 1969—; lectr. Comml. Lending Sch., U. Okla., 1969. Served with AUS, 1942-45. Mem. Robert Morris Assos. (1st v.p.). Presbyn. (past trustee). Mason. Home: 4318 Adrienne Dr Alexandria VA 22309 Office: 515 King St Alexandria VA 22314

FAWZI, MAHMOUD, U.A.R. govt. ofcl.; b. 1900; ed. U. Cairo (Egypt), U. Rome (Italy), U. Liverpool (Eng.), Columbia. Vice consul, N.Y.C., New Orleans, 1926-29; consul, Kobe, Japan, 1929-36; 2d sec., Athens, Greece, 1926-27; consul, then consul-gen., Liverpool, 1937-40; dir. dept. nationalities U.A.R. Ministry Fgn. Affairs, 1940-41; consul-gen., Jerusalem, 1941-44; Egyptian rep. Security Council UN, 1946, then permanent rep.; ambassador to Gt. Britain, 1958-64; mem. Presidency Council, 1962-64; dep. prime minister for fgn. affairs, 1964-67; v.p., pres.'s asst. fgn. affairs, 1967-68; now premier U.A.R.*

FAY, ALBERT BEL, mem. Republican Nat. Com.; b. New Orleans, Feb. 26, 1913; s. Charles Spencer and Marie Dorothy (Bel) F.; B.S. in Geology, Yale, 1936; m. Homoiselle Haden, Feb. 3, 1935; children—Katherine (Mrs. W. Lloyd Lane), Marion (Mrs. Peder Monsen), Albert Bel. With Gray & Wilmerding, 1936-37; exec. v.p., dir. Lacassane Co., Lake Charles, La.; founder, v.p. Eagle Lake Rice Dryer (Tex.); co-founder, v.p., dir. Bel Oil Corp., Lake Charles; partner Quatre Parish Co., Lake Charles; founder, dir. Lake Arthur Rice Dryer (La.), Seabrook Shipyard (Tex.); dir. Swearingen Aircraft, Inc., San Antonio, Panama Canal Co. Mem. Republican Nat. Com. for Tex., 1960-69, mem. Rep. Nat. Finance Com., 1968—. Trustee Mus. Natural Sci. (pres. elect 1970—). Served to lt. (s.g.) USNR, World War II. Mem. Am. Brahman Breeders Assn. (past dir.), Delta Psi. Clubs: St. Anthony, Yale, Cruising of Am. (N.Y.C.); Seawanhaka Corinthian Yacht (Oyster Bay, N.Y.); Houston Country, Tejas, Bayou, Yale of Southeastern Tex., Petroleum (Houston); Galveston Artillery, Galveston Bay Cruising Assn.; Texas Corinthian Yacht (Kemah); N.Y. Yacht. Home: 99 N Post Oak Lane Houston TX 77024 Office: 515 Houston Av Houston TX 77007

FAY, ALBERT HILL, bldg. materials co. exec.; b. Bklyn., Aug. 19, 1911; s. Albert Hill and Clara (Constable) F.; B.Arch., Columbia, 1934, M.S., 1935; m. Leona May Anderson, Sept. 4, 1934. Product mgr., then prodn. mgr. Flintkoke Corp., 1936-50; advt. mgr. Ashestone Corp., New Orleans, 1950-53; dir. product mgmt. Nat. Gypsum Co., Buffalo, 1953-65, v.p. marketing, 1965-69, v.p. research and marketing, 1969—; trustee Niagara Frontier Housing Devel. Corp.; dir. Towne Homes, Inc., Columbus, O. Trustee Housing Center Council, 1969—. Bd. dirs. Brand Names Found. Served to lt. USNR, 1944-46. Mem. Nat. Home Improvement Council (pres.), Asbestos Cement Products Assn. (pres.), Asbestos Information Assn. N.Am. (pres.). Home: 63 Jordan Rd Williamsville NY 14221 Office: 325 Delaware Av Buffalo NY 14202

FAY, CHARLES W., investment banker; b. San Jose, Cal., Sept. 1, 1903; s. Charles W. and Estelle (Lion) F.; student U. Cal., 1926; m. Dorothy Mein, July 7, 1932; children—Frances (Mrs. John G. Bowes), Dorothy (Mrs. Hamilton Robinson, Jr.), Victoria. Contractor, Fay Improvement Co., 1926-32; real estate broker Buckbee-Thorne & Co., 1932-37; pres., chmn. bd. Hooker & Fay, Inc., San Francisco, 1937-63; sr. v.p., mem. exec. com., dir. William R. Staats & Co. (after merger with Hooker & Fay Inc., 1963), 1963-65; sr. v.p., dir. Glore Forgan, Wm. R. Staats Inc. (after merger), 1965-70; sr. v.p. F.I. duPont, Glore Forgan & Co., 1970—; vice chmn. bd. L. Lion and Sons Co., San Jose, Cal., 1936-67, Roos/Atkins, San Francisco; dir. Clear Lake Water Co., Woodland, Cal., 1939-67. Chmn. mgmt. com. U. Cal. Centennial Fund, 1967—; pres. Nob Hill Improvement Assn., 1969—. Chmn. Bay Area Council A.R.C., 1959-64, now mem.-at-large bd. dirs. Golden Gate chpt.; bd. dirs. United Bay Area Crusade, Nat. Pollution Control Found.; trustee, exec., com. U. Cal. Alumni Found.; trustee Garrison Forest Sch., Balt. Served to lt. comdr. USNR, 1942-45. Mem. U. Cal. Alumni Assn. (alumni council, exec. com.), Delta Kappa Epsilon. Clubs: Bohemian, Pacific Union, Burlingame Country, Golf, Commonwealth of Cal. (San Francisco); California (Los Angeles); Racquet and Tennis (N.Y.C.) Home: 1055 California St San Francisco CA 94108 Office: 555 California St San Francisco CA 94104

FAY, DOUGLAS HIGHAM, banker; b. Buffalo, Apr. 25, 1917; s. Seneca Allen and Ethel D. (Higgins) F.; B.S., U. Buffalo, 1940, M.B.A., 1944; m. Martha Jane Hunt, May 29, 1941; children—Arthur Allen, Barbara Jean. Asst. dir. war tng. courses U. Buffalo, 1941; asst. cashier Niagara Nat. Bank (name later changed to First Nat. Bank), Buffalo, 1947-50, comptroller, 1950-55; asst. v.p. Mfrs. & Traders Trust Co., Buffalo, 1955-63, v.p., comml. loan officer, 1963-64; v.p. auditor, 1964—; lectr. finance, accounting State U. N.Y., 1940-68, professorial lectr., 1968—; lectr. Am. Inst. Banking, Canisius Coll., Coll. Life Underwriters. Served to lt. (j.g.) USNR, 1944-46. Mem. Beta Gamma Sigma. Methodist. Mason. Home: 8623 Howard Dr Williamsville NY 14221 Office: M & T Plaza Buffalo NY 14240

FAY, FREDERIC ALBERT, city ofcl.; b. Oneonta, N.Y., July 4, 1911; s. Earl Donovan and Madoline (Lewis) F.; B.S., Syracuse U., 1933; postgrad. Harvard, 1934, U. Va., 1942; m. Wray Hass, Feb. 9, 1936 (dec., 1956); 1 dau., Anne Madoline (Mrs. Albert N. Justice); m. 2d, Virginia Easton Ford, Feb. 11, 1961. Asst. landscape architect Central N.Y. State Parks Commn., Syracuse, 1933-34; asst. landscape architect Nat. Parks Service, Gatlinburg, Tenn., Richmond, Va., 1934-41; tech. dir., asst. exec. dir. Portsmouth (Va.) Redevel. and Housing Authority, 1941-49; architect-engr. George T. McLean Co., Inc., Portsmouth, 1949-50; exec. dir. Richmond Redevel. and Housing Authority, 1950—; mem. slum clearance adv. com. U.S. HHFA, Va. Adv. Legislative Council, 1957; mem. Va. Emergency Resources Planning Com., 1965; mem. jury PHA Honor Awards for Design Excellence Program, 1964. Mem. exec. com. Richmond Symphony; trustee Old Dominion Symphony Council. Named Honorary Citizen Nashville, 1955; New Orleans, 1967, Grant's Pass, Ore., 1967, Portland, Ore., 1967. Fellow Am. Soc. Landscape Architects; hon. mem. A.I.A.; mem. Am. Soc. Planning Ofcls., Am. Inst. Planners, Nat. Assn. Housing and Redevel. Ofcls. (pres., bd. govs.), Sigma Chi. Democrat. Episcopalian. Clubs: Commonwealth, Rotary (Richmond); Golden Horseshoe (Williamsburg). Contbr. articles profl. jours. Home: 801 St Christophers Rd Richmond VA 23226 Office: PO Box 2-AF Richmond VA 23205

FAY, HORACE BYRON, Jr., lawyer; b. Cleve., July 6, 1915; s. Horace Byron and Mable (Keating) F.; student Amherst Coll., 1933-35; A.B., U. Chgo., 1937; LL.B., Western Res. U., 1940; m. Elizabeth Jean Berne, Apr. 30, 1943; children—Gerald Keating, Darcie Hunt, Holly Prentice. Admitted to Ohio bar, 1940, U.S. Supreme Ct., others; asso. firm Fay, Golrick & Fay, Cleve., 1940-51; partner firm Fay & Fay, Cleve., 1951-61; asst. commr. U.S. Patent Office, 1961-65; dir. patent dept. Allied Chem. Corp., 1965—; cons. to firm Fay & Fay, 1965—; lectr. Case Inst. Tech., 1951-52. Trustee Citizens League Greater Cleve., 1957-61, v.p., 1960-62. Councilman, City South Euclid, 1950-53. Served to lt. comdr., aviator, USNR, 1941-45. Mem. Am., Cleve. bar assns., Am., N.Y. (gov.), N.J., Cleve. patent law assns., Heights C. of C. (trustee, pres. 1955-58), Am. Judicature Soc., Mfg. Chemists Assn., Internat. Patent and Trademark Assn., Nat. Assn. Mfrs., U.S. Trademark Assn., Phi Kappa Psi, Phi Delta Phi. Clubs: Cleveland Athletic; Serra. Home: 10 Deer Path Short Hills NJ 07078 also 2853 Fairmont Blvd Cleveland OH 44118 Office: Allied Chem Corp PO Box 70 Morristown NJ 07960

FAY, JAMES ALAN, educator; b. Southold, N.Y., Nov. 1, 1923; s. William Joseph, Jr. and Margaret (Keenan) F.; B.S., Webb Inst. Naval Architecture, 1944; M.S., Mass. Inst. Tech., 1947; Ph.D., Cornell U., 1951; m. Agatha Marie Kelly, Jan. 12, 1946; children—David Anthony, Mark Bernard, Colin Michael, Jamie Martin, Peter Robert, Michele Marie. Research engr. Lima-Hamilton Corp., 1947-49; asst. prof. engring. mechanics Cornell U., 1951-55; mem. faculty Mass. Inst. Tech., 1955, prof. mech. engring., 1960—; cons. to industry, 1950—. Served with USNR, 1942-46. Fellow Am. Acad. Arts and Scis., Am. Phys. Soc. (exec. com. div. fluid dynamics 1964-67); mem. Am. Inst. Aero. and Astronautics (chmn. plasmadynamics com. 1966—), Am. Soc. M.E., Sigma Xi. Author: Molecular Thermodynamics, 1965; also articles. Home: 36 Spruce Hill Rd Weston MA 02193 Office: Mass Inst Tech Cambridge MA 02139

FAY, LEON CONVERSE, clergyman; b. Lynn, Mass., July 5, 1913; s. Leon C. and C. Maude (Robertson) F.; A.B., Tufts U., 1944, S.T.B., 1945; m. Lois Ruth Messenger, Feb. 19, 1944; children—Douglas S., Leon Converse, Jennifer Lee. Asst. to mgr., gen. sales div. Ford Motor Co., 1933-40; ordained to ministry Am. Unitarian Assn., 1945; minister in East and West Bridgewater, Mass., Scituate, Mass. and Nashau, N.H., 1945-57; dir. dept. ministry Am. Unitarian Assn., 1957-61, Unitarian Universalist Assn., 1961-66; minister First Unitarian Ch., Albuquerque, 1966—. Founder, pres. New Eng. Unitarian Ministers Assn., 1950-52; continental pres. Unitarian Ministers Assn., 1952-54; bd. dirs. Am. Unitarian Assn., 1953-57, Soc. Ministerial Relief, 1957-70; mem. N.M. Conf. on Law and Clergy, 1970; settlement dir. Desert Conf. Unitarian-Universalist Chs. and Fellowships, 1969—; pres. Mountain-Desert Unitarian-Universalist Ministerial Assn., 1970—, Bd. dirs. Albuquerque Assn. Mental Health, 1966-70, Bernalillo County Assn. Planned Parenthood, 1967—; mem. bd. N.M. Conf. Social Welfare 1967-70, pres., 1969; mem. bd. N.M. Mental Health Assn., 1968. Mem. of the Am. Acad. of Polit. and Social Sci., Albuquerque Com. Fgn. Relations, Greenfield Group (pres. 1955- 57). Author: The Minister's Security, 1962; Settlement Procedures for Ministers and Churches, 1962; Ordination and Installation in Unitarian Universalist Churches, 1965; Misappropriation of the Laymen's Commitment, 1965. Editor: (with J. W. Brigham) Ministerial Leadership in the Unitarian Universalist Association, 1963. Editor: A Plan of Education for the Unitarian Universalist Ministry, 1962; (with John Crane) Career Hysteria and Professional Autonomy, 1965. Home: 13454 Desert Hills Pl NE Albuquerque NM 87111 Office: 3701 Carlisle Blvd NE Albuquerque NM 87110

FAY, MARION SPENCER, educator; b. New Orleans, July 24, 1896; d. Charles Spencer and Maud (Lobdell) Fay; A.B., Newcomb Coll., Tulane U., 1915; A.M., U. Colo., 1922; Ph.D., Yale, 1925; LL.D., Temple U., Moravian Coll., Hahnemann Med. Coll., 1962; D.Sc., Woman's Med. Coll., Beaver Coll., Elmira Coll., Smith Coll., Wilson Coll.; LL.D., Tulane U. Tchr. history, Kosciusko (Miss.) High Sch., 1916-18; instr. physiol. chemistry, U. Colo., Boulder, 1920-22; adj. prof. and asso. prof. physiol. chemistry, U. of Tex. Med. Br., Galveston, Tex., 1925-35; prof. physiol. chemistry, Woman's Med. Coll. Pa., Phila., 1935—, acting dean, 1943-46, dean, 1946-64, pres., 1959-64, pres., and dean emeritae, 1964-70, acting pres., 1970—. Named Distinguished Dau. of Pa. 1957; recipient Gimbel award, 1959. Mem. Am. Soc. of Biol. Chemists, A.A.A.S., Am. Chem. Soc., Physiol. Soc. of Phila., Sigma Xi, Iota Sigma Pi, Chi Omega. Contbr. articles on biochem. subjects to sci. jours. Home: 3233 Queen Lane Philadelphia PA 19129

FAY, THOMAS F., beverage co. exec. Controller, Canada Dry Corp. Office: 100 Park Av New York City NY 10017*

FAY, WILLIAM EDWARD, Jr., investment banker; b. Joliet, Ill., Feb. 14, 1917; s. William Edward and Helen (Maloney) F.; A.B., Brown U., 1938; m. Margaret Ann Hoover, Feb. 24, 1941; children—Linda Jane (Mrs. David R. Perera), Molly Lou (Mrs. William P. Gottschalk), William Edward III, Lisa Hoover. Sales trainee Halsey, Stuart & Co., Chgo., 1939-41; with Smith, Barney & Co., Inc., Chgo., 1946—, partner, 1958—, v.p., 1964-67, sr. v.p., 1967-69, exec. v.p., 1970—, also mem. mgmt. com., dir. Chmn. bd. dirs. Brain Research Found.; bd. dirs. United Charities Chgo. Served as lt. USNR, 1942-46. Clubs: Old Elm (Highland Park, Ill.); Indian Hill (Winnetka); Shoreacres (Lake Bluff, Ill.); Chicago, University, Racquet (Chgo.). Home: 325 White Oak Lane Winnetka IL 60093 Office: 1 1st Nat Plaza Chicago IL 60670

FAY, WILLIAM MICHAEL, U.S. judge; b. Pittston, Pa.; s. William Morris and Carolyn (Runner) F.; student Georgetown U., 1939; LL.B., Cath. U. Am., 1942; m. Jean Burke, Sept. 8, 1945; 1 son, W. Michael. Admitted to D.C. bar, 1942; asst. counsel atomic energy com. U.S. Senate, 1946; exec. sec. U.S. Senator McMahon, 1946-48; with Chief Counsel's Office, Internal Revenue Service, 1948-61, asst. regional counsel, 1957-61; judge Tax Ct. U.S., 1961—. Served with USNR, 1942-45. Mem. Am. Bar Assn., Bar Assn. D.C., U.S. Senate Assn. Adminstrv. Assts. and Secs. Home: 5809 Highland Dr Kenwood Chevy Chase MD 20015 Office: Tax Ct of US Washington DC 20044

FAYER, MISCHA HARRY, educator; b. N.Y.C., June 6, 1902; s. Max and Sara (Feldman) F.; B.A., U. Minn., 1926, M.A., 1928; Ph.D., Columbia, 1945; Litt. D., Middlebury Coll., 1969; widowed, 1964; m. 2d, Florence L. Kleinman, May 18, 1968. Organizer, head Russian dept. Middlebury (Vt.) Coll., 1943-67, Russian Sch., 1945-67, Inst. Soviet Studies, 1958-67; prof., chmn. dept. Slavic and Oriental langs. U. Ky., 1967—. Mem. Am. Assn. Tchrs. Slavic and Eastern European Langs., Modern Lang. Assn., Am. Assn. U. Profs. Author: Gide, Freedom and Dostoevsky, 1946; Basic Russian I, 1959, 2d edit., 1969; Basic Russian II, 1961; Simplified Russian Grammar, 2d edit., 1963. Home: 2121 Nicholasville Rd Lexington KY 40503

FAYLE, HARLAN DOWNING, educator; b. Hibbing, Minn., July 24, 1907; s. James Robert and Mabel (Downing) F.; B.A., Hamline U., 1931; M.S., U. Minn., 1936, Ph.D., 1963; m. Catherine Marie Hove, Aug. 15, 1936; 1 son, Robert D. Tchr. Eveleth (Minn.) Jr. Coll., 1933-36, Hibbing Jr. Coll., 1936-46, Duluth Jr. Coll., 1946-48, U. Minn., 1948-55; prof. chemistry, chmn. sect. Purdue U. at Hammond, 1956—; cons. to industry. Fellow Am. Inst. Chemists, N.Y. Acad. Scis.; mem. Am. Chem. Soc., A.A.A.S., Am. Assn. Univ. Profs., Kappa Phi Kappa. Methodist (ofcl. bd.). Research on mechanism of Toxic action of cadmium, absorption, distbn. and excretion of cadmium in animals, exptl. cadmium toxicity studies in animals. Home: 7512 Knickerbocker Pkwy Hammond IN 46323

FAZIO, CARL, food co. exec. Chmn. bd. Fisher Foods, Inc.; dir. Midwest Bank & Trust Co. Mem. nat. bd. Am. Com. on Italian Migration; chmn. Cleve. Little Hoover Commn.; bd. dirs. Greater Cleve. Growth Assn., Cleve. Conv. and Visitors Bur.; exec. com. Cleve. Retail Merchants Bd. Trustee Cleve.- Marshall Law Sch.; adv. bd. St. John's Hosp., Cleve. Mem. Nat. Assn. Food Chains (dir.) , Super Market Inst. (dir.) . K.C. (4). Address: 5300 Richmond Rd Bedford Heights OH 44146

FAZIO, JOHN, supermarket exec.; b. Cleve., Jan. 23, 1920; s. Charles and Josephine (Russo) F.; student U. Tulsa, 1944; m. Anita M. Bender, June 4, 1941; children—Charles Walter, John, Janice Jo. Engaged in food bus., 1941—; pres. Fazio's Supermarkets, Cleve., 1957—, Fisher Foods Inc., Cleve., 1965—. Served with AUS, 1943-46. Mem. Supermarket Inst., Asso. Retail Bakers Am. Baptist. Home: 3450 Roundwood Rd Chagrin Falls OH 44022 Office: Fisher Foods 5300 Richmond Rd Bedford Heights OH 44146

FEAGANS, WILLIAM M., univ. dean. Prof., dean Sch. Dentistry, State U. N.Y. at Buffalo. Office: State U NY at Buffalo Buffalo NY 14214*

FEAGIN, ROBERT R., newspaper exec. Pres. Times Union Jour. Address: 400 W Adams St Jacksonville FL 32201*

FEAREY, MORTON, lawyer; b. N.Y.C., Jan. 25, 1913; s. Morton Lazell and Julia (Lawrence) F.; A.B., Yale, 1935, LL.B., 1938; m. Mary Cowham Senior, June 29, 1937; children—Julia L. (Mrs. Robert Habgood), Morton, Mary S., John L.S. Admitted to N.Y. bar, 1939, Dist. Ct., 1946; with firm Davis, Polk & Wardwell, and predecessors, N.Y.C., 1938—, mem., 1951—. Dir., exec. com. Gen. Portland Cement Co. Dallas, North Atlantic Life Ins. Co. Am. Served from lt. (j.g.) to lt. comdr., USNR, 1942-46. Mem. Am., N.Y. State bar assns., Bar Assn. City N.Y. Home: 174 East 80th St New York City NY 10021 Office: 1 Chase Manhattan Plaza New York City NY 10005

FEAREY, ROBERT APPLETON, govt. ofcl.; b. Garden City, N.Y., July 4, 1918; s. Morton L. and Julia (Lawrence) F.; grad. Groton Sch., 1937; A.B., Harvard, 1941; m. Shirley Ann Granum, Oct. 1, 1945; children—Seth G., Barbara L., Ann L., Peter C., Paul L. Pvt. sec. to Am. ambassador, Tokyo, Japan, 1941-42; State Dept. positions in Washington and Tokyo, 1942-50; spl. asst. to Ambassador John F. Dulles, 1950-51; mem. U.S. delegation to NATO, Paris, France, 1951-56; NATO adviser State Dept., 1956-58; student Nat. War Coll., 1958-59; assigned Am. embassy, Tokyo, 1959-61; charge Japanese affairs State Dept., 1961-64, dir. East Asian affairs, 1964-65; polit. adviser to comdr. in chief Pacific, minister, 1966-69; civil adminstr. Ryukyu Islands (Okinawa), minister, 1969—. Mem. Delta Kappa Epsilon. Clubs: Hasty Pudding, Spee (Harvard); Chevy Chase (Md.); Metropolitan (D.C.). Author: The Occupation of Japan, 1950; The United States Versus the USSR—Ideologies in Conflict, 1959. Address: USCAR-CA APO San Francisco CA 96248

FEARING, JERRY, cartoonist. Editorial cartoonist St. Paul Pioneer Press Dispatch. Office: 55 E 4th St St Paul MN 55101*

FEARNS, JOHN M. A., bishop; b. N.Y.C., June 25, 1897; s. Robert Joseph and Margaret Ann (McLaughlin) F.; A.B., St. Joseph's Sem. and Coll., 1918; S.T.D., Propaganda U., Rome, Italy, 1923; student Gregorian U., Rome, 1924-25; LL.D., Fordham U., 1941, Manhattan Coll., 1951. Ordained priest Roman Cath. Ch., 1922, named domestic prelate, 1941, prothonotary apostolic, 1950; asst. in chs., N.Y.C. and New Rochelle, N.Y., 1923; chaplain, instr. catechetics St. Clare's Acad., Hastings, N.Y., 1925-26; asst. Ch. of Resurrection, Rye, N.Y., 1927-30; prof. moral theology and canon law St. Joseph's Sem., Dunwoodie, N.Y., 1930-40; pres. St. Joseph's Coll. and Sem., 1940-56; pastor St. Francis de Sales Ch., N.Y.C., 1956-66, St. Patrick's Ch., Newburgh, N.Y., 1966—; consecreated aux. bishop of N.Y. and titular bishop of Geras, 1957; Episcopal vicar Orange and Rockland Counties, N.Y. Mem. matrimonial ct. Archdiocese N.Y., 1931-38, judge, 1938-40; censor librorum Archdiocese N.Y., 1942-56, bd. consultors, 1948—; chmn. Archdiocesan Liturgical Commn. Mem. Orange County Mental Health Bd. Charter mem. Cath. Theol. Soc. Am. (research com. 1945-51, pres. 1953); mem. Nat. Cath. Edn. Assn. (v.p. sem. sect. 1945, exec. bd. 1946, 53-56), Canon Law Soc., Marian Soc., St. Paul's Guild (Am. rep.), Assn. Bishops English Speaking Countries, Conf. Cath. Am. Bishops (mem. priestly formation com. 1965-70, liaison com. for religious 1966-70, doctrine com.). Address: 55 Grand St Newburgh NY 12550

FEARON, GEORGE RANDOLPH, lawyer; b. Oneida, N.Y., Mar. 12, 1883; s. George and Anna Elizabeth L. Nichol (Charlow) F.; LL.B., Syracuse U., 1905; m. Cora L. Nichols, Nov. 17, 1909; children—Helen (Mrs. Louis E. Ginter), Elizabeth (Mrs. Royal L. O'Day); m. 2d, Katherine P. McBride, Aug. 5, 1953. Admitted to N.Y. bar, 1905, since practiced in Syracuse; sr. mem. Costello, Cooney & Fearon, 1920—. Mem. N.Y. State Assembly, 1916-20; N.Y. State Senate, 1921-36, pres. pro tem and majority leader, 1931-32, minority leader, 1933- 36; mem. N.Y. State Constl. Conv., 1938. Fellow Am. Coll. Trial Lawyers; mem. Am., N.Y. State (v.p. 1952- 56), Onondaga County (past pres.) bar assns. Mason (32, Jester). Clubs: entury, Onondaga (Syracuse); Skytop (Pa.). Home: 770 James St Syracuse NY 13203

FEARON, ROBERT HENRY, banker; b. Oneida, N.Y., Aug. 7, 1900; s. Henry D. and Mary A. (Fuller) F.; B.S., Syracuse U., 1922; m. Ruby J. Kilts, Aug. 27, 1926; chilren—Robert Henry, Patricia A. (Mrs. Richard H. Howarth). With Blair & Co., 1922-24; with Oneida Valley Nat. Bank, 1924—, pres., 1942-71, chmn., 1971—; pres. Sylvan Spring Water Co., Sylvan Beach, N.Y., 1948—, also dir.; treas. Marcellus Lumber Co., Oneida, 1940-68. Trustee N.Y. State Bankers Retirement System. Treas. Madison County council Boy Scouts Am., 1930-58, Oneida City Hosp. Found. Inc. Bd. dirs. Oneida Library, Oneida Area Industries. Served with USNR, 1918. Recipient Silver Beaver award Boy Scouts Am., 1936. Mem. N.Y. State (past chmn. group IV, past treas. assn.), Madison County (past pres.) bankers assns., Delta Kappa Epsilon. Republican. Methodist (past trustee, trustee Central N.Y. Conf.). Elk, Rotarian (past Oneida). Oneida) . Clubs: Seven Oaks Golf (Hamilton, N.Y.). Home: 501 Broad St Oneida NY 13422 Office: Oneida Valley Nat Bank Oneida NY 13422

FEASTER, ESTON KERMIT, coll. pres.; b. Maysville, W.Va., Oct. 14, 1910; s. Albert L. and Stella (Parsons) F.; student Bridgewater (Va.) Coll., 1929-31, Shepherd State Coll., Shepherdstown, W.Va., summer 1931; B.A., Fairmont (W.Va.) State Coll., 1935; M.A., W.Va. U., 1940; Ed.D., George Washington U., 1952; m. Clarice Tucker, Aug. 26, 1937; 1 son, Eston Kenneth. Elementary sch. tchr., Grant County, W.Va., 1931-33, elementary sch. prin., 1933-43, asst. county supt. schs., 1943-44; asst. county supt. schs., Berkeley County, W.Va., 1945-46; dir. tchr. edn. and field service Concord Coll., Athens, W.Va., 1946-49; lectr. edn. George Washington U., 1949; dir. field edn. W.Va. U., 1952-53, acting dean Coll. Edn., 1952-53, dean Coll. Edn., 1953-60; pres. Fairmont State Coll., 1960—. Dir. Survey Ednl. Programs of W.Va. Pub. Schs., 1957. Served with AUS, World War II. Mem. Nat. Soc. Study Edn., A.A.A.S., Phi Delta Kappa, Kappa Delta Pi. Mason, Kiwanian (past lt. gov.). Contbr. ednl. jours. Home: President's Home Fairmont State Coll Fairmont WV 26554

FEATHER, LEONARD GEOFFREY, composer, music critic; b. London, Eng., Sept. 13, 1914; s. Nathan and Felicia (Zelinski) F.; student Univ. Coll. Sch., London, 1920-26, St. Paul's Sch., London, 1926-31; m. Jane Larrabee, May 18, 1945; 1 dau., Lorraine. Came to U.S., 1935, naturalized, 1948. Writer, London Melody Maker, 1933—, Esquire mag., 1943-56, Down Beat, 1951—, Playboy, 1956-62, Internat. Musician, 1961—, Show Mag., 1962—, also for mags. in London, Paris, Stockholm, Berlin; arranger Count Basie, other orchs.; composer lyrics and music various popular singers; emcee radio shows; condr. jazz programs Voice of Am., 1950-52, weekly program 1967—; also broadcasts for B.B.C., London, 1969; producer Jazz Show, KNBC, Los Angeles, 1971; music quiz Platter-brains, ABC Radio Network, 1953—; toured Europe with own prodn. Jazz Club U.S.A., 1954; composer music The Weary Blues for record album of poems, Metro-Goldwyn-Mayer, 1958; cons. Ednl. TV series The Subject is Jazz, NBC, 1958; adv. bd. Newport (R.I.) Jazz Festival; script writer Jazz Scene U.S.A., TV series, 1962-63; commentator at jazz concerts, lectures, 1960—. Mem. Nat. Acad. Rec. Arts and Scis. (bd. govs. 1968-69), A.S.C.A.P., Am. Fedn. Musicians, N.A.A.C.P. Author: Encyclopedia of Jazz, 1955; Book of Jazz, 1957; New Yearbook of Jazz, 1958; New Ency. of Jazz, 1960; Laughter From the

Hip, 1964; The Encyclopedia of Jazz in the '60s, 1966. Contbr. to World Book Ency. and yearbooks, 1955—. Home: 3510 Wrightwood Dr North Hollywood CA 91604

FEATHER, WILLIAM, author, pub.; b. Jamestown, N.Y., Aug. 25, 1889; s. George E. and Henrietta (Hodgson) F.; A.B., Adelbert Coll. (Western Reserve U.), 1910; m. Ruth Presley, Oct. 30, 1912; children—William, Judith. Reporter Cleve. Press, 1910-15; with publicity dept. Nat. Cash Register Co., Dayton, O., 1915-16; organizer, 1916, and past pres. William Feather Co., printers and pubs., Cleve. Author: As We Were Saying, 1921; Haystacks and Smokestacks, 1923; Ideals and Follies of Business, 1927; Business of Life, 1949; Talk About Women, 1960; also articles under title "A Business Man's Philosophy," in newspapers, etc. Editor and pub. The William Feather Magazine, and group of house mags. for indls. cos. Home: 19201 Van Aken Blvd Shaker Heights Cleveland OH 44122 Office: 9900 Clinton Rd Cleveland OH 44144

FEATHERSTON, C. MOXLEY, U.S. judge; b. Jayton, Tex., June 6, 1914; s. William Matthew and Fannie Eva (Roberts) F.; A.B., Hardin-Simmons U., 1935; J.D., George Washington U., 1939; m. Rose Darlington Ross, Dec. 29, 1938; children—Ross Moxley, Neal Roberts, Rose Anne. Admitted to D.C. bar, 1939, Tex. bar, 1940; pvt. practice, Hereford, Tex., 1940; atty. Dept. Agr., 1940-42, War Relocation Authority, 1942-45; asst. gen. counsel Inst. Inter-Am. Affairs, 1949-51; atty. Dept. Justice, 1945-49, 51-67; judge U.S. Tax Ct., 1967—. Mem. Order of Coif, Alpha Chi. Baptist. Home: 2010 Lorraine Av McLean VA 22101 Office: US Tax Ct 12th and Constitution Av Washington DC 20044

FEATHERSTON, ERRETT GLENN, former ednl. adminstr.; b. Callao, Mo., Oct. 15, 1900; s. E.C. and Mattie (Cummingham) F.; student Central Coll., 1920-22; B.S., U. Mo., 1929, M.A., 1931, Ed.D., 1940; m. Sophia Nelle Eubank, Aug. 19, 1931; 1 dau., Jean Ellen. Tchr., prin. high sch., supt. schs., Madison, Mo., 1922-28; prin. high sch., Prairie Hill, Mo., 1928-29; prin. high sch., supt. schs., Huntsville, Mo., 1929-38; dir. research Mo. Dept. Edn., Jefferson City, 1938-41, asst. state supt. schs., 1941-43; with U.S. Office of Edn., 1943-70, successively specialist for pupil transp., asst. dir., dir. adminstrn. br., acting asst. commr. edn., 1943-58, asst. commr. edn., dir. div. state and local sch. systems, 1958-62, dep. asso. commr. research and devel., 1962-65, dep. dir. div. state agy. cooperation, 1965-68, dep. asso. commr. for fed.-state relations, 1968- -. Mem. N.E.A., Am. Assn. Sch. Adminstrs., Am. Ednl. Research Assn., Mo. Tchrs. Assn., Mo. Soc. (pres. Washington 1960-61) . Co-author: Pupil Transportation; also author numerous articles and bulls. on pupil transp. Home: 6427 Quincy Pl Falls Church VA 22042

FEATHERSTONE, ROBERT MARION, educator, pharmacologist; b. Anderson, Ind., Dec. 24, 1914; s. Marion L. and Adah Mary (Brown) F.; B.A., Ball State U., 1940, LL.D., 1962; M.S., U. Ia., 1940, Ph.D., 1954; m. Joyce Amanda Byrum, Aug. 31, 1940; children—David Byrum, Jean, James Byrum, Judith Ann. Instr. biochemistry Med. Coll. of S.C., 1943-44; asst. prof., asso. prof., then prof. pharmacology U. Ia. Coll. Medicine, 1944-57; prof., chmn. dept. pharmacology and exptl. therapeutics U. Cal. Sch. Medicine, San Francisco, 1957—. Chmn. pharmacology tng. program com. NIH, 1963-67. Commonwealth Fund fellow U. London (Eng.), 1965-66. Mem. Am. Soc. Pharmacology and Exptl. Therapeutics (council 1958-61, 64-67, pres. 1968) , Soc. Exptl. Biology and Med., Am. Chem. Soc. (chmn. I. 1947) , N.Y. Acad. of Scis., Tissue Culture Soc., Western Pharmacology Soc. (pres. 1960), Sigma Xi. Author, editor: (with A. Simon) A Pharmacologic Approach to the Study of the Mind, 1959; (with J. Hidalgo) Farmacologia del Sistema Nervioso Autonomo, 1963. Editorial cons. Sci., Biochem. Pharmacology, Molecular Pharmacology. Author research papers. Home: 15 Corlett Way Hillsborough CA 94010 Office: U of Cal Med Center San Francisco CA 94122

FEAVER, JOHN CLAYTON, educator; b. Fowler, Cal., June 24, 1911; s. Ernest Albion and Agnes Katherine (Hansen) F.; A.B., Fresno State Coll., 1933; student San Francisco Theol. Sem. 1934; B.D., Pacific Sch. Religion, 1936; Ph.D., Yale, 1949; m. Margaret Storsand, June 21, 1936; children—John Hansen, Katherine Elaine, Margaret Ellen. Asst., then asso. prof. philosophy Berea Coll., 1941-51; Kingfisher Coll. prof. philosophy religion and ethics U. Okla., 1951—, David Ross Boyd prof. philosophy, 1959—. Chmn. exec. com. Okla. Coll. Continuing Edn.; chmn. exec. com. S.W. Center Human Relations Studies. Mem. Am. Philos. Assn., Southwestern Philos. Soc. (pres. 1960), So. Soc. Philosophy Religion, Am. Acad. Religion, Am. Assn. U. Profs., Phi Beta Kappa, Omicron Delta Kappa. Co-editor: Religion in Philosophical and Cultural Perspective, 1967. Home: 900 E Boyd St Norman OK 73069

FEDER, AARON, physician, educator; b. N.Y.C., May 1, 1915; s. Herman and Fannie (Trenner) F.; student N.Y.U., 1931-34; Exchange scholar, Harvard Med. Sch., 1937; M.D., U. Md., 1938; m. Beatrice Wallance, Dec. 25, 1941; children-Carol (Mrs. S. Elliott Cohan), Jane Louise. Intern Hosp. Joint Diseases, N.Y.C., 1938-40, resident, 1940; practice medicine, specializing in internal medicine, Jackson Heights, N.Y., 1940—; mem. faculty Cornell U. Med. Sch., 1940—, clin. prof. medicine, 1965—; attending physician N.Y. Hosp., L.I. Jewish Med. Center; vis. physician Bellevue Hosp.; cons. physician Booth Meml. Hosp., North Shore Hosp., Long Beach Meml. Hosp.; mem. med. adv. bd. Hebrew U.-Hadassah. Co-chmn. physicians div. United Jewish Appeal Greater N.Y., 1963—; exec. Fedn. Jewish Philanthropies, 1950—. Served from 1st lt. to maj., M.C., AUS, 1942-45; PTO. Fellow A.C.P., Am. Coll. Cardiology, N.Y. Acad. Medicine, N.Y. Acad. Scis., N.Y. Cardiological Soc. (past dir.); mem. Med. Soc. State N.Y. (past sect. chmn.), Harvey Soc., Am. Fedn. Clin. Research, Am. Soc. Tropical Medicine, Am. Heart Assn., Assn. Am. Med. Colls., Royal Soc. Health Gt. Britain, Assn. Mil. Surgeons, A.A.A.S. Contbr. articles profl. jours.. Home: 28 Meadow Woods Rd Great Neck NY 11020 Office: 40-42 75th St Jackson Heights NY 11373

FEDER, DANIEL D., coll. dean; b. Phila., Apr. 12, 1910; s. Jacob and Minnie (Orlovitz) F.; A.B., U. Denver, 1931, M.A., 1931; Ph.D., State U. Ia., 1934; m. Florence Malbin, Sept. 2, 1934; 1 dau., Roberta Louise. Research asst., U. Ia., 1932-34, research asso., 1934-35, asso. in psychology and personnel, 1935-38; asst. dir. personnel bur. and asst. prof. psychology, U. Ill., 1938-42; exec. officer and supr. Ill. State Civil Service, 1942-46; dean of students and prof. psychol., U. Denver, 1946-61, acting dean of acad. adminstrn., 1951-52; chmn. div. psychology, San Francisco State Coll., 1961-63, dean Sch. Humanities and Scis., also prof. psychology, 1963-64, dean acad. planning, 1964—, member adv. com. to counseling service VA, 1952—, chmn., 1970; personnel cons. for numerous colleges and univ.; test cons. and editor Coop. Test Service since 1939; mem. Cal. Adv. Council on Ednl. Research, 1964—; organized and administered personnel bur., U. Ill., and statewide high school testing service for Ill. (over 400 high schs. and 3O colls. cooperating). Pub. mem., trustee Pipe Industry Devel. Fund. 1956-61; pres., dir. Pipe Industry Fund for Scholarships, 1957-61; mem. nat. adv. com. Coop. Plan for Guidance and Admissions, Ednl. Testing Service; bd. dirs. San Francisco Consortium. Served as lt. comdr. USNR, active duty, 1942-45. Pres. Council of Guidance and Personnel Assns., 1947-48. Fellow Am. Psychol. Assn. (diplomate in counseling and guidance) ; mem. Am. Edn. Research Assn., N.E.A., Am. Coll. Personnel Assn. (past pres.) , Nat. Interfrat. Conf. (com. college frat. relations), Am. Personnel and Guidance Assn. (pres. 1960-61), Phi Beta Kappa, Sigma Xi, Phi Delta Kappa. Contbr. psychol., edn. and tech. jours. Address: San Francisco State Coll San Francisco CA 94132

FEDERA, HENRY APPLETON, heavy constn. co. exec.; b. Louisville, May 19, 1913; s. Robert and Marie Edna (Batts) F.; B.A., U. Louisville, 1935, LL.B. magna cum laude, 1937; m. Mary Stafiniak, Sept. 18, 1948; children—Pamela, Danielle, Judith. Admitted to Ky. bar, 1937; atty. Ky. Dept. Revenue, 1937-40; asst. atty. gen. State of Ky., 1940-42; atty. U.S. Steel Corp., Pitts., 1946-50; sec., counsel Orinoco Mining Co., N.Y.C., 1950-52; sec., gen. counsel Raymond Internat., Inc., N.Y.C., 1952—, also dir. Served to capt. AUS, 1942-45. Mem. Am., N.Y. County bar assns., Am. Soc. Corporate Sec., Delta Upsilon (past chmn., pres.). Home: 28 Sherry Hill Lane Manhasset NY 11030 Office: 2 Pennsylvania Plaza New York City NY 10001

FEDERAL, JOSEPH LENNOX, clergyman; b. Greensboro, N.C., Jan. 13, 1910; s. Howard Charles and Margaret Dolores (Keegan) F.; student Niagara U., 1927-29, U. Fribourg, Switzerland, 1929-32, N.Am. Coll., Rome, Italy, 1932-35; Licentiate in Sacred Theology, Gregorian U., 1932; LL.D. (hon.), Niagara U., 1951. Ordained priest, Roman Catholic Ch., 1934; rector Sacred Heart Cathedral, Raleigh, N.C., 1938-51; apptd. Papal Chamberlain, Aug. 1942; consecrated Titular Bishop of Appiaria. and auxiliary to the Bishop of Salt Lake City, 1951, Bishop of Salt Lake City, 1960. Address: 333 East S Temple St Salt Lake City UT 84111

FEDERER, HERBERT, educator, mathematician; b. Vienna, Austria, July 23, 1920; s. Josef and Louise (Schlesinger) F.; B.S., U. Cal. at Berkeley, 1942, Ph.D., 1944; m. Leila Raines, June 30, 1949; children—Andrew, Wayne, Leslie. Came to U.S., 1938, naturalized, 1944. Mem. faculty Brown U., 1945—, prof. Math., 1951—, Florence Pirce Grant U. prof. math., 1966—. Mem. NRC, 1966-69. Served with AUS, 1944-45. Sloan research fellow, 1957-60; NSF sr. postdoctoral fellow, 1964-65. Fellow Am. Acad. Arts and Scis.; mem. Am. Math. Soc. (asso. sec. 1967-68). Spl. research geometric measure theory. Contbr. profl. jours. Home: 287 Elmgrove Av Providence RI 02906

FEDERHOLDEN, DARWIN ERIC educator, biologist; b. Ames, Ia.; B.A., Ia. State U., 1936, M.A., 1937, Ph.D. with honors, 1940; m. Ann Ross, Mar. 23, 1946; children--Edward, Thomas A., Mark. Instr., Ia. State U., 1946-47; asst. prof. biology Johns Hopkins, 1947-50, asso. prof., 1950-62, prof., 1962--, chmn. dept., 1963-69; vis. lectr. Stanford, 1970-71. Active Boy Scouts Am., 4-H Club. Served with AUS, 1940-46. Mem. Am. Soc. Biologists, Md. Soc. Cell Biologists, Am. Soc. Exptl. Biology, Internat. Union Biologists, A.A.A.S., Am. Acad. Arts and Scis., Phi Beta Kappa. Home: 48936 W Hancock Blvd Baltimore MD 20206

FEDERMAN, HENRY ALBERT, watch co. exec.; b. Berlin, Germany, Oct. 25, 1911; s. Hugo and Jenny (Meyer) F.; student bus. coll., Germany; m. Martha Margarete Fink, Feb. 4, 1959; children-Peter, Jenny. Came to U.S., 1940, naturalized, 1946. With Sheffield Watch Co., 1940—, pres., chmn. bd., 1946—. Mem. adv. council Small Bus. Adminstrn. Home: 37 Kellogg St Brookfield CT 06804 Office: 417 Fifth Av New York NY 10016

FEDERSPIEL, WEBER NICHOLAS, steel co. exec.; b. Davenport, Ia., July 26, 1910; s. Henry Pierre and Josephine (Weber) F.; Commerce and Finance, St. Louis U., 1939; m. Lillian Marie Einig, June 10, 1939; children—Mary Jeanne, Judith Ann, Jack Weber. Accountant, Price Waterhouse & Co., C.P.A.'s, St. Louis, 1936-51; controller, asst. sec. Granite City Steel Co. (Ill.), 1951—. C.P.A., Mo. Mem. Financial Execs. Inst. (dir. 1965—, pres. St. Louis 1971), Am. Inst. C.P.A.'s, Am. Iron and Steel Inst., Mo. Soc. C.P.A.'s. Clubs: Mo. Athletic, Glen Echo Country (St. Louis). Roman Catholic. Home: 14 Deer Creek Woods St Louis MO 63124 Office: 20th and State Sts Granite City IL 62040

FEDIN, KONSTANTIN ALEXANDROVICH, novelist; b. 1892. Interned in Germany, 1914-18; returned to USSR, 1918; with Commissariat of Edn., later journalist and war corr.; mem. Secretariat Union Soviet Writers, 1953-; chmn. Moscow Union Soviet Writers, 1955-59; chmn. Soviet-German Cultural and Friendship Soc., 1958- -; 1st sec. Writers Union USSR, 1959—. Decorated Order of Lenin. Mem. USSR Acad. Scis.; corr. mem. Deutsche Akad. der Künste. Author: Anna Timofecvna, 1922; The Waste Lane, 1923; Cities and Years, 1924; Transvaal, 1926; Brothers, 1928; I Was an Actor, 1937; Rape of Europe, 1934; Bakunin in Dresden (play), 1922; Sanatorium Arklur, 1940; Gorky Amoung Us, 1943-44; Return to Leningrad, 1945; Early Joys, 1945; No Ordinary Summer, 1948; Die Flamme, 1962; Dichter, Kunst, Zeit, 1957. Address: Lavrushensky 17 ap 38 Moscow J-17 USSR*

FEE, GEORGE EDWARD, lawyer, corp. exec.; b. Newport, Ky., July 12, 1904; s. George E. and Josephine (McKernan) F.; student Xavier U., Cin., 1922-25; LL.B., U. Cin., 1927; m. Jean Van Horne, Oct. 21, 1933; 1 son, George E. Admitted to Ohio bar, 1927; asso. Dolle, O'Donnell & Cash, Cin., 1927-37; partner Dolle, O'Donnelle & Cash, Cin., 1937-52; sr. partner Dolle, O'Donnell, Cash, Fee & Hahn, Cin., 1952—; prof. law Salmon P. Chase Law Sch., 1935-47; lectr. Coll. Law U. Cin., 1952. Chmn. bd. Lodge & Shipley Co., Cin., 1956-66, dir., 1952-68, gen. counsel, 1952—. Mem. Am., Ohio, Cin. bar assns., Order of Coif. Home: 2200 Victoria Pkwy Cincinnati OH 45206 Office: Central Trust Tower Cincinnati OH 45202

FEE, GEORGE EDWARD, Jr., corp. exec.; b. Norfolk, Va., Dec. 24, 1934; B.A., Tufts U., 1957; J.D., U. Chgo., 1963; m. Joan Fee; children—Sorena, Melinda, Cynthia Grace. With firm Peabody, Arnold, Batchelder and Luther, Boston, 1963; asso. editor law book dept. Little Brown and Co., Boston, 1963-65; dir. placement, asst. U. Chgo. Law Sch., 1965-69, dean students, 1967-69; pres. Fee's Folly, Ltd., Gays Mills, Wis., 1968—; partner William H. Clark Assos., Chgo., 1971—. Served as lt. USMCR, 1957-60. Office: 20 N Wacker Dr Chicago IL 60606

FEE, LEO BERNARD, r.r. exec.; b. Sharon, Pa., June 7, 1909; s. Lawrence and Margaret (Lee) F.; B.S., U. San Francisco, 1931; LL.B., Georgetown Law Sch., 1935; m. Angela C. Patterson, May 14, 1942; children—Lawrence, Christine Elizabeth. Admitted to D.C. bar, 1940; asst. corp. counsel D.C., 1935- 36; examiner, atty. NLRB, 1936-40; asst. mgr. peronnel S. P. Co., 1940- 49; chief examiner Assn. Western Rys., 1949-55; carrier mem. fourth div. Nat. R.R. Adjustment Bd., 1949-55, carrier mem. first div., 1955-56; dir. labor relations N.Y. Central System (co. name changed to Penn Central Co., 1956-57, v.p. employee relations, 1957—, also chmn. bd. pensions; v.p. employee relations Cleve. Union Terminals Co., Lake Erie & Eastern R.R. Co., Chgo. River & Ind. R.R. Co., P. & L.E. R.R., Ind. Harbor Belt R.R.; dir. Can. Southern Ry., Mahoning State Line R.R. Co., Detroit River Tunnel Co., St. Lawrence & Adirondack Ry. Transp. com. Nat. YMCA's. Roman Catholic. Home: 120 Hartsdale Av E Hartsdale NY 10530 Office: 466 Lexington Av New York City NY 10017

FEE, MORTON ELSTON, food co. exec.; b. St. Hyacinthe, Que., Can., Aug. 8, 1915; s. Emerson and Irene (Payan) F.; B.E., McGill U., 1938; m. Pauline Strachan, Sept. 27, 1947; children—Jacqueline Elizabeth, Joan Beverley, Barry Strachan, Shirley Ann. With Can. Starch Co., Ltd., Montreal, 1938—, v.p., 1957-58, exec. v.p., 1958-61, pres., gen. mgr., 1961—; dir. Que. Maple Products, Ltd., Parkwell Ltd., Corn Products Indsl., Ltd., Food, Ltd., La Cantine Mobile, Inc. Served with RCAF, 1943-45. Mem. Canadian Mfrs. Assn., Canadian C. of C., Sigma Chi. Clubs: Montreal Badminton and Squash, St. James (Montreal); St. George's (Sherbrooke, Que.); Kanawaki (Que.) Golf. Home: 5689 Queen Mary Rd Hampstead Montreal 254 Quebec Canada Office: 1 Place du Commerce Nuns Island Montreal 201 Quebec Canada

FEE, ROGER DEXTER, musician, educator; b. Toledo, Ia., Mar. 24, 1918; s. Knight Elias and Minnie Belle (Graves) F.; student Drake U., 1935-37; Mus.B., Am. Conservatory Music, 1939, Mus.M., 1946; Ed.D., U. Denver, 1961; m. Danna Jeanne Atkinson, Nov. 27, 1942; children—Pamela Jo, Daniel Dexter. Theatre, hotel, night club singer, 1939-40; toured with Continental Singers, U.S. and Can., 1940- 41; faculty Ill. Wesleyan U., 1946-48; attended opera workshop Berkshire Music Festival, Tanglewood, Mass.; faculty Drake U., 1948; asst. dir. Lamont Sch. Music, U. Denver, 1949-53, dir., 1952—; opera, oratorio appearances Midwest and Southwest, including appearances with Drake-Des Moines Symphony, Albuquerque Symphony Orch., Denver Symphony Orch.; faculty PauL Chrisiansen Choral Sch., Am. Inst. Normal Methods, 1952—; chorusmaster Central City Opera House Assn., 1952—; dir. music Trinity Meth. Ch. Served as maj. AUS, 1941-46. Mem. Colo. Music Tchrs. Assn. (1st v.p. 1955-57), Music Tchrs. Nat. Assn., Nat. Assn. Tchrs. Singing, Phi Mu Alpha Sinfonia (province gov.), Pi Kappa Lambda, Kappa Kappa Psi. Home: 2786 S Monroe St Denver CO 80210

FEE, WALTER R., historian; b. Steuben Co., Ind., Oct. 29, 1902; s. Shirley Dale and Irene (Gurtner) F.; A.B. Magna cum laude, Ind. U., 1925; A.M., Pittsburgh U., 1928; Ph.D., Columbia, 1933; m. Violet Enterline, Dec. 22, 1928; one dau., Ann Elizabeth. Teacher, Pittsburgh U., Greenville Coll., N.Y. City Coll.; prof., head dept. history. polit. science and social science, Michigan State Univ., 1945-49, head depts. history and social sci., 1949-60, head dept. history, 1945-67, emeritus, 1967—, acting dean basic coll., 1950-51; vis. prof. Silliman U., P.I., 1967-68. Member Assn. for Asian Studies, Asia Soc., Am. Hist. Assn., Am. Oriental Soc. Am. Sociol. Soc., Mich. Acad., Phi Alpha Theta, Phi Beta Kappa, Phi Kappa Phi, Phi Beta Kappa. Assos. Author: The Transition from Aristocracy to Democracy in N.J., 1790-1820. Home: Route 1 Lake Leelanau MI 49653

FEE, WILLIAM EDWARD, Jr., govt. ofcl.; b. Far Rockaway, L.I., N.Y., Mar. 24, 1907; s. William Edward and Victoria Elizabeth (Spillett) F.; A.B., Cath. U. Am., 1929; J.D., Georgetown U., 1932; m. Marie Louise Edmonston, Dec. 27, 1933; children—Marie Louise (Mrs. James A. Young), Jean (Mrs. Anthony D. DiPaola), Jane (Mrs. Paul E. Baker). Legal research, code adminstrn., NRA and Nat. Lumber Code Authority, 1932-35; fed. real estate and procurement Dept. of Agr., 1935-42; adminstr. for personnel, budget and adminstrv. service activities U.S. Office Edn., 1942-45; adminstrv. service nat. soil conservation program Dept. of Agr., 1945-51; adminstrv. operations and procurement world-wide tech. programs Dept. of State, 1952, adminstrv. services, domestic and fgn. operations, 1953-56, dir. office Gen. Services, 1956, dir. Office Spl. Services, 1956-59; staff com. on appropriations U.S. Ho. of Reps., 1959-60; dep. grants adminstr. NSF, 1960-62, head grants office, 1962-70, staff cons., 1970-71; apptd. fgn. service officer, 1956. Pres., chmn. State Dept. Fed. Credit Union, 1959, 60, v.p., 1963—, bd. dirs., 1953—; bd. dirs. D.C. Credit Union League, 1961-64. Recipient commendable service award Dept. State, 1957; superior Service award NSF, 1962. Mem. Phi Kappa. Home: 2820 28th St NW Washington DC 20008 Office: Nat Sci Found Washington DC 20550

FEEHAN, ARTHUR FREDERICK, advt. exec.; b. Detroit, Mar. 29, 1926; s. Robert and Madeline (Meier) F.; m. Eugenia E. Stokes, Apr. 15, 1944; children—Kathleen F., Patrick R., Robert D. Engaged in retailing, 1945-54; with D.P. Brother & Co. advt., Detroit, 1954—, asst. treas., 1961-64, sec.-treas., 1964—. Home: 29800 Bristol Lane Birmingham MI 48010 Office: Gen Motors Bldg Detroit MI 48302

FEEKTISTEV, KONSTANTIN, Russian cosmonaut, scientist; b. Verenezh, Central Russia, 1926; grad. Bauman Higher Tech. Sch., Moscow, 1949; 2 degrees in tech. scis.; m. Galina Feektistev; children—Nikolai, Andrei. Staff various sci. research institutes; mem. three-man team in earth orbit Oct. 1964. Served with Russian Army, World War II. Awarded two orders Red Banner of Labor for contbn. to Soviet sci.*

FEELEY, JOHN JOSEPH, advt. exec.; b. Bklyn., Apr. 22, 1919; s. Michael Joseph and Bridget (Mulrenin) F.; student Coll. City N.Y., 1938-40, N.Y. U., 1941- 42; m. Emily Eileen Egan, June 5, 1943; 1 son, Michael John. Advt. mgr. E.W. Bliss Co., Bklyn., Detroit, Toledo, 1937-50; asst. to pres. Fred Wittner Advt., N.Y.C., 1950-53; pres. Feeley Advt. Agy., Inc., N.Y.C., 1953-67; pres. Feeley & Wheeler, INc., N.Y.C., 1967-69; sr. v.p. Lennen & Newell Inc., N.Y.C., 1970—; dir. Sahlin Co., Detroit. Chmn. Little League, Eastchester, N.Y., 1958-60; pres. Pony League, 1961-62. Club: New York Athletic. Home: 22 Buena Vista Rd Eastchester NY 10709 Office: 370 Lexington Av New York City NY 10017

FEELEY, JOHN PAUL, paper co. exec.; b. Akron, O., July 17, 1918; s. John Joseph and Pauline (Wallace) F.; B.S. in Bus. Adminstrn., U. Akron, 1941; m. Nell King, Feb. 20, 1943; children-Joanne, Suzanne. Civilian with Dept. of Navy, 1946-56, chief Navy Mgmt. Office, 1955-56; sec.-treas. American Colortype Corp., 1956-57; treas. Rapid Am. Corp., 1958-59; asst. controller Remington Rand Co., 1960-62; v.p., dir. APS Paper Corp., 1963-64, Allied Paper Inc., Kalamazoo, 1964—. Served to lt. comdr. USNR, World War II. Home: 5047 Oakland Dr Kalamazoo MI 49001 Office: 1608 Lake St Kalamazoo MI 49001

FEENBERG, EUGENE, educator, physicist; b. Ft. Smith, Ark., Oct. 19, 1906; s. Louis and Esther (Siegel) F.; B.A., M.A., U. Tex., 1929; Ph.D., Harvard, 1933; m. Hilda Rosenberg, May 30, 1940; children—Andrew L., Daniel Richard. Instr. physics Harvard, 1933-35; lectr. physics U. Wis., 1935-36; fellow Inst. Advanced Study, Princeton, 1936-38; mem. faculty Washington Sq. Coll., N.Y.U., 1938-46; micro-wave engr. Sperry Gyroscope Co., 1941-45; mem. faculty Washington U., St. Louis, 1946—, now Wayman Crow prof. Mem. Am. Phys. Soc. Author: (with G. E. Pake) Notes on the Quantum Theory of Angular Momentum, 1953; Shell Theory of the Nucleus, 1955; Theory of Quantum Fluids, 1970. Home: 7128 Kingsbury St University City MO 63130 Office: Washington Univ St Louis MO 63110

FEER, MARK CECIL ISELIN, investment banker; b. N.Y.C. July 31, 1928; s. H. Ernest and Cecile (Iselin) F.; A.B., Dartmouth, 1946-49; postgrad. U. Geneva, 1949-50, Sorbonne, 1950; M.A., Fletcher Sch. Law and Diplomacy, 1951, Ph.D., 1954; m. Helene de Lone, May 31, 1952; children—Camilla H., Barbara S., M. Peter de

L. Econ. cons. Arthur D. Little, Inc., Cambridge, Mass., 1954-55; with First Boston Corp., 1957- 65, asst. v.p., 1961-64, v.p., 1964-65; dep. asst. sec. for financial policy U.S. Dept. Commerce, Washington, 1965-68; asso. Kuhn, Loeb & Co., N.Y.C., 1968, gen. partner, 1969—; dir. Share Australia Mgmt Co. Ltd., Sydney, Pvt. Investment Co. for Asia. Mem. Pvt. Investment Mission to Korea, 1967. Pres. Westchester Chpt. Assn. for Retarded Children, 1958-60. Served AUS, 1955-57. Fulbright grantee, India, 1952- 53. Mem. Council on Fgn. Relations, Asia Soc., Japan Soc., Phi Beta Kappa, Theta Delta Chi. Clubs: India House (N.Y.C.); Fox Meadows Tennis (Scarsdale, N.Y.). Home: 94 Greenacres Av Scarsdale NY 10853 Office: Kuhn Loeb & Co 40 Wall St New York City NY 10005

FEERICK, ROBERT J., gen. mgr. San Francisco. Warriors. Address: 505 Geary St San Francisco CA 94102*

FEFERMAN, SOLOMON, educator. Prof. math. and philosophy Stanford. Office: Dept Math Stanford U Stanford CA 94305*

FEFFER, MELVIN HAROLD, educator; b. Springfield, Mass., Oct. 20, 1923; B.S., U. Mass., 1948; postgrad. (USPHS fellow) Ill. Neuropsychiat. Inst., 1950-51; Ph.D., U. Chgo., 1954; married; 2 children. Asst. in psychology U. Mass., Amherst, 1947-48, U. Chgo., 1949-50; staff psychologist Worcester (Mass.) State Hosp., 1952-56, acting supr. intern tng., 1956-57, resident psychologist, 1957-60; asso. prof. psychology Yeshiva U., 1960-65, prof., 1965—, also chmn. dept.; lectr. Clark U., Worcester, 1956-58, research asso. Inst. Human Devel., 1959-60, cons. psychol. clin., 1958-60. Cons. Worcester State Hosp., 1960—. Served with USAAF, 1943-46. Contbr. articles to profl. jours. Office: Ferkauf Grad Sch Humanities and Social Scis Dept Psy Yeshiva U 55 Fifth Av New York City NY 10033*

FEGEL, ARTHUR CHRISTIAN, metal products co. exec.; b. Perth, N.Y., Aug. 25, 1910; s. Charles Alexander and Villa (Guernsy) F.; B.S., N.Y. State Coll. Forestry, Syracuse U., 1933, M.S., 1934, Ph.D., 1938; m. Virginia Louise Harvey, Dec. 31, 1937; children—Timothy Alan, Robin Douglas, Melinda Louise (Mrs. Daniel Harvey). Teaching fellow N.Y. State Coll. Forestry, 1933-37; engr. Western Electric Co., Kearney, N.J., 1937-42, chief engring. dept., 1942-44, asst. supt., 1944-52, v.p. subsidiary Nassau Smelting and Refining Co., Tottenville, Staten Island, N.Y., 1952-54, pres., dir., 1954—; mem. Staten Island adv. com. Chase Manhattan Bank. Bd. dirs. Econ. Devel. Council N.Y., 1966—, Staten Island C. of C., 1965-69, Staten Island A.R.C., 1964-69. Mem. Am. Soc. M.E., N.Y. Acad. Scis., Newcomen Soc., Sigma Xi, Phi Kappa Phi, Alpha Xi Sigma, Pi Kappa Alpha. Republican. Unitarian. Home: 1895 Lake Av Scotch Plains NJ 07076 Office: 286 Richmond Valley Rd Staten Island NY 10307

FEHER, GEORGE, educator, physicist; b. Bratislava, Czechoslovakia, May 29, 1924; s. Ferdinand and Sylvia (Schwartz) F.; came to U.S., 1947, naturalized, 1953; B.S., U. Cal., Berkeley, 1950, M.S. in Elec. Engring., 1952, Ph.D. in Physics, 1954; m. Elsa R. Rosenvasser, June 1961; children—Laurie Ruth, Shoshanah, Paola. Research physicist Bell Telephone Labs., Murray Hill, N.J., 1954-60; vis. asso. prof. physics Columbia, 1959-60; prof. physics U. Cal., La Jolla, 1960—; vis. prof. biology Mass. Inst. Tech., 1967-68. Bd. govs. Technion, Haifa, Israel, 1968—. Mem. Am. Phys. Soc. (award for inventing and developing ENDOR technique 1960). Office: U Cal Revelle Coll PO Box 109 La Jolla CA 92037

FEHLING, FRED LOUIS, educator; b. Sheboygan, Wis., Oct. 15, 1904; s. Fritz and Albertina (Wilke) F.; B.A., Wartburg Coll., Clinton, Ia., 1926; Ph.D., U. Ia., 1939; m. Evelyn White, Aug. 22, 1936; children—Roberta, Victoria. Mem. faculty U. Ia., 1930—, prof. German lang. and lit., 1930—, chmn. dept., 1960-63. Mem. Nat. Fedn. Modern Lang. Tchrs. Assns. (pres. 1956- 58). Contbr. profl. jours. Home: 424 S Summit St Iowa City IA 52240

FEHNEL, EDWARD ADAM, chemist, educator; b. Bethlehem, Pa., Apr. 22, 1922; s. Edward Franklin and Marguerite (Paull) F.; B.S., Lehigh U., 1943, M.S., 1944, Ph.D., 1946; m. Dorothy Gary Lynn, Oct. 21, 1944; children—Lynn Susan, Gary Edward. Instr. chemistry Moravian Prep. Sch., Bethlehem, 1943-44; chemist Central Research Lab. Allied Chem. & Dye Corp., Morristown, N.J., 1944- 45; research fellow, lectr. U. Pa., 1946-48; asst. prof. chemistry Swarthmore (Pa.) Coll., 1948-57, asso. prof., 1957-66, prof., 1966—; NSF Sci. Faculty fellow U. Cambridge, Eng., 1962; vis. prof. chemistry Ind. U., summer 1968. Mem. Am. Chem. Soc., Phila. Organic Chemists Club Assn. U. Pa. Chemists, Phi Beta Kappa, Sigma Xi, Tau Beta Pi. Mem. editorial bd. Organic Electronic Spectral Data, 1957-60. Contbr. profl. jours. Home: 600 Elm Av Swarthmore PA 19081

FEHR, CARL AUGUST, educator, musician; b. Austin, Tex., Nov. 29, 1907; s. Herman Reno and Selma (Kilian) F.; B.A., U. Tex., 1928, M.A., 1930; Mus.M., U. Mich., 1942; Ed.D. in Music and Music Edn., Columbia, 1950; m. Alice Therese Knippa, June 3, 1933. Tchr., organist St. Paul's Luth. Ch., 1931-33; music instr. Austin pub. schs., 1933-45; mem. faculty Coll. William and Mary, 1945—, prof. music, 1961—; organist, choir dir. in chs., Austin and Williamsburg, 1923-69; musci dir. Common Glory, 1947-67, The Founders, 1957, 58, 64; adjudicator choral festivals, dir. choral workshops in Va., 1947—. Recipient George Washington honor medal Freedoms Found. at Valley Forge, 1969. Mem. Am. Choral Dirs. Assn. (charter), Music Educators Nat. Conf., Va. Music Educators Assn., Pi Kappa Lambda, Phi Mu Alpha Kappa Delta Pi. Home: 108 Spring Rd Williamsburg VA 23185

FEHR, HOWARD FRANKLIN, educator; b. Bethlehem, Pa., Dec. 4, 1901; s. Quincy Howard and Minnie (Patterson) F.; A.B., Lehigh U., 1923, A.M., 1928; Ph.D., Columbia, 1940; m. Gladys Thomas, Dec. 25, 1924; children—Patricia Thomas, Barbara Gladys; m. 2d, Gisele Henle, Sept. 9, 1966; stepson, Gunter. High sch. tchr. maths., Bethlehem, 1923-35, Reading 1925-27, Newark, 1927-34; instr. State Tchrs. Coll., Montclair, N.J. 1934-38, asst. prof., 1937-40, asso. prof., 1940-45, prof., 1946-48; part time instr. Tchrs. Coll., Columbia U., 1946-48, prof. maths., 1948-67, head dept. maths., 1949-67, emeritus, 1967—; exec. sec. InterAm. Conf. Math. Edn., dir. curriculum improvement study, 1965—; part time tchr. Newark Coll. Engring., 1930-35, Newark Sch. of Fine and Indsl. Arts, 1929-30, Rutgers U., 1944-46. Cons. to various communities on math. curricula. Fellow A.A.A.S.; mem. of Assn. State Tchrs. Colls. in N.J. (pres.1941-46); Nat. Council Tchrs. Maths. (bd. mem., pres. 1956- 58), Am. Math. Soc., Assn. Tchrs. Maths. in N.J., Essex County Edn. Assn. (pres. 1945-46), Phi Beta Kappa, Phi Delta Kappa, Republican. Author books including: Secondary Mathematics, A Functional Approach for Teachers, 1951; Algebra Course I and II, 1955; Essential Methematic Series, Book I and II, 1956. Editor: New Thinking in School Mathematics; Synopses for Modern Secondary School Mathematics; Mathematics Today; Teaching Modern Mathematics in the Elementary School, 1967. Contbr. articles to ednl. mags. Home: 165 W 66th St New York NY 10023 ☆

FEHR, KENNETH MANBECK, electronics co. exec.; b. Schuylkill Haven, Pa., Feb. 21, 1928; s. Theodore E. and Eva (Manbeck) F.; B.S., Pa. State U., 1951; M.B.A., U. Pitts., 1953; m. Jean Alice Greenawalt, June 28, 1952; children—K. Craig, Karen Jean, K. Todd. With U.S. Steel Corp., 1951-62, div. controller, 1962; controller Interlake Steel Corp., Chgo., 1962-68; v.p. finance The Hallicrafters Co., 1968—; night sch. tchr. U. Pitts., 1956- 57. Served with USNR, 1945-46. Mem. Financial Execs. Inst., Nat. Assn. Accountants. Mason. Home: 205 Elm Rd Barrington IL 60010 Office: 600 Hicks Rd Rollings Meadows IL 60008

FEHRENBACH, GEORGE JOHN, banker; b. St. Marys, Pa., Apr. 22, 1898; s. George and Elizabeth (Wismeth) F.; student St. Vincent Coll., Latrobe, Pa., 1912- 16; m. Marina L'Abbe, Jan. 20, 1920; 1 son, William G.; m. 2d, Margaret Lynch, Sept. 21, 1936; children—Robert J., Mary Elizabeth. Cost accountant Speer Carbon Co., 1924-32, asst. treas., 1932-44, treas., 1944-58, v.p., 1952-58, exec. v.p., 1958-60, also sec., dir., pres., 1960-64, chmn., 1964-66, dir.; pres. Elk County Bank & Trust Co.; dir. Mid-Continent Telephone Corp., Art Metal, Inc., Speer Carbon Co. of Can. Ltd., St. Marys Nat. Bank, St. Marys Trust Co., Malone Metal Powders, Inc.; dir., exec. com. Home Telephone Co. Mem. bd. adjustment, governing bd. Municipal Authority, Borough of St. Marys; past chmn. Indsl. Council of St. Marys; former mayor, St. Marys. Pres., dir. Boys' Club of St. Marys; dir., treas. Boys' Club Holding Corp.; trustee Andrew Kaul Meml. Hosp., St. Mary's; pres. trustees Warren State Hosp. Decorated Sovereign Mil. Order of Malta, 1961. Mem. Am. Legion, K.C., Elk. Clubs: St. Marys Country; Niagara Falls Country; Penn-Hills Country (Bradford, Pa.); Cuba (N.Y.) Yacht (dir.). Home: Windfall Rd St Marys PA 15857

FEHRENBACHER, DON EDWARD, educator; b. Sterling, Ill., Aug. 21, 1920; s. Joseph H. and Mary (Barton) F.; B.A., Cornell Coll., 1946; M.A., U. Chgo., 1948, Ph.D., 1951; M.A., Oxford U., 1967; D.H.L., Cornell Coll., 1970; m. Virginia Ellen Swaney, Feb. 9, 1944; children-Ruth Ellen (Mrs. Laurence Gleason), Susan Jean, David Charles. Asst. prof. history Coe Coll., Cedar Rapids, Ia., 1949-53; asst. prof. history Stanford, 1953-57, asso. prof., 1957- 62, prof., 1962-66, William R. Coe prof. Am. history, 1966—; Harmsworth prof. Am. history Oxford U., 1967-68; summer teaching Rutgers U., 1959, Northwestern U., 1964, Harvard, 1967, U. B.C., 1970. Served to 1st lt. USAAF, 1943-45. Decorated D.F.C., Air medal with 3 oak leaf clusters. Guggenheim fellow, 1959-60. Mem. Am., So. hist. assns., Cal. Hist. Soc., Orgn. Am. Historians (mem. editorial bd. 1965-68). Author: Chicago Giant: A Biography of Long John Wentworth, 1957; Prelude to Greatness: Lincoln in the 1850s, 1962; The Era of Expansion, 1969. Contbr. articles profl. jours. Home: 625 Salvatierra St Stanford CA 94305

FEIBELMAN, JULIAN BECK, rabbi; b. Jackson, Miss., Mar. 23, 1897; s. Abraham and Eva (Beck) F.; A.B., Millsaps Coll., 1918; LL.D., 1946; rabbi, Hebrew Union Coll., 1926, D.D. honoris causa, 1955; M.A., U. of Pa., 1929, Ph.D., 1939; m. Mary Anna Fellman, Oct. 20, 1938; 1 son, Julian B., Jr. Rabbi, Temple Keneseth Israel, Phila., 1926-36; rabbi Temple Sinai, New Orleans, 1936-68, rabbi emeritus, 1968—; lectr. history of religions Tulane U. 1948-50. Am.-Jewish rep. Internat. Conf. Christians and Jews to study European Anti-Semitism, Switzerland, 1947; city chmn. U.N. Appeal for Children, 1948; mem. exec. bd. of the Central Conf. of Am. Rabbis, 1948, chmn. Interfaith Com. Mem. bd. govs. Hebrew Union Coll. since 1951; pres. combined alumni assn. of Hebrew Union Coll., Cin., and Jewish Inst. Religion N.Y. Mem. Prison Interfaith Bd. Ministers for Parolees; v.p. ch. activity br. La. Safety Assn., 1960; bd. Anti-Defamation League, Vols. Am., Parish Prison Chaplains Commn., Jewish Community Center; pres. New Orleans Rabbinical Council, 1963-64. Mem. bd. Kingsley House, 1963—; hon. life mem. bd. Louise S. Davis School, 1963; mem., 1st vice chmn. lay bd. DePaul Hosp.; bd. dirs. Met. Area Com.; mem. overseers adv. bd. of Hebrew Union Coll. Served U.S. Army, World War I; spl. rep. W.L.B.; chmn. com. home service, field dir., mem. exec. bd., New Orleans Red Cross, World War II. Recipient citation Millsaps Coll., 1967; gold medal St. Mary's Dominican Coll., 1967; Weiss award Nat. Conf. Christians and Jews, 1967; Times Picayune Loving Cup, 1968; Greek Orthodox Ch. spl. merit award, 1970, Mem. Mayor's Adv. Com. New Orleans, 1946. Mem. La. Soc. Mental Hygiene (past pres.), New Orleans Assn. Social Hygiene (past pres.), Nat. Conf. Christians and Jews (Southwestern adviser), New Orleans Urban League (v.p.), Family Service Soc. (pres., 1950), New Orleans Race Relations, Jewish Pub. Soc. Phila. (editorial bd.), New Orleans Fgn. Policy Assn. (exec. bd.), New Orleans TB Assn., Jewish Statis. Bur., United Jewish Appeal Bd., Am. Jewish Com. Bd., Vet.'s Information Center, Boy Scouts (exec. bd.; awarded Silver Beaver 1951), Hebrew Union Coll. Alumni Assn. (pres. 1952), Ch. and Industry Com. (exec. bd.), New Orleans Assn. Commerce. Clubs: Rotary (pres. 1950-51), Athletic (New Orleans), Lakewood Country. Author books. Editor: New Orleans Jewish Ledger, 1940-44. Home: 530 Walnut St New Orleans LA 70118 Office: 6227 St Charles Av New Orleans LA 70118 ☆

FEIBLEMAN, CHARLES B., lawyer; b. Indpls., 1916; A.B., Harvard, 1936, LL.B., 1938. Admitted to Ind. bar, 1938; mem. firm Bamberger & Feibleman, Indpls. Instr. constl. law Ind. Law Sch., 1940-41, partnerships and corp. law, 1947. Served to capt. AUS, 1941-45. Mem. Am., Ind., Indpls. (pres. 1964) bar assns., Lawyers Assn. Indpls. (sec. 1947), Phi Beta Kappa. Mem. bd. editors Harvard Law Rev., 1936-38. Office: 500 Union Fed Bldg 45 N Pennsylvania St Indianapolis IN 46204*

FEIBLEMAN, JAMES KERN, educator, author; b. New Orleans, July 13, 1904; s. Leopold and Nora (Kern) F.; student U. Va., 1924; pvt. study Europe; m. Dorothy Steinam, 1928 (div.); 1 son, Peter Steinam; m. 2d, Shirley Ann Grau, August 4, 1955; children—Ian, Norma, William, Katherine. Asst. mgr. dept. store, 1924-29; v.p., gen. mgr. James K. Feibleman Realty Co., Inc., 1930-54; partner of Leopold Investment Co. 1954—; acting asst. prof. English Coll. Arts and Scis., Tulane U., 1943-44, acting asst. prof. philosophy, 1945-46, grad. prof. since 1946, head dept. philosophy, 1951-56, chmn., 1956-69, W.R. Irby prof. of philosophy, 1969—; lectr., univs., assns., founds. Mem. Charles S. Pierce Soc. (pres. 1948-49), Am. Assn. U. Profs., Am. Philos. Assn. (eastern, pacific and western divs.), Am. Soc. Aesthetics, Art Assn. New Orleans, Assn. for Symbolic Logic, Inst. Applied Logic, Metaphys. Soc. Am., Mind Assn., Modern Lang. Assn. Am., New Orleans Acad. Sci. (pres. 1958-59), Royal Inst. Philosophy, South Central Moderan Lang. Assn., So. Soc. Philosophy and Psychology, Southwestern Philos. Soc., Phi Beta Kappa, Phi Sigma Tau (v.p. 1956-57). Author numerous books, most recent being: The Dark Bifocals, 1952; The Institutions of Society, 1956; The Pious Scientist, 1958; Inside the Great Mirror, 1958; Religious Platonism, 1959; The Foundations of Empiricism, 1962; Biosocial Factors in Mental Illness, 1962; Mankind Behaving: Human Needs and Material Culture, 1963; The Two-Story World, 1966; Moral Strategy, 1967; The Reach of Politics, 1969; The Way of A Man, 1969; The New Materialism, 1960; Great April, 1971; contbr. chpts. to books and numerous book reviews and articles. Home: 12 Nassau Drive Metairie LA 70005 Office: Tulane U New Orleans LA 70118 ☆

FEICHTNER, LEO VINCENT, physician; b. Mahanoy City, Pa., June 1, 1905; s. William and Anna (McAtee) F.; student U. Pa., 1922-25; M.D., Hahnemann Med. Coll., 1929; grad. Med. Field Service Schl., 1943, Spl. Project Sch. Bacteriol. Warfare, 1944; m. Genevieve B. Slattery, Sept. 5, 1936; children—Joan Mary, Anne Lee. Intern Met. Hosp., Welfare Island, 1929-30; resident physician Peekskill (N.Y.) Hosp., 1930-31, attending physician, 1931-42, 46-51, sec. med. staff, 1933-50, bd. dirs., 1946-49; gen. practice medicine, Croton-on-Hudson, N.Y., 1931-42, 46-51; surgeon N.Y. Central R.R.; med. examiner SSS; sr. supr. med. services N.Y. State Edn. Dept., 1951-58, chief bur. health service, 1958—. Hon. bd. dirs. Nat. Aid to Visually Handicapped; med. adv. bd. N.Y. State Commn. for Blind; mem. commn. for children with cardiac limitations N.Y. State Heart Assembly. Chmn. Golden Jubilee celebration founding Village of Croton- on-Hudson; mem. recreation commn. Town of Bethlehem, 1954. Served to maj., M.C., AUS, 1942-46. Decorated Presdl. unit citation, Bronze Star, Distinguished Servide Cross, State of N.Y. Mem. Am. Sch. Health Assn. (pres. 1963-64), N.Y. State Assn. Sch. Physicians (sec. 1955-60, exec. bd. 1960—), Am. Legion. Republican. Roman Catholic. Clubs: University, Aurania (Albany); Lions (pres. 1947; Croton-on-Hudson). Author: Medical Aspects of School Athletics, 1961; The School Physicians, 1959; The School Dentist, 1958; School Health Services, 1959. Asso. editor Jour. Sch. Health. Home: 37 Fernbank Av Delmar NY 12054 Office: NY State Dept of Education Albany NY 12225

FEICK, WILLIAM, Jr., corp. exec.; b. Bklyn., Dec. 12, 1924; s. William and Clara (Nichols) F.; B.A., Amherst Coll., 1947; m. Joan Meeske, Sept. 1, 1950; children—William Kurt, Matthew Fritz, Alexander Nichols. Asst. v.p. Crocker First Nat. Bank of San Francisco, 1948-56; treas. Flintkote Co., N.Y.C., 1956-59, v.p., 1959-62; v.p. MacKay-Shields Financial Corp., N.Y.C., 1963-66, pres., 1966—; dir. Felmont Oil Corp. Served as lt. (j.g.) USNR, 1944-46. Mem. Phi Delta Theta Clubs: Sheorock Shore, University, Country (New Canaan). Republican. Episcopalian. Home: Lambert Rd New Canaan CT 06840 also Stratton VT 05155 Office: 551 Fifth Av New York City NY 10017

FEICKERT, CARL WILLIAM, lawyer; b. Belleville, Ill., Sept. 24, 1906; s. Christian Arthur and Elizabeth (Brosius) F.; LL.B., U. Ill., 1931; m. Emma Joanne Heinl, Apr. 12, 1941; children—Carl A., Elissa Ann, John C. Admitted to Ill., Mo. bars, 1931; practice of law, East St. Louis, also Belleville, 1932-61; atty. regional office HOLC, Chgo., 1934-35; asst. U.S. atty., East St. Louis, 1937-40; U.S. atty. Eastern Dist. Ill., East St. Louis, 1961-69; asst. St. Clair County states atty., 1969—; asso. Jones, Ottesen & Fleming, Belleville, 1969—. Mem. Belleville Twp. High Sch. and Jr. Coll. Bd. Edn., 1957-63, pres., 1960. Pres. United Fund, Belleville, 1959. Served to maj. Judge Adv. Gen.'s Dept. USAAF, 1942-46. Mem. Am., Ill., St. Clair County bar assns., Am. Legion, U.S. (dir. 1938-40), Internat., Ill. (pres. 1939-40) jr. chambers commerce, Belleville C. of C., U. Ill. Alumni Assn., Demolay Legion Honor, Theta Xi, Phi Delta Phi. Democrat. Clubs: Illini, Downtown Optimist (Belleville). Home: 44 N Pennsylvania Av Belleville IL 62220 Office: St Clair County Court House Belleville IL 62220 also 15 Public Sq Belleville IL 62220

FEIDELSON, CHARLES, Jr., educator; b. Savannah, Ga., Feb. 27, 1918; s. Charles and Adeline (Falk) F.; B.A., Yale, 1938, Ph.D., 1948; student Cambridge (Eng.) U., 1938-39; m. Kathryn Van Raalte, Sept. 3, 1947; children—Emily, Anne, John. Mem. faculty Yale, 1947—, prof. English, 1959—; Fulbright vis. prof. U. Rome (Italy), 1960-61. Served with AUS, 1941-45. Guggenheim fellow, 1956- 57. Mem. Modern Lang. Assn. Author: Symbolism and American Literature, 1953. Home: 304 Ridgewood Av Hamden CT 06514 Office: Dept English Yale Univ New Haven CT 06520

FEIDLER, ERNEST REYNOLD, lawyer; b. Superior, Wis., Apr. 15, 1910; s. Ernest William and Agnes Amelia (Swanson) F.; Ed.B. magna cum laude, Wis. State Coll., Superior, 1930; LL.B. cum laude, U. Wis., 1934; Sterling fellow in law, Yale, 1934-35; m. Lydia Keown, July 25, 1936. Admitted to Wis. bar, 1934, D.C. bar, 1946; various capacities Office Gen. Counsel, Treasury Dept., 1935-43, asst. to gen. counsel, 1942-43; sec., gen. counsel The A. W. Mellon Ednl. and Charitable Trust, 1946-51, also sec. Old Dominion Found.; adminstr. Nat. Gallery of Art, Washington, 1954-65, sec., treas., gen. counsel, 1965—70. Member USCG Bd. Review Mil. Justice, 1951-53. Trustee Superior State U. Found., Allentown Art Mus. Served from lt. comdr. to comdr., USCG Res., 1943-46, active, 51-54, rear adm., 1961. Mem. Am., Wis., D.C. bar assns., Chi Phi. Clubs: Army and Navy, National Press, Cosmos (Washington). Contbr. articles legal jours. Home: 1307 N Lynnbrook Dr Arlington VA 22201

FEIDT, WILLIAM ELMER, civil engr.; b. Millersburg, Pa., Apr. 12, 1916; s. William Elmer and Margaret Alice (Lehman) F.; B.S. in Chem. Engring., Northeastern U., 1939; m. Justine Bayles Ganung, June 20, 1942 (dec. July 18, 1968); children—William Bayles, Susan; m. 2d, Alice L. A. Pelissier, Nov. 22, 1969. Cons. civil engr. Thompson & Lichtner Co., Inc., Boston, 1940-47; co-sponsor cons. engrs. firm, Boston, 1948-51; div. engr. residence constrn. Thule Air Base, No. Greenland, 1952-53, also dir. research programs on permafrost constrn., Metcalf & Eddy Engrs., Boston; chief paving founds. and materials br. C.E., 1954-60, also chief engr. ballistic missiles early warning system and dep. dir. Titan 1 missile stas.; airfield expert NATO internat. staff, Paris, France, 1961—. Recipient Meritorious Civilian Service medal U.S. Army, 1960. Registered profl. engr., N.J. Fellow Am. Soc. C.E.: mem. Am. Soc. Mil. Engrs. Mason. Home: 51 Blvd du Souverain Brussels 1160 Belgium Office: USNATO APO New York City NY 09667

FEIEL, GEORGE MELVILLE, steel co. exec.; b. Columbus, O., Aug. 4, 1905; s. George F. and Emily J. (Pengelly) F.; B.S., Ohio State U., 1930; m. Annette F. Berger, Sept. 29, 1928; m. 2d, Elizabeth Gladden, Oct. 16, 1965. Clk. Ralston Steel Car Co., Columbus, 1923-26; pub. accountant Ernst & Ernst, Cleve., 1930-36; accountant Republic Steel Corp., 1936-41, asst. comptroller, 1941-49, comptroller, 1949-60, v.p., comptroller, 1960—. Mem. Am. Iron and Steel Inst., Beta Gamma Sigma, Beta Alpha Psi. Clubs: Union, Cleveland Athletic, Westwood. Home: 21660 Avalon Drive Rocky River OH 44116 Office: Republic Bldg Cleveland OH 44115

FEIERSINGER, SEBASTIAN, tenor; b. Kirchbiehl, Austria, May 5, 1913; s. Peter and Ursula (Bucher) F.; student Musik Akademie, Wien; m. Gertrud Bonnemann, July 8, 1943; children—Manfred, Ursula, Gertrud. First engagement, Saarbrucken, other engagements, Wiesbaden, Graz, Nurnberg, Dusseldorf, Munchen, Berlin; performed Stolzing, Metropolitan Opera Co., 1959, also Wagnerian tenor, San Francisco Opera; operatic performances, S.A., Italy, France, Spain, Portugal. Mem. Tractenverein, Tirol.

FEIFFER, JULES, cartoonist-writer; b. N.Y.C., Jan. 26, 1929; s. David and Rhoda (Davis) F.; student Art Students League, N.Y.C., 1946, Pratt Inst., N.Y.C., 1947- 48, 49-51; m. Judith Sheftel, Sept. 17, 1961; 1 dau., Kate. Asst. to syndicated cartoonist Will Eisner, 1946-51; cartoonist, author syndicated Sunday page, Clifford, engaged in various art jobs, 1953-56; contbg. cartoonist Village Voice, N.Y.C., 1956- -; cartoons pub. weekly in London (Eng.) Observer, 1958-66, London (Eng.) Sunday Telegraph, 1966-69, regularly in Playboy mag., 1959- -; cartoons nationally syndicated U.S., 1959—. Sponsor Nat. Com. Sane Nuclear Policy. Served AUS, 1951-53. Recipient Acad. award for animated cartoon. Munro, 1961; spl. George Polk Meml. award, 1962; Outer Circle Drama Critics award, 1970. Mem. Authors Guild, Dramatists Guild (council), P.E.N. Author: (books) Sick, Sick, Sick, 1959, Passionella and other stories, 1960, The Explainers, 1961, Boy, Girl, Boy, Girl, 1962, Hold Me!, 1962; (mus. revue) The Explainers, 1961; (one act play) Crawling

Arnold, 1961; (novel) Harry, The Rat with Women, 1963; Feiffer's Album, 1963; The Unexpurgated Memoirs of Bernard Mergendeiler, 1965; The Great Comic Book Heroes, 1965; Feiffer's Marriage Manual, 1967; (play) Little Murders (voted best play of yr. by London critics, Obie award, Outer Circle Drama Critics award), 1967; Feiffer on Civil Rights, 1967; (play) God Bless, 1968; (play) The White House Murder Case, 1970; (screenplays) Little Murders, 1971, Carnal Knowledge, 1971; (book) Pictures at a Prosecution, 1971. Office: care Hall Syndicate 30 E 42d St New York City NY

FEIGENBAUM, EDWARD ALBERT, educator; b. Weehawken, N.J., Jan. 20, 1936; s. Fred J. and Sara (Wittman) Rachman; B.S. in Elec. Engring., Carnegie Inst. Tech., 1956, Ph.D. in Indsl. Adminstrn., 1960; m. Nancy Joan DeMaranville, Oct. 4, 1958; children—Janet Denise, Carol Leonora. Asst., then asso. prof. bus. adminstrn. U. Cal. at Berkeley, 1960-64; asso. prof. computer sci., then prof. Stanford U., 1965—, dir. Computation Center, Stanford, 1965-68; cons. to industry, 1957—. Mem. computer and biomath. scis. study sect. NIH, 1968—. Fulbright scholar Gt. Britain, 1959-60. Mem. Assn. Computing Machinery (mem. of nat. council 1966-68), Am. Psychol. Assn., A.A.A.S., Sigma Xi, Tau Beta Pi, Eta Kappa Nu, Pi Delta Epsilon. Author: (with others) Information Processing Language V Manual, 1961. Editor: (with J. Felman) Computers and Thought, 1963. Series editor: McGraw-Hill Computer Science Series, 1966—. Home: 455 Grant Av Palo Alto CA 94306 Office: Computation Center Stanford Univ Stanford CA 94305

FEIGENBAUM, SIMON, ret. engr.; b. nr. Pitts., Mar. 22, 1909; s. Fred and Jennie (Ginsberg) F.; B.S., Carnegie Inst. Tech., 1930, M.E., 1941; m. Pauline Simon, Apr. 16, 1934; children—Fred, David L. With Jones & Laughlin Steel Corp., Pitts., 1930-70, chief indsl. engr., 1955-70. Recipient McKune award Am. Inst. Mining Engrs., 1942. Registered profl. engr., Pa. Mem. Am. Inst. Mining Engrs., Pi Tau Sigma. Mason. Home: 147 Vernon Dr Pittsburgh PA 15228

FEIGHAN, MICHAEL A., congressman; b. Lakewood, O., Feb. 16, 1905; s. John T. and Mary (English) F.; A.B., Princeton, 1928; LL.B., Harvard Law Sch., 1931; m. Florence J. Mathews, June 21, 1930; children—Michael A. (dec.), William Mathews, Fleur. Atty., 1931, mem. 78th-91st Congresses, 20th Dist. Ohio. Democrat. Clubs: Elm (Princeton); Burning Tree, Congressional (Washington). Office: House Office Bldg Washington DC 20515

FEIGHNER, JAMES WILBUR, food co. exec.; b. Marion, Ind., Sept. 17, 1916; s. Harry Wilbur and Lucille (Ferguson) F.; B.S. in Mech. Engring., Purdue U., 1939; grad. Advanced Mgmt. Program, Harvard, 1955; m. Margaret Gordon Richards, Aug. 23, 1941; children—Barrett Gordon, Katherine, James Wilbur. Sales engr. Westinghouse Electric Corp., 1939-41; applications engr. Servel, Inc., 1941-42; with Tom Huston Peanut Co., Columbus, Ga., 1945—, v.p., 1951- 58, pres., 1958—, also dir.; now v.p., dir. of Gen. Mills, Inc., Mpls.; pres., dir. Muscogee Sales Corp., Columbus; dir. First Nat. Bank, Columbus. Trustee Walter Alan Richards Found.; past pres. Muscogee County chpt. A.R.C. Served with USAAF, 1942-45. Mem. Nat. Confectioners Assn. (dir.), Columbus C. of C. (past pres.), N.A.M. (dir.). Home: 1420 Wynnton Rd Columbus GA 31906 Office: 900 8th Av Columbus GA 31901

FEIGL, HERBERT, univ. prof.; b. Reichenberg, Austria-Hungary, Dec. 14, 1902; s. Otto and Camilla (Beck) F.; student Chem. Tech. Sch., Reichenberg, 1917-21, U. Munich, 1921-22; Ph.D., U. Vienna, 1927; m. Maria Kasper, June 30, 1931; 1 son, Eric Otto; came to U.S., 1930, naturalized, 1937. Lectr., People's Inst., Vienna, 1927-30; Rockefeller Research Fellow, Harvard U., 1930-31; lectr. State U. of Ia., 1931-32, asst. prof., 1932-38, asso. prof., 1938-40; Rockefeller Research Fellow, N.Y. and Harvard, 1940; Guggenheim fellow, 1947-48; prof. philosophy U. Minn., 1940—, Regents' prof. philosophy, 1967—; dir. Minn. Center for Philosophy of Sci., 1953-71; Matchette Found. lectr. Purdue U., 1951. Trustee Inst. for Unity of Sci., Boston, also pres., 1967—; Matchette Foundation lectr. Bklyn. Coll., 1956; lectr., panel mem. Internat. Congress Philos, Sci., Zurich, 1954; vis. prof. U. Cal., 1946, 53; U. P.R., 1957; Carnegie vis. prof. Univ. Hawaii, spring 1958; Mead-Swing lectr. Oberlin Coll., 1961; lectr. U. Mexico, 1964; vis. prof. Vienna Inst. Advanced Studies and Sci. Research, 1964-65, Austrian Coll., Alpbach, 1964; Fulbright vis. prof. Australian univs., 1965, U. Hawaii, spring 1971; vis. lectr. Johns Hopkins, 1966, U. Pitts., 1971, Rutgers U., 1971, Boston Colloquium in Philosophy Sci., 1971; Fellow A.A.A.S. (v.p.; chmn. sect. history and philosophy of sci. 1957); mem. Am. Humanist Assn. (dir. 1965-69), Internat. Acad. for Philosophy of Science, Am. Philos. Assn. (pres. Western div. 1962-63), Philosophy of Sci. Assn. (governing bd. 1961-63), Minn. Philosophy Soc. (pres. 1961). Author books including: (with W. Sellars) Readings in Philosophical Analysis, 1949; Readings in the Philosophy of Science, (with M. Brodbeck), 1953; The Mental and the Physical, 1967. Editor: (with others) Current Issues in the Philosophy of Science, 1961. Editorial asso., advisor Philosophy of Science, Internat. Ency. of Unified Science (mem. adv. bd.); asso. editor Philosophical Studies (jour.), 1949—; co-editor Minn. Studies in Philos. Science, 1956, Vol. II, 1958, Vol III, 1962, Vol. IV, 1970, Vol. V, 1970. Home: 5601 Dupont Av S Minneapolis MN 55419 ☆

FEIKENS, JOHN, lawyer, former judge; b. Clifton, N.J., Dec. 3, 1917; s. Sipke and Corine (Wisse) F.; A.B., Calvin Coll., Grand Rapids, Mich., 1939; LL.B., U. Mich., 1941; m. Henriette Dorothy Schulthouse, Nov. 4, 1939; children—Jon, Susan Corine, Barbara Edith, Julie Anne, Robert H. Admitted to Mich. bar, 1942; gen. practice law, Detroit; dist. judge Eastern Dist. Mich., 1960-61. Past co-chmn. Mich. Civil Rights Commn. Alternate del. Rep. Nat. Conv., 1952, 60, del., 1956; chmn. Rep. State Central Com., 1953-57; mem. Rep. Nat. Com., 1953-57. Mem. bd. trustees New Detroit, Inc., 1968—, Calvin Coll. Fellow Am. Coll. Trial Lawyers; mem. Am., Detroit (dir. 1962, past pres.) bar assns., State Bar Mich. (commr. 1965—). Clubs: University of Michigan, Economic, Detroit (Detroit). Home: 743 Pemberton Rd Grosse Pointe Park MI 48236 Office: Penobscot Bldg Detroit MI 48226

FEIN, A. EDWIN, mgmt. co. exec.; b. N.Y.C., Apr. 9, 1898; s. Samuel and Anne (Fine) F.; student N.Y.U., 1919-1925, Columbia, 1925-26. Marketing-tech. cons. Walter Kidde & Co., Bloomfield, N.J., 1934-35; dir. sales DCA Food Industries, N.Y.C., 1936-38; chmn. bd. Research Co. Am., N.Y.C., 1939—; v.p., sec. United Indsl. Corp., N.Y.C., 1959—, also dir.; sec., dir. Affiliated Hosp. Products, Inc., St. Louis; dir. Detroit Stoker Co., Neo Products Co., El Rio Contractors, Inc. Served with U.S. Army, 1918-1919. Fellow Soc. Advancement Mgmt.; Am. Soc. Corporate Secs., Am. Marketing Assn., Am. Legion (comdr. 1931). Author annual editions of Brewing Industry Survey (Annual Advt. award), Basic Marketing Chart of U.S. Contbr. articles profl. jours. Home: 303 E 57th St New York City NY 10022 Office: 660 Madison Av New York City NY 10021

FEIN, BERNARD, investments exec.; b. N.Y.C., Jan. 13, 1908; s. Samuel and Anna (Fine) F.; LL.B., St. Lawrence U., 1929; m. Elaine Schneir, Dec. 26, 1948; children—Kathy Joyce, Lawrence Seth, Susan, Adam, David. Admitted to N.Y. bar, 1931; practice of law, N.Y.C., 1931-41; pres. United Indsl. Internat., Lausanne, Switzerland; pres., chmn. bd. United Indsl. Corp., N.Y.C.; chmn., chief exec. officer Affiliated Hosp. Products, Inc., St. Louis; chmn. bd. Neo Products Corp., Chgo.; dir. Aircraft Armaments, Inc., Balt. Home: 80 Garden Rd Scarsdale NY 10583 Office: 660 Madison Av New York City NY 10021

FEIN, IRVING ASHLEY, TV exec.; b. Bklyn., June 21, 1911; s. Harry and Fannie (Milstein) F.; grad. Colby Acad., 1928; student U. Balt., 1928-29, U. Wis., 1930-32; LL.B., St. Lawrence U., 1936; m. Florence Kohn, Dec. 25, 1941 (dec.); children—Michael Anthony, Patricia Ann; m. 2d, Marion Sheppard Schechter, June 21, 1969. Publicity and advt. dept. Warner Bros., N.Y.C., 1933-36, dir. exploitation and radio, West Coast studios, 1936; asst. publicity dir. Samuel Goldwyn, 1941; dir. exploitation and radio Columbia Pictures, Hollywood, 1946; publicity, advt. dir. Amusement Enterprises, Inc., 1947; with CBS, Inc., 1948-56, dir. exploitation, Hollywood, 1950, dir. publicity and exploitation CBS Radio, Hollywood, 1951-53, dir. pub. relations, 1953-55, v.p. sales promotion, advt., and press information, N.Y.C., 1955-56; pres. J & M Prodns., Inc., Beverly Hills, Cal., 1956-63; exec. v.p. JAC Prodns., 1965—, pres. TV Prodn. Co. Home: 1100 N Alta Loma Rd Los Angeles CA 90069 Office: 9908 Santa Monica Blvd Beverly Hills CA 90212

FEIN, JOHN MORTON, educator; b. Chgo., Dec. 23, 1922; s. Louis Julius and Lola (Dubin) F.; B.A., M.A., Harvard, 1944, Ph.D., 1950; m. Lucille Blumenthal, Sept. 11, 1946; children—David, Judith, Joanna, Laura. Teaching fellow, tutor Harvard, 1944-49, instr., 1949-50; mem. faculty Duke, 1950—, prof. Romance langs., 1963—, chmn. dept., 1964—; vis. prof. U. Chile, U. Catolica (Chile), 1957-58, Ind. U., 1964, Stanford, summer 1965, U. Wyo., summer 1967. Mem. Modern Lang. Assn., Am. Assn. Tchrs. Spanish and Portuguese (exec. com.). Author: Modernismo in Chilean Literature: The Second Period, 1965. Home: 2726 Montgomery St Durham NC 27705

FEIN, NATHANIEL, press rep.; b. N.Y.C., Aug. 7, 1914; s. Herman and Frances (Werth) F.; ed. pub. schs., N.Y.C.; m. Lois Arnold, Nov. 11, 1938; 1 son, David. Mem. staff N.Y. Herald Tribune, 1933-71, news photographer, 1936-71; press rep. Orange and Rochland Utilities, Inc., Spring Valley, N.Y., 1971—; exhbns. of work at Am. Museum Natural History, Mus. Modern Art, Cranbook Mus., Detroit. Served with USAAF, 1943-46. Recipient awards including 1st prize pictorial class, feature class, portrait class, also hon. mention spot news Press Photographers Contest, 1948, 1st prize portrait class, also pictorial class, 1950, hon. mention, 1951, 52, 58, 1st prize, 2 hon. mentions, 1959, William Randolph Hearst trophy, also 1st prize pictorial class, 1960, 1st and 3d prizes, 1963; Pulitzer prize news photography, 1949; Diamond award Graflex Co., 1950; TWA Aviation award, 1950; Freedom award, 1953; Cigar Inst. prize, 1955; 3d prize U.S. Camera mag. contest, 1960; 2d prize A.P. State Contest, 1964, P.B.A. City of N.Y. for graphic portrayal police function, 1966. Mem. N.Y. Press Photographers Assn. Author: Nat Fein's Animals, 1962. Home: 236 Western Hwy Tappan NY 10983 Office: 75 W Route 59 Spring Valley NY 10977

FEINBERG, ABRAHAM, business exec.; b. N.Y.C., Mar. 7, 1908; s. Jacob and Eva (Wolin) F.; student Coll. City N.Y.; LL.B., Fordham U., 1929; LL.M., New York U., 1936; LL.D., Brandeis U., 1961; m. Lillian Farber, Sept. 3, 1929; children—E. Richard, Judith Evelyn. Chmn. exec. com., vice chmn. bd. Am. Trust Co. (co. name changed to Am. Bank & Trust Co. 1966); dir. Beneficial Nat. Life Ins. Co. Mem. N.Y.C. Bd. Higher Edn. Trustee Truman Library, Independence, Mo., John F. Kennedy Library, Eleanor Roosevelt Meml. Found.; Corp. for Israel, 1955; overseer Coll. V.I.; U.S. dir. Nigerian Found. for Ojike Med. Center; bd. dirs. Feinberg Grad. Sch., pres. Am. com. Weizman Inst. Clubs: Harmonie, City Athletic, Manhattan (N.Y.C.); Old Oaks Country (Purchase, N.Y.); Fed. City, Nat. Capitol Democratic (Washington); Caesarea Golf and Country, Ltd. (chmn. bd.) (Israel). Home: 35 Elmsmere Rd Mount Vernon NY 10552 Office: 70 Wall St New York City NY 10005

FEINBERG, GERALD, educator, physicist; b. N.Y.C., May 27, 1933; s. Leon and Florence (Weingarten) F.; B.A., Columbia, 1953, M.A., 1954, Ph.D., 1957; m. Barbara J. Silberdick, Aug. 9, 1968; 1 son, Jeremy Russell. Mem. Inst. Advanced Study, Princeton, N.J., 1956-57; research asso. Brookhaven Nat. Lab., Upton, N.Y., 1957-59, cons., 1960—; prof. physics dept. Columbia, N.Y.C., 1959—. Sloan Found. fellow, 1960-64; Overseas fellow Churchill Coll., Cambridge, Eng., 1963-64. Fellow Am. Phys. Soc.; mem. A.A.A.S., Sigma Xi. Author: The Prometheus Project, 1969. Contbr. articles profl. jours. Home: 535 E 86th St New York City NY 10028

FEINBERG, JOEL, educator; b. Detroit, Oct. 19, 1926; s. Abraham J. and Marion (Tahl) F.; student U. Ill., 1944-45; B.A., U. Mich., 1949, M.A., 1951, Ph.D., 1957; m. Betty Grey Sowers, May 29, 1955; children—Melissa, Benjamin. Instr. philosophy Brown U., 1955-57, asst. prof., 1957-62; asst. prof. Princeton, 1962-64, asso. prof., 1964-66; prof. U. Cal. at Los Angeles, 1966-67; prof. philosophy Rockefeller U., N.Y.C., 1967—. Dir. Pub. Studies Corp.; editorial cons. Dickenson Pub. Co. Served with AUS, 1944-46. Fellow Center for Advanced Study in Behavioral Scis., 1960- 61; liberal arts fellow in law and philosophy Harvard Law Sch., 1963-64. Mem. Am. Soc. Polit. and Legal Philosophy (program chmn. 1963). Author: Doing and Deserving, 1970. Contbg. author: Philosophy in America, 1965. Editor: Reason and Responsibility, 1965; Moral Concepts, 1969. Series editor Contemporary Perspectives in Philosophy, Prentice-Hall Inc., 1963—. Home: 48 Edgewood Av Larchmont NY 10538

FEINBERG, MORTIMER ROBERT, psychologist; b. N.Y.C., Aug. 26, 1922; s. Max and Frieda (Siegel) F.; B.S., Coll. City N.Y., 1944; M.S., Ind. U., 1945; Ph.D., N.Y.U., 1950; m. Gloria Granditer, June 23, 1948; children—Stuart Andrew, E. Todd. Instr. psychology N.Y.U., 1945-50; chief psychologist Research Inst. Am., 1953-58; prof. psychology Bernard M. Baruch Coll., City U., 1958—, acting chmn. psychology dept., 1969-70; pres. BFS Psychol. Assos., 1960—; prin. lectr. Am. Mgmt. Assn.; indsl. psychology cons. psychiatry div. Mt. Sinai Hosp. Research adviser City of N.Y. Exec. Tng. Program, 1959—. Diplomate Am. Bd. Examiners in Indsl. Psychology. Fellow Am. Psychol. Assn., A.A.A.S. Author: Developing People in Industry (with D. Fryer), 1956; Effective Psychology for Managers, 1965. Home: 34 Brook Lane Peekskill NY 10566 Office: 666 Fifth Av New York City NY 10019

FEINBERG, SAMUEL MAURICE, physician; b. Russia, Mar. 28, 1895; s. George and Anna (Shulman) F.; brought to U.S., 1907, naturalized, 1918; B.S., U. Wis., 1917; M.D., Rush Med. Coll., 1919; m. Cecile Stern, Mar. 19, 1922; children—Alan Richard, Robert Herman and Ruth Ann (twins), Helene Rose (Mrs. Pier). Intern Cook County Hosp., Chgo., 1920-21, attending physician, 1926-38; specialist in internal medicine and allergy; emeritus prof. medicine, Northwestern U.; attending physician, dir. Allergy Research Lab., Evanston (Ill.), Hosp. Mem. Res. M.C., U.S. Army, 1918-19. Diplomate in allergy Am. Bd. Internal Medicine. Fellow A.C.P., A.M.A., Internat. Assn. Allergology (past pres.), Am. Acad. Allergy; mem. Ill., Chgo. med. socs., Nat. Inst. for Allergy and Infectious Diseases (past tng. grant com.), Am. Soc. for Study Allergy (past pres.), Chgo. Soc. Internal Medicine, Central Soc. Clin. Research, A.A.A.S., Am. Assn. Immunologists, Peruvian Allergy Assn. (hon.), Chgo. Soc. Allergy (past pres.), also Argentine, Spain, France, Scandinavian, Cuban allergy assns. (all hon.), Phi Beta Kappa, Sigma Xi, Phi Delta Upsilon, Sigma Sigma. Mem. Ref. Jewish Ch. Author: Asthma, Hay Fever and Related DisordersA Guide for Patients, 1933; Allergy in General Practice, 1934; Allergy in Practice, 1944; The Antihistamines, 1950; Allergy: Facts and Fancies, 1951; Living with Your Allergy, 1958; also articles med. jours. Mem. editorial bd. Folia Allergologica, Clinica Europea. Home: 739 Clavey Rd Highland Park IL 60035 Office: 750 Green Bay Rd Winnetka IL 60093

FEINBERG, SHELDON, cosmetic co. exec.; b. Newark, Nov. 14, 1926; s. Louis and Rose F.; B.S., Rutgers U., 1947, LL.B., 1953; C.P.A.; m. Betty Barnhard, July 1, 1951; children—Randi, Dori, Peter, Jami Su. Practice accounting, 1950- 54; treas. J.B. Williams Co., Inc., N.J., 1954-62; v.p., controller Revlon, Inc., N.Y.C., 1962—; dir. Essex County State Bank, Pension Life Ins. Co. Am. Served with USAAF, 1945. Home: 29 Farmstead Rd Short Hills NJ 07078 Office: 666 Fifth Av New York City NY 10019

FEINBERG, WILFRED, U.S. judge; b. N.Y.C., June 22, 1920; s. Jac and Eva (Wolin) F.; B.A., Columbia, 1940, LL.B., 1946; m. Shirley Marcus, June 23, 1946; children—Susan, Jack, Jessica. Admitted to N.Y. bar, 1947; law clk. U.S. dist. judge, 1947-49; asso. firm Kaye, Scholer, Fierman & Hays, N.Y.C., 1949-53; mem. firm McGoldrick, Dannett, Horowitz & Golub, N.Y.C., 1953- 61; dep. supt. N.Y. State Banking Dept., 1958; U.S. judge So. Dist. N.Y., 1961-66; U.S. judge Ct. Appeals, 2d circuit, 1966—. Served with AUS, 1942-45. Mem. Assn. Bar City N.Y., Am. Bar Assn., N.Y. County Lawyers Assn., Am. Judicature Soc., Phi Beta Kappa. Editor-in-chief Columbia Law Rev., 1946. Home: 15 Pasadena Pl Mount Vernon NY 10552 Office: US Courthouse Foley Sq New York City NY 10007

FEINBLOOM, ABRAHAM, business exec.; b. Binghamton, N.Y., 1901. Chmn. bd. Champion Products Inc., Rochester, N.Y.; dir. Central Trust Co., Rochester. Mason, Elk. Home: 820 East Av Rochester NY 14607 Office: 115 Collge Av Rochester NY 14607*

FEINDEL, WILLIAM HOWARD, neurosurgeon, educator; b. Bridgewater, N.S., Can., July 12, 1918; s. Robert Ronald and Annie (Swanberg) F.; B.A., Acadia U., 1939, D.Sc. (hon.), 1963; Rhodes scholar Nova Scotia and Merton Coll., Oxford (Eng.) U., 1939; M.Sc. in Physiology, Dalhousie U., 1942; M.D., C.M., McGill U., 1945; D.Phil. in Neuroanatomy, Oxford (Eng.) U., 1949; m. Faith Lyman, July 28, 1945; children—Christopher, Alexander, Patricia, Janet, Michael, Anna. Demonstrator biology Acadia U., 1937-39; demonstrator physiology Dalhousie U., 1940-42, Banting Found. research grantee, 1941; fellow neuropathology Montreal Neurol. Inst., 1943-44; research asst., demonstrator anatomy Oxford U., 1946-49; demonstrator neurosurgery, then lectr. McGill U. Sch. Medicine, 1951-55; research fellow neurophysiology Montreal Neurol. Inst., 1951-52, Reford postgrad. fellow, 1953-55; prof. surg. U. Sask. Med. Sch., also Univ. Hosp., 1955-59; 1st William Cone prof. neurosurgery McGill U. Med. Sch., 1959-; neurosurgeon-in-chief Montreal Neurol. Hosp., 1963—, founder, dir. Cone Lab. Neurosurg. Research, 1959—; attending neurosurgeon Catherine Booth Hosp., 1950—, Royal Victoria Hosp., 1959—; cons. neurosurgeon Sherbrook Gen. Hosp. NRC grad. fellow, 1940-50; Sigma Xi lectr., 1969; guest lectr. U. Cal. Los Angeles, U. Sask., Yale, Columbia, U. Ore., U. Vt.; dir. 4th Canadian Congress of Neurol. Scis. Bd. curators Osler Library, McGill U., 1965—. Diplomate Am. Bd. Neurol. Surgery. Fellow Royal, Am. (adv. com. neurosurgery 1970) colls. surgeons; mem. Nat. Neurol. Inst. Mex. (hon.), Harvey Cushing Soc., Soc. Neurol. Surgeons, Am. Acad. Neurol. Surgery, Am. Acad. Neurology, A.A.A.S., Am. Neurol. Assn., Royal Soc. Medicine, Anat. Soc. Gt Britain and Ireland, Montreal Neurol. Soc., Canadian Neurosurg. Soc. (v.p. 1966, pres. 1968-69), Vancouver Med. Assn. (hon.), Med.-Chi. Soc., Alpha Omega Alpha. Editor: (with A. Dawson) Prospect and Retrospect in Neurology, 1944; Medical Aspects of Traffic Accidents, 1955. Memory, Learning and LanguageThe Physical Basic of Mind, 1960; Thomas Willis: The Anatomy of the Brain and Nerves, 1965; mem. editorial bd. jour. Stroke. Home: 39 Thornhill Av Westmount Quebec Canada Office: 3801 University St Montreal 2 Quebec Canada

FEININGER, ANDREAS BERNHARD LYONEL, photographer; b. Paris, France, Dec. 27, 1906; s. Lyonel and Julia (Lilienfeld) F.; derivative citizenship; ed. schs. in Germany; studied under Walther Gropius at the Bauhaus, Weimar, Germany, 1922-25; student architecture Staatliche Bauschule in Zerbst, Germany, passed summa cum laude, 1928; m. Gertrud Wysse Hägg, Aug. 30, 1933; 1 son, Tomas G.A. Learned trade of a cabinet maker at the Bauhaus, 1922-25; passed journeyman examination, 1925; practiced architecture, Dessau and Hamburg, Germany, 1928-31; worked with LeCorbusier, Paris, 1932-33; profl. photographer specializing. in archtl. and indsl. photography, Stockholm, Sweden, 1933-39; free lance photographer Black Star Photo Agy., N. Y. C., 1940, under own name, 1941-43; staff photographer Life mag., 1943-62, specializing in "on location" assignments. One-man exhbn. of photographs, Smithsonian Instn., 1963. Charter mem. Am. Soc. Mag. Photographers. Author of books, articles. Research work in telephotography and graphic control processes. Exptl. photography in connection with lenses of very long and very short focal lengths. Home: 18 Elizabeth Lane New Milford CT 06776 ☆

FEINSINGER, NATHAN PAUL, educator; b. Bklyn., Sept. 20, 1902; s. Israel Bernard and Rebecca (Neighstock) F.; A.B., U. Mich. 1926. J.D., 1928; m. Bettie Whitney, Jan. 15, 1940; children—Greg, Ellen, Peter. Sociolegal research, Columbia Law Sch., 1928-29; asst., asso., prof. law U. Wis., 1929—, dir. Center for Teaching and Research in Disputes Settlements, Seminar in Methods of Disputes Settlement, Labor Relations Law; former vis. prof. law univs. of Chgo., Mich., Stanford, 1934, 36, 53, 58. Nat. War Labor Bd., Washington, 1942-46, successively as asso. gen. counsel, dir. nat. disputes and pub. mem.; chmn. Wage Stabilization Bd., 1951- 52. Spl. asst. to atty. gen. and gen. counsel, Wis. Labor Relations Bd., 1937-39; spl. rep. sec. of Labor in labor disputes, 1946-49; chmn. presdl. fact finding bd. in steel, meat packing, airlines labor disputes, 1946, 48. Mem. Am. Bar Assn., Order of Coif, Phi Beta Kappa, Phi Delta Phi (hon.), Druids. Club: University. Author: Stearns on Suretyship, 1937; Cases and Materials on Partnerships, 1939; Cases and Materials on Labor Law, 1940. Home: 1 Langdon St Madison WI 53703 also Box F Aspen CO 81611 Office: Law Sch U Wis Madison WI 53706

FEINSTEIN, ALLEN LEWIS, lawyer; b. N.Y.C., Apr. 18, 1929; s. Jacob and Kate (Goldberg) F.; A.B., Coll. City N.Y., 1949; LL.B., Columbia, 1952; m. Charlesa Joan Wolfe, Dec. 14, 1957. Admitted to N.Y. bar, 1952, Ariz. bar, 1960, U.S. Supreme Ct. bar; practice in N.Y.C., 1953-59, Phoenix, 1960—; law clk. Surrogate Frankenthaler, 1953-55; asso. Proskauer, Rose, Goetz & Mendelsohn, 1955-59; law clk. Supreme Ct. Justice Charles C. Bernstein, Ariz., 1959-61; 1st adminstrv. dir. Supreme Ct. Ariz., 1961-64; pvt. law practice, 1964—. Mem. Phoenix Housing Code Com., 1968; mem. Phoenix Charter Review Com., 1969. Treas., bd. dirs. Meml. Hosp. Phoenix; bd. dirs., mem. exec. com. Paraplegia Found. Ariz.; bd. dirs. Community Council. Served with USAF, 1952-53. Mem. Am. Arbitration Assn., Am., Ariz., Maricopa County bar assns., Am. Judicature Soc., Inst. Jud. Adminstrn., Phoenix Jr. C. of C., Phi Beta Kappa, Phi Delta Phi.

Democrat. Jewish religion. Club: University of Phoenix (pres. bd.). Home: 2110 Encanto Dr S W Phoenix AZ 85007 Office: 114 W Adams St Phoenix AZ 85003

FEINSTEIN, ALVAN RICHARD, educator, physician; b. Phila., Dec. 4, 1925, s. Joel B. and Bella (Ukasz) F.; B.S., U. Chgo., 1947, M.S. in Math., 1948, M.D., 1952; M.A. (hon.), Yale, 1969; m. Linda Louise Marean, Oct. 20, 1968; 1 dau., Miriam Anne. Intern, then resident Yale- New Haven Hosp., 1952-54; research fellow Rockefeller Inst., 1954-55; resident Columbia-Presbyn. Med. Center, N.Y.C., 1955-56; clin. dir. Irvington House, N.Y.C., 1956-62; instr., then asst. prof. N.Y.U. Sch. Medicine, 1956-62; chief clin. pharmacology VA Hosp., West Haven, Conn., 1962-64, chief clin. biostatistics, 1964—; mem. faculty Yale Sch. Medicine, 1962—, prof. medicine and epidemiology, 1969—; chief Eastern Research Support Center, VA, 1967—. Pres. New Haven area chpt. Assn. Computing Machinery, 1968-69. Served with AUS, 1944-46. Recipient Francis G. Blake award for outstanding teaching Yale Med. Sch., 1969. Mem. Assn. Am. Physicians, Am. Soc. Clin. Investigation, A.C.P., Am. Fedn. Clin. Research, Am. Soc. Clin. Pharmacology Therapeutics, Am. Statis. Assn., Assn. Computing Machinery, Biometric Soc., A.M.A., Am. Heart Assn., Am. Assn. History Medicine, Alpha Omega Alpha. Author: Clinical Judgment, 1967; also articles. Mem. editorial bd. Am. Heart Jour., Circulation, Clin. Pharmacology and Therapeutics, Jour. Hist. Medicine. Home: 320 Knollwood Dr New Haven CT 06515 Office: VA Hosp West Haven CT 06516

FEINSTEIN, IRWIN KEITH, educator, mathematician; b. Chgo., Aug. 29, 1914; s. Mike and Rose (Katz) F.; B.S., Ill. Inst. Tech., 1936; M.A., Northwestern U., 1946, Ph.D., 1952; m. Lena S. Zimmerman, July 9, 1954; children—Kate Ann, Ronald Sam. Mem. faculty U. Ill. at Chgo. Circle, 1946—, prof. math., 1962—. Vis. prof. R.I. Coll., 1960, Northwestern U., 1962, Nat. Coll. Edn., 1956-62; cons. in field. Served to lt. USCGR, 1942-46. Mem. Am. Assn. U. Profs., Math. Assn. Am., Nat. Council Tchrs. Math. Club: Men's Mathematics (Chgo.) Mem. B'nai B'rith (dir. educator's lodge 1968-71). Author: Analytic Geometry, 1949; College Algebra, 1957; Accountants Handbook, 1963; New Math I, New Math II, New Math III, 1968-69. Home: 735 Lamon Av Wilmette IL 60091 Office: Univ of Ill at Chicago Circle Chicago IL 60680

FEINSTEIN, SELWYN, reporter; b. N.Y.C., Nov. 5, 1931; s. Jacob and Kate (Goldberg) F.; B.A., Queens Coll., N.Y.C., 1952; M.S. in Journalism, Columbia, 1953; m. Eve Gellerman, June 27, 1954; children—Jeffrey Eliot, Robert Michael. Reporter, United Press, Pitts., 1955-58; asso. editor Tide mag., 1958-59; sr. editor Printers' Ink mag., 1959-61; reporter Wall St. Jour., N.Y.C. 1962-66, in Hong Kong, 1966-67, in Chgo., 1967, now in N.Y.C. Contbg. editor Ency. Americana, 1958-61. Served with AUS, 1953-55. Address: 73 Tompkins Av Hastings-on-Hudson NY 10706

FEIS, HERBERT, historian; b. N.Y.C., June 7, 1893; s. Louis J. and Louisa (Waterman) F.; A.B., Harvard, 1916, Ph.D., 1921; Litt.D., Princeton, 1961; L.H.D., U. Mich., 1966, U. Cin., 1968; m. Ruth Stanley-Brown, Mar. 25, 1922. Instr. econs. Harvard, 1920-21; asso. prof. U. Kan., 1922-25; head dept. econs. U. Cin., 1926-29; vis. prof. history Harvard 1957; Remsen Bird lectr. Occidental Coll.; Univ. lectr. U. Cal. at Berkeley, U. Tokyo; mem. staff Council on Fgn. Relations, 1930-31; econ. adviser Dept. of State, 1931-37; adviser internat. econ. affairs, 1937-43; spl. cons. to Sec. of War, 1944-46; chief tech. adviser Am. delegation, World Econ. and Monetary Conf., London, 1933; spl. adviser Conf. of Am. Republics, Buenos Aires, 1936, Lima, Peru, 1938, Panama, 1939; adviser on Am. indsl. relations, Internat. Labor Office, League of Nations, various periods, 1922-27. Mem. Inst. for Advanced Study, Princeton, 1948-50, 51, 53, 58—; hon. research asso. Harvard, 1967; mem. policy planning staff. Dept. of State, 1950-51. Served in U.S.N.R.F., World War. Guggenheim fellow., 1926; recipient A.L.A. Liberty and Justice award, 1958; Pulitzer prize for history, 1960. Author books including: Seen from E. A., 1947; The Spanish Story, 1948; The Road to Pearl Harbor, 1950; The Diplomacy of the Dollar, 1950; The China Tangle, 1953; Churchill-Roosevelt-Stalin, 1957; Between War and Peace: The Potsdam Conference, 1960; Japan Subdued, 1961; Foreign Aid and Foreign Policy, 1964; Characters in Crisis, 1966; Contest over Japan, 1967; From Trust to Terror, 1970. Contbr. to mags. Home: York ME 03909

FEISS, CARL, educator, city planner; b. Cleve., June 18, 1907; s. Paul Louise and Edith (Lehman) F.; B.F.A., U. Pa., 1931; student Cranbrook Acad. Arts, 1931- 33; M. City Planning, Mass. Inst. Tech. 1938; m. Alleen Kelly, Oct. 10, 1941; children—Caroline Lehman, Alison Kelly Hays. Dir. planning and housing div. Columbia, 1936-42; dir. Denver Planning Commn., 1942-45; dir. sch. architecture and planning, dept. bldg. industry and real estate U. Denver, 1945-47; chief planning and engring. br., div. slum clearance and urban redevel. HHFA, Washington, 1950-54; planning and urban design cons., 1954—; prof. architecture and urban studies U. Fla., 1971—. Planning and devel. cons., Bratenahl, O., Columbia, S.C. State of Ohio, E. Central Fla. Regional Planning Council, Tampa Bay Regional Planning Council, P.R., V.I., others; historic preservation cons., Beaufort, S.C., Charleston, S.C., Columbus, Ga., New Orleans, Washington, others; urban renewal planning and other consultation, Buffalo, Rochester, Syracuse, N.Y., Caracas, Venezuela, others,; cons. Balt. Art Mus., 1970-71, Urban Studies Bur. U. Fla., 1971. Mem. Denver Planning Commn., 1948-50; v.p. Planning Found. Am. Mem. White House Conf. Children and Youth, 1963, White House Conf. on Natural Beauty, 1963. Trustee Denver Art Mus. Recipient grant Nat. Found. on Arts and Humanities, 1966. Fellow A.I.A. (Spl. Services award; mem. Nat. Assn. Housing and Redevel. ofcls., Nat. Housing Conf., Am. Inst. Planners (past dir.), Internat. Housing and Town Planning Assn., Am. Soc. Planning Ofcls. (past dir.), Internat. Commn. on Monuments and Sites (Am. com.), Internat. Union of Architects, Soc. Archtl. Historians, Nat. Trust Historic Preservation (trustee). Club: Cosmos. Author: (with N. S. Keith) Report on the Renewal Possibilities of the Historic Triangle of the City of San Juan, The Future of Buffalo, 1958; A Community Renewal Program for the City of Rochester, N.Y.; co-author With Heritage So Rich, The New City; also contbr. articles profl. jours. Home: 3227 33d Pl NW Washington DC 20008

FEIST, IRVING JONAS, exec. Boy Scouts Am.; b. Newark, Jan. 6, 1907; s. Abram and Irene (Sickle) F.; B.S., Newark Acad., 1925, B.B.S., U. Pa., 1929; LL.D., Monmouth Coll., m. Dorothy Blair, Nov. 30, 1930; children—John Alan, Margaret Louise (Mrs. Claude Foussier). With Feist & Feist, real estate and ins., Newark and N.Y.C., 193O—, v.p., 1930-31, pres., 1931—. Pres. Boy Scouts Am., 1968—. Active fund-raising campaigns, community activities; mem. exec. com., nat. bd. govs. Nat. Conf. Christians and Jews, Inc.; chmn. (finance planning com. World Scouting; nat. adv. council Girl Scouts U.S.A.; bd. dirs. U.S. Found. for Internat. Scouting; adv. bd. Salvation Army, Newark, Nat. trustee, past state chmn. Ducks Unlimited; mem. bd. dirs. Freedoms Found., Valley Forge, Pa.; bd. trustees Sport Fishery Assn. and Found. Comdg. officer N.J. Wing, Civil Air Patrol, 1951-56. Recipient Silver Beaver, Silver Antelope, Silver Buffalo awards Boy Scouts Am. Golden Pheasant, Boy Scouts Japan; golden medalion Korea; Silver Wolf award Brit. Scout Assn., 1967; Silver Tamarow award Boy Scouts Philippines, 1968; Bronze Wolf, World Scouting's highest award, 1969. Mem. Newark, N.Y. real estate bds., Newark C. of C., N.J. Taxpayers Assn., Newark Downtown Assn., Am. Forestry Assn. (dir., hon. v.p.) Am. Soc. Real Estate Counselors, Soc. Indsl. Realtors, Internat. Real Estate Fedn. Clubs: Newark Downtown, Hollywood Golf (past pres.) (Deal, N.J.); Adventurers; St. Hubert's Soc. (founder, chmn. bd.); Wall Street, Madison Square Garden (N.Y.C.); University of Pa., Manasquan Fishing. Home: 200 E 57th St New York City NY 10022 Office: 58 Park Pl Newark NJ 07102 also 100 Park Av New York City NY 10017

FEIT, WALTER, educator, mathematician; b. Vienna, Austria, Oct. 26, 1930; s. Paul and Esther (Blum) F.; B.A., M.S., U. Chgo., 1951; Ph.D., U. Mich., 1954; m. Sidnie Marilyn Dresher, Oct. 26, 1957; children—Paul, Alexandra M. From instr. to asso. prof. Cornell U., 1953-64; prof. math. Yale, 1964—. Served with AUS, 1955-57. Mem. Am. Math. Soc. (Cole prize 1965). Home: 6 Waite St Hamden CT 06517 Office: Yale Univ New Haven CT 06520

FEITEL, ARTHUR, architect; b. New Orleans, June 3, 1891 s. Morris and Sarah (Kahn) F.; B.Arch., Tulane U. 1911; Ecole Nat. Des Beaux-Arts, Paris, France (Architecte Diplomé Par Le Gouvernement), 1922. Architect; designer or asso. designer number of pub. instns., New Orleans. Mem. City Park Commn. Pres. Delgado Art Mus., 1947-57; mem. bd. La. State Museum; chmn. of Vieux Carre Commn. (for preservation of New Orleans French Quarter); dir. Spring Fiesta Assn. Decorated chevalier de l'Ordre National du Merite (France). Fellow A.I.A.; mem. Société Des Architectes Diplomés Par Le Gouvernement, La. Hist. Soc. (mem. bd.), Athenée Louisianais, English Speaking Union (pres. New Orleans br.), New Orleans C. of C., Art Assn. New Orleans (pres. 1940-57), Palmes Academiques (France), Fgn. Relations Assn. New Orleans (dir.). Club: New Orleans Athletic. Home: 515 St Ann St New Orleans LA 70116 Office: Carondelet Bldg New Orleans LA 70130

FEITELBERG, SERGEI, educator, physicist; b. Moscow, Russia, Nov. 13, 1905; s. Arthur and Catherine (Zodicov) F.; M.E. equivalent, Inst. Tech., Berlin Charlottenburg, Germany, 1928; M.D. U. Lausanne (Switzerland), 1939; m. Liesl Ganzel, Oct. 11, 1947. Came to U.S., 1939, naturalized, 1945. Physicist, Mt. Sinai Hosp., N.Y.C., 1939—; mem. faculty Columbia, 1942- 66, asso. clin. prof. radiology (physics), 1959-66; prof. physics Mt. Sinai Sch. Medicine, 1966—. Mem. subcoms. Nat. Com. Radiation Protection, 1950—. Mem. Am. Phys. Soc., Am. Assn. Physicist in Medicine, Sigma Xi. Author: (with others) Radioactive Isotopes in Medicine and Biology, 2d rev. edit., 1963; also articles. Home: 64 E 94th St New York City NY 10728

FEITLER, ROBERT, shoe co. exec.; b. Chgo., Nov. 19, 1930; s. Irwin and Bernice (Gombrig) F.; B.S., U. Pa., 1951; LL.B., Harvard, 1954; m. Joan Elden, May 30, 1957; children—Pamela, Robert, Richard, Dana. Vice pres., gen. mgr. Scott Publs. div. Esquire, Inc., N.Y.C., 1958-64; pres., treas. Weyenberg Shoe Mfg. Co., Milw., 1964—. Trust Smart Family Found. Served with U.S. Army, 1954-56. Jewish religion. Clubs: University, Milwaukee Athletic (Milw.); Harvard (N.Y.C.). Home: 1712 E Cumberland Blvd Whitefish Bay WI 53211 Office: 234 E Resevoir St Milwaukee WI 53201

FEIWELL, MORRIS E., utility exec.; chairman of the board and chief executive officer of the Indianapolis (Ind.) Power & Light Co.; dir. Laclede Gas Light Co., Tecumseh Coal Corp., Stone Container Co. Home: 5555 Everett Av Chicago IL 60637 Office: Indianapolis Power & Light Co 25 Monument Circle Indianapolis IN 46204*

FEJER ANDREW AKOS, engr., educator; b. Budapest, Hungary, June 4, 1913; s. Eugene and Ilona (Haas) F; M.E., Czech Tech. U. 1936; M.S., Cal. Inst. Tech., 1939, Ph.D., 1945; m. Edith Behal, June 12, 1938; children—Theodore William, Mark Eugene, Ilona Anne. Came to U.S., 1938, naturalized, 1948. Mech. engr. Skoda Works, Prague, Czechoslovakia, 1936- 38; research fellow Hydraulics Machinery Lab., Cal. Inst. Tech., 1939- 41, instr. mech. and aero. engring., 1941-45; research engr. aircraft engine div. Packard Motor Car Co., 1945-48; prof., chmn. depts. aero. and mech. engring. U. Toledo, 1948-58; prof., dir. mech. engring. dept. Ill. Inst. Tech. 1958-64, chmn. mech. and aerospace engring. dept., 1964-71; lectr. aeros. U. Mich., 1950-51; engring. cons. Asso. fellow Am. Inst. Aeros. and Astronautics; mem. Am. Assn. Engring. Edn., Am. Soc. M.E., N.Y. Acad. Scis., A.A.A.S., Sigma Xi, Phi Kappa Phi, Tau Beta Pi, Pi Tau Sigma. Home: 122 LeMoyne Pkwy Oak Park IL 60302 Office: 3110 S State St Chicago IL 60616

FELBER, EDWARD RICHARD, utility exec.; b. Chippewa Falls, Wis., May 25, 1896; s. Robert E. and Elizabeth (Misfeldt) F.; B.S. in Mech. Engring., U. Wis., 1922; m. Hazel Norris, June 6, 1926. With Madison Gas and Electric Co. (Wis.), 1922—, chmn. bd., 1966—. Treas. U. Wis. Class of 1922—. Served to 2d lt., inf. U.S. Army, World War I. Registered profl. engr., Wis. (32, Shriner). Home: 38 Fuller Dr Madison WI 53704 Office: 100 N Fairchild St Madison WI 53703

FELBER, EVERETT HENRY FRED, govt. ofcl; b. Ellington, Conn., Dec. 25, 1914; s. Henry and Clara (Voigt) F.; B.A., U. Conn., 1936; m. Dorothea Carolyn Burnham, Sept.26, 1936; children—Carolyn Ann (Mrs. Paul Willis Uber), Everett Craig. With Dept. Agr., 1936—, dir. farmer programs div. Agrl. Stblzn. and Conservation Service, 1962-69, dep. adminstr., mgmt., 1969—. Served to capt. C.E., AUS, 1942-45; PTO Recipient Superior Service award Dept. Agr., 1958. Conglist. Home: 4111 Oliver St Chevy Chase MD 20015 Office: Dept of Agriculture 14th and Independence Av SW Washington DC 20250

FELBERMAYER, ANNY, lyric soprano; b. Vienna, Austria, July 21; d. Hans and Adele (Halmag) Felbermayer; ed. Acad. fur Musik and Darstellende Kunst, Vienna; m. Gustav Szekely, July 2, 1960. Mem. Vienna State Opera, 1950- -; prin. roles include Pamina in Zauberflöte, Marzellina in Fidelio, Zdenka in Arabella, Gretel in Hänsel and Gretel, Annchen in Falstaff, Ighino in Palestrina, Liu in Turandot, Susanna in Figaro; numerous guest appearances Europe, 1957—; recording artist Columbia, London, Vanguard. Vox, Decca, Munich records. Recipient Cebotari prize Mozart Gemeinde, Vienna, 1949; prize, Geneva, Switzerland, 1949, Verviers, Belgium 1950. Home: Wilhelm Buschgasse 32 Vienna 19 Austria Office: Vienna State Opera Vienna 1 Austria

FELD, BERNARD TAUB, physicist; b. Bklyn., Dec. 21, 1919; s. A. Louis and Helen (Taub) F.; B.S., Coll. City N.Y., 1939; Ph.D., Columbia, 1945; m. Eliza McCormick, June 10, 1947; children—Elizabeth T., Ellen D. Physicist, Manhattan Project, Columbia, 1941-42; groupleader Metall. Lab., U. Chgo., 1942-44; physicist Los Alamos Sci. Lab., 1944-46; mem. faculty Mass. Inst. Tech., 1946—, prof. physics, 1957—, chmn. directing com. Lab. Nuclear Sci., 1961-63; vis. prof. U. Rome (Italy), also U. Padua (Italy), 1953-54; vis. scientist European Center Nuclear Research, 1960-61; vis. prof. Ecole Polytechnique (Paris) 1966-67; cons. Brookhaven Nat. Lab.; mem. exec. com. Cambridge Electron Accelerator; chmn. U.S. com. on Pugwash Conf. on Sci. and World Affairs, also mem. internat. continuing com., 1963—. Trustee Asso. Univs., 1958-60; pres. Council for a Livable World, 1963—; adv. council Peace Research Inst., 1960—; bd. dirs. Bull. Atomic Scientists, 1970—. Fellow Am. Phys. Soc.; mem. Fedn. Am. Scientists (vice chmn. 1962), Am. Acad. Arts and Scis. (dir. summer study arms control 1960), Phi Beta Kappa, Sigma Xi. Author: The Neutron Vol. II of Experimental Nuclear Physics, 1954; Models of Elementary Particles, 1969. Editor: Impact of New Technologies on the Arms Race, 1970. Asso. editor Annals of Physics, 1957—; cons. editor Blaisdell-Ginn-Xerox Pub. Co., 1959—. Contbr. articles profl. jours. Home: 42 Arlington St Cambridge MA 02140

FELD, FRITZ, actor, writer, dir.; b. Berlin, Germany, Oct. 15, 1900; s. Heinrich and Martha (Guttman) F.; ed. Gymnasium, Germany, 1907-17; m. Virginia Rickets-Kraft, Nov. 10, 1940; children—Steven, Danny. Came to U.S., 1923, naturalized, 1930. Performer Prof. Max Reinhardt Theaters, Berlin, 1917-23, Century Theatre, N.Y.C., 1923-27; actor, writer dir. Hollywood motion picture studios, 1923—; actor, dir. Nat. Theatre, 1930—, George M. Cohan Theatre, N.Y.C., 1931—; chmn. Am. Nat. Theatre, 1968—. Mem. Screen Actors Guild (dir. 1970-71), ANTA, Acad. Motion Picture Arts and Scis. Address: 12348 Rochedale Lane Los Angeles CA 90049

FELD, JACOB, civil engr.; b. Austria, Mar. 3, 1899; s. Israel and Gussie Rachel (Haarzopf) F.; U.S. citizen by derivation; B.S., Coll. City N.Y., 1918; C.E., U. Cin., 1921, M.A., 1921, Ph.D., 1922; m. Ethel Gold, Jan. 26, 1928; 1 dau., Judith (Mrs. David E. Marrus). Engr. with Dr. D.B. Steinman, Henry Goldmark, Turner Constructors, also L.I. R.R., 1922-26; pvt. practice as cons. engr., 1926—; designer engr. N.Y. Coliseum, Guggenheim Museum, Yonkers Raceway, Bellevue Hosp. Center, Lincoln Center structures, Hudson River Water Pollution Control Plant; vis. prof. Purdue U., Northwestern U., N.C. State U. Spl. engring. cons. USAF, Hdqrs. Civil Engring. Directorate; mem. engring. panel USAF Sci. Adv. Bd., 1965-67; mem. Hwy Research Bd., 1930—; partner firm Feld & Timoney, 1945-68, Feld Kaminetzkey & Cohen, 1966—. Chmn. constrn. economy com., N.Y. Citizens Housing Council, 1936; delegate internat. engring. congresses, 1946—. Bd. dirs. Cejwin Ednl. Camps, PT. Jervis, NY., 1936—; bd. govs. Technion Israel Sch. Tech., Haifa, 1958—. Deocrated Order of Merit (France), 1963; recipient silver medal Soc. Encouragement Progress, France, 1966; Distinguished Engring. Alumnus award Coll. City N.Y., 1969; Distinguished Engring. Coll. Alumnus award U. Cin., 1969; named Met. Engr. of Year, Am. Soc. C.E., 1956, Bklyn. Engrs. Club, 1959. Fellow Am. Soc. C.E., A.A.A.S., N.Y. Acad. Sci. (chmn. div. engring. 1960-61, councillor 1962-63, v.p. and pres. 1964-66); mem. Cons. Engrs. Council, Phi Beta Kappa, Sigma Xi. Tau Beta Pi, Chi Epsilon. Author: Radio Telescope Structures, 1957; Lessons from Concrete Failures, 1964; Construction Failure, 1968. Home: RFD 1 Yorktown Heights NY 10598 Office: 114 E 32d St New York City NY 10016

FELD, NICHOLAS, fgn. service officer; b. Vicksburg, Miss., Dec. 5, 1915; s. Nicholas and Mable (Phillips) F.; A.B. Harvard, 1936, postgrad., 1937-38; m. Cora Helene Hochstein, Dec. 27, 1949; 1 dau., Evelyn Dana. Apptd. fgn. service officer, unclassified, vice consul career, sec. Diplomatic Service, assigned vice consul, Zurich, Switzerland, 1939, Basel, 1939; Fgn. Service Officers Tng. Sch., Dept. State, Washington, 1940; vice consul, Madras, India, 1940; 3d sec., Pretoria, Union South Africa, 1944, 2d sec., 1945; commd. consul, 1948; assigned consul, Dar-es-Salaam, Tanganyika Ty., East Africa, 1948, Geneva, Switzerland, 1950; officer in charge West, Central and East African affairs, Office African Affairs, Dept. State, 1951; consul Singapore, 1954-56; officer charge trusteeship affairs, Office Dependent Area Affairs, State Dept., 1956-60; counselor, Budapest, 1960-62; chief, jr. officer personnel Dept. of State, Washington, 1963-65, acting dir. Office West African Affairs, 1965—; dep. dir. Office Inter-Am. Affairs, Bur. African Affairs, State Dept., 1965—, country dir. for Kenya, Tanzania, Seychelles and Uganda, 1967, U.S. adviser Entente Guaranty Fund, Abidjan, Ivory Coast, 1969. Home: PO Box 62 Chathamport MA 02633

FELD, WERNER JOACHIM, educator; b. Duesseldorf, Germany, Apr. 10, 1910; s. Bruno and Irma (Loebl) F.; student law U. Berlin, 1930-33; Ph.D. in Polit. Sci., Tulane U., 1962; m. Elizabeth Lloyd Tandy, Oct. 1, 1957. Came to U.S., 1938, naturalized, 1944. Dist. mgr. sales E. Edelmann & Co., Chgo., 1938-43, 46; pres. Dixie Specialty Co., Inc., Mobile, 1947-50, 52-61; prof. chmn. dept. polit. sci. and econ. Moorhead (Minn.) State Coll., 1962-65; prof., chmn. dept. polit. sci. La. State U., New Orleans, 1965—; vis. prof. Bologna Center, Johns Hopkins, 1969; adviser to asst. sec. for European affairs State Dept., 1966-68, cons. State Dept., 1965-70. Dir. Civil Def., Mobile, 1955-57. Served with AUS, 1943-46, 50-52. Decorated Army Commendation medal; Fulbright scholar Coll. Europe, Bruges, Belgium, 1968-69. Mem. Am., So. (sec. 1967-68) polit. sci. assns., Internat. Studies Assn. (pres. S. dist.), UN Assn. (pres.). Author: Reunification and West German-Soviet Relations, 1963; The Court of the European Communities: New Dimension in International Adjudication, 1964; The European Common Market and the World, 1967; The Enduring Question of Polities, 1969; Transnational Business Collaboration Among Common Market Countries, 1970. Home: 2362 Killdeer St New Orleans LA 70122

FELDBERG, CHESTER BEN, banker, lawyer; b. N.Y.C., Dec. 16, 1939; s. William and Janet (Mesh) F.; A.B., Union Coll., Schenectady, 1960; LL.B., Harvard, 1963; m. Lynn Lea Uebelhack, Sept. 17, 1963; children—Gregory Howard, Suzanne. Admitted to N.Y. bar, 1963; atty. Fed. Res. Bank of N.Y., N.Y.C., 1964-68, asst. counsel, 1968—, sec., 1969—. Mem. Assn. Bar City N.Y. Club: Harvard (N.Y.C.). Home: 4 Jeffrey Lane Office: 33 Liberty St New York City NY 10045

FELDBERG, STANLEY, bus. exec.; b. 1923; B.A., Dartmouth, 1949. With Zayre, Corp., 1949—, now pres., chief exec. officer, dir. Served with USAAF, 1942-46. Address: 1 Mercer Rd Natick MA 01762*

FELDBERG, SUMNER, bus. exec.; b. 1924; B.A. Harvard, 1947, M.B.A., 1949; m. With Zayre Corp., 1949—, treas., 1956—, sr. v.p., 1965-68, sr. v.p. finance, 1968- 69, exec. v.p., 1969—. Served to lt. USAAF, 1943-46. Address: 1 Mercer Rd Natick MA 01762

FELDER, MILLIE GOLDSTEIN, instn. adminstr.; b. London, Eng., Jan. 29, 1901; d. Harris and Rachel (Pizer) Goldstein; student Coll. City N.Y., New Sch., N.Y.C.; m. Morris Felder, Aug. 5, 1923; children—Jerome Solon, Raoul Lionel. Supt. war plant, food products, Bklyn., 1943-45; exec. dir. Assembly Bklyn. Jewish Women, 1947-49, v.p., coordinator, 1949—; adminstr. Menorah Home and Hosp. for Aged and Infirm, Bkyn., 1949-67; now exec. dir. Active A.R.C.; 1st Bklyn. chmn. March of Dimes; chmn. health ednl. com. Williamburgh- Greenpoint Health Centre; organized 1st day center, also 1st out-patient program in Home for Aged in U.S.A.; mem. N.Y.C. adminstrs. conf. Homes for Aged, 1943—; mem. Govs. N.Y. Com. on Aged; mem. Nat. Conf. Jewish Communal Service, 1958—, Free Nurses Inst. N.Y.C., 1948, Frances Fey Aid 1950—. N.Y. State Welfare Conf., 1956—. Bd. dirs. Neuro-phychiat. Clinic. Recipient citation for service A.R.C., 1944. Mem. Williamburgh Philanthropic Orgn. (pres.), Williamsburgh Helping Hand Assn. (pres.), Nat. Assn. Mentally Retarded Children, Greater N.Y. Hosp. Assn., Asso. Hosp. Puchasing Agts. Greater N.Y. Hosp. Assn. Author profl. articles.

FELDESMAN, WALTER, lawyer, shoe mfg. co. exec.; b. 1917; B.S., N.Y.U., 1937; LL.B., Harvard, 1940; married. Admitted to N.Y. bar, 1941; mem. firm Feldesman & D'Atri, N.Y.C.; sec. Nat. Shoes Inc., Bronx, N.Y., 1970—. Office: Nat Shoes 595 Gerard Av Bronx NY 10451*

FELDMAN, ABRAHAM JEHIEL, rabbi; b. Kiev, Ukraine, June 28, 1893; s. Jehiel and Elka (Rubin) F.; B. Hebrew Lit., Hebrew Union Coll., Cin., 1913, rabbi, 1918, D.D., 1944; A.B., U. Cin., 1917; S.T.D., Trinity Coll., 1953; LL.D., Hillyer Coll., 1953; H.H.D., Hartt Coll. of Music, 1953; Litt.D. (honorary), Parsons Coll., 1969; m. Helen Bloch, June 2, 1918; children—Daniel Bloch, Joan Helen (Mrs. Jerome W. Mecklenburger), Ella (Mrs. Charles Norwood). Rabbi Free Synagogue, N.Y. C. 1918-19, Congregation Children of Israel, Athens, Ga., 1919-20 Ref. Congregation Keneseth Israel, Phila., 1920-25, Congregation Beth Israel, Hartford, Conn., 1925—, now emeritus, 1968—; lectr. in O.T., Hartford Theol. Sem., 1954—; asso. editor English Yiddish Ency. Dictionary, 1910-12; editor Jewish Ledger, 1929—. Dir. Jewish Social Service, Mt. Sinai Hosp., Hartford Jewish Fedn., Julius Hartt Musical Found., Hebrew Home for the Aged; incorporator United War and Community Funds of Conn.; mem. of the exec. bd. Union Am.-Hebrew Congregations, 1945-48, 58-60; trustee, nat. co-chmn. on religious groups People to People Fedn. Recipient Americanism and Civic award Conn. Valley council B'nai B'rith, 1955; George Washington medal of honor Freedoms Found., 1956; Univ. medal U. Hartford, 1968; Nat. Human Relations award Nat. Conf. Christians and Jews, 1969; City of Hartford medal, 1968. Mem. Central Conf. Am. Rabbis (pres. 1947-49), Phi Epsion Pi (nat. chaplain, 1938). Mason (32); mem. B'nai B'rith, K.P. Hon. mem. of several vets. orgns. Founder-regent U. Hartford; dir. Hartt Coll. of Music, Am. Bibl. Ency., Hartford Jewish Community Center; nat. co-chmn. Consultative Council on Desegregation, 1957-59; chmn. Conn. adv. com. to U.S. Commn. Civl Rights, 1958-60; mem. exec. bd. Am. Jewish Com.; mem. bd. of dirs. and exec. com. Nat. Jewish Welfare Board. Clubs: Rotary (pres. 1957-58), Tumble Brook Country. Author numerous books since 1920, latest being; Reform Judaisma Guide, 1953; The American Reform Rabbi-A Profile of a Profession: Words of My Mouth, published in 1969. Contbr. to the Universal Jewish Encyclopedia; the 20th Century Encyclopedia of Religious Knowlege. Home: 145 Ballard Dr Hartford CT 06119 Office: 701 Farmington Av Hartford CT 06119 ☆

FELDMAN, ARTHUR WILLIAM, govt. ofcl.; b. Boston, Sept. 3, 1912; s. Aaron and Dora (Seevak) F.; student Boston Latin Sch., 1926-31, U. de Liege (Belgium), 1931-33; B.S., Colby Coll., 1935; M.A., Harvard, 1941; student U.S. Internat. U., 1969—; m. Lily Wilhelmina Perry, Feb. 16, 1951; 1 son, Bruce. Immigrant insp. Dept. Justice, 1942-44; exec. officer Dept. of State, Alexandria, Egypt, 1944-46; prin. officer, Neuvitas, Cuba, 1946-47, Camaguey, Cuba, 1947-48; cultural affairs officer Sao Paulo, Brazil, 1949-51; dep. prin. officer, Santiago de Cuba, Cuba, 1951-54; consular officer, Montevideo, Uruguay, 1954-57; intelligence research specialist Dept. of State, 1958-59, internat. relations officer, 1959, officer charge Costa Rican affairs, 1960-62; prin. officer, Curitiba, Brazil, 1962-64, Mexicali, Mexico, 1964—; lectr., asst. prof. San Diego State Coll. Calexico Campus, 1967—. Recipient Commendatory Service award Dept. of State, 1954; Award of Distinction, Commn. of Californias, 1970; Outstanding Service award Border Cities Conf., 1970; Cultural Merit medal U. Parana, Brazil, 1964; Distinguished Service award Dept. of Transp., 1971. Home: 2005 Av Pastor Ramos Mexicali Baja California Mexico Office: care Am Consulate Mexicali Baja California Mexico

FELDMAN, BURTON GORDON, advt. exec.; b. Chgo., Dec. 19, 1915; s. Maurice J. and Goldye (Gordon) F.; B.S., Northwestern U., 1933; m. Dorothy Straus, Dec. 28, 1942 (d. 1969); children—Roger, Susan; m. 2d Judith Levinson Miller, 1970. Group copy chief Foote, Cone & Belding, Chgo., 1942-46; v.p. charge Chgo. office Bichanan & Co., 1946-48; exec. v.p. Post, Keyes, Gardner, 1948-59; pres. Burton G. Feldman, Inc., 1959-68; chmn. bd. Feldman & Assos. Advt., Inc., Chgo., 1968—; pres. Phoenix Electric Co., Chgo., 1963-68, dir., 1963—. Pres., James Gordon Grant for Govt., 1962—. Mem. Pi Lambda Phi, Sigma Delta Chi. Home: 175 E Delaware Chicago IL 60611 Office: 919 N Michigan Av Chicago IL 60611

FELDMAN, DAVID, educator, physicist; b. Bklyn., June 16, 1921; s. Isidore and Ida (Dobsevitch) F.; B.S., City Coll. N.Y., 1940; M.S., N.Y.U., 1946; Ph.D., Harvard, 1949; m. Dorothy M. Appel, Aug. 30, 1946; children—Charles A., Robert E. Mem. Inst. for Advanced Study, Princeton, 1949-50; asst. prof. physics U. Rochester, 1950-56; asso. prof. physics Brown U., 1956-59, prof. physics, 1959—; vis. prof. physics U. Paris, France, 1962-63. Mem. adv. panel physics NSF, 1968—. NSF Sr. Postdoctoral fellow, 1962-63. Fellow Am. Phys. Soc.; mem. Italian Phys. Soc., Phi Beta Kappa, Sigma Xi. Editor: Proceedings of the Fifth Annual Eastern Theoretical Physics Conf., 1967. Research, publs. in nuclear physics, quantum field theory, theory of elementary particles. Home: 11 Valentine Dr Barrington RI 02806 Office: Dept Physics Brown U Providence RI 02912

FELDMAN, FRANKLIN ISREAL diversified mfg. co. exec.; b. Cin., May 21, 1910; grad. Phillips Acad., Andover, Mass., 1927; B.S., Princeton, 1931; postgrad. Mass. Inst. Tech., 1931-33; m. Jean R. Holland, June 16, 1935; children--Lois A., Andrew M., James. Salesman, Brown Mfg. Co., Boston, 1932-33; jr. engr. Ball Metals Co., Carson City, Nev., 1933-36, engr., 1936-37, sr. engr., 1937-40; project engr. Kingston Engring. Co., Los Angeles, 1940-43; with dept. engring. City of Denver, 1946-50, dep. head, 1950-52; 2d v.p. Johnson Mfg. Co., Kansas City, Kansas, 1952-54, v.p. for engring., 1954-57; v.p. research Consol. Industries, Inc., South Bend, Ind., 1957-60, exec. v.p., 1960-65, pres., 1965-70, chmn. bd., chief exec. officer, 1970--, also dir.; dir. ABC Chem. Co., 2d Nat. Bank, Country Food Storage Co., Providence Indsl. Corp. Pres., Dewey High Sch., Kansas City, Mo., 1953-54; fund chmn. local div. Salvation Army, 1959-60. Mem. South Bend Republican Com., 1964-68. Bd. dirs. Ind. council Boy Scouts Am., 1969-71; trustee Lovell Found. Served to lt., Corps Engrs., AUS, 1943-45. Decorated Bronze Star medal. Member N.A.M., South Bend C. of C. (v.p. 1963-65, dir. 1965-70), Am. Mgmt. Assn., Ind. Engrs. Soc. (program com. 1961-63), Princeton Alumni Robinson. Sales rep. Ames-Brockton Fabricated Products, Akron, O., 1956-58, sales mgr. Coshocton, Ohio, 1959-61, gen. manager plant, 1961-68, v.p. sales, 1968--. Instr. bus. Coshocton Jr. College, 1968-69. Mem. Coshocton C. of C. (vice president 1967-68, pres. 1969-70), Sales Executives Institute, Phi Beta Kappa, Sigma Chi, Phi Mu. Democrat. Mem. Christian Ch. (lay leader). Mason (32, Shriner). Clubs: Coshocton Country, Coshocton City, Running Deer Country. Home: 2d Av Coshocton OH Office: 3d Av Coshocton OH

FELDMAN, GORDON, eduator; b. Windsor, Ont., Can., Dec. 6, 1928; s. Henry and Veta (Katz) F.; B.A., U. Toronto, 1950, M.A., 1951; Ph.D., U. Birmingham (Eng.), 1953; m. Janet Mary Robson, Mar. 23, 1968. Came to U.S., 1957. Research asst. U. Birmingham, 1953-55; research asso. U. Wis., 1956-57; mem. faculty Johns Hopkins, 1957—, prof. physics, 1964—; vis. prof. Imperial Coll., London, Eng., 1959-60, 62-63, 65-66; mem. Inst. Advanced Study, Princeton, 1955-56. Guggenheim fellow, 1962-63. Contbr. profl. jours. Home: 4832 Keswick Rd Baltimore MD 21210

FELDMAN, HOWARD S., corp. exec.; b. 1918. Engaged in retail liquor business, 1946-59; with Schenley Industries Inc., 1959—, exec. v.p. sales and marketing, 1969— -, also dir. Served with AUS, World War II. Address: 1290 Av Americas New York City NY 10019*

FELDMAN, J. M., corp. co. exec.; b. 1897. Sr. v.p., dir. Witco Chem. Co., Golden Bear Oil Co.; treas., dir. Feldman Co. Trustee City of Hope. Mem. Los Angeles C. of C. (dir.), Western Oil and Gas Assn. (dir.). Home: 2701 McConnell Dr Los Angeles CA 90064 Office: 325 W 8th St Los Angeles CA 90014*

FELDMAN, JACOB, metals co. exec.; b. 1906; s. Moses Feldman. Chmn. bd. Comml. Metals Co., 1932—. Address: 3000 Diamond Park Dr Dallas TX 75247*

FELDMAN, JACOB, educator, mathematician; b. Phila., Jan. 10, 1928; s. Boris and Fannie (Shrager) F.; B.A., U. Pa., 1950; M.A., U. Ill., 1951; Ph.D., U. Chgo., 1954; m. Doreen Stephens, Dec. 31, 1958 (div. Apr. 1970); children—David, Benjamin. Fellow Inst. Advanced Study, Princeton, 1954-56; vis. asst. prof. Columbia, 1956-57; with Bell Telephone Labs., summer 1957; mem. faculty U. Cal. at Berkeley, 1957-, prof. math., 1964-; spl. research functional analysis and probability theory. Mem. Am. Math. Soc. Home: 1179 Glen St Berkeley CA 94705

FELDMAN, JOHN JOSEPH, banker; b. Cleve., June 19, 1932; s. Harold J. and Beatrice (Bolduc) F.; B.A., Dartmouth, 1954; m. Yvonne C. Fournier, Sept. 5, 1959; children—John Joseph, Peter C. with Howard Savs. Instn., Newark, 1954- 65, asst. v.p., 1957-65; v.p. Bank of Commonwealth, Detorit, 1965- 69, sr. v.p., cashier, 1969-70, exec. v.p., cashier, 1970—. Mem. Econ. Club Detroit. Republican. Conglist. Club: Bloomfield (Mich.) Open Hunt. Home: 3812 Mill Spring Rd Bloomfield Hills MI 48013 Office: 719 Griswold St Detroit MI 48226

FELDMAN, JULIAN, educator; b. Chgo., June 14, 1931; s. Harry and Rose (Lipkin) F.; M.A., U. Chgo., 1954; Ph.D., Carnegie-Mellon U., 1959; m. Rita Reva Cohen, Dec. 28, 1951; children—Karin Sue, Tammy Rae, Murray Dov. Asst. prof. bus. adminstrn. U. Cal. at Berkeley, 1959-63, asso. prof., 1963-64; asso. prof. psychology and information and computer sci. U. Cal. at Irvine, 1964-67, prof., chmn. dept. information and computer sci., 1967—. Served with U.S. Army, 1955-56. Home: 2824 Carob St Newport Beach CA 92660 Office: U Cal Dept Information and Computer Sci Irvine CA 92664

FELDMAN, JUSTIN NEWTON, lawyer; b. N.Y.C., May 25, 1919; s. Hyman and Jennie (Zolitarov) F.; A.B., Columbia, 1940, LL.B., 1942; m. Janet Cutting, Apr. 11, 1947; children—Geoffrey C., Diane T., Jane T. Admitted to N.Y. bar, 1942; atty. NPA, 1951-52; adminstrv. asst. U.S. Congress, 1952-55; dir. N.Y.C. office N.Y. State Dept. Commerce, 1956; practice in N.Y.C., 1946-51, 1958—; partner firm Poletti, Freidin, Prashker, Feldman & Gartner, 1964- -. Cons. Dept. Commerce, 1962-64; counsel N.Y. County Democratic Com., 1962-64; spl. counsel N.Y. State Dem. Com., 1962-70; spl. hearing officer Dept. Justice, 1961-68. Mem. labor arbitration panel Am. Arbitration Assn., 1947—, N.Y. State Mediation Bd., 1956—, N.Y. State Pub. Employees Relations Bd., 1967—, N.Y. State Met. Transp. Authority, 1970—; mem. N.Y. Urban Coalition Borough pres. Manattan Community Planning Bd., 1966-70. Served to 1st lt. USAAF, 1943-46. Mem. Am., N.Y. State bar assns., Bar Assn. City N.Y. (chmn. com. adminstrv. law 1958-61). Author: How Tammany Holds Power, 1949. Home: 410 W 24th St New York City, NY 10011. Office: 777 3d Av New York City NY 10011

FELDMAN, LOUIS HARRY, educator; b. Hartford, Conn., Oct. 29, 1926; s. Sam and Sarah (Vine) F.; B.A., Trinity Coll., 1946, M.A., 1947; Ph.D., Harvard, 1951; m. Miriam Blum, Mar. 8, 1966; children—Moshe Yaakov, Sarah Rivkah. Ford found. teaching fellow in classics Trinity Coll., Hartford, Conn., 1951-52, instr., 1952-53; instr. classics Hobart and William Smith Coll., 1953-55; instr. humanities and history Yeshiva and Stern Coll., N.Y.C., 1955-56, asst. prof. classics, Yeshiva Coll., 1956-61, asso. prof., 1961-66, prof., 1966—. Guggenheim fellow, 1963-64, Am. Council Learned Socs. sr. fellow, 1971-72. Mem. Am. Philol. Assn., Phi Beta Kappa. Jewish religion. Author: Scholarship on Philo and Josephus, 1963; Josephus, Jewish Antiquities, Books XVIII-XX, 1965; Prolegomenon, The Biblical Antiquities of Philo, 1971. Asso. editor Classical Weekly, 1955-57; mng. editor Classical World, 1957-59; deptl. editor Greek and Roman writers on the Jews, Ency. Judaica, 1967-71. Contbr. Ency. Brit., classical and religious jours. Home: 915 West End Av New York City NY 10025

FELDMAN, MAURICE, public relations counsel; b. Vienna, Austria, July 24, 1914; s. Samuel and Gisela (von Fiderer) F.; Ph.D. in Econs., U. Vienna, student univs. Stockholm (Sweden) and Geneva (Switzerland). Came to U.S., 1939, naturalized, 1943. Financial and bus. editor Der Tag, Vienna, 1933-38; fgn. trade editor Stockholms Tidningen, Sweden, 1938-39; mem. staff King Features Syndicate, N.Y.C., 1939-40; spl. writer Christian Sci. Monitor, U.S. corr. Public Relations Rev.; lectr. U. St. Gallen (Switzerland), then Central Council Am. Opera Houses, 1966, 67; now owner Maurice Feldman Pub. Relations, N.Y.C. Recipient commendation medals from USAF, Sweden and Austria. Fellow Inst. Directors (London); mem. Pub. Relations Soc. Am., Air Force Assn., Writers Assn. Austria. Author: Economic Barriers of Europe; History of Public Relations; Public Relations in Modern Economy; also articles. Address: 745 Fifth Av New York City NY 10022

FELDMAN, MAX, constrn. co. exec.; b. Gloucester, Mass., Nov. 15, 1923; s. William and Ida (Newmark) F.; B.C.E., Rennselaer Poly. Inst., 1950; m. Frances Larrea, Sept. 29, 1957; children—Mark Joseph, Ian David, Wendy Lisa. Designing engr. D.B. Steinman, cons. engr., N.Y.C., 1950-51; project engr. Tippetts-Abbett-McCarthy-Stratton, engrs., N.Y.C., 1951-59; exec. v.p., dir. Blitman Constrn. Corp., N.Y.C., 1959—. Served with USAAF, 1941-45. Decorated D.F.C., Air medal with 3 oak leaf clusters. Mem. Am. Arbitration Assn., A.I.M. (mem. pres. council 1970—), N.Y. State Soc. Profl. Engrs., Sigma Xi, Tau Beta Pi, Chi Epsilon. Registered profl. engr., N.Y. Home: Woodlands Rd Harrison NY 10528 Office: 101 Park Av New York City NY 10017

FELDMAN, MELVIN STEVEN, glass container mfr.; b. Trenton, N.J., Aug. 9, 1935; s. Sol and Rose (Scull) F.; B.S., U. Pa., 1957, LL.B., 1960; m. Paula Y. Goodman, Mar. 24, 1968; 1 dau., Kimberly D. Admitted to D.C. bar, 1961, N.Y. bar, 1962, Cal. bar, 1969; atty. F.T.C., Washington, 1960-61; asso. Weil, Lee & Bergin, N.Y.C., 1961-64, Amram, Hahn & Sundlun, Washington, 1964-68; asst. sec., asst. gen. counsel Max Factor & Co., Hollywood, Cal., 1968-70; sec., gen. counsel Glass Containers Corp., Fullerton, Cal., 1970—. Mem. Am., Cal., Los Angeles County, Orange County bar assns., Am. Civil Liberties Union. Democrat. Jewish religion. Home: 1814 Toyon Lane Newport Beach CA 92660 Office: 535 N Gilbert Av Fullerton CA 92634

FELDMAN, MORTON, composer, conductor; b. N.Y.C., Jan. 12, 1926; student composition with Wallingford Riegger and Stefan Wolpe. Recording artist for Columbia, Times records. Composer: Projection 2 for flute, trumpet, violin and cello, 1951; Intersection 1, 1951; Marginal Intersection, 1951; Durations for chamber sextet, 1960-61. Office: care NY Philharmonic 111 W 57th St New York City NY 10019

FELDMAN, MYER, lawyer; b. Phila., June, 1917; s. Inrael and Bella (Kurland) F.; student Girard Coll., Phila., 1922-31; B.S. in Econs., Wharton Sch. of U. Pa., 1935, LL.B. (fellow 1938-39), 1938; m. Silva Moskovitz, Oct. 26, 1941; children—Jane Margaret, James Alan. Admitted to Pa. bar, 1938, D.C. bar, 1965, also U.S. Supreme Ct.; pvt. practice, Phila. and D.C. 1939-42, 65—; spl. counsel, exec. asst. to chmn. SEC, 1946-54; counsel banking and currency commn. U.S. Senate, 1955-57; legislative asst. to Senator John F. Kennedy, 1958-61; dep. spl. counsel to Presidents Kennedy and Johnson, 1961-64; counsel to Pres. Johnson, 1964-65; partner firm Ginsburg and Feldman, Washington, 1965-; lectr. law U. Pa., 1941- 42; prof. law Am. U., 1955-56. Pres. Radio Assos., Inc., 1959; partner Key Stas., 1960; chmn. bd. Speer Publs., Capital Gazette Press, Inc., Bay Publs.; dir. Flying Tiger Line, Inc., Flame Hope, Inc. Del. Democratic Nat. Conv., 1968; vice chmn. Congl. Leadership for Future, 1970. Bd. dirs. Weitzman Inst., 1963—; trustee Eleanor Roosevelt Meml. Found., 1963—, Declaration of Independence, House and Library, 1965—, Jewish Publ. Soc., 1966—; bd. overseers Virgin Islands U., 1962—. Served with USAAF, 1942-46. Mem. U. Pa. Law Alumni Assn. Washington (pres. 1952-58), Tau Epsilon Rho (pres. 1938). Author: Standard Pennsylvania Practice, 4 vols., 1958; also articles. Home: 2828 Ellicott St NW Washington DC 20008 Office: 1700 Pennsylvania Av NW Washington DC 20006

FELDMAN, PHILIP, motion picture exec.; b. Boston, Mass., Jan. 22, 1922; s. William and Sarah (Cooper) F.; A.B., Harvard, 1942, student Grad. Sch. Arts and Scis., 1942-43, Grad. Sch. Bus., 1946-47, LL.M., 1949; LL.B., Georgetown U., 1946; m. Ruthe Bergstein, June 27, 1943; children—Dennis Jeffrey, Kenneth Eugene, Gary Richard. Randolph Robert. Prin. owner wholesale and retail dry goods firm, Boston, 1946- 49; admitted to D.C. bar, 1945, Cal. bar, 1950; practice of law, Beverly Hills, Cal., 1950-51; legal counsel Famous Artists Corp., 1951-53; v.p. Hollywood CBS-TV, 1957-60; v.p. Seven Arts Asso. Corp., 1962-66; pres. Phil Feldman Prodns., Inc., 1967- -; exec. v.p. Broadcast Mgmt., Inc., 1960-62; producer You're A Big Boy Now, 1967-68, The Wild Bunch, 1968, The Ballad of Cable Hogue, in 1969; exec. producer Powderkeg, 1970. Served as 1st lt. AUS, 1943-46. Decorated Presdl. Citation of Merit. Home: 806 N Alpine Dr Beverly Hills CA 90210 Office: 1041 N Formosa Av Los Angeles CA 90046

FELDMANCHE, ALBERT diversified mfg. co. exec.; b. Cin., May 21, 1910; grad. Phillips Acad., Andover, Mass., 1927; B.S., Princeton, 1931; postgrad. Mass. Inst. Tech., 1931-33; m. Jean R. Holland, June 16, 1935; children--Lois A., Andrew M., James. Salesman, Brown Mfg. Co., Boston, 1932-33; jr. engr. Ball Metals Co., Carson City, Nev., 1933-36, engr., 1936-37, sr. engr., 1937-40; project engr. Kingston Engring. Co., Los Angeles, 1940-43; with dept. engring. City of Denver, 1946-50, dep. head, 1950-52; 2d v.p. Johnson Mfg. Co., Kansas City, Kansas, 1952-54, v.p. for engring., 1954-57; v.p. research Consol. Industries, Inc., South Bend, Ind., 1957-60, exec. v.p., 1960-65, pres., 1965-70, chmn. bd., chief exec. officer, 1970--, also dir.; dir. ABC Chem. Co., 2d Nat. Bank, Country Food Storage Co., Providence Indsl. Corp. (Ind.), Wilson Investment Co., Inc., Hammond Life Ins. Co., Inc. Pres., Dewey High Sch., Kansas City, Mo., 1953-54; fund chmn. local div. Salvation Army, 19560. Mem. South Bend Republican Com., 1964-68. Bd. dirs. Ind. council Boy Scouts Am., 1969-71; trustee Lovell Found. Served to lt., Corps Engrs., AUS, 1943-45. Decorated Bronze Star medal. Member N.A.M., South Bend C. of C. (v.p. 1963-65, dir. 1965-70), Am. Mgmt. Assn., Ind. Engrs. Soc. (program com. 1961-62), Princeton Alumni Assn. Episcopalian. Home: 6823 Broad Terrace Av South Bend IN 46505

FELDMANN, CHARLES RUSSELL, industrialist; b. Phila., Feb. 8, 1898; s. Charles H. and Eva Adele (Stringfield) F.; ed. N.Y.C. high schs. and evening schs.; m. Charlotte M. Vega, June 14, 1919; children—Carolyn J. A. (Mrs. John F. Otto), Phyllis M. (Mrs. Joseph V. McKee, Jr.), Barbara Jane (Mrs. Spyros S. Skouras). Office boy advancing to service dept. employee auto dealer, N.Y.C., 1913-17; traveling accounting expert installing cost systems in leather cos., 1917-19; owner leather-belting repair and mfg. bus., 1919-25, sold, 1925; indsl. real estate operator, 1925-27; purchased, reorganized and sold Winton Engine Co., Henney Motor Co., VictorPenninsular Co., 1928; founder, pres., dir. Transiton Automobile Radio Corp., 1928-37, sold controlling interest to Philco Corp., 1930; purchased control Simplex Radio Corp., Sandusky, O., 1937, sold to Philco Corp., 1938, pres., dir., 1937-40; purchased control Foster Machine Co., Elkhart, Ind., 1940, co. purchased Internat. Machine Tool Co., Indpls., 1940, Detrola Corp., 1943, co. assumed name Internat. Detrola Corp., 1943, acquired Newport Rolling Mill, Ky., 1946, assumed name Newport Steel Corp., 1949, pres., dir., chmn. bd., 1940-50, holdings sold, 1950; chmn. bd. Strong, Carlisle and Hammond Co., Cleve., 1942-56, interest sold, 1956; chmn. Nat. Union Electric Corp., 1946—, also pres., dir.; acquired by merger Eureka Williams Corp., Bloomington, Ill. div. Nat. Union Electric Corp., 1960; chmn. bd. Napco Plastics, Inc., Napoleon, O., wholly-owned subsidiary, div. Nat. Union Electric Corp., 1960; pres., chmn. Durham Mfg. Corp., Munci, Ind., 1960-64; acquired Emerson Radio and Phonograph Corp. through merger, 1966, now Emerson TV and Radio Co. div. Nat. Union Electric Corp.; dir. Ultra Electronics Holdings Ltd. Mem. pres.'s com. Notre Dame U., 1949—. Methodist. Clubs: Cloud, Sky, Metropolitan (N.Y.C.); Detroit Athletic; Indian Creek Country, Key Largo Anglers, Surf, Jockey (Miami, Fla.). Home: Horse Island Mead Point Greenwich CT 06830 Office: NUE Bldg 66 Field Point Rd Greenwich CT 06830

FELDMANN, EDWARD GEORGE, pharm. chemist; b. Chgo., Oct. 13, 1930; s. Edward Louis and Vera (Arneson) F.; foster mother Helen Whitney Feldmann; B.S. in Chemistry, Loyola U., Chgo., 1952; M.S. in Pharmacy (research fellow Am. Found. Pharm. Edn. 1953-55), U. Wis., 1954, Ph.D. in Pharm. Chemistry- Biochemistry, 1955; postgrad. Northwestern U., 1956, U. Chgo., 1958; m. Mary J. Evans, Aug. 30, 1952; children—Ann Marie, Edward William, Robert, Karen. Teaching asst. Loyola U., Chgo., 1951-52; research asst. U. Wis., 1952-53; sr. chemist Am. Dental Assn., 1955-58, dir. div. chemistry, 1958-59; asso. dir. sci. div. Am. Pharm. Assn., 1959-60, dir., 1960—, asso. exec. dir. for sci. affairs, 1970—, asso. editor sci. edit. assn. jour., 1959-60, editor, 1960; asso. dir. revision Nat. Fomulary, 1959-60, dir. revision, 1960-70; asso. editor Drug Standards, 1959-60, editor, 1960; chmn. Nat. Formulary Bd., 1960-70; editor Jour. Pharm. Scis., 1961—. Mem. adv. panel dental drugs Nat. Formulary, 1955-60; reviewer Internat. Pharmacopeia, World Health Orgn., 1958; spl. lectr. drug standards George Washington U., 1960-64; del. conf. on fellowships Nat. Health Council, 1960; mem. coordinating com. Nat. Conf. Antimicrobial Agts., Soc. Indsl. Microbiology, 1960-63; mem. adv. panel pharm. nomenclature A.M.A.-Am. Pharm. Assn.-U.S. Pharmacopeia, 1961-66, mem. nomenclature com., 1962-66; sec. U.S. Com. Internat. Drug Standards, 1964-65; adv. panel food chems. codex Nat. Acad. Scis.-NRC, 1961-71; liaison rep. to drug research bd. Nat. Acad. Scis.-NRC, 1968—; mem. lab. com. Am. Pharm. Assn. Found., 1961—, com. Ebert prize, 1961—; judge Lunsford-Richardson

Pharmacy Awards, 1962-69; cons. Council on Drugs, A.M.A., 1962; vis. scientist Am. Assn. Colls. of Pharmacy, NSF, 1963-66; mem. expert adv. panel on internat. pharmacopeia and pharm. preparation, World Health Orgn., 1963—; drug cons. Office Sec., U.S. Dept. Health, Edn. and Welfare, 1967-70; nomenclature cons. to Commr., U.S. Food and Drug Adminstrn., 1968—; mem. expert working group Indsl. Devel. Orgn., UN, 1969; mem. organizing com. 31st Internat. Congress Pharm. Scis., 1970-71. Mem. membership com. Revenwood Park Citizens Assn., Falls Church, Va., 1962. Recipient Man of Yr. award Nat. Assn. Pharm. Mfrs., 1970. Life mem. Am. Pharm. Ass.; mem. Am. Chem. Soc., N.Y. Acad. Scis., Nat. Soc. Med. Research (council, 1961-69), Acad. Pharm. Scis., Am. Testing Materials, Council Biology Editors, A.M.A. (affiliate), Fedn. Internat. Pharm., Sigma Xi, Rho Chi, Lambda Chi Sigma. Roman Catholic. K.C. Clubs: Sleepy Hollow Bath and Racquet (Falls Church, Va.). Author articles in field. Mem. editorial adv. bd. Index Chemicus, 1968-. Home: 6203 Cheryl Dr Falls Church VA 22044 Office: 2215 Constitution Av NW Washington DC 20037

FELDMANN, LEONARD G., newspaper editor. Mng. editor Buffalo Courier-Express. Office: 787 Main St Buffalo NY 14240*

FELDMANN, LOUIS GEORGE, lawyer b. Wilkes-Barre, Pa., Sept. 10, 1909; s. John T. and Jessica A. (Cole) F.; B.S., U. Pa., 1933, student Grad. Sch., 1933; LL.B., Duquesne U., 1943; m. Anne R. McKernan, June 3, 1931. Admitted to Pa. bar, 1946; with firm Fahey & Casper, Hazelton, 1946-66, Feldmann & Ciothola, Hazleton, 1966—; dist. atty. Luzerne County, 1951-55. Dir. Northeastern Nat. Bank Pa., dir. Hazleton office dir., pres. Freeland Bldg. & Loan Assn. Tchr. Sch., fed. adult edn. program Penn Treaty Jr. High Sch., 1933; with Pa. Liquor Control Bd., 1933-42, spl. investigator, 1936-39; chief investigator OPA, Pitts., 1942-43; pres. Shemrock Racing Assn., Inc. vice chmn. Pa. Hwy. Commn., 1963-68; v.p., dir. Greater Hazleton Community-Area New Devel. Orgn., Inc.; former mem. pres.'s adv. council Misericordia Coll.; dir. adv. bd. Hazleton Salvation Army; past mem., hon. dir., past pres. Hazleton Cath. Charities; mem. exec. com., past pres. Northeastern Pa. Econ. Devel. Council. Knight of Malta; knight comdr. Holy Sepulchre. Mem. V.F.W., (past nat. comdr.-in-chief), Greater Hazleton C. of C. (past pres., past dir.), Am. Bar Assn., Arms of Friendship (pres., exec. bd.). Republican. K.C. Home: 9 W Diamond Av Hazelton PA 18201 Office: Northeastern Bldg Hazleton PA 18201

FELDMANN, WALTHER HAYNIE ret. mfg. exec.; b. Balt., Jan. 14, 1898; s. August and Marie (Walther) F.; student Balt. Poly. Inst., 1911-15; D.Eng., Newark Coll. Engring.; m. Eleanor Louise McKnew, June 4, 1921; children—Walther Haynie, Beverly Beale (Mrs. Donald B. Edge). Instr. pattern making Balt. Poly. Inst., 1915-16; grad. student Westinghouse Electric & Mfg. Co., East Pittsburgh, Pa., 1916-17; power sales engr. Consol. Gas & Electric Co., Balt., 1917-18, 19-22; regional sales mgr. Electric Machinery Mfg. Co., Mpls., 1922-27, gen. sales mgr., 1927-40, v.p., gen. mgr., later pres. 1940-50; v.p. in charge sales Worthington Corp., Harrison, N.J., 1950-55, exec. v.p., 1955-57, pres., dir., 1957-62, chief exec. officer, 1961-65, chmn. bd., 1962-67; dir. Babcock & Wilcox. Registered profl. engr., N.J. Mem. I.E.E.E., Am. Soc. M.E., Nat. Indsl. Conf. Bd. Presbyn. Clubs: Rotary; Electric Manufacturers, Baltusrol Golf (Springfield, N.J.); Union League (N.Y.C.); LaJolla Country, Cuyamaca (San Diego); U.S. Seniors Golf. Home: 939 Coast Blvd La Jolla CA 92037

FELDMEIR, DARYLE MATTHEW, editor; b. Froid, Mont., Jan. 28, 1923; s. Frank X. and Clara B. (Rhoda) F.; B.A., St. Olaf Coll., 1948; M.A., Harvard, 1949; postgrad. in Am. history, U. Minn., 1951-52; m. Jeanne Elizabeth Meyer, Sept. 24, 1949; children—Ann Laurie, Matthew Joel, Todd Martin, Susan Jeanne. Staff writer, columnist Mpls. Tribune, 1949-55, news editor, 1955-56, mng. editor, 1956-68; mng. editor Chgo. Daily News, 1968-70, exec. editor, 1970-71, editor, 1971—. Mem. bd. Luth. Gen. Hosp. Served as master sgt. USAAF, World War II. Mem. Am. Soc. Newspaper Editors. Lutheran. Home: 824 Boal Pkwy Winnetka IL 60093 Office: 401 N Wabash Av Chicago IL 60611

FELDMEYER, ARTHUR ERNEST, oil co. exec.; b. Asti, Cal., May 25, 1913; s. Clemens A. and Pearl (Sutton) F.; B.A., U. Cal. at Berkeley, 1937; m. Jean Reynolds, May 28, 1938; children—Clemens Roy, Ilma Anne. Geologist Superior Oil Co., 1937- -, geol. investigations, Australia, New Zealand, West Indies, East Indies, Europe, Middle East, N. Africa, Can.; pres., dir. Canadian Superior Old Ltd., Alberta, Can., 1950—; dir. McIntyre Porcupine Mines Ltd. Home: 27 Eagle Ridge Pl Calgary Alberta Canada Office: 355 4th Av SW Calgary Alberta Canada

FELDSTEIN, MARTIN STUART, educator; b. N.Y.C., Nov. 25, 1939; s. Meyer and Esther (Gevarter) F.; A.B. summa cum laude, Harvard, 1961; M.A., Oxford U., 1964, D.Phil., 1967; m. Kathleen Foley, June 19, 1965; 1 dau., Margaret. Research fellow Nuffield Coll., Oxford U., 1964-65, ofcl. fellow Nuffield, 1965-67, lectr. pub. finance, 1965-67; asst. prof. econs. Harvard, 1967-68, asso. prof., 1968-69, prof., 1969—. Mem. Am. Econ. Assn., Econometric Soc., Nat. Inst. Medicine, Phi Beta Kappa. Home: 76 Lincoln St Belmont MA 02178

FELDT, HAROLD WALTER, civil engr.; b. Council Bluffs, Ia., Dec. 8, 1911; s. Walter Soren and Christina (Andersen) F.; B.S. in Civil Engring., State U. Ia., 1932, M.S. in Civil Engring., 1945; student Carnegie Inst. Tech., 1937-39; m. Johnnie Marie McGuire, Mar. 17, 1943; children—Frederick William, John Joseph, Alfred Walter. Engr. on civil works and mil. design and constrn., Corps Engrs., U.S. Army, 1933-57; water resources adviser Panama Govt., State Dept., 1957-59; dir. Servicio Cooperativo Interamericano de Fomento Economica, 1957-59; chief power and telecommunications div. devel. loan fund, State Dept., 1959-61; chief power div., office engring., AID, State Dept. 1961-64; chief regional engr., C.Am. and Panama, AID, 1964-66, chief engineer, Chile, from 1966, now with the Department of State, in Washington. Member of the com. tidal hydraulics C.E., 1954-57. Registered profl. engr., Tex. Mem. Am. Soc. C.E., Am. Geophys. Union, Internat. Assn. Hydraulic Research, Sigma Xi. Lutheran. Office: Dept of State Washington DC 20521

FELICIANO, JOSE, entertainer; b. Larez, P.R., Sept. 10, 1945; s. Jose and Hortencia (Garcia) F.; m. Hilda Perez, Oct. 19, 1963. Folk singer in Greenwich Village, N.Y.C., 1962; recording artist for RCA Records; TV appearances on Bing Crosby show, 1968, Feliciano:-Very Special, 1969; composer most of own material. Recipient Grammy award (2), 1969; voted most promising male vocalist, 1968-69. Home: 8467 Beverly Blvd Los Angeles CA 90048 Office: 9110 Sunset Blvd Los Angeles CA 90069

FELIX, ANTHONY G., Jr., banker; b. Phila., May 8, 1909; s. Anthony G. and Anna Mabel (Young) F.; B.S. in Econs., U. Pa., 1931, LL.B., 1934; m. June R. Spreter, Oct. 28, 1939. Admitted to Pa. bar, 1935; asso. firm Hepburn & Norris, Phila., 1935-42; partner firm Norris, Lex, Hart & Eldredge Co., Phila., 1942- 56; v.p. First Pa. Banking & Trust Co., Phila., 1956-58, v.p., sec., 1958-63, sr. v.p., sec. 1963-68, exec. v.p., sec., 1968—; dir. First Pa. Corp., Asso. Advisers, Inc., Associated Mortgage Cos., Inc., Investors Loan Corp., Indsl. Finance & Thrift Corp. Mem. Banking Bd. Commonwealth Pa., 1964—. Mem. Am., Pa., Phila. bar assns., Am. Law Inst. Clubs: Philadelphia Country, Racquet (Phila.) Home: 1127 Wyndon Av Rosemont PA 19010 Office: First Pa Banking & Trust Co 15th and Chestnut Sts Philadelphia PA 19101

FELIX, HARRY GERARD, banker; b. Washington, Nov. 25, 1930; s. Paul G. and Dorothy (Bride) F.; B.S. in Fgn. Service, Georgetown U., 1953; m. Barbara Ann Lee, Sept. 9, 1961; children—Elissa Ann, Steven Gerard. With Am. Security & Trust Co., Washington, 1955-56; analyst Fed. Res. Bd., Washington, 1956-61; gen. auditor First Va. Corp., 1961-63; sr. v.p. First Va. Bank, Arlington, 1963-71; pres. First Va. Bank of the Peninsula, Hampton, 1971—. Served to 1st lt., inf., AUS 1953-55. Home: 21 Terrell Rd Newport News VA 23606 Office: 1003 W Mercury Blvd Hampton VA 23366

FELIX, ROBERT HANNA, univ. dean; b. Downs, Kan., May 29, 1904; s. Tasso Oliver and Neva Lee (Trusdle) F.; student U. Colo., 1923-26, M.D., 1930, Sc.D. (hon.), 1953; M.P.H., Johns Hopkins, 1942; Sc.D., Boston U., 1953; LL.D., U. Chattanooga, 1957, Ripon Coll., 1959; Sc.D., U. Rochester, 1964; m. Esther R. Wagner, June 18, 1933; 1 dau., Mary Katherine (Mrs. Hoenigman). Intern Col. Gen. Hosp., 1930-31; Commonwealth Fund fellow in psychiatry Colo. Psychopathic Hosp., 1931-33; asst. surgeon USPHS, 1933, passed asst. surgeon, 1936, surgeon, 1943, sr. surgeon, 1944, med. dir., 1945, asst. surgeon gen., 1957; clin. dir. Med. Center for Fed. Prisoners, Springfield, Mo., 1935-36; chief Psychiat. Service, USPHS Hosp., Lexington, Ky., 1937-38, Rockefeller fellow in pub. health, 1941-42; psychiatrist U.S. Coast Guard Acad., 1942-43, sr. med. officer, 1943-44; chief, mental hygiene div. USPHS, 1944-49; dir. Nat. Inst. Mental Health, 1949-64; dean Sch. Medicine, St. Louis U., 1964—. Mem. expert adv. panel on mental health, World Health Orgn., 1952—. Mem. delegation Internat. Congress on Mental Health, London, 1948; chmn. U.S. delegation Mexico City, 1951; mem. delegation, tech. adviser, 2d World Health Assembly, Rome, 1949; mem. Nat. Council on Alcoholism; spl. med. adv. group VA; mem. Mo. Mental Heaalth Commn., St. Louis Joint Bd. Health and Hosps., 1965—. Recipient Rockefeller Pub. Service award, 1961; Nolan D.C.Lewis award, 1963; Edward A. Strecker medal, 1963; Salmon medal, 1963; Bronfman prize, 1964; Rubin award, 1965; D.S.M., 1965; Norlin award U. Colo., 1966. Diplomate Am. Bd. Psychiatry and Neurology. Fellow Am. Pub. Health Assn., A.C.P., Am. Psychiat. Assn. (life; treas. 1958-59, pres. 1960-61), Am. Orthopsychiat. Assn.; mem. A.M.A. (council on mental health 1963-66), World (mem. internat. organizing com. 1961, men. publicity com. 1961, So. (pres. 1946-47) psychiat. assns. Am. Psychol. Assn., Group for Advancement Psychiatry, Royal Medico-Psychol. Assn. (corr.), Canadian Psychiat. Assn. (hon.), Washington Psychoanalytic Soc., Nat. Assn. for Mental Health, S.A.R., Delta Sigma Phi, Phi Chi, Alpha Omega Alpha. Episcopalian. Mason (33). Club: University (St. Louis); Cosmos (Washington). Adv. editor Psychiat. Bull.; mem. adv. editorial bd. Quar. Jour. Studies on Alcoholism; mem. editorial bd. Am. Jour. Psychiatry, 1962-65. Home: 55O Twin Fawns Dr St Louis MO 63131

FELKER, CLAY S., magazine editor; b. St. Louis, Oct. 2, 1928; s. Carl T. and Cora F.; B.A., Duke, 1951. Editor, Duke Chronicle, 1950; reporter Life mag., 1951-57; features editor Esquire mag., 1957-62; cons. editor Viking Press, 1963-66; editor Infinity, Am. Soc. Mag. Photographers mag., 1965-66, Sunday mag. of N.Y. Herald Tribune, 1963-67, Bookweek mag. and Sunday mag. N.Y. World Jour. Tribune, 1966-67; founder, editor New York Mag., 1967—; chmn. NYM Corp., 1967—; dir. Aeneid Equities, 1969—. Mem. Phi Delta Theta, Sigma Delta Chi. Home: 322 E 57th St New York City NY 10022 Office: 207 E 32d St New York City NY 10016

FELKER, JEAN HOWARD, telephone labs. exec.; b. Centralia, Ill., Mar. 14, 1919; s. Henry Adam and Olga Fay (Snider) F. B.S. in Elec. Engring., Washington U., St. Louis, 1941; m. Joan Woodman, Aug. 14, 1943; children—Dittany R., Christopher H. With Bell Telephone Labs., 1945-59; with Am. Tel. & Tel. Co., 1959-62, asst. chief engr., 1960-62; v.p. operations dir. N.J. Bell Telephone Co., 1962-69; bus. cons., 1969-71; v.p. Bell Telephone Labs., 1971—; dir., exec. com. Colonial Life Inst. Co. of Am., Shulman Transport Enterprises. Fellow I.E.E.E. Home: 12 Michael Av Kendall Park NJ 08824

FELKNOR, BRUCE LESTER, pub. co. exec.; b. Oak Park, Ill., Aug. 18, 1921; s. Audley Rhea and Harriet (Lester) F.; student U. Wis., 1939-41; m. Joanne Sweeney, Feb. 8, 1942 (div. Jan. 1952); 1 dau., Susan Harriet; m. 2d, Edith G. Johnson, Mar. 1, 1952; children—Sarah Anne, Bruce Lester II. Reporter, Dunn County News, Menomonie, Wis., 1937-39; freight brakeman Pa. R.R., N.Y.C., 1941, asst. yardmaster, 1942; prodn. coordinator Hwy. Trailer Co., Edgerton, Wis., 1943; radio officer U.S. Maritime Service, 1944-45; flight radio officer Air Transport Command, 1945; pub. relations dept. Am. Airlines, 1945; writer pub. relations dept. I.T. & T., 1946; Southeast regional pub. relations dir. Ford Motor Co., Chester, Pa., 1946-48; free lance pub. relation, N.Y.C., 1948-49; pub. relations exec. Foote, Cone & Belding, Inc., N.Y.C., 1950-53; v.p. Market Relations Network, N.Y.C., 1954-55; exec. dir. Fair Campaign Practices Com., Inc., N.Y.C. 1956-66; asst. to William Benton, chmn. and pub. Ency. Brit., 1966-70, dir. marketing information, internat. div., 1970—; vis. lectr. Hamilton Coll., 1966. Dir. North Castle (N.Y.) Citizens Council, 1959-62, pres., 1960-61; chmn. Citizens Com. for Sch. Centralization in Armonk (N.Y.), 1957-61; mem. North Castle (N.Y.) Adv. Com. on Green Spaces, 1962-63. Mem. Am. Polit. Sci. Assn., Authors League Am., Authors Guild. Democrat. Presbyn. (ruling elder, chmn. com. on religion and race Presbytery Hudson River 1963-67, mem. nat. council on ch. and soc. 1966—). Author: Fair Play in Politics, 1960; State-by-State Smear Study, 1956, You Are They, 1964; (with C.P. Taft): Prejudice & Politics, 1960; Dirty Politics, 1966; also various newspaper, jour. and yearbook articles on politics. Home: 1266 Woodland Dr Deerfield IL 60015 Office: 425 N Michigan Av Chicago IL 60611

FELL, CLARENCE ORVEL, investment exec.; b. Walnut, Ia., Apr. 14, 1901; s. Thomas and Amy Evelyn (Porter) F.; student Coe Coll., 1919-22, So. Ill. U., 1923, Army Flying Cadet Sch., 1925; m. Margaret M. Strauss, Oct. 3, 1949. Sales mgr. James B. Welsh Realty & Loan Co., 1928-34; mortgage investment broker, Kansas City, Mo., 1935-54; ind. oil and gas producer, 194O—; dir. United Funds, Inc., 1942-. Mem. Ind. Petroleum Assn. Am., Alpha Delta Alpha. Home: 59OO N Broadway North Kansas City MO 64118

FELL HOWARD BARRACLOUGH, educator, biol. oceanographer; b. Lewes, Sussex, Eng., June 6, 1917; s. Howard Towne B. and Elsie (Johnston) F.; B.Sc., U. New Zealand, Wellington, 1938, M.Sc., 1939; Ph.D., U. Edinburgh (Scotland), 1941, D.Sc., 1955; A.M. (hon.), Harvard, 1965; m. Irene Clarkson, Oct. 10, 1942; children—Roger Barraclough, Francis Julian, Veronica Irene. Came to U.S., 1964. Sr. lectr. zoology Victoria U., Wellington, 1946-56, asso. prof., 1956-64; curator invertebrate zoology Museum Comparative Zoology, Harvard, 1964—, prof. invertebrate zoology, 1965; hon. lectr. zoology U. Me., 1967—. Pres. New Zealand Assn. Scientists, 1948. Served with Brit. Army, 1941-46. Fellow Am. Acad. Arts and Scis., Royal Soc. New Zealand (Hector medal 1959, Hutton medal 1962); mem. Sigma Xi. Co- author: Treatise on Invertebrate Paleontology, 1966-67; McGraw- Hill Encyclopedia of Science and Technology, 2d edit., 1964; Physiology of Echinoderms, 1966; Deep-Sea Photography, 1967; also numerous articles. Home: 6 Woodland St Arlington MA O2174 Office: Museum Comparative Zoology Harvard Univ Cambridge MA O2138

FELL, JOHN LOUIS, educator, author; b. Westfield, N.J., Sept. 19, 1927; s. Shelby G. and Frances (Hildebrand) F.; A.B., Hamilton Coll., 1950; M.A., N.Y.U., 1954, Ph.D., 1958; m. Suzanne Shillington, Dec. 5, 1958; children—Justine Richmond, John Shillington, Eliza Marritt. Dept. head Film and TV Center, State U. Mont., 1958-60; mem. faculty San Francisco State Coll., 1960—, chmn. film dept., 1967-70, prof. film dept., 1970—; film writer, N.Y.C., 1952-58; musician, N.Y.C., 1950-58. Served with USAAF, 1946-47. Mem. Writers Guild Am., Univ. Film Assn., Soc. Cinema Studies, Am. Fedn. Musicians, Phi Beta Kappa, Kappa Delta Pi, Alpha Epsilon Rho. Author articles in field. Home: 1263 15th Av San Francisco CA 94122

FELL, LAWRENCE GIBSON, bus. exec.; b. Ypsilanti, Mich., June 14, 1897; s. William I. and Frances (Gibson) F.; student Wharton Sch., U. Pa., 1915-20; m. Elizabeth Boos, June 17, 1922; children—Martha (Mrs. Robert G. Pender), Diana (Mrs. James S. Gilmore). With Mich. Carton Co., 1919—, successively treas., v.p., pres., gen. mgr., 1930-58, chmn. bd. and treas., 1958—. Mem. bd. Leila Hosp., Civic Art Centre. Past pres. Community Chest, Community Concert Assn. Mem. Nat. Paperboard Assn. (former bd. mem.) C. of C., Phi Kappa Psi. Epsicopalian (vestryman). Clubs: Tavern (Chgo.): Park (Kalamazoo): Battle Creek Country (past pres.). Home: 200 Wahwahtaysee Way Battle Creek MI 49015 Office: 79 E Foundation St Battle Creek MI 49014

FELLEGARA, VITTORIO, composer; b. Milan, Italy, 1927; studied composition with Luciano Chailly; grad. Conservatory Giuseppi Verdi, 1951. Performed Am. Acad. in Rome, 24th Internat. Festival of Venice, Internat. Soc. Contemporary Music, Internat. Festival, Vienna. Composer: Serenata for Five Instruments. Address: 27 1 go Orazi e Curiaz Rome Italy*

FELLENDORF, GEORGE WILLIAM, assn. exec.; b. Glen Cove, N.Y., Sept. 11, 1925; s. Frederick and Sarah (Bouton) F.; B.S. in Elec. Engring., Union Coll., Schenectady, 1947; B.S. in Mgmt. Engring., M.S., Rensselaer Poly. Inst., 1949; postgrad., edn. of deaf Columbia, 1956-58; m. Hazel Maisey, Nov. 30, 1946; children—Carol Elaine, Linda Jean, Joyce Ellen. Jr. engr. Western Electric Co., 1946-47; project adminstr. Hazeltine Electronics Corp., 1949-51; contracts adminstr. Airborne Instruments Lab., Hicksville, N.Y., 1951-52; v.p. Instruments for Industry, Inc., Mineola, N.Y., 1952-58; pres. Planetronics, Inc., Easton, Pa., 1958-62; exec. dir. Alexander Graham Bell Assn. for Deaf, Washington, 1962—. Mem. President's Com. Employment Handicapped, 1967—, Lutheran Acad. for Scholarship, 1960 Mem. Edn. Press, Council Exceptional Children, Am., Md. speech and hearing assns., I.E.E.E., Nat. Acad. Engring. (subcom on sensory aids), Profl. Rehab. Workers with Adult Deaf. Republican. Lutheran. Kiwanian (bd. dirs. Georgetown, D.C. 1970). Club: Montgomery (Md.) City. Editor: Bibliography on Deafness, 1967; also periodical Volta Rev. Home: 1300 Ruppert Rd Silver Spring MD 20903 Office: 3417 Volta Pl NW Washington DC 20007

FELLER, EDMUND H., educator. Prof. math. U. Wis. at Milw. Office: Dept Math U Wis Milwaukee WI 53201*

FELLER, KARL FRANZ, labor ofcl.; b. Dayton, O., Aug. 6, 1914; s. Karl John and Marie 0Koch) F.; student pub. schs.; m. Virginia K. Snyder, Oct. 9, 1937; children—Karl Richard, Harriet Ann, Natalie Joy, Frances Jean, Judith Lynne. Pres. Brewery Workers local 50, Dayton, 1939, bus. agt., 1940-43; spl. internat. organizer Internat. Union United Brewery, Flour, Cereal, Soft Drink and Distillery Workers Am., Cin., 1943-45; gen. corr. sec., 1945-48, pres., 1948—; founder Ohio-Ky. State Council Brewery Syrup and Soft Drink Workers; mem. exec. bd. C.I.O. Mem. Am. Heritage Found. Roman Catholic. Eagle. Home: 3106 Manning Av Cincinnati OH 45211 Office: 2347 Vine St Cincinnati OH 45219

FELLER, SAMUEL RANDOLPH, lawyer; b. N.Y.C., Sept. 1, 1904; s. Harry and Annie (Rosenthal) F.; A.B., Columbia, 1925, LL.B., 1927; m. Margaret R. Blum, July 12, 1934 (div.); 1 dau., Ann Margaret (Mrs. John L. Oliver). Admitted to N.Y. bar, 1928, since practiced law, N.Y.C.; partner firm Boyle, Feller & Reeves (now Boyle, Feller & Hirsch), 1945—; dir. Am. Consumer Ins. Co., also J.M.L. Trading Corp. Am. Fidelity Fire Ins. Co., Mullins Mfg. Corp. Legislative staff N.Y. State Assembly, 1929-31; 1st dept. N.Y. State Ins. Dept., 1931-35; spl. counsel N.Y. Supt. Ins., 1935-52; spl. counsel N.Y. Supt. Banks, 1939-42. Served as lt. col. Judge Adv. Gen. Dept., AUS 1942-45. Mem. N.Y. County Lawyers Assn., Assn. Bar City N.Y., Phi Beta Kappa. Clubs: Harmonie (N.Y.C.); City Athletic, Author articles in fields ins. and adminstrv. law. Home: 10 Park Av New York City NY 10016 Office: 60 E 42d St New York City NY 10017

FELLERS, JAMES DAVISON, lawyer; b. Oklahoma City, Apr. 17, 1913; s. Morgan S. and Olive R. (Kennedy) F.; student Oklahoma City U., 1930-31; A.B., U. Okla., 1936, LL.B., 1936; m. Margaret Ellen Randerson, Mar. 11, 1939; children—Kay Lynn (Mrs. John T. Pellow) , Lou Ann (Mrs. James B. Street) , James Davisson. Admitted to Okla. State bar, 1936, since practiced in Oklahoma City; partner Fellers, Snider, Baggett, Blankenship & Bailey. Mem. bd. Nat. Legal Aid Assn., 1949-51; mem. adv. bd. Internat. and Comparative Law Center; mem. bd. trustees Southwestern Legal Found. Served as lt. col., USAF Reserve, E.T.O., M.T.O., 8 campaigns, 1941- 45. Decorated Bronze Star medal. Selected outstanding young man of 1948, Oklahoma City C. of C. Fellow Am. Coll. Trial Lawyers, Am. Bar Found.; mem. Am. Bar Assn. (nat. chmn. jr. bar conf. 1946-47, assembly del. House of Dels, 1947-62; chmn. communications com. 1958-59, bd. govs. 1962-65, chmn. house of dels. 1966-68, chmn. constitution and by-laws com. 1969-71) , Nat. Coll. State Trial Judges (dir. 1968-70) , Internat., Inter-Am., Okla. State (pres. 1964) bar assns., Am. Judicature Soc., Am. Law Inst. (com. continuing legal edn., 1947-49), Internat. Assn. Ins. Counsel (v.p. 1955-56) , Phi Kappa Psi. Episcopalian. Clubs: Beacon, Petroleum, Men's Dinner, Cosmpolitan (judge adv. internat. 1941-42) . Mason (Shriner) . Home: 1702 Pennington Way Nichols Hills Oklahoma City OK 73116 Office: First National Bldg Oklahoma City OK 73102

FELLERS, RUFUS GUSTAVUS, coll. dean; b. Columbia, S.C., Sept. 26, 1920; s. Rufus Gustavus and Anna Katherine (LaBorde) F.; B.S. in Elec. Engring., U. S.C., 1941; Ph.D., Yale, 1943; m. Helen B. Bowen, July 15, 1967; children—by 1st marriageRita, Rufus, Gustavus. Instr. elec. engring. Yale, 1943-44; electronic scientist U.S. Naval Research Lab., 1944-45, sect. head, 1950- 55; head dept. elec. engring. U. S.C., 1955-60, former dean Coll. Engring., now prof.; spl. research microwave components and systems, electromagnetic theory, microwave optics, millimeter wave transmission. Registered profl. engr., S.C. Fellow I.E.E.E. (dir.); mem. National Society of Profl. Engrs., Am. Soc. Engring. Edn., Am. Assn. U. Profs., Phi Beta Kappa, Sigma Xi, Tau Beta Pi, Eta Kappa Nu. Contbr. articles profl. jours. Home: 817 Henderson St Columbia SC 29201

FELLINI, FEDERICO, motion picture writer, dir.; b. Rimini, Italy, Jan. 20, 1920; s. Urbano Fellini and Masina, Oct. 30, 1943. Journalist, caricaturist, designer, actor to 1940; scenograph, film script writer, 1940—; writer, dir. pictures Luci del Varieta, le notti di Cabiria, 81/2, others, 1950—, I Vitelloni, Il Bildone, La Strada, La Dolce Vita (won Cannes Film Festival award 1960, N.Y. Film Critics award 1961). Recipient Acad. Awards la Strada, 1957, Le Notta di Cabiria, 1958; 81/2, 1963; Juliet of the Spirits, 1964. Home: Via Margutta 110 Rome Italy Office: Cinecitta Via Tuscolama 1050 Rome Italy

FELLMAN, DAVID, educator; b. Omaha, Sept. 14, 1907; s. Jacob and Brandel (Gubermann) F.; A.B., U. Neb., 1929, A.M., 1930, LL.D., 1966; Ph.D., Yale (grad. fellow in polit. sci. 1931-34), 1934; m. Sara Ann Dinion, Aug. 6, 1933; children—Laura Ann, Michael Dinion. Instr., U. Neb., 1934-39, asst. prof. polit. sci., 1939-43, asso. prof., 1943-47; prof. polit. sci. U. Wis., Madison, 1947—, Vilas prof. polit. sci., 1965—; vis. instr. U. Mo., summer 1938; instr. G.I.U. of Florence (Italy), 1945; Brown and Haley lectr. Coll. Puget Sound, 1959; Gaspar G. Bacon lectr. Boston U., 1963-64; Sperry-Hutchinson lectr. U. S.C., 1965; C.H. Dillon lectr. U. S.D., 1969. Mem. Am. Polit. Sci. Assn. (mem. exec. council, 1952-55; v.p., 1959-60), Am. Assn. U. Profs. (pres. U. Wis. chpt. 1950-51; mem. nat. council 1958-61, 67—, pres. 1964-66), Am. Civil Liberties Union, Midwest Conf. Polit. Scientists (p. 1955-56), Sigma Alpha Mu (nat. scholarship chmn. 1943- 48), Phi Beta Kappa. Author: Problems of the Postwar World (with T.C. McCormick, ed.), 1945; Twentieth Century Political Thought (with J.S. Roucek, ed.), 1946. Editor: Post-War Governments of Europe, 1946; Readings in American National Government, 1947, 2d edit., 1950; The Defendants Rights, 1958; Limits of Freedom, 1959; The Supreme Court and Education, 1960; (with W.B. Graves) State Constitutional Revision, 1960; The Constitutional Right of Association 1963; Religion in American Public Law, 1965; The Defendant's Rights under English Law, 1966; Crime in Urban Soc. (with Barbara N. McLennan, ed.), 1970. Mem. bd. editors Am. Polit. Sci. Rev., 1947-49. Editor: Midwest Jour. Polit. Sci., 1956-59. Contbr. articles to polit. sci., law jours., encys. Home: 1911 Kendall Av Madison WI 53705

FELLNER, WILLIAM JOHN, economist; b. Budapest, Hungary, May 31, 1905; s. Henry and Margaret (Leipziger) F.; student U. Budapest, 1922-23; B.S., Fed. Inst. Tech., Zurich, 1927; Ph.D., U. Berlin, 1929; m. Valerie Korek, Jan. 4, 1936; 1 dau., Anna Valerie (Mrs. Christopher B. Becker). Partner in mfg. firm at Budapest, 1929-38; lectr. econs. U. Cal., Berkeley, 1939-40, asst. prof., 1941-42, asso. prof., 1943-47, prof., 1947-52; prof. econs. Yale, 1952—, Sterling prof. econs., 1959—, chmn. dept. econs., 1962- 64; cons. expert U.S. Treasury Dept., 1945, 49-52; 69—; cons. Nat. Security Resources Bd., 1948-49; vis. Lectr., Havard, 1950-51; Alfred Marshall lectr. U. Cambridge, 1957. Fellow Am. Acad. Arts and Scis.; mem. Am. Econ. Assn. (mem. exec. com. 1955-58, pres. 1969) , Econometric Soc., Phi Beta Kappa (hon.) . Author: A Treatise on War Inflation, 1942; Monetary Policies and Full Employment, 1946, 2d edit., 1947; Competition Among the Few, 1949; Trends and Cycles in Economic Activity, 1956; Emergence and Content of Modern Economic Analysis, 1960; Probability and Profit, 1965. Joint author: Survey of Econtemporary Economics, 1948; Money, Trade and Economic Growth, 1951; Studies in Income and Wealth, Vol. 16, 1954. Joint editor, Readings in the Theory of Income Distribution, 1946; mem. editorial bd. Am. Econs. Review, 1950-52. Contbr. articles to various econs. journs. Home: 131 Edgehill Rd New Haven CT 06525

FELLOW, HAYNES HAROLD, Jr., communications co. exec.; b. N.Y.C., Apr. 10, 1919; s. Haynes Harold and Madeleine Masten (Day) F.; A.B. cum laude, Wesleyan U., Middletown, Conn., 1940; m. Marjorie Mortimer Smith, June 28, 1961; 5 children. With Met. Life Ins. Co. 1940-41; with New Eng. Tel. & Tel. Co., 1946-52, 55- -, v.p., comptroller, 1963-65, v.p. for planning, 1965, v.p. operations, 1965—, also dir.; with Am. Tel. & Tel. Co., 1953-54; corporator Dorchester Savs. Bank (Mass.) ; dir. State Street Bank & Trust Co., Boston. Mem. corp. Boston Mus. Sci. Served to maj. Q.M.C., AUS, 1941-46. Mem. Financial Execs. Inst., Phi Beta Kappa, Delta Kappa Epsilon. Clubs: Downtown, Commercial (Boston) ; Lake Sunapee (N.H.) Yacht. Home: 301 Highland St Weston MA 02193 Office: 185 Franklin St Boston MA 02107

FELLOWS, KENNETH, natural gas co. exec.; b. 1908; B.S., U. Ia., 1931; married. With Libby, McNeill & Libby, 1931-32; reporter Waukon (Ia.) Democrat, 1933-35; owner, publisher Alice (Tex.) Echo, 1935-38; owner Fellow Publishing Co., Keokuk, Ia., 1938-41; with Houston Natural Gas Corp., 1941—, sec., 1951—, v.p., 1956—. Address: Houston Natural Gas Bldg., Houston, TX 77002.*

FELLOWS, OTIS EDWARD, educator; b. Sprague, Conn., Nov. 6, 1908; s. James Franklin and Elisabeth (Merritt) F.; student Amherst Coll., 1926-27; B.A., Am. U., 1930; diplome, Université de Dijon, 1930; M.A., Brown U., 1933, Ph.D., 1936; m. Frances Elaine Young, June 15, 1935; children—Jay Franklin, Elisabeth Merritt (Mrs. Moulton Loyal Andrus). Instr., Brown U., 1934- 39; instr. Columbia, N.Y.C., 1939-43, asst. prof., 1946-50, asso. prof., 1950-58, prof., 1958—, chmn. dept. Italian, 1963-66; vis. prof. U. Pa., 1964,69; Avalon Found. prof. humanities, 197O—. Intelligence officer OWI, London, Paris, 1943-45. Trustee Horace Mann Sch., Lycee de Los Angeles; mem. corp. vis. com. Mass. Inst. Tech. Deocrated chevalier des Palmes Academiques, Officer de l'Academie (France); Guggenheim fellow, 1959-60. Mem. Modern Lang. Assn., Am. Assn. Tchrs. French, Am. Assn. U. Profs., Assn. Internationale des Etudes Francaises, Chi Phi. Author: French Opinion of Molière, 1937; (with Norman L. Torrey) The Age of Englightenment, 1942, rev. edit., 1970; Periodical Press in Liberated Paris, 1948; (with G. N. Laidlaw) Look and Learn Italian, 1966; From Voltaire to 'La Nouvelle Critique": Problems and Personalities, 1970, Editor: Diderot Studies, 1949—; Tournants Dangereux, 1953; A Livre ouvert, 1970. Contbr. to various publs. Home: 106 Morningside Dr New York City NY 10027

FELLRATH, CHARLES JOSEPH, lawyer, ret. automobile mfg. exec.; b. Detroit, July 2, 1909; s. Charles J. and Alice E. (Sweeney) F.; A.B., U. Detroit, 1930; J.D., 1935; m. Dorothy Vail, Aug. 10, 1940; children—Charles VanDyke, Dorothy Vail, Mary Sweeney. Admitted to Mich. bar, 1935, pvt. practice law, Detroit, 1935-45; legal dept. Ford Motor Co., Detroit, 1945-69, sec., 1954-69; practice law with firm Bodman, Longley, Bogle, Armstrong & Dahling, Detroit, 1969—. Trustee Mich. Cancer Found.; adv. bd. Cath. Social Service of Wayne County. Mem. Am. Soc. Corporate Secs. (former nat. pres., nat. dir., State Bar Mich., Detroit Bar Assn. Clubs: Dearborn Country, Detroit. Home: 8162 E Jefferson Av Detroit MI 48214 Office: Buhl Bldg Detroit MI 48226

FELMLY, LLOYD MCPHERSON, ret. journalist, educator; b. Flemington N.J., Jan. 28, 1894; s. Charles Fox and Minnie (Banghart) F.; Ph.B., Lafayette Coll., 1916, Litt.D., 1943; L.H.D., Rutgers, 1956; m. Anna Tallman, Nov. 22, 1919; children—Lloyd McPherson, Janice (Mrs. Wurfel). With Newark News, 1916-59, beginning as reporter, North Jersey editor, 1920-24, state editor, 1924-26, city editor, 1926-33, mng. editor, 1933-44, editor, 1944-59; chmn. English dept. Newark Coll. Engring., 1959-61, prof. English, 1961-64. Bd. mgrs. Howard Savs. Instn.; trustee N.J. Blue Shield; chmn. alumni council Lafayette Coll., 1942-44, alumni trustee, 1946-52, life trustee, 1954-71, pres. bd., 1956-64. Pres. N.J. Safety Council, 1958-61, trustee, 1961—. Served as pvt. to 1st lt. Transp. Corps, AUS, 1918-19; with AEF, 9 months. Mem. Am. Soc. Newspaper Editors, Phi Beta Kappa. Conglist. Clubs: Down Town, Essex (Newark). Home: 110 Osborne St Glen Ridge NJ 07028

FELS, RENDIGS, economist, educator; b. Cin., June 11, 1917; s. Clifford George and Estella Luella (Rendigs) F.; A.B., Harvard, 1939, Ph.D., 1948; A.M., Columbia, 1940; m. Beatrice Carmichael Baker, Dec. 27, 1941; children—Charles Wentworth Baker, Carmichael. Mem. faculty Vanderbilt U., 1948—, prof. econs., 1956—, dir. grad. program econ. devel., 1956- 57, chmn. dept. econs. and bus. adminstrn., 1962-65. Chmn. Univs.-Nat. Bur. Com., 1962-67. Served with USAAF, 1942-46. Mem. Am. (sec.-treas. 1970—), So. (pres. 1967-68), econ. assns. Author: American Business Cycles, 1865-1897, 1959; Challenge to the American Economy, an Introduction to Economics, 1961, 2d edit., 1966; (with C. Elton Hinshaw) Forecasting and Recognizing Business Cycle Turning Points, 1968. Home: 917 Westview Av Nashville TN 37205

FELSENTHAL, LEONARD, fgn. service officer; b. Kaiserslautern, Germany, Jan. 5, 1913; s. Hermann and Caroline (Becker) F.; student U. Berlin, U. Munich (Germany), 1933-34; B.S., U. Cal. at Berkeley, 1938; M.A., U. Chgo., 1940; postgrad. Am. U., 1948-50; m. Floralee Haas, Aug. 14, 1955; children—Mark Edgar, David Louis. Came to U.S., 1934, naturalized, 1939. Economist, U.S. Treasury, Washington, 1940-41; price analyst OPA, Washington, 1941-43; information specialist U.S. Mil. Govt., Munich, Germany, 1945-47; econ. analyst OIR, State Dept. Far Eastern Div., 1948-56; economist Am. embassy, Tokyo, Japan, 1956-60; chief econ. sect. U.S. consul gen., Singapore, 1960-61; spl. asst. to dir. Far Eastern div. Commerce Dept., Washington, 1961-63; economist Office Internat. Trade, State Dept., Washington, 1963-65; counselor econ. affairs U.S. Mission to UN, Geneva, Switzerland, 1965—. Served with AUS, 1943-45. Mem. Am. Econ. Assn., Am. Fgn. Service Assn., Internat. House Japan. Address: US Mission Geneva 80 rue de Lausanne Geneva Switzerland

FELSON, BENJAMIN, physician, educator; b. Newport, Ky., Oct. 21, 1913; s. Solomon and Esther (Bussell) F.; B.S., U. Cin., 1933, M.D., 1935; m. Virginia Raphaelson, Mar. 18, 1936; children—Stephen, Nancy (Mrs. Roderich Walter), Marcus, Richard, Edward. Intern, Cin. Gen. Hosp., 1935-36, resident pathology, 1936-37, resident radiology, 1937-40; fellow in cancer therapy Indpls. City Hosp., 1940-41; practice radiology, Tulsa, 1941-42; asst. prof. radiology U. Cin., 1945-48, asso. prof., 1948-51, prof., dir. radiology, 1951—; radiologist Cin. Gen. Hosp., 1945-48, asso. dir. radiology, 1948-51, dir., 1951—; dir. depts. radiology Holmes, Drake, Children's, Longview, Dunham hosps. (all Cin.). Cons., Wright-Patterson AFB Hosp., Dayton and Cin. VA hosps., USPHS, VA Central Office, Air Force Med. Service, U.S. Army M.C., Surgeon Gen. USAF, Surgeon Gen. AUS, USNR, Walter Reed Hosp., Armed Forces Inst. Pathology. Nat. bd. dirs. Friends of Hebrew U. Israel. Served from capt. to maj. M.C., AUS, 1942-45; ETO. Fellow Am. Coll. Chest Physicians, Am. Coll. Radiology (chmn. commn. on edn. and chancellor 1966-69); mem. Cin. Acad. Medicine, Am. Roentgen Ray Soc., Ohio Med. Assn., Radiol. Soc. N.Am. (1st v.p. 1959), Ohio, Greater Cin. radiol. socs., Alpha Omega Alpha, Pi Kappa Epsilon; hon. mem. Cuban, Brazilian, Colombian and Canadian radiol. socs., Nat. Acad. Medicine Colombia, Med. Soc. Okinawa. Author: Fundamentals of Chest Roentgenology, 1960, 72, Index for Roentgen Diagnoses, 1961; (with A. Weinstein, H.B. Spitz) Principles of Chest Roentgenology, 1965; (with J.F. Wiot) Case of the Day, 1966. Editor: Roentgen Techniques in the Laboratory Animal, 1968; Seminars in Roentgenology, 1966—; corr. editor Annales de Radiologie, 1963—; mem. editorial bd. Chest, 1962—. Contbr. over 100 articles to sci. jours. Home: 3994 Rose Hill Av Cincinnati OH 45229

FELT, ARTHUR FAIRFIELD, Jr., newspaper editor; b. Kansas City, Mo., June 28, 1914; s. Arthur Fairfield and Elizabeth (Osborn) F.; student La. State U., 1932-35; m. Charlottie Mae Yocum, May 5, 1941; children—Melinda Lou, Robert Yocum, Rebecca Goodwin. Sports writer New Orleans Item, 1931-36; mem. staff Times-Picayune, New Orleans, 1936-, city editor, 1945-64, mng. editor, 1964-69, asso. editor, 1969—. Mem. A.P. Mng. Editors Assn., La.-Miss. Asso. Press Assn. (pres. 1969-70), New Orleans C. of C., S.A.R., Sigma Delta Chi, Delta Kappa Epsilon. Club: New Orleans Country. Home: 244 Bellaire Dr New Orleans LA 70124 Office: 3800 Howard Av New Orleans LA 70140

FELT, CHARLES HERBERT, advt. exec.; b. Bremerston, Wash., July 29, 1921; s. Fred William and Genevieve (Murray) F.; student Wayne State U., 1940-42; A.B. in History and Polit. Sci., Mich. State U., 1948; m. Audrey M. Nicholson, May 27, 1967; children by previous marriage—Douglas C., Bradley J., Carole J.; 1 step dau., Margaret von Dedenroth. Advt. copy writer Ross Roy, Inc., Detroit, 1948-52; copy dir. Henry Koltys Co., Detroit, 1952-53, Campbell-Ewald Co., Detroit, 1952-62; sr. v.p., corp. creative dir. MacManus, John & Adams, Bloomfield Hills, Mich. and N.Y.C., 1962-68; sr. v.p., asso. creative dir. Campbell-Ewald Co., Detroit, 1968—. Served with USAAF, 1942-46. Recipient creative advt. awards Detroit Art Dirs. Club, Chgo. Art Dirs. Club, Advt. Club N.Y.C. Club: Recess (Detroit). Home: 8200 E Jefferson St Detroit MI 48214 Office: 3044 W Grand Blvd Detroit MI 48202

FELT, GAELEN LEE, engring. co. exec.; b. Honolulu, Oct. 15, 1921; s. Lee W. and Louise (Hamilton) F.; A.B., Harvard, 1943; M.S., Cal. Inst. Tech., 1948, Ph.D., 1951; m. Margaret Bolt, Nov. 1946; children—Hugh M., John H., E. Suzanne; m. 2d, Leatrice Hasse, Oct. 1957; children—Douglas F., Rebecca L. Group leader, asst. leader J-div. Los Alamos Sci. Lab., 1950-57; mem. tech. staff Space Tech. Labs., 1957-60; with E G & G, Inc., Las Vegas, 1960—, exec. v.p., 1969—, also dir.; dir. CER Geonuclear Corp., Reynolds Elec. & Engring. Co. Mem. Nev. Bd. Edn., 1965-68. Bd. dirs. S.W. Regional Lab. Ednl. Research and Devel. Served with AUS, 1943-46. Mem. Phi Beta Kappa. Republican. Home: 2613 Burton Av Las Vegas NV 89102 Office: P O Box 1912 Las Vegas NV 89101

FELT, HARRY DONALD, bus. cons., ret. naval officer; b. Topeka, June 21, 1902; s. Harry Victor and Grace Greenwood (Johnson) F.; B.S., U.S. Naval Acad., 1923; student Nat. War Coll., 1947-48; m. Kathryn Cowley, Aug. 3, 1929; 1 son, Donald Linn. Commd. ensign USN, 1923, advanced through grades to adm., 1956; gunnery, battleship and destroyer, 1923-29; designated naval aviator, 1929; comdr. dive bomber squadron U.S.S. Lexington, 1939-41; comdr. Saratoga air group, also air officer U.S.S. Saratoga, 1942-43; participated Occupation of Guadalcanal, Battle of Eastern Solomons; comdg. naval air stas., Dayton Beach, Miami, Fla., 1943-44; naval aviation mem. U.S. Mil. Mission to USSR, 1944-45; comdg. carrier U.S.S. Chenango, 1945, participated Okinawa campaign; staff Officer Chief Naval Operations, 1946-47; comdg. U.S.S. Franklin D. Roosevelt, 1948-49; chief staff Naval War Coll., 1950-51; comdr. Naval Middle East Forces, 1951; staff Chief of Naval Operation, 1951-53; comdr. Carrier div. 15 and 3, 1953- 54; asst. Chief of Naval Operations for Fleet Readiness, 1954-56; comdr. 6th Fleet, 1956; vice chief naval operations, 1956-58; comdr.-in- chief in Pacific, 1958-64; dir., chmn. exec. com. Telecheck Internat., Inc.; adv. bd. Crocker Bank Bd. dirs., pres. Hawaii Found. Am. Freedoms. Decorated Navy Cross, Legion Merit, D.F.C., D.S.M. (U.S.); Order White Elephant 1st degree (Thailand); 1st Bronze Anaha Leaf Degree of Chief Comdr. (Philippines); 1st Order Grand Cordon Rising Sun (Japan); Medal of Cloud and Banner with Special Grand Cordon (Republic China); Home: 818 Pueo St Honolulu HI 96816

FELT, IRVING MITCHELL, corp. exec.; b. N.Y.C., Jan. 25, 1910; s. Abraham and Dora (Mandel) F.; B.S., U. Pa., 1929; m. Elaine Edelman, May 20, 1945. Treas., v.p. Felt Found., Inc., N.Y.C., 1941—; chmn. exec. com., dir. Graham-Paige Corp., 1950, pres., 1955—, now chmn.; chmn. exec. com. Sonesta Internat. Hotels Corp. (formerly Hotel Corp. Am.), 1956—; chmn. bd., pres., dir. Madison Sq. Garden Corp.; chmn. N.Y. Rangers Hockey Club, Madison Sq. Garden Boxing, Inc., N.Y. Knickerbockers Basketball Club, Madison Sq. Garden Center, Inc., Holiday-on-Ice Prodns., Roosevelt Raceway, Inc., Arlington Park Race Track, Washington Park Race Track; dir. HCA Food Corp., Mayflower Hotel Corp., Washington, Hotel Corp. La., Hotel Corp. Gt. Britain, Hotel Plaza Corp., N.Y.C., Columbia Pictures Industries, Inc., Laromme Internat. Hotels Corp., Israel, Republic Corp. Pres. Fedn. Jewish Philanthropies, 1963-66; dir. Nat. Conf. Christians and Jews; vice chmn. Greater N.Y. Fund; hon. chmn., past pres. Jewish Child Care Assn. Mem. Madison Sq. Garden Club, Navy League of U.S. (nat. v.p., dir.), N.Y. Conv. and Visitor's Bur. (dir.). Clubs: Wall Street, Harmonie (N.Y.C.); Hollywood Golf (Deal, N.J.). Home: 911 Park Av New York City NY 10021 Office: 410 Park Av New York City NY 10022

FELT, JAMES, city planner; b. N.Y.C., June 29, 1903; s. Abraham and Dora (Mandel) F.; B.S., U. Pa., 1924; m. Sylvia Shapiro, Apr. 17, 1935; children—Rosalind, Henry S. Pres. James Felt & Co., Inc., 1932-55; dir. Home Title Guaranty Co., Pepsi Cola Co.; trustee Excelsior Savs. Bank, Security Mut. Life Ins. Co. Chmn. City Planning Commn., 1956-64. Past v.p. Fedn. Jewish Philanthropies, Mt. Sinai Hosp.; dir. Henry Street Philanthropies, Mt. Sinai Hosp.; dir. Henry Street Settlement, Children's Aid Soc., Henry Kaufmann Found.; past dir. Lavanburg Found. Mem. Urban League N.Y. (past pres.). Home: 101 Central Park W New York City NY 10023 Office: 358 Fifth Av New York City NY 10001

FELT, W. MARK, govt. ofcl.; b. Twin Falls, Ida., Aug. 17, 1913; s. Mark Earl and Rose (Dvgert) F.; B.A., U. Ida., 1935; LL.B., George Washington U., 1940, J.D., 1968; m. Audrey Isabelle Robinson, June 15, 1938; children— Audrey Joan, W. Mark. Admitted to D.C. bar, 1941; U.S. Supreme Ct. bar, 1955; adminstrv. asst. to Senator D. Worth Clark, 1938-41; atty. FTC, Washington, 1941; spl. agt. FBI, 1942—, supr. counterintelligence operations, Washington, 1942-45, agt. charge, Salt Lake City, 1956-58, Kansas City, Mo., 1958-62, asst. dir. insp. div., Washington, 1962-71, dep. asso. dir., 1971—. Home: 3216 Wynford Dr Fairfax VA 22030 Office: FBI Dept Justice 9th and Pennsylvania Av NW Washington DC 20535

FELTENSTEIN, HARRY DAVID, Jr., chem. co. exec.; b. St. Joseph, Mo., Nov. 6, 1920; s. Harry David and Isabel (Rosenhaum) F.; B.S., Harvard, 1942; m. Rosalie Goldstein, Jan. 18, 1945; children—Andre, Martha. Engaged in book pub., 1946-50; with Merrill Lynch, Pierce, Fenner & Smith, 1951-57; with Lithium Corp., Am. Inc., N.Y.C., 1957-69, financial v.p., treas., 1957-58, exec. v.p., treas., 1958-60, pres., treas., 1960-69; pres., dir. Gt. Salt Lake Minerals and Chems. Corp., 1967-69; exec. v.p., dir. Gulf Resources & Chem. Corp., 1967-69; pres. dir. Fuel Mgmt. Corp., Washington, 1970—; pres., dir. Beryllium Metals & Chems. Corps. Served with USNR, 1942-46. Home: Calle Marqués de Salvatierra 5 Ronda (Málaga) Spain Office: 910 17th St NW Washington DC 20006

FELTER, JAMES WARREN, artist; b. Bainbridge, N.Y., Aug. 25, 1943; s. Warren G. and Margaret J. (Carney) F.; B.A., U. So. Fla., Tampa, 1964. One man shows at Town Hall, Walton, N.Y., 1961, Korman Galleries, Tampa, Fla., 1964; exhibited mems. shows Tampa Art Inst., 1962, 63, 138th Ann. Exhbn. N.A.D., 52d Ann. Exhbn. Art Assn. Newport (R.I.); represented in collections Univ. Center Art Collection, U. So. Fla., also pvt. collections in Europe, S.Am. and U.S. Art critic campus edit. Tampa Times. Dir. Galeria de OCEPA, Quito, Ecuador, 1965-66. Peace Corps vol. with Latin Am. Regional Arts and Crafts, 1964-66. Recipient D.A.R. citizenship award, 1958; named WCS Tchrs. Assn. scholar, 1961. Mem. Tampa Art Inst. Contbr. poetry to collections; pub. poems in Spanish. Home: 1108 W Curtis St Tampa FL 33603 Office: Design Dept OCEPA Artesanas del Ecuador Box 2948 Quito Ecuador

FELTES, ROBERT EDWARD, container co. exec.; b. Chgo., Apr. 28, 1928; s. Nicholas R. and Helen (Schabel) F.; B.A., U. Notre Dame, 1949; M.B.A., U. Chgo., 1950; m. Carol Anne O'Bryan, July 20, 1957; children—Robert Nicholas, Anne Virginia, Thomas Ewell. With Container Corp. Am., Chgo., 1954—, asst. controller, 1960-66, controller, 1966—, also v.p., 1969—. Served to 1st lt. USAF, 1950-53. Mem. Financial Execs. Inst. Roman Catholic. Club: University (Chgo.).

FELTIN, MAURICE, clergyman; b. Delle, France, May 15, 1883. Ordained priest, Roman Cath. Ch., 1909; bishop of Troyes, France, 1929-32; archbishop of Sens, France, 1932-35, of Bordeaux, France, 1935-49, of Paris, France, 1949-66. Created cardinal, 1953. Home: 32 rue Barbet de Jouy Paris 7e France

FELTON, JEAN SPENCER, physician; b. Oakland, Cal., Apr. 27, 1911; s. Herman and Tess (Davidson) F.; A.B., Stanford U., 1931, M.D., 1935; m. Janet E. Birnbaum, June 27, 1937; children—Gary, Keith, Robin. Intern Mt. Zion Hosp., San Francisco, 1935-36; resident in surgery Dante Hosp., San Francisco, 1936-38; practice medicine, San Francisco, 1938-40; guest lect. indsl. sociology U. Tenn., Knoxville, 1946-53; med. dir. Oak Ridge Nat. Lab., 1946-53; cons. dept. medicine, prof. dept. preventive medicine, pub. health U. Okla. Med. Sch., 1953-58; cons. indsl. hygiene Okla. State Dept. Health, 1953-58, past cons. VA, St. Louis area; prof. occupational health U. Cal. Schs. Medicine and Pub. Health, Los Angeles, 1958-68; dir. occupational health service, Dept. Personnel, County Los Angeles, 1968- -; cons. occupational health NASA, AEC, San Francisco Area VA, Pub. Health Service, Social Security Adminstrn., 1955- 62; past mem. Youth Service Com. Oak Ridge Welfare Council, 1946-53, Tenn. State Commn. on Children, Welfare Services Dept., chmn., mem. adv. bd. Oak Ridge; past mem. Gov.'s Com. Utilization Physically Handicapped; Pres.'s Com. Employment Handicapped. Served to lt. col., M.C., AUS, 1940- 46; transport surgeon on St. Mihiel and Pres. Pierce between San Francisco and the Orient, 1941; indsl. med. officer Philippines and Japan, Sixth Army, 1945; prepared standard operating procedure of U.S. Army indsl. med. program at San Francisco Port of Embarkation (adopted by the U.S. Army Chief of Transp. for use by all Ports of Embarkation). Awarded Army Commendation Ribbon, 1946; Citation for Excellence in Med. Authorship by Am. Assn. Indsl. Physicians and Surgeons, 1948; Knudsen award Indsl. Med. Assn., 1968. Diplomate Am. Bd. Preventive Medicine. Fellow Am. Coll. Preventive Medicine (pres. 1966-67), Am. Acad. Occupational Medicine, Indsl. Med. Assn. (Mertorious Service award 1965), Am. Pub. Health Assn.; mem. A.M.A. (sec., vice chmn. sect. preventive and indsl. medicine and pub. health, 1949-53, chmn. sect. 1953), Am. Indsl. Hygiene Assn., So.

Cal. Nat. Rehab. Assn. (dir.), So. Cal. Ind. Hygiene Assn. (past pres.). Unitarian. Author: (with A. H. (Katz) Health and Community. Mem. bd. editors Exerpta Medica, Sect. XVII, The Netherlands. Contbr. med. jours. Home: 275 Bellino Dr Pacific Palisades CA 90272 Office: 222 N Grand Av Los Angeles CA 90012

FELTON, LURTON EUGENE, food processing exec.; b. Grand Tower, Ill., Jun 30, 1899; s. Samuel W. and Maude (Norton); B.S., U. Ill., 1923; m. Zola H. Dillavou, Sept. 8, 1923; children—James E., Carol Ann. Certified pub. accountant Albert T. Bacon & Co., Chgo., 1923-26; with Green Giant Co., LeSueur, Minn., 1926- -, successively auditor, controller, treas., sec.-treas., 1926-52, v.p. finance and treas., 1952-58, exec. v.p., 1958-59, pres., treas., 1959- 60, pres., 1960-64, chmn. bd., 1964-69, hon. chmn., 1969—; dir. emeritus Valley Nat. Bank, LeSueur, Employers Mutuals of Warsau. Mem. U. Ill. Found. C.P.A., Ill. Mem. Financial Execs. Inst. Beta Alpha Psi, Beta Gamma Sigma. Home: 76 W Royal Flamingo Dr Sarasota FL 33577 Office: Green Giant Co LeSueur MN 56058

FELTON, M. ROBERT, banker. Auditor, Bank of Del., Wilmington. Office: 300 Delaware Av Wilmington DE 19899*

FELTON, NORMAN, motion picture producer; b. London, Eng., Apr. 29, 1913; s. John Thomas and Gertrude Anne (Francis) F.; came to U.S., 1929, naturalized, 1939; B.F.A., U. Ia., 1939, M.A., 1940; m. Aline Stotts, Sept. 15, 1940; children—Julie Anne, John Christopher, Aline Elizabeth. Dir., St. Paul Civic Theatre, 1940-41, Saginaw (Mich.) Civic Theatre, 1941-42; producer NBC Radio, Chgo., 1944-48; exec. producer central div. NBC TV, 1948-50; dir. Robert Montgomery TV dramatic series, 1950-54; writer, dir. TV dramas, N.Y.C., 1950-56; producer Studio One, CBS-TV, 1957-59; exec. producer CBS West Coast, 1959-60, dir. TV programs, 1960-61; dir. TV films Metro-Goldwyn-Mayer, 1961—; pres. Arena Prodns., 1961—; developed TV series Dr. Kildare, The Eleventh Hour, The Lieutenant, The Man From U.N.C.L.E., Jericho, Strange Report, The Psychiatrist; also produced features To Trap a Spy, 1964, The Spy With My Face, 1965, One Spy Too Many, 1966, The Spy in the Green Hat, 1966, The Karate Killers, 1967, The Helicopter Spies, 1967, How to Steal the World, 1968, God Bless the Children, 1970; exec. producer Strange Report, TV series. Recipient Emmy award for TV direction, 1953; Sylvania award distinuished achievement, 1952, 56; Christopher award, 1954, 56; TV Guide gold medal, 1952; TV Guide award, 1963, 64; Look mag. award, 1954. Mem. Screen Producers Guild (past pres.). Home: 13715 Sunset Blvd Pacific Palisades CA 90272

FELTRINELLI, GIANGIACOMO, indsl. and publishing exec.; b. Milan, Italy, June 19, 1926; s. Carlo and Giannalisa (Gianzana) F. Pres. 1st G. G. Feltrinelli di Studi di Scienze Economiche Politiche e Sociali per la Storia del Socialismo; pub. book Dr. Zhivago. Address: 4 Via Andegari Milan Italy

FELTY, EDWARD BURCHFIELD, banker; b. Altoona, Pa., Sept. 2, 1899; s. Jacob Battorf and North (Burchfield) F.; B.S., Wharton Sch., U. Pa., 1921; m. Mary Louise Plack, July 29, 1929, Engaged in wholesale confectionery and spltys., 1922- 46; pres. Central Trust Co., Altoona, 1946-59, Altoona Trust & Bank Co., 1959-67; pres. Mid State Bank & Trust Co., 1959-67; pres. Mid State Bank & Trust Co., Altoona, 1967-68, chmn. bd., 1968—, also dir.; dir. Blair Hotel Co., Buthcer & Hard Mfg. Co., Altoona Enterprises Inc. Pres., dir. Downtown Area Redevel. Enterprises, Altoona; past pres. Altoona Community Chest, Altoona C. of C. Mem. Sigma Chi. Presbyn. Rotarian. Clubs: Blairmont Country (Hollidaysburg, Pa.); Frankstown Hunt (Altoona); Spruce Creek (Pa.) Rod and Gun. Home: 1108 28th Av Altoona PA 16601 Office: 1230 12th Av Altoona PA 16603

FENDER, DEREK HENRY, educator; b. Hethe, Oxon, Eng., Dec. 4, 1918; s. Wilfrid Henry and Lily (Gray) F.; B.Sc. in Phys. Scis., Reading (Eng.), U. 1939, B.Sc. in Physics, 1947, Ph.D., 1956; m. Marion Gosford Evans, June 3, 1944; children—Michael (dec.), Antony. Came to U.S., 1961 and naturalized, 1971. Sr. lectr. Royal Mil. Coll. Sci., Shrivenham, Eng., 1947-53; lectr. Reading U., 1953-61; sr. research fellow Cal. Inst. Tech., Pasadena, 1961-62, prof. biology and applied sci., 1962—; ednl. cons. Ford Found. (India), Inst. Visual Scis., Electro Optical Systems, Bell Telephone Labs. Dir. research John Tracy Clinic, 1970—. Served to maj. Royal Corps of Signals, Brit. Army, 1939-47. Mem. Photobiology Group, Biol. Engring. Soc., Optical Soc. Am., N.Y. Acad. Scis., Soc. Investigative Ophthalmology, Internat. Soc. Cybernetic Medicine. Author: General Physics and Sound, 1957; Physics to Advanced Level (with others), 1968; (with C.B. Daish) Experimental Physics, 2d edit., 1971. Home: 2227 E Crescent Dr Altadena CA 91001

FENDLER, LUTHER CURT, banker; b. Kennewick, Wash., Nov. 5, 1907; s. George Curt and Anna (Kalinoski) F.; student trust div. Pacific Coast Banking Sch., 1953-54; m. Katherine Marie Kersul, June 12, 1932; children—Norma (Mrs. Roland W. Edens), Paula A. With Old Nat. Bank, Spokane, 1925—, sr. trust officer, 1966—; dir. Davenport Investment Co., Spokane, Oeser Cedar Co., Bellingham, Wash., B.J. Carney & Co., Spokane, Tinling & Powell, Inc., Spokane, Hart & Dilatush, Inc., Spokane. Mem. adv. bd. Spokane Salvation Army, 1950-62, chmn., 1960-61; sec. Ren Rice Found., 1959-71. Trustee Spokane Park and Recreational Found., Spokane Symphony Soc., Eastern Wash. Hist. Soc., YMCA. Mem. Corporate Fiduciaries Assn. Wash. (past pres.). Lutheran. Rotarian. Home: 4807 S Magnolia St Spokane WA 99203 Office: W 428 Riverside Av Spokane WA 99201

FENDLER, MIRIAM OLDEN, (Mrs. Harold A. Fendler), lawyer; b. N.Y.C., d. Max and Ethel (Labowit) Olden; A.B., U. Mich., 1927; LL.B., U. So. Cal., 1929; m. Harold A. Fendler, Mar. 8, 1933; children—Robert H., Douglas M. Admitted to Cal. bar, 1929; practice in Los Angeles, 1929-45, Beverly Hills, 1945—; partner Fendler & Fendler, 1945—. Legislative chmn. P.T.A., Los Angeles, 1949-53. Mem. League Women Voters (pres. Los Angeles, exec. v.p. Cal.), Internat. Fedn. Women Lawyers (hon. life), Delta Sigma Rho, Phi Sigma Sigma (nat. pres.). Home: 735 Bonhill Rd Los Angeles CA 90049 Office: 9465 Wilshire Blvd Beverly Hills CA 90212

FENDLER, OSCAR, lawyer; b. Blytheville, Ark., Mar. 22, 1909; s. Alfred and Rae (Sattler) F.; B.A., U. Ark., 1930, LL.B., Harvard, 1933; m. Patricia Shane, Oct. 26, 1946; children—Tilden P. Wright III (stepson), Frances Shane. Admitted to Ark. bar, 1933; practice in Blytheville, 1933-41, 46—; spl. justice Ark. Supreme Ct., 1965. Mem. Ark. Jud. Council, 1959- 60; pres. Conf. Local Bar Assn., 1958-60; pres. bd. dirs. Ark. Law Rev., 1961-67; mem. Ark. Bd. Pardons and Paroles, 1970-71. Mem. Miss. County Democratic Central Com., 1948—. Served with USNR, 1941-45. Fellow Am. Coll. Probate Counsel, Am. Bar Found.; mem. Am. (chmn. gen. practice sect. 1966-67, mem. council sect. gen. practice 1964—, ho. dels. 1968—, mem. com. edn. about Communism 1966-70, com. legal aid and indigent defendants 1970—), Ark. (chmn. exec. com. 1956-57, pres. 1962- 63), bar assns., Am. Judicature Soc. (dir. 1964-68), Scribes, Nat. Conf. Bar Presidents (exec. council 1963-65), Blytheville C. of C. (past v.p., dir.), Navy League, Am. Legion. Clubs: Blytheville Country, Blytheville Rotary (past pres.), Home: 1062 W Hearn St Blytheville AR 72315 Office: 104 N 6th St Blytheville AR 72315

FENDRICK, ALAN BURTON, advt. exec.; b. Bronx, N.Y., Mar. 22, 1933; s. Louis and Esther (Silberberg) F.; A.B. with honors in Econs., Columbia, 1954; M.B.A., Harvard, 1958; m. Beverly R. Schoenfeld, June 12, 1960; children—Sarah Lin, Lisa Augusta. Asst. sales mgr. splty. div. Hankins Container Co., 1958-60; mgr. bus. adminstrn., operations and engring. NBC, 1960- 67; with Grey Advt. Inc., 1967—, sr. v.p., treas., 1970—. Exec. com. class 1954 Columbia. Dist leader Greenburgh (N.Y.) Town Democratic Com., 1969—. Bd. govs. Orchard Hill Civic Assn. Served with AUS, 1954-56. Mem. Am. Mgmt. Assn., Am. Inst. Mgmt., Advt. Agy. Financial Mgmt. Group, Harvard Bus. Sch. Club N.Y. Home: 30 Canterbury Rd White Plains NY 10607 Office: 777 3d Av New York City NY 10017

FENDT, EDWARD CHARLES, clergyman; b. Michigan City, Ind., Feb. 17, 1904; s. Charles and Mary (Schultz) F.; A.B., Capital U., Columbus, O., 1925, B.D., 1928, D.D., 1943; postgrad. Ohio State U., U. Chgo., 1928-34; LL.D., Pacific Lutheran U., 1958; D.D., Concordia Sem., St. Louis, 1968; Instr. in Bible, Capital U., 1929-36, prof. systematic theology, 1936—, dean Evang. Luth. Theol. Sem., 1946-59, pres., 1959-71. Mem. Soc. Bibl. Lit. and Exegesis. Lutheran. Compiler: What Lutherans are Thinking. Home: 2244 Astor Av Columbus OH 43209

FENERTY, ROBERT L., lawyer; b. Halifax, N.S., Can., Mar. 15, 1911; B.A., U. Alta., LL.B., 1933; B.C.L., Oxford U., 1936. Admitted to Alta. bar 1934; partner firm Fenerty, McGillivray, Robertson, Prowse, Brennan, Fraser, Bell & Code, Calgary, Alta. Mem. Law Soc. Alta., Canadian, Calgary bar assns. Office: 1500 Guinness House Calgary 2 Alberta Canada*

FENICHEL, GERALD M., physician; b. N.Y.C., May 11, 1935; s. Max I. and Sarah (Markowitz) F.; A.B cum laude, Johns Hopkins, 1955; M.D., Yale, 1959; m. Barbara Ross, June 8, 1958; children—Amy, Eric, Adam. Intern Strong Meml. Hosp., Rochester, N.Y., 1959-60; resident NIH, Bethesda, Md., 1960-63, Grace-New Haven Hosp., 1963-64; instr. neurology George Washington U. Sch. Medicine, 1964-67, asst. prof., 1967-69; prof., chmn. dept. neurology Vanderbilt U. Sch. Medicine, 1969—; asso. neurology Children's Hosp. D.C., 1964-69, attending neurologist, 1964-69. Served with USPHS, 1960-63. Richmond S. Paine Meml. lectr. pediatric neurology Children's Hosp. D.C., 1970. Home: 234 Robin Hill Rd Nashville TN 37205

FENIMORE, GEORGE WILEY, electronics co. exec.; b. Bertrand, Mo., Jan. 15, 1921; s. George Wiley and Florence (Bush) F.; B.S., Northwestern U., 1941; LL.B., Harvard, 1947; m. Benetta B. Lindsey, Oct. 27, 1949; children—Lindsey Catherine, Marian Houston, George Wiley III. Asst. to dir. planning Ford Motor Co., 1947-48; exec. asst. to gen. mgr. Hughes Aircraft Co., 1948-53; asst. to pres. Packard Bell Electronics Co., Los Angeles, 1953-55; with TRW, Inc., 1955-64, v.p. internat. operations, 1960-64; v.p. internat. Bunker Ramo Corp., 1964-65; sec. Litton Industries, Inc., Beverly Hills, Cal., 1965—. Sec.-treas. Beverly Hills YMCA. Trustee John Thomas Dye Sch. Served to capt. USAAF, World War II; maj. Res. ret. Mem. Beverly Hills C. of C. (pres.). Mason (Shriner), Rotarian (v.p.). Home: 13187 Chalon Rd Los Angeles CA 90049 Office: Litton Industries 360 N Crescent Dr Beverly Hills CA 90010

FENINGER, CLAUDE, hotel exec.; b. Cairo, Egypt, Jan. 15, 1926; s. Paul and Therese (DeRogatis) F.; student Lausanne (Switzerland) Sch. Hotel Mgmt., 1948, Am. U., Cairo, 1945, Lincoln Sch., Cairo, 1943, Lycee Francais, Cairo, 1935; m. Ruth Lee Rohlfs, July 10, 1965; children—Paul Gordon, Eric. Came to U.S., 1960. With Hilton Internat., 1955-67; product line mgr. Internat. Tel. & Tel., 1967-68; pres. Sheraton Internat., 1968—; cons. in field, 1960—. Mem. Am. Hotel Assn., New Eng. Internat. Center. Home: 80 Beaver Rd Weston MA Office: 470 Atlantic Av Boston MA 02210

FENLON, THOMAS BOLGER, lawyer; b. Long Branch, N.J., Nov. 12, 1904; s. John T. and Elizabeth (Cole) F.; A.B., Georgetown U., 1925; LL.B., Columbia, 1928; m. Juliet O. Ludford, June 30, 1930; children—Mary Ann (Mrs. William V. Knowles), Henry L., Thomas Bolger, Juliet (Mrs. Frederick L. Nagle, Jr.), Lois (Mrs. Michael W. Brinkman). Admitted to N.Y. bar, 1928; partner firm Emmet, Marvin & Martin, N.Y.C., 1942—. Village atty., North Pelham, N.Y., 1933-35; town supr., Pelham, 1942-43; mem. Pelham Bd. Edn., 1945-58, pres., 1955-58. Bd. dirs., mem. exec. 65, acting dir. Office West African Affairs, 1965—; dep. dir. Office of The Pelhams, 1965-68; bd. dirs. United Fund of Westchester, 1969—. Named Man of Year in Pelham, 1967. Mem. Am., N.Y. State (chmn. com. state legislation 1944-46) bar assns., Assn. Bar City N.Y. (chmn. com. state legislation 1944-46), Comml. Law League. Clubs: Pelham Mens (pres. 1952-53); Down Town Assn. (N.Y.C.); Huguenot Yacht (New Rochelle, N.Y.). Home: 72 Clifford Av Pelham NY 10803 Office: 48 Wall St New York City NY 10005

FENN, CHARLES VAN ORDEN, mgmt. exec.; b. Montclair, N.J., Aug. 14, 1908; s. George T. and Frances I. (Geary) F.; M.E., Stevens Inst. Tech., 1929; m. Isabelle Williams, July 2, 1932; children—June Marilyn, William Charles. With Carrier Corp., Syracuse, N.Y., 1929—, successively student engr., mem. constrn. dept., mgr. spl. order shop, dist. mgr. charge sales engring., constrn. and service Southeastern states, mgr. direct dept. covering nat. sales engring., constrn. and service, v.p. and gen. sales mgr. machinery and systems div., 1953-57, gen. mgr. machinery and systems div., 1957-60, v.p. charge corporate staff group, 1960-62, asst. to pres., 1968, exec. v.p. charge all operations, 1968, pres., 1968—, also dir.; pres. Elliot Co. div. Carrier Corp., 1962-68; dir. Mchts. Nat. Bank & Trust Co., Carrier Air Conditioning (Can.) Ltd., Charter N.Y. Corp. Mem. Tau Beta Pi, Beta Theta Pi. Clubs: Century, Onondaga Golf and Country (Syracuse). Home: Marvelle Rd Fayetteville NY 13066 Office: Carrier Corp Carrier Pkwy Syracuse NY 13201

FENN, DAN HUNTINGTON, Jr., educator, govt. ofcl.; b. Boston, Mar. 27, 1923; s. Dan Huntington and Anna (Yens) G.; A.B magna cum laude, Harvard, 1946, student Grad. Sch. Arts and Scis., 1946-48; m. Nancy Ring, Dec. 28, 1946 (div. 1965); children— Peter, Anne, David, Thomas O.; m. Lenore O. Sheppard, Oct. 10, 1969; children—W. Gregory, W. Marie, Christopher G. Asst. dean freshmen Harvard, 1946-49; exec. dir. World Affairs Council Boston, 1949-55; asst. editor Harvard Bus. Rev., mem. faculty, also editor Harvard Bus. Sch. Bull., Harvard Bus. Sch., 1955-61; spl. asst. to Senator Smith, 1961; staff asst. to Pres. Kennedy, 1961-63; mem. U.S. Tariff Commn., 1963-67, vice chmn., 1964- 65; pres. Center Business-Govt. Relations, Inc., Washington, 1967-71; dir. John F. Kennedy Library, Waltham, Mass., 1971—; mem. faculty, lectr. Harvard Grad. Sch. Bus. Adminstrn., also sr. asso. Mass. Inst. Tech-Harvard Joint Center on Urban Studies, 1969- -. Mem. president's Delegation to Algerian Independence Day, 1963. Sec., Lexington (Mass.) Sch. Com., 1957-61; mem. Lexington Town Meeting, 1953-61, 71—. Del. Mass. Democratic Conv., 1954, 56, 58, 60; Dem. nominee for Mass. Legislature, 1952; alternate del.-at-large Dem. Nat. Conv., 1960. Trustee Browne and Nichols Sch., 1959-61. Served with USAAF, 1943-45; ETO. Decorated by Govt. Morocco, 1952. Mem. Phi Beta Kappa. Unitarian. Author: Citizens Guide to International Relations, 1953. Editor: Management Guide to Overseas Operations, 1957; Management in a Rapidly Changing Economy, 1958; Management's Mission in a New Society, 1959; Business Responsibility in Action, 1960; Managing America's Economic Explosion, 1961; co-author: Cases in Business and Government, 1966. Co-editor: Planning the Future Strategy of your Business, 1956; Incentives for Executives, 1962; Management of Materials Research, 1962. Home: 130 Worthen Rd Lexington MA 02173 Office: John F Kennedy Library 380 Trapelo Rd Waltham MA 02154 also Harvard Business School Soldiers Field Boston MA 02163

FENN, HENRY COURTENAY, ret. educator; b. Peking, China, Feb. 26, 1894; s. Courtenay Hughes and Alice Holstein (May) F.; B.A., Hamilton Coll., 1916; M.A., Columbia, 1929, student Tchrs. Coll., 1936-40; m. Constance Latimer Sargent, Jan. 27, 1925; children—Courtenay, Robert, David, Donald. Ednl. Missionary, China, 1920-27; faculty Oak Lane Country Day Sch. of Temple U., Phila., 1929-35, Lincoln Sch. of Tchrs. Coll., N.Y.C., 1935-41, Presidio Hill Sch., San Francisco, 1941-43; faculty dept. Oriental studies Yale, 1943-46, faculty inst. Far Eastern langs., 1949-63, dir., 1953-63, emeritus, 1963- -; mem. faculty Dartmouth Coll., 1964-66; pres. Coll. Chinese Studies Peiping, China, 1946-48; dir. Chinese Lang. Information Center, Modern Lang. Assn. Am., 1963—; faculty dept. Chinese and Japanese, Washington U., St Louis, 1966- 69. Cons. to U.S. Office Edn., 1960-63, N.Y. State Dept. Edn., 1963, Dartmouth, 1963, Nan Yang U., Singapore, New Asia Coll., Hong Kong, 1969. Served as 2d lt. F.A., AUS, 1917-18. Mem. Chinese Lang. Tchrs. Assn., Modern Lang. Assn. Am., Assn. for Asian Studies, Phi Delta Kappa. Clubs: Rotary (China), Yale- in- China (bd. trustees). Author: Syllabus of Chinese History and Culture (with Goodrich), 1951; A Sketch of Chinese History in Yale Romanization, 1952; Speak Mandarin (with Tewksbury), 1968. Contbr. articles profl. publs. Home: 100 Warner Rd North Haven CT 06473

FENN, HOWARD NATHAN, chem. co. exec.; b. Milford, Conn., Nov. 11, 1907; s. Nathan Hartley and Ottilie Josephine (Volkman) F.; B.S. in Chem. Engring., Yale, 1929; m. Mary Eleanor Chesley, Apr. 19, 1948; 1 son, William Hartley. With Dow Chem. Co., 1929-44, prodn. supt., 1942-44; with Dow Corning Corp., Midland, Mich., 1944—, dir. mfg., 1962-63, v.p. mfg., 1963-65, v.p. engring. and mfg., 1965-71, v.p., asst. to pres. and chmn., 1971—. Mem. Am. Chem. Soc., Am. Inst. Chem. Engrs., A.A.A.S., Yale Engring. Assn. Kiwanian. Home: 4401 Gladding Ct Midland MI 48640 Office: Dow Corning Corp Midland MI 48640

FENN, JEAN, opera singer; b. Ill., 1930; d. George Prentice and Maurine (Hansen) Fenn; A.A., Stephens College, 1946; m. to W. T. Farwell. Made professional debut with the Los Angeles Civic Light Opera, 1950; debut with San Francisco Opera Co., 1952, N.Y.C. Center Opera Co., 1953, Met. Opera Co., 1953—, also New Orleans Grand Opera, Kansas City and St. Louis Light Operas, Denver Opera Assn., Seattle Opera Assn., Houston Grand Opera, Tulsa Opera, Inc. Mem. Sigma Alpha Iota. Address: care Met Opera Co Lincoln Center New York City NY 10023

FENN, JOHN BENNETT, educator, chemist; b. N.Y.C., June 15, 1917; s. Herbert Bennett and Jeanette Clyde (Dingman) F.; A.B., Berea Coll., 1937; Ph. D., Yale, 1940; m. Margaret Elizabeth Wilson, June 6, 1939; children—Margaret Marianne, Barbara Leigh, John Bennett. Research chemist Monsanto Chem. Co., Anniston, Ala., 1940-43, Sharples Chems., Inc., Wyandotte, Mich., 1943-45; v.p. Experiment, Inc., Richmond, Va., 1945-52; dir. Project SQUID, Princeton, 1952-62, prof. mech. engring., 1959-63, prof. aerospace scis., 1963-66; prof. applied sci. and chemistry Yale U., 1966—; vis. scientist N.Am. Aviation Sci. Center, 1965-66; dir. Thermal Research & Engring. Corp., 1952-59; sci. liaison officer Office Naval Research, London, 1955; dir. Aero Chem. Research Labs., 1956-60. Mem. Am. Chem. Soc., Am. Inst. Aeros. and Astronautics, A.A.A.S., Am. Inst. Chem. Engrs., Sigma Xi. Editor: (with A.B. Cambel) Transport Properties in Gases, 1958, Dynamics of Conducting Gases, 1960. Home: 226 Pleasant Point Rd Branford CT 06405

FENN, RAYMOND WOLCOTT, Jr., metall. engr.; b. Torrington, Conn., Feb. 4, 1922; s. Raymond W. and Josephine (Mueller) F.; B.Metall. Engring., Rensselaer Poly. Inst., 1943; M.Engring., Yale, 1947, D.Engring., 1949; m. Beatrice Myra Christian, Jan. 19, 1946; children—Carol Louise, Ralph Christian. Metall. engr. Gen. Electric Co., West Lynn, Mass., 1943-44; supr. testing lab., chief testing and instrumentation sect. Metall. Lab., Dow Chem. Co., Midland, Mich., 1949-61; mgr. materials and prodn. systems engring. Space System div. Lockheed Missiles & Space Co., Sunnyvale, Cal., 1961—. Served with USNR, 1944-46. Registered profl. engr., Cal. Mem. Am. Soc. Testing Materials (dir. 1966-69, R.E. Templin award 1961), Am. Inst. Mining and Metall. Engrs., Am. Soc. Metals (trustee 1969-71, chmn., mem. exec. com. Santa Clara Valley chpt. 1966-69), Research Soc. Am., Am. Welding Soc., Soc. Aero. Material and Process Engrs., Nat. Mgmt. Assn., Sigma Xi. Contbr. articles profl. jours. Home: 13428 Carillo Lane Los Altos Hills CA 94022 Office: 1111 Lockheed Way Sunnyvale CA 94088

FENN, WILSON LEE, mfg. exec.; b. Hartford, Conn., Oct. 22, 1912; s. Wilson A. and Frances (Avery) F.; student Deerfield Acad., 1931, Colgate U., 1932, Babson Inst., 1933; m. Virginia Curtis, Sept. 12, 1936; children—Frances Curtis (Mrs. Reese Harvey Harris III), Ardelle Curtis, Wilson Lee. With Fenn Mfg. Co., Newington, 1933—, beginning as machinist, successively v.p. and gen. mgr., treas., former pres. now chmn. bd.; dir. Nickel Cadmium Battery Corp., Amtel Inc. Trustee Emma Willard Sch., Tory, N.Y. Clubs: Brooklawn Country (Fairfield, Conn.); Carlovel Yacht (Clearwater, Fla.); Hartford Gun (Farmington, Connecticut); Hartford Golf (West Hartford, Conn.); Hartford. Home: 60 Sunset Farms West Hartford CT 06007 Office: Fenn Mfg Co Fenn Rd Newington CT 06111

FENNEBERG, DORIS RICHINGS, educator, lawyer; b. Toledo, Nov. 10, 1904; d. Gustave G. and Caroline Maud (Wallace) Fenneberg; A.B., U. Toledo, 1925, A.M., 1927; J.D., U. Mich., 1930. Dir. athletics for women U. Toledo, 1925-27, lectr. sociology, 1944-46, instr. law and law librarian Coll. Law, 1946-49, asst. prof., 1949-53, asso. prof., 1953-56, prof., 1956-69, prof. emeritis, 1969—; admitted to Ohio bar, 1931, Practiced in Perrysburg, Toledo, 1931-37; asst. girls' referee Juvenile Ct., Toledo, 1937-45; atty., adoptive investigator Child and Family Agy., Toledo, 1945-46. Exec. sec. Perrysburg Retail Mchts. Assn., 1931- 33; sec., legal counsel NRA Compliance Bd. for Wood County, O. Sec. Young Democrats of Wood County, 1934-37. Mem. Am., Ohio, Toledo (sec. grievance com. 1953-58, sec. questions and issues com. 1964-65) bar assns., Assn. Am. Indian Affairs, Nat. Assn. Women Lawyers (chmn. com. on profl. ethics 1954-55, 56-57), Am. Assn. Law Libraries (chmn. com. on exchange of duplicates 1954-57, sec. 1957- 60), Ohio Assn. Law Libraries (sec. 1950-52, pres. 1953-54, v.p. 1955-56, mem. exec. com. 1954-55, 56-57), Assn. Am. Law Schs. (chmn. Round Table 1955-56), Am. Judicature Soc., Am. Acad. Polit. and Social Sci., Am. Assn. U. Women, Am. Assn. U. Profs., Am., Nat. philatelic socs., Am. Topical Assn., Nat. Wildlife Fedn., Toledo Zool. Soc., Toledo Animal Shelter Assn., U. Toledo Alumni Assn. (exec. bd. 1930-32, pres. 1932-34), Defenders Wildlife, Smithsonian Assos., Common Cause, Phi Theta Psi (pres. 1923-25), Kappa Beta Pi (province finance officer

1957-60). Democrat. Unitarian. Contbr. articles legal publs. Home: 302 E 2d St Perrysburg OH 44864 Office: University of Toledo Toledo OH 43606

FENNEBRESQUE, JOHN D., corp. exec.; b. Boston, Apr. 11, 1917; s. George W. and Helen (Aubry) F.; B.E., Yale, 1939; student Washington U., 1942; m. Frances Jane Campbell, June 10, 1944; children—John Clark, Kim. Chem. engr. Monsanto Chem. Co., St. Louis, 1939-43; with office rubber dir. WPB, Washington, 1943-44, cons., 1944-46; with Celanese Corp. Am., N.Y.C., 1944-45, v.p., 1951-52, v.p., dir., asst. to pres., 1952-55, gen. mgr. chem. div., 1946-52; v.p., dir. Petrocel Corp., 1951-55, Columbia Cellulose Co., Ltd., 1952-55, Celgar Devel. Co., 1953-55; dir. Canadian Chem. Co., Ltd., 1951-55, v.p., 1953-55; dir. Celanese Mexicana, Celatino, S.A., 1953-55; v.p., asst. to pres. Food Machinery & Chem. Corp., San Jose, Cal., 1955-56, exec. v.p., dir., mem. exec. com., 1956-58; pres., dir., mem. exec. com. Tex. Butadiene & Chem. Corp., 1958- 62, affiliated companies; dir. Societe des Elastomeres de Synthese, 1959-62; pres. Mobil Chem. Co. div. Mobil Oil Corp., 1962- 67; v.p. Mobil Oil Co., 1963-67; dir., mem. exec. com. Jamaica Water & Utilities Corp., (N.Y.), 1968; chmn. bd., chmn. exec. com. Nease Chem. Corp., 1968—; pres. Rolfite Co., 1971 —. Mem. chem. industry adv. com. NPA, 1951-53; petro chem. industry adv. com. OPS, 1951-53; mem. chem. and rubber industry com. Dept. Commerce, 1953—; dir. Mfg. Chem. Assn., 1954-55; mem. exec. com. Rayon and Acetate Yarn Producers Group, 1953-55; with Tech. Indsl. Intelligence Com., 1945, Combined Advance Field Team, 1945. Recipient Yale Engring. award, 1950. Mem. Soc. Chem. Industry, Am. Inst. Chem. Engrs., Internat. Mgmt. Assn. (planning council 1956-59), Am. Chem. Soc., Sigma Xi, Chi Phi. Episcopalian. Clubs: Pinnacle, Twenty-Nine, Yale N.Y. Yacht (N.Y.C.). Home: RFD 3 Chestnutwoods Rd West Redding CT 06876 Office: 111 Prospect St Stamford CT 06901

FENNELL, EDWARD O'BRIEN, airline exec.; b. Washington, Dec. 6, 1925; s. Anthony B. and Madeleine (O'Brien) F.; student U. Md., 1943-44, 45-47; LL.B., Am. U., 1950; m. Barbara E. Duborg, Apr. 15, 1951; children—Karen Ann, Kevin George, Stephen Edward. Admitted to D.C. bar, 1950, Ill. bar, 1957; trial atty. Justice Dept., 1950-51, asst. U.S. atty., 1951-57; with United Air Lines, Inc., 1957—, sr. v.p. legal and pub. affairs, Chgo., 1969—. Mem. Chgo. Crime Commn. Served with USNR, 1944-45. Mem. Am., Chgo., D.C. bar assns. Clubs: International, Congressional Country (Washington); Knollwood (Lake Forest, Ill.). Home: 544 N Fletcher Circle Lake Forest IL 60045 Office: P O Box 66100 O'Hare Internat Airport Chicago IL 60666

FENNELLY, JOHN FAUNTLEROY, investment banker; b. New Orleans, July 18, 1899; s. John Joseph and Alice Janney (Fauntleroy) F.; A.B., Princeton, 1920, AM., 1925, Ph.d., 1928; m. Martha Davis, Dec. 11, 1931 (div. 1955); children—Alison, Anne, Richard; m. 2d, Barbara Potter, May 1957. Reporter, Kansas City (Mo.) Star, 1920; with Hall Baker Grain Co., Kansas City and St. Louis, 1921- 23; instr. econs. Columbia U., 1927-29; economist Nat. City Co., N.Y.C., 1929-31; vice chmn. requirements com. and dir. program bur. WPB, Washington, 1942-43; with Glore, Forgan & Co. and predecessor Field, Glore & Co., 1931—, partner, 1935-65; chmn. policy com. Glore Forgan, Wm. R. Staats, Inc., 1965-70; vice chmn. F.I. duPont Glore Forgan, Inc., 1970—; dir. Stewart- Warner Corp. Exec. dir. Com. Econ. Devel., 1943-44. Chmn. citizens' adv. bd. U. Chgo., 1954-56; pres. bd. trustees Lake Forest Acad., 1945-49. Served as flying cadet USAAF, 1918-19. Vice pres. Investment Bankers Assn. Am., 1948-51. Clubs: Chicago, Commonwealth, Commercial, Attic, LaSalle Street (Chgo.); Old Elm, Onwentsia (Lake Forest, Ill.); Links, Anglers' (N.Y.C.): Flyfishers' (London). Author: (with W.L. Crum) Fiscal Planning for Total War, 1942; Steelhead Paradise, 1963; Memoirs of a Bureaucrat, 1965. Home: 1090 N Edgewood Rd Lake Forest IL 60045 Office: 135 S LaSalle St Chicago IL 60603

FENNELLY, LEO C., lawyer; b. N.Y.C., 1897; A.B., Manhattan Coll., 1919; LL.B., Fordham U., 1922. Admitted to N.Y. bar, 1922; now mem. Fennelly, Douglas, Eagan, Nager & Voohees; asst. U.S. atty., 1934-39; spl. asst. to atty. gen. U.S. 1939-40. Mem. Assn. Bar City N.Y. (jud. com. 1950-52, exec. com. 1953—). Office: 20 Exchange Pl New York City NY 10005

FENNER, DARWIN SCHRIEVER, investment banker, broker; b. New Orleans, 1908; s. Charles E. and Virginia (Shriever) F.; grad. Tulane U., 1929; m. Flora Hardie, 1931; children—Darwin Charles, James Hardie, Flora Sanders (Mrs. Ronald J. French). Clerk for firm Fenner & Beane, 1929-34, partner, 1934- 41; partner Merrill Lynch, Pierce, Fenner & Beane, 1941-57; v.p., dir. Merrill Lynch, Pierce, Fenner & Smith, 1957-70, sr. v.p., 1964-70, also dir. Bd. adminstrs. Tulane U., 1953—, chmn., 1964-69; chmn. Health Edn. Authority La., 1968-71; hon. chmn. New Orleans Ednl. TV Found. Mem. Kappa Alpha. Served as Maj. AC, AUS, 1942- 46. Home: 6123 Marquette Pl New Orleans LA 70118 Office: 1010 Common St New Orleans LA 70112

FENNER, MILDRED SANDISON (Mrs. H. Wolcott Fenner), editor; b. Huntsville, Mo., July 9, 1910; d. John Forte and Minnielee (Holliday) Sandison; B.S., Northwest Mo. State Tchrs. Coll., 1931; M.A., George Washington U., 1938, Ed.D., 1942; Litt.D., Glassboro State Coll., 1962; m. H. Wolcott Fenner, Feb. 1, 1940. With N.E.A. Jour. (now Today's Education), 1931—, beginning as mem. staff. successively asst. editor, mng. editor, 1931- 54, editor, 1954—. Mem. Am. Assn. U. Women, Edn. Press Assn. Am. (sec.-treas. 1951-60; rep. Internat. Ednl. Editors' Workshop, Manila, summer 1956, Amsterdam 1961), Nat. Council Administrv. Women in Edn., Am. Newspaper Women's Club, Horace Mann League (ist woman mem., 2d v.p.), Nat. Communications Club, Pi Lambda Theta, Sigma Sigma Sigma. Methodist. Author: (with Eleanor Fishburn) Pioneer American Educators, 1944; NEA History, 1945; (with H.W. Fenner) The Circus: Lure and Legend, 1970; also articles in field. Home: 530 N St SW Washington DC 20024 Office: 1201 16th St Washington DC 20036

FENNINGER, LEONARD DAVIS, med. educator; b. Hampton, Va., Oct. 3, 1917; s. Laurence and Natalie Ayers (Bourne) F.; A.B., Princeton, 1938; M.D., U. Rochester, 1943; m. Jane Thomas, Mar. 20, 1943; children—David McClure, Anne Randolph. Asso. dean, prof. health services, chmn. dept., prof. medicine U. Rochester, also physician, med. dir., Strong Meml. Hosp., 1961-67; dir. Bur. of Health Manpower, USPHS, 1967-69; asso. dir. for health manpower NIH, 1969—. Diplomate Am. Bd. Internal Medicine. Home: 1430 Woodacre Dr McLean VA 22101 Office: NIH 9000 Rockville Pike Bethesda MD 20014

FENNO, HAROLD O., banker; b. Berlin, N.D., Mar. 29, 1919; s. Edmond Wesley and Chattie (Nichols) F.; m. Ruby Roberta Rockwood, June 18, 1942, children—Gordon Earl, Donald Wayne, Charles Douglas. Asst. cashier James River Nat. Bank, Jamestown, N.D., 1939-43; nat. bank examiner, 1943-49; with Marine Bancorp., Seattle, 1949—, v.p., auditor, 1962—; v.p., auditor Nat. Bank Commerce, Seattle, 1963-69, v.p., gen. auditor, 1969—; gen. auditor Internat. Bank Commerce, Seattle, 1963—. Pres. Puget Sound Conf. Bank Auditors and Comptrollers, 1959-69; bd. govs. Seattle chpt. Inst. Internal Auditors, 1966-67; mem. audit commn. Bank Adminstrn. Inst. Home: 4202 NE 103d Pl Seattle WA 98125 Office: Marine Bancorp 2d Av and Spring St Seattle WA 98125

FENSKE, MERRELL ROBERT, chem. engr.; b. Michigan City, Ind., June 5, 1904; s. William A. and Minna (Glassman) F.; A.B., De Pauw U., 1925, D.Sc., 1946; D.Sc., Mass. Inst. Tech., 1928. Research asso. Mass. Inst. Tech., 1928-29; asst. prof. chmn. engring. Pa. State U., 1929-34, asso. prof., 1934-36, prof., 1936—, in charge Petroleum Refining Lab., 1932, dir. Div. Indsl. Research, 1936-47, head dept. chem. engring., 1959-69; ofcl. investigator and cons. Nat. Def. Research Com., 1941-45; chmn. rev. com. div. chem. engring. Argonne Nat. Lab., 1962-63; cons. NACA, NASA, AEC, Argonne Nat. Lab.; mem. ad hoc com. chem. warfare and biol. warfare programs Dept. Def.; mem. U.S. nat. com. Seventh World Petroleum Congress; mem. air pollution subcom. Nat. Acad. Scis.-Nat. Acad. Engring. Environmental Studies Bd.; dir. Def. Research and Engring., USAF, Baruch Rubber Survey Com., 1942, Metallurgy Lab., U. Chgo., 1944-45. Recipient Naval Ordnance Devel. award, 1945, Certificate of Merit, OSRD, 1945; Nat. award Am. Soc. Lubrication Engrs., 1966; USAF Systems Command certificate of Merit. Fellow Am. Inst. Chemists, Inst. Petroleum (London) (Redwood medal 1964), Royal Soc. Arts; mem. Soc. Chem. Industry, Am. Soc. M.E., Am. Soc. Lubrication Engrs., A.A.A.S., Nat. Acad. Engring, Am. Assn. U. Profs., Am. Petroleum Inst., Am. Chem. Soc. (past chmn. div. indsl. and engring. chemistry), Am. Soc. Engring. Edn., Soc. Automotive Engrs., Am. Inst. Chem. Engrs., Am. Soc. Testing Materials, Phi Beta Kappa, Tau Beta Pi, Sigma Xi, Phi Lambda Upsilon, Sigma Pi Sigma, Alpha Chi Sigma, Alpha Tau Omega. Club: Chemists (N.Y.). Author chpts., tech. papers and various publs. Home: Box 202 State College PA 16801 ☆

FENSTER, MARVIN, mercantile co. exec.; b. Bklyn., Jan. 19, 1918; s. Isaac and Anna (Greenman) F.; A.B., Cornell U., 1938; LL.B., Columbia, 1941; m. Louise Rapoport, Nov. 13, 1954; children—Julie Rose, Mark Andrew. Admitted to N.Y. State bar, 1942; associated with firm Lauterstein, Spiller, Bergerman and Dannett, and successors, New York City, 1941-42, 46-48; atty. R. H. Macy & Co., Inc., N.Y.C., 1948-55, asst. sec., asst. gen. atty., 1955-60, sec., gen. atty., 1960-67, sr. v.p., general attorney, secretary, 1967-; sec., dir. Garden State Plaza Corp., 1960- -, Macy's Bank, 1960—. Served to 1st lt. AUS, 1942-46. Mem. Am. Bar Assn., Assn. Bar City N.Y., Am. Soc. Corporate Secretaries, Phi Epsilon Pi. Home: 535 E 86th St New York City NY 10028 Office: 151 W 34th St New York City NY 10001

FENSTER, SAUL, ednl. adminstr.; b. N.Y.C., Mar. 22, 1933; s. Samuel and Rose (Glass) F.; student Bklyn. Coll., 1949-51; B.Mech. Engring., City U. N.Y., 1953; M.S., Columbia, 1955; student N.Y. U., 1955-56; Ph.D. (Shell fellow 1957- 58), U. Mich., 1958; m. Roberta Schamis, Jan. 11, 1959; children—Deborah, Lisa, Jonathan. Lectr. mech. engring. City U. N.Y., 1953-56; teaching fellow engring. mechanics U. Mich., 1956-57, with univ. Research Inst., 1957-58; research engr. Sperry-Rand Corp., 1959- 62; prof. engring. Fairleigh Dickinson U., Teaneck, N.J., 1962—, chmn. dept. physics, 1962-63, chmn. dept. mech. engring., 1963-70, grad. adminstrv. asst. to dean, 1965-70, asso. dean, 1970-71, exec. asst. to pres., 1971—; cons., 1962—. Mem. Am. Soc. M.E., Am. Soc. Engring. Edn., Am. Assn. U. Profs., Sigma Xi, Pi Tau Sigma. Author: (with Wallace Arthur) Mechanics, 1969. Contbr. chpts. in books, tech. papers. Home: 524 Bernita Dr River Vale NJ 07675 Office: Fairleigh Dickinson Univ Rutherford NJ 07070

FENSTERMAKER, JOHN JOSEPH, wholesale drug co. exec.; b. Columbus, O., Feb. 27, 1918; s. Omar Raymond and F. Louise (Lashley) F.; B.S. in Bus. Adminstrn., Ohio State U., 1940; m. Lucy Satterlee Gay, July 10, 1940; 1 son, John Joseph. Salesman, Midland Mut. Life Ins. Co., Columbus, 1940-42; with Foremost- McKesson, Inc., and predecessor, 1942—, sr. v.p. drug marketing, 1967- -, also v.p.; dir. Pharm. Card System, Inc., Phoenix; occasional guest lectr. Coll. Pharmacy, U. Ill., also Bklyn. Coll. Pharmacy. Mem. 1st nat. marketing adv. council Dept. Commerce, 1967. Trustee Coll. Pharm. Scis., Columbia U. Served with AUS, 1942-45. Mem. Am. Pharm. Assn., Nat. Assn. Retail Druggists, Pharm. Advt. Club N.Y.C., Drug Chem. Allied Trades. Club: Board Room (N.Y.C.). Home: 400 E 56th St New York City NY 10021 Office: 155 E 44th St New York City NY 10017

FENSTERSTOCK, HOWARD WARREN, govt. ofc., lawyer; b. N.Y.C., Aug. 4, 1908; A.B., Coll. City N.Y., 1928; LL.B., Harvard, 1931; m. Elvera Stewart Johnson, June 22, 1946; 1 stepson, John Stewart Johnson. Admitted to N.Y. bar 1932; gen. practice law, N.Y.C., 1932-42, 47-49; asst. counsel-USAF div. Armed Services Renegotiation Bd., 1950-51; atty. Renegotiation Bd., 1951-52, asst. gen. counsel, 1953-56, gen. counsel, 1956—. Served from 1st lt. to lt. col. CWS, AUS, 1942-46; assigned as chmn. Chem. Warfare Price Adjustment Bd., 1945-46. Mem. Fed., Am. bar assns. Clubs: Nat. Press, Nat. Lawyers. Home: 2360 No Quincy St Arlington VA 22207 Office: Renegotiation Bd Washington DC 20446

FENTON, ALAN, artist; b. Cleve., July 29, 1927; s. Morris and Ethel (Beal) F.; B.F.A., Pratt Inst., 1959; student Art Students League, N.Y.C., 1956-57; m. Naomi J. Feigenbaum, July 31, 1955; children—Danielle D., David Efrem. Exhibited group shows Art U.S.A., N.Y.C., 1958, City Center, N.Y.C. (hon. mention), 1959, Am. Inst., Mexico City, 1965, Cleve. Sch. Art. 1950, New Sch., N.Y.C., 1958, N.Y. U., 1958; Mus. Art (1st prize 1960, 61), 1959-61, show San Francisco Mus. Art, 1963, Fed. Pavillion, N.Y. World's Fair, 1964, Larry Aldrich Mus., 1968, Light Show, Conn., 1968, Corcoran Gallery Art, Washington, 1970, Corcoran worldwide touring exhibit, 1971—; exhibited one man show Pace Gallery, N.Y.C., 1964; instr. Pratt Inst., N.Y.C., Housatonic State Coll., Stratford, Conn. Served with U.S. Mcht. Marine, World War II. Home: 408 Riverside Av Westport CT 06880 Studio: 333 Park Av S New York City NY 10010

FENTON, BEATRICE, sculptor; b. Phila., July 12, 1887; d. Thomas Hanover (M.D.) and Lizzie Spear (Remak) Fenton; ed. under governesses; art study, Sch. Indsl. Art, Phila., 1903-04, Pa. Acad. Fine Arts, 1904-11; 2 Cresson European scholarships, 1909,10; A.F.D., Moore Inst. Art, 1954. Principal works: Seaweed Fountain, Fairmount Park, Phila.; Fairy Fountain, Wister Woods, Phila.; bronze meml. tablet to Charles M. Schmitz, Acad. Music, Phila.; Eyre gold medal design Phila. Water Color Club: Nereid Fountain and Boy and Starfish Fountain, private estates; bust of Peter Moran, bust of Thomas H. Fenton and statuette of John F. Huneker, Phila. Art Club; bust of William Penn, Penn Club, Phila.; bust of Marjorie D. Martinet, Martinet Sch. of Art, Balt.; bust of I.P. Strittmater, M.D., Phila.; Wood-Music, Danby Park, Wilmington, Del.; gatepost figure Children's Hosp., Phila.; bust of Felix E. Schelling, U. Pa.; garden sculpture Bacchanale and Leaping Dolphin Fountain; Turner Meml. tablet, Johns Hopkins U.; Ariel Sun-Dial, Shakespeare Garden, U. Pa.; fountain figure Brookgreen Gardens, S.C.; Lizette Woodworth Reese meml. tablet, Pratt Library, Balt.; mem. drinking fountain, Hahnemann Med. Coll., Phila.; meml. sun-dial, Rittenhouse Square, Phila.; two fish fountains, Fairmount Park, Phila. Mem. faculty Moore Inst., ret. Fellow Nat. Sculpture Soc., Fellowship of Pa. Acad. Fine Arts. Winner of McCellan anatomy prize, 1907; Edmund Stewardson prize for sculpture, 1908 (both Pa. Acad. Fine Arts); hon. mention Panama-Pacific Internat. Expn., 1915, Plastic Club, 1916; George D. Widener meml. gold medal Pa. Acad. Fine Arts, 1922; Fellowship of Pa. Acad. Fine Arts prize, 1922; silver medal Plastic Club, 1922; bronze medal Sesquicentennial Internat. Expn., Phila., 1926; winning design for Congl. medal awarded Albin W. Barkley, 1950; hon. mention Woodmere Art Gallery, Chestnut Hill, Pa., 1951, DaVinci Alliance Bronze medal, 1954; Bust Joseph Moore, 1954; Violet Oakley Meml. prize, Woodmere Art Gallery 1962; Percy M. Owens Mem. award, 1967. Club: Art Alliance. Address: 621 Westview St Philadelphia PA 19119 Studio: 311 W Duval St Philadelphia PA 19144

FENTON, EDWARD A., assn. exec.; b. N.Y.C., Nov. 17, 1925; s. Philip and Rose (Poppick) F.; B.Mech. Engring., Coll. City N.Y., 1947; M. Metall. Engring., Polytech. Inst. Bklyn., 1951; m. Elaine B. Schlam, June 27, 1953; children—Ellen, Eliot. Various positions in metall. field in shipbldg., r.r., oil refinery, chem. plant, aircraft industry, 1947-54; mem. staff Am. Welding Soc., Inc., N.Y.C., 1954—, tech. dir., 1957-59, exec. dir., sec., 1969—; cons. engr. industry and govt., 1959—. Author: Marks Handbook for Mechanical Engineers, 1967; Index of Standards From 23 Nations, 1968; The AWS Bibliographies, 1968; also articles; contbr. Book of Knowledge, Ency. Brittanica Jr., World Book, Ency. Internat. Home: 7190 S W 99th St Miami FL 33156 Office: 2501 N W 7th St Miami FL 33125

FENTON, GERALD BATTELLE, business exec.; b. Buffalo, Dec. 8, 1892; s. Clarence Milton and Cora (Battelle) F. student Trinity Sch., N.Y.C., Tome Sch., Ft. Deposit, Md.; student mining engring., Ohio State U.; m. Lelia Timberman, Jan. 14, 1939; one dau., Eleanor (Mrs. Raymond Justus Hanks), step son, Wilbur Alan Smith. With Cherokee Mining & Smelting Co., Pittsburg, Kan., 1915-16, Am. Rolling Mill Co., Columbus, O., 1920-28; treas. Battelle Investment Corp., 1929-63, pres., 1954—; treas. Battelle Devel. Corp., 1949-63; dir. Columbus & So. Ohio Electric Co. Past pres. Columbus Gallery Fine Arts; mem. governing com. Columbus Found., 1955—; trustee Wilson Charitable Found., Columbus; dir. Children's Hosp., Columbus, Children's Mental Health Center, 1951-54; trustee Battelle Meml. Inst., 1925—, treas., 1949-63, vice chmn., 1953—; trustee Harding Hosp., Inc., Worthington, O. Served as capt. 130th F.A., 35th Div. A.E.F., 1916-19. Mem. Sigma Chi. Conglist. Clubs: University; Rocky Fork Hunt and Country; Review; Castalia Trout. Home: 3545 Mann Rd Blacklick OH 43004 Office: 37 W Broad St Columbus OH 43215

FENTON, LEWIS LOWRY, lawyer; b. Palo Alto, Cal., Aug. 20, 1925; s. Norman and Jessie (Chase) F.; B.A., Stanford, 1948, LL.B., 1950; m. Ruth D. Phillips, July 5, 1954; children—Lewis Lowry, Juanita Chase, Daniel Norman. Admitted to Cal. bar, 1950; atty. Cal. Dept. Pub. Works, 1950-52, mem. firm Hoge, Fenton, Jones & Appel, Monterey and San Jose, 1952—. Mem. bldg. com. Community Hosp. Monterey Peninsula, Carmel, 1961-62; found. dir. Monterey Jazz Festival, 1958. Trustee Monterey Peninsula Coll. (pres. 1971), Monterey Inst. Fgn. Studies; pres. trustees York Sch., Monterey, Cal. Served to 2d lt. USAAF, 1942-46. Fellow Am. Coll. Trial Lawyers; mem. Assn. Def. Counsel (pres. 1969), Monterey Bar Assn. (pres. 1963). Episcopalian (vestryman, sr. warden 1956-58). Home: 20 El Caminito Del Norte Monterey CA 93940 Office: PO Box 791 Monterey CA 93940

FENTON, MARTIN, stock broker; b. Washington, Jan. 7, 1908; s. Charles Wendell and Alice (Rochester) F.; grad. St. Mark's Sch., 1925; A.B., Yale, 1929; m. Katharine Elinor Douglas, Oct. 9, 1931; children—Alice D. (Mrs. William C. Kuhns), Martin, Wendell, Edith Douglas (Mrs. Roger Tuckerman), Prudence. Trainee, M.W. Kellogg Co., 1930-31; auditor Nat. City Bank, N.Y.C., 1931-33; mgr. Laird & Co., N.Y.C., 1933-41; partner Laird & Co. (now Laird, Inc.), Wilmington, Del., 1946-56, pres. corp., 1956-64, chmn., 1964-67, now dir.; dir. Christiana Oil Corp., Rollins, Inc., Rollins Internat. Inc., Bank Del.; Ltd. Partner Fenton & Co., Los Angeles. Pres. Orange St. Found. Served to lt. col. USMCR, 1941- 46. Decorated Bronze Star. Episcopalian. Clubs: Cypress Point (Pebbe Beach, Cal.); Wilmington Country (pres. 1957-62), Wilmington; Yale (N.Y.C.). Home: Greenville Wilmington DE 19807 Office: Wilmington Trust Bldg Wilmington DE 19801

FENTON, MERYL MYRON, physician; b. Toronto, Can., Dec. 27, 1908; s. Julius and Rebecca (Ghinasin) F.; B.M., Wayne State U., 1931, M.D., 1932; m. Ruth Colton, Sept. 18, 1938; childrenStuart Victor, Glorianne (Mrs. Walter Siporin), Jerome L. Intern Detroit City Receiving Hosp., 1931-32; resident pediatrics Buffalo Children's Hosp., 1932-33; instr. dep. pediatrics and sensitization U. Mich., 1933-37, chief pediatric sensitization dept., 1938-40; instr. pediatrics Univ. Hosp., Ann Arbor, Mich., 1933-37; asst. prof. Wayne State U.; pvt. practice of medicine, specializing allergy, 1937—; attending staff allergy sect. Sinai Hospital, Detroit; courtesy staff Grace Hosp., Detroit; cons. Brent Hosp., Detroit. Served from capt. to maj., AUS, 1942-45. Fellow Am. Coll. Allergists (past regent, past sec., past 2d vice pres.), A.C.P., Am. Coll. Chest Physicians, Am. Acad. Allergy, Internat. Coll. Alergology, Am. Acad. Pediatrics; mem. N.Y. Acad. Scis., A.M.A., Mich. Allergy Soc. (past pres.), Mich., Wayne County, Maimonides (past pres.) med. socs., Pan Am. Med. Assn. (diplomate), Mexican (hon.), W. Coast allergy socs., Mich. Thoracic Soc., La Sociedad Dealergia y Ciencias (hon.), Phi Lambda Kappa (past pres. Detroit chpt.). Mason (32). Contbr. med. jours. Home: 333 Covington Dr Detroit MI 48203 Office: 15901 W Nine Mile Rd Southfield MI 48075

FENTON, STUART W., educator; b. London, Ont., Can., Apr. 29, 1922; s. William Seabright and Marjorie St. Helene (Bate) F.; B.Sc., Queen's U., 1945, M.S., 1946; Ph.D., Mass. Inst. Tech., 1950; m. Eleanor M. Salisbury, Nov. 11, 1961. Chmn. dept. chemistry, U. Minn. Mem. Am. Chem. Soc., A.A.A.S., Chem. Soc. London, Sigma Xi. Mason. Home: 36 Eagle Ridge Rd North Oaks St Paul MN 55110 Office: Dept Chemistry U Minnesota Minneapolis MN 55455

FENTON, THOMAS EDGAR, Jr., lawyer; b. Orange, N.J., July 23, 1934; s. Thomas Edgar and Maude (Gegenheimer) F.; B.A., Trinity Coll., 1956; LL.B., N.Y.U., 1961; m. Nancy Keahi Iaea, Dec. 18, 1965; children—Tercia, Porcia, Marcia, Jaylen, Thomas Edgar III, Helen Anna. Admitted to Alaska bar, 1962; practice in Ketchikan, 1964, Fairbanks, 1965—; asst. atty. gen. Alaska, 1962-63; dist. atty., Ketchikan, 1964, Fairbanks, 1965—; atty. Alaskan Native Land Claims, 1966—. Mem. Democratic Party Dist. Com., 1966—, parliamentarian, 1970. Pres. bd. Hospitality House, Fairbanks, Fairbanks Alcoholic Rehab. Center; trustee North Star Childrens Home, Dot Lake, Alaska. Mem. Alaska Bar Assn., Am. Civil Liberties Union, Covenant Fellowship. Episcopalian. Home: 276 Yankovich Rd Fairbanks AK 99701 Office: Nerland Bldg Fairbanks AK 99701

FENTON, THOMAS TRAIL, journalist; b. Balt., Apr. 8, 1930; s. Matthew Clark and Beatrice (Trail) F.; A.B., Dartmouth, 1952; m. Simone France Marie Lopes-Curval, Jan. 10, 1959; children—Ariane France, Thomas Trail. Mem. staff Balt. Sun, 1961-70, chief Rome bur., 1966-68, chief Paris bur., 1968-70; reporter-producer CBS News Rome Bur., 1970—. Served with USN, 1952-61. Club: Overseas Press (N.Y.C.). Home: Via Colli della Farnesina 144 Rome Italy

FENTON, WILLIAM NELSON, anthropologist; b. New Rochelle, N.Y., 1908; s. John William and Anna Belle (Nourse) F.; A.B., Dartmouth, 1931; Ph.D., Yale, 1937; LL.D., Hartwick Coll. 1968; m. Olive Louise Ortwine, 1936; children—Elizabeth (Mrs. E. Mayo Snyder), John W., Douglas Bruce, Harry (dec.). Community worker, U.S. Indian Service, N.Y. Agency, in charge Tonawanda and Tuscarora Reservations, 1935-37; instr. sociology and anthropology St. Lawrence U., 1937-38, asst. prof., 1938-39; instr. (summers) Alleghany Sch. Natural History, U. Buffalo, 1938, St. Lawrence U., 1940; vis. prof. Northwestern U., 1947, U. Mich., 1951, U. Ariz., 1963; lectr. Johns Hopkins, 1949-50, Cath. U. Am., 1950-51; asso. anthropologist Bur. Am. Ethnology, Smithsonian Instn., 1939-43, sr. ethnologist, 1943-51, mem. and sec., war com., 1942-44, research asso. Ethnogeographic Bd., 1943- 45; exec. sec. div. anthropology and psychology NRC, 1952-54; dir., asst. commnr. N.Y. State Mus. and Sci. Service, 1954-68; research prof. anthropology State U. N.Y., Albany, 1968—. U.S. del. IV Internat. Congress Anthrop. and Ethnol. Sci., Vienna, 1952; mem. Am. Delegation to VII Internat. Congress on Anthropology and Ethnology, Moscow, 1964. Ethnol. field trips to Iroquois Indian Reservations. Mem. com. on Lang. and Areal Implications, Commn. on Implication of Armed Service Ednl. Programs, Am. Council Edn., 1946. Recipient Cornplanter medal for Iroquois Research, 1965. Fellow A.A.A.S., Royal Anthrop. Inst., Am. Folklore Soc. (pres. 1959-60), Am. Anthrop. Assn. (exec. bd. 1963-65), Am. Ethnol. Soc. (pres. 1959), Am. Indian Ethnohistoric Conf. (pres. 1962), Anthrop. Soc. Washington (former sec., v.p., pres.), Keene Valley Library Assn. (trustee 1970—), Sigma Xi. Episcopalian. Author: Area Studies in American Universities, 1947; Iroquois Eagle Dance, 1953; Indian and White Relations to 1830, 1957; Parker on The Iroquois, 1968; also numerous articles. Home: 7 N Helderberg Pkwy Slingerlands NY 12159 (summer) Keene Valley NY 12943 Office: Dept Anthropology State U N Y Albany NY 12203

FENTRESS, CALVIN, Jr., ins. co. exec.; b. Hubbard Woods, Ill., Oct. 30, 1907; s. Calvin and Paulina Stearns (Lyon) F.; grad. Berkshire Sch., 1926, Princeton, 1931; m. Frances E. Wood, Oct. 1931; children—Audrey, Calvin III, Mary Hardwick, Robert Wood. With Lee, Higginson & Co., investments, 1931-32; with Allstate Ins. Co. and Allstate Fire Ins. Co., 1932—, with investment dept., 1932-36, treas., 1937, v.p. and treas., 1938, exec. v.p. and sec., 1940, pres. and mem. finance com., 1941, pres. and treas., 1944-45, pres., 1945-57, chmn. 1957-66, chmn. finance com., 1966—, also dir.; chmn. finance com., dir. Allstate Life Ins. Co., Allstate Enterprises Inc.; chmn. bd. Baker, Fentress & Co.; dir. Continental Ill. Nat. Bank and Trust Co. of Chgo., No. Ill. Gas Co., Conill Corp., Sears Roebuck & Co. Clubs: Commonwealth, Chicago, Commercial (Chgo.); Onwentsia (Lake Forest, Ill.). Home: 555 Crab Tree Lane Lake Forest IL 60045 Office: 7447 Skokie Blvd Skokie IL 60076

FENWICK-SMITH, BRIAN, indsl. machinery co. exec.; b. Hull, Eng., Aug. 21, 1935; s. John Nicholson and Daisy Ethel (Day) Smith; M.A. in Econs. and Law, St. John's Coll., Cambridge (Eng.) U., 1959; m. Diemut Schoewitz, Sept. 25, 1959; children—Robert, Andrea, Nicola. Articled clk. Peat, Marwick, Mitchell & Co., London, 1959-63; accountant Coulter Electronics Ltd., St. Albans, Eng., 1963-64; chief accountant, sec. Transport Equipment (Thornycroft) Ltd., Basingstoke, Eng., 1964-66; dir. finance USM Corp. (Internat.), Lausanne, Switzerland, 1966-70; controller USM Corp., Boston, 1970—. Mem. Inst. Charted Accountants Eng. and Wales (asso.), Financial Execs. Inst. Home: 90 Gammons Rd Cohasset MA 02025 Office: 140 Federal St Boston MA 02107

FENZI, WARREN EMANUELE, mining co. exec.; b. Santa Barbara, Cal., Aug. 4, 1915; s. Camillo and Dorothy (Redfield) F.; B.S. in Civil Engring., Cal. Inst. Tech., 1937; m. Eleanor Leeds, July 12, 1940; children—Charles C., Louise R., Warren S., Joan F. and David L. (twins). With Phelps Dodge Corp., 1937—, asst. to v.p., gen. mgr. Western div., Douglas, Ariz., 1957-59. asst. to pres., N.Y.C., 1959-62, v.p., 1962-66, exec. v.p., 1966—, dir. Served with USNR, 1944-46; PTO. Mem. Am. Inst. Mining Engrs. Home: 30 Old Post Rd Rye NY 10580 Office: 300 Park Av New York City NY 10022

FEOKTISKOV, KONSTANTIN PETROVICH, Russian cosmonaut; b. Voronezh, Feb. 7, 1926; grad. Bauman Higher Tech. Sch., Moscow, 1949; postgrad. student, Moscow, 1952-55. Intelligence agt., 1941; captured by Germans; engr. factory in Zlatoust, 1949-51; asso. various research establishments, 1955; trainer of cosmonauts, 1961; research physicist aboard space ship Voskhod, 1964. Named Hero of Socialist Labor, 1964; decorated Order Lenin. Gold Star medal, Order Red Banner of Labor (2), medal For Victory Over Germany, Tsiolkovsky Gold medal. Address: care Presidium Acad. Scis. USSR, Lenin Prospekt 14, Moscow, USSR.*

FERBER, DANIEL ARTHUR, coll. dean; b. Painesville, O., Jan. 4, 1929; s. Herman G. and Eva (Eckert) F.; B.A., Wabash Coll., 1951; M.A. (All-U fellow), Ind. U., 1959, Ph.D., 1962; m. Dorothy Anne Reasoner, Nov. 19, 1950; children—Daniel Mark, Matthew Arthur. Pitcher, N.Y. Yankees Baseball System, 1950-52; grad. teaching asst. English, Ind. U., 1952-53, head counselor grad. residence center, 1954, dir. men's reisdence halls, 1954-59, asso. dir. men's and women's residence halls, 1959-62; asso. dir. devel. U. Pitts., 1962-63; dir. devel. and spl. asst. to pres. N.H., 1963-67; dean acad. affairs Gustavus Adolphus Coll., St. Peter, Minn., 1967-70, v.p. acad. adminstrn., dean of Coll., 1970—. Served with USNR, 1945-46. Mem. Nat. Assn. Student Personnel, Am. Personnel and Guidance Assn., Am. Coll. Pub. Relations Assn., N. Central Assn. Acad. Deans, Am. Council Learned Socs., Blue Key, Phi Gamma Delta. Club: Sphinx. Contbr. articles profl. jours. Home: 841 Lower Johnson Circle St Peter MN 56082

FERBER, ROBERT statistician, market analyst, economist, educator; b. N.Y.C., Feb. 13, 1922; s. Samuel and Dinah (Rosenthal) F.; B.S., City Coll. N.Y., 1942; M.A., U. Chgo., 1945, Ph.D., 1951; postgrad. Columbia U. 1946-47; m. Marianne Abeles, Aug. 18, 1946; children—Don Richard, Ellen J. Chief statistician Indsl. Surveys Co., Chgo., 1943-45; economist, statistician I. Devegh Co., N.Y.C., 1945-47; research asso. prof., bur. econ. and bus. research, dept. econs. U. Ill., 1948-57, research prof. bur. econ. and bus. research, and prof. dept. econs., 1957—, prof. dept marketing, dir. survey research lab., 1965—. Recipient award for year's outstanding contbn. to field of marketing Am. Marketing Assn., 1950; named to Hall of Fame in Distbn., 1964. Mem. Am. Statis. Assn., Am. Econ. Assn., Am. Marketing Assn. (pres. 1969-70), Econmetric Soc., Inst. Math. Statistics. Author: Statistical Techniques in Market Research, 1949; A Study of Agregate Consumption Functions; The Railroad Shippers' Forecasts; Factors Influencing Durable Food Purchases: A Basic Bibliography on Market Reasearch (with H.G. Wales); Collecting Financial Data by Consumer Panel Techniques; (with P.J. Verdoorn) Research Methods in Economics and Business, 1962; (with D.F. Blankertz, S.F. Hollander, Jr.) Marketing Research; also articles in research jours. Editor Marketing Research-Selected Literature (with H.G. Wales) 1951; editor Jour. Marketing Research, 1964-69; editor applications sect. Jour. Am. Statis. Assn., 1968—, coordinating editor, 1969—. 606 S Western Av Champaign IL 61820

FERDERBER, JOSEPH, electronics co. exec.; b. Cleve., Oct. 23, 1919; s. Andrew and Anna (Yurkovich) F.; B.S. in Elec. Engring., Case Inst. Tech., 1942; postgrad. Syracuse U., 1945-46; grad. exec. program U. Cal. at Los Angeles, 1958; m. Georgia Lucille Pesek, Sept. 26, 1942 (div. Jan. 1970); children—Lawrence Joseph, Julie Ann, Michael James. Test engr. Gen. Electric Co., Syracuse, N.Y., 1943-44, head test, 1944-46, asst. gen. head test, 1946-48, asst. gen. head inspection, 1948-49; chief prodn. test Hughes Aircraft Co., Culver City, Cal., 1949-50, supt. assembly, 1950- 52, mgr., El Segundo, Cal., 1956-66, v.p. mfg., 1966—, mem. policy bd., 1956—, v.p., 1962—. Bd. dirs. Santa Monica (Cal.) Sheltered Workshop, v.p., 1958-59. Mem. El Segundo C. of C., Western Electronics Mfrs. Assn. (dir. 1963), Sigma Xi, Eta Kappa Nu, Tau Beta Pi. Unitarian (dir., treas.). Home: 7607 St Bernard St Playa del Rey CA 90291 Office: Hughes Aircraft Co Culver City CA 90230

FERDINAND, SISTER MARY, hosp. adminstr.; b. Pitts., Nov. 29, 1906; d. Thomas and Jane (Wherthey) Clark; Ed.D., Duquesne U., 1956. Joined Sisters of Mercy, 1924; tchr. elementary schs., 1927-31; admissions officer Mercy Hosp., Pitts., 1931- 41, bus. mgr., 1941-47, adminstr., 1953—; dir. orgnl. programs St. Paul's Orphanage, Pitts., 1947-53, corporator, 1960—. Mem. rep. com. hosp. adminstrs. Hosp. Planning Assn. Allegheny County, 1960—; mem. nat. tech. adv. com. for devel. pharmacy technicians, div. vocational edn. U. Cal. Trustee Mt. Mercy Coll. Recipient citation for contbn. in field of health to Pitts. community Sun- Telegraph, 1958. Fellow Am. Coll. Hosp. Adminstrs.; mem. Pa. Hosp. Assn. (pres. 1969—, dir. 1970), Hosp. Council Western Pa. (sec., exec. com.), Urban League, Pa. Conf. Catholic Hosps. (sec.), N.A.A.C.P., Am. Mgmt. Assn. Address: 1400-30 Locust St Pittsburgh PA 15219

FEREBEE, STEPHEN SCOTT, Jr., architect; b. Detroit, July 30, 1921; s. Stephen Scott and Caroline (Cheatham) F.; B.Arch. Engring., N.C. State U., 1948; m. Mary Elizabeth Cooper, July 7, 1945; children—Scott III, John, Caroline. Job capt. A.G. Odell, Jr. & Assos., Architects, Charlotte, N.C., 1948-53; partner Higgins & Ferebee, Architects, Charlotte, 1953-59, Ferebee & Walters, Architects, 1959-64; pres. Ferebee, Walters & Assos., Architects/Engrs./Planners, Charlotte, 1964—; dir. Prodn. Systems for Architects and Engrs., Inc., Chgo., 1969—. Pres. N.C. Design Found., 1966-68. Served to capt., 101st Airborne Div., AUS, 1942-46; comdg. gen. 108th Div. (tng.), Charlotte. Decorated Bronze Star, medal, Purple Heart; Croix de Guerre (France and Belgium). Fellow A.I.A. (pres. N.C. 1964 nat. 1st v.p. 1972 chmn. commn. profl. practice 1971), Phi Kappa Phi. Methodist (past chmn. ofcl. bd.). Rotarian. Project have include Tarrytown Mall, Rocky Mount, N.C., 1963-68; cafeteria for U. N.C. at Charlotte, 1969; Raintree Village Community Plan, Charlotte, 1970. Home: 2329 Rock Creek Dr Charlotte NC 28211 Office: 4037 E Independence Blvd Charlotte NC 28205

FERENCE, MICHAEL Jr., physicist; b. Whiting, Ind., Nov. 6, 1911; s. Michael and Ann (Soroka) F.; B.S., U. Chgo., 1933, M.A., 1934, Ph.D., 1936; Dr. Sci. (hon.), Kenyon Coll.; m. Margaret W. Wilfinger, June 19, 1937; children—Lois Ann, Carol Jane, Michele Jean, Michael III, Richard Henry. Instr. physics U. Chgo., 1937-40, asst. prof., 1940-44, asso. prof., 1944-46; civilian cons. Air Force, 1943-46; chief meterol. br. Sig-Corps Eng. Labs., Evans Sig. Lab., 1946-48, chief sci., 1948-51, tech. dir., 1951-53; chief sci. sci. lab. Ford Motor Co., 1953-54, asso. dir., 1954-56, dir., 1957—, exec. dir. sci. lab., 1959-62, v.p. research, 1962—; trustee Rand Corp. Mem. govs. sci. adv. board, Mich.; adv. group weather modification NSF; mem. com. atmospheric scis., tech. panel earth satellite program Nat. Acad. Scis.; research panel Signal Corps. Research and Devel. Adv. Council; mem. President's Air Quality Adv. Bd. mem. Pres.'s Sci. Adv. Com. Trustee Argonne Univs. Assn., Case Western Res. U., Carnegie Instn.; bd. govs. Wayne State U.; bd. dirs. Metal Properties Council. Recipient Quantrell prize U. Chgo., 1943; exceptional civilian service award U.S. Army, 1953. Fellow I.E.E.E.; mem. Nat. Acad. Scis. (geophysics research bd.), Am. Phys. Soc., Soc. Automotive Engrs., Nat. Acad. Engrs., Meteorol. Soc., Geophys. Union, Phi Beta Kappa, Sigma Xi, Club: Cosmos (Washington). Author: Analytical and Experimental Physics, rev. edit., 1957. Contbr. articles tech. jours. Home: 24 Shady Hollow Dearborn MI 48124 Office: Ford Motor Co P O Box 2053 Dearborn MI 48121

FERENDINO, ANDREW JOHN, architect; b. N.Y.C., Apr. 4, 1909; s. John Andrew and Clare (Galatis) F.; B.S. in Arch., U. Fla., 1933; m. Ruth Prevatt, Feb. 4, 1939 (dec.); children—Clare Esther (Mrs. Gerald Gaffney), John Bryant. Architect Russell Pancoast, Coral Gables, Fla., 1936-42; sr. partner Russell T. Pancoast & Assos., 1942-68; partner-in-charge financial adminstrv. design Ferendino, Grafton & Pancoast, Inc., Coral Gables, 1970—, pres., 1970—, chmn. partnership, 1968—; pres. Douglas Village Corp., Miami, Fla., 1968—; chmn. bd. South Bayshore Corp., 1956—. Mem. Dade County Bldg. Code Com., 1946, City of Miami Long Term Capital Improvement Com., 1948-50, Slum Clearance Com., 1951, Citizens Assessment Adv. Com., 1959. Bd. dirs. Florence Crittenton Home of Dade County, Dade chpt. Nat. Found. March of Dimes. Registered profl. architect, Fla. Fellow A.I.A. (pres. Fla. chpt. 1949); mem. Fla. Assn. Architects (bd. dirs. 1959). Contbr. articles profl. jours. Prin. works include Marine Stadium, Miami, 1965, Miami-Dade Jr. Coll., 1963-70, Miami Beach First Nat. Bank, 1970, Mailman Child Devel. Center, U. Miami, 1970. Home: 800 Douglas Rd Coral Gables FL 33134

FERGENSON, A. LEON, cable co. exec.; b. Fitchburg, Mass., Oct. 10, 1912; s. Harry and Lena (Cronson) F.; B.S., U. Pa., 1932; LL.B., Columbia, 1936; m. Constance Elinor Friend, Nov. 9, 1941; children—Arthur F., Anne F. Admitted N.Y. State bar, 1937; pvt. practice law, 1936-46; v.p., gen. counsel Gen. Cable Corp., 1946-66, pres., chief exec. officer, 1966—, chmn. bd., 1971—, also dir., mem. exec. com.; dir. Aluminium Bahrain, Ceat, S.p.A., Italy, Greater N.Y. Mut. Ins. Co., Irving Trust Co., LCA Corp., Phillips Cables Ltd. (Can.), Sun Chem. Corp., W.P. R.R. Co.; trustee Harlem Savs. Bank; adv. dir. Energy Fund, Inc. Bd. dirs. N.Y. div. Am. Cancer Soc. Mem. Assn. Bar City N.Y., Nat. Elec. Mfrs. Assn. (bd. govs.). Clubs: Lotos, Canadian, University (N.Y.C.). Editor Columbia Law Rev., 1934-35. Home: 7 Meadow Pl Larchmont NY 10538 Office: 730 3d Av New York City NY 10017

FERGUS, JOHN CORWIN, automotive exec.; b. Columbus, O., Sept. 18, 1920; s. Corwin A. and Edith (Hoe) F.; A.B., Swarthmore Coll., 1942; F.A.L.S., U. Ill., 1944; J.D., Columbia, 1948; m. Elizabeth D. Owen, June 12, 1948; children—Deborah E., John Corwin, II, Elizabeth F. Admitted to (state?) Ohio bar, 1949; asso. Drugan & Gingher, 1949-51; partner Fergus & Fisher, 1951-55; exec. v.p. Midwestern VW Corp., 1955-60; chmn. bd. dirs. Midvo, Inc., Dublin, O., 1960—; dir. Park Fed. Savs. & Loan Assn., City Nat. Bank & Trust Co., G.O. Corp.; pres., dir. Underwriters Investment Corp. Trustee Central Ohio council Boy Scouts Am., 1967—. Trustee Children's Hosp. Columbus, 1966—, Columbus Gallery Fine Arts, 1971—. Served to 1st lt., AUS, 1942-46. Mem. Columbus Bar Assn., Columbus Area C. of C. (trustee), Episcopalian (vestryman). Mason. Clubs: Kiwanis, Columbus Athletic, Scioto Country (Columbus); Little Traverse Yacht, Wequetonsing Golf (Harbor Springs, Mich.); Hillsboro (Pompano Beach, Fla.); Grosse Point (Mich.) Yacht; North American Yacht Racing Union (N.Y.C.). Home: 4846 Riverside Dr Columbus OH 43220 Office: 5000 Post Rd Dublin OH 43017

FERGUSON, ALAN BLAKELY, brewery exec.; b. Lethbridge, Alberta, Can., Oct. 26, 1926; s. William Blakely and Helen (Sick) F.; B.A. in Econs., U. Wash., 1949; student Siebel Inst. Tech., Chgo., 1950; m. Marjorie Ann Horne, Nov. 6, 1945; children—Helene Louise, Duncan Blakely. Came to U.S., 1940, naturalized, 1945. Sales mgr., asst. gen. mgr. Sicks' Century Brewery, Seattle, 1950- 52; v.p., gen. mgr. Sicks' Rainier Brewing Co., 1952-64, pres., chief exec. officer, 1964—, also dir.; pres. chief exec. officer, 1964—, also mem. board of directors; pres. Rheinlander Brewing Co., Ranier Western, Inc.; dir. People's Nat. Bank. Dir. U.S. Brewers Assn., Wash. Brewers Inst. Seattle Met. chmn. Nat. Alliance Businessmen; v.p. Forward Thrust; co-chairman business advisory com. Seattle Opportunities Industrialization Center; treas. treas. Seattle Urban League, 1963; vice chairman pub. relations com. Seattle World's Fair, 1962. Trustee St. Nicholas Sch. for Girls, Greater Seattle, Inc., King County div. Am. Cancer Soc., Wash. State March of Dimes, Seattle Historical Soc., since 1965—. Served to 2d lt. AUS, 1944-46. Named Seattle's Outstanding Young Man of the Year, Seattle Jr. C. of C., 1961. Mem. Master Brewers Assn. Am., Seattle C. of C. (trustee). Episcopalian. Clubs: Rainier (trustee), Seattle Tennis, Washington Athletic (Seattle). Home: 4347 Hunts Point Rd NE Bellevue WA 98004 Office: 3100 Airport Way S Seattle WA 98134

FERGUSON, ALBERT BARNETT, Jr., physician, educator; b. N.Y.C., June 10, 1919; s. Albert Barnett and Vera (McCreary) F.; B.A., Dartmouth, 1940, student Med. Sch., 1940-41; M.D., Harvard, 1943; m. Louise Enequist, Nov. 20, 1943; children—Sanford, Bruce, Gary, Laurie. Surg. intern Childrens Hosp., Boston, 1943-44, resident pathology, 1947, resident orthopedic surgery, 1948-49, 50-51; surg. intern Peter Bent Brigham Hosp., Boston, 1946-47, resident orthopedic surgery, 1950; resident orthopedic surgery Mass. Gen. Hosp., 1949-50; asst. orthopedic surgery Harvard Med. Sch., Childrens Hosp. and Peter Bent Brighan Hosp., Boston, 1951-53; Silver prof. orthopedic surgery, chmn. dept. U. Pitts. Sch. Medicine, 1953—; cons. St. Francis Rehab. Inst., Green Country Hosp., St. Margarets Hosp.; mem. bd. exec. com. Blue Cross. Served to lt. (s.g.) USNR, 1943- 46. Mem. Am. Acad Orthopedic Surgery (exec. com. 1957, chairman of com. on undergraduate education), Am. Acad. Cerebral Palsy (program chmn. 1959), Orthopedic Research Soc. (program chmn. 1961), Am. Orthopedic Assn., (traveling fellow 1955, sec. 1968—), Am. Coll. Surgeons, Am. Acad. Pediatrics, Am. Acad. Neurology. Author: Orthopedic Surgery in Infancy and Childhood, 2d edit., 1963, 3d edit., 1968; Metals and Engineering in Bone and Joint Surgery, 1959; ABC's of Athletic Injuries and Conditioning, 1964. Home: 14 James Ross Pl Pittsburgh PA 15215

FERGUSON, ALLEN RICHMOND, economist; b. Pawtucket, R.I., Sept. 27, 1919; s. Duncan Hector Campbell and Margaret Esther (Allen) F.; A.B., Brown U., 1941, M.A., 1943; Ph.D., Harvard, 1949; m. Audrey Irene Mitscher, Jan. 12, 1944; children—Allen Richmond, Rondell Audrey, William Duncan, Duncan Campbell. Asst. prof. econs. U. Va., 1949-51; economist OPS, 1951, CIA, 1952; dep. head logistics dept. Rand Corp., 1953-58; dir. research Transp. Center, Northwestern U., 1958-60; sr. economist Rand Corp., 1960-63; coordinator internat. aviation State Dept., 1963-65; dep. mgr. systems econs. div., dir. policy research Planning Research Corp., 1965-71; ind. economist, 1971—; adviser Office Sec. Def., 1958-59; coordinator research Nat. Com. for Effective Congress, 1970—; cons. to Ho. Com. on Banking and Commerce, 1971. Served as 1st lt., pilot USAAF, 1943-45. Decorated D.F.C., Air medal with 2 oak leaf clusters. Mem. Am. Econ. Assn., Econometric Soc., Phi Beta Kappa. Author: The Economic Value of the United States Merchant Marine, 1960; also articles. Home and office: 7902 Park Overlook Dr Bethesda MD 20034

FERGUSON, ARTHUR WILLIAM, former headmaster; b. Norwich, Conn., June 18, 1901; s. John A. and Marie G. (Charbonneau) F.; B.A., Clark U., 1923; M.Ed., Harvard, 1935; m. Janette G. Beckett, June 30, 1925; children—Jane A. (Mrs. Russell E. Andrew), John B. Instr. English, Dean Acad., Franklin, Mass., 1923-27; sr. master, instr. English, Lawrence Acad., 1927-58. Headmaster, 1958-69, ret. Trustee Groton (Mass.) Pub. Library, Nashoba Community Hosp. Mem. Kappa Phi, Cum Laude Soc. Republican. Methodist. Home: Main St Groton MA 01450

FERGUSON, CARL EDWIN, govt. ofcl.; b. Butterfield, Mo., Sept. 18, 1916; s. William Horace and Flora Naomi (Hankins) F.; A.S., Monett (Mo.) Jr. Coll., 1936; B.S. in Agr., U. Mo., 1938, A.M., 1941, Ph.D. in Soil Sci., 1941; m. Faye Westmoreland, May 15, 1943; 1 son, Carl Edwin. Soil surveyor Dept. Agr., Tex., 1941-42; asst. prof. agronomy Tex. A. and M.U., 1946-48, asso. prof. 1948-51; gen. agronomist Office Spl. Rep. ECA, Paris, France, 1949-50; soil scientist Soil Conservation Service, Beltsville, Md., 1951-54; agronomist FOA, Bagdad, Iraq, 1954-56; research agronomist ICA, Port au Prince, Haiti, 1956-59; soils adviser land classification AID, Rabat, Morocco, 1959-62, agrl. officer, Dakar, Senegal, 1963-64, agr. specialist Africa Bur., Washington, 1964-69, food and agr. officer, Rabat, 1969—, mem. study teams, Guinea, 1959, Cameroon, 1961, Senegal River Basin, 1962, Congo, 1968. Served with AUS, 1942-46. Decorated Bronze Star. Fellow A.A.A.S.; mem. Am. Soc. Agronomy, Soil Sci. Soc. Am., Sigma Xi. Author glossaries; Glossaire de la Science des Sols-Anglais-Francais: Francais-Anglais, 1965; Petit Glossaire des Plants, Arbres et Fleurs—A Selactad List of Plants, Trees and Flowers, 2d rev. edit., 1969. Home: 14 Rue d'Azrou Rabat Morocco Office: USAID Am Embassy B P 120 Rabat Morocco

FERGUSON, CHARLES ALBERT, educator, linguist; b. Phila., July 6, 1921; s. Albert T. and Mary (Kohler) F.; A.B., U. Pa., 1942, M.A., 1943, Ph.D., 1945; grad. student Dropsie Coll., Columbia; m. Joanne J. Eichmuller, Sept. 16, 1944 (div. May 1962); children—Lisa Joanna, Christina Mary. Instr. langs. U. Pa., 1943-46; sci. linguist Fgn. Service Inst., State Dept., Washington and Beirut, Lebanon, 1946-55; lectr. Arabic, Georgetown U. 1951-53, linguistics Harvard Center Middle Eastern Studies, 1955-59; vis. prof. linguistics Georgetown U., summer 1955, Deccan Coll., Poona, India, summer 1956; U. Mich., summer, 1960, U. Wash., summers 1962, 63, acad. yr., 1964-65, Ind. U., summer 1964; dir. Fgn. Service Inst. Area and Lang. Sch., Beirut, 1953-55; dir. Center Applied Linguistics, Washington, 1959-66; prof. linguistics, chmn. com. linguistics Stanford, 1967—; cons. to govt. and founds., 1955—. Chmn. com. sociolinguistics Social Sci. Research Council, 1964-70. Mem. Linguistics Soc. Am. (exec. com. 1957-58, pres. 1970), Am. Anthrop. Assn., Am. Oriental Soc., Assn. Asian Studies, (chmn. com. S. Asian langs.), Linguistic Soc. India, Am. Folklore Assn., Linguistic Circle N.Y. Author: (with M. Ani) Lessons in Contemporary Arabic, 1960. Editor: (with J. J. Gumperz) Linguistic Diversity in South Asia, 1960; (with W. A. Stewart) Linguistic Reading Lists for Teachers of Modern Languages, 1963; (with J. A. Fishman and J. Das Gupta) Language Problems of Developing Nations, 1968. General editor: Contrastive Structure series, 1962—; bd. adv. editors Middle Jour., 1955—. Home: 680 Loma Verde Palo Alto CA 94306 Office: Com on Linguistics Stanford Univ Stanford CA 94305

FERGUSON, CHARLES RAY, labor union exec.; b. Dellslow, W.Va., Aug. 25, 1906; s. Charles Edwin and Frances Burnette (Grimm) F.; student pub. schs.; m. Elsie Strolting, Dec. 7, 1928; children—Donald Ray, Charles Edwin. Coal miner, safety dir., asst. mine foreman, 1920-39; sec.-treas. Supervisory Union of Mineworkers, 1939-42; internat. rep. United Mine Workers Am., 1942-48, safety dir., 1948—; dep. adminstr. Def. Solid Fuels Adminstrn., 1950- 52. Mem. Fed. Coal Mine Safety Bd. of Review, 1951—; mem. joint industry safety com. President's Conf. on Occupational Safety, President's Com. on Nat. Employ the Physically Handicapped Week. Served with Naval Air Arm, USN, 1943-45. Mem. Mine Inspector's Inst. Am., Coal Mining Inst. Am., Nat. Mine Rescue Assn., Ill., Ky. mining insts. Moose, Elk, Eagle. Home: 455 Fourth Av New Kensington PA 15068 Office: 1435 K St Washington DC 20005

FERGUSON, CHARLES W., ret. editor, author; b. Quanah, Tex., Aug. 23, 1901; s. Charles Nathaniel Newton and Hannah (Wright) F.; A.B., So. Meth. U., 1923, Litt.D., 1966; postgrad. Union Theol. Sem., New Sch. for Social Research, N.Y.C.; Litt.D., Hillsdale Coll., 1952; m. Victoria Wallace, June 28, 1923 (div.); children—Charles Wallace, Hugh McGinnis. Methodist minister, 1923-25; asso. editor The Bookman and religious editor Doubleday, Doran & Co., 1926-30; sec. Ray Long & Richard R. Smith, Inc., 1930-32; pres. Round Table Press, 1932-34; asso. editor Readers Digest 1934-40, sr. editor, 1940-68 (on leave as cultural relations officer U.S. embassy, London, 1946); vis. lectr. U. Tex., 1969, So. Meth. U., 1972. Mem. Nat. council Boy Scouts Am.; v.p. for pub. information Nat. Safety Council, 1960-67. Recipient Christopher award, 1958. Mem. Sigma Alpha Epsilon. Methodist. Author: The Confusion of Tongues; A Review of Modern Isms, 1927; Pigskin (novel) 1928; Fifty Million Brothers: A Panorama of American Lodges and Clubs, 1937; A Little Democracy is a Dangerous Thing, 1948; Naked to Mine Enemies: The Life of Cardinal Wolsey, 1958; Say It With Words, 1959; Getting to Know the U.S.A., 1963; The Abecedarian Book, 1964; The Male Attitude, 1966; A is for Advent, 1968; Organizing to Beat the Devil: Methodists and the Making of America, 1971. Editor: Religion in America series, 1966—. Home: Apple Tree Hill Mount Kisco NY 10549

FERGUSON, CHESTER HOWELL, lawyer, corp. exec.; b. Americus, Ga., July 1, 1908; s. Sidney Hugh and Barbara (White) F.; student Mercer U., U. Ala.; J.D., U. Fla., 1930; m. Louise Lykes, Dec. 2, 1939; children—Stella Louise, Howell Lykes. Admitted to Fla. bar, 1930; with Macfarlane, Ferguson, Allison & Kelly, predecessors, Tampa, 1930—, mem. firm, 1935—. Chmn. MBS, Inc., 1959-60; v.p., dir. Lykes-Youngstown Corp., 1969—; chmn. Lykes Bros., Inc., 1969—; dir. Lykes Bros. S.S. Co., Inc., Lykes Pasco Packing Co., Knight & Wall Co., Bank of Clearwater, 1st Nat. Bank of Palm Beach, Kennesaw Life & Accident Ins. Co. Dir. civil def. Hillsborough County, also Gulf Coast dist. of Fla., 1947-63. Trustee U. Tampa, 1950—; mem. bd. regents Fla. State U. System, 1969—, chmn., 1965-69. Served from 1st lt. to col., USAAF, 1942-46; asst. chief staff CBI. Decorated Air medal, Legion of Merit, Bronze Star, also Chinese decoration. Mem. Fla., Greater Tampa (bd. govs.) chambers commerce, Am. Legion, Air Force Assn., Mil. Order World Wars, Newcomen Soc., Am., Fla., Tampa bar assns., Am. Coll. Trial Lawyers, Internat. Ins. Counsel Assn., Maritime Law Assn., Am. Coll. of Probate Counsel, Blue Key, Phi Delta Theta, Omicron Delta Kappa. Episcopalian (sr. warden). Clubs: Rotary, University, Tampa Yacht and Country, Palma Ceia Golf and Country, Merrymakers, Ye Mystic Krewe of Gasparilla (Tampa). Home: 5400 Interbay Blvd Tampa FL 33601 Office: 512 Florida Av Tampa FL 33601

FERGUSON, CLARENCE CLYDE, Jr., ambassador; b. Wilmington, N.C., Nov. 4 1924; s. Clarence Clyde and Georgeva (Owens) F.; A.B., Ohio State U., 1948; LL.B., Harvard, 1951; LL.D., Rutgers U., 1966; m. Dolores Zimmerman, Feb. 14, 1954; children—Claire Oberone, Hope Elizabeth, Eve Maria. Admitted to Mass. bar, 1951, N.Y. bar, 1953; asst. dept. gen. edn. Harvard, 1950-52, teaching fellow Law Sch., 1951-52; asso. firm Baltimore, Paulson and Canudo, N.Y.C., 1952-54; asst. U.S. atty. So. Dist. N.Y., 1954-55; prof. law Rutgers U. Law Sch., 1955-63; gen. counsel U.S. Commn. Civil Rights, 1961-63; dean, prof. law Howard U. Law Sch., 1963-69; spl. U.S. coordinator relief to civilian victims of the Nigerian Civil War 1969-70; ambassador to Uganda, 1970—. Civil rights adviser to Gov. Rockefeller of N.Y., 1959-64; mem. several presdl. commns.; cons. to govt., 1955—; U.S. expert UN sub-commn. on discrimination, 1964—. Treas. East Orange (N.J.) Housing Authority, 1959-61. Bd. dirs. legal def. and ednl. fund N.A.A.C.P., 1962- -; trustee Inst. Policy Studies, 1962—. Served with AUS, 1942-46; ETO, PTO. Decorated Bronze Star. Mem. Am., Fed. (nat. council 1963—) bar assns., Assn. Am. Law Schs. (exec. com. 1965—), D.C. Circuit Jud. Conf., Phi Beta Kappa. Author: (with A. P. Plaustein) Desegregation and the Law: The Meaning and Effect of the School Segregation Cases, 2d edit., 1960; Enforcement and Collection of Judgements and Liens, 1961; Secured Transactions, Article IX Uniforms Commercial Code in New Jersey, 1961; also numerous articles, revs. Temporary editor: Materials on Trial Presentation, 1958. Office: Kampala Dept State Washington DC 20521

FERGUSON, DONALD JOHN surgeon, educator; b. Mpls., Nov. 19, 1916; s. Donald Nivison and Arline (Folsom) F.; B.S., Yale, 1939; M.D., U. Minn., 1943, M.S. in Physiology, 1951, Ph. D. in Surgery, 1951; m. Lillian Elizabeth Mack, June 26, 1943; children—Anne Elizabeth, Donald John, Merrill James. Intern, then resident U. Minn. Hosp. 1947-52; asst. prof. surgery U. Minn., 1952-54; asso. prof., 1954-56, prof., 1956-60; prof. surgery U. Chgo., 1960—. Served to capt. M.C., AUS, 1943-46. Mem. A.C.S., Am. Surg. Assn., Soc. U. Surgeons. Contbr. articles in field. Home: 5629 Blackstone Av Chicago IL 60637

FERGUSON, DONALD NIVISON, author, retired educator; b. Waupun, Wis., June 30, 1882; s. Drysdale J. and Emily Agnes (Nivison) F.; B.A., U. Wis., 1904; M.A., U. Minn., 1922; music student, London, Eng., 1905-08; postgrad., U. Vienna, 1929-30; m. Arline Calista Folsom, Sept. 4, 1915; children—Donald John, Mary Barbara, David Lee, Griselda Alice (Mrs. Griselda F. White). Mem. faculty music U. Minn., 1913-50, prof., 1928-50; program annotator Mpls. Symphony Orch., 1930-60; condr. Bach Soc., 1934-50; head, dept. music Macalester Coll., St. Paul, 1950-59. Mem. Minn. Music Tchrs. Assn. (pres. 1925-29), Phi Beta Kappa. Author: History of Musical Thought, 1935; Short History of Music, 1940; Piano Music of Six Great Composers, 1948; Masterworks of the Orchestral Repertoire, 1954; Music as Metaphor, 1960, Chamber Music, 1964; The Why of Music, 1969. Address: 4912 Penn Av S Minneapolis MN 55409

FERGUSON, EDWARD CLIFTON, III, educator; b. Beaumont, Tex., Mar. 11, 1926; s. Edward Clifton and Marie (Meador) F.; B.S., Northwestern U., 1946, B.M., 1949, M.D., 1950. Intern Evanston (Ill.) Hosp., 1950, Cook County Hosp., Chgo., 1951; resident Ill. Eye and Ear Infirmary U. Ill., Chgo., 1954-56; asst. prof. ophthalmology Coll. Medicine U. Ia., 1957-64; asso. prof., chmn. dept. opthalmology U. Tex., 1964-69, prof., chmn. dept. opthalmology, 1969—. Served with USNR, 1944-45, USAF, 1951-53. Diplomate Am. Bd. Ophthalmology. Mem. Am. Acad. Ophthalmology and Otolaryngology, A.M.A., Assn. for Research in Ophthalmology, Soc. Heed Fellows, Am. Coll. Surgeons, Tex., So med. assns., Tex. Ophthalmology Assn., Tex. Soc. Ophthalmology and Otolaryngology, Houston Ophthalmol. Assn., Assn. U. Profs. Ophthalmology, Sigma Xi, Alpha Omega Alpha. Episcopalian.

FERGUSON, ELEANOR ARCHER, librarian; b. Indpls., Mar. 23, 1909; d. George Archer and Lucia (Ray) Ferguson; A.B., Radcliffe Coll., 1930; B.S., Simmons Coll., 1934; M.S. in L.S., Columbia, 1948. Librarian Utica (N.Y.) Pub. Library, 1934-36, Rochester (N.Y.) Pub. Library, 1937-40; chief librarian Prendergast Library, Jamestown, N.Y., 1940-45, Free Library, Council Bluffs, Ia., 1945-48, Dearborn (Mich.) Pub. Library, 1948-55; dir. Library Service Center, Conn. Dept. Edn., Middletown, 1955-57; exec. sec. Assn. of State Libraries, Pub. Library Assn., A.L.A., Chgo., 1957- 69; asst. in pub. library service N.Y. State Edn. Dept., Albany, 1969—. Mem. A.L.A., Pioneers of Ind. Episcopalian. Home: 352 State St Albany NY 12210 Office: 99 Washington Av Albany NY 12210

FERGUSON, ELI HALL, ins. co. exec.; b. Philip, S.D., Oct. 27, 1909; s. Messer A. and Susie Anne (Hall) F.; B.S., S.D. State U., 1932, D.Sc., (hon.) 1963; m. Hazel Mae Bell, Dec. 26, 1934; 1 dau., Faye-Jean (Mrs. David Cartmell). Cattle rancher, 1926-33; fieldman First Nat. Bank, Philip, S.D., 1933-34; various positions U.S. Dept. Agr., Lincoln, Neb., 1934-36; with Equitable Life Assurance Soc. U.S., N.Y.C., 1936—, 2d v.p., 1953-59, charge farm mortgages, 1956-60, v.p., 1959—, v.p. corporate planning on staff of chief exec. officer, 1960-71, sr. v.p. corporate planning, 1971—. Mem. Natural Resources Council, State N.Y. Mem. Am., Western farm econ. assns. Mason. Club: Economic (N.Y.C). Home: 466 Upper Blvd Ridgewood NJ 07450

FERGUSON, FORD M, commodities exec.; b. Powell, S.D., June 15, 1911; s. Edward V. and Frances (Hoffman) F.; B.B.A., U. Minn., 1934; m. Loella Braun, Mar. 1, 1941; children—John Malcolm, Suzanne Gail, James Ford. Asst. v.p. Cargill, Inc., 1934-48; v.p. charge commodity trading The Glidden Co., 1948-52; charge futures, commns. Stratton Grain Co., 1953-63; sr. partner Ferguson Grain Co., 1963—. Mem. Chgo. Merc. Exchange, Chgo. Bd. Trade. Home: 1111 Normandy Lane Glenview IL 60025 Office: Bd of Trade Bldg Chicago IL 60604

FERGUSON, FRANCES HAND, vol. worker; b. N.Y.C., Apr. 9, 1907; d. Learned and Frances (Fincke) Hand; student pvt. sch.; A.B., Bryn Mawr Coll., 1929; M.A. in Psychology, Columbia, 1931, postgrad., 1933-35; m. Robert Munro Ferguson, Nov. 10, 1933; children—Patty M., Robert H.M., Phyllis M. Tchr., Brearley Sch., 1936-38; dir. courses Greater N.Y. chpt. Am. Women's Vol. Services, 1939-40; successively N.Y. pres., nat. chmn. field com., exec. com. Planned Parenthood Assn., 1940-51, pres., 1953- 56; vol. research technician Meml. Hosp., 1941-42; chmn., 1st v.p. Planned Parenthood Fedn. Am., 1959-62; bd. dirs. Internat. Planned Parenthood Fedn., 1953—, v.p., 1959-62, treas., 1970—; bd. dirs. Euthanasia Soc., 1955- 62, Am. Eugenics Soc., 1957-63, Nat. Com. Maternal Health, 1957-63, Human Betterment Assn., 1956-64, Assn. for Vol. Sterilization, 1964—, Assn. for Study of Abortion, 1967-70. Home: 1030 Fifth Av New York City NY 10028

FERGUSON, FRANCIS EUGENE, ins. co. exec.; b. Batavia, N.Y., Feb. 4, 1921; s. Harold M. and Florence (Munger) F.; student Cornell U., 1938-39; B.S., Mich. State U., 1947; m. Patricia J. Reddy, Aug. 11, 1945; children—Susan Lee, Patricia Ann. Asst. sec.-treas. Fed. Land Bank Assn., Lansing, Mich., 1947-48; appraiser Fed. Land Bank, St. Paul, 1948-50; specialist agrl. econs. Mich. State U. Extension, 1951; with Northwestern Mut. Life Ins. Co., Milw., 1951—, specialist, 1951-52, asst. mgr. farm loans, 1952-56, mgr. farm loans, 1956-62, gen. mgr. mortgage loans, 1962-63, v.p. mortgage loans, 1963-67, pres., 1967—. Dir. Cutler Hammer, Inc., Milw., Ralston Purina Co., St. Louis. Gen. campaign chmn. United Fund, 1965; corp. mem. Milw. Children's Hosp.; bd. dirs. Better Bus. Bur. Greater Milw., Milw. Vol. Equal Employment Opportunity Council, Greater Milw. Com., United Community Services Greater Milw., Columbia Hosp. Served to capt. USAAF, 1942-45. Decorated Purple Heart. Mem. Milw. Assn. Commerce (dir.). Republican. Methodist. Clubs: Milwaukee, Milwaukee Country. Home: 1115 W Green Tree Rd Milwaukee WI 53217 Office: 720 E Wisconsin Av Milwaukee WI 53202

FERGUSON, FRANK DANIEL, educator; b. Pleasant City, O., Oct. 4, 1910; s. Henry D. and Missouri (Crewell) F.; B.S., Kent State U., 1948, M.A., 1950; postgrad. Ohio State U., 1950, 52, 53; Ph.D., La. State U., 1958; m. Gertrude Smith, July 19, 1939; children—Janie Elizabeth (Mrs. Robert Neale McBee), Katherine Louise (Mrs. John Hannie). Personnel mgr., instr. Kent State U., 1948-49; head dept. bus. Urbana Coll., 1950-52; faculty La. State U., Baton Rouge, 1952—, prof. secretarial adminstrn., bus. edn., head dept., 1965-69, prof., head dept. office adminstrn., prof. edn., 1969—; vis. prof. N.M. State U., summer 1952; commnr. Accrediting Commn. Bus. Schs. and Colls., Washington, 1969—; cons. pvt. bus. schs. Esso Corp.; chmn. evaluation team for accreditation Bus. Colls. Am., 1957—. Served with AUS, 1944-45. Mem. Nat. Office Mgmt. Assn. (Diamond Merit award 1963, pres. 1959-60), Am. Vocational Assn., N.E.A., Nat. Bus. Tchrs. Assn., Am. Assn. U. Profs., La. Tchrs. Assn. (council mem. 1960-67), Delta Pi Epsilon, Beta Gamma Sigma, Alpha Sigma Lambda, Phi Delta Kappa. Contbr. articles profl. publs. Home: 395 College Hill Dr Baton Rouge LA 70803

FERGUSON, GARY WARREN, pub. relatons exec.; b. Stockton, Kan., May 5, 1925; s. Richard and Nelle (McBee) F.; A.B., Yale, 1946; M.S. in Journalism, Columbia, 1948; m. Doris Drisler, Oct. 2, 1948; children—Arthur Richard, Frances, Robert Warren, Scott William. Reporter, Providence Jour. Bull., 1948-49, Richmond (Va.) News Leader, 1949-52; reporter St. Louis Post-Dispatch, 1954-55, writer, 1955-60; counselor Fleishman-Hillard, Inc., St. Louis, 1961-62, sr. partner, 1962-71; pres. Gary Ferguson, Inc., pub. relations, 1971—. First v.p. St. Louis Newspaper Guild, 1959-60. Mem. council Episcopal Diocese Mo., 1962-66; mem. founding bd. Greater St. Louis Council Alcoholism, 1965, pres., 1966-69, Bd. dirs. Family and Children's Service Greater St. Louis, 1969—. Served with USNR, 1946-47, 52-53. Recipient Bishop's award Episcopal Diocese Mo., 1965. Mem. Pub. Relations Soc. Am., Sigma Delta Chi. Clubs: Noonday, Media (St. Louis). Home: 130 Plant Av Webster Groves MO 63119 Office: 818 Olive St St Louis MO 63101

FERGUSON, GEORGE ANDREW, educator, psychologist; b. New Glasgow, N.S., Can., July 23, 1914; s. Alexander MacN. and Jean (Dennistoun) F.; B.A., Dalhousie U., 1936; M.Ed., U. Edinburgh, 1938, Ph.D., 1940; m. Rowena Sheldon Bellows, May 1955; children—Claudia, Leith. Indsl. psychologist Stevenson & Kellogg, 1945-47; asst. prof. McGill U., Montreal, Que., Can., 1947-49, asso. prof., 1949-52, prof., 1952—, chmn. dept. psychology, 1964—, vice-dean for biol. scis., 1966—. Fellow Royal Soc.; mem. Am., Canadian psychol. assns. Author: Statistical Analysis in Psychology and Education, 3d edit., 1971. Contbr. articles profl. jours. Home: 3003 Cedar Av Montreal 25 Quebec Canada

FERGUSON, GEORGE VICTOR, ret. newspaper editor; b. Cupar Fife, Scotland, Apr. 20, 1897; s. James Thompson and Maud Mant (Martin) F.; student U. Alta., 1915-16, 19-21; B.A., Oxford U., 1924; LL.D., U. New Brunswick, 1950; LL.D., Alta., 1960, McGill U. 1967; m. Mary Simpson Doupe, Dec. 27, 1930; children—David Martin, Stephen Somerville. Deskman, Times of London, 1924; reporter Winnipeg Free Press, 1925-27, editorial writer, 1927-31, news editor, 1931-36, mng. editor, 1936-44, exec. editor, 1944- 46; editor Montreal Star, 1946-58, editor-in-chief, 1958-68, editor emeritus, 1968—. Fellow Royal Soc. Can. Author: John W. Dafoe, a memoir, 1949. Home: 4501 Sherbrooke St W Montreal 215 Quebec Canada Office: 245 St James St West Montreal Quebec Canada

FERGUSON, GLENN WALKER, coll. pres.; b. Syracuse, N.Y., Jan. 28, 1929; s. Forrest Erwin and Mabel Gertrude (Walker) F.; B.A., Cornell U., 1950, M.B.A., 1951; student Georgetown U., 1951-52, U. Santo Tomas, Manila, Philippines, 1952-53, George Washington Law Sch., 1953-55, U. Chgo. Law Sch., 1955-56; LL.B., U. Pitts., 1957; m. Patricia Lou Head, June 22, 1950; children—Bruce Walker, Sherryl Lynn, Scott Sherwood. Staff asso. Govtl. Affairs Inst., Washington, 1954-55; asst. editor, asst. sec.-treas. Am. Judicature Soc., Chgo., 1955-56; adminstrv. asst. to chancellor U. Pitts., 1956-57, asst. dean, asst. prof. pub. adminstrn. Grad. Sch. Pub. and Internat. Affairs, 1957-59, asso. dir. Coordinated Edn. Center, 1959-60; with McKinsey & Co., mgmt. cons., Washington, 1960-61; with Peace Corps, 1961-64, dir. Thailand, 1961-63, asso. dir., 1963-64; dir. Volunteers in Service to Am., Office Econ. Opportunity, Washington, 1964-66; U.S. ambassador to Kenya, 1966-69; chancellor of Long Island U., 1969-70; pres. Clark U., 1970—; consultant to other govtl. agencies, 1959-64; TV moderator fgn. affairs, Pitts., 1957-60. Served to 1st lt. USAF, 1951-53; Korea. Recipient Arthur S. Fleming award, 1968. Member American Soc. Pub. Adminstrn., Am. Polit. Sci. Assn., Am. Fgn. Service Assn., Fed. Bar Assn., Council on Fgn. Relations, Internat. Platform Assn., Psi Upsilon, Phi Delta Phi. Clubs: Internat., Washington Athletic (Washington); Mt. Kenya Safari, Contbr. articles profl. jours. Home: 84 Williams Worcester MA 01610 Office: Clark U Worcester MA 01610

FERGUSON, HARRY, newspaperman; b. Columbia, Mo., Oct. 23, 1903; s. James T. and Caroline (McCasky) F.; B.J., U. Mo., 1925; m. Frances Marriner, Oct. 23, 1933; children—Julie, Frances. Copy editor Miami Herald, 1925-27, Phila. Public Ledger, 1927-29; reporter United Press, 1929-36, sprots editor, 1936-39, asst. gen. mgr., 1939-48, fgn. news editor, 1948-51, exec. editor N.Y. world hdqrs. 1951; now national reporter United Press Internat. Mem. Phi Gamma Delta, Sigma Delta Chi, Kappa Tau Alpha. Address: Nat Press Bld 14th and F St Washington DC 10004

FERGUSON, HOMER, U.S. judge; b. Harrison City, Pa., Feb. 25, 1889; s. Samuel and Margarete (Bush) F.; student U. Pitts., 1910-11; LL.B., U. Mich., 1913, LL.D, 1951; LL.D., Kalamazoo Coll., Detroit Coll. Law, Muhlenberg Coll.; m. Myrtle Jones, June 20, 1913; 1 dau., Amy Margaret (Mrs. Charles Robert Beltz). Admitted to Mich. bar, 1913, and practiced law, 1913-29; circuit judge, 1929-43; U.S. senator from Mich., 1943-54; U.S. ambassador to Philippines, 1955-56; asso. judge U. S. Ct. Mil. Appeals, 1956—; former mem. Senate appropriations, fgn. relations, Republican policy (chmn.) coms. Sat as one-man grand jury, Wayne County, Mich., 1939-42. Prof. law, Detroit Coll. Law. Mem. Am. Mich., Detroit bar assns., Washington Inst. Fgn. Affairs, Am. Judicature Soc., Sigma Delta Kappa. Presbyn. Clubs: Metropolitan (Washington). Home: 5054 Millwood Lane Washington DC 20016 Office: U S Ct Mil Appeals Washington DC 20442

FERGUSON, JAMES, aircraft co. exec.; b. Smyrna, Turkey, Aug. 15, 1913; s. William Christine (Webber) F.; A.A., Fullerton Jr. Coll., 1934; m. Roberta Wilkes, 1950. Commd. 2d lt. USAAF, 1937, advanced through grades to gen., 1966; assigned 405th Fighter Bomb Group, ETO, 1944; with 19th Tactical Air Command, 1944-45; assigned Air Command and Staff Sch., Air U., 1946-47; chief staff A-3 Air Force Mission in Turkey, 1947-50; asst. to vice comdr. Far East Air Force, 1950-51; vice comdr. 5th Air Force, Korea, 1951-52; dep comdr. 9th Air Force, Pope AFB, 1952-55; dir. requirements Dept. Air Force, 1955-59; vice comdr. Air Research & Devel. Command. Andrews AFB, Md., 1959-61; dep. chief of staff Research and Devel., Hdqrs. USAF, 1961-66; comdr. Air Force Systems Command, 1966-70, ret., 1970; v.p. United Aircraft Corp., East Hartford, Conn., 1970—. Decorated D.S.M. with clusters, D.F.C., Legion of Merit with clusters, Air medal with clusters; Croix de Guerre (France), (Luxembourg); Ulchi medal (Korea); Order Brit. Empire. Address: 400 Main St East Hartford CT 06108

FERGUSON, JAMES HENRY, physician; b. Westbury, N.Y., Oct. 4, 1911; s. John Henry and Letitia (Gordon) F.; A.B., U. Pa., 1935, M.D., 1939; m. Marie Louise Miltenberger, May 14, 1949 (dec. April 1968). Intern Presbyterian Hospital, Chicago, 1939-41; pres. Chgo. Lying-In Hosp., U. Chgo. Clinics, 1941-42, 46-47; from instr. to asso. prof. dept. obstetrics and gynecology Tulane U. Sch. Medicine, 1947-55; prof., dept. obstetrics- gynecology U. Miami Sch. Medicine, 1955-68. Chmn. dept., 1955-65; attending staff Jackson Meml. Hosp., Miami, 1955—. Mem. nat. med. council U. Pa. Served from capt. to maj. M.C., AUS, 1942- 46. Diplomate Am. Bd. Obstetrics and Gynecology, Pan Am. Med. Assn. Fellow Am. Assn. Obstetricians and Gynecologists, Am. Coll. Obstetricians and Gynecologists, A.C.S.; mem. Am. Soc. Cytology, Assn. Profs. Gynecology and Obstetrics, A.M.A., So. Atlantic Assn. Obstetricians and Gynecologists, So. Med. Assn., Venezuelan Soc. Obstetrics and Gynecology (hon.), Cuban Soc. Obstetrics and Gynecology (corr.), Alpha Omega Alpha. Home: 8787 Shoreham Dr West Hollywood CA 90069 Office: 9961 SW 66th St Miami FL 33143

FERGUSON, JAMES SHARBROUGH, coll. ofcl.; b. Anguilla, Miss., Dec. 31, 1916; s. James Elbert Jenkins and Delle Prudence (Clark) F.; A.B., Millsaps Coll., 1937; A.M., La. State U., 1940; Ford scholar, Yale, 1952-53; Ph.D., U. N.C., 1953; m. Frances Hardy Cottrell, June 3, 1939; children—Frances Cottrell, Elizabeth Lynn. Instr. math. Amory (Miss.) High Sch., 1937-39; teaching fellow La. State U., 1939-42; Gen. Edn. Bd. fellow U. N.C., 1942-43, instr. history, 1943-44; asst. prof. history Millsaps Coll., 1944-46, asso. prof., 1946. prof., 1947-62, acad. dean, 1954-62, prof. history U. N.C. at Greensboro, 1962—, dean grad. sch., 1962-64, acting chancellor, 1964-65, 66-67, vice chancellor, 1966, chancellor, 1967—; vis. asso. prof. summer session Tulane U., 1947. Dir. Christian Citizenship Seminar, Miss. Meth. Youth Fellowship, 1954. Mem. Am. Assn. U. Profs., So., Miss., Miss. Valley hist. assns., N.C. Lit. and Hist. Assn., Pi Kappa Alpha, Alpha Epsilon Delta, Eta Sigma Phi, Phi Kappa Phi, Pi Kappa Delta, Omicron Delta Kappa. Methodist. Club: Civitan (Greensboro). Contbr. articles hist. jours. Home: 1102 Spring Garden St Greensboro NC 27403

FERGUSON, JO MCCOWN, lawyer; b. Central City, Ky., Apr. 5, 1915; s. Jo Marvin and Willie Mae (Cain) F.; A.B., U. Ky., 1937, LL.B., 1939; m. Margarita Hauser, July 12, 1947; children—Rita, Diane, Jo Frances. Admitted to Ky. bar, 1939, practiced in Central City, 1939-42; asst. atty. gen. Ky., 1948-56, atty. gen., 1956-60; commr. econ. security, 1960-61; partner firm Grafton, Ferguson, Fleischer & Harper, 1961—. Chmn. Gov.'s Com. on Constl. Revision, 1961-62. Served as capt. AUS, ETO, 1944- 47, chief Property Control br. Mil. Govt. Bavaria, 1946-47. Mem. Am., Ky. bar assns., Am.

Legion, V.F.W., So. Attys. Gen. (chmn. 1957- 58). Democrat. Episcopalian. Home: 127 Gibson Rd Louisville KY 40207 Office: 310 W Liberty St Louisville KY 40202

FERGUSON, JOHN BOWIE, textile co. exec.; b. Vancouver, B.C., Can., Sept. 5, 1938; s. John Bowie and Mary Stuart (Howie) F.; grad. high sch.; m. Joan Elizabeth Bate, Sept. 5, 1959; children—Christina, Catherine, John, Joanne. Profl. hockey player Montreal Canadiens, 1963-71; pres. Butternut Enterprises, Ltd., Montreal, Que., 1967—, Double Two Ranch, Montreal, 1971—. Home: 163 Butternut Crescent Dollard Des Ormeaux Quebec Canada Office: 7101 Parl Montreal Quebec 303 Canada

FERGUSON, JOHN BRENDAN, elec. mfg. co. exec.; b. Londonderry, Ireland, May 14, 1923; s. John and Annie (Doherty) F.; came to U.S., 1924, naturalized, 1943; B.S., Duquesne U., 1948; postgrad. U. Pitts., 1952-54; m. Rose Marie Hritzko, May 22, 1954; children—Patricia Ann, John Michael, Sandra Jean, Mark Kevin. With Westinghouse Elec. Corp., 1948—, group comptroller, Pitts., 1962-70, v.p., controller, 1970—. Served with USAAF, 1943-45. Decorated Air medal. Mem. Nat. Assn. Accountants, Financial Execs. Inst., Pitts. C. of C. Club: Edgewood Country (Pitts.). Home: 208 Harwick Dr Pittsburgh PA 15235 Office: Westinghouse Bldg Pittsburgh PA 15222

FERGUSON, JOHN HENRY, educator; b. Lexington, Neb., Aug. 22, 1907; s. Leonard Calvin and Dicie Shirley (Sipes) F.; A.B., Neb. Central Coll., 1929; M.A., U. Pa., 1932, Ph.D., 1937; m. Ruth Arvilla Benton, June 10, 1930; children—Milton O., Richard B., David J., Rachel A. (Mrs. Rider). Prin., tchr. Monroe (Neb.) High Sch., 1929-30; dir. boys work Friends Neighborhood Guild, Phila., 1930-34; instr. polit. sci. Pa. State U., 1934-37, asst. prof., 1937-41, asso. prof., 1941-47, prof., 1947—, head dept., 1947-48, dir. Social Sci. Research Center, 1953-55; dir. Inst. Pub. Adminstrn., Pa. State U., 1959-65, head dept. polit. sci., 1963-65; dean sch. politics New Sch. Social Research, 1948-49; vis. prof. U. Neb., summer 1948; dir. program evaluation Office Gov. of Pa., 1955-56, sec. of adminstrn., 1956-59, budget sec., 1957-59; vis. prof. U. Pa., 1966—. Co- dir. research Pa. Constl. Conv., 1967-68; pres. Better Govt. Assos., Inc., 1967—. Mem. bd. Pub. Service Inst., Commonwealth Pa., chmn., 1963- -; bd. dirs. Lincoln U., 1960—. Dir. Civilian Public Service Camp, Gatlinburg, Tenn., 1943-44. Mem. Am. (exec. council 1951-53), Western, So. polit. sci. assns., Am. Friends Service Com. (adminstrv. asst. 1944-45, exec. bd. 1950-56, 57- 60), Pa. Polit. Sci. and Pub. Adminstrn. Assn. (pres. 1958-60), Am. Soc. Pub. Adminstrn., Am. Acad. Polit. and Social Sci., Am. Assn. U. Prof. Mem. Soc. Friends. Author: American Diplomacy and the Boer War, 1939; (with Dr. Dean E. McHenry) The American System of Government, 11th edit., 1971; The American Federal Government, 11th edit., 1971; Elements of American Government, 9th edit., 1971; (with Dr. Charles F. LeeDecker) Municipally Owned Waterworks in Pennsylvania, 1948, Municipally Owned Electric Plants in Pennsylvania, 1950; (with Drs. Dean E. McHenry and E. B. Fincher) American Government Today, 1951; (with David L. Cowell) The Minor Courts of Pennsylvania, 1962. Home: 555 W Ridge Av State College PA 16801 Office: 601 Payne-Shoemaker Bldg Harrisburg PA 17101

FERGUSON, JOHN HOWARD, pathologist; b. Elmira Heights, N.Y., Sept. 5, 1902; s. John C. and Ina (Fisher) F.; M.D., Syracuse U., 1926; m. Ruth Cadzow, Sept. 3, 1926; children—John Howard, James Cadzow. Fellow in pathology Upstate Med. Center, State U. N.Y. (formerly Syracuse U., Coll. Medicine), 1926-27, instr. in pathology, 1927-29, asst. prof., 1929-32, asso. prof., 1932-42, prof. 1942-69, emeritus, 1969—; attending pathologist Univ. Hosp., 1934-42; pathologist Syracuse Med. Center Hosps., 1942-63; attending pathologist State U. Hosp., 1963-69, sr. attending pathologist, 1969—; county necrotomist, Onondaga County, 1927-50. Mem. adv. council N.Y. State Joint Hosp. Survey and Planning Commn., 1946-61. Mem. Am. Cancer Soc. (mem. exec. com. N.Y. State div.; chmn. fellowship com. 1946-48, chmn. med. service and adv. com. 1948-53), Am. Assn. Pathologists and Bacteriologists, N.Y. State Assn. of Pub. Health Labs. (Pres. 1944-46), Tumor Clinic Assn. of N.Y. State (sec.- treas. 1947—), Syracuse Acad. Medicine, Sigma Xi, Alpha Omega Alpha, Nu Sigma Nu, Phi Kappa Psi. Republican. Contbr. to med. periodicals. Home: 1314 Westmoreland Av Syracuse NY 13210

FERGUSON, JOHN HOWARD, univ. prof.; b. Edinburgh, Scotland, Mar. 1, 1902; s. Howard and Annie (Bowers) F.; B.A., U. of Cape Town, South Africa, 1921; Rhodes Scholar, Oxford, 1923-26, B.A., Oxon, 1925, M.A., 1931; M.D., Harvard, 1928; Licentiate in Medicine and Surgery, Soc. of Apothecaries, London, 1931; D.Sc., Univ. of Cape Town, 1957; m. 1927, and 1955; children—M. Joyce, Phyllis M., Margaret Anne, Helen F., John C., Colin C. Came to U.S., 1931, naturalized, 1941. Lecturer pharmacology, U. of Cape Town, 1922-26, asst. pathology, Harvard U., 1926-28, asst. prof. bacteriol., Cape Town U., 1928-31; instr. physiology, Yale U., 1931-34; asso. prof. physiol. and pharmacol., U. of Ala., 1934-37; asst. prof. pharmacol., U. of Mich., 1937-43, prof. physiol., 1943—, head dept., U. of N.C. Med. Sch., 1943-69. Fellow Am. Coll. Physicians, A.A.A.S.; mem. Am. Physiol. Soc., Soc. Exptl. Biology and Medicine, Internat. Hematol. Soc., Am. Assn. Univ. Profs., Phi Beta Pi, Alpha Omega Alpha. Democrat. Episcopalian. Author: numerous articles in sci. jours. and textbooks. Home: Chapel Hill NC 27514

FERGUSON, JOHN MARSHALL, lawyer; b. Marion, Ill., Oct. 14, 1921; s. John Marshall and Vessie (Widdows) F.; student So. Ill. U., 1939-41, S.E. Mo. Tchrs. Coll., 1941; LL.B., J.D., Washington U., St. Louis, 1948; m. Jeanne Harmon, Sept. 23, 1950; children—Marcia Ann, Mark Harmon, John Scott, Mary Sue. Admitted to Ill. bar, 1949, also U.S. Supreme Ct.; asst. mgr. I.W. Rogers Theaters, Inc., Anna, Ill., 1934-42; atty. U.S. Fidelity & Guaranty Co., St. Louis, 1948-51; asso. firm Baker, Kagy & Wagner, East St. Louis, Ill., 1951-56, partner, 1956-59; partner firm Wagner, Conner, Ferguson, Bertrand & Baker, East St. Louis and Belleville, Ill., 1959—; pres. bd. Arch Aircraft, Inc., 1966—. Precinct committeeman Stookey Twp., St. Clair County (Ill.) Republican Com., 1958-62. Bd. dirs., v.p. East St. Louis chpt. A.R.C. Served to capt. AUS, 1941-45. Mem. Am. Ill., St. Clair County 7th Fed. Circuit (bd. govs.) bar assns., Delta Theta Phi. Mason, Elk. Clubs: East St. Louis City (pres. 1960); Illinois (gov., pres. 1966- 67), St. Clair Country, Missouri Athletic (St. Louis). Home: 12 Oak Knoll Belleville IL 62223 Office: St Clair Nat Bank Bldg Belleville IL 62228

FERGUSON, JOHN ROBERT, Jr., steel co. exec.; b. Berkeley, Cal., Dec. 25, 1915; s. John Robert and Jane (Gray) F.; S.B., Mass. Inst. Tech., 1937; M.B.A., U. Chgo., 1950; m. Dorothy Berry, Dec. 29, 1939; children—Darryl, John Robert III. With Carnegie Ill. Steel Corp., 1940-50; asst. chief engr. Orinoco Mining Co., 1950-54, chief engr. project devel. U.S. Steel Corp., 1954-55; asst. v.p. engring., 1956-63, v.p. design and constrn., 1963-66, v.p. for appropriations, 1966-69; v.p. engring. services USS Engrs. and Consultants, Inc., 1969—. Vice pres. Action Housing, Inc., 1967-68, pres., 1968—; chmn. bd., chmn. exec. com. Allegheny Housing Rehab. Corp., 1968-70, mem. bd. exec. com., 1970—. Mem. Am. Inst. Mining, Metall. and Petroleum Engrs., Engrs., Engrs. Soc. Western Pa., Am. Iron and Steel Inst., Am. Iron and Steel Engrs. Clubs: Allegheny Country, Duquesne, Edgeworth. Home: 335 Grant St Sewickley PA 15143 Office: 600 Grant St Pittsburgh PA 15230

FERGUSON, LEONARD WILTON, psychologist; b. Turlock, Cal., Mar. 2, 1912; s. William Ward and Sara Minium (Kaufman) F.; A.B., Stanford, 1933, M.A., 1935, Ph.D., 1942; m. Edith Beverly Phemister, July 1, 1939; children—Barbara (Mrs. Robert B. Needham), Margaret (Mrs. Benjamin F. Gibson V), Kathryn. Instr. to asst. prof. psychology U. Conn., Storrs, 1939-43; asst. staff supr. Met. Life Ins. Co., 1943-51; research asst. Aetna Life Affiliated Cos., 1951-53; research asso. Life Ins. Agy. Mgmt. Assn., Hartford, Conn., 1953-55, program dir., 1955-63; editor The Journal Press, Provincetown, Mass., 1964-65; prof. psychology Ohio U., Athens, 1966—; sec. com. on tests Life Office Mgmt. Assn. 1940- 47, sec. clerical salary study com., 1943-44, chmn., 1944-49; lectr. N.Y. U., summer 1949, U. Conn. extension div., 1953-54, 54-55. Treas., Joint Council of Psychologists for Legislation in N.Y. State, 1951; mem. adv. com. on job evaluation Nat. Mgmt. Council, 1950. Diplomate in indsl. psychology Am. Bd. Examiners in Profl. Psychology. Mem. N.Y. State (sec. com. on profl. ethics 1950-53), Am., Eastern psychol. assns., Conn. Valley Assn. Psychologists, Sigma Xi. Author: Personality Measurement, 1952; also numerous articles in profl. jours. Editor: Clerical Salary Administration, 1947. Home: 168 Commercial St Provincetown MA 02657 Office: Ohio U Athens OH 45701

FERGUSON, LLOYD NOEL, educator; b. Oakland, Cal., Feb. 9, 1918; s. Noel Swithin and Gwendolyn Louise (Johnson) F.; B.S., U. Cal. at Berkeley, 1940, Ph.D., 1943 D.Sc., Howard U., 1970. m. Charlotte Olivia Welch, Jan. 2, 1944; children—Lloyd Noel, Stephen Bruce, Lisa Annette. Research asst. Nat. Def. Project, U. Cal. at Berkeley, 1941-44; asst. prof. Agr. and Tech. Coll., Greensboro, N.C., 1944-45; faculty Howard U., 1945-65, prof. chemistry, 1955-65, chmn. dept., 1958-65; prof. chemistry Cal. State Coll., Los Angeles, 1965—, chmn. chemistry dept., 1968-71; vis. prof. U. Ore., summers 1958, 60, 63, U. Nairobi, Kenya, 1971-72; govt. chemist Nat. Bur. Standards, Naval Ordnance Lab. and Dept. Agr., summers 1950, 51, 67; vis. scientist, div. chem. edn. Am. Chem. Soc., 1959- -, touring lectr. N.Y. State, 1956; series lectr. Copenhagen, Denmark and Lund, Sweden, 1954. Cons., Coll. Chemistry Consultants Service. Guggenheim fellow Carlsberg Lab., Copenhagen, 1953-54; NSF faculty fellow Swiss Fed. Inst. Tech., Zurich, 1961-62. Fellow Chem. Soc. London, A.A.A.S., Am. Inst. Chemists; Am. Chem. Soc., Am. Assn. U. Profs., Nat. Inst. Sci., Sigma Xi. Author: Electron Structure of Organic Molecules, 1952; Textbook of Organic Chemistry, 1958; The Modern Structural Theory of Organic Chemistry, 1963; also numerous articles. Home: 4221 S Cloverdale Av Los Angeles CA 90008

FERGUSON, MAYNARD, trumpet player; b. Montreal, Que., Can., May 4, 1928. Came to U.S., 1949. Trumpet player Stan Kenton Orch., 1950-53; free-lance musician, Los Angeles, 3 years; formed own touring 13-piece orch., 1957-65; formed sextet, 1965. Address: PO Box 175 Millbrook NY 12545*

FERGUSON, NEIL TAYLOR, investment dealer; b. Alameda, Cal., Mar. 15, 1922; s. Hector Donald and Erna (Taylor) F.; B.A., San Jose State Coll., 1944. Mgr., Fields Store, Campbell, Cal., 1946-48; partner Paul C. Rudolph & Co., San Jose, Cal., 1948-51; pres., dir. Mut. Fund Assos., Inc., Sa Rafael, Cal., 1951—; v.p., dir. Putnam Mgmt. Co., Boston, 1961—; dir. Investors Ins. Assos., Inc., Funded Investors, Inc. Pres. Clear Water Ranch Childrens House, Inc. Served to lt. USNR, 1942-46. Mem. Young Presidents Orgn., UN Orgn. Club: Commonwealth (San Francisco). Home: 7777 Martinelli Rd Forestville CA 95436 Office: 555 Northgate Dr San Rafael CA 94903

FERGUSON, NOEL MOORE, coll. dean; b. East St. Louis, Ill., Dec. 20, 1907; s. Samuel Moore and Anna M. (Gillis) F.; Ph.G., St. Louis Coll. Pharmacy, 1930, Ph.C., 1932, B.Sc., 1933; A.B., Washington U., 1934, M.S., 1935, Ph.D., 1942; m. Marion L. Ash, Dec. 25, 1933; children—Michael Allen, Gary Gene. Asst. chemistry St. Louis Coll. Pharmacy, 1930-32, instr. botany and pharmacognosy, 1932-33, asst. prof., 1933-41, prof., 1941-43; prof. chemistry Ashland Coll., 1943-49; sr. research chemist Dr. Hess Clark, Inc., 1943-49; dean Coll. Pharmacy, U. Houston, 1949—. Cons. to pharm. mfg. industry, 1950—; consultation and study, Europe, Scandinavia, Brit. Isles, 1963-65, Orient, 1968; adviser in pharmacy edn., fed. univs. of Ceara, Paraiba, Rio Grande do Norte, Pernambuco (all Brazil), 1969-70. Mem. Am. Pharm. Assn., Am. Chem. Soc. Author: A Repetitorium of Pharmacognosy, 1932; Laboratory Manual of Phamacognosy, 1955; Textbook of Pharmacognosy, 1956. Home: 11513 Echo Hollow Houston TX 77024

FERGUSON, OLIVER WATKINS, educator; b. Nashville, June 7, 1924; s. John Lambuth and Olive Andrews (Watkins) F.; B.A., Vanderbilt U., 1947, M.A., 1948; Ph.D., U. Ill., 1954; m. Joanne O'Kelly, Aug. 18, 1949; children—John Andrews, Charles Edward. Instr. German, U. Miss., summer 1947; instr. English, U. Ark., 1948-50; instr., then asst. prof. English, Ohio State U., 1954-57; mem. faculty Duke, 1957—, prof. English, 1967—, chmn. dept., 1967—. Served with inf. AUS, 1943-45; ETO. Rotary Internat. Found. fellow, 1952-53; Guggenheim fellow, 1963-64. Mem. Modern Lang. Assn., S. Atlantic Modern Lang. Assn., Am. Assn. U. Profs. Author: Jonathan Swift and Ireland, 1962; also articles. Asso. editor S. Atlantic Quar., 1961—. Home: 1212 Arnette Av Durham NC 27707

FERGUSON, PHIL MOSS, profl. engr.; b. Bartlett, Tex., Nov. 10, 1899; s. William Simpson and Annie Leonora (Moss) F.; B.S. in Civil Engring., U. Tex., 1922, C.E., 1923; M.S., U. Wis., 1924; m. Marion Hicks, Feb. 23, 1939 (div. 1940); 1 son, Yale Hicks. Tutor in physics U. Tex., 1922-23, asso. prof. civil engring., 1928-39, prof., 1939—, chmn. dept. civil engring. 1943-57, Dean T.U. Taylor prof. civil engring., 1968—; structural engr. Dwight P. Robinson & Co., N.Y.C., 1924-28, summer 1930; field insp., designer R.O. Jameson, Dallas, summer 1929; designer bridge div. Tex. Hwy. Dept., summers 1931, 32, 35, 39; designer on Buchanan Dam, S.W. Engring. Co., Austin, Tex., summer 1936. Chmn. bd. U. Coop. Soc., 1952- 54. Recipient research award Am. Soc. C.E., 1961; Distinguished Service citation U. Wis., 1970. Registered profl. engr., Tex. Mem. Am. Concrete Inst. (Wason medal for research 1954, 58, 68, pres. 1959, hon. mem. 1968), Am. Soc. C.E. (pres. Tex. sect. 1967, hon. mem. 1971), Reinforced Concrete Research Council, Comité Européen du Béton, Am. Soc. Engineering Edn., Internat. Assn. Bridge and Structural Engring. (U.S. alternate dir. 1966—), Nat. (dir. 1966-70), Tex. (pres. 1962) socs. profl. engrs., Sigma Xi, Tau Beta Pi, Phi Kappa Phi, Chi Epsilon. Methodist. Author: Plate Girder Theory, rev. 1935; Reinforced Concrete Fundamentals, 1958, 2d edit., 1965; also numerous papers on reinforced concrete and frame analysis. Office: Taylor Hall Austin TX 78712

FERGUSON, ROBERT DOYLE, lawyer; b. New Castle, Pa., Dec. 17, 1905; s. James M. and Floy (Robertson) F.; A.B., Westminster Coll., 1927; LL.B., Harvard, 1931; m. Phyllis S. Marschall, July 20, 1939; children—Phyllis M., James M. Admitted to Pa. bar, 1931; partner Patterson, Crawford, Arensberg & Dunn, 1931-43; v.p. trusts Pitts. Nat. Bank, 1943-70, exec. v.p., 1960-68, chmn. trust com., 1968-70; partner firm Tucker, Arensburg & Ferguson, 1971—; dir. Pitts. Nat. Bank. Vice pres. Magee-Womens Hosp.; trustee Westminster Coll., Bd. Family and Childrens Services. Mem. Am., Pa. bar assns., Am. Bankers Assn. (past pres. trust div.). Republican. Presbyn. Clubs: Duquesne, University, Longue Vue Country. Home: 19 Churchill Rd Pittsburgh PA 15235 Office: 1200 Pittsburgh Nat Bank Pittsburgh PA 15222

FERGUSON, ROBERT GRACEY, air transp. exec.; b. Pitts., Mar. 6, 1905; s. Huber and Caroline (Kraeer) F.; B.S., Washington and Jefferson Coll. (U.Pa.), 1927; m. Madeleine Campbell, Oct. 14, 1930; children—Robert Gracey Sally Jayne (Mrs. Sheridan G. Snyder). With Guaranty Trust Co., N.Y.C., 1928-29; with Pan Am. Airways Corp., 1929—, now sr. v.p. finance, treas., dir. Mem. council financial execs. Nat. Indsl. Conf. Bd. Clubs: Sands Point Golf; Creek, Wings, Treasurers, Sky (N.Y.C.). Home: Piping Rock Rd Locust Valley NY 11560 Office: Pan Am Bldg New York City NY 10017

FERGUSON, ROBERT LEE, educator; b. Plymouth, Ill., Apr. 27, 1921; s. Ira and Beulah (Cox) F.; B.S., Western Ill. U., 1942, M.S., 1947; Ed.D., N.Y. U., 1955; m. Mary Ellen Harwood, Aug. 16, 1941; children—Robert John, Shirlee Rose (Mrs. Garold Keithley), Gerald Paul, Alan Wayne, Mary Edith. Tchr., Gilson, Ill., 1942-43, Griggsville, Ill., 1946-47; prof., chmn., dean Sch. Bus., Ednl. Adminstrn., Western Ill. U., Macomb, 1947—, chmn. bus. edn., 1957- -. Chmn. bd. community Hotel Corp., Macomb; dir. Macomb Savs. and Loan Assn.; bus. cons., 1954—. Grading dir. Nat. Bus. Entrance testing program Nat. Bus. Edn. Assn., 1949—. Served with AUS, 1944-46. Mem. N.E.A., Nat., Ill. bus. edn. assns. Mem. Christian Ch. (elder, chmn. bd.). Home: 212 N Normal St Macomb IL 61455

FERGUSON, ROBERT RICHMOND, Jr., banker; b. Savannah, Ga., Dec. 31, 1923; s. Robert Richmond and Frances (McDonald) F.; B.S. in Bus. Adminstrn., Lehigh U., 1947; student Wharton Sch. of U. Pa., 1948; grad. Stonier Sch. Banking, Rutgers U., 1953; m. Betty Jane King, Nov. 26, 1947; children—Robert Richmond III, James Peter. With Fed. Res. Bank Phila., 1947-49, Fed. Trust Co., Newark, 1949-58; with Nat. State Bank Newark, 1958—, exec. v.p., 1964-66, pres., 1966—, also dir.; pres., dir. First Nat. State Bancorp., Newark, N.J.; dir. Firemen's Ins. Co. of Newark, N.J. Bus. Devel. Corp., Frank W. Egan & Co., Standard Container Corp., Resitoplex Corp. Chmn. trustees Essex County Coll.; trustee Boys Club Newark. Served to capt., USAAF, 1943-46. Mem. Am. Inst. Banking (bd. govs. Essex County chpt.), Phi Beta Kappa, Chi Phi. Club: Essex (Newark); Montclair (N.J.) Golf; Bay Head, Balthusrol (N.J.). Home: 753 Ridge Terrace Smoke Rise NJ 07405 Office: 550 Broad St Newark NJ 07101

FERGUSON, ROWENA, editor, writer; b. Little Rock, Dec. 24, 1904; d. William Benson and Mary (Proudfoot) Ferguson; A.B., Randolph-Macon Woman's Coll., 1925; postgrad. Vanderbilt U. Div. Sch., Columbia Sch. Journalism; D.D. (hon.), Ia. Wesleyan Coll., 1967. Editor, Methodist Pub. House, Nashville, 1930—, dir. dept. youth publs., 1958-71; cons. curriculum Bd. Edn., Meth. Ch. 1958-71; ofcl. recorder World Conf. Christian Youth, Oslo, Norway, 1947, Travancore, India, 1952. Ofcl. del. World Council Christian Edn., Birmingham, Eng., 1957, Toronto, Can., 1950, White House Conf. Children and Youth, 1960. Mem. Tenn. Council on Human Relations, Phi Beta Kappa. Author: Hunger and Hope, 1955; Teen- agers, Their Days and Ways, 1950; Everywhere, The Story of the World- wide Church, 1961; Youth and the Christian Community, 1954; Editing the Small Magazine, 1958; The Church's Ministry with Senior Highs, 1963, rev. edit., 1968. My Life: What Will I Make of It? 1966. Home: 3525 West End Av Nashville TN 37205

FERGUSON, ROY KING, business exec.; b. Paterson, N.J., Dec. 7, 1893; s. Peter Guthrie and Jennie (King) F.; ed. Central High School, Paterson, N.J.; m. Kathleen McMurray, 1916 (dec. 1932); children—Audrey Kathleen (Mrs. James E. Kussmann). Mary (Mrs. Stephen P. Kaptain), Grace (Mrs. Donald K. Hawes), John (dec.), Betty Ann; m. 2d, Leah Conrad, 1944 (dec. 1963); m. 3d, Frances Hurst Mahaffy, 1966. Asst. mgr. Lake Placid Club, N.Y., 1912-17; v.p. Northern N.Y. Securities Co., Watertown, New York, 1917-21; v.p. F. L. Carlisle and Co., N.Y., 1921-32; v.p. and treas., United Corp., N.Y., 1933-34; pres. St. Regis Paper Co., New York, 1934-57, chmn., chief exec. officer, 1957-63; pres. dir. St. Regis Paper Co. (Canada), Ltd. Eastern States Corp. Mem. Am. Mus. Natural History, N.Y., Economic Soc., N.Y. Republican. Clubs: Union League, Metropolitan (New York); Manhassett Bay Yacht (Port Washington); Creek, Pinnacle, North Hempstead Country. Home: Timber Ridge Farm Oyster Bay NY 11771 Office: 150 E 42d St New York City NY 10017

FERGUSON, STANLEY, newspaper editor; b. Worcester, Mass., Apr. 12, 1912; s. M. Howard and Mary (Cowan) F.; student Clark U., 1933-34; m. Phyllis Owens Gregg, Feb. 7, 1953; children—Stephen C., John Otis. Investigator munitions com. U.S. Senate, 1935-36. Com. interstate commerce, 1936-38; with War Dept., 1942; with Jour. of Commerce, N.Y.C., 1942—, editor, 1962—. Home: 5 Peachtree Terrace New City NY 10956 Office: 99 Wall St New York City NY 10005

FERGUSON, STANLEY ANDREW, hosp. adminstr.; b. Chgo., Sept. 10, 1908; s. Andrew P. and Almida (Johnson) F.; Ph.B., U. Chgo., 1929; m. Margaret S. Wragg, Oct. 4, 1952. Bus. mgr.-supt. Chgo. Lying-in Hosp., 1933-48; supt. City Hosp., Cleve., 1948-52; dir. Univ. Hosps., Cleve., 1952—. Bd. overseers Case Western Res. U. Served to capt. Med. Adminstrv. Corps, AUS, 1942-46. Mem. Am. Hosp. Assn. (pres. 1963-64, trustee 1959-62). Fellow Am. Coll. Hosp. Adminstrs. Home: 31000 Landerwood Dr Cleveland OH 44124 Office: 2065 Adelbert Rd Cleveland OH 44106

FERGUSON, THOMAS GRAY, mining co. exec.; b. Charleroi, Pa., May 6, 1909; s. William and Euphemia H. (Gray) F.; B.S., Carnegie Inst. Tech., 1931; m. Faith Hanna, 1935; children—Thomas A., Bruce, Faith A. With Pitts. Coal Co. div. Consolidation Coal Co., 1932-55, v.p., 1951-55; v.p., gen. mgr. Nat. Potash Co., N.Y.C., 1955-60, charge devel. and operation mine and refinery, Carlsbad, N.M., 1960—, pres., chief exec. officer, 1960—; v.p. Freeport Sulphur Co., 1966—. Mem. Carlsbad C. of C. Mason. Home: 1505 Lincoln Dr Carlsbad NM 88220

FERGUSON, TRACY HEIMAN, lawyer; b. Syracuse, N.Y., Sept. 2, 1910; s. George Joshua and Fannie (Heiman) F.; A.B., Syracuse U., 1931; LL.B., Harvard, 1934; m. Babbette R. Oberdorfer, Dec. 22, 1938; children—Babbette Tracy, Earl Mark. Admitted to N.Y. bar, 1934, also U.S. Supreme Ct., other U.S. cts.; practice in Syracuse, 1934—; partner firm Bond, Schoeneck & King, 1947- -; mem. faculty Syracuse U. Coll. Law, 1946-48. Industry mem. N.Y.-N.J. Regional Wage Stblzn. Bd., 1951-52; v.p. citizens Found. Syracuse, 1949-50; nat. vice chmn. jr. div. Am. Jewish Joint Distbn., 1937; chmn. Syracuse Jewish Welfare Fedn., 1950-51, pres., 1951; chmn. Onondaga County chpt. March of Dimes, 1956; mem. labor mgmt. adv. panel N.Y. State Mediation Bd., 1969—; mem. program com. N.Y. U. Inst. Labor Relations, 1968-71. Pres. Republican Citizens Com. Onondaga County, 1962-63. Regent LeMoyne Coll., Syracuse, 1967—; bd. dirs., sec. Community- Gen. Hosp. Greater Syracuse; former bd. dirs. Midtown Hosp., Syracuse, United Community Chest and Council Onondaga County; trustee Onondaga County

Community Coll., 1961-66, Cazenovia Coll., 1965-66, Syracuse Pub. Library, 1965-69, Union of Am. Hebrew Congregations, 1969—. Served as officer USNR, 1943-46. Mem. Am. (chmn. labor relations law sect. 1963- 64, mem. council 1957-66; sect. del. 1965-66), Fed., N.Y. (chmn. labor law com. 1964-66); Onondaga County bar assns., Am. Arbitration Assn. (bd. dirs., former chmn. N.Y. State adv. council). Jewish religion (trustee temple, pres. 1966-71). Clubs: University (Syracuse); Nat. Lawyers (Washington). Contbr. articles legal jours. Home: 218 Brookford Rd Syracuse NY 13224 Office: State Tower Bldg Syracuse NY 13202

FERGUSON, WARREN JOHN, U.S. dist. judge; b. Eureka, Nev., Oct. 31, 1920; s. Ralph and Marian (Damele) F.; B.A., U. Nev., 1942; LL.B., U. So. Cal., 1949; m. E. Laura Keyes, June 5, 1948; children—Faye F., Warren John, Teresa M., Peter J. Admitted to Cal. bar, 1950; mem. firm Ferguson & Judge, Fullerton, Cal., 1950-59; city atty. for cities of Buena Park, Placentia, La Puente, Baldwin Park, Santa Fe Springs, Walnut and Rosemead, Cal., 1953-59; municipal ct. judge, Anaheim, Cal., 1959-60; superior ct. judge, Santa Ana, Cal., 1961-66; U.S. dist. judge, Los Angeles, 1966—. Asso. prof. psychiatry (law), Sch. Medicine, U. So. Cal. Served with AUS, 1942-46. Decorated Bronze Star. Mem. Phi Kappa Phi, Theta Chi. Democrat. Roman Catholic. Office: 312 N Spring St Los Angeles CA 90012

FERGUSON, WHITWORTH, elec. constrn. co. exec.; b. Walcott, Ia., Oct. 30, 1900; s. Charles Andrew and Edna (Whitworth) F.; B.S. in Elec. Engring., Ia. State U., 1921; postgrad. Mass. Inst. Tech., 1921-23; D.Sc. (hon.), Webber Coll., Babson Park, Fla., 1963; m. Dorothy Anger, June 25, 1924; children—Barbara Jean (Mrs. Frederic H. Federlein), Whitworth, Donald Richard. Vice pres. Robertson Electric Co., Buffalo, 1923-35; pres. Ferguson Electric Constrn. Co. Inc., Buffalo, 1935—, Ferguson Electric Equipment Corp., Buffalo, 1953—; v.p., dir. Delnite Mines, Ltd., Timmons, Ont., Can., 1955—; chmn. Buffalo br. Fed. Res. Bank N.Y., 1963- 65; dir. Erie Lackawanna R.R. Co., Buffalo Ins. Co. Vice chmn. N.Y. State Atomic and Space Devel. Authority, 1962—; dep. dir. Erie County Civil Def., 1953—. Chmn. Creative Edn. Found.; pres. Ferguson Found.; past pres. United Fund Buffalo; trustee Hosp. Service Corp. Buffalo, Millard Fillmore Hosp.; bd. regents Canisius Coll.; trustee Buffalo YMCA, Albright Art Gallery; mem. Mass. Inst. Tech. Future Planning Com. Served to col. USAAF, World War II. Recipient Civic Affairs citation U. Buffalo, 1958; Engring. citation Ia. State U., 1963; Man of the Yr. award, Buffalo C. of C., 1968. Mem. Buffalo C. of C. (pres. 1959-60; chmn. nuclear com. 1963—), Newcomen Soc., Def. Orientation Conf. Assn. Presbyn. (elder). Home: 148 Soldiers Place Buffalo NY 14222 Office: 333 Ellicott St Buffalo NY 14203

FERGUSON, WILLIAM CARLISLE, food chain exec.; b. Phila., Dec. 4, 1906; s. William R. and Edith (Carlisle) F.; A.B., Stanford, 1930; m. Katheryne Isobel Kerr, Sept. 23, 1937; children—Katheryne Kerr (Mrs. T. Beuclere Rogers IV); Mary Carlisle (Mrs. David T. Sykes). Traffic statistician traffic dept., City of Phila., 1931-32; field rep., office mgr., pub. relations counsel Household Finance Corp., 1933-36; successively store mgr., buyer, sales and advt. depts. Acme Markets, Inc., formerly Am. Stores Co., 1936-43, dir. tng., 1944-46, dir. personnel, 1947-56, v.p., 1957—. Dir. Phila. YMCA, Penn Center Acad. Mem. St. Andrews Soc., Delta Upsilon. Presbyn. (elder). Clubs: Union League, Poor Richard (Phila.), Merion Cricket (Haverford, Pa.); Rose Tree Fox Hunting (York, Pa.); Winter Harbor (Me.) Yacht. Co-author: Food Marketing, 1950. Contbr. tech. articles merchandising publs. Home: 1200 Remington Rd Wynnewood PA 19096 Office: 124 N 15th St Philadelphia PA 19101

FERGUSON, WILLIAM EMMETT, stock exchange ofcl.; b. Quincy, Mass., Dec. 21, 1902; s. Patrick J. and Margaret (O'Brien) F.; ed. high sch.; m. Loretta Mahon, July 6, 1935. With Thomson & McKinnon, Inc., Chgo. (now Thomson, McKinnon & Auchincloss), 1919—, gen. partner, 1948, now also chm. bd. Formerly member of the board of governors of the vice chmn. exec. com. Midwest Stock Exchange, Chicago. Mem. Bd. Trade City of Chgo., Duluth, Kansas City bds. trade, Memphis Cotton Exchange, Chgo. Merc. Exchange, Winnipeg Grain Exchange, Winnipeg Stock Exchange. Clubs: Beverly Country, Union League (Chgo.). Home: 179 E Lake Shore Dr Chicago IL 60611 Office: 134 S LaSalle St Chicago IL 60603

FERGUSON, WILLIAM MCDONALD, former state official; b. Wellington, Kan., Dec. 2, 1917; s. William McDonald and May (Deems) F.; A.B., U. Kan., 1938; LL.B., Harvard, 1941; m. Harriet Shelden, Sept. 12, 1939; children—Joan, William McDonald III. Admitted to Kan. bar, 1946; city atty., Wellington, 1948-57; gen. Practice law, 1957-61; atty. gen. Kan., 1961-65. Pres. Security State Bank, Wellington, 1959—. Mem. Kan. Ho. of Reps. 69th Dist., 1949-57. Served to lt. (s.g.) USNR, 1942-46. Mem. Am. (ho. dels. 1961-62), Kan. (exec. council 1952-61, v.p., 1961, pres. 1963) bar assns., Am. Legion, Sigma Alpha Epsilon. Republican. Elk. Home: 1023 S Washington St Wellington KS 67152

FERGUSON, WILLIAM MCL., lawyer; b. Newport News, Va., Mar. 4, 1906; s. Homer L. and Eliza Anderson (Skinner) F.; A.B., U. Va., 1927. LL.B., 1930; m. Claire Murray, Oct. 19, 1935 (dec. Dec. 1960); children—Claire Margaret, William, Jr., Charles Anderson, Mary Josephine, David Lane; m. 2d, Shirley Hieatt Hulten, Jan. 12, 1962; children—Faye Lenoir, Graham Scott; stepchildren—Deborah and Holly Hulten. Admitted to N.Y. bar, 1930, and practiced N.Y.C. as asso. law firm Burlington, Veeder, Clark & Hupper, 1930-36; mem. firm Skinner & Ferguson, Newport News. Va., 1940- 45, now Ferguson and Harvell; director Va. Elec. & Power Co. Trustee Mariners' Museum; mem. sch. bd. Warwick Co.; mem. local bds. Boy Scouts, Girl Scouts of Am., Boys' Club. Mem. Va. House Delegates, 1940-46. Trustee of Hampton Roads Academy. Member American, Virginia, and Newport News bar assns., Nat. Rifle Assn., Automobile Assn. Am. (mem. local bd.). Va. Peninsula Sportsmen's Assn., Episcopalian. Clubs: James River Country, Anglers' (N.Y.C.): Lafayette Gun, (Newport News). Elk. Home: 55 Ferguson Lane Blount Point Newport News VA 23606 Office: 225 28th St Newport News VA 23607

FERGUSSON, BERNARD EDWARD, former gov.-gen. New Zealand; b. London, Eng., May 6, 1911; s. Charles and Alice (Boyle) F.; grad. Eton Coll., 1929, Sandhurst Mil. Coll., 1931; m. Laura Grenfell, Nov. 22, 1950; 1 son, George Duncan. Joined Black Watch, British Army, 1931, commd. lt., 1934, advanced through grades to brig., 1943; served in Middle East, Burma, ETO, World War II; served at SHAPE, Paris, France, 1951-53; commander of 153d Highland Brigade, 1955-56, 29th Inf. Brigade, 1957-58; assigned Allied Forces Hdqrs., Port Said, 1956; retired, 1958; gov.-gen. New Zealand, 1962-67; member Internat. Observer Team, Nigeria, 1968-69. Decorated Distinguished Service Order, 1943, Order British Empire, 1950, grand cross St. Michael and St. George, 1962, Royal Victorian Order, 1963. Fellow Royal Geog. Soc., Royal Soc. Lit. Mem. Ch. of Scotland (elder). Clubs: White's (London); New (Edinburgh). Author: Eton Portrait, 1937; Beyond the Chindwin, 1945; Lowland Soldier, (verse), 1945; The Wild Green Earth, 1946; The Black Watch and the King's Enemies, 1950; Rupert of the Rhine, 1952; The Rare Adventure, 1954; The Watery Maze; The Story of Combined Operations, 1961; Wavell, Portrait of a Soldier, 1961; Return to Burma, 1962. Home: Auchairne Ballantrae Ayrshire Scotland

FERGUSSON, FRANCIS, lit. critic; b. Alburquerque, N.M., Feb. 21, 1904; s. Harvey Butler and Clara Mary (Huning) F.; student Harvard, 1921-23; B.A. (Rhodes scholar), Oxford U., 1926; m. Marion Crowne, Jan. 16, 1931 (dec. 1959); children—Harvey, Honora; m. 2d, Peggy Kaiser, July 26, 1962. Asso. dir. Am. Lab. Theatre, N.Y., 1926-30; drama critic The Bookman mag., N.Y., 1930-32; lectr., exec. sec. New Sch. for Social Research. N.Y.C. 1932-34; prof. humanities and drama Bennington, (Vt.) Coll., 1934-47; mem. Inst. for Advanced Study, Princeton, N.J., 1948-49; dir. Princeton Seminars in lit. criticism, 1949-52, adv. bd. humanities program, Princeton, 1952-58; vis. prof. English, Ind. U., 1952-53; mem. editorial bd. Comparative Lit., 1952-60; prof. comparative lit. Rutgers U., 1953-68. Recipient award for lit. Nat. Inst. Arts and Letters, 1953. Mem. Nat. Inst. Arts and Letters. Author books including: The Idea of a Theatre, 1949; Plays of Moliere, Critical Introduction, 1950; Dante's Drama of the Mind, (Christian Gauss award 1953); Aristotle's Poetics, Critical Introduction, 1961; Poems, 1962; Dante, 1966; Shakespeare: The Pattern in His Carpet, 1970; also contrbr. poems to Partisan Review, etc.; Critical Essays; The Human Image, 1957. Gen. editor Laurel Shakespeare, 1957—. Home: Box 143 Kingston NJ 08528 Office: Princeton University Princeton NJ 08540 ☆

FERGUSSON, ROBERT GEORGE, corp. exec., ret. army officer; b. Chgo., May 20, 1911; s. Archibald Campbell and Anne (Sheehan) F.; student Beloit Coll., 1929-32; B.S., U.S. Mil. Acad., 1936; M.A. in Internat. Relations, Boston U., 1959; m. Charlotte Lawrence, Nov. 18, 1937; 1 son, Robert Lawrence (dec.), Commd. 2d lt. U.S. Army, 1936, advanced through grades to maj. gen., 1962; mem. gen. staff 7th Inf. Div., 1943-45; assigned hdqrs. Pacific Base Command, then Hawaii, 1945-46; instr. Command and Gen. Staff Coll., Ft. Leavenworth, Kan., 1946-48; chief dissemination br. intelligence div. Dept. Army, Washington, 1948-49; assigned 8th Inf. Regt., 4th Div., Ft. Ord, Monterey, Cal., 1949, Hdqrs. 8th Army, Korea, 1950-51; chief S.E. Asia br. fgn. mil. affairs Office Sec. Def., Washington, 1952-54; dep. chief staff Hdqrs. U.S. Army Pacific, 1954-55; comdg. officer 14th Inf. Regt., Hawaii, 1955-57; chief army adv. group Naval War Coll., Newport, R.I., 1957-61; asst. div. comdr. 24th Inf. Div., Augsburg, Germany, 1961-62; chief staff Hdqrs. Central Army Group (NATO), Heidelberg, Germany, 1962-65; comdg. gen. U.S. Army Tng. Center, Inf., Ft. Ord, 1965-67; comdr. U.S. Forces, Berlin, 1967-70, retired, 1970; corporate group v.p. manpower planning Dart Industries, Inc., Los Angeles, 1970—. Decorated D.S.M., Legion of Merit with oak leaf cluster, Bronze Star with 3 oak leaf clusters, Purple Heart (U.S.); Knight comdr. Cross with badge and star Order of Merit (Fed. Republic Germany). Mem. of Assn. Grads. U.S. Mil. Acad., Co. Mil. Collectors and Historians, Conseil Internat. de la Chasse (Paris, France), Clan Fergusson Soc., Beta Theta Pi. Home: Box 1016 Pebble Beach CA 93953 Office: 8480 Beverly Blvd Los Angeles CA 90048

FERGUSSON, WILLIE EARL, III, banker; b. Richmond, Va., Apr. 7, 1929; s. Willie Earl, Jr. and Carrie (Holmes) F.; student Va. Poly. Inst., 1946-48; B.S. in Bus. Adminstrn., U. Richmond, 1953; grad. Nat. Trust Sch., Am. Bankers Assn., 1962, NABAC Sch. for Bank Audit, Control and Operation, 1965; m. Jo Lo Jones, May 2, 1952 (div. May 1971); children—Bruce Norwood, Bonnie Lyne; m. 2d, Sara Dianne Smith, July 31, 1971. With State Planters Bank & Trust Co., Richmond, Va., 1948-49, Robert Heard, C.P.A., Columbia, S.C., 1956; plant accountant RECO Tanks, Inc., Columbia, 1956-59; with S.C. Nat. Bank, Columbia, 1960—, gen. auditor, 1962—, v.p., 1966—. Served with AUS, 1954-56. Mem. Nat. Assn. Accountants (pres. Columbia 1965-66, nat. bd. dirs. 1966-68, 70—, nat. v.p. 1969-70, nat. finance com. 1970—), Inst. Internal Auditors (v.p. Piedmont-Carolinas chpt. 1968-69), Bank Adminstrn. Inst. (mem. C.B.A. exam. com. 1970-71), Sigma Phi Epsilon. Presbyn. (elder 1966—, chmn. bldg. commn. 1968, mem. synod. com. on ministers' salaries 1969—). Home: Plantation Oaks Apts Columbia SC 29210 Office: SCN Center Main St Columbia SC 29202

FERLINGHETTI, LAWRENCE, poet; b. Yonkers, N.Y., 1920; s. Charles and Clemence (Mendes- Monsanto) F.; A.B., U. N.C.; M.A., Columbia; Doctorat De L'Université, Sorbonne, 1950; m. 1951; children—Julie, Lorenzo. Founder (with Peter D. Martin) first all paperbound bookstore in U.S., City Lights Books, San Francisco; firm also publishes works of modern poets and writers; widely traveled poetry reader, also painter. Participant (with Allen Ginsberg) Pan Am. cultural conf. U. Concepcion (Chile), 1960. Served with USNR, World War II. Author: (poetry) Pictures of the Gone World, 1955, A Coney Island of the Mind, 1958, Starting from San Francisco, 1961, After the Cries of the Birds, (novel) Her, 1960; Routines; Unfair Arguments With Existence (Plays); The Secret Meaning of Things (poetry); The Mexican Night; Back Roads to Far Places. Editor: City Lights Jour. Address: City Lights Publishing House 1562 Grant Av San Francisco CA 94133

FERM, DEANE WILLIAM, coll. chaplain; b. Lebanon, Pa., May 22, 1927; s. Vergilius T.A. and Nellie (Nelson) F.; B.A., Coll. Wooster, 1949; B.D., Yale, 1952, M.A., 1953, Ph.D., 1954; m. Paulie Swan, June 26, 1949; children—William, Linnea, Robert, Laurie. Ordained to ministry Presbyn. Ch., 1952; minister Fishers Island Union Chapel, N.Y., 1952-54; dir. Sch. Religion, Mont. State U., 1954-59; asst. dir. Danforth Found., 1958; dean Coll. Chapel, Mt. Holyoke Coll., South Hadley, Mass., 1959—; lectr. Smith Coll., 1960-63. Served with USNR, 1945-46. Recipient Danforth Campus Ministry grant, 1965-66; Poulson fellow Am. Scandinavian Found., 1965-66. Mem. Nat. Assn. Coll. and Univ. Chaplains. Author: Responsible Sexuality Now; 1971. Contbr. articles profl. jours. Home: 79 College St South Hadley MA 01075

FERM, ROBERT LIVINGSTON, educator; b. Wooster, O., Jan. 2, 1931; s. Vergilius Ture Anselm and Nellie (Nelson) F.; B.A., Coll. Wooster, 1952; B.D., Yale, 1955, M.A., 1956, Ph.D., 1958; children-Eric Livingston, Alison Flournoy, Mem. faculty Pomona Coll., 1958-69, John Knox McLean prof. religion, 1967-69, chmn. dept., 1963-69; prof. religion Claremont Grad. Sch., 1964-69; prof. religion, chmn. dept. Middlebury Coll., 1969—; ordained minister Presbyn. Ch., 1955. Recipient Wig Distinguished Prof. award Pomona Coll., 1967. Author: Readings in History of Christian Thought, 1964; Issues in American Protestantism, 1969. Home: 5 Green Mountain Pl Middlebury VT 05753

FERM, VERGIL HARKNESS, embryologist; b. West Haven, Conn., Sept. 13, 1924; s. Vergilius T.A. and Nellie (Nelson) F.; A.B., Coll. Wooster, 1946; M.D., Western Res. U., 1948; M.S., U. Wis., 1950, Ph.D., 1955; M.A. (hon.), Dartmouth, 1967; m. Ruth Eleanor Rowe, June 5, 1948; children—Daniel W., David V., Judith N., Susan C. Asst. prof. Ind. U., 1955-57; asso. prof. U. Fla., 1957-61; asso. prof. pathology Dartmouth Med. Sch., Hanover, N.H., 1961- 66, prof. anatomy and embryology, 1966—, also chmn. dept. anatomy. Mem. Am. Assn. Anatomists, Am. Soc. Human Genetics, Teratology Soc. Exptl. Pathology, Phi Beta Kappa, Sigma Xi. Research, publs. on environmental and genetic factors causing birth defects. Home: 20 Valley Rd Hanover NH 03755

FERM, VERGILIUS TURE ANSELM, educator; b. Sioux City, Ia., Jan. 6, 1896; s. Olof Wilhelm and Mathilda (Slattengren) F.; A.B., Augustana Coll., Rock Island, Ill., 1916; B.D., Augustana Theol. Sem., 1919; postgrad. Ia. State U., 1919-22; A.M., Yale, 1923, Ph.D., 1925, postgrad., 1926; m. Nellie Agnette Nelson, June 25, 1919; children—Virginia Annette (dec.), Vergilius Nelson (dec.), Vergil Harkness, Deane William, Jules Robert Livingston. Ordained to Luth. Ch., 1919; pastor, Cedar Rapids, Ia., 1919-22, St. Paul's Ch., Ansonia, Conn., 1922-26; First Ch., West Haven, Conn., 1924-26; prof. philosophy and social scis. Albright Coll., Reading, Pa., 1926-27; asst. prof. philosophy Coll. of Wooster (O.), 1927-28, prof. 1928-64, Compton prof. philosophy, head dept., 1938- 64, prof. emeritus, 1964—, dean of the Coll. summer session, 1940-42, 44; leave for research and writing, 1946-47, 52-53, 56- 57, 61-62; vis. prof. philosophy Sweet Briar (Va.) Coll., 1964-65; vis. prof. Wake Forest (N.C.) U., 1965-68, acting chmn. dept. philosophy, 1966-68; prof. philosophy Ashland (O.) Coll., 1968—; vis. prof. Heidelberg Coll., Tiffin, O., 1968. Elected affiliate mem. Wooster Presbytery, 1949, mem. Lutheran Ministerium of Augustana Synod (now Synod Ohio, United Luth. Ch. Am.). Mem. Am. Philos. Assn., Am. Assn. U. Profs., Am. Theol. Soc. (v.p. 1943-44; pres. 1944-45), Am. Soc. Ch. History, Authors Guild, Phi Beta Kappa. Author of books including: What Can We Believe?, 1948; A Protestant Dictionary, 1951; Their Day Was Yesterday, 1954, Pastoral Psychology, 1955; Pictorical History of Protestantism, 1957; A Brief Dictionary of American Superstitions, 1959; Inside Ivy Walls, 1964; Toward an Expansive Christian Theology, 1964; Basic Philosophy for Beginners, 1969; Memoirs of a College Professor, 1971. Editor: Ency. of Religion, 1945; Religion in the Twentieth Century, 1947; Forgotten Religions, 1949; A History of Philosophical Systems, 1950 (trans. into Japanese, 1956); The American Church, 1952; The Protestant Credo, 1953; Puritan Sage; The Collected Writings of Jonathon Edwards, 1953; Ency. of Morals, 1956; Classics of Protestantism, 1959. Contbg. editor: Dictionary of Philosophy; Philosophic Abstracts; Introduction to A Doctor's Soliloquy, 1953; Questions That Matter Most, 1954; Introduction to the Last Analysis, 1956; Toward an Expansive Christian Theology, 1965, other vols. Contbr. to religious and philos. jours. Home: 1586 Beall Av PO Box 503 Wooster OH 44691 (summer) Mercer Lake Mercer WI 54547 ☆

FERMAN, IRVING, lawyer, educator; b. N.Y.C., July 4, 1919; s. Joseph and Sadie (Stein) F.; B.S., N.Y.U., 1941; J.D., Harvard, 1948; m. Bertha Paglin, June 12, 1946; children—James Paglin, Susan Paglin. Admitted to La. bar, 1948; partner Provensal, Faris & Ferman, New Orleans, 1948-52; dir. Washington office Am. Civil Liberties Clearing House, 1952-54; exec. vice chmn. Pres.'s Com. Govt. Contracts, 1959-60; v.p. Internat. Latex Corp., 1960-66; pres. Piedmont Theaters Corp., 1966-69; adj. asso. prof. mgmt. N.Y.U. Grad. Sch. Bus., 1964-68; adj. prof. law Howard U., 1968-69, prof. law, 1969—. Mem. Am. Com. Cultural Freedom, 1954—; mem. Com. of Arts and Scis. for Eisenhower, 1956; mem. citizens adv. com. U.S. Commn. on Govt. Security, 1957; chmn. Police Complaint Review Bd., 1965—; mem. Dept. Health, Edn. and Welfare Reviewing Authority 1969—. Mem. bd. dirs. New Orleans Acad. Art, 1948-51. Served from cadet to 1st lt., USAAF, 1942-46. Mem. Am., La., New Orleans bar assns. Jewish religion. Clubs: Capitol Hill, International (Washington); Harvard, Caterpillar (N.Y.C.). Contbr. to books and revs. Home: 3818 Huntington St Washington DC 20015

FERMAN, JOSEPH WOLFE, publisher; b. N.Y.C., June 8, 1906; s. Wolfe and Esther (Little) F.; B.C.S., N.Y.U., 1927; m. Ruth L. Eisen, Jan. 29, 1931; 1 son, Edward Lewis. Circulation mgr. Am. Mercury, N.Y.C., 1926-39, bus. mgr., 1939- 44, dir., 1940-50, v.p., sec., 1944-50; dir. Jonathan Press Inc., N.Y.C., 1942-56, v.p., sec., 1944-56; v.p., dir. Fantasy House, Inc., 1949-54, pres., 1954-58, Casebook Publs., Inc., 1950-53; pres. Mercury Publs., N.Y.C., 1954—; pub. mag. Fantasy and Science Fiction, editor, pub. Bestseller Mystery mag., Mercury Mystery mag., 1958-61; treas., dir. Leasehold Assos., 1958-61; dir. Chapin Jr. Corp., 1958—; editor No Limits, 1964; pub. P.S. mag., 1966, Inner Space, Mag. of the Psychic and Occult, 1970; dir. Monroe Gas System. Mem. exec. com. Com. for World Human Rights. Mem. Mag. Pubs. Assn. Clubs: Hundred Million, Nassau County Unity. Home: 20 Addison Place Rockville Centre NY 11570 Office: 347 E 53d St New York City NY 10022

FERMI, LAURA, author; b. Rome, Italy, June 16, 1907; d. Augusto and Costanza (Romanelli) Capon; student U. Rome, 1926-28; m. Enrico Fermi, July 19, 1928 (dec.); children—Nella (Mrs. Nella Weiner), Giulio. Came to U.S., 1939, naturalized, 1944. Author: Atoms in the Family, 1954; Atoms For the World, 1957; Mussolini, 1961; The Story of Atomic Energy (juvenile), 1961; Illustrious Immigrants, 1968; (with Ginestra Amaldi) Alchimia Del Tempo Nostro, 1936; (with Gilberto Bernardini) Galileo and the Scientific Revolution, 1961. Mem. Chgo. Air Pollution Control Com., 1960-68. Bd. govs. Internat. House Chgo., 1955-66; mem. women's bd. U. Chgo. Guggenheim fellow, 1957. Recipient prize Friends of Lit., 1968. Mem. League Women Voters Chgo., Authors' Guild. Home: 5532 South Shore Dr Chicago IL 60637

FERNALD, CHARLES E., business exec.; b. 1902. With Chem. Leaman Tank Lines Inc., Downington, Pa., 1931—, now sec., mem. exec. com., dir. C.P.A., Pa. Office: 520 E Lancaster Av Downington PA 19335*

FERNANDES, JOSEPH EDWARD, supermarket exec.; b. Madeira Island, Portugal, Mar. 12, 1923; s. Jose and Rosa (Teixeira) F.; came to U.S., 1924, naturalized, 1946; B.S. in Bus. Adminstrn., Boston U., 1947; D.Comml. Sci. (hon.), Stonehill Coll., 1964; m. Annabelle Watson, Apr. 24, 1954; children—Joseph, Marcia, Donna Maria. With Fernandes Super Markets, Inc., Norton, Mass., 1948—, pres., treas., 1952—; treas. Fernandes Realty Corp., Brockton East Shopping Plaza, Inc., Fernandes Twin-City Realty Corp.; dir. First Machinists Nat. Bank, Taunton, Mass., Mfrs. Nat. Bank, North Attleboro, Mass., Fall River Line Pier (Mass.). Co-founder, dir. staff Supermarkets Assos., Inc., 1958—. Dir. Annawon council Boy Scouts Am.; regional dir. N.E. Boy Scouts Am., 1971—; former chmn. Portuguese Am. Fedn. U.S. and Can.; cons. Alliance for Progress, Uruguay, 1962. Bd. dirs. Mass. Blue Cross-Blue Shield. Morgan Meml., Boston; chmn. trustees Stonehill Coll; sponsor ann. Portuguese cultural lecture series Wheaton Coll., Norton, 1964—; bd. govs. Acad. Food Distbn., St. Joseph's Coll., Phila. 1969. Served with AUS, 1943-45. Decorated knight St. Gregory the Great; Order Prince Henry the Navigator (Portugal); recipient Man of Year award Nat. Conf. Christians and Jews, Peter Francisco award Portuguese Continental Union, 1966. Mem. Internat. Assn. Chain Stores (pres. 1968-71). Home: Fernandes Circle Norton MA 02766 Office: 380 S Worcester St Norton MA 02766

FERNANDEZ, EUSTASIO, Jr., educator; b. Tampa, Fla., Dec. 11, 1919; s. Eustasio and Carmen (Aguera) F.; B.S., U. Fla., 1941; M.A., U. Md., 1947, Middlebury Coll., 1950; Doctor en Letras, Nat. U. Mexico, 1960; m. Athena Lozos, Dec. 3, 1950; children—Christopher Tasio, Alexandra Athena. Instr. Spanish, U. Tampa, 1951-52, asst. prof., 1952-60, asso. prof., 1960-64, prof. modern langs., 1964—, acting chmn. modern lang. dept., 1958-60, chmn., 1960—. Spanish lang. cons. legal and engring. firms, pub. ofcls. Fla. edn. rep. Fla.-Colombia Alliance, 1965—; chmn. pub. relations Tampa-Barranquilla (Colombia) Sister Com., 1970—. Served with M.I., AUS, 1942-45. Recipient certificate of merit AID, 1970. Inst. Internat. Edn. (N.Y.) fellow U. Havana, 1947; Father Felix Varela fellow U. Havana, 1949. Mem. Am. Assn. Tchrs. Spanish and Portuguese, Modern Lang. Assn., S. Atlantic Modern Lang. Assn., Am. Assn. U. Profs., Tampa World Trade Council, Theta Chi, Phi Delta Kappa. Democrat. Presbyn. Clubs: Sertoma (Tampa, v.p. 1957, pres. 1970); Centro Espanol de Tampa, University Spanish. Author: La Proyeccion Social on las Novelas de Gregorio Lopez y Fuentes, 1960. Home: 104 S Lincoln Tampa FL 33609

FERNANDEZ, LEO, chem. co. exec.; b. 1913; B.S. in Elec. Engring., Newark Coll. Engring., 1940; M.S. in Chem. Engring., Stevens Inst. Tech., 1945; married. With Merck & Co. Inc., 1935—, dir. marketing devel. Merck Sharp & Dohme Internat. div., 1953-54, dir. prodn. and tech. operations, 1954-55, gen. mgr. Latin Am., 1955-57, v.p., 1957-66, sr. v.p. operations, 1966-67, exec. v.p., gen. mgr., 1967-69, pres., 1969—. Office: 128 E Lincoln Av Rahway NJ 07065

FERNANDEZ, MARIANO HUGO, banker; b. Havana, Cuba, Apr. 29, 1939; s. Jesus M. and America (Sire) F.; came to U.S., 1944, naturalized, 1959; standard certificate Am. Inst. Banking, 1965; m. Mary Patricia Demeritt, Aug. 27, 1960; children—Mariano Hugo II, Theresa Marie. With First Nat. Bank Miami, Fla., 1957—, auditor, 1967-68; auditor S.E. Banking Corp., Miami, 1968- -. Served with USCGR, 1959-67. Mem. Bank Adminstrn. Inst. (bd. dirs. S. Fla. chpt. 1968-71). Home: 10190 S W 99th Av Miami FL 33156 Office: 100 S Biscayne Blvd Miami FL 33131

FERNANDEZ, ROYES, dancer; b. New Orleans, July 15, 1929; s. Manuel Paul and Francoise (Blanchin) F.; grad. high sch., New Orleans. Debut, Original Ballet Russe, 1946-47; soloist Markova-Dolin Ballet, 1947-48; soloist Ballet Alicia Alonso, 1948-50, premier danseur, 1952-54; premier danseur Australia's Borovanskv Ballet, 1954-56; soloistAm. Ballet Theatre, 1950- 53, prin. dancer, 1957—, premier danseur, 1962—, also tours sponsored by Dept. State to Europe, 1958, 60, USSR, 1960, 66, Latin Am., 1964; premier danseur London's Festival Ballet, summer 1962; participated Fonteyn World Tour, summer 1963; with Gala Matinee of Ballet, London, Drury Lane Theatre, Royal Acad. Dancing, Dec. 1963; guest artist Australian Nat. Ballet, Sydney and Melbourne, spring 1964, Jacob's Pillow, Lee, Mass., 1961, 62, 63, 64, 66, 70; guest appearances numerous ballet cos., with symphony orchestras and on TV; spl. performance at the White House, 1968; prin. roles include La Sylphide, Nutcracker, Giselle, Sleeping Beauty, La Fille Mal Gardee, Swan Lake, Coppelia, Les Sylphides, also contemporary ballets Etudes, Lilac Garden, Theme and Variations, Lady from the Sea, Aleko, Las Hermanas, Moor's Pavane, The Traitor, Gaite Parisienne. Hon. chmn. La. ballet council La. Council for Music and Performing Arts, 1968—, recipient 1st Ann. award, 1968. Mem. Am. Guild Mus. Artists. Office: American Ballet Theatre 1619 Broadway New York City NY 10019

FERNANDEZ-MORAN, HUMBERTO, biophysicist; b, Maracaibo, Venezuela, Feb. 18, 1924; s. Luis and Elena (Villalobos) F.; M.D., U. Munich (Germany), 1944, U. Caracas (Venezuela), 1945; M.S., U. Stockholm (Sweden), 1951, Ph.D., 1952; m. Anna Browallius, Dec. 30, 1953; children—Brigida Elena, Veronica. Fellow Neurology, neuropathology George Washington U., 1945-46; intern George Washington U. Hosp., 1945-46; resident Serafimerlasarettet, Stockholm, 1946-58; fgn. asst. Neurosurg, Clinic, Stockholm, 1946-48; research fellow Nobel Inst. Physics, Stockholm, 1947-49. Inst. Cell Research & Genetics, Karolinska Institutet, Stockholm, 1948-51, asst. prof., 1952; prof., chmn. dept. biophysics U. Caracas, 1951-58; dir. Venezuelan Inst. Neurology and Brain Research, Caracas, 1954-58; asso. biophysicist neurosurg. service Mass. Gen. Hosp., Boston, 1958-62; vis. lectr. dept. biology Mass. Inst. Tech., 1958-62; research asso. neuropathology Harvard, 1958-62; prof. biophysics U. Chgo., 1962—. Sci. and cultural attache to Venezuelan legations, Sweden, Norway, Denmark, 1947-54; head Venezuelan commn. Atomic Energy Conf., Geneva, 1955; chmn. Venezuelan commn. 1st Inter-Am.-Symposium on Nuclear Energy, Brookhaven, N.Y., 1957; minister of edn., Venezuela, 1958; mem. Orgn. Am. States adv. commn. on sci. devel. in Latin Am., Nat. Acad. Scis., 1958; mem. U.S. Nat. Com. UNESCO, 1957. Recipient Gold medal City Maracaibo, 1968. Fellow Am. Acad. Arts and Sci.; mem. Venezuelan Acad. Medicine (hon.), Academia Ciencias Fisicas y Matematicas (Caracas), Am. Acad. Neurology (corr. mem.), Internat. Soc. Cell Biology, Buenos Aires, Santiago, Lima, socs. Neurology. Buenos Aires, Santiago, Lima, Porto Alegre societies surgery. Electron Microscopy Soc. Am., Am. Nuclear Soc., Pan Am. Med. Assn. Author: The Submicroscopic Organization of Vertebrate Nerve Fibres, 1952; The Submicroscopic Organization of the Internode Portion of Vertebrate Myelinated Nerve Fibers, 1953; Studies of the Submicroscopic Organization of Thalamus, 1955; also numerous sci. papers. Editorial bd. Jour. of Cell Biology, 1961. Home: 5807 Dorchester Av Chicago IL 60637 Office: Dept Biophysics U Chgo 5640 S Ellis Av Chicago IL 60637

FERNBACH, ROBERT DENNIS, lawyer; b. Cheektowaga, N.Y., May 27, 1917; s. Louis P. and Katherine (Kinsella) F.; grad. cum laude U. Notre Dame, 1938; LL.B. with distinction, Cornell U., 1941; m. Beth M. Hager, July 18, 1947; children—Robert Dennis, John P. Admitted to N.Y. bar, 1941; with Moot, Sprague, Marcy, Landy & Fernbach, Buffalo, 1941—, now mem. firm. Sec., dir. Birdair Structures, Inc., Moog, Inc.; dir. Monroe Abstract & Title Corp.; lectr. U. Buffalo Sch. Bus. Adminstrn., 1947-50, Law Sch., 1950-54. Served with USAAF, 1942-45. Decorated Bronze Star medal. Mem. Am., N.Y. State, Erie County bar assns. Republican. Catholic. Home: 117 Hyledge Dr Eggertsville NY 14226 Office: Erie County Bank Bldg Buffalo NY 14202

FERNEAU, ELMER FRANK, educator; b. Tama, Ia., Dec. 7, 1918; s. Frank D. and Adra Elva (Powers) F.; B.S., Ia. State Coll., 1939; M.A., Northwestern U., 1948; Ph.D., U. Chgo., 1954; m. Marie Humphry, Nov. 28, 1942; 1 son, Brett Humphry. Vocational agr. tchr., Bedford, Ia., 1939-41, Audubon, Ia., 1941; dir. adult edn., Chisago City, Minn., 1946-48; grad. asso. Midwest Adminstrn. Center, U. Chgo., 1950-54; asst. prof. edn. Ia. State Tchrs. Coll., 1954- 55; asso. prof. edn. Okla. State U., 1955-57; prof. eds., head dept. U. Tulsa, 1957—, dean Coll. of Education, 1965-70; mem. bd. Children's Med. Center; v.p. board trustees Child Guidance Clinic. Mem. Okla. Commn. Ednl. Adminstrn., Okla. Commn. Tchr. Certification. Served with USNR, 1941-45. Mem. Nat., Okla. edn. assns., Okla. Assn. Sch. Adminstrs. Home: 3207 E 44th St Tulsa OK 74105

FERNLEY, GEORGE ADAMSON, bus. exec. and adviser; b. Phila., June 13, 1891; s. T. James and Harriet (Adamson) F.; B.S., U. Pa., 1912, grad. work, 1912-14; m. Mildred Bougher, Mar. 15, 1916; children—Lois (Mrs. Henry S. McNeil), Robert Clute, Joan Adamson (Mrs. Stewart McCracken). Partner firm Fernley & Fernley, Phila., 1943—. Served as capt., ordnance dept., U.S. Army, 1917-18. Received Award of Merit of Hardware Mchts. & Mfrs. Assn., 1946. Mem. Welsh Pony Soc. Am., S.R., Kappa Sigma. Republican. Episcopalian. Clubs: Riomar Bay Yacht, Riomar Country (Vero Beach, Fla.); Phila. Cricket, Down Town. Home: Crefeld Farm Plymouth Meeting PA 19462 Office: 1900 Arch St Philadelphia PA 19103

FERNLEY, ROBERT CLUTE, trade assn. exec.; b. Phila., Dec. 21, 1922; s. George Adamson and Mildred (Bougher) F.; B.S., U. Pa., 1943; m. Ann Campbell Taylor, June 8, 1946; children—Thomas James III, George Adamson Taylor, John Randolph, Robert Clute, David. Pres., Fernley & Fernley, Inc.; sec., treas. Nat. Welding Supply Assn., 1947—; sec. Am. Brush Manufacturers Assn., 1947—; mng. dir. Nat. Indsl. Distbrs. Assn., 1951—. Mem. S.R. Republican. Episcopalian. Clubs: Racquet, St. Anthony, Sunnybrook Golf. Home: Cartref Plymouth Meeting PA 19462 Office: 1900 Arch St Philadelphia PA 19103

FERNLEY, THOMAS ADAMSON, Jr., trade assn. exec.; b. Germantown, Pa., June 30, 1910; s. Thomas Adamson and Mary Elizabeth (Johnson) F.; A.B., Princeton, 1932; m. Ruth Fielder Allen, Jan. 20, 1934; children—Mary (Mrs. Otis Summerville), Ruth Anne (Mrs. William Sharadin), Thomas Adamson III. Partner Fernley & Fernley, trade assn. exec. 1932-62; chmn. Fernley & Fernley, Inc., 1963—; asst. sec.-treas. Nat. Wholesale Hardware Assn., 1939, exec. sec., 1946, mng. dir., 1958-69, adv. sec., 1969—; Wholesale Jewelers Assn., 1946-68, adv. sec., 1968—; adv. sec. Aviation Distbrs. and Mfrs. Assn., 1948-51, mng. dir., 1951—; adv. sec. Nat. Comml. Refrigerator Sales Assn., 1949—, Woodworking Machinery, Mfrs. Assn., 1947—, Nat. Welding Supply Assn., 1947—, Nat. Assn. Aluminum Distbrs., 1952—, Resistance Welder Mfrs. Assn., 1956—; exec. sec. Copper & Brass Warehouse Assn.; 1957-61, adv. sec., 1961—; adv. sec. Woodworking Machinery Distbrs. Assn., 1959—; exec. dir. Nat. Coil Coaters Assn., 1968—. Republican. Presbyn. Clubs: Philadelphia Cricket, Philadelphia Aviation Country, Terrace, Union League (Phila.); Princeton (Phila., N.Y.C.). Author articles on distbn. and anti-trust laws. Home: 9507 Marstan Rd Chestnut Hill PA 19118 Office: 1900 Arch St Philadelphia PA 19103

FERON, JAMES MARTIN, newspaperman; b. Woodside, N.Y., June 23, 1928; s. James J. and Flora (Trostler) F.; B.A., Marietta Coll., 1950; M.S., Columbia, 1955; m. Jeanne Margaret Clare, Feb. 28, 1953; children—Robert, Michael, Andrew, Margaret. With N.Y. Times, 1952—, beginning as copy boy, successively news clk., radio news writer, gen. assignment N.Y. area corr., UN, 1959- 61, London, 1961-65. Israel, 1965-70, Warsaw, 1970—. Served with Signal Corps, AUS, 1948- 50. Pulitzer travelling fellow, 1955. Contbr. to Ency. Year Book 1963-66. Address. care New York Times 229 W 43d St New York City NY 10036

FERON, LOUIS, sculptor, goldsmith; b. Rouen, France, Aug. 16, 1901; s. Ernest and Louise (Parisot) F.; student Municipal Art Sch., Paris, 1915-20, Ecole Nationale des Arts and Metiers, Paris, 1923-27; courses Collin Rossi, 1918-20. LaGrande Chaumiere Acad., 1923-30; m. Marguerite Schwan, Aug. 6, 1922; m. 2d. (Janet) Leslie Snow, June 9, 1962. Came to the U.S., 1945, naturalized, 1951. Apprentice studio and brass foundry, goldsmith and jewelry works, hammer sculpturing, 1919-26; prof. painting, modeling, decorative arts Pub. Works Sch., Costa Rica, 1935; organizer, dir. Apprenticeship Sch. Pub. Works, Costa Rica, 1939-45; jeweler, goldsmith, sculptor, N.Y.C., 1945—. Named comdr. Ordre du Travail as best craftsman of France, Sorbonne, 1933; recipient Brass Arts, Scis., Lit. medal of France, 1934; Gold Medal for sculpture Internat. Fine Arts Council. Fellow National Sculpture Society (member of council); member St. Luke's Art Guild, Internat. Fine Arts Council. Home: Snowville NH 03877 Office: 10 E 52d St New York City NY 10022

FERRAND, JEAN CLAUDE, oil co. exec.; b. Lyon, France, Feb. 10, 1930; s. Jean A. and Andree (Desire) F.; Engr.'s degree, Ecole de L'Air France, 1952; research asst. Cal. Inst. Tech., 1958-59; advanced mgmt. program Harvard Bus. Sch., 1970-71; m. Bayote Odette, Feb. 20, 1960; children—Jean Pascal, Isabelle, Patrick. Geophysicist in France and Africa for Compagnie Generale de Geophysique, 1955-58; mgr. Compagnie Reynolds de Geophysique, Algeria, 1959-61; adviser to Australian Govt. with French Inst. Petroleum, 1961-63; geophysicist, Australia, then chief geophysicist, asst. to exploration mgr. New Zealand for local subsidiaries Societe Nationale des Petroles d'Aquitaine, 1963-65; exec. v.p., dir. Aquitaine Oil Corp., 1965—; dir. Aquitaine Chems., Inc.; v.p., dir. First Bus. Computing Corp., 1969—. Served as officer French Army, 1951-55. Mem. European Assn. Exploration Geophysicists, Soc. Exploration Geophysicists, Am. Assn. Petroleum Geologists, Ind. Petroleum Assn. Am., Harvard Alumni Assn. Home: 13510 St Mary St Houston TX 77024 Office: 1200 Travis St Houston TX 77002

FERRAND SOSA, VICTOR, consul gen. of Venezuela in Phila. Address: 3 Penn Center Plaza Philadelphia PA 19102*

FERRANTE, ARTHUR, concert pianist; b. N.Y.C.; grad. Julliard Sch. of Music. Faculty theory and composition Julliard Sch. Music to 1947; with Louis Teicher, two piano team, debut performance Toledo Symphony, 1947; on tour U.S., appearing with orchestras, giving recitals; appeared various radio networks, also TV including shows of Ed Sullivan, Dinah Shore, Garry Moore, Steve Allen, Ernie Kovacs, Ding Dong Sch.; recordings for Columbia, Westminster, United Artists; regular appearances with Percy Faith on Woolworth Hour, weekly shows ABC's Piano Playhouse; composed, performed music with original sound effects for motion picture Undersea Conquest. Address: care Larry Penzell 501 Madison Av New York City NY 10022*

FERRANTE, WILLIAM ROBERT, educator; b. Providence, Mar. 9, 1928; s. Pasquale Anthony and Marietta (Fornaro) F.; B.S. in Elec. Engring., U. R.I., 1949; M.S. in Applied Math., Brown U., 1955; Ph.D. in Engring. Mechanics, Va. Poly. Inst., 1962; m. Ann Marie Wharton, Sept. 7, 1968; children—Jennifer, Julia. Faculty math. U. R.I., 1949-50, 56—, prof. mech. engring. and applied mechanics, 1968—, dean Grad. Sch., 1969—; faculty mechanics Lafayette Coll., Easton, Pa., 1952-56; mathematician Boeing Airplane Co., Seattle, summer 1955; research engr. Allis-Chalmers Mfg. Co., summer 1956. Mem. Diocese Providence Commn. Edn., 1968-69. Faculty fellow NSF, 1958-59; Fulbright fellow Al-Hikma U., Baghdad, Iraq, 1963-64. Mem. Am. Soc. M.E., Am. Soc. for Engring. Edn., Math. Assn. Am., Sigma Xi, Tau Beta Pi. Home: PO Box 132 Ferry Rd Saunderstown RI 02874 Office: Grad Sch Kingston RI 02881

FERRARA, WILLIAM A., supermarket co. exec.; b. 1925; B.B.A. in Accounting, Northeastern U., 1952. Mgr., Audio Visual Corp., 1947-52; audit mgr. Price Waterhouse & Co., 1952-64; with First Nat. Stores Inc., 1964—, treas., 1967—. C.P.A., Mass. Served with AUS, 1944-46. Address: 5 Middlesex Av Somerville MA 02145

FERRARI, ENZO, automobile co. exec.; b. Modena, Italy, Feb. 20, 1898; s. Alfredo and Adalgisa (Bisbini) F.; ed. Tech. Profl. Inst., Modena; m. Laura Garello, 1923; 1 son, Alfredo (dec. 1956), Testing engr. Costruzioni Meccaniche Nazionali, Torin and Milan, 1918-20; testing engr., pilot, comml. collaborator Alfa Romeo, 1920-39; dir. Alfa Corse, 1923; pres., gen. dir. Scuderia Ferrari, later Auto Avio Constrn. Ferrari, 1940-60; pres., rep. adminstrv. Ferrari Automobili SpA Sefac, 1960—; builder sports car, grand touring cars, also prototypes that participated in world-wide competitions. Named comdr. for Sport Merits, 1928; knight of labor, 1952; civil engr. Honoris Causa, 1960. Author: My Terrible Joys (autobiography), 1962. Home: Av Trento Trieste 31 Modena Italy Office: Maranello Modena Italy

FERRARI, ROBERT J., savs. bank exec. Comptroller, King's Highway Savs. Bank, Bklyn. Office: 1602 King's Hwy Box 100 Brooklyn NY 11299*

FERRARO, EUGENE THOMAS, educator; b. Paterson, N.J., May 19, 1913; s. Michaelangelo and Giovannia (Ferraro) F.; B.S., Rutgers U., 1937; M.A., New Sch. Social Research, 1941, Ph.D., 1958; m. Victoria S. Saracco, Feb. 13, 1943; children—Eugenia Lu (Mrs. Warren Lewis); Thomas Michael, Philip Alberico. Tchr. social scis., Teaneck, N.J., 1935-41; head social scis. dept. Passaic Valley Regional High Sch., 1941-42; with Curtiss-Wright Corp., Caldwell, N.J., 1942-53, supr. contracts and orders, 1950-52; v.p. logistics Singer-Kearfott div., Fairfield, N.J., 1953-66; dep. under sec. for manpower, asst. sec. U.S. Air Force, 1966-68; pres. Nat. Def. Edn. Inst., 1969—. Vis. lectr. Paterson (N.J.) State Coll., 1947-50; mem. co-adj. faculty Inst. Mgmt-Labor Relations, Rutgers U., 1964-66; indsl. cons. effectiveness industry adv. com. Air Force Weapons Systems, 1963-64. Recipient James Forrestal certificate of merit Nat. Security Indsl. Assn., 1962, Greer award, 1963, hon. life membership, 1966; Exceptional Civilian Service award Dept. Air Force, 1968, Distinguished Alumnus award Paterson State Coll. Alumni Assn., 1969. Author articles edn., tng., manpower, logistics. Home: 30 Wadsworth Rd Glen Rock NJ 07452 Office: New Dutch Lane Fairfield NJ 07006

FERRATER, JOSE MARIA, educator; b. Barcelona, Spain, Oct. 30, 1912; s. Maximiliano and Carmen (Mora) F.; B.A., Institute Maragall (Barcelona), 1932; Licenciado en Filosofia U. Barcelona, 1936. Came to U.S., 1947, naturalized, 1960. Prof. philosophy U. Chile, 1942-47; lectr. philosophy Bryn Mawr Coll., 1949-51, asso. prof., 1951-56, prof., 1956—; vis. prof. Princeton, 1951-52, Johns Hopkins, 1955-56, Temple U., 1970-71; cons. editor Jour. Philosophy, Am. Philos. Quar., Man and World, Jour. Philosophy Religion, Jour. History Philosophy, Abraxas. Guggenheim fellow, 1947-49; Am. Council Learned Socs. fellow, 1963-64. Mem. Institut Internat. de Philosophie (Paris), Am. Philos. Assn., Assn. for Symbolic Logic. Author: Unamuno: A Philosophy of Tragedy, 1962; Man at the Crossroads, 1957; Ortega y Gasset; An Outline of His Philosophy, 1956; Philosophy Today, 1960; Being and Death, 1967; Diccionario de Filosofia, 5th edn. 1967; El Ser y El Sentido, 1968; Investigaciones sobre el lenguaje, 1970. Home: Chetwynd Apts 806 Rosemont PA 19010 Office: Bryn Mawr Coll Bryn Mawr PA 19010

FERRE, FREDERICK POND, educator; b. Boston, Mar. 23, 1933; s. Nels F.S. and Katharine Louise (Pond) F.; student Oberlin Coll., 1950-51; A.B. (Prof. Augustus Howe Buck fellow), Boston U., 1954; M.A., Vanderbilt U., 1955; Ph.D. (Fulbright fellow, Kent fellow), U. St. Andrews (Scotland), 1959; m. Marie Booth, June 8, 1954; 1 dau., Katharine Marie. Asst. prof. philosophy Vanderbilt U., 1958-59; asst. prof. religion Mt. Holyoke Coll., 1959-62; asso. prof. philosophy Dickinson Coll., Carlisle, Pa., 1962-67, Charles A. Dana prof. 1967—; vis. prof. So. Meth. U., 1964-65, Bucknell U., 1965-66, Pitts. Theol. Sem., 1968-69, Princeton Theol. Sem., 1970-71. Nat. Endowment Humanities fellow, 1969-70. Mem. Am. Philos. Assn., Philosophy Sci. Assn. Metaphys. Soc. Am. (program chmn. 1971-72), Am. Theol. Soc. (exec. com. 1970—), Nat. Humanities Faculty, Phi Beta Kappa. Author: Language, Logic and God, 1961; Exploring the Logic of Faith, 1962; Paley's Natural Theology, 1963; Basic Modern Philosophy of Religion, 1967; Comte's Introduction to Positive Philosophy, 1970. Home: 111 S College St Carlisle PA 17013

FERRE, GUSTAVE ADOLF, ednl. adminstr.; b. Gnesta, Sweden, Sept. 11, 1918; s. Frans and Maria (Wichman) F.; came to U.S., 1924, naturalized, 1928; A.B., Boston U., 1943; B.D., Andover-Newton Theol. Sch., 1944; Ph.D., Vanderbilt U., 1957; m. Dorothy Frederick, Sept. 4, 1943; children—Susan, Carl, Loren, Martha, Elizabeth. Ordained to ministry Baptist Ch., 1944; pastor in Belding, Mich., 1945-49; prof. philosophy and religion Rio Grande Coll., 1949-51, Alderson-Broadus Coll., 1951-52; instr. N.T., Vanderbilt U., 1953-57, Ford teaching fellow, 1955-57; asso. editor The Upper Room, 1952-57; dean Cotner Coll., 1957-59; prof. philosophy, head dept. Tex. Christian U., 1959-71; v.p. acad. affairs N. Tex. State U., Denton, 1971—; Wells lectr., 1962; Davies lectr. Phillips U., 1964; Cotner lectr., 1968. Mem. Nat. Assn. Bibl. Tchrs. (editorial staff Encounter jour.), Am., Southwestern (pres. 1969-70) philos. assns. Author: Layment Examines His Faith, 1960; Basic Philosophical Issues, 1962. Home: 1150 Ector St Denton TX 76201

FERRE, JOSE ANTONIO, corp. ofcl.; b. Ponce, P.R., Sept. 13, 1902; s. Antonio and Mary Aguayo (Casals) F.; B.B.A., Boston U., 1924, M.B.A., U. Miami, 1955; m. Florence Salichs, Dec. 31, 1933; children—Maurice, Mary Ann; m. 2d. Joanne Singleterry, Oct. 31, 1961; children—Jo, Noel, Tony; m. 3d, Patricia Christensen, March 29, 1967; children-Emile Antonio, Christina. Salesman P.R. Iron Works, Inc., 1924-34, v.p., 1934—, co-chmn., 1968—; co-chmn. Puerto Rican Cement Co. Inc., 1963—; pres. P.R. Marine Corp., Pan Am. Investment, Inc., P.R. Drydock & Marine, Ferré Devel., Miami Caribe Investments, Fabrica Nacional de Vidrio, Inversiones Ferré, Caribe Panama Investments; co-chmn. P.R. Glass Corp., P.R. Paper & Pulp Corp.; chmn. Maule Industries, Inc., Miami, Fla., 1956—; co-chmn. St. Regis Paper Co. P.R.; dir. Fla. East Coast Ry., Pan Am. Bank of Miami. Hon. consul for Brazil in P. R. Pres. bd. trustees Dr. Phila.'s Hosp., Ponce, 1955-57; trustee Boston U., Pan Am. Hosp., Miami, U. Miami, Catholic U. of P.R., Miami Heart Inst., St. Francis Hosp. Mem. Navy League. Elk. Clubs: N.Y. Athletic, Rotary, Advertising (N.Y.C.); Yacht, Bankers (San Juan). Home: 5 Alcazar Ponce PR 00731

FERRE, LUIS ALBERTO, gov. of Puerto Rico; b. P.R., Feb. 17, 1904; s. Antonio and Mary (Aguayo) F.; B.S., Mass. Inst. Tech., 1924, M.S., 1925; LL.D., Springfield (Mass.) Coll., 1959; D.C.L., U. P.R., 1965, Pace Coll., 1966; D. Hum., Interamerican U. of Puerto Rico, 1966; m. Lorencita Ramirez de Arellano, May 30, 1931; children—Antonio Louis, Rosario (Mrs. Benigno Trigo). With P.R. Iron Works, 1925—; an organiZer P.R. Cement Corp., 1941, now co. chmn. bd., dir.; pres., chmn. several indsl. concerns of Ferre Industries, 1950—; chmn. bd., pres. Ponce Hotel Corp., 1959—; treas. Central Igualdad Inc., 1950—; dir. Banco de Ponce. Gen. chmn. devel. P.R. YMCA, 1950, pres. Fed. YMCA's P.R., 1964; mem. Citizens Adv. Com. Govt. Security, 1957. Rep. candidate for gov. P.R., 1956, 60, 64; mem. P.R. Ho. of Reps. at large, 1952-56; member of the Republican Nat. Com., 1964—; now the governor of Puerto Rico. Organizer Luis A. Ferre Found., 1956. Named P.R. of year Knights of St. John of Chgo., 1958; decorated Order Vasa (Sweden), 1958; Knight of Holy Sepulchre (Pope John XXIII. Mem. C. of C. of P.R. Home: 2 Reina Mora Ponce PR 00731 Office: P O Box 1492 Ponce PR 00731

FERRE, MAURICE ANTONIO, bus. exec.; b. Ponce, P.R., June 23, 1935; s. Jose Antonio and Florence (Salichs) F.; grad. Lawrenceville (N.J.) Sch., 1953; B.S. in Archtl. Engring., U. Miami (Fla.), 1957; m. Maria Mercedes Malaussena, Aug. 25, 1955; children—Mary Isabel, Jose Luis, Carlos Maurice, Maurice Raimundo, Francisco Antonio,

Florence. Pres., Ferre Fla. Corp., downtown properties, Miami, 1960-64, v.p., 1964—; sr. v.p. Maule Industries, Inc., mfr. bldg. materials, Miami, 1961-63, pres., 1964—; dir. P.R. Cement Co., Inc., Empresas Ferre, 1st Nat. Bank of Miami. Mem. Fla. Ho. of Reps., 1967—. Mem. City of Miami Commn., 1968-70. Trustee U. Miami, Barry Coll., Miami. Mem. Young Pres. Orgn. Home: 1643 Brickell Av Miami FL 33129 Office: 100 Biscayne Blvd Miami FL 33132

FERREE, JOHN WILLARD, physician; b. Marion, Ind., Aug. 26, 1904; s. John Daniel and Mary A. (Heaston) F.; A.B., U. Pa., 1925; M.D., Ind. U., 1932; M.P.H., Johns Hopkins, 1939; m. Roberta North, June 10, 1930; children—Barbara, John Daniel, Rebecca. Intern Harper Hosp., Detroit, 1932-33; resident Passavant Meml. Hosp., Chgo., 1933-34, Evanston (Ill.) Hosp., 1934-35; dir. local health administrn. Ind. State Bd. Health, 1936-40, state health commr., 1940-42; dir. ednl. services Am. Social Hygiene Assn., 1946-47; asso. dir. Nat. Health Council, 1947-49, sec., 1961; dir. community service and edn. Am. Heart Assn., 1949-57, asso. med. dir., 1957-59; exec. dir. Nat. Soc. Prevention Blindness, 1959-69. Mem. nat. adv. eye council NIH, 1968-70. Bd. dirs. Am. Found. Overseas Blind, 1968—, Nat. Accreditation Council for Agys. Serving Blind and Visually Handicapped, 1967—, Illuminating Engring. Research Inst., 1960—. Served from lt. comdr. to comdr. M.C., USNR, 1942-46. Diplomate Am. Bd. Preventive Medicine And Pub. Health. Fellow A.C.P., Am. Pub. Health Assn., N.Y. Acad. Medicine; mem. A.M.A., Alpha Omega Alpha, Beta Theta Pi, Nu Sigma Nu. Presbyn. Home: 55 Grandview Av Pleasantville NY 10570

FERREE, MARK, ret. newspaper exec.; b. Marion, Ind., Jan. 19, 1905; s. Evan Harvey and Flora Alice (Cammack) F.; student Ind. U., 1922-25; m. Ruth Gauntt Welborn, Apr. 29, 1930; 1 son, Evan Gauntt. Reporter, editorial writer Marion Chronicle, 1920-22, Ind. U. Daily Student, 1922-25; telegraph editor Evansville Courier, 1925-26; telegraph editor, asst. Sunday editor Miami (Fla.) Herald, 1926-27; publicity mgr. So. Pine Assn., New Orleans, 1927-30, Washington rep., 1930-32; local advt. salesman Washington Daily News, 1932-33, local advt. mgr., 1933-36; advt. dir. Indpls. Times, 1936, bus. mgr., 1937-45; asst. gen. bus. mgr. Scripps-Howard Newspapers, N.Y.C., 1945-49, gen. bus. mgr., 1949-70; exec. v.p., dir., exec. com. E.W. Scripps Co., 1952-70. Mem. staff nat. com. on wood utilization Dept. Commerce, 1930-32; dir. Indpls. Better Bus. Bur., 1939-45, v.p. 1944-45; chmn. bd. govs. Nat. Better Bus. Bur., 1943-45; gov.-at- large Assn. Better Bus. Burs., Inc., 1962-65. Trustee Scripps-Howard Found. Mem. Am. Newspaper Pubs. Assn. (dir. 1955-64, treas. 1957, v.p. 1958-59, pres. 1960-62), Phi Kappa Psi, Sigma Delta Chi. Mem. Soc. of Friends. Clubs: Union League, Sky. Home: South Salem NY 10590 also Stuart FL 33494 Office: 200 Park Av New York City NY 10017

FERRELL, HARRISON HERBERT, educator; b. Chgo., Aug. 28, 1900; s. Harrison Herbert and Susanna (Reed) F.; B.S., Northwestern U., 1924, A.M., 1925, Ph.D., 1928; violin study with Ludwig Becker, Columbia Sch. of Music, Chgo.; L.H.D., Culver Stockton Coll., 1964; LL.D., Marshall U., 1966; m. Emily Miriam Grazia Bell, Sept. 15, 1929. Research fellow Germanic philology Northwestern U., 1924-27; prof., head dept. German, W.Va. State Coll. co-ednl. coll., 1928-66, acting dean, 1930-32, asst. dean, 1932-33, acting registrar, 1934-35, registrar, 1935-37, dean, 1937-66; dir. Upward Bound project, prof. German, Coordinator of instl. studies W.Va. State Coll., Institute 1966-70; adminstrv. asst. Guthrie Center, Spencer State Hosp., State W.Va. Dept. Mental Health, 1970—; violinist; founder and condr. Ferrell Symphony Orch. (founded as memorial to Harrison Herbert Ferrell, Sr.). Pres. Chgo. Music Assn., 1928; dir. W.Va. State College Strings. Trustee, mem. exec. com. W.Va. Soc. Crippled Children and Adults, 1963—. Mem. Modern Lang. Assn., Am. Tchrs. Assn., Nat. Assn. Negro Musicians (adv. bd. 1928-30), W.Va. Fgn. Lang. Assn. (sec. 1935-45), Am. Assn. U. Profs., N.E.A., W.Va. Edn. Assn. (mem. exec. com. 1955-57), W.Va. Assn. Higher Edn. (pres. 1954-55, chmn. program com.), W.Va. Assn. Acad. Deans (pres. 1958- 59, exec. com. 1959-60), W.Va. Arts and Humanities Council, Kappa Alpha Psi, Sigma Pi Phi. Address: 7 Park Av Charleston WV 25302

FERRELL, JAMES K., educator; b. Maryville, Mo., Jan. 18, 1923; s. Harry K. and Susie (Bruce) F.; BS., U. Mo., 1948, M.S., 1949; Ph.D., N.C. State U., 1954; m. Dorothy I. Dobransky, Mar. 23, 1943; children—Janet Marion (Mrs. James Richard Springle), John K. Asst. prof. chem. engring. N.C. State U., Raleigh, 1954-56, head dept. chem. engring., Alcoa prof., 1961—; group leader nuclear div. Martin Co., Balt., 1956-58; sect. chief atomic energy div. Babcox & Wilcox Co., Lynchburg, Va., 1958-61; dir. Hydra Computer Co., Raleigh. Bd. dirs. N.C. Ednl. Computing Service, Research Triangle, N.C. Served to 1st lt., F.A., AUS, 1943-46. Mem. Am. Inst. Chem. Engrs., Am. Chem. Soc., Sigma Xi. Contbr. articles profl. jours. Home: 4205 Rowan St Raleigh NC 27609

FERREN, JACK MAXWELL, indsl. relations exec.; b. Clearfield, Ia., May 21, 1906; s. William Alvah and Edith (Waight) F.; A.B., Parsons Coll., 1927; M.A., U. Mich., 1928; grad. student, Syracuse U., 1930-32; m. Elizabeth Anne Hansen, Aug. 21, 1929; children—John M., Elizabeth Anne, Instr. psychology Parsons Coll., 1928-29. Syracuse U., 1929-33; personnel supr. Standard Oil Co. (Ind.), Kansas City, Mo., 1934-42; supt. services Hercules Powder Co., Lawrence. Kan., 1942-44; dir. personnel Vendo Co., Kansas City, Mo., 1944-46, Stewart-Warner Corp., Chgo., 1946-49; dir. indsl. relations Zenith Radio Corp., Chgo, 1949-56, v.p. indsl. relations, 1956- -. Bd. dirs. Presbyn. Home, Evanston, Ill. Mem. Illinois Mfrs. Assn. (indsl. relations com.). Presbyn. Home: 3214 Park Pl Evanston IL 60201 Office: 1900 N Austin Av Chicago IL 60639

FERRER, JOSE VICENTE, producer, dir., actor; b. Santurce, P.R., Jan. 8, 1912; s. Rafael and Maria Providencia (Cintrón) F.; A.B., Princeton, 1933, M.A. (hon.), 1947; H.H.D. (hon), U. P.R., 1949; m. Uta Hagen, Dec. 8, 1938 (div. 1948); 1 dau., Leticia Thyra; m. 2d, Phyllis Hill, June 19, 1948 (div. 1953); m. 3d, Rosemary Clooney, July 13, 1953 (div. 1967); children—Miguel, Maria, Gabriel, Monsita, Raphael. Asst. stage mgr., playing walkons, Suffern N.Y., 1935; appeared in A Slight Case of Murder, Boy Meets Girl, Spring Dance, Brother Rat, Missouri Legend, Mamba's Daughters, Key Largo, Charley's Aunt, Let's Face It; as Iago to Paul Robeson's Othello, 1943; producer, dir. Strange Fruit, 1945, Stalag 17, Anything Can Happen (motion picture), 1951, The Fourposter, 1951, The Chase, 1952, producer and actor, Cyrano de Bergerac, 1946; played Dauphin to Ingrid Bergman's Joan of Arc, 1948 (motion picture); The Silver Whistle, 1948; produced and acted in Volpone, Angel Street, 4 Chekov 1-act plays, The Alchemists, S.S. Glencaim, The Insect Comedy of N.Y. City Theatre Co.; Twentieth Century, 1950; The Shrike (Pulitzer prize play), 1952; Richard III, Charley's Aunt (all 1953-54). Dir. My Three Angels, 1953, The Dazzling Hour, 1953, Return to Peyton Place, The Chapman Report, gen. dir. N.Y. Theatre Co.; acted in Whirlpool, Crisis, Cyrano de Bergerac (motion pictures), 1950, Moulin Rouge, 1952, Miss Sadie Thompson, 1953, The Caine Mutiny, 1953, Deep in My Heart, 1954, The Shrike, 1954, The Cockleshell Heroes, 1955, I Accuse, 1957, Bay the Moon, 1957, Nine Hours to Rama, 1963. Starred in Lawrence of Arabia, Ship of Fools, The Greatest Story Ever Told. Produced, directed and starred in Edwin Booth (theatre), 1959: directed and co-authored Oh Captain, 1958; directed The Anderson Trial, 1960; starred in play The Girl Who Came to Supper, 1963-64, Man of La Mancha, Broadway, 1966-67; appeared in films Enter Laughing, Cervantes, 1966; did complete live TV prodns. Cyrano de Bergerac, What Makes Sammy Run, complete prodns. Kismet, A Cast of Libel; also TV documentaries and numerous guest appearances. Recipient Motion Picture Acad. Arts and Scis. award as best actor of 1950. numerous other citations and awards. Home: 61 Luisa St Condado PR Office: 2 Pennsylvania Plaza New York City NY 10001

FERRER, MARIE IRENE, physician; b. Elberon, N.Y., July 30, 1915; d. Jose Maria and Irene (O'Donohue) F.; B.A., Bryn Mawr Coll., 1937; M.D., Columbia, 1941; 1 adopted dau., Marianne (Mrs. Legato Killian). Intern, Bellevue Hosp., N.Y.C., 1941-43, resident, 1943-44; clin. prof. med. Coll. Phys. and Surg. Columbia, 1967—; dir. electrocardiographic labs. Columbia. Presbyn. Med. Center, 1956—, Doctors Hosp., 1953—. Bd. dirs. N.Y. Heart Assn. Recipient Salute to Women award Republican Women in Industry and Professions, 1966. Mem. Am. Heart Assn. (council on circulation 1967- -), N.Y. Acad. Med., Am. Soc. Clin. Investigation, Am. Fed. Clin. Research (emeritus). Club: Cosmopolitan (N.Y.C.). Cardiopulmonary research with Dr. A. Cournand and Dr. D. W. Richards (Nobel prize winner 1956). Home: 200 E 66th St New York City NY 10021

FERRER, MELCHOR G., actor, director; b. Elberon, N.J., Aug. 25, 1917; s. Dr. José María and Marie Irene (O'Donohue) F.; grad. Canterbury Prep. Sch., 1935; student Princeton, 1935-37; m. Frances Pilchard, Oct. 23, 1937 (div.; remarried after second marriage); children-Pepa, Mark; m. 2d, Barbara C. Tripp; children—Mela, Christopher; m. 4th, Audrey Hepburn, Sept. 25, 1954 (div.); one son, Sean. Actor (stage) Strange Fruit, 1945, Ondine; (screen) Lost Boundaries, 1949. The Brave Bulls, 1951. Scaramouche, Lilli, 1952, Knights of the Round Table, 1953, War and Peace, The Vintage, 1956, The Sun Also Rises, 0 Fraulein, 1957; The Blood and The Rose, 1960. The Hands of Orlac. 1960. Ladies' Man, 1960, The Longest Day, 1962, The Fall of the Roman Empiere, 1963 (all screen); dir. Girl of the Limberlost, 1945, Cyrano de Bergerac (stage), 1946, The Secret Fury, Vendetta 1950. Green Mansions, 1958. Producer, owner and operator with Gregory Peck and Dorothy McGuire of Lajolla (Calif.) Playhouse Summer Theatre, 1946- 50. also pres. Dir. for Columbia Pictures Corp., pictures; director, co- producer Dome Prodns. Limited: producer Seven Arts Asso. Corp., Assault on a Queen: producer and actor El Greco, 1964; writer, producer, dir. Cabriola, 1964-65; producer Wait Unitl Dark; 1967. Mem. and treas. The Actors Co., theatrical producing co. Author: Tito's Hats, children's book, 1940. Home: Tolochenaz Vaud Switzerland Office: 242 N Canon Dr Beverly Hills CA 90210

FERRI, ANTONIO, educator, engr.; b. Norcia, Italy, Apr. 5, 1912; s. Giovanni B. and Iginia (Sparvieri) F.; Dr. Elec. Engring., U. Rome (Italy), 1934, Dr. Aero. Engring., 1936; m. Renata Mola, July 12, 1937; children—Paul, Rose marie, Joseph. Came to U.S., 1944, naturalized, 1952. Assigned to Direzione Superiore Studi ed Esperienze, Italian Air Ministry, 1935, head supersonic wind tunnel, Guidonia, Italy, 1937-40, head aerodynamics br., 1940-43; asso. prof. U. Rome, 1940-43; head Partisan Brigade Spartaco, 1943-44; with OSS, NACA, 1944-46; research transonic testing techniques, supersonic aerodynamics NACA, 1946-49, head gas dynamics br., Langley Field, Va., 1949-51; prof. aerodynamics Poly. Inst. Bklyn., 1951-54, dir. aerodynamics lab. Poly. Inst. Bklyn., Freeport, N.Y., 1954- 63, head dept. aerospace engring. applied mechanics, Bklyn., 1957-63; exec. v.p. Gen. Applied Sci. Labs., Inc., 1958-60, pres., 1960-67; Astor prof. aerospace scis., dir. Aerospace Lab., N.Y. U., 1964. Mem. adv. group for aero. research and devel. propulsion and energetics panel NATO; mem. research adv. com. on air-breathing propulsion systems NASA; mem. research adv. group engring. scis. Air Force Office Sci. Research; mem. Army Sci. Adv. Panel. Recipient Premio dell'Accademia d, for Science, 1938; sci. achievement award Columbia Civic Clubs N.J., 1954; Akroyd Stuart prize Royal Aero. Soc., 1965; Outstanding Achievement award office Aerespace Research, Dept Air Force, 1970. Fellow Inst. Aero. Scis.; mem. Nat. Acad. Engring., Accademia delle Scienze di Torino of Italy, Internat. Acad. Astronautics. Author: Elements of Aerodynamics of Supersonic Flows, 1949. Author numerous sci. articles. Home: 42 Yukon Dr Woodbury NY 11797 Office: New York Univ 177th St and Harlem River Bronx NY 10453

FERRIER, ILAY CHARLES, plastics co. exec.; b. Juan-Les-Pins, France, August 10, 1927; s. Charles Arthur and Madeleine (Beauvoir) F.; B. Commerce, McGill U., 1948; chartered accountant, Inst. Chartered Accountants Que., 1952; m. Elizabeth Jean O'Brien, June 6, 1953; children—Ilay Ian, John James, Catherine Theresa, Andres Alan, Janet Elizabeth, Mary Alexandra. Accountant, Ernst & Ernst, C.P.A.'s, Montreal, Can., 1951-53; asst. sec.- treas. Tamper Ltd., Montreal, 1953-55; internal auditor, regional accountant Canron Ltd., Montreal and Hamilton, Can., 1955-57, div. controller Tamper div., 1957-64, controller parent company, 1964-68, gen. mgr. plastic pipe div., 1968—, now v.p. operations control. Commnr., St. Leon de Westmount Sch. Commn., 1967-68. Mem. Inst. Chartered Accountants Que., Financial Execs. Inst. Roman Cath. (churchwarden) Home: 428 Lansdowne Av Westmount Quebec Canada Office: 1121 Pl Ville marie Montreal 113 Quebec Canada

FERRIL, THOMAS HORNSBY, poet, editor; b. Denver, Feb. 25, 1896; s. Will C. and Alice Lawton (MacHarg) F.; A.B., Colo. Coll., 1918; hon. M.L., U. Colo., 1934, Litt.D., 1960; hon. doctorate, U. Denver, Colo. Coll.; m. Helen Drury Ray, Oct. 5, 1921; 1 dau., Anne Milroy. Reporter and dramatic editor Denver Times, The Rocky Mountain News, 1919-21; engaged in motion picture advt., Denver, 1921-26; editor Through the Leaves and The Sugar Press (mags. of Great Western Sugar Co.), 1926-68; asso. and contbg. editor Rocky Mountain Herald since 1918; commd. 2d lt. Aviation Sect. Signal Corps, 1918. Awards include; A0 prize by Acad. of Am. Poets, 1939; Ridgely Torrence prize (A0) by Poetry Soc. Am., 1953; A,000 prize, Denver Post, and Perhaps Happiness, 1958; Service to Mankind Award, Sertoma, 1958; Robert Frost (A00) poetry award, Poetry Soc. Am. Contest, 1960. Mem. Am. Hist. Trails Assn. (hon.), The Westerns, Phi Beta Kappa, Phi Delta Theta, Sigma Delta Chi. Clubs: Cactus, Mile High. Denver Press (Denver). Author books including: New and Sleected Poems, 1952; Words for Denver and Other Poems, 1966; (with Mrs. Ferril) The Rocky Mountain Herald Reader, 1966; also poetry, prose and book reviews in many newspapers and mags. Lectr. and mem. Regional Authors' Council of Writers Conf. in The Rocky Mountains, U. of Colo.; lectr. on poetry and Western culture, various univs. Writer of 9 verse texts used in connection with Boettcher murals, Colo. State Capitol. Author: Trial by Time (poems), 1944, I Hate Thursday (prose book), 1946; contbr. Harper's Mag. Author (drama): And Perhaps Happiness, 1957 recipient A,000 award, 1958. One of 31 poets commd. by Steuben Glass Co. to participate in Poetry in Crystal exhbn., N.Y.C., 1963. Home: 2123 Downing St Denver CO ☆

FERRIL, WILLIAM CHARLES, retail grocery co. exec.; b. St. Joseph, June 5, 1931; s. William C. and Ida mae (Williams) F.; B.S., U. Mo., 1957; m. Eleanor L. Hoover, June 21, 1957; children—William C. III, Robert Scott, John David. Pub. accountant Peat, Marwick, Mitchell & Co., Kansas City, Mo., 1957-59; asst. controller Crank Drug Co., Springfield, Mo., 1959-61; controller, treas. Foodtown Super Markets, Inc., Pittsburgh, Kan., 1961-67; controller Red Owl Stores, Inc., Hopkins, Minn., 1967—, treas., 1968—. Served with USAF, 1951-52. Mem. Delta Sigma Pi. Elk. Home: 17225 24th Av N Wayzata MN 55391 Office: 215 E Excelsior Av Hopkins MN 55343

FERRIMAN, JAMES W., ins. co. exec.; b. 1921; B.A., Ohio State U., 1943; LL.B., Cleve. Marshall Law Sch., 1949; married. With Ins. Co. N.Am., Phila., 1948—, asst. sec., 1959-64, sec. claims, 1964-65, sec. policyholders service div., 1965-66, v.p., 1966-67, sr. v.p., 1967—; pres. Gen. Traffic Service, Inc., 1968—. Trustee Magee Meml. Hosp., Phila.; bd. govs. Human Resources Center, Albertson, N.Y. Served with AUS, 1943-45. Office: 1600 Arch St Philadelphia PA 19101

FERRIN, ALLAN WHEELER, book pub.; b. Mt. Vernon, N.Y., Aug. 10, 1921; s. Dana Holman and Eleanor (Wheeler) F.; A.B., Princeton, 1943; m. Barbara Hogate, Sept. 18, 1943; children—Barbara Ann (Mrs. Paul M. Lane), Allan Hogate. Salesman, advt. mgr. F.S. Crofts & Co., book pubs., N.Y.C., 1946-48; with Appleton-Century- Crofts. Inc., N.Y.C., 1949-62, adminstrv. asst. to chmn. bd., 1956-58, v.p., 1958-60, pres., dir., 1960-62; gen. mgr. ednl. div. Meredith Corp., N.Y.C., 1961—, v.p., 1968—, also dir. Gov. Hudson River Country Day Sch., Irvington, N.Y., 1959-61; trustee Scarsdale Pub. Library, 1968—. Served to 1st lt. F.A., AUS, 1943-46. Mem. Phi Beta Kappa (pres. Scarsdale 1959-60). Republican. Episcopalian (vestryman 1964—). Clubs: Scarsdale Golf (Hartsdale, N.Y.); Quaker Hill Country (Pawling, N.Y.). Home: 52 Greenacres Av Scarsdale NY 10583 Office: 750 3d Av S New York City NY 10017

FERRIN, RICHARD ROYCE, violist; b. Hutchinson, Kan., Mar. 5, 1926; s. Fred Arthur and Lurlene Archibald (Haynes) F.; Mus.B., Eastman Sch. Music, 1950, Mus.M., 1951; postgrad. Sibelius Acad. Music (Finland), 1957-58, U. So. Cal., 1966-67, Music Acad. of the West, 1967; m. Lieselotte Gertrud Schmidt-Tuchel, Nov. 10, 1962; children—Genevieve Rebecca, Vanessa Estelle. Violinist, Nat. Symphony Orch., Washington, 1947-48, Rochester (N.Y.) Philharmonic and Civic Orchs., 1949-51, U. Houston Piano Trio, 1953-59, U. Wash. String Quartet, Seattle, 1959-63; prin. viola Seattle Symphony Orch., 1963-66; violist Chgo. Symphony Orch., 1967—, violist Chgo. Symphony Trio, 1969—. Prof. music Tex. Wesleyan Coll., U. Houston, U. Wash., U. Wyo.; vis. prof. U. B.C., San Fernando Valley State Coll., U. Wis.-Milw.; guest lectr. Houston Mus. Fine Arts, 1959, Sibelius Acad. Music, Helsinki, Finland, 1958, U. Ore., 1962. Mem. Cliff Dwellers. Home: 540 Chicago Av Highland Park IL 60035

FERRIS, CHARLES BIRDSALL, civil engr.; b. N.Y.C., Mar. 5, 1904; s. Charles and Florence (Birdsall) F.; B.S., N.Y.U., 1926, C.E., 1927; certificate in Fine Arts, N.Y.U. Sch. Architecture, 1939; m. Laura Soper, Apr. 6, 1929 (div.); m. 2d, Geraldine Beverly, July 18, 1949 (dec. March 1957); m. 3d, Laura Soper Apr. 1958. Engr. Thompson-Starrett Co., 1927-31, Cross & Brown Co., 1931-34; engr. real estate dept. Guaranty Trust Co., 1934-37; in charge archtl. dept. Mut. Life Ins. Co., N.Y.C., 1937-40; v.p. Gramatan Nat. Bank & Trust Co., also Gramatan Co., Bronxville, N.Y., 1946-48; pres. Ferris Constrn. Co., N.Y.C., 1948—, Ferris Constrn. Co., White Plains, N.Y., Charles B. Ferris Inc., N.Y.C., 1951—; sec.-treas. Flagsim Co., Inc., White Plains, 1951-58; propr. Charles B. Ferris Asso. Architects & Engrs., N.Y.C., C.B. Ferris Asso., Geneva, Switzerland, Paris, N.Y.C., 1951—, pres., 1960—. Cons. and dir. operations housing and redevel. bd. charge urban renewal and slum clearance, N.Y.C., 1960-62. Served from pvt. to maj. 102d Engrs., 27th Div. N.Y.N.G., 1925-41, col. C.E. and G.S.C., 1942-46, brig. gen., 1947, comdg. gen. 410th Engr. Brigade, U.S. Army Res., comdg. all engr. troops in res. in N.Y. State; retired 1961. Decorated Legion of Merit with Cluster, Bronze Star Medal, cluster, commendation medal. Registered profl. engr., N.Y. N.J., Mass., Pa., Conn., Wis., Fla; registered architect-engr., Geneva, Switzerland. Mem. Am. Soc. C.E., Soc. Licensed Profl. Engrs., Res. Officers Assn. (past pres. N.Y. chpt.), S.A.R., Am. Legion, Mil. Order World Wars, N.Y. Soc. Mil. Order Fgn. Wars, Sojurners, Am. C. of C. in Paris, Assn. U.S. Army. Episcopalian (warden). Mason. Clubs: Columbia University; Army and Navy. Home: 42 Silverbrook Rd Shrewsbury NJ 07701 Office: 320 E 54th St New York City NY 10022

FERRIS, CHARLES WILLIAM, educator; b. Queens, N.Y., Dec. 24, 1911; s. Charles William and Louise (Gurka) F.; B.A., L.I. U., 1933; M.S., City Coll. N.Y., 1939; Ed.D., Columbia Tchrs. Coll., 1960; m. Katherine Ann McCaig, Jan. 7, 1941; children—Katherine Ann (Mrs. Richard R. Biolsi), Linda Gae, Cheryl Sandra. Purser, S.S. Borinquen, 1937-38, S.S. Exeter, 1939-41; mem. faculty U.S. Mcht. Marine Acad., 1945—, head dept. humanties, 1946—. Served to lt. comdr. USNR, 1942-45. Mem. Am. Assn. U. Profs., Assn. Higher Edn., Phi Delta Kappa, Kappa Delta Pi. Home: 2880 Beltagh Av Wantagh NY 11793 Office: US Merchant Marine Acad Kings Point NY 11024

FERRIS, DEWARD OLMSTED, surgeon, educator; b. Niagara Falls, Ont., Can., Jan. 5, 1907; s. Thomas Elward and Martha (Olmsted) F.; M.D., C.M., Queen's U., Kingston Ont., 1931; M.S. in Surgery, Mayo Found., U. Minn., 1941; m. Edythe Culcheth, Mar. 16, 1938; children—Nancy, William D. Came to U.S., 1937, naturalized, 1943. Intern Kingston Gen. Hosp., 1931, Hamilton Gen. Hosp., 1932; practice gen. medicine, Niagara Falls, Ont., 1933-37; asst. to surg. staff Mayo Clinic, 1937-45, mem. permanent staff 1945—, head surg. sect., 1945—; mem. faculty Mayo Grad. Sch. Medicine, U. Minn., 1947—, prof. clin. surgery, 1962- -. Diplomate Am. Bd. Surgery. Fellow A.C.S.; mem. Am., Minn. med. assns., Central, Western surg. assns., Internat. Soc. Surgery, Soc. Surgery Alimentary Tract, Minn. Surg. Soc., Zumbro Valley Med. Soc., Sigma Xi. Presbyn. Mason. Contbr. articles in field. Home: 706 12th Av SW Rochester MN 55901 Office: 200 1st SW Rochester MN 55901

FERRIS, GEORGE MALLETTE, investment banker,; b. Newtown, Conn., Sept. 25, 1894; s. George B. and Bertha E. (Clark) F.; A.B., Trinity Coll., 1916; LL.D., Gallandet Coll.; m. Charlotte Hamilton, Apr. 14, 1920; children—Gene, Georte M. Engaged in investment banking, 1920—; sr. partner Ferris Co., Washington, 1946—; pres. Ferris & Co., Inc., Washington, 1933-71, chmn. bd., 1971—; dir. Am. Savs. & Loan Assn., DANAC Real Estate Investment Corp. Former chmn. bd. govs. Chevy Chase Village. Mem. N.Y. Stock Exchange. Mem. bd. Sibley Hosp.; trustee, treas. Gallaudet Coll.; trustee Trinity Coll. Mem. Washington Bd. Trade, Alpha Chi Rho. Mason. Clubs: Rotary; Chevy Chase; Columbia; Metropolitan, (Washington); Burning Tree. Home: 5810 Cedar Pkwy Chevy Chase MD 20015 Office: 1720 I St NW Washington DC 20006

FERRIS, GEORGE MALLETTE, Jr., investment banker; b. Washington, Mar. 11, 1927; s. George Mallette and Charlotte (Hamilton) F.; B.S. in Engring. summa cum laude, Princeton, 1948; M.B. A., Harvard, 1950; m. Nancy Strouce, Jan. 25, 1964; children—George Mallette III, Bradley, Kimberly Anne, David Hamilton. Mng. partner Ferris & Co., Washington, 1957—, dir. Axicom Systems, Inc., Credit Card Service Bur., Entron, Inc., Phila.-Balt.-Washington Stock Clearing Corp., Robert-Lynn Assos.,

Ltd., Washington Darts Soccer Club: cons. in field. Mem. Phila.-Balt.-Washington Stock Exchange; mem. regional adv. com., past bd. govs. N.Y. Stock Exchange. Gen. chmn. United Givers Fund campaign, 1966, Nat. Symphony Orch. sustaining fund drive, 1959, 60; chmn. advanced gifts div. United Givers Fund, 1965, bd. dirs., 1967—. Trustee Capitol Inst. Tech., Mt. Vernon Coll.; bd. dirs. D.C. chpt. A.R.C., Washington Drama Soc.; bd. incorporators Washington Hosp. Center; adv. bd. Nat. Capital Area council Boy Scouts Am. Recipient Princeton in Nation's Service award, 1968, Washingtonian award Jr. C. of C., 1959, Order Red Triangle award YMCA Greater Washington, 1966, Silver Beaver award Boy Scouts Am., 1967. Mem. Investment Bankers Assn., (v.p.), Washington Soc. Investment Analysts (past pres.) Washington Execs. assn., Phi Beta Kappa. Rotarian. Clubs: Harvard Business School (past pres., dir.), Metropolitan (Washington); Chevy Chase (Md.). Home: Kirkside Dr Chevy Chase MD 20015 Office: 1720 I St N W Washington DC 20006

FERRIS, JOHN ORLAND, newspaper editor; b. Winchester, Ind., Nov. 7, 1893; s. Charles Elliott and Ethel Mae (Chenoweth) F.; ed. pub. schs.; m. Veda Roller, May 1, 1923 (div. 1929); 1 son. Hugh R.; m. 2d, Esther May Wallace, June 18, 1931 (dec. 1969). Reporter, Winchester Daily News, 1910-11; staff Muncie (Ind.) Evening Press, 1911-18; city editor Muncie Star, 1919-24; mem. editorial dept. Miami (Fla.) Herald, 1924-26; news editor Muncie Star, 1926-35, mng. editor, 1935-60, editor, 1960-. Served with U.S. Army, 1918-19. Mem. Am. Legion. Mason (K.T., 32, shriner). Rotarian. Home: 1500 Linden St Muncie IN 47303 Office: 125 S High St Muncie IN 47302

FERRIS, JULIAN, architect; b. Caracas, Venezuela, July 23, 1921; s. Julian and Maria T. (Betancourt) F.; B.Arch., Syracuse U., 1947; m. Isabel Walli, June 9, 1951; children—Julian, Ana Maria, Gustavo, Leopoldo, Elaisa, Alejandro, Isabel. Pvt. archtl. practice, Caracas, 1949—; pres. Ferris Packing Products; dean Sch. of Architecture, U. Central (Caracas). Pres. Venezuelan Inst. Architects, Found. Arch., 1st Congress Architects Venezuela, Inter-Am. Consortium Study Devel. Trustee Universidad Metropolitana. Decorated Andres Bello, Orden 27 de Junio; recipient nat. archtl. 1st prize for Custom House, Puerto Cabello, Venezuela. Hon. fellow A.I.A.; hon. mem. Coll. Architects of Mexico, Colombia and Peru. Home: 25 El Mirador San Rafael de la Florida Caracas Venezuela South America Office: Centro Prof del Este 62 Sabana Grande Caracas Venezuela South America

FERRIS, MELTON, assn. exec.; b. Modesto, Cal., June 25, 1916; s. Leslie Allen and Georgia (Melton) F.; A.A., Riverside Jr. Coll., 1935; student U. Cal. at Berkeley, 1935-37, Cal. Sch. Fine Arts, 1951-52; m. Mary Jane Kirby, Oct. 9, 1947; children—Kirby, Leslie Allen II, Roxana Winifred Lee. Newspaper reporter, photographer San Jose (Cal.) Mercury Herald, 1937-40, Hilo (Hawaii) Tribune Herald, 1940-41; polit. reporter Internat. News Service, Sacramento, Cal., 1941-42; account exec. Gardner Advt. Co., St. Louis, 1948-50; photography editor San Francisco Chronicle, 1951-53; exec. dir. Cal. council A.I.A., San Francisco, 1954—. Chmn. Marin Parks and Recreation Commn., 1963-69; dir. Cal. Roadside Council, 1967-68, Bolinas Community Inc., 1965—. Served to maj. C.E., USAAF, 1942-48. Mem. A.I.A. (hon.), San Francisco Press Club, Cal., Am. socs. assn. execs. Clubs: Commonwealth of California; Sutter (Sacramento); Inverness Yacht. Home: 8 Hollyhock Ct Mill Valley CA 94941 Office: 1736 Stockton St San Francisco CA 94133

FERRIS, THEODORE PARKER, clergyman; b. Port Chester, N.Y., Dec. 23, 1908; s. Walter Andrew and Eva (Parker) F.; A.B., Harvard, 1929; B.D., Gen. Theol. Sem., N.Y., 1933, S.T.D., 1961; D.D., Rollins Coll., 1944, Middlesbury Coll., 1955, Boston U., 1958, Harvard Coll., 1969; Mus.D., Westminster Choir Coll., Princeton, N.J., 1967. Ordained to ministry Episcopal Ch., 1933; asst. minister Grace Ch., N.Y.C., 1933-37; fellow tutor Gen. Theol. Sem., 1933-37; rector Emmanuel Ch., Balt., 1937-42, Trinity Ch., Boston, 1942—; instr. homilectics Episcopal Theol. Sch., Cambridge, 1943-64. Del. gen. conv. P.E. Ch., 1946, 49, 52, 55, 61, 67; alternate del. First Assembly World Council Chs., Amsterdam, 1948. Trustee Boston Symphony Orch. Author: This Created World, 1944; Go Tell The People, 1951; This is the Day, 1951; The Story of Jesus, 1953; Exposition of the Acts of the Apostles in the Interpreter's Bible, 1954; When I Became a Man, 1957; The New Life, 1961; Book of Prayer for Everyman, 1962; What Jesus Did, 1963; The Image of God, 1965. Home: 233 Clarendon St Boston MA 02116 Office: Trinity Ch Copley Sq Boston MA 02116

FERRIS, WILLIAM HAROLD, pub. utility exec.; b. Madison, Wis., Sept. 26, 1909; s. Albert Eugene and Isabel (Butler) F.; B.S. in Elec. Engring., U. Wis., 1931; m. Margaret Arline Parkin, Dec. 21, 1935; children—Gwen (Mrs. Gerald Splinter), William Harold, Susan (Mrs. Jerry Carter), Sally (Mrs. Glenn Kisch), Mary Katherine (Mrs. Stephen Wickens), Thomas John. With Wis. Power & Light Co., 1937—, chief engr., 1955-65, v.p. engring. and systems operations, 1965- 69, sr. v.p. engring. and systems operations, 1969—. Bd. dirs. Wis. Valley Improvement Assn., 1968—. Atomic Power Devel. Assn., 1968—. Served to lt. USNR, 1943-46. Registered profl. engr., Wis. Asso. mem. I.E.E.E.; mem. Nat., Wis. socs. profl. engrs., Wis. Utilities Assn. (Wis. power liaison officer). Republican. Conglist. (trustee). Home: 4117 Mandan Crescent Madison WI 53711 Office: 122 W Washington Av Madison WI 53703

FERRISS, DAVID PLATT, advt. exec.; b. St. Louis, Jan. 27, 1919; s. Henry Theodore and Edith (Platt) F.; B.A., Yale, 1940; m. Marion Harris Ford, July 9, 1942 (div. July 1951); children—Carol (dec. 1967), Marion; m. 2d. Elizabeth Lashly States, May 17, 1952 (div. July 1963); m. 3d, Jean O. Browne, Jan. 18, 1964. Reporter, St. Louis Star-Times, 1940-41; with Gardner Advt. Co., St. Louis, also N.Y.C., 1946- 70; pres. Ralph Jones Advt., Inc., Cin., 1970—. Former asso. lectr. English, Washington U., 1947-51, George Washington U., 1951-52. Mem. bd. Planned Parenthood, Kidney Found., Cin. Served from pvt. to capt. CIC, AUS, 1941-45, capt. CIA, 1951-52. Mem. Am. Assn. Advt. Agys. (chmn. St. Louis council 1959-60, vice chmn. Cin. council 1971—). Republican. Episcopalian. Clubs: St. Louis Country; Cincinnati Country, Queen City (Cin.); Yale (N.Y.C.). Home: 2835 Ambleside Pl Cincinnati OH 45208 Office: Carew Tower Cincinnati OH 45202

FERROGGIARO, F. A., banker; b. San Francisco, May 12, 1890; s. Natale and Anna (Guinasso) F.; ed. pub. schs., San Francisco; m. Delphine Lerde, Aug. 1, 1916; children—Delphine (Mrs. E. Q. Reed), Fred L. With Bank of Am. NT & SA, San Francisco, 1906, v.p., mgr. Oakland main office, 1931-40, exec. v.p., 1940-49, dir., 1940—, chmn. gen. finance com. 1944—, sr. vice chmn. bd., 1949-54, chmn. bd., 1954—; vice chmn., Bank of Am. Internat.; v.p. Corp. of Am.; v.p., dir. Mchts. Nat. Realty Co.; hon. chmn. bd. chmn. exec. com. Lucky Stores, Inc., San Leandro, Cal. Chmn. bd. dirs. Bank of Am. Giannini Found.; regent St. Mary's Coll. of Cal. Mem. San Francisco C. of C. Republican. Roman Catholic. Elk, Druid, K.C. Clubs: Olympic (San Francisco); Claremont Country (Oakland). Home: 492 Staten Av Oakland CA Office: 300 Montgomery St San Francisco CA 94120 also Lucky Stores Inc 1701 Marine Blvd San Leandro CA 94577

FERRONNIERE, JACQUES, banker; b. Nantes, France, Dec. 2, 1906; s. Lucien and Yvonne (Defline) F.; diplome de l'Ecole Libre des Scis. Politiques, d'Etudes Supérieures de la Faculté de Droit de Paris; m. Marie-Thérse Jalaber, Dec. 9, 1936. Insp. of finances, 1929-35; pres. de la Soc. Générale, 1966—, de la Soc. Anonyme de Credit a l'Industrie Francaise, 1962—, de la Soc. Generale Marocaine de Banques, 1962—; adminstr. Compagnie Bancaire, 1959—, Etablissements J.J. Carnaud et Forges de Basse-Indre, 1962—, Soc. Francaise de Banque et de Dép ôts, 1958—, 1958—, Generale de Banque, 1958—; v.p. de la Soc. Générale Alsacienne de Banque, 1952—. Decorated comdr. Legion of Honor. Home: 1 Av de Camoens Paris 16e France Office: 29 Blvd Haussmann Paris 9e France

FERRUOLO, ARNOLFO BARTHOLOMEW, educator; b. Florence, Italy, Aug. 2, 1915; s. Gaetano and Maria (Fusco) F.; Dottore in Lettere, U. Florence, 1939; m. Clorinda V. Ferruolo, Nov. 8, 1944. Came to U.S., 1950, naturalized, 1956. Adj. prof. English lang. and lit. U. Bologna (Italy), 1947-50; asst. prof. Italian, Harvard, 1950- 56, Cath. U. Am., 1956-57; mem. faculty U. Cal. at Berkeley, 1957—, prof. Italian, 1960—; vis. prof. summer sch. Middlebury (Vt.) Coll., 1968. Decorated cavaliere officiale Dell Ordine al Merito Della Repubblica Italiana. Mem. Modern Lang. Assn. Am., Am. Assn. U. Profs., Am. Assn. Tchrs. Italian, Dante Soc. Am., Renaissance Soc. Am. Author works on Neo-Platonism, Angelo Poliziano, Lorenzo de Medici, Sandro Botticelli, Giordano Bruno, Sir Philip Sidney. Home: 763 Cragmont Av Berkeley CA 94708

FERRY, DAVID RUSSELL, educator; b. Orange, N.J., Mar. 5, 1924; s. Robert Edward and Elsie (Russell) F.; A.B., Amherst Coll., 1948; M.A., Harvard, 1949, Ph.D., 1955; m. Anne Davidson, Mar. 22, 1958; children—Stephen Edward, Elizabeth Emma. Teaching fellow Harvard, 1950-52; instr. Wellesley Coll., 1952-55, asst. prof., 1955-61, asso. prof., 1961-67, prof., 1967—, Sophie Chantal Hart prof., 1971—, chmn. dept. English, 1965-68. Served with AUS, 1943-46. Author: The Limits of Mortality: An Essay on Wordsworth's Major Poems, 1959; (poems) On the Way to the Island, 1960. Editor: The Laurel Wordsworth, 1959. Contbr. poems and essays to periodicals. Home: 8 Ellery St Cambridge MA 02138 Office: Dept English Wellesley Coll Wellesley MA 02181

FERRY, JOHN DOUGLASS, chemist, educator; b. Dawson, Can., May 4, 1912 (parents Am. Citizens) s. Douglass Hewitt and Eudora (Bundy) F.; A.B., Stanford, 1932, Ph.D., 1935; student U. London (Eng.), 1932-34; m. Barbara Norton Mott, Mar. 25, 1944; children—Phyllis Leigh, John Mott. Pvt. asst. Hopkins Marine Sta., Stanford, 1935-36; instr. biochem. scis. Harvard, 1936-38, mem. Soc. Fellows, 1938-41; asso. chemist Woods Hole Oceanographic Inst., 1941-45; research asso. Harvard, 1942-45; asst. prof. chemistry U. Wis., 1946, asso. prof., 1946-47, prof., 1947—, chmn. dept., 1959-67. Chmn. Internat. Com. on Rheology, 1963-68; vis. lectr. Kyoto (Japan) U., 1968. Recipient Eli Lilly award Am. Chem. Soc., 1946, Bingham medal Soc. Rheology, 1953; Kendall Co. award Am. Chem. Soc., 1960. Fellow Am. Phys. Soc. (high polymer physics prize 1966). Am. Acad. Arts and Scis., mem. Nat. Acad. Sci., Am. Chem. Soc., Am. Soc. Biol. Chemists, Soc. Rheology (pres. 1961-63), Internat. Soc. Hematology, Phi Beta Kappa, Sigma Xi, Phi Lambda Upsilon. Alpha Chi Sigma. Rotarian. Author: Viscoelastic Properties of Polymers, 1961, 2d edit., 1970. Co-editor: Fortschritte der Hochpolymeren Forschung. Home: 137 N Prospect Av Madison WI 53705

FERRY, WILBUR HUGH, found. cons.; b. Detroit, Dec. 17, 1910; s. Hugh Joseph and Fay (Rutson) F.; A.B., Dartmouth, 1932; m. Jolyne Marie Gillier, Oct. 23, 1937; children—Lucian (stepson), Denise, Fay (Mrs. Peter B. Crane), Robin. Instr., Choate Sch., 1932-33; engaged as newspaperman, 1933-35, 37-41; dir. publicity Eastern Air Lines, 1936; chief investigator in N.H. for OPA, 1942-44; cons. ILO, 1940-44; dir. pub. relations CIO-Polit. Action Com., 1944; mem. USAF Strategic Bombing Survey, S.W. Pacific Area, 1945; partner Earl Newsom & Co., 1945-54; v.p. Center Study Democratic Instns., 1954-69, cons., 1969—. Author: The Corporation and The Economy, 1959; The Economy Under Law, 1961; Caught on the Horn of Plenty, 1962; What Price Peace, 1963; Masscomm as Educator, 1966; Farewell to Integration, 1967; Tonic and Toxic Technology, 1967; The Police State Is Here, 1969. Home: 1709 Overlook Lane Santa Barbara CA 93103 Office: 906 Garden St Santa Barbara CA 93101

FERST, ROBERT HAROLD, mfg. co. exec.; b. Atlanta, Dec. 17, 1917; s. Monie Alan and Helen (Montag) F.; M.E., Ga. Inst. Tech., 1938; B.S., Yale, 1939; m. Jeanne Rolfe, June 12, 1940; childrenSuzanne (Mrs. Nelson Neiman II), Robin Helen. With M.A. Ferst, Ltd., Atlanta, 1940—, pres., 1956—; chmn. exec. com. Scripto Co., 1955-67, pres., 1967-68, chmn. bd., 1968—; pres. So. Graphote Co., 1954—. Pres. Atlanta Municiple Theatre, 1968, sec., treas., 1953-67; past pres., treas. Atlanta Vis. Nurses Assn., 1956-67. Trustee Atlanta Meml. Arts Alliance, 1963-69, Ga. Inst. Tech. Nat. Alumni Assn., 1957-60, Ga. Inst. Tech. Found., 1961—, Ga. Tech. Research Inst., 1965—, Yale Alumni Assn., 1961-65; sec. chair pvt. enterprise Ga. State Coll., 1964-65, trustee, 1964—. Served with AUS, 1942-44. Mem. Lead Pencil Mfrs. Assn. (sec.-treas. 1964-67), Writing Instrument Assn., Young Pres. Orgn. (regional v.p. 1967), Yale Engring. Soc. Clubs: Stadium (bd. govs. 1967—), Standard, Commerce (Atlanta); Yale (N.Y.C.); Bucks (London). Home: 3585 Woodhaven Rd Atlanta GA 30305 Office: William Oliver Bldg Atlanta GA 30303

FERTIG, INAN JASPER, ins. co. exec.; b. Humphreys, Mo., Nov. 15, 1909; s. John Franklin and Flake (Jackson) F.; extension student U. Minn., 1929; m. Harriet Jane Kimball, Apr. 26, 1937; children—Daniel John, Deborah Ann. Adjuster, then claim mgr. Continental Casualty Co., 1930-35; with St. Paul Fire & Marine Ins. Co., 1935—, asst. sec., 1955-57, sec., 1957—, now sr. v.p. St. Paul Cos., Inc. Served with AUS, 1943-45. Conglist. (trustee 1964-67). Home: 4615 Drexel Av Edina MN 55424 Office: 385 Washington St St Paul MN 55102

FERTIG, JOHN WILLIAM, biostatistian, educator; b. Lebanon, Pa., Oct. 13, 1911; s. Walter E. and Ella J. (Binkley) F.; A.B., Ursinus Coll., 1931; Ph.D., U. Minn., 1935; M.D. (hon.) Faculty Medicine of Uruguay, 1953; m. Dorothy M. Huebner, July 28, 1939 (dec.); children—John, John, Julius. Asso. biometrician Meml. Found. for Neuro-Endocrine Research, Worcester, Mass., 1935-37; research asso. in biostatistics Sch. Hygiene and Pub. Health, Johns Hopkins U., Balt., 1937-40; prof. biostatistics Sch. Pub. Health, Faculty of Medicine, Columbia U., 1940—; vis. lectr. in biostatistics U. Ky., 1938-40; vis. prof. med. statistics N.Y. U., 1943-45, 51-53, Yale, also U. Minn., 1949, sch. tropical medicine U. P.R., 1948-53, prof. biostatists, coll. medicine, 1952; cons. on biostatistics U. Chile, 1953—, U. Saõ Paulo, 1955—, U. Buenos Aires, 1961—, WHO, 1953—; hon. prof. faculty of medicine U. Chile, 1959. Faculty of Medicine, Montevideo, Uruguay, 1953. Who, 1953-55. Fellow A.A.A.S., Am. Pub. Health Assn., Am. Statis. Assn.; mem. Am. Population Assn., Inst. Math. Statis., Am. Statis. Assn., Sigma Xi, Gamma Alpha, Delta Omega. Contbr. articles on math. and med. statistics. Home: 41 Southlawn Av Dobbs Ferry NY 10522 Office: 600 West 168th St New York City NY 10032

FERTIG, LAWRENCE, economist; b. N.Y.C., Mar. 19, 1898; A.B., N.Y. U., 1919; A.M., Columbia, 1920; m. Bertha Alexander, Aug. 1932. Founder Lawrence Fertig & Co., Inc., 1923, pres., 1923-60; syndicated econ. columnist, 1944—. Trustee N.Y U., 1954—, pres. Alumni Fedn., 1950-52; chmn. bd. trustees Found. Econ. Edn. Mem. Phi Beta Kappa. Author: Prosperity Through Freedom, 1961. Home: Port Washington NY 11050 Office: 380 Madison Av New York City NY 10017

FERTIG, WALTER LONGLEY, educator; b. Noblesville, Ind., June 27, 1917; s. Emmet Ross and Alice (Longley) F.; B.A., Wabash Coll., 1(1*; M.A., Harvard, 1941; Ph.D., U. Md., 1952; m. Catharine Bailey, Aug. 26, 1950; children—Lamar, Patricia, Melinda, David. Faculty Wabash Coll., 1940-42, 46-47, 49—, prof., chmn. dept. English, 1957—, Milligan prof., 1957—. Served to lt. (s.g.) USNR, 1942-46. Mem. Modern Lang. Assn., Am. Studies Assn. Home: 1417 W Main St Crawfordsville IN 47933

FERY, JOHN BRUCE, paper mfg. co. exec.; b. Bellingham, Wash., Feb. 16, 1930; s. Carl S. and Margaret (Haack) F.; B.A., U. Wash., 1953; M.B.A., Stanford, 1955; m. Delores L. Carlo, Aug. 22, 1953; children—John Brent, Bruce Todd, Michael Nicholas. Asst. to pres. Western Kraft Corp., Portland, Ore., 1955, prodn. mgr., Albany, Ore., 1955-56; with Boise Cascade Corp. (Ida.), 1957—, asst. to pres., 1957-58, gen. mgr. paper div., Wallula, Wash., 1958-60, v.p. corp., 1960-67, exec. v.p., 1967—, also dir.; dir. Bank Ida. Bd. dirs. Am. Paper Inst.; bd. govs. Paper Industry for Air and Stream Improvement. Served with USNR, 1950-51. Elk. Home: 609 Wyndemere Dr Boise ID 83702 Office: PO Box 200 Boise ID 83701

FESENMYER, FRANCIS WAYNE, petroleum exec.; b. Bradford, Pa., May 17, 1908; s. Frederick W. and Mary D. (Keyes) F.; Student Washington and Lee U., 1927-28; m. Elizabeth Emery Kennedy, Apr. 6, 1933; children—Delevan Kennedy, Natalie Emery. Frederick Wayne, Elaine Emery. Actuarial dept. home office Mut. Life Ins. Co. of N.Y., N.Y.C., 1930; partnership Berwald & Fesenmyer, gen. ins., Bradford, 1931-41; pres. Emery Hotel Corp., Bradford, 1941, gen. mgr., 1942-43; v.p., dir. Lobdell-Emery Mfg. Co., Alma, Mich., 1943-53, pres., dir., 1953-56, chmn. bd., 1956—; pres. Minard Run Oil Co., 1946—; dir. Bradford Nat. Bank. Mem. Pa. Aero. Commn., 1960-70; bd. dirs. Bradford-McKean Airport Commn., 1956-67, chmn., 1966-67; chmn. Bradford Regional Airport Authority, 1967—. Bd. dirs., trustee YMCA, Bradford. Mem. Pa. Oil Producers Assn. (officer Bradford dist. 1946—pres. 1953), Ind. Petroleum Assn. Am. (dir. 1947—, v.p. for Pa. 1950-52, mem. exec. com. 1954-55), Alpha Chi Rho. Republican. Ekl. Clubs: Penhills (dir.), Bradford (Bradford); Quiet Bridmen (Buffalo). Home: 800 Minard Run Rd Bradford PA 16701 Office: Box 18 Bradford PA 16701

FESHBACH, HERMAN, physicist; b. N.Y.C., Feb. 2, 1917; s. David and Ida (Lapiner) F.; B.S., Coll City N.Y., 1937; Ph.D., Mass. Inst. Tech., 1942; m. Sylvia Harris, Jan. 28, 1940; children—Carolyn Barbara, Theodore Philip, Mark Frederick. Tutor, Coll. City N.Y., 1937-38; instr. Mass. Inst. Tech., 1941-45, asst. prof., 1945-47, asso. prof., 1947-55, prof., 1955—, also dir. Center for Theoretical Physics; John Simon Guggenheim Meml. Found. fellow, 1954-55; Ford fellow CERN, Geneva, Switzerland, 1962-63. Cons. AEC. Mem. Am. Phys. Soc. (chmn. div. nuclear physics), Nat. Acad. Scis., NRC, Am. Acad. Arts and Scis. Author: Methods of Theoretical Physics (with P.M. Morse), 1953; also sci. articles tech. jours. Asst. editor Annals of Physics. Home: 5 Sedgwick Rd Cambridge MA 02138 (summer) Dennis MA 02138

FESLER, JAMES WILLIAM, educator, polit. scientist; b. Duluth, Minn., Mar. 14, 1911; s. Bert and Vinnie Leona (King) F.; student U. Cal., 1928-30; A.B cum laude, U. Minn., 1932; A.M., Harvard, 1933, Ph.D., 1935; M.A. (hon.), Yale, 1951; m. Frances Martin, Mar. 15, 1940; children—Janet Martin, James Martin. Research asst. Nat. Resources Com., 1935; asst. prof., U. N.C., 1935-37, asso. prof., 1937-45, prof., 1945-51; Alfred Cowles prof. govt. Yale, 1951—, Ford Research prof., 1961-62, chmn. dept. polit. sci., 1951-55, 57, 62-64; vis. prof. U. Minn., summer 1949, U. Cal., 1949-50; asst. to exec. sec. War Prodn. Bd., 1941-43, chief policy analysis and records br., 1943-45, historian, 1945-46. Mem. staff Pres.'s Com. on Adminstrv. Mgmt., 1936. Research fellow Rockfeller Found., 1937- 38; faculty research fellow Social Sci. Research Council, 1964-65. Fellow A.A.A.S.; mem. Am. Polit. Sci. Assn. (v.p. 1968-69), Nat. Acad. Pub. Adminstrn., Am. Soc. Pub. Adminstrn., Am. Assn. U. Profs., N.E. Polit. Sci. Assn. (pres. 1958-59), Phi Delta Theta. Author: Executive Management and the Federal Field Service, 1937; The Independence of State Regulatory Agencies, 1942; Area and Adminstration, 1949. Editor, contbr. Industrial Mobilization for War, 1947; The 48 States, 1955; The 50 States and Their Local Governments, 1967. Asso. editor Am. Polit. Sci. Rev., 1949-51; editor-in- chief Pub. Adminstrn. Rev., 1958-60. Contbr. to profl. jours. Address: 647 Yale Sta New Haven CT 06520

FESLER, ROBERT L., banker; b. Indpls., Jan. 24, 1937; s. James L. and Irene (Smith) F.; B.S., Ind. U., 1959; m. Judy McFarland, June 13, 1959; children—Kimberly, Kris, Amy. Accountant, K.B. Parrish & Co., C.P.A.'s, Indpls., 1959-62, Inland Container Corp., Indpls., 1963-64; C.P.A., Indpls., 1965-66; controller Merchants Nat. Bank & Trust Co., Indpls., 1967—; tchr. accounting Ind. Central Coll., 1963-65. Mem. Ind. N.G., 1957. Mem. Financial Execs. Inst., Am. Inst. Banking (tchr. 1967), Bank Adminstrn. Inst., Indpls. Jr. C. of C., Sigma Chi. Presbyn. Home: 5415 Susan Dr E Indianapolis IN 46250 Office: 11 S Meridian St Indianapolis IN 46204

FESPERMAN, TOM, newspaper editor; b. Charlotte, N.C., May 14, 1918; s. James Loyd and Catherine (Cartledge) F.; student pub. schs., Charlotte; m. Mary Hewitt, June 3, 1940; children—Lee (Mrs. Donald George Morrison), Thomas David. Reporter, Charlotte (N.C.) News, 1935-42, columnist, 1946-52, city editor, 1953, mng. editor, 1953-56; mng. editor Charlotte Observer, 1956—. Discussion leader Am. Press Inst., Columbia, 1964-69. Bd. dirs. Nat. Conf. Christians and Jews, Mecklenburg County, N.C., 1965-70, United Community Services, 1970—. Served with AUS, 1942-45. Decorated Bronze Star. Mem. AP Mng. Editors Assn. (bd. dirs. 1965-71), Sigma Delta Chi. Home: 1663 Tyvola Dr Charlotte NC 28210 Office: 600 S Tryon St Charlotte NC 28201

FESS, PHILIP EUGENE, educator; b. Troy, O., Nov. 25, 1931; s. Charles E. and Margaret (Furlong) F.; B.S., Miami U., Oxford, O., 1953; M.S., U. Ill., 1955, Ph.D., 1960; m. Suzanne E. Cuthbert, Sept. 17, 1955; children—Linda Marie, Virginia Sue, Martha Ann. Asso. prof. accounting U. Ill. at Urbana, 1953-55, 57-68, prof. accountancy, 1968—. Treas. Champaign County (Ill.) Am. Cancer Soc., 1966-67. Served to 1st lt. USAF, 1955-57. C.P.A., Ill. Mem. Am. Inst. C.P.A.'s, Ill. Soc. C.P.A's, Am., Nat. accounting assns., U. Ill. Alumni Assn. (treas., bd. dirs. 1969—), Phi Beta Kappa, Beta Alpha Psi, Delta Sigma Pi, Omicron Delta Kappa, Beta Gamma Sigma, Sigma Chi. Author: (with C.R. Niswonger) Accounting Principles, 9th and 10th edits., 1969. Home: 2408 Melrose Dr Champaign IL 61820

FESSENDEN, RALPH JAMES, educator; b. Chgo., Oct. 25, 1932; s. Douglas A. and Juliette (Armstrong) F.; B.S., U. Ill., 1955; Ph.D., U. Cal. at Berkeley, 1958; m. Joan Searing, Aug. 13, 1955;

children—Douglas, Bruce. Asst. prof. San Jose State Coll., 1958-63, asso. prof., 1963-67, prof., 1967; prof., chmn. dept. chemistry U. Mont., 1967—. Alfred P. Sloan fellow, 1965-69. Mem. Am. Chem. Soc., N.Y., Mont. acads. scis., Sigma Xi, Alpha Chi Sigma. Author: (with Joan S. Fessenden) The Basis of Organic Chemistry, 1971. Research organosilicon medicinal agts. and detoxication pathways. Home: 111 Takima Dr Missoula MT 59801

FESSENDEN, RUSSELL, fgn. service officer; b. Rochester, N.Y., Apr. 20, 1916; s. George Russell and Marion (Newell) F.; A.B., Oberlin Coll., 1938; Ph.D., Cornell U., 1943; m. Catherine J. Andrus, Oct. 10, 1939; children— Helen, David, Ann, Jean. Mem. faculty Cornell U., 1939-42; with State Dept., 1946-54; joined U.S. Fgn. Service, 1954; assigned NATO Def. Coll., 1955; 1st sec. embassy, Paris, 1955-58; dept. dir., then dir. Office European Regional Affairs, State Dept., 1958-62; dep. chief U.S. Mission to European Communities, Brussels, Belgium, 1962-67; minister, dep. chief mission Am. embassy, Bonn, Germany, 1967-71; dep. asst. sec. state, European affairs, 1971—. Served with AUS, 1943- 46. Home: 186 W College St Oberlin OH 44074 Office: Dept State Washington DC 20520

FEST, THORREL BROOKS, educator; b. Audubon, Ia., Aug. 23, 1910; s. Albert F. and Augusta (Boers) F.; A.B., State Coll. Ia., 1932; M.Ph., U. Wis., 1938, Ph.D., 1952; m. C. Lucille Etzler, June 5, 1934; children—Stephen, Bruce. Tchr. secondary schs., Griswold and Spencer, Ia., 1932-39; asst. prof. U. N.D., 1939-40, Albion Coll., 1940-44; staff Manhattan Project, 1944-45; mem. extension faculty U. Tenn., 1945; asst. prof. U. Colo., 1945-53, asso. prof., 1953-58, prof., 1958—, chmn. dept. speech, 1960- 68; vis. prof. U. Hawaii, 1959, 63, Syracuse U., 1961; vis. lectr. U. New South Wales (Australia), spring 1970. Cons. N.Am. Def. Command Hdqrs. Staff, 1956—, U.S. C. of C., 1959—, Brit. Columbia Tchrs. Fedn., 1968—, Colo. Tax Commn., 1965—; v.p. Nat. Center Communication Arts and Scis., 1965—, program dir., 1966—. Mem. adv. com. Alexander Hamilton Bicentennial Commn., 1956-58. Chmn. bd. trustees Intercultural Sch. Rockies, 1968-71; mem. internat. founding com. Center for Audio Visual Instrn. via Satellite, 1968—. Fellow Internat. Inst. Arts and Letters; mem. Nat. U. Extension Assn., Nat. Collegiate Players, Am. Forensic Assn. (chmn. pub. relations 1951-53), Adult Edn. Assn., Speech Communication Assn. (legislative council 1955-57, exec. council 1957-60, chmn. com. on curricula and certification, 1963-66, legislative council 1963-65, 67-69), Canadian Speech Assn., Colo.-Wyo. Acad. Sci., Am. Edn. Theatre Assn., Am. Assn. U. Profs. (pres. 1960-62), Colo. (pres. state conf. 1962-64), Western (v.p.), Central, So. speech assns., Indsl. Communication Council, Internat. Platform Assn., Internat. Communication Assn. (nat. council 1955-62, nat. pres. 1960-61), Internat. Soc. Gen. Semantics, Izaak Walton League, Delta Sigma Rho (editor Gavel 1949-53, nat. pres. 1953- 57), Lambda Delta Lambda, Kappa Delta Pi, Theta Alpha Phi. Author: (with Martin Cobin) Speech and Theater, 1964; (with R.V. Harnack) Group Discussion: Theory and Technique, 1964; also profl. articles. Home: 1546 Sunset Blvd Boulder CO 80302

FESTGE, OTTO former mayor; b. Cross Plains, Wis., Jan. 1, 1921; s. Otto and Ernestine (Wille) F.; student U. Wis., 1938-42; m. Evelyn Janet Dybdahl, Sept. 4, 1942; children—Michael, Susan, Cynthia. Assessor, Town of Cross Plains, 1945- 52; tchr. Black Earth (Wis.) High Sch., 1946-52; clk. Dane County, Madison, Wis., 1952-65; mayor, Madison, 1965-69; sales rep. Sentry Ins. Co., 1969-71; home sec. Congressman Robert W. Kastenmeier, 1971—. Mem. Wis. County Clks'. Assn. (pres. 1961-62), Wis. League Municipalities, Wis. Alliance Cities (chmn.), Nat. League Cities, U.S. Conf. Mayors, Nat. Farmers Union, Wis. Alumni Assn., Phi Mu Alpha Symphonia. Democrat. Lutheran. Lion. Home: 4310 Herrick Lane Madison WI 53711

FESTINGER, LEON, educator, psychologist; b. N.Y.C., May 8, 1919; s. Alex and Sarah (Solomon) F.; B.S., Coll. City N.Y., 1939; M.A., State U. Ia., 1940, Ph.D., 1942; m. Mary Oliver Ballou, Oct. 23, 1943; children—Catherine, Richard, Kurt; m. 2d, Trudy Bradley, Sept. 7, 1968. Research asso. State U. Ia., 1941-43; instr. U. Rochester, 1943-45; asso. prof. Mass. Inst. Tech., 1945-48; asso. prof. U. Mich., 1948-51; prof. psychology U. Minn., 1951-55, Stanford, 1955-68; Else and Hans Staudinger prof. psychology, grad. faculty New Sch. for Social Research, 1968—. Mem. transnat. social psychology com. Social Sci. Research Council. Fellow Am. Psychol. Assn. (pres. div. 8, 1963; Distinguished Scientist award 1959), Am. Acad. Arts and Scis. Author: Conflict, Decision and Dissonance, 1964. Home: 37 W 12th St New York City NY 10011

FETKOVICH, JOHN GABRIEL, educator, physicist; b. Aliquippa, Pa., June 9, 1931; s. Michael and Anna (Klacik) F.; B.S., Carnegie-Mellon U., 1953; M.S. 1955, Ph.D., 1960; m. Ann Marie Argenziana, Dec. 13, 1958; children—Anne Marie, John Gabriel. Mem. faculty Carnegie-Mellon U., 1960—, prof. physics, 1968—; cons. in field, 1963—. Distinguished appointment Argonne Univs. Assn., 1970-71; vis. scientist Rutherford High Energy Lab., Eng., 1971-72; Served to 1st lt. AUS, 1959-60. Fellow Am. Phys. Soc.; mem. Am. Assn. U. Profs., A.A.A.S., Am. Assn. Physics Tchrs., Sigma Xi, Phi Kappa Phi. Home: 113 Yorkshire Dr Pittsburgh PA 15238

FETRIDGE, WILLIAM HARRISON, corp. exec.; b. Chgo.; s. Matthew and Clara (Hall) F.; B.S., Northwestern U., 1929; LL.D., Central Mich. U., 1954; m. Bonnie Jean Clark, June 27, 1941; children—Bonnie Blakely (Mrs. Harvey H. Bundy III), Clark Worthington. Asst. to dean Northwestern U., 1929-30; editor Trade Periodical Co., 1930-31, Chgo. Tribune, 1931-34, H. W. Kastor & Son, 1934-35, Roche, Williams & Cleary, Inc., 1935-42; mng. editor Republican Mag., 1939-42; asst. to pres. Popular Mechanics mag., 1945-46, v.p., 1946, exec. v.p., 1953-59; v.p. Diamond T Motor Truck Co., Chgo., 1959-61, exec. v.p. 1961-65; pres. Dartnell Corp., Chgo., 1965—. Pres. United Republican Fund of Ill.; alternate del.-at-large Rep. Nat. Conv., 1956; del.-at-large Rep. Nat. Conv., 1968; mem. Rep Nat. Finance Com.; chmn. Midwest Vols. Nixon, 1960; chmn. Rep. Forum, 1958-60; chmn. Nixon Recount Com. Trustee Jacques Holinger Meml. Assn., Am. Humanics Found.; mem. nat. exec. bd., nat. v.p. Boy Scouts Am., 1958—; trustee Lake Forest Coll., Internat. Found. for Scouting; past pres. trustees Latin Sch. Chgo. Recipient Silver Antelope, Silver Beaver, Silver Buffalo, Boy Scouts Am., 1956. Served as lt. comdr. USNR, 1942-45. Mem. Navy League U.S. (past regional pres.), Beta Theta Pi. Clubs: Stevensville Yacht (vice commodore); The Casino, Chicago, Union League, Saddle and Cycle (Chgo.); Capitol Hill (Washington). Editor: The Navy Reader, 1943; The Second Navy Reader, 1944; American Political Almanac, 1950. Home: 2430 Lakeview Av Chicago IL 60614 Office: 4660 Ravenswood Av Chicago IL 60640

FETTER, FRANK WHITSON, economist; b. San Francisco, May 22, 1899; s. Frank Albert and Martha (Whitson) F.; A.B., Swarthmore Coll., 1920; A.M., Princeton, 1922, Ph.D., 1926; A.M., Harvard, 1924; m. Elizabeth Garrett Pollard, Jan. 14, 1929; children—Robert Pollard, Thomas Whitson, Ellen Cole (Mrs. John C. Gille). Instr. econs., Princeton, 1924-25, 27-28, asst. prof., 1928-34; asso. prof. econs. Haverford Coll., 1934-36, prof. 1936-48; prof. econs. Northwestern U., 1948- 67; vis. prof. Dartmouth, 1967-68; lectr. Sch. of Advanced Internat. Studies (Washington); 1945-47, Swarthmore Coll., 1946-47; leave of absence to work with Office Lend-Lease Admistrn. 1943-44; Dept. State 1944-46; vis. prof. U. Wis., 1951-52. Vice pres. Nat. Bur. Econ. Research, 1963-65, chmn., 1965-67, dir., 1950- -. Mem. Am. Commn. of Financial Advisers to govts., 1925-29; editorial writer St. Louis Post-Dispatch, 1930-34. Guggenheim fellow, 1937-38. Decorated Knight Order Polonia Restituta (Poland), 1927; Order of Merit First Class (Ecuador), 1927. Mem. Am. Econ. Assn. (exec. com. 1944-46), Midwest Econs. Assn. (pres. 1952), Academia de Ciencias Economicas (Chile), Phi Beta Kappa. Author books, latest being: Development of British Monetary Orthodoxy. Coauthor books in field. Mem. adv. bd. History of Polit. Economy, 1969—. Contbr. articles on econs. Home: 8 Smith Rd Hanover NH 03755 ☆

FETTER, RICHARD ELWOOD, environmental mgmt. co. exec.; b. Lewisburg, Pa., Feb. 25, 1923; s. Elwood M. and Emily (Rogers) F.; B.S. in Commerce and Finance, Bucknell U., 1947; m. Mary Virginia Gabriel, June 22, 1947; 1 dau., Molly Elizabeth. With Gen. Electric Co., 1947-64, finance mgr. indsl. heating dept., Shelbyville, Ind., 1954-64; controller F.W. Dodge Co. div. McGraw- Hill, Inc. 1964-70, v.p., 1965-67, financial v.p., treas. Standard & Poor's Corp., 1967-70; v.p. finance and adminstr. Research-Cottrell, Inc , Bedminster, N.J., 1970—. Mem. fed. finance com. Ind. C. of C., 1962-63. Bd. dirs. Shelby County United Fund, 1963-64. Served with USAAF, 1945-47. Decorated Air medal. Mem. Financial Execs. Inst., Newcomen Soc., Phi Gamma Delta, Omicron Delta Kappa. Presbyn. (trustee 1960-63). Rotarian (dir. Shelbyville 1960-61). Clubs: Metropolitan (N.Y.C.); Copper Springs Beach and Tennis (Meyersville, N.J.); Fairmont Country (Chatham, N.J.). Home: 49 Van Houton Av Chatham NJ 07928 Office: Research-Cottrell Inc Bedminster NJ 07921

FETTER, ROBERT BARCLAY, educator; b. Berwyn, Ill., May 6, 1924; s. Russell M. and Dorothy (Dupuis) F.; B.S., Va. Poly. Inst., 1947; M.B.A., Ind. U., 1949, D.B.A., 1952; M.A. (hon.), Yale, 1963; m. Audrey Louise Lillard, Feb. 7, 1951; children—Sarah Anne, Robert Alan, Martha Sue. Instr., asst. prof. Ind. U., 1949-53; asst. prof. Mass. Inst. Tech., 1953-58; asso. prof. Yale, 1958-63, prof. adminstrv. scis., 1963—, chmn. adminstrv. scis., 1969—. Cons. Rand Corp., 1963—, E.I. duPont de Nemours & Co., Inc., 1960-, McKinsey & Co., Inc., 1960—; cons. editor R.D. Irwin, Inc., Homewood, Ill., 1960—. Served with USNR, 1944-46. Ford Found. fellow, 1964. Fellow Acad. of Mgmt.; mem. Operations Research Soc. Am., Inst. Mgmt. Scis., A.A.A.S., Econometric Soc., Am. Statis. Assn., Am. Econ. Assn. Home: 21 Barberry Lane Woodbridge CT 06525 Office: 2 Hillhouse Av New Haven CT 06520

FETTER, SHERMAN EVERETT, musician; b. Raytown, Mo., May 4, 1908; s. Sherman and Martha (Hussey) F.; M.B., Ottawa (Kan.) U., 1932; M.M., Kan. U., 1934; student Eastman Sch. of Music, Chgo. Mus. Coll.; m. Thelma Hayes, June 7, 1934; 1 dau., Ann. Dean of music Ottawa U., 1936-42; head music dept., Washburn U., Topeka, Kan., 1946—; condr. Topeka Civic Orch., 1946—; mem. Kan. City Philharmonic, 1933-34. Study and travel, France, 1838 (studied with Pierre Monteux). Served as 1st lt. USAAF, 1942-46. Mem. Music Tchrs. Nat. Assn., Kan. Music Teachers Assn. (pres. 1954). Baptist. Mem. Pi Kappa Lambda, Rotary. Home: 2409 W 19th St Topeka KS 66609

FETTER, THEODORE HENRY, TV producer; b. Ithaca, N.Y.; s. Frank Albert and Martha (Whitson) F.; student The George Sch.; A.B., Swarthmore Coll.; m. Suzanne Merandon Pleven, Apr. 26, 1946; children—Frank Albert II, (foster son) Patrick Alfred Pleven. Actor, Abraham Lincoln, 1929, Garrick Gaieties, 1930, Jubilee, 1935, Many Mansions, 1936; lyric writer The Little Show, 1930, The Show Is On, 1936, Billy Rose's Aquacade, 1939, Cabin in the Sky, 1939; TV prodn., Your Hit Parade, 1950-53, Jack Paar Show, 1954-56, One Man Show, 1969-70, Secret Challenge, 1970-71; v.p., nat. dir. programs ABC TV Network, 1956-68; co-producer of first live intercontinental TV program, U.S. to Europe via satellite, 1962. Mem. A.S.C.A.P., Nat. Acad. Television Arts and Scis., Am. Arbitration Assn. Mem. Soc. of Friends. Published songs include Yours for a Song, Taking a Chance on Love. Home: 19 Haggers Lane Fair Haven NJ 07701 Office: 114 E 71st St New York City NY 10021

FETTERMAN, JOHN DAVIS, journalist; b. Danville, Ky., Feb. 25, 1920; s. John Lawrence and Zora (Goad) F.; B.S., Murray (Ky.) State U., 1948; postgrad. U. Ky., 1949- 50; m. Evelyn Alline Maner, Nov. 2, 1944; children—Phyllis Lee (Mrs. John Terry), Mindy Nelle. Editor Murray Ledger & Times, 1946-47; tchr. Ill. pub. schs., 1948-50; with Nashville Tennessean, 1950-57; writer- photographer Louisville Courier-Jour., 1957-69. Served with USNR, 1942- 45. Recipient Pulitzer prize in journalism, 1969; Nat. Headliner award, 1969; named Outstanding Alumnus, Murray State U., 1971. Author: Stinking Creek, 1967; also articles, photos. Home: 4425 Greenbriar Rd Louisville KY 40207

FETTERMAN, PAUL, lawyer; b. Omaha, Nov. 3, 1906; grad. U. Neb.; LL.B., Creighton U., 1934. Admitted to Neb. bar, 1934, Wash. bar, 1936; now partner firm Halsell, Paul, Fetterman, Todd & Hokanson, Seattle. Mem. Am., Wash. State, Seattle-King County bar assns. Office: Washington Bldg 1325 4th Av Seattle WA 98101*

FETTERS, KARL LEROY, corp. exec., metall. engr.; b. Alliance, O., Nov. 28, 1909; s. Frank K. and Mary (Grimes) F.; B.S., Carnegie Inst. Tech., 1931; D.Sc., Mass. Inst. Tech., 1940; m. Hazel Lower, June 28, 1932 (dec. 1968); children—Norman Craig II, James; m. 2d, Virginia Rhoads Frye, Sept. 5, 1968; stepchildren—Richard C. Frye, Barbara L. Frye, Martha A. Frye. Metall. engr. Nat. Tube Co., Lorain, O., 1933-36; asst. prof. metallurgy Carnegie Tech., 1941-43; asst. v.p. operations Youngstown Sheet & Tube Co. (O.). 1956-59, v.p. research, 1959-70, v.p. planning and tech., 1970-71, v.p. tech. services, 1971—; dir. Sola Basic Industries. Registered engr., Cal., Ohio, Ind., Ill., La., Wyo., Tex., Okla. Mem. Am. Soc. Metals (nat. trustee 1955-56), Am. Inst. Mining, Metall. and Petroleum Engrs. (pres. 1964; pres. Metall. Soc. 1962), Am., W. Scotland, Brit. iron and steel insts., Nat. Acad. Engring., Sigma Xi, Tau Beta Pi, Alpha Sigma Phi. Contbr. tech. papers to profl. jours. Home: 2 Oak Dr Poland OH 44514 Office: Youngstown Sheet & Tube Co P O Box 900 Youngstown OH 44501

FETZER, JOHN EARL, bus., baseball, radio-TV exec.; b. Decatur, Ind., Mar. 25, 1901; s. John Adam and Della Frances (Winger) F.; student Purdue U., 1921; A.B., Andrews U., 1927; student U. Mich., 1929; LL.D., Western Mich. U., 1958; m. Rhea Maude Yeager, July 19, 1926. Pres., owner Fetzer Broadcasting Co., 1930—, Fetzer Television Corp., Kalamazoo-Grand Rapids, Mich., 1970—, Cornhusker TV Corp., Lincoln, Neb., 1954—; pres., owner Fetzer Music Corp., Kalamazoo-Grand Rapids, Fetzer TV, Inc., Cadillac, Mich., 1958—, Detroit Tigers Am. League Baseall Club, 1956—, John E. Fetzer, Inc., 1968—; chmn. Wolverine Cablevision, Inc., 1966—; dir. Am. Nat. Bank & Trust Co., Kalamazoo. Chmn., Maj. League Television Com., 1964—. Asst. dir. U.S. Censorship charge radio, 1944-46; reporting to Gen. Eisenhower, engaged in ETO radio studies in Eng., France, Russia, Germany, Italy and other European countries, 1945; fgn. corr. radio-TV-newspaper mission Europe and Middle East, 1952; mem. mission Radio Free Europe and Middle East, 1952; mem. mission Radio Free Europe, Munich, Germany, and Austrian-Hungarian border, 1956; Broadcasters Mission to Latin-Am., State Dept., 1962, Detroit Tiger Baseball tour of Japan, Okinawa, Korea, under auspices Stat Dept., 1962; mem. adv. bd. N. Am. Service, Radio Diffusion Francaise, Paris, 1946-47. Mem. bd. trustees Kalamazoo Coll., 1954—. Fellow Royal Soc. Arts London; mem. Nat. Assn. Broadcasters (chmn. TV bd. 1957), C. of C. (past pres.); Nat. Geneal. Soc., Acad. Polit. Sci., Am. Soc. Mil. Engrs., I.E.E.E. (life mem.), Internat. Radio and TV Execs. Soc., Broadcast Pioneers, Alpha Kappa Psi. Presbyn. Mason (33, Shriner), Elk. Clubs: Park, Gull Lake Country, Kalamazoo Country (Kalamazoo); Peninsular (Grand Rapids); Economic, Detroit Athletic, Press, Detroit (Detroit); Tucson Country. Author: One Man's Family, 1964. Contbr. Radio and Television Project, Columbia, 1953. Home: 2714 Clovelly Rd Kalamazoo MI 49001 Office: Kalamazoo MI 49001 ☆

FEUDNER, JOHN LLOYD, Jr., dept. store exec.; b. Akron, O., June 20, 1912; s. John Lloyd and Ethel Thay (Harbaugh) F.; B.A., U. Akron, 1934; m. Elsie Barbara Herget, Aug. 22, 1936; children—John Lloyd III, Barbara L. (Mrs. Stephen F. Schaal), Jean E. (Mrs. Gerald F. Ewald). With M. O'Neil Co., Akron, 1935—, exec. v.p., gen. mgr., 1959-63, pres., gen. mgr., 1963-68, chmn, 1969—; v.p. May Dept. Stores, 1960—; dir. Akron Dime Bank, Ohio Edison Co. Trustee Ohio Council Retail Mchts., 1964, v.p., 1969-71. v.p. Akron area council Boy Scouts Am., 1964, pres., 1966-69, exec. com. Region IV, 1969—; v.p. Family Service Soc. Akron, 1964; pres. Parents Assn. Wittenberg U., 1964- 65. Trustee Akron Gen. Hosp., 1964—, Cleve. Muscial Arts Assn., 1970—, Akron Met. Transit Authority, 1969—; trustee Akron Area Progress Bd., 1968—, sec., 1970; mem. bus. adv. com. Akron U., 1964- -, bd. dirs., 1969-70, pres. Akron U. Hilltoppers, 1970; pres. Akron Med. Coll. Found., 1971; exec. dir. Akron Community Trusts, 1971; mem. bus. adv. com. Kent State U., 1964—, Mem. Lutheran Laymen's Movement, Lone Star Frat. (past pres.), Akron Area (pres. 1964), Ohio (dir. 1966—) chambers commerce. Clubs: City (past pres.), Fairlawn Country (past pres.), Sharon Golf, Cascade Men's. 332 Afton Av Akron OH 44313 Office: 226 S Main St Akron OH 44308

FEUER, CY, theatrical and motion picture exec.; b. N.Y.C., Jan. 15, 1911; s. Herman and Ann (Abrams) F.; student Inst. Mus. Art Julliard Found., 1928-32; m. Posy Greenberg, Jan. 20, 1945; children—Robert, Jed. Head music dept. Republic Pictures, 1938-42, 45-47; partner Feuer and Martin Prodns., N.Y.C., 1947—; theatrical prodns. include Where's Charley, 1948, Guys and Dolls, 1950, Can-Can, 1953, The Boy Friend, 1954, Silk Stockings, 1955, Whoop-Up, 1958, How to Succeed in Business Without Really Trying (Pulitzer prize for drama), 1961, Little Me, 1962, Skyscraper, 1965, Walking Happy, 1966, The Goodbye People, 1968; (motion picture) Cabaret, 1971. Home: 158 E 63d St New York City NY 10021 Office: 505 Park Av New York City NY 10022

FEUER, HENRY, educator, chemist; b. Stanislau, Austria, Apr. 4, 1912; s. Jacob and Julia (Tindel) F.; M.S., U. Vienna (Austria), 1934, Ph.D., 1936; m. Paula Berger, Jan. 19, 1946. Came to U.S., 1941, naturalized, 1946. Postdoctoral fellow U. Paris (France), 1939; with dept. chemistry Purdue U., Lafayette, Ind., 1943—, prof. chemistry, 1961—; vis. prof. Hebrew U., Jerusalem, Israel, 1964. Fellow A.A.A.S.; mem. Am. Chem. Soc., Chem. Soc., Am. Inst. Aeros. and Astronautics, Sigma Xi, Phi Lambda Upsilon. Research, publs. in organic nitrogen compounds; discovered new methods for syntheses nitro compounds, cyclic hydrazides; research on mechanism of these reactions. Home: 726 Princess Dr West Lafayette IN 47906 Office: Dept Chemistry Purdue U Lafayette IN 47907

FEUER, LEWIS S., sociologist, educator, philospher; b. N.Y.C., Dec. 7, 1912; s. Joseph and Fannie (Weidner) F.; B.S., Coll. City N.Y., 1931; A.M., Harvard, 1932, Ph.D., 1935; m. Kathryn Jean Beliveau, Oct. 13, 1946; 1 dau., Robin Kathryn. Asst. in philosophy Harvard, 1935-37; instr. philosophy Coll. City N.Y., 1939-42; faculty Vassar Coll., 1946-51, U. Vt., 1951- 57; prof. philosophy and social sci. U. Cal. at Berkeley, 1957-66; prof. sociology U. Toronto, 1966—. Ford fellow for Advancement of Edn., 1954-55; exchange scholar Inst. Philosophy, Soviet Acad. Sci., Moscow, USSR, 1963; recipient Bowdoin medal Harvard, 1935. Mem. Am. Sociol. Assn., Am. Philos. Assn., Cambridge Union U. Tchrs. (sec. 1935-37), Am. Assn. U. Profs. (pres. Vt. chpt. 1955-56). Author: Psychoanalysis and Ethics, 1955; Spinoza and the Rise of Liberalism, 1958; The Scientific Intellectual, 1963; The Conflict of Generations, 1969; Marx and the Intellectuals, 1969. Editor: Marx and Engels, Basic Writings on Politics and Philosophy, 1959. Research, numerous publs. Home: 29 Roxborough St E Toronto 5 Ontario Canada

FEUER, PAULA BERGER, physicist, educator; b. N.Y.C., Feb. 11 1922; d. Morris and Lottie (Greenwald) Berger; B.A., Hunter Coll., 1941; M.S., Purdue U., 1946, Ph.D., 1951; m. Henry Feuer, Jan. 19, 1946. Instr. physics Purdue U., 1946-55, asst. prof. engring. scis., 1955-57, asso. prof., 1957-65, prof. aeros., astronautics and engring. scis., 1965—; vis. prof. physics Hebrew U., Jerusalem, 1964. Mem. Soc. Engring. Sci. (founding dir., treas., 1964-69), Am. Phys. Soc., Sigma Xi, Pi Mu Epsilon, Sigma Pi Sigma. Club: Canadian Alpine. Author articles sci. jours. Home: 726 Princess Dr West Lafayette IN 47906

FEUER, SAMUEL GUSTAVE, physician; b. N.Y.C., July 18, 1903; s. David and Eva (Sher) F.; student Columbia, 1922; M.D., N.Y.U., 1925; m. Ruth Nadelson, Sept. 6, 1926; children—Adele Glaubman, Barbara (Mrs. Donal Keller). Intern, Bellevue Hosp., N.Y.C., 1925-26; pvt. practice medicine, N.Y.C., 1926—; cons. Jewish Chronic Disease Hosp., St. Francis Hosp., Roslyn, L.I.; dir. emeritus phys. medicine and rehab. L.I. Coll. Hosp., Prospect Heights Hosp.; cons. phys. medicine, rehab. VA Hosp., Miami, Fla.; former asso. prof. medicine Downstate U. N.Y. Med. Center. Cons. Police Dept. N.Y.C., 1948-70. Comdr. (M.C.) USNR, 1942-65, active service, 1942-46; ret.; comdr. N.Y. Naval Militia since 1945. Diplomate Am. Bd. Phys. Medicine and Rehab. Fellow Am. Congress Phys. Medicine, Internat. Coll. Angiology, Am. Acad. Compensation Medicine, Am. Geriatrics Soc., A.C.P., N.Y. Acad. Medicine; mem. Am. Soc. Phys. Medicine, A.M.A., N.Y. State, Kings County med. socs., Phi Delta Epsilon (life). Mason. Home: 1327 N Long Beach Rd Rockville Centre NY 11570 also 3901 S Ocean Dr Hollywood FL 33020

FEUER, STANLEY BURTON, manufacturing co. exec.; b. S. Bend, Ind., Oct. 2, 1928; s. Samuel R. and Bess R. (Cohen) F.; grad. Hotchkiss Sch., 1946; B.A., Yale, 1950, LL.B., 1953; m. Frances Schwolsky, Oct. 9, 1955; children—Pamela T., Wendy M., Thomas C. Admitted to N.Y. bar, 1955, Ind. bar, 1957; with firm Breed, Abbott & Morgan, N.Y.C., 1955-57; asst. sec. Studebaker Corp., 1957-63, sec., corp. atty., 1963-67, dir., 1967—; v.p., gen. counsel Studebaker-Worthington, Inc., 1968-71; dir. STP Corp., 1968-71; v.p., gen. counsel GAF Corp., 1971—. Served to lt. (s.g.) USCGR, 1953-55). Mem. Am. Bar Assn. Home: 50 Sinclair Terrace Short Hills NJ 07078 Office: GAF Corp 140 W 51st New York City NY 10020

FEURER, ALEXANDER EUGENE mfg. exec.; b. Lima, O., Apr. 1, 1932; B.S., U. San Francisco, 1954; M.S., Stanford University, 1956; m. Rosemarie Lois Brown, May 15, 1955; 1 son, Anthony Robinson. Sales rep. Ames-Brockton Fabricated Products, Akron, O.,

Knitting Mills, Inc. (Mass.), 1942—. Pres. Union Orthodox Jewish Congregations Am., 1954—; chmn. bd. Torah Umesorah, 1951—; v.p. Hapoel Hamizrachi Am., 1950-51; treas. Nat. Council Young Israel, 1952-53. Mem. Yeshiva Coll. Alumni Assn. (pres. 1942-43). Home: 42 Beech Rd Brookline MA 02147 Office: 303 Eastern Av Malden MA 02148 also Maiden Missl Sales Co 450 7th Av New York City NY 10001

FEUILLE, RICHARD HARLAN, lawyer; b. Mexico City, Mexico, June 10, 1920; s. Frank and Margaret (Levy) F.; B.A. U. Va., 1947, LL.B., 1948; m. Louann Johnston Hoover, Oct. 20, 1948; children—Louann H., Richard H., Robert R., Joseph L. (dec.), James M., Patrick F. (dec.), Margaret J. Admitted to Tex. bar, 1948; asso. firm Jones, Hardie, Grambling & Howell, El Paso, Tex., 1948-53; partner firm Hardie, Grambling, Sims & Feuille, El Paso, 1953-57; sr. partner firm Scott, Hulse, Marshall & Feuille, El Paso, 1957—. Dir. El Paso Nat. Bank, Northgate Nat. Bank El Paso, Gunning-Casteel, Inc. Active United Fund El Paso, 1963—, founder, v.p. trust fund, 1969—, pres., 1968, bd. dirs., 1966—; pres. El Paso Community Concert Assn., 1961-67; mem. adv. council U. Tex. at El Paso, 1968—, mem. exec. com., 1968-70. Bd. dirs. St. Clement's Episcopal Parish Sch., El Paso; trustee YWCA, El Paso. Served to maj. USAAF, 1941-46; PTO. Mem. Am. (estate and gift tax com.), El Paso County (2d v.p.), Tex. bar assns., Greater El Paso Tennis Assn. (bd. dirs.), Order Coif, Phi Beta Kappa, Omicron Delta Kappa. Episcopalian (vestryman, sr. warden). Clubs: Coronado Country, International, El Paso Tennis (El Paso). Home: 1021 Broadmoor St El Paso TX 79912 Office: 11-D El Paso Nat Bank Bldg El Paso TX 79901

FEURT, SELDON DICK, coll. dean; b. Wichita, Kan., Oct. 21, 1923; s. Seldon Ernest and Alice Bouton (Martin) F.; B.S. in Pharmacy, Loyola U., New Orleans, 1949; M.S., U. Fla., 1951, Ph.D. in Pharmacology, 1953; m. Joella Ann Connor, Aug. 8, 1943; children—Dian B., Andi Lee. Instr. pharmacy U. Fla., 1950- 53; asso. prof. pharmacology and pharmacognosy U. Ga., 1953-57, prof., 1958-59; dir. research De Leon Labs., Atlanta, 1954-58; dean Coll. Pharmacy, U. Tenn., 1959—. Mem. Am. Pharm. Assn., Blue Key, Sigma Xi, Phi Kappa Phi, Rho Chi. Mason (Shriner). Co-inventor tranquilizer gun. Author profl. authors. Home: 435 N Mendenhall St Memphis TN 38117

FEWSTER, JOHN DONALD, photog. equipment co. exec.; b. Ontario, N.Y., Sept. 1, 1908; s. Frank L. and Calla Belle (Brandt) F.; B.A., U. Rochester, 1928; M.B.A., Harvard, 1930 m. Alma Hart, Sept 1, 1933; children—Phyllis A. (Mrs. William C. Rosser), Lowell Hart, Janet Alberta. Statistician Eastman Kodak Co., Rochester, N.Y., 1930-35, asst. to treas., 1935-46, asst. treas., 1946- 59, treas., 1959—; dir. Eastman Savs. & Loan Assn., 1953—, v.p., 1957- 60, vice chmn., 1960-68, chmn., 1968—; dir. Security Trust Co., Rochester; trustee Rochester Savs. Bank. Trustee Rochester Area TV Assn., Colgate-Rochester Div. Sch., Rochester Center for Govtl. and Community Research. Mem. Rochester C. of C (trustee, past pres.), Internat. C. of C. (mem. com. on internat. monetary relations), Am. Fianance Assn. Republican. Conglist. Clubs: Harvard Business School, University, City (Rochester). Home: 505 Bonnie Brae Av Rochester NY 14618 Office: 343 State St Rochester NY 14650

FEY, DOROTHY, (Mrs. George J. Jaffe), assn. exec.; b. Chgo., Aug. 5, 1917; d. Charles H. and Lottie (Brousseau) Feyereisen; student Bryant and Stratton Bus. Coll., Chgo. Acad. Fine Arts, also trademark registration N.Y.U.; m. George J. Jaffe, Oct. 1,1957. Account exec. Steve Hannagan Assos., 1943-44; asst. to pres. Don Spencer Co., Inc., 1944-46; sec., dir. pub. relations, media dir. Hiram Ashe Advt. Inc., N.Y.C., 1946-51; exec. sec. U.S. Trademark Assn., 1952-59, exec. dir., 1959—. Mem. Am. Soc. Assn. Execs., N.Y. Soc. Assn. Execs., Internat. Patent and Trademark Assn., Internat. Platform Assn. Home: 535 E 86th St New York City NY 10028 Office: 6 E 45th St New York City NY 10017

FEY, JOHN THEODORE, ins. co. exec.; b. Hopewell, Va., Mar. 10, 1917; s. Raymond B. and Ruth (St. Fultz) F.; student Washington and Lee U., 1935-37; LL.B., U. Md., 1940; M.B.A., Harvard, 1942; J.S.D., Yale, 1952; LL.D., Middlebury Coll., Alma Coll., 1961, U. Vt., 1967; m. Jane K. Gerber, Apr. 5, 1947 (div. May 1964); 1 son, John Theodore; m. 2d, Barbara Jaffee, July 20, 1964. Admitted to Md. bar, 1940, D.C. bar, 1953, Vt. bar, 1959; County atty., Md., 1947-49; faculty Law Sch., George Washington U., 1949-53, dean, 1953-56, professorial lectr., 1956; clk. Supreme Ct. U.S., 1956-58; pres. U. Vt., 1958-64; pres. U. Wyo., 1964-66; pres. Nat. Life Ins. Co., 1966—, also dir.; dir. Burlington Savs. Bank, Union Mut. Fire Ins. Co., New Eng. Guaranty Ins. Co., Equity Services, Inc., Nat. Life Investment Co., Inc., Sentinel Income Fund, Inc. Met. chmn. Nat. Alliance Businessmen; mem. Vt. Municipal Bond Bank. Bd. dirs. New Eng. Council; trustee New Eng. Colls. Fund; bd. govs. Med. Center Hosp. Vt., Burlington; incorporator Central Vt. Hosp. Mem. Md. Legislature, 1946-50. Served to col. USMCR, 1942-46. Mem. Life Ins. Assn. Am. (chmn. bd. dirs., mem. program, personnel coms.; mem. joint com. on econ. policy with Am. Life Conv.), Am. Coll. Life Underwriters (trustee, mem. devel. bd., chmn. adult learning research com.), Life Ins. Agy. Mgmt. Assn. (mem. research steering com.), Marine Corps Assn. (bd. govs.), Order of Coif. Home: 10 Greenock Av Montpelier VT 05602 Office: Nat Life Ins Co Montpelier VT 05602

FEY, LOUIS ANTHONY, univ. adminstr.; b. Utica, N.Y., Apr. 8, 1904; s. Louis A. and Mary A. (Urtz) F.; B.A., St. Joseph's Coll., Princeton, N.J., 1927; grad. Preacher's Inst., Cath. U. Am., 1939; M.S., Fordham U., 1947. Joined Congregation of the Mission, 1927, ordained priest Roman Cath. Ch., 1932; missionary to Panama, 1932-35; prof. math. St. Joseph's Coll., 1935-37; travelling missionary, 1937-41; pastor in Toronto, Can., 1950- 55; treas. St. John's U., 1955—, v.p., 1960—. Served as chaplain USNR, 1942-47; PTO. Mem. Eastern Assn. Coll., Univ. and Bus. Officers. K.C. Address: 81-50 Utopia Pky Jamaica NY 11432.

FEYEREISEN, PAUL ALFRED, army officer; b. Waterloo, Ia., Nov. 26, 1917; s. John Pierre and Grace (Leech) F.; E.E., U. Minn., 1939; B.S., Sophia U., 1952; M.B.A., Harvard, 1954; grad. Command and Gen. Staff Coll., 1943, Nat. War Coll., 1958; m. Leona Anita Stock, Apr. 10, 1943; children—Paul Stock, Nancy (Mrs. Eugene A. Studer), Lawrence Preston, James Andrew. Commd. 2d lt. U.S.Army, 1939, advanced through grades to maj. gen., 1967; dep. chief staff Hdqrs. U.S. Army Materiel Command, Washington, 1962-63, acting chief of staff, 1962, U.S. program/project mgr. MALLARD project, 1966-68, dir. materiel requirements, 1969, dep. comdg. gen. materiel acquisition, 1969—; dep. comdg. gen. U.S. Army Electronics Command, Ft. Monmouth, N.J., 1963-64, dep. comdg. gen. plans and programs, 1964-66, dep. comdg. gen. tactical communication systems, 1967-69; advisor to Mil. Gov. of Ryukyu Islands, 1949-50. Active Boy Scouts Am. Decorated Army Commendation medal with oak leaf cluster, Legion of Merit with 2 oak leaf clusters, D.S.M. with oak leaf cluster; recipient commendations, Japan and France. Mem. I.E.E.E., Armed Forces Communication electronic Assn., Armed Forces Mgmt. Assn. (nat. dir.), Nat. Contract Mgmt. Assn. (nat. dir.), Assn. U.S. Army, Am. Ordnance Assn. (nat. dir.), Pi Tau Sigma. Kiwanian. Home: 1606 Dunterry Pl McLean VA 22101 Office: Hdqrs Army Materiel Command Washington DC 20315

FEYERHERM, HARVEY AUGUST, educator, biologist; b. West Point, Neb., Apr. 27, 1919; s. Frederick Wilhelm and Ida (Kuester) F.; A.B., Neb. Wesleyan U., 1940; M.S., Ia. State U., 1942, Ph.D., 1950; NSF State U. Ia., 1960; m. Ruth Brown, Jan. 17, 1944; children—William H., Ann E., James F. Instr., then asst. prof. zoology Ia. State U., 1942-50; mem. faculty No. Ill. U., DeKalb, 1950-, prof. zoology, 1956—, head dept. biol. scis., 1964-69. Served to capt. San. Corps, AUS, 1943-46. Mem. A.A.A.S., Am. Inst. Biol. Scis., Am. Zool. Soc., Am. Physiol. Soc., Am. Assn. U. Profs., Midwest Coll. Biology Tchrs., Phi Kappa Phi. Home: 808 S 2d St DeKalb IL 60115

FEYNMAN, RICHARD PHILIPPS, physicist; b. N.Y.C. May 11, 1918; s. Melville Arthur and Lucille (Phillips) F.; B.S., Mass. Inst. Tech., 1939; Ph.D., Princeton, 1942. Staff atomic bomb project, Princeton, 1942-43, Los Alamos, 1943-45; asso. prof. theoretical physics, Cornell, 1945-50; prof. of theoretical physcis Cal. Inst. Tech., since 1950. Recipient Einstein Award, 1954; Nobel prize in physics, 1965. Mem. Am. Phys. Soc., A.A.A.S., Royal Soc. (fgn. mem.), Pi Lambda Phi. Contbr. theory of quantum electrodynamics, beta decay and liquid helium. Address: Physics Dept California Institute of Technology Pasadena CA 91109

FFOLLIOTT, JOHN HARVIE, ret. mining co. exec.; b. St. Paul, May 30, 1906; s. Frederick Kerr and Ella (Harvie) F.; E.M. in Geology, U. Minn., 1929; m. Sally Holyoke Locke, Aug. 30, 1930; children—Millicent K. (Mrs. Eliot S. Knight), Kathleen T. (Mrs. Willard F. Enteman II), Charles L. With Tenn. Copper Co., 1929-48, chief mining engr., geologist, 1938-45, asst. to mgr., Copperhill, Tenn., 1946-48; with Miami Copper Co., 1949-60, dir., 1951-60, exec. v.p., 1957-60; v.p. Tenn. Corp., 1960-70, also dir.; pres. Cities Service Minerals Corp., 1967-70. Mem. Am. Inst. Mining Engrs., Metall. Soc. Am., Soc. Econ. Geologists, Am. Mining Congress, Sigma Xi. Clubs: Mining, University (N.Y.C.). Home: PO Box 147 South Orleans MA 02662

FIACCONE, HUBERT NOVELLINO, drug/chem. co. exec.; b. Phila., Feb. 12, 1918; s. Novellino S. and Florence (Ahern) F.; B.S., Syracuse U., 1941; m. Doris Katherine Brewster, June 13, 1943; children—Katherine Ann (Mrs. Daley), William Brewster. Foreman, Gen. Chem. Co., 1941-42; with Merck & Co., Inc., 1942—, dir. operations Rahway, N.J., 1964-65, v.p., gen. mgr. Merck Chem. Mfg. div., 1965-67, sr. v.p., 1967-70, pres. chem. div., Corporate sr. v.p., 1970—. Mem. summit Housing Authority, 1970—. Trustee N.J. Safety Council. Mem. Am. Chem. Soc., Am. Inst. Chem. Engrs., N.J. C. of C. (dir.), Am. Mgmt. Assn. (gen. mgmt. council 1971). Home: 35 Dale Dr Summit NJ 07901 Office: Lincoln Av Rahway NJ 07065

FIALKOV, HERMAN, investment banker; b. Bklyn., Mar. 23, 1922; s. Isidore and Pearl (Heinish) F.; student Coll. City N.Y., 1938-41; B.Adminstrv. Engring., N.Y.U., 1951; m. Elaine Dampf, Nov. 25, 1942; children—Carol Fran, Jay Michael. Engr., Emerson Radio Corp., 1941-47, MBS, 1947-49, Tele-Tone Radio Corp., 1949-51; chief engr. Radio Receptor Co., 1951-54; pres. Gen. Transistor Corp. (merged with Gen. Instrument Corp. 1960), 1954- 60; v.p., dir. Gen. Instrument Corp., 1960-67, sr. v.p., 1967-68; partner Geiger & Fialkov, 1968—; dir. Benrus Corp., Ridgefield, Conn.; chmn. bd. Agora Industries, Inc., Miami; dir. Microsystems Tech., OPCOA, Inc., Valpey Corp., Xynetics Inc. Panelist Am. Arbitration Assn.; turstee Adelphi U., Garden City, 1959-70. Served with AUS, 1943-46. Decorated Bronze Star medal with oak leaf cluster; Conspicuous Service Cross, N.Y. Mem. I.E.E.E., Am. Technion Soc. (dir.). Tau Beta Pi, Alpha Pi Mu. Home: 615 Meryl Dr Westbury NY 11590 Office: 15 Columbus Circle New York City NY 10023

FIBICH, HOWARD RAYMOND, editor; b. Oak Park, Ill., Jan. 6, 1932; s. Raymond Clarence and Vivian (Barrie) F.; B.S., Northwestern U., 1954, M.S., 1955; postgrad. Columbia, 1966; m. Carrol Jean Anderson, June 5, 1954; children—Linda, Steven, Barbara. Reporter, Kokomo (Ind.) Tribune, 1955-56; copy editor Milw. Jour., 1856-64, telegraph editor, 1964, asst. news editor, 1964-67, news editor, 1967—; free lance writer, 1959-63. Mem. Asso. Press Mng. Editors Assn. (new tech. com.), Milw. Press Club, Sigma Delta Chi, Kappa Tau Alpha. Home: 2537 N Swan Blvd Wauwatosa, WI 53226 Office: 333 W State St Milwaukee WI 53201

FICHENBERG, ROBERT GORDON, newspaper editor; b. Phila., Jan. 1, 1920; s. Samuel Harrison and Katherine (Gordon) F.; B.S., Syracuse U., 1940; m. Ruth Pollard, Sept. 14, 1947; children—Ruth Ann, Kathryn Leigh. City editor Adirondack Daily Enterprise, Saranac Lake, N.Y., 1940-42; reporter, copy editor, asst. city editor Binghamton (N.Y.) Press, 1942-57; mng. editor Knickerbocker News, Albany, N.Y., 1957-66, exec. editor, 1966—. Served to 1st lt. Signal Corps, AUS, 1942-46; to capt. U.S. Army, 1951-52. Mem. Am., N.Y. State (pres.) socs. newspaper editors, A.P. Mng. Editors Assn., N.Y. State A.P. Assn. (past pres.), Sigma Delta Chi. Home: Bullock Rd Singerlands RD NY 12159 Office: 24 Sheridan Av Albany NY 12201

FICHTER, JOSEPH H., clergyman, educator; b. Union City, N.J., June 10, 1908; s. Charles J. and Victoria (Weiss) F.; A.B., St. Louis U., 1935, M.A., 1939; Ph.D., Harvard, 1947. Entered Soc. Jesus, 1930; ordained priest Roman Cath. Ch., 1942; instr. Spring Hill Coll., 1935-36; instr. Loyola U., New Orleans, 1944-45, prof., chmn. dept. sociology, 1947-65; vis. prof. sociology Muenster U., Germany, 1953-54; vis. prof. sociology, dir. research Notre Dame U., 1956-57; vis. prof. sociology, dir. research U. Chile, Santiago, 1961-62; vis. prof. sociology U. Chgo., 1964- 65; Stillman prof. Harvard, 1965-70; vis. prof. State U. N.Y., Albany, 1970—. Founder Southeastern. Region Coll. Students Inter-racial Commn., 1948. New Orleans Commn. Human Rights, 1948; member New Orleans Com. Race Relations. Member Nat. Urban League, Am., So. sociol. socs., Soc. Study Social Problems, Am. Assn. U. Profs., Am. Cath. Sociol. Soc., Soc. Sci. Study Religion. Religious Research Assn. Author: Roots of Change, 1939; Man of Spain; Christianity: Social Relations in the Urban Parish: Sociology, 1957; Soziologie der Pfarrgruppen, 1958; Parochial School, 1958; Religion as an Occupation, 1961; Cambios Sociales en Chile, 1962; Priest and People, 1965: America's Forgotten Priests, 1968. Address: 988 Washington Av Albany NY 12203

FICK, ARMIN FREDERICK, mfg. co. exec.; b. St. Louis, Dec. 16, 1917; s. Fred J. and Adele (Beimdick) F.; B.S. in Metall. Engring., U. Mo., 1941, Dr. Engring. (hon.), 1967; M.B.A., U. Chgo., 1956; m. Marian Montgomery, Oct. 9, 1948; 1 son, John F. With Western Electric Co., 1941- -, works mgr., Balt., 1963-65, v.p. mfg. Chgo., 1965—. Dir. Chgo. Crime Commn. Bd. dirs. Community Fund Chgo., Chgo. Boys Clubs. Served to maj. AUS, 1941-46; ETO. Mem. Am. Soc. Metals, Am. Inst. Mining and Metall. Engrs., Ill. C. of C. (dir.), Chgo. Assn. Commerce and Industry (dir.). Office: 20 N Wacker Dr Chicago IL

FICKEN, FREDERICK ARTHUR, educator; b. Moore's Hill, Ind., Aug. 13, 1910; s. Richard Oscar and Grace (Fagley) F.; A.B., Oberlin Coll., 1931; M.A., Ohio State U., 1932; B.A. (Rhodes scholar), Oxford (Eng.) U., 1934; Ph.D., Princeton, 1938; m. Mary Elizabeth Harman, Sept. 11, 1940; 1 son, William Harman. Instr. math. Cornell U., 1938-42; prof. math. U. Tenn., 1942-59; prof. math., chmn. dept. University Heights, N.Y. U., 1959—, dep. chmn., until 1967; cons. to Operations Research Group USN, 1944-45; research asso. Inst. Math. Scis., N.Y.U., 1949-51; cons. Union Carbide Nuclear Co., Oak Ridge, 1946-64. Fellow A.A.A.S. (sec. Sect. A (math. 1969—); mem. Math. Assn. Am., Am. Math. Soc., Am. Assn. U. Profs., Am. Civil Liberties Union, Soc. Indsl. and Applied Math., Phi Beta Kappa, Sigma Xi, Phi Kappa Phi. Author: The Simplex Method of Linear Programming, 1961; Linear Transformations and Matrices, 1967; also articles. Editor Am. Math. Monthly, 1962-66. Home: 14 Benedict Pl Pelham NY 10803 Office: New York U Bronx NY 10453

FICKETT, FRED WILDON, lawyer; b. Galveston, Tex., Dec. 2, 1895; s. Fred W. and Nellie T. (Lord) F.; A.B., U. Ariz, 1917, J.D., 1922; m. Ruth Marjorie Tacquard, July 12, 1921; children—Wildon, Robert C., Howard. Admitted to Ariz. bar, 1922, since practiced in Tucson; asst. U.S. dist. atty. Ariz., 1925-26; asst. city atty., Tucson, 1926-27; judge Superior Ct. Pima County, 1929-34; mem. Supreme Ct. Ariz. 8 different cases, 1929-34; sr. mem. firm Robertson, Molloy, Fickett & Jones, 1971—; lectr. U. Ariz. Law Coll., 1935-37, 42-43; organizer, v.p., dir. Tucson Fed. Savs. and Loan Assn., 1937-70. Pres. Catalina council Boy Scouts Am., 1934; pres. Tucson YMCA, 1943-45; mem. Tucson Sch. Bd., 1935-52, pres., 1938, 41, 52. Republican candidate for U.S. senator, 1944. Trustee U. Redlands, 1932-48, Conservative Baptist Theol. Sem., Denver, 1952-71. Served with U.S. Army, 1917-19. Decorated Purple Heart; recipient award excellence Tucson Edn. Assn. Mem. Am., Ariz., Pima County bar assns., Tucson C. of C., Phi Delta Phi, Alpha Sigma Rho, Phi Kappa Phi. Baptist. Club: Old Pueblo (Tucson). Home: 3448 E Edgemont St Tucson AZ 85716 Office: Tucson Fed Savs Tower Tucson AZ 85701

FICKINGER, WAYNE JOSEPH, business exec.; b. Belleville, Ill., June 23, 1926; s. Joseph and Grace (Belton) F.; B.A., U. Ill., 1949; M.S., Northwestern U., 1950; m. Joan Mary Foley, June 16, 1951; children-Michael, Joan, Jan, Ellen, Steven. Overnight editor U.P., Chgo., 1950-51; spl. project writer Sears-Roebuck & Co., Chgo., 1951-53; account exec. Calkins & Holden Advt. Agy., Chgo., 1953-56; account supr. Foote, Cone & Belding Advt. Agy., Chgo., N.Y.C., 1956-63; sr. v.p. J. Walter Thompson Co., Chgo., 1963—. Fund raising cons. Nat. Mental Health Assn., 1970. Communications counselor Cook County (Ill.) Republican Orgn., 1970. Served with USNR, 1943-46. Recipient Five-Year Meritorious Service award A.R.C., 1963, Service award Mental Health Assn., 1970. Mem. Sigma Delta Chi, Alpha Delta Sigma. Clubs: Exmoor Country (Highland Park, Ill.); Lake Shore Athletic (Chgo.). Home: 1244 Forest Glen Dr S Winnetka IL 60093 Office: 875 N Michigan Av Chicago IL 60611

FICKLEN, JACK HOWELLS, editorial cartoonist; b. Waco, Tex., Apr. 18, 1911; s. Fielding and Bessie (Howells) F.; student So. Methodist U., 1930-32, Dallas Creative Center, 1964—; m. Mary Alice Brown, Oct. 21, 1950; childrenMolly Bess, Jack Howells, Robert F. Copyboy, Dallas News, 1928-35, layout artist, photog. retoucher, 1935-37, sports cartoonist, 1937-40, editorial cartoonist, 1937-40, 46—; syndicated cartoonist Register & Tribune Syndicate, Des Moines, 1940-45. Book illustrator, free lance cartoonist, 1930—, owner, mgr. Avalon Features Syndicate, editorial cartoon service, Dallas, 1960—; work exhibited Archives Am. Art, Detroit, U. Mo. Sch. Journalism, Wayne State U.; permanent exhbn. Assn. Am. Editorial Cartoonists Assn., Dallas Hall of State. Dir. communications Dallas County Civil Def., 1958-60. Served with AUS, 1940-46; ETO. Decorated Bronze Star medal, Croix de Guerre avec paisne (Belgium). Mem. Am. Editorial Cartoonists Assn., Res. Officers Assn. Democrat. Presbyn. Illustrator: Fundamental Principles of Driving, 1945; Self Government by Texans, 1950. Home: 6657 Avalon Av Dallas TX 75214. Office: Dallas Morning News Dallas TX 75202

FICKLING, J.G., union ofcl. Sec., Internat. Air Line Pilots Assn. AFL-CIO. Office: 55th St and Cicero Av Chicago IL 60638*

FIDDES, CLYDE WILLIAM, railroad exec.; b. Mpls., Aug. 26, 1907; s. William Gibson and Mathilde Cecile (Westerman) F.; B.A., U. Minn., 1930, LL.B., 1932; postgrad. advanced mgmt. program Harvard, 1954; m. Alice Elizabeth Culhane, June 30, 1937. Admitted to Minn. bar, 1932, Tex. bar, 1955, Mo. bar, 1946, also U.S. Supreme Ct.; practice in Mpls., 1932-42; with legal service OPA and Office Def., Transp., Washington, 1942-43; with law dept. St. Louis Southwestern Ry. Co., Tyler, Tex., 1946—, gen. solicitor, 1954-57, gen. counsel, 1957—; dir. Memphis Union Sta. Co., St. Louis Southwestern Ry. Co. Tex. Served to capt. AUS, 1943-46. Mem. Nat. Assn. R.R. Trail Counsel, Assn. ICC Practitioners, Nat. Def. Transp. Assn., Phi Delta Phi, Alpha Tau Omega. Roman Catholic. Clubs: Petroleum, Willow Brook Country (Tyler); University, Mo. Athletic (St. Louis). Home: 2114 Hilltop Dr Tyler TX 75701 Office: 1517 W Front St Tyler TX 75701

FIDEL, EDWARD ALLEN, ret. govt. ofcl.; b. Grand Junction, Colo., Nov. 17, 1914; s. Anthony George and Anne Bagley (Allen) F.; student U. Colo., 1932-33; B.S., Georgetown Sch. Fgn. Service, 1937; m. Frances Bean, Jan. 29, 1939; 1 son, Edward Allen II. Fed. agt. U.S. Dept. Interior, 1937-41; with U.S. Dept. State, 1941, successively fgn. service officer Am. embassy, Quito, Ecuador, 3d sec. Am. embassy, Paris, France, 2d sec. Am. embassy, Rome, Italy, econ. adviser Brit. Commonwealth, and N. European affairs div., Washington, 1941-55, 1st sec. Am. embassy, Berne, Switzerland, 1955-57, counselor of embassy for econ. affairs, 1957-59; dir. of exec. staff Econ. Bur., Dept. of State, 1959-61, sr. fgn. service insp., 1961-62, attended sr. seminar in fgn. policy, 1962-63; U.S. consul gen. Trieste, Italy, 1963-66; sr. examiner bd. examiners Dept. State, 1966-70; cons. fgn. econ. affairs, 1970—. U.S. del. adviser Internat. Rubber Study Group Meetings, Rome, 1950, Tin Meetings, 1951. Mem. Am. Fgn. Service Assn., Delta Tau Delta, Theta Nu Epsilon. Club: Propeller (Washington). Home: 8815 Clifford Av Chevy Chase MD 20015 also Ragged Run Etlan VA 22719

FIDELMAN, JOSEF, pianist; b. Tiflis, USSR, 1905; s. Isaac Fidelman; studied Berlin Hochschule. Came to U.S., 1933, naturalized. Piano debut in solo recital at age 5; recital Beethoven centennial, Vienna, 1927, also played Bach, Mozart, Haydn, Brahms festivals; recordings include Josef Fidelman plays Beethoven and Chopin; Bach, Mozart and Scarlatti, 1964; J. Fidelman Plays series. Served from pvt. to maj., AUS, World War II. Recipient 1st prize Bluthner Internat. contest, 1930. Home: Long Island NY 11101 Office: care Lester S Hebbard Jr 1428 Marshall St Elmont NY 11003

FIDLAR, MARION MOORE, utility exec.; b. Vincennes, Ind., June 7, 1909; s. Orville F. and Clara M. (Moore) F.; A.B., Ind. U., 1934, M.A., 1936, Ph.D., 1942; m. Martha E. Thorn, May 9, 1937. Asst. geologist Ind. Geol. Survey, summers 1932-35; asst. geologist, gas supr. Ind. Div. Geology, 1936- 38; dist. geologist Ohio Oil Co., 1938-43; sr. geologist Mountain Fuel Supply Co., Rock Springs, Wyo., 1943-45, chief geologist, 1945-51, mgr. exploration div., 1951-54, v.p., 1954-58, dir., 1956-, exec. v.p., Salt Lake City, 1958-62, pres., 1962—. Dir. First Security Corp. Bd. dirs. Utah Found., U.S. C. of C., Utah Mfrs. Assn. Fellow Geol. Soc. Am., A.A.A.S.; mem. Am. Assn. Petroleum Geologists, Am. Inst. Mining and Metall. Engrs., Ind. Acad. Sci., Wyo. Geol. Assn., Rocky Mountain Oil and Gas Assn. (bd. dirs. 1962—), Pacific Coast Gas Assn. (dir. 1964-69, pres. 1867-68), Am. Gas Assn. (bd. dirs. 1965-69), Phi Beta Kappa, Sigma Gamma

Epsilon. Club: Alta. Author tech. articles. Home: 1040 Vista View Dr Salt Lake City UT 84108. Office: PO Box 11386 Salt Lake City UT 84111

FIDLER, HAROLD ALVIN, educator; b. Phila., Aug. 2, 1910; s. Alvin H. and Mabel (DeWald) F.; B.S., Drexel Inst., 1932, D. Engring.; 1963; M.S., Mass. Inst. Tech., 1934, Sc.D., 1940; m. Lillian E. Saari, Aug. 30, 1939; children—Marjorie, Donald, Richard. Asst. soil mechanics Mass Inst. Tech., 1935-38, instr. civil engring., 1938-40 asst. to engr. charge found. investigation sect., Binghamton dist. U.S. Engrs. Office, 1940-41, engr. charge, 1942, area engr., Berkeley area, Manhattan dist., 1942-45, dep. dir. research div., 1945-46; chief tech. information br. AEC, 1947, chief declassification, 1947-49, area mgr. Berkeley area, 1949-52, dep. mgr. operations office, San Francisco, 1952-54, mgr., 1954-58; asst. dir. Lawrence Berkeley Lab., U. Cal., 1958-60, asso. dir., 1960—. Served as maj. C.E., AUS, 1942-46. Decorated Legion of Merit. Mem. Am. Soc. C.E., Sigma Xi, Tau Beta Pi. Home: 10 Kensington Ct Berkeley CA 94707 Office: Lawrence Berkeley Lab U Cal Berkeley CA 94720

FIDLER, WILLIAM PERRY, assn. exec., educator; b. Birmingham, Ala., July 29, 1906; s. Ora William and Blanche (Perry) F.; A.B., U. Ala., 1928; A.M., Harvard, 1930; Ph.D., U. Chgo., 1947; m. Alice Adeline Gardiner, Jan. 30, 1929; 1 son, David Albert. Instr. to prof. English, U. Ala., 1930-56; staff asso. Am. Assn. U. Profs., 1956-58, gen. sec., 1958-67, dep. gen. sec., 1967—, editor Am. Assn. U. Profs. Bull., 1958-60. Cons. U.S. Employment Office; cons. revision copyright law Library of Congress. Lt. comdr. USNR ret. Mem. Am. Assn. U. Profs., Am. Studies Assn., Am. Civil Liberties Union, Phi Alpha Theta. Club: Cosmos (Washington). Author: Augusta Evans Wilson: A Biography, 1951. Co-editor Comtemporary Southern Prose, 1940. Contbr. profl. jours. Home: 3831 Calvert St NW Washington DC 20007 Office: One Dupont Circle Washington DC 20036

FIEBACH, RALPH PAUL, utilities exec.; b. Coffeyville, Kan., Sept. 7, 1917; s. Ralph P. and Grace Irene (Baker) F.; B.S. in Mech. Engring., Mich. State U., 1941; m. Roberta E. Mitchell, May 12, 1942; children—Gary, Jane, Cathy, Bruce. Sales engr. Multiscope, Inc., Coffeyville, 1946-50; mgr. sales engring. Peelle Co., Bklyn., 1950-55; sales engr. Chester L. Anderson Co., Wichita, Kan., 1955-59; v.p. Kan. Gas & Electric Co., Wichita, 1967, exec. v.p., 1968, pres., 1969—, also dir.; dir. First Nat. Bank of Wichita. Mem. city steering com. Met. Area Planning Commn., 1968—. Bd. dirs. Civic Music Assn., Wichita. Served with USNR, 1941-46. Decorated Bronze Star medal. Mem. Nat. Soc. Profl. Engrs., Kan. C. of C. (dir.), Mo. Valley Electric Assn. (mem. exec. com.), Electric Heating Assn. (dir.), Petroleum Club. Rotarian. Clubs: Wichita (dir.), Wichita Country, Home: 609 N Broadmoor St Wichita KS 67208 Office: PO Box 208 Wichita KS 67201

FIEDLER, ARTHUR, musical condr.; b. Boston, Mass., Dec. 10, 1894; s. Emanuel and Johanna (Bernfeld) F.; student Boston Latin Sch., 1907-10, Royal Acad. of Music, Berlin, 1911-15; hon. M.A., Tufts Coll., 1931; Mus.D., Boston U., 1951, Am. Internat. Coll., 1959; D.F.A., Ripon Coll., 1960; D. Mus., U. Miami, 1963, Music and Arts Inst., San Francisco, 1963, Jacksonville University, 1964; m. Ellen M. Bottomley, Jan. 8, 1942; children—Johanna, Deborah, Peter. Made concert debut at age of 17; organized Boston Sinfonietta, 1924; organized Esplanade Concerts, Boston, 1929, condr., 1929—; condr. Boston Symphony Pops Concerts, 1930—; former conductor Cecelia Society Boston, U. Glee Club, Providence, MacDowell Club Orchestra of Boston; faculty mem. Boston U.; mus. cons. V.A., Boston; guest condr. at San Francisco, N.Y. Philharmonic, Mpls., Chgo., 1923, Montreal, Toronto, Dallas, Seattle N.B.C. Symphony, Portland, Phila. others; conductor RCA Victor Broadcast. Served in U.S. Army, World War. Awarded Croix de l'Officier d'Academie; chevalier Legion of Honor (France), 1954; named number 8 in classical field Top Artists on Campus Poll, 1968. Coll. on staff Gov. of Ky., 1946. Hon. Fire Chief in about 90 cities of U.S. Mem. Harvard Musical Assn., Boston Soc. Recorded Music (pres.). Home: 133 Hyslop Rd Brookline MA 02146

FIEDLER, EDWARD HENRY, lawyer, brewery exec.; b. Chgo., May 7, 1895; s. Henry Fred and Anna Maria (Bittel) F.; LL.B., Chgo.-Kent Coll. Law, 1917; m. Rose Rolleri, June 7, 1924; children—Celeste Bristol, Joan Potts, Barbara Hill, Edward Henry. Admitted to Ill. bar, 1917; with Sears, Meagher & Whitney, 1911- 14, Meagher, Whitney, Ricks & Sullivan, 1914-19, Cooke, Sullivan & Ricks, 1919-24; partner Cooke, Sullivan & Ricks, and Daily, Dines, White & Fiedler, 1924-42; v.p., gen. counsel, dir. Pabst Brewing Co., 1942-57, counsel, dir., 1957-68; v.p., counsel, dir. Hoffman Beverage Co., 1945- 57. Pres., dir. Pabst Breweries Found. 1945-68. Pres., dir. Ill. Beer Industry Com., 1953-68. Mem. Am., Chgo. bar assns., Phi Delta Phi. Address: 311 N Scoville Av Oak Park IL 60302.

FIEDLER, GEORGE, judge; b. Mineral Point, Wis., Sept. 28, 1904; s. Bernard and Dorothy (Gerlach) F.; LL.B., J.D., U. Wis., 1926; m. Agnes Amberg, Nov. 28, 1931; children-Mary (Mrs. John Henry Morgan), John. Admitted to Ill. bar, 1926, since practiced in Chgo.; asso. with Wilson & McIlvaine, 1929- 45; partner firm Fiedler and Amberg, 1945-62; judge Circuit Ct. of Cook County, Chgo., 1962—. Mem. citizens bd. Loyola U. Bd. dirs. Cath. Charities of Chgo.; trustee Calvert Found., Chgo. Indsl. Sch. for Girls. Mem. Am., Ill., Chgo. bar assns., Am. Judicature Soc., Nat. Conf. State Trial Judges, Ill. Jud. Conf. (chmn. 1969-70), Wis. Soc. Chgo., Legal Club of Chgo., Law Club of Chgo., Order of Coif, Delta Sigma Rho, Phi Kappa Phi. Republican. Roman Catholic. Club: University (Chgo.). Author: The Fiedler Family, 1648-1946, 1946; Mineral Point, A History, 1962; also articles on ins., fidelity and surety bonds. Home: 335 Ridge Av Winnetka IL Office: Circuit Ct of Cook County Chicago IL 60602

FIEDLER, HOWARD TAFT, supt. mental hosp.; b. Pitts., Nov. 3, 1908; s. Jay and Sarah (Kaminsky) F.; B.S., U. Pitts., 1926; M.D., Hahnemann Med. Coll., 1930; m. Rosalyn Goldstein, Mar. 23, 1930; 1 dau., Barbara (Mrs. Stanley Edelstein). Intern St. Lukes and Children's Hosp., Phila., 1930-31; asst. physician Westboro (Mass.) State Hosp., 1931-39; sr. asst. physician Phila. State Hosp., 1939-41; asst. supt. Danville (Pa.) State Hosp., 1946-50; supt. Retreat State Hosp., Hunlock Creek, Pa., 1950-55; supt. Allentown (Pa.) State Hosp., 1955—; instr. psychology Lehigh U., Lafayette U. Served to lt. col. M.C., AUS, 1941-46. Diplomate Am. Bd. Psychiatry and Neurology. Fellow Am. (life), Pa. (life) psychiat. assns.; mem. A.M.A. Mason (32, Shriner). Address: Allentown State Hosp Allentown PA 18103

FIEDLER, LESLIE AARON, educator, author; b. Newark, Mar. 8, 1917; s. Jacob J. and Lillian (Rosenstrauch) F.; B.A., N.Y. U., 1938; M.A., U. Wis., 1939, Ph.D., 1941; postdoctoral student Harvard, 1946-47; m. Margaret Ann Shipley, Oct. 7, 1939; children—Kurt, Eric, Michael, Deborah, Jenny, Miriam. Mem. faculty U. Mont., 1941-64, instr. to asso. prof. English, 1941-53, prof., 1953-64, chmn. dept., 1954-56; prof. English, N.Y. State U. at Buffalo, 1965—; vis. prof. U. Rome, 1951-52, U. Bologna and Ca Foscari U., 1952-53, Princeton, 1956-57, Athens, 1961-62, U. Sussex, 1967-68, U. Paris, 1970-71; jr. fellow Ind. U. Sch. Letters, 1951—; asso. fellow Calhoun Yale U., 1969—. Served from ensign to lt. (j.g.), USNR, 1942-46. Rockefeller fellow humanities, 1946-47; recipient Furioso prize for Poetry, 1951; Fulbright fellow, 1951-53; Kenyon rev. fellow in criticism, 1956-57; Christian Gauss lectr., 1956; award Nat. Inst. Arts and Letters, 1957; grant-in-aid Am. Council Learned Socs., 1960, 61; Guggenheim fellow, 1970-71. Mem. English Inst., Modern Lang. Assn., Am. Assn. U. Profs., Dante Soc. Am., P.E.N. Club, Phi Beta Kappa. Author (with others) Leaves of Grass: 100 Years After, 1955; An End to Innocence, 1955; The Art of the Essay, 1959, rev. 1969; The Image of the Jew in American Fiction, 1959; Love and Death in the American Novel, 1960, rev. 1966; No! In Thunder, 1960; Pull Down Vanity (stories), 1962; The Second Stone (novel), 1963; (with J. Vinocur) The Continuing Debate, 1964; Waiting for the End, 1964; Back to China, 1965; (with others) The Girl in the Black Raincoat, 1966; The Last Jew in America, 1966; The Return of the Vanishing American, 1967; Nude Croquet and Other Stories, 1969; Being Busted, 1970; Collected Essays, 1971; The Stranger in Shakespeare, 1972. Editor: Master of Ballantrae, 1951; Waiting for God (S. Weil), 1952; Poems of Whitman, 1959; (with Arthur Zeiger) O Brave New World, 1967; asso. editor Ramparts, 1959-65; contbg. editor Am. Judaism; lit. editor Running Man, 1967-69. Contbr. short stories, poems, articles to jours. U.S. and abroad. Home: 154 Morris Av Buffalo NY 14214

FIEGEL, MELVIN G., banker; b. Ann Arbor, Mich., 1906; grad. U. Mich., 1929. Vice chmn. bd., sr. v.p. Nat. Bank & Trust Co., Ann Arbor; dir. Bradley Chesbrough Agy., Inc. Elk. Home: 1711 Morton Av Ann Arbor MI 48104 Office: 125 S Main St Ann Arbor MI 48107*

FIEKERS, BERNARD ALBERT, clergyman, educator; b. Cambridge, Mass., Jan. 19, 1906; s. Anton and Mary Helen (Schmitt) F.; A.B., Boston Coll., 1927, A.M., 1933, M.S., 1934; student Ignatius Kolleg, Valkenburg, L., Netherlands, 1935-39; Ph.D., Clark U., 1942. Entered Soc. of Jesus, Shadowbrook, Lenox, Mass., 1927; ordained priest Roman Catholic Ch., 1938; philos. and sci. studies Weston (Mass.) Coll., 1930-33; lab. asst. in chemistry, Boston coll., 1933-34, instr. chemistry, 1934-35; student ascetical theology St. Robert's Hall, Pomfret, Conn., 1939-40; instr. chemistry on leave Coll. Holy Cross, Worcester, Mass., and grad. student chemistry Clark U., 1940-42, prof. chemistry Coll. Holy Cross, 1942—, chmn. chemistry, 1942-62. Mem. A.A.A.S., Am. Chem. Soc. (councilor 1955-63, chem. edn. com. council 1957-59), Am. Inst. Chemists, Am. Assn. Jesuit Scientists (pres. 1947-48), New Eng. Assn. Chemistry Tchrs. (hon.), Albertus Magnus Guild, Sigma Chi. Club: Worcester Chemists (pres. 1946). Editor: Jesuit Science Bull., 1948-50, 1956-60, Address: College of the Holy Cross Worcester MA 01610

FIELD, ADELAIDE ANDERSON, publisher; b. Memphis, June 6, 1916; d. Harry Bennett and Patty (Crook) Anderson; A.B., Radcliffe Coll., 1934; m. Donald T. Field, October 7, 1939 (divorced on September 22, 1958); children—Deborah, Martha, Hartry; married 2d, W. Leverett Cummings, Oct. 2, 1960. Freelance writer, 1938; member staff Life Mag., 1937-38; editor Jr. League Mag. of Boston, 1947- 50; editor-in-chief Child Life, 1951-64; v.p. Review Pub. Co., 1964—; sec., dir. Wilevco Corp., 1963-66. Clubs: Country, Junior League, Longwood Cricket. Author: Adventure on the Cloud 9; Mystery on Cape Cod; (a biography) Auguste Piccard, 1969. Home: 8 Warren Terrace Newton Center MA 02159 Office: 16 Warren Terrace Newton Center MA 02159

FIELD, BETTY (Mrs. Raymond L. Olivere), actress; b. Boston, Feb. 8, 1918; d. George Baldwin and Katherine (Lynch) Field; student Am. Acad. Dramatic Art; m. Elmer Rice, Jan. 12, 1942 (dec.); children—John Alden, Judith, Paul; m. 2d, E. Lukas, 1957 (dec. 1966); m. 3d. Raymond L. Olivere, Mar. 22, 1968. Appeared in Fly Away Home, 1934, She Loves Me Not, 1935, Three Men on a Horse, Boy Meets Girl, Room Service, What a Life, The Primrose Path; appeared in Two on an Island, 1941, Flight to the West, 1941, A New Life, 1943; starred in The Voice of the Turtle, 1944, Dream Girl, 1946, The Rat Race, 1949; appeared on Broadway in Ladies of the Corridor, The Fourposter, The Waltz of the Toreadors, A Touch of the Poet, Strange Interlude; appeared off-Broadway in The Sea Gull, The Wild Duck, All Over; with touring company An Evening with Will Shakespeare; appeared in Landscape and Silence, The Birthday Party, Lincoln Center, 1970, The Effect of Gamma Rays in Man in the Moon Marigolds, 1971; starred in plays A Loss of Roses, Where's Daddy, The Little Foxes, The Price; appeared in films What a Life, Seventeen, Of Mice and Men, Shepherd of the Hills, Blues in the Night, Kings Row, Are Husbands Necessary, The Great Gatsby, Tomorrow the World, The Great Moment, Flesh and Fantasy, The Southerner, Bus Stop, Picnic, Bird Man of Alcatraz, Peyton Place, Butterfield 8, Seven Women, Victory, Coogans Bluff, How to Save a Marriage and Ruin Your Life; appeared as guest star on numerous TV series. Recipient Critics Award for Best Performance of 1946-47 Season. Address: care Charles Renthal 641 Lexington Av New York City NY 10022

FIELD, CROSBY, inventor, engr., mfr.; b. Jamestown, N.Y., Mar. 12, 1889; B.S., N. Y. U., 1909; M.E., Cornell U., 1912; M.S. in Elec. Engring., Union Coll., Schenectady, N.Y., 1914; m. Ethel Henriksen, Nov. 23, 1916; children—Margaret Roberta, Dorothy Henrietta, Patricia Crosby. With Gen. Electric Co., 1912-14; in private practice as cons. engr., 1914- 15; chief engr., Standard Aniline Products, Inc., 1915-17; engring. mgr., Nat. Aniline & Chem. Co., in charge all engring. including constrn., maintenance, power plant operating, appraisal and engring. research, 1919-23; v.p., dir. and sec., Brillo Mfg. Co., 1923-45; also with FlakIce Corp., since 1923, Chem. Machinery Corp., 1923-37. Reserve officer. Army Ordnance Dept., since Jan. 1917; served as 1st lt., capt., maj., U.S. Army, 1917-19, acting chief, explosives and loading sect. Inspection Div.; in active service, col., Army Ordnance Dept., AUS, 1942-45, assigned as asst. dir. Safety Office of Chief of Ordnance. Decorated Legion of Merit. Registered profl. engr. Fellow Am. Soc. M.E. (medalist 1953, hon. mem.), I.E.E.E., A.A.A.S., Am. Soc. Heating, Refrigerating and Air Conditioning Engrs. (past pres., hon. mem.); mem. Am. Chem. Soc., Am. Inst. Chem. Engrs. (past mem. council), Am. Inst. Chemists, Nat., N.Y. socs. profl. engrs., Am. Ordnance Assn., Sigma Xi, Phi Beta Kappa Alumni Assn., Phi Beta Kappa Assos., Pi Kappa Alpha, Tau Beta Pi, Pi Tau Sigma. Mason. Republican. Episcopalian. Clubs: Andiron, Engineers, Chemists (N.Y.C.); Union League (Chgo.). Contbr. numerous papers on engring. specialties to sci. orgns. Inventor of the Oxide Film Lightning Arrestor, 1912, and continuous ice ribbon freezing process, 1916, continuous steel wool mfg. process, 1923; over 140 U.S. patents including elec., chem., mech. and refrigeration processes and equipment. Home: 8029 Harbor View Terrace Brooklyn, NY 11209.

FIELD, CYRUS ADAMS, lawyer; b. Fergus Falls, Minn., Oct. 27, 1902; s. Nicolai F. and Ida (Adams) F.; A.B., U. Minn., 1923; LL.B., Harvard, 1926; m. Mary Emily Kutz, Dec. 26, 1953. Admitted to Minn. bar, 1926, since practiced in Fergus Falls; sr. partner Field, Arvesen, Donoho Lundeen & Hoff, 1952—. Dir. Fergus Falls Nat. Bank & Trust Co., Fergus Falls Savs. & Loan Assn. past pres. Fergus Falls Community Chest. Trustee Fergus Falls Salvation Army, Lake Region Hosp. Assn. Mem. Am. (ho. dels. 1963-65), Minn. (pres. 1962-63, bd. govs. 1960-64) bar assns., Fergus Falls C. of C. (past pres.), Harvard Law Sch. Assn., Delta Chi. Conglist. Mason (Shriner), Rotarian (past pres. Fergus Falls), Elk. Club: Harvard of Minn. Home: 334 Alcott Av Fergus Falls MN 56537 Office: Fergus Falls Nat Bank Bldg Fergus Falls MN 56537

FIELD, ELOIS RACHEL, nurse, educator; b. Farnum, Neb., Apr. 19, 1921; d. Joseph Walter and Mary Jane (Johnston) Field; A.A., Jr. Coll. S.E. Colo., 1940; R.N., Baylor U., 1943; B.A., Wheaton Coll., 1945; M. Nursing, U. Wash., 1949; Ph.D., U. Chgo., 1961. Supr. polio epidemic A.R.C., N.W. Tex. Hosp., Amarillo, 1943, pvt. duty nurse, 1943-44, supr. medicine, surgery, 1945, instr. sch. nursing, 1945-46, 50-51; instr. St. Luke's Hosp. Sch. Nursing, Denver, 1946; instr. Baylor Sch. Nursing, Dallas, 1947-48, 54-57, asst. dean, 1951-53; lectr. U. Cal., 1959-60; dir. baccalaureate programs Emory U. Sch. Nursing, Atlanta, 1962-64; dean Sch. of Nursing, U. Ark. Med. Center, 1964. Mem. Am. Nurses Assn., Nat. League Nursing, Am. Assn. U. Women, Sigma Theta Tau, Pi Lambda Theta, Delta Kappa Gamma. Baptist. Author articles profl. jours. Office: Sch of Nursing Univ Ark Med Center 4301 W Markham Little Rock AR 72201

FIELD, FRANK HENRY, educator, chemist; b. Keansburg, N.J., Feb. 27, 1922; s. Frank Aretus and Mary (Fleischmann) F.; B.S., Duke, 1943, M.A., 1944, Ph.D., 1948; m. Elma Louise Randall, June 22, 1944; children—Elaine Bodenheimer (Mrs. L.J. Fitzsimons), Jonathan Randall, Christopher Randall; m. 2d, Doris Helen Baughn, Oct. 10, 1959. Instr. to asst. prof. U. Tex., 1947-52; research chemist to research asso. and sect. head Humble Oil & Refining Co., Baytown, Tex., 1952-66; group leader, research asso., sr. research asso. Esso Research & Engring. Co., Linden, N.J., 1966-70; prof. chemistry Rockefeller U., N.Y.C., 1970—. Guggenheim fellow Leeds (Eng.) U., 1963-64. Mem. Am. Chem. Soc., A.A.A.S., Am. Soc. Mass Spectrometry (v.p. program), Phi Beta Kappa, Sigma Xi, Phi Lambda Upsilon, Unitarian. Author: (with Franklin) Electron Impact Phenomena, 1957. Contbr. articles to profl. jours. Home: 430 E 63d St New York City NY 10021

FIELD, FRANK MCCOY, clergyman, lectr.; b. Mason, Mich., May 4, 1887; s. Isaac H. and Eva C.L.G. (Brewer) F.; A.B., Albion (Mich.) Coll., 1909, D.D., 1936; student Am. Sch. of Oriental Research, Jerusalem, 1930, Am. Univ. Seminar, Washington, 1930; m. Rose Mildred Jenkins, Sept. 21, 1909 (dec. Nov. 1962); children—Doris Isabel (Mrs. Arthur H. Falter), Esther Evelyn (Mrs. Carl Forsberg), Marjorie Rose (Mrs. Charles Hall). Ordained to M.E. ministry, 1909; organizer and pastor Oak Park Ch., Flint, Mich., 1909-13, pastor, 1924-31; pastor successively Gladstone, Plymouth and Holmes Meml. Ch., Detroit, until 1924; dist. supt. Port Huron Dist., 1931-37; pastor East Grand Blvd. Meth. Ch., Detroit, 1937-43; dist. supt. Saginaw Bay Dist. of Meth. Church, 1943-49; pastor, Mt. Clemens, Mich., 1949-53; pres. Holy Land Christian Mission Bd., 1954—; Holy Land Tour condr., 1953- 64; chmn. Baney Dead Sea Expdn. Bd., 1962-68; mem. bd. mgrs. Bd. of Missions and Ch. Extension of Meth. Ch., 1941-53; past pres. conf. Bd. of Missions and Ch. Extension. Lectr. on European scenes and Bible lands (43 lectrs., illustrated). Mem. Gen. Conf. of M.E. Ch., 1936; Jurisdictional Conf. Meth. Ch., 1948. Mem. Internat. Mark Twain Soc., Delta Sigma Rho, Theta Phi. Republican. Mason, Kiwanian. Club: Exchange (past pres.), Author: Bible Lands, syllabus for classes in Bible Land Geography, 1949; Where Jesus Walked, 1951; The New Where Jesus Walked, 1959. Contbr. articles on ch. methods. Asso. editor Holy Land Pictorial News. Home: 336 4th Av N St Petersburg FL 33701.

FIELD, GEORGE, ret. publicist, ednl. and program dir.; b. N.Y.C., Dec. 20, 1904; s. David and Rose (Polay) F.; student N.Y.U., evening sessions, 1926-28, 1931; L.H.D., Pratt Inst., 1970; m. Molly Mass, Mar. 16, 1925; children—Paul, Ellen. Copywriter for Ray D. Lillibridge, Inc., N.Y.C., 1926-28; free lance advt. agency, 1929-32; radio publicity, 1932-36; chmn. bd. Rand Sch. Social Sci., N.Y.C., 1936; radio program dir. Station WEVD, N.Y.C., 1937-40; sec. N.Y. chpt. Com. to Defend Am. by Aiding Allies, 1940-41; dir. WEVD U. of the Air, 1938-63; a founder, sec. Freedom House, 1941-69, exec. dir. emeritus, 1970—; exec. dir. Willkie Meml. Bldg., 1945-70. Dir. Am. tours of Rt. Hon. Herbert Morrison, 1936, 37, 38; dir. Ann. Freedom Award dinners, 1942—. Mem. Am. Polit. Sci. Assn. Club: Overseas Press. Author: American Labor Party Political Handbook (for LaGuardia campaign), 1937. Home: 1237 Old Nassau Rd Jamesburg NJ 08831

FIELD, GEORGE BROOKS, educator; b. Providence, Oct. 25, 1929; s. Winthrop Brooks and Pauline (Woodworth) F.; B.S., Mass. Inst. Tech., 1951; Ph.D., Princeton, 1955; m. Sylvia Farrior Smith, June 23, 1956; children—Christopher Lyman, Natasha Suzanne. Asst. prof. astronomy Princeton, 1957-62, asso. prof. 1962-65; prof. astronomy U. Cal. at Berkeley, 1965—, chmn. dept., 1970—. Mem. astronomy panel Nat. Acad. Scis.-NRC, 1965-68; mem. space scis. panel Pres.'s Sci. Adv. Com., 1966-67; Mem. astronomy panel NSF, 1966-69, chmn., 1967-69; mem. astronomy missions bd. NASA, 1968-70; mem. physics, astronomy survey coms. Nat. Acad. Scis., 1969—, chmn. panel on astrophysics and relativity, 1970—; mem. vis. com. Nat. Radioastronomy Obs., 1967-69. Trustee at large Asso. Univs., Inc., 1969—. Mem. Soc. Fellows Harvard, 1955-57; Guggenheim fellow, 1960-61. Fellow Am. Phys. Soc.; mem. Am. Astron. Soc. (nominating com. 1967-70, chmn. 1969-70, mem. com. on elections 1968-69), Royal Astron. Soc., Astron. Soc. Pacific, Internat. Astron. Union, Am. Assn. U. Profs., A.A.A.S., Sigma Xi. Co-editor: Gordon and Breach Series on Astrophysics and Space Physics, 1968—; editorial bd. Gordon and Breach Sci. Pubs., 1968—; bd. editors Astronomy and Astrophysics: A European Journal; corr. Comments on Astrophysics and Space Physics, 1968—. Home: 48 Senior Av Berkeley, CA 94708.

FIELD, GEORGE REED, educator; b. LaCrosse, Wis., Feb. 23, 1929; s. Donald E. and Lenore (Reed) F.; B.A., Carleton Coll., 1950; M.A., U. Colo., 1953; Ph.D., U. Wis., 1965; m. Marcella Ott, Mar. 1, 1952; children-William, Mary, John, Sarah, Thomas. Asst. to pres., U. Wis., Madison, 1957-62, exec. asst. to pres., 1962-66, v.p. 1966-68; pres. Wis. State U., River Falls, 1968—. Cons. Ford Found., 1965-66; cons. financial aid, Big Ten Conf. Devel. Council, Am. Coll. Pub. Relations Assn., 1962-64; mem. Coll. Scholarship Service, 1964-65. Agy. head Community Chest, U. Wis. 1962-63; mem. Milw. Braves Meml. Scholarship Found., Admistrv. Com. Johnson Found. Served with CIC, AUS, 1951-53. A.C. Neilson Found. grantee, 1965. Mem. Am. Assn. State Colls. and Univs. (internat. com. 1969), Phi Delta Kappa. Contbr. articles profl. jours. Home: 1046 S Fork Dr River Falls WI 54022

FIELD, HENRY, educator; b. Chicago, Ill., Dec. 15, 1902; ed. in Eng.; student Eton Coll., 1916- 21, New Coll., Oxford, 1921-26; B.A., Oxford U., 1925, Diploma in Anthropology, 1926, M.A., 1929, D.Sc., 1937; research U. Heidelberg, 1926; research Peabody Mus., Harvard, 1936-37; m. Julia Rand Allen, Feb. 6, 1953; 1 dau., Juliana Lathrop; (by previous marriage), Mariana. Anthropologist Field Mus. Natural History, 1926-41, asst. curator of phys. anthropology, 1926-36, curator, 1937-41; govt. research on Near East, Library of Congress, Washington, 1941-45. Mem. archaeol. expdn. in Europe, Africa and Southwestern Asia; leader Marshall Field Archaeol. Expdns. to Europe. N. Arabian Desert, Iraq, and others; mem. other expdns. Research fellow phys. anthropology Harvard 1950-69, hon. asso. in phys. anthropology, 1969—; adj. prof. U. Miami, 1966—; Forbes

Hawkes lectr. U. Miami, Lowell Inst., Boston, 1952. Trustee Am. Sch. Prehistoric Research; hon. mem. Glasgow Archaeol. Soc.; corr. mem. several fgn. scientific socs. Mem. U.S. and fgn. profl. and scientific socs. and assns., anthropol., archaeol., and other spl. orgns. Fellow A.A.A.S., Royal Geog. Soc., Royal Central Asian Soc., Royal Asiatic Soc., Royal Anthrop. Inst. of Gt. Brit. and Ireland, Geol. Soc., Zoöl. Soc., Prehistoric Soc., and others; mem. Acad. Arts and Scis. Ams. (pres. 1964—). U.S. del. to internat. congresses and sci. confs. Mem. U.S. mission to Moscow and Leningrad for 220th anniversary of Acad. Scis. USSR, 1945, Internat. Congress, Moscow, 1964, Internat. Geog. Congress, Eng., 1964. Club: Explorers' (N.Y.). Author books on different geog. areas, including: Useful Plants and drugs of Iran and Iraq (with David Hooper), 1937; The Anthropology of Iraq, 1939, 40, 48, 51, 52; Contbns. to the Anthropology of the Caucasus, 1953; The Track of Man, 1953; Los Indios de Tepoztlan, Morelos, Mexico, 1954; Ancient and Modern Man in S.W. Asia, I, 1956, II, 1961; Bibliographies on S.W. Asia I-VII, 1953-61; Anthropological Reconnaissance in West Pakistan, 1959; North Arabian Desert Archaeological Survey, 1925-50, 1960; "M" Project for F.D.R.; Studies on Migration and Settlement, 1962; Physical Anthropology of India, 1970. Editor Peabody Mus. Russian Translation Series, 1960-70. Home: 1960—. Home: 3551 Main Highway Coconut Grove Miami FL 33133 Office: Peabody Museum Cambridge MA 02138 ☆

FIELD, HENRY AUGUSTUS, Jr., lawyer; b. Wisconsin Dells, Wis., July 8, 1928; s. Henry A. and Georgia (Coakley) F.; student Western Mich. Coll., 1946-47; Ph.B., Marquette U., 1950; LL.B., U. Wis., 1952; m. Patricia Ann Young Nov. 30, 1957; children—Mary Patricia, Thomas Gerard, Susan Therese. Admitted to Wis. bar, 1952; asst. U.S. atty. Western Dist. of Wis., 1956-57; asso. Roberts, Boardman, Suhr, Bjork & Curry, 1957-62, jr. partner Roberts, Boardman, Suhr & Curry, 1962-70; partner Boardman, Suhr, Curry & Field, Madison, Wis., 1970—. Dir. Family Service Soc., 1969—, treas., 1971-72. Served with C.I.C., AUS, 1952-55. Mem. Am., Wis. (chmn. negligence sect. 1971-72), Dane County (pres. 1971-72) bar assns., Phi Delta Phi, Sigma Tau Delta, Order of Coif. Republican. Roman Catholic. Elk. Club: Madison. Home: 4410 Keating Terrace Madison WI 53711 Office: 110 E Main St Madison WI 53703

FIELD, JAMES ALFRED, Jr., educator, historian; b. Chgo., Mar. 9, 1916; s. James Alfred and Amy Morehead (Walker) F.; grad. Milton (Mass.) Acad., 1933; S.B., Harvard, 1937, A.M., 1939, Ph.D., 1947; student Trinity Coll., Cambridge (Eng.) U., 1937-38; m. Lila Ruth Breckinridge, Aug. 30, 1941; children—Charles Walker, Mary Breckinridge. Exec. asst. Nat. Resources Com., 1939; teaching fellow Harvard, 1940-42, 47; mem. faculty Swarthmore Coll., 1947—, prof. history, 1958—, chmn. dept., 1963-68; vis. prof. maritime history U.S. Naval War Coll., 1954-55. Mem. hist. adv. com. Dept. of Army, 1964-68. Served with USNR, 1942-46. Mem. Am. Hist. Assn., Orgn. Am. Historians, Am. Studies Assn., U.S. Naval Inst. Club: Great Lakes Cruising (Chgo.). Author: The Japanese at Leyte Gulf, 1947; History of U.S. Naval Operations, Korea, 1962; America and the Mediterranean World, 1969. Home: 612 Hillborn Av Swarthmore PA 19081

FIELD, JAMES BERNARD, physician, educator; b. Ft. Wayne, Ind., May 28, 1926; s. Abraham and Clara (Riddner) F.; M.D. cum laude, Harvard, 1951; m. Dorothy Allison Spivey, Sept. 24, 1954; children—Carolyn Rundle, Nancy Terrell, Douglas Andrew, Susan Tillman. Practice medicine, speciaizing in internal medicine, endocrinology, Bethesda, Md., 1954-62, Pitts., 1962—; sr. asst. surgeon Nat. Inst. Arthritis Metabolic Diseases, NIH, 1954-57, sr. investigator, 1958-62, mem. endocrinology study sect., 1965-69, chmn., 1967-69, mem. diabetes and metabolism tng. grants. com., 1970—; prof. medicine U. Pitts., 1966—; asst. in medicine Diabetic Clinic Kings Coll. Hosp., London, 1957-58; cons. chronic diseases br. USPHS, 1962- 66. Recipient Eli Lilly award Am. Diabetes Assn., 1958, Van Meter prize Am. Goiter Assn., 1961. Mem. Am. Assn. Physicians, Am. Soc. Clin. Investigation, Am. Physiology Soc., Am. Diabetes Assn. (bd. dirs.), Endocrine Soc., Am. Fedn. Clin. Research. Mem. editorial bd. Metabolism, 1960—, editor-in- chief, 1970—; editorial bd. Clinical Research, 1963-64. Contbr. articles profl. jours. Home: 109 Hillcrest Rd Pittsburgh PA 15238

FIELD, JOHN, II, physiologist, educator; b. Phila., May 11, 1902; s. Thomas Rittenhouse and Rachel Lee (Davison) F.; Pierre S. Dupont scholar William Penn Charter Sch., Phila., 1915-19; A.B., Stanford U., 1923, A.M., 1924, Food Research fellow, 1924-25, Ph.D., 1928; m. Sally Miller, Dec. 14, 1929; children—John Austin, Charles Davison, Richard Clark. Mem. faculty, Stanford, 1927-51, prof. physiology, 1942-51 (on leave 1949-51); acting dir. Arctic Research Lab., Office Naval Research, Aug. 1948; head biology br. Office Naval Research, Washington, 1949-51; chmn. dept. physiology U. Cal. Sch. Medicine, Los Angeles, 1951-62, asso. dean Sch. Medicine, 1958-69, prof., asso. dean emeritus, 1969—, prof. med. history and asst. dean, 1969-71; asst. dir. NSF, Washington, cons., 1952—; exec. sec. Arctic Research Lab. Adv. Bd., 1949-51; mem. panel on physiology and panel on Arctic environment Research and Devel. Bd., 1949-51. Mem. steering com. Alaska Sci. Conf., NRC, 1950. Fellow A.A.A.S.; asso. mem. A.M.A.; mem. Am. Physiol. Soc. (editor-in-chief Handbook of Physiology 1955-59), Soc. for Exptl. Biology and Medicine (sec.-treas. Pacific Coast sect. 1936-38), Western Soc. Naturalists, Western Soc. Clin. Research, Cal. Acad. Medicine, Sigma Xi, Phi Rho Sigma. Club: Cosmos (Washington). Mem. editorial bd. Ann. Rev. Physiology, 1951-60. Contbr. articles. Home: 521 S Westgate Av Los Angeles CA 90049

FIELD, JOHN A., Jr., U.S. dist. judge; b. Charleston, W.Va., Mar. 22, 1910; s. John A. and Mayme (Butler) F.; A.B., Hampden-Sydney Coll., 1932; LL.B., U. Va., 1935; m. Elaine Cochran Goode, Apr. 1, 1933; children—John A. III, William Claiborne. Admitted to W.Va. bar, 1935; with firm Brown, Jackson & Knight, Charleston, 1935-43; asso. with George W. Wood in practice, Charleston, 1946-57; tax commnr., W.Va., 1957-59; U.S. judge for So. Dist. W.Va., 1959—. Mem. Charleston City Council, 1947-55, pres., 1951- 55; Rep. candidate for atty. gen. W.Va., 1956. Served to lt. (s.g.) U SNR, 1944-46. Mem. Am., Charleston bar assns., Am. Law Inst., Order of Coif, Chi Phi, Omicron Delta Kappa. Presbyn. Club: Charleston Exchange. Home: 4306 Kanawha Av SE Charleston WV 25306 Office: Federal Bldg Charleston WV 25301

FIELD, JOHN EARLY, textile co. exec.; b. Greensboro, N.C., Oct. 12, 1916; s. Dan B. and Rosa W. (Wells) F.; student U. N.C., 1933-35, Pierce Sch. Bus. Adminstrn., 1935-37; grad. Advanced Mgmt. Program, Harvard, 1948; m. Helen C. Cregier, Sept. 21, 1940; children—John Early, Jane Ellen. Exec. v.p., treasurer, dir. Cone Mills, Inc., N.Y.C. until 1961, pres. dir., 1961—; sr. v.p., dir. Cone Mills Corp., Greensboro. Home: 7 Joan Dr Chappaqua NY 10514 Office: 1440 Broadway New York City NY 10018

FIELD, JOHN LOUIS, constrn. co. exec.; b. Mpls., Jan. 18, 1930; s. Harold David and Gladys Ruth (Jacobs) F.; B.A., Yale, 1952; B. Arch., 1955; m. Carol Helen Hart, July 23, 1961; children—Matthew Hart, Alison Ellen. Apprentice, Skidmore, Owings & Merrill, San Francisco, 1955-57; individual practice architecture, San Francisco, 1959-68; v.p. firm Bull, Field, Volkmann, Stockwell, Architects, San Francisco, 1968—. Guest lectr. Stanford, 1970. Chmn. archtl. council San Francisco Mus. Art, 1969, mem. activities bd., 1969—. Recipient Archtl. Record award, 1961; A.I.A., Sunset mag. awards, 1952, 64, 69, No. Cal. A.I.A., 1967; certificate excellence Cal. Gov.'s Design Awards, 1966; Homes for Better Living awards, 1962, 66, 69. Mem. A.I.A. (exec. com. chpt.), Nat. Council Archtl. Registration Bd., Am. Arbitration Assn. Club: Yale (San Francisco). Works include Arthur Alter House, Rosston Townhouses, Sacramento State Coll. Edn., Taxco Apts., Cascades Apts., Cerberus Theatres. Office: 350 Pacific Av San Francisco CA 94111 Mailing Address Only:

FIELD, JOHN SHAW, lawyer, rancher; b. Boydton, Va., June 3, 1900; s. Bland Randolph and Rinda Alice (King) F.; A.B., U. Va., 1922, LL.B., 1925; m. Alma Cornelius, Mar. 20, 1943. Admitted to Nev. bar, 1927, and since in pvt. practice law, Reno; gen. counsel Nev. State Incorporating & Agy. Co., Steamboat Canal & Irrigation Co., Last Chance Irrigation Co.; Spl. asst. atty. gen. Nev. 1957-60; owner Double F. Ranch. Active Boy Scouts Am.; chpt. chmn. A.R.C., 1945-46, dir., 1942—. Trustee Roanoke River Museum, Prestwould House Found., Va. Served with USN, 1917-19, with USAAF, 1943-44. Mem. Am. (gov., nat. chmn. membership com. corp. sect., council mem., mem. com. on corporate laws; mem. ho. of dels. 1950—; chmn. pub. relations 1961-62), Washoe County (pres. 1944-45) bar assns., State Bar Nev. (pres. interstate bar council 1954), Am. Law Inst., Am. Judicature Soc., Selden Soc. London, U. Va. Law Sch. Alumni Assn. (mem. council). Clubs: The Prospectors, St. Elmo of Va. Home: Double F Ranch S Virginia Rd Reno NV 89502 Office: 328 California Av Reno NV 89502

FIELD, JOHN WARNER, mfg. exec.; b. Bridgeport, Conn., Sept. 14, 1914; s. John and Margaret (Warner) F.; grad. Hotchkiss Sch., 1933; B.A., Yale, 1937; m. Priscilla H. Brown, Apr. 15, 1939; children—Margaret, John Warner, David. Successively an editor Life mag., war corr., war editor, nat. affairs editor, Time, Inc., 1937-46; with Warnaco, Inc., men's and women's apparel retailing and packaging, Bridgeport, 1946—, treas., 1946-49, pres., since 1957—, dir., 1948—; dir. Conn. Nat. Bank, Insilco Co., Meriden, Conn.; trustee People's Savs. Bank, Bridgeport. Trustee Colby Coll., U. Bridgeport. Home: 1450 Hillside Rd Fairfield CT 06430 Office: 350 Lafayette St Bridgeport CT 06604

FIELD, LAMAR, educator, chemist; b. Montgomery, Ala., July 19, 1922; s. Samuel Lamar and Nelle (Brock) F.; S.B., Mass. Inst. Tech., 1944, Ph.D., 1949; m. Betty Leyden, Jan. 1, 1948; children—Patricia Leyden, Brock Lamar. Jr. chemist Merck and Co., 1944-46; Socony-Vacuum fellow Mass. Inst. Tech., 1947-48; mem. faculty Vanderbilt U., 1949—, prof. chemistry, 1959—, chmn. dept., 1961-67; cons., 1955—; cons. NIH, 1965-69; Coulter lectr. U. Miss., 1968. Recipient Boit prize Mass. Inst. Tech., 1941, 42, Roger's award, 1944. Mem. Am. Chem. Soc. (chmn. Nashville sect. 1955, councilor 1960-68, mem. council com. on publs. 1963-68, vis. scientist 1966—, vis. asso. com. profl. tng. 1963—), Tenn. Acad. Sci., Chem. Soc. (London), Sigma Xi (L.C. Glenn award Vanderbilt chpt. 1952), Alpha Chi Sigma, Delta Tau Delta, Contbr. numerous publs. in field chemistry. Office: Box 1507 Station B Vanderbilt U Nashville TN 37203

FIELD, LYMAN, lawyer; b. Kansas City, Mo., Oct. 6, 1914; s. Russell and Gertrude (Brown) F.; A.B., U. Kan., 1936; LL.B., Harvard, 1939; 1 dau. by previous marriage—Kathleen; m. 2d, Jo Ann Straube, Apr. 10, 1965; 1 dau., Jennifer Ann. Admitted to Mo. bar, 1939, since practiced in Kansas City; mem. firm Rogers, Field and Gentry; now partner firm Rogers, Field, Gentry, Benjamin & Robertson; spl. commr. Supreme Ct. of Mo. 1953-54. Dir. Wally F. Findlay Galleries Internat., Inc. Pres. Council Social Agys. Kansas City, Mo., 1951-55; gen. chmn. Citizens Regional Planning Council of Greater Kansas City, 1949-53; pres. Bd. Police Commrs., Kansas City, Mo., 1957-61; mem., chmn. Mo. Council on Arts; gen. chmn. Mayor's Municipal Services Commn., 1951-53; chmn. N.Am. Assembly State and Provincial Art Agencies, 1968-70. Trustee, v.p. Kansas City Philharmonic Orch. Assn.; trustee Samuel H. Kress Found.; bd. dirs. Cross Found. Served from pvt. to maj., USMCR, 1942-46; PTO. Decorated Bronze Star medal. Medal Am., Mo., Kansas City bar assns., Am. Judicature Soc., Internat. Assn. Ins. Counsel, Lawyers Assn. Kansas City, Beta Theta Pi, Phi Delta Phi. Clubs: Kansas City Country, University, Carriage, (Kansas City, Mo.). Home: 5815 State Line Rd Kansas City MO Office: 600 E 11th St Kansas City MO 64106

FIELD, MARSHALL, newspaper pub.; Charlottesville, Va., May 13, 1941; s. Marshall IV and Joanne (Bass) F.; grad. Deerfield Acad., 1959; B.A., Harvard, 1963; m. Joan Best Connelly, Sept. 5, 1964 (div. 1969); 1 son, Marshall. with N.Y. Herald Tribune, 1964-65; pub. Chgo. Sun-Times and Chgo. Daily News; dir. Field Enterprises, Inc., Chgo., 1965—, mem. exec. com., 1966—, also mem. exec. com. of newspaper div.; dir. Field Communications Corp., Field Enterprises Ednl. Corp., First Chgo. Corp., First Nat. Bank of Chgo. Mem. Chgo. com. Chgo. Council Fgn. Relations. Trustee Art Inst. Chgo., Field Mus. Natural History, Rush-Presbyn.-St. Lukes Med. Center, U. Chgo., MacMurray Coll.; bd. dirs. Field Found. of Ill., Jr. Achievement, Lincoln Park Zool. Soc., John Crerar Library; governing bd. mem. Orchestral Assn.; adv. bd. Chgo. area council Boy Scouts Am.; mem. journalism adv. com. Stanford; bd. overseers com. to visit Grad. Sch. Edn., Harvard. Mem. Am. Newspaper Pubs. Assn. (dir. bur. advt.), Nat. Com. Newspaper Pubs. Clubs: River, Brook (N.Y.C.); Fly, Lampoon, Hasty Pudding (Cambridge, Mass.); Chicago Press, Merchants and Manufacturers. Mid-Am., Tavern, Attic, Casino, Racquet, Saddle and Cycle, Chicago (Chgo.); Onwentsia (Lake Forest); Shoreacres (Lake Bluff); McGraw Wildlife (Dundee); Post and Paddock (Arlington Heights, Ill.); Cat Cay (Bahamas). Office: 401 N Wabash Av Chicago IL 60611

FIELD, MICHAEL, research co. exec.; b. N.Y.C., Feb. 21, 1914; s. Max and Hanna (Heller) F.; B.S. in Mech. Engring., Coll. City N.Y., 1937; M.S. in Mech. Engring., Columbia, 1938; Ph.D. in Physics, U. Cin., 1948; m. Ruth V. Clendening, Jan. 24, 1942; children—David, Janice. Research engr. Cin. Milling Machine Co., 1938-48; pres., gen. mgr. Metcut Research Assos., Inc., Cin., 1948—. Active U. Cin., Columbia corporate fund drives, Boy Scouts Am., United Appeal. Named Engr. of Year, Cin., 1966; recipient Gold Medal award Soc. Mfg. Engrs. Phila., 1968, Distinguished alumni award U. Cin., 1969, Joseph Whitworth prize Instn. Mech. Engrs., 1968. Fellow Am. Soc. Metals (William H. Eisenman award 1971), Soc. Exptl. Stress Analysis (chmn. chpt. 1963-65), Soc. Automotive Engrs., Aircraft Industries Assn., Am. Inst. Aeros. and Astronautics, Am. Ordnance Assn., A.A.A.S., Numerical Control Soc., Sigma Xi. Contbr. articles to profl. jours. Home: 9060 Spooky Ridge Lane Cincinnati OH 45242 Office: 3980 Rosslyn Dr Cincinnati OH 45209

FIELD, NOEL MACDONALD, lawyer; b. Providence, Aug. 27, 1904; s. Harold Crins and May (Noel) F.; A.B. cum laude, Brown U., 1926; LL.B. magna cum laude, Harvard, 1929; m. Ellen DeWolf Preston, June 1, 1931; children—Sylvia (Mrs. Jean E. de Valpine), Noel Macdonald. Admitted to R.I. bar, 1929, since practiced in Providence; partner firm Hinckley, Allen, Salisbury & Parsons, and predecessors, 1938—. Past dir. Am. Screw Co., R.I. Textile Co., C.I. Hayes, Inc. Served to capt. USAAF, World War II. Decorated Bronze Star. Fellow Am. Coll. Probate Counsel; mem. Phi Beta Kappa, Alpha Delta Phi. Mem. editorial bd. Harvard Law Rev., 1928-29. Home: 30 Stimson Av Providence RI 02906. Office: Industrial Bank Bldg Providence RI 02903

FIELD, PETER STEWART, Australian diplomat; b. Adelaide, Australia, Mar. 7, 1940; s. Max Stewart and Gwenyth Bernice (Griffiths) F.; B.Ec., U. Adelaide, 1963; m. Anne Michelle DeSalis, Jan. 20, 1967; 1 son, David Stewart. Joined dept. trade and industry Commonwealth Govt. Australia, 1965; 1st comml. sec., Washington, 1967-70, comml. counselor, 1970—. Anglican. Clubs: University (Washington); Royal Adelaide Golf; Guthega Ski. Home: 1335 Lynnbrook Dr N Arlington VA 22201 Office: 1601 Massachusetts Av NW Washington DC 20036

FIELD, RICHARD H., lawyer educator; b. Phillips, Me., May 29, 1903; s. Daniel F. and Clara E. (Hinckley) F.; grad. Phillips Exeter Acad., 1922; A.B., Harvard, 1926, LL.B. magna cum laude, 1929; m. Caroline Crosby, June 28, 1930 (dec. Sept. 1966); children—Mary (Mrs. Rienzi B. Parker, Jr.), Margaret (Mrs. David L. Aronson), Daniel; m. 2d, Laura Shaw, Apr. 19, 1968; stepchildren—Robert, Christopher, Elisabeth, Caleb, Arthur, Caroline. Admitted to Mass. bar, 1929, mem. firm Brown, Field & McCarthy, Boston, 1930-42; asst. counsel spl. comn. on contract and conduct pub. utilities Mass. State, 1929-30; regional atty. O.P.A., Boston, 1942-43, chief legal adviser to adminstr. and acting gen. counsel, Washington, 1943-44, gen. counsel, 1944-46; vis. prof. of law, Harvard Law Sch., 1946-47, prof., 1947—, Story prof., 1968—; vis. Am. prof. Inst. Advanced Legal Studies, 1970-71. Cons. Econ. Stblzn., Adminstrn., 1950-51. Mem. bd. selectmen Town of Weston (Mass.), 1956-58, town moderator, 1962-68. Pres. bd. trustees Cambridge Sch., 1949-55. Mem. Am. Law Inst. (chief reporter div. of jurisdiction between state and fed. courts 1960-68), Mass., Boston, Middlesex bar assns. Permanent sec. Harvard Class of 1926, 1926-51. Author:(with Benjamin Kaplan) Materials for a Basic Course in Civil Procedure, 1953, rev. 1968; (with V.L. McKusick) Maine Civil Practice, 1959, (with V.L McKusick and L.K. Wroth) 2d edit, 1970. Home: 74 Sudbury Rd Weston MA 02193 Office: Harvard Law School Cambridge MA 02138

FIELD, RICHARD LANE, former editor; b. Balt., Sept. 12, 1897; s. Charles Carter and Mary Virginia (Lane) F.; A.B., Johns Hopkins, 1920; m. Camilla L. Chewning, June 25, 1932; children—Richard Lane, William Carter. Reporter, Balt. Sun, 1920-23, night city editor, 1923-24; swing editor Balt. Am., 1925; asst. make-up editor N.Y. Herald-Tribune, 1926, asst. editor, Sunday Mag., 1926-35; a founder, article editor This Week Mag., 1935-45; a founder, asso. editor Holiday mag., 1945-47, mng. editor, 1947-57, prodn. dir., 1957-64; city editor High Springs (Fla.) Herald, 1966; cons., part-time editor The Floridian, St. Petersburg (Fla.) Times Sunday mag. 1966-69. Dir. mag. information O.P.A., Washington, 1945. Served as pvt. U. S. Army, 1918. Mem. Kappa Alpha. Clubs: Dutch Treat, Johns Hopkins, P.E.N. (New York). Contbr. articles to nat. mags. Home: 526 Monterey Blvd Snell Isle St Petersburg FL 33704

FIELD, RON, theatrical dir., choreographer; grad. High Sch. Performing Arts. Profl. debut at age 8 in Lady in the Dark; appeared Broadway plays Kismet, The Boy Friend; mem. Jack Cole Dancers; choreographer Anything Goes, Zorba; dir., choreographer Applause; staged nightclub acts for Liza Minnelli, Carol Lawrence, Chita Rivera, TV dances for Fred Astaire and Angela Lansbury. Recipient Tony award for choreography of Cabaret, and for best dir.-choreographer of Applause. Address: care Palace Theatre Broadway at 47th St New York City NY 10014*

FIELD, RUTH PRUYN, (Mrs. Marshall Field), civic worker; b. N.Y.C., May 5, 1907; d. Robert and Betty (Metcalf) Pruyn; student Brearly Sch.; L.H.D., Hofstra Coll., 1961; m. Marshall Field, Jan. 15, 1936; children—Henry Odgen (dec.), Robert Lansing Phipps, Phyllis (Contesse de Fleurs), Fiona (Mrs. Fiona F. Rust). Dir. The Field Found., Inc., N.Y.C., 1940—, chmn., 1966—. Dir., v.p. Citizens Com. for Children of N.Y.C.; trustee Eleanor Roosevelt Meml. Found., Carnegie Hall Corp.; hon. trustee Sarah Lawrence Coll.; hon. bd. dirs. Wiltwyck Sch. Boys. Office: 136 E 79th St New York City NY 10021

FIELD, SALLY MARGARET, actress; b. Pasadena, Cal., Nov. 6, 1946; d. Richard Dryden and Margaret Joy (Morland) Field; grad. high sch.; m. Steven Craig, Sept. 16, 1968; 1 son, Peter Joshua. Appeared in TV series Gidget, 1965-66, The Flying Nun, 1967-70; appeared in TV films Maybe I'll Come Home in the Spring, Marriage: Year One. Mem. Actors Studio. Address: 1469 Bel Air Rd Los Angeles CA 90024

FIELD, SAMPSON RICHARD, former printer; b. Revere, Mass., July 7, 1902; s. Abraham and Anne (Hirschmann) F.; Harvard, 1923; m. Gantz, June 28, 1930; children—Richard, Barbara. Former pres. Publishers Printing-Admiral Press; chmn. exec. com., treas. Printing Corp. Am., N.Y.C., 1962. Mem. bd. directors of Musician Edn. League N.Y.C.; pres. Musicians Found., Inc.; v.p. Young Audiences, Inc., N.Y.; dir., treas. N.Y. Philharmonic Soc.; dir. Chamber Music Soc. Lincoln Center, Caramoor Art Center. Home: 860 United Nations Plaza New York City NY 10017

FIELD, THOMAS PARRY, educator; b. Waynesburg, Pa, June 6, 1914; s. Frank and Jane (Parry) F.; B.S., E. Tenn. State Coll., 1935; postgrad. U. N.M., 1939; M.A., George Peabody Coll., 1940; Ph.D., U. N.C., 1948; m. Nancie Emerson Davis, July 29, 1944; children—Gwendolynn Parry, Julia Davis (Mrs. Timothy Costich). Tchr. pub. sch., 1935-39, Johnson City, Tenn., Greenville, N.C., 1935- 39; faculty E. Tenn. State Coll., 1940-41, U. Ky., Lexington, 1948—, prof. geography, 1960—. Geog. cons. Dept. Justice, 1968-70, Bur. of Census, 1965—, Office Econ. Opportunity, 1966-68, City-County Planning Commn., Lexington, Ky., 1960—. Served to lt. comdr. USNR, 1942-45: PTO. Named Ky. col., 1961. Presbyn. (elder). Author: A Guide to Kentucky Place Names, 1961; Postwar Land Settlement in Western Australia, 1962. Home: 1014 Castleton Way S Lexington KY 40502

FIELD, THOMAS STEWART, coll. pres.; b. Chgo., June 2, 1915; s. Thomas Robertson and Ann (Stewart) F.; B.S., Wheaton (Ill.) Coll., 1937, D.D., 1957; B.D., Eastern Baptists Theol. Sem., 1941; m. Virginia Margaret Leach, May 20, 1939; children—Melinda (Mrs. Donald Ross Duncan), Rebecca (Mrs. James Edward Montgomery). Ordained to ministry Baptist Ch., 1941; pastor First Bapt. Ch., Quitman, Ga., 1950-52, La Grange, Ga., 1952-57, Lake Charles, La., 1957-60, Springfield, Mo., 1960-70; pres. William Jewell Coll., Liberty, Mo., 1970—. Mem. exec. bd. Ga. Bapt. Conv., 1954-57, La. Baptist Conv., 1958-60, Mo. Baptist Conv., 1961-70, pres., 1967-69; mem. exec. com. So. Bapt. Conv., 1969-70, mem. found. bd., 1965-71, mem. relief annuity bd., 1957-60. Chmn. A.R.C., La Grange, 1956; chmn. adv. bd. Salvation Army, Springfield, 1968-69; mem. exec. com. Community Chest, Lake Charles, 1957; pres. bd. dirs. Ozark Christian Counseling Service, Springfield; v.p. trustees Cox Med. Center, Springfield; chmn. trustees Southwest Bapt. Coll., Bolivar, Mo. Recipient Freedoms Found. award for sermon Let Freedom Ring, 1968. Mem. C. of C. Springfield, Internat. Platform Assn. Rotarian. Home: 510 East Mississippi St Liberty MO 64068

FIELD, WILLIAM BRADHURST OSGOOD, geographer; b. N.Y.C.; Jan. 30, 1904; s. William Bradhurst Osgood and Lila (Sloan) F.; B.S., Harvard, 1926; D.Sc., U. Alaska, 1961; m. Alice Withrow, Apr. 4, 1929 (dec. 1960); children—Diana Sloan, John Osgood; m. 2d, Mary Losey Mapes, 1963. Prodn. edn. and travel motion pictures and geog. studies, 1926-40; research asso. Am. Geog. Soc., 1940-46, head dept. exploration and field research, 1946-69, mem. council, 1970. Chmn. tech. panel on glaciology U.S. Nat. Com. for Internat. Geophys. Year, 1957-58. Served from 1st lt. to capt., Signal Corps, AUS, 1942-46. Recipient medal Explorers Club, 1969; Daly medal Am. Geog. Soc., 1969. Fellow Geol. Soc. Am., Arctic Inst. N.Am.; mem. Am. Geophys. Union (chmn. research com. on glaciers 1948-53), NRC, Assn. Am. Geographers, Glaciological Soc. (hon.). Clubs: Century Assn (N.Y.C.); Explorers; American Alpine (council 1933-38, 48-49; eastern v.p. 1950-52); Camp Fire of Am. Home: 1 W 81st St New York City NY 10024 Office: Am Geographical Soc Broadway at 156th St New York City NY 10032

FIELD, WILLIAM NOE, clergyman, educator; b. Orange, N.J., Dec. 22, 1915; s. William Noé and Marie Natalie (O'Mara) F.; A.B., Seton Hall, 1936; student Immaculate Conception Sem., 1936-40; postgrad. Columbia, 1940-52, M.L.S., 1960. Ordained priest Roman Catholic Ch., 1940; mem. faculty Seton Hall U., South Orange, N.J., 1940-, prof. English, 1940-, dir. libraries, 1963—, dir. devel., 1959-61; lectr. Adult Sch., Chatham, N.J., 1964-66; moderator various employee groups Trustee Cath. Forum, Archbishop Walsh Jr. Coll. Mem. N.J. Library Assn. (pres. elect coll. and univ. div. 1966—), Renascence Soc. (pres. 1971-72, trustee, Serra of Orange moderator 1955—), Cath. Poetry Soc. Am. Editorial bd. Advocate, 1951—. Author: (poetry) Hear My Heart, 1950; also articles, book revs. Address: Seton Hall U South Orange NJ 07079.

FIELD, A. J., business exec.; b. Los Angeles, 1924; B.S. in Civil Engring., Cal. Inst. Tech., 1944; M.S. in Civil Engr., Stanford. With Union Oil Co., 1947-59; with Global Marine Inc., Los Angeles, 1959—, now pres., dir. Served with USNR, World War II. Home: 2520 Nottingham Av Los Angeles CA 90027 Office: 811 W 7th St Los Angeles CA 90017*

FIELDEN, JOHN SEWARD, coll., dean; b. Phila., Nov. 5, 1923; s. William and Elizabeth (MacIlvain) F.; B.S., Wharton Sch., U. Pa., 1945; M.A., Boston U., 1949, Ph.D., 1954; m. Patricia Anne Larkin, Mar. 17, 1945; children—Victoria, Richard, Peter, Michael, Anne, Margaret. Teaching fellow English, Boston U., 1950-52; asst. instr. English, U. Ill., 1952-54; instr., then asst. prof. English, Purdue U., 1954-59; mem. faculty Harvard Grad. Sch. Bus. Adminstrn., 1959-64, asso. editor Harvard Bus. Rev., 1959-64; prof. bus. adminstrn., dean Coll. Bus. Adminstrn., Boston U., 1964—. Dir. Giant Stores Corp., Manhattan Fund, Inc., Liberty Fund, Inc., Hemisphere Fund, Fund, Inc., Fundex, Inc., TMR Appreciation Fund. Bd. govs. Boston Stock Exchange, 1969—. Pres. Newton (Mass.) Mental Health Assn., 1966-67. Served to lt. (j.g.) USNR, 1942- 47. Mem. Am. Assn. Collegiate Schs. Bus. (exec. com. 1967-70). Author articles in field. Home: 90 Hancock St Auburndale MA 02166 Office: 685 Commonwealth Av Boston MA 02215

FIELDER, FREDERICK ALAN, industrialist; b. Ft. Worth, Oct. 23, 1912; s. Hammett H. and Emma Lou (Monaghan) F.; student Civil Engring., U. Ariz., 1931-34; J.D., George Washington U., 1939; m. Virginia A. Robinson, June 18, 1935; children—Carolyn R. Frederick Alan, Sharon P. Pres., dir. CF & I Steel Corp., Denver, 1966-70; pres. Continental Copper & Steels Industries, Inc., 1970—. Admitted to Dist. Columbia bar, 1939. Served as lt. USNR, 1944-45. Mem. Phi Gamma Delta. Presbyn. Clubs: Chicago, Denver. Home: 3106 S Steel St Denver CO 80210 Office: 1755 Glenarm Denver CO 80202

FIELDER, JOHN THOMAS, merchant; b. Austin, Tex., July 13, 1919; s. Hammett Hardy and Emma (Monoghan) F.; B.C.S., Benjamin Franklin U., 1940; student George Washington U., 1940-41; m. Mary Elizabeth Holland, June 20, 1949; children—John Thomas, William Hammett, James Hardy, Elizabeth Holland. Vice pres., dir. Julius Garfinckel & Co., Washington, 1953-59; pres. A. DePinna Co., N.Y.C., 1953-59; v.p., dir. Brooks Bros., N.Y.C., 1953-55; exec. v.p., dir. J.B. Ivey Co., Charlotte, N.C., 1960—. Served to lt., aviator USNR, 1942-46. Office: 127-131 N Tyron St Charlotte NC 28201

FIELDER, PARKER CLINTON, univ. dean; b. Chgo., Oct. 20, 1918; s. Harold Clinton and Adrienne (Parker) F.; B.S. in Commerce, Northwestern U., 1941; LL.B., U. Tex., 1948; m. Marguerite Sparks, June 16, 1943; children—Sydney (Mrs. Joseph Frank Drosihn), Pamela. Accountant-auditor Sears, Roebuck & Co., Chgo., 1941-42; admitted to Tex. bar, 1948, also U.S. Supreme Ct., other fed. cts.; prof. law U. Tex., 1948-53, Williams H. Francis, Jr. prof. law, 1961—; partner firm Turpin, Kerr, Smith & Dyer, Midland, Tex., 1953-61; vis. prof. U. Pa., 1964-65; visiting prof. So. Meth. U., summer 1968; research asso. charge tax project Tex. Legislative Council, 1950. Gen. counsel, dir. Permian Corp., 1959-61. Served to capt. AUS, 1942-46; colonel Res. Mem. Am. Bar Assn., State Bar Tex. (vice chmn. com. continuing legal edn. 1961-64), Am. Judicature Soc., Order of Coif, Phi Delta Phi, Chancellors. Mem. Christian Ch. (mem. bd., tchr.). Author articles in field. Editor in chief Tex. Law Rev., 1947-48. Office: 2500 Red River St Austin TX

FIELDHOUSE, HORACE NOEL, historian; b. Gibraltar, Sept. 10, 1900; s. Henry Warwick and Mary (Edwards) F.; B.A. with honors. U. Sheffield, 1921, M.A., diploma in edn., 1922; B.A. with honors, Queen's Coll., Oxford U., 1924; Litt.D., McGill U., 1969; m. Grace Tinning, Aug. 21, 1942; children—John, Elizabeth. Sr. lectr. modern history U. Sheffield. 1924-28; asst. prof. history U. Man., 1928-30, prof., head dept., 1930-45; Kingsford prof. history McGill U., 1945—, chmn. dept., 1947-62, dean faculty arts and sci., 1947-62, vice principal (academic), 1962-66, sr. research asso., 1969—; vis. prof. Queen's U., 1945, 46, U. B.C., 1949, U. Colo., 1947, 58. Served with Royal Air Force. 1918. Recipient Coronation medal, 1953. Fellow Royal Soc. Can., Internat. Inst. Arts and Letters; mem. Canadian Hist. Assn. (past pres.). Canadian Inst. Internat. Affairs. Contbr. articles hist. jours., publs. Home: 3455 Stanley St Montreal 112 Quebec Canada

FIELDING, ELIZABETH M., govt. ofcl.; b. New London, Conn., May 16, 1917; d. Frederick James and Elizabeth (Martin) Fielding: B.A., Conn. Coll. Women, 1938; M.A., Am. U., 1944. Research writer Republican Nat. Com., 1940, acting dir. research, 1944, asst. dir. research, 1948-53; govt. statistician, personnel clk., economist, 1941-42; research writer, 1942-48; staff writer, spl. cons. several U.S. congressmen, 1944-52; exec. sec., legislative asst. U.S. Senator Alexander Wiley, 1953-54; asso. dir. research Rep. Nat. Com., 1954-57, research, speech writer, 1960-61; legislative analyst, newsletter editor Nat. Assn. Electric Cos., 1957-60; pub. relations dir. Nat. Fedn. Rep. Women, 1961-68; editor Republican Clubwoman, 1961-68; dir. spl. activities women's div. United Citizens for Nixon-Agnew, 1968: finance coordinator Inaugural com., 1968-69; spl. asst. to asst. Postmaster Gen., 1969—; pub. affairs dir. Pres.'s Council on Youth Opportunity, 1970-71; asst. adminstr. for pub. affairs Nat. Credit Union Adminstrn., Washington, 1971—, editor Bull. and Report, 1971—. Recipient Achievement medal Conn. Coll., 1971. Mem. Fed. Editors Assn., Am. Polit. Sci. Assn., Am. Acad. Polit. and Social Sci., A.A.A.S., Am. Newspaper Women's Club, D.C. League Rep. Women, Am. Mgmt. Assn., Am. Soc. Pub. Adminstrn., Am. Soc. for Tng. and Devel., Phi Beta Kappa. Methodist. Clubs: Antique Automobile Am.; Capitol Hill (Washington). Author: A History of the Republican Party, 1854-1948; also party publs., youth manuals. Home: 3 D C Village Lane S W Washington DC 20032 Office: 1325 G St NW Washington DC 20456

FIELDING, GABRIEL, (Alan Gabriel Barnsley), novelist; b. Hexham, Northumberland, Eng., Mar. 25, 1916; s. George and Katherine Mary (Fielding-Smith) Barnsley; B.A., Trinity Coll., Dublin, Ireland, 1940; mem. Royal Coll. Surgeons, licentiate Royal Coll. Physicians, St. Georges Hosp., London, Eng., 1942; D.Litt. (hon.). Gonzaga U., 1967; m. Edwina Eleanora Cook, Oct. 31, 1943; children—Michael Fielding, Jonathan Milne, Mario Simon George Gabriel, Felicity Ann, Mary Gabriel Elizabeth. Physician in gen. practice, Maidstone, Eng., 1948—; part-time med. officer Her Majesty's Tng. Establishment, Maidstone, 1952—; occasional broadcaster BBC, 1961—; author in residence Wash. State U., Pullman, 1966-67, prof. English, 1966—. Served to capt. Royal Army Med. Corps, 1943-46. Hon. librarian Univ. Philos. Soc., Trinity Coll., 1938, recipient Anatomy prize, 1937, Silver medal for oratory, 1938; Journalism award Cath. Press Assn., 1965. Author: (poetry) The Frog Prince and Other Poems, 1952; (novel) Brotherly Love, 1954; (novel) In the Time of Greenbloom, 1956; (novel) Eight Days, 1959; (novel) Through Streets Broad and Narrow, 1961; XXVIII Poems, 1955; The Birthday King, 1963 (W. H. Smith prize 1963; St. Thomas More Soc. gold medal, Chgo.); Gentlemen in their Season, 1966. Roman Catholic. Home: 1811 Monroe St Pullman WA 99163

FIELDING, TEMPLE HORNADAY, author, fgn. corr.; b. N.Y.C., Oct. 8, 1913; s. George Thomas II and Helen Ross (Hornaday) F.; A.B. cum laude. Princeton. 1939; m. Nancy Parker, Oct. 17, 1942; 1 son, Dodge Temple. Profl. writer, 1939—; contbr. articles Reader's Digest. Sat. Eve. Post, Harper's, Life, Coronet, Mademoiselle, Town and Country, 1940—; fgn. corr. Town and Country in Mexico, 1942. Harper's and Reader's Digest in Yugoslavia, 1944. Reader's Digest, Sat. Eve. Post and Cosmopolitan in Europe and Africa, 1946-47; in Ethiopia for Internat. News Service, 1946; corr. for Sat. Eve. Post in Arctic, N.W. Territories, Can., 1948; fgn. corr. 13 S.A. countries for same mags., 1949: newspaper feature writer Internat. News Service, Balt. Sunday Sun, Christian Sci. Monitor, 1940- 49; TV film producer The Fieldings in Europe, series on NBC, 1954; columnist Hall Syndicate, 1956-57; founder, 1958. Since pres. Temple Fielding's Epicure Club of Europe: chmn., pres. Fielding Publs., Inc., 1966—; columnist met. ed. Ladies' Home Jour., 1968-69. Served to maj. AUS. 1941-45. Decorated Information Fund award, knight's cross Haederstegn, knight Royal Order Dannebrog (Denmark); knight's cross Order Queen Isabel La Catolica, comdr. Order Merito Civil. Gold and Silver medals Order Merito Turistico (Spain); Knight Royal Order Vasa (Sweden); Silver medal (Paris). (Copenhagen): Hiio Adoptivo (City of Pollensa); officer Order des Coteaux Commandrie, Silver medal l'Hospitalite (France); gold plaque of merit Federazione Italiana Pubblici Esercizi (Italy): Cross Comdr. Order Merito della Repubblica Italiana: Princeton University Medal of Honor: Flor de Almendro award from Spain: named hon. citizen of Amsterdam and Copenhagen; Knight Tuborg League: Red Badge of Courage, USMC. 1963: spl. citation Pres. Kennedy, 1963; Non Sibi Sed Patria award USMC Res. Officers Assn., 1964. Mem. Union Europeene des Clefs d'Or (hon.), Internat. Platform Assn., Soc. Mag. Writers (past pres.), Soc. Am. Travel Writers, Asso. Corresponsales de Prensa Iberoamericana, Grand Order European Tour Operators (hon.), Artic Inst. (Can.). Adventurers of Denmark (hon.). Clubs: Overseas Press (past gov.), Adventurers (past governor). Travelers Century (Los Angeles); Banshees (New York City); Ski of Great Britain (London); Guild of King Christian IV, Knights of Olefant (Denmark); Flying Dutchmen (Netherlands); Lion Watchers (Ethiopia). Author: A Guide to Fort Bragg, 1942; Fielding's Travel Guide to Europe, annually 1948—; Fielding's Currency Guide to Europe, annually 1951—; Fieldings' Currency Guide to the Far, Near and Middle East, annually, 1967—; Fieldings' World Time Converter. Annually, 1967—; (with Nancy Fielding) The Temple Fieldings Shopping Guide to Europe: annually 1957—, Fielding's Super-Economy Guide to Europe, annually 1967—. Contbr. Deadline Delayed, 1946. Home: Formentor Mallorca Balearic Islands Office: Fielding Publs Inc 105 Madison Av New York City NY 10016

FIELDING, WILLIAM JOHN, author, editor; b. Wharton, N.J., Apr. 10, 1886; s. William and Mary (Mitchell) F.; ed. pub. schs.; m. Elizabeth C. Veale, June 20, 1910 (dec.); children—Elsie (dec.), John Carbis; m. 3d, Mary Burns Cameron, Aug. 29, 1942. Editor Newark Leader, 1915-18; lit. editor N.J. Leader, 1919-22; editor Know Thyself, 1923-24; dramatic editor Golden Rule Mag., 1925-27, Sketch Book Mag., 1927-43; sec.-treas. Louis Comfort Tiffany Found., 1942-68, trustee, 1946-68, hon. life trustee, 1968—; pres. Thomas Paine Found., 1960-70. Named humanist of yr. Humanist Soc. Greater N.Y., 1970. Mem. A.A.A.S., Am. Social Hygiene Assn., Am. Birth Control League, Soc. for Constructive Birth Control and Racial Progress (London), Freethinkers Am. (hon. pres. 1970—), Euthanasia Soc. of Am. (adv. council), Inst. Literaire et Artistique de France, Am. Acad. Polit. and Social Sci., Authors League Am., Ethical Humanist Soc. L.I. (sec. 1950-55), Pi Gamma Mu. Author: Pebbles from Parnassus, 1917; Sanity in Sex, 1920; Psychoanalysis—The Key to Human Behavior, 1921; The Puzzle of Personality, 1922; The Caveman Within Us, 1922; Health and Self- Mastery Through Psycho-Analysis and Autosuggestion, 1923; Autosuggestion—How It Works, 1923; Rejuvenation, 1924; Rational Sex Series, 13 Vols., 1924-25; Teeth and Mouth Hygiene (collaboration), 1925; Dual and Multiple Personalities, 1925; The Cause and Nature of Genius, 1926; Sex and the Love-Life, 1927, rev. 1959; Woman—The Eternal Primitive, 1927; Sex and the Eternal Primitive, Woman—The Criminal, 1928; Woman—The Warrior, 1928; Unconscious Love Elements in Psycho-Analysis, 1929; How the Sun's Rays Give Health, 1930; The Marvels and Oddities of Sunlight, 1930; Boccacio—Lover and Chronicler of Love, 1930; The Art of Love, 1931; Love and the Sex Emotions, 1932; Sex in Civilization (symposia), 1929; The Shackles of the Supernatural, 1938, rev. 1969; Strange Customs of Courtship and Marriage, 1942; Strange Superstitions and Magical Practices, 1945, Self-Mastery Through Psychoanalysis, 1952; Auto-suggestion You Can Use, 1961. Contbr. poems to anthologies. Home: 1393 Long Beach Rd North Rockville Centre NY 11570

FIELDING, T. J., exec. sec. Nat. Labor Relations Bd. Address: 614 Greenbrier Dr Silver Spring, MD 20910.*

FIELDS, CARL RICHMOND, coll. dean; b. Benton, Ky., Nov. 7, 1910; s. John Louis and Verda (Austin) F.; A.B., U. Louisville, 1932, M.A., 1937; Ph.D., U. Ky., 1951; m. Katherine Alice Waller, Feb. 21, 1935; 1 son, Don Richmond Fields. Social worker Louisville and Jefferson County Childrens Home, 1932-33; tchr. Halleck Hall Jr. High Sch., Louisville, 1933-34; mem. faculty Georgetown (Ky.) Coll., 1935—, acad. dean, 1962—. Mem. edn. commn. So. Baptist Assn, 1963—; pres. So. Bapt. Assn. Deans, 1964—. Chmn. bd. John Graves Ford Meml. Hosp., Georgetown, 1958—; mem. bd. Georgetown Pub. Library, 1950—. Mem. Miss. Valley, So. hist. assns., Pi Kappa Alpha, Phi Alpha Theta. Kiwanian (past pres. Georgetown). Club: Filson (Louisville). Home: 300 Hiawatha St Georgetown, KY 40324.

FIELDS, CHARLES WILLIAM, govt. ofcl.; b. Chattanooga, Apr. 26, 1927; s. Charles William and Mamie (Kyle) F.; B.S. in Psychology, Tenn. State U., 1963; m. Vilma Jean Scruggs, Aug. 26, 1950; children—Albert C., DeNeese A., Anthony A., Vincent K. Community counselor Chattanooga pub. schs., 1963-69; mgmt. cons. E.I. DuPont Co., Chattanooga, 1969-70; exec. dir. Chattanooga Urban Coalition, 1970-71; personnel officer TVA, Chattanooga, 1971—. Chmn. bd. Los Gatos' Corp., Hamilton; pres. Vildot's Corp., Chattanooga, 1969—. Mem. Chattanooga-Hamilton County Air Pollution Control Bd., 1969-71; vice chmn. Citizen Non-participation Com., 1971; chmn. Mayor's Manpower Unit, 1971. Served with AUS, 1946-47. Recipient award for pub. relations civic and social orgns. Chattanooga, 1969. Mem. C. of C. (mem. human relations com. 1969), N.A.A.C.P., Kappa Alpha Psi. Roman Catholic. Club: Harambee (Chattanooga). Home: 5031 Mimosa Circle Chattanooga TN 37416 Office: 602 Lupton Bldg 1002 Georgia Av Chattanooga TN 37401

FIELDS, D. WALLACE, lawyer; b. Whitesburg, Ky., Feb. 9, 1910; s. LeRoy Wilson and Belle (Salyer) F.; B.S., Stetson U., 1929, LL.B., 1933; m. Martha Ann Smoth, Aug. 3, 1931; children—Dan Wallace, Rodney S., Robert W. Admitted to Ky. bar, 1933, Fla. bar, 1933; practice in Whitesburg, Ky., 1933-37; partner firm Carlton, Fields, Ward, Emmanuel Smith & Cutler, Tampa, Fla., 1937- -. Dir. Univ. State Bank, Tampa. Fla. rep. Interstate Oil Compact Commn., 1955-60. Mem. Am., Fla., Tampa-Hillsborough County (past treas., dir.) bar assns., Am. Judicature Soc., Sigma Nu. Republican. Episcopalian. K.P. (past chancellor). Home: 3514 Barcelona St Tampa FL 33609 Office: 610 N Florida Av Tampa FL 33602

FIELDS, DONALD EUGENE, ret. librarian; b. Martinsburg, O., Oct. 20, 1901; s. Joseph Cyrus and Etta (McDowell) F.; A.B., Lebanon Valley Coll., 1924; M.A. in Classics, Princeton U., 1928; Ph.D. in Latin, U. Chgo., 1935; M.S. in L.S., U. Mich., 1947; m. Frances Fulton Twaddle, Aug. 1, 1942. Master in Latin, Palmer Inst., Starkey, N.Y., 1924-25, Chestnut Hill (Pa.) Acad., 1926-27; acting prof. Latin, Lebanon Valley Coll., 1928-30; instr. Latin, Ia. State Tchrs. Coll., 1931-32, Muskingum Coll., New Concord, O., 1936-42; asso. librarian Lebanon Valley Coll., 1947-56, librarian, prof. Latin, 1957-70. Served with USAAF, 1942-45. Mem. Am. Philol. Assn., Pa. Library Assn. Home: 46 S Lancaster St Annville PA 17003

FIELDS, DOROTHY, song writer; b. Allenhurst, N.J., July 15, 1905; d. Lew Fields. Writer songs for show at Cotton Club, N.Y.C.; with Jimmy McHugh wrote for Lew Leslie's Blackbirds, 1928, including I Can't Give you Anything But Love, On the Sunny Side of the Street, Don't Blame Me, Lovely to Look At, I'm in the Mood for Love, Exactly Like You; writer scenarios, musical shows with her brother Herbert including Let's Face It, Something for the Boys, Mexican Hayride, Up In Central Park, Annie Get You Gun, Arms and the Girl (words only). Winner Acad. Award for song The Way You Look Tonight (with Jerome Kern), 1936; (play) Sweet Charity, 1966. Office: care ASCAP 575 Madison Av New York City NY 10022

FIELDS, EMMETT B., univ. dean; b. Ft. Smith, Ark., Nov. 19, 1923; s. Emmett B. and Rose Almeda (Black) F.; B.A. magna cum laude, Ouachita Coll., Arkadelphia, Ark., 1948; M.A., Vanderbilt U., 1950, Ph.D. in Am. History, 1953; m. Mary Christine Arnold, Aug. 31, 1947; children—Ross Christopher, Laura Alison, Mary Leslie. Asst., then fellow in history Vanderbilt U., 1950- 52; asso. prof. history Jacksonville (Ala.) State Coll., 1952-54, prof., chmn. dept., 1955-57; dir. summer sessions, asso. dean Coll. Arts and Scis., Vanderbilt U., 1957-60, dean Coll. Arts and Scis., 1960-69; v.p., dean of faculties U. Houston, 1969—. Mem. commn. colls. and univs. So. Assn. Colls. and Schs., 1961-67, chmn., 1964-65, pres., 1969-70, trustee, 1965—. Mem. So. Conf. Acad. Deans, Am., So. hist. assns., Orgn. Am. Historians, Am. Conf. Acad. Deans (exec. council 1969). Presbyn. Home: 459 Westminster Dr Houston TX 77024

FIELDS, JOHN EDWIN, univ. adminstr.; b. Bismarck, N.D., Jan. 20, 1915; s. Paris Ransom and Clara (Collins) F.; B.S., Northwestern U., 1936; student Japanese lang., history, econ. politics, militarism, 1937-43; M.B.A., U. Cal. at Los Angeles, 1960; m. Jean Maxine Rogers, June 21, 1941; children—Christopher Clay, Julie Ransom. Free lance writer, Japan, China, 1937; alumni, pub. relations Northwestern U., 1938-43; acting chief Japan-Korea sect. Pacific bur. psychological warfare (overseas shortwave broadcasting), O.W.I., San Francisco, 1943, chief Japan div., 1944-45; chief Japan sect. internat. broadcasting div. Dept. State, San Francisco, 1945-46; editor, pub. Far East Trader, 1946-49; pres. Farm Implement Co., 1947-48; v.p. U.S. Tractor & Engring Co., 1947-48; dir. devel. U. So. Cal., 1948-52, v.p. charge devel., 1952-56; exec. v.p. Maple Investment, Inc., 1957-66; also partner Valley Vista Investment Co., Phoenix, 1960-68; pres. Apsco Products, Inc. div. Maple Industries, Inc., dir. parent co., 1958-71; v.p. Northwestern U., 1971—; dir. Computer Equipment Corp., Placer County Land Co., G.A. Brakeley & Co., Inc., Mem. Am. Alumni Council (v.p., 1941-42, dir., 1942-43), Am. Coll. Pub. Relations Assn. (v.p. 1953-56), Pub. Relations Soc. Am. (dir. 1952-56. western regional v.p. 1956). Presbyn. Home: 624 Noyes Evanston IL

FIELDS, LEWIS JEFFERSON, ret. marine corps officer; b. Delmar, Md., Oct. 1, 1909; s. Levi Lewis and Annie (Hancock) F.; B.A., St. John's Coll., 1931; m. Mary Elizabeth Packer, June 9, 1937; children—Elizabeth Packer (Mrs. Walter Frederick Roberts, Jr.), Mary Anne. Mem. Md. N.G., 1925-32; enlisted USMC, 1932, commd. 2d lt., 1935, advanced through grades to lt. gen., 1968; various assignments naval and marine bases U.S., 1935-42; bn. comdg. officer 11th Marines, 1st Div., Guadalcanal, 1942-43, Cape Gloucester, 1943; assigned G-3, 1st Marine Div., 1944, participating in seizure of Peleliu and Ngesebus; aide to comdt. Marine Corps, 1945-47; staff Comdr.-in- Chief Atlantic Command and U.S. Atlantic Fleet, 1948; asst. to U.S. rep. North Atlantic Ocean regional planning group NATO; asst. chief staff personnel and adminstrn. Supreme Allied Command Atlantic, 1951; head plans br. G-3 div. Hdqrs. Marine Corps, mem. joint strategic plans com. Joint Chiefs Staff, 1951-53; asst. chief staff G-2, later comdg. officer 11th Marines, Korea, 1953-54; chief plans sect. SHAPE, Paris, 1954-56; asst. chief staff G-3, later chief staff Hdqrs. Fleet Marine Force Atlantic, 1956-57; liaison officer to vice chief naval operations, Washington, 1957; dep. dir. plans and policy Office Joint Chiefs Staff, 1958-60; comdg. gen. Force Troops, Fleet Marine Force Pacific, also comdg. gen. Marine Base, Twentynine Palms, Cal., 1960-62; dir. personnel Hdqrs. Marine Corps, 1962-65; comdg. gen. 1st Marine Div., Fleet Marine Force, Vietnam, 1965-66, 5th Marine Div., Fleet Marine Force, Camp Pendleton, Cal., 1966-67, 4th Marine Div., also Marine Corps Base, Camp Pendleton, 1967-68, Marine Corps Devel. and Edn. Command, Quantico, 1968-70. Decorated D.S.M., Bronze Star, Legion of Merit (U.S.); Vietnam Nat. Order, Vietnam Cross of Gallantry. Episcopalian. Home: 8914 Lynnhurst Dr Fairfax VA 22030

FIELDS, OGDEN WILSON, govt. ofcl.; b. San Francisco, Mar. 4, 1910; s. Ambrose Jackson and Elizabeth (Swearingen) F.; student San Mateo Jr. Coll., 1930-31; A.B., U. Cal. at Berkeley, 1933; postgrad. Columbia, 1938, Maxwell Sch. Citizenship and Pub. Affairs, Syracuse, N.Y., 1938-41; LL.B., George Washington U., 1949; m. Mildred

Peterson Gumaer, Oct. 28, 1940; children-Sarah Mulock (Mrs. John F. Paul), Walter Swearingen, Grace Elizabeth (Mrs. Stephen Woodard). Sales mgr. San Francisco Examiner, Hearst Co., 1927-34; br. mgr. Lucky Lager Brewing Co., 1935; dir. State Unemployment Relief, Plumas County, Cal., 1935; labor coordinator WPA No. Cal., 1936; mgr. Migratory Labor Camp, Marysville, Cal., 1937; field examiner, adminstrv. examiner NLRB, Washington, 1941-51, asst. exec. sec., 1948-51, asso. exec. sec., 1951-60, exec. sec., 1960—; sec. Lake Guymard Devel. Holding Corp. Pres., del. P.T.A., 1951-62; mem. Consumers League, Suburban Md. Fair Housing, 1964-67. Pres. Evanswood Citizens Assn.; v.p. Allied Civic Group; bd. dirs. Suburban Md. Fair Rep. Recipient Commendation award NLRB, 1962, Del. Emeritus award Allied Civic Group, 1960. Mem. Am., Fed. bar assns., Indsl. Relations Research Assn. (past pres. D.C. chpt.), N.A.A.C.P., Urban League, Am. Civil Liberties Union. Home: 614 Greenbriar Dr Silver Spring MD 20910 Office: 1717 Pennsylvania Av NW Washington DC 20570

FIELDS, RALPH RAYMOND, educator; b. Prescott, Ariz., Apr. 29, 1907; s. Ralph Henson and Edna (Holmes) F.; student Phoenix Jr. Coll., 1924-26; A.B., U. Ariz., 1929; A.M., Stanford, 1934, Ed.D., 1940; m. Catherine Julia Tinker, Aug. 24, 1931; children—Ralph Rodney, Kay Louise. Instr., Phoenix Union High Sch., 1930-34, asst. dir. research and guidance, 1934-35; curriculum field sec. Stanford U. Santa Barbara Curriculum Project, 1936-38; asst. prof. edn. Stanford, 1938-41; curriculum dir. San Jose (Cal.) Unified Sch. Dist., 1941-42, asst. supt. schs., 1942-45, supt. schs., 1945-47; asso. supt., chief div. instrn. Cal. State Dept. Edn., 1947-48; exec. officer div. of instrn., prof. edn. Tchrs. Coll., Columbia, 1948-50, dir. div. instrn., prof. edn., 1950-59, asso. dean, 1959-61, prof. higher edn., 1961—; chief party Tchrs. Coll. ICA Mission, East Africa, 1961-62, AID sponsored project in Peru, 1966-68: dir. Office Overseas Projects, 1969-71, chief party Tchrs. Coll. AID sponsored project in Afghanistan, 1971—. Mem. survey staff for P.R. pub. schs., 1948-49; mem. Cal. State Curriculum Commn., 1945-47, chmn. The Cal. Framework Com., 1947-48. Dir. or cons., ednl. workshops and curriculum programs: dir. Community Coll. Study, Pa. Bd. Edn., 1964-65; liaison officer, cons. Asso. Colls. Mid-Hudson Area. Mem. N.E.A., Am. Assn. U. Profs., Am. Assn. Sch. Adminstrs., Am. Ednl. Research Assn., Am. Assn. Jr. Colls. (chmn. com. on curriculum and adult edn. 1952-53). Author: Community College Movement; Interinstitutional Cooperation The Associated Colleges of the Mid-Hudson Area; Community Colleges in Pennsylvania; Kingsborough Community College: Final Report. Contbr. to The Public Junior College, fifty-fifth year-book, Nat. Soc. Study Edn., 1956; articles to profl. jours. Home: Curtis Point Mantoloking NJ 08738 Office: Tchrs Coll Columbia U New York City NY 10028

FIELDS, ROBERT CHARLES, printing co. exec.; b. Tipton, Ia., Aug. 18, 1920; s. Forrest Filson and Frieda (Werling) F.; B.S. in Mech. Engring., Ia. State U., 1949; grad. Advanced Mgmt. Program, Harvard, 1961; m. Velma Mae Ohlsen, Oct. 26, 1941; children—Michael, David. with R.R. Donnelley & Sons Co., 1949—, mfg. div. dir., 1958-63, v.p., 1959-65, dir. sales div., 1963-68, sr. v.p., 1965-71, group dir., 1968—, group v.p., 1971—. Bd. govs. Ia. State U. Found. Served to 2d lt. USAAF, 1942-45. Mem. Newberry Library Assn., Ill. C. of C. (dir.), Art Inst., Field Mus., Book Mfrs. Inst. (v.p.). Clubs: University, Iowa State Univ., Harvard Business (Chgo.); Indianapolis Athletic. Home: 5317 Turvey Ct Downers Grove IL 60515 Office: 2223 King Dr Chicago IL 60616

FIELDS, ROY DUANE, aerospace co. exec.; b. Yakima, Wash., July 27, 1931; s. Orville Roy and Beatrice (Blystone) F.; B.A., San Diego State Coll., 1955; m. Geraldine Worthy, Sept. 10, 1955; children—Karen, Lawrence, Kenneth. With Teledyne Ryan Aero., San Diego, Cal., and predecessor firm, 1955—, v.p. finance, controller, 1969—. Dir. San Diego Taxpayers Assn., 1970-71. Recipient Silver Knight award, Nat. Mgmt. Assn., 1970. Mem. Nat. Mgmt. Assn., Nat. Assn. Accountants, Nat. Contract Mgmt. Assn., Sigma Chi. Home: 1978 Garrison Way El Cajon CA 92020 Office: 2701 Harbor Dr San Diego CA 92112

FIELDS, VICTOR ALEXANDER, vocal research specialist; b. Phila., Pa., Feb. 3, 1901; s. Solomon Alexander and Julia (Ross) F.; student singing, music and dramatics privately, U.S.A. and Europe, Julliard Sch. Music, Teachers Coll., Columbia U., 1919-30; B.S., Coll. City N.Y., 1926; M.A., Columbia U., 1930, Ph.D., 1946; m. Mary Elizabeth Cameron, Jan. 27, 1943. Began musical career in 1919; sang in light opera, oratorio, church and concert; tchr. voice, dramatics and speech; prof. voice and diction City Coll. N.Y., 1926-69, emeritus prof. voice and diction, 1969—, dir. voice and speech clinic, 1932-57, deptl. supr., evening div., 1941-66; vis. prof. U. Ore., summer, 1938. 40, Butler U., 1949. Asst. in speech rehab. of disabled war vets., VA, Army Hall speech Clinic, 1946-49; mem. N.Y. City Bd. Edn. com. surveying handicapped children in pub. schs., 1936-39. Mem. Music Educators Nat. Conf., Assn. for Higher Edn., Nat. Assn. Tchrs. Singing, Music Tchrs. Nat. Assn., Collegiate Chorale N.E. A., Acoustical Soc. Am., Phi Mu Alpha, Phi Delta Kappa. Mason. Author: Training the Singing Voice, 1947; The Singer's Glossary, 1951. Co-author books including: Taking the Stage, 1939; Voice and Diction, 1949. Home: 9400 Atlantic Av Margate NJ 08402 ☆

FIELDS, VICTOR HUGO, chemist; b. Milw., July 11, 1907; s. James Andrew and Willie (Finley) F.; B.A., Fisk U., 1931, M.A., 1935; Ph.D., Marquette U., 1944; m. Carrie Nicholas, May 24, 1941 (div. Feb. 1954); 1 son, Victor Hugo. Instr. Fisk U., 1935-41, asst. prof., 1941-57; prof., chmn. dept. chem. Fla. A. and M. Coll., 1947-49; prof. chemistry, chmn. dept. natural scis. and math. Hampton Inst., 1949—, dir. div. sci. and math., chmn. dept. chemistry, 1967—; cons. Kolmar Labs., Milw., 1944-46. Mem. Am. Chem. Soc., Nat. Inst. Sci., A.A.A.S., Va. Acad. Sci., Beta Kappa Chi, Omega Psi Phi. Mem. Ch. of Christ. Club: Bachelor Benedict (Hampton). Home: 911 Victoria Blvd Hampton Institute Hampton VA 23361

FIELDS, WILLIAM ALBERT, lawyer; b. Parkersburg, W.Va., Mar. 30, 1939; s. Jack Lyons and Grace (Kelley) F.; B.S. magna cum laude, Ohio State U., 1961; postgrad. Harvard Law Sch., 1961-64; m. Prudence Brandt Adams, June 26, 1964. Admitted to Ohio bar, 1964, since practiced in Marietta; partner Strecker & Fields, 1964—; city prosecutor, Marietta, 1964-65; dir. elections Washington County, 1967—. Chmn. Washington County Heart Assn., 1965-67; county chmn. Am. Cancer Soc., 1967; mem. dist. exec. com. Boy Scouts Am., 1967—. Treas. County Republican Exec. Com., 1966- -; county chmn. Nixon for Pres., 1968; county chmn. Saxbe for Senator, 1968. Trustee, Salvation Army. Recipient Meritorious Service award Am. Heart Assn., 1968, Wall St. Jour. award, 1961; named Outstanding Young Man of Marietta, 1968. Mem. Ohio, Washington County bar assns., Marietta Area C. of C. (com. chmn.), Sigma Chi, Beta Gamma Sigma. Rotarian (pres. 1970-71). Club: Marietta Country (trustee). Home: 129 Hillcrest Dr Marietta OH 45750 Office: Peoples Bank Bldg Marietta OH 45750

FIELDS, WILLIAM HENRY, editor; b. Edison, Ga., Mar. 6, 1915; s. Edward Blount and Lura (Rish) F.; student U. Ala., 1931-34; m. Hazel Eugenia Cobb, June 19, 1943; children—William Cobb, Nancy Virginia. Sports editor, gen. assignment reporter Dothan (Ala.) Eagle, 1935; various editorial capacities Dothan Eagle, Nashville Tennesseean, Savannah (Ga.) Morning News, 1935-47; editorial asst. Atlanta Constn., 1947, asso. editor, 1947-51, mng. editor, 1951-64; mng. editor Atlanta Jour., 1964-67; exec. editor Atlanta Jour. and Const n., 1968-70, v.p., 1970—. Served with USMCR, 1942-46. Mem. Am. Soc. Newspaper Editors, Marine Corps Res. Officers Assn., Ga. Press Assn. (bd. mgrs.), Sigma Delta Chi. Home: 565 High Brook Dr N E Atlanta GA 30305 Office: Atlanta Newspapers Inc Atlanta GA 30303

FIELDS, WILLIAM STRAUS, educator, neurologist; b. Balt., Aug. 18, 1913; s. Arthur Mortimer and Lenore (Straus) F.; A.B., Harvard, 1934, M.D., 1938; m. Elizabeth May Ritchie, Dec. 18, 1941; children—Susan Katherine, Anne Ritchie. Intern pathology Nashville Gen. Hosp., 1938-39; intern medicine Children's Meml. Hosp., Montreal, Can., 1939-40; asst. resident medicine Royal Victoria Hosp., Montreal, 1940-41; asst. resident neurology Montreal Neurol. Inst., 1941; resident, fellow neuropsychiatry Washington U. Sch. Medicine, St. Louis, 1946-49; mem. faculty Baylor U. Coll. Medicine, Houston, 1949-65, prof. neurology, 1951-67, chmn. dept., 1959-65; prof. neurology U. Tex., Southwestern Med. Sch., Dallas, 1967-69, U. Tex. Grad. Sch. Biomed. Sci., Houston, 1969-70, U. Tex. Med. Sch., Houston, 1970—. Pres. Houston Acad. Medicine, 1962; mem. med. adv. bd. Myasthenia Gravis Found., chmn., 1969-71. Served with Royal Canadian Navy, 1941-46. Decorated Order Brit. Empire. Diplomate Am. Bd. Psychiatry and Neurology. Mem. Am. Acad. Neurology, Assn. Research Nervous and Mental Diseases, Am. Epilepsy Soc., Am. Neurol. Assn., Am. Assn. Neurol. Surgeons, Canadian Neurol. Soc., A.M.A., Am. Assn. U. Profs., Am. Congress Rehab. Medicine, Houston Neurol. Soc. (pres. 1969-71), La Sociedad Peruana de Psiquiatría, Neurología y Neurocirugía, Sociedad Neurologica de Colombia, Sociedad de Neurología y Neurocirurgía de Montevideo (Uruguay), World Fedn. Neurology, Research Group on Cerebral Circulation, Author 15 books, numerous papers. Home: 225 Stoney Creek Houston TX 77024

FIELDS, WILMER CLEMONT, clergyman; b. Saline, La., Mar. 16, 1922; s. Felder Burkett and Eva Mae (Corbett) F.; B.A., La. Coll., Pineville, 1943; Th. M., So. Bapt. Theol. Sem., Louisville, 1946, Th.D., 1950; m. Rebecca Elizabeth Hagan, June 22, 1946; children—Randall Hagan, Christy Alderson, Rebecca Borden, Student pastor in La., 1940-43; music and ednl. dir. Carlisle Av. Bapt. Ch., Louisville, 1943-48; ordained to ministry Bapt. Ch., 1940; pastor in Louisville, 1948-51, Yazoo City, Miss., 1951-56; editor Bapt. Record, jour. for Miss., 1956-59; pub. relations sec., exec. com. So. Bapt. Conv., 1959—, also press rep., dir. conv. bull. service; editor of the Bapt. Program mag., 1959—; dir. Bapt. Press, SBC News Service, 1959—. Nat. pres. Religious Pub. Relations Council, 1966-67; pres. Asso. Ch. Press, 1967-69. Mem. Pub. Relations Soc. Am., Bapt. Pub. Relations Assn., Bapt. Press Assn., Evang. Press Assn., Pi Kappa Delta, Alpha Chi, Alpha Psi Omega. Author: The Chains Are Strong, 1963; Trumpets in Dixie, 1968. Home: 2223 Woodmont Blvd Nashville TN 37215. Office: 460 James Robertson Pkwy Nashville TN 37219

FIELDSTEEL, HAROLD, liquor co. exec.; b. N.Y.C., Feb. 10, 1922; s. Max and Belle (Rosenfeld) F.; B.B.A., Coll. City N.Y., 1941; student Harvard Grad. Sch. Bus. Adminstrn., 1943; m. Lorena Lewis, Feb. 23, 1946; children—Laura, Danial. With Joseph E. Seagram & Sons Inc., 1941—, controller, 1967—, v.p. finance, 1968—, also dir.; treas., controller Distillers Corp.-Seagrams Ltd., 1971—; dir. P.R. Distillers Corp., Seagram Distillers Ltd. (U.K.), numerous others; instr. controllership Grad. Sch. Bus., Baruch Sch. Bus., 1958- 61. Served to maj. AUS, 1942-46. C.P.A., Tenn. Mem. Am. Inst. C.P.A.'s, Beta Gamma Sigma. Home: 76 Whitehall Blvd Garden City NY 11530 Office: 375 Park Av New York City NY 10022

FIENUP, WILLIAM FRED JOHN, realty co. exec.; b. New Melle, Mo., Dec. 16, 1890; s. Henry Fred and Elise (Hetlage) F.; student City Coll. Law and Finance, St. Louis, also Alexander Hamilton corr. courses; m. Gertrude May Lehr, Oct. 12, 1918; children—Wilbur, Raymond. From office boy to office mgr. Am. Can Co., 1907-22; with R.C. Can Co., St. Louis, 1922-68, exec. v.p., 1961, pres., 1961-68; now pres. Justine Realty Co. Bd. dirs. St. Louis YMCA; sec.-treas. Found. for Jr. Trapshooters. Mem. Nat. Fibre Can and Tube Assn. (pres. 1960-61; bd. dirs. 1961—), N.A.M., U.S., Mo., St. Louis chambers commerce. Lutheran. Mason (32). Inventor easy opening biscuit can, spl. telescope can. Home: Route 2 Box 76 Chesterfield MO 63017

FIERING, MYRON B., educator; b. N.Y.C., Apr. 5, 1934; s. Simon and Elaine (Fox) F.; A.B., Harvard, 1955, S.M., 1958, Ph.D., 1960; m. Jill Marin, Aug. 17, 1957; children—Suzanne Ellen, Lisa Ann. Soils engr. TAMS, Inc., N.Y.C., 1955- 57; asst. prof. engring. U. Cal. at Los Angeles, 1960-61; research fellow engring. Harvard, 1961-62, mem. faculty, 1962—, Gordon McKay prof. engring. and applied math., 1969—. Served with USNR, 1952. Fulbright lectr. Australia, 1964; recipient gold medal for excellence Interam. Assn. San. Engring., 1962. Mem. Am. Soc. C.E., A.A.A.S., Operations Research Soc. Am., Inst. Mgmt. Sci., Sigma Xi. Author: (with M. Hufschmidt) Simulation Techniques for the Design of Water Resource Systems, 1966; Streamflow Synthesis, 1967. Home: 328 Old Lancaster Rd Sudbury MA 01776 Office: Picrce Hall Harvard Univ Cambridge MA 02138

FIERMAN, HAROLD LEE, lawyer; b. N.Y.C., Apr. 1, 1898; s. Morris and Anne (Ackerman) F.; LL.B., Fordham U., 1920; m. Ruth Kaplan, Feb. 15, 1922 (dec.); children—Joan (Mrs. Alan Lerrick), Karel (Mrs. Sigmund Wahrsager); m. 2d, Minnie Ganz Sarnoff, Jan. 27, 1963. Admitted to N.Y. State bar, 1920; sr. partner Kaye, Scholer, Fierman, Hays & Handler, N.Y.C., 1922- -. Chmn. Pacific Coast Properties, Inc.; dir., mem. exec. com. J.W. Mays, Inc.; dir. Petrie Stores Corp. Pres. Fierman Found., Inc.; trustee, v.p., mem. exec. com. Beth Israel Med. Center; trustee Mt. Sinai Sch. Medicine, Brandeis U. Mem. Am. Bar Assn. Clubs: Lawyers, Harmonie (N.Y.C.); Old Oaks Country (Purchase, N.Y.). Home: 700 Park Av New York City NY 10021 Office: 425 Park Av New York City NY 10022

FIERS, ALAN DALE, clergyman; b. Kankanee, Ill., Dec. 17, 1906; s. George Allen and Leah (Grubbs) F.; A.B., Bethany Coll., 1929, D.D., 1945; B.D., Yale Div. Sch., 1935; L.L.D., Tex. Christian U., 1952; L.H.D., Culver-Stockton Coll., 1957; m. Elizabeth Kunz, July 14, 1931; children—Barbara Louise (Mrs. Hugh Edward Joyce), Alan Dale. Ordained to ministry Disciples of Christ Ch., 1929: pastor Shadyside, O., 1929-31, Hamilton, O., 1935-39, Newark, O., 1939-45, Euclid Av. Christian Ch., Cleve., 1945-51; pres. United Christian Missionary Soc., bd. missions and edn. Disciples of Christ, 1951-64; gen. minister, pres. Christian Ch., 1964—; v.p. World Council Christian Edn.; dir unified promotion, mem. council on Christian unity. Mem. bd. Fundamental Edn.; mem. gen. bd. Nat. Council Chs. of Christ in U.S. Bd. dirs. Doctor's Hosp., Cleve.; trustee Bethany Coll., Butler U., Indpls., Christian Theol. Sem., Indpls. Mem. Beta Theta Pi. Republican. Club: Indianapolis Athletic. Author: This is Missions, 1953; Lord Teach Us to Pray, 1960; Prayer and the Great Decisions of Life, 1960; The Christian World Mission, 1966. Home: 5452 University Av Indianapolis IN 46219 Office: 221 Ohmer Av Indianapolis IN 46219

FIERY, BENJAMIN FRANKLIN, lawyer; b. Martinsburg, W.Va., Apr. 19, 1894; s. Samuel V. and Emily (Dukehart) F.; A.B., Washington and Lee U., 1913; LL.B., Harvard, 1916; M. Virginia Biechele, Sept. 13, 1924; 1 dau., Anne (Mrs. Richard C. Byran). Admitted to W.Va. bar, 1916, Ohio bar, 1917, U.S. Supreme Ct., 1921; with firm Banker, Hostetler & Sidlo, Cleve., 1916-17; pvt. sec. to sec. of war Newton D. Banker, 1920-21; mem. firm Baker, Hostetler & Patterson, Cleve., 1925—. Dir. Buckeye Pine Line Co., N.Y.C. Trustee Law Library Assn. Served as 2d lt., air service, U.S. Army, 1917-19. Mem. Am., Ohio, Cleve. bar assns., Am. Judicature Soc., Omicron Delta Kappa. Delta Tau Delta. Clubs: Union, Tavern, Nisi Prius (Cleve.). Home: 2676 Eaton Rd Cleveland OH 44118 Office: Union Commerce Bldg Cleveland OH 44115

FIESENHEISER, ELMER IRVING, educator; b. South Bend, Ind., Aug. 4, 1906; s. Christian G. and Dorothea (Schubert) F.; B.S. with distinction, Purdue U., 1930, C.E., 1945; M.S., Ill. Inst. Tech., 1946; m. Ellen Carlson, Dec. 27, 1930; 1 dau., Ellen Florence. Civil engr. Am. Bridge Co., 1930-35, U.S. Bur. Pub. Roads, 1935-41, Chgo. San. Dist., 1941-42, Arthur G. McKee & Co., 1941-43; faculty Ill. Inst. Te ch., 1943—, prof. civil engring., 1953—, chmn. civil engring., 1953-69; cons. structural engr., 1943—. Fellow Am. Soc. C.E.; mem. Am. Concrete Inst., Am. Soc. Engring. Edn., Structural Engrs. Assn. Ill., Sigma Xi. Author: Versalog, 1951. Home: 10617 S Hoyne Av Chicago IL 60643

FIESER, LOUIS FREDERICK, ret. educator, chemist; b. Columbus, O., Apr. 7, 1899; s. Louis Frederick and Martha Victoria (Kershaw) F.; A.B., Williams Coll., 1920, hon. D.Sc., 1939; Ph.D., Harvard, 1924; postgrad., Frankfort-on-Main, 1924-25, Oxford U., 1925; Dr. honoris causa, U. Paris, 1954; m. Mary A. Peters, June 21, 1932. Asst. and asso. prof. chemistry Bryn Mawr Coll., 1925-30; asst. prof., asso. prof. chemistry Harvard, 1930-37, prof., 1937-39, Sheldon Emery prof. organic chemistry, 1939-68, prof. emeritus, 1968—; scholar in residence State U. N.Y., 1969; Neilson prof. Smith Coll., spring 1968. Engaged in research relating to cancer and chemotherapeutic studies. Mem. Nat. Def. Research Com., 1940-46, Surgeon Gen.'s Adv. Com. Smoking and Health, 1963; cons. on cortisone synthesis mem. Alos Mission, ETO, U.S. Army. Served in O.T.C., 1918. Recipient Katherine Berkan Judd prize for work on cancer-producing hydrocarbons Meml. Hosp., 1941; award for teaching Mfg. Chemists Assn., 1959; Norris award, 1959; Nichols medal Am. Chem. Soc., 1963; Am. Chem. Soc. award in chem. edn., 1967. Fellow Nat. Acad. Sci., 1939. Author: Experiments in Organic Chemistry; (with Mary Fieser) Organic Chemistry, Style Guide for Chemists; Reagents for Organic Synthesis, Vols. 1, 2; also over 300 research papers. Mem. editorial bds. Organic Syntheses, others. Home: 27 Pinehurst Rd Belmont MA 02178

FIEWEGER, WILLIAM HENRY, co. exec.; b. June 14, 1914; m. Marion Heany, Sept. 6, 1948; 5 children. Formerly v.p., dir. Kimberly-Clark Corp., Neenah, Wis.; now pres., dir. George Banta Co., Inc., Menasha, Wis.; dir. Bank of Menasha. Chmn. bd. trustees St. Norbert Coll., West De Pere, Wis. Home: 398 Willow Lane Menasha WI 54952

FIFE, AUSTIN EDWIN, educator; b. Lincoln, Ida., Dec. 18, 1909; s. Robert H. and Mary Elizabeth (Stocks) F.; B.A., Stanford, 1934, Ph.D., 1939; M.A., Harvard, 1937; m. Alta Stevens, Mar. 27, 1934; children—Carolyn (Mrs. David S. Langdon), Marian. Prof. French, Occidental Coll., Los Angeles, 1950-58; specialist for langs. U.S. Office Edn., 1959-60; prof. French, head dept. langs. Utah State U., Logan, 1960—. Served to lt. col. USAF, 1942-45, 51-53. Fulbright exchange prof. French Nat. Museums, 1950-51, Guggenheim fellow, 1958-59. Mem. Modern Lang. Assn. Am., Rocky Mountain Modern Lang. Assn., Am. Folklore Soc. (v.p.). Author: (with Mrs. Fife) Saints of Sage and Saddle, 1956, Borzoi Book of French Folk Tales, 1956, Songs of the Cowboys, 1966, Cowboy and Western Songs, 1968; Ballads of the Great West, 1970; Forms upon the Frontier, 1969; Heaven on Horseback, 1969. Mem. editorial bd. Western Folklore Quar. 1948- -. Contbr. articles profl. jours. Home: 686 E 10th North Logan UT 84321

FIFE, JAMES, ret. naval officer; b. Reno, Jan. 22, 1897; grad. U.S. Naval Acad., 1917; LL.D., U. Nev., 1946. Commd. ensign, U.S. Navy, 1917, and advanced through the grades to admiral, 1955; served in U.S. ships Tacoma, Chicago, Sea Gull, Beaver, Elcano, Monocacy, Idaho, Leary, Hatfield; comdr. U.S.S. Nautilus, 1935- 37, and submarine Div. Twelve, 1937; officer in charge Submarine Sch., New London, Conn., 1938-40; asst. naval attache, Am. Embassy, London, Eng., 1940, assigned to submarine service with Brit. Navy in Eng. and Mediterranean; comdr. Submarine Div. Sixty-two, 1941; chief of staff to comdr. submarines, Asiatic Fleet, 1941 (force operating against Japanese attacks in Philippines Islands and Netherlands East Indies); comdr. submarine squadron, also asst. operating officer on staff of comdr. Southwestern Pacific Force, 1942; comdr. of task force, 1942-44; following duty at hdqrs. Comdr. in chief, U.S. Fleet, returned to Pacific area as comdr. Submarine 7th Fleet; mem. joint strategic survey com. joint chiefs of Staff, Washington; dep. chief U.S. Naval Operations, 1951-53; naval dep. to Comdr. in Chief, Allied Forces, Mediterranean, 1953-55; ret. Decorated D.S.M. with 2 gold stars, Army Distinguished Unit Badge, Navy Unit Commendation, Victory medal with escort clasp; Yangtze Service, Navy Expeditionary, Am. Def. Service with fleet clasp, Asiatic-Pacific Area Campaign and Philippines Def. and Liberation medals; hon. comdr. Military Div., Order Brit. Empire; Grand Officer of Order of Orange-Nassau with Swords (Netherlands). Mason (33). Home: Westerly Rd Stonington CT 06378

FIFIELD, HARRY AMOS, clergyman; b. Schenectady, June 22, 1910; s. Stephen Harvey and Letty (Gates) F.; A.B., U. Fla., 1933; Th.B., Princeton Theol. Sem., 1936; D.D. (hon.), Hampden Sidney Coll., 1953; L.H.D., Oglethorpe U., 1971; m. Margaret Edna McIntosh, Aug. 21, 1937; children—Stephen McIntosh, Margaret Ann (Mrs. James H. Endicott), Harry Ames. Ordained to ministry Presbyn. Ch., 1936; minister in Steelton, Pa., 1936-42, Deland, Fla., 1942-43, Lynchburg, Va., 1946-53, First Presbyn. Ch., Atlanta, 1953—; radio broadcaster. Mem. gen. council Presbyn. Ch., 1960, chmn. com. assembly operations, 1960-67; moderator Atlanta Presbytery, 1964, Synod Ga., 1968-69; mem. exec. bd. Christian Council Met. Atlanta, 1967—; mem. editorial com. Atlanta Minister's Manifesto on Racial Justice, 1957-58. Mem. U.S.O. council Greater Atlanta. Trustee Stillman Coll., Agnes Scott Coll., Columbia Theol. Sem.; bd. dirs. Protestant Radio and TV Center, Presbyn. Center, Met. Atlanta chpt. A.R.C., Atlanta chpt. Am. Assn. UN. Served as chaplain USNR, 1943-46. Recipient Distinguished Service award Anti-Defamation League of B'nai B'rith, 1958. Mem. Delta Tau Delta, Phi Eta Sigma, Kappa Kappa Psi, Blue Key. Kiwanian. Home: 1678 Doncaster Dr N E Atlanta GA 30309 Office: 1328 Peachtree St NE Atlanta GA 30309

FIFIELD, JAMES WILLIAM, Jr., clergyman; b. Chicago, Ill., June 5, 1899; s. James William and Mary Irene (Stoddard) F.; A.B., Oberlin (O.) Coll., 1921; student U. of Wis., summer 1919; M.A., U. of Chicago, 1922: B.D., Chicago Theol. Sem., 1924. D.D., 1934; m. Helen Ramsay, Sept. 30, 1929 (dec.); children—Mary R., H. Ramsay. Ordained to the ministry Conglist. Ch., 1924; minister at

Chamberlain, S.D., 1921-22, Woodstock, Ill., 1922-24. East Ch., Grand Rapids, Mich., 1924-35. 1st Ch., Los Angeles, 1935-67. Lecturer Sch. of Religion, U. of So. Calif., 1937; founder, nat. dir. moblzn. for spiritual ideals, 1935-55, chmn., 1955-57; nat. bd. Crusade for Freedom, 1950; speaker on coast to coast Freedom Story weekly broadcasts. Nat. Hoover Com. for Reorgn. Govt., 1949; now active Freedom Under God Crusade. Mem. bd. dirs. Freedom Library, Inc., Freedom Center, Govt. Research. Inc. Recipient Freedom Found. sermon award, 1947, 50, 51, 53, 55. Served in U.S. Inf., 1919. Mem. bd. Pomona (Cal.) Coll.; trustee Pacific Sch. Religion, Berkeley, Cal.; mem. corporate bd. Yankton Coll. Mem. bd. Am. China Policy Assn., 1950-57; regent Forest Lawn Meml. Pk.; dir. Freedom Clubs Inc. (founder). Mem. Theta Phi Fraternity. Republican. Clubs: Los Angeles Country. Caifornia, Lincoln. Author of magazine articles and books; contributor to religious journals and radio programs; TV program Straight From The Shoulder; TV program The Lighted Window; (book) The Single Path. Home: Freemont Pl Los Angeles CA 90005

FIFIELD, RUSSELL HUNT, educator; b. Readfield, Me., Feb. 21, 1914; s. Charlie Belle and Emma (Hunt) F.; A.B., Bates Coll., 1935, LL.D., 1963; M.A., Clark U., 1940, Ph.D., 1942. Specialist hist. research State Dept., 1944-45; Am. Fgn. service officer, China and Formosa, 1945-47; mem. faculty U. Mich., 1947—, prof. polit. sci., 1954—; Fulbright research prof. U. Philippines, 1953-54; prof. fgn. affairs Nat. War Coll., 1958-59; asso. research E. Asian Research Center, Harvard, 1967-68. Mem. adv. panel E. Asia and Pacific, State Dept., 1966-69; cons. Bur. Intelligence and Research, State Dept., 1953-54, 67-70; sec. gen. XXVII Internat. Congress Orientalists, 1964-67, exec. com. XXVIII and XXIX Congress, 1967. Guggenheim fellow, 1958-59; Council Fgn. Relations fellow, 1959-60; research fellow St. Antony's Coll., Oxford (Eng.) U., 1963-64, Twentieth Century Fund, 1967-69. Mem. Assn. Asian Studies (sec. 1961-63), Am. Polit. Sci. Assn., Am. Hist. Assn. (George Louis Beer prize 1953), Am. Soc. Internat. Law, Detroit Com. Fgn. Relations (chmn. 1970-71), Council Fgn. Relations N.Y., Phi Beta Kappa, Phi Kappa Phi. Club: Cosmos. Author: Woodrow Wilson and the Far East, 1952; Diplomacy of Southeast Asia, 1945-58, 1958; Southeast Asia in U.S. Policy, 1963. Home: 400 Maynard St Ann Arbor MI 48104

FIFIELD, WILLARD MERWIN, assn. exec.; b. Schenectady, Jan. 17, 1908; s. Stephen H. and Letty (Gates) F.; B.S.A., U. Fla., 1930, M.S., 1932; post-grad. Cornell U.; m. Hazel Hook, July 22, 1935. With U. Fla., 1930-62, beginning as grad. asst. Agrl. Expt. Sta., successively asst. horticulturist, horticulturist charge Subtropical Expt. Sta., asst. dir. sta. system, dir., 1930-55, provost for agr., 1955-62; sec., mgr. Fla. Agrl. Research Inst., 1962—. Past chmn. agrl. div. Fla. C. of C. Served to lt. col. USAAF, 1942-46. Recipient Distinguished Service award Fla. Seedmen's Assn., 1953; named Man of Year in Fla. Agr., Progressive Farmer mag., 1955; Ann. Distinguished Service award Fla. Fruit and Vegetable Assn., 1959. Fellow A.A.A.S.; mem. Assn. So. Agrl. Workers (past pres.), Assn. So. Agrl. Expt. Sta. Dir. (past chmn.), Com. of Nine (past chmn.), Fla. Hort. Soc. (pres. 1964), Soil Sci. Soc. Fla., Sigma Xi, Delta Tau Delta, Gamma Sigma Delta, Alpha Zeta, Phi Sigma, Gamma Sigma Epsilon, Fla. Blue Key, Scabbard and Blade. Presbyn. Rotarian. Contbr. articles profl. publs. Home: 1823 NW 7th Av Gainesville FL 32601 Office: 519 N E 1st St Gainesville FL 32601

FIFIELSKI, EDWIN PETER, lawyer; b. Chgo., Oct. 4, 1916; s. Walter A. and Bessie (Dombrowski) F.; LL.B., John Marshall Law Sch., 1940, J.D., 1950; m. Jewel Weglarz, June 18, 1944. Admitted to Ill. bar, 1940, since practiced in Chgo. Chmn. bd. Jefferson State Bank: pres. Spring Realty & Mortgage Co., Emancipator Ins. Agy., Inc. Alderman 45th ward, Chgo., 1963—. Mem. com. Chgo. council Boy Scouts Am., 1958—. Served from pvt. to capt. AUS, 1940-46. Mem. AMVETS (nat. comdr. 1961-62), Jefferson Park C. of C. (pres. 1959-61), Ill. Bar Assn., Am. Judicature Soc., Assn. Life Underwriters, Nat. Advocates Soc., Am. Legion, V.F.W., Chgo. Soc. (pres. 1971). K.C. Club: Jefferson Park Lions (pres. 1966-67). Office: 4758 N Milwaukee Av Chicago IL 60630

FIGEL, JOHN B., savs. and loan exec. Pres., dir. Joliet Fed. Savs. & Loan Assn. (Ill.). Home: 3108 Deer Path Dr Joliet IL 60435 Office: 120 N Scott St Joliet IL 60431*

FIGG, ROBERT MCCORMICK, Jr., lawyer; b. Radford, Va., Oct. 22, 1901; s. Robert McCormick and Helen Josephine (Cecil) F.; grad. Porter Mil. Acad., Charleston, S.C.; A.B., Coll. of Charleston, 1920, Litt. D., 1970; law student Columbia, 1920-22; LL.D., U. S.C., 1959; m. Sallie Alexander Tobias, May 10, 1927; children—Robert McCormick III, Emily (Mrs. Richard A. Dalla Mura), Jefferson Tobias. Admitted to S.C. bar, 1922, practiced in Charleston, 1922-59; circuit solicitor 9th Jud. Circuit of S.C., 1935-47; dean Law Sch., U.S.C., 1959-70; sr. counsel Robinson, McFadden, Moore & Pope, Charleston, 1970. Dir. Palmetto State Life Ins. Co., Home Fed. Savs. & Loan Assn. Mem. S.C. Reorgn. Commn., 1948—, chmn., 1951-55. Mem. S.C. Ho. of Reps., 1933-35. Pres. Coll. of Charleston Found.; trustee Saul Alexander Found. Fellow Am. Coll. Trial Lawyers; mem. Am. Soc. Internat. Law, Am. Acad. Polit. Sci., Am. Law Inst., Am. Judicature Soc., Inter-Am., Charleston County (pres. 1953), Am. (ho. of dels.), S.C. bars assns., S.C. State Bar (pres.), Phi Beta Kappa (hon.), Phi Delta Phi, Blue Key (hon.). Home: 1522 Deans Lane Columbia SC 29205 Office: Jefferson Bldg Charleston SC 29201

FIGGE, FRANK HENRY JOHN, scientist, anatomist; b. Silver Cliff, Colo., Dec. 23, 1904; s. John and Maria Barbara (Schwab) F; A.B., Colo. Coll., 1927, D.Sc. (hon.), 1968; student, Colo. U. Med. Sch., 1928-29; Ph.D., U. of Md. Med. and Grad. Schs., 1934; m. Rosalie Mary Yerkes, June 25, 1932; children—Rosalie Ann, Barbara Elizabeth. Asst. in biology, Colo. Coll., 1925-26, head asst. in biology and comparative anatomy, 1926-28; asst. in anatomy Colo. U. Sch. of Medicine, 1928-29; asst. in anatomy U. of Md. Sch. of Medicine, 1929-30, instr., 1930-34, asso., 1934-35, asst. prof., 1935-36. asso. prof., 1936-47, prof. exptl. anatomy, 1947-49, prof. anatomy, 1949—, head dept., 1955—; chmn. Anatomy Bd. Md., 1955—; vis. prof. anatomy U. Pa., 1948-49; Rockefeller fellow Yale Univ. Med. Sch., 1940-41. Mem. bd. trustees of Biol. Stain Commn., 1947—, pres., 1954-56. Fellow A.A.A.S.; mem. Am. Assn. Anatomists (exec. com. 1953-57), Am. Acad. of Neurology, Am. Cancer Soc. (v.p. 1952-56; Md. div. bd. dirs., mem. exec. com. 1948- -, pres. 1956-62), Am. Genetic Soc., Am. Soc. Naturalists, Histochem. Soc., Soc. Exptl. Biology and Medicine, Am. Assn. for Cancer Research, Marine Biol. Corp., Am. Assn. Med. Colls., So. Soc. Cancer Cytology, Sigma Xi, Delta Epsilon. Club: Torch (pres. Balt. chpt. 1953-54). Author of articles med. subjects to tech. jours. Asso. editor Stain Technology, 1958-65. Am. editor Atlas of Human Anatomy. Address: U Md Med Sch 29 S Greene St Baltimore MD 21201

FIGGIE, HARRY E., Jr., corp. exec.; b. 1923; B.S., Case Inst. Tech., 1947; M.B.A., Harvard, 1949; LL.B., Cleve. Marshall Law Sch.; married; 3 children. Formerly with Western Automatic Screw Machine Co., Parker-Hannifin Corp. and Booz, Allen & Hamiliton; group v.p. indsl. products A. O. Smith Corp., 1962-64; with A-T-O Inc. (formerly Automatic Sprinkler Corp. Am.), 1964—, chmn. bd., chief exec. officer, 1960—, also dir.; pres. Clark Reliance Corp.; dir. Western Union. Trustee Lakewood Hosp., Lakewood, O. Address: 4420 Sherwin Rd Willoughby OH 44094

FIGLEY, MELVIN MORGAN, physician; b. Toledo, Dec. 5, 1920; s. Karl Dean and Margaret (Morgan) F.; student Dartmouth, 1938-41; M.D. magna cum laude (John Harvard fellow), Harvard, 1944; m. Margaret Jane Harris, Mar. 16, 1946; children—Karl Porter, Joseph Dean, Mark Thompson. Intern, resident internal medicine Western Res. U., 1944-46; resident radiology U. Mich., 1948-51, instr., asst. prof., asso. prof. radiology, 1950-58; practice medicine, specializing in radiology, Seattle, 1958—; prof. radiology, chmn. dept. U. Wash., 1958—; mem. radiation study sect. NIH, 1963-67; mem. com. on radiology Nat. Acad. Scis.-NRC, 1964-69, chmn., 1968-69. Bd. dirs. James Piches Found. Served to capt. M.C., AUS, 1946-48. John and Mary R. Markle scholar, 1952-57. Diplomate Am. Bd. Radiology (trustee 1967—). Mem. Assn. U. Radiologists (past pres.), Am. Roentgen Ray Soc. (exec. council 1970—), Radiol. Soc. N.Am., Coll. Radiology, A.M.A., Boylston Med. Soc., Wash. Heart Assn. (past trustee), Soc. Chmn. Acad. Radiology Depts. (exec. council 1969-71), Phi Beta Kappa, Sigma Xi, Alpha Omega Alpha, Sigma Alpha Epsilon. Episcopalian. Contbr. articles profl. jours. Home: 7010 51st St NE Seattle WA 98115 Office: Univ Hosp Dept Radiology Seattle WA 98105

FIHN, JOSEPH ADAM, educator; b. Bac, Austria-Hungary, Apr. 19, 1918; s. Frank and Apollonia (Brochert) F.; student U. Toronto, 1938-39. 43-44; B.A. (hon.), U. Western Ont., 1946; M.A., U. Mich., 1947, Ph.D., 1954; m. Catherine Jean Brunner, Aug. 4, 1945; children—Joseph Thomas, John Michael, Cynthia Ann, Katherine Jean. Mem. faculty U. Detroit, 1947—, prof. Germanic langs., 1961—, chmn. modern lang. dept., 1961-65. Bd. dirs. Modern Lang. Conf. Mich., 1955-60, chmn., 1958-60. Mem. Am. Assn. Tchrs. German (pres. Mich. 1955-56), U. Detroit Acad. Arts and Scis. (pres. 1953-54), Modern Lang. Assn. Am. Contbr. articles on contemporary German lit. Home: 9103 Arnold Detroit MI 48239

FIKE, ED. lt. gov. of Nev.; b. Hopkins, Mo., Feb. 5, 1925; s. Edward Fike;; ed. Westminster Coll., Cornell U.; m. Joann; children—Toni, Mike, Gary, Brian. Founder, pres. Lawyers Title Las Vegas, Inc. (Nev.); pres. Nev. Escrow Service, Inc.; now lt. gov. of Nev. Active Nat. Conf. Christians and Jews; v.p. Boulder Dam Area council Boy Scouts Am.; mem. founders bd. Boys Club. Las Vegas past pres., Nev. pres. Young Republicans; past mem. Nev. Assembly. Mem. Am. Legion. Las Vegas C. of C. (past mem. bd.). Mason, Elk. Office: State Capitol Bldg Carson City NV 89701

FILARET, METROPOLITAN T., pres. synod council bishops Russian Orthodox Ch. Outside Russia. Address: 75 E 93rd St New York City NY 10028 *

FILAS, FRANCIS LAD, educator; b. Cicero, Ill., June 4, 1915; s. Thomas Martin and Emily (Seery) F.; A.B., Loyola U. Chgo., 1937, M.A., 1943; S.T.D., W. Baden (Ind.) Pontifical U., 1952. Joined Soc. of Jesus, 1932, ordained priest Roman Catholic Ch., 1945; tchr. theology U. Detroit, 1946-48; prof. theology Loyola U., Chgo., 1950—, chmn. dept., 1959-67; writer, lectr. Cana Conf., also family counselling; spl. research theology St. Joseph; lectr. radio, TV. Vice pres. Documentation and Research Center, North Am. Soc. of Josephology St. Joseph's Oratory, Montreal, Can., 1952-62, Mem. Cath. Theol. Soc., Am. Acad. Religion, Am. Mariological Soc., Soc. Cath. Coll. Tchrs. Sacred Doctrine, Cath. Bibl. Assn., Holy Shroud Guild (v.p.). Author: The Man Nearest to Christ, 1944; The Family for Families, 1947; Joseph and Jesus, 1952; His Heart in Our Work, 1952; Joseph Most Just, 1956; The Parables of Jesus, 1959; St. Joseph and Daily Christian Living, 1959; Joseph: The Man Closest to Jesus, 1962; Sex Education in the Family 1966; St. Joseph After Vatican II, 1968. Recorded albums on sex edn. and family life, 1964—. Address: 6525 N Sheridan Rd Chicago IL 60626

FILER, JOHN HORACE, ins. co. exec.; b. New Haven, Sept. 3, 1924; s. Harry Lambert and Ehrma (Green) F.; B.A., Depauw U., 1947, LL.D., 1970; LL.B., Yale, 1950; m. Jean Rogers Fairchild, June 25, 1949; children—Susan, Cynthia, Kathryn, Ann. Admitted to Conn. bar, 1950; practice in New Haven, 1950-58; law clk. Carroll C. Hincks, U.S. dist. judge, 1950-51; asso., partner Gumbart, Corbin, Tyler & Cooper, 1951-58; gen. counsel Aetna Life & Casualty Co., Hartford, Conn., 1958-68, exec. v.p., 1968—, also dir.; dir. Conn. Bank & Trust Co. Chmn. Bd. Edn., Farmington, 1963-67; mem. Conn. Commn. to Study Met. Govt., 1966-67. Mem. Conn. Senate, 1957-58. Trustee Kingswood-Oxford Sch., West Hartford, Miss Porter's Sch., Farmington. Served to ensign USNR, 1943-46. Mem. Am., Conn. Hartford County bar assns., Assn. Life Ins. Counsel, Greater Hartford C. of C. (dir.), Conn. Bus. and Industry Assn. (vice chmn.). Episcopalian. Home: Mountain Spring Rd Farmington CT 06032 Office: 151 Farmington Av Hartford CT 06115

FILES, WILMER ROBERT, home mfg. corp. exec.; b. Phila., Oct. 7, 1931; s. Wilmer R. and Mary (Ryan) F.; B.S. in Econs., U. Pa., 1953; m. Patricia Culhane, Apr. 24, 1954; children—Christine, Bryan. Trainee, Gen. Electric Co., 1953-57, traveling auditor, 1957-61, mgr. bus. systems, 1961-65; v.p., controller Nat. Homes Corp., Lafayette, Ind., 1965—. Mem. Financial Execs. Inst. Home: 3513 Cedar Lane Lafayette IN 47904 Office: 401 Earl Av Lafayette IN 47905

FILIATRAULT, ALFRED CHARLES, Jr., maritime soc. exec.; b Duluth, Minn., Jan. 2, 1921; s. Alfred Charles and Alice (Shebetsky) F.; B.S., U.S. Naval Acad., 1943; m. Mary Jane Smith, Sept. 13, 1952. Commd. ensign U.S. Navy, 1943, advanced through grades to comdr., 1958: served in destroyers, S.W. Pacific, World War II; exec. officer, then comdg. officer destroyer escort, Pacific, 1946-48; comdg. officer mine location ship, Fla., 1948-49; aide to comdr. 7th Fleet, Korea, 1950-51; instr. NROTC, U. Minn., 1951-52; comdg. officer, then div. comdr. minesweep ships, Pacific, 1953-56; mil. asst. adv. group, Germany, 1957-59; comdg. officer two destroyers, Pacific, 1959-61; assigned Navy staff, The Pentagon, 1961-65; ret., 1965; nat. exec. sec. Propeller Club U.S., 1965—. Mem. council Am. Master Mariners, 1966—. Trustee, mem. finance com. United Seaman's Service, 1965—; adv. bd. Food and Maritime Trade Sch., N.Y.C., 1965—. Decorated Bronze Star. Mem. N.Y. Soc. Assn. Execs., Navy League, U.S. Naval Acad. Alumni Assn. Mason. Home: 150 West End Av New York City NY 10023. Office: 17 Battery Pl New York City NY 10004

FILION, GERARD, co. exec.; b. Isle-Verte, Que., Can. Aug. 18, 1909; s. Alfred and Philomene (Simard) F.; B.A., Laval U., 1931; M. Commerce, U. Montreal, 1934; m. Francoise Servetre, Jan. 25, 1937; children—Nicole, Monique, Pierre, Jean, Marcel, Morc-André, Louise, Michel, Claudine. Gen. sec. Union Catholique des Cultivateurs, 1935-47; pub. Le Devoir, Montreal, 1947-63; gen. mgr. La Société Générale de Financement (Gen. Investment Corp.), 1963-66: pres. Marine Industries Ltd., 1966—; mayor, St. Bruno. Former pres. County School Board. Home: St Bruno Chambly Co Montreal 2 Quebec Canada Office: 1405 Peel St Montreal 2 Quebec Canada

FILIPPI, FRANK JOSEPH, lawyer; b. San Francisco, Dec. 18, 1907; s. Antonio and Rina (Linqua) F.; A.B., Lincoln U., 1928; LL.B., U. San Francisco, 1932; m. Olivia Cotta, Apr. 30, 1933. Admitted to Cal. bar, 1932, U.S. Supreme Ct. bar; sr. atty. Cal. Compensation Ins. Fund, 1934-44; supt. compensation ins. claims, Cal., 1944-49; now sr. partner Mullen & Filippi with law offices in San Francisco, San Jose, Sacramento; lectr. on ins. law. Served with A.R.C., 1942-46. Mem. Cal. Rep. Central Com., 1946-56. Mem. State Bar Cal., Internat., Inter-Am., Am. (mem. ho. of dels. 1967—, vice chmn. workmen's compensation com.), San Francisco bar assns., Lawyers Club San Francisco (pres. 1959-60, bd. dirs. 1960-70), Am. Bd. Trial Advs., Am. Trial Lawyers Assn., Am. Judicature Soc., Nat. Conf. Bar Presidents, Def. Research Inst., Def. Seminar Assn. San Francisco, Probate Attys. Assn. No. Cal., San Francisco C. of C., Bayview Mchts. Assn. (past pres.), Bay View Civic Club (past pres.), Central Council of Civic Clubs (dir.), Native Sons Cal. Clubs: San Francisco Athletic, Commonwealth of Cal. (San Francisco); Olympic City, Olympic Country. Home: 59 Iris Av San Francisco CA 94118 Office: 315 Montgomery St San Francisco CA 94104

FILL, DENNIS C., pharm. co. exec.; b. 1929; student Inst. Export, London, 1950-52, Borough Poly., 1953; married. Engaged in export and internat. sales Monsanto Chem. Co., 1950-58; Latin Am. area mgr. Olin-Mathieson Chemical Corp. and subsidiaries, 1958-60; partner Internat. Engrs., Washington, 1961-62; regional v.p. Pacific, OlinMathieson Chem. Corp. and subsidiaries, 1962-65; pres. Squibb Internat. Co., 1966-68; group v.p. pharmaceuticals and internat., dir. Equibb Beech-Nut, Inc., 1968—; pres., chief exec. officer E.R. Squibb & Sons, Inc. Address: 745 Fifth Av New York City NY 10022*

FILLER, ROBERT, educator; b. Bklyn., Feb. 2, 1923; s. Alfred Louis and Ethel (Schwab) F.; B.S., City Coll. N.Y., 1943; M.S., U. Ia., 1947, Ph.D., 1949; m. Lael Carol Rosenbloom, Oct. 7, 1945 (dec. 1954); children—Susan, Rebecca, Debby; m. 2d, Miriam G. Holland, Sept. 20, 1959; children—Michael, Daniel. Asst. prof. Union U., 1949-50; postdoctoral research fellow Purdue U., 1950-51; research chemist Wright Air Devel. Center, Dayton, O., 1951-53; instr., asst. prof. Ohio Wesleyan U., 1953-55; asst. prof. Ill. Inst. Tech., 1955-61, asso. prof., 1961-66, prof., 1966—, acting chmn. chem. dept., 1966-68. chmn., 1968—. Research asso. Ben May Lab. for Cancer Research, U. Chgo., 1956-57; cons. U. Ill. Coll. Medicine, 1958-59, I.I.T. Research Inst., 1964-66. Served with AUS, 1944-46. Recipient NIH spl. postdoctoral fellow U. Cambridge (Eng.), 1962-63. Mem. Am. Chem. Soc. (sec.-treas. div. fluorine chemistry 1972—), Chem. Soc. (London), A.A.A.S., Am. Assn. U. Profs., Sigma Xi, Phi Lambda Upsilon. Contbr. articles profl. jours. Home: 6909 S Chappel Av Chicago IL 60649

FILLIUS, MILTON FRANKLIN, Jr., food products co. exec., b. N.Y., Nov. 17, 1922; s. Milton Franklin and Georgiana (Bergh) F.; B.A., Hamilton Coll., 1946; LL.B., U. Mich., 1949; m. Helen C. Fancher, Aug. 24, 1960; children—Julie, Karen, Anthony, Donald. Admitted to Cal. bar, 1950, also U.S. Supreme Ct.; adminstrv. asst. to banker in San Diego, 1949-51; treas., gen. mgr. Nat. Steel and Shipbldg. Co., San Diego, 1951-56, exec. v.p., gen. mgr., 1956-62; exec. v.p. Westgate-Cal. Corp., 1962-65; pres. Vita-Pakt Citrus Products Co., 1966—; dir. Cal. Electric Works, Fever, Dorland & Assos. Bd. dirs. San Diego YMCA, 1957—, San Diego council Boy Scouts Am. 1957—, San Diego County Heart Assn., 1959—, Childrens Home Soc., San Diego, 1959—, Mercy Hosp., San Diego, 1959—. Served with USNR, 1943-46. Mem. State Bar Cal., San Diego County Bar Assn., San Diego C. of C. (pres. 1962-64), Theta Delta Chi, Phi Alpha Delta. Home: 642 S Forestdale West Covina CA 91722 Office: 707 N Barranca St Covina CA 91722

FILMUS, TULLY, artist; b. Bessarabia, Russia, Aug. 29, 1908; s. Mitchel and Evelyn (Gustoff) F.; brought to U.S., 1913, naturalized. 1927; studied with Andre L'hote, Paris: student Pa. Acad. Fine Arts, 1927, N.Y.U., 1931, also Italy, France, Germany: m. Gladys Nodiff, June 18, 1939; children—Michael, Stephen. One man shows ACA Gallery, 1963, 67, 71, ACA, Rome, Italy, 1964, Kenmore Gallery, 1968, Kenmore Gallery, 1971; exhibited group shows ACA Gallery, Am. Acad. Arts and Letters, N.Y.C., Audubon Artists, Whitney Mus., Carnegie Inst., Chgo. Art Inst., Pa. Acad. Fine Arts, Corcoran Gallery, Bklyn. Mus., Denver Mus., State U. Ia., U. Tex., San Francisco Mus. Art, City St. Louis Art Mus., Am. Fedn. Arts, Los Angeles Mus., Mus. Modern Art, Toledo Mus.; represented in permanent collections Whitney Mus., Met. Mus. Art, Mass. Inst. Tech., N.Y.U., N.Y. Hist. Soc., Tel-Aviv (Israel) Mus., Orleans Gavl Inst., Haifa, Fleisher Found., Syracuse U. Mus., Holyoke (Mass.) Mus., Sholem Aleichem Inst., Tel-Aviv, Syracuse U. manuscript collection, others: tchr. painting Am. Artists Sch., 1937-39, Cooper Union, N.Y., 1938-50. Cresson Traveling scholar, 1927. Recipient Fleischer Found. award, 1938; Pa. Acad. Fine Arts fellow, 1948; Saimagundi award Audubon Artists Ann., 1968; Fellowship prize Pa. Acad. Fine Arts. Mem. Artist Equity, Audubon Artists. Author: Paintings and Drawing by Tully Filmus; Tully Filmus-Selected Drawings, 1971. Address: Summer Studio Becket MA 01223 also 17 Stuart St Great Neck NY 11023

FILSON, FLOYD VIVIAN, theologian; b. Hamilton, Mo., Nov. 15, 1896; s. Thomas Anderson and Sarah Zelma (Adams) F.; A.B., Park Coll., Parkville, Mo., 1918, D.D., 1930; B.D., McCormick Theol. Sem., Chicago, 1922; Th.D., U. Basel, Switzerland, 1930; m. Wilma H. Nutt, May 1, 1920; children—Lawrence Edwin, Kirby Ann, Don Paul, Abigail Moulton. Ordained to ministry Presbyn. Ch., June 2, 1922; instr. N.T. Greek, McCormick Theol. Sem., 1923- 30, prof. N.T. lit. and exegesis, 1930-34, prof. N.T. lit. and history. 1934-67, prof. emeritus, 1967—, dean, 1954-67, dean emeritus, 1967—, acting pres. 1956. Moderator of Presbytery of Chgo., 1951-52. Pvt., 2d lt., C.A.C., A.U.S., 1918-19. Pres. Alumni Assn., Park Coll., 1944- 45; mem. Archaeol. Inst. Am., Chgo. Soc. Bibl. research (pres. 1946-47), Soc. Bibl. Lit. and Exegesis (nat. pres. 1949; sec. Midwest sect. 1938-43, pres. 1945- 46), Am. Acad. Religion (pres. 1944). Author: St. Paul's Conception of Recompense (vol. 21 of Untersuchungen zum Neuen Testament), 1931; Origins of the Gospels, 1938; Pioneers of the Primitive Church. 1940; One Lord, One Faith, 1943; Westminster Bible Atlas (co- author with G. Ernest Wright), 1945, rev. edit. 1956; The New Testament Against Its Environment, 1951: Opening The New Testament, 1953; Jesus Christ the Risen Lord, 1956: Three Crucial Decades, 1963; The Gospel According to John, 1963: A New Testament History, 1964; The Gospel for God's People, 1970. Translator of O. Cullmann's Christ and Time, 1950; and also Peter: Disciple, Apostle, Martyr, 1953, rev. edit., 1962; Commentary on II Corinthians, Interpreter's Bible. Vol. X. 1953: Commentary on the Gospel According to St. Matthew, 1960; Yesterday, 1967. Co-translator of Rudolph Otto's book The Kingdom of God and the Son of Man, 1938; Which Books Belong in the Bible, 1957. Co-editor Westminster Study Bible, 1948, N.T. Book Rev. editor, 1950-56. Contbr. Jour. Bibl. Lit., Jour. Bible and Religion. Bible Archaeologist, etc. Mem. Standard Bible Com., 1952—; mem. consultation on Church Union, 1962—. Home: 101 E University Blvd Tucson AZ 85705

FILSON, MALCOLM HAROLD, chemist, educator; b. Chatanooga, Oct. 19, 1907; s. Verdi B. and Gene (Neal) F.; B.S., U. Ky., 1929, M.S., 1931; Ph.D., U. Mich., 1936; grad. student Mich.

State U., 1954-56, Purdue U., 1943; Fellow U. Wis., summer 1959, Cornell U., 1960; m. Elma Hoagbin, May 28, 1960; children by previous marriage—Harolyn Jean (Mrs. Philip Van-Every), Eric Malcolm, Ray Ballard. Chemist, State Ky., 1930; teaching fellow U. Ky., 1929-31, U. Mich., 1931-33; prof. chemistry Ohio No. U., 1933-34; head dept. chemistry, dean summer sch. Miss Womans Coll., 1934-35; mem. faculty Central Mich. U., 1935—, prof. chemistry, 1942—, chmn. dept., 1955—; lectr. Mich. Acad. Scis., Arts and Letters, 1960-62; NSF, fellow Ohio Wesleyan U., summer 1963, U. Fla., summer 1964. Chmn. Isabella County chpt. Nat. Found. Infantile Paralysis, 1938-57, A.R.C., 1950-58; chmn. conservation drives Mt. Pleasant Lions Club; chmn. area Gas Warfare Service, 1943-46, also radiol. com. Civil Def. Mich. Chmn. Isabella County Democratic Party, 1942-53. Recipient Distinguished Service award Jr. C. of C. 1943. Fellow A.A.A.S., Nat. Geog. Soc.; mem. Am. Chem. Soc., Sci. Research Soc. Am., Central Assn. Sci. and Math Tchrs., Nat. Sci. Tchrs. Assn., Ohio. Mich. acads. sci., Am. Mus. Natural History, Sigma Xi (sec. Mich. 1934, pres. Central Mich. U.), Alpha Chi Sigma, Gamma Alpha, Sigma Tau Gamma, Beth Mu Alpha, Phi Eta Sigma. Phi Kappa Phi. Mason (32, K.T.), Old Fellow, Lion. Author: Organic Outline, 1937. Home: 3695 Ridge St Mount Pleasant MI 48858

FINAN, FRANK JOSEPH, ins. co. exec.; b. N.Y.C., Mar. 30, 1916; s. Frank F. and Margaret (Sweeney) F.; student N.Y.U., 1946-56; m. Josephine Hallinan, Oct. 14, 1943; children—Frank J., Jane Louise, Kathleen, Joseph H. With Manhattan Life Ins. Co., N.Y.C., 1937—, successively bookkeeper, asst. treas., 1955, treas., 1959, v.p., 1961. 1st v.p., treas., 1962-66, sr. v.p. investments, 1966—, also dir. Served with AUS, 1942-45. Mem. Am. Inst. Real Estate Appraisers (pres. chpt. 4), N.Y. Soc. Real Estate Appraisers, N.Y. State Soc. Real Estate Appraisers, N.Y. Real Estate Bd., N.Y.C. West Side C. of C., Mortgage Bankers Assn. Am., Tex. Mortgage Bankers Assn., Mortgage Bankers Assn. N.Y. (gov.), Am. Legion, War Vets. Real Estate Assn. (dir.), Newcomen Soc. N.Am. Home: 44 Herman Blvd Franklin Square NY 11010 Office: 111 W 57th St New York City NY 10019

FINAZZO, PAUL J., freight transp. co. exec.; b. 1929; married. Formerly dir. U.S. freight sales Flying Tiger Line Inc.; exec. v.p., dir. Airlift Internat. Inc., Miami, Fla. Office: Airlift Internat Inc Miami Internat Airport Miami FL 33148*

FINCH, CHARLES BAKER, utilities exec.; b. N.Y.C., Mar. 1, 1920; s. Henry LeRoy and Mary (Baker) F.; student Phillips Acad., 1934-37; A.B., Yale., 1941, LL.B., 1943; m. Angela Cobb Sessions, Oct. 22, 1943; children—Charles Baker, William P. Admitted to N.Y. bar, 1943; with Milbank, Tweed & Hope and successor firms, N.Y.C., 1943-54; v.p. Allegheny Power System, Inc., N.Y.C., 1954—, West Penn Power Co.; trustee Broadway Savs. Bank. Bd. dirs. N.Y.C. Mission Soc., Planned Parenthood N.Y. Mem. Municipal Art Soc., St. Nicholas Soc. City N.Y., Am., N.Y.C. bar assns., Nat. Inst. Social Scis., Phi Beta Kappa, Phi Delta Phi, Delta Kappa Epsilon. Clubs: Union, Racquet and Tennis (N.Y.C.); Seabright (N.J.) Beach; Mantoloking (N.J.) Yacht. Home: 167 E 82d St New York City NY 10028 Office: 320 Park Av New York City NY 10022

FINCH, EDWARD CORNELL KIP, lawyer; b. N.Y.C., July 7, 1911; s. James Kip and Lolita Pauline (Mollman) F.; A.B., Columbia, 1933; LL.B., Harvard, 1936; m. Laird Van Winkle, June 25, 1935 (div. Sept. 1950); children—James Kip II, Peter V.W., Margaret L., Sarah Pauline; m. 2d, Ruth Earle Woodward. Nov. 24, 1951; children—Ruth Persis, Earle Kip. With Time Inc., 1936-54, promotion dept., asst. to treas., asst. to pub., gen. mgr. internat. edits. corp. mgmt., 1936-47. asst. to editor-in-chief, 1947-54, war corr., tech. rep. MTO, 1945; admitted to N.Y. bar, 1940, Conn. bar, 1954; pvt. practice law, New Canaan, 1954-58; mem. firm Finch & Makepeace, 1958—. Chmn. bd. dirs. Save the Children Fedn.; dir., mem. exec. com. Aid Refugee Chinese Intellectuals, 1952-70; chmn. A.R.C. Fund, 1950, dir., 1951-53. United Fund, 1955-56; chmn. bd. dirs. Community Devel. Found., Inc. Mem. New Canaan Republican Town Com., 1951-58; mem. Conn. Ho. of Reps., 1959-60; Justice of Peace, New Canaan, 1968—; mem. com. on jud. and govtl. functions. Recipient Ordre de Merite, l'Union International de Protection de l'Enfance, 1967. Mem. Am., Conn., New Canaan (pres. 1964-66), bar assns., Conn. Attys. Title Guaranty Fund (chmn. membership com.), Delta Psi. Republican. Episcopalian. Home: Four Winds Ponus Ridge New Canaan CT 06840 Office: 76 Elm St New Canaan CT 06840

FINCH, EDWIN PERKINS, tobacco co. exec.; b. Henderson, N.C., May 9, 1910; s. Edwin G. and Ida (Fox) F.; A.B., Duke, 1932; m. Lucy Marshall Goode, Feb. 3, 1940; 1 dau., Anne Marshall. With Brown & Williamson Tobacco Corp., Louisville, 1932—, exec. v.p., 1962-64, pres., 1964—, also dir.; dir. Export Leaf Tobacco Co., First Nat. Bank of Louisville; mem. Ky.-Tenn. adv. bd. Liberty Mut. Ins. Co. Mem. council Tobacco Research-U.S.A., 1964; dir. Tobacco Inst., 1965; mem. Pres.'s Nat. Bus. Council for Consumer Affairs. Bd. overseers U. Louisville, Mem. Louisville C. of C., Alpha Tau Omega. Clubs: Louisville Country, Pendennis (Louisville). Home: 4010 Napanee Rd Louisville KY 40207 Office: 1600 W Hill St Louisville KY 40201

FINCH, ERNEST BLISS, educator; b. Edmeston, N.Y., Nov. 1, 1907; s. Adelbert and Nellie (Bliss) F.; A.B., Cornell U., 1928. M.A., 1929, Ph.D., 1951; postgrad. Ithaca Coll., 1936-40. Instr., Syracuse U., 1929-36: asst. prof. Ithaca Coll., 1936-43, dir. drama dept., 1943-47; mem. faculty Alfred (N.Y.) U., 1950—, prof. English, 1953—, chmn. dept., 1950-70. Mem. Modern Lang. Assn., Am. Assn. U. Profs., Phi Beta Kappa, Phi Mu Alpha. Democrat. Research 19th century theatre in Am. and Eng. Home: McHenry Valley Rd Almond NY 14804 Office: Dept English Alfred Univ Alfred NY 14802

FINCH, GLEN, psychologist; b. Portland, Ind., Oct. 23, 1909; s. Selma and Ella (Bockoven) F.; A.B., DePauw U., 1930; A.M., U. Ill., 1931, Ph.D., 1935; m. Jean Mork, 1944; children—Roger J., Alberta Lyons. NRC fellow Johns Hopkins Med. Sch., 1935-36; instr., then asst. prof. Yale, 1936-42; research psychologist USAF, 1942-54; exec. sec. div. behavioral scis. Nat. Acad. Scis., NRC, 1954-65; program mgr. life scis. Air Force Office Sci. Research, 1964—; cons. Dept. Army, Dept. Def. Served from 1st lt. to maj. USAAF, 1942-47; col. Res. Fellow A.A.A.S., Am. Psychol. Assn. Home: 7009 Leesville Blvd Springfield VA 22151 Office: 1400 Wilson Blvd Arlington VA 22209

FINCH, HENRY LEROY, Jr., educator; A.B., Yale; A.M., Ph.D., Columbia. Mem. faculty Sarah Lawrence Coll., 1953—, now prof. philosophy. Address: care Dept. Philosophy, Sarah Lawrence Coll., Bronxville NY 10708 *

FINCH, JAMES AUSTIN, Jr., judge; b. St. Louis, Nov. 13, 1907; s. James Austin and Carrie (Lehman) F.; student Southeast Mo. State Coll., 1925-27; A.B., U. Mo., 1930, J.D., 1932, LL.D., 1966; m. Helen E. Carroll, Aug. 28, 1937; children—Gail Carroll, James Austin III, John David. Admitted to Mo. bar, 1931; asst. atty. gen., Mo., 1932; mem. firm Finch, Finch & Knehans (formerly Finch & Finch), Cape Girardeau, 1933-65; judge Supreme Ct. Mo., 1965—, chief justice, 1971—; pros. atty. Cape Girardeau County, 1941-42. Mem. Mo. Citizens Adv. Com. on Higher Edn., 1956-57, govs. com. Edn. Beyond High Sch., 1958-60; chmn. Gov's Council Higher Edn., 1959-63. Adv. Council Mo. Commn. Higher Edn., 1963-64. Mem. bd. curators U. Mo., 1951-65, pres. bd., 1954-64: trustee Mo. Law School Found., 1952-64, pres. 1958-59. Served as maj. USAAF, 1942-45. Recipient award for contbn. to Mo. edn. Phi Delta Kappa, 1964; Alumni Distinguished Service award U. Mo., 1965; Ann. Law Day award Law Sch., U. Mo. at Kansas City, 1968; Alumni Merit Citation Sch. Law, U. Mo. at Columbia, 1970. Fellow Am. Bar Found.; mem. Am. Law Inst., Am. Judicature Soc. (dir. 1970—), Am. Mo. (chmn. title standards com. 1951-52, chmn. taxation com. 1955-56), Cole County, St. Louis bar assns., Mo. Hist. Soc., Am. Legion, Order of Coif, Inst. Jud. Adminstrn. Acad. Mo. Squires, Phi Beta Kappa Assos., Phi Beta Kappa, Phi Delta Phi, Omicron Delta Kappa, Delta Sigma Rho, Phi Gamma Delta. Republican. Methodist. Clubs: Jefferson City (Mo.) Country, Mo. Athletic (St. Louis). Home: 404 Crystal View Terrace Jefferson City MO 65101 Office: Supreme Ct Bldg Jefferson City MO 65101

FINCH, JAMES HARRISON, architect; b. Atlanta, Dec. 5, 1913; s. Harrison and Anne Cohutta (Gryder) F.; B.S. in Arch., Ga. Inst. Tech., 1936; postgrad. Princeton, 1937-38; m. LewEllyn Grace Lundeen, Jan. 4, 1952; children—LewEllyn, Anne. Draftsman, Hentz, Adler & Shutze, 1938-41; designer Burge & Stevens, 1946-48; partner Finch, Barnes & Paschal, 1948-52, 54-58; partner Finch Alexander Barnes Rothschild & Paschal, Inc., Atlanta, 1958-71, pres., 1971—; v.p. Asso. Space Design, Atlanta, 1965—; asso. prof. arch. Ga. Inst. Tech., 1946-68. Mem. Ga. Commn. Arts, 1964—, chmn. 1966-67; mem. Atlanta Civic Design Commn., 1969—. Trustee, Ga. Conservancy. Served with USMC, 1941-46, 52-54; col. Res. Recipient Ivan Allen award N. Ga. chpt. A.I.A., 1968. Fellow A.I.A. Presbyn. Clubs: Commerce, Piedmont Driving (Atlanta); Principal works include Coco-Cola Co. Bldg., 1969, Atlanta Stadium, 1964, Ga. Power Co. Bldg., 1961, First Nat. Bank Bldg., 1969 (all Atlanta); Riverfront Stadium, Cin., 1971. Home: 37 Inman Circle NE Atlanta GA 30309 Office: Finch Alexander Barnes Rothschild & Paschal 44 Broad St NW Atlanta GA 30303

FINCH, JEREMIAH STANTON, educator; b. Albany, N.Y., Apr. 27, 1910; s. Jeremiah Calvin and Nina (Tree) F.; A.B., Cornell U., 1931, M.A., 1933, Ph.D., 1936; m. Mathilde Effler, July 21, 1937 (div. 1960); children—Jeremiah (dec.), Anne Judith, Abigail Kathryn: m. 2d, Nancy Goheen Wallis, June 28, 1961. Instr. English, Cornell U., 1934-36; with Princeton, 1936—, successively instr. English, asst. prof. pub. speaking, asst. to dean of faculty, asst. dean of coll., lectr. English, asso. dean of coll., 1936-55, dean, 1955-61, prof. English, 1956—, sec. univ., 1966—; study tchr. edn. with James B. Conant, 1961-62; exec. sec. Princeton Program for Servicemen, 1944-48. Trustee Danforth Found., 1964-71, Ripon Coll., 1971—. Mem. Modern Lang. Assn. Am., Charles Lamb Soc., Am. Assn. U. Profs. (council 1946-48), Middle States Assn. (mem. commn. on instns. higher edn. 1958-64, pres. 1970), Phi Kappa Phi. Club: Century Assn. (N.Y.C.). Author: Sir Thomas Browne: a Doctor's Life of Science and Faith, 1950. Contbr. profl. jours. Home: 99 McCosh Circle Princeton NJ 08540

FINCH, JOHN WALLACE, educator; b. Newburgh, N.Y., Dec. 22, 1911; s. Wallace H. and Phebe (Secor) F.; A.B., Wesleyan U., Middletown, Conn., 1933; M.A., Harvard, 1940; m. Madeline Fernandez, Mar. 1, 1952; children—Diana Secor, Marina Sammons, John Fernandez. Instr., tutor Harvard, 1934-39; instr. English, Dartmouth, 1939-42, asst. prof., 1942-52, prof., 1952—, William R. Kenan prof., 1967—, chmn. drama dept., 1968-71; dir. Salsburg Seminar in Am. studies, 1949-50. Mem. Phi Beta. Author: (plays) The Wanhope Building, 1947; The Downstairs Dragon, 1954; The Winner, 1963. Home: 1 Buell St Hanover NH 03755

FINCH, PETER, actor; b. London Eng., Sept. 28, 1916; ed. Sydney, Australia. Stage debut in While Parents Sleep, Australia, 1935; appeared in motion pictures including The Nun's Story, Operation Amsterdam, Kidnapped, Rachel Cade, Trials of Oscar Wilde, No Love for Johnnie, Breaking Point, In the Cool of the Day, Girl With Green Eyes, The Pumpkin Eater, Judith, The Flight of the Phoenix, 10:30 on a Summer's Evening. Address: care Actors Equity Assn 165 W 46th St New York City NY 10036*

FINCH, ROBERT HUTCHISON, govt. ofcl.; b. Tempe, Ariz., Oct. 9, 1925; s. Robert L. and Gladys (Hutchison) F.; B.A. in Polit. Sci., Occidental Coll., 1947, LL.D., 1967; LL.B., U. So. Cal., 1951; LL.D., Lincoln U., 1968, U. Cal. at Los Angeles, 1969, Ohio State U., 1970; m. Carol Crothers, Feb. 14, 1946; children—Maureen, Kevin, Priscilla, Cathleen. Admitted to Cal. bar, 1951, practiced in Los Angeles; partner firm Finch, Bell, Duitsman & Margulis, and predecessor, 1951-66; lt. gov. State of Cal., 1967-69; sec. of health, edn. and welfare, Washington, 1969-70; counsellor to Pres. U.S., 1970—. Organizer, 1st pres. Palos Verdes Savs. & Loan Assn., 1956-58; chmn. bd. Marina Fed. Savs. & Loan Assn., 1958-59. Mem. Pres.'s Cabinet, Domestic Council, Adv. com. on Intergovtl. Relations, Cabinet Com. on Edn., Cabinet Com. on Voluntary Action. Chmn., Cal. Job Tng. and Placement Council, Interagy. Council for Ocean Resources, Electronic Data Processing Policy Com., 1967-69; chmn. Pres.'s Council on Aging, Com. on Retardation, Interdept. Com. on Children and Youth, Air Quality Adv. Bd., Fed. Radiation Council; chmn. Commn. of Californias, 1967-68; vice chmn. Los Angeles County Central Republican Com., 1954-56; del. Rep. Nat. Conv., 1948, 56, 60, 68; Rep. nominee for U.S. Congress, 1952-54; chmn. Los Angeles County Rep. Central Com., 1956-58; trustee Rep. Assos., 1958-66, chmn. exec. com., 1964-65; adminstrv. asst. to Vice Pres. Nixon, 1958-60; campaign dir. for Nixon Presdl. Campaign, 1960; chmn. Senatoral Campaign of George Murphy, 1964; pres. Cal. Senate, 1967-69. Trustee Occidental Coll., 1965-69, Cal. State Colls., 1967-69; regent U. Cal., 1967-69; adv. com. Coro Found., 1962-69; adv. bd. Marymount Coll., 1960-63; bd. dirs. Centinela Valley YMCA, 1954-58; trustee, counsel Palos Verdes Coll., 1953-56; Mem. Legion Lex, Kappa Sigma, Phi Alpha Delta. Clubs: California, Town Hall (Los Angeles); Commonwealth of Cal. Home: 6323 Beachway Dr Falls Church VA 22044 Office: White House Washington DC 20500

FINCH, RONALD M., Jr., savs. and loan exec.; b. Mpls., Jan. 21, 1932; s. Ronald M. and Lynda (Stapel) F.; B.S., U. Fla., 1954; certificate of recognition, Ind. U., 1965; m. Arline Anne Atkins, Sept. 17, 1961. With First Fed. Savs. & Loan Assn., Lake Worth, Fla., 1958—, dir., 1969—, pres., 1970—; dir. Fla. Informanagement Services, Inc., Orlando. Sec., bd. dirs. United Community Fund Lake Worth; bd. dirs. Lake Worth Utilities Authority; trustee Employees Retirement System City Lake Worth, Lake Worth Pub. Library Served as 1st lt. USAF, 1955-58. Mem. Lake Worth C. of C. (past pres. dir.), Am. Savs. and Loan Inst. (past pres. Palm Beach County chpt.), Alpha Tau Omega. Conglist (trustee). Kiwanian. Home: 825 S Palmway Lake Worth FL 33460 Office: 200 Lake Av Lake Worth FL 33460

FINCH, STUART CECIL, med. educator; b. Broadalbin, N.Y., 1921; M.D., U. Rochester, 1944. Surg. intern Balt. City Hosps., 1944-45, asst. resident in pathology, 1945-46; fellow internal medicine Peter Bent Brigham Hosp., Boston, 1948-49, asst. resident in internal medicine, 1949-50; practice medicine, specializing in internal medicine, 1950—; research asso. in internal medicine Evans Meml. Hosp., Mass. Meml. Hosp., Boston, 1950-52; chief of medicine Atomic Bomb Casualty Commn., Japan, 1960-62; attending physician West Haven (Conn.) VA Hosp.; cons. in hematology Laurel Hts. Hosp., Derby, Conn.; from instr. in medicine to prof. Yale, 1952—. Diplomate Am. Bd. Internal Medicine. Mem. A.M.A., Am. Soc. for Clin. Investigation, Am. Fedn. Clin. Research, Sigma Xi. Office: Yale Med Sch 333 Cedar St New Haven CT 06510*

FINCH, STUART MCINTYRE, child psychiatrist; b. Salt Lake City, Aug. 16, 1919; s. Elmer E. and Ann (McIntyre) F.; premed. student U. Utah, 1936-39; M.D., U. Colo., 1944; m. Dorothy Ellen Standish, Sept. 2, 1941; children—Craig Standish, Ellen Stuart. Intern Alameda County Hosp., Oakland, Cal., 1943-44; resident psychiatry Temple U. Hosp. and Sch. Medicine, 1946-49, Phila. Psychoanalytic Inst., 1947-53; instr. psychiatry Temple U. Sch. Medicine, 1949, asso. prof., 1954; attending psychiatrist St. Christopher's Hosp. Children, Phila., 1953-56; mem. faculty U. Mich. Med. Sch., 1956—, prof. psychiatry, chief children's psychiat. service, 1960—. Mem. med. adv. bd. Washtenaw County Planned Parenthood Assn. Diplomate Am. Bd. Psychiat. and Neurology (mem. com. on certification in child psychiatry 1968). Mem. Am. Psychiat. Assn. (chmn. com. psychiatry childhood and adolescence 1964-70), Group Advancement Psychiatry, Am. Orthopsychiat. Assn., A.M.A., Am. Acad. Child Psychiatry, Am. Psychoanalytic Assn. Author: (with O.S. English) Introduction to psychiatry, 3d edit., 1964; Fundamentals of Child Psychiatry, 1960; (with J.F. McDermott) Psychiatry for Pediatricians, 1970. Home: 304 Juniper Lane Ann Arbor MI 48105

FINCH, THOMAS AUSTIN, furniture mfg. co. exec.; b. Thomasville, N.C., Aug. 12, 1922; s. Thomas Austin and Ernestine (Lambeth) F.; grad. Woodberry Forest Sch., 1940; B.S. in Engring., Princeton, 1943; m. Meredith Clark Slane, June 4, 1949; children—Thomas Austin III, John Lambetin, David Slane, Sumner Slane, Meredith Kempton. With Thomasville Furniture Industries, Inc., 1946—, pres., 1961—; sr. v.p. parent co. Armstrong Cork Co., 1968—; dir. Wachovia Bank and Trust Co., Carolina and Northwestern R.R., Integon Corp. Trustee Duke, 1963—, Woodberry Forest Sch., 1967—, Community Gen. Meml. Hosp., Thomasville, 1964—. Served to lt. (j.g.) USNR, World War II. Named Furniture Man of Year, Am. Furniture Mart Corp., 1963. Mem. Phi Beta Kappa. Methodist (past chmn. ofcl. bd.). Rotarian (pres. Thomasville 1958). Home: Pine Needle Lane Thomasville NC 27360 Office: 401 E Main St Thomasville NC 27360

FINCH, WILLIAM CARRINGTON, former coll. pres.; b. Chase City, Va., Dec. 21, 1909; s. Adam Tyree and Bessie Dinwiddie (Morton) F.; A.B., Hampden Sydney Coll., 1929, LL.D., 1955; S.T.B., Bibl. Sem., N.Y.C., 1934; Th.M., Union Theol. Sem., 1936; Ph.D., Drew U., 1940; student Oxford U., U. Zurich, 1937-38; D.Litt., Southwestern U., 1966; m. Lucy Everett Bedinger, Aug. 19, 1937; children—William Tyree, Richard Carrington. Instr. Randolph Macon Acad., 1929-30; master St. Paul's Sch. for Boys, Balt., 1930-31; ordained to ministry Methodist Ch., 1938; minister Meth. Ch., Beulah, 1934-35; asst. minister Presbyn. Ch., Westfield, N.J., 1935-37; asst. prof. religion and philosophy Oklahoma City U., 1938-41, dean students 1940-41; asso. prof., head dept. religion and philosophy Southwestern U., 1941-43, asso. prof. Bible, head dept., 1943-45, prof. Bible, adminstrv. asst., 1945-49, acting pres., 1949-50, pres., 1950-61; dean div. sch. Vanderbilt U., 1961-65; pres. Emory and Henry Coll., Emory, Va., 1965-70. Del. Meth. Ecumenical Conf., Oxford, 1951; So. Central Jurisdictional Conf., 1952; Meth. Gen. Conf., 1960, World Meth. Conf., Oslo, 1961. Co- pres. Tex. Found. Voluntarily Supported Colls. and Univs.; pres. Tex. Council Ch. Related Colls., 1952; treas. Nat. Assn. Colls. and Univs. Meth. Ch., 1954; mem. bd. Edn. of Meth. Ch.; mem. univ. senate United Meth. Ch., 1965—. Mem. bd. edn. Georgetown Independent Sch. System, 1946-49. Served as chaplain (lt.), USNR, 1944-45. Mem. Nat. Assn. Bibl. Instrs., Tex. Meth. Coll. Assn. (pres. 1960-61), S.W. Soc. Bibl. Research, Phi Beta Kappa, Theta Chi, Pi Gamma Mu, Blue Key, Pi Delta Epsilon. Democrat. Methodist. Rotarian. Club: Scholia. Contbr. to religious publs. Home: 6024 Sherwood Dr Nashville TN 37215

FINCH, WILLIAM GEORGE HAROLD, radio engr.; b. Birmingham, Eng., June 28, 1895; s. William Joseph and Amelia (Skelding) F.; came to U.S., 1906; student Woodward High Sch., Cin.; elec. engring. course with Allis-Chalmers, Norwood, O.; radio communication course Marconi Inst. N.Y.C., 1917; completed spl. course radio engring. and patent law, Columbia, 1923; m. Elsie Grace George, Nov. 29, 1916 (dec. May 1967); dau., Eloise Grace (Mrs. Charles Tholen); m. 2d, Helen Stork Ambler, Feb. 1, 1969. Asst. engr. Cleve. Electric Illuminatiing Co., 1916-17; inspecting engr. Nat. Dist. Telegraph Co. (N.Y.C.), N.Y. Compensating Rating Bd., 1917-19; elec. engr. Royal Indemnity Co., 1919- 21; radio engr. and editor Internat. News Service 1921—. Established 1st radiotypewriter press circuit between N.Y.C. and Chgo., 1932, 1st internat. radiotypewriter circuit between N.Y.C. and Havana, 1933. Asst. chief engr. and chief telephone engring. div. FCC and chief engr. fed. investigation telephone cos., 1934-35; pres. Finch Telecommunications, Inc., N.Y.C., 1935-41, Conn. Indsl. Research Corp., Newtown, 1956—; v.p. Sta. WCAE, Pitts.; dir. communications Rowley Newspapers of Ohio, Ashtabula; dir. Telecommunication Cons. Internat. Inc., Washington; patent atty., U.S. and Canada, cons. profl. engr., electronic, facsimile communications and patent engring. Mem. Internat. Radio Consultive Com.; mem. tech. com. on radio and cable communication of Am. Newspaper Pubs. Assn. 1924—; mem. com. on allocation of frequency, Fourth Nat. Radio Conf.; del. to Internat. Telegraphic and Radio Telegraphic Conf., Madrid, 1932, N. Am. Radio Conf., Mexico City, 1933. Mem. 1st F.A., N.Y. Nat. Guard, 1917-18; lt. (s.g.) U.S. Naval Res.; exec. officer U.S. Navy Communication Res., 3d Naval Dist., N.Y.C., 1929- -; also detailed communication officer U.S.S. Wheeling; comdr. USN, 1943- 45; asst. chief, Office Naval Research; capt., 1945-55. Recipient Presdl. Award, Legion of Merit. Registered profl. engr. N.Y., patent atty. Fellow I.E.E.E. (award 1956), Radio Club Am. (dir.); mem. N.Y. Acad. Scis., Armed Forces Communications and Electronics Assn., Mil. Order World Wars, Am. Legion, A.A.A.S., Am. Phys. Soc., Franklin Inst. Episcopalian (vestryman). Mason. Clubs: Lotos, Bankers, Army and Navy, Lotos (N.Y.); Masonic (Buffalo, N.Y.); Army and Navy (Washington); Crown Point Country, Columbia Yacht, N.Y. Athletic; Norwalk Yacht; Candle Wood. Owner of the schooner Night Hawk. Contbr. numerous articles in field; inventor, patentee radio communications. Home: Elfin Newtown CT 06470 Office: P O Box 44 Newtown CT 06470 ☆

FINCHER, JOHN ALBERT, coll. pres.; b. Union, S.C., Sept. 8, 1911; s. Robert C. and Addie (Murphy) F.; B.S., U. S.C., 1933, M.S., 1935; Ph.D., U. N.C., 1939; m. Ruby C. Broom, Aug. 19, 1939; children—Judith Ellen, Janice Manette, John Albert. Prin., Pineview Sch., 1933-34; instr. U. S.C. 1934-35; grad. asst. U. N.C., 1935-39; instr. biology Cumberland Coll., 1939-40; asst., asso. prof. Millsaps Coll., 1940-46; prof., head dept. Samford U., Birmingham, Ala., 1946-57, asst. to pres., 1955-57, dean, 1957-68; pres. Carson-Newman Coll., Jefferson City, Tenn., 1968—. Pres., Mid-Appalachia Coll. Council, 1969—. Chmn. edn. commn. so. Bapt. Conv., 1962-66. Trustee Gorgas Scholarship Found., 1947-68; mem. bd. East End Meml. Hosp., 1958-68, v.p. bd., 1966-68; bd. dirs. Douglas-Cherokee Authority. Fellow A.A.A.S.; mem. Ala. Acad. Sci. (pres. 1952-53), Am. Soc. Zoology, Jefferson City C. of C. (dir.), Am. Assn. for Higher Edn., Tenn. Council Pvt. Colls. (v.p. 1969—), Tenn. Coll. Assn., Phi

Beta Kappa, Sigma Xi, Alpha Epsilon Delta (nat. councilor 1954-60, nat. v.p. 1960-62), Omicron Delta Kappa (province dep. 1968), Pi Kappa Alpha, Beta Beta Beta, Phi Sigma Tau, Kau, Kappa Delta Pi, Blue Key. Democrat. Baptist. Rotarian. Contbr. sci. articles jours. Home: Route 1 Laurel Hills Jefferson City TN 37760

FINCHER, MYRON GUSTIN, veterinarian; b. Corfu, N.Y., Nov. 25, 1898; s. Charles Colby and Cora (Ross) F.; D.V.M., Cornell U., 1920. M.S., 1925: Ph.D. (hon.), U. Thessaloniki, 1958; m. Evelyn N. Davis, June 28, 1924; children—Joyce Edna (Mrs. Donald Coye), Esther Margaret (Mrs. Daniel M. Hays), Myra Jean. Instr. N.Y. Vet. Coll., Cornell U., 1920-25, asst. prof., 1926-38, prof. vet. medicine, 1938-65, head dept. medicine, obstetrics, dir. ambulatory clinic, 1942-65, prof. emeritus, 1965—; faculty vet. medicine, head dept. surgery and medicine, and ambulatory clinic Ahmadu Bello U., Zaria, Nigeria, 1965-67; cons. FDA, Washington, 1967-68, vet. med. officer, 1968-72; Fulbright lectr. vet. coll. U. Thessoloniki, Salonica, Greece, 1958-59; pvt. veterinarian Thoroughbred Horse Farms, Lexington, 1926-27; acting prof. vet. medicine Ohio State U., 1940; cons. diseases of large animals. Dir. N.Y. State Mastitis Control Program, 1946-65. Mem. Am. Vet. Med. Assn. (mem. exec. bd. 1957-65; Borden award 1954), U.S. Livestock San. Assn., N.Y. State Vet. Med. Soc. (pres. 1964, Veterinarian of Year award 1963), Internat. Fertility Assn., Am. Assn. for Study Sterility, A.A.A.S., Sigma Xi, Phi Kappa Phi, Phi Zeta, Gamma Alpha, Omega Tau Sigma. Baptist. Rotarian. Mem. editorial bd. Fertility and Sterility Assn.; editor, contbr. Diseases of Cattle, 1956; 2d edit., 1963. Contbr. 1956 Yearbook of Agr., Animal Diseases. Home: 2000 S Eads St Arlington VA 22202 Office: Parklawn Bldg Rockville MD

FINCK, FURMAN JOSEPH, artist, educator; b. Chester, Pa., Oct. 10, 1900; s. Harry August and Caroline Emma (Smith) F.; student Pa. Acad. Fine Arts, Phila., 1921-24, Ecole des Beaux Arts, Academie Julian, Paris, 1924; studied abroad, 1930, 32, 54, 66, 68, 69, 70; A.F.D. (hon.), Muhlenburg Coll., 1954; m. Mildred Price Smith, June 18, 1938; 1 son, Nicolas. Portrait and landscape artist; emeritus prof. drawing, painting Tyler Coll. Fine Arts, Temple U., Phila,; tchr. Blai Coll., Ocean County Coll.; faculty Cheltenham Art Center, Phila. Mus. Art; chmn. art dept. duCret Sch. Art; lectr. U. London. Exhibited widely in ann., biennial, nat. and internat. group shows; represented in collections Lyman Allyn Mus., New London, Conn., Toledo Mus., State Capitol, Montpelier, Vt., State House, Hartford, Conn., Harvard, Pa., Princeton, Temple, Vt., Yale, L.I., N.C., Ga., Ia., Utah, Wash., Md., Rutgers, Loyola, Mich., Conn., univs., Muhlenburg, Western Md., Ann Arundel, Fla. So. colls., Akron, Drexel insts., Nat. Dem. Club N.Y.C., Union League Club, various hosps. and med. centers, Wyeth Labs., Phila. Coll. Pharmacy, Farragut Med. Bldg., Washington, Berliz Collection, Zurich, John Weinberger, Geneva, Dartmouth House, London, others; works include: Babcock Clinic, composition 34 med. portraits; Burnett Clinic, composition 8 med. portraits; Churchill Clinic, composition 8 med. portraits; Chamberlain Clinic, composition 7 med. portraits; portraits of govt. ofcls. including two Pres. of U.S. U.S. Navy combat artist to the Antarctic, 1961. Recipient Cresson Travelling European Scholarship. Pa. Acad., 1924; Carnegie award Nat. Acad. N.Y.C. 1943; Popular award Worcester Mus., 1945; Krindler prize Salmagundi Club N.Y.C., 1954; 1st Altman prize Nat. Acad., 1955, Am. Acad. Rome, 1966. Mem. Artists Equity, Am. Artists Fellowship, English-Speaking Union, St. George Soc. Club: Dutch Treat, Players, Salmagundi (N.Y.C.). Author: Complete Guide to Portrait Painting. Contbr. articles on art edn. profl. publs., NBC TV U. of Air. Studio: 285 Central Park W New York City NY 10024

FINCKE, MARGARET LOUISE, educator; b. Astoria, N.Y., Oct. 24, 1900; d. Harry Stark and Gertrude (Weeks) Fincke; A.B., Mt. Holyoke Coll., 1921; A.M., Columbia, 1932, Ph.D., 1935. With Synthetic Organic Chem. Mfrs. Assn., N.Y., 1924-28; asst. in chemistry Columbia, 1928-35; asso. prof. foods- nutrition Ore. State U., 1935-43, prof. foods and nutrition, 1943—, head dept., 1944-68, emeritus, 1969—, acting dean home econs., 1963-65; vis. prof., dir. Sch. Home Econs. Hebrew U. Jerusalem, 1969-71; distinguished prof. Ore. State U., 1966. Mem. Food and Nutrition Bd. of NRC, 1948-51, Mem. Am. Inst. Nutrition, Am. Dietetics Assn., Am. Home Econ. Assn., A.A.A.S., Sigma Xi, Phi Kappa Phi, Iota Sigma Pi, Omicron Nu (pres. 1963-65). Episcopalian. Contbr. articles to profl. jours. Home: 124 N W 29th St Corvallis OR 97330

FINDER, THEODORE ROOSEVELT, lawyer; b. N.Y.C., Oct. 28, 1914; s. Henry H. and Wilhelmina (Kirschner) F.; A.B., Columbia, 1936, LL.B., 1938. Admitted to N.Y. bar, 1938; asso. Fearey, Allen, Johnston & Smyth and successor firms, 1938- 42; asso. Beekman & Bogue, N.Y.C., 1945-49, partner, 1950—. Vice pres., asst. sec., dir. B. Fischer & Co., Inc., N.Y.C., 1951-54, asst. sec., dir., 1957-64; pres., dir. Asher Am., Inc., Calgary, Alta., Can., 1952- 53, asst. sec., 1953-58; dir. Redwater Am., Inc., Calgary, 1952-55, pres., 1953, asst., sec., 1953-55; v.p., dir. Gen. Fertilizer Corp., Walla Walla, Wash., 1958-64; asst. sec., dir. Calvan Am., Inc., Calgary, 1951-61, asst. treas., 1952-61; asst. sec., dir. Cola Beverage Corp., Jacksonville, Fla., 1958-64; dir. Studebaker Packard Corp., South Bend, Inc., 1958-60, finance com., 1958- 59, personnel com., 1958-60, exec. com., 1959-60. Served with USAAF, 1942-45, disch. as capt. Decorated D.F.C. (twice), Air medal with clusters, Presdl. Unit Citation with cluster. Mem. Am., N.Y. bar assns., Delta Upsilon. Clubs: Broad Street, Columbia (N.Y.C.); Knickerbocker Country (Tenafly, N.J.). Home: 136 E 76th St New York City NY 10021 Office: 5 Hanover Sq New York City NY 10004

FINDLAY, ALLAN, lawyer; b. Watson, Sask., Can., Aug. 17, 1914; s. Roy Pattullo and Muriel (Stephens) F.; B.A., King's U., 1934; postgrad. Dalhousie U. Law Sch., 1934-35; B.A., Oxford (Eng.) U., 1938, B.C.L., 1939; m. Dorothy Graham Smith, Aug. 9, 1947; children—Marion, Carol, Paul, Allan, Donald. Called to N.S. bar, 1946, Ont. bar, 1946, created Queen's Counsel, 1954; with firm Tilley, Carson & Findlay and predecessor, Toronto, 1946—, partner, 1950—. Served with RCAF, 1941-45. Rhodes scholar for N.S., 1936. Clubs: Toronto, Rosedale Golf (Toronto). Home: 191 Strathgowan Av Toronto 12 Ontario Canada Office: 44 King St W Toronto 1 Ontario Canada

FINDLAY, JAMES FRANKLIN, ret. coll. ofcl.; b. Fort Dodge, Ia., July 25, 1900; s. C.V. and Mabel (Southwick) F.; B.A., Grinnell Coll., 1922, LL.D. 1957; M.A., U. Chgo., 1923; Ph.D., N.Y. U., 1938; L.H.D., Drury Coll., 1964; Litt. D., Coll. of Sch., of Ozarks, 1969; m. Blanche Pritchard, Aug. 25, 1923; children—Cornelia Pritchard, James Franklin. Minister, First Congl. Ch., Cherokee, Ia., 1923-25; dean of men Grinnell Coll., 1925-29, U. Okla., 1929-40; pres. Drury Coll., Springfield, Mo., 1940-64; acad. v.p. The Sch. of Ozarks, Point Lookout, Mo., 1964-69, trustee, 1959-64. Bd. dirs. Chgo. Theol. Sem., 1948-55; mem.-at-large Rd. Home Missions Congl. and Christian Chs., N.Y.C.; commn. on Christian higher edn. Assn. Am. Colls., 1953-56; active Nat. Council Chs. Christ. Active A.R.C. Mem. Nat. Assn. Deans and Advisers of Men (past pres.), Phi Beta Kappa, Alpha Tau Omega, Omicron Delta Kappa. Republican. Congregationalist. Club: Rotary. Contbr. articles to ednl. jours. Address: 2117 E Wayland Springfield MO 65804

FINDLAY, JOHN NIEMEYER, educator, philosopher; b. Pretoria, S. Africa, Nov. 25, 1903; s. John Hudson L. and Elizabeth (Niemeyer) F.; B.A., Transvaal U. Coll., 1922, M.A., 1924; B.A., Balliol Coll., Oxford (Eng.) U., 1926, M.A., 1930; Ph.D., U. Graz (Austria), 1933; m. Aileen May Davidson, Aug. 15, 1941; children—Paul H.D., Rachel Clare. Came to U.S., 1966, Prof. philosophy U. Otago (New Zealand), 1934-44, U. Natal (S. Africa), 1946-48, King's Coll., Newcastle-upon-Tyne, Eng., 1948-51, King's Coll., U. London (Eng.), 1951-66, U. Tex., 1966-67; Clark prof. moral philosophy and metaphysics Yale, 1967—; Gifford lectr. U. St. Andrews (Scotland), 1964-66. Fellow Brit. Acad.; mem. Aristotelian Soc. (v.p. 1956—). Author: Meinong's Theory of Objects and Values, 2d edit., 1963; Hegel: A Re- Examination, 1958; Values and Intentions, 1961; Language, Mind and Value, 1963; The Discipline of the Cave, 1966; The Transcendence of the Cave, 1967; Axiological Ethics, 1970; Ascent to the Absolute, 1970. Translator: Logische Untersuchungen (Husserl), 1970. Home: 470 Whitney Av New Haven CT 06511

FINDLAY, STEPHEN WILLIAM, former headmaster; b. Newark, July 16, 1911; s. Matthew James and Kathryn Agnes (Warner) F.; student St. Anselm Coll., Manchester, N.H., 1929-31; A.B., St. Vincent Coll., Latrobe, Pa., 1934; J.C.D., Cath. U. Am., 1941. Professed Benedictine monk, 1932; ordained priest Roman Cath. Ch., 1937; tchr. Greek. history St. Mary's Sem., Morristown, N.J., 1934-38; tchr. English, St. Benedict's Prep. Sch., Newark, 1941-42; headmaster Delbarton Sch., Morristown, 1942-67, headmaster emeritus, dir. admissions and devel., 1967— dir. Camp Delbarton, Morristown, 1950—; procurator for cause of beatification and canonization Sister Miriam Teresa, 1946—; superior St. Mary's Abbey, Morristown, N.J., 1956- 70, chmn. admissions bd., 1958—. Mem. Canon Law Soc. Am., Nat. Assn. Secondary Sch. Prins., Sister Miriam Teresa League of Prayer (spiritual dir.), Nat. Soc. for Study Edn., Acad. Polit. Sci. Author: Canonical Norms Governing Deposition and Degradation, 1941. Home: Delbarton Sch Mendham Rd Morristown NJ 07960

FINDLAY, WALSTEIN C., Jr., art gallery dir.; b. Kansas City, Mo., 1903; student U. Mo., 1925. Pres., dir. Wally F. Findlay Galleries, Inc., Chgo. and Palm Beach, Wally F. Galleries, Inc., N.Y.C., Wally F. Findlay Galleries Internat., Inc., Chgo., Wally F. Findlay Galleries Internat., SARL, Paris. Clubs: University (Kansas City); Metropolitan, Raffles (N.Y.C.); Beach (Palm Beach). Home: 505 N Lake Shore Dr Chicago IL 60611 Office: 320 S Michigan Av Chicago IL 60604

FINDLEY, PAUL, congressman; b. Jacksonville, Ill., June 23, 1921; s. Joseph S. and Florence Mary (Nichols) F.; A.B., Ill. Coll., 1943; L.H.D., Lindenwood Coll.; m. Lucille Gemme, Jan. 8, 1946; children—Craig Joh, Diane Lillian. Pres., pub. Pike Press. Inc., Pittsfield. Ill., 1947—; mem. 87th-92d congresses 20th Ill. Dist., mem. fgn. affairs com., mem. agr. com. Dir. Federal Union. Inc. Trustee Ill. Coll. Served to lt. (j.g.) USNR, World War II. Mem. Ill. Press Assn. (past dir.). Am. Legion, V.F.W., Navy League, Phi Beta Kappa. Republican. Conglist. Lion. Author: Federal Farm Fable. Home: 306 S Jackson St Pittsfield IL 62363 Office: Rayburn Bldg Washington DC 20515

FINDLEY, THOMAS PALMER, Jr., physician; b. Chgo., Apr. 15, 1901; s. Thomas Palmer and Lyda (Hanna) F.; A.B., Princeton, 1923; B.S., U. Minn., 1925; M.D., U. Chgo., 1928; m. Jean Kver, Apr. 11, 1940; children—Susan, Margaret. Intern U. Hosp., Phila., 1927-29; instr. medicine U. Mich., 1929-32; research fellow pharmacology U. Pa., 1932-35; asst. prof. clin. medicine Washington U., 1935-40; head sect. internal medicine Ochsner Clinic, New Orleans, 1952-54; prof. clin. medicine Tulane U., 1942-54; prof. medicine, dir. Ga. Heart Assn. Lab. for Cardiovascular Research, Med. Coll. Ga., 1954-57, chmn. dept. medicine Med. Coll. Ga., 1957-66, emeritus prof. medicine 1967—; now area coordinator Regional Med. Program; attending physician VA Hosp.; vis. prof. medicine Nat. Def. Med. Center, Taipeh, Taiwan, 1968—. Diplomate Am. Bd. Internal Medicine (sec.-treas. 1955-60). Master A.C.P. (gov. for La. 1950-54, regent 1958. 2d v.p. 1965); mem. Assn. Am. physicians, Am. Clin. and Climatol. Assn., Am. Soc. Clin. Investigation, Central, So. (sec.-treas. 1947-49, pres. 1950) socs. Clin. research. Home: 115 Rosaire Pl NW Cross Creek Pkwy Atlanta GA 30327

FINDLEY, TIMOTHY IRVING, author; b. Toronto, Ont., Can., Oct. 30, 1930; s. Alan Gilmore and Margaret (Bull) F.; ed. pub. schs.; charter mem. Stratford Shakespeare Festival, Ont., 1953; protege Sir Alec Guinness, 1953-54; with H.M. Tennant Prodns., London, 1954-55; appeared in Prisoner, London, 1954. Matchmaker, Berlin and London, 1954-55, Hamlet, Moscow ad London, 1955, Matchmaker, N.Y.C., 1956; on national tour, 1957; writer Last of the Crazy People, 1967, Butterfly Plague, 1969 (novels); scriptwriter Paper People, 1967, Don't Let the Angels Fall, 1969. Recipient Can. Council award for playwriting, 1968. Mem. Author's Guild. Home: Rural Route 1 Cannington Ontario Canada Office: Care Owen Laster William Morris Agy 1350 Av of Americas New York City NY 10019

FINDLEY, WILLIAM NICHOLS, engr., educator; b. ManKato, Minn., Feb. 12, 1914; s. Joseph Stillwell and Florence Mary (Nichols) F.; A.B., Ill. Coll., 1936, D.Sc., 1970; B.S.E. in Math. and Mech. Engring., U. Mich., 1937; M.S. (McMullen scholar), Cornell U., 1939; m. Ruth Woolsey, Aug. 31, 1939; 1 dau., Elizabeth Jo. Instr. engring. George Washington U., 1938-39; instr. engring. U. Ill., 1939-42, asso., 1942-43, asst. prof., 1943-47, asso. prof., 1947-54; prof. engring. Brown U., 1954—, dir. Central Facility for Mech. Testing, 1965-68; mem. sci. adv. council Picatinny Arsenal, Dover, N.J., 1951-62; cons. Lawrence Radiation Lab.; lectr. Colloquium on Fatigue, Stockholm, Sweden, 1955. Mem. organizing com. Joint Internat. Conf. on Creep, 1963; mem. panels on rapid deformation and on European creep practice. Recipient Charles B. Dudley medal Am. Soc. Testing Materials, 1945; prize for paper Soc. Plastics Engrs., 1949, 50; Richard L. Templin award Am. Soc. Testing Materials, 1953, 64. Mem. Am. Soc. Engring. Edn., Am. Soc. Testing Materials, Soc. Exptl. Stress Analysis, Am. Soc. Metals, Am. Soc. M.E., Soc. Rheology, Atlantic Union Com., Sigma Xi, Phi Kappa Phi, Tau Beta Pi. Cons. editor Bull. Mech. Engring. Edn. Contbr. articles to tech. jours., chpts. in books. Home: 35 Mayfair Drive Rumford RI 02916 Office: Barus & Holley Physics and Engring Bldg Providence RI 02912

FINDLY, SARAH ELIZABETH, librarian; b. Winfield, Kan., Apr. 2, 1908; d. Guy H. and Vera Irene (Kindig) Findly; A.B., Drake U., 1929; B.S.L.S., U. Ill., 1934; A.M., U. Mich., 1945. Tchr., jr. and sr. high sch., Geneva, Ia., 1929-33; asst. circulation dept. U. Ia. Library, summer 1934; sr. asst. reference dept. Library, U. Ore., 1934-35, sr. asst. circulation dept., 1935-37, reference dept., 1937-47, head reference librarian, 1947-50, head gen. reference and documents div., 1950-66, head reference librarian, 1966-68, now prof. sch. librarianship. Sec., Wesley Found. at U. Ore., 1938-61. Mem. Am. mem. council 1965-69, Pacific N.W. (2d v.p. 1967-69, chmn. library edn. div. 1970—), Ore. (past pres.) library assns., Am. Assn. U. Profs., Assn. Coll. and Reference Libraries (past sect. chmn.), Pacific N.W. Bibliographic Center (past chmn. bd. mgrs.), Phi Beta Kappa. Methodist. Club: Altrusa. Contbr. profl. jours. Home: 860E 39th Av E Eugene OR 97403 Office: U Ore Library Eugene OR 97403

FINE, BENJAMIN, educator; b. N.Y.C., Sept. 1, 1905; s. Charles and Rebecca (Gulden) F.; B.S., R.I. State Coll., 1928; M.S., Sch. Journalism, Columbia, 1933; M.A., 1935, Ph.D., 1941; Ed.D., Bryant Coll., R.I., 1946, R.I. State Coll., 1950; L.H.D., Yeshiva U., 1949; LL.D., Lebanon Valley Coll., 1951; D.Litt., U. Toledo, 1951; Litt.D., Union Coll., 1952; D.So., Tampa, 1953; m. Lillian Rose Chafetz, Oct. 11, 1936; children—Ellen Sydney, Jill Barbara, Carla Coleman, Janet Eva. Asst., Pulitzer Sch. Journalism, 1932; reporter N.Y. Post, 1933; asst. in pub. relations Tchrs. Coll., Columbia, 1933-36; edn. reporter N.Y. Times, 1937-41, edn. editor, 1941-58; dean Grad. Sch. Edn., Yeshiva U., 1958-60; dean Sch. Journalism, Point Park Coll., 1960-62; headmaster Sands Point (N.Y.) Acad. and Country Day Sch.; head Horizon Sch., Miami, Fla.; edn. editor N.Am. Newspaper Alliance, Bell-McClure Syndicate, 1960—; lectr. edn. Coll. City N.Y., 1944, New Sch. for Social Research; lectr. U. Kansas City, U. Houston, Cornell U., Stetson U., Fla. State U. Past pres. Edn. Writers Assn., Am. Assn. for U.N., exec. council of Ednl. Forum. Recipient Frederick Z. Lewis medal Tchrs. Welfare League of N.Y. State, N.Y. State Tchrs. Assn. commendation, 1948; Pulitzer award N.Y. Times, 1944; Nat. Sch. Bell award for edn. reporting, 1963; others from profl. ednl. assns., orgns. for work in ednl. and sociol. fields. Dir., trustee numerous civic orgns. Mem. Soc. Am. Historians, N.Y. Acad. Pub. Edn., Sigma Delta Pi, Phi Delta Kappa, Kappa Delta Pi. Mason. Author: A Giant of the Press, 1933; College Publicity in the United States, 1941; Educational Publicity, 1943; Democratic Education, 1945; Admission to American Colleges, 1946; Our Children Are Cheated, 1947; Opportunities in Teaching, 1952, Fine's American College Counsellor and Guide, 1955; One Million Deliquents, 1955; The School Administrator and the Press, 1956; The School Administrator and His Publications, 1957; How to be Accepted by the College of Your Choice, 1957; How to Get the Best Education for Your Child, 1958; Modern Family Guide to Education, 1962; Teaching Machines, 1963; Stretching Their Minds, 1964; Profiles of American Colleges, 1964; Your Child and School, 1965; Underachievers-How to Help Them, 1966; also numerous articles and series. Home: 375 Brower Av Rockville Center NY 11570 Office: N Am Newspaper Alliance 1501 Broadway New York City NY 10036 also Sands Point Acad and Day Sch Sands Point NY 12123

FINE, DONALD IRVING, editor, pub.; b. Ann Arbor, Mich., Apr. 19, 1922; s. Morris Seide and Kathleen (Perlis) F.; A.B., Harvard, 1944; grad. student Columbia, 1947; m. Diana Northam, Mar. 30, 1967; 1 son, Stephen Morris. Mng. editor Western Printing & Lithographing Co., 1951-58; editor in chief Popular Library, Inc., 1958-60; v.p., editor in chief Dell Pub. Co., 1960-68; exec. v.p., editor in chief Coward-McCann, Inc., 1968-69; founder, pres., pub. Arbor House Pub. Co., Inc., N.Y.C., 1969—. Active Nassau County Stevenson for Pres., 1952. Served with AUS, 1943-46; PTO. Decorated Presdl. citation with 2 oak leaf clusters. Mem. P.E.N. Club, Western Writers Am., Mystery Writers Am. Club: Harvard (N.Y.C.). Home: 350 E 52d St New York City NY 10022 Office: 15 W 44th St New York City NY 10036

FINE, JOHN VAN ANTWERP, educator; b. Princeton, N.J., Dec. 3, 1903; s. John Burchard and Adele P. (Bohme) F.; A.B., Princeton, 1925; Ph.D., Yale, 1932; m. Elizabeth Bunting, July 6, 1933; 1 son, John Van Antwerp. Instr. classics Yale, 1932-34; asst. prof. classics and history Williams Coll., 1934-40; Andrew Fleming West lectr. in classics Princeton, 1940-41, asst. prof., 1941-46, asso. prof., 1946-49, Ewing prof. Greek langs. and lits., 1949—. Served from capt. to maj. USMCR, 1943-45. Mem. Am. Philol. Assn., Am. Numis. Soc., Am. Assn. U. Profs., Phi Beta Kappa. Author: Horoi: Studies in Mortgage, Real Security, and Land Tenure in Ancient Athens, 1951. Contbr. to Scholarly jours. Home: 112 Rollingmead Princeton NJ 08540

FINE, MORRIS EUGENE, metall. engr., educator; b. Jamestown, N.D., Apr. 12, 1918; s. Louis and Sophie (Berrington) F.; B.Metall. Engring. with distinction, U. Minn., 1940, M.S., 1942, Ph.D., 1943; m. Mildred Eleanor Glazer, Aug. 13, 1950; children—Susan Elaine, Amy Lynn. Instr. U. Minn., 1942-46; mem. tech. staff Bell Telephone Labs., Murray Hill, N.J., 1946-54; prof., chmn. dept. metallurgy Tech. Inst., Northwestern U., 1955-57, chmn. dept. materials sci., 1958-60, prof. and chmn. materials research center, 1960-63, Walter P. Murphy prof. materials sci., 1963—; vis. prof. dept. materials sci. Stanford U., 1967-68. Asso. engr. for Manhattan Project, U. Chgo., also Los Alamos, World War II; mem. materials adv. bd. Nat. Acad. Sci., 1963-68. Named Chicagoan of Year in Sci., 1961. Fellow Am. Phys. Soc., Am. Soc. Metals; mem. A.A.A.S., Am. Ceramic Soc., Am. Assn. Engring Edn. (chpt. chmn. 1963), Am. Assn. U. Profs., Fedn. Am. Scientists, Metall. Soc. of Am. Inst. Metall. Engrs. (chmn. inst. metals div. 1966-68, dir. 1968-71), Sigma Xi, Tau Beta Pi, Alpha Sigma Mu, Sigma Alpha Sigma. Author: Introduction to Phase Transformation in Condensed Systems: also tech. and sci. articles. Home: 1101 Manor Dr Wilmette IL 60091 Office: Northwestern University Evanston IL 60201

FINE, PAUL CHARLES, govt. ofcl.; b. Dallas, June 28, 1915; s. Mose and Susie (Corenbleth) F.; B.A., U. Okla., 1935; M.S., Cal. Inst. Tech., 1936. Ph.D., 1939. Instr. physics U. Ore., 1939. U. Tex., 1939-42; tech. aide OSRD, 1942-45; research fellow Cal. Inst. Tech., 1945-46; asst. dir. sci. panel U.S. del to UN AEC, 1946-47; spl. asst. div. mil. application U.S. AEC, 1948-55, dir. Div. Operations Analysis and Forecasting, 1956—. Recipient Presdl. Certificate of Merit, 1948; Outstanding Service award AEC, 1956. Mem. Phi Beta Kappa. Home: 1220 East West Hwy Silver Spring, MD 20910 Office: AEC Washington DC 20545

FINE, PERLE, artist; b. Boston, May 1, 1908; d. Simon and Sarah (Fine) Fine; studied with Hans Hofmann, Atelier 17; m. Maurice Berezov. One-man shows Marian Willard, DeYoung Mus., Nierendorf, Tanager, Betty Parsons galleries, Graham Gallery, N.Y.C., 1961, 63, 64, 67, Bykert Gallery, Springs, N.Y.; also exhibited nat. group annuals U.S. and abroad: works in permanent collections Whitney Mus., Smith Coll. Mus., Rutgers U., Los Angeles County Mus., Parrish Mus., Brandeis U. Bklyn. Mus. Mus. Non-Objective Art, Mus. Modern Art, Guild Hall, Easthampton, pvt. collections; asso. prof. fine art Hofstra U.; vis. prof. art Cornell U., 1961; tchr., lectr. Provincetown Art Assn., pvt. groups. Recipient Guggenheim scholarship; purchase award for color woodcut Bklyn. Mus., 1956; 1st prize for oil paintings Silvermine Art Guild, 1961, 1st prize, collage, 1963, award for wood collage, 1967; 1st prize for wood collage Guild Hall, Easthampton, 1970. Mem. Am. Abstract Artists, Fedn. Modern Painters and Sculptors, Guild Hall. Contbr. articles on art. Address: 58 3d Av New York City NY 10003 also 538C Old Stone Hwy The Springs NY 11937

FINE, PHIL DAVID, lawyer; b. Brookline, Mass., Aug. 20, 1925; s. Joseph and Ann (Rosenblum) F.; student Northeastern U., 1942-43, 46-47, Norwich U., 1943; LL.B. cum laude, Boston U., 1950; m. Norma Loew, Dec. 28, 1952; children—Susan Ellen, Lauri Joan, Debra Jane. Admitted to Mass. bar, 1950, since practiced in Boston; partner Parker, Coulter, Daley & White, 1955, Peabody, Koufman & Brewer, 1956-58; sr. partner Fine & Ambrogne, 1959—. Vice pres., dir. Hull Coop. Bank (Mass.); exec. v.p., dir. Garden City Trust Co., Newton, Mass., 1959-63; chmn. bd. Commonwealth Bank & Trust Co., Boston, 1964—; dep. adminstr. Small Bus. Adminstrn., 1961-62; dir. Internat. Industries, Inc., Hi-G, Inc., numerous other corps. Vice chmn. Newton Housing Authority; vice chmn. Kennedy for Senator campaign, 1952. Past pres. Mass. Women's Hosp., Parker Hill Med. Center; trustee Newton Free Library, Beaver Country Day Sch.; treas. League Sch. Boston; other charitable corps. Hon. consul Govt. of Costa Rica in Boston. Mem. Nat. Planning Council, Am., Boston bar Assns., Boston U. Law Sch. Alumni Assn. (v.p. 1965-66), Tau Epsilon Rho (supreme council). Home: 42 Annawan Rd Waban MA 02168 Office: 1 State St Boston MA 02109 also 1700 Pennsylvania Av NW Washington DC 20006

FINE, SIDNEY, educator, historian; b. Cleve., Oct. 11, 1920; s. Morris Louis and Gussie (Redalia) F.; B.A., Western Res. U., 1942; M.A., U. Mich., 1944, Ph.D., 1948; m. Jean Schechter, Dec. 5, 1942; children—Gail Judith, Deborah Ann. Mem. faculty U. Mich., 1948—, prof. history, 1959—, chmn. dept., 1969-71; mem. faculty Salzburg Seminar Am. Studies, 1959. Mem. Nat. Archives Adv. Council, 1968—, Rackham predoctoral fellow U. Mich., 1946-48; Guggenheim fellow, 1957-58. Recipient Distinguished Faculty Achievement award U. Mich., 1969. Mem. Am. Hist. Assn., Orgn. Am. Historians, Labor Historians (pres. 1969-71), Am. Assn. U. Profs., U. Mich. Research Club, U. Mich. Sci. Club, Mich. Acad. Scis., Arts, and Letters. Author: Laissez Faire and the General Welfare State, 1956; The Automobile Under the Blue Eagle (Greatest Distinction award U. Mich. Press 1965), 1963; (with G.S. Brown) The American Past, 2 vols., 1961; Recent America, 1962; Sit-Down: The General Motors Strike of 1936-1937, 1969; also articles. Mem. bd. editors Jour. Am. History, 1964-67, Labor History 1963—. Home: 825 Russett Rd Ann Arbor MI 48103

FINE, VIVIAN, composer; b. Chgo., Sept. 28, 1913; d. David and Rose (Finder) Fine; student composition with Ruth C. Seeger, Roger Sessions, piano with Djane Lavoie-Herz, Abby Whiteside; m. Benjamin Karp, Apr. 5, 1935; children—Margaret, Nina. Composer: Race of Life, 1937; Suite for Piano, 1940; Four Elizabethan Songs, 1943; The Great Wall of China, 1947; A Guide to the Life Expectancy of a Rose, 1956; String Quartet, 1957; Concertante for Piano and Orchestra, 1944; Sonata for Violin and Piano, 1952; Alcestis, 1960; My Son, My Enemy, 1964. Works recorded by Imperial Philharmonic Tokyo, Japanese Philharmonic. Mem. faculty Bennington (Vt.) Coll. Vice pres. Am. Composers Alliance, 1961-65. Recipient award A.S.C.A.P., 1967. Mem. A.S.C.A.P. Address: 19 Prospect St New Paltz NY 12561

FINE, WILLIAM CLYDE, paint and chem. co. exec.; b. Aledo, Okla., Nov. 29, 1917; s. Henry Nathan Floyd and Deva Dolores (Campbell) F.; B.S. in Bus. Adminstrn., U. Wichita, 1938; m. Helen Margaret Goodin, Dec. 31, 1938; 1 son, Robert Hayden. With Firestone Tire & Rubber Co., 1938-41; with Sherwin-Williams Co., Cleve., 1941—, sec., 1962—, asst. treas., 1966—, asst. v.p. finance, 1967-68, v.p. financial operations, 1968-70, v.p. finance, 1970—, also dir. Served to lt. (s.g.) USNR, 1943-46. Decorated Commendation medal. Mem. Financial Execs. Inst., Am. Mgmt. Assn., Conf. Bd., Sigma Phi Epsilon. Mason. Home: 3769 E Surrey Ct Rocky River OH 44116 Office: 101 Prospect Av NW Cleveland OH 44115

FINE, WILLIAM MICHAEL, retail exec.; s. Joseph George and Susan (Moss) F.; student Kenyon Coll., Gambler, O.; m. Patricia Purdy, Aug. 22, 1946; children—Brewster William, Douglas Michael, Timothy James; m. 2d, Susan Payson, Dec. 2, 1967. Ge. mgr. of County Press Inc., Westchester (N.Y.) newspaper chain, 1946-47; pub. Bronxville Record and Tuckahoe Record, 1948-50; fashion advt. mgr. McCall's mag., 1950-54; West coast gen. mgr. McCall Corp., 1954-56; pub. Bride & Home, pub. by Hearst Corp., 1955; exec. editor Good Housekeeping mag., pub. by Hearst Corp., 1957; pub. Harper's Bazaar pub. by Hearst Corp., 1960-69, also pub. dir. of Town and Country, House Beautiful; pres. of Bonwit Teller, 1969—; bd. govs. Genesco, Nashville; dir. Sheffield Watch Co., N.Y.C., Greenway Prodns., Hollywood. Trustee Finch Coll. Served with inf., AUS, World War II. Decorated Bronze Star. Mem. Irish Georgia Soc. (dir.), Irish Am. Council N.Y. (dir.), Delta Tau Delta. Club: Country (Darien); Overseas Press (N.Y.C.). Author: That Day With God, 1965. Contbr. articles to mags. Home: 194 Long Neck Point Rd Darien CT 06820 Office: 721 Fifth Av New York City NY 10022

FINEBERG, MEYER HERBERT, ret. hosp. adminstr.; b. Cleve., Sept. 15, 1899; s. Juda and Eva (Brudno) F.; student Harvard, 1917-18; A.B. magna cum laude, Western Res. U., 1921, M.D., 1924; m. Louise Cohen, Feb. 7, 1942; 1 dau., Joyce. Intern Mt. Sinai Hosp., Cleve., 1924-25, mem. vis. staff, 1927-39; resident medicine Montefiore Hosp., N.Y.C., 1925-27; mem. vis. staff Cleve. City Hosp., 1934-39; instr. medicine Western Res. U. Sch. Medicine, 1934-39; asst. dir. Beth Israel Hosp., Boston, 1939-41; chief profl. services, also hosp. dir. Va, 1946-69; dir. Buffalo VA Hosp., 1962-69; asst. clin. prof. medicine State U. N.Y. at Buffalo. Served to col. M.C., Aus, 1941-46. Decorated Army Commendation ribbon. Diplomate Am. Bd. Internal Medicine. Fellow A.C.P., Am. Coll. Hosp. Adminstrs.; mem. A.M.A., Phi Beta Kappa. Contbr. profl. jours. Home: 6 Heritage Dr Salem MA 01970

FINEBERG, SOLOMON ANDHIL, human relations cons.; b. Pitts. Nov. 29, 1896; s. Nathan and Libbie (Landau) F.; A.B., U. Cin., 1917; Rabbi, Hebrew Union Coll., 1920, D.D., 1958; Ph.D., Columbia, 1932; m. Hilda Cohen, 1925. Rabbi, Niagara Falls, N.Y., 1920-24, Pitts., 1924-25, Mt. Vernon, N.Y., 1929-37; community relations cons. Am. Jewish Com., 1939- 64; cons. Nat. Conf. Christians and Jews, 1965—; coordinator N.Y. Interracial Colloquoy, 1966—; exec. dir. Nat. Com. for Commitment to Brotherhood, 1971—; specialist in human relations U.S. State Dept. Internat. Exchange Program in Germany, 1954. Served with USMC, 1917-19. Recipient Am. Heritage Freedom award, 1959. Mem. Central Conf. Am. Rabbis, Nat. Assn. Inter-group Relations Ofcls. (mem. bd. 1954-56), Jewish Community Relations Workers Assn. (pres. 1950-54), U.S. Jewish War Vets. (nat. chaplain 1932-36), Hebrew Union Coll.-Jewish Inst. Religion Alumni Assn. Mem. B'nai B'rith. Author: Biblical Myth and Legend; Project in American Jewish History; Overcoming Anti-Semitism; Punishment Without Crime (Anisfield Wolf Literary award), 1949; The Rosenberg Case; Report on Germany; Deflating the Professional Bigot; Religion Behind the Iron Curtain; Plight of Soviet Jews. Home: 19 William St Mount Vernon NY 10552 (summer) Chesterfield Stage Brattleboro VT 05301 Office: 43 W 57th St New York City NY 10019

FINEGAN, JAMES W., advt. agy. exec. Pres. Gray & Rogers, Inc., Phila. Office: 12 S 12th St Philadelphia PA 19107*

FINEGAN, WILLIAM JAMES, composer, orchestrator; b. Newark, Apr. 3, 1917; s. William Joseph and Christina (Bogle) F.; studied with Rudolph Winthrop and Elizabeth Connolly, 1934-37, Stefan Wolpe, 1946-48, Valerie Soudere, 1948-52; student Paris Conservatory, 1948-52; m. Kathleen Blessing, June 30, 1936; 1 foster son, Thomas Patrick. Orchestra leader, 1935-38; orchestrator Glenn Miller Orchestra, 1938-41, later for Tommy Dorsey, Horace Heidt, other bands; with Geraldo Orchestra, London, Eng., 1949- 51; movie writing 20th Century Fox, motion pictures include Sun Valley Serenade, Orchestra Wives, Fabulous Dorsey's; co-organizer Sauter-Finegan Orchestra, co-leader, 1952—, also orchestrator, composer; recorded for RCA Victor, 1952; orchestrator for NBC, Universal Pictures. Served as pvt. AUS, 1943-45. Mem. Am. Fedn. Musicians, A.S.C.A.P. Home: Narumson Rd Rumson NJ 07760 Office: 425 E 63d St New York City NY 10021

FINELL, MARVIN, ins. co. exec.; b. Chattanooga, July 30, 1924; s. Morris and Rose (Baras) Finkelstein; A.B., Harvard, 1947, LL.B., 1950; m. Karen Kraus, Sept. 9, 1961; children—Steven, Stephanie. Admitted to Cal. bar, 1951, practiced in Beverly Hills; partner firm Wyman, Bautzer, Finell, Rothman & Kuchel, 1952-71; exec. v.p. ins. operations and financial services Nat. Gen. Corp., 1971—, also dir.; chmn. bd. Republic Ind. Co., Gt. Am. Inst. Co., Am. Nat. Ins. Co., Constellation Reins. Co., Gt. Am. Life Ins. Co. Bd. dirs. Cal. Coll. Podiatric Medicine, 1965-68. Served as navigator USAAF, World War II. Mem. Cal. Bar Assn., Phi Beta Kappa. Editor Harvard Law Rev., 1949-50. Home: 1020 Ridgedale Dr Beverly Hills CA 90210 Office: 9601 Wilshire Blvd Beverly Hills CA 90210

FINEMAN, IRVING author; b. N.Y.C., Apr. 9, 1893; s. Joseph and Rebecca Rachel (Blanc) F.; student N.Y. pub. schs.; tech. studies and engrng. jobs, 1912-15; B.S., Mass. Inst. Tech., and Harvard, 1917; m. Helene Hughes, July 7, 1935 (div.); children—Joseph Clinton, Jonathan Peter. Engrng. practice, in various parts of U.S. and Can., 1912-29; taught in Engrng. Sch., U. Ill., 1925-28; turned to literary profession, 1930, when first novel This Pure Young Man won Longmans Green prize; mem. faculty lit. Bennington Coll., 1932-38; cons. RAND Corp., Santa Monica, Cal., 1957. Served as engr. officer USN, 1917-22. Mem. Internat. Platform Assn., Authors League Am., Screen Writers' Guild. Author novels including: Hear Ye Sons, 1933; Doctor Addams, 1938; Akiba, A Child's Play, 1950; Fig Tree Madonna (Stevens award for Drama from Dramatists Alliance, Stanford U. 1951, produced U. Cal. at Los Angeles 1954); (biography) Woman of Valor: The Life of Henrietta Szold, 1961; Lovers Must Learn (made into movie Rome Adventure); Little Red Riding Hood, A Play for Modern Children (produced various schs.). Contbr. short stories, verse lit. criticism and articles to leading mags.; motion-picture stories, and screen-plays for Metro-Goldwyn-Mayer, Warner Brothers, Universal, R.K.O., and Columbia Pictures. Home: Shaftsbury VT 05262

FINERTY, JOHN CHARLES, univ. adminstr.; b. Chgo., Oct. 20, 1914; s. John Lawrence and Hulda (Schulte) F.; A.B., Kalamazoo Coll., 1937; M.S., Kan. State Coll., 1939; Ph.D., U. Wis., 1942; m. Mildred King, Dec. 28, 1940; children—Olivia Lou (Mrs. John L. Moore), Donna Elizabeth (Mrs. James D. Gatewood). Rackham Found. postdoctoral fellow U. Mich., 1942-43, instr. anatomy, 1943-46; asst. prof. anatomy Washington U., St. Louis, 1946-49; asso. prof., then prof. anatomy U. Tex. at Galveston, 1949-56, asst. dean, 1954-56; prof. anatomy, chmn. dept. U. Miami (Fla.) Sch. Medicine, 1956-66, also asso. dean.; prof. anatomy, dean La. State U. Sch. of Medicine, New Orleans, 1966-71, vice chancellor La. State Med. Center, 1971—. Mem. com. pathogenesis cancer Am. Cancer Soc., 1960-63; bd. mem. La. Regional Med. Program, Greater New Orleans Health Planning Council (treas. 1971); anatomy test com. Nat. Bd. Med. Examiners, 1964-68, mem. rev. com. on med. sch. constrn., 1968-70. Fellow A.A.A.S.; mem. Am. Assn. Anatomists (program sec. 1966—), Am. Physiol. Soc., Endocrine Soc., Radiation Research Soc., Soc. Exptl. Biology and Medicine, Tex. Acad. Sci. (pres. 1955-56), Sigma Xi (pres. U. Tex. med. chpt. 1955-56), Phi Kappa Phi, Omicron Delta Kappa. Rotarian. Clubs: Audubon Golf, Coral Gables Country. Home: 5561 Jacquelyn Ct New Orleans LA 70124

FINESHRIBER, WILLIAM H., Jr. motion picture and broadcasting exec.; b. Davenport, Ia., Nov. 4, 1909; s. William H. and Mae (Wallerstein) F.; B.A. summa cum laude, Princeton, 1931; student Sorbonne U., 1931; m. Clotilde Heller, Apr. 12, 1933 (dec.); children—Joy, William H. III (dec.); m. 2d, Ruth Moskin, Aug. 9, 1959. Pub. relations exec. CBS, 1931-34, dir. music, 1937-40, dir. shortwave programs, 1940-43, asst. dir. broadcasts, 1943-46, gen. mgr. program dept., 1946-49; mgr. Carnegie Hall, 1934-37; v.p. in charge programs MBS, 1949-51, exec. v.p. 1951-53, dir., 1952-53; v.p., gen. mgr., radio and TV networks, NBC, 1953, v.p. in charge radio networks, 1954-56; v.p. Television Programs of Am., Inc., 1956-57; dir. internat. operations Screen Gems. Inc. until 1959; v.p. Motion Picture Assn. Am., Motion Picture Export Assn. Am., 1960—. Dir., mem. exec. com. Broadcast Advt. Bur.; chmn. radio and TV com. Am. Jewish Tercentenary. Mem. president's citizen food com. 1947; co-chmn. nat. radio div. Nat. Found. Infantile Paralysis, 1951-55. Mem. Nat. Assn. Broadcasters (program exec. bd.), Radio Diffusion Francaise (adv. com. 1946-48), Nat. Conf. Christians and Jews (commn. mass communications 1951-55), Acad. TV Arts and Scis., Radio and TV Execs. Club, Phi Beta Kappa. Clubs: Radio Pioneers (v.p.), Rockefeller Luncheon, Princeton (N.Y.C.). Author: Stendhal, the Romantic Realist, 1932. Home: 15 E 91st St New York City NY 10028 Office: 522 Fifth Av New York City NY 10036

FINESTONE, ARNOLD BARON, chem. co. exec.; b. N.Y.C., Dec. 19, 1929; s. Irving and Jean (Rosenhaus) F.; B.A., N.Y. U., 1951; Ph.D. in Polymer Chemistry (fellow), Poly. Inst. Bklyn., 1955; m. Susan Frohlich, Aug. 15, 1954; children— Jeanne Lee, Jacqueline Mary, Jessica Carla. Research chemist Westinghouse Research Lab., Westinghouse Electric Corp., Pitts., 1955-56, group leader, 1956-57; group leader long range research Foster Grant Co., Inc., Leominster, Mass., 1957-59, mgr. styrene polymer research, 1959-62, co-dir. research and devel., 1962-64, dir. research and devel. and market devel., 1964-65, v.p., dir. research and devel. and market devel., 1965-68, v.p., dir. planning and devel., 1968-71; exec. v.p. Dart Industries Chem. Group, Paramus, N.J., 1971—. First v.p. Leominster United Fund, 1970-71, Leominster YMCA, 1969-71; pres. Leominster Cancer Found., 1966. Trustee Leominster Library. Mem. Am., Brit. chem. socs., Soc. Plastic Engrs., Soc. Plastic Industries, Mfg. Chemists Assn., Soc. Plastic Industries (chmn. pigment task force), N.Y. Chemist Club, Sigma Xi. Jewish religion. Clubs: Edgewood Country (Rivervale, N.J.); Oak Hill Country (Fitchburo, Mass.). Contbr. articles profl. jours. Patentee in field. Home: 51 Indian Dr Woodcliff Lake NJ 07675 Office: W 115 Century Rd Paramus NJ 07652

FINESTONE, HARRY, educator; b. Atlanta, July 19, 1920; s. Barney and Ida (Schlossman) F.; B.A. in English, Emory U., 1941; M.A. in English Lit., U. Chgo., 1942, Ph.D. in Am. Lit., 1953; m. Mary Eve Israel, Jan. 27, 1955; children—Anne, Stephen, Peter. Instr. U. Va., 1953-56; asst. prof. U. N.C. at Greensboro, 1956-62; asst. prof. English, San Fernando Valley State Coll., Northridge, Cal., 1962—, asst. chmn. dept., 1965-67, chmn. dept., 1967-70, dean academic planning, 1970—; Fulbright lectr. U. Oslo, Norway, 1959-60. Served with USAAF, 1942-45. Mem. Modern Lang. Assn., Cal. Assn. Tchrs. English (bd. dirs. 1967-69), Assn. Depts. of English (dir. nat. seminar English dept. chmn. 1970, 71, coordinator nat. interdisciplinary seminars 1971-72), Cal. State Coll. English Council (pres. 1967-69), Nat. Council Tchrs. English (bd. dirs. 1967-69, speaker convs. 1970, 71). Editor: Bacon's Rebellion: The Contemporary Newsheets, 1956; (with Oliver Evans) The World of the Short Story: Archetypes in Action, 1971. Contbr. Am. Lit. Scholarship, 1964-70. Home: 19200 Itasca St Northridge CA 91324

FINETTE, FLORENCE, nurse educator; b. Aurora, Ill., July 4, 1906; d. Frank Moore and Anna (Madden) Durham; student St. Charles Sch. Nursing, Aurora, 1923-26; B.S., DePaul U., 1941; M.S. U. Chgo., 1947, also postgrad. work; m. Carl G. Finette, Aug. 2, 1938. Instr. St. Charles Sch. Nursing, Aurora, 1927-29; dir., edn. dir. St. Mary Sch. Nursing, Kakakee, Ill., 1929-34; edn. dir., acting dir. Garfield Park Sch. Nursing, Chgo., 1934-39; edn. dir. St. Joseph Mercy Sch. Nursing, Aurora, 1939-44; instr. Loyola U., Chgo., 1944-47; chmn., prof. nursing DePaul U., 1947—. Mem. Nat. League Nursing, Am. Nurses Assn. (past mem. exec. com. of educators, adminstrs. sect.), Ill. (pres. 1955-59, dir.), Chgo. (pres. 1941-45) leagues nursing, Ill. Hosp. Assn. (hon.), Am. Assn. U. Profs., Am. Adult Edn. Assn. Home: 356 Lakelawn Blvd Aurora IL 60506 Office: 2323 N Seminary Chicago IL 60614

FINGER, HAROLD B., Govt. ofcl., space scientist, urbanologist; b. N.Y.C., Feb. 18, 1924; s. Beny and Anna (Perlmutter) F.; B.M.E., City Coll. N.Y., 1944; M.S. in Aero Engring., Case Inst. Tech., 1950; m. Arlene Karsch, June 11, 1949; children—Barbara Lynn, Elyse Sue, Sandra Ruth. With NASA, and predecessor, 1944-69, mgr. joint AEC-NASA Space Nuclear Propulsion Office, 1960-67, dir. nuclear systems NASA, 1961-64, dir. nuclear systems and space power, 1964-67, asso. adminstr. for orgn. and mgmt., 1967-69; dir. space nuclear systems div. AEC, 1965-67; asst. sec. for research and tech. Dept. Housing and Urban Devel., 1969—. Co- recipient Manley Meml. award Soc. Automotive Engrs., 1957; recipient Outstanding Leadership medal NASA, 1966; Jame H. Wyld propulsion award Am. Inst. Aeros. and Astronautics, 1968. Mem. Am. Inst. Aeros. and Astronautics. Home: 6908 Millwood Rd Bethesda MD 20034 Office: Dept Housing and Urban Development Washington DC 20410

FINGER, HOMER ELLIS, Jr., bishop; b. Ripley, Miss., Oct. 8, 1916; s. Homer Ellis and Bertha (Rogers) F.; A.B., Millsaps Coll., Jackson, Miss., 1937; student Emory U., 1938-39; B.D., Yale, 1941; student Union Theol. Sem., N.Y.C., 1946; D.D. (hon.), Centenary Coll. La., 1954; m. Mamie Lee Ratliff, Oct. 6, 1942; children—Homer Ellis, William Ratliff, Elizabeth Ellen. Math. tchr. Aberdeen (Miss.) High Sch., 1937-38; ordained to ministry Meth. Ch., 1941; pastor, Coldwater, Miss., 1941-43, Oxford, Miss., 1946-52; pres. Millsaps Coll., 1952-64; resident bishop Meth. Ch., Nashville, 1964—. Mem. commn. on colls., exec. council So. Assn. Colls. and Secondary Schs.; mem. univ. senate Meth. Ch.; chmn. United Meth. Commn. on Chaplains; mem. bd. Christian social concerns United Meth. Ch.; mem. exec. com. World Meth. Council. Served as chaplain USNR, Air Sta., Pensacola, Fla., 1944-45, with 75th constrn. bn., P.I., 1945-46. Mem. Jackson C. of C. (dir.), Pi Kappa Alpha, Omicron Delta Kappa, Eta Sigma Phi (past nat. pres.). Rotarian (dir. Jackson). Home: 301 Hillwood Dr Nashville TN 37205 Office: 95 White Bridge Rd Nashville TN 37205

FINGER, JOHN HOLDEN, lawyer; b. Oakland, Cal., June 29, 1913; s. Clyde P. and Jennie (Miller) F.; A.B., U. Cal., 1933; m. Dorothy C. Riley, Dec. 30, 1950; 476 Morris Av Rockville Centre NY 11570 bar, 1937; pvt. practice of law, San Francisco, 1937-42; chief mil. commn. sect. Far East Hdqrs. War Dept., Tokyo, 1946-47; partner Hoberg, Finger, Brown & Abramson, San Francisco, 1947-. Dir., 1st Fed. Savs. & Loan Assn. of Fresno, Hampton House Financial Corp., Fresno, trustee Pacific Sch. Religion; mem. bd. dirs. San Francisco Legal Aid Society. San Francisco Legal Aid Soc.; bd. visitors Judge Adv. Gen. Sch., Charlottesville Va., Stanford U. Law Sch. President Laymen's Fellowship, No. California Conference Congl. Churches, 1951-53, moderator, 1954-55. Served to major, judge adv. general corps AUS, 1942-46; col. Res. Decorated Legion of Merit. Fellow Gen. Dept., 1962-64, U.S. Army Judiciary, 1967-68. Decorated Legion of Merit. Fellow Am. Bar Found., Am. Coll. Trial Lawyers; Mem. Am. Judicature Soc., Am. Am. Bar Assn., Bar Assn. San Francisco (dir. 1960-62), Judge Adv. Assn. 1960-62), Judge Adv. Assn. (dir. 1957-, pres. 1964-65), Lawyers Club San Francisco (pres. 1953), State Bar Cal. (bd. govs. 1965-68, pres. 1967-68), Phi Alpha Delta, Sigma Phi Epsilon. Home: 12675 Skyline Blvd Oakland, CA 94610 Office: 703 Market St San Francisco, CA 94103.

FINGER, KENNETH FRANKLIN, scientist, educator; b. Antigo, Wis., Jan. 2, 1929; s. Otto Edward and Elsie (Kuehn) F.; B.S., U. Wis., 1951, M.S., 1953, Ph.D., 1955; m. Lois Eleanor Hoppe, Nov. 16, 1951; 1 son, William Lee. Sr. investigator Chas. Pfizer & Co. Bklyn. 1955-57, 1959-60, research supr., 1960-61, research mgr., 1961-63; asso. prof. Sch. Pharmacy, U. Wis., Madison, 1963-67, prof., 1967-68; dean Coll. Pharmacy, U. Fla., 1968—; guest worker Nat. Heart Inst., 1957-59. Cons. Pfizer Med. Research Labs., 1963-64, A.H. Robins, Richmond, Va. 1965—. Mem. pharmacy review com. Dept. Health Edn. and Welfare; Govs Task Force on Dangerous Drugs, Narcotics and Alcohol Abuse, State of Fla.; profl. edn. com. Fla. div. Am. Cancer Soc. Recipient Teaching award Sch. Pharmacy, U. Wis., 1967. Mem. Am. Soc. Pharmacology and Exptl. Therapeutics. Am. Pharm. Assn., Wis. Acad. Sci., Arts and Letters, Am. Assn. Coll. of Pharmacy, Acad. Pharm. Scis., Am. Chem. Soc., Sigma Xi, Rho Chi. Author publications on adrenergic drugs. Home: 1615 N W 31st Terrace Gainesville FL 32601

FINGER, SEYMOUR MAXWELL, ambassador; b. N.Y.C., Apr. 30, 1915; s. Samuel and Bella (Spiegel) F.; B.S., Ohio U., 1935; postgrad. U. Cin., 1942, Littauer Sch. Pub. Affairs, Harvard, 1953-54; m. Helen Kotcher, Apr. 5, 1956; 1 son, Mark. Branch mgr. Photo Reflex Studios, Inc., 1935-37, 1938-40, regional supr., 1940-43, asst. to v.p., 1945-46; tchr. O'Keefe Jr. High Sch., 1937-38; vice consul Am. embassy, Stuttgart, Germany, 1946-49; 2d sec. Am. embassy, Paris, France, 1949-51; 2d sec., econ. officer Am. legation, Budapest, Hungary, 1951-53; econ. def. officer Am. embassy, Rome, 1954-55; 1st sec. Am. embassy, Vientane, Loas, 1955-56; sr. econ. adv. U.S. Mission to UN, 1956-65; counselor of mission to UN, 1965-67; ambassador, sr. adviser to permanent rep. U.S. Mission to UN, 1967-71; prof. govt. City U. N.Y., S.I. Community Coll., 1971—; sr. adviser policy studies UN Assn. of U.S.A., N.Y.C., 1971—; mem. U.S. delegation to UN Gen. Assembly, 11th- 25th sessions, chmn. security council com. on sanctions in Rhodesia, mem. UN com. on contbrs.; spl. cons. to Brookings Instn., 1964; panel mem. UN Inst. for Tng. and Research. Served as staff sgt. AUS, 1943-45. Mem. Council on Fgn. Relations, Inst. for Mediterranean Affairs (pres. 1971—), Am. Soc. Internat. Law, Acad. Polit. Sci., Am. Acad. Polit. and Social Sci., Phi Beta Kappa, Kappa Delta Pi. Clubs: American (Paris, Rome). Author: The Escape Clause: Its Impact on U.S. Commercial Policy; A New Approach to Colonial Problems at the UN. Home: 476 Morris Av Rockville Centre NY 11570 Office: 799 UN Plaza New York City NY 10017

FINGESTEN, PETER, sculptor; b. Berlin, Germany, Mar. 20, 1916; s. Michel and Bianca (Schiek) F.; B.F.A., Fine Arts Coll., Berlin, 1934, M.F.A., 1935; student Pa. Acad. Fine Arts, 1940-43; married; 1 dau., Alexandra. Came to U.S. 1939, naturalized, 1943. Mem. faculty Coll. Liberal Arts, Manhattan Coll., N.Y.C., 1946-50; lectr. Asia Inst., summer 1950; became asso. in arts Pace Coll., 1950, asso. prof., chmn. art dept., now prof.; vis. prof. Grad. Sch. Music Edn. N.Y. U. Held one man shows in Berlin, Milan, Paris, Phila., Woodstock, N.Y.C., 1935—; represented in permanent collections Galerie Denis René, Paris, Galery Bolaffio, Milan. Recipient first prize Woodmere Art Gallery, Phila., 1942; Internat. Exhbn. Black and White, Milan, 1937;

Louis Comfort Tiffany Found. grant for sculpture, 1948; Commn. for Art of Democratic Living, and Am. Fedn. of Art Nat. Traveling Exhbn., 1951. Served overseas, C.E., Tech. Intelligence, U.S. Army, 1943-45. Mem. Coll. Art Assn., Am. Assn. U. Profs., Am. Soc. for Aesthetics. Mem. Soc. of Friends. Author: Dr. F. Paronelli, Catalogo Delle Opere Di Peter Fingesten (monograph), 1938; Ex Libris by Michel Fingesten (illustrated monograph), 1954; East is East, 1956; The Eclipse of Symbolism, 1970. Contbr. articles art jours. Home: 339 E 18th St New York City NY 10003 Office: Pace Coll 41 Park Row New York City NY 10038

FINHOLT, ALBERT EDWARD, coll. ofcl.; b. Chgo., Jan. 28, 1918; s. Albert E. and Signe (Olsen) F.; A.B., Knox Coll., 1938; postgrad. Purdue U., 1938-39; Ph.D., U. Chgo., 1946; m. Marion Lund, Aug. 9, 1941; children—Joan, Ann, David, Ellen. Research chemist Gen. Printing Ink Co., Chgo., 1939-42; research asst. Manhattan Dist. Signal Corps and CWS, 1942-45; research asso. U. Chgo., 1946-47; chief chemist Metal Hydrides, Inc., Beverly, Mass., 1947-49; prof. St. Olaf Coll., 1949—, chmn. chemistry dept., 1957—, chmn. sci. div., 1959—, dean coll., 1964—, now also v.p.; vis. scientist NSF, 1960-64; NSF faculty fellow Stanford U., 1962-63. Mem. Phi Beta Kappa, Sigma Xi, Tau Kappa Epsilon. Research metal hydrides. Home: 1127 W 2d St Northfield, MN 55057.

FINI, LEONOR, painter; b. Buenos Aires, Argentina, Aug. 30, 1918; s. Ermino and Malvina (Braun) F.; LL.D. (hon.), U. Trieste (Italy). One-man shows include Gallery Zolas, Paris, France, also galleries in N Y C, Milan, Italy, Rome, Italy.

FINK, ARTHUR EMIL, educator; b. Phila., Jan. 20, 1903; s. Johann Christian and Phillipa (Schaefer) F.; student Girard Coll. (elementary and high sch.), 1912-20; A.B., U. Pa., 1924, A.M., 1930, Ph.D., 1936, M.Social Work, Sch. of Social Work, 1937; m. Kathleen Boles, June 13, 1931; children—Susan Boles, Gretchen Boles. Christopher Boles. Instr. sociology U. Pa., 1930-33, 1935-38; headworker Univ. Settlement House, Phila., 1933-34; asst. dir. Inter-Agy. Council for Youth, 1934-35; prof. social work, dir. social work tng. U. Ga., 1938-41; asso. dir., social protection div. Fed. Security Agy., Washington, 1941-45; prof. social work U. N.C., 1945—, dean Sch. Social Work, 1945-65; Fulbright lectr. U. Birmingham (Eng.), 1951-52. Mem. Nat. Assn. Social Workers (chmn. Ga. 1939-41; mem. nat. bd. 1943-46), Nat. Conf. Social Work (chmn. social action sect. 1945-46), Nat. Probation and Parole Assn., Am. Assn. U., Profs., Am. Pub. Welfare Assn., Am. Assn. Schs. Social Work (bd. dirs. 1945-48), So. Sociol. Soc. (v.p. 1941-42), N.C. Conf. Social Service (dir. 1946-49), A.A.A.S. Democrat. Presbyn. Author: Causes of Crime, 1938; The Field of Social Work, 1942, latest rev. edit., 1968. Home: 812 Woodland Av Chapel Hill NC 27514

FINK, DANIEL JULIEN, mfg. exec.; b. Jersey City, Dec. 13, 1926; s. Joseph and Dorothy (Weisberger) F.; student N.Y. U., 1945; B.S., Mass. Inst. Tech., 1948, M.S., 1949; m. Tobie E. Weiss, June 24, 1951; children—Kenneth Wayne, Betsy Ilene, Karen Patrice. Aeromechanics engr. Cornell Aero. Lab., Buffalo, 1948; chief aircraft dynamics Bell Aircraft Corp., Buffalo, 1949-52; with Allied Research Assos., Inc., Concord, Mass., 1952-63, v.p., 1959-63; asst. dir. def. research and engring. (def. systems) Dept. Def., 1963-65, dep. dir. def. research and engring. (strategic and space systems), 1965-67; gen. mgr. space systems orgn., missiles and space div. Gen. Electric Co., 1967-69, v.p., gen. mgr. space div., 1969-69, v.p., gen. mgr. space div., 1968—; spl. aerospace research and devel. dir. Hyperion Industries, Inc., Watertown, Mass., 1961-63. Mem. def. sci. bd. Def. Dept., 1968—. Recipient Distinguished Pub. Service award Dept. Def. Registered profl. engr., Mass. Asso. fellow Am. Inst. Aeros. and Astronautics (chmn. Boston 1962, dir. 1967-69); mem. Am. Ordnance Assn. Club: Cosmos (Washington). Patentee vibration isolation, weapons effects, weapon systems mgmt., aerospace engring. Home: 1154 Norsam Rd Gladwyne PA 19035 Office: PO Box 8555 Philadelphia PA 19101

FINK, DAVID REAM, Jr., univ. ofcl.; b. Red Lion, Pa., Aug. 31, 1928; s. David Ream and Rachel (Heindel) F.; B.A., Dartmouth, 1950; M.S., U. Pa., 1953, Ph.D., 1957; m. Barbara Lee Pickens, July 15, 1950; children—David Ream III, Julianne. Tchr., Fenn Sch., Concord, Mass., 1950-52; mem. faculty U. Me., 1957—, prof. ednl. measurement Coll. Edn., 1957-65, dean Portland campus, 1965- 68, provost, 1968-70, planner, office of chancellor, 1970—. Pres., chmn. bd. Research Inst., Gulf, Me., 1968—. Trustee Portland Pub. Library; bd. dirs. Community Counseling Center. Mem. Am. Ednl. Research Assn., Nat. Council Measurement in Edn., Phi Kappa Phi. Home: 33 Littlejohn Rd Cape Elizabeth ME 04107 Office: 96 Falmouth St Portland ME 04103

FINK, DONALD GLEN, engr., editor; b. Englewood, N.J., Nov. 8, 1911; s. Harold Gardner and Margaret (Glen) F.; B.S., Mass. Inst. Tech., 1933; M.S., Columbia, 1942; m. Alice Marjorie Berry, Apr. 10, 1948; children—Kathleen Marion, Stephen Donald, Susan Carol. Research asst. Mass. Inst. Tech., 1933-34, staff radiation lab., 1941-43, head Loran div., 1943; editorial staff Electronics, 1934-52, editor in chief, 1946-52; bd. dirs. McGraw-Hill Book Co., Inc., 1947-52, cons. editor TV Series, 1949—; vice chmn. Nat. TV System Com., 1950-52, panel chmn. 1950-53; chmn. prep. com. TV, Dept. State, 1951-55; with Philco Corp., 1952-62, dir. research, 1952-58, dir., gen. mgr. research div., 1959-62, v.p.-research, 1961; gen. mgr. I.E.E.E., N.Y.C., 1962—; cons., Belgium, 1952. Expert cons. on radar and electronic nav. Office Sec. War, 1943-45; cons. to comdr. atom bomb tests, Bikini, 1946; mem. com. nav. research and devel. bd. Dept. Def., 1948-51. Recipient Medal of Freedom, 1946; Presdl. Certificate Merit for wartime service, 1948; plaque for contbns. to TV, I.R.E., 1951; Am. Technologists award N.Y. Inst. Tech., 1958; Outstanding Civilian Service medal U.S. Army, 1969; Citation for Outstanding Service to TV, Internat. TV Symposium, Montreux, 1971. Fellow Instn. Elec. Engrs. (London), I.E.E.E. (pres. I.R.E. 1958), Soc. Motion Picture and TV Engrs. (jour. award 1956); mem. Nat. Acad. Engring., Sigma Xi, Tau Beta Pi, Eta Kappa Nu (eminent mem.), Phi Mu Delta. Clubs: Cosmos (Washington); Mt. Kisco (N.Y.) Country: Engineers (N.Y.C.). Author Engineering Electronics, 1938; Principles of TV Engineering 1940; Microwave Radar, 1942; Radar Engineering, 1947; TV Engineering, 1952; Color Television Standards, 1955; Television Engineering Handbook, 1957; Physics of Television, 1960; Computers and the Human Mind, 1966; Standard Handbook for Electrical Engineers, 1968; others. Home: Kitchel Rd Mt Kisco NY 10549 Office: 345 E 47th St New York City NY 10017

FINK, FRANCIS A., editor; b. Ft. Wayne, Ind., Oct. 12, 1907; s. Francis J. and Loretta Ann (Noll) F.; A.B., Notre Dame U., 1930; m. Helen E. Hartman, Feb. 3, 1931; children—John F., William J. James M., Helen Ann, Carol Sue, Thomas M. Reporter, Ft. Wayne News-Sentinel, 1928-29; asso. editor Our Sunday Visitor, 1930-35, mng. editor, 1935, trustee and mem. bd., 1954-68, exec. v.p., 1968. Trustee Cath. Ch. Extension Soc., 1955; founded The Family Digest, 1945; bus. mgr. The Priest, 1944—; v.p., dir. 1st Nat. Bank. First pres. Huntington County Community Chest. Awarded Nat. Family Cath. Action prize, 1948. Mem. Cath. Press Assn. U.S. (pres. 1950-52, St. Francis de Sales award 1971). K.C., Elk, Moose. Clubs: Lafontaine Country, Rotary (Huntington); Country (Ft. Wayne). Compiler: Church in United States History, 1936. Home: 1544 Poplar St Huntington IN 46750 Office: Huntington IN 46750

FINK, FRANK WOLFE, aero. engr.; b. Phila., Jan. 13, 1905; s. Elwood and Gertrude (Wolfe) F.; B.S., U. Colo., 1928; D.Sc., Northrup Inst. Tech., 1963; m. Janet Glendinning, Sept. 12, 1929; children—James Elwood, John Dillon, Susan F. Farrar. Designer, aerodynamicist, project engr. airplane div., Curtiss-Wright Corp., 1928-35; designer, group engr., project engineer, chief prodn. engr., chief engr. Convair div. Gen. Dynamics Corp., 1935-55; v.p. engring. Ryan Aero. Co., San Diego, 1955- 65; pres. San Diego Aircraft Engring., Inc., 1965—; dir. Air Logistics Corp., Pasadena, Cal. Cons. tech. adv. panel aeros. Dept. Def. Bd. dirs. San Diego Soc. Crippled Children, San Diego Child Guidance Clinic, So. Cal. Industry-Edn. Council, U. Colo. Engring. Devel. Found. Registered profl. engineer, State of Cal. Fellow Inst. Aero. Scis.; mem. Am. Rocket Soc., Am. Ordnance Assn., Nat. Mgmt. Assn., Soc. Automotive Engrs. (pres. 1962, bd. dirs.), Aerospace Industry Assn., Nat. Aero. Assn., Army Aviation Assn., Am. Mgmt. Assn., San Diego C. of C. Prebyn. (elder). Clubs: San Diego Yacht, San Diego Lions, San Diego. Contbr. articles engring., trade jours. Home: 550 Gage Lane San Diego, CA 92106 Office: 1730 Kettner Blvd San Diego CA 92101

FINK, GREGORY BURNELL, educator, pharmacologist; b. Outlook, Mont., Aug. 3, 1928; s. Edward N. and Eleanor (Anderson) F.; B.S., Univ. Mont., 1950; Ph.D., U. Utah, 1960; m. Jeaneen R. Harrison, Dec. 28, 1957; children—Lisa, Lynnette, Lori; m. Patricia R. Smith, Oct. 23, 1970. Asst. prof. Wash. State U., 1960-63, U. Kan., 1964; prof. pharmacology Ore. State U., 1964—, head dept., 1964-70. Mem. Ore. Drug Adv. Council. Served with AUS, 1951- 52. Mem. Am. Pharm. Assn., Acad. Pharm. Scis., A.A.A.S., Am. Soc. for Pharmacology and Exptl. Therapeutics, Western Pharmacology Soc., Rho Chi, Sigma Xi. Elk. Home: 2555 Pendleton Pl Corvallis OR 97330

FINK, HERBERT LEWIS, educator, artist; b. Providence, Sept. 8, 1921; s. Harry Harris and Clara (Cohen) F.; student Carnegie Inst. Tech., 1941; B.F.A., R.I. Sch. Design, 1949; M.F.A., Yale, 1956; m. Polly Norton, June 12, 1948; children—Peter, Nicholas Ives, Sarah Elizabeth. Instr. painting and drawing R.I. Sch. Design, 1951-61, Yale, 1956-61; chmn. dept. art So. Ill. U., Carbondale, 1961—; exhbns. include Coll. Print Annual Ohio, 1939, Midwest Exhbn., Omaha, 1958, Am. Color Print Soc., 1959, Phila. Mus. Art, 1959; represented in permanent collections univs. Mich. and Ia., Boston Mus. Art, Md. Inst., Brown U., Library of Congress, Boston Mus. Fine Arts, Smith Coll., Yale Gallery Art, Joslyn Meml. Mus., R.I. Sch. Design, (mural) R.I. Post Office lobby, Providence, (metal sculpture) Sen. Green Airport, R.I., (archtl. screen) Hartford Bank & Trust Bldg. (Conn.). Trustee Tiffany Found. Recipient Chaloner prize, 1951-52, 52-53, Tiffany award, 1958, Ford Fund purchase award, 1959; purchase prizes at Am. Graphic Arts exhbn., 1959, Library of Congress, 1959, Purchase award Washington Ann., 1959; awards Coll. Print Annual Ohio, 1959, Midwest Exhbn., Omaha, 1958, Am. Color Print Soc., 1959, Art Dirs. Annual, 1959; Guggenheim fellow, 1965- 66. Home: 1003 W Hillcrest Dr Carbondale IL 62901

FINK, JOHN, newspaperman; b. Farmington, Ill., Mar. 15, 1926; s. Walter Phillip and Alta Blanche (Payton) F.; B.A., Millikin U., 1949; M.A., U. Ill., 1950; postgrad. U. Wis., 1950-51; m. Eloise Darlene Bradley, Aug. 8, 1949; children—Sara, Joel, Alison. Reporter, City News Bur. Chgo., 1952-53; mem. staff Chgo. Tribune, 1953—, asst. Sunday editor, 1961-67, editor Tribune mag., 1963—. Served USNR, 1944-46. Mem. Chgo. Press Club, Chgo. Headline Club, Sigma Delta Chi. Editor: WGN, a Pictorial History, 1961. Home: 547 Hawthorn Lane Winnetka IL 60093 Office: Chicago Tribune Tribune Tower IL 60611

FINK, LAWRENCE ALFRED, educator; b. N.Y.C., Jan. 20, 1930; s. Merwin Jesse and Claudia (Lowenthal) F.; A.B., Stanford U., 1951; M.A., Columbia, 1958, Ed.D., 1964; m. Barbara Louise Gross, Aug. 30, 1959; children—Laura Alison, James Merwin, Hilary Lynn. Tchr. history New Rochelle (N.Y.) High Sch., 1957-60; instr. TChrs. Coll. of Columbia, 1960-62; asst. prof. edn. Smith Coll., 1963-66, asso. prof., chmn. dept. edn. and child study, 1966-70, prof., chmn. dept., 1970—. Mem. corp. Edn. Devel. Center, Newton, Mass.; cons. Pres.'s Com. Mental Retardation, 1969-70; cons. editor Xerox Coll. Pub. Dir. Hampshire United Fund, Northampton, Mass., 1968—. Trustee Northampton Sch. for Gilrs, Williston Acad. Served with C.I.C., AUS, 1953-55. Mem. Am. Hist. Assn., Nat. Council Social Studies, Orgn. Am. Historians, Am. Ednl. Research Assn., Am. Studies Assn. Author: Honors Teaching in American History, 1969; Crisis in Urban Education, 1971. Home: 96 Maynard Rd Northampton MA 01060

FINK, LYMAN ROGER, engr.; b. Elk Point, S.D., Nov. 14, 1912; s. Willis James and Helen (Black) F.; B.S., U. Cal. at Berkeley, 1933, M.S., 1934, Ph.D., 1937; m. Frances Louise Kelly, Dec. 17, 1937; children—William R., Patricia H., James W. Mgr. electronics lab. Gen. Electric Co., 1947-49, mgr. engr. radio and TV dept., 1949-55, mgr. research application dept., 1955-57, gen. mgr. X-ray dept., 1957-59, gen. mgr. atomic products div., 1959-63, v.p., 1962-63; v.p. Otis Elevator Co., 1963-66; v.p., chief tech. officer The Singer Co., 1966-68, group v.p., 1968-70; exec. v.p., dir. Church's Fried Chicken, Inc., 1970—. Dir., v.p. Atomic Indsl. Forum, 1961-63. Recipient Charles A. Coffin award Gen. Electric Co., 1948. Fellow I.E.E.E.; mem. N.Y. Acad. Scis., A.A.A.S., Sigma Xi, Phi Beta Kappa, Tau Beta Pi, Kappa Delta Rho. Club: Oak Hills Country (San Antonio). Home: 7500 Callaghan Rd San Antonio TX 78229 Office: 35 Spencer Lane San Antonio TX 78284

FINK, RICHARD WALTER, educator, nuclear physicist, chemist; b. Detroit, Jan. 13, 1928; s. Bernard and Ann (Walter) F.; B.S., U. Mich., 1948; M.S., U. Cal. at Berkeley, 1949; Ph.D., U. Rochester, 1953; m. Gunilla Gustafsson, Oct. 4, 1960; children—Kerry Leif, Roger Gunnar. Asso. prof. U. Ark., Fayetteville, 1953-61; prof. dept. physics Marquette U., Milw., 1961-65; vis. prof. Werner Inst. for Nuclear Chemistry, U. Uppsala (Sweden), 1959-60, Inst. for Exptl. Physics, U. Hamburg (Germany), 1963-64; prof. Sch. Chemistry, Ga. Inst. Tech., Atlanta, 1965—; research nuclear chemist Knolls Atomic Power Lab., Schenectady, 1949-50. Cons., Lawrence Radiation Lab., U. Cal., 1961-69, Phillips Petroleum Co., Bartlesville, Okla., 1957-65; chmn. Internat. Conf. on Inner Shell Ionization Phenomena, Atlanta, 1972. Fulbright Travel grantee, 1963-64; Fulbright lectr., Europe, 1964, Nat. Acad. Sci. exchange lectr., Yugoslavia, 1971. Mem. Am. Phys. Soc., Sigma Xi. Contbr. articles to profl. jours. Office: Sch Chemistry Ga Inst Tech Atlanta GA 30332

FINK, ROBERT ORWILL, educator; b. Geneva, Ind., Nov. 4, 1905; s. Orwill Clarkson and Carlista (Andrews) F.; A.B., Ind. U., 1930; M.A., Cornell U., 1931; Ph.D., (Kellogg fellow 1932-34), Yale, 1934; m. Ruth Kuersteiner, June 11, 1935. Instr. classics Yale, 1934-41; asst. prof. Russell Sage Coll. Women, 1941-42; asst. prof., then asso. prof. Beloit Coll., 1942-46; asso. prof., then prof. Kenyon Coll., 1946-66, Emma N. Dempsey prof., 1956-66; prof. classics State U. N.Y. at Albany, 1966—; summer tchr. U. Mich., 1949, U. Colo., 1956, 62, Ohio State U., 1963, Summer Inst. for Latin Tchrs., 1967. Fulbright research fellow Italy, 1956-57; Am. Council Learned Socs. research fellow, 1963-64. Mem. Am. Assn. U. Profs., Am. Philol. Assn., Archaeol. Inst. Am., Am. Soc. Papyrologists, Assn. Internat. de Papyrologues, Phi Beta Kappa. Democrat. Author: (with A.S. Hoey and W.F. Snyder) The Feriale Duranum, 1940; (with C.B. Welles and J.F. Gilliam) The Excavations at Dura-Europos, Final Report V: The Parchments and Papyri, 1959; Roman Military Records on Papyrus, 1971; also articles. Home: 572 Cortland St Albany NY 12208

FINK, ZERA S., educator; b. Holdrege, Neb., Aug. 8, 1902; s. Daniel J. and Nellie M. (Silver) F.; A.B., Grinnell Coll., 1924; M.A., Northwestern U., 1928, Ph.D., 1931; postgrad U. Chgo., summer 1930; m. Lucille McDannell, Mar. 12, 1927; 1 dau., Carlotta L. (Mrs. Carlotta Bogart). Instr. English, Grinnell Coll., 1925-27; instr. English, Northwestern U., 1928-29, 31- 34, asst. prof., 1934-40, asso. prof., 1940-44, prof., 1944-70, (specialist in Milton and English lit. of Romantic period), acting chmn. dept., 1954, 57, summer 1958, 65, 66. Chmn. Newberry Library Renaissance Conf., 1952. Grantee Am. Council Learned Socs., 1959-60. Mem. Modern Lang. Assn. Am., Renaissance Assn. Am., Internat. Assn. U. Profs. English, Phi Beta Kappa. Presbyn. Club: University (Evanston, Ill.). Author: The Classical Republicans, 1945, 2d edit., 1962; The Early Wordsworthian Milieu 1958; also numerous articles. Home: 2414 Hartzell St Evanston IL 60201

FINKBEINER, OTTO KARL, church ofcl.; b. Phila., Jan. 6, 1923; s. Otto and Helen (Betcher) F.; B.S., Temple U., 1947; m. Eileen Ramsay, June 10, 1944; children— Eric, Judith L., Janet L. With Westminster Press, 1947-52; with dept. adminstrn. Gen. Assembly United Presbyn. Ch. in U.S.A., 1953, mgr., 1954- 67, asst. stated clk., 1967—. Served as pilot USAAF, World War II. Mem. Adminstrv. Mgmt. Soc., Assn. Statisticians Am. Religious Bodies (pres. 1960-62). Republican. Home: Montgomery Lane Radnor PA 19087 Office: Witherspoon Bldg Philadelphia PA 19107

FINKE, WALTER WILLIAM, mfg. exec.; b. Mpls., June 16, 1907; s. William and Eva (Schreyer) F.; B.A. cum laude, U. Minn., 1927, LL.B., 1930; m. Lorraine K. Freiberg, July 11, 1932. Exec. v.p. Mpls. C. of C., 1946-51; mgr. ordnance div., asst. to pres. Mpls. Honeywell Regulator Co., 1951-55, v.p. of co., 1958- 67, also pres. electronic data processing div., Wellesley, Mass., 1954- 67; chmn., pres., chief exec. officer Dictaphone Corp., 1967—; dir. Barry Wright Corp., Mite Corp., Honeywell, Inc. U.S. Jr. C. of C., 1941, chmn. N.Y. State Health Planning Adv. Council Bd. mgrs. N.Y. State Communities Aid Assn.; bd. dirs. Medic Alert Found. Internat. Served with USNR, 1942-46; capt. ret, Mem. Bus. Equipment Mfrs. Assn. (past chmn., dir.), Delta Theta Phi, Phi Beta Kappa, Zeta Psi. Mason (Shriner). Clubs: Westchester Country (Harrison, N.Y.); California (Los Angeles); Pinnacle (N.Y.C.). Home: 1 Madison Pl Harrison NY 10528 Office: 120 Old Post Rd Rye NY 10580

FINKEL, DONALD, poet; b. N.Y.C., Oct. 21, 1929; s. Saul A. and Meta (Rosenthal) F.; B.S., Columbia, 1952, M.A., 1953; m. Constance Urdang, Aug. 14, 1956; children—Elizabeth Antonia, Thomas Noah, Amy Maria. Poet-in-residence Washington U., St. Louis, 1965—; cons. prosody Random House Dictionary. Guggenheim fellow, 1966. Mem. Antarctican Soc., Cave Research Found., Authors Guild, P.E.N., Phi Beta Kappa. Author: The Clothing's New Emperor, 1959; Simeon, 1964; A Joyful Noise, 1966; Answer Back, 1968; The Garbage Wars, 1970. Address: 6943 Columbia Pl St Louis MO 63130

FINKEL, LEONARD E., mfg. co. exec.; b. N.Y.C., 1906; LL.B., N.Y.U., 1928; married. With Finkel Umbrella Frame Co., N.Y.C., 1939-65, co. acquired by Aberdeen Mfg. Corp., 1965; pres., dir. Aberdeen Mfg. Corp., N.Y.C., 1965—; dir. Finkel Outdoor Products, Inc., Finkel Outdoor Products Corp., Finkel Outdoor Products of Cal., Inc., Savoy Drapery Corp., Danielson Curtain Co., Diagnostic Research, Inc.; pres., dir. Essex Mfg. Corp., Templar Textile Products, Inc. Mason. Home: 7 Villa Lane Larchmont NY 10538 Office: 16 E 34th St New York City NY 10016*

FINKELSTEIN, ABRAHAM BERNARD, educator; b. N.Y.C., Feb. 11, 1923; s. Samuel and Sophie (Wendrow) F.; B.S., Coll. City N.Y., 1943, M.S., N.Y.U., 1947, Ph.D., 1953; m. Hattie (Bernstein) Aug. 16, 1947; children—Stephen J., Carl J., Susan G. Asst. prof. math. L.I. U., 1948-53; sr. research asso. aero. engring. and applied mechanics Poly. Inst. Bklyn., 1953-57; mem. faculty Pratt Inst., 1957—, prof. math., 1964—, chmn. dept., 1966—. Cons. Eastern Research Group, 1955-60; reviewer NSF, 1960—; editor Regents Pub. Co., 1966- 68; spl. research water wave theory, underwater propulsion systems, transpiration cooling. Served with AUS, 1943-46. Research grantee NSF, 1959-60. Mem. Am. Math. Soc., Math. Assn. Am., Am. Soc. Engring. Edn., Phi Beta Kappa, Pi Mu Epsilon. Home: 992 E 21st St Brooklyn, NY 11210.

FINKELSTEIN, ARTHUR KANARRE, physician, educator; b. Wilmington, Del., Dec. 30, 1906; s. Isaac Bernard and Clara (Statnekoo) F.; B.A., U. Pa., 1927, M.D., 1931; M.S., U. Pa. Grad. Sch. Medicine, 1939; m. Leah Shore, Sept. 11, 1937; children—Dan, Jean. Intern, Jewish Hosp., St. Louis, 1931-32; dir. dept. radiology Grad. Hosp., U. Pa., Phila., 1938—; prof. radiology U. Pa. Grad. Sch. Medicine, 1952—, chmn. dept. radiology, 1956—; prof. radiology U. Pa. Sch. Medicine, 1962; dir. dept. radiology Presbyn.-U. Pa. Med. Center, 1966. Hon. mem. Tex. Radiology Soc., Conn. Roentgen Soc.; mem. Phila. Roentgen Ray Soc. (pres. 1951-52), Pa., Phila. County med. socs., A.M.A., Pa. Radiol. Soc., Am. Roentgen Ray Soc., Radiol. Soc. N.Am., Inter-Am. Radiol. Soc. Home: 33 Righers Mill Rd Narbeth PA 19072 Office: 19th and Lombard Sts Philadelphia PA 19146

FINKELSTEIN, HERMAN N., lawyer; b. Syracuse, N.Y., Aug. 31, 1900; s. Simon J. and Hannah (Breger) F.; B.A., Coll. City N.Y., 1921; LL.B., Columbia, 1924, J.D., 1932; m. Theresa Oakes, Oct. 26, 1926; children—Anne Oakes (Mrs. Stephen Kandel), Michael Oakes. Admitted to N.Y. bar, 1925, since practiced in N.Y.C.; partner firm Finkelstein, Benton & Soll, 1958—. Trustee Eastern Gas and Fuel Assos. Author: Legal Aspects of Commercial Letters of Credit, 1930. Office: Lincoln Park Plaza New York City NY 10001

FINKELSTEIN, JACOB JOEL, educator, Orientalist; b. Bklyn., Mar. 22, 1922; s. Morris and Augusta (Liebhart) F.; B.A., Bklyn. Coll., 1948; Ph.D., U. Pa., 1953; m. Dorothee Metlitzky, Dec. 27, 1956; 1 step dau., Ruth Grdseloff. Research asst. Near Eastern langs. Yale, 1953-55; from asst. prof. to prof. Assyriology, U. Cal. at Berkeley, 1956-63, chmn. dept. Near Eastern langs., 1961-65; William Laffan prof. Assyriology and Babylonian lit. Yale, 1965—. Served with AUS, 1943-46. Guggenheim fellow, 1955-56; fellow Am. Council Learned Socs., 1963-64; sr. fellow Nat. Endowment for Humanities, 1970-71. Mem. Am. Sch. Oriental Research, Am. Oriental Soc. (asso. editor jour., 1961-64). Author articles ancient Mesopotamian law, religion and historiography, also publ. Cuneiform texts. Home: 141 Deepwood Dr Hamden, CT 06517. Office: Hall Grad Studies Yale Univ New Haven CT 06520

FINKELSTEIN, JERRY, industrialist, publisher; b. N.Y.C., Jan. 26, 1916; s. Albert and Ethel (Kaufman) F.; student N.Y. U.; LL.B., N.Y. Law Sch., 1938, LL.D., 1969; m. Shirley Marks, Mar. 29, 1942; children—Andrew Jay Stein, James Arthur. Staff spl. pros. Thomas E.

Dewey, 1935-36; reporter, civil service editor N.Y. Mirror, 1937-39; founder, pub. Civil Service Leader, N.Y., 1939—; chmn. bd., chmn. exec. com. Struthers Wells Corp.; chmn. bd. Struthers Capital Corp., ABC Industries; pres., chmn. bd., N.Y. Law Pub. Co.; chmn. bd. Sci. and Govt. Publs., Inc.; dir. Struthers Sci. and Internat. Corp., Comml. Bank N. Am., N.Y.C. Mem. aviation com. pub. schs., N.Y. State Bd. Regents, 1941; research dir. N.Y. State Senate, 1938-41, ofcl. commn. extension civil service N.Y. State Legislature, 1941; chmn. planning commn., chmn. dept. city planning, N.Y.C., 1950-51. Campaign mgr. mayoralty campaign, N.Y.C., 1949; chmn. N.Y.C. Democratic Com., 1970. Trustee N.Y. Law Sch.; bd. overseers Jewish Theol. Sem. Am.; chmn. fine arts gifts com. Nat. Cultural Center; mem. exec. council Southampton Coll., L.I. U.; mem. pres.'s council Grad. Sch. Pub. Adminstrn., N.Y. U.; mem. bd. visitors U.S. Mil. Acad., West Point, 1969; founder Albert Einstein Coll. Medicine. Served with USCGR, 1943-45. Decorated Knight, Order of Merit (Italy), 1958; recipient Knickerbocker award for outstanding city planning, 1951, seroll for outstanding efforts civic betterment Com. of 1000, 1951. Mem. Am. Jewish Com., Soc. Silurians, Newspaper Reporters Assn. Clubs: National Democratic, Overseas Press, Advertising (N.Y.C.). Home: 812 Park Av New York City NY 10021 Office: 630 Fifth Av New York City NY 10020

FINKELSTEIN, JOSEPH, educator; B.A., Union Coll., 1945; M.A., Ph.D., Harvard. Prof. history and econs. Union Coll., Schenectady. Office: Union Coll Schenectady NY 12308*

FINKELSTEIN, LAWRENCE STANLEY, educator; b. N.Y.C., Mar. 11, 1925; s. Frank and Sylvia (Lemkin) F.; B.A., Columbia, 1944, M.A., 1947, Ph.D., 1970; m. Marina Salvin, Aug. 4, 1951; 1 dau., Susan. Staff div. dependent area affairs Dept. State, 1944-46; trusteeship div. UN Secretariat, 1946-47; research asst., lectr. govt. Columbia, 1947-49, instr. gen. studies govt., 1958-59, vis. lectr. Sch. Internat. Affairs, 1960-61, sr. lectr. polit. sci., 1970, 71-72; staff Council Fgn. Relations, 1949-50, Inst. Pacific Relations, 1950-51; staff Carnegie Endowment Internat. Peace, 1952-65, dir. studies, 1957-62, v.p., 1959-65; dep. asst. sec. def., 1965-66; dir. Case-Western Res. Study, 1966-67; asso. dean acad. adminstrn., acting dean Grad. Sch., Brandeis U., 1967-69; research asso. Center Internat. Affairs, Harvard, 1961-62, sec. center, 1969—; cons. Inst. Def. Analyses, Dept. State, Dept. Def. Mem. Am. Polit. Sci. Assn., Am. Soc. Internat. Law, Council Fgn. Relations, Inst. Strategic Studies London, Internat. Studies Assn. Clubs: Century Assn.; Columbia. Editor: The United States and International Organization: The Changing Setting, 1969. Co- editor Collective Security, 1965; chmn. bd. editors Internat. Orgn. Home: 4 Upland Rd Lexington MA 02173 Office: Center for International Affairs Harvard U Cambridge MA 02138

FINKELSTEIN, LOUIS, sem. adminstr.; b. Cin., June 14, 1895; s. Rabbi Simon J. and Hannah (Brager) F.; A.B., Coll. City of N.Y., 1915; Ph.D., Columbia, 1918; Rabbi, Jewish Theol. Sem. Am., 1919; S.T.D., Columbia, 1944; Litt.D. Boston U., 1950; D.H.L., Dropsie Coll., 1961; LL.D., Temple U., 1963, Manhattan Coll., 1965, Fordham U., 1966; D. Humane Letters, S.E. Mass. Inst. Tech., 1966; S.T.D., N.Y.U., 1967; D.D., Yale, 1967; m. Carmel Bentwich, Mar. 5, 1922; children—Hadassah, Ezra, Faith. Rabbi Congregation Kehilath Israel, N.Y. C., 1919-31; instr. Talmud, Jewish Theol. Sem., 1920-24, Solomon Schechter lectr. in theology, 1924-30, asso. prof. theology, 1930, Solomon Schechter prof. theol. since 1931, asst. to pres., 1934-37, provost, 1937-40, pres., 1940, chancellor, 1951—, pres. Inst. Religious and Social Studies; Ingersoll lectr. Harvard Div. Sch., 1944. Active in ednl. publs. and ednl. coms. and commns. for various gen. and spl. purposes. Ambassador of Pres. Kennedy to Papal Coronation, 1963; hon. chmn. bd. edn. for recruiting young people for preprofl. jobs in war on poverty, 1964; dir. Am. Friends of Hebrew U.; trustee Jewish Tchrs. Coll. Fund; adv. bd. Inst. for Advancement of Cultural and Spiritual Values; Phi Epsilon Pi Fraternity Nat. Service award, 1952; Townsend Harris medal, 1940. Fellow Am. Acad. of Arts and Scis., Acad. of Jewish Research, Jewish Acad. Arts and Scis.; pres. Conf. Sci. Philosophy and Religion. Mem. several assns. and orgns. Author or co-author several books, 1924—, latest being: Abot of Rabbi Nathan, 1950; The Pharisees: The Sociological Background of Their Faith, 1962; New Light on the Prophets, 1969. Editor commentaries, biographies; co-editor numerous symposia; contbr. review and jours. Vice Pres. and mem. editorial bd. Universal Jewish Ency. Home: 340 Riverside Dr New York City NY 10025 Office: 3080 Broadway New York City NY 10027 ☆

FINKELSTEIN, TED, diversified co. exec.; b. Columbus, O., Aug. 26, 1914; s. Mendel and Rachel (Weinberg) F.; B.S. in Bus. Adminstrn., Ohio State U., 1936; m. Jane Florence Frieddenberg, Nov. 18, 1951; children—James Howard, Joel Stephen. With Cooa Industries, Inc., and predecessors, 1931—, corp. treas., 1968—; treas. all subsidiaries. Active United Jewish Fund and Council Columbus, B'nai B'rith, Jewish War Vets., United Appeal. Served with AUS, 1942-66. C.P.A. Mem. Am. Inst. C.P.A.'s, Ohio Soc. C.P.A.'s, Heritage House, Zionist Orgn. Am., Mu Beta Chi. Jewish religion (trustee synagogue 1950-53). Home: 320 S Virginia Lee Rd Columbus OH 43209 Office: 35 N 4th St Columbus OH 43215

FINKL, WILLIAM F., b. Chgo., 1896; grad. Armour Tech. Inst., 1918. Vice chmn., treas. A. Fink & Sons Co. subsidiary of Republic Steel Corp. trustee Ill. Inst. Tech. Address: 2011 N Southport Av Chicago IL 60614

FINKS, JAMES EDWARD, gen. mgr. profl. football club; b. St. Louis, Aug. 31, 1927; s. William T. and Margaret (Hays) F.; B.A., Tulsa U., 1949; m. Maxine Anne Stemmons, Sept. 24, 1951; children—James Edward, Danny, David, Tommy. Quarterback, Pitts. Steelers Profl. Football Club, 1949-55; asst. coach U. Notre Dame, 1956-57; gen. mgr. Calgary (Can.) Canadian Football League, 1957-64; gen. mgr. Minn. Vikings Profl. Football Club, 1964—, also v.p. Home: 7401 Kellogg Av Edina MN 55435 Office: 7809 Southtown Center Bloomington MN 55420

FINLAND, MAXWELL, physician; b. Russia, Mar. 15, 1902; s. Frank and Rebecca (Povza) F.; brought to U.S., 1906, naturalized, 1925; ed. Wendell Phillips Sch., Boston, English High Sch.; B.S., Harvard, 1922, M.D., 1926; D.Sc., Western Res. U., 1964. Asst. resident Boston Sanatorium, 1926-27; med. house officer Boston City Hosp., 1927- 28, resident physician, 1928-29, became jr. vis. physician, 1938, chief IV (Harvard) Med. Service, 1939-62, dir. II and IV (Harvard) Med. Service, 1963-68, head dept. medicine, 1963-68, epidemiologist, 1968—; asst. resident Thorndike Meml. Lab., 1929-32, asst. physician, 1932-41, asso. physician, 1941-50, asso. dir. lab., 1950-63, dir., 1963-68; epidemiologist Boston City Hosp., 1968—; vis. physician Pondville Hosp., 1933-69; successively teaching fellow in hygiene Harvard Med. Sch., 1928-29, asst., 1929-32, Francis Weld Peabody fellow, 1932-37, instr., 1935-37, asso., 1937-40, asst. prof., 1940-46, asso. prof., 1946-62, prof. medicine, 1962-63, George Richard Minot prof. medicine, 1963-68; George Richards Minot Prof. emeritus, 1968—; mem. subcom. infectious diseases NRC, 1946-54, chmn., 1955-59; mem. adv. com. on influenza research USPHS, 1959-63; mem. bacteriol. and mycol. study sect. NIH, 1958-63; asso. mem. commn. acute respiratory diseases Armed Forces Epidemiological Bd., 1950-67, mem. 1967—; mem. drug research bd. Nat. Acad. Scis.-NRC, 1964-71; mem. clin. investigators com. dept. medicine and surgery VA, 1955-69, chmn., 1964-69; chmn. Com. for Lederle Med. Faculty awards , 1952-68. Recipient Charles V. Chapin award City of Providence, 1960; Bristol award Infectious Diseases Soc. Am., 1966; Modern Medicine award, 1969; John Phillips Meml. award A.C.P., 1971; Oscar B. Hunter Meml. award Am. Soc. Clin. Pharmacology and Therapeutics, 1971; Sheen award A.M.A., 1971; named hon. citizen City of Panama, 1970. Master A.C.P.; fellow A.A.A.S.; mem. Mass. Med. Soc., Am. Med. Assn., Soc. for Exptl. Biol. and Medicine, Am. Soc. for Clin. Investigation (councillor 1942-45, v.p. 1947-48), Am. Bd. Internal Medicine, Infectious Diseases Soc. Am. (pres. 1963-64), Am. Assn. Immunologists, Soc. Am. Bacteriol., Am. Acad. Arts and Scis., N.Y. Acad. Scis., Am. Epidemiological Soc. (v.p. 1961-62), Harvard Med. Alumni Assn. (pres. 1971-72), Sigma Xi, Alpha Omega Alpha. Contbr. articles and revs. to sci. jours. and med. text books. Mem. editorial bd. N.E. Jour. Medicine, 1945-68, Applied Microbiology, 1964—, Antimicrobiol. Agents and Chemotherapy, 1960-71, Jour. Infectious Diseases, 1969—. Home: 46 Sycamore Road Squantum MA 02171 Office: Boston City Hospital Boston MA

FINLAY, JAMES CHARLES, univ. dean; b. Roscommon, Ireland, Aug. 29, 1922; s. James Charles and Kathleen (O'Connor) F.; student Fordham Coll., 1940-42; B.A., Loyola U., 1946; M.A., Georgetown U., 1951; S.T.L., L'Immacule Conception, 1955; Ph.D., Duke, 1960 Mem. Soc. Jesus; ordained priest Roman Catholic Ch., 1954; instr. St. Peter's Prep. Sch., 1948-50; instr. polit. sci. Fordham U., 1960-62, asst. prof., 1962-68, chmn. dept., 1963, asso. prof., 1968—, dean Grad. Sch., 1968—. Trustee St. Peter's Coll. French Govt. Postdoctoral grant; Fulbright Travel grant, 1959-60. Mem. Am. Polit. Sci. Assn., N.Y. State Polit. Sci. Assn. (pres. 1969-70), Am. Civil Liberties Union (mem. nat. academic freedom com. 1964—), Phi Beta Kappa, Pi Sigma Alpha. Author: The Liberal Who Failed, 1968. Address: Fordham Univ Bronx NY 10458

FINLAY, WINIFRED LINDSAY, author; b. Newcastle-upon-Tyne, Eng., Apr. 27, 1910; d. James and Susan Lindsay (Crawford) McKissack; B.A., Newcastle U., 1931, D.Th. P.T., 1932, M.A., 1940; m. Evan Finlay, July 25, 1935; 1 dau., Gillian (Mrs. David Hancock). Tchr., Newcastle, Leeds and Stratford-Upon-Avon, 1933-48; lectr., Northampton, Eng., 1950; freelance author, contbr. BBC plays for young people, 1947—. Mem. Soc. Authors. Author 22 books including: Storm over Cheviot, 1955; Folk Tales from the North, 1968; Danger at Black Dyke (best juvenile thriller Mystery Writers Am. 1970), 1968. Address: The Old House Walgrave Northampton England

FINLAYSON, FRANK STANLEY, educator; b. Worcester, Mass., Nov. 6, 1908; s. Frank Morton and Ellen (McPhee) F.; B.S., Worcester Poly. Inst., 1931, M.S., 1945; m. Dorothy Boutwell, June 15, 1935; children—David Frank, Doreen (Mrs. Walter Atwood), Dana Charles. Engr. Norton Co., Worcester, 1936-37; chief engr. L.J. Barrett Co., Worcester, 1937; instr. Worcester Poly. Inst., 1937- 43, asst. prof. mech. engring., 1943-47, asso. prof., 1947-58, prof., 1958—. Cons. to mfrs. air moving, textile, paper making machinery, 1950- -. Registered profl. engr., Mass. Mem. Am. Soc. M.E., Am. Soc. Engring. Edn., Sigma Xi (pres. Worcester chpt. 1954-55). Patentee drives used on paper making machinery. Home: 24 Juniper Rd Worcester MA 01602

FINLAYSON, ROBERT MURRAY, accountant; b. N. Adams, Mass., July 15, 1922; s. Henry George and Jean (Warden) F.; B.B.A., U. Mich., 1946, M.B.A., 1948; m. Louise Swanson, Aug. 31, 1946; children-Ann, Robert, Sarah, Mary, Roderick. With Ernst & Ernst, 1948—, accountant, Detroit, 1948-56, mgr., Saginaw, Mich., 1956-61, mgr., N.Y.C., 1961-63, partner, 1963-68, partner in charge, 1968—. Served with USAF, 1941-45. Decorated D.F.C., Air Medal with three Oak leaf clusters, Purple Heart. C.P.A., Mich., N.Y. Mem. Am. Inst. C.P.A.'s. Clubs: City Midday (N.Y.C.); Indian Hills Country (North Port, N.Y.). Home: 20 Sydney Rd Huntington NY 11743 Office: 140 Broadway New York NY 10005

FINLETTER, THOMAS KNIGHT, lawyer, former ambassador; b. Phila., Nov. 11, 1893; s. Thomas Dickson and Helen (Grill) F.; ed. Episcopal Acad., Phila., 1905-10; A.B., U. Pa., 1915, LL.B., 1920, LL.D., 1950; LL.D., U. Rochester, 1950, Syracuse U., 1950, Coll. St. Joseph, 1951, Rutgers U., 1959; m. Gretchen Blaine Damrosch, July 17, 1920; children—Margot (Mrs. John F.B. Mitchell), Lili (Mrs. Lee O'Neill). Admitted to Pa. bar, 1920, N.Y. bar, 1921; lawyer with Cravath & Henderson, 1920-26; partner Coudert Brothers, 1926-41, 44-50, 53-61; lectr. U. Pa. Law Sch., 1931-41; spl. asst. to sec. of state, Washington, 1941-44; cons. to U.S. delegation to UN Conf. on Internat. Orgn., San Francisco, May 1945; chmn. President's Air Policy Commn., 1947-48; minister in charge E.C.A. Mission to U.K., 1948-49; sec. of Air Force, 1950-53; U.S. ambassador NATO, 1961-65. Capt. F.A., U.S. Army, 1917-19. Mem. Council Fgn. Relations, Bar Assn. City N.Y., Delta Phi. Clubs: River, Knickerbocker, Century (N.Y.); Metropolitan (Washington); Athenaeum (London). Author: Principles of Corporate Reorganization, 1937; Cases on Corporate Reorganization, 1938; The Law of Bankruptcy, 1939; Can Representative Government Do the Job?, 1945; Power and Policy, 1954; Foreign Policy; The Next Phase, 1960; Interim Report, 1968. Home: 151 E 79 St New York City NY 10021 Office: 151 E 79th St New York City NY 10021

FINLEY, CHARLES O., baseball co. exec.; b. Birmingham, Ala., Feb. 22, 1918; s. Oscar A. and Burmah E. (Fields) Finley; m. Shirley McCartney, May 9, 1941; children—Sharon, Charles O., Kathryn, Paul, Martin, Luke, David. From laborer to foreman U.S. Steel Corp. mills, Gary, 1936-41; with Kingsbury Ordnance Plant, 1941-45, div. supt., 1945; pres., owner Charles O. Finley & Co., Inc., gen. ins. brokers, Chgo., 1945—; chmn. bd., pres., owner Oakland (Cal.) Athletic Baseball Club, American League, 1960—; owner Cal. Golden Seals Hockey Team, Oakland, Cal. Named asso. mem. So. Med. Assn. for devel. group ins. for doctors and families, 1960; nat. chmn. Christmas Seal campaign Nat. Tb Assn., 1961. Presbyn. Mason (32, Shriner). Clubs: Chicago Athletic. Home: RR 7 Box 14 La Porte IN 46350 Office: 310 S Michigan Av Chicago IL 60604

FINLEY, DAVID EDWARD, former museum ofcl.; b. York, S.C., Sept. 13, 1890; s. David Edward and Elizabeth Lewis (Gist) F.; A.B., U. S.C., 1910, Litt.D., 1950; LL.B., George Washington Law Sch., 1913, LL.D., 1960; Arts D., Yale, 1946; L.H.D., Georgetown U., 1960; m. Margaret Morton Eustis, June 10, 1931. Practiced law, Phila., 1915-17. Served as 2d lt. U.S. Army, 1917-18; asst. counsel War Finance Corp., 1921-22; mem. war loan staff U.S. Treasury, 1922-27; spl. asst. to sec. treasury, 1927-32; adviser Am. delegation London Financial Conf., July 1931; hon. counselor Am. embassy, London, Eng., 1932-33; practiced law, Washington, 1933-37; dir. Nat. Gallery of Art, 1938-56. Pres. Am. Assn. Museums, 1945-49; chmn. U.S. Commn. Fine Arts, 1950-63; chmn. Nat. Trust for Historic Preservation, 1949-62; v.p. Internat. Council of Museums, 1946-49; chmn. U.S. Nat. Com. on Internat. Cooperation among Museums, 1945-49; vice chmn. Am. Commn. for Protection and Salvage of Artistic and Historic Monuments in War Areas, 1943-46; mem. Nat. Portrait Gallery Commn. and Nat. Collection Fine Arts Commn. of Smithsonian Instn., 1967; mem. Washington Nat. Monument Soc.; trustee Corcoran Gallery of Art. Mem. Com. The People-to-People Program, 1956-60. Recipient Theodore Roosevelt Distinguished Service medal, 1957; Henry medal Smithsonian Instn., 1967. Hon. fellow Nat. Sculpture Soc.; hon. mem. A.I.A.; mem. Assn. Art Museum Dirs., Sigma Alpha Epsilon, Phi Delta Phi, Phi Beta Kappa. Episcopalian. Mason. Clubs: Metropolitan, Alibi, Chevy Chase (Washington); Century (N.Y.). Home: 3318 O St NW Washington DC 20007 also Little Oatlands Loudoun County VA 22124

FINLEY, HAROLD EUGENE, educator, zoologist; b. Palatka, Fla., Nov. 30, 1905; s. Eugene and Lugenia (Bryant) F.; B.S., Morehouse Coll., 1928; M.S., U. Wis., 1929, Ph.D., 1942; m. Eva Elizabeth Browning, Aug. 30, 1929 (dec. 1954); children—Harold Eugene, Eva Kathleen (Mrs. Selvin F. Gumbs); m. 2d, Irene Sealy Pope, Jan. 5, 1957. From instr. to asso. prof. biology W.Va. State Coll., 1929-38; prof. biology, head dept. Morehouse Coll., 1938- 47; exchange prof. biology Atlanta U., 1938-47; prof. zoology Howard U., 1947—, head dept., 1947-69; ind. research investigator Marine Biol. Lab., Woods Hole, Mass., 1930-33; postdoctoral fellow Johns Hopkins, 1955; vis. prof. Ind. U., 1958, U. Wash., 1968, 70, U. Brasilia (Brazil), 1970. Prin. investigator USPHS research grants, 1953—; dir. NSF-Undergrad. Sci. Edn. research participation program, 1959—; U.S. del. IUBS, Montreux, 1967, Washington, 1970. Active Boy Scouts Am. Fellow A.A.A.S., Washington, N.Y. acads. scis.; mem. Am. Microscopical Soc. (pres. elect 1971-72), Washington Electron Microscope Soc. (pres. 1963-64), Soc. Protozoologists (v.p., 1964, pres. 1967), Am. Soc. Zoologists, Nat. Inst. Sci., Electron Microscope Soc. Am., Soc. Gen. Microbiology, Sigma Xi, Beta Kappa Chi, Phi Sigma. Editor trans Nat. Inst. Sci., 1943-53; editorial bd. Jour. Protozoology, 1957-61, Qualified Zool. Taxonomist, 1961—. Contbr. Ency. Brit. Home: 5721 16th St Washington, DC 20011

FINLEY, JAMES DANIELLY, textile co. exec.; b. Jackson, Ga., July 14, 1916; s. Albert C. and Kate (Danielly) F.; B.S. in Textile Engring., Ga. Inst. Tech., 1937; grad. Advanced Mgmt. Program, Harvard, 1951; m. Nancy Butler, June 7, 1941; children—James Danielly, Fred B., William G. With Firestone Tire & Rubber Co., 1938-41; with J.P. Stevens & Co., Inc., N.Y.C., 1945—, v.p., 1958-64, exec. v.p., 1964-65, chmn. bd. 1965—, chief exec. officer, 1969—, dir., 1961—, mem. exec. com., 1962—; dir. Borden Inc., Sperry Rand Corp., Mfrs. Hanover Corp., Mfrs. Hanover Trust Co. Served from 2d lt. to maj. Q.M.C., AUS, 1941-45. Mem. Am. Soc. Corp. Execs., Phi Delta Theta. Episcopalian. Clubs: Rumson (N.J.) Country; Seabright (N.J.) Beach; Weaver (N.Y.C.); Seaview Country; Pine Valley Golf (N.J.). Home: 12 Blossom Cove Rd Red Bank NJ 07701 Office: 1185 Av of Americas New York City NY 10036

FINLEY, JEAN CARSON, geologist, oil co. exec.; b. Cherryvale, Kan., Mar. 29, 1906; s. John Rush and Florence Sarah (Carson) F.; student Kan. U., 1924-29; m. Marjorie Burlingame, Sept. 26, 1943; 1 dau., Lucy Sarah. Geologist, Phillips Petroleum Co., 1929-37; chief geologist Midstate Oil Corp., 1937-48; exploration mgr. Kerr-McGee Oil Industries, Inc., Oklahoma City, 1948-54, v.p. exploration, 1954-58, v.p. fgn. exploration, 1958-67, v.p. staff, 1967—. Mem. Am. Assn. Petroleum Geologists, Tulsa Geol. Soc. Home: 3433 NW 19th St Oklahoma City OK 73107 Office: Kerr-McGee Bldg Oklahoma City OK 73102

FINLEY, JOHN HUSTON, Jr. author, prof.; b. New York, N.Y., Feb. 11, 1904; s. John Huston and Martha Ford (Boyden) F.; prep. edn., Albany (N.Y.) Acad. and Phillips Exeter Acad., Exeter, N.H.; A.B., Harvard, 1925, Ph.D., 1933; Charles Eliot Norton fellow, Am. Sch. of Classical Studies, Athens, 1925-26; studied U. Berlin, 1926-27; Litt.,D., Hamilton Coll. 1961; Harvard 1968, St. Bonaventure, 1969; m. Magdalena Greenslet, June 10, 1933; children—John Huston, 3d, Corinna, Eliot prof. of Greek lit., Master of Eliot House, Harvard, 1942-68; George Eastman prof. Oxford U., 1954-55. Fellow Center for Hellenic Studies, Washington. Mem. Phi Beta Kappa. Episcopalian. Club: Somerset. Author: Thalia, or a Country Day, a masque, in verse, 1929; Thucydides, 1942; co- author: General Education in a Free Society, 1945; Pindar and Aeschylus, 1955; Four Stages of Greek Thought, 1966; Three Essays on Thucydides, 1967. Home: 1010 Memorial Dr Cambridge, MA 02138

FINLEY, JOSEPH EDWIN, lawyer; b. Portageville, Mo., Aug. 7, 1919; s. William V. and Nell (Whitten) F.; B.J., U. Mo., 1942; LL.B., Yale, 1951; m. Joanne E. Otte, July 8, 1950; children—Scott M., Ethan C., Lucinda M., William N. Admitted to D.C. bar, 1951, Ohio bar, 1957; pvt. practice Washington, 1951-61, Cleve., 1957—; atty. Woll, Glenn & Thatcher, 1951-54; gen. counsel AFL, 1951-54; partner Metzenbaum, Gaines, Finley & Stern, 1961—; gen. counsel Office and Profl. Employees Internat. Union AFL-CIO, Internat. Brotherhood Operative Potters AFL-CIO. Pres. Ludlow Community Assn. Served to capt. AUS, 1942-46. Mem. Am., Ohio, Cleve. bar assns. Contbr. articles profl. jours. Home: 243 Pine St Philadelphia PA 19106 Office: Investment Plaza 1801 E 9th St Cleveland OH 44114

FINLEY, MOSES I., educator; b. N.Y.C., May 20, 1912; B.A., Syracuse U., 1927; M.A., Columbia, 1929, Ph.D., 1950; m. Mary F. Thiers, Aug. 9, 1932. Editorial, cons. posts with Ency. Social Scis., 1930-33; mem. faculty Columbia, 1933-34, 37-39, 48-54; then with Inst. Social Research; faculty Coll. City N.Y., 1934-42; exec. posts war relief agys., 1942-47; lectr., asst. prof. history Newark Colls. Rutgers U., 1948-52; lectr. in classics Cambridge U. (Eng.), 1955-64, reader ancient social, econ. history, 1964-70, prof. ancient history, 1970—, chmn. faculty bd. of classics, 1967-69; fellow Jesus Coll., Cambridge, 1957—, coll. librarian, 1960-64; Sather vis. prof. classics U. Cal. at Berkeley, 1972; sec., co- editor Procs. Cambridge Philol. Soc., 1959-65; convener ancient history sect., editor sects. procs. Internat. Econ. History Conf., Aix-en-Provence, 1962, Munich, 1965; sect. chmn. Congressus internationalis antiquitas graeco-romana ac tempora nostra Brno, 1966. Fellow in history Columbia, 1934-35, fellow Am. Council Learned Socs., 1948, Faculty fellow Fund for Advancement Edn., 1951-52. Fellow Brit. Acad.; Mem. Assn. pour les etudes grecques, Joint Assn. Classical Tchrs. (chmn. com. on ancient history 1964-70), Royal Anthrop. Inst., Royal Soc. Arts, Royal Hist. Soc., Soc. For Promotion Hellenic Studies, Soc. for Promotion Roman Studies, Societa Italiana di Storia del Diritto, Royal Hist. Soc., Phi Beta Kappa, Phi Kappa Phi. Author: Studies in Land and Credit in Ancient Athens, 1952; The World of Odysseus, 1954; The Ancient Greeks, 1963; Aspects of Antiquity, 1968; Ancient Sicily, 1968; Early Greece: the Bronze and Archaic Ages, 1970. Editor: The Greek Historians, 1958; Slavery in Classical Antiquity, 1960; Views and Controversies About Classical Antiquity, 1960—; Josephus, 1965; Ancient Culture and Society, 1969—. Editorial com. Comparative Studies in Society and History, 1969—. Contbr. profl. jours. Home: 12 Adams Rd Cambridge England

FINLEY, ROBERT CORPENING, judge; b. Marion, N.C., Nov. 7, 1905; s. Robert Sylvester and Willie Grace (Corpenning) F.; A.B., Duke U., 1930, LL.B., 1934; LL.M., Georgetown U., 1936; m. Werdna Karen Phillips, Dec. 4, 1937; children—Patricia Helen Karen, Robert Andrew, Mary Ellen. Admitted to Wash. bar, 1941, D.C. bar, 1935; atty. Fed. Housing Adminstrn., 1934-35; examiner-atty. Alcohol Control Adminstrn., 1935-37; probation officer U.S. Dist. Ct., Bur. Prisons, Dept. of Justice, Western N.C., 1937-38; alien property, custodian and claims div. Dept. Justice, 1938-40; asst. atty. gen. State Wash., 1940-42; dist. enforcement atty. O.P.A., State

Wash., 1942-44; dir. food enforcement O.P.A., Washington, 1944-45; pvt. law practice, Seattle and Renton, Wash., 1945-51; judge Supreme Ct., State Wash., 1951—, chief justice, 1961-62, 67-68. Mem. Am., Washington State, Seattle bar assns., Order of Coif, Pi Kappa Alpha. Club: Iredell Law (Duke U.). Home: 717 North St Olympia WA 98501 Office: Temple of Justice Olympia WA 98501

FINLEY, STATES RIGHTS GIST, engr.; b. York, S.C., Aug. 30, 1898; s. David Edward and Elizabeth Lewis (Gist) F.; B.S. in Elec. Engring. and M.E., Clemson A. & M. Coll., Clemson Coll., S.C., 1918; LL.D., Clemson U., 1970; m. Grace Isobel Snyder, June 7, 1924; children—States R. (dec.), Kathryn. Jr. engr. Henry L. Doherty & Co., 1919-20; successively engr., dist. supt., v.p., div. mgr., Ohio Pub. Service Co., Massillon, Elyria, Mansfield and Ashland, O., 1920-33; v.p. Faultless Rubber Co., Ashland, 1933-35; chief engr. rural lines, Ohio Farm Bur., Columbus, 1935-37; chief engr. Tenn. Electric Power Bd., Chattanooga, 1937-39, gen. supt., 1937-60, gen. mgr., 1960-63, chmn. 1963-68, honorary chmn., 1968—. Chmn. Ashland County Relief Com., 1930-34; chmn. Tenn. Indsl. Personnel Conf., 1945-46; chmn. Chattanooga Chapter A.R.C., 1942-46; pres. Chattanooga Indsl. Y.M.C.A., 1942-46, Chattanooga Family Service Agy.; nat. vice chmn. A.R.C. Fund Campaign, 1956; pres. Chattannoga Area Heart Assn., 1957-58; dir., sec. Tenn. Heart Assn., 1958-59; pres. Team Evaluation Center, Inc., 1963-67; chmn. bldg. com. Chattanooga-Hamilton County Health Center. Bd. govs. Am. Nat. Red Cross, 1947-50, bd. dirs. Hamilton Co. Meml. Hosp. Assn.; chmn. adv. com. U. Tenn. Sch. Social Work, Hamilton Co. Dept. Pub. Welfare; mem. adv. com. Tenn. Dept. Pub. Welfare. Del. Dem. Nat. Convention, 1960. Served as cpl. U.S.M.C.R. , 1918-19; capt., 6th regt., Tenn. State Guard, 1942-45. Mem. Am. (pres. 1950), Tenn. Valley pub. power assns. (pres., 1947-48), Chattanooga Art Assn., Inc. (bd. dirs.), Sigma Chi. Democrat. Presbyn. Mason. Clubs: Kiwanis (pres., 1947, chmn. internat. com. edn. and fellowship 1955); Chattanooga Automobile (pres. 1951). Home: 925 Scenic Highway Lookout Mountain TN 37350 Office: Elec Power Bldg 6th & Market Sts Chattanooga TN 37402

FINN, BJORN JENSEN, educator; b. Kragero, Norway, Dec. 2, 1909; s. Harald and Signe (Bjornsen) F.; came to U.S., 1930, naturalized, 1937; A.B., U. So. Cal., 1934, M.A., 1935, Ph.D., 1940; m. Julie Ellen Nielsen, Aug. 3, 1946; children—Ronald Bjorn, Barbara Helen, Vicki Greta, Eric. DuPont sr. fellow U. Va., 1935-36; instr. to asst. prof. econs. U. Kan., 1936-42; with U.S. Dept. of State, 1943-46; from asso. prof. to prof. econs. Lehigh U., 1947—, chmn. dept., 1966—. Recipient Medal of Freedom, U.S. Govt., 1946. Mem. Am. Econ. Assn. Author: (with others) Modern Economics, 1952; (with Walter Ingo) The Common Market, 1965; International Economic Relation, 1966. Home: Rd 1 Riegelsville PA 18077 Office: Lehigh Univ Bethlehem PA 18015

FINN, DAVID, pub. relations exec.; b. N.Y.C., Aug. 30, 1921; s. Jonathan and Sadie (Borgenicht) F.; B.S., Coll. City N.Y., 1943; m. Laura Zeisler, Oct. 20, 1945; children—Kathy, Dena, Peter, Amy. Co-founder Ruder & Finn, Inc., 1948, pres., 1956-68, chmn. bd., 1968—; adj. asso. prof. N.Y.U. Paintings exhibited Nat. Acad., Washington, Nat. Acad. Design, N.Y.C., Boston Mus. Art, Westchester County Center, others; one man show New School, N.Y.C. Treas. MacDowell Colony; bd. dirs. City of Hope; chmn. bd. Jewish Mus.; trustee Jewish Theol. Sem. Am., Am. Friends Hebrew U., City Hope, Inst. Advanced Studies in Humanities; adv. bd. Council Study Mankind; grad. adv. bd. Coll. City N.Y.; adv. com. N.Y.C. Office Cultural Affairs. Served to 1st lt., A.C., AUS, 1944. Mem. Pub. Relations Soc. Am., Am. Fedn. Arts, Am. Inst. Graphic Arts (past bd. dirs.), Internat. Pub. Relations Assn., Kappa Tau Alpha (hon.). Author: Public Relations and Management, 1956; The Corporate Oligarch, 1969. Contbr. articles to profl. jours. Photographer: (books) Embrace of Life, 1969, As the Eye Moves, 1970. Home: 90 Wellington St New Rochelle NY 10804 Office: 110 E 59th St New York City NY 10022

FINN, GENE LEROY, govt. ofcl.; b. La Crosse, Wis., Oct. 8, 1932; s. John M. and Irma (Steppen) F.; B.S., U. Wis., 1959, Ph.D., 1961; m. Phyllis Proksch, June 10, 1958; children-Mark, Sean, Kristin. Bd. govs. Fed. Res. System, Econ. Research Service, Dept. Agr.; chief economist SEC, Washington, 1969—. Served with U.S. Navy, 1952-55. Home: 3850 Irongate Lane Bowie MD 20715 Office: 500 N Capitol St Washington DC 20002

FINN, JOHN FRANCIS, food co. exec.; b. Mpls., July 25, 1911; s. John Francis and Mary (Berghaus) F.; B.A., U. Minn., 1933, LL.B., 1936; m. Mary Ann Albrecht, Sept. 29, 1939; children—James Joseph, John Francis III, Thomas William, Kerry Ann. Admitted to Minn. bar, 1936; asso. firm Junell, Dorsey, Fletcher, Colman & Barber, 1936-42; sect. chief counsel OPA, Washington, 1942-44; with Office Counsel, Navy Dept., 1944-46; mem. legal dept. Gen. Mills, Inc., Mpls., 1946—, v.p., sec., gen. counsel, 1962—; dir. Gen. Mills Cereals, Ltd. (Can.), Gold Medal Ins. Co., Imperial Capital Fund, also dir. of Imperial Growth Fund. Pres. Citizens League Mpls. and Hennepin County, 1958-59, also Minn. chpt. Arthritis and Rheumatism Found.; mem. Mpls. Charter Commn., 1959-68. Served to lt. comdr. USNR, 1944-46. Mem. U. Minn. Law Alumni Assn. (pres. 1959-60), Order of Coif, Phi Beta Kappa, Lambda Alpha Psi. Republican. Conglist. Home: 920 E Shady Lane Wayzata MN 55391 Office: 9200 Wayzata Blvd Minneapolis MN

FINN, JOHN MILTON, army officer; b. McCoy, Ore., Aug. 31, 1913; s. John Waldo and Jessie (Davidson) F.; B.S., U.S. Mil. Acad., 1938; grad. Army War Coll., 1954, Nat. War Coll., 1960; m. Mary Kathleen Coberly, Dec. 7, 1945; children—John Milton II, Brian Charles, Mary Kathleen. Commd. 2d lt. U.S. Army, 1938, advanced through grades to maj. gen., 1965; various assignments inf. divs. and sch., U.S., 1938-42; with 7th Inf. Div., PTO, 1942-46; spl. project liaison officer Aberdeen (Md.) Proving Ground, 1946-48; staff officer gen. staff U.S. Army, 1948-51; assigned SHAPE, 1951-52; chief mil. personnel, exec. officer, G-1, Hdqrs. 6th Army, 1954- 55; adviser to sec. def. U.S. army element MAAG Vietnam, 1955-57; chief staff 9th Inf. Div., 1957-59, USARYIS, Okinawa, 1960-62; dep. comdg. gen. USATC, Ft. Polk, La., 1962-64; chief staff 1 Corps, Korea, 1964-65; chief Mut. Security Office, Hdqrs. Army Material Command, 1965-66, dir. internat. logistics, 1966-67; named dep. comdg. gen. USARYIS, Okinawa, 1967; now ret. Decorated D.S.M. with oak leaf cluster, Silver Star with 2 oak leaf clusters, Legion of Merit with 3 oak leaf clusters, Bronze Star, Army Commendation medal with 2 oak leaf clusters, Purple Heart. Home: Star Rt 1 R-1 Moultrie CT Beaufort SC 79902

FINN, L.C., food mfg. co. exec. Sec., Patrick Cudahy, Inc. Office: Cudahy WI 53110*

FINN, ROBERT, music critic; b. Boston, July 13, 1930; s. Edward Anthony and E. Caroline (Seifert) F.; B.A., Boston U., 1952; m. Mary Pacana, Oct. 12, 1957; children—Laurence, Elaine. Staff reporter, music-drama critic New Bedford (Mass.) Standard-Times, 1956-59, Akron (O.) Beacon Jour., 1959- 64; music critic Cleve. Plain Dealer, 1964—; mem. guest faculty Rockefeller Found. project for tng. music critics, 1965, 66. Served with AUS, 1953-56. Mem. Music Critics Assn (exec. bd. 1967-69). Roman Cath. Contbr. Opera News mag. Home: 1211 Blanchester Rd Lyndhurst OH 44124 Office: 1801 Superior Av Cleveland OH 44114

FINN, ROBERT, educator. Prof. math. Stanford. Office: Dept Math Stanford U Stanford CA 94305*

FINN, ROBERT KAUL, educator; b. Wakesha, Wis., May 3, 1920; s. Edward A. and Myrtle (Kaul) F.; B.S., Cornell U., 1941, Chem. Engr., 1942; Ph.D., U. Minn., 1949; m. Lucille M. Rasmussen, Dec. 1949; children—David T., Mary A., Louisa M., Robert J., Heidi R. Research chem. engr. Merck & Co., Inc., Rahway, N.J., 1942-46; asst. prof. chem. engring. U. Ill., Urbana, 1949-55; asso. prof. chem. engring. Cornell U., 1955-61, prof., 1961—. Recipient Fulbright Research award Germany, 1961-62. Fellow A.A.A.S.; mem. Am. Chem. Soc. (past div. chmn.), Am. Inst. Chem. Engrs., Am. Soc. Microbiology. Presbyn. Patentee in field. Home: 107 Oakwood Lane Ithaca NY 14850

FINN, SAMUEL LAWRENCE, lawyer, corp. exec.; b. N.Y.C., June 3, 1890; s. Samuel and Ida (Schwartz) F.; student U. Dayton, 1920-22. H.H.D., 1957; m. Lillian R. Evans, Sept. 15, 1917; children—Chester E., Celeste F. (wife of Dr. Robert Klein). Admitted to Ohio bar, 1914, since practiced in Dayton; partner Estabrook, Finn & McKee, 1920—. Sec., dir. Hewitt Soap Co., Inc.; pres. Chester Investment Co.; pres., dir. Ludlow Realty Co., Dayton; v.p., dir. Nat. Foundry & Furnace Co., Mercer Foundry Co., Harkit Sales Co., Dayton, Victor Realty Co.; treas., dir. Stroop Agrl. Co., Troylon Farms, Inc.; sec., dir. T.K. Bar Cattle Co., Grays Realty Co., Burton Sanford Investment Co., dir., mem. exec. com. Dayton Power & Light Co., mem. bd. dirs. other corps. Past pres. Dayton Community Chest; secretary Metropolitan Community Studies, Inc.; mem. Selective Service Commn. Ohio, World War II. Pres. bd. trustees Dayton U.; trustee Dayton Found. Mem. Am., Ohio, Dayton bar assns. Clubs: Lawyers; Newcomen; Towne, Bicycle. Home: 1200 Amherst Pl Dayton OH 45406 Office: Hulman Bldg 2d and Ludlow Sts Dayton OH 45402

FINN, SIDNEY BERNARD, educator; b. Freedom, Pa., Feb. 2, 1908; s. Abel and Rebecca (Gordon) F.; B.A., Ohio State U., 1930; M.S., U. Rochester, 1940; D.M.D., Harvard, 1934; m. Irma Harriet Rubens, May 7, 1938; children—Catherine Ruth (Mrs. James Fitzpatrick), Andrew Alan. Practice dentistry Rochester, 1935-38; asso. research dentist N.Y. State Dept. Health, 1944-50; prof. dentistry, chmn. dept. pedodontics U. Ala., Birmingham, 1951-58, prof. dentistry, chmn. applied research Inst. Dental Research, Med. Center, 1968—; cons. VA Hosp., Tuskegee, Council on Dental Edn., Am. Dental Assn., Am. Biology Council's Task Force on Contributions of Biol. Scis. to Human Welfare. Mem. dental study sect. NIH, 1964-67; dir. Dental Clinics, Ala. Sch. for Deaf and Blind, Talladega Ala. Carnegie fellow, 1939-40; hon. faculty mem. U. Santo Domingo, 1957—; recipient Fuller award U. Ala. Dental Alumni Assn., 1971; award of excellence Am. Soc. Dentistry for Children, 1968; Distinguished Faculty award U. Ala. Med. Center, 1970. Fellow Am. Coll. Dentists, Am. Pub. Health Assn., Am. Assn. for Advancement Sci., Am. Acad. Pedo.; mem. Am. Dental Assn., Fedn. Dentaire Internationale, Internat. Assn. Dental Research. Club: The Club (Birmingham, Ala.). Author: Clin. Pedodontics, 1957-67. Editor: The Biology of the Dental Pulp Organ, 1968. Co-editor: Year Book of Dentistry, 1967. Home: 2109 Southwood Rd Birmingham AL 35216

FINN, WILLIAM GOEBEL, former govt. ofcl.; b. Burlington, Ky., Mar. 13, 1900; s. Charles A. and Laura I. (Smith) F.; B.S. in Agr. cum laude, U. Ky., 1923; M.S. in Agrl. Econs., Ia. State U., 1927; student advanced econ. studies, Grad. Sch. U.S. Dept. Agr., 1931-33, George Washington U., 1934-36; m. Bernice P. Kirkham, June 9, 1927; children—Susan M. (Mrs. Donald E. Smith), Carole B. (Mrs. David A. Fisher, Jr.). Field agt. U.S. Dept. Agr., 1922-23; asst. prof. agrl. econs. U. Ky., 1924-31; spl. cons. Met. Life Ins. Co., 1930; economist div. statis. and hist. research U.S. Dept. Agr., 1931-35, asst. dir. div. tobacco, sugar, rice and peanuts, A.A.A., 1935-38, dir. E. central div., 1938-42, asst. chief, 1942-46, asst. to adminstr. Prodn. and Marketing Adminstrn., 1946-49; chief tech. assistance br., food and agr., U.S. Del. to Regional Orgns., Paris, France, 1949-54, dep. dir. food and agr., 1954-57, dir., 1957-61; pvt. cons., 1962—; livestock farmer. Bd. dirs., U.S. Dept. Agr. Grad. Sch., 1945-49; mem. coms. Combined Food Bd., World War II; rep. U.S. Dept. Agr. on strategic materials com. U.S. Munitions Bd., 1942-49. Served with U.S. Army, 1918. Named to Hall of Distinguished Alumni, U. Ky.; recipient Presdl. citation for distinguished service to agr. Mem. Am. Farm Econs. Assn., Sigma Nu, Alpha Zeta. Club: American (Paris). Author state univ. bulls., also Dept. Agr. documents, pvt. publs., and contbr. to profl. jours. Address: 2721 Daniel Rd Chevy Chase MD 20015

FINNEGAN, FRANCIS THOMAS, banker; b. Buffalo, Sept. 23, 1915; s. Frank and Margaret (Gazley) F.; A.B., Canisius Coll., 1940; postgrad. Fordham U., 1940-41; LL.B., Harvard, 1948; m. Catherine V. Brady, July 10, 1945; children—Francis, Andrew, Catherine, John, Michael, Mary, Margaret. With Mfrs. and Traders Trust Co., Buffalo, 1948-56; with Depositors Trust Co., Augusta, Me., 1956—, vice chmn. bd., 1968—. Chmn. Augusta Devel. Commn., U. Me. Advt. Council; mem. Gov. Me. Task Force. Pres. Augusta Bd. Trade. Pres., dir. Augusta Gen. Hosp. Served with USAAF, 1941-46. Decorated Bronze Star medal. Mem. Me. C. of C. (pres. 1968). Roman Cath. Home: 10 Summer St Augusta ME 04330 Office: 286 Water St Augusta ME 04330

FINNEGAN, GEORGE BERNARD, Jr., lawyer; b. Nevada City, Cal., June 13, 1903; s. George B. and Margaret (Gillespie) F.; B.S., U.S. Mil. Acad., 1924; postgrad. George Washington Law Sch., 1926-27; J.D., Fordham U., 1929; m. Elisabeth B. Morgan, Oct. 23, 1926; children—Marcus R., George Bernard III, Dana G. Asst. examiner U. S. Patent Office, 1926-27; admitted to N.Y. bar, 1930, since practiced in N.Y.C.; sr. partner Morgan, Finnegan, Durham & Pine, 1939—. Served with U.S. Army, 1924-26, from maj. to col., AUS, 1942-46. Decorated Legion of Merit. Mem. Am. Bar Assn., Am. Judicature Soc., Am., N.Y., N.J. patent law assns., Assn. Grads. U.S. Mil. Acad., West Point Soc. N.Y., West Point Alumni Found. (bd. dirs.), Newcomen Soc., Catholic Lawyers Guild. Clubs: Army-Navy (Washington); Anglers, Downtown Association (N.Y.C.). Co-inventor, licensor Drivo- Trainer. Home: Cove Pl Mountain Lakes NJ 07046 Office: 3451 Park Av New York City NY 10022

FINNELL, MICHAEL HARTMAN, oil co. exec.; b. Los Angeles, Jan. 27, 1927; s. Jules Bertram and Maribel Hartman (Schumacher) F.; student Asheville (N.C.) Sch., 1939-44; B.A., U. Toronto, 1950; M.B.A., Harvard, 1952; m. Grace Vogel, Sept. 11, 1954 (div. June 1964); children—Lesley Hartman, Carter Hartman, Hunter Vogel. Sec.-treas., Triad Oil Co. Ltd., 1952-62, v.p., dir., 1962-66; pres. Devon-Palmer Oils Ltd., 1963-66; v.p. Elwill Devel. Ltd., 1966—; v.p., dir. Canadian Hydrocarbons, Ltd., 1967—; pres. Canadian Hydrocarbons, Ltd., 1971—; dir. Gt. No. Gas Utilities, Ltd., Canadian Homestead Oils, Ltd., Castle Oil & Gas Ltd., Ft. St. John Petroleums Ltd. Served with U.S. Mcht. Marine, 1944-46. Mem. Delta Upsilon (v.p. 1949- 50). Clubs: Ranchmen's, Glencoe, Calgary Petroleum, Calgary Golf and Country; New York Athletic. Home: 2707 Carleton St Calgary Alberta Canada Office: 700 Three Calgary Pl Calgary 1 Alberta Canada

FINNEMORE, DOUGLAS KIRBY, educator; b. Cuba, N.Y., Sept. 9, 1934; s. David Jerome and Mildred (Bosworth) F.; B.S., Pa. State U., 1956; M.S., U. Ill., 1958, Ph.D.,, 1962; m. Faith Romaine Watson, June 16, 1956; children—Martha, Susan, Sara. Mem. faculty Ia. State U., Ames, 1962—, asso. prof. physics, 1965-68, prof., 1968—. Mem. Sigma Xi. Home: 3312 Oakland St Ames IA 50010

FINNEY, ALBERT, actor; b. 1936; student Royal Acad. Dramatic Art; m. Jane Wenham (div.); m. 2d, Anouk Aimée, Aug. 1970. Appeared in Julius Caesar, Henry V, Birmingham Repertory Players; performed roles in Othello, also Coriolanus, Stratford-on-Avon; appeared at Royal Court in Lily-White Boys; dir. School for Scandal, also The Birthday Party, Glasgow, Scotland; co-producer film Night Must Fall; actor motion picture Saturday Night and Sunday Morning, Tom Jones, Two for the Road; actor, dir. Charlie Bubbles; actor Broadway play, Luther; mem. Nat. Theatre Co., 1965-66; played leading role in Joe Egg on Broadway, 1968; lead Scrooge, 1970, Gunshoe, 1971. Recipient Best Actor award Venice Film Festival; Golden Globe award. Address: care Meml Enterprises Ltd Sackville House 40 Picadilly London W 1 England

FINNEY, GEORGE GROSS, physician; b. Balt., Dec. 15, 1899; s. John M.T. and Mary Elizabeth (Gross) F.; grad. Gilman Sch., Inc., 1917; A.B., Princeton, 1921; M.D., Johns Hopkins, 1925; m. Josephine L. Stewart, Sept. 20, 1924; children—George G., Jr., Katharine L. (Mrs. Howard Baetjer II), Redmond C.S., Jervis S. Intern Union Meml. Hosp., 1925-26; asst. resident surgeon, Johns Hopkins Hosp., 1926-29, resident surgeon, 1929-30, staff mem. since 1930, Union Meml. Hosp. since 1931, Hosp. for Women of Md. since 1932; practice medicine specializing in gen. surgery, 1930- 42, 46-69; asst. prof. surgery medical sch. Johns Hopkins, 1938-34, asso. prof. surgery, 1954-65, emeritus, 1965—. Trustee Gilman Sch., Inc., Balt., 1938-68; trustee Princeton U., 1946-69, trustee emeritus, 1969—; bd. dirs. United Fund Central Md., 1970—. Bd. dirs. Balt. br. A.R.C. Served to col., M.C., AUS, 1942-46; P.T.O., 1942-45; cons. to Surgeon Gen. AUS, 1947-62. Decorated Legion of Merit, Bronze Star medal. Fellow A.C.S. (chmn. bd. govs. 1965-67); mem. A.M.A., Am., So. (pres. 1959) surg. assns., Soc. U. Surgs., English Speaking Union (past dir. Balt. br.), Soc. Med. Cons. to Armed Services. Presbyn. Clubs: Maryland (Balt.); Nassau (Princeton, N.J.); Green Spring Valley Hunt (Garrison, Md.); Princeton (N.Y.C.) Home: Stewart Rd Stevenson MD 21153 Office: 5820 York Rd Baltimore MD 21212

FINNEY, NATHANIEL SOLON, newspaper corr.; b. Stewartville, Minn., Oct. 10, 1903; s. Ross Lee and Caroline (Mitchell) F.; A.B., U. of Minn., 1927; m. Flora Edwards, Apr. 5, 1930. Reporter, Minneapolis Star, 1925-26, 1927-29; with Harcourt, Brace & Co., pubs., 1929-30; editor, bldg. trade publ., 1930-33; reporter, Minneapolis Star, 1933-35; city editor, Mpls. Star Jour., 1935- 39, feature editor, 1939-41; Washington corr., Mpls. Star and Tribune, Look Mag., 1941-50; editorial page editor Mpls. Star, 1950-53; chief Washington bur. Buffalo Evening News 1953—. Received Raymond Clapper Memorial Award, 1947; Pulitzer Prize for Nat. Affairs Reporting, 1948. Outstanding Achievement award U. Minn., 1952. Mem. Overseas Writers, White House Corrs. Assn., Chi Phi, Sigma Delta Chi. Club: National Press, The Gridiron (Washington); Chevy Chase. Home: 9131 Aldershot Dr Bethesda MD 20034 Office: Nat Press Bldg Washington DC 20004

FINNEY, REDMOND CONYNGHAM STEWART, ednl. adminstr.; b. Balt., Oct. 19, 1929; s. George G. and Josephine (Stewart) F.; B.A., Princeton, 1951; M.Ed., Harvard, 1959; postgrad. Johns Hopkins, 1959—; m. Jeannette Sheldon Brown, June 12, 1956; children—Jeannette Sheldon, Redmond Conyngham Stewart, Edward Brown, Katharine Elizabeth Finney. With Gilman Sch., Balt., 1954—, faculty adviser discipline and honor, 1963-68, mem. admissions com., 1956-68, asst. dir. summer sch., 1967-68, headmaster, 1968—. Alumni trustee Princeton; trustee St. Timothy's Sch., Keswick Home for Incurables. Served with USNR, 1951-53; PTO. Named Coach of Year, Md. Scholastic Assn., 1968. Mem. Phi Delta Kappa. Presbyn. Home: 5407-A Roland Av Baltimore MD 21210

FINNEY, ROBERT, advt. exec.; b. Summit, N.J., Mar. 15, 1902; s. Frank and Florence (Neat) F.; student Phillips Acad., Andover, Mass., 1919, Yale Sheffield Sci. Sch., 1923; m. Helen Keyes, Oct. 19, 1929; 1 stepson, William G. Johnston. With Summit Herald, 1923; with Street & Finney, Inc., N.Y.C., 1923-68, chmn. bd., 1963-68; chmn. bd. Musius, Wynne-Williams, Inc., N.Y.C., 1968-70, chmn. exec. com., 1971—; dir. Midland Pharmacal Corp., N.Y.C., 1954- 68, Midland Internat. Ltd., N.Y.C., 1962-68, Mentholatum Co., Buffalo, 1968—. Gen. chmn. U.S. Golf Assn., Open Championship, Baltusrol, N.J., 1967. Mem. KOA, Chi Phi. Clubs: Yale (N.Y.C.); Pinehurst (N.C.) Country; Tin Whistles (pres. 1965) (Pinehurst, N.C.); Pine Valley (N.J.) Golf; Short Hills; Baltusrol Golf (pres. 1967-70). Home: 20 Fox Hill Lane Short Hills NJ 07078 Office: 380 Madison Av New York City NY 10017

FINNEY, ROBERT ARTHUR, insurance executive; b. Princeton, Ind., July 16, 1906; s. Charles M. and Mary (Fuhrer) F.; A.B., Butler U., 1928; postgrad. U. Chgo., 1929- 31; m. Gertrude Leitzbach, Aug. 12, 1933; children—Ona, Mary, Paul. Tchr. econs. Allegheny Coll., 1931-34; motor car dealer, Galion, O., 1934-37; breeder Aberdeen-Angus cattle, 1937—; sec., gen. mgr. Humboldt Brick & Tile Co., Kan., 1947-68; pres., dir. Farm & Ranch Life Ins., Wichita, 1968—; dir. Farm & Ranch Financial, Inc., Parklane Nat. Bank, Humboldt National Bank, Humboldt Shale Mining Co., Neosho Valley Oil & Gas Trust Co. Dir. Structural Clay Products Inst. Mem. Kan. Ho. of Reps., 1961-66. Trustee Coll. of Emporia, 1953—; bd. dirs. Wichita Symphony Soc. 1968—. Mem. U. S. (dir., v.p.), Kan. (pres.), Humboldt (past pres.), Wichita (v.p.) chambers commerce, Kan. Assn. Pvt. Univs. and Colls. (trustee). Presbyn. Clubs: Rotary (past pres.), Kansas City, (Mo.); Wichita Country. Home: 23 Huntington Rd Eastborough Wichita KS 67206 Office: 1069 Parklane Wichita KS 67218

FINNEY, ROSS LEE, composer, educator; b. Wells, Minn., Dec. 23, 1906; s. Ross Lee and Caroline (Mitchell) F.; student U. Minn., 1924-25; B.A., Carleton Coll., 1927, L.H.D., 1957; student Harvard, 1929; Nadia Boulanger, 1928. Alban Berg, 1932, Francesco Malipiero, 1937; Mus.D., New England Conservatory of Music; m. Gretchen Ludke, Sept. 3, 1930; children—Ross Lee, Henry C. Prof. music, Smith Coll., 1929-48, Mt. Holyoke Coll., 1940-44, chmn. dept. mus. theory, Hart Sch. of Music, Hartford, 1941-42, Amherst Coll., 1946-47; dir. Northampton Chamber Orch.; composer in residence U. Mich., 1948—, Am. Acad. in Rome, 1960. Chief Paris office Interdeptl. com., OSS, 1944-45. Recipient Purple Heart, Certificate of Merit; Conn. Valley prize, 1935, Guggenheim fellow, 1939, 47, 1939; Boston Symphony award, 1955; Rockefeller Found. Grant, 1956; Acad. of Arts and Letters award, 1956; Brandeis Creative Arts award, 1967. Johnson Foundation fellow, 1927, Pulitzer fellow. Mem. Am. Musicol. Soc., Nat. Inst. of Arts and Letters, Am. Acad. of Arts and Sciences, Phi Beta Kappa, Pi Kappa Lambda, Phi Mu Alpha.

Composer: Piano Sonata, 1933; First String Quartet, 1935; Second String Quartet, 1936; Piano Trio, 1938; Eight Poems by Archibald MacLeish, 1935-37; Sonata for Viola and Piano, 1937; Bleheris, 1937; Fantasy for Piano, 1939; Third String Quartet, 1940: Slow Piece, 1940; Pole Star for This Year, 1939; Symphony Communique, 1942; Third Piano Sonata, 1942; Hymn, Fuguing and Holiday, 1943; Duo for Violin and Piano, 1944; Pilgrim Psalms, 1945; Fourth Piano Sonata, 1945; Poor Richard, 1946: Nostalgic Waltzes, 1947; 4th String Quartet, 1947; Six Spherical Madrigals, 1947; Violin Concerto, 1933-47; Three Love Songs, 1948: Piano Quartet, 1948; Piano Concerto, 1948; 5th String Quartet, 1948; 2d Sonata for Cello and Piano, 1950; 6th String Quartet, 1950; Sonata for Violin and Piano, 1951; 36 Songs (chamber music), 1952; Immortal Autumn, 1952; Variation for Piano, 1952; Piano Quintet; 2d Sonata for Viola and Piano; 3d Sonata for Violin and Piano, 1953; The Express (song), Piano Trio, 1954; 7th String Quartet, Inventions for Piano, Variations for Orchestra, Fantasy for Solo Cello, all 1957; Fantasy for solo violin (command Yehudi Menuhin), String Quintet (commnd. by the Coolidge Foundation), all 1958; 2d Symphony (commnd. by Koussevitsky Found.); Edge of Shadow (commnd. by Grinnell Coll.), 1959; 8th String Quartet (comm'd. by U. Ala.), 3d Symphony, 1960; 2d Piano Quintet (commd. U. S.C.), 1961; Still are New Worlds (May Festival, Ann Arbor), 1962; Sonata quasi una fantasia (Quincy, Ill., Art Festival), 1961; Three Pieces for Strings, Winds, Percusion and Tape Recorder, 1962; Divertimento, 1963; Divertissement (commd. Bowdoin Coll.), 1964; Three Studies in Fours (commd. Poznon Ensemble), 1965; Concerto for Percussion and Orch. (commd. Carleton Coll.), 1965; Nun's Priest's Tale (commd. Dartmouth Coll.), 1965; The Marty's Elegy (commd. U. Mich. Sesquicentennial), 1966; Symphony Concertante (commd. Kansas City Philharmonic), 1967; Organ Fantasies, 1967; 32 Piano Games, 1968; 2d Concerto for Piano and Orch., 1968; The Remorseless Rush of Time, for Chorus and 13 Instruments (commd. Wis. State U.), 1969; Summer in Valley City, for Concert Band (commd. U. Mich. Band), 1969; 24 Inventions for Piano, 1970; 2 Acts for 3 Players, clarinet, percussion and piano (commd. G. LaBlanc Corp.), 1970. Author: The Game of Harmony, 1947. Editor-in-chief Smith Coll. Music Archives, 1935-48, edited, for same, XII Sonatas for Violin and Figures Bass, by Francesco Geminiani, 1935. Editor Valley Music Press. Home: 2015 Geddes Ann Arbor MI Office: Sch Music U Mich Ann Arbor MI 48108

FINNEY, RUTH, (Mrs. Robert Sharon Allen), newspaper corr.; b. Chgo. Mar. 6, 1898; d. John W. and Mary L. (Morrison) Finney; grad. San Jose State (Cal.) Normal Sch. (now San Jose State Coll.), 1918; m. Robert Sharon Allen, Mar. 30, 1929. Reporter, city hall and other polit. assignments, Sacramento (Cal.) Star, 1918-22, city editor, 1922-23; reporter, San Francisco (Cal.) News, 1923; mem. Washington (D.C.) bureau Scripps-Howard Newspaper Alliance, corr. Albuquerque Tribune, other Scripps-Howard papers, 1923—. Mem. Theta Sigma Phi. Club: Women's National Press (Washington). Home: 1525 28th St NW Washington DC 20007 Office: 1013 13th St NW Washington DC 20005

FINNEY, THEODORE M., musician, tchr., author, editor; b. Fayette, Ia., Mar. 14, 1902; s. Ross L. and Caroline (Mitchell) F.; B.A., U. Minn., 1924; studied Conservatoire Americaine, Fontainbleau, France, 1926, Stern Conservatory and U. Berlin, 1927-28; Litt.M., U. Pitts., 1938; Mus. D., Washington and Jefferson Coll., 1947; m. Myrle Greeley, Aug. 1, 1925. Mem. Mpls. Symphony Orch., 1923-25; asst. supr., instr. music, pub. schs., Council Bluffs, Ia., 1925, supr. music, 1933-36; instr. and asst. prof. music, Carleton Coll., Northfield, Minn., 1925-32; mem. faculty Smith Coll. Summer Sch. of Music, Northampton, Mass., 1930-38; prof., head dept. music U. Pitts., 1936-68, prof. emeritus, 1968—; curator Warrington Hymnological collection Pitts. Theol. Sem., 1967; editor, Music Tchrs. Nat. Assn., Vol. of Proceedings and Bulletin; dir. Heinz Chapel Choir, U. Pitts. since 1939. Awarded 1st prize essay Nat. Composers' Congress, 1945. Mem. Music Teachers Nat. Assn., Music Educators Nat. Conf., Internat., Am. musicological socs., Phi Beta Kappa, Phi Mu Alpha-Sinfonia, Phi Alpha Theta, Omicron Delta Kappa, Phi Delta Kappa. Conglist. Author: A History of Music, 1935, rev. 1947; Hearing Music, 1941; We Have Made Music, 1955. Composer, editor chamber music pieces, Pitt Glee Club Series and Pitt Choral Series. Home: 209 Gladstone Rd Pittsburgh PA 15217

FINSTON, HOWARD VIVIAN, educator; b. Tulsa, Dec. 13, 1923; s. Jesse and Pearl M. (Aaronson) F.; A.B. in Econs., A.M., Stanford, 1948, Ph.D., 1953; m. Phyllis Hinckley Moller, Aug. 22, 1958; 1 dau., Felicia Ann. Asst. prof. econs. Humboldt State Coll., Arcata, Call., 1951-52; asst. prof. bus. adminstrn. Loyola U. at Los Angeles, 1952-53; mem. faculty U. N.M., 1953- -, prof. organizational behavior, 1963—, dean Coll. Bus. Adminstrn., 1962-68; mgmt. cons., 1953—; pres. Mgmt. Devel. Systems, Inc. Past dir. S.W. Mgmt. Devel. Program; chmn. Albuquerque Personnel Bd.; mem. small bus. adv. com. Office Econ. Opportunity. Trustee Manzano Sch. Mem. Acad. Mgmt. (pres. S.W. div. 1963-64), Am. Assn. U. Profs. Unitarian (past pres.). Contbr. numerous articles. Home: 8705 La Sala Grande NE Albuquerque NM 87111

FINTEL, NORMAN DALE, ednl. adminstr.; b. Monrovia, Cal., Jan. 21, 1925; s. Ernest A.H. and Nora (Koester) F.; B.A., Wartburg (Ia.) Coll., 1951; M.A., U. Wis., 1959; m. Jeanette Kosbau, June 30, 1953; children—Peggy, William, Barbara. Dir. pub. relations Wartburg Coll., 1951-60; asst. dir., bd. coll. edn. Am. Luth. Ch., 1960-64, exec. dir., 1964—. Pres. Nat. Luth. Campus Ministry, 1966—; ednl. Cons., div. ednl. services Luth. Council in U.S., 1966—. Served with USAAF, 1944-45. Republican. Lutheran. Editor: Evaluating Pub. Relations Results, 1958. Home: 2522 38th Av S Minneapolis MN 55406 Office: 422 S 5th St Minneapolis MN 55415

FINTON, JAMES ROBERT, air force officer; b. Salamanca, N.Y., Sept. 18, 1919; s. Isaac Callin and Gertrude (Sweet) F.; B.S., U. Md., 1941; postgrad. Mass. Inst. Tech., 1942-43; m. Iris Hammer, Oct. 18, 1941; children—James Robert, Thomas Edward, Timothy Christopher. Commd. 2d lt. USAAF, 1941, advanced through grades to col. USAF, 1958; meteorologist U.S. Weather Bur., Washington, 1945-47; dir. avionics engring. Aero. Systems div. Wright- Patterson AFB, O., 1947-68. Decorated Legion of Merit, Air Force Commendation medal. Mem. Am. Meteorol. Soc., I.E.E.E. (v.p. engrng. mgmt. group Dayton). Home: 1317 Merribrook Ct Fairborn OH 45324 Office: Wright-Patterson AFB Dayton OH 45433

FINUCANE, BERNARD EMMET, banker; b. Rochester, N.Y.; June 16, 1889; s. Thomas W. and Mary (Downing) F.; student Phillips Acad., Andover, Mass.; LL.D. (hon.), Niagara U., m. Freda Zimmer, Jan. 29, 1913; children—Frederick T., Mrs. Charles J. Symington, Jr. Began as founder, operator electrical distbg. firm; chmn. bd., dir. Thomas W. Finucane Corp.; dir. Security Trust Co., Rochester, 1930—, pres., 1940-60, chmn. bd., 1960- -; chmn. bd. Security New York State Corp.; dir. Rochester Telephone Corp., Ritter-Pfaudler Corp., Bausch & Lomb Optical Co., Gen. Dynamics Corp., Assn. Dry Goods Corp. Decorated Knight of Malta; received Silver Antelope award Boy Scouts Am., civic achievement award Rotary Club. Mem. N.Y. State Bankers Assn. (past pres.). Home: 91 Douglas Rd Rochester NY 14610 Office: 183 Main St E Rochester NY 14604

FINUCANE, CHARLES CEIL, insurance and investments exec., b. Spokane, Sept. 6, 1905; s. Francis J. and Mary Gertrude (Sweeney) F.; grad. Taft Sch., Watertown, Conn., 1924; B.S. in Indsl. Engring., Sheffield Sci. Sch., Yale, 1928; m. Marion Madeleine Burke, June 20, 1928. Wholesale hardware bus., 1928- 30; v.p. Sweeny Investment Co., 1930-49, pres., 1949-62; v.p. Sunshine Consolidated Mining Co., 1936-38; partner Finucane and Galland, mgrs. comml. bldgs., Spokane, 1946-; 1946—; Spokane and Eastern div. Seattle First Nat. Bank; treas., dir. Jame Smyth Plumbing and Heating Co., Spokane, 1946—; owner Davenport Hotel, Spokane, 1947-53; owner, operator cattle ranches; asst. sec. of army for financial mgmt., 1954-55, under sec. of Army, 1955-58, asst. sec. def., 1958-61; asst. Majority floor leader Wash. Legislature, 1939. Mem. bd. govs. A.R.C., United Service Orgn.; mem. bd. regents Gonzaga U. Dept. Def. rep. on President's com. on Govt. Employment Policy; vice chmn. President's Com. on Fund Raising within Fed. Service. Served from ensign to comdr., USNR, 1932-48; ordnance officer with Northwest Sea Frontier and 13th Naval Dist. and Bur. Ordnance, Washington. Clubs: Racquet and Tennis (N.Y.C.); Spokane Country, Town (Spokane); 1925 F Street, Army and Navy, Metropolitan (Washington); Burning Tree (Bethesda. Md.); Annapolis Yacht. Home: 14 Howard St Spokane WA 99201

FINZI, LEE ALDO, elec. engr., educator; b. Padova, Italy, Dec. 16, 1904; s. Aldo and Giulia (Colorni) F.; M.E.E., U. Naples, 1926; Dr. Ingenieur, Technische Hochschule, Aachen, Germany, 1932; m. Luisa Kaufmann, May 15, 1933. Came to U.S., 1939, naturalized, 1945. Designer Hochspannungs Ges. m.b.H., Cologne, Germany 1927-31; sect. engr. Ente Elettrico Volturno, Naples, Italy, 1931-39; adj. prof. elec. engrng. U. Naples, 1933-38; sr. lab. engr. charge East Pitts. Lightning Lab., Westinghouse Electric Corp., 1940-46; prof. Carnegie-Mellon U., Pitts., 1946—, Buhl. prof. elec. engring., 1955—; cons. elec. mfg. cos. Recipient Borchers Medal, Aachen Hochschule, 1932; Carnegie Corp. award outstanding teaching, 1955. Fellow Inst. Elec. and Electronic Engrs.; mem. Am. Soc. for Engring. Edn., Sigma Xi. Eta Kappa Nu, Tau Beta Pi. Author numerous tech. papers on elec. machinery, magnetic amplifiers, ferromagnetism, super conductivity. Home: 606 South St Circleville Irwin PA 15642

FIORE, LOUIS ROBERT, transp. co. exec.; b. N.Y.C., Oct. 3, 1914; s. John and Mary (Variano) F.; grad. N.Y. State Maritime Coll., 1936; B.S., Hofstra Coll.; M.B.A., N.Y.U.; m. Lily B. MacArthur, June 14, 1941. Asst. prof. U.S. Merchant Marine Acad., 1946-51; asst. to comdt. mgmt. engring. Mil. Sea Transp. Service, 1951-56; with Ohio River Co., Cin., 1956—, pres., 1962—, also dir.; sr. v.p., trustee Eastern Gas and Fuel Assos.; pres. Atlantic Bulk Trading Corp., Mystic Steamship Corp., Boston Towboat Co. Mem. exec. bd. Waterways Transport Assn.; bd. dirs. Water Resources Asso. Served with USNR, 1941-46. Mem. Soc. Naval Architects and Marine Engrs. Home: 5580 Miami Rd Cincinnati OH 45243 Office: Provident Tower Cincinnati OH 45202

FIORE, MARY, editor Photoplay mag. Address: 205 E 42d St New York City NY 10017*

FIORELLI, EDUARDO, violinist, educator; b. Jessup, Pa., July 11, 1926; s. Giovanni and Catherine (Petrucci) F.; student Curtis Inst. Music, 1940-44; B. Mus., Eastman Sch. Music, 1951, M.Mus., 1957. First violinist Rochester Philharmonic Orch., 1949-52; solo recitals, chamber music performances throughout U.S., 1945-52; violin tchr., mem. resident string quartet Coll. Fine Arts, U. Tex., 1952-55; solo recitals, lecture-demonstration performances music clubs, schs. of music, 1955-56; mem. faculty Sch. Music, Northwestern U., 1956—, chmn. prep. stringed instruments dept., violinist Sheridan String Quartet, 1956—; numerous appearances ednl. TV, recordings for Voice of Am. Fulbright grantee, Rome, Italy, 1955. Hon. life mem. Phi Mu Alpha; mem. Pi Kappa Lambda. Home: 609 Sheridan Rd Winnetka IL Office: School of Music Northwestern Univ Evanston IL

FIORENZA, JOSEPH FRANCIS, financial exec.; b. Bklyn., Dec. 16, 1921; s. Dominic and Concetta (Chiusano) F.; B.B.A., Coll. City N.Y., 1947; m. Mary J. Girimonti, Nov. 22, 1958; children—Stephanie, Joseph Francis. Jr. accountant McArdle & McArdle, N.Y.C., 1947-48; overseas resident controller Raymond Internat., Inc., Venezuela, Guatemala, France, Thailand, Brazil and Liberia, 1948-58, accounting mgr., N.Y.C., 1958-62, tax mgr., 1962-64, asst. treas., controller, 1965-68, treas., 1969—. Served with AUS, 1942-45; ETO. Decorated Bronze Star medal, Purple Heart with oak leaf cluster. Mem. Tax Execs. Inst., Flower Hill Civic Assn., Holy Name Soc., 773d Tank Destroyer Bn. Assn. Home: 24 Colony Lane Manhasset NY 11030 Office: 2 Penn Plaza New York City NY 10001

FIORIO, FRANCO EMILIO, Italian diplomat; b. Milan, Italy, June 2, 1912; s. Giovanni B. and Maria (Civita) F.; M.A. in aeroballistics Politecnico Torino, 1937; Ph.D. in Mech. Engring., Politecnico Milano, 1934; m. Maria Lanzillotto, Sept. 12, 1946; children—Gianfranco, Maurizio, Alessandro, Livio. Commd. lt. Italian Air Force, 1936, advanced through grades to col., 1957; tech. asst. to air attache Italian embassy, Washington, 1949-55; head tech sers. Italian Air Fighters Force, 1943-49; retired, 1957; mem. Italian delegation UN Gen. Assembly, sci. adviser to Italian permanent mission, 1958-71; mem. spl. group to investigate Argentine Rocket Range, 1969; consul gen. Republic of San Marino, Washington, 1957-68; sci. counsellor Italian embassy, Washington, 1968—. Dep. head Italian delegation UN Vienna Space Conf., 1968; mem. Italian delegation Conf. Prevention Surprise Attacks, 1959, Disarmament Negotiations, 1960-63; head Italian delegation INTELSAT Preparatory Conf., 1969, dep. head Italian delegation INTELSAT Plenipotentiary Conf., 1969-71; co-founder allied group for aerospace research and devel. NATO, 1952; columnist, 1962-71; corr., 1949-70. Mem. Am. Inst. Aeros. and Astronautics, Am. Astron. Soc. (sr.), A.A.A.S., Am. Space Pioneers Group, Italian Research Nat. Council (rep.), Internat. Astron. Fedn. (com. on application's satellites). Author: Aviazione Moderna, 1964. Editor Italian Missiles and Rocket Mag., 1957-61, Notiziario Fiorio, 1965-71. Contbr. profl. jours. Address: 2600 N Nelson St Arlington VA 22207

FIRESTEIN, ALFRED, cosmetic co. exec.; b. Los Angeles, 1924; legal edn. U. So. Cal. Pres., dir. Max Factor & Co., 1963—, also chief exec. officer. Home: 615 N Trenton Dr Beverly Hills CA 90210 Office: 1644 N McCadden Pl Hollywood CA 90028*

FIRESTEIN, CHESTER, cosmetic co. exec.; b. Los Angeles, July 31, 1930; B.S., U. Cal. at Los Angeles, 1952, M.B.A., 1953; C.P.A., 1954. With Max Factor & Co., Hollywood, Cal., 1955—, exec. v.p., 1968—, also dir. Mem. exec. com., dir. Jewish Fedn.-Council Greater Los Angeles, 1970; bus. and professions chmn. United Jewish Welfare Fund Greater Los Angeles, 1970, gen. campaign chmn., 1971. Recipient Robert Greenberg leadership award, 1961. Mem. Am. Inst. C.P.A.'s, Cal. Soc. C.P.A.'a Zeta Beta Tau, Beta Gamma Sigma. Office: 1655 N McCadden Pl Hollywood CA 90028

FIRESTONE, ARDEN EDSON, co. exec.; b. Akron, O., May 25, 1908; s. Henry E. and Edna M. (Becker) F.; A.B., U. Akron, 1929; J.D., U. Mich., 1932; m. Elizabeth E. Airhart, June 24, 1933; 1 dau., Karen (Mrs. Karen E. Beam). Admitted to Ohio bar, 1932; partner of Hutchison & Firestone, Akron 1932-42; asst. sec. Goodyear Fgn. Operations, Inc., 1947-53; atty. law dept. Goodyear Tire & Rubber Co., 1942-47, sec., 1953-60, v.p., gen. counsel, 1960—, also dir.; dir. The Goodyear Bank. Hon. trustee United Found. Summit County; dir. Summit County chpt. A.R.C.; trustee, v.p. Akron City Hosp. Served as lt. USNR, World War II. Mem. Am., Fed., Ohio, Akron bar assns., Phi Delta Theta. Home: 922 Mayfair Rd Akron OH 44303 Office: 1144 E Market St Akron OH 44316

FIRESTONE, BERNARD, railroad ofcl.; b. N.Y.C., May 1, 1918; s. Martin and Kate (Chariton) F.; B.S. in Civil Engring., Purdue U., 1939; M.A. in Math., Loyola U., Chgo., 1948; m. Sylvia Zussin, Dec. 24, 1939; children—Franklin Joseph, Frances Katherine; m. 2d Bettie Kaplan, Apr. 2, 1961 (div. Nov. 1, 1965); children—Nellisa Lewis, Wendy Lewis, Bethann Firestone. With C. & N.W. Ry., 1939—, asst. comptroller, asst. treas., 1956-62, treas., 1962—, also dir.; treas. Northwest Industries, Inc., 1968—. Served to lt. (j.g.) USNR, 1944-46. Mem. Am. Ry. Engring. Assn., Assn. Am. Railroads, Ry. Systems and Procedures Assn. Home: 2106 St Johns Av Highland Park IL 60035 Office: 400 W Madison St Chicago IL 60606

FIRESTONE, CHARLES E., banker. Sr. v.p., also cashier City Nat. Bank, Beverly Hills, Cal. Office: City Nat Bank 400 N Roxbury Dr PO Box 1141 Beverly Hills CA 90213*

FIRESTONE, HARVEY SAMUEL, Jr., rubber co. exec.; b. Chgo., Apr. 20, 1898; s. Harvey Samuel and Idabelle (Smith) F.; grad. Asheville (N.C.) Sch., 1916; A.B., Princeton, 1920; LL.D., U. Akron, Stetson U.; m. Elizabeth Parke, June 25, 1921; children—Elizabeth Chambers (Mrs. Firestone Willis), Martha Parke (Mrs. William C. Ford), Harvey Samuel III (dec.), Anne Idabelle (Mrs. John F. Ball). Actively asso. Firestone Tire and Rubber Co., dir., 1919-69, v.p., 1929-41, pres., 1941-46, pres., chief officer, 1946-48, chmn., chief exec. officer, 1948-63, chmn., 1963-66, hon. chmn., hon. dir. 1966—; v.p. Firestone Plantations Co. (with rubber plantations in Liberia, West Africa), 1926-32, pres., chmn., 1932-67. Founder Am. Assn. Against Addiction; nat. chmn. U.S.O., mem. internat. com. YMCA; mem. Nat. Com. Washington Cathedral. Mem. nat. council United Negro Coll. Fund; trustee, dir. Episcopal Ch. Found., Asheville Sch., U. Liberia, Ohio Found. Ind. Colls., Inc.; charter trustee Princeton; trustee Thomas Alva Edison Found. (v.p.). Served in Naval Aviation, 1918. Decorated Dept. Def. medal for distinguished pub. service; Officer Legion of Honor (France); Comdr. Order Isabella the Catholic (Spain); Grand Band Order of Star of Africa, also Grand Cordon of the Most Venerable Order Knighthood of Pioneers of Republic of Liberia; Comdr. of the White Rose (Finland); Comdr.'s Cross Order Merit (Germany). Mem. Am. Bible Soc. (v.p.), UN Assn. U.S.A. (dir.), Nat. Conf. Christians and Jews. Republican. Episcopalian. Author: Man on the Move, The Story of Transportation. Home: 50 Twin Oaks Rd Akron OH 44313 also Ocean Lawn Cliff Av Newport RI 02840

FIRESTONE, LEONARD KIMBALL, tire and rubber mfr.; b. Akron, O., June 10, 1907; s. Harvey Samuel and Idabelle (Smith) F.; student, the Hill Sch., Pottstown, Pa., 1927, Princeton U., 1931; LL.D., U. So. Cal., 1965; L.H.D., Okla. Christian Coll., 1970; m. Polly Curtis, Sept. 14, 1932; children—Kimball Curtis, Anthony Brooks, Lendy Stewart (Mrs. Samuel C. Register); m. 2d, Barbara Heatley, Mar. 4, 1966. Pres., Firestone Tire & Rubber Co. of Cal., 1943-70, dir.; dir. Wells Fargo Bank, Firestone Tire & Rubber Co., Akron, O. Mem. nat. exec. bd. Boy Scouts Am. Trustee U. So. Cal., Grad. Theol. Union; dir. Cal. Community Found.; pres. Richard Nixon Found. Served as lt. USNR, 1942-43. Decorated grand band Order Star of Africa. Episcopalian. Clubs: Hillcrest Country, Los Angeles Country (Los Angeles); Bohemian, Pacific-Union (San Francisco); Thunderbird Country (Palm Springs, Cal.); Cypress Point (Pebble Beach, Cal.). 10375 Wilshire Blvd Los Angeles CA 90024

FIRESTONE, NEIL EUGENE, heating and cooling co. exec.; b. Ft. Wayne, Ind., Sept. 26, 1915; s. Ross E. and Hazel R. (Shaw) F.; student Franklin Coll., 1932-34, LL.D. (hon.), 1962; student Purdue U., 1943-44; m. Merle A. Yelton, June 22, 1946; children—Douglas, Thomas, Nancy. Partner in automotive equipment distbn., 1935-42; with Gen. Electric Co., 1942-61, gen. mgr. flight propulsion div., 1958-61; v.p. mfg. and facilities world-wide, Internat. Tel. & Tel. Corp., 1961-66; pres. Turner Corp., 1966-69, now dir.; pres., dir. Burnham Corp., 1969—; dir. Betham Corp. Pres. Bruce Museum Assn., Greenwich. Trustees Franklin Coll., 1963—. Mem. Newcomen Soc. North Am., Internat. Platform Assn., Soc. Automotive Engrs., Cin. Engrs. Club, Nat. Def. Transp. Assn., Air Force Assn., Greenwich C. of C. Clubs: Queen City (Cin.); Wings (N.Y.C.); Burning Tree Golf (Greenwich). Home: Calhoun Dr Greenwich CT 06830 Office: 2 Main St Irvington NY 10533

FIRESTONE, RAYMOND CHRISTY, rubber co. exec.; b. Akron, Ohio, Sept. 6, 1908; s. Harvey S. and Idabelle (Smith) F.; student The Hill Sch., Pottstown, Pa.; A.B., Princeton 1933; LL.D., U. Akron, 1957; H.H.D., U. Liberia, 1960; m. Laura An Lisk, Aug. 25, 1934 (dec. July, 1960); children—Christy An (Mrs. Geoffrey A. Gordon-Creed), Judith An (Mrs. Dale K. Thiel); m. 2d, Jane Allen Messler, April 28, 1962. Joined sales dept., The Firestone Tire & Rubber Co., 1933, Firestone store 1934, dist. store supr., Los Angeles, 1934, asst. mgr. Southeastern sales zone, Akron, 1934-35, dist. mgr., Richmond, Va., 1935- 36, staff Firestone plant at Memphis, 1936, pres. subsidiary, 1937-49, dir. parent co., 1942—, exec... v.p., 1954-57, pres., 1957-63, pres., chief exec. officer, 1963-64, chief exec. officer, chmn. exec. com., 1964—, chmn. bd., 1966—; dir. The Firestone Bank. Mem. Akron Area Council Boy Scouts Am. Chmn., Future Farmers Am. Found., 1951; dir. Le Bonheur Children's Hosp., Inc., Memphis; trustee City Hosp. Akron. Dir. Nat. Indsl. Conf. Board. Served as major USAF, 1942-44. Recipient Humanitarian Service award Eleanor Roosevelt Found., 1961; Grand Band Order Star of Africa. Mem. Am. Ordnance Assn., Soc. Automotive Engrs. Episcopalian. Clubs: Detroit Athletic, Recess (Detroit); Union Tavern, Chagrin Valley (Cleve.); Rolling Rock (Ligonier, Pa.); Indpls. Athletic; Genesee Valley, Rochester Country (Rochester N.Y.); Country of N.C., Pinehurst. Home: Lauray Farms Bath OH 44210 Office: Akron OH 44317

FIRESTONE, RICHARD FRANCIS, educator; b. Canton, O., June 18, 1926; s. Lester Ellis and Elizabeth (Corkran) F.; A.B., Oberlin Coll., 1950; Ph.D., U. Wis., 1954; m. Olwen Margaret Huskins, Aug. 21, 1954; children—William, Mark, Robert. Resident research asso. Argonne Nat. Lab., 1954-56; asst. prof. chemistry Western Res. U., 1956-60; asso. prof. Ohio State U., 1961-66, prof., 1967—, chmn. dept. chemistry, 1971—. Served with USNR, 1944-46. Fellow A.A.A.S.; mem. Am. Chem. Soc., Am. Inst. Physics, Am. Assn. U. Profs. Home: 820 Old Woods Rd Worthington OH 43085 Office: 140 W 18th Av Columbus OH 43210

FIRFER, ALEXANDER, economist; b. Paterson, N.J., Apr. 6, 1919; s. Louis and Mary (Suratt) F.; B.A. cum laude, N.Y.U., 1940; postgrad. Columbia, 1940-41; m. Amy Ross Weston, Sept. 6, 1947. Economist, OPA, 1942-47; on loan to sec. war for U.S. Strategic Bombing Survey in Europe, 1945; econs. instr. N.C. State Coll., 1947; pub. utility cons., Washington, 1947; economist FCC, 1948-51, 53-54, Small Defense Plants Adminstrn., 1951-53; cons. economist Econ.

Devel. Adminstrn. P.R., 1954-58; indsl. devel. expert UN Tech. Assistance Bd., Caracas, 1958-62; industry devel. economist Govt. of Republic of China, Taiwan, for ICA, 1960; dir. AID mission in Bolivia, 1962-65, Dominican Republic, Santo Domingo, 1965-68; dep. dir. CORDS, Danang, Vietnam, 1968-70; dir. AID mission in Panama, 1970—. Home: 4345 Hawthorne St NW Washington DC 20016

FIRKUSNY, RUDOLF, pianist; b. Napajedla, Czechoslovakia, Feb. 11, 1912; s. Rudolf and Karla (Sindelarova) F.; student coll. Brno and Bucovice, 1922-1930, Conservatory of Music, Brno, Praha; m. Tatiana Nevolova; children— Veronique, Igor. First appeared with Czech. Philharmonic Orchestra, 1922; made concert tours, Europe, 1930-39; toured U.S. with symphony orchestra, including N.Y. Philharmonic, Boston, Phila., Chgo., Nat. Detroit, Mpls., Cleve., San Francisco, Los Angeles, Toronto, Montreal; played in recitals in all sects. U.S.; S.Am. tours, 1943—, annual tours in Europe, 1950—, tour of Australia and Far East, 1959. Composer piano concerto (performed in Praha, Czechoslovakia); piano pieces, songs. Home: Staatsburg NY 12580

FIRMILIAN, FIRMILIAN, bishop Mid-West diocese Serbian Orthodox Ch. in U.S. and Can. Address: 8347 W Summerdale Av Chicago IL 60656*

FIRMIN, PETER ARTHUR, Jr., univ. dean; b. Meeker, La., Feb. 24, 1924; s. Peter Arthur and Charlotte (Aucoin) F.; B.S., La. State U., 1943; M.B.A., U. Cal. at Berkeley, 1948; Ph.D., U. Mich., 1957; m. Jean Cameron Nash, Sept. 3, 1959; children—William C., Renee, Therese, Kathryn, David A., Peter N., Michael C. Staff accountant Montgomery Ward & Co., Oakland, Cal., 1946-47; instr. St. Mary's Coll. (Cal.), 1947-49; asst. prof. accounting Tulane U., New Orleans, 1949-57, asso. prof., 1957-63, prof., 1963—, W.R. Irby prof. accounting, 1966—, dean Grad. Sch. Bus. Adminstrn., 1968—. Mem. Met. New Orleans Goals Found. Council, 1970-71; dir. Met. Crime Commn., New Orleans, 1971-72, Interracial Council for Bus. Opportunity, 1971-72. Served to 1st lt. AUS, 1943-46. Ford Found. fellow for study math. for application to bus., 1959-60. Mem. Am. Accounting Assn. (v.p. 1967-68), Am. Inst. C.P.A.'s, Nat. Assn. Accountants, Financial Execs. Inst. Democrat. Roman Catholic. Author: (with Hector R. Anton) Contemporary Issues in Cost Accounting, 1965; (with others) University Cost Structures and Behavior, 1967. Home: 1700 Mirabeau Av New Orleans LA 70122

FIRMINGER, HARLAN IRWIN, pathologist, educator; b. Mpls., Dec. 31, 1918; s. Harry and Emily (Irwin) F.; A.B., Washington U., St. Louis, 1939, M.D., 1943; m. Jane Ryder Hollings, Sept. 14, 1942; children—Ann Laura (Mrs. Kenneth Leon Howard, Jr.), Carol Jean, Barbara Lynn. Intern Barnes Hosp., St. Louis, 1943; resident pathology Mass. Gen. Hosp., Boston, 1946-47; pathologist Nat. Cancer Inst., Bethesda, Md., 1948-51; practice medicine, specializing in pathology, Kansas City, Kan., 1951-57, Balt., 1957—; asst. prof., prof. pathology U. Kan., 1951-57; prof. chmn. dept. pathology U. Md., 1957-67, prof. pathology, 1967—; dir. Univs. Asso. for Research and Edn. in Pathology, 1964-71, scientist-asso., 1971—; mem. sci. adv. bd. Armed Forces Inst. Pathology, 1965-70; mem. com. on pathology, div. med. scis. Nat. Acad. Scis.-NRC, 1966—. Pres. Md. div. Am. Cancer Soc., 1967-68. Served to capt. M.C., AUS, 1943-46. Diplomate Am. Bd. Pathology, Mem. Am. Soc. Exptl. Pathology, Am. Assn. Pathologists and Bacteriologists, Internat. Acad. Pathology, Am. Assn. Cancer Research, Soc. Mayflower Descendants (gov. Md. chpt. 1967-70), Md. Soc. Pathologists (pres. 1969-71), Alpha Omega Alpha. Editor: Atlas of Tumor Pathology, 1966—. Contbr. articles profl. jours. Home: 512 Goucher Blvd Towson MD 21204 Office: 660 W Redwood St Baltimore MD 21201

FIRST, JOSEPH MICHAEL, pub. and communications co. exec.; b. Phila., Apr. 1, 1906; s. Louis and Sarah (Selig) F.; B.S. in Econs. cum laude, Wharton Sch., U. Pa., 1927, J.D. cum laude (case ed. U. Pa. Law Rev. 1929-30), 1930, LL.M. (Gowen fellow 1930-32), 1932; m. Helen Gross, Dec. 27, 1931; children—Elsa, Abigail (Mrs. Roger E. Farber), Jonathan. Admitted to Pa. bar, 1930; v.p., sec., gen. counsel Triangle Publns., Inc., 1940—; dir. Central Penn. Nat. Bank, Phila., C.P. Financial Corp., Phila. First pres., hon. pres., bd. dirs. Albert Einstein Med. Center, 1951—; v.p., sec. Annenberg Sch. Communications, 1958—, M.L. Annenberg Found., 1944—; sec., treas. Annenberg Fund, Inc., 1951—; bd. dirs. Merion Civic Assn., Fedn. Jewish Philanthropies Phila., Phila. chpt. Am. Friends Hebrew U., Phila. chpt. Am. Friends Technion U.; trustee Temple U., 1966—, also mem. exec. com., chmn. ednl. policies com.; trustee Dropsie Coll., 1950-53; asso. trustee U. Pa., 1968—; hon. trustee Akiba Hebrew Acad. Recipient Outstanding Alumnus award McKean Law Club, U. Pa., 1959, alumni award of merit, 1958. Mem. Brandeis Lawyers Soc. (bd. dirs.) Am., Pa. (editor quar. 1941-68, emeritus editor 1968—), chmn. publns. com. 1960-67; Distinguished Service award 1961; spl. citation 1968), Phila. bar assns., Soc. TV Pioneers, Jewish Publ. Soc. (pres. 1966-69), Am. Arbitration Assn. (nat. panel arbitrators), Order of Coif. Scribes. Jewish religion (life trustee temple). Home: 230 Orchard Way Merion PA 19066 Office: 250 King of Prussia Rd Radnor PA 19088

FIRST, WESLEY, newspaper editor; b. Erie, Pa., Feb. 18, 1920; s. Orson John and Pearle (Unger) F.; student U. Mich., 1937-40; B.S., Columbia, 1958; M.A., New Sch. for Social Research, 1963; m. Margaret Elizabeth Whittlesey, Apr. 3, 1943; children—Karen Lee, Michael; m. 2d, Maryellen Ward, June 22, 1967. Engaged as reporter, Erie Dispatch, 1943- 47, asst. city editor, 1947-48, asst. to editor, 1948-50; with N.Y. World-Telegram and Sun, N.Y.C. 1950-63, successively copyreader, night news editor, 1950-57, asst. mng. editor, 1957-60, mng. editor, 1960-63; prof. journalism Ohio State U., 1963-65; dir. univ. relations Columbia, N.Y.C., 1965-67; asst. to pres. Sarah Lawrence Coll., 1967-68; asst. to pres. Juilliard School, N.Y.C., 1968-69; editor Travel Weekly, 1969—; guest lectr. newspaper design and makeup Fordham U.; instr. journalism Finch Coll., N.Y.C. Rep. to newspaper design and makeup seminar Am. Press Inst., 1957. Served with USAAF, 1944-46. Woodrow Wilson Fellow, 1959. Mem. U. Mich., Columbia U. alumni assns., Phi Beta Kappa, Kappa Tau Alpha, Sigma Delta Chi. Editor: Columbia Remembered; University on the Heights. Home: 348 W 15th St New York City NY 10011

FIRTH, EVERETT JOSEPH, timpanist; b. Winchester, Mass., June 2, 1930; s. Everett Emanuel and Rosemary (Scandura) F.; Mus.B. with distinction, 1952; m. Olga Kwasniak, June 22, 1960; children—Kelly Victoria, Tracy Kimberly. Solo timpanist Boston Symphony Orch., 1952—, Boston Pops Orch., 1952—; with Boston Symphony Chamber Players; faculty head New Eng. Conservatory, 1950—; mem. faculty Berkshire Music Center, 1956—. Mfr. custom line of timpani and drum sticks. Mem. Phi Kappa Lambda, Phi Mu Alpha Sinfonia. Recs. with RCA Victor, Mercury, Columbia, Cambridge, Deutsche Grammophon. Home: 3 Pine Wood Rd Dover MA 02030 Office: Symphony Hall Boston MA 02115

FIRTH, ROBERT E., educator; b. Duluth, Minn., Dec. 19, 1921; s. William E. and Loa (Budd) F.; B.A., Union Coll., Lincoln, Neb., 1948; M.A., U. Neb., 1950, Ph.D., 1960; m. Morna Y. Leguier, Aug. 28, 1943; children—Francis E., Holly (Mrs. Danny L. Howell). Accountant, asst. mgr. Maplewood Acad., Hutchinson, Minn., 1949-52; mem. faculty Union Coll., Lincoln, 1948-49, 52-64, asso. prof. bus. adminstrn. 1956-60, prof., 1960-64; prof. Andrews U., Berrien Springs, Mich., 1964—, also head bus. adminstrn. dept. Served with M.C., AUS, 1942-46. Decorated Bronze Star, Combat Medic badge. Mem. Am. Bus. Law Assn., Acad. Mgmt., Midwest Bus. Adminstrn. Assn., Delta Mu Delta. Author: Public Power in Nebraska, 1962. Home: 133 N George St Berrien Springs MI 49104

FIRTH, RODERICK, educator; b. Orange, N.J., Jan. 30, 1917; s. Leo Earl and Ida (Lake) F.; B.S., Haverford Coll., 1938; M.A., Harvard, 1940, Ph.D., 1943; m. Maria Lee Goodwin, June 10, 1943; 1 son, Roderick. Instr. philosophy and psychology Coll. William and Mary, 1943-45; instr. to asso. prof. philosophy Swarthmore Coll., 1945-53; asso. prof. philosophy Harvard, 1953-58, prof., 1958—, chmn. dept., 1957-63. Guggenheim fellow, 1952- 53; fellow Am. Council Learned Socs., 1959-60, Center for Advanced Studies Behavioral Scis., 1964-65, 67-68. Mem. Am. Philos. Assn., Am. Acad. Arts and Scis., Council for Philos. Studies, Phi Beta Kappa. Mem. Soc. of Friends. Home: 2 Patriots Dr Lexington MA 02173 Office: Harvard University Cambridge MA 02138

FISCH, CHARLES, educator; b. Tolkiew, Poland, May 11, 1921; s. Leon and Janette (Deutscher) F.; A.B., Ind. U., 1942, M.D., 1944; m. June Spiegal, May 23, 1943; children—Jonathan, Gary, Bruce. Intern St. Vincent's Hosp., Indpls., 1945; resident internal medicine VA Hosp., Indpls., 1948-50; fellow gastroenterology Marion County Gen. Hosp., Indpls., 1950-51, fellow cardiology, 1951-53; asst. prof. medicine Ind. U. Med. Sch., 1953-59, asso. prof., 1959-63, prof., 1963—, dir. cardiovascular div., 1963—, dir. Krannert Inst. Cardiology, 1960—. Served to capt., M.C., AUS, 1946-48. Diplomate Am. Bd. Internal Medicine, Am. Bd. Cardiovascular Medicine. Fellow A.C.P., Am. Coll. Cardiology (dir.); mem. Am. Fedn. Clin. Research, Central Soc. Clin. Research, Am. Physiol. Soc. Co-editor: Digitalis, 1969; contbr. articles to med. jours.; editorial bd. Am. Heart Jour., 1967—, Am. Jour. Cardiology, 1967—, Am. Jour. Electrocardiology, 1967—, Coer et Medicine Interne, 1970—. Home: 7901 Morningside Dr Indianapolis IN 46240

FISCHANG, ALBERT CHARLES, banker; b. Waterbury, Conn., Aug. 14, 1927; s. Albert A. and Esther (Anderson) F.; student Bentley Sch. Accounting, 1949, U. Wis., 1967; m. Rosetta Davidson, May 10, 1952; children—Jean, Nancy, Carol. With Citizens & Mfrs. Nat. Bank, 1949-59; with Colonial Bank & Trust Co., Waterbury, 1959—, now v.p. office of controller. Served with USNR, 1945-46. Mem. Nat. Assn. Accountants (v.p. Waterbury chpt.). Episcopalian (treas.). Home: 158 Lakeview Av Waterbury CT 06705 Office: Colonial Bank & Trust Co Waterbury CT 06702

FISCHBACH, ALLEN DANIEL, elec. contracting co. exec.; b. N.Y.C., July 26, 1917; s. Henry F. and Beatrice (Adelman) F.; student Rensselaer Poly. Inst., 1935-37; m. Sheila Kay Gilmore, Sept. 26, 1959; children—Frederick, Patricia Dee, Allen Daniel, Jonathan Henry, Virginia, Stuart Edmond. Pres., dir. F & M of Alaska, Inc., 1950—, J. L. Wilson Co., 1953—, v.p., dir. Fischbach & Moore of Can., 1959—, Fischbach, Moore and Morrissey, 1946—; pres. Fischbach & Moore Inc., 1956-67, vice chmn., chief exec. officer, chmn. exec. com., 1967—. Founder Albert Einstein Coll. Medicine, 1957. Trustee Acad. Religion and Mental Health. Served to 2d lt. USAAF, World War II. Decorated Air medal. Home: Lincoln Av Purchase, NY 10577. Office: 545 Madison Av New York City NY 10022

FISCHBACH, HENRY, govt. ofcl.; b. N.Y.C., May 2, 1914; s. Morris and Molly (Glatt) F.; B.A. in Chemistry, Ind. U., 1935, M.A., 1936, Ph.D., 1938; m. Jean Elizabeth Comstock, Nov. 9, 1935 (dec.); children—Lee Clark, Peter William, Jeffrey Stephen; m. Dorothea Schramm, Aug. 1, 1970. Asst. chemistry Ind. U., 1935-38; dir. ednl. program Joseph E. Seagrams & Co., 1939; food and drug insp. U.S. FDA, New Orleans, 1939-41, research chemist food div., Washington, 1941-45, charge chem. research antibiotics and alkaloids, div. pharm. chemistry, 1945-56, dir. planning for new hdqrs. bldg., 1955- 59, asst. to dir. bur. biol. and phys. scis., 1956-59, dir. food div., 1959-69, dir. pesticides div., 1969, dir. Office of Pesticides, 1970—, dir. Office of Sci., 1971—. Research chemist OSRD, Navy Dept., 1944; sec. com. lab. supplies and equipment Fed. Supply Bd., 1949-53; panel mem. Bd. U.S. Civil Service Examiners, 1957- -; adv. panel NRC, Nat. Acad. Scis., 1961—, also mem. com. on analytical chemistry. Recipient Superior Service award Dept. Health, Edn. and Welfare, 1959; Distinguished Service Award, 1967. Fellow Assn. Ofcl. Analytical Chemists; mem. Am. Chem. Soc., Internat. Union Pure and Applied Chemistry (chmn. trace substance com. 1964—), Internat. Union Pure and Applied Chemistry (chmn. trace commn. 1965), Nat. Acad. Scis. (chmn. specifications com. food chems. codex 1961—), Inst. Food Tech., Sigma Xi, Phi Lambda Upsilon. Unitarian. Author articles in field. Home: 5627 Bradley Blvd Alexandria VA 22311 Office: US Food and Drug Adminstrn Washington DC 20204

FISCHEL, WALTER JOSEPH, univ. prof.; b. Frankfurt am Main, Germany, Nov. 12, 1902; s. Hugo and Zerline (Kahn) F.; student U. Heidelberg, 1921-22; Dr. Rer. Pol., U. Frankfurt, 1924; Ph.D., U. Giessen, 1925; m. Irene Markrich, June 1954; 1 dau., Corinne. Tchr. and lectr. Rabbinical Coll., Frankfurt, 1922-24; asst., research fellow and lectr. Hebrew U., Sch. Oriental Studies, Jerusalem, 1926—; mem. sci. expdns. Syria, Turkey, Iraq, Kurdistan, Persia, 1930, 36; guest lectr. various univs. S.A., 1938, S. Africa, 1940, in U.S. and Can., 1943-44; vis. prof. Semitic langs. and lit. U. Cal. at Berkeley, 1945-46, prof. Semitic langs. and lit. 1946—, chmn. dept. Nr. Eastern langs., 1948-58; Guggenheim Fellow, 1959-60; Fulbright Fellow, 1963-64. Mem. 18th, 19th, 21st, 23d, 25th Internat. Orientalists' congresses. Fellow Am. Acad. Jewish Research, Royal Asiatic Soc. Gt. Brit. and Ireland; mem. Soc. Bibl. Lit. Pacific Coast (pres. 1948-51), Am. Oriental Soc., Soc. Bibl. Research and Lit., Am. Assn. Jewish Edn. (bd. govs.). Author numerous books, most recent being: Ibn Khaldun in Mamluk Egypt, 1951; Semitic and Oriental Studies, 1951; Ibn Khaldun and Tamerlane, 1952; The City in Islam, 1955; New Light on the Dead Sea Scrolls, 1956; Studies on the History of Jews in Persia, 1956; Ibu Khaldun's Autobiography, 1956; The Jews in India, Their Contribution to the Economic and Political Life, 1960; also articles sci. and learned jours. Mem. editorial staff Middle Eastern Affairs chmn. editorial bd. U. Cal. publs. in Semitic Philology. Home: 2954 Russell St Berkeley CA 94705 ☆

FISCHER, ALFRED GEORGE, educator, natural scientist; b. Rothenburg, Germany, Dec. 12, 1920; s. George Erwin and Thea (Freise) F.; came to U.S., 1935; student Northwestern Coll., Watertown, Wis., 1935-37; B.A. in Geology, U. Wis., 1939, M.A., 1940; Ph.D., Columbia, 1950; m. Winnifred Varney, Aug. 26, 1939; children—Joseph Fred, George William, Lenore Ruth. Instr., Va. Poly. Inst., 1941-48; petroleum geologist Stanolind Oil & Gas Co., 1943- 46; instr. U. Rochester, 1947-48; from instr. to asst. prof. U. Kan., 1948-51; petroleum geologist Internat. Petroleum Co., 1951-56; mem. faculty Princeton, 1956—, prof. geology, 1963—. NSF sr. fellow, 1962- 63, Guggenheim fellow, 1969—. Mem. Geol. Soc. Am., Am. Assn. Petroleum Geologists, Paleontol. Soc. Am., Soc. Econ. Paleontologists and Mineralogists, Palaeontologische Gesellschaft, Geologische Vereinigung, Sigma Xi. Author: (with others) Invertebrate Fossils, 1952; (with others) The Permian Reef Complex, 1953; (with others) Electron Micrographs of Limestones and their Nannofossils, 1967. Home: 544 Alexander Rd Princeton NJ 08540

FISCHER, ANNIE, pianist; b. Budapest, Hungary; ed. Franz Liszt Conservatory; student of Arnold Szekeley and Ernst von Dohnanyi; m. Aladar von Toth, 1937. Debut in Budapest, then in Zurich, in U.S., 1961; appearances in Paris, Brussels, Amsterdam, Vienna, Prague, Munich, Frankfurt, Berlin, London, Cleve., Chgo., St. Louis, also Canada; tchr. Acad. Music, Budapest, 1941- 46; recording artist of Beethoven, Liszt and Bartok. Office: care Colbert Artists Mgmt 850 7th Av New York City NY 10019

FISCHER, ARTHUR AARON, advt. exec.; b. N.Y.C., Sept. 2, 1923; s. Sol and Lillian (Gilman) F.; B.A., U. N.C., 1943; m. Ruth Greenberg, June 20, 1948; children—Harold, Sally. With Blackstone Advt., N.Y.C., 1948-51; with Cole, Fischer and Rogow, Inc., N.Y.C., 1951—, pres., then chmn. exec. com., 1955—; dir. Western Union CandyGrams. Served with AUS, 1943-46. Club: Friars (bd. govs.) (N.Y.C.). Home: 17 E 96th St New York City NY 10028 Office: 655 Madison Av New York City NY 10021

FISCHER, AUGUST OWEN mfg. exec.; b. Lima, O., Apr. 1, 1932; B.S., U. San Francisco, 1954; M.S., Stanford University, 1956; m. Rosemarie Lois Brown, May 15, 1955; 1 son, Anthony Robinson. Sales rep. Ames-Brockton Fabricated Products, Akron, O., 1956-58, sales mgr. Coshocton, Ohio, 1959-61, gen. manager plant, 1961-68, v.p. sales, 1968--. Instr. bus. Coshocton Jr. College, 1968-69. Secretary Coshocton YMCA, 1960-61; active Boy Scouts of America. Named Man of Year, Coshocton Junior Chamber of Commerce, 1968. Mem. Coshocton C. of C. (vice president 1967-68, pres. 1969-70), English Speaking Union, Coshocton Sertoma Club, Nat. Assn. Mfrs., Sales Executives Institute, Phi Beta Kappa, Sigma Chi, Phi Mu. Democrat. Mem. Christian Ch. (lay leader). Mason (32, Shriner). Clubs: Coshocton Country, Coshocton City, Running Deer Country. Home: 2d Av Coshocton OH Office: 3d Av Coshocton OH

FISCHER, BRUCE ELWOOD, mental health mgmt. cons.; b. Wahpeton, N.D., June 10, 1930; s. George Joseph and Minnie (Mathiesen) F.; B.S., Concordia Coll., Moorhead, Minn., 1955; grad. student U. Minn., 1955-57; m. Sally Anderson, Nov. 25, 1950; children—Bruce Ellwood, Brent Anderson, Rebecca Jill, George Bradley. Teller, Wahpeton Nat. Bank, 1949-50; auditor Mcht.'s Nat. Bank, Fargo, N.D., 1953-55; adminstrv. resident hosp. adminstrn. Syracuse (N.Y.) Meml. Hosp., 1956-57; adminstr. Onondaga County Home and Hosp., Syracuse, N.Y., 1957-62, Anoka (Minn.) State Hosp., 1962-69; exec. dir. Hennepin County Mental Health and Mental Retardation, 1970; pres. Bruce Fischer Assos., mental health mgmt. consultants, 1970—; v.p., dir. Century Mobil Homes Sales, Inc., Sacramento, Cal.; v.p. Roger Rathrock and Co., N.Y.C. Mem. Minn. Purchasing Com., 1964—; pres. adminstrv. study group Minn. Hosps. for Mentally Ill and Mentally Retarded, 1964—; spl. cons. Nat. Inst. Mental Health, 1968-70. Served with AUS, 1951-52. Mem. Assn. Mental Health Adminstrs. (chmn. nat. com. community mental health 1968-70). Methodist. Mason (Shriner), Kiwanian. Address: 7712 N Mississippi Lane Minneapolis MN 55430

FISCHER, C. RUTHERFORD, educator; b. N.Y.C., June 21, 1934; s. Samuel and Anna (Kurtz) F.; B.S., Coll. City N.Y., 1954; M.S., Yale, 1955, Ph.D., 1960; m. Janet Zevator, Dec. 9, 1962; 1 dau., Lois Karen. Asst. prof. physics N.M. State U., 1959-61, Adelphi U., Garden City, N.Y., 1961-64; asso. prof. physics Queens Coll., Flushing, N.Y., 1964-69, prof., 1970—; cons. U.S. Army Research Office, Durham, N.C., 1970-71. Contbr. articles to sci. jours. Home: 21 Manor Rd N Greenlawn NY 11740

FISCHER, CARL, photographer, artist; b. N.Y.C., May 3, 1924; s. Joseph Albert and Irma (Schwerin) F.; student Cooper Union Sch. Art, 1948, Central Sch. Arts, London, Eng., 1952; m. Marilyn Wolf, Oct. 30, 1949; children—Kim Alison, Douglas James, Kenneth Lee. Designer, Columbia Records, 1948; designer Look Mag., 1949-51; asst. art dir. William H. Weintraub & Co., 1952-54; art dir. Sudler & Hennessey, 1954-56; art dir. Grey Advt., 1956-58; owner Carl Fischer Photography, N.Y.C., 1958—; owner Carl Fischer Prodns., Inc., 1965—; exhbt. Mus. Modern Art, 1965; contbg. editorial photogrpaher Esquire, Redbook, McCalls, and New York mags., Nova, London Sunday Times; TV, film cons. Served with AUS, 1942-45; PTO. Recipient Fulbright grant, 1951, Art Dirs. Club N.Y. Gold medal, 1960, Profl. Achievement citation Cooper Union, 1966; St. Gaudens Medal, 1969. Mem. Dirs. Guild Am., Am. Soc. Mag. Photographers. Office: 121 E 83d St New York City NY 10028

FISCHER, CARL CASTLE, pediatrician, educator; b. Phila., Oct. 13, 1902; s. John Adolph and Millie (Leupold) F.; B.S., Princeton, 1924; M.D., Hahnemann Med. Coll. and Hosp., Phila., 1928, M.A. (hon.), 1938; m. Mae Adelaide Charles, Mar. 7, 1931; children—Elaine Lois (Mrs. Alexander Marshak), Charles Thomas, John William. Intern Hahnemann Hosp., Phila., 1928-29, chief dept. pediatrics, 1945-67, asso. dir. med. affairs, 1967-69; pvt. practice pediatrics, Phila., 1930-58; cons. pediatrician St. Vincents, Misercordia, St. Lukes, Childrens hosps., Phila., Crozer Hosp., Chester, Pa., Meml. Hosp., Pottstown, Pa.; faculty Hahnemann Med. Coll., 1930—, prof. pediatrics, head dept., 1945-67, emeritus prof. pediatrics, 1967—; dir. health service Girard Coll., Phila., 1958-67. Chmn. Gov. Pa. Com. Children and Youth, 1956-59; mem. Gov. Pa. Com. Handicapped, 1959-60. Fellow A.M.A., A.C.P.; mem. Am. Acad. Pediatrics (pres. 1961-62), Pa. Heart Assn., Heart Assn. of Southeastern Pa. (dir., past pres.), Phi Chi, Alpha Omega Alpha. Unitarian. Author: The Role of the Physician in Environmental Pediatrics, 1960. Editor: The Handicapped Child, 1958. Home: Oak Hill Apt Narberth PA 19072 Office: 230 N Broad St Philadelphia PA 19102

FISCHER, CARL HAHN, educator, actuary; b. Newark, Aug. 22, 1903; s. Carl H.H. and Minnie (Hahn) F.; B.S., Washington U., St. Louis, 1923; M.S., U. Ia., 1930, Ph.D., 1932; m. Kathleen Kirkpatrick, Sept. 25, 1925; children—Patrick Carl, Michael John. Spl. engr. Am. Steel Foundries, 1923-26; instr. math. Beloit (Wis.) Coll., 1926-29; asst. U. Ia. 1929-32; instr. U. Minn., 1932-33; spl. research asst. Northwestern Nat. Life Ins. Co., 1933-34; instr. Wayne U., 1934-37, asst. prof., 1937-41; mem. faculty U. Mich., 1941—, prof. ins. and actuarial math., 1950—; vis. prof. U. Cal. at Berkeley, 1951, U. Hawaii, 1955. Hebrew U., Jerusalem, 1965, 67, Netherlands Sch. Econs., Rotterdam, 1966; cons. actuary, 1939- -. Trustee Ann Arbor Employee Retirement System, 1948—; actuary Tchrs. Retirement Fund N.D., 1939—; mem. Adv. Council Social Security Financing, 1957-58; chmn. study com. Mil. Retired Pay for U.S. Senate, 1960-61. Mem. Ann Arbor Bd. Edn., 1957-60. Fellow Soc. Actuaries, Conf. Actuaries in Pub. Practice (v.p. 1970—), Fraternal Actuarial Assn.; mem. Am. Acad. Actuaries, Inst. Actuaries (Eng.), Am. Risk and Ins. Assn., Am. Statis. Assn., Math. Assn. Am., Mich. Actuarial Soc., Internat. Platform Assn., Acacia, Sigma Xi, Beta Gamma Sigma. Mason. Author: (with P.R. Rider) Mathematics of Investment, 1951; (with W.O. Menge) Mathematics of Life Insurance, 1965. Home: 1706 Morton Av Ann Arbor MI 48104

FISCHER, CLARE, pianist, composer; b. Durand, Mich., Oct. 22, 1928; s. Cecil Harold and Luella (Roussin) F.; Mus.B., Mich. State U., 1951, Mus.M., 1955; children—Brent Sean Cecil, Tahila Georgienne Marguerite Bianca, Lee Clare. Recordings for or with Hi-Lo's, Dizzy Gillespie, George Shearing, Cal Tiader, World Pacific, Columbia Records; tour Argentina, 1964; pvt. tchr., 1959—; condr. concerts and clinics at univs., 1962—. Served with AUS, 1953-54. Mem. Am. Fedn. Musicians, Nat. Acad. Radio Arts and Scis., Phi Kappa Phi. Composer: String quartet, 1951; Piece for woodwinds and strings, 1950; Septet for string quartet, trumpet, oboe and clarinet, 1949; Rhapsody for alto saxophone and Chamber Orch., 1955; Piece for woodwinds and soft brass, 1965. Address: 5417 Fulton Av Van Nuys CA 91401

FISCHER, EDWARD GEORGE, mech. engr.; b. N.Y.C., Mar. 31, 1916; s. Edward George and Bertha Augusta (Saegert) F.; B.S., Copper Union, 1936; M.S., U. Pitts., 1939, Ph.D., 1946; postgrad. (Westinghouse-Lamme scholar), Columbia, 1941-42; m. Helen Betty Miller, Sept. 9, 1944; children—Mary Louise (Mrs. Bernard Smith), Robert Edward, William James, Thomas Paul. Cons. engr. Westinghouse Electric Corp. Research Labs., Pitts., 1936—. Instr., U. Pitts. Grad. Sch., 1946-59. Recipient certificate of appreciation Army C.E. dynamics cons. on ABM System, 1970. Mem. Am. Soc. M.E., Am. Nat. Standards Inst., Soc. Exptl. Stress Analysis, Seismol. Soc. Am., Inst. Environmental Scis. Contbr. articles to profl. jours. Patentee in field. Home: 5525 3d St Verona PA 15147 Office: Westinghouse Research Labs Pittsburgh PA 15235

FISCHER, EMIL C., architect, coll. adminstr.; b. Elizabeth, N.J., Dec. 29, 1907; s. Theodore C. and Lillian (Koch) F.; A.B., Columbia, 1929, B.Arch., 1932, M.S., 1933; m. Ruth Minarcik, May 2, 1936; children—Craig, Keith. Archtl. practice, 1934—; instr. design Columbia U. Archtl. Atelier, 1933-37, condr. seminars on residential architecture, 1934-37; asst. prof. dept. architecture Pratt Inst. Bklyn., 1937-41, dir. summer session, 1943; lectr., cons. residential design, bldg. material devel. Flintkote Co., N.Y.C., 1937-42; vis. prof. design Cornell U., 1943-44, U. Mich., summers 1948-51; prof. dept. architecture Ohio State U., 1945-55, dir. design sch. architecture, 1951- 55; head dept. architecture and allied arts Kan. State U., 1955-63, dean coll. architecture and design, 1963-70, dir. grad. program architecture and design, 1971—. Adviser, Kan. Art Center Found. Mem. Manhattan (Kan.) City Commn., 1952-62; mayor, Manhattan, 1962-64. Trustee Environmental Research and Devel. Found., Kansas City. Member A.I.A. (pres. Columbus chpt. 1954-65, mem. exec. com. Kan. chpt. 1958, ednl. com., 1958-63), Soc. Archtl. Historians, Internat. Platform Assn., Archtl. Soc. London, Alpha Rho Chi, Tau Sigma Delta (grand chpt. master 1964-71), Phi Kappa Phi, Sigma Lambda Chi. Rotarian. Home: 805 Wildcat Ridge Manhattan KS 66502

FISCHER, FREDERICK GEORGE, accountant; b. New Haven, Feb. 19, 1924; s. Frederick F. and Katherine (Greiner) F.; grad. cum laude, Williston Acad., 1941; B.S. in Econs., Wharton Sch. of U. Pa., 1948; m. Ann Balzer, June 17, 1950; children—Pamela, Frederick. Comptroller, Conn. Med. Service, New Haven, 1949-51; partner Baker, Goodyear & Co., C.P.A.'s, New Haven, 1951-58; firm merged with Ernst & Ernst, C.P.A.'s, 1958, partner charge New Haven office, 1961—; lectr. New Haven Coll., 1951-65. Regional chmn. com. for greater Pa., U. Pa., 1963—. Mem. budget com. United Fund. Treas., bd. dirs. Cheshire Youth Center, 1963—; bd. dirs. Jr. Achievement New Haven, 1963—; mem. gen. alumni bd. U. Pa., 1965-70; mem. exec. com. Family Service, 1969—. Served to 1st lt. AUS, 1942-46; MTO. C.P.A., Conn., 7 other states. Mem. Am. Inst. C.P.A.'s, Conn. Soc. C.P.A.'s, Conn. Assn. Credit Mgmt. (pres. 1966), New Haven Assn. Credit Men (counselor 1966), New Haven C. of C. (chmn. local govt. com. 1966—, chmn. Operation Native Son 1967-70, v.p. 1967-71, chmn. 1971—), Am. Arbitration Assn. (mem. panel). Clubs: New Haven Country, U. Pa. Alumni (pres. 1958-66), Grad. Assn., U. Pa. Football (New Haven); Branford (Conn.) Yacht. Home: 920 Bethany Mountain Rd Cheshire CT 06410 Office: 900 Chapel Sq New Haven CT 06509

FISCHER, GEORGE DRENNEN, corp. exec.; b. Des Moines, Nov. 19, 1925; s. Charles R. and Naomi (Drennen) F.; student U. Ia., 1945, Drake U., 1945-46, U. No. Ia., 1946-49; grad. study Ia. State U., Drake U.; children—Charles J., Dan J. Cowboy, Utah, 1948; coach, Macksburg, Ia., 1945-46; miner, Colo., 1949: farmer, Ia., 1950-60; tchr. drafting, English, math. Des Moines Tech. High Sch., 1956-67; chmn. bd., chief exec. officer Ednl. Facilities Corp., Chgo. Mem. Norwalk (Ia.) Bd. Edn., 1957-64, pres., 1960-64. Mem. N.E.A. (mem. exec. com. 1964—, pres. 1969-70), Des Moines Edn. Assn. (pres. 1961-65), Epsilon Pi Tau. Home: 1255 N State Pkwy Chicago IL 60610 Office: 625 N Michigan Av Chicago IL 60611

FISCHER, GERALD J., food and beverage co. exec.; b. Wilkes-Barre, Pa., Sept. 14, 1917; s. John Conrad and Olive (Straup) F.; A.B., Rutgers U., 1939, postgrad., 1939-40; postgrad. Princeton, 1940-41; m. Helen Beth Buckley May 31, 1941; children—Gerald John, Kenneth Christian, Norman Charles. Martha Anne, Research asst. Nat. Bur. Econ. Research, N.Y.C., 1941-42; head statis, analysis br. U.S. Maritime Commn., Washington, 1942-44; bus. analyst ECA, Washington, 1948-50; mgr. investment analysis dept. Ford div. Ford Motor Co., 1950-55, asst. controller Ford div., 1955-60, controller automotive assembly div., 1960-65; v.p. overseas credit operations Ford Motor Credit Co., 1965-67; v.p., controller Pepsico, Inc., 1967—. Pres. Plymouth (Mich.) Bd. Edn., 1962-67, Plymouth Symphony Soc., 1953-57; mem. nat. adv. bd. Interlochen Center for the Arts (Mich.), 1968. Served to lt. j.g. USNR, 194446. Princeton fellow in econs. Mem. Am. Statis Assn., Am. Mgmt. Assn., Phi Beta Kappa. Presbyn. (elder). Co-author; Ships for Victory, 1949. Home: 71 Delafield Island Rd Darien CT 06820 Office: 500 Park Av New York City NY 10022

FISCHER, HAROLD ROBERT, banker; b. Kewanee, Ill., Aug. 28, 1902; s. Emil and Sarah (Hodge) F.; student U. Chgo., 1920-21, Am. Inst. Banking, Grad. Sch. Banking, Rutgers U., 1945; m. Goldie Gamble, May 21, 1925; children—James Robert, Nancy Jean and Sally Ann (twins). Bookkeeper, asst. cashier and trust officer Union State Savs. Bank & Trust Co., Kewanee, Ill., 1922-31; asst. receiver Ill. State Bank Liquidation, 1931- 42; asst. cashier First Granite City Nat. Bank, 1942-44, v.p., 1944-46, pres. 1946-68, chmn. bd., 1968-71, vice chmn., 1971—. Chmn., dir. Tri-Cities Port Authority. Bd. dirs. United Fund, YMCA; past chmn. Tri- Cities chpt. A.R.C., Tri-Cities Community Chest, Cahokia council Boy Scouts Am.; chmn. bd. trustees So. Ill. U., Tri-City Regional Park Dist. Mem. Tri-Cities C. of C. Methodist. Elk. Club: Granite City Optimist. Home: 2725 Madison Av Granite City IL 62040 Office: Box 428 Granite City IL 62040

FISCHER, HARVEY A., lawyer; b. Detroit, 1900; A.B., U. Mich., 1922, LL.B., 1924. Admitted to Mich. bar, 1924; now mem. firm Fischer, Franklin & Ford, Detroit Mem. Am., Detroit bar assns., State Bar of Mich. Office: Guardian Bldg Detroit MI 48226

FISCHER, HELEN MARIE, state legislator; b. Sleepy Eye, Minn., June 2, 1912; d. William J. and Anna L. (Nelson) Schmid; student Northwest Coll. Speech, 1931; m. Edward A. Fischer, June 10, 1934; children—Richard W., David A., Linda A. A founder Operation Statehood, nonpartisan orgn. working for statehood for Alaska, 1952; del. Alaska Constl. Conv., 1955-57; mem. Alaska Territorial Ho. of Reps., 1956-58, mem. Alaska Ho. of Reps., 1958-60, 70—. Mem. nat. bd. Eleven Western State Democratic Com., 1956- -; vice chmn. 13 Western States Dem. Conf., 1960-63, chmn. fgn. trade com., 1961-62; Dem. nat. committeewoman for Alaska, 1956-63; del. to Dem. Nat. Conv., 1960; mem. Alaska Centennial Commn., 1964—. State dir. U.S. Savs. Bonds div. Treasury Dept.; chmn. Mrs. Alaska Com., 1966-67, Alaska Centennial Com., 1965—. Treas., Greater Anchorage, Inc. Nat. bd. mem. Woman's Med. Coll. Pa., mem. univ. council Alaska Methodist U. Named One of Outstanding Living Alaskans, Alaska Press Club; elected to Alaska Hall of Fame. Mem. Alaska Mental Health Assn., League Women Voters, Bus. and Profl. Women, Operation Statehood, 55 Club (mem. Constl. Conf.). Clubs: Woman's, Democratic Women's (Anchorage); Emblem; Alaska Press (gov.). Address: 2023 Wildwood Lane Anchorage AK 99503

FISCHER, HELEN R., assn. exec.; b. Bklyn., Aug. 6, 1926; d. Abraham and Fannie (Goldberg) Nadelson; A.B., Bklyn. Coll., 1948; m. William A. Fischer, July 25, 1953. Tchr. pub. schs., N.Y.C., 1951-53; tchr. Arabian Am. Oil Co., Dhahran, Saudi Arabia, 1953-56; exec. sec. Am. Psychoanalytic Assn., N.Y.C., 1956—. Home: 60 Matlock St Lido Beach NY 11101 Office: 1 E 57th St New York City NY 10022

FISCHER, HENRY GEORGE, mus. curator; b. Phila., May 10, 1923; s. Henry G. and Agnes Beatrice (Hurdman) F.; B.A., Princeton, 1945; Ph.D., U. Pa., 1955; m. Eleanor Armstrong Teel, Dec. 15, 1951; 1 dau., Katherine Fraser. Instr. English, Am. U. Beirut (Lebanon), 1945-48; asst. Egyptian sect. U. Pa. Mus. 1949-56; mem. univ. expdn. to Mit Rahineh (Egypt), 1955, 56; asst. prof. Egyptology, Yale Grad. Sch., 1956-58; asst. curator Egyptian art Met. Mus. Art, 1958-63, asso. curator, 1963-64, curator, 1964-70, Lila Acheson Wallace curator in Egyptology, 1970—; adj. asst. prof. fine arts Inst. Fine Arts, N.Y.U., 1962-64, adj. asso. prof., 1964- 66, adj. prof. 1966—; vis. lectr. art history and archaeology Columbia, 1960-61. Secretary-treas. Am. Com. to Preserve Abu Simbel, 1964-70. Trustee Am. Research Center in Egypt, 1955-66; bd. dirs. Ams. Middle East Understanding. Guggenheim fellow, 1956-57. Mem. Am. Inst. Archaeology, Egypt Exploration Soc. (London), Phi Beta Kappa; corr. mem. German Archaeol. Inst. Author: Inscriptions from the Coptite Nome: Dynasties VI-XI, 1964; Ancient Egyptian Representations of Turtles, 1968; Dendera in the Third Millennium B.C., 1969.

FISCHER, HERMAN ARTHUR, lawyer; b. Wheaton, Ill., Aug. 25, 1882; s. Herman A. and Julia Waters (Blanchard) F.; A.B., Wheaton Coll., 1903; LL.B., Harvard, 1908. Admitted to Ill. bar, 1908, since practiced in Chgo.; mem. firm Fischer, Guy & Jacobson, and predecessor law firms, 1915—. Pres. Gary-Wheaton Bank, 1931-52, chmn. bd., 1952-66; v.p., dir. Cuneo Press, Inc. Trustee emeritus Wheaton Coll. Mem. Am., Ill., Chgo., Du-Page County bar assns., Am. Legion. Republican. Conglist. Club: Union League. Home: 805 E Liberty Dr Wheaton IL 60187 Office: 1 N LaSalle St Chicago IL 60602

FISCHER, JAMES ADRIAN, clergyman; b. St. Louis, Oct. 15, 1916; s. John and Agnes (Henke) F.; A.B., St. Mary's Sem., Perryville, Mo., 1941; S.T.L., Cath. U. Am., 1949; S.S.L., Pontifical Bib. Inst., Rome, Italy, 1951; LL.D. (hon.), Niagara U., 1968. Joined Congregation of Mission, 1936, ordained priest Roman Cath. Ch., 1943; prof. sacred scripture St. John's Sem., San Antonio, 1943-45, St. Mary's Sem., Houston, 1951-56, St. Mary's Sem., Perryville, 1958-62; provincial Western province Vincentian Fathers, 1962—. Chmn. trustees De Paul U., Chgo., 1962—. Mem. Cath. Bib. Assn., Nat. Cath. Edn. Assn. Address: 1849 Cass St St Louis MO 73106

FISCHER, JO, cartoonist; b. Chgo., Dec. 18, 1904; s. Abraham and Anna (Silverberg) F.; student Chgo. Acad. Arts, 1920-21, Chgo. Art Inst., 1921-22; m. Caroline Meis, Jan. 1, 1943; 1 son, Joal. Staff artist, sports cartoonist Chgo. Hearst Newspapers, 1922-42; asst. to cartoonist Jimmy Hatlo, King Features Syndicate, N.Y.C., 1942-49; nat. syndicated cartoonist, From 9 to 5, Publishers-Hall Syndicate, 1944—; judge annual cartoon contest, 1960-61, also Art Project Nat. Hospitalized Vets.; tours vets. hosps., Alaska and Europe, 1951, 53, 54, 56, 58. Recipient citations Dept. Def., 1953, 54; named Press Vet. of Year, Chgo. Press Vets. Assn., 1963. Mem. Nat. Cartoonists Soc., Chgo. Press Vets. Assn. Club: Chgo. Press. Home: 1082 Lincoln Av S Highland Park IL 60035 Office: 401 N Wabash Av Chicago IL 60611

FISCHER, JOHN, editor and writer; b. Texboma, Okla., Apr. 27, 1910; s. John S. and Georgia (Caperton) F.; student U. Okla., 1928-32; Rhodes scholar Oxford (Eng.) U., 1933-35; LL.D., Kenyon Coll., 1954, Bucknell U., 1954; D.H.L., U. Mass., 1956; m. Elizabeth Wilson, 1936; children—Nicolas, Sarah. Reporter, Daily Oklahoman, Oklahoma City, Amarillo Globe-News, Amarillo, Tex., and other newspapers in Okla. and N. Mex., 1928-33; reporter U.P.I., Eng. and Germany, 1933-35, A.P., Washington, 1935-37; with U.S. Dept. of Agr., 1937-42; various positions with Bd. Econ. Warfare, Washington, Jan. 1942-July 1943; chief rep. Bd. Econ. Warfare and Fgn. Econ. Adminstrn. in India, July 1943-June 1944, in charge econ. intelligence and lend-lease; with Fgn. Econ. Adminstrn., Washington, June-Oct. 1944; asso. editor Harper's Mag., 1944-47, editor in chief, 1953-67, contbg. editor, 1967—. Vis. fellow Yale. Mem. Presdl. Commn. on Rural Poverty, 1966—. Trustee Brookings Instn.; bd. dirs. Nat. Ednl. TV Network, Nat. Municipal League. Mem. Am. Soc. Mag. Editors, Council Fgn. Relations, Am. Polit. Sci. Assn., Phi Beta Kappa. Club: Century Assn. Author: Why They Behave Like Russians, 1947; Master Plan, U.S.A., 1951; The Stupidity Problem, 1964. Contbr. articles New Yorker, Harper's Reader's Digest, Life, etc. Home: Shell Beach Rd Guilford CT 06437 Office: care Harper's Mag 2 Park Av New York City NY 10016

FISCHER, JOHN HENRY, coll. pres.; b. Balt., July 16, 1910; s. Henry and Minnie (Muth) F.; Diploma, Md. State Tchrs. Coll., 1930; B.S., Johns Hopkins, 1940; M.A., Columbia Tchrs. Coll., 1949, Ed.D. (Shankland Meml. Scholar), 1951, L.H.D., 1964; LL.D., Morgan St. Coll., 1955, Goucher Coll., 1959, U. Akron, 1963; Litt.D., Jewish Theol. Sem. Am., 1968, Muskingum Coll., 1969; L.H.D., Cleve. State U. 1968; m. Norma Frederick, Nov. 28, 1934; children—David Hackett, Miles Pennington. Tchr. Balt. Pub. Schs., 1930- 35, vice prin., 1935-38; spl. asst. charge Benjamin Franklin Jr. High Sch., Balt., 1938-42, dir. sch. attendance and child guidance, 1942-45, asst. supt. for gen. adminstrn., 1945-52; dep. supt. schs., Balt., 1952-53, supt. pub. instrn., 1953-59; dean Tchrs. Coll., Columbia U., 1959-62, pres., 1962—. Dir. Cowles Communications, Inc. Mem. Nat. Adv. Council on Edn. Disadvantaged Children, 1965-69, Pres.'s Commn. on Sch. Finance, 1970-72; Mem. nat. exec. bd. Boy Scouts Am.; trustee Ednl. Testing Service, chmn., 1971-72; pres. Balt. Council Social Agys., 1957-59, Md. Prisoners Aid Assn., 1952. Trustee Johns Hopkins U., 1965-71, Inst. for Ednl. Devel., Center for Urban Edn., Met. Applied Research Center. Recipient Silver Beaver, Silver Antelope, Silver Buffalo awards Boy Scouts Am. Mem. Md. Tchrs. Assn. (pres. 1945), Am. Assn. Sch. Adminstrs., N.E.A., Phi Delta Kappa, Kappa Delta Pi. Clubs: University, Century Assn., Columbia (N.Y.C.); Johns Hopkins (Balt.). Contbr. articles ednl. jours. Home: 503 W 120th St New York City NY 10027

FISCHER, LOUIS, coll. dean; b. Seattle, Aug. 18, 1905; s. August and Wilhelmine (Renner) F.; B.S., U. Wash., 1926, Ph.C., 1926, M.S., 1928, Ph.D., 1933; m. Marion Margaret Christenson, June 29, 1929; children—Marion Elaine (Mrs. George J. Hiester), Brian Louis. Asst. state chemist, Wash., 1929-35; instr. pharmacy U. Wash., 1935-37, asst. prof. pharm. chemistry, 1937- 41, asso. prof., 1941-45, prof., 1945—, chmn. dept. pharm. chemistry, 1949—, asst. to Dean, 1949-60, asso. dean, 1960—. Research chemist Nat. Canners Assn., 1936-37, salmon examiner, 1941; med. rep. Consol. Dairy Products, 1940; marketing specialist food distbn. agy., U.S. Dept. Agr., 1942, ofcl. grader dairy products, 1942—; research chemist Wash. Liquor Bd., 1943-44. Adv. com. Nat. Formulary; mem. NIH Medicinal and Organic Chemistry Fellowship Rev. Panel. Mem. Univ. Research Soc., Am. Pharm. Assn., A.A.A.S., Inst. Food Techs. Mason. Contbr. profl. articles to pharm. jours. Mem. revision com. U.S. Pharmacopia, 1950-70. Home: 4853 N E 85th St Seattle WA 98115

FISCHER, LOUIS ENGELMANN, real estate co. exec.; b. St. Louis, Jan. 21, 1930; s. Chester O. and Grace Lucille (Nelson) F.; grad. Lawrenceville Sch., 1948; B.A., Brown U., 1952; m. Beryl Molyneux Mostrom, July 11, 1953; children—Lise, Kurt, Carl. Gen. sales mgr. Techbuilt, Inc., Cambridge, Mass., 1954-58; agt./broker Mass. Mut. Life Ins. Co., 1958-61; mgmt. cons. Anderson-Nichols & Co., Inc., Boston, 1961-68; pres. Levitt & Sons, Inc., Lake Success, N.Y., 1968—; exec. v.p. ITT-Levitt & Sons, Inc., 1968—; dir. Fibre-Optics Industries, Palm Beach, Fla., R.I. CATV, Providence. Mem. R.I. Air N.G., 1952-54. Served as 1st lt. USAF, 1951-52. Home: 741 Remsens Lane Oyster Bay NY 11771 Office: Lakeville Rd and Marcus Av Lake Success NY 11040

FISCHER, LOUIS THEODORE, advt. exec.; b. Des Plaines, Ill., Apr. 1, 1913; s. Theo. H. and Augusta (Klein) F.; diploma in commerce, Northwestern U., 1939; m. Edith W. Hesemann, Sept. 1, 1945; children—James L., Stephen F. Mem. research staff Blackett Sample Hummert, Chgo. 1939-42; with Dancer Fitzgerald Sample, Inc., N.Y.C., 1945—, asst. account exec., 1945-46, time buyer, 1946-49, media dir., 1949-55, v.p., 1955-66, sr. v.p. for media, 1966—; instr. advt. N.Y. Advt. Club, media seminars for Advt. Age. Mem. bd. Taxpayers Orgn. Yonkers. Served to lt. AUS, 1941-45. Decorated Bronze Star. Mem. Media Dirs. Council (pres. 1967). Lutheran (pres., bd. mem.). Club: Wykagyl Country (New Rochelle, N.Y.). Home: 51 Harvard Av Yonkers NY 10710 Office: 347 Madison Av New York City NY 10017

FISCHER, MAURICE, pub. relations cons., b. Chgo., Mar. 22, 1903; s. Abraham and Anna (Silverberg) E.; B.A., U. Ill., 1924; m. Elvera Mary Lampe, Sept. 1, 1942. Staff, City News Bur., Chgo., 1925-27; with Chgo. Daily News, 1927-68, beginning as financial news asst., successively real estate editor, night city editor, asst. day city editor, 1927-58, city editor, 1958-64, asst. mng. editor, 1964-65, asst. to editor, 1966-68; asst. mgr. met. dept. Field Newspapers, 1965; mng. editor Arlington Day, 1965; now pub. relations cons. Lay trustee Mundelein Coll.; bd. dirs. Cath. Interracial Council of Chgo., Cath. Charities Chgo.; mem. Mayor's Commn. for Rehabilitation of Persons. Served with USAAF, 1942-43. Mem. Chgo. Press Vets, Assn. (bd. dirs.) Pan Am. Council Chgo. (pres. 1969-71), Sigma Delta Chi. Clubs: Chicago Headline (exec. sec.), Chicago Press (pres. 1965), Ill. Athletic, City (v.p., bd. dirs.). Home: 2328 N Cleveland Av Chicago, IL 60614.

FISCHER, MAURICE E., pres. United Factors, U.M. & M. Credit Corp., U.M. & M. Financial; exec. v.p. dir. United Mchts. & Mfrs., Inc. Address: 1407 Broadway New York City NY 10018

FISCHER, RAYMOND P., business exec.; b. Wheaton, Ill., Oct 15, 1900; s. Herman A. and Julia (Blanchard) F.; student Wheaton Coll., 1918-20; A.B., Pomona Coll., 1922; LL.B., Harvard, 1925; m. Marita McMillan, June 18, 1932; 1 dau., Elizabeth Christine. Admitted Ill. bar, 1925; practiced, Chgo., Ill.; chmn. Asso. Consultants, bus. cons., investment adviser. Episcopalian. Clubs: Chicago Golf; University (N.Y.C. and Chgo.); North Shore Country (Neenah, Wis.). Office: 799 Roosevelt Rd Chicago IL 60137

FISCHER, ROBERT GEORGE, educator, microbiologist; b. St. Paul, Oct. 17, 1920; s. Fred F. and Agnes (Cooney) F.; B.A., U. Minn., 1942, M.S., 1947, Ph.D., 1948; m. Margaret Mary Roddy, June 28, 1947; children—Mary, John, James. Research asso. U. Minn., 1946-48; mem. faculty U. N.D. Med. Sch., 1948—, prof. microbiology, 1955—, chmn. dept., 1962—. Served to capt., Med. Service Corps, AUS, 1942-45; ETO. Diplomate Am. Bd. Microbiology. Fellow Am. Acad. Microbiology; mem. Am. Soc. Microbiology. Research on transmission of viruses by anthropod vectors; murine and avian leukemia virus transmission. Home: 447 Campbell Dr Grand Forks ND 58201

FISCHER, THOMAS V., mfg. co. exec.; b. 1929; A.B., DePauw U., 1951; LL.B., U. Mich., 1956; married. Admitted to bar, with firm Stevenson, Conaghan, Hackert, Rooks & Pitts., 1956-63; sec., counsel North Am. Car Corp., 1963-65; sec., counsel A.E. Staley Mfg. Co., 1965-69, v.p. law and adminstrn., 1969—, dir., mem. exec. com., 1970. Address: A E Staley Mfg Co Eldorado at 22D St Decatur IL 62525

FISCHER, WALTER MARVIN, investment co. exec.; b. Chgo., Oct. 31, 1919; s. Harold and Betty (Plax) F.; student DePaul U., 1936-38; m. Anne Zeiner, Aug. 8, 1957; children—Theodore, Andrea Sue (Mrs. Richard Wollock), Laurence, Harold. Engaged as accountant, 1939-43; gen. agt. Prudence Life Ins. Co., Kansas City, Mo., 1947-55; v.p. Waddell & Reed, Inc., Chgo., 1955-65; exec. v.p. Allen Steadman & Co., 1965-69, Steadman Security Corp., Washington, 1965-69, Steadman Planning Corp., 1965-69, Steadman Sci. and Growth Fund, Inc., 1965-69, Steadman Investment Fund, Inc., 1965-69, Steadman's Shares in Am. Industry, Inc., 1965-69; sr. cons. U.S. Investment Services, Ltd., London, Eng., 1969—; adv. bd. USI Group, Inc., Novato, Cal., 1969—; dir. Baxter, Blyden, Selheimer & Co., Inc., Washington, 1970—. Bd. dirs. Mut. Fund Council of Million Dollar Producers 1968—; fellow president's council A.I.M., 1969—. Served with AUS, 1943-46; PTO, ETO. Decorated Bronze Star. Mem. Soc. Financial Counselling (bd. govs. 1969—), Nat. Assn. Securities Dealers, Am. Legion (past post. comdr.). Jewish religion. Club: Internat. (Washington). Home: 64 Green Bay Rd Highland Park IL 60035 also 970 Iris Ct Marco Island FL 33937 Office: 1775 K St NW Washington DC 20006

FISCHER, WILLIAM AUGUST, geologist; b. Litchfield, Ill., Jan. 6, 1919; s. August Ernst and Juliette Marie (Niemeyer) F.; B.S., McKendree Coll., Lebanon, Ill., 1940; student U. Ill., 1940-41; m. L. Blanche Youngblood, Sept. 8, 1941; children—Judith Lynn (Mrs. Court Soloff), William Jeffrey. Tchr. chemistry, physics Christopher (Ill.) High Sch., 1941; with U.S. Geol. Survey, 1941-44, 46-66, chief photogeology sect., 1950-60, charge lunar probe photometric analyses, 1960-62, research geologist charge remote sensing project, 1962-66, research coordinator Earth Resources Observation Satellite Program, Dept. Interior, 1966—, prin. lectr. pilot course aerial surveys for geology UN, Tokyo, Japan, 1961. Rep. Dept. Interior orgn. meeting Orgn. Europeenen d'Etudes Photogrammetriques Experimentales, Brussels, Belgium, 1952; chmn. U.S. delegation UN seminar aerial survey methods, Bangkok, Thailand, 1960; chief U.S. rep Orgn. meeting UNESCO conf. intergrated surveys, Paris, France; 1963; chief U.S. delegation Internat. Congress Photogrammetry, 1964; mem. com. remote sensing environment Nat. Acad. Scis., 1964—. Served as officer USNR, 1944-46. Fellow A.A.A.S. (rep. council 1957-58), Am. Soc. Photogrammetry (pres. 1964-65, also dir., mem. exec. com.), Dept. Interior Recreation Assn. (pres. 1961). Club: Cosmos (Washington). Author numerous papers and maps. Home: 228 Norland St Falls Church VA 22046 Office: U S Geol Survey Washington DC 20242

FISCHER-DIESKAU, DIETRICH, baritone; b. Berlin, Germany, May 28, 1925; s. Albert and Dora (Klingelhoffer) Fischer-D.; student high sch., Berlin; studied music with Georg A. Walter, Herman Weissenborn; m. Irmgard Poppen, Feb. 10, 1949 (dec. Dec. 1963); children—Mathias, Martin, Manuel. Sang lyrical and title role baritone Municipal Opera, Berlin, 1948; extensive concert tours, Europe, U.S.; appearance festivals, including Edinburgh, Vienna, London, Paris, Netherlands, Munich, Berlin, Salzburg; mem. Vienna State Opera, 1957—. Served with German Army, World War II; prisoner of war. Recipient award Internat. Gramophone Record, 1955, 57, 58, 60, 61, 64, 65, 68; art award, Berlin, 1950; Golden Orpheus, Mantua, 1955; Federal medal for distinguished services, 1st class, 1958; Naras award 1962; Mozart-Medaille Wien, 1963; Ehrenmitgliedschaft Konzerthausgesellschaft Wien, 1963; Byerischer Kammersänger, 1959, Berliner, 1963; Edison award, 1962, 64, 67. Mem. Acad. Arts, Internat. Mahler Soc. Vienna, Internat. Music Council (German sect.). Chief roles include Wolfram, Jochanaan, Alamavive, Marquis Posa, Don Giovanni, Dr. Faust, Falstaff, others. Address: Lindenallee 22 1 Berlin 19 Germany

FISCHETTE, RICHARD LOUIS, banker; b. Rochester, N.Y., Mar. 26, 1924; s. Rocco M. and Mary (Buttaccio) F.; student U. Toronto, 1943-44; grad. Rochester Bus. Inst., 1950, Am. Inst. Banking, 1960, Bank Adminstrn. Inst., U. Wis., 1965; m. Angeline P. Alesso, Feb. 9, 1946; children-Ann Marie, Jeanne Marie and Jane Ellen (twins), Richard J. With Eastman Kodak Co., 1946-48; with Central Trust Co., Rochester, 1950—, asst. auditor, 1961-65, br. mgr., 1966-69, auditor, 1969—; tchr. Am. Inst. Banking. Committeeman 21st Ward Republican Com., 1968—. Served with M.C., AUS, 1943-46. Mem. Am. Inst. Banking (past pres.), Bank Adminstrn. Inst., Am. Legion (past post comdr.). Home: 40 Dalkeith Rd Rochester NY 14609 Office: 44 Exchange St Rochester NY 14614

FISCHETTI, JOHN, cartoonist; worked on animated films for Walt Disney; drew his 1st editorial cartoons for Chgo. Sun (now Sun-Times); did illustrations for Coronet, Esquire, Sat. Eve. Post, Collier's N.Y. Times; became syndicated cartoonist Newspaper Enterprise Assn., 1950, staff cartoonist N.Y. Herald Tribune, 1962; later cartoonist Publishers' Newspaper Syndicate (now subsidiary Field Enterprises Inc.); now chief editorial cartoonist Chgo. Daily News; with Pub.'s Hall syndicate. Served with Signal Corps, AUS. Recipient Pulitizer Prize, 1969; named Best Editorial Cartoonist, Nat. Cartoonist Soc., 4 times. Office: 401 N Wabash Av Chicago IL 60611

FISCHNA, CARMINE MICHAEL, chem. co. exec.; b. Bklyn., July 23, 1924; s. Mario and Antoinette (Novellino) F.; B.B.A., St. John's U., 1944; m. Joan Virginia Martin, Aug. 27, 1957; children—Diane, Robert. With Reichold Chems. Inc., 1950- -, asst. treas., 1959-65, treas., 1965—; treas. Bluebeard's Castle, Inc. Served with USNR, 1943-46. Home: Leland Av Pleasantville NY 10570 Office: 525 N Broadway White Plains NY 10630

FISCHOFF, EPHRAIM, educator, clergyman; b. N.Y.C., Oct. 2, 1904; s. Aaron and Betty (Gunsberg) F.; A.B., Coll. City N.Y., 1924; M.H.L., Jewish Inst. Religion, 1928; D.Social Sci., New Sch. Social Research, 1942; m. Marion Judson, Dec. 28, 1943; children—Aronel, Gabriel and Raphael (twins), Michael, Bettina, Daniel. Rabbi, 1928; ministry, religious edn. group work, 1928-42; lectr. sociology, Pa. State U. 1935; lectr. Jewish Tchrs. Sem., N.Y., 1937-42; editorial cons. World Jewish Congress, 1941-45; lectr. New Sch. Social Research, 1942-51, Hunter Coll., Coll. City N.Y., 1942-46; asst. editor Jour. Legal and Polit. Soc., 1943-45; acting exec. dir. Conf. Jewish Relations, 1946; head dept. sociology Am. Internat. Coll., 1946-54; lectr. various univs. and orgns. Dir. B'nai B'rith Hillel Found. U. Cal., Berkeley, 1954, Hillel Found., Yale, 1954-58; prof. humanities and social sci., dir. honors program Lynchburg Coll., 1960-69; now prof. sociology Wis. State U., Stevens Point, also U. Wis., Marathon; vis. prof. Coll. William and Mary, 1969, Sir George Williams U., Montreal, Que., Can., 1970; Ford Found. fellow Asian studies U. Va., 1963-65; vis. prof. Hollins Coll., U. Va., 1965-67. Exec. bd. A.R.C., Family Service Soc., Pres.'s Com. Employing Physically Handicapped. Nat. Conf. Christians and Jews; mem. Marathon Adv. Com. on Aging. Fellow Am. Sociol. Assn., Soc. for Applied Anthropology; charter mem. Nat. Assn. Social Workers, Acad. Religion and Mental Health; mem. Acad. Certified Social Workers, Am. Acad. Religion, Am. Studies Assn., Philosophy of Edn. Soc., Am., S.E. psychol. assns., Central Conf. Am. Rabbis, Am. Oriental Soc., Internat., Am. polit. sci. assns., Nat. Soc. for Study Edn., Am. Soc. for Legal and Polit. Philosophy, Soc. for Psycholog. Study Social Issues, Assn. for Asian studies, Am. Assn. U. Prof., Modern Lang. Assn., Soc. Study Social Problems, Soc. Sci. Study Religion, Va. Social Sci. Assn. (hon. v.p.), Am. Bibliog. Soc., Soc. Bibl. Lit. and Exegesis, Nat. Assn. Jewish Communal Service, Nat. Council Jewish Edn., Société Européenne de Culture, and others. Editor, translator: Sociology of Religion (Max Weber). Contbr. articles profl. publs. Home: 918 Franklin St Wausau WI 54401

FISH, CHARLES JOHN, biol. oceanographer; b. Fall River, Mass., May 13, 1899; s. Charles Frederick and Emily Victoria (Teale) F.; grad. Durfee High Sch. and Textile Inst., Fall River, 1917; Ph.B., Brown U., 1921, Sc.M., 1922, Ph.D., 1923; Sc.D., U. R.I., 1966; m. Marie Dennis Poland, Feb. 10, 1923; 1 dau., Marilyn Poland (Mrs. J. Barnes Munro Jr.). Sci. asst. U.S. Bur. Fisheries, 1922-24, asso. hydrobiologist, 1924-27; dir. Buffalo Mus. Sci., 1928-34; asst. prof. zoology R.I. State Coll., 1934, asso. prof., 1935-36, prof. zoölogy, 1937, chmn. dept., 1938-48, prof. marine biology, 1948-62, prof. oceanography, 1962-66, prof. emeritus, 1966—, acting dean grad. sch. of oceanography, 1961- 62, dir. Narragansett Marine Lab., 1937-46, 48-66, adv. emeritus dir., 1966—. Mem. council Yenching U., China, 1934—; cons. marine biology, 1946-48; asso. in marine biology Woods Hole Oceanographic Inst., 1946-64, hon. staff, 1964—; mem. fisheries adv. com. N.Y. World's Fair, 1939; mem. Atlantic Fisheries Biologists, 1940—; mem. Gov.'s adv. council on R.I. Div. of Fish and Game, 1939-52; mem. North Atlantic Fisheries Commn., 1942-43; mem. internat. com. on oceanography Internat. Council of Sci. Unions, 1946-55; mem. U.S. com. on oceanography of the Pacific, N.R.C., 1947- 55; sci. adviser U.S. State Dept. Delegation Indo-Pacific Fisheries Council, Bangkok, 1954. Mem. econ. adv. com. N.E. Council Econ. Devel. and Regional Cooperation, Bd. dirs. R.I. Wildlife Fedn. Served with USNRF, 1918; from lt. comdr. to capt USNR, 1942-46. Decorated Legion of Merit; Officer d'Academie (France), 1947; recipient Stamford Mus. award for sci. achievement, 1963; Charles J. Fish Oceanographic Lab. dedicated at U. R.I., 1960. Fellow A.A.A.S.; mem. R.I. Acad. Sci.; mem. Audubon Soc. R.I. (v.p. 1937-43), Am. Society Limnology and Oceanography, Phi Sigma, Phi Kappa Phi, Phi Beta Kappa, Sigma Xi, Theta Delta Chi. Episcopalian. Club: Kiwanis (hon.). Editor oceanographic sect. Am. Geophys. Union, 1944-47. Address: 1291 Kingstowne Rd Kingston RI 02881

FISH, HAMILTON, Jr., congressman; b. Washington, June 3, 1926; s. Hamilton and Grace (Chapin) F.; grad. Kent Sch., 1944; A.B., Harvard, 1949; LL.B., N.Y. U., 1957; postgrad. John F. Kennedy Sch. Pub. Adminstrn.; m. Julia Mackenzie (dec. Mar. 1969); children—Hamilton III, Julia Alexandria, Nicholas S., Peter L. Admitted to N.Y. bar; vice consul to Ireland, 1951-53; with firm Alexander and Green, N.Y.C., 1957-64; practice in Poughkeepsie and Milbrook, N.Y., 1964—; mem. 91st-92d congress from 28th Dist. N.Y., mem. Jud. Com. Mem. Franklin Delano Roosevelt Meml. Commn. Mem. exec. com. Dutchess County council Boy Scouts Am. Served with USNR, 1944-46. Republican. Mason, Elk; mem. Improved Order Red Men. Home: Millbrook NY 12545 Office: House Office Bldg Washington DC 20515

FISH, JAMES STUART, advt. exec.; b. Mt. Pleasant, Ia., Sept. 8, 1915; s. Don Ellsworth and Belle (Osborn) F.; B.A., U. Minn., 1937; postgrad., Northwestern U. Sch. Bus. Adminstrn., 1937-38; m. Dorothea Merritt, Nov. 3, 1941; children—James Stuart, Richard Merritt, Nancy Osborn. Summer worker Minn. State Fair, 1931-40; advt. dept. Nat. Tea Co., Chgo., 1937-38; advt. dept. Gen. Mills, Inc., Mpls., 1938-40, staff premium dept., grocery products advt. products mgr., 1940-43, advt. mgr. home appliance dept., 1946-53, asst. dir. advt., 1953-55, dir. advt., 1955—, v.p., 1956—. Spl. cons. sec. treasury, 1966-67; mem. Atty. Gen.'s Consumer Protection Adv. Council, Minn., Minn. Atty. Gen.'s Citizens Adv. Council Bd. dirs. Advt. Research Found., Better Bus. Bur., Council Better Bus. Bur., Advt. Council, Mpls. People to People; trustee KTCA-TV (ETV). Served as lt. USNR, 1943-46. Mem. Assn. Nat. Advertisers, Brand Names Found., Am. Advt. Fedn. Am. (chmn. bd. 1959-61, bd. dirs.), Advt. Council (dir.), Citizens Com. Pub. Education. Clubs: Wayzata Country; Minneapolis Advertising (pres. bd. dirs.). Conglist. (trustee; moderator). Home: 19005 12th Av N Wayzata MN 55391 Office: 9200 Wayzata Blvd Minneapolis MN 55440

FISH, MARIE POLAND, (Mrs. Charles John Fish), oceanographer; b. Paterson, N.J., May 22, 1902; d. Addison Brown and Mary (Dennis) Poland; B.A. cum laude, Smith Coll., 1921; Sc.D., U. R.I., 1966; m. Charles John Fish, Feb. 10, 1923; 1 dau., Marilyn (Mrs. J. Barnes Munro Jr.). Hydrobiologist U.S. Bur. Fisheries, 1922-27; curator ichthyology Buffalo Mus. Sci., 1928-31; ichthyologist Arcturus Oceanographic Expdn., 1925, Pacific Oceanic biology project Woods Hole Oceanographic Instn., 1946-50; research asso. Internat. Passamaquoddy Investigations, 1931-33, U.S. Nat. Mus., 1944-46; research asso. Narragansett Marine lab. U. R.I., Kingston, 1937-39; biol. oceanographer charge Office Naval Research Project Underwater Sound Biol. Origin, 1948- -, instr., 1942-43; ichthyologist State R.I., 1942-43; research oceanographer U. R.I. Chmn. Kingfish com. USN, 1954-64; dir. U.S. Navy Reference Library Underwater Sounds, 1954-70, U.S. Navy Simultaneous Data Sta. Program, 1963-67, R/V TRIDENT Bioacoustics Program, 1962-66; rep. various cons. USN; cons. USN Atlantic Fleet Tng. Center, Newport, R.I., 1960, Submarine Forces Pacific Fleet, Hawaii and Cal., 1960. Mem. Kingston Improvement Assn.; instr. first aid A.R.C., Narragansett, 1942-46, chmn. Servicemen's Center, 1943-44; pres. Am. Youth Hostel, Wyoming, R.I., 1942-48, bd. dirs. R.I., 1939-48; pres. Kingston Players, 1936-38. Recipient Women's Centennial Congress award, 1940; Stamford Mus. Distinguished Sci. award, 1963, Sophia Smith Distinguished Alumna award Smith Coll., 1964, Distinguished Pub. Service award USN, 1965. Mem. Am. Inst. Biol. Scis., A.A.A.S., Am. Soc. Ichthyologists and Herpetologists, Soc. Woman Geographers, N.Y. Zool. Soc. (research asso.), Jr. League Providence, League Women Voters, Cocumscussoc, Pettaquamscutt hist. assns., South County Art Assn., Smith Coll. Alumnae Assn., Nat. Fedn. Bus. and Profl. Women's Club (woman of year award 1966- 67), Am. Soc. Limnology and Oceanography, Phi Beta Kappa, Sigma Xi, Phi Sigma. Republican. Presbyn. Clubs: Triangle (Kingston, R.I.), South County Art (South Kingston, R.I.), Dunes (Narrangansett, R.I.). Author: Sonic Fishes of the Pacific, 1948; Marine Mammals of the Pacific with Particular Reference to the Production of Underwater Sound, 1949; Sounds of Western North Atlanta Fishes, 1970; also films and taped recordings of marine animal sound prodn., articles. Home: 1291 Kingstowne Rd Kingston RI 02881 Office: Narrangansett Marine Lab U R I RI 02881

FISH, MARJORIE, occupational therapist; b. St. Louis, Oct. 20, 1905; d. Edwards Russell and Ida (McBride) Fish; B.A., Swarthmore Coll., 1927; M.A., Columbia, 1952; postgrad. Boston Sch. Occupational Therapy, 1932. Organizer occupational therapy depts. Columbia, 1941-51, hosps. and tng. centers, Australia, 1948-50; exec. dir. Am. Occupational Therapy Assn., N.Y.C., 1951-64; cons. in occupational therapy, div. of tng., Vocational Rehab. Adminstrn., 1964—. Mem. panel President's Commn. on Health Needs of the Nation, 1951-52; U.S. del. World Fedn. Occupational Therapists, 1954-62; cons. rehab. Phys. Medicine and Rehab. Service, VA, 1955-60; adv. panel on rehab. WHO, 1957—; tech. adv. com. Office Vocational Rehab., 1956-57; com. Internat. Exchange of Persons for Fulbright lecturing and research awards, 1957-62. Mem. Internat. Soc. for Welfare Cripples (U.S. com. 1950-59), Am. (chmn. council edn. 1945- 46, v.p. 1946-49), N.Y. (pres.) occupational therapy assns. Author: (with Holland Hudson) Occupational Therapy in the Treatment of the Tuberculosis Patient, 1943; also articles in field. Home: 503 6th St S E Washington DC 20003 Office: Vocational Rehab DHEW Washington DC 20201

FISH, RICHARD RAMSDELL, lawyer; b. N.Y.C., Mar. 10, 1921; s. Willard Hayes and Florence L. (Smith) F.; B.S., Columbia, 1944; LL.B., U. Ariz., 1950; m. Margaret Gibbons, Apr. 3, 1969; step-children-Judith A. (Mrs. Milton Alexander Stumpff, Jr.), John Gibbons Callender. Admitted to Ariz. bar, 1950, since practiced in Tucson; partner firm Spaid, Fish, Briney & Duffield, Tucson, 1963—. Pres. So. Ariz. Estate Planning Council, 1959-60. Served with AUS, 1942-43. Mem. Ariz., Pima County bar assns., Am. Bd. Trial Advocates (pres. Tucson chpt 1970-71), Alpha Kappa Psi (pres. Chi chpt. 1942), Phi Delta Phi. Presbyn. (clk. of session 1968-69). Mason (Shriner). Clubs: Old Pueblo, Country (Tucson). Home: 6138 San Leandro Dr Tucson AZ 85715 Office: Transamerica Building Tucson AZ 85701

FISHBACH, J. KARL, retail stores exec.; b. Bklyn., Feb. 27, 1909; s. Alexander S. and Sarah R. (Friedman) F.; B.B.A., Coll. City N.Y., 1930; graduate Columbia Bus. Sch., 1931, Cooper Union, 1932; m. Evelyn Stern, June 16, 1935; children—Philip D., Richard A. With Loeb & Troper, Katz, Zucherman & Co., also Homes & Davis, C.P.A. firms, 1926-34; asst. corp. controller R.H. Macy & Co., Inc., 1934-50; controller City Stores Co., 1950-60, corp. controller, 1960—, chmn. capital authority com., 1958-63; pres., treas., dir. City Stores Credit Corp. Mem. adv. panel to comptroller Office Chief Staff, U.S. Army, 1949-51. Treas., dir. City Stores Found. C.P.A., N.Y. Mem. Am. Arbitration Assn. (nat. panel arbitrators), Financial Execs. Inst. (bd. dirs. N.Y.C. 1954-56, chmn. com. capital assets and related reserves 1954-56; adv. panel nat. com. fed. taxation 1952-66, taxation com. 1966—; chmn. subcom. LIFO. 1968—; admissions com. N.Y.C. chpt. accounting prins. and practices com.), Nat. Retail Merchants Assn. (credit com., pension and social security com., taxation com. Dir. 1966 Controllers Congress (past chmn. standardization com.; retail com. on accounting principles), Am. Inst. C.P.A.'s, Am. Accounting Assn., Met. Controllers Assn. (past bd. dirs.), Am. Acad. Polit.and Social Sci. Contbr. profl. jours. Home: 8101 19Oth St Jamaica NY 11423 Office: 500 Fifth Av New York City NY 10036

FISHBEIN, MORRIS physician, editor; b. St. Louis, Mo., July 22, 1889; s. Benjamin and Fanny (Glück) F.; B.S., U. Chgo., 1910; M.D., Rush Med. Coll., 1912; D. Pharmacy (hon.), Rutgers U., 1942; LL.D., Fla. So. Coll., 1957; D.Sc., Chgo. Med. Sch., 1965; m. Anna Mantel, July 7, 1914; children—Barbara Fishbein Friedell, Morris (dec.), Marjorie Fishbein Clavey, Justin Mantel. Fellow in pathology Rush Med. Coll., 1912; with Jour. of A.M.A., 1913-49; editor of Hygeia until 1949; editor Bull. of Soc. of Med. History, Chgo.; contbg. editor Postgrad. Medicine, 1950-70; mem. chief bd. editors Exerpta Medica, 1949-71; chmn. sci. adv. bd. Municipal Tb San. and City of Hope; prof. emeritus medicine U. Ill. Coll. Medicine, U. Chgo.; editor med. sect. Britannica Book of Year; contbg. editor McCall's, 1959-67. Decorated knight comdr. Order of Crown of Italy, Nat. Order of Merit of Carlos J. Finlay (Cuba); Certificate of Merit from Pres. Truman, 1948; Comdr. Civil Order Health (Spain), 1952; Officer's Cross Order Orange-Nassau, Netherlands, 1954; comdr. cross Royal Order of Phoenix (Greece), 1967; recipient Jesse L. Rosenberger medal for achievements in pub. medicine and med. edn., 1968. Mem. several profl., advt. coms. and orgns. Fellow Am. Pub. Health Assn.; mem. A.A.A.S., Phi Delta Epsilon, Alpha Omega Alpha, Sigma Delta Chi. Clubs: Variety, Lotos, Chgo. Literary, Quadrangle, The Tavern, Standard, Arts. Author numerous books, 1925—, later ones include: Joseph Bolivar DeLee; Crusading Obstetrician (with Sol Theron DeLee), 1949, Handy Home Medical Adviser, 1957. Editor numerous books and reports, later ones include: Modern Family Health Guide, 1967; Heart Care, 1960; Modern Home Medical Adviser, 1969; Morris Fishbein, MD—An Autobiography, 1969. Editor World-Wide Abstracts of General Medicine, 1958-67; Medical World News, 1960—. Home: 5454 South Shore Dr Chicago IL 60615 ☆

FISHBERG, ARTHUR MAURICE, physician; b. N.Y.C., June 17, 1898; s. Maurice and Bertha (Cantor) F.; A.B., Columbia, 1919, M.D., 1921; m. Irene Levin, June 16, 1933. Intern City Hosp., 1921-22; adj. and asso. physician Mt. Sinai Hosp., 1926-46; physician-in-chief Beth Israel Hosp., 1946—; cons. physician St. Joseph's Hosp., 1944—; cons. Army Med. Center, Washington, 1947—; clin. prof. med. N.Y. U., 1947—; cons. physician Mount Vernon Hosp., 1957—; clin. prof. medicine Mt. Sinai Sch. Medicine, 1966—. Pres. Dazian Found. for Med. Research, 1956. Mem. Am. Soc. for Clin. Investigation, A.M.A., Am. Heart Assn., N.Y. Acad. of Medicine; hon. mem. Buenos Aires Med. Soc., Brazilian Cardiological Soc. Jewish religion. Author: Hypertension and Nephritis, 1930; Heart Failure, 1937. Contbr. numerous articles dealing with cardiovascular and renal disease. Conducted extensive investigations on cardiovascular and renal disease. Address: 1136 Fifth Av New York City NY 10028

FISHBURN, HOWARD DEWITT, physician, educator; b. Burr Oak, Kan., Nov. 27, 1909; s. Charles Davis and Estella Emma (Haworth) F.; M.D., U. Colo., 1935; m. Alma Gayle Lackner, June 17, 1935; 1 son, John Howard. Intern USPHS, Seattle, 1935-36; commd. USPHS, 1936, asst. surgeon gen., 1961; mil. duty with USCG, 1945-46; chief surgery USPHS Hosp., Boston, 1948-51, USPHS Hosp., Balt., 1951- 61; chief med. service with rank rear adm. USCG, 1961-71; asso. prof. surgery Georgetown U. Sch. Medicine, 1971—. Recipient Meritorious Service medal USPHS, 1962; Presdl. Legion of Merit, 1967; USPHS Distinguished Service medal, 1970. Diplomate Am. Bd. Surgery. Mem. A.C.S., A.M.A., Assn. Mil. Surgeons, Coast Guard Acad. Alumni Assn., Phi Rho Sigma. Presbyn. Home: 4007 Danbury Ct Bethesda MD 20014 Office: Georgetown Univ School of Medicine Washington DC 20005

FISHEL, LESLIE HENRY, Jr., coll. pres.; b. N.Y.C., Nov. 14, 1921; s. Leslie Henry and Thelma R. (Minzie) F.; A.B., Oberlin Coll., 1943; A.M. Harvard, 1947, Ph.D., 1954; Litt.D., Lakeland Coll., 1969; m. Barbara G. Richards, June 30, 1943; children—Ruth (Mrs. John R. Barry), Timothy, Lesley (Mrs. Gregg R. Hanson), Andrew, John. Mem. faculty Mass. Inst. Tech., 1948-55; lectr. history Oberlin Coll., 1956- 59, exec. dir. Alumni Assn., 1955-59; pres. Heidelberg Coll., Tiffin, O., 1969—; research asso. Nat. Sci. Fedn. History Sci. Project, 1953-55. Cons., Bancroft Library, U. Cal. at Berkeley, 1967; chmn. Wis. Capitol Exec. Residence Bd., 1968-69; adv. com. Library of Congress Nat. Union Catalogue of Manuscripts, 1967—; mem. Wis. Council Social Studies, 1969—; Chmn. sponsoring com. Madison Friends Urban League, 1961-67. Sec. Wis. Hist. Found., 1959-69; sec. Wis. Civil War Centennial Commn., 1959-66; exec. v.p. Historic Sites Found. Wis., 1960-69; sec. Lincoln Fellowship Wis., 1962-69; mem. Wis. Vets. Meml. Commn., 1959-69; chmn. Gov. Wis. Com. Portage Canal, 1964-66; mem. Gov. Wis. Portage Canal Implementation Com., 1966-69, 1962-69, Wis. Hist. Soc., 1959-69, Nat. Ry. Mus., 1959-69, Roadstead Found., 1961-70; mem. nat. council Nat. Endowment for the Humanities, 1970—. Bd. dirs. Univ. YMCA, Madison, 1962-69; Served lt. (j.g.) USNR, 1943-46. Mem. Am. Assn. State and Local History (gov. council 1964-70), Tiffin Area C. of C. (dir. 1971—), Oberlin-Shansi Meml. Assn. (past trustee), Orgn. Am. Historians. Ch. of Christ (past trustee, moderator). Clubs: Harvard (N.Y.C.); Mohawk Golf. Author: (with B. Quaries) The Black American: A Documentary History, 1967, rev. 1970; also articles. Home: Route 1 Tiffin OH 44883

FISHER, ADRIAN SANFORD, lawyer, univ. dean; b. Memphis, Jan. 21, 1914; s. Hubert Frederick and Louise (Sanford) F.; A.B., Princeton, 1934, LL.D., 1965; LL.B., Harvard, 1937; m. Laura Graham, Jan. 12, 1945; children—Laura Donelson, Louise Sanford. Admitted to Tenn. bar, 1938; law clk. to Supreme Ct. Justice Brandeis, 1938, Justice Frankfurter, 1939; atty. various govt. agys., 1939-41; asst. chief. Fgn. Funds Control div. U.S. Dept. State, 1941-42; asst. to asst. sec. of war, 1944; solicitor U.S. Dept. Commerce, 1947-48; gen. counsel AEC, 1948-49; legal adviser Dept. State, 1949-53; dep. dir. U.S. Arms Control and Disarmament Agy., 1961-69; pvt. law practice, former asso. Covington & Burling; v.p., counsel Washington Post Co.; prof. internat. law and internat. trade, Georgetown U. Law Center, dean, 1969—; legal adviser to U.S. Delegation to UN, Paris, 1952; mem. Pres.'s Commn. on Immigration and Naturalization; mem. U.S. Panel Permanent Ct. Arbitration. Tech. adviser to U.S. judges, Internat. Mil. Tribunal, Nuremberg, Germany, 1946. Served to capt. USAAF, 1942-43, 45. Awarded Legion of Merit. Mem. Am. Law Inst., Am. Bar Assn., Bar Assn. D.C., Phi Beta Kappa. Democrat. Presbyn. Club: Metropolitan (Washington). Home: 2721 N St N W Washington DC 20007 Office: 506 E St N W Washington DC 20001

FISHER, AIKEN WOOD, mfg. exec.; b. Pitts., Mar. 19, 1908; s. Chester G. and Margaret R. (Aiken) F.; grad. Shady Side Acad., 1925; B.S., Yale, 1929; m. Jane I. Marshall, Feb. 25, 1933; children—Joan (Mrs. John J. Humphrey), Constance (Mrs. E. Fisher Humphrey). With Fisher Sci. Co., Pitts. 1929- -, beginning as trainee, successively salesman, mgr., v.p., 1929-50, pres., 1950-65, chmn. bd., 1965—, dir., 1932—; dir. Granie City Steel Co., Mellon Nat. Bank and Trust Co., Latrobe Steel Co., Equitable Life Assurance Soc.; trustee Dollar Savs.

Bank. Mem. Carnegie Hero Fund Commn.; chmn. bd., trustees Carnegie-Mellon U.; trustee Shady Side Acad. (hon.), Western Pa. Hosp. Mem. Am. Chem. Soc., Soc. Chem. Industry. Clubs: Duquesne (Pitts.); Rolling Rock (Ligonier, Pa.); Pike Run Country (Jones Mills, Pa.); Yale (N.Y.C.). Home: Chatham Towers Pittsburgh PA 15219 Office: 711 Forbes Av Pittsburgh PA 15219

FISHER, ALAN, fgn. service officer; b. Bklyn., Jan. 20, 1913; s. Reuben and Lila (Hodes) F.; grad. Bklyn. Tech. High Sch., 1931; m. Florence Kalm, Jan. 20, 1935; 1 dau., Stephanie Nair. Staff photographer N.Y. World Telegram, 1933-40, PM, 1940-42; lectr., writer on press photography, 1935-42; writer-photographer for coordinator Inter-Am. Affairs in S.A., 1942-44, war corr. in Italy, 1944-45; joined U.S. Fgn. Service, 1945; motion picture officer, Rio de Janeiro, Brazil, 1946-48, asst. information officer, asst. attache, 1948-50, motion picture officer, 1950-53; transferred to USIA, 1953; motion picture officer, Paris, France, 1956-58, Saigon, Viet-Nam, 1958-60; assigned Washington, 1960; chief domestic prodn. div. Motion Picture Service, 1961-63, chief fgn. prodn. div., 1963-66; pub. affairs officer, Sao Paulo, Brazil, 1966—. Decorated Medalha de Guerre, Medalha de Campanha (Brazil). Mem. Press Photographers Assn. N.Y., Brazilian Press Assn., Press Photographers Assn. Rio de Janeiro (a founder, hon. mem.), Soc. Motion Picture and TV Engrs. Address: Am Consulate Gen Sao Paulo Brazil

FISHER, ALLAN CARROLL, Jr., editor; b. Cumberland, Md., Feb. 17, 1919; s. Allan C. and Ella (Rees) F.; A.B., U. Md., 1941; m. Mary Alice MIchael, Jan. 20, 1944; children—Suzanne de Cessna (Mrs. Roger A. Eichholz), Martha Rees. Staff writer Washington Post, 1941, Balt. Sun, 1941-43; editorial staff N.Y. bur. A.P., 1943-47; N.Y. pub. relations rep. Kaiser-Frazer Corp., 1947- 48; v.p. Booke & Fisher, Inc., pub. relations, Houston, 1948-49; asso. Hammond Assos., pub. relations, Balt., 1949-50; mem. staff Nat. Geog. Mag., 1950—, asst. editor charge articles, 1963-65, sr. asst. editor, 1965-70, sr. asst. editor, staff adminstrn., 1971—. Recipient James J. Strebig Meml. award Aviation Writers Assn., 1956, 60. Mem. Aviation/Space Writers Assn., Nat. Assn. Sci. Writers, Nat. Aero. Assn., A.A.A.S. Democrat. Episcopalian. Clubs: Nat. Space (bd. govs. 1961-62), Nat. Press. Nat. Aviation, Aero, Clipper (Washington); Annapolis Yacht. Contbr. numerous articles Nat. Geog. Mag. Home: Beaumaris Bywater Rd Annapolis MD 21401 Office: Nat Geog Soc 17th and M Sts N W Washington DC 20036

FISHER, ALTON KINDT, dentist, pathologist, educator; b. Abrams, Wis., Nov. 1, 1905; s. Fred Ward and Edith Bertha (Kindt) F.; student U. Wis., 1925-32; D.D.S., Marquette U., 1935; B.S., Loyola U., 1948; grad. study Tulane U., 1948- 49; m. Marcella Coad Neff, Aug. 15, 1931. Asst. anthropology Milw. Pub. Mus., 1927-32, research asso. since 1937; intern Milw. Children's Hosp., 1935-36; pvt. dental practice, Milw., 1936-40; instr. histology Marquette U., 1937-40; attending dentist St. Joseph's Hosp., 1937-40; asst. prof. pathology Loyola U., New Orleans, 1945-47, prof., 1947-49; prof., chmn. dept. oral pathology U. Ia., 1949—, prof., head dept. of stomatology, 1958-65; vis. dental surgeon Charity Hosp. La., New Orleans, 1946-49; cons. VA Hosp., Des Moines, 1951—, VA Hosp., Iowa City. Served to comdr. USN, 1940-46; rear adm. Res. ret. Recipient Lapham medal Wis. Archeol. Soc., 1946. Fellow Am. Coll. Dentists, Am. Acad. Oral Pathology, Am. Anthrop. Assn., A.A.A.S.; mem. Internat. Acad. of Pathology, Am. Dental Assn., Fedn. Dentaire Internationale, Soc. Exptl. Biology and Medicine, Am. Soc. Clin. Pathology, Internat. Assn. Dental Research, Wis. Archeol. Soc., Archaeol. Inst. Am., Arctic Inst. N.Am., Am. Polar Soc. Sigma Xi, Omicron Kappa Upsilon. Episcopalian. Mason. Author articles pathology. Research normal and pathologic tissue respiration, 1951—; arctic animals Naval Arctic Research Lab., Point Barrow, 1958-59, 68, 69-71. Home: 60H24 Stewart Rd Route 6 Iowa City IA 52240

FISHER, ANDREW, business exec.; b. Richmond, Va., Dec. 17, 1920; s. Marion Nimmo and Sarah Randolph (Talcott) F.; B.A., Amherst Coll., 1943; M.B.A., Harvard, 1947; m. Cornelia Johnson, Oct. 10, 1942; children—Peter R., Carolyn, Andrew R. Dir. indsl. relations Internat. Braid Co., Providence, 1947; with N.Y. Times, 1947—, v.p., 1963-70, exec. v.p., 1971—; pres. Chatham Holdings, Inc.; dir. Compusamp, Inc. Trustee Albany Med. Coll., Russell Sage Coll. Served to capt. AUS, 1942-46. Clubs: Harvard Bus. Sch. (dir., sr. v.p.) (N.Y.C.); Troy (N.Y.) Country. Home: 601 E 20th St New York City NY 10028 also Kinderhook Lane RD 2 Nassau NY 12123 Office: Chathamn Holdings Inc Warren St Hudson NY

FISHER, ARNOLD, lawyer; b. 1929; A.B., Columbia Coll., 1950; M.A., Columbia, 1954; LL.B., Fordham U., 1957. Admitted to N.Y. bar, 1957, U.S. Supreme Ct. bar, 1961, N.J. bar, 1965; partner firm Lowenstein, Sandler, Brochin, Kohl and Fisher, Newark; atty. interpretative div. Office Chief Counsel, 1957-60, legislation and regulation div., 1960-61; atty. Office of Tax Legislative Counsel, U.S. Treasury Dept., 1961-63. Mem. Am., N.J. State, Essex County bar assns. Office: 744 Broad St Newark NJ 07102*

FISHER, ARTHUR JOHN, glass fiber mfg. co. exec.; b. London, Eng., Sept. 13, 1913; s. John Edward and Elizabeth (Dickinson) F.; student Eltham Coll., Kent, Eng., 1922-29; certificate in Elec. Engring. North Staffordshire Tech. Coll., Eng., 1935; m. Dorothy Edith Hipkin, Dec. 27, 1937; children—Gillian, Peter, Hugh, Valerie. With Callenders Cable & Constrn. Co., Eng., 1932-36, Johnson & Phillips, Ltd., Eng., 1936-39, Atomic Research Establishment, Harwell, Eng., 1945-48; plant mgr. Fiberglas Can., Ltd., Sarnia, Ont., 1948-51, gen. mgr., Toronto, Ont., 1951-55, v.p. mfg. and engring., 1955-67, pres., 1967—, also dir.; chmn. bd., dir. N.Am. Caledonian Mining Co., Pitts.; dir. Dominion Explorers, Ltd., Toronto, Vermiculite Insulations, Ltd., Montreal. Vice pres. Canadian Arthritis and Rheumatism Soc. Served as lt. col., arty., Brit. Army, 1939-45. Decorated U.S. Legion of Merit. Registered profl. engr., Ont. Mem. Inst. Elec. Engrs. Eng., Engring. Inst. Can. (mem. Canadian-Am. com.), Soc. Plastics Industry Can. (dir.). Home: 8 Maytree Rd Willowdale Ontario Canada Office: 48 St Clair Av W Toronto 195 Ontario Canada

FISHER, BENJAMIN REEVES, mfg. co. exec.; b. Pitts., Apr. 5, 1916; s. Chester G. and Margaret (Aiken) F.; B.S., Yale, 1938; m. Lilian C. Hall, Apr. 10, 1939; children—Margaret Aiken (Mrs. Paul F. McKean), Coburn Hall, Benjamin Reeves, Christine Chase. With Fisher Sci. Co., Pitts., 1938—, pres., chief exec. officer, 1965—, also dir.; dir. Fisher Sci. Co. Ltd. (Can.). Trustee Children's Hosp. Pitts., Ellis Sch., Pitts. Mem. Sci. Apparatus Makers Am. (bd. dirs. 1957-64), Sigma Xi (asso.). Presbyn. (trustee). Home: 5565 Northumberland St Pittsburgh PA 15217 Office: 711 Forbes Av Pittsburgh PA 15219

FISHER, CARL, ins. co. exec.; b. Newkirk, Okla., Nov. 21, 1911; s. Raymond Glen and Mollie (Diel) F.; B.S. in Bus. Adminstrn., U. Okla., 1932; m. Janice Smith, Oct. 29, 1965. Ins. agt., Okla.,1932-34; mgr.gen. agy., Okla., 1934-38; with Nat. of Hartford Group, 1938-55, sec., 1953-55; with Pacific Indemnity Co., Los Angeles, 1955—, exec. v.p., 1961-65, pres., 1965—, also dir., mem. exec. com.; dir. The Chubb Corp., Fed. Ins. Co., Vigilant Ins. Co., Tex. Pacific Indemnity Co., Northwestern Pacific Indemnity Co. Dir., v.p. Cal. Ins. Fedn., 1963—; pres. Pacific Ins. and Surety Conf., 1961. Bd. dirs., mem. exec. com. Cal. Traffic Safety Found., 1963—, pres., 1970; dir. mem. exec. com. Greater Los Angeles Safety Council, 1962—; dir., mem. exec. com. Western Ins. Information Service, 1961—, pres., 1964; mem. Gov. Cal. Com. Traffic Safety, 1966—; bd. councilors Cal. Hosp. Med. Center. Served to lt. comdr. USNR, 1942-45; PTO. Decorated spl. commendation sec. navy, 1945. Mem. Blue Goose, Alpha Tau Omega. Episcopalian. Clubs: University (N.Y.C.). Jonathan (Los Angeles). Home: 3278 Wilshire Blvd Los Angeles CA 90005 also 9 S La Senda Pl South Laguna CA 92677 Office: 3200 Wilshire Blvd Los Angeles CA 90054

FISHER, CARL FREDERICK, mfg. co. exec.; b. Tiffin, O., June 12, 1924; s. Lawrence F. and Margaret (LaFountain) F.; B.S. in Bus. Adminstrn., Ohio State U., 1949; m. Kathleen Griffith Denman, Dec. 18, 1948; 1 son, Kurt Denman. With Gen. Motors Corp., 1949-51, Ford Motor Co., 1951-54, Chrysler Corp., 1954- 58, Chrysler de Venezuela, 1958-60; v.p., treas. Garrett Corp., Los Angeles, 1960-67; chmn. bd., pres. Signal Equities Co., 1967- 70; sr. v.p. Tracor, Inc., Austin, Tex., 1970—. Served with USAAF, 1943-45. Club: Austin Country. Home: 7705 Shadyrock Dr Austin TX 78731 Office: 6500 Tracor Lane Austin TX 78721

FISHER, CHARLES HAROLD, research adminstr.; b. Hiawatha, W.Va., Nov. 20, 1906; s. Lawrence D. and Mary (Akers) F.; B.S., Roanoke Coll., 1928; M.S., U. Ill., 1929, Ph.D., 1932; D.Sc., Tulane U., 1953; Sc.D. (hon.), Roanoke College, 1963; m. Elizabeth Dye, Nov. 4, 1933 (dec. 1967); m. 2d, Lois Carlin, July 1968. Teaching asst. chemistry U. Ill., 1928-32; instr. Harvard, 1932-35; asso. organic chemist U.S. Bur. Mines, Pitts., 1935-40; head carbohydrate div. E. Regional Research Lab., Dept. Agr., 1946-50, became chief So. Utilization Research Br., Dept. Agr., New Orleans, 1950, now dir. So. Marketing and Nutrition Research div. U.S. Dept. Agr. Pres. New Orleans Sci. Fair, 1967-69. Recipient So. Chemists award, 1956, Herty medal, 1959; Chem. Pioneer award Am. Inst. Chemists, 1966. Mem. Am. Inst. Chemists (pres. 1962-63), Sci. Research Soc. Am., Oil Chem. Soc., New Orleans C. of C., Am. Chem. Soc. (bd. dirs. region legion IV); Am. Assn. Textile Chemists and Colorists, Sigma Xi, Alpha Chi Sigma, Gamma Alpha, Phi Lambda Upsilon. Clubs: Round Table, Internat. House (New Orleans); Cosmos (Washington); Chemists (N.Y.C.). Office: 1100 Robert E Lee Blvd PO Box 19687 New Orleans LA 70119

FISHER, CHARLES NEWELL, investment banker; b. Pitts., June 29, 1905; s. Charles Andrew and Ritchie (Newell) F.; grad. Shady Side Acad., 1923; A.B., Williams Coll., 1927; m. Dorothy Gleeson, May 24, 1930 (dec.); children—Charles Newell, Richard E. Bookkeeper, Aluminum Co. Am., 1929-30; statistician Union Trust Co., 1930-35; municipal dept. mgr. Singer, Deane & Scribner, (both Pitts.), 1934-41, partner, 1941—; dir. Duquesne Slag Products, Pitts. Past pres. met. bd. YMCA; chmn. bd. trustees, bd. dirs., trustee, past pres. Playhouse Sch. Theatre. Served as lt. USNR, OSS, 1942-45. Mem. Investment Bankers Assn. Am. (past governor), Securities Traders Assn. Pitts. (past pres.). Clubs: Fox Chapel Golf, Bond (past pres.), Harvard-Yale-Princeton, Duquesne (Pitts.); Williams (N.Y.C.); Coral Beach (Bermuda); Sea View Country (Absecon, N.J.); Port Royal Beach, Hole-in-the-Wall (Naples, Fla.); Stone Harbor Yacht (Stone Harbor, N.J.). Home: Highland Rd Fox Chapel Pittsburgh PA 15238 Office: Union Trust Bldg Pittsburgh PA 15219

FISHER, CHARLES THOMAS, III banker; b. Detroit, Nov. 22, 1929; s. Charles Thomas, Jr. and Elizabeth Jane (Briggs) F.; A.B. in Econs., Georgetown U., 1951; M.B.A., Harvard, 1953; m. Margaret Elizabeth Keegin, June 18, 1952; children—Margaret Elizabeth, Charles Thomas IV, Curtis William, Lawrence Peter II, Mary Florence. With Touche, Ross, Bailey & Smith, C.P.A.'s, Detroit, 1953-58; asst. v.p. Nat. Bank Detroit, 1958-61, v.p., 1961-66, sr. v.p., 1966-69, exec. v.p., 1969—, also dir.; dir. Internat. Bank of Detroit, Detroit Edison Co., Prime Securities Corp., Hiram Walker-Gooderham & Worts, Ltd., Am. Broadcasting Co., Am. Airlines. Mem. Mackinac Bridge Authority; treas. Greater Detroit Area Hosp. Council. Trustee Mt. Elliott Cemetery, Detroit. Named Detroit Young Man of Year, Detroit Jr. Bd. Commerce, 1961. C.P.A., Mich. Mem. Am. Inst. C.P.A.'s, Mich. Assn. C.P.A.'s. Republican. Roman Cath. Clubs: Bloomfield Hills (Mich.) Country; Country of Detroit (Grosse Pointe); Detroit Athletic, Detroit, Recess, Yondotega (Detroit); Links (N.Y.C.); Union (Cleve.). Home: Grosse Pointe MI 48236 Office: National Bank Detroit Detroit MI 48232

FISHER, CHESTER LEWIS, Jr., lawyer, ins. exec.; b. Maplewood, N.J., May 30, 1911; s. Chester Lewis and Katherine Barton (Riddle) F.; grad. Mercersburg Acad., 1929; A.B., Princeton, 1933; J.D., Cornell U., 1936; m. Grace Annette Tainsh, Nov. 23, 1943; children—Chester Lewis III, Jane Alison. Instr. phys. edn. Cornell U., 1933-36; admitted N.Y. bar, 1937, P.I. bar, 1945, N.J. bar, 1947; practiced law, N.Y.C., 1936-39; atty. Met. Life Ins. Co. 1939-57, asst. v.p., asst. to pres. and chmn., 1957-60, 3d v.p., 1960-63, 2d v.p., 1963-65, v.p., 1965-70, v.p. and dir. urban and environmental affairs, 1970—. Village trustee, Briarcliff Manor, 1969-71, mayor, 1971—. Served from 1st lt. to col. USAAF, 1940- 46; col. USAF Res. ret. Decorated Legion Merit. Mem. Assn. Life Ins. Counsel (past pres.), Am. Bar Assn., S.A.R. Mason. Episcopalian (warden). Club: Sleepy Hollow Country. Home: 164 Pine Rd Briarcliff Manor NY 10510 also 10 Old Way Rd Landing NJ 07850 Office: 1 Madison Av New York City NY 10010

FISHER, CLYDE PALMER, coll. dean; b. Blackwell, Okla., Aug. 15, 1920; s. Charles Webster and Sarah Rose (McCrady) F.; A.B., U. Okla., 1942; A.M., U. So. Cal., 1947, Ph.D., 1955; m. Helen Frances Motsenbocker, June 14, 1942; children—Clyde Palmer, Margaret Ellen. Teaching asst. math. U. So. Cal., 1946-47; mem. faculty Cal. State Poly. Coll., 1947—, dean coll., 1960- 61, dean applied scis., 1961-70, dean sci. and math., 1970—. Chmn. finance com. Mercy Bowl Football Game, 1961. Pres. bd. Cal. Poly. Student Meml. Fund. Served to capt. AUS, 1942-46; lt. col. Res. Mem. A.A.A.S., Nat. Geog. Soc., Am. Sci. Affiliation. Mem. Church of Nazarene (dir. music, trustee, Sunday sch. tchr.) Home: 297 Marlene Dr San Luis Obispo CA 93401

FISHER, DALE JOHN, chemist; b. Omro, Wis., June 4, 1925; B.S., Wis. State U., Oshkosh, 1947; Ph.D. (U. fellow), Ind. U., 1951; m. Ruth J. Laird, Apr. 27, 1957; 1 dau., Shelley Dale. Staff mem. Inst. Paper Chemistry, Appleton, Wis., 1945; chemist city Oshkosh, Wis., summers 1947-49; chemist ionic analyses group Oak Ridge National Lab., 1951-52, group leader analytical instrumentation group, 1952—. Mem. Am. Chem. Soc. (award chem. instrumentation), Polarographic Soc., Tenn. Archaeol. Soc., Sigma Xi, Phi Lambda Upsilon. Conceives and directs research programs for devel. of and select and apply physiochem., mech., electronic and optical principles in design of instrumentation and for new or improved instrumental methods. Home: 22 Outer Dr Oak Ridge TN 37830 Office: P O Box X Oak Ridge TN 37830

FISHER, DAVID KIRKPATRICK ESTE, Jr., architect; b. Balt., Feb. 2, 1892; s. D. K. Esté and Sally Jones Milligan (McLane) F.; Litt. B., Princeton, 1913; B.S. in Architecture, Mass. Inst. Tech., 1916; m. Jean Bellingham (Small), Feb. 18, 1933 (dec. July 1969); stepsons—Samuel Small (dec.), George Latimer Small. Archtl. draftsman, N.Y., 1916-17, Balt., 1919-24; partner Parker, Thomas & Rice, Balt., 1924-27, Taylor & Fisher and successors, 1927—. Served as 1st lt., 6th F.A., 1st div., A.E.F., later instr. Saumur F.A. Sch., 1917-19, and capt. F.A. Res., 1919-29. Fellow A.I.A. (pres. chpt. 1937-38); life mem. Am. Mus. Natural History, Balt. Mus. of Art, Soc. of Cin. in N.J. Democrat. Episcopalian (chmn. diocesan dept. religious art 1960-65). Clubs: Maryland, Elkridge. Home: 3908 N Charles St Baltimore MD 21218 Office: 130 W Hamilton St Baltimore MD 21201

FISHER, DONALD WIENER, lawyer; b. Sandusky, O., Jan. 27, 1923; s. Albert Livingston and Orpha (Wiener) F.; B.S., Ohio State U., 1947, J.D., 1949; m. Jeanne Marie Bolan, Oct. 4, 1952; children—Sarah Jeanne, Laura Laskey, John Bolan, Andrew Donald, Martha Emily. Admitted to Ohio bar, 1949, D.C. bar, 1970; practiced in Toledo, 1949—; asso. Mulholland, Hickey & Lyman and predecessor firm, 1949- -, partner, 1956—; atty. NLRB, ICC; asst. gen. counsel Sheet Metal Workers Internat. Assn. Served with AUS, 1943-45; PTO. Mem. Am., Ohio, Toledo bar assns. Home: 3003 Kenwood Blvd Toledo OH 43606 Office: Nat Bank Bldg Toledo OH 43604

FISHER, EDDIE (Edwin Jack Fisher), singer; b. Phila., Aug. 10, 1928; s. Joseph and Kate (Minicker) F.; student pub. schs., Philadelphia; m. Debbie (Mary Frances) Reynolds, Sept. 26, 1955 (div. 1959); children—Carrie F., Todd; m. 2d, Elizabeth Taylor, May, 1959 (div.). Began as singer, Phila., 1942, on Skipper Dawes' radio shows; prdn. singer Capacabana, 1946. Grossinger's Resort, 1948-49; various other engagements; toured with Eddie Cantor, 1949; under contract RCA Victor, 1949—; TV nightclub bookings, 1949-51; star of Coke Time TV show, 1953—; began motion picture Bundle of Joy, 1956; co-starred in Butterfield 8. Served as pvt. tank corps AUS, 1951-52, vocalist AUS Band, Ft. Meyer, Va., 1952-53. Received Jr. Achievement award; Interfaith award, 1955. Mem. Vets. Fgn. Wars. Home: Beverly Hills CA 90213

FISHER, EDWARD, author, artist; b. Franklin, Mass., Nov. 20, 1902; s. James Edward and Catherine (Morrison) F.; S.B. magna cum laude, Harvard, 1924, A.M., 1926; postgrad. U. Paris, France, 1928-29, Carnegie Inst. Tech. Pitts., Arts Coll., 1932-34, Corcoran Sch. Art, 1948-49; m. Betty King Ward, July 17, 1950; 1 son by previous marriage, Alan Edmund. Instr. English, Carnegie Inst. Tech., 1926-35, instr. psychology and edn., 1932-35; dir. Key West (Fla.) Players, also editor Key West Guide, 1934- 35; curator Martello Gallery, 1948-49; play adaptor for Jed Harris, 1936- 38; spl. ast. to Harry Hopkins, 1938-40; exhbns. include Pitts. Asso. Artists, Carnegie Inst., Corcoran Gallery, Martello Gallery, others. Adviser fgn. war relief A.R.C., 1941; cons. USPHS, 1938, S.E. Asia Found., 1945. Served to maj. AUS, 1941-45. Recipient Sci. Book Choice award, 1936; named to honor roll Am. Short Story, 1931, 32, 33, 34,35; recipient award Best Brit. Short Stories, 1931. Mem. MacDowell Assn., MacDowell Colonists, A.A.A.S., Am. Psychol. Assn., Retired Officers Assn. Club: Harvard (Washington). Author: To The Sun, 1929; Marriage in Blue, 1931; Requiem, 1933; (with Paul Karlson) The World Around Us, 1936; (with Harry Sinclair Drago) The Moon and the Wind, 1937; Amazon Key, 1961; Shakespeare & Son, 1962; Love's Labour's Won, 1963; The Best House in Stratford, 1965. Contbr. nat. magazines, anthologies. Home: 3133 Connecticut Av Washington DC 20008

FISHER, EDWARD F., business exec.; b. Norwalk, O., 1891. Chairman, dir. Gar Wood Industries, Inc.; v.p., dir. Fisher & Co., Inc., Detroit; dir. Gen. Motors Corp. Home: 3300 Ricket Rd Brighton MI 48116 Office: Fisher Bldg Detroit MI 48202

FISHER, EDWIN SHELTON, publisher; b. Memphis, May 7, 1911; s. Lester Alan and Edna (Shelton) F.; student Columbia, 1929-30; B.S., U.S. Naval Acad., 1934; D.Litt., Westminster Coll., 1968; LL.D., Susquehanna U., 1968; m. Louise Tait, June 27, 1936; children—Shelton Tait, Anthony Kent, Anne Louise (Mrs. Jonathan Colby), Christopher Alan. With Curtis Pub. Co., 1935-38, McCann-Erickson Advt., 1938-40; joined McGraw-Hill Pub. Co. (now McGraw-Hill, Inc.) 1940, promotion mgr. Business Week, 1940-42, asst. pub. Science Illustrated, 1946-49, pub. Power, 1949-57, Fleet Owner, 1954-58; 1954-58, Elec. Merchandizing, 1957-59, sr. v.p. McGraw Hill Pubs. 1958-62, pres., 1963-65, pres. McGraw-Hill, Inc., 1966—, chief exec. officer, 1968—, also dir.; dir. Borden, Inc., Sperry-Rand Corp. Bd. dirs. Av. of Americas Assn.; trustee U.S. Naval Acad. Found., Westminster Coll. Served as lt. comdr. 1942-46. Mem. UN Assn. U.S.A. (trustee), Internat. C. of C. (trustee), Delta Kappa Epsilon. Clubs: University (N.Y.C.); Wee Burn Country. Office: 330 W 42d St New York City NY 10036

FISHER, ELMER HOWARD, utility co. exec.; b. Pomeroy, Wash., Nov. 21, 1906; s. Ora Elmer and Margaret Anna (Diehl) F.; student Cal. Inst. Tech., 1923-26; A.B. in Engring., Stanford, 1928, E.E., 1929; m. Margaret S. Stone, Mar. 19, 1932; 1 dau., Margaret Leatrice (Mrs. Marcello Cresti). Elec. engr. Coast Counties Gas & Electric Co., Santa Cruz, Cal., 1930; supt. Coast Indsl. Gas Co., also Coast Natural Gas Co., Pittsburg, Cal., 1930-39, mgr., San Francisco, 1939-44; mgr. natural gas div. Pacific Pub. Service Co., San Francisco, 1944- 51; mgr. gas supply and control Coast Counties Gas & Electric Co., San Francisco, 1951-54; gen. supt. pipe line operations Pacific Gas & Electric Co., San Francisco, 1954-60, v.p. charge gas operations, 1960—; v.p. Alberta Natural Gas Co.; pres., dir. Standard Pacific Gas Line, Inc.; v.p., dir. Alta. & So. Gas Co., Gas Lines, Inc., Natural Gas Corp. of Cal., Pacific Gas Transmission Co. (all San Francisco). Mem. Pacific Coast Gas Assn., Pacific Coast Elec. Assn., Am. Gas Assn., Western Gas Processors and Oil Refiners Assn., Sigma Xi, Tau Beta Pi. Clubs: Engrs., Electric, World Trade (San Francisco). Home: 123 Camino Pablo Orinda CA 94563 Office: 245 Market St San Francisco CA 94106

FISHER, EVERETT, lawyer; b. Greenwich, Conn., May 23, 1920; s. Henry Johnson and Alice Gifford (Agnew) F.; grad. Phillips Acad., 1937; B.A., Yale, 1941, LL.B., 1948; m. Catherine Gray Marshall, Aug. 21, 1943; children—Catherine (Mrs. W. John Funk II), Emily Trenholm. Admitted to Conn. bar, 1948, N.Y. State bar, 1949; asso. Littlefield, Miller & Cleaves, N.Y.C., 1948- 51; partner Pullman, Comley, Marshall & Parker, Grenwich, 1951- 58, Parker, Badger & Fisher, 1958—. Dir., sec., mem. exec. com. Popular Sci. Pub. Co.; adv. bd. dirs. Union Trust Co. Mem. bd. of estimate and taxation, Greenwich. Trustee Greenwich Country Day Sch. Vice pres., dir. Greenwich Boys' Club; dir. of Boys Clubs of Am. Mem. Internat., Am. bar assns., State Bar of Conn., English-Speaking Union, Phi Delta Phi. Republican. Clubs: Pine Valley Golf (Clementon, N.J.); Royal and Ancient Golf (St. Andrews, Scotland); Round Hill (dir., past pres), Field (Greenwich); Yale (N.Y.C.); Royal St. George's Golf (Sandwich, Eng.); Honourable Company of Edinburgh Golfers (Muirfield, Scotland). Home: Pecksland Rd PO Box 1158 Greenwich CT 06830 Office: 49 W Putnam Av Greenwich CT 06830

FISHER, FRANCIS DUMMER, govt. ofcl., lawyer; b. Winnetka, Ill., June 23, 1926; s. Walter Taylor and Katharine (Dummer) F.; A.B., Harvard, 1947, LL.B., 1951. Admitted to Ill. bar, 1951; with firm Tenney, Sherman, Bentley & Guthrie, Chgo., 1953-62; asst. gen. counsel for Far East, AID, 1962-64; dep. dir. AID mission to Colombia, 1965-67; regional adminstr. U.S. Dept. Housing and Urban

Devel., 1967-70, spl. asst. to sec. housing and urban devel., 1970—. Chmn. Com. Ill. Govt., 1957; bd. dirs. Chgo. Met. Planning and Housing Council, 1961; exec. com. Chgo. Welfare Council, 1960-61. Candidate for Alderman, Chgo., 1959. Served with USNR, 1944-46; PTO. Office: Office of Sec Housing and Urban Devel Washington DC 20410

FISHER, FRANK BERTMAN, banker; b. Lisbon, O., July 11, 1921; s. Frank B. and Elsie (Rigby) F.; B.A., Hiram Coll., 1943; M.B.A., U. Pa., 1947; grad. Stonier Sch. Banking, Rutgers U., 1958; m. Norma M. Larsen, June 21, 1947; children—Donald, Kathryn, Jeffrey, Douglas. With Continental Bank & Trust Co., N.Y.C., 1947-48, Comml. Nat. Bank, Middletown, N.Y., 1950-63; with County Nat. Bank, Middletown, N.Y., 1950-63, exec. v.p., 1960-63; pres., chief exec. officer Capital Nat. Bank, Cleve., 1963—; instr. Am. Inst. Banking, Orange Community Coll., Middletown, 1960. Chmn. Am. Cancer Soc., Cleve., 1970. Pres. trustees Cleve. Plan; trustee Euclid Av. Assn. Mem. Cleve. Council World Affairs, Bank Pub. Relations and Marketing Assn., U. Pa. Alumni Assn. Presbyn. (pres. bd. trustees). Rotarian. Clubs: Union, Commerce (Cleve.); Country (Pepper Pike, O.). Home: 3701 Greenwood Dr Pepper Pike OH 44124 Office: 1101 Euclid Av Cleveland OH 44115

FISHER, FRANKLIN MARVIN, educator; b. N.Y.C., Dec. 13, 1934; s. Mitchell Salem and Esther (Oshiver) F.; A.B. summa cum laude Harvard U., 1956, M.A., 1957, Ph.D., 1960; m. Ellen Jo Paradise, June 22, 1958; children—Abraham Samuel, Abigail Sarah, Naomi Leah. Asst. prof. economics U. Chgo., 1959-60; asst. prof. economics Mass. Inst. Tech., 1960-62, asso. prof., 1962-65, prof. 1965—; dir., cons. Charles River Assos. Inc.; cons. Arthur D. Little Inc.; Faculty Research fellow, 1966-67; NSF fellow, 1962-63. Fellow Econometric Soc. Am., Am. Acad. Arts and Scis., mem. Am. Economic Assn. Editor Econometrica, 1968—. Home: 197 Holden Wood Rd Concord MA 01742 Office: E52-359 50 Memorial Dr Mass Inst Tech Cambridge MA 02139

FISHER, GAIL ANN, actress; b. Orange, N.J., Aug. 18; d. William Isaac and Ona (Brown) Fisher; grad. Am. Acad. Dramatic Arts, 1958, Lincoln Center Repertoire Theater, 1964; m. John Levy, Mar. 23, 1964; children—Samara Lynn, Jole Ann. Roles include Simply Heaven (Broadway and TV), 1958; Danton's Death (1st prodn. in Vivian Boumount Theater, Lincoln Center), 1965; roles in TV prodns. include The Doctors, 1959, The Defenders, 1960, My Three Sons, 1967, Mannix, 1968-71. Goodwill ambassadress Easter Seal drive, 1970, 71; mem. Malfundi Inst., Los Angeles, 1970-71, T.E.A.C.H. Found., Los Angeles, 1970-71; chmn. Woman's Div. Los Angeles County Christmas Seals, 1971. Recipient Image award N.A.A.C.P., 1969, Emmy award, 1970, Golden Globe award, 1971; named Business Woman of Year Los Angeles dist. Cal. Fedn. Bus. and Profl. Women's Clubs, Inc., 1971. First black to do spoken nat. TV commercial, 1961. Address: 5451 Marathon St Hollywood CA 90038

FISHER, GEORGE B., investment banker; b. Colo. Springs, Colo., Aug. 23, 1915; s. John Dow and Barbara (Ballingall) F.; B.A., Colo. Coll., 1937; M.B.A., Northwestern U., 1940; m. Carmen A. Hennebach; children-Carol Ann, Scott B. Sr. v.p., Bosworth Sullivan & Co., Inc., Denver, 1946—; dir. One Hundred Fund, One Hundred One Fund. Served with USAAF, 1942-46. Charted financial analyst. Mem. Investment Bankers Assn. Am. (gov. 1968-70), Denver Soc. Security Analyst (pres.). Home: 3300 E Kentucky Denver CO 80209 Office: 660 17th St Denver CO 80202

FISHER, GERALD SAUL, restaurateur; b. Bronx, N.Y., Mar. 24, 1931; s. Abraham Samuel and Rose (Richards) F.; B.B.A., Clark U., 1952; LL.B., Boston U., 1955; m. Sue Louise Chidakel, Apr. 7, 1957; children—Steven Lawrence, A. Jody, David Scott. Admitted to Mass. bar, 1955, D.C. bar, 1962, also U.S. Supreme Ct.; atty.-adviser div. corp. finance SEC, 1956-58; with Small Bus. Adminstrn., 1958-67, asst. dep. adminstr. investment, 1963-65, asst. dep. adminstr. procurement and mgmt. assistance, 1965-67; adminstrv. v.p. internat. foods div. Internat. Industries; pres. Copper Penny Family Restaurants, an Internat. Industries Co., 1969—. Capt., Clark U. Alumni Fund Dr., 1963-65; chmn. incentive award com. Small Bus. Adminstrn., 1966, mem. adv. council to adminstr.; v.p. Small Bus. Adminstrn. Recreation Assn., 1966, coordinator for Pres.' Youth Opportunity campaign 1966. Bd. dirs. Men's Club, Hebrew Home for Aged, 1964—. Recipient awards for outstanding service to govt. Mem. Am. Bar Assn., Phi Theta Kappa. Author articles in field. Sr. editor Boston U. Law Rev. Home: 4450 Callada Pl Tarzana CA 91356 Office: 4942 Vineland Av North Hollywood CA 91601

FISHER, GRANVILLE CHAPMAN, artist; b. Nashville, Apr. 11, 1906; s. Henry Gordon and Blanche (Dickens) F.; Ph.B., U. Chgo., 1944, A.M., 1946, Ph.D., 1949; B.D., Meadville Theol. Sch., 1945; F.D., Boswell Soc., Chgo.; m. Ijourie Bernice Stocks, Oct. 7, 1941; children—Douglas, April. Cartoonist, So. Bapt. Pub. Bd., Nashville, 1922-24; archtl. draftsman Asmus & Clark, 1925-28; ordained to ministry Baptist Ch., 1928; pastor, 1928-34; art dir. Surf Club, Miami Beach, Fla., 1932-42; Unitarian minister, 1942—; dir., actor profl. theatre, 1935-37; psychologist Cook County Criminal Ct., Chgo., 1945-46; prof. psychology U. Miami, 1946-71, chmn. dept., 1948-60. Founder, owner Granville Galleries, Coral Gables; one-man show Rudolph Galleries, Coral Gables, 1954, Bass Mus., Miami Beach, 1965; chmn. Fine Arts Commn. City Miami. Recipient Outstanding Tchr. award U. Miami, 1968; First Poetry award Fla. Poetry Festival, 1968; also numerous awards in painting, local and nat. Fellow Gerontol. Soc.; mem. Am., Fla. psychol. assns., Am. Assn. U. Profs., Sigma Xi, Psi Chi. Contbr. articles to jours. Home: 3925 Ponce de Leon Blvd Coral Gables FL 33134

FISHER, HAROLD H., lawyer; b. Armenia, Jan. 21, 1900; student Rutgers U.; LL.B., Columbia, 1924. Admitted to Fla. and N.J. bars; practice of law, Newark; mem. firm Shanley & Fisher. Spl. asst. pros., Newark, 1928-32; asso. counsel N.J. Bd. Pub. Utility Commrs. and dep. atty. gen. State of N.J., 1943-46; spl. counsel to Gov. Meyner, 1954-55. Mem. N.J. Essex County bar assns. Asso. editor N.J. Law Jour., 1942—. Office: 744 Broad St Newark NJ 07102*

FISHER, HARVEY IRVIN, educator, zoologist; b. Edgar, Neb., June 15, 1916; s. Fred Herman and Mary Blanche (Baker) F.; B.S., Kan. State U., 1937; Ph.D., U. Cal. at Berkeley, 1942; m. Mildred Leone Hoch, July 11, 1937; children—Fred Harvey, George Karl, James Rilan. Tech. curator Mus. Vertebrate Zoology, U. Cal. at Berkeley, 1942-45; asst. prof. zoology U. Hawaii, 1945-48; exchange prof. U. Nev., 1947-48; asso. prof. U. Ill., 1948-55; prof. zoology So. Ill. U., Carbondale, 1955—, chmn. dept., 1955-71. Recipient Carl Schurz award Kan. State U., 1937. Fellow A.A.A.S., Internat. Acad. Zoology, Am. Ornithol. Union; mem. Soc. Study Evolution, Am. Inst. Biol. Scis., Cooper Ornithol. Soc., Am. Assn. U. Profs., Wilson Ornithol. Soc., Ill. Acad. Sci., Sigma Xi, Phi Delta Kappa, Phi Kappa Phi. Rotarian. Club: Exchange (Urbana, Ill.). Asst. editor Condor, 1942-45; editor The Auk, 1948-52, Pacific Sci., 1947-48, Ill. Biol. Monographs, 1952-55. Trans. Ill. Acad. Sci., 1955-59. Home: Hillcrest Dr Carbondale IL 62901

FISHER, HERMAN GUY, retired toy mfg. co. exec.; b. Unionville, Pa., Nov. 2, 1898; s. Elwood and Mary (Zimmerman) F.; B.A., Pa. State U., 1921; m. Suzanne Edwina Greist, Sept. 24, 1932 (dec.); children—Susan (Mrs. Victor W. Lavenstein), Rachel (Mrs. J. Steven Renkert), John Burgis; m. 2d, Elizabeth F. Abbott, Feb. 1, 1969. Vice pres., gen. mgr. All Fair, Inc., Churchville, N.Y., 1926-30; pres., gen. mgr. Fisher-Price Toys, Inc., East Aurora, 1930-66, chmn. bd., 1964-69; dir. Liberty Nat. Bank & Trust Co., Buffalo. A founder, pres. Boys' Club, East Aurora. Home: 861 Chestnut Hill Rd East Aurora NY 14052 Office: 21 S Grove St East Aurora NY 14052

FISHER, ILO DOLORES, librarian; b. Springfield, O., Oct. 18, 1913; d. Thomas Guy and Lilian (Chapman) Fisher; A.B., Wittenberg U., Springfield, O., 1935; B.L.S., U. Ill., 1940, M.S., 1951. Tchr. Springfield (O.) pub. schs., 1935-36; cataloger Wittenberg U. Library, 1939-43, head library sci. program, 1945—, head librarian, 1946-65, chief of tech. services, 1965-67, spl. projects librarian, 1967—; head catalog and order dept. Warder Pub. Library, 1943-46. Mem. Comprehensive Mental Health Planning Com., Clark County; pres. Clark County Mental Health Assn., 1964-66, Friends of Warder Public Library, 1967-69. Mem. Am. Assn. U. Profs., Spl. Libraries Assn., Clark County Historical Society, Women's Nat. Book Assn., A.L.A. (council 1954-56), Am. Assn. Coll. and Reference Libraries, Ohio Library Assn., Ohio Valley Regional Catalogers Assn., Ohio Assn. of Sch. Librarians, Beta Phi Alpha. Republican. Club: Altrusa (Springfield). Contbr. mags. Home: Detrick-Jordan Rd Springfield OH 45502 Office: Wittenberg U Library Springfield OH 45502

FISHER, JAMES LEE, coll. pres.; b. Decatur, Ill., June 2, 1931; s. Morris Lee and Vera (Brant) F.; B.S., Ill. State U., 1956, M.S., 1957; Ph.D., Northwestern U., 1963; student U. Mich., summer 1964; m. Barbara E. McCammon, Sept. 3, 1952; children—Kerry Brant, Kathryn Sue, Curtis James, John Benson. Grad. asst. Ill. State U., 1956-57, dir. student financial aids, asst. dir. admissions, 1960-63, asso. prof. psychology, 1963-69, asst. to pres. 1963-65, exec. asst. to pres., 1965-66, v.p., dean information and research services, 1966-69; tchr. Rich Twp. High Sch., Park Forest, Ill., 1957-59; asst. dir. admissions Northwestern U., 1959-60; pres. Towson (Md.) State Coll., 1969—. Cons., White House on campus tensions, 1970-71. Sec. treas. Ill. State U. Found., 1960-63. Served with USMCR, 1951-54. Mem. Assn. Higher Edn. (Eastern regional council), Am. Psychol. Assn., N.E.A., Pi Gamma Mu, Phi Eta Sigma, Phi Delta Kappa. Home: 628 Hastings Rd Towson MD 21204

FISHER, JAMES WILLIAM, med. educator, pharmacologist; b. Startex, S.C., May 22, 1925; s. Ernest Amaziah and Mamie V. (Turner) F.; B.S., U.S.C., 1947; Ph.D., U. Louisville, 1958; m. Carol Barbara Brodarick, June 5, 1947; children—Candis Loreen (Mrs. Phillip Rush), Patricia E., Richard W., William E., John C., Elaine M. Pharmacologist, Armour Pharm. Research Labs., Chgo., 1950-53, Lloyd Bros., Cin., 1954-56; instr. pharmacology U. Tenn., 1958-60, asst. prof., 1960-62, asso. prof., 1962-66, prof., 1966-68; prof., chmn. dept. pharmacology Med. Sch., Tulane U., 1968—; lectr. in field. Mem. com. erythropoietin Nat. Heart and Lung Inst., 1971-74. Served to lt. (j.g.) USNR, 1943-46; PTO. Mem. Am. Soc. Pharmacology and Exptl. Therapeutics, Soc. Exptl. Biology and Medicine, Am. Soc. Nephrology, Am. Soc. Hematology, Assn. Med. Sch. Pharmacology, A.A.A.S, Am. Assn. Univs. Profs., Sigma Xi. Author: Readings on the History of Pharmacology. Editor: Kidney Hormones, 1971; Renal Pharmacology, 1971; cons. editor Erythropoletin, 1968; mem. editorial review bd. of Blood, 1969—, Jour. Lab. Clin. Medicine, 1967—, Sci., 1969—. Editorial bd. Proc. Soc. Exptl. Biology and Medicine, 1971—. Contbr. articles to profl. jours. Research on effects of drugs on kidney erythropoietin prodn., anemia and kidney disease, kidney transplantation. Patentee antirheumatic drug. Home: 4025 Pin Oak Av New Orleans LA 70114

FISHER, JASPER WILLIAM, mfg. exec.; b. Marshalltown, Ia., July 30, 1914; s. Jasper Henry and Florence Edna (Baughman) F.; student Ames Coll., 1933; m. Dorothy Meyer, Sept. 14, 1941; children—Russell William, Christine-Ellen. Pres., dir. Fisher Control Co., Marshalltown, Iowa, 1944—, also chmn.; dir. Mchts. Nat. Bank, Cedar Rapids, Ia., Mons Co. Bd. dirs. Met. Opera; bd. govs. Ia. State U. Home: 410 N 6th St Marshalltown IA 50158 Office: Fisher Controls Co Marshalltown IA 50158

FISHER, J.B., business consultant; b. Bradford, Pa., May 29, 1899; s. Joseph Fischer and Lucy A. (Diebolt) F.; A.B. cum laude, Harvard, 1920; m. Christine Jean Schonblom, Mar. 2, 1931; children—Louis Antony, Helen Louise. With mfg. dept. Kendall Refining Co., 1920; purchasing agt. and gasoline sales mgr., 1926-27, dir., asst. treas., 1927-32, asst. treas., sec., 1932-38, exec. v.p., 1938-43, pres., 1943-66; v.p., dir. Witco Chem. Corp., 1966-70; cons. Witco Chem. Corp.-Kendall Refining Co. Div., 1970—; dir. Bradford Nat. Bank (Pa.), Bradford Community Indsl. Corp. Dir. Bradford Hosp. Mem. Nat. Petroleum Refiners Assn. (bd. dirs.). Clubs: Bradford, Penhills (Bradford, Pa.). Home: 54 Stone Av Bradford PA 16701 Office: 77 N Kendall Av Bradford PA 16701

FISHER, JEROME BONAPARTE, publs. exec.; b. Jamestown, N.Y., Apr. 19, 1910; s. Jerome Bonaparte and Imogene (Partidge) F.; A.B., Hamilton Coll., 1932; LL.B., Yale, 1935; m. Patricia Graves, Jan. 1, 1939; children—Jerome B., Wendy Patridge. With Publ. Corp. and affiliates, 1936—, sec., 1950-54, dir., 1952—, pres., then chmn., dir., 1954—. Trustee Knapp Found., Inc. Club: University (N.Y.C.). Home: Madison CT 06443 Office: 640 Fifth Av New York City NY 10019

FISHER, JEROME KEARNEY, Jr., physician; b. Derry, Pa., Nov. 11, 1901; s. Jerome Kearney and Ada Myrtle (Shomo) F.; Ph.G., U. Pitts., 1923; postgrad. U. Cal. at Los Angeles, 1930-33; A.B., Stanford, 1934, M.D., 1938; Sc.D., Columbia, 1943; m. Isobel Wells Yealy, June 12, 1937; children—Nancy Wells, Jerome Kearney III. Intern, resident dermatology Los Angeles County Gen. Hosp., 1937-40; teaching fellow dermatology Vanderbilt Clinic, Columbia Med. Center, N.Y.C., 1940-43; practice medicine, specializing in dermatology, N.Y.C., 1945-47, Pasadena, Cal., 1947—; asso. clin. prof. dermatology U. So. Cal., 1947-66, clin. prof. dermatology emeritus, 1966—. Med. researcher NRC, 1944. Diplomate Am. Bd. Dermatology. Fellow Am. Acad. Dermatology (past dir. teaching course), A.C.P., A.M.A., Pacific Dermatol. Assn.; mem. Los Angeles Dermatol. Soc. (past pres.), Am. Dermatol. Assn., Los Angeles County Med. Assn. Mason, Rotarian. Home: 1116 Lorain Rd San Marino CA 91108 Office: 960 E Green St Pasadena CA 91106

FISHER, JOHN, educator; B.S., Ph.D., Columbia. Prof. langs., chmn. lang. dept. Fairleigh Dickinson U., Rutherford, N.J. Office: Lang Dept Fairleigh Dickinson U Rutherford NJ 07070*

FISHER, JOHN ANDREW, librarian; b. Rawlins, Wyo., May 1, 1928; s. Ernest and Dorothy (Stines) F.; B.A., U. Wyo., 1949; M.L.S., Rutgers U., 1956. Library asst. Phila. Free Library, 1953, stack supr., 1954-56; asst. demonstration librarian Lower Ark. Valley Demonstration Library, Las Animas, Colo., 1959; demonstration librarian N.E. Colo. Regional Library, Yuma, 1959-61; area library supr. Colo. State Library, Denver, 1961-63; librarian Wyo. State Library, 1963-67; library services program officer Region VIII, U.S. Office of Edn., Denver, 1968-70; free-lance library cons., 1970—. Mem. Am. (mem. council 1965-68), Mountain Plains, Wyo. library assns., Spl. Libraries Assn., Assn. State Libraries (v.p. 1967-68). Address: Centennial WY 82055

FISHER, JOHN HURT, educator; b. Lexington, Ky., Oct. 26, 1919; s. Bascom and Franke (Sheddan) F.; B.A., Maryville Coll., 1940; M.A., U. Pa., 1942, Ph.D., 1945; L.H.D., Loyola U., Chgo., 1970; Litt.D., Middlebury Coll., 1970; m. Jane Elizabeth Law, Feb. 21, 1942; children—Janice Carol (Mrs. R.B. Lowe), John Craig, Judith Law. Instr. English, U. Pa., 1942-45, Yale, summer 1944; instr. English, N.Y. U., 1945-48, asst. prof., 1948-55; instr. English, U. Mich., summer 1956; asso. prof. Duke, 1955-58, prof., 1958-60; prof. English, Ind. U., 1960-62, N.Y. U., 1962—. Mem. Modern Lang. Assn. Am. (exec. sec. 1963-71, editor PMLA 1963-71), Medieval Acad. Am., Linguistic Soc. Am., Nat. Council Tchrs. English, Coll. English Assn. Clubs: Century, Cosmos. Author: John Gower: Moral Philosopher and Friend of Chaucer, 1964; The College Teaching of English, 1965. Editor: The Medieval Literature of Western Europe, 1966. Contbr. articles medieval lit., English linguistics, English edn. Home: 346 Park St Upper Montclair NJ 07043 Office: 19 University Pl New York City NY 10003

FISHER, JOHN MORRIS, assn. ofcl., editor; b. Fairhaven, O., Apr. 20, 1922; s. Marion Hays and Bessie (Morris) F.; A.B., Miami U., Oxford, O., 1947; student Bklyn. Law Sch., 1950-51, Northwestern U. Grad. Sch., 1954-55; m. Thelma Lucille Ison, Feb. 2, 1947; children—Steven Roger, Linda Lucille. With Belden Mfg. Co., Richmond, Ind., 1941; spl. agt. FBI, 1947-53; exec. trainee Sears, Roebuck & Co., Chgo., 1953, exec. staff asst. to v.p. charge personnel and employee relations, 1953-57, chmn. security com., 1957-61; operating dir. Am. Security Council, 1956-57, pres., chief exec. officer, 1957—; organizer, pres. Fidelifax, Inc., investigative orgn., 1956-57. Pres., chief exec. officer Inst. Am. Strategy, 1962—, chmn. merc. div. Nat. Safety Council, 1959-60, 1st vice chmn. trades and services sect. 1961; pres. Am. Research Found., 1961—; chmn. Chgo. Retail Safety Conf., 1959-60; spl. adv. Ill. Supt. Pub. Instrn., 1963- 64; cons. to Gov. Fla.; cons. to chmn. com. cold war edn. Nat. Gov's Conf., 1962-65; Ill. Civil Def. Adv. Council, 1965—. Bd. visitors Freedoms Found., 1964-65. Served to 1st lt. USAAF, 1943-45. Decorated Air Medal with clusters; recipient Tenth Anniversary Medal and Scroll, Assembly Captive European Nations. Mem. Am. Soc. Indsl. Security (bd. dirs. 1959-62), Phi Kappa Tau. Republican. Presbyn. Mason. Clubs: Tower; Culpeper (Va.) Country. Home: 1 S 512 Bayberry Lane Wheaton IL 60187 also Boston VA 22713 Office: 123 N Wacker Dr Chicago IL 60606

FISHER, JOHN P., banker. Vice pres., auditor Detroit Bank & Trust. Office: Fort St at Washington St Detroit MI 48231*

FISHER, JOHN WASHBURN, fgn. service officer; b. Stevensville, Mont., Jan. 4, 1920; s. Roy Washburn and Mattie (Gardner) F.; B.S., Mont. State Coll., 1941; student Yale Law Sch., 1946-47; m. Dorothy Margaret Hansen, Oct. 15, 1949; children—Beverly Ann, Richard Hanse, John Washburn. Joined U.S. fgn. service, 1947; assigned Guatemala City, Guatemala, 1947-50, Barranquilla, Colombia, 1951-52, State Dept., 1953-56; assigned Vienna, Austria, 1956-61, 1st sec. embassy, 1959-61, sr. seminar fgn. policy, Washington, 1961-62, dep. dir. Office C.Am. and Panama Affairs, 1962-64, counselor of embassy, Tegucigalpa, Honduras, 1964-66; counselor of embassy, dep. chief mission, La Paz, Bolivia, 1966-70; country dir. Bolivia and Chile affairs Dept. State, 1970—. Served to capt. inf. AUS, 1941-46. Mem. Phi Kappa Phi, Sigma Alpha Epsilon. Home: 8509 Fenway Rd Bethesda MD 20034 Office: Dept State ARA-BC Washington DC 20520

FISHER, JOSEPH JEFFERSON, U.S. judge; b. San Augustine County, Tex.; s. Guy B. and Lula (Bland) F.; student Stephen F. Austin Coll., 1929; LL.B., U. Tex., 1936; m. Kathleen Clark, Sept. 22, 1938; children—Leila (Mrs. Leila F. Thomas), Joseph Jefferson, John Clark, Guy Cade, Kathleen Anne (Mrs. Fred Thomas Winslow). Admitted to Tex. bar, 1936; served as county atty. San Augustine County, 1936-39; dist. atty. 1st Jud. Dist. Tex., 1939-46, dist. judge, 1956-59; partner firm Fisher, Tonahill & Reavley, Jasper, Tex., 1947-56; U.S. dist. judge Eastern Dist. Tex., 1959—, chief judge, 1967—. Mem. Am. (chmn. jud. sect. 1957), 1st Jud. (pres. 1956), Tex. bar assns., State Bar Tex. (legislative and exec. coms. 1957-59), Am. Judicature Soc., Tex. Hist. Assn., Sons of the Republic of Tex., Ex-Student Assn. U. Tex. (life), Delta Kappa Epsilon. Methodist. Mason, Lion (dist. gov., internat. dir., mem. exec. com. 1952-59). Home: 130 Central Caldwood Dr Beaumont TX 77707 Office: Box 88 Beaumont TX 77704

FISHER, JOSEPH LYMAN, economist; b. Pawtucket, R.I., Jan 11, 1914; s. Howard Colburn and Caroline (Nash) F.; B.S., Bowdoin Coll., 1935; postgrad. London Sch. Econs., 1935-36; M.A., Harvard, 1938, Ph.D. (teaching fellow 1946-47), 1947; M.A. in Edn., George Washington U., 1951; D.Sc., Bowdoin, 1965; LL.D., Allegheny Coll., 1966; m. Margaret Saunders Winslow, June 21, 1942: children—H. Benjamin, Caroline, Robert W., William B., Elizabeth, James H., Barbara W. Instr. econs. Allegheny Coll., 1938-40; planning tchr. Nat. Resources Planning Bd. 1939-43; economist Dept. State, 1943; economist, exec. officer Council Economic Advisers, Washington, 1947-53; asso. dir. Resources for the Future, Inc., Washington, 1953-59, pres., 1959—; trustee Analytic Services, Inc.; vis. prof. U. Colo., 1957, U. Cal., 1971; staff dir. Cabinet Com. Energy Supplies and Policies, 1955; cons. to govt. agys. Mem. Arlington County Bd., 1964—, chmn., 1965, 71. Trustee Unitarian Universalist Assn., 1961-65, moderator, chmn. bd. trustees, 1965—; trustee Tchrs. Ins. and Annuity Assn., 1966—, United Planning Orgn., 1966—; bd. dirs. Met. Washington Council of Govts., 1966—, pres. 1969, chmn., 1970; bd. overseers Bowdoin Coll. Served with inf. AUS, 1943-46. Mem. Am. Forestry Assn. (dir.), Am. Econ. Assn., Am. Soc. Pub. Adminstrn., A.A.A.S. Regional Sci. Assn., Arctic Inst. N.Am., Phi Beta Kappa, Phi Delta Kappa. Club: Cosmos (Wash.). Author: (with others) Resources in America's Future; World Prospects for Natural Resources, Contbr. chpts. in books, articles to profl. jours. Home: 2608 N 24th St Arlington VA 22207 Office: 1755 Massachusetts Av N W Washington DC 20036

FISHER, KENNETH ROBINSON, flouring mill co. exec.; b. Seattle, Dec. 12, 1906; s. William Peter and Estelle (Meeker) F.; B.A., U. Wash., 1928; M.B.A., Harvard, 1930; m. Margarett Olivia Lewis, Oct. 29, 1930; children—Phelps Kenneth, Ann Estelle (Mrs. Peter Charles Hanson). With Fisher Flouring Mills Co., Seattle, 1930—, dir., 1949—, asst. gen. mgr., treas., 1952-60, v.p., gen. mgr., treas., 1960-65, pres., gen. mgr., 1965—; dir. Co., White-Dulany Gallatin Valley Milling Co., Fisher-White-Henry Co., Fisher's Blend Sta., Inc., Societe Candy Co., Magic Prodns., Inc., O.W. Fisher Co., Burr Fisher Corp., Seattle First Nat. Bank, Western Internat. Hotels, Safeco Corp., Millers Nat. Fedn. Finance chmn. Wash. State Citizens for Abortion Reform, 1968-70. Mem. King County Republican Finance Com. and Wash. Central Finance Com., 1964—. Bd. dirs. Seattle Found., Planned Parenthood Center of Seattle, Camp Brotherhood, Inc., Wash. Internat. Trade Fair, Seattle-King County Safety Council, Seattle World Trade Center; mem. vis. com. Grad. Sch. Pub. Affairs, trustee, mem. adv. com. Grad. Sch. Bus. Adminstrn. U. Wash.

Recipient Gulick award Campfire Girls, 1956, Man of Year award Planned Parenthood Center, Seattle, 1969. Mem. Pacific Millers Assn., Poor Richard Investors, Beta Theta Pi. Conglist. Clubs: Rainier, Harbor, Broadmoor Golf, Seattle Golf, Tennis, 49, Harvard Business School (Seattle). Home: 1920 Shenandoah Dr E Seattle WA 98102 Office: 3235 16th Av SW Seattle WA 98134

FISHER, LEON HAROLD, coll. dean, physicist; b. Montreal, Que., Can., July 11, 1918; s. Jacob and Rachel (Haimowitz) F.; brought to U.S., 1920, naturalized, 1925; B.S., U. Cal. at Berkeley, 1938, M.S. 1940, Ph.D., 1943; m. Phyllis Kahn, Dec. 21, 1941; children—Robert Alan, Lawrence Edgar, Carol Lee, David Bruce. Instr. physics U. Cal. at Berkeley, 1943, vis. physics prof., summers 1949, 51, 55; instr. physics U. N.M., 1944; physicist Los Alamos Sci. Lab., 1944-46; asst. prof. physics N.Y. U., 1946-50, asso. prof., 1950-57, prof. physics, 1957-61; vis. physics prof. U. So. Cal., summer 1948; mgr. plasma physics, Lockheed, Missiles and Space Co., 1961- 62, sr. mem. electronic scis. lab., 1963-67, 69-70, asst. mgr. lab., 1967-69, sr. mem. electro optical scis. lab., 1969-70; head plasma physics Gen. Telephone Electric Labs., 1962-63; prof. elec. engring., head dept. information engring. U. Ill. at Chgo. Circle, 1971; prof. physics, dean Sch. Sci., Cal. State Coll., Hayward, 1971—. Cons. Edgerton, Germeshausen & Grier, 1954-55, Radiation Research, 1957-58, Harry Diamond Labs., Wash., 1958-61, Xerox Corp., Rochester, N.Y., 1958- 61, Army Research Office, Durham, N.C., 1958-64, Re-Entry Physics Panel, Nat. Acad. Scis., 1965-66, Monsanto Enviro-Chem. Systems, Inc., 1971—; chmn. Gaseous Electronics Conf., 1948, 67, 68. Fellow Am. Phys. Soc., A.A.A.S.; mem. Am. Assn. Physics Tchrs., I.E.E.E., Phi Beta Kappa, Sigma Xi, Pi Mu Epsilon. Asso. editor Phys. Rev., 1955-58. Contbr. articles profl. publs. Home: 102 Encinal Av Atherton CA 94025 Office: 25800 Hillary St Hayward CA 94542

FISHER, LESLIE HAWES, ret. govt. ofcl.; b. Kansas City, Mo., Aug. 11, 1910; s. Leslie E. and Hulda (Hawes) F.; A.B., U. Kan., 1932; J.D., Washington U., 1936; m. Helen Willis, July 10, 1940; children—Leslie Hawes, Mary Catherine, Laurie Willis. Admitted to Mo. bar, 1934; practice in St. Louis 1934-41; sr. mem. Fisher, Bohn & Durham, 1938-41; atty. FDIC, Washington, 1954-62, asst. gen. counsel, 1962-66, dep. gen. counsel, 1966-70, gen. counsel, 1968-70. Served with USNR, 1941-46; comdr. Res. ret. Mem. Am. Bar Assn., Sigma Phi Epsilon. Methodist. Home: 6141 Beachway Dr Falls Church VA 22041

FISHER, LESTER EMIL, zoo dir.; b. Chgo., Feb. 24, 1921; s. Louis and Elizabeth (Vodicka) F.; V.M.D., Ia. State U., 1943; m. Elizabeth Jane, Oct. 2, 1948; children—Jane Serrita, Katherine Clark. Supr. animal care program Northwestern U. Med. Sch.,1946-47; attending veterinarian Lincoln Park Zoo, Chgo., 1947-62, dir. zoo, 1962—; owner, dir. Berwyn (Ill.) Animal Hosp., 1947-68; producer, moderator ednl. closed circuit TV for nat. vet. meetings, 1949-66; asso. prof. dept. biology DePaul U., 1968—. Mem. citizens com. U. Ill.; chmn. zoo and wildlife div. Morris Animal Found. Served to maj., Vet. Corps, AUS, 1943-46. Recipient Alumni Merit Award, Ia. State Univ., 1968. Mem. Am. Animal Hosp. Assn. (regional dir.; outstanding Service award, 1969), Am. Vet. Med. Assn., Nat. Recreation and Park Assn., Internat. Union Dirs. Zool. Gardens, Am. Assn. Zoo Veterinarians (pres. 1966-69), Am. Assn. Zool. Parks and Aquariums (v.p.), Theta Xi. Clubs: Adventures (pres.), Execs. of Chgo. (bd. dirs. 1968—), Arts. Asso. editor Brit. Small Animal Jour. and Small Animal Clinician, 1958—. Home: 2242 Lincoln Park W Chicago IL 60614 Office: Lincoln Park Zool Garden Chicago IL 60614

FISHER, LINDALE CARSON, banker; b. Wyoming, Del., Jan. 16, 1899; s. William Lindale and Grace May (Carson) F.; student U. Del., 1918-20; B.S., U. Pa., 1923; grad. Army Finance Sch., 1943; m. Mary Valliant Short, June 28, 1924. Accountant James L. Wilson & Co., Phila., 1923-26; accountant balance sheet div., accounting dept. E.I. duPont de Nemours & Co., Wilmington, Del., 1926-29; bank examiner State Banking Dept. of Del., 1929-36, dep. bank commr. of Del., 1936-37, chief dep. bank commr., 1941-42, 44-46; asst. to v.p. Union Nat. Bank, Wilmington, 1937-41; v.p., dir. Farmers Bank State of Del., Dover, 1946-66, also sr. v.p.and pres. Georgetown office. Dir. Milford (Del.) Meml. Hosp. Served as capt., finance dept., AUS, 1942-44. Mem. Am., Del. (mem. exec. com.; pres. 1966) bankers assns., Am. Inst. Banking, Kappa Alpha (So.), Episcopalian (past sr. warden, vestryman, treasurer). Clubs: Sussex Pines Country (Georgetown, Del.); Georgetown-Millsboro Rotary (pres. 1954-55). Home: 209 S Bedford St Georgetown DE 19947

FISHER, LLOYD EDISON, Jr., lawyer; b. Medina, O., Oct. 23, 1923; s. Lloyd Edison and Wanda (White) F.; B.S., Ohio State U., 1947, J.D., 1949; m. Twylla Dawn Peterson, Sept. 11, 1949; children—Karen S., Kirk P. Admitted to Ohio bar, 1950; practice in Columbus, 1962—; mem. gen. hearing bd. Ohio Dept. Taxation, 1950-53; trust officer Huntington Nat. Bank, Columbus, 1953-62; partner firm Alexander, Ebinger, Holschuh & Fisher, Columbus, 1962—; adj. prof. law Ohio State U., 1967-69. Bd. dirs. Seal of Ohio council Girl Scouts U.S., 1969—. Served with AUS, 1943-45. Mem. Am., Ohio, Columbus bar assns., Order of Coif. Methodist (trustee). Home: 174 DeSantis Dr Columbus OH 43214 Office: 17 S High St Columbus OH 43215

FISHER, LOUIS JOSEPH, lawyer, orgn. exec.; b. Waterbury, Conn., Mar. 13, 1901; s. Louis and Philomena (de Zinno) F.; student N.Y.U., 1921, U. N.C., 1925; m. Ethel McMullan, Dec. 29, 1931; children—Louis Joseph III, John Reed, David Kendall. Admitted to N.C. bar, 1925, since practiced in High Point; asst. county atty. Guilford County, 1932-43; pros. atty. High Point Municipal Ct., 1946-51, 60—. Mem. Amateur Athletic Union U.S., 1936—, pres. Carolinas Assn., 1942-50, nat. publicity chmn., 1950, nat. chmn. law and legislation com., 1951-57, mem. exec. com. fgn. relations, 1948—, trustee surplus funds, 1955—, chmn. championships awards, 1959- 60, 1st v.p., 1959-61, pres., 1961—; charter Mercury Athletic Club, High Point, 1941, pres., 1941-43; chmn. High Point Boxing and Wrestling Commn., 1941—; bd. dirs. U.S. Olympic Assn., 1952-56, 56-60, 60—, mem. games coms., 1952—, womens swimming com., 1952—, U.S. rep., 1956-60; U.S. rep. Internat. Amateur Athletic Fedn., 1962—. Sec. Guilford County Rd. Elections, 1933-46; govt. appeal agt. local SSS. 1940—. Vice chmn. Guilford County Dem. Exec. Com., 1931-33; chmn. High Point Township Dem. Exec. Com., 1931-33; mem. N.C. Dem. Com., 1940-46; del. Nat. Dem. Conv., 1944; mayor Pinehaven Village N.C., 1954-56. Trustee Col. Harry B. Henshell Found. Recipient citations and certificates for SSS service; named High Pointer of Week, High Point Enterprise, Dec. 1961; Tar Heel of Week, Raleigh News and Observer, Apr. 1962; citation for sportsmanship for Mo. Legislature; Louis J. Fisher award established by Carolinas assn. U.S. Amateur Athletic Union, 1956. Fellow Internat. Soc. Barristers; mem. Am., N.C., 18th Jud. High Point (pres. 1951-52; award for distinguished service 1951) bar assns., N.C. Bar (mem. council), Amateur Athletic Union (chmn. nat. adv. com., counsellor N.C.), High Point C. of C. Comml. Law League Am., Am. Judicature Soc., Fed. Bar Assn., Delta Theta Phi. Elk. Home: Box 242 Skeet Club Rd High Point NC 27261 Office: 111 Hayden Pl High Point NC 27260

FISHER, LOUIS MCLANE, architect; b. Ruxton, Md., Aug. 3, 1901; s. David Kirkpatrick Este and Sally Jones Milligan (McLane) F.; A.B., Princeton, 1923, M.F.A., 1926; m. Betty Tailer Griswold, Sept. 7, 1934. Employed archtl. offices, N.Y.C., 1926-28, Balt., 1928; in charge design of alterations and additions U.S. Legation, Prague, Czechoslovakia, 1931-32; with Palmer & Lamdin, architects, Balt., 1933-41, asso. partner, 1939-41; chief zone architect QMC, U.S. Army, 1941; partner Fisher, Nes, Campbell & Assos., architects, Balt., and successor firms, 1945—. Mem. Md. Archtl. Registration Bd., 1947-52; mem. Art Commn., City of Balt., 1950- 55. Mem. grad. council Princeton, adv. council Sch. Architecture. Served from capt. to lt. col. constrn. div. C.E., AUS, 1942-45. Fellow A.I.A. (pres. Balt. 1956). Club: Century Assn. (N.Y.C.). Home: Cockeysville MD 21030 Office: 2120 N Charles St Baltimore MD 21218

FISHER, LOWELL BURDETTE, educator; b. Pearl, Ill., Jan. 17, 1909; s. Robert Lee and Olive Mae (Bowen) F.; B.E., Western Ill. U., 1932; M.A., Columbia Tchrs. Coll., 1938; Ed.M., U. Ill., 1947; LL.D., Bradley U., 1956; Litt.D., Jackson Coll., Honolulu, 1958; m. Frances Marie Ferro, Aug. 15, 1934; children—Franca F., Toni Lee. Pub. sch. tchr., Ill., 1932-34, pub. sch. adminstr., 1934-43; asst. high sch. visitor U. Ill., 1943-46, coordinator univ.-sch. relations, prof. edn., 1956-65, univ. coordinator sch. and coll. relations, 1966—. State chmn. North Central Assn. Colls. and Secondary Schs. of Ill., 1945—, exec. sec. com. on admissions secondary schs., 1946-56, coordinator school and univ. relations; mem. Nat. Commn. Study Role of Ind. Schs., 1955-57. Mem. bd. edn., Urbana, 1951—, pres., 1958—; v.p. Nat. Safety Council, 1953—, vice chmn. bd. dirs., 1957—; chmn. Champaign County Devel. Council Found., 1965—. Cons. Am. Overseas Schools for Army and Navy, Eng., Europe, Africa, Greece, Turkey, 1953, 57-60. Mem. Ill. Assn. Sch. Bds. (dir. 1970—). North Central Assn. (chmn. commn. secondary schs. 1952-54, exec. com. 1952-59, v.p. 1956-57, pres. 1957-58), Urbana Assn. Commerce (pres. 1957- 59), Kappa Delta Pi, Phi Delta Kappa. Presbyn. Mason, Moose, Elk, Kiwanian. Author jour. articles. Editor: Your Life Plans and the Armed Forces, 1955. Home: 711 Delaware Av Urbana IL 61801

FISHER, LYLE HARRIS, mfg. exec.; b. Gilby, N.D., Dec. 8, 1912; s. Henry Aiken and Anna Rebecca (Pratt) F.; B.S., Northwestern U., 1935; m. Shirley Ann Larson, July 31, 1937; children—Susan (Mrs. David Ristau), Katherine (Mrs. James Hunter III), Ann (Mrs. David Pheil). With Minn. Mining & Mfg. Co., St. Paul, 1942—, dir. indsl. relations, 1942—, dir. personnel relations, 1954—, v.p. personnel and indsl. relations, 1958-70, v.p. pub. affairs and personnel relations, 1970—; dir. Eastern Heights State Bank, Mut. of Omaha Growth Fund, Mut. Omaha Income Fund. Mem. adv. council Minn. Dept. Employment Security; employer adviser for U.S., Internat. Labor Conf., Geneva, Switzerland, 1969. Past pres. Greater St. Paul United Fund, Inc.; mem. indsl. relations adv. council U. Minn. Trustee Twin City Area Ednl. TV Corp., Mounds Park-Midway Hosp., Children's Hosp. Recipient citation for community service; N.D. Sci., and Industry award, 1965. Mem. N.A.M. (indsl. relations com.), Am. Mgmt. Assn. (personnel planning council, bd. dirs.), U.S. (labor relations com.), St. Paul (dir.) chambers commerce, St. Paul Employers Assn. (past pres.), Delta Tau Delta. Presbyn. Clubs: Gyro, Somerset Country, St. Paul Athletic, Minn. (past pres.); Royal Poinciana Golf (Naples, Fla.). Home: 1624 Edgcumbe Rd St Paul MN 55116 Office: 3M Center St Paul MN 55101

FISHER, MICHAEL ELLIS, educator, math. physicist, chemist; b. Trinidad, W.I., Sept. 3, 1931; s. Harold Wolf and Jeanne Marie (Halter) F.; B.S. with 1st class honors in Physics, King's Coll., London, Eng., 1951, Ph.D., 1957; m. Sorrel Castillejo, Dec. 12, 1954; children—Caricia J., Daniel S., Martin J., Matthew P.A. Lectr. math. RAF, 1952-53; lectr. theoretical physics King's Coll., 1958-62, reader physics, 1962-64; prof. physics U. London, 1964-66; prof. chemistry and math. Cornell U., 1966—; guest investigator Rockefeller Inst., 1963-64; vis. rof. applied physics Stanford, 1970-71; Buhl lectr. theoretical physics Carnegie-Mellon U., 1971. Guggenheim fellow, 1970-71. Fellow Royal Soc. (London); mem. Phys. Soc. London, Am. Phys. Soc. (Langmuir prize chem. physics 1970), Soc. Indsl. and Applied Math., Math. Assn. Am. Author: (with D.M. MacKay) Analogue Computing at Ultra-High Speed, 1962; The Nature of Critical Points, 1964; The Theory of Equilibrium Critical Phenomena, 1967. Asso. editor Jour. Math. Physics, 1963-68; adv. bd. Jour. Theoretical Biology, 1972—. Contbr. articles to profl. jours. Office: Baker Lab Cornell Univ Ithaca NY 14850

FISHER, MILTON JAMES, hosp. adminstr.; b. Hoquiam, Wash., Jan. 6, 1923; s. Milton S. and Myrtle H. (Johnson) F.; student U. Wash., 1942-44; B.S. in Occupational Therapy, U. Puget Sound 1952; M.P.A., Cornell U., 1963; m. Louise Knepley Trump, June 24, 1944; children—Milton Samuel, James Clyde, Michael John, Joseph Patrick, Stephen Paul. Occupational therapist St. Elizabeth's Hosp., Washington, 195254; dir. rehab. therapy Utah State Hosp., Proud, Utah, 195457; activity program coordinator Allentown (Pa.) State Hosp., 195761, asst. supt., 196364; hosp. adminstr. Rochester (Minn.) State Hosp., 1964—. Served to ensign USNR, World War II. Mem. Am. Coll. Hosp. Adminstrs., Am., Minn. hosp. assns. Clubs: Kiwanis (bd. dirs.) Toastmasters (Rochester). Home: 822 8th Av SW Rochester MN 55901 Office: 2110 E Center St Rochester MN 55901

FISHER, O. CLARK, congressman; b. nr. Junction, Tex., Nov. 22, 1903; s. Jobe B. and Rhoda (Clark) Fisher; student U. Tex.; LL.B., Baylor U., 1929; m. Marian DeWalsh, Sept. 12, 1927; 1 dau., Rhoda. Admitted to Tex. bar, 1929; county atty. Tom Green County, 1931-35; state rep., 1935-37; dist. atty. 51st Jud. Dist., 1937-43; mem. 78th to 92d Congresses from 21st Dist. Tex. Democrat. Mem. Acacia. Mason, K.P., O.E.S., Rotarian. Author: It Occurred in Kimble, 1937; (with others) Great Western Indian Fighters, 1960; Texas Heritage of the Fishers and the Clarks, 1964; King Fisher: His Life and Times, 1966. Home: Watergate East Apts Washington DC 20013 Office: Rayburn Office Bldg Washington DC 20510

FISHER, PAUL LESLIE, Jr., educator; b. Fairhaven, Mass., Dec. 8, 1918; s. Paul Leslie and Lettie (Jenny) F.; A.B., U. Mo., 1941, M.A., 1946, Ph.D., 1950; m. Kathryn Potter, Aug. 12, 1942; children—Carley Georganna, Paul Leslie III. Mem. faculty U. Mo., 1952—, prof. journalism, 1956—; dir. Freedom of Information Center, Columbia, 1958—; operator press of Crippled Turtle, 1948—; cons. in field, 1952—. Chmn. Mid-Mo. chpt. Am. Civil Liberties Union, 1968—, chmn. acad. freedom com. Eastern Mo. chpt., 1967—. Served with AUS, 1942-45. Mem. Internat. Center Typographic Arts, Am. Inst. Graphic Arts, Am. Assn. U. Profs., Internat. Council Indsl. Editors. Methodist. Editor: Freedom of Information Digest, 1958—; Freedom of Information in the Marketplace, 1966; Race and News Media, 1967. Home: 1501 W Boulevard Ct Columbia MO 65201

FISHER, PHILIP SYDNEY, ret. publisher; b. Montreal, Can., Mar. 31, 1896; s. Roswell Corse and Mary Field (Ritchie) F.; A.B., McGill Univ., 1916, LL.D., 1962; D.C.L., Bishop's U., 1957, Waterloo Lutheran U., 1966; m. Margaret Linton Southam, June 8, 1920; children—Syndey Mary (Mrs. Rudolph Duder), Guy Southam, Margaret Claire (Mrs. Peter Frederick Kerrigan), John Philip, Gordon Neil, Martha June (Mrs. Hugh Hallward). With real estate firm Walter Molson & Co., Montreal, 1919-20; statis. dept. Royal Securities Corp., 1920-21; with Southam Press, Ltd., 1924-71, pres., 1945-61, chmn. bd., 1961-71. Served in Royal Naval AS, lt., 1917, flight comdr., 1917. Decorated Distinguished Service Order, D.S.C., comdr. Order British Empire (1946); service medal Order of Canada. Mem. Canadian Council on Social Devel. (past pres.), Montreal Council Soc. Agys. (past Pres.), Montreal Red Feather Services (past pres.), Can. Daily Newspapers Assn. (pres. 1946), Can. C. of C. (past chmn. exec. com., 1934-36). Clubs: Royal St. Lawrence Yacht, Royal Automobile, St. James's, Canadian, Montreal Flying, Delta Upsilon (life). Home: 3130 Cedar Av Montreal 218 Quebec Canada

FISHER, RALPH TALCOTT, Jr., educator; b. Washington, Apr. 5, 1920; s. Ralph Talcott and Margaret (Merriam) F.; certificate U. Montpellier (France), 1938; B.A., U. Cal. at Berkeley, 1942, M.A. 1948; certificate Russian Inst., Columbia, 1950, Ph.D. in History, 1955; m. Ruth Paroni Meads, Dec. 20, 1942; children—Ralph Talcott III, Margaret Manson, Albert Meads. From asst. in instrn. to asst. prof. history Yale, 1950-58; asso. prof. history U. Ill., 1958-60, prof. history, dir. Center Russian Lang. and Area Studies, 1960—; research asst. Am. Museum Natural History, 1949; vis. lectr. Russian history U. Cal. at Berkeley, summer 1954. Served to capt. Inf., AUS, 1942-46; China. Grantee Social Sci. Research Council, 1951; Rockefeller Found. fellow, 1956; Fulbright-Hays grantee, 1964; grantee Am. Council of Learned Socs., 1965; Danforth Asso. Mem. Am. Hist. Assn. (chmn. conf. on Slavic and East European history 1969), Am. Assn. Advancement Slavic Studies (sec. 1960-69), Phi Beta Kappa, Alpha Delta Phi. Conglist. Author: Pattern for Soviet Youth: A Study of the Congresses of the Komsomol, 1918-1954, 1959. Editor: (with G. Vernadsky and S. Pushkarev) Dictionary of Russian Historical Terms, 1970. Mem. editorial board Russian Review, 1959—, Slavic Rev., 1969—. Home: 2115 Burlison Dr Urbana IL 61801 Office: Dept History Univ Illinois Urbana IL 61801

FISHER, RAYMOND GEORGE, mfg. exec.; b. Heber City, Utah, June 30, 1911; s. John David and Maude (Van Wagoner) F.; B.S. with honors, U. Utah, 1934; postgrad. George Washington U., 1936-38, Am. U., 1938-39; m. Ruth Bitner, July 27, 1935; 1 son, Stephen Bitner. Jr. economist Bur. Labor Statistics, 1934-35; asst. economist Central Statis. Bd., 1935-39; research adv. U.S. Housing Authority, 1939-40; asst. chief munitions br. W.P.B., 1940-42, asst. to prodn. v. chmn., 1942-43; dir. program control div. Combined Chiefs Staff, 1943-44; adv. mil. programs Office of War Moblzn. and Reconversion, 1944-45; dir. reports and statistics Office of Mil. Govt. for Germany, 1945-46; asst. to bd. dirs. R.F.C., 1946; economist Rockefeller Office, 1946-52; on leave as asst. prodn to dir. Def. Mobilization, 1951; dir. econ. research Continental Can Co. 1952- 58, v.p. marketing for co., 1958-62, v.p., gen. mgr. flexible packaging, 1962-65, v.p., gen. mgr. Central metal div., 1965-67, group v.p. diversified products group, 1967-71, exec. v.p., 1971—; dir. Tee-Pak, Inc., DeLuxe Engraving Co. Adv. formulation European Recovery Program, 1948, Point Four Program, 1949-50. Served as capt. AUS, 1944. Decorated Medal for Freedom, Army Commendation Ribbon. Mem. Am. Statis. Assn., Owl and Key, Pi Kappa Alpha. Clubs: Fairfield Hunt (Westport, Conn.); Pinnacle (N.Y.C.); Weston (Conn.) Gun; Greenwich Country. Home: Deer Park Ct Greenwich CT 06830 Office: 633 3d Av New York City NY 10017

FISHER, RICHARD JULIUS, mfg. co. exec.; b. Avon, Minn., July 10, 1927; s. George and Flora (Hanover) F.; LL.B., Cornell U., 1955; LL.M., N.Y.U., 1956. Profl. baseball player with Cleve. Indians, 1951; labor counsel, asst. gen. counsel M.A. Hanna Co., 1956-60; labor counsel, asst. gen. counsel, dir. labor relations Wis. Gas Co., div. Am. Natural Gas Co., 1960-62; with Cutler-Hammer, Inc., Milw., 1962—, sec.-treas., 1963—, gen. counsel, 1965—; dir. Hubshman Fund. Mem. Wis. Legislative Advisory Com. on Securities Laws, Citizens Govtl. Research bus. Mil. Bd. dirs. St. Joseph's Hosp., Milw., Goodwill Industries Milw., Xavarian Father's Milw., Jr. Achievement Milw., United Community Services, Milw., Pub. Expenditure Survey, Milw., Chgo. Symphony Orch., United Performing Arts Fund, Inc., Milw. Mem. Am. Soc. Corporates Secs., Financial Execs. Inst., Machinery and Allied Products Inst. Home: 1121 N Waverly Pl Milwaukee WI 53202 Office: 4201 N 27th St Milwaukee WI 53216

FISHER, RICHARD VIRGIL, educator; b. Whittier, Cal., Aug. 8, 1928; s. Frank Albert and Aileen (Miller) F.; B.A., Occidental Coll., 1952; Ph.D., U. Wash., 1957; m. Beverly Joyce Taylor, May 2, 1947; children—Susan Lee (Mrs. Robert Plourde), Richard Michael Dianne Elaine, Peter Martin. Acting instr. U. Cal. at Santa Barbara, 1955-57, instr., 1957-58, asst. prof., 1958-63, lectr., 1963-65, asso. prof., 1965-69, prof., 1969—, chmn. dept. geol. scis., 1969—; vis. asso. prof. dept. geosciences and asso. geologist Hawaii Inst. Geophysics, 1965-66. Prin. investigator NASA Apollo 12 lunar samples. Mem. adv. com. Archeol. Research, Inc. Served with AUS, 1946-47. Fellow Geol. Soc. Am. (sec. cordilleran sect. 1961-65); mem. Internat. Assn. Planetology, Hawaii Inst. Geophysics (research affiliate 1965—), Am. Geol. Inst. (vis. lectr. 1970), Sigma Xi. Contbr. articles profl. jours. Home: 6553 Camino Venturoso Goleta CA 93017 Office: Dept Geol Scis U Cal Santa Barbara CA 93106

FISHER, ROBERT DEAN, found. exec.; b. Warsaw, N.Y., July 22, 1903; s. Addison Washburn and Pearl (Nettleton) F.; A.B., Oberlin Coll., 1926; J.D., Western Res., 1931; LL.D., Cal. Coll. Medicine, 1954, Whittier Coll., 1969; m. Elizabeth Gould Woodruff, Dec. 23, 1929; children—Martha Joan (Mrs. Donald L. Winston), Rowland Addison, John Woodruff. Statistician N.Y. Bell Telephone Co., 1926; practice law, Painesville, O., 1931-34; office counsel Western Res. U., 1934-36, sec., 1936-43, v.p.; 1940-43; sec. Cleveland-Cliffs Iron Co., Cliffs Corp. and affiliated cos., 1943-46; financial v.p. U. So. Cal. 1946-58; v.p., dir. Cyprus Mines Corp., 1958-62; financial cons. 1962-68; chmn. Seeley G. Mudd Fund, 1968—. Pres. Sch. Bd. Palos Verdes, 1950-52; chmn. Palos Verdes Good Schs. Assn., 1953-54; mem. citizens Com. on Reorgn. Com. Chest, Los Angeles, 1950-52; profl. adv. com. on restudy needs of Cal. in Higher Edn., 1953-54; charter mem., sec. Assn. Independent Cal. Colls. and Univs., 1955-58, trustee, 1955- 58, 62—; mem. evaluation com. Air Pollution Fedn., Los Angeles, 1956-57; nat. council Pomona Coll., 1964—; mem. adv. bd. Hoover Instn. at Stanford; mem. Pres.'s Commn. on Fed. Statistics, 1970-71. Conglist. Club: California (Los Angeles). Home: 17 Portuguese Bend Rolling Hills CA 90274 Office: 523 W 6th St Los Angeles CA 90014

FISHER, ROBERT JOHN, sugar exec.; b. Buffalo, May 23, 1915; s. Albert J. and Elizabeth (Kulow) F.; B.S., Southeastern U., 1940; student econs., grad. sch. Dept. Agr., 1940-43; m. Alice Lindhurst, June 22, 1940; children—Linda, Janet, Norman, Elizabeth, Judith. Employed as sports writer for the Buffalo Courier-Express, 1932-34; agrl. economist Dept. Agr. and War Food Adminstrn., Washington, 1934-44; asst. to pres. Gt. Western Sugar Co., Denver, 1945-50, treas., 1950-66, v.p., 1961—; v.p. No. Ohio Sugar Co., Denver. Treas., Am. Sugar Beet Industry Policy Com., 1946—. Treas., Colo. Council Chs., 1950-52. Bd. dirs. Luth. Hosp. of Wheatridge, Colo. Mem. Denver C. of C. (dir. 1951-53). Home: 1065 Jackson St Denver CO 80206 Office: Sugar Bldg Denver CO 80217

FISHER, ROBERT SEYMOUR, bus. exec.; b. Hackensack, N.J., Oct. 13, 1907; s. Frederick T. and Adele (Blakeney) F.; A.B., Colgate U., 1930; m. Ruth Jones, Aug. 6, 1930; 1 dau., Lynn. Accountant Corn Products Refining Co., N.Y.C., 1930- 31; lab., plant worker Hubinger

Co., Keokuk, Ia., 1931-33, asst. purchasing agt., 1933-34, v.p., treas., 1934-35, exec. v.p., treas.,1935-46, pres., 1946-54, chmn. bd., chief exec. officer, 1954—; pres. The Hubinger Found.; dir. State Central Savs. Bank. Bd. dirs. Keokuk YM-YWCA (pres. 1968-70); trustee Corn Refiners Assn. (chmn. bd. trustees 1966-68); trustee Graham Hospital. Served as 1st lt. Civil Air Patrol, Anti Submarine Patrol, 1942-43; capt. USAAF, 1943-45, USAF Res., 1945-53. Decorated Air Medal. Mem. S.R., Nat. Pilots Assn., Sigma Nu. Episcopalian (vestryman). Clubs: Bob O'Link Golf, Union League, Tavern, Mid-America (Chgo.); Wings (N.Y.C.); Rotary (pres. 1953-54), Keokuk Country; Philadelphia Gun. Home: Starhaven Keokuk IA 52632 Office: 601 Main St Keokuk IA 52632

FISHER, ROGER DUMMER, lawyer, educator; b. Winnetka, Ill., May 28, 1922; s. Walter Taylor and Katharine (Dummer) F.; grad. N. Shore Country Day Sch., Winnetka, 1939; A.B., Harvard, 1943, LL.B. magna cum laude, 1948; m. Caroline Speer, Sept. 18, 1948; children—Elliott Speer, Peter Ryerson. Admitted to Mass. bar, 1948, D.C. bar, 1950; asst. to gen. counsel, then asst. to dep. U.S. spl. rep. ECA, Paris, 1948-49; with firm Covington & Burling, Washington, 1950-56; asst. to solicitor gen. U.S., 1956-58; lectr. law Harvard Law Sch., 1958-60, prof. law, 1960—; vis. prof. internat. relations dept. London Sch. Econs., 1965-66; cons. pub. affairs editor WGBH-TV, Cambridge, 1969; originator, 1st exec. editor The Advocate series on pub. TV, 1969-70, moderator, 1970-71. Trustee Hudson Inst. Served to 1st lt. USAAF, 1942-46. Guggenheim fellow, 1965-66. Fellow Am. Acad. Arts and Scis.; mem. Am. Soc. Internat. Law (mem. exec. council 1961-64, 66-69), Am. Bar Assn.; Commn. to Study Orgn. of Peace, Council of Fgn. Relations. Club: Metropolitan (Washington). Author: International Conflict for Beginners, 1969. Editor, co- author: International Conflict and Behavioral Science-The Craigville Papers, 1964; asso. editor Jour. Conflict Resolution. Contbr. articles on disarnament and internat. law. Home: 12 Ash Street Pl Cambridge MA 02138

FISHER, ROY MAC, coll. dean; b. Stockton, Kan., Sept. 5, 1918; s. Carey A. and Alice (Bales) F.; B.S., Kan. State U., 1940; Nieman fellow, Harvard, 1950-51; m. Anne Fallon, June 12, 1948; children—Leslie Anne, Patricia Alice, Mary Margaret, Sarah Harkin. Reporter, Hastings (Neb.) Tribune, 1940, Pratt (Kan.) Tribune, 1940-41; reporter Chgo. Daily News, 1945-52, asst. city editor, 1952-56, features editor, 1956-58, editor, 1966-71; dean Sch. Journalism, U. Mo. at Columbia, 1971—; asst. mng. editor World Book Ency., Field Enterprises Ednl. Corp., 1958-60, mng. editor, 1961-64, exec. editor, v.p., 1964-66; lectr. Medill Sch. Journalism, 1950-55. Trustee Garrett Theol. Sem., Chgo. Wesley Hosp., Adler Planetarium. Served to lt. comdr. USNR, 1941- 45; PTO. Named outstanding Young Man of Chgo., 1953; recipient Nat. Headline award, 1953, Page One award, 1952; Sigma Delta Chi award, 1949. Mem. Am. Soc. Newspapers Editors, Sigma Delta Chi. Methodist. Clubs: Press, Tavern (Chgo.); Media (St. Louis). Office: Sch Journalism Univ Missouri Columbia MO 65201

FISHER, RUSSELL ARDEN, educator; b. Ludington, Mich., Sept. 11, 1904; s. Charles McKinley and Sarah Allen(Judge) F.; B.A., U. Mich., 1927, Ph.D., 1931; m. Helen Foster, Aug. 20, 1929. Instr. physics Northwestern U., 1931- 32, asst. prof. 1932-37, asso. prof., 1937-42, prof., 1946—, chmn. dept. physics, 1950-57, acting chmn., 1960-61; tech. cons. govt. agys. Served with AUS, 1942-46. Decorated Bronze Star medal (U.S.); Order Brit. Empire. Mem. Am. Phys. Soc., Optical Soc. of Am., Phi Beta Kappa, Sigma Xi, Phi Kappa Phi, Alpha Kappa Lambda, Gamma Alpha. Contbr. articles tech. jours. Home: 810 Edgewood Lane Glenview IL 60025

FISHER, STERLING WESLEY, mag. exec.; b. at San Antonio, Texas, May 24, 1899 son of Sterling and Sue (Harper) F.; student So. Meth. U., 1916-18; A.B., U. of Tex., 1919; student Sch. of Journalism, Columbia, 1921-22; A.M., U. of Calif., 1924; m. Jean Alice Callahan, Nov. 28, 1923; children—Sterlin, William Murray. Instr. in English, Himeji (Japan) Middle Sch., 1919-21; instr. Ga. Sch. of Tech., 1922-23; prof. of English, U. and Western Japan, Kobe, 1924-29; editorial work Springfield (Mass.) Rep., 1929, Asso. Press, N.Y. 1930; Far Eastern expert and corr. N.Y. Times, 1930-37; represented publisher of N.Y. Times at inauguration of Philippine Govt., Manila, 1935, toured China, Japan and Manchuria for The Times, 1935-36; dir. of Edn., CBS, 1937-42; asst. pub. service counselor, NBC, 1942-48, mgr. pub. affairs and edn. dept., 1948-50; gen. mgr. for Far East, Reader's Digest, 1950-56, dir. public affairs Reader's Digest, 1956-67; now exec. dir. Reader's Digest Found.; chmn. bd. World Press Inst. Macalester Coll. Adv. broadcasting, U.S. Dept. State, 1942-47. Mem. U.S. Com. on Internat. Intellectual Cooperation, Fed. Radio Edn. Com., 1940-42 and 48-50. Served as mayor of Tarrytown, N.Y., 1947- 49. Served with U.S. MC, 1918. Pres. Am. C. of C. in Japan 1951-52; v.p. Am.-Japan Soc. (Tokyo), 1951-56; dir. Internat. House (Tokyo). Mem. U.S. Ednl. Commn. for Japan. Dir. Joseph C. Grew Found., 1952-56. Recipient award of Nat. Sch. Broadcast Conf. for promotion of better relations between North and South Am. by the use of radio, 1941; Magazine Digest Award for outstanding pub. service, 1946. Methodist. Club: Overseas Press. Contbr. to periodicals. Home: 2 Manor Close Sleepy Hollow Manor North Tarrytown NY 10591 Office: Reader's Digest Pleasantville NY 10570 ☆

FISHER, SYDNEY NETTLETON, educator; b. Warsaw, N.Y., Aug. 8, 1906; s. Addison Washburn and Pearl Ellen (Nettleton) F.; A.B., Oberlin Coll., 1928, M.A., 1932; Ph.D., U. Ill., 1935; postgrad. Princeton, 1935, U. Brussels, 1938; m. Elizabeth Evelyn Scipio, Sept. 3, 1938; children—Alan Washburn, Robert Lynn, John Logan, Margaret Ellen. Tutor math. Robert Coll., Istanbul, Turkey, 1928- 31, tutor English, 1936-37; instr. history Denison U., 1935-36; instr. history Ohio State U., 1937-42, asst. prof., 1942-47, asso. prof., 1947-54, prof., 1954—, coordinator Grad. Inst. World Affairs, 1961-65; asso. chief econ. analysis Bd. Econ. Warfare, 1943, Fgn. Econ. Adminstrn., 1943-44; country specialist comml. policy div. Dept. State, 1944-46; lectr. Chautauqua Inst., 1940-42; vis. prof. Stetson U., 1949, U. So. Cal., 1954, 61. Dir. publs. Middle East Inst., 1952-53. Grantee Am. Council Learned Soc., 1935, 38, Social Sci. Research Council, 1958- 59. Fellow Royal Hist. Soc. (London), Ordinario, Accademia del Mediterraneo (Rome, Italy); mem. Am. Hist. Assn., Ohio Acad. History, Phi Beta Kappa, Phi Alpha Theta, Phi Kappa Phi. Presbyn. Author: The Foreign Relations of Turkey, 1481-1512, 1948; Evolution in the Middle East: Revolt, Reform and Change, 1953; Social Forces in the Middle East, 1955; The Middle East: A History, 1959, rev. edition, 1968; The Military in the Middle East, 1962; France and European Community, 1965; New Horizons for the United States in World Affairs, 1966. Editor Middle East Jour., 1952-53. Home: 560 Oxford St Worthington OH 43085

FISHER, SYLVIA GWENDOLINE VICTORIA, (Signora U. Gardini), opera singer; d. John and Margaret (Frawley) Fisher; student St. Joseph's Coll., Kilmore, Australia, also Conservatorium of Music, Mellbourne; m. Ubaldo Gardini, 1954. Operatic debut in Cadmus and Hermoine, 1932; Covent Garden debut in Fidelio, 1948; appeared as Sieglinde, Rome, Italy, 1952, as Isolde, Cagliari, Sardinia, Italy, 1954, as Gutrune, Bologna, 1955, as Brunnhilde, Covent Garden, London, 1956, in Der Rosenkavalier, Frankfurt Opera House, Germany, 1957; on tour, Australia, 1955; now prin. soprano Royal Opera House, London. Winner Sun Aria competition, Melbourne, 1936, Internat. Celebrity Concert, Australia, 1947. Address: 24 Dawson Pl London W2 England*

FISHER, WALTER, corp. exec.; b. 1918; student Pa. State U., also Northwestern U. married. Buyer, Montgomery Ward & Co., 1946-52, appliance mdsg. mgr. Asso. Mdsg. Corp., 1952-54; v.p. sales Norge Sales Corp., 1954-61; with Zenith Sales Corp., div. Zenith Radio Corp., 1961—, pres., 1968—; v.p. marketing Zenith Radio Corp., 1968—. Address: 1900 N Austin Av Chicago IL 60639*

FISHER, WALTER S., bank exec. Auditor, Security Trust Co., Rochester, N.Y. Office: 1 East Av Rochester NY 14604*

FISHER, WALTER TAYLOR, lawyer; b. Chgo., Feb. 20, 1892; s. Walter Lowrie and Mabel (Taylor) F.; grad. Chgo. Latin Sch., 1909; A.B., Harvard, 1913; student law U. Chgo., 1910-15; LL.B., Harvard, 1917; m. Katharine Dummer, Aug. 21, 1915 (dec. 1961); children—Walter, Ethel, John, Roger, Francis, Gerard Henderson; m. 2d, Margaret W. Rieser, Jan. 25, 1962. Law clk. with Matz, Fisher & Boyden, Chgo., 1917; admitted to Ill. bar, 1918, and practiced law in Chgo.; counsel Bell, Boyd, Lloyd, Haddad & Burns. Chmn. Ill. Commerce Commn., 1949-53. Asst. gen. counsel War Finance Corp., Washington, 1921-22; pres. Amalgamated Trust & Savs. Bank, Chgo., 1926-29. Counsel for Chgo. agy. RFC, 1932-33; alternate pub. mem. Nat. Def. Mediation Bd., 1941; mem. Pres.'s Emergency Bds. in nat. nonoperating railway employees case, 1943, and other cases; also mediator, arbitrator or permanent umpire for various labor disputes. Trustee U. Ill., 1929-31. Pres. Chgo. Council Fgn. Relations, 1944-46; lectr. Northwestern U. Law School, 1962. Mem. Am. (chmn. com. on lawyer referral service 1956-57), Ill. State, Chgo. (chmn. com. initiating lawyer reference plan for low-cost legal service 1939-43) bar assns. Clubs: Law, Legal (pres. 1936-37), City (pres. 1925- 27), University, Attic. Home: 877 Dean Av Highland Park IL 60035 Office: 135 S LaSalle St Chicago IL 60603

FISHER, WAYNE H., Jr., corp. exec.; b. 1920; B.A., Pomona Coll., 1942; postgrad. Harvard, 1943, Stanford, 1945-66; married. Pres. Owl Drug Co., Los Angeles, 1947-62; with Lucky Stores, Inc., 1962—, exec. v.p. 1968-71, pres., 1971—, also dir. Served with AUS, 1943-45. Address: 1701 Marine Blvd San Leandro CA 94577*

FISHER, WILBER CLINTON, banker; b. Bedford, Ky., Sept. 3 1901; s. John Joseph and Bettie (Andrews) F.; LL.B., Jefferson Law Sch., 1926; m. Verna Fruechlenicht, Aug. 15, 1928; 1 son, Wilbur C.. With Liberty Nat. Bank & Trust Co., Louisville, 1928—, v.p., cashier, 1939-64, pres., 1964-68, also chmn. bd., dir. Dir. Louisville Water Co. Pres. Louisville Sinking Fund, 1948. Home: 2136 Woodford Pl Louisville KY 40205 Office: 416 W Jefferson St Louisville KY 40201

FISHER, WILLIAM EARL, telephone co. exec.; b. Lonedell, Mo., July 4, 1920; s. Arthur W. and F. Maudie (Lewis) F.; student exec. courses St. Louis U., 1952, Williams Coll., 1958, Dartmouth, 1961; m. Frances Jean Johnson, Dec. 23, 1942; 1 dau., Judith Ann. With Southwestern Bell Telephone Co., 1940-63, v.p., gen. mgr. Mo.-Ill. area, 1962-63; v.p. operation and engring. Chesapeake & Potomac Telephone Cos., 1963—, also dir. Bd. dirs. Boys Club Greater Washington. Served with USMCR, 1942-46, 51-52. Mem. Met. Washington Bd. Trade, Armed Forces Communications and Electronics Assn. Rotarian. Clubs: Army and Navy, Congressional Country (Washington). Home: 9617 Old Spring Rd Kensington MD 20795 Office: 1710 H St NW Washington DC 20006

FISHER, WILLIAM THOMAS, educator; b. Central Falls, R.I., Mar. 15 1918; s. William L. and Sarah (Foley) F.; B.S. with high honors, Am. Internat. Coll., 1949; M.Ed., Boston U., 1951; Ph.D., U. Conn., 1956; postgrad. Clark U., 1954, Columbia, 1957; m. Mary Rowena Donnelly, Dec. 26, 1949; 1 son, William Thomas. Prodn. planner Belding Heminway Corp., Putnam, Conn., 1938-42; prin. Templeton (Mass.) Sch., 1949-50, Tourtelotte High Sch., Thompson, Conn., 1950-57; instr. Becker Jr. Coll., Worcester, Mass., 1955-57; asso. prof. U. State N.Y. at Albany, 1957; asst. dean Sch. Ins., U. Conn., 1957—; adminstrv. dir. Hartford M.B.A. program, 1957-64; vis. prof. Ohio U., summer 1962; dir. Advanced Ins. Industry Sch., IBM Corp., 1960—. Mem. Conn. State Ins. Com. And Conn. State Ins. Purchasing Bd., 1963—, chmn. bd., 1971—; past pres., now dir. Conn. Assn. Municipal Devel. Commns.; mem. Conn. adv. council Small Bus. Adminstrn., 1964-70, chmn., 1967; chmn. evaluation com. Greater Hartford Council Econ. Edn., 1958-60, 62-64, chmn. lectr. com., 1965-66; mem. Thompson Bd. Finance, 1963—; chmn. Thompson Indsl. and Devel. Com., 1964-70, 71—; pres. Thompson Indsl. Found., 1965-66; co-chmn. Quinebaug Valley Indsl. Devel. Council, 1962-64; mem. Gov.'s Conf. on Human Rights and Opportunities, 1967; Thompson Community Devel. Action Program, 1968-69. Organizer Conn. small bus. div. Businessmen for V.P. Humphrey, 1968. Trustee Am. Internat. Coll.; chmn. adv. bd. govs. Conn. Library Service Center, Willimantic, 1964-68, mem. exec. com., 1968- -; past trustee, past pres. Thompson Library; corporator Day Kimball Hosp., Putnam, Conn. Served with AUS, 1942-45. Award of Yr., Hartford Assn. Ins. Women, 1969; Presdl. Certificate Appreciation, Conn. Assn. Municipal Devel. Commns., 1968. Mem. Nat., Conn. edn. assns., Am. Assn. Sch. Adminstrs., Am. Risk and Ins. Assn. (fellowship 1960-62), Ins. Co. Edn. Dirs. Soc., Internat. Platform Assn., Life Ins. Agy. Mgmt. Assn., Northeastern Indsl. Developers Assn., Conn. Council Advancement Econ. Edn., Am. Legion, Phi Delta Kappa, Delta Pi Epsilon. Contbr. profl. jours. Home: Chase Rd Thompson CT 06277 also 187 N Oxford St Hartford CT 06105 Office: 39 Woodland St Hartford CT 06105

FISHER, YULE, assn. exec.; b. Edwardsville, Ill., Jan. 15, 1912; s. Martin Hamilton and Marguerite Wheeler (Metcalfe) F.; A.B., Am. U., 1932; LL.B., J.D., George Washington U., 1935; m. Genevieve Wilder Marsh, June 3, 1949; children—David Yule, Genevieve Cutler, Charles Martin. With Nat. Hwy. Users Conf., Washington, 1934-69, dir. research counsel, 1968-69; exec. v.p. Hwy. Users Fedn. for Safety and Mobility, Washington, 1970—. Bd. dirs. Home Bldg. Assn., Washington; bd. mgmt. Camp Letts, YMCA. Chmn., Nat. Com. on Uniform Traffic Laws, 1964—. Served to lt. comdr. USNR, 1942-45. Recipient Alumni award Am. U., 1964, citation for Distinguished Service Nat. Com. Uniform Traffic Laws, 1971, Silver Beaver award Boy Scouts Am., 1939. Mem. Hwy. Research Bd., Alpha Tau Omega. Contbr. articles to profl. lit. Home: 5514 Center Chevy Chase MD 20015 Office: 1776 Massachusetts Av Washington DC 20036

FISHER OF LAMBETH, MOST REV. AND RT. HON. LORD GEOFFREY FRANCIS, former archbishop Canterbury; b. Higham Rectory, Nuneaton, Eng., May 5, 1887; s. Rev. Henry and Katharine (Richmond) F.; student Marlborough Coll., 1901-06; B.A., Exeter Coll., Oxford, 1910, M.A.,1913; D.D. Oxford, 1933, Cambridge, 1946, Princeton, 1946, Edinburgh, 1953, Seabury- Western Theol. Sem., 1954, Trinity Coll., 1961; LL.D., U. Pa., Columbia, 1946, London, 1948, Manchester Univ., 1950, Yale, 1954, U. British Columbia, 1954; D.S.T., Northwestern U., Evanston, 1954; Th.D. (hon.), General Theol. Sem. N.Y.C., 1957; D.C.L., Assumption U., Windsor, Canada, 1962; m. Rosamond C. Forman, April 12, 1917; 6 sons. Ordained to the ministry of the Ch. of Eng., deacon 1912, priest 1913; consecrated bishop, 1932; asst. master Marlborough Coll., 1911-14; headmaster Repton Sch., Derbyshire, Eng., 1914-32; bishop of Chester, 1923-39, bishop of London, 1939-45; dean of Chapels Royal, Prelate of Order of British Empire, Archbishop of Canterbury, 1945-61. Privy Councillor, 1939—. Prelate Order of St. John of Jerusalem. Pres. World Council Chs., 1946-54. Royal Victorian Chain, 1949. Recipient Grand Cross Order of Redeemer (Greece), Grand Cross of St. Olav (Norway), Order of White Lion, 2d Class (Czechoslovakia); Freeman of Cities of London and Canterbury, 1952; Knight Grand Cross of Royal Victoria Order, 1953. Honorary fellow Exeter Coll. Oxford, 1939. Pres. World Council Chs., 1946. Address: Trent-Rectory Sherborne Dorsetshire England

FISHMAN, ABRAHAM, lawyer; b. Evansville, Ind., Jan. 23, 1909; s. Myer and Rose (Belgrade) F.; B.S., Northwestern U., 1929, J.D., 1932; m. Florence Cooper, June 30, 1935. Admitted to Ill. bar, 1931; practice in Chgo., 1932—; partner firm Sonnenschein, Levinson, Carlin, Nath & Rosenthal, 1949—; lect. N.Y.U. Inst. Federal Taxation, 1960. Trustee, sec. Chgo. Planetarium Soc. Served with AUS, World War II. Mem. Am., Ill., Chgo. bar assns., Order of Coif, Tau Epsilon Rho. Club: Standard (Chgo.). Home: 3150 Lake Shore Dr Chicago IL 60657 Office: 69 W Washington St Chicago IL 60602

FISHMAN, ERWIN, educator; b. Cleve., Nov. 7, 1927; s. Herman B. and Rosanna (Feingold) F.; A.B., Oberlin Coll., 1950; Ph.D., Brown U., 1954; m. Lois Lyman, June 24, 1950; children—Stephen, Sarah, Rebecca, Elizabeth, Ellen. Research asso. U. Ill., 1954-55; prof. chemistry Syracuse U., 1955-69, U. Bordeaux (France), 1960; prof., chmn. dept. chemistry Union Coll., Schenectady, 1969—. Served with AUS, 1945-46. Mem. Am. Chem. Soc., Am. Inst. Physics, Am. Assn. Univ. Profs., A.A.A.S., Sigma Xi. Home: 1234 Lowell Rd Schenectady NY 12308

FISHMAN, JOSHUA AARON, educator, sociologist; b. Phila., July 18, 1926; s. Aaron S. and Sonia (Horwitz) F.; B.S., M.S. (Mayor Phila. competitive scholar 1944-48), U. Pa., 1948; Ph.D., Columbia, 1953; Ped.D. (hon.), Yeshiva U., 1968; m. Gella Jeanne Schweid, Dec. 23, 1951; children—M. Manuel, David Elliot, Avrom. Tchr. elementary and secondary Jewish secular schs., 1945-50; ednl. psychologist, sr. research asso. dept. research and experimentation Jewish Edn. Com. N.Y., 1951-54; from lectr. to vis. prof. psychology Coll. City N.Y., 1955-58; research asso. to dir. research Coll. Entrance Exam. Bd., 1955-58; asso. prof. human relations and psychology U. Pa., 1958-60; prof. psychology, dean Grad. Sch. Edn., Yeshiva U., 1960-66, prof. psychology, sociology, Distinguished U. Research prof. social scis. Ferkauf Grad. Sch. Humanities and Social Scis., 1966—; sr. specialist Inst. Advanced Projects, East-West Center, U. Hawaii, 1968-69. Com. on sociolinguistics Social Sci. Research Council. Adviser, cons. Am. Jewish Congress, Nat. Scholarship Service and Fund for Negro Students, Coll. Entrance Exam. Bd., Am. Assn. Jewish Edn., Ministry of France, Republic of Ireland. Pres.'s scholar E.C. Morris fellow Columbia Tchrs. Coll., 1952- 53; postdoctoral research tng. fellow Social Sci. Research Council, 1954- 55; NSF European Conf. Grant, 1960; Social Sci. Research Council European Conf. grant, 1961; fellow Center Advanced Study Behavioral Scis., 1963-64; Nat. Inst. Mental Health grant, Latin Am., 1963, 66; NSF grantee, Europe, 1966. Fellow Am. Psychol. Assn., Am. Sociol. Assn., A.A.A.S.; mem. Am. Anthrop. Assn., Am. Ednl. Research Assn., Linguistic Soc. Am., Yivo Inst. Jewish Research, Am. Assn. U. Profs. Author: Language Loyalty in the United State; Readings in the Sociology of Language; Bilingualism in the Barrio; Language Problems of Developing Nations; Sociolinguistics; The Sociology of Language; Advances in the Sociology of Language; Yiddish in America; also numerous prof. publs. Asso. editor Jour. Ednl. Sociology, 1963-65; editor Jour. Social Issues, 1964-69, Yivo Bleter, 1970—, Yivo Annual, 1970—. Home: 3340 Bainbridge Av New York City NY 10467 Office: 55 Fifth Av New York City NY 10003

FISHMAN, MEYER H., business exec.; b. Russia, 1892; married. With M.H. Fishman Co., Inc., N.Y.C., 1917—, now chmn. bd., dir. Mason (Shriner). Home: 115 Central Park West New York City NY 10023 Office: 300 Park Av S New York City NY 10010

FISHMAN, RALPH HENRY, lawyer; b. New Orleans, Feb. 8, 1915; s. Abraham Leon and Anna (Campell) F.; J.D. cum laude, Loyola U. of the South, 1941; m. Elise Ruth Yarrut, Dec. 28, 1938; children—Louis Y., Ann C. Admitted to La. bar, 1941; law clk. La. Supreme Ct., 1941-42; chief rent atty. OPA, New Orleans, 1942-44; partner Yarrut & Fishman, New Orleans, 1944-48, Fishman, Reuter, Rosenson & D'Aquin, New Orleans, 1949-58, Sessions, Fishman, Rosenson, Snellings & Boifontaine, New Orleans, 1958—. Dir. Bank New Orleans, Central Savs. & Loan Assn. New Orleans., Equity Industries, Inc., New Orleans. Exec. com. Combined New Orleans Tourist Commn., 1971. Trustee Community Chest, Children's Bur. New Orleans, Jewish Welfare Fedn., New Orleans Home for Jewish Aged. Jewish Community Center; bd. dirs. Children's Bur. New Orleans. Mem. Am., La., New Orleans bar assns., Blue Key, Alpha Sigma Nu. Home: 400 Audubon Blvd New Orleans LA 70125 Office: Bank New Orleans Bldg New Orleans LA 70112

FISHMAN, ROBERT ALLEN, educator, neurologist; b. N.Y.C., May 30, 1924; s. Samuel Benjamin and Miriam (Brinkin) F.; A.B., Columbia, 1944; M.D., U. Pa., 1947; m. Margery Ann Satz, Jan. 29, 1956; children—Mary Beth, Alice Ellen, Elizabeth Ann. Mem. faculty Columbia Coll. Phys. and Surg., 1954-66, asso. prof. neurology, 1962-66; asst. attending neurologist N.Y. State Psychiat. Inst., 1955-66; asst. attending neurologist Neurol. Inst. Presbyn. Hosp., N.Y.C., 1955-61, asso., 1961-66; co-dir. Neurol. Clin. Research Center, Neurol. Inst., Columbia-Presbyn. Med. Center, 1961-66; prof. neurology, chmn. dept. U. Cal. Med. Center, San Francisco, 1966—; cons. neurologist San Francisco Gen. Hosp., San Francisco VA Hosp., Letterman Gen. Hosp Nat. Multiple Sclerosis Soc. fellow, 1956-57; John and Mary R. Markle scholar in med. sci., 1960-65. Mem. Am. Neurol. Assn., Am. Fedn. for Clin. Research, Harvey Soc., Assn. for Research in Nervous and Mental Diseases, Am. Acad. Neurology (v.p. 1971-72), N.Y. Neurol. Soc., Assn. U. Profs., Neurology, A.A.A.S., Am. Epilepsy Soc., N.Y. Acad. Scis., A.M.A. (sec. sect. on nervous and mental diseases 1964-67, v.p. 1967-68, pres. 1968-69). Contbr. articles profl. jours. Home: 26 Southridge E Tiburon CA 94920 Office: U Cal Med Center 794 Herbert C Moffitt Hosp San Francisco CA 94122

FISHMAN, WILLIAM SAMUEL, corp. exec.; b. Clinton, Ind., Jan. 26, 1916; s. Max and Fanrie (Dumes) F.; student Sch. Internship Polit. Sci., Washington, 1934-35; B.A. with highest honors in Polit. Sci., U. Ill., 1936; postgrad. U. Chgo., 1936-37; D.Bus. Adminstrn., Bryant Coll., 1968; LL.D., Lincoln Meml. U., 1969; m. Clara K. Silvian, June 28, 1936; children—Alan L., Fred B., David J. Exec. v.p. Automatic Mdsg. Co., Inc., Chgo., 1942-56, pres., 1956-59; sr. v.p. ARA Services, Inc., Phila., 1959-63, exec. v.p., 1963-64, pres., 1964—; dir. Versafood Services, Ltd., Can., Fidelity Bank, Phila. Chmn. automatic merchandising division Combined Jewish Appeal Chgo., 1959, Allied Jewish Appeal Phila., 1963-71; pres. Jewish Publ. Soc. Am.; v.p. Big Bros. Am. Fellow Brandeis U.; trustee Bryant Coll.; bd. dirs. Phila. Orch. Assn., Robin Hood Dell Concerts, ACES, Phila. Crime Commn.; chmn. bd. dirs. Phila. Music Acad. Mem. Nat. Restaurant Assn., Nat. Automatic Mdsg. Assn. (dir., exec. com., pres.

1958-59), Phi Beta Kappa, Phi Kappa Phi, Delta Sigma Rho. Jewish religion (past pres. synagogue). Clubs: Standard (Chgo.); Harmonie (N.Y.C.); Palm Beach (Fla.) Country; Locust, Ashbourne Country (Phila.). Home: 2124 Delancey Pl Philadelphia PA 19103 Office: ARA Services Inc Independence Sq W Philadelphia PA 19146

FISHPAW, KENNETH B., dairy products co. exec.; b. Pickerington, O., Aug. 24, 1910; s. Jesse F. and Cora B. (Lawyer) F.; B.S., Ohio State U., 1932; m. Ednah B. Young, Mar. 28, 1936; 1 dau., Anita (Mrs. Evan Bukey). Accountant, Ernst & Ernst, C.P.A.'s, Cleve., 1932-33; treas. Banks-Baldwin Law Pub. Co., Cleve., 1933-40; with Kraftco Corp., 1941—, comptroller, 1964—, v.p., 1971—. C.P.A., Ohio. Mem. Am. Inst. C.P.A.'s, Financial Execs. Inst. Clubs: Union League (N.Y.C.); Country (Darien). Home: 10 Haskell Lane Darien CT 06820 Office: 260 Madison Av New York City NY 10016

FISHWICK, JOHN PALMER, r.r. exec.; b. Roanoke, Va., Sept. 29, 1916; s. William and Nellie (Cross) F.; A.B., Roanoke Coll., 1937; LL.B., Harvard, 1940; m. Blair Wiley, Jan. 4, 1941; children—Ellen Blair, Anne Palmer, John Palmer. Admitted to Va. bar, 1939; asso. Cravath, Swaine & Moore, N.Y.C., 1940- 42; asst. to gen. solicitor N. & W. Ry., Roanoke, Va., 1945-47, asst. gen. solicitor, 1947-51, asst. gen. counsel, 1951-54, gen. solicitor, 1954-56, gen. counsel, 1956-58, v.p., gen. counsel, 1958-59, v.p. law, 1959-63, sr. v.p., dir., then pres., chief exec. officer, dir., 1963—; former chmn., chief exec. officer Erie Lackawanna Ry. Co.; former pres., chief exec. officer Del. and Hudson Ry. Co., Dereco, Inc., now dir.; dir. Trailer Train Co., Akron, Canton & Youngstown R.R., Va. Commonwealth Corp., Pocahontas Land Corp., Va. Holding Corp. Pres., United Fund of Roanoke Valley, 1960, dir., 1959-62, campaign chmn. 1959. Trustee Roanoke Coll., Salem, Va.; bd. dirs. Roanoke Fine Arts Center. Served as lt. comdr. USNR, 1942-45. Mem. Am., Va. (exec. com. 1959-62), Roanoke bar assns., Am. Law Inst., Newcomen Soc. N.A., Va. (dir. 1959-62, 65—), Roanoke (pres. 1958) C.'s of C., Kappa Alpha, Tau Kappa Alpha. Episcopalian. Clubs: City Tavern Assn. (Georgetown); Commonwealth, Shenandoah (Roanoke); Duquesne (Pitts); Metropolitan (Washington). Home: 535 Market St Salem VA 24153 Office: 106 N Jefferson St Roanoke VA 24011

FISK, JAMES BROWN, physical scis. research exec.; b. West Warwick, R.I., Aug. 30, 1910; s. Henry James and Bertha (Brown) F.; B.S., Mass. Inst. Tech., 1931, Ph.D., 1935; M.A. (hon.), Harvard, 1947; D.Sc., Carnegie Inst. Tech., 1956, Williams Coll., 1958, Newark Coll. Engring., 1959, Columbia, 1960, Colby Coll., 1962, N.Y.U., 1963, Rutgers, the State U., 1967; D.Engring., U. Mich., 1963, U. Akron, 1963; Lehigh U., 1967, Ill. Inst. of Tech., 1967; D.Sc. (hon.), Drew U., Harvard U., 1969; Litt.D. (hon.), Newark State Coll., 1969; m. Cynthia Hoar, June 10, 1938; children—Samuel, Zachary, Charles. Research asst. aero. engring., Mass. Inst. Tech., 1931; Proctor travelling fellow, Trinity Coll., Cambridge, Eng., 1932-34; teaching fellow physics Mass. Inst. Tech., 1934-36; Soc. of Fellows, Harvard, 1936-38; asso. prof. of physics U. N.C., 1939; electronics research engr., asst. dir., phys. research Bell Telephone Labs., 1939-47, dir., 1949-51, dir. research-phys. scis., 1952-54, v.p. research, 1954-55, exec. v.p., 1955-58, dir., 1955—, pres. Bell Telephone Labs., 1959—; dir. Cummins Engine Co., Am. Cyanamid Co., Equitable Life Assurance Soc., Sandia Corp., Am. Nat. Bank & Trust. Gordon McKay prof. applied physics, Harvard, 1947-49, sr. fellow, Soc. Fellows, 1949; dir. div. research AEC, 1947-48, mem. gen. adv. com., 1952-58; mem. President's Sci. Adv. Com., 1957-60, cons., 1960—. Mem. Mass. Inst. Tech. Corp.; trustee John Simon Guggenheim Meml. Found., Alfred P. Slaon Found.; bd. overseers Found. for Advancement of Grad. Study in Engring., Newark Coll. Engring., Harvard U., 1961-67. Recipient Indsl. Research Inst. Medal, 1963; citation Midwest Research Inst., 1968; Washington award Western Soc. Engrs., 1968; Presdl. certificate of Merit, World War II. Fellow Am. Phys. Soc. Am. Acad. Arts and Scis., I.E.E.E.; mem. of Nat. Acad. Engring., Nat. Acad. Sci., Am. Philos. Soc., Sigma Xi, Tau Beta Pi. Clubs: Harvard (N.Y.C.); Ausable (St. Huberts, N.Y.); Somerset Hills. Asso. editor Phys. Rev., 1945-48. Contbr. articles of profl. periodicals. Home: Lee's Hill Rd Basking Ridge NJ 07920 Office: Bell Telephone Labs Murray Hill NJ 07974

FISK, MCKEE, educator; b. Alton, Ill., Feb. 4, 1900; s. Elmer McReynolds and Maud Ella (McKee) F.; A.B., Oklahoma City U., 1923; A.M., U. So. Cal., 1926; Ph.D., Yale, 1936; m. Laura R. Best, Nov. 26, 1931; children—Donald M., Karolus A., Patricia Ann. Tchr. Denison (Tex.) High Sch., 1923-25; instr. Santa Ana (Cal.) Coll., 1925-26, dean, 1926-35; instr. Yale, 1935-36; prof. bus. edn. Okla. State U., 1936-40, U. N.C. at Greensboro, 1940-43; chief bus. and sales tng. div. vocational rehab. and edn. Central Office VA, 1943-45; editor bus. edn. McGraw-Hill Book Co., 1945-48; prof. bus. adminstrn., dean sch. bus. Fresno State Coll., 1948- -69, dean emeritus, 1969—, accreditation com. Bus. Sch., 1950- 68; prof. bus. adminstrn. Grad. Sch. Bus., U. Santa Clara, 1969—; AID adviser, cons. to dean bus. adminstrn. faculty and dir. Inst. Bus. Adminstrn., U. Karachi, Pakistan, 1962, 64; prof. U.So. Cal., Bitburg, Germany, 1970; mem. of bus. profl. adv. com. Cal. Dept. Edn., 1952-56; chmn. adv. com. San Joaquin Valley Council on Econ. Edn., 1952-55; mem. bd. Inst. of Antiquity and Christianity. Recipient Distinguished Service award United Bus. Schs. Assn. Collegiate Schs. Bus., 1968, Cal. Bus. Edn. Assn., 1969; Am. Vocational Assn. Award, 1966. Mem. Nat. Bus. Tchrs. Assn. (hon.), Cal. Bus. Edn. Assn. (pres. 1952-53), Nat. Bus. Edn. Assn. (hon.), Blue Key, Phi Chi Theta (hon.), Delta Pi Epsilon (nat. pres. 1939-41), Phi Kappa Phi, Alpha Kappa Psi, Sigma Alpha Epsilon, Beta Gamma Sigma. Conglist. Author: (with W.E. Grimes) Farm Accounting, 1938; (with D.A. Pomeroy) Applied Business Law, 1944, rev., 1950, (with J.C. Snapp), 1955, rev. edit., 1960. 66; Introduction to Business Law, 1957, rev. edit., 1962, 67. Editor: Nat. Bus. Tchrs. Assn. Yearbook 1940, 41, 42, 43. Home: 880 W Cliff Dr Santa Cruz CA 95060

FISK, ROBERT SATTERLEE, educator; b. Coleraine, Minn., Oct. 7, 1913; s. Frank Satterlee and Ada (Kremer) F.; B.A., Grinnell Coll., 1935; M.A., U. Minn., 1940; Ed.D., Columbia, 1943; m. Jeanne H. Bishop, June 18, 1939; children—Elizabeth, John, Paul. Tchr., prin., Minn., 1935-41; confidential sec. of mem. N.Y.C. Bd. Edn., 1942-43, 46; tchr. sch. adminstrn. U. Minn., summer 1946, N.Y. State Coll. for Tchrs., 1946-48, Syracuse U., 1948-53; dean Sch. of Edn., dir. summer session State U. N.Y., BUffalo, 1953-67, prof. ednl. studies, 1968—; prin. Milne Sch., Albany, 1946-48; cons. secondary edn., tchr. edn. Govt. Pakistan, 1957; vis. scholar Inst. Edn., U. London, 1967-68; Fulbright lectr. Haifa U. Coll., 1968. Chmn. Nat. Conf. of Profs. Ednl. Adminstrn., 1952-53. Served with USNR, 1943-46. Mem. Phi Delta Kappa. Unitarian-Universalist. Contbr. articles profl. jours. Home: 4200 Harris Hill Rd Williamsville NY 14221 Office: State U NY at Buffalo BUffalo NY 14214

FISK, SHIRLEY CARTER, physician; b. N.Y.C., June 25, 1910; s. Arthur Lyman and Alice Bowie (Carter) F.; grad. Hill Sch., 1927; B.A., Yale, 1931; M.D., Columbia, 1935; m. Mary Averell Harriman, Apr. 29, 1940; children—Robert Carter, Kathleen Lawrence, Averell Harriman. Intern Presbyn. Hosp., N.Y.C., 1935- 37, asso. attending physician, 1958—; pvt. practice internal medicine, N.Y.C., 1937-63; attending physician VA Hosp., Kingsbridge Rd., N.Y., 1945-63; cons. Tuxedo Meml. Hosp., Tuxedo Park, N.Y., 1951-63; asso. clin. prof. medicine Columbia, 1958—, asso. dean Coll. Physicians and Surgeons, 1967—, asso. prof. clinical medicine, 1967—, dep. asst. sec. def. for manpower, health and med., Dept. Def., 1963-67; Mem. Health Resources Adv. Com.; ex-officio mem. Nat. Adv. Health Council, 1963-67. Served to maj., M.C., AUS, 1941-45. Diplomate Am. Bd. Internal Medicine. Mem. Soc. Med. Cons. Armed Forces, A.M.A., A.C.P., N.Y. County Med. Soc., N.Y. Acad. Medicine, Alpha Omega Alpha. Club: Century Assn. (N.Y.C.). Home: 180 East End Av New York City NY 10028 Office: 630 W 168 St New York City NY 10032

FISK, WILLIAM LYONS, coll. adminstr.; b. Newark, O., Feb. 24, 1921; s. William L. and June (Lyons) F.; A.B., Muskingum Coll., 1941; M.A., Ohio State U., 1944, Ph.D., 1946; m. Beatrice Sprague, Aug. 1, 1962; children—Elizabeth Sprague, John Lyons. Asst. prof. history Muskingum Coll., 1946-47, asso. prof., 1947-55, prof., 1955—, chmn. dept., 1957-67, v.p. acad. affairs, 1968—. Mem. Am. Hist. Assn. Rotarian. Home: 159 Harper St New Concord OH 43762

FISKE, DONALD WINSLOW, educator, psychologist; b. Lincoln, N.H., Aug. 27, 1916; A.B., Harvard, 1937, A.M., 1939; Ph.D., U. Mich., 1948; m. Barbara Page; children—Alan, Susan. Instr., Cambridge Jr. Coll., 1939-41; asst. Harvard, also Radcliffe Coll., 1939-40; research asso. Phillips Acad., 1940-42; instr. Wellesley Coll., 1941; from asst. project dir. to instr. U. Mich., 1946-48; mem. faculty U. Chgo., 1948—, prof. psychology, 1960—, asso. chmn. dept., 1963-68. Mem. study panel in mental health Nat. Inst. Mental Health. Served with USNR, 1942-43, 46; with OSS, 1944-45. Fellow A.A.A.S.; mem. Am. (chmn. com. psychol. tests 1957-58, conv. com. 1964-65), Midwestern (sec.-treas. 1955-58, pres. 1962-63) psychol. assns., Am. Assn. U. Profs., Soc. Multivariate Exptl. Psychology (pres. 1968-69), Sigma Xi. Author: (with others) Assessment of Men, 1948; (with E.L. Kelly) The Prediction of Performance in Clinical Psychology, 1951; (with S. Maddi) Functions of Varied Experience, 1961; Measuring the Concepts of Personality, 1971; also articles. Home: 5711 Blackstone Av Chicago IL

FISKE, KENNETH MORTON, lawyer; b. Chgo., June 16, 1894; s. John T. and Jennie (Frazier) F.; LL.B., Chgo.-Kent Coll. Law, 1916, J.D., 1917; m. Eunice Van Dyne, Sept. 29, 1923; children—Kenneth Van Dyne, Mary Virginia. Admitted to Ill. bar, 1916, since practiced in Chgo.; partner Defrees, Fiske, Voland, Alberts & Hoffman, corp. real estate and probate law. Served as ensign, Overseas Transport Service, USN, World War I. Mem. Am., Ill., Chgo. bar assns., Am. Legion, Phi Alpha Delta. Republican. Methodist. Mason. Clubs: Union League; Dairymen's Country; Woodstock Country. Home: 530 Devonshire Lane Crystal Lake IL 60014 Office: 72 W Adams St Chicago IL 60603

FISKE, LAWRENCE FARRIMOND, steamship co. exec.; b. N.Y.C., Nov. 2, 1911; s. John W. and Marie (Dawson) F.; B.A., Colgate U., 1934; grad. Advanced Mgmt. Program, Harvard, 1961; m. Jacqueline Barker, Apr. 22, 1938; children—Michael John, Terry (Mrs. Perrett), Lawrence, Susan Barker. With Am. Can Co., 1936-37; successively gen. mgr., asst. to pres., sec., dir. Seas Shipping Co., 1937-57; with Moore-McCormack Lines, Inc., 1957—, sr. v.p., 1965-68, exec. v.p., 1968-70, pres., 1970-71, also dir.; exec. v.p. Moore and McCormack Co., Inc., 1965-70, pres., 1970, vice chmn. bd., 1971—; former exec. v.p., dir. Trident Leasing, now pres., chmn. bd.; dir. Tidewater Terminals Inc., U.S. Hydrofoils. Clubs: Wee Burn Country (Darien, Conn.); India House, New York Athletic (N.Y.C.). Home: 14 Dorechester Rd Darien CT 06820 Office: 2 Broadway New York City NY 10004

FISKE, VIRGINIA MAYO, educator; b. Bklyn., Sept. 21, 1910; d. Virginius J. and Lois (Waterbury) Mayo; B.A., Mt. Holyoke Coll., 1932, M.A., 1934; Ph.D., Radcliffe Coll., 1939; m. George Farrington Fiske, Sept. 17, 1938; children—John Mayo, George Farrington, Katharine Reid. Asst. Mt. Holyoke Coll., 1932-34; tchr. Dana Hall Sch., Wellesley, Mass., 1934-37; tchr. sci. Winsor Sch., Boston, 1937-38, 39-41, 42-43; research asst. Harvard, 1938-39; research endocrinology Pratt Diagnostic Clinic, Boston, 1942; mem. faculty Wellesley Coll., 1943—, prof. zoology and physiology, 1964—, chmn. dept. biol. scis., 1964-67. Mem. Sherborn School Com., 1955-61. Sr. Postdoctoral fellow NSF, 1956-57; recipient Alumnae award Radcliffe Coll. Grad. Assn., 1966. Mem. Phi Beta Kappa, Sigma Xi. Author articles in field. Home: 27 Hollis St Sherborn MA 01770 Office: Dept Biol Sciences Wellesley Coll Wellesley MA 02181

FISTER, GORDON BRONG, newspaper editor; b. Allentown, Pa., June 8, 1911; s. William Trexler and Mary (Brong) F.; student Muhlenberg Coll., 1929-33; m. Caroline Miles Sherrill, Sept. 21, 1934; children—Barbara Ann (Mrs. David M. Graf), Sarah Way (Mrs. Charles H. Van Auken). Reporter, Call-Chronicle Newspapers, Allentown, 1931-49, asst. mng. editor, 1949-50, promotion dir., 1950-60, asso. editor, 1960-66; editor Morning Call, 1966—; pub. relations dir. Muhlenberg Coll., editor Alumni Mag., 1937-49. Sec. Phoebe Apts., Inc. Mem. Lehigh Valley Hosp. Planning Council, 1966—; coordinating dir. Lehigh Valley Sci. Fair, 1952-70; chmn. Internat. Sci. Fair Council, 1961-64. Vice pres. Lehigh County Hist. Soc.; trustee Sci. Service, Inc., Lehigh Count Homemaker Service. Mem. Pa. Soc. Newspapers Editors, Pi Delta Epsilon. Republican. Mem. United Ch. of Christ. Rotarian. Author: Allentown Hospital Half Century, 1949. Home: 2343 Allen St Allentown PA 18104 Office: 101 N 6th St Allentown PA 18105

FITCH, ALVA REVISTA, mil. editor; b. Amherst, Neb., Sept. 10, 1907; s. John Albert and Gertrude (de la Barre) F.; B.S., U.S. Mil. Acad., 1930; grad. U.S. Army Arty. Sch., 1935, Command and Gen. Staff Sch., 1946, Strategic Intelligence Sch., 1947, Armed Forces Staff Coll., 1951, Army War Coll., 1954; m. Carolyn Shaw, Oct. 3, 1935; children—Carolyn (Mrs. Thomas N. Weiskirch, Jr.), John Albert. Commd. 2d lt. U.S. Army, 1930, advanced through grades to lt. gen., 1964; various assignments U.S. and Philippines, 1930-42; provisional battalion and group comdr. Philippine Army, 1942; prisoner of war, 1942-45; instr. Command and Gen. Staff Sch., 1946-47; army attache, El Salvador, 1948-50; chief Latin Am. sect. G-2, Dept. of Army, 1951, asst. chief prodn. div. G-2, 1951-52; exec. officer IX Corps arty., Korea, 1952-53; exec. officer G-2, Dept. of Army, 1954-55, dep. asst. chief staff G-2, 1955; comdg. gen. 3d Armored Div. arty., 1955-57; chief Mil. Assistance Adv. Group, Brussels. Belgium, 1957-59; dep. asst. chief of staff for intelligence Dept. of Army, 1959-61; asst. chief of staff for intelligence Dept. of Army, 1961- 64; dep. dir. Def. Intelligence Age., 1964-66; mil. editor Kiplinger Washington Editors, 1966—. Decorated D.S.C., Silver Star, Legion of Merit, Bronze Star medal, Purple Heart, D.S.M. Mem. Assn. U.S. Army, Armor Assn., Assn. Grads. U.S. Mil. Acad. Mil. Order Caraboa, Legion of Valor. Clubs: N.Y. Anglers; Army and Navy (Washington); Rolling Rock (Ligonier, Pa.). Home: 217 Gibbon St Alexandria VA 22314 Office: 1729 H St NW Washington DC 20006

FITCH, COY DEAN, physician, educator; b. Marthaville, La., Oct. 5, 1934; s. Raymond E. and Joey (Youngblood) F.; B.S., U. Ark., 1956, M.S., 1958, M.D., 1958; m. Rachel Farr, Mar. 31, 1956; children—Julia Anne, Jaquelyn Kay. Intern, U. Ark. Sch. Medicine, 1958-59, resident, 1959-62, instr. biochemistry, 1959-62, asst. prof. medicine and biochemistry, 1962-66, asso. prof., 1966-67, dir. Honors Med. Student Research Program, 1965- 67; asso. prof. internal medicine and biochemistry St. Louis U. Sch. Medicine, 1967—, head sect. metabolism, 1969—; practice medicine, specializing in internal medicine, Little Rock, 1962-67, St. Louis, 1967—; dir. Diabetic Clinic, U. Ark. Med. Center, 1962-67, head sect. metabolism and endocrinology, 1966- 67; mem. nutrition study sect. div. research grants NIH, 1967-71. Served from capt. to lt. col., M.C., AUS, 1967-69. Recipient Lederle Med. Faculty award, 1966-67; Russell M. Wilder-Nat. Vitamin Found. fellow, 1959-62. Diplomate Am. Bd. Internal Medicine. Fellow A.C.P.; mem. Am. Diabetes Assn., Am. Fedn. Clin. Research, Am. Inst. Nutrition, Central Soc. Clin. Research, So. Soc. Clin. Investigation, Phi Beta Kappa, Sigma Xi. Asso. editor: Nutrition Revs; 1964. Contbr. articles profl. jours. Office: 1325 S Grand Blvd St Louis MO 63104

FITCH, DAVID ROBNETT, educator; b. Brookfield, Mo., Dec. 10, 1921; s. Donald Colt and Helen Morton (Robnett) F.; B.A. in Econs., Tex. A. and M. U., 1942; M.S. in Econs., U. Wis., 1948; Ph.D., U. Okla., 1956; m. Doris Griffin Stephenson, Aug. 1, 1952; children—Cynthia, Robin, Susan. Asso. prof. Tex. A. and M. U., College Station, 1949-56, prof., 1956-60; prof., chmn. dept. finance, ins. and real estate N. Tex. State U., Denton, 1960—. Served to capt. F.A., AUS, 1942-47. C.L.U., Tex. Mem. Am. Finance Assn., Am. Econ. Assn., Am. Risk and Ins. Assn., Assn. C.L.U.'s, Southwestern Finance Assn. (pres.), Phi Delta Theta, Delta Sigma Pi, Beta Gamma Sigma. Home: 2719 Crestwood Denton TX 76201

FITCH, EDWARD THOMAS, mfg. co. exec.; b. Roscoe, Pa., Dec. 19, 1912; s. John and Etta (Moore) F.; grad. Pitts. Sch. Accountancy, 1934; student Duquesne U. Evening Sch. Bus. Adminstrn., 1938-43; m. Claire Fritsch, July 18, 1938; children—Mary Claire, Dorothy Ann, Betty Lou, Patty Jo. With Dravo Corp., Pitts., 1928—, successively clk., asst. sec., asst. treas., controller, 1953-60, v.p. finance, 1960-67, sr. v.p., 1962—, also dir., mem. exec. com.; v.p., Dravo-Doyle, Co., Union Barge Line, subsidiaries, 1955—, also Potomac Sand & Gravel, 1960—; v.p., dir., mem. exec. com. Dravo of Can., Ltd., Dravo Constrn., Ltd. Board trustees Seton Hall Coll., Greensburg, Pa; dir., mem. exec. com. Western Pa. Multiple Sclerosis Soc. Mem. Nat. Assn. Accountants (past pres. Pitts. chpt., nat. dir.), Financial Execs. Inst. (past pres. Pitts. control, nat. dir. 1963—), Newcomen Soc. Clubs: Duquesne, Chartiers Country (Pitts.); Whispering Pines Country (Pinehurst, N.C.). Home: 724 Osage Rd Pittsburgh PA 15216 Office: Dravo Corp Neville Island Pittsburgh PA 15225

FITCH, ELIOT G., banker; b. Milw., Mar. 12, 1895; s. Grant and Eliza (Eliot) F. St. Paul's Sch., Concord, N.H., 1910-14, B.A., Yale, 1918; M.A. in Econs., U. Wis., 1921; m. Janet Margaret Fell, July 15, 1922 (div. Apr. 4, 1941); children—John Grant, Janet Margaret, Jared Eliot; m. 2d, Ruth Bartlett Jones, Sept. 10, 1943. Began with The Nat. Exchange Bank of Milwaukee (now Marine Nat. Exchange Bank), 1923, and held progressively positions as asst. cashier, cashier, v.p., pres., chmn. bd., 1942—, dir. 1925—, also chmn. bd.; chmn. Marine Capital Corp.; pres., dir., chmn. bd. Marine Corp.; pres., dir. Polaris Corp.; dir. Jared Corp., Norway-Gravure, Inc., Braun-Hobar Co., Brownberry Ovens, Inc., Nordberg Mfg. Co., Northwestern Nat. Ins. Co. Commd. 1st lt. F.A., and overseas during World War I with 110th F.A., 29th Div. trustee, chmn. bd. govs. Menninger Found.; bd. dirs. Milw. Children's Hosp.; mem. adv. bd. Milw. Boys Club. Citizens Bur. Milw.; treas. Ole Evinrude Found. Mem. Res. City Bankers Assn., Psi Upsilon. Clubs: Milwaukee, University, Country. Home: 1241 No Franklin Place Milwaukee WI Office: 1 Marine Plaza Milwaukee WI 53202

FITCH, FRANK WESLEY, pathologist, educator; b. Bushnell, Ill., May 30, 1929; s. Harold Wayne and Mary Gladys (Frank) F.; M.D., U. Chgo., 1953, S.M., 1957, Ph.D., 1960; m. Shirley Dobbins, Dec. 23, 1951; children—Mary Margaret, Mark Howard. USPHS postdoctoral research fellow, 1954-55, 57-58; faculty U. Chgo., 1957—, prof. pathology, 1967—; Markle Found. scholar, 1961-66; Commonwealth Fund fellow U. Lausanne (Switzerland) Institut de Biochimie, 1965-66. Recipient Borden Undergrad. Research award, 1953, Lederle Med. Faculty award, 1958-61. Mem. Am. Assn. Immunologists, Am. Assn. Pathologists and Bacteriologists, Am. Soc. Exptl. Pathology, Chgo. Path. Soc., Radiation Research Soc., Reticuloendothelial Soc., Sigma Xi, Alpha Omega Alpha. Contbr. chpts. to books, articles profl. jours. Home: 5449 Kenwood Av Chicago IL 60615

FITCH, FREDERIC BRENTON, educator; b. Greenwich, Conn., Sept. 9, 1908; s. Ashbel Parmelee and Josephine Hoyt (Smith) F.; B.A., Yale, 1931, Ph.D., 1934, Sterling fellow, 1935-36; DuPont fellow U. Va., 1934-35; m. Marguerite Bailey Rea, Sept. 9, 1933; children—Susan Howell (Mrs. William Bradley Price), Mary Hoyt (Mrs. Elwyn LaVerne Simons). Research asst. Yale, 1936-37, mem. philosophy dept. 1937—, prof., 1951—, acting dir. grad. studies philosophy, 1949-50, 71-72, dir., 1950-56; cons. logic IBM, 1956, 68, Bell Telephone Labs., 1957-63. Guggenheim fellow, 1945-46. Mem. Am. Math. Soc., Philosophy of Scr. Assn., Metaphys. Soc Am., Am. Philos. Assn., Assn. Symbolic Logic (v.p. 1956-58, pres. 1959-61). Author: Mathematico- Deductive Theory of Rote Learning (with others), 1940; Symbolic Logic, An Introduction, 1952. Editor: (with Robert Feys) Dictionary of Symbols of Mathematical Logic, 1968. Cons. editor Jour. Symbolic Logic; editorial bd. Jour. Philos. Logic. Contbr. profl. jours. Home: 307 Lawrence St New Haven CT 06511

FITCH, JAMES A., banker. Pres., dir. South Chgo. Savs. Bank. Office: 2959 E 92d St Chicago IL 60617*

FITCH, JAMES MARSTON, educator; b. Washington, May 8, 1909; s. James Marston and Ellen Cromwell (Payne) F.; student U. Ala., 1925-26, Tulane U. Sch. Architecture, 1927-28, Columbia, 1950-52; m. Cleopatra Rickman, Feb. 7, 1936. Chief designer Herbert Rodgers, Nashville, 1929-33; research Tenn. Planning Commn., 1933-34; low-cost housing analyst FHA, 1935-36; asso. editor Archtl. Record, 1936-41; tech. editor Archtl. Forum, 1945-49; lectr. Sch. Architecture, Columbia, 1948-52, asso. prof., 1954-60, prof., 1960—; archtl. editor House Beautiful, 1949-53; vis. prof. Salzburg Seminars in Am. Studies, 1964, U. Ill., Chgo., 1968, Internat. U. Art, Florence-Venice, 1969—. Pres. Rockland Found., 1956-58; dir. Internat. Design Com., Aspen, Colo., 1952-54; mem. nat. com. Internat. Commn. Sites and Monuments, 1964—; mem. Rome Center standing com. Adv. Council on Historic Preservation, 1970—. Served with USAAF, 1942-45. Mem. Archtl. League, Am. Acad. Polit. and Social Sci., A.A.A.S., Victorian Soc. (dir.), Municipal Art Soc. N.Y.C. (dir.), Soc. Archtl. Historians (dir. 1970—), Assn. for Preservation Tech. (founding mem.). Episcopalian. Author: Tennessee Population Trends, 1935; American Building: The Forces that Shape It, 1948; (with F.F. Rockwell) American Gardens, 1957; Walter Gropius, 1960; Architecture and The Esthetics of Plenty, 1961; American Building, 2 vols., 2d edit., 1966; Vier Jahrhunderte Bauen in USA, 1968. Home: Collaberg Rd Stony Point NY 10980 also 232 E 5th St New York City NY 10003 Office: Sch Architecture Columbia U New York City NY 10027

FITCH, LEE OSCAR, lawyer; b. New Boston, O., Oct. 16, 1915; s. Lawrence and Cynthia (Field) F.; student U. Mich., 1934-35, Ohio U., 1946-47; LL.B., Ohio State U., 1950; m. Marguerite Virginia Beard,

May 28, 1936; children— Sandra Louise (Mrs. William Robert Lemons), Cynthia Lou (Mrs. George Lurrett Robinson). Admitted to Ohio bar, 1950, since practiced in Portsmouth; partner Miller, Searl & Fitch, 1955—. Trustee So. Hills Hosp. Served with USNR, 1944-46. Mem. Am., Ohio, Portsmouth bar assns., Internat. Assn. Ins. Counsel, Am. Judicature Soc., Assn. Ins. Attys., Def. Research Inst., Ohio Def. Assn., Portsmouth Bar and Law Library Assn. (past pres.). Republican. Methodist. Mason (Shriner), Elk, Kiwanian. Home: 1657 Coles Blvd Portsmouth OH 45662 Office: Masonic Bldg Portsmouth OH 45662

FITCH, LYLE CRAIG, adminstr., economist; b. Merriman, Neb., May 22, 1913; s. Fred B. and Frances (Logsdon) F.; B.S., Chadron (Neb.) State Coll., 1935; M.A., U. Neb., 1938; Ph.D., Columbia, 1946; m. Violet Vaughn, Sept. 4, 1937; 1 dau., Linda (Mrs. Peter Andrews). Econ. depts. Bklyn. Coll., Columbia, Wesleyan U., 1939-50; cons. mgmt. and finance, N.Y.C., P.R., 1950-53; asso. prof. econs. Columbia, 1953-54; sr. mgmt. econs. Office of Mayor, City N.Y., 1954-56, 1st dep. city adminstr., 1957-60, acting city adminstr., 1960, city adminstr., 1960-61; dir. fiscal research Inst. Pub. Adminstrn., 1956-57, pres., 1961—. Economist, U.S. Treasury Dept. 1942; spl. asst. to Gov. Conn., 1949-50; cons. govts. of Venezuela, Peru, Dominican Republic, Western Nigeria, UAR, also fed. depts. of housing and urban devel., transp., health edn. and welfare, and also state and municipal govts. Mem. Am. Econs. Assn., Nat. Tax Assn., Am. Soc. Pub. Adminstrn., Am. Polit. Sci. Assn., Regional Sci. Assn., Internat. Pub. Finance Assn., Tax Inst., Com. on Urban Econs. Club: Century. Author and editor: (with Horace Taylor) Planning for Jobs, 1946. Author: Taxing Municipal Bond Income, 1950; (with Robert Haig, Carl Shoup) The Financial Problem of the City of New York, 1952; (with Carl Shoup, others) The Fiscal Systems of Venezuela, 1958; Urban Transportation and Public Policy, 1964; (with Annmarie Hauk Walsh) Agenda for a City, 1970; other books, numerous articles and reviews. Contbr. to Ency. Brit. Home: 121 Red Hill Rd Princeton NJ 08540 Office: 55 W 44th St New York City NY 10021

FITCH, MORGAN LEWIS, Jr., patent lawyer; b. Chgo., Nov. 21, 1922; s. Morgan Lewis and Marian (Ringer) F.; B.S. in Chem. Engring., Ill. Inst. Tech., 1943; student Princeton, 1943, Mass. Inst. Tech., 1943-44; J.D., U. Mich., 1948; m. Helen Shearer, June 9, 1945; children—Ruth Ann, Mary Louise, Morgan Lewis, Frederick Shearer. Admitted to Ill. bar, 1948, since practiced in Chgo.; partner firm Fitch, Even, Tabin & Luedeka, 1953—. Nat. chmn. sea explorer com. Boy Scouts Am. Trustee Tri-State Coll., Angola, Ind., La Rabida Children's Hosp. and Research Center. Served to lt. (s.g.) USNR, 1943-46. Recipient Distinguished Pub. Service award sec. Navy, 1960, 65. Mem. Am., Ill., Chgo. bar assns., Chgo. Patent Law Assn., Navy League U.S. (pres. 1965- 67), U.S. Naval Sea Cadets Corps (pres. 1963-65), Naval Commandery, Naval Res. Assn. Clubs: Legal, Executives (Chgo.). Home: 4640 Clausen St Western Springs IL 60558 Office: 135 S LaSalle St Chicago IL 60603

FITCH, ROBERT ELLIOT, educator; b. Ningpo, China (parents Am. citizens), Jan. 25, 1902; s. Robert Ferris and Isadore (Kloss) F.; A.B., Yale, 1923; B.D., Union Theol. Sem., 1926; student U. Paris, 1926-27; A.M., Columbia, 1929, Ph.D., 1935; m. Marion W. De Witt. Mar. 26, 1931; children—John Elliot, Robert De Witt, Shelley Annette. Instr. philosophy U. Va., summer 1929, Coll. City of N.Y., 1929-30, Columbia, 1930-31, U. Tex., 1931-32; prof. philosophy Pacific U., 1932-38, Occidental Coll., 1938-49, dean faculty, 1946-49; prof. Christian ethics Pacific Sch. Religion, 1949—, acting dean, 1950-51, dean, 1951-67. Ordained ministry Congl. Ch., 1936. Served as chaplain U.S.N.R., 1944-46. Mem. Am. Philos. Assn., Modern Lang. Assn., Shakespeare Assn. Am., Pacific Coast Theol. Discussion Group, Phi Beta Kappa. Author: Voltaire's Philosphic Procedure, 1935; A Certain Blind Man, 1944; Preface to Ethical Living, 1947; The Kingdom Without End, 1950; The Limits of Liberty, 1952; The Decline and Fall of Sex, 1957; Odyssey of the Self-Centered Self, 1961; Shakespeare: The Perspective of Value, 1969; Of Love And Of Suffering, 1970. Home: 1941 Skycrest Dr Walnut Creek CA 94595 Office: Pacific School of Religion 1798 Scenic Av Berkeley CA 94709

FITCH, VAL LOGSDON, physicist; b. Merriman, Neb., Mar. 10, 1923; s. Fred B. and Frances Marion (Logsdon) F.; B.Eng., McGill U., 1948; Ph.D., Columbia, 1954; m. Elise Cunningham, June 11, 1949; children—John Craig, Alan Peter. Instr., Columbia, 1953; instr. physics Princeton, 1954-56, asst. prof., 1956-59, asso. prof., 1959-60, prof., 1960—; cons. AEC, Dept. of Def. Mem. Pres.'s Sci. Adv. Com., 1970—. Sloan fellow, 1960. Trustee Asso. Univ., Inc., 1961-67. Served with AUS,1943-46. Recipient Research Corp. award, 1967; E.O. Lawrence award, 1968. Fellow Am. Phys. Soc., Am. Acad. Arts and Sci., A.A.A.S.; mem. Nat. Acad. Sci. Home: 292 Hartley Av Princeton NJ 08540

FITCH, WILLIAM CHESTER, educator; b. Billings, Mont., Nov. 12, 1916; s. Harry Davis and Grace E. (McCormick) F.; B.S. in Indsl. Engring., Mont. State Coll., 1938; M.S. in Engring. Valuation, Ia. State U., 1939, Ph.D., 1950; m. Manzella Lucille Groth, Feb. 23, 1946; 1 son, David Paul. Tchr. engring. Ia. State U., 1939-45; asst. prof. indsl. engring. Mont. State Coll., 1945- 46; lectr. mech. engring. U. Cal. at Berkeley, 1946-47; asso. prof. Ia. State U., 1947-52; asst. dir. valuation div. Gannett Fleming Corddry & Carpenter, cons. engrs., Harrisburg, Pa., 1952-58, 59-64; prof., head mech. engring. dept. Utah State U., 1958-59, Mich. Tech. U. 1964-68; prof., chmn. engring. and tech. dept. Western Mich. U., 1968—; cons. engr., 1952—. Registered profl. engr., Ia., Pa. Mem. Am. Soc. M.E., Am. Soc. Engring. Edn., Nat. Soc. Profl. Engrs., Am. Inst. Indsl. Engrs., Tau Beta Pi, Phi Kappa Phi, Pi Mu Epsilon, Pi Tau Sigma, Lambda Chi Alpha. Presbyn. (elder). Rotarian (bd. dirs. Houghton, Mich., 1966-68). Home: 2408 Waite Av Kalamazoo MI 49001

FITCHEN, JOHN FREDERICK, III., architect, educator; b. Ithaca, N.Y., May 24, 1905; s. John Frederick, Jr. and Ruth (Williams) F.; B.A., Yale, 1927; M.Arch., Harvard, 1932; m. Mary Elizabeth Nelson, June 23, 1934; children—Allen Nelson, Leigh Williams, John Hardy. Mem. dept. fine arts Colgate U., Hamilton, N.Y., 1934-71, emeritus, 1971—, chmn. dept., 1950-65; cons. architect N.Y. State Emergency Housing Project, 1946-47. Chmn. Friends of Colgate U. Library, 1962-65. Recipient Citation of Merit, Central N.Y. chpt. A.I.A. for design of Phi Kappa Tau fraternity house Colgate U., 1951. Mem. A.I.A., Soc. Archtl. Historians, Central N.Y. Archtl. Historians (past pres.), Internat. Center of Medieval Art, Assn. for Preservation Tech. Author, illustrator: The Construction of Gothic Cathedrals, 1961; The New World Dutch Barn, 1968. Editor: Philobiblon, 1962-65. Contbr. articles archtl. jours. Address: Colgate U Hamilton NY 13346

FITE, ALAN CRAIG, mfg. co. exec.; b. Washington Court House, O., Dec. 18, 1917; s. Ed and Susan (Cockerill) F.; student Northwestern U., 1935-36; B.S., Ohio State U., 1939; m. Ina Ziegenhorn, Nov. 5, 1944; 1 dau., Susan Elizabeth. With Procter & Gamble Co., Cin., 1939—, mgr. finance and accounting internat. divs., 1958-64, treas., 1964—; treas. Procter & Gamble Internat. Co., Procter & Gamble Distbg. Co., Procter & Gamble Mfg. Co., Procter & Gamble Comml. Co., Buckeye Cellulose Corp., D.H. Food Co., Folger Coffee Co., Charmin Paper Products Co. Mem. program and allocations com. Cin. United Appeal; exec. com., treas. Ohio Valley chpt. Arthritis Found. Mem. asso. bd. lay trustees Coll. Mt. St. Joseph on the Ohio. Mem. Financial Execs. Inst., Cin. Council World Affairs, Beta Alpha Psi, Beta Gamma Sigma. Methodist. Clubs: Kenwood Country, Cin. Bankers. Home: 2500 Oak Ridge Dr Cincinnati OH 45237 Office: 301 E 6th St Cincinnati OH 45202

FITE, ARTHUR FREEMAN, Jr., lawyer; b. Jasper, Ala., Jan. 6, 1919; s. Arthur Freeman and Margaret (Sprott) F.; B.A., U. Ala., 1946, LL.B., 1948; m. Mary Ann Gilder, June 18, 1943; children—Arthur Freeman III, John Gilder. Admitted to Ala. bar, 1948; practice in Jasper, 1948-65, Hamilton, 1965—; circuit ct. judge, 1954-56. Mem. Ala. Ho. of Reps., 1950-54. Served with USAAF, 1941- 45. Decorated Air Medal, Croix de Guerre. Mem. Am. Bar Assn., Am. Trial Lawyers Assn., Phi Delta Theta, Phi Delta Phi. Mason (Shriner). Club: Civitan (Hamilton). Address: P O Box 157 Hamilton AL 35570

FITE, DANIEL HARLEY, savs. and loan exec.; b. nr. Watertown, Tenn., Feb. 24, 1902; s. Ernest and Violet Brilla (Jennings) F.; B.S., State Coll., Murfreesboro, Tenn., 1927; A.M., Peabody Coll., 1931, Ph.D., 1942; m. Esther Robinson, Sept. 30, 1922; children—Lila, Esther, Bettye Ruth. Prin. scs., Auburntown, Bradyville, Sixteenth Modd (all Tenn.), 1922-26; asst. headmaster Memphis U. Sch., 1927-31; dir. tchr. edn. Austin Pealy State Coll., 1931-41, dean, 1942-46; edn. cons. TVA, 1946-47; head dept. edn. State Teachers Coll., Florence, Ala., 1947-48; pres. Carson-Newman Coll., Jefferson City, Tenn., 1948-68; vis. prof. edn. Peabody Coll., summer 1931, 45; dir. ednl. found. Am. Edn. Life Ins. Co.; v.p. Morristown Savs. and Loan Assn., 1968—; bd. dirs. Univ. Parks Am., 1968—. Mem. curriculum com., State Dept. Edn., 1956-62; steering com. for improvement of instrn. Tenn. Bd. Edn., 1938- 42; spl. work in curriculum, Ala., 1947-48; mem. edn. commn. So. Bapt. Conv., 1963-67. Recipient Distinguished Alumnus award State Coll. Mem. N.E.A., Am. Assn. Sch. Adminstrs., Tenn. Edn. Assn., Tenn. Pub. Schs. Officers Assn., So. Assn. Bapt. Colls. (past pres.), C. of C. (pres. 1955), Tenn. Coll. Assn. (pres. 1960), Phi Delta Kappa, Alpha Tau Alpha. Baptist. Club: Civitan (lt. gov. Appalachian dist., 1954). Contbr. to edn. jours. Home: 105 W King St Jefferson City TN 33760

FITE, DEAN PICKERING, corp. exec.; b. Washington Court House, O., July 29, 1912; s. Ed and Susan (Cockerill) F.; Comml. Engr., U. Cin., 1935; m. Norma Conard, June 13, 1936; children—David C., Nancy L. (Mrs. Peter Stockmann). Employed as asst. mgr. The Henking-Bovie Co., wholesale grocery, 1935-37; accountant The Buckeye Cotton Oil Co. (subsidiary Procter & Gamble Co.), 1937-45; staff comptroller's div. Procter & Gamble Co., 1945-58, comptroller, 1958-61, v.p., comptroller, 1961, v.p.-corporate affairs, dir., 1961—; dir. Cin. Milagron Co. Mem. adv. bd. on policy Cin. Council on World Affairs. Chmn. bd. trustees Cin. Mus. Natural History. Served to maj. AUS, 1942-45. Mem. Financial Execs. Inst., Am. Enterprise Inst. (trustee). Council Financial Execs., Nat. Indsl. Conf. Bd. Presbyn. Clubs: Queen City, Bankers. Home: 6915 Winding Way Cincinnati OH 45236 Office: PO Box 599 Cincinnati OH 45201

FITE, GILBERT COURTLAND, univ. pres., author; b. Santa Fe, O., May 14, 1918; s. Clyde and Mary (McCardle) F.; student Wessington Springs (S.D.) Coll., 1935-37; B.A., M.A., U. S.D., 1941; Ph.D., U. Mo., 1945, Litt.D., Seattle Pacific Coll., 1962; m. Alberta June Goodwin, July 24, 1941; children—James Franklin, Jack Preston. Dir. pub. relations Wessington Springs Coll., 1941-42; instr. history U. Mo., 1943-45; prof. history U. Okla., 1945-71, research prof., 1958-71, chmn. dept., 1955-58; pres. Eastern Ill. U., Charleston, 1971—; prof. Am. history Jadavpur U., Calcutta, India, 1962-63; dir. Am. Studies Research Centre, Hyerabad, India, 1967-70; summer vis. prof. U. Mo., 1950, 51. Vanderbilt U., 1955, U. Ill., 1959. Cons. Nat. Park Service, 1950. Trustee Wessington Springs Coll., 1960—. Ford fellow, 1954-55; Guggenheim fellow, 1964. Mem. Agrl. History Soc. (pres. 1960-61), Am. Assn. State and Local History (mem. council), Orgn. Am. Historians (exec. com. 1958-61), So. Hist. Assn. (mem. exec. council 1967-70), S.W. Social Sci. Assn., Econ. History Assn., Phi Beta Kappa (hon.), Phi Alpha Theta. Mem. Disciples of Christ Ch. Author: Peter Norbeck Prairie Statesman, 1948; Mount Rushmore, 1952; Readings in American History (with others), 1952; George N. Peek and the Fight for Farm Parity, 1954; (with Ladd Haystead) The Agricultural Regions of the United States, 1955; (with H.C. Peterson) Opponents of War, 1917-18, 1957; (with Jim E. Reese) An Economic History of the United States, 2d edit., 1965; Farm to Factory: A History of the Consumers Cooperative Association, 1965; The Farmer's Frontier, 1865-1900, 1966; (with others) A History of the United States, 2 vols., 1970; (with J. Carrol Moody) The Credit Union Movement, 1971; also articles. Address: Eastern Illinois Univ Charleston IL 61920

FITE, ROBERT HUNTER, utilities exec.; b. Nashville, July 26, 1902; s. Robert Hunter and Alma (McCarthy) F.; B.E., Vanderbilt U., 1923; m. Mary Josephine Cotton, May 14, 1932; children—Peter Hunter, Robert Cotton. With Gen. Electric Co., 1923-25; head rate dept. to gen. sales mgr. Fla. Power & Light Co., Miami, 1926-36; with Ebasco Services, Inc., N.Y.C., 1936-45, as sales sponsor, head sales dept., mgr. Washington office; with Fla. Power & Light Co., 1945—, successively v.p. and dir., v.p. and gen. mgr., pres. and gen. mgr., 1954-68, pres., chief exec. officer, 1968-69, now vice- chmn. Mem. Beta Theta Pi. Clubs: Miami (Fla.), Kiwanis (Miami); Riviera Country (Coral Gables, Fla.). Home: PO Box 3100 Miami FL 33101 Office: Florida Power & Light Co Miami FL 33101

FITT, ALFRED BRADLEY, univ. ofcl.; b. Highland Park, Ill., Apr. 12, 1923; s. Frank and Harriett (Bradley) F.; B.A., Yale, 1946; J.D., U. Mich., 1948; m. Patricia Hewitt, May 20, 1944; children—Cathleen, Benjamin, Ann, Craig. Admitted to Mich. bar, 1948; with firm Lewis and Watkins, Detroit, 1948- 54, partner, 1952-54; legal adviser to gov. Mich., 1954-60, asso. counsel subcom. adminstrv. practice, U.S. Senate Judiciary Com., 1960- 61; chief counsel spl. com. FAA adminstrv. procedures, 1961; dep. under sec. manpower Dept. Army, 1961-63, dep. asst. sec. def. for civil rights, 1963-64; gen. counsel Dept. Army, 1964-67; asst. sec. of defense for manpower, 1967-69; spl. adviser to the pres. Yale U., 1969—. Served with U.S. Army, 1943-46. Home: 121 Deepwood Dr Hamden CT 06517 Office: Yale U New Haven CT 06520

FITTERER, GEORGE RAYMOND, educator; b. Newark, O., Apr. 10, 1901; s. John Wesley and Josephine Grace (Richardson) F.; B.S. in Chem. Engring., Rose-Poly. Inst., 1924, D.Sc. (hon.), 1962; M.S., Carnegie Inst. Tech. Metall. Engring., 1927; Ph.D., U. Pitts., 1930; D. Eng., Universidad Federico Santa Maria, 1965; Dr. Honoris Causa, Universidad Catolica de Cordoba (Argentina), 1967; m. Katherine Evans, Feb. 5, 1925; 1 son, Charles Evans. Metallurgist Highland Iron & Steel Co., Terre Haute, Ind., 1924-25; metallographer Stanley Works, 1925-26; research fellow Carnegie Inst. Tech., U.S. Bur. Mines, 1927-31, asso. metallurgist, head metall. dept., 1931- 33; Pres. Fitterer Pyrometer Co., Inc., Pitts., 1933-38; pres. Fitterer Engring. Assos., Inc., 1969—; lectr. U. Pitts., 1930-38, prof. and head metall. engring. dept., 1938-51, dir. engring. research div., 1950, dean Schs. Engring. and Mines, 1951-63, 1st distinguished prof. metall. engring., 1963—, also dir. Center Study Thermodynamic Properties of Materials. U.S. del. UN, Econ. Commn. for Latin Am., Bogata; del. steel conf. UN Econ. Commn. for Latin Am., Sao Paulo, 1956; dir. research Acid Open Hearth Research Assn., Inc.; supr. War Prodn. Bd. Research Project, Office Sci. Research and Devel. Contract, USN contracts; dir. ICA contract Engring. Edn., Chile, S.Am.; cons. AID, Argentina, 1967. Campbell Meml. lectr. Am. Soc. Metals; 1st Herty Meml. lectr. Am. Inst. Mining, Metall. and Petroleum Engrs.; Carnegie lectr., 1961. Recipient Frontiers of Process Metallurgy award Am. Inst. Mining, Metall. and Petroleum Engrs., 1967. Fellow Am. Inst. Chemists; mem. Am. Soc. Metals, Am. Inst. Mining, Metall. and Petroleum Engrs., Brit. Iron and Steel Inst., Am. Soc. Engring. Edn., Am. Assn. U. Profs., Sigma Xi, Sigma Tau, Sigma Gamma Epsilon, Tau Beta Pi, Theta Xi. Mason. Clubs: University (Pitts.); Oakmont Country; Cosmos (Washington). Contbr. tech. jours. Patentee. Home: 825 12th St Oakmont PA 15139

FITTERER, JOHN ANGUS, assn. exec.; b. Ellensburg, Wash., July 1, 1922; s. C.J. and Violet C. (McMillan) F.; A.B., St. Louis U., 1945, M.A., 1947, Ph.L., 1948; S.T.B., Gregorian U., Rome, Italy, 1951, S.T.L., 1954. Joined Soc. of Jesus, 1940, ordained priest Roman Cath. Ch., 1953; dean Coll. Arts and Scis., Seattle U., 1956-65, asso. prof. classical lang. and philosophy, 1958-63, pres. Univ., 1965-71, chancellor, 1970-71; pres. Assn. Jesuit Colls. and Univs., Washington, 1971—. Address: 1717 Massachusetts Av NW Washington DC 20036

FITTON, STUART MASSEE, lawyer; b. Hamilton, O., Nov. 3, 1906; s. Sam D. and Irene (Massee) F.; A.B., Oberlin Coll., 1929; J.D., U. Cin., 1933; m. Jeannette Hidy, Aug. 15, 1936; children-Heidi, Terry (Mrs. John F. Dammann), Sam T. Admitted to Ohio bar, 1933; since practiced in Hamilton; pvt. practiced, 1933-36; U.S. Govt. sr. atty. HOLC, 1936-44; partner Millikin, Reister, Fitton, Latimer, Persson & Irwin, 1944—; lectr. bus. law Miami U., 1969-70. Dir. Krauth & Benninghofen, Pauline F. Schwartz Co. Chmn. Ohio State Bar Examining Com., 1952-57. Bd. dirs. Planned Parenthood Assn., Westover Retirement Residence, Tb. Assn.; trustee Western Coll. for Women. Fellow Am. Coll. Probate Counsel, Ohio Bar Found. Methodist. Mem. Barrett Exploring Expdn. in Himalaya Mountains, 1924-25. Home: 106 Tenney Ct Oxford OH 45056 Office: Rentschler Bldg Hamilton OH 45011

FITTS, DONALD DENNIS, educator, chemist; b. Concord, N.H., Sept. 3, 1932; s. Russell P. and Elisabeth (Reille) F.; A.B., Harvard, 1954; Ph.D., Yale, 1957; m. Beverly Hoffman, July 11, 1964; children—Robert K., William R. NSF postdoctoral fellow U. Amsterdam, Netherlands, 1957-58; research fellow Yale, 1958-59; mem. faculty U. Pa., 1959—, asso. prof. chemistry, 1964-69, prof. chemistry, 1969—, asst. chmn. dept., 1965-72. Cons. Am. Cyanamid Co., 1959-63. Mem. Am. Phys. Soc., Am. Chem. Soc., Assn. Harvard Chemists, Faraday Soc., Yale Chemists Assn. Author: Nonequilibrium Thermodynamics, 1962; also articles. Research on theory of optical activity, statis.-mech. theory of transport processes, nonequilibrium thermodynamics, molecular quantum mechanics. Home: 634 Revere Rd Merion Station PA 19066 Office: Dept Chemistry Univ Pa Philadelphia PA 19104

FITTS, OSMER C., lawyer; b. Brattleboro, Vt., Oct. 21, 1905; s. Clarke Cushing and Maud (Emerson) F.; B.S. Dartmouth, 1926; J.D., Harvard, 1929; J.D. (hon.), Suffolk U., 1960; m. Dorothy D. Moore, June 28, 1930. Admitted to Vt. and Mass. bars; partner law firm Sargent, Chase & Fitts, Ludlow, Vt., 1930-39, Fitts & Olson, Brattleboro, 1954—; atty. pvt. practice, Brattleboro, 1939-54; reporter of decisions Supreme Ct. Vt., 1940-42. Dir., gen. counsel, exec. com. Vt. Nat. Bank. Mem. Vt. Library Bd., 1970—. Exec. com. New Eng. Law Inst., 1955—. Bd. govs. Springfield Shriners Hosp. Crippled Children, 1963—. Served as lt. col. AUS, 1942-46. Mem. Am. (gov. 1954-57; chmn. ho. of dels. 1960-62), Vt. (pres. 1949) bar assns., Am. Coll. Trial Lawyers (regent 1954), Am. Coll. Probate Counsel (regent 1963—), Judge Advs. Assn. (dir. 1943-44, 47—, pres. 1970—). Conglist. Home 10 Chestnut Hill Brattleboro VT 05301 Office: 16 High St Brattleboro VT 05301

FITTS, WILLIAM COCHRAN, Jr., corp. exec., lawyer; b. Mobile, Ala., Mar. 7, 1905; s. William Cochran and Eleanor Langley Hyde, June 28, 1930; children—William Cochran, Holland, Harriet, Miriam, Marjorie, Robert. Admitted to Ala. bar, 1929, and began practice in Birmingham, Ala.; partner firm Fitts & Fitts; atty. TVA. Knoxville, Tenn., 1934-44, asst. gen. solicitor, 1935-36, asst. gen. counsel, 1936, solicitor, 1937-39, gen. counsel and sec., 1939-44; mem. firm Cates, Smith, Long & Fitts, Knoxville, Tenn., 1945; asso. with James Lawrence Fly, N.Y. City, 1945—; mem. firm Fly, Fitts & Shuebruk, 1945- 50; mem. legal dept. CBS, 195O-69, dir. labor relations, 1952-69, v.p., 1954-69; v.p., dir. labor relations and employee relations Allied Maintenance Corp., N.Y.C., 1969—. Democrat. Episcopalian. Home: 304 S Barry Av Mamaroneck NY 10543 Office: 2 Pennsylvania Plaza New York City NY 10001

FITTS, WILLIAM THOMAS, Jr., surgeon, educator; b. Jackson, Tenn., Oct. 6, 1915; s. William Thomas and Carrie (Burrus) F.; A.B., Union U., Jackson, 1937; M.D., U. Pa., 1940; m. Barbara Kinsey Willits, Oct. 29, 1942; children—Barbara Hayden, Catherine Austin, Michael Andrew. From intern to resident surgery U. Pa. Hosp., 1940-47, asso. surgeon, 1947, exec. officer surg. service, 1948- 56, chief surg. ward service, div. II, 1956-65, chief surg. service div. B, 1965—, asst. chief dept. gen. surgery, 1957-59, asso. chief, 1959—; asst. vis. surgeon thoracic surgery Phila. Gen. Hosp., 1951-53; mem. vis. staff Children's Hosp., Phila., 1954-56; cons. VA Hosp., Phila., 1955—; mem. faculty U. Pa., 1945—, prof. surgery, 1956—; vis. prof., med. edn. program Honolulu, 1965. Served to capt., M.C., AUS, 1942- 45. Recipient Spencer Morris prize U. Pa., 1940, Alumni medal, 1940, Ob- Gyn prize, 1940, Lindback Teaching award, 1964. Mem. A.M.A., Phila. County, Pa. med. socs., Soc. U. Surgeons, Am. Assn. Surgery of Trauma (pres. 1965), A.C.S. (sec. Phila. com. trauma 1955-67, chmn. Phila. regional com. trauma 1958-60, vice chmn. com. trauma 1965-66), Am. Surg. Assn., John Morgan Soc., Phila. Acad. Surgery (sec. 1957-59), Phila. Coll. Physicians, Halsted Soc., Soc. Surgery Alimentary Tract, Eastern Surg. Soc., Soc. Internat. de Chirurgie, Am. Assn. U. Profs., U. Pa. Research Club, Sigma Xi, Phi Chi; hon. mem. Anchorage Med. Soc. Co-author: Open Reduction Common Fractures; (with William S. Blakemore) Management of the Injured Patient, 1969; also chpts. in textbooks. Editor Jour. of Trauma, 1968. Contbr. profl. jours. Office: U Pa Hosp 3400 Spruce St Philadelphia PA 19104

FITZ, ELBERT HARVEY, banker, b. Callendar, Ia., May 5, 1905; s. Harvey J. and Lora B. (Reynolds) F.; B.S., U. Cal. at Berkeley, 1927, m. Mabel W. Gould, Aug. 6, 1932. With Bank of Am., 1927-47, asst. v.p., 1944-47; with First Nat. Bank Nev., Reno, 1947—, pres., 1966-67, mem. bd. dirs. cons., 1968—. Mem. Nevada Planning Bd., 1955—, chmn., 1961- 62, 67—; mem. nat. adv. bd. invest-in-Am. Nat. Council, 1962—. Mem. U.S., Reno C.'s of C. Am. (exec. council 1966—), Nev. (past pres.) bankers assns., Delta Phi Epsilon. Clubs: Rotary (past pres.). Prospector's, Elks (Reno). Home: 600 Hunter Pl Reno NV 89502 Office: 1 E 1st St Reno NV 89504

FITZ, JOHN ALLEN, ednl. adminstr.; b. Hampton, Ia., June 8, 1908; s. Stephen Roberts and Edna May (Watson) F.; A.A., Santa Ana (Cal.) Jr. Coll., 1928; A.B., U. Cal. at Berkeley, 1930, M.A., 1937; student U. So. Cal., 1945-50; Ed.D., U. Denver, 1955; m. Helen Ann Scott, June 15, 1933; children—Marilyn Ann (Mrs. Mark McClure),

Jonelle (Mrs. Nathan L. Simmons), Stephen Scott. Secondary sch. tchr., 1931-38; curriculum coordinator, 1938-39; supt. schs., 1939-50; univ. prof., 1952-58; joined U.S. Fgn. Service, 1955; inservice tchr. ednl. adviser, Ethiopia, 1955- 57; edn. adviser, Iran, 1958-60; chief edn. adviser Salisbury, Rhodesia, 1961-62, Washington, 1963-66; program co-ordinator State Tech. Services Act Programs at U. Cal. at Los Angeles, 1967—; field worker Rocky Mountain Sch. Study Council, 1951-52. Mem. Assn. Supervision and Curriculum Devel., Nat. Soc. Study Edn., Am. Assn. U. Profs., African Studies Assn., Am. Fgn. Service Assn., Soc. Internat. Devel., Phi Delta Kappa. Home: 1155 Quartz Way Hemet CA 92343 Office: 601 E Florida Hemet CA 92343

FITZ, REGINALD HEBER, physician, educator; b. Boston, Oct. 28, 1920; s. Reginald and Phoebe Marion (Wright) F.; grad. Milton (Mass.) Acad., 1938; A.B., Harvard, 1942, M.D., 1945; m. Edna Wilmot Woelfel, Sept. 10, 1946; children—Reginald, Tracy, Grahame W., Ralph W. Intern, Faulkner Hosp., Jamaica Plain, Mass., 1945-46; med. resident U. Colo. Med. Center, 1948- 50; mem. faculty U. Colo. Sch. Medicine, 1950-61, asso. prof. medicine, 1961, asso. dean, 1959-61; prof. medicine, dean Sch. Medicine, U. N.M., 1961-68; dir. N.M. Regional Med. Program, 1966—. Mem. N.M. and Mid Rio Grande Comprehensive Health Planning Councils, 1968—. Mem. nat. adv. dental research council Nat. Inst. Dental Research, 1963-65; mem. exec. com. N.M. Comprehensive Health Planning Council, 1968—; vice chmn. Mid-Rio Grande Health Planning Council, 1968—. Bd. dirs. Albuquerque United Community Fund, 1964-70. Served to capt. M.C., AUS, 1946-48. Diplomate Am. Bd. Internal Medicine. Fellow A.C.P. (bd. govs. N.M. 1963-69), A.A.A.S.; mem. Am. Clin. and Climatol. Assn., Assn. Am. Indian Affairs, Am. Fedn. Clin. Research, Assn. Am. Med. Colls., Am., Bernalillo County med. assns., N.M. Med. Soc. Contbr. articles profl. jours. Mem. editorial bd. Jour. Med. Edn., 1964-69. Home: 1505 Stanford NE Albuquerque NM 87106 Office: 920 Stanford NE Albuquerque NM 87106

FITZER, JOSEPH B., banker; b. Chgo., 1906. Sr. v.p., cashier Continental Ill. Nat. Bank & Trust Co., Chgo., v.p., dir. Continental Ill. Safe Deposit Co.; dir. Continental Internat. Finance Corp., Continental Bank Internat. Home: 7535 N Hoyne Av Chicago IL 60645 Office: 231 S LaSalle St Chicago IL 60604

FITZGERALD, CHARLES PATRICK, financial exec.; b. Kingston, N.Y., Aug. 13, 1930; s. Francis X. and Anne (Daly) F.; B.S., Babson Inst., 1956; M.B.A., Western Res. U., 1962; m. Mary E. Onions, Aug. 31, 1957; children-Elizabeth, Timothy, Pamela, Michael, Daniel, Scott. Teller, First Nat. Bank, Binghamton, N.Y., 1947- 50; auditor Glidden Co., Cleve., 1956-59, cost accountant, 1959-61, mgr. corporate accounting, 1961-64, div. controller, 1964-65, corporate asst. controller, 1965-68; controller Capitol Industries, Hollywood, Cal., 1968-70, treas., 1970—. Group chmn. Cleve. United Appeal, 1966-67. Served to 2d lt. U.S. Army, 1951-53. Mem. Budget Exec. Inst. (past pres. Cleve chpt.), Financial Execs. Inst. Home: 4520 Park Livorno Calabasas CA 91302 Office: 1750 N Vine St Hollywood CA 90028

FITZGERALD, CLIFFORD LLEWELYN, advt. exec.; b. St. Louis, Oct. 10, 1903; grad. The Principia, St. Louis, 1923; student Dartmouth Coll., 1923-24; m. Isabel Hanway, Dec. 31, 1924; children—Shirley Hanway Gately, Joan Hughes Gardner, Clifford Llewelyn. Advt. writer,. 1924; founder chmn. Dancer-Fitzgerald-Sample, Inc., 1961—. Pres. The Fitzgerald Found. Mem. Advt. Council, Inc. N.Y. dir., U.S. Sr. Golf Assn., Alpha Delta Phi, Dragon (Dartmouth). Clubs: Blind Brook (Portchester, N.Y.); Round Hill (Greenwich); Clove Valley Rod and Gun (Lagrangeville, N.Y.); Raquet (Chgo.); Anglers (N.Y.C.). Home: Field Point Circle Greenwich CT 06830 Office: 347 Madison Av New York City NY 10017

FITZ-GERALD, DANIEL MICHAEL, mfg., agrl. and mdsg. exec.; b. N.Y.C., Feb. 6, 1910; s. Richard and Elizabeth (O'Connor) Fitz-G.; student Walsh Inst. Accountancy, Wayne U.; m. Grace Elizabeth Prier; children—Eve M. (Mrs. Nick Barris), Sandra L. (Mrs. Walter Pfander), Richard Michael. Staff Lybrand, Ross Bros. & Montgomery, 1930-42; comptroller Wickes Bros., Wickes Boiler Co., 1942- 49; treas. Wickes Corp., 1949-56, exec. v.p., 1956-64, pres., 1964-69, chmn. bd., 1969—; dir. Mich. Nat. Bank, Consumers Power Co., Alodex Corp. Bd. fellows Saginaw Valley Coll.; bd. dirs. Boy Scouts Am., United Fund Saginaw County. Mem. Mich., Saginaw chambers commerce, Am. Inst. Accountants, Mich. Assn. C.P.A.'s. Home: 2375 Williamson Rd Saginaw MI 48601 Office: 515 N Washington Av Saginaw MI 48607

FITZGERALD, DESMOND JAMES, educator; b. Toronto, Ont., Can., Jan. 18, 1924; s. John Henry and Gertrude Elizabeth (Chadwick) F.; B.A., U. Toronto, 1946, M.A., 1947; M.A., U. Cal. at Berkeley, 1950, Ph.D., 1954; m. Evelyn Critelli, June 16, 1947; children—Cynthia, Brian. Came to U.S., 1948, naturalized, 1955. Admission officer Canadian Dept. External Affairs, 1947-48; mem. philosophy dept. U. San Francisco, 1948—; participant reporter Canadian press World Press, Nat. Endl. TV, 1969—. Fulbright research scholar, Italy, 1966-67. Mem. Am. Assn. U. Profs., Am., Am. Cath. philos. assns., History Sci. Soc. Home: 230 Stonecrest Dr San Francisco CA 94132

FITZGERALD, EDMOND JAMES, artist; b. Seattle, Aug. 19, 1912; s. Maurice F. and Elizabeth (Norton) F.; student Eustace P. Ziegler and Mark Tobey; m. Mary Louise Streets, Sept. 7, 1940; children—Desmond, Ryder O'Bannon. One-man shows include Seattle Art Mus., 1941, Grand Central Gallery, 1946; murals include Trail to Ore., Ontario, Ore., 1937, Pathfinders, Colville, Wash., 1939, Battle of Bear River, Preston, Ida., 1940, Normandy Invasion, Nat. Maritime Union's Curran Plaza Bldg., Man and the Land, Am. Mus. Nat. History, 1949, Pasteur, Kenilworth, N.J., murals for Union First Nat. Bank (N.J.), 1958, Cranford (N.J.) Jr. Coll., 1959, Jamaica (N.Y.) Savs. Bank, 1964, Chem. Constrn. Co., N.Y.C., 1961; represented in permanent collections White House, George Washington U., Swope Mus., Terre Haute, Ind., New Britain (Conn.) Mus., Seattle Art Mus., Frye Mus., Seattle, Wash. State Coll., U.S. Naval War Coll., IBM, Nat. Cash Register Co.; lectr., tchr. Recipient grand prize Art USA, 1958, Ranger Fund purchase N.A.D., 1963, Am. Artists Profl. League prize, 1955; anonymous watercolor prize, 1959, Club prize, 1961, Frank B. Williams prize, 1958, Salmagundi Club; gold medal of honor Hudson Valley Art Assn., 1952, 58, 60, also Jane Peterson prize for oil painting, 1962; Famous Artists' Sch. award, 1969; Washington Sch. Art award, 1970. Served as officer USNR, 1942- 46; comdr. Res. ret. Asso. N.A.D.; mem. Allied Artists Am. (pres.; Jane Peterson prize 1956, Robert S. Brush award 1959), Am. Watercolor Soc. (v.p., dir.; Herb Olsen prize 1961), Nat. Soc. Mural Painters (first prize 1946). Club: Salmagundi (N.Y.C.). Author: Painting and Drawing in Charcoal and Oil, 1959. Home: 175 Larchmont Av Larchmont NY 10538 Office: 94 Post Rd Larchmont NY 10538

FITZGERALD, EDMUND BACON, elec. co. exec.; b. Milw., Feb. 5, 1926; s. Edmund and Elizabeth (Bacon) F.; B.S. in Elec. Engring., U. Mich., 1946; m. Elisabeth McKee Christensen, Sept. 6, 1947; children—Karen, Kathleen, Edmund Greer, Rogers Christensen. With Cutler-Hammer, Inc., Milw., 1946—, v.p. charge engring., 1959-61, adminstrv. v.p., 1961-63, pres., 1964-69, now chmn. and chief exec. officer, also dir.; dir. Kimberly-Clark Corp., Outboard Marine Corp., Snap-On Tools Corp., First Wis. Trust Co., First Wis. Nat. Bank, First Wis. Bankshares Corp., Milw. Brewers Baseball Club, Inc.; trustee Northwestern Mut. Life Ins. Co. Bd. dirs. Nat. Indsl. Conf. Bd., Greater Milw. Com.; trustee Milw. Children's Hosp. Com. for Econ. Devel. Served to capt. USMCR, 1943-46, 51-52. Named Man of Year, Milw. Jr. C. of C., 1956. Mem. Nat. Elec. Mfrs. Assn. (pres. 1968), Nat. Indsl. Conf. Bd., Machinery and Allied Products Inst. Home: 7644 N Beach Dr Milwaukee WI 53217 Office: 4201 N 27th St Milwaukee WI 53216

FITZGERALD, EDWARD EARL, editor, author; b. N.Y.C., Sept. 10, 1919; s. Francis J. and Mary Leona (Morgan) F.; m. Libuse P. Ostruk, June 6, 1942; children—Eileen Frances, Kevin Paul. Reporter, Westchester County Pubs., Inc., 1937-42; editor Macfadden Pubs., Inc., 1946-60, editor-in-chief Sport mag., 1951-60, editorial dir. men's group, 1952-60, asst. to pres., 1958-60; editor-in- chief Lit. Guild of Am., 1960-64; v.p. Doubleday & Co., Inc., gen. mgr. book club div., 1964-67, sr. v.p. in charge book club div., pub. div., book shop div., 1967-68; pres., chief exec. officer McCall Publishing Co., 1968-71; v.p. Book-of-the-Month Club, 1971—. Served with infantry, AUS, 1942-46. Club: Overseas Press (N.Y.C.). Author: (with Lou Boudreau) Player-Manager, 1949; (with Althea Gibson) I Always Wanted to be Somebody, 1958; (with Genevieve Caulfield) The Kingdom Within, 1960; (with Yogi Berra) Yogi, 1961; (with Mel Allen) You Can't Beat the Hours, 1964; (with John Unitas) Pro Quarterback. Home: 26 Claudet Way Eastchester NY 10709 Office: 280 Park Av New York City NY 10017

FITZGERALD, EDWIN ROGER, educator, physicist; b. Oshkosh, Wis., July 14, 1923; s. James C. and Edwina (Brown) F.; B.S. in Elec. Engring., U. Wis., 1944, M.S. in Physics, 1950, Ph.D. in Physics, 1951; m. Carolyn H. Johnson, Aug. 30, 1946; children—Lucia Edwina, Margaret Mary, William Maurice, Alice Ann, Roger Edwin, Douglas Brendan, Thomas Michael, Jane Carolyn. Physicist, Phys. Research Lab., B.F. Goodrich Co., 1944-46; Project asso. chemistry U. Wis., 1951-52; faculty Pa. State U., 1952-61, prof. physics, 1959-61; prof. mechanics Johns Hopkins, 1961—; spl. research mech. and dielectric properties solids. Fellow Am. Phys. Soc. (exec. com., chmn. high polymer Physics 1958-59); mem. Acoustical Soc. Am., Sigma Xi, Eta Kappa Nu. Author: Particle Waves and Deformation in Crystalline Solids, 1966. Contbr. numerous tech. articles, sects. in books. Home: 1409 Walnut Hill Lane, Baltimore, MD 21204

FITZGERALD, ELLA, singer; b. Newport News, Va., Apr. 25, 1918; m. Ray Brown (div. 1953) 1 son, Ray, Jr. Began singing with Chick Webb Orchestra, 1934-39; tours throughout U.S., Japan, Europe with Jazz at the Philharmonic troupe, 1948—, with An Evening of Jazz troupe in Sweden, Denmark, Norway, France, Belgium, Switzerland, Germany, Italy, 1957; recording artist for Decca, 1936-55, Verve, 1956—; motion picture in Pete Kelly's Blues, 1955; numerous nightclub appearances, 1956—. Recipient numerous popularity awards from Down Beat mag., Metronome mag., Musicians Poll, JAY Award Poll; named number 1 female singer 16th Internat. Jazz Critics Poll, 1968.

FITZGERALD, EUGENE FRANCIS, life ins. co. exec.; b. Jersey City, Mar. 15, 1925; s. Arthur Gregory and Anna (O'Rourke) F.; B.S. in Bus. Adminstrn., Georgetown U., 1949; m. Ellen M. O'Connor, Sept. 1, 1951; children—Timothy, Mary Ellen, Eugene Francis, Maura, John, Ann, Katherine. Spl. agt. FBI, 1951-52; mgr. Prudential Ins. Co. Am., Newark, 1953-63; agy. v.p. K.C., New Haven, 1965-67; v.p. Minn. Mut. Life Ins. Co., St. Paul, 1967-70; exec. v.p. Southland Life Ins. Co., Dallas, 1970—, also dir.; dir. Nathan Hale Life Ins. Co. Served with USMCR, 1943-45. Decorated Bronze Star. Mem. Nat. Assn. Life Underwriters, Sales and Marketing Execs. Internat. Catholic. Clubs: St. Paul Tennis; Las Colinas Country (Dallas). Home: 4630 Heatherbrook Dr Dallas TX 75234 Office: 1800 Southland Center Dallas TX 75201

FITZGERALD, GEORGE LESLIE, apparel industry exec.; b. Beardsley, Minn., July 1, 1903; s. Julian and Louise (Kortsch) F.; B.S. in Engring., U. Minn., 1926; m. Mary O'Reilly, Sept. 7, 1934. With Nelly Don, Inc., Kansas City, Mo., 1937—, v.p., gen. sales mgr., 1942-54, pres., 1954-59, dir., 1954—, chmn. bd., 1959- -; chmn. bd. Texmo Corp., Dallas, 1956—. Mem. adv. com. Women's Working Apparel Industry WPB, 1942. Mem. Kan. State, Kansas City C.'s of C., Chgo. Nat. Apparel Assn. (bd. dirs.), Kansas City Advtg. Club, Lambda Chi Alpha. Clubs: The Carriage, Kansas City (Kansas City, Mo.). Home: 1216 W 63d St Kansas City MO 64113 Office: 1600 Swift Av North Kansas City MO 64416

FITZGERALD, HAROLD ALVIN, newspaper publisher; b. St. Johns, Mich., Aug. 3, 1896; s. Howard Harold and Zylpha Irene (Shaver) F.; A.B., U. Mich., 1917; LL.D., Oakland U.; m. Elizabeth Millis, June 16, 1923; children—Howard Harold II, Nancy E. Connolly, Richard Millis. With Pontiac (Mich.) Daily Press since 1919, as telegraph editor and bus. mgr. to 1930, editor and mgr., 1930-44, pub., 1944-66, ret. as chmn.; 1st v.p. Asso. Press, 1951-54, dir., 1954-63; dir. Grand Trunk Ry., Fed. Home Loan Bank Ind.-Mich., 1950-59; v.p. of Hillsdale (Mich.) News. Former trustee Kingswood, Cranbrook, Brookside Schs., Bloomfield Hills, Mich.; dir. Mich. Soc. for Crippled Children. Mem. Mich. Constl. Commn., 1942; vice chmn. Cranbrook Found., Bloomfield Hills. Bd. dirs. Ams. Found.; chmn. Univ. Oakland Found. Served as 2d Lt., Air Service, U.S. Army, 1917-18. Hon. alumnus Mich. State U. Mem. Am. Soc. of Newspaper Editors, Inter-Am. Press Assn. (dir. 1957-68, hon. life dir.), Am. Legion, Alpha Delta Phi, Sigma Delta Chi. Episcopalian (former vestryman). Rotarian. Clubs: Bloomfield Hills Country (past pres.); Orchard Lake Country; Univ. of Mich. (Ann Arbor); Marco Polo (N.Y.C.). Contbr. to Sat. Eve. Post, Am. Mag., Look mag., others. Home: 48 Ottawa Dr Pontiac MI 48053

FITZGERALD, HOWARD HAROLD, II, former newpaper exec.; b. Pontiac, Mich., July 1, 1924; s. Harold Alvin and Elizabeth (Millis) F.; student U. Ia., 1943-44, U. Mich., 1946-47; m. Jean Craig, June 28, 1947; children—Ann C., Craig M., Harold A. II, Katherine B. Exec. v.p. Pontiac Press Co., 1960-66, pub., pres., 1966-70, gen. mgr., dir., 1951-70; pres. Chief Pontiac Photo Engraving, 1959-70, Oakland Graphic, until 1970. Vice pres. Met. Detroit Citizens Devel. Authority, 1968—. Active Mich. United Fund, Mich. Emotionally Disturbed Children; treas. Inter Am. Press Scholarship Fund. Bd. dirs. Cranbrook Inst. Sci. Served with AUS, 1943-45. Mem. InterAm. Press Assn., Internat. Press Inst. Rotarian. Home: 4820 Echo Rd Bloomfield Hills MI 48013

FITZGERALD, JAMES JOSEPH, Jr., lawyer; b. Omaha, Aug. 26, 1903; s. James Joseph and Katie A. (O'Rourke) F.; A.B., Creighton U., 1925, J.D., 1927; m. Helen Muriel Robinson, June 3, 1933; children—Thomas R., Robert H., James E., Elizabeth H. (Mrs. Quinn). Admitted to Neb. bar, 1927; sr. partner Fitzgerald, Brown, Leahy, McGill & Strom, Omaha, 1936—; sec., dir. Fitzgerald Co., Globe Realty Co.; officer, dir. Standard Warehouse Co.; dir. Nat. Am. Ins. Co., Neb. Feeding Co., Foxley & Co., Comml. Savs. & Loan Assn. Mem. Am., Neb., Omaha (pres. 1966) bar assns., Am. Judicature Soc., C. of C., Alpha Sigma Nu. Roman Catholic. Clubs: Kiwanis (pres. 1943), Omaha, Omaha Country, Omaha Athletic (Omaha). Home: 652 N 59th St Omaha NB 68132 Office: Continental Bldg Omaha NB 68102

FITZGERALD, JOHN FRANCIS, fgn. service officer; b. Phila., Oct. 25, 1913; s. John F. and Lavinia (Brennan) F.; student U. Pa., 1935-42, Cornell U., 1942; m. Harriett Fitch, Sept. 7, 1940; children—Gail, Karen, Gwen. With State Dept., 1942- -, Am. vice consul, Medellin, Colombia, 1942-44, Tijuana, Mexico, 1944-45, Bilbao, Spain, 1945-47, Tunis, Tunisia, 1948-49; Am. consul, Valletta, Malta, 1950-51; 2d sec. Am. embassy, Brussels, Belgium, 1951- 53; lst sec. Am. embassy, Cairo, Egypt, 1954-56; fgn. service insp., 1957-59; assigned Nat. War Coll., Washington, 1959-60; 1st sec. Am. embassy, Buenos Aires, 1960-61, counselor of embassy for polit. affairs, 1961-63; chief conf. program staff State Dept., 1963-66, dep. coordinator Cuban affairs, 1966-67, coordinator Cuban affairs, 1967-69; consul gen. Tijuana, Mexico, 1969—. Address: PO Box 1358 San Ysidro CA 92073

FITZGERALD, JOHN WOOD, editor; b. Pontiac, Mich., Aug. 5, 1917; s. Harry Yerkes and Grace Wood (Lynch) F.; grad. Kiski Prep. Sch., 1935, Babson Inst., 1937; m. Mary Elizabeth Emery, Dec. 18, 1941; children—Julie, Susan. Photog. chief Pontiac Press Co. (Mich.) 1945-50, picture editor, 1950-54, asst. editor, 1954-56, editor, 1956-69, exec. v.p., dir., until 1969. Served with Signal Corps. AUS, 1941-45, Photog. Center, Long Island City, N.Y. Mem. Mich. Asso. Press Mng. Editors. Am. Soc. Newspaper Editors. Mich. Press Assn. Roman Catholic. Clubs: Orchard Lake Country (Birmingham, Mich.); Rotary, City (Pontiac, Mich.). Home: 155 Point Circle Jupiter FL 33458

FITZGERALD, JOSEPH HAROLD, airline co. exec.; b. Los Angeles, Mar. 20, 1909; s. Joseph Harold and Mildred (Anderson) F.; A.B. in Econs., U. Mont., 1934; B.A. in Jurisprudence, Oxford (Eng.) U., 1934, B.C.L., 1935; m. Ruth Knowles Milliken, Nov. 1935; children—Helen (Mrs. Robert Cserr), Jean (Mrs. Thomas P. Jackson), Joseph Knowles, Susan. Admitted to Mass. bar, 1936, and practiced in Boston until 1942; with Bd. Econ. Warfare, and successor agencies, 1943-46; atty. CAA, 1947-51; dir. Alaska office CAB, 1951-53; dir. bur. air operations, 1953-58; gen. mgr. Ozark Air Lines, St. Louis, 1958-59, pres., 1959-63; exec. dir. Alaska Pub. Service Commn., also coordinator Alaska Reconstrn. and Devel. Commn., Anchorage, 1964—; chmn. Fed. Field Com. for Devel. Planning in Alaska. Mem. Air Transp. Assn. Am. (dir.), Assn. Local Transport Airlines (dir.). Home: 632 W 6th Av Anchorage AK 99503

FITZGERALD, JOSEPH JOHN, lawyer, lumber co., exec.; b. Maple Park, Ill., Sept. 21, 1904; s. James and Teresa (McGirr) F.; student U. Ill., 1922-24, Northwestern U. Law Sch. 1925-26; m. Dorothy Poss, Dec. 26, 1938; children—Susan (Mrs. Donald Rice, Jr.), Gail (Mrs. Gerald James); Anne (Mrs. Joseph O'Neill). Admitted to Ill. bar, 1929; with Edward Hines Lumber Co., Chgo., 1932—, gen. atty., 1945—, exec. v.p., 1963—, also dir.; pres., dir. So. Mineral Corp.; dir. Neb. Bridge Supply & Lumber Co. Recipient Citizenship award Lumber Industry, 1965. Mem. Am., Ill. bar assns., Nat. Forest Products Assn. (dir.), Newcomen Soc. Home: 2334 Central Park Evanston IL 60201 Office: 200 S Michigan Av Chicago IL 60604

FITZ GERALD, LESLIE MAURICE, oral surgeon; b. Cresco, Ia., Aug. 18, 1898; s. Edward A. and Emma (Daly) Fitz G.; D.D.S., U. Ia., 1919; D.Sc., Loyola U., 1954, Temple U., 1957; m. Marcelle Meis, Oct. 8, 1921 (dec. 1970); children—Shirley Ann (Mrs. F.D. Gilloon, Jr.), Patricia (Mrs. J.A. O'Brien III), Jacqueline (Mrs. F. Benjamin Merritt II). Instr. U. Ia., 1919-20; resident oral surgery U. Ia. Hosp., 1919-20; pvt. practice oral surgery, Dubuque, 1920—; chief oral surgery St. Joseph, Finley, Xavier hosps., cons. oral surgery Central Office VA, also Surgeon Gen. USN; v.p. Dubuque Thrift Plan Indsl. Bank, 1931-63, pres., 1963—; dir. Dubuque Savs. & Loan Assn., First Nat. Bank of Dubuque. Chmn. dental adv. com. to Am.-Korean Found., 1954. Pres. Boy's Club, Community Chest, Dubuque, 1931-32; v.p. Centralia Community Fire Dept., 1947—. Served as lt. comdr. Dental Corps, USN. Recipient Arnold K. Maislen Meml. award N.Y.U., 1958; Thomas P. Hinman award, Atlanta; Distinguished Service award State U. Ia., 1969, Am. Soc. Oral Surgeons, 1970. Hon. col., staff Gov. of N.M., Co- founder, diplomate, sec. Am. Bd. Oral Surgery. Fellow Am. Coll. Dentists (chmn. com. oral surgery), Internat. Coll. Anesthetists, Acad. Internat. Dentistry, Internat. Coll. Dentists; hon. mem. Alaska, Hawaii, P.R. dental socs.; mem. Nat. Inter-Assn. Council on Health, 1954; mem. Am. Dental Assn. (pres. 1953-54, chmn. bur. econ. research and statistics 1943-51; chmn. sect. oral surgery 1948, mem. editorial bd. Jour. Oral Surgery 1950-56; chmn. council on dental edn.), Ia. (pres. 1942-43, past trustee), Dubuque (pres. 1920-21, 32-33), Chgo. dental socs., Am. Soc. Oral Surgeons (Pres. 1941-42, 42-43), Dubuque County Med. Soc., Fedn. Dentaire Internat., Jr. C. of C. (pres. 1923-24), Dubuque C. of C. (dir. 1924-30), U. Ia. Coll. Dentistry Alumni Assn. (pres. 1931-32), Am. Legion, 40 and 8, Farm Bur., Guernsey Breeders Assn., Omicron Kappa Upsilon, Xi Psi Phi. Roman Catholic. Elk, Rotarian (pres. 1930-31). Asso. editor Kruger Textbook of Oral Surgery; Oral Surgery Directory of World. Contbr. articles dental, medical publs. Lectr. in many states and before univs. Home: 450 Villa Court Dubuque IA 52001 Office: 988 W 3d Dubuque IA 52001

FITZGERALD, MARK JAMES, educator; b. Olean, N.Y., May 28, 1906; s. Edward W. and Helen M. (York) F.; A.B., U. Notre Dame, 1928; M.B.A., Harvard, 1931; Ph.D., U. Chgo., 1950; student St. Bonaventure's Coll., 1925-26, Holy Cross Coll., 1936- 40. Ordained priest Congregation Holy Cross, Roman Catholic Ch., 1940; mem. faculty econs. U. Notre Dame, 1940—, dir. indsl. relations sect., 1953- -, prof., 1956—, mem. grad. council, 1956-59, president's com. for acad. appointments, 1958-61. Pub. panel mem. 6th regional WLB, World War II; arbitration panels Fed. Mediation and Conciliation Service; pres. Holy Cross Ednl. Conf., 1955. Mem. Cath. Econ. Assn. (pres. 1957), Cath. Assn. Internat. Peace (v.p. 1958-61), Nat. Acad. Arbitrators (research and edn. com. 1961-65), Am. Arbitration Assn. (arbitration panel). Author: Britain Views Our Industrial Relations, 1955; The Common Market's Labor Programs, 1966. Address: Dept Economics Univ Notre Dame Notre Dame IN 46556

FITZGERALD, RICHARD A., lawyer, airline exec.; b. Franklin, O., July 29, 1913; s. John P. and Florence (Wolfe) F.; A.B., Western Mich. U., 1936; J.D., George Washington U., 1940; m. Dorothy E. Ell, Aug. 26, 1940; children—David, Margaret. Admitted to D.C. bar, 1940; clk. Covington, Burling, Rublee, Washington, 1938-40; atty. Dept. Agr., 1940-41; asso. Denning & Cross, Washington, 1941-47; partner Cummings, Stanley, Truitt & Cross, Washington, 1947-55; asst. v.p. Nat. Airlines, 1955-57, v.p., 1957-61; asst. gen. counsel Air Transport Assn. Am., 1961; v.p. Seaboard World Airlines, 1961-62, sec.-gen. counsel Frontier Airlines, Denver, 1962-63, v.p. legal, sec., 1963-66 sr. v.p., gen. counsel, sec., 1966—. Served with USNR, 1943-45. Mem. Tau Kappa Alpha, Phi Alpha Delta, Order Coif. Clubs: Nat. Aviation, Kenwood Country (Washington); Valley Country (Denver). Home: 487 Oswego St Aurora CO 80010 Office: 5900 E 39th St Denver CO 80207

FITZGERALD, RICHARD DAVID, accountant; b. Aurora, N.Y., Mar. 28, 1926; s. Dennis Francis and Alice (Maloney) F.; A.B. cum laude, Dartmouth, 1946, M.C.S. with distinction, Amos Tuck Sch., 1949; m. Kathryn McGeary Lynch, Aug. 14, 1954; children—Stephen J., Roseann, Denise F. With Price Waterhouse & Co., C.P.A.'s, N.Y.C., also Hartford, Conn., 1949—, partner, 1963—. Served as Officer USNR, 1946- 48. C.P.A., N.Y., Conn. Mem. Am. Inst. C.P.A.'s, Conn. Soc. C.P.A.'s, Greater Hartford C. of C., Phi Beta Kappa, Sigma Alpha Epsilon. Roman Catholic. Clubs: Hartford, Hartford Golf, Exchange; Stamford Yacht. Contbr. profl. jours. Home: 164 Ox Yoke Dr Wethersfield CT 06109 Office: 799 Main St Hartford CT 06103

FITZGERALD, ROBERT G., corp. exec.; b. 1927; B.A., U. Portland, 1950; married. With Tektronix Inc., 1950—, exec. v.p. internat. and U.S. operations, 1966—, also dir. Served with U.S. Merchant Marine, 1944-46. Address: PO Box 500 Beavertown OR 97005*

FITZGERALD, ROBERT STUART, writer; b. Geneva, N.Y., Oct. 12, 1910; s. Robert Emmet and Anne Montague (Stuart) F.; grad. Choate Sch., Wallingford, Conn., 1929; A.B., Harvard, 1933; student Trinity Coll., Cambridge (Eng.) U., 1931-32; m. Sarah Morgan, Apr. 19, 1947; children—Hugh Linane, Benedict Robert Campion, Maria Juliana, Peter Michael Augustine, Barnaby John Francis, Caterina Maria Teresa. Reporter, N.Y. Herald Tribune, 1933-35; writer Time mag., 1936-49; instr. lit. Sarah Lawrence Coll., 1946-53, Princeton, 1950-51; fellow Sch. Letters, Ind. U., 1952—; vis. prof. U. Notre Dame, 1957, U. Wash., 1961, Mt. Holyoke Coll., 1964, Harvard, 1964-65; Nicholas Boylston prof. Harvard, 1965—. Guggenheim fellow, 1953; recipient Shelley award Poetry Soc. Am., 1955; grantee creative writing Ford Found., 1959; recipient Bollingen prize for translation, 1961. Fellow Am. Inst. Arts and Letters (award 1957), Am. Acad. Arts and Scis., Acad. Am. Poets (chancellor 1968). Roman Catholic. Club: Harvard (N.Y.C.). Author: Poems, 1935; A Wreath for the Sea, 1943; In the Rose of Time, 1956; Spring Shade, 1971. Translator: (with Dudley Fitts) Alcestis (Euripides), 1935; Antigone (Sophocles), 1939; Oedipus Rex (Sophocles), 1949; Oedipus at Colonus (Sophocles), 1941; Odyssey (Homer), 1961; Chronique, Birds (St. John Perse), 1961-66. Address: San Fortunato Della Collina Perugia Italy also 20 Bryant St Cambridge MA 02138

FITZGERALD, THOMAS ROLLINS, univ. adminstr.; b. Washington, Feb. 23, 1922; s. Thomas Rollins and Bessie (Sheehy) F.; B.A., Woodstock (Md.) Coll., 1945, M.A., 1948; S.T.L., Facultes St. Albert de Louvain (Belgium), 1953; Ph.D., U. Chgo., 1957. Joined Soc. of Jesus, 1939, ordained priest Roman Catholic Ch., 1952; instr. classics Novitiate St. Isaac Jogues, Wernersville, Pa., 1957-58, dean studies, asst. prof. classics, 1958-64; dean Coll. Arts and Scis., Georgetown U., 1964-66, acad. v.p., 1966—. Mem. adminstrv. com. Consortium of Univs., Washington, 1968—. Trustee Gonzaga High Sch., Washington, 1969—; chmn. bd. trustees St. Peter's Coll., Jersey City, 1969—. Mem. Am. Philol. Assn. Democrat. Address: Georgetown Univ 37th and O Sts NW Washington DC 20007

FITZGERALD, WENDELL THOMAS, lawyer; b. Thistle, Utah, Sept. 21, 1898 s. Thomas Joseph and Mary Margaret (Freece) F.; A.B., U. Mich., 1922, J.D., 1924; m. Elizabeth Church, Dec. 13, 1943; children—Kirk (foster), Wendell Thomas. Admitted to Cal. bar, 1925, since practiced in San Francisco; mem. firm Morrison, Foerster, Holloway, Clinton & Clark, 1940—. Mem. San Francisco Estate Planning Council. Sec.-treas. standing com. Alexander F. Morrison Found.; bd. dirs. San Francisco Legal Aid Soc. Served with F.A., U.S. Army, 1918-19. Fellow Am. Bar Found.; mem. Am., San Francisco (pres.) bar assns., State Bar Cal. (v.p. 1964-65, bd. govs.), Am. Judicature Soc., Am. Legion, Phi Delta Phi, Phi Gamma Delta. Clubs: Lawyers University Michigan, Bohemian (San Francisco). Home: 128 Fey Dr Burlingame CA 94010 Office: 120 Montgomery St San Francisco CA 94104

FITZ GERALD, WILLIAM AMBROSE, librarian; b. Boston, Jan. 28, 1906; s. Martin Leo and Margaret Lillian (Shea) F.G.; A.B., Boston Coll., 1927, M.A., 1928; Ph.D., Fordham, 1934; B.S. in L.S., Columbia, 1938; m. Julia Frances Morris, Aug. 15, 1936; children—Priscilla, Benedict Fenwick, Stephanie Margaret. Librarian-archivist Bklyn. Prep. Sch., 1928-44; lectr. library edn. Boston Coll., summers 1933, 1934, 1937, Georgetown U., 1936; vis. prof. library sci. Villanova U., summers 1939, 40, 41; instr. library sci., history and govt. St. John's U., 1942-45; librarian and asst. prof. med. history, sch. medicine St. Louis U., 1944-48; dir. library sch. and prof. library sci. George Peabody Coll. for Tchrs., Nashville, 1948-63; dir. libraries, prof. library sci. Marquette U., Milw., 1963-71; prof. library sci., chmn. grad. library sci. dept. Villanova U., Phila., 1971—; library cons. to ICA, Mut. Security Mission to China, Taipei, Taiwan, 1956-58; library cons. Govt. Libya, Tripoli, 1961-63; library services adviser to govts. of Sierra Leone and Liberia, 1962; cons. U.S. Peace Corps, Milw. Civil Service Commn. Mem. Nat. Conf. Christians and Jews. Mem. Newman Fedn. (Cath. faculty adviser Gulf States sect. 1952- 55), Chinese Library Assn., Coll. and Research Libraries Assn., Am. Assn. U. Profs., Assn. Am. Library Schs. (pres. library edn. div. 1956-57), Cath. Commn. Intellectual and Cultural Affairs, Gallery Living Cath. Authors (pres. 1941-49), Am., Cath. (pres. 1939- 41), Southeastern, Med., Mo., Wis., Tenn. library assns., Spl. Libraries Assn. Compiler: Family Bookshelf, 1948, rev. edit., 1955. Adv. editor New Library Cath. Knowledge, 12 vols., 1963-65. Contbr., adviser Cath. Youth Ency., 1965; contbr. to library jours. Home: The Cambridge Alden Park Philadelphia PA 19144

FITZGERALD, WILLIAM FRANCIS, savs. and loan assn. exec.; b. Omaha, Jan. 20, 1908; s. James J. and Katherine (O'Rourke) F.; student Creighton U., 1926-27; B.S. in Mech. Engring., Ia. State Coll., 1931; m. Mary Allingham, Sept. 29, 1934; children—Mary Frances (Mrs. J. Emmet Root), William A., Katherine A. (Mrs. A. R. Grandsaert, Jr.). With Comml. Savs. & Loan Assn., Omaha, 1932—, sec., 1942-50, pres., 1950—, also dir.; dir. Hennen Realty Co., United Seed Co., Temperature Supply Co., Air Conditioning Equipment Co., Fitzgerald Co., Omaha Apts. Co., Wynn Co.; vice chmn., dir. Fed. Home Loan Bank, Topeka, 1960-64. Mem. Fed. Savs. and Loan Adv. Council, Washington, 1962-63. Chmn. Creighton U. Alumni Fund drive, 1960-61. Bd. dirs. United Community Fund, Omaha, 1958-61; bd. regents Creighton U., 1961-68, mem. pres.'s council, 1968—, mem. pres.'s research council, 1967—, Mem. U.S. Savs. and Loan League (bd. dirs. 1955-57), Omaha C. of C. (bd. dirs. 1958-61), Beta Gamma Sigma (hon.). Clubs: Omaha Country, Omaha; Kiwanis (charter, bd. dirs., past pres. South Omaha). Home: 685 N 57th St Omaha NB 68132 Office: 4501 Dodge St Omaha NB 68101

FITZ GERALD, WILLIAM HENRY GERALD, corp. exec.; b. Boston, Dec. 23, 1909; s. William Joseph and Mary Ellen (Smith) Fitz G.; B.S., U.S. Naval Acad., 1931; student Harvard Law Sch., 1934-35; D.Sc., Adelphi U., 1962; m. Annelise Petschek, July 2, 1943; children—Desmond, Anne. With Borden Co., N.Y.C., 1936-41; personal bus. interests, Mexico, 1946-47; organized Metall. Research & Devel. Co., Washington, 1947, v.p., treas., 1947-56, pres., 1956-58, 60—, chmn., 1960—; chmn. bd. Nat. Metallizing Corp., Trenton, N.J., 1956-58, The Cottages, Ltd., Jamaica, B.W.I., 1960—, Linden Corp., Washington, 1962-70, N.Am. Housing Corp., Washington, 1971—; chmn. Supramar, Ltd., Lucerne, 1963-69, dir., 1970—; pres. Nat. Media Analysis, Inc., Washington, 1968-70, chmn., 1970—; partner Hornblower & Weeks, Hemphill-Noyes, 1970; dir. Cosmadent, Ltd., Zurich, Switzerland, Pyrotector, Inc., Hingham, Mass., Avemco Corp. Cons. to dir. ICA, Washington, 1957; dep. dir. for mgmt. ICA, Dept. State, 1958-60; dir. Inst. Inter Am. Affairs, 1958-60; mem. nat. council Fgn. Policy Assn. Trustee Fed. City Council, Wash. Inst. fgn. Affairs. Trustee Fgn. Student Service Council, 1963—, Oblate Coll. (Cath. U.). Served as ensign USN, 1931-34, from lt. (j.g.) to comdr., 1941-46. Decorated Order Militar de Ayacucho (Peru); master knight Sovereign Mil. Order Malta; knight grand cross Order Holy Sepulchre. Mem. Soc. Naval Architects and Marine Engrs., Am. Soc. Naval Engrs., Acad. Polit. Sci., Nat. Inst. Social Scis., Newcomen Soc. N.AM. Roman Catholic. Clubs: Army-Navy Country; University, Internat. (Washington); Harvard, Racquet and Tennis (N.Y.C.); Essex County (Manchester, Mass.). Home: 2305 Bancroft Pl Washington DC 20008 Office: 1875 Connecticut Av Washington DC 20009

FITZGERALD, WILLIAM TERRENCE, lawyer; b. North Vernon, Ind., Oct. 21, 1902; s. William and Lida (Kelley) F.; Ph.B., Notre Dame, 1923; grad. study Yale, 1924; LL.B., Georgetown U., 1927; m. Marie Catherine Thieman, Oct. 21, 1937; children—Kathleen, Patricia, Maureen. Admitted to Ind. bar, 1927; mem. Fitzgerald & Fitzgerald at North Vernon, 1927-37; judge 6th Jud. Circuit, 1937-43; mem. firm Fitzgerald, Buthod, Bowers, Harrison & Kent; city atty. of Evansville, 1948-51. Pres., Evansville-Vanderburgh Levee Authority Dist. Mem. Ind. State Senate, 1935-37. Fellow Am. Coll. Trial Lawyers; mem. Am. (ho. of dels. 1953-54). 7th Fed. Circuit (gov. 1954- 55), Ind. (pres. 1953-54) bar assns., Ind. Judges' Assn. (past pres.), Phi Alpha Delta. Elk. Club: Evansville Country. Home: 398 S Alvord Blvd Evansville IN 47714 Office: Permanent Savs Bldg Evansville IN 47708

FITZ-GIBBON, BERNICE, (Mrs. Herman Block), adtv. exec.; b. Waunakee, Wis.; d. William and Nora (Bowles) Fitz- Gibbon; student Sacred Heart Acad., Madison, Wis., 1903-13; B.A., U. Wis., 1918; m. Herman Block, July 6, 1925; children—Peter, Elizabeth Bowles. High sch. tchr. English, Chippewa Falls, Wis., 1918-19; staff Rockford (Ill.) Register-Gazette, 1920; with Marshall Field & Co., Chgo., 1921, R. H. Macy, N.Y.C., 1923-35; advt. dir. Wanamaker's, 1936- 40, Gimbel Bros., 1940-54; pres. Bernice Fitz-Gibbon, Inc., 1954—. Named woman of year in bus. Asso. Press Editors, 1955; one of top 7 bus. women Fortune mag., 1956. Coined slogan "It's smart to be thrifty" for Macy's and "nobody but nobody undersells Gimbels." Office: 720 Fifth Av New York City NY 10019

FITZGIBBON, JOHN R., banker; b. Tobias, Neb., 1922; student U. Neb. Exec. v.p., dir. Ia-Des Moines Nat. Bank; dir. Northwest Internat. Bank. Home: 721 54th St Des Moines IA 50312 Office: Ia-Des Moines Nat Bank 6th and Walnut Sts Des Moines IA 50309*

FITZGIBBON, RICHARD DILLON, Jr., U.S. atty.; b. St. Louis, May 9, 1925; s. Richard Dillon and Grace (Devine) F.; grad. U.S. Merchant Marine Acad., 1945; student Sch. Commerce, St. Louis U., 1946-47, LL.B., 1950; m. Susan Blumeyer, Sept. 1, 1948; children—Susan Antoinette, Richard David, Peggy Marie, Mary Blumeyer, Arthur Blumeyer. Admitted to Mo. bar, 1950; practice in St. Louis, 1950-62; U.S. atty. Eastern Dist. Mo., 1962—. Dist. activities chmn. Boy Scouts Am. Bd. dirs. Big Bros. Orgn. Served with U.S. Merchant Marine, 1943-46. Mem. Am., Fed., St. Louis bar assns., Delta Theta Phi. Home: 13 Aberdeen Pl St Louis MO 63105 Office: 1114 Market St St Louis MO 63101

FITZ GIBBON, ROBERT LOUIS CONSTANTINE, author; b. Lenox, Mass., June 8, 1919; s. Francis Lee-Dillon and Georgette (Folsom) F.; student Wellington Coll., 1933-35, U. Munich and Sorbonne, 1935-37, Exeter Coll., Oxford U., 1937-39; m. Marjorie Steele; 1 dau., Oohagh; 1 son by previous marriage, Francis. Tchr., Saltus Grammar Sch., Bermuda, 1946-47; profl. writer, 1947—. Served with Brit. Army, 1939-42, with AUS, 1942-46. Author: (fiction) The Arabian Bird, 1948, The Iron Hoop, 1949, Dear Emily, 1952, The Holiday, 1953, The Fair Game, 1956, Paradise Lost and More, 1959, Watcher in Florence, 1959, When the Kissing Had to Stop, 1960, Going to the River, 1963, High Heroic, 1969; (non-fiction) Miss Finnigan's Fault, 1953, Norman Douglas: A Pictorial Record, 1953, (with Giles Playfair) The Little Tour, 1954, 20 July, 1956, The Blitz, 1957, The Life of Dylan Thomas, 1966, Selected Letters of Dylan Thomas, 1967, Through the Minefield, 1967, Denazification, 1969, Out of the Lion's Paw, 1969; London's Burning, 1970; Red Hand: The Ulster Colony, 1971. Address: St Ann's Killiney Hill Rd Dublin Ireland

FITZGIBBON, RUSSELL HUMKE, educator; b. Columbus, Ind., June 29, 1902; s. Thomas Francis and Frances A. (Moore) F.; A.B., Hanover Coll., 1924; LL.D., 1952; A.M., Ind. U., 1928; Ph. D., U. Wis., 1933; m. Irene Cory, July 6, 1929; children—Alan Lee, Katherine Irene (Mrs. David G. Lilly). Research asst. polit. sci. U. Wis., 1931-33; instr., asst. prof., asso. prof., prof. history and polit. sci. Hanover Coll., 1924- 36; asst. prof. polit. sci. U. Cal. at Los Angeles, 1936-42, asso. prof., 1942-48, chmn. dept., 1942-43, 1948-50, prof., 1948-64, dir. Center Latin Am. Studies, 1959-62, acad. asst. to the pres., 1962-64, 1967-68; prof. polit. sci. U. Cal., Santa Barbara, 1964—; Del Amo Found. fellow, Latin Am., 1943-44, Spain, 1959, Doherty Found. Social Sci. Research Council fellow, Latin Am., 1951; sr. polit. analyst Office Inter-Am. Affairs, Washington, 1944-45; vis. prof. polit. sci (summers) Ohio State U., 1952, U. Neb., 1954, U. Ill., 1956, Ind. U., 1960, Georgetown U., 1963, 64. Fulbright research grantee, Italy, 1958-59. Decorated Order of Don Cristóbal Colón (Dominican Republic). Mem. Am. Polit. Sci. Assn. (bd. editors 1946-47), Western Polit. Sci. Assn. (exec. council 1951-53, 57-58, pres. 1956-57), Phi Delta Theta (nat. editor 1931-36), Pi Sigma Alpha (exec. council 1948-50), Pi Gamma Mu, Alpha Phi Gamma. Presbyn. Author: Cuba and the United States, 1935; Outline of Latin American History, 1937; Uruguay; Portrait of a Democracy, 1954; Latin America: A Panorama of Contemporary Politics, 1971. Co-author: Latin America, Past and Present, 1946. Editor: The Civilization of the Americas, 1938; Forty Years on Main Street (editorials of William Allen White), 1938; Global Politics, 1944; Tie Constitutions of the Americas, 1948. Mem. bd. contbg. editors: Handbook of Latin American Studies, 1941-45; bd. editors Inter-Am. Econ. Affairs 1949—; internat. adv. bd. Hispanic Am. Report, 1949-62. Contbr. articles profl. publs. Home: 1201 N Ontare Rd Santa Barbara CA 93105

FITZGIBBONS, DAVID JOHN, drug co. exec.; b. Paterson, N.J., Jan. 18, 1906; s. David John and Elizabeth (Hynes) F.; grad. Drake Bus. Coll., Paterson, 1925, Pace Inst., 1928; m. Eleanor Corry Kelly, Feb. 22, 1941; children—Robert Anton, David James. Office mgr., sec. Standard Plumbing & Heating, Inc., 1928-35; with Price, Waterhouse & Co., C.P.A.'s 1935-37; chief accountant Am. Ferment Co., 1937-39; v.p., treas. Sterling Products Internat., Inc., 1939—, Sydney Ross Co., 1939—, Winthrop Products, Inc., 1949—; v.p., Sterling Drug. Inc., 1960-61, exec. v.p., 1961-63, pres., 1963—, also dir. Bd. dirs. Nat. Fgn. Trade Council. Club: Essex Country (W. Orange, N.J.). Home: 100 Essex Rd Summit NJ 07901 Office: 90 Park Av New York City NY 10016

FITZGIBBONS, EDWARD SPENCE, shoe co. exec.; b. Brockton, Mass., Aug. 19, 1921; s. Harold Edward and Angeline (Spence) F.; grad. Milton Acad., 1940; A.B., Harvard, 1943; m. Patricia Ann May, Feb. 11, 1956; children—Edward Spence, Lisa Ann, Caroline M., Stephen M. With Blanchard Bro. & Lane, Newark, 1947-58, pres., 1956-58; v.p. Hanover Shoe, Inc. (Pa.), 1958-62, pres., 1962—; dir. Nat. Bank & Trust Co. Central Pa. Pres., dir. Upholstery Leather Group, Inc., 1952-58; bd. dirs. Tanners Council Am., 1958, Leather Industries Am., 1956-57. Mem. Nat. Footwear Mfrs. Assn. (dir. 1965—). Republican. Roman Cath. Home: 235 Highland Av Hanover PA 17331 Office: 118 Carlisle St Hanover PA 17331

FITZGIBBONS, JOHN P., business exec. Vice pres., treas., controller B. Gertz, Inc. Office: 162-10 Jamaica Av Jamaica NY 11432*

FITZHENRY, ROBERT IRVINE, publisher; b. N.Y.C., Apr. 10, 1918; s. Irvine and Margaret (Lane) F.; B.A., U. Mich., 1939; m. Hilda Anderson, Jan. 20, 1949; children—Sharon (Mrs. Robert Rinkoff), Bridget, Hollister. Reporter, editor, night mgr. United Press Assn., Cleve. and Columbus, O., 1939-41; from salesman, sales mgr. to dir. gen. sales Harper & Row, Pubs., N.Y.C., 1946-66; co-founder, 1966, since pres. Fitzhenry & Whiteside Ltd., publishers, Don Mills, Ont., Can., 1966—; Chmn. Pound Ridge Democratic party, 1960-64. Served with USAAF, 1941-45. Mem. Am. Book Pubs. Council (chmn. book distbn. com. 1946-48). Home: 62 Mill St Uxbridge Ontario Canada Office: 150 Lesmill Rd Don Mills Ontario Canada

FITZHUGH, EDWIN A., editor, writer; b. Phoenix, July 30, 1909; s. Edwin C. and Gustina (Thiesen) F.; grad. Phoenix High Sch., 1925; m. Meryal Meadows, Feb. 13, 1937; children—Lee, Meryal Lee, Reporter. deptl. editor Phoenix Gazette, San Francisco News, Sacramento (Cal.) Bee, Los Angeles Examiner, 1925-31; editor El Centro (Cal.) Imperial Valley Press, 1931- 43; owner, pub. El Centro Weekly, 1943-46; pub. El Centro Imperial Valley Press and Morning Post, 1946-51; editor Chgo. Sun-Times Syndicate, 1951-56; editorial writer Indpls. Star, 1956-58; editor The Phoenix Gazette, 1958—. Mem. Am. Soc. Newspaper Editors, Sigma Delta Chi, Ariz. Acad., Newcomen Soc. N.Am., Nat. Conf. Editorial Writers, Internat. Press Inst. Author syndicated newspaper column Close to Home,'1950-60; short stories. Home: 7810 N 14th St Phoenix AZ 85021 Office: The Phoenix Gazette Phoenix AZ 85004

FITZHUGH, GILBERT WRIGHT, life ins. co. exec.; b. Bklyn., July 8, 1909; s. Herbert W. and Ethel (Gilbert) F.; B.S., Princeton, 1930; LL.D., Carroll Coll., 1966; m. Lea Van Ingh, June 17, 1933; children—Gilbert Van Ingh, Lea Armistead. With Met. Life Ins. Co., 1930—, various positions actuarial and group divs., 1930-58, asst. gen. mgr. Canadian head office, 1946, 47, v.p. charge planning and devel., N.Y.C., 1958- 60, v.p., gen. mgr. for Can., 1960-61, exec. v.p., N.Y.C., 1962-63, pres., chief exec. officer, 1963-66, chmn. bd., chief exec. officer, 1966—; dir. Singer Co., Met. Life Ins. Co. Chmn., Pres. Nixon's Blue Ribbon Def. Panel, 1969-70. Trustee YMCA Retirement Fund, Nat. Indsl. Conf. Bd., The Conf. Bd. Fellow Soc. Actuaries, Casualty Actuarial Soc.; mem. Am. Acad. Actuaries, N.Y. C. of C. (chmn. exec. com., pres.), Inst. Life Ins. (chmn.), Phi Beta Kappa. Clubs: Blind Brook, The Links, Union League University, Princeton (N.Y.C.); Rideau, Ottawa Hunt and Golf (Ottawa, Can.); Adirondack Mountain (Lake Placid, N.Y.); Seigniory (Montebello, Can.); California (Los Angeles); Pacific-Union (San Francisco). Home: 16 Sutton Pl New York City NY 10022 Office: 1 Madison Av New York City NY 10010

FITZ-HUGH, GLASSELL SLAUGHTER, otolarynogologist, educator; b. Charlottesville, Va., May 1, 1907; s. Glassell and Orie (Slaughter) Fitz-H.; student Augusta Mil. Acad., 1925- 27; M.D., U. Va., 1933; m. Dorothea Minor Meredith, Sept. 9, 1937; children—Glassell Slaughter, George Meredith, Elizabeth Morrison. Intern, resident Charity Hosp., New Orleans, 1933-35, U. Va. Hosp., Charlottesville, 1935-37; faculty sch. medicine U. Va. since 1937, prof. otolaryngology since 1951, chmn. dept. since 1951. Former mem. communicative disorder research tng. com. NIH. Served as capt. to lt. col. M.C., A.U.S., 1942-46. Diplomate Am. Bd. Otolaryngology. Fellow A.C.S.; mem. A.M.A., So. Med. Assn., Med. Soc. Va., Va. Soc. Ophthalmology and Otolaryngology, Am. Acad. Ophthalmology and Otolaryngology, Am. Laryngol. Rhinol. and Otological Soc. (pres. 1967), Am. Acad. Facial Plastic and Reconstructive Surgery, Am. Otological Soc., Am. Laryngol. Assn., Am. Assn. U. Profs., U. Va. Alumni Assn., Am. Soc. Head and Neck Surgery, Soc. U. Otolaryngologists, Va. Acad. Scis., Va. Hearing Found., Am. Council Otolaryngology, Nat. Rehab. Assn., Alpha Omega Alpha. Club: Centurian. Presbyn. Rotarian. Home: 2003 Spottswood Rd Charlottesville VA 22903 Office: 1400 Jefferson Park Av Charlottesville VA 22903

FITZHUGH, HOWARD NAYLOR, beverage co. exec.; b. Washington, Oct. 31, 1909; s. William H. and Lillian (Naylor) F.; B.S. cum laude, Harvard, 1930, M.B.A., 1933; postgrad. Columbia, 1939-41, Am. U., 1959-61; LL.D., Va. State Coll., 1970; m. Thelma E. Hare, June 11, 1938; children—Howard Naylor, Richard H., Judith Ellen (Mrs. Sylvester Rice). Mem. faculty Howard U., 1934-65, asst. prof. marketing, 1946-65, co-organizer Small Bus. Guidance and Devel. Center, 1963, chmn. adv. com., 1963-69; v.p. spl. markets Pepsi Cola Co., Purchase, N.Y., 1965—. Organizer, exec. dir. Affiliated Bus. Assns. Washington, 1946-49; cons. Adult Distributive Ednl. Program, Washington, 1950-52, Moss H. Kendrix Orgn., Washington, 1953-60, Spl. Markets Resources, Washington, 1961-65; mem. nat. marketing adv. com. Commerce Dept., 1968-70; coordinator advt. council nat. adv. program A.R.C., 1969-71; mem. bus. adv. com. Columbia Sch. Bus., 1970—. Bd. dirs. Burgundy Farms Sch., Alexandria, Va., 1949-51, Coop. Fedn., Washington; bd. mgmt. Washington YMCA, Interracial Council Bus. Opportunity, N.Y.C. Recipient award Advt. Age, 1970. Mem. Nat. Bus. Edn. League (past pres.), Nat. Assn. Market Devel. (co-founder, 1st exec. dir., past pres.), Am. Marketing Assn. (v.p.). Author articles in field. Editor: proc. Annual Social Science Conference, 1957; proc. National Conference Small Business, 1962. Home: 51 Carver Terrace Yonkers NY 10710 Office: Pepsi Cola Co Anderson Hill Rd Purchase NY 10577

FITZHUGH, WILLIAM WYVILL, Jr., advt. exec.; b. Bklyn., June 27, 1914; s. William Wyvill and Portia (Starr) F.; A.B., Dartmouth, 1935; B.A., Trinity Coll., Cambridge U., 1937, M.A., 1938; m. Florence Hardy, Dec. 13, 1941; children—William, Priscilla, John, Portia. Fellow Carnegie Endowment Internat. Peace, 1938-39; sec.-rapporteur Internat. Studies Conf., League of Nations, 1938-39; instr. govt. Columbia, 1939- 42; exec. v.p. William W. Fitzhugh, Inc., N.Y.C., 1945—; pres. New Haven Board & Carton Co., Inc., N.Y.C., 1960-64; partner Dalsemer, Fitzhugh & Catzen, N.Y.C., 1964-66; pres. Newspaper Preprint Corp., N.Y.C., 1966—. Chmn. Chappaqua Orchestral Assn. Served to lt. USNR. Mem. Gravure Tech. Assn. (past pres.), Folding Paper Box Assn. Am. (past pres. met. N.Y. group), Label Mfrs. Assn. (past dir.), Bklyn. C. of C. (past dir.), Phi Beta Kappa, Sigma Chi. Republican. Episcopalian. Home: Hog Hill Rd Chappaqua NY 10514 Office: 750 3d Av New York City NY 10017

FITZMAURICE, GERALD GRAY, justice Internat. Ct. Justice; b. Storrington, Sussex, Eng., Oct. 24, 1901; s. Maurice Swynfen and Mabel Gertrude (Gray) F.; student Malvern Coll., 1914-19; B.A., LL.B. (scholar of coll. 1923, hon. fellow 1961), Gonville and Caius Coll., Cambridge U.; m. Evelina Alexandra Sandberg, Sept. 15, 1933; children—James Alexander Swynfen, Maurice Evelyn Forbes. Called to English Bar at Gray's Inn, 1925 (elected bencher 1961); practiced in London, 1925-29; joined U.K. Fgn. Service as legal adviser, 1929; legal adviser Minister Econ. Warfare, 1939-43; dep. legal adviser Fgn. Office, 1945-53, chief legal adviser, 1953-60; named Queen's Counsel, 1957; judge Internat. Ct. of Justice, The Hague, 1960—. Legal adviser numerous U.K. delegations at pre-war and post-war internat. confs., also for U.K. Govt. in cases before Internat. Ct. Justice; mem. internat. law com. UN, 1955-60, pres., 1959. Decorated companion Order St. Michael and St. George, 1945, knight comdr., 1954, knight grand cross, 1960. Mem. Inst. Internat. Law, Internat. Law Assn., Am. Soc. Internat. Law, British Inst. Internat. Law, Grotius Soc. (pres. 1956-60). Home: 3 Gray's Inn Sq Holborn London WC 1 England Office: Internat Court of Justice The Hague Netherlands

FITZPATRICK, BERCHMANS TANNER, lawyer; b. Washington, July 13, 1907; s. James Frederick and Mary Madeline (O'Brien) F.; A.B., Dartmouth, 1930; LL.B., Harvard, 1933; m. Georgiana Mary DeWolfe, Oct. 10, 1936; children—Barry Morgan, Robert Brian, James Frederick. Atty., PWA, 1933-37; spl. counsel Mpls.-St. Paul San. Dist. Project, 1935-37; regional atty. U.S. Housing Authority, 1938-42; asst. and asso. gen. counsel Nat. Housing Agy., 1942-46, gen. counsel, 1947; asst. adminstr. and gen. counsel HHFA, 1947-49, dep. adminstr., gen. counsel, 1949-54, gen. counsel, 1954; vice chmn., dir. Fed. Nat. Mortgage Assn.; v.p., dir. Def. Homes Corp.; gen. counsel First Nat. Redevel. Corp.; counsellor at law and housing cons., 1955—. Dir. Nat. Housing Conf.; exec. sec. Mayor's Com. for Better Housing of City N.Y.; sec. McNamara's Com. on Mil. Housing Policy and Programs, 1967; cons. to various groups. Recipient Honor award HHFA, 1955; Honor award Nat. Housing Conf., 1970. Mem. Alpha Tau Omega. Democrat. Roman Catholic. Home: 22 W Irving St Chevy Chase MD 20015 Office: 1250 Connecticut Av NW Washington DC 20036

FITZPATRICK, EDWIN J., securities broker; b. N.Y.C., Ap. 15, 1910; s. James E. and Anna (Gallagher) F.; A.B., Cornell U., 1932; m. Betty C. Roney, July 5, 1940; children—Edwin J., Anne Roney. Asst. instr. econs. Cornell U., 1932-33; v.p. charge sales Clapp's Baby Foods, Inc., 1933-41; asst. chief food div. W.P.B., 1941-42; pres. Chef Boy-ar-dee Foods, Inc., Milton, Pa., 1946-49; also dir., v.p. Am. Home Foods, Inc., N.Y.C., 1946-49; pres. Permacel Tape Corp., New Brunswick, N.J., 1949-55; gen. partner Orvis Bros. & Co., N.Y.C., 1955—. Cons. bus. and def. service adminstrn. Dept. Commerce, 1954-55. Served as maj. to col. Q.M.C., ETO, U.S. Army, 1942-46. Decorated Legion of Merit, Bronze Star. Mem. Phi Beta Kappa, Chi Phi, Quill and Dagger. Clubs: Genesee Valley (Rochester, N.Y.); Plainfield (N.J.) Country; University (N.Y.C.). Home: 1734 Sleepy Hollow Lane Plainfield NJ 07060 Office: 15 Broad St New York City NY 10005

FITZPATRICK, FRANCIS J., lawyer; b. Wilmington, Del., Feb. 23, 1904; A.B., Williams Coll., 1925; LL.B., Fordham U., 1928. Admitted to N.Y. bar, 1929; partner firm Boal, McQuade & Fitzpatrick, N.Y.C. Mem. Westchester County Bar Assn. Office: 116 John St New York City NY 10038*

FITZPATRICK, FRANCIS JOHN, naval officer; b. Salt Lake City, Feb. 3, 1916; s. John Francis and Margaret (Mockler) F.; student U. Wyo., 1934-35; B.S. in Elec. Engring., U.S. Naval Acad., 1939; student U.S. Naval Postgrad. Sch., Monterrey, Cal., 1943-44, Indsl. Coll. Armed Forces, 1957-58; M.S. in Bus. Administrn., George Washington U., 1963-64; m. Kathleen Ellen Binet, Oct. 19, 1941; children—Kathleen Ellen (Mrs. Joseph D. Stewart), Tara Mairead (Mrs. Mariano Echevarria), Francis John, Brigid Canice (Mrs. Thomas C. Ruland), Moira Eileen, Michael Kevin. Commd. ensign USN, advanced through grades to rear adm., 1966; service in N. Atlantic convoys, also with 3d and 5th fleets, PTO, World War II; comdr. destroyer, Korean War; also comdr. attack transport and USS Wright; dep. dir. communications, electronics Office of Joint Chiefs Staff, Washington, 1966-68, asst. chief naval operations for communications and cryptology, 1968—. Decorated Bronze Star medal, Legion of Merit. Mem. Armed Forces Communications and Electronics Assn. (nat. v.p. 1968—), Sigma Nu. Roman Catholic. Home: 6224 Nelway Dr McLean VA 22101 also 1303 7th St Coronado CA 92118 Office: Chief of Naval Operations The Pentagon Washington DC 20350

FITZPATRICK, JAMES HENRY, hosp. adminstr., clergyman; b. Bklyn., Oct. 12, 1922; s. James Henry and Mary Agnes (Schell) F.; grad. Cathedral Coll. Prep. Sem., Bklyn., 1942; grad. Sem. of Immaculate Conception, Huntington, N.Y., 1948. Ordained priest Roman Catholic Church, 1948, elevated to papal chamberlain, 1962; asst. pastor 14 Holy Martyrs Ch., Bklyn., 1948-50; asso. dir. div. health and hosps., Cath. Charities, Diocese Bklyn., 1950-66, dir. div. health and hosps., 1966—. Moderator of Catholic Physicians Guild Bklyn. Bd. dirs., also coms. Greater N.Y. Hosp. Assn.; v.p., dir. Hosp. Council Greater N.Y.; mem. N.Y. State Cath. Welfare Com., Mayor N.Y.C. Task Force Orgn. Med. Services; adv. bd. N.Y. State Employment Service, United Hosp. Fund N.Y.-Queens County chmn.; mem. N.Y. State Hosp. Rev. and Planning Council, 1967—; chmn. com. long term care, trustee Am. Hosp. Assn.; v.p. Greater N.Y. Hosp. Assn., 1967—). Mem. Cath. Hosp. Assn. U.S. and Can. (pres. 1963—), Queensboro Jamaica C.'s of C. Home: 152-11 89th Av Jamaica NY 11432 Office: 345 Adams St Brooklyn NY 11201

FITZPATRICK, JOHN J., lawyer; b. Toronto, Ont., Can., Sept. 1, 1914; s. John J. and Agnes (Wray) F.; B.A., U. Toronto, 1939; LL.B., Osgoode Hall; m. Joan Elizabeth Cowie, Aug. 25, 1945; children—John, James, Kathleen, Margaret Ann, Moira, Janet, Sheila, Joan. Admitted to Ont. bar, 1948; partner firm Gardiner, Roberts, Anderson, Conlin, Fitzpatrick, O'Donohue & White, Toronto, 1960—. Dir. Nat. Sewer Pipe Ltd. Served with RCAF, World War II. Mem. Canadian Bar Assn., Internat. Assn. Ins. Counsel, Lawyers Club Toronto, Sigma Chi, Phi Delta Phi. Roman Catholic. Clubs: Toronto Cricket; Skating and Curling; Queens; National; Osler Bluff Ski; Muskoka Lakes Golf and Country. Office: Canadian Imperial Bank of Commerce Bldg Toronto 1 Ontario Canada*

FITZPATRICK, JOSEPH EDWARD, food service co. exec.; b. Auburn, N.Y., Oct. 14, 1931; s. Joseph E. and Stella (Bannon) F.; B.B.A., LeMoyne Coll., 1953; m. Jean M. Cuddy, May 1, 1954; children—Michael, Kevin, Brian, Mary Jo. Staff accountant Price Waterhouse & Co., N.Y.C., 1955-58, sr. accountant, Rochester, N.Y., 1958-61, audit mgr., Bogota, Colombia, S.A., 1961-63, Phila., 1963-64; v.p., controller Saga Adminstrv. Corp., Menlo Park, Cal., 1964—. Active Boy Scouts Am., Little League. Served to cpl., AUS, 1953-55. C.P.A., N.Y. Mem. Am. Inst. C.P.A.'s, N.Y. State Soc. C.P.A.'s. Democrat. Roman Catholic. Home: 600 Guadalupe Dr Los Altos CA 94022 Office: 1 Saga Lane Menlo Park CA 94025

FITZPATRICK, JOSEPH MARK, patent lawyer; b. Jersey City, May 27, 1925; s. Joseph Francis Stephen and Meave (Wilson) F.; M.E., Stevens Inst. Tech., 1945; J.D., Georgetown U., 1951; m. Elizabeth Anne Keane, June 18, 1949; children—Elizabeth A., Susan E., Christopher M., Stephen R. Examiner, U.S. Patent Office, 1946-50; admitted to Va. bar, 1950, N.Y. bar, 1954; trial atty., anti-trust div. Dept. Justice, 1951-52; mem. firm War, McElhannon, Brooks & Fitzpatrick, N.Y.C., 1954-70, Fitzpatrick, Cella, Harper & Scinto, N.Y.C., 1970—. Served with USNR, 1943-46. Mem. Am., N.Y., Va. bar assns., N.Y. Patent Law Assn. Clubs: City Midday; Manasquan River Yacht. Home: 17 Oak Lane Scarsdale NY 10583 Office: 277 Park Av New York City NY 10017

FITZPATRICK, MARGEE GRACE, mem. Republican Nat. Com.; b. St. John, N.B., Can., Feb. 16, 1918; d. Archie and Margaret (Tiplady) Albin; grad. Kings County Sch. Nursing, Bklyn., 1939; m. James J. Fitzpatrick, Dec. 13, 1947; 1 dau., Jeanne K. (Mrs. Richard Bishop). Committeewoman Alaska Rep. Party, 1962; finance chmn. Southcentral dist., 1962; mem. Rep. Nat. Com. for Alaska, 1968—. Candidate for Alaska Ho. of Reps., 1962, 64. Mem. Alaska Commn. Status Women, 1968—. Served to 1st lt., Nurse Corps, AUS, 1941-45. Mem. Anchorage Med. Aux. (pres. 1959). Home: 2407 Cottonwood St Anchorage AK 99504 Office: Box 4-2050 Anchorage AK 99503

FITZPATRICK, PAUL EARLY, corp. exec.; b. Buffalo, Sept. 25, 1897; s. William H. and Clara (Hillery) F.; C.E., Cornell U., 1921; LL.D., Canisius Coll., 1956; m. Marion Agnes Lenahan, Sept. 28, 1921; children—Clairose (Mrs. Jerome B. Magee), Ella (Mrs. Francis J. Haley). Pres., dir. W. H. Fitzpatrick & Sons, Inc., 1925—; pres. Am. Lubricants, Inc., 1935-55, now chmn.; pres. Fitzpatrick Donahy, Inc., 1938—, El Clair, Inc., 1945—; dir. Harkin, Inc. (Ft. Lauderdale), El Clair Projects, Inc. Past commr. State Ins. Fund N.Y. Past Dem. chmn. Erie County and N.Y. State; del. Dem. Nat. Conv., 1940, 44, 48, 52. Trustee Cornell U.; bd. regents Canisius Coll. Served with naval aviation USN, World War I. Mem. Cornell Engring. Soc., Knight of Malta, K.C. Clubs: Cornell Buffalo, Buffalo; Cherry Hill Country (Ridgeway, Ont.); Cornell (Buffalo and N.Y.C.). Home: 253 Woodbridge Av Buffalo NY 14214 Office: 1575 Clinton St Buffalo NY 14606

FITZPATRICK, PETER, lawyer; b. Hilltown, County Down, North Ireland, June 26, 1906; s. James and Mary (McCrickard) F.; brought to U.S., 1907, naturalized, 1919; A.B., Loras Coll., 1926; LL.B., Chgo.-Kent Coll. Law, 1933, LL.M., 1934; m. Alma Berard, July 19, 1937; children—James, Maureen (Mrs. John W. Hauch), Elaine (Mrs. Thomas A. Smuczynski), Joseph, Michael, Colleen (Mrs. John Brandeburg), Yvonne (Mrs. Thomas L. Mullins), Robert, Thomas, Rita, Barbara, John, William, Dorothy, Catherine, Margaret Mary. Admitted to Ill. bar, 1933, since practiced in Chgo.; mem. firm Fitzpatrick & Gulbranson. Mem. Jud. Adv. Council of Cook County, 1961—; mem. com. on jury instrns. Ill. Supreme Ct., 1957-62; mem. com. to revise Ill. Civil Practice Act and Rules of Ct., 1950-56; chmn. Chgo. Commn. on Human Relations, 1967—. Bd. dirs. Ill. Bar Found.; trustee Calvert Found. Fellow Am. Coll. Trial Lawyers, Am. Bar Found.; mem. Am., Ill. (pres. 1965-66), Chgo. (bd. mgrs. 1952-54) bar assns., Bar Assn. 7th Fed. Circuit, Ill. Soc. Trial Lawyers, Nat. Conf. Bar Assn. Presidents. Democrat. Roman Catholic. Club: Union League (Chgo.). Contbr. articles to legal publs., law revs. Home: 10532 S Hoyne Av Chicago IL 60643 Office: 10 S LaSalle St Chicago IL 60603

FITZPATRICK, THOMAS BERNARD, educator, physician; b. Madison, Wis., Dec. 19, 1919; s. Joseph J. and Grace (Lawrence) F.; B.A. with honors, U. Wis., 1941; M.D., Harvard, 1945; fellow Mayo Found., 1948-51; Ph.D., U. Minn., 1952; fellow Commonwealth Fund, Oxford, 1958-59; m. Beatrice Devaney, Dec. 27, 1944; children—Thomas B., Beatrice, John, L. Scott, Brian. Intern 4th (Harvard) Med. Service, Boston City Hosp., 1945-46; biochemist Army Med. Center, Md., 1946-48; asst. prof. dermatology U. Mich. Med. Sch., 1951-52; prof., head div. dermatology U. Ore. Med. Sch., 1952- 58; Edward Wigglesworth prof. dermatology, head dept. Harvard Med. Sch., also chief dermatology service Mass. Gen. Hosp., Boston, 1959—; Sigmund Pollitzer lectr. dept. dermatology N.Y. U. Med. Sch., 1962; Internat. Exchange lectr. on dermatology, Japan, 1969; spl. cons. USPHS, NIH; cons. dermatology Peter Bent Brigham Hosp., 1962- -; dept. dermatology Multnomah Hosp., also Children's Hosp., 1952-58. Dir. J.J. Fitzpatrick Lumber Co., Madison. Mem. adv. bd. Robert F. Kennedy Miss. Project. Pres. Dermatology Found., 1971. Recipient Mayo Found. Alumni Research award, 1951; Outstanding Achievement award Bd. Regents, U. Minn., 1964; Myron Gordon award 6th Internat. Pigment Cell Conf., 1965. Diplomate Am. Bd. Dermatology, Fellow Am. Acad. Dermatology and Syphilology (past dir.), Royal Soc. Medicine; mem. Am. Acad. Arts and Scis., Soc. Investigative Dermatology (pres. 1959-60, Stephen Rothman award 1970), Am. Soc. Exptl. Pathology, Am. Dermatol. Assn., Boylston Med. Soc., Western Assn. Physicians, A.M.A., Am. Soc. for Clin. Investigation (emeritus 1965), Irish and Am. Pediatric Soc., S. African Dermatol. Soc. (hon.), Sigma Xi, Alpha Omega Alpha; hon. mem. fgn. profl. socs. Democrat. Roman Catholic. Author: Handbook of Medical Emergencies, 1947; Dermatologic Differential Diagnosis (with Sheldon A. Walker), 1962; also articles. Editor: Handbook of Medical Emergencies, 1947; chief editor Dermatology in General Medicine, 1971. Editorial bd. New Eng. Jour. Medicine, 1961-69; asso. editor Jour. Investigative Dermatology, 1961-64. Home: 138 Wellesley St Weston MA 02193 Office: Mass Gen Hosp Boston MA 02114

FITZPATRICK, WILLIAM FRANCIS, lawyer; b. Owasco, N.Y., Apr. 7, 1902; s. David J. and Mary A. (McGarr) F.; LL.B., Syracuse U., 1927; LL.D., Le Moyne Coll., Syracuse, N.Y., 1966; m. Margaret M. Shortt, June 28, 1936; children—William F., Francis X., James D., Mary M. Admitted to N.Y. bar, 1928, since practiced in Syracuse; partner firm Bond, Schoeneck & King, 1946—. Dir. Lincoln Nat. Bank and Trust Co., Syracuse. Bd. regents LeMoyne Coll., Syracuse; bd. visitors Syracuse U. Coll. Law. Fellow Am. Coll. Trial Lawyers, Am. Bar Found.; mem. Am., N.Y. State (chmn. trial lawyers sect. 1957, pres. 1963), Onondaga County (pres. 1951) bar assns. Republican. Catholic. Clubs: Onondaga Golf and County (Fayetteville, N.Y.); University (Syracuse). Home: 201 Croyden Rd Syracuse NY Office: State Tower Bldg Syracuse NY 13202

FITZPATRICK, WILLIAM HENRY WALTER, editor; b. New Orleans, May 23, 1908; s. Harry William and Clara Mary (Bertel) F.; student Rugby Acad. (New Orleans), Tulane; m. Francis Westfeldt, Aug. 31, 1940; children—William Whitfield, Peter Bryan, Victor Vaughan Owen, Francis James Gasquet. Reporter, New Orleans Item, 1933-35, Times-Picayune, 1935-40; city editor New Orleans States, 1940-41, mng. editor, 1941-45, editor, 1945- 52; v.p., dir. The Times-Picayune Pub. Co., 1948-52; dir. Internat. House, New Orleans, 1949-50; asso. editor Wall Street Jour., 1952-60; editor Norfolk-Portsmouth (Va.) Ledger-Star, 1960-71; exec. editor, v.p. Landmark Communications, Inc., pubs. of Virginian-Pilot and Ledger-Star, Norfolk (Va.), Roanoke (Va.) Times, World News, and Greensboro (N.C.) Daily News and Record, 1971—. Bd. Visitors Tulane, 1953-64; mem. La. selection com. for Root-Tilden scholarships at N.Y. U. Sch. of Law, 1950-52. Served from lt. to lt. comdr. USNR, 1942-45; duty in U.S. ships Enterprise, Intrepid and Hancock in assault and capture of Gilberts, Marshalls and Okinawa, and raids on Wake, Truk and Japan. Awarded Commendation Ribbon by Adm. Nimitz for courage under fire; recipient Pulitzer prize for distinguished editorial writing, 1950; Freedoms Found. medal, 1952. Mem. S.A.R., Am. Soc. Newspaper Editors, La., N.Y. (council 1956-58), socs. colonial wars, Beta Theta Pi, Sigma Delta Chi. Roman Catholic. Clubs: Louisiana, Boston, Wrong Day Duck (New Orleans); Racquet and Tennis (N.Y.C.); Biltmore (N.C.) Forest Country; Cedar Point; Princess Anne Country. Home: 1321 W Princess Anne Rd Norfolk VA 23504 Office: 150 W Brambleton Av Norfolk VA 23510

FITZ RANDOLPH, JOHN ANDERSON, investment banker; b. Bklyn., Apr. 30, 1892; s. George B. and Elizabeth (Anderson) Fitz R.; A.B., Columbia, 1913, LL.B., 1915; m. Grace Farrar, Mar. 19, 1920. 1 dau., Mary Elizabeth (Mrs. Arthur M. Hettich). pub. relations E.I. duPont de Nemours & Co., Inc., 1916-18; gen. mgr. Melville Shoe Corp., 1918-28; dir. sales. advt., pub. relations J. C. Penney Co., 1929-52; v.p. J. Walter Thompson Co., 1952-60; partner Frances I. duPont & Co., N.Y.C., 1960—; dir. Melchers, Inc., Am. Far Eastern Corp., Airkem, Inc. Trustee Packer Collegiate Inst., Bklyn. Home: Sunset Rd Stamford CT 06903 Office: 1 Wall St New York City NY 10005

FITZSIMMONS, ARTURO QUIROZ, banker. Gen. mgr. Banco de Chile, Santiago. Office: 251 Ahumada St Santiago Chile*

FITZSIMMONS, FRANK E., labor union exec.; b. 1908. Gen. vice pres. Internat. Brotherhood of Teamsters. Address: 1050 Harvard St Grosse Pointe MI 48236*

FITZSIMONS, MATTHEW ANTHONY, educator; b. N.Y.C., July 1, 1912; s. Andrew and Helen (Murray) F.; A.B., Columbia, 1934, M.A., 1938; B.A., Oriel Coll., Oxford, 1937; Ph.D., U. Chgo., 1947; m. Frances Schlosser, Sept. 8, 1937; childrenRobert, Carol, Gerald, David. Instr. history U. Notre Dame, 1937-55, prof., 1955—. Mem. Cath. Commn. on Intellectual and Cultural Affairs, Am. Hist. Assn., Midwest Conf. Brit. Hist. Studies, Phi Beta Kappa. Roman Catholic. Author: (with James A. Corbett) Christianity and Civilization, 1947; Foreign Policy of the British Labour Government, 1945-51, 1953; Empire by Treaty, 1964. Co-editor: The Catholic Church in World Affairs, 1954; The Development of Historiography, 1955; What America Stands For, 1959; Diplomacy in a Changing World, 1959; The Image of Man, 1959; editor: The Catholic Church Today: Western Europe, 1969. Cons. editor Rev. Politics, 1942-55, editor, 1955—. Home: 3109 McKinley St South Bend IN 46615 Office: Box B Notre Dame IN 46556

FITZWATER, OTTIS TEASLEY, utilities exec.; b. Ky., Jan. 22, 1906; s. Henry Elliott and Amy (Bastin) F.; ed. pub. schs.; m. Paula Leigeber, Sept. 30, 1926; children—Donald E., Richard E. With Indpls. Power & Light Co. (and predecessor firm), 1923—, beginning as timekeeper, successively mem. gen. accounting dept., asst. treas., treas., v.p., 1923-57, pres., 1957-66, chmn. bd., pres., 1966-67, chmn. bd., chief exec. officer, 1967-71, chmn. exec. com., 1971—, also dir.; dir. Indpls. Life Ins. Co., Mchts. Nat. Bank & Trust Co., Indpls., Indpls. Union Ry., Inc. Bd. dirs. Indpls. United Fund, Central Ind. council Boy Scouts Am., Indpls. Center for Advanced Research; trustee Ind. Central Coll. Member Ind. (bd. dirs.), Indpls. (bd. dirs.) chambers of commerce, Financial Execs. Inst. Mem. Ch. of God. Mason (Shriner). Clubs: Columbia, Meridian Hills Country, Indianapolis Athletic, Indianapolis Country, Press (Indpls.) Home: 402 Kessler Blvd W Dr Indianapolis IN 46208 Office: 25 Monument Circle Indianapolis IN 46206

FIVES, FRANK MICHAEL, mfg. co. exec.; b. Dunmore, Pa., Dec. 25, 1917; s. Thomas F. and Mary T. (Ginley) F.; B.S. in Mech. Engring., Carnegie Inst. Tech., 1939; m. Nancy J. Clark, Sept. 25, 1943; children—Ellen Mary (Mrs. Charles F. Combs), Kathy, Michael, Nora, Mark, Christopher. With Carrier Corp., Syracuse, N.Y., 1945—, product specialist, 1957-58, sales mgr. indsl. compresser, 1958- 59, v.p., 1969—, group v.p. indsl. machinery, 1971—; with Elliott Co. div. Carrier Corp., Jeannette, Pa., 1959—, asst. gen. sales mgr., 1960-61, v.p., gen. sales mgr., 1961-67, exec. v.p., 1967-68, pres., 1968—; pres. Elliott Overseas Corp., 1969—, Compactor Corp., 1969—. Bd. dirs. Westmoreland County Mental Health Assn., 1968. Served to lt. comdr. USNR, 1942-45. Decorated Silver Star. Clubs: Lakeview (W.Va.) Country; Greensburg (Pa.) Country. Home: 48 Woodland Av Greensburg PA 15601 Office: Elliott Co Jeannette PA 15644

FIXMAN, MARSHALL, educator, chemist, b. St. Louis, Sept. 21, 1930; s. Benjamin and Dorothy (Finkel) F.; A.B., Washington U., St. Louis, 1950; Ph.D., Mass. Inst. Tech., 1954; m. Marian Ruth Beatman, July 5, 1959 (dec. Sept. 1969); children—Laura Beth, Susan Ilene, Andrew Richard. Jewett postdoctoral fellow chemistry Yale, 1953-54; instr. chemistry Harvard, 1956-59; sr. fellow Mellon Inst., Pitts., 1959-61; prof. chemistry, dir. Inst. Theoretical Sci., U. Ore., 1961-64, prof. chemistry, research asso. inst., 1964-65, prof. chemistry Yale, New Haven, 1965—. Served with AUS, 1954-56. Fellow Alfred P. Sloan Found., 1961-63; recipient Governor's award Ore. Mus. Sci. and Industry, 1964. Mem. Am. Acad. Arts and Scis., Am. Chem. Soc. (award pure chemistry 1964), Am. Phys. Soc., Fedn. Am. Scientists. Asso. editor Jour. Chem. Physics, 1962-64, Jour. Phys. Chemistry, 1970—, Macromolecules, 1970—. Address: Dept of Chemistry Yale New Haven CT 06504

FIXX, JAMES FULLER, editor; b. N.Y.C., Apr. 23, 1932; s. Calvin Henry and Marlys (Fuller) F.; student Ind. U., 1950-52; B.A., Oberlin Coll., 1957; m. Mary J. Durling, June 11, 1957; children—Paul, John, Elizabeth and Stephen (twins). Reporter, Sarasota (Fla.) Jour., 1957-58; feature editor Saturday Rev., 1958-66; exec. editor McCall's, N.Y.C., 1966-67, editor, 1967-69; editorial cons. to N.Y. Times, other publs., 1969—; gen. editor Great Contemporary Issues books, pub. by N.Y. Times, 1970—; contbg. editor Christian Herald, 1970—; articles editor Audience mag., 1971—. Mem. Sch. Bd. 23, N.Y.C., 1966. Bd. dirs. Greenwich (Conn.) Fair Housing, 1967—, Episcopalian mag., 1967—. Served with U.S. Army, 1952-54. Mem. U.S. Lawn Tennis Assn. Contbg. editor Christian Herald, 1970—. Home: 5 Chapel Lane Riverside CT 06878 Office: 241 1/2 E 32d St New York City NY 10016

FIZDALE, ROBERT, pianist. With Arthur Gold, performs as classical duo-pianist. Address: care Columbia Artists Mgmt Inc Andre Mertens Div 165 W 57th St New York City NY 10019*

FIZZELL, ROBERT BRUCE, lawyer; b. Taylorville, Ill., Sept. 20, 1889; s. James Albert and Martha Catherine (Allen) F.; A.B., U. Ill., 1910; LL.B., Harvard, 1913; m. Florence Edith Hoover, Nov. 27, 1916 (dec. 1963); children—Robert Bruce, Dorothy Florence; m. 2d, Vera L. Hagen, July 10, 1965. Admitted to Mo. bar, 1913, and since practiced in Kansas City; now mem. Stinson, Mag, Thomson, McEvers & Fizzell. Trustee Kansas City Art Inst., Friends of Art of Kansas City (pres. 1937-39). Chmn. Jackson County Charter Commn., 1948. Mem. Am., Mo. State and Kansas City bar assns., Lawyers Assn. of Kansas City (pres. 1947), Phi Beta Kappa, Delta

Sigma Rho. Democrat. Clubs: University, Kansas City Country. Home: 1228 W 68th Terrace Kansas City MO 64113 Office: 2100 Ten Main Center Kansas City MO 64127

FJELDE, PAUL, sculptor; b. Minneapolis, Minn., Aug. 12, 1892; s. Jacob H. G. and Margarethe Veronica (Madsen) F.; student Minneapolis Sch. of Fine Arts, 1908-10, State Normal Sch., Valley City, N.D., 1912, Studio of Lorado Taft, 1913-16, Beaux Art Inst. of Design, N.Y., 1922-23, Art Students League, N.Y., 1923-24, Royal Acad., Copenhagen, 1924-25, Acad. de la Grande Chaumiere, Paris, 1925-26; m. Amy Nordstrom, 1918; 1 son, Rolf Gerhard. Began as sculptor, 1912; teacher sculpture, Carnegie Inst. Tech., 1928-29; asso. prof. figure, design and sculpture Pratt Inst., 1929-59, emeritus. Principle works: Lincoln Monument, Oslo Norway; Col. Heg. Monument, Lier, Norway and Madison, Wis.; panels Westinghouse Monument, Pittsburgh; numerous memorial tablets, busts, reliefs and medals; also archtl. sculpture in Eastern cities. Fellow Am. Scandinavian Foundation, Nat. Sculptures Soc.; mem. Allied Artists Am., Am. Artists Profl. League. Grand Central Art Galleries, Nat. Acad. Design. Studio: 161 Emerson Pl Brooklyn NY 10005

FJELLMAN, CARL GUSTAF, coll. pres.; b. Cedar Rapids, Ia., May 7, 1919; s. Anders Gustaf and Huldah Cornelia (Johnson) F.; student State U. Ia., 1937-38; B.A., Augustana Coll., Rock Island, Ill., 1941, L.H.D., 1967; B.D., Augustana Theol. Sem., 1945; student U. Cal. at Berkeley, 1946; Ph.D., Drew U., 1955; m. Carolyn Elizabeth Schock, June 28, 1945; children—Susan Babette, Thomas Conrad. Ordained to ministry Lutheran Ch., 1945; pastor, Alameda, Cal., 1945-47; mem. faculty Upsala Coll., East Orange, N.J., 1947—, v.p., dean coll., 1951-65, acting pres., 1965-66, pres., 1966—. Mem. Am. Assn. U. Profs. Office: Upsala Coll East Orange NJ 07019

FJELSTAD, RALPH SYLVESTER, polit. scientist; b. Emmons, Minn., Nov. 12, 1915; s. Rudolf Malvin and Gena (Loken) F.; B.A., Concordia Coll., 1937; student U. Minn., 1938-39; Ph.D., Northwestern U., 1948; m. Margaret Dorothy Haugseth, Dec. 30, 1941; children—Mary, Carol, Paul. Dir. personnel ordnance dept. Ill. Ordnance Plant, Carbondale, Ill., 1941-43; Edward C. Congdon Found., prof. govt., Carleton Coll., 1948—. Cons. Small Bus. Adminstrn., 1958; chmn. state Constl. Revision Com., 1962-63; cons.-examiner and mem. Commn. on Instns. Higher Edn., N. Central Assn., 1970—. Mem. Northfield Community Chest. 1954-57, pres., 1956-57; sec. Northfield City Charter Commn., 1958-61; mem. Northfield Sch. Bd., 1963-69. Classification specialist, USAAF, 1943-46. Norman Walt Harris fellow polit. sci. Northwestern U., 1939-41; faculty fellow Fund for Advancement Edn., 1952-53; study Norwegian Parliament under travel grant Louis W. and Maude Hill Family Found., 1961. Mem. Am. Polit. Sci. Assn., Midwest Conf. Polit. Scientists. Republican. Home: 909 S Division St Northfield MN 55057

FLACK, JAMES MONROE, business exec.; b. Baxterville, Miss., Aug. 29, 1913; s. Jesse James and Lenora (Lucas) F.; B.S., Miss. Delta State Coll., 1935; B.D., Yale, 1942; student Harvard, 1952; m. Hertha E. Eisenmenger, Aug. 30, 1941; children—James Monroe, Sonya Karen, Robert Frank, Suzanne Margaret. Prin. Shaw (Miss.) High Sch., 1935-39; employee relations dept. Standard Oil Co. of N.J., 1946; officer, dir. subsidiaries Textron, Inc., 1946- 53; vice pres., dir. Indian Head, Inc., 1953—; chmn. bd. ABA Textile Mills, Ltd. Ltd. comdr. USN, 1942-45. Mem. Newcomen Soc. Clubs: Town Tennis; N.Y. Athletic; Red Fox Country; Tyron (N.C.) Country. Home: 1030 Fifth Av New York City NY 10028 Office: Indian Head Inc 111 W 40th St New York City NY 10018

FLACK, JOE FENLEY, ins. co. exec.; b. Menard, Tex., Feb. 23, 1921; s. Frank H. and Evelyn (Fenley) F.; B.B.A., U. Tex., 1943; m. Ann Tarry, Jan. 21, 1945; children—Kate T., Joan E., Joe Fenley, Sr. accountant Ernst & Ernst, C.P.A.'s, Houston, 1946-47; with Am. Gen. Ins. Co., 1947—, treas., 1951- -, sr. v.p., 1968—, also dir.; partner John L. Wortham and Son, Houston, 1947-65; auditor Hawaiian Life Ins. Co.; v.p., dir. Channing Financial Corp., Md. Casualty Co.; v.p. Me. Bonding & Casualty Co.; v.p., treas., dir. Md. Am. Gen. Ins. Co., Nat. Standard Ins. Co., Agrl.-Livestock Finance Corp., Atlas Realty Corp., Knickerbocker Corp.; dir. Constat Services, Inc., Am. Gen. Investment Corp., Am. Gen. Realty Co. Chmn. finance com. Boy Scouts Am. Mayor pro-tem city Bunker Hill Village (Tex.), 1959-61, mayor, 1961-63. Trustee, v.p. sch. bd. Spring Branch Ind. Sch. Dist.; bd. dirs. Kappa Sigma Found., U. Tex., Houston chpt. Salvation Army. Served to lt. USNR, 1943-45. C.P.A., Tex. Clubs: River Oaks Country Petroleum (Houston). Methodist. Home: 301 Mayerling Dr Houston TX 77024 Office: P O Box 3247 Houston TX 77001

FLAGELLO, EZIO, opera singer; bass; b. Bronx, N.Y.C., Jan. 28, 1931; s. Dionisio Flagello and Geneveffa (Casiello) Flagello; Mus.B., Manhattan Sch. Music, 1952; postgrad. U. Perugia, Italy, 1954; studied with Frederick Schorr, John Brownlee; m. Ann J. Mione, Dec. 26, 1954; children—Genoveffa, Dante, Josine, Christine. Violinist; performed as soloist at the world premier of Christopher Columbus, Carnegie Hall in 1952; appeared in Boheme, Ellenville Music Festival, 1955; European debut in Elixer of Love. Rome, Italy, 1956; Metropolitan Opera debut, 1957. mem. co., 1957—, as jailer in Tosca, Leporello in Don Giovanni; v.p. Scope Recording Co. Recipient Oscar Award musical competition, U.S. Army, 1954; Fulbright scholar, 1955; Met. Auditions of the Air award, 1957; named outstanding alumnus of the year Evander Childs High Sch., 1959. Recording artist. Office: 147 W 39th St New York City NY 10018

FLAGELLO, NICOLAS, composer, conductor; b. N.Y.C., Mar. 15, 1928; s. Dionisio and Genoveffa (Casiello) F.; Mus.B., Manhattan Sch. Music, 1949; Mus. M., 1930; superior studies Acad. S. Cecilia, Rome, Italy, 1936; m. Dianne Danese, July 18, 1953; children—Donis, Vittorio. Solo pianist Longines Symphonette, 1930-51; mem. conducting staff Chgo. Lyric Opera, 1961; tchs. composition and conducting Manhattan Sch. Music, 1950-; head composition dept. Curtis Inst. Opera, 1967; cons. summer session N.C. Sch. Music, Phila., 1964-65; debut as condr. with N.Y.C. Opera, 1967; Arts, Siena, Italy; condr. symphonies and operas throughout U.S., Europe, S. Am.; recording artists for Scope, Columbia, Serenus, 20th Century records; dir., founder Festival of the Amalfi Coast, Italy. Fulbright fellow, 1955; recipient citation from Pius XII for choral and orchestral work Pentaptych, 1953; N.Y. Music Critics Circle award nomination for Tristis Est Anima Mea, 1960. Mem. A.S.C.A.P. (annual award), Nat. Assn. Am. Composers and Conductors (program chmn. 1961-64). Am. Guild Am. Composers. Composer 5 operas, 6 concerti, 3 symphonies, orchestral and chamber works. ‡

FLAGG, JEWETT TAYLOR, clothing mfg. exec.; b. Buffalo, Dec. 31, 1900; s. George Benjamin and Madeleine Taylor (Smith) F.; diploma, The Lomis Sch., Windsor, Conn., 1920; student Lowell (Mass.) Tech. Inst., 1920-23, M.S. (hon.), 1953; m. Charlotte Brooks, Apr. 10, 1926; childrenMary Louise (Mrs. William S. Flanagan), Nancy Ann (Mrs. John Patrick Kern). Chmn. bd. dir. chmn. exec. com. Flagg-Utica Corp.; chmn. bd., dir. Mutual Box Board Co., Mpls. Knitting Works; pres., dir. Amwool Financial Corp.; dir., chmn. exec. com. Am. Woolen Co.; dir. Indian Head Mills, Inc., First Nat. Bank of Florence, Alabama, S. H. Kress & Co. Honorary prof. at Lowell Tech. Inst. Mem. bd. trustees council The Loomis Sch. Mem. N.Y. Cotton Exchange, Underwear Inst. (dir., mem. exec. com.), Phi Psi. Episcopalian (parish treas.). Mason, Elk. Clubs: Union League, Merchants, Garden City Country (N.Y.C.), Algonquin (Boston); Wianno, Oysters Harbors (Osterville on Cape Cod); Capitol City (Atlanta); Florence (Ala.) Golf and Country. Home: 129 Norwood Ct Florence AL 35630 also Union League Club New York City NY 10001 Office: 350 Fifth Av New York City NY 10001

FLAGG, MILDRED BUCHANAN (Mrs. Francis John Flagg), writer, lectr.; b. Moravia, N.Y., May 1, 1886; d. B. Frank and Julia (McCormick) Buchanan; A.B., Syracuse U., 1908; A.M., Boston U., 1927; D.Sc.O. (hon.), Curry Coll., 1958; Litt.D. (hon.), Boston U., 1963; L.H.D. (hon.), Portia Law School, 1965; m. Francis John Flagg, Oct. 7, 1914; children—David Buchanan (dec.), Julia Buchanan (Mrs. Kenneth A. Williams), Nancy Ferard (Mrs. Robert E. Gibney). Head English dept. high sch., Palmyra, N.Y., 1911-13, Watertown, N.Y., 1913-14; in ednl. work and active as lectr. and writer since 1914; dir. Am. Students Abroad, 1929-33; dir. Flagstaff Radio Hour (sta. WCOP), Boston, 1935-37. Dir. United Cerebral Palsy Assn. of Mass., 1947-54, Boston U. Women's Council, 1931-34, Com. on Pub. Health, Newton Council for Better World Order, nat. chmn. Books for Norway, 1947-49; chmn. Celebrity Breakfasts, 1945-62; sponsor Caney Creek Community Center, Pippa Passes, Ky., 1925-62; mem. N.E. com. Anatolia Coll., Greece; vice-comdr. Women's Field Army for Control of Cancer; trustee Flora Koralsky Scholarship Fund, 1955-60; dir. Writers Workshop, Nat. Found. for Study of Aging; trustee Brusch Med. Research Center, Inc.; trustee and mem. corp. Curry Coll., 1963-67. Mem. Mass. State Teachers Fdn. (pub. relations com.), N.E. Women's Press Assn. (pres. 1931-33), Am. Assn. U. Women (state pres. 1930-32, state chmn. TV-radio 1948-52), English-Speaking Union (mem. bd. Syracuse), The Pres.' Club of Mass. (pres. 1937-38), Boston-Syracuse Alumnae Assn. (pres. 1920-37), Boston U., Grad. Sch. Alumni Assn. (pres. 1935-37), Newton Center Woman's Club (lit. chmn. 1945-48), Women's City Club of Boston, Am. Numismatic Assn., Y.W.C.A., Nat. Fedn. Bus. and Profl. Women's Clubs, N.E.A. (hon. life), Authors League (pres. Central N.Y.), Profl. Women's League, Boar's Head, Phi Beta Kappa, Theta Sigma Phi, Delta Kappa Gamma. Republican. Conglist. Clubs: Professional Women's (pres., 1931-33), Boston Authors (pres., 1947-49, 64—, dir. 1950-52); National League American Pen Women (pres. Boston br., nat. lectrs. chmn., 1954-56); Boston Travel; Zonta, Onaway (Syracuse, N.Y.). Author: Community English, 1921; Camera Adventures in Africa, 1935; Plymouth Maid, 1937; Boy of Salem, 1939; Celebrity Chatalogs, 1945; A Lad of Old Nantucket, 1947; Approaching Old Age, 1955; Uncle Sam's Forgotten Children, 1956; Notable Boston Authors, 1965; Boston Authors Now and Then, 1966; also articles various publications. Editor: Study Outlines in Pocket Classics (6 vols.), 1921-33; A Certain Rich Man (William Allen White), 1923, 30. Home: 753 James St Syracuse NY 13203

FLAGLE, CHARLES DENHARD, educator; b. Scottdale, Pa., Apr. 23, 1919; s. Charles D. and Marie Elizabeth (Denhard) F.; B.Engring., Johns Hopkins, 1940, M.Sc., 1954, D.Engring., 1955; m. Lois Hagaman, July 3, 1946 (dec. Mar. 1963); children—Charles Lawrence, Judith Ellen, Douglas Anderson; m. 2d, Janet Sayward Waters Dryden, Mar. 27, 1965; 1 stepdau., Elizabeth Hooper Dryden. Devel. and design engr. Westinghouse Elec. Corp., 1940-46; with Henry C. Robinson Co., Hartford, Conn., 1946-47, John E. Sjostrom Co., Phila., also Wayne Iron Works (Pa.), 1947-50; mem. faculty Johns Hopkins, 1950—, research asso. instr. Coop. Research, 1954—, prof. operations research and indsl. engring., 1962—, prof. pub. health adminstrn., 1963—, dir. operations research Johns Hopkins Hosp., 1956- -: cons. USPHS, VA; spl. asst. to surgeon gen. of USPHS. Mem. Nat. Adv. Com. Epidemiology and Biometry, 1963-66. Mem. Operations Research Soc. Am. (chmn. edn. com. 1965-66), Am. Pub. Health Assn., Inst. Mgmt. Scis., Tau Beta Pi. Unitarian. Clubs: Johns Hopkins (bd. govs. 1962-65), Sierra (Balt.). Editor: (with W. H. Huggins and R. H. Roy) Operations Research and Systems Engineering, 1960. Mem. editorial bd. Health Services Research, 1965—. Home: 1822 Circle Rd Ruxton MD 21204 Office: Sch Hygiene and Pub Health Johns Hopkins Baltimore MD 21205

FLAHERTY, DANIEL LEO, clergyman, editor; b. Chgo., July 29, 1929; s. Daniel Leo and Marguerite (Pauly) F.; student Xavier U., 1950-51; A.B., Loyola U., Chgo., 1952, M.A., 1957; Ph.L., West Baden (Ind.) Coll., 1954, S.T.L., 1961; postgrad. Northwestern U., 1959-60. Joined Soc. of Jesus, 1947, ordained priest Roman Catholic Ch. 1960. Book editor America, 1962- 65, exec. editor, 1965-71; sec. America Press, Inc., 1969-71; mem. bd. Catholic Book Club, 1962-71; exec. dir. Loyola U. Press., Chgo., 1971—; mem. selection bd. Campion award, 1962-71. Bd. dirs. John La Farge Inst., 1970-71; trustee Loyola U., Chgo., 1970—, U. Detroit, 1970—. Author: (with W.D. Ciszek) With God in Russia, 1964. Address: 3441 N Ashland Av Chicago IL 60657

FLAHERTY, EUGENE DEWEY, ocean shipping cons.; b. N.Y.C., Apr. 9, 1898; s. William Patrick and Ella Barbara (Fisher) F.; student Los Angeles Coll. Law, 1927-31; m. Georgiana Boenau, July 16, 1923; children—Robert, Mary Eileen, William. Office mgr. Beh & Herter, N.Y.C., 1916-18; clk. U.S. ICC, Washington, 1918; sec. to dir. gen. U.S. R.R. Adminstrn., 1918-20; sec. W.G. McAdoo, N.Y.C. 1920-22; gen. office mgr. McAdoo, Neblett & O'Connor, Los Angeles, 1922-31; dir., sec. Seaboard Dev. Co., Seaboard Realty Co., Los Angeles, 1923-38; gen. office mgr., sec. Am. Pres. Lines, 1938-48, v.p. operations, 1949- 50, v.p. S.W. div. 1950-63; pres., gen. mgr. Marine Exchange of Los Angeles, Long Beach Harbor, Inc., 1963-68; dir., sec. Jameson Petroleum Co., Los Angeles, 1923-38; dir., pres. Culver City Airport, Culver City, Cal., 1928-32; dir., sec. State Consol. Oil Co. 1932-34. Mem. Los Angeles (Cal.) World Affairs Council. Capt., USNR, ret.; comdg. officer U.S. Naval Armed Guard Center, Pacific, 1941-46, Vol. Composite (Armed Guard) Unit 12-30, Treasure Island, Cal., 1949-50. Recipient Sec. of Navy Commendation ribbon for services in World War II. Mem. Los Angeles S.S. Assn. (hon. life), Japan-Am. Soc. (life), Cal. Nat. Def. Transp. Assn. Democrat. Roman Catholic. Clubs: SKAL (Los Angeles); Army-Navy (Washington); Propeller (bd. govs.). Home: 1812 Parkside Av Burbank CA 91506

FLAHERTY, FRANK, (John Francis), journalist; b. Caledon, Ont., Can., Dec. 18, 1903; s. James and Anne (Wallace) F.; B.A., U. Toronto, 1925, M.A., 1928; student Osgoode Hall Law Sch., 1925-28; m. Dorothy Eva Rhodes, Aug. 28, 1934; childrem—Mary Anne (Mrs. Hubert Dittmann), Helen Theresa (Mrs. John Dempster), Roderick John, Kathleen Dorothy. Reporter, Toronto Daily Star, 1925-26; reporter, wire-editor, Parliamentary corr. Canadian Press, 1927-45; Parliamentary corr. Toronto Globe and Mail, 1946-47; Canadian corr. Chgo. Daily News, 1947-69; pub. nat. bus. news report Buchanan's Bull., 1945-69; pres., mgr. Nat. Editorial Bur., 1965—. Organized pub. relations and information services for Marian Congress Ottawa. Mem. Canadian Inst. Internat. Affairs, Canadian C. of C. (first Parliamentary Press Gallery, Sigma Delta Chi. Club: Nat. Press Can. (past pres.). Home: 539 Hilson Av Ottawa Ontario Canada Office: 150 Wellington St Ottawa Ontario Canada

FLAHERTY, J.L., bishop; b. Norfolk, Va., May 13, 1910; s. Charles E. and Mary (Ferris) F.; A.B., Holy Cross Coll., 1922; S.T.L., U. Gregoriana, Rome, 1937; Ph.D. in Edn., Cath. U. Am., 1950. Ordained priest Roman Cath. Ch.; supt. schs. Diocese Richmond, Va., 1949-61; founding pastor St. Luke's Parish, McLean, Va., 1961-62; rector St. John Vianney Sem., 1963-65; bishop of Richmond, 1966—. Served as chaplain AUS, World War II. Decorated Silver Star; recipient Nat. Brotherhood citation Nat. Conf. Christians and Jews, 1967. Mem. Am. Legion (chaplain Va. 1946-47), Cath. War Vets. (nat. chaplain ladies aux. 1952-53). Home: 909 Rennie Av Richmond VA 23227 Office: 807 Cathedral Pl Richmond VA 23220

FLAHERTY, JOSEPH ANTHONY, univ. pres.; b. Phila., June 13, 1916; s. James A. and Mary I. (Bradley) F.; A.B., St. Joseph's Coll., Phila., 1938, L.H.D., 1965; M.A. in English, Cath. U. Am., 1944; Ph.D., Harvard, 1949; Pd.D., LaSalle Coll., Phila., 1966; Litt.D., Merrimack Coll., N. Andover, Mass., 1967. Joined Order of St. Augustine, 1938, ordained priest Roman Cath. Ch., 1943; chmn. dept. English, Merrimack Coll., 1949-64, dir. part-time div., 1951- 64; v.p. acad. affairs Villanova U., 1964-65, pres., 1965—. Mem. Phila. Commn. Higher Edn., 1965—, Phila. Crime Commn., 1967—. Bd. visitors USAF Acad., 1966—; bd. dirs. WHYY, Phila. Ednl. TV Assn., 1965—. Mem. Nat. Council Tchrs. English, Assn. Higher Edn., Modern Lang. Assn., Commn. Ind. Colls. and Univs., Phila. C. of C. Address: Villanova Univ Villanova PA 19085

FLAHERTY, PETE F., mayor; b. Pitts., June 24, 1925; s. Pete and Anne (O'Toole) F.; LL.B., Notre Dame U., 1951; M.P.A., U. Pitts., 1967; m. Nancy Houlihand, Aug. 29, 1958; children—Shawn, Pete, Brian, Maggie, Greg. Admitted to Pa. bar; asst. dist. atty. Allegheny County, 1957-64; city councilman, Pitts., 1966-69; mayor, Pitts., 1970—. Served to capt. USAAF, 1942-46. Decorated Air medal. Mem. Am., Pa. bar assns. Home: 5033 Castleman St Pittsburgh PA 15232 Office: City County Bldg Pittsburgh PA 15219

FLAHIE, CHARLES EDWARD, utility co. exec.; b. Cygnet, O., July 15, 1907; s. Edward J. and Anna L. (Connelly) F.; B.S., U. Mich., 1931; M.A., U. Detroit, 1960; m. Helen Mae Moninger, Apr. 14, 1931; children—Felicia (Mrs. Amer J. Dodge), Monica (Mrs. John Katzenberger), Mary Cecilia (Mrs. John Prior), Regina Marie (Mrs. Kent Johnson), John Patrick. Jr. engr. Pub. Service Co. Colo., Denver, 1931-35; engr. Toledo Edison Co., 1935-46, supt. underground dept., 1946-47, supt. meter dept., 1947-50, transmission and distbn. engr., 1950-59, chief elec. engr., 1959-62, v.p., 1962-65, exec. v.p., 1964—. Mem. I.E.E.E., Am. Mgmt. Assn., C. of C. Roman Catholic. Home: 4364 Northmoor Rd Toledo OH 43615 Office: Toledo Edison Co 300 Madison Av Toledo OH 43652

FLAHIFF, GEORGE BERNARD, archbishop; b. Paris, Ont., Can., Oct. 26, 1905; s. John James and Eleanor Rose (Fleming) F.; B.A., St. Michael's Coll., U. Toronto, 1926; student U. Strasbourg (France), 1930-31; Dipl. Archiviste-Paleographe, Ecole Nat. des Chartes, Paris, France, 1935; hon. degree in law U. Seattle, 1965, U. Notre Dame, 1969, U. Man., 1969, U. Windsor, 1970. Ordained priest Roman Catholic Ch., 1930; prof. medieval history Pontifical Inst. Medieval Studies and U. Toronto, 1935-54, sec. inst., 1943-51; superior-gen. Basilian Fathers, 1954-61; archbishop of Winnipeg, Can., 1961—; named to Coll. Cardinals, 1969; mem. Sacred Congregation for Religious, Sacred Congregation for Edn. Home: 39 Bishop's Lane Charleswood R3R 0A8 Manitoba Canada Office: 50 Stafford St Winnipeg R3M 2V7 Manitoba Canada

FLAHIVE, LAWRENCE MATTHEW, mfg. co. exec.; b. Chgo., Apr. 21, 1916; s. John and Adelaine (Smith) F.; student Armour Inst. Tech., 1935-36, Northwestern U., 1936-37; div.; children—Lawrence J., James P., Thomas M., Gerald E., Patrick D., Daniel R. Mgr. Fiddes-Moore Co., Ft. Wayne, Ind., 1949-57; company acquired by Evans Products Co., 1959, pres. subsidiary Plywall Products Co., 1957-63, v.p., gen. mgr. Plywall div., 1963-65, dir., 1964—, exec. v.p., gen. mgr. bldg. products group, then sr. exec. v.p. marketing, 1965—. Bd. dirs. Corona (Cal.) Boys Club. Served with USAAF, 1943-46. Mem. Riverside C. of C. Home: 6979 Palm Ct Riverside CA 92506 Office: 1346 Railroad St Corona CA 91720

FLAMSON, RICHARD JOSEPH, III; banker; b. Los Angeles, Feb. 2, 1929; s. Richard J. and Mildred (Jones) F.; B.A., Claremont Men's Coll., 1951—; certificate Pacific Coast Banking Sch., U. Wash., 1962; m. Arden Black, Oct. 5, 1951; children—Richard Joseph IV, Scott Arthur, Michael Jon, Leslie Arden. With Security Pacific Nat. Bank, Los Angeles, 1955—, v.p., 1962-69, sr. v.p., 1969-70, exec. v.p. corporate banking dept., 1970—. Trustee Claremont Men's Coll. Served to 1st lt. AUS, 1951-53. Mem. Bankers Assn. for Fgn. Trade, Robert Morris Assos., Town Hall, Stock Exchange Club. Clubs: Balboa Bay, Balboa Yacht (Newport Beach, Cal.). Home: 2000 Kewamee Dr Corona del Mar CA 92625 Office: 561 S Spring St Los Angeles CA 90013

FLANAGAN, BARBARA, journalist; b. Des Moines; d. John Merrill and Marie (Barnes) Flanagan; student Drake U., 1942-43; m. Earl S. Sanford, 1966. With promotion dept. Mpls. Times, 1945-47; reporter Mpls. Tribune, 1947-58; women's editor, spl. writer Mpls. Star and Tribune, 1958-65; columnist Mpls. Star, 1965—. Bd. dirs. Minn. Orchestral Assn. Mem. Mpls. Soc. Fine Arts (life), Mpls. Inst. Arts (founding mem. Minn. Arts Forum), Kappa Alpha Theta, Sigma Delta Chi. Episcopalian. Home: 17 S 1st St Minneapolis MN 55401 Office: Mpls Star 5th and Portland Sts Minneapolis MN 55415

FLANAGAN, BERNARD JOSEPH, church bishop; b. Proctor, Vt., Mar. 31, 1908; s. John B. and Alice (McGarry) F.; student Holy Cross Coll., North American Coll., Rome; J.C.D., Cath. U. Am., 1943. Ordained priest Roman Cath. Ch., 1931; sec. to bishop, chancellor of diocese, Burlington, 1943-53, named 1st bishop Norwich diocese, 1953; now bishop of Worcester, Mass., 1959—. Address: Bishop's House Worcester MA 01602

FLANAGAN, DANIEL V., union ofcl. Dir. Region 22 Dept. Orgn. AFL-CIO. Office: 995 Market St San Francisco CA 94103*

FLANAGAN, DENNIS, editor; b. N.Y.C., July 22, 1919; s. John Richard and Nan (Apotheker) F.; A.B., Mich., 1941; m. Geraldine A. Lux, Jan. 9, 1948; children—Cara Louise, John Gerard; m. 2d, Ellen Raskin, Oct. 17, 1966. Staff writer Life mag., 1941-47; mng. editor Scientific Am., 1947-50, editor, 1950—. Home: 20 E 9th St New York City NY 10003 Office: 415 Madison Av New York City NY 10017

FLANAGAN, EDWARD MICHAEL, Jr., army officer; b. Saugerties, N.Y., July 13, 1921; s. Edward Michael and Marie (Sinnott) F.; B.S., U.S. Mil. Acad., 1943; grad. U.S. Army Command and Gen. Staff Coll., Ft. Leavenworth, Kan., 1946, Armed Forces Staff Coll., Norfolk, Va., 1955, U.S. Army War Coll., Carlisle Barracks, Pa., 1959; M.A., Boston U., 1960; m. Marguerite Farrell, Dec. 26, 1945; children—Edward Michael III, Maureen Ann, Terrence Girard, Patricia Marie and Kathleen Mary (twins). Commd. 2d lt. U.S. Army, 1943, advanced through grades to maj. gen. 1970; comdg. gen. U.S. Army John F. Kennedy Center for Mil. Assistance and comdt. U.S. Army Inst. or Mil. Assistance, Ft. Bragg, N.C., 1968-71; comdg. gen. 1st Inf. Div., Ft. Riley, Kan., 1971—. Decorated D.S.M., Legion of Merit with oak leaf cluster, Bronze Star, Air medal with oak leaf cluster, Army Commendation medal; Vietnam Nat. Order of Merit (knight class), Vietnam Army Distinguished Service Order 1st class, Vietnam Gallantry Cross with gold star, Vietnam

Medal of Honor. Roman Catholic. Author: The Angels, A History of the 11th Airborne Division, 1948. Contbr. rticles profl. jours. Home: 1 Barry Av Fort Riley KS 66442 Office: Office Comdg Gen Fort Riley KS 66442

FLANAGAN, JOHN CLEMANS, research inst. exec.; b. Armour, S.D., Jan. 7, 1906; s. Charles Gibbons and Gertrude (Clemans) F.; B.S., U. Wash., 1929. M.A., 1932; Ph.D., Harvard, 1934; m. Katherine Ross, Jan. 18, 1930; children—John Ross, Scott Calhoun; m. 2d, Ruth Colonna, June 21, 1962. Tchr. sci. and maths. Renton (Wash.) High Sch., 1929-30; tchr. math. Cleveland High Sch., Seattle, 1930-32; asst. in edn. Harvard, 1934-35; lectr. Columbia Tchrs. Coll., 1936-41; asso. dir. Coop. Test Service, N.Y.C., 1935-41; prof. psychology U. Pitts., 1946—; chmn. bd. dirs. Am. Inst. Research, Pitts., 1946—, also mem. bd. Served to col. USAAF, 1941- 46; dir. aviation psychology program. Decorated Legion of Merit, 1946; recipient Raymond F. Longacre award Aero. Med. Assn., 1954. Diplomate in personnel psychology Am. Bd. Examiners in Profl. Psychology. Mem. A.A.A.S. (chmn. edn. sect.), Am. Ednl. Research Assn., Am. Psychol. Assn. (pres. div. evaluation and measurement 1956-57, pres. div. mil. psychology 1961-62, pres. div. gen. psychology 1963-64, pres. div. ednl. psychology 1969-70), Am. Statis. Assn., N.Y. Acad. Scis. (v.p. 1936), Psychometric Soc. (pres. 1952), Sigma Xi. Home: 8 Arastradero Rd Portola Valley CA 94025 Office: P O Box 1113 Palo Alto CA 94302

FLANAGAN, JOHN JOSEPH, stock broker; b. Bklyn., Mar. 25, 1915; s. John J. and Ellen (O'Sullivan) F.; ed. pub. schs.; m. Jane Elizabeth Savage, June 12, 1946; childrenJohn Joseph, Daniel George, Patricia Hawley, James Michael, Thomas Jere, Mary Jane. With Josephthal & Co., N.Y.C., 1929-. Bd. govs. N.Y. Stock Exchange, 1965—. Served to maj., inf., AUS, 1941- 45. Home: 264 Oak Ridge Av Summit NJ 07901 Office: 120 Broadway New York City NY 10005

FLANAGAN, JOHN THEODORE, educator; b. St. Paul, Jan. 15, 1906; s. John Joseph and Emma (Hamm) F.; B.A., U. Minn., 1927, M.A., 1928, Ph.D., 1935; m. Virginia McGuigan, July 24, 1929; children—Sheila Virginia (Mrs. Richard H. Paulsen), Moira Ellen (Mrs. Leo J. Harris), Cathleen Coyla. Instr. English, U. N.D., 1928-29; instr., asst. prof. U. Minn., 1929-45; prof. English, So. Methodist U., 1945-46; asso. prof. English, U. Ill., Urbana, 1946-49, prof., 1949—. Vis. prof. Ind. U., summer 1949, Kyoto U., summer 1952; Fulbright lectr. U. Bordeaux, 1952-53, Univs. Liege, Ghent, Brussels, 1960-61; vis. lectr. U. Moscow, U. Leningrad, 1963. Newberry Library fellow, 1943-44; Guggenheim fellow, 1943-44. Mem. Modern Lang. Assn., Am. Folklore Soc., Am. Studies Assn., Minn. (life), Ill. (life) hist. socs., Soc. Midland Authors, Phi Beta Kappa. Republican. Clubs: Caxton (Chgo.); Dial (Urbana). Author: James Hall, Literary Pioneer of the Ohio Valley, 1941; The American Way, 1953. Editor: America Is West, 1945; (with Arthur Palmer Hudson) Folklore in American Literature, 1958; (with Clarence Brown) American Literature, A College Survey, 1961; Profile of Vachel Lindsay, 1970. Mem. editorial bd. American Literature, 1968-71. Contbr. articles and revs. to lit. and hist. jours. Home: 705 W Michigan Av Urbana IL 61801

FLANAGAN, THOMAS JOHN, airline exec.; b. Somerville, Mass., Nov. 15, 1920; s. Michael and Delia (McCarthy) F.; A.B. in Physics, Boston Coll., 1942; student Oxford (Eng.) U., 1955, Columbia Grad. Sch. Bus., 1967; m. Jane Frances Erickson, Oct. 22, 1949; children—Thomas John, Elizabeth Anne. With Pan Am. World Airways, 1942—, sr. v.p. operations, 1969—. Clubs: N.Y. Athletic, Wings, Sky (N.Y.C.); Waccabue Country (South Salem, N.Y.). Home: 59 West Lane Ridgefield CT 06877 Office: Pan Am World Airways Kennedy Internat Airport Jamaica NY 11430

FLANAGAN, WILLIAM ROBERT, naval officer; b. Athens, Ga., Apr. 23, 1921; s. William Grady and Tallie Serena (Jennings) F.; student U. Ga., 1938-40; B.S., U.S. Naval Acad., 1943; postgrad. Naval War Coll., 1960-61. Commd. ensign U.S. Navy, 1943, advanced through grades to rear adm., 1969; gunnery officer U.S.S. Phoenix, 1943-45; project officer devel. Navy attack aircraft, 1948-50; air squadron comdr., pilot, 1946-58; plans officer 7th Fleet, Far East, 1961-62; comdg. officer U.S.S. Constellation, 1967-68; dep. comdr. Naval Forces, Vietnam, 1969-70; dir. East Asia and Pacific Region for Internat. Security Affairs Dept. Def., 1970—. Decorated D.S.M., Legion of Merit, Air medal, Navy Commendation medal; Nat. Order Vietnam, Vietnam Gallantry Cross. Clubs: Ponle Vedra (Fla.); Army-Navy (Washington). Home: PO Box 323 Athens GA 30601 Office: Office Asst Sec Def ISA Washington DC 20301

FLANAGIN, NORRIS CORNELIUS, ins. exec.; b. Chgo., Feb. 7, 1904; s. Cornelius Alfredo and Edna (Elden) F.; Ph. B., U. Chgo., 1924; m. Virginia Riddell, Apr. 25, 1928; children—Neil, Charles R., William E.; m. 2d, Mary Humphrey Cranage, May 10, 1968. Western mgr. Theatre mag., 1925-29; account exec. Matthew G. Pierce, 1930-32, Doremus & Co., 1932-34; chmn. bd., dir. Fidelity Life Assn., Fed. Kemper Life Assurance Co., Empire State Mut. Life Ins. Co.; dir. Economy Fire & Casualty Co., Am. Mfrs. Mut. Ins. Co., Fed. Mut. Ins. Co., Am. Motorists Ins. Co., Lumbermens Mut. Casualty Co., Kemper Co. Served as lt. USNR, World War II. Mem. Alpha Delta Phi. Clubs: Chicago, Tower (Chgo.); Glen View (Golf, Ill.); Hole-in-the-Wall, Yacht (Naples, Fla.). Home: 1410 Sheridan Rd Wilmette IL 60091 Office: 20 N Wacker Dr Chicago IL 60606

FLANDERS, HELEN HARTNESS, author, ballad collector, lectr.; b. Springfield, Vt., May 19, 1890; d. James and Lena (Pond) Hartness; grad. Dana Hall, Wellesley, Mass., 1909; M.A., Middlebury Coll., 1942; m. Ralph E. Flanders, Nov. 1, 1911 (dec. Feb. 1970); children—Helen Elizabeth (Mrs. William Whitney Ballard), Anna Hartness (Mrs. Henry P. Balivet, Jr., dec.), James Hartness. Fellow Internat. Inst. Arts and Letters; mem. Am. Northeast folklore socs., Soc. Ethnomusicology, Internat. Folk Music Council, Internat. Congress Ethnol. and Anthrop. Scis., A.A.A.S., poetry socs. Am. and Vt., Washington Lit. Soc. D.A.R., Nat. League Am. Pen Women. Conglist. Clubs: Altrurian, Sulgrave (Washington). Author books; also ballad collections (with others) Vermont Folk-Songs and Ballads, 1931; A Garland of Green Mountain Song, 1934; Country Songs of Vermont, 1937; New Green Mountain Songster, 1939; Vermont Chapbook, 1941; Ballads Migrant in New England, 1953; (poetry anthology) Green Mountain Verse, 1943; Ancient Ballads Traditionally Sung in New England, Vol. I, 1960. Vol. II, 1961, Vol. III, 1963, Vol. IV, 1965; Country News Items and other Poems, 1965. Home: Smiley Manse Springfield VT 05156 also 2701 O St NW Washington DC 20007 ☆

FLANDERS, JACK DUANE, mfg. co. exec.; b. Dowagiac, Mich., Mar. 16, 1931; s. Claire and Naomi (Ferris) F.; B.B.A., Western Mich. U., 1957; m. Mary E. McMahon, Sept. 3, 1955; children—Jo Ann, Patricia M. Staff accountant Lawrence Scudder & Co., Kalamazoo, Mich., 1951-61, partner, 1961-65; treas. Allen Electric & Equipment Co., Melville, N.Y. 1965—. Past dir. Kalamazoo Assn. for Retarded Children. Served with USAF, 1951-54. C.P.A., Mich. Mem. Am. Inst. C.P.A.'s. Nat. Assn. Accountants (past dir. Kalamazoo). Republican. Presbyn. Home: R D 1 Box 316A Scotts MI 49088 Office: 534 Broad Hollow Rd Melville NY 11746

FLANIGAN, DONALD FRANCIS, lawyer; b. Glendale, Cal., Sept. 12, 1928; s. Byrnes F. and Anna Mae (Pefly) F.; student U. Cal. at Los Angeles, 1946-48; A.B., Stanford, 1954, LL.B., 1956; m. Joan E. Parsons, Mar. 26, 1953; children—Susan K., Bruce K. Admitted to Cal. bar, 1956; staff atty. Convair div. Gen. Dynamics Corp., San Diego, 1956-59, asso. counsel, asst. sec., 1959-61; atty. Ampex Corp., Redwood City, Cal., 1961-69, asst. sec., 1961—, gen. counsel, 1969—. Served with USNR, 1948-53. Decorated Air Medal. Mem. Am., Fed. bar assns., State Bar Cal. Home: 90 Bear Gulch Dr Portola Valley CA 94025 Office: Ampex Corporation 401 Broadway St Redwood City CA 94063

FLANIGAN, JOHN, brewery exec.; b. N.Y.C., Apr. 7, 1922; s. Horace C. and Aimee (Magnus) F.; grad. Portsmouth Priory Sch.; student Mass. Inst. Tech., 1940-42, Princeton, 1942, 47; m. Carlota Busch, June 21, 1948 (div.); children—John August, Karen Clark, Michael Magnus, Kathleen Chouteau. With Anheuser-Busch, Inc., 1948—, beginning in purchasing and sales depts., v.p. Pacific region, dir., 1954—. Served from pvt. to 1st lt. AUS, 1942-46; PTO. Clubs: California, Los Angeles Country (Los Angeles); Pacific Union, Bohemian (San Francisco). Office: PO Box 2113 Los Angeles CA 90054

FLANIGAN, PETER MAGNUS, govt. ofcl.; b. N.Y.C., June 21, 1923; s. Horace C. and Aimee (Magnus) F.; grad. cum laude, Portsmouth Priory, R.I.; B.A. summa cum laude, Princeton, 1945; m. Brigid Snow, Nov. 27, 1954; children—Brigid Snow, Sheila Magnus, Timothy, Megan, Robert. With Dillon, Read & Co., Inc., 1947-69, v.p., 1954-69; asst. to President U.S., 1969—. Financial analyst ECA Mission to U.K., 1949-50. Clubs: Recess (gov., v.p.), Links (N.Y.C.); Round Hill (Greenwich, Conn.); Clove Valley (North Clove, N.Y.). Home: 4801 Indian Lane Washington DC 20016 Office: White House Washington DC

FLANIGAN, ROBERT LEE, singer; b. Greencastle, Ind., Aug. 22, 1926; s. Minter Lee and Nellie (Fodrea) F.; student Arthur Jordan Conservatory, Indpls., 1947; m. Mary L. Scott; children—Stephen, Debra, Jennifer, Julie, Jill, Scott Lee. Mem. vocal group Four Freshmen, 1948—, now lead singer, also trombone and base player; appearances at colls. and univs. throughout U.S., also Europe and Far East; recording artists for Capital Records, 1950—; recording artists for Liberty Record, 1968—; v.p. Viscount Internat. Prodns., Ken- Bob Music, Ross-Don Music. Served with AUS, 1945-46. Group has won awards from Playboy, Readers Poll, All Star Poll, Downbeat mag., Metronone mag., Billboard mag., Cash Box, Record Whirl, also Melody Maker award in Eng. Mem. A.S.C.A.P., Tau Kappa Epsilon. Office: 8720 Woodley Av Sepulveda CA 91343

FLANNELLY, JOSEPH F., bishop; b. N.Y.C., Oct. 22, 1894; ed. Cathedral Coll., N.Y.C., St. Joseph Sem., Dunwoodie, Yonkers, N.Y. Ordained priest Roman Cath. Ch., 1918; adminstr. St. Patrick's Cathedral, N.Y.C., since 1939; named titular bishop of Metelis, auxiliary bishop of N.Y., 1948; consecrated, 1948. Home: 460 Madison Av New York City NY 10022

FLANNER, JANET, writer; b. Indpls., Mar. 13, 1892; d. Frances and Mary-Ellen (Hockett) Flanner; student Tudor Hall, Indpls., U. Chgo.; Litt.D. (hon.), Smith Coll., 1958. Fgn. corr. New Yorker mag., writer Letter from Paris, 1925- -. Decorated Legion of Honor. Mem. Nat. Inst. Arts and Letters. Author: (novel) The Cubical City, 1926; (collected New Yorker Profiles) American in Paris, 1940; (art monographs) Men and Monuments, 1957; Paris Journal, 1944-65 (Nat. Book award 1966). Translator; Claudine a L'Ecole and Cheri (by Colette); Ma Vie avec Maeterlinck (by Mme. Georgette Le Blanc). Home: Hotel Ritz Place Vendome Paris France Office: care New Yorker Magazine 25 W 43d St New York City NY 10036

FLANNERY, HARRY WILLIAM, writer, lectr.; b. Greensburg, Pa., Mar. 13, 1900; s. John V. and Catherine (Flynn) F.; Ph.B. in Journalism, U. Notre Dame, 1923; m. Ruth Carmody, July 5, 1937 (dec. July 1968); 1 dau., Patricia Ann; m. 2d, Mary Moriarty Heinemann, Aug. 18, 1969, 1 son, William L. Heinemann. Reporter Hagerstown (Md.) Mail, Balt. Sun, Chgo. City News Bur. and Albany Evening News, 1916-25; sec. to J.P. McEvoy, 1925-26; editor Hoosier Observer, Ft. Wayne, Ind., 1931-32; radio news editor WOWO, Ft. Wayne, 1932-33; news editor and analyst KMOX, St. Louis, 1935-40; Berlin corr. CBS, 1940-41; A.T.C. to Europe, Far East and Near East, 1945; news analyst CBS, Los Angeles, 1942-48; makeup editor Los Angeles Examiner, 1948-49; mem. editorial staff Catholic Digest, 1951; editor AFL News Reporter, 1952-56; radio coordinator AFL-CIO, 1956-66; now lectr. Inst. Indsl. Relations, U. Cal. at Los Angeles. Mem. Cath. Assn. Internat. Peace (pres. 1956-63), Los Angeles Archdiocesan Com. on Papal Peace Proposals. Nominated for Peabody Award, radio news analysts, S. Cal. region, 1946. Mem. council R.W.G., 1948-49; organizer Cath. Labor Inst., Leo XIII Sch. Social Action. Mem. Authors Guild, Broadcast Pioneers. Roman Catholic. Author: Assignment to Berlin, 1942; Off Mike, chpt. on Analyzing Analysts, 1944. Co-author: The Church and the Workingman, 1965; Which Way Germany?, 1967. Editor: Pattern for Peace, 1962. Home: 1105 N Bundy Dr Los Angeles CA 90049

FLANNERY, JOHN FRANCIS, lawyer; b. Chgo., Oct. 15, 1928; s. Edward J. and Ellen (Brennan) F.; B.S. in Elec. Engring., U. Ill., 1950; postgrad. Northwestern U., 1953- 54; J.D., Loyola U., Chgo., 1959; m. Marjorie Ann Tuohy, June 5, 1954; children-Colleen, John, Erin, Kevin, Brian, Patrick. Admitted to Ill. bar, 1959, since practiced in Chgo., partner firm Anderson, Luedeka, Fitch, Even & Tabin, 1962—. Served with AUS, 1951-53. Mem. Am., Ill., Chgo. bar assns., patent Law Assn. Chgo., Am. Legion, Eta Kappa Nu. Phi Alpha Delta. Roman Cath. K.C. Club: Evanston (Ill.) Golf. Home: 6720 N Le Mai Lincolnwood IL 60646 Office: 135 S LaSalle St Chicago IL 60603

FLANNERY, JOHN SARSFIELD, Jr., financial co. exec.; b. Chgo., Dec. 16, 1923; s. John Sarsfield and Lucille (Thurnes) F.; B.S.C., DePaul U., 1948; m. Ann O'Brien, June 16, 1944; children—John Sarsfield III, Dennis, Brian, Terrance, Timothy, Mary, Ann. Asst. controller Automatic Electric Co., Northlake, Ill., 1955-59, controller, 1959—. Mem. commerce adv. com. DePaul U. Served with AUS, 1944-46. C.P.A., Ill. Mem. Financial Execs. Inst., Am. Inst. C.P.A.'s. Roman Catholic. Home: 895 Appletree Ct Northbrook IL 60062 Office: 400 N Wolf Rd Northlake IL 60164

FLANNERY, ROBERT GENE, railroad ofcl.; b. Washington, Ind., Sept. 14, 1924; s. Allen H. and Nellie Jane (White) F.; B.S. in Civil Engring., Purdue U., 1948; m. Barbara Ann Angell, Feb. 23, 1952; children-Julia Ann, Jennifer Ann, Amy Lynn. With N.Y.C. R.R., 1948-68, gen. mgr. Syracuse, N.Y., 1965, asst. v.p. transp., N.Y.C., 1965, v.p. systems devel., 1967-68; v.p. systems devel. Penn Central Co., 1968-69, v.p. operations, Phila., 1969-70; exec. v.p. Penn Central Transp. Co., 1970, v.p. operations, 1970—. Served with USNR, 1943-45. Mem. Pi Kappa Alpha. Democrat. Mason. Home: 910 Stony Lane Gladwyne PA 19035 Office: 6 Penn Center Plaza Philadelphia PA 19104

FLANNERY, THOMAS, polit. cartoonist; b. Carbondale, Pa., Dec. 16, 1919; s. James A. and Clare (Reap) F.; student Pratt Inst., 1939-40, U. Scranton, 1946-47; m. Donna Hossack, Dec. 26, 1952; children—Shawn, Sharon, Janine, David. Polit. cartoonist Lowell (Mass.) Sun, 1947-57, Balt. Evening Sun, 1957—. Served with USAAF, World War II; staff cartoonist Yank mag., 1943-45. Decorated Bronze Star. Mem. Am. Soc. Editorial Cartoonists. Home: 506 Orkney Rd Baltimore MD 21212 Office: 500 Calvert St Baltimore MD 21201

FLANNERY, THOMAS AQUINAS, U.S. atty.; b. Washington, May 10, 1918; s. John J. and Mary (Sullivan) F.; LL.B., Columbus U., 1940; m. Rita Sullivan, Mar. 3, 1951; children-Thomas Aquinas, Irene M. Admitted to D.C. bar, 1940; practice in Washington, 1940-42, 45-48; trial atty. Dept. Justice, Washington, 1948-50; asst. U.S. Atty. Washington, 1950-62; partner Hamilton and Hamilton Washington, 1962-69; U.S. atty for D.C., Washington, 1969—. Served with USAF, 1942-45. Fellow Am. Coll. Trial Lawyers; Mem. Am., Fed., D.C. bar assns. Home: 5607 Jordan Rd Washington DC 20016 Office: United States Court House Washington DC 20001

FLANNERY, WILLIAM LOUIS, educator; b. Jamestown, N.D., Dec. 22, 1922; s. William Louis and Frances (Duchscher) F.; B.A. with honors, U. N.D., 1948; student N.D. State U., 1948-50; Ph.D., U. Md., 1953; m. Ruth Elaine Kjerstad, June 14, 1948; 1 son, Kevin Michael. Bacteriologist, Dept. Agr., Beltsville, Md., 1953; instr. Baylor U. Coll. Medicine, 1953-54, asst. prof. microbiology, 1954-56; med. edn. adviser ICA, San Salvador, El Salvador, 1956-59; prof. microbiology El Salvador Med. Sch., 1956-59; prof., head dept. microbiology U. Southwestern La., 1959—. Served with M.C., AUS, 1943-46. Mem. Am. Soc. Microbiology, A.A.A.S., Am. Assn. U. Profs., Soc. Gen. Microbiology, Sigma Xi, Sigma Alpha Omicron, Alpha Tau Omega, Phi Kappa Phi. Contbr. articles profl. jours. Home: 148 River Rd Lafayette LA 70501

FLASK, ANTHONY B., former mayor of Youngstown, O. Address: 515 Carlotta Dr Youngstown OH 44504*

FLATT, ERNEST ORVILLE, dancer, choreographer; b. Denver, Oct. 30, 1918; s. Ernest Scorrow and Della May (Allen) F.; grad. high sch. Dancer films including An American in Paris, Singin' in the Rain; choreographer film Anything Goes; choreographer TV shows Your Hit Parade, 1955-58, Garry Moore Show, 1958-63, Carol Burnett Show, 1968—; asso. producer TV spl. Julie and Carol at Carnegie Hall; dir.-choreographer Carol and Co., Calamity Jane.; dir. Ernatt Corp. Bd. dirs. Am. Sch. Dance. Served with AUS, 1941-45. Recipient Emmy award for Garry Moore Show, for Julie and Carol at Carnegie Hall, and in 1971. Mem. A.F.T.R.A., Actors' Equity, Soc. Dirs. and Choreographers. Home: 1240 N Wetherly Dr Los Angeles CA 90069 Office: care CBS Studio Center 4024 Radford Studio City CA 91604

FLATTO, LEOPOLD, educator, mathematician; b. Antwerp, Belgium, Aug. 20, 1929; s. Abraham and Martha (Gradom) F.; came to U.S., 1941; B.S., City Coll. N.Y., 1950; M.A., Johns Hopkins, 1951; Ph.D., Mass. Inst. Tech., 1955; m. Zehava Krumholz, Apr. 20, 1966; children—Sharon Helen, David. Mathematician, Reeves Instrument Corp., 1955-57; prof. math. Bklyn. Poly. Inst., 1957-60; mathematician IBM, 1960-61; prof. math. Yeshiva U., 1961—. NSF grantee, 1963-70. Mem. Am. Math. Soc. Contbr. articles profl. jours. Home: 3850 Hudson Manor Terrace Bronx NY 10463 Office: Belfer Graduate School of Science 186th St and Amsterdam Av New York City NY 10033

FLAVIN, JAMES WILLIAM, actor; b. Portland, Me., May 14, 1906; s. James William and Katherine Louise (Rice) F.; B.S., U.S. Mil. Acad., 1926; m. Lucile Browne, Sept. 17, 1933; 1 son, William James. Actor Jefferson Stock Co., Portland, 1927, Broadway stage, 1928-31; under contract Universal Studios, 1931-32; appearances motion pictures and TV, 1931—, including Broadway revival Front Page, 1969-70. Mem. Acad. Motion Picture Arts and Scis. Home: 3073 Patricia Av Los Angeles CA 90064 Office: c/o Velvet Amber 6308 Quebec Rd Hollywood CA 90028

FLAVIN, JOSEPH B., mfg. co. exec.; b. St. Louis, Oct. 16, 1928; s. Joseph B. and Mary E. (Toomey) F.; m. Melisande Barillon, 1946; children—Patrick Brian, Shawn Elaine. Accountant, Cawley Aircraft Supply Co., 1953; with IBM World Trade Corp., 1953-67, controller, 1965-67; group v.p. Xerox Corp., Rochester, N.Y., 1967-70, exec. v.p., dir., 1970—; dir. Ginn & Co. Served with USMCR. Mem. Financial Execs. Inst., Budget Execs. Inst. Club: Economics (N.Y.C.). Home: 8 Kingsbury Ct Rochester NY 14618 Office: Xerox Sq Rochester NY 14603

FLAVIN, THOMAS J., govt. ofcl.; b. Boston, July 13, 1906; s. John and Bridget (O'Gara) F.; A.B., Boston Coll., 1926, A.M., 1927; LL.B., Georgetown U., 1932; m. Ann E. Jackson, Feb. 1, 1941; children—Thomas J., Patricia Ann, Deborah Peck. Instr., asst. prof. classical lit. Georgetown U., 1927-32; admitted to D.C. bar, 1932, Mass. bar, 1933, practiced in Boston, 1932-34; atty. U.S. Dept. Agr., 1934-42, jud. officer, 1942—. Mem. Adminstrv. Conf. U.S., 1962, 68—. Home: 4800 Dover Rd Washington DC 20016 Office: US Dept Agr Washington DC 20515

FLAX, ALEXANDER HENRY, aero. engr.; b. Bklyn., Jan. 18, 1921; s. David and Etta (Schenker) F.; B.Aero. Engring., N.Y. U., 1940; Ph.D. in Physics, U. Buffalo, 1958; m. Ida Leane Warren, Aug. 25, 1951; 1 dau., Laurel Elizabeth. Structure, vibration engr. airplane div. Curtiss-Wright Corp., 1940-44; chief aerodynamics and structures Piasecki Helicopter Corp., 1944-46; asst. head aeromechanics dept. Cornell Aero. Lab., 1946-49, head aerodynamics dept., 1949-55, asst. dir., 1955-56, v.p., tech. dir., 1956-59, 61-63; chief scientist USAF, 1959-61; asst. sec. Air Force for research and devel., 1963-69; v.p. for research Inst. for Def. Analysis, Arlington, Va., 1969, pres., 1969—. Mem. com. aerodynamics NACA, 1952-54, subcom. highspeed aerodynamics, 1954- 58; adv. com. aircraft aerodynamics NASA, 1958-62; mem. coms. various govtl. orgns., 1970—. Recipient Air Force Exceptional Civilian Service awards, 1961, 69; NASA Distinguished Service medal, 1968. Fellow Am. Inst. Aeros. and Astronautics (Lawrence Sperry award 1949, Wright Bros. lectr. 1959); mem. Nat. Acad. Engring., Sigma Xi. Club: Cosmos (Washington). Contbr. sect. to book, numerous articles to profl. jours. Home: 9007 Belmart Rd Potomac MD 20854 Office: Inst Def Analysis 400 Army-Navy Dr Arlington VA 22202

FLAX, SERENE (Mrs. Donald Flax), artist; b. Chgo., May 25, 1925; d. Walter and Florence (Zimmerman) Gottstein; grad. Chgo. Acad. Fine Arts, 1943; student Northwestern U., 1944-45, Art Inst. Chgo., 1946, Inst. Design, Chgo., 1946-47; m. Donald Flax, Feb. 15, 1948; children—Robert, Carole, Patrice. Art dir. advt. agys., Chgo., 1946-48; contbr. to art rental and sales Art Inst. Chgo., 1964—; exhibited one man shows Ontario-East Gallery, Chgo., 1966, Mundelein Coll., Chgo., 1967, Kaumerman Gallery, Racine, Wis., 1962, Barat Coll., Lake Forest, Ill., 1970, Madison (Wis.) Art Center, 1970; exhibited group shows, nat. competitions including Drawings, U.S.A., St. Paul, 1963, Allied Artists Am., N.Y.C., 1963-64, Audubon Soc. Artists, N.Y.C., 1963-64, Am. Water Color Soc., 1964—, Miss. Valley Artists Invitational, Springfield, Ill., 1965, Ill. State Mus. Invitational, Springfield, 1968; Butler Inst. Am. Art, Youngstown, O., 1962—; rep. permanent collections Caravan Gallery, Tulsa, Bocour collection, N.Y.C., also many pvt. collections throughout U.S. Chmn.

Old Orchard Festival, Skokie, Ill., 1965, chmn. exhbns., 1965—; vol. mem. human relations group Lake Forest (Ill.) chpt. Panel Am. Women, 1966—. Recipient travel awards Am. Watercolor Soc., 1963, 64, 65, 66, 67, Cal. Watercolor Soc. and Watercolor U.S.A., 1967-68; Bruggers Merit award for transparent watercolor Cal. Watercolor Soc., 1964; 1st prize Evanston (Ill.) Women's Club, 1964; purchase award Watercolor U.S.A., Springfield (Mo.) Art Mus., 1966; Municipal Art League award Chgo. Art Inst., 1969; 1st award for painting Deer Path Art League, 1970; hon. mention Old Orchard Festival, 1969. Mem. Am., Cal. watercolor socs. Contbg. author profl. mags. Address: 268 Moraine Rd Highland Park, IL 60035.

FLAXMAN, SEYMOUR LAWRENCE, educator, b. N.Y.C., Dec. 15, 1918; s. Aaron and Ida (Levine) F.; B.S., N.Y.U., 1938; M.A., Columbia, 1939, Ph.D., 1950; m. Ruth Krantz, Oct. 2, 1944; children—Carol Thalia, Amy Madeline. Lecturer Sch. Gen. studies, Columbia, 1941-42, 46-50; mem. faculty Univ. Coll., N.Y.U., 1946-62, asso. prof. Germanic langs., 1956-62, dir. summer session in Europe, 1960-62; prof. Germanic langs. State U. N.Y. at Stony Brook, 1962-67, chmn. dept., prof., City Coll., City U. N.Y., 1967—; exec. officer, comparative lit., also Germanic langs. and lit. Grad. Cntr., City U. N.Y., 1968—, dir. summer lang. program, 1970—; vis. prof. Columbia, 1971-72. Served with AUS, 1942-45; MTO. Traveling fellow in Scandinavia, Inst. Intercontinental Studies, 1950; Fulbright research scholar, Amsterdam, 1954-55. Mem. Modern Lang. Assn., Internat. Comparative Lit. Assn., Am. Comparative Lit. Assn., Am. Assn. U. Profs., Am. Assn. Tchrs. German, Fedn. Internat. des Langues et Lit. Modernes, Modern Humanities Research Assn., Internat. Vereinigung für germanische Sprache und Literaturwissenschaft. Republican. Jewish religion. Author: Herman Heijermans and His Dramas, 1950. Editor: Reports of the Northeast Foreign Language Conference, 1961. Home: 3850 Hudson Manor Terrace New York City NY 10463 Office: Grad Center City U NY 33 W 42d St New York City NY 10036

FLEAGLE, ROBERT GUTHRIE, educator; b. Woodlawn, Md., Aug. 16, 1918; s. Benjamin Edward and Frances Taylor (Guthrie) F.; A.B., Johns Hopkins, 1940; M.S., N.Y. U., 1944, Ph.D., 1949; m. Marianne Diggs, Dec. 19, 1942; children—Robert Guthrie, John B. Asst. prof. U. Wash., 1948-51, asso. prof., 1951-56, prof., 1956—, chmn. dept. atmospheric scis., 1967—. Cons. various bus., instns., govt. agys. Tech. asst. Office Sci. and Tech., Exec. Office of Pres., 1963-64; mem. Nat. Acad. Scis. Com. on Atmospheric Scis., 1962—, chmn., 1969—; mem. panel on oceanography Pres.'s Sci. Adv. Com., 1965-66; mem. U.S. Com. Global Atmospheric Research Program, 1968—; mem. NATO adv. panel on meteorology, 1970—. Trustee Univ. Corp. for Atmospheric Research, 1970—, chmn. council mems., 1966-67. Served from pvt. to capt. AUS, 1942-46. NSF fellow Imperial Coll., London, 1958-59. Fellow Am. Geophys. Union, Am. Meteorol. Soc. (Meisinger award 1959, Cleveland Abbé award 1971); mem. Sigma Xi. Author: (with J.A. Businger) An Introduction to Atmospheric Physics, 1963. Editor: Weather Modification: Science and Public Policy, 1968. Contbr. articles to sci. jours. Home: 7858 56th Pl N E Seattle WA 98115

FLECK, BENJAMIN ARMSTRONG, fgn. service officer; b. Pa., May 10, 1923; s. G. Dare and Mabel (Stewart) F.; B.A., U. Pitts., 1943; M.I.A., Columbia, 1948; m. Marjorie Cooper, Aug. 17, 1952; children—Alan Armstrong, Kenneth Stewart, David Cooper. Assigned Diplomatic Service, Dept. State, 1948; 3d sec., Caracas, Venezuela, 1949-51, 2d sec., 1951; assigned Dept. State, 1951, South Asian lang. area study Fgn. Service Inst., U. Pa., 1951; 2d sec., vice consul, New Delhi, India, 1952-54; vice consul, Madras, 1954-56, cons., 1956-57; internat. relations officer Dept. State, 1957-58, officer charge India, Nepal, Ceylon affairs, 1958-61; 2d sec., Seoul, Korea, 1961-62. 1st sec., 1962-65; officer charge Korean affairs Dept. State, 1965-66, country dir. for Korea, 1966-68; student Nat. War Coll. 1968-69; dep. chief Mission, Rangoon, Burma, 1969—. Served with AUS, 1943-46. Mem. Am. Fgn. Service Assn., Am. Oriental Soc. Home: 220 Lee Av NE Winter Haven FL 33880 Office: Am Embassy Rangoon Burma

FLECK, GUSTAV PETER, banker, corp. exec.; b. Amsterdam, The Netherlands, 1909; s. Richard and Anna (Stein) F.; grad. Amsterdam Lyceum, 1927; D.H.L. (hon.), Starr King Sch. for Minstry; m. Ruth Alice Irene Melchior, June 1, 1939; children—Ann (Mrs. Michael L.C. Henderson), Andrea (Mrs. John Clardy), Marjorie (Mrs. Scott K. Withers). Came U.S., 1941, naturalized, 1945. With Erlangers, Ltd., London, 1928-29, Banque des Pays de L'Europe Centrale, Paris, 1929-30, Bank fur Auswartigen Handel, Berlin, 1930-31; with Continental Handelsbank, Amsterdam, 1931-40, v.p., 1936-40; organized Amsterdam Overseas Corp., N.Y.C. 1947, pres., 1947-67, chmn., 1967—; chmn. New Court Securities Corp., pres., dir. Five Arrows Securities Co., Ltd., Toronto, Can., Five Arrows Securities Co. Curacao N.V.; dir. N.M. Rothschild & Sons, Ltd., London, Banque Rothschild, S.A. Paris, Compagnie Lambert, Brussels, Brit. Nfld. Corp., Ltd., Montreal, Internat. Flavors and Fragrances, N.Y.C., Magnum Fund, Toronto, Jefferson Ins. Co. N.Y. Trustee The Gill Sch., Bernardsville, N.J.; chmn. Meadville Theol. Sch. of Lombard Coll., Chgo., Netherlands-Am. Found. Decorated officer Order Oranje Nassau. Mem. Netherlands C. of C. in U.S. (bd. dirs.), Am. Arbitration Assn. (panel arbitrators). Council Fgn. Relations. Home: Campbell Rd Bernardsville NJ 07924 Office: 70 Pine St New York City NY 10005

FLECK, HENRIETTA (Mrs. Henrietta Fleck Houghton), educator; b. Papillion, Neb., Sept. 22, 1903; d. John Peter and Wilhelmina (Prinz) Fleck; student Peru (Neb.) Tchrs. Coll., 1921-23; B.S., U. Neb., 1928; M.S., Columbia, 1932; Ph.D., Ohio State U., 1944; m. Dale Houghton, June 6, 1956. Home econs. tchr. Neb. high schs., 1923-27; dietitian in charge metabolic div. Santa Barbara (Cal.) Cottage Hosp., 1928-29; head dept. foods and nutrition U. Del., 1932-42; research asst., bur. ednl. research Ohio State U., 1942-44; chmn. home econs. dept. Ill. State Normal, 1944-46, N.Y.U. since 1946; cons. edn. procedures N.Y. Dept. Edn., bus. corps., social orgns. since 1946. Mem. N.E.A. (pres. home econs. dept. 1953-55), Am. Home Econ. Assn., A.A.A.S., Am. Dietetic Assn., Am. Edn. Research Assn., Nat. Council Family Relations, Am. Assn. U. Profs., Nat. Soc. Study Edn., Omicron Nu, Pi Lambda Theta. Author: A Recipe Primer, 1949; How to Evaluate Students, 1953; Introduction to Nutrition, 1962, 2d edit., 1971; The Co-ed Cookbook, 1967; Toward Better Teaching of Home Economics, 1968. Co-author: Everybody's Book of Modern Diet and Nutrition, 1955; Exploring Home and Family Living, 1959, 3d edit., 1971; Living With Your Family, 1965. Editor Macmillan series coll. home econs. text books, 1957-63. Contbr. editor Forecast Mag. for Home Economists, 1949-62; ednl. and curriculum adviser, contributor to Forecast magazine, 1963—. Contbr. profl. jours. Home: 157 E 18th St New York City NY 10003 Office: 100 Washington Sq New York City NY 10003

FLECK, STEPHEN, educator, psychiatrist; b. Frankfurt/Main, Germany, Sept. 18, 1912; s. Georg and Anna (Beer) F.; student J.W. Goethe U., Frankfurt/Main, 1931- 33, U. Amsterdam (The Netherlands), 1933-35; Physikum Exam., Germany, 1935; M.D., Harvard, 1940; m. Louise Harlan, Oct. 13, 1945; children—Anna-Lou Jacobs, Stephen Harlan, Carra Ruth. Came to U.S., 1935, naturalized, 1941. Intern, Beth Israel Hosp., Boston, 1940-41; resident psychiatry Johns Hopkins Hosp., 1946-48; instr. medicine and psychiatry Johns Hopkins Med. Sch., 1948-49; instr. psychiatry, then asst. prof. U. Wash. Med. Sch., 1949-53; chief psychiatrist outpatient dept. King County Hosp., Seattle, 1949-53; cons. VA Hosp., Seattle, 1951-53; mem. faculty Yale Med. Sch., 1953—, psychiatrist-in-chief Yale Psychiat. Inst. and Conn. Mental Health Center, prof. psychiatry and pub. health, 1963—, dep. chmn. psychiatry dept., 1968—; cons. VA Hosp., West Haven, Conn., Conn. State Hosp., Middletown, 1953, Family Service New Haven, 1953-57. Bd. dirs. health edn. com. Hamden (Conn.) Pub. Schs. Past pres. Hamden P.T.A. Council. Served to maj. AUS, 1942-46; ETO. Diplomate Nat. Bd. Med. Examiners, Am. Bd. Psychiatry and Neurology. Mem. A.M.A., Am. Psychiat. Assn., Am. Psychosomatic Soc., Am. Fedn. Clin. Research, Am. Soc. Gerontology, Nat. Council Family Relations, Group for Advancement Psychiatry, N. Pacific Soc. Neurology and Psychiatry, Am., Conn. pub. health assns., W. New Eng. Psychoanalytic Soc. and Inst., Unitarian Soc. New Haven (past pres.), Sigma Xi. Author monograph; contbr. articles to profl. jours. Home: 18 Ardmore St Hamden CT 06514 Office: 333 Cedar St New Haven CT 06510

FLEECE, EUGENE LOUIS, former banker; b. Indpls., July 16, 1903; s. Joseph Benjamin and Emma (Williams) F.; student Purdue U., 1922-23, Ind. U., 1924-27; m. Martha Emily Mauck, June 7, 1942; 1 son, Eugene Louis. With Ernst & Ernst, Indpls., 1925-36; dep. auditor state accounting State Ind., 1936-42; with Ind. Nat. Bank, Indpls., 1945-68, sr. v.p., loan adminstr. until 1968; dir. C.P. Lesh Paper Co. Mem. Ind. N.G., 1926-29; served to lt. col. USAAF, 1942- 45; Mem. Phi Gamma Delta. Republican. Presbyn. Club: Indianapolis Athletic. Home: 3200 W 42d St Indianapolis IN 46208

FLEECE, GEORGE ALLEN, former coll. pres.; b. Louisville, Dec. 2, 1909; s. Hugh Berry and Annabell (Fox) F.; A.B., Washington and Lee U., 1931, D.D., 1938; B.D., Columbia Theol. Sem., 1934; m. Isabel Berry, July 30, 1934; children—Anne Berry, David Fox, Ned (dec.). Ordained to ministry, Presbyn. Ch., 1934; pastor First Ch., Covington, Ga., 1934-35, Central Ch., Chattanooga, Tenn., 1936-37, Westminster Ch., 1948-51; mem. faculty Columbia Bible Coll., 1938-43, 46-47, 51-52, pres. 1953-69; faculty Moody Bible Inst., Chgo., 1944-45; dir. Ben Lippen Conf. Center, Asheville, N.C. Pres. bd. trustees Ben Lippen Sch., Asheville; mem. exec. bd. West Indies Mission. Home: Monticello Rd Columbia SC 29203

FLEEGE, URBAN H., educator; b. Dubuque, Ia., Nov. 4, 1908; s. William B. and Dora (Kellner) F.; B.S., U. Dayton, 1932; Ph.D., Cath. U. Am., 1940; m. Virginia B. Hansen, Aug. 31, 1948; children—William, Kathleen, Richard, Robert, Maureen, Michael. High sch. tchr. English and math., Chgo., 1932-34; athletic dir. Cathedral High Sch., Belleville, Ill., 1934-36, prin., 1941-44; tchr. McBridge High Sch., St. Louis, 1937; asst. prof. edn. St. Mary's U., San Antonio, 1940-41; lectr. psychology Loyola U., Chgo., 1944; asst. prof. secondary edn. and adolescent psychology Catholic U. Am., 1944-46, chmn. dept. edn. summers 1945, 46; dean N.M. Highlands U., 1946-47; co-dir. Nat. Workshop Adminstrs. of Women's Colls., Denver, 1947; dir. guidance clinic, coordinator vets. affairs, prof. edn. Marquette U., 1947-48; edn. and cultural relations adviser State Dept. to U.S. High Commr. in Germany, 1948-51; dir. ednl. instns. div. FCDA, 1951-52; chief UNESCO Tech. Mission to P.I., 1953-56; asso. sec. Nat. Cath. Edn. Assn., Washington, 1952-53, 56-57; chmn. dept. edn. DePaul U., Chgo., 1957-62, v.p. univ. charge planning and research, 1962-63, asso. v.p., 1963—; pres. Midwest Montessori Tchr. Tng. Center, 1964—. Mem. Ill. Adv. Council on Edn.; mem. curriculum council Chgo. Bd. Edn.; rector edn. faculty Lincoln Acad. Ill.; bd. advisers St. Mary's Coll. Notre Dame, 1969—. Mem. tech. adv. bd. Chgo. Anti-Poverty Campaign. Mem. N.E.A., Nat. Cath. Edn. Assn., Am. Council on Edn., Am., Am. Cath. psychol. assns., Am. Assn. U. Profs., Am. Acad. Polit. and Social Sci., Am. Assn. Sch. Adminstrs. K.C., Elk, Rotarian. Author: Personal Problems of Modern Adolescents, 1940; Self- Revelation of the Adolescent Boy, 1945; The Community School, 1956; Problems in Education, 1956; Mental Health for Teachers, 1960; Building the Foundations for Creative Learning, 1965; Issues Confronting the Church, 1967; Montessori Preschool Education, 1968. Contbr. profl. jours. Home: 831 Fair Oaks St Oak Park IL 60302 Office: DePaul U Chicago IL 60614

FLEER, ROLAND, lawyer; b. Sea Isle City, N.J., July 13, 1903; s. Frederick Henry and Elsabet (Landgraf) F.; A.B. cum laude, Harvard, 1924, LL.B., 1928; m. Doris Helene Runge, Oct. 8, 1932; children—Elsabet (Mrs. Russell K. Thomson, Jr.), Roland. Admitted to Pa. bar, 1928, since practiced in Norristown; sr. partner Waters, Fleer, Cooper & Gallagher, 1961—. Solicitor, Local Bd. Sch. Dirs., 1936-56; pres. Local Borough Council, 1938-46; mem. adv. com. Decedents Estates Laws to Joint State Govt. Commn. Gen. Assembly of Commonwealth Pa., 1945-69. Chmn. Main Line br. United World Federalists, Phila, 1960-62. Recipient Bronze plaque for preserving existence Borough of Narberth as self-governing community, 1936. Mem. Montgomery County Bar Assn. (pres. 1962). Editor: M.P. Smith) Fiduciary Review, 1932-41; Montgomery County Law Reporter, 1938-42. Home: 1508 Spring Mill Lane, Villanova, PA 19085. Office: 512 Swede St Norristown PA 19401

FLEESON, WILLIAM, univ. dean; b. Sterling, Kan., May 21, 1915; s. William H. and Eva Lynn (Seward) F.; A.B. (Summerfield scholar), U. Kan., 1937; M.D., Yale, 1942; postgrad. Advanced Mgmt. Program Harvard, 1964; m. Beatrice Riedel, Mar. 26, 1943; children—William, Breck, Lucinda, Peter, Elizabeth. Intern, U. Hosps., Mpls., 1942-43; asso. psychiatrist Manhattan Project, Oak Ridge, 1945-46; asso. psychiatrist, dir. child guidance div. Minn. Psychiat. Inst., Mpls., 1946-55; staff psychiatrist Elizabeth Kenny Inst., Mpls., 1953-56; Nat. Found. fellow U. Minn., Mpls., 1956, asst. prof. psychiatry and phys. medicine, 1957-61, MEND coordinator Coll. Med. Scis., 1959-63, lectr. Law Sch., 1960-63, asso. prof. psychiatry, 1961-63, asst. dean Coll. Med. Scis., 1960-63; asso. dean, prof. psychiatry Sch. Medicine, U. Conn., Hartford, 1963—, lectr. Sch. Social Work, 1967—, acting head dept. psychiatry U. Conn., 1967-68; lectr. psychiatry Sch. Medicine, Yale, 1965—; supr. psychotherapy Inst. for Living, Hartford, Conn., 1965-67. Cons. psychiatry child study div. Mpls. Bd. Edn., 1957-63. Served to capt. AUS, 1943-46. USPHS fellow child psychiatry Judge Baker Guidance Center, Boston, 1950-51. Fellow Am. Psychiat. Assn.; mem. Assn. Am. Med. Colls. (sec.-treas. Northeastern group for student affairs 1970—), Conn. Psychiat. Soc. (council 1966-68), Hartford Med. Soc. Club: Graduate (New Haven). Contbr. book revs. to Jour. Am. Psychiat. Assn., Sci. Books. Home: 37 Wendy Lane West Hartford CT 06117 Office: U Conn Sch Medicine 1280 Asylum Hartford CT 06105

FLEGENHEIMER, ALBERT, sugar industry exec.; b. Schwäbisch-Hall, Germany, July 4, 1890 (parents Am. citizens); s. Samuel and Lisette (Rothschild) F.; ed. in Germany; m. Helen Stern, Dec. 21, 1920; children—Ruth (Mrs. Henry H. Herzog), Ernest. Comml. apprentice, Karlsruhe, Germany, 1905-07; various positions sugar industry, Germany, Italy, Rumania, Bulgaria, 1907-37, also mem. mgt. Sueddeutsche Zucker A.G., Mannheim, Germany; organized beet sugar factory, Man., Can., 1939-41; pres. Waverly Sugar Co. (Ia.), 1941-48, Menominee Sugar Co., Green Bay, Wis., 1952-57; dir. Mich. Sugar Co., Saginaw, 1961—, chmn., 1963—. Club: Rotary (Waverly, Ia.). Home: 300 Central Park W New York City NY 10024 Office: 42 Broadway New York City NY 10004

FLEGENHEIMER, ERNEST, sugar co. exec.; b. Zurich, Switzerland, Jan. 30, 1927; s. Albert and Helen (Stern) F.; came to U.S., 1942, naturalized, 1943; grad. Lake Forest (Ill.) Acad., 1945; student N.Y. U., 1946-48, Middlebury (Vt.) Coll., 1948-49, Grenoble (France) U., 1949-50; m. Marjorie McGinn, June 7, 1952; children—Ellen, Lauren, Eric Jon, Mark Steven. With Domestic Concentrates, Inc., imports-exports, N.Y.C., 1950-54, Menominee Sugar Co., Green Bay, Wis., 1954-62, Bend Southall McBratnie Co., sugar brokers, Green Bay, 1962-63; pres., chief exec. officer, dir. Mich. Sugar Co., Saginaw, 1963—; dir. 2d Nat. Bank of Saginaw. Bd. dirs. Internat. Sugar Research Found. Mem. Farmers and Mfrs. Beet Sugar Assn. (pres., bd. dir.), U.S. Beet Sugar Assn. (trustee). Home: 4660 Ashland Dr Saginaw MI 48603 Office: Second Nat Bank Bldg Saginaw MI 48607

FLEGER, PHILLIP ARTHUR, ret. utilites exec.; b. Chgo. June 3, 1903; s. Philipp and Marie (Becker) Pfleger; student U. Ill., 1921-22; LL.B., U. W.Va., 1926; m. Margaret Rodgers, June 22, 1933; children—Louise (Mrs. Samuel A. Bishop), Linda. Past chmn., pres. Duquesne Light Co., Pitts., 1950-68, now dir.; emeritus dir. Mellon Nat. Bank & Trust Co.; past pres. Edison Electric Inst. Past pres. United Fund Allegheny County; past chmn. Regional Ind. Devel. Corp. Devel. Fund. Bd. dirs. Western Pa. Hosp.; trustee Carnegie-Mellon U. Recipient award for leadership in mgmt. Duquesne U., 1956; named Man of Year in Bus., Pitts. Jr. C. of C. 1958; others. Mem. Law Club, Phi Delta Phi, Alpha Chi Rho. Clubs: Duquesne, Golf, Fox Chapel Golf (Pitts.); Rolling Rock, Laurel Valley (Ligonier, Pa.); Lyford Cay (Nassau, Bahamas). Home: Jefferson School Rd Ligonier PA 15658

FLEIG, OTTO JAMES, ins. co. exec.; b. Bklyn., Jan. 30, 1910; s. Otto and Elizabeth (Whitford) F.; B.C.S., N.Y.U., 1932; m. Melicent L. Hovey, Nov. 1, 1941; 1 dau., Melissa A. With Larkin & Jennys Investment Bankers, 1927-30; with Ames, Emerich & Co., investment bankers, 1930; with Met. Life Ins. Co., N.Y.C., 1931—, v.p. securities, 1965-69, v.p., treas., 1969—; mem. Chem. Bank-Lower Midtown Adv. Bd. Served to Comdr. USNR, 1942-45. Club: Nassau Country (Glen Cove, N.Y.). Home: 93 Gaynor Av Manhasset LI NY 11030 Office: 1 Madison Av New York NY 10010

FLEISCHAKER, BETTY JANE, civic worker; b. Terre Haute, Ind., Sept. 9, 1920; d. David Henry and Helen (Steiner) Spritz; student Smith Coll., 1938-39, U. Cin., 1939-41; B.A. (with honors), U. Louisville, 1968; m. Leopold Fleischaker, Nov. 29, 1941 (div. 1965); children—David Spritz, Jon Leopold, Marc Leopold, Elizabeth. Dir. manpower program Louisville and Jefferson County Community Action Commn., 1968-71, adminstr. external operations, 1971—. Pres. Louisville sect. Nat. Council Jewish Women, 1953-55, pres. So. interstate region, 1959-61, nat. chmn. pub. affairs com., 1961-65, nat. v.p., 1965- -; pres. Louisville Women's Com. Civil Rights, 1963-64; state coordinator Women in Community Service, 1964-65; sec. Louisville and Jefferson County Community Action Commn., 1965-66, Louisville and Jefferson County Youth Commn., 1964-65; chmn. com. pub. accommodations Louisville Human Relations Commn., 1962-64; bd. dirs. Women in Community Service, 1965-69, Louisville Area Mental Health Center, 1964-65, Ky. chpt. Nat. Conf. Christians and Jews, 1955-61; chmn. edn. com., bd. dirs. Louisville League Women Voters, 1949-53 Recipient Community Service award Mt. Lebanon Baptist Ch. Women, Louisville, 1964: Hannah E. Solomon award Nat. Council Jewish Women, 1966. Home: 2326 Broadmeade Louisville KY 40205 Office: 1213 W Broadway Louisville KY 40203

FLEISCHAKER, JOSEPH, retail electric appliance exec.; b. Louisville, Jan. 9, 1910; s. Siegfried and Sophie (Lippold) F.; B.S. in Bus. Adminstrn., U. Miami (Fla.), 1932; extension courses N.Y. U.; m. Marie Sales, June 14, 1937; children—Carol R. (Mrs. Alvin G. Westerman), Susan (Mrs. Eliot Lee Silbar), Joan (Mrs. Henry T. Evers III). Dist. sales mgr. Orbon Stove Co., Belleville, Ill. Mem. treas. com. Jefferson County Republican Campaign Fund. Bd. dirs. Jewish Hosp. Louisville, Hebrew Home for Aged, Old Peoples Home, St. Louis, Annie Maloney Home, St. Louis. Served from lt. (j.g.) to lt. comdr. USNR, 1941-46. Mem. Nat. Appliance Radio-TV Dealers (pres. 1958- 59), Ky. Retail Appliance Dealers (pres. 1954-56), Urban League, Am. Jewish Com., Nat. Conf. Christians and Jews, Am. Legion, Brandeis U. (asso. fellow and life mem.), Phi Epsilon Pi, Rho Beta Omicron. Jewish religion (temple pres. 1952-55). Kiwanian. Club: Standard Country (v.p., chmn. house com. 1954-58) (Louisville). Home: 665 S Skinker Blvd St Louis MO 63105 Office: Will Sales Bldg Louisville KY 40201

FLEISCHBEIN, MARGIE OPHELIA EASTER, former orgn. exec.; b. Amelia, Va., Sept. 18, 1923; d. Lewis and Nettie Bell(Keener) Easter; student Smithdeal-Massey Bus. Coll., Richmond, Va., also George Washington U.; m. Reuben Richard Fleischbein, June 30, 1956; 1 dau., Christina Jean. Sec., Phila. Ordnance Dist., Richmond, 1942-46, Mil. Air Transp. Service, Washington, 1946-51, FCDA, Washington, 1951- 54, ICA mission to Tripoli, Libya, 1954-57; exec. sec. Fedn. Am. Scientists, Washington, 1963-70. Mem. Nat. Secs. Assn. (v.p. Presdl. chpt. 1959-61). Home: 3605 Pinetree Terrace Falls Church VA 22041

FLEISCHER, HEINRICH RUDOLF, organist, educator; b. Eisenach, Germany, Apr. 1, 1912; s. Ernst Rudolf and Margarete (Grellmann) F.; student U. Jena, 1930-32, State Music Acad., Weimar, 1930-32; diploma in Ch. Music, State Music Acad., Leipzig, 1934; Ph.D., Leipzig U., 1940. Came to U.S., 1949, naturalized, 1956. Prof. organ State Acad. Music, Leipzig, 1937-48; univ. organist Leipzig U., 1937-48; prof. music Valparaiso (Ind.) U., 1949-57; univ. organist U. Chgo., 1953-59; prof. music, univ. organist U. Minn., Mpls., 1959—; organ recitals in U.S.A., Can., Europe. Fellow Am. Guild Organists. Home: 123 Warwick St SE Minneapolis MN 55414

FLEISCHER, HERBERT OSWALD, wood technologist; b. Lake Geneva, Wis., June 22, 1913; s. Herman Albert and Alma (Treichel) F.; B.A., Northwestern Coll., Wis., 1935; B.S., U. Mich, 1938, M.F., 1938; Ph.D. (Sheffield fellow), Yale, 1952; m. Dorothy V. Groth, June 7, 1941 (dec. 1965); children—Christine (Mrs. David Flagler), Cornelia D. (Mrs. Robert Mutel). m. 2d, Bertha B. Wachholz, Sept. 9, 1967. Forester, Lake States Forest Expt. Sta., U.S. Forest Service, 1938, Nicolet Nat. Forest, 1939, Consol. Water Power & Paper Co., 1939-40; wood technologist Forest Products Lab. U.S. Forest Service, Madison, Wis., 1942-64, chief div. solid wood products research, 1957-64, dir. Forest Products Lab., 1967—, dir. forest products and engrng. research, forest service U.S. Dept. Agr., Washington, 1964-67. Civilian research service U.S. Army, USAAF, USN, NACA, 1943-45; tech. cons. Fgn. Econ. Adminstrn. Europe, 1945; lectr. forest products U. Wis., 1950—; chmn. wood-based panel products com. UN FAO, 1965—; mem. com. research evaluation U.S. Dept. Agr., 1956; chmn. forest products sect. Internat Union Forestry Research Orgns., 1967—. Bd. dirs. Bethesda Lutheran Home; trustee Wis. Evang. Luth. Synod. Recipient Patriotic Civilian Service award Dept. Army, 1951. Fellow Internat. Acad. Wood Sci.; mem. Forest

Products Research Soc. (pres. 1964, past chmn.), Soc. Wood Sci. and Tech., Soc. Am. Foresters, Am. Soc. Testing Materials, Sigma Xi. Home: 2508 Santa Maria Ct Middleton WI 53562 Office: Forest Products Lab Madison WI 53705

FLEISCHER, JULIUS CHRISTIAN AUGUST, Norwegian diplomat; b. Fredrikstad, Norway, Sept. 8, 1907; s. Johan Christian Severin and Karen Amalie (Christiansen) G.; student in Germany and France, also fgn. diplomatic exam.; m. Magnhild Othilie Sundby, Mar. 22, 1941; children—Christian August, Anne-Carine, Vibeke Cecilie, Marit Benedicte Sophie. Engaged in pvt. bus., 1927-37; sec. Royal Norwegian Ministry Fgn. Affairs, 1937; attache legation, Warsaw, Poland, 1937-39; sec., 1939-40; sec. legation, Stockholm, Sweden, 1940-47; counsellor, chief sect. Ministry Fgn. Affairs, 1947-51; charge d'affaires, Athens, Greece, summer 1949; consul gen. in Cape Town, S. Africa, 1951-58; ambassador to Buenos Aires, also minister to Asuncion and Montevideo, 1958-62; consul gen. in N.Y.C., 1962-70; ambassador to Switzerland, 1970—. Decorated comdr. order St. Olva, Order Vasa (Sweden), grand Ocross Order de Mayo (Argentina), Queen Elizabeth Coronation medal in silver. Home and office: Norwegian Embassy Bern Switzerland

FLEISCHER, RICHARD O., film dir.; b. Bklyn., Dec. 8, 1916; B.A., Brown U.; M.F.A., Yale. Former stage dir.; joined RKO Pathe, 1942; writer-producer Flicker Flashbacks; writer-dir. This is America; co-producer Design for Death; dir. Child of Divorce, Banjo, So This Is New York, Bodyguard, Follow Me Quietly, The Clay Pigeon, Narrow Margin, The Happy Time, Arena, 20,000 Leagues Under the Sea, Violent Saturday, Girl in The Red Velvet Swing, Bandido, Between Heaven and Hell, The Vikings, These Thousand Hills, Compulson, Crack in the Mirror, The Big Gamble, Barabbas, Fantastic Voyage, Doctor Dolittle, Boston Strangler. Address: care Columbia Pictures Corp 711 Fifth Av New York City, NY 10022.*

FLEISCHER, ROBERT LOUIS, physicist; b. Columbus, O., July 8, 1930; s. Lee H. and Rosalie (Kahn) F.; A.B., Harvard, 1952, A.M., 1953, Ph.D., 1956; m. Barbara L. Simons, June 10, 1954; children—Cathy Ann, Elizabeth Lee. Asst. prof. metallurgy Mass. Inst. Tech., 1956-60; physicist Gen. Elec. Research Lab., Schenectady, 1960—. Sr. research fellow physics Cal. Inst. Tech., 1965-66; adj. prof. physics and astronomy Rensselaer Poly. Inst., 1967-68; cons. U.S. Geol. Survey, 1967-70. Pres., Zoller Sch. P.T.A., 1968-69; mem. com. on candidates Schenectady Citizens Conv. for Sch. Bd., 1969—, chmn., 1969-70. Bd. dirs. Schenectady Citizens' League. Recipient awards Indsl. Research, 1964, 65, Spl. award Am. Nuclear Soc., 1964, Ernest O. Lawrence award U.S. Atomic Commn., 1971, Gen. Elec. Silver medallion Inventor's award, 1971. Fellow Am. Phys. Soc., Meteoritical Soc.; mem. Am. Geophys. Union, Am. Astron. Soc., A.A.A.S., Sigma Xi. Asso. editor 1st and 2d Lunar Sci. Conf. Procs., 1970-71. Contbr. articles to profl. lit. Research in charged particle tracks in solids and their use in several fields, including cosmic ray and meteorite sci., geochronology, and nuclear physics; defects in solids and their effects on mech. properties and superconducting properties. Home: 1356 Waverly Pl Schenectady NY 12308 Office: Gen Elec Research Lab Schenectady NY 12301

FLEISCHMAN, ALVIN, mfg. co. exec.; b. Phila., Dec. 9, 1922; s. Samuel and Florence (Frank) F.; grad. Pa. State U.; grad. student Wharton Sch. Financee and Commerce, U. Pa.; m. Doris Trachtmau, June 4, 1950; children—Larry, Marc. With Seagram Distillers, 1951—, exec. v.p. marketing House of Seagram, Montreal, 1968—. Served with AUS, World War II. Mem. Pi Lambda Phi. Jewish religion. Home: 45 Glebmord Rd Hampstead Quebec Canada* Office: 1430 Peel St Montreal Quebec Canada*

FLEISCHMAN, HENRY LEONARD, mfg. co. exec.; b. N.Y.C., Apr. 19, 1907; s. Charles and Emma (Loewenthal) F.; B.S., N.Y. U., 1927; LL.B., N.Y. Law Sch., 1933; m. Gertrude M. Selig, Aug. 9, 1936; children—Charles D., Daniel L. Pub. accountant, 1927-29; admitted to N.Y. bar, 1933; C.P.A., N.Y., 1939; asso. firm Adolph Henry Bloch, N.Y.C., 1939-43; with Lily-Tulip Cup Corp. (merged into Owens-Ill., Inc. 1968) N.Y.C., 1943-68, sec., 1949-68, gen. counsel, 1958-68; asst. sec. Owens- Ill., Inc., 1968-70; legal counsel Lily-Tulip div., 1968-70; sec. Red River Paper Mills, Inc., 1961-70, Lily Cups Ltd., 1952-70, Danadyne, Inc., Auto Pak, Inc.; dir., sec. Lily Tulip Internat. Corp.; dir. Old Town Pulp Products, Inc., 1957-70; pvt. practice law, N.Y.C., 1970—; partner Freyr Groves, 1961—; sec., dir. Firebird Groves, Inc. Trustee, sec., treas. Henry Nias Found., Inc., 1957—; treas., trustee Larchmont Temple, 1970—. Recipient Townsend Wandel medal N.Y. Law Sch., 1933. Mem. Assn. Bar City N.Y., N.Y. State Soc. C.P.A.'s, Am. Soc. Corp. secs. Home: 639 Seney Av Mamaroneck NY 10543 Office: 122 E 42d St New York City NY 10017

FLEISCHMAN, MARK H., leisure time co. exec.; b. Great Neck, N.Y., Feb. 1, 1940; s. Martin and Sylvia (Zausner) F.; B.S., Cornell U., 1961. Exec. dir., owner Forest Hills (N.Y.) Inn, 1965-67; prin. in exec. hotel and design, A Quiet Little Table in the Corner, 1967—; partner Monark Shrimp Corp., 1967-68; pres. Davos, Inc., leisure time and foods, N.Y.C., 1968—. Chmn. econ. adv. com. 6th Congl. Dist. Served to lt. USNR, 1962-64. Mem. Young Presidents Orgn. Home: 36 E 38th St New York City NY 10016 Office: 66 Park Av New York City NY 10016

FLEISCHMAN, WILLIAM JOHN, editor; b. St. Louis, Aug. 26, 1919; s. William Victor and Rosella (O'Keeffe) F.; student Washington U., St. Louis, 1937-40, Sam Houston State Coll., 1944; m. Frances Wyatt, Dec. 28, 1951; children—Mary, Catherine, Patricia, William. Reporter St. Louis Star-Times, 1940-43, chief copy editor, sports editor, 1946-48, asst. mng. editor, 1949-51; news editor Mid-Pacific edit. Stars & Stripes, 1945; sports editor St. Louis Globe-Democrat, 1951—. Mem. St. Vincent de Paul Soc., 1960—. Served with AUS, 1943-46. Mem. Sigma Delta Chi. Contbr. articles to mags. Home: 11066 Saginaw St St Louis MO 63136 Office: 12th and Delmar blvds St Louis MO 63101

FLEISCHMANN, ADELBERT, lawyer; b. Hamburg, N.Y., Nov. 20, 1912; s. Simon and Laura (Justice) F.; B.A., U. Buffalo, 1934; LL.B., Harvard, 1937; m. Helen White, Sept. 11, 1945; children—Peter, Lisa, Laura. Admitted to N.Y. bar, 1937, since practiced in Buffalo; partner Fleischmann Bros., 1937-40; partner Fleischmann & Augspurger and successor firms, 1945-54; partner Jaeckle, Fleischmann, Kelly, Swart & Augspurger, 1955-70, Jaeckle, Fleischmann & Mugel, 1971—. Lectr., Sch. Medicine State U. N.Y. at Buffalo, 1950—. Chmn. bd. dirs. Heart Assn. Erie County. Served to maj. AUS, 1941-45. Mem. Am., N.Y. State, Erie County bar assns. Clubs: Buffalo, Marshall (pres. 1952), Lawyers of Buffalo (pres. 1955). Home: 564 Lafayette Av Buffalo NY 14222 Office: Liberty Bank Bldg Buffalo NY 14202

FLEISCHMANN, GLEN HARVEY, artist, author; b. Manley, Neb., Feb. 23, 1909; s. Frederick Ferdinand and Sarah Montgomery (Taylor) F.; student Vogue Sch. of Art, Chgo., 1929- 30; m. Evelyn Grace Fitzpatrick, Feb. 10, 1931. From apprentice to ad creator (layout, copy, finished art) Meyer Both Advt. Co., Chgo., 1932- 37; exec. artist R. H. Macy & Co., N.Y.C., 1937-39; author, artist, contbr. to nat. mags., 1939—, including Sat. Eve. Post, Good Housekeeping, Collier's, Woman's Home Companion, American, Field and Stream, Outdoor Life, Sports Afield, This Week, Nation's Business. Served with Dept. Tng. Publs., C.E., AUS, 1943-45. Mem. Authors Guild, Authors League Am. Author: While Rivers Flow, 1963; The Cherokee Removal (Jr. Lit. Guild selection), 1971; The Artist: His Markets and His World, 1971. Office: 1160 Midland Av Bronxville NY 10708

FLEISCHMANN, MANLY, lawyer; b. Hamburg, N.Y., July 15, 1908; s. Simon and Laura (Justice) F.; A.B., Harvard, 1929; LL.B., U. of Buffalo, 1933; m. Lois Marseilles, Aug. 25, 1933; 1 daug., Alison. Admitted to N.Y. Bar; partner Fleischmann Bros., Buffalo, 1933-41, sr. partner Fleischmann, Augspurger, Henderson & Campbell, Buffalo, 1946-50; asst. gen. counsel W.P.B., 1941-43; gen. counsel Fgn. Liquidation Bd., State Dept., 1946; cons. on Asiatic affairs E.C.A., 1950; gen. counsel N.P.A., Dept. Commerce, 1950-51, administrator, 1951; adminstr. D.P.A., 1951-52; mem. law firms Webster, Sheffield, Fleischmann, Hitchcock & Brookfield, N.Y.C., and Jaekle, Fleischmann, Kelly, Swart and Augspurger, Buffalo. Dir. Sierra Research Corp., Am. Airlines, Equitable Life Assurance Co. of U.S.; operating receiver Sterling Engine Co., Buffalo, 1948-50; lecturer internat. law, Law Sch., U. Buffalo, 1950, Trustee State U. N.Y., Albright-Knox Art Gallery, Asso. Councils of the Arts. Served as lt. USNR, 1943-45. Deocrated Bronze Star; Presidential Unit Citation, Peace Medal (Siam). Mem. Am. Law Inst., Am., N.Y., Erie Co. bar assns., Am. Coll. Trial Lawyers, Bar Assn. N.Y.C. (exec. com.), Buffalo Council World Affairs. Clubs: Buffalo; Harvard (N.Y.C.). Author: War Production Board—Administrative Policies and Procedures, 1944 (with John Lord O'Brian); Trails Through the Washington Jungle, 1953. Home: 33 Oakland Pl Buffalo NY 14222 Office: 1 Rockefeller Plaza New York City NY 10020 also Liberty Bank Bldg Buffalo NY 14202

FLEISCHMANN, PETER FRANCIS, mag. pub. exec.; b. N.Y.C., Jan. 27, 1922; s. Raoul H. and Ruth (Gardner) F.; grad. Hotchkiss Sch., 1940; B.A., Yale, 1944; m. Nancy Montgomery, 1948 (div.); children—James R., Ruth G., Stephen G.; m. 2d, Jeanne Cowles Wilson, May 1964. Staff New Yorker Mag., Inc., N.Y.C., 1955—, treas., dir., 1956—, exec. v.p., 1965-68, pres., 1968—. Served as capt. AUS, 1945. Office: New Yorker Magazine Inc 25 W 43d St New York City NY 10036

FLEISCHMANN, WOLFGANG BERNARD, educator; b. Vienna, Austria, July 10, 1928; s. Walter and Gertrude (Furth) F.; B.A., St. John's Coll., 1950; A.M., U. N.C., 1951, Ph.D., 1954. Came to U.S., 1940, naturalized, 1950. Instr. English, U. N.C., 1957-59; asst. prof. comparative lit. U. Okla., 1959-61; asst. prof., also asso. prof. Emory U., 1961-63; faculty U. Wis., Milw., 1963-66, prof., chmn. comparative lit. dept., 1964-66; vis. prof. romance langs. Princeton, 1966-67; prof., chmn. comparative lit. dept. U. Mass., Amherst, 1967-70; dean Sch. Humanities, prof. comparative lit. Montclair State Coll., Upper Montclair, N.J., 1970—; also lectr., critic. Mem. bd. vis. and govs. St. John's Coll., Annapolis, Md. and Santa Fe, N.M., also now sec. Served with U.S. Army, 1953-55. Inst. Research in Humanities fellow U. Wis., 1965-66. Mem. Modern Lang. Assn. (chmn. 1965, 67), Am. Comparative Lit. Assn. (editor Newsletter 1968—). Author: Lucretius and English Literature 1680-1740, 1964; gen. editor: Ency. of World Lit. in the 20th Century, vol. 1, 1967, vol. 2, 1969, vol. 3, 1971; mem. editorial bds. Books Abroad, 1959—, James Joyce Quart, 1964—, Dimension, 1966—. Home: 462 W 23d St New York City NY 10011 Office: Montclair State Coll Upper Montclair NJ 07043

FLEISHER, GERARD ADALBERT, educator, biochemist; b. Dresden, Germany, Nov. 10, 1911; s. Siegbert and Else (Prast) F.; diploma chemistry Friedrich Wilhelm U., Berlin, Germany, 1934; Ph.D., Technische Hochschule, Danzig, 1936; m. Gisela Nolte, Jan. 21, 1937; children—Thomas Arthur, Christian Andrew. Came to U.S., 1937, naturalized, 1944. Research chemist Schering Corp., Bloomfield, N.J., 1937-42; research asso. medicine Cornell U. Med. Coll., 1942-44; research chemist Gelatin Products Corp., Detroit, 1944- 45; cons. biochemistry Mayo Clinic, 1945—; prof. biochemistry Grad. Sch., U. Minn., 1964—; spl. research chemistry progesterone and adrenal hormones, isolation prolactin and gonadotropin, enzyme kinetics, characterization enzymes and changes asso. with disease, mechanisms enzyme turnover in body. Fellow A.A.A.S.; mem. Am. Soc. Biol. Chemists, Am. Chem. Soc., Am. Assn. Clin. Chemists, Soc. Exptl. Biology and Medicine, Alumni Assn. U. Minn., Sigma Xi. Home: 833 11th St SW Rochester MN 55901

FLEISHER, LEON, concert pianist; b. San Francisco, July 23, 1928; s. Isidor and Bertha (Mittelman) F.; ed. privately; pupil Artur Schnabel, Lago di Como, Italy, N.Y.C., 1938-48; m. Dorothy Druzinsky, 1951 (div. Mar. 1962); children—Deborah, Richard, Leah; m. 2d, Risselle Rosenthal, Apr. 1, 1962; children—Paula Beth, Julian. First recital, San Francisco, 1935; concert debut with San Francisco Orch., 1943; N.Y.C. debut with N.Y. Philharmonic, 1944; recitalist, soloist maj. orchestras in U.S., Can., S.Am., Europe; AssociacioÉ Leon Fleisher founded, Buenos Aires, Argentina; rep. U.S. Brussels World's Fair, 1958; due to paralysis of right hand has performed only compositions for left hand, 1965—; music dir. Theatre Chamber Players, Washington, 1968—; debut as condr. N.Y. Chamber Orch.'s Mostly Mozart Festival, 1970; condr. Annapolis (Md.) Symphony, 1970—; prof. piano Peabody Conservatory of Music, Balt., 1959—; recordings Columbia Masterworks, Epic Records. Bd. dirs. Walter W. Naumburg Found. First Am. winner Concours Internat. Reine Elisabeth de Belgique, 1952. Mem. Am. Assn. U. Profs. Address: c/o Columbia Artists Mgmt Inc 165 W 57th St New York City NY 10019

FLEISHER, WILFRID, radio rep., corr., author; b. Phila., Nov. 20, 1897; s. Benjamin Wilfrid and Marie Blanche (Blum) F.; student Charterhouse, Eng., 1911-14; Litt. B., Sch. Journalism, Columbia, 1921; m. Greta Sundberg, May 19, 1923; children—Eric Wilfrid, Benita Saga (Baroness Claes Ramel), Frederic Elliott. Corr. Japan Advertiser and N.Y. World with A.E.F. in Siberia, 1918-19; with Paris Bur. United Press Assn. (corr. at 2d League Assembly, Geneva, 1922), 1921-23; bus. mgr. Japan Advertiser, Tokyo, and corr. N.Y. Times in Japan, 1923-25; Washington corr. N.Y. Times, 1925-28; mng. editor Japan Advertiser (Am. daily newspaper), Tokyo, 1929-40, and corr., N.Y. Herald Tribune in Japan, 1931-40; corr. N.Y. Herald Tribune, Washington, 1940-42; spl. writer for N.Y. Herald Tribune Syndicate, radio comentator for ABC, 1942-46; toured Scandinavian countries for N.Y. Herald Tribune, 1946; chief corr. CBS in Scandinavian countries, 1947-48; press attaché, 1st sec. Am. Embassy, Stockholm, 1949- 53; rep. CBS for Scandinavia, 1954—; also corr. Washington Post. Mem. U.S. Ednl. Commn. in Sweden. Decorated Knight of North Star by King of Sweden. Mem. Internat. Platform Assn. Clubs: Nat. Press, Overseas Writers, P.E.N. (N.Y.C.). Author: Volcanic Isle, 1941; Our Enemy Japan, 1942; What to do With Japan, 1945; Sweden, The Welfare State, 1956. Address: 18 Sturegatan Stockholm Sweden also CBS News 524 W 57th St New York City NY 10019

FLEISHHACKER, MORTIMER, Jr., mfg. exec.; b. San Francisco, May 3, 1907; s. Mortimer and Bella (Gerstle) F.; A.B., U. Cal., 1927; m. Janet L. Choynski, May 1, 1929; children—Delia (Mrs. John Ehrlich), Mortimer, David. Vice pres. Anglo Cal. Nat. Bank, San Francisco, 1931-40; pres. Chemicals, Inc., 1940-56; v.p. Lord Baltimore Press of Cal. (formerly Fleishhacker Paper Box Co.). San Francisco, 1953-60; chmn. bd. Precision Instrument Co., 1960- 70; v.p., dir. Natomas Co.; Ltd. partner Golden Gateway Center; dir. Crocker-Citizens Nat. Bank. Chmn. Bay Area Edn. TV Assn.; v.p. San Francisco Symphony Assn.; trustee San Francisco Mus. Art, World Affairs Council of No. Cal., Asia Found.; regent U. San Francisco; v.p., dir. Internat. House, Berkeley; bd. dirs. Cal. Theatre Found. Served as lt. comdr. USNR, World War II. Home: 2600 Pacific Av San Francisco CA 94115 Office: One Maritime Plaza San Francisco CA 94111

FLEISHMAN, ALFRED, pub. relations exec.; b. St. Louis, June 16, 1905; s. Samuel Isaac and Sara (Spetner) F.; B.Pharm., St. Louis Coll. Pharmacy, 1926; m. Lucylle Elizabeth Magid, Oct. 9, 1928. Supt. recreation, St. Louis, 1933-35; chief dep. clk. St. Louis Circuit Ct., 1935-42; spl. cons. on pub. relations to sec. def., 1946; sr. partner Fleishman-Hillard, Inc., St. Louis, 1946—; dir. Brentwood Bank. Lectr. pub., human relations St. Louis U., Washington U., U. Mo., So. Ill. U. Past pres. St. Louis Urban League, St. Louis Jewish Fedn., St. Louis Jewish Community Relations Council; mem. Mo. Bd. Tng. Schs., 1947, Mo. regional adv. bd. Anti- Defamation League B'nai B'rith. Bd. dirs. St. Louis Area council Boy Scouts Am., U.S. Com. Sports for Israel, Jewish Community Centers Assn., Council Jewish Fedns. and Welfare Fund; past chmn bd. dirs. St. Louis Symphony Soc., Gov.'s Task Force on Role Pvt. Higher Edn. in Mo. Served from 2d lt. to maj. AUS, 1942-46. Decorated Legion of Merit. Recipient Distinguished Service medal for civic achievement U.S. Jr. C. of C., 1935, Americanism medal V.F.W., 1934. Mem. USCG Aux., N.A.A.C.P., Advt. Club, Jewish War Vets. U.S., St. Louis C. of C. (dir.), Pub. Relations Soc. Am. (past pres. St. Louis chpt.). Clubs: Media, Stadium, Washington U. Faculty. Author: Sense and Nonsense, A Study in Human Communication, 1971. Mem. adv. com. newspaper St. Louis Jewish Light. Home: 4 Twin Oaks St St Louis MO 63124 Office: 1 Memorial Dr St Louis MO 63102

FLEISHMAN, BERNARD ABRAHAM, educator, mathematician; b. N.Y.C., June 15, 1925; s. Saul and Anna (Reingold) F.; B.A. cum laude, City Coll., N.Y., 1944; M.S. in Physics, N.Y.U., 1948, Ph.D. in Math., 1952; m. Ruth Dreizin, June 17, 1950; children—Daniel, Nina, Leo. Spl. linguistic instr. Oriental langs. U. Pa., 1943-44; research mathematician Applied Physics Lab., Johns Hopkins, 1952-55; mem. faculty Rensselaer Poly. Inst., 1955—, prof. math., 1961—; vis. prof. U.S. Army Math. Research Center, U. Wis., 1961-62; cons. to industry, 1956, 58. Mem. bd. edn. Brittonkill Central Schs., 1963—, pres., 1967-69; pres. Rensselaer County Sch. Bds., 1970; mem. Rensselaer County Charter Commn., 1970; Democratic candidate for N.Y. State Senate, 1970. Served with AUS, 1944- 46. Mem. Am. Math. Soc., A.A.A.S., Am. Civil Liberties Union, Am. Assn. U. Profs. (pres. Rensselaer Poly Inst. chpt. 1960-61). Jewish religion (bd. dirs. temple 1966—). Contbr. numerous papers applied math. Home: Colehamer Av Troy NY 12180

FLEISHMAN, EDWIN ALAN, psychologist, author; b. N.Y.C., Mar. 10, 1927; s. Harry E. and Sera (Weinblatt) F.; B.S., Loyola Coll., Balt., 1945; M.A., U. Md., 1949; Ph.D., Ohio State U., 1951; m. Pauline S. Utman, Feb. 9, 1949; children —Jeffrey B., Alan R. Dir. Skill Components Research Lab., USAF, San Antonio, 1951-56; prof. indsl. adminstrn. and psychology Yale, 1957-63; Guggenheim fellow, vis. prof. Israel Inst. Tech., 1962-63; sr. v.p., dir. Washington office American Inst. Research. Cons. to govt., ednl. instns. and industry, 1957—; mem. adv. panel social sci. Office Sec. Def., 1959-61; mem. adv. panel behavioral scis. Office Surgeon Gen. Army, 1964—. Served with USNR, 1945-46. Fellow Am. Psychol. Assn.; mem. A.A.A.S., Internat. Assn. Applied Psychology (Am. rep. exec. com. 1964-), Am. Assn. Health, Phys. Edn. and Recreation, Psychometric Soc., Sigma Xi. Club: Cosmos (Washington). Author: Studies in Personnel and Industrial Psychology, 2d edit., 1967; (with R. Gagne) Psychology and Human Performance, 1959; Structure and Measurment of Physical Fitness, 1964; (with others) Leadership and Supervision in Industry; also numerous articles, chpts. in books, encys. Asso. editor Personnel Psychology, 1961—, Organizational Behavior and Human Performance, 1966- -. Editor in chief: Jour. Applied Psychology. Home: 8201 Woodhaven Blvd Bethesda MD 20034 Office: 8555 16th St Silver Spring MD 20910

FLEMING, ALLAN FOSTER, naval officer; b. Iowa City, Ia., Dec. 14, 1912; s. Burton Percival and Florence (Foster) F.; B.S., U.S. Naval Acad., 1936; grad. Army Arty. Sch., 1948, Naval War Coll., 1954; m. MacGregor Gray, June 6, 1938; children-Allan Foster, Skye MacGregor, Leslie Mitchell. Commd. ensign U.S. Navy, 1936, advanced through grades to rear adm., 1963; designated naval aviator, 1939; served in various squadrons and aircraft carriers, World War II; mem. staffs comdr. U.S. 8th Fleet, 1946, U.S. 2d Task Fleet, 1946-47; comdr. U.S. Naval Radar Tng. Sch. and Naval Air Sta., St. Simons Is., Ga., 1945-46, Air Devel. Squadron 4, 1950-51, U.S.S. Pine Island, 1958-59, U.S.S. Saratoga, 1959-60; staff comdr. in chief U.S. Naval Forces Eastern Atlantic and Mediterranean, 1956-58; dep. chief staff (plans) Allied Hdqrs., Malta, 1962-64; comdr. attack carrier striking force U.S. 6th Fleet, 1964-65, carrier div. 4, 1964-65; dir. strategic plans div. Office Chief Naval Operations, 1966-67; asst. dep. chief naval operations (policy and plans), 1967-69; comdr. Fleet Air Med., Comdr. anti-sub. warfare forces U.S. 6th Fleet, comdr. maritime air med. NATO. Decorated Legion of Merit, Purple Heart, D.S.M. Episcopalian. Clubs: Chevy Chase (Md.); Outrigger Canoe (Honolulu); Royal Henley Regatta (U.K.). Home: 107 Via Marechiaro Naples Italy Office: COMFAIRMED/COMASWFORSIXTHFLT FPO NY 09521

FLEMING, BRICE NOEL, educator; b. Hutchinson, Kan., July 29, 1928; s. Augustus Brice and Anna (Noel) F.; B.A., Harvard, 1950; D.Phil., Oxford (Eng.) U., 1961; m. Barbara Warr, Dec. 20, 1965. Asst. lectr. Manchester (Eng.) U., 1956-57; instr. Yale, 1957-59, 1960-62; asst. prof. U. Cal. at Santa Barbara, 1962-65, asso. prof., 1965-69, prof., 1969—. Served with AUS, 1951-53. Office: Dept Philosophy U Cal Santa Barbara CA 93106

FLEMING, DAVID G., physiologist, educator; b. N.Y.C., July 3, 1926; s. Samuel and Sadie (Gurock) F.; A.B., U. Cal. at Berkeley, 1948, Ph.D., 1952; m. Elyse S. Schwartz, Jan. 30, 1949; 1 son, Neil S. Asso., U. Cal. at Berkeley, 1952- 53; asst. prof. physiology U. Kan., 1953-58; research physiologist Gen. Electric Co., Cleve., 1958-60; now prof. biomed. engring. Case Western Res. U., Cleve. Chmn. Conf. on Engring. in Medicine and Biology, 1964; mem. U.S. Nat. Com. for Engring. in Medicine and Biology, 1966-67. Served with USNR, 1944-46. Mem. Am. Physiol. Soc., I.E.E.E. (chmn. group on engring. in medicine and biology 1968-70), A.A.A.S., Biophys. Soc. (chmn. joint com. on engring. in medicine and biology 1966-67), Alliance for Engring. in Medicine and Biology (mem. council 1969-70), Am. Soc. Engring. Edn. (chmn. biomed. engring. com. 1968-70). Editor CRC Critical Revs. in Bioengring. Contbr. profl. jours., Voice Am. Forum Series on Bioengring. Patentee ion generator. Office: Case Western Reserve University Cleveland OH 44106

FLEMING, DENNA FRANK, educator; b. Paris, Ill., Mar. 25, 1893; s. Albert and Eleanor (McCormick) F.; grad. Eastern Ill. State Coll., 1912, Pe.D., 1949; A.B., U. Ill., 1916, A.M., 1920, Ph.D., 1928; student Columbia, 1928; m. Doris Sigrid Anundsen, June 29, 1929.

Prin. high sch., Hume, Ill., 1912-14. tchr. high sch., Freeport, 1916-17, Walla Walla, Wash., 1917; prin. high sch., Tonica, Ill., 1919-21, and Colfax, 1921-22; asst. prof. social sci. Monmouth Coll., 1922-23, asso. prof., 1923-24, prof., chmn. dept., 1924-27; asst. prof. polit. sci. Vanderbilt U., 1928, asso. prof., 1930, prof., 1938, chmn. dept., 1940, research prof., 1951-61, prof. emeritus, 1961—; research asso. Stanford U., 1966; vis. prof. U. Ariz., 1964, 66, Cal. State Coll. Los Angeles, 1965, Simon Fraser U., Vancouver, B.C., 1968-69. Instr., Ia. State Tchrs. Coll., summers 1926-27, Middle Tenn. State U., 1970; Penfield traveling scholar, 1932-33, 1938-39; mem. Inst. for Advanced Study, Princeton, 1946, 48, 49; adviser atomic energy sect. State Dept., 1946. Fgn. editor Nashville Evening Tennessean, 1934-37; fgn. commentator WSM, 1939-47; radio commentator Woodrow Wilson Found., 1944-46, dir., 1950-55; Fulbright lectr. Conf. on Am. Studies, Cambridge U., 1954, Sch. Internat. Studies, New Delhi, 1959-60. Served with AEF, World War I. Mem. Am. Assn. U. Profs. (mem. exec. council), Am. Com. in Geneva Staff, 1932, Am. Acad. Polit. and Social Sci., Internat. Platform Assn., Am. (v.p. 1943), So. (pres. 1941) polit. sci. assns., Phi Beta Kappa Assos., Acacia, Delta Sigma Rho, Kappa Delta Pi, Phi Beta Kappa, Phi Kappa Phi. Democrat. Methodist. Mason. Club: Nashville Round Table (pres. 1937). Author: The Treaty Veto of the American Senate, 1930; The United States and the League of Nations (1920-33), 1938; Can We Win the Peace? 1943; While America Slept, 1944; The United States and the World Court, 1945; The Cold War and its Origins (1917-1960) Vols. I and II, 1961; The Origins and Legacies of World War I, 1968; America's Role in Asia, 1969; The Issues of Survival, 1971. Home: 4721 Sewanee Rd Nashville TN 37220

FLEMING, DONALD HARNISH, educator, historian; b. Hagerstown, Md., Aug. 7, 1923; s. Donald Harnish and Luciphene (Beery) F.; A.B., Johns Hopkins, 1943; A.M., Harvard, 1944, Ph.D., 1947. With Brown U., 1947-58, successively lectr., asst. prof., asso. prof., 1953-55, prof. history, 1955-58; prof. history of sci. Yale, 1958-59; vis. prof. Harvard 1958-59, prof. history, 1959-70, Jonathan Trumbull prof. Am. history, 1970—. Fellow Am. Acad. Arts and Scis.; mem. Am. Hist. Assn., History of Sci. Soc., Am. Assn. History Medicine. Democrat. Author: John William Draper, 1950 (Beveridge prize Am. Hist. Assn.); William Henry Welch and the Rise of Modern Medicine, 1954. Co-editor; Perspectives in American History, 1967—, The Intellectual Migration: Europe and America 1930-1960, 1969. Home: 221 Mt Auburn St Cambridge MA 02138

FLEMING, EDWARD J, clergyman; b. Montclair, N.J., Mar. 29, 1920; s. Timothy Joseph and Agnes (Gannon) F.; student Seton Hall Prep. Sch., South Orange, N.J., 1932-36; A.B., Seton Hall U., 1940, M.A., 1948, LL.D., 1970; student Immaculate Conception Sem., Ramsey, N.J., 1936-40; S.T.L., Cath. U. Am., 1944; Ph.D., St. John's U., Bklyn., 1955. Ordained priest Roman Catholic Ch., 1944, elevated to papal chamberlain, 1963; priest St. Teresa's Church, Summit, N.J., 1944-49; became prof. ednl. psychology Seton Hall U., 1949, dir. student affairs, 1950, dean coll., 1952, exec. v.p., 1961-69, acting pres., 1969-70; pastor Our Lady of Blessed Sacrament Ch., Roseland, N.J. 1970—. Archdiocesan clergy examiner. Mem. Army Adv. Panel ROTC Affairs; mem. Edn. Commn. States. Trustee Greater Newark Black and White Opera Co. Recipient Alpha Epsilon Mu award, 1956; Sapientiae Christianae award, 1956; named Irishman of Year, Friends of Brian Boru, Inc., 1970. Mem. Eastern Assn. Coll. Deans and Advisers of Men, Nat. Cath. Edn. Assn. (pres. Eastern unit 1965-66), N.J. Hist. Soc. (com. of 125); Cath. Theol. Soc. Am. Address: 28 Livingston Av Roseland NJ 07068

FLEMING, EDWARD MCCLUNG, mus. adminstr.; b. Kasauli, India, May 29, 1909 (parents U.S. citizens), s. Daniel Johnson and Elizabeth (Cole) F.; student Ecole Alsacienne, Paris, France, 1923-24, Hill Sch., Pottstown, Pa., 1925-26; B.A., Yale, 1930; M.A., Columbia, 1934, Ph.D., 1943; m. Patricia Crew, Sept. 14, 1940; children—Malcolm McClung, Daniel Johnson III, Elizabeth, Bruce. History faculty Forman Christian Coll., Lahore, India, 1930-32; fellow in history Columbia, 1935-36; instr. history dept. Coll. City N.Y., 1936- 42, chmn. dept. history, sch. bus. and civic adminstrn., 1942-43; prof. history, dean of coll. Park Coll., Parkville, 1947-55; head edn. div. Henry F. DuPont Winterthur Mus., 1955—, adj. prof. history U. Del., 1963—. Chmn. zoning subcom. Parkville Planning Commn., 1951-53. Am. del. Anglo-Am. Conf. World Student Christian Fedn., also World Youth Peace Congress, Eerde, Holland, 1928; mem. Continuing Conf. on Gen. Edn. and Social Scis., 1950-52; student adminstrv. com. West Central Area Bd. YMCA; gov. Council World Affairs, Greater Kansas City; trustee Tatnall Sch. 1st lt. AUS, 1944-47, information edn. officer Combat Tng. Command. Fellow Nat. Council Religion in Higher Edn.; mem. Am. Studies Assn. (treasurer assn. 1962-65), North Central Assn. (commn. univs. and colls. 1953-56), Mo. State Tchrs. Assn. (pres. div. higher edn. 1953-54), Am. Hist. Assn., N.Y. State, Platte Co. hist. socs., Am. Assn. of U. Profs., also mem. Am. Assn. Museums (chmn. edn. sect. 1960-61), Analytical Psychology Club of N.Y. (exec. com. 1936- 38, v.p. 1938), Phi Beta Kappa. Presbyn. (elder). Clubs: Parkville Rotary (pres.); Torch, Yale (Del.). Author: R.R. Bowker; Militant Liberal, 1952. Contbr. articles, book reviews to profl. jours. Home: 196 Brecks Lane Wilmington DE 19807 Office: Henry Francis DuPont Winterthur Museum Winterthur DE 19735

FLEMING, FOY BURWELL, lawyer; b. Sparta, Ga., Oct. 13, 1921; s. Thomas Farrar and Ava Butler (West) F.; A.B., U. Tex., 1947; LL.B., U. Miami, 1949; m. Joanne Louise Tait, Apr. 15, 1948; children-Victoria Ann, Paula Joan, Roger Tait. Admitted to Fla. bar, 1949, since practiced in Ft. Lauderdale; partner firm Fleming, O'Bryan & Fleming, 1949—. Chmn. Am. Nat. Bank and Trust Co., Ft. Lauderdale, 1962—, Sunrise Am. Nat. Bank, Ft. Lauderdale, 1963- -. Bd. dirs. United Fund Broward County, 1955; trustee Nova U. of Advanced Tech., 1966-70, Pine Crest Prep. Sch., 1967-69. Served to lt. (j.g.) USNR, 1943-46. Mem. Am., Fla. bar assns., C. of C. of Greater Ft. Lauderdale (bd. dirs. 1967—). Home: 1625 SE 1st St Fort Lauderdale FL 33304 Office: 1415 E Sunrise Blvd Fort Lauderdale FL 33304

FLEMING, GEORGE MCMILLAN, hosp. adminstr.; b. Flagstaff, Ariz., Mar. 26, 1919; s. George A. and Mary (McMillan) F.; B.A., Ariz. State U., 1940; M.Ed., U. Houston, 1949, Ed.D., 1957; m. Mary Kathryn Matthews, May 20, 1944; children—George Matthews, Scott Matthews. Lectr. U. Houston, 1957-61, dir. Research and Statist. sect. VA Regional Office, Houston, 1946-51, rehabilitation splst., 1951-54, personnel dir. VA Hosp. and Regional Office, Houston, 1954-61, adminstr. Galveston County Meml. Hosp., La Marque, Tex., 1961-67; asso. adminstr. edn. The Methodist Hosp., Houston, 1967-70; adminstr. Santa Rosa Med. Center, San Antonio, Tex., 1970—. Council health and safety officer Bay Al-ea council Boy Scouts Am., 1961-67, chmn. Mainland dist., 1966-67, dir., 1961-67. Served to capt. USAAF, 1942-45. Fellow Am. Coll. Hosp. Adminstrs.; mem. Tex. League Nursing (treas. 1967-69), Tex. Hosp. Assn. (chmn. council on pub. edn. 1966-69), Houston Area Hosp. Assn. (chmn. personnel com. 1965-66), Am. Hosp. Assn., Phi Delta Kappa. Home: 11102 Whisper Ridge San Antonio TX 78230 Office: PO Box 7330 Station A San Antonio TX 78207

FLEMING, HAROLD STEDMAN, govt. ofcl.; b. New Haven, Apr. 21, 1932; s. Harold Stedman and Edith May (Wormley) F.; A.B., Brown U., 1953; M.A., Columbia, 1955; m. Elizabeth Labarre Smith, Sept. 27, 1969; children—Douglass, Craig, Harold. Dir. field and data processing Forbes Inc., N.Y.C., 1957-63; exec. v.p. Decision Information Group, Inc., N.Y.C., 1963-65; v.p. Grudin Research subsidiary Screengems, N.Y.C., 1965-66; spl. asst. Office Adminstr. Peace Corps, Washington, 1966-67, dir. pub. affairs, 1967-68, dir. Peace Corps, Ivory Coast, 1968—. Partner Decision Information Group, Inc.; lectr. City U. N.Y. Mem. Market Research Trade assn. (dir. chmn. awards com. 1960-64), Ten Inc. (founding mem., pres. 1958-66). Office: care Am Embassy Abidjan Ivory Coast

FLEMING, HOWARD ALLBRIGHT, coll. dean; b. Los Angeles, Sept. 12, 1919; s. Isaac and Mabel Lee (Hustace) F.; A.B., U. Cal. at Los Angeles, 1947, Ph.D., 1952; m. Jean Voorvaart, Feb. 5, 1943; 1 son, Howard Allbright. From asst. prof. to asso. prof. history Los Angeles State Coll., 1949-58; mem. faculty San Fernando Valley State Coll., 1958—, prof. history, chmn. dept., 1960- 64, asso. dean letters and sci., 1964-69, dean acad. adminstrn., 1969—. Served to captl F.A., AUS, 1941-45; PTO. Mem. Am. Hist. Assn., Civil War Round Table So. Cal., Phi Alpha Theta. Author: Canada's Arctic Outlet; A History of the Hudson Bay Railway, 1957; also articles, revs. Home: 17303 Lassen St Northridge CA 91324

FLEMING, JAMES DOUGLAS, business exec.; b. San Bernardino, Calif., Dec. 30, 1896; s. James and Elida (Wagner) F.; student Cutler Sch. for Boys, N.Y., 1910-11, Hitchcock Mil. ACad., San Rafael, Calif., 1913-14; A.B., Stanford U. 1918; m. Grace Willson, June 20, 1927. Asso. with Grinnell Co. of the Pacific, Los Angeles, 1919, as contracting engr., then branch mgr., San Francisco and Oakland branches, v.p. and mgr., 1937-40; v.p. and sales mgr. Grinnell Co. hdqrs., Providence, R.I., 1940-42; exec. v.p., 1942-48, dir. since 1944, pres., 1948-68, now chmn.; dir. Industrial Trust Co., Gorham Mfg. Co., Automatic Fire Alarm Co. of N.Y. and Delaware, Holmes Electric Co. (N.Y.), Davol Rubber Co., Eaton Paper Corp.; dir., mem. exec. com. Indsl. Nat. Bank; chmn. bd. dirs. Am. District Telegraph Co. Member board of trustees Rhode Island Hosp. Served as naval aviator, World War I. Mem. Phi Gamma Delta. Episcopalian. Clubs: Bohemian, San Francisco; Agawam Hunt, Turks Head, Hope, Providence, Union League (N.Y.). Home: 330 Blackstone Blvd Providence RI 02906 Office: 260 W Exchange St Providence RI 02903

FLEMING, JAMES R., lawyer, pub.; b. Henry Co., Ind., Nov. 8, 1881; s. George R. and Sarah (Cummins) F.; LL.B., U. of Mich., 1904; m. Jennie Adair, Dec. 24, 1906; children—Marian (Mrs. James Abromson), Virginia. Pros. atty. 58th Jud. Circuit, Ind., 1906-10; U.S. dist. atty. for northern Dist. of Ind., 1933-41; resigned to enter private practice, 1941; chmn. bd., pres., pub. Ft. Wayne Journal-Gazette. Mem. Ind. Ho. of Reps., 1913-15, Ind. Senate, 1915-19; mem. Dem. State Central Com., 1922-26. Chairman Governor's Commission on the Arts; mem. UN Ednl., Scientific and Cultural Orgn.; mem. Mayor's Youth Council, Ft. Wayne, Ind. Mem. Am., Ind., Allen County bar assns., Ind. Soc. of Chgo., Ind. Hist. Soc., Am. Soc. Newspaper Editors. Presbyterian. Mason. Elk. Clubs: Nat. Press (Washington); Fort Wayne Country, Press (Ft. Wayne, Indiana); Olympia; Columbia (Indpls.); Indianapolis Athletic. Home: 4520 Old Mill Rd Fort Wayne IN 46807 Office: Journal-Gazette Bldg 701 S Clinton St Fort Wayne IN 46802

FLEMING, JOHN GUNTHER, educator; b. Berlin, Germany, July 6, 1919; B.A., Oxford U., 1939, M.A., 1941, Ph.D., 1948, D.C.L., 1959; m. Valerie Joyce Beall, Apr. 16, 1946; children—Anthony, Barbara, Colin, Stephen. Came to U.S., 1960. Admitted to English bar, 1947; lectr. in law King's Coll., London, 1946-48; prof., dean faculty law Australian Nat. U., 1949-60; prof. law U. Cal., Berkeley, 1957-58, 60—. Served with Royal Armoured Corps, Brit. Army, 1940-45. Mem. Am. Law Inst. Author: Law of Torts, 1971; Introduction to the Law of Torts, 1967. Editor-in-chief Am. Jour. Comparative Law, 1971—. Home: 836 Spruce St Berkeley CA 94707

FLEMING, JOHN WEST, lawyer; b. Sparta, Ga., May 1, 1920; s. Thomas Farrar and Ava Butler (West) F.; A.B. cum laude, U. Fla., 1941; student Harvard Bus. Sch., 1941-42, LL.B. cum laude, U. Miami (Fla.), 1949; m. Mary Emma McBrayer, Feb. 11, 1950; children—Mary Ann, Ellen Teresa, John West, Jody McBrayer, Ava Cile, Peter Aubrey. Dispatcher, navigator Pan Am. World Airways, 1942-45; admitted to Fla. bar, 1949; partner firm Fleming, O'Bryan & Fleming, Ft. Lauderdale, 1950—. Fellow Am. Coll. Trial Lawyers; mem. Am., Fla., Broward County (pres. 1957-58) bar assns., Internat. Assn. Ins. Counsel, Blue Key, Phi Kappa Phi, Chi Phi, Phi Alpha Delta. Presbyn. Republican. Club: Lauderdale Yacht; Coconut Grove (Fla.) Sailing. Home: 407 S E 25th Av Fort Lauderdale FL 33301 Office: American Nat Bank Bldg Fort Lauderdale FL 33304

FLEMING, JOSEPH BENEDICT, newspaperman; b. N.Y.C., Jan. 29, 1919; s. Joseph Benedict and Eleanor (Kane) F.; B.S., Coll. City N.Y., 1941. Staff Portsmouth (N.H.) Herald, 1942, Stars and Stripes, 1943-45, Chattanooga Times, 1946-47; with U.P.I., 1948—, bur. mgr., Berlin, 1950—. Club: Overseas Press. Home: Roedern Allee 144 1 Berlin 26 West Germany

FLEMING, LAWRENCE DURWOOD, univ. pres.; b. Sulphur Springs, Tex., Aug. 9, 1914; s. John Payne and Alice Lucile (Rash) F.; B.A., So. Meth. U., 1937, B.D., 1940; D.D., McMurry Coll., 1957; m. Lurlyn January, Mar. 19, 1940; children—Jon Hugh, Pamela, Martha Ann. Ordained to ministry Meth. Ch., 1940; pastor, Caddo-Mills-Salem, Tex., 1940-42, Dallas, 1942-44, Eastland, Tex., 1944-45; founding pastor St. Luke's Meth., Houston, 1945-61; pres. Southwestern U., Georgetown, Tex., 1961—. Former pres. Tex. Council Ch.- Related Colls.; del. World Meth. Council, 1960, 64, 66, gen., jurisdictional confs., 1960, 64, 68; mem. Tex. Conf. Chs.; mem. Commn. on Ecumenical Affairs Tex. Conf. United Meth. Ch. Mem. Tex. Planning Commn., Gov.'s Adv. Council for Lang. Handicapped Children. Bd. dirs. Tex. United Community Services. Recipient Distinguished Alumnus award So. Meth. U., 1965. Mem. Tex. Meth. Coll. Assn., Am. Assn. Ind. Coll. and U. Presidents, Philos. Soc. Tex., Assn. Colls. and Univs. for Internat.- Intercultural (dir.). Mason, Rotarian. Home: 111 Taylor Rd Georgetown TX 78626

FLEMING, MACK GERALD, lawyer; b. Hartwell, Ga., May 3, 1933; s. Mack Judson and Dessie Leola (Vickery) F.; B.S., Clemson (S.C.) U., 1956; J.D., Am. U., Washington, 1966; m. Elizabeth McClellan, Mar. 30, 1963; 1 dau., Katharine Lee Fleming. Asst. dir. prodn. control Woodside Mills, Simpsonville, S.C., 1959-60; adminstrv. asst. to Rep. W.J. Bryan Dorn, 1960-64; staff asst. on adminstrs. staff VA, Washington, 1965-66, dir., counsel Congl. Liaison Office, 1966-68, spl. asst. to adminstr., 1968-69; adminstrv. asst., counsel to Rep. Dorn, 1969-70; pvt. practice law, Washington, 1970—. Served to 1st lt. U.S. Army, 1956-58. Mem. Nat. Textile Mfrs. Soc., Am., Fed., S.C. bar assns., Phi Psi, Delta Theta Phi. Democrat. Baptist. Home: 121 5th St N E Washington DC 20002 Office: 1750 Pennsylvania Av NW Washington DC 20006

FLEMING, NEAL BOND, coll. Dean; b. Canon, Ga., June 18, 1910; s. James William and Tinie (Bond) F.; A.B., Emory U., 1933, B.D., 1936; S.T.M., Boston U., 1937, Ph.D., 1941; postdoctoral student Harvard, 1953-54; m. Mary Louise Dunn, Aug. 27, 1939; children—Mary Dell, Jane Ellen, John Howard, Rebecca Bond. Ordained to ministry Methodist Ch., 1936; pastor in New Eng., 1938-45; prof. philosophy Millsaps Coll., 1945-62; acad. dean Centenary Coll., Shreveport, La., 1962-66; dean, div. exec. Oxford (Ga.) Coll., Emory U., 1966—. Nat. rep. Woodrow Wilson Fellowship Found., 1960-61; Ford scholar, 1953-54. Mem. Sigma Chi. Kiwanian. Home: 1205 Wesley St Oxford GA 30267

FLEMING, NED NELSON, wholesale food distbr.; b. Lyndon, Kan., Jan. 18, 1900; s. Oliver Albert and Edith May (Hollingsworth) F.; student Washburn U., 1917-19, D. Bus. Adminstrn., 1963; B.S. in Econs., U. Pa., 1921; m. Marjorie Virginia Miller, Oct. 15, 1923; children—Marilyn Jean (Mrs. Richard D. Harrison), James B., Stephen M. With Fleming Co., Inc., Topeka, 1921—, treas., gen. mgr., 1922-33, v.p., gen. mgr. 1933- 45, pres., 1945-64, chmn. bd., chief exec. officer, 1964-66, chmn. bd., 1966—; dir. Gas Service Co., Kansas City, Southwestern Bell Telephone Co., St. Louis, First Nat. Bank of Topeka, Unitog Co., Kansas City, Mo. Trustee Washburn Coll., Midwest Research Inst.; exec. com. Menninger Found., Topeka. Mem. Phi Delta Theta. Clubs: Kansas City, River (Kansas City, Mo.); Topeka Country; Paradise Valley (Ariz.) Country. Home: R F D 8 Topeka KS 66604 also 5315 E Solano Dr Paradise Valley AZ 85253 Office: 820 Quincy St Topeka KS 66612

FLEMING, PETER DONNELL, psychoanalyst; b. N.Y.C., Nov. 18, 1917; s. Irvin Henry and Dorothea (Grosmann) F.; A.B., U. Ala., 1937; M.D., Washington U., 1941; grad. Topeka Psychoanalytic Inst., 1958; m. Vivian Lucille Doggette Mar. 3, 1946; children—John Lawrence, Richard Lewis, Elizabeth Jane, Christopher Andrew. Intern, Deaconess Hosp., Cin., 1941-42; resident Winder VA Hosp., Topeka, 1946-48; psychiatrist Topeka Mental Hygiene Clinic, 1948-49; mem. staff Menninger Found., Topeka, 1949-55, sect. leader clinic, 1955-58, sr. cons. to clin. services, 1968—; mem. exec. com. Menninger Sch. Psychiatry, 1956-68, instr., 1964—; sr. psychiatrist, asst. dir. C.F. Menninger Meml. Hosp., Topeka, 1958-63, dir. 1963-68. Examiner, USIA, 1959. Served to maj., parachute inf. AUS, 1942-46; PTO. Fellow Am. Psychiat. Assn. (central inspection bd. 1959-61); mem. A.M.A., A.A.A.S., Kan., Shawnee County med. socs., Topeka Psychoanalytic Soc., Am. Internat. psychoanalytic assns., Am., So. psychol. assns., Mid-Continent Psychiat. Assn., Kan. Psychiat. Soc., Central Neuropsychiat. Hosp. Assn. (pres. 1967-68, councilor), Am. Geriatric Soc., Am. Hosp. Assn. (adv. panel on psychiat. hosps.), Am. Assn. Suicidology, Am. Group Psychotherapy Assn., World Futures Soc., Internat. Soc. Gen. Semantics. Home: 235 Greenwood St Topeka KS 66606 Office: 3617 W 6th St Topeka KS 66606

FLEMING, PETER JAMES, clergyman; b. St. Paul, Jan. 4, 1935; s. Frank P. and Josephine (Foy) F.; B.A., St. Paul Sem., 1961; J.C.D., Catholic U., Washington, 1964. Ordained priest Roman Catholic Ch., 1961; asst. pastor St. Paul Cathedral, 1961; vice chancellor Archdiocese, St. Paul, 1962-63; asso. presiding judge Archdiocesan Tribunal, St. Paul, 1964—; Episcopal vicar for religious for Archdiocese, 1967—; asst. pastor St. Luke's Parish, St. Paul, 1964-70. St. Peter's Parish, Mendota Heights, Minn., 1970—. K.C. Home: 1940 Lexington Av S Mendota Heights MN 55118 Office: 226 Summit Av St Paul MN 55102

FLEMING, PHYLLIS JANE, physicist, coll. dean; b. Shelbyville, Ind., Oct. 9, 1924; d. Russell P. and Grace (Wheeler) Fleming; B.A., Hanover Coll., 1946; M.S., U. Wis., 1948, Ph.D., 1954. Instr. physics Mt. Holyoke Coll., 1948-50; instr. dept. physics Wellesley Coll., 1953-55, asst. prof., 1955-61, asso. prof., 1961-67, prof. physics, 1967—, dean, 1968—. Mem. Am. Phys. Soc., Am. Assn. Physics Tchrs., Am. Assn. U. Profs., Sigma Xi. Roman Catholic. Contbr. articles to profl. jours. Home: 668 Washington St Wellesley MA 02181

FLEMING, RICHARD, chem. co. exec.; b. N.Y.C., June 15, 1924; s. James and Caroline (Jung) F.; B.Chem. Engring., Pratt Inst., 1944; M. Chem. Engring., N.Y. U., 1949; m. Roberta Marie Seeber, Apr. 8, 1945; children—Richard James, Robert Carleton, Kathleen Teresa Mary. Devel. engr. Air Reduction Co., Stamford, Conn., 1946-48; design engr. Tex. Co.-N.Y., N.Y.C., 1948-50; devel. engr. Rohm & Haas Co., Bristol, Pa., 1950-52; asst. mgr. corp. devel. Lukens Steel Co., Coatsville, Pa., 1952-54; sect. mgr. research and devel. Sun Oil Co., Marcus Hook, Pa., 1954-59, asst. dir. research and engring., Phila., 1959-62; pres. Avisum Corp., Phila., 1962- 69; group v.p. Air Products & Chems., Inc., Allentown, Pa., 1969—. Mem. Greater Phila. C. of C. (chmn. research and devel. com. 1969—), The Franklin Inst. Served with USNR, 1942-46. Mem. Am. Inst. Chem. Engrs., Am. Chem. Soc., Am. Mgmt. Assn., Mfg. Chemists Assn., Commd. Chem. Devel. Assn. Home: Country Club Rd Phoenixville PA 19460 Office: P O Box 538 Allentown PA 18105

FLEMING, ROBBEN WRIGHT, univ. pres.; b. Paw Paw, Ill., Dec. 18, 1916; s. Edmund Palmer and Emily Jeannette (Wheeler) F.; B.A., Beloit Coll., 1938; LL.B., U. Wis., 1941; LL.D., Mich. State U., U. Mich., Wayne State U., U. Wis., Cleve. State U., Western Mich. U., Mich. Technol. U., U. Ill., Beloit Coll., No. Mich. U.; m. Aldyth Louise Quixley, Apr. 3, 1942; children—Nancy Jo, James Edmund, Carolyn Elizabeth. Admitted to Wis. bar, 1941; atty. reorg. div. SEC, Washington, 1941-42, War Labor Bd., Washington, 1942; dir. Indsl. Relations Center, U. Wis., 1947-52; exec. dir. nat. WSB, Washington, 1951; dir. Inst. Labor and Indsl. Relations, U. Ill., 1952-58, prof. law, 1958-64; prof. law chancellor U. Wis., 1964-67; prof. law, pres. U. Mich., Ann Arbor, 1968—; exchange prof., Germany, summer 1950, Norway and Sweden, winter 1956; arbitrator indsl. disputes; indsl. arbitrator Fed. Mediation and Concilation Service, Am. Arbitration Assn., mem. Atomic Energy Labor-Mgmt. Relations Panel, 1958—; exec. dir. Armour Automation Com., 1960- 61. Co-chmn. task force on edn. White House Conf. on Youth, 1971. Served with AUS, 1942-46. Mem. Indsl. Relations Research Assn., Nat. Acad. Arbitrators (past pres.), Phi Beta Kappa, Order of Coif, Beta Theta Phi. Presbyn. Contbr. articles indsl. relations. Co-editor; Emergency Disputes and National Policy, 1955; The Politics of Wage-Price Decisions, A Four-Country Analysis, 1965; The Labor Arbitration Process, 1966. Home: 815 S University Ann Arbor MI 48104

FLEMING, ROBERT HENRY, govt. ofcl.; b. Madison, Wis., Jan. 30, 1912; s. Robert H. and Mabel Clair (Scanlan) F.; B.A., U. Wis., 1934; Nieman fellow, Harvard, 1950; m. Jean Elizabeth Heitkamp, June 27, 1936; children—Robert Henry, Frederick Heitkamp. Reporter, Madison Capital Times, 1931-43, Milw. Jour., 1945-53; Midwest bur. chief Newsweek mag., 1953-57; corr. ABC, 1957-61, chief Washington bur., 1961-65; dep. press sec. to Pres. U.S., 1966-68; asst. dir. USIA, 1968-69; staff Ho. of Reps., 1969—. Served as officer, inf. AUS, 1943-45. Recipient Distinguished Service award U. Wis., 1959. Mem. Radio-TV Corrs. Assn. (Pres. 1962), Radio-TV News Dirs. Assn., Broadcasters Club, Sigma Delta Chi. Presbyn. (deacon). Clubs: Nat. Press, Internat. (Washington); Chicago Press (treas.

1956). Contbr. Ency. Brit., Nieman Reports. Home: 2711 Jenifer St N W Washington DC 20015 Office: House of Reps Cannon Office Bldg Washington DC 20515

FLEMING, ROBERT JOHN, Jr., business exec., ret. army officer; b. Fort Robinson, Neb., Jan. 13, 1907; s. Robert John and Augusta MacArthur (Grimes) F.; grad. Phillips Exeter Acad., 1924; B.S., U.S. Mil. Acad., 1928; M.S. in Mech. Engring., Mass. Inst. Tech., 1931; grad. Army Engrs. Sch., 1935, Nat. War Coll., 1951; m. Eleanor Marion Canby, May 27, 1930; children—Patricia Anne (Mrs. Benjamin B. Beasley), Eleanor Augusta (Mrs. John C. Pace). Commnd. 2d lt., Corps Engrs., U.S. Army, 1928, advanced through grades to maj. gen., 1961; dep. adminstr. WPA, So. Cal., 1935-39; dep. chief staff Central Pacific Area, 1941-43; engr. XXII Corps., also asst. chief engr. Europe, 1944-47; asst. chief engrs. for mil. operations, also engr. Army Field Forces, 1948-53; dist. engr., Phila., 1954; div. engr., New Eng., 1955-57; comdg. gen. Theatre Army Support Command, Europe, 1957-60; div. engr. Army Engrs. Div. Southwestern, 1960-61; gov. Canal Zone, also pres. Panama Canal Co., 1962-67; retired, 1967; v.p. Anderson Nichols & Co., Boston, 1967—. Decorated Legion of Merit, Bronze Star medal, Army Commendation medal; comdr. Order White Lion (Czechoslovakia); Order Fatherland (Russia); officer Legion of Honor (France); Grand Cross Nunez de Balboa (Panama). Mem. Am. Soc. C.E., Soc. Am. Mil. Engrs. Home: Boston MA 02101 Office: care Anderson Nichols & Co Boston MA 02101

FLEMING, ROBERT THOMAS, lawyer; b. Normal, Ill., June 19, 1923; s. Birney F. and Carrie (Brown) F.; B.S., Ill. Wesleyan U., 1945; J.D., Northwestern U., 1949; m. Myra King, Nov. 1, 1952; children—Elizabeth, Nancy, Robert Thomas, Steven. Admitted to Ill. bar, 1949, since practiced in Bloomington; mem. firm Fleming, Messman & Lapan, 1949—. Dir. First Nat. Bank Normal. Corp. counsel, Town of Normal, 1951-70; asst. atty. gen. Ill., 1968-70. Mem. Am., Ill., McLean County bar assns., Am. Judicature Soc., Phi Delta Phi, Sigma Chi. Republican. Presbyn. (trustee). Mason, Rotarian (past pres. Normal), Toastmaster (past pres. Bloomington). Home: 7 Kent Dr Normal IL 61761 Office: 217 E Washington St Bloomington IL 61701

FLEMING, ROBERT WRIGHT, investment banker; b. Washington, Aug. 26, 1918; s. Robert Vedder and Alice Listen (Wright) F.; grad. Lawrenceville Sch., 1937; B.A., George Washington U., 1941; m. Martha Wills Schoenfeld, Nov. 21, 1942; children—Margaret Johanna, Robert Vedder II, Bruce Wright. Washington rep. Pan. Am. Airways, 1946-48; became v.p., sec., dir. Folger, Nolan, Fleming, Douglas, Inc., Washington, 1948, now exec. v.p., sec., dir.; dir. Steadman Am. Industry Fund, Steadman Fiduciary Investment Fund, Prudential Bldg. Assn., Acacia Mut. Life Ins. Co., Security Storage Co.; adv. bd. Riggs Nat. Bank, Washington. Mem. Washington Bd. Trade, N.Y., Am. stock exchanges. chmn. endowment and investment com. Community Chest Fedn.; chmn. adv. com. Pub. Service Commn. D.C. Treas., Nat. Citizens for Eisenhower Congl. Com. Bd. dirs., treas. D.C. Crippled Children's Soc.; bd. dirs. Washington Heart Assn., D.C. chpt. A.R.C.; trustee Boys Club of Washington, Washington Hosp. Center. Served as lt. comdr. USNR, 1941-46. Mem. Friendly Sons St. Patrick, Nat. Assn. Security Dealers (bd. govs.), Assn. Stock Exchange Firms, Investment Bankers Assn., Phila.-Balt. Exchange, Nat. Geog. Soc. (finance com.), Kappa Alpha, Omicron Delta Kappa. Rotarian. Clubs: Burning Tree (Bethesda, Md.); Chevy Chase (Md.); Metropolitan, National Press, Alfalfa (Washington). Home: 5106 Cammack Dr Spring Hill Washington DC 20016 Office: 725 15th St Washington DC 20005

FLEMING, ROGER W., farm orgn. exec.; b. Dinsdale, Ia., July 9, 1915; s. Lester G. and Mabel Mary (Dinsdale) F.; student Ia. State Tchrs. Coll., 1933-35; B.S., Ia. State Coll., 1938; m. Jeanne Virginia Jacobs, Aug. 18, 1938; 1 dau., Barbara Jean (Mrs. Klaus V. Luehning). Served on staff Ia. Farm Bur. Fedn., 1938-48; dir. Washington office Am. Farm Bur. Fedn., 1948—, sec.-treas., 1949—; sec.-treas. Am. Agrl. Marketing Assn., Am. Farm Bur. Service Co.; v.p., pres. Am. Mgmt. Bd, Inc.; sec. Am. Agrl. Mut. Ins. Co. Served with supply corps USNR, 1943-46. Mem. Phi Kappa Phi. Home: Layhill Rd Silver Spring MD 20906 Office: 425 13th St N W Washington DC 20004

FLEMING, SAMUEL M., banker; b. Franklin, Tenn., Apr. 29, 1908; s. Samuel M. and Cynthia Graham (Cannon) F.; student Battle Ground Acad., 1919-24; A.B., Vanderbilt U., 1928; m. Josephine Cliffe, Dec. 10, 1930; children—Joanne Cliffe (Mrs. Toby S. Wilt), Daniel Milton. Asst. credit mgr. N.Y. (City) Trust Co., 1928- 31; with Third Nat. Bank, Nashville, 1931—, dir. 1947—, pres., 1950- 70, chmn. bd., 1970—; dir. Williamson Co. Bank, L. & N. R.R. Co., Jack Daniel Distillery, Genesco, Inc., Tenn. Tufting Co., Murray-Ohio Mfg. Co., Ky. Fried Chicken Corp., Nat Life & Accident Ins. Co.; pres. NLT Corp. Trustee Battle Ground Acad., Vanderbilt U., Meharry Med. Coll. Served to lt. comdr. USNR, 1942-45. Mem. Res. City Bankers Assn., Robert Morris Assos., Am. Bankers Assn. (pres. 1961), Tenn. Hist. Soc. (treas.), Tenn. Hist. Commn., S.A.R., Sigma Alpha Epsilon (past hon. eminent supreme archon). Presbyn. (elder). Clubs: Nat. Golf (Augusta, Ga.); Cumberland, Belle Meade Country Richland Golf (Nashville); Links, University (N.Y.); U.S. Seniors Golf. Home: 810 Jackson Blvd Nashville TN 37205 Office: Third Nat Bank Nashville TN 37219

FLEMING, SCOTT, govt. ofcl.; b. Twin Falls, Ida., Oct. 17, 1923; s. John Scott and Anna Laura (Bascom) F.; student U. Nev., 1941-42, U. Chgo. Law Sch., 1936-47; A.B., U. Cal. at Berkeley, 1948, LL.B., 1949; grad. Advanced Mgmt. Program, Harvard, 1964; m. Alma Geneva Skinner, Mar. 5, 1954; children—India Christie, Hilari Lanice. Admitted to Cal. bar, 1949; bus. and tax law practice, San Francisco, 1949-52; atty. Henry J. Kaiser Co., Oakland, Cal., 1952-55; with Kaiser Found Health Plan and Kaiser Found. Hosps., Oakland, 1955-71, exec. v.p., sec., 1970-71; dep. asst. sec. policy devel. Office Asst. Sec. Health and Sci. Affairs, Dept. Health, Edn. and Welfare, 1971—. Life mem., past chmn. river conservation com., past bd. dirs. legal def. fund Sierra Club. Served to 1st lt. AUS, 1943-46. Mem. Am. Mgmt. Assn., Order of Coif. Democrat. Home: 6938 Blaisdell Rd Bethesda MD 20034 Office: 330 Independence Av SW Washington DC 20201

FLEMING, STUART REID, engring. and constrn. co. exec.; b. West Orange, N.J., Aug. 25, 1909; s. Joseph and Anne E. (Reid) F.; B.S., Mass. Inst. Tech., 1932; m. Alice J. Glannan, Sept. 13, 1935; children—Isabel Ann (Mrs. Richard S. Millward), Patricia Anne (Mrs. Robert E. Jester). Vice pres., sr. constrn. mgr. Stone & Webster Engring. Corp., 1965—, also dir.; v.p., dir. Stone & Webster Atlantic Corp.; dir. Stone & Webster Internat., Inc., Stone & Webster Constrn. Co., Stone & Webster India Corp. Registered profl. engr., N.Y., N.J., Ill., Miss., Tenn., Wash., Ore., Cal., Ariz., Fla., Mass., Ohio, B.C., Alta. Fellow Am. Soc. C.E.; mem. Am. Soc. M.E., Nat. Soc. Profl. Engrs., Am. Arbitration Assn., Tau Beta Pi, Sigma Nu. Presbyn. Clubs: University (Pitts.); Mass. Institute Technology Alumni; Down Town (Boston). Home: 34 Windsor Rd Dover MA 02030 Office: 225 Franklin St Boston MA 02107

FLEMING, THOMAS CRAWLEY, physician; b. Chgo., June 16, 1921; s. Frederic Sydney and Margaret (Moore) F.; student Cal. Inst. Tech., 1940-42; M.D., Columbia Coll. Phys. & Surg., 1945; m. Katherine Slaughter, Oct. 14, 1949; children—Sandra Lee, Wendy, John Gregory, Margot, Frederic Scott. Intern St. Luke's Hosp., N.Y.C., 1945-46; instr. physiology Coll. Phys. & Surg., Columbia, 1948-50; engaged in clin. research Hoffmann La Roche, 1950-57; dir. clin. research Mead Johnson, 1957-59; med. dir. Warner Chilcott, 1959-60; exec. v.p., med. dir. Robert E. Wilson, Inc., 1960-62; chief, chronic medicine Bergen County Hosp., Paramus, N.J., 1952-54, also dir. med. edn.; v.p., med. dir. Sudler & Hennessey, Inc., N.Y.C., 1954—; asst. prof. medicine U. Tenn. Sch. Medicine, 1958-59. Bd. dirs. Emergency Medicine. Served to capt. M.C. AUS, 1946-48. Fellow Am. Coll. Angiology, N.Y. Acad. Scis., Royal Soc. Health (London); mem. A.A.A.S. Contbr. articles med. jours. Home: 183 S Mountain Av Montclair NJ 07042 Office: 130 E 59th St New York City NY 10022

FLEMING, THOMAS JAMES, writer; b. Jersey City, July 5, 1927; s. Thomas James and Katherine (Dolan) F.; A.B., Fordham U., 1950, postgrad. Sch. Social Work, 1950-51; m. Alice Mulcahey, Jan. 19, 1951; children—Alice, Thomas, David, Richard. Reporter, Yonkers (N.Y.) Herald Statesman, 1951; asst. to Fulton Oursler, 1951-52, lit. executor estate, 1953; asso. editor Cosmopolitan mag., 1954-58, exec. editor, 1959-61; writer, 1961—. Recipient Achievement award in communication arts Fordham U., 1961, Encaenia award, 1965; Mass Media award Nat. Conf. Christians and Jews, 1963. Mem. N.Y. Hist. Assn., Soc. Mag. Writers (pres. 1966-67), Am. PEN (pres. 1971—), Soc. Am. Historians. Clubs: Coffee House, Dutch Treat (N.Y.C.). Christopher award, 1970. Author: Now We Are Enemies, 1960; All Good Men, 1961; The God of Love, 1963; Beat the Last Drum, 1963; One Small Candle, 1964; King of the Hill, 1966; A Cry of Whiteness, 1967; Affectionately Yours, George Washington, 1967; West Point, The Men and Times of the U.S. Military Academy, 1969; The Man from Monticello, 1969; Romans Countrymen Lovers, 1969; The Sandbox Tree, 1970; The Man Who Dared the Lightning, 1971; also various TV scripts, articles, short stories. Editor: Lights Along the Shore (Oursler), 1953. Home: 315 E 72d St New York City NY (summer) Westbrook CT 06498

FLEMING, THOMAS PAUL, librarian; b. Massillon, O., Aug. 27, 1907; s. Thomas P. and Mary Cecelia (Schmader) F.; A.B., Western Reserve U., 1929, B.S., 1930, M.S., 1932; m. Ilene Lovica Evans, July 1, 1932; children—David Strong, Thomas Evans. Gen. asst. in charge dept. libraries, Western Reserve U., 1930- 32; head, order and binding dept., U. of Minn. library, and instr., bibliography and library methods, div. library instruction, U. of Minn., 1932-37; librarian, Coll. of Physicians and Surgeons, Columbia U., 1937- 44; asst. dir. Columbia U. Libraries, 1944-48; prof. library service, librarian medical-natural sciences at Columbia, 1948- -; vis. prof. Japan Library Sch., Keio U., Tokyo, 1963. Chmn., Joint Com. on Importations; A.L.A. com. on public documents; cons. republication program, Office Alien Property Custodian; British zone representative. Library of Congress Mission, Germany, 1946. Mem. Renaissance Soc. Am., Am. Assn. History of Medicine, Am. Library Assn. (exec. bd.), 1944-48), Assn. of Coll. and Reference Libraries, Bibliographical Soc. of Am., History of Sci. Soc., Med. Library Assn., N.Y. Library Assn., Soc. for the Advancement of Edn., Special Libraries Assn., Minn. Library Assn. Theta Kappa Psi. Democrat. Episcopalian. Clubs: Foil and Mace, Grolier (New York). Author: Guide to the Literature of Science, 1957; Guide to the Literature of the Medical Sciences, 1961. Contbr. articles to profl. journals. Home: 396 Highwood Av Leonia, NJ 07605. Office: Coll Physicians and Surgeons Columbia Univ New York City NY 10032

FLEMING, WENDELL HELMS, educator, mathematician; b. Guthrie, Okla., Mar. 7, 1928; s. James Lucian and Helen (Helms) F.; B.S., Purdue U., 1948, M.S., 1949; Ph.D., U. Wis., 1951; m. Florence Tatum, Apr. 4, 1948; children—Randall, Daniel, William. Mathematician, RAND Corp., 1951-55, cons., 1960-65; asst. prof. Purdue U., 1955-58; mem. faculty Brown U., 1958—, prof. math., 1963—, chmn. dept., 1965-68. Nat. Sci. Found. fellow, 1968-69. Mem.-at-large Conf. Bd. Math. Scis. Fellow A.A.A.S.; mem. Am. Math. Soc., Math. Assn. Am., Soc. Indsl. and Applied Math. Author: Functions of Several Variables, 1965. Editor: SIAM Rev. Editorial cons. Math. Reviews, 1963-65. Home: 3 Colley Ct Barrington, RI 02806. Office: Math Dept Brown Univ Providence RI 02912

FLEMING, WILLARD C., dental educator; b. Sausalito, Cal., Oct. 11, 1899; s. Willard Stephen and Effie (Urquhart) F.; D.D.S., U. Cal., 1923; D.Sc., U. So. Cal., 1947; LL.D., U. Toronto, 1959; m. Carlotta Heid, Nov. 11, 1924; 1 dau., Gail Allison. Practice of dentistry, Oakland, Cal., since 1923; also mem. faculty, Coll. of Dentistry, U. Cal., since 1923, as instr., 1923-30, asst. clin. prof., 1943-49, prof. operative dentistry 1949—, vice provost, 1958-64, dean students, 1965-66, chancellor U. Cal. Med. Center, 1966-69. Commr. Western Interstate Commn. Higher Edn., 1956-58; mem. commn. Survey of Dentistry, Am. Council Edn.; mem. Nat. Adv. Dental Research Council, USPHS; mem. dental adv. council W. K. Kellogg Found. Served as pvt. and cpl., A.U.S., World War I. Fellow Am. Coll. Dentists (pres. 1951-52), A.A.A.S. (v.p. 1954); mem. Am. Dental Assn., Am. Assn. Dental Schs. (pres., 1946-47), Sigma Xi, Psi Omega, Epsilon Alpha, Omicron Kappa Upsilon. Home: 5924 McAndrew Dr Oakland CA 94611 Office: Office of Chancellor Univ of Cal San Francisco CA 94122

FLEMING, WILLIAM, educator; b. Berlin, Germany, Feb. 15, 1907; s. Sigmar and Margarete (Alexander) F.; student U. Berlin, 1925-28; Dr. Juris Utriusque magna cum laude, U. Freiburg, Germany, 1934; postgrad. Columbia, 1942-46, Ph.D., 1959; m. Edith Schlesinger, Mar. 9, 1935 (dec. 1968); 1 son, Andrew P.; m. 2d, Suzanne Wahl, July 3, 1969; 1 dau., Bettina V. Came to U.S., 1940, naturalized, 1945. Faculty, Ripon (Wis.) Coll., 1947—, prof. polit. sci., 1960- -, chmn. dept., 1947—. Vis. prof. Northwestern U., summer 1956. Asst. dir. Am. Assembly conf. on Am. Sec. State, 1961; mem. nat. adv. bd. Young Ams. for Freedom, 1964—; adv. assembly Am. Conservative Union, 1964—; bd. advisers Wis. Acad. Conf. Student Govts., 1969—; mem. nat. adv. bd. Nat. Inst. for Law/Order/Justice, 1969—; charter sponsor Univ. Centers for Rational Alternatives, N.Y.C., 1969. Bd. dirs., v.p. Citizens United for Responsible Edn. Recipient Harold and May Severy award excellence teaching, 1959. Mem. Am. Polit. Sci. Assn., Acad. Polit. Sci., Am. Soc. Internat. Law, U. Profs. for Acad. Order (charter), Alpha Phi Omega (certificate appreciation 1967). Republican. Contbr. numerous articles to profl. jours. Contbg. editor: Dictionary of Polit. Scci. Philos. Library); Ency. Brit. Home: 503 Watson St Ripon WI 54971

FLEMING, WILLIAM ADAM, govt. ofcl.; b. Battle Creek, Mich., Apr. 14, 1921; s. William and Greta Jane (Wolf) F.; B.S., Purdue U., 1943; m. Evelyn Alice Lasch, Oct. 20, 1945; children—Jack William, Janice Lynne. Engaged in jet engine and rocket research Lewis Research Center NASA, Cleve., 1943-60, staff tech. asst. space flight program planning, coordination, Washington, 1960-61, dir. program review div., 1961-70, dep. dir. office analysis and evaluation, 1970—. Asso. fellow Am. Inst. Aeros. and Astronautics (past chmn. Cleve.-Akron sect.); mem. Pi Tau Sigma, Pi Kappa Alpha. Home: 6611 Meldoy Lane Bethesda, MD 21134. Office: NASA Hdqrs Washington DC 20546

FLEMING, WILLIAM CARY, physician; b. Lee Hall, Va., Jan. 16, 1918; s. Thomas Hayes and Martha (Kirby) F.; B.S. in Chemistry, U. Va., 1942, M.D., 1945; m. Mabel Clare Green, Mar. 19, 1944; children—Martha Frances, Sharon Anne, Joan Marie. Intern Delaware Hosp., Wilmington, 1945-46; gen. practice, Glasgow, Va., 1948-49; mem. staff student health U. Kan., 1949-51; indsl. physician E. I. duPont de Nemours & Co., Inc., Waynesboro, Va., 1951-53; resident phys. medicine and rehab. VA Hosp.-Med. Coll. Va., Richmond, 1953-56; phys. medicine and rehab. physician VA hosps., Richmond, 1956-58. Pitts., 1959, Coral Gables, Fla., 1959-64, Birmingham, Ala., 1970—; prof. phys. medicine and rehab. U. Ala. Med. Sch., 1964—, chmn. dept., 1964-70; physiatrist in chief Univ. Hosp., Birmingham, 1964-70, now physiatrist; med. dir. Spain Rehab. Center Birmingham, 1964-69, physiatrist, 1969—; dir. U. Ala. Rehab. Research and Tng. Center, 1966-69; cons. staff Childre's, St. Vincent's hosps., 1965—; spl. research rehab. aspects stroke, emphysema, kidney disease, heart disease, spinal cord injury, electromyography. Dir. chronic illness project Dade County, Fla., 1962-63; mem. adv. bd. N. Ala. Rehab. Center, 1966-70. Served to capt. M.C., AUS, 1946-48. Diplomate Am. Bd. Phys. Medicine and Rehab. Mem. Am., So. (chmn. sect. 1966-67) med. assns., Am. Congress Rehab. Medicine, Am. Acad. Phys. Medicine and Rehab., So. Soc. Phys. Medicine (chmn. 1970—), Raven Soc., Alpha Chi Sigma, Nu Sigma Nu. Home: 3528 Belle Meade Way Birmingham, AL 35223.

FLEMING, WILLIAM COLEMAN, educator, author, music critic; b. Pomona, Cal., Aug. 3, 1909; s. William Thomas and Theodora (Loney) F.; student Pomona Coll., 1927-28; studied piano and music lit. with Paolo Gallico, N.Y.C., 1928-30, Artur Schnabel, Berlin, Germany, 1930-33, Tobias Matthay, London, Eng., 1934; M.A., Claremont Grad. Sch., 1939, Ph.D., 1941; D.F.A. hon. causa, Monmouth Coll., 1959. Concert pianist, Europe, Am., 1932-40; Am. debut Carnegie Hall, 1937; instr. music, philosophy Pomona Jr. Coll., 1940-45; asso. prof. fine arts Syracuse U., 1945-47, founder dept. fine arts Coll. Liberal Arts, 1947, prof., chmn. dept. fine arts, 1947-69, Centennial prof. fine arts, 1969—, Ford Found. faculty fellow, 1953-54; music critic, Post-Standard, Syracuse, New York, 1952—. Fellow Royal Soc. Arts; mem. Coll. Music Soc., Am. Musicological Soc., Am. Soc. Aethestics, Am. Assn. U. Profs., Coll. Art Assn. Author: Arts and Ideas, 1955, 3d edit., 1968; (with Abraham Veinus) Understanding Music, 1958, rev., 1971; Art, Music and Ideas, 1970 Contbr. Ency. Brit., World Book Ency., numerous biographies. Home: 112 Hillcrest Rd Syracuse, NY 13224.

FLEMING, WILLIAM DAVID, stockbroker; b. San Mateo, Cal., July 8, 1910; s. William J. and Maude (Lockie) F.; student pub. schs.; m. Barbara Trotter, Oct. 20, 1934; children—Gerald S., Richard D. With Blyth & Co., San Francisco, Los Angeles, 1929-45; with Walston & Co., Inc., Los Angeles, 1945- 52, partner, N.Y.C., 1952-57, sr. v.p., Chgo., 1957-64, pres., N.Y.C., 1964—. Mem. Chgo. Bd. Trade. Clubs: Bond, Broad Street (N.Y.C.); Bond (Chgo.); Winged Foot Golf (Mamaroneck, N.Y.). Home: 21 Carriage House Lane Mamaroneck NY 10543 Office: 77 Water St New York City NY 10005

FLEMING, WILLIAM LEROY, physician, educator; b. Morgantown, W.Va., Aug. 29, 1905; s. Walter Lynwood and Mary (Boyd) F.; A.B., Vanderbilt U., 1925, M.S., 1927, M.D., 1932; m. Beatrice Heathcote, Apr. 28, 1934; children—Elizabeth, Anne, Mary, Jane. Interne Bellevue Hosp., N.Y.C., 1933-34; asst. resident and resident in medicine Vanderbilt U. Hosp., 1934-37; Milbank fellow Johns Hopkins Hosp., 1937-39; staff mem. Internat. Health Div. of Rockefeller Found., N.Y.C., 1939; research prof. syphilogy Sch. Pub. Health, U. N.C., 1939-45; asso. prof. medicine Boston U. Sch. Medicine, 1946-48, prof. preventive medicine, 1948-52; physician Mass. and Evans Meml. Hosps., 1946-52; prof. preventive medicine U. N.C., 1952—, chmn. dept., 1952-70, asst. dean sch. medicine, 1957-70; dir. gen. clinic, N.C. Meml. Hosp., 1952-64. Fellow Am. Pub. Health Assn.; mem. Am. Soc. Clin. Investigation, A.M.A., Am. Venereal Disease Assn. (past pres.), Internat. Epidemiological Assn., Assn. Tchrs. Preventive Medicine (pres. 1959-60), Am. Coll. Preventive Medicine, Sigma Xi. Contbr. to med. and sci. periodicals. Home: Morgan Creek Rd Chapel Hill NC 27514 Office: N C Meml Hosp Chapel Hill NC 27514

FLEMINGS, MERTON CORSON, educator; b. Syracuse, N.Y., Sept. 20, 1929; s. Merton Corson and Marion (Dexter) F.; B.S., Mass. Inst. Tech., 1951, M.S., 1952, Sc.D., 1954; m. Elizabeth Goodridge, Sept. 6, 1956; children—Anne, Peter. Asst. prof. metallurgy Mass. Inst. Tech., 1956-61, asso. prof., 1961-69, Abex Corp. prof. metallurgy and materials sci., 1969—; cons. Monsanto Chem. Corp., Latrobe Steel, Hitchiner Corp., Balfour Co., Norton Co., U.S. Govtl. Agencies. Trustee Leicester Jr. Coll. Am. Exchange lectr., Brussels, 1958; Simpson Gold medal Am. Foundrymen's Soc., 1961; Hoyt Meml. lectr., 1964; AIME Mathewson Gold medal, 1969. Mem. Am. Foundrymen's Soc., Am. Inst. Metall. Engrs., Am. Soc. Metals, Inst. Metals, Am. Inst. Metall. Engrs. (metals div. solidification com. 1960—, awards and lecture com. 1969—). Author: Foundry Engineering, 1959. Home: 15 Percy Rd Lexington MA 02173 Office: 77 Massachusetts Av Cambridge MA 02139

FLEMISTER, LAUNCELOT JOHNSON, physiologist, educator; b. Atlanta, Dec. 11, 1913; s. Launcelot Johnson and Willie (Moore) F.; A.B., Duke, 1935, M.A., 1939, Ph.D., 1941; m. Sarah Elizabeth Culbreth, Dec. 25, 1941. Instr., Med. Sch. George Washington U., 1941-42; research asso. Sharp & Dohme, Phila., 1946-47; asst. prof. Swarthmore Coll., 1947-51, asso. prof., 1951-66, prof. zoology, 1966—. Cons. NSF, 1963-64. Fulbright fellow, Peru, 1959-60. Served to lt. USNR, 1942-46. Fellow A.A.A.S.; mem. Am. Physiol. Soc., Am. Soc. Zoologists, Sigma Xi. Office: P O Box F Swarthmore PA 19081

FLEMMING, ARTHUR SHERWOOD, univ. pres.; b. Kingston, N.Y., June 12, 1905; s. Harry H. and Harriet (Sherwood) F.; A.B., Ohio Wesleyan U., 1927, LL.D., 1941; A.M., American U., 1928, LL.D., 1942; LL.B., George Washington U., 1933; hon. degrees from 37 instns. in the U.S.; m. Bernice Virginia Moler, Dec. 14, 1934; children—Elizabeth Anne (Mrs. George Speese), Susan Harriet (Mrs. John Parker), Harry Sherwood, Arthur Henry and Thomas Madison (twins). Instr. govt., debate Coach Am. U., 1927-30, dir. Sch. Pub. Affairs, 1934-39, exec. officer, 1938-39; editorial staff U.S. Daily (now U.S. News and World Report), 1930-34; editor Uncle Sam's Diary (weekly current events paper for high school students), 1932-35; mem. U.S. Civil Service Commn., 1939-48; pres. Ohio Wesleyan U., 1948- 53, 57-58; sec. Health, Education and Welfare, 1958-61; pres. U. Oregon, 1961—; chief labor supply, Labor Division, OPM, 1941-42; mem. Manpower Survey Board, Navy Dept., 1943-44; chmn. mgmt.- labor policy com. War Manpower Commn., 1942-45; mem. adv. council, Retraining and Reemployment Adminstrn., Dept. of Labor, 1944-47; mem. Commn. on Orgn. Exec. Branch of the Govt., 1947-49, 53-55; chmn. adv. com. on personnel mgmt. AEC, 1943-53; mem. Internat. Civil Service Adv. Bd., 1950-64; mem. Pres's. Adv. Com. on Govt. Orgn., 1953-61, chmn., 1950-61; mem. nat. adv. com. Peace Corps, 1961—. Awarded travelling fellowship Washington branch English-speaking Union, 1928; Medal of Freedom, 1957; Alexander Meiklejohn award for acad. freedom, 1962. Chmn. Pres,'s Commn. on Polit. Activity of Govt. Personnel. Trustee Theodore Roosevelt Memorial Assn.; v.p. Nat. Council Chs. of Christ in Am., 1950- 54, 64-66, pres., 1967—. Mem. Ore. Council

Chs. (pres. 1964—), Alpha Sigma Phi, Delta Sigma Rho, Omicron Delta Kappa. Republican. Methodist. Home: 2315 McMorran Dr Eugene OR 97403

FLEMMING, HARRY S., govt. ofcl.; b. Washington, Sept. 15, 1940; s. Arthur S., and Bernice (Molar) F.; Ohio State U.; Am. U., m. Sonya Moose, Dec. 27, 1961; children—Harry Todd, Janis Lea. Vice pres. Madigan Electronic Corp., Farmingdale, N.Y., 1965-69; pres. and dir. No. Va. Communications Co., Arlington, spl. asst. to Pres. Nixon, Washington, 1969—. Councilman city Alexandria (Va.). Chmn. Va. Nixon-Agnew campaign, 1968; asst. to chmn. Rep. Nat. Com., 1968. Home: PO Box 1355 Alexandria VA 22313 Office: White House Washington DC 20050

FLES, JAMES HERMAN, trucking co. exec.; b. Muskegon, Mich., Aug. 25, 1912; s. Isaac Jacob and Lutena (Boonstra) F.; A.B., Calvin Coll. and Sem., 1935; M.B.A., U. Mich., 1937; m. N. Lucile Noordewier, June 16, 1937; children—James H., William D. With Asso. Truck Lines, Inc., Grand Rapids, Mich., 1937—, exec. v.p., 1946-59, pres., 1959-70, chief exec. officer, chmn., 1970—; dir. Union Bank & Trust Co., Grand Rapids. Mem. Gov. Mich. Spl. Commn. on Traffic Safety, 1964—, Mich. World Trade Adv. Council, 1965—; chmn. Pres.'s Adv. Com. Central States Motor Freight Bur., 1963—; vice chmn. econ. research com. Regular Common Carrier Conf. Vice pres., trustee Mich. Colls. Found., 1964—. Pres., Grand Rapids Christian High Schs. Ednl. Found., 1965—. Recipient Distinguished Alumni award Calvin Coll. and Sem., 1971. Mem. Am. (exec. com. 1960, bd. govs. regular common carrier conf., charter mem. nat. accounting and finance council, hon. life mem. Mich. chpt.), Mich. (exec. com., past pres.) trucking assns., Trucking Employers (exec. policy com. 1963), Greater Grand Rapids (chmn. nat. affairs com. 1966), Mich. chambers commerce. Mem. Christian Ref. Ch. Clubs: Peninsular, University (Grand Rapids). Home: 1051 Monterey Dr S E Grand Rapids MI 49506 Office: Vandenberg Center Grand Rapids MI 49502

FLESCH, RUDOLF, author; b. Vienna, Austria, May 8, 1911; s. Hugo and Helen (Basch) F.; Dr.Jur., U. Vienna, 1933; Ph.D., Columbia, 1943; m. Elizabeth Terpenning, Sept. 6, 1941; children—Anne Sutherland (Mrs. Peter Wares), Hugo Walter, Gillian Ruth, Katrina Woodburn, Abigail Allan, Janet Amalia. Came to U.S., 1938, naturalized, 1944. Author: The Art of Plain Talk, 1946; The Way to Write (with A.H. Lass), 1947; The Art of Readable Writing, 1949; The Art of Clear Thinking, 1951; How to Make Sense, 1954; Why Johnny Can't Read, 1955; The Book of Unusual Quotations, 1957; A New Way to Better English, 1958; How to Write, Speak and Think More Effectively, 1960; How to Be Brief, 1962; The ABC of Style, 1965; The Book of Surprises, 1965; The New Book of Unusual Quotations, 1966. Home: 24 Belden Av Dobbs Ferry NY 10522

FLESHEIM, SYLVESTER WOLF, bldg. co. exec.; b. Cleve., Apr. 13, 1889; s. Isaac and Fanny (Wolf) F.; m. Erma Hexter, Oct. 17, 1911; children—Clementine Hexter (Mrs. H. Reitman), Emily Louise (Mrs. Ben Hibshman, Jr.). With Master Builders Co., Cleve., 1909—, pres., chmn. bd., 1953-56, chmn., 1953—; chmn. S. M. Hexter Co., Cleve., 1930-56. Pres. Mt. Sinai Hosp., Cleve. Home: 19015 Van Aken Blvd Shaker Heights, OH 44122. Office: 2490 Lee Blvd Cleveland OH 44118

FLESHOOD, ARNOLD PENDLETON, coll. dean; b. LaCrosse, Va., Sept. 11, 1923; s. Otis Arnold and Josephine (Roberts) F.; B.A., U. Richmond, 1950; M.S., Va. Poly. Inst., 1954; Ed.D., Columbia, 1961; m. Carrie Louise Allen, Dec. 27, 1950; children—William Arnold, Martha Louise. Tchr. English, Martinsville (Va.) High Sch., 1950-53; prin. Joseph Martins Sch., Martinsville, 1953-56; gen. supr. Martinsville Sch., 1956-58, dir. instrn., 1958-60; dir. instrn., asst. supt. Lynchburg (Va.) City Sch. System, 1961-65; prof., head dept. elementary edn. Richmond (Va.) Profl. Inst., 1965-68; dean Sch. Edn., Va. Commonwealth U., Richmond, 1968—; vis. prof. Randolph Macon Womans Coll., Lynchburg Coll., 1960-61, Dalhousie U., Halifax, N.S., Can., summers 1963-64. Mem. bd. edn. Va. Meth. Conf., 1968-70. Bd. visitors Buford Acad. Served with USNR, 1943-46. Recipient Outstanding Community Service award Martinsville Exchange Club, 1961. Mem. Phi Delta Kappa, Theta Chi. Club: Richmond Exchange (pres.). Home: 204 Roslyn Hills Dr Richmond VA 23229

FLETCHALL, EUGENE DALTON, meat packer; b. Poseyville, Ind., Aug. 19, 1908; s. Eugene Dalton and Perle (Robinson) F.; B.S., Ind. U., 1932, LL.B., 1934; m. Jane Malcolm, Aug. 10, 1935; 1 dau., Ann. Admitted to Ind. bar, 1934; salesman refinery dept. Swift & Co., 1934-46, plant mgr. Winona, Minn., 1946-48, asst. mgr., St. Paul, 1948-51, mgr., San Francisco, 1951-53, asst. to exec. v.p., Chgo., 1953-55, v.p., 1955—, exec. v.p., 1964—, also dir. Mem. Phi Gamma Delta, Phi Delta Phi. Conglist. Home: 919 Country Club Dr LaGrange IL 60525 Office: 115 W Jackson Blvd Chicago IL 60604

FLETCHER, ALAN GORDON, univ. dean; b. Gibson's Landing, B.C., Can., Jan. 2, 1925; s. William G. and Florence (Smith) F.; B.A. in Sci., U. B.C., 1948; M.S., Cal. Inst. Tech., 1952; Ph.D. (Walter P. Murphy fellow), Northwestern U., 1965; m. A. Irene Flynn, Aug. 6, 1949; children—Christopher Lee, Lynn Patricia, Elizabeth Joan. Engr.-in-tng. B.C. Electric Co., Ltd., Vancouver, 1948- 52, hydraulic designer, 1952-56; supr. hydro planning B.C. Engring. Co., Vancouver, 1956-59; asst. prof., asso. prof. civil engring. U. Ida., 1959-62; asso. prof. civil engring. U. Utah, 1964-69; dean U. N.D. Coll. Engring., Grand Forks, 1969—. Pres. bd. Vancouver-Central YMCA; bd. govs. Vancouver Met. YMCA. Danforth asso., 1965—. Registered profl. engr., B.C. Mem. Am. Soc. C.E.s, Engring. Inst. Can., Am. Soc. Engring. Edn., N.D. Acad. Sci., Sigma Xi, Chi Epsilon. Presbyn. (elder). Rotarian. Home: 3117 Olson Dr Grand Forks ND 58201

FLETCHER, ALBERT LEWIS, clergyman; b. Little Rock, Ark., Oct. 28, 1896; s. Thomas M. and Helen (Wehr) F.; A.M., Little Rock Coll., 1917; student St. John's Home Mission Sem. (Little Rock), 1917-20. Ordained priest Roman Catholic Ch., 1920; asst. prof. Little Rock Coll., 1920-23, pres. 1923-25; mem. faculty of St. John's Sem., 1925-39; chancellor of Little Rock Diocese, 1926-33; apptd. vicar gen. Little Rock Diocese, 1933; made papal chamberlain, 1929, and domestic prelate of papal household, 1934; elected to titular see of Samos, 1939, and apptd. auxiliary bishop of Little Rock; consecrated auxiliary bishop, 1940; apptd. bishop of Little Rock by Pope Pius XII, Dec. 7, 1946. Apptd. pres. of Diocesan Publ. Soc., 1937. Home: 4605 Crestwood Dr 72207 Office: 305 West 2d St Little Rock AR 72201

FLETCHER, ANDREW, business exec.; b. N.Y.C., Feb. 6, 1895; s. Andrew and Jean L. (Drummond) F.; ed. Yale, 1916; E.D. (hon.), U. Mo., 1949, Mont. Sch. Mines, 1964; LL.D., St. Frances Xavier U., 1953, Seton Hall U., 1957; m. E. Dorothea Camp, Oct. 19, 1918. Shipyard mechanic Harlan and Hollingsworth, Wilmington, Del., until 1917; foreman Balt. Dry Dock Co., 1917-18; sec. W. and A. Fletcher Co., Hoboken, N.J., 1918-24; in charge Fletcher shipyard 1924-29, when plant merged with 6 other N.Y. shipyards under title United Dry Docks, Inc.; v.p., treas., dir. St. Joseph Lead Co., 1929-46, exec. v.p., 1946-47, pres., 1947-60, chmn. bd., 1960-67, hon. chmn. bd. trustees, chmn. finance com., 1967—; past pres. Meramec Mining Co., 953 Fifth Av. Corp. Mayor, Mendham, N.J., 1964-70. Past pres. United Engring. Trustees; trustee Engring. Found. Bd. (N.Y.). Hon. mem. Am. Mining Congress. Mem. Am. Inst. Mining Metall. and Petroleum Engrs. (past pres.), Soc. Naval Architects and Marine Engrs., Lead Industries Assn. (past pres., dir.), Am. Zinc Inst., Mining and Metall. Soc., Inst. of Metals (London), Australasian Inst. Mining and Metallurgy (hon.), Yale Engring. Assn. Mason. Clubs: Yale, Mining, University (N.Y.C.). Home: Three Fields Cherry Lane Mendham NJ 07945 Office: 250 Park Av New York City NY 10017

FLETCHER, ARTHUR ALLEN, govt. ofcl.; b. Phoenix, Dec. 22, s. Andrew A. and Edna (Miller) F.; B.A., Washburn U., 1950; postgrad. Kan. State U., 1953-54, San Francisco State Coll., 1964-65; m. Bernyce Hassom, May 5, 1965; children—Phyliss, Sylvia,, Arthur Allen, Paul, Phillip. Tchr. pub. schs., Berkeley, Cal., 1960-65; dir. Wash. Manpower Devel. Project, Pasco, 1965-66; employee relations specialist Hanford Automic Energy Facility, Richland, Wash., 1967-69; spl. asst. gov. State of Wash., Olympia, 1969; now with Dept. Labor, Washington. Mem. city council, Pasco, 1968-69; state vice chmn. Kan. Republican State Com., 1954-56, vice chmn. Schwanee Young Reps., 1956-57; Chmn. adv. com. on civil rights Cal. Rep. Assembly, 1962-64; committeeman Alameda County (Cal.) Central Com., 1962-65; candidate lt. gov. Wash., 1968, 17th Assembly Dist. Cal., 1962; community organizer East Pasco Self-Help Coop., 1968-69. Served with AUS, 1943-45. Recipient Nat. Freedom Found. award, 1968. Mem. Kan., Cal. tchrs. assns., Am. Legion, N.A.A.C.P., Northwest Assn. Personnel Officers. Home: 874 Azalea Dr Rockville MD 20850 Office: Dept Labor 14th and Constitution Sts Washington DC

FLETCHER, CHARLES HENRY, Jr., banker; b. Detroit, Aug. 26, 1924; s. Charles Henry and Cara (Van Campen) F.; B.S., Cornell U., 1945; M.B.A., U. Detroit, 1961; m. Mary Elizabeth Cosgrove, Apr. 7, 1947; children—Ben G. (stepson), Susan Anne, Charles Henry III. Sales engr. Westinghouse Electric Corp., 1946-59, mgr. sales tng., 1959-60; with Mellon Nat. Bank & Trust Co., Pitts., 1960—, sr. v.p., 1968—. Mem. Adv. council President's Plans for Progress, 1964-69. Bd. dirs. Urban League, Psychol. Services Pitts., Jr. Achievement S.W. Pa. Mem. Am. (chmn. sub-com. tng.), Pa. (chmn. employee relations task force) bankers assns., Pitts. Personnel Assn. (pres. 1965-66). Home: 60 East Dr Sewickley PA 15143 Office: Mellon Nat Bank and Trust Co Mellon Sq Pittsburgh PA 15230

FLETCHER, CHARLES LOREN, hotel co. exec.; b. Kinbrae, Minn., Dec. 21, 1902; s. Charles E. and Nora (Bickley) F.; B.S., U. Ill., 1929; postgrad. Loyola U. Chgo., 1937-38, Columbia, 1953; m. Violet Root, Oct. 22, 1923; children—Barbara, Charles, James, William. Accountant, Harris, Kerrr, Forster & Co., Chgo., 1931-42, Houston, 1943-48, Los Angeles, 1948-52, partner, 1944-52; financial v.p. Hilton Hotels Corp., Chgo., 1952-68, treas., 1959—, sr. financial v.p., 1968—; treas. Hilton Credit Corp., Los Angeles, 1959-65, exec. v.p., 1961-63, chief exec. officer, 1962-63, dir., 1961-65; v.p., treas. Hotel Waldorf-Astoria Corp., N.Y.C., 1954—, Hilton Hotels Internat., Inc., N.Y.C., 1952-64, Statler Hotels Del. Corp., Chgo., 1954-64; Hilton Inns, Inc., Chgo., 1958—, Hilton-Burns Hotels Co., Inc., Honolulu, 1961—, Hotel Equipment Corp., 1967—, Hilton Rent-A-Car Corp., 1969-71, Hilton Service Corp., 1964—; dir. v.p. Savoy-Plaza, Inc., N.Y.C., 1957-58. C.P.A., Ill., Cal., Tex. Mem. Am. Inst. C.P.A.'s, Ill. Soc. C.P.A.'s. Home: 1731 E Ridgewood Lane Glenview IL 60025 Office: 720 S Michigan Av Chicago IL 60605

FLETCHER, CHARLES WILLIAM, army officer; b. Mpls., May 11, 1920; s. John Wilkinson and Mary (McLaughlin) F.; B.S., U.S. Mil. Acad., 1941; M.A., George Washington U., 1963; m. Johnnie Dillard, Oct. 16, 1946; children—Suzanne E., Charles W., Mary K., James E., Margaret A., Anne R. Commd. 2d lt. F.A., U.S. Army, 1941, advanced through grades to brig. gen., 1968; served in Europe, World War II; assigned to Office Chief of Staff, U.S. Army, 1961-63; comdr. arty. units in Europe, 1963-65, Korea, 1967-68; dir. ground ammunition Office Asst. Sec. Def., Installation and Logistics, Washington, 1968-71, dir. indsl. moblzn. planning and munitions prodn., 1971—. Decorated Bronze Star, Silver Star with oak leaf cluster, Air medal, Joint Services Commendation medal. Roman Catholic. Home: 4205 Cordell St Annandale VA 22003 Office: Office Asst Secretary Defense (I and L) Washington DC 20310

FLETCHER, COLIN, author; b. Cardiff, Wales, Mar. 14, 1922; s. Herbert Reginald and Margaret Elizabeth (Williams) F.; student West Buckland Sch., North Devon, Eng.; m. twice (2 divorces). Emigrated to Kenya, 1947; mfr.'s rep., Nairobi, mgr. hotel, Kitale, 1947-48; farmer, nr. Nakuru, 1948-52; road builder on estate, nr. Inyanca, So. Rhodesia, 1952-53; with mining cos., Can., summers 1953-56; head janitor Polyclinic Hosp., San Francisco, 1957-58; free-lance writer, San Francisco, 1958—; profl. lectr. Served to capt. Royal Marine Commandos, 1940-47. Mem. Wilderness Soc., Nat. Audubon Soc. Club: Sierra. Author: The Thousand-Mile Summerin Desert and High Sierra, 1964; The Man who Walked Through Time; Complete Walker, 1968. Contbr. articles to Reader's Digest, Field and Stream, other mags. in U.S., Can., Gt. Britian, Africa. Office: care Brandt & Brandt 101 Park Av New York City NY 10017

FLETCHER, CYRIL SCOTT, mgmt. cons.; b. Sydney, Australia, July 28, 1904; s. Michael Scott and Sara Anne (Davies) F.; student Newington Coll., 1917-21; D.P.E.C., Sydney U., 1925; D.H.L., Southwestern at Memphis; Litt.D., U. Akron, 1962; m. Olga Noreen Brigg, Oct. 23, 1929; children—Barbara, Douglas, Wendy. Came to U.S., 1929, naturalized 1941. Studebaker agt. Cayce Paul Motors, Ltd., Sydney, 1922-26; advt. mgr. Studebaker Corp., Australia, 1926-29, spl. Austalasia rep. at head office, U.S., 1929, successively spl. rep., W.I., dir. Far East agys., mng. dir. and factory rep., Australasia, regional supr., South Africa, gen. sales mgr., Can., 1932-35, Studebaker Corp., 1937-41; asso. mem. faculty sch. bus. Ind. U., 1939-41; dir. field devel. Com. for Econ. Devel., 1942-44, exec. dir., 1944-46, trustee, 1946-51; pres. Ency. Brit. Films, 1946-51; pres. Fund for Adult Edn. of Ford Found., 1951-61; dir. Fund for Advancement Edn. of Ford Found., 1951-60; cons. ECA, 1949-50. Pres., chmn. exec. com., dir. Community Ednl. TV Found. South Fla., 1967—. Trustee, China Inst. Am., 1947-51; bd. dirs. Ednl. TV and Radio Center, 1952-57. Mem. Nat. Assn. Ednl. Broadcasters (dir.), Nat. Audubon Soc., Omicron Delta Kappa. Clubs: Miami Rod and Reel; Stuart Sailfish (Fla.). Author: Education for Public Responsibility, 1961; Education, The Challenge Ahead, 1962. Home: Route 1 Box 108 Sewalls Point Rd Jenson Beach FL 33457

FLETCHER, DEAN CHARLES, educator; b. Logan, Utah, June 14, 1921; s. Calvin and Susette (Ricks) F.; B.S. in Physiology, Utah State U., 1943, M.S., 1948; Ph.D. in Chemistry, U. Del., 1951; m. Ann Louise Barber, Apr. 5, 1944; children—Louise, Susette Barber, Ellen Jean, Instr. physiology Utah State U., 1943, 48-49, research, teaching asst., 1946-48; research asso. Biochem. Research Found., Franklin Inst., 1949-51; research biochemist E.I. du Pont de Nemours & Co., Inc., 1951-57; dir. research Washoe Med. Center, Reno, 1957-61; Allie M. Lee research prof. biol. scis. U. Nev., Reno, 1961-70, coordinator health scis., health physicist, 1970—, also dir. student affairs Sch. Medicine; asst. clin. prof. U. Utah Sch. Medicine; cons. biochemistry Washoe Med. Center, St. Mary's Hosp., Reno, Lamar Chem. Co., Reno VA Hosp. Bd. dirs. Talent, Inc.; bd. dirs. Center for Learning Resources, U. Ky. Med. Center, Lexington, 1972—. Mem. Gov. Nev. Com. Med. Edn., Pres. U.S. Com. on Youth, Nev. Cancer Coordination Com., Nev. Med. Basic Sci. Bd., Gov.'s Com. Med. Edn., Gov.'s Com. Emergency Patient Care, Gov.'s Com. Title IX. Bd. dirs. Reno Cancer Center. Served with AUS, World War II. Decorated Commendation medal. Mem. Am. Chem. Soc., N.Y. Acad. Scis., Fed. Socs. Biology and Medicine, Internat. Acad. Forensic Scis., Am. Acad. Forensic Scis., Sigma Xi, Phi Delta Kappa, Gamma Sigma Delta. Mem. Ch. of Jesus Christ of Latter-Day Saints (bishop, pres. stake). Home: PO Box 8011 Reno NV 89507

FLETCHER, DOUGLAS BADEN, investment co. exec.; b. Pleasant Ridge, Mich., Mar. 25, 1925; s. Ernest H. and Gladys (Marthan) F.; B.A., Princeton, 1949; m. Sally Wittenberg, Sept. 9, 1950; children—David, Christopher, James, Jonathan. Security analyst Walston & Co., N.Y.C., 1949-53; mem. underwriting dept. Blyth & Co., Los Angeles, 1953-62; pres., dir. Shareholders Mgmt. Co., Los Angeles, 1962—, Harbor Fund, Inc., Los Angeles, 1962—, Enterprise Fund, Inc., Los Angeles, 1962—, Fletcher Fund, Inc., Los Angeles, 1966—; pres. Shreholders Capital Corp., 1968—. Served with AUS, 1943-46. Mem. Inst. Chartered Financial Analysts, Los Angeles Soc. Financial Analysts (pres. 1960-61). Club: Princeton of So. Cal. (pres. 1962-64). Home: San Marino CA 91108 Office: 1888 Century Park E Century City Los Angeles CA 90067

FLETCHER, EDWARD ABRAHAM, educator; b. Detroit, July 30, 1924; s. Morris and Lillian (Protes) F.; B.S., Wayne State U., 1948; Ph.D. (DuPont fellow), Purdue U., 1952; m. Roslyn Silber, June 15, 1948; children—Judith Ellen, Deborah Gail, Carolyn Ruth. Head propellant chemistry and flame mechanics sects. NASA, Cleve., 1952-59; asso. prof. U. Minn., Mpls., 1959-60, prof., 1960—; vis. scientist Byellorussian Acad. Scis., 1964; vis. Fulbright prof. U. Poitiers, 1968. Participant adv. group for aero. research and devel. NATO Confs., 1961. Served with USNR, 1943-46. Recipient NASA Spl. award, 1961; Outstanding Ski Patrolman of Wetern Region award Nat. Ski Patrol, 1969-70. Mem. Combustion Inst. (bd. advisers, sec. Central States sect. 1967—), Am. Chem. Soc., A.A.A.S., Sigma Xi. Editor: Isotopes, 1958-59. Home: 3909 Beard Av S Minneapolis MN 55410

FLETCHER, FERDINAND THUM, lawyer; b. San Diego, June 5, 1911; s. Ed and Mary (Batchelder) F.; student Stanford, 1929-31, 33-34; B.S., U. Ore., 1933; LL.B., Hastings Coll., 1935; m. Virginia P. English, Sept. 9, 1939; children—Ferdinand E., Robert C., Victoria S. Admitted to Cal. bar; asst. counsel San Francisco Select Sabbath Com., House of Congress Investigations, 1935- 36; practice of law, San Diego, 1936-37; asst. city pros., San Diego, 1937-38; partner Higgs, Jennings, Fletcher & Mack, 1939—. Dir. Bill Jack Sci. Instrument Co. Chmn. ho. of dels. Easter Seal Soc. Cripplied Children and Adults of Cal.; dir., vice chmn. ho. of dels. Nat. Easter Seal Soc. Crippled Children and Adults; chairman com. mgmt. San Diego Armed Services YMCA, 1959—; trustee Hastings Law Sch. Alumni Assn., Salk Inst. Biol. Studies, San Diego. Served to lt. (s.g.) USNR, 1943-46. Mem. San Diego Bar Assn. (past dir., past pres.). Episcopalian. Rotarian (pres. San Diego 1962-63). Home: 459 Tavara Pl San Diego CA 92106 Office: 2250 3d Av San Diego CA 92101

FLETCHER, FRANK UTLEY, lawyer; b. Sparta, N.C., Feb. 7, 1912; s. Alfred J. and Elizabeth (Utley) F.; student N.C. State Coll., 1927-29; LL.B. cum laude, Wake Forest Coll., 1932; postgrad. Duke, 1932-34; m. Elizabeth Dalrymple, 1935 (dec. 1955); children—Frank Utley, Alfred Dalrymple, Anne; m. 3d, Nelle Wood Crowell, Oct. 3, 1961. Admitted to N.C. Bar, 1933, D.C. bar, 1939; atty. FCC, 1934-39; asso. Spearman & Roberson, Washington, 1939-42, now sr. partner Fletcher, Heald, Rowell, Kenehan & Hildreth; pvt. practice, 1945-53. Co-owner radio sta. WARL, Arlington, Va., 1946-51. Chmn. communications industry com. Adv. Council on Fed. Reports; mem. planning council World Peace Through Law Center; mem. Bus. Adv. Council on Fed. Reports; chmn. Com. on Communications Industry. Served from 1st lt. to capt., ordnance dept. AUS, 1942-45. Mem. Nat. Assn. Broadcasters, Am., Fed., D.C. bar assns., Fed. Communications Bar Assn. (pres. 1960, exec. com. 1954-55), Am. Judicature Soc. Mason (32). Clubs: Variety, International, Congressional Country, Columbia Country; National Communications. Home: 8600 Fenway Dr Bethesda MD 20034 Office: 1225 Connecticut Av N W Washington DC 20036

FLETCHER, GILBERT HUNGERFORD, radiotherapist; b. Paris, France, Mar. 11, 1911; s. Walter Scott and Marie (Boudol) F.; B.A., U. Paris, 1929; B.A. in Engring., U. Louvain (Belgium), 1932; M.S. in Math., U. Brussels, 1935, M.D., 1941; m. Mary Critz, June 10, 1943; children—Walter Scott, Thomas. Rotating intern U. Brussels Hosp., 1939-41; intern obstetrics French Hosp., N.Y.C., 1942- 43; asst. resident radiology N.Y. Hosp., 1942-43, resident radiology, 1943-44; fellow radiotherapy Royal Cancer Hosp., London, Eng., Curie Found., Paris, France, 1947-48; head dept. radiotherapy M.D. Anderson Hosp., Houston, 1948—; prof. radiotherapy U. Tex. Grad. Sch. Biomed. Scis., Houston, 1965—, cons. radiotherapy Hermann, St. Joseph hosps., Baylor U. Coll. Medicine, Houston, Santa Rosa Med. Center, San Antonio; nat. cons. to surgeon gen. USAF, 1968—. Served from 1st lt. to capt. M.C., AUS, 1944-47. Diplomate Am. Bd. Radiology. Fellow Am. Coll. Radiology; mem. Inter-Am. Coll. Radiology, Radiol. Soc. N.Am., Am. Soc. Therapeutic Radiologists (pres. 197-68), Am. Radium Soc. (treas. 1959-61, pres. 1962-63, Janeway lectr. 1970), Am. Roentgen Ray Soc., Tex. Radiol. Soc., N.Y. Acad. Scis., A.M.A., Harris County Med. Soc., Royal Soc. Medicine London, French Soc. Radiotherapists Paris. Home: 2215 Dorrington St Houston TX 77025 Office: M D Anderson Hosp Houston TX 77025

FLETCHER, HARRIS FRANCIS, educator b. Ypsilanti, Mich., Oct. 23, 1892; s. Azro and Elizabeth (Lambie) F.; B.Pd., Mich. State Normal Coll., 1912; A.B., U. Mich., 1914, A.M., 1923, Ph.D., 1926; Litt.D., U. Ill., 1961, Olivet Coll., 1962; L.H.D., Eastern Mich. U., 1962; m. Dorothy Bacon; children—Mary Elizabeth, Dorothy Priscilla, Charlotte Anne. Tchr. in high sch., Wyandotte, Mich., 1912-13; supt. schs., Algonac, Mich., 1914-18; instr. rhetoric U. Mich., 1923-26; asst. prof. English, U. Ill., 1926-31, asso. prof., 1931-38, asso. dean Coll. Liberal Arts and Scis., 1931-38, prof., 1938—. Fellow A.A.A.S. Presbyn. Author: studies on Milton's works; facsimile and critical text edit. of Milton's Poetical Works, Vol. I, 1943, Vol. II, 1945, Vols. III, IV, 1948; The Intellectual Development of John Milton, Vol. I, 1956, Vol. II, 1961. Contbr. Jour. English and Germanic Philology, Studies in Philology, Modern Lang. Notes, etc. Home: 705 Indiana Av Urbana IL 61801

FLETCHER, HARVEY, coll. dean, physicist; b. Provo, Utah, Sept. 11, 1884; s. Charles E. and Elizabeth (Miller) F.; B.S., Brigham Young U., 1907; Ph.D., U. Chgo., 1911; D.S. (hon.), Columbia, 1935, Kenyon Coll., Stevens Inst., Case Sch., U. Utah, 1944, Brigham Young U.; m. Lorena Chipman, Sept. 9, 1908; children—Phyllis, Stephen Harvey, James Chipman, Robert Chipman, Harvey J., Paul C. Head dept. physics Brigham Young U., 1911-16, dir. research, 1952—, dean Coll. Phys. and Engring. Scis., 1953—; engring. staff research dept. Bell Telephone Labs., 1916-48, dir. phys. research, 1933-49; prof. elec. engring. Columbia, 1949-52. Recipient Louis Edward Levy medal for phys. measurements of audition, 1924, Gold medal Soc. Motion

Pictures Engrs., 1949; Gold medal Audio Engring. Soc., 1958; Founders award and medal I.E.E.E., 1967. Fellow Am. Phys. Soc. (pres. 1945), A.A.A.S. (v.p. 1937-38), Am. Inst. E.E.; mem. Am. Soc. Hard of Hearing (pres. 1929-30), Nat., Utah (pres. 1915-16) acads. scis., Acoustical Soc. Am. (pres. 1929-30; Gold medal 1957), Phi Beta Kappa, Sigma Xi; hon. mem. Am. Otological Soc. Author: Speech and Hearing, 1929; Speech and Hearing in Communications, 1952. Contbr. papers in field. Research on audition. Home: 1615 N Willow Lane Provo UT 84601

FLETCHER, JAMES CHIPMAN, govt. ofcl.; b. Millburn, N.J., June 5, 1919; s. Harvey and Lorena (Chipman) F.; A.B., Columbia, 1940; Ph.D., Cal. Inst. Tech., 1948; D.Sc., U. Utah, 1971; m. Fay Lee, Nov. 2, 1946; children—Virginia Lee, Mary Susan, James Stephen, Barbara Jo. Research physicist Navy Dept. Bur. Ordnance, 1940-41; spl. research asso. Cruft Lab., Harvard, 1941-42; instr. Princeton, 1942-45; teaching fellow Cal. Inst. Tech., 1945-48; instr. U. Cal. at Los Angeles, 1948-50; dir. theory and analysis lab. Hughes Aircraft Co., 1948-54; asso. dir. guided missile lab., dir. electronics guided missile research div., later in space tech. labs. Ramo-Wooldridge Corp., 1954-58; organizer, pres. Space Electronics Corp., 1958-60; organizer, pres. Space-Gen. Corp. subsidiary Aerojet-Gen. Corp., 1961-62, chmn. bd. subsidiary, 1962-64, v.p. systems Aerojet-Gen. Corp., 1962-64; pres. U. Utah, 1964-71; adminstr. NASA, Washington, 1971—. Mem. subcom. on stability and control NACA, 1950-54; chmn. ad hoc com. to rev. Skybolt Program, 1959; cons. Office Sec. Def., 1959-64; cons. to asst. sec. USAF, 1961-64, Arms and Control Disarmament Agy., 1962-64, Aerojet-Gen. and Space-Gen. Corps., 1960-64; cons., then mem. Pres.'s Sci. Adv. Com., 1958-70, mem. com. rev. minuteman Command and Control System, 1961; mem. command, control and intelligence com. Dept. Def., 1961-62; mem. Air Force Sci. Adv. Bd., 1963-67; summer study group arms control, Woods Hole, Mass., 1962; chmn. physics panel rev. com. NIH, 1962-64; mem. strategic weapons panel Pres.'s Sci. Adv. Com., 1959-61, command, control and intelligence panel, 1962-64, mil. aircraft panel, 1964-67, chmn. naval warfare panel, 1967-71; mem. Pres.'s Nat. Crime Commn., 1966. Trustee Aerospace Edn. Found. Fellow I.E.E.E.; mem. Am. Phys. Soc., Am. Inst. Aeros. and Astronautics, A.A.A.S., Nat. Space Club (bd. govs.), Nat. Acad. Engring., Assn. Western Univs. (chmn. exec. com. 1968-71), Sigma Xi. Club: Cosmos. Author classified papers, sci. papers, chpts. in books. Bd. editors Addison-Wesley Pub. Co., 1958-64. Home: 7721 Falstaff Rd McLean VA 22101 Office: 400 Maryland Av SW Washington DC 20546

FLETCHER, JAMES E., pub. co. exec.; b. Chgo., Oct. 4, 1921; s. Wallace and Gunnil (Gornson) F.; student Ill. Wesleyan U., 1940-41; B.S., Northwestern U., 1948; m. Margaret N. Kelley, Sept. 1, 1945; children—Barbara Ann (Mrs. E. Craig Oursler), James A., Michael W., Mark A., Patricia A. Staff auditor David Himmelblau & Co., Chgo., 1948-50; asst. to CHA audits and procedures Inland Steel Co., Chgo., 1950-52; controller Midwest Mortgage Co., Miami, Fla., 1952-53; with Field Enterprises Educational Corp., Chgo., 1953—, v.p., 1959—; pres. Field Enterprises, Inc., Chgo., 1970—; dir. Nat. Boulevard Bank of Chgo. Bd. dirs. The Ravinia Festival Assn., Southwest Suburban Cook County Mental Health Assn., The Howard V. Phalin Found. Grad. Study. Served with USAAF, 1942-46. Mem. Ill. Soc. C.P.A.'s, Am. Acctg. Assn., Am. Inst. Mgmt., Northwestern U. Alumni Assn. (dir. 1969-71), Ill. Wesleyan U. Alumni Assn., Phi Gamma Delta. Clubs: Northwestern Univ. (dir. 1967-69), Tavern, Chicago, Club 71, Skyline (Chgo.). Home: 5000 Lawn Av Western Springs IL 60558 Office: 401 N Wabash Av Chicago IL 60611

FLETCHER, MRS. JOHN GOULD, see Simon, Charlie May.

FLETCHER, JONATHAN MOSS, savs. and loan assn. exec.; b. Des Moines, Oct. 28, 1914; s. Clyde Beals and Jennie (Moss) F.; A.B., U. Ia., 1935; postgrad. Drake U., 1937-38; m. Virginia Jane Votruba, Mar. 21, 1941; children—Gary Stephen, John Wise, Virginia Ann, Katherine Jean. With U.S. Dept. Agr., 1935-37; with Home Fed. Savs. & Loan Assn., Des Moines, 1937—, successively treas., sec. and treas., exec. v.p., sec. 1937-58, pres., 1958—, dir., 1938—; treas., dir. Fletcher Corp., 1956—, pres., 1963—; dir. Fed. Home Loan Bank Des Moines, 1964-67, vice chmn., 1967; dir. Ia. Bus. Devel. Credit Corp., Ia. Kemper Mut. Ins. Co., FHLB of Des Moines. Mem. savs. and loan adv. com to U.S. sec. of treasury, 1966—. Gen. chmn. United Campaign, 1958. Mem. Greater Des Moines Com., 1957—, pres., 1968; mem. City Planning and Zoning Commn., Des Moines, 1950-59, chmn., 1957. Treas. Ia. Central Com. Rep. Party, 1955-57. Bd. control athletics U. Ia., 1960-66; bd. trustees Drake U. Served to capt. AUS and USAAF, 1942-45. Recipient Des Moines Tribune Community award, 1959. Savs. and Loan Found. (trustee 1954-56), U.S. (exec. com. 1956-58) Mem. Ia. (pres. 1950), savs. and loan leagues Des Moines C. of C. (pres. 1954, bd. dirs. 1952—); Nat. Planning Assn. (nat. council 1970—), Delta Upsilon. Conglist. Clubs: Rotary, Des Moines; Wakonda, Prairie; Bradenton (Fla.) Country; University Athletic (Iowa City). Home: 701 54th St Des Moines IA 50312 Office: 601 Grand Av Des Moines IA 50307

FLETCHER, JOSEPH FRANCIS, III, educator, clergyman; b. Newark, Apr. 10, 1905; s. Joseph Francis, II and Julia (Davis) F.; A.B., W.Va. U., 1925; B.D., Berkeley Divinity Sch., 1929, D.D., 1969; student Grad. Sch., Yale, 1930, London U., 1930-32; S.T.D., Kenyon Coll., 1939; D.Litt., Ohio Wesleyan U. Delaware, m. Forrest Hatfield, Sept. 5, 1928; children—Joseph Francis, Jane Elizabeth. Ordained to ministry of P.E. Ch., 1929; positions with several chs., 1929-39; dean, Grad. Sch. of Applied Religion, Cin., 1936-44; lectr. in labor history and Bibl. lit., U. Cin., 1940-44; prof. pastoral theology and Christian ethics, Episcopal Theol. Sch., Cambridge, Mass., 1944-70; vis. prof. med. ethics U. Va., Charlottesville, 1970—, lectr. Harvard Divinity Sch., 1964-65; supr. Episcopal summer tng. program in W.I., 1955; Lilly vis. prof. Internat. Christian U., Tokyo, Japan, 1963-64; St. Andrews U., 1966; vis. fellow Clare Coll., Cambridge U., Eng., 1967-67; dir. Musser Seminar, Harvard Bus. Sch. Dir. Japan Internat. Christian U., also Assn. Study Abortion, Ins. Pastoral Care. Mem. World Peace Council (Am. observer 1950), Soviet-Am. Friendship Soc., Am. Sociol. Soc., Planned Parenthood Fedn., Episcopal League for Social Action, Mass. Council of Chs. (mem. research and planning com.), Association of Professors of Social Ethnics (pres.), Cambridge Family Soc. (dir.), Human Betterment Assn. Am. (pres.), U.S. C. of C. Clubs: Faculty (Harvard); Twenty (Boston); Dartmouth House (London). Author: The Church and Industry, 1930; Christianity and Property, 1947; Morals and Medicine, 1954; Mission to Main Street, 1961; William Temple; A Theological Portrait, 1963; Situation Ethics, 1966; Moral Responsibility, 1967; (with H. Cox) Situation Ethics Debate, 1968; Hello Lovers, 1970. Contbr. to Schaff-Herzog Ency. of Religious Knowledge, 1955; Die Religion in Geschichte und Gegenwart, 1956; The Crisis in American Medicine. Asso. editor Anglican Theol. Rev., Jour. of Pastoral Care, Christendom (English), The Witness, The Churchman. Home: Morea Sprigg Lane Charlottesville VA 22903 Office: Med Sch U Va Charlottesville VA 22903

FLETCHER, KIM, savs. and loan exec.; b. Los Angeles, 1927; grad. Stanford, 1950. Pres., mgr. Home Fed. Savs. & Loan Assn., San Diego; dir. 1st Fed. Savs. & Loan Assn. Hollywood. Home: 3000 Sandy Lane Del Mar CA 92014 Office: 7th St and Broadway PO Box 2070 San Diego CA 92112*

FLETCHER, LLOYD, commr. U.S. Court Claims; b. Amarillo, Tex., Jan. 5, 1915; s. Lloyd and Florence (McKenzie) F.; B.B.A., U. Tex., 1936; J.D., George Washington U., 1939; m. Lola Slaight, Apr. 25, 1940; children—Diane, Bruce. Admitted to D.C. bar, 1940; pvt. practice, Washington, 1940-59; professorial lectr. law Am. U., 1946—; commr. U.S. Ct. Claims, Washington, 1960—. Served to lt. (j.g.) USCGR, World War II. Mem. Am., D.C., Fed. bar assns., The Barristers (Washington), Order of Coif, Phi Kappa Psi. Mason (Shriner). Contbr. articles legal jours. Home. 4851 Maury Lane Alexandria VA 22304 Office: U S Court Claims Washington DC 20543

FLETCHER, LOUIS DUBOIS, lawyer; b. Newburgh, N.Y., June 29, 1899; s. Louis DuBois and Clara Louise (Smith) F.; E.E., Rensselaer Poly. Inst., 1922; LL.B., George Washington U., 1925; m. Louise Ann Thomas, Sept. 27, 1927; children—Linda Louise, Louis DuBois. Asst. examiner U.S. Patent Office, 1922-25; admitted to N.Y. bar, 1928, Supreme Ct. U.S., 1938; asso. Darby & Darby, N.Y.C., 1925-70, mem., 1930-70, sr. partner, 1950-66. Dir. Westchester Heart Assn. Mem. Am. Inst. E.E., Am., N.Y. Patent law assns., Phi Delta Theta, Alpha Tau Omega. Home: 12 Rutland Rd Scarsdale NY 10583

FLETCHER, MAX ELLIS, educator; b. Preston, Ida., Aug. 23, 1921; s. Sam H. and Marian (Ellis) F.; B.A. magna cum laude, U. Wash., 1946; M.A., U. Ida., 1949; postgrad. London Sch. Econs., 1954-55; Ph.D., U. Wis., 1957; m. Ann Barrows, Dec. 14, 1954; children—Cody, Justin. With Equitable Life Assurance Soc., N.Y.C., Los Angeles, 1949-52; instr. econs. Marquette U., 1955-56; asst. prof. econs. Humboldt State Coll., 1957-58; asst. prof., prof. econs. U. Ida., Moscow, 1958—, chmn. dept. econs., 1968—. Served with USNR, 1939- 45, 47-48. Fulbright scholar, 1954-55, Ford Found. fellow, 1956-57. Mem. Am., Western econ. assns., Am. Assn. U. Profs., Econ. Hist. Assn., Assn. Evolutionary Econs., Phi Beta Kappa, Beta Gamma Sigma. Contbr. articles profl. jours. Home: Route 1 Viola ID 83872 Office: Dept Econ U Ida Moscow ID 83843

FLETCHER, NORMAN COLLINGS, architect; b. Providence, Dec. 8, 1917; s. Robert C. and Lily (Wilcock) F.; B.F.A. in Architecture, Yale, 1940; m. Jean Bodman, Sept. 23, 1944 (dec. Sept. 1965); children—Judith, Jon B., Jeremy B., Mollie H., Rebecca H., Katrina H.; stepchildren—Lucas B. Hoak, Damon O. Houk; m. 2d, Marjorie Taplin, Oct. 10, 1970. Designer Skidmore, Owings and Merrill, N.Y.C., 1943-44, Searinen, Swanson & Assos., Washington, Birmingham, Mich., 1944-46; prin. The Architects Collaborative Inc., Cambridge, Mass., 1946—. instr. architecture Grad. Sch. Design, Harvard, 1949-52; vis. critic Sch. Architecture, Mass. Inst. Tech., 1957-58, Sch. Architecture, Yale, 1956—, U. Tucman (Argentina), 1954—; mem. jury Higher Edn. Facilities Design Award Program, Dept. Health, Edn. Welfare; 1966; mem. com. Rotch Travelling Fellowship, 1964-66, mem. preliminary jury, 1969; mem. architecture com. Boston Arts Festival, 1955-57, Yale Arts Assn., 1965—, pres., 1970. Recipient numerous awards, including citation Progressive Architecture Design awards for Chem. Lab., Tufts U., Medford, Mass., 1963, for IBM fed. systems div., Gaithersburg, Md., 1964, 1st prize Nat. House competition, 1945, 1st prize Smith Coll. dormitory competition, 1946; honor award for YMCA, Roxbury, Mass., New Eng. regional council A.I.A., 1966, nat. honor award for dormitory and dining commons Clark U., Worcester, Mass., A.I.A., 1967, dormitory and dining commons complex 2, central Mass. A.I.A., 1970, for Worcester Found. for Exptl. Biology, Shrewsbury, central Mass. A.I.A., 1970; Merit award for Roxbury YMCA, HUD, 1968; Architecture and Allied Arts award Tau Sigma Delta, 1970; Alice Kimball English travelling fellow, 1940. Fellow A.I.A., mem. Nat. Acad. Design (asso. mem.), Boston Soc. Architects (pres. 1966-67 Mass. Assn. Architects (exec. com. 1963-68). Home: 36 Moon Hill Rd Lexington MA 02173 Office: 46 Brattle St Cambridge MA 02138

FLETCHER, PARIS, lawyer; b. Middlebury, Vt., June 19, 1903; s. John Albert and Sophia (Warner) F.; grad. Phillips Andover Acad., 1920; B.S., Middlebury Coll., 1924; LL.B., Harvard, 1927; m. J. Marion Stoddard, Apr. 18, 1936; children—Patricia Allen, Warner Stoddard, Allen Waring. Admitted to Mass. bar, 1927; partner Gage, Hamilton & June, Worcester, 1936-51, June, Fletcher & Whipple, 1952—. Home: 11 Monmouth Rd Worcester MA 01609 Office: 340 Main St Worcester MA 01608

FLETCHER, RALPH ANDREW, civil engr.; b. Westford, Mass., Nov. 24, 1895; s. Herbert E. and Carrie D. (Hill) F.; B.S., Mass. Inst. Tech., 1916; m. Priscilla Kennard, May 19, 1923 (div.); children—Cynthia (Mrs. Peter B. Robinson), Ralph Andrew, Hasbrouck (dec.), Emerson Kennard; m. 2d, Sibyl L. Baxter, Sept. 22, 1950; children—John Herbert, Samuel Hill, Rebecca Ann. Chmn. bd. dirs. H.E. Fletcher Co., granite prodn.; dir. Allied Concrete Co., Boston; treas. Lovejoy Granite Co., 1925—, Allied Minerals, Inc., 1942—; dir. Union Nat. Bank of Lowell, Mass. Served as lt., U.S.N.R.F., 1917-19. Mem. Am. Soc. Testing Materials, Am. Inst. Mining Engrs., Smaller Bus. Assn. N.E., Inc. Clubs: Yorick (Lowell, Mass.); Tennis and Racquet (Boston); Country (Brookline, Mass.); Santee. Office: West Chelmsford MA 01824

FLETCHER, RAYMOND RUSSWALD, Jr., airlines exec., lawyer; b. Schenectady, June 7, 1929; s. Raymond Russwald and Elsie (Hovemeyer) F.; B.Chem.Engring., Rensselaer Poly. Inst., 1949; LL.B., Harvard, 1956; m. Elsa Ellen Tillema, Dec. 20, 1949; children—Raymond Russwald III, Nicholas Henry, Pamela Louise, William Edward, Catherine Ann. Admitted to N.Y. bar, 1956; asso. atty. Chadbourne, Parke, Whiteside & Wolff, N.Y.C., 1956-63; with Trans World Airlines, Inc., 1963—, v.p., gen. counsel, 1969—. Served as aviator USN, 1949-53; Korea. Decorated Air medal. Mem. Am., N.Y. State bar assns., Assn. Bar City N.Y. Democrat. Presbyn. Home: RD 1 Mount Kisco NY 10549 Office: 605 3d Av New York City NY 10016

FLETCHER, ROBERT DAWSON, meteorologist; b. Lampacitos, Mexico, Feb. 11, 1912; s. Edmond McC. and Grace (Dawson), F.; B.S. in M.E., Cal. Inst. Tech., 1933, M.S. in M.E. (Aero), 1934, M.S. in Meteorology, Mass. Inst. Tech., 1935, D.Sc. in Meteorology, 1941; m. Elsie Walser, June 1, 1953; children—Robert Dawson, John E. Meteorologist Am. Airlines, Inc., 1935-39; instr. meteorology U. Cal. at Los Angeles, 1940- 42; meteorologist U.S. Weather Bur., 1940-50, supervising forecaster, 1941-46, chief hydrometeorol. sect., 1946-50; with USAF Air Weather Service, 1950—, cons., 1950-52, dir. sci. services, 1952-64, dir. of aerospace scis., 1964—, Tech. cons. OSRD, 1944, USAAF in CBI and Caribbean, 1944-45; U.S. del. World Meteorological Orgn. (UN), 1952—; USAF and NRC del., Manila, 1952, Bangkok, 1957, adv. group aero. research and devel. NATO Conf. Polar Meteorology, Oslo, Norway, 1956, Australian Conf. Tropical Storms, Brisbane, 1956; mem. meteorology panel U.S. Nat. Com. on Internat. Geophys. Year, 1955-64; liaison rep. com. on high altitude rocket and balloon research Nat. Acad. Scis., 1963- -, mem. panel on edn., 1963-. Pres. Bannockburn (Md.) Citizens Assn., 1951-52. Recipient of USAF decoration for exceptional civilian service, 1962; Robert M. Losey award Am. Inst. Aeronautics and Astronautics, 1969; Charles Franklin Brooks award Am. Meteorol. Soc., 1970. Fellow Am. Meteorol. Soc. (pres. 1956-57); asso. fellow Am. Inst. Aeros. and Astronautics (chmn. tech. com. on atmospheric environment 1964-65); mem. Am. Geophys. Union, Royal Meteorol. Soc., Sigma Xi. Contbr. articles profl. jours. Home: 135 Roger Dr Lebanon IL 62254 Office: Scott AFB IL 62225

FLETCHER, ROBERT IRVING, financial cons.; b. Malone, N.Y., Feb. 27, 1899; s. Ernest Tilden and Mary Helene (Conley) F.; B.S., U. Pa., 1921; m. Gladys Caroline Ruhberg, Nov. 24, 1928; 1 dau., Marjorie. Staff accountant Price Waterhouse & Co., N.Y.C., 1924-28; comptroller Central Hudson Gas & Elec. Corp., Poughkeepsie, N.Y., 1929-33, Long Island (N.Y.) Lighting Co., 1934-36; mng. accountant R.G. Rankin & Co., N.Y. City, 1937-38; comptroller Newport News (Va.) Shipbldg. and Dry Dock Co., 1939-53, v.p., 1947-53, financial v.p., 1953-66, dir.; former dir., comptroller Newport News Shipbldg. Co. Found., comptroller Newport News Shipbldg. & Dry Co. Pension Fund. Dir. Va. and Peninsula Heart Assns. C.P.A., N.Y., 1928. Served in S.A.T.C., U. of Pa., 1918. Fellow Va. Soc. Pub. Accountants; mem. Inst. Accountants, Financial Execs. Inst., N.Y. Soc. C.P.A.'s, Am. Inst. C.P.A.'s. Clubs: U. Pa. (N.Y.C.); James River Country (Newport News). Home: 21 Douglas Dr Newport News VA 23601 Office: PO Box 1786 9296 Warwick Blvd Newport News VA 23601

FLETCHER, ROBERT P., Jr., fisheries exec.; b. Wilmington, Del., Dec. 7, 1898; s. Robert P. and Mary M. (Cox) F.; ed. Friends School, Wilmington, Del.; Peekskill (N.Y.) Mil. Acad.; B.S. in E.E., U. of Delaware, 1922; m. Elizabeth E. Hastings, 1924; children—Robert P., Daniel H., James C. Purchasing agent, E. I. du Pont de Nemours and Co., 1923-25; pres., Interstate Amiesite Co., 1925-33; chmn. Booth Fisheries Corp. div. Consol. Foods Corp., Chgo., also dir., exec. and finance coms. parent co.; pres. Booth Fisheries Canadian Co., Ltd., and also Booth Fisheries de Mexico S.A. de C.V., Booth Fisheries de Nicaragua S.A.; pres. and dir. Booth Cold Storage Co., Mo.; dir. Mid Am. National Bank. MacLean Fogg Lock Nut Co., Szabo Food Service Co. Mem. Sigma Nu. Clubs: Skokie Country, Chicago, Chicago Curling (Chgo.). Home: 55O South Av Glencoe IL 60022 Office: 2 Riverside Plaza Chicago IL 60606

FLETCHER, STEPHEN HARVEY, utilities exec.; b. Provo, Utah, Nov. 20, 1911; s. Harvey and Lorena (Chipman) F.; student Brigham Young U., 1928-30; A.B., Columbia, 1932, LL.B., 1935; m. Dorothy Lillian Roberts, June 5, 1937; children—Elizabeth Jean, William Stephen, Richard Curtis. Admitted to N.Y. bar, 1936, D.C., 1951; atty. Am. Tel. & Tel. Co., 1935-40, 45-49; atty. N.Y. Telephone Co., 1940-45, asst. gen. atty., 1949, gen. atty., 1949-51; gen. counsel Chesapeake & Potomac Telephone Co. of Va., Washington, Md., and W.Va., 1951-57, v.p., 1955-57; gen. atty. Am. Tel. & Tel. Co., 1958—; v.p., dir., gen. counsel Western Electric Co., Inc., 1963—; dir. Teletype Corp. Mem. N.Y. Lawyers Club, Am. (chmn. pub. utility sect. 1961-62), N.Y. State, D.C. bar assns., Assn. Gen. Counsel, Am. Law Inst., Am. Soc. Internat. Law, Am. Judicature Soc., Acad. Polit. Sci., Newcomen Soc. N.Am. Clubs: Columbia Country (Chevy Chase, Md.); Metropolitan (Washington); Canoe Brook Country. Home: 7 Byron Rd Short Hills NJ 07078 Office: 195 Broadway New York City NY 10007

FLETCHER, STEWART GAILEY, steel co. exec.; b. Wilkinsburg, Pa., Jan. 20, 1919; s. C.T. and Ruth (Gailey) F.; B.S., Carnegie Inst. Tech., 1938; Sc.D., Mass. Inst. Tech., 1943; m. Helen M. Bennett, June 27, 1942; children—Fred B., Nancy G., Sherrill A., Stewart Gailey. Research asso. Mass. Inst. Tech., 1942-45; chief metallurgist Latrobe Steel Co. (Pa.), 1947-58, v.p., tech. dir. 1958—. Mem. NRC, 1967—. Fellow Am. Soc. Metals (pres. 1965-66; Howe medal 1945, 49); mem. Am. Iron and Steel Inst., Am. Inst. Mining, Metall. and Petroleum Engrs., Am. Soc. Testing Materials, Iron and Steel Inst. (London), Soc. Automotive Engrs., Pa. Material Adv. Panel. Presbyn. (elder). Home: 7 Saxman Dr Latrobe PA 15650

FLETCHER, THOMAS WILLIAM, city ofcl.; b. Portland, Ore., Mar. 1, 1924; s. Irving A. and Florence (Cooper) F.; B.S. in Bus. Adminstrn., U. Cal. at Berkeley, 1951; m. Margerie Frances Muller, Dec. 27, 1945; children—Thomas William, Heidi, Dean. Asst. to city mgr., San Leandro, Cal., 1951-52; city adminstr., Davis, Cal., 1952-55; asst. to city mgr., San Diego, 1955-61, city mgr., 1961-66; pres. Franchise Corp., 1966-67; dep. asst. sec. Dept. Housing and Urban Devel., 1967; dep. mayor of Washington, 1967-69, city mgr. San Jose, Cal., 1969—. Mem. Little Hoover Commn. for Washington, 1970-71. Vice pres. San Diego County council Boy Scouts Am., 1959—; mem. adv. bd. San Jose State Coll. Bd. dirs. San Diego YMCA, 1961-64, San Jose YMCA. Served with AUS, 1943-46. Named Outstanding Young Man of Year in San Diego, San Diego Jr. C. of C., 1960. Mem. League Cal. Cities (pres. city mgrs. dept. 1965-66, chmn. electronic data processing com. 1965-67), Western Govt. Research Assn. (pres. 1963-64), Am. Soc. Pub. Adminstrn. (pres. San Diego 1960-61), Internat. City Mgrs. Assn., Nat. League Cities (chmn. nat. joint com. uniform traffic control devices 1965-66), Nat. Municipal League (mem. council), Inst. Local Self Govt., Nat. Acad. Pub. Adminstrn. Kiwanian, Rotarian. Contbr. articles in field. Home: 1595 Chambers Dr San Jose CA 95118 Office: City Hall 801 N 1st St San Jose CA 9511O

FLETCHER, WALTER D., lawyer; b. Heuvelton, N.Y., Apr. 28, 1896; s. Everett H. and Sarah (Wheater) F.; A.B., Columbia, 1918, M.A., 1922, LL.B., 1922, LL.D., 1965; LL.D., Alfred Univ., 1957; m. Eleanor Langley. Admitted to N.Y. bar, 1922, and since practiced in N.Y. City; mem. firm Davis Polk & Wardwell and predecessor firms; dep. atty. gen. N.Y., 1923; dir., mem. exec. com. City Investing Co.; chmn. bd., dir. Torsion Balance Co.; dir. U.P. R.R., Ore. Short Line R.R. Co., Los Angeles & Salt Lake R.R. Co., Merchant-Sterling Corp., Orama Securities Corp., Ore.-Wash. R.R. & Navigation Co., Sterling Iron & Ry. Co. Volunteer spl. counsel Am. Nat. Red Cross, counsel Greater N.Y. A.R.C. Trustee emeritus Columbia U.; trustee St. John's Guild City of N.Y. (hon.), N.Y. Racing Assn.; gov. Fed. Hall Meml. Assos., Inc.; pres., dir., mem. Dom Mocquereau Found. Served as pilot AC USNRF, World War I. Mem. Am., N.Y. bar assns., N.Y. County Lawyers Assn., Bar Assn. City N.Y. Clubs: Links, Turf and Field, Downtown Assn., Union. Home: 150 E 69th St New York City, NY 10021. also November Hill Farm 1108 Charlottesville VA 22902 Office: 1 Chase Manhattan Plaza New York City NY 10005

FLETCHER, WENDELL S., aviation corp. exec.; b. Otego, Ill., 1899; Santa Barbara State Coll., 1939. Pres. Fletcher Aircraft Co., San Marino, Cal. Mason (Shriner). Home: San Marino CA 91108

FLEUELLING, LEWIS EDWARD, automobile equipment mfg. co. exec.; b. St. Thomas, Ont., Can., Aug. 24, 1920 (parents Am. citizens); s. James Arthur and Elsie (Bate) F.; B.S. in Engring., U. Mich., 1947; m. Joyce Corbeille, Aug. 31, 1944; children—Anne, Paul, Nancy. Project engr. Monroe Auto Equipment Co. (Mich.), 1947-49, asst. to sales mgr. mfrs. sales, 1949-51, sales mgr. mfrs. sales, 1951-64, v.p., gen. mgr., dir., 1964—; dir. Monroe-Acme Ltd., Toronto, Ont. Pres., Monroe County United Fund, 1956. Served with USAAF, 1942-45. Decorated D.F.C., Air medal with three oak leaf clusters. Mem. Soc. Automotive Engrs., Engring. Soc. Detroit, Automotive Old Timers. Club: Monroe Golf and Country (pres. 1961). Home: 225 Maywood Av Monroe MI 48161 Office: 1426 E 1st St Monroe MI 48161

FLEWELLEN, WILLIAM CRAWFORD, Jr., univ. dean; b. Eufaula, Ala., Aug. 31, 1918; s. William Crawford and Lena Kendrick (Hurt) F.; B.S., U. Ala., 1940, M.S., 1947; Ph.D., Columbia, 1956; m. Tommie Sue Kendrick, Aug. 31, 1941; children—Susan, Mary Jane. Asst. prof., prof. accounting U. Ala., 1946-61; prof. accounting, dean Coll. Bus. and Industry, Miss. State U., 1961-68; prof. accounting, dean Coll. Bus. Adminstrn., U. Ga., Athens, 1968—. Dir. Found. Growth Stock Fund, Inc., Continental Mut. Investment Fund Inc. Served to maj. USAAF, 1942-46; lt. col. Res. Recipient Algernon Sidney Sullivan award U. Ala., 1961. Mem. Am. Accounting Assn., Nat. Assn. Accountants (chpt. pres. 1965-66), Am. Assn. Collegiate Schs. Bus. (chmn. com. on cooperation with collegiate jr. colls. 1964-71, bd. dirs. 1971—), Accounting Careers Council (nat. chmn. 1965-66), So. Bus. Adminstrn. Assn. (pres. 1966-67), Financial Execs. Inst. (nat. coms. edn. and taxation 1964-68), Delta Sigma Pi, Beta Alpha Psi, Omicron Delta Kappa, Blue Key, Beta Gamma Sigma, Phi Kappa Phi. Home: 140 Mal Bay Rd Athens GA 30601

FLEWELLING, RALPH CARLIN, architect; b. St. Louis, Mich., May 4, 1894; s. Ralph Tyler and Jennie (Carlin) F.; grad. Cambridge Latin Sch., 1912; B.S., Wesleyan U., 1916; postgrad. Mass. Inst. Tech., 1916-17; m. Katherine B. Agard, Aug. 10, 1951; 1 son, Ralph Hunter. With various archtl. offices, Los Angeles, 1920-25; practicing architect, Cal., 1926—; chmn. bd. dirs. Flewelling & Moody, Los Angeles, 1962—; pres. Flewelling Assos.; works include Mudd Hall of Philosophy, Fisher Gallery of Fine Arts and Lab. Med. Research, all of U.So. Cal., Central Engring. Bldg. of Jet. Porpulsion Lab. and Millikan Meml. Library, both of Cal. Inst. Tech., 1st Meth. Ch. of Glendale, Mudd Meml. Library of Claremont Colls. Mem. Emerald Bay Archtl. Bd., 1932-41, Pasadena City Planning Commn., 1965-69. Mem. Palos Verdes Art Jury, 1935-42. Served from 2d lt. to capt. inf., U.S. Army, 1917-19. Recipient House Beautiful prize, 1930, 33, Better Homes in Am. prize, 1933, 35. Fellow A.I.A. (pres. So. Cal. chpt. 1937-38); mem. Am. Soc. Mil. Engrs., Precast Concrete Inst. Clubs: Los Angeles University, Annandale Golf (Pasadena), DeAnza Desert Country (Borrego Springs, Cal.). Home: 855 Holly Vista Dr Pasadena CA 91105 Office: 766 Colorado Blvd Los Angeles CA 90041

FLEXNER, JAMES THOMAS, author; b. N.Y.C., Jan. 13, 1908; s. Simon and Helen (Thomas) F.; grad. Lincoln Sch. of Tchrs. Coll., Columbia, 1925; B.S. magna cum laude, Harvard Coll., 1929; m. Beatrice Hudson, 1950; 1 dau., Helen Hudson. Reporter, N.Y. Herald Tribune, 1929-31; exec. sec. Noise Abatement Commn., N.Y.C. Dept. of Health, 1931-32; Guggenheim fellow, 1953. Cons. Colonial Williamsburg, 1956-57; adv. com. The Papers of George Washington. Recipient Library of Congress grant-in-aid for studies history of Am. civilization, 1945; Life in America Prize, 1946; Benjamin Franklin fellow Royal Soc. Arts. Fellow Soc. Am. Historians (exec. bd.); mem. P.E.N. (pres. 1954-55, hon. v.p. 1963-66), Phi Beta Kappa. Clubs: Century, Coffee House. Author: several books including Doctors on Horseback: Pioneers of American Medicine, 1937; The Pocket History of American Painting, 1950; The Traitor and the Spy, 1953; American Painting: The Light of Distant Skies, 1954; Treason, 1780 (TV drama), 1954; Gilbert Stuart, 1955; Mohawk Baronet: Sir William Johnson of N.Y., 1959; That Wilder Image: The Painting of America's Native School from Thomas Cole to Winslow Homer, 1962 (awarded Parkman prize); George Washington: The Forge of Experience, 1732-1775, 1965; The World of Winslow Homer, 1966; America's Old Masters, rev. edit., 1967; George Washington in the American Revolution, 1968; George Washington and the New Nation, 1970; Ninteenth Century American Painting, 1970. Contbr. to mags. and newspapers. Lectr. on history of Am. art and civilization. Address: 530 E 86th St New York City NY 10028

FLEXNER, LOUIS BARKHOUSE, scientist, educator; b. Louisville, Jan. 7, 1902; s. Washington and Ida (Barkhouse) F.; B.S., U. Chgo., 1923; M.D., Johns Hopkins, 1927; m. Josefa Barba Gosé, Aug. 23, 1937. Fellow medicine Johns Hopkins Hosp., 1928-29; resident physician U. Chgo. Clinics, 1929-30; instr. and asso. anatomy Johns Hopkins Med. Sch., 1930-39; with dept. physiology Cambridge (Eng.) U., 1933-34; staff mem. dept. embryology Carnegie Instn. Washington, 1939-51, research asso., 1951—; prof. anatomy Sch. Med. U. Pa., 1951—, chmn. dept., 1951-67, dir. Inst. Neurol. Scis., 1953-66. Sci. adv. bds. USPHS, United Cerebral Palsy, Nat. Council to Combat Blindness, Nat. Paraplegic Soc., NRC, Nat. Found. Mem. Am. Assn. Anatomists, Nat. Acad. Scis., Am. Physiol. Soc., Am. Soc. Biol. Chemists, Nat. Acad. Arts and Scis. Contbr. profl. jours. Home: 4631 Pine St Philadelphia, PA 19143.

FLEXNER, WILLIAM WELCH, educator, mathematician; b. N.Y.C., Oct. 5, 1904; s. Simon and Helen (Thomas) F.; B.S., Harvard, 1926; Ph.D., Princeton, 1930; m. Elizabeth Anne Wrey, Oct. 11, 1946. Research and teaching asst. Princeton, 1929-31; lectr. Bryn Mawr Coll., 1931-33; asst., then asso. prof. Cornell U., 1934-48; with Statis Office, UN 1948-65, asst. dir., 1963-65; mem. faculty Cooper Union Sch. Engring. and Sci., 1965-70, prof. math., 1969-70, acting head dept., 1969; retired, 1971. With UNRRA, 1944-46, European Central Inland Transp. Orgn., 1946-47; cons. President's Com. Fgn. Aid, 1948. Mem. Am. Math. Soc., Am. Statis. Assn., Am. Assn. U. Profs., London math. Soc. Author papers in field. Address: 9 Paultons St London SW 3 England

FLICK, CYRUS BRUCE, cement co. exec.; b. Wheeling, W.Va., Dec. 5, 1899; s. Cyrus P. and Alice (Alger) F.; B.S.C., U. Cal., 1922; m. Elizabeth Wiltshire, Mar. 22, 1926; children—Alice (Mrs. Alice Ahmed), Elizabeth (Mrs. Howard L. Swinehart). Vice pres., treas., dir. Pacific Portland Cement Co., San Francisco, 1946-51; treas. Ideal Basic Industries, Inc., Denver, 1952- 56, sec.-treas., dir., 1956-64, v.p. finance, dir., 1964-68; v.p. finance Ideal Basic Industries, Inc., 1968-70, vice chmn. bd., treas., 1970—; dir. Am. Crystal Sugar Co. Trustee Boettcher Found. C.P.A., Cal. Mem. Kappa Alpha, Beta Gamma Sigma, Beta Alpha Psi. Episcopalian. Home: 155 Marion St Denver, CO 80218. Office: 821 17th St Denver CO 80202

FLICK, JOHN EDMOND, newspaper exec.; b. Franklin, Pa., Mar. 14, 1922; s. Edmond Leroy and Mary M. (Weaver) F.; student U. Pa., 1945; LL.B., Northwestern U., 1948; m. Lois Anna Lange, Apr. 20, 1946; children—Gregory Allan, Scott Edmond, Lynn Ellen, Ann Elizabeth. Commd. 1st lt. Judge Adv. Gen. Corps, U.S. Army, 1950, advanced through grades to lt. col. Res., 1968; res. active duty, 1963; faculty U.S. Mil. Acad., 1954-57; instr. Judge Adv. Gen. Sch., U. Va.; admitted to Ill. bar, 1948, Cal. bar, 1971; counsel, dir. contracts Litton Industries, Beverly Hills, Cal., 1963-67; sr. v.p., sec., gen. counsel, dir. Bangor Punta Corp., 1967-69; sr. v.p., sec., dir. Cosmodyne Corp., 1970; v.p., sec., gen. counsel Times Mirror Co., Los Angeles, 1970—; dir. Piper Aircraft. Recipient Am. Bar Assn. Academic award, 1961. Mem. Am., Fed., Ill. bar assns., State Bar Cal. Home: 23680 Park Sevilla Calabasas Park CA 91302 Office: Times Mirror Sq Los Angeles CA 90053

FLICK, SOL EDWARD, watch co. exec., lawyer; b. N.Y.C., May 4, 1915; s. Joseph and Anna (Mednick) F.; B.A., Bklyn. Coll., 1937; LL.B., St. Lawrence U., 1939; m. Stella Hurwitz, Jan. 14, 1940; children—Susan, Jonathan. Admitted to N.Y. bar, 1941; practice in N.Y.C., 1941—; sec. Bulova Watch Co., Inc., 1958-63, dir., 1963—, exec. v.p., 1964—; sec. Bulova Watch Co. Ltd. (Can.), 1959—, also dir.; sec. Bulova Internat., Ltd., 1960—, vice chmn., 1963—, dir., 1960—; sec., dir. Bulova U.K., Ltd., 1963—; exec. v.p., dir. Atlantic Time Products Corp., (Am. Virgin Islands), 1965—; v.p., dir. Chelsea Nat. Bank, N.Y.C.; dir. Bulova Watch S.P.A. (Italy), Bulova Toyo Corp., Taiwan, Bulova de Mexico S.A. de C.V., Bulova-Citizen Co., Ltd., Japan, Manufacture des Montres Universal Perret Freres S.A. (Switzerland) dir. exec. v.p. Pacific Time Corp., Am. Samoa. Chmn. scholarship com. Bklyn. Coll., 1963-64. Sec. J. Bulova Sch. Watchmaking, 1958-64, trustee, 1960—; bd. dirs. Bulova Watch Co. Found., 1963—, also sec., asst. treas.; bd. dirs. Booth Meml. Hosp., N.Y.C. Mem. Am. Bar Assn. Clubs: Nat. Lawyers (Washington); Twenty-Four Karat (N.Y.C.). Home: 55 Percheron Lane Roslyn Heights NY 11577 Office: 630 Fifth Av New York City NY 10020

FLICKINGER, GLENN WHITWELL, food distbg. co. exec.; b. Buffalo, June 25, 1902; s. Smith M. and Louise (Nassal) F.; A.B., Harvard, 1923; m. Beatrice Awdry Griffith, Oct. 4, 1930; children—Thomas Radcliffe, William Smith. With S. M. Flickinger Co. Inc., Buffalo, 1923—, exec. v.p., treas., 1939-45, mem. exec. com., 1945-61, chmn. exec. com., 1961-65, chmn. bd., mem. exec. com., 1965-71, chmn. emeritus, 1971—, also dir. Bd. dirs. mem. exec. com. Buffalo Philharmonic Orch. Mem. Cult of White Buffalo. Clubs: Buffalo, Buffalo Country, Saturn, Midday, Harvard (Buffalo). Home: 144 Middlesex Rd Buffalo NY 14216 Office: 45 Azalea Dr Buffalo NY 14225

FLICKINGER, THOMAS L., hosp. adminstr.; b. Carroll, Ia., Apr. 22, 1939; s. Leslie Winfred and Evelyn (Hanson) F.; B.B.A., U. Ia., 1961, M.A., 1963; m. Marjorie Ellen Madison, Apr. 19, 1970. Adminstrv. asst. Presbyn.-St. Luke's Hosp., Chgo., 1963-64; asst. adminstr. 1 Creighton Meml. St. Joseph Hosp., Omaha, 1964-66, asso. dir., 1966-68, adminstr., 1968—. Mem. Omaha Hosp. Assn. (pres. 1971), Am. Coll. Hosp. Adminstrs., Phi Kappa Psi. Home: 311 S Happy Hollow Blvd Omaha NB 68132 Office: 2305 S 10th St Omaha NB 68108

FLIEGEL, FREDERICK CHRISTIAN, educator; b. Edmonton, Alta., Can., Apr. 3, 1925; s. John Carl and Ruth Friedeborg (Aastrup) F.; came to U.S., 1928, naturalized, 1935; student Moravian Coll., 1942-43; B.A., U. Wis., 1949, M.A., 1952, Ph.D., 1955; m. Thellyn Ruth Haller, Aug. 25, 1955; children—Frederick M., Ruth E., David C., Johanna C. Asst. prof. to asso. prof. Pa. State U., 1955-65; asso. prof. Mich. State U., 1966-67; prof. sociology U. Ill., 1968—, head dept., 1970—; vis. prof. U. Wis., summer 1963. Served with USMC, 1943-46. Fellow Am. Sociol. Assn.; mem. Rural, Midwest sociol. socs., A.A.A.S., Am. Assn. Univ. Profs. Author: (with Roy, Sen and Kivlin) Agricultural Innovations in Indian Villages, 1968, Agricultural Innovation Among Indian Farmers, 1968, Communication in India: Experiments in Introducing Change, 1968. Editor of Rural Sociology, 1970-72. Home: 606 W Church St Champaign IL 61820 Office: Lincoln Hall Univ Illinois Urbana IL 61820

FLIEGER, HOWARD WENTWORTH, editor; b. Denver, Oct. 11, 1909; s. Sterling N. and Florence (Milliken) F.; student pub. schs.; m. Dorothy Kathryn James, Apr. 7, 1927; children—Howard Wentworth, Kenneth Hugh. Reporter, city editor Shawnee (Okla.) Morning News, 1929-33; with A.P.; St. Louis, 1933-35, night news editor, Kansas City, Mo., 1935-37, bur. chief, Jefferson City, 1937-43, White House Corr., Washington, 1943-45; mng. editor World Report, Washington, 1945-48; directing editor world staff U.S. News and World Report, 1948-58, asst. exec. editor, 1958- 65, asso. exec. editor, 1965-69, exec. editor, 1969—, Member of the White House Corrs. Assn. Clubs: Nat. Press, F. Street (Washington). Home: 6818 Selkirk Dr Bethesda MD 20034 Office: US News and World Report Washington DC 20407

FLIEGERS, SERGE, fgn. corr.; b. Sept. 10, 1921; S. Peter Fliegers. Washington Corr. Reuters; chief regional rep. UN Agy. for Middle East, Africa; radio commentator WWDC, Washington; contbr. editor American Mercury; editor Inter-Continental Press; Rome corr. Internat. News Service, spl. corr. Middle East and Mediterranean, chief International News Service Bureau, Moscow; now European bureau chief Hearst Newspapers, and chief European correspondent MBS. Clubs: Harvard, Overseas Press (N.Y.C.); Harvard (Boston). Home: Harvard Club New York City Office: care Press Wireless Rue Edouard VII Paris 9e France

FLIEGLER, LOUIS AARON, educator; b. N.Y.C., Sept. 3, 1917; s. Philip and Pearl (Spodek) F.; B.B.A., Coll. City N.Y., 1945; M.A., N.Y. U., 1947, Ph.D., 1954; m. Dorothy Scherr, June 29, 1945; children—Gail, Susan. Tchr., sch. psychologist San Francisco pub. schs., 1947-53; instr. psychology and edn. U. Wyo., also Wyo. Community Coll., 1954; research psychologist U. Colo. Med. Center, 1954-55; mem. faculty U. Denver, 1955-66, prof., coordinator spl. edn., 1960-66; prof., chmn. spl. edn. Kent (O.) State U., 1966—. Adv. bd. Montgomery Inst., Akron, O., 1966—. Served with AUS, 1946-47. Recipient merit award service spl. edn. Colo., 1966. Mem. Am. Edn. Research Assn., Am. Psychol. Assn., Am. Assn. Mental Deficiency, N.E.A., Council Exceptional Children (pres. div. tchr. edn. 1965-66), Assn. Gifted (pres. 1966-67), Phi Delta Kappa. Editor: Curriculum Planning for the Gifted, 1961. Home: 1827 Kingsley Av Akron OH 44313 Office: Kent State U Kent OH 44240

FLINCHUM, JAMES M., Jr., newspaper editor; b. Shawnee, Okla., Nov. 5, 1916; s. James M. and Frances (Shawver) F.; student U. Okla., 1939; m. Nancy Reynolds, Mar. 17, 1948; children—Nancy, Suzy. Successively staff corr., bur. mgr., Mountain States news editor, bus. rep., U.P.I., 1939-61; editor Wyo. State Tribune, Cheyenne 1961—. Wyo. civilian aide to sec. of army. Served with AUS, 1942-45. Decorated Bronze Star. Republican. Rotarian. Home: 1627 Maple Ct Cheyenne WY 82001 Office: 110 E 17th St Cheyenne WY 82001

FLINDT, FLEMMING OLE, Danish ballet dancer; b. Sept. 30, 1936; ed. Royal Danish Ballet Sch. Salet dancer, 1955—; solo dancer Royal Theatre, Copenhagen, Denmark, 1957-60; dancer Etoile Theatre Nat. de l'Opera, Paris, France, 1960—; dir. Royal Danish Ballet, Copenhagen, 1965—. Guest artist Royal Ballet Covent Garden, 1963, Bolshoi Theatre, Moscow, Opera, Vienna, Opera, Rome; guest choreographer Met. Opera House, N.Y.C., La Scala, Milan, Italy, 1965, Western Theatre Ballet, 1967, 68, City Center Joffrey Ballet, 1968, Nat. Ballet, Washington, 1968; choreographed La Lecon (Ionesco) (Grand Prix Italia), 1963. Le Jeune Homme a Marier (Ionesco), 1964, The Three Musketeers, 1966, the Miraculous Mandarin, 1967, Tango Chikane, Sacre du Printemps, 1968, La Triomphe de la Mort (Ionesco), 1971. Decorated knight Order of Dannebrog (Denmark). Address: Bulowsvej 26 Copenhagen Denmark

FLINK, EDMUND BERNEY, physician, educator; b. Isanti, Minn., Jan. 27, 1914; s. John Leonard and Huldah (Swenson) F.; M.B., U. Minn., 1937, M.D., 1938, Ph.D., 1945; m. Marian Richard, June 12, 1940; children—Charles, Alice, James, Paul. Intern, teaching fellow U. Minn., 1937-42, instr., 1942-43, asst. prof., 1943-50, asso. prof., 1950-57, prof. medicine, 1957-60; research asst. biol. chemistry dept. Harvard Med. Sch., 1948-49; chief med. service Mpls. VA Hosp., 1952-60; vis. prof. Seoul Nat. U., Korea, 1957-58; prof. medicine, chmn. dept. W.Va. U. Med. Sch., 1960—. Commonwealth Fund fellow, 1948-49. Mem. Am. Soc. Clin. Investigation, A.C.P., Endocrine Soc., Central Soc. Clin. Research, A.M.A., Assn. Am. Physicians, Soc. Exptl. Biology and Medicine, Sigma Xi, Alpha Omega Alpha. Home: 303 Sylvan Pl Morgantown WV 26505

FLINK, SALOMON J., economist; b. Neumarkt, Germany, Dec. 22, 1906; s. Samuel and Freda (Stein) F.; M.B.A., Coll. Commerce, Berlin Germany, 1927; M.A., Columbia, 1928, Ph.D., 1931; m. Florence Rothman, May 23, 1937; children—Noami, Jonah, Rachel. Came to U.S., 1927, naturalized, 1936. Instr. economics Coll. City N.Y., 1930-34; asst. prof. econs. U. Newark, 1934-39, asso. prof., 1939-45; prof., chmn. econs. dept. Rutgers U. Sch. Bus. Adminstrn., 1946—; economist Esquire's Apparel Art, 1945-53; Fulbright prof. U. Vienna, Austria, 1955-56; vis. prof. Inter Am. Univ. Puerto Rico 1968. Dir. postwar planning Research Inst. Am., 1943-44; cons. Fgn. Econ. Adminstrn., Washington, 1944; dir research Housing Inst., 1945-46; cons. U.S. Mission to NATO, 1956, 57; chief econ. cons. N.J. Gen. Assembly, 1958-59. Mem. Am. Econ. Assn., Am. Assn. U. Profs. Author: Your Business After the War, 1943; the First Year of the Housing Room, 1945; the American Economy, 1948; others. Editor of Review of New Jersey Business 1951—. Home: 6 Lenox Pl Maplewood NJ 07040 Office: 18 Washington PL Newark NJ 07102

FLINN, PAUL ANTHONY, educator, metall. engr.; b. N.Y.C., Mar. 25, 1926; s. Richard A. and Anna (Weber) F.; A.B., Columbia, 1948, M.A., 1949; Sc.D., Mass. Inst. Tech., 1952; m. Mary Ellen Hoffman, Aug. 20, 1949; children—Juliana, Margaret, Donald, Anthony, Patrick. Asst. prof. Wayne U., 1952-54; staff mem. Westinghouse Research Lab., Pitts., 1954-63; mem. faculty Carnegie Inst. Tech., 1963-67, prof. physics and metall. engring., 1964-67; prof. physics, metall. engring., materials sci. Carnegie-Mellon U., Pitts., 1967—; vis. prof. U. Nancy (France), 1967-68; Argonne Univs. Assn. Distinguished appointment, 1971-72; cons. metal physics. Fellow Am. Phys. Soc.; mem. A.A.A.S., Am. Inst. Metall. Engring., Phi Beta Kappa, Sigma Xi, Tau Beta Pi. Contbr. articles to sci. jours. Investigation of local atomic arrangements in alloys; contbns. to theory of strengthening mechanisms in alloys; applications of Mossbauer effect to study of alloys. Home: PO Box 51 Murrysville PA 15668 Office: Carnegie-Mellon U Schenley Park Pittsburgh PA 15213

FLINNER, CHARLES FREDERICK, govt. ofcl.; b. Leavenworth, Kan., Jan. 17, 1920; s. Max and Florence (Hampel) F.; B.S., U. Kan., 1941; m. Betty Goodwin, Oct. 26, 1946; children—Linda Charlene (Mrs. James Benson), Charles Frederick, Margaret Anne. Accountant, Aetna Fed. Savs. and Loan Assn., Topeka, 1941; accountant VA, Chgo. and Washington, 1946- 50; dep. chief accountant Office U.S. High Commr. for Germany, Frankfurt and Bonn, 1950-52; comptroller Det. Material Procurement Agy., London, Eng., 1952-54; with ICA, AID, Washington, 1954—, controller, 1964—. Served to capt., Finance Corps, AUS, 1942-46. Mem. Fed. Govt. Accountants Assn., Alpha Kappa Psi. Club: Lakewood Country (Rockville, Md.) Home: 2004 Glen Ross Rd Silver Spring MD 20910 Office: AID Dept State Washington DC 20523

FLINT, CALVIN CHARLES, coll. pres.; b. Payette, Ida., May 5, 1906; s. Herbert Charles and Mary Elizabeth (Johnson) F.; A.B., Stanford, 1928, M.A., 1931, Ed.D., 1954; student Sorbonne U., 1928-29, 32-33, London Sch. Econs., 1929-30; m. Lenore Dean, June 22, 1945. Dean of men Santa Ana Jr. Coll., 1934-42; pres. Monterey Peninsula Coll., 1947-58; pres., supt. Foothill Coll., 1958—. Served to lt. col. USAAF, 1942-46. Rotarian. Home: 444 Fir Lane Los Altos CA 94022 Office: Foothill Coll 12345 El Monte Av Los Altos Hills CA 94022

FLINT, EMILY PAULINE RIEDINGER, editor; b. N.Y.C., Apr. 1, 1909; d. Louis and Emma Therese (Schaufele) Riedinger; A.B., Barnard Coll., 1930; M.A., Tufts, 1932; B.S., Columbia Sch. Library Service, 1935; L.H.D. (hon.), New Eng. Coll., 1967; D. Litt (hon.), Franklin Pierce Coll., 1969; m. Paul H. Flint, Aug. 18, 1935; 1 son, Paul H. Teaching fellow English, Tufts Coll., 1930-32; instr. Tufts U. Writers' Workshop, summer 1954; library staff Mt. Vernon (N.Y.) Pub. Library, 1932-34, Columbia Library, 1934-35; humanities librarian Mass. Inst. Tech., 1935-44; editorial asst. Atlantic Monthly, 1945-47, research editor, 1948-51, mng. editor, 1951-70, contbg. editor, 1970—, editor Peabody Museum, Harvard U., 1970—; pres. Creative Editing, Inc., 1970—; asso. editor Alma Mater mag., 1971—; instr. div. journalism Boston U., 1948-51. Trustee Medford (Mass.) Pub. Library; alumna trustee Barnard Coll., 1965-69. Mem. New Eng. Women's Press Assn. (bd. dirs. 1958, 1961-69, pres. 1967-69), Boston Center Adult Edn. (dir. 1948-50, 58- 70, 71—, pres. 1949-50, 60-65, v.p. 1959-60). Club: Zonta (Medford). Editor: (with Edward Weeks) Jubilee: 100 Years of the Atlantic, 1957. Home: 26 Edison Av Medford MA 02155 Office: 8 Arlington St Boston MA

FLINT, GEORGE SQUIRE, lawyer, corp. exec.; b. Ft. Wayne, Ind., Oct. 28, 1930; s. A. Verne and Alberta (Minor) F.; A.B., U. Mich., 1952, J.D., 1955; m. Emily Gregg McLees, Nov. 23, 1968; children by previous marriage—Julia M., Melissa A., Anthony E. Admitted to N.Y. bar, 1956; asso., then sr. asso. firm Fulton, Walter & Duncombe, N.Y.C., 1955-65; with Tenneco Chems., Inc., 1965—, v.p., sec., gen. counsel, 1965—; v.p., treas. Moorgate Corp. (Del.); asst. sec. Tenneco Inc., Tenneco Internat. Inc.; dir. Crown Gen. Internat. S.A. (Belgium). Served with USNR, 1955-57. Mem. N.Y. State Bar Assn., Am. Arbitration Assn. (panel arbitrators), Assn. Bar City N.Y., Order of Coif. Home: 114 E 90th St New York City NY 10028 Office: 280 Park Av New York City NY 10017

FLINT, JOHN GARDINER, investment banker; b. Milw., Aug. 17, 1902; s. Wyman K. and Jennie L. (Ray) F.; A.B. cum laude, Harvard, 1923; m. Eleanor Musgrave, June 6, 1925; children—John Gardiner, Mrs. Jean M. Putnam. With Stone & Webster, Inc., 1923-26, Stone & Webster and Blodget, Inc., 1927-31; joined Kidder, Peabody & Co., Inc., Boston, 1931, partner, 1936-64, v.p., 1964—; trustee Suffolk Franklin Savs. Bank, Boston; dir. N.H. Ball Bearings, Inc. Chmn. Mass. Victory Fund Com., U.S. Treasury, 1942-43. Chmn., dir. Better Bus. Bur. of Eastern Mass., Inc., mem. corp. Children's Hosp.; mem. bd. mgrs. Adams House. Mem. Investment Bankers Assn. Am. (gov. 1943-46). Clubs: Somerset, Union (Boston); Myopia Hunt (Hamilton, Mass.). Home: 1 Hart St Beverly Farms MA 01915 Office: 75 Federal St Boston MA 02110

FLINT, MELVIN COLBY, chem. co. exec.; b. St. Louis, June 6, 1920; s. Luther Wesley and Bernice (Kramer) F.; B.S., U. Mo., 1942; postgrad. U. Wash., 1942-43, Georgetown U., 1946-47; LL.B., So. Meth. U., 1950; m. Audrey Jean Case, July 24, 1943; children—Melvin Colby, Barbara IMrs. Barry Scoville). Admitted to Tex. bar, 1950, Pa. bar, 1951; patent atty. Atlantic Regining Co., Phila., 1947-53; corporate sec. Minerals & Chems. Philipp Corp., Menlo Park, N.J., 1953-67, v.p. minerals and chems. div., 1964-67; corporate sec., v.p. minerals and chems. div. Engelhard Minerals & Chems. Corp., Edison, N.J., 1967—; dir. Porocel Corp., Chemstone Corp., Cuyahoga Lime Co., Eastern Magnesia Talc Co., Served with USNR, 1943-46. Mem. Am. Bar Assn., Bar State Tex., Bar commonwealth Pa., Am., N.J. patent law assns., Am. Soc. Corporate Secs., Phi Kappa Phi, Tau Beta Pi. Mason. Home: RD 1 Far Hills NJ 07931 Office: Menlo Park Edison NJ 08817

FLINT, PAUL HARRY, educator; b. Methuen, Mass., Apr. 3, 1908; s. Harry Deane and Mary Ann (McClellan) F.; A.B., Harvard, 1930, A.M., 1937, Ph.D., 1947; A.M., Tufts Coll., 1932; m. Emily Pauline Riedinger, Aug. 18, 1935; 1 son, Paul Harry. Teaching fellow English, Tufts U., 1930-32, instr. to asso. prof. English, 1935-38, prof., 1958—, asst. dean Grad. Sch. Arts and Scis., 1951-59, acting dean, 1959-60, dean, 1960—69, dir. Tufts Workshop in Tech. Writing, 1956-58, 60, asso. dir., 1959: asst. to pres. Doble Engring. Co., 1932-35, cons., 1946-57. Served as officer USNR, World War II; capt. Res. Fellow A.A.A.S.; mem. Soc. Tech. Writers (founder, Pres. 1954- 55), Soc. Tech. Writers and Editors (exec. bd. 1957-60), Modern Lang. Assn., Soc. Tech. Writers and Pubs. Am. Soc. Engring. Edn., Medieval Acad., Am. Assn. U. Profs., Res. Officers Assn., New Eng. Conf. Grad. Edn. (pres. 1967-68). Unitarian. Home: 26 Edison Av Medford MA 02155

FLINT, RICHARD FOSTER, geologist; b. Chgo., Mar. 1, 1902; s. Nott William and Edith Burnham (Foster) F.; B.S., U. Chgo., 1922, Ph.D., 1925; A.M. (hon.), Yale, 1945; Sc.D. (hon.), U. Dublin, 1963; Sc.D. (hon.), U. Wroclaw, Poland, 1966; m. Margaret Cecil Haggott, Dec. 29, 1926; 1 dau., Anne R. Ogilvy. Asst. in geology U. Chgo., 1922-25; instr., asst. prof., prof. Yale, 1925-56, Henry Barnard Davis prof., 1957- 70, emeritus, 1970—, dir. grad. studies in geology, 1951-57, chmn. dept., 1957-64; chmn. adv. bd. Yale Geochronometric Lab., 1953-60; exchange prof. The Sorbonne, lectr. U. Cambridge, Joly lectr. Trinity Coll. (Dublin), 1951; Bownocker lectr. Ohio State U., 1967; temp. geologist U.S. Geol. Survey and other geol. surveys; served as sr. scientist Boyd Arctic expdn., 1937; cons. Research and Devel. Bd., 1946-53, Army Engrs., 1949-63; chmn. compilation com. Glacial Map of N.A., NRC, 1939-45, Glacial Map U.S., 1956-59; mem. com. on Carbon 14 Am. Anthrop. Assn., 1949-51. Pres. 7th Congress Internat. Quaternary Assn., 1965. Maj., intelligence, USAAF, 1943-45; lt. col. CE, USAR, 1949-53. Guggenheim fellowship, 1965-66; recipient Albrecht Penck medal German Quaternary Assn., 1966. Fellow A.A.A.S., Geol. Soc. Am., Arctic Inst. N.Am. (gov. 1945, chmn. 1950), Am. Acad. Arts and Scis.; mem. Am. Geophys. Union, Glaciol. Soc., hon. fgn. mem. geol. societies Edinburgh, London, Stockholm, Finland, and Argentina, Phi Beta Kappa, Sigma Xi. Author of: Glacial Geology and the Pleistocene Epoch, 1947; Glacial and Pleistocene Geology, 1955; Glacial and Quaternary Geology, 1971. Co-author: Physical Geology, 1932, 37, 48, 69; Introduction to Physical Geology, 1955, 62. Asso. editor Am. Jour. Sci., Quaternary Research, Zeitschr. f. Geomorphologie, Quaternaria; co-editor Radiocarbon. Contbr. articles in field. Home: 265 Bradley St New Haven CT 06510

FLINT, ROBERT BRYAN, lawyer; b. Washington, Mar. 10, 1939; s. Einar Philip and Adele (Cavanagh) F.; B.A., Yale, 1960; LL.B., Georgetown U., 1963; m. Virginia May Bagby, June 8, 1963; children—Christopher Edward, Bryan David, Kevin James. Admitted to Alaska bar, 1964, since parcticed in Anchorage; asst. atty. gen. Alaska, 1964-65; asst. dist. atty., 1965; pvt. practice, 1965-66; legislative asst. for Rep. Howard W. Pollock, 1967- 68; partner McGrath, Wohlforth & Flint, 1969—. Orgn. chmn. South Central Republican Com., 1966. Mem. Alaska, Anchorage bar assns. Roman Catholic. Home: 2515 Telequana Dr Anchorage AK 99503 Office: 825 W 8th Av Anchorage AK 99501

FLINT, SAM HALL, food mfg. co. exec.; b. Mt. Airy, Ga., Mar. 7, 1920; s. Samuel Hall and May (Harbin) F.; A.B., Piedmont Coll., 1941; m. Jerry Macmillan, Dec. 25, 1943; 1 dau., Cynthia Hall. Asst. traffic mgr. Tallulah Falls Ry., 1941- 43; dir. transp. Ga. Pub. Service Commn., 1946-53; gen. traffic mgr. Quaker Oats Co., Chgo., 1953-64, v.p., 1964-70, corporate v.p. distbn. and operations research, 1970—. Admitted to Ga. State bar, 1952. Hon. aide de camp Gov. of Ga. Mem. Assn. ICC Practitioners (pres. 1959-60). Am., Ga., bar assns., Nat. Indsl. Traffic League, Nat. Freight Traffic Assn. (pres. 1971—), Mchts. and Mfrs. Episcopalian. Clubs: Union League, Traffic (Chgo.); Medinah Country. Home: 550 Banbury Rd Arlington Heights IL 60005 Office: Quaker Oats Co Merchandise Mart Chicago IL 60654

FLINTOFT, JAMES, paper co. exec.; b. Montreal, Can., Nov. 18, 1919; s. Edward Percy and Felicia (Howitt) F.; B.Sc., Bishop's U., 1940; LL.B., Osgoode Hall Law Sch., 1948; m. Joan Baird Mitchell, Dec. 27, 1946; children—Sandra Felicia, Virginia Frances, Jane Mitchell. Called to Ont. bar, 1948, created Queen's counsel, 1966; asst. solicitor Canadian Pacific Ry. Co., 1948-54; legal officer Abitibi Paper Co. Ltd., 1954-65, sec., 1965—. Bd. govs. Lakefield Coll. Sch., 1955—, Bishop Strachen Sch., 1966—. Served with Canadian Army, 1941-45; ETO. Decorated Mil. Cross. Mem. Canadian Bar Assn., Alpha Delta Phi. Clubs: Toronto Golf, University (pres. 1964) (Toronto). Home: 11 Ormsby Crescent Toronto 7 Ontario Canada Office: Box 21 Toronto-Dominion Centre Toronto 1 Ontario Canada

FLINTON, EDGAR WILLIAM, ret. univ. adminstr.; b. Ballston Spa, N.Y., Nov. 19, 1905; s. Edward and Ellen (Straight) F.; B.S. in Edn., Boston U., 1929; Ed.M., Harvard, 1947, Ed.D., 1952; m. Doris S. Holt, Apr. 16, 1932; children—Suzanne Fogelson, Jennifer S., John H. Tchr. math. Williamstown (Mass.) High Sch., 1929-37; founder, headmaster Pine Cobble Sch., Williamstown, 1937-43, trustee, 1945-71, trusteee emeritus, 1971—; operations analyst planning cons. USAAF, 1944-45; asst. to dean, registrar Grad. Sch. Edn., Harvard, 1945-49; research asso. N.Y. State Dept. Edn., 1949-52; dir. grad. studies State U. N.Y., Albany, 1952-63, dean grad. studies, 1963-71, dean emeritus, 1971—, spl. asst. to pres., 1960. Mem. staff Commn. Study N.H. Ednl. System, 1946, staff Commn. Study Buffalo Pub. Schs., 1950. Recipient Certificate of Commendation, 2d Air Force, 1945; award distinction studies Harvard chpt. Phi Delta Kappa, 1947. Mem. Assn. Higher Edn., Phi Delta Kappa. Home: 20 Cranberry Rd East Dennis MA 02641

FLIPCHENKO, LT. COL. ANATOLI V., Russian cosmonaut; b. 1928. Mem. Russian Air Force for nineteen years; qualified test pilot; flight comdr. of space craft Soyuz 7, 1969. Address: care Scientific Research Inst Petrovsky Park Moscow USSR*

FLIPSE, MATHEW JAY, physician; b. Passaic, N.J., Nov. 16, 1896; s. Martin and Maggie (Pfanstiehl) F.; A.B., Hope Coll., 1917, M.S. (hon.), 1919; M.D., U. Cin., 1921; m. Alice Raap, Aug. 18, 1921; children—Thomas E., Robert Frank. Intern, resident Cin. Gen. Hosp., 1921-23; pvt. practice medicine, Miami, Fla., 1923—; mem. courtesy staff various hosps. in Miami and Miami Beach area; pres. staff Jackson Meml. Hosp., Miami, 1938; clin. asso. prof. medicine U. Miami Sch. Medicine emeritus. Fellow A.M.A. (past chmn. sect. diseases chest 1959), Am. Coll. Chest Physicians (pres. 1960-61), A.C.P. (life), Am. Coll. Cardiology, Am. Heart Assn., Am. Geriatrics Soc., Am. Acad. Compensation Medicine, Am. Coll. of Angiology, Am. Coll. of Allergy, Acad. Internat. Medicine; life mem. So., Fla., Dade County (past pres.) med. assns.; mem. Am. Thoracic Soc., Am. Therapeutic Soc., Nat. Tb Assn. (dir. 1939-40), Am. Acad. General Practice, Am. Diabetic Soc. Contbr. articles med. jours. Home: 715 NE 93d St Miami Shores FL 33153 Office: 550 Brickell Av Miami FL 33131

FLITTIE, EDWIN GILBERT, educator; b. Brookings, S.D., Mar. 10, 1924; s. Theodore I. and Grace (Gilliland) F.; B.A. magna cum laude, U. Colo., 1946; M.A., Stanford, 1947; Ph.D., Northwestern U., 1955; m. Mary Josephine Fowler, June 11, 1949 (div. Apr. 1970). Instr. sociology U. Wyo., Laramie, 1947-51, asst. prof., 1957-60, asso. prof., 1960-64 asst. dean Coll. Arts and Scis., 1961-63, chmn. dept. sociology, anthropology and geography, 1963-66, prof. sociology, 1964—, chmn. dept. sociology, 1966—, also mem. faculty senate; program officer Inst. Inter-Am. Affairs, Bogota, Colombia, 1952-54; asst. prof. sociology San Jose (Cal.) State Coll., 1955-57; chmn. Wyo. sect. Mountain States Regional Med. Program, 1968—, also mem. steering com. and exec. com. Fellow Am. Sociol. Assn. Democrat. Contbr. articles profl. jours. Home: 223 Corthell Rd Laramie WY 82070

FLITTIE, WILLIAM JORGEN, lawyer, educator; b. Brookings, S.D., Nov. 23, 1919; s. Theodore Ignatius and Grace Eliza (Gilliland) F.; student S.D. State Coll., 1937- 38, U. So. Cal., 1938-39; B.S., U. Minn., 1946; LL.B., Columbia, 1947; m. Elizabeth Lorraine Hanten, Mar. 26, 1951; 1 son, William Hanten. Admitted to S.D. bar, 1947, Colo. bar, 1954, Tex. bar, 1963; practiced in Huron, 1947-48; asst. atty. gen., dep. indsl. commr. State of S.D., 1948-53, ex-officio commr. labor, 1948-53; atty. Denver div. Texaco, Inc., 1953- 61; prof. law So. Meth. U., 1961—; Served as lt. comdr. USNR, 1940-45. Address: Sch of Law Southern Methodist U Dallas TX 75222

FLOAN, ALBERT EDWARD, airline exec.; b. St. Paul, Minn., May 6, 1900; s. Albert C. and Andrea (Leveroos) F.; A.B., Princeton, 1922; LL.B., U. Minn., 1925; m. Helen Dean, Dec. 29, 1934; children—Laura Dean, Alice Dean, Christina. Admitted to Minn. bar, 1925, practiced in St. Paul, 1925-35; with West Pub. Co., 1935-40; with Northwest Airlines, Inc., 1940—, now v.p., dir., sec., counsel. Clubs: University, Somerset Country (St. Paul). Home: 360 S Lexington Pkwy St Paul MN 55105 Office: St Paul-Mpls Internat Airport St Paul MN 55111

FLOBERG, JOHN FORREST, lawyer; b. Chgo., Oct. 28, 1915; s. Frederick Oscar and Emily (Jurney) F.; grad. Loyola Acad., 1932; A.B., Loyola U., 1936; LL.B., Harvard, 1939; m. Cecelia Elizabeth Spencer, Jan. 8, 1944. Admitted to Ill. bar, 1939, D.C. bar, 1953, Ohio bar, 1961, practiced with Kirkland, Fleming, Green, Martin & Ellis, Chgo., 1939-41, 46-49, Washington, 1953-57; sec., gen. counsel, v.p., dir., mem. exec. com. Firestone Tire and Rubber Co.; mem. AEC, 1957-60; asst. sec. Navy for Air, 1949-53. Commd. ensign USNR, 1941, advanced through grades to lt. comdr., 1945; exec. and comdg. officer U.S.S. S.C. 770, 1943; gun officer U.S.S. Goss, 1944-45; exec. and comdg. officer U.S.S. Bivin, 1945-46; mem. Air Coordinating Com., 1951-53; mem. Research and Devel. Bd., 1951- 53; cons. 2d Hoover Commn., 1953-54; dir., mem. exec. com. Atomic Indsl. Forum, 1961-63; trustee Research Analysis Corp. Mem. Akron—Canton Airport Authority, 1965—. Trustee Barberton Citizens Hosp., Ursuline Coll., Cleve.; pres. bd. dirs. Akron Art Inst., 1966. Mem. Am. Nuclear Soc., Am. Inst. Aeros. and Astronautics, Soc. Naval Architects and Marine Engrs., Am. Ordnance Assn. (life), Nat. Security Indsl. Assn. (life), Am., Ill., Chgo., Ohio, Akron bar assns., Bar Assn. D.C., Am. Judicature Soc., Harvard Law Sch. Assn., Assn. of Gen. Counsel, U.S. C. of C. Clubs: Firestone Country, Sharon, Portage Country (Akron); Harvard, Wings (N.Y.C.); Lake Shore (Chgo.); Army-Navy, Metropolitan, Burning Tree, 1925 F Street (Washington). Mem. editorial bd. Harvard Law Rev., 1937-39. Home: 4240 Ira Rd Bath OH 44210 Office: 1200 Firestone Pkwy Akron OH 44317

FLOCH, JOSEPH, artist, painter; b. Vienna, Austria, Nov. 5, 1895; s. Samuel and Jeanette (Mauksch) F.; ed. Acad. Fine Arts, Vienna; m. Hermine Frankl, May 12, 1934; children—Jenny Eva, Suzanne Marguerite. Came to U.S., 1941, naturalized, 1952. Works owned by M.H. De Young Mus., San Francisco, Toledo Mus. Art, Mus. Modern Art, Paris, Jeu de Paume, Paris, William Rockhill Nelson gallery, Kansas City, Mo., Mus. Vienna, Smithsonian Instn., Washington, Herron Mus., Indpls., Albertina Mus., Vienna, Mus. Lille, France, Mus. Lyon, France, Mus. City of Paris, Springfiled Mus. Fine Arts, Montclair Art Mus., Mus. Mulhouse, France, Mus. Tel Aviv, Met. Mus. Art, others; faculty mem. New Sch. Social Research. Recipient Gold medal Paris Internat. Exhbn., 1937; Lippincott prize Pa. Acad. Fine Arts, 1945; award Nat. Inst. Arts and Letters, 1951; Breevoort-Eickemeyer prize, Columbia, 1955; Wm. Palmer Meml. prize, Nat. Acad., N.Y.C., 1960, gold medal of merit, 1968, Palmer meml., 1969; Chevalier French Order Arts and Letters; Isidor Meml. gold medal Nat. Acad.; Clara Obrig prize Nat. Acad.; Saltus gold medal for merit, 1967; Andrew Carnegie award, 1969. Mem. Salon d'Automne (Paris), Fedn. Modern Painters and Sculptors, Nat. Acad., Salon des Tuileries (Paris); 1st prize Eastern States Art Exhibits Springfield Mus., 1966. Home: 61 W 74th St New York City NY 10023 Office: care Forum Gallery 1018 Madison Av New York City NY 10021

FLOCK, EUNICE VERNA, biochemist; b. Kellogg, Ida., Aug. 20, 1904; d. Abraham Lincoln and Florence Louise (Ashby) Flock; B.S., U. Wash., 1926; M.S., U. Chgo., 1931; Ph.D., U. Minn., 1935. Fellow physiol. chemistry Mayo Found., 1933- 36; cons. biochemistry Mayo Clinic, 1936; faculty Mayo Found., Grad. Sch. U. Minn., 1936-69, prof. biochemistry, 1957-69, emeritus prof. biochemistry, 1969—; vis. scientist Nat. Inst. Arthritis and Metabolia Diseases, Phoenix Indian Med. Center, 1971—. Spl. research phosphorus compounds in liver and muscle, amino acids of brain, metabolism thyroid hormones. Fellow A.A.A.S.; mem. Am. Chem. Soc., Am. Soc. Biol. Chemists, N.Y. Acad. Sci., Alumni Assn. Mayo Found., Am. Thyroid Assn., Sigma Xi. Home: 6315 N 16th St Phoenix AZ 85016 Office: 4212 N 16th St Phoenix AZ 85016

FLOCKHART, ROBERT SEATON, clergyman; b. Plymouth, Eng., Jan. 15, 1889; s. John and Mary (Edwards) F.; ed. State Normal Sch., Springfield, S.D., also Sioux City Business Coll. until 1909; Friends U., Wichita, 1909-11, Gen. Theol. Sem., 1911-14; D.D., Tabor (Ia.) Coll., 1927; m. Marguerite Alice Meyer, Jan. 10, 1917; 1 dau., Mary Louise (Mrs. John Windsor Persse). Ordained deacon P.E. Ch., 1914, priest, 1915, rector Grace Ch., Chanute, Kan., 1914-15; asso. rector All Saints Ch., Omaha, 1915-17; successively rector Ch. Resurrection, Fernbank, Cin., Ch. Ascension, Cin., St. Thomas Ch., Sioux City, Ia., St. John's Ch., Western Run, Balt., 1929, St. Thomas's Ch. New Haven, 1934-50, Trinity Ch., Lime Rock, Conn., 1917-58; retired. Nat. crusader, N.D., 1927; asso. sec. field dept. Nat. Council P.E. Ch., 1928-32, dep. Gen. Conv., Washington, Cleve., 1943; mem. Coll. Preachers, Washington, 1928-33; diocesan missioner, Washington, 1930, 32; dir. Diocesan Ch. Mission of Help, 1929-33; mem. City Mission Staff, Balt.; mem. faculty Racine Conf., 1931; leader clergy confs. Diocese Me., 1931; chaplain Hannah More Acad., Balt., 1933-34; instr. Md. Diocesan Normal Sch., 1933-34; pres. New Haven Clerical Assn., 1935-37; mem. faculty Pomfret Summer Conf., Diocese Conn., 1936-40, mem. com. old age benefits, 1937; pres. New Haven Missionary Assn., 1935-38; mem. Church Scholarship Soc.; chmn. New Haven Archdeaconry Div. Budget and Program, 1941-43; mem. Diocesan Dept. Budget and Program, 1941-43; mem. diocesan dept. missions and mem. standing com. Diocese Conn., 1943-50, mem. exec. council, 1948-50. Rotarian. Home: Ambassador Apts Canterbury Rd and 39th St Baltimore MD 21218

FLOCKS, RUBIN H., urologist, educator; b. N.Y.C., May 7, 1906; s. Morris and Rose (Blackman) F.; A.B., Johns Hopkins, 1926, M.D., 1930. Resident house officer Johns Hopkins Hosp., 1930-31; practice of medicine, urology, Iowa City, 1932—; asst. instr., asso. in urology U. Ia., 1932-37, asst. prof. urology, 1937-39, asso., 1939-46, prof., 1946-49, prof., head dept. urology, 1949—. Mem. NRC, 1965—, Nat. Adv. Cancer Council, 1965- -. Diplomate Am. Bd. Urology (pres. 1963—). Fellow A.C.S.; mem. A.M.A. (sec. urology sect. 1954), Am. Urol. Assn. (sec. 1962—, pres. N. Central sect. 1954; pres. 1967-69), Johnson County Med. Soc. (pres. 1944), Clin. Soc. Genito-Urinary Surgeons, Am. Assn. Genito-Urinary Surgeons, Phi Beta Kappa, Alpha Omega Alpha, Sigma Xi. Author: Surgical Urology, 1954. Contbr. sects. med. books. Home: 514 Grandview Ct Iowa City IA 52240 Office: University Hosp Iowa City IA 52240

FLOE, CARL FREDERICK, educator, cons. metallurgist; b. Dawson, Yukon Terr., Can., Jan. 1, 1908; s. Iver Stefan and Caroline (Ulvestad) F.; B.S., Wash. State Univ., 1930, M.S, 1932; Sc.D., Mass. Inst. Tech., 1935; m. Margaret Proctor, Aug. 30, 1935; children—Carol Sherwood, Joan Proctor; m. 2d, Beverly Brooks, June 21, 1954; children—Charles Pennell, Jonathan Tyndall. Mem. faculty Mass. Inst. Tech., 1939—, prof. phys. metallurgy, 1950—, asst. provost, 1952-56, asst. chancellor, 1956-57, administrv. vice chancellor, 1957-59, v.p. research adminstrn. 1959-69; cons. metallurgist, 1932—; dir. Walworth Co., White Pigment Corp., Nitralloy Corp., Abex Corp., B.T.U. Engring. Corp., Univ. Corp. Atmospheric Research, Inc. Fellow Am. Acad. Arts and Scis.; mem. Am. Inst. Mining and Metall. Engrs., Am. Soc. for Metals, Iron and Steel Inst. (London), Inst. of Metals (London), Sigma Xi, Tau Beta Pi, Phi Kappa Phi, Sigma Tau, Phi Sigma Kappa. Clubs: St. Botolph, Algonquin (Boston); University (N.Y. City). Home: 40 Howells Rd Belmont MA 02178 Office: Mass Inst of Tech Cambridge MA 02139

FLOERSHEIMER, ALBERT, Jr., motion picture communications co. exec.; b. N.Y.C., Apr. 14, 1917; s. Albert and Fannie (Markwell) F.; student N.Y. U., 1934, Columbia, 1935; m. Adriana Musa, Nov. 11, 1956; 1 dau., Adrienne. Reporter various newspapers, 1934-42; v.p. pub. relations and catering Walter Reade, Inc., 1955-58; dir. pub. relations Theatre Owners of Am., N.Y.C., 1958-62; pres. AMPA, N.Y.C., 1961-62; dir. advt. and publicity Walter Reade Orgn., Inc., Oakhurst, N.J., 1963-64, adminstrv. asst. to pres., sec., asst. treas., 1966—. Mem. Middletown (N.J.) Tercentennial Commn., 1968; chmn. Walter Reade Employees Fund; sec. Walter Reade Found., Walter Reade Employees Pension Plan. Served to capt. Signal Corps, AUS, 1941-46. Mem. Assn. Motion Picture Advertisers (pres.). Democrat. Jewish religion. Home: 49 Bamm Hollow Rd Middletown NJ 07748 Office: Mayfair House Deal Rd Oakhurst NJ 07755

FLOERSHEIMER, STEPHEN HELMUTH, investment banker; b. Frankfurt, Germany, Mar. 21, 1925; s. Walter David and Charlotte (Salomon) F.; came to U.S., 1939, naturalized, 1946; B.A., U. Mo., 1949; Ph.D., St. Catherine's Coll., U. Oxford (Eng.), 1952; m. Eliane Goldmuntz, June 15, 1954; children—Barbara, Daniel M., Mark W. With Sutro Bros. & Co., N.Y.C., 1952—, partner, 1955-62, mng. partner, 1962—; dir. Devel. Corp. Am., 1958-60, N.Y., Susquehanna & Western R.R., 1956-62, Crescent Corp., 1963-65, Am. Snowblast Corp.; chmn. bd., dir. Nat. Equipment Rental, Inc., 1962-65. Bd. govs. 92 St. YM-YWHA. Mem. N.Y. Cocoa Exchange, N.Y. Mercantile Exchange, N.Y. Stock Exchange, Am. Stock Exchange. Home: 1049 Park Av New York City NY 10028 Office: 80 Pine St New York City NY 10005

FLOERSHEIMER, WALTER D., banker; b. Wehrheim, Germany, Mar. 11, 1900; s. David F. and Fanny (Rosenthal) F.; student U. Frankfurt; Ph.D., U. Wurzburg; m. Charlotte Saloman, May 21, 1931; 1 son, Stephen F. V.p. Dresdner Bank, Germany, partner E.J. Meyer Banking House, Berlin; now sr. partner Sutro Bros. & Co. Mem. N.Y. Stock Exchange, N.Y.C. Clubs: Bankers (N.Y.C.); North Shore Country (Glen Head, L.I.); Palm Beach (Fla.) Country. Home: Palm Beach FL 33480 Office: 80 Pine St New York City NY 10005

FLOM, EDWARD LEONARD, steel co. exec.; b. Tampa, Fla., Dec. 10, 1929; s. Samuel Louis and Julia (Mittle) F.; B.C.E., Cornell U., 1952; m. Beverly Boyett, Mar. 31, 1956; children—Edward Louis, Mark Robert, Julia Ruth. With Fla. Steel Corp., Tampa, 1954—, v.p. sales, 1957-64, pres., dir., 1964—; adv. bd. Founders Life Assurance Co. Fla.; dir. Exchange Nat. Bank of Tampa, Exchange Bancorp. Tampa, I.W. Phillips & Co., Tampa. Mem. Eagle Scout Bd. Rev. Dir., mem. exec. com. United Fund Tampa; adv. com. St. Joseph's Hosp., Tampa; bd. dirs. Family Service Assn. Tampa, Jewish Welfare Fedn. Tampa; exec. com. Com. of 100, Tampa. Served with C.E., AUS, 1952-54. Mem. Young Pres.'s Orgn., Fla. Engring. Soc. Jewish religion (bd. dirs. temple). Rotarian (bd. dirs. Tampa). Clubs: University, Palma Ceia Golf and Country, Tampa Yacht, Gasparilla Krewe. Home: 4516 Sylvan Ramble Tampa FL 33609 Office: 1715 Cleveland St Tampa FL 33601

FLOM, JOSEPH HAROLD, lawyer; b. Balt., Dec. 20, 1923; s. Isadore and Fannie (Fishman) F.; student Coll. City N.Y., LL.B. (cum laude), Harvard, 1948; m. Claire Cohen, Nov. 14, 1958; children—Peter Lesie, Jason Robert. Admitted to N.Y. bar, 1949, since practiced in N.Y.C. Spl. counsel to subcom. of Com. on Ways and Means on Adminstrn. of Internal Revenue Laws, 1951, 52. Mem. N.Y.C. Bar Assn. Editor Harvard Law Rev., 1947-48. Co-editor: Disclosure Requirements of Public Corporations and Insiders, 1967; Texas Gulf Sulphur, 1968. Home: 31 E 79th St New York City NY 10021 Office: 919 3d Av New York City NY 10017

FLOM, SAMUEL LOUIS, steel co. exec.; b. Lithuania, June 10, 1901; s. Morris and Sarah (Notes) F.; came to U.S., 1906, naturalized, 1939; C.E., Lehigh U., 1921; m. Julia Mittle, June 1, 1927; children—Joann (Mrs. Harry G. Greenberg), Edward, Mary Sue (Mrs. Frederick M. Rothenberg). Br. mgr. Truscon Steel Co., Tampa, Fla., 1925-37; sec.- treas. Fla. Steel Products, Inc., Tampa, 1937-56; sec.-treas. Fla. Steel Corp., Tampa, 1956-59, pres., 1959-64, chmn., 1964—; dir. Crestview Realty Co. Trustee Univ. Community Hosp., Tampa. Mem. Am. Iron and Steel Inst. Mason, Rotarian. Clubs: Palma Ceia Golf and Country, University, Tampa Yacht and Country (Tampa). Home: 5001 Shorecrest Circle Tampa FL 33609 Office: P O Box 23328 Tampa FL 33601

FLOOD, DANIEL J. congressman; b. Hazleton, Pa., Nov. 26, 1904; s. Patrick F. and Sarah (McCarthy) F.; A.B., Syracuse U., 1924; postgrad. Harvard, 1925-26; LL.B., Dickinson Sch. Law, 1929; m. Catherine H. Swank, Sept. 24, 1949. Admitted to Pa. bar, 1930, since in gen. practice law, Wilkes-Barre, Pa.; Luzerne County atty. HOLC, 1933; dep. atty. gen. Commonwealth Pa., counsel Pa. Liquor Control Bd. 1936-41, dir. bur. pub. assistance State Treasury Dept., exec. asst. to state treas. Commonwealth Pa., 1941-44; spl. ambassador to Peru, 1945; mem. 79th, 81st, 82d, 84th-92d Congresses 11th Pa. Dist., mem. spl. com. investigation Katyn Massacre. 1951-52, house appropriations com., def. sub-com., chmn. appropriation subcom. labor HEW, 1967. Dir. State Bank Pa. Democratic nat. committeeman Pa. Young Democrats. Active A.R.C., Community Welfare, Civilian Def., War Loan drives, Local Draft Board (all Wilkes-Barre). Trustee Misericordia Coll., Dallas, Pa.; bd. dirs. Wilkes-Barre Cath. Charities, Cath. Youth Center, Mercy Hosp.; bd.

visitors U.S. Naval Acad., Annapolis, Md. Decorated comdr. Cross of Carlos Cespedas (Cuba); Cross Polonia Restituta (Polish Govt. in Exile, London); Distinguished Service award Pres.'s Com. on Employment Handicapped, 1971; Children's Asthma Inst. award, Los Angeles, 1969. Mem. Am., Pa., Luzerne County bar assns., Sigma Alpha Epsilon, Delta Sigma Rho. Lion, Elk, Owl, Eagle, Moose, K. of Columbus. Clubs: Harvard; Greater Pittston (Pa.) Friendly Sons (hon. life). Author: The Dreyfus Affairs, 1925; 3 One-Act Plays 1936. Home: 460 N Pennsylvania Av Wilkes-Barre PA 18702 Office: United Penn Bank Bldg Wilkes-Barre PA 18701 also Cannon House Office Bldg Washington DC 20515

FLOOD, MERRILL MEEKS, math. scientist, indsl. engr.; b. Seward, Neb., Nov. 28, 1908; s. James Francis and Lydia Jane (Meeks) F.; A.B., U. Neb., 1929, A.M., 1930; Ph.D. in Math., Princeton, 1935; m. Alice Mae Wikoff, Sept. 20, 1932 (dec. Feb. 1969); children—Susan Rojeane (Mrs. Harold A. Judd), Merrill Meeks, Walter Wikoff, James Francis II, Michael John, Robert Hallam; m. 2d, Ingeborge Kammler Van Buren, May 20, 1970. Instr. math. U. Neb., 1929-31; faculty Princeton, 1931-45, dir. applied math. group, 1944-45; research supr. N.J. Dept. Instns. and Agys., 1935; dir. Princeton br. Frankford Arsenal, 1943-44; owner Merrill Flood & Assos., photogrammetric engrs., 1942-49; asst. dep. dir. research and devel. Dept. Army, 1947-48; exec. dir. Am. Statis. Assn., 1948-49; project officer logistics RAND Corp., 1949-52; faculty Columbia, 1953- 56; dir. Inst. Research Mgmt. Indsl. Prodn., 1954-56; prof. indsl. engring. U. Mich., 1956-68, head Willow Run labs., 1956-58, sr. research mathematician Mental Health Research Inst., 1959-68, prof. math. biology in dept. psychiatry, 1960- 68; prin. scientist System Devel. Corp., Santa Monica, Cal., 1968-69; owner Merrill Flood & Assos., computer services, Santa Monica, Cal., 1969—. Vis. prof. bus. adminstrn., vis. research economist space scis. lab. U. Cal. at Berkeley, 1963-64; vis. prof. mgmt. Mass. Inst. Tech., 1965-66; Regents lectr. U. Cal. at Irvine, 1968. Pub. finance cons. Social Sci. Research Council, 1937-40; tech. adviser Gov. W.Va., 1937-40; adminstrv. cons. Harvard Grad. Sch. Edn., 1940; ofcl. investigator OSRD, 1940-46, field service cons., 1944; cons. guided missiles com. U.S. Joint Chiefs Staff. 1944; expert cons. sec. war, 1946-47; cons. to librarian of Congress, 1961-62; also cons. to corps., others; mem. sci. information council NSF, 1965-67, chmn., 1966-67; mem. operations research adv. council to mayor N.Y.C., 1967-68; cons. Office Sci. and Tech., Exec. Office Pres., 1965-68. Trustee Community Systems Found., Ann Arbor, Mich. Fellow A.A.A.S., Royal Econ. Soc.; mem. Am. Inst. Indsl. Engrs. (sr., v.p. 1962-66), Inst. Mgmt. Scis. (pres. 1955), Operations Research Soc. Am. (pres. 1961-62), Assn. Computing Machinery, Sigma Xi, Pi Mu Epsilon, Alpha Pi Mu (hon.). Presbyn. Clubs: Cosmos (Washington). Author: (with G.W. King, others) Automaton and the Library of Congress, 1963. Contbr. articles to profl. jours. Office: 1505 4th St Santa Monica CA 90401

FLOOD, ROBERT F., mfg. co. exec.; b. N.Y.C., 1912; ed. Mass. Inst. Tech., 1935; m. Catherine Byrnes; children—Maurice, Pauline, Robert F., Kathleen, Timothy, Patricia, Marian. Vice pres. Union Carbide Corp. Clubs: University (N.Y.C.); Winged Foot Golf; Pine Valley Golf. Home: 20 Flint Av Larchmont NY 10538 Office: 270 Park Av New York City NY 10017

FLORA, CHARLES JERRY, coll. pres.; b. Wabash County, Ind., Nov. 16, 1928; s. Roscoe R. and Velma (Dyson) F. B.S., Purdue U., 1950; M.Ed., U. Fla., 1955, Ed.D., 1957; m. Amelia Rosemary Germain, Dec. 28, 1950; children—Deva Marie, Christopher Lee, John Kimberly, Lisa Ann. Mem. faculty Western Wash. State Coll., Bellingham, 1957—, prof. zoology, 1964-66, acad. dean, 1966-68, acting pres., 1967-68, pres., 1968—. Mem. Wash. council Nat. Council on Crime and Delinquency. Served with AUS, 1951-53. Recipient Golden Mike award Am. Legion Aux., 1963. Mem. A.A.A.S., N.Y. Acad. Sci., Am. Council Edn., Assn. State Colls. and Univs., Wash. Council Higher Edn., Northwest Assn. Secondary and Higher Schs. (commr.), Wash. Council State Coll. and Univ. Pres.'s (chmn. 1971-72). Rotarian. Author: (with Eugene Fairbanks) The Sound and the Sea, 1966. Home: 6618 Lunde Rd Everson WA 98247

FLORA, DONALD H., oil co. exec.; b. Greybull, Wyo., 1924; LL.B., U. Denver, 1950. Sec., gen. atty. Husky Oil Co., Husky Oil Ltd. Home: 1000 Canyon Av Cody WY 82414 Office: P O Box 380 Cody WY 82414

FLOREEN, DAVID ALFRED, ins. co. exec.; b. Chgo., Oct. 24, 1910. With Automobile Ins. Co., Hartford, Conn., 1934-42; marine mgr. Home Ins. Co., Detroit office, 1942- 46; with Atlantic Mut. Ins. Co., 1946—, sr. exec. v.p., 1965-66, pres., 1966-69, chmn. bd., 1970—. Clubs: India House (N.Y.C.); Houston; University (Mexico); New York Yacht. Home: 20 Beckman Pl New York City NY 10022 Office: 45 Wall St New York City NY 10005

FLORES, JOSEPH S., educator; b. Salamanca, Spain, May 10, 1908; s. Anthony S. and Beatrice (Gomez) F.; brought to U.S., 1920, naturalized, 1932; A.B., U. Minn., 1932, M.A., 1933; student U. Madrid, 1933-34; Ph.D., U. Ill., 1941; m. Iren L. Erickson, June 23, 1934; children—Phillip E., Carmen R. (Mrs. Charles Moore), Camille I. (Mrs. Robert Madix). U. Ill., Mem. faculty at Urbana, 1935—, prof. Spanish, 1961—; vis. prof. N.M. Highlands U., summers 1955, 1957; dir. classrooms abroad U. Madrid, summer, 1966. Mem. Am. Assn. Tchrs. Spanish and Portuguese, Modern Lang. Tchrs. Assn., Am. Coll. Tchrs. Fgn. Langs., Am. Assn. U. Profs., Sigma Delta Pi. Home: 116 W Pennsylvania Av Urbana IL 61801

FLORES-BANUET, FERNANDO, publisher; b. San Jose, Costa Rica, July 14, 1908; s. Enrique Flores Vargas and Berta Banuet de Flores; student Kucei de Costa Rica, 1924; Heald Coll., Oakland, 1928; m. Gloria Flores; 1 daughter, Rima Maria. Export executive, Prentice Bros. and Company, San Francisco, 1929; vice consul Costa Rica, San Francisco, 1930-42; consul gen. Los Angeles, since 1942; secretary to the Costa Rican Delegation United Nations Organization, San Francisco, 1945; economic advisor, Ministry of Finance, Costa Rica,1946; coordinatio Nat. Recovery Program, 1946; delegate govt. loan negotations with Import and Export Bank, Washington, 1946; delegate U.N. Gen. Assembly, Lake Success, N.Y., 1947; on several diplomatic missions to various countries in C.Am. Pres. Preservo, S.A. treas. Picado Minerals S. A.;dir. Costa Mar Ltd. (all in Costa Rica, Commr., Inter-Am. Tropical Tuna Commn.; extraordinary ambassador to Spain on special mission, 1967. Cal. rep. National Newspaper Assn. of Mexico. Commd. major, Army of Costa Rica, 1943, lt. col., 1944, now col. Recipient Presidential Medal of Merit, Govt. Nicaragua, Nov. 15,1934; knight comdr. Order Isabel la Catolica (Spain). Catholic. Clubs: Union, San Jose, Costa Rica. Co-author, editor, pub. several books; pub., Pesca Marina, Marine and Fisheries Dictionary, Fernando Flores Ltd. Pub. Co., Los Angeles. Editor, pub. Index International, U.S. rep. Edimar, S.A. (pub. co.). Home: 527 N Las Palmas Av Los Angeles, CA 90004.

FLOREY, ROBERT, film dir.; b. Paris, France, Sept. 14, 1900; ed. France and Switzerland; came to U.S., 1921. Began motion picture career with Gaumont, Pathe, in France, later dir. Columbia, Tiffany, Universal, others in U.S.; dir. 1st Paramount sound films, L.I., N.Y. Directed motion pictures including: Hotel Imperial, Magnificent Fraud, Till We Meet Again, Desert Song, God Is My Co-Pilot, Danger Signal, Johnny One Eye, Vicious Years; dir. TV programs including: Four Star Playhouse,, 1952-53, Letters to Loretta, 1953-54, Schlitz Playhouse of Stars, Disneyland, Four Star Playhouse, 1954-55, Wire Service, Meridian, Four Star, 1956, Telephone Time, Zane Grey Theatre, Joseph Cotten Show, Jane Wyman Theatre, Wagon Train, Alfred Hitchcock Presents, Barbara Stanwyck Theatre, June Allyson, Checkmate, Michael Shayne, The Untouchables, Twilight Zone, Adventures in Paradise, Dick Powell Theatre, Going My Way. Author books on motion picture technique. Address: 11411 Ayrshire Rd Los Angeles CA 90049

FLORINSKY, MICHAEL, author, teacher; b. Kieff, Russia, Dec. 27, 1894; s. Timothy and Vera (Florinsky-Kremkoff) F.; student U. of Kieff Law Sch., 1913-14 and 1918-19, Michael Arty. Sch., Petrograd, 1914-15, London Sch. of Economics, 1920-21, King's Coll., London, 1922-23; M.A., Columbia, 1927, Ph.D., 1931; m. Louise Ligott Dear, Sept. 5, 1946. Associate editor Economic Social History of the War, Carnegie Endowment for Internat. Peace, 1921-32; asso. in economics, Columbia, 1931-36, lecturer 1937-46, asst. prof. 1947-53, asso. prof., 1953-56, professor economics, 1956-63, professor emeritus, 1963—. Served as junior officer in the 31st Regiment F.A., Russian Army, 1915-18; wounded in action, 1916. Mem. Council Fgn. Relations, Am. Hist. Association. Awarded four Russian Army decorations. Member of the Russian Greek Church. Author several books on Europe, also Russia: A History and an Interpretation, 1953; Integrated Europe, 1955; Russia: A Short History, 1964, revised edit., 1969. Co-author: Contemporary Europe, 1941. Editor of Commercial and Tariff History, 1939-41, McGraw Hill Ency. on Russia and the Soviet Union, 1960-61; editor paper back div. Russian series Crowell-Collier. Contbr. econ. articles to mags. Home: 14 Quai Perdonnet 1800 Vevey Switzerland

FLORIO, LLOYD JOSEPH, physician, fgn. service officer; b. Batavia, N.Y., Mar. 9, 1910; s. Flavio and Ida (Lindinann) F.; A.B., Cornell U., 1931; M.D., U. Rochester, 1935; Dr. P.H., Harvard, 1941; fellow tropical medicine Tulane U., 1942; study tissue culture U. Toronto, 1948; D.Sc. (hon.), Far Eastern U., Manila, P.I., 1966; m. Madeline Carey, June 24, 1937; children—Barbara, Marcia, David. Intern Buffalo Gen. Hosp., 1935- 36; fellow W. K. Kellogg Found., Battle Creek, Mich., 1937-40; asso. prof. pub. health U. Colo. Sch. Medicine, 1941-46, prof. pub. health, 1946-47, prof., head dept. preventive medicine and pub. health, 1947-57, mgr. health and hosps., 1952-59, clin. prof., 1957-59; fellow tropical medicine, Costa Rica, 1941, WHO, 1949; cons. USPHS Communicable Disease Center, Atlanta, 1948-57, pub. health in Korea, Am.-Korean Found., 1954, medicine Denver Gen. Hosp., to 1959, pub. health Children's Hosp., Denver, to 1959; chief health div. U.S. Operations Mission, Manila, 1959- 66; hon. prof. U. San Tomas, Manila, 1966; regional health adviser Near East and S. Asia, AID, 1967-68, human resources officer, Lima, Peru, 1968-69, asst. dir. (pub. health), Saigon, Vietnam, 1969—. Member bd. Nat. Tb Assn., 1947-59, v.p., 1956-57; editorial bd. Pub. Health Reports, 1954-57. Diplomate Am. Bd. Preventive Medicine and Pub. Health, 1949. Mem. Assn. Profs. Preventive Medicine (pres. 1950-53), Am., Colo. (pres. 1945-47) pub. health assns., A.M.A., Colo., Denver med. socs., A.C.P., Soc. Exptl. Biology and Medicine, A.A.A.S., Sigma Xi. Contbr. Profl. Publs. Address: USAID-ADPH APO San Francisco CA 96243

FLORIT, EUGENIO, educator, poet; b. Madrid, Spain, Oct. 15, 1903; s. Ricardo and Maria Sanchez, de Fuentes F.; B.A., Inst. La Habana (Cuba), 1922; LL.D., U. Havana, 1926. Came to U.S., 1940, naturalized, 1960. Mem. Cuban Consular Service, 1927-45; instr. Spanish, Columbia, 1942-45; prof. Spanish, Barnard Coll. and Grad. Sch. Columbia, 1945-69, prof. emeritus of Spanish, 1969. Mem. Hispanic Soc. Am., Modern Lang. Assn. Author several books poetry, anthologies, articles. Editor Revista Hispanica Moderna, 1960-69. Home: 440 Riverside Dr New York City NY 10027

FLOROVSKY, GEORGES, clergyman, educator; b. Odessa, Russia, Aug. 28, 1893; s. Basil and Claudia (Poprouzhenko) F.; diploma grad. studies, U. Odessa, 1916, research fellow, 1916-19; D.D., St. Andrews U. (Scotland), 1937; S.T.D., Boston U., 1950; Th.D., U. Salonica, 1959; LL.D., Notre Dame U., 1966; m. Xenia Simonov, Apr. 27, 1922. Came to U.S., 1948, naturalized, 1954. Lectr. philosophy U. Odessa, 1919-20; lectr. philosophy of law Russian Faculty Law, Prague, 1922-26; prof. patristics Orthodox Theol. Inst., Paris, 1926-48; ordained priest Greek Orthodox Ch., 1932; prof. divinity St. Vladimir's Orthodox Theol. Sem., N.Y.C., 1948-55, dean, 1950-55; adj. prof. history and theology Eastern orthodoxy Union Theol. Sem; adj. prof. religion Columbia, 195O-55; asso. prof. Greek Archdiocese Holy Cross Theol. Sch., Brookline, Mass., 1955-59; prof. eastern ch. history Harvard Divinity Sch., 1956-64, prof. emeritus, 1964—; sr. vis. fellow council humanities, vis. prof. religion and Slavics, Princeton, 1963- -; prof. patristic theology and philosophy of religion Holy Cross Theol. Sch., Brookline, Mass., 1963-65; also vis. lectr. church history Boston U., 1954-55. Mem. acad. council Ecumenical Inst. for Advanced Theol. Studies, Jerusalem, 1945—. Fellow Am. Acad. Arts and Scis.; mem. Royal Acad. of Athens (Greece) (corr. mem.), Am. Soc. Ch. History, World Council Chs. (mem. provisional com. 1938-46; assembly del. 1948, 54, 61, 68; central and exec. coms., del confs., 1937, 52, 63), Nat. Council Chs. Christ U.S.A. (v.p. 1954-57), Am. Hist. Assn., Am. Assn. for Advancement Slavic Studies. Home: 2 Nassau St Princeton NJ 08540

FLORSHEIM, LILLIAN HYMAN, (Mrs. Irving Florsheim), sculptor; b. New Orleans, May 17, 1896; d. Harris and Clara (Newman) Hyman; B.A., Smith Coll., 1916; m. Irving Florsheim, Feb. 14, 1918; children—Mary (Mrs. Mary Jones), Nancy (Mrs. Bertrand Goldberg). Exhibited in one man shows at Main St. Gallery, Chgo., 1966, No. Ill. U., 1966, Galerie Krugier, Geneva, Switzerland, 1967, Galerie Denise Rene, Paris, France, 1968, Galerie Denise Rene-Hans Mayer, Krefeld, Germany, 1969. Home: 1328 N State Pkwy Chicago IL 60610

FLORSHEIM, RICHARD ABERLE, artist; b. Chgo., Oct. 25, 1916; s. Leonard S. and Bertha (Aberle) F.; grad. cum laude, Chgo. Latin Sch., 1934; student U. Chgo., 1934-36; pvt. art studies, Europe and Near East, 1936-38; m. Helen Porfirieff, Feb. 14, 1948. Painter, printmaker, Chgo., 1938-42, 46—, tchr., lectr., 1946- -; one man shows Art Inst. Chgo., Inst. Nacional de Bellas Artes (Mexico), New Sch. Social Research, Milw. Art Inst., pvt. galleries; works represented permanent collections Mus. Modern Art, Met. Mus., Art Inst. Chgo., Cin. Art Mus., Library of Congress, Mus. of Modern Art Paris, Rome, Sao Paolo, Lima, Bibliothèque Nationale (Paris), others U.S. and abroad. U.S. del. Internat. Assn. Plastic Arts, 1963; mem. Ill. Arts Council, 1965—. Served as lt. USNR, 1942-46; mem. Res. Asso. Nat. Acad. Design; mem. Artists Equity Assn. (pres. 1954-55, hon. pres. 1955—), Soc. Am. Graphic Artists, Audubon Soc. Artists, Renaissance Soc. U. Chgo., Arts Club Chgo., Provincetown Art Assn. (hon. v.p., trustee), Provincetown Acad. Living Arts (trustee). Clubs: Lotos, Century (N.Y.C.); Beachcombers (Provincetown, Mass.). Painting Night City reproduced in Eliot's 300 Years of Am. Painting, 1958. Home: 5 E Ontario St Chicago IL 60611 also 651 Commercial St Provincetown MA 02657 Office: care ACA Galleries 25 E 73d St New York City NY 10021

FLORSHEIM, THOMAS W., shoe mfg. co. exec.; b. 1930; B.A., Wabash Coll.; M.A., U. Chgo., 1955; married. Sales mgr., v.p. Florsheim div. Internat. Shoe Co., 1955-64; pres. Weyenberg Shoe Mfg. Co., Milw., 1964-68, chmn. bd., chief exec. officer, 1968—; dir. Bowers Printing Co. Inc. Office: 234 E Reservoir Av Milwaukee WI 53201*

FLORY, ARTHUR LOUIS, artist, tchr.; b. Lima, O., Aug. 14, 1914; s. Louis and Lydia (Badowska) F.; student Phila. Mus. Sch. Art; m. Jane Trescott, Sept. 29, 1941; children—Cynthia, Christine, Erika. Exhibited in nat. exhbns., also Europe, Japan; represented in permanent collections Pa. Acad. Fine Arts, Phila. Mus. Art, New Britain (Conn.) Mus., Albany (N.Y.) Mus., Butler Art Inst., Youngstown, O., William Rockhill Nelson Mus., Kansas City, Mo., Nat. Gallery Art, Washington, Rosenwald collections, Tel Aviv Mus. Israel, Bibliotheque Nationale, Paris, Art Gallery New South Wales, Sydney, Australia, Bridgestone Gallery, Tokyo, Japan; numerous others; instr. paintings, graphics Tyler Sch. Fine Arts, Temple U., 1950-68; adviser lithography Phila. Coll. Art, 1968-70. Served with USCGR, 1942-44. Recipient 1st prize in painting Phila. Regional Art Exhbn., 1951; Purchase prize Albany Print Club, 1952; U.S. Govt. purchase prize, 1940; Eyre medal Pa. Acad. Fine Arts, Phila. Water Color Club. Rockefeller grantee to establish lithography workshop in Tokyo, 1960-61. Mem. Phila. Water Color Soc., Phila. Art Alliance, Artists Equity, Soc. Am. Graphic Artistists, Am. Color Print Soc., Phila. Print Club Rosenwald prize 1961), Print Council Am., Boston Printmakers, Phila. Water Color Club (dir.). Home: 1814 Beech Av Melrose Park PA 17752

FLORY, HARRY RUSSELL, newspaperman; b. Maysville, O., June 11, 1899; s. John and Mary Alice (Hess) F.; B.A., Coll. of Wooster, 1920; B.Litt., Columbia U., 1922; L.H.D., Coll. of Wooster, 1943; m. Florence King Gilman, Jan. 22, 1925; children—Harry R. (dec.), Marjorie Anne, Stewart Gilman. Worked as newsboy, printer's devil, pressman, reporter Wooster Daily News while attending high sch., coll.; reporter Akron Times, summer 1920; acting city editor Wooster Daily Record, summer 1921; staff corr. Internat. News Service, N.Y. City, Kansas City, Indianapolis, Chicago, Paris and London, 1922-26, Paris bureau mgr., 1926-28, London bureau mgr., 1928- 31; staff corr. United Press, London, 1931-34, asst. European News mgr., London, 1934-38, European news mgr. 1938-43 (hdqrs. transferred to N.Y. City, Dec. 1940), fgn. news mgr., dir. communications, 1943-52; gen. manager communications, 1952-64; communications cons. to Am. Newspaper Pubs. Assn., N.Y.C., 1964—. Established special communications arrangements between London and Amsterdam bureaus of United Press, Oct. 1939. Observer Internat. Telecommunications Conf., Cairo, 1938. Served as 2d lt. U.S. Army, Sept.-Dec. 1918. Trustee, Coll. of Wooster, 1948- 51. Mem. Phi Beta Kappa, Phi Sigma Kappa, Sigma Delta Chi. Club: University (N.Y.C.). Home: 47 E 87th St New York City NY 10028 also River Rd Newcastle ME 04553 Office: 750 3d Av New York City NY 10017

FLORY, JOHN, motion picture exec.; b. Cleve., July 28, 1910; s. Walter LeRoy and Julia Hall (McCune) F.; A.B., Yale, 1932; m. Elizabeth Harding, Dec. 25, 1944; 1 son, Jack Harding. Prodn. asst. This Is Am., 1932-33; producer, dir. author Mr. Motorboat's Last Stand, 1934; prodn. staff Paramount Pictures Inc., Hollywood, Cal., 1934-36; v.p. in charge prodn., distbn. Standard Films Cal., Hollywood, 1936-38; prodn. mgr. The City, Carnegie Corp., 1938; v.p. in charge prodn., distbn. Motion Picture Corp. Am., N.Y.C., 1939; producer, dir. Song Of A City for Cleve. Trust Co., 1940-41; exec. v.p. in charge prodn., distbn. Grant, Flory & Williams Inc., N.Y.C., 1941-47; pres. Flory Films Inc., N.Y.C., 1948-50; adviser non-theatrical films Eastman Kodak Co., Rochester 1950-65, cons. motion picture and edn. markets div., 1965- -. Chmn. 1st Internat. Film Cataloging Conf., 1951; mem. com. Bible Visualization Nat. Council Chs. Christ in U.S.A., 1953; mem. com. for radio and audio-visual edn., 1953—. Trustee Reynolds Library Found.; v.p., trustee U. Film Found. Fellow Soc. Motion Picture and TV Engrs.; mem. Internat. Radio and TV Execs., Nat. Inst. Audio-Visual Selling (bd. govs. 1953-54), N.E.A., Assn. for Ednl. Communications and Tech., Am. Sci. Film Assn., U. Film Assn., Ednl. Film Library Assn., Ednl. Film Producers Assn. (sec.), Nat. Audio-Visual Assn., Information Film Producers Assn. Am. (Jay E. Gordon Meml. award 1962), Nat. Advertisers (chmn. films com. 1951-56), Audio-Visual Council for Pub. Information, Council on Internat. Non.-Theatrical Events (pres. 1962-63, v.p. 1966-68), Soc. Am. Archivists, Audio Engring. Soc., A.A.A.S., Advt. Council Rochester, Soc. Cinephiles, Rochester C. of C., Rochester Audiovisual Assn. (pres. 1970), Zeta Psi, Delta Kappa Alpha (hon.). Clubs: Sales Executives (Rochester); Xale (N.Y.C.). Author: Films For Learning, 1968. Co-author: Designing New Apparatus For Learning, 1963. Editor: The Dollars and Sense of Business Films, 1954. Contbr. articles to profl. jours. Home: 36 Dogwood Glen Rochester NY 14625 Office: 343 State St Rochester NY 14650

FLORY, PAUL JOHN, educator; b. Sterling, Ill., June 19, 1910: s. Ezra and Martha (Brumbaugh) F.; B.S., Manchester Coll., 1931, Sc.D. (hon.), 1950; M.S., Ohio State U., 1931, Ph.D., 1934, Sc.D., 1970; m. Emily Catharine Tabor, Mar. 7, 1936; children—Susan, Melinda, Paul J. Engaged in research on synthetic fibers, synthetic rubber and other polymeric substances, DuPont Exptl. Sta., Wilmington, Del., 1934-38, U. Cin., 1938-40, Standard Oil Devel. Co., Elizabeth, N.J., 1940-43; dir. fundamental research Goodyear Tire & Rubber Co., Akron, O., 1943-48; prof. chemistry, Cornell U., 1948-57; exec. dir. research Mellon Inst., Pitts., 1956-61; prof. chemistry Stanford, 1961—, now chmn. chemistry dept. Recipient Sullivant medal Ohio State U., 1945; Baekeland award Am. Chem. Soc., 1947; George Fisher Baker non-resident lectureship in chemistry Cornell U., 1948; Peter Debye award in phys. chemistry Am. Chem. Soc., 1968. Mem. Am. Chem. Soc., Nat. Acad. Scis., A.A.A.S., Am. Acad. Arts and Scis., Am. Phys. Soc., Sigma Xi. Author: Principles of Polymer Chemistry and of Statistical Mechanics of Chain Molecules. Contbr. to sci. publs. Pioneered research on constitution and properties of substances comprised of giant molecules (rubbers, plastics, fibers, films, proteins, etc.). Home: 210 Golden Oak Dr Portola Valley CA 94025 Office: Stanford U Stanford CA 94305

FLORY, WALTER S. Jr., geneticist, botanist; born at Bridgewater, Va., Oct. 5, 1907; s. Walter Samuel and Ella May (Reherd) F.; A.B., Bridgewater Coll., 1928, Sc.D. (hon.), 1953; A.M., U. Va. (Blandy fellow, 1928-31), 1929, Ph.D., 1931; Nat. Research fellow in biol. scis. and research asso., Harvard, 1935-36; m. (Nellie) Maude Thomas, Apr. 24, 1930 (dec. 1971); children—Kathryn Sue (Mrs. Walter Maier), Walter Samuel, and Thomas Reherd. In charge of technical work Shaver Brothers, Incorporated, Jacksonville and Tampa, Fla., 1931-32; instr. in sci., Greenbrier Coll., Lewisburg, W.Va., 1932-34; prof. biology, Bridgewater Coll., 1934-35; horticulturist, Tex. Agrl. Expt. Sta., 1936-44, Va. Agrl. Expt. Sta., 1944-47; prof. exptl. horticulture U. Va., 1947-63; vice dir., mgr. Blandy Exptl. Farm, 1947-63, vis. prof., summer 1964; curator O. E. White Research Arboretum, 1955-63; mem. board directors Winston-Salem Nature Sci. Center, 1964-69, treas., 1965-66; Babcock professor botany Wake Forest Univ., Winston-Salem, N.C., 1963—; dir. Reynolda Gardens, 1964—; instnl. lectr. Piedmont University Center, 1965-70; collaborator to the United States Dept. Agr., 1945-48. Trustee of Bridgewater Coll. Del. Internat. Botany Congress, Paris, 1954,

Montreal, 1959, Edinburgh, 1964; mem. Internat. Genetics Congress, Montreal, 1958, Tokyo, 1968, Internat. Hort. Congress, 1966. Trustee, mem. exec. com. Highlands Biological Sta. (pres. 1969-71). Recipient J. Shelton Horsley Research award Va. Acad. Sci., 1949; Pres. and Visitors Research prize U. Va., 1951; Bridgewater Coll. Alumni award, 1956; I.F. Lewis distinguished service award Va. Acad. Sci., 1969. Fellow A.A.A.S.; mem. Am. Soc. Hort. Sci., Genetics Soc. Am., Am. Genetics Assn., Soc. Study Evolution, Bot. Soc. Am. (chmn. southeastern sect. 1951-52), Assn. Southeastern Biologists (pres. 1962-63), Am. Boxwood Soc. (co-founder, treas., editor 1961-63), Am. Assn. Bot. Gardens and Arboretums (editorial bd. 1962-64), Am. Begonia Soc. (hon.), Fairchild Tropical Garden (life), So. Appalachian Bot. Club (v.p. 1962), Am. Plant Life Soc., Va. Acad. Sci. (pres. 1956; chmn. long range planning com. 1960-62, chmn. biology sect., 1962-63), La. Soc. Hort. Research (hon.), Am. Magnolia Soc. (v.p. 1968-71), Phi Beta Kappa, Sigma Xi (chpt. pres. 1970), Tau Kappa Alpha, Phi Sigma. Democrat. Mem. Ch. of Brethren. Club: Torch (local pres. 1970). Contbr. articles on genetics, cytology and hort. subjects in profl. jours. and mags. Home: 2025 Colonial Pl Winston-Salem NC 27104

FLORY, WILLIAM EVANS SHERLOCK, educator; b. Canton, O., Apr. 25, 1914; s. Wilson Reese and Frances (Sherlock) F.; A.B., Coll. Wooster, 1935; A.M., Duke, 1938, Ph.D., 1941; m. Anne Randolph Putney, June 4, 1938; children—William, Anne. Various teaching positions Ohio and Ga., 1935-39; analyst Princeton U. govt. surveys, 1940; dir. research N.J. Municipal Aid Adminstrn., Trenton, 1940-42; analyst N.Y. Joint Legislative Economy Commn. Albany, 1942-43, Bur. Budget, Washington, 1943-44; dep. asst. to under-sec. State, Washington, 1944-50; econ. policy adviser to sec. Interior, Washington, 1950-53; staff economist Office Bur. Mines and Minerals and Solid Fuels, Washington, 1953-61, dir., 1961-69; asso. prof. marketing Am. U. Sch. Bus. Adminstrn., Washington, 1969—. Cons. investments. Commr., Prince William County Hist. Commn., Manassas, Va., 1969—. Mem. Am. Soc. Internat. Law, Am. Marketing Assn. Democrat. Episcopalian. Author: Prisoners of War, 1941, Restoration of Historic Bel Air Plantation. Contbr. to govt. publs. Home: Bel Air Planation 14313 Minnieville Rd Woodbridge VA 22191 Office: School Business Adminstrn The American Univ Washington DC 20016

FLORY, WILLIAM R., hotel exec.; b. Rockingham County, Va., Mar. 26, 1897; s. George William and Leila Abbie (McKinney) F.; A.B., Juniata Coll., Huntingdon, Pa., 1921. President, dir. Grenoble Hotels, Inc., Harrisburg, Pa., 1933—, operating chain of 23 hotels; pres., dir. Chambersburg (Pa.) Hotel Corp. since 1943, Va. Operating Co., Portsmouth, 1945—, Tenn. Hotels, Inc., Cleveland, 1954- -; dir. Am. Hotels Corp., N.Y.C., Richard McAllister Realty Corp., Hanover, Pa., Radford (Va.) Hotel Corp., Asso. Hotels, Inc., Whiteville, N.C., Asso. Va. Hotels, Inc., Wytheville, Va. Hotel Operators, Inc., Radford. Trustee Juniata Coll. Mem. Am. Hotel Assn. (past nat. chmn. smaller hotels com.). Mason (32,Shriner). Home: 8 Clemson Dr Cedar Cliff Camp Hill PA 17011 Office: State St Bldg Harrisburg PA 17101

FLOTT, FREDERICK WILLIAM, fgn. service officer; b. Chgo., May 8, 1921; s. Frederick William and Anna Wills (Fleming) F.; B.A., Carleton Coll., 1942; M.A., Sch. Advanced Internat. Studies, 1947; student Escola Livre de Sociologia e Politica, Sao Paulo, Brazil, summer 1941, Georgetown U. Sch. Langs. and Linguistics, 1952-53. Joined U.S. Fgn. Service, 1947; vice consul Am. embassy, Paris, France, 1947-51; assigned European hdqrs. ECA, Paris, 1951-52, Tehran, 1954-56; 2d sec. Am. embassy, Bonn, Germany, 1957-59, Geneva, Switzerland, 1959-62, State Dept., 1962-63; 1st sec. embassy, Saigon, Viet-Nam, 1963-66; assigned Bur. East Asian and Pacific Affairs, Dept. State, 1966, spl. asst. to dep. under-sec. for econ. affairs, 1969-70, spl. asst. to asst. sec. for East Asian and Pacific affairs, 1970—. Mem. Phi Beta Kappa. Home: 2301 E St NW Washington DC 20037 Office: Dept State Washington DC

FLOWER, BARDWELL HASTINGS, physician; b. Rupert, Vt., Apr. 27, 1902; s. Albert H. and Mary E. (Roberts) F.; A.B., Wesleyan U., Middletown, Conn., 1923; M.D., Harvard, 1928; D.Sc., Assumption Coll., Worcester, Mass., 1970; m. Maveret E. Hughes, Aug. 9, 1927; children—Constance (Mrs. Robert L. Porter), Martha Hughes (Mrs. William J. Stromer), David Albert (dec.), Bardwell Hastings (dec.). Intern Worcester (Mass.) City Hosp., 1929-30; sr. physician Worcester State Hosp., 1931-34; asst. supt. Grafton State Hosp., North Grafton, Mass., 1934- 38; asst. commr. Mass. Dept. Mental Health, 1938-41; supt. Worcester State Hosp., 1941-69; cons. forensic psychiatry Vt. State Hosp., Waterbury, 1970—. Diplomate Am. Bd. Psychiatry and Neurology. Mem. A.M.A., Mass., Worcester Dist. med. socs., Am. Psychiat. Assn., New Eng. Soc. Psychiatry, Vt. Psychiat. Assn. Clubs: Rotary, Torch (Worcester). Address: West Rupert VT 05776

FLOWER, JOHN ARNOLD, educator; b. Aberdeen, Wash., Feb. 4, 1921; s. Lloyd Edwin and Linda (Nelson) F.; B.A., U. Wash., 1948; Mus. M., U. Mich., 1951, Ph.D., 1956; certificate, Conservatoire Americaine, Fontainebleau, France, 1955; m. Lanette Sheaffer, Feb. 1, 1951; children—Jill Tenwick, John Arnold II. Instr. music U. Mich., 1952-62, prof. music, asso. dean music, 1962-66; prof., asso. provost Kent (O.) State U., 1966—; dean Blossom Festival Sch. of Cleve. Orch. and Kent State U.; harpsichordist U. Mich. Baroque Trio, 1963-65; cons. U.S. Office Edn.; cons., examiner N. Central Assn. Colls. Bd. dirs. Ohio Outdoor Theater Assn., Cleve. Ballet Guild, Peninsula Valley Heritage Assn., Western Res. Found. Served to capt. USAAF, 1942-46. Mem. Internat. Assn. Fine Arts Deans, Pi Kappa Lambda, Pi Kappa Delta. Contbr. articles profl. jours. Home: Wellgate Hudson OH 44236 Office: Coll Fine and Profl Arts Kent State U Kent OH 44240

FLOWER, MILTON EMBICK, educator; b. Harrisburg, Pa., Feb. 27, 1910; s. C. Guiles and Lenore (Embick) F.; A.B., Dickinson Coll., 1931; A.M., Columbia, 1937, Ph.D., 1946. Research historian Army Information Sch., 1946-47; faculty Dickinson Coll., 1947—, prof. polit. sci., 1957—, chmn. dept., 1961- 69, Robert Blaine Weaver prof., 1968—; vis. prof. diplomatic history Am. U., fall 1950; vis. prof. Am. studies Faculte des Lettres, U. Dijon (France), 1955-56; spl. research Am. primitive art; lectr. as Am. specialist for U.S. Dept. State in Japan, S.E. Asia, India and Pakistan, 1962-63. Mem. Gov.'s Adv. Commn. Elections and Election Laws. Sec. Carlisle Municipal Planning and Zoning Commn. Grantee Am. Assn. State and Local History, 1961. Mem. Am. Polit. Sci. Assn., Am. Hist. Assn., Acad. Polit. Sci., Am. Assn. U. Profs., Am. Studies Assn., Pi Gamma Mu. Lutheran. Author: (with Lenore E. Flower) This is Carlisle, 1944; Life of James Parton, 1951; Carpenter's Companies and Carlisle Architecture, 1955; also monographs. Editor: Dear Folks at Home: Civil War Letters . . ., 1963. Contbr. articles profl. jours. Home: 166 W Pomfret St Carlisle PA 17013

FLOWER, WALLACE MCFARLAND, investment banker; b. Chgo., Oct. 1, 1903; s. Jewell and Louise (McFarland) F.; A.B., U. Mich., 1924; M.B.A., Harvard, 1926; m. Ruth Kreutzer; 1 son by previous marriage—Wallace; 1 dau., Elizabeth; step- children—Keith, Daniel. Partner William Blair & Co., Chgo., 1944—; dir. S & C Electric Co., A.M. Castle Co., Chgo., Fansteel Co., Chgo. Trustee Hull House. Clubs: University, Saddle and Cycle (Chgo.) Home: 1085 Sheridan Rd Winnetka IL 60093 Office: 135 S LaSalle St Chicago IL 60603

FLOWERREE, ROBERT EDMUND, paper co. exec .; b. New Orleans, Jan. 4, 1921; s. Robert E. and Amy (Hewes) F.; B.A., Tulane U., 1942; m. Elaine Dicks, Sept. 22, 1943; children—Robert E. III, Ann D., John H., David R. Vice pres. Georgia- Pacific Corp., 1956-63, exec. v.p. pulp, paper and chem. operations, 1963—, also dir.; hon. director Nat. Security Bank, Toledo, Ore. Knight of Malta. Clubs: Arlington, Waverly Country (Portland); Boston (New Orleans); Canadian (N.Y.C.). Home: 02425 S W Military Rd Portland OR 97219 Office: Georgia-Pacific Corp 900 SW 5th Av Portland OR 97204

FLOWERS, CHARLES ELY, Jr., physician, educator; b. Zebulon, N.S., Can., July 20, 1920; s. Charles Ely and Carmen (Poole) F.; B.S., The Citadel, 1941; M.D., Johns Hopkins, 1944; m. Juanita Bays, Nov. 23, 1944 (dec.); children—Charles Ely III, Carmen Eva. Intern Johns Hopkins Hosp., 1944, resident, 1945-50; instr. State U.. N.Y., 1950-51, asst. prof., 1951-53; asso. prof. U. N.C., 1953-61, prof., 1961-66; prof., chmn. dept. obstetrics and gynecology Baylor U. Med. Sch., 1966-69, U. Ala. Med. Center, Birmingham, 1969—; obstetrician and gynecologist in chief U. Ala. Hosp., 1969—. Cons. NIH; mem. adv. com. oral contraceptives Internat. Planned Parenthood; mem. nat. clin. adv. com. United Cerebral Palsy Assn.; chmn. 6th World Congress Gynecology and Obstetrics, 1970. Served to capt. M.C., AUS, 1946-48. Mem. A.M.A., Continental Gynecol. Soc., Am. Gynecol. Soc., Am., Central assns. obstetricians and gynecologist, A.C.S., Am. Coll. Obstetricians and Gynecologists (chmn. com. obstetrics anesthesia and analgesia), Internat. Coll. Anesthetists. Mem. editorial bd. Obstetrics and Gynecology. Home: 3757 Rockhill Rd Birmingham AL 35223

FLOWERS, CHARLES HOWARD, author; b. Knoxville, Tenn., Nov. 12, 1942; s. Howard Fischer and Rose Sullins (Canup) F.; A.B. magna cum laude, Harvard, 1964. Reporter Chattanooga Times, summers 1961-64, book reviewer, 1966-71; head English dept. Catalina Island Sch., Avalon, Cal., 1965-67; drama coach Palmdale (Cal.) Sch., 1967-68; audiovisual coordinator Fremont Sch., Los Angeles, 1968-69. Recipient Thomas R. Coward prize novel award, 1970. Fellow MacDowell Artists' Colony, Bread Loaf Writers' Conf. Mem. Authors Guild. Club: Monday Malcontents Soc. (N.Y.C.). Author: It Never Rains in Los Angeles, 1970. Home: 12 E 10th St New York City NY 10003 Office: care Lucy Kroll Agy 119 W 57th St New York City NY 10019

FLOWERS, PAUL ABBOTT, journalist, educator; b. Trenton, Tenn., Mar. 30, 1905; s. F. C. and Louise (Dance) F.; student La. Coll., Pineville, 1925-26; B.A., Ohio State U., 1940, M.A., 1942; D.Litt., Erskine Coll., 1960; m. Louise Templeton, Dec. 26, 1936; 1 son, Frank Templeton. Reporter, Lake Charles (La.) Am.-Press, 1922-25, Alexandria (La.) Town Talk, 1926-27, Shreveport (La.) Times, 1927-28; copyreader Birmingham (Ala.) News, 1928; telegraph editor Age-Herald, Birmingham, 1929, also news editor Lake Charles Am. Press; feature writer, photographer The Enterprise, Beaumont, Tex., 1929-30; reporter Comml. Appeal, Memphis, 1931, The Times, El Paso, Tex., 1931; copyreader News and Age-Herald, Birmingham, 1933-37; telegraph editor Ohio State Jour., Columbus, 1937-41; asst. prof. journalism W.Va. U., 1941-43; columnist, book editor The Comml. Appeal, Memphis, 1943-71; instr. creative writing Southwestern U., 1945; asso. prof. polit. sci. Memphis State Coll., 1946-47; asst. prof. polit. sci. Sch. Nursing U. Tenn. Extension, 1948—; asst. prof. journalism Miss. State Coll. for Women, Columbus, 1964- 66. Mem. exec. com., dir. Memphis Heart Assn. Mem. Sigma Delta Chi, Kappa Tau Alpha. Presbyn. Home: 30 N Highland St Memphis TN 38111 Office: Joint Univ Center 127 Madison Av Memphis TN 38103

FLOWERS, WALTER, congressman; b. Greenville, Ala., Apr. 12, 1933; s. Walter W. and Ruth (Swaim) F.; A.B., U. Ala., 1955, LL.B., 1957; Rotary Found. fellow, U. London, 1957-58; m. Margaret V. Pringle, Aug. 21, 1958; children—Vivian Victoria, Walter Winkler III, Victor Woodley. Admitted to Ala. bar, 1957, Miss. bar, 1960; sr. partner firm Flowers and Shelby, Tuscaloosa, Ala., 1961-68; mem. 91st to 92d Congresses, 5th Dist. Ala. Past mem. Black Warrior council Boy Scouts Am., Tuscaloosa YMCA; former mem., chmn. Tuscaloosa Civil Service Bd.; past pres. Tuscaloosa County Mental Health Assn. Past bd. dirs. Tuscaloosa County chpt. A.R.C., Tuscaloosa Tb Assn. Served to 1st lt. U.S. Army Res., 1958-59. Mem. Am., Miss., Ala., Tuscaloosa County bar assns., U. Ala. Alumni Assn. (past pres. Tuscaloosa County), Phi Beta Kappa, Omicron Delta Kappa, Jasons Soc., Phi Delta Phi, Sigma Alpha Epsilon. Democrat. Episcopalian. Rotarian. Home: 2111 14th St Tuscaloosa AL 35401 Office: House of Representatives Washington DC 20515

FLOWERS, WILLIAM HOWARD, Jr., food co. exec.; b. Thomasville, Ga., Nov. 14, 1913; s. William Howard and Flewellyn Evans (Strong) F.; B.S. in Bus. Adminstrn., Washington and Lee U., 1933; m. Fontaine Maury Tice, June 22, 1936; children—Fontaine (Mrs. Thomas Garcin Parker), Maury, Daphne (Mrs. C. Martin Wood III), Taliaferro. With Flowers Baking Co. div. Flowers Industries, Inc., Thomasville, Ga., 1933-68, chmn. bd., chief exec. officer, 1965-68; chmn. bd., chief exec. officer Flowers Industries, Inc., Thomasville, 1968—; pres., Container Industries, Inc., Jacksonville, Fla. 1950—; dir. Am. Heritage Life Ins. Co., Jacksonville, Fla. Mem. spl. adv. com. on pub. opinion U.S. Dept. State, 1970—. Mem. Thomas County Sch. Bd., 1953-58, Madeira Sch. Corp., Greenway, Va., 1960-68. Mem. Ga. Senate, 1964-68; city commr., Thomasville, 1941. Trustee William Howard Flowers Found., John D. Archbold Meml. Hosp., Thomasville. Named Man of Year, Thomas County C. of C., 1964. Mem. N.A.M. (dir. 1962-66), Young Presidents' Orgn., Chief Execs. Forum, Ducks Unltd. (nat. trustee 1967—), Kappa Alpha. Episcopalian. Clubs: Lyford Cay (Nassaua); Sapphire Valley Country, Wildcat Cliffs Country (Highlands, N.C.); Farmington Country (Charlottesville, Va.). Office: Home: Merrily Plantation Thomasville GA 31792

FLOYD, CARL M., banker; b. Atlanta, 1907. Sr. v.p. Fulton Nat. Bank, Atlanta. Home: 5660 Lake Forest Dr NW Atlanta GA 30305 Office: PO Box 4387 Atlanta GA 30302*

FLOYD, CARLISLE, composer, educator; b. Latta, S.C., June 11, 1926; s. Carlisle Sessions and Ida (Fenegan) F.; Mus.B., Syracuse U., 1946, Mus. M., 1949; m. Kay Reeder, Nov. 28, 1957. Mem. faculty Sch. Music Fla. State U., Tallahassee, 1947—, now prof. music; composer Slow Dusk (mus. play), 1949, Susannah (mus. drama), 1954, Pilgrimage, 1955, Sonata For Piano, 1957, Wuthering Heights (mus. drama), 1958, The Mystery, 1960, The Passion of Jonathan Wade (mus. drama), 1962, The Sojourner and Mollie Sinclair (comedy-drama), 1963, Markheim (mus. drama), 1965, Of Mice and Men (mus. drama), 1970. Recipient Citation of Merit, Nat. Assn. Am. Composers and Condrs., 1957, N.Y. Music Critics Circle award, 1957; named one of ten Outstanding Young Men, U.S. Jr. C. of C., 1959; Guggenheim fellow, 1956. Mem. A.S.C.A.P., Am. Guild Mus. Artists, Pi Kappa Lambda, Phi Mu Alpha, Delta Omicron. Democrat. Episcopalian. Home: 806 Middlebrook Circle Tallahassee FL 32303

FLOYD, EDWIN EARL, educator; b. Eufaula, Ala., May 8, 1924; s. John Quincy and Ludie (James) F.; B.A., U. Ala., 1943; Ph.D., U. Va., 1948; m. Marguerite Stahl, May 11, 1945; children—Judith L., Sally J., William J. Instr. math. Princeton, 1948-49; mem. faculty U. Va., 1949—, prof. math., 1956- -, Robert Taylor prof., chmn. dept., 1966-69; mem. Inst. Advanced Study, 1958-59, 63-64. Sloan Research fellow, 1962-64. Author: (with P.E. Conner) Differentiable Periodic Maps, 1964; also articles. Home: 144 Bennington Rd Charlottesville, VA 22901.

FLOYD, EUGENE HARLOW, coll. ofcl.; b. Caney, Kan., Aug. 23, 1910; s. Harry E. and Anna May (Hosford) F.; Ph.B., Washburn Coll., Topeka, 1935; A.M., Boston U., 1939, S.T.B., 1940; m. Ruth Marie Winship, Dec. 18, 1939. Dir. placement Hamline U., 1941-42; exec. sec. U. Neb. YMCA, 1943-44; asso. sec. Penn State Christian Assn., 1946; asst. to pres. Washburn U., 1946-49; asst. to pres. Boston U., 1949-59, coordinator univ. functions, 1959-60; dean adminstrn. Western New Eng. Coll., Springfield, Mass., 1961-64, asst. to pres., 1964-65, dean of students, 1965-67, dir. financial aid, 1967—, asst. dean Sch. Law, 1970—. Served to lt. (s.g.) USNR, 1944-46. Mem. Eastern Assn. Student Financial Aid Adminstrs., Nat. Assn. Fgn. Student Affairs, Mass. Assn. Student Financial Aid Adminstrs., Kan. Hist. Soc., Am. Personnel and Guidance Assn., Am. Coll. Personnel Assn., Pi Gamma Mu, Alpha Phi Omega. Home: 97 Forest Park Av Springfield, MA 01108.

FLOYD, GEORGE CROSBIE, steel co. exec.; b. Butte, Mont., Dec. 20, 1904; s. John and Jessie (Smith) F.; A.B. in Chemistry, U. Mont., 1927; Ph.D. in Chemistry, Cornell U., 1933; m. Marie A. Gebel, Nov. 23, 1935; children—James G., David G., Linda G. Metallurgist stainless steel Republic Steel Corp., Massillon, O., 1933-36; supt. alloy dept. Allegheny Ludlum Steel Corp., West Leechburg, Pa., 1936-40, plant mgr., 1940-47; v.p. operations Thomas Steel Co., Warren, O., 1947-52; v.p., dir. Vandium Corp. Am., N.Y.C., 1952-60, sr. v.p., 1960-63; v.p., asst. to pres. Sharon Steel Corp. (Pa.), 1963-70. Mem. Am. Chem. Soc., Am. Soc. Metals, Am. Inst. Mining, Metall. and Petroleum Engrs., Am. Iron and Steel Inst. Club: Duquesne (Pitts.). Home: 2107 Arms Dr Girard OH 44420

FLOYD, JAMES C., aviation consultant; b. Eng., Oct. 20, 1914; s. James and Annie Elizabeth (Wilkinson) F.; Higher nat. certificate Manchester Coll. Tech., 1935; m. Irene Habbeshaw, July 8, 1940; children—David, Noel, Michael, Paul. Training aircraft engring. A. V. Roe & Co., Manchester, Eng., 1930-46, chief project engr., 1944-46; chief design engr. Avro Aircraft Ltd., Malton, Ont., 1946, chief engr., 1952-55, v.p. engring., 1955-59, designer Avro Jetliner (N.A.'s 1st jet transport); with advanced projects group Hawker Siddeley Aviation, Ltd., 1959-62; chief cons. J.C. Floyd & Assos., Epsom, Surrey, Eng., 1962—. Recipient Wright Bros. medal, Soc. Automotive Engrs., 1950; McCurdy Award, Canadian Aero. Inst., 1958, George Taylor gold medal, Royal Aero. Soc., 1962. Fellow Royal Aero. Soc., Canadian Aero. Inst., Inst. Aero. Scis. (chmn. Toronto br. 1948-49). Author tech. papers. Address: Lloyd's Bank Chambers Epsom Surrey England

FLOYD, JAMES WHITNEY, forester, univ. dean; b. Bloomington, Ida., May 11, 1903; s. Lyman Harvey and Charlotta Maretta (Nelson) F.; student Brigham Young U., 1923- 24, Ida. State Coll., 1929-31, Ricks Coll., Rexburg, Ida., 1924-25; B.S., Utah State Agrl. Coll., 1935; M.S., U. Calif., 1942; m. Virginia Payne, May 14, 1934; children—Darrell Whitney, Lyman John, Beverly, Dianne. Instr. in forestry, Utah State U., 1935-36, asst. prof., 1936-42, asso. prof., 1942-45, prof. forestry, 1945—, head dept. forest mgmt., 1949-65, acting dean Coll. Forest, Range and Wildlife Management, 1959-61, dean, 1961—, extension forester, 1935-45; dean of Coll. of Natural Resources; chief forester-fire warden, Utah, 1942-61; forestry cons. to ICA, Iran, 1955. State coordinator, Fire Fighters Orgns. of Utah. Chmn. state governor fire prevention com., 1946-48. Fellow Soc. Am. Foresters (chmn. program com. 1946); mem. A.A.A.S., Am. Forestry Assn., Assn. State Foresters (chmn. program com. 1950, pres. 1958), Zi Sigma Pi. Club: Kiwanis (mem. agrl. com., 1946, lt. gov., Utah- Ida. dist. 1947). Home: 1270 E 19th N North Logan UT 84321 Office: Utah State Univ Logan UT 84321

FLOYD, MARQUETTE LAVERNE, dist. ct. judge; b. Winnsboro, S.C., Oct. 14, 1928; s. Clinton L. and Bernice (Floyd) Brown; B.S., N.Y.U., 1958; LL.B., Bklyn. Law Sch., 1960; m. Helen E. Young, May 7, 1948; children—Stafford, Jonathan, Braxton. Admitted to N.Y. bar, 1961, also U.S. Dist. Ct.; practicing atty., 1961-69; dist. ct. judge Suffolk County, N.Y., 1969—. Pres. Ronek Park Civic Assn., 1961-64; chmn. ACE Opportunity Center Poverty Agy., Amityville, N.Y. Pres. North Amityville Rep. Club, 1964-66. Dir. Sunrise Psychiat. Hosp. Served to sgt., USAAF, 1948-54. Named man of year, County Line Guild Career Women, 1970. Mem. Suffolk County Magistrates Assn., Suffolk County Bar Assn., Suffolk County Criminal Bar Assn. Home: 621 N Broadway Amityville NY 11701 Office: Veterans Memorial Hwy Haupauge NY

FLOYD, MORRIS, business exec.; b. Jeffersonville, Ind., Sept. 5, 1901; s. Irwin and Grace (Morris) F.; A.B. (Rector scholar), DePauw U., Greencastle, Ind., 1924; m. Jane Frazer Wiglesworth, Oct. 18, 1931; 1 son John A. Patton. Salesman, Wood Conversion Co., Cloquet, Minn., 1925-28; v.p. Gen. Iron Works Co., Cin., 1929-32; mgr. div. Edwards Mfg. Co., Cin., 1932-33; pres. Morris Floyd & Con., mfrs. agts., 1933-45; pres., treas. Floyd & Co., Inc., Cin., 1945—; pres., pub. Palm Beach (Fla.) Illustrated, 1958-60; dir. Conrad Spring Co.; devel. and market research cons. Peerless div. Dover Corp. Active fund raising drives. Bd. dirs. Citizen's Devel. Com.; pres. bd. trustees Mus. Nat. Hist., 1946-64, now hon. life trustee. Vice chmn. Longview Hosp. Citizens Com.; mem. Gov.'s Natural Resources Commn., 1963-64. Served as seaman USNRF, 1917-19. Mem. Am. Soc. Heating. Refrigerating and Air Conditioning Engrs., A.I.M. (pres.'s council), Gas Equipment Assn. (pres. 1949-51), D.A.V., Am. Legion, Sigma Nu, Delta Nu Epsilon, Theta Un Epsilon. Clubs: Queen City, University (Cin.); Everglades, Beach (charter Palm Beach); Pendennis (Louisville); Optimist; Tequesta. Owner, breeder thoroughbred race horses. Home: 254 Golf View Dr Tequesta FL 33458 Office: Executive Bldg Tequesta FL 33458

FLOYD, RAYMOND, golfer; b. Ft. Bragg, N.C., Sept. 14, 1942; s. Loren B. and Edith (Brown) F.; student U. N.C., 1940. Profl. golfer, 1961—, winner PGA tournament, 1963, 1969, others; mem. Ryder Cup team, 1969. Served with AUS, 1961-63. Named Rookie of Year Golf Mag., 1963. Club: Preston Trail Golf (Dallas). Home: 20 E Cedar Apt 2D Chicago IL 60611 Office: 1 Erieview Plaza Suite 1300 Cleveland OH 44114*

FLUCKEY, EUGENE BENNETT, naval officer; b. Washington, Oct. 5, 1913; s. Isaac Newton and Luella (Snowden) F.; B.S., U.S. Naval Acad., 1935; student design engring., U.S. Naval Postgrad. Sch., 1943; grad. Nat. War Coll., 1960; m. Marjorie Palmer Gould, June 6, 1937; 1 dau., Barbara Ann (Mrs. Charles Bove, Jr.). Commd. ensign U.S. Navy, 1935, advanced through grades to rear adm., 1960; comdr. U.S.S. Barb, World War II; aid to Adm. Nimitz, 1946-47; naval attache, Lisbon, Portugal, 1950-53; comdr. S. Atlantic Amity Force, 1961, Submarine Force, U.S. Pacific Fleet, 1964-66; dir. naval intelligence, 1966-68; comdr. Iberian Atlantic Area (NATO), Lisbon,

Portugal, 1968—. Decorated Congl. Medal of Honor, Navy Cross (4); Legion of Merit (2), Portugese Medalha Militar, unit citations and area ribbons. Home: Quintas Dos Golfinhos Dourados Rua Rio Da Bica 34 São Pedro Da Sintra Portugal Office: Comdr Iberian Atlantic Area Oeiras (Lisbon) Portugal

FLUETSCH, JOHN FOSTER, savs. and loan assn. exec.; b. Merced, Cal., Feb. 13, 1936; s. John Jay and Helen (Shaffer) F.; B.A., Stanford, 1953-57; m. Jimi Lou Cargil, Apr. 13, 1957; children—Timmy, Tommy, Margaret, Barbara, Diane, Michael. Trainee, 1st Western Bank, Redwood City and Merced, 1957-59; asst. mgr. Stanislaus-Merced Savs. & Loan, Merced, 1959-62, mgr., 1963-65; exec. v.p., sr. loan officer State Savs. & Loan, Stockton, Cal., 1965-70, exec. v.p., mng. officer, 1970—, also dir.; pres., dir. San Goronio Savs. & Loan, Stockton, 1968-70. Bd. dirs. Merced United Crusade, 1962-65. Mem. Am. Mgmt. Assn., Pres.'s Assn., C. of C., Savs. and Loan Inst., Alpha Sigma Phi. Kiwanian. Club: Big Valley Ad (pres., dir. 1967) (Stockton). Home: 11342 N Alpine Rd Stockton CA 95205 Office: 222 N El Dorado St Stockton CA 95201

FLUG, MARTIN RAPHAEL, mgmt. cons.; b. N.Y.C., Jan. 6, 1931; s. Samuel S. and Evelyn (Raphael) F.; B.A., Harvard, 1952, M.B.A., 1957; LL.B., Yale, 1955; m. Elaine Allen, Aug. 26, 1951 (div.); 1 son, Jeremy Jay. Admitted to N.Y. bar, 1955; chmn., treas. Flug Rowley Assos., Inc. mgmt. cons., N.Y.C., 1957—, Columbia TV Co., Inc., N.Y.C., 1962—; chmn. bd. Mahon Tech. Group, Inc., N.Y.C.; vice chmn. Atlas Pacific Engring. Co., Emeryville, Cal.; pres. RCM Corp., N.Y.C.; dir. Maloney-Crawford Tank Corp., Tulsa. Office: 60 E 42d St New York City NY 10017

FLUNO, ROBERT YOUNGER, educator; b. Appleton, Wis., Nov. 27, 1916; s. Arthur Swetland and Elsie (Younger) F.; A.B., Rollins Coll., 1938; postgrad. Am. U., 1938-40, London (Eng.) Sch. Econs., 1950-51; Ph.D., U. Minn., 1952; m. Ruth Lilja, Jan. 18, 1944. Civil servant U.S. Govt., Washington, 1938-42, 45; instr. polit. sci. U. Minn., 1946-48; asst. prof. Mount Union Coll., Alliance, O., 1948-52; asso. prof. Whitman Coll., Walla Walla., Wash., 1952-56, prof. polit. sci., 1956-60, Miles C. Moore prof., 1960—; reader polit. sci. U. Rajshahi, Pakistan, 1957. Adv. com. Wash. Civil Liberties Unions, 1957-58, 62-68; exec. bd. Wash. Citizenship Clearing House, 1954-67. Served from ensign to lt., USNR, 1942-45. Mem. Am., Western, Pacific N.W. (pres. 1970-71) polit. sci. assns., Am. Assn. U. Profs., Am. Acad. Polit. and Social Sci. Author: (with Chester C. Maxey) The American Problem of Government, 1957; The Democratic Community, 1971. Home: 725 Valencia St Walla Walla, WA 99362.

FLUOR, JOHN ROBERT, engr.; b. Santa Ana, Cal., Dec. 18, 1921; s. Peter E. and Margaret (Fischer) F.; grad. U. So. Cal., 1946; m. Lillian Marie Breaux, May 17, 1944; children—John Robert II, Peter. With Fluor Corp., 1946—, successively mgr., v.p. and gen. mgr. mfg., v.p. in charge mfg., exec. v.p., 1952-62, pres., 1962-68, chmn., chief exec. officer, 1968—, dir., 1952—; dir. Cal. Canadian Bank, Crown Zellerbach Corp., United Financial Corp. Cal. Trustee U. So. Cal. Served as 1st lt. USAAF, 1941-45. Mem. N.A.M. (dir.). Clubs: California, San Gabriel Country; Sky (N.Y.); Sleepy Hollow Country (Hudson-on-Bay); De Caza Y Pesca Las Cruces (Baja, Cal.); Eldorado Country (Palm Desert, Cal.). Home: 1245 Hillside Rd Pasadena CA 91105 Office: 2500 S Atlantic Blvd Los Angeles CA 90022

FLUSSI, HARRY VALENTINE, hosp. adminstr.; b. Hilldale, Pa., Feb. 14, 1918; s. Sam and Josephine (Baldinucci) F.; B.A., U. Scranton, 1939; postgrad. Bucknell U., 1939-42; m. Mary Martha Dinis, Apr. 8, 1944; children—Diane Marie (Mrs. John W. Gittinger, Jr.), Claire Denise. Social worker Pa. Dept. Pub. Assistance, 1939-41; officer mgr. SSS, Plains, Pa., 1941-43; with VA, 1946—, dir. VA Center, Togus, Me., 1965-70, VA Hosp., Lebanon, Pa., 1970—; high sch. tchr. St. Thomas High Sch., Scranton, 1939. Chmn. U.S. Civil Service Commn. Interagy. Bd., Augusta, Me., 1966-68, Combined Fed. Campaign for Me., 1966—; mem. action panel Dept. Agr., 1968—; mem. regional health services com. Augusta-Gardiner Area Community Council, 1966—. Served with C.E., AUS, 1943-46. Recipient citations and awards of merit Am. Legion, V.F.W., Am. Vets. World War II; letters of commendation VA and other govt. agencies; VA Sustained Superior Performance award manager's commendation. Mem. Nat. Inter-Agy. Inst. Fed. Hosp. Adminstrs., U.S. Postoffice Mail Users Council, Lambda Alpha Phi. Address: Quarters 100 VA Hosp Lebanon PA 17042

FLYNN, COLIN PETER educator, physicist; b. Stockton-on-Tees, Eng., Aug. 18, 1935; s. Francis Johnson and Edith (Mercer) F.; B.S., U. Leeds, Eng., 1957, Ph.D., 1960; M.A., Cambridge U., Eng., 1966; m. Marilyn Louise Jacobs, July 2, 1961; 1 son, James Edward. Came to U.S., 1960. Research asso. U. Ill. at Urbana, 1960-62, mem. faculty, 1962—, prof. physics, 1968—; fellow Christs Coll., Cambridge (Eng.) U., 1966-68; cons. Atomic Energy Research Establishment, Harwell, Eng. Fellow Am. Phys. Soc. Author: Point Defects and Diffusion, 1971; also articles. Home: 1510 W Green St Champaign IL 61820 Office: Physics Dept U Ill Urbana IL 61801

FLYNN, EDWARD JAMES, chocolate co. exec.; b. Coldwater, Mich., 1906; s. Edmond and Kinney F.; grad. Loyola U., 1933; m. Hilah Bloomquist, Nov. 6, 1935; one dau., Jeannine. With Cook Chocolate Co., Chgo., 1935—, exec. v.p., dir., 1957—; pres. Stewart Bldg. Corp., Chgo.; dir. Kinney Printing Co., Chgo. Mem. Loyola U. Alumni Assn., Exec. Mgmt. Alumni Assn. (Columbia). Home: Post and Rail Farm Palos Park, IL 60464. Office: 2521 W 48th St Chicago IL 60632

FLYNN, FRANCIS J., ret. coll. adminstr.; b. McCloud, Cal., Apr. 20, 1908; s. Michael F. and Mary (Scanlon) F.; A.B., U. So. Cal., 1931, M.A., 1935, Ed.D., 1951; m. Jessica H. Heber, Nov. 26, 1932; children—Gary E., Nancy Ann. Tchr., Big Pine (Cal.) High Sch., 1933-35; prin. Owens Valley Union High Sch., Independence, Cal., 1935-39; vice prin. South Pasadena (Cal.) Jr. High Sch., 1939-43, 46-50; lectr., bus. mgr., dean students, exec. dean devel. Cal. State Coll., Long Beach, 1950-71. Chmn. bldg. com., bd. dirs. local council Girl Scouts Am., 1964—. Served to lt. USNR, 1943-46. Mem. Phi Kappa Tau, Phi Kappa Phi, Phi Delta Kappa. Mason. Clubs: Rotary; Torch; Commonwealth of Cal. Home: 5511 La Pasada Long Beach CA 90815

FLYNN, FRANCIS MARION, newspaper exec.; b. Mt. Ayr, Ia., Jan. 25, 1903; s. John F. and Sara (Long) F.; B.J., U. Mo., 1924, LL.D., 1962; m. Margaret Barnes, July 21, 1924 (dec.); children—Jack Francis Arthur (dec.), Margaret Maureen. Advt. mgr. E.W. Stephens Pub. Co., Columbia, Mo., 1924-26; gen. mgr. Japan Advertiser Press, also corr. for London Express and rep. N.Y. Times World Wide Photo Service, Tokyo, Japan, 1926-29; asst. to bus. mgr. N.Y. News, 1929-31; bus. mgr. Detroit Mirror, 1931- 33; asst. bus. mgr. N.Y. News, 1933-38, bus. mgr., 1938-46, dir., 1941—, gen. mgr., 1946-55, pres., 1947—, pub., 1955—, chmn. bd., 1970—; chmn. bd., dir. TV sta. WPIX, Inc., Conn. Broadcasting Co.; sr. v.p., dir. Tribune Co.; v.p., dir. N.Y. News Charities, Inc.; dir. Chgo. Tribune Co., WGN Continental Broadcasting Co., Ill. Atlantic Co., The Ontario Paper Co. Ltd., Quebec North Shore Paper Co., Manicouagan Power Co., Gore Newspapers Co., Sentinel Star Co. Mem. Alpha Tau Omega, Sigma Delta Chi, Kappa Tau Alpha. Clubs: Union League, Pinnacle (N.Y.C.); Pelham (N.Y.) Country; Lyford Cay (Nassau, Bahamas). Home: 4 Priory Lane Pelham Manor NY 10803 Office: 220 E 42d St New York City NY 10017

FLYNN, GEORGE T., business exec.; b. New Rochelle, N.Y., 1906. Partner, mem. exec. com., mgr. syndicate dept. Hornblower & Weeks, N.Y.C. Adv. council St. Johns U.; bd. lay trustees Iona Coll. Mem. Friendly Sons of St. Patrick. K.M. Clubs: Recess, Stock Exchange Lunch, Wykagyl Country. Home: 257 Oxford Rd New Rochelle NY 10804 Office: 8 Hanover St New York City NY 10004

FLYNN, GEORGE W., newspaper exec; Business mgr. Pacific Coast edition. Wall St. Jour. Office: 1701 Page Mil Rd Palo Alto CA 94304*

FLYNN, J. WALTER, editor, pub., artist; b. Bayonne, N.J., Dec. 16, 1910; s. Walter Joseph and Alice Gertrude (Molloy) F.; grad. Cooper Union Coll., 1928; m. Ruth L. Simmons, May 28, 1932; children—Francine Ruth, Maureen Mary. Successively promotion art dir. Conde Nast Publs., art editor Asia mag., exec. art editor Street & Smith Publs., asso. editor, v.p. Triangle Publs., asso. editor Hearst Mags., asso. editor Liberty Mag., editor in chief Everywoman's Mag., N.Y.C., 1950-58; editor N.M. State Mag., Santa Fe, 1959-62; creative printing cons. Precision Press, Inc., Dallas, 1962-64; editor, pub. La. Forests and People mag., 1964-66; editor Arkansas State Mag., Little Rock, 1966-68; editor, pub. Fla. State Mag., Longwood, 1968-71; pub., editor Carte Blanche mag., Los Angeles, 1971—; artist, works exhibited Berkshire Gallery, Roerich Mus., Art Students League, Art Dirs. Club, Soc. Illustrators, Met. Mus. Art, N.Y.C., Grand Central Art Galleries. Recipient citation U.S. Treasury Dept., World War II; 1st award for editorial achievement Indsl. Marketing Assn.; award for distinctive merit Nat. Exhbn. Advt. and Editoral Art, Art Dirs. Club N.Y.; certificate of excellence Am. Inst. Graphic Arts; Graphic Arts award Printing Industries Am., 1969. Mem. Soc. Illustrators, Soc. Typographic Arts Chgo., Art Dirs. Club N.Y., Regional Pubs. Assn., Fla. Mag. Assn., Soc. Publ. Designers. Clubs: The Lambs (N.Y.C.); Westport Artists, Inc. (Conn.). Home: 1107 California Av Santa Monica CA 90403 Office: 3460 Wilshire Blvd Los Angeles CA 90005

FLYNN, JACQUES, lawyer; b. St. Hyacinthe, Que., Can., Aug. 22, 1915; s. Francis and Jeanne (Lussier) F.; B.A., Laval U., 1936, LL.L., 1939; m. Renee des Rivieres, Feb. 14, 1942; children—Marie, Francis. Called to bar, Que., 1939; pracice in Quebec City, 1948—; partner Flynn, Rivard, Jacques, Cimon, Lessard & LeMay, 1948—; enforcement counsel Wartime Prices and Trade Bd. Eastern Que., 1942-45. Dir. Can. Cement Lafarge, Ltd., Trans- Pub. Advt. Co., Ltd., Savs. & Investments Trust Co., Savs. & Investments Group, Savs. & Investments Mut. Fund, Savs. & Investments-Am. Mut. Fund, Valcartier Industries, Inc., Le Pret Hypothecaire, F.F. Soucy, Inc. Mem. Ho. of Commons, 1958-62, dep. speaker, chmn. coms., 1960, minister Mines and Tech. Surveys, 1961; mem. Senate, 1962—, leader of opposition, 1967. Roman Catholic. Clubs: Circle Universitaire, Garrison (Quebec). Home: 1086 Thornhill Park Sillery Quebec 6 Canada Office: 2 Chauveau Av Quebec 4 Quebec Canada

FLYNN, JOSEPH ANTHONY, actor; b. Youngstown, O., Nov. 8, 1924; s. Joseph Anthony and Grayce Ann (McGraw) F.; student U. Notre Dame, 1942-43; A.B., U. So. Cal., 1950; m. Shirley J. Haskin, Nov. 12, 1955; children—Tony, K. C. Appeared motion pictures including The Love Bug, 1968, The Barefoot Executive, 1970, The Million Dollar Duck, 1971, Now You See Him, Now You Don't, 1972; star television series McHale's Navy, 1962-66. Art commr. State of Cal., 1966-68; mem. Mayor's Community Adv. Com., Los Angeles, 1962—. Bd. dirs. Cal. Epilepsy Soc. Served with AUS, 1943-46. Mem. Screen Actors Guild (dir.). Democrat. Home: 257 N Bentley Av Bel Air CA 90049 Office: care Wm Morris Agy 151 El Camino Dr Beverly Hills CA 90212

FLYNN, RICHARD JEROME, mfg. co. exec.; b. Albia, Ia., Jan. 4, 1924; s. William Alfred and Elizabeth (Mahoney) F.; B.S., Coll. of Holy Cross, Worcester, Mass., 1947; LL.B., Georgetown U., 1949; m. Ellen Francis McGarty, May 3, 1952; children—Bernard M., Elizabeth A., Mark W., Mary R., Richard R., Patricia J., Matthew J. Admitted to D.C. bar, 1950; law clk., bd. govs. Fed. Res. System, 1950; asso. Mulholland, Robie & Hickey, Washington, 1950-51; atty. Raytheon Co., Waltham, Mass., 1951-56; gen. atty., v.p. finance of subsidiary, treas. Collins Radio Co., Dallas, 1956-62; v.p. Ling-Temco-Vought, Dallas, 1962-64, exec. v.p. Continental Electronics Mfg. Co., Dallas, 1964-69; pres., chief exec. officer, dir. Riley Stoker Corp., Worcester, Mass., 1969—; dir. Scam Instrument Corp. Served with USNR, 1943-46. Home: Fiske Hill Sturbridge MA 01566 Office: 9 Neponset St Worcester MA 01600

FLYNN, THOMAS DAVID, accountant; b. Los Angeles, Feb. 19, 1913; s. John T. and Alice (Bell) F.; A.B. in Econs., Princeton, 1935; M.S. in Accounting, Columbia, 1939; m. Harriet Howland, July 13, 1940; children—Susan, Christine, John. Staff asst. U.S. Senate Commn. Interstate Commerce, 1935-38; accountant FTC, 1939-40; partner Arthur Young & Co., N.Y.C., 1940—. Bd. dirs. Nat. Bur. Econ. Research. C.P.A., N.Y. Mem. Am. Inst. C.P.A.'s (pres. 1964-65), N.Y. State Soc. C.P.A.'s Am. Accounting Assn. (v.p. 1960), Phi Beta Kappa, Beta Gamma Sigma. Home: 35 Cornwell's Beach Rd Sands Point, NY 11050. Office 277 Park Av New York City NY 10017

FLYNN, THOMAS E., labor union ofcl.; b. Chgo., July 1, 1906; s. Patrick P. and Katherine (Nolan) F.; m. Mildred Wanetta Brandeberry, June 16, 1923; children—Robert Thomas, Jerome Patrick, Colleen (Mrs. Robert S. Schwenger) and Maureen (Mrs. John P. Treanor) (twins). Mem. Internat. Brotherhood of Teamsters, 1923—, internat. dir. Eastern conf., 1953-69, internat. v.p., 1957-69, gen. sec.-treas., 1969—. Democrat. Roman Catholic. Home: 7808 Renoir Ct Potomac MD 20854 Office: 25 Louisiana Av NW Washington DC 20001

FLYNN, THOMAS WILLIAM, lawyer; b. Chgo., Aug. 20, 1914; s. Thomas William Sr. and Katharine T. (O'Brien) F.; Ph.B., Nortre Dame U., 1935; J.D., DePaul U., 1939; m. Ruth I. Duay, Oct. 17, 1942; one dau., Marie-Adele (now Mrs. Terrence G. O'Hara). With Federal Life Ins. Co., Chgo., 1936-39, Travelers Ins. Co., Chgo., 1939-41; with FBI, Dept. Justice, 1941-45; pub. prosecutor, Honolulu, 1945-46; gen. practice of law, Honolulu, 1946, 52—; dep. atty. gen., 1946-52. Dir. Pioneer Savs. & Loan Assn., Hawaii, 1952—, pres., 1962-63, 65—, chairman of the board, 1964; sec., mem. bd. directors Oahu Constrn. Co., Ltd., 1953—. Mem. Hawaii adv. com. U.S. Commn. on Civil Rights; chmn. Hawaii Subversive Activities Commn.; exec. bd. Aloha council Boy Scouts Am., 1954—; mem. Honolulu chpt. Nat. Council Crime and Delinquency; mem. adv. com. U.S. Regional Med. Program. Adv. bd. St. Francis Hosp., 1949—. Mem. Am., Ill. bar assns., Bar Assn. Hawaii (pres. 1962), Navy League U.S., Soc. Former Spl. Agts. FBI, Inc., Delta Theta Phi, Pi Gamma Mu. Democrat. K.C. (grand knight 1962-63). Clubs: Pacific, Waialae Country (dir. 1965- -) (Honolulu). Home: 4764 Aukai Av Honolulu HI 96815 Office: 116 S King St Honolulu HI 96813

FLYNN, WILLIAM H., business exec.; b. Oklahoma City, 1926; grad. U.S. Naval Acad., 1947. With Central Power & Light Co., 1947-48; chief engr. Port of Brownsville, Brownsville Nav. Dist., 1948-53; ltd. partner Marchant Bros. & Balay, 1953-54; with J. Ray McDermott & Co. Inc., 1954-56; v.p., dir. Trans Gulf Off-Shore Drilling Inc., 1956-60; asst. to exec. v.p. Mandrel Industries Inc., 1960-65; pres. Zapata Norness Inc., Houston, 1966-69, chmn. bd., chief exec. officer, 1969—; dir. Southdown, Inc., Tex. Tenn. Industries. Served with USNR, 1943-47. Home: 12431 Cobblestone Dr Houston TX 77024 Office: Zapata Norness Southwest Tower Houston TX 77002*

FLYNN, WILLIAM PATRICK, banker; b. Indpls., Mar. 10, 1899; s. John W. and Catherine C. (Kelley) F.; student St. Anthony's Sch., Indpls.; m. Mable Hurst Flynn, Nov. 25, 1920; children—Barbara (Mrs. F.B. Quinn), Marjory (Mrs. R. J. Gastineau), Patricia (Mrs. Joseph F. Sexton), Carolyn (Mrs. Flynn Fay), Suzy (Mrs. William D. Stuhldreher), Mary Kay (Mrs. William Blair Bowling). Asst. nat. bank examiner, Chgo., 1918-30; messenger boy, clerk, teller Ind. Nat. Bank of Indpls., 1915-18, v.p. 1930- 44, exec. v.p., dir., 1944-52, pres., 1952-57, chmn., 1957-64, chmn. exec. com., 1964—; dir. Indpls. Power & Light Co., Continental Steel Corp., Inland Container Corp., State Life Ins. Co., Ind. Bell Telephone Co. Treas., dir. Indpls. chpt. A.R.C.; trustee Indpls. Found., William E. English Found.; mem. Brebeuf Prep. Sch., Indpls. Mem. C. of C. (dir.). Roman Catholic. K.C., Knight of St. Gregory. Clubs: Columbia, Athletic (Indpls.). Home: 7320 Holliday Dr W. Indianapolis, IN 46260. Office: 3 Virginia Av Indianapolis IN 46204

FLYNT, JOHN JAMES, Jr., congressman; b. Griffin, Ga., Nov. 8, 1914; s. John James and Susan Winn (Banks) F.; student Ga. Mil. Acad.; A.B., U. Ga., 1936; postgrad. Emory U., 1937-38; LL.B., George Washington U., 1940; grad. Command and Gen. Staff Sch., Air Corps Advanced Flying Sch., Brooks Field, Tex.; m. Patricia Irby Bradley, Feb. 7, 1942; children—Susan, John James III, Crisp. Admitted to Ga. bar, 1938; asst. U.S. atty. No. Dist. Ga., 1939- 41, 45-46; mem. Ho. of Reps., Ga., 1947-48; solicitor gen. Griffin Jud. Circuit, 1949-54; mem. 83d-88th Congresses, 4th Ga. Dist., and 89th-92d Congresses from 6th Ga. Dist. Served in U.S. Army, 1936-37, 41-45; ETO; col. Res. Decorated Bronze Star medal. Mem. Am., Ga. (pres.) bar assns., Am. Legion, V.F.W., Phi Delta Phi, Sigma Alpha Epsilon. Democrat. Methodist (chmn. bd. stewards). Mason (Shriner), Kiwanian. Home: Griffin GA 30223 Office: House Office Bldg Washington DC 20515

FLYNT, RALPH COMER MICHAEL, former govtl. adminstr.; b. Washington, Ga., Sept. 6, 1904; s. Carl Z. and Cornelia Florence (Smith) F.; B.S., U. Va., 1928, M.S., 1931; postgrad. Princeton, 1931-33; m. Bonnie Frost, July 26, 1934; children—Anne Cornelia (Mrs. Robert Amory III), Richard Adams. High sch. prin., Sardis, Ga., 1924-25, Thomson, 1925-26; master in history Shenandoah Valley Acad., Winchester, Va., 1928- 29; instr. history U. Va., 1929-31; Proctor fellow Princeton, 1931-33; ednl. adviser. div. C.C.C. Camp edn. U.S. Office Edn., 1934-38, asst. dir., 1938-40, asso. dir., 1940-42; specialist in higher edn., div. higher edn., 1942-45; asst. dir. div. central services, 1945-48; exec. asst. to U.S. commr. edn., 1948-50; dir. div. Spl. Edn. Services, U.S. Office Edn. 1950, dir., gen. and liberal edn. 1952-53, dir. higher edn. program br., 1954-58, asst. U.S. commr. edn., 1958-59, asst. commr. edn. for legislation and program devel., 1959-62, asso. commr. edn. for research and devel., 1962-65, asso. U.S. commr. for internat. edn., 1965-68, dept. asst. sec. for internat. edn. Office Sec., Dept. Health, Edn. and Welfare, 1968-69. Mem. U.S. delegation Internat. Study Conf., Atlantic Community, Oxford, 1952, Copenhagen, 1953; vice chmn. study group on role of sch., Paris, 1954; bd. govs. Atlantic Union Com., 1953-63, chmn. com. to draft constn. Atlantic Treaty Assn., London, 1954, chmn. U.S. delegation to constnl. conv., The Hague, 1954, to assemblies, Paris, 1955, 56, vice chmn. assn., 1955-57; vice chmn. Am. Council on NATO, 1954-56, dir.; chmn. Atlantic Treaty Assn., 1958, U.S. del. 8th to 11th assemblies, 1962-65; mem. U.S. delegation World Conf. on Literacy, 1965, U.S. delegation 14th Conf. UNESCO, 1966; vice chmn. Commn. on Sci. and Tech. Personnel OECD, 1967—. Fellow Am. Geog. Soc.; mem. Assn. for Higher Edn., Am. Acad. Polit. and Social Sci., Am. Hist. Assn., Atlantic Council U.S. (dir.), Phi Beta Kappa, Phi Beta Kappa Assos. Episcopalian (vestryman). Clubs: Cosmos (Washington); Princeton (N.Y.C.). Home: 2201 Woodmont Rd Alexandria VA 22307

FOA, JOSEPH VICTOR, educator, aero. engr.; b. Turin, Italy, July 10, 1909; s. Ettore and Lelia (DellaTorre) F.; Dr.Ing., Politecnico di Torino, 1931, U. Rome, 1933; m. Lucy Bouvier, June 27, 1942; children—Lelia, Sylvana, Eugenie, Gay. Came to U.S. 1939, naturalized, 1944. Project engr. Piaggio Aircraft Co., Italy, 1933-35, 37-39; chief engr. Caproni Engring. Center, Studi Caproni, Italy, 1935-37; project engr. Bellanca Aircraft Corp., 1939-40; cons., chief engr. Am. Aeromarine Co., 1942; head aero. design research Curtiss Wright Corp., 1943-45; head propulsion br. Cornell U. Aero. Lab., 1945-52; prof. aero. engring. Rensselaer Polytech. Inst., 1952-70, head dept., 1958-67; prof. engring. and applied sci. George Washington U., 1970—; cons. aircraft companies. Recipient development award and certificate for exceptional service Navy Ordnance Dept. of 1945, certificate of appreciation Dept. of Army, 1951. Asso. Fellow Am. Inst. Aeros. and Astronautics; mem. Am. Soc. M.E. Author: Flight Propulsion, 1960; co-author other engring. books. Contbr. articles profl. jours. Patentee. Home: 3404 Thornapple St Chevy Chase MD 20015

FOA, PIERO PIO, physician; b. Torino, Italy, Apr. 13, 1911; s. Carlo and Eloisa (Errera) F.; M.D. cum laude, U. Milano, 1934, Ph.D. in Chemistry, 1938; m. Naomi Levin, Apr. 6, 1941; children—Helen, Richard. Intern medicine U. Milano Hosp., 1936-37, intern surgery, 1937-38; asst. prof. physiology U. Pavia, 1938-39; research fellow surgery U. Mich., 1939-42, fellow medicine, 1942-43; asst. prof. physiology and pharmacology Chgo. Med. Sch., 1944-45, asso. prof., 1946-51, chief endocrine and metabolic clinic, 1944-47, prof., 1951-61; prof. physiology Wayne State U., 1962- -; chmn. dept. research Sinai Hosp., Detroit, Rizzi fellow biochemistry, 1939; Dazian research fellow physiology Yale, 1939. Recipient silver medal Ill. Med. Soc., 1953, M. L. Parker award for meritorious research Chgo. Med. Sch., 1953, Merit award Chgo. Tech. Socs. Council, 1961. Mem. Am. Physiol. Soc., Soc. Exptl. Biology and Medicine (pres. Ill. 1954, 55, nat. council 1954, 55), Endocrine Soc., Am. Diabetes Assn., Am. Fedn. Clin. Research, Am. Chem. Soc., A.A.A.S., N.Y. acads. sci., Chgo. Heart Assn. (gov. 1957), Royal Soc. Medicine, Mich. Diabetes Assn. (gov. 1966—), Venzuelan Assn. Advancement Sci., Sigma Xi. Home: 12917 Wales St Huntington Woods MI 68070 Office: 6767 Outer Dr Detroit MI 68235

FOBES, DONALD EDWARDS, lawyer; b. Ridgewood, N.J., Sept. 23, 1910; s. Hiram and Carrie (Edwards) F.; grad. Loomis Sch., 1928; B.A., Yale, 1932; LL.B., Columbia, 1935; m. Nancy W. Garoutte, Dec. 29, 1950; children—David L., Katherine F. (Mrs. Edward S. Gilfillian III), Alison F. Admitted to N.Y. bar, 1935, practiced in N.Y.C.; asso. Cadwalader, Wickersham & Taft, 1935-36; asso. Cravath, Swaine & Moore, 1936-42; with Asiatic Petroleum Corp., 1942-69, formerly v.p., sec., dir. Home: Main Rd Chesterfield MA 01012

FOBES, JOHN EDWIN, internat. orgn. ofcl.; b. Chgo., Mar. 16, 1918; s. Wilfred and Mable (Skogsberg) F.; B.S. cum laude (Clarion Dewitt Hardy scholar), Northwestern U., 1939; M.A., Fletcher Sch. Law and Diplomacy, 1940; m. Hazel Ward Weaver, June 7, 1941; children—Patricia Cleveland, John Geoffrey Weaver. With Bur. of Budget, Washington, 1942; secretariat prep. commn. of UN, London, 1945; exec. sec. UN adv. group of experts on adminstrn., personnel and budgetary questions, 1946; with Bur. of Budget, 1946-48; adviser Pan Am. Union, 1947-48; with E.C.A., Marshall Plan, 1948-52; attache U.S. delegation to NATO and OEEC, Paris, 1952-55; dir. office Internat. Adminstrn., Dept. of State, Washington, 1955-59; spl. asst. to asst. sec. of state, 1959-60; asst. dir. Tech. Cooperation Mission to India, 1960-62; dep. dir. U.S. Agy. Internat. Devel. Mission to India, 1962-64; asst. dir. gen. UNESCO, Paris, 1964-70, dep. dir. gen., 1970—. Vis. research scholar Ind. U., Harvard, 1970. Pres. Am. Library in Paris, 1968-70. Mem. adv. com. UN Gen. Assembly, 1955-60. Served as maj. USAAF 1942-46. ETO. Mem. Am. Soc. Pub. Adminstrn., Phi Beta Kappa, Phi Gamma Delta. Home: La Celle les Bordes 78 France Office: UNESCO Place de Fontenoy Paris France

FOBES, MELCHER PRINCE, educator; b. Portland, Me., Sept. 18, 1911; s. Leon Melcher and Anne Prince (Burgess) F.; A.B., Bowdoin Coll., 1932; M.A., Harvard, 1933, Ph.D., 1947; student U. Chgo., 1939-40; m. Frances Mary Simpson, June 4, 1942. Instr. math. Bryn Mawr Coll., 1938-39; mem. faculty Coll. Wooster, 1940—, prof. math., 1947—, chmn. dept., 1948—, Johnson prof., 1955—. Mem. Math. Assn. Am., Phi Beta Kappa. Author: (with Ruth B. Smyth) Calculus and Analytic Geometry, 1963. Home: 1560 Hawthorne Dr Wooster OH 44691

FOCH, NINA actress; b. Leyden, Netherlands, Apr. 20, 1924; d. Dirk and Consuelo (Flowerton) Fock; came to U.S., 1928; grad. Lincoln Sch., 1939; m. James Lipton, June 6, 1954; m. 2d, Dennis R. Brite, Nov. 27, 1959. Appeared in motion pictures Song to Remember, My Name is Julia Ross, Undercover Man, Dark Past; Spartacus, 1960, Cash McCall, Executive Suite, An American in Paris; appeared Broadway plays including John Loves Mary, 1947, Twelfth Night, 1949, King Lear, 1950, Taming of the Shrew and Measure for Measure, Am. Shakespeare Festival, 1956; Second String, 1960; actress TV 1947—, including Pulitzer Playhouse, Playhouse 90, Playwrights 56, Producer's Showcase, also panel shows. Nominated for Acad. Award for supporting performance Executive Suite, 1954. Address: c/o Arthur Kennard Assos 8776 Sunset Blvd Los Angeles CA 90069 ‡

FOCK, JENO, Hungarian govt. ofcl.; b. Kispest, Hungary, 1916; student Acad. Econs. and Tech.; m. Judit Sztanko, 1945; children—Judit, Jeno. Dist. sec. Hungarian Communist Party, 1945-47, later dep. head, dept. party com., Budapest; dep. minister metallurgy and machine industry, 1951; comml. counsellor, 1954-55; mem. Parliament, 1945-47, 58-67, 71—. Decorated Silver grade of Hungarian Order of Freedom, Gold grade of medal for Merit HPR, Order of Red Banner of Labour, Order of Socialist Motherland. Author: The Hungarian People's Economy on the Road of the Building of Socialism, 1963. Office: Parliament Budapest Hungary

FOCKE, ALFRED BOSWORTH, educator, physicist; b. Cleve., Sept. 30, 1906; s. Theodore Moses and Anne (Bosworth) F.; B.S., Case Western Res. U., 1928; Ph.D., Cal. Inst. Tech., 1932; m. Alice Beatrice Cook, Sept. 17, 1928; 1 son, Alfred Bosworth; m. 2d. Katherine Crawford, Aug. 12, 1944; children—Alice Anne, Theodore William, Francis George, Karl Crawford, Louis Ross. Instr. surveying Case Sch. Applied Sci., 1928; inst. fellow Cal. Inst. Tech., 1932-33; Nat. Research Council fellow, Yale, 1933-34; instr. physics Brown U., 1934-38, asst. prof., 1938-45; physicist U.S. Dept. of Navy, 1940-45; physicist USN Electronics Lab., San Diego, Cal., 1945-53; dir. U. Cal. Marine Phys. Lab., 1954-58; tech. dir. Pacific Missile Range, Point Mugu, Cal., 1958-59; prof., chmn. dept. physics Harvey Mudd Coll., Claremont, Cal., 1959—. Sci. dir. Operation Wigwam, USN, 1954-56; cons. naval applications to industry and A.E.C., Naval Ordnance Lab., Lawrence Radiation Lab. Bd. dirs. San Miguel Sch., San Diego. Fellow A.A.A.S.; mem. Acoustical Soc. Am., Am. Phys. Soc., Am. Inst. Physics, Am. Assn. Physics Tchrs., Seismol. Soc. Am., Coll. Fed. Council So. Cal. Home: 550 W 12th St Claremont CA 91711

FOCKE, ARTHUR BERNARD, lawyer, govt. ofcl.; b. Dayton, O., Aug. 12, 1911; s. Bernard Matthias and Stella (McFadden) F.; student U. Dayton, 1929-32; LL.B., Georgetown U., 1936; student Cath. U. Am., 1938-40; m. Marianne Kernan, Aug. 24, 1935; children—Michael, Marian. Admitted to D.C. bar, 1935, also U.S. Supreme Ct. bar; claims examiner, atty. U.S. Gen. Accounting Office, 1935-42; atty. Bur. Budget Office Mgmt. and Budget, Exec. Office of Pres., 1946-51, legal adviser, 1951-58, gen. counsel, 1958—. Served to comdr. USNR, 1942- 46. Mem. Am., Fed. bar assns. Clubs: Nat. Press, Edgemoor, National Lawyer's. Home: 5619 Western Av Washington, DC 20015. Office: Office Mgmt and Budget Exec Office of Pres Washington DC 20503

FOCKE, THEODORE BROWN, corp. exec.; b. Cleve., Sept. 16, 1904; s. Theodore Moses and Anne (Bosworth) F.; B.S., Case Inst. Tech., 1926; D.Sc., U. Nancy (France), 1928; m. Mary duPont; children—William B., H. Elizabeth, Mary L. Engr., Perfection Stove Co., 1929-42; factory mgr., gen. mgr. Curtiss- Wright Corp., 1946-49; v.p., gen. mgr. Wright Aero. Corp., 1949-52; pres., dir. Nat. Radiator Co., 1952-55, Nat.-U.S. Radiator Corp., 1955- 60; v.p., gen. mgr. plumbing, heating, air conditioning group Crane Co., 1960; v.p. finance and adminstrn. The Mitre Corp., Bedford, Mass., 1961- 63; pres., dir. The Better Tire Sales Co., Johnstown, Pa., 1963—, Wm. K. Stamets Co., Pitts., 1964—. Served with Bur. Aeros., USN, 1942-46. Mem. Am. Soc. Metals, Am. Soc. Heating and Air Conditioning Engrs. Home: 930 Windan Lane Johnstown PA 15905 Office: 338 S Main St Columbiana OH 44408

FODERARO, ANTHONY HAROLDE, educator, physicist; b. Scranton, Pa., Apr. 3, 1926; s. Edward and Myrtha (Bachman) F.; B.S., U. Scranton, 1950; Ph.D., U. Pitts., 1955;m. Rita Lacey, May 4, 1953; children—Anthony Edward, John Keith, Diana Lacey. Supervisory scientist Westinghouse Bettis Lab., Pitts., 1954-56; sr. nuclear physicist Gen. Motors Research Labs., Warren Mich., 1956-60; asso. prof. nuclear engring. Pa. State U., 1960-63, prof., 1963—; cons. Def. Atomic Support Agy.; cons. to industry. Served with inf., AUS, 1943-46; ETO. Mem. Am. Phys. Soc., Am. Nuclear Soc., Am. Assn. Physics Tchrs., Am. Soc. Engring. Edn., Am. Assn. Univ. Profs., Sigma Xi. Author: The Elements of Neurton Interaction Theory, 1971; Engineering Compendium on Radiation Shielding, 1968; (with others) Planning Atomic Shelters: a Guidebook for Architects and Engineers, 1961; (with others) Reactor Shielding Design Manual, 1956. Home: 301 S Gill St State College PA 16801 Office: Sackett Bldg University Park PA 16802

FODOR, EUGENE, editor, publisher; b. Léva, Hungary, Oct. 14, 1905; s. Gyula Mátyás and Malvin (Kürti) F.; Baccalaureat, Lucenec, Czechoslovakia, 1924; Licencie ès Econ. Politique, Faculté de Droit, U. Grenoble (France), 1927; postgrad. U. Hamburg (Germany), London (Eng.) Sch. Econs.; m. Vlasta Maria Zobel, Dec. 4, 1948. Came to U.S., 1938, naturalized, 1942. Travel corr. Prague Hungarian Jour., 1930-33; travel editor European Travel Guides, London, 1934-38; fgn. editor Query mag., London, 1937-38; editor, pub. Fodor's Modern Guides, Inc., Paris, France, 1949-64; pres. Fodor's Modern Guides, Inc., Litchfield, Conn., 1964—; chmn. bd. Fodor's Modern Guides, Ltd., London, 1964—. Served to capt. AUS, 1942-47.Recipient Grand prix de Littérature de Tourisme, 1959; award Caribbean Tourist Assn., 1960; Spl. award Pacific Area Tourist Assn., Hong Kong, 1962; Austrian Govt. Honor medal, 1970; others. Mem. Nat. Assn. Travel Orgns. (award 1966), Soc. Am. Travel Writers, Internat. Union Ofcl. Travel Orgns., Fedn. Internat. des Journalistes et Ecrivains de Tourisme, Pacific Area Travel Assn., S.Am. Travel Orgn., Caribbean Tourist Assn. Editor 42 travel books pub. annually, 1950— (trans. French, German, Italian, Dutch, Spanish, Hungarian). Home: Blue Swamp Road Litchfield CT 06759 Office: P O Box 784 Litchfield CT 06759

FOEHL, CHARLES ALLEN, Jr., coll. adminstr.; b. Sewickley, Pa., May 15, 1909; s. Charles Allen and Clara (Hamilton) F.; B.A., Williams Coll., 1932; LL.B., Harvard, 1935; m. Mary Mason, Dec. 27, 1932; children—Charles Allen III, William C., John H., Stephen M. Admitted to N.J. bar, 1936; asso. Lindabury, Depue & Faulks, Newark, 1935-40; partner firm Young, Shanley & Foekl, 1940-50; treas. William Coll., Williamstown, Mass., 1950—, also v.p. for adminstrn. Dir. Berkshire Life Ins. Co., Pittsfield, Mass., Nat. Securities & Research Corp., N.Y.C. Served to lt. col. AUS, 1942-46. Decorated Bronze Star. Mem. Eastern Assn. Coll. and Univ. Bus. Officers (exec. com. 1957). Conglist. Home: Bulkley St Williamstown MA 01267

FOEHL, RICHARD E., former v.p. operations, treas. First Pa. Banking & Trust Co. Address: 15th and Chestnut Sts Philadelphia PA 19101*

FOELBER, CHARLES HEPBURN, ins. co. exec.; b. Fort Wayne, Ind., Nov. 20, 1924; s. Herbert Jacob and Marie (Roesner) F.; student U. Mich., 1947-48; B.A., Valparaiso U., 1949; m. Lois Ann Rieck, July 1, 1950; children—Charles R., John T., Susan M., Michael D. With U.S. Fidelity & Guaranty Co., Balt., 1951—, sr. exec. v.p., 1970—, Md. Nat. Bank; Bd. dirs. Balt. Luth. High Sch. Assn., Jr. Achievement Met. Balt.; exec. bd. Balt. Area council Boy Scouts Am.; trustee Commn. Govt. Efficiency and Economy. Served with AUS, 1943-44, to 2d lt. USAAF, 1944-45. Mem. Rho Lamda Tau. Republican. Lutheran. Kiwanian. Clubs: Merchants (Balt.); Maryland. Home: 222 Solway Ct Timonium MD 21093 Office: U S Fidelity & Guaranty Co Calvert and Redwood Sts Baltimore MD 21203

FOELLINGER, HELENE R., newspaper pub.; b. Fort Wayne, Ind., Dec. 12, 1910; d. Oscar G. and Esther Anna (Deuter) Foellinger; A.B., U. of Ill., 1932; Litt D. (hon.), Tri-State Coll. With editorial dept. News Pub. Co., publs. of News-Sentinel, Fort Wayne, 1932-36, pres., gen. mgr., 1936—; pres. Ft. Wayne Newspapers, Inc., News-Sentinel Broadcasting Co., Inc.; dir. Lincoln Nat. Bank & Trust Co. Mem. Ft. Wayne Tennis Commn. Bd. dirs. Ft. Wayne Better Bus. Bur., Conv. Bur., Ft. Wayne-Allen County United Community Services, Ft. Wayne Horse Show Assn., Ft. Wayne Light Opera Festival, Allen County Tb Assn., Allen County chpt. Nat. Found. Infantile Paralysis, Allen County unit Ind. Cancer Soc., Fort Wayne chpt. A.R.C., Jr. Achievement Ft. Wayne Art Sch., Ft. Wayne Philharmonic Orch., Fine Arts Found., Legal Aid Soc., Ft. Wayne Zool. Soc., Ft. Wayne Found., Taxpayers Research Assn.; trustee Tri-State Coll., Allen County War Meml. Coliseum. Mem. C. of C. (dir.), Am. Newspaper Assn., Ft. Wayne Exec. Club, Phi Beta Kappa, Pi Beta Phi, Pi Mu Epsilon, Mortar Board, Psi Iota Xi. Republican. Lutheran. Clubs: Altrusa, Fort Wayne Country. Home: 4415 Old Mill Rd Fort Wayne IN 46807 Office: 600 W Main St Fort Wayne IN 46802

FOELSCH, CHARLES BEREND, clergyman; b. Ottumwa, Ia., Mar. 31, 1891; s. Rev. Henry and Caroline (Wagner) F.; A.B., Wartburg Coll., 1909; grad. Chgo. Luth. Sem., 1915; Ph.D., U. Pitts., 1924; D.D. (hon.), Newberry Coll., 1934, Carthage Coll., 1943; m. Pauline Gray, May 4, 1920; children—Carolyn, Charles Berend (M.D.), Donald. Ordained to ministry, Luth. Ch., 1915; pastor, Wilkinsburg, Pa., 1920-27, Charleston, S.C., 1927-34, Sunbury, Pa., 1934- 40, Washington, 1940-42; pres. Chgo. Luth. Theol. Sem., 1942-47; pastor Holy Trinity Ch., N.Y.C., 1947-52; pres. Pacific Luth. Theol. Sem., Berkeley, Cal., 1952-61, pres. emeritus, 1961—; pastor Christ the King Luth. Ch., Chgo., 1961-63; co-pastor Seamen's Center, N.Y.C., 1963-66; minister-in-charge Christ Ch., N.Y.C., 1966—. Chmn. com. on moral and social welfare United Luth. Ch., 1932-36, chmn. dept. evangelism, 1938-40, mem. bd. Am. missions, pres. bd., 1952-56; mem. exec. bd. United Luth. Ch. in Am., 1940-48, 56-62, Sec. of Court of Adjudication, 1962—; councilor Nat. Luth. Council, 1950-60. Mem. Hymn Soc. Am. (chmn. exec. com. 1968—), Soc. Luther Research. Author: A Mighty Fortress, 1924; His Word for My Way, 1962; also monthly essay, Landmark Churches of our Faith, in the L.B. Bond, 1956- -. Co-author: Epistle Messages, 1934. Editor: The Day's Worship Book of Devotions, 1935; The New Day's Worship, 1966. Address: 450 E 20th St New York City NY 10009

FOERSTER, BERND, educator; b. Danzig, Dec. 5, 1923; s. Joseph and Martha (Brumm) F.; came to U.S., 1947, naturalized, 1954; student Columbia, 1948-49; B.S. in Architecture, U. Cin., 1954; M.Arch., Rensselaer Poly. Inst., 1957; m. Enell Dowling, May 13, 1950; children—Kent, Mark. Worked for Govt. Netherlands, 1945-47; with various engrs. and architects offices, 1950- 59; ch. bldg. cons., design cons., 1954—; instr. architecture U. Cin., 1954; instr. architecture Rensselaer Poly. Inst., Troy, N.Y., 1954-56, asst. prof., 1956-62, asso. prof., 1962-65, prof., 1965-71; prof., dean Coll. Architecture and Design, Kan. State U., Manhattan, 1971—. Cons. archtl. and community surveys N.Y. State Council on Arts for Arts, 1962-71; cons. Albany Hist. Sites Commn., 1967-71; v.p. Mohawk-Hudson Council on Ednl. TV, 1968-69; co-chmn. Conf. on Rensselaer County, 1966; pres. Rensselaer County Council for Arts, 1963-64, 66-67. Bd. dirs. Albany Inst. History and Art, 1967-71; trustee Olana Historic Site, 1969-71. Mem. A.I.A., Nat. Trust for Historic Preservation, Nature Conservancy, Am. Assn. U. Profs. (past chpt. pres.), Assn. Collegiate Schs. Architecture, Soc. Archtl. Historians, Sierra Club, Audubon Soc. Author: Man and Masonry, 1960; Pattern and Texture, 1961; Architecture Worth Saving in Rensselaer County, N.Y., 1965; (films) Man and Masonry, 1961; What Do You Tear Down Next?, 1964; Earth and Fire, 1964; Assault on the Wynantskill, 1967. Home: 1415 Normandy Pl Manhattan KS 66502

FOERSTER, NORMAN, educator; b. Pitts., Apr. 14, 1887; s. Adolph Hartin and Henrietta M. (Reineman) F.; A.B., Harvard, 1910; A.M., U. Wis., 1912; Litt.D., U. South, 1931, U. N.C., 1948; D.H.L., Grinnell Coll., 1946; m. Dorothy Haskell, Feb. 21, 1911; children—Donald Madison, David Bruce. Instr. English, U. Wis., 1911-14; asso. prof. English, U. N.C., 1914-19, prof., 1919-30; dir. Sch. of Letters, prof. English, U. Ia., 1930-44; vis. prof. English, Duke U., 1948-51. Mem. Coll. English Assn. (pres. 1941), Modern Lang. Assn. Am. (exec. council 1939-42), Modern Humanities Research Assn., Soc. Am. Historians, Phi Beta Kappa (hon. mem. 1949). Author: Outlines and Summaries, 1915; (with J.M. Steadman, Jr.) Sentences and Thinking, 1919, 23, Writing and Thinking, 1931, 41, 52; Nature in American Literature, 1923; American Criticism, 1928; The American Scholar, 1929; Toward Standards, 1931; The American State University, 1937; The Future of the Liberal College, 1938; The Humanities and the Common Man, 1946; co-author: The Reinterpretation of American Literature, 1928; The Intent of the Critic, 1941; Literary Scholarship, 1941; The Humanities After the War, 1944. Editor: (with F.A. Manchester and Karl Young) Essays for College Men, 1913, 2d series, 1915; (with Will D. Howe) Selected Literary Essays from James Russell Lowell, 1914; Chief American Prose Writers, 1916, 19, 31; (with W.W. Pierson, Jr.) American Ideals, 1917; (with G.R. Elliott) English Poetry of the 19th Century, 1923; American Poetry and Prose, 1925, 34, 47, 52, 57; Humanism and America, 1930; American Critical Essays, 1930. Contbr. to various jours. Home: 1480 San Leandro Park Rd Santa Barbara CA 93103

FOERSTNER, GEORGE C., refrigeration co. exec. Pres. Amana Refrigeration, Inc. Office: Amana Refrigeration Inc Amana IA 52203*

FOERY, WALTER A., bishop; b. Rochester, N.Y. July 6, 1890; student St. Andrews Prep. Sem., St. Bernards Sem., Rochester. Ordained priest Roman Catholic Ch., 1916; curate, 1916-22; pastor Mt. Carmel Ch., Rochester, 1922-32, Holy Rosary Ch., Rochester, 1932-37; consecrated bishop of Syracuse, 1937. Dir. Rochester Catholic Charities, 1930-37. Nat. Cath. Welfare Conf. rep. Internat. Conf. on Social Welfare, London, 1936. Address: 1234 James St Syracuse NY 13202

FOFT, JOHN WILLIAM, physician, educator; b. Los Angeles, May 13, 1928; s. Wilford L. and Mary E. (McMahon) F.; B.S., U. Neb., 1951, M.D., 1954; m. Marianne T. Deibler, Mar. 12, 1957; children—John, Christine. Intern Mpls. Gen. Hosp., 1954-55; asst. prof. pathology, dir. clin. chemistry U. Chgo., 1965-67; asso. prof. clin. pathology U. Ala., 1968-70, dir. pediatric-clin. pathology lab., 1968-70, asst. prof. pediatrics, 1968—, also clin. pathologist Center for Developmental and Learning Disorders of U. Ala. Med. Center, 1969—; dep. chmn. research clin. pathology U. Ala., 1969-70, prof., chmn. dept. clin. pathology, 1970—; acting chief clin. labs. VA Hosp. Served as capt. AUS, 1955-57, USAF, 1961-64. Nat. Heart Inst. fellow U. Minn. Hosps., 1959-61; Am. Cancer Soc. scholar Argonne Cancer Research Hosp., 1968. Mem. N.Y. Acad. Sci., Am. Assn. Pathologists and Bacteriologists, A.A.A.S., Coll. Am. Pathologists, A.M.A., Ala. Assn. Pathologists, Jefferson County Med. Soc., Birmingham Acad. Medicine, Assn. Advancement Med. Instrumentation, Sigma Xi, Alpha Omega Alpha. Research on nucleic acid metabolism in developing lymphoid cells and in virus infected cells. Home: 3529 Spring Valley Ct Birmingham AL 35223

FOGARTY, ANNE, designer; b. Pitts., Feb. 2, 1919; d. Robert and Marion (Bosoranoff) Whitney; student Allegheny Coll., 1936-37, Carnegie Tech., 1937-38, E. Hartman Sch. Design, 1939; m. Thomas E. Fogarty, Jr., Aug. 10, 1940; 1 son, 1 dau. Began career in advt., modeling; fashion stylist Dorland Internat., 1947-48; fashion designer Youth Guild, 1948-50, Margot Dresses, Inc., 1950-57; designer for Saks 5th Avenue, 1958-62; designer, pres. Anne Fogarty, Inc., N.Y.C., 1960—; created modern full-skirt petticoated feminine fashions; designer lingerie, costume jewelry, shoes, hats, coats, suits. Recipient merit award Mademoiselle, 1951; fashion award Bonwit Teller, 1951; award Am. Fashion Critics, 1951; fashion award Neiman-Marcus, 1953; 20th Century world of fashion award Phila. Fashion Group, 1953; Internat. Silk Assn. award, 1955; Cotton Fashion award, 1957; Sports Illustrated Magazine Designer of Year award, 1960; Am. Express Annual Fashion award in 1962. Member of Council Fashion Designers of Am. (charter mem.), Fashion Group, Am. Fedn. of Radio Artists. Republican. Roman Catholic. Author: Wife Dressing, 1959. Contbr. publicity articles popular mags., newspapers, U.S. and Europe. Office: Anne Fogarty Inc 530 7th Av New York City NY 10018

FOGARTY, CHARLES FRANKLIN, mining co. exec; b. Denver, May 27, 1921; s. Charles Franklin and Mabel Still (Bowman) F.; E.M., Colo. Sch. Mines, 1942, D.Sc., 1952; m. Wilma Marguerite Wells, Oct. 14, 1943; children—Charles M., Harry W., Patricia Ann, Mary E., Catherine Sue, Joan M., Paul T., Theresa E. Exploration geologist Socony Vacuum Oil Co. of Colombia, S.A., 1946-50; geologist Tex. Gulf Sulphur Co., 1952-53, asst. mgr. exploration dept., 1953-54. mgr. exploration dept., 1954-57, v.p., mgr. exploration dept., 1957-61, sr. v.p., 1961-64, exec. v.p., 1964-68, pres., 1968—, dir., 1962—; pres., dir. Ecstall Mining, Ltd., 1966—; dir. Compania Exploradora del Istmo. S.A., Mexico, Sulphur Export Corp. Served to maj. C.E., AUS, 1942-46. Registered profl. engr., Tex. Recipient Distinguished Achievement medal Colo. Sch. Mines, 1962; Hal W. Hardinge award, 1969. Mem. Mining and Metall. Soc. Am. (pres. 1967-68), Am. Inst. Mining and Metall. Engrs., Am. Assn. Petroleum Geologists, Canadian Inst. Mining and Metallurgy, Soc. Exploration Geophysicists, Houston Geol. Soc., Am. Petroleum Inst., Newcomen Soc. N. Am., Tau Beta Pi, Sigma Gamma Epsilon, Kappa Sigma, Scabbard and Blade. Roman Catholic. Clubs: Board Room, Mining, Sky, Economic (N.Y.C.); Alta (Salt Lake City); Westchester Country, University. Home: Holly Lane Rye NY 10580 Office: 200 Park Av New York City NY 10017

FOGARTY, JAMES WILLIAM, orgn. exec.; b. Bklyn., Aug. 3, 1913; s. Michael James and Elizabeth (O'Doherty) F.; A.B., Fordham Coll., 1935, M.A., Sch. Social Service, 1938; student Cath. U. Am., 1940-41, Collegio Manuel Nobrega, Brazil, 1943; doctoral candidate Center for Human Relations Studies, N.Y.U., 1958; m. Barbara Schumann, Jan. 11, 1944; children—Barbara M.E., James M.W., Carol A., Catherine E. Social worker Bklyn. Cath. Charities, 1935- 38, N.Y.C. Dept. Pub. Welfare, 1938-40, Juvenile Ct., Washington, 1940- 42; asst. to dir. Cath. Charities, Syracuse, N.Y., 1945-48; exec. sec. Council Social Agencies, Greenboro, N.C., 1948-51; S.E. regional rep. United Community Def. Services, 1951-54; dean, prof. social work Fordham U. Sch. Social Service, 1954-62; community surveys, Williamsport, Pa., 1951, Lawrence, Mass., 1953, Scranton, Pa., 1955, Wilkes-Barre, Pa., 1958; exec. dir. Community Council Greater N.Y., 1962- -; mem. adv. council on pub. welfare U.S. Dept. Health, Edn. and Welfare. Mem. bd. N.Y.C. Dept. Welfare. Nat. Com. on Aging. Served from ensign to lt. comdr. USNR, 1942-45. Mem. Nat. Conf. Cath. Charities (v.p. 1952-53), Am. Sociol. Soc. Council Social work Edn. Nat. Assn. Social workers, Nat. Social Welfare Assembly (ho. of dels.), N.E.A., Assn. Higher Edn., Internat., Pan Am. (v.p. 1957) confs. social work. Democrat. Roman Catholic. Clubs: Rotary (N.Y.C.); Bayside Yacht. Home: 4002-221 St Bayside NY 11361

FOGARTY, JOHN FRANCIS, investment co. exec.; b. Des Moines, Sept. 9, 1921; s. John F. and Cathryn (Gallagher) F.; B.S., Rockhurst Coll., Kansas City, Mo., 1943; m. Mary Louise Ernst, Jan. 8, 1944; children—Kathy, Patricia, Michael, Terry, Janet, Jo Ellen, Daniel. Vice pres. Soden-Zahner & Co., Kansas City, Mo., 1947-52; exec. v.p. Zahner & Co., Kansas City, Mo., 1952-56; pres., v.p. Stern Bros. & Co., Kansas City, Mo., 1956—; chmn. bd. Country Club Bank, Kansas City, Mo., 1966-68. Pres. bd. edn. Cure of Ars Catholic Sch., Leawood, Kan., 1967-68; chmn. investment com. Rockhurst Coll., 1967—. Served to lt. USNR, 1942-46; PTO. Mem. Investment Bankers Assn. (gov. Southwestern group 1966-69), Kan. Bond Adv. Council (chmn. 1959, pres. 1960), Kansas City Security Traders Assn.

(pres. 1959), Rockhurst Coll. Alumni Assn. (pres. 1958). Home: 9713 Mohawk Lane Leawood KS 66206 Office: 1009-15 Baltimore Av Kansas City MO 64199

FOGEL, EPHIM GREGORY, educator; b. Odessa, Russia, Nov. 15, 1920; s. Harry Gregory and Elizabeth (Mitnik) F.; B.A., City Coll. N.Y., 1941; M.A., N.Y.U., 1947; Ph.D., Ohio State U., 1958; m. Charlotte Finkelstein, May 17, 1941; children—Daniel, David, Rebecca, Jessica. Asst. instr. English, Ohio State U., 1946-47; mem. faculty Cornell U., 1949—, dir. grad. studies in English, 1963-65, prof. English chmn. dept., 1966-70; mem. supervisory com. Cornell Concordances, 1961—; chmn. bd. editors Cornell Studies in English, 1966-70; hon. adviser Joint Com. for Summer Schs. U.K. Chmn. selection com. George Jean Nathan award for dramatic criticism, 1966, 69. Served with AUS, 1942-46. Univ. fellow English, Ohio State U., 1947-48; Nat. Endowment for Humanities grant, 1967. Mem. Am. Assn. U. Profs., Modern Lang. Assn., Renaissance Soc. Am., Shakespeare Assn. Am., Nat. Council Tchrs. English, Am. Civil Liberties Union, Phi Beta Kappa. Democrat. Jewish religion. Club: Statler (Ithaca). Author: (with David V. Erdman) Evidence for Authorship, 1966; also articles. Home: 812 Triphammer Rd Ithaca, NY 14850.

FOGEL, ERNEST JAMES, hosp. supt., psychiatrist; b. Rochester, Pa., Mar. 2, 1906; s. Charles and Mary (Reader) F.; B.S., Geneva Coll., 1934; M.D., U. Pa., 1937; m. Jean Fornear, Nov. 26, 1939; children—E. James, Mary K. Intern Allegheny Gen. Hosp., Pitts., 1937-38; resident psychiatry Warren (Pa.) State Hosp., 1938-41; with VA, 1946-58, chief psychiatry and neurology VA Hosp., Indpls., 1958; supt. Logansport (Ind.) State Hosp., 1958-67; chief staff VA Hosp., Murfreesboro, Tenn., 1967—; asso. prof. Ind. U. Med. Sch., 1956-67. Served to comdr. USNR, 1941-45. Decorated Navy Commendation ribbon. Fellow Am. Psychiat. Assn. Rotarian. Contbr. profl. jours. Address: VA Hosp Murfreesboro TN 37130

FOGEL, NORMAN, educator; b. Chgo., May 20, 1924; s. Jacob and Gussie (Leon) F.; B.S., U. Ill., 1950; M.S., U. Wis., 1951, Ph.D., 1956; m. Joane Patricia Moran, Dec. 9, 1960; children—Nancy, Dara. Instr. U. Wis. Extension, 1951-56; mem. faculty U. Okla., 1956—, prof. chemistry, 1968—. Served with AUS, 1943-46. Mem. Am. Chem. Soc., Sigma Xi, Phi Lambda Upsilon. Home: 2509 Beaurue Dr Norman OK 73069

FOGEL, ROBERT WILLIAM, educator, economist; b. N.Y.C., July 1, 1926; s. Harry Gregory and Elizabeth (Mitnik) F.; A.B., Cornell U., 1948; A.M., Columbia, 1960; Ph.D., Johns Hopkins, 1963; m. Enid Cassandra Morgan, Apr. 2, 1949; children—Michael Paul, Steven Dennis. Instr., Johns Hopkins, 1958-59; asst. prof. U. Rochester, 1960-64; Ford Found. vis. research prof. U. Chgo., 1963-64, asso. prof., 1964-65, prof. econs., 1965-69, prof. econs. and history, 1970—; prof. econs. U. Rochester, fall 1968—. Chmn. com. math. and statis. methods in history Math. Social Sci. Bd. Faculty Research grantee Social Sci. Research Council, 1966; Gilman fellow, 1957-60; fellow Social Sci. Research Council, 1960; NSF Grant, 1967, 70; Arthur H. Cole prize, 1968; Fulbright grant, 1968; Ford Found. faculty research fellow, 1970. Mem. Am. Econ. Assn., Royal Econ. Soc., Econometric Soc., Econ. History Assn., Am. Hist. Assn., Agrl. History Soc., Phi Beta Kappa. Author: The Union Pacific Railroad: A Case in Premature Enterprise, 1960; Railroads and American Economic Growth: Essays in Econometric History, 1964; (with others) The Reinterpretation of American Economic History, 1971. Home: 5710 S Blackstone Av Chicago, IL 60637; also 110 University Park Rochester NY 14620

FOGELMAN, LAZAR, editor; b. Newish, Russia, May 27, 1891; s. Simha and Adele (Sacker) F.; J.D., Imperial U., Warsaw, Poland, 1912; student Psychoneurol. Inst., Petrograd, Russia, 1913-15; LL.D., Fordham U., 1927; m. Sarah Belle Damesek, Nov. 23, 1920 (dec. Dec. 1963); 1 son, Edwin; m. 2d, Elsie Botwinik, Dec. 27, 1965. Came to the U.S., 1921, naturalized, 1927. Dir. Jewish Tchrs. Sem., N.Y.C., 1924-27; editorial and feature writer Jewish Daily Forward, N.Y.C., 1921—, editor, 1962—; editor Zukunft, Yiddish mag., 1939-41. Pres. Jewish Writers Union, 1933-35; treas. Workmens Circle, 1943-46; mem. World Meml. Jewish Martyrs, Jewish Labor Com., Jewish Culture Congress. Author: (biography) Paul Axelrod, 1928, Booker T. Washington, 1930; (history) Workmen's Circle, 1931. Home: 135 Ocean Pkwy Brooklyn NY 11218 Office: 175 E Broadway New York City NY 10007

FOGELQUIST, DONALD F., educator; b. Sioux City, Ia., Aug. 23, 1906; s. Frederick C. and Anna (Lundgren) F.; B.A., Wash. State U., 1930, M.A., 1933; Ph.D., U. Wis., 1941; m. Helen Rasmussen, July 1, 1939; children—Alan Frederick, Mark Stephen, James Donald. Mem. faculties Wash. State U., U. Miami, U. Fla., 1938-42; prof. Spanish, U. Cal. at Los Angeles, 1948—; dir. Paraguayan- Am. Cultural Center, Asuncion, Paraguay, 1945-46; lectr. in Latin Am. under auspices State Dept., 1959. Served to lt. comdr. USNR, 1942-45. Fulbright fellow, 1962-63. Mem. Inst. Internat. de Lit. Iberio-americana, Am. Assn. Tchrs. Spanish and Portuguese. Juan Ramón Jiménez (Vida Obr. Bibliografiá, Espaoles de Amèrica y Americano de Espaa.). Home: 326 Mt Holyoke St Pacific Palisades CA 90272 Office: Chmn Spanish Dept Univ California Los Angeles CA 90024

FOGELSON, DAVID, lawyer; b. Netcong, N.J., Mar. 15, 1903; s. Reuben and Sarah (Peshkin) F.; B.C.S., N.Y. U., 1923; LL.B., Fordham U., 1926; m. Gertrude Edelman, July 10, 1930; children—Ellen (Mrs. Arthur Liman), James H. Admitted to N.Y. bar, 1928; with Nathan Burkan, N.Y.C., 1926-36; mem. firm Schwartz & Frohlich, N.Y.C., 1936-68. Trustee Joe and Emily Lowe Found. C.P.A., N.Y. Mem. Assn. Bar City N.Y. Home: 980 Fifth Av New York City NY 10021 Office: 720 Fifth Av New York City NY 10021

FOGERSON, HARRY B., chain store exec.; b. Aurora, Mo., Nov. 18, 1906; s. William E. and Willa E. (Grammer) F.; student Springfield (Mo.) Bus. Coll., 1926; m. Georgia M. Franz, Jan. 27, 1934; children—Harriet Ann (Mrs. Richard H. Bird), George Edgar, Linda Edel. With F. W. Woolworth Co., N.Y.C., 1926- -, v.p., 1960—, dir., 1963—. Mem. Newcomen Soc. Conglist. Home: 2110 Seward Dr Scotch Plains NJ 07076 Office: 233 Broadway New York City NY 10007

FOGG, GORDON, lawyer; b. Sioux City, Ia., Sept. 25, 1908; s. Maurice Adams and Hope Scott (Peters) F.; B.S., U. Va., 1930; J.D., U. Mich., 1934; m. Doris Heloise Cross, Feb. 22, 1936; 1 son, Gordon Cross. Admitted to Tex bar; atty. legal dept. Shell Oil Co., Houston, 1934-42; practice in Dallas, 1946—; partner firm Locke, Purnell, Boren, Laney & Neely, and predeccessors, 1949—. Served to capt. AUS, 1943-46. Mem. Am., Tex., Dallas bar assns., Am. Judicature Soc., Jefferson Soc., Theta Delta Chi, Pi Kappa Delta. Baptist (deacon). Mason. Club: Brookhaven Country. Author: (with Julian J. Pickrel) An Economic Survey of Winchester and Frederick County, Virginia, 1930. Home: 3705 Shenandoah Av Dallas, TX 75205. Office: Republic Nat Bank Tower Dallas TX 75201

FOGG, JOHN MILTON, botanist; b. Phila. Nov. 8, 1898; s. John Milton and Grace (Kirby) F.; B.S., U. Pa., 1925; Ph.D., Harvard, U. 1929; Sc.D., LaSalle Coll., 1949; m. Helen Biggs, June 27, 1930; children—Sonia, Felicia. Instr. botany U. Pa., 1925-32, asst. prof. of botany, 1932-41, asso. prof., 1941-44, prof., 1944—, dean coll. arts and scis., 1941-44, vice provost, 1944-53, dir. Morris Arboretum, 1954-67, curator Herbarium, 1922—; dir. Barnes Arboretum, 1967—. Mem. bd. mgrs. N.Y. Bot. Gardens, 1954-65, vis. com. Arnold Arboretum, 1957-67; trustee Ludwick Inst. (pres. 1955—). Served S.A.T.C., 1918. Fellow A.A.A.S.; mem. Phila. Bot. Club, Pa. Acad. Sci., Bot. Soc. Pa., Bot. Soc. Am., Torrey Bot. Club, New Eng. Bot. Club, Faculty Club (U. of Pa.), Phi Beta Kappa, Sigma Xi. Home: 6807 Quincy St Philadelphia PA 19119 ☆

FOGG, PHILIP SHEARER, engring. exec.; b. Battle Creek, Mich., July 28, 1903; s. Alvah Lemont and Delia (Shearer) F.; A.B. cum laude, Stanford, 1925; M.B.A. magna cum laude, Harvard, 1929; m. Jean Adix, July 30, 1935; children—Jonathan, James. Chief statistician Rand McNally & Co., San Francisco, 1925-27; investment analyst Tri-Continental Corp., N.Y.C., 1929-30; lectr. Am. Inst. Banking, Los Angeles, 1932-38, Inst. Govt., U. So. Cal., Los Angeles, 1937, Cal. Sch. Design, Pasadena, 1937-41; prof. bus. economics, registrar Cal. Inst. Tech., Pasadena, 1930-41; treas. Consolidated Electrodynamics Corp., Pasadena, 1937-41, exec. v.p., 1941- 45, chmn. bd., 1945-65, pres., 1945-61; vice chmn. Bell & Howell Co., 1961-66, now dir.; dir. Royal Industries, Inc., Security Pacific Nat. Bank of Los Angeles; chmn. exec. com. Lear Siegler, Inc., 1965—, dir., 1954—. Trustee Harvey Mudd Coll., Claremont, Cal.; dir. Pasadena Found. Med. Research Spl. adviser AEC, 1947-49. Mem. C. of C. (pres. 1948-49), Cal. Inst. Tech. Assos., Stanford Assos., Phi Beta Kappa. Republican. Clubs: Rotary (pres. 1950-51), Lincoln, Twilight (pres. 1966- 67), Annadale Golf (Pasadena, California); Harvard (N.Y.C.); Valley (Montecito, Cal.). Author articles on taxation, fed. finance. Home: 720 S San Rafael Av Pasadena CA 91105 Office: 3171 S Bundy Dr Santa Monica CA 90406

FOGLE, RICHARD HARTER, educator; b. Canton, O., Mar. 8, 1911; s. James Underhill and Amanda (Harter) F.; B.A., Hamilton Coll., Litt.D. (hon.), 1967; M.A., Columbia, 1936; Ph.D., U. Mich., 1944; m. Catherine Pace Cox, Sept. 6, 1939; children—Catherine Harter, Faith Underhill. Instr. English, U. Rochester, 1939-40; instr. U. Mich., 1943- 46; asst. prof., prof., Tulane U., 1946-54, head dept. English, 1954-63, chmn., 1957-60, 63-66; prof. English, U. N. C., Chapel Hill, 1966-68, Univ. Distinguished prof. English, 1968—; mem. editorial bd. Keats-Shelley Jour., Am. Lit. Fellow Melville Soc. (pres. 1961); mem. Modern Lang. Assn. Am., So. Atlantic Modern Lang. Assn., Internat. Assn. U. Profs. English, Modern Humanities Research Assn., Keats-Shelley Assn. Author: The Imagery of Keats and Shelley, 1949; John Keats, Selected Poetry and Letters, 1951; Hawthorne's Fiction, 1952, rev. edit. 1964; Melville's Shorter Tales, 1960; The Idea of Coleridge's Criticism, 1962; The Romantic Movement in American Writing, 1966; Romantic Poets and Prose Writers, 1967; Hawthorne's Imagery, 1969. Home: 511 E Rosemary St Chapel Hill NC 27514

FOGLEMAN, JOHN ALBERT, judge; b. Memphis, Nov. 5, 1911; s. John Franklin and Julia (McAdams) F.; student U. Ark., 1927-31; LL.B., U. Memphis (now Memphis State U.), 1934; m. Annis Adell Appleby, Oct. 24, 1933; children—John Albert, Annis Adell (Mrs. Henry M. Rector), Mary Barton (Mrs. Charles L. Williams, Jr.). Admitted to Ark. bar, 1934; dep. circuit ct. clerk Crittenden County, 1933-34; pvt. practice of law, 1934-44; partner Hale & Fogleman, West Memphis, 1944-66; dep. pros. atty., Crittenden County, 1946-57; asso. justice Ark. Supreme Ct., 1967—. Mem. State Bd. Bar Examiners, 1960-63; chmn. Ark. Judiciary Commn., 1963-65; mem. Ark. Constl. Revision Study Commn., 1967, Fed.-State Jud. Council, Ark., 1971—. Active Ark. and Crittenden County Democratic central coms. Served from pvt. to 1st 1t. AUS, 1944-45. Fellow Am. Coll. Trial Lawyers; mem. Ark. (past pres.), N.E. Ark., Crittenden County bar assns. Mason, Rotarian. Home: 67 Cherry St Marion AR 72364 Office: Justice Bldg Little Rock AR 72201

FOGLEMAN, JULIAN BARTON, lawyer; b. Memphis, Apr. 17, 1920; s. John Franklin and Marie Julia (McAdams) F.; B.S., U. Ark., 1941, LL.B., 1943, J.D., 1969; m. Melba Margaret Henderson, Aug. 11, 1950; children—Margaret Elisabeth, Julian Barton, John Nelson, Jennifer Leigh, Frances Lorie. Admitted to Ark. bar, 1943; practiced in Marion, 1946-54, West Memphis, 1954—; pvt. practice, 1946-52; asso. Hale & Fogleman, 1952-66, partner, 1967—; city atty., Marion, 1951—; dep. pros. atty., 1957-64. Chmn. finance drive Crittenden Dist.-Chickasaw council Boy Scouts Am., 1969, mem. exec. bd. Chickasaw council, 1970-71. Served with inf., AUS, 1943-45: ETO. Decorated Combat Inf. Badge. Mem. Am., Ark., N.E. Ark. (pres.), Crittenden County (past pres.) bar assns., Phi Alpha Delta, Sigma Chi. Methodist. Home: 84 Turner Av Marion AR 72364 Office: 626 E Broadway West Memphis AR 72301

FOIL, ROBERT RODNEY, educator; b. Bogalusa, La., Aug. 12, 1934; s. Earl Odell and Rose A. (Green) F.; B.S. in Forestry, La. State U., 1956, M.F., 1960; D.Forestry, Duke, 1965; m. Patti Sue Thomas, Jan. 20, 1959; children—Jerry Thomas, Allison. Forester, Union Camp Corp., Ga., 1956; instr., then asst. prof. La. State U., 1959-67, asso. specialist, specialist Coop. Extension Service, 1967-69; prof., head dept. forestry Miss. U., 1969—; cons. in field. Pres. Jr. C. of C., Homer, La., 1967. Served with AUS, 1956-58. Named Outstanding Young Man Homer, La., 1967. Mem. Soc. Am. Foresters (chmn. Gulfstate sect. 1969), Miss., La. (dir. 1969) forestry assns., Sigma Xi, Xi Sigma Pi, Alpha Zeta, Gamma Sigma Delta, Phi Kappa Phi. Contbr. articles profl. jours. Home: Box 4650 State College MS 39762

FOISIE, JACK, journalist; b. Seattle, Apr. 21, 1919; s. Francis Patrick and Winifred Amanda (Shaw) F.; student U. Wash., 1938-39, U. Cal., Berkeley, 1940-41; m. Florence Mildred McTighe, Apr. 8, 1944; children—Kathleen Florence, Franklin Sean, Patricia Abbie. Sports reporter Seattle Post- Intelligencer, 1937; jr. reporter Seattle Times, 1938; reporter San Francisco Chronicle, 1940, 45-64, corr., Korean War, 1953, Vietnam War, 1962; bur. chief in Saigon Los Angeles Times, 1964-66, Bangkok, 1966—; tech. adviser movie story of G.I. Joe, 1944. Served with AUS, 1941-45. Decorated Legion of Merit for combat coverage of campaign in Sicily; Nieman fellowship, 1946-47; recipient Overseas Press Club award, 1966. Contbr. to Sat. Eve. Post and other nat. mags. Home: PO Box 2159 Bangkok Thailand Office: Los Angeles Times Fgn Bur Times Mirror Sq Los Angeles CA 90053

FOISIE, PHILIP MANNING, journalist; b. Seattle, Mar. 14, 1922; s. Francis Patrick and Wynifred (Shaw) F.; B.A., Harvard, 1947; m. Margaruitte van Tschurin, Apr. 3, 1948; children—Gregory, Geoffrey, Christina, Timothy. City editor China Press, Shanghai, 1948-49; reporter, telegraph editor Santa Rosa (Cal.) Press-Democrat, 1949-53; copy editor Louisville Courier-Jour., 1953-56; cable editor Washington Post, 1956-60, fgn. editor, 1960-68, asst. mng. editor, 1968—. Served with AUS, 1942-46. Home: 812 Timber Branch Pkwy Alexandria VA 22302 Office: Washington Post 1515 L St NW Washington DC 20005

FOKMA, JAN JELLE, lawyer; b. Barradeel, Netherlands, Apr. 2, 1900; s. Frans and Joukje (Fenema) F.; LL.D., Leiden U., 1925; m. Aleida Bosman, Feb. 27, 1934; 4 sons, Frans, Aleidus, Jan. Ruurd. Practice of law, 1925—; with Drs. v.d. Hoeven, Fokma, Kaulingfreks, Mijs, Korthals, Altes & van Schifgaarde, Rotterdam, 1930—. Chmn. Holland-Am. Line, United Ropeworks, Rotterdamsch Nieuwsblad (all Rotterdam), Maatschappij van Berkel's Patent N.V., Rotterdam; supervisory dir. Christiani & Nielsen, The Hague, Nehterlands. Decorated officer Order Orange Nassau. Home: 31 Groene Wetering Rotterdam Netherlands Office: 184 Mathenesserlaan Rotterdam Netherlands

FOLCH-PI, JORDI, physician; b. Barcelona, Spain, Mar. 25, 1911; s. Rafael Folch Capdevila and Maria Pi Ferrer; B.S., Instituto Balmes, Barcelona U., 1927; M.D., U. Barcelona, 1932; M.S. (hon.), Harvard, 1951; D.Sc., U. Montpellier, 1967; M.D., U. Chile., 1969; m. Willa G. Babcock, June 23, 1945; children—Raphael Charles, Diana Maria, Frederic Albert. Came to U.S., 1936, naturalized, 1947. Student intern dept. gen. surgery Hosp. Clinico, Barcelona, Spain, 1930-33, asst. resident physician dept. metabolic disease, 1933-35; Rockefeller Found. fellow, vol. asst. Rockefeller Inst. Hosp., N.Y.C., 1935-37, asst., 1937-42, asso., 1942- 44; asst. prof. biol. chemistry Harvard Med. Sch., 1944-51, asso. prof., 1951-55, prof. neurochemistry, 1956—; dir. sci. research McLean Hosp., Belmont, Mass., 1944—. Chmn. bd. sci. counselors Nat. Inst. Mental Health, 1960—; chmn. sci. rev. com. Kennedy labs. Mass. Gen. Hosp. Boston, 1961—. Mem. Am. Soc. Oil Chemistry, A.A.A.S., Am. Soc. Biol. Chemists. Harvey Soc., Soc. Research Mental and Nervous Disorders, Am. Acad. Arts and Scis., Acad. Neurology, Internat. (sec. 1967—), Am. (sec. 1969—) socs. neurochemistry, Am. Neurol. Assn. Club: Harvard (Boston). Editor Jour. of Neurochemistry. Author sci. papers. Home: 228 Marlborough St Boston MA 02116 Office: McLean Hosp Belmont MA 02178

FOLDES, ANDOR, pianist, condr.; b. Budapest, Dec. 21, 1913; s. Emil and Valerie (Ipolyi) F.; B.A., Royal Hungarian Music Acad., Budapest, 1932; m. Lili Rendy, July 1, 1940. Came to U.S., 1939, naturalized, 1948. Piano student since age 5; profl. debut at age 8, Royal Philharmonic Orch., Budapest; concert, pianist, Vienna, Milan, Paris, London, Stockholm, Oslo, Copenhagen, Amsterdam, 1933-39; Am. debut NBC, 1940; concerts throughout U.S., 1940-48, including appearances with N.Y. Philharmonic Symphony Orch., Los Angeles Philharmonic, Detroit Symphony, Utah State Symphony, others; tours Western Europe, 1948—, appearing with London Symphony Orch., Royal Philharmonic Orch., London, Lamoureux Orch., Paris, Berlin Philharmonic, Stockholm, Konsertforeningen, Danish State Radio Symphony, Oslo Philharmonic, Brussels Radio Symphony, Orch. de la Suisse Romande, Geneva, San Carlo Symphony, Naples, others; concert tour South Africa; conducted in Germany, Belgium, Switzerland, Luxembourg, Norway, Finland, Great Britain, Denmark, Australia, New Zealand, Japan; world tour, 46 concerts in India, Australia, New Zealand, Indonesia and Japan, 1959; third concert tour around the world in 1969; Andor Foldes Festival, Grison, Switzerland, 1969; spl. master classes Hochschule für Musik in Saarbrucken, Germany, 1958-65; recording artist for DEMI-Angel Records. Mem. Kuratorium for rebuilding Beethoven Hall, Bonn, Germany, 1954—. Recipient prize Franz Liszt internat. piano competition, Budapest, 1933; grand prix du Disques in Paris for complete Piano Works of Bela Bartok, 1957; Silver medaille City of Paris, 1971; decorated Order of Merit First Class, West Germany, 1956; grand cross Order of Merit, West Germany, 1964; officier Merite Culturel et Artistique, France, 1964; Comdr. Merite Culturel et Artistique, France, 1968. Mem. Phi Mu Alpha. Author: Keys to the Keyboard, 1948 (pub. Eng., 1950; also pub. in Norwegian, Italian, Portuguese, Dutch, Finnish, German); Is There a Contemporary Beethoven Style, 1964. Address: Herrliberg/ZH Switzerland

FOLDI, ANDREW HARRY, singer, educator; b. Budapest, Hungary, July 20, 1926; s. Alexis and Ann (Rothman) F.; came to U.S., 1939, naturalized, 1947; Ph.B., U. Chgo., 1945, M.A., 1948; pvt. student singing and piano; m. Leona Levy, Aug. 10, 1947; children—David John, Nancy Susanne. Leading bass La Scala, Milan, Vienna Staatsoper, Teatro San Carlo, Naples, Vienna Festival, Grand Theátre, Geneva, Theátre Royale de la Monnaie, Brussels, Am. Nat. Opera, Cin. Opera, Stadttheater Zurich, Teatro Comunale, Genoa, Nederlandsche Opera, Amsterdam, San Francisco Opera Co., Lyric Opera Chgo., Santa Fe Opera, Sociedad Pro Arte Mus., Havana, Cuba; guest soloist Vienna Festival, Bavarian State Radio, Munich, Concertgebouw Orch., Amsterdam, Orch. de la Suisse Romande, Geneva, Nat. Orch. Monte Carlo, Pitts. Symphony Orch., Clarion Concerts, N.Y., Gulbenkian Found., Lisbon, Concerti sinfonici, Genoa, Aldeburgh Festival, Lucerne Festival, Lausanne Festival, Chgo. Symphony Orch., Little Orch. Soc. N.Y., Rochester, Kansas City (Mo.) Philharmonic orchs., Radio Sottens, Geneva, Radio Beromunster, Zurich, Grant Park Concerts, Chgo., Indpls. Symphony Orch., Internat. Soc. Contemporary Arts, also numerous recitals, radio and TV appearances; rec. for Guilde Internationale de Disque. Faculty U. Chgo., 1947-49, dept. adult edn., 1951-61; instr., dir. opera workshop DePaul U., 1949-57; vis. instr. voice Augustana Coll., 1950-51; pvt. tchr. voice, 1949-61; cantor, mus. dir. Temple Isaiah Israel, Chgo., 1948-61, English-speaking Jewish Community of Geneva; faculty apprentice tng. program Santa Fe Opera, 1959, 64, stage dir. Mem. Am. Musicological Soc., Nat. Assn. Tchrs. Singing, Soc. Am. Musicians, Internat. Soc. Contemporary Music, Am. Guild Mus. Artists. Author: (recorded text) An Introduction to Music, 1959; also criticism, program notes. Office: 11 Ch de Crets de Champel Geneva Switzerland

FOLDS, CHARLES WESTON, merchandising exec.; b. Pitts., Oct. 22, 1910; s. George Robert and Camilla (McKey) F.; A.B., Yale, 1932; m. Suzanne Lord, Apr. 10, 1948; 1 dau., Suzanne Dewar. With Marshall Field & Co., 1932—, v.p., 1957-70, sr. v.p., gen. mgr., 1970—. Bd. dirs. Children's Meml. Hosp. Served as comdr. Supply Corps, USNR, 1941-46; supply officer Mediterranean Forces, 1945. Decorated Bronze Star medal. Mem. Chgo. Assn. Commerce and Industry (dir.). Clubs: Chicago, University, Economic, Executives, Yale (Chgo.); Glen View (Golf, Ill.); Yale (N.Y.C.). Home: 81 Woodley Rd Winnetka IL 60093 Office: 111 N State St Chicago IL 60690

FOLDS, THOMAS MCKEY, museum dean edn.; b. Connellsville, Pa., Aug. 8, 1908; s. George R. and Camilla W. (McKey) F.; A.B., Yale, 1930, B.F.A., 1934; m. Katharine L. Atwater, June 22, 1935; children—Charles Weston, David Atwater. English instr. Phillips Exeter Acad., 1934-35; art dir., 1935-46; chmn. and prof. dept. of art, Northwestern U., 1946-60; dean edn. Met. Mus. N.Y., 1960—; art cons. Pres. bd. trustees Sch. Art League N.Y.C. Mem. Coll. Art Assn., Internat. Council Museums (pres. internat. edn. and cultural action 1965-68). Contbr. profl. jours. Lectr. on art. Home: 535 E 86th St New York City NY Office: Metropolitan Museum New York City NY 10028

FOLDY, LESLIE LAWRANCE, educator; b. Sabinov, Czechoslovakia, Oct. 26, 1919; s. Leonard and Helen (Lustig) F.; B.Sc., Case Inst. Tech., 1941; Ph.M., U. Wis., 1942; Ph.D., U. Cal. at Berkeley, 1948; m. Roma Bisgyer, Nov. 25, 1944; children—Seth Leonard, Erica Gabrielle. Mem. faculty Case Western Res. U. and predecessor, 1948—, prof. physics, 1953—, Inst. prof., 1966—; vis. scientist Bohr Inst. Theoretical Physics, Copenhagen, Denmark, 1953- 54, CERN, Geneva, Switzerland, 1963-64, Brookhaven Nat. Lab., summers. NRC predoctoral fellow, 1946-48; Guggenheim fellow, 1953-54; Fulbright fellow, 1953-54; NSF sr. postdoctoral fellow, 1963-64. Fellow Am. Phys. Soc., Acoustical Soc. Am.; mem. Am. Assn. U. Profs., Fedn. Am. Scientists, Sigma Xi. Spl. research theoretical atomic, nuclear and elementary particle physics. Home: 2232 Elandon Dr Cleveland Heights OH 44106 Office: Case Western Res Univ Cleveland OH 44106

FOLEJEWSKI, ZBIGNIEW, educator; b. Wilno, Poland, Oct. 18, 1910; s. Joseph and Bronislawa (Hajkowska) F.; M.A., Wilno U., 1934; Ph.Licentiste, Uppsala (Sweden) U., 1948, Ph.D., 1949; m. Ulla K. Lindberg, Jan. 6, 1946; children—Peter J., Anna K., Vanda I. (Mrs. William Bidwell), Christina M., Louise B. Lectr. Cath. Coll., Harbin, Manchuria, 1935-37, U. Stockholm (Sweden), 1937-47; lectr. Uppsala U., 1947-49, docent, 1949-53; mem. faculty U. Wis.-Madison, 1951-65, chmn. Slavic dept., 1960-62; prof. Slavic, comparative lit. U. Ill., Urbana, 1965-67; prof. Slavic langs., chmn. comparative lit. U. B.C., 1967—; vis. prof. U. Cal. at Berkeley, 1953, 56, U. Colo., 1962, U. Toronto, 1962-63, Pa. State U., 1963-64; cons. Nobel prize com. Swedish Acad., 1958, Standard Med. Dictionary, 1960—, Can. Council, 1968—, Humanities Research Fund, 1968—. U. Wis., Pa. State U. rep. 600th Anniversary, Jagellonian U., Cracow, Poland, 1964. Mem. Am. (adv. bd. 1962-64, 64-67; conf. nat. standards in comparative lit., N.Y.C. 1964), Internat. (Am. del. 2d internat. congress Chapel Hill, N.C., 1958, 4th internat. congress Fribourg, Switzerland 1964), Canadian (chmn. Canadian com. Slavists, rep. internat. com. Slavists, 1969—) comparative lit. assns., Modern Lang. Assn. Am., Am. Assn. Tchrs. of Slavic and East European Langs., Canadian Assn. Slavists (chmn. editorial bd. Canadian Slavonic Papers 1968—), Phi Kappa Phi. Editor: Studies in Russian and Polish Literature in Honor of W. Lednicki, 1961; editor Svio-Polonica, 1937-47; editorial bd. proc. Modern Lang. Assn., 1959-64, 64-69, Polish Rev., 1956-61; asso. editor Slavic and East European Jour., 1956—, Books Abroad, 1964—. Home: 4103 W 11th Av Vancouver 8 British Columbia Canada

FOLEY, ADRIAN M., Jr., lawyer; b. Bartlett, N.D., Jan. 16, 1922; B.S. cum laude, Seton Hall U., 1943; LL.B., Columbia, 1947. Admitted to N.J. bar, 1948; mem. firm Hughes, McElroy, Connell, Foley & Geiser, Newark. Surrogate, County of Essex, 1954-58; pres. N.J. Constl. Conv., 1966. Fellow Am. Bar Found.; mem. Am. (mem. projects com. 1957), N.J. State (trustee 1957-58, treas. 1958-61, 2d v.p. 1961-62, 1st v.p. 1962-63, pres. 1964-65), Montclair-West Essex, Hudson County, Essex County (mem. practice and procedure in probate cts. com. 1956-58) bar assns., Am. Coll. Probate Counsel. Office: 24 Commerce St Newark NJ 07102*

FOLEY, ARTHUR DAVID, fgn. service officer; b. Palmer, Mass., Aug. 9, 1919; s. Henry Michael and Rosemary (O'Neill) F.; A.B. in Polit. Sci., U. Mich., 1941; m. Anne Nichols, Sept. 14, 1946; children—Anne O'Neill, Kathleen Nichols, Frances Donnelly, Elizabeth Kerrigan. With U.S. Rubber Co., 1941; joined U.S. Fgn. Service, 1946; 3d, then 2d sec. embassy, Rio de Janeiro, Brazil, 1946-49; 2d sec. embassy, Caracas, Venezuela, 1949-52; consul, Bremen, Germany, 1952-55; assigned Office Munitions Control State Dept., 1955-58; 1st sec. U.S. Mission to NATO, Paris, France, 1958-62; div. chief European regional affairs, bur. intelligence and research, State Dept., 1962-65, Austrian-Swiss affairs, 1965-67, special asst. politico-mil. affairs, 1967—. Served to captain AUS, 1942-46. Mem. Kappa Sigma. Address: Dept of State Washington DC 20525

FOLEY, DONALD LESLIE, educator; b. Hamilton, N.Y., Aug. 22, 1916; s. Roy William and Jessie (Ross) F.; A.B., Colgate U., 1938; M.A., U. Chgo., 1942; Ph.D., Washington U., St. Louis, 1948; m. Katharine Averill, Dec. 27, 1941; children—Thomas, William, Margaret, Judith. Planning analyst St. Louis City Planning Commn., 1946-48; asst. prof. sociology U. Rochester, N.Y., 1948-53; research asso. Bur. Applied Social Research, Columbia, 1953; lectr. U. Cal. at Berkeley, 1953-55, asso. prof. city planning, architecture, 1955-63, prof., 1963—, chmn. dept. city and regional planning, 1964-67. Dir. Berkeley Area Community Chest and Council, 1954- 59, Bay Area Welfare Planning Fedn., 1958-59. Served from ensign to lt., Supply Corps, USNR, 1942-45. Fellow Am. Sociol. Assn.; mem. Am. Inst. Planners, Population Assn. Am., Regional Sci. Assn. Author: Controlling London's Growth, 1963. Contbr. articles profl. jours. Home: 1050 Mariposa Av Berkeley CA 94707

FOLEY, DUNCAN CHRISTOPH chemist, educator; b. Chicago, 1928; B.S. in Physics, Yale, 1950; Ph.D. in Chemistry, Harvard, 1956; m. Sally Ann Jones, July 5, 1957; children--Kenneth J., Nancy A. Chemist, Acme Chem. Co., Blue Island, Ill., 1950-51; director of Research Lab., Indsl. Chemicals Corp., Cambrige, Mass., 1956-60; project coordinator environmental sect. Steinmetz Assos., Chgo., 1960-61; v.p. for research Bauer Bros. Chem. Co., Inc., Memphis, 1961-64; asst. prof. chemistry Washington U., St. Louis, 1964-66, asso. prof., 1966-70, prof., 1970--, head of chemistry dept., 1970-71. Vis. prof. So. Ill. U., summer 1967, U. of Ore., 1969. Bd. dirs. Rest Haven Home for Elderly, 1960-61; trustee of the Lutheran Hosp., 1965-71. Served from lt. to capt., AUS, 1951-53. Mem. Am. Chem. Soc., Sci. Research Soc. Am. (chpt. treas. 1967), Sigma Xi. Author: (with others) Basic Inorganic Chemistry, 1971. Home: Fairfax Apts 7291 Windermere Dr University City MO 63105 Office: Dept Chemistry Washington University St Louis MO 63130

FOLEY, EDWARD H., lawyer, executive; b. Syracuse, N.Y., May 23, 1905; s. Edward H. and Josephine (Mullin) F.; LL.B., Fordham U., 1929; m. Emily Ligon Bowdoin, Aug. 16, 1941. Admitted to N.Y. Bar, 1930, U.S. Supreme Ct., 1936, D.C. bar, 1946; mng. clerk and atty. Hawkins, Delafield & Longfellow, N.Y., 1926-32; atty. R.F.C., Washington, 1932-33; asst. gen. counsel and gen. counsel Fed. Emergency Adminstrn. Pub. Works, Washington, 1933-37; asst. gen. counsel Treas. Dept., Washington, 1937-38, gen. counsel, 1939-42 (atty. gen's com. on bankruptcy adminstrn., 1939; bd. legal examiners for Civil Service Commn., 1941-43); U.S. del. and chmn. Inter-Am. Conf. on Systems of Econ. and Financial Control, 1942. Asst. sec. Treasury Dept.,j 1946- 48, under sec., 1948-53; mem. Foley & Lynch, Washington, 1953-62, Corocoran, Foley, Youngman & Rowe, 1962—; dir. Ionics, Inc. Mem. Pres. Temporary Commn. on Employee Loyalty, 1946-48; mem. Joint Commn. on Coinage, 1967—. mem. Commn. Exec., Legis. and Jud. Salaries, 1968—. Bd. trustees Nat. Found. for Infantile Paralysis, Inc., and Ga. Warm Springs Found., 1952—; bd. trustees John Fitzgerald Kennedy Library; bd. dirs. Franklin D. Roosevelt Found., 1953—; gen. chmn. Community Chest campaign Met. Washington, 1947. Gen. chmn. Presidential Inauguration, 1961; hon. vice chmn. Presidential Inauguration, 1965. Served from lt. col. to col. Army U.S., 1942-45, legal adviser to Q.M. Gen., 1942-43; served as joint dir. finance subcommn., Allied Control Commn. Italy, 1943-44; gen. counsel, Office of Contract Settlement, 1944-46. Awarded Bronze Star Medal, Legion of Merit, Grand Officer Order of Merit (Republic Italy). Mem. Bar Assn. City N.Y., N.Y. State and Am. bar Assns., Am. Law Inst., Order of Coif (hon.). Democrat. Roman Catholic. Clubs: Chevy Chase, Metropoiltan (Washington); Brook, Recess (N.Y.C.); Spouting Rock Beach Association, Reading Room, Clambake, Newport Country (Newport). Contbr. articles to law revs. Home: 2340 Wyoming Av Washington DC 20008 also 5 Red Cross Av Newport RI 02840

FOLEY, EUGENE PATRICK, govt. ofcl.; b. Wabasha, Minn., Nov. 22, 1928; s. John Robert and Ellen Monica (Brennan) F.; B.A., St. Thomas Coll., St. Paul, 1952; student Inst. European Studies, Vienna, Austria, 1952; LL.B., U. Minn., 1955; m. Frances Dillon, June 19, 1954; children—Anne Doris, Robert Dillon, Margaret Mary, Paul Hubert. Admitted to Minn. bar, 1955; with firm Foley & Foley, Rochester and Wabasha, 1955-59; legal counsel small bus. com. U.S. Senate, 1959-61; dep. asst. sec. commerce for domestic affairs, also adminstr. Bus. and Def. Services Adminstrn., 1961-62; dep. to sec. commerce, 1962-63; adminstr. Small Bus. Adminstrn., 1963-65; asst. sec. commerce, dir. economic devel., 1965—; pres. Internat. Ore & Fertilizer Corp., 1967-69. Democratic candidate for Congress, 1958; exec. asst. to Senator Humphrey in Wis. and W. Va. presdl. primaries, 1960. Named Govt. Man of Year, Nat. Bus. League, 1964, Internat. Boss of Year, Nat. Secs. Assn. Internat., 1965; Arthur S. Flemming award, 1965. Mem. Fed. Bar Assn., Philos. Soc. Washington. Author: The Achieving Ghetto.

FOLEY, FRANCIS DRAKE, naval officer; b. Dorchester, Mass., July 4, 1910; s. Paul and Josephine Frances (Drake) F.; B.S., U.S. Naval Acad., 1932; grad. Naval War Coll., 1953; m. Martha McCullough, Nov. 22, 1941 (dec. Nov. 1965); children—Josephine Drake, Jamie Harlan Vogel, William Raymond Vogel, Timothy James Vogel, Frederick John Vogel; m. 2d, Clair O'Neill Vogel, Aug. 20th, 1966. Commd. ensign USN, 1932; designated aviator, 1936, advanced through grades to rear adm., 1957; assigned to squadrons VS-41, VO-4, VP-31, VN-15, 1936-42, U.S.S. Hornet, 1942; mem. staffs CTF-65, ComAirSolomons, also COMFAIRSOUTH, 1943; head officers flying sect. Office Naval Operations, 1944-45; navigator, air officer, then exec. officer U.S.S. Franklin D. Roosevelt, 1945-47; mem. staff CNATRA, 1947- 49; comdg. officer helicopter squadron 2, 1949-50; with aviation plans br. Office Naval Operations, 1950-52; mem. staff SACLANT, 1953-55; comdg. officer U.S.S. Salisbury Sound, 1955-56, U.S.S. Shangri-La, 1956- 57; asst. chief staff plans CINCPAC, 1957-60, ComCarDiv 1, 1960-61, also comdr. attack carrier force, 7th Fleet, 1960; asst. chief programs mgmt., Bur. Weapons, Navy Dept., 1961-62; dep. asst. chief staff plans and policy SACEUR, 1962-65; asst. chief naval operations (fleet operations and readiness), 1965-67; comdt. Third Naval Dist., also commdr. naval base, N.Y.C., 1967-71; sr. mem. UN Command Mil. Armistice Commn., Korea, 1971—. Former Navy mem. mil. liaison com. AEC. Decorated Legion of Merit, Bronze Star with combat V, Joint Services Commendation medal, Sec. Navy Commendation medal with combat V, various area and campaign medals. Mem. U.S. Naval Inst., Am. Helicopter Soc., Am. Ordnance Assn., Nat. Geog. Soc., Caterpillar Soc. Clubs: N.Y. Yacht; Army-Navy (Washington); Army-Navy Country (Arlington, Va.). Home: Jacksonville FL Office: United Nations Command Seoul Korea APO San Francisco CA 96301

FOLEY, FRANK CLINGAN, geologist; b. Ont., Can., Aug. 8, 1906; s. Herbert Walter and Annie Laura (Clingan) F.; B.A. with honors, U. Toronto, 1929; Ph.D., Princeton, 1938; m. Adelaide Bowler Kirk, Jan. 31, 1934; 1 dau., Barbara Kirk. Came to U.S., 1929, naturalized, 1937. Instr. geology Dartmouth, 1929-30; grad. asst. Princeton, 1930-33; instr. U. N.D., 1933-35, asst. prof., 1935-38, prof., 1938-41, head dept. geology, also state geologist, N.D., 1938-41; geologist U.S. Geol. Survey, Utah and Wyo., 1941-42, dist. geologist, Wis., 1946-51; geologist, head ground water div. Ill. Geol. Survey, 1951-54; research prof. geology U. Ill., 1951- 54; state geologist, dir. Kan. Geol. Survey, 1954-70; prof. geology U. Kan., 1954—, head dept., 1957-63. Cons. on water supply for mil. cemeteries Am. Battle Monuments Commn.; field geologist Canadian and Newfoundland geol. surveys, 1927-36; chmn. governor's water res. factfinding com., Kan., 1954; hydrogeologist UN, West Africa, East Africa, 1968, 71. Served as maj., C.E., AUS, 1942-45. Decorated Bronze Star medal. Fellow Geol. Soc. Am.; mem. Am. Geophys. Union, Soc. Econ. Geologists, A.A.A.S., Am. Water Resources Assn., Nat. Water Well Assn., Internat. Assn. Hydrogeologists (v.p. 1957-61), Sigma Xi, Sigma Gamma Epsilon, Lambda Chi Alpha. Conglist. Home: 1203 W 20th St Terrace Lawrence KS 66044

FOLEY, HAROLD SCANLON, mfg. exec.; b. Mpls., Sept. 9, 1900; s. Jeremiah and Marie (Scanlon) F.; B. Commerce, U. Notre Dame, 1921; LL.D., U. B.C., 1957, St. Mary's U., 1958; m. Frances C. Burrowes, Sept. 29, 1927; two daughters. Salesman Brooks-Scanlon, Inc., Eastport, Fla., 1922-25; part owner Dunan Lumber Co., Brandenton, Fla., 1925-28; pres. Foley Lumber Co., Jacksonville, Fla., 1928-29; v.p. Brooks-Scanlon, Inc., Foley, Fla., 1929-36; exec. v.p. Powell River Co., Ltd., Vancouver, B.C., 1936-40, pres., 1940-55, chmn. bd., 1955—, also dir.; chmn., dir. Powell River Sales Co., Ltd., 1938—; vice chmn. bd., dir. MacMillan, Bloedel & Powell River, Ltd., 1960-61; v.p., dir., mem. exec. com. Bank of Montreal; dir. Union Oil Co. of Can. (Calgary), Harbor Park Devels. Ltd. (Vancouver), Bank of Montreal (Cal.), San Francisco. Hon. pres. B.C. Cancer Found.; hon. chmn. B.C. and Yukon div. Canadian Cancer Soc.; hon. v. p. Red Cross Soc. Bd. dirs. Nat. Heart Found.; bd. lay trustees, finance com. U. Notre Dame. Decorated Knight of St. Gregory; recipient Human Relations award Can. Council Christians and Jews, 1958. Mem. Canadian Assn. Sovereign Order Malta. Roman Catholic. Clubs: Vancouver, Shaughnessy Golf and Country, Faculty (Vancouver); Bohemian (San Francisco); Mount Royal (Montreal). Home: 1503 Angus Dr Vancouver British Columbia Canada Office: 603-626 W Pender St Vancouver British Columbia Canada

FOLEY, HARRY JOHN PATRICK, naval officer; b. Trenton, N.J., June 7, 1916; s. Harry Patrick and Anna (Joyce) F.; B.S., U.S. Naval Acad., 1938; grad. Naval War Coll., 1947; m. Jane Otto, Feb. 14, 1942; children—J. Michael, Robert P., Barbara J. Commd. ensign U.S. Navy, 1938, advanced through grades to rear adm., 1964; gen. line duties U.S.S. Quincy, 1938-40; mem. staff Destroyer Div. 66, 1941-42; asst. supply officer U.S.S. Lexington, 1942-44; staff Naval Air Advanced Tng. Command, 1945-46; comdg. officer Aviation Supply Depot, Pearl Harbor, 1947-49; dir. supply div. Bur. Aero., 1950-53; supply officer U.S.S. Coral Sea, 1953-54; dir. stock control and plans Aviation Supply Office, 1954-58; supply officer Naval Air Sta., San Diego, 1958- 60; force supply officer, comptroller Naval Air Force, Pacific Fleet, 1960-63; comdg. officer Naval Supply Depot, Seattle, 1963-64; asst. chief transp. and facilities Bur. Supplies and Accounts, 1964-66; comdg. officer Navy Aviation Supply Office, 1966-70; comdg. officer Naval Supply Center, San Diego, 1970—. Mem. Mayor Seattle Maritime Com., 1963-64. Bd. dirs. Seattle YMCA, 1964. Fellow Soc. Logistics Engrs.; mem. Nat. Def. Transp. Assn. (pres. Phila 1966-69), Naval Hist. Found. Clubs: Cuyamaca, Koni Kai (San Diego); Army-Navy Country (Arlington, Va.). Home: 1419 Catalina Blvd San Diego CA 92107 Office: Naval Supply Center 937 N Harbor Dr San Diego CA 92133

FOLEY, HENRY ELLIOTT, lawyer; b. Boston, Mar. 30, 1902; s. Henry J. and Ella J. (Carroll) F.; A.B., Boston Coll., 1922; LL.B., Harvard, 1925, S.J.D., 1926; m. Catherline E. Sullivan, Sept. 10, 1931; children—Carol Liston, Henry Elliott. Admitted to Mass. bar, 1925, practiced in Boston, 1925—; partner firm Foley, Hoag & Eliot 1938—; corp. counsel, City of Boston, 1934-38; chmn. Overseers of Pub. Welfare, 1950-52. Prof. Boston Coll. Law Sch., 1930-40, acting dean, 1938-39; clerk of corp. Northeast Airlines, Inc. Bd. dirs. Boston Municipal Reseaech Bur. Boston Citizens Council, Inc., 1954—. The Edgartown (Mass.) Reading Room; mem. Mass. Bd. of Regional Community Colls., trustee Eastern Gas & Fuel Assos. Mem. Boston Port Protective Com., Am. Judicature Soc., Newcomen Soc. Assn. ICC Practitioners, Am. Law Inst., Am., Mass., Boston bar assns. Knight of Malta. Clubs: Lyford Cay (Bahamas); Algonquin, Union, Saint Botolph, Downtown (Boston); Edgartown (Mass.) Yacht; Wings, The Leash (N.Y.C.). Home: 166 Beacon St Boston MA 02116 Office: Ten Post Office Sq Boston MA 02109

FOLEY, HENRY MICHAEL, educator; b. Palmer, Mass., June 1, 1917; s. Henry Michael and Rosemary (O'Neill) F.; B.S., U. Mich., 1938, M.S., 1939, Ph.D., 1942; m. Margaret Moore, Mar. 27, 1943 (div. 1959); children—David, Barbara; m. 2d, Barbara Mallard, Apr. 1959. Teaching asst. U. Mich., 1939, Coffin fellow, 1940-42, research for OSRD, 1942-43; research on proximity fuse for OSRD, Washington, 1944-45; instr. physics advancing to prof. Columbia, 1946—, chmn. dept. physics, 1957-60; research atomic and nuclear physics; Guggenheim fellow, 1954-55; Fulbright lectr., Netherlands, 1955; U.S. Office Naval Research, London, 1968-69. Fellow Am. Phys. Soc. (vice chmn. div. electron and atomic physics 1971); mem. Am. Assn. Physics Tchrs. Home: 460 Riverside Dr New York City NY 10027

FOLEY, JAMES THOMAS, U.S. dist. judge; b. Troy, N.Y., July 9, 1910; s. Thomas David and Mary (Malone) F.; A.B., Fordham U., 1931; LL.B., Albany Law Sch., 1934; m. Eleanor Marie Anthony, July 16, 1953; 1 dau., Mary Jude. Admitted N.Y. bar, 1934; engaged in private practice law, Troy, 1935- 42; sec. to Supreme Ct. Justice William H. Murray, 1939-42, 46-49; judge U.S. Dist. Ct., No. Dist. N.Y., 1949-63, chief judge, 1963—. served as lt. USNR, 1942-45. Mem. Am., N.Y. bar assns., Vets. Fgn. Wars, Am. Legion. K.C., Elk. Home: R F D 1 Rensselaer NY 12144 Office: Federal Post Office Bldg Albany NY 12207

FOLEY, JEAN COLEMAN, author, lit. agt.; b. Stafford Springs, Conn., Feb. 10, 1929; s. Francis John and Kathryn Maureen (Cummiskey) C.; B.A., Barry Coll., 1950; m. Joseph J. Foley, June 7, 1952. Publicity worker Burl Ives, N.Y.C., 1950-51; writer TV, radio commls. Videocast Prodns./Nat. Farm Network, N.Y.C., 1951-54; lt. agt. Donald MacCampbell Agy., N.Y.C., 1954-56, The Foley Agy., 1956—. Mem. Beta Kappa Kappa. Author (with husband): The Hangover Cookbook, 1968; The Finger and Fork Snack Book, 1970. Home: New York City NY 10016 also Simmons Rd Madison MD 21648 Office: 34 E 38th St New York City NY 10016

FOLEY, JOHN MARTIN, lawyer; b. N.Y.C., Nov. 16, 1925; s. John Joseph and Valentina E. (Clark) F.; B.C.E., Manhattan Coll., 1945; LL.B., Fordham U., 1948; m. Eileen M. Mahoney, July 3, 1948; children—Eileen, Kevin John. Admitted to N.Y. bar, 1949; law sec., Chief Judge S. J. Ryan, U.S. Dist. Ct., So. Dist. N.Y., 1947-50; asst. U.S. atty. So. Dist. N.Y., 1950-53; practice of law, New York City, 1949—; partner in the law firm of Foley, Hickey, Gilbert & Currie; counsel borough pres. Bronx, 1956-59; spl. counsel Bd. Higher Edn., N.Y.C., 1953-54. Mem. Am., N.Y. State bar assns., Bronx County Lawyers Assn., Cath. Lawyers Guild, Friendly Sons of St. Patrick. Clubs: Manhattan, N.Y. Athletic (N.Y.C.). Home: 5220 Arlington Av New York City, NY 10071. Office: 70 Pine St New York City NY 10005

FOLEY, JOSEPH MICHAEL, physician; b. Boston, Mar. 9, 1916; s. Michael and Hannah (O'Sullivan) F.; A.B., Coll. Holy Cross, 1937, Sc.D. (hon., 1962; M.D., Harvard, 1941; m. Alice Marie Corcoran, Aug. 23, 1944; children—Susan, Joseph Michael, Celia, Stephen Corcoran, Martha, George Bartlett. Intern Bellevue Hosp., N.Y.C., 1941-43; Rockefeller spl. asst. neurology Boston City Hosp., 1946-48; asst. prof. neurology Boston U. Sch. Medicine, 1948-51; vis. physician neurology Boston City Hosp., 1955- -, also neuropathologist; asst. prof. Harvard Med. Sch., 1951-60; prof. neurology Seton Hall U., 1959-61; prof. neurology Case Western Res. U., 1961—, coordinator postgrad. med. edn., 1968—; dir. neurol. service Jersey City Med. Center, 1960-61; neurologist-in- chief U. Hosps., Cleve. Med. adv. bd. Nat. Multiple Sclerosis Soc., nat. cons. USPHS. Mem. Cath. Commn. on Intellectual and Cultural Affairs. Mem. adv. bd. Ursuline Coll., Cleve.; trustee Cleve. Med. Library Assn., Coll. Holy Cross. Served with USNR, 1943-46. Decorated Bronze Star. Mem. Am. Acad. Neurology (pres. 1963-65), Am. Neurol. Assn., Am. Assn. Neuropathologists. Home: 2869 Berkshire Rd Cleveland Heights OH 44121 Office: U Hosps Cleveland OH 44106

FOLEY, LEO ALBERT, educator, assn. exec.; b. Boston, Mar. 25, 1916; s. Leo A. and Mary M. (Cady) F.; student Marist Fathers Sem., 1934-43; M.A., Cath. U. Am., 1944, Ph.D., 1946 Joined Soc. of Mary, 1937, ordained priest Roman Cath. Ch., 1943; faculty Cath. U. Am., 1946—, prof. philosophy, 1960—; research theory nuclear physics and radioastronomy Cambridge (Eng.) U., 1955-56. Mem. Am. Cath. Philos. Assn., 1946—, sec., 1959-64, editor proceedings, 1959—. Author: Cosmology: Philosophical and Scientific, 1962. Mem. Am. Philos. Assn., A.A.A.S. Contbr. profl. pubs. Home: 220 Taylor St NE Washington DC 20017

FOLEY, MARTHA, editor, writer, educator; b. Roston, d. Walter and Margaret Millicent (McCarty) Foley; educated Girls Latin Sch., Boston, Boston U. 1 son David. Formerly newspaperwoman on staff Am. newspapers as reporter, editor, fgn. corr.; co-founder of magazine Story, and co-editor The Story Press, 1931-42; editor The Best Am. Short Stories 1915-65, 1965; lectr. on short story, Columbia, 1945—. Contbr. short stories and articles to mags. Home: 29 Bank St New York City NY 10014 Office: Columbia U New York City NY 10027

FOLEY, PAUL, advt. exec.; b. Pontiac, Mich., Mar. 12, 1914; s. Raymond M. and Mary (Hautekeur) F.; B.A. magna cum laude, U. Notre Dame, 1937; m. Sophye Balicki, Oct. 31, 1937; children—Susan Mary, Peter Michael, Jane Celeste. Reporter, Chgo. Evening Am., 1937-38; editorial staff Pontiac (Mich.) Press, 1938-39; copywriter Grace & Bement, Inc., advt. agy., 1940-43; exec. v.p., dir. MacManus, John & Adams, Inc., 1946-56; sr. v.p., dir. McCann-Erickson, Inc., N.Y.C., 1956-71, vice chmn. bd. dirs., 1963-65, chmn. bd. dirs., 1965-71, also chief exec. ofcr.; pres., chief exec. officer Interpub. Group Cos., 1971—. With OWI, N.Y.C., 1943, bur. chief, Instanbul, Turkey, 1944-45. Mem. Hist. Soc. Pa., Detroit Hist. Soc. Clubs: Bloomfield Open Hunt (dir. Bloomfield Hills, Mich.); Detroit Athletic, Recess, Players (Detroit). Home: 1211 Willow Lane Birmingham MI 48009 also 6 E 81st St New York City NY 10028 Office: 485 Lexington Av New York City NY 10017

FOLEY, THOMAS STEPHEN, congressman; b. Spokane, Wash., Mar. 6, 1929; s. Ralph E. and Helen Marie (Higgins) F.; student Gonzaga U., 1947-50; B.A., U. Wash., 1951, LL.B., 1957; m. Heather Strachan, Dec. 1968. Admitted to Wash. State bar; partner firm Higgins & Foley, 1957-58; dep. pros. atty. Spokane County, Spokane, 1958-60; asst. atty. gen. State of Wash., Olympia, 1960-61; spl. counsel interior and insular affairs com. U.S. Senate, Washington, 1961-64; mem. 89th-92d Congresses 5th Dist. Wash. Instr. law

Gonzaga U., 1958-60. Mem. Phi Delta Phi. Democrat. Home: 524 7th Av Spokane WA 99202 Office: Longworth Bldg Washington DC 20510

FOLEY, WILLIAM EDWARD, govt. ofcl., b. Danbury, Conn., Feb. 7, 1911; s. Edward L. and Hertha (Braun) F.; A.B., Harvard, 1932, LL.B., 1935, A.M., 1939, Ph.D., 1940; m. Marguerite M. Pratt, June 5, 1951; children—William, Christopher, Anne, Richard, Jonthan, David, Carl. Admitted to Mass. bar, 1935; practiced in Boston, 1935-40; chief internal security fgn. agts. registration sect. Dept. Justice, 1948-54, exec. asst. internal security div., 1954-58, 1st asst. criminal div., 1958-64; dep. dir. Adminstrv. Office U.S. Cts., 1964—, sec. com. on rules of practice and procedure. Served to lt. comdr. USNR, 1942-46; capt. Res. Mem. Am. Law Inst., Am., Fed. bar assns., Am. Judicature Soc. Home: 5 E Melrose St Chevy Chase MD 20015 Office: Supreme Ct Bldg Washington DC 20544

FOLEY, WILLIAM THOMAS, educator, physician; b. N.Y.C., Oct. 30 1911; s. Edmund Leo and Sarah (O'Loughlin) F.; B.A., Columbia, 1933; M.D., Cornell U., 1937; m. Barbara Ball, June 29, 1946; children—Caroline Ball, Lucy L., Claire E., Laura D.; m. 2d, Regula von Murait, Apr. 25, 1970. Instr. anatomy Hong Kong U., 1939-41; organizer Fong Pin Hosp., Canton, China, 1940; mem. pub. health survey Orient for Navy, 1941; research fellow Pekin Union Med. Coll., 1941; prisoner of war Japanese, 1941-45; comdg. officer Prisoner of War Camp Sendai II; mem. staff N.Y. hosp., 1946—; asso. attending physician, chief vascular clinic, asso. prof. medicine Cornell U. Med. Sch.; cons. physician N.Y. Infirmary, Mary Walsh Home, Southampton, Prospect Heights, St. Barnabas, Beckman Downtown hosps.; mem. med. bd. Doctors Hosp Del. Internat. Heart Congress, Paris, 1950, Buenos Aires, 1952, Basel, 1954, Stockholm 1956, Brussels, 1958, Mexico, 1962, Barcelona, 1967, London, 1970; mem. U.S. nat. commn. USPHS. Served as 1t. (j.g.), USN, 1937-38, comdr., 1941-46. Decorated D.S.M. (Navy), Bronze Star, Purple Heart; recipient A.R.C. citation for heading relief work beri beri epidemic, Canton, China, 1940. Diplomate Am. Bd. Internat. Medicine. Fellow A.C.P., N.Y. Acad. Medicine, Am. Coll. Cardiology; mem. Am. Fedn. Clin. Research, A.M.A. (cons. to council pharm. and chemistry), Am.Acad. Compensation Medicine (v.p.), Am. Heart Assn. (circulation bd.), N.Y. Physicians Sci. (pres.), Internat. Council Health and Travel, Harvey Soc., Beta Theta Pi. Clubs: Dutch Treat, Racquet and Tennis, Piping Rock, Seawanhaka Yacht, Beaver Dam Winter Sports. Author: Vascular Diseases, 1947; Colored Atlas and Management of Vascular Diseases, 1959; co-author: Diseases of the Heart and Blood Vessels, 1964; also articles in med. jours. Asso. editor Angiology. Home: 120 East End Av New York City NY Office: New York Hospital Doctors Bldg 441 E 68th St New York City NY 10021

FOLGATE, HOMER EMMETT, Jr., lawyer; b. Rockford, Ill., Nov. 10, 1920; s. Homer Emmett and Hazel J. (Grissinger) F.; J.D., U. Ill., 1948; m. Letty Rae Huber, Apr. 28, 1944; children-Randall Lind, Jill, John Ernest. Admitted to Ill. bar, 1948; asst. states atty., Winnebago County, Ill., 1948-55; partner firm Reno, Zahm, Folgate & Skolrood, Rockford, Ill., 1955—. Chmn. Winnebago County Republican Central Com., 1955-64. Served with AUS, 1943-46. Decorated Purple Heart, Silver Star. Maon. (Shriner). Home: 1042 Lundvall Av Rockford IL 61107 Office: Camelot Tower Rockford IL 61108

FOLGER, JOHN CLIFFORD, ex-ambassador; b. Sheldon, Ia., May 28, 1896 s. Homer and Emma (Funston) F.; B.S., State Coll. of Washington, 1917. M.S., 1918; m. Mary Kathrine Dulin, Nov. 2, 1929; children—John Dulin, Lee Merritt. Chmn. bd. Folger, Nolan, Fleming & Co., Inc., Piedmont Mortgage Co., Washington; dir. Hiram Walker-Gooderham & Worts, Ltd., Ont., IBM, Va. Industries, Inc., World Banking Corporation, Ltd. (Nassau); American ambassador to Belgium, 1957-59. Mem. bd. govs. New York Stock Exchange. Chmn. Rep. Nat. Finance Com. 1955-57, 60-61. Gen. chmn. Washington Community Chest, 1940; chmn. D.C. chpt. A.R.C., 1942, now hon. chmn.; mem. Washington Cathedral. Pres. Investment Bankers Assn. Am., 1943-45. Mem. Nat. Inst. Social Sci. Republican. Clubs: Alfalfa, The Brook, Chevy Chase, Metropolitan, 1925 F Street (Washington); Down Town Assn. (New York City); Lyford Cay (Nassau); Everglades, Bath and Tennis (Palm Beach). Home: 2991 Woodland Dr NW Washington DC 20008 Office: 725 15th ST NW Washington DC 20005

FOLGER, JOHN DALTON MURPHY, govt. ofcl.; b. Thunderbolt, Ga., Oct. 15, 1915; s. William Clayton and Lilly May (Doane) M.; A.B., Emory U., 1951, M.L.S., 1954; m. Florence Mary Schloss, Feb. 15, 1947. Librarian Ga. State Library, Atlanta, 1951- 56; asst. state librarian Ga., Atlanta, 1956-59, state librarian, 1959—. Served as med. lab. technician AUS, 1942-46; ret. sgt. Res. Mem. A.L.A., Am. Assn. Law Librarians. Home: 1861 Boulderview Dr SE Atlanta, GA 30316. Office: Jud Bldg 40 Capitol Sq SW Atlanta GA 30334

FOLGER, JOHN KENNETH, state ofcl.; b. Atlanta, Mar. 13, 1924; s. Dagnall Frank and Vivian (Rowland) F.; student W. Ga. Coll., Carrollton, 1940-42; A.B., Emory U., 1943; M.A., U. N.C., 1950, Ph.D., 1951; m. Marjorie Bullock, July 27, 1947; children—Karen, John Kenneth, Carol Anne; m. 2d, Mary J. Harrison, May 10, 1958; children—Susan, Dagnall, James. Chief tech. services Human Resources Research Inst., USAF, Montgomery, Ala., 1951-53; research asso. So. Regional Edn. Bd., Atlanta, 1953-57, asso. dir., 1957-61; dean Grad. Sch., Fla. State U., Tallahassee, 1961-65, 67-68; director Tenn. Commn. Higher Education, 1968—; director Commn. on Human Resources, Nat. Acad. Scis., 1965-67. Mem. tech. adv. com. 1960 and 1970 Census. Served lt. (j.g.) USNR, 1944-46. Fellow Am. Sociol. Assn.; mem. Am. Statis. Assn., Population Assn. Am. Author: Education of the American Population, 1967; Human Resources and Higher Education, 1969. Home: 5437 Camelot Rd Brentwood TN 37027

FOLINSBEE, JOHN FULTON, landscape painter; b. Buffalo, N.Y., Mar. 14, 1892; s. Harrison Davis and Louise (Mauger) F.; ed. Gunnery Sch., Washington, Conn.; studies Art Students' League (N.Y.), Woodstock Sch. Art, Ulster County, N.Y.; pupil of John Carlson, F.V. Du Mond and Birge Harrison; m. Ruth Baldwin, 1914; children—Elizabeth (Mrs. E.W. Wiggins), Joan Baldwin (Mrs. Peter G. Cook). Awarded numerous prizes since 1916; the most recent ones are Jennie Sesman gold medal, Pa. Acad. Fine Arts, 1931; 2d Altman prize, N.A.D., 1936, 1st prize, 1951 and 1950; Century Club medal, 1950; Palmer Marine prize, N.A.D., 1952; Cooper prize Conn. Acad. Fine Arts, 1955; Charles K. Smith prize Woodmere Gallery, Phila., 1961; Oakley Memorial prize Woodmere Gallery, 1961; Century Assn. medal, 1962; Phillips Mill patrons prize, 1963; Pennational prize, 1965; Portrait medal Century Assn., 1966; Nat. Art Club Silver medal, 1969; Artists Fellowship Gold medal, N.Y.C., 1970. Represented in Corcoran Gallery (D.C.), Syracuse Mus., Nat. Arts Club, Grand Rapids Art Assn., Phila. Art Club, R.I. Sch. of Design, Reading (Pa.) Mus., Mus. Fine Arts (Houston), Pa. Acad. Fine Arts, Century Club, N.Y.C., New Britain Mus., Library U. at Beirut; (murals) in postoffice, Freeland, Pa., courthouse, Paducah, Ky. Mem. Nat. Inst. Arts and Letters, Conn. Acad. Arts, A.N.A., 1919, N.A., 1928. Clubs: Nat. Arts, Century (N.Y.C.). Home: New Hope PA 18938

FOLK, OLIVER HAROLD, govt. cons.; b. Moselle, S.C., Dec. 26, 1915; s. Oliver Perry and Ursula (O'Quinn) F. B.S., Clemson U., 1937; M.A., U. Va., 1938; fellow Econ. Devel. Inst.; m. May Day Wyatt, Nov. 14, 1940; children—May Day, Ruth, Frances. Agrl. economist U.S. Dept. Agr., Washington, 1938-40; asst. exec. SSS, Washington, 1940-47; loan officer Internat. Bank for Reconstrn. and Devel., Washington, 1947-61; chief devel. adviser Govt. Saudi Arabia, Riyadh, 1961-63; cons., Washington, 1963-64, 69—; dep. asst. adminstr. AID, Washington, 1964-69; dir. Resource Devel. Corp. Comdg. officer Selective Service Army Res. Unit, Washington. Pres., Washington Council Presbyn. Men, 1951-52; chmn. dept. finance Washington Fedn. Chs., 1951-53, v.p. Internat. Christian Leadership, 1947-52, Fellowship Found., 1948-54. Bd. dirs. Presbyn. Lay Com. Washington, Sr. Research Inst. Arts and Scis. Served to col. AUS, 1940-46. Mem. Clemson U. Alumni Assn. (chpt. pres. 1948-49), Res. Officers Assn. (pres. Lewis B. Hershey chpt. 1964-65), Soc. Internat. Devel., Am. Finance Assn., Am. Econ. Assn., Am., Inter-Am. statis. assns., Am. Acad. Polit. and Social Sci., A.A.A.S., Acad. Polit. Sci., Am. Fgn. Service Assn., Nat. Planning Assn., Population Assn. Am., World Future Soc., Mil. Order World Wars, U. Va. Alumni Assn., Iran-Am. Soc., UN Assn., Order Lafayette, Mason (32, Shriner). Presbyn. (elder). Clubs: International of Washington, National Economist's, Foreign Service Officers, Sphinx. Author: White House Task Force Proposal on Urban Development Bank. Home: 3351 Stephenson Pl NW Washington DC 20015 Office: 5480 Wisconsin Av Washington DC 20515

FOLKEMER, LAWRENCE DANIEL, clergyman; b. Balt., Sept. 21, 1916; s. Paul Israel and Laura (Becker) F.; A.B., Gettysburg Coll., 1937; B.D., Lutheran Theol. Sem., Gettysburg, 1940; S.T.M. Hartford (Conn.) Theol. Sem., 1941, Ph.D., 1946; m. Anna Burger, Oct. 20, 1943; children—Lawrence Daniel, Gordon Christian, Mary Ellen. Ordained to ministry Luth Ch., 1942; minister in Lansdowne, Md., 1942-47; head dept. religion prof. George Washington U., 1947-54, professorial lectr. religion, 1954-56; minister Luth Ch. Reformation, Washington, 1954-60; prof. theology Luth. Theol. Sem., Gettysburg, 1960—; Knubel-Miller lectr. Luth. Ch. Am., Can. and U.S., 1959. Mem. bd. higher edn. United Luth. Ch. Am., 1950-62, pres., 1956- 62; pres. bd. coll. edn. and ch. vocations Luth. Ch. Am., 1962—; del. nat. assembly Nat. Council Chs., 1957-60, 63-66; spl. guest Fed. German Republic, 1960. Mem. Washington Ministerial Assn., Phi Beta Kappa, Eta Sigma Phi, Theta Sigma. Democrat. Author: Christianity and Modern Paganism, 1959. Home: Seminary Ridge Gettysburg PA 17325

FOLKERS, KARL AUGUST, chemist; b. Decatur, Ill., Sept. 1, 1906; s. August William and Laura Susan (Black) F.; B.S., U. of Ill., 1928; Ph.D., U. of Wis., 1931; post- doctorate research Yale U., 1931-34; D.Sc., Phila. Coll. Pharmacy and Science, 1962; Pharm.D., U. Uppsala, Sweden, 1969; D.Sc., U. Wis.; m. Selma Leona Johnson, July 30, 1932; children—Cynthia Carol, Richard Karl. With Sherwin-Williams Co., Chicago, summer 1928. Commercial Solvents Corp., Terre Haute, Ind., summer, 1930. Merch & Co., Inc., Rahway, N.J., summer 1933; with Merck & Co., Inc., since June 1934, asst. director of research, 1948-45, dir. organic and biochemical research since 1945, asso. dir. research and development 1951-53, dir. organic & biol. chem. research, 1953-56, exec. dir. Fundamental Research, 1956-62, vice president exploratory research, 1962-63; pres. Stanford Research Inst. Menlo Park, Cal., 1963-68; courtesy prof. chemistry Stanford 1963-68; prof., dir. Inst. Biomed. Research U. Tex., 1968—. Baker non-resident lecturer in chemistry Cornell, 1953; regents lecturer Univ. of Cal. at Los Angeles, 1960; courtesy appointment as a lecturer of vitamin chemistry U. Cal. Berkeley, 1963—; mem. sci. adv. com. Institute Microbiology, Rutgers, Chairman adv. council dept. chemistry Princeton, 1958-64. Recip. Am. Chem. Soc. award in pure chemistry, 1941. Spencer Award, 1959; Julius Sturmer Lecture award 1957; Perkin Medal, Soc. Chem. Industry, 1960; Nichols medal N.Y. section Am. Chemical Soc., 1967. Mem. Nat. Acad. Sci., Am. Chem. Soc. (pres., 1962), Am. Soc. Biol. Chemistry, Am. Inst. Nutrition, Society Exptl. Biology, medicine, N.Y. Acad. Science Am. Soc. Biol. Chemistry, Am. Inst. Nutrition, Soc. Exptl. Biology and Medicine, A.A.A.S., Am. Inst. Chemists, Royal Swedish Acad. Engring. Scis. (fgn. mem.), Societa Italiana di Scienze Farmaceutiche (hon.), Sigma Xi, Phi Lambda Upsilon (hon.), Alpha Chi Sigma, Rho Chi. Methodist. Contbr. sci. jours. on organic chemistry. Home: 6406 Mesa Dr Austin, TX 78731.

FOLKMAN, MOSES JUDAH, surgeon; b. Cleve., Feb. 24, 1933; s. Jerome Daniel and Bessie (Schomer) F.; B.A., Ohio State U., 1953; M.D., Harvard, 1957; m. Paula Prial, June 26, 1960; children—Laura Elizabeth, Marjorie. Resident surgery Mass. Gen. Hosp., Boston, 1957-65; practice medicine, specializing in surgery, Boston, 1965—; instr. surgery Med. Sch., Harvard, 1965, prof. surgery, 1967, Julia Dyckman Andrus prof. pediatric surgery, 1968—; research career awardee Nat. Cancer Inst., 1965—; surgeon-in-chief Childrens Hosp. Med. Center, 1967—. Served to lt., M.C., USN, 1960-62. Named one of Ten Outstanding Men, Boston Jr. C. of C., 1967. Diplomate Am. Bd. Surgery, Am. Bd. Thoracic Surgery. Mem. Soc. Univ. Surgeons, Soc. Academic Surgeons, N.Y. Acad. Scis., Phi Beta Kappa, Alpha Omega Alpha. Home: 18 Chatham Circle Brookline, MA 02146. Office: 300 Longwood Av Boston MA 02115

FOLLAND, HAROLD FREEZE, educator; b. Salt Lake City, Oct. 1, 1906; s. William H. and Grace (Freeze) F.; A.B., Harvard, 1929, M.A., 1932, Ph.D., 1940; m. Helen Budge, July 3, 1946; 1 son, Gerald. Instr. English, tutor div. modern langs. Harvard, 1930-38; instr. English, U. Utah, 1938-39, asst. prof., 1939-43, asso. prof., 1943-49, prof., 1949-65, prof. English and theatre and ballet, 1965—, head dept., 1961-64. Actor U. Utah Theatre, including summer musicals, 1946-69; frequent narrator Utah Symphony; active ednl. TV. Served to 2d lt. AUS, 1942-45. Mem. Modern Lang. Assn., Harvard Mus. Soc., Soc. Theatre Research (London), Phi Beta Kappa, Theta Alpha Phi, Phi Kappa Phi. Editorial bd. Western Humanities Rev., 1949-71. Author: (with J. Adamson) The Shepherd of the Ocean, 1969. Home: 1571 Harvard Av Salt Lake City UT 84105

FOLLETT, DWIGHT WALCOTT, publisher, author; b. Chgo., May 28, 1903; s. Charles Walcott and Edyth (Benepe) F.; A.B., U. Ill., 1925; m. Mildred Johnson, May 15, 1926; children—Robert J.R., Nancy Elizabeth (Mrs. Richard A. Waichler), Ariel Edith (Mrs. J. Philip O'Hara). Chmn. bd., pres. Follett Corp., Chgo., 1958—, Follett Pub. Co., Chgo., 1952—; dir. Theta Delta Chi Press. Pres. Oak Park (Ill.) Community Lectrs., 1958-68, Chgo. Book Clinic, 1949; chmn. Chgo. area People-to-People book drive, 1959; mem. Ill. Ednl. Facilities Authority, 1970—; regional v.p. Nat. Municipal League, 1969—. Trustee Oak Park Village Mgr. Assn., 1952—, pres., 1953; pres. Oak Park Planning Commn., 1958-68. Chmn. bd. trustees Columbia Coll., Chgo., 1967—. Served to lt. comdr. USNR, 1942-45. Decorated Purple Heart; recipient Good Am. award, 1963. Mem. Theta Delta Chi. Clubs: Explorer's (N.Y.C.); River Forest Tennis (past pres.). Author: Trains, 1936; Boats, 1937; Gunner and the Dumbo, 1946; Story of Maps, 1948; Little Creek, Big River, 1962. Co-author: Exploring the New World, 1953; Exploring the Old World, 1955; Exploring Regions Near & Far, 1961; Exploring Regions of the New World, 1965; Exploring World Communities, 1969. Home: 244 Forest St Oak Park IL 60302 Office: 1000 W Washington St Chicago IL 60607

FOLLETT, GARTH B., publishing co. exec.; b. Assumption, Ill., 1905. Vice pres., dir. Follett Corp., Chgo. Home: 1440 Park Av River Forest IL 60305 Office: 1000 W Washington Blvd Chicago IL 60607*

FOLLETT, ROBERT JOHN RICHARD, publisher; b. Oak Park, Ill., July 4, 1928; s. Dwight W. and Mildred (Johnson) F.; A.B., Brown U., 1950; postgrad. Columbia, 1950-51; m. Nancy L. Crouthamel, Dec. 30, 1950; children—Brian L., Kathryn R., Jean A., Lisa W. Editor Follett Pub. Co., Chgo., 1951-55, sales mgr., 1955-58, gen. mgr. ednl. div., 1958-68, pres., 1970—; pres. Follett Ednl. Corp.; pres., chmn. bd. Instructional Systems Corp.; v.p., dir. Follett Corp.; v.p. United Learning Corp.; pub. Big Table Books; dir. Ednl. Systems Corp. Pres. Alpine Research Found., 1968—; bd. dirs. Village Mgr. Assn., 1964, Community Found. Oak Park and River Forest, 1959—; trustee Inst. Ednl. Data Systems, 1965—. Served to sgt., AUS, 1951-53. Mem. Assn. Am. Publishers, Am. Ednl. Research Assn., Assn. Supervision and Curriculum Devel., Assn. Ednl. Data Systems. Clubs: Cliff Dwellers, Caxton (Chgo.); Sierra; River Forest Tennis. Author: Your Wonderful Body, 1961. Home: 508 N Oak Park Av Oak Park IL 60302 Office: 1010 W Washington Blvd Chicago IL 60607

FOLLEY, A.J., lawyer; b. Oletha, Tex., Nov. 28, 1896; s. George Washington and Rebecca Ann (Roberts) F.; A.B., Baylor U., 1921, LL.B., 1925; m. Blance Bass, May 28, 1929 (dec. 1960); 1 dau., Frances F. Notestine; m. 2d, Rowena Jones Cowan, July 28, 1962. Tchr. English and mathematics Frederick (Okla.) High Sch., 1921-23; teacher history Baylor Univ., 1922- 24; admitted to Tex. bar, 1925, in gen. practice of law, Floydada, Tex., 1925-35; dist. atty. 110th Judicial Dist. of Tex., 1929-34; dist. judge, 1934-37; asso. justice Court of Civil Appeals, Amarillo, Tex., 1937-43; judge Commn. of Appeals Tex. Supreme Court, 1943-45; asso. justice Supreme Court of Tex., 1945-49; now member firm Folley, Snodgrass & Calhoun. Trustee Baylor U., 1948-62. Fellow Am. Coll. Trial Lawyers, Am. Bar Found.; mem. Am. Bar Assn. (ho. of dels. 1962-66), State Bar Tex. (pres. 1959-60). Presbyn. Rotarian. Home: 3004 S Hughes Amarillo TX 79109 Office: American National Bank Bldg Amarillo TX 79101

FOLLEY, JARRETT HARTER, educator, physician; b. Syracuse, N.Y., Aug. 25, 1913; s. John Frederick and May (Harter) F.; A.B., Hamilton Coll., Clinton, N.Y., 1934; M.D., Harvard, 1938; m. Barbara Hope, June 3, 1938; children—Hilda Pamela (Mrs. Sidney C. Miller). Jarrett Harter, Gillian Hope. Intern Mary Hitchcock Meml. Hosp., Hanover, N.H., 1938-40, mem. clin. staff, 1941—, pres. staff bd. govs., 1964—; sr. medicine New Haven Hosp., 1940-41; fellow gastroenterology Univ. Hosp., Phila., 1941; cons. VA Hosp., White River Junction, Vt., 1946—; pres. Hitchcock Clinic, Hanover, 1964—; mem. faculty Dartmouth Med. Sch., 1941—, clin. prof. medicine, 1969—. Trustee Conn. & Passumpsic Ry. Assn. Med. dir. Atomic Bomb Casualty Commn., Japan, 1950-52. Trustee Mary Hitchcock Meml. Hosp., Hitchcock Found. Diplomate Am. Bd. Internal Medicine. Fellow A.C.P. (gov. N.H. 1962-68); mem. N.H., Grafton County med. socs. Author papers in field. Home: Main St Norwich VT 05055 Office: 2 Maynard St Hanover NH 03755

FOLLIN, JAMES WIGHTMAN, ret. engr.; b. Washington, D.C., May 19, 1892; s. John Madison and Georgia (Dorsey) F.; student, Harvard, 1909-10; B.C.E., U. Mich., 1913, M.S.E., 1916; m. Maud Mills, June 23, 1917; children—James Wightman, Katherine (Mrs. Peter G. Sulzer), Elizabeth Ann (Mrs. F.R. Jones). Asst. san. engr., State of Mich., 1915-16; held several engring. positions; mng. dir., Producers' Council (nat. orgn. mfrs. of bldg. materials), 1939-46; dep. adminstr. Fed. Works Agy., 1946-49; spl. asst. to adminstr. Gen. Services Adminstrn., 1949-51, dir. office of contract settlement, Gen. Services Adminstrn., also chmn. subcommittee on construction, conservation division ODM, 1951-53; dir., div. slum clearance and urban development Housing and Home Finance Agy.,, 1953-54, commr. urban renewal adminstrn., 1954-56; urban renewal cons. and consulting engr., 1957—. Mgr. Renovize Phila. and Renovize R.I. campaigns to create useful employment, 1933. Served AUS, San Corps, 1917-19. Fellow Am. Soc. C.E. (pres. Phila. 1932); mem. A.I.A. (hon.), U. Mich. Alumni Assn. (dir. 1935), Chi Phi, Sigma Xi, Tau Beta Pi frats. Clubs: Columbia Country (Washington). Address: 3917 Aspen St Chevy Shase MD 20015

FOLLIS, RALPH GWIN, business exec.; b. San Francisco, Feb. 1, 1902; s. James Henry and Mary Bell (Gwin) F.; student Phillips Acad., Andover, Mass., 1916- 18; B.S., Princeton, 1924; D.Sc., U. So. Cal., 1968; m. Opal Ann Young, June 1, 1929; children—Mary Bell, James Gwin. With Standard Oil Co. of Cal., San Francisco, as engr. helper, 1924-25, crude still operator, 1925-26, specialist research dept., 1926-27, refinery supt., 1928-32, cracking plants mgr., 1933-36, mfg. dept. mgr., 1937-42; dir. since 1942, vice pres., 1942-45, pres., 1945-47, vice chmn., 1948-49, chmn. bd., 1950-66; dir. Del Monte Corp., Fund Am. Cos., Broadway-Hale Stores, Inc., Crocker Nat. Bank. Trustee emeritus Princeton U.; trustee Asia Found; bd. dirs. Stanford Research Inst., M.H. de Young Meml. Mus. Mem. Am. Petroleum Inst., 25- Year Club Petroleum Industry (pres. 1955), Clubs: Burlingame (Cal.) Country: Pacific-Union, Bohemian (San Francisco). Home: 3690 Washington St San Francisco CA 94118 Office: 555 Market St San Francisco CA 94120

FOLLMER, FREDERICK VORIS, judge; b. Milton, Pa., Dec. 13, 1885; s. Dr. John Samuel and Elizabeth B. (Voris) F.; A.B., Bucknell U., 1906, D.C.L. (hon.), 1956; LL.D. (hon.), Lycoming Coll., 1959; m. Ella Brown, May 30, 1921; 1 dau., Mary Elizabeth (Mrs. Robert E. LaCroix). Admitted to Pa. bar, 1910, practicing in Milton; asst. dist. atty. Northumberland County, 1911-14; U.S. atty. for Middle Dist. Pa., 1935-46; U.S. dist. judge, Eastern, Middle and Western dist., Pa., 1946-55; U.S. dist. judge Middle dist. Pa., 1955—. Mem. Phi Beta Kappa. Democrat. Mason (33). Club: Rotary (past pres.) Home: 635 E Broadway Milton PA 17847 Office: US Courthouse Lewisburg PA 17837

FOLMAR, LAURIE WORTH, petroleum co. exec.; b. Goshen, Ala., Dec. 19, 1919; s. Benjamin Herbert and Beulah (Floyd) F.; student Pan Am. Coll., 1937-39; B.S., U. Tex., 1947; m. Elizabeth Jane Bean, Aug. 24, 1943; children—Ruth Elizabeth (Mrs. Robert Joseph Ross), Martha Ann. With Texaco, Inc., N.Y.C., 1947—, gen. mgr. producing Eastern Hemisphere, 1965-67, v.p., 1967-70, sr. v.p. producing, dir., 1970—; dir. Arabian Am. Oil Co. Bd. dirs. Nat. Fgn. Trade Council, Near East Found. Served to capt. USAAF, 1941-45; PTO. Decorated Air medal with oak leaf cluster. Mem. Am. Inst. Mining, Metall. and Petroleum Engrs. (chmn. Ft. Worth sect. 1956). Home: 222 Corlies Av Pelham NY 10803 Office: 135 E 42d St New York City NY 10017

FOLSOM, GEORGE K., lawyer; b. Irvington, N.J., Apr. 3, 1919; B.S., U. Cal. at Berkeley, 1941; LL.B., U. Denver, 1956. Admitted to Nev. bar, 1957; partner firm Woodburn, Forman, Wedge, Blakey, Folsom and Hug, Reno. Mem. Am., Washoe County bar assns., State Bar Nev., Phi Delta Phi. Office: First Nat Bank Bldg Reno NV 89501*

FOLSOM, JAMES CANNON, psychiatrist; b. Sweetwater, Ala., Oct. 11, 1921; s. Douglas Lawrence and Lillian (Hart) F.; student Livingston State Coll., 1939-41, U. Ariz., 1941, U. Ala., 1942-44; M.D., Washington U., 1946; postgrad. U. Vienna, Austria, 1948; m. Ruth Elizabeth Becton, Aug. 14, 1947 (div. 1950); 1 dau., Ivy (Mrs. John Ernest Gary Simpson); m. 2d, Geneva Rose Scheihing, Dec. 29,

1958; 1 dau., Lisa Kay. Intern Jefferson-Hillman Hosp., Birmingham, Ala., 1946-47; psychiatrist Hill Crest Sanitarium, Birmingham, 1949; resident psychiatry Timberlawn Sanitarium, Dallas, 1950-52, staff psychiatrist, 1952; resident psychiatry Menninger Sch. Psychiatry, VA Hosp., Topeka, 1952-53; admission physician VA Hosp., Topeka, 1953-55, chief phys. medicine rehab. service, 1955-60; clin. dir. Mental Health Inst., Mt. Pleasant, Ia., 1960-62; chief of staff VA Hosp., Tuscaloosa, Ala., 1962-66; hosp. dir., 1966—; clin. prof. psychiatry Menninger Sch. Psychiatry, 1953-60; asso. clin. prof. psychiatry U. Ala. Sch. Medicine, 1963—; teaching roster Med. Assn. State of Ala., Montgomery, 1968—; cons. Ala. Dept. Mental Health and state hosps., 1969—. Mem. Interagency bd. U.S. Civil Service Examiners for N. Ala., 1966—; mem. Ala. Gov.'s Com. on Employment of Handicapped, 1967-69; mem. steering com. Comprehensive Mental Health Center Program, Bibb, Pickens and Tuscaloosa counties, 1967-70. Bd. dirs. Ala. Assn. for Mental Health, Tuscaloosa County Assn. for Mental Health, Tuscaloosa County Boys Club, United Fund Tuscaloosa County; bd. mgmt. Tuscaloosa County YMCA; mem. adv. bd. Tuscaloosa County Salvation Army, Mental Health Bd. Bibb, Pickens and Tuscaloosa counties; bd. advisers Ala. Womens Hall of Fame. Served to capt. M.C., AUS, 1943-46. Recipient Dir.'s Commendation awards VA Hosp., Topeka, 1960, VA Hosp., Tuscaloosa, 1965, Superior Performance award VA Central Office, 1969, Adminstr.'s Commendation medal VA Central Office, 1969; named Boss of Year, VA Hosp. Secs. Assn., 1970. Diplomate Am. Bd. Psychiatry and Neurology. Fellow Am. Geriatric Soc., Am. Psychiat. Assn. (com. chmn., editor Newsletter Ala. Dist. br.), Am. Coll. Psychiatrists; mem. A.M.A., Menninger Sch. Psychiatry Alumni Assn. (editor bull., past pres.), Tuscaloosa County Med. Soc., Ala. Acad. Neurology and Psychiatry (past pres.), Assn. Regional Planning Dirs. and Adminstrs., Assn. Med. Supts. of Mental Hosps., Am. Hosp. Assn. (gov. council psychiat. hosp. sect. 1968—), Phi Gamma Delta. Unitarian. Contbr. articles profl. jours. Home: Quarters 8 VA Hosp Tuscaloosa AL 35401

FOLSOM, JOHN ROY, savs. and loan exec.; b. Hartsville, S.C., Dec. 30, 1918; s. William Arthur and Flora (Newsom) F.; B.A., Furman U., 1940; m. Anita Anderson, Oct. 18, 1941; children—Anita Marie (Mrs. Harold A. Boney, Jr.), Dale (Mrs. Reginald Davies Heinitsh, Jr.), John William, George Anderson. With Aiken Loan and Security Co., Florence, S.C., 1940-41, Surety Life and Liberty Life Ins. Co., Greenville and Columbia, S.C., 1941-43, 46-60; with Home Fed. Savs. & Loan Assn., Columbia, S.C., 1960- -, pres., 1963—, also mem. exec. com. loan com., dir.; dir. Investors Nat. Life Ins. Co. Mem. financial adv. com. Erskine Coll. Trustee United Fund Columbia, 1966—; past treas., vice chmn., bd. dirs. chmn. S.C. Heart Assn., 1968—; bd. dirs., campaign chmn. Musical Arts; trustee Research Devel. and Ednl. Found. Columbia Hosp. Mem. Citizens Com., Bd. Adminstrs., Richland County, 1968—. Recipient Good Egg award S.C. Heart Assn. Mem. S.C. Savs. and Loan League (pres. 1968- 69), Columbia C. of C. (dir., v.p. indsl. devel.), Furman U. Alumni Assn. (pres. 1953-54, mem. athletic council, 1955), Columbia Real Estate Bd., Columbia Real Estate Appraisers, Columbia Home Builders Assn., Univ. Assos. U. S.C. (v.p.), Sigma Alpha Epsilon. Methodist (chmn. finance com., bd. dirs.). Rotarian, Lion. Clubs: Palmetto, Forest Lake, Spring Valley Country (Columbia). Home: 1515 Adger Rd Columbia SC 29205 Office: 1500 Hampton St Columbia SC 29201

FOLSOM, MARION BAYARD, former sec. health, edn. and welfare; b. McRae, Ga., Nov. 23, 1893; s. William B. and Margaret Jane (McRae) F.; A.B., U. Ga., 1912; M.B.A., Harvard, 1914; LL.D., U. Rochester, 1945, Hobart and William Smith Colls., 1951, Syracuse U., Tufts U., 1955, Brown U., 1957, Swarthmore Coll., 1957, Hamilton Coll., 1962; D.C.L. Rollins Coll., 1957; D.C.S., N.Y. U., 1950; D.P.S., Springfield Coll., 1962; D.Sc., Albany Med. Coll., 1966; m. Mary Davenport, Nov. 16, 1918; children—Jane McRae (dec.), Marion Bayard, Frances. With Eastman Kodak Co., 1914, treas., 1935-53, dir., 1947-52, 58-68; pres. Eastman Savs. & Loan Assn., 1947-52; trustee Rochester Savs. Bank, 1931-49, 58-63; dir. Lincoln-Rochester Trust Co., 1929-52, 58-63; under sec. treas., 1953-55; sec. Dept. Health, Edn. and Welfare, 1955-58. Staff dir. spl. com. postwar econ. policy and planning U.S. Ho. Reps., 78th-79th Congress. Mem. Pres.'s Adv. Council Econ. Security, 1934-35; pres. Rochester Council Social Agys., 1934- 36; U.S. employer del. Internat. Labor Conf., Geneva, 1936; mem. Fed. Adv. Council Social Security, 1937-38; div. exec. Nat. Adv. Def. Commn., 1940-41, vice chmn. Pres.'s Adv. Com. Mcht. Marine, 1947-48; mem. social security adv. council U.S. Senate Finance Com., 1948; mem. Regional War Manpower Commn., 1942-45; mem. N.Y. State Adv. Council Unemployment Ins., 1935-50; mem. Bus. Council 1936—; chmn. adv. com. personnel study USPHS, 1961-62; dir. U.S. C. of C., 1942-48; trustee Com. Econ. Devel., 1942—, chmn. trustees, 1950-52, vice chmn., 1960-68; chmn. Nat. Commn. Community Health Services, 1962-67; mem. Fed. Hosp. Council, 1965-68, Fed. Adv. Council Social Security, 1963-65, N.Y. State Hosp. Rev. and Planning Council, N.Y. State Adv. Health Planning Council, 1969, Pres.' Commn. Heart Disease, Cancer and Stroke, Fed. Adv. Council Employment Security, 1966-70, Nat. Health Adv. Council, 1970—; Health Council Monroe County, 1961-67; vice chmn. White House Conf. Health, 1967. Bd. dirs. Nat. Bur. Econ. Research, Monroe Community Coll., Brookings Instn., 1958-63, Rochester Community Chest, Genesee Regional Hosp. Council, Rochester Bur. Municipal Research; trustee Rochester C. of C. (past pres.); trustee U. Rochester 1948-63, chmn. exec. com., 1957-63; bd. overseers Harvard Coll., 1951-57; Served with U.S. Army, 1917-19. Recipient Albert Einstein medal citizenship, 1958; Bronfman prize pub. health achievement, 1963; Edward Mott Moore award Monroe County Med. Soc., 1970. Hon. fellow Am. Coll. Hosp. Adminstrs., Acad. Medicine Rochester; mem. Am. Hosp. Assn. (hon.), N.E.A. (hon. life), Acad. Arts and Scis., Phi Beta Kappa Assos. (dir.), Phi Beta Kappa, Sigma Nu. Presbyn. Clubs: University, Rochester Country, Genesee Valley, Pundit (Rochester); Harvard (N.Y.C.); Metropolitan (Washington). Home: 106 Oak Lane Rochester NY 14610

FOLSOM, RICHARD GILMAN, ret. coll. pres.; b. Los Angeles, Feb. 3, 1907; s. Harry Gilman and C. Mabel (Hazard) F.; B.S., Cal. Inst. Tech., 1928, M.S., 1929, Ph.D., 1932; m. Carroll Greene, Aug. 24, 1929; children—Geranne, Ronald Gilman, Margaret. Teaching asst. Cal. Inst. Tech., 1928-32; engr. water dept., City of Pasadena, Cal., 1932-33; teaching asst. U. Cal., Berkeley, 1933- 34, instr., 1934-37, asst. prof., 1937-41, asso. prof., 1941-47, prof. mech. engring., 1947-53, chmn. div. mech. engring., 1949-53; dir. Engring. Research Inst., prof. mech. engring., U. Mich., 1953-58; pres. Renssaelaer Poly. Inst., 1958-71; dir. Air Reduction Co., Arthur D. Little, Inc., Bendix Corp., Am. Electric Power Co., Potter Instrument Co., Research Analysis Corp. Registered profl. engr., N.Y., Cal. Hon. mem. Am. Soc. M.E., Am. Soc. Engring. Edn.; mem. Am. Inst. Chem. Engrs., Am. Inst. Aeros. and Astronautics, Soc. History Tech., Nat. Acad. Engring., Newcomen Soc. N.Am., Sigma Xi, Tau Beta Pi. Rotarian. Contbr. Engring. Jours. Home: 585 Oakville Crossroad Napa CA 94558

FOLSOM, SARAH BLANTON, educator; b. Notasulga, Ala., Oct. 22, 1915, d. Alza Ernest and Bessie (Lanier) Blanton; A.B., Judson Coll., Marion, Ala., 1936, L.H.D., 1966; M.A., Auburn U., 1941, LL.D., 1966; m. Douglas L. Folsom, Jr., Aug. 10, 1940; children—Douglas L. III, James Blanton. Tchr. elementary and secondary schs., also coll., Ala., 1936-43; supt. Yavapai County Schs., Prescott, Ariz., 1953-64; supt. pub. instrn. Ariz., 1965-69; mem. Ariz. Bd. Edn., 1963-69. Mem. Ariz. Acad., Am. Assn. U. Women, Bus. and Profl. Women's Club, Am. Assn. Sch. Adminstrs., Nat. Ariz. Edn. Assns., P.T.A. (life). Home: 236 S Mount Vernon Prescott AZ 86301 Died June 11, 1969.

FOLSOM, VICTOR CLARENCE, lawyer; b. Dallas, Dec. 31, 1909 s. Clarence S.T. and Mildred (Johnson) F.; student U. Tex., 1929-33; LL.B., Pacific Coast U., 1935; m. Maude A. Ward, Dec. 23, 1933 (div.) children—Georgia, Dale John, Glen Victor, Alan Lynn; m. 2d, Victoria Vancza, 1948. Law clk. Gordon & McCall, Los Angeles, 1933-35; admitted to Cal. bar, 1935. N.Y. bar, 1942, Mass. bar, 1960; practicing atty. Mawhew & Folsom, Los Angeles, 1935-40; fgn. dept. Reid & Priest, New York City, 1940-42; fgn. legal cons. U.S. Alien Property Custodian, 1942-44; fgn. counsel Sterling Drug Inc., New York City, 1944-59; v.p. Sterling Products Internat., Inc., 1956-59; gen. counsel, mem. mgmt. com. United Fruit Co., Boston, 1960-61, v.p., gen. counsel, 1961-70, dir., 1962-70, legal adviser, 1970—; chairman advisory bd. internat. and comparative law center Southwestern Legal Foundation, Dallas, 1968-70, also member of faculty. Member of World Trade Adv. Commission Dept. of Commerce. Legal adviser U.S. Missions to various Latin Am. countries. Mem. adv. bd. World Tax Series, Harvard Law School; chmn. advisory committee international legal studies program University of Texas School of Law. Recipient gold medal Inter-Am. Bar Assn., 1967. Member Am. (ho. of dels.) Inter-Am. (exec. com.; U.S. council rep.), Fed., Cal., N.Y. State, Mass., Boston bar assns., Assn. Gen. Counsel, Am. Fgn. Law Assn. (council), Am. Soc. Internat. Law, Acad. Polit Sci., Pan-Am. Soc. Internat. C. of C., Proprietary Assn., Nat. Fgn. Trade Council (dir.), Controllers Inst. Am. (internat. operations com. New York City Control), Internat. Bar Assn., American Judicature Soc., Council on Foreign Relations, Nat. Lawyers Club, Bolivarian Soc. U.S. Republican. Methodist. Clubs: Forest Hill Field (Bloomfield, N.J.); University (Boston); Charles River Country. Contbr. profl. jours. Office: Prudential Center Boston MA 02199

FOLTZ, EDWIN JOSEPH, internat. adminstr.; b. Ft. Smith, Ark., Dec. 31, 1915; s. Dr. James Arthur and Janie (Price) F.; LL.B., Washington and Lee U., 1940; m. Dorothy Deane Mitchell, Dec. 31, 1941; children—Edwin Joseph, Dorothy and Deane (twins). Admitted to Va. bar, 1940. Ga. bar, 1947, Ark. Bar, 1948, Ohio bar, 1952. U.S. Supreme Ct., 1945; pvt. practice of law, 1940- 41; spl. agt. FBI, 1941-50, an adminstrv. asst. to dir., 1944-46, spl. agt. charge 3 divisions, 1946-50; dir. indsl. and pub. relations Pesco products div. Borg-Warner Corp., also sec. and asst. to pres. Wooster div. Borg-Warner Corp., 1950-53; asst. dir. personnel adminstrn. Campbell Soup Co., 1953-55, dir. personnel adminstrn., 1955-58, v.p. personnel, charge corporate labor and personnel relations, 1958-60, v.p. internat., 1960—; pres. Campbell's Soups Internat., 1960—; chairman of the bd. Campbell's de Mex., S.A. de C.V. (Mex.); pres. dir. Campbell's Soups Inter-America, Inc.; mem. bd. of dirs. Godiva Chocolatier, Inc., Campbell Soup Co., Ltd. (Can.), Campbell's Soups, Ltd. (U.K.), Campbell's Soups (Australia) Pty., Ltd., Campbell's Soups S.P.A. (Italy), Les Industries Alimentaires S.A., Biscuits Delacre S.A., Soc. Francaise des Biscuits Delacre S.A. Conducted labor relations, personnel relations seminars for Am. Mgmt. Assn. Trustee Gladwyne Free Library, 1962—, pres. 1962-63; mem. Am. Mgmt. Assn. (dir. 1960-64, member world council, 1960—, vice president world council 1968—, dir. 1968—), Am. Inst. Fgn. Trade (dir. 1964—). Episcopalian (vestryman) Home: 917 Black Rock Rd Gladwyne PA 19035 Office: Campbell Soup Co Camden NJ 08101

FOLTZ, RICHARD HARRY, pub. relations exec.; b. Frackville, Pa., Apr. 11, 1924; s. John Boyd and Blanche (Price) F.; student extension center Pa. State Coll., 1941; B.A., Harding Coll., 1949; m. Margie Alexander, June 6, 1948; children—Richard Gary, Karen Lynn, Terri Nan. Chief inspector's office Glenn L. Martin Co., Balt., 1941-42; adminstrv. insp. Far East Air Forces, 1942-45; writer lectr. dept. nat. edn. Harding Coll., 1945-49; with Freedoms Found., Valley Forge, Pa., 1949—, v.p. pub. relations, 1952-62, sr. v.p., 1962-65, exec. v.p., Western region, since 1965—; dir. Schuylkill Valley Lines, Inc. Past pres. Upper Merion Twp. Sch. Bd. Mem. bd. Northwestern Inst. Christian Edn.; bd. counselors Pepperdine Coll. Mem. nat. pub. relations com. Boy Scouts Am. Mem. Pub. Relations Soc. Am. New York City Advt. Club; Republican. Mem. Ch. of Christ. Author articles on citizenship. Home: 4041 Palos Verdes Dr S Palos Verdes Peninsula CA 90274 Office: Western Regional Office Freedoms Found 2727 W 6th St Los Angeles CA 90057

FOLZ, RICHARD E., lt. gov. Ind.; b. Evansville, Ind., Jan. 14, 1922; s. Frank J. and Mary (Metzger) F.; student Georgetown U., 1938-41, Ind. U., 1941; LL.D., Vincennes U., 1970. Treas. F.J. Folz Co., Evansville, 1946—; dir. Nat. City Bank, Evansville; lt. gov. Ind., 1969—. Dir. Ind. Dept. Commerce, 1969—. Treas. Ind. Republican Central Com., 1968. Served with USNR, 1942-46. Mem. Am. Legion. Elk. Clubs: Petroleum, Press (Evansville); Columbia (Indpls.) Home: 1725 W Franklin St Evansville IN 47712 Office: State House Indianapolis IN 46204

FONCK, CHARLES MARIE, international economic and financial adviser; b. Brussels, Belgium, May 9, 1897; s. Jean Henri and Marie Francoise (Bernard), F.; M. Philosophy and Letters, U. of Brussels, 1922, LL.D., 1925, spl. degree for criminal law in Dutch, 1925; licentiate in Econs. and Finance, Solvay Bus. Sch., U. Brussels, 1927; student N.Y.U., 1943; diploma in investment and security analysis N.Y. Inst. Finance, 1954. Came to U.S., 1940. Personal asst. to sec. gen., Pub. Welfare Adminstrn., Brussels, 1917-20; chief of cabinet, Adolphe Max, Minister of State and Burgomaster of Brussels, Belgium, 1920-36; dir. City of Brussels, 1936; dir. gen. Palais Du Centenaire, Brussels, 1936-, organizer of gen. mgr. several world's fairs; adviser on orgn. world and internat. trade fairs, 1936—; also sample fairs and expns.; prof. internat. trade Inst. Belgian Journalists 1937-40; director conference division UN, 1946-50, organized and liquidated 3d General UN Assembly, Paris, 1948-49, chief administrative officer Havana Conf., 1947; dir. Internat. Center Pub. Adminstrn., 1950; dir. fellowships and scholarships div., and chmn. selection coms. for fellowships in econ. development, pub. adminstrn., social welfare, Tch. Assistance Adminstrn., 1951-52; chmn. bd. cons. Internat. Fair Cons., Inc., New York City, 1960—. Dir. Maison de l'Amerique Latine (Brussels), Recipient numerous awards from govts. including Belgium, Brit. Empire, Italy and others, also pvt. assns. Tech. adviser to Belgian minister of health, 1939; commr. of evacuation Belgian Dept. Health and Nat. Defense, 1940; head Am. div. Belgian Commn. for Study of Post-War Problems, New York City, 1941-45; spl. adviser in U.S., Belgian Dept. of Edn., 1945-46; Belgian del. to Conv. on Coops., Washington, 1944; sec. gen. and tech. adviser of Belgian delegation Internat. Labor Conf., Phila., 1944; radio lectr. Mem. Rotary,; A.I.M., Soc. Advancement Management, Assn. of Exhibit Mgrs., Am. Soc. Planning Officials, Belgian C. of C. in U.S. Author numerous articles and pamphlets in many languages; editor, Transit, internat. trade mag., 1939. Internat. econ. and financial adv., Investment Banker.†

FONDA, AVERY HUNT, banker; b. Brevard, N.C, Apr. 5, 1921; s. Earl Avery and Fanny (Hunt) F.; B.S., U. N.C., 1944; spl. banking courses Northwestern U., 1950, Rutgers U., 1955; m. Sarah Elizabeth Warner, May 5, 1951. Asst. cashier 1st Union Nat. Bank of N.C., Asheville, 1947-49, asst. v.p., 1950-52, v.p., sec., 1952-58, sr. v.p., 1958-59; sr. v.p. S.C. Nat. Bank, Greenville, 1959-69; exec. v.p. Liberty Nat. Bank & Trust Co., Buffalo, 1969-70, pres., chief exec. officer, 1970—, dir., 1969—; pres., dir. United Bank Corp. N.Y., Albany. Mem. faculty Carolina Bankers Conf., U. N.C., 1953; lectr. Mgt. Inst. for N.C. Distributive Edn. Service, Asheville, 1957; lectr. nat. conf. Financial Pub. Relations Assn., Fla., 1955; mem. bus. execs. adv. com. Sch. Bus. Adminstrn., U. N.C., 1957. Dir. Asheville Agrl. Devel. Council, 1951-59; chmn. Asheville and Buncombe County United Fund, 1955; dir. United Appeal, 1956-58; dir. Asheville Jr. Achievement, 1956-58, Buncombe County Family and Child Council, 1951-53, Salvation Army, 1951-52; chmn. Greenville Area Com. for Tech. Edn., 1963-69, Greenville County Com. for Higher Edn., 1967-69; dir. Greater Buffalo Devel. Found., 1970—, Downtown Buffalo Devel. Corp., 1971—. Trustee Rosary Hill Coll., United Fund Buffalo and Erie County. Mem. Nat. Assn. Bank Auditors and Comptrollers (pres. Western N.C. chpt. 1951, dir. 1951-53), Am. Inst. Banking (pres. Asheville chpt. 1949), Bank Marketing Assn. (nat. dir. 1959-62), Soc. Advancement Mgmt. (chpt. dir. 1954-55), Buffalo C. of C. (past dir.), Phi Beta Kappa, Beta Gamma Sigma. Clubs: Asheville Civitan (dir. 1956-59), Asheville Country (treas. 1954-57), Mountain City of Asheville (dr. 1959). Home: 78 Le Brun Circle Buffalo NY 14226 Office: 424 Main St Buffalo NY 14240

FONDA, HENRY actor; b. Grand Island, Neb., May 16, 1905; s. William Brace and Herberta (Jaynes) F.; student U. of Minn., 1923-25. Began as actor, Community Playhouse, Omaha, 1925; appeared with other little-theater and touring companies; appeared in The Farmer Takes a Wife, New York City, 1934, Blow Ye Winds, N.Y. City, 1938; in motion pictures since 1935. Motion pictures: The Farmer Takes a Wife, 1935; Trail of the Lonesome Pine, 1936; You Only Live Once, 1937; Wings of the Morning, 1937; Jezebel, 1938; Jesse James, 1939; Young Mr. Lincoln, 1939; Grapes of Wrath, 1940; Lady Eve, 1940; Male Animal, 1941; Ox Bow Incident, 1942; My Darling Clementine, 1946; The Long Night, The Fugitive, A Miracle Can Happen, 1947. On legitimate stage in Broadway prodn. Mr. Roberts (later in film of same name), 1949, Point of No Return, 1952, Caine Mutiny Court Martial, 1953. 12 Angry Men, Tin Star, 1957; Stage Struck, 1958; Warlock, 1959; The Longest Day, How the West was Won, 1963; Fail Safe, The Best Man, 1964; Sex and the Single Girl, 1965; In Harm's Way, 1965; Battle of the Bulge, 1965; The Rounders, 1965; The Dirty Game, 1966; A Big Hand for the Little Lady, 1966; Yours, Mine and Ours, 1967; The Boston Strangler, 1968; Madigan, 1968; stage plays Two For the Seesaw, 1958; A Gift of Time, 1962; Generation. TV appearances. Enlisted as seaman 1st class USN, 1942; attended quartermaster sch., Naval Tng. Base, San Diego, Cal.; disch. as lt., 1945. Home: 151 E 74th St New York City NY 10021

FONDA, JANE, actress; b. N.Y.C., Dec. 21, 1937; d. Henry and Frances (Seymour) Fonda; student Vassar Coll.; m. Roger Vadim; one child. Appeared on Broadway stage in There Was A Little Girl, 1960, The Fun Couple, 1962; in Actor's Studio prodn. Strange Interlude, 1963; appeared in films Tall Story, 1960, A Walk on the Wild Side, 1962, Period of Adjustment, 1962, Sunday in New York, 1963, In the Cool of the Day, 1963, The Love Cage, 1963, La Ronde, 1964, Barbarella, They Shoot Horses, Don't They?, 1969, Klùte, 1970, others. Address: Ashley Famous Agy 9255 Sunset Blvd Los Angeles CA 90069*

FONDA, PETER, actor; s. Henry Fonda. Film appearances include The Wild Angeles; The Trip; Easy Rider. Address: 151 E 74th St New York City NY*

FONDAHL, JOHN WALKER, educator; b. Washington, Nov. 4, 1924; s. John Edmund and Mary (DeCourcy) F.; B.S., Thayer Sch. Engring., Dartmouth, 1947, M.S. in Civil Engring., 1948; m. Doris Jane Plishker, Mar. 2, 1946; children—Lauren Valerie, Gail Andrea, Meredith Victoria, Dorian Beth. Instr., then asst. prof. U. Hawaii, 1948-51; constrn. engr. Winston Bros. Co., Mpls., 1951-52; project engr. Nimbus Dam and Powerplant project, Sacramento, 1952-55; mem. faculty Stanford, 1955—, prof. civil engring., 1966—; pres. Constrn. Data Systems Corp., Stanford; dir. Scott Co. Cal., Oakland, 1963—; cons. Nev. test site AEC, 1965—. Bd. dirs. Project Mgmt. Inst., Drexel Hill, Pa. Served with USMCR, 1943-46. Mem. Am. Soc. C.E., Am. Soc. Engring. Edn., Phi Beta Kappa, Sigma Xi, Lambda Chi Alpha. Republican. Patentee, author reports in field. Home: 12810 Viscaino Dr Los Altos Hills CA 94022 Office: Dept Civil Engring Stanford Univ Stanford CA 94035

FONER, PHILIP S., educator; b. N.Y.C., Dec. 14, 1910; s. Abraham and Mary (Smith) F.; A.B., Coll. City N.Y., 1932; M.A., Columbia, 1933, Ph.D., 1941; m. Roslyn Held, 1939; children—Elizabeth, Laura. Began as tchr., 1933; pub., mem. firm, Citadel Press, N.Y.C., 1945-66; prof. history Lincoln U. (Pa.), 1967—. Mem. Am. Hist. Assn., Phi Beta Kappa. Author: Business and Slavery, 1941; Jack London, American Rebel, 1947; The Fur and Leather Workers Union, 1950; History of Labor Movement in the United States, Vol. 1, 1947, Vol. 2, 1955, Vol. 3, 1964, Vol. 4, 1965; The Life and Writings of Frederick Douglass, 1949-52; Mark Twain, Social Critic, 1958; History of Cuba and its Relations with the United States, 2 vols., 1962-63; The Case of Joe Hill, 1965; The Letters of Joe Hill, 1965; The Haymarket Autobiographies, 1969; The Black Panthers Speak, 1970; W.E.B. Du Bois Speaks, 2 vols., 1970; American Labor and the War in Indochina, 1971. Compiler writings Thomas Jefferson, Thomas Paine, Abraham Lincoln, George Washington, Frederick Douglass. Office: Dept History Lincoln U Lincoln University PA 19352

FONG, HIRAM L., U.S. senator; b. Honolulu, Oct. 1, 1907; s. Lum Fong and Chal Har Lum; grad. with honors, U. Hawaii, A.B., 1930, LL.D., 1953; LL.B., Harvard, 1935; LL.D., Tufts U., 1960, Lafayette U., 1960, Lynchburg Coll., 1970, Lincoln U., 1971; L.H.D., L.I. U., 1968; m. Ellyn Lo; children—Hiram, Rodney, Merie-Ellen and Marvin-Allan (twins). With supply dept. Pearl Harbor Navy Yard, later with Suburban Water System; founder law firm Fong, Miho, Choy & Robinson; chmn. bd. Finance Factors, Grand Pacific Life Ins. Co., Finance Realty, Finance Investment Co., Market City, Ltd.; dir. numerous firms, Honolulu; former mem. Hawaiian Legislature, speaker three terms; mem. U.S. Senate, 1959—. U.S. del. 150th Anniversary Argentine Independence, Buenos Aires, 1960, 55th Interparliamentary Union (World) Conf., 1966, Ditchley Found. Conf. 1967, U.S.-Canada Inter-Parliamentary Union Conf., 1961, 65, 67, 68; U.S. del. Mex.-U.S. Inter-Parliamentary Conf., 1968. Active in civic and service orgns. Vice pres. Territorial Constl. Conv., 1950; del. Rep. Nat. Conv., 1952, 56, 60, 64, 68. Asst. judge adv. World War II; now col. USAF Res. ret. Recipient Nat. Assn. Christians and Jews award, 1960; Horatio Alger award, 1970; citation for outstanding service Japanese Am. Citizens League, 1970; award Nat. Acad. Achievement, 1971. Mem. Am. Legion, V.F.W., Phi Beta Kappa. Republican. Home: 1102 Alewa Dr Honolulu HI 96817 Office: New Senate Office Bldg Washington DC 20515

FONG, WEN CHIH, educator, author; b. Shanghai, China, Dec. 9 1930; s. Tse-tsing and Jen- yen (Sha) F.; came to U.S., 1948, naturalized, 1961; A.B., Princeton, 1951, M.F.A., 1954, Ph.D., 1957. m. Constance Chih-ming Tang, Aug. 29, 1953; children—Laurence T., Peter C., Serena M. Research asst. Cleve. Mus. Art. 1953; instr., then asst. prof. Princeton, 1955-60; vis. curator Oriental art Yale Art Gallery, 1958-59; mem. faculty Princeton, 1960—, prof. art and archaeology, curator Oriental art, 1967—, chmn. Ph.D. program Chinese and Japanese art and archaeology, 1964—, chmn. dept. art and archaeology, 1970—. Hon. fellow Inst. Oriental Studies Hong Kong U., 1961-62, Inst. Advanced Chinese Studies, Taiwan, Republic China, 1966—; spl. cons. in Far Eastern affairs Met. Mus. Art, 1971—. Bollingen Found. fellow, 1956-57. Guggenheim fellow, 1961-62; Am. Council Learned Socs. fellow, 1965-66; McCosh Faculty fellow Princeton, 1965-66; Am. Council Learned Socs. fellow, 1969-71. Mem. Am. Coll. Art Assn., Chinese Art Soc. Am. Author: (with Sherman E. Lee) Streams and Mountains Without End, 2d edit, 1966, Lohans and a Bridge to Heaven, 1958; Problem of Forgeries in Chinese Painting, 1963; also articles. Home: 38 Adams Dr Princeton NJ 08540

FONTAINE, ANDRE LUCIEN, journalist; b. Paris, Mar. 30, 1921; s. Georges Louis and Blanche (Rochon-Duvigneaud) F.; licencié ès lettres, U. Paris, also licencié en droit, and diplomes d'etudes superieures de droit pub. et d'economie politique; m. Isabelle Cavaillé, June 15, 1943; children—Jean-Marc, Agnés, Laurent. Asst. editor Temps present, 1946-47; with Le Monde, 1947- -, fgn. editor, 1951-69, chief editor, 1969—. Decorated officer Order Vasa (Sweden), Lion of Finland; knight Crown of Belgium, of Danebrog (Denmark); recipient prix de la communauté atlantique. Author: L'alliance atlantique a l'heure du dégel, 1960; History of the Cold War, 2 vols., 1968, 69; La Guerre Civile froide, 1969. Home: 6 rue Gounod Paris France 17 Office: 5 rue des Italiens Paris France 9

FONTAINE, ARMAND LOUIS, assn. exec.; b. Sorel, Que., Can., Apr. 24, 1924; s. Louis Phillip and Angelina (Villandre) F.; student U. Americas, 1947, McGill U., 1948; B.S., U. So. Cal., 1949; postgrad. U. Paris, 1950; m. Barbara Jones, Aug. 7, 1953; 1 son, George Robert. Came to U.S., 1926, naturalized, 1949. Exec. v.p. Am. Bldg. Contractors Assn., 1955—; pres. Western Adminstrs., 1955—; v.p. Nat. Home Improvement Council, 1960—; dir. Cal. Compensation Ins. Fund. Served with AUS, World War II; CBI. Mem. Lambda Chi Alpha, Delta Phi Epsilon. Club: Vikings (Los Angeles). Office: 3345 Wilshire Blvd Los Angeles CA 90010

FONTAINE, ATHANAS PAUL, aircraft exec.; b. Ludlow, Mass., Aug. 1, 1905; s. Clovis and Oliva (Lavoie) F.; B.S., N.Y.U., 1930; D.Sc. in Engring., Wayne State U., 1962; D.B.A. (hon.), U. Mich., 1968; m. Arline McGrath, Oct. 20, 1930; children—John Clovis, Edward, Thomas, Anne. Project engr. Republic Aircraft Corp., Farmingdale, N.Y., 1936-39; aircraft designer Fairchild Aircraft Corp., Hagerstown, Md., 1935-36; chief engr. Convair's Stinson div. Vultee Aircraft, Inc., Wayne, Mich., 1938-40, Convair's Vultee field div., 1940-42, asst. dir. engring. Consol. Vultee Aircraft Corp., 1942-44, exec. v.p., 1951-52; dir. exptl. aircraft div. Bendix Aviation Corp., Detroit, 1944-45, staff exec. eastern group, 1952- 54, dir. engring., Detroit, 1954-55, v.p. engring., 1955-60; exec. v.p. Bendix Corp., 1960-65, chmn., chief exec. officer, 1965-68, 71—, chmn., pres., 1968-71; dir. Aero. Research Center, U. Mich., 1945-51; dir. Rohr Corp., Nat. Bank Detroit, Uniroyal, Inc. Mem. Econ. Devel. Corp. Greater Detroit; Mich. chmn. U.S. Savs. Bond Program, 1971-72. Trustee Traffic Safety Council Mich., Citizens Research Council Mich.; bd. dirs. U. Mich. Devel. Council; mem. corp. Merrill-Palmer Inst.; exec. com. Air Found. Recipient Distinguished Alumnus award N.Y. U., 1961; Mich. Wolverine award, 1961; named Alumnus of Yr., N.Y. U. Coll. Engring., 1962. Mem. N.A.M. (dir.), Conf. Bd. Club: Economic (dir.) (Detroit). Office: Bendix Corp Bendix Center Southfield MI 48076

FONTAINE, JOAN, (born de Havilland), actress; b. Tokyo, Japan, Oct. 22, 1917; m. Brian Aherne, Aug. 20, 1939 (div. 1944); m. 2d, William Dozier, May 2, 1946; 1 dau., Deborah Leslie, adopted dau., Martita Valentina Caideron; m. 3d Collier Young, Nov. 10, 1952 (div. 1961); m. 4th, Alfred Wright, Jr. Feb. 1964. Has appeared in numerous motion pictures since 1937; pictures include: Rebecca, 1939 (N.Y. Critics award); Suspicion, 1940 (Acad. award): The Unafraid, 1948: You Gotta Stay Happy, 1948; September Affair, 1949; Born to be Bad, 1949: Something to Live For, 1950; Darling How Could You, 1950; Ivanhoe, 1951; Decameron Nights, 1952; Casanova, 1953; broadway debut in Tea and Sympathy, 1954; Until We Sail, 1957; A Certain Smile, 1958; Tender Is the Night: The Devils Own, 1966. Home: care Ashley Famous Artists 1301 Av of Americas New York City NY 10019

FONTAINE, THOMAS DAVIS, chemist; b. Utica, Miss., Apr. 12, 1916; s. Thomas Davis and Emma (Lloyd) F.; A.B., Miss. Coll., 1937; Ph.D. in Chemistry, U. Pitts., 1942; m. Louise Sutton Lean, Dec. 26, 1941; children—Lynn Louise, Thomas Davis. Grad. asst. chemistry U. Pitts., 1937-38; fellowship asst. Mellon Inst., Pitts., 1938-41; from research chemist to head biologically active compounds div. Dept. of Agr., 1941-55; adminstrv. asst. to U.S. Senator Stennis, 1955-57; head fellowship sect. NSF, 1957- 65, dir. div. grad. edn. in sci., 1965-66, asso. dir. (edn.), 1966-69, dep. asst. dir. (edn.), 1969-71; asst. dir. div. sponsored research U. Fla., Gainesville, 1971—. Recipient Superior Service award Dept. of Agr., 1949; Distinguished Service award NSF, 1970. Mem. Am. Chem. Soc., Am. Soc. Biol. Chemists, Alpha Chi Sigma. Club: Cosmos (Washington). Author numerous articles, also chpt. in book. Co-discoverer glycosidal alkaloid, tomatine, in tomato plant. Office: Division of Sponsored Research Univ of Fla Gainesville FL 32601

FONTANA, CARL CHARLES, trombonist; b. Monroe, La., July 18, 1928. Played with Woody Herman, Lionel Hampton and Stan Kenton in 1950's; played show bands and jazz combos, Las Vegas; appeared in Las Vegas Jazz Festival, 1962, with Benny Goodman in Las Vegas, 1966; European tour with Woody Herman, 1966. Address: 1705 Willowbrook St La Vegas NV*

FONTANA, MARS GUY, educator, engr.; b. Iron Mountain, Mich., Apr. 6, 1910; s. Dominic and Rosalie (Amico) F.; B.S., U. Mich., 1931; M.S., 1932, Ph.D., 1935; m. Elizabeth Frances Carley, Aug. 21, 1937; children—Martha Jane, Mary Elizabeth, David Carley, Thomas Edward. Research asst., dept. engring. research U. Mich., 1929-34; metall. engr., group supervisor engring., dept. duPont Co., Wilmington, Del., 1934-45; prof., chmn. dept. metall. engring., Ohio State U., 1945—, Regents professor, 1967—, Duriron prof., 1970—, dir. Corrosion Center, supr. metall. research; research NASA, USN, USAF, Nat. Sci. Found., Alloy Casting Inst.; cons. engr. several pvt. and govtl. orgns. Recipient distinguished alumnus citation, University Mich., 1953, Sesquicentennial award, 1967; Frank Newman Speller Award in corrosion engineering, Nat. Assn. Corrosion Engrs., 1956; Native Son award Iron Mountain (Mich.) Rotary Club, 1969. Fellow Am. Soc. Metals (hon. mem.), Am. Inst. Mining, Metall. and Petroleum Engrs.; mem. Nat. Assn. Corrosion Engineers (pres., 1952, editor Jour. Corrosion, 1962—), Electrochem. Soc., Nat. Acad. Engring., Nat. Soc. Profl. Engrs., Am. Inst. Chem. Engrs., Am. Soc. Engring. Edn. (award for excellence in engring. instrn. 1969), Sigma Xi, Tau Beta Pi, Alpha Chi Sigma, Iota Alpha, Phi Eta Sigma, Phi Lambda Upsilon, Sphinx, Texnikoi. Clubs: Port au Villa (pres. 1967—) (Naples, Fla.); Faculty, University Golf. Author: Corrosion: A Compilation, 1957; Corrosion Engineering, 1967. Contributor column Industrial and Engring. Chemistry, 1947-56; also other tech. publs. Patentee on corrosion testing and recording devices, also iron ore reduction and corrosion resistant alloys. Home: 2086 Elgin Rd Columbus OH 43221

FONTANA, MICOL, fashion designer; b. Parma, Italy, Nov. 8, 1913; d. Giovanni and Amabile (Dal Co) Fontana; ed. pvt. tutoring; m. Dr. Fernando Caldiero, Sept. 6, 1959. Owner with sisters Sorelle Fontana, Rome, 1944—; clients include Queen of Egypt, Queen of Persia, Queen of Afghanistan, Princess Borghese, Princess Ruspoli, Princess Belmonte, Princess Torlonia, Princess Caracciolo, also stage and screen stars; seasonal fashion shows, Venice, Italy, Berne, Zurich, Lausanne, Switzerland, London, Eng., Brussels, Belgium, Brazil, Uruguay, Argentina, Chgo., San Francisco, Dallas, New York City, Washington, Los Angeles. Home: Piazza Monte Savello 30 Rome Italy also Hotel Plaza New York City NY 10019

FONTANA, PAUL JOHN, marine corps officer; b. Lucca, Italy, Nov. 27, 1911 (father Am. oitizen); s. Ralph and MariAnna (Luporini) F.; B.S. in Elec. Engring., U. Nev., 1934; grad. Nat. War Coll., 1953; m. Claire R. Lockwood, July 2, 1938 (dec. May 1954); children—Susan Anne, Ann Paola, Mary Frances, Paul John; m. 2d, Beth G. Gilchrist, July 16, 1955. Commd. 2d lt. USMC, 1936, advanced through grades to maj. gen., 1964; fighter squadron comdr., Guadalcanal, 1942-43; group comdr., Korea, 1950-51; dep. dir. J- 3, Joint Staff, Joint Chiefs Staff, 1960-62; comdg. gen. 2d Marine Aircraft Wing, 1963-64, 1st Marine Aircraft Wing, 1964-65; dir. Marine Corps Ednl. Center, Marine Corps Schs., Quantico, Va., 1965-68; dep. comdg. gen. Fleet Marine Force, Pacific, 1968-70; comdr. Marine Corps Air Bases, Eastern Area, comdg. gen. Marine Corps Air Sta., Cherry Point, N.C., 1970—. Decorated Navy Cross, Silver Star, Legion of Merit, D.F.C., Bronze Star, Air medal, Navy Commendation medal. Mem. Marine Corps Assn., Am. Fighter Ace Assn., Order of Daedalions. Home: 317 Jefferson Dr Marine Corps Air Station Cherry Point NC 28533 Office: Marine Corps Air Station Cherry Point NC 28533

FONTANA, ROBERT EDWARD, educator, ret. air force officer; b. Bklyn., Nov. 26, 1915; s. Valentino and Secondina (Lesca) F.; B.Elec. Engring., N.Y. U., 1939; M.S., U. Ill., 1947, Ph.D., 1949; m. Victoria E. Mauriello, Dec. 2, 1945; children—Robert Edward, Thomas Paul, Mary Joan. Commd. 2d lt. USAAF, 1942, advanced through grades to col. USAF, 1959, ret. 1969; research scientist Sandia Corp., 1949-54; spl. asst. nuclear devel. Hdqrs. USAF, 1954-58; head nuclear applications Air Research and Devel. Command, 1958-61; dir. Aerospace Research Labs., Wright-Patterson AFB, O., 1961-66; chmn. dept. elec. engring. Air Force Inst. Tech., Wright-Patterson AFB, 1966—. Pres. Honors Seminars Met. Dayton, 1966—. Decorated Legion of Merit with oak leaf cluster. Mem. I.E.E.E. (chmn. Dayton sect. 1971, editor edn. group newsletter 1970—), Am. Soc. Engring. Edn. (editor elec. engring. div. newsletter 1970—), Sigma Xi, Tau Beta Pi, Eta Kappa Nu. Home: 6663 Celestine St Dayton OH 45424 Office: AFIT Dept Elec Engring Wright-Patterson AFB OH 45433

FONTANNE, LYNN, actress; b. London, Eng., d. Jules Pierre Antoine and Frances Ellen (Thornley) Fontanne; L.H.D., Dartmouth, 1954; hon. degrees Temple U., Brandeis U., N.Y.U., Beloit Coll., Art Inst. Chgo., Emerson Coll., Yale, Carroll Coll., Vassar Coll., St. Thomas Aquinas Coll., Russell Sage Coll.; m. Alfred Lunt. Made first stage appearance as a child at the Drury Lane Pantomime; first London appearance, 1909; first New York appearance as Harriett Bludgeon in "Mr. Preedy and the Countess," Nov. 7, 1910; played Gertrude in "Milestones" on tour and later in the revival; small parts in "My Lady's Dress"; then followed, "The Wooing of Eve," "Harp of Life," "Out There," "Happiness," "Dulcy," "In Love With Love," "The Guardsman," "Elizabeth," "Design for Living," "Reunion in Vienna," "Point Valaine," "Idiot's Delight," "Amphitryon," "The Sea Gull," "Taming of the Shrew," "There Shall Be No Night," "The Pirate," "O Mistress Mine," "I Know My Love," Quadrille, 1954, The Great Sebastians, 1956; The Visit, 1958-59. Played in motion picture The Guardsman with Alfred Lunt. Recipient Presdl. Medal of Freedom, 1964; Antoinette Perry award; Emmy award. Home: Theatre Guild 245 W 52d St New York City NY 10019

FONTENROSE, JOSEPH, educator; b. Sutter Creek, Cal., June 17, 1903; s. Antone and Alice Laura (Eddy) F.; A.B., U. Cal. at Berkeley, 1925, M.A., 1928, Ph.D., 1933; m. Marie Holmes, June 22, 1942; children—Jane (Mrs. Robert Cajma), Robert, Anne. Instr. classics Cornell U., 1931-33; asst. prof. Greek and Latin, U. Ore., 1934; mem. faculty U. Cal. at Berkeley, 1934—, prof. classics, 1955-70, emeritus, 1970—, chmn. dept., 1962-66; vis. prof. classics Brandeis U., 1971. Fellow Am. Council Learned Societies, 1935- 36; sr. fellow classics Am. Acad. Rome, 1951-52; Guggenheim fellow, 1958- 59. Mem. Am. Philol. Assn., Philol. Assn. Pacific Coast, Modern Lang. Assn., Am. Folklore Soc., Archaeol. Institute America, Am. Fedn. Tchrs., Dickens Fellowship, William Morris Soc., Fabian Soc. (London, Eng.). Mem. Socialist Party. Author: Python: A Study of Elphic Myth and Its Origins, 1959; The Cult and Myth of Pyrros at Delphi, 1960; John Steinbeck: An Introduction and Interpretation, 1963: The Ritual Theory of Myth, 1966. Home: 823 San Luis Rd Berkeley, CA 94707.

FONTEYN, DAME MARGOT see Arias, Dame Margot Fonteyn de

FONTRON, JOHN, state justice; b. McPherson, Kan., Dec. 2, 1903; s. John F. and Bess A. (Penney) F.; LL.B., Kan. U., 1926; m. Dorothy A. Randles, Apr. 10, 1946; children—Elizabeth Ann, Carol Ann, Leo Warren. Admitted to Kan. bar, 1926, since practiced in Hutchinson; dist. judge 40th Jud. Dist., 1953- 64; judge Kan. Supreme Ct., 1964—. County atty. Reno County, Kan., 1947-51. Served with Judge Adv. Gen.'s Dept. AUS, 1942-46. Mem. Am., Kan. Reno County bar assns., Am. Judicature Soc., Inst. Jud. Adminstrn., Order of Coif, Beta Theta Pi, Phi Alpha Delta. Methodist. Rotarian. Home: 2710 Boswell St Topeka KS 66611 Office: State Capital Bldg Topeka KS 66612

FONT SALDANA, JORGE, sec. of treasury P.R.; b. Havana, Cuba, Jan. 14, 1907; s. Jorge Font Ruiz and Maria Luisa Saldana; m. Carmen Maria Gonzalez Olivieri; children—Alma, Marta, Maria Eugenia, Jorge. Mem. bd. editors El Imparcial, La Democracia, El Mundo, also P.R. Illustrado, 1932-47; editor mag. Bohemia Puertorriquena, 1963; formerly adminstrv. asst. to treas. P.R. exec. asst. to gov. P.R., chmn. bd. dirs. P.R. Cement Corp., mem. Indsl. Com. P.R., supt. ins. P.E., sec. senate P.R., pres. P.R. Finance Commn, vice speaker P.R. Ho. of Reps.; now sec. treas. P.R. and chmn. bd. dirs. Govt. Devel. Bank Rep. of P.R. to Jose Marti Centennial, Havana, 1953, Pro-Democracy and Liberty Congress, Maracay, Venezuela, 1960; formerly sec. commn. on preamble and sec. commn. style P.R. Constl. Conv. Mem. central com. and presdl. commn. Popular Democratic Party. Recipient Journalism award Inst. P.R. Lit., 1939, 53. Mem. P.R. Soc. Pub. Adminstrn. (pres. 1964-65), P.R. Atheneum (bd. dirs.), Royal Spanish Acad., P.R. Acad. Arts and Scis., P.R. Soc. Journalists, Lion (past pres. San Juan) Home: 706 Paz St Miramar Santurce PR Office: Dept of Treasury San Juan PR 00901*

FONVILLE, ROBERT EARL, utilities exec.; b. Belzoni, Miss., Dec. 13, 1918; s. Early M. and Maggie (Putnam) F.; M.B.A., Harvard, 1954; m. Beth Gulledge, June 21, 1953; children—Philip Murray, Gregory DuBois. Sec.-treas. Amurex Oil. Co., 1958-62; sec. Tex. Utilities Co., Dallas, 1962—. Served as capt. AUS, World War II. Home: 3619 Princeton St Dallas TX 75205 Office: 1506 Commerce St Dallas TX 75205

FOODY, WALTER M., Jr., ins. co. exec.; b. Chgo., 1921; B.S., U. Chgo., 1942; M.A., Loyola U., Chgo., 1948; married. Instr. math. Loyola U., Chgo., 1946-50; sr. v..p. Continental Assurance Co., Chgo., 1969—; sr. v.p., dir. Continental Casualty Co.; v.p. Transp. Ins. Co. Home: 10203 S Wood St Chicago IL 60643 Office: 310 S Michigan Av Chicago IL 60604

FOONBERG, JAY G., lawyer, accountant; b. Chgo., Oct. 29, 1935; s. Hyman J. and Esther (Leon) F.; B.S., U. Cal. at Los Angeles, 1957, J.D., 1963; m. Lois Alpin, Aug. 31, 1958; children—Alan Marshall, David Jeffrey Steven Mark. Auditor Cal. Bd. Equalization, 1957-59; accountant Seidman & Seidman, C.P.A.'s, Beverly Hills, Cal., 1959-60, Lever & Anker, C.P.A.'s, 1960-63; partner law firm Foonberg & Frandzel, Beverly Hills, 1970—. Mem. Mens Club of Cedars-Sinai Med. Center, Speakers Bur., 1966, also dir. Served with USAF, 1958-64. Mem. Am. Assn. Atty.-C.P.A.'s (charter sec., pres., dir.), Cal. Assn. Atty.-C.P.A.'s (dir. sr. v.p.), Cal. Soc. C.P.A.'s, Beverly Hills Bar Assn. (adviser to bd. govs.), Phi Alpha Delta, Phi Epsilon Phi Contbr. articles to profl. jours.; lectr. in field. Home: 349 S Palm Dr Beverly Hills CA 90212 Office: 8530 Wilshire Blvd Beverly Hills CA 90210

FOOSE, RICHARD MARTIN, educator; b. Lancaster, Pa., Oct. 9, 1915; s. Leon K. and Grace (Leinbach) F.; B.S. Franklin and Marshall Coll., 1937; M.S., Northwestern U., 1939; Ph.D., Johns Hopkins, 1942; M.A. (hon.), Amherst Coll., 1964; m. Dorothy Jane Kell, Feb. 11, 1943; children—Michele Leslie, Michael Peter, Stephan, Terry. Instr., Northwestern U., 1937- 39; prof. and head dept. geology Franklin and Marshall Coll., 1946-57; sr. geologist Stanford Research Inst., 1957-63, chmn. dept. earth scis.; prof., chmn. dept. geology Amherst (Mass.) Coll., 1963—; asst. geologist Pa. Geol. Survey, 1939-42, asso. geologist, 1942-43, sr. geologist, 1943- 46; geologist Pa. Turnpike Commn., 1941; cons. geologist, 1942—; Ford Found. fellow, research asso. Stanford, 1955-56; NSF sr. postdoctoral fellow Eldg. Technische Hochschule, Zurich, Switzerland, 1962-63; Nat. Acad. Sci. fellow USSR, 1969; U.S. govt. del. Internat. Geol. Congress, 1968; mem. NRC, 1969—. Fellow A.A.A.S., Geol. Soc. Am., Am. Geog. Soc.; mem. Soc. Econ. Geologists (councillor 1954-57), Am. Inst. Mining Engrs. (chmn. div. indsl. minerals 1950-51, vice chmn. mineral econ. div. 1953-54, del. internat. geol. congress 1952, 56, 60, chmn. com. mineral econs. 1962- 63; asso. editor Indsl. Minerals and Rocks, 1960), Yellowstone Bighorn Research Assn. (v.p. 1955), Pa. Acad. Sci. (pres. 1949-50), Am. Geol. Inst., Assn. Geol. Tchrs. (del. internat. geol. congress 1956), Am. Geophys. Union, Am. Inst. Profl. Geologists (charter; sec. 1968), Geochem. Soc., Phi Beta Kappa, Sigma Xi. Club: Torch (Lancaster). Contbr. articles profl. jours. Office: Amherst Coll Amherst MA 01002

FOOSHEE, IRB HASKELL, former chem. co. exec.; b. Glen Rose, Tex., Sept. 7, 1908; s. John Grover Cleveland and Nola Margaret (Griffey) F.; B.S. in Chem. Engring., Tex. A. and M. Coll. 1929; m. Etna Lea Morgan; children—Jeralea Morgan Fooshee Hesse, John Morgan (dec.), Richard Cleveland, Nola Rebecca. With Gulf Oil Corp., 1929-42; v.p. Neches Buthane Products Co., Pt. Neches, Tex., 1945-46; with Allied Chem. Corp., N.Y.C., 1947—, exec. v.p., then pres. gen. chem. div., 1957-59, v.p. mfg., 1959, exec. v.p., 1965-70, also dir., mem. exec. com.; dir. Allied Chem. Can., Ltd. Mem. Am. Inst. Chem. Engring., Mfg. Chem. Assn. (v.p., dir.). Rep. (pres. Tenafly). Episcopalian (vestry). Clubs: Downtown Athletic, Regency Whist (N.Y.C.); Knickerbocker Country (Tenafly); Englewood (N.J.) Field. Home: 16 Park St Tenafly NJ 07670 Office: 61 Broadway New York City NY 10006

FOOSHEE, MALCOLM, lawyer; b. Charleston, Tenn., Oct. 1, 1898; s. Joseph Crockett and Lillian (Powell) F.; A.B., U. South, Sewanee, 1918; LL.B., Harvard, 1921; B.C.L., Christ Church, Oxford University (Rhodes scholar), 1924; m. Clare Fraser Murray, May 6, 1930 (died 1951); children—Joan Murray (Mrs. Shepard A. Spunt) (dec.), Clare Fraser (Mrs. Robert D. Childres); m. 2d, Wynne Byard Taylor, 1953. Admitted to N.Y. bar, 1922, since practiced in New York City; with Murray, Aldrich & Roberts, 1921-22, Davis, Polk, Wardwell, Gardiner & Reed, 1925-43; mem. Donovan, Leisure, Newton & Irvine, New York City and Washington, since 1943; legal work, Europe and Japan. 1928, 35, 49, 50; mem. Inner Temple (Inns of Court), English bar, London, since 1925. Mem. legislative com. Citizens Union, N.Y.C., 1926-27; mem. Rye (N.Y.) Planning Commn., 1943-45, Rye Sch. Consolidation Commn., 1943-44; mem. Diocesan Commn. Coll. Work, New York City, 1951-58. Pres. Rye Free Reading Room, 1950-53, trustee, 1948- 59; trustee Rye Country Day Sch., 1947-51, trustee U. of South, 1953- 56. Mem. Am. delegation to Atlantic Congress, London, 1959. Mem. Harvard Naval Unit, 1918; Squadron A Cav., N.Y. N.G., 1926-29. Asso. officer Order St. John Jerusalem. Mem. Am. (chmn. sect. corp., banking and bus. law 1951-52), Internat. N.Y. State bar assns., Assn. Bar City N.Y., Am. Law Inst., Am. Judicature Soc., Assn. Am. Rhodes Scholars (dir. 1949—), Huguenot Soc. Am., S.R., Phi Beta Kappa, Kappa Sigma. Democrat. Episcopalian. Clubs: Century, Harvard, Down Town Assn., Church (N.Y.C.); Quaker Hill Country (Pawling, N.Y.). Contbr. to legal publs. Office: 2 Wall St New York City NY 10005

FOOT, MICHAEL, Brit. govt. ofcl.; b. July 23, 1913; s. Isaac Foot; ed. Wadham Coll., Oxford U.; m. Jill Craigie, 1949. Asst. editor Tribune, 1937-38; acting editor Eve. Standard, 1942; editor Tribune, 1948-52, 55-60, now mng. dir.; polit. columnist Daily Herald, 1944-64; book critic Eve. Standard, 1964—; pres. Oxford Union, 1933; mem. Parliament from Deevounport div. Plymouth, 1945-55, Ebbw Vale div. Monmouthshire, 1960—. Author: Armistice 1918-1939, 1940; Trial of Mussolini, 1943; Brendan and Beverley, 1944; Still at Large, 1950; Full Speed Ahead, 1950; (with Mervyn Jones) Guilty Men, 1957; The Pen and the Sword, 1957; Parliament in Danger, 1959; Aneurin Bevan, Vol. 1, 1897-1945, 1962. Address: care Tribune, 24 St John St London E.C.1, England*

FOOTE, ALFRED SHERMAN, former banker; b. N.Y.C., Apr. 13, 1906; s. Arthur E. and Edith (Palmer) F.; grad. Phillips Acad.; A.B., Yale, 1928; m. Jane Zevely, Sept. 4, 1936; children—Sally (Mrs. C.M. Pettus), Missy (Mrs. T.A. Cunningham), Peter. With Farmers Loan & Trust Co., 1928-41; with J.P. Morgan & Co., Inc., N.Y.C., 1941-59; former sr. v.p. Morgan Guaranty Trust Co., 1959-71, former chmn., pres. 15 Broad St. Resources Corp.; dir. Penn Virginia Corp., dir. Chesebrough-Pond's, Inc., Union Camp Corp., Abex Corp., Peerage Properties Inc. Clubs: Mid Ocean, Bedford Golf and Tennis. Home: RD 1 Mt Kisco NY 10549

FOOTE, CHRISTOPHER SPENCER, educator; b. Hartford, Conn., June 5, 1935; s. William J. and Dorothy (Bennett) F.; B.S. magna cum laude, Yale, 1957; Fulbright scholar, U. Gottingen, 1957-58; A.M.., Harvard, 1959, Ph.D., 1961; m. Stefanie von Susich, Sept. 10, 1960; children—Jonathan, Thomas. Nat. Sci. Found. predoctoral fellow Harvard, 1958-61; instr. chemistry U. Cal. at Los Angeles, 1961-62, asst. prof., 1962-66, asso. prof., 1966-69, prof., 1969—; cons. to panel on polycyclic organic matter Nat. Research Council of Nat. Acad. Scis., 1970; cons. Proctor & Gamble Co., Sloane fellow, 1965-67; Guggenheim fellow, 1967-68. Mem. Am. Chem. Soc., Chem. Soc. London, A.A.A.S., Phi Beta Kappa, Sigma Xi, Phi Lambda Upsilon. Mem. hon. editorial adv. bd. Photochemistry and Photobiology Jour., 1970. Home: 416 20th St Santa Monica CA 90402 Office: Dept Chemistry Univ California Los Angeles CA 90024

FOOTE, EMERSON, corp. exec.; b. Sheffield, Ala., Dec. 13, 1906; s. James Adonijah and Ruth (Penn) Foote; student pub. schs.; D.Pub. Service, Brigham Young U., 1965; m. Sabina Fromhold, Apr. 18, 1938; children—Florence Ann, Katherine Penn, James Adair, Jennifer Brouhgton. With bldg. and loan assn., automobile distbg. co., life ins. co., 1923-31, Leon Livingston Advt. Agy., San Francisco, 1931-35, Yeomans & Foote, 1935-36, J. Stirling Getchell, Inc., N.Y.C., 1936-38; with Lord & Thomas, 1938-42, exec. v.p., 1942; co-founder Foote, Cone & Belding, 1942, pres., 1942-50; with McCann-Erickson, Inc., 1951-64, pres., 1960-63, chmn. bd., 1962-64; 1st chmn. Nat. Interagy. Council on Smoking and Health, Washington, 1964-67; chmn. Campaign to Check Population Explosion, 1967-69; dir. Nat. Liberty Corp., Valley Forge, Pa., 1969—, chmn. bd. DeMoss Assos., Inc. subsidiary, 1969—. Mem. Pres. Johnson's Commn. on Heart Disease, Cancer and Stroke, 1964-65; adviser to Govt. India on Family Planning, 1969; mem. U.S. Senate Panel Consultants on Cancer, 1970-71. Trustee or bd. dirs. various non-profit orgns. including Menninger Found., Am. Cancer Found., N.Y. Sch. Psychiatry, Inst. for Advancement Med. Communication, others. Recipient Clement Cleveland medal for cancer work, 1953. Clubs: Metropolitan, Players (N.Y.C.). Home: 185 E 85th St New York City NY 10028 Office: DeMoss Assos Valley Forge PA 19481

FOOTE, FRANK W., Jr., pathologist, educator; b. Hattiesburg, Miss., 1911; M.D., U. Va., 1935. Spl. fellow tumor pathology Nat. Cancer Inst., Meml. Hosp., New York City, 1939-40, attending staff pathology; instr. to asst. prof. pathology U. Va., 1935-39; prof. pathology Sloan-Kettering div. Cornell U. Med. Coll., Chmn. dept. pathology Meml. Center Cancer and Allied Diseases, New York City; cons. pathologist Valley Hosp., Ridgewood, N.J.; asso. attending pathologist N.Y. Hosp. Diplomate path. anatomy Am. Bd. Pathology, 1942. Mem. Am. Assn. Pathologists and Bacteriologists. Home: 444 E 68th St New York City NY 10021

FOOTE, FRANKLIN MANLEY, pub. health physician; b. Dannemora, N.Y., Apr. 15, 1908; s. Wilbur Ephraim and May Etta (Manley) F.; B.S., Yale, 1930, M.D., 1933, Dr. P.H., 1935; m. Doris Brewer Humphrey, June 24, 1933; children—Patricia Beverly, Susan Eleanor, Franklin Humphrey. Physician USPHS Hosp., Norfolk, Va., 1933-34; co. health officer, Tenn., 1935-37; chief div. local health administrn. Conn. State Dept. Health, 1937-41; dist. health officer, N.Y.C., 1941-46; med. dir., later exec. dir. Nat. Soc. Prevention Blindness, N.Y.C., 1946-59; asst. prof. pub. health and preventive medicine, Cornell U. Med. Sch., 1941-52; commr. Conn. State Dept. Health, 1959—; lectr. in epidemiology, pub. health Yale, 1959—; Chmn. Conn. Drug Adv. Council; sec. Nat. Health Council, N.Y.C., 1957-59. Recipient Fones medal Conn. Dental Assn., 1965; Winslow medal Conn. Pub. Health Assn., 1967. Served as maj. M.C., AUS, 1942-46. Decorated Army Commendation medal. Fellow Am. Pub. Health Assn.; mem. A.M.A., Conn. Med. Soc., Harvey Soc., Am. Sch. Health Assn., Assn. Research Ophthalmology, Pan-Am. Assn. Ophthalmology, Internat. Assn. Prevention Blindness, Nat. Conf. Cooperation in Health Edn., Am. Assn. State Hosp. Constrn. Authorities (pres.). Author sci. articles. Home: 300 Russell Rd Wethersfield CT 06109 Office: 79 Elm St Hartford CT 06106

FOOTE, FREEMAN, educator, geologist; b. Orange, N.J., Nov. 8, 1908; s. Will Howe and Helen (Freeman) F.; grad. Phillips Exeter Acad., 1926; B.A., Princeton, 1931; postgrad. Columbia, 1931-37; m. Sally Newnham Carlton, July 22, 1939; 1 dau., Nancy Newnham. Asst., Columbia, 1933-37; mem. faculty Williams Coll., 1937—, prof. geology, 1956—, Edward Burst prof. geology and mineralogy, 1968—, chmn. dept., 1964-67; asso. prof. Columbia, summers 1952, 53, Wesleyan U., Middletown, Conn., summer 1955; tchr. Mr. Greylock High Sch. Ecology Inst., Williamstown, 1967. Mem. fellowship selection panel NSF, 1964, 65, 68. Vice chmn. Williamstown Republican Com., 1952-60; mem. Williamstown Finance Com., 1970—. Vice pres. Greylock Found., 1964- -. Served to lt. comdr. USNR, 1942-45. Fellow Geol. Soc. Am.; mem. A.A.A.S., Nat. Assn. Geology Tchrs. (sec. 1958-60), Sigma Xi. Home: Cold Spring Rd Williamstown MA 01267

FOOTE, MRS. HENRY D., Jr., vice chmn. bd. govs. Am. Nat. Red Cross. Address: care Am. Nat. Red Cross, 17th and D Sts Washington, DC.*

FOOTE, HORTON, writer; b. Wharton, Tex., Mar. 14, 1916; s. Albert Horton and Hallie (Brooks) F.; student Pasadena (Cal.) Playhouse Sch. Theatre, 1933-35, Tamara Daykarhanova Sch. Theatre, New York City, 1937-39; m. Lillian Vallish, June 4, 1945; children—Barbarie Hallie, Albert Horton, Walter Vallish, Daisy Brooks. Mem. writers guilds Am. East, West Dramatists Guild, Authors Guild Am. Author: (motion pictures) To Kill a Mockingbird (Acad. award best screenplay based on material another medium, Writers Guild Am. screen award best written Am. Drama), 1962-63, The Traveling Lady, 1964-65, The Chase, 1965; (plays) The Chase, 1952, Trip to Bountiful, 1953; The Traveling Lady, 1954; (TV) The Trip to Bountiful, 1953, Young Lady of Property, 1953, John Turner Davis, 1953, The Oil Well, 1953, Roots in a Parched Ground, 1961; (collected TV plays) Harrison, Tex., 1956; (novel) The Chase, 1956; Three Plays, 1962: (screenplay) The Stalking Moon, 1968.

FOOTE, JAMES HAROLD, cons. profl. engr; b. Jackson, Mich., Nov. 21, 1891; s. James Berry and Rebecca Eliza (Tuttle) F.; B.S. in Civil Engring., Mich. State U., 1914; D.Sc. in Engring. (hon.), Wayne State U., 1958; m. Marie D. Dinius, Oct. 12, 1915; children—James Harold, Barbara Marie (Mrs. Joseph A. Crain). Surveyor, engr., constrn. engr. Fargo Engring. Co., Consumers Power Co., and asso. cos., Jackson, 1914-23; elec. engr. charge sta. and transmission line engring. Commonwealth Power Corp. of Mich., and successors, 1924-31; supervising engr. charge elec. engring. No. div. Commonwealth & So. Corp. N.Y., 1932-36, charge engring., 1936-49; v.p., dir. Commonwealth Services, Inc. N.Y., 1949-61, dir. engring., 1958-61; pres., dir. Commonwealth Assos., Inc., Jackson, 1949-58, chief engr., 1958-61, dir., 1958-60; pres., dir. Commonwealth Bldgs., Inc., Jackson, 1955-61; pvt. practice profl. engring. electricity supply systems and equipment, 1962—; pres. dir. Waupakisco Realty Co. Battle Creek Mich., 1937-43; v.p., dir. Miller Plating Corp., Jackson, 1963-69. Mem. Internat. Conf. Large Electrical High Tension Systems; tech. adviser U.S. nat. com. Internat. Electrotech. Commn., 1955-70, del. tech. coms., 1955-58; mem. Mich. Bd. Registration Architects, Profl. Engrs. and Land Surveyors, 1943-50, chmn., 1950. Vice pres., Mich. Council Chs. and Religious Edn., 1949. Trustee Olivet (Mich.) Coll., 1943- 50, Adrain (Mich.) Coll. 1956-59. Recipient Centennial award Mich. State U., 1955, distinguished alumni award, 1961; named Mich. Engr. Year, 1960, Mich. Soc. Profl. Engrs. Registered profl. engr., Mich. Fellow A.A.A.S., I.E.E.E. (pres. 1959-60; Edison and John Fitz medal coms. 1960-63); mem. Am. Forestry Assn., Mich. Assn. Professions, Am. Inst. Cons. Engrs., Am. Soc. Engring. Edn., Am. Soc. Testing Materials (chmn. com. elec. conductors 1938-50, adminstry. com. standards 1953-60, hon. mem. 1962), U.S.A. Standards Inst. (dir. 1956-63, mem. elec. and electronics standards bd. 1952-70; Howard Coonley medal 1960), Nat., Mich. (dir. 1950-53) socs, profl. engrs., Mich. Engring. Soc. (pres. 1944-45; hon. mem.), Tau Beta Pi, Eta Kappa Nu, Pi Tau Sigma. Republican. Methodist. Author in field. Spl. work long transmission line corona tests, improved electric excitation systems and control, novel designs wood and steel transmission structures, coordination insulation strengths electric systems and equipment. Address: Brethren MI 49619

FOOTE, MARCELLE K., librarian; b. Albion, Ind., Nov. 12, 1910; d. George Loomis and Lelia (Kitt) Foote; A.B., Ind. U., 1932; B.L.S., Western Res. U., 1933. Librarian, Albion (Ind.) Pub. Library, 1933-36, Connersville (Ind.) Pub. Library, 1937-56; cons. Ind. State Library, Indpls., 1956-60, head extension div., 1960-67, dir., 1967—. Sec. Ind. Commn. Pub. Records, 1967- -, Ind. Certification Bd., 1967—, Am. Revolution Bicentennial Commn., 1971—; mem. Ind. Commn. Aging Edn. Com., 1969- -. Chmn. Fayette County chpt. Am. Cancer Soc., 1952-54; mem. Fayette County Adult Edn. Council, 1949-52. Named Librarian of Year, Ind. Library Trustee Assn., 1966. Mem. Am. (chmn., trustee citation com. 1962), Ind. (pres. 1951-52) library assns., Am. Assn. State Libraries (sec. 1963-64), Ind. Sch. Libraries Assn., Ind. Hist. Soc., Am. Legion Aux., Am. Assn. U. Women, Delta Zeta. Presbyn. (deaconess). Mem. Order Eastern Star. Club: Altrusa (dist. gov. 1957-59, internat. 2d v.p. 1961-63). Home: 3611 Washington Blvd Indianapolis IN 46205 Office: 140 N Senate Av Indianapolis IN 46204

FOOTE, NELSON NORTHRUP, educator, sociologist; b. Newcastle, Neb., Mar. 27, 1915; s. La Rue Lee and Georgia (Northrup) F.; B.S., Cornell U., 1939, Ph.D., 1956; m. Geraldine Roach, June 8, 1940; children—Kathleen Ellen, Jefferson. Program analyst Dept. Agr., 1941-43; research, editor Mich. Indsl. Union Council, Detroit, 1943-45; instr. Wayne U., 1945-47, Cornell U., 1947-51; asst. prof., dir. Family study Center, U. Chgo., 1951-56, with Gen. Elec. Co., 1956-70; prof., chmn. dept. sociology Hunter Coll., 1970—. Mem. Am. Sociol. Soc., Indsl. Relations Research Assn., Am. Assn. Pub. Opinion Research, Market Research Council. Author (with L. S. Cottrell) Identity and Interpersonal Competence, 1955; (with others) Household Decision-Making, 1961; (with others) Housing Choices and Constraints, 1960. Home: Hillside Pl Tarrytown NY 10591 Office: 695 Park Av New York City NY 10021

FOOTE, NORMAN LANDON, bishop; b. Saratoga Springs, N.Y., Nov. 30, 1915; s. Leroy H. and Amy V. (Close) F.; A.B., Princeton, 1937; S.T.B., Gen. Theol. Sem., 1940, S.T.D., 1957; D.D., Church Div. Sch. of the Pacific, 1957; m. Carolyn H. Swayne, June 1, 1940; children—Margaret, Judith, Leroy, Ralph. Ordained to ministry of P.E. Ch., deacon, priest, 1940; missionary, Mont., 1940- 43, archdeacon, 1943-50; dir. Nat. Town and Country Church Inst. Parkville, Mo., 1950-57; bishop of Ida., 1957—. Home: 6830 McMullen St Boise ID 83705 Office: Box 2188 Boise ID 83701

FOOTE, ROBERT LAKE, lawyer; b. Evanston, Ill., Dec. 4, 1914; s. Roger Lee and Margaret (Lake) F.; grad. Hill Sch., Pottstown, Pa., 1934; B.A., Yale, 1938; LL.B., Harvard, 1941; m. Barbara Austin, June 14, 1941; children—Markell Brooks, Marion Roberts, Helen Lake. Admitted to Ill. bar, 1941; with firm Sidley & Austin, Chgo. and predecessor firm, 1941—, partner, 1951—. Dir. A.C. Nielsen Co., Northwest Engring. Co., Erdco Engring. Co., Grant Pub. Co. Trustee Village of Glencoe, Ill., 1952-60, mem. zoning bd., 1950—; sec. Chgo. Ednl. TV Assn. Bd. dirs. Chgo. Council Community Nursing; endowment trustee A.L.A.; trustee Hoover Found. Served with USNR, 1942-45. Mem. Am., Ill., Chgo. bar assns. Mem. Union Ch. Clubs: Law, Legal, Economic, Chicago, University (Chgo.) Skokie County (Glencoe); Wausaukee (Wis.). Home: 587 Longwood St Glencoe IL 60022 Office: 11 S LaSalle St Chicago IL 60603

FOOTE, ROBERT THADDEUS, food co. exec.; b. Newton Center, Mass., Oct. 25, 1917; s. Edward Thaddeus and Laura (Stedman) F.; B.S., Cornell U., 1939; m. Barbara Brumder, Mar. 30, 1940; children—Robert Thaddeus, Barbara Chapin. Prodn. foreman Procter & Gamble Co., Chgo., 1939-41; with Red Star Yeast & Products Co. (name changed to Universal Foods Corp.), Milw., 1941—, exec. v.p., dir., 1957-66, pres., chief exec. officer, dir., 1966-68, chmn. bd., pres., chief exec. officer, 1968—. Mem. Met. Study Commn., 1957-60; dir. Milw. County Zool. Soc., Friends of Mus., Greater Milw. Com.; sec. Citizens Govt. Research Bur., 1962-64, pres., 1964-65, now trustee; mem. council Cornell U. Mem. Assn. Commerce (pres. 1971—), Gyro Internat., Chi Psi. Republican. Rotarian. Home: Route 1 Nashotah WI 53058 Office: 433 E Michigan St Milwaukee WI 53201

FOOTE, SHELBY, author; b. Greenville, Miss., Nov. 17, 1916; s. Shelby Dade and Lillian (Rosenstock) F.; student U. N.C., 1935-37; m. Gwyn Rainer, Sept. 5, 1956; children—Margaret Shelby, Huger Lee. Playwright in residence Arena Stage, Washington, 1963-64; novelist in residence U. Va. Nov. 1963, Guggenheim fellow, 1955-57; Ford Found. fellow, 1963-64, Mem. Am. Hist. Soc. Author: (novels) Tournament, 1948, Follow Me Down, 1949, Love in a Dry Season, 1950, Shiloh, 1951, Jordan County, 1952; (history) The Civil War, A Narrative: Vol. I, Fort Sumter to Perryville, 1958, Vol. II, Fredericksburg to Meridian, 1963.

FOOTE, WILLIAM JENKINS, editor; b. New Haven, Apr. 27, 1905; s. Harry Ward and Martha (Jenkins) F.; student Phillips Acad., 1921-23; B.S., Yale, 1927; m. Dorothy Hope Bennett, June 4, 1932; children—Christopher, Edward, William, Mary. Reporter, N.Y. Herald Tribune, 1928-30; editorial writer Hartford (Conn.) Courant, 1930-41, asst. mng. editor 1941-49, mng. editor, 1949-67, editor editorial page, 1967—. Past pres. Conn. Children's Aid Soc., Hartford Orphan Assylum. Mem. Conn. Circuit Asso. Press (pres.) Am. Soc. Newspaper Editors, A.P. Mng. Editors Assn., Berzelius. Clubs: Elizabethan, University (Hartford.) Home: 114 Steele Rd West Hartford CT 06107 Office: 285 Broad St Hartford CT 06105

FORBATH, THOMAS PAUL, chem. co. exec.; b. Budapest, Hungary, Nov. 25, 1921; s. Emeric and Olga (Popper) F.; B.S., Columbia, 1942, Chem. Engr., 1942; m. Pauline Buirski, June 4, 1944; children—William Emeric, Theodore Charles. Came to U.S., 1940, naturalized, 1946. Chem. engr. Am. Cyanamid Co., 1943-46, Chem. Constrn. Corp., 1946-56; with Am. Cyanamid Co., 1956—, gen. mgr. comml. devel. div., 1959-65, v.p., 1965—, also dir; dir. First Nat. Bank N.J., Totowa. Mem. adv. com. Newark Coll. Engring.; engring. council Columbia U. Mem. Am. Inst. Chem. Engrs., Am. Chem. Soc., Soc. Chem. Industry, Sigma Xi, Tau Beta Pi, Phi Lambda Upsilon. Clubs: Chemists, Hemisphere (N.Y.C.). Home: 933 E Saddle River Rd Ho-Ho-Kus NJ 07423 Office: 859 Berdan Av Wayne NJ 07470

FORBES, ALEXANDER COCHRANE, hotel exec.; b. Needham, Mass., Nov. 3, 1909; s. Francis Murray and Marjorie (Cochrane) F.; grad. Groton Sch., 1928; B.A., Harvard, 1932; m. Irene Helen Robbins, Feb. 10, 1934; children—Alexandra, Stewart, Felicity. Vice pres. Ritz Carlton Hotel, Boston. Home: PO Box 54 South Dartmouth MA 02714

FORBES, ANTHONY HENRY, educator; b. N.Y.C., Nov. 17, 1910; s. James and Ada (Fischer) F.; student Princeton, 1929-31; LL.B. cum laude, Bklyn. Law Sch., 1935; postgrad. Columbia, 1940-41; A.B., U. Cal. at Los Angeles, 1955, Ph.D. in History, 1960; m. Marion MacKinnon, Aug. 13, 1952; 1 son, James Forbes. Admitted to N.Y. bar, 1936, also U.S. Supreme Ct., 1948; with firm Conner & Chopnick, N.Y.C., 1935-48; partner David L. Anderson & Assos., pub. relations, San Diego, 1948-51; lectr. history U. Cal. at Los Angeles, 1959-63; mem. faculty No. Mich. U., 1963-69, prof. history, 1966-69, head dept., 1964-67, dir. summer session, asst. to v.p., 1967- 69; dean letters and sci. Wis. State U., Superior, 1969—. Served with USAAF, 1942-45. Mem. Am., Am. Cath. hist. assns., Medieval Acad. Am., Am. Soc. Ch. History, Conf. British Studies, Conf. Recusant History, Philonomic Council, Phi Beta Kappa. Rotarian. Contbr. profl. jours. Home: PO Box 363 Superior WI 54880

FORBES, ARCHIBALD FINLAYSON, banker; b. Johnstone, Scotland, Mar. 6, 1903; s. Charles and Elizabeth (Robertson) F.; student Glasgow U.; m. Angela Gertrude Ely, Nov. 9, 1943; (dec. 1969); children—Angela Clare, Alasdair Charles, Cynthia Rose. With Thompson McLintock & Co., 1931-35; with Spillers, Ltd., London, Eng., 1935—, now pres.; with Air Ministry, Ministry Aircraft Prodn., Brit. Govt. Service, 1940-45; chmn. Iron and Steel Bd., 1946-49, 53-59, Central Mining and Investment Corp., Ltd., 1959-64, Midland Bank Ltd., London, 1964—; dir. Dunlop Rubber Co., Ltd., Shell Transport & Trading Co. Ltd.; chmn. Midland & Internat. Banks, Ltd. Pres., Fedn. Brit. Industries, 1951-53, Epsom Coll.; hon. treas. Caldecott Community, League Hosp. Friends; mem. governing body Imperial Coll. Decorated knight bachelor, knight Grand Cross Brit. Empire. Clubs: Brook's; Pratt's; Royal Thames Yacht. Home: 26 Orchard Ct Portman Sq London W1 England Office: 27/32 Poultry London EC2 England

FORBES, BRENDA, (Mrs. Merrill Shepard), actress; b. London, Eng.; student Old Vic. First Broadway appearance in the Barretts of Wimpole Street, later appeared in Romeo and Juliet, Lucrece, Candida, Flowers of the Forest; starred in The Rivals, The Cocktail Party, Heartbreak House at Goodman Theatre, Chgo., also in The Misanthrope, U. Chgo. profl. theatre; played in motion pictures including Mrs. Miniver, White Cliffs of Dover, This Above All; in TV programs including Studio One, Alcoa Hour, Producers' Showcase Kraft Theatre, U.S. Steel Hour, Four Star Playhouse, Hallmark Hall Fame; also Cocteau's La Voix Humaine on ednl. TV; appeared in Broadway prodns. Yesterday's Magic, Jane (Theatre Guild), Ring Round the Moon, The Reluctant Debutante, Quadrille (with the Lunts), The Loves of Cass McGuire, (costar) Darling of the Day; starred with Chgo. Symphony Orch. as Joan of Arc in Honegger's Jeanne d'Arc au Bucher. Home: 81 E Elm St Chicago IL 60611

FORBES, BRYAN, actor, writer, director; b. London, Eng., July 22, 1926; s. William Theobald Clarke and Judith Kate Helen (Seaton) F.; student Royal Acad. Dramatic Art, London, 1941-42; m. Constance Smith, Feb. 19, 1951 (div. 1955); m. 2d, Nanette Newman, Aug. 27, 1955; children—Sarah Kate Amanda, Emma Katey. Entered profl. theatre, 1942; debut in The Corn is Green, London, 1942; other stage appearances include Flare Path, 1943, Gathering Storn, 1948, September Tide, 1948, The Holly and the Ivy, 1950, Tobias and The Angel, 1953, A Touch of Fear, 1956; film appearances include The League of Gentlemen, 1959. The Baby and the Battleship, 1955, The Wooden Horse, 1948. An Inspector Calls, 1954, The Key, 1957; dir. films Whistle Down the Wind, 1961, The L-Shaped Room, 1962, Seance on a Wet Afternoon, 1963, King Rat, 1964, The Wrong Box, 1965, The Whisperers, 1966, Deadfall, 1967; dir. The Madwoman of Chaillot, 1968; writer, dir. The Raging Moon, 1970; fiction critic The Spectator, 1951-52; chief cons. editor King mag. Mem. of gen. adv. council British Broadcasting Corp., 1969-71. Mng. dir., head prodn. Asso. Brit. Prodns. Ltd. Served with British Army, 1943-48. Mem. British Screenwriters Guild (mem. council, treas. 1960-63), British Actors Equity, Screen Actors Guild, Writers Guild Am., Directors Guild Am., Assn. Cinema Technicians. Author: (short stories) Truth Lies Sleeping, 2d edit., 1950; (screenplays) The Angry Silence (British Acad. award), 1959, The League of Gentlemen, 1959, Only Two Can Play (British Acad. award), 1962, The L-Shaped Room, 1962, Seance on a Wet Afternoon (British Acad. award, Edgar award, Best Screenplay award San Sebastian Film Festival), 1964. Home: care Beaver Films Ltd Beaver Lodge The Green Richmond Surrey England

FORBES, CLARENCE ALLEN, educator; b. Colebrook, N.H., Sept. 6, 1901; s. Allen Allison and Mamie (Corcoran) F.; A.B., Bates Coll., 1922; A.M., U. Ill., 1924, Ph.D., 1928; m. Florence Gertrude Lemaire, Sept. 1, 1924; children—Jacqueline (Mrs. William Kehoe), Charmian (Mrs. Richard Wright), Rodney, Roland, Joyce (Mrs. Frank Nolan). Instr., U. Cin., 1925-27; instr. to prof. U. Neb., Lincoln, 1927-48; prof. classics Ohio State U., Columbus, 1948—. Mem. Am. Philol. Assn., Am. Inst. Archaeology, Am. Assn. U. Profs., Am. Classical League, Classical Assn. Middle West and South (pres. 1951), Phi Beta Kappa. Democrat. Roman Catholic. Author: Greek Physical Education, 1929; Neoi, 1933; Teachers' Pay in Ancient Greece, 1942; (with H.S. Wilson) Gabriel Harvey's Ciceronianus, 1945; The Teaching of Classical Subjects in English, 1958; Firmicus Maternus, The Error of the Pagan Religions, 1969. Home: 33 E Torrence Rd Columbus OH 43214

FORBES, DOUGLAS WARREN, oil exec.; b. Little Rock, Nov. 26, 1899; s. James William and May Chadbourne (Bovey) F.; student U. Tex., 1918; m. Josephine Selecman, Feb. 6, 1929; children—Betty (Mrs. John M. Anderson), Sarah (Mrs. John Rex Wayland), Carolyn (Mrs. Earle E. Norwood). Asst. cashier Repub. Nat. Bank, Dallas, 1921-32, v.p., mem. exec. com., 1932-47; dir. Consumers Gas Co., Carmi, Ill. Bd. dirs. Dallas Symphony Orch. Mem. Am. Petroleum Inst., Ind. Petroleum Assn., Dallas Art Assn., Dallas Hist. Assn., Sigma Chi. Methodist. Mason (Shriner). Home: RFD 1 Plano TX 75074 Office: Republic Bank Bldg Dallas TX 75201

FORBES, EDWARD COYLE, diversified machinery co. exec.; b. Bangalore, India, Sept. 5, 1915 (parents Am. citizens); s. Sherman Guy and Bertha (Coyle) F.; grad. Phillip Exeter Acad., 1934; B.S. in Elec. Engring., Auburn U., 1938; B.S. in Aero. Engring., Air Force Aero. Inst., 1945; m. Maria Victoria Herran, July 11, 1955; children—Christina, Lucien, Alexandra, Edward, Alvaro. Various positions Gen. Electric Co., 1939-41, sales engr. Internat. Gen. Electric Co., 1946-51, dist. office mgr., Oporto, Portugal, 1951-52, gen. mgr., 1952-55, gen. mgr. producer products operations, Argentina, 1955-63; v.p. corporate planning Worthington Corp., Harrison, N.J., 1963-64, v.p. group exec., 1964; now chmn. Alco

Products, Inc., Harrison, Alco Locomotive, Inc., MLW-Worthington, Ltd.; corporate v.p. Studebaker-Worthington, Inc. Founder, Argentine Inst. for Devel. Execs., 1959-63. Served to maj. USAAF, 1941-46. Registered profl. engr. N.J., Ohio. Mem. Acad. Polit. Sci. Clubs: Balturol Golf (Springfield, N.J.); University (New York City); Estoril (Portugal) Golf; American Men's (past pres.) (Lisbon, Portugal). Home: 100 Hepburn Rd Clifton NJ 07102 Office: 401 Worthington St Harrison NJ 07029

FORBES, ELLIOT, educator; b. Cambridge, Mass., Aug. 30, 1917; s. Edward Waldo and Margaret (Laighton) F.; B.A., Harvard, 1941, M.A., 1947; m. Kathleen Brooks Allen, June 7, 1941; children—Diana, Barbara Anne, Susan. Tchr., Santa Barbara (Cal.) Sch., 1941-43, Belmont Hill Sch., 1943-45; asst. prof. music Princeton, 1947-54, asso. prof., 1954-58; dir. Harvard Glee Club and Radcliffe Choral Soc., Harvard, 1958-70, prof. music, 1958-61, Fanny Peabody prof. music, 1961—. Mem. Am. Musicol. Soc., Coll. Music Soc., Am. Acad. Arts and Scis. Revised and edited: Thayer's Life of Beethoven, 1964. Home: 182 Brattle St Cambridge MA 02138

FORBES, GILBERT BURNETT, physician, educator; b. Rochester, N.Y., Nov. 9, 1915; s. Gilbert DeLeverance and Lillian Augusta (Burnett) F.; B.A., U. Rochester, 1936, M.D., 1940; m. Grace Moehlman, July 8, 1939; children—Constance Ann (Mrs. Joseph F. Citro), Susan Young (Mrs. William A. Martin). Intern, Strong Meml. Hosp., Rochester, 1940-41; resident St. Louis Children's Hosp., 1941-43; practiced medicine, specializing in pediatrics, Los Alamos, 1946-47, Rochester, 1954—; instr. pediatrics Sch. Medicine Washington U., St. Louis, 1943- 46, asst. prof., 1947-50; prof. pediatrics, chmn. dept. Southwestern Med. Sch., Dallas, 1950-53; asso. prof. pediatrics Sch. Medicine U. Rochester, 1953-57, prof. 1957-68, prof. pediatrics, prof. radiation biology, 1968—, chmn. faculty council, 1969-70; cons. Nat. Inst. Child Health and Human Devel.; mem. sci. adv. com. Nutrition Found., 1963-66; mem. Nat. Council on Radiation Protection; mem. com. infant nutrition, com. dietary allowances NRC, 1960-63; vis. research fellow U. Oxford, Eng., 1970-71. Recipient Research Career award USPHS, NIH, 1962—, Borden award Am. Acad. Pediatrics, 1964. Mem. Am. Pediatric Soc. (council), Soc. Pediatric Research (past pres.), A.M.A., Soc. Explt. Biology and Medicine, A.A.A.S., Am. Acad. Pediatrics, U. Rochester Med. Alumni Assn. (past pres.), Sigma Xi, Alpha Omega Alpha, Theta Chi. Rotarian. Author numerous articles in field. Asso. editor: Am. Jour. Diseases Childhood, 1964—; Nutrition Revs., 1961—. Home: 2021 Westfall Rd Rochester NY 14618 Office: 260 Crittenden Blvd Rochester NY 14620

FORBES, JAMES WENDELL, marketing exec.; b. Evansburg, Alta., Can., Oct. 8, 1923; s. Prescott and Alvira (MacLean) F.; B.Commerce, U. B.C., 1948; m. Carolyn J. Irvine; children—James, Wendell, Elizabeth MacLean. With Time Inc., 1948-70, circulation dir. Life mag., 1962-64, adminstr. book pub. div., 1964-68; asst. planning dir. Time-Life Books, 1969; asst. to mng. dir. Time-Life Records, 1970; mgmt., marketing adviser, Ridgefield, Conn., 1970—. Chmn. bd. Direct Mail Advt. Assn., 1964-65. Served with RCAF, 1943-45. Address: 87 Peacable Hill Rd Ridgefield CT 06877

FORBES, JOHN DOUGLAS, educator; b. San Francisco, Apr. 9, 1910; s. John Franklin and Portia (Ackerman) F.; A.B., U. Cal. at Berkeley, 1931; M.A., Stanford, 1932; A.M., Harvard, 1936, Ph.D., 1937; m. Margaret Funkhouser, Feb. 4, 1937; children—Pamela (Mrs. Louis McLane), Peter. Accountant J.F. Forbes & Co., C.P.A.'s, San Francisco, 1937-38, 42-43; asst. to dir., curator paintings San Francisco World's Fair, 1938-40; chmn. dept. fine arts U. Kansas City (Mo.), 1940-42; faculty history Bennington Coll., 1943-46; asso. prof. history and fine arts Wabash Coll., 1946-50, prof., 1950-54; prof. bus. history U. Va., 1954—. Served as 2d lt. AUS, 1942. Decorated Ordre des Palmes Académiques (France). Mem. Am. Hist. Assn. (life), Coll. Art Assn. (life), Mystery Writers Am., Soc. Archtl. Historians (pres. 1962-64; life), Colonial Soc. Mass., Am. Assn. U. Profs., A.I.A. (hon.), Audubon Soc., Nat. Trust for Historic Preservation, Wilderness Soc. (life), Sierra Club (life), Nature Conservancy (life), Mechanics Inst. (life), Victorian Soc., Cal. Hist. Soc., Friends of Sea Otter, Tamalpais Conservation Club (life), Am. Kitefliers Assn., Phi Beta Kappa. Clubs: Rolls-Royce Owners; Colonnade; (life), Pacific-Union (San Francisco), Farmington Country (Charlottesville); Cambridge (Mass.) Boat. Author: Israel Thorndike, Federalist Financier, 1953; Victorian Architect, 1953; (with C.C. Abbott, L.A. Thompson) The Executive Function and Its Compensation, 1957; Murder in Full View, 1968; Death Warmed Over, 1971. Editor Journal Society Archtl. Historians, 1953-58. Adv. editor industry, Ency. Brit., 1956-58. Home: Box 3607 University Station Charlottesville VA 22903 (summer) 1250 Jones St San Francisco CA 94109

FORBES, JOHN GEORGE, lawyer; b. N.Y.C., Oct. 19, 1919; s. George and Hazel (Mavricos) F.; B.S.S., Coll. City N.Y., 1940; LL.B., Harvard, 1943; m. Demetra Ramos, May 6, 1950; 1 son, John George. Admitted to N.Y. bar, 1943, since practiced in N.Y.C.; partner firm Battle, Fowler, Stokes & Kheel, 1967—; lectr. Practising Law Inst., 1959—; instr. Tax Workshop Sch., 1954-56. Dir., sec., gen. counsel Unimusic, Inc.; dir. Central Securities Corp. Trustee, sec.-treas. Inst. Mus. Art City N.Y.; trustee Christian A. Johnson Endeavor Found. Mem. N.Y. N.G., 1944-47. Mem. Assn. Bar City N.Y., Am. Bar Assn. Contbr. legal jours. Editor Harvard Law Rev., 1942-43. Home: 111-20 73d Av Forest Hills NY 11375 Office: 280 Park Av New York City NY 10017

FORBES, JOHN RIPLEY, ecucator, museologist; b. Chelsea, Mass., Aug. 25, 1913; s. Rev. Kenneth Ripley and Ellen Elizabeth (Barker) F.; spl. student U. Ia., 1933-34, Bowdoin Coll., Me., 1934-35; m. Margaret Sanders, Dec. 10, 1951; children—Ripley, Anne. Founder, dir. Stamford (Conn.) Mus., 1935-36; ornithologist, taxidermist Lee Mus. Biology, MacMillan-Arctic Expdn. to Labrador and Baffin Island, 1937; founder, dir. William T. Hornaday Meml. Found., 1938-50; organizer, dir. Kansas City (Mo.) Mus., 1939- 41; founder Nashville Children's Mus., acting dir., 1945-46; exec. dir. Jacksonville (Fla.) Children's Mus., 1945, Fernbank Children's Nature Mus., Atlanta, 1946; organizer, dir. Ore. Mus. Sci. and Industry, Portland, 1947-49; founder Sacramento Jr. Mus., Sacramento, dir., 1951- 53, co-founder, dir. operations Nature Centers for Young Am., 1959- 60; founder, pres. Natural Sci. for Youth Found., N.Y.C., 1961—; founder Nat. Found for Jr. Mus., N.Y.C., dir. 1951-60; founder, pres. William T. Hornaday Meml. Trust, Conn., 1961; founder Mid-Fairfield County Youth Mus., Westport, Conn., 1958, pres., 1963-66; founder Am. Youth Mus. Assn., 1964; co-founder, v.p. Aspetuck Land Trust, Fairfield County, Conn. Pres., St. John's on the Lake Assn., 1963-64. Served with M.C., USAAF, 1942-45. Mem. Am. Assn. Museums (chmn. children's mus. sec. 1965), conservation Edn. Assn., Nat. Audubon Soc. (life), Am. Nature Study Soc., Nature Conservancy, Wilderness Soc., Am. Ornithologist Union (life), N.Y. Zool. Soc., Nat. Wildlife Fedn., Conn. Conservation Assn. (pres. 1969—), N.H. Audubon Soc. (trustee 1970). Clubs; Explorers (N.Y.C.); Dunwoody Country (Atlanta); Mazamas (Portland) Ore.; Sierra (Cal.). Home: Ball Mill Creek Rd Atlanta GA 30319 Office: 763 Silvermine Rd New Canaan CT 06840

FORBES, MALCOLM STEVENSON, publisher, ex-state senator; b. N.Y.C., Aug. 19, 1919; s. Bertie Charles and Adelaide (Stevenson) F.; grad. cum laude, Lawrenceville Acad., 1937; A.B., Princeton, 1941; L.H.D., Nasson Coll., 1966; m. Roberta Remsen Laidlaw, Sept. 21, 1946; children—Malcolm Stevenson, Robert Laidlaw, Christopher Charles, Timothy Carter, Moira Hamilton. Owner, pub. Fairfield Times, weekly, Lancaster, O., 1941; est. Lancaster Tribune, weekly, 1942; asso. pub. Forbes Mag. Bus., N.Y.C., 1946-54, pub., editor 1954-57, pub., editor-in-chief 1957—; v.p. Forbes Inc., N.Y.C., 1947-64, pres., 1964—; chmn. bd. 60 Fifth Av. Corp.; chmn. bd., pres. Investors Adv. Inst., Slegers-Forbes Inc.; pres. Forbes Internat. Inc., Forbes Trinchera Inc.; founder Nations Heritage, bi-monthly, pres., pub., 1948-49; chmn. bd. Sangre de Cristo Ranches Inc.; v.p. Investors Adv. Inst., Inc., 1948-54, pres. 1954-56, dir., 1960—. Chmn. bd. trustees Nassau Sovereign, Princeton undergrad. mag. Mem. Borough Council Bernardsville, N.J.; state senator, 1952-58. Campaign chmn. A.R.C., Somerset Hills, N.J., 1949. Republican candidate for gov. N.J., 1957; N.J. del.-at-large 1960 Rep. Nat. Conv. Served with inf. AUS 1942-45. Decorated Bronze Star, Purple Heart. Named Young Man of Year, N.J. Jr. C. of C., 1951. Mem. St. Andrew's Soc., 84th Inf. Div. Assn., Navy League, Assn. U.S. Army, Def. Orientation Conf. Assn., N.J. Hist. Soc., Confrerie des Chevaliers du Tastevin. Episcopalian (vestryman). Clubs: Princeton; Essex Fox Hound; New York Racquet and Tennis, New York Yacht; Lyford Cay; Coral Beach; Links; Staniel Cay; Jockey; Salmagundi. Home: Timberfield Far Hills NJ 07931 Office: 60 Fifth Av New York City NY 10011

FORBES, RICHARD E., advt. exec.; b. Larchmont, N.Y., Sept. 21, 1915; s. George P. and Charlotte (Ricketson) F.; B.A., Williams Coll., 1936; m. Phinina Gagliardi, June 22, 1946; children—Mary C., Richard E. With Macy Westchester Papers, 1937-42; appliance advt. mgr., staff cons. Gen. Electric Co., 1948-56; dir. advt. Chrysler Corp., 1956—. Bd. dirs. Advt. Research Found., Adcraft Club Detroit, Detroit Advt. Assn. Home: 80 Cranbrook Rd Bloomfield Hills MI 48013 Office: Chrysler Corp PO Box 1919 Detroit MI 48226

FORBES, ROBERT BRIEDWELL, educator, geologist; b. Aberdeen, Wash., Mar. 14, 1924; s. Robert Walston and Hope (Briedwell) F.; student U. Ore., 1941-42, 46-48; B.S., U. Wash., 1949, Ph.D., 1959; m. Norma Evelyn Smart, Aug. 22, 1953; children—Robert Lyle, John Bruce. Geologist, Juneau Icefield Research Project, Coast Range, Alaska, 1949-50; cons. U.S. Army, 1951-52; chief field observation br. R. and D div. U.S. Army Washington, 1952-54, asst. chief research br., 1954-56; research asso. geology dept. U. Wash., Seattle, 1956-59; asst. prof. geology U. Alaska, College, 1959-61, asso. prof., 1961-64, prof., chmn. geology dept., 1965-69, prof. geology, petrologist Geophys. Inst. and geology dept., 1969—. Apptd. to U.S. Geol. Survey, 1969—. Served to 1st lt. AUS, 1942-46. NSF fellow. sci. faculty Tokyo U., 1963-64. Fellow Arctic Inst. N.Am., A.A.A.S., Geol. Soc. Am; mem. Am. Geophys. Union (v.p. volcanology geochemistry and petrology sect. 1970-71), Am. Assn. Petroleum Geologists, Am. Polar Soc., Sigma Xi. Club: American Alpine. Home: Box 162 Red Fox Dr College AK 99701

FORBES, ROBERT CHARLES, army officer; b. Camden, N.J., July 22, 1917; s. Charles Ryan and Caroline (Shay) F.; B.A., U. Pa., 1939; grad. Command and Gen. Staff Coll., 1950, Army War Coll., 1959; m. Anne Catherine Eckenrode, May 16, 1942; children—John David, Robert Charles, Elizabeth Anne (Mrs. Michael Carter), Michael Edward. Commd. 2d lt. U.S. Army, 1942, advanced through grades to maj. gen., 1968; comdg. officer 1st Battalion, 255th Inf. Regt., France and Germany, 1944-45; assigned War Dept., 1945-46; instr. Command and Gen. Staff Coll., 1950-53; liaison officer Brit. Staff Coll., 1953-55; asst. sec. gen. staff Dept. Army, 1955-58; sr. adviser 15th Div., Korea, 1959-60; comdg. officer 4th Tng. Regt., Ft. Dix, N.J., 1960-62; dep. sec., sec. Joint Chiefs Staff, 1962-66; asst. div. comdr. 9th Div., 1966-67; chief staff II FFV, Vietnam, 1967; comdg. gen. 199th Inf. Brigade, Vietnam, 1967-68; asst. chief staff J-1 USMACV, 1968; dir. internat. logistics, dir. requirements, dir. personnel, tng. and force devel. Army Material Command, Washington, 1968-71; chief staff Allied Land Forces South Eastern Europe, 1971—. Decorated D.S.M., Silver Star (2), Legion of Merit (2), Air medal (14), Bronze Star (3); Nat. Order Vietnam 5th class, Vietnam Army Distinguished Service Order, Vietnam Cross Gallantry with palm, Nat. Polit. Service medal Vietnam 1st class. Mem. Lambda Chi Alpha, Eta Sigma Phi. Home: 5111 S 8th Rd Arlington VA 22204 Office: Hdqrs ALFSEE APO New York City NY 09224

FORBES, THEODORE MCCOY, Jr., lawyer; b. Atlanta, Oct. 28, 1929; s. Theodore M. and Mary (Christie) F.; B.S. in Chemistry, Ga. Inst. Tech., 1950; LL.B., U. Va., 1953; m. Margaret Paty, Dec. 12, 1953; children—Theodore McCoy III, Margaret Paty. Instr., Culver (Ind.) Summer Naval Sch., 1950; admitted to Ga. bar, 1952, since practiced in Atlanta; asso., then partner firm Gambrell, Russell, Killorin, Wade & Forbes, 1953—. Bd. dirs. Ga. chpt. Arthritis Found., 1961-68. Mem. Am., Atlanta bar assns., State Bar Ga. (chmn. adminstrv. law sec. 1967-68), Am. Judicature Soc., Order of Coif, Alpha Tau Omega, Sigma Nu Phi, Alpha Chi Sigma. Presbyn. (deacon). Kiwanian. Club: Capital City. Home: 284 Camden Rd NE Atlanta GA 30309 Office: First Nat Bank Bldg Atlanta GA 30303

FORBES, THOMAS ROGERS, anatomist; b. N.Y.C., Jan.5, 1911; s. James Bruff and Stella (Rogers) F.; B.A. cum laude, U. Rochester, 1933, Ph.D., 1937; M.A. (hon.) Yale, 1962; m. Helen Frances Allen, June 19, 1934; children—Thomas R., William M. Fellow anatomy U. Rochester, 1933-37; asst. anatomy Johns Hopkins, 1937-38, instr., 1938-42; instr. anatomy Yale, 1945-46, asst. prof., 1946-51, asso. prof., 1951-62, prof., 1962- -, asst. dean, 1948-60, asso. dean Sch. Medicine, 1960-70; fellow Branford Coll., Yale, 1951—. Tech. aide, div. med. scis. NRC, OSRD, 1942-45. Guggenheim fellow, 1942. Fellow A.A.A.S.; mem. Am. Assn. Anatomists, Soc. Exptl. Biology and Medicine, Endocrine Soc., Am. Assn. Hist. Med., Royal Soc. Medicine (London), Am. Soc. Zoologists, Faculty Hist. Pharmacy and Med., Worshipful Soc. Apothecaries (London), Conn. Acad. Arts and Scis., Soc. Social History of Medicine (London), Phi Beta Kappa, Sigma Xi, Psi Upsilon. Club: Beaumont (New Haven). Author: The Midwife and the Witch, 1966; Chronicle from Aldgate, 1971. Bd. editors Jour. History of Medicine, 1956-68, pres. bd. mgrs., 1958—, acting editor, 1960-62, editor, 1962-63. Contbr. research papers on endocrinology, history of medicine. Home: 86 Ford St Hamden CT 06517

FORBES, WILLIAM EUGENE, univ. regent; b. Anoka, Neb., May 30, 1906; s. Robert Bruce and Laura (Forbes) F.; B.A., U. Cal. at Los Angeles, 1928; m. Ann Fontron, Sept. 6, 1930; children—Julie, Allison. Exec. asst. to pres. CBS, Hollywood and New York City, 1937-44; TV supr. Young & Rubicam, Inc., New York City, 1944-51; pres. So. Cal. Music Co., 1951—. Bd. regents U. Cal. Mem. Beta Theta Pi, Beta Gamma Sigma. Republican. Presbyn. Clubs: University, Annandale Golf (Pasadena). Home: 1500 Chelsea Rd San Marino CA 91108 Office: 637 S Hill St Los Angeles CA 90014

FORBIS, WILLIAM HUNT, writer; b. Missoula, Mont., Feb. 4, 1918; s. Clarence Jenks and Josephine (Hunt) F.; B.A., U. Mont., 1939; m. Marie Vincent Dec. 12, 1943 (dec. Aug. 1969); children—Peter Vincent, Steven Jenks, Barbara Belle; m. 2d, Deborah Hall, Sept. 19, 1970; 1 son, William Hall. With Time mag., 1949-67, writer, N.Y.C., 1951-58, sr. editor, 1958-67; chief S.Am. corr. Time-Life News Service, 1967-69; tchr. mag. writing U. Mont., Missoula, 1969-70. Home: 118 Takima Dr Missoula MT 59801

FORBUSH, DASCOMB RAMSEY, educator; b. N.Y.C., Feb. 18, 1920; s. Dascomb Edmund and Anne (Ramsey) F.; A.B., Oberlin Coll., 1940; M.B.A., Harvard, 1942, M.A., 1948, Ph.D., 1954; m. Dorothy Louise Fitts, Sept. 7, 1946; children—Dascomb David, Maudellen, Daniel Henry. Asst. prof. bus. econ. Northwestern U., 1948-54, asso. prof., 1954-65; prof., chmn. dept. econ. Clarkson Coll. Tech., Potsdam, N.Y., 1965—; vis. prof. U. Wash., 1960; cons. Ford Found. to Jordan Devel. Bd., Amman, 1961-62. Served to capt. AUS, 1942-46. Mem. Am. Econ. Assn., Am. Statis. Assn., Am. Assn. U. Profs. (past local pres.), Am. Civil Liberties Union, Phi Beta Kappa. Club: Century. Unitarian. Author: Problems of Corporate Power, 1960; Managements' Relationships with its Publics, 1960; (with M. Colberg and G. Whitaker) Busniess Economics, 3d edit., 1964; 4th edit., 1970 (with Dorothy Forbush) Study Guide for Economics, 1969. Home: 89 Market St Potsdam NY 13676

FORBUSH, SCOTT E., math. physicist; b. Apr. 10, 1904; B.S., Case Inst. Tech., 1925, D.Sc. (hon.), 1962; postgrad. Johns Hopkins, 1931-32, George Washington U.; m. Clara Lundell, July 29, 1929 (dec. Sept. 1967). Teaching asst. Ohio State U., 1925-26; jr. physicist Bur. Standards, 1926-27; observer dept. terrestrial magnetism Carnegie Instn., Washington, 1927-42, math. physicist, 1942-57, chmn. analytical statis. geophys. sect., 1957—. Civilian with Naval Ordnance Lab., 1940-44, OSRD, 1944-45, Operations Research Office, Johns Hopkins, 1951-52. Recipient J.A. Fleming medal, Sir Charles Chree prize. Mem. Am. Geophys. Union, Operations Research Soc., Nat. Acad. Sci. Club: Cosmos (Washington). Research in terrestrial magnetism, cosmic radiation statistics, operations research. Home: 7208 Brennon Lane Chevy Chase MD 20015 Office: Carnegie Instn of Washington 5241 Broad Branch Rd NW Washington DC 20015

FORCE, ELIZABETH SCULTHORPE, family life cons.; b. Sea Bright, N.J., Mar. 25, 1902; d. Willis Middleton and Sophie (Worthley) Sculthorpe; B.S., N.Y. U., 1939, M.A., 1947; postgrad. Mills Coll., 1941; m. Herman Force, Feb. 5, 1929. Tchr. English, Toms River (N.J.) Jr. High Sch. and Sr. High Sch., 1934-41; tchr. social behavior, family relationships Toms River High Sch., 1941-57; family life cons., mem. edn. div. staff Am. Social Health Assn., N.Y. C., 1957, dir. div. family life edn., 1962, 71—. Bd. dirs. Nat. Council on Family Relations, Mpls., 1958-68, pres., 1968. Named Citizen of Year, Toms River Kiwanis Club, 1953. Montclair State Tchrs. Coll., 1957. Mem. Am. Assn. U. Women (state 2d v.p. 1946- 48). Author textbooks, papers, articles in field. Home: 2 Horatio St New York City NY 10014 Office: 1740 Broadway New York City NY 10019

FORCHHEIMER, RUDOLPH, metal co. exec.; b. Nuremberg, Germany, June 5, 1918; s. Jacob and Dina (Neu) F.; student McGill U.; m. Hilda U. Noymer, Oct. 7, 1945; children—Audrey P., Constance J. Came to U.S., 1954, naturalized, 1965. With Anglo Metal Co., London, England, 1935, A/B Ferrolegeringar, Stockholm, Sweden, 1936-39, Govt. of Canada, 1943-44, H.F. Pollock & Co., Ltd., Montreal, 1944-45; pres. Philipp Bros. (Canada) Ltd., Montreal, 1946-54, v.p. Philipp Bros., Inc., N.Y.C., 1954-60; v.p. Philipp Bros. div. Minerals & Chems. Philipp Corp., 1960-67; v.p. Minerals and Chems. Philipp Corp., N.Y.C., 1965-67; v.p., asst. sec. Engelhard Minerals & Chems. Corp., 1967—. Clubs: Brae Burn Country (Purchase, N.Y.); Scarsdale Town. Home: 1 Oakstwain Rd Scarsdale, NY 10583. Office: 299 Park Av New York City NY 10017

FORD, ALLEN HUNTINGTON, corp. exec.; b. Cleve., July 29, 1928; s. David K. and Elizabeth (Brooks) F.; B.A., Yale, 1950; M.S., Case Inst. Tech., 1964; m. Constance Towson, Feb. 19, 1954; children—Hope, Sarah, James T. With Pickands Mather & Co., Cleve., 1953-69, v.p. finance, 1967-69; treas. Diamond Shamrock Corp., Cleve., 1969, v.p. finance, 1969—; dir. Motch & Merryweather Machinery Co., Elwell-Parker Electric Co. Pres., trustee Cleve. Mental Health and Rehab., Inc.; treas., trustee Welfare Fedn. Cleve., Laurel Sch., Shaker Heights, O.; trustee Federated Ch. Chagrin Falls, O, Western Res. Hist. Soc., Cleve. Served with U.S. Army, 1950-52. Clubs: Union, Cleveland Racquet, Tavern (Cleve.). Home: 50 Mill Hollow Dr Chagrin Falls OH 44022 Office: Union Commerce Bldg Cleveland OH 44115

FORD, AMOS WEEKS, educator; b. Bellevue, Tex., Sept. 18, 1901; s. Joseph Brown and Beulah (Weeks) F.; B.A., Baylor U., 1922; M.A., U. Chgo., 1926; m. Elizabeth Clark, Aug. 1, 1928; children—Clark, Diane. Sch. prin., Bellevue, 1922- 25; asst. prof. bus. Bradley Poly. Inst., Peoria, Ill., 1926-28; prof. bus. Southwestern Coll., Winfield, Kan. 1928-29; prof. econs. La. Poly. Inst., Ruston, 1929-45, dir. pub. relations, 1945-49, prof. bus. adminstrn., 1955-69. Commr., Ouachita Valley council Boy Scouts Am., 1941—. Mem. Ruston C. of C. (past pres.), Beta Gamma Sigma, Delta Sigma Pi. Democrat. Baptist. Kiwanian. Home: 1410 Maple St Ruston, LA 71270.

FORD, ARCHIE W., state ofcl.; b. Wooster, Ark., Jan. 25, 1906; s. Thomas N. and Minnie (Clements) F.; B.E., Ark. State Tchrs. Coll., 1928; M.S., U. Ark., 1948; LL.D., Ouachita Bapt. Coll., Arkadelphia, Ark., 1962. m. Ruby Lee Watson, Dec. 24, 1927; children—Justin Turner (dec.) Harold Watson (dec.), Joe Thomas. Formerly tchr. and ednl. adviser Civilian Conservation Corps; staff Ark. State Dept. Edn. since 1941, commr. edn. since 1953. Mem. N.E.A. Ark. Edn. Assn. Council Chief State Sch. Officers (pres. 1962-63), Phi Delta Kappa, Kappa Delta Pi. Democrat. Baptist. Mason, Contbd. nat. profl. mags. Home: 1221 Mitchell St Conway AR 72032 Office: Education Bldg Little Rock AR 72201

FORD, BENSON, business exec.; b. Detroit, July 20, 1919; s. Edsel Bryant and Eleanor (Clay) F.; student Hotchkiss Sch., 1935-38, Princeton, 1938-40; m. Edith McNaughton, July 9, 1941; children—Benson, Lynn McNaughton. Asst. purchasing agt. Ford Motor Co., 1940-41, asst. supt., 1941-42, dir. parent co. and subsidiaries; became v.p. Ford Motor Co., gen. mgr. Lincoln-Mercury div., now v.p., chmn. dealer policy bd. Ford Motor Co.; mem., trustee Edison Inst.; dir. Seaboard Properties Co. Protestant co-chmn. Nat. Conf. Christians and Jews, 1951-55; chmn. Automotive Safety Found., 1964-66, Traffic Safety Assn. Detroit, 1959-66. Mem., trustee Ford Found.; mem., trustee, pres. Henry Ford Hosp., Detroit; trustee Dermatology Found.; bd. dirs. Detroit Symphony Orch., Traffic Safety Assn. Detroit, United Community Funds and Councils Am., Hwy. Users Fedn. for Safety and Mobility; hon. chmn., bd. dirs. Detroit United Found. Served as capt. USAAF, World War II. Republican. Episcopalian. Clubs: Country of Detroit, Detroit, Detroit Athletic, Economic, Grosse Pointe, University, Cap and Gown. Home: 635 Lake Shore Rd Grosse Pointe Shores MI 48236 Office: American Rd Dearborn MI 48121

FORD, BYRON EDWARD, lawyer; b. Columbus, O., Apr. 22, 1901; s. William John and Amanda Ella (Evans) F.; B.A., Ohio State U., 1923, LL.B., 1925; m. Marion Waldron, Aug. 26, 1932; children—Byron Edward, Charles W. Admitted to Ohio bar, 1925, since practiced in Columbus; partner firm Vorys, Sater, Seymour &

Pease. Dir. Va. Homes, Inc.; dir., sec. New Albany Savs. & Loan Assn. Trustee Columbus YMCA, Harding Hosp. Fellow Am. Bar Found. Am. Coll. Trial Lawyers; mem. Am., Ohio, Columbus bar assns., Am. Judicature Soc., Internat. Assn. Ins. Counsel. Methodist. Home: 5050 Kitzmiller Rd New Albany OH 43054 Office: 52 E Gay St Columbus OH 43215

FORD, CHARLES ALFRED, psychologist, editor; b. Columbus, O., Jan. 19, 1901; s. Charles and Florence (Kendall) F.; B.S., Ohio State U., 1923, M.A., 1926, Ph.D., 1930; m. Marion Lingo, Feb. 3, 1923; children—Charles Douglass, Robert Stanley. With Am. Rolling Mills Co. in employment dept. 1923-24; prin. Antwerp (O.) High Sch., 1924-25; supt. schs. Brown Twp., Miami County, O., 1925- 27; dir. research State Bur. Juvenile Research, Columbus, O., 1927- 29; prof. psychology Temple U., 1929-41, head dept., 1937-41, dir. Evening Coll. Liberal Arts and Evening Extension Div., 1935-41, adminstrv. asst. to pres., 1936-41; dean Temple U. Community Coll. and Tech. Inst., 1946-48; editor in chief, John C. Winston Co., 1948-52; v.p., editor-in-chief F.E. Compton Co., 1952—, chmn. editorial adv. bds. coordinator for Area Number 1, Penna Area Coll. Center Program, 1946-49; organized and operated Martin Coll., Rittenhouse and Sproul Colls. as emergency colls. Served as capt. USNR, 1941-46. Decorated Legion of Merit. An incorporator, bd. dirs. Philatelic Mus.; bd. mem. Naples Civic Assn., 1967-71, pres., 1968-70; trustee Edison Jr. Coll., Ft. Myers, Fla. Fellow Am., Pa., Ill. psychol. assns.; mem. A.A.A.S., N.Y. Acad. Scis. Presbyn. (elder 1969-70). Clubs: Skokie Country (Ill.); Franklin Inn (Phila.); Cliff Dwellers (Chgo.); Naples Athletic, Country (dir.; v.p. 1969-70), Royal Poinciana Golf, Naples Yacht (Naples, Fla.) Home: 400 Park Shore Dr Naples FL 33940 Office: 425 N Michigan Av Chicago IL

FORD, CLELLAN STEARNS, educator; b. Worcester, Mass., July 27, 1909; s. Leroy Stearns and Fanny Benedicta (Fisher) F.; Ph.B., Yale, 1931, Ph.D., 1935; m. Edna Sheppard Yates, June 10, 1932; children—Thomas Fisher, John Yates. B.P. Bishop mus. fellow, 1935-36; research asst. sociology Inst. Human Relations, Yale, 1936-39, dir. cross-cultural survey, 1946—. asst. prof. anthropology, 1940-46, asso. prof., 1946-51, prof., 1951—; asst. dir. Strategic Index of Americas, 1942-43; exec. dir. central orgn. Human Relations Area Files, Inc., 1949—, now pres. Prin. cons. peoples and problems of Pacific, Bd. Econ. Warfare. Served as lt. USNR, 1943-45; research mil. govt. activities Pacific. Decorated Bronze Star. Mem. Am. Anthrop. Assn., Eastern Sociol. Soc., Soc. Applied Anthropology, NRC, A.A.A.S., Am. Ethnol. Soc., Am. Acad. Polit and Social Sci.,Nat. Acad. Sci. (com. research in problems of sex), Sigma Xi. Author: Smoke From Their Fires, 1941; A Comparative Study of Human Reproduction, 1945; (with F.A. Beach) Patterns of Sexual Behavior, 1951; Contbr. articles profl. pubs. Home: 422 Whitney Av New Haven CT 06511

FORD, CORNELIUS WILLIAM, savs. and loan assn. exec.; b. Bingham, Utah, Oct. 16, 1918; s. John W. and Esther (Jones) F.; ed. pub. schs., Bingham; m. Anne Pecoraro, Jan. 18, 1945; children—Leanna Jo, William Douglas, John Christopher. Exec. v.p. Santa Maria Savs. & Loan Assn. (Cal.), 1947-56; pres. Central Savs. & Loan Assn., San Luis Obispo, Cal., 1956-60; exec. v.p. First Savs. & Loan Assn., Oakland, Cal., 1960-61, pres., dir., 1961-70; pres., dir. Gt. Western Financial Corp., Beverly Hills, Cal., 1964—, Gt. Western Savs. & Loan Assn., Los Angeles, 1964—; dir. Gt. Western Savs. & Loan So. Cal., Los Angeles, Gt. Western Savs. & Loan No. Hollywood, Great Western Savs. San Diego, First City Savs., Los Angeles. Served to 1st lt. USAAF, World War II; prisoner of war. Decorated Air medal, Purple Heart. Mem. Cal. Savs. and Loan League (past bd. dirs.) Home: 126 N Rockingham Rd Los Angeles CA 90049 Office: 9601 Wilshire Blvd Beverly Hills CA 90210

FORD, DENNIS B., Jr., educator; b. Decatur, Tex., Nov. 4, 1922; s. Dennis B. and Bertha (wheelock) F.; B.B.A., Tex. A. and I. U., 1948; M.B.A., Tex. Technol. U., 1950; Ph.D., U. Tex., Austin, 1958; m. F. LaNelle Brigance, Sept. 11, 1943; children—Betty Kathryn, Linda Frances. Instr., U. N.D., 1950-51; instr. W.Tex. State U., 1951-54; asst. prof., asst. dean Coll. Bus. Adminstrn., U. Tex., Austin, 1956-58; prof., dean Sch. Bus. Adminstrn., Tex. A. and I. U., Kingsville, 1958—. Served with inf., AUS, World War II; ETO. Found. for Econ. Devel. fellow, 1956. Mem. Beta Alpha Psi. Sigma Iota Epsilon, Delta Sigma Pi, Alpha Chi. Kiwanian. Baptist (chmn. bd. deacons). Home: 1226 W Henrietta St Kingsville TX 78363

FORD, DONALD HAINLINE, lawyer; b. Chgo., Dec. 5, 1906; s. Matthew Henry and Ethel (Griffith) F.; B.S., Ore. State U., 1929; J.D., U. Mich., 1932; m. Siri Ann Enegren, Aug. 22, 1934; children—Carol Ann (Mrs. Raymond D. McMullin), Barbara Jean (Mrs. Robert A. Harrington), Richard Donald. Admitted to Cal. bar, 1933; park ranger Lassen Volcanic Nat. Park, 1931-32; asso. firm Overton, Lyman & Prince, Los Angeles, 1933-41, partner,1941—. Exec. v.p., dir. Earle C. Anthony, Inc. Glacier Park Inc.; dir. W/W. Henry Co. Served with USAAF, 1941-46. Decorated Bronze Star. Presbyn. Home: 4079 Punta Alta Dr Los Angeles CA 90008 Office: 550 S Flower St Los Angeles CA 90017

FORD, DONALD HERBERT, psychologist, educator; b. Sioux City, Ia., Aug. 15, 1926; s. Herbert Owen and Esther (Sanow) F.; B.S., Kan. State U., 1948; M.S., 1951; Ph.D., Pa. State U., 1955; m. Carol Clark, May 30, 1948; children—Russell, Martin, Douglas, Cameron. Counselor, Kan. State U., 1948-52; asst. prof. psychology Pa. State U., University Park, 1955-64, asso. prof., 1964-67, asso. prof. human devel., 1967—, asst. dir. div. counseling, 1956-59; dir., 1959-67, dean Coll. Human Devel., 1967—. Served with USAAF, 1944-45. Mem. A.A.A.S., Am. Eastern, Pa. psychol. assns. Author: Systems of Psychotherapy; A Comparative Study, 1963. Contbr. chpt. to Ann. Rev. Psychology, 1966—. Home: Branch Rd Lemont, PA 16851. Office: Coll Human Devel Pa State U University Park PA 16802

FORD, EDWARD COFFIN, steel co. exec.; b. Pitts. Jan. 14, 1918; s. William Wallace and Edith Viola (Coffin) F.; B.S., Yale, 1939; LL.B., U. Pitts., 1942; m. Sarah Hosack Parrish, Nov. 4, 1950; children—William Parrish, Deborah Parrish, Thomas Coffin II, Isabel Jane, Edward Coffin. Admitted to Pa. bar, 1942; law clk. U.S. Dist. Ct., 1946-47; with Jones & Laughlin Steel Corp., 1948—, asst. sec., 1949-64, sec., 1964—, gen. counsel, 1971—. Dir. Ednl. Products Information Exchange, Councilman, Rosslyn Farms Borough. Served to 1st lt. AUS, 1942-45. Mem. Pitts. C. of C. (dir.), Allegheny County, Am., Pa. bar assns., Am. Iron and Steel Inst., Order of Coif, Phi Delta Phi. Presbyn. (elder). Clubs: Duquesne, University (Pitts.); Chartiers Country. Home: 94 Pilgrim Rd Rosslyn Farms Carnegie PA 15106 Office: 3 Gateway Center Pittsburgh PA 15230

FORD, ERNEST JENNINGS, entertainer; b. Bristol, Tenn., Feb. 13, 1919; s. Clarence and Maude (Long) F.; student Cin. Conservatory Music, 1939; m. Betty Jean Heminger, Sept. 18, 1942; children—Jeffrey Buckner, Brion Leanard. Pres. TEF, Inc., Bet. Ford Corp., San Francisco; TV show NBC Network, 1955-61; daytime TV show ABC, 1962-65; rec. artist Capitol Records, 1949—, outstanding records include 16 Tons. Served to lt. USAAF, World War II. Named col. personal staff Gov. of Tenn. Home: 819 Mitten Rd Burlingame CA 94010

FORD, F. RICHARDS, III, banker, lawyer; b. N.Y.C., June 12, 1928; s. Frank Richards and Cornelia W. (Burchell) F.; grad. cum laude, The Hotchkiss Sch., 1946; A.B., Princeton, 1950; LL.B., U. Va., 1952; grad. Comml. Bank Mgmt. Program, Columbia; m. Mary Hope Lewis, June 24, 1950; children—Emily Van Orden, Madison Lewis, F. Richard IV, Christopher Peale, Maria Hope. Admitted to Conn. bar, 1952; atty. firm Cummings & Lockwood, Stamford, Conn., 1953-60; cons. U.S. Dept. Def., Geneva, Switzerland, 1960-61; cons. Dept. State, Washington, 1961, U.S. Arms Control and Disarmament Agy., 1961-63; sec. State Nat. Bank of Conn., Bridgeport, 1962, v.p., sec., 1962-64, sr. v.p., sec., 1964—, head fiduciary div., 1967—. Chmn. Community Planning Com., Stamford, 1961; chmn. civil def. sub-com. Greenwich Citizens Com., 1962-63; mem. Joint Civilian Orientation Conf. #39, 1969; mem. dist. 11 Rep. Town Meeting, Greenwich, 1964. Trustee, Stamford br. U. Conn., 1960; mem. adv. bd. Homemaker Service, Stamford, 1963-66; pres. bd. trustees Greenwich Acad. Parents, 1963-66; trustee Rumsey Hall Sch., Washington, Conn., 1968-70. Mem. Am. Conn. bar assns. Presbyn. (ruling elder 1968-71). Clubs: Princeton (N.Y.C.), Round Hill, Greenwich Skating (Greenwich); Contemporary, Ausable. Home: Doubling Rd Greenwich CT 06830 Office: The State Nat Bank of Conn 2834 Fairfield Av Bridgeport CT 06605

FORD, FRANCIS J.W., judge; b. Boston, Mass. Dec. 23, 1882; s. Cornelius J. and Josephine (Murphy) F.; grad. Boston Latin Sch. 1900, Harvard Coll. 1904, Harvard Law Sch., 1906; m. Ann Cresswell, Mar. 6, 1916; 1 dau., Barbara Ford Carter. Admitted to Mass. bar, 1906, since practiced in Boston; mem. Boston City Council, 1917-22, pres. 1919; apptd. U.S. dist. atty. for Mass., Sept. 22, 1933; apptd. U.S. District Judge for Mass., June 27, 1938. Mem. Am., Boston bar assns., Am. Judicature Soc., Jud. Conf. U.S. Democrat. Catholic. Clubs: Harvard Varsity, Harvard (Boston). Home: 276 Marlborough St Boston MA 02116 Office: Federal Bldg Boston MA 02110

FORD, FRANKLIN LEWIS, educator, historian; b. Waukegan, Ill., Dec. 26, 1920; s. Frank Leland and Dorothy Elsey (Lewis) F.; A.B., U. Minn., 1942; M.A., Harvard, 1948, Ph.D., 1950; m. Eleanor Rose Hamm, Jan. 8, 1944; children—Stephen Joseph, John Franklin. Mem. faculty Bennington Coll., 1949-52; mem. faculty Harvard, 1953—, prof. history, 1959—, McLean prof. ancient and modern history, 1968—, dean faculty arts and scis., 1962-70. Fulbright research fellow, France, 1952-53; Guggenheim fellow, Germany, 1955-56; fellow Center Advanced Study Behavioral Scis., 1961-62. Trustee Bennington Coll. Served with OSS, AUS, 1943-46. Fellow Am. Acad. Arts and Scis.; mem. Am. Hist. Assn., Mass. Hist. Soc., Signet Soc., Phi Beta Kappa. Clubs: Harvard (N.Y.); Examiner (Boston). Author: Robe and Sword, 1953; Strasbourg in Transition, 1958; Europe, 1780-1830, 1970. Co- editor: Traditions of Western Civilization, 1966. Home: 12 Clifton St Belmont MA 02178

FORD, FREDERICK SLOANE, business exec.; b. Wyandotte, Mich., Jan. 27, 1899; s. John Battise and Helen (Sloane) F.; student U. of Mich., 1919-20; m. Esther Caulkins, June 16, 1921. Serving as member board directors Libby Owens Ford Co., Toledo, O. Trustee Detroit Citizens Research Council. Home: 275 Lakeshore Rd Grosse Pointe Farms MI 48236 Office: Ford Bldg Detroit MI 48226

FORD, FREDERICK WAYNE, lawyer; b. Bluefield, W.Va., Sept. 17, 1909; s. George Michael and Annie Laurie (Linn) F.; A.B., W.Va. U., 1930, J.D., 1934; m. Virginia Lee Carter, Aug. 12, 1933 (dec. Feb. 1958); 1 dau., Mary Carter; m. 2d, Mary Margaret Mahony, Oct. 11, 1959; 1 son, Frederick Wayne. Admitted to W.Va. Bar, 1934; D.C. bar, 1968; jr. partner Stathers & Cantrall, Clarksburg, 1934-39; atty. FSA, 1939-42, OPA, 1942, 46-47; atty. FCC, 1947-53, mem. FCC, 1957-65, chmn. 1960; 1st asst. to asst. atty. general Office Legal Counsel, Dept. Justice, 1953-56, acting asst. atty. gen. Office Legal Counsel, 1956-57; asst. dept. atty. gen. U.S., 1957; pres. Nat. Community TV Assn., 1965-69; sr. partner Pittman, Lovett, Ford, Hennessey and White, 1970—. Mem. Harrison County Republican Exec. Com., 1936. Served as maj. USAAF, 1942-46. Mem. Am., Fed. Communications bar assns., W.Va. State Bar, Am. Law Inst., Alexandria Assn. (pres. 1950-53), Phi Delta Phi, Sigma Chi, Scabbard and Blade. Episcopalian. Clubs: Young Republican of Harrison County (pres. 1939); Congressional Country; Capitol Hill. Editorial staff W.Va. U. Law Quar., 1932-33. Home: 316 Duke St Alexandria VA 22314 Office: 1819 H St NW Washington DC 20006

FORD, GEORGE BURT, lawyer; b. S. Bend, Ind., Oct. 1, 1923; s. George W. and Florence (Burt) F.; B.S. in Engring. Law, Purdue U., 1946; LL.B., Ind. U., 1949; m. Charlotte Ann Kupferer, June 12, 1948; children-John, Victoria, George, Charlotte. Admitted to Ind. bar, 1949, since practiced in S. Bend; partner firm Jones, Obenchain, Johnson, Ford & Pankow, 1953—; gen. counsel, dir. Shippers Dispatch, Inc.; atty. Bd. Aviation Commnrs. St. Joseph County, Ind., Humane Soc. St. Joseph County. Bd. dirs. Cancer Soc. St. Joseph County, 1965—, treas., 1969—; bd. dirs. Robert P. and Clara I. Milton Home. Served with AUS, 1943-45. Fellow Am. Coll. Probate Counsel; mem. Am., Ind., St. Joseph County bar assns., Phi Gamma Delta, Phi Delta Phi. Presbyn. (trustee 1966-68, elder 1967-70). Home: 1340 E Colfax Av South Bend IN 46617 Office: Am Nat Bank Bldg South Bend IN 46601

FORD, GEORGE HARRY, educator; b. Winnipeg, Canada, Dec. 21, 1914; s. Harry and Gertrude (Burgess) F.; B.A., U. Manitoba, 1936; M.A., U. Toronto, 1938; Ph.D., Yale, 1942; m. Patricia Murray, May 4, 1942; children—Leslie Margaret, Harry Seymour, Asso. prof. U. Cin., 1946-54, prof. 1954-58; vis. prof. U. Chgo., 1948, Johns Hopkins, 1949, U. B.C., 1953; prof. English, U. Rochester, 1958—, chmn. dept. 1960—. Served from lt. capt., Canadian Army, 1942-45. Recipient of a Guggenheim fellowship. Fellow Am. Council Learned Socs.; mem. Internat. Assn. Profs. English, Literary Club Cin., English Inst. Episcopalian. Author: Dickens and His Readers, 1955; The Norton Anthology of English Literature, 1962; Double Measure: D.H. Lawrence, 1965. Home: 2230 Clover St Rochester NY 14618

FORD GERALD R., congressman; b. Omaha, Neb., July 14, 1913; s. Gerald R. and Dorothy (Gardner) F.; A.B., U. Mich., 1935; LL.B., Yale, 1941; LL.D., Mich. State U., Albion Coll., Aquinas Coll., Spring Arbor Coll.; m. Elizabeth Bloomer, Oct. 15, 1948; children—Michael, John, Steven, Susan. Admitted to Mich. bar, 1941; practiced law at Grand Rapids, 1941-49; mem. law firm Buchen and Ford; mem. 81st-92d U.S. Congresses, 5th Dist. Mich., elected minority leader, 1965. Del. to Interparliamentary Union, Warsaw Poland, 1959, Belgium, 1961, Bilderberg Group Conf., 1962. Served as lt. comdr. USNR, 1942-46. Recipient Grand Rapids Jr. C. of C. Distinguished Service award, 1948; Distinguished Service Award as one of ten outstanding young men in U.S. by U.S. Jr. C. of C., 1950; Silver Anniversary All-Am., Sports Illustrated, 1959; Distinguished Congl. Service award Am. Polit. Sci. Assn., 1961. Mem. Am., Mich. State, Grand Rapids bar assns., Delta Kappa Epsilon, Phi Delta Phi. Republican. Episcopalian. Mason. Clubs: University, Peninsular (Kent County). Home: 1624 Sherman St SE Grand Rapids MI 49506 also 514 Crown View Dr Alexandria VA 22314 Office: US Capitol Bldg Washington DC 20515 also 425 Cherry St SE Grand Rapids MI 49502

FORD, GLENN (Gwyllyn Samuel Newton Ford), actor; b. Que., Can., May 1, 1916; s. Newton and Hannah Ford; ed. high sch., Santa Monica, Cal.; m. Eleanor Powell, Oct. 23, 1943 (div.); 1 son, Peter Newton; m. 2d, Kathryn Hays, March 27, 1966. Acting debut at age 4 in Tom Thumb's Wedding; stage mgr. Wilshire Theater, 1934; stage mgr., actor The Children's Hour, 1935, Golden Boy; on tour with John Beal in Soliloquy, 1938; actor Heaven with a Barbed Wire Fence, Twentieth Century-Fox Studio, 1939; with Columbia Pictures Corp., 1939-43, 45-53, free lance, 1953-55, Metro-Goldwyn Mayer, 1955—; films include The Desperados, Destroyer, 1943, A Stolen Life, 1946, Framed, 1947, Return of October, 1948, Interrupted Melody, 1955, Blackboard Jungle, 1955, Don't Go Near the Water, 1957, Imitation General, Cowboy, 1958, Torpedo Run, 1958, Trial, The Teahouse of the August Moon, Cimarron, 1961, Cry for Happy, 1961, The Courtship of Eddie's Father, 1963, The Rounders, 1965, Is Paris Burning?, 1966, The Money Trap, 1968, Rage, 1966. Served with USMCR, 1942-45. Named Number One Box Office Star in Am., ann. poll Motion Picture Herald, 1958. Home: 911 Oxford Way Beverly Hills CA 90210

FORD, H. ERNEST, banker. Vice pres. Fed. Res. Bank Richmond (Va.). Office: 9th and Franklin Sts Richmond VA 23213*

FORD, HAMILTON, physician; b. Goldthwaite, Tex., 1908; M.D., U. Tex., 1931. Intern, Charity Hosp., New Orleans, 1931-32; intern, John Sealy Hosp., 1932-33, now neuropsychiatrist; resident Galveston State Psychopsychiatry Hosp., 1933-35; fellow neurology sect. Mayo Clinic, Rochester, Minn., 1935; neuropsychiatrist St. Mary's Infirmary; past prof. neuropsychiatry U. Tex., chmn. dept. neurology and psychiatry Med. Br. Served as maj., M.C., AUS, 1942, Diplomate Am. Bd. Psychiatry and Neurology, 1939. Fellow Am. Psychiatry Assn. (past. speaker assembly dist. brs.); mem. A.M.A. (chmn. council mental health), So. Psychist. Assn. Address: 2501 Fairwood Dr La Marque TX 77568

FORD, HARRY XAVIER, coll. pres.; b. Seymour, Ind., Jan. 12, 1921; s. John William and Emma (Gibo) F.; A.B., U. Cal. at Los Angeles, 1949; M.A., Sacramento State Coll., 1953; grad. student higher edn., U. Cal. at Berkeley, 1962-67; m. Celeste K. C. deBaca, Aug. 8, 1945; children—John Damian, Anthony Alexius. Tchr. Placer Union High Sch., Auburn, Cal., 1950-53, Stuttgart (Germany) Am. High Sch., 1953-58; chmn. dept. tchr. edn. Cal. Coll. Arts and Crafts, Oakland, 1958-59, pres., 1959—. Adv. bd. Coordinating Council Higher Edn. Cal., 1966—. Chmn. Oakland-Piedmont Arts Council, 1966-68; mem. Alameda County Art Commn., 1966—; gov. bd. Oakland Museums Assn., 1966—, Oakland Repertory Theatre Assn., 1967-68. Museum West of Am. Craftsman Council, 1967-68. Served to capt. USAAF, 1942-45; maj. Res.; ETO. Decorated Air medal, Bronze Star; recipient 1st award watercolor AAUW competition, Auburn, Cal., 1953. One man show State Dept. Amerika Haus, Stuttgart, 1957; exhbns. include Kingsleey Art Show at Crocker Art Gallery, Sacramento, 1950. Mem. DeYoung Museum Soc. Democrat. Roman Cath. Home: 382 Admas St Oakland, CA 94610.

FORD, HENRY II, automobile mfr.; b. Detroit, Sept. 4, 1917; s. Edsel and Eleanor (Clay) F.; grad. Hotchkiss Sch., Lakeville, Conn., 1936; student Yale, 1936-40; m. Anne McDonnell, July 13, 1940 (div.); children—Charlotte, Anne, Edsel Bryant II; m. 2d, Marie Cristina Vettore Austin, Feb. 19, 1965. With Ford Motor Co., 1940—, v.p., 1943, exec. v.p., 1944-45, pres., 1945, chmn., chief exec. officer, 1960—, also dir. Chmn. Nat. Alliance of Businessmen, 1968-69; chmn. Nat. Center for Voluntary Action, 1970; mem. Bus. Council. Trustee Ford Found. Home: Grosse Pointe Farms MI 48236

FORD, HOWARD EGBERT, ret. utility exec.; b. Chgo., May 26, 1906; s. Reginald and Maude (Egbert) F.; B.S., U. Ill., 1927; m. Mary Dixie Brown, Mar. 16, 1946; children—Mary Dixie, Leslie Bearden. With No. Ill. Gas Co., and predecessors, Aurora, Ill., 1927-71, v.p., 1958-69, sr. v.p., 1969-71. Served from lt. (j.g.) to lt. USNR, 1943-45. Mem. Western Soc. Engrs., Chgo. Assn. Commerce and Industry. Clubs: Economic (Chgo.); River Forest Tennis. Home: 914 Keystone Av River Forest IL 60305

FORD, JAMES DAYTON, moving co. exec.; b. Harrisburg, Ill., May 31, 1924; s. J. Dayton and Anna (Dorris) F.; B.B.A., U. Mich., 1948, M.B.A., 1948; LL.B., 1951; m. Alice Maria Evans, June 9, 1944; children—Lynn Alice (Mrs. L. E. Frase), Katherine Anne, Anne Maria, Elizabeth Ellen, Jamie LaCene. Admitted to Ill. bar, 1952. Ariz. bar, 1960; tax. atty. U.S. Steel Corp. subsidiaries in Duluth, Minn. and Pitts., 1951-54; tax mgr. M. W. Kellogg Co., N.Y.C., 1954-58, Comml. Solvents Corp., N.Y.C., 1958-59; partner firm Hull, Terry & Ford, Tucson, 1960-66; gen. counsel Allied Van Lines, Broadview, Illinois, 1966-68, executive vice president, 1968- -. Served with Army of U.S., 1943-46. Mem. Am., Ariz., Pima County bar assns., Nat. Def. Transp. Assn., Nat. Rifle Assn., Delta Sigma Pi. Republican. Mem. Christian Ch. Clubs: Traffic (Chgo.); Civitan. Home: 144 Canary Rd Lombard IL 60148 Office: Allied Van Lines 25th Av and Roosevelt Rd Broadview IL 60153

FORD, JAMES LAWRENCE COLLIER, educator; b. Foochow, China, Apr. 7, 1907; (parents Am. citizens); s. Eddy Lucius and Effie (Collier) F.; A.B., Lawrence Coll., 1928; A.M., U. Wis., 1939; student Stanford, 1940, 41; Ph.D. (Coffman Meml. fellow 1945), U. Minn., 1948; m. Elsa Grimmer, Dec. 23, 1929; childrenJames Lawrence Collier, Frederick Eddy. Cable editor N.Y. bur. Chgo. Tribune, 1928-30; writer Fairchild Publs., N.Y., 1930; wire editor and cable editor N.Y. bur. U.P.I., 1931-37; asst. prof. U. Ore., 1939-40; instr., asst. prof. U. Cal., 1940-42; cable editor A.P., San Francisco, 1941-42; dean, prof. journalism Mont. State U., 1942-54; prof. journalism, dir. mag. sequence and creative writing workshop Sch. Communications, So. Ill. U., 1955—. Cons. editor Focus/Midwest mag. Mem. Am. Council on Edn. for Journalism, 1946. Mem. Am. Assn. U. Profs. (chpt. pres. 1947-48), Assn. Accredited Schs. and Depts. Journalism (nat. council on edn. for journalism, 1946) Internat. Assn. Bus. Communications, Phi Beta Kappa, Sigma Delta Chi, Phi Delta Kappa, Pi Delta Epsilon, Sigma Phi Epsilon, Kappa Tau Alpha. Methodist. Co-author: An Outline Survey of Journalism, 1937; Careers for Journalism, rev. edit., 1956; New Survey of Journalism, rev. edit., 1959; Magazines for Millions-the Story of Specialized Publications, 1969. Contbr. articles profl. publs., short stories to mags. Home: 807 Skyline Dr Carbondale IL 62901

FORD, JESSE HILL, writer; b. Troy, Ala., Dec. 28, 1928; s. Jesse Hill and Lucille (Musgrove) F.; B.A., Vanderbilt U., 1951; M.A., U. Fla., 1955; postgrad. (Fulbright scholar), U. Oslo (Norway), 1961-62; Litt.D. (hon.), Lambuth Coll., 1968; m. Sarah Anne Davis, July 20, 1951; children—Jay, Charles Davis, Sarah Ann, Elizabeth. Reporter, The Nashville Tennessean, 1950- 51; news writer Gen. Extension Div. of Fla., 1953-55; dir. pub. relations Tenn. Med. Assn., 1955-56; asst. dir. pub. relations A.M.A., Chgo., 1956- 57; fiction writer, Humboldt, Tenn., 1957—; vis. fellow Center for Advanced Study, Wesleyan U., Middletown, Conn., 1965; writer-in-residence, Memphis State U., 1969-71. Chmn. Nat. Library Week Tenn., 1968. Trustee Reelfoot Regional Libraries. Served with USNR, 1951-53. Atlantic grantee, 1959; Guggenheim fellow, 1966; included in O. Henry Prize Collection Short Stories, 1961-66, 67. Mem. Writers Guild Am. Episcopalian. Author: Mountains of Gilead, 1961; The Liberation of

Lord Byron Jones, 1965, screenplay (with Stirling Silliphant), 1969; The Feast of St. Barnabas, 1969; (short story collection) Fishes, Birds and Sons of Men, 1967; (play) The Conversion of Buster Drumwright, 1963. Address: Canterfield Farm Humboldt TN 38343

FORD, JOHN, (Sean O'Feeney), dir. motion pictures; b. Cape Elizabeth, Me., Feb. 1, 1895; s. Sean and Barbara (Curran) O'Feeney; Dr. Fine Arts. U. Me., 1939; M.A., Bowdoin Coll., Brunswick, Me., 1947; L.H.D., Brandeis U.; m. Mary McBryde Smith July 3, 1920; children—Patrick Roper, Barbara Nugent. Began as property man, Universal City, Cal., 1914; later became dir.; has directed more than 80 pictures for Universal-Fox, Metro-Goldwyn-Mayer, United Artists, Radio-RKO, latest being How the West Was Won, Seven Women. Served from lt. comdr. to capt., USNR, World War II, to rear adm., Korean War. Recipient N.Y. Critics Award 1935, 39, 40, 41; Acad. Motion Picture Arts and Sci. directorial award, 1935, 40, 41, 53; Acad. Awards for two documentaries made for Govt. while in Navy, "Midway," "December 7th." Decorated Legion of Merit, Purple Heart, Air medal; Chevalier Crown of Belgium; Knight Comdr. Italian Republic; Knights of Malta Legion of Honor. Democrat. Catholic. K.C. Clubs: Army and Navy (Washington and Manila, P.I.). Address: 321 S Beverly Dr Beverly Hills, CA 90212.

FORD, JOHN AMBROSE, automobile co. exec.; b. New Haven, June 21, 1920; s. John A. and Mabelle (Loomis) F.; B.A., Yale, 1941; M.A., State U. Ia., 1948; m. Virginia Anderson, Dec. 18, 1948; children—Cynthia, Gail, Marian, Thomas, John, James. Instr. communications and journalism State U. Ia., 1946-53; asst. dir. pub. relations dept. Pillsbury Co., Mpls., 1953-58; asst. dir. pub. relations Am. Cyanamid Co., Wayne, N.J., 1958-61, gen. mgr. pub. relations div., 1961-63; v.p. pub. relations Chrysler Corp., 1963—. Bd. dirs. United Found., Detroit, Cranbrook Sch., Bloomfield Hills, Mich. Mem. Pub. Relations Soc. Am. Clubs: Oakland Hills Country; Detroit Athletic; Yale (N.Y.C.). Home: 1081 Country Club Dr Bloomfield Hills MI 48013 Office: Chrysler Corp Detroit MI 48231

FORD, JOHN ANSON, former state ofcl.; b. Waukegan, Ill., Sept. 29, 1883; s. Rev. James Tooker and Sarah (Holmes) F.; A.B., Beloit Coll., 1907, LL.D., 1952; H.H.D. (hon.), Los Angeles Conservatory Music and Art, 1950; m. Lois Goldsmith, 1911; 1 son, John Arnold. Newspaper reporter, editor, 1911- 19; news writer Dept. Agr., Washington, 1919-20; mem. Hogg and Ford, advt. and pub. relations, 1920-27; head John Anson Ford Co., advt. and pub. relations, 1927-34; sr. mem. Ford-Long Co., Los Angeles, 1949-52; dir. pub. information for radio KRHM, 1959. Mem. Los Angeles Co. Bd. Suprs., 1934-58, chmn. bd., 1952-54, 57; pres. Los Angeles Coliseum Commn., 1952; acting chmn. Civic Center Authority, 1952; chmn. Cal. Fair Employment Practices Commn., 1959-63, commr., 1963-68. Mem. El Pueblo State Hist. Monument Commn. Chmn. co. central com. Democratic Party, 1936-38, mem. state central com., 1942-50, nat. committeeman from Cal., 1952-53; del. nat. convs., 1944, 48, 52, 56. Cal. chmn. Kefauver-for-Pres., 1952. Hon. dir. Hollywood Bowl, Los Angeles Art Inst., Las Fiestas de las Americas. Recipient Foundacion Internacional Eloy Alfaro medal for Inter-Am. friendship, 1950; judge Hollzer bronze award for inter-racial good-will, 1950; Golden Anniversary award Los Angeles Ch. Fedn., 1960; citation Japan Am. Citizens League, 1965. Mem. Japan Am. Soc. (pres. 1960-61), Death Valley 49ers (pres. emeritus), Sigma Chi, Delta Sigma Rho, Pi Sigma Alpha. Conglist. Author: Thirty Explosive Years in Los Angeles County, 1961. Home: 1976 N Normandie Av Los Angeles CA 90027.

FORD, JOHN BATTICE, Jr., corp. dir.; b. Wyandotte. Mich., Mar. 3, 1897; s. John Battice and Helen (Sloane) F.; ed. Sheffield Sci. Sch., Yale, 1918; LL.D., Wayne State U., 1956; m. Katherine Tanner, Oct. 4, 1920 (dec. May 1953); children—John B. III, Gordon T.; m. 2d. Mary Holland Sept. 12, 1956. Dir. Nat. Bank Detroit. Chmn. bd. dirs. Detroit Symphony Orch., Little Traverse Hosp. Assn.; trustee Henry Ford Hosp. Clubs: Detroit, Yondotega, Country (Detroit); Grosse Pointe; New York Yacht; Jupiter Island (Hobe Sound, Fla.). Home: 16638 E Jefferson Av Grosse Pointe MI 48236 Office: Ford Bldg Detroit MI 48226

FORD, JOHN JOSEPH, govt. ofcl.; b. Archibald, Pa., Mar. 30, 1927; s. John James and Florence Ruth (Caffrey) F.; B.A. with honors, George Washington U., 1950; m. Betty Boyle, Nov. 10, 1951; children—Sean Joseph, Brendan James. Served as congl. corr. Army Times Pub. Co., 1955-1965; exec. com. Periodical Press Gallery, U.S. Capitol, 1957-65; mem. profl. staff Subcom. for Spl. Investigations, Com. on Armed Services, U.S. Ho. Reps., 1965-66, profl. staff mem. Com. Armed Services, 1966—. Chmn. commn. on future govt. of Vienna, Va., 1959-60; mem. Town Council, Vienna, 1960-63. Served with USNR, 1945-46. Mem. Phi Delta Epsilon. Club: Nat. Press (Wash.). Author: The Ramparts We Watch, 1964. Home: 1110 Westbriar Ct NE Vienna VA 22180 Office: Rayburn Bldg Washington DC 20525

FORD, JOHN THOMAS, r.r. ofcl.; b. N.Y.C., May 15, 1923; s. John Thomas and Josephine (Corkill) F.; B.S. cum laude, U. Notre Dame, 1947; m. Mary Elizabeth Gleason, Sept. 23, 1950; children—Ann Gleason, Mary Elizabeth, John Thomas III, Margaret Ellen. Sr. accountant Haskins & Sells, C.P.A.'s, N.Y.C., 1947-51; with C. & O. Ry., 1951-63; dep. comptroller B. & O. R.R., 1963-64; comptroller C.& O. B. & O. R.R., Balt., 1964-67, asst. v.p., 1968—. Served with USAAF, World War II. Decorated Air medal with four oak leaf clusters. Home: 21 St Ives Dr Severna Park MD 21146 Office 2 N Charles St Baltimore MD 21201

FORD, JOHN WILLIAM, govt. ofcl.; b. Louisville, Ky., May 19, 1920; s. John M. and Leila (Waters) F.; student U. Louisville. 1939-40, Jefferson Law Sch., Louisville, 1940-42, 46-47. FBI Acad., Quantico, Va., 1943; grad. Nat. War Coll., 1961; m. Mercedes Barreda, Jan. 13, 1945; children—John Henry, Douglas William, Walter Paul, Richard Anthony, Glen Michael, Robert James. With FBI, Dept. Justice, 1939-44, 46-47; attache U.S. embassy, Caracas, Venezuela, 1947-49, Mexico City, 1949-50, Paris, France, 1950-51; asst. chief, then chief div. security Dept. State, 1952, dir. Office of Security, 1953; attaché Am. embassy, Manila, 1954- 55, 1st sec., consul, 1955-56; 1st sec., consul Mexico City, 1956- 60, assigned to Dept. State, Washington. 1960—, exec. sec. policy planning council, 1962-64, dir. Office Inter-Am. Polit. Affairs, 1967-70; consul gen., Barcelona, Spain, 1964-67; minister counselor U.S. Permanent Mission to OAS, Washington, 1971—. Alternate U.S. mem. Inter-Am. Peace Com., 1967-70, Inter-Am. com. Alliance for Progress, 1970—. Served with C.I.C., U.S. Army, 1944-46. Recipient Commendable Service award Dept. State, 1958, 61, Meritorious Service award, 1964; Cruz y Placa, Defensores de la Republica y Sus Descendientes, Mexico, 1960. Home: 104 W Myrtle St Alexandria VA 22301

FORD, JOSEPH, educator; b. Asheville, N.C., Dec. 18, 1927; s. Charles R. and Belle (Feagle) F.; B.S., Ga. Inst. Tech., 1952; Ph.D., Johns Hopkins, 1956; m. Mary Caroline Lindsay, Nov. 23, 1951; children—Diane, Mark Lindsay, James Michael. Research physicist Union Carbide Co., Niagara Falls, N.Y., 1956-58; asst. prof. U. Miami, Coral Gables, Fla., 1958-60; vis. prof. Johns Hopkins, 1960-61; asso. prof. Ga. Inst. Tech., Atlanta, 1961-66, prof., 1966—; cons. Oak Ridge Nat. Labs., 1964—. Served with USNR, 1946-48. Fellow A.A.A.S.; mem. Am. Phys. Soc., Am. Assn. U. Profs. Contbr. articles profl. jours. Home: 1073 Northcliffe Dr NW Atlanta GA 30318

FORD, JOSEPH BRANDON, educator, sociologist; b. Los Angeles, Jan. 20, 1918; s. William Joseph and Cecilia (Chambers) F.; B.A. with highest honors, U. Cal. at Los Angeles, 1937; M.A., U. So. Cal., 1941; M.A., Harvard, 1947; Ph.D., U. Cal. at Berkeley, 1951; m. Marjorie Henshaw, Dec. 11, 1948; children—Anabel Deirdre, Cecelia Elinore, Stephen Joseph Jerome. Social worker, later social service supr. and supr. Cal. Bur. Personnel Audits, 1939-40; vocational counsellor VA, 1946; spl. agt. War Assets Adminstrn., 1946-48; real estate broker, later v.p., dir. Morgage Credit Corp., 1948-50; instr. Los Angeles City Coll., 1948-49; asst. prof. to prof. Los Angeles State Coll., 1950-58; prof. sociology San Fernando Valley State Coll., Northridge, Cal., 1958—, chmn. dept. sociology and anthropology, 1958-65; vis. prof. U. Cal. at Berkeley, 1951, U. Cal. at Santa Barbara, 1955, U. Rome, 1955-56, U. Vienna, 1958-59, Nat. U. Mexico, 1960; Fulbright fellow, vis. prof. U. Madrid, 1961-62, Am. U. Beirut (Lebanon), 1965-66; cons. Inacasa Housing program, Italy, 1956; commr. city planning City of Los Angeles, 1961-63; sociol. adv. com. Cal. Dept. Edn., 1963—. Served to lt. USNR, 1942-46. Fulbright fellow, 1955-56, 58-59, 61-62, 65-66; NSF Instnl. grant for urban research, 1965; recipient East-West program grant for research in Poland, Ford Found and Inst. Internat. Edn., summer 1959. Fellow Am. Sociol. Soc., Institut Internat. de Sociologie (councillor, mem. governing bur. 1963—; exec. sec. internat. sci. commn., treas. 1967—), Internat. Sociol. Assn., Pacific Sociol. Soc., Instituto de Estudies Politicos U. Madrid, Phi Beta Kappa, Alpha Kappa Delta. Author: (with others) Contemporary Sociology, 1958; (with others) Contemporary American Sociology, 1961; (with C. C. Zimmerman) Sociology of Change, 1965; (with Allen, Toynbee, others) Sorokin in Review, 1963; Bibliographic Introduction to Urban Sociology, 1964; Comte and Positivism, 1968; Historical Statistics: Uses, Limits, Potentials, 1968; Toward Humanistic Science, 1968; Methodology of Macrosociology, 1969; Work of Sorokin, 1969. Regional editor for N.Am.; Sociologia Internationalis. Contbr. sci. articles profl. jours. Home: 18247 Ludlow St Northbridge CA 91324

FORD, JOSEPH FRANCIS, educator; b. Phila., Mar. 16, 1919; s. John Joseph and Anne (Schneider) F.; B.S. in Commerce with highest honors, Drexel Inst. Tech., 1941; M.B.A. magna cum laude, U. Pa., 1950; m. Janet Bruce Weiler, Apr. 18, 1942; children—Emille Louise, Linda Jean. With Curtis Pub. Co., 1938, Scott Paper Co., 1939, Joseph H. McGrath & Co., C.P.A.'s, Phila., 1940- 41; mem. faculty Drexel U., 1946—, prof. accounting, 1952—, dir. M.B.A. program, 1951-66, asso. dean Coll. Bus. Adminstrn., 1966—, acting dean, 1970-71. Vice pres. Home and Sch. Assn. Drexel Hill Sch. Served to lt. col. AUS, 1941-46; ETO. Decorated Bronze Star. C.P.A., Pa. Mem. Am., Pa. insts. C.P.A.'s, Financial Execs. Inst., Res. Officers Assn., Scabbard and Blade, Phi Kappa Phi, Beta Gamma Sigma, Sigma Rho. Republican. Presbyn. (pres. trustees). Author: (with others) Principles of Accounting, 1954. Home: 1221 Cornell Av Drexel Hill PA 19026 Office: Drexel Univ 32d and Chestnut Sts Philadelphia PA 19104

FORD, KENNETH W., mfg. exec.; b. Asoton, Wash., Aug. 4, 1908; s. Clair H. and Ora (Randolph) F.; student pub. schs.; m. Hallie E. Brown, June 16, 1936; children—Carmen, Allyn. Owner and pres. Roseburg Lumber Co., 1936—. Mem. Ore. Trade Mission to Japan, 1964. Pres. Hosp. Bd.; past mem. adv. bd. local Salvation Army; bd. dirs., treas. Linfield Coll.; trustee Ore. Grad. Center. Mem. C. of C. (past pres.), Am. Plywood Assn. (past dir.), Nat. Lumber Mfrs. Assn. (com. indsl. needs), Western Wood Products Assn. (v.p. bd. govs. dist. 6). Elk, Rotarian. Home: 415 W Madrone Av Roseburg OH 45362 Office: Roseburg Lumber Co Roseburg OH 45362

FORD, KENNETH WILLIAM, physicist, educator; b. West Palm Beach, Fla., May 1, 1926; s. Paul Hammond and Edith (Timblin) F.; student John Carroll U., 1945, U. Mich., 1945-46; A.B., Harvard, 1948; Ph.D., Princeton, 1953; m. Joanne Baumunk, June 9, 1962; children—Paul T., Sarah E. (by previous marriage), Caroline, Adam, Jason, Lucas; 1 stepdau., Nina. Research asst. Los Alamos Sci. Lab., 1950-51; research asso. Princeton, 1951-52; research asso. Ind. U., 1953-54, asst. prof., 1954-1957, asso. prof., 1957-58; asso. prof. Brandeis U., 1958-1961, prof., 1961-64; prof. physics U. Cal. at Irvine, 1964-70, chmn. dept., 1964-68; prof. physics U. Mass., Boston, 1970—. Served USNR, 1944-46. Fulbright fellow Max Planck Inst., Germany, 1955-56; NSF Sr. Postdoctoral fellow Imperial Coll., London, also Mass. Inst. Tech., 1961- 62. Fellow Am. Phys. Soc., A.A.A.S.; mem. Am. Assn. Physics Tchrs. (pres. 1972), Fedn. Am. Scientists (commr. coll. physics 1968-71). Author: The World of Elementary Particles, 1963; Basic Physics, 1968. Bd. editors Phys. Rev., 1960-62. Contbr. articles on nuclear physics and field theory to tech. publs. Home: 27 Newton St Weston MA 02193 Office: Physics Department University Mass Boston MA 02116

FORD, LOGAN, lawyer; b. Dallas, Oct. 19, 1906; s. George Brown and Laura Louise (Maddox) F.; A.B. in Chemistry and Math., So. Methodist U., 1927, LL.B., 1930; m. Catherine McBride, Nov. 1, 1934; children—Catherine Lee (Mrs. A.L. Pierce, Jr.), Virginia Ann (Mrs. Bartholow), Jane Logan (Mrs. Steven L. Davis). Admitted to Tex. bar, 1930, since practiced in Dallas; now mem. firm Burford, Ryburn & Ford, and predecessor. Mem. Am. Coll. Trial Lawyers, Am., Tex., Dallas bar assns., Tex. Assn. Def. Attys., Internat. Assn. Ins. Counsel, Lambda Chi Alpha, Delta Theta Phi. Author articles. Home: 3908 Shannon Lane Dallas TX 75205 Office: Fidelity Union Life Bldg Dallas TX 75201

FORD, LYMAN SEDGWICK, social worker, orgn. exec.; b. Baldwinsville, N.Y., Jan. 28, 1909; s. George Lyman and Katherine (Sedgwick) F.; A.B., Denison U., 1931; M.A., Ohio State U., 1937, L.H.D., 8 children—Barbara Elizabeth (Mrs. Edmund J. Thelen), James Lyman. Pub. relations dir. Community Fund and Council Social Agys., Columbus, O., 1932- 33; exec. sec. Community Chest, Kansas City, Kan., 1933-38; exec. sec. Community Chest, Council Social Agys., Evanston, Ill., 1938-42; dir. health and welfare planning United Community Funds and Councils Am., 1942-50, asso. exec. dir., 1950-60, exec. dir., 1960-70. Trustee Denison U.; bd. dirs. Nat. Information Bur. Recipient Alumni citation Denison U., 1953. Mem. Nat. Assn. Social Workers, Nat. Conf. Social Welfare (exec. com. 1957-59), Kappa Sigma. Club: Scarsdale (N.Y.) Golf. Address: 518 Caswell Rd Chapel Hill NC 27514

FORD, MORGAN, judge U.S. Customs Ct.; b. nr. Wheatland, N.D., Sept. 8, 1911; s. Morgan J. and Mary (Langer) F.; B.A., U. North Dakota, 1935; LL.B., Georgetown U., 1938; m. Margaret Duffy, July 30, 1955; children—William, Patrick and Michael (twins), Mary Ellen. Tchr., Dist. 102, Everest Twp., Cass Co., N.D., 1933-34; state mgr., Royal Union Fund, Des Moines, Ia., 1938-39; in gen. law practice, Fargo, N.D., 1939-49; pres. Surety Mut. Health & Accident Ins. Co., Fargo, 1939- 49; v.p., 1st State Bank of Casselton, N.D., 1941-49; judge U.S. Customs Ct., 1949—. City atty., Casselton, 1942-48; mem. adv. bd. for registrants in selective service, 1942. Address: US Customs Court 1 Federal Plaza New York City NY 10007

FORD, NEVIL, investment banker; b. Boston, Apr. 18, 1891; s. Edwin and Anne Paddock (Hopkins) F.; student Chestnut Hill (Mass.) Sch., 1903, Volkmann Sch., Boston, 1909; B.S., Harvard, 1913; m. Louise McAlister, Aug. 6, 1917. Factory worker and salesman, A. H. Davenport Co., Boston, 1914; securities salesman, Jackson & Curtis, 1915-20; with First Boston Corp., 1921-60, mem. exec. com., 1935-56, sr. v.p., 1950-56, dir., 1935-60; pres., dir. Huntington Purchase, Inc., 1945-69; dir. and chmn. bd.; mem. exec. com. Huntington Fed. Savs. & Loan Assn.; dir., treas., mem. exec. com. Fgn. Bondholders Protective Council, Inc.; v.p., dir. 825 Fifth Av. Corp. Trustee, mem. exec. and finance coms., chmn. audit com., N.Y.U.- Bellevue Med. Center; chmn. N.Y. Univ.-Bellevue Med. Fund, 1947-51. Pres., dir. Peoples Symphony Concerts, N.Y. Dir. North Suffolk chpt. A.R.C.; bd. dirs., mem. exec. com. Netherlands-Am. Found. Served as lt. (j.g.), U.S. Naval Flying Corps. 1918-19. Served as state adminstr. for Defense Saving0; staff N.Y., U.S. Treas. Dept., 1941. Exec. mgr. War Finance Com., N.Y. U.S. Treas. Dept., 1942-43, chmn., 1944-45. Chmn. and dir. Armed Forces Convalescent Services, Huntington, since 1945. Mayor Village Lloyd Harbor, 1950-58. Dir., pres. Pub. Health Research Inst. City of N.Y., Inc., L.I. Biol. Assn. (chmn., dir., mem. exec. com.). Dir. Huntington Township YMCA; chmn. trustees com. Univ. Hosp., 1964-66; adv. com. Pub. Health Practice Research Center, N.Y.C. Dept. Health; bd. dirs. Better Bellevue Assn.; overseers vis. com. for biology Harvard Coll., 1964-70. Mem. Med. and Health Research Assn. N.Y.C. (dir. until 1970), N.Y. Panel Arbitrators, N.Y. Stock Exchange (dir.), Nat. Assn. Securities Dealers, Assn. Crippled Children (dir.; exec. com., chmn.), Am. Shakepeare Festival Theater and Acad. (dir.), Nat. Health Council (dir.), Council on Fgn. Relations, Italy-Am. Soc. (dir.), PanAm. Soc., Philharmonic Symphony Soc. of N.Y. (dir.), Huntington (N.Y.) C. of C. Clubs: Huntington (N.Y.) Country; Harvard (Boston); Lloyd Neck Bath (Huntington, N.Y.), Harvard (N.Y.C.); Bankers of Am., Bond (former pres.; N.Y. City). Home: PO Box 67 Cold Spring Harbor NY 11724 also 825 Fifth Av New York City NY 10021 Office: care First Boston Corp 20 Exchange Pl New York City NY 10005

FORD, NEWELL F., educator; b. Portland, Ore., Mar. 10, 1912; s. Olin F. and Esma (Newell) F.; B.A., Reed Coll., 1936; M.A., Harvard, 1938; Ph.D., U. Cal. at Berkeley, 1945; m. Alysoun Huntley, Mar. 21, 1941 (div. 1967). Mem. faculty Stanford, 1945—, prof. English, 1963—. Mem. Modern Lang. Assn., Keats-Shelley Assn. Author: The Prefigurative Imagination of John Keats, 2d edit., 1966; also articles. Home: 244 Santa Rita Palo Alto CA 94301 Office: Stanford Univ Stanford CA 94305

FORD, O'NEIL, architect; b. Pink Hill, Tex., Dec. 3, 1905; s. Bert and Lula Belle (Sinclair) F.; student N. Tex. U., 1924-26; D.F.A. (hon.), Trinity U., 1967; m. Wanda Graham, Aug. 29, 1940; children—Wanda (Mrs. Philip Childs), Michael O'Neil, Linda (Mrs. Terrence Loughrey), John Douglas. Draftsman David R. Williams, Dallas, 1926-30; pvt. practice architecture, 1930-33; with Rural Resettlement Adminstrn., 1933-36; architect Ford & Swank, Dallas, 1936-39, Ford & Rogers, San Antonio, 1939-53, O'Neil Ford & Assos., San Antonio, 1953-65; partner Ford, Powell & Carson, San Antonio, 1965—; dir. Citizens Nat. Bank; Ward-Lucas lectr. Carleton Coll., 1971; cons. Corps of Engrs., 1967—; prin. works include campus site and bldgs. Skidmore Coll., Trinity U., Tower of Americas, concept design U. Tex. at San Antonio. Mem. Nat. Council on the Arts, 1968—; chmn. bd. dirs. 1st Repertory Theatre, San Antonio, 1971-72. Mem. vis. com. Harvard, 1953-61, Mass. Inst. Tech., 1959-62. Served with USAAF, 1942-45. Thomas Jefferson Meml. fellow U. Va., 1967. Fellow A.I.A. Club: Argyle (San Antonio). Home: 7 Willow Way San Antonio TX 78214 Office: 528 King William St San Antonio TX 78204

FORD, PAUL, actor; b. Balt., Nov. 2, 1901; s. Louis Clarence and Effie (Ford) Weaver; m. Nell Campbell, Dec. 27, 1924; children—Paul, Jean (Mrs. Harold Priest), Katherine (dec.), Lois (Mrs. Jean Goehrig), Donald. Broadway appearances include Decision, Another Part of the Forest, Command Decision, Thurber Carnival, Teahouse of the August Moon, Never Too Late, Bascom Barlow; motion picture appearances include House on 92d Street, Lust for Gold, The Matchmaker, Teahouse of the August Moon, Advise and Consent, Music Man, Never Too Late, Big Hand for the Little Lady, The Russians Are Coming, The Russians Are Coming, The Comedians, Help Stamp out Fairplay; various television appearances, including The Bilko Show, others; pres. Grandandy Prodns., Inc., N.Y.C., 1964—. Mem. Actors Equity (past mem. council), Screen Actors Guild, A.F.T.R.A. Club: Players (N.Y.C.). Address: 37 W 12th St New York City NY 10011.

FORD, PAUL CHARLES, elec. co. exec.; b. Flora, Ind., Apr. 15, 1915; s. Charles C. and Eva (Miller) F.; student DePauw U., 1935; B.S., Purdue U., 1937; m. Katherine Farquhar, Aug. 3, 1940. With Wagner Electric Corp., St. Louis, 1937—, successively transformer engr., supr. unit substa. and dry type transformer engring., asst. mgr. transformer engring. dept., chief elec. engr., exec. engr., 1937-58, v. p. engring., 1958-66, exec. v. p., 1966—. Mem. Am. Inst. E.E., Soc. Automotive Engrs., Assn. Iron and Steel Engrs., Am. Ordnance Assn., Engrs. Club St. Louis, Beta Theta Pi. Methodist. Home: 6 Burroughs Lane Ladue MO 63124 Office: 6400 Plymouth Av St Louis MO 63133

FORD, QUINTON U., banker. Sr. v.p. investment dept. Bankers Trust Co., N.Y.C. Office: 280 Park Av New York City NY 10017*

FORD, R. H., steel co. exec.; b. 1924; B.S.L., U. Minn., 1948, J.D., 1949. Admitted to N.D. bar, 1950, Ill. bar, 1951; law clk. firm Meagher, Gier & Markham, 1949; asso. prof. U. N.D. Law Sch., 1949-51; asso. firm Levinson, Becker & Peebles, 1951-56; sr. partner Peebles, Greenberg, Keeles, Lunn & Ford, 1957-69; pres., chief exec. officer Fansteel Inc., North Chicago, Ill., 1969—, also dir. Served with USNR, 1942-43, USMCR, 1943-46. Office: One Tantalum Pl North Chicago IL 60064*

FORD, RICHARD, lawyer; b. Ypsilanti, Mich., Nov. 22, 1903; s. Richard Clyde and Grace Augusta (Cogshall) F.; student U. Montpellier (France), 1922; A.B., Eastern Mich. U., 1923; J.D., U. Mich., 1926; m. Janet Hankinson, Sept. 21, 1931; children—Thomas Clyde, Janet Grace (Mrs. Donald J. Campbell), Mary Ainslie (Mrs. Neal A. Talbot). Admitted to Mich. bar, 1926, since practiced in Detroit; partner firm Fischer, Franklin & Ford, 1942—; instr. Detroit Coll. Law, 1957—. Mem. Am., Detroit (bd. dirs. 1956-62), Oakland County bar assns., State Bar Mich., Am. Coll. Trial Lawyers. Republican. Methodist. Contbr. legal publs. Home: 4555 Pickering Rd Birmingham MI 48010 Office: Guardian Bldg Detroit MI 48226

FORD, RUBYE LOUISE, banker; b. Buhl, Ala.; d. Samuel Emmett and Maude (Gramling) Food; student Florence State Normal, 1923; standard certificate Am. Inst. Banking, 1957; m. William Wilson Peebles, July 5, 1931 (div. May 1935). With Bank for Savs. & Trust, Birmingham, Ala., 1924-63, asst. treas., 1941-43, treas., 1943-63; cashier Birmingham Trust Nat. Bank, 1963—. Mem. Nat. Assn. Bank Women, Am. Inst. Banking (past pres., v.p., treas., dir.), Women's Jr. Co. of C. (past pres., v.p., treas., finance chmn., dir.). Baptist. Clubs:

Women's Com. of 100 for Birmingham (treas. 1964- 70), Downtown, Relay House. Home: 508 Town House 2008 8th Av S Birmingham AL 35233 Office: PO Box 2554 Birmingham AL 35202

FORD, T. MITCHELL, corp. exec.; b. Albany, N.Y., Apr. 27, 1921; s. Clarence Edwin and Alice (Mitchell) F.; grad. Hotckiss Sch., 1939; A.B., Harvard, 1943; LL.B., Yale, 1948; m. Mimi Parsons, Oct. 4, 1944; children—Kyle (Mrs. L.B. Schutz), Mitchell P. Admitted to Conn. bar, 1949; with firm Becket & Wagner, Lakeville, Conn., 1948-52; asst. gen. counsel CIA, 1952-55; gen. counsel Naugatuck Valley Indsl. Council, Waterbury, Conn., 1955-58; with Emhart Corp., and predecessor Am. Hardware Corp., Hartford, Conn., 1958—, gen. counsel 1960-64, v.p., 1964-67, pres., 1967—, also dir.; dir. Hartford Nat. Bank & Trust Co., Hartford Nat. Corp., Terry Corp. of Conn. Steam Turbine Co., United Aircraft Corp., Block Island Power Co., Veeder Industries, Inc. Bd. dirs. Mfrs. Assn. Hartford County; bd. corporators Hartford Hosp., Inst. for Living of Hartford, New Britain Hosp. Served with AUS, 1943-45; ETO. Clubs: Shuttle Meadow Country; New Britain. Home: 45 Windsor Rd New Britain CT 06052 Office: PO Box 1620 Hartford CT 06102

FORD, THOMAS ROBERT, ret. air force officer; b. Edgetts, Mich., Nov. 4, 1914; s. Thomas W. and Alma (Goldammer) F.; student Ferris Inst., Big Rapids, Mich., 1932, Mich. State Normal Sch., Ypsilanti, 1934-37; B.A. in Bus. Administrn., Mich. State Coll., 1938; grad. primary and basic flying tng., Randolph Fields, Tex., 1939, advanced tng., Kelly Field, Tex., 1939, Armed Forces Staff Coll., 1951; m. Mariiyn June Gunnell, Nov. 29, 1939; children—Thomas Robert, Jacqueline Kay, Barbara Ann. Commd. 2d lt. USAAF, 1939, advanced through grades to maj. gen., 1965; various assignments U.S., Panama and Dutch W. Indies, 1939-43; operations officer Hdqrs. 416th Bomb Group, Lake Charles, La., 1943, dep. comdr., Laurel, Miss., 1943, dep. comdr., ETO. 1944; group comdr. Hdqrs. 409th Bomb Group, ETO, 1944- 45, group comdg. officer, Westover Field, Mass., 1945; base comdg. officer, Lake Charles, 1945-46; dep. operations Hdqrs. 9th Air Force. Biggs AFB, also Greenville AFB, S.C., 1946-47; chief combat tng. br. TUSAFG, Ankara, Turkey, 1947-48; chief air tng. div. 1140th USAF FM group, Ankara, 1948-50; mem. Joint Adv. Planning Staff, Ankara, 1950; chief TAC air. br., commands div., dep. chief staff operations Hdqrs. USAF, 1951, asst. chief commands div., 1951-52; dep. chief operations plans div. Hdqrs. USAF, 1952-54; wing comdr. Hdqrs. 461st Bomb Wing, Hill AFB, Utah, 1954-56, wing comdr., Blytheville AFB, Ark., 1956-58; div. comdr. 837th Air Div., Shaw AFB, S.C., 1958-60; dep. for operations 9th Air Forces, Shaw AFB, 1960-61; comdr. 41st Air Div., Johnson Air Sta., Japan. 1961-62, 6100th Support Wing, Iachikawa Air Base, Japan, 1962-64; dep. chief staff material Hdgrs. Air Def. Command, Ent. AFB, Colo., 1964-69; ret., 1969. Decorated D.S.M., Legion of Merit, D.F.C., Air medal with 4 oak leaf clusters, Bronze Star; Croix de Guerre (France and Belgium). Mem. Order Daedalians. Home: 500 Camino Del Bosque N W Alburquerque NM 87114

FORD, THOMAS ROBERT, educator, sociologist; b. Lake Charles, La., June 24, 1923; s. Gervais w. and Alma (Weil) F.; B.S., La. State U., 1946, M.A., 1948; Ph.D., Vanderbilt U., 1951; m. Harriet Lowrey, Aug. 13, 1949; children—Margaret Erin, Janet Patricia, Mark Lowrey, Charlotte Elizabeth. Instr. sociology La. State U., 1948-49; asst. prof. U. Ala., 1950-53; supervisory analytical statistician (demography) USAF Personnel and Tng. Research Center, Maxwell AFB, Ala., 1953-56; faculty U. Ky., Lexington, 1956—, prof. sociology, 1960—, chmn. dept., 1966-70. Research dir. So. Appalachian Studies, Inc., 1957-62. Mem. Pres.'s Nat. Adv. Com. on Rural Poverty, 1966-67; sr. adviser Colombian Assn. Faculties Medicine, Bogota, 1970—. Bd. dirs. Council So. Mountains. Served with USAAF. 1943-45. Decorated Air medal with 6 oak leaf clusters. Guggenheim fellow, 1962. Mem. A.A.A.S. Am. Sociol. Assn., Population Assn. Am., Rural (v.p. 1966-67). So. sociol. socs. Author: Man and Land in Peru, 1955; Health and Demography in Kentucky 1964. Editor: The Southern Appalachian Region: A Survey, 1962; The Revolutionary Theme in Contemporary America, 1965; (with Gordon DeJong) Social Demography, 1970. Home: 1107 Eldemere Rd Lexington KY 40502

FORD, WENDELL HAMPTON, state govt. ofcl.; b. Owensboro, Ky., Sept. 8, 1924; s. Ernest M. and Irene (Schenk) F.; student U. Ky., 1942-43; grad. Md. Sch. Ins., 1947; m. Jean Neel, Sept. 18, 1943; children—Shirley Jean, Steven. Partner Gen. Ins. Agy., Owensboro, 1959—; chief asst. to gov. (Ky.), 1960; mem. Ky. Senate, 1966-67; lt. gov. Ky., 1967—. Chmn. Legislative Research Commn., Ky.; mem. Ky. Property and Bldgs. Commn., Ky. Turnpike Authority. Served with AUS, 1944-46; Ky. Nat. Guard, 1949-62. Mem. Ky. (pres. 1954-55), U.S. jr. chambers commerce (pres. 1956-57), Jr. C. of C. Internat. (v.p. N.Am. 1958-59), U.S. C. of C. (bd. dirs. 1956-57). Democrat. Baptist, Elk. Home: 333 Maple St Owensboro, KY 42301. Office: State Capitol Bldg Frankfort KY 40601

FORD, WILLIAM CLAY, motor exec.; b. Detroit, Mar. 14, 1925; s. Edsel Bryant and Eleanor (Clay) F.; B.S., Yale, 1949; m. Martha Firestone, June 21, 1947; children—Martha, Sheila, William Clay, Elizabeth. Sales and advt. staff Ford Motor Co., 1949, indsl. relations, labor negotiations with U.A.W., 1949, quality control mgr. gas turbine engines Lincoln-Mercury div., Dearborn, Mich., 1951, mgr. spl. product operations, 1952, v.p., 1953, gen. mgr. Continental div., 1954, group v.p. Lincoln and Continental divs., 1955, v.p. prodn. planning and design, 1956—, dir., 1948- -. Pres., owner Det. Lions Profl. Football Club; chmn. Edison Inst., Edsel B. Ford Inst. for Med. Research; trustee Thomas A. Edison Found.; sec.-treas. Henry Ford Hosp.; dir. Dearborn Y.M.C.A.; mem. bd. Girl Scouts Am. Mem. Soc. Automotive Engrs. (asso.), Automobile Old Timers, Phelps Assn., Psi Upsilon. Mason (K.T.). Home: Grosse Pointe MI 48236 Office Ford Motor Co Dearborn MI 48121

FORD, WILLIAM DAVID, lawyer, congressman; b. Detroit, Aug. 6, 1927; s. Robert Henderson and Jean Bowie (McGhee) F.; student Neb. Tchrs. Coll., Peru, 1946, Wayne State U., 1947-48; B.S., U. Denver, 1949, LL.B., 1951; L.H.D., Westfield State Coll., 1970; children—William David, Margaret, John P. Admitted to Mich. bar, 1951; practice law, 1951—; mem. 89th to 92d Congresses, 15th Dist. Mich.; justice of peace, Taylor, Mich., 1955-57, twp. atty., 1957-64; city atty., Melvindale, Mich., 1957- 59; congl. adviser to UNESCO, 1971—. Del. Mich. Constl. Conv., 1961-62; mem. Mich. Senate 21st Dist., 1962-64. Served with USNR, 1944-46. Recipient Distinguished Service award; Outstanding Young Man of Yr. award, Taylor, Mich., 1962. Mem. Am., Mich. Downriver (pres. 1961-62) bar assns., Taylor Businessmen's Assn., Am. Legion, Phi Delta Phi. Mason. (Shriner), Eagle, Elk, Moose. Club: Rotary (pres. 1961-62). Home: 24329 Filmore Taylor MI 48180 Office: House Office Bldg Washington DC 20515

FORDHAM, CHRISTOPHER COLUMBUS, III, med. educator; b. Greensboro, N.C., Nov. 28, 1926; s. Christopher Columbus, Jr. and Frances Long (Clendenin) F.; student U. N.C., 1943-45, 47; M.D., Harvard, 1951; m. Barbara Byrd, Aug. 16, 1947; children—Pamela (Mrs. William Richey), Susie, Betsy. Intern Georgetown U. Hosp., 1951-52; resident Boston City Hosp., 1952-53, N.C. Meml. Hosp., Chapel Hill, 1953-54; fellow in medicine U. N.C. Sch. Medicine, 1954-55, instr. medicine, 1958-60, asst. prof., 1960-64, asso. prof., asst. dean Sch. Medicine, 1964-68, prof., asso. dean Sch. Medicine, 1968-69; prof. medicine, v.p. for medicine, dean Sch. Medicine, Med. Coll. Ga., Augusta, 1969-71; prof. medicine, dean Sch. Medicine, U. N.C., Chapel Hill, 1971—; practice medicine, specializing in internal medicine, Greensboro, N.C., 1957-58. Served with USAF, 1955-57. Fellow A.C.P.; mem. So. Soc. Clin. Investigation, Am. Soc. Nephrology, Am. Fedn. Clin. Research, N.Y. Acad. Sci., Sigma Xi. Home: 412 Morgan Creek Rd Chapel Hill NC 27514

FORDHAM, JEFFERSON BARNES, lawyer, educator; b. Greensboro, N.C., July 8, 1905; s. Christopher Columbus and Maggie Shepherd (Barnes) F.; A.B., U. N.C., 1926, A.M., J.D. with honors, 1929, LL.D., 1953; J.S.D., Yale, 1930; LL.D., Franklin and Marshall Coll., 1960; L.H.D., U. Pa., 1970; m. Rebecca Jane Norwood, Sept. 6, 1930 (dec. 1962); children—Robert, William; m. 2d, Rita Ennella, Mar. 21, 1964. Admitted to N.Y., Ohio, Pa. bars; Sterling Research fellow, Yale Law Sch., 1929-30; mem. law faculty, W.Va. Univ. and faculty editor, W.Va. Law Quar., 1930-35; spl. asst. to U.S. Sec. of Labor, 1935; asso. law firm, Reed, Hoyt & Washburn, N.Y.C., 1935-38; rev. counsel U.S. Pub. Works Adminstrn., Washington, 1938-39, counsel, chief bond atty., 1939-40; prof. law, La. State U., 1940-46, Vanderbilt U., 1946-47; dean, prof. law, Ohio State U., 1947-52; dean, prof. law, U. Pa. 1952-70, univ. prof. law, 1970—; Edward Douglass White lectr. La. State U., 1954; Benjamin N. Cardozo lectr. Assn. Bar City N.Y., 1957; Frank Irvine lectr. Cornell U., 1970; William H. Leary lectr. U. Utah, 1971. Mem. Pres.'s Adv. Panel on Conflicts of Interest and Ethics in Govt., 1961. Served USNR, 1942-45, Mem. Am. (chmn. sect. municipal law 1949-51, 1st chmn. sect. individual rights and responsibilities 1966- 68), Pa. bar assns., Assn. Bar City N.Y., Am. Law Inst. (council), Assn. Am. Law Schs. (pres. 1970), Phi Beta Kappa, Order of Coif. Democrat. Club: Century Assn. (N.Y.C.). Author: Coursebook on Local Government Law; co-author; Coursebook on Legislation. Contbr. legal publs. Home: 1507 Mt Pleasant Rd Villanova PA 19085

FORDTRAN, HENRY C., banker; b. Chgo., July 25, 1904; s. Henry and Emma (Schmitt) F.; B.S., Northwestern U., 1925; m. Blanche Dorsett McGregor, Sept. 7, 1929; children—Anne Fayette (Mrs. John Terrence Flynn), Nancy Renee (Mrs. Bruce Ian McPhee). Asst. cashier Wilmette State Bank, (Ill.) 1928-34; div. controller Montgomery Ward & Co., Chgo., 1934-52; financial v.p. Wilson Jones & Co., Chgo., 1952-56; v.p., controller Nat Blvd. Bank of Chgo., 1956-61, exec. v.p., dir., 1961—. Pres., bd. dirs. Gt. Lakes Region Health and Edn. Found.; treas., bd. dirs., mem. exec., finance and investment coms. Presbyn. Home, Evanston: bd. dirs., mem. exec. and finance coms. Lawson YMCA, Chgo. Mem. Am. Inst. Banking, Ill. Bankers Assn., Bankers Club Chgo., Execs. Club Chgo., Chgo. Athletic Assn., Chgo. Assn. Commerce. Presbyn. (trustee). Clubs: Exmoor Country (Highland Park); Arts (Chgo.). Home: 441 Lakeside Manor Rd Highland Park IL 60035 Office: 410 N Michigan Av Chicago IL 60611

FORDYCE, CLIFTON POWELL, lawyer; b. Little Rock, Mar. 15, 1901; s. John Rison and Lillian (Powell) F.; grad. Philips-Exeter Acad., 1919; A.B., Harvard, 1923, LL.B., 1926; m. Ruth O'Reilly Fordyce, Oct. 12, 1941; children—Nancy Fordyce (Mrs. Thomas Oliver Nevison, Jr.), Cameron P., Robert O'Reilly. Admitted to Mo. bar, also U.S. Supreme Ct.; mem. firm Fordyce, Mayne, Hartman, Renard & Stribling and predecessor firms, St. Louis. Mem. Am. (coms. on taxation, real property, probate and trust law). Mo., St. Louis bar assns., C. of C. Met. St. Louis (taxation and legislation com.). Methodist. Contbr. articles to legal publs. Home: 27 Lenox Pl St Louis MO 63108 Office: 818 Olive St St Louis MO 63101

FORDYCE, JAMES PAUL, life ins. exec.; b. Wichita, Kan., Aug. 1, 1892; s. Jesse Harvey and Lucy (Allen) Wash.; m. Roberta Leonard, Jan. 21, 1915 (div. 1933); 1 dau., Audrey Marie; m. 2d, Margaret Monahan, June 15, 1935; 1 son, Donald Michael. Salesman Western Union, Spokane, Wash., 1911-14; dir. agencies New World Life Ins. Co., Seattle, Wash., 1915-22; gen. agent State of Wash., Lincoln Nat. Life Ins. Co., 1923-29; v.p., dir. agys. United Pacific Life Ins. Co., 1930-31; agy. supt. No. Life Ins. Co., 1932-33; dir. agys. Manhattan Life Ins. Co., N.Y. C., 1934-36, v.p., dir. agys., 1936-39, pres., 1939-50, chmn. bd., 1950-66, chmn. exec. com., 1966-70, hon. chmn. bd., 1970—. Dir. N.Y. Bd. Trade. Lay trustee Gilmour Acad., Gates Mills, O. Mem. U.S., N.Y. State chambers commerce, Am. Life Conv., Life Presidents Assn. Republican. Club: Metropolitan. Home: 1900 S Ocean Dr Fort Lauderdale FL 33316 Office: 111 W 57th St New York City NY 10019

FOREE, ROBERT L., oil producer; b. Dallas. May 9, 1899; s. Kenneth and Edna (Fisher) F.; student So. Methodist U., 1917-19; m. Della Keith. Oct. 16, 1927; children—Robert L., Barbara Ann (Mrs. Reagan M. Waskom, Jr.), Elizabeth Keith (Mrs. J. D. Flickinger), Nancilee (Mrs. John Pearcy). Engaged in oil bus., 1919—; organizer Seminole Supply Co. (Okla.). 1919-35; ind. oil producer, Dallas, 1935—; pres. Foree Drilling Co.; dir. Lone Star Steel Co. Dir. prodn. Petroleum Adminstrn. for Def., 1952; mem. Nat. Petroleum Council, 1965—, Chmn. bd. trustees Scott and White Meml. Hosp., Temple, Tex. Mem. Tex. Ind. Producers and Royalty Owners Assn. (pres. 1950-52, exec. com.), Mid-Continent Oil and Gas Assn. (dir.), Ind. Petroleum Assn. Am. (dir.). Baptist. Clubs: Dallas Petroleum (pres. 1951); Brook Hollow Country. Home: 10140 Gaywood Rd Dallas TX 75229 Office: First Nat Bank Bldg Dallas TX 75202

FOREHAND, JACK MARION, freight co. exec.; b. Savannah, Ga., Feb. 27, 1921; s. Walter F. and Blanche G. (Hill) F.; B.B.A., U. Ga., 1946; m. Loraine M. Baugnet, June 30, 1945; children—Jack Marion, Robert, Michael, William, Raymond II, Mary Anne. Staff accountant Price Waterhouse & Co., Atlanta, 1946-50; chief accountant Newport Industries, Inc., Pensacola, Fla., 1950-57; controller Tenneco Chem. Corp., N.Y.C., 1957-64, Great Dane Trailers, Inc., Savannah, 1964-69; treas. U.S. Freight Co., N.Y.C., 1969—. Served with AUS, 1943-45. Mem. Alpha Tau Omega. Club: Savannah Yacht. Home: Orchard Hill Rd Westport CT 06880 Office: 711 3d Av New York City NY 10017

FORELL, GEORGE WOLFGANG, educator; b. Breslau, Germany, Sept. 19, 1919; s. Frederick J. and Madeleine (Kretschmar) F.; came to U.S., 1939, naturalized, 1945; student U. Vienna, 1937-38; B.D., Lutheran Theol. Sem., Phila., 1941; Th.M., Princeton Theol. Sem., 1943; Th.D., Union Theol. Sem., N.Y.C., 1949; D.D. (hon.), Wartburg Theol. Sem., 1967; m. Elizabeth Jean Rossing, June 14, 1945; children—Madeleine Helene (Mrs. Gary Marshall), Mary Elizabeth (Mrs. Christopher Davis). Ordained to ministry Luth. Ch., 1941; pastor in N.J. and N.Y., 1941-47; asst. prof., then asso. prof. philosophy Gustavus Adolphus Coll., St. Peter, Minn., 1947-54; asst. prof., then asso. prof. theology U. Ia., 1954-58; prof. systematic theology Luth. Sch. Theology, Chgo., 1958-61; prof. religion U. Ia., 1961—, dir. Sch. Religion, 1965- 71; vis. prof. U. Hamburg (Germany), 1957-58, All Africa Theol. Seminar, Marangu, Tanzania, 1960, Japan Luth. Coll., Tokyo, 1968. Mem. Am. Philos. Assn., Am. Soc. Ch. History, Am. Soc. Reformation Research (pres. 1959), Soc. Religion in Higher Edn., Omicron Delta Kappa. Democrat. Lutheran. Author: Faith Active in Love, 1954; Ethics of Decision, 1955; The Protestant Faith, 1960; The Christian Year, 1964-65; Understanding the Nicene Creed, 1965; Christian Social Techings, 1966; The Augsburg Confession, A Contemporary Commentary, 1968. Home: 10 Bella Vista Iowa City IA 52240

FOREMAN, CARL, film writer, director, producer; b. Chgo., July 23, 1914; s. Isadore and Fanny (Rozin) F.; student U. Ill., 1932-33, Northwestern U., 1935-36, John Marshall Law Sch., 1936-37; m. Evelyn Smith; children—Carla, Jonathan Amanda, Eliot. Motion pictures include: Champion, 1948; Home of the Brave, 1948; The Men, 1949; Cyrano de Bergerac, 1950; High Noon, 1951; The Key, 1957; The Mouse That Roared, 1960; The Guns of Navarone, 1961; The Victors, 1964; Born Free, 1965; Mackenna's Gold, 1969; exec. producer Otley and The Virgin Soldiers, 1969, Living Free and Young Winston, 1971; mng. dir. Open Road Films, Ltd., London, Eng., 1952—. Bd. govs. Brit. Film Inst., 1965-71, Nat. Film Sch. Served with AUS, World War II. Named comdr. Royal Order Phoenix (Greece), Most Excellent Order Brit. Empire; recipient award for distinguished service to writers Brit. Writers' Guild, 1968. Fellow Royal Soc. Arts; mem. Writers Guild Am. (Laurel award 1969), Writers Guild Gt. Britain (pres. 1968—), Israel Screen Writers Guild (hon. pres.). Clubs: Savile, Garrick (London). Address: 25 Jermyn St London SW1 England

FOREMAN, CLARK H., assn. exec.; b. Atlanta, Feb. 19, 1902; s. Robert Langdon and Effie Park (Howell) F.; A.B., U. Ga., 1921; Ph.D., Columbia, 1932; student Harvard, London Sch. Econs.; m. Mairi Elizabeth Fiona Fraser, July 26, 1933; children—Shelagh Alexandra (Mrs. David E. Wolfe), Joan Fraser (Mrs. Dietrick Klakow), Hugh (dec.). Soc. Ga. Com. for Interracial Coopn.; asst. to dir. Phelps-Stokes Fund; dir. studies Julius Rosenwald Fund; adviser on econ. status of negroes to sec. of interior; spl. counsel to sec. of interior; dir. power div. P.W.A.; dir. defense housing. Fed. Works Adminstrn.; scientist operational research, for U.S. Navy Dept.; asst. prof. Black Mountain Coll.; dir. tng. program Bur. of Applied Social Research, Columbia; pres. Southern Conf. Human Welfare; dir. emeritus Emergency Civil Liberties Com. Democrat. Club: Cosmos (Washington). Author several books. Home: Adjuntas PR Office: 421 Seventh Av New York City NY 10001

FOREMAN, CLYDE MELVIN, educator; b. Akron, O., Apr. 27, 1920; s. Clyde C. and Frances (Mac- Geary) F.; B.A., Seattle Pacific Coll., 1942; S.T.B., Bib. Sem. N.Y.C., 1945; M.A., U. Wash., 1955, Ph.D., 1957; m. Sylvia Marie Ahnlund, Sept. 4, 1946; children—Dale Melvin, Jan Marie, Jerild Curtis. Ordained to ministry Free Methodist Ch., 1945; dean Los Angeles Pacific Coll., 1946- 48; prof. sociology Seattle Pacific Coll., 1948-64, 71—, dean instrn., 1964- 70; research fellow Yale Div. Sch., 1970-71. Fellow Am. Sociol. Assn. Home: 2922 5th St W Seattle WA 98119

FOREMAN, EDGAR FRANKLIN, Jr., former congressman; b. Portales, N.M., Dec. 22, 1933; s. Edgar Franklin and Lillian (Childress) F.; student Eastern N.M. U., 1951-53; B.S. in Civil Engring., N.M. State U., 1955; m. Barbara Lynn Southard, Aug. 26, 1955; children—Preston Kirk, Rebecca Lynn. Petroleum engr. Philips Petroleum Co., 1955-56; v.p., gen. mgr. Foreman Brine Sales & Service, Inc., Odessa, Tex., 1956-62; v.p. Hickerson Trans., Inc., Odessa, 1956- 62; pres. Drill Aid, Inc., Odessa, 1956-62; pres. Valley Transit Mix, Inc., Foreman Oil, Inc., New Mexico Petroleum Co., Inc.; mem. 88th Congress 16th Dist. Tex.; mem. of 91st Congress, at-large New Mexico; now cons. Dept. Interior, Washington. Bd. dirs. Permian Basin Oil Show, 1958—, parade chmn., 1958, 60, 62; chmn. Ector County Heart Fund Council, 1961. Bd. dirs. N.M. Heart Assn. Served with USNR, 1956-57. Named Outstanding Young Man Odessa, 1960, one of five Outstanding Young Men Tex., 1962; recipient Distinguished Service award Odeasa Jr. C. of C., 1960; Boss of Year award Howdy Pardner chpt. Am. Bus. Women's Assn., 1961. Mem. U.S. Odessa (dir.), Midland, El Paso Las Cruces chambers commerce, Tex. Mid-Continent Oil and Gas Assn. (past chmn. Ector County oil information com.), Am. Soc. C.E., Am. Petroleum Inst., N.M. Home Builders Assn. (dir.), N.M. Bus. and Mfrs. Assn. (dir.), N.M. Sand, Gravel and Concrete Assn. (dir.). Republican. Methodist (bd. stewards). Mason (Shriner), Rotarian. Home: 2245 Thomas Dr Las Cruces NM 88001 Office: PO Drawer L Las Cruces NM 88001

FOREMAN, JAMES DAVIS, mfg. co. exec.; b. Barnesville, O., Mar. 13, 1925; s. J. Harrison and Freda (Davis) F.; B.S. magna cum laude, Syracuse U., 1949; M.B.A., U. Pa., 1956; C.P.A., Conn., 1954; m. Helen Laura Bolon, Nov. 27, 1943; children—James Bolon, Barbara Jean, Helen Marie. With Arthur Young & Co., C.P.A.'s, N.Y.C., 1950-51, Ernst & Ernst, C.P.A.'s, Hartford, Conn., 1951-55; mgr. accounting and adminstrn. Xerox Corp., 1955-60; v.p., controller Olivetti Corp., 1960—. Office: 500 Park Av New York City NY 10017

FOREMAN, LAWTON DURANT, clergyman; b. Sebastian Co., Ark., Mar. 8, 1913; s. Jess Jonathan and Willie Ann (Mathews) F.; Grad. Bible. Missionary Bapt. Sem., 1936, Master Bible, 1937, Dr. Bible, 1939; m. Mary Opal Henry, June 21, 1936; children—Rebekah, Lynn, Priscilla, Betty Jane. Ordained to ministry Bapt. Ch., 1935; faculty mem. Missionary Bapt. Sem., Little Rock. Ark., 1939, dean, 1945, pres., 1946-66; pastor First Bapt. Ch., Cave City, Ark., 1939-42, Sheridan, Ark., 1942-47, Antioch Ch., Little Rock 1947- 66, Woodhaven Bapt. Ch., Little Rock, 1966—. Co-founder Foreman-Payne Publishers, Inc. Mem. Am. Bapt. Assn. (mem. Sunday sch. and ch. publs. com. 1940—, pres. 1950-51, v.p. 1963), State Assn. Bapt. Chs. Ark. (moderator 1949-51), States' Rights Council Ark. (dir. 1958- 59, United Comml. Travelers (chaplain council 167; chaplain grand council). Mem. Masons (32, KT, KCCH, grand orator 1946-47, right illustrious grand chaplain grand council 1955-56, eminent comdr. of Hugh de Payens Commandery 1957). Author: Bible in Eight Ages, 1942; Handbook on Ordinations, 1952; A Study Course in the Gospel of John, 1953; Biblical Proofs for Identifying the True Church, 1955; Ministerial Practicalities, 1961; Life of Christ (18 sermons). Co-author: Life and Works of Bogard, 3 vols.; The Golden Key to Bible Analysis. Editor: Credenda, 1951; Missionary Bapt. World (monthly publ.). Home: 12313 Sardis Rd Mabelvale AR 72103 Office: 10225 Mabelvale W Mabelvale AR 72103

FOREMAN, PERCY, lawyer, lectr.; b. Polk County, Tex., June 21, 1902; s. Ransom Parson and William Pinckney (Rogers) F.; LL.B., U. Tex., 1927; m. Marguerite Obert, Apr. 21, 1957; children—William Pinckney Rogers III, Marguerite. With Nat. Lyceum, then Chautauqua lectr.; admitted to Tex. bar, 1927, since practiced in Houston. Mem. Am., Tex., Houston bar assns., Nat. Assn. Def. Lawyers Criminal Cases (pres. 1963-64). Home: 200 Carnarvon St Houston TX 77024 Office: First Nat Life Bldg 806 Main Houston TX 77002

FOREMAN, WALTER CYRIL, educator; b. Moline, Ill., Sept. 3, 1910; s. Walter Cyril and Helen (Rothwell) F.; B.A., Union Coll., Lincoln, Neb., 1933; M.A., U. Neb., 1937; Ph.D., U. Cal. at Berkeley, 1948; m. Clayoma I. Engel, June 4, 1936; 1 son, Walter Cyril. Instr. English, U. Neb., 1937-40; teaching asst. U. Cal. at Berkeley, 1942-48; mem. faculty Ore. State U., 1948—, prof. English, 1958—, chmn. dept., 1965—; cons. in field, 1937—; Marjorie Balley meml. lectr. Inst. Renaissance Studies, Ashland Shakespeare Festival, 1966. Recipient

Outstanding Tchr. award Ore. State U., 1956. Mem. Am. Assn. U. Profs., Nat. Council Tchrs. English, Modern Lang. Assn., Renaissance Soc. Am., Corvallis C. of C., Phi Kappa Phi. Democrat. Clubs: Triad, Century (Corvallis). Author: Exercises in Writing and Thinking, 1952; editor, author: English in Oregon Secondary Schools, 1963. Home: 3720 SW Country Club Dr Corvallis OR 97330

FORER, LOIS GOLDSTEIN, (Mrs. Morris Leon Forer), lawyer; b. Chgo., Mar. 22, 1914; d. Harry and Lorraine (Beilman) Goldstein; A.B., Northwestern U., 1935, J.D., 1938; m. Morris Leon Forer, June 30, 1940; children—Sturart, John, Hope Abigail. Admitted to Ill. bar, 1938, Pa. bar, 1942; mem. legal staff U.S. Senate Com. on Edn. and Labor, 1938-39, Rural Electrification Adminstrn., 1940- 41; law clk. U.S. Ct. of Appeals, 3d Circuit. Phila., 1942-46; mem. legal staff OPS, Phila., 1950-51; practice law in Phila., 1946—; dep. atty. gen. State of Pa., Harrisburg, 1954-63; atty. in charge Community Legal Services, Inc., Office for Juveniles, Phila., 1966-68; lectr. law U. of Pa., 1953-59. Cons. White House Conf. Children and Youth, 1970. Mem. Am. Civil Liberties Union (dir. Phila. 1952—, also mem. nat. bd.), Am. (Ross Eassay prize 1953), Pa., Phila. bar assns. Democrat. Author: No One Will Lissen: How Our Legal System Brutalizes the Youthful Poor, 1970. Address: 622 W Hortter St Philadelphia PA 19119

FORER, RAYMOND, sociologist, educator; b. New Brunswick, N.J., Feb. 12, 1915; s. Solomon and Celia G. (Jelin) F.; B.A., U. Denver, 1947; M.A., Yale, 1951, Ph.D., 1955; m. Valeria Jean Trimble, Sept. 25, 1945; children—Susan Gretel, Alice Rebekah. Instr., New Haven Coll., 1950-52; asst. in instrn. sociology Yale, 1949-52, research asst. psychiatry, 1953-56; instr. sociology and anthropology U. Conn., 1953-57; research sociologist Conn. Dept. Mental Health, 1957-60; prin. investigator Conn. Commn. Alcoholism Vocational Rehab. Project, 1960; dir. behavioral scis. program Ky. Dept. Health, 1960-61, also adj. asst. prof. U. Ky. Med. Center; prof. sociology, head dept. sociology and anthropology U. Me., 1961-63; chief behavioral scis. activities Communicable Disease Center, USPHS, 1963-66; prof. sociology Emory U., 1963-66, State U. N.Y., Albany, 1966—; research cons. 1950—. Served with USAAF, 1942-45. Fellow Am. Sociol. Assn., Soc. Applied Anthropology; mem. Eastern Sociol. Soc., A.A.A.S., Am. Assn. U. Profs., Phi Beta Kappa, Pi Gamma Mu, Alpha Kappa Delta. Contbr. profl. jours. Home: 29 Bennock St Orono ME 04473 Office: State U NY Albany NY 12203

FORESMAN, BOB, newspaperman; b. Tulsa, July 20, 1912; s. Frank and Mabyl (Weldon) F.; A.B., U. Tulsa, 1934; m. Betty Louise McDaniel, Dec. 15, 1940; 1 dau., Elizabeth Ann. With Tulsa Tribune, 1935—, bus. editor, 1958—, writer weekly column Okla. Business. Founder, Tulsa Tribune Send-a-Kid-to-Camp Fund, 1936; fund chmn. Tulsa Expressway Beautification Co., 1963-64. Bd. dirs. Fort Washita Commn. Served to lt. condr. USNR, 1943-46; PTO, ETO. Recipient Sol. Merit award Okla. Pub. Expenditure Council, 1955. Mem. Tulsa Press Club (past pres.), Okla. Hist. Soc. (dir.) Navy League, Sigma Delta Chi, Lambda Chi Alpha. Methodist. Clubs: University Tulsa Lettermens, Petroleum, University, Indian Springs Country (Tulsa). Home: 2347 S Delaware Pl Tulsa OK 74114 Office: 315 S Boulder Av Tulsa OK 74102

FOREST, HERBERT LEON, govt. ofcl.; b. Arlington, Mass., Apr. 20, 1910; s. Joseph Michel Henry and Rose Ella (Quinn) F.; B.S., U. Mass., 1932; grad. student Harvard, 1932-35; m. Anna Katherine Digney, June 10, 1935; 1 dau., Anna Katherine. Analyst Office Fed. Milk Market Adminstr., Boston, 1935; with U.S. Dept. of Agr., 1935—, beginning as economist dairy br., successively head lend-lease and fgn. requirements div., asst. dep. dir. charge civilian activities, asst. dep. dir. dairy br., dep. dir. dairy br., dir. dairy div. consumer and marketing service, 1954—. Recipient Superior Service award U.S. Dept. Agr., 1970. Mem. Am., Farm econ. assns., Phi Sigma Kappa, Phi Kappa Phi. Home: 1208 Shenandoah Rd Alexandria VA 22308 Office: US Dept of Agr Washington DC 20250

FORESTER, JOHN EVERETT, trustee; b. Wauwatosa, Wis., Apr. 8, 1913; s. John L. and Ethel (Moss) F.; B.A., U. Wis., 1933, LL.B., 1936; m. Betsy Quarles, Sept. 24, 1938; children—John Moss, Charles Quarles, Richard Gordon; m. 2d, Alice Richardson Woodson Hagge, Nov. 12, 1964. Admitted to Wis. bar, 1936; trust officer First Wis. Trust Co., Milw., 1945-46; spl. agt. F.B.I., 1943-45; atty., mng. trustee, 1946—; pres., dir. Forewood, Inc.; sec.-treas., dir. Wis. Valley Trust Co., Wausau; sec., dir. The Aytchmonde Woodson Found., Inc., Wausau, Wis.; pres., treas., dir. Woodson Fiduciary Corp., Wilmington, Del.; pres., dir. Forewood, Inc.; v.p., dir. Mont.-Dakota Utilities Co., Bismarck, N.D., Central Wis. Bankshares, Inc., Marathon Electric Mfg. Corp., Marathon Electric Found., Inc. (both in Wausau, Wis.), Marathon Electric Research of Can., Ltd., Toronto, Ont., MCI-North Central States, Inc., Mpls.; chmn. bd. dir. Mosinee Paper Mills Co. Wis., Wausau Paper Mills Co., Brokaw, Wis.; dir. Masonite Corp., Chgo., Wausau Theatres Co., Bay West Paper Co., Green Bay, First Am. Nat. Bank, Wausau, Employers Ins. of Wausau, Longview Fibre Co., Wash. Sec., dir. Wausau Hosps., Inc.; treas., dir. YMCA Found., Inc., Wausau; sec.-treas., dir. Wausau Cemetery Assn. Mem. Marathon County Hist. Soc. (v.p., dir.), Wis. Taxpayers Alliance (dir.), Delta Upsilon. Home: Franklin Hill Wausau WI 54401 Office: First Am State Bank Bldg Wausau WI 54401

FORGAN, JAMES RUSSELL, investments exec.; b. Evanston, Ill., Mar. 12 1900; s. David Robertson and Agnes (Kerr) F.; grad. St. Mark's Sch., Southboro, Mass., 1918; B.A., Princeton, 1922; m. Ada Rand Johnson, Dec. 2, 1922; children—Joan Berwick (Mrs. Joan Parks), Florence (Mrs. Henry P. Wheeler), James Russell, Ada J. (Mrs. Whitney Addington). Clerk, Nat. City Bank Chgo., 1922-24, asst. cashier, 1924-25, asst. v.p. Nat. Bank Rep. Chgo., 1925-27; v.p. Brokaw & Co., 1927-30; partner Glore, Forgan & Co. (formerly Field, Glore & Co.,) Chgo. and N.Y.C., 1931- 65; chmn., chief exec. officer Glore, Forgan, Wm. R. Staats Inc., 1965- 70; chmn. du Pont Glore Forgan, Inc., 1970—; dir. Interco, Inc., Borg Warner Corp., Nat. Distillers & Chem. Corp.; mem. adv. com. Bankers Trust Co. Vice chmn. Joint Emergency Relief Fund, Chgo.; vice chmn. U.S. Navy Relief Soc. Past trustee Princeton U. Served from lt. col. to col. AUS, World War II; comdg. officer OSS, E.T.O., 1945. Decorated D.S.M., Legion of Merit, Legion of Honor; Croix de Guerre with palm; Order British Empire; Order of Leopold (Belgium); comdr. Order Dannebrog (Denmark); Cross of Liberation (Czechoslovakia); Gen. Wm. J. Donovan award, Vets. Strategic Services. Presbyn. Clubs: Links, Racquet and Tennis, Recess, Princeton (N.Y.C.); Links Golf; Travellers (Paris); Buck's, Special Forces (London); Lyford Cay (Nassau). Home: 640 Park Av New York City NY 10021 Office: One Wall St New York City NY 10005

FORKER, DAVID MATTHEWS, Jr., valve co. exec.; b. Cin., Jan. 17, 1904; s. David M. and Anna (McClure) F.; B.S., Yale, 1926; m. Margaret Elizabeth Nichols, Oct. 18, 1934; children—Margaret, David III. Chmn. bd., dir. Wm. Powell Co., Cin.; dir. Cin. Bell, Inc., Cin. Equitable Ins. Co., Eagle-Picher Industries, Inc. Trustee Children's Hosp. Med. Center. Home: 2243 Grandin Rd Cincinnati OH 45208 Office: 2503 Spring Grove Av Cincinnati OH 45214

FORKER, LEE R., refinery exec.; b. Oil City, Pa.; grad. Cornell U., 1928. Formerly pres., dir. Quaker State Oil Refining Corp., Oil City, Pa., now bd. chmn., chief exec. officer, dir.; pres., dir. Quaker State, S.A., Quaker State Oil Refining Co. of Can., Ltd.; sec. treas., dir. McCoy Natural Gas Co., Tionesta Gas Co.; mem. exec. com., dir. Northwest Pa. Bank & Trust Co.; dir. Brockway Glass Co., Pa. Grade Crude Oil Assn., James B. Berry Sons' Co. Mem. Am. Petroleum Inst. (dir.), Nat. Petroleum Refiners Assn. Home: 417 W 3d St Oil City PA 16301 Office: 11 Center St Oil City PA 16301

FORKEY, LEO ORVILLE, educator; b. Malone, N.Y., Mar. 12, 1915; s. Joseph Edward and Célina (La-Pierre) F.; B.A., U. Ala., 1938; Ph.D., Johns Hopkins, 1942; postgrad. Sorbonne, Paris, France, 1951-52. Instr., then asst. prof. French, Johns Hopkins, 1946-51; head dept. French, U. Redlands (Cal.), 1952-53; asso. prof. Romance langs., head dept. Drake U., 1953-60, prof., 1959—, chmn. dept. fgn. lang., 1960-68. Served to capt. AUS, 1942-45. Mem. Modern Lang. Assn. Am., Phi Beta Kappa. Episcopalian. Author: French Comedy in the Seventeenth Century, 1947; also articles. Home: 3523 University Av Des Moines IA 50311

FORKOSCH, MORRIS DAVID, educator, author; b. N.Y.C., Feb. 26, 1908; s. Samuel and Yetta (Heimowitz) F.; LL.B., St. John's Law Sch., 1930, LL.M., 1932; B.A., N.Y.U., 1936, M.A., 1938, J.S.D., 1948; Ph.D., New Sch. Social Research, 1952, M.S.Sc., 1956; m. Selma Milner, Nov. 29, 1934 (dec. Aug. 1958); children—Joel Anton, Jonathan Andrew. Admitted to N.Y. bar, 1931, U.S. Supreme Ct., 1939, Supreme Ct. of Philippines, 1946; practice in N.Y.C., 1931-44; 46—; prof. law, chmn. dept. pub. law Bklyn. Law Sch., 1949—; mem. faculty U. Internat. de Scis. Comparees, Luxembourg, summer 1962, 71, L'Enseignement du Droit Compare, Trieste, Italy, summer 1963, Liege, Belgium, summer 1965, Uppsala, 1966, Desert Sun Sch., Western U. Law Sch., 1968, San Diego Law Sch., 1969, Conf., Center for Study Democratic Instns., Santa Barbara, Cal., 1969, New Sch. for Social Research, 1970-71, Tokyo Law Sch., 1970, Basel, Switzerland, 1970, City Coll., N.Y.C., 1971, Free U. West Berlin, 1971; lectr. Police Acad., Inst., Police Tng. Officers, 1958. Dir., gen. counsel Anti-Nazi League to Champion Human Rights, 1939-41; pres. sect. VI, Congres Internat. de Droit Compare, Hamburg, Germany, 1962, v.p. sect. V, Uppsala, Sweden, 1966; cons. NLRB, 1963-64, chmn. coms. 2d region confs., 1960, 61, 62; mem. local sch. bds. dists, 21 and 22, N.Y.C. Bd. Edn., 1962-64, mem. local sch. bd. dist. 13, 1965- -; served as spl. trial examiner N.Y. State Labor Relations Bd., 1953- 54; panel arbitrators Am. Arbitration Assn., 1949—, N.Y. region Fed. Mediation and Conciliation Agy., 1949—; mem. Nat. Pub. Employment Disputes Settlement Panel, 1969—; hearing officer N.Y.C. Dept. Transp., 1971—; mediator Ombudsman's Office, N.Y.C., 1971—. Served with AUS, 1944-46. Mem. Am. Soc. Legal History (pres. 1958-61, nat. bd. dirs. 1961—, br. pres. Northeastern states 1962—), Internat. Soc. Legal History, Am. Assn. U. Profs., Assn. Bar City N.Y., Am. Hist. Assn., Am. Econ. Assn., Am. Polit. Sci. Assn., Indsl. and Labor Relations Research Assn., Acad. Polit. Sci., Internat. Assn. Lawyers. Author: A Treatise on Labor Law, 1953, second edit., 1965; The Political Philosophy of Arnold Brecht, 1954; A Treatise on Adminstrative Law, 1956; Antitrust and the Consumer, 1956; Carmody's New York Practice, 1956; Constitutional Law, 1963, 2d edit., 1969; Carmody-Forkosch New York Practice, 8th edit. 1963, with ann. supplements; Essays in Legal History in Honor of Felix Frankfurter, 1965; also numerous articles. Home: 250 Joralemon St Brooklyn NY 11201

FORLEY, MAURICE, assn. exec.; b. Indpls., Sept. 19, 1910; s. Morris and Mildred (Mayerstein) Feuerlicht; student Ohio State U., 1927; Ph.B., Yale, 1931; J.D., Northwestern U., 1934. Admitted to Ill., Ind. bars, 1935, also U.S. Supreme Ct. bar; practiced in Chgo., Indpls., 1934-37; various assignments U.S. Govt. agys., U.S. Senate com. staffs, Washington, also N.Y.C., 1937-43; mgr. 16mm film div. Paramount Internat. Pictures, N.Y.C., 1947; exec. asst. to mayor Los Angeles, 1948- 49; sec. Mikron Instruments, Inc., Pasadena, Cal., 1950; dir. personnel and pub. relations Hunt Foods, Inc., Fullerton, Cal., 1952-54; v.p. Internat. Brewing Corp., also cons. W.R. Staats & Co., Los Angeles, 1954- 56; adminstrv. counsel Toastmasters Internat., Santa Ana, Cal., 1956-58, exec. dir., 1958-68. Asso. prof. speech dept. Cal. State Coll., Fullerton, 1961-67; sec., dir. Anglo-Am. Aviation Co., Inc., Burbank, Cal., 1956- 66. Mem. nat. com. St. John's Colls., Annapolis, Md., Santa Fe. Bd. dirs Big Brothers Orange County. Served to 1st lt. JAG, AUS, 1943-46. Mem. Am. Soc. Assn. Execs., Orange County chambers of commerce, Speech Assn. Am. Author: Public Speaking Without Pain, 1965; Practical Guide to Public Speaking, 1970; (with S.A. Fessenden) A Guide to Better Listening, 1965. Contbr. articles law revs. and popular mags. Address: 1824 Altivo Way Los Angeles CA 90026

FORM, WILLIAM H., educator; b. Rochester, N.Y., June 2, 1917; s. Anthony and Mary (Conet) F.; A.B. cum laude, U. Rochester, 1938, A.M., 1940; Ph.D., U. Md., 1944; children—Catherine Louise, Helen. Asst. prof. Kent (O.) State U., 1945-47; prof. Mich. State U., Lansing, 1947—, asso. dir. research and planning Sch. Labor and Indsl. Relations, 1959-61, acting dir., 1963-64, chmn. dept. sociology, 1965-68, research prof., 1962—. Cons., NSF, 1964—, U.S. Dept. Labor, 1965—, U.S. Dept. Health, Edn. and Welfare, 1968—. Recipient Distinguished Prof. award Mich. State U., 1965. Mem. Am. Sociol. Assn. (council 1968—), Ohio Valley Social. Soc. (pres. 1953), Indsl. Relations Research Assn., Am. Assn. U. Profs., Internat. Sociol. Soc. Author: Community in Disaster, 1958; Industry, Labor and Community, 1960; Industrial Sociology, 1964; Influentials in Two Border Cities, 1965; Comparative Perspectives on Industrial Society, 1969; also numerous articles. Home: 2111 Galen St Champaign IL 61820

FORMAN, CHARLES WILLIAM, educator; b. Gwalior, India, Dec. 2, 1916 (parents U.S. citizens); s. Henry and Sallie (Taylor) F.; B.A., M.A., Ohio State U., 1938; Ph.D., U. Wis., 1941; B.D., Union Theol. Sem., N.Y.C., 1944, S.T.M., 1947; m. Helen Janice Mitchell, Mar. 12, 1944; children—David, Sarah, Harriet. Ordained to ministry Presbyn. Ch., 1944; prof., N. India United Theol. Coll., Saharanpur, 1945-50; sec. program emphasis Nat. Council Chs., 1951-53; mem. faculty Yale Div. Sch., 1953—, D. Wills James prof. missions, 1961—. Chmn. theol. edn. fund World Council Chs., 1963-70; mem. commn. ecumenical mission United Presbyn. Ch., 1962—, chmn., 1965- -. Mem. bd. edn., Bethany, Conn., 1957-66. Author: A Faith for the Nations, 1958; The Nation and The Kingdom, 1964; Christianity in the Non- Western World, 1967. Home: Downs Rd Bethany CT 06525 Office: 409 Prospect St New Haven CT 06511

FORMAN, DAVID GREENE, corp., exec., b. Buffalo, June 24, 1913; s. Howard A. and Georgia Mead (Greene) F.; grad. Hill Sch. Pottstown, Pa. 1934; m. Elizabeth Clark, Oct. 16, 1935; children—David Greene, James Clark, Sally Lester (Mrs. George Strawbridge, Jr.), Frances Elizabeth (Mrs. Alfred J. Yardley, Jr.), Patricia Elizabeth. Exec. asst. to pres., asst. sec. and mgr. Helicopter div. Bell Aircraft Corp., 1935-51; pres. subsidiary Bell Aircraft Supply Corp., 1947-51; v.p. Umont Mining, Inc., 1954—, also dir.; chmn. adminstrv. and finance com. Transcontinent TV Corp., 1956- -, also dir.; pres., treas. Ont. Marine, Inc., 1961—, dir. Amherst India Corp., 70 Niagara St. Services, Inc. Mem. Buffalo and Ft. Erie Pub. Bridge Authority, 1966—. Bd. dirs. Buffalo Soc. Natural Scis., Erie County Soc. Prevention Cruelty to Animals. Clubs: Buffalo Country, Mid Day, Saddle and Bridle (Buffalo); Explorers (N.Y.C.); Jockey of Fort Erie (dir.); Caughnawana Fishing and Hunting (Toronto, Ont., Can.). Home: 240 Cayuga Rd Williamsville NY 14221 Office: 70 Niagara St Buffalo NY 14202

FORMAN, HARRISON, explorer, author, lectr.; b. Milw., June 15, 1904; student Chgo. Acad. Fine Arts, 1922-23; Layton Sch. Art, Milw., 1923- 24; B.A., U. Wis., 1929; m. Selmah Holcombe (Sandra Carlyle Forman, profl. name), Aug. 10, 1934; children—Brenda Lu, John Holcombe. In Mexico, 1929; instr. navigation and meterol., United Sch. Aeros., San Francisco, 1930; tech. dir. Columbia Pictures Corp., Hollywood, 1936-37; expdn. across Gobi Desert of Mongolia, 1937; 3rd expdn. Tibet (interview and motion pictures of Jamv Japa, 4th in the hierarchy of Living Buddhas of Tibet), 1937; made motion pictures of Chinese Communist Red Army, 1937, of bombardment of Shanghai (released through March of Time), 1937, of Russo-Japanese hostilities at Changkufeng Hill on Siberia-Manchuria-Korea border, 1938, bombardment of Warsaw, 1939; Japanese invasion Indo-China, 1940; China War Theatre, 1941-45; Battle of the Yangtze and Communist capture of Shanghai, 1949; anti-communist wars in Malaya and Indo-China, 1950; Dutch withdrawal from Indonesia, 1950; visited and reported from East and Nr. East countries and S.A., 1950-54; interviewed Dalai Lama of Tibet, 1959; expdns. to N. Philipines, Malaya, Island of Komodo in S. Seas, 1955-56, Afghanistan, Middle East, 1957, Indonesia, Nepal, 1958, Russia, Central Asia, 1959, South East Asia, Celebes, Moluccas, 1960, Siberia and Mongolia, 1964, W. Africa and Central Africa, 1965, Pakistan and Nepal, India, 1969, South Pacific, S. Am., 1969, Thailand, Tanzania, Iran (ruins of Persepolis, ancient capital of Darius the Great), 1967; tech. dir. Lost Horizon (Acad. award); fgn. corr. Far East for N.Y. Times, London Times, and NBC; lectr. internat. relations; ednl. photog. assignments Far East, 1960, Iron Curtain Countries of Europe, Africa, Timbuktu in Sahara Desert, 1961, also Siberia and Outer Mongolia, 1964; pres. Harrison Forman World Travel, Inc., N.Y.C. Mem. Soc. Mag. Writers (founder-mem.). Clubs: Explorers (life), Clipper, Overseas Press. Author books, Through Forbidden Tibet, 1935; Horizon Hunter, 1940; Report from Red China, 1945; Changing China, 1948; Blunder in Asia, 1950; How to Make Money with your Camera, 1951; The Land and People of Nigeria, 1964. Contbr. to mags. Home: 40 Central Park S New York City NY 10019 Office: 500 Fifth Av New York City NY 10036

FORMAN, HENRY CHANDLEE, educator, architect; b. N.Y.C.; s. Horace Baker, Jr. and Elizabeth (Chandlee) F.; A.B., Princeton, 1926; M.Arch., U. Pa., 1931, Ph.D. in Fine Arts, 1942; m. Caroline Biddle Lippincott, Sept. 28, 1929; children—Elizabeth (Mrs. Bryant Harrell, Jr.), Richard Townsend Turner, Lawrence Thorne. Pvt. practice architecture as H. Chandlee Forman, Easton, Md., 1931-35, 52—; chief architect Jamestown (Va.) Archaeol. Project, 1935-36; editor nat. records Historic Am. Bldgs. Survey, 1936-37; lectr. fine arts Haverford Coll., 1937-39; instr. art Rutgers U., 1939-40; lectr. history art U. Pa., 1940-41; Chatherine L. Comer prof. fine arts Wesleyan Coll. of Ga., 1941-45; prof. art, head dept. Agnes Scott Coll., 1945-52; cons. architect Ga. Hist. Commn., 1952-60. Adviser city commn., St. Mary's, 1965-69; mem. Md. Archaeol. Commn., 1968—; sec. bd. dirs. Soc. Preservation Md. Antiquities, 1952-58; lectr. throughout world for State Dept., 1964. Recipient George Barnard White prize Princeton, 1926; Carnegie Found. fellow creative painting, 1947. Fellow A.I.A.; mem. Talbot County (Md.) Hist. Soc. (bd. dirs., co-organizer, 1st curator), Soc. Colonial Wars. Author numerous books, including: Early Manor and Plantation Houses of Maryland, 1934; Jamestown and St. Mary's, 1938; The Architecture of the Old South, The Medieval Style, 1948; Virginia Architecture in the 17th Century, 1957; Early Nantucket and its Whale Houses, 1966; Old Buildings, Gardens and Furniture in Tidewater Maryland, 1967. Address: PO Box 807 Easton MD 21601

FORMAN, JAMES, formerly exec. sec. Student Nonviolent Coordinating Com. Leader in Nat. Black Econ. Devel. Conf.*

FORMAN, JONATHAN, internist, editor, author; b. Austinburg, O., Sept. 30, 1887; s. Cassius Clay and Alice Florence (Coup) F.; A.B., Ohio State U., 1910; M.D., Starling-Ohio Med. Coll., 1913; grad. work Harvard, summers 1912-16; m. Doris Marie Andrews, Nov. 1, 1923; children—Alice Ann, Cynthia Louise, Jonathan. Asst. in anatomy and physiology, Ohio State U., 1910- 11; asst. in pathology, Starling-Ohio Med. Coll., 1911-13; asst. in pathology, Coll. Medicine Ohio State U., 1913-14, instr. 1914-16, asst. prof., 1916-19; Austin teaching fellow, Harvard, 1919-20; practiced medicine, Columbus, O., 1920—; spl. lectr. allergy Ohio State U., 1933-34, lectr. medicine 1934—; prof. history of medicine 1945—, now emeritus; has served as pathologist and gastroenterologist several hosps. and clinics. Served as dir. lab. div. U.S. Naval Hosp., Naval Operating Base, Hampton Roads, 1917-19. Chmn. Friends of the Land, 1952-60. Recipient Louis Bromfield gold medal, 1961; Clemens von Pirquet gold medal, 1964; Phi Rho Sigma Ainsley Griffin gold medal. Diplomate Am. Bd. of Internal Medicine. Fellow Am. Coll. Allergy (pres. 1949-50), Am. Acad. Allergy, Internat. Assn. Allergists, Soc. Tech. Editors and Pubs.; hon. mem. Argentine Soc. for Study of Allergy; mem. profl. and tech. assns. and socs. including A.M.A., Internat. Corr. Soc. of Allergists (dir.-gen.), Alpha Omega Alpha, Sigma Delta Chi, Phi Rho Sigma, Sigma Tau Delta. Editor: Directory of Physicians Interested in Clin. Allergy, 1948, 54. Author: Hist. of the First Hundred Yrs. of the Coll. of Med. of Ohio State U., 1934. Editor or co-editor bulls., jours. and proceedings various orgns. 1916—, including Ohio State Med. Jour., 1953-57. Editor-in-chief Clinical Physiology, 1956-65; editorial bd. World-Wide Abstracts, Vox Medica, Rev. Allergy and Applied Immunology. Editor: Archives Clin. Ecology. Contbr. numerous articles to med. jours. Home: 4425 Olentangy Blvd Columbus OH 43214 Office: 139 S Grant Av Columbus OH 43215

FORMAN, MILOS, film dir.; b. Feb. 18, 1932; ed. film faculty Acad. Music and Dramatic Art, Prague, Czechoslovakia. Dir., Laterna Magika, Prague, 1958-62; mem. artistic com. Sebor-Bor Film Producing Group; dir. films including Talent Competition, Peter and Pavla (Czechoslovak Film Critics' award 1963, Grand Prix 17th Internat. Film Festival, Locarno 1964), The Knave of Spades, A Blonde in Love, Episode in Zruc. Address: Mjr Schramma 31 Prague Czechoslovakia *

FORMAN, PHILLIP, judge; b. N.Y. City, Nov. 30, 1895; s. Morris and Tilly (Peters) F.; LL.B., Temple U., 1919; m. Pearl Edith Karlberg, April 12, 1937. Admitted to N.J. bar, 1917; practiced in Trenton; mem. Forman & Levy, 1919-32; asst. U.S. atty., Dist. N.J., 1923-28, U.S. atty., 1928- 32; judge, U.S. Dist. Ct., N.J., 1932-59, chief judge, 1951-59; judge U.S. Ct. Appeals. 1959-61, sr. judge, 1961—. Trustee emeritus Rutgers U. Jewish religion. Home: 5 Belmont Circle Trenton NJ 08618 Office: US Court House Trenton NJ 08607

FORMAN, SIDNEY, librarian; b. Bklyn., Mar. 16, 1915; s. Alexander and Bertha (Weintraub) F.; B. Social Sci., Coll. City N.Y., 1936; M.A., Columbia, 1939, Ph.D., 1949, M.S. in L.S., 1959; m. Belle Schaeffer, Dec. 1, 1940; children—Charles Robert, Phillip Alexander. Staff archivist, historian U.S. Mil. Acad., 1946-62, librarian, 1957-62; prof. history Ladycliff Coll., Highland Falls, N.Y., 1946-62; prof. edn., librarian Tchrs. Coll., Columbia, 1962—, asso. Inst. of Adult Edn.,

1964-66; also library planning consultant. Treas., trustee Constitution Island Assn., 1954-62, Ladycliff Coll., Highland Falls, N.Y., 1969—. Served from pvt. to sgt., AUS, 1942-46. Recipient grant Fund for Advancement Edn., 1966-69. Mem. Am. Hist. Assn., Assn. Am. Archivists, Spl. Library Assn., A.L.A. (chmn. Dana awards com. 1964-65), Am. Mil. Inst. Author: The Story of the Five Towns, 1941; West Point, 1950; Fort Sumter, 1961; English as a Second Language, 1967. Research editor School Libraries, 1966-69. Home: 501 W 120th St New York City NY 10027 Office: 525 W 120th St New York City NY 10027

FORMAN, WILLIAM JOEL, former lawyer; b. Versailles, Mo., Dec. 15, 1899; s. William and Mary (Vaughn) F.; LL.B., U. Cal., 1924; m. Corinne Newkom, Jan. 16, 1926; 1 son, William Newkom. Admitted to Nev. bar, 1923; practiced in Reno, 1930-71; mem. firm Woodburn, Forman, Wedge, Blakey, Folsom & Hug; dep. atty. gen. Nev., 1925-30. Mem. State Bar Nev. (pres. 1946-47, past bd. govs.). Home: 751 Marsh Av Reno NV 89502 Office: 1 E 1st St Reno NV 89501 Died Jan. 31, 1971

FORMAN, WILLIAM N., lawyer; b. San Francisco, Dec. 12, 1930; B.A., U. Nev., 1952; LL.B., U. Utah, 1955. Admitted to Nev. bar, 1955; partner firm Woodburn, Forman, Wedge, Blakey, Folsom and Hug, Reno; legislative bill drafter, 1957; spl. dep. atty. gen., 1959-62. Mem. Am. (state chmn. jr. bar div. 1961), Washoe County bar assns., State Bar Nev., Phi Alpha Delta. Office: First Nat Bank Bldg Reno NV 89501*

FORNESS, MILDRED M., librarian; b. Allegany, N.Y., Sept. 23, 1902; d. John Joseph and Ernestine (Green) Forness; student Geneseo State Normal Sch., 1920-22; B.A., St. Bonaventure U., 1927; postgrad. Syracuse U., 1930, Columbia, 1940; M.A., Northwestern U., 1937. Asst. librarian Edinboro (Pa.) State Normal Sch., 1922-25; tchr. jr. high schs., Allegany, 1925-27; librarian Edinboro State Coll., Edinboro, Pa., 1927-66, dir. library edn., 1966-69, ret., 1969, also organizer, chmn. dept. library sci., dir. library edn. Mem. Am., Pa. library assns., N.E.A., Delta Kappa Gamma, Alpha Pi Omega, Alpha Delta Iota (adviser). Home: Box 195 Edinboro PA 16412

FORNEY, JOHN MCLAUGHLIN, advt. exec.; b. Los Angeles, June 4, 1927; s. John McLaughlin and Kathleen (Foster) F.; B.A., U. Ala., 1948; m. Margaret Pride Binger, Oct. 21, 1951; children—Rutledge, Burke, Cornelia, John, Pride. Staff and sports announcer, also producer radio sta. WAPI, Birmingham, Ala., 1948-49; TV Producer and copywriter Batton, Barton, Durstine & Osborn, N.Y.C., 1949-51, Biow Co., N.Y.C., 1951-52; exec. Keegan Advt. Agy., Birmingham, 1952-54; exec. v.p. Robert Luckie & Co., Birmingham, 1954— (now Luckie & Forney, Inc.); v.p., sec. Agy. Land Co., Birmingham. Mem. bd. Nat. Advt. Agy. Network, 1963-65. Chmn. publicity Jefferson County United Appeal, 1961. Bd. dirs. Children's Aid Soc., Birmingham, 1960—, Crippled Children's Clinic, 1970—. Served with USNR, 1945-46. Named Ala. Sportscaster of Year, 1960. Mem. U. Ala. Alumni Assn. (pres. Jefferson County 1959), S.A.R., Nat. Assn. Sportswriters and Sportscasters, Phi Delta Theta. Omicron Delta Kappa. Clubs: Birmingham Country, Birmingham Quarterback (bd. dirs. 1962-63, pres. 1971). Home: 3212 Salisbury Rd Birmingham AL 35213 Office: 120 Office Park Dr Birmingham AL 35223

FORNOF, JOHN RENCHIN, newspaper pub.; b. Streator, Ill., June 23, 1889; s. John W. and Sarah Jane (Seavey) F.; B.A., U. of Ill., 1910; m. Helen Honeywell, Sept. 14, 1910; children—Elizabeth Jane, John Honeywell. Reporter and mgr. Free Press, Streator, 1910-23, owner and pub., 1923-27; v.p. Times Press Pub. Co., 1927—; v.p., dir. Union Nat. Bank; dir. Citizens Loan & Investment Co., Eby-Cullen Co. Past pres., dir. La Salle County Tb Sanitarium; trustee Riverview Cemetery Assn. Mem. Streator C. of C. (dir. and past pres.), Phi Kappa Psi. Republican. Universalist. Mason, Elk, Odd Fellow. Clubs: University (Chicago); Streator (Streator). Home: 301 Court St Streator IL 61364 Office: 122 S Bloomington Streator IL 61364

FORNOFF, CHARLES WRIGHT, lawyer, educator; b. Pana, Ill., June 25, 1900; s. John Henry and Grace (Wright) F.; A.B., U. Ill., 1922, M.A., 1923, Ph.D., 1926, J.D., 1932; m. Inda Wilson, June 14, 1928; 1 dau., Jane. Admitted to Ill. bar, 1932; instr. history State U. Ia., 1924-25; asst. history, polit. sci. U. Ill., 1925-28; asst. prof. history, polit. sci. U. Ark., 1928-30, asst. prof. law, 1936-37; partner Fornoff & Fornoff, Pana, 1932-36; asst. prof. law U. Utah, 1937-38; asso. prof. law U. Ida., 1938-39, U. Toledo Coll. Law, 1939—, acting dean, 1942-46, dean, 1946-60. Mem. Am. Assn. U. Profs., Am., Ohio bar assns., Am. Judicature Soc., Assn. of Am. Law Schs. (mem. numerous councils and coms.), League Ohio Law Schs. (sec.-treas. 1946-51, pres. 1951-52), Phi Beta Kappa, Order of Coif. Author articles in law jours. Co-author: Anatomy of Modern Legal Education, 1961. Home: 2249 Meadowwood Dr Toledo OH 43606

FORRER, GORDON RANDOLPH, physician; b. Balt., Apr. 1, 1922; s. William Gordon and Blanche (Shules) F.; student State Tchrs. Coll., Towson, Md., 1939-41, Johns Hopkins, 1941-42; B.A., U. Md., 1945, M.D., 1947; m. Carol Lucille Hanke, May 26, 1951; children—Jane Elizabeth, Susan Ellen, John Gerritt. Intern U.S. Marine Hosp., Balt., 1947-48; psychiat. resident Ypsilanti (Mich.) State Hosp., 1948-50, Wayne County (Mich.) Mental Health Clinic, 1950-51; clin. dir. Northville (Mich.) State Hosp., 1954-60; pvt. practice psychiatry, Detroit, 1960—; chief psychiatry Mt. Carmel Mercy Hosp.; mem. staff St. Mary Hosp., Livonia, Mich., Detroit Rehab. Inst.; clin. asst. prof. Wayne U. Med. Sch. 1955-68. Introduced atropine coma therapy for treatment psychoses, 1950; devel. psychoanalytic theory hallucination, psychoanalytic theory placebo. Served to capt., M.C., AUS, 1952-54. Diplomate Am. Bd. Psychiatry and Neurology. Mem. Mich. State, Wayne County med. socs., Mich. Soc. Psychiatry and Neurology (Research award 1953), Am., Pan-Am. med. assns., Am. Psychiat. Assn. Trustee Schoolcraft Coll., Livonia, 1963-67. Author: Weaning and Human Development, 1969; also articles in field. Home: 45995 W Main St Northville MI 48167 Office: 20141 James Couzens Hwy Detroit MI

FORREST, EDWARD JOHN, coll. dean; b. Reynoldsville, Pa., Dec. 27, 1917; s. B. William and Amelia (Marta) F.; B.S., U. Pitts., 1939, D.D.S., 1941, M.S., 1949, Ph.D., 1953; m. Alice E. Hamerlick, May 15, 1944; children—Edward J., Alice Cynthia, Thomas D. Gen. practice dentistry, Ambridge, Pa., 1941-42; practice orthodontics, Sewickley, Pa., 1948—; mem. faculty and adminstrn. U. Ill., Chgo., 1957-61, dir. USPHS dental assistance program, 1957-61, asso. prof. orthodontics, 1957-59; mem. faculty and adminstrn. U. Pitts., 1952-57, 58—, dir. teaching edn. program, 1959-61, dean Sch. Dental Medicine, 1961—, prof. orthodontics, 1960—; cons. USPHS, 1957-68, Commonwealth Pa., 1956-69, testing program Am. Dental Assn., 1958-61, dental assn. certification bd. testing Psychol. Center N.Y., 1958-61, VA Oakland and Leech Farm, Pitts., 1961—. Mem. adv. council central office VA, 1969—. Pres. Ambridge Bd. Edn., 1951-56. Bd. dirs. Kane Hosp. for Aged, Pitts.; trustee Presbyn.-Univ. Hosp., Pitts., 1966-67. Served with AUS, 1942-46. Diplomate Am. Bd. Orthodontics. Fellow Acad. Gen. Dentistry, Am. Coll. Dentists, Acad. Consulting Dentistry; mem. Am. Dental Assn. (del. from Pa. 1964-68), Pa. Dental Assn. (del. from 10th dist. 1961-69), Odontological Soc. Western Pa. (former pres.), Am. Orthodontics Soc., Internat. Assn. Dental Research, Sigma Xi, Psi Omega, Omicron Kappa Upsilon. Contbr. profl. jours. Moderator series Ask Yor Dentist, WQED-TV, Pitts., 1962-64. Home: Oliver Rd Sewickley PA 15143 Office: 3500 Terrace St Pittsburgh PA 15213

FORREST, FREDERICK AUGUST, educator; b. Buenos Aires, Argentina, Dec. 27, 1914; s. Santiago Noe and Desiderata (La Tullerie) F.; Bachelor Humanities, Colegio Nacional Bartolome Mitre, 1933; student Institute de Estudios Libres; A.A., San Mateo Jr. Coll., 1942; student U. Cal. at Berkeley, 1942-43, M.A. in L.S., 1955; B.A., San Jose State Coll., 1947; M.A., Stanford, 1948, Ph. D., 1952; m. Alice Elizabeth Brown, June 17, 1955 (div. 1967); m. 2d, Lorain June McClintock, 1967. Came to U.S., 1940, naturalized, 1943. Playground dir., Argentina, 1934-39; teaching asst. Stanford, 1949-50; lectr. modern U.S. history Ateneo de la Juventud, 1949-50; travel fellow Inst. Internat. Edn., for collection data on constl. history of Argentina, 1952-53; bibiliographer, social sci. cataloguer Long Beach State Coll., 1955-58, head librarian, 1958-60; asst. prof. history So. Ill. U., 1959-60; dean libraries and communication arts Inter-Am. U., San German, P.R., 1960-64; curator Hispanic Am. collections Yale, 1964-65; asso. prof. library sci. Denver U., 1965-68; chmn. dept. library sci. Queens Coll. City U. N.Y.; also spl. lectr. econs.; lectr. Latin Am. history peace corps, Ecuador, 1962. Bd. dirs. Eurico Corp., mfrs. x-ray plates, Mayaguez, P.R. Mem. Latin Am. Council. Served with USAAF, 1943-46; PTO. Research editor Inst. Press, New Haven. Address: Queen Coll City U NY Flushing NY 11367

FORREST, LEONARD JOSEPH, mfg. co. exec.; b. Shelton, Wash., Dec. 8, 1906; s. James and Helen (Carstairs) F.; m. Claribel Raasch, Sept. 16, 1937; children—Judith Ann, William Morgan. Dir. Polson Logging Co., Hoquiam, Wash., 1943-47; with ITT Rayonier, Inc. (name change due to merger 1968), 1947—, mgr. N.W. timber div., 1958-61, v.p., mgr. div., Hoquiam, 1961—; chmn. bd., dir. Timbermen's Nat. Bank of Hoquiam; dir. Western Forest Industries, Ltd., National Bank of Washington. Pres. Assn. Wash. Industries, 1960-62; pres., dir. Indsl. Forestry Assn. Mason (32, Shriner), Rotarian, Elk. Home: 547 Fairway Dr Aberdeen WA 98520 Office: PO Box 539 Hoquiam WA 98550

FORREST, MATTHEW GALBRAITH, naval architect; b. Johnstone, Scotland, July 8, 1906; s. John and Jean (Galbraith) F.; brought to U.S., 1906, naturalized, 1912; B.S., U. Mich., 1927; postgrad. Bklyn. Poly Inst., 1935-36; certificate in Celestial Navigation, Weems Sch. Navigation, 1937; m. Elizabeth Dickinson, July 28, 1937; children—Matthew Dickinson, Jonathan Lee. With Fed. Shipbldg. & Dry Dock Co., Kearny, N.J., summers 1925-26; jr. sci. dept. N.Y. Shipbuilding Co., Camden, N.J., 1927; marine technician marine dept. Gulf Refining Co., N.Y.C., 1928; designer, engr. Gibbs & Cox, Inc., N.Y.C., 1928-34, asst. naval architect, 1934-52, v.p. naval architecture, 1956-67, exec. v.p., 1967-71, sr. cons., 1971—. Mem. Internat. Conf. for Safety of Life at Sea, 1960. Mem. Bd. Edn., Chatham, N.J., 1947-54. Co-founder, past v.p., bd. dirs. Morris County (N.J.) Assn. Mental Health; past pres. bd. trustees Chatham Pub. Library. Served with USNR, World War II; PTO. Decorated Naval Certificate Commendation; recipient Capt. Joseph H. Linnard prize Soc. Naval Architects and Marine Engrs., 1948, Distinguished Alumnus citation U. Mich., 1953; David W. Taylor medal Soc. Naval Architects and Marine Engrs., 1968. Registered profl. engr., N.Y. Mem. Soc. Naval Architects. and Marine Engrs. (pres. 1965-66, chmn. publs. com. 1968-70, hon. mem.), Am. Soc. Naval Engrs. Presbyn. Home: Guinea Hollow Rd Califon NJ 07830 Office: 21 West St New York City NY 10006

FORREST, STEPHEN PAUL, educator, dentist; b. Reynoldsville, Pa., July 23, 1912; s. B. William and Amelia (Marta) F.; B.S., U. Pitts., 1936, D.D.S., 1936, M.S., 1938; m. Eleanor R. Conrady, 1940; children—Eleanor Ruth, Mary Kaaren, Stephen Paul. Pvt. practice of dentistry, specializing in prosthetics, 1936—; prof. prosthetic dentistry, dir. dept. Baylor U. Sch. Dentistry, 1948- 56, prof. prosthetic dentistry Baylor U. Grad. Sch., 1948-56; asso. dean St. Louis U. Sch. Dentistry, 1956-57, prof. prosthetic dentistry, dir. dept., faculty Grad. Sch., 1956—, dean Sch. Dentistry, 1957—; cons. U. Mo., Crippled Children's Service, Cardinal Glennon Hosp.; cons. VA Central Dist. Lab., Dallas, 1952-57, VA Hosp., Big Spring, Tex., 1953-57, VA Domiciliary Center, Bonhomme, Tex., 1953-57, VA Hosp., Dallas, 1951-57, VA Hosp., McKinney, Tex., 1952-57, U. Saigon, Vietnam; dentist, St. Mary's and Firmin Desloge hosps., St. Louis U.; cons. prosthodontics John Cochran VA Hosp., St. Louis. Mem. Sci. adv. com., Strontium 90 Baby Tooth Survey; trustee Dr. Tom Dooley Edn. Found.; nat. adv. dental research council Dept. Health, Edn. and Welfare. Served to major AUS, World War II. Recipient of Mo. Dental Assn. Centennial award; U. Pitts. distinguished alumnus award, 1969. Fellow Am. Coll. Dentists, A.A.A.S., Internat. Coll. Dentists, Am. Pub. Health Assn.; mem. N.Y. Acad. Sci., Gerontol. Soc., Am. Dental Assn., Am. Cleft Palate Assn., Am. Assn. Cleft Palate Rehab. (pres. 1958), Am. Assn. U. Profs., Am. Assn. Dental Schs. (chmn. legislative com.), Internat. Assn. Dental Research, Mo. Dental Assn. (del. to Am. Dental Assn.), Greater St. Louis Dental Soc. (cons. TV Com., chmn. legislative com.), Am. Acad. History Dentistry (exec. com., pres. 1966), Internat. Congress on Cleft Palate (adviser to secretariat), Am. Assn. History Medicine, Am. Assn. Dental Editors, Fedn. Dentaire Internat., Am. Assn. Mil. Surgeons, Southwestern Soc. Denture Prosthesis, Southwestern Soc. Dental Medicine, Am. Prosthodontic Soc., St. Louis Soc. Dental Sci., Odontol. Soc. Western Pa., Tex. Acad. Sci., Am. Name Soc., St. Apollonia Guild, Omicron Kappa Upsilon, Delta Sigma Delta. Roman Catholic. Editor: Current Therapy in Dentistry, vol. I, 1964, vol. II, 1966, vol. III, 1968. Contbr. articles dental jours. Home: 1501 Windridge Dr St Louis MO 63104

FORREST, WILLIAM A., Jr., corp. exec.; b. 1929; B.A., U. Va., 1951, LL.B., 1956; married. With firm McGuire, Woods, King, Davis & Patterson, 1956-65, partner 1961-65; with A.H. Robins Co. Inc., 1966—, sec., asst. gen. counsel, 1966-69, sec., gen. counsel, 1969—; dir. Capital Savs. and Loan Assn. Pres. Richmond Tennis Patrons Assn., 1969—; trustee Crippled Children's Hosp., 1970—; bd. dirs. Team Progress, 1970—. Served with AUS, 1951-53. Address: 1407 Cummings Dr Richmond VA 23220

FORREST, WILLIAM RICHARD, advt. exec.; b. Scarborough, Eng., Apr. 7, 1906; s. William Hill and Mary Ellen (Croft) F.; brought to U.S., 1907, naturalized, 1913; B.S., U. Wis., 1928; postgrad. Northwestern U., 1941-43; m. Ruth Margaret Baker, Dec. 6, 1930; children—Richard Baker, Nancy Lee (Mrs. Ronald Gough). With Wallace Press & Columbian Engraving Co., Chgo., 1928-32, Brown & Bigelow, South Bend, Ind., 1932-36; creative dir. The H. M. Gousha Pub. Co., Chgo., 1936-43; market research Foote, Cone & Belding Advt. Agy., 1943-45, account exec., 1945-47, exec. asst., 1947- 49, account supr., 1949-51, v.p., 1951-56, dir., 1955-67, sr. v.p., 1956- 67, chmn. plans bd., 1957-67; pres. Win-Par, Inc., Winter Park, Fla., 1967—, Golfside Devel. Co., Chgo., 1967—; dir. Armour-Dial, Inc., Chgo. Mem. Newcomen Soc. N.Am., Delta Phi Delta, Scabbard and Blade. Episcopalian. Clubs: Oak Park Curling, Oak Park (Ill.) Country; Tavern (Chgo.). Home: 1040 Lake Shore Dr Chicago IL 60611 Office: 401 N Michigan Av Chicago IL 60611

FORRESTAL, DANIEL JOSEPH, Jr., pub. relations exec.; b. St. Louis, Sept. 2, 1912; s. Daniel Joseph and Kathryn Cecilla (Otto) F.; student St. Louis U., 1930-34; grad. Advanced Mgmt. Program, Harvard Bus. Sch., 1948; m. Esther Witte, Oct. 5, 1940; children—Daniel Joseph III, Patrick George, Elizabeth Kathryn. Newspaperman, 1927-46; staff St. Louis Globe-Democrat, 1933-46, asst. mng. editor, 1941-46, war corr. for N. Am. Newspaper Alliance, 1945; with Monsanto Co., St. Louis, 1947—, mgr. pub. relations, 1951-58, dir. pub. relations, 1958—. Chmn. pub. relations com. St. Louis U., 1959-68. Recipient Alumni Merit award St. Louis U., 1960. Mem. Pub. Relations Soc. Am. (pres. 1957), Mfg. Chemists Assn. (pub. relations com. chmn. 1965-67), Sigma Delta Chi. Clubs: Overseas Press Am. (asso.); Harvard Business School (pres. 1961-62); The Saint Louis, Bellerive Country (gov. 1962-66) (St. Louis). Co-author: Public Relations Handbook, 1969. Home: 17 Bellerive Country Club Grounds St Louis MO 63141 Office: 800 N Lindbergh Blvd St Louis MO 63166

FORRESTAL, MICHAEL VINCENT, lawyer; b. N.Y.C., Nov. 26, 1927; s. James Vincent and Josephine (Ogden) F.; grad. Philips Exeter Acad., 1945; student Princeton, 1949; LL.B., Harvard, 1953. Admitted to N.Y. bar, 1954, since practiced in N.Y.C.; partner firm Shearman & Sterling, 1960—. Spl. asst. to Averell Harriman, dir. Marshall Plan, 1948-50; sr. mem. White House Nat. Security Staff, 1962-65; sec. tripartite Naval Commn., Berlin, 1946; asst. U.S. naval attache, Moscow, USSR, 1946-47. Chmn. Met. Opera Guild, 1967—; bd. dirs. Met. Opera Assn., 1965—, Nat. Opera Inst., 1971—; trustee Aiken (S.C.) Prep. Sch., 1959—; exec. sec. adv. com. Kennedy Inst. Politics, Harvard, 1967—; trustee Inst. Advanced Study, Princeton, N.J., 1970—. Mem. Am. Bar Assn., Assn. Bar City N.Y., Council on Fgn. Relations. Episcopalian. Clubs: Racquet and Tennis, Links (N.Y.C.); Metropolitan (Washington); Travellers (Paris, France). Home: 25 Central Park West New York City NY 10023 Office: 53 Wall St New York City NY 10005

FORRESTAL, MILLARD J., Jr., assn. exec. Pres., Met. Opera Guild Inc., N.Y.C. Office: 1865 Broadway New York City NY 10023*

FORRESTER, ALVIN THEODORE, physicist; b. Bklyn., Apr. 13, 1918; s. Joseph D. and Rose (Kissen) F.; A.B., Cornell U., 1938, A.M., 1939, Ph.D., 1942; m. June Doris Berg, Oct. 5, 1956; children—Bruce H., David A., Cheri J., William C., Susan J. Research asso. U. Cal. at Berkeley, 1942-45; physicist RCA Labs., Princeton, N.J., 1945-46; asst. physics U. So. Cal., Los Angeles, 1946- 51, asso. prof., 1951-54; vis. asso. prof. physics U. Pitts., 1954-55; physicist Westinghouse Research Labs., Pitts., 1955-58; nuclear spl. Atomics Internat., Los Angeles, 1958-59; dept. mgr. Electro-Optical Systems, Pasadena, Cal., 1959-65; prof. U. Cal. at Irvine, 1965-67, at Los Angeles, 1967—. Fellow Am. Phys. Soc., I.E.E.E.; mem. Am. Rocket Soc. (Research award 1962, chmn. electrostatic propulsion panel 1960- 61), Am. Inst. Aeros. and Astronautics, A.A.A.S., Am. Assn. U. Profs., Am. Assn. Physics Tchrs., Am. Optical Soc., Sigma Xi, Phi Kappa Phi. Research in photoetoelectric mixing of light, ion propulsion, isotope separation, superconductivity, physics, laser scattering. Home: 519 N Roxbury Dr Beverly Hills CA90210

FORRESTER, BRUCE MILLAR, U.S. judge; b. Kansas City, Mo., Dec. 26, 1908; s. James M. and Bertha (Wilkinson) F.; J.D., U. Mo., 1935; m. Anne Lee Broaddus, Nov. 9, 1937; children—Anne Norris, Jean Bruce, Bruce Millar. Admitted to Mo. bar, 1935, practiced in Kansas City, 1935-57; mem. firm Watson, Ess, Groner, Barnett & Whittaker (now Watson, Ess, Marshall & Enggas); judge U.S. Tax Court, Washington, 1957—. Trustee Holton-Arms School, Washington. Served with AUS, 1944-45; instr. ROTC. Mem. Fed., Am., Mo., Kansas City bar assns., Lawyers Assn. Kansas City, Am. Law Inst., Am. Judicature Soc., Sigma Alpha Epsilon (past pres., trustee). Episcopalian. Home: 7017 Beechwood Dr Chevy Chase MD 20015 Office: 1111 Constitution Av Washington DC 20004

FORRESTER, JAMES, coll. pres.; b. Edinburgh, Scotland, May 15, 1909; s. John and Agnes (McLean) F.; B.A., Queen's U. (Can.), 1938; M.A., U. So. Cal., 1951, Ph.D., 1958; LL.D., Whitworth Coll., 1949; D.D., Sterling Coll., 1949; m. Melba Ismay, Nov. 10, 1939; children—Lynne, Jimmy. Came to U.S., 1926, naturalized, 1944. Field sec. Inter-Varsity Fellowship, Toronto, 1937-39; asst. to pres. Whitworth Coll., 1939-42; pres. Westmont Coll., Santa Barbara, Cal., 1947-50; ordained to ministry Baptist Ch., 1942; pastor in Cal., 1946-47, 54-58; v.p. Whitworth Coll., 1958-60; pres. Gordon Coll and Gordon Div. Sch., Wenham, Mass., 1960—. Bd. dirs. Council Advancement Small Colls. Served as chaplain USAAF, 1943-46. Mem. Acad. Religion and Mental Health, Ariz. Acad., Am. Sci. Affiliation. Rotarian. Author book reviews, articles. Home: 44 Alan Rd South Hamilton MA 01982 Office: Gordon Coll Wenham MA 01984

FORRESTER, JAMES DONALD, ednl. adminstr., mining engr.; b. Salt Lake City, Apr. 6, 1906; s. James Gillon and Diana (George) F.; B.S., U. Utah, 1928, Geol.E., 1956; M.S., Cornell U., 1929, Ph.D., 1935; m. Lisle Keele, Sept. 27, 1929; 1 dau., Lisle Jean. Mining geologist Anaconda Copper Mining Co., Butte, Mont., 1929-32, 1935-39; instr. geology Cornell U., 1928-29, 34-35; prof. geol. engring. U. of Ida., 1939-44, head dept. geology, 1939-44; geologist U.S. Geol. Survey, intermittently 1943-45; prof. mining engring., chmn. dept. Mo. Sch. of Mines and Metallurgy, 1944-54, chmn. com. on grad. study, 1944-54; dean coll. mines U. Ida., 1954-56; dir. Ida. Bur. Mines and Geology, 1954-56; dean coll. mines U. Ariz., 1956-70; dir. Ariz. Bur. Mines, 1956-70; dir. div. environmental engring. and research Phelps Dodge Corp., 1970—. Mem. adv. com. on engring. U.S. Civil Service Commn., 1950—; mem. council Engrs. Council for Profl. Devel., 1963-69. Registered profl. engr., Mo. Fellow Geol. Soc. Am., Soc. Econ. Geologists, Am. Inst. Mining Engrs. (chmn. geology sub-div. mining geology, geophysics div. 1952; chmn. mining, geology and geophysics div. 1954-55, dir. 1957-60, western regional v.p. 1957-60, chmn. council on edn. 1960), Ariz. Acad., Mining and Metall. Soc. Am. (mem. council 1963-68). Am. Soc. Engring. Edn.; mem. Sigma Xi, Pi Kappa Alpha, Theta Tau, Tau Beta Pi, Phi Eta Sigma. Presbyn. Rotarian. Clubs: Old Pueblo (Tucson); Mining of the Southwest. Author several books on geology. Home: 5719 E 8th St Tucson AZ 85711

FORRESTER, JAY WRIGHT, educator; b. Anselmo, Neb., July 14, 1918; s. Marmaduke M. and Ethel Pearl (Wright) F.; B.Sc., U. Neb., 1939, D. Engring. (hon.), 1954; M.Sc., Mass. Inst. Tech., 1945; D.Sc. (hon.), Boston U., 1969; D.Engring. (hon.), Newark Coll. Engring., 1971; m. Susan Swett, July 27, 1946; children—Judith, Nathan Blair, Ned Cromwell. Tchr., X-ray equipment research Mass. Inst. Tech., 1939-40, co-founder servomechanisms lab., 1940, devel. electric and hydraulic servomechanisms for gun mounts and radar, 1940-44, asso. dir. servomechanisms lab., also supr. Whirlwind I digital computer devel., 1944-51, founder Digital Computer Lab., dir., 1951-56, div. head Lincoln Lab. for Air Def., 1951-56; prof. mgmt. Sloan Sch. Mgmt., Mass. Inst. Tech., 1956—; partner Forrester Cattle Ranch, Anselmo, Neb. Dir. ALZA Corp. Recipient Inventor of Yr. award, Geo. Washington U., 1968; Valdemar Poulsen Gold medal Danish Acad. Tech. Scis., 1969. Fellow I.E.E.E., Am. Acad. Arts and Scis., Acad. Mgmt., mem. Nat. Acad. Engring., Inst. Mgmt. Scis., Am.

Phys. Soc., Assn. Computing Machinery, Eta Kappa Nu, Sigma Xi, Sigma Tau. Patentee in servomechanisms, digital information storage, indsl. control. Lectures and tech. papers on digital computers and indsl. mgmt.; also dynamics indsl. and econ. behavior. Author: Industrial Dynamics, 1961; Principles of Systems, 1968; Urban Dynamics, 1969; World Dynamics, 1971. Home: King Lane Concord MA 01742 Office: Mass Inst Tech Cambridge MA 02139

FORRESTER, MAUREEN KATHERINE STEWART, contralto; b. Montreal, Que., Can., July 25, 1930; d. Thomas and Mae (Arnold) F.; student of Sally Martin, Frank Rowe, Bernard Diamant; m. Eugene J. Kash, July 1954; children—Paula, Gina, Daniel, Linda. Debut in Can., at Town Hall, N.Y.C., 1956; concert appearances with N.Y. Philharmonic, orchs. in Chgo., Pitts., Detroit, Boston, San Francisco, New Orleans, Mpls., numerous others; festival appearances with Empire State Festival, also in Berlin, Holland, Monteaux, Bournemouth. Edithburgh Internat. Festival, numerous others U.S., Can. and Europe; operatic appearances with Am. Opera Soc.; title role in Orfeo, Toronto. 1961; recording artist for RCA Victor. Home: 338 Roslyn St Westmount Montreal Quebec Canada Office: care Ingpen & Williams Ltd 14 Kensington Ct London W8 England

FORRESTER, WILLIAM RAY, dean, lawyer; b. Little Rock, Ark., Jan. 14, 1911; s. William Thomas and Mary Louise (Lucas) F.; A.B., U. Ark., 1933, LL.D., 1963; J.D., U. Chicago, 1935; m. Celine Mortee Penn, Oct. 31, 1942; children—William Ray, Catherine Lucas, David. Stephen. Admitted to Ill. bar, 1936, N.Y. bar, 1970; mem. legal div., trust dept., 1st Nat. Bank, Chgo., 1935; atty., Defrees, Buckingham, Fiske & O'Brien, Chgo., 1935-41; asst. prof. law, Tulane U., 1941-43, prof. law, 1943-49, sec. law faculty. 1942-46, dean and prof. law, 1952-63, faculty editor Tulane Law Review, 1942-46; dean and prof. law Vanderbilt U., 1949-52, Cornell U. Law Sch., Ithaca, N.Y., 1963—; mem. summer faculty U. Wis., 1943, U. Miss., 1948. U. N.C., 1954, Stanford, 1955, Tex. Tech., 1968; vis. prof. Yale Sch. Law. fall 1956, U. P.R., summer 1958; Walker-Ames prof. law U. Washington, summer 1962; faculty Hastings Coll. Law, U. Cal., summer 1966; vis. prof. U. Ryukyus (Okinawa), summer 1969. Pub. mem. Regional WSB, 1950-52; permanent arbitrator Internat. Havester and UAWCIO, 1951- 52; Interim chmn. Bd. of Conciliation and Arbitration of U.S. Steel and United Steelworkers of Am.; 1949-51; cons. proposed revision of La. Constitution, 1947-50; commr. on Uniform State laws for La., 1957-63; mem. New Orleans Mayor's Com. Law Enforcement, 1963. Mem. bd. govs. Nat. Acad. Arbitrators, 1949-50. Trustee Metairie Country Day Sch., 1955-61, pres. bd., 1959-61; mem. vis. com. Vanderbilt Law Sch., 1969—. Mem. Am. Bar Assn., N.Y. State Bar, Order of Coif, Kappa Delta Phi (hon.), Sigma Nu (comdr. 1932), Omicron Delta Kappa, Phi Delta Phi, Tau Kappa Alpha. Club: Boston (New Orleans). Author: Forrester's Edition of Dobie and Ladd, Federal Jurisdiction and Procedure, 1950; Cases and Materials on Constitutional Law, 1959, Supplement, 1966; (with Currier) Federal Jurisdiction and Procedure, 1962, 2d edit. (with Currier and Moye, 1970. Contbr. to various legal publs. Home: 218 Fall Creek Dr Ithaca NY 14850

FORROW, BRIAN DEREK, lawyer, corp. exec.; b. N.Y.C., Feb. 6, 1927; s. Frederick George and Doris (Williams) F.; A.B., Princeton, 1947; J.D., Harvard, 1950; m. Eleanor Reid, Mar. 8, 1952; children—Lisa Coggins, Brian Lachlan, Catherine Frances, Derek Skylstead. Admitted to N.Y. bar, 1950; asso. firm Cahill, Gordon. Sonnett, Reindel & Ohl, and predecessors, 1950-64, mem. firm, 1964-68; v.p., gen.counsel Allied Chem. Corp., 1968—, dir., 1969—. Served to 1st lt. USAF, 1951-53. Mem. Am., Internat., Conn., N.Y. State bar assns., Bar Assn. City N.Y., Am. Soc. Internat. Law, Fgn. Tax Assn. Republican. Episcopalian. (sr. warden). Author articles. Home: 704 Lake Av Greenwich CT 06830 Office: 1411 Broadway New York City NY 10018

FORRY, JOHN EMERSON, aerospace co. exec.; b. Coweta, Okla., Feb. 13, 1920; s. Fred Emerson and Elizabeth (Ingram) F.; B.S. in Mech. Engring., Okla. State U., 1939; LL.B., George Washington U., 1953; m. Marion Carlotta MacArthur, May 24, 1941; children—John Ingram, Anne Elizabeth. Asst. chief engr. Piper Aricraft Corp., 1939-41; project engr. CAA, Kansas City, Mo., 1942; head aircraft design research br. Bur. Aero., U.S. Navy, 1946-54; asst. dir. Office Aircraft and Marinecraft, Dept. Def., 1954-57; with McDonnell Aircraft Corp., St. Louis, 1957—, v.p., controller, 1968—; dir. McDonnel Douglas Astronautics Co. Mem. bishop's vestry P.E. Diocese Mo., 1968—. Alderman, Warson Woods, Mo., 1960-62. Bd. dirs. Webster Groves (Mo.) YMCA, 1960-64. Served to lt. USNR, 1943-46. Admitted to D.C. bar, 1953, Mo. bar, 1960; rgistered prof. engr., D.C. Mem. Sigma Tau, Phi Delta Phi. Home: 921 Masonridge Rd St Louis MO 63141 Office: PO Box 516 St Louis MO 63166

FORSBERG, CARL J., utilities exec.; b. Chgo., Feb. 11, 1903; s. Charles J. and Sigrid (Stahlberg) F.; B.S., U.S. Naval Acad., 1926; m. Marion L. Felt, Oct. 6, 1926; 1 dau., Carol L. Sales engr. Pub. Service Co. No. Ill., Chgo., 1928-34; indsl. engr. Wis. Power & Light Co., Madison, 1934-42, various exec. positions, 1946-54, chmn., 1965—; dir. Sentry Life Ins. Co., First Wis. Bankshares. Commd. ensign U.S. Navy, 1926; served as comdr. USNR, 1942-46. Home: 3212 Bluff St Madison WI 53705 Office: 122 W Washington Av Madison WI 53701

FORSBERG, FRANKLIN S., pub. co. exec.; b. Salt Lake City, Oct. 21, 1905; s. Charles E. and Anna (Olson) F.; B.S., U. Utah, 1930; M.B. A., N.Y.U. Grad. Sch. of Bus. Adminstrn.; m. Ann Routree. January 15, 1944; children—Kristin, Lars, Erik. Research and sales analyst for Reuben H. Donelley, N.Y.C., 1936-37; gen. mgr. Street & Smith Pubs., Inc., N.Y.C., 1937-42, v. p., 1946-47; pres. Forsberg, Merrit & Harrity, Inc., N.Y.C., publs. counselors, 1947-48; pres. and pub., Liberty mag., 1948-50; Forsberg & Church, mgmt. cons., 1950-52; operations v.p. Popular Mechanics Co., 1955-59; exec. v.p. Holt, Rinehart & Winston, 1959—, also dir. Served as col. in charge of information and education activities (Yank, The Army Weekly, Army News Service, Camp Newspaper Service, NEWSMAP, Fgn. Lang. Unit, Radio and Music Sects.; Stars and Stripes), U.S. Army, 1942-46. Decorated D.S.M. (U.S.); Order of Brit. Empire; Royal Order of Vasa (Sweden). Mem. Mag. Pubs. Assn. (dir.), Swedish C. of C. U.S.A. (dir.), Pi Kappa Alpha. Clubs: Chicago (Chgo.); Dutch Treat (dir.), Lochinvar (N.Y.C.); Question. Home: 465 Lake Av Greenwich CT 06830 Office: 383 Madison Av New York City NY 10017

FORSBERG, ROBERT LEE, utility exec.; b. Columbus, O., May 20, 1916; s. Frederik and Martha (Vorpe) F.; B.S.C., Miami-Jacobs Bus. Coll., Dayton, O., 1939; m. Janet L. Blakley, Jan. 27, 1942; children—Terry Lee, James Lind. Successively budget dir., comptroller, dir. market research Airtemp div. Chrysler Corp., 1936-58; with G.E. Schumacher, Dayton, 1958-61; with Ariz. Pub. Service Co., Phoenix, 1961—, treas., 1963—, asst. sec., 1963—, financial v.p., 1967-71, exec. v.p. finance and control, 1971—. Bd. dirs. United Fund, 1963- 69, treas., 1966, pres., 1967, 1968; treas. Phoenix operation Guide Dogs for Blind, 1964-68; mem. financial com., adv. bd. Theodore Roosevelt council Boy Scouts Am., 1964-66. Served with AUS, 1944-46. Mem. Am., Pacific Coast (chmn. exec. com., adminstrv. services sect. 1968) gas assns., Phoenix Soc. Financial Analysts (pres. 1968-69), Financial Execs. Inst., Financial Analysts Fedn., Nat. Assn. Accountants, Pacific Coast Elec. Assn., Edison Electric Inst., Newcomen Soc. N. Am., Phoenix C. of C., Ariz. Acad., Phi Theta Pi. Home: 2820 E Cinnabar Av Phoenix AZ 85028 Office: PO Box 21666 501 S 3d Av Phoenix AZ 85036

FORSEE, AYLESA, author; b. Kirksville, Mo.; d. Edward W. and Lena (Moore) Forsee; B.S., S.D. State U.; Mus.B., MacPhail Coll. Music, Mpls., 1938; M.A., U. Colo., 1939. Instr. history music, Rochester, Minn., 1939-45; tchr. history and music U. Ia., 1945-46, U. Denver, 1946-49; mem. staff writers conf. Temple Buell Coll., 1967, 68. Mem. adv. bd. Nat. Writers Club. Recipient Helen Fish award, 1955. Mem. Colorado Author's League. Christian Scientist. Author: The Whirly Bird, 1955; Miracle for Mingo, 1956; Too Much Dog, 1957; American Women Who Scored Firsts, 1958; Louis Agassiz: Pied Piper of Science, 1958; Frank Lloyd Wright: Rebel in Concrete, 1959; Women Who Reached for Tomorrow, 1960; My Love and I Together, 1961; Beneath Land and Sea, 1962; Albert Einstein, 1963; William Henry Jackson, 1964; Pablo Casals: Cellist for Freedom, 1965; Men of Modern Architecture, 1966; Headliners, 1967; Famous Photographers, 1968; Artur Rubinstein: King of the Keyboard, 1969. Address: 1845 Bluebell Av Boulder CO 80302

FORSHAM, PETER HUGH, physician; b. New Orleans, Nov. 15, 1915; s. John S. and Augusta (Kahnweiler) F.; B.A., Cambridge U., 1937, M.A., 1941; M.D. cum laude, Harvard, 1943; m. Constance Campbell, Aug. 2, 1947; children—Barbara (Mrs. Thomas G. Cheetham), Elizabeth, Ann. Intern, resident research fellow Peter Bent Brigham Hosp., Boston, 1944-51, also instr. Harvard, 1950-51; asso. prof. medicine and pediatrics U. Cal., 1952-57, prof., 1957—, also dir. metabolic research unit, 1952—, chief endocrinology dept. medicine, 1957—; dir. Gen. Clin. Research Center of U. Cal. Hosps., 1963—; mem. nat. adv. council on health research socs. NIH; cons. Oak Knoll, Naval, San Francisco VA hosps. Fellow N.Y. Acad. Sci.; mem. A.M.A., Mass., Cal., San Francisco med. assns., Endocrine Soc., Am., San Francisco (past pres.), No. Cal. (pres.) diabetes assns., Western Assn. Physicians, Cal. Soc. Internal Medicine, Assn. Am. Physicians, Am. Soc. Clin. Investigation, Am. Fedn. Clin. Research (pres. San Francisco br. 1956), Laurentian Hormone Conf., Western Soc. Clin. Research, A.A.A.S., Soc. Exptl. Biology and Medicine, Sigma Xi. Mem. editorial bd. of Diabetes, 1961-71; Metabolism, 1962-69. Contbr. articles profl. jours., chpts. in books. Home: 267 Hillside Av Mill Valley CA 94941 Office: University of California Hospitals San Francisco CA 94122

FORSHEW, JOHN HILDRETH, III, former advt. exec.; b. Scranton, Pa., Nov. 12, 1911; s. Charles Pierpont and Geraldine (Wright) F.; student Lehigh U., 1928-31; night courses, N.Y.U., Fla. So. Coll.; m. Charlotte Jacobus, Jan. 9, 1935; children—Diana S., Frank C., Elizabeth C., Dawn W., Charles P. II. Sales rep. system survey and machine installation IBM Corp., 1931-34, Remington-Rand, Inc., 1934-35; founder, owner Forshew & Jacobus, 1935- 42; mgr. research dept. Young & Rubicam, 1944-46; account exec. Indsl. Surveys, 1946-48; v.p., account rep., dir. consumer panel J. Walter Thompson Co., 1948-54; sr. v.p., mem. exec. com., dir. Campbell-Ewald Co., 1954-69, ret., 1969. Bd. dirs. Western Coll. for Women, Bloomfield Country Day Sch. Served with USAAF, 1942-44. Mem. Am. Marketing Soc., Market Research Council, Alpha Delta Sigma. Presbyn. Home: 1530 Glengarry Rd Birmingham MI 48010 Office: General Motors Bldg Detroit MI

FORSLUND, HERMAN CARL, educator; b. Puyallup, Wash., Sept. 13, 1911; s. Carl Eric and Amelia (Lindberg) F.; B.S., Wash. State U., 1938, M.S., 1940; m. Esther M. Kaufman, June 11, 1939; children—Doreen J. (Mrs. Ed Corwin), Charles H. Mem. faculty Wash. State U., 1938-40, Ida. State Coll., 1940-45; mem. faculty Ore. State U., 1945-, prof., pharmacy, 1956-, head dept. pharmacy adminstrn. Sch. Pharmacy, 1960—, asst. dean Sch. Pharmacy, 1968—; Fulbright lectr., cons. Alexandria (Egypt) U., 1960- 61. Mem. nat. bd. higher edn. Methodist Ch., 1956-60. Mem. Ore. Pharm. Assn., Sigma Xi, Kappa Psi (nat. pres. 1961-63), Rho Chi. Elk. Home: 1737 Beca Corvallis OR 97330

FORSON, NORMAN RAY, corp. exec.; b. Port Arthur, Tex., July 12, 1929; s. Hollis G. and Annie (Butler) F.; B.A., Baylor U., 1952; M.B.A., U. Houston, 1961; m. Nancy McAnelly, Dec. 6, 1952; 1 son, James Hollis. Sales engr. Magcobar, New Orleans and Houston, 1956-57; buyer Transcontinental Gas Pipe Line, Houston, 1957-61; supr. Ernst & Ernst, Houston, 1961-65; v.p., treas. Gulf & Western Industries, Inc., N.Y.C., 1965—. Served to 1st lt. USAF, 1952-56. Mem. Am. Inst. C.P.A.'s, U.S. Handball Assn. Club: New York Athletic. Office: 1 Gulf and Western Plaza New York City NY 10023

FORSSMANN, WERNER, surgeon, urologist; b. Berlin, Germany, Aug. 29, 1904; s. Julius and Emmy (Hindenberg) F.; grad. Askanisches Gymnasium, Berlin; postgrad. Friedrich-Wilhelm U., Berlin; m. Elsbet Engel, Dec. 7, 1933; children—Klaus, Knut, Jörg, Wolf, Bernd, Renate. Former asst. physician Auguste-Viktoria Hosp., Eberswalde, Germany, surg. clinic Charite Hosp., Berlin, surg. clinic Municipal Hosp., Mainz, Germany, chief resident physician urol. clinic Municipal Rudolf-Virchow Hosp., Berlin, surg. clinic Municipal Hosp., Dresden-Friedrichstadt, Germany, 3d Surg. Univ. Clinic, Robert Koch Hosp., Berlin; gen. practitioner, 1945-50; head physician dept. urology Diakonie Insts., Bad Kreuznach, Germany, 1950-57; head phys. dept. surgery Evangel Hosp., Düsseldorf, Germany, 1958-70; prof. surgery Johann-Gutenberg U., Mainz; hon. prof. surgery Universitad Nacional-Cordoba (Argentina) 1961, U. Düsseldorf, 1964. Served as surgeon, capt. German Army, 1939-45. Recipient Leibniz medal Germany Acad. Scis., 1954; co-recipient Nobel prize in medicine and physiology, 1956. Hon. fellow Indian Acad. Scis.; mem. German Soc. Surgery, German Soc. Urology (hon.), Am. Coll. Chest Physicians, Svensk Förenning for Cardiologi (hon.), Brit. Med. Assn. (fgn. corr.), Acad. Scis. Country of Nordrhein-Westfalen.

FORST, MARION FRANCIS, bishop; b. St. Louis, Sept. 3, 1910; s. Frank A. J. and Bertha T. (Gulath) F.; grad. Kenrick Sem., Webster Groves, Mo., 1934. Ordained priest Roman Catholic Ch., 1934; consecrated bishop Dodge City, Kan., 1960; pastor St. Mary's Cathedral, Cape Girardeau, Mo., 1949-60; vicar gen. Diocese of Springfield-Cape Girardeau, 1956-60; Kan. chaplain K.C., 1964—. Served with Chaplains Corps, USNR, World War II. Address: 910 Central Av Box 849 Dodge City KS 67801

FORSTALL, WALTON, mech. engr., educator; b. Rosemont, Pa., June 26, 1909; s. Walton Sr. and Ednah (Logan) F.; B.S., Lehigh U., 1931, M.S., 1943; M.E., 1951; Sc.D., Mass. Inst. Tech., 1949; m. Jean Elizabeth Riegel, Jan. 15, 1942; children—Douglas Walton, Keith William. Asst. test engr. Delaware sta. Phila. Electric Co., 1930; sci. staff Franklin Inst., Phila., 1932-34; engring. asst. Phila. Gas Works Co., 1934-40; instr., asst. prof. mech. engring. Lehigh U., 1940-44; project engr. Tenn.-Eastman Corp., Manhattan Dist. Project, Oak Ridge, Tenn., 1944-45; research asso. Mass. Inst. Tech., 1946-49; asso. prof. mech. engring. Carnegie-Mellon U., 1949-57, asst. dean engring. and sci., 1955-57, George Tallman Ladd prof. mech. engring., 1957—, asso. head dept. mech. engring., 1963—. Sec. Beaumaris Land Co., Ltd. Pres. bd. sch. dirs. West Jefferson Hills Sch. Dist., 1961-63, 69—. Mem. Indsl. Standards Bd. Consultants Pa. Registered profl. engr., Pa. Mem. Am. Soc. M.E. (chmn. Pitts. sect. 1958-59; regional sec. 1962-66, v. p. 1966-70), Franklin Inst., Am. Soc. Engring. Edn. (nat. council 1957-59), Am. Phys. Soc., Phi Beta Kappa, Sigma Xi, Tau Beta Pi, Pi Tau Sigma, Psi Upsilon. Presbyn. Home: 124 Woodland Dr Pittsburgh, PA 15236.

FORSTER, ARNOLD, lawyer, author; b. N.Y.C., June 25, 1912; s. Hyman Lawrence and Dorothy (Turits) Fastenberg; LL.B., St. John's Coll., 1935; m. May Kasner, Sept. 29, 1940; children—Stuart William, Jane E. Admitted to N.Y. bar, 1935, also U.S. Supreme Ct.; gen. practice law, 1935-40; dir. law dept. Anti- Defamation League of B'nai B'rith, 1940-46, gen. counsel, dir. civil rights, 1946—, gen. counsel Internat. Council, 1960—; police justice N.Y. State, 1954-57. Mem. bd. edn., New Rochelle, N.Y., 1962-66. Author: Anti-Semitism in the United States, 1947; A Measure of Freedom, 1950; (with B. R. Epstein) The Troublemakers, 1952; Cross-Currents, 1956; Some of My Best Friends . . . , 1962; Danger on the Right, 1964; (with B.R. Epstein) Report on the Ku Klux Klan, 1965; Report on the John Birch Society, 1966; Radical Right: Report on the John Birch Society and its Allies, 1967; Report From Israel, 1969. Home: 79 Wykagyl Terrace New Rochelle NY 10804 Office: 315 Lexington Av New York City NY 10016

FORSTER, FRANCIS MICHAEL, physician, educator; b. Cin., Feb. 1 1912; s. Michael Joseph and Louise Barbara (Schmid) F.; student Xavier U., Cin., 1930-32, LL.D., 1955; B.S., U. Cin., 1935, B.M., 1936, M.D., 1937; m. Helen Dorothy Kiley, June 15, 1937; children—Denis, Susan, Kathleen, Mark, Gabrielle. Rotating intern Good Samaritan Hosp., Cin., 1936-37; house officer neurology and neurosurgery Boston City Hosp., 1937-38, resident neurology, 1939-40; fellow psychiatry Pa. Hosp., Phila., 1938-39; asst. neurology Harvard Med. Sch., 1939-40; Rockefeller Found. research fellow physiology Yale Sch. Medicine, 1940-41; instr. neurology Boston U. Sch. Medicine, 1941-43; asst. prof. neurology Jefferson Med. Sch., 1943-47, asso. prof. neurology, 1947-50; prof. neurology, dir. dept. Georgetown U. Sch. Medicine, 1950-58, dean Sch. Medicine, 1953-58; prof., chmn. dept. neurology, U. Wis. Sch. Medicine, 1958—; cons. neurology. Diplomate Am. Bd. Psychiatry and Neurology (dir.). Mem. A.M.A. (chmn. nervous and mental diseases sect. 1952-53), D.C. Med. Soc. (chmn. sect. neurology and psychiatry 1955-56), Am. Acad. Neurology (chmn. survey com. 1948-51; pres. 1957-59), Am. Neurol. Assn. (chmn. com. internat. collaboration 1954-55), Am. Epilepsy League (pres. 1951-52), Assn. Research Nervous and Mental Diseases, Am. Physiol. Soc., Am. Psychiat. Assn., Am. Assn. Electroencephalographers, A.A.A.S., Am. Assn. U. Profs., Mass. Med. Soc., State Med. Soc. Wis., N.Y. Acad. Scis., Acad. Medicine Washington, Sigma Xi, Alpha Omega Alpha. Club: Cosmos (Washington). Author: Synopsis of Neurology, 1962, 66. Editor: Modern Therapy in Neurology, 1957; Evaluation of Drug Therapy, 1961. Home: 4020 Co M Middleton WI 53562 Office: U Hosp U Wis Madison WI 53705

FORSTER, ISAAC, UN judge of Senegal; b. 1903; ed. Lyceé Hoch, Versailles, also U. Paris. Gen. state counsel dept. for French West Africa, 1930; dep. judge, Dakar, 1933, dep. to pros., Conakry, Guinea, 1933; judge, St. Denis, Reunion, then Madagascar, 1941; judge of court, Guadeloupe, 1945, French West Africa, 1947; pres. of Chamber, Dakar, 1957; sec.-gen. of govt., Senegal, 1958-60; pres.-gen., Dakar, 1959; 1st pres. Supreme Ct. of Senegal, 1960-64; judge Internat. Ct. of Justice, The Hague, 1964, now UN. Asso. mem. Inst. Internat. Law. Recipient numerous decorations. Address: Judge of Senegal Internat Ct of Justice UN New York City NY 10017*

FORSTER, JAMES FRANKLIN, mfg. exec.; b. Higginsville, Mo., May 20, 1908; s. James Franklin, Sr. and Emma (Higgins) F.; B.S., U.S. Naval Acad., 1930; M.B.A., Harvard, 1936; Ph.D., Clarkson Coll. Tech., 1969; m. Kathleen Allen, Sept. 18, 1936; children—James Franklin III, Patricia Ann (Mrs. Cameron S. Avery). Staff accountant Arthur Andersen & Co., 1936-39; with Sperry Rand Corp., 1939—, dir., 1964—, pres., 1965- -, pres., chmn., chief exec. officer, 1967—, with Sperry Gyroscope Co., 1939-41, treas., exec. v.p., pres. Vickers, Inc., Detroit, 1941-64, pres. Univac div., N.Y.C., 1964-66; dir. No. Natural Gas, Borden, Inc., Continental Can Co., Inc., NL Industries, Inc. Trustee the Conf. Bd., Com. Econ. Devel. Mem. Am. Inst. C.P.A.'s, Am. Soc. M.E. Clubs: Country of Detroit, Burning Tree, Blind Brook, Laurel Valley Golf. Home: 200 E 66th St New York City NY 10021 Office: 1290 Av Americas New York City NY 10019

FORSTER, ROBERT, educator; b. N.Y.C., June 7, 1926; s. Theodore and Elise (Strobel) F.; B.A., Swarthmore Coll., 1949; M.A. in Modern European History, Harvard, 1951; Ph.D., Johns Hopkins, 1956; m. Elborg Hamacher, July 8, 1955; children—Marc Richard, Thomas Theodore. Instr. modern European history Johns Hopkins, 1956-57; Blissing fellow U. Toulouse (France), 1957-58; asst. prof. U. Neb., 1958-62, asso. prof. Dartmouth, 1962-65; prof. history Johns Hopkins, 1966—. Served with AUS, 1944-46. French Govt. fellow, 1953-55; Research fellow, France, 1962, 64; recipient Prix Gaussail Acad. Toulouse. Mem. Phi Beta Kappa. Author: The Nobility of Toulouse in the 18th Century, 1960; The House of Saulx-Tavanes: Versailles and Burgundy, 1700-1830, 1971; also articles. Home: 208 Oakdale Rd Baltimore MD 21210

FORSTER, ROBERT ELDER, II, physiologist, educator; b. St. Davids, Pa., Dec. 23, 1919; s. John Montgomery and Gladys (Jameson) F.; B.S., Yale, 1941; M.D., U. Pa., 1943; grad. student Harvard, 1947; m. Elizabeth Hilbert Day, June 26, 1947; children—Julia Bacon, Jameson, John Montgomery, Elizabeth Richards. Intern internal medicine Peter Bent Brigham Hosp., Boston, 1944, asst. resident, 1947-48; mem. faculty U. Pa., 1950—, prof. physiology div. grad. medicine, 1958—, chmn. dept., 1959—, prof. physiology in surgery Sch. Medicine, 1961—, Isaac Ott prof. physiology, 1959—; cons. pulmonary physiology Children's Hosp., Phila., Phila. Naval Hosp.; clin. physiologist U. Pa. Hosp.; physiologist Phila. Gen. Hosp. Mem. cardiovascular study sect. Nat. Heart Inst., 1960-63. Served to capt., M.C., AUS, 1944-46. Mem. Am. Physiol. Soc. (council, publs. com. 1963-65, pres. 1966-67), Am. Soc. Clin. Investigation, Biophys. Soc., Physiol. Soc. Phila., Am. Fedn. Clin. Research, Mass. Med. Soc., Sigma Xi. Editorial bd. Am. Soc. Clin. Investigation, 1962—, Am. Physiol. Soc., 1961—. Home: 501 Oakley Rd Haverford PA 19041 Office: Dept Physiology Div Grad Medicine U Pa Philadelphia PA 19104

FORSTER, ROY PHILIP, educator, physiologist; b. Milw., Sept. 28, 1911; s. Frank M. and Adele M. (Schatz) F.; B.S., Marquette U., 1932; Ph.M., U. Wis., 1935, Ph.D., 1938; M.A. (hon.), Dartmouth, 1948; m. Dorothy F. Seegers, Aug. 31, 1935; 1 dau., Peggy (Mrs. Charles L. Ffolliott). Faculty mem. Dartmouth Coll., Hanover, N.H., 1938—, prof., 1948-64, Ira Allen Eastman prof., 1964—, chmn. zoology dept., 1950-56, chmn. sci. div., 1947-51, lectr. physiology Med. Sch., 1964—; cons. research VA Center, White River Junction, Vt., 1963—; cons. research lab. sci. medicine VA, 1964- 66; dir. regulatory biology program NSF, 1959-60; dir. Mt. Desert Island Biol. Lab., summers 1940-47, v.p., 1960-63, pres., 1963-70; John Simon Guggenheim Meml. Found. fellow, Cambridge U. and various European biol. labs., 1948-49. Developed techniques for evaluation of kidney function, research on hemodynamics and cellular physiology of kidney: mem. Conf. Renal Function of Josiah Macy, Jr. Found., 1949- 54; John Simon Guggenheim Meml. Found. fellow for travel and study abroad,

1955-56. Trustee Mt. Desert Island Biol. Lab., 1940- -, Corp. Bermuda Biol. Sta. for Research: mem. sci. rev. com. Health Research Facilities NIH, 1964-66, med. biology rev. com., 1966-67, comparative pharm. com., 1966, pharm.-toxicology rev. com., 1969—. Fellow A.A.A.S.; mem. Am. Heart Assn. (council circulation), Am. Soc. Zoologist, Am. Physiol. Soc., N.H. Acad. Sci. (exec. com. 1945-48), Am. Soc. Nephrology, Internat. Soc. Nephrology, Soc. Gen. Physiologists, Sigma Xi, (pres. Darmouth chpt. 1968-69), Gamma Alpha, Alpha Sigma Nu, Delta Sigma Rho, Phi Sigma. Author articles profl. jours. Editor kidney sect. Biol. Abstracts, 1947—; asso. editor Jour. Gen. Physiology, 1960-68; editorial bd. Am. Jour. Physiology, Jour. Applied Physiology, 1960-66, 70—, Jour. Gen. Physiology, 1968—. Home: 18 Hemlock Rd Hanover NH 03755

FORSTER, WALTER LESLIE, cons.; b. Leeds, Eng., June 30 1903; s. John Mark and Margaret (Forster) F.; B.Sc., Leeds U., 1924; m. Lorna Bonstow, Feb. 3, 1936; 1 son, John. Engr., Royal Dutch-Shell Group, Mexico, Venezuela, Roumania, Egypt, 1925-40, gen. mgr., Colombia, 1946-47, Venezuela, 1947-50; cons. 1951—; dir. Canadian Petrofina, Ltd., Gen. Star, Inc., others. Served as col. British Army, 1940-46. Decorated Comdr. Order Brit. Empire, Legion of Merit (U.S.). Fellow Inst. Petroleum London. Home: 61 Summit Crescent Westmount Quebec Canada Office: 235 Saint James Street West Montreal Quebec Canada

FORSTER, WALTER OTTO, educator; b. Chesterfield, Mo., Sept. 14, 1913; s. John Frederick and Mathilda (Merz) F.; diploma Concordia Coll., Milw., 1931; B.D., Concordia Sem., St. Louis, 1935; M.A., Washington U., St. Louis, 1936, Ph.D., 1942; m. Lydia Treichel, July 12, 1937; children—Vivian (Mrs. Ronald W. Baumann), Constance (Mrs. Ronald P. Wilcox). Engaged as teacher at St. Paul's School, San Antonio, Tex., 1933-34; news editor, announcer radio sta. WIL, St. Louis, 1935-40; ordained to ministry Lutheran Ch., 1944; corr. Am. Credit Indemnity Co., St. Louis, 1941-42; adminstrv. asst., tng. officer St. Louis Engr. Dist., C.E., 1942-46; mem. faculty Purdue U., 1946—, prof. history, 1956—, head dept. history, govt. and philosophy, 1961-64, head dept. history, 1964-69. Mem. Am. Hist. Assn., Orgn. Am. Historians, Am. Polit. Sci. Assn., Am. Acad. Polit. and Social Sci., Ind. Acad. Social Sci. Author: Zion on the Mississippi, 1953; (with George H. Mayer) The United States and the Twentieth Century, 1958. Home: 321 Laurel Dr West Lafayette IN 47906

FORSTER, WILLIAM BLAIR, hosp. cons; b. Martin's Ferry, O., July 1, 1911; s. Emmett Reed and Pearle (Stewart) F.; A.B., Mt. Union Coll., 1933; m. Christeen Lanning, Mar. 6, 1938. Bookkeeper, Alliance (O.) City Hosp., 1929-33; asst. adminstr. Elyria (O.) Meml. Hosp., 1933-38; asst. adminstr. St. Lukes Hosp., Cleve., 1938-42, Akron (O.) City Hosp., 1942-56; adminstr. Bexar County Hosp. Dist., San Antonio, 1956-67; adminstr. Harris County Hosp. Dist., Houston, 1967-69; adminstrv. cons. Methodist Hosp. Houston, 1969—; preceptor Trinity U. Grad. Sch. Hosp. Adminstrn. Course. Mem. adv. council on health aspects of civil def. Tex. Dept. Health, 1964-. Recipient Modern Hosp. Gold medal for significant contbn. to hosp. lit., 1942. Fellow Am. Coll. Hosp. Adminstrs.; mem. Am., Tex. (past pres.) hosp. assns., Nat. League Nursing (past Tex. bd.). Contbr. articles to profl. jours. Home: 7819 Prestwood Houston TX 77036 Office: 6516 Bertner Dr Houston TX 77025

FORSTMAN, HENRY JACKSON, educator; b. Montgomery, Ala., June 15, 1929; s. Joseph Carl and Kate Gertrue (Kelley) F.; B.A., Phillips U., 1949; B.D., Union Theol. Sem., N.Y.C., 1956, Th.D., 1959; m. Shirley Marie Cronk, June 3, 1950; children—David Jackson, Valerie Marie, Paul Frederick. Asst. prof. Randolph-Macon Woman's Coll., 1958-60, Stanford, 1960-64; mem. faculty Vanderbilt U., 1964—, prof. religion, 1968—, chmn. grad. dept. religion, 1969—, acting dean Div. Sch., 1970. Kent fellow, 1957-58; postdoctoral fellow for cross disciplinary studies Soc. Religion in Higher Edn., 1966-67. Mem. Soc. Religion in Higher Edn., Am. Soc. Ch. History, Am. Acad. Religion, Am. Assn. U. Profs., Assn. Disciples Theol. Discussion, New Haven Discussion Group. Author: Word and Spirit, 1962; Christian Faith and the Church, 1965. Home: 3913 Kimpalong St Nashville TN 37205

FORSYTH, ALFRED SMITH, lawyer; b. St. Davids, Pa., June 21, 1907; s. James Porter and Mabel (Peck) F.; A.B., Columbia, 1929, LL.B., 1931; m. Mary Sholes Bryan, June 26, 1933; children—Mary B., Alfred Smith, William J.B. Admitted to N.Y. bar, 1932, since practiced in N.Y.C.; mem. firm Wheaton & Forsyth, 1940-56, Cabell, Medinger & Forsyth, 1956- 58, Cabell, Medinger, Forsyth & Decker, 1958-66, Medinger, Forsyth & Decker, 1967-68, Forsyth, Decker & Murray, 1968—; dir., gen. counsel U.S. Tobacco Co. Served to maj. USMCR, 1943- 45. Mem. Assn. Bar City N.Y. Clubs: University, Sierra (chmn. Atlantic chpt.; v.p. 1970) (N.Y.C.). Home: 15 LeRoy Pl Chappaqua, NY 10514. Office: 51 W 51st St New York City NY 10019

FORSYTH, GEORGE HOWARD, Jr., art historian, educator; b. Highland Park, Ill., Sept. 2, 1901; s. George Howard and Sarah (Brockunier) F.; grad. Lawrenceville (N.J.) Sch., 1919; A.B., Princeton, 1923; M.F.A., 1927; student Inst. for Advanced Study, Princeton, 1935-36, 1945; m. Eleanor Marquand, Feb. 5, 1927; children—Eleanor, Mary Blaikie, George Allan; m. 2d, Mary Isom Hayes, August 18, 1942 (dec. Nov. 1958); 1 dau., Hope Gifford; m. 3d, Ilene Eleanor Haering, June 4, 1960. Instr. and later asst. prof., dept. art and archaeology, Princeton, 1927- 42; prof. history of art U. Mich., 1947-, chmn. dept., 1947-61, dir. Kelsey Mus. Archaeology, 1961-69, research prof. archeology, 1969—; dir. survey and excavation, Ch. St. Martin, Angers, France (project supported by Princeton, Am. Council Learned Socs., Carnegie Found.), 1929-36; field dir. Mich., Princeton, Alexandria Univs. archeol. expedition to Mt. Sinai, Egypt, 1958, 60, Mem. bd. of scholars Dumbarton Oaks Research Library and Collection, Harvard; research asso. at the Freer gallery Smithsonian Inst., 1954, 56, 60. Served as lt. USNR, 1942-45. Recipient traveling fellowship, Mediaeval Acad. Am., 1924-25, Haskins medal, 1955; Rockefeller Found. Research Grant, 1946; Guggenheim fellow, 1953. Life mem. Société française d'archéologie; mem. College Art Assn. (dir. 1949, 54), Phi Beta Kappa, Phi Kappa Phi. Clubs: Century Association (N.Y.C.); C.): Cosmos (Washington). Author: Church of St. Martin at Angers, 1951; contbr. art publs. Home: 5 Geddes Heights Ann Arbor MI 48104

FORSYTH, GLADYS M., savs. and loan assn. exec.; b. Folsom, Cal., July 12, 1894; d. Edward and Sarah (Seiboldt) McCue; A.B., Stanford, 1916; m. Evald M. Forsyth, Dec. 15, 1915; 1 dau., Rena (Mrs. John E. Dean). With First Fed. Savs. and Loan Assn., Lincoln, Neb., 1935—, pres., 1947—; past dir. FHLB Topeka. Past mem. bd. advisers Small Adminstrn.; past pres. Midwest Savs. and Loan Conf., Southwestern Savs. and Loan Conf. Past sec. Lancaster County chpt. A.R.C.; mem. adv. com. aerospace project Lincoln pub. schs., 1966—; hon. chmn. 1965 Radio Free Europe Fund. Past vice chmn. Lancaster County Republican Party; hon. chmn. Goldwater in Neb., 1964; past mem. Neb. Rep. Central Com. Trustee Lincoln Gen. Hosp., 1954- -, pres., 1960-62. Recipient Newcomen Soc. Recognition for Neb., 1970, Outstanding Bus. Women award Axis Bus. and Profl. Women of Lincoln, 1970. Mem. U.S. Savs. and Loan League, Am. Assn. U. Women (past pres. Lincoln), Lincoln C. of C. (past bd. dirs.), Neb. Real Estate Assn., Joslyn Meml. Art Mus., Neb. Art Assn., Neb. CowBelles; hon. mem. Rho Epsilon. Clubs: University, Altrusa (hon.), Lincoln Country. Home: 900 Fall Creek Rd Lincoln NB 68510 Office: 1235 N St Lincoln NB 68501

FORSYTH, WILLIAM DOUGLASS, ret. Australian govt. ofcl.; b. Casterton, Victoria, Australia, Jan. 5, 1909; s. James Douglass and Martha Alice (Lambourne) F.; B.A., Melbourne U., 1929, M.A., 1931; Litt.B., Balliol Coll., Oxford U., 1939; m. Thelma Joyce Sherry, Dec. 1935; children—Julian Douglass, Katherine, Valerie. History tchr. Victorian High Sch., Australia, 1930-35; with Australian Govt. Dept. Information, 1941-42, Australian Dept. External Affairs 1942-69; adv. U.N. Conf. on Internat. Orgns., San Francisco, 1945, also other confs.; rep. Far Eastern Commn., Tokyo, Japan, 1946, also other internat. orgns.; mem. Trusteeship Council, 1947-48, 51-55; Australian del., adviser U.N. Gen. Assembly, 1946-48, 51-58; sec.-gen. S. Pacific Commn., 1948-51; Australian permanent rep. UN, 1951-56; asst. sec. Dept. External Affairs, Australia, 1956-59; Australian ambassador Vietnam, 1959-61, minister Laos, 1959-60; asst. sec. Dept. External Affairs, Canberra, Australia, 1961-63; sec.-gen. S. Pacific Commn., 1963- 66; Australian ambassador, Beirut, Lebanon, 1967-69. Rockefeller fellow, 1936-37, 39; research fellow Melbourne U., 1938, 40. Decorated Officer Brit. Empire, 1955. Author: Governor Arthur's Convict System, 1935, reprinted 1970; The Myth of Open Spaces, 1942. Editor of Australasiatic Bulletin, 1940. Address: 88 Banks St Yarralumia Canberra 2600 Australia

FORSYTHE, CARL STANFORD, lawyer; b. Jackson, O., Jan. 29, 1910; s. Carl F. and Clara (Evans) F.; student Princeton Prep. Sch., 1927-28; A.B., U. Mich., 1932, J.D., 1935; m. Virginia Cluff, July 6 1936; 1 son, Carl S. Admitted to N.Y. bar, 1935; asso. O'Connor & Farber, N.Y.C., 1935-37; partner Townley, Updike & Carter, 1937-51, Forsythe, McGovern, Pearson & Nash, 1951—; dir. Crompton & Knowles Corp., Worcester, Mass., 1955—, chmn. bd., 1970—; dir. John M. Maris Co., Inc., Peters, Griffin, Woodward, Inc., McCorquodale Process, Inc., McCorquodale Color Card Co. Served as 1st lt., OSS, AUS, 1944-45. Decorated Certificate of Merit, Bronze Star (U.S.), Golden medal of Vaza (Sweden). Mem. Judge Adv. Gen.'s Assn., Am. Legion, N.Y. Bar Assn., Assn. Bar City of N.Y., Sigma Delta Chi. Republican. Methodist. Clubs: Union League (N.Y.C.), Greenwich Countru, Indian Harbor Yacht (Greenwich). Home: Dingletown Rd Greenwich CT 06830 Office: 345 Park Av New York City NY

FORSYTHE, EDWIN B., congressman; b. Westtown, Pa., Jan. 17, 1916; s. Albert H. and Emily (Matlack) F.; grad. high sch.; m. Mary McKnight, Aug. 24, 1940; 1 dau., Susan. Gen. mgr. Locust Lane Farm Dairy, Moorestown, N.J., 1933-60, sec.-treas., 1960—; mem. 91st-92d congresses from 6th N.J. Dist. Sec. Bd. Adjustment, Moorestown, 1948-52, mem. Bd. Health, 1953-62, mayor, 1957-62, chmn. Planning Bd., 1962-63; committeeman Moorestown Twp., 1953-62; mem. N.J. Senate, 1964-70. Mem. bd. N.J. Legaue Municipalities, 1958-62. Del., Republican Nat. Conv., 1968. Bd. dirs. Burlington C. YMCA. Recipient Citizen of Year award Combined Service Clubs Moorestown, 1962; named Legislator of Year, N.J. Assn. Chosen Freeholders, 1968. Mem. South Jersey Milk Dealers Assn. (pres. 1958-61), N.J. Milk Industry Assn. (pres. 1960-62). Mem. Soc. of Friends. Home: 265 West 2d St Moorestown NJ 08057 Office: Cannon Bldg Washington DC 20515

FORSYTHE, GEORGE ELMER, educator; b. State College, Pa., Jan. 8, 1917; s. Warren Ellsworth and DeEtta (Brodie) F.; A.B., Swarthmore Coll., 1937; M.S., Brown U., 1938, Ph.D., 1941; m. Alexandra Illmer, June 14, 1941; children—Warren Louis, Diana Elizabeth. Instr. math. Stanford, 1941-42, prof. math., 1957-64, prof., chmn. computer sci., 1961—; research engr. Boeing Aircraft Co., Seattle, 1946-47; asst. prof. meteorology U. Cal. at Los Angeles, 1947-48, research mathematician, 1954-57; mathematician Nat. Bur. Standards, 1948-54. Fellow A.A.A.S., Brit. Computer Soc.; mem. Am. Math. Soc., Assn. Computing Machinery (pres. 1964-66), Soc. Indsl. and Applied Math. (trustee), Math. Assn. Am., Am. Assn. U. profs. Sierra Club. Home: 835 Lathrop Dr Stanford CA 94305

FORSYTHE, GEORGE IRVIN, army officer; b. Butte, Mont., July 21, 1918; s. George Irvin and Victoria (Davis) F.; B.A., U. Mont., 1939; grad. U.S. Army Command and Staff Coll., 1951, Armed Forces Staff Coll., 1953, Air War Coll., 1957; m. Mary Elizabeth Barnett, July 27, 1942; 1 son, George Barnett. Commd. 2d lt. U.S. Army, 1939, advanced through grades to lt. gen., 1969; comdg. officer 2d Bn., 22d Inf., Germany, 1951-52, regimental exec. officer, 1952; asst. chief Progress Evaluation br. Office Comptroller of Army, Washington, 1953-54; chief Personnel Mgmt. br. Office Sec. Army, Washington, 1954-55; White House liaison officer, chief Coordination Group, Office Chief of Staff U.S. Army, Washington, 1955-56; chief 101st Airborne Div. Planning Group; Doctrine and Test Group, Ft. Campbell, Ky., 1956; comdg. officer 502 Airborne Inf., comdr. 1st Airborne Battle Group 502d Inf., Ft. Campbell, 1956-57; dep. chief Combat Arms Tng. Orgn., Mil. Assistance Adv. Group U.S. Army Element, Saigon, Vietnam, 1958-59, sr. adviser to field command Vietnamese Army, 1959; dep. asst. chief staff G3, Ft. McPherson, Ga., 1959-60, dep. chief staff Hdqrs. 3d Army, 1960; chief presentation analysis and coordination sect. Coordination Group, chief policy coordination div. Office Chief Staff, Washington, 1960-62; exec. officer, sr. aide to Chief of Staff U.S. Army, Washington, 1962-63; asst. div. comdr./maneuver 25th Inf. Div., Schofield Barracks, Hawaii, 1963-64, asst. div. comdr./support, 1964-65; asst. comdt. U.S. Army Inf. Sch., Ft. Benning, Ga., 1965-66; asst. chief staff G3, U.S. Army Pacific, Ft. Shafter, Hawaii, 1966-67; asst. dep. to COMUSMACV for civil operations and revolutionary devel. support Hdqrs. U.S. Mil. Assistance Command. Saigon, 1968-69; comdg. gen. 1st Air Cavalry Div., Camp Evans, Vietnam, 1969; comdt. U.S. Army Inf. Sch. comdg. gen. Ft. Benning, Ga., 1969; comdg. gen. U.S. Army Combat Devels. Command, Ft. Belvoir, Va., 1969-70; project mgr. Modern Vol. Army, Washington, 1970—. Decorated Distinguished Service medal with oak leaf cluster, Legion of Merit with two oak leaf clusters, D.F.C., Bronze Star medal with three oak leaf clusters, Air medal with 31 oak leaf clusters, Army Commendation medal with two oak leaf clusters; Croix de Guerre (French) with palm; Croix de Guerre (Belgium) with palm; Nat. Order Vietnam, Distinguished Service Order Vietnam, Gallantry Cross Vietnam. Mem. Assn. U.S. Army, Airborne Assn., Sigma Chi. Rated Army Aviator and Senior Parachutist. Episcopalian. Address: Quarters 4 Fort McNair Washington DC 20024

FORSYTHE, JOHN, actor; b. Penn's Grove, N.J., Jan. 29, 1918; student U. N.C.; also N.Y. Actor's Studio; m. Parker McCormick (div.); m. 2d, Julie Warren; children—Dall, Page, Brooke. Motion picture debut in Destination Tokyo, 1944, other films include Escape from Fort Bravo, 1953, Trouble with Harry, 1956, Ambassador's Daughter; In Cold Blood, 1968; Topaz, 1969; Happy Ending, 1970; on tour with play Mr. Roberts, then on Broadway, later dir. City Center (N.Y.) revival, 1956; Broadway play Weekend, 1968; TV debut, 1947, appeared numerous dramatic shows; role TV series Bachelor Father; on Broadway in Teahouse of August Moon, All My Sons, Yellow Jack; appeared in Madame X, 1966; host sports show Hollywood Park Feature Race, 1971. Home: 11560 Bellagio Rd Los Angeles CA 90049

FORSYTHE, JOHN EVANS, lawyer; b. Media, Pa., Nov. 27, 1905; s. John Evans and Helen Lucretia (MacDonald) F.; B.A., Haverford Coll., 1927; LL.B., Yale, 1930; m. Margaret Pancost Longaker, Sept. 30, 1933; children—Felicia, Alice Mary. Admitted to Pa. bar, 1930; since practiced in Phila., 1930—; partner MacCoy, Evans & Lewis, 1943—, Twp. solicitor Lower Merion Twp., Montgomery County; solicitor Lower Merion Twp., Bd. Health, 1943—; chmn., legal counsel Pa. State Assn. Twp. Commrs. Treas., trustee, dir. Bryn Mawr Coll., 1953—; treas. Haverford Friends Sch., 1947—. Mem. Am., Pa., Phila. bar assns., Phi Beta Kappa, Phi Delta Phi. Mem. Soc. of Friends. Clubs: Haverford, Merion Cricket (Haverford); Vespers (Phila.). Home: 418 Penn Rd Wynnewood PA 19096 Office: 2 Penn Center Philadelphia PA 19102

FORSYTHE, MARGARET JEANNE, univ. dean; b. Flint, Mich., May 28, 1923; d. William Ray and Genevieve (Lancashire) Forsythe; B.A., Oberlin Coll., 1945; certificate bus. adminstrn. Radcliffe Coll., 1946; M.A., Syracuse U., 1951; Ed.D., Western Res. U., 1963. Adminstrv. asst. pub. relations Central Nat. Bank Cleve., 1946-49; editor Cleve. Banker, publ. Fed. Res. Dist., 1948-49; residence hall dir., Panhellenic adviser Kan. State Coll., Manhattan, 1951- 53; faculty Kent State U., 1953-63, dean of women, 1959-63, asst. prof. spl. edn., 1962-63; dean of women U. Cin., 1963-65; dean of women Ohio Wesleyan U., Delaware, 1965-70, dean student devel., 1970—. Adviser dist. 1 Alpha Lambda Delta, 1963-65. Mem. Nat. Edn. Assn., Am. Coll. Personnel Assn. (exec. council 1962-63, secretary 1963-65), Assn. Higher Edn., Nat. Assn. Women Deans and Counselors (v.p. 1969-71), Am. Personnel and Guidance Assn., Am. Assn. U. Women, Ohio Assn. Women Deans, Adminstrs., and Counselors (pres. 1960-62), League Women Voters, Pi Lambda Theta. Home: 10 Orchard Lane Delaware OH 43015

FORSYTHE, RICHARD HAMILTON, food co. exec.; b. Griswold, Ia., Dec. 9, 1921; s. Piercy and Alice (Hamilton) F.; B.S., Ia. State Coll., 1943, Ph.D., 1949; m. Charlotte Langworthy, Mar. 20, 1943; children—Charlynn, Lesley Kay, Patricia. Asst. prof. poultry products tech. Ia. State U., 1949-51; asso. dir. food research Armour & Co., 1951-53; dir. central labs., v.p. Henningsen Foods, Inc., Springfield, Mo., 1953-60; prof., head dept. poultry sci. Ia. State U., 1960-68; v.p. food research Henningsen Foods, Inc., 1968- -. Chmn. com. civil def. Inst. Food Technologists, 1956-62; exec. com. research council Inst. Am. Poultry Industries, 1954—. Recipient Mo. 4-H Alumni award, 1958; Research award Inst. Am. Poultry Industries, 1958; named Poultry Industry Man of Year, 1970. Mem. Am. Chem. Soc., Poultry Sci. Assn., Worlds Poultry Sci. Assn. (pres. U.S.A. br. 1970—), A.A.A.S., Inst. Food Technologists, Am. Assn. Cereal Chemists, Am. Poultry Hist. Soc. (dir. 1970-71). Presbyn. Mason, Kiwanian. Author articles, chpts. in books. Asso. editor Food Tech. Home: 2851 S Glendale Springfield MO 65804 Office: Henningsen Foods Inc 2501 College Springfield MO 65801

FORSYTHE, ROBERT AMES, lawyer; b. Menomonie, Wis., Oct. 22, 1921; s. Robert Alvin and Elvera (Hovlid) F.; B.A., St. Olaf Coll., 1947; J.D., U. Minn., 1949; student Cambridge (Eng.) U., 1945-46; m. Mary MacCornack, July 18, 1942; children—Robert Ames, Mary Pauline, Jean Louise, Ann, Joan. Instr. speech, dir. forensics Coll. St. Catherine, St. Paul, 1947-53; claims adjuster Aetna Casualty Co., Mpls., 1948-50; admitted to Minn. bar, 1949, also U.S. Supreme Ct.; pvt. practice, Mpls., 1950-53; chief counsel U.S. Select Com. on Small Bus., 1953-55; adminstrv. asst. to U.S. Senator Thye, 1955-59; congl. liaison officer Dept. Health, Edn. and Welfare, 1959, became asst. sec., 1959; state chmn. Rep. Party State Minn.; mem. Rep. Nat. Com. Mem. Pres.'s Commn. on Voter Registration and Participation, 1963—. Bd. regents Augustana Coll. Served to capt. USAAF, 1942-46; ETO. Decorated Bronze Star. Mem. Minn., Hennepin County bar assns., Pi Kappa Delta, Phi Delta Phi. Lutheran. Home: 4605 Edina Blvd Edina MN 55424 Office: 1600 Parklawn Minneapolis MN 55435

FORT, ADA, nurse, educator; b. Stafford, Ala., Oct. 5, 1914; d. Joseph Elias and Maggie D. (Bland) Fort; tchrs. certificate Ala. State Tchrs. Coll., 1933; diploma nursing S. Highlands Infirmary, 1936; B.S., George Peabody Coll., 1940; A.M., Columbia, 1943, Ed. D., Teachers Coll., Columbia 1960; L.H.D., Wesleyan Coll., Macon, Ga., 1958. Asst. night supr. S. Highland Infirmary, Birmingham, Ala., 1936-37, dir. nursing edn. Sch. Nursing, 1944-46; staff nurse operating room Selma (Ala.) Bapt. Hosp., 1937; staff nurse U.S. VA Hosp., Columbia, S.C., 1938-39, pub. health nursing Lee Co. Health Dept. and E. Ala. Tng. Center, Opelika, 1941-42; instr. nursing arts, Hartwick Coll., Oneonta, N.Y., 1943-44, sch. nursing Emory U., Ga., 1946-47, asso. dean, 1947-50, acting dean, dean sch. nursing, 1950—; spl. cons. to U.S. Pub. Health Service, 1957. Mem. bd. collegiate review, Nat. Nursing Accreditation Service, 1954-58, chmn. 1956-57; adv. com. Diuguid Fellowship Program, 1969-71; mem. Gov.'s Commn. Nursing, 1970. Bd. dirs., Met. Atlanta chpt. A.R.C. vis. com. Tuskegee Sch. Nursing, Tuskegee Inst. Ala., 1969—. Mem. Ga. State League for Nursing (pres. 1953-55, 1st v.p. 1961-63), So. Regional Edn. Bd. (regional com. nursing 1953; chmn. regional com. grad. edn. and research nursing, 1959), Am., Ga. nurses assns., Nat. League Nursing Edn. (chmn. Nutting awards com.), Nat. Orgn. Pub. Health Nursing, N.E.A., Am. Assn. U. Profs., Am. Assn. Deans Coll. and Univ. Schs. Nursing (sec. 1969—), Sigma Theta Tau, Soc. Golden Key. Methodist. Home: 1261 Amanda Circle Decatur GA 30033

FORT, DANIEL MATHEWS, dept. store exec.; b. Burlington, Wis., Oct. 14, 1921; s. Joyce Vincent and Delinia (Jacobson) F.; B.S., The Citadel, 1943; M.B.A., U. Chgo., 1962; J.D., John Marshall Law Sch., 1971; m. Jeanne Wood, Sept. 1, 1946; 1 dau., Linda Ann. With Carson Pirie Scott & Co., Chgo., 1946—, divisional mdse. mgr., 1963-67, asst. sec., 1967-70, sec., 1970—; sec., dir. Carson Internat., Inc. Mem. adv. com. Civic Fedn., Chgo., 1969—. Served with AUS, 1943-46, ETO, 1951-53, Far East. Decorated Combat Inf. Badge. Mem. Am. Soc. Corporate Secs. Episcopalian. Club: Executive Program of U. Chgo. Home: 246 Belden Pl Munster IN 46321 Office: 1 S State St Chicago IL 60603

FORT, RUFUS E., Jr., ins. exec.; b. Nashville, Aug. 29, 1910; s. Rufus E. and Louise (Clark) F.; B.S. in Elec. Engring., Va. Mil. Inst., 1931; m. Agnes M. Stokes, June 17, 1933; children—Agnes S., Julia G., Eugenia W., Louise C. Instr. elec. engring. Va. Mil. Inst., 1931-32; with Nat. Life & Accident Ins. Co. of Nashville, 1932-66, life ins. agt., Detroit, supt., mgr., Nashville, asst. mgr. ordinary life dept., agy. sec., mgr. manpower devel. div., supt. agencies, 1932-53, v.p. charge field research planning and devel., 1953-62, sr. v.p. selling and servicing, 1962-64, sr. v.p. spl. assignments, 1964-66, dir. 1940—, mem. exec. com. 1959—. Trustee, vice chmn. bd. Tenn. Retirement System, 1949—; trustee Checkwood- Tenn. Bot. Garden and Fine Arts Center. Served as 2d lt. AUS, 1942-46. Adj. gen. Tenn., 1946. Named mem. Exec. and Profl. Hall of Fame. Mem. Life Ins. Agy. Mgmt. Assn., Life Underwriters Tng. Council. Episcopalian. Elk. Clubs: Belle Meade Country, Cedar Creek, Cumberland, Exchange (Nashville); Capital City (Atlanta); Internat. (Chgo.); University (N.Y.C.). Home: 116 Jackson Blvd Nashville TN 37205 Office: PO Box 2641 Nashville TN 37219

FORTAS, ABE, lawyer, former asso. justice U.S. Supreme Ct.; b. Memphis, June 19, 1910; s. William and Ray (Berson) F.; A.B., Southwestern Coll., Memphis, 1930; LL.B., Yale, 1933; m. Carolyn Eugenia Agger, July 9, 1935. Asst. prof. law Yale, 1933-37; asst. chief, legal div. A.A.A., 1933-34; asst. dir. corporate reorgn. study SEC, 1934-37, cons. 1937-38, asst. dir. Pub. Utilites Div., 1938-39; gen. counsel PWA, 1939-40, bituminous coal div., 1939-41; dir. div. of power Dept. Interior, 1931-42, undersec. dept., 1942-46; past mem. firm Arnold, Fortas & Porter, Washington; asso. justice U.S. Supreme Ct., 1965-69. Acting gen. counsel Nat. Power Policy Com. 1941; mem. bd. legal examiners Civil Service Commn., 1941-43; mem. Pres.'s Com. to Study Changes in Organic Law P.R., 1943; adviser U.S. delegation to UN, San Francisco, 1945, London 1946. Vis. prof. law Yale, 1946-47; mem. adv. council Johns Hopkins Sch. Advanced Internat. Studies. Dir. Federated Dept. Stores, Inc., Festival Casals, Inc., SuCrest Corp. Trustee Carnegie Hall Corp., John F. Kennedy Center for Performing Arts. Mem. Fed., Am., FCC bar assns., Order of Coif, Omicron Delta Kappa. Asso. editor Jour. Psychiatry. Contbr. to legal, other periodicals. Address: 1054 31st St NW Washington DC 20007

FORTENBAUGH, CHARLES ELMER, assn. exec.; b. Cleve., Apr., 1909; s. Charles Henry and Helena Theodora (Boll) F.; student Case Inst. Tech., 1930-31, Western Res. U., 1938, 42, Cleve. Coll., 1944, 46; m. Edna Marion Jackson, Apr. 20, 1934; children—Marian (Mrs. R. Barrett), Ann (Mrs. William Kingzett), Charles P., Kathleen, Thomas. Jr. engr. City Cleve., 1937-41; indsl. engr. Republic Steel Corp., 1941-44, Cleve., 1944-50; cost engr., asst. supt. Diamond Shamrock, Painesville, U., 1950-65; sr. project estimator Lummus Co., Houston, 1967—; exec. dir. Am. Assn. Cost Engrs., Houston, 1970—. Home: 5806 Wigton Dr Houston TX 77035

FORTENBAUGH, SAMUEL BYROD, Jr., lawyer, bus. exec.; b. London, Eng., Mar. 2, 1902; (parents Am. citizens); s. Samuel Byrod and Florence (Cowden) F.; B.S., Union Coll., 1923; LL.B., Harvard, 1926; m. Katherine F. Wall, Dec. 29, 1926; children—Samuel Byrod III, William Wall. Admitted to Pa. bar, 1926, since practiced Phila.; partner Clark, Ladner, Fortenbaugh & Young; pres., dir. Wisteria Hosiery Mills, Saluda, N.C., Vale Hosiery Corp., Lincolnton, N.C.; chmn. bd., treas., dir. Wall Industries, Inc., NYHM Transp. Co., Wall Rope Works, Beverly, N.J.; dir. Central- Penn Nat. Bank, Phila., Pub. Finance Service, Inc., Phila., Mrs. Paul's Kitchens, Phila. Chmn. bd. trustees Union Coll., Schenectady. Mem. Am., Pa., Phila. bar assns., Phila. Maritime Soc. (past pres.), Phi Beta Kappa, Beta Theta Pi. Clubs: India House, Harvard (N.Y.C.); Racquet (Phila.); Merion Golf (Ardmore, Pa.); Bay Head (N.J.) Yacht. Home: King of Prussia Rd Radnor PA 19087 Office: Widener Bldg Philadelphia PA 19107

FORTENBERRY, CHARLES NOLAN, educator; b. Oakvale, Miss., Sept. 18, 1908; s. John Morgan and Eliza Cornelia (Parkman) F.; B.A., M.A., U. Miss., 1931; Ph.D., U. Ill., 1937; m. Mae Edwards, Aug. 28, 1938; children—Charles Nolan, Joseph Edwin. Instr. social scis. Oakvale High Sch., 1931-32, 33-34, Clinton (Miss.) High Sch., 1933-34; grad. teaching asst. polit. sci. U. Ill., 1935-36; instr. govt. Edinburg (Tex.) Coll. (now Pan Am. Coll.), 1937-39, Tex. A. and M. Coll., 1939-40; asst. prof. govt. N. Tex. State Coll., 1940-42, asso. prof., 1942-46; asso. prof. polit. sci. U. Miss., 1946-49, prof., 1949-68, acting dean Grad. Sch., 1957-58, chmn. dept. polit. sci., 1958- 68; prof. polit. sci., head dept. polit. sci. Auburn U., Auburn, Ala., 1968—; vis. prof. U. Ala., summer 1957. Served to capt. USAAF, 1942-46. Mem. Am., So. polit. sci. assns., Pi Kappa Alpha, Pi Sigma Alpha, Omicron Delta Kappa, Phi Kappa Phi. Democrat. Episcopalian. Rotarian. Author: A Guidebook of the Chancery Clerk, 1949; A Handbook for Mississippi Legislators, 7th edit., 1968; (with R. B. Highsaw) Municipal Government in the South, 1952, The Government and Adminstration of Mississippi, 1954; also numerous articles profl. jours. Contbr. Yesterday's Constitution Today, 1960; Power in American State Legislatures, 1967; others. Home: Box 1102 Auburn AL 36830

FORTER, ELIZABETH TUSTEN, educator; b. Wichita, Kan., Nov. 19, 1922; d. Cecil Alfred and Elizabeth (Tusten) Forter; B.A., U. Wichita, 1943; M.A., U. Wis., 1945, Ph.D., 1955. Instr. English, U. Wichita, 1945-47, 52-53; mem. faculty Lawrence Coll., 1953—, chmn. dept. English, 1959-64, prof., 1963—, Edwards-Alexander prof. English, 1962—. Mem. Am. Assn. U. Profs., Modern Lang. Assn., Nat. Council Tchrs. English. Co-editor: The Comic in Theory and Practice, 1960; editor Caesar and Cleopatra (G. B. Shaw), 1965; Major Barbara (G. B. Shaw), 1971. Home: 119 S Meade St Appleton WI 54911

FORTESS, KARL EUGENE, lithographer, painter; b. Antwerp, Belgium, Oct. 13, 1907; s. David and Sara (Jukowska) F.; student Chgo. Art Inst., Art Students League N.Y., Woodstock Sch. of Painting; m. Lillian Fine. Came to U.S., 1915, naturalized, 1923. Faculty Art Students League, Bklyn Mus. Art Sch., La. State U., Am. Art Sch., now prof. Boston U. Sch. Fine and Applied Arts; works exhibited Nat. Inst. Arts and Letters, Art Inst. Chgo., Carnegie Inst., Whitney Mus. Am. Art, Corcoran Gallery Art, Mus. Modern Art, Nat. Acad. Design, Pa. Acad.; one-man shows Asso. Am. Artists Galleries, N.Y.C., Ganso Gallery, N.Y.C., Vose Galleries, Boston, Krasner Gallery, Mirski Gallery, also others; represented in permanent collections Butler Inst. Am. Art, Nat. Collection Fine Arts Smithsonian Instn., Munson-Williams-Proctor Inst., Newark (N.J.) Mus., Brooklyn Mus., Mus. Modern Art (print collection). Hudson Walker, other pvt., pub. collections. Recipient E. Keith Meml. award Woodstock Artists Assn., 1935; hon. mention Carnegie Inst., 1941. Guggenheim fellow, 1946. Mem. Artist Equity Assn., Coll. Art Assn., Art Students League N.Y. (life), Soc. Am. Graphic Artists, Am. Assn. U. Profs., Brit. Film Inst., Mus. Modern Art. Contbg. author: The Funnies: An American Idiom, 1963. Contbr. articles to profl. jours. Home: 96 Bay State Rd Boston MA 02215

FORTH, STUART, librarian; b. Manistee, Mich., Aug. 13, 1923; s. Wade S. and Nan (Rumans) F.; B.A., U. Mich., 1949, M.A. in L.S., 1950; Ph.D. in History, U. Wash., 1961; m. Pearl Brown, Dec. 24, 1951. Catalog librarian Ore. State U., 1950-52, adminstrv. asst. to dir. libraries, 1952-54; reference librarian Seattle Pub. Library, 1954-59; undergrad. librarian U. Kan., 1959-61, asso. dir. libraries, 1961-65; dir. libraries U. Ky. 1965—, v.p. for student affairs, 1968-70; teaching fellow history U. Wash., 1954-55, 57-58; tchr. dept. Western civilization U. Kan., 1960-65. Mem. Kan. Library Com., 1964-65. Served with USAAF, 1942-45; PTO. Mem. Am. Assn. U. Profs. (pres. U. Kan. chpt. 1965), Am. Hist. Assn., Orgn. Am. Historians, Bibliog. Soc. Am., Pacific Northwest (sec. 1953-54), Kan. (chmn. coll. and univ. library sect. 1963-64), Ky., Am. library assns., Am. Civil Liberties Union. Democrat. Episcopalian. Clubs: Caxton (Chgo.); Filson (Louisville). Contbr. to profl. jours. Home: 1277 Colonial Dr Lexington, KY 40504.

FORTHMANN, ANDREW KEATING, soap co. exec.; b. Los Angeles, Aug. 27, 1910; s. John A. and Elvira (Keating) F.; A.B., U. So. Cal., 1933, M.A., 1934; LL.B., 1939; m. Gerturde Ingli, Apr. 26, 1947; children—Andrea Marie, Andrew Keating, Christopher, DruAnne, Angele. Admitted to Cal. bar, 1946; with firm Dockweiler & Dockweiler, Los Angeles, 1946-; with Los Angeles Soap Co., 1942—, chmn. bd., 1956—, also dir.; with White King Soap Co., Los Angeles, 1947—, pres., 1955—, also dir.; pres., director of Cal. Rendering Co., 1947-62, chairman of the board, 1962-66; v.p., sec. of Forthmann Estate Co., 1950—. Served from 1st lt. to capt., USAAF, 1942- 46. Mem. Am., Cal., Los Angeles bar assns., Soap and Detergent Assn. (v.p. Western div. 1954-58, 61-65, national pres. 1958-61), Southern California Wine and Food Soc. Clubs: California, Los Angeles (Los Angeles). Home: 913 N Roxbury Dr Beverly Hills CA 90210 Office: 617 E 1st St Los Angeles CA 90012 also 210 W 7th St Los Angeles CA 90014

FORTIN, LUIS HORACIO, banker; b. Buenos Aires, Argentina, Feb. 14, 1920; s. Louis Alexandre and Isabel (Garcia) F.; Nat. Pub. Accountant, U. Buenos Aires, 1952; M.B.A., Columbia, 1962, Ph.D., 1967; m. Blanca Isabel Pascual, Sept. 8, 1947. Airline captain, Argentine Airlines, 1946-61; operations dir., 1952-53; prof. finance U. Buenos Aires, 1967-68; investment officer IFC, Washington, 1968-69; minister plenipotentiary financial affairs Argentine embassy, Washington, 1969-70; investment officer IFC, Washington, 1971—. Served as pilot French Air Force in Royal Air Force, 1941-45. Decorated Legion of Honor, Croix de Guerre with 3 palms (France); Distinguished Flying Cross (Eng). Home: 2230 47th St NW Washington DC 20007 Office: 1818 H St Washington DC 20433

FORTSON, BENJAMIN WYNN, Jr., Ga. sec. state; b. Tignall, Ga., Dec. 19, 1904; s. Benjamin Wynn and Lillie (Welborn) F.; student Emory U., 1919-20, Starkes U., 1920-23, Ga. Inst. Tech., 1923-24; LL.D., John Marshall Law Sch., 1949; m. Mary Cade, May 15, 1926 (dec.); 1 dau., Ann McNeill (Mrs. George Mandus). With Citizens Nat. Bank, Washington, Ga., 1924-25, Atlanta and Lowry Nat. Bank, 1925-26; asst. cashier Washington Loan and Banking Co., 1927-29; sec. state State of Ga., Atlanta, 1946—. Sec., treas. Wilkes County chpt. A.R.C., pres. Ga. Soc. for Crippled Children, 1954-56. Mem. Ga. Senate, 1939-40, 41-42; mem. Ga. Ho. of Reps., 1943-46. Trustee, Mary Willis Library. Mem. Nat. Assn. Secs. of State (pres. 1954), Alpha Kappa Psi (hon.), Pi Sigma Alpha (hon.), Demonsthenian Lit. Soc. U. Ga. (hon. life). Democrat. Methodist. Mason, Moose. Home: Box 428 Washington GA 30673 Office: State Capitol Atlanta GA 30334

FORTUNE, PHILIP ROBERT, metal mfg. co. exec.; b. Gouverneur, N.Y., Feb. 14, 1913; s. Robert J. and Mary (Cain) F.; B.A., St. Joseph's Coll., 1933; M.A., Niagara U., 1939; m. Margaret E. Burns, Apr. 15, 1944; children—Joanne, Terence, David, Christopher, Stephen. Instr., Niagara U., 1938-40; with N.Y. Air Brake Co., (merged with Gen. Signal Corp. 1967), Watertown, 1940—, gen. mgr., 1955-63, v.p., 1959-65, group exec. 1961-65, pres., 1965-67, chmn. exec. com., 1967—, dir.; dir. Hamworthy Hydraulics Ltd., 1963—, chmn. bd., 1971; trustee Watertown Savs. Bank. Served to lt. col. AUS, World War II; ETO. Mem. Watertown C. of C. Home: 18 Stonehouse Rd Scarsdale NY 10583 Office: 280 Park Av New York City NY 10017

FORTUNE, PORTER LEE, Jr., ednl. adminstr.; Old Fort, N.C., July 2, 1920; s. Porter and Eunice (Ross) F.; B.A., U. N.C., 1941, Ph.D., 1949; M.A., Emory U., 1946; m. Mary Elizabeth Cummings, Oct. 15, 1944; children—Philip Lee, Peggy Jean, Janet Cummings, Carey Ross. Instr. Emory U., 1946; teaching asst. U. N.C., 1946-47; faculty Miss. So. Coll., 1948-61, successively asst. prof. history, asso. prof., dean Basic Coll., 1948-57, prof., dean Coll. and Grad. sch., 1957-61; nat. exec. sec. Nat. Exchange Club, 1961- 68; chancellor U. of Miss., 1968—. Exec. bd. Yocona Area Council, Boy Scouts Am.; bd. dirs. So. Univ. Conf. Served as lt. (s.g.), USNR, 1942-46. Decorated Bronze Star medal; recipient Freedoms Found. Geo. Washington honor medal, 1966. Mem. N.E.A., Miss. Hist. Soc. (bd. dirs.), So. Assn. Land-Grant Colls; and State Univs. (pres.), Miss. Council Devel. Marine Resources, So. Regional Edn. Bd. (exec. com.), Orgn. Am. Historians, So. Hist. Assn., C. of C., Phi Alpha Theta, Pi Kappa Delta, Omicron Delta Kappa, Phi Kappa Phi, Pi Gamma Mu, Phi Delta Kappa, Pi Tau Chi, Kappa Alpha, Kappa Delta Pi. Methodist. Club: Exchange (past pres. Hattiesburg, past pres. Miss. chpt.; nat. regional v.p., chmn. nat. edn. com., nat. bd. control; Golden award for service 1968). Address: Chancellor's Office U Miss University, MS 38677.

FORTUNE, WILLIAM BROOKS, pharm. co. exec.; b. Holmesville, O., July 2, 1913; s. Richard Lee and Alba (Simmons) F.; B.S., Mt. Union Coll., 1934, D.Sc. (hon.), 1966; M.S., Purdue U., 1936, Ph.D., 1938, D.Sc. (hon.), 1966; m. to Joan Whitlock, Mar. 1, 1941; children—Susan Ann, Robert William, John Bradley. With Eli Lilly & Co., 1938-41, 46—, exec. dir. biochem. and biol. prodn., 1961-62, v.p., 1963-65, group v.p. 1965- -,also dir., 1964—. Mem. Com. Revision U.S. Pharmacopeia, 1960-70, Com. Nat. Formulary, 1960-70. Served to lt. col. AUS, 1941-46. Decorated Legion of Merit. Mem. Am. Chem. Soc., Am., Ind. pharm. assns., Royal Soc. Health. Presbyn. (trustee). Contbg. author: Analytical Absorption Spectroscopy, 1950. Patentee in field. Home: 7898 Ridge Rd Indianapolis, IN 46240. Office: Eli Lilly & Co Indianapolis IN 46206

FORTUNE, WILLIAM JAN, govt. ofcl.; b. Pottsville, Pa., Nov. 24, 1926; s. Robert Joseph and Blanch (Rauch) F.; B.S., Pa. State U., 1949; M.B.A., U. Pa., 1950; postgrad. U. Pitts., 1953-54, N.Y.U., 1954-60; m. Donna T. Martin, June 20, 1953; 1 son, Jan Eric. Supr. purchase analysis Westinghouse Air Brake Co., 1953-54; adminstrv. asst. to v.p. mfg. WAD div. Curtiss- Wright Co., 1954-58; mgmt. cons. A.T. Kearney & Co., Chgo., 1958-60; mfg. mgr. Conley Electronics Co., Skokie, Ill., 1960; prin. mgmt. engr. Martin Marietta Co., Orlando, Fla., 1961-69; mgmt. planner Girl Scouts Am., 1969; adminstr. Southeastern Power Adminstr., Dept. Interior, Elberton, Ga., 1969—; tchr. Rollins Coll. Grad. Sch. Bus. Adminstrn., Fla. So. Coll. Mem. Fla. Ho. of Reps. from Seminole and Orange counties, 1963-65, 67-68; chmn. Seminole County Republican Com., 1965-67. Served to 1st lt., Signal Corps, U.S. Army, 1950-53. Mem. Tau Beta Pi, Sigma Tau, Alpha Pi Mu. Home: 533 Rhodes Dr Elberton GA 30635 Office: Southeastern Power Adminstrn Elberton GA 30635

FORTUNE, WILLIAM LEMCKE, state ofcl.; b. Indpls., Dec. 6, 1912; s. Russell and Elinor (Lemcke) F.; A.B., Princeton, 1935; m. Jane Hennessy, Nov. 26, 1938; children—Janie, Pamela, William Lemcke, Richard Hennessy. Reporter Ft. Wayne (Ind.) Jour. Gazette, 1936; reporter, polit. writer Indpls. Times, 1937-38; pub. Dunkirk (Ind.) News, 1938-40, Waveland (Ind.) Independent, 1941; accountant. Mem. Ind. Gen. Assembly, 1947-48; treas. State of Ind., 1951-53; revenue commr. Ind., 1965-69. Spl. legislative corr. for 48 newspapers; lectr. state tax problems. Campaign dir. Marion County March of Dimes, 1961-62. Contbr. articles on state taxes and internat. trade to newspapers and mags. Served from pvt. to sgt. AUS, 1942-46. Home: Indianapolis IN 46206 Office: Zionsville IN 46077

FORWARD, CHARLES HAMILTON, lawyer; b. Pitts., Mar. 19, 1886; s. John F. and Ella F. (Dillon) F.; student U. Cal., 1904-05, 11-13, U.S. Coast Guard Acad., 1906-09; m. Zella E. Saint, June 24, 1914; 1 son, Charles H. Admitted to Cal. bar, 1911, since practiced in San Diego; partner Luce, Forward, Hamilton & Scripps. Captain of port, San Diego, Cal. Served as lt. Comdr., USCGR, 1943-46. Mason. Clubs: Cuyamaca, University. Home: 3353 Goldsmith St San Diego CA 92106 Office: Electronics Capital Bldg San Diego CA 92101

FOSBURGH, JAMES WHITNEY, artist; b. N.Y.C., Aug. 1, 1910; s. James B. A. and Leila (Whitney) F.; A.B., Yale, 1933, M.A., 1935; student Royal U., Rome, 1933-34; m. Mary Cushing, 1953. Lectr., Frick Collection, N.Y.C., 1935-54; tchr. painting Parsons Sch. Design, 1952; paintings exhibited group shows, pvt. collections, galleries; exhibited one-man show Durlacher Bros., 1952, 55, 57, San Francisco Palace Legion of Honor, 1955, Los Angeles County Mus., 1955, Kennedy Galleries, 1968; lectr. Nat. Gallery Art, Yale, Met. Mus. Art, 1950-60; represented in collections Met. Mus. Art, Boston Mus. Fine Arts, Pa. Acad. Fine Arts, Toledo Mus. Fine Arts, pvt. collections. Chmn., Com. for Paintings for White House, 1961-63; mem. Landmarks Preservation Commn., N.Y.C., 1962—, Com. for Preservation White House, 1964—. Served in USAAF, 1942-46. Contbr. to profl. publs. Home: 32 E 64th St New York City NY 10021

FOSCUE, HENRY ARMFIELD, furniture mfr.; b. Jamestown, N.C., Mar. 9, 1904; s. John Edward and Vera (Armfield) F.; B.B.A., U. N.C., 1926, D.Hum., Raleigh, 1964, D.H.L., Greensboro, 1966; L.H.D., N.C. State U., 1964; m. Valworth McMillan, Dec. 22, 1933; children—Ellen Valworth, Henry Armfield. Sales dept. Globe Furniture Co., High Point, N.C., 1926-35, sec., sales mgr., 1935-50, pres., 1950—; founder, pres. Colony Tables, Inc., Henry of High Point; pres., chmn. So. Furniture Expn. Bldg.; dir. Hatteras Yacht Co., High Point; dir., chmn. trust com. Wachovia Bank & Trust Co., High Point; mem. adv. bd. Founders Life Assurance Co. of Carolina, High Point. Pres. N.C. Indsl. Council, 1951-52; mem. Exec. Mansion Fine Arts Commn. of N.C.; mem. exec. com. Assn. of Governing Bds. of Univs. and Colls. Founder, pres. Furniture Found., Inc.; dir. Home Econs. Found., Bus. Found., U. N.C.; dir. N.C. Engring. Found., N.C. State U.; trustee, mem. exec. com. Consol. U. N.C., 1953—. Selected Man of Yr. in Furniture Industry, 1948; recipient Brotherhood citation Nat. Conf. Christians and Jews, 1965. Mem. So. Furniture Mfrs. Assn. (chmn. ednl. com.; past. dir., mem. exec. com., pres. and chmn.), N.A.M. (dir. 1951-54). Club: Co- founders (pres.) (Med. Sch. U. N.C.). Home: 1026 Rockford Rd High Point NC 27262 Office: So Furniture Expn Bldg High Point NC 27261

FOSDICK, LLOYD DUDLEY, educator; b. N.Y.C., Jan. 18, 1928; s. Eugene O. and Janet (Goldstein) F.; Ph.B., U. Chgo., 1946, B.S., 1948; Ph.D., Purdue U., 1953; m. Erica Ross, Dec. 19, 1958; children-Sarah, Aaron. Research asso. Control Systems Labs., U. Ill., 1953; asst. head computer div. Midwestern Univs. Research Assn., Madison, Wis., 1956-57; prof. computer soil U. Ill., 1957-70; prof., chmn. computer sci. Colo. U., 1970—. Served with AUS, 1954-56. prof., chmn. computer sci. Colo. U., 1970—. Served with AUS, 1954-56. Guggenheim fellow, 1964-65. Mem. Assn. Computing Machinery (gov. bd. spl. interest group numerical math.; editor for communications), Soc. Indsl. and Applied Math., Am. Assn. U. Profs., Sigma Xi. Home: 276 Acorn Lane Boulder CO 80302

FOSHAY, ARTHUR WELLESLEY, educator; b. Oakland, Cal., July 23, 1912; s. Arthur Wellesley and Amelia Gertrude (Brazill) F.; A.B., U. Cal, 1934; Ed.D., Columbia, 1949; m. Irene Finette Partridge, Aug. 26, 1938; children—Constance Finette, Wellesley Robinson. Tchr., prin., guidance cons. Oakland pub. schs., 1936-46; asst. prin. Horace-Mann-Lincoln Sch., N.Y.C., 1946-48; asst. and asso. prof. edn., research asso. Horace Mann- Lincoln Inst. Sch. Experimentation, Tchrs. Coll., Columbia, 1948-52, prof. edn., dir. Horace Mann-Lincoln Inst. 1957-66, dir. research and field service, 1961-64, asso. dean research and field services, 1964-68, prof. edn. Tchrs. Coll., Columbia, 1968—; prof. edn. dir. Bur. Ednl. Research, Ohio State U., 1952-57; cons. to school systems and pvt. firms on curriculum development; program specialist Ford Found., Iran, 1960-61; dir. UNESCO Inst. Edn. Study, 1962. Bur. mem. Internat. Assn. Evaluation Ednl. Attainment, 1970 —. Mem. Assn. Supervision and Curriculum Devel. (chmn. 1957 yearbook com.; pres. 1960-61), N.E.A., A.A.A.S., Am. Ednl. Research Assn. Author: Education in the Elementary School (with H.L. Caswell), 1950, rev. edits. 1950, 57; Children's Social Values, An Action Research Study (with K. D. Wann and assos.), 1954; Curriculum for the 70's, an Agenda for Invention, 1970. Editor: Research for Curriculum Improvement, 1957; Handbook of Education, 1963; The Professional as Educator, 1970. Contbr. articles mags., chpts. to yearbooks. Home: 17 Cherry St Tenafly, NJ 07670; also Rowe MA 01367 Office: Tchrs Coll Columbia U New York City NY 10027

FOSHAY, WILLIAM WARD, lawyer; b. Port Chester, N.Y., Sept. 14, 1910; s. William Briggs and Lydia Marie (Ward) F.; A.B., Harvard, 1931, LL.B., 1935; student Merton Coll., Oxford (Eng.) U., 1931-32; m. Ella Dunlevy Milbank, Feb. 24, 1938; children—William Ward, Katharine Fowler (Mrs. John F. Horn), Barbara Briggs (Mrs. Anthony D. Duke, Jr.), Ella Milbank (Mrs. Michael B. Rothfeld). Admitted to N.Y. bar, 1935; with firm Sullivan & Cromwell, 1935-41, partner, 1945—; counsel Bur. Ships, U.S. Navy, 1942-45. Dir. Marine Midland Banks, Inc., Internat. Nickel Co. Can., Ltd., Pitney-Bowes, Inc., Russell, Burdsall & Ward Bolt and Nut Co. Pres., U.S. Srs. Golf Assn. Trustee Arthritis and Rheumatism Found., 1963—. Served with USNR, World War II. Decorated Legion of Merit. Home: 1 E 66th St New York City NY 10021 Office: 48 Wall St New York City NY 10005

FOSHEE, JOHN G., pipe mfg. co. exec.; b. 1921; B.Sc., B.A., U. Ala., 1943, M.Sc., 1948; married. With Ernst & Ernst, 1948-56; asst. treas. Am. Cast Iron Pipe Co., Birmingham, Ala., 1956-60, treas., dir., 1960—. Served with AUS, 1943-46. C.P.A., Ala. Office: Am Cast Iron Pipe Co Box 2603 Birmingham AL 35202*

FOSS, LUKAS, composer, condr., musician; b. Berlin, Germany, Aug. 15, 1922; s. Martin and Hilde (Schindler) F.; student Lycee Pasteur, 1932-37; grad. Curtis Inst. Music, 1940; spl. study Yale, 1940-41; pupil of Paul Hindemith, Julius Herford, Serge Koussevitzky, Fritz Reiner, Isabelle Vengerova, Randal Thompson, Rosario Scalero, Felix Wolfes; LL.D., Los Angeles Conservatory of Music, 1956, others; m.; 2 children. Came to U.S., 1937, naturalized, 1942. Former prof. U. Cal. at Los Angeles in charge orch. and advanced composition; former condr., music dir. Buffalo Philharmonic; faculty Harvard, 1970-71; composer, condr., pianist; orchestral compositions performed by many major orchs.; best known works include (opera) The Jumping Frog; The Prairie; Piano Concerto No. 2; Song of Songs; Parable of Death; Griffelkin (opera in 3 acts); Psalms; Baroque Variations; Paradigm; Geod; piano pieces, ballets; works commd. by Kulas Found., League of Composers and Koussevitzky Music Found., NBC opera on TV. Founder, co-dir. Center Creative and Performing Arts, Buffalo U.; pres. Lukas Foss New Music Found. Guggenheim fellow, 1945. Pulitzer scholar for Suite to the Tempest of Shakespeare, 1942; N.Y. Critic Circle citation for Prairie, 1944, Soc. for Pub. Am. Music award for String Quartet in G, 1948; Rome prize, 1950; Horblit award for Piano concerto No. 2, 1951, Naumburg Rec. award for Song of Songs, 1957; Creative Music grant Inst. Arts and Letters, 1957; N.Y. Music Critics Circle award for Time-Cycle orch. songs, 1961, for Echoi, 1963. Mem. Nat. Inst. Arts and Letters. Address: 4 E 95th St New York City NY 10028

FOSS, OLIVER, artist; b. Hanover, Ger., Oct. 17, 1920; s. Martin and Hilda (Schindler) F.; B.A., Janson de Salily Coll., Paris, France, 1934-36; student Art Students League, N.A.D. 1937-38, Jacobi-Annot Sch. Art, 1937-39; B.S., Elizabethtown Coll., 1942;

student U. Basel, 1946-48, Ecole Nat. Superieure des Beaux Arts, 1948-50; m. Marcelle Bertier, Oct. 19, 1946 (div.); 1 son, Marc; m. 2d, Fides Maria Rankl, Mar. 5, 1960; children—Rahel Maria, Jean-Ulrich, René Waldemar. Began career as designer with Seagram Distillers, Esquire magazine, Feltman Co., Inc., Adolphe Hurst Co., 1938-39; exhibitor paintings, 1938-; one man show Riverside Mus., N.Y.C., 1938, New Sch. Social Research, 1939, Galerie Landy, Paris, 1949 (canvas Madeleine purchased by French govt.), Galerie Herve, Paris, 1950, Van Dieman-Lilienfeld Galleries, N.Y.C., 1951; Galerie Drouant David, 1952; Galerie de l'Art Moderne, Paris, 1956, 57, 58, also several exhbns. in Switzerland, 1964; group exhbns. Gallery Durant-Ruel, Paris, 1957, Ecole de Paris, Charpentier, 1957, Peintres-Témoins de leur temps, Musée Gallieria, Paris, 1958-62; lab. technician, instr. bacteriology Women's Hosp., Phila. 1939-40; prof. fine arts Elizabeth Town Coll., 1940-42; instr. French, Lafayette Coll., 1942-43; paintings represented permanent collections in various museums. Served with AUS, Europe, 1942-46. Recipient 1st prize Nat. Art Exhbn., Monte Carlo, 1949; award Soc. des Artistes Francais, 1950; silver medal Ville de Paris, 1955; prize Festival of Aix en Provence, 1958; recipient of Paris-Medaille de Vermeil, 1964; elected officer du Mérite Culturel Nat., 1965; Silver medal Merite Nat. Francais, 1966; 1st prize Salon Populiste, 1966; Croix de Chevalier of Etoile du Bien, Paris, 1966; officers cross of Devouement Francas, Paris, 1967. Fellow Internat. Inst. Arts and Letters; mem. Entreaide des Artistes, Soc. Artistes Francais, Salon des Independents Paris, Ecole de Paris, Peintres Temoins De Leur Temps. Founder Doctrine Visionism. Address: 96 Av des Ternes Paris 17, France

FOSS, PHILLIP OLIVER, polit. scientist, educator; b. Maxbass, N.D., May 18, 1916; s. Oliver Olson and Petra (Elton) F.; B.A., U. Wash., 1947; M.S., U. Ore., 1953, Ph.D., 1956; m. Dorothy Marie Hansen, May 31, 1941; children—Coral Lee, Phyllis Ann, Phillip Oliver Jr., Thorvald C. Instr. U. Ore., 1955-57; asst. prof. San Francisco State Coll., 1957-61, asso. prof., 1961-62; asso. prof. Colo. State U., 1962-64, prof., 1964-71, chmn. dept. polit. sci., 1965-71, chmn. Natural Resources Center, 1964-67; cons. Bur. Land Mgmt., U.S. Dept. Inteerior, 1964-65, 69, Nat. Acad. Scis., 1969-70. Served witth USAAF, 1942-46, USAF, 1951-53. Recipient outstanding service award San Francisco State Coll., 1960, distinguished service award Colo. State U., 1970. Mem. Am., Western (exec. council 1967-69, v.p., pres. elect 1970-71; recipient outstanding dissertation award 1957) polit. sci. assns., Am. Soc. Pub. Adminstrn. Author: Politics and Grass, 1960; Federal Agencies and Outdoor Recreation, 1962; Education in Natural Resources, 1964; Politics and Policies 1970; Public Land Policy, 1970; Outdoor Recreation, 1971; Politics and Ecology, 1971. Contbr. articles profl. jours. Home: 3019 Moore Lane Fort Collins CO 80521

FOSS, ROBERT EDWIN, oil exec.; b. Glendale, Cal., July 7, 1910; s. Raymond P. and Mary Ann (Peters) F.; B.S., Cal. Inst. Tech., 1932; m. Olive Lorene Easley, July 13, 1935; children—David Easley, Dixon Keith. Jr. engr. Barnsdall Oil Co., 1935-40, chief engr., 1940-42, gen. supt., 1942-45, v.p. in charge Cal. prodn., 1945-49; joined Sunray Oil Corp. (Sunray-Barnsdall merger), 1950, v.p., 1950, v.p. in charge exploitation and prodn., Tulsa, 1952- 55, co. merged with Mid-Continent Oil Corp., 1955, v.p., mgr. production dept. Sunray DX Oil Co., 1955-59, sr. v.p. prodn., 1959-63, exec. v.p., directing mfg. and marketing, 1963-68, pres., 1964-68, dir., 1958-68;, co. merged with Sun Oil Co., 1968, exec. v.p., dir., 1968—; dir. 1st Nat. Bank Tulsa. Nat. chmn. central com. on tng., nat. chmn. exec. com. on standardization of oilfield equipment and materials Am. Petroleum Inst. (dir.). Mem. Twenty-Five Year Club Petroleum Industry. Home: 3310 Fairmount Dallas TX 75201

FOSS, WILLIAM FRANCIS, mfg. co. exec.; b. Mpls., Aug. 5, 1917; s. Peter and Lucinda (Larson) F.; student St. Thomas Coll., St. Paul, 1935-36, U. Minn., 1941-42; m. Kathryn Bolduc, Feb. 22, 1941; children—Thomas W., Jeffrey J., Kathleen, Timothy, Ann Marie, William F. II (dec.). With Mpls. Moline Inc., Hopkins, Minn. 1941-67, mng. dir. Mpls.-Moline Turk Traktor, 1954-57, controller, v.p., asst. to pres., 1957-59, v.p., treas., 1959-61, sr. v.p., treas., permanent chmn. operating com., 1961-62, pres., chief exec. officer, dir., 1962-67, v.p. White Motor Corp., 1965-67; pres., chief exec. officer, dir. Fabri-Tek, Inc., Mpls., 1967-70; pres., dir. Applied Power Industries, Inc., Milw., 1970—; dir. Tel-E-Lect, Inc. Apache Corp., Gelco IVM Leasing Co. (all Mpls.). Pres., treas. William F. Foss II Meml. Found. Mem. Mpls. C. of C. (pres. 1966, dir.), Nat. Assn. Accountants. Clubs: Minneapolis; Wayzata (Minn.) Country; Union League (Chgo.); University (Milw.). Home: 5157 N Lake Dr Milwaukee WI 53217 Office: Box 3100 Milwaukee WI 53218

FOSSE, BOB, choreographer; b. Chgo., June 23, 1927; s. Cyril K. and Sarah (Stanton) F. Choreographer for musical plays, 1956—, Pajama Game, 1956—, Damn Yankees, 1957, Bells Are Ringing, 1958, New Girl in Town, 1958; choreographer, dir. play Redhead, 1959; mus. staging How To Succeed in Business Without Really Trying; choreographer, co.-dir. Little Me. Recipient Tony award for, Pajama Game, 1956, Damn Yankees, 1957, Redhead, 1959; Donaldson award for Pajama Game, 1956, Dance Mag. and Tony award for Little Me, 1963. Home: 91 Central Park West New York City NY 10023

FOSSETT, CARROLL ATWOOD, banker; b. Albany, N.Y., Aug. 28, 1917; s. Richard Leigh and Ethel (Berry) F.; student Albany Acad., 1928-35; B.Sc., Yale, 1939; m. Mary Jane Mackey, Nov. 13, 1943; children—Judith Bliss (Mrs. Joseph D. Rodgers), Carroll Atwood, John Nichols, Benjamin Leigh, Roger Mackey. Asst. buyer Jordan Marsh Co., Boston, 1939-41; chief accountant Univ. Club, Boston, 1941; account mgr. Arthur Andersen & Co., Boston, 1945-52; controller Tech. Operations, Inc., Arlington, Mass., 1952-56; asst. gen. mgr. Campbell & Hall, Inc., Boston, 1956-57; sr. asst. treas. Raytheon Co., 1957-66; v.p. adminstrn. J. Henry Schroder Banking Corp., N.Y.C., 1966-68; sr. v.p., controller Nat. Shawmut Bank, Boston, 1968—. Served to lt. comdr. USNR, 1941-45. C.P.A., Mass. Mem. Am. Inst. C.P.A.'s, Financial Execs. Inst. Conglist. Clubs: Wellesley; Wellesley Country; Yale (Boston); Bay. Home: Sabrina Farm Rd Wellesley MA 02181 Office: 40 Water St Boston MA 02109

FOSSUM, KYLE KINGMAN, banker; b. Mobridge, S.D., Sept. 21, 1918; s. Alex E. and Maybelle (Kyle) F.; B.B.A., U. Minn., 1941; postgrad. Grad. Sch. Banking, Rutgers U., 1951-53; m. Ruby Mennes, Sept. 9, 1950; children—Kyle Kingman, David G., Mary A. With Fed. Res. Bank of Mpls., Helena, Mont. br., 1941-68, sr. v.p., 1966-68; 1st v.p. Fed. Res. Bank of Atlanta, 1969—. Mem. U.S. Delegation to Center for Latin Am. Monetary Studies, Buenos Aires, Argentina, 1965. Served to col. AUS, 1941-47; ETO. Mem. Robert Morris Assos., Alpha Delta Phi. Rotarian. Office: 104 Marietta St NW Atlanta GA 30303

FOSTER, ADRIANCE S., educator; b. Poughkeepsie, N.Y., Aug. 6, 1901; s. Raymond and Alice (Adriance) F.; B.S., Cornell, 1923; S.M., Harvard, 1925, Sc.D., 1926; m. Helen N. Vincent, July 29, 1930; 1 son, Richard V. Prof. botany U. Cal. at Berkeley, also chmn. dept. botany, prof. botany emeritus 1968—. Mem. Internat. Soc. Plant Morphologists (pres. exec. council 1970—), Am. Inst. Biol. Sci., A.A.A.S., Bot. Soc. Am., Acad. Arts and Sci., Sigma Xi. Author: Practical Plant Anatomy, 2d edit.; (with E.M. Gifford, Jr.) Comparative Morphology of Vascular Plants, 1959. Contbr. articles to sci. jours. Home: 57 Poplar St Berkeley CA 94708

FOSTER, ALAN HERBERT, automobile mfg. co. exec.; b. Somerville, Mass., Nov. 7, 1925; s. Herbert and Margaret J. (Griffin) F.; B.S., B.A., Boston Coll., 1951; M.B.A., Harvard, 1953; m. Cynthia Ann Brooks, June 26, 1954; children—Mark Brooks, Andrew Herbert. With Sylvania Electric Products, Inc., 1953-63; with Am. Motors Corp., 1963—, corp. dir. financial planning and analysis, 1963-67, treas., 1967-68, v.p., treas., 1968—; v.p., treas., dir. Am. Motors Pan-Am. Corp., Am. Motors Sales Corp., AM Data Systems Corp.; v.p. Holmes Foundry Ltd., Evart Products Co.; treas., dir. Jeep Corp., Jeep Sales Corp., Jeep Internat. Corp.; treas. AM Gen. Corp., Amland Corp., Financiera de Am., S.A., A.M.C. de Venezuela, C.A.; dir. Devel. Credit Corp., Permanente S.A.C.y.F., Am. Motors Can. Ltd., Ensambladora Centroamericana de Costa Rica S.A., Rambler Motors (AMC) Ltd., Vehiculos Automotores Mexicanos, S.A. Served with USNR, 1945-46. Mem. Commanderie de Bordeaux, Financial Execs. Inst., Baker Street Irregulars (v.p. Detroit chpt.), Speckled Band Boston, Inst. Mgmt. Scis. (past nat. chmn. coll. planning). Clubs: Harvard (N.Y.C. and Boston); India House (N.Y.). Author: Practical Business Management, 1962; also articles. Home: 2200 Fuller Rd Ann Arbor MI 48105 Office: 14250 Plymouth Rd Detroit MI 48232

FOSTER, ALFRED LEON, educator, mathematician; b. N.Y.C., July 13, 1904; s. Henry and Josephine (Sonnen) F.; B.S., Cal. Inst. Tech., 1926, M.S., 1927; Ph.D., Princeton, 1931; m. Else Wagner, Sept. 19, 1930; children—Wilfred, Erwin, Elsbeth (Mrs. Jose Ramos), Toni-Ann. Research fellow math. Princeton, 1931; Internat. research fellow U. Göttingen (Germany), 1932- 33; mem. faculty U. Cal. at Berkeley, 1933-, prof. math., 1950-. Mem. Am. Math. Soc., Assn. Symbolic Logic. Author numerous research papers. Home: 954 Keeler Av Berkeley CA 94708

FOSTER, ARCHIBALD MCGHEE, advt. exec.; b. East Hampton, N.Y., Aug. 22, 1915; s. Albert V. and Margaret (Baxter) F.; grad. St. Mark's Sch.; A.B., Harvard, 1938; m. Joan Bersbach, Sept. 23, 1938; 1 son, Archibald McGhee. Promotion dir. Conde Nast Publs., 1940; account exec. A.W. Lewin Co., advt., 1946-51; v.p. Cecil & Presbrey, advt., 1951-54; with Ted Bates & Co., Inc., 1954- -, pres., chief exec. officer, 1965-71, chmn. bd., chief exec., 1971—. Served with USMCR, 1940-45. Mem. Am. Assn. Advt. Agys. (chmn. 1970-71). Home: 925 Park Av New York City NY 10028 Office: 1 Astor Plaza New York City NY 10019

FOSTER, ARTHUR KEY, Jr., lawyer; b. Birmingham, Ala., Nov. 22, 1933; s. Arthur Key and Vanceil (Oden) F.; B.S., Princeton, 1955; LL.B., U. Va., 1960; m. Jean Lyles, Jan. 7, 1967. Admitted to Ala. bar, 1960, Since practiced in Birmingham; mem. firm Martin, Balch, Bingham, Hawthorne & Williams, 1960—, partner, 1965—. Mem. Republican County Exec. Com., 1968—. Bd. dirs. YMCA; trustee Epsicopal Found. Jefferson County, Ellen H. Douglas Home. Served to lt. (j.g.) USNR, 1955-57. Mem. Am., Birmingham bar assns., princeton Alumni Assn. Ala. (treas.). Home: 3234 Carlisle Rd Birmingham AL 35213 Office: 600 N 18th St Birmingham AL 35203

FOSTER, ARTHUR ROWE, engring, educator; b. Peabody, Mass., Apr. 22, 1924; s. Francis Joel and Helen Almira (Rowe) F.; B.S. in Mech. Engring., Tufts U., 1945; M. Engiring. in Mech. Engring., Yale, 1949; m. Nettie Claire Pease, July 12, 1947; children—Jackson Judd, Cynthia Grace. Engr. material devel. lab. Pratt & Whitney aircraft div. United Aircraft Corp., 1947-48; mem. faculty Northeastern U., 1949—, prof. mech. engring., chmn. dept., 1961- -. Served to ensign USNR, 1945-46. Registered profl. engr., Mass. Mem. Am. Soc. M.E., Am. Soc. Engring. Edn., Am. Nuclear Soc., Delta Tau Delta, Pi Tau Sigma, Tau Beta Pi. Author: (with R. L. Wright, Jr.) Basic Nuclear Engineering, 1968. Home: 28 Strathmore Circle Braintree, MA 02184. Office: Northeastern U Boston MA 02115

FOSTER, CEDRIC, pub. relations exec; b. West Hartford, Conn., Aug. 31, 1900; s. Arthur Leon and Josephine (Wilkinson) F.; student Dartmouth Coll., 1920- 21, 1922-23; D.Litt., Southwestern U., Georgetown, Tex., Carthage (Ill.) College; LL.D. (hon.), John Brown U. m. Marguerite Lane, Dec. 12, 1921; children—Shirley Plummer (Shirley Foster Fields), Sarah Ann H. (Mrs. Peter Carpenter). With Hartford (Conn.) Courant and Asso. Press, San Francisco, 1923-25; Conn. mgr. United Press, 1925-26; with New Britain (Conn.) Herald, Waterbury (Conn.) Am. and Providence Jour., 1926-29; financial editor Hartford (Conn.) Times, 1929-35; mgr. radio sta. WTHT, Hartford, 1935-41; news commentator MBS, 1940-67; news commentator radio sta. KTLN and Intermountain Network, Denver, 1967-69, KFML, 1969-70; pub. relations Farland-Buell Chrysler Plymouth, Denver, also Glenco Devel. Corp., Evergreen and Glenwood Springs, Colo, 1970—. Decorated Comdr. of the Royal Order Phoenix, comdr. of the Royal Order of King George I (Greece); Order of Homayoun (Iran); officer of the Royal Order Orange-Nassau (The Netherlands); recipient plaque for 25 years distinguished service to broadcasting Nat. Assn. Broadcasters, 1963. Mem. Phi Sigma Kappa, Sigma Delta Chi, Order Ahepa. Club: Denver Press. Address: 550 E 12th Av Denver CO 80203

FOSTER, CHARLES ADDISON, Jr., petroleum co. exec.; b. Tacoma, Apr. 27, 1912; s. Charles Addison and Gertrude (Childs) F.; student San Mateo (Cal.) Jr. Coll., 1928-29; m. Hannah Cox Wight, June 15, 1940; 1 son, Hugh W. With Shell Oil Co., 1929- -, v.p. marketing Shell Oil Co. Can., Ltd., 1958-62, v.p. central marketing region parent co., 1962-65, v.p. Western marketing region, 1965-68, v.p. pub. relations N.Y.C., 1968-70, v.p. pub. affairs, 1970—; asst. mgr. Caracas (Venezuela) Anglican Ch. Mission, 1947, San Francisco area Boy Scouts Am., 1951, Atlanta Community Chest, 1952, Albany (N.Y.) Arthritis and Rheumatism Found., 1956-57. Served to lt. comdr. USNR, 1941-45. Mem. Am. Petroleum Inst. Clubs: Pacific Union (San Francisco); Burlingame Country; Hemisphere, Links (N.Y.). Home: 521 Park Av New York City, NY 10021. Office: 50 W 50th St New York City NY 10020

FOSTER, CHARLES ALVIN, govt. ofcl.; b. Vancouver, Can., Sept. 28, 1913; (parents Am. citizens); s. Albert Walter and Marion Alice (Wells) F.; A.B., Linfield Coll., 1935; A.M., Harvard, 1940; Ph.D., 1950; S.M., Georgetown U., 1937; Docteur de l'Universite de Paris, summa cum laude, 1949; m. Marie Brigitte David, July 8, 1946; children—Caroline, Anne, Denis. Mem. faculty Harvard, 1949-50; asst. dir. Mid-Europe Study Center, Nat. Com. Free Europe, N.Y.C., also sec. Free Europe U. in Exile, Paris, France, 1950-52; European dir. Inst. Internat. Edn., Paris, 1952-53; chief div. edn. internat. understanding UNESCO, 1954-55; cons., then acting dir. Presidents Com. Edn. Beyond High Sch., 1956-57; cons. internat. div. RCA, 1958-61; dep. mission dir. Agy. Internat. Devel., Laos, 1961, acting dir., 1961-63, dir. of employee devel., 1963-66, mgr. Am. Schs. and hosps. abroad program, adviser edn. and manpower planning, 1966-68; tech. assistance adviser Bur. for East Asia, 1968; chief edn. adviser U.S. Mission to Korea, 1969—. Bd. govs. U.S. Found. of U. Paris; chmn. dirs. Am. Sch. Vientiane. Served with USAAF, 1942-46; ETO. Decorated Croix de Guerre (France). Fellow Pierpont Morgan Library. N.Y. Mem. Am. Fgn. Service Assn., Coll. Art Assn. Am., Assn. Guillaume Budé (Paris). Clubs: Harvard, Grolier (N.Y.C.); University (Paris). Author: Television the new tool, 1958. Contbr. to profl. publs. Home: 21 rue du Cherche Midi Paris VI France Office: AID Dept State Washington DC 20523

FOSTER, CHARLES HOWELL, educator; b. Elizabeth, N.J., Aug. 3, 1913; s. Raymond and Alice (Adriance) F.; ed. The Peddie Sch., Hightstown, N.J., 1927-32; B.A., Amherst Coll., 1936; M.A., U. Ia., 1937, Ph.D., 1939; m. Doris Van Denbergh; children—John W., Thomas H., Mary A., David A. Instr. English, U. Ia., 1939-42, asst. prof., 1942-44; asso. prof. U. Colo., 1944-47; prof. English, Grinnell Coll., 1947-58; prof. English, U. Minn., 1958—; vis. prof. Bowdoin Coll., 1964-65. (Am. Council Learned Socs.) fellow, 1952. Mem. Am. Studies Assn. (exec. council 1968-71), Phi Beta Kappa. Clubs: Ampersand, Gown-in-Town (Mpls.). Author: Emerson's Theory of Poetry, 1939; The Rungless Ladder: Harriet Beecher Stowe and New England Puritanian, 1954, 70; Beyond Concord: Selected Writings of David Atwood Wasson, 1965. Bd. editors The New Eng. Quar., 1958—. Home: Martin Rd Luray VA 22835

FOSTER, CHESTER W., mfg. co. exec.; b. Milw., 1908; grad. U. Wis., 1931. Pres. Nordberg div. Rex Chainbelt, Inc., Milw., also corporate dir.; dir. Marine Nat. Exchange Bank, Milw., Twin Disc Inc., Boston Mfrs. Mut. Ins. Co., Machinery & Allied Products, Inc. Home: 34947 Fairview Rd Oconomowoc WI 53066 Office: 3070 S Chase Av Milwaukee WI 53207

FOSTER, DAVID HENRY, electronics exec.; b. Cedar Rapids, Ia., July 15, 1927; s. Wayne J. and Edna (Westfall) F.; B.A., State U. Ia., 1950, J.D., 1952; m. Barbara Sue Burrell, June 8, 1950; children—Sarah, Kathleen, Robert. Asso. law firm Lynch, Dallas, Smith & Harman, Cedar Rapids, 1952-56; asst. to pres. H.A. Wagner Co., Van Nuys, Cal., 1956-58; head contracts Stromberg- Carlson, San Diego, 1958-59; sec., gen. atty. Collins Radio Co., Dallas, 1959, now v.p., sec.; dir. First Nat. Bank, Richardson, Tex. Served with USNR, 1945-46. Mem. Order of Coif, Phi Beta Kappa. Methodist (ofcl. bd.). Home: 7440 Stonecrest Dr Dallas, TX 75240. Office: Collins Radio Co Dallas TX 75207

FOSTER, DAVID RAMSEY, soap co. exec.; b. London, Eng., May 24, 1920 (parents Am. citizens); s. Robert Bagley and Josephine (Ramsey) F.; student econs. Gonville and Caius Coll., Cambridge (Eng.) U., 1938; m. Anne Firth, Aug. 2, 1957; children—Sarah, Victoria. With Colgate-Palmolive Co., and affiliates, 1946—, v.p. gen. mgr. Europe, Colgate-Palmolive Internat., 1961-65, v.p., gen. mgr. household products div. parent co., N.Y.C., 1965-68, exec. v.p., 1968-70, pres., 1970—, chief exec. officer, 1971—, also dir. Served to lt. comdr. Royal Naval Vol. Res., 1940-46. Decorated Distinguished Service Order, Distinguished Service Cross with bar. Mem. Am. Soc. in Britain. Clubs: American (London); Hawks (Cambridge U.); Royal Ancient Golf (St. Andrews, Scotland); Garden City (N.J.) Golf; Economic, Pinnacle (N.Y.C.); Half Moon-Rose Hall (Jamaica, W.I.); Sankaky Head Golf. Home: 165 E 66th St New York City NY 10021 Office: 300 Park Av New York City NY 10022

FOSTER, DEAN, educator; b. Bellflower, Ill., June 22, 1919; s. John J. and Bessie (Smith) F.; A.B., Ind. U., 1942; Ph.D., Cornell U., 1949; m. Maxine Pace, Oct. 18, 1942; children—Thornton, Janne (Mrs. James Robinson), Lance, Lianne. Dir. labs., dir. research U.S. Testing Co., Hoboken, N.J., 1952-61; research dir. Sleep Research Found., Lexington, Va., 1956—; prof. psychology Va. Mil. Inst., 1961—. Mem. Parsippany (N.J.) Sch. Bd., 1958-59. Mem. Am. Psychol. Assn., Sigma Xi. Club: Va. Mil. Inst. Faculty. Home: Rt 5 Box 161 Lexington VA 24450

FOSTER, DONALD LEE, corp. exec.; b. Bloomington, Ind., Dec. 23, 1932; s. Wayne and Marie (Butcher) F.; B.S., Ind. U., 1954; m. Janet Faye Lentz, Feb. 25, 1955; children—Julie Ann, Donald Lee, Thomas Gordon. Sr. accountant Arthur Young & Co., Chgo., 1954-61; gen. auditor Internat. Minerals & Chem. Corp., Skokie, Ill., 1961-64, group finance mgr., 1964-69; treas., asst. sec. Bergen Brunswig Corp., Los Angeles, 1969-71; gen. auditor Abbott Labs., North Chicago, Ill., 1971—. Served to 1st lt. U.S. Army, 1955-57. C.P.A., Ill. Mem. Kappa Delta Rho. Club: Toastmasters (past pres.) (Skokie). Office: Abbott Labs Abbott Park North Chicago IL 6064

FOSTER, ELIZABETH READ, educator, historian; b. Chgo., June 26, 1912; d. Conyers and Edith (Kirk) Read, A.B., Vassar Coll., 1933; A.M., Columbia, 1934; Ph.D., Yale, 1938; m. Richard Wingate Foster, Dec. 31, 1938; children—Richard Coulson, Timothy, Benjamin Read, Daniel Wingate, Instr., then asso. prof. history Ursinus Coll., Collegeville, Pa., 1953-65; asso. prof. U. Del., 1962-63; acting dir. Yale Parliamentary Diaries project Yale, 1965-66; dean Grad. Sch. Arts and Scis., prof. history Bryn Mawr Coll., 1966—. Mem. Conf. British Studies, Am. Hist. Assn. Editor: Proceedings in Parliament 1610, 2 vols., 1966. Home: 205 Strafford Av Wayne PA 19087 Office: Bryn Mawr Coll Bryn Mawr PA 19010

FOSTER, FRANKLIN LEROY, engr.; b. Avon, Mass., Dec. 22, 1902; s. William F. and Julia M. (Cherrington) F.; S.B. in Mining Engring., Mass. Inst. Tech., 1925; S.M., 1930, Sc.D., 1939; m. Evelyn S. Taylor, Sept. 20, 1930; children—Richard S., Alden T. with Mass. Inst. Tech., Cambridge, 1925—, asst. instr. dept. mining engring. to asst. prof., 1925-40, asst. dir. div. indsl. coop., 1939-52, asso. dir., 1952-54, dir., 1955-56, dir. div. sponsored research, 1956-68, spl. asst. to v.p. and treas., 1968—. Dir. Lowell Inst. Sch., 1959—. Mem. Am. Inst. Mining, Metall. and Petroleum Engrs., Am. Soc. Engring. Edn. (chmn.. engring. coll. research council 1968-70, v.p. 1968-70), Tau Beta Pi. Mason. Home: 100 Memorial Dr Cambridge, MA 02142.

FOSTER, GEORGE BUCHANAN, lawyer; b. Montreal, Can., Aug. 19, 1897; s. George G. and Mary Maud (Buchanan) F.; B.C.L., McGill U., 1921; m. Barbara MacDougall, Nov. 1928; children—Hilda Margot, Joan Elizabeth. Admitted to Quebec bar, 1921, sr. partner Foster, Leggat, Colby, Ridoux & Malcolm, Montreal 1940—; dir., pres. Dominion Wire Rope & Cable Co. Ltd., Mount Royal Metal Co. Ltd.; dir. Travelers Ins. Co., Montreal Trust Co., Superheater Co. Ltd. Mem. Legislative Council Province Quebec 1946—. Home: 116 Aberdeen Av Westmount Quebec Canada Office: 901 Victoria Square Montreal 1 Quebec Canada

FOSTER, GEORGE MCCLELLAND, Jr., anthropologist; b. Sioux Falls, S.D., Oct. 9, 1913; s. George McClelland and Mary (Slutz) F.; B.S., Northwestern U., 1935; Ph.D., U. Cal. at Berkeley, 1941; m. Mary Fraser LeCron, Jan. 6, 1938; children—Jeremy, Melissa (Mrs. William C. Bowerman). Began career as instr. Syracuse U., 1941-42; lectr. U. Cal. at Los Angeles, 1942-43, vis. prof. at Berkeley, 1953-55, prof. anthropology, 1955-, chmn. dept. 1958-61, acting dir. Mus. Anthropology, 1955-57, lectr. pub. health, 1955-64; anthropologist Inst. Social Anthropology, Smithsonian Instn., 1943-52, dir., 1946-1952; field research Cal. Indians, 1937, Spain, 1949-50, Mexico, 1940—; adviser AID, India-Pakistan, 1955, Afghanistan, 1957, Zambia, 1961, 62, Nepal, 1965. Recipient Guggenheim fellow, 1949, Wenner- Gren fellow, 1949; fellow Center for Advanced Studies in Behavioral Scis; 1969-70; Fellow Am. Anthrop. Assn. (pres. 1970), Am. Sociol. Assn. Club: Cosmos (Washington). Author: Traditional Cultures and the Impact of Technological Change, 1962;

Tzintzuntzan: Mexican Peasants in a Changing World, 1967; Applied Anthropology, 1969; monographs, articles. Home: 790 San Luis Rd Berkeley, CA 94707

FOSTER, GERALD LEN, architect; b. Maud, Tex., Apr. 3, 1931; s. James Young and Katie (Morgan) F.; B.S., U. Houston, 1953; m. Joan Arlone Grimes, Aug. 20, 1965; children—Barry Young, Michael Vernard. Archtl. draftsman MacKie & Kamrath, Houston, 1957-58, Reinheimer & Cox, Texarkana, Tex., 1958-60, Wiener, Morgan & O'Neal, Shreveport, Ia., 1960-61, George R. Rodgers, Marshall, Tex., 1961-65; pvt. archtl. practice, Longview, Tex., 1965—. Served with USAF, 1953-57. Mem. A.I.A. (sec.-treas. N.E. Tex. chpt. 1969-70). Club: Lions (bd. dirs. Longview). Home: 1407 Dartmouth St Longview TX 75601 Office: First National Bank Bldg Longview TX 75601

FOSTER, GORDON WILLIAM, apparel co. exec.; b. Binghamton, N.Y., Aug. 10, 1913; s. Clarence Harrison and Flossie (Burgess) F.; student Purdue U., 1932-35; m. Margaret Watts Gray, Nov. 18, 1942; children—Gordon William, Edward Irvine, Margaret Cabell, Nancy Lee, Mech. engr., then factory mgr. E. C. Brown Co., Rochester, N.Y., 1935-38; staff exec. Grand Union Co. N.Y.C., 1946-50; treas. Food Mart Inc., El Paso, Tex., 1950-52, pres., 1952-65; chmn. bd. Shop Rite Foods Inc., El Paso, 1965-66, dir., 1970—; v.p., dir. Farah Mfg. Co., El Paso, 1966—, El Paso Terminal & Storage Co., 1963—; chmn. bd. Fed. Res. Bank El Paso, 1965-70. Pres. El Paso Better Bus. Bur., 1954; mem. El Paso City Planning Commn., 1956-61. Trustee Providence Meml. Hosp., El Paso, 1963-. Served to maj., F.A., AUS, 1941-45; ETO. Decorated Bronze Star (2). Clubs: El Paso (dir.), Coronado Country (El Paso). Address: 5011 Vista Del Monte El Paso TX 79922

FOSTER, HARRY SCHUYLER, fgn. affairs specialist; b. Somerset, Mass., June 17, 1905; s. Harry Schuyler and Florence Josephine (Grady) F.; B.S., Dartmouth, 1925; M.A., Harvard, 1928; Ph.D., U. Chgo., 1932; m. Doris Giller, July 29, 1933; children—Gwyneth (Mrs. John N. Dukes), Bronwen (Mrs. Ronald W. Lee). Instr. English and history Mass. Inst. Tech., 1925-26; instr. polit. sci. Ohio State U., 1929-35, asst. prof. polit. sci., 1936-43; instr. govt. Harvard, 1935-36; Social Sci. Research Council fellow, 1937-38; asso. prof. polit. sci. W.Va. U., summer 1941, Denison U., spring 1942; pub. opinion analyst Dept. of State, 1943-51, chief pub. studies div., 1951-60, dir. pub. opinion studies staff, 1960-66, pub. opinion adviser, 1966—. Mem. World, Am. assns. pub. opinion research, Am. Polit. Sci. Assn., Phi Beta Kappa, Delta Sigma Rho. Contbr. articles to fgn. affairs, pub. opinion jours. Home: 3933 Livingston St Washington DC 20015 Office: Dept of State Washington DC 20520

FOSTER, HARVEY GOODSON, airline exec.; b. Indpls., Oct. 11, 1912; s. E. V. and Blanche Louise (Dodge) F.; student U. Ky., 1932-33; LL.B., U. Notre Dame, 1939; m. Mable Louise Mahler, Aug. 3, 1936; children—John D., Daniel G. Admitted to Ind. bar, 1939, N.Y. bar, 1962, also U.S. Supreme Ct.; with FBI, 1939- 62, spl. agt. in charge, Indpls., 1957-58, spl. agt. in charge, N.Y.C., 1958-62; v.p., gen. mgr. Dallas Smith Transp. Corp., Phoenix, 1962-63; dir. Sweet Mfg. Co., W. Mansfield, Mass., 1962-70; dir. security Gen. Telephone & Electronics Corp., 1963-64; v.p. audits and security Am. Airlines, Inc., N.Y.C., 1964-66, v.p. Chgo., 1966- -; dir. Merc. Nat. Bank. Mem. N.Y. State Municipal Police Tng. Council, 1959-62; exec. bd. Greater N.Y. council Boy Scouts Am., 1959-62, also chmn. health and safety com., adv. bd. Theodore Roosevelt council, Phoenix, 1962-63, exec. bd., commr. Greater New York council, 1963-66, mem. exec. bd. Chgo. Area council, 1966—. Mem. adv. bd. Mercy Hosp.; bd. govs. U. Notre Dame, 1964—. Named Notre Dame Man of Year in Indpls., 1952, N.Y. State pistol champion, 1959; named Hoosier of Year in N.Y., Sons of Ind. of N.Y., 1961. Mem. Sons of Indiana (bd. govs. 1964—), Notre Dame Nat. Alumni Assn. (pres. 1952), Nat. Rifle Assn. (life), Internat., N.J., N.Y. State assns. chiefs police, Nat. Law Enforcement Assn., Am. Bar Assn., Soc. Former Agts. FBI (chmn. ins. com. 1964), Am. Soc. Indsl. Security, Cal., Tex. peace officers assns., Fed. Bus. Assn. (v.p. Greater N.Y. area 1959-60), Chgo. Conv. and Tourism Bur., Cosmopolitan C. of C. (mem. adv. bd.), Chgo. Assn. Commerce and Industry, Am. Soc. Travel Agts., Clubs: Notre Dame (bd. govs. 1964—) (N.Y.C.); Nat. Monogram (Notre Dame U.). Home: 1012 S Hamlin St Park Ridge IL 60068 Office: Am Airlines Inc 10 S LaSalle St Chicago IL 60603

FOSTER, JACK, newspaperman; b. St. Joseph, Mo.; June 29, 1906; s. J. W. and Delia (Smith) F.; attended Western Reserve U., 1923-24; m. Frances Mangum, Aug. 30, 1938. Began as newspaper reporter with Cleve. Press, 1923; reporter Cleve. Press, 1923-26; reporter Rocky Mountain News, 1926- 29; asst. exec. editor N.Y. World-Telegram, 1929-40; editor Rocky Mountain News, 1940-70; ret. Address: 11 Upland Rd Colorado Springs CO 80906

FOSTER, JAMES WILLIAM, Jr., art mus. dir.; b. Balt., Jan. 4, 1920; s. James William and Dorothy Madison (Brown) F.; student Johns Hopkins, 1938-41; B.A., Am. U., 1947; m. Mary Page Ruth, Apr. 2, 1945; children—John Robinson, Page Nelson, Dorothy Madison. Exec. asst. Balt. Mus. Art, 1947-52, asst. dir., 1952- 57; dir. Santa Barbara (Cal.) Mus. Art, 1957-63, Honolulu Acad. Arts, 1963—. Served to lt. USNR, 1941-45. Mem. Assn. Art Mus. Dirs., Am. Assn. Museums, Western Assn. Art Museums. Club: Pacific. Home: 2377 Makiki Heights Dr Honolulu HI 96822 Office: 900 S Beretania St Honolulu HI 96814

FOSTER, JOHN MORRILL, glass co. exec.; b. Evanston, Ill., May 20, 1898; s. Adelbert M. and Lillian (Ragley) F.; A.B., Williams Coll., 1920; m. Eleanora Lutz, Jan. 30, 1932; children—John Joseph, Robert Lutz. With Foster-Forbes Glass Co., Marion, Ind., 1920-70, treas., 1929-35, pres., 1935-65, chmn. bd., chief exec. officer, 1965-70, ret.; dir. First Nat. Bank, Marion, Ind., Nat. Can Corp., Chgo. Trustee Marion YMCA; Marion, Ind., Nat. Can. Corp., Chgo. Trustee Marion YMCA; active fund drive Marion Gen. Hosp. Served with U.S. Navy, 1918. Mem. Glass Container Mfrs. Inst. (past pres., trustee) Zeta Psi. Republican. Conglist. Rotarian. Home: 210 Northwood Ct Marion IN 46952 Office:

FOSTER, JOHN STUART, Jr., physicist; b. New Haven, Sept. 18, 1922; s. John Stuart and Flora (Curtis) F.; B.Sc. with honours, McGill U., 1948; Ph.D., U. Cal. at Berkeley, 1952; m. Barbara Anne Wickes, May 23, 1946; children—Susan (Mrs. Patrick Duffy), Bruce, Scott, John. Civilian air force cons., MTO, 1942-45; with NRC, Chalk River, Ont., Can., summers 1946, 47; mem. staff Lawrence Radiation Lab., Berkeley, 1948-52, asso. dir., 1961-65; mem. staff Lawrence Radiation Lab., Livermore, 1952-65, asso. dir., 1958-61, dir., 1961-65; dir. def. research and engring. Dept. Def., 1965—. Mem. Air Force Sci. Adv. Bd., until 1956, Army Sci. Adv. Panel, until 1958, Panel Cons. President Sci. Adv. Com., 1959-65. Recipient Ernest O. Lawrence award AEC, 1960; Distinguished Pub. Service medal Dept. Def., 1969; 1969 James Forrestal Meml. award, 1970. Mem. Nat. Acad. Engring., Sigma Xi, Theta Delta Chi. Home: 6382 Lakeview Dr Falls Church VA 22041 Office: Office of Sec Def Washington DC 20301

FOSTER, JOSEPH C., mfg. co. exec.; b. 1906; married. Pres., chief exec. officer Foster Grant Co. Inc., Leominster, Mass., 1943-69, chmn. bd., chief exec. officer, 1969—, also dir. Office: 289 N Main St Leominster MA 01453*

FOSTER, JOSEPH FRANKLIN, biochemist, educator; b. Marion, Ind., May 17, 1918; s. DeWitt L. and Grace (Cameron) F.; B.S., Ia. State U., 1940, Ph.D., 1943; m. Ruth E. Hobson, June 8, 1940; children—Ann E., Gregory H., Michael C. Postdoctoral fellow Med. Sch., Harvard, 1943-45; research chemist Am. Maize Products Co., Roby, Ind., 1945-46, cons., 1948-59; faculty Ia. State U., 1946-54; mem. faculty Purdue U., Lafayette, Ind., 1954—, prof., 1957—, head dept. chemistry, 1967—; cons. Central Research Labs. Gen. Foods Corp., 1960-63, NIH, 1962-66, Army Q.M.C., 1963-64. Mem. Am. Chem. Soc., Am. Soc. Biol. Chemistry, Biophys. Soc., A.A.A.S., Am. Assn. U. Profs., Sigma Xi. Author: (with S.W. Fox) Introduction to Protein Chemistry, 1957. Contbr. articles profl. jours. Home: 328 Laurel Dr West Lafayette IN 47906 Office: Dept Chemistry Purdue U Lafayette IN 47907

FOSTER, KENNETH COLLEY, ins. co. exec.; b. Augusta, Me., Jan. 31, 1913; s. Earle Brown and Glenys (Young) F.; A.B., U. Me., 1934; M.S., Columbia, 1936; J.D., Rutgers U., 1940; m. Alice Good, Oct. 31, 1942; children—Grace Ann, Catherine. With Prudential Ins. Co. Am., Newark 1938—, dir. agys., 1947-50, v.p., 1950- 58, sr. v.p., 1958-65, sr. v.p. charge Western operations, 1965-66, exec. 1967-70, pres., dir., 1970—; pres., dir. PRUCO, Inc.; chmn. bd. Prudential Property and Casualty Ins. Co.; dir. Prudential's Gibralter Fund, Nabisco. Mem. nat. gen. services pub. adv. com. Gen. Services Adminstrn.; co-chmn. N.J. region Nat. Conf. Christians and Jews; mem. Nat. Bus. Council for Consumer Affairs. Bd. dirs. Widows' Consultation Center, Boys' Clubs Am.; trustee, past pres. Boys' Clubs of Newark; mem. adv. council Grad. Sch. Bus., Columbia; trustee Ednl. Broadcasting Corp. Served to capt. AUS, 1941-45. C.L.U. Mem. Nat. Planning Assn. (nat. council), Am. Soc. C.L.U., Nat. Assn. Life Underwriters. Clubs: Essex, Essex County Country; Economic (N.Y.C.). Contbr. to ins. handbooks and periodicals. Home: Llewellyn Park West Orange NJ 07052 Office: Prudential Plaza Newark NJ 07101

FOSTER, LEE BYRON, corp. exec.; b. Titusville, Pa., July 4, 1882; s. Aaron and Lena (Sable) F.; student Iron City Bus. Coll.; m. Pauline L. Livingston, June 10, 1909; children—Adrienne (Mrs. Milton Porter), Jay L. Sr. partner L. B. Foster Co., Pitts., 1903-18, pres., 1918-52, chmn. 1953, now vice chmn. bd., chmn. finance com. and dir.; hon. chmn. bd., dir. Copperweld Steel Co., Pitts.; v.p. Foster Export Co., N.Y.C., Foster Internat. Co. Chmn. Montfiore Hosp. Research Inst.; dir. Montefiore Hosp.; mem. bd. Pitts. YM and YWHA. Clubs: Concordia, Westmoreland Country (mem. bd.), One Hundred (Pitts.); Harmonie (N.Y.C.); Montauk (N.Y.) Yacht. Home: 5119 Penton Rd Pittsburgh PA 15213 Office: Frick Bldg Pittsburgh PA 15219

FOSTER, LUTHER HILTON, coll. pres.; b. Lawrenceville, Va., Mar. 21, 1913; s. Luther Hilton and Daisy (Poole) F.; B.S., Va. State Coll., 1932, LL.D., 1959; B.S., Hampton Inst., 1934; M.B.A., Harvard, 1936; M.A., U. Chgo., 1941, Ph.D., 1951; Dr. Pub. Service, Adams (Colo.) State Coll., 1957; LL.D., U. Liberia, 1958, U. Mich., 1967, Colby Coll., 1971; H.L.D., Loyola U., Chgo., 1970; m. Vera Chandler, Aug. 27, 1941; children—Adrienne Maria, Luther Hilton III. Budget officer Howard U., 1936-40; bus. mgr. Tuskegee Inst., 1941-53, pres., 1953—. Mem. bd. So. Regional Council; chmn. Race Relations Information Center; mem. adv. com. dept. and Grad. Sch. Edn., U. Chgo.; mem. Am. Revolution Bicentennial Commn.; Overseas Devel. Com.; mem. vis. com. Air U.; mem. adv. council Air Force Acad. Dir. United Negro Coll. Fund; trustee George Washington Carver Found., Coll. Retirement Equities Fund; bd. dirs. Council on Financial Aid to Edn., Assn. Am. Colls. (chmn. 1970), Resources for Future, Inc. Recipient Alumni award Hampton Inst., 1954. Mem. Phi Delta Kappa, Alpha Kappa Mu, Alpha Phi Alpha, Sigma Pi Phi Boule. Home: Tuskegee Institute Tuskegee AL 36088

FOSTER, MARGERY SOMERS, coll. dean; b. Boston, Mar. 27, 1914; B.A., Wellesley Coll., 1934; Ph.D. in social Sci. (Barrett fellow), Radcliffe Coll., 1958; Litt.D., Russell Sage Coll. Asst. to actuary New Eng. Mut. Life Ins. Co., 1934-43; dep. comptroller and dir. devel. Wellesley Coll., 1946-54; lectr. econs. Harvard Sch. Bus. Administrn., 1956-58; lectr. econs., sec. coll. Mt. Holyoke Coll., 1958-64; prof. econs., dean coll. Hollins Coll., 1964-67; prof. econs., dean coll. Douglass Coll. of Rutgers U. 1967—. Mem. Commn. on Tests Coll. Entrance Exam. Bd., 1966-70. Served to lt., Women's Res., USNR, 1943-46. Mem. Am. Econ. Assn., Econ. History Assn., Econometric Soc., Econ. History Soc., Assn. Am. Colls. (mem. commn. on internal affairs 1969—). Clubs: Appalachian Mountain, Cosmopolitan. Author: Out of Small Beginnings, an Economic History of Harvard College in the Puritan Period, 1962. Spl. research Am. colonial history, history edn., fiscal policy, pub. Finance. Address: 23 Nichol Av New Brunswick NJ 08901 *

FOSTER, MARK GARDNER, educator; b. Winfield, Kan., Mar. 17, 1914; s. Everett Kin and Harriet (Gardner) G.; B.A., Miami U., Oxford, O., 1935; Ph.D., Cal. Inst. Tech., 1939; m. Louella Estelle Turney, June 29, 1939; children—Mary Ann (Mrs. Gregory F. Mihalic), Charles, John. Teaching fellow Cal. Inst. Tech., 1935-39; physicist Champion Paper & Fibre Co., 1939-41, Naval Ordnance Lab., 1941-45, Curtiss-Wright Corp., 1945; head various depts. Cornell Aero. Lab., Inc., 1946-56; dir research Crosley div. AVCO Mfg. Co., 1956- 57; prin. physicist Cornell Aero. Lab., Inc., 1957-60; faculty U. Va., Charlottesville, 1960—, Willis Johnson prof. elec. engring., 1960—, chmn. dept., 1960-67. Mem. fellowship evaluation panels NSF, 1964-68. Recipient Meritorious Civilian Service pin Navy Dept., 1945. Mem. I.E.E.E., Am. Phys. Soc., A.A.A.S., Phi Beta Kappa, Sigma Xi, Tau Beta Pi, Sigma Pi Sigma, Eta Kappa Nu, Phi Mu Alpha. Methodist (trustee). Home: 10 Orchard Rd Charlottesville VA 22901

FOSTER, MINARD IRWIN, govt. ofcl.; b. Miami, Fla., Dec. 8, 1915; s. Irwin Bell and Mary (Johnstone) F.; B.B.A., U. Miami, 1950, M.A., 1951; Ph.D., U. Fla., 1953; m. Margaret Freeman, Mar. 30, 1946; children—Mary (Mrs. Josiah Jackson Harrison, Jr.), Michael Bruce, Robert Freeman. Asst. prof. econ. U. Miami, 1953-54; with TVA, 1954—, economist, supr. borrowing, and investment, 1958-62, chief navigation resources br., 1962-67, dir. navigation devel. and regional studies, Knoxville, Tenn., 1967—. Lectr., U. Chattanooga, 1954-63. Mem. U.S., internat. commns. Permanent Internat. Assn. Navigation Congresses. Served with USAAF, 1943-45. Mem. So. Econ. Assn., Order of Artus, Phi Beta Kappa, Alpha Kappa Psi. Home: 5205 Shady Dell Trail Knoxville TN 37914 Office: 501 Arnstein Building Market St Knoxville TN 37902

FOSTER, RAYBURN L., lawyer; b. Carthage, Mo., Sept. 15, 1894; s. James Thomas and Ada (Givens) F.; LL.B., U. Okla., 1916; m. Alma Clark, May 12, 1917; children—Charles Rayburn, James Richard, Carol. Admitted to Okla. bar, 1916; practiced in Henryetta, Okla., 1916-28, staff atty. Ind. Oil & Gas Co., Tulsa, 1928-30; staff atty. and asst. gen. atty. Phillips Petroleum Co., Bartlesville Okla., 1930-39, gen. atty., 1939-44, asst. gen. counsel, 1944-50, v.p., gen. counsel, dir., 1951-61, lawyer and cons., 1961—. Regent, U. Okla., 1951-57, pres., 1956-57; mem. Okla. Library Bd., 1965-67. Recipient Distinguished Service citation U. Okla., 1963. Mem. Am., Okla., Washington County bar assns., Mid-Continent Oil and Gas Assn., Order of Coif, Phi Delta Phi, Sigma Chi. Home: 1417 Hillcrest Dr Bartlesville OK 74003

FOSTER, RICHARD BAILEY, lawyer; b. Lansing, Mich., Feb. 25, 1908; s. Walter S. and Lena (Bailey) F.; A.B., U. Mich., 1930, LL.B., 1932; m. Frances Arbaugh, 1931; children—Richard Bailey, Walter S. II. Admitted to Mich. bar, 1932, since practiced in Lansing; mem. Foster, Campbell, Lindemer & McGurrin, 1946—; pros. atty., Ingham County, 1928-42. Served to maj. AUS, 1942- 45. Mem. Am., Ingham County (pres. '954-55) bar assns., State Bar Mich. Home: 3 Locust Lane Lansing MI 49001 Office: American Bank & Trust Bldg Lansing MI 48933

FOSTER, ROBERT PORTER, coll. pres.; b. Warrensburg, Mo., May 24, 1917; s. Robert Porter and Oda M. (Long) F.; B.S., Central Mo. State Coll., 1939; M.Ed., U. Mo., 1951, Ed.D., 1960; m. Virginia Ann Mutz, Mar. 26, 1943; children—Robert Porter III, Douglas Kemp. Tchr., Carrollton (Mo.) High Sch., 1939-40, prin., 1940-41; engaged in pvt. bus., Maryville, Mo., 1946-48; registrar N.W. Mo. State Coll., Maryville, 1948-59, dean adminstrn., 1959-64, pres., 1964—. Research asst. for Gov. of Mo. Council Higher Edn., 1958—; state rep. to nat. and regional commn. Tchr. Edn. and Profl. Standards, 1955—. Mem. exec. council Pony Express council Boy Scouts Am., 1960, pres., 1967, 68, 69, also mem. nat. council; bldg. chmn. Wesley Found. Mo. Conf., 1959; chmn. Blood Bank Nodaway County chpt. A.R.C., 1946. Trustee So. Meth. U. Served with USNR, 1942-45. Recipient Silver Beaver award Boy Scouts Am., 1963, Man of Year award for outstanding community service Maryville C. of C., 1968. Mem. N.E.A., Am., Mo. (past pres.) assns. collegiate registrars and admissions officers, Mo. Tchrs. Assn., Am. Legion (past post comdr.), Phi Delta Kappa. Mason (K.T.), Lion (pres. Maryville). Home: 703 College Av Maryville MO 64468

FOSTER, TED, univ. dean; b. Seward, Neb., Dec. 23, 1903; s. Charles Delmer and Bertha Hope (Daves) F.; LL.B., Oklahoma City U., 1937; LL.D., Cleveland- Marshall Law Sch., 1962; m. Alma Bernice Collier, Oct. 11, 1924; children—Ted, Olive Hope (Mrs. Dan T. Gray). Dep. sheriff Okla. Country, 1928-38; admitted to Okal. bar, 1937; practice in Oklahoma City, 1938- 56; instr. Office Civil Def., 1940-45; prof. Sch. Law, Oklahoma City U., 1956-60, dean, 1968—. Dir., gen. counsel Jamco, Inc. Chmn. Oklahoma City Bd. Adjustment; mem. Oklahoma County Excise and Equalization Bd., 1970; mem. Gov. Okla. ADv. Com. Law Enforcement, 1934-36. Mng. trustee Meml. Park Cemetery Assn., 1950—. Mem. Am., Okla., Oklahoma County (bd. dirs. 1948) bar assns., Am. Judicature Soc. Mason (32, Jester). Author- editor: Municipal Taxation, 1965. Home: 416 N W 44th St Oklahoma City OK 73118

FOSTER, THOMAS ARNOLD, pharmacist; b. Camp Hill, Ala., Jan. 26, 1895; s. William Thomas and Eugenia (McLendon) F.; student Howard Coll., Birmingham, Ala., 1911-12; Ph.G., Wilson Sch. Pharmacy, 1916; m. Mary Reeves, Sept. 30, 1919 (dec. Jan. 2, 1942); children—Mary Virginia (Mrs. J. Richard Roberts), Thomas Arnold; m. 2d, Katherine Verschoor, Dec. 8, 1945. Practice pharmacy, Birmingham, Ala., 1917; retail pharmacist, co-owner drug stores, Birmingham, 1919-32; commd. pharmacist USPHS, 1933, advanced through grades to pharmacist dir., 1960; adminstrv. officer, 1933-42, chief supply service hdqrs. Hosp. div., Washington, 1942-44, chief supply officer Office Surgeon Gen., 1944-50, assigned div. civilian requirements, health supplies liaison officer ODM, 1958-60; medical supply cons., Washington, 1960-70; cons. to Office Emergency Planning, Exec. Office Pres., 1964—. Gen. chmn. convention Assn. Mil. Surgeons, Washington, 1955; Am. Pharm. Assn. del. Conv. Internat. Pharm. Fedn., London, Eng., 1955. Served with U.S. Army, 1917-19. Recipient Founders medal Assn. Mil. Surgeons U.S., 1955, Andrew Craigie award, 1960; medal Swedish Ministry Health, 1959; H.A.K. Whitney award Am. Soc. Hosp. Pharmacists, 1960. Fellow Royal Soc. Health Eng. (life); mem. Am. Pharm. Assn. (chmn. spl. com. Project Hope 1961-62, hon. pres. 1963, chmn. standing com. on disaster preparedness and nat. security 1963, chmn. standing com. govtl. pharm. service 1964, rep. to surgeon gen.'s profl. adv. com. emergency health preparedness, 1963-64), Am. Soc. Hosp. Pharmacists (chmn. com. laws, legislation and regulations 1967-70), assn. Mil. Surgeons U.S., Am. Legion, Commd. Officers Assn. Pub. Health Service, Am. Surg. Trade Assn. Chgo. (hon. life), Med-Surg. Mfrs. Assn. (hon. life). Home: 3900 Cathedral Av NW Washington DC 20016

FOSTER, WALTER HERBERT, lawyer; b. LaGrange, Me., Mar. 31, 1880; s. Ernest Montgomery and Caroline (Banton) F.; ed. Harvard Coll.; LL.B., U. of Me., 1905; LL.M., 1914; m. Gertrude Sullivan, Oct. 23, 1901; children—Daphne (Mrs. George Maes Henderson), Walter Herbert Jr., Richard Channing. Mem. law firm MacPherson & Foster, also atty. for Boston Elevated Ry. Co., 1907-10; mem. firm Foster & Colby, 1910-18; individual practice, Boston, 1919-42; acted as spl. asst. to atty. gen. of Mass.; chmn. Center Boston Cancer Control Com. (affiliated state bd. of health), 1940-42; mem. Draft Adv. Bd.; Chief Compliance Commr. W.P.B., Washington, 1942-45, Civilian Prodn. Adminstrn., 1945-46, Office of Housing Expediter, 1946- 47; resumed practice of law, Boston, 1948; asst. atty. gen. Commonwealth of Mass., and counsel to State Housing Bd. Vets. Housing Program, 1948-49; chief hearing commn. NPA, Washington, 1951-53; private practice of law, Boston, 1953-. Mem. Soc. Colonial Wars. Republican. Episcopalian. Clubs: Union, Harvard (Boston). Author Administrative Procedure WPB; Promoters' Liability to the Corporation. Home: Mistover South Lyndeborough NH 03082 (winter) Bayou Louise Siesta Key Sarasota FL 33581 Office: 53 State St Boston MA 02109

FOSTER, WILLIAM CHAPMAN, ret. govt. ofcl.; b. Westfield, N.J., Apr. 27, 1897; s. Jed S. and Anna Louise (Chapman) F.; student Mass. Inst. Tech., 1918; LL.D., Syracuse U., 1957, Rutgers U., 1968, Bowdoin U., 1968, Yale, 1969; D. Pub. Service George Washington U., 1963; H.L.D., Kenyon Coll., 1968; m. Beulah Robinson, May 9, 1925; 1 son, Seymour Robinson. Officer and dir. Pressed and Welded Steel Products Co., Inc., 1922-46; under- sec. commerce, 1946-48; dep. U.S. spl. rep. ECA, 1948-49, dep. adminstr., 1949-50, adminstr., 1950-51; dep. sec. of defense, 1951-53; pres. Mfg. Chemists Assn., Inc., 1953-55; exec. v.p., dir. Olin Mathieson Chem. Corp., 1955-58, dir., v.p., sr. adviser, 1958-61; chmn. bd., pres. United Nuclear Corp., 1961; dir. U.S. Arms Control and Disarmament Agy., 1961-69, recipient Distinguished Honor award, 1969. Chief U.S. rep. 18th-Nation Disarmament Conf., 1962-69; U.S. del. UN, 1964-66, 68, U.S. rep. UN Disarmament Commn., 1965. Served with U.S. Army, World War I; dir. purchases div. Army Services Forces and spl. rep. Under-sec. of War on procurement for USAAF, World War II. Decorated U.S. Medal for Merit; commendations for civilian service from War Dept. Def. Mem. Bus. Council (hon.). Clubs: University (N.Y.C.); Metropolitan, Chevy Chase (Washington). Home: 3304 R St NW Washington DC 20007

FOSTER, WILLIAM FITZ-WALTER, mfg. co. exec.; b. Revelstoke, B.C., Can., Oct. 25, 1908; s. William W. and Olive (Stewart) F.; m. Jeanie Alexander, Apr. 9, 1938; children—Susan, William A., Stephanie, Frances. With Evans, Coleman & Evans, Ltd., 1934-57, gen. mgr., 1949-57, also dir. co. and subsidiaries; company merged with B.C. Cement Co. Ltd. to form Ocean Cement & Supplies Ltd., 1957, exec. v.p., 1959-60, pres., 1960—, also pres. subsidiaries dir. Royal Gen. Ins. Co. Can. Clubs: Vancouver, Shaughnessy Golf and Country, Lawn Tennis and Badminton (Vancouver). Home: 1607 W 49th St Vancouver British Columbia Canada Office: Ocean Cement & Supplies Ltd 1060 One Bentall Centre Vancouver British Columbia Canada Canada

FOSTER, WILLIAM JAMES, III, lawyer; b. Schenectady, June 20, 1923; s. William James, Jr. and Ruth (Seltzer) F.; A.B., Amherst Coll., 1946; LL.B., Cornell U., 1949; m. Suzanne E. Nichols, Nov. 30, 1944; children—Caroline N., William James IV, Andrew McE., Douglas R. Admitted to N.Y. bar, 1949; practiced in N.Y.C., 1949-67; atty. Naylon, Foster, Shepard & Aronson, 1949-50; atty. Gen. Electric Co., Schenectady, 1950-53, Abex Corp., N.Y.C., 1953- 67; sec., gen. counsel Ex-cell-O Corp., Detroit, 1967—. Served to lt. (j.g.) USNR, 1943-46. Mem. Assn. Bar City N.Y., Mich., Detroit bar assns., Phi Gamma Delta, Phi Delta Phi. Republican. Conglist. Clubs: N.Y. Yacht; Am. Yacht (Rye, N.Y.). Home: 712 Fairfax St Birmingham MI 48009 Office: 14310 Hamilton Av Highland Park MI 48232

FOTOS, JOHN THEODORE, educator, author, editor; b. Montreal, Can., July 7, 1906; s. Theodore John and Marie (Bousiotes) F.; B.A. with 1st class honors, McGill U., 1924; M.A., U. Chgo., 1929; Ph.D. in Romance Langs. and Lit., 1945; m. Virginia Mary Cummings, July 11, 1931; children—Consuela Cummings (Mrs. Richard E. Grace), Genevieve Cummings (Mrs. Clifford D. Martin), Theodore John, Henry Cummings. Came to U.S., 1925, naturalized, 1931. Teaching fellow romance langs. U. Chgo., 1925; instr. modern langs. Purdue U., 1927-28, asst. prof., 1929-33, asso. prof., 1934-37, prof., 1938, chmn. French dept., 1947-59; vis. Smith-Mundt prof. Am. culture and linguistics Nat. U. of Nicaragua, 1959; cons. linguist and lang. coordinator Peace Corps, Washington, 1961; chmn. European langs. U. Hawaii, Hilo campus, 1964-66, chmn. humanities, 1965-66; prof., chmn. dept. modern langs. Parsons Coll. Fairfield, Ia., 1966-68; head dept. modern fgn. langs. Edinboro (Pa.) State Coll., 1968-70. Adv. editor Charles Scribner's, 1935-38; directing editor Crowell's Modern Lang. Series, 1939-54; gen. editor Haywood Modern Lang. Series and Book Dept., 1954-59. Mem. Am. Assn. Tchrs. French (chmn. Ind. chpt. 1929, 35, chmn. exec. com. 1936-40, program chmn. 1946-53, del. ann. nat. meetings 1951- 64), Central States Modern Lang. Tchrs. Assn. (1st v.p. 1956-58, pres. 1958-60, exec. com. 1960-65), Nat. Fedn. Modern Lang. Tchrs. Assns. (exec. com. 1965-68), Ind. Fgn. Lang. Tchrs. Assn. (organizer, pres. 1951, 52, exec. bd. 1962), Modern Lang. Assn. Am., Am. Assn. U. Profs., Internat. Comp. Lit. Assn., Assn. Int. des Etudes Francaises, Assn. des Profs. Francais en Am. Mason (32, Scottish Rite), Elk. Author: (with J.L. Cattell) Essentials of French Pronunciation, 1934, Practical Modern French Grammar, 1935; German Grammar for Chemists and Other Science Students, 1939; Introductory Readings in Chemical and Technical German, 1940; Advanced Readings in Chemical and Technical Germany, 1940; Alexandre Dumas' Les Trois Mousquetaires, 1940; (with E.P. Shaw) Dix Contes, 1961. Editor: Spanish Review Grammar by Castellano and Brown, rev. edition, 1956, others; also translations into French, Spanish and Portuguese various publs. Home: 210 Harrison St West Lafayette IN 47906

FOU, TS'ONG, concert pianist; b. Shanghai, China, Mar. 10, 1934; s. Lai and Mei (Chu) F.; student Yunan U., 1954, Warsaw Conservatoire, 1959; m. Zamira Menuhin, Dec. 17, 1960 (div.), 1 son, Fou-Lin-Siao. Appeared with Cin. Symphony Orch., N.Y. Philharmonic, Honolulu Symphony; numerous concerts in Europe and Brit. Isles, 1955—; condr. chamber orchs. Recipient prizes Internat. Bucharest competition, 1954, Internat. Chopin competition, Warsaw, Poland, 1955. Home: 28 Rosecroft Av London NW3 England

FOUBERT, EUGENE F., indsl. relations exec.; b. Berkeley, Cal., May 10, 1914; s. Eugene C. and Marie (Gallegher) F.; B.S., U. Cal. at Berkeley, 1938; m. Patricia Ryon, Dec. 24, 1941; children—David Harrison, Suzanne Mary. Staff, dept. employment placement office State of Cal., 1938-41; mgr. indsl. relations Nordstrom valve div. Rockwell Mfg. Co., 1941-47, dir. indsl. relations, 1947-55, v.p. indsl. relations, 1955—. Dir., past pres. Vocational Rehab. Center. Mem. Pitts. Personnel Assn. (dir., past pres.), Phi Sigma Kappa. Club: Valley Brook Country (Pitts.). Home: 2490 Huntington Dr Pittsburgh, PA 15241. Office: 400 N Lexington Av Pittsburgh PA 15208

FOUCH, GEORGE EDGAR, govt. ofcl.; b. Mt. Vernon, O., Apr. 11, 1909; s. Rollin James and Nellie Elizabeth (Mitchaux) F.; B.Sc., Ohio State U., 1931, M.B.A., 1937; m. Beulah Clarinda Snyder, June 29, 1940; children—Gregory George, Roger Brent, Barbara Nell. Asst. prof. bus. adminstrn. Wittenberg U., 1935-36; dir. comml. research Goodyear Tire & Rubber Co., 1937-42; asst. to gen. mgr. Goodyear Aircraft Corp., 1942; v.p., gen. mgr. Sterrett Motors, 1947-48; planning and logistics support Berlin Airlift, Mil. Air Transport Service, 1948; chief spl. projects div. Exec. Office Sec. Navy, 1949-52; mgr. subcontracting J-47 Program, Gen. Electric Co., 1952, gen. mgr. jet engine dept., 1953-54, gen. mgr. Evendale operations, aircraft gas turbine div., 1955-57, gen. marketing cons. pres.'s office, 1957-62; dep. asst. sec. for equipment maintenance and readiness, installations and logistics, Dept. Def., 1962-68, dep. asst. sec. for logistics mgmt. systems and programs, installations and logistics, 1968-. Served to comdr. USNR, 1943-46. Recipient Distinguished Pub. Service award Dept. Navy, 1956; Distinguished Service award Soc. Am. Value Engrs., 1965; Engring. News Record mag. citation, 1966. Mem. Am. Ordnance Assn., Soc. Am. Value Engrs. (hon. v.p. 1968), Am. Soc. Zero Defects (chmn. of the adv. bd.), Inst. Aero. Scis., Soc. Automotive Engrs. Author: Graphic Management Control, 1943. Home: 6859 Tulip Hill Terrace NW Washington DC 20016 Office: The Pentagon Washington DC 20301

FOUCHE, JACOBUS JOHANNES, South African govt. ofcl.; b. Wepener, Orange Free State, South Africa, June 6, 1898; s. Jacobus Johannes and Maria (Steynberg) F.; student Grey Coll., 1913-14, Victoria Coll., 1917; Ph.D., U. Stellenbosch, 1966; m. Letta Rhoda McDonald, Mar. 31, 1920; 1 son, Jacobus Johannes. State President Republic of South Africa, 1968—; mem. Parliament for Smithfield, 1941-50, adminstr. Orange Free State Province, 1951-59, Minister of Defense, 1959-66, mem. Parliament Bloemfontein West, 1960-68, Minister Agrl. Tech. Service and of Water Affairs, 1966-68; Freeman South African cities of Virginia, Vanderbijlpark, Kroonstad, Bloemfontein, Johannesburg, Paarl, Kokstad, Pietermaritzburg. Mem. Dutch Reformed Ch. Home: State President's Residence Pretoria South Africa Office: State President's Residence Republic of South Africa Pretoria South Africa

FOUCHE, JAMES W., physician. Dir., State Park Health Center. Office: State Park Health Center State Park SC 29147*

FOUDY, JOHN T., educator; b. San Francisco, Oct. 1, 1913; s. Denis D. and Anne (O'Looney) F.; A.B., St. Patrick's Sem., 1936; Ph.D., Cath. U. Am., 1945. Ordained priest Roman Cath. Ch., 1940; asst. supt. schs. Archdiocese San Francisco, 1945-57, supt. schools, 1957-66, archdiocesan sec. for edn., 1966—; archdiocesan cons., 1959- -; domestic prelate, 1962-; pastor St. Agnes Church, San Francisco, Cal.; mem. summer sch. faculty Cath. U. Am., 1947-56. Mem. Cal. del. White House Conf., 1955. Mem. bd. trustees Coll. Entrance Exam. Bd. Mem. Nat. Cath. Edn. Assn. (sec. supts. dept.). Home: 1025 Masonic Av San Francisco, CA 94117. Office: 443 Church St San Francisco CA 94114

FOULIS, RONALD JAMIESON, lawyer; b. St. Louis County, Mo., Apr. 1, 1904; s. Robert and Amanda Martha (Eilenberger) F.; LL.B., Washington U., St. Louis, 1927; m. Maxine Ford Bray, June 22, 1929; children-Saralee Martha (Mrs. Saralee F. Irwin), Ronald Jamieson. Admitted to Mo. bar, 1926, D.C. bar, 1953; with firm Koerner, Fahey & Young, St. Louis, 1926-29, Thompson, Mitchell, Thompson & Young, 1929-40; mem. firm Orr, Pflager, Foulis & Andreas, St. Louis, 1941-52; atty. Southwestern Bell Telephone Co., 1944- 53, Am. Tel. & Tel. Co., 1953-69; counsel Morgan, Lewis & Bockius, Washington. Chief dist. price atty. OPA, 1942-43; mem. Air Force Evaluation Bd., 1944-45; sec. U.S. Territorial Expansion Meml. Commn., 1957—; v.p. Jefferson Nat. Expansion Meml. Assn., 1949-53, vice chmn., 1953—; mem. Ladue (Mo.) Sch. Bd., 1947-53. Chmn. bd. trustees Hawthorne Sch., Washington, 1958-64; dir. Am. Bar Endowment, 1950—, pres. 1965- 67. Life fellow Am. Bar Found.; mem. Am. Bar Assn. (ho. dels. 1939-44 asst. sec. 1945-47, state del. 1950-53, chmn. Jr. Bar Conf. 1938-39, del. Assembly 1960-70), Am. Judicature Soc. (dir. 1942-51), Bar Assn. St. Louis (chmn. com. on jud. selection and tenure, treas. 1936-39), Am. Law Inst., D.C., Fed., Fed. Communications, Inter-Am. bar assns., Sigma Nu, Phi Delta Phi, Kappa Phi Sigma. Clubs: Columbia Country (Chevy Chase, Md.); Metropolitan, Capitol Hill (Washington). Home: 4432 Edmunds St NW Washington DC 20007 Office: 1140 Connecticut Av NW Washington DC 20036

FOULKE, WILLIAM GREEN, banker; b. Whitemarsh, Pa., Nov. 20, 1912; s. Walter Longfellow and Helen (Pardee) F.; grad. St. Paul's Sch., Concord, N.H., 1930; A.B., Princeton, 1934; m. Louisa Lawrence Wood, Nov. 2, 1934; children—Louisa Lawrence (Mrs. William Ver P. Newlin), Walter Longfellow, William Green. Asst. treas. Provident Trust Co., Phila., 1940-41, trust officer, 1945-50, v.p., 1950-57; sr. v.p. charge trust div. Provident Tradesmens Bank and Trust Co., Phila., 1957-60, exec. v.p. 1960-62, pres., 1962-64; pres. Provident Nat. Bank, Phila., 1964-69; chmn. chief exec. officer, 1969—; chmn., chief exec. officer Provident Nat. Corp., 1969—; v.p., dir. Pardee Co., dir. Provident Mut. Life Ins. Co. of Phila., Pardee & Curtin Lumber Co., East Tenn. & West N.C. Transp. Co. (and subsidiaries), VF Corp., Commonwealth Land Title Ins. Co. Bd. mgrs. Pennsylvania Hospital; bd. dirs. Ch. Found. P.E. Diocese Pa., Charles E. Ellis Sch. for Girls, Old Phila. Devel. Corp.; trustee Fairmount Park Art Assn. Served to lt. comdr. USNR, 1941-45. Mem. Pa. Bankers Assn. (pres. 1970-71), Am. Bankers Assn. (exec. council), Greater Phila. C. of C. (dir.), Assn. Res. City Bankers. Episcopalian. Clubs: Racquet, Philadelphia (Phila.); Gulph Mills Golf (King of Prussia, Pa.); Ivy (Princeton); Pine Valley Golf (Clementon, N.J.). Home: 452 W Chestnut Hill Av Philadelphia, PA 19118. Office: Provident Nat Bank Broad and Chestnut Sts Philadelphia PA 19101

FOULKES, HOWARD TALLMADGE, lawyer; b. Fond du Lac, Wis., Oct. 14, 1888; s. Edward and Virginia (Tallmadge) F.; grad. Phillip's Acad., Andover, Mass., 1907; B.A., Yale, 1911; LL.B., U. Wis., 1913; LL.D., Nashotah (Wis.) House, 1946; m. Helen Esther Joerns, Oct. 4, 1919 (dec. Aug. 1946); children—Elisabeth Wood (Mrs. Richard E. Phillipson), Cornelia (Mrs. Donald A. Austin). Admitted to Wis. bar, 1913, since practiced in Milw.; partner firm Borgelt, Powell, Paterson & Frauen, and predecessors, 1913- -. Chmn. group work div. Milw. Community Fund, 1945-46; chancellor Episcopal Diocese Milw., 1945-65, dep. to gen. conv. from diocese, 1943- 69; sec., mem. chpt. All Saints Cathedral, Milw., 1930—, canon chancellor, 1965—; mem. Unity Commn. Episcopal Ch., 1943-61. Bd. dirs. St. Luke's Hosp., Milw., 1954—; trustee Nashotah House, 1943—; sec., bd. dirs. Stark Hosp., Milw., 1932—; pres. St. Luke's Hosp. Medically Indigent Found. Served as 1st lt., Q.M.C., U.S. Army, 1918-19. Mem. Am., Wis., Milw. (past chmn. real estate div.) bar assns., Order of Coif, Beta Theta Pi, Phi Alpha Delta. Republican. Club: University (Milw.). Home: 2840 N Prospect Av Milwaukee WI 53211 Office: 828 N Broadway Milwaukee WI 53202

FOULKES, LLYN, artist, educator; b. Yakima, Wash., Nov. 17, 1934; student Central Wash. Coll., 1952-53, U. Wash., 1954, Chouinard Art Inst., 1957-59; m. Katie Foulkes; 1 dau., Laurey. Prof. art U. Cal. at Los Angeles. Recipient Los Angeles County Mus. Purchase grant, 1963; 1st prize (gold medal) Paris Biennale, 1967. Exhibited group shows: Los Angeles County Mus. Art, 1960, 61, 63. Pomona (Cal.) Coll., 1961, San Francisco Mus. Art, 1961, 63, Pasadena (Cal.) Art Mus., 1964, 68, 70, Saõ Paulo, Brazil, 1964, Allan Frumpkin Gallery, Chgo., 1964, N.Y. Worlds Fair, 1965, Mus. 20th Century, Vienna, 1965, Guggenheim Mus., 1966, Mus. Modern Art, N.Y.C., 1966, Whitney Mus., N.Y.C., 1967, 69, 70, 71, Robert Frazier Gallery, London, 1966. Sao Paulo Biennale, 1968, Paris Biennale, 1967, Mus. Modern Art, Paris, 1967, Seattle Art Mus., 1968, Portland (Ore.) Art Mus., 1968, San Francisco Mus., 1968, Brandeis U., 1968, traveling exhbn. Found. Maeght, France, 1968, Art Council London (Eng.), 1968, U. Nev. 1969, Va. Mus., Richmond, 1970, others; one-man shows: Nelson Gallery, 1963, 64, Oakland (Cal.) Art Mus., Ferus Gallery, 1961, Pasadena Art Mus., 1962 Rolf, 1964; Rolf Nelson Gallery, Los Angeles, 1966, David Stuart Gallery, Los Angeles, 1969, Galerie Danthea Speyer, Paris, 1970; represented in permanent collections: Mus. 20th Century, Vienna, LaJolla (Cal.) Mus. Art, Los Angeles County Mus. Art, Oakland Art Mus., Pasadena Art Mus., Whitney Mus., Mus. Modern Art, N.Y.C. and Paris, Stanford, Palo Alto, Chgo. Art Inst. Served with AUS, 1954-56. Address: 6010 Eucalyptus Lane Los Angeles CA 90042

FOULKES, WILLIAM WILKINSON, Jr., banker; b. Arvonia, Va., Aug. 1, 1910; s. William Wilkinson and Emma (Jones) F.; student Va. Poly. Inst., 1931, Duke, 1946, Stonier Grad. Sch. Banking, Rutgers U., 1954; m. Hazel F. Killoch, Mar. 16, 1934; childrenn-William Wilkinson III, Joyce (Mrs. James Weir), Jane. Vice pres. Hudson Trust Co., Union City, N.J., 1946-56; sr. v.p. First Jersey Nat. Bank, Jersey City, 1956—; meem. legislative com. Interbank; thesis adviser Sch. Consumer Banking, U. Va., Stonier Grad. Sch. Banking, Rutgers U. N.J. chmn. Bankers Polit. Action Com., 1970. Trustee Garden State Credit Bur., Sch. Consumer Banking C.B.A., Washington. Served to maj., finance dept., AUS, 1942-46. Mem. Eastern State Bankcard Assn. (dir., mem. exec. com.), N.J. Bankers Assn. Club: Knickerbocker Country (trustee, past pres.) (Englewood, N.J.). Home: 59 Everett Rd Demarest NJ 07627 Office: 1Exchange Pl Jersey City NJ 07303

FOULKROD, HARRY ELLSWORTH, mgmt. exec.; b. Williamsport, Pa., Nov. 15, 1903; s. Royden and Mabel (Shultz) F.; A.B., Pa. State Coll., 1925; postgrad. Columbia, Johns Hopkins; m. Margaret Price, Nov. 27, 1925; children—Jay Martin, Daniel Price. Automobile dealer, 1938-52; marketing mgr. Packard Motor Car Co., 1953; gen. sales mgr. Fruehauf Trailer Co., Detroit, 1958, exec. v.p., 1959, past sr. exec. v.p.; pres. Foulkrod Assos., Mgmt. Cons., Ft. Lauderdale; dir. Dean Research Corp., Kansas City. Chmn. Wray Meml. Found., Ft. Lauderdale; bd. dirs. Nat. Safety Council. Bd. trustees Leelanau Schs. Mem. Nat. Indsl. Conf. Bd., Am. Mgmt. Assn., Am. Ordnance Assn., Sales Execs. Club (dir.), Sales Marketing Internat. (dir., award as marketing exec. 1966), Sales Marketing Detroit (v.p.), Alpha Tau Omega. Rotarian. Clubs: Detroit Athletic, Grosse Pointe Yacht, Detroit Golf; Coral Ridge Country (Ft. Lauderdale). Home: The Fountainhead 3900 Ocean Dr Fort Lauderdale FL 33308 Office: Lauderdale Beach Bank Bldg Lauderdale by the Sea FL 33308 33308

FOUNTAIN, GUION HILLMAN, hosp. exec.; b. Plainfield, N.J., May 26, 1889; s. George Henry and Mary Augusta (Hillman) F.; student Yale, 1910-12, Am. Inst. Banking, 1916; m. Florence Prior, Oct. 21, 1916; children—Elizabeth (wife of Rev. Merrel P. Callaway), Joyce (Mrs. James F. Clingen), Audrey (Mrs. Hugh B. Jordan). Asst. cashier Nat. City Bank, N.Y.C., 1917-22; v.p., trust officer, dir. First Nat. Bank & Trust Co., Summit, N.J., 1934-36; pres., treas., dir. 87th St. and East End Av. Corp., N.Y.C., 1927-30; a founder Doctors Hosp., N.Y.C., 1927, v.p. charge operations, 1930—. Chmn. twp. com., Chatham, N.J., 1929-41, chmn. bd. health, 1932-36, mem. bd. edn., 1923-39; chmn. fund raising drives A.R.C., 1923-50. Bd. dirs. Summit YMCA, 1930-37, Morris County YMCA, 1937-48; a founder Long Hill Chapel (Chatham). Mem. Book and Gavel Soc. Yale Law Sch., Yale Law Sch. Alumni Assn., Huguenot Soc. Am. Baptist Church. Club: Yale of Central New Jersey. Home: 805 Fairmount Av Chatham, NJ 07928. Office: 170 East End Av New York City NY 10028

FOUNTAIN, LAWRENCE H., congressman; b. Leggett, N.C., Apr. 23, 1913; s. Lawrence H. and Sallie (Barnes) F.; A.B., U. N.C. (Wiley P. Mangum Oratorial medal), 1934, J.D. (Mary D. Wright Debate medal 1935), 1936; m. Christine Dail, May 14, 1942, 1 dau., Nancy Dail. Admitted to N.C. bar, 1936; reading clerk N.C. Senate, 1936-41; v.p. Coastal Plains Broadcasting Co., radio sta. WCPA, Tarboro; mem. 83d-92d congresses from 2d N.C. dist., mem. ho. fg. affairs com., chmn. inter-govtl. relations subcom. of govt. operations com.; mem. U.S. delegation 22nd session UN Gen. Assembly, 1967. Mem. exec. com. East Carolina council Boy Scouts Am. State senator, 4th Senatorial Dist., Gen. Assembly, 1947-52. Pres. Edgecombe Young Democratic Club, 1940, eastern organizer Young Dem. Clubs of N.C., 1941, past chmn. exec. com. 2d Congl. Dist. Trustee St. Andrews Presbyn. Coll., Laurinburg, N.C. Served from pvt. to maj. AUS, 1942-46. Elected Tarboro's Man of Yr., 1948; recipient citation for distinguished pub. service N.C. Citizens Assn., 1971. Mem. Am., N.C., Edgecombe County bar assns., N.C. Farm Bur., N.C. Grange, Am. Legion. Democrat. Presbyn. (elder). Elk, Kiwanian (past pres. Tarboro, lt. gov. 6th N.C. div.). Home: Tarboro NC 27886 Office: PO Bldg Tarboro NC 27886

FOUNTAIN, PETER DEWEY, Jr., (Pete), clarinet player; b. New Orleans, July 3, 1930. Played clarinet in sch. band, 1942; with Jr. Dixieland Jazz Band, 1948-49, Phil Zito, 1949-50, Basin Street Six, 1950-54; appeared New Orleans, also Jazz Ltd., and Blue Note in Chgo., 1949-53; formed group Pete Fountain and His Three Coins, 1954-57; leader Dixieland combo Lawrence Welk Orch., ABC-TV series, 1957-59; owner Pete Fountain's Inn, New Orleans. Address: 231 Bourbon St New Orleans LA 70150

FOUNTAIN, WALTER JAMES, finance and ins. co. exec.; b. Pearlington, Miss., Sept. 26, 1906; s. Noah Webster and Angeline (Favre) F.; B.B.A., Tulane U., 1932; m. Frances Katherine Jordan, Sept. 6, 1936; children—Linda, Sandra (Mrs. Robert R. Winn), James. Vice pres. Mossler Acceptance Co., New Orleans, 1932-42; self engaged in pub. accounting, New Orleans, 1942-48; v.p., part owner Gen. Credit Co., Shreveport, 1948-51; pres., dir. Allen Parker Co., Houston, 1951—; chmn. bd., dir. Standard Casualty Co., Houston, 1967—, L.W. Life Ins. Co., Houston, 1968—; dir. Lane Wood, Inc., Dallas. Mem. adv. com. Tulane U. Grad. Sch. Bus. Adminstrn. C.P.A., La., Tex., Miss. Mem. Am. Inst. C.P.A.'s, La. Soc. C.P.A.'s, Nat. Assn. Accountants, Beta Gamma Sigma, Sigma Nu. Home: 2929 Buffalo Speedway Houston TX 77006 Office: 3701 Kirby Dr Houston TX 77006

FOUNTAIN, WINFIELD STEINNER, univ. dean; b. St. Maries, Ida., Mar. 2, 1918; s. William Windover and Viola (Steinner) F.; student Gonzaga U., 1938; B.A., North Ida. Coll. Edn. 1939; M.Ed., U. Wash., 1953, Ed.D., 1956; m. Louise Arlynne Zwicker, Dec. 30, 1939; children—Molly Michelle (Mrs. William Dey), Constance Kevin (Mrs. Barclay Rogers), Heather Anne, Timothy Winfield, Barry Brett. Jr. high sch. tchr., St. Maries, 1939-42; high sch. tchr., Raymond, Wash., 1947-50; sch. adminstr., Richland, Wash., 1950-54, Moses Lake, Wash., 1954-57; prof. sch. adminstrn. Seattle U., 1957-63; dean Sch. Edn., 1963—. Vis. prof. U. R.I., 1968-69; cons. in field, 1955—. Adv. mem. Preparation Wash. Community Coll. Tchrs., 1967—, Wash. Tchr. Certification, 1957—; adminstr. credentials evaluation Wash. State, 1957; mem. vis. teams Nat. Council Accreditation Tchr. Edn., 1966-. Served with AUS, 1942-46. Mem. Am. Assn. Sch. Adminstrs., Am. Assn. Colls. Tchr. Edn., Nat., Wash. (pres. 1955-56) edn. assns. Roman Catholic. Kiwanian (pres. Broadway club. Seattle 1961). Author: Development Planning of Big Bend Community College, 1956: Pluralism in American Education, 1963. Home: 145 39th Av E Seattle, WA 98102

FOURACRE, MAURICE HAMILTON, educator; b. Jackson, Mich., Jan. 4, 1912; s. Charles and Elizabeth (Grieve) F.; A.A., Jackson Jr. Coll., 1933; A.B., U. Mich., 1935, A.M., 1940, Ph.D., 1942; m. Mary M. McClure, July 24, 1936; children—Mary Ellen, John S., Linda W. Prin. Scottville (Mich.) High Sch., 1937-40, Birmingham (Mich.) Quarton Elementary Sch., 1941-42; prof., head dept. edn. for exceptional children, Milw. State Tchrs. Coll., 1942-46; prof., head dept. edn. for handicapped children N.Y. State Coll. Tchrs., Buffalo, 1946-52; prof., head dept. spl. edn. Columbia Tchrs. Coll., 1952-62; dir. St. John's Child Devel. Center, Washington, 1962—. Pres. Council for Exceptional Children, N.E.A., 1957-58. Mem. Phi Kappa Phi. Club: Cosmos (Washington). Home: 4000 Cathedral Av N W Washington, DC 20016. Office: 5005 MacArthur Blvd NW Washington DC 20016

FOURAKER, LAWRENCE EDWARD, educator; b. Bryan, Tex., Oct. 28, 1923; s. Leroy L. and Laura (Broach) F.; B.A. Tex. A. and M. Coll., 1947, M.S., 1948; Ph.D., U. Colo., 1951; M.A. (hon.), Harvard, 1963; m. Patricia Orr, June 14, 1949; children—Senter Elizabeth, Lawrence Anderson. Instr., U. Wyo., 1948-49; from asst. prof. to prof. Pa. State U., 1951-61; faculty Harvard Bus. Sch., 1961—, prof. bus. adminstrn., 1962—, dir. div. research, 1968-70, George Fisher Baker prof. bus. adminstrn., 1970—, dean Bus. Sch., 1970—. Acting program dir., econs. program NSF, 1960-62. Served with AUS, 1943-46. Author: (with S. Siegel) Bargaining and Group Decision Making, 1960, Bargaining Behavior; (with H. Bierman and R. Jaedicke) Quantitative Analysis for Business Decisions, 1961. Home: Dean's House Harvard Business School Boston MA 02163

FOUR FRESHMEN, singing group, see Albers, John Kenneth; Barbour, Ross; Comstock, William Collins; Flanigan, Robert Lee; Reynolds, Dick.

FOURIE, GEORGE KARL, baritone; b. Johannesburg, S. Africa, Oct. 25, 1929; s. Tobias Johannes and Christina (Nel) F.; pvt. student of singing, drama and opera in Johannesburg, London, Vienna, Berlin and Milan; diploma with highest honors, Vienna State Acad. Music and Performing Arts, 1958. First operatic role at age of seventeen in Magic Flute; mem. Sadlers Wells Opera, 1955-57; first prin. baritone

Graz (Austria) Opera House, 1958- 63; mem. Kominsche Opera, 1963-65; guest artist in S. Africa, 1960-61, 63-64; U.S. debut in Boston, 1966; numerous concert tours, 1958—; recording artist for Decca, RCA records. Recipient Richard Tauber meml. scholarship, London, 1957. Mem. Am. Guild Mus. Artists. Home: 2109 Broadway New York City, NY 10023 Office: Care Eric Simon Assos 111 W 57th St New York City NY 10019

FOURNET, JOHN BAPTISTE, ret. judge; b. St. Martinville, La., July 27, 1895; s. Louis Michel and Marcelite (Gauthier) F.; grad. La. State Normal, 1915; LL.B., Louisiana State U. 1920, LL.D., 1956; m. Rose M. Dupuis, Feb 1, 1921 (div.); children—Lela Mae Ann (Mrs. Roger Vincent), John Dupuis; m. 2d, Sylvia Ann Fournet. Admitted to La. bar, 1920; practice law, St. Martinville, 1920, Baton Rouge, 1921-22, Jennings, 1922; served as mem. La. Ho. of Reps., and as speaker, 1928-32; lt. gov. of La., 1932-35; asso. justice Supreme Ct. of La., 1935-49, chief justice Sept. 1949-70. Served as pvt., U.S. Army, 1918. Mem. Am. and La. bar assns., Am. Judicature Soc., Conf. of Chief Justices, Order of Coif, Gamma Eta Gamma, Phi Alpha Delta, Pi Lambda Beta, Pi Gamma Mu. Democrat. Mason (32, Shriner). Clubs: Lamplighters (gov.) New Orleans Country, Lamplighter (bd. govs.) (New Orleans). Home: 200 Kings Rd Lafayette LA 70501

FOURNIER, CATHARINE, food co. exec., author, calligrapher; b. Bklyn., Dec. 28, 1908; d. William Henry and Mabel Laura (Trumpbour) Fournier; B.A., St. Joseph's Coll., Bklyn., 1930. Asst. sec. Kraftco Corp., 1953—; writer, 1960—, calligrapher, 1956—; exhbns. include Mus. Contemporary Crafts, N.Y.C., Allentown (Pa.) Mus., Peabody Inst. Library, Balt. (all 1961), Inst. Arts and Scis., N.Y.C., 1959, Gen. Theol. Sem., N.Y.C., 1963, Peabody Inst. Library, 1965, Donnell Library Center, 1966. Mem. Guild Book Workers, Am. Inst. Graphic Arts. Author: The Coconut Thieves (N.Y. Herald Tribune Children's Spring Book Festival award), 1964. Adapter: (Maria Konopnicka) The Golden Seed, 1962. Office: 260 Madison Av New York City NY 10016

FOURNIER, FERDINAND ERNEST, hosp. supt.; b. Akali, Hungary, Nov. 2, 1913; s. Nandor and Margit (Kiss) F.; M.D., Royal Hungarian Pazmany Peter U., Budapest, 1939; M.A., U. Colo., 1947; Ph.D., Ind. U., 1943; m. Helena Ifsitts, Apr. 1941. Came to U.S., 1957, naturalized, 1962. Intern Univ. Hosp., Budapest, 1937-39, Queen Mary Vet. Hosp., Montreal, Can., 1952-54, Pontiac (Mich.) State Hosp., 1957-60; supt. Sagamore Hills Children's Psychiat. Hosp., Northfield, O., 1967—. Home: 436 W Twinsburg Rd Northfield OH 44067 Office: Box 345 Northfield OH 44067

FOURNIER, PIERRE, concert artist; b. Paris, France, June 24, 1906; s. Gaston and Gabrielle (Morice) F.; grad. French Nat. Conservatory Music, Paris; m. Lydia Antik, July 16, 1936; 1 son, Jean Pierre. Concert artist, 1935—; soloist European, Am. orch.; tchr. Normal Sch. Music, Paris, Paris, 1938- 39; tchr. cello master class French Nat. Conservatory Music, 1941-49; concert tours Europe, U.S., S.A., Far East, South Africa. Decorated officer Legion of Honor. Home: 14 Parc Chateau Banquet Geneva, Switzerland.

FOURNIER, SERGE RAYMOND-JEAN, orch. conductor; b. Mayet, France, Sept. 28, 1931; s. Raymond and Genevieve (Brisset) F.; grad. Conservatoire Nat. Superieur de Musique, Paris, 1956; student Berkshire Music Center, 1961-62, Friedelind Wagner's Master Class, 1963. Came to U.S., 1961, naturalized, 1969. Flutist, Lamoureux Orchestra, France, 1958-60; conductor Compagnie Madeleine Renaud and Jean Louis Barrault, Theatre de France, 1960; asst. to Leonard Bernstein conductor N.Y. Philharmonic Orch., 1962, 63; music dir., conductor Toledo Symphony Orch., 1964—; guest appearances Radio Diffusion and Television Francaise, Paris, 1963, Orch. Grand Casino de Vichy, 1957, 58, Berkshire Music Festival, 1961; guest conductor in Europe, U.S., Japan and Can. Served in French Army, 1952-54. Recipient Premiere Medaille de Solfege, 1948, Premier Prix de Flute, 1949, Premier Prix d'Histoire de la Musique, 1951, Premier Prix d'Ensemble Instrumental, 1952, Premier Prix de Direction d'Orchestre, 1956, Deuxieme accessit de Contrepoint, 1956, Koussevitzky Memorial Conducting prize, 1961; named One of Ten Outstanding Young Men, Toledo C. of C., 1965. Rotarian. Home: 640 N Lallendorf Rd Oregon OH 43616 Office: Toledo Symphony Orchestra One Stranahan Square Toledo OH 43604

FOUST, ALAN SHIVERS, educator; b. Dublin, Tex., June 26, 1908; s. Charles George and Carrie E. (Lattimore) F.; B.S., U. Tex., 1928, M.S., 1930; Ph.D., U. Mich., 1938; m. H. Elizabeth Aigler, Nov. 29, 1939; children—H. Patricia, Alan S., Carolyn E., Charles William. Chemist, Magnolia Petroleum Co., Beaumont, Tex., 1930-32; devel. engr., Tex. Pacific Coal & Oil Co., 1932; asso. prof. chemistry Tex. Coll. Mines, 1935-36; instr. chem. engring. U. Mich., 1937-39, asst. prof., 1939-46, asso. prof., 1946-48, prof. chem. engring., 1948-52; prof. chmn. engring. Lehigh U., Bethlehem, Pa., 1952—, head dept., 1952-62, dean Coll. Engring., 1962-65, McCann prof. chem. engring., 1965—. Dir. Bowen Engring. Co., North Branch, N.J., Served to lt. col., Chem. Corps, AUS, 1942-46. Decorated Legion of Merit. Member Am. Soc. Engring. Edn., Am. Inst. Chem. Eng. Sigma Xi, Delta Kappa Epsilon, Tau Beta Pi, Phi Lambda Upsilon, Phi Kappa Phi. Mason (Shriner), Rotarian. Author: (with G.G. Brown and others) Unit Operations, 1950; Evaporation and Crystallization, 1955; (with others) Principles of Unit Operations, 1960; also articles. Home: 917 Prospect Av Bethlehem, PA 18018

FOUST, JOHN W., oto-rhinolaryngologist; b. Lexington, N.C., Nov. 17, 1930; s. John Wesley and Annie (Smith) F.; B.S. in Medicine, U. N.C., 1952, M.D., 1955; m. Doris Teachey, Oct. 1, 1955; children—John Phillip, Steven Wesley, Newton Douglas, Kenneth Ross, Laura Anne. Chief oto- rhinolaryngology Charlotte (N.C.) Meml. Hosp., 1965—; chief ophthalmology and otolaryngology Presbyn. Hosp., Charlotte, 1967—; clin. instr. oto-rhinolaryngology U. N.C. Med. Sch., 1965—. Served with AUS, 1957-59. Mem. A.M.A., N.C. So., Mecklenburg County med. socs., Am. Assn. Study Headaches, Am. Acad. Opthalmology and Oto-Rhinolaryngology, Am. Rhinol. Soc., N.C. Acoustical Soc., N.C. Eye, Ear, Nose and Throat Soc. Republican. Lutheran. Home: 2511 Inverness Rd Charlotte NC 28209 Office: 1850 E 3d St Charlotte NC 28204

FOUST, ROSCOE THORNTON, counselor; b. Washington, May 23, 1901; s. Noah and Pearl (Lord) F.; grad. Harvard Coll., 1921; B.S., Hobart Coll., 1923; S.T.B., Gen. Theol. Sem., 1926; grad. student N.Y. U. and Columbia; D.D., Kenyon Coll., Gambier, O., 1948; m. Mary Edith Sparks, June 9, 1926; children—Roscoe Thornton, Michael Sparks, Barbara Willis, Cornelia; m. 2d, Mabel H. Schubert, July 31, 1957. Ordained to ministry of Protestant Episcopal Ch., 1926; rector Trinity Ch., Cranford, N.J., 1928-32; chaplain, U.S. Mil. Acad., West Point, N.Y., 1932-37; dean and rector, Cathedral Ch. of the Nativity, Bethlehem, Pa., 1937-45; rector, Ch. of the Ascension, N.Y.C., 1945-54; pastoral counselor, psychotherapist; dir. dept. of religious, social and spl. services for the Seamens Ch. Inst., N.Y.C. Certificate William Alanson White Inst. Psychiatry, Psychoanalysis and Psychology. Mem. Phi Beta Kappa, Kappa Alpha. Club: Harvard (N.Y.C.). Mem. editorial bd. of The Witness. Address: 2781 N Ocean Blvd Boca Raton FL 33432

FOUTS, JOHN DAVID, physician; b. Benge, Ky., Mar. 9, 1910; s. John Calvin and Kittie (Cornett) F.; B.S., Eastern Ky. U., 1932; M.D., U. Louisville, 1936; M.P.H., Columbia, 1948; m. Margaret Elizabeth Griffin, May 24, 1944; children—Nancylee (Mrs. Malcolm Fowler), Susan Cornett (Mrs. Henry Tilman), Martha Craft. Intern McKeesport (Pa.) Gen. Hosp., 1936-37; county health officer Laural County, Ky., 1938-41; dir. venereal disease control Louisville and Jefferson County Health Dept., 1941-43; USPHS officer in charge venereal disease program and hosps., Ark., Washington, Columbia, S.C., Seattle, 1943-45; dir. King County Health Dept., King County Tb Sanitorium, Seattle, 1945-47; dist. health officer Northwestern Wash., dir. Whatcom County Hosp. and Indigent Med. Care Program, Whatcom and San Juan Counties, 1948-62; chief pub. health div. AID Mission to Ghana, State Dept., 1962-64, provincial dir. health, Ethiopia, 1964-69, dep. dir. pub. health div. CORDS, 3d Regional Assistance Command, Vietnam, 1969—. Instr. pub. health and preventive medicine U. Louisville Sch. Medicine, 1941-43; asst. prof. preventive medicine and pub. health U. Wash., 1946-62; cons. No. State Hosp., Sedro Wooly, Wash., 1960-62. Served from capt. to maj. USPHS, 1943-46, now col. Res. Tropical medicine fellow Tulane U., 1964. Diplomate Am. Bds. Preventive Medicine and Pub. Health. Fellow Am. Pub. Health Assn.; mem. A.M.A., Wash., Whatcom County med. socs., Commd. Officers Assn. USPHS, Fgn. Service Club Washington, Am. Fgn. Service Assn., Phi Beta Pi. Republican. Baptist (deacon 1950-60). Clubs: Washington, Yacht, Country (Bellingham). Active participant Sauk polio vaccine nat. field trials, 1954-55; Leishmaniasis study, Ethiopia, 1967-68. Home: 504 Fieldston Rd Bellingham WA 98225 Office: 3d Regional Assistance Command Office CORDS Gia Dinh Vietnam ADV TM 44 APO San Francisco CA 96243

FOWKES, FREDERICK MAYHEW, educator; b. Chgo., Jan. 29, 1915; s. Wm. Herbert and Eleanor (Seley) F.; B.S., U. Chgo., 1936, Ph.D., 1938; m. Royce Berkeley Budge, Sept. 3, 1937; children-Gordon Seley, Joan Berkeley (Mrs. David R. Pitkin), Mary Elisabeth, Virginia Mayhew. Research supr. Shell Devel. Co., Emeryville, Cal., 1947-62; dir. research Sprague Electric Co., North Adams, Mass., 1962-68; prof., chmn. chemistry dept. Lehigh U., Bethlehem, Pa., 1968—; adj. prof. Rensselaer Poly. Inst., 1967-68. Served from lt. to maj., F.A., AUS, 1942-46; PTO. Decorated Silver Star medal, Mem. Am. Chem. Soc. (past div. chmn.), Electrochemical Soc., Faraday Soc. Contbr. articles profl. jours. Patentee in field. Home: 18 Pleasant Dr RD 3 Bethlehem PA 18015

FOWKES, ROBERT ALLEN, educator; b. Harrison, N.Y., Apr. 7, 1913; s. William Robert and Elizabeth (Allen) F.; A.B., N.Y.U., 1934, M.A., 1935; Ph.D., Columbia, 1947; student U. Bonn (Germany), 1936-37; m. Angela M. Vescio, June 17, 1939; children—Robert Allen, Richard Owen, William Ivor. Mem. faculty N.Y. U., 1936-37, 38—, prof. German, 1959—, chmn. dept. Germanic langs., 1957-68; asst. Columbia, 1937-38, lectr. Sanskrit, 1947-60; civilian linguist C.E., AUS, 1942-45. Guggenheim fellow, 1950-51; recipient Great Tchr. award N.Y.U., 1964. Mem. Linguistic Soc. Am., Modern Lang. Assn. Am., St. David's Soc. (pres. N.Y. State 1956-58), Linguistic Circle N.Y. (pres. 1958), Phi Beta Kappa. Author: Gothic Etymological Studies, 1949; Literarische Auswahl, 1960; Pagine Scelte, 1960; also articles. Home: 632 Van Cortlandt Park Av Yonkers, NY 10705. Office: New York Univ Bronx NY 10453

FOWLE, FRANK FULLER, lawyer; b. Chgo., May 28, 1908; s. Frank Fuller and Alice Edna (Cowper) F.; A.B., William Coll., 1929; LL.B., Harvard, 1932; M.A., Columbia, 1946; m. Elisabeth Sloan Ballard, June 27, 1938; children—Elizabeth Sloan, Susan Rankin, Margaret Duryee, Frank Fuller, William Cowper II. Admitted to Ill. bar, 1932; asso. firm McKinney, Lynde & Grear, Chgo., 1932-34; with legal div. NRA, Washington, 1934-35, PWA, Washington, 1935-37; asso. firm Mayer, Meyer, Austrian & Platt, Chgo., 1937-40; mem. firm Pope, Ballard, Kennedy, Sheppard & Fowle, and predecessors, Chgo., 1940—. Mem. Cook County Rent Adv. Bd., 1952-53; pres., dir. Winnetka Community Chest, 1958-61; pres. combined bd. Winnetka PTA, 1952-53; chmn. Ill. Jr. Coll. Bd., 1965—; mem. Ill. Bd. Higher Edn., 1965—. Bd. dirs. Nat. Soc. Prevention Blindness, 1957-66; pres., trustee Ill. Soc. Prevention Blindness, 1956- -, Rheumatic Fever Research Inst., Chgo., 1955-58; v.p., trustee Library Internat. Relations, Chgo., 1948-53; gov. mem. Glenwood Sch. Boys, 1949- 64. Served to lt. comdr. USNR, 1942-45. Mm. Am., Chgo. law insts. Am., Ill., Chgo., (bd. mgrs. 1964-66) bar assns., Chgo. Hist. Soc., Chgo. Zool. Soc., Chgo., Mus. Natural History, Chi Psi. Episcopalian (past vestry). Clubs: Law, Legal, University (dir. 1954-57, sec. 1957) (Chgo.). Home: 125 Enid Lane Northfield IL 60093 Office: 69 W Washington St Chicago IL 60602

FOWLE, JAMES LUTHER, clergyman; b. Washington, N.C., Oct. 14, 1897; s. Samuel Richardson and Mary (Payne) F.; student Randolph Macon Acad., Bedford City, Va., 1913- 14; A.B., Davidson Coll., 1918; student Johns Hopkins, 1918; B.D., Union Theol. Sem., 1921 (Hoge fellowship 1921-22); S.T.M., Princeton Theol. Sem., 1923; D.D., Westminster Coll., Fulton, Mo., 1928, Davidson Coll., 1928; LL.D., U. Chattanooga, 1942; Litt. D., King Coll., 1949; m. Katharine Ferguson, Jan. 26, 1925 (dec. May 1950); 1 dau., Mary Payne. Ordained Presbyn. ministry, 1923; pastor Central Presbyn. Ch., St. Louis, 1923-29, First Presbyn. Ch., Chattanooga, 1929-67; active in adminstrn. of Presbyteries, 1927—, commr. gen. assemblies, mem. councils of ch.; joint moderator Gen. Assembly Presbyn. Church U.S., 1951, and mem. bd. of ch. extension, 1948-56, mem. bd. of annuities and relief, 1956-62, 66—, vice chmn. 1966—, chmn. permanent nominating com., v.p.; spl. tchr. U. Chattanooga, 1948-68. Chaplain, City of Chattanooga, 1944—. Pres. Chattanooga Community Chest, 1936-46, mem. exec. com. 1946- 56; active in exec. adminstrn. community civic activites such as clinics, hosps., Boy Scouts, YMCA, YWCA, USO, Traveler's Aid, and others; v.p. Tenn. div. Am. Cancer Soc., 1953-56, pres. Tenn. div., 1956- 57; mem. bd. Girls Clubs, Opportunity Home for Girls, Greater Chattanooga United Fund. Pres. of Chattanooga Bible Inst., 1934—; trustee King Coll., Bristol, Tenn., Calsted Home (chmn. bd. 1970-71), Girls Prep. Sch., Chattanooga, Bachman Home, Colored Orphans Home, U. Chattanoogaa, Hillandale; trustee Montreat Assn., 1934-56; gen. council Presbyn. Ch., 1949-53; exec. com. Assn. Services for Armed Forces. Mem. Chattanooga Pastors Assn., Kappa Alpha, Omicron Delta Kappa, Alpha Phi Omega. Clubs: Civitan (chaplain), Kiwanis (hon.), Rotary (hon.), Chattanooga Golf and Country. Author: So Many People, 1943; Planned Services for Church Groups, 1946. Received Kiwanis award for social service, 1947. Home: 209 Windmere Dr Shepherd Hills Chattanooga TN 37411 ☆

FOWLE, PERCY FRANK, mfr. sheet metal products; b. Montreal, Can., Nov. 12, 1909; s. O. Percy Frank and Gladys (Brown) F.; ed. high sch., Montreal; grad. Advanced Mgmt. Program, Harvard; m. Gladys Marjorie Tucker, July 15, 1934; children—Norman Brian, Gail Virginia. With Bank of Montreal, 1926-29, Pitfield, Scott & Co., 1929-31; with Westeel Products, Ltd. (co. name changed to Westeel-Rosco Ltd.), Toronto, Can., 1931—, pres., 1956-65, chmn. bd., 1965—; associated with the corporate sales dept. Crown Trust Co. Mem. Anglican Church. Clubs: Nat., High Park (Toronto). Home: 17 Brunhamthorpe Park Blvd Islington Ontario Canada Office: 302 Bay St Toronto Ontario Canada

FOWLE, WILSON FARNSWORTH, Jr., mfg. co. exec.; b. Nov. 23, 1926; s. Wilson F. and Lenora Helen (Clark) F.; B.A., U. Va., 1948; m. Audrey Loux Smith, Sept. 9, 1950; children—Wilson Farnsworth III, Sara Loux. With Vick Chem. Co., 1948-52, Mennen Co., 1952-55, Benton & Bowles Advt., Inc., 1955-60; with Colgate- Palmolive Co., 1960-67, v.p., marketing dir. Toilet Articles div., 1964- 67, v.p. marketing Royal Crown Cola Co., Columbus, Ga., 1967—. Served with USNR, 1944-46. Mem. Am. Horse Show Assn., Phi Kappa Psi. Episcopalian. Clubs: Ox Ridge Hunt (Darien, Conn.); Columbus Country; Atlanta Polo; Midland (Ga.) Hunt. Home: Still Creek Farm Old Warm Springs Rd Midland, GA 31820 Office: Box 1440 Columbus GA 31906

FOWLER, ALEXANDER MURRAY, educator; b. Cape Town, South Africa, Mar. 23, 1905; s. Alexander Duguid and Katherine (Walker) F.; B.A., U. Minn., 1927; M.A., U. Ore., 1929; Ph.D., Harvard, 1940; m. Barbara Hughes, July 14, 1956; children—Jane Alexandra, Emily Hughes. Faculty U. Wis., Madison, 1947—, chem. dept. linguistics, 1948-65, prof. linguistics, 1965-. Home: 1102 Sherman Av Madison, WI 53703.

FOWLER, BEN B., lawyer; b. Hopkinsville, Ky., Mar. 9, 1916; s. William Thomas and Ila (Earle) F.; B.S. in Commerce, U. Ky., 1937; LL.B., U. Va., 1940; m. Eleanor Randolph, Oct. 19, 1940. Admitted to Ky. bar, 1940; atty. firm Fowler & Fowler, Lexington, 1940-41; asst. atty. gen., Ky., 1945-47; mem. firm Daily & Fowler, Frankfort, Ky., 1948—; city solicitor, Frankfort, 1958-60; chief counsel Ky. Civil Code Com., 1953; chmn. Ct. Appeals Adv. Com. Civil Rules Procedure, 1953—. Vice pres., gen. counsel, dir. Frankfort & Cin. R.R.; pres., dir. Community Service, Inc. Vice chmn. Gov.'s Commn. Economy and Efficiency, 1963-64. Republican candidate for atty. gen. 1955. Mem. Am. Judicature Soc., Am. (ho. of dels. 1955-60) Ky. (bd. bar commrs. 1953-60, pres. 1959-60; Outstanding Service award 1954), Franklin County (pres. 1969) bar assns., Frankfort C. of C. (pres. 1957-58, chmn. indsl. devel. 1958- 59), Delta Tau Delta, Phi Alpha Delta. Presbyn. (deacon 1947-53, elder 1953—). Clubs: Rotary (pres. Frankfort 1952-53), Frankfort Country (dir. 1953-56, v.p. 1955). Home: 110 Reservoir Dr Frankfort KY 40601 Office: McClure Bldg Frankfort Ky 40601

FOWLER, CHARLES ALBERT, electronics engr.; b. Centralia, Ill., Dec. 17, 1920; s. Clarence J. and Bess (Maxwell) F.; B.S. in Engring. Physics, U. Ill., 1942; m. Kathryn Elizabeth Grimes, Oct. 23, 1943; children—Patricia Ann, Mary Catherine. Mem. staff radiation lab. Mass. Inst. Tech., 1942-45; head radar systems dept. Airborne Instruments Lab., Deer Park, N.Y., 1946-66; dep. dir. (tactical warfare) def. research and engring. Dept. Def., 1966-70; v.p., mgr. equipment devel. labs. Raytheon Co., Sudbury, Mass., 1970—. Mem. sch. bd., East Norwich, N.Y., 1955-61, library bd., 1956-62. Fellow I.E.E.E.; asso. fellow Am. Inst. Aero. and Astronautics; mem. Am. Ordnance Assn., A.A.A.S. Author articles in field. Home: 15 Woodberry Rd Sudbury MA 01776 Office: Raytheon Co Sudbury MA 01776

FOWLER, CHARLES ALLISON EUGENE, archtl. engring. co. exec.; b. Halifax, N.S., Can., Jan. 24, 1921; s. Charles Allison and Mildred (Crosby) F.; B.Sc., Dalhousie U., 1942; B.Eng., McGill U., 1944; B.Arch., U. Man., 1948; m. Dorothy Christine Gràham, Aug. 30, 1947; children—Graham Allison, Beverly Anne. With C.A. Fowler, Bauld & Mitchell, Ltd., Halifax and predecessor firms, Halifax, 1946—, sr. partner, 1966-70, pres., 1970—. Mem. adv. com.. Sch. Architecture N.S. Tech. Coll., Halifax, 1961—, mem. senate, 1962—; pres. N.S. Mus. Fine Arts, Halifax, 1969—. Bd. dirs. Royal Archtl. Inst. Can. Found. Served with Canadian Army 1943-45. Fellow A.I.A. (hon.), Royal Archtl. Inst. Can. (pres. 1965); mem. Engring. Inst. Can., Assn. Profl. Engrs. N.S., N.S. Assn. Architects (past pres.). Mem. United Ch. Clubs: Halifax, Saraguay (Halifax). Projects include Mineers Mus., Glace Bay, N.S., 1968, Victoria Gen. Hosp. expansion, Halifax, 1964-68, Dalhousie U. Fine Arts Center, 1970, univ. centers Acadia U., St. Francis Xavier U., Acad. Center at Mt. St. Vincent U. Home: 2 Hall's Rd Halifax Nova Scotia Canada Office: Duke St Tower Halifax Nova Scotia Canada

FOWLER, CHARLES ARMAN, Jr., educator; b. Salt Lake City, Apr. 23, 1912; s. Charles A. and Beatrice (Buckle) F.; A.B., U. Utah, 1933, M.S., 1934; Ph.D., U. Cal., 1940; m. Inez Hanson, Aug. 4, 1934; children—Scott Wellington, Craig Huntington. Instr. physics U. Cal. at Berkeley, 1940-42, asst. prof., 1943-46, faculty, summers 1951, 53, 55, 62; asso. prof. Pomona Coll., Claremont, Cal., 1947- 49, prof., chmn. dept. physics, 1950—. NSF sr. postdoctoral fellow for research Fourier Inst., U. Grenoble (France), 1960-61; NSF Sci. Faculty fellow, 1967-68; participant Internat. Conf. on Magnetism, Grenoble, 1970. Mem. Am. Phys. Soc. (com. on coll. physics facilities 1962-65), Am. Assn. Physics Tchrs., A.A.A.S., Am. Assn. U. Profs., Phi Beta Kappa, Sigma Xi. Contbr. chpt. to Magnetic Material Digest for 1961, author sect. Magnetic Domains, 1964, Magnetism and Magnetic Domains, 1965; contbr. to sci. publs. Home: 366 Blaisdell Dr Claremont CA 91711

FOWLER, CODY, lawyer; b. Arlington, Tenn., Dec. 8, 1892; s. Orin Scott and Maud (Cody) F.; student U. Mo., 1911-12; LL.B., Cumberland U., 1913, LL.D.; LL.D., U. Miami; H.H.D., U. Tampa; m. Maude Stewart, Apr. 28, 1915; children—Betty (Mrs. Stanley P. Campbell), Maude (Mrs. Lee F. Pallardy, Jr.), Cody (Mrs. James O. Davis, Jr.). Admitted to Tenn. bar, 1913, Fla. bar, 1914, Okla. bar, 1916; practiced in Jacksonville, Fla., 1914-16, Oklahoma City, 1919-24; with Macfarlane, Pettingill, Macfarlane & Fowler, Fowler, Tampa, Fla., 1924-35; pvt. practice law, Tampa and Miami, Fla., 1935-43; with Fowler, White, Humkey, Burnett, Hurley & Banick, Miami, Flowler, White, Gillen, Humkey, Kinney & Boggs and predecessor firms, Tampa, St. Petersburg, 1943—. Chmn. bd. dir., First Fed. Savs. & Loan Assn., Tampa; dir. City Nat. Bank of Miami. Served with F.A., U.S. Army, 1917-19. Recipient Human Relations award Fla. Anti-Defamation League of B'nai-B'rith, 1961; Distinguished Service award Stetson U. Mem. Am. Bar Assn. (ho. of dels., life mem., bd. govs. 1946-52, pres. 1950-51) Am. Coll. Trial Lawyers (past pres.), Fla. State, Hillsborough County, Dade County, Inter-Am. (past pres.), Internat. bar assns., Am. Law Inst., Am. Judicature Soc., Maritime Law Assn. U.S., Tampa chambers commerce, Am. Legion, Order of Coif, Phi Delta Theta. Democrat. Epsicopalian. Elk, Mason (Shriner, K.T.), Rotarian. Clubs: Propeller, Gasparilla Krewe, Yacht and Country, University (Tampa); Miami; Century Assn., Wall Street (N.Y.C.). Home: 84 Davis Blvd Tampa FL 33606 Office: First Federal Bldg Tampa FL 33602 also City Nat Bank Bldg Miami FL 33130 also Fla Office Bldg St Petersburg FL 33701

FOWLER, C.W., utility exec. Controller, Mich. Consol. Gas Co., Detroit. Office: 1 Woodward Av Detroit MI 48226*

FOWLER, DANIEL EISON, lawyer; b. Hopkinsville, Ky., Nov. 20, 1908; s. William Thomas and Ila (Earle) F.; B.A., U. Ky., 1932, J.D., 1933; m. Louisa Bickel, Apr. 14, 1932; 1 son, Robert Bickel. Admitted to Ky. bar, 1933, since practiced in Lexington; partner Fowler & Fowler, 1933-52, Fowler & Bell, 1952-54, Fowler, Bell, Cox & Hancock, 1958-59, Fowler, Rouse, Measle & Bell, 1959- -. Sec. F. & C. R.R. Co., 1933-60, Old Lewis Hunter Distillery Co., 1935- 1935-42; pres. Landholders, Inc., Properties, Inc.; sec. Spindletop Research,

Inc. County judge Fayette County, 1954-58. Served to lt. comdr. USNR, 1942-45. Mem. Ky. Soc. S.R., Am., Ky. bar assns., Delta Tau Delta, Phi Delta Phi. Presbyn. (deacon). Kiwanian. Club: Thoroughbred of America (Lexington). Home: 409 Bristol Rd Lexington KY 40502 Office: 141 N Upper St Lexington KY 40507

FOWLER, DOROTHY GANFIELD, educator; b. Green Bay, Wis., July 2, 1902; d. William Arthur and Clara (Boardman) Ganfield; student Ky. Coll. Women, 1915-20, Mt. Holyoke Coll., 1920-21; B.A., Carroll Coll., 1923, LL.D., 1946; M.A., U. Wis., 1926, Ph.D., 1928; m. Emmett Fowler, Dec. 31, 1929. Tchr., Appleton (Wis.) High Sch., 1923-25; asst. U. Wis., 1925-28; prof. history Mo. Valley Coll., Marshall, 1928-30; faculty Hunter coll. of City U. N.Y., 1930—, prof. history, 1956-72, prof. emeritus, 1972, chmn. dept., 1962-68. Fulbright vis. prof. Instituut voor Geschiedenis der Rijksuniversiteit te Utrecht, 1968-69. Mem. N.Y. bd. Protestant Student Work, 1952-55, vice chmn., 1954-55. Mem. Am. Assn. U. Women (dir. N.Y. 1955-57), Am. Hist. assn., Orgn. Am. Historians, Am. Assn. U. Profs. Republican. Presbyn. (elder). Author: The Cabinet Politician; Postmasters General, 1829-1909, 1943; John Coit Spooner. Defender of Presidents, 1961. Contbr. articles to profl. jours. Home: 460 W 24th St New York City NY 10011

FOWLER, EARLE CABELL, educator, physicist; b. Bowling Green, Ky., June 10, 1921; s. William Earle and Reba (Brownfield) F.; B.S. in Chemistry, U. Ky., 1942; A.M. in Physics, Harvard, 1947, Ph.D., 1949; m. Marjorie Jane Land, Oct. 25, 1950; children—Marjorie Anne, Walter Earle, Thomas Land. Asso. physicist Brookhaven Nat. Lab., Upton, N.Y., 1949-52, cons., 1952—; acad. staff Yale, 1952-62; prof. physics Duke, Durham, N.C., 1962-71; prof. physics, head dept. Purdue U., 1971—; cons. Oak Ridge Inst. Nuclear Studies, 1962—. Sr. Fulbright lectureship to U.K., 1958-59, U. Rome (Italy), 1967-68. Fellow Am. Phys. Soc.; mem. Phi Beta Kappa, Sigma Xi, Sigma Pi Sigma, Delta Tau Delta. Author: (with Robert K. Adair) Strange Particles, 1963. Research in application electronic computers to automatic film data analysis, high energy physics, in cosmic radiation and with large accelerators; helped to develop 1st high pressure diffusion cloud chambers. Office: Dept Physics Purdue Univ West Lafayette IN 47907

FOWLER, EDMUND ROY, mfg. co. exec.; b. Rockford, Ill., Mar. 7, 1928; s. Roy Eugene and Vera (Alderson) F.; B.S. in Bus. Adminstrn., Northwestern U., 1950, M.B.A., 1958; m. Mary Janet Boggs, June 12, 1949; children-Debra Ann, David Edmund, Pamela Dale. Buyer, investment analyst Northwestern U., 1951-54; credit mgr. C.E. Niehoff, Chgo., 1954-60; credit mgr. Square D Co., Park Ridge, Ill., 1960-64, asst. corporate controller, 1964-67, asst. sec., 1967-69, corporate sec., 1969—. Served with AUS, 1946-48, 50-51. Mem. Am. Soc. Corporate Secs., Park Ridge C. of C. Methodist. Home: 906 S Western Av Park Ridge IL 60068 Office: Square D Co 205 S Northwest Hwy Park Ridge IL 60068

FOWLER, FRANCIS E., Jr., corp. exec.; b. St. Louis, Sept. 24, 1891; s. Francis E. and Mary A. (Harig) F.; student St. Vincent's Sem., 1900-03, Notre Dame U., 1903-04, St. Louis U., 1904-11; m. Emily Robins Riddle, Apr. 29, 1916; children—Francis E., Truman Riddle, Philip Fouke. Organized Caligrapo Co., flavoring extract mfrs., 1918, sole owner until 1937; organizer, pres. Midland Distilleries, Inc. since 1937, So. Comfort Corp. since 1937; pres. Francis E. Fowler, Jr. Found. (and museum). Clubs: University (St. Louis); Home: 288 N Saltair Av Los Angeles CA also 7683 Hillside Dr La Jolla CA 19030 also 19030 Pacific Coast Hwy Malibu CA 90265 Office: Southern Comfort Corp Bldg 150 Barrington Pl Los Angeles CA 90049 90049.

FOWLER, GILES MERRILL, film and drama critic; b. Kansas City, Mo., Jan 3, 1934; s. Richard Brosing and Elinor (Montgomery) F.; B.A., Westminster Coll., Fulton, Mo., 1955; M.S. in Journalism, Columbia, 1956; m. Jane Pecinovsky, Jan. 17, 1959; 1 son, Stephen Carr. Reporter, Kansas City (Mo.) Star, 1956- 57, 58-62, motion picture editor, 1962—, drama and film editor, 1964—; reporter Times of London (Eng.), 1957-58. Mem. film com. Mo. Council on Arts, 1965—; mem. Friends of Art, Kansas City, 1971—; mem. Mayor Kansas City Theatre Planning Com., 1965-66; film adv. com. Kan. Cultural Arts Commn., 1968—. Mem. Motion Picture Assn. Kansas City, Beta Theta Pi, Phi Alpha Theta (pres. Westminster chpt. 1955), Pi Delta Epsilon. Home: 6825 Cherry St Kansas City MO 64131 Office: 1729 Grand Av Kansas City MO 64108

FOWLER, HAROLD LEES, coll. dean; b. Boston, Sept. 11, 1907; s. Herbert Lees and Sybil Gertrude (Major) F.; A.B., Dartmouth, 1928; M.A., Harvard, 1930, Ph.D., 1934; m. Theodosia Jeannette Marshall, Dec. 26, 1934. Instr., West Nottingham Acad., Colora, Md., 1928-29; asst. in history Harvard, 1930-34; faculty coll. William and Mary, Williamsburg, Va., 1934—, prof. history, 1946—, head dept., 1959-64, dean faculty, 1964—, dir. Am. studies Program, 1960. Vis. prof. U. N.C., summers 1951-52, Cal. Inst. Tech., 1956-57. Served as lt. USNR, 1943-46. Mem. Inst. Early Am. History and Culture (council 1960-63), Am. So. hist. assns., Am. U. Profs., Cum Laude Soc., Flat Hat Club Soc., Phi Beta Kappa, Lambda Chi Alpha, Omicron Delta Kappa, Kappa Phi Kappa, Tau Kappa Alpha. Episcopalian (sr. warden). Home: 140 Chandler Ct Williamsburg VA 23185

FOWLER, HARRY WINTHROP, banker; b. N.Y.C., Dec. 26, 1920; s. Robert Ludlow and Charlotte Winthrop (Cram) F.; grad. St. Paul's Sch., 1939; B.A., Harvard, 1943; m. Grace Montgomery, Feb. 26, 1949; children—Cecily Fowler Grand, Harry Winthrop, Angela Wilmerding, Lucius Ludlow. With Fiduciary Trust Co. of N.Y., N.Y.C., 1947—, successively investment officer, asst. v.p., v.p., 1951-56, exec. v.p., 1956-60, pres., 1960-70, chmn. bd., 1970—, dir.; dir. Penryn, Inc. (Montclair, N.J.); trustee N.Y. Bank Savs. Trustee Coll. Retirement Equities Fund, N.Y.C., Miss. Hall's Sch., No. Westchester Hosp.; trustee, mem. finance com. Am. Schs. Oriental Research; pres. Correctional Assn. N.Y.; vice chmn. U.S.A. investment adv. com. Employers-Comml. Union Cos. Served to capt., King's Royal Rifle Corp., Brit. Army, 1941-46. Clubs: Knickerbocker (gov.), Down Town Assn. (trustee) (N.Y.C.). Home: Hook Rd Katonah NY 10536 Office: 1 Wall St New York City NY 10005

FOWLER, HENRY HAMILL, investment banker; b. Roanoke, Va., Sept. 5, 1908; s. Mack Johnson and Bertha (Browning) F.; A.B., Roanoke Coll., 1929; LL.B., Yale, 1932, J.S.D., 1933, LL.D., 1962; LL.D., William and Mary Coll., 1966, Wesleyan U.; 1966; m. Trudye Pamela Hathcote, Oct. 19, 1938; children—Mary (now Mrs. Roy C. Smith IV), Susan (now Mrs. James Gallagher), and Henry Hamill (dec.). Admitted Va. bar, 1933, D.C. bar, 1946; counsel TVA, 1934-38, asst. general counsel, 1939; spl. asst. to atty. gen. as chief counsel subcom. Senate Com. Edn. and Labor, 1939-40; spl. counsel Fed. Power Commn., 1941; asst. gen. counsel O.P.M., 1941, W.P.B., 1942-44; econ. advisor U.S. Mission Econ. Affairs, London, Eng., 1944; spl. asst. to adminstr. Fgn. Econ. Adminstrn., 1945; dep. adminstr. N.P.A., 1951, adminstr., 1952; adminstr. Defense Prodn. Adminstrn., 1952-53; dir. ODM, mem. Nat. Security Council, 1952-53; sr. mem. Fowler, Leva Hawes & Symington, Washington, 1946-51, 1953-61, 64-65; undersec. of Treasury, 1961-64; mem. law firm Fowler, Leva, Hawes & Symington, Washington, 1964-65, U.S. sec. of Treasury, 1965-68; gen. partner Goldman, Sachs & Co., N.Y.C., 1969—. Trustee Roanoke Coll. Funds, P.E. Ch. Diocese of Va. Del. Dem. Nat. Conv., 1956; mem. nat. commn. on money and credit; alternate Dem. Nat. Convention, 1960. Recipient distinguished alumni award Tau Kappa Alpha, 1958. Mem. Council on Foreign Relations, also Yale Law Sch. Assn. Washington (pres. 1955), Pi Kappa Phi, Phi Delta Phi. Democrat. Episcopalian. Clubs: Pinnacle, Links (N.Y.C.); Nat. Capital Democratic (pres. 1958-60), Metropolitan (Washington). Home: 209 S Fairfax St Alexandria VA 22314 also 825 Fifth Av New York City NY 10021 Office: 55 Broad St New York City NY 10004

FOWLER, JAMES ALEXANDER, Jr., lawyer; b. Clinton, Tenn., Feb. 27, 1897; s. James Alexander and Lucy Ellen (Hornsby) F.; A.B., U. Tenn., 1916; LL.B., Harvard, 1919; m. Hilleda Thomas, July 17, 1920; children—James Alexander III, Ann Astelle (Mrs. D.L. Walters). Admitted to N.Y. bar, 1920, since practiced in N.Y.C.; counsel Bur. of Naval Personnel, 1942-44; with Cahill, Gordon, Sonnett, Reindel & Ohl, 1921—, partner, 1927—. Nat. chmn. Harvard Law Sch. Fund, 1955-57; dir. N.Y. Assn. for Blind, Sheltering Arms Children's Service. Fellow Am. Coll. Trial Lawyers, Am. Bar Found; mem. N.Y. Practicing Law Inst. (chmn.; trustee), Am. Law Inst., Am., N.Y. bar assns., Assn. Bar City N.Y., N.Y. County Lawyers Assn., Harvard Law Sch. Assn. (pres. 1961-63). Clubs: University, Down Town Assn. Home: 140 E 72d St New York City NY 10021 Office: 80 Pine St New York City NY 10005

FOWLER, JAMES EDWARD, oil co. exec., lawyer; b. Boise, Ida., Dec. 8, 1931; s. Jim and Beulah (Cazer) F.; A.B. summa cum laude Princeton U., 1953; LL.B., Yale Law Sch., 1959; m. Carolyn Elizabeth Jacobus, Aug. 16, 1958; children—Barbara Ann, Thomas Edward. Admitted to N.Y. bar, 1960; asso. firm Debevoise, Plimpton, Lyons & Gates, N.Y.C., 1959-68; corp. counsel Mobil Oil Corp., N.Y.C., 1968-69; gen. counsel Mobil East Inc., N.Y.C., 1969—. Mem. Chappaqua (N.Y.) Sch. Dist. Bd. Edn., 1970—. Served with AUS, 1953-56. Mem. Assn. Bar City N.Y., N.Y. State, Am., Internat. bar assns., Am. Soc. Internat. Law, Yale Law Sch. Assn. N.Y.C. (v.p., sec. 1971), Phi Delta Phi. Conglist. (chmn. bd. deacons 1969-70, moderator 1970-71). Bd. editors Yale Law Jour., 1958-59. Home: 10 Danny Lane Chappaqua NY 10514 Office: 150 E 42d St New York City NY 10017

FOWLER, JAMES RANDLETT, govt. ofcl.; b. Boulder, Colo., Dec. 11, 1920; s. Samuel Ross and Louise White (Randlett) F.; B.A. magna cum laude (Kiwanis scholar), U. Colo., 1943; B.A. (Rhodes scholar), Oxford U., 1949; m. Margaret Williamson, Apr. 19, 1947; children—Pamela Leighton, Deborah Randlett, Michael Ross. Instr. English, U. Colo., 1946-47; with Bur. for UN, Office Dependent Area Affairs, Dept. State, 1950-53; with internat. div. Bur. Budget, 1953-56; with Office Dep. Dir. for Planning, ICA, 1956-58, with Office Far East Affairs, 1960-61, with Office Dep. Coordinator for Mut. Security, Dept. State, 1958-60; dep. asst. adminstr. for Far East, AID, 1961-63, mission dir., Bogota, Colombia, 1964-67; dep. U.S. coordinator Alliance for Progress, Dept. State, Washington, 1967-70, spl. asst. to adminstr. AID, 1970, detailed to Sr. Sem. in Fgn. Policy, Dept. State, 1970-71, spl. asst. to adminstr. AID, exec. dir. Com. on Environment and Devel. AID, 1971—. Served to 1st lt., inf., AUS, 1943-46. Mem. Am. Acad. Polit. and Social Scis., Am. Assn. Rhodes Scholars. Democrat. Episcopalian. Club: Gibson Island (Md.). Home: 8 W Irving St Chevy Chase MD 20015 Office: Dept State Washington DC 20523

FOWLER, JOHN RUSSELL, chain dept. store exec.; b. Pontiac, Mich., Apr. 4, 1918; s. John Tasker and Amy (Hurlburt) F.; B.A, Amherst Coll., 1940; m. Dorthalene Borthwick, Oct. 5, 1924; children—John Russell, James Borthwick. With Jacobson Stores Inc., Jackson, Mich., 1946—, exec. v.p., 1962-68, pres., 1968—; dir. Nat. Bank Jackson, Tecumseh Products Co. (Mich.) Camp Realty Co., Jackson. Chmn. Torch drive, Jackson, 1956, Community Chest, 1957, City Planning Commn., 1970; Chmn. citizens com. Bd. Edn., Jackson, 1960-61. Bd. dirs. Mercy Hosp., Jackson. Served to lt. comdr. USNR, 1941-45. Decorated D.F.C., Air medal. Clubs: Town, Country of (Jackson); Otsego (Gaylord). Home: 1115 S Higby St Jackson MI 49203 Office: 1200 N West Av Jackson MI 49202

FOWLER, JOSEPH WILLIAM, amusement park exec.; b. Monmouth, Me., July 9, 1894; s. William and Jennie (Larkin) F.; grad. Monmouth (Me.) Acad., 1911; B.S., U.S. Naval Acad., 1918; M.S., Mass. Inst. Tech., 1921; grad. U.S. Naval War Coll., 1929; m. Marguerite Turner, April 13, 1918; 1 son, Joseph William. Commd. ensign, U.S.-Navy, 1917, and advanced through the grades to rear admiral, 1946; prodn. officer Navy Yard, Mare Island, Calif., 1940-42; asst. indsl. mgr. (naval work in pvt. yards). San Francisco, Calif., 1942-45; became comdr. San Francisco, Calif. Naval Shipyard Oct. 1945; dir. indsl. survey, Office Sec. Navy, 1946-48; dir. Def. Supply Mgmt. Agy., 1952; now v.p. Disneyland, Anaheim, Cal., Walt Disney Productions, Burbank, Cal. Decorated World War I Victory Medal and clasp. Yangtze Service Medal; World War II, Legion of Merit. Commendation Ribbon Victory Medal, Pre-Pearl Harbor and Am. Theatre ribbons (M.S.); Al Merito (Chile). Mem. Soc. Naval Engrs. Clubs: Army-Navy Country (Arlington, Va.); Army Navy (Washington); Bohemian (San Francisco); Balboa Bay (Newport Beach, Cal.). Home: Los Gatos CA also 46 Shorecliff Rd Corona del Mar CA 92625 Office: Disneyland Anaheim CA 92802 ☆

FOWLER, SISTER MARY CHARLOTTE, coll. pres.; b. Mechanicsville, Md., Aug. 26, 1899; d. Thomas Henry and Charlotte (Burch) Fowler; student St. Mary's Acad., Leonardtown, Md., 1916-17, 18-19, U. Ky., summers 1921-25, Sisters' Coll., Washington, 1926- 1926- 27; Ph.D., Cath. U. Am., 1938. Joined Congregation Sisters of Charity of Nazareth, 1920; tchr. high sch. to 1933, coll. math., 1937—; faculty Nazareth Coll. (name changed to Catherine Spalding Coll.), 1937-61, head dept. math., 1950-61, pres., 1961—. Mem. Math. Assn. Am., Am. Math. Soc. Address: Catherine Spalding Coll Louisville KY 40203

FOWLER, MELVIN LEO, educator; archeologist; b. Gordon, Neb., Dec. 3, 1924; s. George Lincoln and Velma (Baber) F.; student Graceland Coll., 1942-43; B.S., Purdue U., 1946; M..A., U. Chgo., 1949, Ph.D., 1959; m. Dorothy Mae Mills, Mar. 26, 1948; children—Michael Q., Erika Jae, Kirstin Angela, Arthur Lincoln. Civil engr. CAA, Dubuque, Ia., 1946; curator anthropology Ill. State Mus., Springfield, 1949-59; asst. prof. anthropology U. Mus., So. Ill. U., 1959-64, asso. prof., 1964-66; prof. anthropology U. Wis., Milw., 1966—. Dir. Ill. Archeol. Survey, Wis. Archeol. Survey, Archeol. Research, Inc. Served with USMCR, 1943-45. NSF sr. postdoctoral fellow, 1964-65. Fellow Am. Anthrop. Assn., A.A.A.S. Home: 3253 N Summit St Milwaukee WI 53211

FOWLER, PAUL CLIFTON, educator; b. Hastings, Neb., Feb. 9, 1922; s. Thomas John and Esther (Edna) F.; B.A., Chadron (Neb.) State Coll., 1943; M.A., U. Colo., 1947; Ph.D., Ind. U., 1956; m. Alice Swaum, May 29, 1949; children—Mary Ruth, Elizabeth Anne, Barbara Lee. Instr., Gen. Motors Inst., 1947-49; teaching fellow, then instr. Ind. U., 1951-56; prof. polit. sci. Ind. State U., 1956—, chmn. dept., 1965—. Treas. M.S. Hope Chest of Vigo County; mem. legislative com. Ind. Council Chs. Served to lt. (j.g.) USNR, 1943-46. Mem. Am., Midwest polit. scis. assns., Ind. Acad. Social Sci. Home: RR 1 West Terre Haute IN 47885 Office: Dept Polit Sci Ind State U Terre Haute IN 47809

FOWLER, RAY WARREN, educator; b. Stanley, N.D., Apr. 20, 1905; s. George Warren and Hattie A. (Ward) F.; B.A., Union Coll., Lincoln, Neb., 1929; M.S. U. Ida., 1941; Ph.D., U. Neb., 1951; m. Alice Elizabeth Carr, July 24, 1929. Mathematics instr. Maplewood Acad., 1929-35; prin. Shevenne River Acad., 1935-41; prof. bus. adminstrn. Union Coll., 1941-51; prin. Auburn Acad., 1951-54; dean Pacific Union Coll., 1954-55, pres., 1955-63; bus. mgr. Union Coll., Lincoln, Neb., 1963-64, pres., 1964-70; tchr. dept. bus. and econs. Walla Walla Coll., part-time, 1970—. Rotarian. Office: Walla Walla Coll College Place WA

FOWLER, RAYMOND DALTON, Jr., educator, psychologist; b. Jasper, Ala., Dec. 22, 1930; s. Raymond Dalton and Willie (Sanders) F.; student Vanderbilt U., 1948-50; B.A., U. Ala., 1952, M.A., 1953; Ph.D., Pa. State U., 1957; m. Nancy Allebach, Aug. 13, 1955; children—Karen Sidney, Derek Tyson, Michael Alan. Mem. faculty U. Ala., 1956—, dir. psychol. clinic, 1958-65, prof. psychology, chmn. dept., 1965-70; mem. nat adv. com. on alcoholism Dept. Health, Edn. and Welfare; cons. Ala. Dept. Mental Health div. alcoholism, Ala., Vocational Rehab. Assn., VA, Ga. Dept. Mental Health, Roche Labs. Vice chmn. bd. dirs. Rehab. Research Found.; mem. profl. adv. bd. Ala. Assn. Mental Health; mem. faculty past chmn. bd. Southeastern Sch. Alcohol Studies; v.p. Ala. Council Human Relations; mem. Ala. Bd. Examiners Psychology. Diplomate Am. Bd. Examiners Profl. Psychology. Fellow Soc. Personality Assessment; mem. Am. (counsel reps.), Ala. (past pres.) psychol. assns., Am. Assn. U. Profs., A.A.A.S., Southeastern Psychol. Assn. (mem. exec. bd. Pres. elect), Sigma Xi, Phi Kappa Phi. Developed method interpreting p personality tests by computer, Home: 10 Hillcrest St Tuscaloosa AL 35401. Office: PO Box 6234 University AL 35486

FOWLER, REX H., lawyer; b. Ottawa, Ill., Aug. 27, 1893; grad. Drake U., 1917. Admitted to Ia. bar, 1917; mem. firm Bradshaw, Fowler, Proctor & Fairgrave, Des Moines. Mem. Am., Ia., Polk County bar assns., Internat. Assn. Ins. Counsel. Office: Des Moines Bldg Des Moines IA 50309*

FOWLER, RICHARD BROSING, newspaper editor; b. Sedalia, Mo., Aug. 15, 1902; s. Richard Dillon and Mathilda Geyer (Brosing) F.; student Westminister Coll., Fulton, Mo., 1919-21, U. Mo., 1926-27; B.S. in Commerce, Washington U., St. Louis, 1923; m. Elinor Carr Montgomery, Feb. 9, 1924; children—Richard Brosing, Lee Montgomery, Giles Merrill. Mem. staff Kansas City (Mo.) Star, 1930- -, editor editorial page, 1954-60, dir., 1958—, editor, 1960-67, pres., -, roving corr., 1968-. Trustee Childrens Mercy Hosp.; bd. dirs. Midwest Research Inst. Mem. Sigma Delta Chi, Beta Theta Pi. Author: Leaders in Our Town, 1952. Co-author: City of the Future, 1950. Home: 810 W 57th St Kansas City MO 64113 Office: Kansas City Star 18th and Grand Sts Kansas City MO 64108

FOWLER, RICHARD GILDART, physicist; b. Albion, Mich., June 13, 1916; S. Rufus Alexander and Ethel Alberta (Gildart) F.; A.B., Albion Coll., 1936; M.S., U. Mich., 1939, Ph.D., 1942; postgrad. Christ Ch. (Oxford, Eng.), 1953-54; m. Frances Mirian Holmes, Aug. 26, 1930; children—Lynne Carol, Nancy Barbara, Patricia Anne, Richard Gerald. Research asst. Dow Chem. Co., 1936-38; grad. research asst. U. Mich., 1938-42, research physicist, 1943-46; asst. prof. physics N.C. State Coll., 1942; asst. to asso. to prof. U. Okla., Norman, 1946-61, research prof., 1961—, chmn. dept. physics, 1955-59, 66-68, chmn. Sch. Engring. Physics, 1948-53, 55-62, v.p. Research Inst., 1962-64. Carroll fellow U. Sydney (Australia), 1963; Fulbright lectr., 1963; chmn. physics fellowship panel NSF 1959-61. Guggenheim fellow Oxford U., 1952-3. Fellow Okla. Acad. Scis., Am. Phys. Soc. (chmn. fluid dynamics div. 1968), Phys. Soc. London; mem. A.A.A.S., Am. Assn. U. Profs., Am. Inst. Physics (regional counsellor 1964-66), Phi Beta Kappa, Sigma Xi, Sigma Pi Sigma (hon.), Sigma Tau, Delta Tau Delta, Gamma Alpha, Asso. editor Physics of Fluids, 1964-68. Address: Dept Physics Univ Okla 440 W Brooks Norman, OK 73069.

FOWLER, ROBERT DUDLEY, physicist, chemist, sculptor; b. San Francisco, June 27, 1905; s. Frank Duthan and Anna Violet (de Groot) F.; B.S., U. Cal., 1926; M.S., U. Mich., 1928, Ph.D., 1931. Instr. chemistry, U. of Cal., 1930-35; instr. chemistry Johns Hopkins, 1936, asso. in chemistry, 1936-40, asso. prof., 1940-43, prof., 1943-52, chmn. dept. chemistry 1947-52; asso. leader, div. chemistry and metallurgy Los Alamos Sci. Lab., 1952- 56, leader CMF div., 1956-70, research adviser, 1970-71. Chem. engring research pilot plant devel. for NDRC and Manhattan District, U.S. Engrs., 1941-45. Mem. bd. trustees, and sci. adv. bd. brookhaven Nat. Lab. of AEC, 1946-49. Mem. Am. Chem. Soc., Am. Phys. Soc., Phi Beta Kappa, Alpha Chi Sigma, Phi Lambda Upsilon, Gamma Alpha, Sigma Xi. Republican. Unitarian. Contbr. research papers to tech. jours. Sculptor portrait bust Surf Rider. Home: 735 46th St Los Alamos NM 87544

FOWLER, ROBERT HOWARD, mag. editor; b. Monroe, N.C., July 2, 1926; s. James Wiley and Stella (Mundy) F.; student Guilford (N.C.) Coll., 1946-48; A.B., U. N.C., 1950; M.S. in Journalism , Columbia, 1954; m. Beverly Jeanne Utley, June 30, 1950; children—Wade Utley, Alyce Mundy, Robert Howard; Susanna Jeanne. Reporter, Reidsville (N.C.) Rev., 1950; reporter, asst. city editor Greensboro (N.C.) Daily News, 1950-55; city editor St. Petersburg (Fla.) Times, 1955-56; editorial writer Harrisburg (Pa.) Patriot-News, 1956-60; founder, editor Civil War Times Illustrated, 1959—; Am. History Illustrated, 1966—; v.p., sec. Hist. Times, Inc., 1960-69, pres., 1968—. Dir. People-to-People book drive, 1959. Served with USNR, 1944-46. Recipient prizes for editorial and pub. service Pa. Newspaper Publ. Assn. Mem. Am. Soc. Mag. Editors, Nat. Hist. Soc. (founder, pres.), pres.), Company Mil. Historians, Sigma Delta Chi. Democrat. Methodist. Author: Album of the Lincoln Murder, 1965; also articles. Home: 703 Hilltop Dr New Cumberland PA 17070 Office: Am History Illustrated Cameron and Kelker Sts Harrisburg PA 17105

FOWLER, ROBERT LAWRENCE, fgn. service officer; b. Roanoke, La., Sept. 16, 1910; s. Warren Robert and Mary Lorena (McNabb) F.; A.A., Los Angeles Jr. Coll., 1931; A.B., U. Cal. at Los Angeles, 1934, M.A., 1935; Ph.D., U. Neb., 1941; m. Oletha E. Paul, Aug. 1939 (div. Sept. 1952); 1 dau., Bobette M. Instr. botany Colo. State U., 1936- 38; sr. tchr. agr. Manzanar War Relocation Authority, 1942-43; agrl. research adviser Office Fgn. Agrl. Relations Dept. Agr., Ecuador, 1943-52; adviser tropical horticulture FOA, Brazil, 1952-59, Colombia, 1959-60; asst. chief Latin Am. br. ICA, Washington, 1960-62; asst. chief agr. and rural devel., tech. adv. staff East Asia AID, 1962-65, chief, 1965-68; dep. asst. dir. agr. USOM, AID, Bangkok, Thailand, 1968—. Recipient USOM meritorious service citation, 1959. Fellow A.A.A.S.; mem. Internat. Devel. Soc., Asia Soc., Sigma Xi, Beta Beta Beta. Rotarian. Contbr. articles profl. jours. Home: 2674 Olive St Huntington Park CA 90255 Office: USOM APO San Francisco CA 96346

FOWLER, ROBERT MACLAREN, lawyer, assn. exec.; b. Peterborough, Ont., Can., Dec. 7, 1906; s. Edward Bruce and Genevieve Winnifred (Amey) F.; B.A. with honors, U. Toronto, 1928; grad. Osgoode Hall Law Sch., 1931; LL.D., U. Montreal, 1961; m. Sheila Gordon Ramsay, June 23, 1934; children—Diana, Robert, Bruce, Philip, Robin. Admitted to Ont. bar, 1931; with McMaster, Montgomery, Fleury & Co., Toronto, 1931-37; legal sec. Royal Commn. on Dominion Provincial Relations, 1937-39; with McCarthy & McCarthy, Toronto, 1939-45; gen. counsel, sec. Wartime Prices and Trade Bd., Ottawa, Can., 1942-45; asso. firm Gowling & Henderson, Ottawa, 1945—. Chmn. Royal Commn. on Broadcasting, 1955-57. Recipient Medal of Service, Order of Can., 1967. Mem. Canadian Pulp and Paper Assn. (pres. 1945—), Econ. Council of Canada, Canadian Inst. Internat. Affairs (pres. 1945-50), Canadian C. of C. (past chmn. exec. council). Clubs: Mt. Royal, St. James' (Montreal); University (Toronto); Seigniory (Montebello, Que.). Home: 36 Summit Circle Westmount Quebec Canada Office: Sun Life Bldg Montreal Quebec Canada

FOWLER, SAMUEL BENJAMIN, physician; b. Nashville, Dec. 5, 1913; s. Charles Clark and Elizabeth (Love) F.; student Vanderbilt U., 1931-34; M.D., U. Tenn., 1937; m. Adelaide Bellan, July 7, 1945; children—Elizabeth Love, Barbara, Adelaide, Samuel Benjamin III. Intern Nashville Gen. Hosp., 1938-39; resident Los Angeles Orthopedic Hosp., 1939-42; surgeon Douglas Aircraft, Eritrea, East Africa, 1942-43; pvt. practice medicine, specializing in orthopedic surgery, Nashville, 1947—; clin. prof. orthopedic surgery Vanderbilt U. Served to maj. AUS, 1944-47. Mem. Am. Orthopedic Assn., Am. Acad. Orthopedic Surgery (past pres.), Clin. Orthopedic Soc. (past pres.), Am. Soc. Surgery of Hand (past pres.), A.C.S., Nashville Surg. Soc. (past pres.), So. Med. Assn. (past chmn. orthopedic sect.). Presbyn. Clubs: Belle Meade Country; Blue Grass Country. Contbr. articles to med. jours. Home: 3800 Woodlawn Dr Nashville TN 32703 Office: 1919 Hayes St Nashville TN 32715

FOWLER, STEWART HAMPTON, educator; b. St. Paul, July 20, 1922; s. Talbert Bass and Doris Ernestine (Blitch) F.; B.S.A., U. Fla., 1947; M.S., Auburn U., 1950; Ph.D., Tex. A. and M. U., 1954; m. Rachel Ann Summerford, Mar. 18, 1950; children— Stewart Hampton, James Jackson, Amy Margaret. Livestock feed salesman John W. Eshelman & Sons, Tampa, Fla., 1947; livestock buyer Lykes Bros., Tampa, 1947-48; grad. teaching asst., instr. Auburn U., 1848-51; grad. teaching asst., instr. Tex. A. and M. U., 1951-54; asst. prof. animal sci. U. Md., 1954-55; asso. prof. animal sci. Wash. State U., 1955-58; prof. animal sci. La. State U., 1958-69; head dept. animal sci. Miss. State U., 1969—. Asst. dir. Stockmen's Sch., Phoenix. Tribal chief, nation chief YMCA Indian Guide Program for Boys, 1962-65. Served with USNR, 1943-46. Recipient Outstanding Tchr. award La. State U. chpt. Gamma Sigma Delta, 1962; Distinguished Tchr. award Am. Soc. Animal Sci., 1970. Fellow A.A.A.S.; mem. Am. Soc. Animal Sci., Soc. Study Reprodn., Am. Genetics Assn., Am. Soc. Range Mgmt., Sigma Xi, Gamma Sigma Delta, Phi Kappa Phi, Alpha Zeta. Methodist (bd. mem.). Author: The Marketing of Livestock and Meat, 1957; Beef Production in the South, 1969. Home: 905 Poplar Rd Starkville MS 39759

FOWLER, WARD SCOTT, physiologist; b. Summerfield, Kan., Oct. 24, 1915; s. John Joseph and Leila (Moore) F.; A.B., Swarthmore Coll., 1937; M.D., Harvard, 1941; m. Joan Kelley, Sept. 4, 1940; children—Robert Scott, Thomas Richard. Research fellow A.C.P., 1947-48. USPHS, 1948-50; faculty dept. physiology U. Pa. Grad. Sch. Medicine, 1946-51. asso. prof. physiology, 1951; cons. physiology Mayo Clinic, Rochester, Minn., 1952—; prof. physiology Mayo Found., U. Minn. Grad. Sch., 1956—. Mem. anesthesiology tng. com. NIH, 1966-68. Served to capt., M.C., AUS, 1942-46. Mem. Am. Physiol. Soc., Am. Soc. Clin. Investigation, Central Soc. Clin. Research, Soc. Exptl. Biology and Medicine. Mem. editorial bd. Am. Soc. Clin. Investigation, 1953-58, Am. Physiol. Soc., 1956-62. Home: 713 13th Av SW Rochester MN 55901 Office: Mayo Clinic Rochester MN 55901

FOWLER, WILLIAM ALFRED, physicist; b. Pitts., Aug. 9, 1911; s. John McLeod and Jennie Summers (Watson) F.; B. Eng. Physics, Ohio State Univ., 1933; Ph.D., Cal. Inst. Tech., 1936; m. Ardiane Olmsted, Aug. 24, 1940 children—Mary Emily, Martha Summers. Research fellow Cal. Inst. Tech., Pasadena, 1936-39, asst. prof. physics, 1939-42, asso. prof. 1942-46, prof. physics, 1946-70, Inst. prof. physics, 1970—. Fulbright lectr. Cavendish lab. U. Cambridge, 1954-55; Guggenheim fellow, 1954-55; Guggenheim fellow St. John's Coll. and dept. applied math. and theoretical physics U. Cambridge, 1961-62, vis. fellow Inst. Theoretical Astronomy, summers 1967-71; asst. dir. research, div. 3, NDRC, 1941- 45; tech. observer. office of field service OSRD, (South Pacific Theatre), 1944; sci. dir., project VISTA, dept. Defense, 1951-52; mem. nat. sci. bd. NSF, 1968—; mem. space sci. bd. Nat. Acad. Scis., 1970—; mem. space program adv. council NASA, 1971; sometime named lectr., univs., colls. Bd. dirs. Am. Friends of Cambridge U., 1970—. Recipient Naval Ordnance Devel. award U.S. Navy, 1945, Medal of Merit, 1948; Lamme medal Ohio State U., 1952; Liége medal U. Liége, 1955; Barnard medal for contbn. to sci. Columbia, 1965; Apollo Achievement award NASA, 1969. Benjamin Franklin fellow Royal Soc. Arts. Fellow Am. Phys. Soc. (Tom W. Bonner prize, 1970), Am. Acad. Arts and Scis., Royal Astronom. Soc.; mem. Nat. Acad. Scis., A.A.A.S., Am. Inst. Physics, Am. Astron. Soc., N.Y. Acad. Scis., Am. Assn. U. Profs., Am. Philos. Soc., Soc. Royal Sci. Liege (corr. mem.), Brit. Assn. Advancement Sci., Sigma Xi, Tau Beta Pi, Tau Kappa Epsilon. Democrat. Clubs: The Athenaeum (Pasadena); Cosmos (Washington). Contbr. numerous articles to profl. jours. Home: 1565 San Pasqual St Pasadena CA 91109

FOWLER, WILLIAM EDWARD, Jr., lawyer; b. Pitts., Apr. 20, 1919; s. William Edward and Helen (Kerr) F.; grad. Phillips Exeter Acad., 1938; B.S., Yale, 1942; J.D., U. Mich., 1948; m. Jean Louise Moore, Apr. 24, 1943; children—Mary Jane, John Moore, William Edward III, James Kerr. Admitted to Ohio Bar, 1948, since practiced in Youngstown; partner firm Harrington, Huxley & Smith, 1955—. Mem. Ohio Bd. Bar Examiners, 1965-70. Active Youngstown Community Chest; mem. Boardman Kical Sch. Dist. Bd. Edn., 1960—; mem. Yale Alumni Bd., 1958—. Served to lt. USNR, World War II. Fellow Am., Ohio bar founds.; mem. Am., Ohio (council dels.; exec. com. 1963-66) Mahoning County (sec.-treas. 1956-58) bar assns., Pa.-Ohio Yale Alumni Assn. (sec.-treas.). Home: 50 Forest Hill Rd Youngstown OH 44512 Office: Mahoning Bank Bldg Youngstown OH 44503

FOWLER, WILLIAM GEORGE exec.; b. Lima, O., Apr. 1, 1932; B.S., U. San Francisco, 1954; M.S., Stanford University, 1956; m. Rosemarie Lois Brown, May 15, 1955; 1 son, Anthony Robinson. Sales rep. Ames-Brockton Fabricated Products, Akron, O., 1956-58, sales mgr. Coshocton, Ohio, 1959-61, gen. manager plant, 1961-68, v.p. sales, 1968--. Instr. bus. Coshocton Jr. College, 1968-69. Secretary Coshocton YMCA, 1960-61; active Boy Scouts of America. Named Man of Year, Coshocton Junior Chamber of Commerce, 1968. Mem. Coshocton C. of C. (vice president 1967-68, pres. 1969-70), English Speaking Union, Coshocton Sertoma Club, Nat. Assn. Mfrs., Sales Executives Institute, Phi Beta Kappa, Sigma Chi, Phi Mu. Democrat. Mem. Christian Ch. (lay leader). Mason (32, Shriner). Clubs: Coshocton Country, Coshocton City, Running Deer Country. Home: 2d Av Coshocton OH Office: 3d Av Coshocton OH

FOWLES, GRANT ROBERT, educator, physicist; b. Fairview, Utah, Sept. 19, 1919; s. Jacob T. and Elodia (Allred) F.; B.S., U. Utah, 1941; Ph.D., U. Cal., 1950; m. Martha J. Garrett, Dec. 30, 1942; children—Robert Earl, Janice Louise, Richard Garrett, Marilyn Elizabeth. Asst. prof. physics U. Utah, 1950-55, asso. prof., 1955-62, prof., 1962—. Served to lt. USNR, 1942-46. Mem. Am. Inst. Physics, Optical Soc. Am., Am. Assn. Physics Tchrs., N.Y. Acad. Scis. Author: Analytical Mechanics, 1962; Introduction to Modern Optics, 1968. Home: 1864 Princeton Av Salt Lake City UT 84108

FOWLES, JOHN, author; b. Essex, Eng., Mar. 31, 1926; s. Robert and Gladys (Richards) F.; honours degree in French, Oxford U., 1950; m. Elizabeth Whitton, Apr. 2, 1954. Author: The Collector, 1963; The Aristos, 1964; The Magus, 1966; The French Lieutenant's Woman, 1969. Address: care Jonathan Cape 30 Bedford Sq London WC 1 England

FOWLIE, WALLACE, author, literary critic; b. Brookline, Mass., Nov. 8, 1908; s. Wallace Bruce and Helen (Adams) F.; A.B., Harvard, 1930, A.M., 1933, Ph.D., 1936. Fellow Ezra Stiles Coll., Yale; faculty French lit. Yale, 1940-45, U. Chgo., 1945-49, Bennington (Vt.) Coll., 1950-62; James B. Duke prof. French, Duke, 1964—. Guggenheim fellow, 1948-49. Author: Sleep of the Pigeon, 1948; Pantomime, 1951; Age of Surrealism, 1953; Mallarmé, 1953; Paul Claudel; Studies in Modern European Literature and Thought, 1957; A Guide to contemporary French Literature: From Valéry to Sartre, 1957; Dionysus in Paris, 1960; A Reading of Proust, 1964; André Gide: His Life and Art, 1965; Rimbaud: A Critical Study, 1965; Jean Cocteau: The History of a Poet's Age, 1965; Climate of Violence: The French Literary Tradition from Baudelaire to the Present, 1967; The French Critic: 1549- 1967, 1968. Translator: The Journals of Jean Cocteau, 1955; Seamarks (Saint-John Perse), 1958; Two Dramas of Claudel, 1960; Complete Works of Rimbaud, 1966; many other French works. Fgn. editor Poetry mag., 1950-70. Home: 17-D Valley Terrace Durham NC 27707

FOWLKES, JOHN GUY author, educator; b. Greenville, Mo., July 8, 1898; s. John Thomas and Lola (Burroughs) F.; A.B. Ouachita Coll., Ark., 1916; A.M. Columbia, 1921, Ph.D., 1922; m. Dec. 27, 1917 (wife dec. 1925); m. 2d. Helen Agatha Karlen, May 20, 1928; children—Sarah Anne, Nancy Lee. Asst. in mathematics, Ouachita Coll., 1914-16; tchr., high sch. prin., and headmaster in Ark. and N.Y., 1916-22; asst. prof. edn. U. Wis., 1922-24, asso. prof., 1924-26, prof., 1927-66, C.J. Anderson prof. ednl. adminstrn., 1966—, dir. summer session, 1942-54, dean sch. edn., 1947- 54; vis. prof. U. Cal. Berkeley, 1926-27; ednl. adviser Ministry Edn. India, 1954-56. Dir. of Wis. Improvement Programtchr. edn. and local school systems, 1959—. Mem. Miss., Va., Nev. State Educational Survey staffs; dir. surveys including Pasadena, Fort Worth, Flint, Kan City, Fellow A.A.A.S.; mem. N.E.A., Am. Assn. Sch. Adminstrs., Am. Assn. U. Profs., Am. Ednl. Research Assn., Phi Delta Kappa, Alpha Kappa Lambda. Conglist. Mason. Clubs: Maple Bluff Country, University. Author: School Bonds; Financial Accounting for Schools; several textbooks, including Heathy Life Series; also series of charts Democracy at Work and bulls. of Bur. Ednl. Research, U. Wis.; (with Knezevich) Business Management of Local School Systems, 1960. Mem. cons. editorial bd. The Nation's Schools; editorial adviser A. J. Nystrom & Co.; adv. editor Exploration Series in Edn., Harper & Row. Home: 529 Woodward Dr Madison WI 53704 ☆

FOWLKES, RICHARD WILLIAMSON, physician; b. Martinsville, Va., Sept. 26, 1893; s. Williamson Dickerson and Sara Alice (Lawrence) F.; grad. Danville Sch. for Boys, 1911; A.B., Washington and Lee U., 1951; M.D., U. Va., 1920; m. Louise Fishburn, Nov. 15, 1930 (div. July 15, 1934); 1 dau., Louise Fishburn; m. 2d, Ferebee Fenner, Mar. 1, 1940. Interne, U. Va., Hosp., 1919-20, Bellevue Hosp., 1921, Chgo. Health Bd., 1922; instr. in dermatology and syphilology Columbia, 1922-24; in pvt. practice, specializaing in dermatology and syphilology, Richmond, Va., 1925—; asso. prof. Med. Coll. Va., 1939-47, prof. dermatology and syphilology, 1947-59, clin. prof. dermatology, 1959—; cons. Med. Coll. Va. Hosp., Johnston-Willis Hosp. Mem. Am. Dermatol. Assn., Soc. Investigative Dermatology, A.M.A., So. Med. Assn. (vice chmn. sect. on dermatology and syphilology 1940, chmn. 1948), Va. Med. Soc., Richmond Acad. Medicine, Balt.and Washington Dermatol. Soc., Gen. Alumni Assn. of Washington and Lee U. (pres. 1940), S.R., Phi Beta Kappa, Phi Kappa Sigma, Phi Chi, Omicron Delta Kappa. Episcopalian. Club: Commonwealth (pres. 1955- 57). Home: 1418 Park Av Richmond VA 23220 Office: Professional Bldg Richmond VA 23219

FOX, ABLIAH UPSON, investment exec.; b. Bklyn., Jan. 20, 1905; s. Abijah Charles and Helen Manlove (Shawhan) F.; Litt.B. cum laude, Rutgers U., 1926; m. Isabel Place Sullivan, Nov. 26, 1935; children—Abijah Shawhan, Jarvis Powell, Suzanne Angevine. Accountant and pro-mgr. Nat. City Bank, Tokyo, Japan, 1926-34; partner Swan, Culbertson & Fritz, investment bankers and brokers, Shanghai, Hongkong and Manila, 1934-41; dep. dir. fgn. funds control U.S. Treasury Dept., Washington, 1941-44, dir. Office of Surplus Property, 1945, dep. dir. finance div. Mil. Govt., Germany, 1945-46; chmn. and dir. Mahieson Chem. Corp., N.Y.C., 1946-48; treas. Am. Thread Co., 1948-59, dir., 1949-59, v.p., 1950-59; gen. partner investment firm Hayden, Stone & Co., 1959-62; v.p. Hayden, Stone, Inc., 1962—. State rep. 152d dist. Conn. Gen. Assembly, 1968—. Episcopalian. Clubs: Union League (N.Y.C.); Belle Haven, Indian Harbor Yacht (Greenwich, Conn). Home: 200 North St Greenwich CT 06830 Office: 2 Greenwich Plaza Greenwich CT 06830

FOX, BERTRAND, economist; b. Williams Bay, Wis., Feb. 28, 1908; s. Philip and Ethel Lillian (Snow) F.; A.B., Northwestern, 1929; A.M., Harvard, 1933, Ph.D., 1934; m. Mary Kent Ziegler, Dec. 21, 1935 (div. 1950); children—Philip, Thomas, Kenneth; m. 2d, Patricia Noyes O'Neill, Jan. 20, 1951; children—Ann Snow, Peter Noyes, Joan Pallen. Statistician Harvard Econ. Soc., 1929-32; instr. Harvard, 1931-35, prof. bus. adminstrn. Grad. Sch. Bus. Adminstrn., 1949-55, Edsel Bryant Ford prof. bus adminstrn., 1955- 67, Jacob H. Schiff prof. investment banking, 1967—, dir. research, 1953- 68; asst. prof. econ. Williams Coll., 1935-40, asso. prof., 1940-45, prof. econ., 1945-49; dir. mil. div. W.P.B., Washington, 1941-44, dir. program and statis, bur., 1944-45. Cons. Army-Navy Munitions Bd., 1946- 50, NSRB, 1947-48; econ. adviser to counsel in Underwriters Anti-trust Suit, Sullivan and Cromwell et al, 1948-53; spl. cons. ODM, 1953-58; mem. program com. Office Emergency Preparedness, 1956—; cons. Nat. Shawmut Bank, 1953- 56; dir. Eberstadt Fund 1966—, Chem. Fund, 1969—, Internat. Assos., 1964. Adminstr. Merrill Found. for Advancement Financial Knowledge, Inc., 1947-62; research dir. Nat. Commn. on Money and Credit, 1958-62. Mem. Am. Econ. Assn., Phi Beta Kappa, Sigma Xi. Author: Research Report for Committee on Economic Development on Monetary and Fiscal Policy, 1919- 39, 1948. Contbr. to Explorations in Economics, 1938. Contbr. articles to Econ. Statis., 1931-39. Home: 18 Edgewood Rd Lexington MA 02173 Office: Harvard Business School Soldier's Field Boston MA 02163

FOX, BYRON LESTER, educator; b. Toledo, Jan. 7, 1906; s. Ammon Lester and Josephine (Krieghaum) F.; B.A., B.S. in Edn., Ohio State U., 1928; M.A. in Sociology, 1930, Ph.D., 1947; m. Nancy Littell, Dec. 5, 1966; 1 dau., by previous marriage, Caroline Jo (Mrs. Jack E. Heck). Tchr. English, Berea (O.) High Sch., 1928-29; asst. prof. sociology and econs. Bethany (W. Va.) Coll., 1932-36; asst. prof. sociology and anthropology Ohio Wesleyan U., 1936-40; field supr. Nat. Youth Adminstrn., Cleve., 1940- 42; personnel and adminstrv. officer Office Emergency Mgmt., Cleve., 1942-44; personnel and adminstrv. officer State Dept., 1944-46, adviser social sci., div. internat. exchange persons, 1946-47; asso. prof. sociology Syracuse U., 1947-65, acting chmn. dept., 1958-59, faculty adviser Internat. Student Orgn., 1961-64, prof. sociology No. Ariz. U., 1965-67; prof., chmn. dept. sociology and anthropology Carleton Coll., Northfield, Minn., 1967-71. Pres. Onondaga Consumers Coop., Inc., Syracuse, 1949-52. Vice chmn. Syracuse Peace Council, 1955-57. Fellow Am. Sociol. Assn.; mem. Soc. Study Social Problems (pres. 1957-58, chmn. com. standards and freedom of teaching, research and publ. 1968-69), Midwest, Eastern sociol. socs., Am. Assn. U. Profs., United World Federalists, Phi Beta Kappa (past pres. Syracuse U. chpt.), Alpha Kappa Delta (v.p. 1959-60). Democrat. Unitarian. Mason. Contbr. The New Sociology, also profl. Jours. Home: Mountainview Box 3426 West Sedona AZ 86340

FOX, CAROL, opera producer; b. Chgo., June 15, 1926; d. George Edward and Virginia (Scott) Fox; grad. Girls Latin Sch., Chgo.; pvt. voice studies with Giovanni Martinelli, Edith Mason, Vittorio Trevisan, Virgilio Lazzari, also studied in Italy; Mus.D. (hon.), Chgo. Conservatory, 1955; LL.D., Rosary Coll., 1958; L.H.D., Lake Forest Coll., 1961; m. Dr. C. Larkin Flanagan, June 22, 1957; 1 daughter, Victoria. Founder Lyric Theatre of Chgo. (became Lyric Opera of Chgo.), 1952, pres., gen. mgr., 1952-56, gen. mgr., 1956—. Mem. women's bd. U. Chgo., Loyola U. Decorated Cavaliere al Merito della Republica Italiana; Commendatore nell' Ordine Al Merito della Republica Italiana; recipient Chgo. medal merit, 1958; Internat. Achievement award World Peace, Trade Fair and Chgo. Assn. Commerce and Industry, 1959; Chicagoan Yr. Arts, Jr. Assn. Commerce and Industry, 1961. Mem. Chgo. Jr. League. Office: 20 N Wacker Dr Chicago IL 60606

FOX, CHARLES RALPH, selective service ofcl.; b. Nicholas County, W.Va., Nov. 16, 1912; s. Joseph Bud and Amma (Walker) F.; student elec. engring., Internat. Corr. Sch., 1935-40; grad., honors, Indsl. Coll. Armed Forces, 1962; course nuclear physics, Johns Hopkins, 1946; m. Vernise Jane Pritt, Feb. 9, 1935; children—Charles Warren, Janice Lynn, Roger Neill, Mark William. Pressman, Am. Fork and Hoe Co., Charleston, W.Va., 1932- 37; central office repairman Chesapeake & Potomac Tel. Co. of W.Va., Charleston, 1937-41. Enlisted W.Va. N.G., Sept. 1930, 2d lt. inf. June 1936; called to active duty with U.S. Army, Jan. 1941; attended Air Corps Advanced Flying Sch., Tex., 1941-42; rated Aircraft Observer; served with 14th A.F., China, 1944-45; duty Hdqrs. A.A.F. Washington, D.C., plans div., rank lt. col., Dec. 1945-July 1946; adj. gen. State of W.Va., rank of maj. gen., 1946-57; state dir. Selective Service, W.Va., 1948-57; state dir. civil def. W.Va., 1949-57; chief commn. and records div., nat. hdqrs. SSS, 1957-70. Decorated Bronze Star medal, Air medal, Cloud and Banner medal (Chinese Govt.), Pilot Wings (hon.), Chinese Air Force and 10 service and theatre ribbons and medals for World War II and Vietnam. Mem. Air Force Assn. (charter mem.), N.G. Assn. of U.S., Adjutants Gen. Assn. U.S. (pres. 1953-56), Am. Legion, Mil. Order World Wars (comdr. of D.C. chpt. 1966-67, sr. vice comdr. in chief 1966-69), Assn. U.S. Army, Reserve Officers Assn. (pres. D.C. dept. 1963-64), 14th Air Force Assn. Democrat. Presbyn. Mason (32, Shriner). Home: 5606 Chesterbrook Rd Washington DC 20016 Office: 5480 Wisconsin Av Chevy Chase MD 20015

FOX, CHARLES WELFORD, ret. naval officer; b. Balt., Dec. 5, 1894; s. Henry William and Mary Ella (Gressitt) F.; ed. in pub. schs., Balt., m. Aida Moore Smith, Apr. 30, 1919; children—Virginia Rachael (Mrs. K.C. Wydler), Mary Ellen, Charles Welford, Jr. Enlisted in U.S. Navy, 1913, apptd. pay clk., 1917; commd. ensign supply corps, Dec. 12, 1918, advanced through grades to vice admiral; Served at Naval Air Sta., Moutchic, Lacanau, 1918, also with No. Bombing Group, Autiques, Pas de Calais, U.S. Naval Tng. Camp, Deer Island, Mass., 1918-19, Naval Air Sta., Cape May, N.J., 1919-20; charge aviation supply div. Bur. Supplies and Accounts, Washington, 1942- 44; asst. aviation supply officer Aviation Supply Office, Phila. Pa., 1944-45; supply officer in command Navy Supply Depot, Mechanicsburg, 1945-48; apptd. dep. and asst. chief Bur. Supplies and Accounts, Navy Dept., 1948, chief and paymaster gen., 1949-51, chief of naval material, 1951-53, ret. Pres. emeritus bd. trustees St. Luke's and Children's Med. Center, Phila. Decorated Legion of Merit (with gold star). Republican. Episcopalian. Home: 5117 Bangor Dr Kensington, MD 20795.

FOX, DONALD E., chemist, coll. dean; b. Elberon, Ia., Jan. 1, 1905; s. John W. and Anna (Ludvicek) F.; A.B., U. Ia., 1927, M.S., Ph.D., 1936; postgrad. U. Neb., 1930; m. Viola C. Wiemers, Jan. 1, 1965. Instr. sci. Holdrege (Neb.) High Sch., 1927-35; instr. chemistry, head dept. chemistry, chmn. div. sci. and math., dean Sch. Natural and Social Scis., Kearney (Neb.) State Coll., 1936—. Mem. Am. Chem. Soc. (sect. chmn.) N.E.A., Phi Lambda Upsilon. Home: 10 E 30th St Kearney NB 68847

FOX, DONALD LEE, food co. exec.; b. Newport, Ky., Feb. 20, 1921; s. Stuart Charles and Eleanor (Pfirman) F.; B.A., Va. Mil. Inst., 1943; m. Elizabeth Ann Berry, May 23, 1943; children—Donald Lee II (dec.), Stuart Charles, Marion Berry. With Super Food Services, Inc., 1967—, chmn., chief exec. officer, 1968—; chmn. bd. Fame Marketing Corp., 1968—; adviser to chmn. and pres. MBS, 1968—; dir. Fisher Cheese Co., Wapakoneta, O., Ind. Grocers Alliance Distbg. Co., Chgo. Mem. Pres. Com. on Mental Retardation, 1970—; dist. chmn. Citizens for Eisenhower-Nixon, 1956; chmn. Montgomery County (O.) Republican Finance Campaign, 1952-53; mem. Ohio Rep. Resources Com., Ohio Rep. Finance Com. Vice pres., trustee Loren M. Berry Found., Dayton, O. Served to capt. AUS, 1943-46. Mem. Exec. Order Ohio Commodores. Episcopalian. Clubs: Dayton Country; Racquet Internat. (Miami Beach, Fla.); Cap d'Antibes (France); Palm Bay (Biscayne Point, Miami, Fla.). Home: 224 Grandon Rd Dayton OH 45419 Office: 3185 Elbee Rd Dayton OH 45439

FOX, EDWARD ALEXANDER, engring. educator; b. N.Y.C., Aug. 7, 1920; s. Samuel A. and Rebecca (Serber) F.; grad. Fieldston Sch., 1937; B.S., Harvard, 1941; B.S., Columbia, 1947, Ph.D., 1958; m. Sally Wister Ingersoll, Jan. 29, 1949; children—Deborah (dec.), Patricia, Susan, Barbara. Engaged as constrn. engr., 1947-51; mem. faculty Rensselaer Poly Inst., 1954—, prof. mechanics, 1963—. Served as officer USNR, 1942-46. Mem. Am. Soc. M.E., Am. Assn. U. Profs., N.A.A.C.P., Sigma Xi. Author: Mechanics, 1967. Home: 1429 Dean St Schenectady NY 12309. Office: Dept Mechanics Rensselaer Poly Inst Troy NY 12181

FOX, EDWARD GEORGE, mining engr.; b. Pottsville, Pa., Dec. 27, 1900; s. Jacob W. and Jennie M. (Kennedy) F.; student Mercersburg Acad.; E.M., Pa. State Coll., 1924; m. Eleanor R. Jones, Nov. 21,

1926; children—Marcia (Mrs. Richard B. Ryon), Edward George. Gen. mgr. Madeira, Hill & Co., 1936, Colonial Collieries Co., 1937-43; gen. supt., later pres. Phoenix Contracting Co., 1943-46; pres. Shen-Penn Prodn. Co., Shenandoah, Pa., Co., Phila., 1947-51; pres., 1951-56, also pres. dir. subsidiaries; pres. Bituminous Coal Operators' Assn., Washington, 1956-68; now cons. in engring. Pottsville, Pa.; chmn. bd. Wagner Assos., Inc.; dir. Pa. Nat. Bank & Trust Co., Pottsville, Pa. Mem. Am. Inst. Mining Engrs., Mine Insps. Inst. Am., Pa. Profl. Engrs., Rocky Mt. Coal Mining-Inst., Am. Ming Congress (dir.), Nat. Safety Council (dir.), Phi Gamma Delta. Presbyn. Clubs: Union of Cleve.; University (Washington); Duquesne (Pitts.); Pottsville. Home: 1507 Mahantongo St Pottsville PA 17901 Office: World Center Bldg 16th and K Sts NW Washington WA 20006

FOX, EDWARD INMAN, educator, author; b. Nashville, Aug. 22, 1933; s. Herbert Franklin and Ladye (Inman) F.; B.A., Vanderbilt U., 1954. M.A., 1958; student U. Montpellier (France), 1956-57; A.M., Princeton, 1959, Ph.D., 1961. Teaching asst. Vanderbilt U., 1957-58; preceptor European lit. Princeton, 1959; asst. prof. Romance langs. Vanderbilt U., 1960-64, acting dir. admissions, 1960-61, asso. prof. Spanish, 1964-66; asso. prof. Romance langs. U. Mass., 1966-67; prof. Hispanic studies, chmn. dept. Vassar Coll., 1967—, acting dean faculty, 1971-72; bd. dirs. Internat. Inst. Spain, 1967- -; cons. Library of Congress on Spanish newspapers. Served to lt. (j.g.), USNR, 1954-56; comdr. Res. Woodrow Wilson fellow, 1956-57; Fulbright scholar France, 1956-57; Herbert Montgomery Bergen fellow Princeton, 1958-59; grantee Am. Philos. Soc., 1963, 68; Fulbright research scholar Spain, 1965-66; Guggenheim fellow, 1970-71. Mem. Assn. Princeton Grad. Alumni (bd. govs.), Internat. Assn. Hispanists, Modern Lang. Assn. (mem. exec. and nominating com. Spanish 4, 1965-68, chmn. Spanish 5, 1968), Phi Beta Kappa, Omicron Delta Kappa, Sigma Alpha Epsilon. Author: Azorin as a Literary Critic, 1962; also articles, translations poetry. Editor: La voluntad, 1969; Antonio Azorin, 1970; co-editor; Spanish Thought and Letters in the Twentieth Century, 1966. Address: Vassar Coll Poughkeepsie NY 12601

FOX, EDWARD JACKSON, educator; b. St. Thomas, Ont., Can., Sept. 9, 1913; s. Jay and Anne (Jackson) F.; B.A. with honors in Econs. and Polit. Scis., U. Western Ont., 1935; M.Sc. in Econs., U. London (Eng.), 1937; Ph.D. in Econs., U. Cal. at Berkeley, 1950; m. Ruth Chesler, Sept. 9, 1959; children—Brenda Steinman (Mrs. Dennis Morgan), Gary Devenow, Sanford Lee Steinman, Lisa Terry. Came to U.S., 1953, naturalized, 1963. With OPA, 1940-41, Canadian Wartime Prices and Trade Bd., 1941-47; mem. faculty U. Western Ont., 1948-54, prof. bus. adminstrn., 1949-54, dir. bur. bus. research, 1950-53; prof. marketing U. Miami (Fla.), 1954—, chmn. dept. 1956-69; prof. marketing IMEDE Mgmt. Devel. Inst., 1968-69, Marketing Execs. Program, 1971; marketing and econ. cons. practice, 1948—. Vice pres. Jewish Vocational Service, Dade County, Fla., 1964-67; mem. Fla. adv.bd. Anti-defamation League, 1963-65; bd. dirs. Miami chpt. Am. Jewish Com., 1965-69; pres. Miami Beach chpt. UN Assn., 1956-57, Coral Gables chpt., 1962-63; bd. govs. Am. Histadrut Cultural Exchange Inst., 1965-66, mem. bus. adv., com., 1967; tech. adv. com. Nat. Jewish Population Study, 1965-67; dir. 1st Internat. Health Securities Fund, Ltd., 1969—. Fellow Brookings Instn., 1940; fellow to U. Cal.-Ford Found. workshop, 1964. Mem. Am., So. econ. assns., Am. (pres. Miami chpt. 1965-67), So. marketing assns., Sales and Marketing Execs., Alpha Kappa Psi, Alpha Delta Sigma, Beta Gamma Sigma. Order Artus. Jewish religion (bd. dirs. temple 1963-65, trustee 1966). Editor: (with David Leighton) Marketing in Canada, 1958; editorial bd. So. Jour. Bus., 1969—. Home: 7855 S W 70th St South Miami FL 33143 Office: Marketing Dept Univ Miami Coral Gables FL 33146

FOX, ELDON E., business exec.; b. Greeley, Colo., July 3, 1918; s. Austin Eugene and Ina (Ramsay) F.; B.A. cum laude, Dartmouth, 1940; postgrad. Harvard Sch. Bus., 1941; m. Nancy Kilmartin, May 1967; children—Jeffery Dennis, Gregory Alan, Lorrie Jean. Account exec. Young & Rubicam, Inc., N.Y.C., 1946-51; dir. advt., sales promotion Mpls.-Honeywell, Mpls., 1951-56; advt. mgr. Edsel div. Ford Motor Co., Dearborn, Mich., 1956-58, Edsel advt. and sales promotion M-E-L div., 1958-59; v.p., asso. mgr. Batten, Barton, Durstine & Osborn, Inc., Mpls. and St. Paul, 1959-61; v.p. Bendix Corp., Detroit, 1961-69; v.p. AMF, Inc., N.Y.C., 1969—. Served to maj. F.A., AUS, 1942-46. Decoraed Bronze Star medal. Mem. Pub. Relations Soc. Am. Clubs: Sleepy Hollow (Scarborough, N.Y.); Pinnacle (N.Y.C.). Home: 4 Sunset Dr Chappaqua NY 10514 Office: 261 Madison Av New York City NY 10016

FOX, EUGENE JACKSON, coll. dean; b. Drumright, Okla., July 14, 1914; s. Jacob Harold and Gertrude (Jackson) F.; B.S., Central State Coll., Okla., 1938; M.A., Okla. U., 1944; Litt.D., U. Nacional de Mexico, 1951; m. Margaret Halley Dec. 24, 1942; 1 son, Steven H. Tchr.-coach Tryon (Okla.) High Sch., 1938-41; instr. Spanish, Okla. Mil. Acad., Claremore, 1944-48; asst. prof. Spanish, N.M. Mil. Inst., 1948-59; faculty Eastern N.M. U., 1959—, prof. modern langs., 1964—, dean gen. coll., 1967—; cons. in field, 1938—. Mem. N.G., 1936-38; served with USAAF, 1942-44. Recipient Fulbright award, 1958; Pres.'s Faculty award Eastern N.M. U., 1965. Mem. Modern Lang. Assn., Rocky Mountain Lang. Assn. (co-chmn. standards com. 1964), N.E.A., Phi Delta Kappa. Author: Guide for College Students, 1968; also poems, articles, fiction. Home: 129 New Mexico Dr Portales NM 88130

FOX, FRANCIS HENRY, educator, veterinarian; b. Clifton Springs, N.Y., Mar. 11, 1923; s. Henry Sylvester and Alma (Lindner) F.; D.V.M., N.Y. State Vet. Coll., 1945; m. Mildred Genevieve Cullen, Aug. 6, 1946; children—Rosanna, Laurinda, Teresa, Henry. Research asst. N.Y. State Vet. Coll.-Cornell U., 1945-46, mem. faculty, 1947—, prof. vet. medicine and obstetrics, 1953—; instr. surgery Vet. Coll., Ohio State U., 1946-47. Mem. Am. (exec. bd.mem. dist. I, 1966—). So. tier (sec.-treas. 1957-62) vet. med. assns., N.Y. State Vet. Med. Soc., N.Y.State Assn. Professions, Am. Assn. Bovine Practitioners (pres. elect 1970-71), Sigma Xi, Alpha Psi, Phi Zeta, Phi Kappa Phi. Omega Tau Sigma. Author articles in field. Home: 11 Muriel St Ithaca NY 14850

FOX, FRANK, govt. ofcl.; b. Johnstown, N.Y. Jan. 11, 1908; s. Gross and Catharine (Smith) F.; student Williams Coll., 1925; A.B., Cornell U., 1929; 1 son, James Stewart. With Chase Manhattan Bank of N.Y., 1929-31, N.Y. Trust Co., 1931-37; with 2d Nat. Bank of New Haven, 1937-41, trust officer, 1941; entered govt. service, 1946; Army mem. War Contracts Price Adjustment Bd., 1950, chmn., 1952; mem. Armed Services Renegotiation Bd., 1950, vice chmn. Army div., 1950; spl. asst. under-sec. of army, chief renegotiation affairs br., 1952-54; spl. asst. to adminstr. gen. services, 1954-56; treas. East Coast Aeronautics, Inc., 1956-58; Republic Indsl. Corp., 1957-58; financial adviser to premier of N.S., 1958-59; propr. Lebanon Farms (Conn.), 1959-62; chief of resources mgmt. State of Conn., 1962-63; finance officer U.S. Dept. Housing and Urban Devel., 1963, dir. finance for met. devel., 1968—. Served to maj. AUS, 1942-46. Home: 4817 14th St S Arlington VA Office: 451 7th St SW Washington DC

FOX, GEORGE LEWIS, bus. cons.; b. Stockton, Cal., Mar. 28, 1899; s. George William and Lillie Ann (Graves) F.; student U. Cal. at Berkeley, 1922; m. Mildred Florence Brescia, July 26, 1930 (dec. July 1965); 1 son, George Lewis; m. 2d, Edith Harris, Nov. 4, 1967. Reporter, editor Stockton Daily Ind., 1919-22; mgr. indsl. dept. Stockton C. of C., 1924-37; indsl. and traffic dir. Parr-Richmond Terminal Corp., 1937-43; mgr. indsl. dept. San Francisco C. of C., 1943-48, v.p., gen. mgr., 1948-62, exec. v.p., 1962-64; v.p., dir. Parr Indsl. Corp., 1964-71, Indio Properties, Inc.; cons. 1964—; pres. Western States Council, 1955-56. Acting chmn. German-Am. C. of C. Pacific Coast, -. Mem. Cal. C. of C. Mgrs. (hon. life mem.; past dir.), Central and No. Cal. C. of C. Execs. (past pres.), Phi Kappa Psi Alumni Assn. Clubs: Rotary, Press, Commercial, Commonwealth. Home: 161 Havenside Dr San Francisco CA 94132 Office: 555 California St San Francisco CA 94104

FOX, GORDON KINGSLEY, ins. co. exec.; b. Winnipeg, Man., Can., Mar. 31, 1913; s. Charles Harry and Ivy (Hind) F.; B.A., U. Man., 1935; m. Hazel Jean Gore, Aug. 9, 1941; 1 dau., Heather (Mrs. David George Fuller). With Imperial Life Assurance Co. of Can., Toronto, Ont., 1935—, exec. asst., 1952-64, exec. v.p., 1964-67, pres., mng. dir., 1967—; dir. IMPCO Properties, Ltd. Served with Royal Canadian Navy, 1941-45. Fellow Soc. Actuaries, Canadian Inst. Actuaries. Conservative. Mem. United Ch. Kiwanian. Clubs: Granite (Toronto), Toronto. Home: 3 Otter Crescent Toronto 12 Ontario Canada Office: 95 St Clair Av W Toronto 7 Ontario Canada

FOX, HALE DRURY, newspaper exec.; b. Los Angeles, Aug. 23, 1926; s. Walter Saxelby and Ethel (Drury) F.; student Butler U., 1950-51; B.B.A. cum laude, U. Miami (Fla.), 1953; m. Helen Caldwell, June 19, 1951; children—Hale Caldwell, Carol Drury. Staff accountant Price Waterhouse & Co., C.P.A.'s, Pitts., 1952-58; with Wheeling-Pitts. Steel Co., 1958-70, comptroller, 1966-70, officer, dir. several subsidiaries; comptroller The Ogden Newspapers, Inc., 1970—; lectr. accounting Wheeling Coll., 1958—. Bd. dirs., sec. Wheeling Home, 1957—; bd. dirs., treas. Wheeling Country Day Sch., 1967—. Served with USNR, 1944-46. C.P.A., W.Va. Mem. Nat. Assn. Accountants, Am. Inst. C.P.A.'s, Kappa Sigma. Episcopalian. Home: Hubbard Lane Wheeling WV 26003 Office: 1500 Main St Wheeling WV 26003

FOX, HENRY JACKSON, lawyer; b. Milw., Jan. 21, 1911; s. John J. and Rose (Kohn) F.; A.B., U. Wis., 1932, LL.B., 1934, S.J.D., 1937; LL.M., Harvard, 1936; m. Charlotte F. Kahn, Nov. 30, 1939; children—Leslie Ann, Robert Irving, Linda Ellen. Admitted to Wis. bar, 1934, Fla. bar, 1941, D.C. bar, 1942; partner Arent Fox Kinter Plotkin & Kahn, Washington, 1942—; faculty law sch. U. Wis., 1936-37, U. Ky., 1937-38, Stetson Law Sch., 1939-41; sr. bill Draftsman Wis. State Legislature, 1937, 1939; Wis. dir. U.S. Atty. Gen. Survey Release Procedures, atty. Nat. Labor Relations Bd., 1937-38, Dept. Justice, 1941-42, Ind. panel mem. 3d Regional War Labor Bd., 1945; pres. Concord Devel. Co., Inc., Capitol Enterprises, Inc.; dir. U.S. Ceramic Tile Co. Mem. Fla., Wis., D.C. (mem.. adminstrv. law council, chmn. adminstrv. law sect.; mem. of bd. of dirs.), Fed. (chmn. of internat. law and trade council, mem. council), Am. bar assns., Wis. Law-Alumni Assn. (pres. Washington), Order of Coif, Phi Kappa Phi, Phi Eta Sigma. Clubs: Wisconsin Alumni, Harvard Alumni (Washington). Author: Problems and Aids in Drafting Legislation; also author legal articles. Home: 4201 Cathedral Av Washington DC 20016 Office: Fed Bar Bldg Washington DC 20006

FOX, IRVING, lawyer; b. N.Y.C., June 11, 1909; s. Herman and Sadie (Low) F.; B.S., N.Y. U., 1930, J.D., 1932; m. Lenore Galowitz, Aug. 6, 1933; children—Eric Roger, Steven Andrew. Admitted to N.Y. bar, 1933, since practiced in N.Y.C.; mem. firm Netter, Lewy, Dowd, Fox, Ness & Stream, 1962—. Nat. treas. Thanks to Scandinavia, Inc., Phi Sigma Delta Found. Trustee Charles Kriser Found. Served to lt. USNR, 1944-46. Mem. N.Y. State Bar Assn., N.Y. Country Lawyers Assn. Home: 70 E 10th St New York City NY 10003 Office: 660 Madison Av New York City NY 10021

FOX, IRWIN SONNY, TV performer, producer; b. Bklyn., June 17, 1925; s. Julius A. and Gertrude (Goldberg) F.; B.A., N.Y.U., 1947; m. Gloria Benson, May 1, 1953; children-Christopher, Meredith, Dana, Tracy. Host, Let's Take a Trip, CBS, 1955-58; host, asso. producer Wonderama, WNEW-TV, 1959-67; exec. producer, host On Your Mark, ABC, 1961; exec. producer Cowboy and Tiger, 1963; host The New Yorkers, WNEW-TV, 1967-68; host, Movie Game, syndicated, 1969; chmn. bd. Nat. Acad. TV Arts, Scis., 1970-72; bd. dirs. Internat. Acad., 1968—. Bd. dirs. Conn. Assn. Children With Learning Disabilities, 1968—, League for Parent Edn., 1969—; chmn. spl. projects Muscular Dystrophy Assn. Am., 1965-67. Served with inf., AUS, 1943-45; ETO. Decorated Purple Heart, Combat Infantry badge. Mem. Asia Soc. (mem. Korea Adv. council 1967—). Author: Jokes and How to Tell Them, 1966. Home: Weston CT 06880 Office: 59 E 54th St New York NY 10022

FOX, J. RONALD, educator; b. Binghamton, N.Y., Dec. 11, 1929; s. John C. and C. Frances (Lilly) F.; B.S, LeMoyne Coll., 1951; M.B.A., Harvard, 1959, M.A., 1967, Ph.D., 1968; m. Dorris A. Campbell, June 25, 1968. Vice pres., gen. mgr. Mgmt. Systems Corp., Cambridge, Mass., 1960-63; dep. asst. sec. Air Force, Washington, 1963-65; asso. prof. bus. adminstrn. Harvard, 1965-69, now prof.; asst. sec. Army, Washington, from 1969. Served with USN, 1953-57. Recipient Air Force Exceptional Civilian Service award, 1965, sec. Army distinguished civilian service award, 1971; Pres. Korea Order Nat. Security Merit, 1970. Mem. Armed Forces Mgmt. Assn. (pres. 1969-70, dir.), Nat. Contract Mgmt. Assn. Exhibited sculpture Washington galleries, 1970, 71. Home: 180 Kent Rd Newton MA 02168 Office: Grad Sch Bus Adminstrn Harvard Boston MA 02163

FOX, JACK VERNON, newspaperman; b. St. Joseph, Mo., Nov. 28, 1918; s. Forest R. and Josephine (Halley) F.; B.J., U. Mo., 1940; m. Feryle Dawson, Feb. 17, 1941; children—Stephen Patrick, Linda. With United Press, 1940—, successively writer, Kansas City, Denver, staff war cable desk, N.Y.C., rewrite desk, N.Y.C., corr., London, 1949-51, bur. mgr., 1951-53, feature editor, N.Y.C., 1954-58, roving corr., 1958-63, 66—, news feature editor, 1963-66, corr. Los Angeles, 1968—. Mem. Sigma Delta Chi. Home: 6716 Los Verdes Dr Palos Verdes Peninsula CA 90274 Office: 205 S Broadway Los Angeles CA 90012

FOX, JACOB LOGAN, lawyer; b. Chgo., Apr. 20, 1921; s. Jacob Logan and Sarah (Schutz) F.; B.A., U. Chgo., 1942, J.D., 1947; m. Mary S. Livingston, May 19, 1956; children—Jay, Katherine, Laura. Admitted to Ill. bar, 1947, since practiced in Chgo.; mem. firm Brown, Fox & Blumberg, Chgo., 1947—. Chmn. bd. Weil-McLain Co., Inc., Republic Industries, Inc.; dir. Inlander-Steindler Paper Co., Advt. Metal Display Co., Fasano Pie Co., Financial Marketing Services Co. Bd. dirs. Chgo. Youth Centers, O'Hara Found. Served with AUS, 1942-46. Mem. Am., Ill., Chgo. bar assns. Club: Standard (Chgo.). Home: 422 Arlington Place Chicago IL 60614 Office: 72 W Adams St Chicago IL 60603

FOX, JAMES G., Jr., chem. mfg. co. exec.; b. Downington, Pa., Apr. 20, 1905; s. James G. and Emma (Strickler) F.; B.S., Yale, 1926; m. Edna Ziegler, Sept. 15, 1930; children—James G. III, Phyllis Z. (Mrs. R.F. Silver). Chemist, mfg., engring., research Gen. Chem. div. Allied Chem. Corp., 1926-58, v.p. mfg., v.p. engring. and research, 1956-58, exec.. v.p. Nat. Aniline div., 1958, pres., 1959—. Mem. Mfg. Chemists Assn., Am. Mgmt. Assn. Clubs: Downtown Athletic, Whitehall (N.Y.C.). Home: 244 Gregory Av West Orange NJ 07052 Office: 40 Rector St New York City NY 10006

FOX, JEAN DEWITT, neurosurgeon, editor; b. Santa Ana. Cal., July 25, 1918; s. Mark I. and Ruth Page (Carmichael) F.; graduate Glendale Academy, 1935; B.A., Columbia Coll., 1944; M.D., Loma Linda U., 1945; M.S. Surgery, U. Mich., 1954; LL.D., Far East Theological Seminary, 1968; m. Evelyn Snyder, July 21, 1940; children—Jean DeWitt, Evelyn, Jere. Intern surgery Henry Ford Hosp., Detroit, 1945-46, resident neurosurgeon, 1953-58; resident surgery Vets. Hosp., Los Angeles, 1948-49; fellow oncology and cancer research White Meml. Hosp., 1949; editor Life and Health Mag., Review & Herald Pub. Assn., Washington, 1949—; attending neurosurgeon Glendale Hosp., Behrens Meml. Hosp., Meml. Adventist Hosp., Meml. Hosp., Cal. Hosp. (Los Angeles), Hollywood (Cal.) Presbyn. Hosp. Capt., M.C., AUS, Brooke and Letterman gen. hosp., 1946-48. Recipient $1000 M & R award Am. Acad. Gen. Practice, 1951. Diplomate Nat. Bd. Med. Examiners, Am. Bd. Surgery, Am. Bd. Neurol. Surgery; licentiate Med. Council of Canada. Fellow Am. C. S.; mem. of World, Am., Cal., Los Angeles med. assns., Am. Assn. Neurol. Surgeons, Am. Med. Writers Assn., Nat. Sci. Writers Assn., Am. Med. Authors Assn., Coll. of Physicians and Surgeons (Can.), Am. Legion, Congress Neurol. Surgeons, Am. Acad. Neurology, A.A.A.S., Am. Pub. Health Assn. Clubs: Kiwanis, Verdugo, Oakmont Country (Glendale, Cal.); Nat. Press (Washington). Author: The Best of Life and Health, 1955; The Doctor Prescribes, 1956; How to Keep Well, 1966; Why Not Smoke?, 1968. Contbr. med. articles lay mags. Home: 717 Avonglen Terrace Glendale, CA 91206 Office: Neurologic Center 7080 Hollywood Blvd Los Angeles CA 90028

FOX, JOHN, banker; b. Little Rock, Ark., Sept. 1, 1905; s. Marmaduke and Eleanor (Hagel) F.; student Bradley U., 1925-26, U. Mich., 1926-27; A.B., Washington U., 1930, A.M., 1932; grad. Sch. Banking, 1942; m. Geraldine D. Jones, Oct. 17, 1938; children—Jerry D., John Nancy, Patricia, Mary L., Joseph Clark, Susan. Sec. to pres. Mercantile Trust Co., St. Louis, 1933-36, asst. cashier, 1938-43, asst. v.p., 1943-45, v.p., 1945-55, sr. v.p., 1955-62, pres., 1962-67, chmn., chief exec. officer, 1967-70, ret.; ret.; fed. adv. council Fed. Res. System, 1967-69; lectr. Grad. Sch. Banking, 1955-64; dir. Pott Industries, Inc., St. Louis County Water Co., Midland Shoe Co., Mo.-Kansas-Texas R.R. Co., Mercantile Trust Co., Mercantile Commerce Commerce Trust Co., Hydraulic Press Brick Co.; chmn. Group Hosp. Service, Inc., 1961- 63. Bd. St. Louis Bur. Mem. exec. bd. Boy Scout council; treas. Mo. Pub. Expenditure Survey, 1965, 70. Bd. dirs. Cath. Charities of St. Louis; chmn. exec. com. Civic Center Redevel. Corp.; trustee Govtl. Research Inst.; adv. bd. Harris Tchrs. Coll., Maryville Coll. Sacred Heart. Mem. Robert Morris Assos., Bankers Assn. Fgn. Trade, Assn. Res. City Bankers, C. of C. of Met. St. Louis. Clubs: Racquet, Bellerive Country, Noonday; St. Louis; Media. Author: Banking in Mexico. Home: 6128 Waterman Av St Louis MO 63112

FOX, JOHN FRENCH, wholesale food co. exec.; b. Weston, W.Va., Aug. 20, 1922; s. French and Josephine (Hale) F.; student Wharton Sch., U. Pa.; divorced; children—Kathryn, John French, Marguerite. With Fox Grocery Co., Belle Vernon, Pa., 1947—, pres., 1961—; dir. Foodland-Clover Farm Co. Bd. dirs. Mon Valley Progress Council, Inc.; mem. adv. com. Office Emergency Preparedness. Campaign chmn. United Fund, 1967-68; past mem. bd. edn. Served with AUS, 1942-46. Recipient certificate of merit Pitts. Food Brokers Assn., 1968. Mem. Am. Wholesale Grocers Assn. (pres.), Young Pres. Orgn. Home: Box 342-B RD 3 Belle Vernon PA 15012 Office: Box 29 Belle Vernon PA 15012

FOX, JOHN GASTON, physicist, educator; b. Biggar, Saskatchewan, Can., Mar. 5, 1916; s. Jacques Gaston and Lulu Margaret (Connell) F.; B.Sc., U. Saskatchewan, 1935, M.Sc., 1937; Ph.D., Princeton, 1941; m. Constance Mary Sullivan, July 15, 1947; children—Wendy Elizabeth, Grant Sullivan, Paul John. Came to U.S., 1940, naturalized, 1955. Physicist Hercules Powder Co., 1941- 45, Los Alamos Sci. Lab., U. Cal., 1945-46, asst. prof. physics Carnegie Inst. Tech., 1946-49, asso. prof., 1949-56, asst. head dept., 1950-56, prof., 1956—, head dept., 1956-61; vis. prof. Indian Inst. Tech., Kanpur, India, 1967-69, 71-72. Physicist, Laboratoire Joliot-Curie de Physique Nucleaire, Orsay, France, 1962-63. Fellow Am. Phys. Soc.; mem. Am. Assn. U. Profs., Am. Assn. Physics Tchrs., Soc. Nuclear Medicine, Sigma Xi, Phi Kappa Phi. Author numerous articles. Home: 415 11th St Oakmont PA 15139 Office: Carnegie-Mellon U Pittsburgh PA 15213

FOX, JOHN GEORGE, lawyer; b. Ansted, W.Va., Apr. 27, 1923; s. Lorah O. and Emily (Vawter) F., A.B., Washington and Lee U., 1948, LL.B., 1949; m. Millicent B. Hill, Sept. 29, 1946; children—John George, Claudia Mildred, David Vawter, Nancy Rudisill. Admitted to W.Va. bar, 1949; with Mahan, White & Higgins, Fayetteville, 1949-52; atty. gen. W.Va., 1952-57; atty. Am. Tel. & Tel. Co., 1957-58, asst. v.p. atty, 1961—; became gen. atty. Chesapeake & Potomac Telephone Co. W.Va., 1958. Mem. W.Va. Ho. of Dels., 1950. Served as sgt. AUS, 1942-45, with 1st Army, ETO. Mem. Am. W.Va., Fayette Co. bar assns., Am. Legion, Am. Law Inst. Episcopalian. Moose, Odd Fellow. Home: 3723 Cardiff Rd Chevy Chase MD 20015 Office: 2000 L St N W Washington DC 20036

FOX, JOHN MICHAEL, corp. exec.; b. Esher, Eng., Dec. 28, 1912; s. James and Grace (Blott) F.; brought to U.S., 1913, naturalized, 1918; A.B., Colgate U., 1934; m. Floy Binkley, Mar. 16, 1938; children—Marcia Carol, Byron Michael, Susan, John Stephen, Br. sales mgr. Internat. Bus. Machines, Worcester, Mass., 1935-43; v.p. Nat. Research Corp., Cambridge, 1943-45; pres., dir. Minute Maid Corp., Orlando, 1945-61; exec. v.p. United Fruit Co., Boston, 1961-65, pres., chief exec., 1965-67, chmn., chief exec. officer, 1967-70; pres. United Brands Co., 1969-71, now dir., cons.; dir. Fed. Res. Bank Boston. Trustee Com. Economic Devel., dir. Am. Found. Religion and Psychiatry; trustee Colgate U., Tabor Acad., mem. Sales Execs. Club of N.Y. (hon. mem., past pres.). Home: 770 Boylston St Boston MA 02199 Office: Prudential Center Boston MA 02199

FOX JOHN PATRICK Jr., lawyer; b. Chgo., Dec. 14, 1918; s. John Patrick and Irene (Boyle) F.; A.B., Loyola U., Chgo., 1941, J.D. 1949. Admitted to Ill. bar, 1948; atty. law dept. Beatrice Foods Co., Chgo., 1949-65 gen. atty., chief corporate legal officer, 1965—, gen. counsel, 1969—; dir., counsel Boyle Ice Co. of Delaware, Chgo., 1950—. Served to lt. USNR, 1942-46. Mem. Am., Chgo. bar assns., Alpha Delta Gamma (pres. 1949-50). Clubs: Evanston Golf; Pinehurst (N.C.) Country; Pickwick Golf (Glenview, Ill.). Home: 201 Kedzie St Evanston IL 60202 Office: 120 S La Salle St Chicago IL 60303

FOX, JOHN PERRIGO, educator, physician; b. Chgo., Nov. 10, 1908; s. John S. and Myrtle (Perrige) F.; B.S., Haverford Coll., 1929; M.D., Ph.D., U. Chgo., 1936; M.P.H., Columbia, 1948; m. Helen Duffell, July 14, 1934; children—Judith M., John D., Haigh P., Joanne M. With No. Trust Co., Chgo., 1929- 31; fellow, later asst. dept. pathology U. Chgo., 1933-36; intern Evanston (Ill.) Hosp., 1937-38; staff internat. health div. Rockefeller Found., 1938-49; prof. epidemiology Sch. Medicine Tulane U., 1949-58, Wm. Hamilton Watkins prof. epidemiology, dir. div. grad. pub. health, 1958-60, vis. prof. epidemiology, 1960-70; chief dept. epidemiology, mem. Pub. Health Research Inst. City of N.Y., Inc., 1960-65; adj. prof. epidemiology Columbia Sch. Pub. Health, 1960-65, N.Y.U. Sch. Medicine, 1960-65; prof. preventive medicine Med. Sch., U. Wash., 1965-70, prof. epidemiology and internat. health, asso. dean Sch. Pub. Health and Community Medicine, 1970—. Cons. Communicable Disease Center, USPHS, mem. rickettsial disease commn. Armed Forces Epidemiological Bd., 1955—; mem. virus and rickettsial study sect. NIH, 1958-64, chmn. 1962-64, mem. bd. sci. counselors div. standards, 1962-64, chmn., 1964, mem. com. epidemiology and biometry tng. grants, 1965-69; mem. bd. sci. counselors Nat. Inst. Allergy and Infectious Disease, 1969—; cons. expert com. rabies, WHO, 1958—. Recipient Howard Taylor Ricketts prize U. Chgo., 1936. Diplomate Am. Bd. Preventive Medicine. Fellow Am. Pub. Health Assn. (governing council, 1958-62), N.Y. Acad. Sci., A.A.A.S., Royal Belgian Soc. Tropical Medicine (hon.); mem. Am. Soc. Tropical Medicine and Hygiene, Am. Soc. Bacteriologists, Harvey Soc., Am. Coll. Preventive Medicine, Internat. Epidemiological Soc., Assn. Tchrs. Preventive Medicine (exec. com. 1957-60), Soc. Exptl. Biology and Medicine, Am. Assn. Immunologists, Am. Epidemiological Soc. (pres. 1969), Am. Acad. Microbiology, Club: Cosmos. Author: (textbook) Epidemiology: Man and Disease. Editor Am. Jour. Epidemiology, 1964-69, asst. mng. editor, 1969—. Contbr. articles to sci., med. jours. Home: 16529 41st Av N E Seattle WA 98155

FOX, JOSEPH, shoe co. exec.; b. Schenectady, Apr. 19, 1911; s. Morris and Rebecca (Rabinsky) F.; m. Annabelle Garrison, Apr. 19, 1941; children—Garrison J., Robert Norman, Judy Ann. With Senack Shoes, div. Consol. Retail Stores, 1942—, mdse. mgr., buyer, 1948-56, pres., 1959—, v.p. parent co., 1956-59; pres. Internat. Retail Shoe Co., 1965—; v.p., dir. Interco, Inc.; dir. Cowden Mfg. Corp., Lexington, Ky. Clubs: Media, Meadowbrook Country, Mo. Athletic. Home: 4501 Lindell Blvd Lindell Terrace St Louis MO 63108

FOX, JOSEPH P., business exec.; b. Rochester, N.Y., 1914; grad. U. Notre Dame, 1936, Harvard Bus. Sch., 1938. Pres., dir. Champion Products, Inc., Rochester; dir. Central Trust Co., Rochester. Home: 57 Hickory Ridge Rd Rochester NY 14625 Office: 115 College Av Rochester NY 14607*

FOX, KARL AUGUST, economist; b. Salt Lake City, July 14, 1917; s. Feramorz Young and Anna Teresa (Wilcken) F.; B.A., U. Utah, 1937, M.A., 1938; Ph.D., U. Cal., 1954; m. Sylvia Olive Cate, July 29, 1940; children—Karl Richard, Karen Anne. Economist U.S. Dept. Agr., 1942-54, head div. statis. and hist. research, Bur. Agrl. Econs., 1951-54; economist Council Econ. Advisers, Washington, 1954-55; head dept. of econs. and sociology Ia. State U., 1955-66, head dept. econs., 1966—, Distinguished prof. scis. and humanities, 1968—. Bd. dirs. Social Sci. Research Council, 1963-67, mem. com. econ. stability, 1963-66, chmn. com. areas social and econ. statistics, 1964-67; mem. Com. Reg. Accounts, 1963-68. Recipient superior service medal Dept. Agr., 1948, award for outstanding pub. research Am. Agrl. Econ. Assn., 1952, 54, 57, for outstanding doctoral dissertation, 1953. Fellow Econometric Soc., Am. Statis. Assn., A.A.A.S.; mem. Am. (research and publs. com. 1963-67), Am. Agrl. v.p. 1955-56) econ. assns., Phi Beta Kappa, Phi Kappa Phi, Gamma Sigma Delta. Author: Econometric Analysis for Public Policy, 1958; (with M. Ezekiel) Methods of Correlation and Regression Analysis, 1959; (with others) The Theory of Quantitative Economic Policy, 1966; Intermediate Economic Statistics, 1968; (with J. K. Sengupta) Economic Analysis and Operations Research, 1969; (with W.C. Merrill) Introduction to Economic Statistics, 1970. Co- editor; Readings in the Economics of Agriculture, 1969; Economic Models Estimation and Risk Programming (essays in honor of Gerhard Tintner), 1969. Home: 3610 Woodland St Ames IA 50010

FOX, KENNETH LEE., newspaper editor; b. Kansas City, Mo., Mar. 18, 1917; s. Henry Hudson and Margaret Patience (Kiely) F.; A.B., Washington U., St. Louis, 1939; student U. Kansas City, 1939-40. With Kansas City Star, 1938—, asso. editor, 1966—; news analyst radio sta. WDAF, Kansas City, 1948-53; war corr., Vietnam, 1964. Served to lt. col. AUS, 1940-46. Recipient 1st place editorial div. nat. aviation writing contest, 1957, 58, 59, 60, 67; named Aviation Man of Year for Kansas City, 1959. Mem. Am. Legion, 40 and 8, Res. Officers Assn., Mil. Order World Wars, Phi Beta Kappa, Beta Theta Pi, Pi Sigma Alpha, Sigma Delta Chi. Club: Kansas City Press. Home: 310 W 49th St Kansas City MO 64112 Office: Kansas City Star Kansas City MO 64108

FOX, KENNETH RUSSELL, consultant; b. Lowell, Mass., Feb. 14, 1916; s. Russell Metcalf and Minnie B. (Callahan) F.; B.S. in Textile Engring., Lowell Tech. Inst. 1938, M.S. (hon.), 1951, Sc.D. (hon.), 1954; S.M., Mass. Inst. Tech., 1940; m. Eleanor Pihl, June 19, 1941; children—Karen Elisabeth (Mrs. Francis C. Evans), Stephen R., Linda P. (Mrs. Kenneth K. Kugel), Janet W. (Mrs. Robert J. Fleming). Research asst. Mass. Inst. Tech., 1940-41, instr., 1941-43, asst. prof., 1943-45; pres. Lowell Textile Inst., 1945-50; v.p., tech. dir. Burlington Mills Corp., 1950-53; past pres. Lowell Textile Asso., Inc., (Mass.); dir. Fabric Research Labs., Inc., Dedham, 1942—, vice chmn., 1967-70, chmn., 1970—; dir. Troy Mills Inc. (N.H.). Mem. materials adv. board, Dept. Def., 1959-62. Mem. Tech. Intelligence Indsl. Com. to study textile edn. in Germany, 1945. Mem. Higher Edn. Facilities Commn., Mass., 1966-70. Dir. Lexington Red Cross, 1956—; Industry Aids to Edn., Inc.; trustee Mass. State Colls., 1966-70, chmn. bd., 1966-69. Recipient scholastic medal Am. Assn. Cotton Mfrs., 1938. Fellow Brit. Textile Inst. Mem. Nat. Council Textile Sch. Deans; mem. Nat. Edn. Assn. of U.S.A.; mem. State Recess Commn. to Study Higher Edn. in Mass., 1948. Nat. councillor Am. Assn. Textile Chemists and Colorists; pres. Internat. Inst., Lowell, Mass., 1950. Registered profl. engr., Mass. Mem. Boston Microchem. Soc. (past pres.), Am. Assn. Textile Chemists and Colorists, Am. Phys. Soc., Am. Assn. Textile Technologists, Lowell Tech. Inst. Alumni Assn. (dir. 1953-62), Lowell Tech. Inst. Library Assn. (pres. 1958-63), Newcomen Soc., Am. Soc. M.E., Textile Research Inst., Sigma Xi, Tau Epsilon Sigma, Omicron Pi. Republican. Conglist. Clubs: Chemists (N.Y.C.); Rotary. Contbr. to Textile Research, Am. Dyestuff Reporter, Rayon Textile Monthly, A.S.T.M. Bull., Modern Textiles, Daily News Record. Home: 8 Oakmount Circle Lexington MA 02173 Office: 1000 Providence Hwy Dedham MA 02023

FOX, LAWRENCE AARON, govt. ofcl.; b. N.Y.C., Mar. 9, 1923; s. Aaron and Celia (Goldstein) F.; A.B. summa cum laude, Clark U., 1944; M.S. (Maxwell fellow), Syracuse U., 1945; Littauer fellow, Harvard, 1946-47; LL.B., George Washington U., 1951; m. Dorothy Louise Schwartz, Dec. 26, 1948; children—Rebecca, Judith, Joshua Aaron. Internat. affairs analyst Bur. of Budget, 1945-49; adviser Am. mission for aid to Greece, 1948; internat. economist Dept. Commerce, 1949-61; consul, comml. attache, Geneva, Switzerland, 1961-62; with Dept. Commerce, 1962—, dir. Bureau of Internat. Commerce, 1965-69, dep. asst. sec. commerce for trade policy, 1968-70, dep. asst. sec. commerce internat. econ. policy, 1970—; adj. prof. econs. George Washington U., 1964—; lectr. Fgn. Service Inst., 1958—; lectr. Am. Mgmt. Assn., 1965—. Alternate mem. bd. Fgn. Service U.S., 1965—; mem. U.S. delegation numerous internat. econ. confs. Admitted to D.C. bar, 1951. Recipient Meritorious Service award Dept. Commerce, 1961, also recipient of gold medal, 1967. Mem. Fed. Bar Assn. Club: American (sec. 1961) (Geneva). Contbr. profl. jours. Home: 6508 Lakeview Dr Falls Church VA 22041 Office: Dept of Commerce 14th and Constitution Av NW Washington DC 20230

FOX, LOUIS, wholesale grocery exec.; b. N.Y.C., Aug. 16, 1917; s. Pincus and Gussie (Gordon) F.; student Am. U., 1950-52; m. Dora Levin, June 18, 1939; children—Irene (Mrs. Martin Goodman), Helen (Mrs. Daniel Guckenheimer). Vice pres. Dist. Grocery Stores, Washington, 1948-50, pres., 1950-56; operations mgr. Asso. Wholesale Grocers, Inc., Kansas City, Kan., 1956-57, gen. mgr., 1957-68, pres., chief exec. officer, 1968—; chmn. bd. Shurfine-Central Corp., Northlake, Ill.; pres. Beaver Valley Canning Co., Grimes, Ia., Mo. Valley Food Distbrs., Supermarket Investment Co., Inc., Super Market Developers, Inc.; 1st v.p. Coop. Food Distbrs. Am., Chgo.; dir. City Nat. Bank, Kansas City. Bd. councilors Menorah Med. Center, Kansas City, Mo. Home: 4900 W 85th St Overland Park, KS 66207. Office: 1601 Fairfax Trafficway Kansas City KS 66115

FOX, LOUIS JOSEPH, automobile co. exec., orgn. ofcl.; b. Balt., June 8, 1911; s. Robert and Sylvia (Miller) F.; grad. Balt. City Coll., 1929; m. Dorothy Goldsmith Newman, Sept. 11, 1933; 1 dau., Shirley Mae (Mrs. Paul A. Scholder). Pres. Fox Chevrolet Sales, Inc., Balt., 1933—. Pres. Council Jewish Fedns. and Welfare Funds, 1966-69; asso. Jewish Charities and Welfare Fund Balt., 1956-69; mem.-at-large Balt. Jewish Council, 1958; chmn. legacy and endowment fund com. Council Jewish Fedns. and Welfare Funds, 1964—; mem. United Jewish Appeal Cabinet, 1966-70; chmn. meml. gifts div. S. Balt. Gen. New Hosp. Fund, 1965-69; mem. exec. com. United Jewish Appeal, 1967; nat. Israel bond chmn. for communal resources, 1970—. Bd. dirs. Jewish Telegraphic Agy. Bd. dirs. Joint Distbn. Com.; adv. bd. Israel Edn. Fund; trustee, chmn. devel. com. U. Balt. Home: 7706 Seven Mile Lane Baltimore, MD 21208. Office: 2020 S Hanover St Baltimore MD 21230

FOX, MARVIN, educator; b. Chgo., Oct. 17, 1922; s. Norman and Sophie (Gershengorn) F.; B.A., Northwestern U., 1942, M.A., 1946; Rabbi, Hebrew Theol. Coll. Chgo., 1942; Ph.D., U. Chgo., 1950; m. June Elaine Trachtenberg, Feb. 20, 1944; children—Avrom Baruch, Daniel Jonathan, Sheryl Deena. Instr. philosophy Ohio State U., 1948-52, asst. prof., 1952-56, asso. prof., 1956-61, prof., 1961—; vis. prof. Hebrew Theol. Coll. Chgo., summer 1955, Hebrew U. of Jerusalem, 1970-71; mem. exec. com. Conf. Jewish Philosophy, 1963—; asso.' Columbia Seminar on Israel and Jewish Studies. Served with USAAF, 1942-46. Fellow Am. Council Learned Socs., 1962-63; Elizabeth Clay Howald postdoctoral fellow, 1956-57. Mem. Nat. Commn. B'nai B'rith Hillel Founds., Assn. Jewish Studies (dir. 1970—), Am. Assn. U. Profs., Am. Philos. Assn., Medieval Acad. Am., Metalphys. Soc. Am., Am. Acad. Jewish Research, Conf. Jewish Philosophy. Editor: Kant's Fundamental Principles of the Metaphysic of Morals, 1949; cons. editor Jour. of History of Philosophy, 1970—; editorial bd. Library of Living Philosophers, Inc., 1946—, Judaism, 1953—. Contbr. articles profl. jours. Home: 128 S Ardmore Rd Columbus OH 43209

FOX, MORTIMER JOSEPH, Jr., pharm. co. exec.; b. N.Y.C., Nov. 28, 1909; s. Mortimer J. and Helen (Morgenthau) F.; certificate Lincoln Sch., Teachers Coll., 1926; Ph.B., Yale, 1930; M.B.A., Harvard, 1933; m. Mary Lou Yoder, Feb. 17, 1945; children—James William, Philip Henry, Robert Louis, Barbara Frances. Asst. to gen. agt. FCA, 1933-34; chief div. research and statistics FDIC, 1934-36; economist, financial analyst Tri-Continental Corp., 1936-41; research adviser automotive br. WPB, 1941-42; treas., controller, dir. Indian Motocycle Co., 1946-49; asst. to pres. Schering Corp., 1949-50, treas., 1950-63, v.p., 1956-63, v.p. finance and planning, 1963-68, v.p. finance, 1968—; dir. Schering Corp., Ltd., Montreal, Schering Corp. Panama. Trustee, treas. Schering Found.; trustee Med.-Surg. Plan N.J. and Bloomfield Coll. Served to capt. AUS, 1942-46. Mem. Nat. Assn. Bus. Economists, Am. Pub. Health Assn., Financial Execs. Inst., Pharm. Mfrs. Assn. (past chmn. financial sect.). Clubs: Yale (N.Y.C.); Harvard Business School No. N.J. (past pres.); Nat. Press (Washington); Montclair Golf. Home: 88 Upper Mountain Av Montclair NJ 07042 Office: 60 Orange St Bloomfield NJ 07003

FOX, NOEL PETER, U.S. dist. judge; b. Kalamazoo, Aug. 30, 1910; s. Charles K. and Caroline C. (Kokx) F.; Ph.B., Marquette U., 1933, J.D., 1935; m. Dorothy A. McCormick, Aug. 1, 1934; children—Maureen (Mrs. Maureen Fox Reiss), Noel Joseph, Virginia Lynn. Admitted to Wis. bar, 1935, Mich. bar, 1935, also U.S. Supreme Ct.; asso. firm Bunker & Rogoski, 1935-39, Fox & Beers, 1945-49; pvt. practice, 1935-44, 1946-51; asst. pros. atty., Muskegon County, 1937-39; circuit judge 14th Jud. Circuit of Mich., 1951-62; U.S. dist. judge Western Dist. Mich., 1962—, chief U.S. dist. judge, 1971—. Served with USNR, World War II. Mem. Mich. Judges Assn. (past pres.), State Bar Mich. (past chmn. ct. adminstrn. com.), Nat. Jesuit Scholastic and Hon. Soc., Fed., Am., Muskegon, Grand Rapids bar assns., Jud. Conf. Com. Trial Practice and Techniques, Am. Judicature Soc. Home: 2162 Robinson Rd SE Grand Rapids MI 49506 Office: Federal Bldg Grand Rapids MI 49502

FOX, PAUL HARRIS, aluminum co. exec.; b. Sevierville, Tenn., Mar. 29, 1915; s. James Manker and Sarah Katherine (Walker) F.; B.A., Maryville (Tenn.) Coll., 1938; m. Mary Frances Beasley, June 13, 1942; 1 dau., Susan Frances. With O. P. Jenkins Furniture Co., Knoxville, Tenn., 1939-41; with Reynolds Metals Co. and affiliates, 1941—; exec. v.p. sales and marketing Reynolds Internat., Inc.; dir. Westeel-Rosco Co. Ltd., O'Hare Internat. Bank. Clubs: North Shore Country (Glenview, Ill.); Peachtree Golf, Commerce (Atlanta). Home: Berkshire Apts 300 W Franklin St Richmond VA 23220 Office: 6603 W Broad St Richmond VA 23213

FOX, RAYMOND BERNARD, educator; b. Woodstock, Minn., Feb. 8, 1926; s. Fred Joseph and Esther (Short) F.; B.S., Mankato State Coll., 1949; M.A., Colo. Coll., 1952; Ed.D., U. Cal. at Berkeley, 1957; m. Gudelia Agnes Utz, Jan. 27, 1950; 1 dau., Jacalyn Ann. Tchr., English and dramatics Springfield (Minn.) High Sch., 1949-50, Reno (Nev.) Sr. High Sch., 1950-53; tchr. social studies Pittsburg (Cal.) Sr. High Sch., 1953-57; asst. prof. edn. St. Cloud State Coll., 1957-59; prof. edn., head edn. dept. No. Ill. U., 1959-65, asso. dean Coll. Edn., 1965-69, prof. edn., 1969—. Dir., Am. Sch. Project, Addis Ababa, Ethiopia. Served with USNR, 1943-46. Mem. Assn. for Supervision and Curriculum Devel. (bd. dirs.), Ill. Assn. for Supervision and Curriculum Devel. (pres. elect), Ill. Curriculum Council (exec. bd.), Am. Assn. Colls. for Tchr. Edn. (instl. rep.), Am. Ednl. Research Assn., Nat. Soc. College Tchrs. Edn. Contbr. articles profl. jours. Home: 527 S 4th St DeKalb, IL 60115.

FOX, RICHARD K., hosp. adminstr.; b. Hayward, Wis., Apr. 2, 1909; s. Charles William and Rose (Schon) F.; student Duluth (Minn.) Bus. U., 1927-28, U. Chgo., 1928- 30; m. Frances H. Kolocollins, Oct. 20, 1934; children—Richard, Judith, James. With St. Luke's Hosp., Duluth, 1928—, adminstr., 1955—. Vice chmn. trustees Minn. Blue Cross, 1954—, Minn. Indemnity Inc., 1965—; trustee Arrowhead Regional Planning council Upper Midwest Hosp. Assn., 1951-54. Mem. Minn. Hosp. Assn. (pres. 1952), Duluth C. of C., Nat. Office Mgrs. Assn. (pres. Duluth 1942). Rotarian. Clubs: Kitchi Gammi, Ridgeview Country (Duluth). Home: 3816 E Superior St Duluth MN 55804 Office: 915 E 1st St Duluth MN 55805

FOX, ROBERT ALAN, constrn. materials co. exec.; b. Phila., Dec. 31, 1929; s. Frederic and Zena (Witlin) F.; B.S.; U. Pa., 1952; m. Esther Grossman, June 22, 1953; children—James, Debra, Nancy, Amy, Kenneth. Co-founder Fox Bilt Homes, Phila., 1953, partner, 1953-63; pres. Warner Co., Phila., 1963—, also dir.; dir. Continental Bank, Indsl. Valley Title Co. Trustee Albert Einstein Med. Center. Mem. Phila. Homebuilders Assn. (pres. 1962, chmn. bd. 1963). Home: 943 Coates Rd Meadowbrook PA 19046 Office: 1721 Arch St Philadelphia PA 19103

FOX, ROBERT JOHN, clergyman; b. N.Y.C., Apr. 18, 1930; s. John Bernard and Margaret (Dunleavy) F.; B.A., St. Joseph's Sem. and Coll., 1953; M.S.W., Nat. Cath. Sch. Social Services, 1958. Ordained priest Roman Cath. Ch., 1955; parish asst. Holy Family Ch., Manhattan, 1955-56; student placement Monroe County Welfare, Rochester, N.Y., 1957, Family and Children's Soc., Balt., 1958; asso. dir. Family Service, Cath. Charities, N.Y.C., 1958-61; Fulbright lectr. social work, Montevideo, Uruguay, 1961-63; coordinator Spanish community action Archdiocese of N.Y., 1963-70; dir. Full Circle Assos., N.Y.C., 1970—; asso. prof. theology Marymount Coll., 1967—; dir. Inst. Intercultural Communication, N.Y.C., 1959-61. Vice chmn. Archdiocesan Social Justice Task Force, N.Y.C., 1970—; founder, dir. Summer in the City, N.Y.C., 1964—; initiator The Thing in the Spring, 1967, Mansight, 1971. Trustee CIDOC, Guernavaca, Mexico, 1967—. Home: 158 E 103d St New York City NY 10029 Office: 426 E 119th St New York City NY 10035

FOX, ROBERT KRIEGBAUM, mfr.; b. Covington, O., Apr. 1, 1907; s. Ammon L. and Josephine (Kriegbaum) F.; A.B., Ohio State U., 1929, M.A., 1930, Ph.D., 1932; m. Dorothy Carroll Bush, Aug. 28, 1934; children—Susan, Hannah, Robert L. Chemistry instr. Bethany Coll., W.Va., 1932-36; chmn. faculty Hiram Coll., O., 1936-41; partner Fox Chemical Co., Coshocton, O., 1941-45; pres. Lancaster Glass Corp., 1945—, Indiana Glass Co., 1956—; v.p., treas. Lancaster Colony Corp., 1962—; dir. Hocking Valley Nat. Bank. Mem. Sigma Xi, Phi Lambda Upsilon. Mason (Shriner), Rotarian. Home: Amanda Rd Lancaster OH 43130 Office: 220 W Main St Lancaster OH 43130

FOX, ROBERT WILLIAM, educator; b. Montreal, Que., Can., July 1, 1934; s. Kenneth and Jessie (Glass) F.; B.S. Mech. Engring., Rensselaer Poly. Inst., 1955; M.S., U. Colo., 1957; Ph.D., Stanford, 1961; m. Beryl Williams, Dec. 15, 1962; children—David, Lisa. Instr. mech. engring. U. Colo., Boulder, 1955-57; research asst. Stanford (Cal.) U., 1957-60; mem. faculty Purdue U., Lafayette, Ind., 1960—, asso. prof., 1963-66, prof., 1966—; cons. Owens-Corning Fiberglass Co., Education Services Inc., Nelson Mfg. Co., Peoria, Ill., B. Offien Co., Chgo., Agard Co., Johns-Marsville Co., Richmond, Ind. Named Standard Oil Outstanding Teacher, Purdue, 1967. Mem. Am. Soc. Mech. Engrs., Am. Soc. Engring. Edn., Am. Inst. Aero., Astronautics, Sigma Xi, Pi Tau Sigma, Tau Beta Pu, Delta Tau Delta. Home: 921 Hall Rd West Lafayette IN 47906 Office: Sch Mech Engring Purdue U Lafayette IN 47907

FOX, RUSSELL V., banker; b. W. Milton, O., 1891; ed. Miami-Commercial Coll., 1911. Dir. emeriti 1st Nat. Bank Dayton (O.); dir. Anchor-Rubber Co. Trustee Ashland Coll. Mason (Shriner). Home: 2616 Salem Av Dayton OH 45406 Office: 112 W 2d Av Dayton OH 45402

FOX, SAMUEL, lawyer, educator; b. Chgo., Mar. 18, 1905; s. M. Bert and Sara (Nestor) F.; Ph.B., U. Chgo., 1924, M.B.A., 1947; J.D., Loyola U., Chgo., 1927, LL.M., 1928; Ph.D., U. Notre Dame, 1950; m. Genevieve Kubreener, Mar. 29, 1928; children—Stanley K., Lawrence Nestor, Stephen Richard. Admitted to Ill. bar, 1927; practice in Chgo., 1927-39; atty. Luster & Luster, Chgo., 1927; partner Fox & Fox, 1928-39; U.S. regional enforcement atty. Chgo. region, 1943-46; budget accountant U.S. Rubber Co., 1940-41; inventory controller Bendix Aviation Corp., 1941-42; controller Bell & Thorn, Inc., 1942-43; mgmt. cons. H.B. Maynard & Co., Pitts., 1967; lectr. law Loyola U., Chgo., 1928-32; prof. accountancy, managerial jurisprudence U. Ill. at Chgo. Circle, 1946—; lectr. accounting control Ill. Inst. Tech., Chgo., 1949-53; vis. prof., lectr. mgmt. Am. U., Beirut, Lebanon, lectr. Beirut Mgmt. Coll., 1963; Fulbright-Hayes vis. prof. Al-Hikma U., Baghdad, Iraq, 1966-67; lectr. accounting, curriculum cons. to pres. Peruvian U. Sci. and Tech., cost accounting specialist Peruvian Army and Navy, AID, U.S. Dept. State, Lima, Peru, 1967; mem. accounting curriculum com. c.p.a. accreditations Wis. State U. at Eau Claire, 1967, vis. prof., acting chmn. dept. accounting, 1968. Fellow Internat. Acad. Law and Sci., Intercontinental Biographical Assn.; mem. Am. Inst. C.P.A.'s, Tax Inst. Am., Smithsonian Inst., Acad. Mgmt., A.A.A.S., Am. (exec. v.p. 1963-64), Chgo. (organizer 1957, pres. 1957-59) bus. law assns., Ill. Bar Assn., Am. Accounting Assn. (chmn. membership 1970-72), Nat. Assn. Accountants, Am. Econ. Assn., Internat. Platform Assn., Wis. Soc. C.P.A.'s, Am. Judicature Soc., Am. Soc. Engring. Edn. Author: Law of Decedents' Estates, 1938; Fundamental Cost Accounting Stipes, 1958; Advanced Cost Accounting, 1959; Management and the Law, 1966. Home: 175 E Delaware Pl Chicago IL 60611

FOX, SIDNEY ALBERT, ophthalmologist; b. Russia, Jan. 30, 1898; s. Dr. Louis Asir and Rebecca (Albert) F.; brought to U.S., 1904, naturalized, 1912; A.B., Brown U., 1919; M.D., St. Louis U., 1931; Sci.M., U. Pa., 1935; m. Dorothea Doctors, 1931. Resident, Bellevue Hosp., N.Y.C., 1934-35; in practice opthalmology, N.Y. C., since 1935; clin. prof. N.Y. U. Sch. Medicine; asso. attending ophthalmologist U. Hosp.; attending opthalmologist of Bellevue Hosp.; cons. opthalmologist Goldwater Meml. Hosp., VA Hosp., Hosp. for Joint Disease. Mem. opthal. adv. com. Commr. Health N.Y.C., 1956-58. Lt. col. M.C., A.U.S., 1943—. Awarded Legion of Merit. Diplomate Am. Bd. Ophthalmology. Fellow A.C.S., N.Y. Acad. Med., Am. Acad. Ophthalmology and Otolaryngology, Pan-Pacific Surg. Assn.; mem. A.M.A., Alpha Omega Alpha. Jewish religion. Author: Your Eyes, 1944; Opthalmic Plastic Surgery, 4th edit., 1970; Affections of the Lids, 1964; Surgery of Ptosis, 1968. Contbr. to various sci. publs. Address: 11 E 90th St New York City, NY 10028

FOX, SIDNEY WALTER, educator, chemist; b. Los Angeles, Mar. 24, 1912; s. Jacob and Louise (Burmon) F.; B.A., U. Cal., 1933; Ph.D., Cal. Inst. Tech., 1940; m. Raja Joffe, Sept. 14, 1937; children—Jack Lawrence, Ronald Forrest, Thomas Oren. Technican, Rockefeller Inst., 1934-35; research asst. Cal. Inst. Tech., 1935-37, teaching fellow, 1937-39; research chemist Cutter Labs., 1940-41, F. E. Rooth Co., 1942-43; Upjohn Co. grant U. Mich., 1941-42; asst. prof. chemistry Ia. State Coll., 1943-46, asso. prof., 1946-47, prof., 1947-55, head chem. sect. Ia. Agrl. Expt. Sta., 1949-54; dir., prof. Oceanographic Inst., Fla. State U., 1955-61, dir., prof. Inst. for Space Bioscis., 1961-64; dir., prof. Inst. Molecular Evolution, U. Miami, Coral Gables, Fla., 1964—; cons. AEC, 1947- 55, Staley Mfg. Co., 1954-60, NASA, 1960—. USA-USSR interacademy lectr., 1969. Chmn. subcom. nomenclature of biochemistry NRC, 1956-57; mem. Nat. Sci. adv. panel, systematic biology NSF, 1958-60. Recipient of Honors medal and citation as Outstanding Scientist Fla., Fla. Acad. Scis., 1968; Tex. Christian U. Distinguished Scientist of Yr., 1968. Mem. Am. Chem. Soc. (chmn. div. biol. chemistry 1958-59, nat. councilor 1955-58), Internat. Union Biochemistry (U.S. nat. com. 1956-59, sec. 1957-59), Internat. Soc. Study of Origin of Life (v.p. 1970—), Internat. Assn. Geochemistry and Cosmochemistry, Am. Soc. Naturalists, Am. Soc. Biol. Chemists, Geochem. Soc., Am. Astron. Soc. Soc. for Study Evolution, Am. Soc. Cell Biologists, Sigma Xi. Author: Introduction to Protein Chemistry (with Joseph F. Foster), 1957. Editor: Origins of Prebiological Systems, 1965; asso editor Chem. Rev., 1956-58; adv. bd. editors Currents in Modern Biology, 1965—. Contbr. sci. jours. Home: 7721 SW 50th Ct Miami FL 33143

FOX, SIV CEDERING, (Mrs. David Lawrence Fox), poet; b. Overkalix, Sweden, Feb. 5, 1939; d. Hilding and Elvy (Wikstrom) Cedering; brought to U.S., 1953; naturalized, 1958; David Lawrence Fox, children—Lisa, Lora, David. Poems published in several literary periodicals, including N.Y. Quarterly, The Literary Rev., The Colo. Quarterly, The So. Poetry Rev., The Quarterly Rev. Literature, others. Recipient William Marion Reedy award Poetry Soc. Am., 1970, John Masefield Narrative Poetry award, 1969; The Annapolis Fine Arts Festival poetry prize Md. Fine Arts Council 1968, Photography prize Sat. Rev., 1970. Mem. Poetry Soc. Am., Acad. Am. Poets. Address: Polly Park Rd Rye NY 10580

FOX, TERRY J., bus. exec.; b. Bklyn., Jan. 1, 1938; B.S., N.Y.U., 1960, student Grad. Sch. Bus., 1962; student Latin Am. Inst., 1960. Registered rep. Gruntal & Co., mems. N.Y. Stock Exchange, N.Y.C., 1959-63; sales exec. Am. Flange & Mfg. Co., N.Y.C., 1963-64; v.p. Internat. Breweries, Buffalo, 1965, chmn. bd., chief exec. officer, 1965—; chmn. bd., chief exec. officer Iroquois Industries, Inc., 1968-; vice chmn. Lincoln Nat. Bank Buffalo, 1968-71. Past pres., chmn. bd. Henry St. Settlement Jr. Bd. Former trustee Immaculata Coll.; chmn. investment bankers com. Rosary Hill Coll. regional coordinator White House Conf. on Children and Youth. Served with AUS, 1960-61. Mem. Young Pres. Assn. Clubs: Silver Springs Country (Ridgefield, Conn.); Goldens Bridge Hunt (North Salem); Downtown Athletic (N.Y.C.), Investor, designer, patentee Sam Sam Snead hand strengthener. Home: Hunt Lane North Salem NY 10560 Office: Rand Bldg Lafayette Sq Buffalo NY 14203

FOX, THOMAS G., Jr., research chemist; b. Union Deposit, Pa., Feb. 19, 1921; s. Thomas G. and Kathryn (Fasnacht) F.; B.S. in Chemistry, Physics and Mathematics, Lebanon Valley Coll., Annville, Pa., 1940, D.Sc. (hon.), 1967; Ph.D. in Phys. Chemistry, Columbia, 1943; m. Joyce Arlene Cake, June 21, 1941; children—Joyce Melinda, Margaret Leigh, Mary Louise. Asst. chemistry Columbia, 1940-43; Allied Chem. & Dye Co. fellow, 1942-43; research chemist Goodyear Tire & Rubber Co., 1946-48; research asso. Cornell U., 1948-50; research chemist Rohm & Haas Co., 1950-57; asst. dir. research Mellon Inst., Pitts., 1957-61, dir. research, 1961-62, staff fellow, 1962—, also mem. adv. bd.; prof. chemistry, polymer sci. Carnegie-Mellon U.; spl. research phys. chemistry polymers, intrinsic viscosities and thermodynamics of polymer solutions, molecular weights of polymers, melt viscosities and 2d order transitions polymers, crystallization in polymers, kinetics of polymerization, polymer structures. Science adviser to gov. of Pa., 1965—. Chmn. Pa. Sci. and Engring. Found. Fellow Am. Phys. Soc.; mem. Am. Chem. Soc., Soc. Rheology,, Sigma Xi, Phi Lambda Upsilon. Editor Jour. Polymer Sci., 1965- Office: Mellon Inst 4400 5th Av Pittsburgh PA 15213

FOX, THOMAS WALTON, educator; b. Pawtucket, R.I., Mar. 21, 1923; s. Thomas Mathew and May (Walton) F.; B.S., U. Mass., 1949, M.S., 1950; Ph.D., Purdue U., 1953; m. Jean Dorothy Manning, June 6, 1948; children—Cynthia Jean, Sandra Jane. Teaching fellow U. Mass. at Amherst, 1949-50, instr., 1952-53, prof., head dept. poultry sci., 1954-64, head dept. vet. and animal scis., 1964—; research asst. Purdue U., Lafayette, Ind., 1950-52; cons. Pilch Poultry Breeding, Inc., Hazardville, Conn., 1967-70. Mem. Amherst-Pelham Regional Sch. Com., 1963-69, chmn. region, 1968, 69; mem. Amherst Sch. Com., 1963-69. Served to sgt. AUS, 1943-45. Decorated Purple Heart with one oak leaf cluster. Fellow A.A.A.S.; mem. Am. Inst. Biol. Scis., Poultry Sci. Assn., World's Poultry Sci. Assn., Am. Genetic Assn., Genetic Soc. Am., Sigma Xi, Phi Kappa Phi. Contbr. articles profl. jours. Research in poultry genetics and applied poultry breeding, poultry physiology. Home: 676 E Pleasant St Amherst MA 01002

FOX, VERNON BRITTAIN, educator, criminologist; b. Boyne Falls, Mich., Apr. 25, 1916; s. John Lorenzo and Ethel (Hamilton) F.; A.B., Mich. State U., 1940, certificate in social work, 1941, M.A., 1943, Ph.D., 1949; m. Laura Grace Ellerby, Mar. 22, 1941; children—Karen, Vernon, Loraine. Caseworker and athletic dir. Starr Commonwealth, Albion, Mich., 1941-42; psychologist State Prison So. Mich., 1942-46, dep. warden, 1949-52; psychologist Cassidy Lake Tech. Sch., Mich. Dept. Corrections, 1946-49; prof. Sch. Social Welfare, Fla. State U., Tallahassee, 1952-64, prof., chmn. dept. criminology, 1964—, also dir. Delinquency Control Inst. Mem. Fla. Adv. Council on Adult Corrections and Prison Industries; cons. U.S. Law Enforcement Assistance Adminstrn. Served with AUS, 1945-46. Mem. Am. Correctional Assn., Am. Sociol. Soc., Fla. Psychol. Clubs: Capital City Country, Exchange (Tallahassee). Author: Violence Behind Bars, 1956; Guidelines for Corrections Programs in Community and Junior Colleges, 1969. Mem. internat. bd. editors Abstracts in Criminology, 1959-71. Home: 644 Voncile Av Tallahassee FL 32303

FOX, VIRGIL, (Keel), organist; b. Princeton, Ill., May 3, 1912; s. Miles S. and Birdie E. (Nichols) F.; Artist's Diploma, Peabody Conservatory Music, 1932; Mus.D. (hon.), Bucknell U., 1963; student of Wilhelm Middelschulte, 1928-29, Marcel Dupre, 1932-33. Profl. debut, Cin., 1926; debut in London, Eng., 1933, N.Y.C., 1933; head organ dept. Peabody Conservatory Music, 1938- 42; performed Library of Congress, 1946; organist Riverside Ch., N.Y.C., 1946-65; 1st organ soloist Lincoln Center, N.Y.C., 1963; dir. organ series Gallery Mod. Art, N.Y.C., 1965-66; concert tours throughout U.S., Can. and Europe, 1933—; rep. U.S. 1st Internat. Conf. Sacred Music, Bern, Switzerland, 1952; soloist with N.Y. Philharmonic, Phila., Boston, Balt., Rochester, Detroit, Dallas, Grand Rapids, CBS Symphony, Los Angeles Festival orchs.; recording artist for Kapp, Columbia, RCA Victor, Capitol, Command, Decca. Served with USAAF, 1942-46. Winner Nat. Fedn. Music Clubs biennial contest, 1929; named most popular organist Choral and Organ Guide mag., 1952; recipient Distinguished Alumni award Peabody Conservatory Alumni Assn., 1964. Mem. Am. Guild Organists, Phi Mu Sinfonia. Address: 394 E Palisade Av Englewood NJ 07631

FOX, W.F., electric co. exec.; b. 1910; E.E., U. Cin.; married. Formerly gen. mgr. operations electric div. Avco Corp.; v.p. mfg. div. North Electric Co., Galion, O., 1964-68, exec. v.p., 1968—. Office: 553 S Market St Galion OH 48833*

FOX, WILLIAM JOSEPH, retail corp. exec.; b. Bklyn., Apr. 13, 1921; s. Adolph W. and Margaret E. (Brill) F.; B.S. in Chemistry, Holy Cross Coll., 1941, M.S., 1942; LL.B., Bklyn. Law Sch., 1949, LL.M., 1962; m. Ethel Brennan, May 3, 1944; children—Patricia, William Joseph. Research chemist Am. Cyanamid Co., 1945-47; chemistry Pratt Inst., 1947-49; with Dorr- Oliver, Inc., Stamford, Conn., 1949-68, v.p. domestic operations, 1959- 62, exec. v.p., 1962-66, pres., 1966-67, chmn. bd., chief exec. officer, 1967-68; pres. Whitlock Corp., 1971—; dir. Preload Internat. Inc. Admitted to N.Y. and Conn. bars, 1949. Served to lt. (s.g.) USNR, 1941-45. Mem. Process Equipment Mfrs., Assn. (dir.), Am. Bar Assn., N.Y. Patent Law Assn., Am. Chem. Soc. Club: Burning Tree Country (past pres.) (Greenwich). Home: 59 Burning Tree Rd Greenwich CT 06830

FOX, WILLIAM THORNTON RICKERT, educator; b. Chgo., Jan. 12, 1912; s. John Sharpless and Myrtie Leah (Perrigo) F.; B.S., Haverford Coll., 1932; M.A., U. Chgo., 1934, Ph.D., 1940; m. Annette Baker, Sept. 3, 1935; children—Carol Perrigo (Mrs. Morton Foelak), and Merritt Baker. Instr. polit. sci. Temple U., 1936-41; instr., conf. dir. Sch. Pub. and Internat. Affairs, Princeton, 1941-43; research asso. Inst. Internat. Studies, Yale, 1943- 51, asst. dir., 1948-50, asso. prof. polit. sci., 1946-50; prof. internat. relations Columbia, N.Y.C., 1950-68, James T. Shotwell prof. internat. relations, 1968—, dir. Inst. War and Peace Studies, 1951—. Chmn. nat. security policy research com.. Social Sci. Research Council, 1953-64. Fellow Am. Acad. Arts and Scis., Hudson Inst.; mem. Am. Polit. Sci. Assn. (v.p. 1965-66, council 1956-58), Nat. Research Council, Council Fgn. Relations. Author: The Super-Powers, 1944; The American Study of International Relations, 1968. Editor, co-author: Theoretical Aspects of International Relations, 1959; co-author NATO and The Range of Am. Choice; mng. editor World Politics, 1948-53; mem. editorial bd., 1948- 61, 62—. Home: 18 Lake Dr Riverside CT 06878. Office: Inst War and Peace Studies Columbia U New York City NY 10027

FOX, WILLIAM WALTER, psychiatrist; b. Winnipeg, Man., Can., June 24, 1924; s. William Joseph and Edith (MacDonald) F.; M.D., U. Man., 1948; M.S. in Adminstrv. Medicine, Columbia, 1965; m. Margaret Elizabeth Livingston, Dec. 16, 1949; children—Tannis Lillian, Jennifer Colleen. Came to U.S., 1952, naturalized, 1957. Intern Winnipeg Gen. Hosp., 1947-48; resident Winnipeg Gen. Hosp., also Norton Psychiat. Unit, Louisville, 1949-54; practice medicine, specializing in psychiatry, Winnipeg, 1950-51, Louisville, 1954-65, New Orleans, 1965-66, Mt. Pleasant, Ia., 1966—; staff psychiatrist Winnipeg Psychopathic Hosp., 1951-52; cons. psychiatry Dept. Mental Health, Commonwealth Ky., 1954-55, research on problems of aged, 1955; clin. dir. Central Hosp., Louisville, 1955-56, supt., 1956-65; asst. prof. dept. psychiatry Faculty Medicine, U. Louisville, 1952-65; asst. prof. dept. psychiatry Tulane Med. Sch., 1965- 66; supt., area dir. mental health Mental Health Inst., 1966—; cons. Mental Health Clinic of Rock Island and Mercer Counties, Rock Island, Ill.; spl. cons. to Nat. Inst. Mental Health. Mem. tech. com. health White House Conf. Aging, 1971. Diplomate Am. Bd. Psychiatry and Neurology. Fellow Am. Psychiat. Assn.; mem. Assn. Med. Supts. of Mental Hosps. (past pres.), A.M.A., Ia. Med. Assn., Ia. Psychiat. Soc., Henry County Med. Assn., Am. Hosp. Assn. (mem. governing council psychiatric facilities sect.). Home: RFD 1 Box 191A Salem IA 52649 Office: Mental Health Inst Mount Pleasant IA 52641

FOX-MARTIN, MILTON, sales exec.; b. Kansas City, Mo., May 14, 1913; s. Asa Earl and Anna Elizabeth (Fox) M.; diploma Haverford Sch., 1931; B.A., Yale, 1935; m. Mary Warner, June 25, 1938 (div. Aug. 1950); children—Elizabeth Fay (Mrs. Peter C. Funk), Ludlow; m. 2d, Isabel Fountain Brackett, Aug. 26, 1950 (div. June 1960); 1 child—Belle; m. 3d, Ferle Hoffman, July 22, 1960 (div. Dec. 1967); m. 4th, Nancy Verkuil, Jan. 13, 1968; 1 child, Shana. Sales executive U.S. Indsl. Chemicals, Inc., Transfilm Inc., McArthur Advt. Corp., Martin Sales Devel. Corp., N.Y. Herald Tribune, 1935-51; mgr. mut. fund dept. Kidder, Peabody & Co., 1951-54; mgr. dealer relations Wellington Co., 1954-58; pres. Broad St. Sales Corp., 1958-60; v.p. sales Hugh W. Long & Co., Inc., 1961-62, pres., 1962-64; pres. underwriting div., v.p. Anchor Corp., 1964-68; internat. marketing cons., 1969—. Treas. church extension com. Presbytery N.Y.C.; class agt. Yale Alumni Fund. Republican. Presbyn. (elder). Author: (with Lawrence Madison) Life With Baby, Trout Lore, 1942; Sales Bullets series, 1960—; Positive Attitude Posters series, 1965—; Selling Mutual Funds, 1970—. Address: Leidsegracht I Amsterdam C Holland

FOXON, N. CONANT, hosp. adminstr. Adminstr. Center Gen. Hosp. Office: Box 1 Howard RI 02834*

FOXWORTHY, JAMES ERNEST, univ. adminstr.; b. Los Angeles, Feb. 23, 1930; s. James Norwood and Mary (Stone) F.; B.E., U. So. Cal., 1955, M.S., 1958, Ph.D., 1965; m. Peggy Lou Jones, Aug. 20, 1950; children—Michael D. Paula C., John E., Maryellen, Timothy M., Stephen J., Brian J. Research asso. U. So. Cal., Los Angeles, 1957-58; mem. faculty, adminstrn. Loyola U. Los Angeles, 1958—, prof., chmn. dept. civil engring., 1959-69, Dean Engring., 1969—; cons. sanitation dists. Los Angeles County, 1966—, Allan Hancock Found., Los Angeles, U. So. Cal., 1962—. Mem. Mayor's Council on Environmental Mgmt., Los Angeles, 1970-71, vice chmn., 1970—. Served with Engr., AUS, 1950-52; Mem. Am. Soc. Engring. Edn., Am. Soc. C.E., Am. Assn. Profs. Sanitary Engring., Sigma Xi, Phi Kappa Phi, Tau Beta Pi, Chi Epsilon. Research in marine pollution. Home: 27953 Alaflora Dr San Pedro CA 90732 Office: 7101 W 80th St Los Angeles CA 90045

FOXWORTHY, JOHN PAUL, pediatrician; b. Franklin, Ind., Nov. 22, 1925; s. Paul and Margaret (Thompson) F.; A.B., Johns Hopkins, 1948, M.D., 1952; m. Lois Fotos, Aug. 5, 1959; children—Linda, Don. Resident pediatrics John Hopkins Hosp., 1952-55; pvt. practice pediatrics, Grand Rapids, Mich., 1956—; mem. staff Blodgett Meml. Hosp. Mem. planning com. Johns Hopkins. Served to lt. (j.g.) USNR, 1943-46. Mem. Am. Acad. Pediatrics, Phi Gamma Delta, Alpha Omega Alpha. Home: 2537 Indian Trail SE Grand Rapids MI 49506. Office: 50 S College St Grand Rapids MI 49503

FOY, FRED CALVERT, former chem. mfr.; b. S.F., Jan. 28, 1905; s. John M. and Emma (Squires) F.; A.B., U. Cal., 1928; m. Elizabeth Hamilton, Sept. 28, 1929; chidren—Ann (Mrs. Stuart R. Gunn), Sara (Mrs. John Iversen Dixon), Fred Calvert. Asst. mgr. pub. relations San Joaquin Light & Power Corp., Fresno, Cal., 1928-30; account rep. J. Walter Thompson Co., S.F., 1930-31, mgr., Los Angeles, 1932-33, v.p., Detroit, 1945-48; asst. gen. mgr. Seattle Gas Co., 1931-32; advt. mgr. Shell Oil Co., S.F., N.Y.C., 1933-38; v.p. Wilding Pictures, N.Y.C., 1938-40; account rep. Young & Rubicam, 1940-42; v.p. sales Koppers Co., Inc., Pitts., 1948-50, v.p., gen. mgr. tar products div., 1950-55, dir., 1954—, pres., chief exec. officer, 1955-58, chmn., pres., 1958-60, chmn., chief exec. officer, 1960-67, chmn., 1968-70, ret., 1970; dir. Mellon Nat. Bank & Trust Co., H.K. Porter Co., Inc., Nat. Cash Register Co. Trustee Carnegie Inst.; chmn. bd. trustees Carnegie-Mellon U. Commd. lt. col. AUS, 1942, col., Gen. Staff Corps., Dec. 1942; asst. dir. purchase div., Army Service Forces, 1942- 44, dir., 1944-45; spl. rep. Under Sec. War on procurement for A.A.F., 1942-45; disch. 1945. Awarded Legion of Merit. Mem. Bus. Council, Nat. Indsl. Conf. Bd. (sr. mem.). Republican. Episcopalian. Clubs: Duquesne (Pitts.); Laurel Valley Golf, Rolling Rock (Ligonier, Pa.); Bohemian (San Francisco). Home: Star Route Rector PA 15677

FOY, JOE HARDEMAN, utility exec., lawyer; b. Henderson, Tenn., Aug. 16, 1926; s. C.M. and Carrie (Hardeman) F.; student Freed Hardeman Coll., 1942-44, Ga. Tech. Inst., 1944-45; B.A., Vanderbilt U., 1948, J.D., 1950; m. Martha Lowe Overall, May 28, 1949; children—Joe H., Melissa Haynes. Admitted to Tenn. and Tex. bars, 1950; city atty., San Angelo, Tex., 1951-53; partner firm Hardeman, Smith & Foy, San Angelo, 1953-65; v.p., gen. counsel Houston Nat. Gas Corp., 1965-69, sr. v.p., gen. counsel, 1969—, also dir.; dir. Main Bank, Houston. Chmn. adv. com. transp. Tex. R.R. Commn., 1964—; pres. Houston Opera Assn., 1971—. Mem. sch. bd., San Angelo, 1961-64, pres., 1964-65; mem. city council, Bunker Hill Village, Tex., 1967-71. Served to ensign USNR, 1945-48. Mem. Tex. Bar Assn. (chmn. pollution law com.), Order of Coif, Tau Beta Pi, Delta Kappa, Alpha Tau Omega, Omicron Delta Kappa, Phi Delta Phi. Democrat. Mem. Ch. Christ. Author articles. Home: 11731 Winshire Circle Houston TX 77024 Office: PO Box 1188 1200 Travis St Houston TX 77001

FOY, JOSEPH GERARD, food distbn. co. exec.; b. Quincy, Mass., Mar. 5, 1910; s. Robert Edward and Ellen (Hassett) F.; A.B., Holy Cross Coll., 1931; student Boston U., 1931-33; m. Geraldine Marie Kelly, Sept. 2, 1933; children—Joseph Gerard, Nancy Louise (Mrs. Robert A. Meisenheimer), Peter Dudley, Thomas Gerald, Judith Eleanor. Tchr.-coach. N. Quincy High Sch., 1933-42; dir. processed foods rationing OPA, 1942-43; dir. research and edn. Nat. Assn. Retail Grocers, 1946-48; pres., gen. mgr. Spartan Stores, Inc., Grand Rapids, Mich., 1948; pres., dir. Market Devel. Corp., 1961—, Beaver Valley Canning Co., 1952-68, dir. Pacific Merc. Corp., 1959- -; dir. Grand Rapids Coffee Co., 1951—, Shufine-Central Corp., 1951, pres., 1962-65; treas., dir. United Wholesale Grocery Co., 1950—. Chmn. Food Industry Council, 1965. Served with USNR, 1943-46. Named Food Statesman of Year, Coop. Food Distbrs. Am., 1965; Distinguished Service award, Western Mich. U., 1968. Hon. life mem. Nat. Assn. Retail Grocers; mem. Coop. Food Distbrs. Am. (bd. dirs., past pres.), Super Market Inst., Mich. Food Dealers Assn., Pa. Grocers Assn. (hon.). Home: 2117 Leffingwell NE Grand Rapids, MI 49505 Office; 1111 44th St SE Grand Rapids MI 49508

FOY, LEWIS WILSON, steel co. exec.; b. Somerset County, Pa., Jan. 8, 1915; s. George Martin and Nellie (Speicher) F.; student Duke, 1933-34, George Washington U., 1943-44, Lehigh U., 1947-49; LL.D., Moravian Coll., 1971; m. Marjorie Werry, May 9, 1942; children—Susan (Mrs. F. Arnold Heller), Jane (Mrs. Joseph W. Karaman). with Bethlehem Steel Corp., 1936—, v.p. purchasing, 1963-70, exec. v.p., 1970, pres., 1970—, dir. 1963—; dir. Brinco Ltd., Fluoruros, S.A. Trustee Moravian Coll, Bethlehem. Served AUS, 1941-46. Mem. Pa. Soc., Am. Iron and Steel Inst. Clubs: Economic, Union League, Links (N.Y.C.); Saucon Valley Country, Bethlehem (Pa.); Laurel Valley Golf, Rolling Rock, (Ligonier, Pa.). Home: Kenridge Farms E Macada Rd Bethlehem PA 18017 Office: 701 E 3d St Bethlehem PA 18016

FOY, NORMAN WARD, bus. exec.; b. Balt., July 25, 1895; s. Joseph Franklin and Winifred (Wroten) F.; ed. pub. schs. and high sch., Balt. and Cambridge, Md.; m. Marie Elmont Browning, June 7, 1916; children—Norman Ward, Constance Browning; m. 2d, Madelyn Marie Burns, Oct. 16, 1930; children—Patricia (Mrs. Paul B. Allodi), Brian Burns. With Carnegie Steel Co., 1912-17; salesman and dist. sales mgr., Republic Iron & Steel Co., Phila., Buffalo, Boston, and Birmingham, 1919-30; with Republic Steel Corp., 1930—, gen. mgr. of sales, 1937-53, v.p. in charge of sales, 1953-61, dir., 1956-62; chmn. bd. dirs. Pioneer Engring. & Mfg. Co., Detroit; trustee First Union Realty Trust, Cleve.; dir. McDowell-Wellman Engring. Co. With the steel div. of the War Prodn. Bd. 1941-44, dir. steel div., Apr.-Nov. 1944; active in initiating and developing controlled materials plan for budgeting and distribn. of steel, copper and aluminum for war purposes; asst. adminstr. N.P.A., Washington, 1951, in charge of metals and minerals bur. Served as 1st lt., C.E., U.S. Army, World War I. Mem. Am. Iron and Steel Inst., Clubs: Union, Pepper Pike, Country (Cleve.). Home: Roundwood Rd Daisy Hill Farms Chagrin Falls OH Office: 1515 E Ohio Bldg Cleveland OH

FOYE, ARTHUR BEVINS, accountant; b. Bklyn., June 20, 1893; s. Frank Melvin and Sarah (Bevins) F.; B.C.A. magna cum laude, N.Y.U., 1914; m. Emma Graham, Oct. 7, 1914; 1 dau., Barbara Bricknell (Mrs. Wiley Washington Merryman, Jr.). Instr. accounting N.Y.U., 1915-17; mem. Haskins & Sells, 1923—, sr. partner, 1945-56; chmn. Haskins and Sells Found. Mem. overseas econ. operations task force Hoover Commn. Trustee N.Y.U. C.P.A., N.Y., N.J., Cal., Ill., Ia., Ky., La., Tenn., Pa., N.C., Washington; pub. accountant, Fla. Mem. Far East-Am. Council of Commerce and Industry (past pres.), Am. Inst. C.P.A.'s (past pres.), Accountants Club of Am. (past pres.), Pilgrims U.S., Inst. of Dirs. (Eng.), Saint George Soc., The Acad. Polit. Sci., Internat. C. of C. (trustee U.S. council), Council Fgn. Relations, Am. Accounting Assn., Nat. Assn. Accountants, state socs. of C.P.A.'s of N.Y. (past pres.), N.J., Cal., Pa., La. Episcopalian. Clubs: Arcola Country, Downtown Athletic, Paris Am., Long Island Country, Skytop, Union League, N.Y.U., Opera, Harbor View (N.Y.C.). Home: 345 Manor Rd Ridgewood NJ 07460 Office: 2 Broadway New York City NY 10004

FRACCI, CARLA, dancer; b. Milan, Italy, Aug. 20, 1936; d. Luigi and Santa Laura (Rocca) Fracci; student Teatro alla Scala Ballet Sch., Milan, 1946-55; m. Beppe Menegatti, Oct. 7, 1964; 1 son, Francesco. Solo dancer La Scala Ballet, 1956-58, prima ballerina, 1958—; guest artist London Festival Ballet, 1959, 62, Royal Ballet, 1963, Ballet teatro del l'Opera, Rome, 1964-67, Stuttgart Ballet, 1965, Am. Ballet Theatre, 1967-69, Montecarlo Ballet, 1967, 68, Houston Ballet, 1967, Royal Danish Ballet, 1967, Royal Swedish Opera Ballet, 1969; leading roles in La Loup, Coppelia, The Seagull, The Macheths, Pas de quatre, Daphnis et Cloe, also Le Palais de Cristal, Serenade, Concerto barocco, Bourree fantasque, Balletto imperial, Allegro brillante, Les Sylphides, Excelsior, Cinderella, Romeo and Juliet, Coppelia, Swan Lake (Act 2), Giselle, Sleeping Beauty, Francesca de Rimini, Don Juan, La Strada, Nutcracker, Pantea, Madness for Ophelia, La Sylphide, Egyptian Nights, others. Named Woman of Year. Mademoiselle mag., 1961; recipient Anna Pavlova prize Parts U. of Dance, 1962; Dance mag. award, 1968. Address: care Dr Dino Meucci 57 V le Coni Zugna 20144 Milan, Italy.

FRACKELTON, WILLIAM HAMILTON, educator, plastic surgeon; b. Milw., Apr. 5, 1911; s. Albert and Grace (Hamilton) F.; M.D., Harvard, 1936; m. Jane Rohn Love, June 18, 1938, (dec. July 1971); children—William Hamilton (dec.), William Hamilton II, Susan Love. Intern Columbia Hosp., Milw., 1937; resident Passavant Meml. Hosp., Chgo., 1938-40; mem. faculty Med. Coll. Wis., 1941—, clin. prof. plastic surgery, 1958—, head dept., 1958-70; med. lectr. Milw. Downer Coll., 1952—; pres. Newberry Pubs., Inc. Milw., 1951—. Corp. mem. Boys Club Milw., Milw. Symphony League; bd.

dirs. Found. Am. Soc. Plastic and Reconstructive Surgery. Served to col., M.C., AUS, 1941-46. Decorated Legion of Merit. Mem. Am. Assn. Plastic Surgeons (pres. 1961-62), Am. Assn. Surgery Trauma, Am. Assn. Physicians and Surgeons, Am. Cleft Palate Assn., A.C.S. (gov. 1967-69), Am. Soc. Plastic and Reconstructive Surgery, Am. Acad. Orthopaedic Surgeons (hon.), Nat. Rehab. Assn., Am. Soc. Surgery Hand (pres. 1952), Pan Pacific Surg. Assn., Wis. Surg. Soc., Wis., Midwestern assns. plastic surgeons, Wis. Soc. Plastic Surgeons (pres. 1964). Club: Wis. Harvard (pres. 1963). Home: 1919 N Summit Av Milwaukee WI 53202 Office: 2266 N Prospect Av Milwaukee WI 53202

FRACKIEWICZ, RYSZARD, Polish diplomat; b. Sielec, Poland, Apr. 22, 1931; s. Antoni and Maria (Wyszkiewicz) F.; B.A., Central Sch. Planning and Stats., Warsaw, 1952; M.A., Inst. Fgn. Ser., Warsaw, 1954; postgrad. Inst. Social Sci., Warsaw, 1954-57; m. Maja Motyl, July 22, 1954 (div. 1964); 1 dau., Anna-Maja; m. 2d, Krystyna Kedzierski, Dec. 26, 1968; 1 dau., Karina Natalia. Clk., Comml. Bank, Warsaw, 1948-51; asso. prof. Warsaw U., 1952-54; press attache, 1st sec., Washington, 1960-64; dep. dir. Press Office and N. Am. Office, Ministry Fgn. Affairs, Warsaw, 1964-69; counselor, dep. chief mission, Washington, 1969—. Councelor, biweekly Swiat i Polska, 1957-58; fgn. editor weekly Forum, 1966-69. Pub. relations expert Polish United Workers Party central com., 1957-60. Home: 2939 Van Ness NW Washington DC 20008 Office: 2640 16th St Washington DC 20009

FRADON, DANA, artist; b. Chgo., Apr. 14, 1922; student Art Inst. Chgo., also Art Students League, N.Y.C.; m. Ramona Dom, Sept. 20, 1948; 1 dau., Amy. Regular contbr. cartoons to New Yorker mag., Look mag., Sat. Rev., Sat. Eve. Post, other nat. mags.; rep. permanent collection Library of Congress. Sec. Newtown (Conn.) Zoning Bd. Appeals, 1965-67. Served with USAAF, 1942-45. Democrat. Author: Breaking the Laugh Barrier, 1961; My Son the Medicine Man, 1964. Address: RFD 2 Brushy Hill Rd Newtown, CT 06470.

FRAENKEL, GEORGE KESSLER, chemist; b. Deal, N.J., July 27, 1921; s. Osmond Kessler and Helene (Esberg) F.; B.A., Harvard, 1942; Ph.D., Cornell U., 1949; m. Johanna- Maria Herzog, June 30, 1951 (div. Aug. 1965); m. 2d, Elizabeth R. Rosen, Nov. 11, 1967. Research group leader National Def. Research Com., 1943- 46; instr. chemistry Columbia, N.Y.C., 1949-53, asst. prof., 1953-57, asso. prof., 1957-61, prof., 1961—, chmn. dept. chemistry, 1966-68, dean grad. sch. arts and scis., 1968—; mem. postdoctoral fellowship com. Nat. Acad. Sci.-NSF, 1964-65; chmn. Gordon Research Conf. Magnetic Resonance, 1967; mem. Arts Coll. adv. council Cornell U., 1964—. Trustee Columbia U. Press, 1968-71. Recipient Army-Navy certificate of appreciation, 1948. Fellow Am. Phys. Soc.; mem. Am. Chem. Soc., A.A.A.S. Asso. editor: Jour. Chem. Physics, 1962-64. Mem. adv. editorial bd. Chemical Physics Letters, 1966-71, editorial bd. Jour. Magnetic Resonance, 1969—. Home: 450 Riverside Dr New York City NY 10027

FRAENKEL, GOTTFRIED SAMUEL, biologist, educator; b. Munich, Germany, Apr. 23, 1901; s. Emil and Flora (Weil) F.; came to U.S., 1948, naturalized, 1953; Ph.D. in Zoology, U. Munich, 1925; m. Rachel Sobol, Dec. 15, 1928; children—Gideon, Dan. Asst., Hebrew U., Jerusalem, 1928-30; privatdozent U. Frankfurt (Germany), 1931-33; lectr. Imperial Coll., London, Eng., 1935-48; prof. entomology U. Ill. at Urbana, 1948—. Mem. Nat. Acad. Scis. Author: (with D.L. Gunn) The Orientation of Animals, 1940; Decorative Music Title Pages, 201 Examples from 1500 to 1800, 1968. Home: 606 W Oregon St Urbana IL 61801

FRAENKEL, STEPHEN JOSEPH, engring. and research exec.; b. Berlin, Germany, Nov. 28, 1917; s. Max S. and Martha (Plessner) F.; B.S. in Civil Engring. with distinction, U. Neb., 1940, M.S. in Civil Engring., 1941; Ph.D., Ill. Inst. Tech., 1951; m. Josephine Rubnitz, June 28, 1941; children—Richard Mark, Charles Matthew, Martha Ann. Came to U.S., 1938, naturalized, 1943. Engr., Pitts.- Des Moines Steel Co., 1941-44, Link Belt Co., 1944-46; with Ill. Inst. Tech. Research Inst., successively research engr., supr., dept. mgr., head dept. propulsion and structural research, 1953-55; dir. research and devel. Stanray Corp., Chgo., 1955-62; dir. research engring. Continental Can Co., 1962-64; gen. mgr. research and devel. Container Corp. Am., Chgo., 1964—; adviser effects nuclear weapons Dept. Def., 1950—; cons. space flight programs ABC. Recipient certificate of achievement for atomic test Greenhouse, U.S. Joint Task Force Three. Registered structural and profl. engr., Ill. Mem. Soc. Exptl. Stress Analysis, Am. Ordnance Assn., Am. Mgmt. Assn., T.A.P.P.I. (chmn. Chgo. sect. 1968-69, dir. 1969—, chmn. acad. adv. group 1071—), Am. Inst. Aeros. and Astronautics (pres. Chgo. sect. 1958-59; mem. bd. dirs. 1959—), Navy League, Sigma Xi, Sigma Tau, Tau Beta Pi, Chi Epsilon. Contbr. profl. jours. Home: 1252 Spruce St Winnetka IL 60093 Office: 500 E North Av Carol Stream IL 60103

FRAENKEL-CONRAT, HEINZ, research biochemist; b. Breslau, Germany, July 29, 1910; s. Ludwig Fraenkel and Lili Conrat; student Univs. Breslau, Munich, Vienna, Geneva; Dr. Med., U. Breslau, 1933; Ph.D. in Biochemistry, U. Edinburgh, 1936; m. Jane Opermann, July 14, 1939 (div.); children—Richard, Charles; m. 2d, Bea A. Singer, 1964. Came to U.S., 1936, naturalized, 1941. Research, Rockefeller Inst., N.Y.C., 1936-37; crystallization of rattlesnake venom neurotoxin Inst. Butantan, Sao Paulo, Brazil, 1937-38; chemistry and biology pituitary hormones Inst. Exptl. Biology, U. Cal. at Berkeley, 1938-42; research methods protein modification Western Regional Research Lab., Dept. Agr., Albany, Cal., 1942-49; Rockefeller fellow, Eng., Denmark, 1950; staff virus lab., prof. virology U. Cal. at Berkeley, 1951—, also prof. molecular biology, also research degradation and reconstitution tobacco mosaic virus, chem. research protein and nucleic acid of viruses. Recipient (with Schramm and Hershey) Lasker award, 1958; named scientist of the year, Cal., 1958. Mem. Am. Soc. Biol. Chemists, Am. Chem. Soc., Soc. Exptl. Biology and medicine, Brit. Biochem. Soc. Sigma Xi. Author: Design and Function at the Threshold of Life: the Viruses, 1962; the Chemistry and Biology of Viruses, 1969. Home: 870 Grizzly Peak Blvd Berkeley CA 94708

FRAGER, ALBERT S., retail food co. exec.; b. Boston Dec. 29, 1922; s. Oscar and Anna (Polterak) F.; student Dartmouth Amos Tuck Sch., 1943; B.S. in Bus. Adminstrn., Northeastern U., 1944; m. Marion Nathan, June 15, 1950; children—Owen R., Bonnie L., Laurie J., Sherri L. Internal revenue agt. Internal Revenue Servi^e, 1945-56; v.p., controller Stop & Shop, Inc., Boston, 1956-67, treas., 1967—, financial v.p., 1969—, also dir. Served with USRN, 1943-44. Mem. Am. Inst. C.P.A.'s, Mass. Soc. C.P.A.'s, Tax Execs., Inc. Jewish religion (v.p., dir. temple). Home: 45 Ferncroft Rd Waban MA 02168 Office: 393 D St Boston MA 02210

FRAGER, MALCOLM, pianist; b. St. Louis, Jan. 15, 1935; s. Alfred and Florence (Friedman) F.; ed. by tutors, N.Y.C., 1949-53; B.A., Columbia, 1957; pupil Carl Freidberg, 1949-55; m. Morag Macpherson, Oct. 19, 1962; children—Andrew Monroe, Melanie. Town Hall debut, 1952; concert tours U.S. and Europe, 1959—, USSR, 1963, South and Central Am., 1963, 65, 68, 70, Japan and Asia, 1968, Australia, 1969; also performed at the White House, 1960; recordings for RCA Victor. Recipient Michaels Meml. Music award, Chgo., 1956; Career award Nat. Soc. Arts and Letters, 1958; Leventritt award N.Y.C., 1959; 1st prize from Queen Elisabeth of Belgium, Internat. Piano Competition, Brussels, 1960. Mem. Phi Beta Kappa. Address: 165 W 57th St New York City NY 10019

FRAGOMEN, AUSTIN THOMAS, capital goods co. exec.; b. Hoboken, N.J., Feb. 24, 1919; s. August and Mary (Firmin) F.; student Cornell U., 1944; B.S. in Sci. and Physics, Seton Hall U., 1946; student at Rensselaer Poly. Inst., 1945; m. Ann E. Duffy, June 22, 1942; children—Austin Thomas, Ann E., Maryanne. Constrn. supt. Babcock & Wilcox Co., N.Y. area, 1942-43, supt. shop assembly mobile power plants, 1943, supt. charge constrn. Phila. Electric Southwark Sta., 1946-48, mgr. constrn., Chgo., 1950-59, mgr. constrn. dept., Barberton, O., 1960-63, v.p. mfg., 1963-69; dist. mgr. constrn. A. M. Lockett Co., New Orleans, 1948-49; corporate v.p. Diebold, Inc., Canton, O., 1969—. Trustee Area Devel. Summit County Ohio. Served with USNR, 1943-45. Mem. Ohio Mfg. Assn. (trustee). Club: Brookside Country. Home: 2624 Dunkeith NW Hills and Dales Canton OH 44708 also 8 Curtis Point Dr Mantoloking NJ 08738 Office: Diebold Inc 818 Mulberry Rd SE Canton OH 44702

FRAHM, H.W., telephone co. exec. Pres., Gen. Telephone Co., Madison, Wis. Office: 18 S Thornton Av Madison WI 53703*

FRAIBERG, LOUIS BENJAMIN, educator; b. Detroit, Sept. 18, 1913; s. Meyer and Anna (Lazner) F.; B.A., Wayne State U., 1937, M.A., 1939; M.S.W., U. Mich., 1946, Ph.D., 1956; m. Selma Horwitz, Mar. 11, 1945; 1 dau., Lisa. Instr., Wayne State U., 1953-57; lectr. U. Mich., 1957-58; asst. prof., then asso. prof. La. State U., New Orleans, 1958-63; prof. English U. Toledo, 1963- -, chmn. dept., 1963-66. Mem. Modern Lang. Assn., Nat. Council Tchrs. English, Am. Assn. U. Profs. Author: Psychoanalysis and American Literary Criticism, 1960. Bd. adv. editors Hartford Studies in Literature, 1969—. Home: 2888 Bayridge Dr Ann Arbor, MI 48103.

FRAIN, ANDREW DENNIS, security agy. exec.; b. Chgo., Jan. 28, 1936; s. Andrew T. and Lillian (Warner) F.; student Loyola U., Chgo., 1955; U. Miami (Fla.), 1957-59, DePaul U., 1960; m. Janet L. Remus, July 7, 1956; children—Kimberly, Bridgette, Shawn, Colleen. With Andy Frain, Inc., 1949—, pres., 1962—; pres. ADF Enterprises, Inc., 1968—; dir. Consol. Concession Corp. Bd. dirs. Chgo. Conv. Bur. Home: 3284 Deerfield Rd Riverwoods Deerfield IL 60015 Office: 737 N LaSalle St Chicago IL 60610

FRAIN, FRANK LORD, aircraft exec.; b. Houston, Aug. 7, 1912; s. Rito and Dorothy (Stautberg) F.; grad. Am. Inst. Banking; grad. advanced mgmt. program Harvard, 1949; m. Phyllis Thomas, May 1, 1938; children—Lee, Pamela, Marilyn. Loan officer Union Bank & Trust Co., Los Angeles, 1935-42; treas. Lockheed Aircraft Corp., Burbank, Cal., 1942—, v.p., 1961-70, sr. v.p. finance, 1970—, dir., 1970—; dir. Lockheed Aircraft Internat., Inc., Lockheed Western Export Co., Lockheed Aircraft (Australia) Pty., Ltd., MFB Mut. Ins. Co.; trustee Lockheed Shipbldg. & Constrn. Co., Seattle. Bd. dirs. AMCAP Fund, Inc., Los Angeles. Clubs: Long Beach Yacht; Pinnacle (N.Y.C.); Jonathan (Los Angeles). Home: 1040 Corsica Dr Pacific Palisades CA 90272 Office: Lockheed Aircraft Corp Burbank CA 91503

FRAINE, HAROLD GEORGE, educator; b. Newark, Oct. 16, 1900; s. Walter and Ada Louise (Ineson) F.; student Miami U., Oxford, O., 1919-20; Comml. Engr., U. Cin., 1926; Ph.D., U. Minn., 1937; m. Mary Katherine Wallace, Dec. 27, 1926. Asst. prof. bus. U. Ind., Bloomington, Ind., 1937-39; financial analyst SEC, N.Y.C., 1939-40, head capital markets research sect., Washington, 1941, head research sect., Phila., 1942-47; asst. dir. investment research Life Ins. Assn. Am., N.Y.C., 1947-48; prof. bus. U. Wis., Madison, 1948-70, prof. emeritus, 1971—, dir. research project valuation rules for life ins. cos., 1958-62. Asso. dir. corporate bond research project Nat. Bur. Econ. Research, 1939-41. Mem. Am. Finance Assn. (dir. 1953, 65, 66), Financial Analysts Phila. (pres. 1945), Minn. Statis. Assn. (sec.-treas. 1934), Am. Econ. Assn., Mid-West Finance Assn., Finance Mgmt. Assn., Alpha Kappa Psi, Beta Alpha Psi. Episcopalian. Clubs: Blackhawk Country (Madison). Author: Valuation of Security Holdings of Life Insurance Companies, 1962; also articles. Editor Jour. Finance, 1956-57, 60-63. Home: 1651 Capital Av Madison WI 53705

FRAINE, JOHN NORMAN, ry. exec.; b. Medicine Hat, Alberta, Apr. 9, 1912; s. John Denton and Bertha Grace (Squance) F.; B.Sc. in C.E., U. Manitoba, 1939; Bus. Adminstrn., U. Western Ont., 1950; m. Audrey Eleanor Hook, Oct. 14, 1939; children—John Denton, Thomas Edward. With C.P. Ry., 1935—, beginning as asst. supt., Lethbridge, North Bay, Schreiber, Toronto, successively supt. Laurentian div., Montreal, gen. mgr. Que. Central Ry., Sherbrooke, Que., asst. to v.p., gen. supt., Calgary, gen. mgr., Toronto, 1943-57, v.p., gen. mgr. Vancouver, 1957-59, v.p., gen. mgr. Pacific region, 1959-64, v.p. rail operations, Montreal, 1963-67, senior regional v.p., Vancouver, 1966-; pres. Houlton Branch R.R. Co., 1964-. Member U. Manitoba Alumni Soc., Most Venerable Order Hosp. St. John of Jerusalem. Mem. United Ch. of Can. Mason (Shriner). Home: 1549 W 34th Av Vancouver 13 British Columbia Canada Office: Cpr Sta 601 W Cordova St Vancouver British Columbia Canada

FRAKER, ELMER L., assn. exec.; b. Hazelton, Kan., Nov. 18, 1896; s. John C. and Sarah Frances (Smith) F.; B.A., U. Okla., 1920, M.A., 1938; m. Edna M. Stuerke, June 5, 1923; children—Carolyn (Mrs. M.L. Atkinson III), Robert Vincent. Head, English dept. Cherokee High Sch., 1921-25; prin. high sch. Chickasha, Okla., 1926-39; pres. Mangum Jr. Coll., 1939-45; state adj. bus. mgr. Am. Legion Okla., 1945-55; adminstrv. sec. Okla. Hist. Soc., 1955—; mem. council Am. Assn. State and Local History, 1960—. Vice pres. N. Am. Historic Sites Commns. Assn., 1957-58; founder, 1st chmn. State History Adminstrs., 1968-69. Editor Okla. Legionnaire, 1945-55; mem. publ. bd. Chronicles of Okla., 1955—. Mem. State Pardon and Parole Bd., 1942-45. Mem. Okla. City Schs. Policy Com., 1953. Mem. Oklahoma City adv. com. Salvation Army. Dir. Civil Def., Southwestern Okla.; State Salvage Com. World War II; mem. State Edn. Adv. Com., 4th Corps Army Area Civilian Adv. Com., State Vets. Employment Adv. Com. Candidate Democratic nomination U.S. Senate, 1944. Mem. U. Oka. Alumni Assn. (pres. 1942), Am. Legion (state comdr. 1935-36), Internat. Platform Assn., Sigma Nu. Methodist. Mason, Odd Fellow, Rotarian. Clubs: Oklahoma City Men's Dinner. Author workbooks U.S. History, 1931, World History, 1933. Home: 2712 Drakestone Oklahoma City OK 73120 Office: Oklahoma Hist Soc Oklahoma City OK 73102

FRALEY, JOHN, business exec. Asst. supt. Rhyne House Mfg. Co., 1939-40; sec., treas., gen. mgr., dir. Bucknit Processing Co., 1945; with Carolina Freight Carriers Corp., 1949—, asst. gen. sales mgr., 1951-53, exec. v.p., 1953- 70, pres., dir., 1970—. Office: Carolina Freight Carriers Corp Cherryville NC 28021*

FRALICK, FRANCIS BRUCE, physician; b. Northport, Mich., Apr. 8, 1903; s. Francis J. and Elizabeth (Bruce) F.; M.D., U. of Mich., 1927, M.S., 1935; m. Mary Ellen Appleton, June 8, 1929; children—Margaret, Elizabeth, Marion, Martha Jane. Intern, 1927-28; asst. resident ophthalmology Univ. Hosp., U. Mich., 1928-29; pvt. practice medicine, specializing in ophthalmology, Ann Arbor, 1933—; instr. ophthalmology U. Chgo., 1931-32; instr. ophthalmology U. Mich., 1929-31, asst. prof.; 1932-33, asso. prof., 1933- 38, acting head dept. ophthalmology, 1936-38, prof. ophthalmology, 1938-69, prof. emeritus, 1969—, chmn. dept., 1938-68. Diplomate Am. Bd. of Ophthalmology (cons. 1960-63, 64, 68, chmn. bd. 1957-58). Fellow A.C.S.; mem. A.M.A., Am. Acad. Ophthal. and Otol., Assn. Research in Ophthal., Am. Ophthal. Soc., Nat. Soc. Prevention Blindness, Southwestern Mich. Triological Soc., Washtenaw County Med. Soc., Michigan Ophthal. Soc., Galen Med. Soc., Sigma Xi, Alpha Omega Alpha, Phi Chi. Methodist. Club: Detroit Ophthalmological. Home: 11332 Algonquin Dr Pinckney MI 48169 Office: North Outpatient Bldg U Med Center Ann Arbor MI 48104

FRAME, CLARENCE GEORGE, banker; b. Dakota County, Minn., July 26, 1918; s. George and Helen (Hunter) F.; A.B., U. Minn., 1941; LL.B., Harvard, 1947. Admitted to Minn. bar, 1947; with 1st Nat. Bank, St. Paul, 1947—, asst. cashier, 1953-54, cashier, 1954-57, v.p., cashier, 1957-59, v.p., 1959-61, sr. v.p., 1961-68, exec. v.p., 1966—; dir. Cornelius Co. (Anoka, Minn.), Webb Pub. Co., J.L. Shiely Co., Northland Co., (all St. Paul), Rosemount Engring. Co., Mpls., Ravenhorst Corp., Mpls. Trustee Children's Hosp., St. Paul, Minn. Orchestral Assn. (Mpls.), Mpls. Soc. Fine Arts. Served from ensign to lt. comdr., USNR, 1942-46, to comdr., 1951-53. Mem. Assn. Res. City Bankers. Clubs: Somerset Country; Minnesota (St. Paul); Minneapolis. Home: 334 Cherokee Av St Paul, MN 55107. Office: 332 Minnesota St St Paul MN 55101

FRAME, DONALD MURDOCK, educator; b. N.Y. C., Dec. 14, 1911; s. James Everett and Jean (Loomis) F.; A.B., Harvard, 1928-32; A.M., Columbia, 1935, Ph.D. 1941; m. Katharine Mailler Wygant, June 7, 1941; children-James Wygant, Donald Murdoch. Techr. Loomis Sch., Windsor, Conn., 1932-34; instr. French, Columbia, 1938-46, asst. prof., 1946-50, prof., 1950—; vis. prof. N.Y.U., 1961, U. Pa., 1964-66, Fordham., U., 1968, Rutgers U., 1969-70; bd. mem. Nat. Humanities Faculty, 1968—. Served to lt. USNR, 1943-46. Mem. Modern Lang. Assn. Am. (editorial com. 1958-68), Am. Assn. U. Profs., Am. Assn. Tchrs. French, Phi Beta Kappa (vis. scholar 1967-68). Democrat. Club: Century Assn. (N.Y.C.). Author: Montaigne in France, 1812-1852, 1940; Montaigne's Discovery of Man, 1955; Montaigne: A Biography, 1965; Montaigne's Essais: A Study, 1969. Translator from Montaigne (Complete Works,1957) Voltaire, Prevost, Moliere. Home: 401 W 118th St New York NY 10027

FRAME, EDGAR OLAN, leisure activities co. exec.; b. Sutton W.Va., July 16, 1924; s. Edgar Olan and Hazel (Carder) F.; B.S., Morris Harvey Coll., Charleston, W.Va., 1952; student San Fernando Valley State Coll., Northbridge, Cal., 1962-64; m. Maria Anita Diehl, Sept. 1, 1946; 1 son, Edgar Olan III. Pres. Beckley Vending Co. (W.Va.), 1952-55, with Host Internat., Inc., 1955—, treas., 1963—; treas. Jim Dandy Fast Foods, Inc. Served with USAAF, 1943-48. Mem. Am. Soc. Ins. Mgmt., Kappa Sigma Kappa. Home: 20731 Ingomar St Canoga Park CA 91306 Office: Host Internat Inc Pico at 34th St Santa Monica CA 90406

FRAME, JAMES SUTHERLAND, mathematician; b. N.Y.C., Dec. 24, 1907; s. James Everett and Jean Herring (Loomis) F.; student Ecole Nouvelle, Lausanne, 1921-22, Horace Mann Sch., N.Y.C., 1922-23, Loomis Sch., Windsor, Conn., 1923-25; A.B. summa cum laude, Harvard, 1929, A.M., 1930, Ph.D., 1933; Rogers traveling fellow from Harvard, univs. of Göttingen and Zurich, 1933-34; m. Emily Rogert Boyce, June 25, 1938; children—Barbara Boyce, Paul Sutherland, Roger Everett, Lawrence Henry. Instr. in maths. Harvard, 1930-33; instr. Brown U., 1934-38, asst. prof., 1938-42, adviser to freshmen, 1936-37, mem. bd. counselors, 1937-42; asso. prof. and head math. dept. Allegheny Coll., 1942-43; prof. math. Mich. State U., 1943-63, prof. math. and engring. research, 1963—, head of dept., 1943-60; mem. Inst. Advanced Study, Princeton, 1950-51; project dir. Conf. Bd. of Math. Sci., 1961-62; cons. Univ. Devel. Commn., Bangkok, Thailand, 1968; cons. Ford Found., Bangkok, 1970. Mem. E. Lansing Bd. Edn., 1948-52. Recipient Distinguished Faculty award, Mich. State U., 1967. Mem. A.A.A.S. (council mem. 1963-65), Mich. Edn. Assn., Nat. Council Tchrs. Maths., Am. Math. Soc., Math. Assn. of Am. (gov. 1950- 52, 58-60; vis. lectr. 1960), Am. Assn. U. Prof. (mem. nat. council 1948-51), Mich. Acad. Sci. Arts and Letters (pres. 1958-59), Phi Beta Kappa Assos., Sigma Xi, Pi Mu Epsilon (nat. dir. gen. 1957-66), Phi Kappa Phi. Conglist. Kiwanian (local pres. 1969). Clubs: Harvard of Central Mich. (pres. 1968-69); U & I (pres. 1970-71) (Lansing) Author: General Mathematics (with C. H. Currier and E. E. Watson), 1939; Solid Geometry, 1948; Buildings and Facilities for the Mathematical Sciences, 1963. Asso. editor Am. Math. Monthly, 1942-46, Pi Mu Epsilon Journal, 1949-57. Abstractor, Math. Reviews, 1940—; abstractor Zentralblatt für Math., 1967—. Contributor articles to sci. jours. Researcher in theory of representations of finite groups, continued fractions, approximate computations, matrix theory in systems analysis. Home: 136 Oakland Dr East Lansing, MI 48823.

FRAMPTON, GEORGE THOMAS, lawyer and educator; b. N.Y.C., Mar. 24, 1917; s. Harry Vinton and Mary Louise (Fottrell) F.; A.B., Duke, 1938, LL.B., 1941; m. Margaret Anne Raup, May 2, 1941; children—George Thomas, Mary Louise. Admitted to N.Y. bar, 1942, Ill. bar, 1956, also U.S. Supreme Ct.; with firm Cravath, deGersdorff, Swaine & Wood, N.Y.C., 1941- 42, OPA, Washington, 1942-43; firm Fulton, Walter & Halley, N.Y.C., 1945- 53; teaching fellow Harvard Law Sch., 1953-54; mem. faculty U. Ill. Coll. Law at Champaign, 1954—, prof., 1957—, vice chancellor campus affairs, Urbana-Champaign, 1970—; vis. summer prof. N.Y.U., 1954, Stanford, 1957, Salzburg (Austria) Seminar Am. Studies, 1965; vis. prof. U. Cal. at Berkeley, 1959-60, N.Y. U., 1967- 68. Dir. Nat. Provisioner, Inc., 1952—. Cons., Joint Congl. Com. Atomic Energy, 1963, Nat. Council Radiation Protection, 1961- 63, project corp. debt financing Am. Bar Assn., 1963-65. Mem. Democratic County Com., Westchester County, N.Y., 1946-53, Champaign County, Ill.,1960-70. Served with AUS, 1943-45; ETO. Mem. Am., Fed. Ill. bar assns., Assn. Bar City N.Y., Am. Trial Lawyers Assn., Am. Arbitrarion Assn. (panelist). Club: Nat. Lawyers (Washington). Author: (with E.R. Latty) Basic Business Associations, 1963. Home: 304 W Michigan Av Urbana, IL 61801. Office: Univ Ill Coll Law Champaign IL 61820

FRAMPTON, MERLE ELBERT, educator; b. Smithfield, W.Va., Sept. 15, 1903; s. Clark Sylvester and Ethel Pearl (Von Betzer) F.; B. Religious Edn., Boston U., 1925, A.M., 1927, M.S., 1928; A.M., Harvard, 1935, Ph.D., 1935; LL.D., Coll. of the Ozarks, Ark., 1932; Litt. D., Mo. Valley Coll., Marshall, Mo., 1940; m. Iris Coldwell, Dec. 30, 1923; children—Scott Athearn, Iris Merle, Diane Joyce. Bus. asso. to dean, Boston U., 1925-29; boys worker Chgo. Commons Settlement House, 1921-23; prof. of econ., Coll. of the Ozarks, 1930-33, v.p., 1930-33; dir. Westminster Found., Boston, 1933-35; prof. edn. and head dept., Tchrs. Coll., Columbia, 1935-44; prof. edn. Hunter Coll., 1952—; dir. N.Y. Inst. for Edn. of Blind, 1935—; vis. prof. Hunter Coll., N.Y.C.; dir. Am. Printing House for Blind, Soc. for the Prevention of Cruelty to Children, Westminster Found. Mem. or chmn. several spl. coms. or orgns. on edn., tng. and employment of blind persons including: chmn. policy com. Nat. Com. for Employment of Handicapped, dir. of study for U.S. House Reps. Com. on Edn. and Labor, Spl. Edn. and Rehab.; mem. exec. com. Bronx Council Social Agys.; vice chmn. pres. Com. on Employment of the Handicapped. Deocrated Nat. Order of Merit (Republic Paraguay). Mem. N.E.A., Am. Sociol. Soc., Am. Assn. of Instrs. and Workers for Blind and others. Commd. comdr. H.(S) USNR. Republican. Presbyn. Clubs: National Arts (Harvard), National Republican, University (N.Y.C.); Rotary, N.Y. Athletic. Author several books, including: Camping for Blind Youth; The Residential School, 1954; Tragedy, 1968; Forgotten Children, 1969. Editor: Special Education for the Exceptional, Vols. I, II, III (Porter Sargent), 1956. Sec. treas. Internat. Jour. of the Blind. Contbr. articles on edn. of handicapped to jours. Home: 999 Pelham Pkwy Bronx NY 10469 ☆

FRANC, HARRY L., investment banker; b. Toledo, Feb. 9, 1907; s. Harry L. and Sadie (Gans) F.; B.S., Harvard, 1928; m. Ruth C. Glasser, Oct. 23, 1934; 1 son, Terry Franc. With Scherck, Stein & Franc, Inc., and predecessors, 1928—, now chmn. exec. com. Mem. N.Y., Midwest stock exchanges. Home: 6414 Forsyth St St Louis MO 63105 Office: 506 Olive St St Louis MO 63101

FRANCA, CELLA, dir., choreographer, dancer; b. London, Eng., June 25, 1921; d. Solomon Franks; student Guildhall Sch. Music, Royal Acad. Dancing; LL.D., U. Windsor, 1959, Mt. Allison U., 1966; D.C.L., Bishop's U., 1966; m. James Morton, Dec. 7, 1960. Debut in corps de ballet in Mars in The Planets, Tudor, Mercury Theatre, London, 1936; soloist Ballet Rambert, London, 1936-38, leading dramatic dancer, 1938-39, guest artist, 1950; dancer Ballet des Trois Arts, London, 1939, Arts Theatre Ballet, London, 1940, Internat. Ballet, London, 1940; leading dramatic dancer Sadler's Wells Ballet, 1940-46; guest artist, choreographer Sadler's Wells Theatre Ballet, London, 1946-47; dancer, tchr. Ballets Jooss, Eng., 1947; ballet mistress, leading dancer Met. Ballet, London, 1947-49; dancer Ballet Workshop, London, 1949-51; founder, artistic dir. Nat. Ballet of Can., 1951—; co-founder, artistic adviser Nat. Ballet Sch., Toronto, 1959—; prin. roles include Girl with Red Stockings in Bake's Progress, Russian Ballerina in Gala Performance, Swanhilda in Coppelia, Young Girl in Specter of the Rose, Woman in His Past in Lilac Garden; title roles in Giselle, Le Festin de l'Araignée, Lady from the Sea; choreographer ballets, including: Midas, London, 1939; Cancion, London, 1942; Khadra, London, 1946; Dance of Salome, BBC Television, 1949; The Eve of St Agnes, BBC Television, 1950; Afternoon of a Faun, Toronto, 1951; Le Pommier, Toronto, 1951; Casse-Noisette, 1955; Princess Aurora, 1960; the Nutcracker, 1964; Ehl. 1967; Cinderella, 1968. Recipient Woman of the Year award, B'nai B'rith, 1958; Medal of Service, Order of Can., 1967. Home: 1187 Glenrose Av Toronto 7 Ontario Canada Office: 157 King St E Toronto 1 Ontario Canada

FRANCAIX, JEAN, composer; b. Le Mans, France, May 23, 1912; studied with Nadia Boulanger, Paris, 1922, Isidor Philipp at Paris Conservatory. Am. debut with N.Y. Philharmonic Symphony, 1938; opera La Main de Gloire received world premiere, Bordeaux Music Festival, France, 1950; other compositions include: Bagatelles (string quartet and piano), 1931, Conception for Piano and Orchestra, 1932, Sonata for Two Violins and Cello, 1933, Concerto for Piano and Orchestra, 1936, Le Diable Boiteux, 1937, Quintet (woodwind); (ballets) Le Roi Nu, 1935, Le Jeu Sentimental, 1936, Le Jugement du Fou, 1938, A la Francaix, 1951; (operas) L'Apostrophe, 1940, La Main de Gioire, 1948, others. Address: 10 Av Ernest-Bousson Chatou, France.

FRANCE, BEULAH SANFORD, editor, health educator; b. Redding, Conn., Oct. 18, 1891; d. George Turney and Florence May (Hill) Sanford; grad. Centenary Collegiate Inst., 1907, St. Luke's Hosp. Sch. of Nursing and Sloane Hosp. for Women, N.Y.C., 1920; grad. work Columbia, 1921-23, George Peabody Coll., 1925-26, Pratt Inst., 1927; Litt.D., Hartwick Coll., 1961; m. Harry C. France, Mar. 26, 1927; 1 dau., Mrs. Winifred Osborn Carriere. Pub. health nurse, Larchmont, N.Y., 1920-21; S. and W. field supervisor pub. health nurses Met. Life Ins. Co., 1921-26; writing, radio broadcasting N.Y. City Dept. Health, 1930-32; health edn. work E. R. Squibb and Sons, 1932-44; free lance advt.-writing, broadcasting, TV, lecturing, 1934-60; child-care editor Curtis Pub. Co. Country Gentleman (later called Better Farming) until publ. ceased; organizer, condr. child care courses The Brides' Sch. of Sci. Housekeeping, N.Y.C., 1932-42. Lectr. on health and child care before student bodies and women's clubs, 1932-46. R.N. Trustee Centenary Coll. Hackettstown, N.J. Fellow Am. Pub. Health Assn., Royal Soc. of Health (London, Eng.); mem. of Pub. Health Assn. N.Y.C., Maternity Center Assn., League of Women Voters (child welfare chmn. 1930-32), St. Luke's Alumnae Assn. (bus. mgr. bulletin 1930-54), American Nurses Assn., Internat. Council of Nurses, Nat. Soc. Daus. of Founders and Patriots of Am., Nat. Soc. Colonial Dames Am. Methodist. Contbr. on health to mags., U.S., Can., Latin Am., England; column Child Care appears in leading papers six days a week with circulation including U.S., Can., P.I.; editorial dir. Am. Baby Mag., 1940-63, editor emeritus, 1963-; free lance writer. Author: The Expectant Mother; Your Baby from Birth to One Year; How to Have a Happy Child, 1953; The Expectant Mother Month by Month; Ask Beulah France, R.N.; How to Raise A Healthy Happy Baby, 1964. Address: 186 Riverside Dr New York City NY 10024

FRANCE, HARRY CLINTON, financial writer, lectr.; b. Richmondville, N.Y., July 17, 1890; s. s. Julius Henry and Ellen Rocelia (Leonard) F.; A.B., Wesleyan U., Middletown, Conn., 1913; grad. student U. Pa., 1915-17, Columbia, 1923-25; grad. Sch. Oratory, Northwestern U., 1918; Litt.D. (hon.), Hartwick Coll., 1958; D.Pedagogy, Houghton Coll., 1965; m. Beulah Sanford Osborn, Mar. 26, 1927; 1 stepdau., Winifred Osborn. Rural sch. tchr., Seward, N.Y., 1908-09; head English dept. Banks Business Coll., Phila., 1915-17; dir. YMCA pub. speaking courses, Chgo., 1917-18; pub. relations successively with Govt. Loan Orgn. of U.S. Treasury, Guaranty Trust Co., Hamilton Nat. Bank, N.Y.C., 1919-26; sec.-treas. Holmes-France Security Corp., Detroit, 1926-30; financial writer, lectr., adviser, 1931—; lectr. Columbia, N.Y.U., Wayne U. 1919—; lectr., finance Rochester Bus. Inst., 1943. writer of weekly financial column syndicated Gen. Features Corp., 1933—; lectr. Town Hall, socs., bankers Treas. N.Y. Deaconess Assn.; pres., trustee bd. Ch. of St. Paul and St. Andrew, 1945-46, Mem. Beta Theta Pi. Clubs: Faculty (Columbia); Quill (pres. 1945-46) (N.Y.C.). Author: The Ethics of Capitalism Careers in Finance; Making Money with Investments, 1957; Your Financial Serucity, 1960; Dollars That Grow, 1962; Managing Money, 1966. Home: 186 Riverside Dr New York City NY 10024

FRANCE, ROBERT RINEHART, economist, univ. ofcl.; b. Massillon, O., Aug. 12, 1921; s. Karl Anthony and Jennie (Fields) F.; A.B., Oberlin Coll., 1947; Ph.D., Princeton, 1952; m. Jean Charmion Reitsman, Jan. 31, 1948; children—Robert Karl, Virginia Grace, Cornelia Reitsman. Asst. prof. dept. econs. Princeton, 1952-56, research asso. indsl. relations sect., 1952-55; asso. prof. dept. econs. U. Rochester, 1956-62, prof., 1962-, asso. dean Coll. Arts and Sci., 1962-63, asso. provost univ., 1963-70, v.p. planning, 1970—; impartial arbitrator labor-mgmt. disputes, 1953—. Commr., chmn. housing com. Human Relations Commn., Monroe County. Bd. dirs. Health Council of Monroe County; bd. dirs. Rochester Family Service. Served to capt. USAAF, 1942-46; lt. col. Res. Mem. Am. Econ. Assn., Am. Arbitration Assn., Indsl. Relations Research Assn., Nat. Acad. Arbitrators. Contbr. articles profl. publs. Home: 25 Hardwood Hill Rd Pittsford NY 14534.

FRANCE, ROBERT WILLIAM, food co. exec.; b. Chgo., May 30, 1912; s. Joseph John and Caroline (Tuch) Zak; student Northwestern U., 1931-33; m. Jane Sherman July 6, 1946; children—Richard D. Sampson, Jr., Robert Sherman France, John Cameron France, William Graham France. With Beatrice Foods Co., Chgo., 1933—, treas., 1956—. Served to capt. AUS, 1943-46. Mem. Delta Upsilon. Clubs: Glen View (Golf); Chicago Curling. Home: 1436 Overlook Dr Golf IL 60029 Office: 120 S LaSalle St Chicago IL 60603

FRANCELLO, JOSEPH ANTHONY, educator; b. Glasco, N.Y., Mar. 1, 1926; s. Antonio and Erminia (Castiglione) F.; B.A., State U. N.Y. at Albany, 1949, M.A., 1950; Ph.D., Syracuse U., 1960; m. Mary Lois O'Neil, Apr. 9, 1950; children—Mark Joseph, Lois Ann. Tchr. social studies Victor (N.Y.) Central Sch., 1950-57; grad. teaching asst. Syracuse U., 1957-59; prof. social studies Edinboro (Pa.) State Coll., 1960-68; prof., head dept. sociology and anthropology Muhlenberg Coll., Allentown, Pa., 1968—. Served with USNR, 1944-46. Mem. Am. Assn. Univ. Profs. (pres. Muhlenberg chpt. 1970-71). Research on Seneca Indians. Home: 28 Sunrise Av RD 2 Allentown PA 18103

FRANCESCATTI, ZINO RENE, concert violinist; b. Marseille, France, Aug. 9, 1902; s. Fortuné and Ernesta-Feraud F.; m. Yoland de la Briere, Jan. 2, 1930. Appeared in concerts throughout Europe with leading condrs. and orchs., 1928- 38; concert tour in South Am., 1938, 47, 52; first tour in U.S., 1939, and since appeared with leading orchs.; tours of South Am. and Mexico, 1947, 52, Europe, yearly; concert performances in Israel, 1949- 56, 58, 63, 66. Decorated Officer de Legion d'Honneur; commandeur de l'Ordre de Leopold (Belgium). Roman Catholic. Address: 165 W 57th St New York City NY 10019

FRANCIOSA, ANTHONY, actor; b. N.Y.C., Oct. 25, 1928; s. Anthony and Jean (Franciosa) Papaleo; ed. high sch., N.Y.C.; studied drama with Joseph Geiger; scholarship Dramatic Workshop, New Sch. Social Research; studied Actor's Studio; m. Beatrice Bakalyar, 1952 (div. Apr. 1957); m. 2d, Shelley Winters, May 5, 1957 (div. Nov. 1960); m. 3d, Judy Balaban, Jan. 1, 1962. Waiter, U.S.S. Pres. Cleveland; worked with drama groups including Off Broadway, Inc., N.Y. Repertory Theatre; on Broadway in End as a Man, 1953, Wedding Breakfast, 1954-55, A Hatful of Rain, 1955; performed in numerous motion pictures, the latest being Wild is the Wind, Long, Hot Summer, 1958, Naked Maja, 1959, Career, 1959, Story on Page One, 1960, Go Naked in the World, 1960; Senilita, 1961; Period of Adjustment, 1962; appeared in Assault on a Queen, 1966, A Man Could Get Killed, 1966; The Swinger, 1966. Recipient Count Volpe Di Misurata cup Venice Film Festival. Address: care A Morgan Maree Jr 6363 Wilshire Blvd Los Angeles CA 90048

FRANCIS, ALEX W., Jr., business exec.; b. 1912; B.S., U. Okla.; married. Pres. Nat. Tank Co., Tulsa, Okla., 1937—; v.p., dir. Combustion Engring. Co., Inc. Office: Charles Page Blvd 31 West Av Tulsa OK 74101

FRANCIS, ARLENE, (Mrs. Martin Gabel), actress; b. Boston, Mass.; d. Aram and Leah (Davis) Kazanjian; student Covent of Mt. St. Vincent, Finch Finishing Sch., and Theatre Guild Sch.; m. Martin Gabel, May 14, 1946; 1 son, Peter. Appeared in: (plays) The Women, 1937; Orson Welles' Mercury Theatre prodn. of Horse Eats Hat, and Danton's Death, 1938; All That Glitters, 1938; Michael Drops In, 1938; Young Couple Wanted, 1939; Journey to Jerusalem, 1940; The Walking Gentleman, 1942; The Doughgirls, 1942; The Overtons, 1945; The French Touch, 1945; The Cup of Trembling, 1948; (in translation of French play) L'Empereur de Chine, 1949; The Little Blue Light, 1951, Once More with Feeling; (TV) Whats My Line, Home, Arlene Francis Show Soldier Parade; (radio) emcee on What's My Name, and Blind Date (movie) All My Sons; One, Two, Three, 1961; The Thrill of it All, 1963; appeared in play Mrs. Dally, 1965, Dinner at Eight, 1966. Bd. dirs. 721 Corp. Member Am. Fedn. of Radio Artists, Actors Equity Assn., Screen Actors Guild. Author: That Certain Something, 1960.

FRANCIS, CHARLES DRIVER, Jr., mfg. co. exec.; b. Bklyn., Aug. 6, 1914; s. Charles Driver and Maude (Sprague) F.; B.A., Yale, 1936; LL.B., Bklyn. Law Sch., 1939; m. Barbara Thomas, May 23, 1942; children—Hilary, Thomas, Robert. Admitted to N.Y. bar, 1939, Ohio bar, 1946; mgr. employee relations N.J. Zinc Co., 1947- 58; with Celanese Corp., N.Y.C., 1958—, v.p., 1963—. Served with USNR 1940-45. Clubs: Yale (N.Y.C.); Canoe Brook Country (Summit, N.J.). Home: 78 Woodwild Way Berkeley Heights NJ 07922 Office: 522 Fifth Av New York City NY 10036

FRANCIS, CLARENCE, corp. exec.; b. Port Richmond, S.I., N.Y., Dec. 1, 1888; s. Clarence Southar and Helen Annett (Hawes) F.; B.S., Amherst Coll., 1910, LL.D., 1955; D.C.S., N.Y.U., 1950; LL.D., Trinity Coll., 1955, L.I. U.; m. Grace Abbott Berry, May 5, 1914; children—Richard Hawes (dec.), John Berry, Barbara. With sales dept. Corn Products Refining Co., N.Y.C., 1910-19; nat. sales mgr. cereal div. Ralston Purina Co., St. Louis, 1919-24; domestic sales mgr. Postum Co., N.Y.C., 1924; v.p., dir. Post Products, N.Y.C., 1924- 27, pres., 1927-29; v.p. in charge sales Gen. Foods Corp., 1929- 31, exec. v.p., 1931-35, pres. 1934-43, chmn. 1943-54, dir., mem. exec. com., 1954-58; mem. bd. Studebaker-Packard Corp., 1958—, chmn. and chief exec. officer, 1961-63; chmn. Lillard Syndications, Inc., 1964-65; chmn. Francis-Lillard Assos., Inc., 1968—; dir. Lehman Corp., Mead Corp., Air Reduction Co., Inc., N.P. Ry., Gen. Foods Corp., Mut. Life Ins. Co., Smith Corona Marchant, Inc. bd. govs. Fed. Res. Bank of N.Y. Pub. gov. N.Y. Stock Exchange. Chmn. bd. dirs., mem. exec. com. Fund for Adult Edn. The Ford Found.; bd. trustees Nutrition Found., Lawrence Hosp., Bronxville, N.Y., Eisenhower Exchange Fellowships, Inc.; finance chmn., dir., chmn. devel. com. Lincoln Center for Performing Performing Arts; chmn. adv. com. Inst. Nutritional Sci. Columbia; Am. rep. European Productivity Agy. pres., dir. Econ. Devel. Com., N.Y.C.; chmn. Citizens Com. for Hoover Report; bd. trustees Com. for Econ. Devel. Sometime mem. numerous fed., state and local govtl. adv. bodies. Mem. planning group Moffett Program in agr. and bus. Harvard. Dep. sheriff Westchester County, N.Y. Lt. cal. cal. N.Y. State Guard, 1913-14. Named Man of the Year, N.A.M., 1953; recipient recipient U.S. C. of C. award, 1954; Hall of Fame, Boston Conf. on Distbn., 1950; Gold Brotherhood distinguished service award Nat. Conf. Christians and Jews, 1953; Henry Laurence Gantt gold medal award, 1954; Order of Cruzeiro do Sul (Brazil), 1954; Advt. award for pub. service, 1955; Clarence Francis chair for sociology Amherst Coll., 1968. Mem. Am. Assembly (chmn. policy (com.), Am. Assn. for UN (past pres. UN Week), Am. Korean Found. (dir.), Sales Execs. Club U.S. C. of C. (past dir.), Delta Upsilon. Republican. Mem. Dutch Ref. Ch. Clubs: Union League, Sky (N.Y.C.); Bronxville Derby, Siwanoy Country (Bronxville); Blind Brook (Port Chester, N.Y.); Am. Yacht. Yacht. Author: A History of Food and Its Preservation, 1937. Home: 9 Westway Bronxville NY 10708 Office: 250 Park Av New York City NY 10017

FRANCIS, DARRYL ROBERT, banker; b. Ridgeway, Mo., Aug. 21, 1912; s. Leonard F. and Cora (Young) F.; B.S. in Agr., U. Mo., 1936; m. Loretta Smyth, Feb. 26, 1938; children—Darryl Robert II, Linda (Mrs. Robert E. Northrip), Marilyn (Mrs. Fred W. Obermiller). Research asst. dept. of agrl. econs. U. Mo., 1936-39; sec.-treas. Ozark Prodn. Credit Assn., Springfield, Mo., 1939-42, St. Joseph Prodn. Credit Assn. (Mo.), 1942-44; agrl. economist Fed. Res. Bank St. Louis, 1944-49; v.p. Nat. Bank Commerce, Memphis, 1949-52, Boatmen's Nat. Bank, St. Louis, 1953; v.p. Fed. Res. Bank St. Louis, 1953-59, mgr. Memphis br., 1954-59, 1st v.p., 1960-66, pres., 1968—. Mem. Alpha Gamma Sigma, Gamma Sigma Delta. Home: 7400 Woodland Way St Louis, MO 63121. Office: 411 Locust PO Box 442 St Louis MO 63166

FRANCIS, DAVID LIVINGSTON, coal co. exec.; b. Charlottesville, Va., Sept. 29, 1914; s. James Draper and Permele Crawford (Elliott) F.; grad. Hill Sch., 1933; B.A., Yale, 1937; M.B.A., Harvard, 1939; student mining W.Va. U., 1937; LL.D., Davis and Elkins Coll., 1961, Marshall U., 1963; m. Nancy Lindberg, Aug. 11, 1945; children—James Draper II, Kathy Anne, Anna Barbour. V.p., gen. mgr. Princess Elkhorn Coal Co., David, Ky., 1940-42, pres., 1946- 59; pres. Princess Coals, Inc. (merger Princess Elkhorn, Powellton, Sycamore and Cinderella coal cos.), 1959-63, chmn. bd., 1963-68; pres. Princess Coal Sales Co., 1946-68, chmn. bd., 1968—; pres. Mallory Stores, Inc., Huntington, W.Va., 1946-63; dir. Appalachian Coals, Inc. Dir., v.p. So. States Indsl. Council, 1950—; chmn. W.Va. Adv. Com. Manpower Utilization; mem. W.Va. Rehab. Adv. Council, 1961—; active Cancer, United Fund-A.R.C. campaigns, Tri-State area council Boy Scouts Am. Councilman, City of Huntington, 1956-61, mayor, 1960-61; chmn. Huntington Charter Bd., 1964-. Trustee, past pres. Huntington Clin. Found.; trustee Com. Econ. Devel. N.Y.C., 1958—, Davis and Elkins Coll.; bd. dirs. W.Va. Found. Ind. Colls. Served to lt. comdr. USNR, 1942-45. Mem. U.S. C. of C. (dir. 1956-64, v.p. 1961-64), Nat. Coal Assn. (dir. 1958-, treas. 1960-61), So. Coal Producers Assn. (dir. 1958—, exec. com.), Am. Inst. Mining and Metall. Engrs., N.A.M., Chi Psi. Presbyn. (elder). Mason. Clubs: Guyan Golf and Country, Engineers (Huntington); University (Washington). Address: PO Box 1210 Huntington WV 25714 ☆

FRANCIS, E. LEE, lt. gov. of N.M.; b. Seboyeta, N.M., Mar. 16, 1913; m. Ethel Gottleib; 3 daus., 2 sons. Agt., Continental Oil Co., Western Valencia County, N.M., 1945—; dealer Internat. Harvester Co., 1941—; distbr. B.F. Goodrich Tire Co., 1950—; lt. gov. of N.M., 1967—; cattle rancher, Cubero, N.M., Sheep, Colo. Exec. com. Nat. Lt. Govs. Conf., 1966-69, vice chmn. Western region, 1969—. Mem. N.M. Fair Commn.; finance chmn., chmn., Valencia County, exec. bd. Kit Carson council Boy Scouts Am. County chmn. Valencia County; mem. N.M. Republican State Central Com., N.M. Rep. Party State Exec. Com.; coordinator dist. N.M. Rep. Party. Mem. Valencia County Fair Assn. (past dir.), N.M. Cattle Growers Assn., N.M. Wood Growers Assn., Valencia County Farm Bur. K.C. (4). Home: Cubero NM 87014 Office: State Capitol Bldgs Santa Fe NM 87501

FRANCIS, EMILE, v.p., gen. mgr. N.Y. Rangers. Address: 307 W 49th St New York City NY 10019•

FRANCIS, SIR FRANK, (Chalton), librarian, mus. dir.; b. Liverpool, Eng., Oct. 5, 1900; s. Frank W. and Elizabeth (Chalton) F.; B.A., U. Liverpool, 1923; M.A., U. Cambridge, 1925; Litt. D. (hon.), U. B.C., 1960, Trinity Coll., Dublin, 1962, U. of Liverpool, 1963, U. Exeter, 1966, U. Leeds, 1967, U. N.B., 1967, U. Oxford, 1968, U. Cambridge, 1968, U. Wales, 1968; m. Katrina F. McClennon, Apr. 20, 1927; children—Jane, Jeremy J. F., Guy. Asst. master Holyhead County Sch., 1925-26; asst. keeper British Mus., 1926-46, sec., 1946-47, keeper dept. printed books, 1948-59, dir., prin. librarian, 1959-68; lectr. bibliography Univ. Coll., London, 1945-59; David Murray lectr. U. Glasgow (Scotland), 1957. Chmn. Internat. Com. Library Experts, UN, 1948, Council British Nat. Bibliography, 1949-59; v.p. internat. adv. com. bibliography UNESCO, 1954-60, Hon. fellow Emmanuel Coll., Cambridge U., also Pierpont Morgan Library. Decorated as a Knight Comdr. of the Bath (Eng.). Fellow Soc. Antiquaries, Museums Assn. (pres. 1965-66), Library Assn. (pres. 1965); mem. Internat. Fedn. Library Assns. (pres. 1964-69), Anglo-Swedish Soc. (chmn. 1964-68), Mass. Hist. Soc. (corr.), Bibliog. Soc. (hon. sec. 1938-64, pres. 1964-66), Kungl. Gustav Adolfs Akademien Sweden (hon.), Inst. de France (corr.), Oxford, Cambridge, Edinburgh, and American bibliog. socs., Assn. Spl. Libraries and Information Bur. (pres. 1957-59); hon. foreign mem. Am. Acad. Arts and Sci. Club: Grolier (hon.). Author: Robert Copland, Sixteenth Century Printer and Translator, 1961; also articles in field. Editor: The Library, 1936-53, The Bibliographical Society 1892-1942, Studies in Retrospect, 1945; Facsimile of The Compleat Catalogue, 1680, 1956. Co- editor: Jour. of Documentation, 1947—. Home: The Vine Nether Winchendon Aylesbury Bucks England Office: Council on Library Resources Inc One Dupont Circle Washington DC 20036

FRANCIS, JOHN DARRELL, banker; b. Campbell, Tex., Feb. 3, 1904; s. William Foster and Rachel Tennesse (Yancey) F.; student pub. schs., Greenville, Tex.; m. Martha Elizabeth Jordan, Mar. 17, 1932; children—Darrell Shannon, John Foster, Robert Connor, Raymond Edwin, Martha Elizabeth. With Merc. Nat. Bank, Dallas, 1925—, jr. officer, 1927-39, v.p., 1939-51, sr. v.p., 1951- 57, exec. v.p., 1957-61, pres., 1961-65, chmn. bd., chief exec. officer, 1966-69, chmn. exec. com., chief exec. officer, 1969—; dir. Republic- Financial Services, Inc., Dallas, Allied Finance Co., Lomas & Nettleton Financial Corp., Gen. Telephone Co. of the Southwest, Dallas Airmotive, Inc., Capital Southwest Corp., Summers Electric Co., Strickland Transp. Co., Republic Nat. Life Ins. Co., Burrus-Mills, Inc., Dallas Power & Light Co., Rangaire Corp., Cleburne, Tex. Bd. dirs. Dallas Citizens Council, Tex. Research League; trustee Southwestern Med. Found. Mem. Assn. Res. City Bankers, C. of C. (dir.). Mason (33, Shriner). Clubs: City, Dallas Athletic, Dallas Country, Chaparral, Petroleum. Home: 3604 Lexington Av Dallas TX 75205 Office: Mercantile Nat Bank Dallas TX 75201

FRANCIS, JOHN JOSEPH, state judge; b. Orange, N.J., June 19, 1903; s. Theodore Thomas and Mary (Moran) F.; LL.B., Rutgers U., 1925, LL.D., 1959; LL.M., N.Y.U., 1947; m. Penelope Connolly, Dec. 26, 1933; children—John J., Cynthia, Hugh. Admitted to N.J. bar, 1926; asso. law firms, Newark, 1926-37; mem. firm Foley & Francis, 1937-47; adv. master Ct. of Chancery, 1947-48; judge Essex County Ct., 1948-53, appellate div. Superior Ct., 1953-57; asso. justice Supreme Ct. of N.J., 1957—. Mem. adv. com. on drafting model probation and parole act; chmn. Supreme Ct. coms. on reconciliation and sentencing problems. Democratic candidate 11th Congl. Dist., 1944. Recipient award meritorious services Rutgers Law Alumni Assn. Mem. Am., N.J., Essex County (pres. 1942-43) bar assns., Inst. Jud. Adminstrn., Rutgers Law Alumni Assn. Club: Bay Head (N.J.) Yacht, Essex County Country. Asso. editor New Jersey Law Journals, 1943-47. Contbr. articles profl. jours. Home: 9 Keasby Rd South Orange NJ 07079 Office: 520 Broad St Newark NJ 07102

FRANCIS, MARION SMITH, lawyer; b. Slater, Mo., July 17, 1905; s. Marion L. and Annie Marian (Smith) F.; student Kemper Mil. Sch., 1923-24; A.B., U. Mo., 1927, J.D., 1929; m. Jewel M. Brandenberger,

May 26, 1943; 1 son, James Ashby. Admitted to Mo. bar, 1928; practice of law, Mexico, Mo., 1929-38; pub. adminstr. Audrain Co., Mo., 1931-33; mem. Pub. Service Commn. Mo., Jefferson City, 1938-41; asso. Bryan, Cave, McPheeters & McRoberts, St. Louis, 1942-50, partner, 1951—; dir. A. Brandenberger Drug Co. (Jefferson City, Mo.). Past trustee Mo. U. Law Sch. Found. Served from 2d lt. to maj., judge adv. gen. dept. AUS, 1943-46, served with 70th inf. div. 7th army, E.T.O. Mem. St. Louis, Mo. State, Am. bar assns., S.A.R., Judge Advocates Assn., Phi Gamma Delta, Phi Delta Phi. Clubs: Missouri Athletic, Bellerive Country (St. Louis). Home: 14 Willow Hill Rd LaDue MO 64758 Office: 314 N Broadway St Louis MO 63102

FRANCIS, MURIEL BULTMAN, publicity and personal rep.; b. New Orleans; d. A. Fred and Pauline (Geschwind) Bultman, Jr.; B.A., U. Ala., 1928; student Sorbonne, Paris, France, 1928-29; m. Harold Owen Francis, Aug. 9, 1932 (dec. 1943). Promotion rep. Grace Denton, Chgo., 1934; publicity rep. New Orleans Philharmonic Symphony Orch., 1936-37; personal rep. for Hollywood Workshop of Max Rheinhardt, 1930-40; pres. Pioneer Assurance Co., New Orleans, 1940-43; account exec. for radio and TV programs Earl Ferris Assos., N.Y.C., 1943-45; publicity and personal rep. Muriel Francis Assos., N.Y.C., 1946-61; head artists div. Nat. Concerts and Artists Corp., 1962-64; pres. Bultman Mortuary Service, Inc., New Orleans, 1964- -; cons. Edgar Vincent Assos., 1961—. Mem. President Eisenhower's Person to Person Music Com., 1956-62. Pres., Isaac Delgado Mus. Art, New Orleans, 1968-69; bd. dirs. New Orleans Philharmonic Symphony Orch., New Orleans Opera House Assn., New Orleans Opera House Found., Cultural Attractions Fund, Orleans Gallery, New Orleans Spring Fiesta Assn., New Orleans Speech and Hearing Center, English Speaking Union New Orleans. Mem. Phi Beta Kappa, Delta Zeta. Roman Cath. Home: 116 E 65th St New York City, NY 10021; also 1525 Louisiana Av New Orleans LA 70115 Office: 3338 St Charles Av New Orleans LA 70115

FRANCIS, RALPH E., banker; b. Iroquois, Ill., May 8, 1901; s. Samuel and Laura (Nosker) F.; B.S., Ill. State Normal U., 1924; grad. student Columbia, 1926-27; m. Dorothy Erickson, Sept. 3, 1927; children—Ydeen, Ralph E. Sec. Kankakee Citizens System, 1927-35, exec. v.p., 1935-44, pres., 1944—; pres. Kankakee Citizens, Inc., 1950—; treas., dir. Hotel Kankakee. Chmn. adv. com. Kankakee County, Ill. Pub. Aid. Commn.; pres. Kankakee Co. Community Chest, 1943-44; past. dir. A.R.C., YMCA. Mem. Ill. Citizens Edn. Com., 1957—; Ill. Governor's Commn. on Abraham Lincoln sesquicentennial observance; com. on Lincoln-Douglas debates centennial Knox Coll., 1959; area pres. Nat. Conf. Christians and Jews, 1961—. Area chmn. Kankakee Community Coll. Devel. Com.; chmn. Kankakee County Human Relations Commn., 1964, Mayor's Com. Econ. Opportunity, 1965; adv. edn. com. Kankakee Bd. Edn., 1963; chmn. Ill. Hist. Soc. Sesquicentennial Com.; mem. Ill. Council on Articulation for Colls. and Univs., 1968—; mem. Gov.'s Council on Ill. Degree Granting Instns., 1969—; chmn. Kankakee County commn. on Ill. SesquiCentennial. Mem. bd. trustees Asso. Colls. of Ill., 1965—; pres. bd., trustee Kankakee Community Coll. Recipient Human Relations award for B'nai B'rith. Mem. Am. (pres. 1954-55, hon. dir.-at-large), Ill. (pres. 1938) indsl. bankers assns., Ill. C. of C., (chmn. sch. finance com. 1954—). Kankakee C. of C. (chmn. edn. com. 1963), Ill. (pres. 1956-57, chmn. endowment com.), Kankakee County (pres. 1947-54) hist. socs. Methodist. Rotarian.

FRANCIS, RICHARD LOUIS, psychiatrist, state sch. dir.; b. Millerton, N.Y., Oct. 10, 1919; s. Champ Carter and Irene Virginia (Harris) F.; B.S., Howard U., 1941, M.D., 1944; m. DeWreathe Valores Green, Sept. 14, 1943; children—DeWreathe Valores Sarah, Irene Daisy. Intern Sydenham Hosp., 1945; psychiat. resident Vets. Hosp., Tuskegee, Ala., 1947-49, Harlem Valley State Hosp., Wingdale, N.Y., 1955-57; resident physician N.Y.C. Farm Colony, Staten Island, 1945-47; neuropsychiatrist VA Hosp., Tuskegee, 1947-53; sr. physician Harlem Valley State Hosp., 1955; supervising psychiatrist, 1955-61, asst. dir., 1961-67; dir. Sunmount State Sch., Tupper Lake, N.Y., 1968—. Mem. adv. com. North Country Community Coll., Saranac Lake, N.Y., 1968—. Served to capt. M.C., AUS, 1953-55. Mem. Am. Psychiat. Assn. (sec. Mid-Hudson dist. br. 1963-67), A.M.A., N.M.A., Franklin County, N.Y., Saranac Lake med. socs., Am. Assn. Mental Deficiency. Rotarian. Address: Sunmount State Sch Tupper Lake NY 12986

FRANCIS, ROBERT, author; b. Upland, Pa., Aug. 12, 1901; s. Ebenezer Fisher and Ida May (Allen) F.; A.B., Harvard, 1923, Ed.M., 1926; L.H.D. (hon.), U. Mass., 1970. Co-recipient Shelley Meml. award, 1938; recipient Golden Rose award New Eng. Poetry Club, 1942, Jennie Tane Poetry award Mass. Rev., 1962; Phi Beta Kappa poet Tufts U., 1955, Harvard, 1960; Rome fellow Am. Acad. Arts and Letters, 1957-58; Amy Lowell poetry travelling scholarship, 1967-68. Hon. mem. Phi Beta Kappa. Author: (poems) Stand With Me Here, 1936, Valhalla and Other Poems, 1938, The Sound I Listened For, 1944, The Face Against the Glass, 1950, The Orb Weaver, 1960; Come Out Into the Sun, 1965; (fiction) We Fly Away, 1948; (essays) The Satirical Rogue on Poetry, 1968; (autobiography) The Trouble With Francis, 1971. Address: Fort Juniper 170 Market Hill Rd Amherst, MA 01002.

FRANCIS, ROGER BRYANT, library dir.; b. Taunton, Mass., Sept. 10, 1915; s. Percy F. and Alice (Warren) F.; A.B., Brown U., 1938; B.S. in Library Sci., Columbia, 1940; m. Eleanor F. Stringer, Oct. 12, 1940; 1 son, Christopher M. Reference asst. N.Y. Pub. Library, 1940-43, gen. asst., 1946-48, exec. asst., 1948- 52; dir. South Bend (Ind.) Pub. Library, 1952—. Mem. Internat. Relations Council, South Bend, 1956—, Human Relations Council, 1956—; mem. edn. com. YMCA, 1954-65; asst. treas., dir., v.p. Council of Chs., 1963-69, pres., 1969—; dir. Community Coalition, 1969. Served with AUS, 1943-46; ETO. Mem. Am. (past sect. chmn.), Ind. (past pres., com. chmn.) library assns., Am. Civil Liberties Union. Rotarian. Contbr. articles to profl. jours. Home: 51783 Lilac Rd South Bend IN 46628. Office: 122 W Wayne St South Bend IN 46601

FRANCIS, ROY GUSTAF, educator, sociologist; b. Portland, Ore., Dec. 25, 1919; s. Carl and Edla M. (Olson) F.; A.B. magna cum laude, Linfield Coll., McMinnville, Ore., 1946; A.M. with honors, U. Ore., 1948; Ph.D., U. Wis., 1950; postdoctorate student math., Harvard, 1952-53; m. Lillie G. McCormick, Dec. 16, 1950; children—Roy G., Virginia Marr. Asst. prof., research asso. Tulane U., 1950-57; from asst. prof. to prof. U. Minn., 1952-66; dean Coll. Letters and Sci., prof. sociology U. Wis.-Milw., 1966-69, Brittingham prof. sociology, 1969—; owner Research Assos., St. Paul, 1957-66; dir. research Tri-county Mental Health Center, Grand Rapids, Minn., 1962-65, KSTP-Radio-TV, Twin Cities, Minn., 1957-66; psychol. cons. VA, Mpls., 1959-66. Co-chmn. Citizens for McCarthy, Milw., 1968. Bd. dirs. Planned Parenthood Milw., 1969—, Calhoun Beach Manor, Mpls., 1964-66. Served with USAAF, 1942-45. Recipient prize Howard Soc., 1946; Jerome Meml. plaque, 1946; fellow Social Sci. Research Council, 1952-53; dept. fellow U. Wis., 1949. Mem. Am. Sociol. Assn., Midwest Sociol. Soc. (pres. 1969), Am. Civil Liberties Union. Democrat. Author books and articles in field. Home 4748 N Wilshire Rd Whitefish Bay, WI 53211 Office: Univ Wis-Milw Milw Milwaukee WI 53201

FRANCIS, SAM, artist; b. San Mateo, Cal. 1923; B.A., U. Cal. at Berkeley, 1949, M.A., 1950; m. Mako Idemitsu; one son, Osamu. Exhibited one man shows Galerie Nina Dausset, Paris, 1952, Galeri Rive-Droite, Paris, 1954, Martha Jackson Gallery, N.Y.C., 1956, 57, 58, 63, Dusanne Gallery, Seattle, 1957, Phillips Gallery, Washington, 1958, San Francisco Mus. Art, 1959, Seattle Art Mus., 1959, Dayton Art Inst., Pasadena Mus. Art, 1959, Kornfeld & Klipstein, Bern, Switzerland, 1966, Pierre Matisse, N.Y.C., 1967, San Francisco Art Mus., 1967, Mus. Fine Arts, Houston, 1967. Center Nat. Contemporary Art, Paris, France, 1969, also exhibited London, Eng., Stockholm, Tokyo and Osaka, Japan, Dusseldorf, Germany; numerous exhbns. U.S. including Carnegie Internat., 1955, Dunn Internat., 1963, Brussels World's Fair, Biennale, Sao Paulo, also Paris, Rome, other European cities; represented collections Guggenheim Mus., N.Y.C., Mus. Modern Art, Albright Art Gallery, Tate Gallery, London, others. Recipient prize Internat. Exhibit, Tokyo, 1956, 1st prize Internat. Print Exhibit, 1961. Address: 345 W Channel Rd Santa Monica CA 90402

FRANCIS, WILLIAM JUSTUS FLETT, chem. co. exec.; b. Sunderland, Eng., Jan. 8, 1915; s. William Henry and Edith M. (Flett) F.; brought to U.S., 1921, naturalized, 1929; B.S., U. Cal. at Berkeley, 1936, M.S., 1937; m. Alice M. Burke, June 10, 1939; children—Burke W. F., Valerie K., Gary T., Deborah A. Dist. sales mgr. Cal. Spray-Chem. Corp., 1937-43; Western sales mgr., also Western gen. sales mgr. Pennsalt Chems., Inc., 1943-52; gen. sales mgr. Am. Potash & Chem. Corp., Los Angeles, 1952-55, v.p. marketing, 1955—, also mem. bd. dirs., 1964—. Mem. industry adv. coms. WPB and OPS, Washington, 1950-52. Mem. Potash Export Assn. (dir.), Am. Potash Inst. (dir.), Entomol. Soc. Am. Republican. Episcopalian. Home: 748 Amalfi Dr Pacific Palisades CA 90272 Office: 3000 W 6th St Los Angeles CA 90005

FRANCIS, WINTHROP NELSON, educator; b. Phila., Oct. 23, 1910; s. Joseph Sidney and Kate Winthrop (Nelson) F.; grad. William Penn Charter Sch., 1927; A.B., Harvard, 1931; M.A., U. Pa., 1935, Ph.D., 1937; m. Anne Poage Funkhouser, Nov. 25, 1939 (div. 1967); children—John W.N., Samuel Hopkins; m. 2d, Nearlene J. Burkley Bertin, July 1, 1967. From instr. English to prof., Franklin and Marshall Coll., 1937-62, chmn. dept., 1958-62; prof. linguistics and English, Brown U., 1962—, chmn. dept. linguistics, 1968—; Fulbright sr. research fellow Leeds (Eng.) U., 1956-57; vis. prof. Summer Inst. Linguistics, U. Tex., 1960; hon. research fellow Univ. Coll., London, 1965; Fulbright vis. prof., Japan, summer 1967; cons. in field, 1954—. Mem. adv. coms. Coll. Entrance Exam. Bd., Center Applied Linguistics, Nat. Council Tchrs. English, Modern Lang. Assn., U.S. Office Edn.; dir. Brown-Tougaloo English Lang. Project, 1965-69. Served to lt. USNR, 1943- 46. Mem. Modern Lang. Assn., Linguistic Soc. Am., Nat. Council Tchrs. English, Internat. Linguistic Assn., Am. Dialect Soc. Author: The Structure of American English, 1958; The English Language, an Introduction, 1965; (with Henry Kucera) Computational Analysis of Present Day American English, 1967; also articles. Editor: The Book of Vices and Virtues. Home: 45 Appian Way West Barrington, RI 02890. Office: Box E Brown Univ Providence RI 02912

FRANCISCO, CLYDE TAYLOR, educator; b. Virgilina, Va., June 2, 1916; s. Luther T. and Nancy (Firesheets) F.; A.B., U. Richmond, 1939, D.D., 1962; Th.M., So. Baptist Theol. Sem., 1924, Th.D., 1944; m. Nancy Lee Anderson, Dec. 26, 1940; children—Don Richard, Carol Lee. Ordained to ministry Bapt. Ch., 1940; pastor in Va. and Ky., 1936-44; interim pastor in Ky. and W.Va., 1953- 61; mem. faculty So. Bapt. Theol. Sem., 1944—, John R. Sampey prof. O.T. interpretation, 1951—. Mem. Soc. Bib. Lit. and Exegesis, Am. Acad. of Religion, Intern. Platform Assn., Phi Beta Kappa. Author: Introducing the Old Testament, 1950; Studies in Jeremiah, 1961; The Book of Deuteronomy, 1964; Broadman Bible Commentary, 1970. Translator; Proverbs, New Berkeley Version of the Bible, 1970. Home: 640 Upland Rd Louisville KY 40206

FRANCISCO, PETER YATES, stockbroker; b. Rome, N.Y., Sept. 5, 1907; s. Jesse Peter and Augustine (Saunders) F.; grad. Utica (N.Y.) Acad., 1926; m. Margaret Allen, Feb. 1, 1956. With Otis & Co., N.Y.C.,1928-31; partner Pershing & Co., and predecessor, N.Y.C., 1933-. Mem. Am. Stock Exchange, 1951-, bd. govs., 1964—. Republican. Episcopalian. Club: Sleepy Hollow Country (Scarborough-on-Hudson, N.Y.). Home: 60 Judson Av Dobbs Ferry, NY 10522 Office: 120 Broadway New York City NY 10005

FRANCISCUS, JAMES GROVER, actor; b. Clayton, Mo., Jan. 31, 1934; s. John Allen and Loraine (Grover) F.; B.A., Yale, 1957; m. Kathleen Kent Wellman, Mar. 28, 1960; children—Jamie, Kellie. Appeared TV series Naked City, 1958, Mr. Novak, 1963-65, Longstreet, 1971; films include The Outsider, 1962, Youngblood Hawke, 1963, Hell Boats, 1968, Marrooned, 1969, Beneath the Planet of the Apes, 1969, Cat and Nine Tails, 1970; v.p., producer Omnibus Prodns. Inc., Ltd., 1968; prodns. include Heidi, 1969, David Copperfield, 1970, Jane Eyre, 1971, Kidnapped, 1972. Home: 12549 Addison St North Hollywood CA 91607 Office: care Internat Famous Ag Inc 9255 Sunset Blvd Los Angeles CA 90069

FRANCK, AUGUST ALBERT, mfg. co. exec.; b. Antwerp, Belgium, Nov. 26, 1910; s. Jules and F. (Van Straetan) F.; m. Hilda Vandaman, Aug. 19, 1936; children—Walter A., Robert, Greta. With Soc. Generale de Belgique group, 1935—; now pres., chmn. exec. com. GenStar Ltd. (formerly Sogemines Ltd.); vice chmn., dir. Union Miniere Can. Ltd.; dir. Indussa Corp., Atlantic Overseas Corp., Fraser Companies, Ltd., Rathesay Paper Corp., BACM Industries, Ltd. Past pres. Am. Inst. Imported Steel; bd. dirs. Belgian-Am. C. of C., N.Y. C. of C. Decorated chevalier de l'Ordre de la Couronne (Belgium.) Roman Cath. Clubs: St. James's, Mount-Royal, Royal Montreal Golff, Montreal, St.-Denis (Montreal); Seigniory (Que.). Home: 1455 Sherbbrooke St W Montreal Quebec Canada Office: 1 Pl Ville Marie Montreal 113 Quebec Canada*

FRANCK, CHARLES, corp. exec.; b. Berlin, Germany, Nov. 21, 1881; s. Gustav Franck; grad. high sch.; m. 1912; children—Carl G., Ruth (Mrs. H.A. Van Collie). With Holophane Co., Inc., 1915—, formerly exec. v.p., now chmn. bd. Mem. Illuminating Engring. Soc. Home: 900 NE 100th St Miami Shores Miami FL 33153 Office: 1120 Av Americas New York City NY 10036

FRANCK, FREDERICK SIGFRED, artist, dental surgeon, author; b. Maastricht, Netherlands, Apr. 12, 1909; s. Daniel and Helen (Foyer) F.; student U. Amsterdam, 1926-31; Chirurgien Dentiste, Antwerp Dental Sch., 1935; L.D.S., Royal Coll. Surgeons, Edinburgh, Scotland, 1937; D.D.S., U. Pitts., 1942; Dr. of Fine Arts (hon.), U. Pitts., 1963; m. Claske Berndes Franck, July 15, 1960; 1 son, Lukas van Witsen Franck. Came to U.S., 1939, naturalized, 1945. Practice of dentistry, London, Eng., 1937-39; resident oral surgery U. Pitts., 1942-44; anaesthetist Elizabeth Steel Magee Hosp., staff Children's Hosp., Pitts., 1942-44; service cons. Netherlands East Indies govt., 1944-46; dentist, N.Y.C., 1946-66; vis. staff Albert Schweitzer Hosp., 1958-60. One-man shows Contemporary Arts Gallery, Lilienfield Galleries, Passedoit Gallery (all N.Y.C.), Albert Landry Gallery, 1959, 60, Saginaw (Mich.) Mus., Doll & Richards Gallery, Boston, M.H. De Young Mus., San Francisco, Waddell Gallery, Far Gallery (both N.Y.C.), others; shows in Paris, Amsterdam, Geneva, London, Rotterdam, Brussels, Rome, Japan 1971: Tokyo, Kyoto; group shows Met. and Whitney museums, Corcoran Biennale, also Indpls., Mpls.; works rep. collections M.H. de Young Memorial Mus., Fogg Art Museum San Francisco Mus., U. Ill., Mus. Modern Art, Vatican, Rome, Tokyo Nat. Mus., Nat. Collection Fine Arts, Washington, museums Santa Barbara, Amsterdam, Eindhoven, Maastricht, N.Y. Pub. Library, Seattle Mus., Dartmouth, Cornell U., Aschenbach Found., Georgia Mus., Whitney Mus., others; traveling exhbn. to 12 univs. and colls. Midwest, 1970-71; contributor articles, drawings to various magazine and periodicals; chief mission Med. Internat. Coop., 1958. Recipient purchase prize U. Ill., Am. Inst. Arts Letters, Living Arts Found.; 1st prize Carnegie Inst.; prize Musees Nationaux Francais; medal for drawings, Pope John XXIII, 1963. Fellow Internat. Inst. Arts and Letters, Foundation for the Arts, Religion and Culture; mem. Am. Dental Assn., Artists Equity Assn. (hon. dir. N.Y.). Author: Open Wide, Please, 1957; Au Pays du Soleil, 1958; Days with Albert Schweitzer, a Lambarene Landscape, 1959; My Friend in Africa (juvenile), 1960; African Sketchbook, 1961; My Eye is in Love (Art Am. 50th Anniversary spl. citation 1963), 1963; Au Fil de L'Eau, 1964; Outsider in the Vatican, 1965; Met Het Oog Op Het Vatican, 1965; I Love Life (juvenile), 1967; Exploding Church, 1968; Open Book, 1967, Croquis Parisien, 1969; Tutte le Strade portano a Roma, 1969; Le Paris de Simenon, 1969; Simenon's Paris, 1970. Built Pacem In Terris, Warwick, N.Y., 1965. Home: Route 1 Covered Bridge Rd Warwick NY 10990

FRANCK, THOMAS MARTIN, educator; b. Berlin, Germany, July 14, 1931; s. Hugo and Isle (Rosenthal) F.; naturalized Canadian citizen, 1945; B.A., U. B.C., 1952, LL.B., 1953; LL.M., Harvard, 1954, S.J.D., 1956. Asst. prof. law U. Neb., 1956-57; mem. faculty N.Y.U., 1957—, prof. law, 1960, dir. Center Internat. Studies, 1965—; vis. prof. Stanford, 1963, U. East Africa, 1964, 65. Cons. U.S. AID Dept. State, 1970-71. Constl. adviser govts. Tanganyika, 1963, Zanzibar, 1963, 64, Mauritius, 1965; mem. Sierra Leone Govt. Commn. Legal Edn., 1964; mem. Nat. Liberal Adv. Council Can., 1952-53. Served to lt. Canadian Army, 1953. Mem. African Studies Assn., African Law Assn., Assn. Am. Law Schs. Author: Race and Nationalism, 1960; The United Nations in the Congo, 1963; East African Unity Through Law, 1965; Comparative Constitutional Process, 1968; The Structure of Impartiallity, 1968; Why Federations Fail, 1968; A Free Trade Association, 1968. Contbr. books. Home: 15 Charlton St New York City NY 10014

FRANCK, WILLIAM FRANCIS, Jr., knitting co. exec.; b. Fayetteville, N.C., July 17, 1917; s. William Francis and Martha Elizabeth (Lawhon) F.; B.A., Duke, 1939; m. Carolyn Ann Pannill, Nov. 29, 1941; children—Martha (Mrs. Overman Rollins), William Francis III, Carolyn Ann, John M. Salesman, Belk Leggett Co., Durham, N.C., 1935-40; cost clk. DuPont Co., Martinsville, Va., 1940-43; personnel mgr. Pannill Knitting Co., Martinsville, 1946-50; v.p. gen. mgr. Sale Knitting Co., Martinsville, 1950-53, pres., chief exec. officer, 1953—; pres. Kings Mill Inc., King's Mountain, N.C., 1966—; dir. Piedmont Trust Bank, Am. Furniture Co., Graves Supply Co. (all Martinsville). Bd. mem. Martinsville YMCA, 1959-61, Boy Scouts Am., Roanoke, 1969—, Martinsville Sch. Bd., 1957-61; fund chmn. Meml. Hosp. drive, 1966-67, bd. mem. 1963—; mem. Martinsville Sch. Bd., 1956-61; mem. Blue Ridge Airport Authority, 1962—. Served to 1st lt. Q.M.C., AUS, 1943-46; ETO. Mem. Martinsville C. of C. (1st pres. 1959-61). Presbyn. (elder 1954—). Rotarian. Club: Chatmoss Country. Home: Route 6 Box 391 Martinsville VA 24112 Office: Box 5191 Martinsville VA 24112

FRANCKE, DON EUGENE, educator, pharmacist; b. Athens, Pa., Aug. 28, 1910; s. Edward Owen and Margaret Carmalita (Kinney) F.; B.S., U. Mich., 1936, M.S., 1948; D.Sc. (hon.), Purdue U., 1951, U. Mich., 1967; m. Maxine Hafey, Aug. 18, 1937; children—Markay, Stephanie, David, Michele, Jon; m. 2d, Gloria Niemeyer, Apr. 15, 1956. Dir. pharmacy service U. Mich. Hosp., 1944-63; dir. sci. services Am. Soc. Hosp. Pharmacists, 1963-66; cons. hosp. pharmacy Surg. Gen. Army, 1947—, VA 1951—; lectr. hosp. pharmacy U. Mich. Coll. Pharmacy, 1948-51, asst. prof. pharmacy, 1951-62, asso. prof. pharmacy, 1962-63; pharmacy adviser WHO, 1959-; prof., chmn. dept. hosp. pharmacy Coll. Pharmacy, U. Cin., 1967- 71, dir. Inst. Studies Hosp. Pharmacy, 1967—; dir. pharmacy service Cin. Gen. Hosp., 1967-71, VA Central Office, 1971—; dir. Aud-Pharm. Service in Hosp., USPHS grant, 1956-59, dir. hosp. pharmacy technician study, 1970-73. Mem. Am. Pharm. Assn. Mission to Japan, Supreme Command Allied Powers, 1949; mem. Mich. Bd. Pharmacy, 1950-52; mem. revision com. U.S. Pharmacopiela, 1950-60. Lt. comdr. USPHS Res., 1949; pharmacist dir. Res., 1954. Recipient J. Leon Lascoff Meml. Found. award for contbns. pharmacy, 1947, J. Leon Lascoff Memorial award, 1948, H.A.K. Whitney lecture award, 1953, Remington Hon. medal, 1970. Fellow A.A.A.S.; mem. Am. Chem. Soc., Am. Hosp. Assn., Am. Pharm. Assn. (dir. div. hosp. pharmacy 1949-56, council, 1948-56, chmn. com. on publs., 1951-56, pres. 51-52), Am. Soc. Hosp. Pharmacists (pres. 1943-46, editor jour. 1944-66), Am. Assn. U. Profs., Am. Acad. Polit. and Social Sci., Mich. Acad. Pharmacy (dir. 1947-57), Internat. Pharm. Fedn. (council 1953—, v.p. 1958-66, pres. sect. press and documentation), N.Y. Acad. Scis., Am. Med. Writers Assn., Sociedada de Farmacia e Quimica de Sao Paulo, Brazil (hon.), Associacion Farmaceutica y Bioquimica Argentina (hon.), Japanese Pharm. Assn. (hon.), Drug Information Assn. (pres. 1969), Am. Inst. History Pharmacy, Rho Chi, Phi Delta Chi. Club: Cosmos (Washington). Author: Hospital Formulary of Selected Drugs; (co-author) Art of Compounding, Remingon's Practice of Pharmacy; Report of Audit of Pharmaceutical Services in Hospitals; sr. author Mirror to Hospital Pharmacy, 1964. Editor: Formulary U. of Mich. Hosp.; co-editor: Perspectives in Clinical Pharmacy, 1971; asso.. editor: U. Mich. Med. Bull., 1950-58; editor Internat. Pharm. Abstracts, 1964-66, Drug Intelligence, Drug Information Bull., 1967-71. Contbr. articles pharmacy and hosp. jours. Home: Cosmos Club 22d and Massachusetts Av Washington DC Office: Pharmacy Service VA Central Office Vermont Av Washington DC 20008

FRANCO, HERMAN BENJAMIN, lawyer; b. Montgomery, Ala., Jan. 26, 1929; s. Simanto and Zelda (Sarfati) F.; B.S., U. Ala., 1951, LL.B., 1956. Admitted to Ala. bar, 1956, since practiced in Montgomery; partner Emmet & Franco, 1956-61, Hobbs, Copeland, Franco, Riggs & Screws, 1966—. Served with inf., U.S. Army, 1954-56. Mem. Am., Ala., Montgomery County bar assns., Am. Trial Lawyers Assn., Am. Judicature Soc., Ala. Law Inst. Lion. Home: 2460 Price St Montgomery AL 36111 Office: 444 S Perry St Montgomery AL 36101

FRANCO, MICHAEL J., banker; b. Phila., 1911; grad. U. Pa., 1935. Pres., dir. City Nat. Bank Miami (Fla.); dir. City Nat. Bank Miami Beach, City Nat. Bank Coral Gables. Home: 1480 NE 101st St Miami FL 33138 Office: 25 W Flagler St PO Box 3280 Miami FL 33132

FRANCO, RALPH ABRAHAM, lawyer; b. Montgomery, Ala., Dec. 27, 1921; s. Abraham and Matilda (Habib) F.; B.S., U. Ala., 1943, LL.B., 1948. admitted to Ala. bar, 1948, since practiced in Montgomery; asso. Hill, Hill, Stovall & Carter, 1948-54, partner, 1954-68; partner Hill, Hill, Stovall, Carter & Franco, 1968—; prof. Jones Law Sch., Montgomery, 1957-67. State chmn. Employ the

Physically Handicapped Week, 1950. Pres., bd. dirs. Jewish Fedn. Montgomery; trustee Blue and Gray. Served from 2d lt. to capt.,inf.,AUS, 1943-46, Judge Adv. Gen. Corps, U.S. Army, 1951-52. Mem. Am., Ala. (com. chmn.), Montgomery County bar assns., U. Ala. Law Sch. Alumni Assn. (past pres.) Jewish religion. Lion. Home: 607 E Patton Av Montgomery AL 36111 Office: Hill Bldg P O Box 116 73 Washington Av Montgomery AL 36104

FRANCO BAHAMONDE, FRANCISCO, head of Spanish State; b. El Ferrol, Prov. of Corunna, Spain, Dec. 4, 1892; s. Nicolas Franco Salgado-Araujo and Pilar Bahamonde Pardo; grad. Inf. Acad., 1907; attended course for officers of various nations, Paris and Verdun, France, 1930; m. Carmen Polo y Martinez de Valdes, Oct. 16, 1923; 1 dau., Carmen (Marquesa de Villaverde). Entered mil. career with rank of 2d lt. inf.; advanced to brig. gen., 1926; served with distinction in Africa; pres. of commn. which organized Gen. Mil. Acad. of Saragossa, 1927, dir. of the acad., 1928-31 (when it was supressed by the Republic); comd. 15th Inf. Brigade, Corunna, 1932; apptd. mil. comdr. of the Balearics, 1933; promoted maj. gen., 1934; comdr. in chief of the forces in Morocco, Feb.-May 1935, chief of gen. staff, May 1935, comdr. in chief Canary Islands, 1936. Assumed leadership of mil. forces in Africa which rebelled against the Republican govt. in Spain, and conducted campaign in continental Spain, 1936; by degree of Council of Nat. Def., apptd. head of Spanish State and Generalissimo of Land, Sea and Air Forces, Sept. 1936, and served as such during Spanish Civil War, 1936-39 and 1940—; reorganized parliament under name of Cortes Españolas, 1942; approved Spain's Constl. Charter, 1945; by general referendum the law of succession to headship of the state was approved, 1947. Decorated Gran Cruz Laureada de San Fernando, Medalla de Sufrimientos por la Patria. Curz del Mérito Naval con distintivo rojo. Cruz del Mérito Militar con distintivo rojo. Cruz y Placa de la Real y Militar Order de San Hermenogildo, and numerous other mil. and civil awards (Spain); also decorations and high honors from the govts. of other countries throughout the world. Address: Madrid Spain

FRANCOEUR, SISTER MARY PETRONILLIA, former coll. pres.; b. Martinton, Ill., Nov. 20, 1905; d. Leopold D. and Eugenie (Barrassa) F.; B.A., Desales Coll., Toledo, 1928; M.A., U. Detroit, 1931; Ph.D., U. Mich., 1944, vis. scholar, 1962; grad. student U. Miami (Fla.). Cath. U. Am., Harvard Inst. Adminstrs. Joined Order of St. Dominic, 1923; tchr. in kindergarten, coll. and grad. schs., 1924-65; chmn. grad. div. Barry Coll., Miami, Fla., 1960-65; pres. Siena Heights Coll., Adrian, Mich., 1965-69; speaker classical convs. Mem. Classical Assn., Am. Assn. Tchrs. French, Assn. Coll. and Univ. Pres., Assn. Ind. Colls. Mich., Am. Assn. U. Women, Nat. Cath. Ednl. Assn. Address: Verro Beach FL

FRANCOIS-PONCET, ANDRE, diplomat; b. Provins, France, June 13, 1887; student lycées Carnot and Henry IV; laureat at gen. examinations, l'Ecole Normale Suérieure, 1907; m. Mlle Dillais; children—Louis, Henri, Bernard, Jean. Geneviéve. Collaborator journal l'Opinion, 1911; lecturer l'Ecole Polytechnique, 1913; with French Embassy, Berne, 1917-18; mem. Internat. Econ. Mission to U.S.; del. of French Govt. to confs. at Genoa and Ruhr, 1919; founded The Buelletin, daily publ. of Soc. for Studies and Econ. Information, 1920; mem. dirs. com. Rep. Dem. Alliance; elected deputy from 17th Arrondissement of Paris, 1924, 1928; mem. Commn. of Finances; under-sec. of state for Beaux-Arts, for technique instrn.; participated in numerous internat. confs. until 1931; named ambassador of France to Berlin, 1931-1938, ambassador to The Quirinal, 1938, returned to France June 1940; deported and interned by Gestapo, 1943; diplomatic councilor of French Govt., Dec. 1948. High Commr. of French Republic in Germany 1949-55. Served as lt. of infantry, French Army, 1914-16. Pres. French Red Cross, 1955—; pres. permanent commn. of Internat. Red Cross as successor to Count Bernadotte, 1949. Received first standing in examination for German fellowship, 1910. Roman Catholic. Published a first work on Les affinitiés électives, by Goethe, 1910. Author: Ce que pense la jeunesse allemande, a study, 1913; Souvenirs d'une Ambassade à Berlin, 1946; De Versailles à Potsdam, 1946. Elected mem. Académie francaise, 1952. Home: 92 rue du Ranelagh Paris, XVI France

FRANDSEN, ARDEN N., educator; b. Redmond, Utah, Feb. 4, 1902; s. Niels and Algie (Anderson) F.; B.S., U. Utah, 1927, M.S., 1929; Ph.D., U. Minn., 1932; m. Phyllis J. Jorgenson, Sept. 1933; 1 dau., Julia Ann. Clin. psychology Minn. Bd. Control, 1932-33; asst. prof. psychology U. Utah, 1933-36; prof. dept. psychology Utah State U., 1936—, head of dept., 1936- 65; vis. prof., summer sessions, San Jose State Coll., U. Ill., Cornell U., N.Y.U. Coll. Edn., Plattsburg, Diplomate clin. psychology Am. Bd. Examiners Profl. Psychology. Fellow Am. Psychol. Assn.; mem. Nat. Soc. Study Edn., Sigma Xi. Author: How Children Learn, 1957; Educational Psychology, 1961, rev. edit., 1967; also sci. articles. Home: 550 E 6th N Logan UT 84321

FRANDSEN, JULIUS, news exec.; b. Moscow, Ida., July 12, 1907; s. Julius Herman and Mattie (Madsen) F.; A.B., U. Neb., Lincoln, 1927; m. Eleanor Cameron, Sept. 1, 1931 (dec. 1953); m. 2d, Ruth Gmeiner, Aug. 8, 1954; 1 son, Jon Christian. Editorial work on the Springfield (Mass.) Republican, 1927-29; with United Press (now United Press Internat.) in reportorial and managerial capacities, N.Y.C. and Washington, 1929—, news editor Washington Bur., 1939-60, Washington mgr., 1961-65, v.p., Washington mgr., 1966—. Dir., Nat. Press Bldg. Corp. Chmn., Sigma Delta Chi Found. of Washington, Thomas L. Stokes Award Com., 1966—. Mem. Delta Upsilon, Sigma Delta Chi (chmn. nat. freedom information com. 1964- 65). Clubs: Gridiron (pres. 1962, sec. 1965—), Internat., Nat. Press (Washington). Home: 5134 Worthington Dr Washington DC 20016 Office: National Press Bldg Washington DC 20004

FRANJEH, SULEIMAN, pres. Lebanon; b. Zgharta, June 14, 1910; ed. Coll. at Antoura, Lebanon; m.; five children. Elected to Lebanese parliment 1960, 64; Minister of Interior, 1968; Minister of Justice; Minister of Econ.; Minister of Pub. Works; Minister of Nat. Econ., 1969-70, pres. Lebanon, 1970—. Address: Office of Pres Beirut Lebanon*

FRANK, ABERT EUGENE, fgn. service officer; b. Marengo, Ill., Feb. 24, 1918; s. Robert Worth and Grace (Haun) F.; student Wabash Coll., 1934-36; B.A., Coll. Wooster, 1938; M.A., U. Minn., 1941; postgrad. Woodrow Wilson Sch., Princeton, 1960-61; m. Nancy Ballard, May 25, 1942; children—Chana, Worth, Nancy, Morley. Instr., Highlands U., 1946, Morgan Park Jr. Coll., 1946-47; joined U.S. fgn. service, 1947; vice consul, Sydney, Australia, 1947-1950; 2d sec. Am. embassy, Ottawa, Can., 1950-1952; officer State Dept., 1952-56; 2d sec. Am. embassy, Rome, 1956-60; officer State Dept., 1961-65; 1st sec. Am. embassy, Mogadisio, Somali Republic, 1965-68, Paris, France, 1968-71; adviser Dept. State Office Telecommunications, Washington, 1971—. Served with USN, 1941-46. Mem. Am. Fgn. Service Assn. Presbyn. Home: 3319 Fessenden St NW Washington DC 20008 Office: Dept of State Washington DC 20025

FRANK, ANTHONY MELCHIOR, financial and real estate exec.; b. Berlin, Germany, May 21, 1931; s. Lothar and Elisabeth (Roth) F.; came to U.S., 1937, naturalized, 1943; B.A., Dartmouth, 1953, M.B.A., 1954; postgrad. finance, U. Vienna, 1956; m. Gay Palmer, Oct. 16, 1954; children—Tracy, Randall. Asst. to pres., bond portfolio mgr. Glendale Fed. Savs. Assn. (Cal.), 1958-61; v.p., treas. Far West Financial Corp., Los Angeles, 1962; adminstrv. v.p., v.p. savs. First Charter Financial Corp., Beverly Hills, Cal., 1962- 66; pres. State Mut. Savs. and Loan Assn., Los Angeles, 1966-68, Titan Group, Inc., N.Y.C. and Los Angeles, 1968-70; pres. INA Properties, Inc., 1970—; group v.p. charge real estate and health care INA Corp., Los Angeles, Phila., 1970—; chmn. Fed. Home Loan Bank San Francisco; trustee Larwin Mortgage Investors Fund; dir. Capital Guardian Trust, AID, Inc., Data Corp., WDC Services, Inc.; former pub. interest dir. Nev. Savs. and Loan Assn., Las Vegas; former dir., cons. State Mut. Savs. and Loan Assn., Los Angeles; mem. adv. com. financial instns., exec. tng. program U. Cal. extension. Chmn. econs. sect., gov. Town Hall, Los Angeles, 1968- 71. Del. Cal. Democratic Conv., 1968. Served with AUS, 1954-56. Mem. Twentieth Century Round Table, Young Pres. Orgn. (sec.). Clubs: Dartmouth So. Cal.; University (Los Angeles). Home: 4310 Chevy Chase Dr La Canada CA 91011 Office: 4050 Wilshire Blvd Los Angeles CA 90010

FRANK, CHARLES RAPHAEL, Jr., economist; b. Pitts., May 15, 1937; s. Charles Raphael and Lucille (Briscoe) F.; B.S., in Math., Rensselaer Poly. Inst., 1959; M.A. in Econs., Princeton, 1961, Ph.D. in Econs., 1963; m. Susan Patricia Backman, Mar. 9, 1963; children—Elizabeth Grace, Stephen Raphael. Sr. research fellow East African Inst. Social Research Makerere U. Coll., Kampala, Uganda, 1963-65; asst. prof. econs. Yale, 1965-67; asso. prof. econs. and internat. affairs Princeton, 1967-70, prof., 1970—; operations research analyst U.S. Steel, summers 1960, 61; cons. in field, 1964—; research adv. AID; asso. dir. research program econ. devel. Woodrow Wilson Sch., Princeton 1967-70, dir., 1970—. Mem. Econometric Soc., A.A.A.S., Council Fgn. Relations, Am. Econ. Assn. Author: Production Theory and Indivisible Commodities, 1969; The Sugar Industry in East Africa, 1965; (with Brian Van Arkadie) Economic Accounting and Development Planning, 2d edit., 1969; Debt and The Terms of Aid, 1970; statistics and Econometrics, 1971. Home: 59 Cedar Lane Princeton NJ 08540

FRANK, CLINTON EDWARD, advt. exec.; b. St. Louis, Sept. 13, 1915; s. Arthur A. and Daisy Marian (Irwin) F.; grad. Lawrenceville Acad., 1934; A.B., Yale, 1938; m. Frances Calhoun Price, July July 25, 1941 (div. 1967); children—Marcia Case, Clinton Edward, Laurie Anne, Cynthia Calhoun, Arthur A. III; m. 2d Margaret Rathje Mullins, May 24, 1967. Account exec. Blackett-Sample- Hummert, 1938-41. Dancer-Fitzgerald-Sample, 1947-48; sales promotion mgr. E. J. Brach & Sons, Chgo., 1948-49; v.p., treas., partner Price-Robinson & Frank, Inc., 1949-53; pres. Clinton E. Frank, Inc., Chgo., 1954-67, chmn. exec. com., dir., 1967—; dir. Stanray Corp., Mdse. Nat. Bank Chgo. Bd. dirs. Passavant Meml. Hosp. Served with USAAF, 1941-45 aide to Lt. Gen. James H. Doolittle, exec. officer 98th Bomb Group, Africa, Italy; ret. as lt. col. Clubs: Chicago, University, Commonwealth, Glen View, Indian Hill. Home: 28 Bridlewood Rd Northbrook IL Office: 120 S Riverside Plaza Chicago IL 60606

FRANK, CURTISS E., lawyer, orgn. exec.; b. N.Y.C., Nov. 13, 1904; s. Augustus A. and Mary (Fowler) F.; A.B., Colgate U., 1925, L.L.D., 1969; L.L.B., Columbia, 1928; m. Grace Watkins, Oct. 11, 1929 (dec. Nov. 1957); children—Anne Fairfield (Mrs. Arthur DuBois), Curtiss Ely; m. 2d, Lila Bonhus Shaw, Dec. 13, 1958. Admitted to N.Y. bar, 1928; asso. Hughes, Schurman & Dwight, 1928-37; asst. U.S. atty. So. Dist. N.Y., 1931-32; partner Hughes, Hubbard & Ewing, 1937-49; v.p., gen. counsel Reuben H. Donnelley Corp., 1949-51, exec. v.p., 1952-55, pres., 1956- 61, chmn. bd., chief exec. officer, 1961-66; pres. Dun & Bradstreet, Inc., 1966-67, vice chmn., 1968-69; pres. Council Financial Aid Edn., 1970—; dir. Dun & Bradstreet, Inc., Reuben H. Donnelley Corp., Southeastern Pub. Service Co., ACF Industries, Willcox & Gibbs, Inc.; mem. adv. com. Bankers Trust Co. Mem. cons. panel to comptroller gen. U.S., 1967-69. Councilman City of Yonkers, 1942-43, mayor, 1944-49. Trustee Nat. Council on Crime and Delinquency; chmn. bd. trustees Colgate U.; v.p. Nat. Municipal League. Presbyn. Clubs: Union League, Blind Brook; Round Hill (Conn.) Country. Home: Winding Lane Greenwich CT 06830 Office: 6 E 45th St New York City NY 10017

FRANK, ELKE, educator; b. Hamburg, Germany, May 27, 1934; s. Rudolf and Margarethe (Daehn) F.; came to U.S., 1953, naturalized, 1965; B.A. cum laude, Fla. State U., 1957, M.A., 1959; Ph.D., Harvard, 1964. Asst. prof. polt. sci. Fla. State U., 1961-66, Hunter Coll., 1966-69; asso. prof. Am. U., 1968-70; acad. dean, prof. polit sci. Mary Baldwin Coll., Staunton, Va., 1970—. Brookings Instn. guest scholar, 1964. Mem. Am., So. polit. sci. assns., So. Assn. Colls. and Schs., Assn. Deans So. Colls., Phi Beta Kappa, Phi Kappa Phi, Pi Sigma Alpha, Phi Alpha Theta, Alpha Lambda Delta. Author: Law Makers in a Changing World, 1966; John F. Kennedy, a Political Biography, 1968; (with Marian Irish) A Theory of Comparative Politics, 1972; also articles, book revs. Mem. editorial bd. Jour. Politics, 1969—. Home: 509 E Beverly St Staunton VA 24401

FRANK, ELL, Jr., lawyer; b. Balt., Aug. 29, 1902; s. Eli and Rena (Ambach) F.; B.A., Johns Hopkins, 1922; LL.B., Harvard, 1925; m. Amy Heilbronner, May 7, 1928; children—Marcia (Mrs. Franz Allina), Victoria (Mrs. Leonard D. Albert). Admitted Md. bar, 1925; asso. firm Beeuwkes, Skeen & Oppenheimer, Balt., 1925-34; chief counsel U.S. Bur. Customs, 1934-36; asst. gen. counsel Treasury Dept., 1936; partner firm Laucheimer & Frank, Balt., 1936-55, Frank, Bernstein, Conaway & Kaufman, 1943-66, Frank, Bernstein, Conaway and Goldman, 1966—. Mem. rules com. Md. Ct. Appeals, 1946-54; mem. Appellate Ct. Jud. Commn. Md., 1971—. Dir. S. Kann Sons Co., The Savings Bank of Baltimore; sec. Penguin Books, Inc. Mem. bd. sch. commnrs. Balt. City, 1957-62, pres., 1962-67; commr. Edn. Commission of the States, 1966-68. Trustee Johns Hopkins, 1959-; chmn. trustees Johns Hopkins Fund, 1961-66. Mem. Am., Md. (pres. 1969-70) bar assns., Am. Law Inst., Bar Assn. Balt. City, Harvard Law Sch. Assn. Md. (pres. 1967-68). Clubs: Johns Hopkins, Suburban Country, 14 West Hamilton St. (Balt.). Home: 5415 Greenspring Av Baltimore MD 21209 Office: Mercantile Bank and Trust Bldg 2 Hopkins Plaza Baltimore MD 21201

FRANK, ERNST L., metal ore co. exec.; b. Strassbourg, Germany, Aug. 15, 1905; s. Paul G. and Ida (Bendix) F.; came to U.S., 1926, naturalized, 1934; M.A., New Sch. For Social Research, 1954; m. Elfriede Hartung, Oct. 11, 1933; children—Eva Maria (Mrs. Hans E. Tausig), Ernest H., Sybil Ann. With Ore & Chem. Corp., 1926-38, W.R. Grace & Co., 1938-48; with Philipp Brox. div. Minerals & Chems. Philipp Corp., N.Y.C., 1948; now sr. v.p. Engelhard Minerals & Chems. Corp., Newark; v.p., dir. Minerals & Chems. Philipp Corp. C.P.A., N.Y. Mem. Am. Inst. Mining and Metall. Engrs., N.Y. Soc. C.P.A.'s, Commodity Exchange. Club: Marco Polo. Home: 85-19 Abingdon Rd Kew Gardens, NY 11415; also 28 India St Nantucket MA 02554 Office: 113 Astor St Newark NJ 07114

FRANK, EUGENE MAXWELL, bishop; b. Cherryvale, Kan., Dec. 11, 1907; s. Ade W. and Emma W. (Maxwell) F.; B.S., Kan. State Tchrs. Coll., 1930; B.S., Garrett Bib. Inst., 1932; D.D., Baker U., 1947; LL.D., Central Coll., 1957; D.D., St. Paul School of Theology, Methodist, 1962; m. Wilma A. Sedoris, June 20, 1930; children—Wilmagene (Mrs. Lewis C. Noonan), Gretchen (Mrs. J. Harrison Beal), Susan (Mrs. Michael Pomerantz), Thomas Frank. Ordained to ministry Meth. Ch., 1932; pastor, Tonganoxie, Kan., 1932, Americus, Kan., 1933-36, Olathe, Kan., 1936-42, Kansas City, Kan., 1942-48, Topeka, Kan., 1948-56; consecrated bishop, 1956; bishop of Mo., St. Louis, 1956—. Pres. Council of Bishops of Meth. Ch., 1968—; mem. bd. missions; chmn. pub. relations and Meth. information; exec. com. World Meth. Council; mem. coordinating council Meth. Ch. Pres. bd. trustees St. Paul Sch. Theology Methodist. Mem. Kappa Delta Pi, Pi Kappa Delta, Phi Mu Alpha, Tau Kappa Epsilon. Address: 835 Oleta Dr St Louis MO 63105

FRANK, EVELYN, educator; b. Chgo.; Ph.D., Northwestern U., 1945. Instr. Northwestern U., Evanston, Ill., 1942-46; prof. math. U. Ill. at Chgo. Circle, 1946—. Mem. Am. Math. Soc., Math. Assn. Am., Soc. Indsl. and Applied Math., Phi Beta Kappa, Sigma Xi. Author articles in field. Address: P O Box 361 Evanston IL 60204

FRANK, EVERETT, business exec.; b. Paris, Tex., Aug. 12, 1893; s. William and Wilhelmina (Fried) F.; grad. Philips Exeter Acad., 1911; A.B., Princeton 1915; m. Ruth Long, Oct. 17, 1921 (dec. Dec. 1963); children—Everett, Jr., and Ruth Elizabeth (Mrs. Milton Pelovitz); m. 2d, Mrs. Alice Crabtree, Feb. 24, 1968. With National City Co., 1915-17, Dillon Read and Co., 1919-30; v.p. and pres. Keswick Corp., 1930-45; chmn. bd. Childs Co. 1947—. Served with U.S. Army, 1917-19. Clubs: Princeton, City Midday (New York). Home: 14 Woodfield Dr Short Hills NJ 07078 Office: 39 Broadway New York City York City NY 10006

FRANK, FICE ALEXANDER, savs. and loan assn. exec.; b. Elmhurst, N.Y., June 19, 1916; s. Daniel and Julia (Weiss) F.; B.A., Amherst Coll., 1937; M. in Govt. and Internat. Relations, Columbia, 1938, LL.B., 1941. Admitted to N.Y. bar, 1942; practice in N.Y.C., 1946—; counsel, dir., mem. exec. com. Woodside Savs. and Loan Assn. (N.Y.), 1946-65, chmn. bd., 1965—, pres., 1969—. Patron Met. Opera Assn.; active urban renewal work, Bklyn. and Bronx, N.Y. Served with AUS, 1942-46. Mem. Nat. League Ins. Savs. and Loan Assns., Savs. Assn. League N.Y. (chmn. legislative com., alternate dir.), U.S. Savs. and Loan League, Am. Savs. and Loan Inst., Queens County C. of C., Am., Queens County bar assns. Home: 515 E 89th St New York City NY 10028 Office: 60-20 Woodside Av Woodside NY 11377

FRANK, GEROLD, author: Deed, 1963; The Boston Strangler (Edgar Allan Poe award), 1967. Address: care Mystery Writers of Am 151 W 48th St New York City NY 10036*

FRANK, HARRY P., publisher Elizabeth (N.J.) Journal. Address: care Elizabeth Journal Elizabeth NJ 07202*

FRANK, HENRY SORG, chemist; b. Pitts., Aug. 6, 1902; s. Austin Cleis and Alma (Sorg) F.; B. Chemistry, U. Pitts., 1922, M.S., 1922; Ph.D., U. Cal. (DuPont fellow and China Med. Bd. fellow), 1928; L.H.D., Geneva Coll., 1969; m. Martha Elizabeth Griggs, June 15, 1927; children—Austin C., Alice (Mrs. Edwin P. Brown), Marian (Mrs. Arnold Zeitlin). Instr., later asst. prof. of physics Lingnan U., Canton, China, 1922-25, asso. prof. chmistry, 1928-33, prof. chemistry, 1933-51, chmn. dept. chemistry, 1933-47, dean coll. sci., 1938-51, vice provost, 1946-48, provost, 1948-51; grad. asst. U. Cal., 1925-26, instr. chemistry, 1927-28, lectr., 1942-45; research Inst. of Phys. Chemistry, Copenhagen (Denmark), 1933-34; interned by Japanese, Hong Kong, China, Jan.-June 1942; head China sect., div. cultural cooperation, Dept. of State, 1945-46; vis. prof. U. Pitts., 1939-40, prof., head dept. chemistry, 1951-63, prof., 1963—; adj. sr. fellow Mellon Inst., 1963-71; cons. Oak Ridge Nat. Lab., 1966—; Boomer Meml. lectr. dept. chemistry, U. Alta., Edmonton, Can., 1967, adviser, spl. chair prof. chemistry Research Center, Nat. Taiwan U., 1968; researcher Max Planck Inst., Göttingen, Germany, 1957; ICA cons., vis. prof. Inst. Nuclear Sci., Nat. Tsinghua U., Taiwan, summer 1959. Mem. of the bd. trustees Lingnan U. (N.Y.C.). Fellow A.A.A.S.; mem. Am. Chem. Soc. (Pitts. award 1964), Chinese Chem. Society (hon.), Phi Beta Kappa, Sigma Xi, Phi Lambda Upsilon, Alpha Chi Sigma. Contbr. profl. jours. Home: 4 Olympia Pl Pittsburgh PA 15217

FRANK, ILYA MIKHAILOVICH, Russian scientist; b. Leningrad, Oct. 23, 1908; s. Mikhail Lyudvigovich and Yelizaveta Mikhailovna (Gratsianova) F.; grad. Moscow U., 1930; m. Ella Abramovna Beilikhis, 1937; 1 son, Alexander. Research photoluminescence of solutions, photo chemistry, optical dissociation of molecules; staff Lebedev Inst. of Physics USSR Acad. Scis., 1934—, research atomic nucleus physics, head atomic nucleus physics lab. until 1970; faculty Moscow U., prof., head of chair, 1944—, dir. lab. neutron physics Joint Inst. for Nuclear Research, 1957—. Recipient (with P.A. Cerenkov, I. E. Tamm) Nobel prize in physics for discovery and interpretation of Cerenkov effect, 1958. Mem. USSR Acad. Scis. Address: Joint Inst for Nuclear Research Head Post Office PO Box 79 Moscow Russia

FRANK, IRA, Jr., banker. Adminstrv. v.p. Am. Nat. Bank & Trust Co., Chgo. Office: LaSalle St at Washington St Chicago IL 60690*

FRANK, ISAIAH, educator, economist; b. N.Y.C., Nov. 7, 1917; s. Henry and Rose (Isserles) F.; B.S., Coll. City N.Y., 1936; M.A. in Econs., Columbia, 1938, Ph.D. in Econs., 1960; m. Ruth Hershfield, Mar. 23, 1941; children—Robert E., Kenneth D. Research asso. Columbia U. Council for Research in Social Scis., 1936-39; teaching fellow, instr. Amherst Coll., 1939-41; Carnegie fellow Nat. Bur. Econ. Research, 1941-42; cons. W.P.B., 1942; sr. economist OSS, 1942-44; various positions Dept. State, 1945-63, dir. Office Internat. Trade, 1957-59, dir. Office Internat. Financial & Devel. Affairs, 1961-62, dep. asst. sec. for econ. affairs, 1962-63; William L. Clayton prof. internat. econs. Sch. Advanced Internat. Studies, John Hopkins, 1963—. Cons. U.S. Dept. State, Treasury Dept., Internat. Bank for Reconstrn. and Devel. Mem. Industry-Govt. Iron and Steel Mission to Europe, 1947; adviser U.S. delegation Econ. Commn. of Europe, 1948; dep. dir. fgn. resources div., Pres.'s Materials Policy Commn., 1951-52; mem. U.S. delegation 10th Inter-Am. Conf., Caracas, Venezuela, 1954, Inter-Am. Conf. Ministers of Finance and Economy, Rio de Janeiro, 1954; head U.S. Delegation Conf. on Dollar Liberalization, OEEC, Paris, 1955-56; del. Conf. of Ministers Paris, 1957; chmn. U.S. delegation, Gen. Agreement on Tariffs and Trade, Geneva, 1958; alternate U.S. rep. Fourth Meeting Devel. Assistance Group, London, 1961; chmn. U.S. delegation to preparatory com. UN Conf. Trade and Devel., Geneva, 1963—; U.S. rep. Spl. Trade Conf. OAS, Alta Gracia, Argentina, 1964; exec. dir. President's Commn. on Internat. Trade and Investment Policy, 1970-71; adv. com. UN Trade and Devel. Bd.; adviser Com. Econ. Devel. Served to 1st lt., AUS, 1944-45. Recipient Rockefeller Pub. Service Award, 1959-60; Ford Found. Research grant. Mem. Council Fgn. Relations, Am. Econ. Assn., Phi Beta Kappa. Club: Cosmos (Washington). Author: The European Common Market: An Analysis of Commercial Policy. Contbr. profl. publs. Home: 3102 Hawthorne St NW Washington, DC 20008. Office: 1740 Massachusetts Av NW Washington DC 20036

FRANK, JEROME DAVID, psychiatrist, educator; b. N.Y.C., May 30, 1909; s. Jerome W. and Bess (Resenbaum) F.; A.B. summa cum laude, Harvard, 1930, A.M., 1932, A in Psychology, 1934, M.D. cum laude, 1939; m. Elizabeth Kleeman, Jan. 4, 1948; children—Deborah, David, Julia, Emily. Research asso. group psychotherapy research project VA, 1946-49; instr. Washington Sch. Psychiatry, 1947-49; clin. asso. prof. Howard U., 1948-49; instr. Johns Hopkins Med. Sch., 1942-46, 49—, prof. psychiatry, 1959—; psychiatrist-in-charge psychiat. out-patient dept. Johns Hopkins Hosp., 1951-64, dir. clin. services Henry Phipps Psychiat. Clinic, 1961-63, acting chief dept. psychiatry, 1960-61, 62- 63; staff mem. Center Study Dem. Instns., 1966. Adv. bd. Patuxent Instn., 1954—; mem. adv. coms. Nat. Inst. Mental Health, 1951-55, 57- 58, 59-61, 68-69, mem. task force on homosexuality, 1967-69; mem. social sci. adv. bd. U.S. Arms Control and Disarmament Agy., 1969—; mem. adv. com. phychiatry and neurology service Dept. Medicine and Surgery, VA Central Office, 1960-64; bd. dirs. Met. Balt. Assn. Mental Health, 1952—. Bd. dirs. Nat. Com. Sane Nuclear Policy. Bd. dirs. Council for a Livable World, 1963—. Recipient Tenth Emil A. Gutheil award Assn. for Advancement Psychotherapy, 1970. Fellow Center Advanced Study Behavioral Scis., Palo Alto, Cal., 1958-59; Praelector in Psychiatry, Faculty Medicine, U. St. Andrews, Dundee, Scotland, 1967; H.B. Williams Travelling prof. psychiatry, Australia and New Zealand, 1971. Served to maj., AUS, 1943- 46. Recipient Emil A. Gutheil award Assn. Advancement Psychotherapy, 1970. Fellow Am. Psychiat. Assn., Am. Psychol. Assn., Soc. for the Psychol. Study of Social Issues (pres. 1965-66), Am. Coll. Psychiatrists, Am. Group Psychotherapy Assn., World Acad. of Art and Sci.; mem. Am. Psychopathol. Assn. (pres. 1963), A.M.A., Am. Assn. U. Profs., Phi Beta Kappa, Sigma Xi, Alpha Omega Alpha. Author: Persuasion and Healing; A Comparative Study of Psychotherapy, 1961; (with Florence Powdermaker) Group Psychotherapy: Studies in Methodology of Research and Therapy, 1953; Sanity and Survival: Psychological Aspects of War and Peace, 1967; also articles. Home: 603 W University Pky Baltimore MD 21210 Office: Phipps Clinic Johns Hopkins Hosp Baltimore MD 21205

FRANK, JOHN PAUL, lawyer, author; b. Appleton, Wis., Nov. 10, 1917; s. Julius Paul and Beatrice (Ullman) F.; B.A., U. Wis., 1938, M.A., LL.B., 1940; J.S.D., Yale, 1946; m. Lorraine Weiss, May 11, 1944; children—John Peter, Gretchen, Karen, Andrew, Nancy Jo. Admitted to Wis. bar, 1940, D.C. bar, 1966, Ariz. bar, 1954, also U.S. Supreme Ct.; law clk. U.S. Supreme Ct. Justice Hugo L. Black, 1942; asst. to sec. interior, 1943, to atty. gen., 1944-45; asst. prof. law Ind. U., 1946-49; asso. prof. law Yale, 1949-54; vis. lectr. law U. Wash., 1966, U. Ariz., 1967; with firm Covington & Burling, Washington, 1947, Arnold & Porter, Washington, 1948, 53; mem. firm Lewis & Roca, Phoenix, 1954—. Mem. adv. com. civil procedure Jud. Conf. U.S., 1960-70. Democratic precinct committeeman, 1956—; counsel Ariz. Dem. Party, 1962-65. Mem. Am., Maricopa County bar assns., Am. Law Inst. Clubs: Press, University, Lawyers (Phoenix). Author: Mr. Justice Black, 1949; Cases on Constitutional Law, 1950; Cases on the Constitution, 1951; My Son's Story, 1952; Marble Palace, 1958; Lincoln as a Lawyer, 1961; Justice Daniel Dissenting, 1964; The Warren Court, 1964; American Law: The Case for Radical Reform, 1969; also articles. Home: 5829 E Arcadia Lane Phoenix AZ 85018 Office: 114 W Adams St Phoenix AZ 85003

FRANK, JOSEPH, educator; b. Chgo., Dec. 20, 1916; s. A. Richard and Gertrude (Greenbaun) F.; B.A., Harvard, 1939, M.A., 1947, Ph.D., 1953; m. Margery Goodkind, Feb. 1, 1941; children—Thomas, Peter, Andrew; m. 2d, Florence Stanton Clark Zartman, Jan. 24, 1969. From instr. to prof. English, U. Rochester, 1948-67; prof., chmn. dept. English, U. N.M., 1967-69; prof., head English dept. U. Mass., Amherst, 1969—. Pres. Genesee Valley, Am. Civil Liberties Union, 1965, mem. N.M. bd., 1967-69. Served with Am. Field Service, 1943; AUS, 1943-45. Huntington Library fellow, 1955-56, Guggenheim fellow, 1958-59, 61, Folger Shakespeare Library fellow, 1962. Mem. Modern Lang. Assn., Am. Assn. U. Profs., Renaissance Soc., Milton Soc., Assn. Depts. of English (mem. exec. bd., past pres.). Author: The Levellers, 1955; The Beginnings of the English Newspaper, 1961; Hobbled Pegusus, 1968. Editor: Literature From the Bible, 1963; Modern Essays in English, 1966; The New Look in Politics, 1968. Home: 166 Lincoln Av Amherst MA 01002

FRANK, MILTON HENRY, cons.; b. Niles, Mich., July 23, 1888; s. Bishop Quesnel and Nancy Jane (White) F.; B.S., Purdue U., 1912, E.E., 1915; m. Hazel Shadley, Aug. 29, 1917. Clk. N.Y.C. R.R., Elkhart, Ind., 1909-10; apprentice Ft. Wayne (Ind.) Electric Works, 1911; various engring. positions, Ind., Ill., Mich., 1912-18; local mgr. Eastern Wis. Electric Co., Fond du lac, 1918- 22, div. mgr., 1922-30; asst. to v.p. Wis. Power & Light Co., Madison, 1930-33, So. div. mgr., 1933-34, asst. to pres., 1935-36, v.p., 1936-46, exec. v.p., 1946-53; v.p. Franklin Van Sant Assos., Inc., 1954-63; pres. M.H. Frank Co., 1964-70. Mem. Newcomen Soc., Nat. Assn. Life Underwriters (million dollar round table life mem.), Wis. Utilities Assn. (past pres.), Wis. Union (life), Pub. Relations Soc. Am. (pres. Wis.; nat. v.p. central dist. 1954), YMCA, Purdue Alumni Assn., Iron Key, Acadia, Tau Beta Pi, Republican. Conglist. Mason. Rotarian. Clubs: Maple Bluff, Madison, Technical (Madison); Union League (Chgo.). Home: 302 Walnut St Madison WI also 2101 E Maryland Av Phoenix AZ 85016 Office: 202 State St Madison WI 53701

FRANK, NATHANIEL HERMAN, educator, physicist; b. Boston, Mar. 18, 1903; s. Abraham and Fannie Katherine (Goldberg) F.; S.B., Mass. Inst. Tech., 1923, Austin fellow, 1925, Sc.D., in Physics, 1926; m. Louise Elizabeth Temme, 1929 (dec.); 1 son, Christopher T.; m. 2d, Evalyn, F. Jacobs, 1964 (dec.). With Mass. Inst. of Tech., 1924—, successively asst. elec. engring., instr. physics, asst. prof., asso. prof., 1924-44, prof., 1944-68, prof. emeritus, 1968—, served as head dept., 1952-62; fellow, Munich, 1929, Inst. Advanced Study, 1936. With NDRC; expert cons. Office Sec. War. Fellow Am. Phys. Soc., Assn. Physics Teachers, Am. Acad., A.A.A.S. (v.p., chmn. physics sect.); mem. Am. Soc. for Engring. Edn., Sigma Pi Sigma, Alpha Mu. Author: Introduction to Mechanics and Heat; Introduction to Electricity and Optics; Introduction to Theoretical Physics, Mechanics and Heat; Introduction to Electricity and Optics; Introduction to Theoretical Physics, Mechanics, Electromagnetism (with J. C. Slater). Research in electron theory of metals, theory of design of electronuclear accelerators.†

FRANK, REUVEN, journalist; b. Montreal, Que., Can., Dec. 7, 1920; s. Moses Zebi Reichenstein and Anna (Rivenovich) F.; came to U.S., 1940, naturalized, 1943; student Univ. Coll., U. Toronto, 1937-40; B.S. in Social Scis., Coll. City N.Y., 1942; M.S. in Journalism, Columbia, 1947; m. Bernice Kaplow, June 9, 1946; children—Peter Solomon, James Aaron. Reporter, Newark Evening News 1947-49, night city editor, 1949-50; mem. staff NBC News, 1950-67, exec. v.p., 1967-68, pres., 1968—; news editor Camel News Caravan, 1951-54; producer polit. conv., 1956, polit. convs. and elections, 1960, elections, 1962; producer Huntley-Brinkley Report, 1956- 62, exec. producer, 1963-65; exec. producer polit. convs. and elections, 1964; writer-producer Berlin-Window on Fear, 1953, The Road to Spandau, 1954, Outlook (series), 1956-59, Time Present (series), 1959-60, Chet Huntley Reporting (series), 1960-63, IsraelThe Next Ten Years, 1958, The S-Bahn Stops at Freedom, 1958, The American Stranger, 1958, The Requiem for Mary Jo, 1959, The Big Ear, 1959, Our Man in the Mediterranean, 1959, Where is Abel, Your Brother?, 1960, Our Man in Hong Kong, 1961, The Land, 1961, The Many Faces of Spain, 1962, Our Man in Vienna, 1962, Clear and Present Danger, 1962, The Tunnel, 1962, A Country Called Europe, 1963, The Problem with Water is People, 1963. Trustee, Edwin E. Aldrin Fund State of N.J., 1970—. Recipient Sigma Delta Chi award news writing for TV, 1955; Robert E. Sherwood award, 1958, 59; George Polk award L.I. U., 1961; Columbia Journalism Alumni award distinguished service, 1961; First Person award Inst. Edn. by Radio-TV, Ohio State U., 1963; Emmy award best news program, 1958, 59, 60, 61, 62, 64, best documentary program, 1963, program of year, 1963. Poynter fellow Yale, 1970. Mem. Writers Guild Am. (organizing com. 1954-56), Am. Newspaper Guild (Newark News organizing com. 1948-50), Nat. Acad. TV Arts and Scis., Radio and TV Corr. Assn. (asso. non-resident). Office: 30 Rockefeller Plaza New York City NY 10020

FRANK, ROBERT EDWIN, hosp. adminstr.; b. St. Louis, Nov. 30, 1926; s. Edwin J. and Genevieve (Graeff) F.; B.S., St. Louis U., 1950, M.A., 1962; m. Mary Catherine Porter, Sept. 10, 1949; children—Michael, Nancy. Asst. personnel dir. Gen. Cable Corp., St. Louis, 1950-53; personnel dir. De-Paul Hosp., St. Louis, 1953-61; intern hosp. adminstrn. Barnes Hosp., St. Louis, 1961, asst. dir., 1961-64, asso. dir., 1964-65, acting dep. dir., 1965, dep. dir., 1965-66, acting dir., 1966, dir., 1966—; asst. prof. Washington U. Sch. Medicine Program in Hosp. Adminstrn. Mem. Mo. Adv. Council on Heart, Stroke and Cancer, 1966—. Served with AUS, 1945-46. Mem. Mo. Hosp. Assn. (trustee). Roman Catholic. Home: 10300 Badgley St St Louis, MO 63126. Office: Barnes Hosp Plaza St Louis MO 63110

FRANK, ROBERT STEPHEN, securities broker; b. N.Y.C., Nov. 7, 1912; s. Matthew and Ruth (Mayer) F.; B.S., N.Y.U., 1934, LL.B., 1938; m. Eleanor S. Goldberger, May 29, 1940; children—Robert Stephen, Matthew Harold. Mem. Am. Stock Exchange (formerly N.Y. Curb Exchange), 1938—, formerly mem. and vice chmn. bd. govs.; admitted to N.Y. bar, 1939. Home: 255 W. 88th St New York City, NY 10024. Office: 86 Trinity Pl New York City NY 10006

FRANK WALTER NILS, stock broker; b. Bklyn., Apr. 22, 1908; s. Louis and Selma (Persson) F.; student N.Y.U., 1924-26; Dr. Comml. Sci. (hon.), Suffolk U., Boston, 1967; m. Ruth E. Carlson, Apr. 22, 1931; children—Judith Evelyn, Walter Nils. Partner, Marcus & Co., N.Y.C., 1937—. Mem. N.Y. Stock Exchange, mem. board of govs., 1959—, vice chmn. bd. govs., 1962-65, chmn., 1965- 67. Chmn. bd. govs. N.Y. Stock Exchange; trustee, mem. devel. council Wagner Coll.; trustee Valley Hosp., Ridgewood, New Jersey, Presbyterian (elder). Clubs: Madison Square Garden, Pinehurst Country, Ridgewood Country. Home: 13 Deerhill Dr Hohokus NJ 07423 Office: 61 Broadway New York City NY 10006

FRANKE, ALLYN J., lawyer; b. Springfield, Ill., Nov. 20, 1918; A.B., U. Chgo., 1941, LL.B., 1942. Admitted to Ill. bar, 1942; mem. firm Norman and Billick and predecessor firms, Chgo. Mem. Am., Ill., Chgo. bar assns., Phi Alpha Delta. Club: Legal (Chgo). Office: 69 W Washington St Chicago IL 60602*

FRANKE, ANN, indsl. designer; b. Bound Brook, N.J., Oct. 29, 1897; d. Otto M. and Marie (Lehn) Franke; student N.Y. Sch. Applied Design for Women, 1916- 19, Winold Reiss Sch. Art, 1919-21, N.Y. Textile Eve. Sch., 1931-33; m. Pedro Manuel Gonzalez, Aug. 18, 1923 (dec.); 1 dau., Anita. Designer Willich Embroidery Studios, 1919-22; partner, designer Willich-Franke Studios, since 1922; instr., mem. bd. trustees Design Lab., 1934-36; instr. Cooper Union, 1936-52; cons., designer manual industries div. P.R. Indsl. Devel. Corp., 1945-46; stylist, designer upholstery div. Cohn Hall Marx, 1949-50, Golding Decorative Fabrics, 1951-53; stylist furniture fabrics Collins & Aikman 1953—. Exhibited works N.Y. World's Fair, San Francisco Fair, Met. Mus., Toledo Mus., Cleve. Mus., N.Y. Mus. Sci. and Industry, Phila. Art Alliance, Grand Central Palace; mem. adv. bd. N.Y. State Inst. Applied Arts and Sci., 1949-50. Recipient medal for excellence in Textile design, Am. Designer Inst. (nat. bd. trustees, treas. N.Y. chpt. chmn. membership and competitions com., nat. sec.), Indsl. Designers Assn. Am., Manhattan Miniature Camera Club. Contbr. articles profl. publs. Home: 446 E 66th St New York City NY 10021 Office: B Altman & Co Fifth Av New York City NY 10016

FRANKE, FREDERICK RAHDE, physician; b. Pitts., Oct. 14, 1918; s. Frederick Ferdinand and Louise Anna (Rahde) F.; B.S., U. Pitts., 1941, M.D., 1943; M.S., U. Pa., 1950, D.Sc., 1952; m. Nancy Olive Digby, Mar. 22, 1943; children—Suzanne, Paula, Frederick Rahde, Paul D., John C., Virginia N. Intern, then resident St. Francis Hosp., Pitts., 1943-45, research asso. physiology, 1947-52, physician-in-chief charge therapeutics, 1953-56; pvt. practice, Pitts., 1952—; asst. prof. medicine Sch. Medicine U. Pitts., 1953-56; chief medicine St. Clair Hosp., South Side Hosp., St. Margaret Hosp., 1955-63; mem. faculty Sch. Medicine Johns Hopkins, 1960-61; sr. cardiologist charge cardiovascular-pulmonary lab., chief div. medicine Western Pa. Hosp., 1963-69, medical dir., 1967—. Bd. dirs. Health Research Services Found. Served with M.C., USNR, 1945-46. Diplomate Am. Bd. Internal Medicine (cardiovascular diseases). Fellow A.C.P., Council Clin. Cardiology, Am. Heart Assn.; mem. Pa. Heart Assn. (past pres., com. chmn.; Meritorious Service award 1962), Soc. Exptl. Biology and Medicine, Am. Therapeutic Soc., Am. Soc. Human Genetics, A.M.A., Sigma Xi, Republican. Presbyn. Clubs: University (Pitts.); Rolling Rock Ligonier, Pa.). Author articles, chpts. in books. Home: 19 Glen Ridge Lane Pittsburgh PA 15216 Office: 4800 Friendship Av Pittsburgh PA 15224

FRANKE, PAUL, tenor; studied in Boston and N.Y.C. Mem. Radio City Music Hall chorus, later made soloist; debut with Met. Opera as the youth in L'Amore dei Tre Re, 1948; numerous roles in four langs., including role of captain in Wozzek. Address: care Metropolitan Opera 147 W 39th St New York City NY 10018*

FRANKEL, ANDREW J., corp. exec.; b. N.Y.C., 1932; ed. Columbia, 1955. Exec. v.p., dir. Kinney Nat. Service Inc., N.Y.C.; dir. Nat. Cleaning Cons. Inc.; v.p., dir. Security Maintenance Services, Inc., Bldg. Maintenance Corp.; dir. Cleaning Supplies Corp.; v.p., dir. Realty Maintenance Corp.; sec., treas., dir. Nat. Cleaning Co.; dir. Maintenance Services Inc., Exterminating Service Corp., Realty Services Inc. Vice pres., Dir. Nat. Cleaning and Affiliates Found. Home: 19 Heathcore Rd Larchmont NY 10583 Office: 60 Madison Av New York City NY 10010*

FRANKEL, CHARLES, educator, author; b. N.Y.C., Dec. 13, 1917; s. Abraham Philip and Estelle Edith (Cohen) F.; A.B. with honors in English and Philosophy, Columbia, 1937, Ph.D., 1946; student Cornell U., 1937-38; LL.D., Mercer U., 1968; m. Helen Beatrice Lehman, Aug. 17, 1941; children—Susan, Carl. Mem. faculty Columbia, 1939—, prof. philosophy, 1956-70, Old Dominion prof. philosophy and pub. affairs, 1970—; asst. U.S. sec. state ednl. and cultural affairs, 1965-67; host TV program The World of Ideas, CBS, 1959; cons. Orgn. for Econ. Cooperation and Devel., 1969—. Co-chairman of Nat. Assembly for Teaching Prins. Bill of Rights, 1962-65. Chmn. U.S. delegation UNESCO Gen. Conf., 1966; mem. N.Y. State Commn. on Quality, Cost and Financing Edn., 1969—. Pres. bd. trustees Rockland Country Day Sch., Congers, N.Y., 1959-64; bd. dirs. N. State Civil Liberties Union, 1960-65, Commn. on Acad. Affairs Am. Council on Edn. Recipient Woodbridge prize philosophy Columbia, 1947; Guggenheim fellow, 1953-54; Fulbright prof. U. Paris (France), 1953-54; Carnegie Corp. reflective year fellow, 1959-60. Served to lt. USNR, 1942-46. Fellow Am. Acad. Arts and Scis.; mem. Am. Philos. Assn., Am. Assn. U. Profs. (chmn. com. profl. ethics 1956-59), Authors League Am., P.E.N., Council Fgn. Relations, Phi Beta Kappa. Club: Century Association (N.Y.C). Author: The Faith of Reason, 1948; The Bear and the Beaver, 1951; The Case for Modern Man, 1956; The Democratic Propect, 1962; The Love of Anxiety and Other Essays, 1965; The Neglected Aspect of Foreign Affairs, 1966; Education and the Barricades, 1968; High on Foggy Bottom, 1969. Principal author: The Power of the Democratic Idea, 1960. Gen. editor: Introduction to Contemporary Civilization in the West, 1941. Editor: (Rousseau) Social Contract, 1947; The Uses of Philosophy, 1955; Issues in University Education, 1959; The Golden Age of American Philosophy, 1960. Editor-at-large Saturday Rev., 1968—. Contbr. articles profl. publs. Home: 317 Phillips Hill Rd New York City NY 10956

FRANKEL, JACOB PORTER, coll. dean; b. Phila., Sept. 7, 1923; s. Harold Aaron and Ceil (Porter) F.; M.S., U. Cal. at Berkeley, 1947; Ph.D., U. Cal. at Los Angeles, 1951; m. Helen Bruce, Jan. 27, 1946; children—Martha Jean, Molly, David Alan, Deborah, Robert Aaron. Instr., then asst. prof. engring. U. Cal. at Los Angeles, 1948-52; lead metallurgist Cal. Research and Devel. Co., 1952- 54; asso. prof. Northwestern U., 1954-56; asso. prof., then prof. U. Cal. at Los Angeles, 1957-66; asso. dean, prof. Thayer Sch. Engring., Dartmouth, 1966-68; dean faculty Harvey Mudd Coll. Sci. and Engring., 1968—. Pres. Fgn. Resource Services, Inc., 1963—; cons. systems engring., 1956—; cons. sci. and engring. edn. to govts. India, Republic of China, 1970. Chmn. Livermore (Cal.) Recreation Bd., 1953-54. Served to lt. (j.g.) USNR, 1944-51. Mem. Am. Soc. Engring. Edn., Soc. Hist. Tech., Amateur Yacht Research Soc., Phi Beta Kappa, Sigma Xi. Author: The Principles of the Properties of Materials, 1957; also articles. Home: 1852 Antioch Rd Claremont CA 91711

FRANKEL, JAMES ANDREW, reporter; b. Cleve., May 1, 1923; s. Henry and Lillian (Ray) F.; B.A., Yale, 1945; m. Marilyn Roebuck, Aug. 7, 1949; children-Susan Daniel. Mem. staff Cleve. Press, 1947—, showtime editor, 1970—. Served with USAAF, 1943-46. Home: 4087 Lambert Rd South Euclid OH 44121 Office: 901 Lakeside Av Cleveland OH 44114

FRANKEL, JAMES ROBERT, lawyer; b. Milw., Sept. 3, 1919; s. Andrew H. and Fay (Gordon) F.; B.A., U. Mich., 1941, J.D., 1943; m. Florence Davis, Apr. 19, 1947; children—Mark Andrew, Wendy, Terry, Julie. Admitted to Ill. bar, 1943; asso. firm DeFrees, Fiske, O'Brien & Thompson, Chgo., 1943-45, Cobbey & Brussel, Chgo., 1945-50; partner firm Mulder & Frankel, Chgo., 1950-55, 60-64, Wolff, Frankel, Pennish & Orlikoff, Chgo., 1955-60, Ettelson, O'Hagen, Ehrlich & Frankel, Chgo., 1964—, Dir. Merc. Nat. Bank Chgo., Republic Packaging Corp. Mem. sch. bd. Highland Park (Ill.) Sch. Dist. 108, 1962-67. Mem. Ill., Chgo. bar assns. Club: Downtown (Chgo.). Home: 1666 Old Briar Rd Highland Park IL 60035 Office: 208 S LaSalle St Chicago IL 60604

FRANKEL, JOSEPH JEROME, hosp. dir.; b. Phila., Aug. 4, 1912; s. Victor and Rebecca (Gross) F.; B.S., Temple U., 1933, M.D., 1936; m. Reba Robins, July 8, 1937; children—Marsha (Mrs. Malcolm N. Blumenthal), Sheila (Mrs. Robert Goldman). Intern Mt. Sinai Hosp., Phila., 1936-37; asst. physician Pa. Tb Sanitarium, Mt. Altom, 1937-38; pvt. practice, Phila., 1938-39; tng. VA Hosp., Oteen, N.C., 1939-40; ward officer VA Hosp., Outwood, Ky., 1940; from ward officer to asst. chief medicine Hines VA Hosp., 1940-50; chief medicines VA Hosp., Wilkes-Barre, Pa., 1950-53; chief staff West Side VA Hosp., Chgo., 1953-59, Hines VA Hosp., 1959-61; dir. West Side VA Hosp., 1961-63, Coral Gables (Fla.) VA Hosp., 1963-64, Indpls. VA Hosp., 1964-67, West Side VA Hosp., 1967—; prof. medicine Chgo. Med. Sch., 1954-69; lectr. medicine U. Ill., 1967-69, prof. medicine, asst. dean for Vet. Hosp. affairs, Abraham Lincoln Sch. Medicine, 1969—. Mem. Council Teaching Hosps., Ill. Regional Med. Program, 1967—; mem. ad hoc planning com. West Side Hosp., 1968—; mem. Fed. Exec. Bd. and Commn. Intergovtl. Relations, 1967—. Served to lt. col., M.C., AUS, 1942-46. Diplomate Am. Bd. Internal Medicine. Fellow A.C.P., Am. Coll. Hosp. Adminstrs., Inst. Medicine Chgo.; mem. A.M.A., Ill., Chgo. med. socs., Chgo. Soc. Internal Medicine, Assn. Mil. Surgeons, Chgo. Heart Assn., D.A.V. Mason (Shriner). Home: 2400 Lakeview Av Chicago IL 60614 Office: VA West Side Hosp 820 S Damen Av Chicago IL 60612

FRANKEL, LARRY, educator; b. N.Y.C., July 8, 1928; s. Charles and Sally (Goldleyer) F.; B.S. cum laude, Bklyn. Coll., 1950; M.A., Columbia, 1952; Ph.D., U. Neb., 1956; m. Anita Schachter, May 24, 1950; children—Roberta, Nina, Sara. Geologist, AEC, 1954-55; mem. faculty U. Conn., Storrs, 1955—, prof. geology, 1968—; tech. officer Geol. Survey Can., summers 1956, 57, 59, 60, 61. Cons. geologist. Fellow Geol. Soc. Am.; mem. Am. Assn. Petroleum Geologists, Paleontol. Soc., Soc. Econ. Paleontologists and Mineralogists, A.A.A.S. Home: Hunting Lodge Rd Storrs CT 06268

FRANKEL, MARVIN, educator, ecomonist; b. Oakland, Cal., Mar. 28, 1924; s. Joseph and Mathilde (Sewelson) F.; A.B. in Econs., U. Cal. at Berkeley, 1947, Ph.D., 1953; student London Sch. Econs., 1950-51; m. Matilda Shoenberg, Sept. 23, 1951; children—Karen, Kenneth Alan, David Paul. From asst. prof. to asso. prof. Bur. Econs. and Bus. Research, U. Ill. Urbana, 1952-57, asso. dean Grad. Coll., 1963-66, prof. econs., 1961—, chmn. dept., 1967—; vis. prof. U. Colo. summer 1966; vis. asso. prof. Stanford, 1957-58; cons. to govt. and industry, 1957—. Served to 1st lt., pilot, USAAF, 1943-46. Mem. Am. Econ. Assn., Am. Assn. U. Profs., Phi Beta Kappa. Bd. editors So. Econ. Jour., 1967-69; editor Quar. Rev. Econs. and Bus., 1952-63. Contbr. profl. jours.

FRANKEL, MARVIN E., U.S. judge; b. N.Y.C., July 26, 1920; s. Charles and Anne (Brody) F.; A.B., Queens Coll., 1943; LL.B., Columbia, 1949; m. Betty Streich, June 20, 1945 (div. 1965); 1 dau., Eleanor; m. 2d, Alice Kross, Aug. 22, 1965; 1 dau., Mara. Admitted to N.Y. bar, 1948, also U.S. Supreme Ct.; asst. to U.S. solicitor gen., 1952-56; mem. firm Proskauer Rose Goetz & Mendelsohn, 1956-62; prof. law Columbia, 1962-65; vis. prof. Coll. City N.Y., 1968; U.S. dist. judge So. Dist. N.Y., 1965—. Dir. Legal Def. Fund Civil Rights Inst., 1964-65. Served with AUS, 1942-46. Mem. Am., N.Y. State bar assns., Bar Assn. City N.Y. Editor-in-chief Columbia Law Rev., 1948. ‡

FRANKEL, MAX, journalist; b. Gera, Germany, Apr. 3, 1930; s. Jacob A. and Mary (Katz) F.; came to U.S., 1940, naturalized, 1948; A.B., Columbia, 1952, M.A. in Polit. Sci., 1953; m. Tobia Brown, June 19, 1956; children—David M., Margot S., Jonathan M. Mem. staff N.Y. Times, 1952—, chief Washington corr., 1968—. Served with AUS, 1953-55. Mem. Council Fgn. Relations, Phi Beta Kappa. Home: 5607 Montgomery St Chevy Chase, MD 20015. Office: 1920 L St NW Washington DC 20036

FRANKEL, SAMUEL BENJAMIN, ret. naval officer; b. Cin., July 14, 1905; s. Jonas and Bertha (Sass) F.; B.S., U.S. Naval Acad., 1929; m. Tellervo von Hellens, June 2, 1938; 1 dau., Susan von Hellens. Commd. ensign USN, 1929, advanced through grades to rear adm., 1959; assigned cruisers, destroyers U.S. and Asiatic waters; asst. naval attache, Murmansk, USSR, 1941-44; naval attache, China, 1948-50;

mem. U.S. delegation Council Fgn. Ministers, Moscow, 1947; mem. U.S. delegation Surprise Attack Conf., Geneva, 1958; dep. dir. Naval Intelligence, Washington, 1961; chief staff Def. Intelligence Agy., 1961-64; ret., 1964; dept. mgr. System Devel. Corp. until 1970, ret., 1970. Dir. Tulsioy Found. Decorated Distinguished Service medal. Home: Box 314A Bluemont VA 22012

FRANKEL, STANLEY ARTHUR, corp. exec.; b. Dayton, O., Dec. 8, 1918; s. Mandel and Olive (Margolis) F.; B.S. with high honors, Northwestern U., 1940; student Columbia, 1940, U. Chgo., 1946-49; m. Irene Baskin, Feb. 20, 1946; children—Stephen, Thomas, Nancy. Reporter Chgo. News Bur., 1940; publicist CBS, 1941; asst. to pres. Esquire and Coronet mags., N.Y.C., 1946-56; pres. Esquire Club, 1956-58; with McCall Corp., N.Y.C., 1958- 61, asst. to pres. and pub., 1958-61, v.p., 1959-61; v.p., dir. corporate devel. Ogden Corp. subsidiary Luria Bros. & Co., Inc., 1961—; v.p. Ogden Corp., 1962- -; v.p., dir. Michaelis Prodns., Inc.; dir. Rockwood Corp., 1955, Careful Office Service Inc., Western Cal. Canners Corp., Internat. Terminal Operating Co., Inc., Ogden Am. Corp. Mem. Pres.'s Adv. Council on Peace Corps, 1965—, Pres.'s Adv. Council on Youth Opportunity; Chancellor's panel State U. of N.Y., 1970—; bd. mem., exec. com. Nat. Council Crime and Delinquency; bd. mem., vice chmn. Nat. Businessmen's Council. Exec. bd. Writers for Stevenson, 1952, 56, for Kennedy, 1960; pub. relations dir. Stevenson-for-President, 1956; chmn. Writers for Senator Humphrey Presdl. campaign, 1964; exec. bd. Businessmen for Humphrey-Muskie, 1968; chmn. N.Y. Writers for Humphrey-Muskie, 1968. Bd. dirs., v.p., mem. exec. com. YMCA of Greater N.Y., Westchester County Community Service, Pub. Relations Bd., Inc., N.Y. and Chgo., Bedford Stuyvesant Project (T.R.Y.). Served to maj. AUS, 1940-46. Decorated 2 Presdl. Citations, 3 Bronze Stars; recipient Peabody award for TV Series Adlai Stevenson Reports, 1961-63; Northwestern U. Alumni Merit award, 1964. Mem. Ohio Soc. of N.Y., Scarsdale P.T.A. (mem. bd.), Am. Mgmt. Assn. (chmn. pub. relations course 1971), Phi Beta Kappa. Clubs: Northwestern U. of N.Y. (pres. 1964); Overseas Press (N.Y.C.); Scarsdale (N.Y.) Town (bd. govs.). Author: History of 37th Division, 1947. Contbr. articles to popular mags. Home: 109 Brewster Rd Scarsdale NY 10583 Office: 161 E 42d St New York City NY 10017

FRANKEL, WILLIAM VICTOR, service corp. exec.; b. N.Y.C., Sept. 3, 1903; s. Louis and Julia (Koch) F.; grad. Hamilton Inst., N.Y.C., 1921; extension student Columbia, 1922-23; m. Selma F. Rentner, Apr. 3, 1930; children—Andrew J., Linda (Mrs. Cahill). Salesman, European Chinaware Co., 1924-26; with Nat. Cleaning Contractors, 1926—, pres., 1950-64, chmn. bd., 1964—; chmn. bd. Kinney Service, Inc., 1966—. Mem. Exec. Assn. Greater N.Y. (pres. 1953-55). Clubs: Harmonie, Manhattan, Governor's (N.Y.C.); Fairview Country (Greenwich, Conn.); Boca Raton Golf, Boca Rio Golf (Boca Raton, Fla.). Home: 33 E 70th St New York City NY 10021 Office: 10 Rockefeller Plaza New York City NY 10020

FRANKENA, WILLIAM KLAAS, educator; b. Manhattan, Mont., June 21, 1908; s. Nicholas Auke and Gertie (Vander Schaaf) F.; A.B., Calvin Coll., Grand Rapids, Mich., 1930; A.M., U. of Mich., 1931; Ph.D., Harvard, 1937; m. Sadie Gusta Roelofs, June 23, 1934; children—Karl Roelofs, Mark William. Instr. in philosophy, U. of Mich., 1937-40, asst. prof., 1940-46, asso. prof., 1946-47, prof. of philosophy, 1947—, chmn. dept. of philosophy, 1947-61; vis. lectr. Harvard, 1941-42; Guggenheim fellow, 1948-49; vis. prof. Columbia, 1953, U. Tokyo, 1954, Harvard, 1955, 62-63, Princeton, 1960. Mem. Am. Philos. Assn., Am. Acad. Arts and Scis., Mich. Acad. of Sci., Arts and Letters, Nat. Acad. Edn., Am. Soc. Polit. and Legal Philosophy, Phi Beta Kappa, Phi Kappa Phi. Author of essays in The Philosophy of G. E. Moore (ed. by P. A. Schilpp), 1942; in Philosophical Analysis (ed. by M. Black), 1950; in Language, Thought, and Culture (ed. by P. Henle), 1958; in Religion and the State University (ed. by E. A. Walter), 1958; in Essays in Moral Philosophy (ed. by A. I. Melden), 1958; Social Justice (ed. Richard B. Brandt), 1962; Law and Philosophy (ed. Sidney Hook), 1964; Contemporary American Philosophy (ed. J.A. Smith), 1970. Author: Ethics, 1963; Philosophy of Education, 1965; Three Historical Philosophies of Education, 1965; Some Beliefs About Justice, 1966. Contbr. articles and review in philos. journals. Home: 1 Hillside Ct Ann Arbor MI 48104

FRANKENBERG, LLOYD, poet, critic; b. Mt. Vernon, N.Y., Sept. 3, 1907; s. Henry and Helen (Conklin) F.; student Columbia, 1924-29; m. Loren MacIver. Mem. editorial bd. Decision, 1942. Tiger's Eye, 1947-48; dir. poetry readings Mus. Modern Art, 1950-52; mem. poetry jury Nat. Book Award, 1951; Fulbright lecturer in France, 1961-62. Recipient Spenser award, 1938, Guggenheim Found. fellowship, 1940, Carnegie grant, 1942, Acad. Arts and Letters award, 1947, Rockefeller Found. fellowship, 1952. Author: The Red Kite (poems), 1939; Pleasure Dome: On Reading Modern Poetry, 1949; Invitation To Poetry, 1956; A Round of Poems (recording), 1956. Editor: Pleasure Dome (audible anthology modern poetry, read by its creators), 1949; A James Stephens Reader, 1962; James Stephens: a Selection, 1962; James Seumas and Jacques: Unpublished Writings of James Stephens, 1964; Poems of William Shakespeare, 1966; Poems of Robert Burns, 1967. Contbr. articles, poems, profl. and popular publs. Home: 61 Perry St New York City NY 10014

FRANKENBERGER, NORBERT, ret. naval officer, ednl. adminstr.; b. Washington, Jan. 11, 1918; s. Hugo and Beatrice (McCandless) F.; B.S., U.S. Naval Acad., 1940; M.S., Mass. Inst. Tech., 1945; m. Suzanne Sullivant Chase, Apr. 2, 1942; children—Diane (Mrs. James R. Wilson), Nancy (Mrs. Edward A. Dunn), John Norbert. Commd. ensign U.S. Navy, 1940, advanced through grades to rear adm., 1967; assigned U.S.S. Ranger, 1940-43, Norfolk Naval Ship Yard, 1945-47, U.S.S. Coral Sea, 1947-48, Pearl Harbor Naval Ship Yard, 1948-51, U.S. Naval Acad., 1951-54; staff comdr. Service Force Atlantic, 1954-56; assigned Bur. Ships, 1956-60, Naval War Coll., 1960-61, Mare Island Naval Ship Yard, 1961-65; staff comdr. Service Force Pacific, also staff comdr. in chief Pacific Fleet, 1965-68; comdr. San Francisco Bay Naval Ship Yard, 1968-70, ret., 1970; dir. planning and devel. State Tech. Inst. at Memphis, 1970—. Decorated Legion of Merit. Home: 18 S Yates Rd Memphis TN 38117 Office: State Tech Inst at Memphis 5983 Macon Cove Memphis TN 38128

FRANKENHEIMER, JOHN MICHAEL, drama director; b. N.Y.C., Feb. 19, 1930; s. Walter Martin and Helen Mary (Sheedy) F.; grad. LaSalle Mil. Acad., 1947; B.A., Williams Coll., 1951; m. Carolyn Diane Miller, Sept. 22, 1954 (div. 1961); children—Lisa Jean, Kristi; m. third, Evans Evans, 1964. Actor, 1950 and 1951; director of the CBS-TV, 1954-59 dir. programs You Are There, Danger, Climax, Studio One, Playhouse 90; programs directed include Forbidden Area, The Comedian, The Last Tycoon, Clash by Night, The Days of Wine and Roses, A Town has Turned to Dust, Old Man, Face of a Hero, For Whom the Bell Tolls; dir. motion picture Young Stranger, RKO, 1959, Broadway play, The Midnight Sun, 1959; free-lance dir. The Browning Version, DuPont Show of the Month, 1959, Ingrid Bergman in Turn of the Screw, 1959; motion pictures The Young Savages, Birdman of Alcatraz, All Fall Down, The Manchurian Candidate; dir., The Train, 1965, Seconds, 1966. Recipient of the Christopher award, 1954; grand prize for best film dir., Lacarno Film Festival, 1955; Critics award for best direction of year, 1956-59; dir. The Comedian (winner Emmy award as outstanding program of year), 1958; Brotherhood award, 1959; Acapulco Film Festival award, 1962. Office: care Creative Mgmt Assos 9465 Wilshire Blvd Beverly Hills CA 90012

FRANKENSTEIN, ALFRED, art critic; b. Chgo., Oct. 5, 1906; s. Victor Samuel and Irma (Rosenthal) F.; Ph.B., U. Chgo., 1932 (attended intervals between 1925-32); Yale, 1930; m. Sylvia Lent, Apr. 18, 1935; children—John, David. Music editor, Review of Reviews Corp., 1930-32; asst. to Herman Devries, music editor Chgo. American, 1930-34; instr. music U. Chgo., 1932-34; music critic San Francisco Chronicle, 1934-65, art critic, 1934—; program editor San Francisco Symphony Orch., 1935- 63; lectr. Am. art U. Cal., 1950—; instr. Harvard, summer 1951, 52, 67; tchr. Salzburg Seminar in Am. Studies, 1962, 64; lectr. in Am. studies Mills Coll., 1955-70; adj. prof. Am. art N.Y. U. 1969-70. Awarded Guggenheim fellowship for research on William Michael Harnett, Am. still life painter, 1947. Mem. Newspaper Guild, Am. Fedn. Musicians, Am. Studies Assn., Internat. Assn. Art Critics, Am. Musicol. Soc. Author: Two Journeyman Painters (with Arthur K. D. Healy); After the Hunt, 1953, 1969; Angels Over the Altar, 1961; The Royal Visitors, 1963; A Modern Guide to Symphonic Literature, 1967. Co-author: The World of Copley, 1970. Office: care San Francisco Chronicle San Francisco CA 94119 ☆

FRANKENSTEIN, LESTER ECKMANN, clothing mfr.; b. Ft. Wayne, Ind., Nov. 5, 1921; s. Solly K. and Julia (Eckmann) F.; B.S., Northwestern U., 1945, LL.B., 1947; m. Anabel Cahn, July 12, 1947; children—Laura, William, Ellen. Admitted to practice law before Ind. bar, 1947; practiced law, Ft. Wayne, Ind., 1947-52; credit mgr. B. Kuppenheimer & Co., Inc., Chgo., 1952-54, v.p., 1954-59, pres., 1959-63, also dir.; pres. Michael Stern & Co., Inc., Rochester, N.Y., 1964—, also dir.; adv. com. Amal. Ins. Fund. Chmn. retirement edn. com. Mayor's Commn. on Sr. Citizens, 1962-64. Mem. adv. com. Civic Fedn., 1959-64; dir. Chgo. Crime Commn., 1955-64; chmn. Midwest Chgo. Boys Club, 1952-64, West Central Assn., 1955-63, Midwest Community Council, 1956-63; treas. Sr. Centers Met. Chgo., 1962-64; chmn. dept. of aging Council of Social Agencies; treas. Harley School; trustee U. Chgo. Cancer Research Found., 1959- 64; bd. dirs. Sidney Hillman Health Center, Rochester. Served as navigator USAAF, 1943-45. Decorated Air medal with 5 clusters, Purple Heart. Mem. Young Pres.'s Orgn. Clubs: Rochester, Irondequoit, Rotary, Hunt Hollow (Rochester); Mid-Day; Economic, Executive (Chgo.). Home: 3487 East Av Rochester NY 14618 Office: 87 Clinton Av N Rochester NY 14602

FRANKENSTEIN, RICHARD JOHN, Jr., lawyer; b. Effingham, Ill., May 16, 1903; s. Richard John and Margaret E. (Weltz) F.; LL.B., Chgo.-Kent Coll. Law, 1924; m. Dorothy Ahern, June 23, 1928 (div. June 1962); m. 2d, Marie M. La Croix, Dec. 29, 1962. Admitted to Ill. bar, 1924, asso. Chapman and Cutler, Chgo., 1921-40; partner McDermott, Will & Emery, Chgo., 1940- -. Dir. Low's, Inc. Mem. Ill. Pension Laws Commn., 1956- -, vice chmn., 1962. Mem. adv. com. Ill. Inst. Tech., Chgo.-Kent Coll. Law. Mem. Am., Ill., Chgo. bar assns. Office: 111 W Monroe St Chicago IL 60603

FRANKENTHALER, HELEN, painter; b. N.Y.C., Dec. 12, 1928; d. Alfred and Martha (Lowenstein) Frankenthaler; B.A., Bennington Coll., 1949; L.H.D. Skidmore Coll., 1969; m. Robert Motherwell, Apr. 6, 1958. One man shows include Tibor de Nagy Gallery, N.Y.C., 1951-58, Andre Emmerich Gallery, 1958-69, Jewish Mus., N.Y., 1960, Everett Ellin Gallery, Los Angeles, 1961, Galerie Lawrence, Paris, 1961, 63, Bennington Coll., 1962, Galleria dell'Ariete, Milan, 1962, Kasmin Gallery, London, 1964, David Mirvish Gallery, Toronto, 1965, 71, retrospective Whitney Mus. Am. Art, 1969, Whitechapel Gallery, London, Eng., 1969, Kongress-Halle, Berlin, Kunstverein, Hannover; exhibited in group shows including Whitney Mus., 1958, Carnegie Internat., Pitts., 1958, 1961, Columbus Gallery Fine Arts, 1960, Guggenheim Mus., 1961, Seattle World's Fair, 1962, Art Inst. Chgo., 1963, San Francisco Mus. Art, 1963, Krannert Mus. of Ill., 1963, Washington Gallery Modern Art, 1963, Pa. Acad. Fine Arts, 1963, N.Y. World's Fair, 1964, Am. Fedn. Arts Circulating Exhbn., 1964, U. Austin Art Mus., 1964, Rose Art Mus. Circulating Exhbn., 1964, Detroit Inst. Arts, 1965, also Japan, Germany, Brazil, Eng.; rep. permanent collections Met. Mus. Art, N.Y.C., Pasadena (Cal.) Mus., Mus. Modern Art, N.Y.C., Whitney Mus., Carnegie Inst., Knox- Albright Art Gallery, Buffalo, Milw. Art Inst., Wadsworth Atheneum, Hartford, Newark Mus., Yale Art Gallery, U. Neb. Art Gallery, Carnegie Inst., Pitts., Detroit Inst. Art, Balt. Mus., Univ. Mus., Berkeley, Cal.; tchr. Yale, 1966, 67, 70, Hunter Coll., 1970, Princeton, 1971; Yale Grad. Sch. U.S. rep. Venice Biennale, 1966. Trustee Bennington Coll., 1967—. Fellow Yale U., 1968—. Recipient 1st prize for painting Paris Biennale, 1959; gold medal Pa. Acad. Fine Arts, 1968; Great Ladies award, Fordham U., Thomas Moore Coll., 1969; Spirit of Achievement award, Albert Einstein Coll. Medicine, 1970. Home: 173 E 94th St New York City NY 10028

FRANKFURT, STEPHEN OWEN, advt. exec.; b. Bronx, N.Y., Dec. 17, 1931; s. Milton A. and Blanche (Muller) F.; B.F.A., N.Y.U., 1951; student Pratt Inst., 1954; m. Suzanne Allen, Nov. 21, 1956; children—Peter, Jamie. Staff designer NBC, 1953- 54, CBS, 1954-55; staff art dir. U.P.A., 1954-55; mem. faculty Pratt Inst., 1958-60; sr. vice pres. Young & Rubicam, Inc., 1964-68, pres. domestic operations, 1968—. Exhibited in USIA 1963 Exhbn. in Iron Curtain countries. Recipient Gold medal N.Y. Art Dirs. Club, 1958, 59, 61, 62, 63, 66, 67, Spl. Gold medal award outstanding TV advt., 1960; Sylvania TV award, 1956; TV Age award, 1958; Cannes Film Festival award, 1958; N.Y. TV Film Festival award, 1958-64; Detroit Art Dir. Club medal, 1958; Los Angeles Art Dirs. Club medal, 1959; winner TV category Venice Film Festival, 1964; Am. TV Commercials Festivals Clio, 1966. Films exhbt. Museum of Modern Art, 1959-60; designer book Art Direction, 1956. Mem. N.Y. Art Dirs. Club (chmn. TV exhbn. 1960; Gold medal 1954, 55, Distinctive Merit award 1954-64), Nat. Art Dirs. Soc. (nominated art dir. of year 1962, 64). Home: 163 E 80th St New York City NY 10021 Office: Young & Rubicam 285 Madison Av New York City NY 10017

FRANKHAUSER, MAHLON MUNDELL, investment banker; b. Shillington, Pa., Sept. 20, 1931; s. Earl M. and Dorothy (Mundell) F.; A.B., Albright Coll., 1954; LL.B., U. Pa., 1957; m. Joan F. Callahan, Aug. 24, 1958; children—Scott, Gregory, Victoria. Admitted to D.C. bar, 1958; legal counsel Office Gen. Counsel, SEC, Washington, 1957-61, chief Office Criminal Reference div. trading and markets, 1961-64, asst. div. dir., 1964-66, regional adminstr., N.Y.C. Office, 1966-69; v.p., gen. counsel CBWL-Hayden Stone, Inc., 1970—. Vice pres. N.Y. Stock Exchange, 1969-70. Mem. Fed. Exec. Bd. Pres. North Springfield Civic Assn.; pres. Salem Ridge Civic Assn., Ridgewood, N.Y. Recipient Arthur Fleming award to outstanding men in govt., 1967, 68; and named One of Outstanding Young Men Am., 1965; One of Outstanding Civic Leader Am., 1968. Mem. Fed., N.Y. bar assns., City Bar Assn. N.Y. Home: 525 E Saddle River Rd Ridgewood NJ 07450 Office: 767 Fifth Av New York City NY 10022

FRANKL, PETER, concert pianist; b. Budapest, Hungary, Oct. 2, 1935; s. Tibor and Laura (Rodosi) F.; grad. Franz Liszt Music Acad., Budapest, 1956; m. Annie Feiner, Sept. 9, 1958; children—Judith, Andrew. Concert tours in Europe, South Africa, South Am., Australia, 1958—; U.S. debut, Dallas, 1965; Carnegie Hall debut, 1967; first Am. tour, 1967. Winner internat. competitions in Paris, France, 1957. Munich, Germany, 1957, Rio de Janeiro, Brazil, 1959; recipient Franz Liszt award for distinguished musicians, Budapest, 1958; named hon. citizen of Rio de Janeiro, 1960. Address: 5 Gresham Gardens London NW 11, England.

FRANKL, VIKTOR E., psychiatrist, author; b. Vienna, Austria, Mar. 26, 1905; s. Gabriel and Elsa (Lion) F.; M.D., U. Vienna, 1930, Ph.D., 1949; LL.D., Loyola U., Chgo., 1970, Edgecliff Coll., 1970; m. Eleonore Katharina Schwindt, July 18, 1947; 1 dau., Gabriele Vesely. Editor jour. Man in Everyday Life, 1927; founder, head Youth Adv. Centers, Vienna, 1928-38; staff. Neuropsychiatric Univ. Clinic, 1930-38; specialist neurology and psychiatry, 1936—; head neurological dept. Rothschild Hosp., Vienna, 1940-42; head Neurol. Poliklinik Hosp. of Vienna, 1946-70; asso. prof. neurology and psychiatry U. Vienna, 1947-55, prof., 1955—; prof. logotherapy U.S. Internat. U., San Diego, 1970—; vis. prof. Harvard Summer Sch., 1961, So. Meth. U., 1966; founder sch. logotherapy or existential analysis. Lectr. U.S. and fgn. countries. Internat. council Internat. Center Integrative Studies; bd. internat. cons. Religion in Edn. Found. Imprisoned in concentration camps, 1942- 45. Recipient Austrian State prize for pub. edn. (1st non-Am.); West Va. Wesleyan Coll. Founders award; citation Religion in Edn. Found.; citation Indianapolis Pastoral Counseling Center; also Austrian Cross of Honor for Science and Art; Wash. Coll. Distinguished Lectr. award, 1970; City Vienna prize for scientific achievement, 1970. Mem. Austrian Soc. for psychotherapy (pres. 1950—), Internat. Federation of Medical Psychotherapy (exec. board), Acad. Human Rights (adv.); hon. mem. Argentine Soc. Med. Anthropology, Peruvian Soc. Neuropsychiatry and Legal Medicine, Peruvian Soc. Geriatrics, Spanish Soc. of Clinical and Exptl. Hypnosis. Author: The Doctor and the Soul, an Introduction to Logotherapy, 1955; Man's Search for Meaning, 1962; psychotherapy and Existentialism, 1967; The Will to Meaning, 1969. Others pub. Portuguese, German, Polish, Japanese, Dutch, Spanish, Italian, Swedish, Norwegian, Danish, French, Chinese, Hebrew. Editor: (with V.E. von Gebsattel, J. H. Schultz) Ency. of Psychotherapeutics (5 vols.). Home: Mariannengasse 1 Vienna A-1090 Austria Office: Logotherapy Inst US Internat U San Diego CA 92124

FRANKLAND, CHARLES F., banker; b. Seattle, June 17, 1900; s. Charles W. and Pauline J. Frankland; B.B.A., U. of Washington, 1922; m. Edith H. Levis, Jan. 24, 1924; children—Charles William, Nancy Jane. Hotel operator, 1923-26; entered banking bus., 1926; joined Pacific Nat. Co., affiliate of Pacific Nat. Bank, 1929; v.p. The Pacific Nat. Bank of Wash. (formerly known as Pacific Nat. Bank of Seattle), 1936-45, pres., 1945-65, chmn. bd., 1965- -; dir. athletics U. Wash., 1933-36. Served with U.S. Navy, World War I. Mem. Beta Theta Pi. Clubs: Rainier, Seattle Golf and Country (Seattle). Home: 2110 Waverly Way E Seattle WA 98102 Office: Second Av at Marion Seattle WA 98111

FRANKLIN, ALAN DOUGLAS, physicist; b. Glenside, Pa., Dec. 10, 1922; s. Benjamin Jr. and Adrienne (Kenyon) F.; A.B., Princeton, 1946, Ph.D., 1950; m. Phoebe Perry Taylor, May 8, 1943; children—Adrienne Kenyon, Christopher Perry; m. 2d, Katherine Ann McMurdie, Apr. 14, 1960; 1 dau., Mary Louise. Research engr. Franklin Inst. Labs., Phila., 1949-55, chief magnetics sect., 1954-55; group leader ferroelectricity group Nat. Bur. Standards, 1955-59, chief inorganic solids div., 1959-63, asst. to dir. Inst. Materials Research, 1963-65, research chemist, 1965-66, dep. dir. material office Advanced Research Projects Agy., 1966-67, chemist Nat. Bur. Standards, 1967—. Fellow Am. Inst. Chemists, Am. Ceramic Soc., Am. Phys. Soc.; mem. A.A.A.S., Am. Chem. Soc., Phi Beta Kappa, Sigma Xi. Home: 6510 Ridge Dr Washington, DC 20016. Office: Nat Bur Standards Washington DC 20234

FRANKLIN, ALBERT ERNST, Brit. diplomat; b. Nov. 28, 1914; s. Albert John Henry and Ann (Leitzgen) F.; B.A., St. John's Coll., Oxford (Eng.) U., 1937; m. Henrietta Irene Barry, July 22, 1944; children—Anne Maria (Mrs. Kirit Vaidya), Sally Jane. Joined Brit. Fgn. Service assigned Peking, 1937-39, Yunnanfu, 1939-40, Chungking, 1940-42, Calcutta, 1943, Algiers, 1943-44, Marseilles, 1944-45, Fgn. Office, London, 1945-47, Amoy, 1947, Tientsin, 1947-49, Fgn. Office, 1949-51, Kabul, 1951-53, Basle, 1953-55, Tamsui, 1955-58, Dusseldorf, 1958-66; consul gen., Los Angeles, 1966—. Decorated comdr. Order Brit. Empire; comdr. Victorian Order. Home: 450 S June St Los Angeles CA 90005 Office: 3324 Wilshire Blvd Los Angeles CA 90005

FRANKLIN, ARETHA, singer; b. Memphis, Mar. 25, 1942; d. Clarence L. and Barbara (Siggers) Franklin. First recording at age 12; recording artist Columbia Records, N.Y.C., 1961, now with Atlantic records; albums include The Electrifying Aretha Franklin, Laughing on the Outside, Runnin' Out of Fools, Unforgettable, Lady Soul, Aretha Now, Aretha in Paris, others; also concert tours, U.S., Europe. Named top female vocalist, 1967; number 1 female singer (talent deserving of wider recognition) 16th Internat. Jazz Critics Poll, 1968. Address: Columbia Records 51 W 52d St New York City NY 10019*

FRANKLIN, BERNARD W., transportation co. exec.; b. Anderson, S.C., Apr. 14, 1911; s. George A. and Anne (Carney) F.; LL.B., U. Ga., 1934; m. Josephine Lee Maguire, Aug. 14, 1942; children—Bernard W., Josephine Anne, Margaret Lee, George Alfred. With Nat. City Lines, Inc., Chgo., 1938—, now exec. v.p., dir.; dir. Auto Carriers, Inc., Los Angeles-Seattle Motor Express, Inc. Mem. Alpha Tau Omega. Home: 72 Martinique Davis Island FL 33601 Office: 1701 N West Shore Blvd Tampa FL 33607

FRANKLIN, CARL MASON, univ. adminstr.; b. Spokane, Wash., Feb. 27, 1911; s. Charles and Lucille Gertrude (DeForde) F.; A.B., U. Wash., 1931; M.A., Stanford, 1935, Columbia, 1939; M.B.A. (Baker scholar), Harvard, 1940; LL.B. (Dupont scholar), U. Va., 1948; J.S.D. (Sterling fellow internat. law), Yale, 1956; m. Carolyn D. Craig, June 11, 1944; children—Allan, Sterling, Laurence, Priscilla. Instr. comml. subjects Chehalis (Wash.) High Sch., 1931-33; instr. accounting and econs. U. Alaska, 1933-34, registrar, comptroller, 1935-38; asst. to pres., dir. academic budget Ohio State U., 1941-46; lectr. constl. law U. Va., 1947; exec. v.p., prof. law U. Okla., 1948-53; prof. law U. So. Cal., 1953—, v.p. financial affairs, 1960—; vis. prof. U. Cal. at Berkeley, 1954, Los Angeles, 1956; hon. chmn. internat. law Naval War Coll., Newport, R.I., 1959-60; attendant Hague Acad. Internat. Law, 1959. Bd. govs., past pres. Town Hall, Los Angeles; trustee Idyllwild Arts Found. Served from lt. (j.g.) to lt. comdr. USNR, 1942-45. Mem. Assn. Am. Law Schs. (chmn. com. internat. law 1951, 52), Am. Soc. Internat. Law, Am. Acad. Polit. Sci., Internat. Law Assn., Phi Beta Kappa, Phi Kappa Phi. Mason. Home: 5966 Abernathy Dr Los Angeles CA 90045

FRANKLIN, CHARLES BENJAMIN, lectr. mgr.; b. Jefferson County, Kan., Oct. 15, 1891; s. Joseph Manning and Lucy Virginia (Kunkel) F.; A.B., Washburn Coll., 1913; student Columbia U., 1924; A.M., Harvard, 1927; D.H.L., Washburn Coll., 1967; m. Elizabeth Turner, Aug. 20, 1929 (div.); 1 dau. Elizabeth Logan Burg; m. 2d, Margaret Lavona Barnum, Jan. 20, 1940; children—Margaret Lee, Benjamin Barnum. Pres., Asso. Chautauquas, 1919-32; pub. Jayhawk

Mag., 1922-23; state bus. mgr. of Kan., 1933- 36; pres. Knife and Fork Club. Internat. and Asso. Clubs, 1938—; dir. Am. Platform Guild, 1945-47. Pres. Native Sons of Kans., 1928-29, Rotary Club of Topeka, 1929-30. Served as 2d lt., Air Service, World War I. Recipient award Internat. Platform Assn., 1965, 67, 70. Mem. Internat. Platform Assn. (bd. govs.), Am. Legion, 40 and 8. Republican. Conglist. Mason (Shriner). Editor: Famous After Dinner Speeches, 1949; The Dinner Club Movement, 1954. Home: 4808 West Hills Dr Topeka KS 66606 Office: New England Bldg Topeka KS 66603

FRANKLIN, EDWARD WARD, controls co. exec., lawyer; b. N.Y.C., Sept. 23, 1926; s. Albert Ward and Edith (Meyers) F.; A.B. magna cum laude, Harvard, 1947, LL.B., 1950; m. Joan Rice, Aug. 25, 1956; children—Caroline, Melissa, Edward Ward. Admitted to N.Y. bar, 1950; asso. Cadwalader, Wickersham & Taft, N.Y.C., 1950-56; gen. counsel N.Y. Air Brake Co., 1956-67, v.p. internat. and legal, 1962-67; v.p., gen. counsel Gen. Signal Corp., N.Y.C., 1967—, sec., 1969—, also dir., mem. exec. com.; dir. Gen. Signal of Can., Ltd., Hamworthy Hydraulics, Ltd., Poole, Eng., N.Y. Air Brake Co. of Can., Ltd., Rexdale, Ont., Regina Corp., Edwards Co., Inc., Cin. Time Recorder Co. Trustee, Town Sch., Inc., Carnegie Hill Neighborhood Conservation Project. Served with USAAF, 1945. Mem. Am. Bar Assn., Assn. Bar City N.Y., Phi Beta Kappa. Clubs: Whist, Cloud, Board Room, Harvard, Regency (N.Y.C.); Mesquamicat (Watch Hill, R.I.). Home: 1170 Fifth Av New York City NY 10029 Office: 280 Park Av New York City NY 10017

FRANKLIN, FREDERIC, dancer; b. Liverpool, Eng., June, 1914; s. Frederick and Florence Mabel (Brown) F.; studied dancing with Shelagh Elliott Clarke, 1926-31; passed elementary, intermediate exams. Assn. Operatic Dancing (now Royal Acad. Dancing); studied with Nicholas Legat, 1933-35, Lydia Kyasht, 1935-37, Mme. Anna Pruzina, 1936-38. Child dancer, appeared in clubs, cabarets, dramatic prodns., Liverpool, Eng., 1927-31; mem. English dancing troupe, Lancashire Lads, also revue Casino de Paris, 1931; appeared in musical comedies, danced with Wendy Toye at Grosvenor House, London; appeared in Ballerina, 1933; guest artist Vic-Wells Co., 1934; mem. Markova-Dolin Co., 1935-37; debut with Ballet Russe in Monte Carlo as Baron in Gaite Parisienne, in London as Spirit of Creation in Beethoven's 7th Symphony; other prin. roles as knight in St. Francis, slave in Scheherazade, king of the dandies in Le Beau Danube, prince in Prince Igor, beggar in Devil's Holiday, 1939, Franz in Copelia, 1939-40, musical comedy dancing role in ballet The New Yorker to music of George Gershwin. Danced the Trepak, Casse Noisette, staged by Monte Carlo, 1939- 40; appeared in Song of Norway, 1944, Maitre de Ballet, Ballet Russe de Monte Carlo, 1944-52, 54—; premier danseur, co-dir. Slavenska-Franklin Ballet, 1952-53; roles, 1944— include Johnny in Ruth Page's ballet Frankie and Johnny, prin. part Stravinsky-Balanchine's Dances Concertantes, prin. part Balanchine's Mozartiana, the Poet in Balanchine's Night Shadow, Albrecht in Giselle, Billy in Ruth Page's Billy Sunday. Address: 231 E 51st St New York City NY 10022

FRANKLIN, GENE FARTHING, educator; b. Banner Elk, N.C., July 25, 1927; s. B.D. and Delia (Farthing) F.; B.S. in Elec. Engring., Ga. Inst. Tech., 1950; M.S., Mass. Inst. Tech., 1952; D.Engring. Sc., Columbia, 1955; m. Gertrude Stritch, Jan. 3, 1952; children—David Michael, Carole Lea. Asst. prof. Columbia, 1955-57; mem. faculty Stanford, 1957—, prof. elec. engring., 1961—, asso. provost for computing, 1971—; cons. to industry, 1957—; cons. editor Holden-Day Pub. Co., 1963—. Served with USNR, 1945-47. Mem. I.E.E.E., Soc. Indsl. and Applied Math., Eta Kappa Nu, Tau Beta Pi. Democrat. Methodist. Author: (with J. R. Ragazzini) Sampled-Data Control Systems, 1958. Home: 820 Santa Fe Av Stanford CA 94305

FRANKLIN, GEORGE S., Jr., orgn. exec.; b. N.Y. City, Mar. 23, 1913; s. George Small and Elizabeth (Jennings) F.; student U. Grenoble, 1931-32; A.B., Harvard, 1936; LL.B., Yale, 1939; m. Helena Edgell, June 24, 1950; children—Helena, George III, Cynthia, Sheila. Law clk. Davis, Polk, Wardwell, Gardiner & Reed, 1939; asst. Nelson A. Rockefeller, 1940; div. world trade intelligence Dept. State, 1941-44; asso. with Council on Fgn. Relations, 1945—, asst. exec. dir., 1951-53, exec. director, 1953—. Trustee Internat. House, N.Y.C., Robert Coll., Istanbul, Turkey, Brearley Sch., Atlantic Council U.S., Am Ditchley Found., Commn. Atlantic Colls., Salzburg Seminar Am. Studies. Presbyn. Clubs: Century, River, Harvard (N.Y.C.). Home: 1220 Park Av New York City NY 10028 also Cove Neck Rd Osyter Bay NY 11771 Office: 58 E 68th St New York City NY 10021

FRANKLIN, GORDON PELTON, dept. store exec.; b. N.Y.C., Nov. 10, 1915; s. Leo A. and Carolyn (Hastings) F.; student N.Y. U., nights 1934-37; m. Gwendolyn Kenny, July 4, 1956; stepchildren—Haughton, Christopher Randolph. With Saks Fifth Av., N.Y.C., 1933—, v.p., 1968-69, pres., 1969—; dir. Gimbel Bros., 1172 Corp. Active local Boy Scouts Am., Lighthouse for Blind, Anti-Defamation League, City of Hope. Served to lt. comdr. USNR, World War II. Decorated Bronze Star, Navy Commendation medal. Clubs: N.Y. Athletic; E. Hampton (L.I.) Yacht. Home: 1172 Park Av New York City, NY 10028. Office: 611 Fifth Av New York City NY 10022

FRANKLIN, JAMES B., airline exec.; b. Jefferson City, Tenn., May 4, 1909; s. James Ernest and Maude (Williams) F.; student Carnegie Inst. Tech.; m. Jean Schmidt, 1935; children—George B., Stanley M., Barbara J. With Capital Airlines, and predecessors, 1934—, successively co-pilot and capt., dir. maintenance and engring., operations dir., 1934-48, sr. v.p. operations, 1948; capt. United Air Lines after merger with Capital Airlines; pres., chief exec. officer Airlift Internat., Inc., 1961—; dir. Fairfax County Nat. Bank, Seven Corners, Va. Mason. Clubs: LaGorce Country (Miami Beach, Fla.); Pinnacle (N.Y.C.). Home: 3020 W Ox Rd Herndon VA 22070 Office: PO Box 535 Miami FL 33148

FRANKLIN, JOE LOUIS, Jr., educator, chemist; b. Natchez, Miss., Aug. 11, 1906; s. Joe Louis and Katherine Hunt (Balfour) F.; B.S., U. Tex., 1929, M.S., 1930, Ph.D., 1934; postgrad. Mass. Inst. Tech., 1930-31; m. Mildred Louise Selkirk, Dec. 22, 1935; children—William Selkirk, James Balfour, Robert Ainsworth. Research chemist Humble Oil & Refining Co., 1934-38, sec. head, 1938-45, asst. div. head, 1945-47, research asso., 1947-63; originator, coordinator Humble lectr. scis., engring., 1946-63; guest scientist Nat. Bur. Standards, 1957-58; Welch vis. scholar Rice U., Houston, 1961-62, Welch prof. chemistry, 1963—; Wiley lectr. Purdue U., 1957. Recipient Publs. award S. Tex. sect. Am. Inst. Chem. Engrs., 1949, Distinguished Service award, 1962; S.W. award Am. Chem. Soc., 1962, Southeastern Tex. sect. award, 1970. Registered profl. engr., Tex. Fellow Am. Phys. Soc., Am. Inst. Chemists; mem. Am. Soc. Mass Spectrometry (pres. 1969-70; dir.-at-large), Houston Philos. Soc., A.A.A.S. (councilor), Am. Chem. Soc. (mem. exec. bd., councilor, chmn. S.E. Tex. sect. 1955), Am. Inst. Chem. Engrs. (tech. program chmn. 1955, chmn. S. Tex. sect. 1949), Faraday Soc., Am Soc. Testing Materials (chmn. com. mass spectrometry 1968-69), Am. Petroleum Inst., Combustion Inst. Author: Electron Impact Phenomena and Properties of Gaseous Ions, 1957. Contbr. articles profl. jours. Home: 3627 S Braeswood St Houston TX 77025

FRANKLIN, JOEL NICHOLAS, educator, mathematician; b. Chgo., Apr. 4, 1930; B.S., Stanford, 1950, Ph.D., 1953; 1 dau., Sarah Jane. Research asso. N.Y.U., 1953-55; asst. prof. math. U. Wash, 1955; mem. faculty Cal. Inst. Tech., 1957—, prof. applied sci., 1966-69, prof. applied math., 1969—, asso. dir. Willis Booth Computing Center, 1966-69; cons. to govt. and industry, 1955—. Mem. Am. Math. Soc., Assn. Computing Machinery, Phi Beta Kappa, Sigma Xi. Author Matrix Theory, 1968; also articles. Home: 1763 Alta Crest Altadena CA 91001 Office: California Inst Tech Pasadena CA 91001

FRANKLIN, JOHN CURTIS, mfg. co. executive; b. Palo Alto, Cal., Dec. 8, 1904; s. Edward Curtis and Effie June (Scott) F.; B.A. in Physics, Stanford, 1926; M.B.A., Harvard, 1929; m. Francis Snyder, Apr. 1, 1933 (div. July 1963); children—Peter Scott, Edward Curtis; m. Ruth Walgreen Stephan, Feb. 11, 1966. With Trans World Airlines, 1929-47, v.p. engring. and maintenance, 1942-47; mgr. AEC, Oak Ridge, 1947-49; v.p., dir. Gen. Aniline & Film Corp., 1949-55; gen. partner Lazard Freres & Co., N.Y.C., 1957-66; v.p. corp. devel. Gen. Dynamics Corp., N.Y.C., 1966—. Home: 2 Washington Square Village New York City, NY 10012; also Khakum Wood Greenwich CT 06830 Office: 1 Rockefeller Plaza New York City NY 10020

FRANKLIN, JOHN FRANCIS, Jr., ret. army officer; b. Manila, Philippines, Jan. 4, 1911; s. John Francis and Satilla Grace (Moran) F.; grad. Stanton Prep. Sch., Cornwall on Hudson, N.Y.; B.S., U.S. Mil. Acad., 1934; grad. Command and Gen. Staff Coll., 1941, Army War Coll., 1953; m. Jean Williamson (dec. May 1962); 1 son, John Francis III; m. 2d, Dorothy Weill, Oct. 30, 1962; 1 foster son, Theodore S. Hatzfeld III; 1 adopted dau., Cynthia J. Commd. 2d lt., U.S. Army, 1934, advanced through grades to maj. gen., 1962; unit officer, mem. staff, faculty Command and Gen. Staff Coll., Ft. Leavenworth, Kan., 1934-41; participated Guadalcanal campaign, 1942-43; mem. operations div. War Dept. Gen. Staff, 1944-46; exec. officer Marshall Mission, China, 1946-51; comdr. 44th Tank Bn., 82d Airborne Div., later G-3 XVIII Airborne Corps, 1951-52; chief staff 3d Inf. Div., Korea, 1953; sec., dir. instrn., then chief staff Command and Gen. Staff Coll., 1954-58; dep. chief staff for personnel, hdqrs. U.S. Continental Army Command, Ft. Monroe, Va., 1959-61; asst. div. comdr. 3d Armored Div., Germany, 1961; dep. chief staff logistics and orgn. Allied Forces Central Europe, NATO, Fontainebleau, Francce, 1962; comdg. gen. 4th Armored Div., Germany, 1962-64; chief staff 7th U.S. Army, 1964; U.S. comdr., Berlin, 1964-67; dep. comdg. gen. Sixth U.S. Army, 1967-70, ret., 1970; dir. devel. San Francisco Symphony Assn., 1970—. Decorated D.S.M. with cluster, Legion Merit with 2 clusters, Bronze Star; spl. breast Order of Yun Hui (China); Ulchi Distinguished Service medal (Korea). Mem. U.S. Army Armor Assn., Assn. U.S. Army, Army-Navy Country, Mil. Council Cath. Men in Europe (pres. 1963-64). Office: San Francisco Symphony Assn 107 War Meml Vets Bldg San Francisco CA 94102

FRANKLIN, JOHN HOPE, educator, author; b. Rentiesville, Okla., Jan. 2, 1915; s. Buck Colbert and Mollie (Parker) F.; A.B., Fisk U., 1935; A.M., Harvard, 1936, Ph.D., 1941; LL.D., Morgan State Coll., 1960, Va. State Coll., 1961, Lincoln University, 1961; A.M., Cambridge (England) University, 1962; LL.D., Tuskegee Inst., 1964, Lincoln Coll., 1965, Hamline U., 1965, Fisk U., 1965, R.I. Coll., 1967, Dickinson Coll., 1968, Howard U., 1968, Johnson C. Smith Coll., 1968; Litt.D., Tougaloo Coll., 1967; L.H.D., U. Mass., 1964; L.H.D., L.I. U., 1964; others; m. Aurelia E. Whittington, June 11, 1940; 1 son, John Whittington. Instr. history Fisk U., 1936-37; prof. history St. Augustine's Coll., 1939-43, N.C. Coll. at Durham, 1943-47, Howard U., 1947-56; chmn. dept. history Bklyn. Coll., 1956-65; prof. Am. history U. Chgo., 1964—, chmn. dept., of history, 1967-70, John Matthews Manly Distinguished Service prof., 1969—; William Pitt prof. Am. history and instns. Cambridge U., 1962-63; vis. prof. Harvard, U. Wis., Cornell U., Salzburg Seminar, U. Cal., Cambridge U. Chmn. Bd. of Fgn. Scholarships, 1966-69. Chmn. bd. of trustees Fisk U., 1968—. Edward Austin fellow, 1937-38; Rosenwald fellow, 1937-39; Guggenheim fellow, 1950-51; Pres.'s fellow Brown U., 1952-53; Fulbright prof., Australia, 1960; mem. bd. dirs. Salzburg Seminar. Mem. bd. trustees Fisk U., Am. Council Learned Socs. Fellow of Am. Acad. of Arts and Scis.; mem Am., So. (pres. 1970-71) hist. assn., Orgn. Am. Historians, Assn. for Study Negro Life and History, Am. Studies Assn. (past pres.), Am. Assn. State and Local History, Am. Assn. of U. Profs., Assn. of Social Science Tchrs., Phi Beta Kappa (mem. senate 1966—), Phi Alpha Theta. Author: Free Negro in North Carolina, 1943; Civil War Diary of James T. Ayers, 1947; From Slavery to Freedom: A History of American Negroes, 3d edit., 1967; Militant South, 1956; Reconstruction After the Civil War, 1961; The Emancipation Proclamation, 1963; (with others) Land of the Free, 1966. Editor: A Fool's Errand (by Albion Tourgee), 1961; Army Life in a Black Regiment (by Thomas Higginson), 1962. Editorial bd. Jour. Negro History, Jour. Am. History. Home: 5805 S Blackstone Av Chicago, IL 60637.

FRANKLIN, JOSEPH AMOS, univ. adminstr.; b. Madison Co., Ind., July 5, 1904; s. Pierce and Emma (Zetta) F.; B.S., Ind. U., 1927; m. Beatrice Long, June 9, 1926; children—Richard, Zetta Ann (Mrs. Anderson), Janet (Mrs. Carrell), Joseph. Accountant, auditor Ind. U., 1927-34, chief accountant, 1934-37, asst. comptroller, 1937-42, asst. treas., 1942-46, treasurer, 1946-48, v.p., treas., 1948—. Trustee Lions Cancer Control Fund of Indiana, Inc.; mem. Ind. Med. Edn. Found.; bd. dirs. United Student Aid Funds, Nat. Myasthenia Gravis Found., Indiana Purdue Found., Ft. Wayne. Mem. Nat., Central assns. of coll. and univ. business officers, James Whitcomb Riley Meml. Assn. (life gov.,) C. of C., Hoosier Salon Patrons Assn., Assn. Univs. for Research in Astronomy (v.p.), Ind. U. Alumni Assn. (life), Ind. Union (life), Beta Alpha Psi, Beta Gamma Sigma, Acacia. Mem. Church of Christ (elder). Clubs: Lions, Columbia, Bloomington Country. Author articles on bus. adminstrn. Home: Rural Route 1 Box 174F Unionville IN

FRANKLIN, LEO ISAAC, lawyer; b. Detroit, Jan. 26, 1904; s. Leo M. and Hattie M. (Oberfelder) F.; A.B., U. Mich., 1924, J.D., 1926; m. Ethel Eleanor Arie, Dec. 28, 1946; 1 son, John F. Admitted to Mich. bar, 1926, since practiced in Detroit; mem. firm Fischer, Franklin & Ford, and predecessors, 1926—; instr. Law Sch. Wayne State U., 1929-42; chief Mich. counsel U.S. OPA, 1942; chief counsel price adjustment bd. U.S. Army-Air Force Central Procurement Dist., 1942-43. A founder Common Pleas Ct. Detroit. Chmn, Wayne State U. Found., 1955; commr. Detroit House Correction, 1961- 69. Bd. dirs. Boys Republic, Civic Searchlight, Inc., Tb and Health Soc. Wayne County, Montefiore Home For Aged, Cleve. Mem. Am., Mich. (past commr., sec.), Detroit (past dir., pres.) bar assns., Am. Judicature Soc. Club: Great Lakes (past pres.). Home: 17155 Muirland Av Detroit, MI 48221. Office: Guardian Bldg Detroit MI 48226

FRANKLIN, LINDLEY MURRAY, Jr., church ofcl.; b. Flushing, N.Y., Aug. 5, 1910; s. Lindley Murray and Magdelaine (Weed) F.; B.A., Williams Coll., 1933; LL.D., St. Augustine's Coll., 1963; m. Eleanor Wooley, June 21, 1935 (dec. Dec. 25, 1968); children—Janet (Mrs. Thomas R. Peifer), Maddalena, Nina; m. 2d, Helen McConaughy, Dec. 26, 1970. Asst. manager Brooklyn Trust Co., 1933-43; asst. treas. Domestic and Fgn. Missionary Soc. P.E. Ch. U.S. (Exec. Council P.E. Ch.), 1946-58, treas., since 1958; treas. Seabury House of P.E. Ch., Episcopal Service for Youth, Inc.; bd. dirs., mem. exec. com. Seabury Press. Police commr., Darien, Conn., 1965—. Treas. Am. Council St. Luke's Internat. Med. Center, Tokyo; bd. dirs., exec. com. Episcopal Ch. Found.; bd. dirs., exec. com., chmn. finance com. Japan Internat. Christian U.; treas. bd. trustees of fgn. parishes P.E. Ch. in U.S., St. James' Am. P.E. Ch., Florence, Italy, St. Paul's Am. P.E. Ch., Rome. Served with AUS, 1943-46. Mem. Church Assn. for Seamen's Work (treas.), Darien Hist. Soc. (pres. 1960-62), Psi Upsilon. Episcopalian. Clubs: Noroton Yacht; Church (N.Y.C.). Home: 80 Nearwater Lane Noroton CT 06820 Office: 815 Second Av New York City NY 10017

FRANKLIN, MARC ADAM, educator; b. Bklyn., Mar. 9, 1932; s. Louis A. and Rose (Rosenthal) F.; A.B., Cornell, 1953, LL.B., 1956; m. Ruth E. Korzenik, June 29, 1958; children—Jonathan, Alison. Admitted to N.Y. bar, 1956; atty. firm Proskauer Rose Goetz & Mendelsohn, N.Y.C., 1956-57; law clk to Hon. Carroll C. Hincks, New Haven, 1957-58, to Earl Warren U.S. Supreme Ct., Washington, 1958-59; prof. law Columbia, 1959-62, Stanford, 1962—. Fellow Center for Advanced Study in the Behavioral Scis., 1968-69. Author: Biography of a Legal Dispute, 1968; Dynamics of American Law, 1968; Injuries and Remedies: Cases and Materials on Tort Law and Alternatives, 1971. Home: 30 Pine Ridge Way Portola Valley CA 94025 Office: Stanford Law Sch Stanford CA 94305

FRANKLIN, MICHAEL HAROLD, orgn. exec.; b. Los Angeles, Dec. 25, 1923; A.B., U.. Cal. at Los Angeles, 1948; LL.B., U. So. Cal., 1951; m. Georgia Hanni, June 14, 1964; children—Barbara, John, James, Robert. Admitted to the Cal. bar, 1951; practice in Los Angeles, 1951-52; pvt. practice, 1951-52; atty. CBS, 1952-54; atty. Paramount Pictures Corp., 1954-58; exec. dir. Writers Guild Am. West, Inc., 1958-. Served with C.E., AUS, 1942-46. Mem. Am. Civil Liberties Union, Los Angeles Copyright Soc., Order of Coif. Home: 17153 Adlon Rd Encino, CA 91316. Office: 8955 Beverly Blvd Los Angeles CA 90048

FRANKLIN, MITCHELL, educator; b. Montreal, Que., Can., Feb. 19, 1902; s. Adolphe and Emma (Franklin) F.; A.B., Harvard, 1922, J.D., 1925, S.J.D., 1928; m. Virginia Frances Wesler, June 25, 1922. Law sec. to Supreme Jud. Ct. of Mass., 1925-28; engaged in practice of law, N.Y. C., 1928-30; W.R. Irby prof. of law Tulane U., New Orleans, 1930-67, now emeritus; vis. prof. State U. N.Y. at Buffalo, 1967-68, prof. law, philosophy of law, 1968-69, prof. philosophy, prof. law, 1969—. Served as pvt. U.S. Army, World War I; maj. to lt. col. World War II. Recipient of Franklin D. Roosevelt award, 1958. Legal adviser, UN Relief and Rehab. Adminstrn., Southwestern Europe, Middle East, hdqrs. Rome, 1946. Legal officer UN Secretariat, 1948. Rosenwald fellow, Paris, 1939; Guggenheim fellowship, 1948-49. Mem. N.Y., La., bar assns. U.S. reporter at Congresses of Comparative Law, The Hague, also London, Paris. Contbr. legal publs. Home: 675 Delaware Av Buffalo NY 14202 Office: Law Sch State Univ NY at Buffalo Buffalo NY 14202 also Tulane U New Orleans LA 70118

FRANKLIN, OMER W., Jr., judge; b. Valdosta, Ga., 1914; A.B., U. Ga., 1936, LL.B., 1939. Admitted to Ga. Bar, 1939; sr. partner firm Franklin, Barham, Coleman, Elliott & Blackburn, Valdosta, 1961-69; judge Superior Cts., So. Jud. Circuit, Valdosta, Ga., 1969—. Mem. rules com. Ga. Supreme Ct., 1961—, Fed. Jud. Council, 1961—. Fellow Am. Coll. Trial Lawyers, Am. Coll. Probate Counsel; mem. Am., Valdosta (pres. 1959-60) bar assns., State Bar Ga. (chmn. com. rules of practice and procedure, 1964- 65; pres. 1966-67), Am. Judicature Soc., Internat. Assn. Ins. Counsel, Phi Delta Phi. Address: Lowndes County Courthouse Valdosta GA 31601

FRANKLIN, OWEN ELLSWORTH, social service adminstr.; b. Vincennes, Ind., Oct. 27, 1924; s. Court M. and Zoe (Day) F.; B.S., Ind. U., 1950, M.A., 1952; m. Dicy Lou Morrow, Sept. 16, 1946; children—Randall M., Mark A., Jeffrey W., Rebecca A. Sch. social worker Indpls. Pub. Schs., 1952-55; child welfare cons. State Welfare Dept., Indpls., 1956; asst. dir. Nat. Child Welfare div. Am. Legion, Indpls., 1957-59; dir. social services Woodward (Ia.) State Hosp.-Sch., 1959-64, supt., 1969—. Mem. com. Mental retardation Dept. Health, Edn. and Welfare, Washington, 1965-67; co-chmn. com. on mental retardation U.S. Childrens Bur., 1965-68. Served with AUS, 1943-46. Decorated Bronze Star (5) with bronze arrowhead. Mem. Am. Assn. on Mental Deficiency, Nat. Assn. Social Workers. Address: Woodward State Hosp-Sch Woodward IA 50276

FRANKLIN, RICHARD EWELL, ry. ofcl.; b. Birmingham, Ala., Dec. 3, 1919; s. William F. and Mary (Cunningham) F.; student Internat. Corr. Schs., 1937-40; m. Frances Stevens, Oct. 19, 1940; children—R. Miles, Elaine (Mrs. Donald E. Love), Frances Mabel. With So. Ry.Co., 1937-61, 64-65, supt. maintenance equipment, Charlotte, N.C., 1952-55, asst. v.p. mech., Washington, 1956- 61, chief mech. officer 1963-64, v.p., asst. to pres., v.p. operations, 1964, sr. v.p., 1965; v.p. engring., prodn. and research Ry. Maintenance Corp., Pitts., 1961-62; dir. indsl. engring. Pa. Ry. Co., Phila., 1962- 63, v.p. transp., maintenance, 1966-67; asst. pres. Central of Ga. Ry., Savannah, 1967-68, pres., 1968—, dir., 1967—, mem. exec. com., 1967—; pres., dir. mem. exec. com. Ocean Steamship Co. Savannah, Savannah & Atlanta Ry. Co., South Western R.R. Co., Wrightsville & Tennille R.R. Co.; pres., dir. Albany Passenger Terminal Co., 1967—, Central of Ga. Motor Transport Co., 1967—, Chatham Terminal Co., 1967—, Empire Land Co., 1967—; dir. Augusta & Summerville R.R. Co., C & S Nat. Bank adv. bd., Savannah, Ga., 1967—. Dir. So. States Indsl. Council, 1968-; mem. Savannah Regional Export Expansion Council, 1968—. Bd. dirs. A.R.C., Savannah, 1968—, Savannah YMCA, 1968—; chmn. Savannah area U.S. Savs. Bonds campaign, 1969; chmn. div. A, United Community Appeal, 1969 —; mem. Savannah Council on Youth Opportunity, Coastal Empire council Boy Scouts Am., 1968—. Trustee Ga. Coll. Found., Milledgeville, 1969- -, Historic Savannah Found., 1969—. Served with AUS, 1944-46. Mem. Ga. C. of C. (dir. 1968—), Savannah Area C. of C. (dir. 1968—, pres. 1969). Served with AUS, 1944- Baptist. Rotarian. Clubs: Savannah Golf, Savannah Yacht; Chatham; Forest City Gun; Savannah Inn and Country; Kenwood Golf and Country (Washington). Home: 2 Woodhull Circle The Bluff Savannah, GA 31404. Office: 227 W Broad St Savannah GA 31401

FRANKLIN, ROBERT DUMONT, library adminstr.; b. Memphis, Sept. 15, 1908; s. Dumont and Grace Fulton (Campbell) F.; student Southwestern Coll., 1926-27; B.A., U. Tenn., 1933; B.S., Columbia, 1934; m. Mary McFarland Wilson, Aug. 9, 1934; children—Linda Campbell, Robert McFarland. Library page and asst., Memphis and Knoxville, 1925-33; credit clk. Procter & Gamble Co., Memphis, 1928-30; library asst. N.Y. Pub. Library, 1934-36; librarian Am. Mcht. Marine Library Assn., N.Y.C., 1936-38; dir. Shelby County Libraries, Memphis, 1938-46; asst. dir. Toledo Pub. Library, 1946-55, dir., 1955-71; dir. Charlottesville-Albemarle County (Va.) Pub. Library, 1971—; lectr. grad. library sci. Toledo U., others. Mem. A.L.A., Va. Library Assn., United World Federalists (pres. Toledo 1952-53). Clubs: Toledo Tennis, Rotary (Toledo). Lyricist: (with Elizabeth Gould) Declaration for Peace, 1955. Contbr. articles to profl.

periodicals, book rev. newspapers. Home: 2716 Northfield Rd Charlottesville VA 22901 Office: McIntire Pub Library Charlottesville VA 22901

FRANKLIN, THOMAS CHESTER, educator, chemist; b. Birmingham, Ala., Feb. 5, 1923; s. Chester S. and Irene (Tibbetts) F.; B.S., Howard Coll., 1944; Ph.D., Ohio State U., 1951; m. Nellie Louise Friel, June 26, 1946; children—Irene Elise, Margaret Elaine, Janice Carol, Thomas Edward. Instr., Howard Coll., 1946-48; asst. instr. Ohio State U., 1948-51; asst prof. U. Richmond, Va., 1951-54; research asso. Va. Inst. for Sci. Research, Richmond, 1951-53; faculty Baylor U., Waco, Tex., 1954—, prof. chemistry, 1964—. Mem. Am. Chem. Soc., Electrochem. Soc., Am. Electroplaters Soc., Internat. Com. Electrochem. Thermodynamics and Kinetics, Sigma Xi. Author: (with John Xan) A Lab Manual for Semimicroqualitiative Analysis, 1948. Studies, publs. of electrochem. and catalytic properties of metal surfaces in contact with solutions using absorption of hydrogen as a measure of active area; studies of electrodeposition, catalytic and electrolytic oxidations and reductions of organic compounds. Home: 1312 Guthrie Dr Waco TX 76703

FRANKLIN, WILLIAM BALFOUR, chem. engr.; b. Natchez, Miss., Oct. 7, 1908; s. Joe Louis and Katherine Hunt (Balfour) F.; B.S. in Chem. Engring., U. Tex., 1930, M.S., 1931, Ph.D. in Phys. Chemistry, 1934; m. Geraldine Slaughter, Sept. 6, 1933; children—Joan Marie (Mrs. A.J. Phipps), Carol Jean (Mrs. J.M. Heller). Instr. phys. chemistry, also chem. engring. U. Tex., 1930-34; with Humble Oil & Refining Co., 1934—, mgr. tech., and research, 1957-58, mgr. tech., 1958-69, head of math. computing and systems, 1969—. Mem. Tex. Atomic Energy Adv. Com., 1964—; charter mem. adv. council Engring. Found., U. Tex., 1957-63, chmn., 1962, mem. vis. com. dept. chem. engring., 1961-70. Mem. bd. Baytown and E. Harris County Community Chest. Registered profl. engr., Tex. Fellow Am. Inst. Chem. Engrs. (chmn. awards com. 1959-60, nat. dir. 1959-61, v.p. 1964, pres. 1965; adv. com. Chem. Engring. Progress 1957-61; alternate dir. Engrs. Joint Council 1964; Distinguished Service award S. Tex. sect. 1960; Founders award 1968); mem. Am. Chem. Soc., Sigma Xi, Tau Beta Pi, Phi Lambda Upsilon. Methodist (ofcl. bd.). Home: 5005 Glen Haren Baytown TX 77520 Office: PO Box 2180 Houston TX 77001

FRANKLIN, WILLIAM HENRY, mfr.; b. Chgo., Jan. 30, 1909; s. Edward T. and Helen (Willett) F.; grad. Phillips Exeter Acad., 1927; B.A., Princeton, 1931; m. Mary Haas, Apr. 19, 1937; children—William Henry, Ann Elizabeth, Mary Josephine, Robert Edward. Auditor Price, Waterhouse & Co., Chgo., 1934-41; asst. controller Caterpillar Tractor Co., Peoria, Ill., 1941-44, controller, 1944-52, v.p., 1952-62, exec. v.p., 1962-66, pres., 1966—, also dir.; dir. Standard Oil Co. (N.J.), Fed. Res. Bank Chgo., Carson Pirie Scott & Co., Toledo, Peoria & Western R.R. Trustee Com. for Econ. Devel., Bradley U. C.P.A., Ill. Mem. Nat. Assn. Accountants (past nat. v.p.), Am. Inst. Accountants, Peoria Assn. Commerce. Clubs: Country of Peoria, Creve Coeur (Peoria). Home: 500 Miller Rd Peoria IL 61614 Office: 600 Washington St Peoria IL 61611

FRANKLIN, WILLIAM MCHENRY, historian; b. Cin., Sept. 6, 1913; s. Ward and Hazel (McHenry) F.; B.A., U. Cin., 1934, M.A., 1935; exchange student U. Koenigsberg, 1935-36; Ph.D., Fletcher Sch. Law and Diplomacy, 1941; m. Alicelia Hoskins, May 25, 1939; children—Hayward H., Charles E. Research sec. Council Fgn. Relations, 1939-40; div. asst. State Dept., 1941-46, asst. chief hist. div., 1947-62, dir. Hist. Office, 1962—; professorial lectr. diplomatic history Georgetown U., 1964—. Served to lt. USNR, 1943-45. Recipient Meritorious Service award State Dept., 1963. Mem. Am. Hist. Assn., Am. Polit. Sci. Assn., Am. Soc. Internat. Law, Phi Beta Kappa. Author: Protection of Foreign Interests, 1947; also articles. Editor: Documents on Conferences of World War II. Home: 6617 Barnaby St NW Washington, DC 20015. Office: Historical Office State Dept Washington DC 20520

FRANKOVITCH, MIKE J., film producer; b. Bisbee, Ariz., Sept. 29, 1910; B.A., U. Cal. Producer, commentator on radio, 1934-38; author screenplays for Universal Studios, 1938, Republic Pictures, 1940-49; producer Fugutive Lady; Lucky Nick Kane; Thief of Venice; Decameron Nights; Malaga; Footsteps in the Fog; Joe Macbeth; mng. dir. Columbia Pictures Corp. Ltd., 1955-59, chmn., 1959-67; v.p. Columbia Pictures Internat. Corp., 1955-67; head Columbia Pictures Internat. Prodns., 1958-67; 1st v.p. charge world prodn. Columbia until 1967; dir. BLC Films; chmn. Screen Gems Ltd.; independent producer, 1967—. Served with AUS, World War II. Club: Variety (chief banker Tent 36).*

FRANKS, CHARLES LESLIE, banker; b. Columbus, Miss., Jan. 21, 1934; s. Leslie J. and Almeda (Morris) F.; B.S. magna cum laude, Miss. State U., 1956; m. Cecil Alice Cronovich, Feb. 7, 1959; children—Carolyn Anne, Charles Christopher. Accountant, Arthur Andersen & Co., Houston, 1959-61; mgr. internal audit dept. Bank of S.W., Houston, 1961—; instr., speaker various Bank Adminstrn. Inst. seminars, meetings and convs. Served to capt. USAF, 1956-59. Mem. Tex. Soc. C.P.A.'s (sec. Houston chpt. 1971-72), Bank Adminstrn. Inst. (v.p. Gulf Coast chpt. 1971-72), Am. Inst. Banking, Inst. Internal Auditors, Houston C. of C., Arnold Air Soc., Phi Eta Sigma, Chi Lambda Rho, Phi Kappa Phi, Alpha Kappa Psi. Roman Catholic. Home: 6106 Cheena St Houston TX 77035 Office: PO Box 2629 Houston TX 77001

FRANKS, JOHN RICHARD, lawyer; b. Goldendale, Wash., Nov. 12, 1910; s. Oscar and Emma (Johanson) F.; LL.B., U. Ariz., 1934; m. Lena B. Scholey, May 9, 1936; children—Gladys Marie (Mrs. David B. Montgomery), Pamela J. Admitted to Ariz. bar, 1935; practice in Prescott, 1935-53, Phoenix, 1953—; partner Murphy, Posner & Franks, 1962—; atty. Yavapai County, 1942-43; city atty., Phoenix, 1959-62; chief counsel Indsl. Commn. Ariz., 1953-59. Mem. Ariz. Senate, 1948-52. Served as lt. (j.g.) USNR, 1943-45. Mem. State Bar Ariz., Am., Fed. bar assns., Am. Judicature Soc., Lawyer's Club Phoenix, Phi Delta Phi. Democrat. Conglist. Kiwanian. Club: Phoenix Country. Home: 41 E Marlette Rd Phoenix AZ 85012 Office: Towne House Tower Phoenix AZ 85013

FRANKS, LUCINDA LAURA, journalist; b. Chgo., July 16, 1946; d. Thomas Edward and Lorraine Lois (Leavitt) F.; B.A., Vassar Coll., 1968. Journalist specializing youth affairs, civil strife in No. Ireland, U.P.I., London, 1968—. Recipient Pulitizer prize nat. reporting, 1970; Nat. Headliners award, Soc. Silurians award journalism. Home: 60 Riverview Gardens London SW 13 England Office: U P I 220 E 42d St New York City NY 10017*

FRANKS, OLIVER SHEWELL, (Lord Franks of Headington), educator; b. Birmingham, Eng., Feb. 16, 1905; s. Robert Sleightholme and Katharine (Shewell) F.; B.A., Oxford U., 1927, M.A., 1930, D.C.L. (hon.), 1952; m. Barbara Mary Tanner, July 3, 1931; children—Caroline Lesley (Mrs. John R. Dinwiddy), Alison Elizabeth. Fellow, tutor Queens Coll., Oxford U., 1927-37; prof. moral philosophy Glasgow (Scotland) U., 1937-45; permanent sec. Ministry Supply, 1939-46; provost Queens Coll., 1946-48; British ambassador to U.S., 1948-52; chmn. Lloyds Bank Ltd., London, 1954-62; provost Worcester Coll., Oxford U., 1962—. Mem. Nat. Econ. Devel. Council until 1964; chmn. Com. on Ofcl. Secrets, sect. 2. Trustee Pilgrim Trust; chmn. trustees Wellcome Trust. Found. Fellow Brit. Acad. Address: Worcester Coll Oxford England

FRANKUM, JAMES EDWARD, airlines co. exec.; b. Vincennes, Ind., Feb. 25, 1921; s. Hubert and Pearl (Evans) F.; student Vincennes U., 1940-41, Northwestern U., 1955, Stanford, 1959, Advanced Mgmt. Program, Harvard Graduate School of Business, 1966; LL.D., Vincennes U., 1967; m. Madalene Tharp, June 6, 1943; children—Stephanie Anne, Barbara Ellen, James Edward. With Trans World Airlines, Inc., 1942—, v.p. transp., 1961-68, v.p. flight operations, 1968—; dir. Grand Av. Bank, Kansas City, Mo. Mem. Air Transport Assn. (exec. com.), Internat. Air Transport Assn. (chmn. technical com.). Clubs: Wings, Pinnacle (N.Y.C.); Kansas City, Mission Hills Country (Kansas City, Mo.); Nassau Country, Manhasset Bay Yacht (L.I.). Home: 841 Park Av Manhasset NY 11030 Office; 605 3d Av New York City NY 10016

FRANQUIZ, JOSE ANTONIO, educator; b. Yauco, P.R., Oct. 15, 1906; s. Miguel and Hortensia (Ventura-Morales) F.; student U. P.R., 1926-27; B.A., Colgate U., 1930; B.S.T., Boston U., 1933, Ph.D., 1940; m. Frieda F. Haynes, Dec. 6, 1933; 1 dau., Arline (Mrs. Eugene R. Marteney). Psychologist, profl. adviser Dist. Penitentiary of San Juan (P.R.), 1934-36; prof. philosophy, psychology, sociology Inst. Free Studies, Athenaeum of P.R., San Juan, 1936-38; instr. philosophy U. P.R., Rio Piedras, 1936-40, asst. prof., 1940-46; prof., chmn. dept. philosophy W.Va. Wesleyan Coll., Buckhannon, 1946—. Participant 1st through 7th inter-Am. congresses philosophy, 1941-70, 1st Inter-Am. Congress Psychology, 1953, 12th through 15th internat. congresses philosophy, 1958—, other congresses. Mem. Am., Am. Cath. philos. assns., Am. Soc. Aesthetics, Metaphys. Soc. Am., Am. Acad. Religion, So. Soc. for Philosophy Religion (pres. 1965-66), Philos. Soc. W.Va. (co-founder, past pres.), Latin Am. Studies Assn., Soc. Puerto Rican Authors, Internat. Soc. for Study Medieval Philosophy, Soc. Sci. Study Religion, Coll. Poetry Guild Am., Pi Epsilon Theta, Phi Upsilon Kappa. Methodist. Rotarian. Author: Lilies and Jasmines (poetry), 1925; Interminable Blue (poetry), 1932; Introspection as Fundamental Method in Psychology and Philosophy, 1935; Nature of Human Mind, 1935; Delinquency in Puerto Rico in Light of Sociology and Psychology, 1935; Borden P. Bowne's Treatment of the Problem of Change and Identity, 1942; others. Contbr. numerous articles, essays to profl. jours. Home: 9 Latham St Buckhannon WV 26201

FRANTZ, CHARLES, educator; b. Rocky Ford, Colo., Apr. 22, 1925; s. Osee Clark and Blanche (Talhelm) F.; A.B., Earlham Coll., 1950; A.M., Haverford Coll., 1951; Ph.D., U. Chgo., 1958; m. Charlotte Stutzman, June 8, 1950; children—Marina, Trevor Kelly, Corinne. From instr. to prof. anthropology Portland (Ore.) State U., 1953-64, chmn. dept., 1960-64; vis. prof. U. Toronto, 1964-65; dir. African Studies program Howard U., 1965-67; exec. sec. Am. Anthrop. Assn., 1966-68; prof. anthropology State U. N.Y. at Buffalo, Amherst, N.Y., 1968—; on leave as prof., head dept. sociology Ahmadu Bello U., Zaria, Nigeria, 1970—. Chmn. N.W. Anthrop. Conf., 1963. Grantee Am. Council Learned Socs., 1964- 65, Wenner-Gren Found., 1960, Am. Friends Service Com., 1956-58. Fellow Am. Anthrop. Assn., African Studies Assn.; mem. Soc. Applied Anthropology, Am. Ethnol. Soc., Internat. African Inst., Am. Sociol. Assn. Author: (with C. A. Rogers) Racial Themes in Southern Rhodesia, 1962; The Student Anthropologist's Handbook, 1971; also articles. Office: 4242 Ridge Lea Rd Amherst NY 14226

FRANTZ, HARRY WARNER internat. reporter; b. Cerro Gordo, Ill., Nov. 5, 1891; s. John S. and Ada (Carver) F.; student Stanford, 1913-19; m. Kathleen Hargrave, February 15, 1924; 1 daughter, Jean (Mrs. Eric A. Blackall). International Correspondent, 1917—; dir. publicity Yellowstone Nat. Park, 1923; press dir. Office Inter-Am. Affairs, 1941-44; information officer with asst. sec. state for Am. Republics, 1944-45; information staff Chapultepec, San Francisco confs., 1945; with U.P.I., 1920— (except war years), staff fgn. dept., 1920—. Explored Mountain Province, Luzon, 1916; ambulance driver French Army, Orient, 1917; sec., inspector, historian Commn. to Serbia, A.R.C., 1917-19. Decorated service medal with group citation French Army; Red Cross medal (Serbia); Order of White Eagle (Yugoslavia); Order of Southern Cross (Brazil); Order of Merit Eloy Colon Alfaro medal (Ecuador); Maria Moors Cabot gold medal for journalism Columbia, 1957; Jane N. Smith life mem. Nat. Geog. Soc., with citation from bd. trustees for coverage pioneer air flights S.A., Pacific, Atlantic; certificate of merit Internat. House, New Orleans; gold medal U.S. Antarctic Service. Mem. National Geographical Soc., Am. Geophys. Union, Antarctican Soc. of Washington. Episcopalian. Club: Overseas Writers'. Contbr. articles news mags., jours. Spl. guest Pres. Manuel Quezon, P.I. Commonwealth, in recognition 14 years reporting P.I. independence campaign before U.S. Congresses, 1936. Home: 807 Triphammer Rd Ithaca NY 14850

FRANTZ, JOE BERTRAM, educator; b. Dallas, Jan. 16, 1917; s. Ezra A. and Mary Lavanna (Buckley) F.; B. Journalism, U. Tex., 1938, M.A., 1940, Ph.D., 1948; fellow bus. history, Harvard, 1948-49; m. Helen Boswell, Sept. 3, 1939; children—Jolie, Lisa. Asst. prof. history, then asso. prof. U. Tex., 1949-59, prof. history, chmn. dept., 1959-65; dir. Tex. State Hist. Assn., 1966—, dir. oral history project, 1968—; cons. Borden Co., N.Y.C., 1956-58. Mem. National Hist. Publs. Commn., 1964-69. Com. on Internat. Exchange of Persons. Ford Found. fellow, 1953-54; Social Sci. Research Council fellow, 1953- 54; E.D. Farmer fellow, 1959. Mem. adv. bd. Nat. Park Service, 1964-70; mem. hist. adv. com. NASA, 1967-69. Served to lt. (s.g.) USNR, 1943-46. Fellow Tex. Hist. Assn. (dir. 1966—), Tex. Inst. Letters (pres. 1967-69); mem. Philos. Soc. Tex., Am., Miss. Valley (exec. council 1962-64), Western (exec. council 1965-68), So. (exec. council 1961-63) hist. assns., S.W. Social Sci. Assn. (pres. 1963-64), Bus. Hist. Soc., Phi Alpha Theta (nat. councilor 1956-58, pres. 1962-64). Club: Cosmos. Author: Gail Borden, Dairyman to a Nation (Tex. Inst. Letters award 1951), 1951; (with J.E. Choate) The American Cowboy: Myth or Reality, 1955. Co-author: Historians of the American Frontier, 1965. Editor: An Honest Preface and Other Essays, 1959; (with Cordia S. Duke) 6000 Miles of Fence, 1961; (with others) Readings in Am. History, 1964, Three Historians on the American Frontier, 1965; Violence in America, 1969. Home: 4301 Edgemont Austin, TX 78731.

FRANTZ, LEROY, bus. exec.; b. Wilmington, Del., Apr. 28, 1888; s. Jacob Frick and Gertrude Lavina (Osborne) F.; Litt.B., Princeton, 1910; m. Henrietta Beiler Glossbrenner, Apr. 21, 1914; children—Doris Osborne (Mrs. Robert Winslow Carrick), Jeanne (Mrs. Earl B. Douglass, Jr.), Leroy. Pres. Dentist's Supply Co., N.Y. C., 1944-49; pres. Leroy Frantz, Inc., 1949—; dir. emeritus 1st Westchester Nat. Bank, New Rochelle; hon. dir. Internat. Flavors & Fragrances, Inc., N.Y.C. Past dir. Huguenot YMCA. Mem. C. of C. Republican. Clubs: Princeton (N.Y.C.); Cap and Gown (Princeton, N.J.); Lauderdale Yacht (Ft. Lauderdale, Fla.); Larchmont Yacht, N.Y. Yacht. Home: Sans Souci Davenport Neck NY 10805 Office: 271 North Av New Rochelle NY 10801

FRANTZ, WELBY MARION, motor carrier co. exec.; b. Atlanta, Ill., Oct. 27, 1912; s. Marion C. and Jennie (Brandt) F.; student Ill. State U.; m. Frances C. Mitchell, Mar. 9, 1940; 1 dau., Melana Susan. With Brandt's Truck Line, Bloomington, Ill., 1930-33; terminal mgr. Decatur Cartage Co., Danville and Peoria, Ill., also Terre Haute, Ind., 1933-46; with Eastern Express, Inc., Terre Haute, 1946—, exec. v.p., 1946-62, pres., 1962-70, vice chmn. bd., 1970—; dir. Terre Haute 1st Nat. Bank. Life bd. govs. Regular Commo Carriers Conf., 1961- -. Mem. Ind. Com. Bus. Edn. Past. bd. dirs. Terre Haute Community Chest; mem. adv. council Ind. State Univ.; overseer Sheldon Swope Art Gallery; bd. assos. Rose-Hulman Inst. Tech.; dir., chmn. finance com. Union Hosp., Terre Haute, Ind.; trustee Ind. State Univ.. Found. Served as capt., Transp. Corps, AUS, 1942-46. Named Terre Haute Man of Week, Dec. 1954, Transp. Man-of-Yr., 1964; recipient U.S. Air Force Exceptional Service award. Mem. Am. Trucking Assns. (life sr. v.p., pres. 1960, chmn. bd. 1961), Nat. Def. Transp. Assn. (nat. pres., 1967-70, chmn. bd. 1971), A.I.M., (pres. council), Transp. Assn. Am. (dir., vice chmn. hwy. panel), Nat. Safety Council (v.p.), Internat. Platform Assn., Eastern Central Motor Carriers Assn. (chmn. bd. trustees 1954-64, life chmn. 1964—), U.S. C. of C. (dir.; chmn. transp. com.). Mason (Shriner), Elk. Clubs: Kiwanis; Terre Haute Country; Marco Polo (N.Y.C.); N.Y. Traffic; Columbia (Indpls.); Tamarac Country (Ft. Lauderdale, Fla.). Home: 250 Kean Lane Terre Haute IN 47803 Office: 1450 Wabash Av Terre Haute IN 47807

FRANZ, EDWARD L., banker; b. Bklyn., 1911. Sr. v.p. Bank of Commerce, N.Y.C. Home: 100 Park Terrace New York City NY 10034 Office: 56 E 42d St New York City NY 10017*

FRANZ, JOHN BAPTIST, clergyman; b. Springfield, Ill., Oct. 29, 1896; s. Fridolin and Louisa (Reisch) F.; A.M., Quincy Coll., 1917; student Kendrick Sem., 1917-20, Apostolic Mission House, Cath. U. Am., 1920-21. Ordained priest Roman Cath. Ch., 1920; asst. pastor St. Joseph's Ch., Granite City, Ill., 1920- 27; pastor St. Mary's Ch., Farmersville, Ill., 1927-35, Cathedral Immaculate Conception, 1935-51; officialis Roman Cath. Diocese of Springfield, 1930-51, consultor, 1936-51, adminstr. sede vacante, 1948- 49; 1st bishop Diocese of Dodge City (Kan.), 1951-59; bishop Diocese of Peoria (Ill.), 1959-71. K.C. Home: 2223 W Heading Av Peoria IL 61604

FRANZ, PAUL JUSTUS, Jr., univ. adminstr.; b. Phila., May 24, 1924; s. Paul Justus and Eleanor S. (Herrmanns) F.; B.A. in Bus. Adminstrn., Lehigh U., 1944, M.A., 1955; m. Jean E. Pope, Mar. 25, 1950; children—Helen G., Peter E. Mem. staff Lehigh U., 1944—, asst. to pres., 1949-62, v.p. devel. and pub. relations, 1962—. Bd. dirs. Am. Alumni Council, 1957-61, dir. devel. programs, 1960-61, chmn. ednl. fund raising com., 1961. Mem. financial adv. com. Urban Coalition. Trustee Kings Coll., Wilkes-Barre, Pa.; member board of directors of Wiley House, Bethlehem, Pennsylvania. Co- recipient Alfred Noble Robinson award Lehigh U., 1957. Mem. Phi Beta Kappa, Delta Tau Delta, Pi Delta Epsilon, Phi Alpha Theta, Beta Gamma Sigma. Episcopalian (vestry). Home: 37 E Church St Bethlehem, PA 18018.

FRANZ, RICHARD PETER, financial exec.; b. Milw., Jan. 2, 1924; s. Walter A. and Lenore (Sievers) F.; B.B.A., U. Wis., 1948; m. Marjorie Elaine Mandt, Aug. 28, 1948; children—Richard Peter, Steven C., Gary M. With Arthur Young & Co., 1948- 51; mgr. tax dept. Miller Brewing Co., 1951-57; with Edw. F. Jennick & Co., pub. accountants, 1957-58; sec. treas. Johnson Service Co., Milw., 1958—. Served with USNR, 1943-46. Mem. Am. Inst. C.P.A.'s, Wis. Soc. C.P.A.'s, Nat. Assn. Accountants, Financial Execs. Inst. Home: 403 E Carlisle Av Milwaukee WI 53217 Office: 507 E Michigan St Milwaukee WI 53202

FRANZEN, EARL THEODORE, civil engr.; b. Palisade, Minn., Jan. 7, 1915; s. Emil Ferdinand and Jennie (Anderson) F.; B.Civil Engring. with high distinction U. Minn., 1937; m. Irene Helen Super, Oct. 28, 1944; children—Robert, Thomas, Jonathan. Asst. bridge engr. G.N. Ry., St. Paul, 1937-55; structural engr. Wis. Hwy. Dept., 1955; bridge engr. Rock Island R.R., Chgo. 1955-63; structural engr. Alfred Benesch & Assos., cons. engrs., Chgo., 1963-64; chief engr. M.P. R.R., St. Louis, 1964—. Mem. Am. Soc. C.E., Am. Ry. Engrs. Assn., Am. Ry. Bridge and Bldg. Assn., Roadmasters and Maintenance of Way Assn. Am. Mason. Home: 83 Webster Woods Webster Groves MO 63119 Office: 210 N 13th St St Louis MO 63103

FRANZEN, ERIC THORGNY, ins. co. exec.; b. Newark, Oct. 2, 1920; s. Eric Thorgny and Leonie (Dieffenbach) F.; B.S., Yale, 1942; M.B.A., Harvard, 1947; m. Nancy Mason, Aug. 20, 1943; children—Eric Thorgny III, Douglas, James. With Phoenix Mut. Life Ins. Co., 1947—, coordinator staff coordination work, 1956-57, 2d v.p. charge ins. service dept., 1957-60, v.p., 1960-67, sr. v.p. adminstrn., dir., 1967—. Mem. West Hartford Bd. Finance, 1963-65; active Greater Hartford Community Chest, Greater Hartford Community Council. Bd. dirs. Conn. Blue Cross, 1968. Served to lt. USNR, 1942-45. Decorated Navy Cross, Air medal with three oak leaf clusters. Mem. Life Office Mgmt. Assn. (dir. 1965-68), Phi Beta Kappa. Clubs: Hartford Golf; Country Greenfield. Home: 465 Colrain Rd Greenfield MA 01301 Office: 1 American Row Hartford CT 06115

FRANZEN, GOSTA, educator; b. Soderkoping, Sweden, June 14, 1906; s. Frans and Amalia (Svensson) F.; Fil. Kand., Uppsala U., Sweden, 1927, M.A., 1929, Ph.D., 1937; postgrad. U. Heidelberg, 1926, U. Marburg, 1939; m. Karin Franson, Aug. 5, 1939; children—Lars, Ingrid. Came to U.S., 1941. Docent Scandinavian langs. Uppsala U., 1937-43; dir. information bur. Swedish Consulate, San Francisco, 1943-44; instr. Swedish, U. Cal., 1943-44; asso. prof. Scandinavian langs. and literature U. Chgo., 1944-56, prof., dir. Scandinavian studies, 1956—. Decorated Knight Order of Vasa, Knight Order of North Star (Sweden), Knight Order of St. Olaf (Norway); research fellow Am. Scandinavian Found., 1941-43; recipient grants Am. Philos. Soc., Sweden, 1950, Iceland, 1960, Faroe Islands, 1964, West Indies, 1969. Mem. Soc. Advancement Scandinavian Study (pres. 1958-59), Royal Swedish Acad. Sci. Uppsala, Royal Gustavus Adolphus Acad., Royal Acad. Humanities Uppsala, Uppsala Place Name Soc., Icelandic Soc. Uppsala. Author: Vikbolandets by och gardnamn, 1937; Amerikansk kateder och svensk, 1947; Runo ortnamn, 1959, Laxdoelabygdens ortnamn, 1964; Faroiska batnam, 1966; Prose and Poetry of Modern Sweden, 1969. Co-editor of Swedish Dialect Atlas, 1938-41, Scandinavian Studies, 1946-48. Home: 5703 S Maryland Av Chicago IL 60637

FRANZEN, JOHN EMIL, paper co. exec.; b. Maplewood, N.J., July 29, 1916; s. Eric T. and Leonie (Dieffenbach) F.; B.S., U. Pa., 1938; M.B.A., Harvard, 1940; m. Pearl Hazel Peterson, Aug. 29, 1943; children—John Emil III, Peter B., Erica M., Iver C. Salesman, DuPont Film Mfg. Co., 1940-41; with Hammermill Paper Co., 1946—, gen. sales mgr., Erie, Pa., 1959-60, v.p. marketing, 1960-66, exec. v.p., 1966-69, sr. v.p., 1969—, mem. bd. dirs., 1962—; mem. bd. dirs. Erie Brewing Co., Carter-Rice Storrs and Bement, Inc., Boston, Mass. Cons. pulp-paper and board div. Civilian Prodn. Adminstrn., 1946; dep. dir. pulp-paper div. NPA, Dept. Commerce, Washington, 1951; mem. exec. res. Bus. and Def. Service Adminstrn., Washington, 1956—. Bd. dirs. Salvation Army, Humane Soc. of Northwestern Pa., (pres. 1969-70). Served to maj. AUS, 1941-46. Mem. Friars Soc., Newcomen Soc., N.Y. Paper Club, Southerners, Quartermasters Assn. (past v.p.), Beta Theta Pi. Presbyn. (trustee). Clubs: Erie, Erie Yacht, Mantoloking Yacht, Aviation Country, Kahkwa (past pres.),

Erie Ski, Mask and Wig, University Pa. Alumni (v.p., past treas., exec. bd.). Home: 5604 Bonaventure Dr E Erie PA 16505 Office: Hammermill Paper Co Erie PA 16507

FRANZEN, ULRICH, architect; b. Germany, Jan. 15, 1921; s. Erich and Elizabeth (Hallersberg) F.; came to U.S., 1936, naturalized, 1943; B.A., Williams Coll., 1942; B.Arch., Harvard, 1948; m. Josephine Burgess; children—Peter H., David M., J. April. Head firm Ulrich Franzen & Assos., N.Y.C., 1955—; lectr. Cornell U., Yale, U. R.I., U. Minn., Columbia; vis. critic Washington U., St. Louis, Carnegie Inst. Tech., Harvard, Yale; prin. works include Philip Morris Research Center, Richmond, Va., 1959, Castle residence, 1961, New London Towers residence, 1960, Philip Morris Operations Center, Richmond, 1963, Agronomy Bldg., Cornell U., New Alley Theatre, Houston, Residence Hall and Dining Hall at U. N.H., Watchtower Bible and Tract Society, Brooklyn Heights, N.Y.; work exhibited Boston Arts Festival, Yale, travelling exhibition of the Museum of Modern Art. Chairman bd., bd. archtl. rev., Rye, N.Y., 1959-62. Served with AUS, World War II. Decorated Bronze Star; Croix de Guerre with palms (Belgium); recipient award excellence for design Archtl. Record, 1956, 57, 59, 60, 62, 63-68, award excellence design and constrn. House & Home mag., 1957, 60, 1st prize excellence design and constrn. Queens C. of C., 1958; award architecture Boston Arts Festival, 1961, 62; Brunner Meml. prize architecture Nat. Inst. Arts and Letters, 1962. Mem. A.I.A. (com. on design; award of merit 1959, 62, 64, Homes for Better Living award 1966, 1st honor award 1970, 71), Archtl. League N.Y. (pres. 1966; Gold medal hon. mention 1962), N.Y. State Assn. Architects. Home: 975 Park Av New York City NY 10028 Office: 555 Madison Av New York City NY 10022

FRANZHEIM, KENNETH, U.S. ambassador to New Zealand. Address: care American Embassy, Wellington, New Zealand.*

FRANZI, MARIO, Italian diplomat; b. Naples, Italy, Feb. 4, 1916; s. Enrico and Sofia (Galli) F.; law degree U. Naples, 1937; m. Padula Carmela, Oct. 18, 1941; children—Giovanni, Fabrizio. Italian rep. ECOSOC, 1961-64, 70; dep. permanent rep. Italy to UN, 1964—. Home: 970 Park Av New York City NY 10028 Office: Italian Mission to UN 809 UN Plaza New York City NY 10017

FRANZINI, JOSEPH BERNARD, educator; b. Las Vegas, N.M., Nov. 10, 1920; s. Joseph Bernard and Mary (Widmann) F.; B.S., Cal. Inst. Tech., 1942, M.S., 1943; Ph.D., Stanford, 1950; m. Gloria Ruth Place, Aug. 24, 1946; children—Joseph Bernard, Robert J., Marilyn R., Cheryl A. Teaching asst. Cal. Inst. Tech., 1942-44; teaching asst. Stanford, 1946-49, mem. faculty, 1949—, prof. civil engring., 1962—, asso. head dept., 1963—; spl. cons. George S. Nolte Co., Cons. Civil Engrs., Inc., San Jose, Cal., 1958—. Served with USNR, 1944-46. Mem. Am. Soc. C.E., Am. Geophys. Union, Am. Soc. Engring. Edn., Soil Sci. Soc. Am., Sigma Xi. Author: (with R.K. Linsley) Water-Resources Engineering, 1964; (with R.L. Daughtery) Fluid Mechanics with Engineering Applications, 1965. Home: 2915 S Court Palo Alto CA 94306 Office: Civil Engring Dept Stanford Univ Stanford CA 94305

FRANZ JOSEPH, reigning prince of Liechtenstein; b. Frauenthal, Aug. 16, 1906; s. Alois and Elisabeth, Archduchess of Austria; student Schottengymnasium Wien, Hochschule für Bodenculture, Wien; m. Georgine, Countess Wilczek, Mar. 7, 1943; children—Hans, Philipp, Nikolaus, Nora, Franz. Succeeded grand-uncle, Prince Francis I, as reigning prince of Liechtenstein since 1938. Address: Vaduz Liechtenstein

FRASCA, JOHN ANTHONY, newspaperman; b. Lynn, Mass., May 25, 1916; s. Michele A. and Mary (Jordan) F.; B.A., Miss. Coll., 1940; m. Louise Cummings, Dec. 20, 1948; children—Charlotte (Mrs. Gene Krupa), Sydney (Mrs. Vincent Giovenco), Karen, Michele, John Anthony. Free-lance polit. analyst, cons. weekly newspapers, also radio commentator, 1958-64; mem. staff Tampa (Fla.) Tribune, 1964—. Recipient award for best feature of year in Tex., A.P., 1954; Pa. Mental Health Bell award, 1956; Phila. Good Citizenship award, 1956; Pa. Optimist Club award, 1957; Best Writing of Year award Phila. Press Assn., 1956; 2d prize campaign series, My Ten Days in a Mental Hosp., Pa. Newspaper Pubs. Assn., 1956, best campaign series Children Who Walk Alone, 1957, best feature award Inside Israel, 1957, 2d award ct. coverage Injustice for Our Kids, 1957, hon. mention spot news White Woman Unknown, 1957; Pulitzer prize, also Heywood Broun award for Robert Lamar Watson series, 1966. Author: The Mulberry Tree (spl. Edgar Allen Poe award Mystery W Writers Am. 1968), 1967; Con Man or Saint?, 1969; A Sharecropper's Best S Stories, 1970. Home: 4517 Vasconia St Tampa FL 33609

FRASCONI, ANTONIO, artist; b. Montevideo, Uruguay, Apr. 28, 1919; s. Franco and Armida (Carbonai) F.; student Circulo de Bellas Artes, Montevideo; scholarship Art Students League, N.Y.C., 1954-46, New Sch. Social Research, 1947-48; m. Leona Pierce, July 18, 1951; children—Pablo, Miguel. Came to United States, 1945. Art faculty New School Social Research, 1951-57; artist- resident U. Hawaii, Honolulu, in 1964; one man shows Montevideo, Mexico, Brooklyn Mus., Pasadena Art Inst., Pan American Union, Va. Mus. Fine Arts, Balt. Mus. Art, Witte Meml. Mus., San Antonio, Wehye Gallery, N.Y.C., Art Alliance, Phila., others; retrospective shows Montevideo, Uruguay, 1961, Balt. Mus. of Art, 1963, Brooklyn Mus. (N.Y.), 1964; group shows Europe, S.Am., U.S., including Nat. Acad. N.Y.C., U. Minn., Library Congress, Seattle Art Mus., Pa., Acad. Art, San Francisco Mus. Art, Memphis Acad. Art, others; represented permanent collections Mus. Modern Art, Cleve. Mus. Art, San Diego Mus. Art, N.Y.C. Pub. Library, R.I. Sch. Design, Newark Mus., Detroit Mus. Art, Art Inst. Chgo., several univs., others. Recipient purchase prize Bklyn. Mus., 1946, U. Neb., 1951; prize Phila. Print Club, 1951; Erickson award Soc. Am. Graphic Arts, 1952; Yaddo scholarship 1952; Guggenheim fellowship, 1952-53; prize Pa. Acad. Fine Arts; Nat. Inst. Arts and Letters award, 1954; winner competition to design postage stamp honoring Nat. Acad. Sci., 1963; Joseph H. Hirshorn Found. prize Soc. Am. Graphic Artists, 1963; W. H. Walker prize Print Club Phila., 1964; prize 2d Biennale d'Art Graphique, Brno, Czechoslovakia, 1966, Salon Nacional de Bellas Artes, Montevideo, 1967; Grand Premio Exposition de la Habana, Cuba, 1968; Tamarind Lithography grantee, 1962. Author: 12 Fables of Aesop, 1954; See and Say, 1955; Frasconi Woodcuts, 1957; The House that Jack Built, 1958; Birds from My Homeland, 1958; The Face of Edgar Allen Poe, 1959; A Whitman Portrait, 1960; (film) The Neighboring Shore (Grand Prix award Venice Film Festival 1960), 1960; (books) Known Fables, 1964, The Cantilever Rainbow, 1965 (both chosen as one of Fifty Books of Year, Am. Inst. Graphic Arts); Unstill Life, 1969; Overhead The Sun, 1969; Elijah the Slave, 1970; On the Slain Collegians, 1971. Home: 26 Dock Rd South Norwalk CT 06854

FRASER, ALEXANDER STEWART, educator, scientist; b. London, Eng., Dec. 24, 1923; s. Thomas Stewart and Christina (Allan) F.; B.S., U. New Zealand, 1943, M.S., 1944; Ph.D., U. Edinburgh (Scotland), 1950; m. Eila Anne Soper, Mar. 15, 1950; children—Alan, Andrew, Alexis, Annette, Alistair, Aileen. Came to U.S., 1962. Research asst. New Zealand Inst. Wheat, Christchurch, 1944-45; asst. chemist New Zealand Dept. Agr., Hamilton, 1945-46; research asst. Massey Agrl. Coll., Palmerston, New Zealand, 1946-49; research fellow Inst. Animal Genetics, Edinburgh, 1949-52; sr. prin. research officer Commonwealth Sci. and Indsl. Research Orgn., Sydney, Australia, 1952-62; prof. genetics U. Cal. at Davis, 1962-67, chmn. dept., 1963-65, animal husbandry, 1966-67; head dept. biol. scis. U. Cin., 1967—. Served with New Zealand Army, 1942-44. Fellow Australian Acad. Scis. Author: Heredity Genes and Chromosomes, 1966. Co-author: Computer Models in Genetics, 1970. Home: 110 Hosea Av Clifton Cincinnati, OH 45220

FRASER, ANTONIA, author; b. London, Eng., Aug. 27, 1932; d. Frank and Elizabeth (Harman) Pakenham (Earl and Countess of Langford); ed. St. Mary's Convent (Eng.); grad. Lady Margaret Hall, Oxford (Eng.) U., 1953; m. Hugh Fraser, Sept. 25, 1956; children—Rebecca, Flora, Benjamin, Natasha, Damian, Orlando. Mem. Arts Council Gt. Britain. Author: Dolls, 1963; History of Toys, 1966; Mary Queen of Scots (James Tait Black prize for biography 1969), 1969; King Arthur (Juvenile), 1970; Robin Hood, 1971. Lectr.; radio and TV appearances. Home: 52 Campden Hill Sq London W8 England

FRASER, ARCHIE CHARLES, lawyer; b. Cleve., June 16, 1902; s. Archie Reed and Alma Marie (Gruis) F.; student Detroit City Coll., 1921-23; LL.B., Detroit Coll. Law, 1934, J.D., 1970; m. Melba Margaret Fleming, June 18, 1925; children-Jeanette Aleen (Mrs. Charles F. Willingham), Geraldine Melba (Mrs. Paul M. Shields). Admitted to Mich. bar, 1934; practice in Lansing, 1950—; partner Hon. Wilber M. Brucker, 1934-36; asso. Clark, Klein, Brucker & Waples, 1937-41; asst. atty. gen. Mich. charge Detroit Office, 1941-42; asst. atty. gen. and state pub. adminstr., 1947-48; asst. atty. gen., gen. counsel Mich. Pub. Service Commn., 1948-50; partner Fraser, Trebilcock, Davis & Foster and predecessor firm, 1950—. Mem. estate planning council Alma Coll., 1969-70. Republican nominee U.S. Congress, 15th Dist. Mich., 1938-40. Pres. United Community Chest Greater Lansing, Greater Lansing Urban League. Served from capt. to lt. col., USAAF, 1942- 47; ETO. Decorated Legion of Merit, Bronce Star medal, Officer Order Brit. Empire; recipient award for exceptional civilian Service Dept. Army, 1959. Mem. Am., Ingham County (past pres.) bar assns., State Bar Mich., Am. Legion (past post comdr.), Order Demolay for Boys (past master councillor, mem. Legion of Honor). Presbyn. (elder, chmn. bd. trustees), Mason (K.T., Shriner); mem. Order Eastern Star. Clubs: City (past pres.), Automobile (Lansing). Home: 4685 Woodcraft Rd Okemos MI 48864 Office: 1018 Michigan Nat Tower Lansing MI 48933

FRASER, ARTHUR MCNUTT, educator; b. Hamiota, Man., Can., Dec. 29, 1915; s. James Moss and Marie (McNutt) F.; B.A., U. Man., 1945; M.A., Columbia, 1947, Ed.D., 1951; m. Ruth Irvine Gordon, Sept. 12, 1942; children—Loran, Bruce, Susan. Came to U.S., 1949, naturalized, 1966. Asst. prof. Whitworth Coll., Spokane, 1951-54; asso. prof. Howard Coll., Birmingham, Ala., 1954-55; prof., dir. Sch. Music, Montevallo (Ala.) State Coll. Liberal Arts, 1955-63; prof. music, head dept. U. S.C., 1963—; conductor Huntsville (Ala.) Orch., 1955-59, Columbia Philharmonic Orch., 1964—. Maj. Canadian Armored Corps, 1942-46. Mem. Music Tchrs. Assn., Am. Symphony Orch. League, Southeastern Choral Conductors Conf. (pres.), Columbia Art Museum, S.C. Arts Commn. (exec. com.). Home: 2822 Sheffield Rd Columbia, SC 29208

FRASER, DONALD HINES, legislator; b. Hinesville, Ga., Feb. 27, 1906; s. Donald and Beulah Lee (Hines) F.; student Mercer U., 1923-25; LL.B., U. Fla., 1927; m. Evelyn Hughey Green, July 13, 1933; one dau., Jane Evelyn (Mrs. William E. Bowen). Admitted to the Georgia bar and to the Fla. bar, 1928; judge city ct., Darien, Ga., 1943-45, Hinesville, Ga., 1933-49; solicitor gen. Atlantic Jud. Circuit, 1950-51; asst. U.S. atty. So. Dist. Ga., 1951-61, U.S. atty., 1961-69. Mem. Ga. Gen. Assembly from Liberty County, 1930-31, 70—; mem. Hinesville City Council, 1931-33. Mem. Ga. Bar Assn. (bd. govs. 1950), St. Andrews Soc. Savannah, S.A.R. Democrat. Methodist. Club: Savannah Exchange. Home: 503 Oglethorpe Hwy Hinesville GA 31313 Office: PO Box 979 Savannah GA 31402

FRASER, DONALD MACKAY, congressman; b. Mpls., Feb. 20, 1924; s. Everett and Lois (MacKay) F.; B.A. cum laude, U. Minn., 1944, LL.B., 1948; m. Arvonne Skelton, June 30, 1950; children—Thomas Skelton, Mary MacKay, John DuFrene, Lois MacKay, Anne T. (dec.), Jean Skelton. Admitted to Minn. bar, 1948; practice in Mpls., 1948-62; partner firm Lindquist, Fraser & Magnuson, and predecessors, 1950-62; mem. Minn. Senate, 1954-62, sec. Senate Liberal Caucus, 1955-62; mem. 88th-92d Congresses 5th Dist. Minn. Vice chmn., dir. Mpls. Citizens Com. on Pub. Edn., 1950-54. Sec. Minn. delegation Democratic Nat. Conv., 1960; chmn. Minn. Citizens for Kennedy, 1960; mem. platform com. Dem. Nat. Conv., 1964; chmn. nat. com. tithing in investment; vice chmn. Com. Dem. Selection Presdl. Nominees, 1968; chmn. Democratic Study Group Congress, 1969-71; chmn. Commn. on Party Structure and Del. Selection Dem. Party, 1971—; mem. Fgn. Affairs Com., D.C. Com. Congress; mem. Anglo-Am. Parliamentary Conf. on Africa, 1964—. Served as lt. (j.g.) USNR, 1944-46. Mem. Mpls. Fgn. Policy Assn. (pres. 1952-53), Citizens League Greater Mpls. (sec. 1951-54), Minn., Hennepin County bar assns., U. Minn. Law Alumni Assn. (dir. 1958-61), Univ. Dist. Improvement Assn. (pres.). Home: 813 7th St SE Minneapolis 14, MN ; 1253 4th St SW Washington DC 20024 Office: House Office Bldg Washington DC 20515

FRASER, DONALD R., lawyer, state legislator; b. Toledo, May 21, 1927; s. Malcolm W. and Elizabeth (Ross) F.; B.S., U. Toledo, 1952; J.D., George Washington U., 1954; m. Caroline Ann Pilliod, Aug. 26, 1952; children—Donald R., Marguerite Ann. Patent engr. U.S. AEC, 1952-54; admitted to D.C. and Ohio bars, practice in Toledo; patent agt. Kaiser Aluminum & Chem. Co., 1954-57; pvt. practice patent, trademark and copyright law, 1957—; mem. Ohio Ho. of Reps., 1968—. Served with C.E., AUS, 1944-47; MTO. Mem. Am., Lucas County, Toledo bar assns., Am., Toldeo patent law assns., Phi Kappa Psi. Republican. Clubs: University, Patent Lawyers (past pres.), Kenwood Golf and Country (Washington); Inverness Country (Toledo). Home: 4719 Springbrook St Toledo OH 43615 Office: Nat Bank Bldg Toledo OH 43604

FRASER, EDWARD SMITH, bridge and iron co. exec.; b. E. Orange, N.J., Dec. 9, 1917; s. Edward S. and Ethel M. (VanWart) F.; B.S. in Civil Engring., U. Ill., 1939; grad. student Ill. Inst. Tech., 1946-47, U. Utah, 1950-52, U. Chgo., 1959-60; m. Elsie M. Thomas, Feb. 4, 1938; children—Louise M. (Mrs. George F. Gray), William T., Mary A. (Mrs. Jeffery Morey). With Chgo. Bridge & Iron Co., 1939—, mgr. central region, 1961—, v.p. corporate planning, 1964-66, v.p. for research, 1966-71, now cons. Bd. dirs. Chgo. Bridge Found. until 1971. Served to capt. USAAF, 1940-46. Registered profl. engr., Utah, Ill., Fla.; registered structural engr., Ill. Mem. Am. Welding Soc. (past dist. chmn.), Am. Soc. Testing Materials, Am. Soc. C.E., Chgo. Assn. Commerce and Industry, Ill. C. of C., Am. Mgmt. Assn., Sigma Xi, Phi Eta Sigma, Chi Epsilon, Tau Beta Pi, Phi Kappa Phi. Presbyn. Clubs: Palmetto-Pine Country (Cape Coral, Fla.); Ruth Lake Country (Hinsdale, Ill.). Home: 63 Baybrook Lane Oak Brook IL 60521 Office: 901 W 22d St Oak Brook IL

FRASER, GEORGE BROADRUP, educator; b. Washington, May 9, 1914; s. George B. and Florence M. (Hillyard) F.; A.B., Dartmouth, 1936; LL.B., Harvard, 1939; LL.M., George Washington Univ., 1941; m. to Phebe E. Bandy, Dec. 20th, 1965. Admitted to D.C. bar, 1939, Okla. bar, 1952; practice in Washington, 1939-41; asso. atty. Boise (Ida.) regional office, VA, 1946; acting prof. law, then prof. law U. Ida., 1946-49; prof. law U. Okla., 1949—, Boyd prof., 1959—; vis. prof. George Washington U., summers 1948, 51, 58, U. Ill., 1959-60; vis. prof. of law Univ. of Michigan, spring 1964, Hastings Coll. Law, U. Cal., San Francisco, 1966. Served to lt. comdr. USNR, 1941-45. Mem. Am., Okla., Cleveland County bar assns., Am. Judicature Soc., Order of Coif, Phi Delta Phi. Author articles, chpts. in books.

FRASER, HARVEY REED, coll. pres.; b. Elizabeth, Ill., Aug. 11, 1916; s. James Hiram and Ethel M. (Reed) F.; B.S., U.S. Mil. Acad., 1939; M.S., Cal. Inst. Tech., 1948; Ph.D., U. Ill., 1956; diploma grad. Von Karman Inst. Fluid Dynamics, Brussels, Belgium, 1961; grad. U.S. Command and Gen. Staff Coll., 1953; m. Jean A. Mueller, July 31, 1940; children—Harvey Reed, Janet (Mrs D.R.E. Hale), Joan K. Commd. 2d St. U.S. Army, 1939, advanced through grades to brig. gen., 1965; served in PTO, ETO, also Am. theatre with C.E.; mem. faculty U.S. Mil. Acad., 1948-65, prof. mechanics, 1952-56, acting head dept., 1958-59; retired, 1965; dean engring. S.D. Sch. Mines and Tech., Rapid City, 1965-66, pres., 1966-. Asso. dir. Marine Midland Bank S.E. N.Y., 1962-65. Dir., v.p. St. John's McNamara Hosp., Rapid City, 1965—. Decorated Bronze Star with cluster, Legion of Merit with cluster; Croix de Guerre (France); recipient certificate of merit for ednl. study report in Ethopia, 1964. Mem. Am. Soc. Engring. Edn. (exec. com. mechanics div. 1960-64), Soc. Am. Mil. Engrs., U.S. Mill Acad. Assn. Grads. (trustee 1960-65), Sigma Xi. Clubs: Army-Navy Country (Arlington, Va.); Arrowhead Country (Rapid City). Author articles. Home: 3107 Flint Dr Rapid City, SD 57701

FRASER, HENRY S., lawyer; b. Oswego, N.Y., July 11, 1900; s. Hector A. and Minnie (Salmon) F.; A.B., Haverford Col., 1922; J.D., Cornell, 1926; m. Myrtle Gosse, June 15, 1937; children—Bruce, Rosene, Roger. Admitted to N.Y. State bar, 1927; tech. adviser, League of Nations Com. of Experts for Progressive Codification of Internat. Law, 1927; chief of research staff, N.Y. State Constnl. Conv., 1938; chmn. N.Y. State Uniform Law Commn., 1948-70; chief counsel U.S. Senate, Spl. Com. Investigating Petroleum Resources, 1945-47; pvt. practice, Syracuse, N.Y., since 1927. Fellow Am. Coll. Probate Counsel; mem. Am. Law Inst., Am., N.Y. State N.Y. City bar assns., Phi Beta Kappa, Chi Phi. Rotarian. Club: Century. Author various legal publs. Home: Presdl Plaza Syracuse NY 13202 Office: Midtown Plaza Syracuse NY 13210

FRASER, HUGH RUSSELL, author, columnist; b. Cornwall-on-the-Hudson, N.Y., Feb. 16, 1901; s. Rev. Hugh Russell and Jessie E. (Hough) F.; student Mt. Hermon Sch.; m. Agnes Hines, Feb. 16, 1931 (died 1950). Copy boy N.Y. World, 1919; news classifier N.Y. Times, 1920-21; editor Shenendoah Valley News, Waynesboro, Va., 1922-24; rep. Washington Herald, 1925-26; staff Buffalo Courier-Express, 1927-29; columnist Albany (N.Y.) Evening News, 1930-31; associate editor Real America Mag., 1933-49; author weekly newspaper column Inside Washington, 1939-45; asso. editor Pathfinder mag., Washington, 1946-52, columnist Daily Comm. News, San Francisco, 1958-62, Los Angeles Times, 1961-62, Columbia Features Syndicate, 1962—; editorial commentator Ga. TV Network, 1967—. Co-author with Dr. Allan Nevins, of Pulitzer-prize winning N.Y. Times history test Apr. 1943, given 7,000 college Freshmen in 36 colleges. Author: Democracy in the Making: The Jackson-Tyler Era, 1938. Contbr. World Book Ency., 1957—; contbr. Harpers, True and other mags. Home: 811 Oakdale Rd NE Atlanta, GA 30307. Office: 811 Oakdale Rd NE Atlanta GA 30307

FRASER, HUGH WILSON, Jr., former banker; b. Monticello, Fla., Feb. 4, 1904; s. Hugh Wilson and Katherine Archer (Parkhill) F.; B.S., U. of South, 1924; m. Nancy Foster, June 18, 1932; children—Nancy (Mrs. Hugh O. Pearson), Hugh Wilson III. With Citizens & So. Nat. Bank, Atlanta, 1924—, successively asst. cashier, Savannah, Ga., asst. comptroller, Atlanta, asst. to pres., v.p. and comptroller, 1938-59, v.p. Citizens & So. Nat. Bank, exec. v.p. Citizens and So. Holding Co., pres. Citizens and So. Capital Corp., gen. v.p., 1960-70, ret., 1970; dir. Citizens & So. Nat. Bank, Citizens & So. Bank of Albany, Dublin, Newman, LaGrange, Thomaston; dir. Pamlico, Inc. Mem. Financial Execs. Inst. (nat. dir. 1962-64, So. Area v.p. 1964), Council of Profit Sharing Industries (nat. dir. 1966-67), Soc. Colonial Wars, Kappa Sigma. Clubs: Capital City, Commerce (Atlanta); Oglethorpe (Savannah, Ga.); Plantation (Hilton Head, S.C.). Home: 2 N Caliboque Cay Hilton Head Island SC 29928

FRASER, JOHN DICKIE, brewing co. exec.; b. Toronto, Ont., Can., Jan. 30, 1915; s. John Dickie and Margaret (Birnie) F.; m. Eileen Verna McColeman, May 19, 1934; children—Glenn Bruce, John Davidson, Eloise Marlene. With Canadian Breweries, Ltd., 1933—, treas., 1960-68, v.p., treas., 1968—. Masn (32, Shriner). Home: 3416 Pinesmoke Cr Mississauga Ontario Canada Office: 79 St Clair Av E Toronto 7 Ontario Canada

FRASER, JOSEPH T., Jr., former dir. Pa. Acad. Fine Arts; b. Phila., Sept. 15, 1898; B.S. in Architecture, U. Pa., 1922; m. Mary Isabel Chism, Oct. 10, 1926; children—Joseph Thompson III, Sarah Ann. Practicing registered architect State of Pa., 1922-34; curator summer sch. Pa. Acad. Fine Arts, 1934; curator winter, summer sch., 1935-38, sec., dir. 1938-69, ret., 1969. Recipient Gold Medal of Honor, Pa. Acad. Fine Arts, 1955. Bd. dirs. Phila. Art Alliance, Fairmount Park Art Assn. Fellow A.I.A.; mem. Mus. Council of Phila., Metropolitan Mus. Art, Phila. Mus. Art, Mus. Modern Art N.Y.C., Phi Delta Theta. Republican. Protestant Episcopalian. Clubs: Orpheus; Franklin Inn. Home: 330 South Camac St Philadelphia PA 19107

FRASER, LORNE DONALD, oil co. exec.; b. Ottawa, Can., Apr. 1, 1911; s. Lorne and Jennie Ingram (Nicol) F.; student Glebe Collegiate Sch., Ottawa, Westmount Acad., Montreal; Ph.D., (hon.), Sherbrooke U.; m. Edythe Helen Irving, Dec. 31, 1932; one daughter Helen Diane (Mrs. John H. Ovenden). With Imperial Oil, Ltd., 1928—, beginning as jr. clk., successively resident mgr., Ottawa, div. mgr., Winnipeg, 1939-52, gen. mgr. marketing, 1952-57, v.p., 1960- -, sr. v.p., 1969—, also dir., 1957—. Mem. Am. Petroleum Inst., Canadian Arthritis and Rheumatism Soc. (past pres.), Newcomen Soc., Royal Canadian Inst. Clubs: St. James (Montreal); Seigniory (Quebec); University, Granite, National (Toronto); Manitoba (Winnipeg). Home: 111 St Clair Av W Toronto 7 Ontario Canada Office: 111 St Clair Av W Toronto Ontario Canada

FRASER, SIR ROBERT, Brit. TV exec.; b. Adelaide, South Australia, Sept. 26, 1904; s. Reginald and Thusnelda (Homburg) F.; B.A., Trinity Coll., U. Melbourne, 1926; B.Sc. in Econs., U. London, 1930; m. Betty Harris, Jan. 17, 1931; 1 dau., Rosalind. Leader writer Daily Herald, London, 1930-39; with empire div. Ministry Information, 1939-41, dir. pubs. div., 1941-45, controller prodn., 1945-46; dir. gen. Central Office Information, 1946-54, Ind. TV Authority, 1954-70; chmn. Ind. TV News, 1971—. Created knight, 1949; decorated Order Brit. Empire, 1944. Hon. fellow London Sch.

of Econs.; mem. of Royal Inst. Pub. Adminstrn. (v.p.). Club: Athenaeum. Home: 5M Portman Mansions Chiltern St London W 1 England Office: 48 Wells St London WIP 3FE England

FRASER, ROBERT P., lawyer; b. Saskatoon, Sask., Can., Oct. 10, 1929; B.A., U. Sask., 1949, LL.B., 1952. Admitted to Alta. bar, 1953; now partner firm Fenerty, McGillivray, Robertson, Prowse, Brennan, Fraser, Bell & Code, Calgary. Mem. Canadian, Calgary (pres. 1963) bar assns., Law Soc. Alta. Office: 15000 Guinness House Calgary 2 Alberta Canada*

FRASER, RUSSELL ALFRED, educator, author; b. Elizabeth, N.J., May 31, 1927; s. Roger John and Mary Louise (Narden) F.; A.B., Dartmouth, 1947; M.A., Harvard, 1949, Ph.D., 1950; m. Eleanor Jane Phillips, May 31, 1947; children—Karen Mildred, Alexander Varennes. Instr. English, U. Cal. at Los Angeles, 1950; postgrad. study, Eng., 1951-52; instr., then asst. prof. English, Duke, 1952-56; asst. prof., then asso. prof. English, Princeton, 1956- 65, asso. dean Grad. Sch., 1962-65; prof., chmn. English, Vanderbilt U., Nashville, 1965-68; prof., chmn. English, U. Mich., 1968—. Grantee Am. Council Learned Societies, 1951, 52, 60, 68, Am. Philos. Soc., 1951-52, 60, 68, Dartmouth, 1951-52; jr. fellow Council Humanitires, Princeton, 1960; NSF grantee, 1964-67. Served with USNR, 1944-46. Mem. Am. Assn. U. Profs., Modern Lang. Assn., Renaissance Soc. of Am., Shakespeare Assn. Am. Author: Shakespeare's Poetics, 1962. Editor: The Court of Venus, 1955; The Court of Virtue, 1961; King Lear, 1963; Oscar Wilde, 1969; The War Against Poetry, 1970. Home: 2105 Toumy Rd Ann Arbor MI 48104

FRASER, THOMAS AUGUSTUS, Jr., bishop; b. Atlanta, Apr. 17, 1915; s. Thomas Augustus and Lena Lee (Connell) F.; B.A., Hobart Coll., 1938, S.T.D., 1965; B.D., Va. Theol. Sem., 1941, D.D., 1960; spl. student U. Jena (Germany), 1937; D.D., U. of South, 1960; D.D., Wake Forest Coll., 1961; m. Marjorie Louise Rimbach, May 29, 1943; children—Thomas Augustus III, Constance Louise. Ordained to ministry Episcopal Ch. as deacon, 1941, priest, 1942, bishop, 1960; missionary Diocese L.I., N.Y., 1941-42; sec., chaplain Bishop of L.I., 1942; sr. asst., N.Y.C., 1942-44; rector in Alexandria, Va., 1944-51, Winston-Salem, N.C., 1951-60; bishop coadjutor Diocese of N.C., Raleigh, 1960-65, bishop, 1965—. Mem. editorial com. Anglican Congress, Toronto, Can., 1963; chmn. Joint Commn. on Edn. Holy Orders Episcopal Ch., 1963—. Mem. Community Nursing, Alexandria, 1944-50, Winston-Salem, 1951-60, Alcoholic Rehab., Winston-Salem, 1954-59, United Fund, Winston-Salem, 1957-60, Family and Child Welfare, Winston-Salem, 1955-57, Childrens Psychol. Clinic, Winston-Salem, 1955-57. Trustee U. of South, Va. Theol. Sem., St. Mary's Jr. Coll., Raleigh, N.C., St. Augustine's Coll. Mem. exec. com. Gov.'s Commn. on Piedmont Crescent, 1964—, sec. Commn. Priesthood, 1968; Lambeth Conf., London, Eng. Mem. Tau Kappa Alpha, Sigma Chi. Home: 1200 Glen Eden Dr Raleigh, NC 27609. Office: 201 St Albans Dr Raleigh NC 27609

FRASSINELLI, ATTILIO, lt. gov. Conn.; b. Stafford, Conn., Aug. 7, 1908; s. John D. and Josephine (Agnese) F.; ed. LaSalle U.; m. Mildred M. McLagan; five children. Engaged in ins. and real estate bus.; mem. Stafford Sch. Bd., 194048; chmn. Stafford Town Com., 1944-48; mem. Conn. Ho. of Reps., 1946-50; selectman, Stafford, 1947-59; commnr. food and drugs Conn., 1955-59; commnr. consumer protection Conn., 1959 66; lt. gov. Conn., 1966—. Democrat. Address: 63 Grant Av Stafford Springs, CT 06076.*

FRASURE, CARL MAYNARD, educator; b. Oakland, O., Jan. 15, 1903; s. Nelson and Minnie (Valentine) F.; B.A., Ohio State U., 1924, M.A., 1925, Ph.D., 1928; summer student U. Chgo., 1925, 26; student Cambridge (Eng.) U., 1929-30; LL.D., Morris Harvey Coll., Charleston, 1966; m. Louise Durham, Dec. 26, 1930; children—Carl Maynard, Robert Conway. Instr. polit. sci. and history W.Va. U., 1927-29, asst. prof. polit. sci., 1930-35, asso. prof., 1935-40, prof., 1940—, chmn. dept., 1935-40, chmn. dept., 1940- 61, dir. bur. Govt. Research, 1949-61, dean Coll. Arts and Scis., 1961- 69. Cons. exec., and legislative depts. W.Va., 1933-69; dir. W.Va. Merit System, 1940-41, OPA for W.Va., 1942-43; chmn. W.Va. Commn. Interstate Coop., 1944-66; dir. OPS for W. Va., 1951; spl. asst. to regional, nat. dirs. OEP, 1958; chmn. com. on state ofcls. on drafting suggested state legislation Council State Govts., Chgo., 1965. Mem. Am., So. polit. sci. assns., Am. Assn. U. Profs., Kappa Delta Rho. Democrat. Episcopalian. Author: British Policy on War Debts and Reparations, 1940; co-author: West Virginia State and Local Government, 1963. Home: 490 Pythian St Morgantown WV 26505

FRATCHER, WILLIAM FRANKLIN, educator; b. Detroit, Apr. 4, 1913; s. Vernon Claude and Ethel Stuart (Thomas) F.; A.B. with distinction, Wayne U., 1933, A.M., 1938; J.D. with distinction, U. Mich., 1936, LL.M., 1951, S.J.D., 1952; grad. Command gnd Gen. Staff Sch., U.S. Army, 1944; spl. study U. Paris, 1945; m. Elsie Florene Briscoe, Aug. 22, 1941; 1 dau., Agnes. Admitted to Mich. bar, 1936; asso., mem. Lewis & Watkins, 1936-41; asso. prof. law U. Mo., 1947-49, prof., 1949—, R.B. Price distinguished prof. law, 1971—, chmn. faculty com. on tenure, 1970—; research dir. spl. com. model probate code sect. real property, probate and trust law Am. Bar Assn., 1962-63; research counsel N.Y. Temporary State Commn. Estates, 1963; vis. prof. law U. Mich., summer 1952, N.Y.U., 1954-55, summer 1963, 65; Ford Found. Law Faculty fellow Inst. of Advanced Legal Studies, also hon. mem. Faculty of Laws, King's Coll., U. London (Eng.), 1963-64; research asso. U. Mich., summer 1953; research grantee of Nat. Conf. Commrs. on Uniform State Laws at U. Mich., summer 1966, U. Colo., summer 1967; research grantee of Internat. Assn. of Legal Sci. at U. Oxford, Eng., summer 1969; chmn. joint com. on cooperation between Assn. Am. Law Schs. and Am. Assn. Law Libraries, 1969. Mem. adv. com. to Sec. of State on UNIDROIT Draft Conv. to Establish Internat. Form of Will. Commd. capt., Judge Adv. Gen.'s Dept., U.S. Army, 1941; served as chief, control br., Office Judge Advocate Gen., War Dept., 1942, exec. to asst. judge adv. gen. in charge civil matters, 1943-44, chief, miscellaneous br., Mil. Justice div., Br. Office The Judge Adv. Gen., E.T.O., Paris, 1945; chief, war crimes br., legal div., Office Mil. Govt. U.S., Berlin, 1945-46 (U.S. commr. and chmn. Internat. Commn. for Control of Central Registry of War Criminals and Security Suspects, 1946); staff judge adv., Berlin Dist. and hdqrs. command, U.S. Forces, E.T.O., 1946; (reviewed Kronberg Castle jewel theft cases); lt. col. Res., 1947, col., 1957. Decorated Legion of Merit, Commendation, ribbon. Acad. fellow Am. coll. Probate Counsel, 1971. Mem. Am. Bar Assn. (mem. spl. com. mil. justice 1959-61, 64-71, vice chmn. 1970-71), Mo. Bar (chmn. mil. law com. 1967-68, mem. council probate and trusts com. 1969—), Judge Advocates Assn., Res. Officers Assn. of the U.S., Selden Soc. (Mo. corr.), Soc. Pub. Tchrs. Law, Brit. Inst. Internat. and Comparative Law, Am. Soc. Legal History, Scribes, Order of Coif. Presbyn. Author: Perpetuities and Other Restraints, 1954; (with Lewis M. Simes) Cases and Other Materials on Fiduciary Administration, 1956; Trusts and Estates in England, 1968; Cases and Materials on Veterinary Jurisprudence, 1968; (with others) Landmark Papers on Estate Planning, Wills, Estates and Trusts, 1968, Planning Large Estates, 1968. Editor pocket parts Simes and Smith, The Law of Future Interests, 1961, 65, 67, 69, 71; govt. publs. on mil. law. Mem. editorial bd. Manual for Courts-Martial, U.S.A., 1949; reporter Uniform Probate Code, 1963-70; gen. reporter on trusts Internat. Ency. Comparative Law, 1966—. Contbr. to Ency. Brit., 1971. Contbr. articles. Office: U Mo Tate Hall Columbia MO 65201 ☆

FRAUTSCHI, STEVEN CLARK, educator, physicist; b. Madison, Wis., Dec. 6, 1933; s. Lowell Emil and Grace (Clark) F.; B.A., Harvard, 1954; Ph.D., Stanford, 1958; m. Mie Okamura, Feb. 16, 1967; 1 dau., Laura. Research fellow Kyoto U., Japan, 1958-59, U. Cal. at Berkeley, 1959-61; mem. faculty Cornell U., 1961-62; mem. faculty Cal. Inst. Tech., Pasadena, 1962—, prof. theoretical physics, 1966—. Guggenheim fellow, 1971-72. Mem. Am. Phys. Soc. Author: Regge Poles and S-Matrix Theory, 1963. Research, publs. on Regge poles, bootstrap theory. Home: 1561 Crest Dr Altadena CA 91001 Office: 1201 E California Blvd Pasadena CA 91109

FRAUTSCHI, WALTER ALBERT, contract and publ. printing co. exec.; b. Madison, Wis., Dec. 4, 1901; s. Emil John and Ida (Parman) F.; B.A., U. Wis., 1924; m. Dorothy Jones, Aug. 10, 1927; children—John Jones, Walter Jerome. Chmn. bd. Webcrafters, Inc., Madison, 1959—, Westport Paper Co., Madison, 1959—, Waldorf Corp., Madison, 1960—; pres. DERS, Inc., Madison, 1945—; treas., dir. Frautschi's Inc., Madison, 1950—; dir. First Nat. Bank, Madison. Campaign chmn. Madison United Givers Fund, 1938. Trustee and pres. Wis. Alumni Research Found.; trustee estate William F. Vilas; chmn., trustee Brandenburg Found. Mem. Wis. Acad. Sci., Arts and Letters, Wis. Alumni Assn. (pres. 1948). Sigma Nu, Sigma Delta Chi, Phi Kappa Phi. Presbyn. (trustee). Rotarian (pres. Madison 1955). Home: 29 Fuller Dr Madison, WI 53704. Office: Box 1148 Madison WI 53701

FRAWLEY, ERNEST DAVID, publisher; b. Brockton, Mass., Apr. 17, 1920; s. Arthur Henry and Viola (Morse) F.; A.B., Middlebury Coll., 1942; student Bread Loaf Grad. Sch. English, summers 1940, 41; m. Natalie Pingree, Oct. 29, 1948 (dec. Dec. 30, 1962); children—Betsy, Cynthia, Susan; m. 2d, Elizabeth von Thurn, Nov. 19, 1965. Staff mem. N.E. regional magazine Boston Transcript, 1946; with advertising dept. Dewey & Almy Chemical Co., Cambridge, Mass., 1947-48, Green Mountain Pubs., baseball publs., Boston, 1948-49; pub., treas., dir. Child Life mag., 1949-56; circulation dir., asst. bus. mgr. Harvard Bus. Review, Harvard Grad. Sch. Bus. Adminstrn., 1956-63, controller, 1963—; trustee, adminstr. Internat. Marketing Inst., 1960-70, treas., 1961-70; dir. Comml. Bank & Trust Co. (Wilmington, Mass.), 1962-65; cons. U.S. Dept. State, 1960-70, Dept. Commerce, 1960-66. Sec. Boston Conf. on Distribution, 1961-64. Trustee Thayer Pub. Library, Braintree. Served as lt. (s.g.), USNR, 1942-45. Mem. Am. Marketing Assn., Delta Kappa Epsilon. Club: Harvard. Office: Grad Sch Bus Adminstrn Harvard U Soldiers Field Boston MA 02163

FRAWLEY, JAMES, film dir.; b. Houston, Sept. 29, 1936; s. James J. and Marjorie (Strauss) F.; grad. Peddie Sch., 1955; student drama Carnegie Inst. Tech., 1956-57; m. Jill Hill, Jan. 24, 1964. Appeared in Off-Broadway prodns. Becket, 1959-60, The Premise (also London), 1962-63, Arturo Ui, 1965, Anyone Can Whistle, 1965; TV roles, 1966-67; film dir. Shoot the Actor, 1964, J-24 (winner San Francisco Film Festival), 1965; dir. film The Monkees (Emmy award), 1967. Address: 2062 Glencoe Way Los Angeles, CA 90028

FRAWLEY, JOHN F., metal co. exec.; b. Troy, N.Y., 1917; s. Michael and Mary (Fisher) F.; grad. Albany (N.Y.) Bus. Coll.; m. Elizabeth Shortsleeve, 1942; children—Elizabeth Carol (Mrs. John L. Haggerty), Jeanne Elizabeth. With Gen. Electric Co., 1936-64, gen. mgr., 1962-64; with Am. Metal Climax Inc., 1964—, controller, 1967, v.p., 1968—, group v.p.; also. pres. Amax Petroleum. Home: 336 Hollow Tree Ridge Rd Darien, CT 06820. Office: 1270 Av Americas New York City NY 10020

FRAWLEY, PATRICK J., Jr., chmn. bd. Eversharp, Inc. Address: 5933 W Slauson Av Culver City CA 90230

FRAWLEY, THOMAS FRANCIS, physician; b. Rochester, N.Y., June 27, 1919; s. Thomas J. and Mary (Leddy) F.; A.B., U. Rochester, 1941; M.D., U. Buffalo, 1944; m. Marigrace Cecelia Gould, Feb. 23, 1946; children—Thomas Joseph II, Colleen, Brian. Intern, St. Mary's Hosp., Rochester, N.Y., 1944-45; resident Buffalo Gen. Hosp., 1945-48; research fellow Harvard Med. Sch., 1948-52; resident Peter Bent Brigham Hosp., Boston, 1948-52; chief endocrinology and metabolism Albany (N.Y.) Med. Sch., 1952-58, asso. prof. medicine, 1952-58, prof. medicine, 1960-63; research asso. NIH, 1958-60; prof., chmn. dept. internal medicine St. Louis U. Sch. Medicine, 1963—; physician-in-chief St. Louis U. Hosp., 1963—. Mem. drug efficacy study panel Nat. Acad. Scis., 1966-69; med. adv. com. Cath. Hosp. Assn., 1966-69; scientific rev. com. NIH, 1970—. Served to capt., M.C., AUS, 1946-47; surgeon USPHS, 1958-60. Diplomate Am. Bd. Internal Medicine. Fellow A.C.P. (gov. Mo. 1971—), N.Y. Acad. Scis.; mem. Assn. Am. Physicians, Endocrine Soc., Central Soc. Clin. Research, So. Soc. Clin. Investigation, Am. Thyroid Assn., Am. Diabetes Assn., Am. Clin. and Climatol. Assn., Sigma Xi, Alpha Omega Alpha. Author articles, books in field. Home: 23 Williamsburg Estates St Louis MO 63131 Office: 1325 S Grand Blvd St Louis MO 63104

FRAZER, GEORGE ENFIELD, lawyer; b. Amber, Ia., Feb. 1, 1889; s. George Henry and Alzora (Stephens) F.; A.B., State U. of Ia., 1909; J.D., U. of Wis., 1912; LL.D., Rockford (Ill.) Coll., 1938, Washburn Coll., Topeka, Kan., 1940; D.H.L., Kenyon Coll., 1942; m. Helen James, June 9, 1915; children—Edmund James, George (dec.), Richard Symons. Admitted to Wis. bar, 1912, Ill. bar, 1916; prof. pub. accounting and comptroller, U. of Ill., 1913-15; devised Ill. state financial system, 1917; professorial lectr., U. Chgo., 1917-19; asst. dir. finance, U.S. Army, 1918; gen. counsel to gov. and legislature, reorgn. State of Ohio, 1921; sr. partner, Frazer & Torbet, accountants, N.Y.C. and Chgo., 1917- 52; chmn. Nat. Transitads, Inc., 1940-54. Trustee Rockford (Ill.) Coll., Kanyon (O.) Coll. C.P.A., Wis. Mason. Clubs: University, Sunset Ridge Country, Chicago (Chgo.); Accountants (N.Y.); Athenaeum (Pasadena). Author of numerous technical papers. Home: 435 Sheridan Rd Winnetka IL 60093 Office: 120 S LaSalle St Chicago IL 60603

FRAZER, JAMES NISBET, lawyer; b. Cedartown, Ga., Oct. 1, 1903; s. James Newton and Willie (Nisbet) F.; student Oglethorpe U., 1924; LL.B., Atlanta Law Sch., 1926; m. Rebecca Young, July 7, 1937; children—James Nisbet, Rebecca Young. Admitted to Ga. bar, 1926, since practiced in Atlanta; mem. firm Powell, Goldstein, Frazer & Murphy, since 1937. Chmn. bd., dir. Atlanta & St. Andrews Bay Ry. Co.; dir. Citizens & So. Nat. Bank, Citizens & So. Capital Corp., Chmn. Bd. Cerebral Plasy Soc. Ga., 1960—. Mem. Am., Ga., Atlanta bar assns., Lawyers Club Altanta. Presbyn. (deacon, trustee). Clubs: Piedmont Driving, Capital City, Commerce (Atlanta); Oglethorpe (Savannah, Ga.). Home: 565 W Wesley Rd NW Atlanta GA 30305 Office: Citizens & So Nat Bank Bldg Atlanta GA 30303

FRAZER, JOHN RONALD, coll. dean; b. Ottawa, Ontario, Canada, July 17, 1923; s. Sidney R. And Mabel (Louttit) F.; came to U.S., 1942, naturalized, 1960; B.M.E., Clarkson Coll., 1945; M.S., Iowa State U., 1950, Ph.D., 1954; m. Doris C. Arbogast, Aug. 28, 1948; children—Kathryn, Patricia, Michael, Judith, Bruce. Instr., then asst. prof. Iowa State U., 1946-53; instr. Clarkson Coll., Potsdam, N.Y., 1945-46, asst. prof. indsl. mgmt., 1953-54, asso. prof., 1954-60, prof. 1960-70, dept. chmn., 1960-70, dean Sch. Mgmt., 1960—; cons. Gen. Motors Corp., 1958-60, Aluminum Co. Am., 1955-57. Reg. profl. engr., Ia. Mem. Am. Soc. Engring. Edn., Am. Inst. Indsl. Engrs., Acad. Mgmt., Delta Upsilon. Author: Applied Linear Programming, 1968. Home: 18 Grant St Potsdam NY 13676

FRAZER, KEENER CHAPMAN, univ. prof.; b. Eufaula, Ala., Mar. 6, 1901; s. John Stanley and Stanley and Mary Ella (Chapman) F.; A.B., Wofford Coll., 1920; A.M., U. of N.C., 1921; 1921; grad. study, Johns Hopkins, 1921, 23; Dr. Polit. Sci., Inst. Internat. Internat. Studies, U. Geneva, Switzerland (Carnegie fellow in internat. law), 1931- 1931-32; 32; L.H.D., Birmingham-Southern Coll., 1957; hon. grad. U.S. Naval War Coll.; m. Virginia Randolph McIlwain, Sept. 12, 1936. Instr. history, U. of N.C., 1922-24, instr. polit. sci., 1924, asst. prof., 1926-30, asso. prof., 1930-36, prof. 1936—; vis. asst. prof. U. Va., 1925; vis. Nimitz prof. internat. politics, U.S. Naval War Coll., 1955-57. Dir. Conf. Relations of Atlantic Nations, Nations, Chapel Hill, N.C., 1970; chairman com. internat. So. U. Congress, 1948-51. Served as lt. comdr., U.S. Navy, 1943-45; duty 12th Fleet Hdqrs. liaison duty hdqrs. U.S. Army, Supreme Hdqrs., A.E.F., A.E.F., Staff chief Naval Operations. Mem. Am., So. (pres. 1939), polit. sci. assns., Southern Council on Internat. Relations Relations (dir. (dir. since 1939), Am. Soc. Internat. Law, Alpha Tau Omega. Democrat. Methodist. Pub. The South and World Affairs, 1939-48. Contbr. articles articles on internat. law and internat. relations to various pubs. Mem. bd. editors Sprunt Studies in History and Polit. Sci. Home: Chapel Hill NC 27514

FRAZER, MAURICE DOYLE, physician; b. Utica, Neb., Apr. 2, 1911; s. David J. and June (Doyle) F.; B.Sc., U. Neb., 1936, M.D., 1937; m. Margaret Clare Underwood, Sept. 17, 1935; children—Betty Lou, Patricia Jane. Intern Methodist Hosp., Omaha, 1937-38; practice of medicine, 1938—, specializing radiology, 1940—; asso. prof. U. Neb. Coll. Medicine; attending in radiology Bryan Meml. Hosp., Lincoln, Neb., 1955—; former chmn. Neb. Bd. Health; cons. radiologist Neb. State Hosp. Mem. radiation adv. council Neb. Dept. Health. Mem. A.M.A., Am. Coll. Radiology, Radiol. Soc. N.Am. (pres.), Am. Radium Soc., Neb. Med. Assn., Lancaster County Med. Soc. Home: 1774 S 58th St Lincoln NB Office: 5145 O St Lincoln NB 68510

FRAZER, ROBERT WALTER, eduator; b. Sacramento, Dec. 19, 1911; s. Walter and Orilla Daisy (Stanfield) F.; B.A., U. Cal. at Los Angeles, 1936, M.A., 1940, Ph.D., 1941; m. Marian Eloise Burnett, Apr. 11, 1941. Teaching asst. U. Cal. at Los Angeles, 1937-40; asst. prof. Adams State Coll., Alamosa, Colo., 1940-42; service engr. Northrop Aircraft, Inc., Hawthorne, Cal., 1942- 46; prof. U. Wichita, 1946-66; prof. history Cal. State Coll., Long Beach, 1966—, head dept. history, 1956-64; vis. prof. U. Cal. at Los Angeles, 1961-62, Cal. State Coll., Long Beach, 1964-65. Member of Western History Assn., Miss. Valley Hist. Assn., Hispanic Am. Soc., Conf. Latin Am. History, Am. Geog. Soc., Kappa Alpha, Pi Gamma Mu, Phi Alpha Theta. Author: Mansfield on the Condition of the Western Forts, 1963; Forts of the West, 1965. Contbr. articles and reviews hist. jours. Home: 2410 S Gaffey St San Pedro CA 90731 Office: History Dept Cal State Coll Long Beach CA 90804

FRAZER, WILLIAM ROBERT, educator, physicist; b. Indpls., Aug. 6, 1933; s. William Jay and Mildred (Dahlman) F.; A.B., Carleton Coll., 1954; Ph.D., U. Cal. at Berkeley, 1959; postgrad. U. Utrecht, Netherlands, 1956-57; m. Jane Zaiser, July 31, 1954; children—Bruce, Katherine. Mem. Inst. Advanced Study, Princeton, N.J., 1959-60; mem. faculty U. Cal. at San Diego, 1960—, prof. physics, 1967—, acting provost Third Coll., 1969-70. Mem. Am. Phys. Soc. Author: Elementary Particles, 1966; also articles. Research on theory of interaction of elementary particles, principally strong interactions responsible for nuclear force. Home: 407 W Spruce St San Diego CA 92103 Office: U Cal at San Diego La Jolla CA 92037

FRAZIER, JAMES BERIAH, Jr., ex-congressman; b. Chattanooga, June 23, 1890; s. James Beriah and Louise Douglas (Kieth) F.; student U. Va.; LL.B., Chattanooga Coll. Law, 1914; m. Elizabeth Hope, Mar. 30, 1939; 1 dau., Elizabeth Hope. Admitted to Tenn. bar, 1914; mem. Frazier and Frazier, Chattanooga, 1919—; apptd. U.S. atty. Eastern Dist. Tenn., 1933, reappointed, 1937-41; resigned, 1948; mem. 81st-87th Congresses, 3d Dist. Tenn. Served to maj. U.S. Army, World War I. Democrat. Methodist. Home: 211 Glenwood Dr Chattanooga TN 37404

FRAZIER, JAMES TAYLOR, machinery distbr.; b. Pocahontas, Va., Mar. 10, 1905; s. Charles s. Charles C. and C. and Bertha E. (Wood) F.; B.S. in Bus. Adminstrn., U. Richmond, 1926; m. m. Dorothy M. Connally, June 21, 1928; children—Betty C. (Mrs. Frank M. M. Winterholler), James Taylor, Reva M. Pres. Bluefield Supply Co. (W.Va.), (W.Va.), 1956-67, chmn. bd., pres., 1967—; pres. Monte Vista Park Cemetery, Bluefield, 1950—; pres. Rish Equipment Co., Bluefield, 1960-67; chmn. chmn. bd., pres., 1967—; pres. Skyland, Inc., Bluefield, 1962—, Skyland Skyland Hosp. Supply, Bluefield, chmn. bd., pres. Dixie Appliance Co., Virginian Electric, Inc.; dir. Flat Top Nat. Bank, S & S Machinery Co., Inc., Richlands, Va. Past dir. local A.R.C., Boy Scouts Am., Salvation Army, Community Chest; dir. Bluefield Area Devel. Corp. Mem. Am. Automobile Assn. (past dir.), Bluefield (past pres.; dir.), U.S. chambers commerce, Bluefield Assn. Credit Men (past pres.), Bluefield Auto Club (past pres.; dir.), Pi Kappa Alpha. Methodist. C (Bluefield); Ponte Vedra (Fla.). Home: 1004 Heatherwood Rd Bluefield WV 24701 Office: Bluefield Supply Co Bluefield WV 24701

FRAZIER, JOE, prize fighter; b. Beaufort, S.C., Jan. 17, 1944; s. Dolly and Rubin F. Prize fighter, 1958—; heavyweight champion, N.Y., Mass., Ill., Me., 1968, 70; winner fight with Muhammad Ali, 1971; also head rock-blues singing group. Baptist.*

FRAZIER, JOHN EARL, chem. engr.; b. Houseville, Pa., July 4, 1902; s. Chauncey E. and Mary Ellen (Gibson) F.; B.S., Washington and Jefferson Coll., 1922, achievement citation award, 1954; grad. student chem. engring. practice, Mass. Inst. Tech., 1922-24, S.M., 1924; Sc.D., U. Brazil, 1938; m. Frances Sprague Lang, June 23, 1936; children—John Earl II, Thomas Gibson. Chemist and engr. Berney Bond Glass Co. (now Owens-Ill. Glass Co.), 1924-26; fuel engr. Simplex Engring. Co., 1926-28, asst. sec., asst. treas., 1928-30, sec., treas., 1930-38; v.p., treas. Frazier-Simplex, Inc., 1938-45, pres., sec., 1945—; mem. adv. bd. Pitts. Nat. Bank (Washington County br.); past pres., dir. Washington Union Trust Co., Washington County Motor Club. Trustee, pres. Western State Sch. and Hosp., Canonsburg; trustee, sec., treas. Washington Hosp. (chmn. property com.); life trustee, asst-sec. bd. Washington and Jefferson Coll.; bd. dirs. Ceramic Camera Club (past pres.); past chmn. Pa. Economy League (Washington County br.); past pres. Washington (Pa.) C. of C.; past pres. Nat. Soc. Am. Comp. Shooters. Recipient Distinguished Citizen award Washington (Pa.) City Council, 1960; named Kappa Sigma Fraternity Man of Year, 1964; named to Bus. and Profl. Hall of Fame. Fellow Royal Soc. Arts Eng., Am. Inst. Chemists, A.A.A.S., Am. Ceramic Soc. (Albert V. Bleininger Meml. award), (v.p. 1967-68, treas. 1968-69, chmn. Orton Meml. lecture com. 1968),

Intercontinental Biog. Assn. (life), Soc. Glass Tech. of Eng.; mem. Pa. Ceramic Assn. (past pres., dir.), Ind. Heating Equipment Assn. Washington (past dir.), Am. Chem. Soc., Am. Soc. Mil. Engrs., Nat. Soc. Profl. Engrs., Am. Soc. Heating, Refrigeration and Air-Conditioning Engrs., Am. Soc. Testing Materials, Nat. Inst. Ceramic Engrs. (PACE award judge 1962), Pa. Soc. of N.Y.C., Nat. Rifle Assn. of Am., Pictorial Photographers of Am., Royal Photog. Soc. of Eng., Photog. Soc. Am., Am. Legion, Pa. Atomic Scientists, Pa. Acad. Sci., Keramos (Greaves-Walker roll of honor), Phi Beta Kappa, Sigma Xi, Phi Chi Mu, Kappa Sigma. Republican. Presbyn. Mason (Shriner, Jester), Lion (named Lion of Year). Clubs: Mass. Inst. Tech. of Western Pa., also New York, Inc.; Druids, University (Pitts.); Chemists (N.Y.C.); University; Varsity Letermen's; Fortnightly, Bassett (Washington, Pa.); Lions, Elks. Author: Kilns for Nat. Ency.; co-author: Glass Sand and a Glass Industry in Puerto Rico; Glass Industry for Venezuela; also other papers for trade and sci. publs. Frazier-Keramos Library at Pa. State U. named in his honor. Home: 36 Morgan Av Washington PA 15301 Office: 436 E Beau St PO Box 493 Washington PA 15301

FRAZIER, JOHN PEDEN, Jr., ins. co. exec.; b. Phila., Feb. 6, 1914; s. John Peden and Ethel (Hooper) F.; B.S., U. Pa., 1936; m. Rosalind Scheer Williams, Feb. 13, 1937; children—John Peden III, Heather F. (Mrs. Adin Tooker). With The Travelers Ins. Co., Hartford, Conn., 1936—, asst. comptroller, 1947-55, comptroller, 1955—. Pres., Hartford Hearing League, 1956-57. Mem. Financial Execs. Inst. (nat. dir. 1962-65, adv. council 1968, 69-71, area v.p. 1967-68), Theta Delta Chi. Clubs: Hartford; Dauntless (Essex, Conn.). Home: 150 Ridgewood Rd West Hartford CT 06107 Office: One Tower Sq Hartford CT 06115

FRAZIER, OWSLEY BROWN, distillery exec.; b. Louisville, May 7, 1935; s. Harry S. and Amelia (Brown) F.; B.S. in Law, U. Louisville, 1958, J.D., 1960; m. LaVera Anne Hatten, Aug. 4, 1956; children—Laura Lavera, Catherine Amelia, Anne Owsley. Admitted to Ky. bar, 1960; with Brown-Forman Distillers Corp., Louisville, 1955—, sec., 1964-68, v.p., sec., 1968—, exec. dir. personnel and corp. services, 1966—, also dir.; sec., dir. Early Times Distillery Co., Jos. Garneau Co., Brown Forman Industries; dir. G. Bittner and Sons, Inc., Asso. Industries Ky. Chmn. bd. dirs. Arthritis Found. Ky.; bd. dirs. Internat. Center at U. Louisville, United Appeal-Community Chest; sec., trustee Louisville Country Day Sch.; trustee Law Alumni Found. at U. Louisville. Mem. Am. Mgmt. Assn., Am., Ky., Louisville bar assns., Am. Judicature Soc., Louisville Corp. Counsel Assn., U Louisville Assos. (pres.), Beta Theta Pi, Phi Alpha Delta. Clubs: Louisville Country, Pendennis, Harmony Landing Country (Louisville); Ocean Reef (North Key Largo, Fla.). Home: 123 Arrowhead Rd Louisville KY 40207 Office: 1908 Howard St Louisville KY 40210

FRAZIER, ROBERT G., assn. exec.; b. Oak Park, Ill., Apr. 16, 1923; s. Cecil Austin and and Harriet (Greenleaf) F.; Ph.B., U. Chgo., 1943; B.S., 1945, M., 1947; 1947; m. Ruth Ann Johnson, nov. 25, 1950; children—Stephen, Thomas, Carolyn. Carolyn. Intern Grace-New Haven Community Hosp., 1947-48; resident pediatrics U. Chgo. Clinics, 1948-50; instr. pediatrics U. Colo. Med. Sch., 1950-52; 1950-52; asst. prof. pediatrics State U. Ia. Med. Sch., 1954-58; sec. Am. Acad. Acad. Pediatrics, 1958-67, exec. dir., 1967—. Served to 1st lt., M.C., AUS, AUS, 1952-54. Home: 1539 Spencer St Wilmette IL 60091 Office: 1801 Hinman Av Evanston IL 60204

FRAZIER, ROBERT HAINES, lawyer; b. Greensboro, N.C., Jan. 8, 1899; s. Cyrus Pickett and Lucetta (Churchill) F.; student Guilford Coll., 1917-18; A.B., U. N.C., 1922; student Columbia Grad. Sch., 1929; LL.D., N.C. Agrl. and Tech. State U., 1970; m. Florence Hyde. Admitted to N.C. bar, 1922, D.C. bar, 1947; pvt. practice, Greensboro, 1922-25; partner Frazier & Frazier, 1925—; sr. atty. OPA, 1943, chief counsel Office Export-Import, 1944-47. With Am. fgn. service, 1918-20, Oslo, Norway, Murmansk, Russia, and Havre, France; vice consul, Oslo, 1920. Dir. in orgn. N.C. Broadcasting Company, 1929. Mem. Am. Friends Service Com., chmn. Southeastern region, 1948-54; mem. Guilford County Bd. Health, 1951-55; mem. permanent bd. N.C. Yearly Meeting of Friends, 1940-64, Friends World Com., 1953—, rep. Friends World Conf., Oxford, Eng., 1952, Gilford, N.C., 1967; chmn. John Motley Morehead Meml. State Commn., 1959—. Councilman, mayor pro-tem. City of Greensboro, 1949-51, mayor, 1951-55 (rep. U.S. Conf. Mayors at Internat. Conf. Mayors, Rome, Italy, 1955). Chmn. bd. Greensboro Pub. Library, 1941-49; pres. Greensboro Community Chest, 1950; dir. Greensboro YMCA, 1952-55; trustee Guilford Coll. (chmn. 1950-69), N.C. Agrl. and Tech. State Univ. (chmn. 1957-70), Oak Ridge Acad. Found., Wooglin Found. Recipient Charles A. Cannon Hist. award, 1955. Fellow Am. Bar Found., Am. Coll. Probate Counsel (regent 1967—); mem. N.C. Soc. Preservation Antiquities (dir., v.p. 1954-69), Greensboro Travelers Aid Soc. (pres. 1937-43), Fed., Internat. (presented paper London Conf. 1950), Am. (chmn. sect. on real property, probate and trust law 1961-62, mem. ho. dels. 1962-64), N.C. (chmn. exec. com. and v.p. 1953-54), Greensboro (pres. 1950-51) bar assns., S.A.R. (pres. Gen. Green chtp. 1949), Am. Judicature Soc., Nat. Conf. Christians and Jews (pres. Greensboro chpt. 1949), Am. Judicature Soc. (dir. 1966-69), Am. Acad. Polit. and Social Sci., Am. Soc. Internat. Law, Am. Law Inst., Beta Theta Pi (nat. trustee, v.p. 1936-42), Phi Delta Phi. Mem. Soc. of Friends. Clubs: Greensboro Barristers (pres. 1928), Greensboro Merchants and Manufacturers (pres. 1929, 33), Greensboro Country; University (Washington). Author: A Christmas City—Christiana, Norway, 1926; Nantucket and North Carolina, 1936 (monographs); Coltrane and Frazier Genealogy, 1961; various legal briefs. Editor U. N.C. Law Review, 1922. Home: 620 Woodland Dr Greensboro NC 27402 Office: Southeastern Bldg Greensboro NC 27402

FRAZIER, ROBERT LEWIS, hosp. supt., physician; b. New Philadelphia, O., Aug. 9, 1910; s. Robert Lewis and Esther Alice (Eggenberg) F.; A.B., Ohio State U., 1934, M.D., 1938; m. Martha Beathard, Aug. 18, 1947; children—Robert Lewis, Lucy, Columbus State Hosp., 1952-55; mem. staff Orient (O.) State Inst., Columbus State Hosp., 1952-55; mem. staff Orient (O.) State Inst., 1939—, supt., 1955—. Mem. Am., Ohio med. assns., Am. Psychiat. Assn., Am. Assn. Mental Deficiency, Columbus Acad. Medicine, Neuropsychiat. Assn. Central Ohio, Am. Genetic Assn. Contbr. articles to profl. jours. Address: Orient State Inst Orient OH 43146

FRAZIER, SHERVERT HUGHES, Jr., educator, psychiatrist; b. Shreveport, La., June 12, 1921; s. Shervert Hughes and Mary (Lowman) F.; student Baylor U., 1936-39; B.S., U. Ill. at Chgo., 1941, M.D., 1943; M.S. in Psychiatry, U. Minn., 1957; certificate psychoanalytic medicine, Columbia Coll. Phys. and Surg., 1963; m. Gloria Barger, July 20, 1947; children—Elise, Alan, Rosalie, Stephen. Intern U. Ill. Research and Ednl. Hosp., 1943-44; fellow internal medicine Mayo Found., 1951-52, fellow psychiatry, asst. to staff, 1954-56; pvt. practice, Harrisburg, Ill., 1946-50, 53; adminstr. Harrisburg Med. Found., 1948-51; cons. sect. psychiatry Mayo Clin. St. Marys Hosp., also Meth. Hosp., Rochester, Minn., 1956-58; chief research scientist internal medicine N.Y. State Psychiat. Inst., 1958-61; asso. psychiatry, then asst. prof. psychiatry Columbia Coll. Phys. and Surg., 1958-62; Joske asst. prof. psychiatry Columbia Coll. Phys. and Surg., 1958-62; asst. attending psychiatrist Presbyn. Hosp., N.Y.C., 1958-63, dir. inpatient cons. service in psychiatry, 1961-62; prof. psychiatry, chmn. dept. Baylor U. Coll. Medicine, 1962-68; prof. psychiatry Columbia U. Coll. of Phys. and Surg., 1968—; attending psychiatrist Presbyn. Hosp. N.Y.; dep. dir. N.Y. State Psychiat. Inst.; dir. Houston Psychiat. Inst., 1962-65; psychiatrist in chief Ben Taub Gen. Hosp., Houston, 1962- 68; cons., VA Hosp., Houston, 1962-68; sr. attending Meth. Hosp., Houston, 1962-68; cons. Rice U., 1963-68; commr. Mental Health and Mental Retardation for Tex., 1965-67. Served as officer, M.C., USNR, 1944-46; PTO. Diplomate Am. Bd. Psychiatry and Neurology (bd. dirs. 1965). Fellow N.Y. Acad. Medicine, Am. Psychiat. Assn. (chmn. program com. 1965-67); mem. Am., N.Y., Tex. med. assns., N.Y. County, Harris County med. socs., Am. Psychosomatic Soc., A.C.P., Am. Soc. Human Genetics, Houston Psychiat. Soc., Am. Assn. (chmn. program com. 1965-68), Am. Soc. Human Genetics, Assn. of Psychoanalytic Medicine, Coll. Am. Psychiatrists, Central Neuropsychiat. Assn., Assn. Research Nervous and Mental Disease, Sigma Xi, Alpha Omega Alpha. Author numerous articles in field. Home: 26 Thatcher Rd Tenafly NJ 07670 Office: 722 W 168th St New York City NY 10032

FRAZIER, WALTER STEPHEN, architect; b. Aurora, Ill., Oct. 29, 1895; s. Walter S. and Clara (Pfrangel) F.; student U. Ill., 1913-15; B.S. in Architecture, Mass. Inst. Tech., 1915-19; student Ecole des Beaux Arts, Paris, 1919-20. With Holabird & Root, Chgo., 1920-24; pvt. practice, 1924—; partner Frazier, Orr, Fairbank & Quam, Inc., architects, Geneva, Ill., 1945—. Served to 2d lt., Air Corps, U.S. Army, 1917-19; to lt. col. USAAF, 1943-46. Fellow A.I.A. Clubs: Tavern, Arts (Chgo.). Home: 102 S Bennett St Geneva IL 60134 Office: 223 E State St Geneva IL 60134

FRAZIER, WARREN DAYLE, editor; b. Duncan Falls, O., June 24, 1897; s. Cassius C. and Alta (Eckelberry) F.; student pub. schs., Zanesville, O.; m. Emily J. Thomas, June 24, 1918; 1 son, Dayle. Reporter Zanesville (O.) Signal, 1915-16, Parkersburg (W. Va.) News, 1916-17, Canton (O.) Daily News, 1917, Columbus (O.) Monitor, 1917-18; reporter, city editor Columbus (O.) Citizen, 1918-35; copy editor Washington Post, 1935; asst. to dir. F.H.A., 1935; asst. city editor, news editor Columbus Dispatch, 1937-51, mng. editor, 1951-61, exec. managing editor, 1961-66, exec. editor, 1966-67, dir.; pres. Dispatch Features Syndicate. Member board trustees Columbus Town Meeting radio and television forum. Columbus Conv. Bur.; adv. bd. Salvation Army. Member of Ohio Legislative Corr. Assn. Am. Soc. of Newspaper Editors, Sigma Delta Chi. Methodist. Mason (32, Shriner). Home: 105 Northmoore Pl Columbus OH 43214

FRAZIER, WILLIAM COLEMAN PRIEST, cement co. exec.; b. Chgo., Dec. 18, 1910; s. William Coleman Priest and Laura Ragland (McFerran) F.; student Howard U., 1929, Tulane, 1947; m. Mildred Hudson. With Lone Star Cement Corp., N.Y.C., 1935-66, sales mgr., Seattle, 1957-60, v.p. sales, 1960-66; v.p. Marquette Cement Mfg. Co., Chgo., 1966-69. Mason, Rotarian. Club: International House (New Orleans). Office: 20 N Wacker Dr Chicago IL 60606

FREAD, SIDNEY, financial cons.; b. N.Y.C., June 9, 1916; s. Louis and Sarah (Lichtzer) F.; B.S.S., Coll. City N.Y., 1936; M.B.A., Harvard, 1938; m. Olga S. Horwitz, Sept. 18, 1949 (dec. May, 1966); children—Monica R., Deborah H.; m. 2d, Carol Hiberger, 1968. Asst. controller Maiden Form, 1938-41; asst. to pres. Malden Mills (Mass.), 1941-45; controller Publix Shirts, 1945-49; treas. Internat. Latex Corp., Dover, Del., 1949- 55; v.p. finance, Controller, dir. Joseph E. Seagram & Son's, Inc., 1955-59, v.p., treas., dir. Revlon, Inc., 1959-67; pres. Lehigh Valley Industries, Inc., 1967-69; v.p. finance, dir. Loew's Theatres Inc., 1969-70; now financial cons.; dir. Vivonex Corp.; dir. Thomas Doran & Co.; ltd. partner Brimberg & Co. Mem. Harvard Bus. Sch. Assn., Inst. Gen. Semantics, Am. Marketing Assn., Controllers Inst., Phi Beta Kappa. Home: 42 Meadow Rd Scarsdale NY 10583

FREAR, JOSEPH ALLEN, Jr., former govt. ofcl.; b. Rising Sun, Del., Mar. 7, 1903; s. Joseph and Clara (Lowber) F.; B.S., U. of Del., 1924; m. Esther Viola Schauer, Feb. 11, 1933; children—Fred, Clara, Louise. Agriculturist, Dover, Del. since 1922; U.S. senator from Del., 1949-61; mem. Securities and Exchange Commn., 1961-63. State commr. Del. State Coll. 1936-41, Old Age Welfare, 1937-48, Del. State Hosp. 1946-48; dir. Fed. Land Bank, Baltimore, since 1938 (chmn. of bd. 1946-48), Farmer's Bank, Dover, Del., Baltimore Trust Co., Camden, Del., Fruit Grower's Nat. Bank of Smyrna, Del.; pres. Kent Gen. Hosp., Dover, Del. Veteran World Wars I and II; maj. Officers' Res. Corps, World War II. Mem. C. of C., Am. Legion, Am. Hosp. Assn., Del. State Farm Bur., Sigma Nu. Democrat. Conglist. Mason (K.T., Shriner). Clubs: Dover Rotary, Delaware Motor, Maple Dale Country; Wilmington (Del.); Metropolitan (Washington). Home: 3601 Connecticut Av Washington DC 20008

FREBERG, CARL ROGER, engring. educator; b. Hector, Minn., Mar. 17, 1916; s. Charles and Bertha (Boock) F.; B.Mech. Engring., U. Minn., 1938, M.S. in Mech. Engring., 1940; Ph.D., Purdue U., 1943; m. Virginia Clawson, June 11, 1941; children—Charles Alan, Barbara Ann. Draftsman, Cereal Engring. and Constrn. Co., 1939; instr. machine design U. Minn., 1939-40; instr. mech. engring., then asst. prof. mech. and aero. engring. Purdue U., 1940-45; research engr. Carrier Corp., 1945-46; head engring. div. So. Research Inst., 1946-49; dir. equipment research U.S. Naval Civil Engring. Lab., 1949-52; asso. dir. Borg-Warner Research Center, 1952-57; prof., head mech. and aerospace engring. U. So. Cal., 1957-66, prof. mech. engring., 1966—. Mem. Am. Soc. M.E., Am. Soc. Engring. Edn., Am. Soc. Metals, Am. Assn. U. Profs., Sigma Xi, Tau Beta Pi, Pi Tau Sigma. Author: Elements of Mechanical Vibrations, 2d edit., 1949; Aircraft Vibration and Flutter, 1944. Home: 846 S Hudson Av Los Angeles CA 90005

FREBERG, STAN, (Stanley Victor Freberg), satirist; b. Pasadena, Cal., Aug. 7, 1926. Started as radio and record comedian; later organized Freberg, Ltd., specializing in satirical advertising; writer, performer numerous satirical recordings. Address: 911 N Beverly Dr Beverly Hills CA 90210

FRECCIA, MASSIMO, conductor; b. Florence, Italy, Sept. 19, 1906; s. Lazzaro and Porzia (de'Rossi) F.; student Cherubini Conservatory; Dr. Music (hon.), Tulane Univ., 1950; m. Maria Luisa Azpiazu, Sept. 20, 1945. Came to U.S., 1937, applied for citizenship. Conductor symphony orchestras since 1928; conducted major orchestras in Rome, Milan, Florence, Turin, Genoa, Budapest, Vienna, Paris, Prague and Warsaw; guest engagements in U.S. and Can. include N.Y Philharmonic-Symphony (stadium concerts), Phila. Orchestra (Robin Hood Dell), Cleveland Orchestra, Montreal Concerts Symphoniques, Chicago Symphony (Ravinia Park); musical dir. Havana (Cuba) Philharmonic, 1939-43, New Orleans (La.) Symphony Society, 1944-50; condr. concerts, Detroit Symphony Orchestra, 1947; NBC Symphony Orchestra, N.Y. City; condr. Houston Symphony Orchestra, 1948; guest condr. NBC Symphony Orchestra, since 1948; San Francisco Symphony, 1951; musical dir. New Orleans Symphony Orchestra, 1944-52; condr., music dir. Baltimore Symphony, 1952-58; conductor of European orchestras; chief condr. Rome RAI Symphony Orch., 1957-63; condr. RAI Radiotelevisione Italiana, 1959—. Decorated Order of Star of Italian Solidarity. Home: 230 Via Appia Antica Rome, Italy. Office: Columbia Artists Mgmt 165 W 57th St New York City NY 10019

FRECHETTE, VAN DERCK, ceramic engr.; b. Ottawa, Ont., Can., Jan. 5, 1916; s. Howells and Lena D. (Derick) F.; student U. Toronto, 1934-36; B.S., Alfred U., 1939; M.S., U. Ill., 1940, Ph.D., 1942; m. Sarah W. Houghton, Apr. 4, 1940; children—William G.H., Howells Van Derck, Christopher J., Margaret Kathleen, Judith L. Research physicist Corning Glass Works, (N.Y.), 1942-44; prof. ceramic sci. State U. N.Y. Coll. Ceramics, Alfred U., 1944—; guest prof. U. Göttingen (Germany), 1955-56, Max Planck Inst., Würzburg, 1965-66; cons. on fractology, ceramic problems and microscopy. Pres. Alfred Delta Sig Corp., 1971—. Bd. dirs. Alfred U. Research Found. Recipient Gordon Research Conf. award, 1955, Western Elec. award, 1969. Fulbright fellow, 1955. Registered profl. engr., N.Y Fellow Am. Ceramic Soc.; mem. Swedish Royal Acad. Arts and Scis., Sigma Xi, Delta Sigma Phi, Phi Kappa Phi. Author: Microscopy of Ceramics, 1955. Editor: Noncrystalline Solids, 1960, Kinetics of Reactions in Ionic Systems, 1970, Applied Mineralogy Series, 1971—. Home: 22 S Main St Alfred NY 14802

FRECHIE, MEYER JACK, steamship exec.; b. Phila., Mar. 24, 1907; s. Jacob M. and Bessye (Blum) F.; hon. grad. Wharton Sch. U. Pa., 1932; m. Henrietta Weil, Aug. 16, 1931; 1 son, Allen M. Traffic mgr. Phila. & Norfolk S.S. Co., 1936-41; v.p. Newtex S.S. Co., 1945-55; exec. v.p. Am. Hawaiian S.S. Co., N.Y.C., 1955—, also dir.; dir. Ore Transport, Inc., Hawaiian Trading Co., Transport, Trading & Terminal Corp. Served as col. Transportation Corps, AUS, 1942-46; dir. operational movements, ETO. Decorated Legion of Merit, Bronze Star Medal. Mem. Am. Soc. Traffic and Transp. (a founder).

FRECHTLING, LOUIS EARL, govt. ofcl.; b. Hamilton, O., June 19, 1913; s. Louis Henry and Elsie (Cebernick) F.; B.A., Miami U., Oxford, O., 1934; M.A., Fletcher Sch. Law and Diplomacy, 1935; student U. Heidelberg (Germany), summer 1935; D.Phil., U. Oxford (Eng.), 1939; m. Mary Louise Porch, Sept. 6, 1940; children—Douglas Carleton, Susan Rice. Instr., Miami U., 1939-40; research asso. Fgn. Policy Assn., N.Y.C., 1940-42; chief Near East sect. Bd. Econ. Warfare, 1942-43; asst. chief, then chief div. research Near East and Africa, State Dept., 1946-51; student Nat. War Coll., 1951-52; spl. asst. Office Coordinator Mut. Security Affairs, State Dept., 1952- 61; mem. program coordination staff AID, 1961-63; asst. dir. Office Internat. Adminstrn., State Dept., 1963-66, dir., 1966—. Adviser U.S. delegations to confs. FAO, UNESCO, IMCO, 1963-68. Served to lt. USNR, 1943-46. Decorated sec. navy letter of commendation; Rhodes scholar, 1936-39; Rockefeller fellow, 1940. Mem. Phi Beta Kappa, Omicron Delta Kappa, Phi Delta Theta. Conglist. Home: 5623 Newington Rd Washington, DC 20016. Office: Dept of State Washington DC 20520

FRECKLETON, FRANK ROBERT, pub. health physician; b. N.Y.C., Aug. 2, 1921; s. Frank and Marguerite (Magill) F.; A.B., Columbia Coll., 1941; M.D., Tulane U., 1944; M.P.H., Columbia Sch. Pub. Health, 1947; m. Elaine Lucile Kidwell, May 29, 1962; children—Michael, William. Intern, Grasslands Hosp., Valhalla, N.Y., 1944- 45; resident Hartford (Conn.) Hosp., 1945-46; dep. health commr. Rensselaer (N.Y.) County, 1947-50; health commr. Columbia (N.Y.) County, 1950-52, Boston, 1960-62; joined USPHS, 1952, med. dir., 1959—; chief immunization program Nat. Communicable Disease Center, Atlanta, 1963-70; med. officer in charge USPHS, Am. Embassy, London, Eng., 1970—; lectr. Harvard Sch. Pub. Health, 1960-62. Served with AUS, 1943-44. Diplomate Am. Bd. Preventive Medicine. Fellow Am. Pub. Health Assn.; mem. A.M.A., U.S.-Mexico Border Pub. Health Assn. Home: 9 Clarence Gate Gardens London NW1 England Office: Am Embassy 24 Grosvenor Sq London W1A IAE England

FRED, EDWIN BROUN, educator; b. Middleburg, Va., Mar. 22, 1887; s. Samuel Rogers and Catherine Conway (Broun) F.; prep. edn., Randolph Macon Acad., Front Royal, Va., 1902-03; B.S., Va. Poly. Inst., 1907, M.S., 1908; Ph.D., U. of Göttingen, Germany, 1911, recipient "Golden Diploma," 1961; LL.D., Lawrence Coll., 1945, Northwestern U., 1947, Mich. State Coll., 1955; D.Sc., Marquette U., 1945; Beloit Coll., U. N.C., Northland Coll., Ashland, Wis., 1946; U. Wis., 1958; m. Rosa Helen Parrott, June 21, 1913; children—Ann Conway, Rosalie Broun (Mrs. Thomas Moffatt). Asst. bacteriology Va. Poly. Inst., 1907-08, asst. prof. bacteriology, 1912-13; asst. prof. U. Wis., 1913-14, asso. prof., 1914-18, prof., 1918-58, dean Grad. Sch., 1934-43, dean Coll. of Agr. and dir. Agr. Expt. Sta., 1943-45, pres. U. Wis., 1945-58, pres. emeritus, prof. emeritus, 1958—. Apptd. as 1st lt. Chem. Warfare Service, U.S. Army, 1918. Awarded Medal for Merit for services during World War II. Recipient meritorious service citation Va. Poly. Inst. Chem. Adv. Com. Biol. Warfare of Nat. Acad. of Scis., 1941-43. Mem. Nat. Adv. Health Council, 1945-50; bd. trustees, Nutrition Foundation, 1945-50, Carnegie bd. trustees, 1946-58; U.S. Adv. Commn. on Ednl. Exchange 1949-54; NSF Bd., 1950-56; mem. nat. adv. and infectious diseases council NIH, 1956-57; adv. com. for biology and medicine AEC, 1956-57; Am. Council on Edn. Commn. on Edn. and Internat. Affairs, 1958-61; Pres.'s Internat. Devel. adv. bd., 1959. Trustee Vilas Trust, 1961—; mem. U. Wis. Found., 1961—. Fellow A.A.A.S.; mem. Nat. Acad. Sci., Am. Philos. Soc., Soc. Am. Bacteriologists (pres. 1932), Sigma Xi, Phi Beta Kappa, Alpha Sigma Epsilon, Gamma Alpha, Phi Sigma, Epsilon Sigma Phi, Phi Kappa Phi. Democrat. Co-author: Textbook of Agricultural Bacteriology (with F Löhnis), 1933; Laboratory Manual of Microbiology (with S. A. Waksman), 1928; Root Nodule Bacteria and Leguminous Plants (with Baldwin and McCoy), 1932. Home: 10 Babcock Dr Madison WI 53706

FREDENBERGER, WILLIAM E., union ofcl. Pres., Internat. Brotherhood Firemen and Oilers AFL-CIO. Office: 200 Maryland Av Washington DC 20002*

FREDERICK, ANTHONY PETER, educator; b. New Memphis, Ill., Jan. 14, 1900; s. George F. and Anna (Wirtner) F.; B.A., U. Dayton, 1925; M.A., St. Louis U., 1935. Tchr. St. Joseph High Sch., Victoria, Tex., 1920-24, St. Mary's Acad., San Antonio, 1924-27; tchr., registrar McBride High Sch., St. Louis, 1927- 35; prof. English, St. Mary's U., 1935—, chmn. dept., 1937-61, dean arts and scis., 1961-64. Gen. chmn. St. Mary's U. self study So. Assn. Colls. and Schs. Evaluation Program, 1961-62. Mem. student loan and Piper Scholars com. Minnie Stevens Piper Found. Brother, Soc. of Mary. Mem. Nat. Council Tchrs. English (dir. 1953-68, charter mem. commn. on the profession 1958-62, Tex. chmn. achievement awards program 1960-63, chmn. com. Am. lit. landmarks 1965-68), Tex. Council Tchrs. English (v.p. 1964-65, dir. 1965-68), Modern Lang. Assn., So. Central Modern Lang. Assn., Tex. Conf. Coll. Tchrs. English, San Antonio (Tex.) Council Internat. Relations. Author: The Term Paper in Theory and Example, rev. edit., 1962. Compiler: This They Wrote, 1953. Contbg. author: (essay collection) Why I Became a Brother, 1954. Editorial chmn. Annotated Index to English Jour. 1944-63, 1964. Contbr. articles to various mags. Home: 2700 Cincinnati Av San Antonio, TX 78228.

FREDERICK, GEORGE RICHARDSON, candy mfr.; b. Nokomis, Ill., June 1, 1908; s. Henry George and Inez (Gelly) F.; student pub. schs. Nokomis, Clevaland Coll.; m. Mary Cushman, Oct. 14, 1936; children—Nancy, George Richardson, Robert Lovell. With Fred Harvey, Chicago, 1925-33; pres. Herz Candy Co., St. Louis, 1934-38, Busy Bee Candy Co., 1938-40; v.p. Loft Candy Corp., Long Island

City, N.Y., 1941-49, pres., 1949-57, vice chmn. bd., 1957-64, pres., chmn. board, 1964-65, chairman of the board, 1965-69; pres. of Music Inc., Sarasota, Fla. Mem. Assn. Retail Confectioners U.S. (preo.), Assn. Mfrs. Confectionery and Chocolate (v.p.). Home: 113 Fillmore Dr Sarasota FL 33577 Office: NY Athletic Club New York City NY 10001

FREDERICK, HAL CHRISTOPHER, actor; b. N.Y.C.; s. Christopher and Helen (Peters) F.; student Am. Theatre Wing, 1956; N.Y.U., 1956-59. Appeared roles movies Violent Secret, 1963; The Baker of Venice, 1964; prodn. asst. Fellini's Guilietta di Spiriti, 1965; prin. role in premier performance in Paris of Leroy Jones Putchman, 1965-66; co-star film Two Gentlemen Sharing, 1968; appeared roles TV series FBI, Ironsides, Movie of the Week, Felony Squad, World Premiere; star on Interns, CBS-TV, 1970-71. Served with AUS, 1953-55. Recipient Danny Kaye Community Service award, 1952; Irene Beck Meml. Scholarship, 1956; Robert Helpman-Michael Benthal Old Vic Scholarship, 1957. Mem. Negro Indsl. and Economic Union. Home: 8910 Holly Pl Los Angeles CA 90046 Office: care Gregory Thomas Ltd 9523 Sunset Blvd Los Angeles CA

FREDERICK, HAROLD ANTON, lawyer; b. LaCrosse, Wis., Oct. 18, 1923; s. Albert E. and Elnora (Geier) F.; B.S., U. Wis., 1949, J.D., 1951; m. Grace E. Bowen, Aug. 27, 1949; children—Michael, Mark, Mary Jo, Martin. Admitted to Wis. bar, 1951, Ariz. bar, 1968; practiced in LaCrosse, 1951-54, Phoenix, 1968—; asso. Johns, Roraff, Pappas & Flaherty, 1951-54; adjuster Western Adjustment & Investigation Co., 1954-56, Fireman's Fund Ins. Co., 1956-60; claims mgr. Nat. Union Ins. Co., 1960-68; partner Black, Robertshaw & Frederick, 1968—. Tchr. law for everyday use LaCrosse Vocational Sch., 1952-55. Served with USCGR, 1942-46. Recipient Distinguished Service award Am. Ins. Assn. and Am. Mut. Ins. Alliance, 1966. Mem. Ariz. Claimsmen's Assn. (past pres.), Claims Mgrs. Council (past pres.). Home: 3040 N 53d Pkwy Phoenix AZ 85031 Office: 3003 N Central Av Phoenix AZ 85012

FREDERICK, JOSEPH FRANCIS, Jr., hotel exec.; b. Luzerne, Pa., July 13, 1933; s. Joseph Francis and Emma (Sabtini) F.; B.S., Pa. State U., 1956; m. Joanne Agnes Pollock, July 23, 1955; 1 dau., Joelle Ann. Exec. trainee Waldorf-Astoria Hotel, N.Y.C., 1956-57, asst. front office mgr., 1962-63; service mgr. Statler Hilton, N.Y.C., 1963-65; dir. sales Hartford (Conn.) Hilton, 1965-68; resident mgr. Dallas Statler Hilton, 1968-69; gen. mgr. Hartford Hilton, 1969; gen. mgr. Netherland Hilton, Terrace Hilton hotels, Cin., 1969—. Mem. bd. dirs. Conv. and Visitors Bur., Cin. Served with USAF, 1957-62. Mem. YMCA, Pa. State Alumni Assn., Sigma Pi Eta, Sigma Pi. Address: Netherland Hilton Hotel Cincinnati OH 45202

FREDERICK, PAULINE, radio and TV news correspondent; b. Gallitzin, Pa.; d. Matthew Phillip and Susan (Stanley) Frederick; A.B., Am. U., Washington, also A.M.; m. Charles Robbins, State Dept. corr. U.S. News; radio editorial asst. H. R. Baukhage, Blue Network and ABC; free-lance Western Newspaper Union, North Am. Newspaper Alliance, also news commentator ABC, 1946-53; news corr. NBC, 1953—, also UN corr. ABC, NBC; radio anchor man Dem. and Rep. Convs., NBC, 1956. Recipient Headliner award Theta Sigma Phi, Alfred I duPont award, George Foster Peabody award for contbn. to internat. understanding, Golden Mike award for outstanding woman in radio-TV, McCall's; voted radio's woman of the year Radio-TV Daily poll; Univ. of Missouri School of Journalism medal; voted outstanding woman of the year Women's Advt. Club of Phila., special citation for UN coverage, National Federation of Women's Clubs, East-West Center award, 1966; Journalism Achievment award, U. So. Cal., 1967; First Pennsylvania Journalism Achievment award; Carr Naw Anda award Ohio U. Sch. Journalism, 1971. Mem. UN Corrs. Assn., Assn. Radio and Television Analysts, Radio-TV Corrs. Assn. Author: Ten First Ladies of the World, 1968. Office: 30 Rockefeller Plaza New York City NY 10020

FREDERICKS, ALANSON ROSWELL, ins. co. exec.; b. Syracuse, N.Y., Apr. 9, 1910; s. Roswell T. and Florence (Leighton) F.; B.A., Amherst Coll., 1931; LL.B., Syracuse U., 1934; m. Lilian Gertrude Price, July 16, 1938; children—Sian Roberts, Kerry Leighton. Admitted to N.Y. bar, 1934, practiced in Syracuse, 1934- 36; legal dept. Am. Surety Co., 1936-63, successively asst. gen. counsel, gen. counsel, 1936-55, v.p., gen. counsel, 1957-63, past. mem. bd. dirs.; asst. gen. counsel Md. Casualty Co., 1963-65, gen. counsel, 1955-68, v.p. and gen. counsel, 1968—; past v.p., dir., gen. counsel Am. Life Ins. Co., Surety Fire Ins. Co.; gen. counsel No. Ins. Co. of New York, Assurance Co. of Am., Autopian Ins. Co. Mem. bd. reps., Stamford, Conn., 1953- 59; Republican minority leader, 1955-59. Mem. Am. Bar Assn., Internat. Assn. Ins. Counsel, Theta Delta Chi, Phi Delta Phi. Mason (Shriner, K.T.). Club: Mt. Washington. Contbg. author: Property and Liability Insurance Handbook, 1965. Home: 4300 N Charles St Baltimore, MD 21218. Office: 701 W 40th St Baltimore MD 21203

FREDERICKS, JACOB WAYNE, found. ofcl.; b. Wakarusa, Ind., Feb. 26, 1917; s. William J. and Flossa E. (Walters) F.; B.S. in Engring. with honors, Purdue U., 1938; m. Anne R. Curtis, Jan. 19, 1952; children—Maria Loring, William Curtis. Asst. mgr. fgn. mfg. div. Kellogg Co., 1938-40, 46-51, 54-56; analyst aircraft div. U.S. Strategic Bombing Survey, German and Japan, 1946; with Dept. Def., 1951-54; program asso. pub. affairs program, Ford Found., 1956- 58, asso. dir. overseas devel. program for Asia, 1958-61, head Middle East and African program, 1967—; dep. asst. sec. state for African affairs, 1961-67. Trustee Lincoln U., Phelps-Stokes Fund, Adlai Stevenson Inst. Internat. Affairs. Lt. col. USAAF, 1941-46; lt. col. Res. Decorated Legion of Merit, D.F.C., Bronze Star; Order British Empire; Croix de Guerre (France); recipient Superior Honor award Dept. State, 1965, Distinguished Honor award Dept. State, 1967. Mem. Council Fgn. Relations, African Studies Assn., Air Force Assn. (dir. 1958-60), Sigma Xi. Club: Federal City. Home: 4530 Lowell St NW Washington DC 20016 Office: Dept of State Washington DC 20525

FREDERICKS, JOHN DONNAN, clay products mfg. exec., lawyer; b. Los Angeles County, Cal., Sept. 7, 1900; s. John Donnan and Agnes (Blakeley) F.; J.D., Stanford U., 1923; m. Elizabeth Watt, Nov. 10, 1921; children—John Donnan (dec.), Mary (Mrs. John W. Downs, Jr.), Thomas Anthony (dec.); m. 2d, Charlotte Rayner, Mar. 31, 1934. Admitted to Cal. bar, 1923; mem. Fredericks & Fredericks, Los Angeles, 1923-50; pres. Pacific Clay Products, 1950-65, chmn. bd., chief exec. officer, 1965-70, chmn. bd., 1970—, also dir.; former dept. com., dir. Fed. Res. Bank San Francisco. Served with USN, World War I. Mem. Mchts. and Mfrs. Assn. Los Angeles (past dir.), Los Angeles C. of C. (past dir.), Alpha Delta Phi, Phi Delta Phi. Roman Catholic. Home: 956 Mariposa Lane Santa Barbara CA 93103 Office: 1255 W 4th St Los Angeles CA 90017

FREDERICKS, MARSHALL MAYNARD, sculptor; b. Rock Island, Ill., Jan. 31, 1908; s. Frank A. and Frances Margaret (Bragg) F.; student John Huntington Poly. Inst., Cleve.; grad. Cleve. Sch. Art, 1930; student Heimann Schule, Schwegerle Schule, Munich, Germany, Academie Scandinav, Paris, France, pvt. studios Rome and London, Carl Milles' Studio, Stockholm, Sweden, Cranbrook Acad. Art, Bloomfield Hills, Mich.; m. Rosalind Bell Cooke, Sept. 9, 1943; children—Carl Marshall and Christopher Matzen (twins), Frances Karen Bell, Rosalind Cooke, Suzanne Pelletreau. Faculty Cleve. Sch. Art, 1931, Cranbrook Acad. Art, Kingswood Sch., Cranbrook, 1932-42; Royal Danish consul. for Mich.; local, nat., internat. exhbns. art since 1928 include: Carnegie Inst., Cleve. Mus., Pa. Acad., Chgo. Art Inst., Whitney Mus., Detroit Art Inst., Denver Mus., Phila. Internat. Invitational, N.Y. World's Fair Am. art exhbn., Modern Sculpture Internat. Exhbn. Detroit, Internat. Sculpture Show Cranbrook Mus., A.I.A., Nat. Sculpture Soc., Archtl. League of N. Y., Mich. Acad., Brussels, Belgium, others; commns. include; N.Y. World's Fari Baboon Fountain; Levi Barbour Meml. Fountain, Rackham Meml. Bldg., Fort Str. Sta., Vets. Meml. Bldg., Detroit; adminstrn. bldg. war meml. U. Mich., Louisville Courier-Jour. Bldg., Jefferson Sch., Wyandotte, Mich., Holy Ghost Sem., Ann Arbor, Mich., union bldg. Ohio State U., Ford Rotunda, Marc Joslyn Meml., Alvan Macauley Meml. City-County Bldg., Ford Auditorium, Detroit Zool. Garden, also the Indian River Shrine, State Dept. Fountain, Washington; Cleve. War Meml. Fountain, Milw. Pub. Mus. Sculpture, N.Y. World's Fair permanent sculpture, Fed. Bldg. sculpture, Cin., Community Nat. Bank, Pontiac, Mich., Sir Winston Churchill Meml., Freeport, Bahamas, J.L. Hudson's Eastland, Northland, and Flint (Mich.) Mall, Two Sister fountain, Cranbrook, Michigan, Dallas Library sculpture, many others; portrait commns. include Senator Arthur Vandenburg, Willard Dow, Midland, Mich., George G. Booth Meml., Cranbrook, Mrs. Horace Rackham Meml., Pres. John F. Kennedy, Yoshita, others; works included numerous museums, pvt., civic collections. Mem. Pres.'s Com. for Employment of Handicapped; mem. Gov.'s State Capitol Com.; co-founder, dir. DIADEM Program for Internat. Exchange of Handicapped. Served with C.E., U.S. Army, 1942-44, lt. col. 20th bomber command; 8th Air Force, Okinawa, 1944-45. Decorated Knight Order of Dannebrog; recipient of 1st prize Cleve. Mus. Art, 1931; Anna Scripps Whitcomb prize Detroit Inst. Arts, 1938; 1st prize internat. exhbn. Dance Internat., Rockefeller Center, N.Y.C., 1st prize Barbour Meml. nat. competition, medal Mich. Inst. Architects, fine arts gold medal A.I.A., 1952, gold medal honor Mich. Acad. Arts. Letters, Sci., 1953; Achtl. League of N.Y.; Golden Plate award Am. Acad. Achievement; citation Mich. Assn. Professions, Am. Inst. Decorators, Nat. Soc. Crippled Children and Adults, State of Mich., U. of Detroit, others. N.A. Fellow of Internat. Inst. of Arts and Letters; mem. Mich. Soc. Architects, Federation Internationale de la Medaille, A.I.A., St. Dunstans Dramatic Guild, Mich. Acad. Sci., Arts, Letters, C. of C. Nat. Acad. Design, Am. Inst. Decorators, Nat. Soc. Interior Designers, Beta Sigma Phi, Alpha Beta Delta. Clubs: Royal Swedish Yacht; Orchard Lake Country; Architectural League N.Y. (N.Y.C.); Prismatic (Detroit); Royal Norwegian Yacht; Royal Danish Yacht. Home: 440 Lake Park Dr Birmingham MI 48009 Studio: 4113 N Woodward Av Royal Oak MI 48053 also East Long Lake Road Bloomfield Hills MI 48013

FREDERICKSON, ARMAN FREDERICK, minerals co. exec.; b. Winnipeg, Man., Can., May 5, 1918; s. Albert F. and Ethel M. (Wilton) F.; came to U.S., 1923, naturalized, 1940; B.S. in Mining Engring., U. Wash., 1940; M.S. in Metall. Engring., Mont. Sch. Mines, 1942; Sc.D. in Geology, Mass. Inst. Tech., 1947; m. Mary Maxine Stubblefield, Sept. 23, 1943; children—Mary Christene, Clover Diane, Penny Kathlene, Kimberly Mei, Sigrid. Mining engr., chief geologist Cornucopia Gold Mines, (Ore.), 1939-40; instr. mineral dressing Mont. Sch. Mines, 1941; research asst. Mass. Inst. Tech., 1942-43; prof. geology Washington U., St. Louis, 1947-55; organizer, supr. geol. research Pan Am. Petroleum Corp., Tulsa, 1955-60; prof. geology, chmn. dept. earth and planetary sci., dir. oceanography U. Pitts., 1960-65; sr. v.p., dir. research, mgr. mining prospecting and mineral programs King Resources Co., Denver, 1965-71; pres. Denver Research Corp., 1966—, N. Am., Fertilizer Corp., 1966—; v.p. Rocky Mountain Mineral Corp., 1967—; cons. in mining and petroleum exploration, 1971—. Organizer, past chmn. clay minerals com. Nat. Acad. Sci.-NRC. Served with USNR, 1943-45. Fellow Geol. Soc. Am., Mineral Soc. Am.; mem. Am. Inst. Mining, Metall. and Petroleum Engrs., Am. Assn. Petroleum Geologists, Soc. Econ. Geologists, Geochem. Soc. Am., Underwater Soc. Am. Author papers in field. Patentee fertilizer, oil and water pollution processes and products; and geochemistry. Home: 10027 Bayou Glen Houston TX 77042 Office: 1946 W Grey Houston TX

FREDERICKSON, EDWARD ARTHUR, educator, geologist; b. Madison, Wis., Sept. 23, 1908; s. Edward Arthur and Rose (Fertig) F.; B.A. in Econs., U. Wis., 1930, Ph.D. in Geology, 1942; m. Bernice Elizabeth Bliss, Sept. 6, 1938; children—Toni Anne, Jeannine. Teaching asst. U. Wis., 1937-40; mem. faculty Okla. U., 1940- 64, prof. geology, 1951-64; prof. geology, chmn. dept. Kent State U., 1964—; with Wis. Geol. Survey, summers 1937, 39; part-time geol. investigation Okla. Geol. Survey, 1940—; cons. in field, 1948—; spl. research Cambrian paleontology and stratigraphy, Okla. geology, Colo. geology, trilobites, maps. Served to lt. col. USAAF and USAF, 1942-46, 51-53; col. Res. ret. Fellow Geol. Soc. Am.; mem. Am. Assn. Petroleum Geologists, Paleontol. Soc., Soc. Econ. Geologists, Paleontologists and Mineralogists, A.A.A.S., Ohio Acad. Sci., Am. Assn. U. Profs., Sigma Xi (pres. Okla. chpt. 1950-51; pres. Kent State 1968-69), Sigma Alpha Epsilon, Sigma Gamma Epsilon (v.p. Central province 1952-59; (nat. pres. 1960-65). Republican. Episcopalian. Lion. Club: Twin Lakes Country (Kent). Contbr. profl. jours. Home: 715 Doramor St Kent OH 44240

FREDINE, CLARENCE GORDON, biologist; b. St. Paul, Aug. 15, 1909; s. Andrew Clarence and Hulda (Anderson) F.; B.S. in Biology, Hamline U., 1932; grad. student zoology, U. Minn., 1932-35, Purdue, U., 1941-43; m. Edith Louise Handy, June 7, 1934; children—John Gordon, Patricia Ann. Ranger-naturalist Nat. Park Service, Yellowstone, Park, Wyo., 1934; asso. biologist Minn. Emergency Conservation Work, St. Paul, 1935-36; chief biologist, game and fish cons., game and fish div. Minn. Conservation Dept., 1936-41; asst. prof. wildlife conservation dept. forestry and conservation, Agrl. Expt. Sta., Purdue U., 1941-47; with Dept. Interior, 1947—, prin. park planner mission 66, Nat. Park Service, 1960-62, chief div. extension services, 1962-64, chief div. of internat. affairs, since 1964—. Charter mem. Wildlife Soc., 1937, exec. sec., 1960-63, pres. Washington chpt., 1964- 66, hon. mem. Served to lt. (s.g.) USNR, 1943-46; PTO. Recipient distinguished service award Department of the Interior, 1967. Member Ecological Soc. of Am., Am. Fisheries Soc., Washington Biologists Field Club, Student Conservation Assn., Nature Conservancy, Soc. Am. Foresters (asso.), Internat. Assn. Game, Fish and Conservation Commrs., Theta Chi. Unitarian. Authors govt. bulls., articles. Home: 5921 Anniston Rd Bethesda, MD 20034. Office: Nat Park Service Interior Bldg Washington DC 20240

FREDLAND, JOHN ROGER, educator; b. Lincoln, Me, Dec. 1, 1916; s. Arthur and Ethel (Swasey) F.; A.B., Bates Coll., 1936; Ph.D. Am. U., 1956; postgrad. Princeton, 1936-38; m. Dorothy Halliday Staples, Aug. 3, 1940; children—Eric, Peter, Kurt, Robert, Mark. Instr. Pa. State U., 1938-41; mem. faculty U.S. Naval Acad., Annapolis, Md., 1941—, prof. econs., 1956—, chmn. dept., 1948—; lectr., prof. Am. U., 1956-58, George Washington U., 1960-62, Anne Arundel Community Coll., Annapolis, Md., 1961-71. Mem. Annapolis City Council, 1957-61, Annapolis Planning and Zoning Commn., 1959-61. Served to lt. USNR, 1943-45; PTO. Found. for Econ. Edn. fellow, 1951. Mem. Am. Econ. Assn., Am. Assn. U. Profs., Phi Beta Kappa. Democrat. Episcopalian. Club: Army-Navy (Washington). Author: (with E.B. Potter and others) U.S. and World Sea Power, 1956; (with E.B. Potter) Sea Power: A History, 1960; (with M. Ulmer) Economics: A Handbook, 1965. Home: 100 Old Crossing Lane Annapolis MD 21401

FREDRICK, LAURENCE WILLIAM, educator, astronomer; b. Stroudsburg, Pa., Aug. 27, 1927; s. Ishmeal T. and Grace (Slider) F.; B.A, Swarthmore Coll., 1952. M.A., 1954; Ph.D., U. Pa., 1959; m. Frances I. Schwenk, Feb. 5, 1949; children—Laura Grace, Theodore David, Rebecca Lyn. Research asst. Sproul Obs., Swarthmore, Pa., 1952-56; research asso. Flower and Cook Obs., Malvern, Pa., 1957-59; astronomer Lowell Obs., Flagstaff, Ariz., 1959-63; mem. faculty U. Va., 1963—, prof. astronomy, 1965—, chmn. dept., dir. Leander McCormick Obs., 1963—; cons. in field. Served with USNR, 1945-48. Named Alumnus of Year, Milton Hershey Sch., 1961. Mem. Am. Astron. Soc. (sec.), Internat. Astron. Union, Sigma Xi. Co-author: An Introduction to Astronomy, 8th edit., 1967; Astronomy, 9th edit., 1970. Home: 2602 Bennington Rd Charlottesville VA 22901

FREDRICKSEN, CLEVE JOHN, mfg. co. exec.; b. Bklyn., Aug. 24, 1917; s. John A. and Laura A. (Olsen) F.; student St. John's U., 1937-40; m. Harriet Ingrid Johnsen, Dec. 7, 1940; children—Cleve Laurance, Brian Harold, Thomas Mark. Asst. sec., asst. treas. AMP, Inc., Harrisburg, Pa., 1941-42, dir., 1942—, sec., asst. treas., 1942-56, sec.-treas., 1956-59, v.p., treas., 1959- 68, v.p., chief financial officer, 1968—; dir. Pamcor, Inc., San Juan, P.R., 1952—; sec.-asst. treas., 1952-56, sec.-treas., 1956- 59, v.p., treas., 1959-68, v.p., chief financial officer, 1968—; dir. Dauphin Deposit Trust Co., Harrisburg, Harsco Corp. Bd. dirs. Harrisburg Polyclinic Hosp., U. Center Harrisburg; trustee Kline Found. Presbyn. Mem. Pa. Society. Clubs: West Shore Country (Camp Hill); Coral Beach and Tennis (Paget, Bermuda). Home: 345 N 27th St Camp Hill PA 17011 Office: Eisenhower Blvd Harrisburg PA 17111

FREDRICKSON, ARNOLD GERHARD, educator, chem. engr.; b. Fairbault, Minn., Apr. 11, 1932; s. Gerhard and Anna (Quamme) F.; student Augsburg Coll., Mpls., 1950-51; B.S., U. Minn., 1954, M.S., 1956; Ph.D., U. Wis., 1959. With Archer-Daniels- Midland Co., 1957; mem. faculty U. Minn., 1958—, prof. chem. engring., 1966—; cons. to govt., 1967—. Mem. Am. Inst. Chem. Engrs., Soc. Rheology, Am. Chem. Soc. (honor scroll indsl. and engring. chemistry div. 1967), Sigma Xi, Tau Beta Pi, Phi Lambda Upsilon. Author: Principles and Applications of Rheology, 1964. Home: 501 4th St SE Minneapolis MN 55418

FREDRICKSON, DONALD SHARP, med. scientist; b. Canon City, Colo., Aug. 8, 1924; s. Charles Arthur and Blanche (Sharp) F.; student U. Colo., 1942-43; B.S., U. Mich., 1946, M.D., 1949; m. Henriette Priscilla Dorothea Eekhof, Sept. 5, 1950; children—Eric Henderikus, Rurik Charles. Intern Peter Bent Brigham Hosp., Boston, 1949-50; house staff mem., fellow Peter Bent Brigham and Mass. Gen. hosps., 1950-53; mem. sr. research staff lab. cellular physiology and metabolism Nat. Heart and Lung Inst., Bethesda, Md., 1955-61, clin. dir. inst., 1961-66, head sect. molecular diseases lab. metabolism, 1962-66, dir. inst., 1966-68, chief molecular disease br., 1966—, dir. intramural research, 1968—; clin. instr. medicine George Washington U. Sch. Medicine, 1956-59; spl. lectr. internal medicine, 1959—; lectr. preventive medicine Georgetown U. Sch. Medicine, 1963—. Mem. cardiovascular study sect. NIH, 1959-62; mem. com. fats, food and nutrition bd. NRC, 1961-67; mem. nutrition research adv. com. Nat. Dairy Council, 1961-63; med. adv. bd. FAA, 1965-67, Nat. Tay-Sachs Found., 1965-67. Served with AUS, 1943-45. Recipient Gold Medal award Am. Coll. Cardiology, 1967, Internat. award James F. Mitchell Found. for Med. Edn. and Research, 1968, Distinguished Achievement award Modern Medicine, 1971; Superior Service award Dept. Health, Edn. and Welfare, 1970, Distinguished Service award, 1971; McCollum award Am. Soc. Clin. Nutrition and Clin. div. Am. Inst. Nutrition, 1971. Fellow Am. Coll. Cardiology; life fellow A.C.P.; mem. A.A.A.S., Am. Heart Assn. (exec. com. council arteriosclerosis), A.M.A., Am. Oil Chemists Soc., Am. Physiol. Soc. (chmn. publs. com.), Am. Soc. Clin. Investigation (sec.-treas.), Am. Soc. Human Genetics; Assn. Am. Physicians, Internat. Soc. Cardiology (exec. com.), Med. Soc. Sweden, Soc. Pediatric Research, Washington Soc. Pathologists, Inst. Medicine Brit. Cardiac Soc. (corr.), Phi Beta Kappa, Phi Kappa Phi, Alpha Omega Alpha. Editor: (with others) The Metabolic Basis of Inherited Disease, 3d edit., 1971. Contbr. articles profl. jours. Home: 6615 Bradley Blvd Bethesda MD 20034 Office: Nat Heart and Lung Inst NIH Bethesda MD 20014

FREDRICKSON, HAROLD M., lawyer; b. Davenport, N.D., Nov. 21, 1912; B.A., U. Minn., 1936, LL.B., 1936. Admitted to Minn. bar, 1945, U.S. Supreme Ct. bar; mem. firm Fredrickson, Byron, Colburn Ltd., Mpls. Instr. wills, trusts and estates U. Minn., 1951-52, 54-57. Mem. Am., Minn. (bd. govs. 1966-68), Hennepin County bar assns., Am. Judicature Soc., Phi Alpha Delta. Mem. editorial bd. Minn. Law Rev., 1934-35, recent case editor, 1935-36. Office: 1460 Northwestern Bank Bldg Minneapolis MN 55402*

FREDRICKSON, WILLIAM RUSSELL, physicist; b. Chgo., June 28, 1903; s. Andrew William and Augusta (Johnson) F.; B.S., U. Chgo., 1924, M.S., 1926, Ph.D., 1928; m. Linnea Nelson, Aug. 16, 1930; children—Donald, Lenore. Tchr. sci. Lockport (Ill.) High Sch., 1924-25; instr., Syracuse (N.Y.) U. 1928-30, asst. prof. physics, 1930-35, asso. prof., 1935-38, prof. physics 1938-71, chmn. dept. of physics 1939-65. Fellow Am. Phys. Soc.; mem. Am. Assn. Physics Teachers, Phi Beta Kappa, Sigma Xi. Presbyn. Home: 202 Halton Rd Syracuse, NY 13224

FREDRIKS, GERRITT JAMES, lawyer; b. Cincinnati, May 24, 1882; s. Gerritt Jacobis and Sophia Emily (Oehlmann) F.; student U. Cin., Solomen P. Chase Coll.; m. Texanna Peacock, Jan. 1, 1908; children—Ruth Arkana (Mrs. Arwood Liggett), Ella Emily (Mrs. Robert D. Williamson). Admitted to Ohio bar, 1907, since practiced in Cin.; with Thorndyke, Frederiks & Cappelle, 1907-12, Fredriks & Huffman, 1912-16; pvt. law practice since 1916; now sr. mem. firm Fredricks & Liggett, Cin.; title officer Title Guaranty & Trust Co., 1908-09; gen. mgr. Bankers Surety Co., 1907-17. Pres. Federated Civic Assns. Hamilton Co.; chmn. bd. Food and Home Show. Lt. Inf., U.S. Army, World War I. Mem. Am. (past mem. house of dels.), Ohio State (pres. 1939-40) Cin. bar assns., Zool. Soc. Cin. (trustee, past pres.). Republican (past sec. Blaine club and past pres. Federation Republican clubs, Hamilton Co.). Mason (Shriner; past monarch, past thrice potent master; hon. mem. Sovereign Grand Insps. Gen. of 33). Club: Hyde Park Businessmen's (past pres.). Home: 2527 Ritchie Av Cincinnati OH 45208 Office: 1st Nat Bank Bldg Cincinnati OH 45202

FREDRIKSON, ROGER L., clergyman, educator; b. Mission City, Can., Nov. 27, 1920; s. Alfred L. and Elvira M. (Michaelson) F.; came to U.S., 1925; B.A., Ottawa (Kan.) U., 1942, D.D. (hon.), 1958; B.D., Andover-Newton Theol. Sch., 1948, S.T.M., 1949; m. Ruth Beaver, June 1, 1944; children—Randall Stuart, Miriam Sue, Joel Richard. Pres. Nat. Baptist Youth Fellowship, 1944-46; ordained to ministry Bapt. Ch.; head dept. religion and philosophy Ottawa U., 1949-54; pastor First Bapt. Ch., Ottawa, 1954-59, First Bapt. Ch., Sioux Falls, S.D., 1959—; v.p. Am. Bapt. Conv., 1960-61, pres. bd. edn. and publs.,

1961-62, chmn., 1963-70, pres., 1970-71. Trustee Sioux Falls Coll., Central Bapt. Theol. Sem. Recipient Distinguished Service award U.S. C. of C., 1955. Mem. Sioux Falls Ministerial Assn. (pres. 1964-65). Author: It Costs Your Life. Home: 1516 S Park Av Sioux Falls SD 57105 Office: First Baptist Ch Sioux Falls SD 57104

FREE, JOSEPH PAUL, educator, archeologist; b. Cleve., Oct. 11, 1911; s. Joseph LaVerne and Enna Edith (Lamb) F.; A.B., Princeton, 1932, A.M., 1933, Ph.D., 1935; postgrad. student Oriental Inst. U. Chgo., 1940-48; m. Ruby Aldrich, Aug. 20, 1935; children—Alice Anita, David Paul. Asst. prof. archeology Wheaton Coll., 1935-40, asso. prof., 1940-43, prof. archeology, dir. archeol. studies, 1943-66, Fred McManis prof. archeology, 1955-67; staff Am. Sch. Oriental Research, excavating at Dibon in Arab Palestine, 1951, 52; dir. Wheaton archeol. expdn., excavating site of ancient Dothan in Arab Palestine, 1953-60, 62, 64—; exec. dir. Nr. E. Sch. Archaeology, Mt. of Olives, Jerusalem, Jordan, 1962—; archeol. editor Sunday School Times, 1942—; prof. archaeology and history Bemidji State Coll., Minn., 1966—. Member Soc. Bibl. Lit., Nat. Assn. Bible Instrs., Nat. Soc. Arts and Letters (nat. lit. chmn. 1966—). Author: Archeology and Bible History, rev. edit., 1969. Author articles on Bibl. archeology. Home: Freehaven Park Rapids, MN 56470.

FREE, RICHARD HENRY, army officer; b. Davenport, Ia., Jan. 8, 1914; s. Henry Rudolph and Anna (Eckhardt) F.; M.E., George Washington U., 1935; B.S. in Engring., U.S. Mil. Acad., 1940; M.S. in Engring., Cornell U., Ithaca, N.Y., 1948; grad. Indsl. Coll. Armed Forces, 1959; m. Margaret Elizabeth Hatke, July 20, 1940; children—Kendall R., Beth Ann (Mrs. Daniel V. James, Jr.), Noel K., Susan Lee (Mrs. John T. Ward), Holly Margaret. Commd. 2d lt. U.S. Army, 1940, advanced through grades to maj. gen., 1967; combat engr. comdr. 26th Inf. Div., World War II; assigned Manhattan Project, 1946-47; spl. weapons group comdr. Armed Forces Spl. Weapons Project, 1949-52; combat engr. group comdr., Korea, 1952-53; assigned Army Staff, Japan, 1953-55; exec. sec. mil. liaison com. to AEC, 1955-58; mem. logistics staff Supreme Hdqrs. Allied Powers, Europe, 1959-60, exec. to supreme allied comdr., 1961-62; army dist. engr., Norfolk, Va., 1962-64; engr. Southwestern div., Dallas, 1964-66, U.S. Army Engr. Div. S. Atlantic, Atlanta, 1969—; dir. research, devel. and engring. Hdqrs. Army Material Command, 1966-69. Decorated D.S.M., Silver Star medal, Legion of Merit with oak leaf cluster, Bronze Star medal, Purple Heart; officer Order of Crown with palms, Croix de Guerre with palms (Belgium); War Cross (Czechoslavakia); The Pacificator (Brazil). Registered profl. engr., D.C., Tex. Mem. Assn. U.S. Army, Am. Soc. Mil. Engrs. Rotarian. Home: 15-W Wheeler Dr Fort McPherson GA 30330 Office: 30 Pryor St S W Atlanta GA 30303

FREEBAIRN-SMITH, THOMAS, TV exec.; b. Walton, Surrey, Eng., Nov. 5, 1900; s. Thomas and Theresa (Rees) F.; student Kings Coll., Cambridge U., 1918-20; m. Mary Elizabeth Peers, Jan. 20, 1929; children—Ian Peers, Roderick Thomas. Came to U.S., 1924, naturalized, 1945. Purser, Brit. Mcht. Marine, 1922-26; radio pioneer sta. KGW, Portland, Ore., 1926-29; announcer, writer radio sta. KEX, 1929; chief announcer radio sta. KJR, Seattle, 1929-32; chief announcer, dir. KNX-CBS, Hollywood, Cal., 1933-37; radio dir. Ruthrauff & Ryan, 1937-43, Foote, Cone & Belding, 1944-47; program dir. KFWB, 1947- 50; TV operations mgr., program dir. WCAU-TV, Phila., 1950-52; exec. dir. Nat. Acad. TV Arts and Scis., 1952—. Served as piper London Scottish bn., Brit. Army, 1916-18. Recipient Sylvania TV award, 1952; citation as best announcer Am. Acad. Arts and Letters, 1933. Mem. Episcopal Theatre Guild (pres. 1955), British United Services Club (pres. 1943). Episcopalian. Club: Hollywood Cricket (pres. 1957, 65). Home: Sherman Oaks CA 91413 Office: 7188 Sunset Blvd Los Angeles CA 90046

FREEBURNE, CECIL MAX, educator; b. Sublette, Kan.; Aug. 19, 1918; s. Cecil Stanley and Beatrice Montez (McCollum) F.; B.S. in Edn., Emporia (Kan.) State Tchrs. Coll., 1940; M.A., State U. Ia., 1941, Ph.D., 1948; m. Edna Louise Fleming, Aug. 10, 1941; children—Anne-Kathleen, Brian Craig. Profl. musician full time, 1936-41, part-time, 1941-58; prin., band instr., Andrew, Ia., 1941-42; supr. instrumental music, Washburn, Wis., 1942; teaching asst. psychology State U. Ia., 1946-48; mem. faculty Bowling Green State U., 1948—, prof. psychology, 1961—, chmn. dept., 1960-64; lectr. Ohio Acad. of Sci. Vis. Scientist Program. Served with USAAF, 1942-46. Mem. Philosophy Sci. Assn., Am. Assn. of U. Profs., Am., Midwestern, Ohio psychol. assns., Sigma Xi, Psi Chi, Phi Kappa Tau. Contbr. articles profl. jours. Home: 14217 Wintergarden Rd Bowling Green OH 43402

FREED, ARTHUR, motion picture producer, composer; b. Charleston, S.C., Sept. 9, 1894; s. Max and Rose (Grossman) F.; grad. Phillips Exeter Acad., 1914; m. Renee Klein, Mar. 14, 1923; 1 dau., Barbara (Mrs. Marvin Saltzman). Producer motion pictures, 1938—, including Meet Me in St. Louis, 1944, Easter Parade, 1948, On the Town, 1949, Annie Get Your Gun, 1950, Show Boat, 1951, An American in Paris, 1951, Singin' in the Rain, 1952, The Band Wagon, 1953, Brigadoon, 1954, It's Always Fair Weather, 1955, Kismet, 1955, Silk Stockings, 1957, Gigi (Acad. award best motion picture, SPG award best theatrical film, Photoplay award most popular picture of yr., Hollywood Fgn. Press award best musical, Downbeat award best musical motion picture), 1958, Bells Are Ringing, 1960, Subterreans, 1960, Light in the Piazza, 1962. Decorated chevalier Legion of Honor (France); recipient Acad. award best motion picture of 1951, An American in Paris; Irving Thalberg Meml. award, 1951; award for superlative and distinguished service to the acad. Acad. Motion Picture Arts and Scis., 1968. Mem. Royal Hort. Soc. (Eng.), A.S.C.A.P., Am. Orchid Soc., Acad. Motion Picture Arts and Scis. (pres. 1963-67). Composer: Temptation, Wedding of the Painted Doll, Broadway Melody, Pagan Love Song, Singin' in the Rain, I Cried for You, Fit as a Fiddle, This Heart of Mine, Coffee Time. Home: 634 Stone Canyon Los Angeles CA 90024 Office: care Metro-Goldwyn-Mayer Studio Culver City CA 90230

FREED, BERT, actor; b. N.Y.C., Nov. 3, 1919; s. Ely and Hannah (Fried) F.; B.S., Pa. State U., 1940; m. Nancy Lee Waring, Feb. 12, 1956; children—Carl Robert, Jennifer. Broadway debut Johnny 2X4, 1942; subsequent appearances include counterattack, One Touch of Venus, Day Before Spring, Joy to the World, Annie Get Your Gun, Paths of Glory, Halls of Montezuma, Wild in the Streets, There Was a Crooked Man, In The Matter of J. Robert Oppenheimer, Pres. Brentwood Democratic Club, 1968-69. Mem. Acad. Motion Picture Arts and Scis. (mem. com. fgn. films 1968—), Screen Acctors Guild (dir. 1970—). Jewish religion (dir. temple). Home: 418 N Bowling Green Way Los Angeles CA 90049 Office: Jack Fields and Assos 9255 Sunset Blvd Los Angeles CA 90069

FREED, FRED, TV news producer; b. Portland, Ore., Aug. 25, 1920; s. Edgar and Elise (Oberdorfer) F.; B.A., Princeton, 1941; children—Lisa, Kayce. With Esquire mag., 1946-48, CBS, 1948-56, 57-61; with NBC, 1956-57, 61—, exec. producer NBC News, 1961—. Served USNR, 1942-46. Recipient Emmy awards, 1963-64, 65-66, 67-68, 70-71, Peabody award, 1966, 70; Dupont Columbia award, 1969-70. Author: (with Len Giovannitti) The Decision to Drop the Bomb, 1965. Home: 120 E 62d St New York City NY 10021 Office: NBC 30 Rockefeller Plaza New York City NY 10020

FREED, HIRSH, lawyer; b. Fitchburg, Mass., Jan. 13, 1910; s. Meyer and Esther Rose (Skolnick) F.; A.B. cum laude, Harvard, 1930, LL.B., 1936; m. Rosalind Bloom, June 17, 1934; children—Justin Michael, Kenneth Lawrence. Admitted to Mass. bar, 1936; asst. corp. counsel, Boston, 1939-45; commnr. Mass. Dept. Pub. Utilities, 1946-47; partner firm Brown, Rudnick, Freed & Gesmer, 1948—. Mem. examining com. Boston Pub. Library, 1953-54; mem. Boston com. Am. Jewish Tercentenary; mem. Harvard 1930 Class Com.; sec., counsel 25th reunion com., 1955, class agt., 1970—. Trustee Combined Jewish Philanthropies, Boston. Mem. Mass., Boston bar assns., Phi Beta Kappa, Kappa Nu. Democrat. Jewish religion (bd. dirs. temple). Mem. B'nai B'rith. Club: Belmont (Mass.) Country. Home: 111 Perkins St Jamaica Plain MA 02130 Office: 85 Devonshire St Boston MA 02109

FREED, VIRGIL HAVEN, educator; b. Mendota, Ill., Nov. 18, 1919; s. Jay R. and Olive (Edgell) F.; B.S., Ore. State U., 1943, M.S., 1948; Ph.D., U. Ore., 1959; m. Anna May Carlson, Jan. 30, 1944; children—Kathleen, John, Linda, David. Asst. prof. agrl. chemistry and farm crops Ore. State U., Corvallis, 1944-48, asso. prof., 1948-54, asso. prof. chemistry, 1954-59, prof., 1960—, head agrl. chemistry dept., 1961—; mem. environmental health tng. com. USPHS, 1965-68; lectr. Dupont Seminar Series and Gordon Conf. Mem. Sch. Bd., Corvallis, 1964—. Bd. dirs. Community Coll. Fellow A.A.A.S., Am. Inst. Chemists (N.W. Scientist award 1971), Soc. of Toxicology, Am. Soc. Biol. Chemists, Am. Sci. Affiliation; mem. Am. Chem. Soc. (chmn. symposium), Weed Soc. Am., Sigma Xi, Alpha Zeta, Phi Sigma, Phi Lambda Upsilon. Baptist. Kiwanian. Home: 11 Edgewood Way Corvallis OR 97330

FREEDBERG, A. STONE, physician; b. Salem, Mass., May 30, 1908; s. Hyman and Rachel Leah (Freedberg) F.; A.B., Harvard, 1929; M.D., U. Chgo., 1935; m. Beatrice Gordon, Aug. 29, 1935; children—Richard Gordon, Leonard Earl. Intern Mt. Sinai Hosp., Chgo., 1934-35, Mass. Meml. Hosp., Boston, summer 1935; resident Cook County Hosp., Chgo., 1935-36; house officer pathology R.I. Hosp., 1936-37; practice medicine, specializing in internal medicine, Boston, 1946—; asst. in medicine Beth Israel Hosp., 1938-40, jr. vis. physician, 1940-46, asso. in med. research, 1940-50, asso. vis. physician, 1946-48, vis. physician, 1949-63, asso. dir. med. research, 1950-63, sr. Ziskind fellow, 1956, physician, 1964—, dir. cardiology unit, 1964—; research fellow medicine Med. Sch. Harvard, 1941-42, asst. in medicine, 1942-46, instr. medicine, 1946-47, asso. in medicine, 1947-50, asst. prof., 1950- 57, asso. prof., 1958-69, prof., 1969—, adminstrv. bd. faculty medicine, 1958-62; cons., com. mem. med. div. Oak Ridge Inst. Nuclear Studies, 1955-56; spl. cons. metabolism study sect. USPHS, 1956-60; mem. sr. cons. staff Nuclear Medicine Inst., 1966-67; Guggenheim fellow Oxford U., 1967-68. Diplomate Am. Bd. Internal Medicine (cardiology). Fellow Am. Heart Assn. (bd. dirs.; mem. council clin. cardiology); mem. Mass. Heart Assn. (dir., past pres., com. chmn.), Am. Thyroid Assn. (v.p.); Mass., Charles River Dist. med. socs., Am. Soc. Clin. Investigation, Am. Physiol. Soc., Assn. Am. Physicians, Royal Soc. Medicine (London), New Eng. Cardiovascular Soc. (pres. 1971-72). Mem. editorial bd. Circulation, 1956-60, 62-67. Contbr. articles profl. jours. Home: 111 Perkins St Jamaica Plain Boston MA 02130 Office: 330 Brookline Av Boston MA 02215

FREEDBERG, SYDNEY JOSEPH, educator; b. Boston, Nov. 11, 1914; s. Samuel and Lillian (Michelson) F.; A.B. summa cum laude, Harvard, 1936, A.M. 1939, Ph.D., 1940; m. Anne Blake, Jan. 15, 1942 (div. 1950); 1 son, William Blake; m. 2d, Susan Pulitzer, April 10, 1954 (dec. June 1965); children—Kate Pulitzer, Nathaniel Davis; m. 3d, Catherine Blanton, June 24, 1967. Mem. faculty of Harvard, 1938-40, 53—, prof. fine arts, 1960—, chmn. dept., 1959-63; asst. prof. art, then asso. prof. Wellesley Coll., 1946-54; vis. lectr. Inst. Modern Art, Boston, 1947; spl. research 16th Century Italian art. Vice chmn. Nat. Exec. Com. Rescue Italian Art. Served to maj. AUS, 1942-46. Guggenheim fellow, 1949- 50, 54-55; fellow Am. Council Learned Socs., 1958-59, 66-67; recipient Faculty prize Harvard U. Press, 1961; Morey Book prize Coll. Art Assn., 1965; decorated Order Brit. Empire, Grand officer Order of Star of Italian Solidarity. Fellow Am. Acad. of Arts and Scis.; mem. Coll. Art Assn. (dir. 1962-66), Phi Beta Kappa. Author: Parmigianino, His Works in Painting, 1950; Painting of the High Renaissance, 1961; Andrea del Sarto, 1963; Painting in Italy, 1500-1600, 1971. Home: 5 Channing Pl Cambridge MA 02138

FREEDHEIM, EUGENE H., lawyer; b. Leadville, Colo., Mar. 16, 1900; s. Alfred A. and Carrie (Heitler) F.; A.B., U. Colo., 1921; LL.B., Harvard, 1924; m. Mina Koperlik, Mar. 2, 1927; children—Joan (Mrs. Laurence G. Kraus), Donald K., David E. Admitted to Ohio bar, 1925, since practiced in Cleve.; partner Hahn, Loeser, Freedheim, Dean & Wellman. Dir. Akro Corp., Wickman Corp., Work Wear Corp., Bobbie Brooks, Inc. Trustee Mt. Sinai Hosp. (Cleve.), Cleve. Community Chest, Welfare Fedn. Cleve., 1952- 57 (chmn. case work council 1949-50), Family Service Assn., 1953-62, Youth Bur., 1952-58, Jewish Community Fedn.; trustee Jewish Family Service Assn. Cleve., 1935-53, pres., 1945-49; pres. Family Service Assn. Am., 1957-59; dir. Nat. Council for Homemaker-Home Health Aide Services, 1965—, treas., 1969—, exec. com., 1967; mem. Lawyer's Com. for Civil Rights Under Law, 1966—, dir., 1967—; mem. nat. bd. Nat. Conf. Social Welfare, 1966-68; trustee Cleve. Playhouse; vis. com. Sch. Law, Western Reserve U., 1958-68. Recipient distinguished service award Cleve. Community Chest, 1956; Eisenman award Jewish Community Fedn., 1970. Fellow Am. Bar Found.; mem. Cleve. (pres. 1955-56), Am. (rep. to Nat. Conf. Lawyers and Social Workers 1961-70) bar assns., Am. Law Inst., Am. Arbitration Assn. (dir. 1965-69), Am. Bar Assn. Phi Beta Kappa Assos. (life mem.). Jewish religion. Clubs: Oakwood, City, Commerce (Cleve.). Home: 2925 Eaton Rd Shaker Heights OH 44120 Office: Nat City East 6th Bldg Cleveland OH 44114

FREEDMAN, ABRAHAM E., lawyer; b. Phila., Aug. 25, 1907; s. Barnett and Rebecca (Rowling) F.; LL.B., Temple U., 1933; m. Roz B. Schneider, June 15, 1930; children—Joan Phyllis (Mrs. Herbert C. Meyer), Barbara Dee (Mrs. A. G. Sassoon). From engr. to asst. sect. engr. transit dept. City Phila., 1925-32; admitted Pa. bar, 1933, N.Y. bar, 1964; practice in Phila., 1933—; sr. partner Freedman, Landy & Lorry, 1944—, successor firm Freedman, Borowsky & Lorry, 1964—. Mem. adv. com. Supreme Ct. U.S. on Admiralty Rules, 1960—, adv. com. on civil rules 1964—; permanent mem. 3d Jud. Conf.; lectr. Am. Law Inst., 1959, Practicing Law Inst., 1960. Fellow Am. Coll. Trial Lawyers, Internat. Acad. Trial Lawyers (past pres.); mem. Internat., Fed., Am., Pa., N.Y., Phila. bar assns., Am. Trial Lawyers Assn. (chmn. admiralty sect. 1950—), 4th Jud. Conf. Home: 413 Meadow Lane Merion PA 19066 Office: Lafayette Bldg Philadelphia PA 19106

FREEDMAN, ALFRED MORDECAI, physician; b. Albany, N.Y., Jan. 7, 1917; s. Jacob A. and Pauline (Hoffman) F.; A.B., Cornell U., 1937; M.B., U. Minn., 1941, M.D., 1942; m. Marcia Kohl, Mar. 24, 1943; children—Paul, Daniel. Intern Harlem Hosp., N.Y.C., 1941-42; resident psychiatry Bellevue Hosp., N.Y.C., 1948- 50; dir. psyhiatry Flower and Fifth Av. Hosps., 1960—, Met. and Bird S. Coler Hosps., 1960—; prof. psychiatry N.Y. Med. Coll., N.Y.C., 1960—, also chmn. dept. and dir. Community Mental Health Center, Met. Hosp., 1965—, bd. dirs. Walden Sch., N.Y.C., 1957-61; founding mem. bd. trustees Center Urban Edn., N.Y.C., 1965-70. Served to maj., M.C., AUS, 1942-46. Recipient Henry Wisner Miller award Manhattan Soc. Mental Health, 1964. Diplomate Am. Bd. Psychiatry and Neurology. Fellow Am. Orthopsychiat. Assn. (bd. dirs. 1962-64, mem. editorial bd. jour. 1964—); mem. Am. Acad. Child Psychiatry, N.Y. Acad. Medicine, Am. Psychopathol. Assn. (pres. 1971), Collegium Internat. Neuro-Psychopharmacologicum, Am. Coll. Neuro-Psychopharmacology (pres. elect 1971), Am. Psychiat Assn., N.Y. Soc. Clin. Psychiatry (pres. 1967), Anthros Academy (treas.). Club: Cornell of New York. Author: (with H. I. Kaplan), Comprehensive Textbook of Psychiatry, 1967; (with J. Zabin) Psychopathology of Adolescence; also articles. Home: 161 W 86th St New York City NY 10024 Office: 5 E 102d St New York City NY 10029

FREEDMAN, BENEDICT, writer; b. New York, N.Y., Dec. 19, 1919; s. David and Beatrice (Goodman) F.; student of Columbia, 1934-37; Curtiss-Wright Tech. Inst., Glendale, Calif.; m. Nancy Mars, June 29, 1941; children—Johanna, Michale Hartley, Deborah. Writer for Al Jolson radio program and M.G.M. studios, 1939; comedy writer for Red Skelton radio show since 1941; instr. Curtiss-Wright Tech. Inst., Glendale Cal., 1942-43; lectr. math., chmn. gen. studies program Occidental Coll. Author: (with Nancy Freedman) Back to The Sea, Viking (novelette), 1942; Mrs. Mike (selection of The Literary Guild), 1947; This and No More, 1950; The Spark and The Exodus, 1954; Lootville, 1957; Tresa, 1959, The Apprentice Bastard, 1967, Cyclone of Silence, 1969. Address: 315 Via de la Paz Pacific Palisades CA 90272

FREEDMAN, BETTY L., advt. exec.; b. N.Y.C., Sept. 18, 1930; d. Jack and Ruth (Fleischer) Freedman; B.S. in Edn., City Coll. N.Y., 1951; M.A. in English Lit., 1953; m. Albert Barsom, June 25, 1968; children—Joseph R. Schwartz, Alexandra L. Schwartz. Copy supr. Foote, Cone & Belding, 1966-68; v.p., copy group head Kenyon & Eckhardt, 1968-69; v.p., creative dir. Grey Advt., N.Y.C., 1969—. Mem. Copy Club N.Y., Fashion Group. Home: 165 West End Av New York City NY 10023 Office: 777 3d Av New York City NY 10023

FREEDMAN, DANIEL X., educator, psychiatrist; b. Lafayette, Ind., Aug. 17, 1921; s. Harry and Sophia (Feinstein) F.; B.A., Harvard, 1947; M.D., Yale, 1951; grad. Western New Eng. Inst. Psychoanalysis, 1966; m. Mary C. Neidigh, Mar. 20, 1945. Intern pediatrics Yale Hosp., 1951-52, resident psychiatry, 1952-55; from instr. to prof. psychiatry Yale; chmn. dept. U. Chgo., 1966—, Louis Bloch prof. biol. scis.; 1969—; career investigator USPHS, 1957-66; dir. psychiatry and biol. sci. tng. program Yale, 1960-66; cons. Nat. Inst. Mental Health, 1960—, U.S. Army Chem. Center, Edgewood, Md., 1965-66. Chmn. panel psychiat. drug efficacy study Nat. Acad. Sci.-NRC, 1966; mem. adv. com. FDA, 1967—. Dir. Founds. Fund for Research in Psychiatry, 1969—. Served with AUS, 1942-46. Fellow Am. Psychiat. Assn. (pres. New Haven-Middlesex chpt. 1965-66, counselor Conn. br. 1963-64), Am. Coll. Neuropsychopharmacology (pres. 1970—); mem. Ill. Psychiat. Soc. (pres. 1971-72), Social Sci. Research Council (dir. 1968-69), Chgo. Psychoanalytic Soc., Western New Eng. Psychoanalytic Inst., Am. Soc. Pharmacology and Exptl. Therapeutics, A.A.A.S., Am. Psychopathol. Assn., Group Advancement Psychiatry, Psychiat. Research Soc., Am. Pub. Health Assn., Am. Psychosomatic Soc., Soc. Biol. Psychiatry, Sigma Xi, Alpha Omega Alpha. Author: (with N.J. Giarman) Biochemical Pharmacology of Psychotomimetic Drugs, 1965; (with F. C. Redlich) The Theory and Practice of Psychiatry, 1966. Home: 4950 S Chicago Beach Dr Chicago IL 60615 Office: 950 E 59th St Chicago IL 60637

FREEDMAN, DAVID NOEL, educator; b. N.Y.C., May 12, 1922; s. David and Beatrice (Goodman) F.; student Coll. City N.Y., 1935-38; A.B., U. Cal. at Los Angeles, 1939; Th.B., Princeton Theol. Sem., 1944; Ph.D., Johns Hopkins, 1948; m. Cornelia Anne Pryor, May 16, 1944; children—Meredith Anne, Nadezhda, David, Jonathan. Ordained to ministry Presbyn. Ch., 1944; supply pastor in Acme and Deming, Wash., 1944-45; teaching fellow, then asst. instr. Johns Hopkins, 1946-48; asst. prof., then prof. Hebrew and O.T. lit. Western Theol. Sem., Pitts., 1948-60; prof. Hebrew and O.T. lit., Pitts. Theol. Sem., 1960-61, James A. Kelso prof., 1961-64; prof. O.T., San Francisco Theol. Sem., 1964-70, Gray prof. Hebrew exegesis, 1970-71, dean of faculty, 1967-70, acting dean of sem., 1970-71; prof. O.T., Grad. Theol. Union, Berkeley, Cal., 1964- 71; prof. dept. Nr. Eastern langs. U. Mich., 1971—. Danforth vis. prof. Internat. Christian U., Tokyo, Japan, 1967; dir. Am. Sch. of Oriental Research, Jerusalem, 1969-70. Recipient prize in N.T. exegesis Princeton Theol. Sem., 1943, William H. Green fellow O.T., 1944; William S. Rayner fellow Johns Hopkins, 1946, 47; Guggenheim fellow, 1959; fellow Am. Assn. Theol. Schs., 1963; Am. Council of Learned Socs. grant-in-aid, 1967. Mem. Soc. Bib. Lit., Am. Oriental Soc., Am. Schs. Oriental Research, Bib. Colloquium. Author: (with J. D. Smart) God Has Spoken, 1949; (with F. M. Cross, Jr.) Early Hebrew Orthography, 1952; (with John M. Allegro) The People of the Dead Sea Scrolls, 1958; (with R. M. Grant) The Secret Sayings of Jesus, 1960; (with F. M. Cross, Jr.) Ancient Yahwistic Poetry, 1964; (with M. Dothan) Ashdod I, 1967. Editor: (with G. E. Wright) The Biblical Archaeologist, 1961; (with E. F. Campbell, Jr.) The Biblical Archaeologist Reader 2, 1964, The Biblical Archaeologist Reader 3, 1970; (with W. F. Albright) The Anchor Bible, 1964—, including Genesis, 1964, James, Peter and Jude, 1964, Jeremiah, 1965, Job, 1965, Proverbs and Ecclesiastes, 1965, I Chronicles, II Chronicles, Ezra-Nehemiah, 1965, Psalms I, 1966, John I, 1966, Acts of the Apostles, 1967, II Isaiah, 1968, Psalms II, 1968, John II, 1970, Psalms III, 1970, Esther, 1971, Matthew, 1971, Ephesians, 1971; (with J. Greenfield) New Direction in Biblical Archaelogy, 1969. Asso. editor of Jour. Bib. Lit., 1952-54, editor, 1955-59; cons. editor Interpreter's Dictionary of the Bible, 1957-60. Contbr. numerous articles profl. jours. Home: 120 Seminary Rd San Anselmo, CA 94960. Office: 2 Kensington Rd San Anselmo CA 94960

FREEDMAN, ELISHA CHAIM, city ofcl.; b. Hartford, Conn., Aug. 12, 1926; s. Joseph D. and Dorothea (Simons) F.; student U. Conn., 1946-48, Trinity Coll., summer 1947; A.B. cum laude, Syracuse U., 1949, M.P.A., 1955; m. Adeline Kaufman, Feb. 11, 1951; children—Jonathan, Noah, Jeremy, Anne. With Hartford Redevel. Agy., 1952-53, Fed. Rent Control Office, Hartford, 1951-52, Conn. Employees Assn. 1951; supr. budget and research, Hartford, 1955-59, exec. sec. to city mgr., 1959-63, city mgr., 1963-71; chief adminstrv. officer Montgomery County, Md., 1971—; town controller, Manchester, Conn., 1959. Mem. Conn. Temporary Commn. Study Municipal Collective Bargaining, 1964-65, Conn. Planning Com. Criminal Adminstrn., 1968—. Recipient Louis Brownlow award for outstanding contbrn. to lit. of pub. adminstrn., 1967. Mem. Am. Soc. Pub. Adminstrn. (pres. Conn. 1967), Internat. City Mgmt. Assn. (pres. Conn. 1969; chmn. Task Force on Sense of Community Mng. for Neighborhood Identity 1970). Home: 258 Kenyon St Hartford CT 06105 Office: County Office Bldg Rockville MD

FREEDMAN, FRANK HARLAN, mayor; b. Springfield, Mass., Dec. 15, 1924; s. Alvin Samuel and Ida (Rosenberg) F.; student Springfield Coll., 1942-43, Trinity Coll., 1943- 44; LL.B., Boston U., 1949, LL.M., 1950; LL.D., Western New Eng. Coll., 1970; m. Eleanor

Edith Labinger, July 26, 1953; children—Joan Robin, Wendy Beth, Barry Alan. Admitted to Mass. bar, 1950; councillor-at-large, Springfield, 1962-67, councilman, 1960-61; asst. atty. gen. Mass., 1963-67; mayor of Springfield, 1968—. Chmn. Muscular Dystrophy county drive, 1962; chmn. Leukemia drive, 1970. Del. Republican Nat. Conv., 1964, 68. Bd. dirs. Susan Auchter Meml., 1966-67. Served to lt. U.S. Navy, 1943-46. Mem. Hampden County Bar Assn., Jewish War Vets., Lewis Marshall Club Jurisprudence (pres. 1963). Jewish religion. Elk; mem. B'nai B'rith. Home: 9 Normandy Rd Springfield, MA 01106. Office: 1421 Main St Springfield MA 01103

FREEDMAN, MRS. ISIDOR, organization exec.; b. New York City, Feb. 9, 1888; d. Max I. and Lina (Klein) Lefkowitz; ed. pub. schs., New York City; m. Isidor Freedman, Mar. 27, 1906; children—Milton, Linore (Mrs. Jess Ward), Harriett (Mrs. Carl Marcus), David. Became a charter mem. and a founder of the Women's branch Union of Orthodox Jewish Congregations Am. and Can. (nat. vice pres., 1924-38, pres. 1938-46, hon. nat. pres. since 1946); a founder Hebrew Teachers Training Sch. for Girls, 1928 (recording sec. since 1928), mem. Nat. Jewish Welfare Bd. since 1941 (chmn. religious activities com. of Greater N.Y. Army and Navy com. since 1941, mem. exec. com. of women's div. since 1941); vice chmn. Jewish Council for Russian War Relief, 1942-47; mem. nat. steering com. and nat. exec. bd. Supplies for Overseas Survivors Collection (mem. national council, Joint Distbn. Com. since 1946); delegate to First World Congress for Hebrew Literature and Culture, Jerusalem, Israel, 1950; v.p. Fedn. Jewish Women's Organizations, Inc.; Sisterhood of Congregation of the Path of Life, since 1936; recording sec. Jewish Braille Inst. of America; member Nat. Conf. Jews and Christians, Nat. Council of Jewish Women. Permanent del. to Am.-Jewish Conf. since 1944; del. 1st World Conf. Ashkenasi and Sephardic Synagogue Jews, Jerusalem, January, 1968; member organizing com. U.S.O. Canteen, Temple Emanu-El World War War II. Recipient citations, Nat. Jewish Welfare Bd., U.S. Treasury Dept. (for furthering sale of bonds through affiliated groups of Women's Br., Union of Orthodox Jewish Congregations of Am.), Hebrew Teachers Training Sch. for Girls, Council for Russian War Relief, Women's Br. Union of Orthodox Jewish Congregations of Am. Financial sec. League for Safeguarding the Fixity of the Sabbath, since 1930. Home: 115 W 86th St New York City NY 10024

FREEDMAN, LEON DAVID, educator; b. Balt., July 19, 1921; s. Samuel and Jennie (Greenberg) F.; A.B., Johns Hopkins, 1941, M.A., 1947, Ph.D., 1949; m. Myrle Florence Neistadt, June 23, 1945; children—Carl Howard, Jean Rose. Analytical chemist USPHS, 1941-44; organic chemist USPHS, 1949-61; asso. prof. chemistry N.C. State U., Raleigh, 1961-65, prof., 1965—; dir. Organic Electronic Spectral Data, Inc. Served with USNR, 1944-46. Fellow A.A.A.S.; mem. Am. Chem. Soc., Phi Beta Kappa, Sigma Xi, Phi Lambda Upsilon. Author: (with George O. Doak) Organometallic Compounds of Arsenic, Antimony and Bismuth, 1970. Editor: (with J.P. Phillips, J.C. Craig) Organic Electronic Spectral Data, vol. VI, 1970. Home: 2006 Myron Dr Raleigh NC 27607

FREEDMAN, MAX, columnist Daily News Washington, 1962—. Recipient Internat. Freedom award, Internat. Freedom Festival, Windsor, Ont. Address: 1642 29th St Washington DC 20007*

FREEDMAN, MERVIN BURTON, psychologist, educator; b. N.Y.C., Mar. 6, 1920; s. Eli and Rose (Weithorn) F.; B.S., Coll. City N.Y., 1940; Ph.D., U. Cal. at Berkeley, 1950; m. Marjorie Ellingson, Feb. 16, 1952; children—Eric, Kristin, Rolf, Anne Marie. Lectr. dept. psychology U. Cal. at Berkeley, 1950-53; research asso. Mellon Found. for Advancement Edn., Vassar Coll., 1953- 58; dir. Mellon Found., 1958-60; research asso. Inst. for Study Human Problems, Stanford, 1962-63, asst. dean undergrad. edn., 1963-65; chmn. dept. psychology San Francisco State Coll., 1965-68, Prof. psychology, 1968—; dean grad. div. Wright Inst., Berkeley, 1969—; sr. Fulbright research scholar U. Oslo, 1961-62; fellow Center for Advanced Study Behavioral Sci., 1960-61; higher edn. editor Jossey-Boss Pub. Co. Vice pres. San Francisco Am.-Scandinavian Found. Served with AUS, 1941-45. Decorated Bronze Star. Fellow Am. Psychol. Assn.; mem. Western Cal. psychol. assns. Author: The College Experience, 1967; (with others) Search for Relevance, 1969. Home: 866 Spruce St Berkeley CA 94707 Office: Wright Inst 2728 Durant Av Berkeley CA 94704

FREEDMAN, MONROE HENRY, educator, lawyer; b. Mt. Vernon, N.Y., Apr. 10, 1928; s. Chauncey and Dorothea (Kornblum) F.; A.B. cum laude, Harvard, 1951, LL.B., 1954, LL.M. (Faculty fellow), 1956; m. Audrey Willock, Sept. 24, 1950; children—Alice Beth, Sarah Martha Louise, Caleb Reuben, Judah Elijah. Admitted to Mass. bar, 1954, Pa. bar, 1957, D.C. bar, 1960, also U.S. Supreme Ct., Ct. of Claims, ICC; faculty asst. Harvard Law Sch., 1954-56; asso. firm Wolf, Block, Schorr & Solis-Cohen, Phila., 1956-58; prof. law Nat. Law Center, George Washington U., 1958—; partner Freedman & Temple, Washington, 1968—; legislative cons. to Senator McClellan, 1959; cons. U.S. Commn. Civil Rights, 1960-64, Ednl. Testing Service, 1954-68, Neighborhood Legal Services Project, 1970; dir. Stern Community Law Firm, Washington, 1970-71; counsel in civil liberties cases, 1958—. Chmn. Am. Civil Liberties Union, Nat. Capitl area, 1965-66, mem. exec. bd. and litigation planning com., 1964—; chmn. com. on privacy, Am. Civil Liberties Union, 1966-67; mem. nat. adv. bd. Law Students Civil Rights Research Council, 1963—; co-dir. Criminal Trial Inst., Washington, 1965-66; founding mem. D.C. Lawyers' Com. (co-chmn. 1968—); radio commentator Cases and Controversies, Sta. WBAI, 1968-69. Mem. Am. Arbitration Assn. (mem. nat. panel, and nat. community disputes settlement panel), Am. (panel speaker on legal ethics), Fed. (chmn. com. on profl. disciplinary standards and procedures 1969-70), D.C. bar assns. Democrat. Jewish religion (trustee temple 1962-64). Author: Cases on Contracts, 1964, 2d edit., 1967; also articles. Home: 7723 Curtis St Chevy Chase MD 20015

FREEDMAN, NANCY MARS, writer; b. Evanston, Ill., July 4, 1920; d. Hartley Farnum and Brillie Jellet (Hintermeister) Mars; student Los Angeles City Coll., 1937-39; m. Benedict Freedman, June 29, 1941; children—Johanna, Michael Hartley, Deborah. Appeared in role of Grazia in Death Takes a Holiday; on tour in Max Reinhardt productions of The Miracle, Faust, and Six Characters in Search of An Author; summer stock in Main, Benedict and Nancy Freedman collection established Mugar Library, Boston U. Author: (with Benedict Freedman) Back to the Sea, Viking, 1942, Mrs. Mike, 1947, This and No More, 1950, The Spark and The Exodus, 1954, Lootville, 1957, Tresa, 1950, The Apprentice Bastard, 1967, Cyclone of Silence, 1969. Home: 4859 Stratford Rd Pacific Palisades CA 90042

FREEDMAN, PHILIP, educator, physician; b. London, Eng., June 25, 1926; s. Myer and Mildred (Frankel) F.; M.B., B.S., (honors) Univ. Coll. Hosp. Med. Sch., London, 1948, M.D., 1951; m. Jean Kennis Cunningham, Dec. 21, 1954; children—Simon John, Marion Rose, Mark Alexander, Paul Daniel, Adam James. House surgeon Univ. coll. Hosp., 1948; sr. house physician Chase Farm Hosp., 1949; med. registrar Univ. Coll. Hosp., 1953-56; research asst. professorial med. unit, 1956-57, Bilton Pollard fellow, 1957-59; 1st asst. physician St. George's Hosp., London, 1959-60; cons. to Woolwich Hosp. Group, London, also Redhill Hosp. Group, Surrey, Eng., 1960-63; came to U.S., 1963, naturalized, 1970; chief Chgo. Med. Sch. Service, Div. Medicine, also dir. renal unit Cook County Hosp., Chgo., 1963-66; chmn. dept. medicine Mt. Sinai Hosp. Med. Center, Chgo., 1966—, prof., chmn. dept. medicine Chgo. Med. Sch., 1967—. Mem. Ill. Inst. Health and Pub. Health Adv. Com. Served with M.C., Brit. Army, 1951-53. Fellow A.C.P.; mem. Am. Soc. Nephrology, Assn. Profs. Medicine, Chgo. Heart Assn. (bd. govs.), Brit. Soc. Immunology, Royal Coll. Physicians, Central Soc. Clin. Investigation, Inst. Medicine, Chgo., Internat. Soc. Nephrology, Med. Research Soc. London, Med. Soc. London, Soc. Med. History of Chgo., Soc. Exptl. Biology and Medicine, Sigma Xi, Alpha Omega Alpha (faculty mem.). Contbr. articles profl. jours. Home: 2808 Knollwood Lane Glenview IL 60025 Office: Mt Sinai Hosp 15th and California Av Chicago IL 60608

FREEDMAN, RONALD, educator; b. Winnipeg, Man., Can., Aug. 8, 1917; s. Isador and Ada (Greenstone) F.; came to U.S., 1924, naturalized 1920; B.A., U. Mich., 1939, M.A., 1940; Ph.D., U. Chgo., 1947; m. Deborah Gail Selin, May 4, 1941; children—Joseph Selin, Jane Ilene. Mem. faculty U. Mich., 1946—, prof. sociology, 1954—, research asso. Survey Research Center, 1954—, dir. Population Studies Center, 1962-67, 68—; co-dir. Taiwan Populations Studies Center, 1962-64; cons. to govt., 1962—. Mem. Tech. Adv. Com. 1970 Census of Population, 1965, Pres.'s Adv. Com. on Population and Family Planning. Dir. Beth Israel Center, Ann Arbor, 1950- 54. Served with USAAF, 1942-45. Recipient award excellence on teaching U. Mich. Class of 1952, Distinguished Faculty Service award U. Mich., 1970. Guggenheim fellow, 1957-58; Fulbright fellow, 1957-58; fellow Center for Advanced Study in Behavioral Scis., 1970. Mem. Population Assn. Am. (pres. 1964-65), Internat. Union Study Population (v.p. 1966—), Am. Sociol. Assn., Am. Statis. Assn., Asian Studies Assn., Sociol. Research Assn., Phi Beta Kappa. Author: The Sociology of Human Fertility, 1960; (with others) Family Planning, Sterility and Population Growth, 1959; (with others) Principles of Sociology, 1952; (with others) Family Planning in Taiwan, 1969; also articles and monographs. Home: 1404 Beechwood Rd Ann Arbor, MI 48103.

FREEDMAN, SAMUEL, judge; b. Russia, April 16, 1908; s. Nathan and Ada (Foxman) F.; migrated to Can., 1911; B.A. (hons.), U. Man., 1929; LL.B., Man. Law Sch., 1933; LL.D., U. Windsor, 1960, N.D. State U., 1965, U. Toronto, 1965, Hebrew U. Jerusalem, 1964, U. Man., 1968, Brock U., 1968, McGill Univ., 1968, Dalhousie U., 1971, Queen's U., 1969, York U., 1971; D.C.L., St. John's Coll., Winnipeg, 1967; m. Claris Brownie, June 29, 1934; children—Martin H., Susan R., Phyllis C. Called to Canadian bar, 1933; created Queen's counsel, 1944; mem. firm Steinkopf, Lawrence & Freedman, 1933-45, Freedman & Golden, 1946-52; judge Ct. of Queen's Bench of Man., 1952-60; judge Ct. of Appeal Man., 1960—, chief justice, 1971—; lectr. Man. Law Sch., 1941-59; chancellor U. Man., 1959-68. Pres. YMHA of Winnipeg, 1936-37, Winnipeg Lodge B'nai B'rith, 1943-44; chmn. Rhodes Scholarship Selection Com. Man., 1956-66; co-chmn. central div. Canadian Council Christians and Jews, 1955-58; chmn. Winnipeg chpt. Canadian Friends of Hebrew U., 1953-68. Trustee John W. Dafoe Found., 1955—; bd. govs. Hebrew U. Jerusalem, 1955—. Hon. pres. U. Man. Students Union, 1949-50; recipient Man of Year award Sigma Alpha Mu, 1957. Mem. Man. Bar Assn. (pres. 1952), Medico-Legal Soc. Man. (pres. 1954-55), Law Soc. Man. (bencher 1949-52). Home: 425 Cordova St Winnipeg 1 Manitoba Canada Office: Law Cts Winnipeg 1 Manitoba Canada

FREEDMAN, SELMA G., fgn. service officer; b. Washington, July 28, 1919; d. Joseph and Sara (Brown) Freedman; A.B., George Washington U., 1940; postgrad. Harvard, 1958-59. Formerly with OPA; economist Dept. State, 1945-55; mem. Fgn. Service, 1955—; 2d sec. Am. embassy, Ottawa, Can., 1950-61, Paris, France, 1965-69, with Dept. State, 1961-64; sr. seminar in Fgn. Policy, 1964-65; with Dept. State, 1969—. Office: Dept of State Washington DC 20525

FREEDMAN, SOLOMON, govt. ofcl.; b. Phila., Nov. 8, 1909; s. Jacob and Sarah (Zinman) F.; B.S., U. Pa., 1931, LL.B., 1934; m. Gladys Schwartz, Oct. 8, 1939; children-Jerrold F., David A., Sara E. Admitted to Pa. bar, 1935; practice in Phila., 1935-38; atty. Pa. Pub. Utility Commn., 1938-41; atty. div. pub. utilities SEC, 1942-52, asst. dir. div. corporate regulation, 1952-61, asso. dir., 1961-64, dir., 1964—. Home: 4501 Middleton Lane Bethesda MD 20014 Office: 500 N Capital St Washington DC 20549

FREEDMAN, STANLEY ARNOLD, lawyer; b. N.Y.C., Oct. 3, 1922; s. David A. and Ruth (Silverstein) F.; A.B., Harvard, 1942, LL.B., 1949; m. Martha Taintor Thomas, May 2, 1943; children—Ann, Lucy, David, Edith. Admitted to N.Y. bar, 1949, Ohio bar, 1959; practice in N.Y.C., 1949-58, Dayton, O., 1958—; partner firm Smith & Schnacke, 1961—. Served to 1st lt. USAAF, 1943-46. Decorated Air medal. Mem. Am., Ohio, Dayton bar assns., Assn. Bar City N.Y. Home: 1011 W Rahn Rd Dayton OH 45429 Office: 390 Talbott Tower Dayton OH 45402

FREEDMAN, WALTER S., retail co. exec.; b. N.Y.C., Sept. 13, 1925; s. Abraham and Florence (Sherman) F.; B.B.A., Coll. City N.Y., 1947; m. Jacqueline Mond, Sept. 7, 1947; 1 dau., Cathy. Sr. accountant Touche, Ross, Bailey & Smart, C.P.A.'s, N.Y.C., 1951-56; controller Alexander's, Inc., New York City, 1956-67, financial v.p., 1967—, also dir. C.P.A., N.Y. Mem. Met. Controllers Assn., Controllers Congress, N.Y. State Soc. C.P.A.'s, Nat. Retail Merchants Assn. Home: 200 E 57th St New York City NY 10022 Office: Alexander's Inc Lexington Av and 58th St New York City NY 10022

FREEHAFER, EDWARD GELER, former librarian; b. Reading Pa., Feb. 11, 1909; s. Edward Franklin and Martha Frances (Weitzel) F.; A.B., Brown U., 1930, L.H.D., 1955; B.S., Columbia Sch. Library Service, 1932; L.H.D., Hamilton Coll., 1970; m. E. Isabel Houck, July 7, 1934; 1 son, John Geier. Student asst. Columbia Sch. Bus. Library, 1931-32; reference asst. main reading room and econs. div. N.Y. Pub. Library, 1932-36, gen. asst., 1936-41, chief Am. history and genealogy div., 1941-44, acting chief acquisition div., 1942-44; asst. librarian Brown U. Library, 1944- 45; exec. asst. N.Y. Pub. Library, 1945-47; chief personnel office, 1947-53, chief reference dept., 1954, dir., 1954-70; ret. 1971. Mem. A.L.A., N.Y. Library Assn., Kappa Sigma. Clubs: Century Assn., N.Y. Library, Grolier, Brown (N.Y.C.). Home: 137 Corlies Av Pelham NY 10803

FREEHAFER, LYTLE JUSTIN, univ. adminstr.; b, Texhoma, Okla., Feb. 9, 1910; s. Franklin E. and Bertha (Krieg) F.; B.A. cum laude, De Pauw U., 1931; m. Ruth V. Ward, Oct. 14, 1933; children—Ann (Mrs. Donald K. Andersen), Lucy (Mrs. Richard T. Wold), John (dec.). Auditing, fiscal adminstrv. offices State of Ind., 1933-39, 47-48, dir. budget, 1949-52; asst. comptroller Purdue U., 1953, comptroller, asst. bus. mgr., 1954, bus. mgr., asst. treas., 1955-60, v.p., treas., 1961—; pres. Purdue Aero. Corp.; dir. Lafayette Life Ins. Co. Treas. Ind.- Purdue Found. of Ft. Wayne. Served from maj. to col., AUS, 1940-46. Recipient Good Govt. award Ind. Jr. C. of C., 1950. Mem. Midwestern Univs. Research Assn., Nat., Central assns. coll. and univ. bus. officers, Blue Key, Sigma Delta Chi, Lambda Chi Alpha, Omicron Delta Kappa. Methodist. Rotarian. Contbr. articles profl. jours. Home: 15 Hitching Post Rd West Lafayette IN 47906 Office: Purdue U Lafayette IN 47909

FREEHAN, BILL, catcher for Deteroit Tigers Profl. Baseball Team. Address: care Tiger Stadium, Detroit, MI 48216.*

FREEHLING, NORMAN, stockbroker; b. Chgo., Oct. 15, 1905; s. Isaac and Pearl (Eichberg) F.; A.B., U. Mich., 1927; J.D., Chgo. Kent Coll. of Law, 1932; m. Edna Wilhartz, Feb. 14, 1934; children—William W., Paul E. Mem. Chgo. Stock Exchange, 1927-49, Midwest Stock Exchange, 1949—; partner Norman Freehling & Co., 1936-47, Freehling, Meyerhoff & Co., 1947-63, Freehling & Co., 1963—. Formerly chmn. bd. govs. Midwest Stock Exchange. Clubs: Standard (Chgo.); Northmoor Country (past pres.) (Highland Park, Ill.). Home: 399 Fullerton Parkway Chicago, IL 60614. Office: 120 S LaSalle St Chicago IL 60603

FREEHLING, STANLEY MAXWELL, investment banker; b. Chgo., July 2, 1924; s. Julius and Juliette (Stricker) F.; student U. Chgo., 1942-43, Ind. U., 1943-44, U. Stockholm (Sweden), 1946-47; m. Joan Steif, Jan. 26, 1947; children—Elizabeth, Robert Stanley, Margaret J. With First Nat. Bank Chgo., 1947-52; partner Freehling & Co., mems. N.Y. Stock Exchange, Chgo., 1960—, Freehling Bros., real estate, Chgo., 1948—; dir. G.R.I. Corp., Republic Capital Corp., DPA, Inc., Dallas Compumatics, Inc., Chgo., Dukeland Packing Co., Balt. Mem. Ill. Pub. Employees Pension Laws Commn., 1962-66. Chmn. Ravinia Festival Assn., 1967—; pres. men's council Art Inst. of Chgo., 1962- 65, trustee, 1962-65; trustee Glenwood (Ill.) Sch. for Boys, 1967—, Highland Park (Ill.) Hosp., 1958—; mem. Chgo. citizen bd., mem. vis. com. to the humanities U. Chgo.; mem. Chgo. com., past treas. Council on Fgn. Relations; chmn. bd. Ill. Arts Council. Chmn. Ill. Arts Found.; bd. dirs. Research Found., Goodman Theatre; governing mem. Orchestral Assn., Art Inst. Chgo. Mem. Chgo. Assn. Stock Exchange Firms (bd. govs.). Clubs: Arts, Bond, (Chgo.); Lake Shore Country (Glencoe, Ill.); Mid-Day. Home: 121 Belle St Highland Park IL 60035 Office: 120 S LaSalle St Chicago IL 60603

FREEHLING, WILLIAM WILHARTZ, educator, historian; b. Chgo., Dec. 26, 1935; s. Norman and Edna (Wilhartz) F.; A.B., Harvard, 1958; M.A., U. Cal. at Berkeley, 1959, Ph.D., 1964; m. Natalie Paperno, Jan. 27, 1961 (div. Apr. 1970); children—Alan Jeffrey, Deborah Ann; m. 2d, Alison Goodyear, June 19, 1971. Woodrow Wilson fellow U. Cal. at Berkeley, 1961-63; instr. history Harvard, 1963-64; mem. faculty U. Mich. , 1964—, asso. prof. history, 1967-70, prof. history, 1970—. Nat. Humanities Found. fellow, 1968; Guggenheim fellow, 1970; recipient Allan Nevins History prize, 1965, Bancroft History prize, 1967. Mem. Am., So. hist. assns., Phi Beta Kappa. Author: Prelude to Civil War: The Nullification Controversy in South Carolina, 1816-1836, 1966. Home: 2555 Devonshire Rd Ann Arbor MI 48104

FREEHOF, SOLOMON BENNETT, rabbi; b. London, Eng., Aug. 9, 1892; s. Isaac and Golda (Blonstein) F.; naturalized U.S. citizen, 1916; A.B., U. of Cin., 1914; rabbi, D.D., Hebrew Union Coll., Cin., 1916, D.H.L., 1944; D.H.L., Jewish Inst. of Religion, 1945; m. Lillian Simon, Oct. 29, 1934. Prof. of rabbinics, Hebrew Union Coll., 1915-24; rabbi, K.A.M. Temple, Chgo., 1924-35, Rodef Shalom Temple, Pitts., since 1934. Chaplain, rank of 1st lt., A.E.F., World War I. Past pres. Central Conf. Am. Rabbis. Chmn. Comm. on Jewish Edn.; former chmn. div. religious activities Nat. Jewish Welfare Bd.; hon. life pres. World Union Progressive Judaism. Author books including: Preface to Scripture, 1950; Reform Jewish Practice, Vol. 2, 1952; The Book of JobA Commentary; Responsa Literature, 1955; Reform Responsa, 1960. Home: 128 N Craig St Pittsburgh PA 15213 Office: 4905 5th Av Pittsburgh PA 15213

FREELAND, H. THEODORE, securities co. exec.; b. Alexandria, Va., 1915. Formerly exec. v.p., now pres. Am. Securities Corp., N.Y.C., also dir. Home: Hamilton Rd Morristown NJ 07960 Office: 25 Broad St New York City NY 10004*

FREELING, NICOLAS, author: Strike out Where Not Applicable; This is the Castle; Because of the Cats; Criminal Conversation; Death in Amsterdam; Double Barrel; Dresden Green, King of the Rainy Country (Edgar Allan Poe award 1967); Question of Loyalty; Tsing-Boom. Address: Care Harper and Row Publication 1180 Av Americas New York City NY 10036*

FREEMAN, ALBERT CORNELIUS, Jr., actor; b. San Antonio, Mar. 21; s. Albert Cornelius and Lottie Brisette (Coleman) F.; student Los Angeles City Coll.; m. Sevara E. Clemon, Jan. 8, 1960. Actor various theatres in U.S., 1960—; appeared in The Long Dream, 1960, Kicks & Co., 1961, Tiger Tiger Burning Bright, 1962, The Living Premise, 1963, Trumpets of the Lord, 1963, Blues for Mister Charlie, 1964, Conversations at Midnight, 1964, The Slave, 1964, Dutchman, 1965, Measure for Measure, 1966, Camino Real, 1968, The Dozens, 1969, Look to the Lilies, 1970. Served with USAF. Named Outstanding Drama Student, Los Angeles City Coll., 1957; recipient Russwurm award, Golden Gate award; Emmy award nominee. Home and office: 10 W 66th St New York City NY 10023

FREEMAN, ALWYN VERNON, lawyer; b. Detroit, Dec. 11, 1910; s. Alexander and Sadie (Jacobs) F.; A.B. cum laude, U. Mich., 1930; LL.B., Harvard, 1933; Diplomé, inst. U. Hutes Etudes Internationales, 1938; Dr. es Sci. Politiques, U. Geneva, 1938; grad. study Hague Acad. Internat. Law (Carnegie fellow), 1934-35; m. Grenna Sloan, Nov. 7, 1948; 1 dau., Janne Sloan. Admitted to Mich. bar, 1934; with Asso. Press Bur., Geneva, Switzerland, 1935; counsel U.S. sect. U.S.-Mexico Agrarian Claims Commn., 1939-40; with U.S. Maritime Commn., 1941-42; asst. legal advisor Dept. State, 1946-47, legal counsel, 1951-53; cons. Foreign Relations Com., U.S. Senate, 1953-58 dep. rep. Internat. Atomic Energy Agy. at UN Hdqrs., 1958-62; U.S. agt. Jones Arbitration between Norway and U.S., 1952; lectr. internat. law Am. U., Washington, 1946-47; lectr., Academie de Droit Internat., Hague, 1955; asso. prof. Law Ohio State U., 1947-49; vis. prof. internat. law U. Cal. at Los Angeles Law Sch., 1960, U. Mich. Law Sch., 1963, Johns Hopkins Sch. Advanced Internat. Studies, 1965-68. Del. Am. Bar Assn. to 4th Inter-Am. Bar Conf., Santiago, Chile, 1945; mem. Am. delegation to Far Eastern Commn., 1946-47; Am. Del. Conf. Govt. Experts for Revision Geneva Conventions on Prisoners of War, 1947; apptd. by Pres. as U.S. mem. Inter-Am. Juridical Com., 1949-50; U.S. del. 1st meeting Inter-Am. Council Jurists, Rio de Janeiro, 1950; U.S. rep., chief delegation 4th Inter-American Council Jurists, Santiago, Chile, 1959; mem. adv. bd. Am. Law Inst. Restatement Fgn. Relations Law; mem. Harvard Law Sch. Adv. Com. for draft codification on responsibility of states; mem. U.S. delegation Xth General Assembly UN; Internat. Atomic Energy Agy. del. to UN Prep. Commn. Special Fund, to 13th to 16th Gen. Assemblies, UN; dir. research centre, Hague Acad. Internat. Law, 1957-58. Dir. Bank of the Commonwealth (Detroit), vice chmn. bd., 1964-65, U.S. mem. Canadian-Am. Lake Ontario Claims Arbitration Tribunal, 1966-68. Served as captain office Judge Adv. Gen., U.S. Army, 1942-46. Mem. Am., Mich. State bar assns., Am. Soc. Internat. Law (exec. council 1949-52, 56-59), Soc. Comparative Legislation Internat. Law. Order of the Coif. Mason. Clubs: Hillcrest Country (Beverly Hills); Racquet (Palm Springs); Harvard, Great Lakes (Detroit, Michigan); Cosmos (Washington, D.C.). Author of: The International Responsibility of States for Denial of Justice, 1938; Responsibility of States for Unlawful Acts of Their Armed Forces,

1956. Contbr. articles internat. law journals. Member of the bd. editors Am. Jour. Internat. Law. Office: Ford Bldg Detroit MI 48226 also Beverly Hills CA 90213

FREEMAN, BUD, See Freeman, Lawrence Bud.

FREEMAN, CLARENCE CALVIN, financial exec.; b. Lancaster, Pa., July 2, 1923; s. Clarence Calvin and Margaret (Hollinger) F.; A.B. cum laude, Franklin and Marshall Coll., 1951; m. B. Virginia Miller, Aug. 26, 1944; children—Margaret Ann, Elizabeth Ann, Martha Suzanne. Asst. bookkeeper Battery & Brake Service Co., Lancaster, 1941-42; supr. inventory records and receiving Armstrong Cork Co., Lancaster, 1946-48; accountant Internat. Latex Corp., Dover, Del., 1951-52; accountant Ebasco Services, Inc., Holtwood, Pa., 1952-53; office mgr., accountant A.O. Smith Corp., Leola, Pa., 1953-54; office mgr., plant accountant Sybron-Permutit div., Lancaster, 1954-57; div. controller BCA div. Fed. Mogul Corp., Lancaster, 1957-64; controller Fed. Mogul Corp., Southfield, Mich., 1964—; owner accounting service, 1953-64; owner Dairy Queen, 1956-60; lectr. Franklin and Marshall Coll., 1957-58, Wayne State Grad. Sch., 1966-67; guest speaker Nat. Assn. Accountants. Mem. Oakland County Planning Commn., 1967-68; adviser Jr. Achievement, 1957-58. Served with AUS, 1943-46; PTO. Mem. Nat. Assn. Accountants, Financial Execs. Inst., Phi Beta Kappa (v.p. Detroit), Pi Gamma Mu. Republican. Presbyn. (elder, deacon). Mason, Kiwanian, Elk. Home: 30865 Lincolnshire W Birmingham MI 48010 Office: Lahser Rd and Northwestern Hwy Southfield MI 48075

FREEMAN, DAVID HUGH, educator; b. Washington, Nov. 14, 1924; s. David and Grace (Kern) F.; B.A., Calvin Coll., 1947; M.A., U. Pa., 1952, Ph.D., 1958; m. Iren Klara Enyedi, July 26, 1950; children—Iren Grace, Diana B., John D. Chmn. dept. philosophy Wilson Coll., Chambersburg, Pa., 1952-57; prof. philosophy U. R.I., Kingston, 1957—, chmn. dept., 1957-58, 66—. Editor, Presbyn. Reformed Pub. Co., 1952—. Served with AUS, 1942-45. Decorated Purple Heart. Mem. Am. Philos. Assn., Metaphys. Soc. Author: Recent Studies in Philosophy and Theology, 1962; A Philosophical Study of Religion, 1964; Logic: The Art of Reasoning, 1967. Home: 136 Oakwood Dr Peace Dale RI 02879 Office: Dept Philosophy U R I Kingston RI 02881

FREEMAN, EDWARD, newspaper editor; b. Vanndale, Ark., Mar. 11, 1914; s. C. K. and Mary (Craig) F.; A.B., Murray State Coll., 1937; m. Lois Aline Farley, July 31, 1939; children—Edward Michael, Mary Elizabeth. Editor, Ledger & Times, Murray, Ky., 1937-40, Inland Empire News, Richland, Wash., 1940; reporter Nashville Tennessean, 1940-43, then city editor, now mng. editor. Served to lt. USNR, 1944-46. Mem. Sigma Delta Chi. Home: 4960 Stillwood Dr Nashville TN 37220 Office: 1100 Broadway St Nashville TN 37203

FREEMAN, FRANK SAMUEL, psychologist; b. St. Louis, Oct. 11, 1898; s. Isaac and Anna (Levine) F.; B.S., Harvard, 1920, Ed.D., 1926; m. Esther E. Worthington, June 19, 1928. Psychologist and dir. of edn., Mass. State Infirmary, Tewksbury, 1921-23; mem. faculty, Cornell, 1925-65, instr. in edn., 1925-28, asst. prof., 1928-35, prof. of edn., 1935-40, prof. of psychology, 1940- 65; vis. prof., U. Denver, summer, 1948, U. So. Cal., summer 1949, Ore. Coll. Edn., summer 1967; vis. prof. U. Hawaii, 1963-64; practicing psychologist since 1925. Ednl. cons. Bur. of Aeros., USN, 1942; cons. in psychology to several nat. ednl. socs. Mem. div. on human devel. Am. Council on Edn., U. Chgo., 1939-40; chmn. N.Y. State Bd. Examiners of Psychologists, 1956-60, mem. bd., 1960- 62. Mem. Am., N.Y. (v.p. 1934-45, exec. com. 1951-53, dir. 1956-57), Fla. psychol. assns. Author: Theory and Practice of Psychological Testing, 1950, 3d edit., 1962, others; also articles and book reviews. Home: 1414 N Lakes Shore Dr Sarasota FL 33579

FREEMAN, FRANKIE MUSE, (Mrs. Shelby T. Freeman, Jr.), lawyer; b. Danville, Va.; d. William B. and Maud B. (Smith) Muse; student Hampton Inst., 1933-36; LL.B., Howard U., 1947; m. Shelby T. Freeman; 1 dau., Shelbe Patricia. Admitted to D.C. bar, 1947, Mo. bar 1948; instr. bus. law Sampson Coll., 1947-48; gen. practice law, St. Louis, 1949-56; asst. atty. gen. Mo., 1955-56; asso. gen. counsel St. Louis Housing and Land Clearance Authorities, 1956—. Mem. Commrs. Commn. on Civil Rights. Bd. mgrs. Herbert Hoover Boys Club; bd. dirs. Human Devel. Corp. Met. St. Louis, Greater St. Louis council Girl Scouts U.S.A., Health and Welfare Council Met. St. Louis, Family and Childrens Service. Named outstanding citizen Mound City Press Club, 1953, woman of achievement Nat. Council Negro Women, 1956, woman of achievement in pub. affairs St. Louis Globe Democrat, 1965; recipient Centennial medallion Hampton Inst., May 1968. Mem. Am. Bar Assn., Lawyers Assn. St. Louis, Nat. Assn. Housing and Redevelopment Ofcls., Nat. Housing Conf., N.A.A.C.P., Nat. Council Negro Women, Delta Sigma Theta (nat. pres. 1967—). Baptist. Home: 5391 Waterman St Louis, MO 63112. Office: 1300 Delmar Blvd St Louis MO 63103

FREEMAN, FULTON, coll. pres.; b. Pasadena, Cal., May 7, 1915; s. Robert and Margery (Fulton) F.; student Lingnan U., 1934-35; A.B., Pomona College, 1937, LL.D., 1963; postgrad. Princeton, 1937- 38, Nat. War Coll., 1950-51; LL.D., Occidental Coll., 1966, Monmouth Coll., 1967; H.H.D., U. of Americas, Mexico City, Mexico, 1967; m. Phyllis Towne Eaton, Oct. 8, 1938; children—Margery Ellen, Carol, Jean. Apptd. fgn. service officer, vice consul, career sec. diplomatic service, 1939; vice consul, Mexico City, 1939; assigned Fgn. Service Sch., Dept. State, 1940; lang. officer, Peiping, China, 1940; interned Dec. 1941-June 42; spl. study U. Cal., 1942, 3d sec., Chungking, China, 1943, 2d sec., 1945; consul, Peiping, 1946; assigned Dept. State, asst. chief div. Chinese affairs, 1948; 1st sec., Rome, Italy, 1951-55; dir. politico-mil. affairs Hdqrs. Supreme Allied Comdr. Atlantic, Norfolk, Va., 1955-57; sr. fgn. service insp., 1957-58; dep. chief mission, Brussels, Belgium, 1959-61; U.S. ambassador to Colombia, 1961-64, Mexico, 1964-69; pres. Monterey (Cal.) Inst. Fgn. Studies, 1969—. Home: 25835 Rio Vista Dr Carmel CA 93921 Office: 425 Van Buren St Monterey CA 93940

FREEMAN, GAYLORD AUGUSTUS, Jr., banker; b. Chgo., Jan. 19, 1910; s. Gaylord A. and Pauline A. (Miser) F.; A.B., Dartmouth, 1931, LL.D., 1962; LL.B., Harvard, 1934; m. Frances Lee Tollerton, Dec. 23, 1931; children—Nancy Lee (Mrs. Norman Ellett), Linda Jane (Mrs. Richard Strubel), Clara. Admitted to Ill. bar., 1934; atty. First Nat. Bank of Chgo., 1940-50, v.p. corr. bank div., 1950-53, gen. v.p., 1953-60, pres., dir., 1960-62, vice chmn., from 1962, now chmn. bd., chief exec. officer, also dir.; chmn. 1st Chgo. Corp.; dir. Caterpillar Tractor Co., Clearing Indsl. District, Inc., Time, Inc., N.W. Industries, Inc., Borg-Warner Corp., Marcor, Inc. Trustee, Northwestern U.; bd. dirs. Aspen Inst. Humanistic Studies, Infant Welfare Soc.; trustee Com. Econ. Devel. Mem. Am., Ill., Chgo. bar assns. Conglist. Clubs: Chicago, Bankers, Mid-Day, Commercial, Mid-Am. (Chgo). Home: White Thorn Rd Wayne IL 60184 also 1040 Lake Shore Dr Chicago IL 60611 Office: 38 S Dearborn St Chicago IL 60603

FREEMAN, GEORGE CLEMON, Jr., lawyer; b. Birmingham, Ala., Jan. 3, 1929; s. George Clemon and Annie Laura (Gill) F.; B.A., Vanderbilt U., 1950; LL.B., Yale, 1956; m. Anne Colston Hobson, Dec. 6, 1958; children—Anne Colston, George Clemon III, Joseph Reid Anderson. Admitted to Ala. bar, 1956, Va. bar, 1958; law clk. Justice Hugo L. Black, U.S. Supreme Ct., 1956; practiced in Richmond, Va., 1957—; mem. firm Hunton, Williams, Gay, Powell & Gibson, 1957—, partner, 1963—. Pres. Va. chpt. Nature Conservancy, 1962-63; mem. Capitol Region Park Authority, Va., 1969-70. Chmn. Richmond City Democratic Com., 1969—. Sec., bd. dirs. Richmond Symphony, 1960-63, bd. dirs. Hand Work Shop, 1962—, Am. the Beautiful Fund of Natural Areas Council, 1967—. Served to lt. (j.g.) USNR, 1951-54. Mem. Am. (chmn. law library congress com. 1968—, chmn. trade assns. com. of corp., banking and bus. law sect. 1969—), Va., Richmond bar assns., Am. Law Inst., Am. Judicature Soc., Phi Beta Kappa, Phi Delta Phi, Omicron Delta Kappa, Alpha Tau Omega. Episcopalian. Clubs: Country of Virginia, Deep Run Hunt, 2300 (Richmond); Knickerbocker (N.Y.C.). Contbr. articles profl. jours. Home: 10 Paxton Rd Richmond, VA 23226. Office: 700 E Main St Richmond VA 23212

FREEMAN, GEORGE LESTER, assn. exec.; b. Detroit, Feb. 16, 1928; s. Jasper Wooten and Marie (Lester) F.; B.A., Vanderbilt U., 1951; m. Mary Grace Roderick, July 16, 1954; children—Thomas Lester, Helen Roderick, Martha. With So. Bell Telephone Co., Jacksonville, Ft. Lauderdale and Miami, Fla., 1952-68, asst. to v.p., 68; exec. v.p. Greater Miami C. of C., Miami, Fla., 1968—. Mem. Orange Bowl Com., 1968—, mem. United Fund of Dade County, 1961—, Hearing and Speech Center Fla., 1969—; v.p. 3d Century U.S. Corp., 1969—; met. dir. Nat. Alliance Businessmen, 1968—. Bd. dirs. S. Fla. Community TV, Inc., 1965—, pres., 1967-68; bd. dirs. Salvation Army, Jr. Achievement Greater Miami; bd. trustees Super Bowl Corp., Greater Miami Progress Found. Served with C.E., AUS, 1946-48. Recipient Civic Salesman of Year award Sales and Marketing Execs. Assn. S. Fla., 1966. Mem. Am. C. of C. Execs. Methodist. Clubs: Miami; Victor's Carriage (Miami Beach). Home: 7350 S W 108th Terrace Miami FL 33156 Office: 1200 Biscayne Blvd Miami FL 33132

FREEMAN, GORDON MYRON, labor union exec.; b. Portsmouth, O., Nov. 15, 1896; s. Charles S. and Mollie (Demaris) F.; ed. pub. schs., Portsmouth; m. Virginia Cryer, Apr. 26, 1920; 1 son, Robert M. Mem. Internat. Brotherhood Elec. Workers, 1913—, internat. rep., 1930-44, internat. v.p. 4th dist., 1944-55, internat.pres., 1955—; v.p. bldg. trades dept., metal trades dept., indsl. union dept. AFL-CIO. Vice chmn. President's Com. Employment Handicapped, 1955—; mem. Adv. Com. Social Security, 1963-65. Served with U.S. Army, World War I; AEF in France. Recipient Distinguished Service award President's Com. Employment Handicapped; Civil Rights award Anti-Defamation League. Home: 10103 E Bexhill Dr Kensington, MD 20795. Office: 1270 15th St NW Washington DC 20005

FREEMAN, GRAYDON LAVERNE, pub. co. exec.; b. LaGrange, O., Aug. 30, 1904; s. G. Simeon and Lena (Goodman) F.; B.E., Cortland State Coll., 1923; B.S., Syracuse U., 1925; M.A., Cornell U., 1927, Ph.D., 1929; m. Ruth Lazeare Sunderlin, June 22, 1929; children—James Lazeare, John Crosby, Peter Sunderlin. High sch. prin., Marathon, N.Y., 1926-27; Sage research fellow, Edminster tutor, Cornell U., 1928-29; fellow Nat. Research Found., Yale, 1930-31; successively instr., asst. prof., asso. prof., prof. psychology Northwestern U., 1932-45, lab. dir. psycho-physiology, dir. gen. edn. Univ. Coll., 1937-42; vis. prof. New Sch. Social Research, 1949; pres. Century House Publishers, 1949-69; nat. syndicated lectr. Colson Leigh Bur., 1952-58; dir. retirement research USPHS, Western Res. U., 1955-57; exec. dir. Am. Life Found., Watkins Glen, N.Y.; vis. fellow Med. Research Council, Applied Med. Psychology Unit, Cambridge and London U., Eng., 1962-70. Served as comdr. USNR, 1942- 45, dir. naval officer procurement, service sch. selection. Guggenheim fellow, 1945-46. Author: Physiological Psychology, 2d edit., 1947; Energetics of Human Behavior, 1948, 71; Fields of Psychology, 1948; How to Pick Leaders, 1950; Motivation and Morale in Industry, 1951; Self-Management for Management Men, 1958; Vocation and Avocation, 1968, Louis Prang of Boston , Giant of a Man, 1971, other books on psychology; Light on Old Lamps, Cavalcade of Toys, American Victorian Silver, Nursery Americana, The Merry Old Mobiles, One Collector's Luck, The Melodies Linger On; Hobby Handbooks for Retirement; How To Buy and Sell Old Books. Editor: The Am. Life quar., 1962-68, Next Horizons, 1969—. Home: Yorker Yankee Village Old Irelandville PO Watkins Glen NY 14891 Office: Watkins Glen NY 14891

FREEMAN, HAL MACKENZIE, retina surgeon; b. Camrose, Alta., Can., Mar. 25, 1929; s. Harry Newell and Ethel Christine (MacKenzie) F.; M.D., U. Alta., 1956; student U. B.C., 1952, Harvard, 1958, U. Ill., 1961. Came to U.S., 1958. Intern Holy Cross Hosp., Calgary, Alta., 1956-57; resident ophthalmology Ill. Eye and Ear Infirmary, Chgo., 1958-60; research asso. Tufts U., 1958; instr. ophthalmology U. Ill. Med. Sch., 1960-61; fellow Mass. Eye and Ear Infirmary, 1961-66, research asst. to dir. dept. retina research, 1966—, asst. ophthalmology, 1966—; asso. Retina Found., Boston, 1964-66, instr. ophthalmology Harvard Med. Sch., 1967—; cons. to ophthalmology Mass. Gen. Hosp., 1967—. Fellow A.C.S.; mem. Am. Acad. Ophthalmology and Otolaryngology, Assn. Research Ophthalmology, Jules Gonin Club (Switzerland), Gold Key Soc., Retina Soc., New Eng. Ophthal. Soc. Author articles in field. Asso. editor A.M.A. Archives Ophthalmology, 1966-69. Devel. technique eye surgery with patient suspended face down on table above surgeon, instrumentation and technique of vitreous surgery. Home: One Emerson Pl Boston MA Office: 100 Charles Plaza Cambridge St Boston MA

FREEMAN, HAROLD BENEDICT, Jr., steel co. exec.; b. Butler, Pa., July 18, 1918; s. Harold Benedict and Blanche (Welsh) F.; student Temple U., Phila., 1949-51; m. Jane Ullman Miller, Dec. 12, 1941; children—James Robert, Linda Kay. With Phoenix Steel Corp., Claymont, Del., 1938—, sr. v.p., 1965-68, exec. v.p., 1968-69, chmn. bd., chief exec. officer, pres., 1969—; dir. S.E. Nat. Bank of Pa., Chester. Mem. Schuylkill Twp. Sch. Dist. Authority, 1964-68. Served to maj., F.A., AUS, 1941-46. Mem. Am. Iron and Steel Engrs. Home: 1578 Valley Forge Rd Phoenixville PA 19460 Office: 4001 Philadelphia Pike Claymont DE 19703

FREEMAN, HARROP ARTHUR, lawyer; b. Elyria, O., Nov. 7, 1907; s. Glenn and Lena (Goodman) F.; student Cortland Normal Sch., 1920-25; A.B., Cornell U., 1929, LL.B., 1931, S.J.D., 1945; m. Ruth N. St. John, June 11, 1930; 1 son, Norman D. Admitted to N.Y. State bar, 1931; practiced as asso. with firm Cohn, Chorman & Franchot, later Franchot, Runals, Robillard & Cohen, then Franchot, Runals, Cohen, Taylor & Rickert, Niagara Falls, N.Y., 1930-42; in pvt. practice, specializing in taxation and pub. law, Phila. and Ithaca, N.Y., since 1942. Exec. dir. Pacifist Research Bur., Phila.; prof. law, Coll. of William and Mary, Williamsburg, Va., 1942-45; prof. Law Sch., Cornell U., since 1945; lectr. on internat. affairs and law. Candidate U.S. Ho. of Reps., 33d N.Y. Dist., 1962. Fellow Center Study Dem. Instns., Santa Barbara. Mem. Am. Bar Assn., Internat. Law Assn., Fellowship of Reconciliation, War Resisters League, Phi Beta Kappa. Mem. Soc. of Friends. Author: Road to Peace, 1947; Administrative Law of India, 1960; Dear Mr. President, An Open Letter on Foreign Policy, 1961; Legal Interviewing and Counseling, 1964; Counseling, 1965; Counseling in the United States, 1966. Contbr. law reviews and mags. Home: 103 Needham Pl Ithaca NY 14850 Office: Myron Taylor Hall Ithaca NY 14850

FREEMAN, HARRY, journalist; b. N.Y.C., Mar. 2, 1906; s. Isaac and Stella (Lvovitch) F.; A.B., Cornell, 1926; student Columbia, 1928; m. Vera Shapiro, Oct. 7, 1927. Reporter, various N.Y.C. newspapers, 1926-39; corr. for Tass agy., 1929-30, asst. mgr. and mng. editor, Am. Bur., Tass agy., since 1930. Mem. standing com., UN Corrs., 1946-48. Mem. Fgn. Press Assn. (v.p., 1946-48), UN Corrs. Assn., Acad. Polit. Sci., Phi Beta Kappa, Phi Kappa Phi. Club: National Press (Washington). Contbr. to New Times, Life Abroad, Internat. Affairs, other fgn. publs. Home: 22 E 89 St New York City NY 10028 Office: 50 Rockefeller Plaza New York City NY 10020

FREEMAN, HARRY BOIT, banker; b. Newton, Mass., Oct. 17, 1896; s. Franklin W. and Helen (Boit) F.; grad. Cheshire Acad.; student U. Wash., 1915-16, Yale, 1919; m. Theodora Hollander, Oct. 10, 1925; children—Harry R., Willard C., Peter B. With Harris Forbes & Co., 1920-33; resident partner Whiting, Weeks & Knowles, 1933-42; trust officer Providence Nat. Bank, 1942-45, v.p., 1945-47; pres. Phenix Nat. Bank, 1947-52; dir., exec. v.p. Rhode Island Hosp. Trust Co., 1953-57; pres., 1958-63, chmn. bd., 1963-69; chmn. bd. Providence Jour. Co.; dir. Providence Gas Co., Providence Mutual Ins. Co., Fields PT Manufacturing Co. Chairman Community Fund, 1952; v.p. United Fund, 1954-56, pres., 1959-61. Served with Air Corps, U.S. Army, World War I. Home: 100 Alumni Av Providence RI 02906 Office: Rhode Island Hospital Trust Co Providence RI 02903

FREEMAN, HARRY BOIT, Jr., financial exec.; b. Providence, June 14, 1926; s. Harry Boit and Theodora (Hollander) F.; grad. Middlesex Sch., 1944; B.A., Yale, 1949; M.B.A., N.Y.U., 1952; m. Leslie Stires, June 14, 1947; children—Tracy Clark, Harry Boit III. With City Bank Framers Trust Co., N.Y.C., 1949- 52; v.p. Tchrs. Ins. & Annuity Assn., also Coll. Retirement Equities Fund, N.Y.C., 1953-59; gen. partner Wood, Struthers & Winthrop, and predecessor, N.Y.C., 1959-67; v.p. Englehard Hanovia, Inc., Newark, N.J., 1967-70; pres., dir. Van Strum & Towne, Inc., also The Channing Funds, N.Y.C., 1970—; dir. Patriot Life Ins. Co., No. Ins. Co. N.Y., Variable Annuity Life Ins. Co. Am. Served with USMCR, 1944-45. Mem. Am. Finance Assn. Clubs: Racquet and Tennis, Down Town Assn., City Midday (N.Y.C.); Rumson (N.J.). Home: 176 E 77th St New York City, NY 10021. Office: 280 Park Av New York City NY 10017

FREEMAN, HARRY LYNWOOD, accountant; b. Los Angeles, May 5, 1920; s. Edward Church and Mildred Eaton (Noyes) F.; B.S., U. Cal. at Los Angeles, 1942; m. Ruth Turner, Feb. 14, 1941; children—Tracy Ruth (Mrs. Richard W. Flatow), Martin Harry. With Price Waterhouse & Co., C.P.A.'s, 1942—, partner, Mexico City, 1956—. Chmn. auditing com. Am. British Cowdray Hosp., 1962-68. Bd. dirs., treas. YMCA of Mexico, Inst. Mexicano- Norteamericano de Relaciones Culturales. Served with AUS, 1944- 46. C.P.A., 7 states. Mem. Am. Inst. C.P.A.'s, Cal. Soc. C.P.A.'s, Am. C. of C. Mexico (past pres.), U.S. C. of C. (mem. Mexico-U.S. com., internat com.), Assn. Am. C.'s of C. in Latin Am. (past pres.). Clubs: American; Bankers, University (Mexico City); Wings (N.Y.C.); Chapultepec Golf (Lomas, Mex.). Home: Sierra Paracaima 855 Mexico 10, Mexico. Office: Paseo de la Reforma 243 Mexico 5 DF Mexico

FREEMAN, HERBERT, educator; b. Frankfurt-Main, Germany, Dec. 13, 1925; s. Leo and Johanna (Friedmann) F.; brought to U.S., 1938, naturalized, 1943; B.E.E., Union Coll., 1946; M.S., Columbia U., 1948, Dr. Engring. Sc., 1956; m. Joan Sleppin, Nov. 24, 1955; children—Nancy, Susan, Robert. Tchg. asst. Columbia U., 1946-48; project engr. Sperry Gyroscope Co., Great Neck, N.Y., 1948-57, head advanced studies and data processing depts. 1957-60; vis. asso. prof. Mass. Inst. Tech., 1958-59; asso. prof. N.Y.U., 1960-64, prof., 1965—, chmn. dept. elec. engring., 1968—; vis. prof. Swiss Fed. Inst. Tech., Zurich, Switzerland, 1966; cons. engr. Dir. Cybex Assos. Inc. Vice-chmn. U.S. Com. for IFIP Congress, Edinburgh, Scotland, 1968, chmn., 1971; chmn. Congress Com. Internat. Fedn. for Information Processing, 1970—. Registered Profl. Engr., N.Y. Fellow I.E.E.E.; mem. Assn. for Computing Machinery, A.A.A.S., N.Y. Acad. Sci., Soc. for Information Display, Sigma Xi, Eta Kappa Nu. Author: Discrete-Time Systems, 1965. Patentee computers and computer graphics. Home: 50 Shelley Lane Great Neck NY 11023 Office: NYU Bronx NY 10453

FREEMAN, HOWARD EDGAR, educator; b. N.Y.C., May 28, 1929; s. Herbert M. and Rose (Herman) F.; B.A., N.Y.U., 1948, M.A., 1950, Ph.D., 1956; m. Sharon Kleban, Aug. 7, 1953; children—Seth Richard, Lisa Jill. Social scientist RAND Corp., 1955-56; research asso. Harvard Sch. Pub. Health, 1956-62; now Morse prof. urban studies Florence Heller Grad. Sch. Advanced Studies Social Welfare, Brandeis U., 1960—; sociologist Russell Sage Found., N.Y.C., 1966—. Cons. to govt. and communities, 1956—; mem. career devel. com. Nat. Inst. Mental Health; cons. Inst. Nutrition, Bogota, Colombia, research adviser Inst. Nutrition Central Am. and Panama. Served to 1st lt. USAF, 1952-53. Fellow WHO, Eng., 1962; recipient Hofheimer prize Am. Psychiat.Assn., 1963. Author: The Mental Patient Comes Home, 1963; The Clinic Habit, 1967; Social Policy and Social Research, 1970; Social Problems, 1970. Editor: The Handbook of Medical Sociology, 1963, 2d edit., 1971; American's Troubles, 1969, 2d edit., 1972; The Dying Patient, 1970. Asso. editor Am. Sociol. Rev., 1962-66, Social Problems, 1961-66, Jour. Community Mental Health, 1963- -; asso. editor Jour. Health and Social Behavior, 1966-69, editor, 1969- -. Contbr. numerous articles in field. Home: 15 Park Av Newton, MA 02158. Office: Brandeis U Waltham MA 02154 also Russell Sage Foundation 230 Park Av New York City NY 10017

FREEMAN, HYMAN B., lawyer; b. Syracuse, N.Y., Sept. 3, 1904; s. Levi and Rebecca (Catcherman) F.; LL.B., Albany Law Sch., 1926; m. Lilian E. Tarsches, Nov. 24, 1932; children—Arthur L., Ruth (Mrs. David B. Claus); Admitted to N.Y. bar; practice in Rochester; partner firm Wiser, Shaw, Freeman, VanGraafeiland, Harter & Secrest. Mem. Rochester City Council, 1955-67 vice mayor, 1966-67. Mem. Monroe County Bar Assn. (pres. 1953-54). Jewish religion (pres. Congregation 1957-60). Home: 280 Berkeley St Rochester, NY 14607. Office: Midtown Tower Rochester NY 14604

FREEMAN, IRA HENRY, author, journalist; b. N.Y.C., Aug. 12, 1906; s. Arthur J. and Rachel (Abrams) F.; B.Litt., Columbia, 1928; m. Beatrice Oppenheim, Sept. 21, 1937. Staff writer N.Y. Times, 1928-61; now free-lance writer. Instr. journalism Coll. City N.Y., 1950-51; corr. Yank, army weekly, U.S., Europe and Middle East, 1943-45. Recipient George Polk award for nat. reporting L.I.U., 1951. Mem. Am. Newspaper Guild (charter). Author: White Sails Shaking, 1949; Out of the Burning, 1960; (with Beatrice Freeman), Careers and Opportunities in Journalism, 1965. Contbr. to Yank, the GI Story of the War, 1947; Great Reading from Life, 1960; The Death Penalty in America, 1964; Detail and Pattern, 1969, also numerous mag. articles, short stories. Home: Harkaway Woodbury NY 11797

FREEMAN, J. RUSSELL, ins. co. exec.; b. Sabula, Ia., Jan. 26, 1913; s. W. J. and Margaret (Maloney) F.; B.A., Loras Coll., Dubuque, Ia.; m. Margaret Hilsinger, Feb. 17, 1941; children—Mary, Julie, James, William, Richard, John. Sr. v.p., dir. Old Republic Life Ins. Co., Chgo.; sr. v.p., dir. Old Republic Life Ins. Co. N.Y., N.Y.C.; v.p. Old Republic Assurance Co. Phoenix, Old Republic Ins. Co., Greensburg, Pa., Old Republic Internat. Corp., Motors Beneficial Ins. Co., Chgo. Mem. Am. Legion. Elk. Clubs: Ill. Athletic (Chgo.); Glen Flora Country. Home: 1414 N Sheridan Rd Waukegan IL 60085 Office: 307 N Michigan Av Chicago IL 60601

FREEMAN, JAMES LEO, editor; b. Jersey City, N.J., Dec. 2, 1908; s. Alfred J. and Mary E. (Clancy) F.; certificate journalism, N.Y. U., 1938; m. Mary E. Campbell, Feb. 10, 1934 (dec. 1948); children—James Leo, Paricia Ann (Mrs. Arthur C. Lehmann), Linda Jane (Mrs. Thomas A. Kenzik); m. 2d, Mary E. Valente, June 6, 1953; children—Kevin Thomas, Elizabeth Ann. Editorial asst. Bell Syndicate, 1926-38; night editor N.Am. Newspaper Alliance, 1938-43; editor NBC, 1943-44; asst. editor Popular Sci. mag., 1944-46; mng. editor United Feature Syndicate, 1946—. Home: 31 Ramapo Lane Hillsdale, NJ 07642. Office: 220 E 42d St New York City NY 10017

FREEMAN, JEREMIAH PATRICK, educator; b. Detroit, Aug. 3, 1929; s. Bartholomew Joseph and Agnes (Ryan) F.; B.S., U. Notre Dame, 1950; M.S., U. Ill., 1951, Ph.D., 1953; m. Mary Elizabeth Mifflin, June 13, 1953; children—Thomas M., Christopher R., John A., Mary Susan, James A., Kathleen Anne. Sr. chemist Rohm & Haas Co., Huntsville, Ala., 1953-57, group leader, 1957-64; asso. prof. U. Notre Dame, 1964-68, prof., 1968—, asst. chmn. dept. chemistry, 1964-70, chmn., 1970—. AEC fellow, 1951-53; A.P. Sloan fellow, 1966-68. Mem. Am. Chem. Soc. (sec., treas. div. organic), Chem. Soc. London, A.A.A.S., Sigma Xi, Phi Beta Kappa. Home: 17806 Edgewood Walk South Bend IN 46635

FREEMAN, JOHN, English diplomat; b. London, Eng., Feb. 19, 1915; s. Horace and Beatrice (Craddock) F.; student Brasenose Coll., Oxford, 1933-37; m. Catherine Dove, 1961; children—Matthew John Aylmer, Thomas Alexander, Lucy Catherine. Advt. cons., 1937-40; mem. Parliament, 1945-55; journalist and broadcaster, 1955-65; British high commr. in India, 1965-68; British ambassador to U.S, Washington, 1968-71. Served with Brit. Army, 1940-45. Mem. H. M. Privy Council. Address: c/o Barclay's Bank 58 Southampton Row London WC1 England

FREEMAN, JOHN D., Jr., clergyman; b. Alleene, Ark., Feb. 25, 1884; s. John D. and Mecha Catherine (Wright) F.; A.B., U. Ark., 1910; A.M., Trinity Coll., Durham, N.C., 1913; Th.M., So. Baptist Theol. Sem., 1916; D.D., Union U., Jackson, Tenn., 1925, Ouachita Coll., Arkadelphia, Ark., 1935, Georgetown Coll., Ky., 1944; L.H.D., U. Ark., 1950; m. Landis Barton, Oct. 9, 1918; children—Georgia May (Mrs. C. Frank Fielden, Jr.), Lucy Katherine (Mrs. Perry M. White, Jr.). Tchr. sci. and history, Warren (Ark.) High Sch., 1910-11; prin. Ashdown (Ark.) High Sch., 1911-12; ordained to ministry So. Bapt. Ch., 1914; missionary S.W. Ark., 1916-18; pastor, Springfield, Ky., 1918-23, Belmont Heights Ch., Nashville, 1923-25; editor Baptist and Reflector, Nashville, 1925-33; exec. sec., treas. Tenn. Bapt. Conv., 1933-42; editor Western Recorder, Louisville, 1942-46; sr. minister Belmont Heights Bapt. Ch., 1960—. Field sec. rural dept. So. Bapt. Home Mission Bd., 1946-50; recording sec. So. Bapt. S.S. Bd., 1936-42; pres. Nashville Bapt. Hosp. Bd., 1925-28; v.p. bd. dirs. Union U., 1927-33; recording sec. Am. Bapt. Theol. Sem., Nashville, 1924-42; pres. So. Bapt. Press Assn., 1928-33; del. Bapt. World Congress, Toronto, 1929, Berlin, Germany, 1934, Atlanta, 1939; v.p. United Dry Forces Tenn., 1934-38; chmn. Tenn. Interracial Com., 1937-42; past mem. bd. dirs. Nat. Temp. Movement also So. Bapt. Hosp.; recording sec. bd. dirs., Ky. Bapt. Found., 1944-46; field sec. rural life dept. Bapt. Home Mission Bd., 1946-50; instr. Bapt. Bible Inst., Graceville, Fla., 1952-54; chmn. Mid-Tenn. Bapt. Historic Soc., 1966-67. Mason (Shriner, K.T.). Author: When The West Was Young (novel); The Mystic Symbol (theology); More than Money; the Country Church, Its Problems and Their Solution; Time's Character Gauge; Buried- Living; Death Loses The Game; Shadow Over America, 1956; co-author: Zondervan's Pictorial Bible Dictionary, 1963. Address: 615 Bowling Av Nashville TN 37215

FREEMAN, JOHN GEORGE, physician; b. Willmar, Minn., Nov. 11, 1918; s. George Herman and Mata (O'Neill) F.; B.A. cum laude, Gustavus Adolphus Coll., 1940; M.B., U. Minn., 1943, M.D., 1944; fellow neurology and psychiatry, Mayo Found., 1944-45, 48-50; 1 son, Michael J. First asst. psychiatry Mayo Clinic, 1950-51; clin. dir. Fergus Falls (Minn.) State Hosp., 1951-54; clin. dir., asst. supt. Jamestown (N.D.) State Hosp., 1954-59; research psychiatrist U. Neb. Med. Sch. and Neb. Psychiat. Inst., 1959-61; supt. Mont. State Hosp., 1961-63; asst., then asso. supt. Stockton (Cal.) State Hosp., 1963-67; med. dir. DeWitt (Cal.) State Hosp., 1967-70; med. dir. local programs Dept. Mental Hygiene No. Cal. Region, 1970—. Served to capt., M.C., AUS, 1945-47. Fellow Am. Psychiat. Assn.; life mem. A.A.A.S. Contbr. articles to profl. jours. Home: Route 2 Box 2527 Auburn CA 95603 Office: 2817 D St Sacramento CA 95816

FREEMAN, JOHN HENRY, lawyer; b. San Antonio, Oct. 23, 1886; s. James D. and Rose (Phelps) F.; student U. Chgo., 1908-10; LL.D., Baylor U., 1950; m. Edna Stewart, Dec. 5, 1912; children—Winifred (Mrs. R. L. Davis, Jr.), John Henry. Admitted to Tex. bar, 1913, Supreme Ct. U.S., 1928, since practiced in Houston; partner, Campbell, Myer & Freeman, 1916-23; mem. Fulbright, Crooker & Freeman, 1923-42, Fulbright, Crooker, Freeman, Bates & Jaworski, 1942—; city atty. Houston, 1928-29; bd. dirs., chmn. trust com. First City Nat. Bank, Houston. Trustee M. D. Anderson Found., Houston, 1936—, pres., 1940—; trustee Tex. Med. Center, Shrine Crippled Children's Hosp. Mem. Am., Tex. State, Houston, City N.Y. bar assns. Clubs: Ramada, River Oaks Country (Houston). Home: 6159 Willer's Way Houston TX 77027 Office: Bank of SW Bldg Houston TX 77002

FREEMAN, JULIAN, business exec., architect; b. Bklyn., Oct. 17, 1897; s. Abraham Louis and Rae (Waldman) F.; student Crane Coll., 1914-16, Art Inst. Chgo., 1914-16; m. Esther Freeman, August, 9, 1924 (dec. June 1958); 1 dau., Janet (Mrs. Maurice Cooper); m. 2d, Belle Kline Dobrowitz, August 14, 1960. Tchr. manual tng. Chgo. Pub. Schs. 1916-17; architect 1919—; pres. Freeman Store Equipment Co., Inc., 1933-63; gen. mgr. Freeman Building Corp., 1952—. Pres. Council Jewish Fedns. and Welfare Funds, 1950-55, past nat. chmn. com. for achieving stable and unified nat. fund raising, chmn. commn. to study Jewish Cultural Agys. U.S.; bd. dirs. Community Chests and Councils Am., also mem. nat. budget com.; past pres. Indpls. Jewish Welfare Fedn., East Central States Region Council Jewish Fedns. and Welfare Funds; bd. dirs., past v.p. Indpls. Jewish Community Center Assn.; past mem. bd., exec. Com. Indpls. Community Fund; chmn. com. on middle east Nat. Community Relations Adv. Council, also vice chmn. council. Chmn. bd. Nat. Found. Jewish Culture; former overseer Jewish Theol. Sem. Served as 1st lt. F.A., AUS, 1917-19. Mem. United Synagogue Am. (bd. dirs., past v.p., past chmn. nat. com. philosophy and program conservative movement), United Service for New Americans (bd. dirs.), American Jewish Congress (v.p., chmn. com. internat. affairs), Joint Distbn. Com., Am. Jewish Com., Am. Legion. Jewish religion (past pres. temple, now hon. pres.). Mason, B'nai B'rith. Home: 5514 Washington Blvd Indianapolis IN 46220 Office: 1300 W 29th St Indianapolis IN 46208

FREEMAN, LAWRENCE BUD, musician; b. Chgo., Apr. 13, 1906; s. Louis Milton and Emily (Fermetto) F.; ed. high sch., pvt. tutors. Tenor soloist with Tommy Dorsey, Benny Goodman and Eddie Condon, 1936-47; tenor saxaphonist. Winner jazz poll, 1936, Metronome and Downbeat mags.; named soloist of Year, Life mag., 1938. Composer: The Erl. Member A.S.C.A.P., Federation of Musicians. Address: 65 E 96th St New York City NY*

FREEMAN, LUCY, author; b. N.Y.C., Dec. 13, 1916; d. Lawrence S. and Sylvia (Sobel) Greenbaum; A.B., Bennington Coll., 1938; m. William Freeman, Oct. 7, 1946 (div. Nov. 1948). Reporter, N.Y. Times, 1941-52. Author: Fight Against Fears, 1951; Hope for the Troubled, 1953; Before I Kill More, 1955; Hospital in Action, 1956; Search for Love, 1957; So You Want to Be Psychoanalyzed, 1958; Troubled Women, 1959; Story of Psychoanalysis, 1960; Emotional Maturity in Love and Marriage, 1961; The Abortionist, 1962; Children Who Kill, 1962; Remember Me to Tom, 1963; Chastise Me with Scorpions, 1964; The Wandering Husband, 1964; Why People Act That Way, 1965; The Two Assassins, 1965; Lords of Hell, 1967; The Mind, 1967; The Available Woman, 1968; The Cry for Love, 1969; Farewell to Fear, 1969; The Ordeal of Stephen Dennison, 1970; I Hate My Parents, 1970; The Search for Serenity, 1970; Celebrities on the Couch, 1970; The Dream, 1971. Recipient of the New York Newspaper Women's Club award, 1948, N.Y. chpt. Theta Sigma Phi award, 1950. Mem. Nat. Assn. Sci. Writers, Mystery Writers (mem. nat. bd.), Authors Guild, Nat. Probation and Parole Assn. (editorial bd. 1958—), Soc. Mag. Writers. Address: 120 Central Park S New York City NY 10019

FREEMAN, MASON B., naval officer; b. Chgo., Feb. 8, 1914; s. A. Jay and Harriet Ann (Kerr) F.; B.S., U.S. Naval Acad., 1935; m. Marion Jean Wright; children—Jean M., Robert J., Mason W. Commd. ensign U.S. Navy, 1935, advanced through grades to rear adm., 1963; assigned U.S.S. Oklahoma, 1935-36, U.S.S. Zane, 1936-39, U.S.S. St. Louis, 1939-41, Postgrad. Sch., Annapolis, 1941-42, ammunition sect. Bur. Ordnance, 1942-43, U.S.S. New Orleans, 1942-45; ammunition officer staff comdr. in chief U.S. Pacific Fleet, 1945-46, staff comdr. Service Force Pacific, 1946-47; flag. sec. comdr. in chief Pacific, 1947-48; comdr. destroyer U.S.S., Rush, 1948-49; assigned Naval War Coll., 1949-50; ammunition procurement officer Bur. Ordnance, 1949-52; comdr. U.S.S. Conecuh, 1952-54; armament officer staff comdr. Operational Devel. Force, 1954-56; assigned Nat. War Coll., 1956-57; dep. chief staff to comdr. 2d Fleet, 1957-60; comdr. destroyer squadron 16, 1960-61; dir. electronic warfare div. Office Chief Naval Operations, 1961-62, naval command and control systems exec., 1962-63; comdr. cruiser-destroyer flotilla 2, also anti-submarine warfare group Charlie, 1963-64; asst. chief naval personnel for edn. and tng. Navy Dept., 1964-67; comdr. cruiser-destroyer force U.S. Pacific Fleet, 1967- 70; vice dir. Joint staff Joint Chiefs of Staff, 1970—. Decorated D.S.M., Bronze Star with combat V, numerous unit and area ribbons. Home: 1421 S 22d St Arlington VA 22202 Office: Joint Chiefs of Staff Washington DC 20350

FREEMAN, MAURICE TRACY, investment exec.; b. Somerville, Mass., Feb. 8, 1904; s. Maurice James and Catharine (Tracy) F.; B.S., Mass. Inst. Tech., 1925; M.B.A., Harvard, 1927; m. Ruth Moulton, Sept. 12, 1931; children—Louise, Elizabeth Jane, Ruth Moulton, Jean Tracy. Staff research dept. Loomis, Sayles & Co., Inc., 1927-42, dir. investment research dept., 1942-63, exec. v.p., 1958-63, pres., 1963-68, chmn. bd., chief exec. officer, 1968-69; trustee Winchester Savings Bank; dir. First Nat. Stores, Standard Shares, Inc. Centennial life fellow Mus. Fine Arts. Trustee Winchester Hosp. Home: 11 Lorena Rd Winchester MA 01890 Office: 28 State St Boston MA 02109

FREEMAN, MAX HERBERT, educator, author, lectr.; b. Poland, Oct. 12, 1907; s. Samuel and Ida (Potash) F.; B.S., N.Y.U., 1930, M.A., 1931, Ph.D., 1942; m. Dora R. Tuchman, Aug. 25, 1934; children—Alice R., Carol J. Tchr. bus. Somerville High Sch., (N.J.); tchr., chmn. bus. dept., Hastings-on-Hudson, N.Y., 1936-39; tchr. bus., placement dir. Westside High School, Newark, 1939-43; prof., chmn. bus. dept. Paterson (N.J.) State Coll., 1943-54; prof., dir. grad. studies Montclair (N.J.) State Coll., 1954—; pvt. accounting practice, 1924—. Cons. to AID on Ohio State U. team in India, 1963-65. Pres. Sherwood Sch. Bus., Paterson, 1951-68. Mem. Delta Pi Epsilon (nat. pres. 1952-54). Co-author: Practical Bookkeeping, 1943; Medical Secretary, 1947; Methods of Teaching Business Subjects, 1949, 57, 65; Bookkeeping Simplified, 1953, 58; Briefhand, complete Course, 1957; Bookkeeping and Accounting Advanced, 1958; Gregg Bookkeeping and Accounting, 1963; Bookkeeping 1 and 2 Data Guides, 1963; Metodos Para La Ensenanza De Materias Comerciales, 1965; An Experience in Teacher Education in India, 1965; Accounting 0/2, 1968; Gregg Accounting Advanced Course, 1969. Editor: Fundamentals in Business Training, 1940. Home: 113 Buckingham Rd Upper Montclair NJ 07043

FREEMAN, MEREDITH NORWIN, coll. pres.; b. Elvins, Mo., June 1, 1920; s. William J. and Zelpha (McGuire) F.; B.S., S.E. Mo. State Coll., Cape Girardeau, 1949; M.Ed., U. Mo., 1951, Ed.D., 1955; m. Helen Lorene Larkin, Aug. 3, 1941 (dec. Nov. 1970); children—James Michael, Judith Ann. Rural sch. tchr., St. Francis County, Mo., 1940-41; elementary tchr., also prin., New Haven, Mo., 1941- 42, 46-47, high sch. sci. tchr., prin., 1947-50; supt. schs., Wright City, Mo., 1951-52, New Haven, Mo., 1952-54; tchr. chemistry and physics Hickman High Sch., Columbia, Mo., 1954-55; asso. prof. edn. Ft. Hays (Kan.) State Coll., 1955-57; dir. spl. services, prof. edn. Mankato (Minn.) State Coll., 1957-64, asst. acad. dean, 1964-66, acad. dean, 1966-67; pres. Black Hills State Coll., Spearfish, S.D., 1967—. Mem. exec. com. Minn. Assn. Colls., 1964-67; sec. S.D. Council Coll. and Univ. Presidents, 1967—; mem. S.D. Indian Scholarships Com., 1967—. Served with AUS, 1942-46. Mem. Nat., S.D. edn. assns., Spearfish C. of C., Phi Delta Kappa (past faculty sponsor Epsilon Iota chpt.), Sigma Tau Gamma. Methodist. Mason, Lion. Home: 1015 Sunset St Spearfish SD 57783

FREEMAN, MILTON VICTOR, lawyer; b. N.Y.C., Nov. 16, 1911; s. Samuel and Celia (Gelfand) F.; A.B., Coll. City N.Y., 1931; LL.B., Columbia, 1934; m. Phyllis Young, Dec. 19, 1937; children—Nancy Lola, Daniel Martin, Andrew Samuel, Amy Martha. Admitted to the N.Y. bar, 1934, D.C. bar, 1946; with general counsel's office SEC, 1934-42, asst. solicitor, 1942-46; staff securities div. FTC, 1934; with firm Arnold & Porter, Wash., and predecessor firms, 1946—; lectr. Georgetown U. Law Sch., 1952. Mem. Am., Fed. bar assns., Bar Assn. D.C. Contbr. articles to profl. jours. Home: 3405 Woodlsey Dr Chevy Chase MD 20015 Office: 1229 19th St NW Washington DC 20036

FREEMAN, MONROE EDWARD, army officer; b. Washington, Apr. 1, 1906; s. Edward M. and Grace D. (Studeman) F.; B.S., U. Minn., 1928, M.S., 1929, Ph.D., 1931; m. Christina Gray Clinch, Aug. 30, 1939; children—Mary Gray (Mrs. John B. Kelly), Monroe Edward. Instr. chemistry U. Ariz., 1929-30; asst. prof. bio-chemistry U. Me., 1930-36; research prof. chemistry U. Mass., 1936-45; resident prof. research chemistry, 1945-47; chief chem. Walter Reed Army Inst. Research, 1947-53; asst. chief Med. Service Corps, Office Surgeon Gen., 1950-54; research coordinator Army Gen. Staff, 1953-56; comdg. officer European Research Office, U.S. Army, 1956-60; Advanced Project Research Agy. Office Sec. Def., 1960-61; ret., 1961; dir. Sci. Information Exchange, Smithsonian Instn., 1961- -. Served to maj. AUS, 1942-45, to col. U.S. Army, 1947-61. Decorated Army Commendation medal, Legion of Merit. Fellow Am. Assn. Clin. Chemists (pres. 1954), Am. Bd. Clin. Chemists (bd. dirs. 1958- 64); mem. A.A.A.S., Soc. Exptl. Biology and Medicine, Internat. Union Pure and Applied Chemistry, Internat. Commn. Clin. Chemistry (sec. 1958- 60, pres. 1960-64), Washington Acad. Medicine, Washington Acad. Sci., Internat. Fedn. Clin. Chemists (pres. (196O-64), Sigma Xi, Delta Upsilon. Episcopalian. Club: Cosmos (Washington). Contbr. profl. jours. Home: 1280 21st St NW Washington DC 20036 Office: 1730 M St N W Washington DC 20036

FREEMAN, MONTINE MCDANIEL, museum trustee; b. Forrest City, Ark., Apr. 19, 1915; d. Louis and Montine (Kirkpatrick) McDaniel; B. Design, Newcomb Coll., 1936; student Tulane U., 1946-48; m. Richard W. Freeman, Oct. 15, 1936; children—Richard W., Louis McDaniel, Tina Louise. Bd. trustees Isaac Delgado Mus. Art, New Orleans, 1959-66, treas. 1961, sec. bd. trustees, 1964, now hon. mem. museum; bd. dirs. La. State Mus., 1961—, New Orleans Philharmonic Symphony, 1949—; trustee Greater New Orleans United Fund, 1956- 58, sec., 1958, Chmn., Women's div., 1956; bd. dirs. New Orleans YWCA, 1954-60, v.p., 1959; mem. Community Volunteer Service Bd., 1953- 59. New Orleans Neighborhood Center Bd., 1950-60, Pre-Sch. for Blind, 1954- 57; chmn. women's com. Internat. House, New Orleans, 1956-58; v.p. New Orleans Jr. League, 1953-54; bd. regents Kenmore Assn., Inc., Fredericksburg, Va.; adv. bd. Home Good Shepherd, 1965-67. Mem. Garden Club Am. (dir. 1969—), Phi Beta Phi. Presbyn. Clubs: Orleans, Petit Salon (New Orleans). Address: 295 Walnut St New Orleans LA 70118

FREEMAN, NEAL BLACKWELL, editor; b. N.Y.C., July 5, 1940; s. Malcolm T. and Virginia (Neal) F.; grad. Phillips Exeter Acad., 1958; B.A. magna cum laude, Yale, 1962; m. Jane Louise Metze, Mar. 19, 1966; children—Malcolm Trowbridge II, James Bragdon. Asst. to pres. Washington Star Syndicate, 1965-66; asso. producer Firing Line TV Show, 1966-67; exec. editor King Features Syndicate, N.Y.C., 1967—; cons. Nat. Ednl. Television Network; dir. King Features Television Prodns., Inc.; commentator WBAI-FM. Bd. dirs. Nat. Right to Privacy Com., Hist. Research Found. Mem. Nat. Press Club, Colony Found., Zeta Psi. Club: Yale (N.Y.C.). Office: 235 E 45th St New York City NY 10706

FREEMAN, NELSON WRIGHT, corp. exec.; b. Charleston, Ill., Aug. 6, 1908; s. Ernest and Mabel (Wright) F.; student U. Ill.; m. Norma Greenlese, Sept. 11, 1928; children—Nancy (Mrs. Henry Hughes), Jody Greenwood. Br. mgr. Univeral Credit Corp., Detroit, 1929-34; pres., gen. mgr. Freeman & Riesen Motor Co., Milw., 1934-38; mgr. Assos. Investment Co., Houston, 1938-42; personnel and safety dir. Lummus Co., 1942-43; mgr. personnel dept. Tenn. Gas Transmission Co. (co. name now Tenneco. Inc.), 1943-47, asst. to pres., 1947-5O, v.p., 195O-54, sr. v.p., 1954-59, pres., dir., 1966—, also chief exec. officer, 1968—; pres. Midwestern Gas Transmission Co., 1954- 61; natural gas cons., 1962-64; pres., dir. Houston Nat. Bank, 1964-66, dir., chmn. exec. com., 1966—; chmn. bd., dir. J. I. Case Co., Newport News Shipbldg. & Dry Dock Co. Tenneco Corp., Midwestern Gas Transmission Co., East Tenn. Natural Gas Co., Channel Industries Gas Co.; dir. Tenneco Oil Co., Tenn. Gas Transmission Co., Packaging Corp. of America, Tenneco Internat., Inc., Heggblade-Marguleas-Tenneco, Inc., Tenneco West, Inc., Tenneco Properties, Inc., Tenneco Realty, Inc., Tenneco Walker Mfg. Co.; pres., dir. Houston Nat. Co.; dir. Petro-Tex Chem. Corp., Phila. Life Ins. Co., Tenn. Life Ins. Co., Farmers Nat. Bank, Brenham, Tex.; adv. dir. Bayshore Nat. Bank, LaPorte, Tex. Bd. dirs. U. St. Thomas, Houston; trustee United Fund of Houston and Harris County; chmn. 1970 and 1971 Payroll Savs. Bond Drive (Houston-Harris County). Mem. Houston C. of C. (dir.). Clubs: River Oaks, Ramada (Houston); Links, Board Room (N.Y.); Chicago; Burning Tree (Washington). Home: 1233 Post Oak Park Dr Houston TX 77002 Office: Tenneco Bldg Houston TX 77002

FREEMAN, ORVILLE LETHROP, corp. exec.; b. Mpls., May 9, 1918; s. Orville E. and Frances (Schroeder) F.; B.A., magna cum laude, U. Minn., 194O, LL.B., 1946; m. Jane C. Shields, May 2, 1942; children—Constance Jane, Michael Orville. Admitted to Minn. bar, 1947; mem. Larson, Loevinger, Lindquist and Freeman, Mpls., 1947-55; gov. of Minn., 1955-61; U.S. sec. of agr., 1961- 69; pres. E.D.P. Technology Internat. Inc., 1969-70, Bus. Internat. Corp., N.Y.C., 1970—. Asst. to major of Mpls. charge veterans affairs, 1945-49; chmn. Mpls. Civil Service Commn., 1946-49; sec. Minn. Democratic Farm Labor Party, 1946- 48, chmn., 1948-5O; candidate for atty. gen., 195O, for gov., 1952; moderator Minn. Forum TV Program. Dir. Mpls. Family and Children's Service. Lt. col. USMC Res. Mem. Am. Judicature Soc., Mem. Minn. Assn. Claimants Compensation Attys. (past pres.). Minn. Bar Assn., Co-op Services, Inc., Minn. UN. Nat. Congress Parents and Tchrs., U. Minn. Alumni Assn., Am. Vets. Com., Vets. Fgn. Wars, Am. Legion, Disabled Vets. Am., Marine Corps League, Iron Wedge, Phi Beta Kappa. Delta Sigma Rho. Served from 2d lt. to maj. USMCR, 1941-45. Decorated Purple Heart. Lutheran (deacon). Moose Eagle. Club: Minnesota M. (Mpls.). Home: New York City NY 10021 Office: 757 3d Av New York City NY 10017

FREEMAN, PAUL DOUGLAS, symphony conductor; b. Richmond, Va., Jan. 2, 1936; s. Louis H. and Louise (Willis) F.; Mus.B., Eastman Sch. Music, 1956, Mus.M., 1957, Ph.D., 1963; Fulbright scholar, Hochshule für Musik, Berlin, Germany, 1957-59; m. Cornelia Perry; 1 son, Douglas Cornel. Dir. Hochstein Music Sch., Rochester, N.Y., 1960-66; founder, conductor Faculty-Community Orch., also music dir. Opera Theatre, Rochester, 1961-66; dir. San Francisco Community Music Center, 1966-68; conductor San Francisco Conservatory Orch., 1966-67; music dir. San Francisco Little Symphony, 1967-68; asso. conductor Dallas Symphony, 1968-69, 69-70; conductor-in-residence Detroit Symphony Orch., 1970—; numerous guest appearances in U.S. and Europe. First v.p. Nat. Guild Community Music Schs., 1964-66; bd. dirs. N.Y. State Opera League, 1963-66; music adv. com. San Francisco chpt. Young Audiences, 1966—; mem. Cal. Framework Com. for Arts and Humanities, 1967-68. Recipient prize Dimitri Mitropolous Internat. Conductor's competition, 1967—; Spoleto award Festival of Two Worlds, 1968. Home: 1300 Lafayette E Detroit MI 48207 Office: Detroit Symphony Ford Auditorium Detroit MI 48226

FREEMAN, PAUL LAMAR Jr., retired army officer, business exec.; b. Manila, P.I., June 29, 1907; s. Paul Lamar and Emma Rosenbaum F.; B.S., U.S. Mil. Acad., 1929; grad. Nat. War Coll., 1952; LL.D. (Honoris Causis), Norwich 1967; m. Mary Anne Fishburn, Aug. 18, 1932; 1 dau., Anne Sewell (Mrs. Roy G. McLeod). Commd. 2d lt., inf., U.S. Army, 1929, advanced through grades to gen., 1962; served in CBI, 1941-43, in Philippine liberation campaigns; participant Combined Chiefs of Staff Confs., London and Quebec, 1944; mem. Joint Brazil-U.S. Mil. Commn. in Brazil, 1945-47; chief Latin Am. br., plans and operations div., Army Gen. Staff and U.S. Army mem. Joint

Brazil-U.S. Def. Commn., Washington, 1948-50; comdr. 23d Inf. Reg. 2d Div., Korea, Aug. 1950 until wounded, Feb. 1951; dep. dir. Plans and Operations, U.S. European Command; comdr. 2d Inf. Div., 1955-57; sr. army mem. Weapons System Evaluation Group, Sec. of Def., Washington, 1957-58, comdt. Inf. Sch., comdg. gen. Inf. Center, Ft. Benning, Ga. 1958-60; dep. comdg. gen. for res. forces, Ft. Monroe, Va., 196O-62; comdr. Joint Task Force Four, Ft. Monroe, 1961-62; comdr-in-chief U.S. Army, Europe, also comdr. Central Army Group (NATO), 1962-65; comdg. gen. U.S. Continental Army Command, comdr.-in-chief U.S. Army Strike Command and U.S. Army Atlantic, Ft. Monroe, Va., 1965-67; ret., 1967; v.p. operations planning Mellonics div. Litton Industries, 1968-70; spl. cons. Litton Industries, 1971—; dir. McCulloch Aircraft Corp. Decorated D.S.C., D.S.M., Legion of Merit, Silver Star with oak leaf cluster, Bronze Star with 3 oak leaf clusters, Air medal, Purple Heart, comdr. Legion of Honor, Croix de Guerre with palm (France); Ordem do Merito (Brazil); Grand Cross Order of Merit (Germany); Grand Cross Order Mil. Merit (Spain), Gen. Staff insignia (Argentina). Clubs: Army Navy Country (Arlington, Va.); Presidio Golf (San Francisco); Monterey Peninsula Country (Pebble Beach, Cal.). Home: 3445 Martin Rd Carmel CA 93921 Office: 1001 W Maude Av Sunnyvale CA 94086

FREEMAN, RALPH MCKENZIE, U.S. dist. judge; b. Flushing, Mich., May 5, 1902; s. Horace B. and Laura D. (McKenzie) F.; LL.B., U. Mich., 1926; m. Emmalyn E. Ellis, Aug. 13, 1938. Admitted to Mich. bar, 1926; pvt. practice law, Flint, 1926- 27, 33-54; mem. Freeman, Bellairs & Dean, 1953-54; asst. pros. atty. Genesee County, Mich., 1928-30, pros. atty., 1931-32; U.S. judge Eastern Dist. Mich., 1954— now chief U.S. dist. judge. Mem. Flint (Mich.) Bd. Edn., 1933-49, pres., 1938-39, 48-49. Mem. Am. Bar Assn., State Bar Mich., Am. Bar Found., Phi Kappa Tau, Sigma Delta Kappa. Mason, Elk. Clubs: Circumnavigators; Economic (Detroit); Birmingham Country. Home: 2274 Northlawn Birmingham MI 48009 Office: Federal Bldg Detroit MI 48226

FREEMAN, RICHARD C., lawyer, city ofcl.; b. Atlanta, Dec. 14, 1926; A.B., Emory U., 1950, LL.B., 1952. Admitted to Ga. bar, 1953, since practiced in Atlanta; mem. firm Haas, Holland, Freeman, Levison & Gibert, 1955-58, partner, 1958—. Alderman City of Atlanta, 1962—. Mem. Am., Ga., Atlanta bar assns., Lawyers Club Atlanta, Am. Judicature Soc., Chi Phi, Phi Delta Phi. Office: First Nat Bank Tower Atlanta GA 30303 also Office of the Aldermen City Hall Atlanta GA 30303

FREEMAN, RICHARD WEST, beverage mfr.; b. New Orleans, Jan. 4, 1913; s. Alfred Bird and Ella Moore (West) F.; B.B.A., U. Tulane U., 1934; m. Montine McDaniel, Oct. 15, 1936; children—Richard W. Louis, Tina. Salesman Milw. Coca-Cola Bottling Co., 1934-35; asst. to pres. Great Lakes Coca Cola Bottling Co. 1936-38; pres. Wis. Coca Cola Bottling Co., also plants in Mich., Ohio, 1938-42; dir. Coca Cola Co., Chgo., 1938-42, 58-61; asst. to pres. La. Coca Cola Bottling Co., Ltd., 1946-47, pres., 1947-70, chmn. bd., 1970—; dir. Hibernia Nat. Bank, Coca Cola Co., Middle States Utilities, Delta Air Lines, Inc., New Orleans Pub. Service, Inc. Mem. bd. adminstrs. Tulane U.; dir. YMCA, New Orleans. Mem. Miss. River Bridge Commn., 1954-65; bd. La. Dept. HWys., 1952-56; pres. New Orleans Community Chest, 1952. Trustee Alton Ochsner Med. Found.; dir. United Fund, 1953-55, La. div. Am. Cancer Soc., 1947- 55, New Orleans chpt. A.R.C., 1948-5O; Mem. bd. Liquidation, City Debt. (New Orleans). Mem. S.A.R., Sons Colonial Wars, C. of C., Phi Delta Theta. Democrat. Presbyn. Clubs: International House, Louisiana, Boston, Picwick. Stratford, New Orleans Country, Southern Yacht (New Orleans). Home: 295 Walnut St New Orleans LA 70118 Office: PO Box 50400 New Orleans LA 70150

FREEMAN, ROBERT TURNER, Jr., mgmt. cons.; b. N.Y.C., Apr. 25, 1918; s. Robert Turner and Eva (Boyd) F.; B.A., Lincoln (Pa.) U., 1941; student N.Y.U. Grad. Sch., 1941- 42; m. Mary Frances Jones, Nov. 28, 1942; children—Veronica (Mrs. Wisdom F. Coleman, Jr.), Robert Turner III. Econ. statistician WBB, 1942-45; v.p., actuary United Mut. Life Ins. Co., N.Y.C., 1945-55; founder, mng. dir. Ghana Ins. Co. Ltd., Accra, 1955-62, Ghana Gen. Ins. Co., Ltd., Accra, 1959-62; cons. actuary Providence Ins. Co., Monrovia, Liberia, 1958-59, Nigerian Broadcasting Corp., Lagos, 1964-65; founder, dir. Great Nigeria Ins. Co. Ltd., Lagos, 1960-63; mng. dir. Ghana State Ins. Corp., Accra, 1962-65; asso. dir. for mgmt. Peace Corps, 1965-66; cons. minority affairs USIA, 1966-68; pres. Freeman, Cole and Assos., Inc., Washington, 1966-68; dir. office capital devel. and finance Bur. Africa, AID, 1968—; dir. Ghana Nat. Investment Bank, 1962-65, First Ghana Bldg. Soc., 1958-63, Lafayette Fed. Credit Union, Washington, 1966—. Dir. Commn. Ednl. Exchange between U.S. and Ghana, 1964-65; mem. Fulbright Scholarship Com., Accra, 1960-61; mem. Bus. Community Scholarship Com., Accra, 1958-61; co-chmn. United Negro Coll. Fund, Bklyn., 1952; cons. Korry com. on Africa, Dept. State, 1966. Trustee Phelps-Stokes Fund. Mem. Lincoln U. Alumni Assn. (pres. N.Y.C. 1952-55), Alpha Phi Alpha. Rotarian (pres. Ghana 1963-65). Home: 3001 Veazey Terrace NW Washington DC 20008 Office: Bureau for Africa AID Washington DC 20523

FREEMAN, ROGER ADOLF, economist; b. Vienna, Austria, Sept. 2, 1904; s. Samuel F. and Emma (Ferber) F.; diploma Vienna Sch. Bus. Administrn., 1927; LL.D (hon.), Brigham Young U., 1966; m. Emily Georgia Harpster, Aug. 10, 1944 (div. 1971); children—Mary Christine, Roger Charles Montague. Came to U.S., 1940, naturalized, 1945. With mdse. dept. Delka, Inc., Vienna, 1927-39; mdse. mgr. W. L. Douglas Shoe Co., N.Y.C., 194O-42; buyer, dept. mgr. L. Bamberger & Co., Newark, 1943-45; asst. to pres. Shoe Corp. Am., Seattle, 1945-49; spl. asst. to gov. Wash., 1950-55; asst. White House office, 1955-56; fiscal adviser Govt. Bolivia, 1957; v.p. Inst. Social Sci. Research, Washington, 1957-6O; research dir. Inst. Studies in Federalism, Claremont Men's Coll., 1960-62; sr. fellow Hoover Instn. Stanford, 1962—, on leave as spl. asst. to Pres. U.S., 1969-70. Member co-chmn. state and local govt. adv. com. U.S. Bur. Census, 1952-56; cons. sch. finance White House Conf. Edn., 1955; research adviser edn. comm. U.S. Commn. Intergovtl. Relations, 1954-55. Chmn. task force fed. revenue Sharing, Republican coor. com., Rep. Nat. Com., 1967. Recipient Distinguished Research award Govtl. Research Assn., 1959; George Washington Honor medal award Freedoms Found. Valley Forge, 1967; named knight comdr. Equestrian Order Holy Sepulchre at Jerusalem, 1964. Mem. Nat. Tax Assn. (chmn. com. financing pub. edn. 1957-6O, exec. com. 1961- 64), Tax. Inst. Am. (adv. bd. 1955-61), Am. Econ. Assn., Am. Soc. Pub. Administrn. Author: Federal Aid to Education-Boon or Bane?, 1955; School Needs in the Decade Ahead, 1958, Taxes for Schools, 196O; Crisis in College Finance?, 1965; Socialism and Private Enterprise in Equatorial Asia, 1968; also chpts. in books, articles. Home: 1824 Ok Creek Dr Palo Alto CA 94304 Office: Hoover Instn Stanford CA 94305

FREEMAN, ROGER MORSE, Jr., ins. co. exec.; b. N.Y.C., July 20, 1921; s. Roger Morse and Mary (Bradstreet) F.; student Phillips Andover Acad., 1938-39, Chancy Hill Sch., Boston, 1939-40; B.S., Mass. Inst. Tech., 1947; m. Elizabeth Taft, Apr. 13, 1942; children—Roger Morse III, Elizabeth C., Marianna B., Hayward T. With Mfrs. Mut. Fire Ins. Co., Providence, 1947-68, v.p., 1955-62, exec. v.p., 1962-63, pres., chief exec. officer, 1963-68; pres., dir., exec. com. successor firm MFB Mut. Ins. Co., Providence, 1968—; dir. R.I. Hosp. Trust Nat. Bank, Nicholson File Co., Am. Mut. Reins. Co. (Chgo.), Affiliated FM Ins. Co., FM Ins. Co., Ltd. (London), Factory Service Corp. Treas. R.I. Pub. Expenditure Council, 1968—; mem. Nat. Commn. Fire Prevention and Control, 1970—. Served to 1st lt. USAAF, 1942-45; ETO. Mem. Am. Mgmt. Assn.; Greater Providence C. of C. (past dir.), Providence Engring. Soc., Nat. Fire Protection Assn. Home: 57 Hazard Av Providence RI 02906 Office: 150 S Main St Providence RI 02904

FREEMAN, ROSEMARY, educator, writer, lectr.; b. London, Eng., Dec. 9, 1913; d. George S. and Adela Mary G. (Field) Freeman; scholar St. Paul's Girls Sch., 1924- 33; scholar Girton Coll., 1933-37, Ottilie Hancock fellow, 1954-55; B.A., Cambridge U., 1936, M.A., 1938, Ph.D., 1940. Supr. Girton Coll., 1938-40; lectr. Queen Mary Coll., London U., 1941-47, Birkbeck Coll., London, 1940-64; sr. lectr. Birkbeck Coll., 1964—; instr. English univ. vacation courses, Lille and Toulouse, France, 1945-46; sr. tutor, dir. vacation courses Am. students, London U., 1948-5O; broadcast reviews BBC, 1950; chmn. bd. examiners English lit. Inst. Edn., London U. Adminstrv., academic appointment fgn. refugees British Council, 1940- 45. Bd. govs. Maria Assumpta Tng. Coll., London. Recipient John W. Watson prize, 1932. Gamble prize, 1939, Rose M. Crawshay prize British Acad., 1951; fellow Smith Coll., 1937-38. Mem. Nat. Arts Collections Fund. Author: English Emblem Books, 1948: Edmund Spencer, 1957, rev., 1962, reprinted, 1968; The Faerie Queene: A Companion for Readers, 1969, also revs. lit. jours. Home: 187 Queen's Gate SW 7 London England

FREEMAN, RUTH BENSON, nursing adminstr.; b. Methuen, Mass., Dec. 5, 1906; d. Wilbur Milton and Elsie (Lawson) F.; grad. Mt. Sinai Hosp. Sch. Nursing, 1927; B.S., Columbia, 1934; A.M., N.Y.U., 1939, Ed.D., 1951: m. Anselm Fisher, Sept. 6, 1927; 1 dau., Nancy Ruth. Staff nurse and supr., Vis. Nurse Service of N.Y., 1928-37; instr. edn., N.Y.U., 1937-41; prof. pub. health U. Minn., 1941-46; adminstr. Nursing Services, A.R.C., 1946-50, chief nursing sect., NSRB, 1948-49; asso. prof. pub. health adminstrn. Johns Hopkins, 1950-62, prof. pub. health, 1962-71; mem. citizens com., adv. panel on nursing WHO, also Tech. Com. on Pub. Health Nursing. Mem. Nat. Health Council (pres. 1959-60); mem., v.p., state bd. nurse examiners Minn., 1943-46. Fellow Am. Pub. Health Assn. (chmn., nursing sect., 1947-48); mem. Nat. League Nursing (pres. 1955-59), Am., Minn. (pres. 1944-46) nurses assns., Am. Nat. Soc. Health Edn. Pub. (bd. dirs. 1963). Author numerous books including: Public Health Nursing Practice, 1950. rev. 1962; (with E.M. Holmes) Administration of Public Health Services, 1960; Community Health Nursing Practice, 1970. Home: 616 Massachusetts Av NE Washington DC 20002

FREEMAN, THEODORE MURRAY, financial exec.; b. N.Y.C., Dec. 13, 1930; s. Abraham and Betty (Levinson) F.; B.B.A., Coll. City N.Y., 1951; postgrad. U. Cal. at Los Angeles, 1956-68; m. Selma Messinger, Apr. 19, 1959; children—Michael S., Robin D. Staff accountant Price Waterhouse & Co., Los Angeles, 1954-56; divisional controller Paramount Pictures, Los Angeles, 1956-59; v.p. finance, sec., treas. Royal Industries, Pasadena, Cal., 1959—. Served with USMC, 1951-53. Mem. Am. Inst. C.P.A.'s, Cal. Soc. C.P.A.'s, Nat. Assn. Accountants. Home: 13820 Victory Blvd Van Nuys CA 91104 Office: 980 S Arroyo Pkwy Pasadena CA 91109

FREEMAN, VERNE CRAWFORD, asso. dean; b. Bentonville, Ind., Dec. 25, 1900; s. Charles Willard and Nettie May (Crawford) F.; B.S.A., Purdue U., 1923, M.S.A. 1926; m. Mary Phyllis Dean, June 26, 1926; 1 son, Richard Dean. Tchr. sci., high sch., Fairview, Ind., 1923-25; asst. to dean, instr. animal husbandry, Purdue U., 1926-35, asst. dean Sch. Agr., 1935-39, asst. prof. animal husbandry, 1938-42, asso. dean Sch. Agr., 1939—, prof. animal husbandry 1942—, dir. resident instrn., prof. animal sci., 1957-69, emeritus, 1969—; faculty rep. Intercollegiate Conf., 1945- 69; chmn. council cons. Bd. Fundamental Edn.; mem. gen commn. Ind. Bd. Edn., 1948-57; adviser Lafayette Community House; Trustee Lafayette Home Hosp., 1941-61, Harrison Trails council Boy Scouts Am.; bd. dirs. Lafayette YMCA. Recipient nat. gold medal award Kappa Delta Pi, 1969. Fellow Am. Soc. Animal Sci.; mem. N.E.A., Adult Edn. Assn., Am. Council Edn., Am. Farm Econ. Assn., Am. Assn. U. Profs., Am. Forestry Assn., Am. Inst. Biol. Scis., Alpha Tau Alpha. Alpha Gamma Rho (past nat. pres.), Alpha Zeta (past nat. pres.), Phi Eta Sigma, Kappa Delta Pi, Pi Chi Omega, Sigma Delta Chi. Mem. Christian Ch. (elder) Mason (33). Clubs: Torch, Kiwanis, John Purdue, Purdue Glee. Home: 518 Hillcrest West Lafayette IN 47906

FREEMAN, WARREN SAMUEL, educator; b. Boston, Nov. 11, 1911; s. Samuel James and Eleanor (Cohan) F.: Mus.B., Boston U., 1932, M. Ed., 1937, Ed.D., 1955; postgrad. Harvard, 1938; m. Phyllis J. Brown. June 1, 1935 (div.); 1 son, Donald C.; m. 2d, Gene Seymour, May 29, 1944 (div.); children—James A., Peter W.; m. 3d, Ruth Collar, July 23, 1966; 1 child, Raines C. Dir. music edn. pub. schs., Haverhill, Mass., 1932-35, State Tchrs., Coll., Hyannis, Mass., 1935-37, Belmont, Mass., 1937-46; exec. alumni sec., Boston U., 1946-49, dean Coll. Music, 1949-52; chmn. music edn. dept. Boston Conservatory Music; ednl. cons. sch. systems throughout U.S.; producer music festivals, Detroit, Milw., Lowell, Vienna, Austria, and elsewhere; mgr. Eastern Music Camp, 1933-34, State Normal Sch., Presque Isle, Me., summer session, 1938, Hyannis State Tchrs. Coll., 1937-39, U. Me., 1949- 50; headmaster Barrington Sch., Gt. Barrington, Mass., 1960, Am. Acad., Aguas Buenas, P.R., 1961, Kingsley Hall Sch., Westbrook, Conn., 1961—. Dir. N.E. Philharmonic Orch.; Boston Esplanade Children's Concerts, 1940; N.E. Opera Theatre; All Newton Music Sch.; N.E. Music Festival Assn., dir. Ted Mack Camp, Barrington, Mass.; exec. dir. Internat. Sch. Band Festival, Vienna; dir. Project Learn, Madison, Con Exec. dir. Ted Mack Found. for Young Americans: trustee Cape Cod Conservatory Music, Ashemere Acad., Western Mass. Econ. Council, Music Mountain, Salisbury, Conn. Served to lt. comdr. USNR, 1942-46. Mem. Mass. Music Educators Assn., Music Educators Nat. Conf., Musicians Protective Assn., Nat. Assn. Secondary Sch. Prins., Mass. Schoolmasters Club, Phi Mu Epsilon, Phi Delta Kappa, Sinfonia. Author: Story of Music, 1937; The Key, 1941; How to Teach Children to Know Music, 1940; Children's Record Book. 1944; Recordings for Elementary Schools, 1949; Songs to Sing, 1946; Time and Tune, 1938; Children's Book of Composers, 1951; Adventures in Singing, 1951; Great Composers, 1952; Music Everywhere, 1954. Contbr. to music edn. jours. Home: Post Rd Westbrook CT 06498 Office: Kingsley Hall Sch Westbrook CT 06498

FREEMAN, WILLIAM E., food mfg. co. exec. Sr. v.p. Frito Lay, Inc., Dallas. Office: Frito Lay Tower Dallas TX 75235*

FREEMAN, WILLIAM ERNEST, Jr., architect; b. Greenwood, S.C., Apr. 11, 1913; s. William Ernest and Julia (Griffin) F.; B.S. in Architecture, Clemson U., 1934; m. Othella Leonard, Dec. 11, 1937; children—William Ernest III, Allen Leonard, John Thomas. Draftsman, designer William R. Ward, Architect, Greenville, S.C., 1935-39; archtl. examiner FHA, Columbia, S.C., 1939-40; owner W.E. Freeman, Jr. & Assos., Greenville, 1940-65; partner Freeman, Wells & Major, Architects, Greenville, 1965—; dir. First Fed. Savs. & Loan Assn., Greenville; v.p., dir. Freeman's, Inc., Greenville. Mem. S.C. Bd. Archtl. Examiners, 1954-59, Greenville; Archtl. Commn., 1967-70, Gov. S.C. Beautification and Community Devel. Bd., 1969—; chmn. Greenville Planning and Zoning Bd. Adjustments, 1953-60. Pres., trustee Archtl. Found., Clemson U., 1955-59, mem. engring. adv. bd., 1954-55. Fellow A.I.A. (nat. dir. 1962-65, pres. S.C. chpt. 1951-52, regional dir. 1962-65); mem. Greenville C. of C. (dir. 1959-61), Greenville Art Assn. (pres. 1956-57). Baptist (deacon). Rotarian. Club: Greenville Country. Archtl. works include Hillcrest High Sch., 1957, St. Mark Meth. Ch., Seneca, 1960, 1st Bapt. Ch., Valdese, N.C., 1965, Northwood Sch., 1966, St. Mathew Meth. Ch., Greenville, 1967, Visitor's Center, Kedwee-Toxaway Nuclear Devel., 1969. Home: 22 Kenwood Lane Greenville SC 29609 Office: 226 W Washington St Greenville SC 29601

FREEMAN, WILLIAM MISER, constrn. co. exec.; b. Chgo., May 5, 1919; s. Gaylord Augustus and Pauline Angeletta (Miser) F.; B.A. cum laude (Rufus Choate scholar 1941), Dartmouth, 1941; grad. Advanced Mfgmt. Program, Harvard, 1958; m. Winifred Carol Stevens, Nov. 1, 1941; children—Carol Jean, James Stevens, Margaret Pauline. With Chgo. Bridge & Iron Co., 1941—, v.p., gen. mgr. Internat. div., 1964-66, v.p., gen. sales mgr., 1966-70, sr. v.p. finance, treas., 1970—, also dir.; dir. Gary Wheaton Bank, Wheaton, Ill., Standard Am. Financial Corp., Horton Steel Works Canada, Horton Argentina. Chicago Bridge Ltd. (London), Chicago Bridge (Netherlands), Chgo. Bridge (Deutschland), Chgo. Bridge Italiana Montaggi, Chgo. Bridge (Phillippines). Trustee Summit (N.J.) Library Assn., 1957-64; bd. dirs. Summit United Campaign, 1959-64. Served to lt. comdr. USNR, 1942-46, Mem. Am. Mgmt. Assn., Am. Petroleum Inst., British-Am. C. of C. Clubs: Oak Brook Polo; Hinsdale Golf. Home: 425 E 17th St Hinsdale IL 60521 Office: 901 W 22d St Oak Brook IL 60523

FREEMAN, WILLIAM RAYMOND, lighting equipment mfr.; b. Lewisburg, W.Va., Dec. 4, 1905; s. Charles Minot and Suzanne (Goheen) F.; student Fla. So. Coll., 1922-25; m. Dorothy R. Ade, Jan. 18, 1925; children—William R., Robert M., Joan (Mrs. J. J. McKew), Barbara (Mrs. Richard Forrest), Nancy (Mrs. William E. Russell, Jr.). Editor, Montclair (N.J.) Times, 1925-32; v.p., gen. mgr. Ladnew Corp., Jersey City, 1932-36; v.p., sales mgr. Birdseye Electric Co., Gloucester, Mass., 1936-39; sales and advt. mgr. Manning Bowman Co., Meriden, Conn., 1939- 41; v.p. sales Wabash Corp., Bklyn., 1941-47; v.p. Lustra Corp. Am. and affiliate Amplex Corp., 1947-59, exec. v.p., 1959-65; pres. Amplex Corp., 1965-67; pres. Amplex div., exec. v.p. Lustra div., chmn. bd. Internat. Tel. & Tel. Illumination Corp., 1967-69, sr. adv. cons. ITT Illumination div., 1969—. Mem. Illuminating Engring. Soc., Nat. Fed. Sales Exec., Am. Mgmt. Assn., Nat. Elec. Photographic Mfrs. and Distbrs. Assn. (v.p.), Nat. Assn. Photographic Mfrs., Am. Hotel Assn., N.Y. Sales Execs. Club, Elec. Assn. Club: Hempstead Country (past pres.). Home: Commodore Apts Galt Ocean Mile Fort Lauderdale FL 33308

FREESE, CARL GATES, banker; b. Framingham, Mass., Dec. 23, 1892; s. John Perley and Grace Eva (Gates) G.; A.B., Harvard, 1915; m. Dorothy H. Clapp, May 3, 1924; children—Carl Gates, Nancy Jackson (Mrs. Boardman Brown). Rep., So. Ry., Argentina and Uruguay, 1914; joined R.L. Day & Co., investment bankers, Boston, and N.Y. City, 1919, partner, 1928-43; v.p. Conn. Savs. Bank, New Haven, 1944, pres. and treas., 1948-62, chmn., 1962-67, vice chmn. and trustee, 1967—. dir., treas. Conn. Med. Service (Blue Shield): formerly dir. U. S. Casualty Co., New Amsterdam Casualty Co., Security Ins. Co., Francestown Water Co., New Haven Gas Co. Member Savings Banks Railroad Bond Com., 1949-55. Member finance com. New Haven Hosp. until 1971; chmn. war finance com. World War II; chmn. Citizens Action Commn., 1954-57; director New Haven Boys Club. Served as sgt. U.S. Army A.S. with French Army, 1917-18; attached to Peace Commn., Paris, 1918. Decorated Croix de Guerre (France). Mem. Savs. Banks Assn. Conn. (pres. 1947-48), Nat. Assn. Mut. Savs. Banks (pres. 1951-52), New Haven C. of C. (pres. 1947- 49). Conglist. Clubs: Harvard (Conn. and N.Y. City); Lawn, Graduates, Kiwanis (New Haven); Author banking articles in trade mags.; speeches in N.Y. Times and other papers. Home: PO Box Nangate Francestown NH Office: 47 Church St New Haven CT 06510

FREESE, RAYMOND WILLIAM, educator; b. Forstell, Mo., Dec. 17, 1934; s. Herman E. and Lydia (Giessmann) F.; B.S. in agr., U. Mo., 1956, B.S. in edn., 1958, M.A., 1958, Ph.D., 1961; m. Celia Ann Staubach, Aug. 10, 1957; children—Carl Herman, William Charles, Timothy Carl. Instr. mathematics U. Mo., 1958-61; asst. prof. mathematics St. Louis U., 1961-64, asso. prof., 1964-67, prof., 1967—, chmn. dept., 1971—. Vice pres. Francis Howell Sch. Dist. Bd. Edn., 1967-69; mem. exec. com. Mo. Sch. Bds. Assn., 1968-70. Gregory fellow, 1957-58; Nat. Sci. Found. Coop. Grad. fellow, 1959-61; recipient 4-H Alumni Award, 1970. Mem. Mo. Mathematics Assn. Advancement Tchr. Tng. (pres. 1971-72), Math. Assn. Am. (chmn. Mo. sect. 1964-65), Am. Math. Soc., Pi Mu Epsilon, Sigma Xi, Phi Eta Sigma, Phi Delta Kappa. Mem. United Ch. of Christ (mem. Mo. conf. council). Contbr. articles profl. jours. Home: Rt 1 Foristell MO 63348 Office: 221 N Grand Blvd St Louis MO 63103

FREESTON, WILLIAM DENNEY, ins. co. exec.; b. Camden, N.J., Oct. 30, 1910; s. George Denney and Harriet (Harding) F.; B.S. in Engring., Princeton, 1932, C.E. 1933; m. Dorothy Elizabeth Mirtz, Mar. 1, 1941. With Prudential Ins. Co. Am., Newark, 1933—, sec., 1961—, v.p., 1962—. Trustee, past pres. N.J. Safety Council. Served to lt. USNR, 1943-45. Mem. N.J. Hist. Soc. (trustee). Clubs: Princeton (N.Y.C.); Edgartown (Mass.) Yacht; Baltusrol Golf (Springfield, N.J.); Essex (Newark). Home: Old Farm Rd Bernardsville NJ 07924 Office: 745 Broad St Newark NJ 07101

FREI, EMIL, III, physician; b. St. Louis, 1924; M.D., Yale, 1948; m., five children. Intern St. Mary's Group Hosps., St. Louis, 1948-49; resident pathology Barnes Hosp., St. Louis, 1952-53; resident internal medicine St. Louis U., 1953-54, VA Hosp., St. Louis, 1954-55; chief gen. medicine br. Nat. Cancer Inst., Bethesda, Md., 1955-65; head devel. therapeutics, asso. dir. MD Anderson Hosp. and Tumor Inst., Houston, 1965—. Served as lt. (j.g.). M.C., USNR, 1950-52. Diplomate Am. Bd. Internal Medicine, 1957. Mem. A.M.A. Home: 4939 Valkeith St Houston, TX 77035. Office: 6723 Bertner Houston TX 77025

FREIBERG, ALBERT DANIEL, customer researcher; b. Stanton, Neb., Feb. 9, 1904; s. Albert Fred and Frieda Hoffmeyer F.; A.B., North Central Coll., 1926; Ph.D., Cornell U., 1936; m. Harriet Winthrop Hall, Jan. 1, 1937; children—Susan Lane (Mrs. Thomas R. Coolidge), Ann Hall Freiberg. Instr., Mich. State Coll., 1929-33; staff Psychol. Corp., N.Y.C., 1935-58, sec., 1940- 44, v.p., 1944-47, dir. market research, 1944-58, dir., 1946-60, 1st v.p., 1947-58; pres. Profl. Research Assn., Inc., 1958—, Profl. Marketing Assos. Mem. Market, Copy Research councils, Am. Eastern, N.Y. State psychol. assns., A.A.A.S., Am. Marketing Assn., Am. Assn. Pub. Opinion Research, Sigma Xi. Clubs: Cornell, Greenwich Country. Home 4 Putnam Hill Greenwich CT 06830 Office: 283 Greenwich Av Greenwich CT 06830

FREIDBERG, SIDNEY, real estate devel. co. exec., lawyer; b. N.Y.C., Jan. 20, 1914; s. David and Tillie (Friedman) F.; B.S., N.Y.U., 1933; LL.B., Yale, 1936; m. Edith L. Hebald, June 11, 1962; children—David, Emily; stepchildren—Selian Hebald, Anne Hebald. Admitted to N.Y. bar, 1936, D.C. bar, 1945; practice in N.Y.C., 1936-42, 45-68; partner firm Arent, Fox, Kintner, Plotkin & Kahn, Washington, 1945-54; in research and analysis div. OSS, 1942-43; counsel printing and pub. div. WPB, Washington, 1943-45; counsel Ho. of Reps. select com. on newsprint and paper supply, Washington, 1948-49; commr. Fgn. Claims Settlement Commn., Washington, 1968-70; exec. v.p., gen. counsel Nat. Corp. for Housing Partnerships, Washington, 1970—; pres. Morning Side Realty Property Assn., 1960-62. Mem. alumni bd. visitors N.Y.U., 1959-61; mem. founders com. Am. Symphony Orch., 1942—; Trustee Lincoln Square Neighborhood Center, 1964-68. Mem. Am., Fed., Inter-Am., N.Y. State, City N.Y. bar assns., Am. Soc. Internat. Law, Am. Judicature Soc., World Peace Through Law Center, Phi Beta Kappa. Democrat. Clubs: Federal City, Nat. Press, Nat. Lawyers (Washington); Yale (N.Y.C. and Washington). Contbr. articles to profl. jours. Home: 1832 24th St NW Washington DC 20008 Office: 1133 15th St NW Washington DC 20005

FREIDEL, FRANK BURT Jr., historian; b. Bklyn., May 22, 1916; s. Frank Burt and Edith (Heacock) F.; B.A., U. So. Cal., 1937, M.A., 1939; Ph.D., U. Wis., 1942; M.A., Oxford U., 1954, Harvard, 1955; m. Elisabeth Margo, 1938 (div. 1955); children—Linda Beth, Dorothy Edith, David Alan, Charles Robinson; m. 2d, Madeleine Bicskey, Feb. 23, 1956; children—Philip (dec.), Paul Christine, Irene. Faculty, asso. prof. Shurtleff Coll., 1941-43; asst. prof. U. Md., 1943-45, Pa. State Coll., 1946-48, Vassar Coll., 1948-49; asst. prof. U. Ill., 1949-52, asso. prof., 1952-53; asso. prof. Stanford, 1953-55; Harmsworth prof. Am. history Oxford U., 1955-56; prof. Harvard, 1955—; tchr. summers George Washington U., 1946, 49, Mich. State U., 1948, Columbia, 1952, U. Cal., 1959; lectr. Salzburg (Austria) Seminar in Am. Studies, 1955-56; fellow Center for Advanced Study in Behavioral Scis., 1959-60. Cons. Office Naval Research, summer 1949; historian NSF, summer 1951. Served with USNR, 1943-46. Guggenheim fellow, 1964-65. Author: Francis Roosevelt: The Apprenticeship, 1952; Roosevelt: The Ordeal, 1954; Roosevelt: The Triumph, 1956; The Splendid Little War, 1958; America in the Twentieth Century, 1960; Over There, 1964; The Presidents of the United States, 1964; F.D.R. and the South, 1956; Our Country's Presidents, 1966. Co- author: A History of the United States, 1939; America, A Modern History of the United States, 1970; Dissent in Three American Wars, 1970. Editor: The Golden Age of American History, 1959; The New Deal and the American People. 1964; Union Pamphlets of the Civil War, 1967; American Epochs series. Co- editor: Builders of American Institutions, 1963; American Issues in the Twentieth Century 1966. Home: 74 Hillcrest Rd Belmont MA 02178 Office: Harvard U Cambridge MA 02138

FREIDIN, RICHARD GERALD, financial cons.; b. N.Y.C., July 27, 1930; s. Philip William and Edith (Aronowitz) F.; B.S., N.Y. U., 1951; LL.B., Harvard, 1956; m. Yona Simberkoff, Jan. 29, 1957; children—Jonathan, Marian, David. Admitted to N.Y. bar, 1956; tax supr. Touche, Ross, Bailey & Smart, C.P.A.'s, N.Y.C., 1956-61; with May Dept. Stores, St. Louis, 1961-68, asst. treas., 1964-67, treas., 1967-68; partner Richard G. Freidin & Co., N.Y.C., 1968-70; partner Touche Ross & Co., Newark, 1970—. Served with USNR, 1951- 53. C.P.A., N.Y., N.J., Mo. Home: 15 Carolyn Pl Armonk NY 10504 Office: 60 Park Pl Newark NJ 07102

FREIDIN, SEYMOUR KENNETH, columnist and author; b. N.Y.C., Apr. 27, 1917; s. Irving H. and Fay (Meyer) F.; B.A., Columbia, 1936, student U. Vienna (Austria), 1945-46; m. Lillian Stiva Berger, Mar. 21, 1950; children—Joshua John and Nicholas William (twins). Mem. staff N.Y. Herald Tribune, 1936-49, 61- 66, covered Battle of Berlin, 1945, coup in Czechoslavakia, 1948, exec. editor fgn. news, 1961-66, author fgn. news commentary, 1949-66; with Collier's mag., 1949-51; author sydicated column fgn. affairs from Europe, 1931-61; syndicated fgn. affairs columnist, 1966—. Recipient Centennial Founders award Lehigh U., 1963. Mem. Authors Guild. Club: Overseas Press (N.Y.C.). Author: The Forgotten People (best book fgn. affairs Overseas Press Club), 1962; also numerous articles. Author; The Experts, 1968. Co-author; The Fatal Decisions, 1956. Home: Seven Maples Hopkinton NH 03301 also Neapishead Norfolk England Office: 60 Ormonde Gate London SW 3 England

FREIDMANN, EUGENE ALVIN, educator; A.B., U. Chgo., 1947, A.M., 1949, Ph.D., 1953. Now prof. sociology and anthropology, head dept. Kan. State U. Address: Dept Sociology and Anthropology Kansas State U Manhattan KS 66502*

FREIDSON, ELIOT LAZARUS, educator, sociologist; b. Boston, Feb. 20, 1923; s. Joseph and Grace (Backer) F.; student U. Me., 1941-42; Ph.B., U. Chgo., 1947. M.A., 1950, Ph.D., 1952; m. Judith Lorber, Aug. 9, 1966; 1 son, Matthew Aaron; children by previous marriage—Jane Beatrice, Oliver Eliot. Postdoctoral fellow U. Ill., 1952- 54; asst., then asso. prof. sociology Coll. City N.Y., 1956-61; mem. faculty N.Y.U., 1961—, prof. sociology, 1963—; cons. in field, 1956—. Adviser div. research grants NIH, 1963-66; adviser joint research program Social Security Adminstrn. and Social Rehab. Service, Dept. Health, Edn. and Welfare, 1968-70. Served with inf. AUS. 1943-46; ETO. Decorated Bronze Star. Fellow Am. Sociol. Assn. (chmn. med. sociol. sect. 1963-64), Am. Anthrop. Assn.; mem. Soc. Study Social Problems, Am. Assn. U. Profs., A.A.A.S., Internat. Sociol. Assn. (pres. com. research med. sociology 1967-70). Author: Patient's Views Medical Practice, 1961; Profession of Medicine, 1970; Professional Dominance, 1970; also articles. Editor; Student Government, Student Leaders and American Colleges, 1955; Hospital in Modern Society, 1963; Jour. Health and Social Behavior, 1966-69. Co-editor: Med. Men and Their Work, 1972. Home: 110 Bleecker St New York City NY 10012

FREILICHER, JANE, artist; b. Bklyn., Nov. 29, 1924; d. Martin and Bertha (Cummings) Niederhoffer; B.A. Bklyn. Coll., 1947; M.A., Columbia, 1949; postgrad, Hans Hofmann Sch., 1947; m. Joseph Hazan, Feb. 17, 1957; 1 dau., Elizabeth. Exhibited in 13 one-man shows at Tibor Denagy Gallery, N.Y.C., 1952-71; represented in permanent collections at N.Y.U., Bklyn. Mus., Brandeis Art Mus., Mus. Modern Art, R.I. Mus., Parrish Art Mus. Winner Hallmark Competition, 1960. Vis. artist U. Pa. Grad. Sch. Fine Arts, 1968, 71, Skowhegan Sch. Art, 1968, Tanglewood Inst., 1968. Illustrator: Turandot and Other Poems, 1954; Paris Review Portfolio, 1965; Poets of the New York School, 1969. Home: 51 Fifth Av New York City NY 10003 also: Watermill NY 11976

FREIMAN, DAVID GALLAND, pathologist; b. N.Y.C., July 1, 1911; s. Leopold and Dorothy (Galland) F.; A.B., Coll. City N.Y., 1930; M.D., L.I. Coll. Medicine, 1935; A.M. (hon.), Harvard, 1962; m. Ruth Schein, Sept. 2, 1949; children—Nancy (Mrs. Stephen Schultz), Leonard. Intern, resident pathology Montefiore Hosp., 1938-43; practice medicine, specializing in pathology, Boston, 1944-50, 56—, Cin., 1952-56; asst. pathologist Mass. Gen. Hosp., 1944- 50; attending pathologist Cin. Gen. Hosp., Drake Meml. Hosp., 1952-56; pathologist-in-chief, dir. labs. Beth Israel Hosp., 1956—; cons. Pathologist VA, Hosps., Cin., Ft. Thomas, Ky., 1954-56, Boston, 1962—; instr. pathology Med. Sch. Tufts U., 1947-48; instr. pathology Med. Sch. Harvard, 1949-50, clin. prof. pathology, 1956-62, prof., 1962—, Mallinckrodt prof. pathology, 1969—; asst. prof. pathology Coll. Medicine U. Cin., 1950-52, asso. prof., 1952-56; lectr. pathology Simmons 1962—; cons. pathology Cambridge Hosp., 1968—. Recipient Stratford prize Coll. City N.Y., 1931, Alumni prize L.I. Coll. Medicine, 1935. Mem. Am. Assn. Pathologists and Bacteriologists, Am. Soc. Exptl. Pathology, Internat. Acad. Pathology, Histochem. Soc., Am. Soc. Clin. Pathologists, A.A.A.S., Mass. Med. Soc., New Eng. Soc. Pathologists, Phi Beta Kappa, Sigma Xi, Alpha Omega Alpha. Mem. editorial bd. Am. Jour. Pathology, 1961—, Circulation, 1962-67, Human Pathology, 1969—; mem. editorial adv. com. Atlas of Tumor Pathology, 1966—. Contbr. articles to profl. jours. Home: 182 Homer St Newton Centre MA 02159 Office: 330 Brookline Av Boston MA 02215

FREIMARK, ROBERT, artist; b. Doster, Mich., Jan. 27, 1922; s. Alvin O. and Nora (Shinaver) F.; Ed. B., U. Toledo, 1950; M.F.A., Cranbrook Acad. Art, 1951; m. Lillian Tihlarik; 1 dau., Christine Gay. Numerous one-man shows including Minn. Inst. Arts, Toledo Mus. Art, Salpeter Gallery, Morris Gallery, N.Y.C., Des Moines Art Center, Santa Barbara Mus.; group shows Art Inst. Chgo., 1952, Pa. Acad. Fine Arts, 1952 (Lambert Fund prize), 1953, Detroit Inst. Arts, 1956, Mich. State U., 1956, N.A.D., 1956, Bklyn. Mus., Mus. Modern Art. New Talent in U.S.A., 1957; represented in collections Pa. Acad. Fine Art, Butler Inst. Am. Art, Canton Art Inst., Daytona Beach Art Center, Albion Coll., Ford Motor Co., South Bend Art Assn., Joslyn Art Mus., Seattle Art Mus., Georgia Mus., Massillon Mus., U. Toledo, Marietta Coll., Colo. Coll., W. Va. Wesleyan Coll., Huntington Gallery, U. N.D., Ore. State Coll., U. Okla. City, Des Moines Art Center, Smithsonian Inst., Library Congress, Los Angeles County Art Inst., others; guest artist Joslyn Meml. Mus., 1961; instr. painting and drawing Ohio U. 1955-59; artist in residence Des Moines Art Center, 1959-63; dir. Crystal Lake Art Center, Frankfort, Mich., 1955-57; guest lectr., one man show Columbia, 1963; cultural exchange exhibit Northamerican Cultural Inst., Mexico City, 1963; guest artist Riverside Art Center, 1964; asst. prof. art San Jose State Coll., 1964—; Wiche prof. Soledad State Prison, 1967; Recipient 2d award for oil Northwest Territorial exhibit, 1954, Roulet medal Toledo Mus. Art, 1957; 1st award print exhbns., 1958; Ohio U. research grant, 1958-59; purchase award Midwest Biennial and Northwest Printmakers; Cal. State Coll. grant to create spl. edit. serigraphs; Western Interstate Commn. for Higher Edn. grant, 1967; San Jose State Coll. Found. grants, 1966, 67, 68, 69-70, 71. Served with USNR, 1939-46. Contbr. to profl. publs. Home: Route 2 Box 539A Morgan Hill CA 95037 Office: Art Dept San Jose State Coll San Jose CA 95114

FREI MONTALVA, EDUARDO, former pres. Chile; b. Santiago, Chile, Jan. 16, 1911; s. Eduardo Frei and Victoria Montalva; ed. Catholic U. Chile, 1933; m. Maria Ruiz Tagle; children—Maria Irene, Carmen, Eduardo, Isabel Margarita, Jorge, Francisco Javier. Editor daily paper El Tarapaca, Chile, 1935-37; titular prof. labour law, philosophy of law Catholic U. Chile, 1937-45; founder Chilian Christian Democrat Party, 1935, pres., 1940-45; minister pub. works, 1945; senator provinces Atacama and Coquimbo, 1949; Chilean del. to UN, 1950; chmn. com. economists Fgn. Ministers Conf., Rio de Janeiro, 1954; senator province Santiago, 1957; pres. First World Christian Dem. Congress, 1961; now pres. Republic Chile; lectr. U. Notre Dame, Columbia, Georgetown U. Author: The Regime of Fixed Salaries and its Possible Abolition; Unknown Chile; Now is the Time; Politics and the Spirit; The History of Chilean Political Parties; Truth Has Its Hour; Political Meaning and Form; Thought and Action; America Latina tiene un destino. Home 683 Hindenburg Santiago, Chile.

FREIN, JOSEPH PETER, constrn. cons.; b. St. Louis, May 22, 1904; s. Jacob Peter and Mary Ellen (Sullivan) F.; engring. extension student, Washington U. St. Louis; m. Margaret Mary Peters, June 8, 1929; children—Michael James, Elizabeth Margaret. Office engr., chief survey party, also insp., div. sewers and paving, City St. Louis, 1925-30; engr. W. E. Callahan Constrn. Co., St. Louis, 1930-43; with Morrison-Knudsen Co., Inc., 1943- 69, chief engr., Boise, Ida., 1951-60, v.p. charge engring., 1960-68, v.p. fgn., 1968-69, dir., 1959-70; v.p. Morrison Knudsen Internat. Co., Inc., 1968-69; now ind. constrn. cons. Mem., past chmn. constrn. subcom. U.S. Com. on Large Dams, Internat. Commn. on Large Dams, 1969-71. Mem. Am. Arbitration Assn. (nat. panel arbitrators 1968—). Contbg. author, asso. editor: Handbook of Construction Management and Organization, 1972. Co-inventor, patentee deep bridge pier founds. Home: 4312 Edgemont St Boise ID 83704

FREINKEL, NORBERT, physician, educator; b. Mannheim, Germany, Jan. 26, 1926; s. Adolf and Veronika (Kahn) F.; A.B., Princeton, 1945; M.D., N.Y. U., 1949; m. Ruth Kimmelstiel, June 19, 1955; children—Susan Elizabeth, Andrew Jonathan, Lisa Ann. Intern, asst. resident medicine Bellevue Hosp., N.Y.C., 1949- 50; from research fellow to asst. prof. medicine Harvard Med. Sch. and Thorndike Meml. Lab., Boston City Hosp., 1952-66; Kettering prof. medicine, chief sect. endocrinology, metabolism and nutrition, dir. Endocrine Clinics, Northwestern U. Med. Sch., 1966—. Mem. metabolism study sect. NIH; mem. adv. com. on alcoholism Nat. Inst. Mental Health; cons. surg. gen. U.S. Army. Served with USNR, 1943-45, AUS, 1950-52. Am. Cancer Soc. fellow, 1953-55, Nat. Found. fellow, 1955-56. Mem. Assn. Am. Physicians, Am. Soc. Clin. Investigation, Am. Physiol. Soc., Endocrine Soc. (council, 1969—), Am. Thyroid Assn., Am. Diabetes Assn. (Lilly award and medal 1966, bd. dirs. 1968—), Soc. Exptl. Biology and Medicine, Alpha Omega Alpha, Phi Beta Kappa, Sigma Xi; hon. mem. High Table, King's Coll., Cambridge, Eng. Editorial bd. Jour. Clin. Endocrinology and Metabolism, Jour. Lab. and Clin. Medicine, Annual Rev. Medicine, Jour. Clin. Investigation. Contbr. articles to profl. jours., chpts. in textbooks. Home: 938 Edgemere Ct Evanston IL 60202 Office: 303 E Chicago Av Chicago IL 60611

FREISER, HENRY, educator, chemist; b. N.Y.C., Aug. 27, 1920; s. Abraham and Henrietta (Graubard) F.; B.S., Coll. City N.Y., 1941; M.A. in Organic Chemistry, Duke, 1942, Ph.D. in Phys. Chemistry, 1944; m. Edith Schwartz, Aug. 22, 1942; children—Emanuel, Deborah Jean, Ben Sherman. Instr. N.D. State Coll., 1944-45, Coll. City N.Y., 1945; research fellow Mellon Inst., 1945-46; instr., then asso. prof. U. Pitts., 1946-58: prof. chemistry faculty U. Ariz., 1958—, chmn. dept., 1958-67; cons. in field, 1950—. Fellow Chem. Soc. (London, Eng.); mem. Am. Chem. Soc. (chmn. analytical div. 1971-72; rep. to intersoc. com. on manual of methods for air sampling and analysis 1971—), Am. Soc. Testing Materials. Author: (with G. H. Morrison) Solvent Extraction in Analytical Chemistry, 1957; (with Q. Fernando) Ionic Equilibria in Analytical Chemistry, 1963. Co-editor: International Series Monographs in Analytical Chemistry. Editorial bd. Analytical Chemistry, 1967-70; editorial adv. bd. Talanta, 1963—. Home: 6911 E Big Bear Dr Tucson AZ 85715

FREITAG, DOROTHEA, composer, arranger, mus. dir., pianist; b. Balt., Dec. 2, 1914; d. William and Belle (Hackett) Freitag; student Curtis Inst., 1930-33; tchrs. certificate, Peabody Conservatory, 1934; student Ecole Normale, Paris, 1934-36; pupil of Alexander Sklarevski and Nadia Boulanger, also Bohuslav Martinu, and Mario Castelnouvo-Tedesco; m. Charkes Yuki, Mar. 16, 1931; (marriage dissolved); two sons. Due pianist recital Town Hall, N.Y.C., 1946; composer ballet music for Windy City, 1946; pianist, vocal arranger Lend and Ear, 1948; composer music for Veracuzana, also Jazz in Five Movements, 1950; pianist Courtin' Time, 1951; arranger dance music, pianist High Time, 1953; pianist Phoenix, '55, 1955; mus. dir., pianist Annie Get Your Gun, 1956; composed music, mus. arranger, played own piano compositions in Autobiography, 1956; mus. dir., arranger, pianist Shoestring '57, 1956; mus. dir., pianist Out of This World, 1957. The Wizard of Oz, 1957; mus. dir., arranger, pianist Mask and Gown, 1957; mus. dir., pianist The King and I, 1959; mus. dir., arranger, pianist Oh, Kay, 1960; composed dance music, additonal arrangements pre- Broadway tryouts Kicks and Co., 1961; ballet District Storyville, 1962; additional dance music for Tovarich, 1963; TV appearance in District Storyville, 1962; arranger night club show Medium Rare, 1960, also for solo performers; pianist No Strings, 1962. Address: care Am Fedn Musicians 261 W 52d St New York City NY 10019*

FREITAG, ROBERT FREDERICK, govt. ofcl.; b. Jackson, Mich., Jan. 20, 1920; s. Fred J. and Beatrice (Paradise) F.; B.S.E. in Aero. Engring., U. Mich., 1941; postgrad. Mass. Inst. Tech., 1941-42; m. Maxine Pryer, Apr. 13, 1941; children—Nancy Marie (Mrs. Stephen Sprague), Janet Louise (Mrs. Richard Wasserstrom), Fred John II, Paul Robert. Commd. ensign USNR, 1941, lt. comdr. U.S. Navy, 1946, advanced through grades to capt., 1960; various guided missile programs, 1941-55; project officer Jupiter and Polaris intermediate range ballistic missiles, Chief Naval Operations, 1955-57; range planning officer, also spl. asst. to comdr. Pacific Missile Range, Point Mugu, Cal., 1957-59; astronautics officer Bur. Naval Weapons, 1959-63; ret., 1963; dir. launch vehicles and propulsion NASA, 1963, dir. Manned Space Flight Field Center Devel., 1963—. Mem. NACA Com. Propellers, 1944-46, Sec. Def. Spl. Com. Adequacy Range Facilities, 1956-58, Joint Army-Navy Ballistic Missile Com., 1955-57, NACA Spl. Com. Space Tech., 1958-59, re-adv. com. missile and spacecraft aerodynamics NASA, 1960-63, joint Def. Dept.-NASA-Astronautics Coordinating Bd. on launch vehicles panel, 1960-64. Decorated Legion of Merit, 1959; recipient Spl. Commendation from Comdr.- in-Chief U.S. Pacific Fleet, 1953. Spl. Commendation from Sec. Def., 1958, Sec. Navy Commendation medal, 1959; recipient Distinguished Alumnus award U. Mich., 1957, Sesquicentennial medal and certificate, 1967, NASA Exceptional Service medal, 1969. Fellow Royal Aero. Soc.; asso. fellow Am. Inst. Aeros. and Astronautics (pres. Central Cal. sect. 1958-59, bd. dirs. Washington sect. 1964-65, 69). Author tech. papers. Home: 4110 Mason Ridge Dr Annandale VA 22003 Office: 600 Independence Av SW Washington DC 20546

FREITAS, GEORGE ERNEST, corp. exec.; b. Honolulu, Dec. 2, 1905; s. Henry and Mary (Lewis) F.; B.S. in Civil Engring., U. Dayton, 1929; L.H.D., Chaminade Coll., Honolulu; m. Flora Cabral, Aug. 6, 1938; children—Gail, Alan. Pres., chief exec. Hawaii Corp., 1962-69; founder, 1938, chmn., dir. Pacific Constrn. Co. Ltd., 1938-69; founder Pacific Contractors, 1957. chmn., dir. 1958- 69; chmn., dir. Von Hammn-Young, Inc., 1962-69, Pacific Investment Inc., 1962-69, Johnston & Buscher, Inc., 1962-69, VHY Pty. Ltd. (Australia), 1964—, Pacific-Peru Constrn. Corp., 1965-69, Amelco Engrs. Pty. Ltd. (Australia), 1970—; pres., chmn., dir. Pacific Devel. Co., Ltd., 1951—, Pacco, Ltd., 1962-69; v.p., dir. Moanalua Manor Shopping, Inc., Rosalei Apts., Inc.; dir. First Hawaiian Bank, Hawaiian Western Steel, Ltd., Hawaii Corp., 1962—. Mem. Territorial Bd. Health Civil Service Commn., 1937-40; bd. govs. Hawaii Employers Council, 1962-68; lay bd. mem. Marianist Province Pacific; patron Smithsonian Instn.; bd. dirs. Aloha United Fund, 1967-69; v.p., bd. dirs. St. Louis-Chaminade Ednl. Center; chmn. bd. regents Chaminade Coll.; life mem. Queens Hosp., Honolulu Acad. Arts, U. Hawaii Found. (trustee 1962-68). Recipient Outstanding Alumnus award St. Louis High Sch., 1970. Mem. Honolulu C. of C. (bd. dirs. 1962-64), Navy League U.S., Nat. Planning Assn., Air Force Assn., St. Louis Coll., U. Dayton alumni assns., Gen. Contractors Assn. Hawaii (pres. 1947). Clubs: Pacific, Outrigger Canoe, Oahu Country, Waialae Country (Honolulu). Home: 3049 Noela St Honolulu HI 96815 Office: Amfac Bldg Honolulu HI 96813

FREKING, FREDERICK WILLIAM, bishop; b. Heron Lake, Minn., Aug. 11, 1913; s. August and Rosa (Oberbroeckling) F.; A.B., St. Mary's Coll., 1934, LL.D., 1958; student North Am. Coll., Rome. 1934-39; S.T.B., Gregorian U., 1937; J.C.D., Cath. U. Am., 1948. Ordained priest Roman Cath. Ch., 1938; asst. pastor St. John's Ch., Rochester Minn., 1940-43; supt. Lourdes High Sch., Rochester, 1941-43; pastor St. John's Ch., Winona, Minn., 1943-45; 1st editor Winonan edit. Our Sunday Visitor, 1943-45; sec. to Bishop Leo Binz. Winona, 1948-50; mem. Civil Corp., Diocese of Winona. 1943-53. sec. corp., 1950-53; sec. Diocesan Matrimonial Tribunal. Diocese of Winona. 1948-50; defender of marriage bond, 1950-53; vice chancellor Diocese of Winona. 1950-51, chancellor. 1951-53, diocesan dir. cemeteries. 1950-53; pastor Holy Cross Ch., Dakota. Minn., 1950-51, also with mission at Precious Blood Ch., LaMoille, Minn.: pastor St. Mary's Ch., Minnieska, Minn., 1951-53, also with mission. St. Paul's Ch., Minnesota City; spiritual dir. North Am. Coll., Rome, 1953-57; named papal chamberlain by Pope Pius XII, 1949, domestic prelate, 1954. Bishop of Salina. 1958-65, bishop of La Crosse (Wis.) diocese, 1965—. Adv. bd. Boy Scouts Am., 1958—, Marymount Coll., Salina, 1958—. Decorated Knight Comdr. Holy Sepulchre, 1958. Mem. Nat. Cath. Rural Life Conf. (pres.). Phi Kappa Theta. K.C. (4). Address: 421 Country Club Rd Salina KS 67401

FRELINGHUYSEN, PETER, H.B., congressman; b. N.Y.C., Jan. 17, 1916; s. Peter H. B. and Adaline (Havemeyer) F.; A.B. magna cum laude, Princeton, 1938; LL.B., Yale, 1941; m. Beatrice S. Procter, Sept. 7, 1940; children—Peter, Beatrice, Rodney, Adaline, Frederick. Investment bus., N.Y.C.; dir. Am. Nat. Bank and Trust Co. Morristown; mem. 83-92d Congresses, 5th N.J. Dist. Bd. mgrs. Howard Savs. Instn., Newark. Served as lt. USNR, World War II. Republican. Episcopalian. Home: Sand Spring Lane Morristown NJ 07960 Office: Rayburn Office Bldg Washington DC 20515

FRELLESVIG, PER WELSCH, Danish diplomat; b. Holstebro, Denmark, Feb. 17, 1921; s. E. and Antoinette (Welsch) F.; degree in econs. (cand. econ.), U. Aarhus, 1947; m. Else F. Hansen, June 3, 1949 (dec. 1963); children—Hans, Anne; m. 2d, Lis-Vibeke Nordlien, June 2, 1967; children— Sten, Eva. Joined Danish Fgn. Service, 1947, served in Ankara and The Hague, then chief NATO Dept., Ministry Fgn. Affairs, 1963-66; minister counselor in Paris, 1966-70; consul gen. in San Francisco, 1970—. Home: 2108 Washington St San Francisco CA 94109 Office: Alcoa Bldg One Maritime Plaza San Francisco CA 94111

FRELONG, FRIZ, exec. v.p. DePatie-Frelong Enterprises, Inc. Address: 527 Lexington Av New York City NY 10017*

FREMONT, ERNEST HOAR Jr., lawyer; b. Glenwood, Minn., Nov. 19, 1925; s. Ernest Hoar and Olga (Ostlund) F.; B.A., U. Minn., 1950; J.D., U. Mo. at Kansas City, 1956; m. Johanne M. Ravenholt, Dec. 27, 1947; children—Paula Marie, Alicia Ann. Admitted to Mo. bar, 1956; partner firm Popham, Popham, Conway, Sweeny &

Fremont, Kansas City, 1956—. Chmn. Mo. Adv. Com. Free Press-Fair Trial, 1968-70; chmn. Supreme Ct. (Mo.) Com. on Profl. Ethics and Responsibility, 1969-71. Pres. law found. U. Mo. at Kansas City, 1965- 66, trustee, 1962-66; trustee Kansas City U. Conservatory Music. Served with USNR, 1944-46; served to 1st lt. AUS, 1951-53. Recipient Alumni Achievement award U. Mo. at Kansas City, 1965; named Distinguished Alumnus of Yr., Powell Inn, Phi Delta Phi, 1970. Hon. fellow Harry S. Truman Library Inst.; fellow Internat. Soc. Barristers; mem. Am. (chmn. standing com. pub. relations 1965-68), Mo. (bd. govs. 1964—, mem. control council 1963—, chmn. pub. information com. 1962-64, pres. 1971-72), Kansas City bar assns., Powell Inn (exchequer 1952-53), Nat. Planning Assn. (mem. nat. council 1970—), Internat. Platform Assn., Fedn. Ins. Counsel, Phi Delta Phi. Conglist. (trustee 1966-68, chmn. 1967-68). Home: 659 Romany Rd Kansas City MO 64113 Office: Commerce Bank Bldg Kansas City MO 64106

FREMONT-SMITH, FRANK, physician; b. St. Augustine, Fla., Mar. 19, 1895; s. Frank and Dorothea M. (Grossman) F.-S.; grad. Groton (Mass.) Sch., 1913; student Mass. Inst. Tech., 1915-16; M.D., Harvard, 1921; m. Frances Eliot, June 5, 1920 (div. 1935); children—Paul, Kenneth, Eliot; m. 2d, Hazel Crockett, July 25, 1935; 1 son, Nicholas. Intern, Peter Bent Brigham Hosp., Boston, 1921-22; mem. dept. neuropathol. Harvard Med. Sch., 1925-36; instr., 1926-29, asst. prof., 1929-36; med. dir. Josiah Macy, Jr., Found., 1936-60; vis. prof. clin. psychiatry Temple U., 1962-70; dir. inter-disciplinary conf. program Am. Inst. Biol. Scis., 1960-64; dir. inter-disciplinary communications program N.Y. Acad. Sci., 1964-68; spl. cons. Nat. Inst. Child Health and Human Devel., 1963-66; cons. Dept. Def., 1958—; adviser to surgeon-gen. U.S. Army; co-chmn. World Mental Health Yr., 1960. Cons. sec. of war, assigned office insp. gen., 1944-45; sr. monitor Radiol. Safety Sect., Operation Crossroads, Bikini, June, July, 1946; cons. mental health, gerontol., surg.-gen. USPHS, 1946-47; expert cons. to air surgeon in psychology and neurology, 1948-51. Trustee Communication Research Inst., St. Thomas, V.I., 1961-65, Acad. Religion and Mental Health, 1961—; mem. corp. Congress Scientists on Survival, 1963-65; bd. dirs. Scientists on Survival, 1963- 65. Served with USNR, 1917-18. Fellow N.Y. Acad. Sci., N.Y. Acad. Medicine, Royal Soc. Medicine (London), Am. Psychiat. Assn. (life); mem. Am. Orthopsychiat. Assn., World Med. Assn. (U.S. com.), Group for Advancement of Psychiatry, A.A.A.S. (com. cooperation among scientists), A.M.A., Am. Neurol. Assn., World Fedn. Mental Health (past pres., chmn. gov. bd. 1960—; incorporator 1962), Acad. Psychoanalysis (asso.), Nat. Assn. Sci. Writers (hon.) Am. Soc. Clin. Investigation, Assn. Am. Physicians, Assn. Research in Nervous and Mental Diseases, Mass. Med. Soc., Soc. Study Growth and Devel., Soc. Research in Child Devel., N.Y. Acad. Medicine, Am. Soc. Research in Psychosomatic Problems, Nat. Com. Mental Hygiene (v.p., 1944-50 chmn. joint adv. com. with Am. Assn. Psychiat. Social workers to War Office Psychiat. Social Work 1945-46), NRC (com. on selection and tng. aircraft pilots, bd. on clin. psychology, com. on mental hosps.), Am. Hosp. Assn., N.Y. Psychiat. Soc., Am. Psychonalytic Assn. (hon.), Gerontological Soc. Inc. U.S. vice pres. Internat. Com. for Mental Hygiene, 1947-48. Club; Cosmos. Co-author: Cerebro-Spinal Fluid, 1937. Address: 149 Brewster Rd Massapequa NY 11758 ☆

FRENCH, A. JAMES, physician; b. Van Houten, N.M., Sept. 3, 1912; s. A. P. and Elizabeth (Williams) F.: A.B., U. Colo., 1933, M.A., 1936, M.D., 1936; m. Genevieve Fetter, July 19, 1937; 1 dau., Patricia Sue. Intern Kansas City Gen. Hosp., Mo., 1936-37; resident pediatrics Children's Hosp., Denver, 1937-38; resident pathology St. Louis City Hosp., 1938-40; resident, instr. pathology U. Mich. Hosp., 1940-41, chief clin. labs., 1952—; asst. prof. pathology U. Mich. Med. Sch., 1946-47, asso. prof., 1947-53, prof., 1953—, chmn. dept., 1956—, also editor Med. Bull., 1955-57; pathologist Surgeon Gen.'s Office, Washington and Far East, 1941-46, cons., 1947-50; cons., mem. pathology adv. council VA Hosp., Ann Arbor, also Wayne County Gen. Hosp., 1959—. Dir. Mich. Maternal Tissue Registry, 1957- -; mem. sci. adv. bd. Armed Forces Inst. Path., 1965-70, chmn., 1968-70; mem. etiology com. Am. Cancer Soc., 1962-65. Col. AUS Res. Diplomate Am. Bd. Pathology (trustee 1962—, sec.-treas. 1964—). Fellow A.C.P.; mem. Mich. Pathol. Soc. (pres. 1953), Internat. Acad. Pathology (council 1957-60, pres. 1966), Am. Soc. Clin. Pathology, Am. Assn. Pathologists and Bacteriologists (mem. council 1970, sec.-treas. 1971—), Coll. Am. Pathologists (chmn. acad. sect. 1960-61, gov. 1964-70, sec.-treas. 1969-70), Am. Acad. Oral Pathology (hon.). A.M.A. (sec. treas. sect. on pathology 1972—), Frederick A. Coller Surg. Soc. (hon.). Contbr. med. jours. Home: 356 Ausable Pl Ann Arbor MI 48104 Office: 1335 E Catherine St Ann Arbor MI 48104

FRENCH, ANTHONY PHILIP, physicist, educator; b. Brighton, Eng., Nov. 19, 1920; s. Sydney James and Elizabeth Margaret (Hart) F.; B.A. with honors, Cambridge (Eng.) U., 1942, M.A., 1946, Ph.D., 1948; m. Naomi Mary Livesay, Oct. 6, 1945; children—Martin Charles, Gillian Ruth. Came to U.S., 1955. Mem. atomic bomb projects Tube Alloys and Manhattan Project, 1942-46; demonstrator, lectr. physics Cambridge U., 1948-55, fellow Pembroke Coll., 1950-55; prof. physics U. S.C., 1955-63, chmn. dept., 1956-62; vis. prof. Mass. Inst. Tech., 1962-64, prof. 1964—. Mem. Am. Phys. Soc., Am. Assn. Physics Tchrs., Sigma Xi, Sigma Pi Sigma, Blue Key. Author: Principles of Modern Physics, 1958; Special Relativity, 1968; Newtonian Mechanics, 1971; Vibrations and Waves, 1971; also articles. Office: Mass Inst Tech Cambridge MA 02139

FRENCH, BRUCE HARTUNG, economist, lawyer; b. Canton, O., May 2, 1915; s. Garnett Bruce and Marie (Hartung) F.; A.B., Haverford Coll., 1937; A.M., U. Pa., 1940, Ph.D., 1946; postgrad. Princeton, 1941-42; LL.B., Rutgers U., 1945; m. Jeanne Adrienne Aeberhard, June 27, 1942 (div. 1969); children—Robert Adrain, David Adrain; m. 2d, Dorothy S. Fleming Gorman, Nov. 29, 1969. Asst. in govt. Haverford Coll., 1937-39; instr. politics Princeton, 1941-42, 46-47; asst. prof. econs. U. Coll., Rutgers U., 1947-53, asso. prof. econs., 1953—, chmn. dept. econs., 1951—; admitted to N.J. bar, 1948; partner law firm French & Cook, Princeton, N.J. 1950-59; pvt. practice law, 1959—; pres. Estate Owners, Inc.; Bar Harbor Property Owners Corp.; exec. dir., counsel Housing Authority Borough Princeton, 1949-58, Hightstown, 1958—; pres. Princeton Community Chest, 1950; mem. N.J. Tercentenary Adv. Com., 1960. Bd. dirs. Haverford Coll. Served to lt. comdr. USNR, 1942-46; as liaison officer with fgn. govts., officer-in-charge USN Internat. Aid Office, N.Y.C. Mem. Princeton Hist. Soc. (past pres.), N.J., Mercer County, Princeton bar assns., S.A.R., Huguenot Soc., War of 1812, St. Nicholas Soc., Soc. Colonial Wars, Phi Beta Kappa. Mem. Soc. of Friends. Republican. Clubs: Nassau (past pres.), Pretty Brook Tennis (Princeton): Union, Princeton (N.Y.C.); Athenaeum, Racquet (Phila); Pot and Kettle, Bar Harbor (Bar Harbor, Me.); Founders (Haverford Coll.). Author: Banking and Insurance in New Jersey-A History, 1965. Contbr. articles profl. jours. Home: 73 Castle Howard Ct Princeton NJ 08540 Office: 192 College Av New Brunswick NJ 08901 also: 10 Nassau St Princeton NJ 08540

FRENCH, CHARLES CLEMENT, educator; b. Phila., Oct. 24, 1901; s. Harry Sailer and Gertrude Comly (MacMillan) F.; B.S., U. Pa., 1922, M.S., 1923, Ph.D., 1927; LL.D., U. Punjab, Lahore, Pakistan, Whitworth Coll.; Litt.D., Pacific Luth. U., Tacoma; LL.D., Wash. State U.; m. Helen Augusta Black, Dec. 25, 1925; children—Jane French Blaisdell, Richard Clement. Instr. chemistry U. Pa., 1922-30; prof. chemistry, chmn. dept. Randolph-Macon Woman's Coll., 1930-49, acting dean, 1936-37, dean Coll., 1937-49; v.p. and acting dir. grad. studies Va. Polytech. Inst., 1949-50; dean Coll., Tex. A. and M. Coll., 1950-52; pres. Wash. State U. 1952-66; chmn. Wash. Constl. Revision Com., 1968-69. Pres. Assn. Va. Colls., 1942- 44. Sec.-treas. conf. Acad. Deans So. States, 1940-42, chmn., 1942- 45; sec. Am. Conf. Acad. Deans, 1946-47, chmn., 1947-49. Chmn. com. on standards, 1950-52, So. Assn. Colls. and Secondary Schs. (v.p. 1951-52); mem. exec. com. bd. trustees Va. Episcopal Sch., 1943-50, exec. com. Am. Assn. Land-Grant Coll. and State Univs., 1955-58, pres., 1958-59, chmn. exec. com., 1959-60; 1st v.p. Am. Council on Edn., 1957-58, exec. com., 1958-61. Adv. panel ROTC Affairs to res. forces policy bd. Dept. Def., 1956-65, Air Force ROTC Adv. Panel, 1960-66; ednl. adv. com. VA, 1958-59; commr. for Wash., Western Interstate Commn., 1956-66, chmn., 1961-62. Bd. overseers Whitman Coll., Walla Walla, Wash. Mem. Nat. Council Accreditation Tchr. Edn., Sigma Xi, Alpha Chi Sigma, Tau Beta Pi, Tau Kappa Alpha. Omicron Delta Kappa, Phi Kappa Phi, Pi Kappa Delta, Pi Eta Sigma. Episcopalian. Mason. Home: 305 Sunset Dr Pullman WA 99163 Office: French Adminstrn Bldg Wash State U Pullman WA 99163

FRENCH, CHARLES EZRA, economist, educator; b. Smithville, Mo., Apr. 7, 1923; s. Charley E. and Ruth (Downs) F.; student Washington U., St. Louis, 1943; B.S., U. Mo., 1948, M.A., 1949; Ph.D., Purdue U., 1951; postgrad. U. Cal. at Berkeley, 1957; m. Dolores Eloise Albers, Aug. 31, 1947; children—Ned Carleton, Hugh Nathan, Sarasue. Asst. prof. agrl. econs. Purdue U., Lafayette, Ind., 1951-54, asso. prof., 1954-57, prof. agrl. econs., 1957-58, asst. head dept. agrl. econs., 1958-65, acting head dept., 1965-66, head dept., 1966—. Mem. agrl. bd. NRC, Nat. Acad. Scis.; adviser U.S. Dept. Agr., Dept. State, Dept. Health, Edn. and Welfare; cons. Ford Found., Dept. State in Latin Am. Served to capt. USAAF, 1943-46. Decorated Air medal with clusters. Mem. Am., Canadian agrl. econs. assns., Western Farm Econs. Assn., Agrl. Marketing Assn., A.A.A.S., Internat. Platform Assn., Internat. Assn. Agrl. Economists, Sigma Xi, Alpha Gamma Sigma, Alpha Zeta, Phi Eta Sigma, Gamma Sigma Delta, Alpha Phi Zeta. Methodist. Author: (with others) Organization and Competition in Midwest Dairy Industries, 1970. Contbr. articles profl. jours. Home: 329 Leslie Av West Lafayette IN 47906 Office: Krannert Bldg State St Lafayette IN 47907

FRENCH, CHARLES FERRIS, Jr., banker; b. N.Y.C., Jan. 4, 1918; s. Charles F. and Alma (Young) F.; A.B. in Bus. Adminstrn., Duke, 1939; grad. Rutgers U. Grad Sch. Banking, 1955; m. Martha Jane Williams, June 29, 1940; 1 dau., Christie C. with Mfrs. Trust Co., N.Y.C., 1939-58; v.p., 1955-58; pres. First Nat. Iron Bank N.J., Morristown, 1963—. Vice chmn. Morristown chpt. A.R.C., 1966- -. Bd. dirs. Morristown Meml. Hosp., 1966—; trustee Morristown Sch., 1967—. Mem. Robert Morris Assoc. (pres. N.Y.C. chpt., 1957-58), N.J., Morris County (past pres.) bd. dirs., Chi Phi. Alpha Kappa Psi. Rotarian (past pres. Morristown). Club: Rockaway River Country (past pres.) (Denville). Home: Norris Rd Denville, NJ 07834. Office: 22 South St Morristown NJ 07960

FRENCH, CHARLES STACY, scientist; b. Lowell, Mass., Dec. 13, 1907; s. Charles Ephraim and Helena (Stacy) F.; student Loomis Inst., Windsor, Conn., 1921-25; B.S., Harvard, 1930, A.M., 1932, Ph.D., 1934; m. Margaret Wendell Coolidge, Dec. 10, 1938; children—Helena Stacy, Charles Ephraim. Asst. in gen. physiology Harvard, 1930-33; research fellow Cal. Inst. Tech., 1934-35; guest worker with Otto Warburg, Kaiser Wilhelm Inst., Berlin-Dahlem, Germany, 1935-36; Austin teaching fellow in biochemistry Harvard Med. Sch., 1936-38; instr. (research) in chemistry with James Franck, U. Chgo., 1938- 41; asst. prof. dept. botany U. Minn., 1941-45, asso. prof., 1945-47; dir. div. plant biology Carnegie Instn. of Washington at Stanford U. 1947—, prof. (by courtesy) Stanford. Mem. Am. Soc. Plant Physiologists (chmn. Western Sect. 1954), Bot. Soc. Am., Nat. Acad. Scis., Am. Acad. Arts and Scis., Am. Soc. Biol. Chemists, Soc. Gen. Physiologists (v.p. 1954, pres. 1955-56), A.A.A.S., Biophys. Soc., Deutsche Akademie der Naturforscher Leopoldina. Club: Am. Alpine. Contbr. sci. jours. on plant physiology. Home: 11927 Rhus Ridge Rd Los Altos Hills CA 94022 Office: Carnegie Institution Stanford CA 94305

FRENCH, DAVID MARVIN, coll. dean; b. Los Angeles, Mar. 30, 1909; s. Samuel H. and Mabel A. (Marvin) F.; B.A., Pomona Coll., 1931; B.A., Oxford U., 1933, B.Litt., 1934; M.A., Harvard, 1936, Ph.D., 1940; m. Mary Ruth Oldt, Sept. 10, 1938; children—Margaret E., Mary M., Sarah H. Instr. polit. sci. Western Res. U., 1936-37, U. Mich., 1937-41; asst. and asso. prof. polit. sci. Mills Coll., 1941-49, dean faculty, 1941-46, dir. grad. study, 1946-48; internat. adminstrn. officer Dept. State, 1949-56; dean Flint Coll., U. Mich., 1956—. Adviser U.S. Delegation Gen. Assembly UN, 1949; mem. U.S. delegations Internat. Civil Aviation Orgn., 1950-54, World Health Assembly, 1955. Mem. Am. Polit. Sci. Assn., Am. Fgn. Service Assn., Phi Beta Kappa, Phi Kappa Phi, Phi Delta Kappa. Rotarian. Club: University (Flint). Home: 602 S Lynch St Flint MI 48503

FRENCH, DEXTER, educator; b. Des Moines, Feb. 23, 1918; s. Raymond Albert and Minnie Emily (Ormerod) F.; A.B., U. Dubuque, 1938, D.Sc., 1960; Ph.D., Ia. State U., 1942; m. Mary Catherine Martin, June 17, 1939; children—Alfred, David, Walter, Barbara (dec.), Jean, Nancy, Carol. Research chemist Corn Products Co., 1945; mem. faculty Ia. State U., 1946—, prof. chemistry, 1955—, prof. biochemistry, 1960—, chmn. dept. biochemistry and biophysics, 1963-71. Postdoctoral fellow phys. chemistry Harvard Med. Sch., 1942-44; sr. postdoctoral fellow NSF, London and Paris, 1962-63. Mem. Am. Chem. Soc., Am. Soc. Biol. Chemists. Home: 3521 Ross Rd Ames IA 50010

FRENCH, GEORGE THANET, farm and indsl. equipment mfr.; b. Davenport, Ia., Oct. 6, 1911; s. George Decker and Dorothy (Lischer) F.; grad. Phillips Andover Acad., 1929; A.B., Yale, 1933; m. Nancy Rendleman, Feb. 26, 1945 (div. Apr. 1959); children—George R., Lucia Ann, William D.; m. 2d, Caroline Wagoner, Nov. 6, 1960, With Deere & Co., Moline, Ill., 1934-71, dir., 1951—, v.p. implement prodn. div., 1956-60, v.p. mfg., 1960-63, sr. v.p., 1963-68, sr. v.p. overseas div., 1968-70, sr. v.p. indsl. products, 1970-71; past dir. Central Engring. Co., Davenport, Ia. Bd. Dirs. U.S.A. Standards Inst., trustee funds and property Diocese of Quincy. Home: 1230 36th Av Rock Island IL 61201

FRENCH, ISABELLE FRANCES, electronics engr.; b. Swampscott, Mass., Feb. 16, 1924; d. Abram and Grace Benton (Seward) French; B.S. in Radio Engr., Tri-State Coll., Angola, Ind., 1944; grad. student Boston U., Northeastern U.; D. Engring. (hon.), Tri-State College, 1966. Jr. engr. Sylvania Electric Products Inc., 1944-52; engr. Capehart-Farnsworth Corp., 1952-54; asso. mem. tech. staff Bell Telephone Labs., Allentown, Pa., 1954—. Mem. East Allen Twp.-Northampton County Planning Commn., chmn., 1970-71; chmn. Zoning Hearing Bd., 1971. Recipient Alumni Distinguished Service award Tri-State Coll., 1962. Mem. Soc. Women Engrs. (treas. 1953-55, sec. 1961-63, v.p. 1963-64, pres. 1964- 66), I.E.E.E. Club: Allentown Altrusa (corr. sec. 1967-69, v.p. 1969-71, pres. 1971-72). Home: Box 462-C R D 2 Bath PA 18014 Office: 555 Union Blvd Allentown PA 18103

FRENCH, JOHN DOUGLAS, surgeon, educator; b. Los Angeles, Apr. 11, 1911; s. John Rollin and Effie (Douglas) F.; A.B., U. Cal. at Los Angeles, 1933; M.D., U. So. Cal., 1937; m. Dorothy Kirsten, July 18, 1955. Intern internal medicine U. Cal. Hosp., San Francisco, 1937-38; intern surgery Strong Meml. Hosp. and U. Rochester Sch. Medicine, 1938-39; successively asst. resident surgery, asso. resident neurosurgery, chief resident surgeon Strong Meml. Hosp., 1939-43, asst. surgeon, 1943-46; asst. prof. neurol. surgery U. Rochester Sch. Medicine and Dentistry, 1943-46; fellow U. Ill. Neuropsychiat. Inst., 1946-47; chief neurosurgery VA Hosp., Long Beach, Cal., 1948-58, asso. dir. profl. services for research, 1950-58, chief cons. neurosurgery, 1958—; clin. prof. surgery-neurosurgery U. Cal. Sch. Medicine, Los Angeles, 1949—, prof. anatomy, 1960—, dir. Brain Research Inst., 1960—. Mem. biosci. tng. com. NIH, 1958-63, biosci. subcom. Office Space Sci. and Application, NASA, 1960—, com. bioastronautics Nat. Acad. Scis.-Armed Forces- NRC, 1958-62. Mem. adv. com. Big Bros. Los Angeles. EPI-HAB LA. Diplomate Am. Bd. Surgery, Am. Bd. Neurol. Surgery. Mem. Am. Neurol. Assn., Am. Acad. Neurol. Surgery, Am., Cal., Los Angeles med. assns.; Harvey Cushing Soc., Los Angeles Soc. Neurology and Psychiatry, Pacific Coast Surg. Assn., Soc. Neurol. Surgeons, Soc. U. Surgeons, So. Cal. (pres. 1957-58), Western (pres. 1969) neurosurg. socs., Sigma Xi, Alpha Omega Alpha. Author, editor: Frontiers in Brain Research, 1962. Editor; (with R. W. Porter) Basic Research in Paraplegia, 1962. Contbr. to books. Home: 12841 Sunset Blvd Los Angeles, CA 90049.

FRENCH, JOHN HENRY, Jr., banker, b. Detroit, July 2, 1911; s. John Henry and Elsie (Mott) F.; grad. Swarthmore (Pa.) Prep. Sch., 1930; A.B., Brown U., 1933; M.B.A., Babson Inst., 1934; m. Katharine Baker, Sept. 15, 1934; children—John Henry III, Dainforth Baker, Henry Welling. With City Nat. Bank of Detroit, 1949—; pres., dir. 1953—, chmn. bd., 1970—; dir. Higbie Mfg. Co., Rochester. Pres. Detroit Clearing House, 1967—. Bd. dirs. Central Bus. Dist. Assn. Mem. Am. Bankers Assn. (exec. council 1958), Greater Detroit C. of C. (dir.). Episcopalian. Club: Economic (treas.) (Detroit). Home: 130 Merriweather Rd Grosse Pointe Farms MI 48236 also Goslow Rd Gaylord MI Office: Penobscot Bldg Detroit MI 48226

FRENCH, LYLE ALBERT, surgeon; b. nr. Worthing, S.D., Mar. 26, 1915; s. Leslie V. and Bernice M. (McKinney) F.; student Macalester Coll., 1933-35; B.S., U. Minn., 1936, M.B., 1939., M.D., 1940, M.S., 1946, Ph.D., 1947; m. Gene F. Richmond, Sept. 13, 1941; children—Frederick E., Eldridge T., Barbara Gene. Intern U. Hosp., Mpls., 1939-40; instr. neurosurgery U. Minn., St. Paul, 1947-49, asst. prof., 1949-52, asso. prof., 1952-57, prof., 1957- -, chmn. dept. neurol. surgery, 1960—, v.p. health scis., 1970—; chief staff Univ. Hosps., Mpls., 1968—; cons. neurosurgery Surgeon Gen., U.S. Army, 1962—; spl. cons. Central Office, VA, 1968—. Served from lt. to maj. AUS, 1941-45. Diplomate Am. Bd. Neurol. Surgery. Mem. Am. Soc. Research in Stereoencephalotomy (pres. 1968—), Minn. Soc. Neurol. Scis. (pres. 1963), Neurosurg. Soc. Am. (pres. 1958), Mpls. Acad. Medicine (pres. 1960). Contbr. articles in field. Home: 85 Otis Lane St Paul MN 55455.

FRENCH, MERTON BYRON, univ. prof.; b. Topeka, Kan., Nov. 17, 1905; s. Shirley S. and Mary (Brown) F.; A.B., Washburn Coll., 1929; A.M., Brown U., 1931, Ph.D., 1935; m. Elizabeth Louise Hale, July 26, 1939; children—Mrs. John Perry, Sarah Frances (Mrs. Glenn Collins). Prof. religion Elon (N.C.) Coll., 1935-46; prof. of philosophy and religion Washburn Municipal U., Topeka, Kan., 1946-71, prof. emeritus, 1971—, chmn. dept. philosophy, 1952-71, chmn. humanities div., 1958-71. Mem. Am. Acad Religion, Soc. Bibl. Lit. and Exegesis, Am. Oriental Soc., Gallahue Seminar in Religion and Psychiatry (Menninger Found.), Phi Pi Phi, Phi Beta Kappa, Pi Gamma Mu, Tau Delta Pi, Pi Kappa Delta. Republican. Conglist. Home: 1306 High St Topeka KS 66604

FRENCH, ORVAL C, univ. prof.; b. Genesco, Kan., Jan. 3, 1908; s. Oliver Collins and Nina Mabel (Gilkison) F.; B.S., Kan. State Coll., 1930, M.S. in argl. engring., 1931; m. Helen Jane Pembleton, May 29, 1932; children—Nina LuEllen, Byron Thomas. Agrl. engr. Black-Sivalls & Bryson Mfg. Co., 1930; instr., U. Cal. at Davis, 1931-40, asst. prof., 1941-47, asso. prof. 1947; prof. agrl. engring. and head of dept. Cornell U., 1947—; mem. adv. com. Thor Research Center, Marengo, Ill., 1957-60; vis. prof. agrl. engring. U. Philippines, 1958. Trustee Village of Cayuga Heights, 1961-65. Mem. coll. conf. bd., United Cooperatives, Inc. Treas. Westminster Found., 1961-65. Fellow A.A.A.S., Am. Soc. Agrl. Engrs. (chmn. N. Atlantic sect. 1959-60, pres. 1966-67); mem. Am. Soc. Engring. Edn., Tau Beta Pi, Sigma Xi, Gamma Sigma Delta, Phi Kappa Phi. Presbyn. (elder). Rotarian. Home: 404 Highland Rd Ithaca NY Office: 104 Riley-Robb Hall Cornell U Ithaca NY 14850

FRENCH, PRENTISS, landscape architect, land planner; b. Chgo., June 26, 1894; s. William Merchant Richardson and Alice (Helm) F.; A.B., Williams Co..., 1917; M. Landscape Architecture, Harvard, 1921; m. Helen Louise Douglass, Nov. 30, 1927; 1 dau., Pamela. Asst. prof. landscape architecture U. Mass., 1924-25; landscape architect, Venice, Fla., 1926-27; pvt. practice of landscape architecture, including broad-scale planning, Fla., Mass., Cal., 1927—; design gardens, other pvt. projects, also master plans for mil. establishments Ft. Richardson, Alaska, Fitzsimons Army Hosp., Denver, coll. campuses Loyola U., Los Angeles. Served as lt. F.A., U.S. Army, 1917-18; sr. landscape architect, Office Chief Engrs., AUS, World War II. Fellow Am. Soc. Landscape Architects (trustee 1945, 57-59); mem. Am. Planning and Civic Assn. Home: 2659 Filbert St San Francisco CA 94123 Office: 414 Mason San Francisco CA 94102

FRENCH, RAYMOND, realtor; b. Milw., June 14, 1920; s. Sydney and Mabel (Gamble) F.; grad. Mercersburg Acad., 1939, Yale, 1943, U.S. Merchant Marine Acad., 1946; m. Joan Foy, Dec. 27, 1947; children—Pamela Farquhar, Christina Chrysler, Wendy Collison. Vice pres. Webb & Knapp, Inc., N.Y.C., 1957-62; pres., dir. Canal-Randolph Corp., N.Y.C., 1962—; pres., dir. United Stockyards Corp.; dir. Peninsula Terminal Co., Sioux Falls Stock Yards Co., Sioux City Terminal Co., Fargo, Union Stock Yards Co., Blue Ridge Real Estate Co., Split Rock Lodge, Inc., Am. Union Ins. Co. N.Y.; trustee Dollar Sav. Bank. Mem. Downstate Med. Center State U. N.Y., 1965—. Trustee, chmn. Hofstra U.; pres., bd. dirs. Pro Arte Symphony Orch. Clubs: Piping Rock Creek (Locust Valley, N.Y.); Yale (N.Y.C.); Quogue (N.Y.) Field. Home: Piping Rock Rd Locust Valley NY 11560 Office: 277 Park Av New York City NY 10017

FRENCH, REGINALD FOSTER, educator; b. West Lebanon, N.H., May 23, 1906; s. Ernest E. and Florence (Hilliard) F.; A.B., Dartmouth, 1927; M.A., Harvard, 1928, Ph.D., 1935; postgrad. U. Rome, 1929; M.A. (hon.), Amherst Coll., 1949; m. Rachel E. Clapp, Aug. 11, 1930; children—Rebecca, Richard, Polly. Instr. U. Mo., 1930-31, prof., summer 1938; instr. Williams Coll., 1931-35; asst. prof. U. Neb., 1935-37; asso. prof. Romance langs. Amherst Coll., 1937-49, prof., 1949—, acting chmn., 1943-48. Chmn. coll. com. Amherst Bicentennial. Mem. curiatorial bd. Sturbridge Village. Trustee Amherst Acad. Mem. Amherst Hist. Soc., Modern Lang. Assn.

(chmn. Italian sect. 1946), Pewter Collectors Club Am. (editorial bd.), Phi Beta Kappa, Alpha Sigma Phi. Episcopalian. Contbr. profl. and antiquarian jours. Home: 657 S Pleasant St Amherst MA 01002

FRENCH, RICHARD FREDERIC, educator; b. Randolph, Mass., June 23, 1915; s. Herbert F. and Edith (Macgregor) F.; grad. Philips Exeter Acad., 1933; B.S., Harvard. 1937, M.A., 1939. Asst. prof. music Harvard, 1947-51; dir. publs., v.p. Asso. Music Pubs., 1951-59; pres. N.Y. Pro Musica, 1959-70, dir., 1959—; Robert S. Tangeman prof. sacred music Union Theol. Sem., N.Y.C., 1965—. Trustee Bklyn. Music Sch. Served with USAAF, 1942-45. Decorated Bronze Star medal. Mem. Am. Musicol. Soc., Internat. Soc. Contemporary Music (treas. U.S. sect.). Club: Harvard (N.Y.C.). Contbr. articles to books, mags. Home: 15 W 81st St New York City NY 10027 Office: Union Theol Sem 3041 Broadway New York City NY 10027

FRENCH, ROBERT HOUSTON, lawyer; b. Dayton, O., Dec. 12, 1904; s. Edward Houston and Moile B. (Nevin) F.; A.B. with honors, Ohio State U., 1927, J.D. summa cum laude, 1927; m. Dorothy M. Duff, July 22, 1933; children—Mary F. Sweet, Nancy Louise, Robert Houston. Admitted to Ohio bar, 1927, since practiced in Cin.; asst. U.S. atty. So. Dist. Ohio, 1928-31; spl. counsel to Atty. Gen. Ohio, 1938; mem. firm Pogue, Hoffheimer & Pogue, 1931-37, Pogue, Helmholz, Culbertson & French, 1937—; spl. counsel City of Piqua, 1948- 68. Pres. Ohio Valley chpt. Arthritis Found., 1957-60, 65-66, nat. bd. govs., mem. exec. com., 1962—, v.p., 1965-68, sec., 1970—. Recipient Distinguished Service award Nat. Arthritis Found., 1960, 66. Fellow Ohio, Am. bar assn. founds.; mem. Jud. Conf. of U.S. Ct. Appeals for Sixth Circuit, Am., Fed., Ohio (exec. com.), Cin. (v.p. 1959-63, pres. 1963-64) bar assns., Legal Aid Soc. (trustee Cin. 1963-64), Phi Beta Kappa, Order Coif, Phi Delta Phi. Republican. Mason. Clubs: University, Lawyers (Cin.). Home: 8862 Raiders Run Dr Cincinnati OH 45236 Office: First Nat Bank Bldg Cincinnati OH 45202

FRENCH, ROBERT WARREN, educator; b. South Bend, Ind., May 8, 1911; s. Robert Warren and Lura (Keller) F.; A.B., U. of Mich., 1932, M.A., 1933, Ph.D., 1937; fellow Brookings Instn., 1934-35; m. Dorothy Louise Smith, July 8, 1934; children—Nancy Alice (Mrs. Neil McWhorter), Judith Kay (Mrs. Donald B. Lowe, Jr.). Teaching fellow econs. U. Mich., 1937-41; asso. prof. internat. trade dir. bur. bus. research, Coll. Commerce, La. State U. 1941-46. Prof. internat. trade, dir. bur. bus. research, coll. bus. adminstrn. U. Tex., 1946-49; prof. econs., dean sch. bus adminstrn. Tulane U. 1949-55, vice pres., 1953-56; dir. Port of New Orleans, 1956- 60; pres. Tax Found., Inc., 1960-63; dir. exec. programs, prof. mgmt. Grad. Sch. Bus. Adminstrn., U. So. Cal., 1963-65; staff asso. office of pres. U. Ill., Chgo., 1965-68, prof. econs. and mgmt. Coll. Bus. Adminstrn., 1965-70, acting dean Coll. of Bus. Adminstrn., 1966-68; asst. to pres. U. Ala., Birmingham, 1970—, prof. econs. and bus. adminstrn. Div. Bus., 1970—; exec. dir. Pub. Affairs Research Council La., 1950-54. Cons. Nat. Indsl. Conf. Bd., 1963, Assn. Western Rys., 1966-67, U.S. Gen Accounting Office, 1968—. Trustee Dillard U.; bd. mgmt. Flint Goodridge Hosp., 1959-60; bd. councilors Grad. Sch. Bus. Adminstrn. U. So. Cal., 1961-63. Mem. Am. Soc. Pub. Adminstrn. (Member editorial board, 1959-65), Am., Southern economic assns., also Phi Kappa Phi, Pi Gamma Mu, Omicron Delta Kappa, Beta Gamma Sigma. Editor: La. Bus. Rev., 1941-46; Tex. Bus. Rev., 1946-49. Contbr. Am. Peoples Ency., 1952-57, The Tax Exec., Vol. VIII, Tulane Tax Inst., 1951, Basics for Business, 1968, others. Home: 2717 Highland Av Birmingham AL 35205 also Box 108 Buchanan MI 49107

FRENCH, S. ROY, Jr., lawyer, corp. exec.; b. N.Y.C., Sept. 12, 1929; s. S. Ray and Mary (Howard) F.; grad. Fordham Prep. Sch., N.Y.C., 1947; B.S. cum laude Georgetown U. Sch. Fgn. Service, 1951; LL.B., Fordham U., 1956; m. Eileen Joan Leahy, May 14, 1960; children—Robert, Virginia, Elizabeth, Karen, Teresa, Catherine,, Steven. Admitted to N.Y. bar, 1956, since practiced in N.Y.C.; asso. firm Wilkie Farr & Gallagher, 1956-60; staff atty. Cerro Corp., 1960-65, asst. sec., 1965—, asst. gen. atty., 1968—. Served to 1st lt. AUS, 1951-53. Mem. Am. Bar Assn., Assn. Bar City N.Y. Home: RFD 1 Lyon Ridge Rd Katonah NY 10536 Office: 300 Park Av New York City NY 10022

FRENCH, SAMUEL WILLIAM, medical educator; b. Milw., Aug. 7, 1926; s. Samuel Lorenzo and Mary Cecil (Church) F.; A.B., U. Cal. at Berkeley, 1949; M.D., U. Cal. at San Francisco, 1952; m. Rosalie Greer, Feb. 12, 1952 (div. May 1965); children—Linda Greer, William Scott, Leslie Carol; m. 2d, Barbara Alan Black, Sept. 24, 1965; children—Samuel Wheeler, Christopher Alexander. Intern U. Cal. at San Francisco, 1952-53, instr. 1956-60, asst. prof., 1960-64, asso. prof., 1965-67; resident pathology New Eng. Deaconess Hosp., Boston, 1953-55; practice medicine specializing in pathology, San Francisco, 1956-67, Los Angeles, 1967-71, Vancouver, B.C., 1971—; instr. Tulane Med. Sch., New Orleans, 1955-56; asso. prof. U. Cal. at Los Angeles, 1967-69, prof., 1969-71; prof. U. B.C. at Vancouver, 1971—; chief pathology service Harbor Gen. Hosp., Torrance, Cal., 1969-71; mem. staff Vancouver Gen. Hosp., 1971—. Served with USNR, 1944-46. Mem. Internat. Acad. Pathology, N.Y. Acad. Sci., Am. Nutritional Inst., A.A.A.S., Am. Assn. U. Profs., Am. Soc. Exptl. Pathology, Soc. Exptl. Biol. Medicine. Research in acute and chronic toxcity of alcohol. Home: 3100 Blanca Vancouver British Columbia Canada

FRENCH, WILLIAM HAROLD, newspaper editor; b. London, Ont., Can., Mar. 21, 1926; s. Harold Edward and Isabel (Brash) F.; B.A., U. Western Ont., 1948; Nieman fellow Harvard, 1954-55; m. Margaret Jean Rollo, June 23, 1951; children—Jane, Mark, Paul, Susan. With The Globe and Mail, Toronto, Ont., Can., 1948—, lit. editor, 1960—; instr. journalism Ryerson Poly. Inst., 1955—; asso. fellow York U., 1969—; broadcaster Canadian Broadcasting Corp., 1964—; cons. Can. Council, 1969—. Recipient President's medal U. Western Ont., 1966. Author: A Most Unlikely Village, 1960. Home: 78 N Hills Terrace Don Mills Ontario Canada Office: 140 King St W Toronto 110 Ontario Canada

FRENCH, WILLIAM MARSHALL, educator; b. Bodine, Pa., Feb. 18, 1907; s. Harry Hiram and Mary (Pray) F.; A.B., N.Y. State Coll. for Tchrs., 1929; Ph.D., Yale, 1934; m. Florence M. Smith, Apr. 9, 1936; 1 son, Geoffrey Smith. Tchr., Grosse Pointe, Mich., 1929-32; instr. edn. Yale, 1932-34, State Coll., Albany, 1934-38, asst. prof., 1938-39; dean Muskingum Coll., 1939-43; pres. Hastings (Neb.) Coll., 1943-52; prof. Macalester Coll., 1953; prof. edn. Muhlenberg Coll., 1953—; vis. prof. edn. Ohio State U., 1941. Recipient distinguished alumnus award, State U. N.Y., 1969. Mem. History of Edn. Soc., Phi Delta Kappa, Kappa Phi Kappa, Pi Gamma Mu, Kappa Delta Rho. Lutheran. Author: (with Florence French) College of the Empire State, 1944; Education for All, 1955; American Secondary Education, 1957; America's Educational Tradition, 1965. Home: 2605 Greenleaf St Allentown PA 18104

FRENCH, WILLIAM TAYLOR, marketing exec.; b. Detroit, June 22, 1912; s. Francis Raymond and Harriet (FitzGerald) F.; student U. Pa., 1931-32; LL.B., George Washington U., 1942; m. Concetta Vitullo, Feb. 5, 1944; children—Victoria, Stephanie, Deborah, William Taylor. Dir. fire def., Office Civilian Def., then adminstrv. officer OPA, 1940-43; with Vick Chem. Co., 1946-50, asst. to pres., 1949-50; advt. mgr., asst. to pres., Sealtest div., Nat. Dairy, 1951-56; with Lever Bros., N.Y.C., 1956-59, dir. corp. devel., 1956-57, marketing, v.p., 1958-59; pres., chief exec. officer, dir. Asso. Merchandising Corp. N.Y.C., 1960-66, chmn. bd., chief exec. officer, 1966-70; dir. Pillsbury Co., Mpls., Burlington Industries, Inc., Greensboro, N.C., Quincy Assos., N.Y.C., Internat. Farm Systems, Streator, Ill., Mgmt. Horizons, Columbus, O.; adv. bd. Mfrs. Hanover Trust Co. Mem. nat. adv. council Hampshire Coll., Amherst, Mass. Served to lt. USNR, 1943- 46. Mem. Fgn. Policy Assn. (nat. council), Sigma Chi. Clubs: Anglers; Economic; Wee Burn Country; Union League, Sky. Home: Stephanie Lane Darien CT 06820

FRENETTE, EDMOND, business exec.; b. Nouvelle, Que., Can., 1907; grad. U. Montreal (Can.), 1932. Treas., Dupuis Freres, Ltd., Montreal, Que.; dir. Slater Shoe Co. (Can.) Ltd.; chmn. Assumption Mut. Life Ins. Co.; chmn., pres. Librairie Beauchemin Limitee. Home: 3020 Graham Blvd Mount Royal Quebec Canada Office: 865 St Catherine St E Montreal 24 Quebec Canada

FRENI, MIRELLA, soprano; b. Modena, Italy, Feb. 27, 1935; d. Ennio and Gianna (Circelli) Freni; student of Campogalliani and Magiera. Debut as Micaela at Modena Communal Theatre, 1957; appeared Italian theatres Bologne Communla, 1958, Massimo of Palermo, 1959, San Carlo of Naples, 1960, 65, Carlo Felice in Genoa, 1965; appearences in Germany, Holland, London, Spain; sang at Glyndebourne Festival, 1960, La Scala, 1962, 63, 64, 65, Palermo, Spain, 1963: debut Vienna Staatsoper, 1963. Address: Rua Muro 68 Modena, Italy.

FRENKIL, VICTOR, bldg. constrn. exec.; b. Balt., Sept. 14, 1908; s. Isaac and Jennie (Goldscheider) F.; student Johns Hopkins, 1929-31; D. Engring. (hon.), Steed Coll. Tech., Johnson, Tenn.; m. Margaret Panzer, Feb. 15, 1932; children—Janet, Vida, Victor, Leonard. Started home improvement bus., 1931; now chmn. bd., chief exec. officer Balt. Contractors, Inc.; dir. Devel. & Constrn. Co., Inc., Jarvis Steel & Lumber Co., Inc., Citizens Nat. Bank of So. Md., Progress Fed. Savs. and Loan Assn. Life mem. Am. Cancer Soc. Md. Mem. bus. adv. com. UN. Dir. Balt. Civic Opera Co., Balt. Symphony Orch.; trustee State Colls. State Md., N. Charles Gen. Hosp. Recipient gold key for indsl. leadership Balt. Inst., 1953. Mem. Assn. Commerce, Am. Soc. C.E., Mil. Engrs., Phi Alpha. Mason (Shriner), Rotarian; mem. B'nai B'rith. Clubs: Engineers, Advertising (Balt.). Created first nat. TV play award. Office: 711 S Central Av Baltimore MD 21202

FRENSLEY, HERBERT JAMES, engr., constrn. co. exec.; b. Duncan, Okla., Sept. 25, 1906; s. Charles F. and Daisy (Deane) F.; student So. Meth. U., 1926-27, U. Tex., 1927- 29; m. Evelyn Sundberg, Mar. 28, 1935; 1 dau., Joan Elaine. Asst. dir. cigarette tax div., comptroller pub. accounts. Austin, Tex., 1933-36; with Tex. Unemployment Compensation Commn., 1936-42; with Brown & Root, Inc., 1942—, pres., chief exec. officer, dir., 1963—; pres., chief exec. officer, dir. Brown & Root, Ltd., Brown & Root S.A., Houston Exec. Air Service, Southwestern Pipe, Inc., Highlands Ins. Co.; v.p., asst. sec., dir. Joe D. Hughes, Inc.; dir. Gibralter Savs. Assn., Fannin Gen. Ins. Agy., Halliburton Co., Tex. Eastern Transmission Corp., 1st City Nat. Bank Houston, Gordon Jewelry Corp., Armco Steel Corp., Highland Resources; Inc. Chmn. Tex. Game and Fish Commn., 1953-59. Bd. dirs. Tex. Med. Center, Inc.; trustee Baylor Coll. Medicine; mem. Arts and Scis. Found., U. Tex. Brown Found., Inc. C.P.A., Tex. Mem. Am. Inst. Accountants, Tex. Soc. C.P.A.'s, Houston C. of C. (bd. dirs.). Methodist. Clubs: River Oaks Country, Petroleum, Houston, Ramada (bd. dirs.). Home: 2001 Maconda Lane, Houston, TX 77027. Office: PO Box 3 Houston TX 77001

FRENZ, HORST, educator; b. Oberlauringen, Germany, June 29, 1912; s. Paul and Betty (Oestreicher) F.: student U. Breslau, 1930-31, U. Heidelberg, 1931-32, U. London, 1933-34; Ph.D., U. Göttingen, 1936; fellow Allegheny Coll., 1937-38; M.A., U. Ill., 1939; m. Evelyn Anna Haerting, Dec. 23, 1939; children—Paul Dieter, Sigrid Insull. Came to U.S., 1937, naturalized, 1948. Asst., U. London, 1933-34; research, teaching asso. U. Ill., 1938- 40; instr. English, Ind. U., 1940-45, asst. prof. English, 1945-49, asso. prof., 1949-54, prof. English, 1954-64, prof. English and Comparative lit., asso. dir. Sch. of Letters, 1964—, Distinguished prof. English and Comparative lit., 1969—, chmn. comparative lit. program, 1949—; vis. prof. U. Wis., 1947-48, N.Y.U. summers 1950, 60, U. Hamburg, 1954- 55, 59, 63, U. Göttingen, 1962-63, U. Erlangen, 1969. Grantee Am. Council Learned Socs., Am. Philos. Soc.; fellow Fund Advancement Edn., Ford Found., 1952-53; Guggenheim fellow, 1968-69. Mem. Internat. (v.p. 1961- 64), Am. (v.p. 1968-71, pres. 1971—) comparative lit. assns., Modern Lang. Assn., Am. Soc. Theatre Research, Am. Assn. U. Profs., Nat. Council Tchrs. English (chmn. comparative lit. com. 1955-65), Theatre Library Assn., ANTA. Author: Soziales Drama in England, 1938; Eugene O'Neill, 1965. Editor: Whitman and Rolleston: A Correspondence, 1951; Writers of the Western World, rev. edit. 1967; Amerikanische Dramaturgie, 1962; American Playwrights on Drama, 1965; Nobel Prize Lecture in Literature, 1901-1967, 1969; (with others) Comparative Literature: Method and Perspective, rev. edit., 1971. Co- editor: Yearbook of Comparative and Gen. Lit., 1952-60, editor-in-chief, 1960—. Contbr. Am. and fgn. publs. Home: 421 Blue Ridge Dr Bloomington IN 47401

FRENZEL, BILL, congressman; b. St. Paul, July 31, 1928; s. Paul and Paula (Schlegel) F.; B.A., Dartmouth, 1950, M.A.A., 1951; m. Ruth Purdy, June 6, 1952; children—Deborah, Pamela, Melissa. Pres. Mpls. Terminal Warehouse Co., 1966-70, No. Waterway Terminals Corp., 1965-70; mem. 92d Congress 3d Dist. Minn. Mem. adv. com. Nat. Rivers and Harbors Congress, 1967-70, Minn. Dept. Employment Security, 1965-70; dir. transp. Hennepin County Civil Def., 1964-70; mem. bd. Indsl. Relations Center, U. Minn., 1968-70. Mem. Minn. Ho. Reps., 1962-70. Trustee Nat. Cystic Fibrosis Found. Served to lt. USNR, 1951-54; Korea. Named One of Outstanding Young Men, U.S. Jaycees, 1964; One of Outstanding Suburban Legislators, Suburban Sun Newspapers, 1967. Republican. Rotarian. Club: Minneapolis. Home: 6310 Stoneham Lane McLean VA 22101 Office: Longworth House Office Bldg Washington DC 20515

FRENZEL, CHARLES HERMAN, Hosp. adminstr.; b. Jersey City, Sept. 6, 1919; s. Charles H. and Carolyn (Reichert) F.; A.B., Duke, 1941, certificate hosp. adminstrn., 1951; m. Virginia LeGlise, Jan. 6, 1945; 1 son, James Charles. Dir. N.C. Hosp. Study Commn., 1951-52, S.C. Hosp. Care Study, 1952-53; adminstr. Bedford County Meml. Hosp., Bedford, Va., 1953-56; asst. dir. Duke Med. Centre, 1956-58, dir., 1958-68; prof. hosp. adminstrn. Duke, 1962—, dir. grad. program hosp. adminstrn., 1958-64, 67—. Dir. Central Carolina Bank, Durham. Mem. curriculum task force on hosp. orgn. and mgmt. A.U.P.H.A.; mem. Gov.'s Adv. Com. on Med. Assistance; mem. hosp. adv. com. N.C. Regional Med. Programs. Served to 1st lt. AUS, 1941-46. Fellow Am. Coll. Hosp. Adminstrs. (com. on scholarship and loans); mem. Am. Hosp. Assn. (del.), Nat. Rehab. Assn., Nat. League for Nursing (exec. com. N.C. league), Durham C. of C. (chmn. health services). Rotarian. Author: Hospital Care of the Indigent in South Carolina, 1953, also articles. Home: 3950 Bristol Rd Durham NC 27706 Office: Duke Univ Med Center Durham NC 27706

FRENZEL, OTTO NICHOLAS, banker; b. Indpls., May 6, 1899; s. Otto Nicholas and Caroline (Goepper) F.; student Cornell U., 1918-20; LL.D., Ind. Central Coll.; m. Eleanor Terhune Dickson, May 6, 1925; children—Eleanor Dickson, Otto Nicholas III. With Merchants Nat. Bank & Trust Co. (merger in 1953 of Merchants Nat. Bank and Ind. Trust Co.) 1920—, beginning as bank clerk and advancing through positions to pres., 1945—, chmn. bd., 1966—; became pres. Ind. Trust Co., 1930, then chmn. bd., 1945, chmn. exec. com., 1970; dir. Lykes-Youngstown Co., Am. States Life Ins. Co., Am. States Ins. Co., Am. States Fire Ins. Co., Indpls. Power & Light Co., Am. United Life Ins. Co., Stokely-Van Camp, Inc. Served with USNR. 1918. Dir. United Fund of Greater Indpls., United War Fund; chmn. financial div. Ind. War Finance Com. for 6th and 7th War Loan Drives. Trustee YMCA, Butler U.; dir. Riley Meml. Hosp., Indpls. Mem. Ind. C. of C. (treas., dir.), Indpls. Civic Progress Assn., Indpls. C. of C. (dir.), Bankers Assn., Delta Kappa Epsilon. Clubs: Country Woodstock, Columbia, Indpls. Athletic, Dramatic (Indpls.); Traderspoint Hunt; Indiana Society (Chgo.); Chicago Yacht; Athenaeum, University, Keeneland, Meridian Hills Country; Indianapolis Country. Home: Hobby Horse Farm Spring Mill Rd Carmel IN 46032 Office: care Mchts Nat Bank & Trust Co Indianapolis IN 46204

FRERE, CECIL HOWSON BUTLER, lawyer; b. London, Eng., May 5, 1907; s. Gilbert H.B. and Alice (Coe) F. brought to Can., 1914; LL.B., U. Saskatchewan, 1928; m. Gladys Vera Cockburn, Dec. 24, 1936 (div. Oct. 1960); 2 daus., Leslie Joan, Janet Louise; m. 2d, Grace Breen, Mar. 23, 1964. Called to bar Sask., 1930; admitted as solicitor, B.C., 1938, Que., 1967; barrister, B.C., 1958; pvt. practice law, Kindersley, Sask., 1931-36; with legal div. Consol Mining & Smelting Co. of Can., Ltd., (name now changed to Cominco, Ltd.), 1959—, gen. solicitor, 1949-66, gen. counsel, 1966—, sec., 1968- -. Dir. W. Kootenay Power & Light Co., Ltd., Trail, B.C., Pine Point Mines, Ltd., Trail. Mem. Law Soc. B.C., Can. Bar Assn. Home: 23 Easton Av Montreal W Quebec Canada Office: Cominco Ltd 630 Dorchester Blvd W Montreal 101 Quebec Canada

FRERET, DOUGLASS VINCENT, architect; b. New Orleans, Oct. 6, 1903; s. Vincent Rillieux and Emma Regina (Kiefer) F.; B.Arch., Tulane, 1925; M.Arch., Cornell U., 1926; student Ecole Fountainebleau des Beaux Arts, 1923, 55; postgrad. Res. Officers Naval Architecture Group, U.S. Naval Acad., 1943; m. Elizabeth Hughes, Feb. 19, 1927; 1 dau., Elizabeth Hughes (Mrs. Carl Daniel Webster Luke); m. 2d, Ruth Jahncke, Feb. 20, 1964. With Favrot & Livaudias, architects, 1921-33, Bryant Fleming, 1925, York & Sawyer, N.Y. C., 1926; pvt. practice architecture, New Orleans, 1933-42; partner Freret & Wolf, New Orleans 1946—; pres. Andrew Jackson Apts., Inc.; projects include U.S. Post Office, New Orleans, Tulane U. Delta Regional Primate Research Center, Covington, La., Convent of Good Shepherd, Westwego, La., Christ Ch. Cathedral-ancilary bldgs. Tchr. design and drawing Tulane; drawings exhibited Delgado Mus. Art, 1956-57. Vice chmn. bd. Charity Hosp. of La. at New Orleans, 1940-57; pres. Kingsley House and New Orleans Day Nursery, 1961—; bd. visitors Tulane U. Served to lt. comdr. USNR, 1942- 45, Finalist, Rome prize in architecture, 1926; recipient Labouisse prize Tulane, 1923-24. Mem. A.I.A. (pres. New Orleans 1952), Constrn. Ind. Assn. (pres. 1964), Tulane Alumni Assn. (pres. 1967), New Orleans C. of C., La. Architects Assn., Gargoyle, Pi Kappa Alpha, Phi Kappa Phi. Clubs: Boston, Stratford, Pickwick, Louisiana, Southern Yacht, Round Table (New Orleans). Home: 1300 Philip St New Orleans LA 70130 Office: 630 Gravier St New Orleans LA 70130

FRERICHS, ERNEST SUNLEY, educator; b. S.I., N.Y., Apr. 30, 1925; s. Ernest V. and Eva (Sunley) F.; A.B., Brown U., 1948; A.M., Harvard, 1949; S.T.B., Boston U., 1952, Ph.D., 1957; m. Sarah Hazel Cutts, Aug. 20, 1949; children—John Allen, David Sunley, Elizabeth Ann. Ordained to ministry Methodist Ch., 1951; mem. faculty Brown U., 1953—, prof. religious studies, 1965—, chmn. dept., 1964—, asst. dean coll., 1958-59. Bd. dirs. R.I. Council Chs., 1960-62. Mem. region 1 and 11 selection com. Woodrow Wilson Found., 1959-68; mem. R.I. Com. Children and Youth, 1959- -. Served with inf. AUS, 1943-46. Beebe fellow Boston U., 1952-53; Lilly postdoctoral fellow Heidelberg (Germany) U., 1962-63. Mem. Am. Acad. Religion (pres. New Eng. 1970-71), Phi Beta Kappa (sec. Brown U. chpt. 1964-68). Home: 16 John St West Barrington RI 02890 Office: Dept Religious Studies Brown U Providence RI 02912

FRESCO, JACQUES ROBERT, biochemist, educator; b. N.Y.C., May 30, 1928; s. Robert and Lucie (Asseo) F.; B.A., N.Y. U., 1947, M.S., 1949, Ph.D., 1953; m. Rosalie Sarah Bernstein, Dec. 22, 1957; children—Lucille Deborah, Suzette Josie, Linda Hannah. Postdoctoral fellow Sloan Kettering Inst. for Cancer Research, N.Y.C., 1952-54; instr. biochemistry N.Y. U. Coll. Medicine, 1953-54, instr. pharmacology, 1954-56; sr. research fellow dept. chemistry Harvard, 1956-60, tutor biochem. scis., 1957-60; vis. fellow Cavendish Lab., Cambridge, Eng. and Institut de Biologie Physico-Chimique, Paris, France, 1957; asst. prof. dept. chemistry Princeton, 1960-62, asso. prof., 1962-65, prof., 1965—, acting chmn. biochem. scis., 1965-66, prof. dept. biochem. scis., 1970—; mem. adv. bd. biopolymers, 1963-70; cons. sci. adv. com. Helen Hay Whitney Found.; vis. scientist MRC Lab. Molecular Biology, Cambridge, Eng., 1969-70. Recipient Am. Scientist Writing award A.A.A.S., 1962. NIH fellow, 1952-54, Lalor Found. fellow, 1957; established investigator Am. Heart Assn., 1958-63; Guggenheim fellow, 1969-70. Mem. Am. Chem. Soc., Am. Soc. Biol. Chemists, Sigma Xi. Mem. editorial bd. Jour. Phys. Chemistry, 1963-70, Analytical Biochemistry, 1969—. Home: 282 Hartley Av Princeton NJ 08540

FRESE, WALTER FREDERICK, educator; b. Denison, Ia., May 21, 1906; s. Rev. William and Elizabeth (Bosecker) F.; A.B., U. Ia., 1928; M.A., U. Ill., 1930: LL.D., Southeastern U., Washington, 1956; M.A. (hon.), Harvard, 1957; m. Mildred Smith, Sept. 2, 1935; children—Mary Ann, Wayne Frederick, Martha Eileen. Mem. accounting faculty U. Ill., 1928-35, asst. prof. accountancy, 1937-38, also pub. accounting practice; with U.S. Treasury Dept., 1936-48, various capacities including asst. chief accountant Bur. of Accounts, spl. treas., rep. Stblzn. Bd. of China, spl. asst. to fiscal asst. sec. of treasury; dir. accounting systems div. U.S. Gen. Accounting Office, 1948-56; vis. prof. Harvard Grad. Sch. Bus. Adminstrn., 1956-57, prof., 1957—, Lovett-Learned prof., 1968-70, Arthur Lowes Dickinson prof., 1970—; adviser, instr. exec. devel. programs various univs. and assns. Cons. to comptroller gen. U.S., mem. adv. panel, 1966—. Mem. C.P.A. Examination Appraisal Commission, 1959—. C.P.A., Illinois. Mem. Am. Inst. C.P.A.'s. American Accounting Assn., Fed. Govt. Accountants Assn. (past pres.; Robert W. King Meml. medal 1969), Phi Beta Kappa, Beta Gamma Sigma, Beta Alpha Psi, Alpha Kappa Psi, Kappa Sigma. Order of Artus. Lutheran. Mem. editorial adv. bd. Jour. of Accountancy, 1960-62. Home: 16 Clifton St Belmont MA 02178 Office: Harvard Grad Sch of Bus Adminstrn Soldiers Field Boston MA 02163

FRESE, WALTER WENZEL, publisher: b. Mt. Vernon, N.Y., Sept. 28, 1909; s. Walter Adolf and Clara Wenzel) F.: student Columbia, 1927-31; m. Margaret Penny, June 20, 1931; children—Alan David Rogers, Frederick Wenzel, Diana Elaine. With Archtl. Book Pub. Co., Inc., 1927—, v.p. 1930-53, pres. 1953—; founder, pres., Hastings

House, pubs., 1936—, Archives Pub. Co. of Pa., Inc., 1945-56; partner, Arnold & Frese, securities, 1936-39. Dir. Knickerbocker Growth Fund, Inc. Pres. Stamford (Conn.) Hills Assn., 1945-48. Mem. Conn. adv. com. on UN Orgn. Hdgrs. Site. Mem. Am. Inst. Graphic Arts (pres. 1945-47). Episcopalian. Clubs: Coffee House, Columbia University (N.Y.); Stamford Yacht (vice commodore 1970—, dir.), Dutch Treat (gov.), Pilgrims. Home: 268 Dogwood Lane Stamford CT 06903 Office: 10 E 40th St New York City NY 10016

FRESHLEY, DWIGHT LOWELL, educator; b. Homeworth, O., June 27, 1924; s. Palmer Warren and Dora Ann (Unger) F.; A.B., North Central Coll., 1950; M.A., Northwestern U., 1951; Ph.D. Ohio State U., 1955; m. Ruth Jean Reinhart, Nov. 10, 1950; children—Philip, Bruce, Douglas, Dina. Instr. speech, debate coach Lehigh U., 1951-53; asst.. prof. speech to asso. prof., dir. forensics Vanderbilt U., 1955-63; prof., chmn. dept. speech communication, U. Ga. at Athens, 1963—. Served as sgt. 1st class AUS, 1943-46; ETO. Decorated Commendation medal; recipient distinguished service award, So. Speech Assn. Fulbright grantee, Athens, Greece. Mem. Tenn. (pres. 1960), So. (exec. sec. 1963-66) speech assns. Democrat. Methodist (adminstrv. bd. 1968-71). Author: Interpersonal and Organizational Communication, (with R. Huseman and C. Logue), 1969. Editor So. Speech Jour., 1969-72. Home: 110 St George Dr Athens GA 30601

FRETTER, WILLIAM BACHE, educator; b. Pasadena, Cal., Sept. 28, 1916; s. William Albert and Dorothy (Bach) F.; A.B., U. Cal. at Berkeley, 1937, Ph.D., 1946; m. Grace Powles, Jan. 1, 1939; children—Travis D., Gretchen, Richard Brian. Research engr. radar counter-measures Westinghouse Electric Co., 1941-45; mem. faculty U. Cal. at Berkeley, 1946—, prof. physics, 1955- -, dean Coll. Letters and Sci., 1962-67; spl. research cosmic rays, high- energy particle physics. Fulbright scholar, France, 1952-53, 60-61; Guggenheim fellow. 1960-61; decorated chevalier Legion of Honor (France), 1964. Fellow Am. Phys. Soc. Author: Introduction to Experimental Physics, 1955; (with David S. Saxon) Physics for the Liberal Arts Student, 1971. Home: 1120 Cragmont Av Berkeley CA 94708.

FRETWELL, ELBERT KIRTLEY, Jr., coll. pres.; b. N.Y.C., Oct. 29, 1923; s. Elbert Kirtley and Jean (Hosford) F.; A.B. with distinction, Wesleyan U., Middletown, Conn., 1944; A.M. in Teaching, Harvard, 1948; Ph.D., Columbia, 1953; m. Dorrie Shearer, Aug. 25, 1951; children—Barbara Alice, Margaret Jean, James Leonard, Katharine Louise, Corr., A.P., 1942-44; staff writer A.R.C., 194-45; vice consul Am. embassy, Prague, Czechoslovakia, 1945-47; tchr. Brookline (Mass.) pub. schs., 1948, Evanston (Ill.) Township High Sch. and Community Coll., 1948-50; adminstrv. sec. John Hay Fellowships, John Hay Whitney Found., 1951-53; asst. prof., asst. to dean Tchrs. Coll., Columbia U., 1955-56, asso. prof., 1956; asst. commr. for higher edn. N.Y. State Edn. Dept., 1956-64; summer faculty U. Cal. at Berkeley, 1964; dean acad. devel. City U. N.Y., 1964-67; pres. State U. N.Y. Coll. at Buffalo, 1967—. Trustee of Erie County Savings Bank. Organizer N.Y.C. meeting White House Conf. Edn., 1955; cons. Pres.'s Com. Edn. Beyond High Sch., 1956; assisted in James B. Conant Study Edn. Am. Tchrs., 1962; mem. commn. higher instns. Middle State Assn., 1965—; trustee Carnegie Found. for Advancement Teaching, 1968—; chmn. planning committee 17th National Conf. Higher Edn., 1962; trustee Wesleyan U., 1967-70, Nichols Sch., Buffalo, Canisius Coll.; exec. dir. com. on edn. N.Y. State Const. Conv., 1967; vice chmn. N.Y. State Revolutionary War Bicentennial Commn.; mem. exec. bd. Buffalo chpt. Nat. Conf. Christians and Jews; bd. dirs. Greater Buffalo Devel. Found.; trustee United Fund Buffalo and Erie County; hon. mem. Buffalo Fine Arts Acad. Recipient ann. award N.Y. State Assn. Jr. Colls., 1962; Carnegie Corp. grantee, 1964. Mem. Am. Assn. Higher Edn. (exec. com. 1962- 66, nat. pres. 1964-65), A.A.A.S., Am. Acad. Polit. and Social Sci., Assn. Am. U. Profs., Am. Soc. Pub. Adminstrn., Buffalo and Erie County Hist. Soc. (bd. mgrs.), Buffalo Soc. Natural Scis. (bd. mgrs.). Clubs: University (Albany); Rotary (Buffalo); Harvard (N.Y.C.); Adirondack Mountain. Author: Founding Public Junior Colleges, 1954; also articles, chpts. in yearbooks. Home: 152 Lincoln Pkwy Buffalo NY 14222

FREUD, ANNA, psychoanalyst; b. Vienna, Austria, Dec. 3, 1895; d. Sigmund and Martha (Bernays) F.; grad. Cottage Lyzeum, Vienna, 1912; LL.D., Clark U., 1950; Sc.D. Jefferson Med. Coll., 1964; LL.D., U. Sheffield (Eng.), 1966; Sc.D., U. of Chicago, 1966, Yale, New Haven Conn., 1968. Chairman of Inst. Psycho-Analysis, Vienna, until 1938; organizer exptl. day nursery, Jackson Nursery, Vienna, 1937-38, residential war nursery for homeless children, London, Eng., 1940-45; practicing psychoanalyst, London, 1938—; dir. Hampstead Child Therapy Course and Clinic. London, 1952—, Decorated comdr. Order of the Brit. Empire. Member of the British Psychoanalytical Society and Institute. Author numerous books; also numerous articles professional journals. Address: 20 Maresfield Gardens London NW 3 England

FREUDENHEIM, MILTON, dir. fgn. service Chgo. Daily News, Paris, France. Address: care Chgo Daily News 401 N Wabash Av Chicago IL 60611*

FREUDENSTEIN, FERDINAND, educator; b. Frankfurt, Germany, May 12, 1926; s. George Gerson and Charlotte (Rosenberg) F.; came to U.S., 1942, naturalized, 1945; student N.Y.U., 1942-44; M.S., Harvard, 1948; Ph.D., Columbia, 1954; m. Leah Schwarzchild, July 5, 1959 (dec. May 1970); children—David George, Joan Merle. Devel. engr. instrument div. Am. Optical Co., 1948-50; mem. tech. staff Bell Telephone Labs., 1954; mem. faculty Columbia, 1954—, prof. mech. engring., 1959—, chmn. dept., 1958-64; cons. to industry, 1954—; spl. research kinematics, mechanisms, engring. design. Served inf. AUS, 1944-46. Recipient Gt. Tchr. award Soc. Older Grads. Columbia, 1966; Guggenheim fellow, 1961-62, 67-68. Fellow N.Y. Acad. Scis.; mem. Am. Soc. M.E. (Jr. award 1955), Harvard Soc. Engrs. and Scientists, Columbia Engring. Soc., N.Y. Acad. Scis., Sigma Xi. Home: 435 W 259th St Riverdale, NY 10471.

FREUDENTHAL, ALFRED MARTIN, educator, engr.; b. Stryj, Poland, Feb. 12, 1906; s. Simon and Gustafa (Mueller) F.; Civil Engr., Technische Hochschule, Prague, Czechoslavakia, 1929, D.Sc. in Engring., 1930; M.Sc. in Theoretical Physics, Charles U., Prague, 1930; m. Mary Ann Silberstein, Feb. 9, 1939; m. 2d, Maria Ronay, Aug. 24, 1962; 1 son, Pierre Simon. Came to U.S., 1947, naturalized, 1953. Design engr. reinforced concrete and steel, Prague, 1930-34; cons. eng., Warsaw, Poland, 1934-35; from structural engr. to resident engr. Port of Tel Aviv, Palestine, 1935-45; cons. to chief engr., British Army, Palestine, and Transjordan, 1941-44; cons. engr. Tel Aviv, 1945-47; lectr., later prof. civil engring. Hebrew Inst. Tech., Haifa, Palestine, 1937-49; vis. prof. theoretical and applied mechanics U. Ill., 1947-48; lectr. and research cons. Columbia, 1948-49, U. Ill., 1948-57; prof. civil engring. Columbia, 1949-69, dir. Inst. Fatigue and Structural Reliability, 1962-69; prof. civil and materials engring. George Washington U., 1969—, dir. Inst. Materials Engring. and Structural Reliability, 1969—, chmn. dept. civil, mech. and environmental engring., 1970—; vis. prof. Fed. Inst. Tech., Zurich, Switzerland, 1970—. Recipient Norman medal Am. Soc. C.E., 1948, 57, medal Royal Swedish Aero. Soc., 1956, von Karman medal Am. Soc. C.E., 1971. Fellow Am. Soc. C.E.; mem. Inst. Aeros. and Astronautics, Soc. Rheology, Internat. Assn. Bridge and Structural Engrs., Internat. Assn. Navigation Congresses, Sigma Xi, Tau Beta Pi. Author: Verbundstuetzen f. Hohe Lasten (Berlin), 1933; Inelastic Behavior of Engineering Materials and Structures, 1950; Introduction to Mechanics of Solids, 1966. Editor: Fatigue in Flight Structures, 1956; Elevated Temperature Design, 1964; Structural Reliability, 1971. Contbr.: Handbook of Physics, 1958; also tech. and science papers civil engring., applied mech. and materials. Office: Sch Engring and Applied Sci George Washington U Washington DC 20006

FREUND, CHARLES GIBSON, holding co. exec.; b. Chgo., Oct. 8, 1923; s. Charles and Jewl (Gibson) F.; B.S., Aeronautical, U. Chgo., 1948; LL.B., John Marshall Law Sch., 1956; m. Ann L. Schiera, June 8, 1947; children—Mark, Eric, Kurt, Scott, Pamela. Stress analyst Northrup Aircraft Co., Hawthorne, Cal., 1949; with Natural Gas Pipeline Co. of Am., Chgo., 1949—, asst. sec., 1957-61, sec., 1961-66, v.p. finance, 1966-69, sec.-treas., 1969—; v.p., sec., treas. Peoples Gas Co., Chgo., 1969—; sec., treas. Peoples Gas Light & Coke Co., N. Shore Gas Co. Dir. United Cerebral Palsy of Chgo., 1959—, also v.p.; dir. Chgo. Council on Alcoholism, 1968—; mem. sr. bd. Nat. Conf. Christians and Jews, 1965- -, nat. trustee, 1969—, nat. gov., 1970—. Trustee, Village of Lincolnshire, Ill. Served with USAAF, 1942-45. Decorated Purple Heart, Air medal. Mem. Am., Ill., Chgo. bar assns., Am. Soc. Corp. Secs., Am. Gas Assn., Ind. Natural Gas Assn. Am., Tex. Mid-Continent Oil and Gas Assn., Am. Legion, Ill., Chgo. chambers commerce. Democrat. Roman Catholic. Club: Executives, Chgo. Athletic Assn. (Chgo.). Home: 30 Plymouth Ct Lincolnshire Deerfield IL 60015 Office: 122 S Michigan Av Chicago IL 60603

FREUND, CLEMENT JOSEPH, mech. engr., coll. dean; b. Appleton, Wis., Aug. 7, 1895; s. Alois John and Ottilia (Lenz) F.; A.B., Campion Coll., Prairie du Chien, Wis., 1916; M.E., Marquette U., 1922; m. Mabelle Gertrude Ziegler, Aug. 21, 1926; children—Mary Elizabeth, Paul Clement (dec.), Louis James (dec.). With Falk Corp., 1922-32, ednl. dir., 1926-32; instr. evening tech. courses, Milw. Vocational Sch., 1924-32, supr. same, 1926-30; spl. lectr. Coll. Engring., Marquette U., 1930-32; dean Coll. Engring. U. Detroit, 1932-62, prof., 1962—; cons. higher tech. edn., West Pakistan, 1958-60; cons. engring. edn., Pakistan Commn. on Nat Edn., 1958-60; cons. Minn. State Coll. Bd. S.W. Minn. State Coll. Mem. conf. bd. Asso. Research Councils, Com. on Fulbright Awards in Engring., 1955- 58. Mem. Gov.'s Seaway Commn., Mich., 1954. Served from 2d to 1st lt. U.S. Army, World War I. Fellow Am. Soc. M.E.; mem. Am. Foundrymen's Soc. (hon.), Am. Soc. Engring. Edn. (past pres., past chmn. ethics com., rep. Am. Council on Edn. 1955-58), Engring. Soc. Detroit (distinguished mem. 1971—, past pres.), Engrs.' Council Profl. Devel. (chmn. com. on ethics, 1955-58; engring. manpower com.), Mich. Soc. Profl. Engrs. (past chmn. long range planning com.), Mich. Engring. Soc. (hon.), Tau Beta Pi, Alpha Sigma Nu, Pi Tau Sigma, Crown and Anchor. Roman Catholic. Contbr. profl. jours. Home: 17597 Oak Dr Detroit MI 48221

FREUND, ERNEST HANS, educator; b. Berlin, Germany, June 10, 1905; s. Ernst and Margarete (Philippi) F.; student U. Berlin, 1924-25, U. Marburg, 1925-28; Ph.D., U. Freiburg, 1932; m. Marjorie Alderfer, Sept. 30, 1942; children—George, Howard, Peter. Came to U.S., 1940, naturalized, 1943. Lectr. philosophy, instr. lang. Pendle Hill Sch., Wallingford, Pa., 1941- 43, 45-46; faculty philosophy Pa. State U., 1946—, prof., 1957—, head dept., 1954-58. Pres. State College (Pa.) Council Chs., 1956-58; chmn. bd. dirs. Pa. State U. Christian Assn., 1958-59; with Am. Friends Service Com., Berlin. 1959-60. Served with AUS, 1943-45. Mem. Am. Philos. Assn., Am. Assn. U. Profs., Phi Delta Kappa. Mem. Soc. of Friends. Author: Ontologische Untersuchungen zum Cantorschen Mengenbegriff, 1933; The Balanced Life, 1959; The Ground of Self-Frustration, 1971. Co-editor: Problems of Philosophy, 1964. Translator: The Great Promise (Karl Barth), 1963; co-translator: Discourse On Thinking (Martin Heidegger) 1966. Home: 667 Glenn Rd State College PA 16801 Office: Pa State U University Park PA

FREUND, GERALD, coll. dean; b. Berlin, Germany, Oct. 14, 1930; came to U.S., 1940, naturalized, 1946; s. Kurt and Anneliese (Josephthal) F.; B.A., Haverford Coll., 1952; D. Phil. magna cum laude (fellow), Oxford (Eng.) U., 1955; m. Jane Bicker Shaw Trask, Sept. 29, 1956 (div. Sept. 1970); children—Jonathan Gerald, Matthew Trask, Andrew Josephthal. Research asst. Inst. Advanced Study, Princeton, 1956-57; fellow Council Fgn. Relations, 1957-59; asst. prof. Haverford Coll., 1958-60; from asst. dir. to asso. dir. social scis., humanities, arts Rockefeller Found., 1960-69; asst. to pres. Yale, 1969-70; exec. v.p. Film Soc. of Lincoln Center, 1970-71; acting dean humanities and arts, prof., dir. Arts Center, Hunter Coll., 1971—; cons. Washington Center of Fgn. Policy Research, 1959-60, Annenberg Center, Phila., 1970-71; lectr., TV and radio activities. Mem. Charter Revision Commn., Stamford, Conn., 1964-65, planning commn. coms., 1965-67; mem. Com. on Orgn. of Peace, 1963—. Vice pres. Democratic Party, N. Stamford, Conn., 1962-64. Trustee Woodstock (Vt.) Country Sch.; bd. dirs. Inst. Current World Affairs, N.Y.C. Recipient Fulbright award, 1952-54; Rockefeller Found. grantee 1956-57, 59-60. Mem. Am. Polit. Sci. Assn., Am. Hist. Assn. Jewish religion. Author: Unholy Alliance; German Russian Relations 1917-1926, 1957, 1958; Germany Between Two Worlds, 1961. Home: 3 E 75th St New York City NY 10021 Office: 695 Park Av New York City NY 10021

FREUND, MAX, lawyer; b. N.Y.C., Jan. 10, 1909; s. Oscar and Rose (Mukasey) F.; B.S. magna cum laude, N.Y. U., 1929; LL.B. cum laude, Harvard, 1932; m. Serena Lewis, July 14, 1940; children—Elizabeth Amy (Mrs. Robert Green), Alice Laura. Admitted to N.Y. bar, 1933, since practiced in N.Y.C.; sr. partner firm Rosenman, Colin, Kaye, Petschek, Freund & Emil, and predecessors, 1943—. Past dir. Republic Pictures Corp., Textile Realty Corp. Bd. dirs. Linden Hill Sch., Westchester County, N.Y. Served to 1st lt. AUS, 1944-45. Recipient Sears prize Harvard Law Sch., 1931. Mem. Am., N.Y. State bar assns., N.Y. County Lawyers Assn., Assn. Bar City N.Y. (exec. com. 1967-71), Phi Beta Kappa. Jewish religion. Clubs: Harmonie (past gov.) (N.Y.C.); Sunningdale Country (pres., gov.) (Westchester County, N.Y.). Editor Harvard Law Rev., 1930-32. Home: 29 E 64th St New York City NY 10021 Office: 575 Madison Av New York City NY 10022

FREUND, MIRIAM KOTTLER, (Mrs. Milton Freund), clubwoman; b. N.Y.C., Feb. 17, 1906; d. Harry and Rebecca (Zindler) Kottler; B.A., Hunter Coll., 1925; M.A., N.Y.U., 1927, Ph.D., 1936; m. Milton Freund, July 3, 1927; children—Mathew, Harry. Tchr. pub. high schs., N.Y.C., to 1944; nat. bd. Hadassah, Women's Zionist Orgn. Am., 1940—, v.p., 1953-56, nat. pres., 1956-60, national youth activities com., 1943-48, nat. vocational edn. chmn., 1948-53, chmn. nat. youth Aliyah, 1953-56; actions Com. World Zionist Orgn., 1956—; chairman exec. com. Am. Zionist Council, 1960—; nat. v.p. Am. Zionist Fedn., 1970—. Del. Am. Jewish Conf., 1942; co-chmn. Am. Zionist Youth Commn., 1944-49; founder, charter mem., Brandeis Youth Found., 1944; nat. bd. Jewish Nat. Fund and Keren Hayesod, 1947-48. Nat. v.p. women's com. Brandeis U. Recipient citation Jewish Book Council Am., 1954. Mem. Am. Assn. U. Women, Am. Jewish Hist. Soc. World Council Synagogues (dir.). Author: Jewish Merchants in Colonial America, 1936; Jewels for a Crown; the Editor; Hadassah mag. Home: 200 E 71st St New York City NY 10021 Office: 65 E 52d St New York City NY 10022

FREUND, PAUL ABRAHAM, educator; b. St. Louis, Feb. 16, 1908; s. Charles and Hulda (Arenson) F.; A.B., Washington U., 1928, LL.D., 1956; LL.B., Harvard, 1931, S.J.D., 1932; LL.D., Columbia, 1954, U. Louisville, 1956, U. Chgo., 1961, Boston U., 1964, Queen's U., Ont., 1970; L.H.D., Hebrew Union Coll., 1961; Litt.D., Cornell Coll., 1968; D.C.L., Union Coll., 1968. Admitted to D.C. bar, 1935, Mass. bar, 1947; law clerk to Mr. Justice Brandeis, 1932-33; legal staff Treasury Dept. and R.F.C., 1933-35, spl. asst to atty. gen., Office of Solicitor Gen., Justice Dept., 1935-39, 1942-46; lectr. law, Harvard Law Sch., 1939-40, prof. law, 1940-50, Charles Stebbins Fairchild prof., 1950-57; Royall prof. law Harvard U., 1957-58; Carl M. Loeb U. prof. Harvard, 1958—; Pitt. prof. Am. history and institutions Cambridge U., 1957-58, fellow Trinity Coll., 1957-58; fellow Center for Advanced Study in Behavioral Scis., 1969-70. Mem. adv. com. Civil Liberties Union, Mass.; dir. Salzburg Sem. Am. Studies. Trustee Washington U. Fellow Am. Acad. Arts and Scis. (past pres.); mem. Am. Judicature Soc., Mass. Hist. Soc., Am. Philos. Soc., Am. Bar Assn., Am. Law Inst., Harvard Soc. Fellows, Signet Soc., Phi Beta Kappa, Pi Sigma Alpha. Club: St. Botolph (Boston). Author: On Understanding the Supreme Court, 1949 (Rosenthal lectures, Northwestern U.): The Supreme Court of the U.S., 1961; On Law and Justice, 1968. Editor: Experimentation with Human Subjects, 1970. Co-editor: Cases on Constitutional Law, 1962. Editor- in-chief: History of Supreme Court. Contbr. Ency. Brit., Ency. Social Sci., legal periodicals. Home: 1010 Memorial Dr Cambridge MA 02138

FREUND, RICHARD ALAN, photog. equipment co. exec.; b. N.Y.C., Nov. 14, 1924; s. Mortimer and Lillian Adele (Straus) F.; A.B., Columbia, 1947, M.S., 1949; m. Valerie Audrey Lorna Tancock, Nov. 27, 1963. Staff cons. quality assurance Eastman Kodak Co., Rochester, N.Y., 1949—. Served with USAAF, 1942-46. Recipient Lansdale Service award YMCA, 1967. Fellow Am. Soc. Quality Control (Brumbaugh award 1960, 62, pres. elect 1971-72), Am. Statis. Assn., A.A.A.S.; mem. Am. Soc. Testing and Materials. Asso. editor Technometrics, 1963-66; mem. editorial bd. Indsl. Quality Control, 1962-66. Office: Kodak Park Division MSDD Bldg 56 Rochester NY 14650

FREUND, TIBOR, artist; b. Budapest, Hungary, Dec. 29, 1910; s. Dezso and Margit (Honig) F.; diploma in architecture Fed. Tech. U., Zurich, Switzerland, 1932; student with Vilmos Aba-Novak Art Sch., Budapest; m. Barbara Horvat, Feb. 23, 1938 (dec. 1962); 1 son, Alexander. Came to U.S., 1953, naturalized 1958. Originated motion paintings, 1957; one-man shows include: Galerie Norval, N.Y.C., 1960, Contemporaries Gallery, N.Y.C., 1965, 67, Bertha Schafer Gallery, N.Y.C., 1969; Am. Fedn. Arts traveling exhibits, 1963-65, 66-67, 71-72; represented in permanent collections museums. Recipient top prize Silvermine Guild award 19th Ann. New Eng. Exhbn., 1968. Registered architect, N.Y. Fellow Royal Soc. Arts (London). Created moving murals Univeral Dissemination of Knowledge, Seaton Falls Sch., N.Y.C., Vehicle of Progress, I. Sch. 162, N.Y.C. Studio: 34-57 82d St Jackson Heights NY 11372

FREUNDLICH, AUGUST LUDWIG, artist, univ. dean; b. Frankfort, Germany, May 9, 1924 (parents Am. citizens); s. Julius and Erni (Keller) F.; B.A., Antioch Coll., 1949; M.A., Columbia Tchrs. Coll, 1950; Ph.D., N.Y.U., 1960; m. Lillian Grace Thomson, Dec. 26, 1948; children—Mary, Jeffrey Paul, Heidi, Christopher Thomson. Art edn. specialist Antioch Lab. Sch., 1949- 50, U. Ark., 1950-53, South Plainfield and New Paltz (N.Y.) State Tchrs. Coll., 1953-54; head dept. art Eastern Mich. U., 1954-58; chmn. arts div., Sullivan prof. arts edn. George Peabody Coll., 1958-64; dir. Joe and Emily Lowe Art Gallery and chmn. art dept. U. Miami, Coral Gables, Fla., 1964-70; dean Sch. of Art, Syracuse U., 1970—; exhbns. in competitions Tenn., Ark., Ohio, Ky., N.J., Mich., N.M. Pres. Nashville Arts Council, 1961-63; mem. exec. com. Inst. for Study Art in Edn., 1964-69; v.p. S.E. Mus. Conf., 1969, editor bull., 1968-70. Trustee, cons. Everson Mus. Served with USMCR, 1942-46. Recipient U. Miami research grant, 1967. Mem. Western Arts Assn. (council 1954-62, pres. 1958-60), Mich., Tenn., Ohio, N.Y., Ark. art edn. assns., Coll. Arts Assn., Nashville Artist Guild (pres. 1960-61), Nat. Com. Art Edn. (council asso. 1951—), S.E. Coll. Art Assn. (pres. 1969-70), Nat. Art Edn. Assn. (council 1956-62), Tenn. Fine Arts Center (mem. bd.), Nashville Mus. Council, Tenn. Mus. Assos., Am. Assn. Museums, Fla. Art Mus. Dirs. Home: Duguid Rd Manlius NY 13104

FREW, WILLIAM M., banker. Pres., dir. Citizens Bank & Trust Co., Park Ridge, Ill. Home: 319 Rosalie Lane Palatine IL 60067 Office: 1 Northwest Hwy Park Ridge IL 60068

FREY, ALBERT, architect; b. Zurich, Switzerland, Oct. 18, 1903; s. Albert and Ida (Meyer) F.; diploma architecture, Kantonales Technikum, Winterhur- Zurich, 1924. Came to U.S., 1930, naturalized, 1941. With Le Corbusier, architect, Paris, France, 1929; with architects' offices, N.Y.C., Washington and U.S. Dept. Agr., 1930-34, Palm Springs, Cal., 1934-37; with Philip L. Goodwin, architect on design Mus. Modern Art, 1937-39; designer Palm Springs City Hall, North Shore Beach and Yacht Club, others. Fellow A.I.A. Author: In Search of a Living Architecture, 1939. Office: 686 Palisades Dr Palm Springs CA 92262

FREY, ALEXANDER HAMILTON, prof. law; b. L.I. City, N.Y., June 2, 1898; s. Walter Guernsey and Susan Baker (Hamilton) F.; student Columbia, 1915-17, A.M., 1920; A.B., Yale, 1919, LL.B., 1921, J.S.D., 1925; student Oxford U., 1921-23; m. Alice Field Hubbard, Feb. 2, 1930; children—Alice, Alexander, Charles, Richard, Susan. Admitted to Conn. bar, 1921, N.Y. bar, 1922, Pa. bar, 1934; asst. prof. Law Sch., Yale, 1926-30; prof. Law Sch., U. Pa. 1932-68, Ferdinand Wakeman Hubbell prof. law, 1950-64, Algernon Sydney Biddle prof. law, 1964-68, Algernon Sydney Biddle prof. emeritus, 1968—; vis. prof. law schs. Columbia, 1929, U.N.C., 1939, Yale, 1946, U. Kan., 1949, U. Tex., 1950, U. Utah, 1952, U. Ariz., 1957, U. Colo. (Charles Inglis Thomson Guest professorship), 1958; mem. law faculty Salzburg (Austria) Seminar in Am. Studies, 1961, 66; vis. prof. Duke, 1931-32, U. Va., 1967. Conciliator-cons. Equal Employment Opportunity Commn., 1968; counsel David Berger, P.A., Phila., 1971. Chmn. Pa. Minimum Wage Bd. for Hotel Industry, 1938, Phila. Citizens Council on Dem. Rights, 1949-51. Mem. U.S. Minimum Wage coms., 1941-42; frequent arbitrator of labor disputes. Chmn. Phila. Good Neighbor League, 1936, Phila. Civil Liberties Com., 1936-40; pres. Greater Phila. br., Am. Civil Liberties Union, 1953-56, 65,67, Pa. chpt., 1955-62, mem. bd. dirs. nat. orgn., 1954-56; 1st chmn. univ. senate U. Pa., 1952-53. Pub. mem., chmn. mediation panels Nat. War Labor Bd.; pub. mem. 3d Regional War Labor Bd., vice chmn., 1943-44; pub. mem. 3d Regional WSB, 1945-47. Past v.p. Indsl. Relations Research Assn. Served as seaman, USNRF, 1918. Mem. Assn. Am. Law Schs. (exec. com. 1947-48), Am. Assn. U. Profs. (past pres. U. of Pa. chpt.), Nat. Acad. Arbitrators, Pa., Phila. bar assns., Juristic Soc. (Phila.), City Policy Com. (Phila.), Order of Coif, Delta Upsilon. Democrat. Quaker. Author: Frey's cases and Statutes on Business Association, 1935; Cases on Labor Law, 1941; Cases and Materials on Corporations and Partnerships, 1951. Editor: (with others) Labor Relations and the Law, 1953, 60; (with C. Robert

Morris and Jesse Chaper) Cases and Materials on Corporations, 1966. Contbr. legal and other periodicals. Home: R D 2 Phoenixville PA 19460 Office: U Pa Law Sch 3400 Chestnut St Philadelphia PA 19104 ☆

FREY, BRICE A., Jr., ins. co. exec.; b. N.Y.C., Mar. 31, 1915; A.B., Harvard. Asst. mgr. N.Y.C. office Indemnity Ins. Co. N.Am., 1939-54; v.p. Gen. Reins. Corp., N.Y.C., 1954-68, sr. v.p., 1968—; pres., dir. Herbert Clough Inc., 1970—. Mem. Newcomen Soc. N.Am., Casualty and Surety Club, Mayflower Soc. Clubs: City Midday, Tuxedo (N.Y.C.). Home: Tuxedo Park NY 10987 Office: 400 Park Av New York City NY 10022

FREY, CARL, assn. exec.; b. N.Y.C., Feb. 1, 1927; s. Adolph and Lina (Heilmann) F.; B.M.E., N.Y. U., 1948; M.A., Columbia, 1952; m. Iris Ihde, Feb. 12, 1955; children—Thomas, Douglas, Clifford. Dir. Nat. Engrs. Register, N.Y.C., 1963-65; exec. sec. Engring. Manpower Commn., N.Y.C., 1960-65; exec. dir. Engrs. Joint Council, N.Y.C., 1965—; mem. exec. com., treas. World Energy Conf. Adviser Labor Dept., 1964—; del. internat. confs.; mem. Exec. Res. Office of Pres., 1964—. Mem. Am. Soc. for Engring. Edn., Am. Inst. Aeros. and Astronautics, A.A.A.S., Internat. Soc. Gen. Semantics, Audubon Soc., Soaring Soc. Am. Club: Engineers (N.Y.C.). Pub. engr. mag. Home: 19 Harding Lane Westport CT 06880 Office: Engrs Joint Council 345 E 47th St New York City NY 10017

FREY, DAVID GROVER, zoologist; b. Hartford, Wis., Oct. 10, 1915; s. Grover Cleveland and Henrietta (Zimmerman) F.; B.A., U. Wis. 1936, M.A., 1938, Ph.D., 1940; m. Sarah Elizabeth Jones, Jan. 24, 1948; children—Karl Frederich, Barbara Louise, Katharine Elizabeth. Study Columbia River salmon, U.S. Fish and Wildlife Service, 1940-42, Chesapeake Bay oysters, College Park, Md., 1942-45; asso. prof. dept. zoology U. N.C., 1946-50; asso. prof. dept. zoology Ind. U., 1950-55, prof., 1955—; instr. 4th Internat. Inland Fisheries Tng. Center, Bogor, Java, 1955. Served as ensign USNR, 1945-46; survey fresh water conditions, Pacific Islands; survey war damage to fisheries of P.I.; Southampton Island Expdn., 1957; Nat. Acad. Scis. exchange visit to Soviet Union, 1962; research Brit. Mus. Natural History, London, 1962-63; Ford cons. Mindanao State U., 1967-68. Fulbright research fellow to Austria; Guggenheim fellow, 1953-54. Mem. Internat. Union Quarternary Research, Brit. Freshwater Biol. Assn., British Ecol. Soc., Am. Soc. Limnology and Oceanography (pres. 1955), Internat. Assn. Theoretical and Applied Limnology, Ecol. Soc. Am., Am. Soc. Zoologists, Soc. Systematic Zoology, Am. Micros. Soc. (v.p. 1970), Ind. Acad. Sci., Phi Beta Kappa, Sigma Xi. Founder Jour. Limnology and Oceanography, editor, 1956-59. Home: Route 3 Smith Rd Bloomington IN 47401

FREY, DONALD NELSON, mfg. co. exec., engr.; b. St. Louis, Mar. 13, 1923; s. Muir Luken and Margaret Bryden (Nelson) F.; student Mich. State Coll., 1940- 42; B.S., U. Mich., 1947, Ph.D., 1950; m. Margaret Kingsley Wirth, Mar. 27, 1942 (div. 1970); children—Donald Nelson, Judith Kingsley, Margaret Bente, Catherine, Christopher, Elizabeth; m. 2d, Mary Elizabeth Cameron, June, 1971. Research asso. Engring. Research Inst., U. Mich., 1947-49, instr. metall. engring., 1949-50, asst. prof. chem. and metall. engring., 1950-51; research engr. Babcock & Wilcox Tube Co., Beaver Falls, Pa., summer 1951; supr. metall. dept. sci. lab. Ford Motor Co., 1951, mgr. metall. dept., 1951-55, asso. dir. sci. lab., 1955-57, dir. engring. research, 1957-58, exec. engr. car product engring. Ford div., 1958-59, asst. chief engr. car product engring., 1959-61, product planning mgr., 1961-62, asst. gen. mgr. Ford div., 1962-65, gen. mgr., 1965-68, co. v.p., 1965-67, v.p. for product devel., 1967-68; pres. Gen. Cable Corp., N.Y.C., 1968-71; chmn. bd. Bell & Howell Co., Chgo., 1971—; dir. McCord Corp., Babcock & Wilcox Co., Clark Equipment Co., 20th Century Fox Film Corp. Mem. devel. council U. Mich., 1963—; trustee Salk Inst. Biol. Studies. Served with AUS, 1943-46. Named young engr. of year Engring. Soc. Detroit, 1953; recipient Russell Springer award Soc. Automotive Engrs., 1956; named outstanding alumni Coll. Engring., U. Mich., 1957; outstanding young man of the year Detroit Jr. Bd. Commerce, 1958; selected as potential leader in bus. Esquire mag., 1958. Mem. Am. Inst. Mining, Metall. and Petroleum Engrs. (chmn. Detroit 1954; chmn., editor Nat Symposium on Sheet Steels 1956), Am. Soc. Metals, Nat. Acad. Engring., Engrs. Joint Council (dir.), Am. Soc. M.E., Soc. Automotive Engrs. (vice chmn. Detroit 1958), Detroit Engring. Soc. (dir. 1962—), Nat. Elec. Mfrs. Assn. (dir.), Sigma Xi, Phi Kappa Phi, Tau Beta Pi, Phi Delta Theta. Unitarian. Home: 1500 Lake Shore Dr Chicago IL 60610 Office: 7100 McCormick Rd Chicago IL 60645

FREY, EDWARD JOHN, banker; b. Grand Rapids, Mich., July 3, 1907; s. John Edward and Stella (Reeves) F.; A.B., U. Mich., 1932; grad. Rutgers U. Grad. Sch. Banking, 1940; m. Frances Taliaferro, Nov. 7, 1936; children—Mary Caroline, John Monroe, David Gardner, Edward John. With Union Bank and Trust Co., N.Am., Grand Rapids, 1933—, now chmn. bd., also dir.; faculty Rutgers U. Grad. Sch. Banking; dir. Mich. Mut. Liability Co., Detroit, Foremost Ins. Co., Asso. Truck Lines (all Grand Rapids), mem. Downtown Devel. Com. Grand Rapids. Bd. dirs. United Community Services of Grand Rapids and Kent County; trustee, chmn. finance com. Grand Valley Coll., Grand Rapids. Served to lt. comdr. USNR, 1943-46; PTO. Mem. Am. (state legislative com.), Mich. (exec. council) bankers assns., U.S. (taxation and finance com.), Grand Rapids (dir., past pres.) chambers commerce. Episcopalian (vestryman, sr. warden). Rotarian (past pres.). Clubs: Peninsular (past pres.), Kent Country (Grand Rapids); River (N.Y.C.); Kinne Creek; University. Home: 180 Greenwich Rd NE Grand Rapids MI 49506 Office: 200 Ottawa Av NW Grand Rapids MI 49502

FREY, FREDERICK WARD, educator; b. Cleve., June 16, 1929; s. Frederick H. W. and Helen (Simpson) F.; student Ohio Wesleyan U., 1946-47; A.B., Western Res. U., 1951; A.B. (Rhodes scholar 1951), Balliol Coll., Oxford (Eng.) U., 1953; Ph.D., Princeton, 1962; m. Patricia Ann Evans, Dec. 16, 1967. Mem. faculty Mass. Inst. Tech., 1960—, prof. polit. sci., 1966—, sr. staff mem. Center Internat. Studies, 1960—, dir. Behavioral Research Service, 1967—; fellow Center for Advanced Study in Behavioral Scis., Stanford, 1971-72; cons. AID, 1962—, Mass. Commn. Against Discrimination, 1963—. Served with AUS, 1953-55. Mem. Am. Polit. Sci. Assn. (Pi Sigma Alpha award), Am. Sociol. Assn., Am. Assn. Pub. Opinion Research, Middle East Inst., Phi Beta Kappa (jr.), Phi Kappa Psi. Author: The Turkish Political Elite, 1965; also articles. Home: 26 Blossom St Lexington MA 02173 Office: Mass Inst Tech Cambridge MA 02139

FREY, GERARD LOUIS, bishop; b. New Orleans, May 10, 1914; s. Andrew and Marie Therese (DeRose) F.; D.D., St. Joseph's Sem. at St. Benedict"s La., 1933; student Notre Dame Sem., New Orleans. Ordained priest Roman Cath. Ch., 1938; asst. pastor, Taft, La., 1938-46; asst. dir. Confraternity Christian Doctrine, Archdiocese New Orleans, also asst. St. James Ch., New Orleans, 1946; dir. Confraternity Christian Doctrine, Archdiocese New Orleans, also asst. pastor St. Leo the Great Paris, 1946-47; founding pastor St. Frances Cabrini Ch., New Orleans, 1952-63; pastor St. Frances de Sales Parish, Houma, La., 1962-67; clergy rep. 2d Vatican Council, 1964; dir. Diocesan Friendship Corps, New Orleans, 1966; bishop of Savannah, Ga., 1967—; Episcopal moderator Theresians Am., 1968—. Recipient Bishop Tracy Vocation award St. Joseph's Sem. Alumni Assn., 1959. Address: PO Box 8789 225 Abercorn St Savannah GA 31402

FREY, HENRY S., savs. bank exec. Vice pres., auditor Citizens Comml. & Savs. Bank, Flint, Mich. Office: 328 S Saginaw St Flint MI 48502*

FREY, JAMES MCKNIGHT, govt. ofcl.; b. Mattoon, Ill., Dec. 7, 1932; s. Raymond Matthew and Virginia Laurel (McKnight) F.; A.B., Harvard, 1954, M.B.A., 1956; m. Jean Meyer, June 18, 1954; children—Katherine Marie, Nancy Elizabeth, With Bur. of Budget, 1954-62, 1965-70, mgmt. analyst internat. programs, 1960-62, dir. internat. programs div., 1970; asst. to spl. asst. to President U.S., also staff mem. Nat. Security Council, 1962-64; spl. asst. for policy coordination to asst. sec. state inter-Am. affairs, also policy planning officer Bur. Inter-Am. Affairs, State Dept., 1964-65; chief internat. programs div. U.S. Office Mgmt. and Budget, Washington, 1970—. Mem. President's Task Force Govt. Reorgn., 1964. Mem. Am. Acad. Polit. and Social Sci. Clubs: Harvard, Harvard Business School (Washington). Home: 11717 Devilwood Dr Potomac MD 20854 Office: Exec Office of The President Office Mgmt and Budget Washington DC 20503

FREY, JOHN JOSEPH, magazine pub.; b. N.Y.C., Mar. 30, 1919; s. Charles L. and Marion E. (Campbell) F.; B.S., Fordham U., 1942; student Columbia Grad. Sch. Bus., 1946-48; m. Barbara Gerlach, Feb. 8, 1947; children—Jeffery Paul, Stephanie Joan, Judith Anne, Mark Lawrence, Barbara Jean. With Gen. Motors Corp., 1941-47, Ernst & Ernst, C.P.A."s. N.Y.C., 1947-48; with Time, Inc., 1948—, gen. mgr. Fortune mag., also Archtl. Forum mag. to 1960, House and Home mag., 1962-64, asst. pub. Time mag., 1964-67, asso. dir. corp. development, 1967, dir. central services, 1967—. Member council bd. of trustees Fordham U., 1968-, adminstrv. com. of council, 1969—; mem. national publicity com. Freedoms Found. Clubs: Hemisphere: Sleepy Hollow Country (trustee) (Scarborough-on-Hudson, N.Y.). Home: 25 Browning Dr Ossining NY 10562 Office: Time-Life Bldg Rockefeller Centre New York City NY 10020

FREY, JOSEPH RICHARD, banker; b. Secor, Ill., Jan 2, 1897; s. Clarence W. and Geneva (Colburn) F.; B.S., U. Ill., 1919; m. Hilda Kohl, Nov. 5, 1921; 1 son, Richard Kohl. State bank examiner, 1923-29; v.p. Lake Shore Trust & Savs. Bank, 1929; pres., dir. Lake Shore Nat. Bank, 1933-52, pres., chmn., 1952-62, chmn., chief exec. officer, 1962—; mem. board of directors Fed. Life Ins. Co. (Chgo.). Standard Rate & Data Service (Skokie, Ill.), C.W. Frey & Sons, (Bloomington, Ill.), Merrill Co. Pubs. (Chgo.), Greater N. Mich. Av. Assn. Dir. Blue-Cross-Blue Shield; treas., dir. Rehabilitation Institute Chicago; mem. bd. dirs. A.R.C. Mem. American (state legislative com. mem. council), Ill. (pres. 1950-51) bankers assns., Tau Kappa Epsilon. Mason (32 K.T., Shriner). Clubs: University, Executives, Arts, Commercial (Chgo.): Chicago Curling (Northbrook, Ill.); Indian Hill (dir., treas.) (Winnetka, Ill.). Home: 915 Shabona Lane Wilmette IL 60091 Office: 605 N Michigan Av Chicago IL 60611

FREY, KENNETH, drug store co. exec.; b. 1928; B.A., Pa. State U., 1952; married. Sr. accountant Touche, Ross & Co., C.P.A.'s, 1952-59; with Gray Drug Stores Inc., 1959—, treas., 1968—. Served with USNR, 1946-48. C.P.A., Ohio. Mem. Am. Inst. C.P.A.'s, Ohio Soc. C.P.A.'s. Address; care Gray Drug Stores Inc Euclid Bldg Cleveland OH 44114*

FREY, LOUIS, Jr., congressman; b. Rutherford, N.J., Jan. 11, 1934; s. Louis and Mildred (Engel) F.; B.A. cum laude, Colgate U., 1955; J.D. with honors, Mich. Law Sch., 1961; m. Marcia Turner, Nov. 1956; children—Julia, Lynn, Louis, Lauren. Admitted to Fla. bar, 1961; practice in Orlando; asst. county solicitor, 1963; asso., partner firm Gurney, Skolfield & Frey, Winter Park, 1963-67; partner firm Mateer, Frey, Young & Harbert, Orlando, 1967; mem. 91st-92d Congresses 5th Dist. Fla.; mem. Sci., Astronautics Mct. Marine and Fisheries coms.; Republican Com. on Population and Environment; leader Republican Task Force on Campus Unrest. Acting gen. counsel Fla. Turnpike Authority, 1966-67. Past mem. Fla. Republican State Exec. Com.; past treas., chmn. Fla. Fedn. Young Reps.; legal counsel Nat. Fedn. Young Reps., 1965-66. Bd. dirs. Winter Park Youth Center, Am. Cancer Soc. Orange County; mem. asso. bd. Fla. Symphony. Served to lt. (j.g.) USNR, 1955-58; comdr. Res. Mem. Order of Coif, Phi Gamma Delta, Phi Delta Phi. Lutheran. Home: 139 Genius Dr Winter Park FL 32789 Office: 1315 Longworth House Office Bldg Washington DC 20515

FREY, MICHAEL J., newspaper pub.; b. Wallhalla, N.D., Aug. 28, 1898; s. John and Leopoldina (Schuster) F.; m. Adelaide Wilson, June 20, 1922 (dec.); children—J. Richard, Marilyn S., m. 2d. Rosemary Dwyer, Nov. 19, 1949. With The Oregonian 1915—, country circulation mgr., 1923-32, circulation promotion mgr., 1932-34, circulation mgr. 1934-39, bus. mgr. 1939-46 gen. mgr. 1946-53. pub. 1953-68, now pres. Oregonian Publishing Co. Former dir. Better Bus. Bur.; pres. Pacific Northwest Newspaper Assn. Member Sigma Delta Chi, Alpha Delta Sigma. Republican. Presbyterian. Clubs: Waverly Country, Arlington, Multnomah Athletic. Home: 16350 SW Phantom Bluff Rd Lake Oswego OR 97034 Office: The Oregonian Portland OR 97201

FREY, OTTO, diplomat; b. Prague, Nov. 24, 1907; s. Maurice Elsa Frey; LL.D., Prague Univ., 1931; research Univ. Frankfurt on Main, 1931-32, Paris U., 1932, London Sch. Econ., 1933-34; m. Heda Fantova, Jan. 12, 1946; m. 2d, Phyllis Ruth Nayer, July 12, 1961. Entered Czechoslovak civil service 1934; govt. sec. to Minister for Pub. Works, 1934-35; transferred to diplomatic service, 1935; counsellor Czechoslovak Embassy, London, since 1938; chief of cabinet, Czechoslovak fgn. minister, 1941-45; mem. secretariat U.N. 1945, chief sect. in security council dept. UN, N.Y.C., 1946—, also joint sec. UN Disarmament Commn. and Sub-Com., dep. spl. rep. of sec.-gen. of UN to Geneva Disarmament Conf. Home: 85 East End Av New York City NY 10028 also: Sherman CT 06784

FREY, RICHARD KOHL, banker; b. Chgo., June 2, 1928; s. Joseph Richard and Hilda (Kohl) F.; A.B., Dartmouth, 1946-50; student Northwestern U. Law Sch., 1950-51; J.D., Chgo. Kent Coll. Law, 1958; m. Mary Johnson, Aug. 20, 1959; children—Martha Mary, Susan Hillary. With Lake Shore Nat. Bank, Chgo., 1955—, v.p., chmn. bus. devel., 1961-67, sr. v.p., 1967-69, exec. v.p., 1969—, dir., 1970—. Treas., bd. dirs. Mus. Contemporary Art, Chgo., 1971—; bd. dirs. Tim Russell Charitable Found. Served to lt. (j.g.) USNR, 1951-55. Mem. Bank Marketing Assn. (treas. 1969—). Clubs: Indian Hill (Winnetka); Press, University, Economics, Executive (dir. 1971—) (Chgo.). Home: 318 Rosewood St Winnetka IL 60093

FREY, ROBERT KETTERMAN, investment analyst; b. York, Pa., Feb. 25, 1910; s. Harvey W. and Ida (Ketterman) F.; Grad. Balt. City Coll., 1926; m. B. Lazetta Eberhart, Oct. 7, 1937; children—Ruth L., Martha E. With Nat. Bank Balt., 1926-29; with Mercantile-Safe Deposit & Trust Co., Balt., 1929—, v.p., 1952—, charge investment research and analysis, 1956-67, financial analysis, 1967—; dir. Am. Disinfectant Co., Balt. & Annapolis R.R. Co. Mem. N.Y. Soc. Security Analysts, Balt. Security Analysts Soc. (pres. 1957- 58). Lutheran. Home: 704 Dryden Dr Baltimore, MD 21229. Office: 2 Hopkins Plaza Baltimore MD 21201

FREYBERG, RICHARD HAROLD, educator, physician; b. Goshen, Ind., Aug. 14, 1904; s. William E. and Mary (Houk) F.; A.B., U. Mich., 1926, M.D., 1930, M.S. in Nutrition, 1935; m. Helen Beckman, Sept. 3, 1932; children—Joanne (Mrs. David R. Moss), Thomas R. Intern, then resident internal medicine U. Mich. Hosp., 1930-34; instr., then asst. prof. internal medicine U. Mich. Med. Sch., 1934-44, dir. Rackham Arthritis Research Unit, 1937-44; mem. faculty Cornell U. Med. Coll., 1944—, emeritus clin. prof. medicine, 1970—, chief sect. rheumatic diseases, 1944-70; dir. dept. rheumatic diseases Hosp. Spl. Surgery, N.Y.C., 1944-70. Bd. dirs. Arthritis Found., 1948-70, v.p., 1970—; pres. Pan-Am. League Against Rheumatism, 1952-56. Recipient Floyd B. Odlum award N.Y. chpt. Arthritis Found., 1966; Sesquicentennial award U. Mich., 1967; citation meritorious service N.Y. Hosp.-Cornell U. Med. Coll., 1969. Mem. A.M.A., A.C.P., Am. Soc. Clin. Investigation, Central Soc. Clin. Research, Am. (pres. 1949-50), N.Y. (pres. 1961-62) rheumatism assns., Harvy Soc. Home: 9 Horseguard Lane Scarsdale NY 10583 Office: 449 E 68th St New York City NY 10021

FREYHAN, FRITZ ADOLF, physician; b. Berlin, Germany, Nov. 24, 1912; s. Max and Clara (Gottschalk) F.; M.D., U. Berlin, 1937. Came to U.S., 1937, naturalized, 1943. Pathol. tng. Sydenham Hosp., N.Y.C., 1939, rotating intern, 1939- 40; mem. staff Del. State Hosp., Farnhurst, 1940-50, clin. dir., dir. research, 1950-60; dir. dept. psychiatry and neurology Del. Hosp., Wilmington, 1954-61; cons. psychiatry VA Hosp., Wilmington, Del., 1954- 61; dep. chief charge clin. studies, clin. neuropharmacology research center, Nat. Inst. Mental Health, 1961-66; dir. clin. studies, clin. and behavioral studies center St. Elizabeths Hosp., Washington, 1961-66; from asso. to adj. asso. prof. psychiatry U. Pa. Sch. Medicine, 1950-61; clin. prof. psychiatry George Washington U. Sch. Medicine, 1960-66; mem. faculty Washington Sch. Psychiatry, 1962-66; dir. research dept. psychiatry St. Vincent's Hosp., N.Y.C., 1966—; asso. clin. prof. psychiatry N.Y.U. Med. Center, 1966—. Diplomate Am. Bd. Neurology and Psychiatry. Fellow Am. Coll. Neuropsychopharmacology, N.Y. Acad. Medicine, Am. Psychiat. Assn., A.A.A.S.; mem. A.M.A., Medical Soc. D.C., Am. Psychopathol. Assn. (pres. 1969), Collegium Internationale Neuro-Psychopharmacologicum (councilor), Assn. Nervous and Mental Diseases, Soc. Biol. Psychiatry, Soc. Medico-Psychologique (asso.), Deutsche Gesellschaft fur Psychiatrie und Nervenheikunde (corr.), Societa Italiana di Neuropsicofarmacologia (corr.), Societe Royale de Medecine Mentale de Belgique (hon.). Club: Cosmos (Washington). Editor Comprehensive Psychiatry, 1960—; co-editor International Pharmacopsychiatry, 1967—. Home: 11 Riverside Dr New York City, NY 10023. Office: Cronin Research Bldg St Vincent's Hosp New York City NY 10011

FREYRE, GILBERTO DE MELLO, writer, social anthropologist; b. Brazil, 1900; ed. Colegio Americano, Recife, Brazil; Baylor U., Columbia; B.A., M.A., D.Litt.; Aggregatus of Sociology (hon.), Buenos Aires (Argentina) U.; Dr. h.c. (hon.), Columbia, Recife U., Bahia (Brazil) U. Prof. sociology Pernambuco (Brazil) State Normal Sch., 1928-30; author, 1934—; prof. sociology, founding prof. sociol anthropology Rio de Janeiro (Brazil) U., 1935-38; founder Recife Inst. for Research in Social Scis., 1949; supr. N.E. Brazil Social and Ednl. Research Centre, 1957—. Mem. Fed. Council Culture Brazil, 1967—. Del. UN Gen. Assembly. N.Y.C., 1949; tech. adviser Dept. for Protection Hist. and Artistic Monuments, UN Com. on Race Relations in S. Africa, 1954. M.P., Brazil, 1954-56. Recipient Filipe d'Oliveira award, 1934. Amsfield-Wolf award Princeton, 1957. Aspen award for outstanding contbn. in humanities, 1967. Mem. Am. Sociol. Soc., Brazilian Hist. and Geog. Inst. (both hon.), Portuguese, Ecuadorean, Colombian hist. acads. Am. Anthrop. Assn., Lisbon Geog. Soc., Am. Philos. Soc. Author: Casa-Grande e Senzala, 1934, (in English as The Masters and the Slaves, Vol. I); Sobrados e Mucambos, 1936, (in English as The Mansions and the Shanties, Vol. II); Sociologia, Problemas brasileiros de Antropologia, 1945; Ingleses no Brazil, 1948; Aventura e Rotina, 1953; Vida Social no Brasil nos Meades do Seculo XIX, Dona Sinha e o Filho Padre (in English Mother and Son) 1964. Address: Apipucos Recife Brazil*

FRIAR, GEORGE EDWARD, lawyer, state ofcl.; b. Claiborne Co., Tenn., Aug. 18, 1916; s. George Allen and Ida Mae (Crutchfield) F.; student Maryville Coll., 1932-34; LL.B., U. Tenn., 1937; grad. study Vanderbilt U., Princeton; m. Mary Edna Ball, Nov. 26, 1940; 1 son, George Edward. Admitted to Tenn. bar, 1938; dir. parole and probations Tenn., 1939-40, chief personnel and tng., 1942; adminstrv. asst. to Gov. Tenn., 1940; chief clk. Tenn. Ho. of Reps., 1941-43; sr. partner Friar. Lockett and Mahood, Knoxville, 1946- 54, sr. partner Friar, Vineyard and Reynolds, 1959—; now v.p., gen. counsel Performance Systems, Inc.; pres. Corporate Concepts, Inc.; gen. counsel Tenn. R.R. and Pub. Utilities Commn., 1949-51: chief counsel freight rate cases So Govs. Conf., 1950-51; sec. State Tenn., 1953-57. Chmn. Tenn. delegation Young Democratic Nat. Conv., 1947, 49; exec. dir. Tenn. Dem. Exec. Com., 1952- 58; del. Inter-Am. Congress of Municipalities, 1954. Chmn., U.S. Dist. Ct. Land Condemnation Commn. Dir. A.R.C., Traveller's Aid, Community Chest. Served as combat officer USNR. World War II. Mem. Am. Legion, Vet. Fgn. Wars, Phi Delta Phi, Sigma Phi Epsilon. Elk. Home: 3314 West End Av Park Rd Apts Nashville TN 37203 Office: 2708 Franklin Rd Nashville TN 37204

FRICK, FORD CHRISTOPHER, newspaperman, past nat. commr. baseball; b. Wawaka, Ind. Dec. 19, 1894; s. Jacob and Emma (Prickett) F.; B.A., De Pauw U., 1915, L.H.D., 1955; LL.D., Fla. So. Coll., 1952, Colo. Coll., 1958; m. Eleanor Cowing, Sept. 15, 1916; 1 son, Frederick Cowing. Asst. prof. English, Colo. Coll., Colorado Springs, 1915-17; supr. tng. Vets. Bur., Denver, 1918-19; mem. staff Colorado Springs Telegraph, 1919-21, N.Y. Jour., 1921-34; radio news commentator, 1930-34; pres. Nat. League of Profl. Baseball Clubs, 1934- 51, nat. commr. of baseball, 1951-65. Manpower cons. Econ. Devel. Council of N.Y.C. Trustee Babe Ruth Found.; chmn. bd. Nat. Baseball Hall of Fame. Received Thomas Jefferson award for advancement of demoncracy (pub. relations div.), 1948; named to Nat. Baseball Hall of Fame, 1970. Civilian lectr. in orientation course, U.S. Army. Trustee De Pauw U. Mem. Advt. Club Am., Am. Legion, Sigma Delta Chi, Phi Kappa Psi. Episcopalian. Clubs: St. Andrews Golf (Hastings); Siwanoy Golf (Bronxville). Home: 16 Edgewood Lane Bronxville NY 10708

FRICK, GOTTLOB, operatic and oratorio bass; b. nr. Stuttgart, Germany; gen., tech. edn. in Germany; scholarship student opera-sch. Städtische Opera, Stuttgart Landestheater, 1928-33; m. Margaret Bayen. Adminstrv. positions in tool- making factory; mem. family choir, appearing concerts as boy high- baritone; mem. opera co. Landestheater, Coburg, 1933-36, became prin. bass, appearing numerous Wagner parts, including Fasolt and Fafner, Hunding and Hagen, Henry the Fowler, Landgrave, Daland and Burnemanz; mem. Freiburg Opera Co., 1936-38, Königsberg Co., 1938-40, Dresden Opera. East Germany, 1940-50: mem. resident co. Deutsche Oper, West Berlin, 1950-52; debut in Hunding and Hagen, Metropolitan Opera. N.Y.C., 1951; appeared at Wagner Festival. Bayreuth,

1952-59; debut La Scala, Milan, 1952; other appearances Covent Garden, London, Teatro dell'Opera. Rome, also Naples, Florence, Bologna: roles of Khan Kontchak in Prince Igor, opera in Vienna; recordings including Walküre, 1955. Entführung, 1957, Rocco in Fidelio, Sarastro in Die Zauberflöte, Commendatore in Don Giovanni, Daland in Flying Dutchman, Pogner in Meistersinger, Herman in Tannhäuser, Henry the Fowler in Lohengrin, Kecal in Bartered Bride.

FRICK, KENNETH EUGENE, govt. ofcl.; b. Bakersfield, Cal., Apr. 30, 1920; s. Forrest Abraham and Ruth McKay (Finlayson) F.; B.S., U. Cal., Berkeley, 1941; m. Margaret Ann Janes, Feb. 9, 1946; children-Linda Ann, Gail, David. Owner, Ken-Mar Farms, Arvin, Cal., 1945-69; exec. v.p. CCC, U.S. Dept. Agr., 1969—, adminstr. Agrl. Stblzn. and Conservation Services, 1969—. Past dir. Calcot, Ltd., Bakersfield. Mem. Nat. Cotton and Cottonseed Research Adv., 1961-63. Mem. Sch. Bd., Arvin, 1955-65. Served with USAAF, 1941-45. Republican. Rotarian. Home: 4201 Cathedral Av NW Washington DC 20016 Office: US Dept Agr Agrl Stblzn and Conservation Service 14th and Independence Av SW Washington DC 20250

FRICK, PHILIP WILLIAM, utilities exec.; b. L.I., N.Y., July 26, 1925; s. John P. and Gertrude (Sparks) F.; student U. Minn., 1945; B.A., St. Johns U., 1948; postgrad. Pace Coll., 1952, U. Mich., 1958; m. Anna Mae Minett, Oct. 1, 1950; 1 son, Gary. Treas., Pitts Group Cos.-Columbia Gas System, Inc., 1966-69; treas. Columbia Gas System, Inc., 1969; v.p. finance, treas. Columbia Gas System Service Corp., Wilmington, Del., 1969—; treas. Columbia Gas Transmission Corp., Columbia LNG Corp., Columbia Gas Devel. Corp., Columbia Gas Devel. Can., Ltd. Served with AUS, 1944-46. Home: 8 Pelham Rd Welshire Wilmington DE 19803 Office: 20 Montchanin Rd Wilmington DE 19807

FRICK, RAYMOND AUGUSTUS, mfg. co. exec.; b. Bloomfield, N.J., Jan. 16, 1919; s. William French and Gertrude Mable (Small) F.; B.S. in Econs., U. Pa., 1941: m. Betsy Ann Osborne, Sept. 25, 1941; children—Raymond Augustus, Gregory Osborne, Stephen Louis, Tracey Gertrude. With Abex Corp., 1942—, gen. works mgr., 1952-54, v.p., 1954-61, exec. v.p. r.r. products div., 1961- -. Served as bomber pilot USAAF, 1942-45. Mem. Sigma Chi. Presbyn. (trustee). Club: University (N.Y.C.). Home: Anthony Wayne Rd Route 48 Morristown NJ 07960 Office: 530 Fifth Av New York City NY 10036

FRICK, THOMAS CORWIN, oil co. exec.; b. Caney, Kan., Apr. 20, 1909; s. William Ralph and Lena (Huggins) F.; B.S., U. Tulsa, 1933; student Mo. Sch. Mines, 1929-30; m. Aina Fransworth, Nov. 3, 1934; children—Martha F. (Mrs. Bradley A. Pigeon), Charles M. Engr., clk. Phillips Petroleum Co., Bartlesville, Okla., 1933-36; asso. prof. petroleum engring. U. Tulsa, 1936-41; various positions oil prodn. Atlantic Richfield Co., Dallas, 1941-61, mgr. natural gas div. 1961-66, mgr. natural gas dept., 1966-67, v.p. Central region, 1967—; dir., v.p. McKamie Gas Cleaning Co., 1954-58. Named to Hall of Fame, U. Tulsa Coll. Engring. and Phys. Scis., 1968. Mem. Am. Inst. Mining, Metall. and Petroleum Engrs. (dir. 1956-58, v.p. 1958-59, pres. 1965, hon. mem.), A.A.A.S., Am. Petroleum Inst., Am. Gas Assn., Mid-Continent Oil and Gas Assn., Kappa Alpha. Presbyn. Clubs: Chaparral; Las Colinas Country. Editor: Handbook of Petroleum Production, 1961. Home: 6516 Park Lane Dallas TX 75225 Office: Box 2819 Dallas TX 75221

FRICKE, RICHARD IRVIN, ins. co. exec.; b. Buffalo, Mar. 25, 1922; s. Richard F. and Julia S. (Cooper) F.; A.B., Cornell U., 1943, J.D. with distinction (editor Law quar. 1946-47), 1947; grad. Advanced Mgmt. Program, Harvard, 1965; m. Jeanne Hines, July 22, 1943 (dec.); children—Richard J., Diane L., Kathryn J. David R.; m. 2d, Ruth Byerly Tinker, March 26, 1967; children—Mark C., Michael A., Jodie P., John H. Admitted to N.Y. bar, 1947; asso. atty. Kenefick, Cooke, Mitchell, Bass & Letchworth, Buffalo, 1947-52; asst. prof., then asso. prof. law Cornell U. Law Sch. 1952-57; asso. counsel Ford Motor Co., 1957-62; v.p. gen counsel Mut. Life Ins. Co. N.Y., 1962-67, sr. v.p., 1967-69, exec. v.p., 1969—; trustee MONY Mortgage Investors. Mem. speakers bur. Buffalo Council World Affairs, 1952; cons. N.Y. State Law Revision Commn., 1952-57. Mem. adv. council Cornell Law Sch., Cornell U. Council; trustee Cornell U. Served with field arty. AUS and USAAF, 1943-45. Fellow Am. Bar Found.; mem. Am. Fed. of N.Y., N.J. and Conn. (v.p. 1956) bar assns., Assn. Bar City N.Y., Cornell Law Assn. (pres. 1965-67), Order of Coif, Am. Judicature Soc., Phi Kappa Phi, Phi Delta Phi. Clubs: University (N.Y.C.); Wee Burn Country. Home: 45 Birch Rd Darien CT 06820 Office: 1740 Broadway New York City NY 10019

FRICKE, ROBERT ELMER, physician; b. Milw., May 10, 1892; s. William A. and Elma (Winegardiner) F.; A.B., Johns Hopkins, 1916, M.D., 1920; m. Gertrude B. Hax, April 10, 1924. Mem. staff, Howard A. Kelly Hosp., 1920-27; cons. emeritus dept. therapeutic radiology Mayo Clinic, Rochester, Minn.; in charge of radium therapy Mayo Clinic; instr. radium therapy, Grad. Sch. Medicine, U. Minn., 1927-37, asst. prof., radiology, 1937-43, asso. prof., 1943-57; emeritus asso. prof. radiology Mayo Found.; specializing in treatment of cancer. Served in Med. Enlisted R.C., U.S. Army, 1917-18. Former mem. Rochester dist. exec. com., chmn. health and safety com. Boy Scouts Am. Diplomate Am. Bd. Radiology. Fellow Am. Coll. Radiology; mem. A.M.A. Am. Radium Soc. (sec. 1953-56), Pan Pacific Surg. Assn., Am. Roentgen-Ray Soc., Radiol. Soc. N.Am., Am. Therapeutic Soc. (v.p., 1943), Minn. Radiol. Soc. (pres. 1946), Minn. State Med. Assn., Johns Hopkins Surg. Soc., Alumni Assn. Mayo Found., Am. Soc. for Control of Cancer, Zumbro Valley Med. Soc. (exec. sec. 1958—), Am. Club Therapeutic Radiologists (founding mem.), Rochester C. of C., Sigma Xi. Republican. Clubs: Rochester Kiwanis (pres. 1941, bd. dirs. 8 yrs., treas., 6 yrs.); Johns Hopkins (Balt.). Author chpts.: Gynecology (Howard A. Kelly), 1928; The Science of Radiology, 1933; Surgical Clinics of North America, Mayo Clinic Number, 1935; Medical Clinics of North America, Mayo Cancer and Allied Diseases, 1964. Contbr. numerous articles to med. jours. Home: Knob Hill Apts 410 6th Av SW Rochester MN 55901 Office: Mayo Clinic Rochester MN 55901

FRICKE, THEODORE PAUL, former ch. ofcl.; b. Detroit, Dec. 21, 1904; s. Adolf and Martha (Koehne) F.; B.A., Capital U., Columbus, O., 1926, D.D., 1945; B.D., Lutheran Theol. Sem., Columbus, 1929; S.T.M., Princeton Theol. Sem., 1932; S.T.D., Wartburg Sem., 1945; m. Selma Reece, Oct. 9, 1933; children—Timothy, Priscilla (dec.). Ordained to ministry Luth. Ch., 1929; pastor in Detroit, 1929-31, St. Mary's, Ohio, 1932-37, Washington, 1937-43; exec. sec. world missions Am. Luth. Ch., 1943-60, asso. dir., 1960-62, exec. dir., 1963-70. Author: We Found Them Waiting, 1945. Home: 6821 Creston Rd Minneapolis MN 55435

FRICKER, PETER RACINE, composer, educator; b. London, Eng., Sept. 5, 1920; s. Edward Racine and Deborah (Parr) F.; student Royal Coll. Music, London, 1937-41: Mus.D. (hon.), U. Leeds (Eng.), 1958; m. Helen Clench, Apr. 17, 1943. Came to U.S. 1964. Dir. music Morley Coll., London, 1953-64; prof. music Royal Coll. Music, London, 1956-64; prof., chmn. music dept. U. Cal. at Santa Barbara, 1964- -; conductor, lectr., 1948—. Bd. dirs. Santa Barbara Symphony Assn. Served to flight lt. RAF, 1941-46. Decorated Order of Merit (West Germany), 1965; recipient Freedom City London, 1962. Fellow Royal Coll. Organists; asso. Royal Coll. Music; mem. Composer"s Guild Great Britain (chmn. 1955), Royal Philharmonic Soc. London, Soc. Promotion New Music, Am. Music Center, Am. Guild Organists, Am. Assn. U. Profs., Am. Soc. Univ. Composers, Royal Acad. Music (hon.). Compositions include four symphonies, oratorio, 2 violin concertos, piano concerto, viola sonata, cello sonata, 12 studies for piano, also vocal, guitar and organ music, music for films and radio. Home: 6155 Verdura Av Goleta, CA 93017. Office: Music Dept U California Santa Barbara CA 93106

FRICKER, SYLVIA, Canadian folk singer, appearing with Ian Tyson, billed as Ian and Sylvia. Address: care Internat Talent Assos 65 E 55th St New York City NY 10022*

FRIDAY, CHARLES BOSTWICK, educator; b. Fort Collins, Colo., Aug. 6, 1921; s. Carl Bostwick and Cleta Mae (Rubart) F.; B.A., U. Colo., 1943, M.A., 1947, Ph.D., 1950; m. Jean Brewer, July 23, 1944; children—Kathryn Ann, Deborah Jean, John Charles. Instr. econs. U. Colo., 1947-50; faculty Ore. State U., 1950—, prof. econs. 1957—, chmn. dept., 1957-67. Mem. adv. council Small Bus. Adminstrn., Fed. Govt., 1962-68. Served with AUS, 1943-45. Mem. Am., Western (mem. exec. com. 1963—, pres. 1970) econs assns., Econ. History Assn., Am. Studies Assn., Am. Assn. U. Profs., Assn. for Evolutionary Econs., Phi Beta Kappa, Pi Gamma Mu. Author: (with B.H. Wilkins) The Economists of the New Frontier, 1963. Home: 1006 N 31st St Corvallis OR 97330

FRIDAY, F.P., insurance co. exec.; b. Stevens Point, Wis., Jan. 16, 1924; s. A.V. and Susan Friday; B.S., U.So. Cal.; m. Shirley Murphy, June 18, 1949; children—Denise, Kathleen, Kimpatrick, Daniel. With Continental Casualty Co., 1949-52, Charles O. Finley Co., Inc., 1952-61; with Kansas City Athletics Baseball Club (Mo.), 1961-65, former v.p. gen. mgr., dir.; v.p. dir. Finley & Friday, Inc. div. Charles O. Finley Co., Inc. Served with AUS, 1943-46. Office: 310 S Michigan Av Chicago IL 60604

FRIDAY, HERSCHEL HUGAR, lawyer; b. Lockesburg, Ark. Feb. 10, 1922; s. Herschel Hugar and Rose Lee (Scarborough) F.; student Little Rock U. 1939-41, U. Minn, 1943; J.D., U. Ark., 1947; m. Nancy Elizabeth Hammett, Feb. 26, 1943; children—Gregory David, Steven Herschel, Pamela. Admitted to Ark. bar, 1947; sec. law clk. U.S. judge, Western dist., Fort Smith, Ark., 1947- 52; lectr. law U. Ark., 1951-52; mem. firm Smith, Williams, Friday & Bowen, and predecessor firm, Little Rock, 1952—. Mem. Ark. Bd. Law Examiners, 1960-66. Legal adviser to bd. Ark. Children"s Colony, 1957- -; mem. Gov.'s Com. on Mental Retardation, 1962-66; pres. Ark. Assn. Retarded Children, 1967-69. Trustee Ark. Children's Hosp., 1954—, pres., 1962-64. Served with USAAF, 1943-46. Fellow Am. Bar Found.; mem. Am. (ho. of dels. 1954—, mem. com. bill of rights, 1961-66, mem. bd. govs. 1968—), Ark. (exec. com. 1954-68, chmn. 1963-64), Pulaski County bar assns., Am. Judicature Soc. Baptist. Clubs: Exchange of Little Rock (pres. 1955-56), Pleasant Valley Country (pres. 1963- 64), Little Rock. Contbr. articles law revs. Home: 172 Pleasant Valley Dr Little Rock AR 72207 Office: Boyle Bldg Little Rock AR 72201

FRIDAY, WILLIAM CLYDE, univ. pres.; b. Raphine, Va., July 13, 1920; s. David L. and Mary E. (Rowan) F.; student Wake Forest Coll., 1937. LL.D., 1957; B.S., N.C. State Coll., 1941; LL.B., U. N.C., 1948; LL.D., Belmont Abbey Coll., 1957; LL.D., Duke, 1958; LL.D., Princeton, 1958; LL.D., Elon Coll., 1959, Davidson Coll., 1961, U. Ky., 1970; m. Ida Howell, May 13, 1942; children—Frances H. Mary H. Ida E. Admitted N.C. bar, 1948; asst. dean student U.N.C., 1948-51, asst. to pres., 1951-55, sec. of univ. 1955-56, acting pres., 1956, pres., 1956—. Trustee Carnegie Found. for Advancement of Teaching Urban Inst., chmn., 1971; mem. Carnegie Commn. Future Higher Edn.: vice chmn. So. Regional Edn. Bd., 1967-69; chmn. President's Task Force on Education, 1966-67; mem. Commn. White House Fellows: dir., mem. Markle Found.; bd. visitors Davidson Coll. Served as lt. USNR, World War II. Mem. Assn. Am. Univ. (pres. 1971). Democrat. Baptist. Home: 402 E Franklin St Chapel Hill NC 27514

FRIDE, EDWARD THEODORE, lawyer; b. Duluth, Minn., Jan. 8, 1927; s. Edward T. and Lina (Wick) F.; A.A., Duluth Jr. Coll., 1947; B.S. in Law, U. Minn., 1949, J.D., 1951; m. Nancy Jean McHaffie, June 13, 1952; children—Edward O., Nancy E., Mark R., Scott D., Gail E., William A. Admitted to Minn. bar, 1951; partner firm Sullivan, Hanft, Hastings, Fride & O'Brien, Duluth, 1956—. Dir. Minn. and Man. R.R. Co., Mid-Continent Warehouse Co., Andresen-Ryan Coffee Co.; pres. Arco Bldg. Corp.; instr. bus. law U. Minn., 1951-53, now lectr. Continuing Legal Edn. Center. Vice pres. Duluth Bd. Edn., 1964-68; pres. Duluth Rehab. Center, 1958-60. Served with U.S. Mcht. Marine, 1944-46, USNR, 1944-46. Fellow Internat. Soc. Barristers; mem. Duluth, Minn., Am. bar assns., Nat. Assn. Rd. Trial Counsel, Internat. Assn. Ins. Counsel, Maritime Law Assn. U.S., Fedn. Ins. Counsel. Home: 3910 Gladstone St Duluth MN 55804 Office: 1200 Alworth Bldg Duluth MN 55802

FRIDGE, BENJAMIN WALL, govt. ofcl.; b. Alexandria, La., Aug. 28, 1916; s. Herbert Eldon and Mary (Wall) F.; B.S., La. State U., 1938; m. Bettye Barnum, Oct. 3, 1942; children—Marsha, Richard, Stephen. Chem. engr. Ethyl Corp., 1939- 47; owner, operator wholesale farm machinery bus., San Jose, Cal., 1947- 55; v.p. dir. engring. Menlo (Cal.) Research Lab., 1957; dep. for res. and ROTC affairs Office Sec. Air Force, 1957-60; asst. to pres. William H. Singleton Co., Inc. Springfield, Va., 1960-61; spl. asst. for manpower, Personnel and res. forces Office Sec. Air Force, 1961—. Served to col. USAAF, 1941-45; brig. gen. Res. Decorated D.S.C., Soldiers medal, Air medal with oak leaf cluster. Mem. Air Force Assn., Res. Officers Assn., Legion of Valor, Order Daedalians, Nat. Aviation Club. Home 1900 S Eads Arlington, VA 22202. Office: Sec Air Force The Pentagon Washington DC 20330

FRIDLEY, RICHARD MARC, life ins. co. exec.; b. Oelwein, Ia., Apr. 5, 1927; s. Marc Lincoln and Emma (Notbohm) F.; student Ia. State Tchrs. Coll. 1948-49; B.S. in Bus. Adminstrn., Drake U., 1952; m. Doris Evelyn Baer, Aug. 6, 1949; children—Richard Marc, Anne Carol. Actuarial research Guarantee Mut. Life Co., Omaha, 1952-53; actuarial v.p. Automotive Life Ins. Co., New Orleans, 1953-56; with Pan Am. Life Ins. Co., New Orleans, 1957—, chief actuary, 1961, v.p., chief actuary, 1962, v.p. acturial and adminstrv., 1963—, also dir. Vice pres., Social Welfare Planning Council. Bd. dirs., treas. Childrens Bur. of New Orleans. Served to lst lt. USAAF, 1945-48. Fellow Soc. Actuaries; mem. New Orleans C. of C., Am. Arbitration Assn., Am. Acad. Actuaries, Internat. House New Orleans, Delta Sigma Pi, Kappa Mu Epsilon. Lutheran (pres.). Clubs: Actuaries of Southwest (past pres.), VistaShores (New Orleans); Century; American (Mexico City). Home: 6262 Pratt Dr New Orleans LA 70122. Office: 2400 Canal St New Orleans LA 70119

FRIDLUND, HILMER MAURICE, lawyer; b. Sioux City, Ia., Apr. 11, 1896; s. Magnus and Hilma (Bergman) F.; A.B., Grinnell Coll., 1918, LL.D., 1970; J.D., (Perkins scholar), Harvard, 1921; Sheldon traveling fellow Faculte de Droit, Sorbonne, Paris, 1921-22, Jurist Schule, Berlin, 1922-23; postgrad. Inst. Internat. Law, Paris, 1921-22, Berlin Law Sch., Germany, 1922-23; m. Edith St. John, Dec. 24, 1923 (dec. 1965); children—Elaine (Mrs. Roger Lester), Norman St. John, Alice (Mrs. Warren Hance). Admitted to N.Y. bar, 1923, since practiced in N.Y.C.; with Kirlin, Campbell & Keating, 1923—, partner, 1934—, sr. mng. partner, 1964-69, counsel, 1969—. Vis. prof. polit. sci. Grinnell Coll., 1968-70, Kan. Wesleyan U., 1970- 71. Pres. Tenafly (N.J.) Bd. Health, 1944-56, Bergen County Pub. Health and San. Assn., 1946-56, Commn. on World Service and Finance, Newark Conf. Methodist Ch., 1948-56; observer at World Council Chs. Amsterdam Assembly, 1948, Uppsala, 1968. Pres. Commn. on Interpretation and Support World Council Chs. in U.S., 1956-69. Mem. adv. council Grinnell Coll. Mem. Am., N.Y. State bar assns., Maritime Law Assn. U.S., Phi Beta Kappa. Republican. Clubs: Harvard, India House (N.Y.C.); Knickerbocker Country (Tenafly). Contbr. profl. jours. Home: Washington NH 03280 Office: 120 Broadway New York City NY 10005

FRIED, ALEXANDER, music and art critic; b. N.Y.C., May 21, 1902; s. Henry and Sarah (Perils) F.; A.B., Columbia, 1923, A.M., 1924; m. Edith Trumpler, Jan. 28, 1949; children—Madelyn Natalie, Harriet. Mng. editor Musical Digest, N.Y., 1924-25; music editor, then art editor, San Francisco Chronicle, 1926-34; music and art editor San Francisco Examiner 1934—. Hebrew religion. Home: 22 Crown Terrace, San Francisco CA 94114 Office: San Francisco Examiner San Francisco CA 94119

FRIED, BURTON DAVID, educator, physicist; b. Chgo., Dec. 14, 1925; s. Albert O. and Bertha (Rosenthal) F.; B.S., Ill. Inst. Tech., 1947; M.S., U. Chgo., 1950, Ph.D., 1952; m. Sally Rachel Goldstein, Aug. 17, 1947; children—Joel Ethan, Jeremy Steven. Instr. physics Ill. Inst. Tech., 1947-52; research physicist Lawrence Radiation Lab. of U. Cal., 1952-54; sr. staff physicist TRW Systems, Los Angeles, 1954—; prof. physics U. Cal. at Los Angeles, 1963—; dir. research lab. Ramo-Wooldridge Computer Div., Los Angeles, 1961-63. Served with USNR, 1944-46. Mem. Am. Phys. Soc., Sigma Xi. Research and publs. on theoretical elementary particle and plasma physics. Home: 1119 Las Pulgas Pl Pacific Palisades CA 90272 Office: 405 Hilgard St Los Angeles CA 90024

FRIED, CHARLES, legal educator; b. Prague, Czechoslovakia, Apr. 15, 1935; s. Anthony and Marta (Wintersteinova) F.; came to U.S., 1941, naturalized. 1948; grad. Lawrenceville Sch., 1952; A.B., Princeton, 1956; B.A. Juris., Oxford (Eng.) U., 1958, M.A., 1961; LL.B., Columbia, 1960; m. Anne Sumerscale, June 13, 1959; children—Charles Gregory, Antonia Catherine. Admitted to D.C. and Mass. bars; law clk. to asso. justice John M. Harlan, U.S. Supreme Ct., 1960; mem. faculty Harvard Law Sch., 1961—, prof. law, 1965—; vis. prof. U. Cal. at Berkeley, 1968; vis. prof. philosophy Mass. Inst. Tech., 1969. Dir. Metric, Inc., Urban Systems, Inc. Asso. reporter model code prearraignment procedure Am. Law Inst. 1965—; spl. cons. Treasury Dept., 1961-62. Guggenheim fellow, 1971-72. Mem. Am. Soc. Polit. and Legal Philosophy (v.p.), Phi Beta Kappa. Author: An Anatomy of Values, 1970. Contbr. legal and philos. jours. Office: Harvard Law Sch Cambridge MA 02138

FRIED, HELEN FEINER, (Mrs. Albert Fried), educator, religious worker, pub. speaker; b. Port Chester, N.Y., Mar. 6; d. Joseph and Rose (Boehm) Feiner; B.C.S., N.Y. U., 1934, M.A., 1938; m. Albert Fried, June 30, 1935; children—Arthur William, J. Michael. Tchr., Rhodes Sch., N.Y.C., 1935-42; pub. speaker, 1956—; faculty speech and drama dept. Coll. City N.Y., 1967-. Bd. dirs., mem. commn. Jewish Life Synagogue Council Am., 1962—, del. to UN, 1968—; dir., mem. overseas bd. dirs. Jewish Theol. Sem. Am., 1960—; exec. com. Jewish Braille Inst., 1958—; exec. com. dir. World Council Synagogues, 1960; br. pres. Nat. Women's League United Synagogues Am., 1950-52, nat. pres., 1962-66, now hon. pres. Bklyn. br., also dir. Active A.R.C., Israel Bonds, United Jewish Appeal; participant White House Conf. Edn. 1965, White House Conf. Civil Rights, 1966. Committeewoman N.Y.C. Liberal Party; hon-govtl. orgn. del. to UN, 1966—. Named Woman of Achievement, Jewish Theol. Sem. Am.; recipient Nat. Community Leadership award, 1965. Contbr. articles to profl. jours. Home: 2071 E 35th St Brooklyn NY 11234

FRIED, HERBERT DANIEL, advt. exec.; b. Chgo., May 27, 1928; s. Herbert D. and Beatrice (Frank) F.; student U. N.M., 1946-48, U. Ill., 1948; m. Ninon Connart, Mar. 7, 1953; children—Bruce M., William F. Account exec. Foote, Cone & Belding, Chgo., 1948-54, Weiss & Geller, Chgo., 1954-55; account exec., gen. mgr. W.B. Doner & Co., Balt., 1955-56, v.p., 1956-68, pres., 1968—. Div. chmn. Community Chest-A.R.C.-United appeal, 1964; Served with USNR, 1946. Recipient award Chgo. Federated Advt. Club, 1959. Mem. Am. Assn. Advt. Agencies (bd. govs. Chesapeake council 1960, regional dir. 1963), Advt. Club Balt., C. of C., Kappa Sigma. Club: Suburban of Baltimore County (Pikesville, Md.) Home: 3505 Round Hollow Rd Baltimore MD 21208 Office: 2305 N Charles St Baltimore MD 21218

FRIED, JOSEF, chemist, educator; b. Przemysl, Poland, July 21, 1914; s. Abraham and Frieda (Fried) F.; student U. Leipzig, 1934-37, U. Zurich, 1937-38; Ph.D. Columbia, 1941; m. Erna Werner, Sept. 18, 1939; 1 dau., Carol Frances. Came to U.S., 1938, naturalized, 1944. Eli Lilly fellow Columbia, 1941-43; research chemist Givaudan, N.Y., 1943; head dept. antibiotics and steroids Squibb Inst. Med. Research, New Brunswick, N.J., 1944-59, dir. sect. organic chemistry, 1959-63; prof. chemistry, biochemistry and Ben May Lab. Cancer Research, U. Chgo., 1963—; mem. med. chem. study sect. NIH, 1963-67, 68-72, chmn., 1971; mem. com. arrangements Laurentian Hormone Conf., 1964-71; Knapp Meml. lectr. U. Wis. 1958. Recipient N.J. Patent award, 1968. Fellow A.A.A.S., N.Y. Acad. Scis.; mem. Am. Chem. Soc., Nat. Acad. Scis., Am. Soc. Biol. Chemists, Brit., Swiss chem. socs., Sigma Xi. Mem. bd. editors Jour. Organic Chemistry, 1964-69, Steroids, 1966—. Contbr. articles profl. jours. Patentee in field. Home: 5715 S Kenwood Av Chicago IL 60637

FRIED, MORTON HERBERT, educator, anthropologist; b. N.Y.C., Mar. 21, 1923; s. Norton and Sally (Solomon) F.; B.S., Coll. City N.Y., 1942; Ph.D., Columbia, 1951; m. Martha Nemes, June 22, 1945; children—Nancy, Elman Steven. Mem. faculty Columbia, 1949—, prof. anthropology, 1961—, chmn. dept. anthropology, 1966-69; vis. prof. U. Mich., 1960-61, Nat. Taiwan U., 1963-64, Yale, 1965-66. Bd. dirs. Social Sci. Research Council, 1965-68. Served with AUS, 1943-45. Guggenheim fellow, 1963-64; NSF grantee, 1964-66, 65—. Mem. Am. Anthrop. Assn. (mem. exec. bd. 1970—), Asian Studies Assn., Am. Ethnol. Soc., A.A.A.S. Author: Fabric of Chinese Society, 1953; Readings in Anthropology, 1959; The Evolution of Political Society, 1967; The Study of Anthropology, 1971; others. Home: 117 Leonia Av Leonia NJ 07605 Office: Dept Anthropology and East Asian Inst Columbia U New York City NY 10027

FRIED, WALTER JAY, lawyer; b. N.Y.C., May 27, 1904; s. Joseph and Flora V. (Shamberg) F.; B.A. magna cum laude, Harvard, 1924; LL.B., Columbia, 1928; m. Louise E. Goldman, June 8, 1934; 1 son, Michael W.; m. 2d Brita Digby-Brown, July 8, 1948. Admitted to N.Y. bar, 1929, since practiced in N.Y.C., admitted to D.C. bar, 1966; mem. firm Fried, Frank, Harris, Shriver & Jacobson; mem. faculty Bklyn. Law Sch., 1931-39. Dir. Bergdorf & Goodman Co., Salant Corp. Pres. bd. dirs. Am. Chess Found.; bd. dirs. Elida B. Langley Charitable Trust. Served to maj. AUS, 1942-45. Decorated Legion of Merit. Mem. Am., N.Y. State bar assns. Assn. Bar City N.Y., N.Y.

County Lawyers Assn. N.Y. Law Inst., Assn. Harvard Chemists, N.Y. Cipher Soc., Phi Beta Kappa, Clubs: Harvard Bankers Am., Manhattan Chess (dir.) (N.Y.C.). Home: 14 E 75th St New York City NY 10021 also Lily Pond Lane East Hampton NY 11937 Office: 120 Broadway New York City NY 10005

FRIEDAN, BETTY NAOMI, author, feminist leader; b. Peoria, Ill., Feb. 4, 1921; d. Harry and Miriam (Horwitz) Goldstein; B.A. summa cum laude, Smith Coll., 1942; m. Carl Friedan, June 1947 (div. May 1969); children—Daniel, Jonathan, Emily. Research fellow U. Cal. at Berkeley, 1943; lectr. feminism univs., women's groups, polit. groups in U.S. and Europe; founder Nat. Orgn. for Women, 1st pres., 1966-70, now chairwoman adv. com. Organizer Nat. Women's Polit. Caucas, 1971. Mem. P.E.N., Soc. Mag. Writers, Assn. Humanistic Psychology, Phi Beta Kappa. Author: The Feminine Mystique, 1963; columnist McCall's mag., 1971; contbr. Harper's, Social Policy, N.Y. Times drama sect. Address: 31 W 93d St New York City NY 10025

FRIEDBERG, ARTHUR LEROY, educator, ceramic engr.; b. River Forest, Ill., Mar. 25, 1919; s. Oscar and Fannie (Blumenthal) F.; B.S. in Ceramic Engring., U. Ill., 1941, M.S., 1947, Ph.D., 1952; postgrad. U. Chgo., 1943-44; m. Marian Davis, Feb. 4, 1944; children—Richard Charles, Anne. Mem. faculty U. Ill., 1946- -, prof. ceramic engring., 1957—, head dept. 1963—. Served to lt. (s.g.) USNR, 1943-46. Mem. Am. Ceramic Soc., Soc. Glass Tech., Am. Soc. Testing Materials, A.A.A.S., Am. Assn. U. Profs., Canadian Ceramic Soc., Am. Soc. Engring. Edn. Home: 1118 Waverly Dr Champaign IL 61820 Office: U Illinois Urbana IL 61801

FRIEDBERG, M. PAUL, landscape architect; b. Bklyn., Oct. 11, 1931; s. Morris and Mary (Bennett) F.; B.S. in Landscape Architecture, Cornell U., 1954; m. Esther Louise Hidary, Jan. 21, 1962; children—Mark, Allen Jeffry. Ladscape architect with Arthur Hoffman, Hartford, Conn., 1954, with Joseph Gangemi, N.Y.C., 1954, 56-58; propr. M. Paul Friedberg and Assos., landscape architects, N.Y.C., 1960—; vis. critic, lectr. U. Pa., 1967, Syracuse U., 1967, Carnegie Inst. Tech., 1967, Harvard, 1966, others; faculty mem. Pratt Inst., Columbia U., New Sch. for Social Research; prin. works include Carver House Plaza, N.Y.C., 1964, Riis Houses Plaza, N.Y.C., 1966, Buchanan Sch., Washington, Pub. Sch. 166, N.Y.C., Bklyn. Bedford-Stuyvesant Superblock; landscape architect Spanish Pavilion, N.Y. World's Fair, 1965. Del White House Conf. Natural Beauty, 1965, N.Y. State Conf. Natural Beauty, 1966, Urban Am. Conf., 1966. Recipient awards Am. Assn. Nurserymen, 1964; Albert S. Bard award, 1965, 67; Honor award Housing Urban Devel. (2), 1966; award citation A.I.A., 1969, Honor award, 1967; bronze plaque and merit award N.Y. Municipal Arts Soc., 1967. Mem. Am. Inst. Planners, Municipal Art Soc. N.Y. (bd. dirs.), Am. Soc. Landscape Architects (Honor awards 1965, 68, 70, Merit awards 1965, 67, 68, 69), Parks Assn. N.Y.C., N.Y.C. Council for Parks and Recreation (Art award 1967), Archtl. League. Home: 116 W 88th St New York City NY 10024 Office: 4 W 62d St New York City NY 10023

FRIEDBERG, SIMEON ADLOW, physicist, educator; b. Pitts., July 7, 1925; s. Emanuel B. and Lillian (Adlow) F.; A.B., Harvard, 1947; M.S., Carnegie Inst. Tech., 1948, D.Sc., 1951; m. Joan Brest, Sept. 4, 1950; children—Elizabeth B., Aaron L., Susan A. Fulbright grantee U. Leiden, Netherlands, 1951-52; research physicist Carnegie Inst. Tech., Pitts., 1952-53, mem. faculty, 1953-67, prof. physics, 1962-67; prof. physics Carnegie-Mellon U., Pitts., 1967—. Westinghouse fellow, 1950-51; Alfred P. Sloan Found. research fellow, 1957-61; Guggenheim fellow Imperial Coll., London, Eng., 1965-66. Fellow Am. Phys. Soc.; mem. Sigma Xi, Tau Beta Pi, Phi Kappa Phi, Pi Mu Epsilon. Contbr. chpt. Methods of Experimental Physics, 1959. Research, numerous publs. in low temperature solid state physics, thermal and magnetic properties of coupled spin systems, thermal and transport properties in certain metals, semi-conductors, insulators. Home: 1220 S Negley Av Pittsburgh PA 15217

FRIEDBERG, WALLACE, educator; b. N.Y.C., Apr. 12, 1927; s. Isidor and Mae Doris (Lobman) F.; student L.I. U., 1944-45; A.B., Hope Coll., 1949; M.S., Mich. State U., 1951, Ph.D., 1953; m. Mary Elizabeth House, Aug. 17, 1957; children—Susan, Jacqueline, Daniel. Research asso. Children's Hosp., Phila., 1954-55; research asso. Oak Ridge Nat. Lab., 1955-56, asso. biologist, 1958-59, biologist, 1959-60, loanee, 1969—; chief, radiobiology research FAA, Civil Aeromed. Inst., Oklahoma City, 1960—; asso. in biology Oklahoma City U., 1968—; asst. prof. research biochemistry U. Okla., 1961-64, asso. prof., 1964-69, prof. research biochemistry and molecular biology, 1969—, research prof. parasitology and lab. practice, 1969—, adj. prof. zoology, 1971—. Served with USNR, 1945-46. USPHS fellow Ind. U., 1953-54, USPHS fellow Oak Ridge Nat. Lab., 1957-58. Mem. Am. Chem. Soc., Soc. Exptl. Biology and Medicine, Am. Physiol. Soc., Transplantation Soc., Sigma Xi, Sigma Pi Sigma, Phi Lambda Upsilon. Home: 7805 N W 26th St Bethany OK 73008

FRIEDE, REINHARD LEOPOLD, neuropathologist, educator; b. Jaegerndorf, Czechoslovakia, May 12, 1926; s. Reinhard and Hilde (Rosner) F.; M.D., U. Vienna, 1951; m. Editha R. Franzen, Dec. 22, 1953; children—Reinhard H., Gerd R. Came to U.S., 1957, naturalized, 1962. Intern City Hosp., St. Poelten, Austria, 1951- 52; resident dept. neurology U. Vienna (Austria), 1953, Clinic of Neurosurgery Freiburg, Germany, 1953-57; mem. staff Aero Med. Lab., Wright Air Devel. Center, Dayton, O., 1957-59; faculty U. Mich., Ann Arbor, 1959-65; prof. neuropathology Case Western Res. U., Cleve., 1965—. Mem. Am. Assn. Neuropathology. Author: A Histochemical Atlas of Tissue Oxidation in the Brain Stem of the Cat, 1961; Topographic Brain Chemistry, 1966. Contbr. numerous articles on histochemistry, neuropathology to med. jours. Home: 2923 Drummond St Shaker Heights Cleveland OH 44120 Office: Institute of Pathology 2085 Adelbert Rd Cleveland OH 44106

FRIEDEL, SAMUEL NATHANIEL, congressman; b. Washington, Apr. 18, 1898; s. Philip and Rose (Franklin) R.; student pub. schs., Balt.; m. Regina B. Johnson, Mar. 8, 1939. Mem. 83d-91st Congresses, 7th Dist. Md., chmn. house adminstrn. com., chmn. transp. and aeronautics subcom, vice chmn. joint com. on printing, vice chmn. joint com. on library. Mem. Md. Ho. Dels., 1934-38; mem. Balt. City Council, 1939, 43, 51. Mem. Mt. Washington Improvement Assn., Balt. Democrat. Elk. Home: 2201 South Rd Baltimore MD 21209.

FRIEDELL, HYMER LOUIS, radiologist; b. St. Petersburg, Russia, Feb. 6, 1911; s. Harry and Rachel (Wien) F.; came to U.S., 1911, naturalized, 1915; B.S., U. Minn., 1931, M.B., 1935, M.D., 1936, Ph.D., 1939; m. Miriam Lipser, Feb. 16, 1935; children—Carol Ann, Janet Leslie, Richard Alan Anthony. Teaching fellow U. Minn., 1936-39; Nat. Cancer Inst. fellow, Chgo. Tumor Inst., Meml. Hosp. N.Y., and U. Cal. Hosps., 1939-41; research fellow in radiation lab., instr. radiology U. Cal., 1941-42; dir. dept. radiology Univ. Hosps. of Cleve., also prof. radiology Case Western Res. U., Cleve., 1946—. Served as lt. col., C.E., AUS, 1942-46; exec. officer and dep. chief Medical div., Manhattan Dist., 1942-46. Mem. central adv. com., radioisotope sect., research and edn. service VA, 1947-60; formerly mem. com. radiobiology NRC, reactor safeguard com., AEC, chmn. exec. bd. council of insts. Argonne Nat. Lab.; past chmn. radiation study sect. NIH; now mem. Plowshare adv. com. AEC; former mem. vis. com. Brookhaven Nat. Lab. Fellow Am. Coll. Radiology; mem. Am. Roentgen Ray Soc. (mem. exec. council), Radiation Research Soc. (pres. 1961-62), Radium Soc., Radiol. Soc. N.Am., A.A.A.S., Soc. Exptl. Biology and Medicine, A.M.A., Sigma Xi, Alpha Omega Alpha. Home: 2895 Sedgewick Rd Shaker Heights OH 44120 Office: 2065 Adelbert Rd Cleveland OH 44106 ☆

FRIEDEN, BERNARD JOEL, educator; b. N.Y.C., Aug. 11, 1930; s. George and Jean (Harris) F.; B.A., Cornell U., 1951; M.A., Pa. State U., 1953; M.C.P., Mass. Inst. Tech., 1957, Ph.D., 1962; m. Elaine Leibowitz, Nov. 23, 1958; 1 dau., Deborah Susan. Asst. prof. urban studies and planning Mass. Inst. Tech., 1961-65, asso. prof., 1965-69, prof., 1969—. Research mem. Mass. Inst. Tech.-Harvard Joint Center for Urban Studies, 1960-70, dir., 1971—; cons. U.S. Dept. H.U.D., 1966-68, Nat. Inst. Mental Health, 1968-70, U.S. Dept. H.E.W., 1968; staff Pres. Johnson's Task Force Urban Problems, 1965; mem. Pres. Nixon's Task Force Urban Problems, 1968, White House Task Force Model Cities, 1969; trustee Nat. Assembly Social Policy and Devel., 1970—; bd. dirs. Citizens Housing and Planning Assn., 1966—. Served with AUS, 1952-54. Mem. Am. Inst. Planners, Planners Equal Opportunity, Regional Sci. Assn., Ams. Dem. Action. Jewish religion. Author: The Future of Old Neighborhoods, 1964; Metropolitan America, 1966; Urban Planning and Social Policy, 1968; Shaping an Urban Future, 1969. Editor of Jour. Am. Inst. Planners, 1962-65. Contbr. to The Metropolitan Enigma, 1970, The State and the Poor, 1970. Home: 83 Washington Av Cambridge MA 02140

FRIEDEN, CARL, educator, biochemist; b. New Rochelle, N.Y., Dec. 31, 1928; s. Alexander and Evelyn (Gutman) F.; B.A., Carleton Coll., 1951; Ph.D., U. Wis., 1955; m. Sari Anne Schneider, Dec. 20, 1953; children—Amy, Eric, Karen. Faculty dept. biochemistry Washington U., St. Louis, 1957—, prof. biol. chemistry, 1963—; chmn. St. Louis Biochemistry Group, 1961-62. Mem. Am. Soc. Biol. Chemists, Am. Chem. Soc., A.A.A.S., Sigma Xi. Editorial bd. Jour. Biol. Chemistry, 1963-68. Research, publs. on mechanism of enzyme action including correlation of protein structure to catalytic function; devel., application of kinetic theory with respect to enzymes. Home: 7452 Wellington Way St Louis MO 63105

FRIEDEN, EARL, educator, biochemist; b. Norfolk, Va., Dec. 31, 1921; s. Simon and Sarah (Bluestein) F.; B.A. in Chemistry, U. Cal. at Los Angeles, 1943; M.S. U. So. Cal., 1947, Ph.D. in Biochemistry, 1949; m. Esther Handleman, Dec. 31, 1942; children—Carol Joan, James Anthony. Instr., U. So. Cal., 1948; chem. lab. supr. synthetic rubber program U.S., Rubber Co., 1943-46; mem. faculty Fla. State U., Tallahassee, 1949—, prof. chemistry, 1957—, chmn. dept., 1962-68. Postdoctoral fellowship rev. panel NSF, 1968- 70. Labor fellow inst. enzyme research U. Wis., 1955; spl. USPHS postdoctoral fellow Carlsberg Labs., Copenhagen, Denmark, 1957-58. Recipient Distinguished Prof. award Fla. State U., 1969-70. Mem. Am. Chem. Soc. (exec. com. biol. chem. div., 1968—, Fla. award 1968), Am. Soc. Biol. Chemists, Phi Beta Kappa, Sigma Xi, Phi Lambda Upsilon. Editorial bd. Biochem. Preparations, Endocrinology. Home: 1921 Country Club Dr. Tallahassee FL 32301.

FRIEDEN, EDWARD HIRSCH, biochemist, educator; b. Norfolk, Va., Jan. 4, 1918; s. Simon and Sarah (Bluestein) F.; A.B., U. Cal., Los Angeles, 1939, M.A., 1941, Ph.D., 1942; m. Betty Barnett, June 29, 1941; children—Ray Allan, Jeanne E., Robert E., Robert S., Joyce S. Lalor Found. fellow U. Tex., 1942-43, instr., research asso. Med. Sch., 1943-46; research fellow Harvard, 1946-52, instr. Med. Sch., 1948-52; faculty Tufts U. Med. Sch., 1952-64, asso. prof. biochemistry, 1962-64; research coordinator, dir. Rotch Lab., Boston Dispensary, 1957-64; prof. chemistry Kent (O.) State U., 1964—. Biochem. cons. Hynson, Westcott & Dunning, Balt., 1950-70. Guggenheim fellow U. Cal. at Los Angeles, 1953-54. Mem. Am. Chem. Soc., Am. Soc. Biol. Chemists, Endocrine Soc., Soc. for Exptl. Biology and Medicine, A.A.A.S. Contbr. articles profl. jours. Home: 359 Wilson Av Kent OH 44240

FRIEDENBERG, EDGAR Z., educator; b. N.Y.C., Mar. 18, 1921; s. Edgar M. and Arline (Zodiag) F.; B.S., Centenary Coll., 1938; M.A., Stanford, 1939; Ph.D., U. Chgo., 1946. Instr., then asst. prof. U. Chgo., 1946-53; asst., then asso. prof. Bklyn. Coll., 1953-64; prof. sociology U. Cal. at Davis, 1964-67; prof. sociology and edn. State U. N.Y. at Buffalo, 1967-70; prof. edn. Dalhousie U., Halifax, N.S., Can., 1970—. Mem. Am. Sociol. Assn., Am. Civil Liberties Union, Phi Delta Kappa. Author: The Vanishing Adolescent, 1959; Coming of Age in America, 1965; The Dignity of Youth and Other Atavisms, 1965. Home: Conrad Rd Hubbards Nova Scotia Canada Office: Dalhousie U Halifax Nova Scotia Canada

FRIEDENBERG, RICHARD MYRON, educator, physician; b. N.Y.C., May 6, 1926; s. Charles and Dorothy (Steg) F.; A.B., Columbia, 1946; M.D., L.I. Coll. Medicine, 1949; m. Gloria Geshwind, Jan. 22, 1950; children—Lisa, Peter, Amy. Intern in medicine Maimonides Hosp., Bklyn., 1949-50; resident radiology Bellevue Hosp., N.Y.C., 1950-51, Nat. Cancer fellow, 1951-52; fellow radiology Columbia-Presbyn. Hosp., 1952-53; cons. radiologist 3d Air Force, London, Eng., 1953-55; asst. prof. radiology Albert Einstein Coll. Medicine, 1955-66, asso. clin. prof. radiology, 1966-68; dir., chmn. dept. radiology Bronx Lebanon Hosp. Center, 1957-68; prof., chmn. dept. radiology N.Y. Med. Coll., 1968—; dir. radiology Flower Fifth Av. Hosp., Met. Hosp. Center, Bird S. Coler Hosp., N.Y.C. Diplomate Am. Bd. Radiology. Fellow Am. Coll. Radiology, N.Y. Acad. Medicine; mem. Assn. U. Radiologists, Radiol. Soc. N.Am., Am. Roentgen Ray Soc., N.Y. Acad. Scis., Assn. Am. Med. Colls., A.M.A., Soc. Chmn. Acad. Radiology Depts. (sec.), N.Y. Roentgen Soc. (v.p.). Author: (with Charles Ney) Radiographic Atlas of the Genitourinary System, 1966. Contbr. articles profl. jours. Home: 48 Winding Brook Rd New Rochelle NY 10804 Office: 1249 Fifth Av New York City NY 10029

FRIEDENBERG, WALTER DREW, editor; b. Meriden, Conn., Dec. 22, 1928; s. Gustav Edward and Adela (Drews) F.; B.A., Wake Forest U., 1949; A.M., Harvard, 1956; postgrad. U. Chgo., summer 1959; m. Ramona Avila, May 29, 1965; children—Christopher Drew, Eric Avila. Reporter, Rocky Mount (N.C.) Evening Telegram, 1949-50, Winston-Salem Jour., 1950, Richmond (Va.) Times-Dispatch, 1954, Buffalo Evening News, summer 1956; fellow Inst. Current World Affairs, N.Y. in Indian subcontinent, 1956-60; stringer Chgo. Daily News, Fgn. News Service, 1960; reporter Pitts. Press, 1960-61; fgn. corr. in Europe, Africa and Asia, Scripps-Howard Newspaper Alliance, Washington, 1961-66, editorial writer, 1966-69; editor Cin. Post and Times-Star, 1969- Served to 2d lt. U.S. Army, 1951-53. Mem. Nat. Press Club Washington, Phi Beta Kappa, Omicron Delta Kappa. Club: Queen City (Cin.). Home: 3475 Vista Av Cincinnati OH 45208 Office: 800 Broadway Cincinnati OH 45202

FRIEDENTHAL, JACK HARLAN, legal educator; b. Denver, Sept. 22, 1931; s. Alfred Leo and Rena (Singer) F.; A.B., Stanford, 1953; LL.B. magna cum laude, Harvard, 1958; m. Jo Anne Marder, June 15, 1958; children-Ellen, Amy, Mark. Admitted to Cal. bar, 1959; acting dep. dist. atty., Ventura County, Cal., 1961 mem. faculty Stanford Law Sch., 1958—, prof. law, 1964—; cons. in field. Bd. dirs. San Francisco Neighborhood Legal Sevices Found. Served with AUS, 1953-55. Mem. Cal. Bar Assn., Am. Assn. U. Profs. (pres. Stanford chpt. 1970-71). Co-author: Civil Procedure, 1968; Pleading-Joinder-Discovery, 1968. Home: 930 Lathrop Pl Stanford CA 94305

FRIEDERICH, WERNER PAUL, educator; b. Thun, Switzerland, June 2, 1905; s. Robert and Catherine (Reusser) F.; student Sorbonne, Paris, 1925-27; M.A., Harvard, 1929, Ph.D., 1932; Schweizerisches Staatsexamen, U. Bern, 1931; m. Molly I. Heuberger, Dec. 27, 1935 (dec. July 1958); 1 daughter, Nicolette; m. 2d, Iris Wilcock, Feb. 12, 1960. Mem. faculty U. N.C., 1935—, prof. German and comparative lit., 1948-70, prof. emeritus, 1970—, chmn. comparative lit. dept. 1956-67; vis. prof. Am. lit. U. Bern, 1938; research Sevilla and Florence, 1950; Fulbright prof. U. Melbourne, Australia, 1955, 64, Perth U., 1964; vis. prof. U. Hawaii, 1959, U. Zurich, 1960, U. Cal. at Berkeley, 1962, U. Colo., 1963, Duke, 1966-68, U. So. Cal., 1968; Kenan prof. German. comparative lit., 1959—. Mem. Am. Comparative Lit. Assn. (pres. 1959-62), Modern Lang. Assn. (founder comparative lit. sect. 1947), Internat. Comparative Lit. Assn. (sec.-gen. 1955-58, pres. 1958-61), Modern Humanities Research Assn. (exec. com. 1959-65). Author: Outline-History of German Literature. 1948: Bibliography of Comparative Literature (with Fernand Baldensperger), 1950; Dante's Fame Abroad, 1350- 1850. 1950; Outline of Comparative Literature from Dante Alighieri to Eugene O'Neill, 1954; Australia in Western Imaginative Prose Writings. 1600-1960, 1967; The Challenge of Comparative Literature and other Addresses, 1970. Founder, editor U.N.C. Studies in Comparative Literature, 1950-66. Yearbook of Comparative and General Literature, 1952-60; co-founder, since co-editor Comparative Literature, 1949; editorial board Revue de Littérature comparée (Paris). Home: 698 Gimghoul Rd Chapel Hill NC 27514

FRIEDEWALD, WILLIAM FRANK, physician; b. St. Louis, June 3, 1912; s. William H. and Albertine (Eilers) F.; B.S. St. Louis U., 1931, M.D., 1935; m. Mary L. Wright, May 29, 1937; children—William T., Jeannette A., James W., Richard W. Interne, St. Louis City Hosp., 1935-36, asst. resident and resident in medicine, 1936-38; asst. in pathology and bacteriology Rockefeller Inst. for Med. Research, 1938-42; mem., staff Internat. Health div., Rockefeller Found., 1942-45; prof. bacteriology and immunology Emory U. Sch. Medicine, 1945-51, asso. prof. medicine 1945—; pvt. practice internal medicine, allergy, 1951- -; profl. cons. internal medicine to Surgeon 3d U.S. Army, 1958-68; chief staff St. Joseph's Hosp., Atlanta, 1968—. Mem. Soc. Exptl. Biol. and Medicine, Fulton County Med. Soc. Ga., Am. Soc. Exptl. Pathology. Author articles on med. and bacteriol. subjects. Home: 250 Robin Hood Rd NE Atlanta GA 30309 Office: 1293 Peachtree NE Atlanta GA 30309

FRIEDHOFF, ARNOLD, med. scientist; b. Johnstown, Pa., Dec. 26, 1923; s. Abraham M. and Stella (Beerman) F.; B.A., U. Pa., 1944, M.D., 1947; m. Frances Wolfe, Feb. 24, 1946; children—Lawrence, Nancy, Richard. Intern, Western Pa. Hosp., 1947-48; resident psychiatry U.S. Army, 1952-53, Bellevue Hosp., N.Y.C., 1953-55; instr., prof. psychiatry N.Y. U. Sch. Mediicine, 1956—, head psychopharmacology research unit, 1956-63, co-dir. Center for Study Psychotic Disorders, 1963-69, dir., 1970—, dir. Millhauser Labs., 1970- -; mem. clin. projects research review com. Nat. Inst. Mental Health. Served to 1st lt. M.C., U.S. Army, 1951-53. Recipient Career Scientist award Nat. Inst. Mental Health, 1967. Diplomate Am. Bd. Psychiatry and Neurology. Fellow Am. Coll. Neuropsychopharmacology (v.p.), Am. Psychiat. Assn., Am. Soc. Clin. Pharmacology and Therapeutics; mem. Am. Chem. Soc., Internat. Soc. Neurochemistry, Royal Medico-Psychol. Assn., Assn. for Research in Nervous and Mental Diseases (past asst. sec.- treas.), Am. Psychopath. Assn. (treas.). Co-editor Yearbook of Psychiatry and Applied Mental Health, 1968—; mem. adv. bd. Biological Psychiatry, 1969—. Home: 32-25 168th St Flushing NY 11358 Office: 550 1st Av New York City NY 10016

FRIEDKIN, JOSEPH FRANK, govt. ofcl.; b. Bklyn., Oct. 18, 1909; s. Joel and Irene (Hedden) F.; B.S. in Mining Engring. with honors, Tex. Western Coll., 1932; student hydrology and soil mechanics, Miss. State Coll., 1944; m. Nellie May Berry, Mar. 21, 1937; children—Jonnell, Kim K. Hydraulic engr. Internat. Boundary Commn., El Paso, Tex., 1934-42; resident engr. charge San Diego office Internat. Boundary and Water Commn., 1946-52, prin. engr., El. Paso, 1952-62, commnr., 1962—. Chmn. govt. div. El Paso United Fund, 1963; chmn. phys. edn. com. El Paso YMCA, 1962—. Mem. engring. adv. com. Tex, Western Coll., 1961—. Served to maj., C.E., AUS, 1942-46. Named Civil Servant of Year, 1958, Outstanding Engr. of Year, 1959, Conquistador of El Paso, 1961. Fellow Am. Soc. C.E.; mem. Am. Soc. Mil. Engrs., Am. Geophys. Union. Author: A Laboratory Study of the Meandering of Alluvial Rivers,1945. Home: 3821 Hillcrest Dr El Paso TX 79902. Office: 300 Main Dr El Paso TX 79901

FRIEDKIN, MORRIS ENTON, educator, biochemist; b. Kansas City, Mo., Dec. 30, 1918; s. Benjamin and Anna (Lapatuchin) F.; B.S., Ia. State Coll.,1940, M.S., 1941; Ph.D., U. Chgo., 1948; m. Roberta Vanocur, Sept. 1943; children—Noah, Susanna, Deborah. Chemist. Penicillin project. World War II; postdoctoral research fellow U. Copenhagen (Denmark), 1948-49; instr. then asso. prof. pharmacology U. Washington, St. Louis, 1949-58; prof. pharmacology, chmn. dept. Tufts U. Med. Sch., 1958-67, prof. biochemistry, chmn. dept., 1967-69; prof. biology U. Cal., San Diego, 1969—. Fellow A.A.A.S.; mem. Am. Acad. Arts and Scis. Am. Soc. Biol. Chemists, Am. Soc. Pharmacology and Exptl. Therapeutics, Am. Chem. Soc. Office: care Dept Biology 4080 Basic Sci Bldg Univ California San Diego La Jolla CA 92037

FRIEDKIN, WILLIAM, film dir.; b. Chgo., Aug. 29, 1939; s. Louis and Rae (Green) F. Dir. films Good Times, 1966, The Night They Raided Minsky's, 1967, The Birthday Party, 1968, The Boys in the Band, 1969, The French Connection, 1971. Address: care Internat Bus Mgmt 1901 Av of the Stars Los Angeles CA 90067

FRIEDL, ERNESTINE, (Mrs. Harry L. Levy), anthropologist; b. Cegled, Hungary, Aug. 13, 1920; d. Nicholas and Ethel (Neudorfer) Friedl; brought to U.S., 1922, naturalized, 1927; A.B. Hunter Coll., 1941; Ph.D., Columbia, 1950; m. Harry L. Levy, Sept. 27, 1942. Lectr., Bklyn. Coll., 1942-44, 46-47; instr. Wellesley Coll., 1944- 46; instr. Queens Coll., 1947-55, asst. prof., 1956-60, asso. prof., 1960-64, prof., 1965—, chmn. dept. anthropology-sociology, 1964-68; exec. officer Ph.D. program in anthropology City U. N.Y., 1969-70. NSF grantee, 1963-65; recipient Fulbright Research (Greece) award, also Research award Wenner-Gren Found., 1955-56. Fellow Am. Anthropl. Assn., A.A.A.S.; mem. Soc. Applied Anthropology, Am., Eastern sociol. socs., Am. Ethnol. Soc. (sec-treas. 1951-52, pres. 1967), Northeastern Anthrop. Assn. (pres. 1970), Phi Beta Kappa. Author: Vasilika, a Village in Modern Greece, 1962. Home: 345 E 69th St New York City NY 10021 Office: Graduate Center City U NY 33 W 42d New York City NY 10036

FRIEDL, FRANCIS PETER, coll. pres.; b. Waterloo, Ia., Nov. 26, 1917; s. Philip and Mary (Schares) F.; B.A., Loras Coll., 1939; postgrad. Mt. St. Mary Sem., U. Notre Dame, summer 1947; M.A., Cath. U. Am., 1952, Ph.D., 1954. Ordained priest Roman Cath. Ch., 1943; curate Nativity Ch., Dubuque, 1943; instr. Loras Acad.,

1947-50; asst. prof. psychology, dir. pub. relations Loras Coll., 1954; v.p., 1956, exec. v.p., 1963—, acad. dean, 1965-71, pres., 1971—, prof., 1970—. Mem. Sigma Xi. K.C. Address: Loras Coll Dubuque IA 52001

FRIEDLAENDER, FRITZ JOSEF, educator; b. Freiburg/Breisgau, Germany, May 7, 1925; s. Ludwig and Frieda (Murzynski) F.; B.S., Carnegie Inst. Tech., 1951, M.S., 1952, Ph.D., 1955; m. Gisela Triebe, Aug. 7, 1969; 1 son, Daniel F. Came to U.S., 1947, naturalized, 1953. Asst. prof. Columbia, 1954-55; asst. prof. Purdue U., Lafayette, Ind., 1955-59, asso. prof., 1959-62, prof. elec. engring., 1962—; guest prof. Max-Planck Institut für Metallforschung, Tech. U. Stuttgart, Germany, 1964-65; cons. Gen. Electric Corp., Ft. Wayne, Ind., 1956-58, Components Corp., Chgo., 1959-61, Lawrence Radiation Lab., U. Cal. at Livermore, 1967-69. Fellow I.E.E.E. (revs. editor trans. Magnetics 1965-67, editorial bd. jour. 1968—, chmn. awards magnetics group 1966—); mem. Am. Phys. Soc., Am. Soc. Engring. Edn., Arbeitsgemeinschaft Magnetismus, Sigma Xi, Phi Kappa Phi, Tau Beta Pi, Eta Kappa Nu, Beta Sigma Rho. Contbr. articles profl. jours. Research in magnetics, magnetic devices and memories. Home: 151 Colony Rd West Lafayette IN 47906

FRIEDLAND, DAVID THEODORE, chain food store exec.; b. Newark, Aug. 25, 1906; s. Philip and Badonna (Horowitz) F.; grad. Newark State Normal Sch., 1932: m. Sylvia Leavitt. Oct. 27, 1935; children—Helene (Mrs. Helene Durst), Judith (Mrs. Robert Norinsberg), Ronald. With Food Fair Stores, Inc., Phila. 1933—, v.p. store operations, 1955—. Mem. Super Market Inst., Nat. Assn. Food Chains. Jewish religion Mason. Home: Latches Lane Apts Old Lancaster Rd Merion PA 17235 Office: 3175 John F Kennedy Blvd Philadelphia PA 19104

FRIEDLAND, LOUIS LEIF, educator; b. Paterson, N.J., Oct. 28, 1908; s. Jacob and Helen (Goldman) F.; B.A., U. Wis., 1932; M.A., U. Cin., 1933, Ph.D., 1949; m. Minna Blumberg, Oct. 15, 1939; children—Hope Ellen (Mrs. Jacques Palmer), Justin Jeffrey. Chief of placement Ohio Bur. Employment Security, Cin., 1934-41; asst. dir. Mich. War Manpower Commn., Detroit, 1943-45; regional rep. U.S. Govt., Dept. Labor, Cleve., Washington, 1941-43, 45- 47; from asst. prof. to prof. Wayne State U., Detroit, 1947—, asso. dean liberal arts, 1965—; dir. Fair Employment Practices Commn. State of Mich., Lansing, 1955-56; research dir. Mich. Reapportionment Commn., Lansing, 1963; cons. Detroit Met. Regional Study, Doxiadis & Assos., 1965-70. Legislative cons. Com. on Reorganization State Govt. Mich., Lansing, 1952-53. Recipient Legislative citation State of Mich., 1953. Spelman Fund fellow, 1935-36. Mem. Am. Polit. Sci. Assn., Am. Soc. Pub. Adminstrn., World Soc. for Ekistics, Phi Beta Kappa. Author: Governmental Organization for Metropolitan Southeast Michigan, 1965; Regional Governmental Manpower Needs-Southeast Michigan, 1965. Contbr. to Growth and Emergence of a Metropolitan Area, Vol. 1, 1968, Vol. 2, 1969. Home: 27630 Aberdeen St Southfield MI 48075 Office: Mackenzie Hall Wayne State U Detroit MI 48202

FRIEDLANDER, GERHART, chemist; b. Munich, Germany, July 28, 1916; s. Max O. and Bella (Forchheimer) F.; B.S., U. Cal. at Berkeley, 1939, Ph.D., 1942; m. Gertrude Maas, Feb. 6, 1941 (dec. 1966); children—Ruth Ann, Joan Claire. Came to U.S., 1936, naturalized, 1943. Instr. U. Ida., Moscow, 1942-43; staff Los Alamos Sci. Lab., 1943-46; research asso. Gen. Electric Co. Research Lab., Schenectady, 1946-48; vis. lectr. Washington U., St. Louis, 1948; chemist Brookhaven Nat. Lab., Upton, N.Y., 1948-52, sr. chemist, 1952—, chmn. chemistry dept., 1968—. Chmn., Gordon Research Conf. on Nuclear Chemistry, 1954; mem. adv. com. for chemistry Oak Ridge Nat. Lab., 1966-70. Fellow Am. Phys. Soc., Am. Inst. Chemists; mem. Am. Chem. Soc. (chmn. div. nuclear chemistry and tech. 1967, award for nuclear applications in chemistry 1967), A.A.A.S. Author: (with J.W. Kennedy) Introduction to Radiochemistry, 1949: Nuclear and Radiochemistry, 1955. (with J.M. Miller), 1964; also articles. Asso. editor Ann. Rev. Nuclear Sci. 1958-67. Research on chem. effects of nuclear transformations, properties of radioactive isotopes, mechanisms of nuclear reactions, especially those induced by protons of very high energies. Home: 18 Arthur Av Blue Point, NY 11715. Office: Brookhaven Nat Lab Upton NY 11973

FRIEDLANDER, JEROME MILTON, lawyer; b. Cleve., Aug. 24, 1900; s. Jacob and Mary (Lustig) F.; LL.B. magna cum laude, Baldwin Wallace Coll., 1921; LL.D., Cleve. Marshall Law Sch., 1967; m. Marian Mendelson, Sept. 14, 1942; children—Suzanne (Mrs. Herbert H. Miller), Jerome Milton, Tom A. Admitted to Ohio bar, 1921, since practiced in Cleve.; sr. mem. firm Benesch. Friedlander, Mendelson & Coplan, 1939—. Sec., dir. Capital Nat. Bank: exec. dir Fenway Hall Hotel Corp., South Park Manor Co.; dir. Moritz Steel Co., Anzac Industries, Inc. Trustee Schnumann Foundation, also Soc. Crippled Children, Burdett-Oxygen Found and Charitable Trust; trustee, sec. Montefiore Home for Aged. Mem. Ohio, Cleve. bar assns. Jewish religion Clubs: Commerce, Oakwood Country (Cleve.). Home: 1 Bratenahl Pl Bratenahl, OH 44108. Office: Citizens Bldg 850 Euclid Av Cleveland OH 44114

FRIEDLANDER, PAUL JOSEF CROST, newspaperman; b. Utica, N.Y., July 17, 1910; s. Jacob and Rebecca (Crost) F.; B.A., Hamilton Coll., Clinton, N.Y. 1931; m. Hilda Harris, Oct. 11, 1935; children—Susan Syra (Mrs. Richard F. Gutow), Rebecca Crost (Mrs. Sidney H. Shaw). With Utica (N.Y.), Daily Press, 1932-41, city editor, 1937-41; rewrite man, reporter N.Y. Post, 1941; feature editor-writer A.P. Feature Service, N.Y.C., 1941-43; Sunday mag. deskman, writer N.Y. Times, 1943-46, travel editor, 1946-70, travel columnist, 1970—. Mem. Environmental Commn., Village of East Hills, 1971—. Decorated officer Ordre National du Merite (France); recipient awards for aviation and travel reporting, including Trans World Airlines awards, 1961, 62, 63, 68, Strebig-Dobben Meml. award, 1967. Mem. N.Y. Travel Writers Assn. (founder pres. 1967-69). N.Y. Travel Research Assn. Sigma Delta Chi. Democrat. Jewish religion. Home: 113 Magnolia Lane East Hills NY 11577 Office: 229 W 43d St New York City NY 10036

FRIEDLANDER, RAYMOND NATHAN, lawyer, clothing co. exec.; b. Chgo., Apr. 16, 1926; s. Benjamin and Lillian (Rosenthal) F.; student U. Ill., 1944, 46-48; J.D., DePaul U., 1951; m. Sonia Treger, Jan. 29, 1950; children—David, Mark. Admitted to Ill. bar, 1951; practiced in Chgo., 1951-62; partner Friedlander & Weisz, 1951-62; house counsel Aldens, Inc., 1962-67, v.p., sec., gen. counsel, 1967—; dir. Gamble Alden Life Ins. Co. Bd. dirs. Ill. Retail Mchts. Assn. Served to 2d lt. AUS, 1944-46. Mem. Am., Ill., Chgo. bar assns. Mem. B'nai B'rith. Home: 9650 N Keeler St Skokie IL 60076 Office: 5000 W Rosevelt St Chicago IL 60607

FRIEDLANDER, SHELDON KAY, educator; b. Bronx, N.Y., Nov. 17, 1927; s. Irving and Rose (Katzewitz) F.; B.S., Columbia, 1949; M.S., Mass. Inst. Tech., 1951; Ph.D., U. Ill., 1954; m. Marjorie Ellen Robbins, Aug. 17, 1958; children—Eva Kay, Amelie Elise, Antonia Zoe, Josiah. Asst. prof. chem. engring. Columbia, 1954- 57; asst. prof. then asso. prof. Johns Hopkins, 1957-62, prof. chem. engring., 1962-64; prof. chem. engring. and environmental health engring. Cal. Inst. Tech., 1964—. Mem. environmental sci. and engring. study sect. B, USPHS, 1965-68; mem. com. on colloid and surface chemistry Nat. Acad. Scis.-NRC, 1968—; chmn. panel on particulate emissions, com. on air quality mgmt. NRC-Nat. Acad. Engring., 1970—. Served with AUS, 1946-47. Fulbright scholar, 1960-61; Guggenheim fellow, 1969-70. Mem. Am. Chem. Soc., Am. Inst. Chem. Engrs. (Colburn award 1959), Sigma Xi, Tau Beta Pi. Mem. editorial adv. bd. Environmental Sci. and Tech. 1967-70, Jour. Colloid and Interface Sci., 1967-70, Jour. Aerosol Sci., 1969—. Originator theory self-preservating size spectra, aerosol filtration theory. Home: 1591 Oakdale St Pasadena CA 91106

FRIEDLICH, HERBERT AARON, lawyer; b. Rochester, N.Y. Dec. 21, 1893; s. Abraham and Nettie (Bloch) F.; student Phillips Exter Acad., 1910-11; A.B., Harvard, 1915, LL.B., 1917; m. Margaret H. Becker, Mar. 10, 1923; children—John, Mary. Mem. legal com. War Industries Bd., 1918; admitted to Ill. bar, 1919. since practiced in Chgo.; mem. firm Mayer, Friedlich, Spiess, Tierney, Brown & Platt, until 1969. With U.S. Army, 1918; spl. asst. to under sec. of war, 1942; commd. lt. col., U.S. Army, 1942, detailed to Office of Under-Sec. of War, Washington; chief Contracts and Facilities div., Office of Under Sec. of War., 1944; col. Judge Adv. Gen's dept., AUS, 1945. Overseer Harvard Law Rev., 1966—. Decorated Legion of Merit, 1945; recipient Silver medal Carnegie Hero Fund, 1922. Mem. Am. Bar Found., Am., Ill., Chgo. bar assns. Ind. Republican. Reformed Jewish religion. Clubs: Mid-Day (Chicago); Lake Shore Country (Glencoe, Ill.). Home: 2424 St Johns Av Highland Park IL 60035

FRIEDLUND, JOHN ARTHUR, lawyer; b. Chgo., July 1, 1898; s. John Peter and Hannah (Nelson) F.; LL.B., U. Mich., 1922; m. Frances Garetson, Nov. 27, 1941; children—John E. Elizabeth C., (Mrs. John McCracken), Ann S. Admitted to Ill. bar. 1922, since practiced in Chgo.; now counsel Leibman, Williams, Bennett, Baird and Minow. Chmn. of exec. com., dir., gen. counsel Automatic Canteen Co. Am., 1937—; gen. counsel N.Y. Yankees Baseball Club: dir. W.F. Hall Printing Co., Wirtz, Haynie & Ehrat, Inc., Forman Realty Corp., Am. Furniture Mart Corp., Bismarck Hotel Co., Franklin Says. Assn., Casualty Mut. Ins. Co., Hubshman Factors Corp., Comml. Discount Corp. Treas., Counsel, trustee endowment fund Swedish Retirement Assn., Evanston, Ill.; trustee Folke Bernadotte Meml. Found., St. Peter,Minn. Served to 2d lt., inf., U.S. Army, World War I. Mem. Chgo. Bar Assn. Phi Alpha Delta. Clubs: Chgo. Athelic, Mid-Day, Taver, Swedish, Saddle and Cycle Chgo. Home: 1420 Lake Shore Dr Chicago IL 60610 Office: 208 S LaSalle St Chicago IL 60604

FRIEDMAN, ALEXANDER HERBERT, educator, neuropharmacologist; b. Yonkers, N.Y., July 26, 1925; s. Simon and Esther (Hertz) F.; B.A., N.Y.U., 1948; student Yale, 1951-52, 53-54, U. Paris (France), 1952-53; M.S., U. Ill., 1956, Ph.D., 1959; m. Gertrud Schaffner, July 14, 1961; children—Susan Marie, Simon Hilary. Lab. technician St. John's Riverside Hosp., Yonkers, N.Y., 1948-51, instr. med. tech., 1949-51; research asst. Yale, 1954, U. Ill., 1955-59; instr. dept. pharmacology U. Wis. Med. Sch., 1959-62; asst. prof., 1962-64, acting chmn., 1963-64; asst. prof. dept. pharmacology and exptl. therapeutics Stritch Med. Sch., Loyola U., Chgo., 1964-66, asso. prof., 1966—; vis. prof. U. Wis. Med. Sch., 1965, 66, 67. Cons. Council on Drugs, A.M.A., 1964—. Served with AUS, 1946-47; PTO. Recipient Lederle Med. Faculty award, 1966-69. Mem. N.Y. Acad. Scis., A.A.A.S., Am. Soc. Pharmacology and Exptl. Therapeutics, William T. Salter Society, Internat. Soc. for Biochemical Pharmacology, Sigma Xi (Research prize 1958). Spl. research neuropharmacology Parkinsonism, other diseases causing motor dysfunction; modulator effects drugs and circadian rhythms as basis for drug action; influence radiation on life processes and drug action. Home: 400 E 33d St Chicago IL 60616 Office: Loyola U Stritch Sch Medicine Hines IL 60141

FRIEDMAN, ALVIN, lawyer; b. Bklyn., June 19, 1931; s. Isidor and Freda (Yanuck) F.; B.A. with honors in polit. sci., Cornell U., 1952; LL.B. cum laude (editor Law Jour. 1956-57), Yale, 1957; m. Maryann Kallison, Mar. 27, 1955; children—Alan K., Margot N. Admitted to Tex. and D.C. bars, 1957; asso. firm Covington & Burling, 1957-63; spl. asst. to gen. counsel Dept. Def., 1962-64, spl. asst. to asst. sec. def. for def. for internat. security affairs, 1964, dep. asst. sec. def. for internat. security affairs Far East and Latin Am., 1964-66; partner Ginsburg & Feldman, Washington, 1966-67, Epstein and Friedman, Washington, 1967-70, Epstein, Friedman & Duncan, 1970—. Custodian, Telluride Assn., 1962-64. Served to 1st lt. USAF, 1952-54. Mem. Am., Tex., D.C. bar assns. Home: 3460 Roberts Lane, Arlington, VA 22207. Office: 1001 Connecticut Av NW Washington DC 20036

FRIEDMAN, ARNOLD D'ARCY, publisher; b. Plumerville, Ark., July 24, 1900; s. Saul and Ida (Adelman) F.; B.A., Columbia, 1922; m. M. Judith Scheinberg, Feb. 29, 1932; children—J. Roger, Elisabeth, John. Co-founder, 1925, since pub. Chain Store Age; pub. Discount Store News, Supermarket Sales Man, Nat. Restaurant News; pres. Chain Store Pub. Corp., Business Guides, Inc., Lebhar-Friedman Publs., Inc., 1942—; founder Large Size Week, Nationally Advt. Brands Week, Multi-Unit Food Service Operators Conf., also seminars; chmn., pres. L-F Telecom. N.Y., Lake County Cablevision, Inc. Fla.; chmn. Leesburg Cablevision Inc., (Fla.). Club: City Athletic (N.Y.C.). Home: 923 Fifth Av New York City NY 10021 Office: 2 Park Av New York City NY 10016

FRIEDMAN, ARNOLD PHINEAS, physician, educator; b. Portland, Ore., Aug. 25, 1909: s. Carl and Lena (Levy) F.; B.A., U. So. Cal., 1932; M.A., 1934; M.D., U. Ore., 1939; m. Sara Fritz, July 10, 1939; 1 dau., Carol. Intern, then resident neurology Los Angeles County Hosp., 1939-42; asst. physician Boston Psychopathic Hosp., 1942; resident charge head injury project, also research asso. Boston City Hosp., 1943-44; fellow neurology Harvard Med. Sch., 1943-44; pvt. practice, N.Y.C., 1946—, physician-in-charge headache unit Montefiore Hosp. and Med. Center, N.Y.C., 1949—, attending physician div. neurology, 1949—; asso. attending physician Neurol. Inst., Presbyn. Hosp., N.Y.C., 1949—; clin. prof. neurology Columbia Coll. Physicians and Surgeons, 1967—. Cons. Nat. Inst. Neurol. Disease and Blindness, NIH, 1961—; chmn. research group headache and migraine World Fedn. Neurology, 1967—; hon. surgeon N.Y.C. Police Dept., 1961—. Recipient Am. Acad. Gen. Practice award A.M.A. exhibit, 1968; Rush silver medal, 1969. Diplomate Am. Bd. Neurology and Psychiatry (bd. dirs. 1964, pres. 1971—). Fellow Am. Acad. Neurology, A.M.A. (chmn. sect. nervous and mental diseases 1962-63: Billings silver medal 1959), Am. Psychiat. Assn., N.Y. Acad. Medicine, A.C.P.; mem. Am. Assn. Neuropathologists, Am. Neurol. Assn., Internat. Coll. Allergilocicum, U.S. Pharmacopeia (adv. panel neurol. disease therapy), Psi Chi. Author: Modern Headache Therapy, 1951; co- author, editor: Headache: Diagnosis and Treatment, 1959. Author numerous articles in field Office: 71 E 77th St New York City NY 10021

FRIEDMAN, ARTHUR, educator; b. Maroa, Ill., Dec. 13, 1906; s. Samuel Arthur and Catherine (Edmunds) F.: A.B., U. Cal. at Los Angeles. 1928; Ph.D., U. Chgo. 1938; m. Natalie Pannes. 1936; m. 2d, Marchia Meeker, 1943 (div. 1953); children—Arthur Meeker, Margaret Lois. m. 3d, Ann B. Heekin, 1957. Mem. faculty U. Chgo., 1932—, successively research asst. English, instr. humanities, instr. English, asst. prof., asso. prof., 1932-52, prof. English, 1952-71, distinguished service prof. English, 1971—, chmn. dept. English, 1960-63. Recipient Guggenheim fellowship, 1957-58. Mem. Modern Lang. Assn. Clubs: Quadrangle (Chgo): Les Cheneaux Yacht (Cedarville, Mich.). Author: (with others) English Literature. 1660-1800: A Bibliography of Modern Studies (3 vols.). 1950, 52, 62. Editor: Collected Works of Oliver Goldsmith (5 vols.), 1966; She Stoops to Conquer (Goldsmith), 1968. Editor Modern Philology. 1967—. Contbr. articles learned jours. Home: 5744 Blackstone Av Chicago IL 60637

FRIEDMAN, AVNER, educator, mathematician; b. Petah-Tikvah, Israel, Nov. 19, 1932; s. Moshe Simcha and Hanna (Rosenthal) F.; M.Sc., Hebrew U., Jerusalem, Israel, 1954, Ph.D., 1956; m. Lillia Lynn Kelly, July 7, 1959; children—Alissa, Joel, Naomi, Tamara. Came to U.S., 1956, naturalized, 1963. Research asso. Kan. U., Lawrence, 1956-57; lectr. U. Ind., 1957-58; vis. asst. prof. U. Cal. at Berkeley, 1958-59; asso. prof. U. Minn., 1959-61; vis. asso. prof. Stanford, 1961-62; prof. Northwestern U., 1962—; vis. prof. Tel Aviv (Israel) U., 1966-67, 70-71. Alfred P. Sloan fellow, 1962-65; Guggenheim fellow, 1966-67. Mem. Am. Math. Soc. Author: Generalized Functions and Partial Differential Equations, 1963; Partial Differential Equations of Parabolic Type, 1964; Partial Differential Equations, 1969; Foundation of Modern Analysis, 1970; Advanced Calculus, 1971; Differential Games, 1971. Contbr. articles profl. jours. Home: 2669 Orrington Av Evanston IL 60201

FRIEDMAN, BAYARD HARRY, banker; b. Fort Worth, Tex., Oct. 7, 1926; s. Harry Bavard and Mavme (Potishman) F.; LL.B., U. Tex., 1950; m. Cornelia Cheney, June 10, 1950; children—Harry Bavard II, Walker Cheney, Alan Douglas, Cornelia. Admitted to the Tex. bar, 1950; partner firm Stone, Parker, Snakard, Friedman and Brown, Fort Worth, 1950-65; sr. v.p. Fort Worth Nat. Bank, 1965-71, exec. v.p., 1971—; also adv. dir.; adv. dir. Fort Worth Nat. Corp. Mem. Pres.'s Nat. Adv. Council on Minority Bus. Enterprise. Vice Pres. Nat. Municipal League, 1966—; mem. Joint Dallas-Fort Worth Airport Bd., 1965—; mem. Harold Brunn Soc. Med. Research Harold Brunn Inst. Mt. Zion Hosp. and Med. Center, San Francisco. Mem. Fort Worth City Council, 1962-65; mayor of Fort Worth, 1963-65. Vice chmn. bd. trustees Tex. Christian U. Research Found.; trustee Tex. Christian U.; bd. dirs. Radiation and Med. Research Found. of Southwest, Fort Worth. Served with AUS, 1945-46. Named Fort Worth Salesman of Year, Sales and Marketing Execs. Fort Worth, 1965; Fort Worth Outstanding Citizen, B'nai B'rith, 1965; recipient Golden Deeds award Fort Worth Exchange Club, 1966; Royal Purple award Tex. Christian U., 1967; Distinguished Citizen's award Nat. Municipal League, 1968. Mem. Am., Fort Worth, Tarrant County bar assns. State Bar Tex. Home: 5100 Crestline Rd Fort Worth TX 76107 Office: P O Box 2050 Fort Worth TX 76101

FRIEDMAN, BENJAMIN, physician; b. Vilna, Russia, Aug. 30, 1900; s. Hyman and Bertha (Haytin) F.; M.D., N.Y. U., 1924; m. Bassami Raskin, Dec. 22, 1925; children—Mrs. Ronnie Woog, Mrs. Ellin Grossman, Came to U.S., 1905, naturalized, 1914. Intern, Bellevue Hosp., N.Y.C., 1924-25; postgrad. tng. Knapp Meml. Eye Hosp., N.Y.C., also State Eye Hosp., Budapest and Pecs, Hungary; practice medicine, specializing in ophthalmology, N.Y.C., 1926—; dir. ophthalmology Flower and Fifth Ave. Hosp., 1956—, Met. Hosp. 1956—, Bird S. Coler Hosp., 1956—; prof. emeritus ophthalmology N.Y. Med. Coll., 1967—. Served with U.S. Army, 1918; to comdr. M.C., USNR, 1943- 46. Fellow A.C.S.; mem. Am. Acad. Ophthalmology and Otolaryngology, N.Y. Soc. Clin. Ophthalmology, N.Y. Acad. Medicine. Contbr. numerous articles on ophthalmology to med. jours. Home: 8 E 96th St New York City NY 10028. Office: 3 E 74th St New York City NY 10021

FRIEDMAN, BERNARD HARPER, writer; b. N.Y.C., July 27, 1926; s. Leonard and Madeline (Uris) F.; B.A., Cornell U., 1948; m. Abby Noselson, Mar. 6, 1948; children—Jackson, Daisy. With Cross & Brown Co., 1949-50; v.p. dir. Uris Bldgs. Corp., N.Y.C., 1950-63. Lectr. creative writing Cornell U., 1966- 67. Trustee Whitney Mus. Am. Art, Am. Fedn. Arts. Served with USNR, 1944- 46. Author: Circles, 1962 (reprinted as I Need to Love, 1963); (monograph with Barbara Guest) Robert Goodnough, 1962; Yarborough, 1964; (monograph) Lee Krasner, 1965. Editor: School of New York, 1959. Contbr. articles mags. U.S., Eng., Japan. Home: 237 E 48th St New York City NY 10017

FRIEDMAN, BERNARD SAMUEL, chemist; b. Chgo., Jan. 4, 1907; s. Nathan and Fannie (Baskin) F.; A.B., U. Ill., 1930, Ph.D. in Organic Chemistry, 1936; m. Estelle B. Freund, June 12, 1938; children—Richard F., Alice Joyce. High sch. tchr., Streator, Ill., 1930-33; instr. chemistry U. Ill., 1933-36; research chemist Universal Oil Products Co., Riverside, Ill., 1936-45; dir. chem. lab. QMC Research and Devel., 1947-48; asso. dir. organic research div. Sinclair Research Labs., Inc., 1948-59, research asso., 1959-69; professorial lectr. chem. dept. U. Chgo., 1969—. Mem. Chgo. Bd. Edn., 1962—. Mem. Mayor Chgo. Commn. Sch. Bd. Nominations, 1961-62; gen. chmn. Greater Chgo. Careers Conf., 1950. Mem. Am. Chem. Soc. (chmn. Chgo. 1959), Chgo. Tech. Socs. Council (pres.; Merit award 1963), Am. Inst. Chemists (chmn. Chgo. 1952; Honor scroll 1958), Phi Beta Kappa, Sigma Xi, Zeta Beta Tau. Author articles, chpts. in books. Patentee in field. Home: 7321 South Shore Dr Chicago IL 60649 Office: Chemistry Dept Univ of Chicago Chicago IL 60637

FRIEDMAN, BRUCE JAY, author, editor; b. N.Y.C., Apr. 26, 1930; s. Irving and Molly (Liebowitz) F.; B.Journalism, U. Mo., 1951; m. Ginger Howard, June 13, 1954; children—Josh Alan, Drew Samuel, Kipp Adam. Editorial dir. Mag. Mgmt. Co., mag. publishers, N.Y.C., 1953-66; frequent contbr. Esquire, Harpers, N.Y. Times Book Rev. Served as 1st lt. AUS, 1951-53. Mem. Kappa Tau Alpha, Sigma Delta Chi. Author: Stern, 1962; Far From The City of Class, 1963; A Mother's Kisses, 1964; Black Angels, 1966; The Dick, 1970; (play) Scuba Duba, 1968, Steambath, 1970. Home: 11 Gateway Dr Great Neck NY 11021

FRIEDMAN, DONALD ERNEST, jazz pianist, composer; b. San Francisco, May 4, 1935; s. Edward and Ann (Lowie) F.; student Los Angeles City Coll., 1953-55. Pianist, Buddy de Franco Quintet, 1956-57; free-lance pianist, N.Y.C., 1959-63; mem. Herbert Mann Sextet, 1963-65; tour Europe with Jimmie Giuffre Trio, 1965; solo piano piano concert U. Kan., 1965; pianist, leader quartet concert Hart House, U. Toronto, 1966; participant as pianist, composer, arranger Berlin (Germany) TV Workshop, 1967: recording artist for Orpheum Prodns., Prestige Records. Recipient Down Beat critics poll as pianist most deserving wider recognition, 1964. Composer: Circle Waltz, 1963; Sea's Breeze,1963; Flashback, 1964; Spring Signs, 1965; Contrasts, 1967; Spring Signs II, 1967. Address: 3777 Independence Av Bronx NY 10463

FRIEDMAN, EDMUND, civil engr.; b. Nashville, Nov. 10, 1897; s. Bernard and Lottie (Whitelaw) F.; B.Engring. summa cum laude, Vanderbilt U., 1918. Asst. city engr., Jackson, Miss., 1925; city engr., Coral Gables, Fla., 1925-29, city mgr. 1929-31; county engr., Dade County, Fla., 1932-42; chmn. bd. Cornell Assos., Inc., cons. engr., also partner Connell, Pierce, Garland & Friedman, architects-engrs., Miami. Fla., 1945—. Served to maj., C.E., AUS, 1942-45. Recipient Distinguished Service to Engring. Profession award, Fla. Engring.

Soc. award, 1963, Engr. of Yr. award, 1964. Registered profl. engr., 8 states. Fellow Am. Soc. C.E. (nat. pres. 1962-63), Fla. Engring. Soc.(Engr. of Yr., Miami sect. 1964); mem. Soc. Am. Mil. Engrs., Fla. Bd. Engr. Examiners (pres. 1936-40), Am. Road Builders Assn. (v.p. So. Dist. County Hwy Ofcls. div. 1942), Am. Inst. Cons. Engrs., Nat. Soc. Profl. Engrs., Inst. Traffic Engrs., Tau Beta Pi. Home: 3031 Segovia St Coral Gables FL 33134. Office: 315 NW 27th Av Miami FL 33135

FRIEDMAN, EDWARD DAVID, lawyer; b. Chgo., May 2, 1912; s. Joseph C. and Bessie (Levison) F.; A.B., U. Chgo., 1935, J.D. cum laude. 1937; m. Mary Louise Melia, Nov. 1, 1947; children—Michael, Daniel, Mary Eleanor, Elizabeth. Admitted to Ill. bar. 1937; law clk. to fed. master in chancery. Chgo., 1937-38; with firm Rosenberg, Toomin & Stein, Chgo., 1938-39; mem. gen. counsel staff SEC, 1939-42; chief counsel OPA, 1942-43; spl. asst. to solicitor Dept. Labor, 1943-48; chief law officer 5th regional office, also asst. gen. counsel, NLRB, 1948-60; labor counsel to Senator John F. Kennedy, 1960-61. Senator Wayne Morse, 1961-65, U.S. Senate Labor and Pub. Welfare Com., 1961-65: counsel to majority and minority floor mgrs. Senatros Clark and Case on Civil Rights Bill, 1964; spl. asst. fgn. farm labor program sec. labor, 1964, dep. solicitor of labor, 1965-69. Partner firm Bernstein, Alper. Schoene & Friedman, 1969-. U.S. delgate OECD, Paris, France, 1968. Mem. town council, Garrett Park, Md., 1954- 58. mayor, 1960-66. James Nelson Reymond fellow, 1937. Mem. Am., Fed. bar assns. Order of Coif. Asso. editor U. Chgo. Law Rev., 1936-37. Home: 10702 Wevmouth St Garrett Park, MD 20766 Office: 818 18th St NW Washington DC 20006

FRIEDMAN, EDWARD LUDWIG, author, lectr.; b. Reynoldsville, Pa., Oct. 26, 1903; s. Sol and Fannie (Stein) F.; student U. Colo., 1922-23, U. Mo., 1923-25; m. Bertha Leiser, Sept. 1, 1935; 1 dau., Linda (Mrs. Howard E. Robinson). Reporter, Pueblo (Colo.) Chieftain, 1920-22; mem. editorial staff N.E.A. Service, Cleve., 1925-28, Pueblo Star-Jour., 1928-31; editor Radio Features Service, 1931-34; dir. Nat. Reference Library, Cleve., 1934—; pres. Library Asso. Services, Inc., 1959—, Jewish religion. Author: Speechmaker's Complete Handbook, 1955; Toastmaster's Treasury, 1960; Better Communication Guide and Manual, 1963; The Speaker's Handy Reference, 1967. Lectr., condr., communication workshops; developer mnemonic heart method of memory recall, also word picture communication. Home: 13855 Superior Rd Cleveland OH 44118. Office: 1468 W 9th St Cleveland OH 44113

FRIEDMAN, EMANUEL A., med. educator; b. N.Y.C., June 9, 1926; s. Louis and Pauline (Feldman) F.; A.B., Bklyn. Coll., 1947; M.D., Columbia, 1951, Med. Sc.D., 1959; M.A., Harvard, 1969; m. E. Judith Salomon, June 6, 1948; children—Lynn Alice, Meryl Ruth, Lee Martin. Intern Bellevue Hosp., N.Y.C., 1951-52; resident Columbia-Presbyn. Hosp., N.Y.C., 1952-57; instr. Columbia Coll. Phys. and Surg., 1957-59, asst. prof., 1960-62, asso. prof., 1962-63; prof., chmn. dept. obstetrics and gynecology Chgo. Med. Sch., 1963-69; chmn. dept. obstetrics and gynecology Michael Reese Hosp., Chgo., 1963-69; prof. obstetrics and gynecology Harvard, 1969—; obstetrician-gynecologist-in-chief Beth Israel Hosp., Boston, 1969—. Served with USNR, 1944-46. Recipient Joseph Mather Smith research prize Columbia, 1958, Distinguished Alumnus award Bklyn Coll., 1964, Bicentennial commemorative silver medallion award Columbia, 1967. Diplomate Am. Bd. Obstetrics and Gynecology. Fellow A.C.S., N.Y. Acad. Medicine; mem. N.Y. Acad. Scis., Soc. Exptl. Biology and Medicine, Soc. Investigative Gynecology, Am. Assn. U. Profs., A.A.A.S., Alpha Omega Alpha. Author: Labor: Clinical Evaluation and Management, 1967; Rh-Isoimmunization and Erythroblastesis Fetalis, 1969; Lymphatic System of Female Genitalia, 1971. Home: 212 Grant Av Newton Centre MA 02159 Office: 330 Brookline Av Boston MA 02215

FRIEDMAN, EPHRAIM, physician, univ. dean; b. Rural Belvedere, Cal., Jan. 1, 1930; s. Solman and Libe (Lipson) F.; B.A. with honors in Zoology, U. Cal., Los Angeles, 1950; M.D., U. Cal., San Francisco, 1954; m. Dagmar Benioff, Aug. 22, 1955; children—Deborah, David, Jonathan, Karen. Intern San Francisco City and County Hosp., 1954-58; research fellow Hadassah Hosp., Jerusalem Hebrew U. Sch. Medicine, 1958; president Ophthalmology Mass. Eye and Ear Infirmary, Boston, 1959-61; research fellow Howe Lab. Ophthalmology, Harvard Med. Sch., 1961-65, instr. ophthalmology, 1964-65; prof., chmn. dept. ophthalmology Boston U. Sch. Medicine, 1965-71, prof., dean Sch. Medicine, 1971—. Bd. mgrs. Mass. Eye and Ear Infirmary; bd. dirs. Mass. Soc. Preventive Blindness, Inc. Served to capt. USAF, 1956-58. Diplomate Am. Bd. Ophthalmology. Fellow Am. Acad. Ophthalmology and Otolaryngology; mem. A.M.A., Mass. Med. Soc., Assn. Univ. Profs. Ophthalmology, Am. Assn. U. Profs., Am. Assn. Med. Colls., Microcirculatory Soc., Mass., New Eng. ophthal. socs., Alpha Omega Alpha. Researcher in field; developer methods of quantitating ocular blood flow. Home: 281 Otis St West Newton MA 02165

FRIEDMAN, GERALD MANFRED, educator, geologist; b. Berlin, Germany, July 23, 1921; s. Martin and Frieda (Cohn) F.; student U. Cambridge (Eng.), 1938-39; B.Sc., U. London (Eng.), 1943; M.A., Columbia, 1950, Ph.D., 1952; m. Sue Tyler, June 27, 1948; children—Judith Fay, Sharon Mira, Deborah Paula, Eva Jane, Wendy Tamar. Came to U.S., 1946, naturalized, 1950. Lectr., Chelsea Coll., London, 1944-45; analytical chemist E.R. Squibb & Sons, New Brunswick, N.J., also J. Lyons & Co., London, 1945-48; asst. geology Columbia, 1950; temporary geologist N.Y. State Geol. Survey, 1950; instr., then asst. prof. geology U. Cin., 1950-54; cons. geologist Sault Ste. Marie, Ont., Can., 1954-56; mem. research dept. Pan Am. Petroleum Corp., Tulsa, 1956-64, sr. research scientist, 1956-60, research asso., 1960-62, supr. sedimentary petrological research, 1962-64; Fulbright vis. prof. geology Hebrew U., Jerusalem, Israel, 1964—; prof. geology Rensselaer Poly. Inst., 1964—, adviser Judo Club, 1964—; research scientist Hudson Labs., Columbia, 1965, 66-69, research asso. dept. of geology, 1968- -; vis. prof. U. Heidelberg (Germany), 1967; cons. scientist Inst. Petroleum Research and Geophysics (Israel), 1967-71; vis. scientist Geol. Survey of Israel, 1970. Mem. phys. edn. com. Tulsa YMCA, 1958-63. Bd. dirs. Troy Jewish Community Council, 1966—. Fellow Mineral. Soc. Am. (mem. nominating com. for fellows 1967-69), Geol. Soc. Am., A.A.A.S.; mem. Geochem. Soc., Am. Chem. Soc., Am. Assn. Petroleum Geologists (chmn. carbonate rock com. 1965-69, mem. research com. 1965—, lectr. continuing edn. program 1967—), Soc. Econ. Palentologists and Mineralogists (nat. v.p. 1970-71, sect. pres. 1967-68), Assn. Geology Tchrs. (nat. treas. 1951-55, pres. Okla. 1962-63), Assn. Earth Sci. Editors (chmn. 1971—). Author articles in field. Editor: Jour. Sedimentary Petrology (Best Paper award 1961), 1964-70; sect. editor Chem. Abstracts, 1962-69; editorial bd. Sedimentary Geology, 1970. Co-editor, contbr. Carbonate Sedimentology in Central Europe, 1968; editor, contbr. Depositional Environments in Carbonate Rocks, 1969. Home: 32 24th St Troy NY 12180

FRIEDMAN, HANS ADOLF, architect; b. Hamburg, Germany, June 10, 1921; s. Sally and Erna (Samson) F.; B.Arch., Ill. Inst. Tech., 1950; m. Maxine Oppenheimer, May 31, 1952; children—Eric, Katy, John, Paul. Came to U.S., 1939, naturalized, 1942. Chief architect firm DeLeuw, Cather & Co., Chgo., 1951-61; sr. partner Friedman, Omarzu, Zion & Lundgoot, Chgo., 1961; pres. A.M. Kinney Assos., Inc., Chgo., 1961—; partner A.M. Kinney Assos.-William Rabon, Cin., 1961—. Lectr., So. Ill. U., 1959. Served with AUS, 1942-46. Recipient Distinguished Bldg. awards Chemplex Co., Rolling Meadows, Ill., 1969, S.C. Johnson & Sons, Wind Point, Wis., 1969. Mem. A.I.A., Nat. Trust for Historic Preservation. Club: Cliff Dwellers (Chgo). Editor Inland Architect, 1958-64. Home: 1024 Judson Av Evanston IL 60202 Office: 4747 Dempster St Skokie IL 60076

FRIEDMAN, HAROLD, religious assn. exec. Pres. United Hias Service, Jewish Congregations. Address: 200 Park Av S New York City NY 10003*

FRIEDMAN, HERBERT, physicist; b. N.Y.C., June 21, 1916; s. Samuel and Rebecca (Seligson) F.; B.A. Bklyn. Coll., 1936; Ph.D. in Physics, Johns Hopkins, 1940; m. Gertrude Miller, 1940; children—Paul, Jon. With U.S. Naval Research Lab., 1940—, supt. atmosphere and astrophysics div., 1958—, chief scientist E.O. Hulburt Center Space Research, 1963—; part-time prof. physics U. Md.; spl. research V-2 rocket, satellite launchings, solar cycle variations X-ray and ultra-violet radiations from sun; produced 1st X-ray and ultra-violet photographs, also discovered hydrogen geocorona, measured ultraviolet fluxes of early-type stars. Chmn. COSPAR working group II, Internatl. Quiet Sun Year; mem. Gen. Adv. Com. on Atomic Energy, 1968—; pres. Interunion Com. on Solar-Terrestrial Physics, 1967—; chmn. com. on solar-terrestrial research Nat. Acad. Scis.-NRC, 1968—; mem. geophysics research bd. Nat. Acad. Scis., 1969—, mem. adv. com. int. orgns. and programs, 1969—, mem. com. sci. and pub. policy, 1967—. Recipient Distinguished Service award Navy Dept., 1945, R.D. Conrad medal Navy Dept., 1964, Distinguished Achievement in Sci. award 1962; medal Soc. Applied Spectroscopy, 1957; Distinguished Civilian Service award Dept. Def., 1959; Janssen medal French Photographic Soc., 1962; Eddington medal Royal Astron. Soc., 1964; Presdl. medal for distinguished fed. service, 1964; Space Sci. award Am. Inst. Aeros. and Astronautics 1963; Rockefeller Pub. Service award, 1967; Nat. medal Sci. 1969. Fellow Am. Phys. Soc., Am. Optical Soc., Am. Geophys. Union (pres. sect. on solar-planetary relationships, 1967—), Am. Astronautical Soc., Am. Inst. Aeros and Astronautics; mem. Nat. Acad. Scis. (exec. com. space sci. bd.), Am. Acad. Arts and Scis., Internat. Acad. Astronautics, Am. Philos. Soc. Club: Cosmos. Home: 2643 N Upshur St Arlington VA 22207 Office: Code 7100 Naval Research Lab Washington DC 20390

FRIEDMAN, HOWARD W., corp. exec.; b. Bklyn., Aug. 21, 1925; s. Harry and Bertha (Wang) F.; B.B.A., Coll. City N.Y., 1945; m. Regina Lee Hazen, Mar. 22, 1952; children—Ira, Debra Ann, Patti, Jane. Sr. accountant, N.Y.C., 1945-51; pvt. accounting practice, N.Y.C., 1951-57; partner Schoenfeld-Friedman Co., N.Y.C., 1957-61; dir. Amrep Corp., N.Y.C., 1961—, pres., 1968—. Trustee Howard and Lee Friedman Found.; dir. Martha Graham Found. C.P.A., N.Y. Jewish religion (officer, dir. temple). Home: 1036 Channel Dr Hewlett Harbor NY 11557 Office: 16 W 61st St New York City NY 10023

FRIEDMAN, IRVING SIGMUND, internat. economist; b. N.Y.C., Jan. 31, 1915; s. Sigmund and Sara (Tobor) F.; A.B., City U. N.Y., 1935; M.A., Columbia, 1937, Ph.D., 1940; m. Edna M. Edelman, Sept. 27, 1938; children—Barbara Ellen (Mrs. Reid Peyton Chambers), Kenneth Sigmund, John Stephen. Asst. to trade commr. Govt. India, 1940-41; div. monetary research U.S. Treasury, 1941-46, asst. dir., 1946; act. financial attaché U.S. Embassy, Chunking, acting as financial adviser U.S. Army Hdgrs. Chungking, spl. missions to India and Egypt. 1944; chief U.S.-Can. div. Internat. Monetary Fund, 1946-48, asst. to dep. mng. dir., 1948-50, dir. Exchange restriction dept., 1950—; chmn. econ. com., mem. pres.'s council, econ. adviser to pres. Internat. Bank for Reconstruction and Development, 1964—; vis. fellow Yale, also All Soul's Coll., Oxford, 1970-71; guest lectr. Vatican univs. Spl. responsibility for staff work Nat. Adv. Council Internat. Monetary and Financial Problems. Mem. Internat. Devel. Soc. (councillor, treas., mem. exec. com.), Am. Econ. Assn. Unitarian. Author: British Relations with China, 1931-39, 1940; Post-war U.S. Economic Policy (with M.G. deVries), 1948; Foreign Exchange Controls, 1959; also financial and econ. articles. Home: 6620 Fernwood Ct Bethesda MD 20034 Office: 1818 H St NW Washington DC 20006

FRIEDMAN, IZCHAK, coll. dean; b. Berehovo, Czechoslovakia, Aug. 3, 1920; s. Eliahu and Wilma (Rothbart) F.; came to U.S., 1952, naturalized, 1956; B.S., Coll. City N.Y., 1959; M.S., Pratt Inst., 1962; postgrad., Polytech. Inst. Bklyn., 1962—; m. Estelle Yudkin, Jan. 28, 1951; children—Jonathan, Wilma. Plant mgr. Micron Plastics Corp., Bklyn., 1954-61; instr. Pratt Inst., Bklyn., 1962-64, asst. prof., 1965-67, asso. prof. chemistry, 1968—, acting dean, 1970-71, dean Sch. Engring. and Sci., 1971—. Served with Palestine Underground Army, 1940-48. Mem. Am. Assn. U. Profs. Home: 600 W 239th St Riverdale NY 10463

FRIEDMAN, JEROME ISAAC, educator, physicist; b. Chgo., Mar. 28, 1930; s. Selig B. and Lillian (Warsaw) F.; A.B., U. Chgo., 1950, M.S., 1953, Ph.D., 1956; m. Gina I. Spadaro, May 3, 1956; children—Sandra, Seth, Joel. Research asso. Fermi Inst., U. Chgo., 1956-57; with High Energy Physics Lab., Stanford, Palo Alto, Cal., 1957-60; mem. faculty physics Mass. Inst. Tech., 1960—, asso. prof., 1964-67, prof., 1967—. Mem. adv. coms. Cambridge (Mass.) Electron Accelerator, 1965-67, Princeton (N.J.)-Pa. Accelerator, 1967-70, Stanford Linear Accelerator Center, 1971—. Fellow Am. Phys. Soc.; mem. Phi Beta Kappa. Contbr. articles profl. jours. Home: 33 Wachusett Dr Lexington MA 02173 Office: 77 Massachusetts Av Cambridge MA 02139

FRIEDMAN, JOSEPH, industrialist; b. Phila., June 28, 1906; s. William and Etta (Middleman) F.; student Benton Coll. Law, St. Louis, 1925-27; m. Lily Mae Brody, Nov. 15, 1926; children—Carol Ellen (Mrs. Irvin Goldfarb), Stephanie Joan, William Hersh. Sales exec. E.A. Friedman Co., Madison, Ill., 1924- 33, v.p., dir. 1930—; sales mgr. Chgo. dist. Band Box Corp., St. Louis, 1933-36, v.p., gen. mgr., 1936-39; individual dry cleaning unit sales mgr. U.S. Hoffman Machinery Corp., 1939-44, gen. export, lend lease sales dir., 1944-46, v.p. merchandising mgr., 1946-53, lst. v.p., 1953-55, exec. v.p., 1955-57; pres. Chromalloy-Am. Corp., 1958-59, chmn. bd., chief exec. officer, 1959—; pres. Investment Exchange, Inc., St. Louis, 1958—; chmn. bd. Cardionics Corp., Belgium, Valley Lines Co. Mem. Nat. Conf. Christians and Jews, Zionist Orgn. Mem. B'nai B'rith. Clubs: Friars, Bankers (N.Y.C.); Mo. Athletic; Wings. Home: 69 Berkshire St Louis MO 63117 Office: 120 Broadway New York City NY 10005

FRIEDMAN, JOSEPH BIVENS, lawyer; b. Caldwell, O., June 30, 1911; s. Joseph Henry and Minnie (Bivens) F.; A.B., Coll. Wooster, 1932; J.D., Ohio State U., 1935; m. Mary Elizabeth Brown, Dec. 24, 1933; children— Jane, Robert Brown. Admitted to Ohio bar, 1935, U.S. Supreme Ct. bar, 1939, D.C. bar, 1946, N.Y. bar, 1948; atty. Office Gen. Counsel, U.S. Treasury, 1935-48, chief counsel Office Internat. Finance, also asst. gen. counsel treasury, 1945-48. Adviser to minister finance Republic of Ecuador, 1942-44; asst. exec. dir. War Refugee Bd., 1944; mem. U.S. delegation Allied-Swiss negotiations regarding German external assets, 1946; legal adviser U.S. delegation 1st and 2d annual meetings bds. govs., Internat. Monetary Fund and Internat. Bank Reconstrn. and Devel., 1946, 47; cons. Internat. Monetary Fund, adviser Central Bank Philippines, 1950, spl. counsel, 1954; legal adviser. U.S. Econ. Survey Mission to Philippines, 1950. Decorated Order Al Merito (Ecuador), 1943. Mem. Am., Fed., D.C. bar assns., Phi Beta Kappa, Order of Coif. Home: 3315 Quesada St NW Washington DC 20015 Office: 1028 Connecticut Av NW Washington DC 20036

FRIEDMAN, LAWRENCE MEIR, educator; b. Chgo., Apr. 2, 1930; s. I. M. and Ethel (Shapiro) F.; A.B., U. Chgo., 1948, J.D., 1951, LL.M., 1953; m. Leah Feigenbaum, Mar. 27, 1955; children—Jane, Amy, Mem. faculty U. Wis., 1961-68; prof. law Stanford, 1968—; David Stouffer Meml. lectr. Rutgers U. Law Sch., 1969. Served with U.S. Army, 1953-54. Mem. Law and Soc. Assn. (trustee). Author: Contract Law in America, 1965; Government and Slum Housing, 1968. Co-editor: Law and the Behavioral Sciences, 1969. Contbr. articles profl. jours. Home: 724 Frenchman's Rd Stanford CA 94305

FRIEDMAN, MAE HEGBY FRED, physiologist, educator; b. Montreal, Can., Apr. 28, 1909; s. Zelig Alex and Aide (Clayman) F.; B.Sc., McGill U., 1929, Ph.D., 1937; M.A., U. Western Ont., 1932; m. Carol Michaels, Sept. 8, 1938; children—Stephen Arthur, Linds Carol, Frederick Michael Douglas. Came to U.S., 1938, Research worker Atlantic Biol. Sta., New Brunswick, Can., summers 1929- 33. demonstrator zoology McGill U., 1929-30, U. Western Ont., 1930-32; research fellow physiology then research asso. physiology McGill U., 1932-38; research asso. (instr.) physiology Wayne U. Coll. Medicine, 1938-41; mem. faculty Jefferson Med. Coll. Phila., 1941—, prof. physiology, 1954—. head dept. 1957—. Mem. A.A.A.S., Am., Phila. Detroit, Canadian physiol. socs. Am. Soc. Zoologists, Soc. Exptl. Biology and Medicine, Am. Gastroenterol. Assn., Belgian Gastroenterol. Soc. (hon. fgn. mem.), Gastroenterol. Soc. Brazil. Assn. Am. Med. Colls., A.M.A., Sigma Xi. Author numerous sci. articles, monographs Asso. editor Am. Jour. Digestive Diseases. Home: 2420 Greenhill Rd Landsowne PA 19050. Office: 1025 Walnut St Philadelphia PA 19107

FRIEDMAN, MARK WILLARD, hotel and real estate developer; b. Chgo., Aug. 30, 1924; s. Percy S. and Florence (Josephson) F.; student U. Ill., 1942, DePaul U., 1945-46; m. Anne Worbioff, May 15, 1952 (div. 1967); children—Peter Lee, Matthew. Pres., Transam Properties, Chgo., 1962—; pres. Mark IV Mgmt. & Realty, Friedman Enterprises, Inc.; chmn. Metroam. Hotels Corp. including Knickerbocker Hotel, Sheraton-O'Hare Motor Inn, Oxford House, Sheraton Oakbrook (all Chgo.); dir. Sheraton Inns, Inc., Fed. Bake Co.; pres., dir. Elgin Gas & Power Co. Chmn. hotel div. Chgo. March of Dimes, 1968, real estate div. Chgo. Combined Jewish Appeal, 1967, hotel-restaurant div. Heart Fund Assn., 1966-69. Named to Hospitality Mags. Hall of Fame. Mem. Greater Chgo. Hotel and Motel Assn. (dir.), Chgo. Real Estate Bd. (dir.), Greater N. Mich. Av. Assn. (dir.), Chgo. Conv. Bur. Jewish religion. Mem. B'nai B'rith. Clubs: Covenant, Variety (Chgo.); Jockey (Miami). Contbr. articles periodicals. Home: 1000 Lake Shore Plaza Chicago IL 60611 Office: 225 N Wabash Chicago IL 60601

FRIEDMAN, MARTIN, museum dir.; b. Pitts., Sept. 23, 1925; s. Israel and Etta (Louik) F.; student U. Pa., 1943-45; B.A., U. Wash., 1947; M.A., U. Cal. at Los Angeles, 1949; postgrad. Columbia, 1956-57, U. Minn., 1958-60; m. Mildred Shenberg, September 3, 1949; children—Lise, Ceil, Zoe. Instr. art, curriculum cons. Los Angeles City Schs., 1949-56; instr. art U. Cal. Extension, Los Angeles, 1950-51; fellow Bklyn. Mus., 1956-57; grantee Belgian-Am. Ednl. Found., Brussels, 1957-58; curator Walker Art Center, Mpls., 1958-60, dir. 1961—; Ford Found. fellow, 1961-62; Am. fine arts commr. Sao Paulo Bienal, 1963—. Mem. Nat. Collection Fine Arts Commn.; mem. Commn. on Founds. and Pvt. Philanthropy, Mem. adv. bd. on environmental planning Bur. Reclamation, 1965-69; arts adv. group Bus. Com. for Arts, 1970—; dir. Guthrie Theatre Found. Served with USNR, 1943-46. Fellow Am. art U. Minn., 1959-60. Mem. Coll. Art Assn., Assn. Am. Mus. Dirs. Author books, catalogues internat. contemporary art. Contbr. articles mags. Home: 1505 Mount Curve Av Minneapolis MN Office: Vineland Pl Minneapolis MN 55403

FRIEDMAN, MARTIN, mfr. metal products; b. Cleve., Sept. 27, 1908; s. Samuel and Rebecca (Singer) F.; B.S., Case Inst. Tech., 1928, C.E., 1928; m. Lucille D. Weiner, Apr. 17, 1932; children—Ellen Shari (Mrs. Marvin Persky), Michael D. Civil engr., 1928-30; steel salesman Lake Erie Steel & Blanking Co., Cleve., 1930-42; owner, chmn. bd. Momart Steel Corp., Cleve., 1942—; v.p. Harvard Mfr., Cleve., 1953—; chmn. bd. Rusco Industries, Inc., (formerly F. C. Russell Co.), Columbiana, O., 1961-67. Trustee Mt. Sinai Hosp. Jewish religion (pres., trustee temple). Mason. Club: Beechmont Country (Cleve.). Home: 19601 Van Aken Blvd Shaker Heights OH 44120 Office: 235 E 131st St Cleveland OH 44108

FRIEDMAN, MARTIN JAY, advt. exec.; b. Bklyn., Apr. 8, 1929; s. Milton and Doris (Greenfield) F.; A.B., Syracuse U., 1950; M.B.A., N.Y.U., 1964; m. Pamela Margaret Green, Dec. 13, 1959; children—Mark Andrew, Adam Michael. Mdsg. account exec. Benton & Bowles, 1953-59; with Dancer-Fitzgerald-Sample, 1959—, sr. v.p. marketing services, 1967—. Served with AUS, 1951-53. Republican. Jewish religion. Home: 43 10 Kissena Blvd Flushing NY 11355 Office: 347 Madison Av New York City NY 10019

FRIEDMAN, MAURICE DE LAN chemist, educator; b. Chicago, 1928; B.S. in Physics, Yale, 1950; Ph.D. in Chemistry, Harvard, 1956; m. Sally Ann Jones, July 5, 1957; children--Kenneth J., Nancy A. Chemist, Acme Chem. Co., Blue Island, Ill., 1950-51; director of Research Lab., Indsl. Chemicals Corp., Cambrige, Mass., 1956-60; project coordinator environmental sect. Steinmetz Assos., Chgo., 1960-61; v.p. for research Bauer Bros. Chem. Co., Inc., Memphis, 1961-64; asst. prof. chemistry Washington U., St. Louis, 1964-66, asso. prof., 1966-70, prof., 1970--, head of chemistry dept., 1970-71. Vis. prof. So. Ill. U., summer 1967, U. of Ore., 1969. Bd. dirs. Rest Haven Home for Elderly, 1960-61; trustee of the Lutheran Hosp., 1965-71. Served from lt. to capt., AUS, 1951-53. Mem. Am. Chem. Soc., Sci. Research Soc. Am. (chpt. treas. 1967), Sigma Xi. Author: (with others) Basic Inorganic Chemistry, 1971. Home: Fairfax Apts 7291 Windermere Dr University City MO 63105 Office: Dept Chemistry Washington University St Louis MO 63130

FRIEDMAN, MILTON, economist; b. Bklyn., July 31, 1912; s. Jeno Saul and Sarah Ethel (Landau) F.; A.B., Rutgers U., 1932, LL.D., 1968; A.M., U. Chgo., 1933; Ph.D., Columbia, 1946; LL.D., St. Paul's (Rikkyo) U., 1963, Kalamazoo Coll., 1968, Lehigh U., 1969, Loyola U., 1971, Bethany Coll., 1971, Rochester U., 1971; L.H.D. (hon.), Rockford Coll., 1969; m. Rose Director, June 23, 1938; children—Janet, David. Asso. economist Nat. Resources Com., Washington, 1933-37; mem. research staff Nat. Bur. Econ. Research, N.Y., 1937-46, 1948—; vis. prof. economics U. Wis., 1940-41; prin. economist, tax research div., U.S. Treasury Dept., 1941-43, asso. dir. research, statis. research group, war research div., Columbia, 1943-45; asso. prof. economics and statistics U. Minn., 1943-46; asso. prof. economics U. Chgo., 1946-48, prof. economics, 1948-62; Paul

Snowden Russell prof. econs., 1962—; Fulbright lectr. Cambridge U., 1953-54; vis. Wesley Clair Mitchell Research prof. econs. Columbia, 1964-65; fellow Center for Advanced Study in Behavioral Sci. Pres.'s Commn. All-Volunteer Army, 1969. Recipient John Bates Clark medal Am. Econ. Assn., 1951. Fellow Inst. Math. Statis., Am. Statis. Assn., Econometric Soc.; mem. Am. Econ. Assn. (member exec. com. 1955-57, pres. 1967), Am. Enterprise Inst. (adv. bd.), Royal Economic Soc., Am. Philos. Soc., Mont Pelerin Soc. (bd. dirs. 1958- 61, pres. 1970—). Club: Quadrangle. Author: Taxing to Prevent Inflation (with Carl Shoup and Ruth P. Mack), 1943; Income from Independent Professional Practice (with Simon S. Kuznets), 1946; Sampling Inspection (with Harold A. Freeman, Frederic Mosteller, W. Allen Wallis), 1948; Essays in Positive Economics, 1953; A Theory of the Consumption Function, 1957; A Program for Monetary Stability, 1960; Price Theory, 1962; (with Rose D. Friedman) Capitalism and Freedom, 1962; (with Anna J. Schwartz) A Monetary History of the United States, 1867-1960, 1963; Inflation: Causes and Consequences, 1963; (with Anna J. Schwartz) The Great Contraction, 1965, Monetary Statistics of the United States, 1970; (with Robert Roosa) The Balance of Payments; Free vs. Fixed Exchange Rates, 1967; Dollars and Deficits, 1968; The Optimum Quantity of Money and Other Essays, 1969; (with Walter W. Heller) Monetary vs. Fiscal Policy, 1969. Editor: Studies in the Quantity Theory of Money, 1956. Bd. editors Am. Econ. Rev., 1951-53, Econometrica, 1957-68; columnist Newsweek mag., 1967—, contbg. editor, 1971—. Contbr. articles to profl. jours. Home: 5825 Dorchester Av Chicago IL 60637 Office: Dept Econs U Chgo Chicago IL 60637

FRIEDMAN, MILTON, physician; b. Newark, Sept. 13, 1903; s. Samuel and Sarah (Goldberg) F.; M.D. George Washington U., 1926; m. Marian M. Mendelson, 1928 (div., 1946); 1 dau., Susan; m. 2d, Elna Linborg, 1947; m. 3d, Marianne Schener, 1967; 1 son. Matthew. Interne, Newark Hosp., 1926-28, resident Bellevue Hosp., New York City, 1922-29, research fellow, 1930-32, now vis. radiation therapist; asso. prof. radiology N.Y.U. School Medicine, now prof.; attending radiotherapist Hosp. for Joint Diseases, New York City; attending radiologist N.Y.U. Hosp., Cons. Nat. Bur. Standards on radiation protection also USPHS on supervoltage radiation; cons. Walter Reed Army Hosp.; area cons. VA; chmn. brachytherapy radiation AEC; med. dir. Lila Motley Cancer Found; mem. Hosp. Rev. and Planning Com. State N.Y., 1965—; cons. N.Y. Dist. Selective Service, 1969, Israel-American Medical Center; member of executive com. N.Y.C. Cancer Adv. Com.; mem. com. for radiation therapy studies NRC; mem. Am. Joint Com. for Classification Tumors; chmn. Coop. Project for Chemotherapy plus Radiation; Am. delegate Internat. Congress of Radiology, 1965. Served as lt. col. AUS, chief radiation therapy sect. Walter Reed Gen. Hosp., 1942-45. Decorated Legion of Merit; recipient awards and prizes for exhibts by various socs., and for research in supervoltage radiation in cancer of bladder and testis, cancer chemotherapy and enhancement; lst Ann. award Acad. Medicine N.J., 1968. Diplomate Am. Board Radiology, Fellow Am. Coll. Radiology (com. on internat. affairs); mem. Am. Radium Soc. (treas. 1964, pres-elect 1965, president 1966), Soc. Head and Neck Surgeons, N.Y. Roentgen Soc. (treas. 1964), radiol. socs. N.Am. (spl. lectr. refresher courses), N.J., N.Y. Cancer Soc. (pres. 1959-60), N.J. Assn. Tumor Clinics, Am. Assn. Cancer Research, Am. Assn. for Study Neoplastic Diseases, A.M.A., Am. Radiotherapy Soc. (pres. 1961-62), Soc. Nuclear Medicine, Sigma Xi. Author: Tumors of the Skin (with J.S. Eller); Gynecological Roentgenology (with J. Jarcho); Roentgens, Rad, and Riddles, A Report on Supervoltage and Gamma Beam Teletherapy; also monographs, other sci. paper. Editor: American Lectures in Radiation Therapy. Address: 566 1st Av New York City NY 10016 ☆

FRIEDMAN, RALPH, financial exec.; b. N.Y.C., Jan. 11, 1904; s. Uri Mark and Mary (Behman) F.; student, Coll. City of N.Y., 1921, N.Y.U., 1922-24; m. Ruth J. Emrich, Feb. 11, 1933; children—Peter R., Robert E. Sr. gen. partner Friedman & Co., mem. N.Y. Stock Exchange, 1933-46; chmn. bd. dirs. Met. Body Co., 1940-48, Standard Milling Co., Kansas City, Mo., 1931-63; dir. Bank Leumi Le Israel-Tel Aviv and N.Y., 1963—; chmn. exec. com., dir. Israel Bank & Trust Co., N.Y.; chmn. finance com., dir. Eastern Life Ins. Co. N.Y. Trustee Hillside Hosp., N.Y.C., Montefiore Hosp., Menninger Found., Topeka. Friedman Found., N.Y.C. Mem. cave expedition to Mexico for N.Y. Zool. Soc., 1940; mem. Friedman-Anthony Alaska Expdn. for Am., Mus. Natural History, U.S. Nat. Park Service, 1948; mem. Friedman- Mozambique Expdn. for Am. Mus. of Natural History, 1968, S.W. Africa Expdn. for Am. Mus. Natural History, 1970; chmn. Am. Jewish Com., 1964-66; dir. Nat. Park Found., 1968-70. Mem. N.Y. Acad. Scis., Linnean Soc., Am. Geog. Soc., Am. Mus. of Natural History (patron), N.Y. Zool. Soc. (life), N.Y. State Forestry Assn., Am. Acad. Polit. Sci. Clubs: Explorers, Bankers, Economic Research Round Table; Union Interallie (Paris, France). Home: 14 E 75th St New York City, NY 10021. Office: 598 Madison Av New York City NY 10022

FRIEDMAN, ROBERT EUGENE, petroleum exec.; b. Eufaula, Ala., Feb. 1, 1913; s. Bernhardt and Mathilda (Mayer) F.; A.B., Tulane U., 1934, LL.B., 1935; LL.M., Harvard (research fellow), 1938. Admitted to La. bar, 1935, Cal. bar, 1961, U.S. Supreme Ct. bar, 1941; law clerk to U.S. Circuit Ct. Judge, New Orleans, 1935-36; atty. with Titche and Titche, New Orleans, 1936-37, U.S. Housing Authority, Washington, 1938, Office of Solicitor, U.S. Dept. Interior, Washington, 1938-41; asst. chief counsel Office of Petroleum Co-ordinator, Washingtn. 1941-43; dir., supply and transportation div., Petroleum Adminstrn. for War, 1945- 46; asso. dir. oil and gas div. U.S. Dept. Interior, 1946, dir. 1948; asst. to pres. Trunkline Gas Supply Co., 1949-50; asst. to exec. v.p. Gen. Petroleum Corp., Los Angeles, 1950-60; counsel Mobil Oil Co., Los Angeles, 1960—. Served as lt. comdr., USNR, 1943-46. Mem. Order of Coif, Phi Beta Kappa Assos., Zeta Beta Tau. Cluubs: Petroleum (Los Angeles); Harvard (So. Cal.). Editor Tulane Law Rev. 1933-35. Home: 975 Dolores Dr Altadena CA 91001 Office: 612 S Flower St Los Angeles CA 90017

FRIEDMAN, ROBERT JOSEPH, elec. machinery co. exec.; b. Bethpage, L.I., N.Y., Feb. 19, 1913; s. Morris and Grace (Ross) F.; B.S. in Aero. Engring., Auburn U., 1936; m. Judith Richardson, Oct. 2, 1963; children—Robert Joseph, Douglas William. Mem. F.A. Res., 1933-35; commd. 2d lt., F.A., U.S. Army, 1935, advanced through grades to lt. gen. USAF 1965; dep. chief staff material 3d Air Div., Thetford, Eng., also air insp. 95th Bomb Wing, World War II; dir. programming Far East Air Force, Korea, 1950- 52; assigned Air War Coll., 1952-53; comptroller Air Def. Command, Colorado Springs, Colo., 1953-56; dir. budget Dept. Air Force, 1956-61; comptroller Air Force Systems Command, 1961-63; dir. aerosapce programs Dept. of Air Force, Washington, 1963-64, asst. dep. chief staff programs and requirements, 1964-65, dep. chief staff programs and resources, 1965-67; chief of staff UN Command, Korea, 1967-69; vice comdr. Air Force Logistics Command, Wright-Paterson AFB, 1969-70; ret. 1970; v.p. Fairchild Semiconductor Products, Inc., 1970—. Decorated Air Medal (Air Force), Legion of Merit with three oak leaf clusters, D.S.M. with 2 oak leaf clusters, D.S.M. (Army); Most Noble Order Crown (Korea). Mem. Air Force Assn., Auburn Alumni Assn. Office: Fairchild Semiconductors Products Inc 464 Ellis St Mountain View CA 94040

FRIEDMAN, ROBERT SIDNEY, educator; b. Balt., Mar. 1, 1927; s. Harry N. and Eva (Cohen) F.; B.A., Johns Hopkins, 1948; M.A., U. Ill., 1950, Ph.D., 1953; m. Renee Cohen, Aug. 11, 1953; children-Helene, David. Research asst. Bur. Govt. Research, Md., 1953-55; instr. govt. and politics U. Md., 1955-56; from instr. to asso.. prof. govt. La. State U., 1956-61; research asso. Inst. Pub. Adminstrn., U. Mich., 1961-67, acting dir., 1967-68; asso. prof. polit. sci. U. Mich. 1961-66, prof., 1966-68; prof., head dept. polit. Pa. State U., 1968—. Mem. bd. Pa. Civil Liberties Union, 1969-72. Served with AUS, 1945-46. Mem. Am., Midwest, So. polit. sci. assns., Am. Soc. for Pub. Adminstrn., Pi Sigma Alpha. Co-author: Local Government in Maryland, 1955; Government in Metropolitan New Orleans, 1959; Political Leadership and the School Desegration Crisis in New Orleans, 1963; author: The Michigan Constitutional Convention and Adminstrative Organization: A Case Study in the Politics of Constitution-Making, 1963. Contbr. to Politics in the American States, 1965; also jours in field. Home: 1136 Westerly Pkwy State College PA 16801 Office: Sparks Bldg Pa State U University Park PA 16802

FRIEDMAN, SIDNEY, banker, lawyer; b. N.Y.C., Dec. 1, 1907; s. William and Sarah (Silver) F.; LL.B., Yale, 1931; M.A., Brown U., 1931, Ph.B., 1928; m. Blanche Banner, Apr. 6, 1930; children—Nancy (Mrs. Paul Friedman), Stuart, Susan Elaine (Mrs. Emilios Dimitris). Admitted to N.Y. bar, 1932; asso. firm Kaufman, Weitzner & Celler, N.Y.C., 1931-33; asst. to justice N.Y. Supreme Ct., 1933; counsel RFC, Washington, 1933-35; partner Cole, Friedman & Deitz, N.Y.C., 1935-64; chmn. bd. Nat. Bank N. Am., N.Y.C., 1964—; chmn. exec. com. Trust Co. N. Am., 1955-57, Comml. Bank N. Am., 1957-60; dir. CIT Financial Corp. Bd. dirs. Mitchell Field Devel. Corp., Nassau Citizens Devel. 1967—. asso. trustee North Shore Hosp., Manhasset, N.Y., 1965—; treas., mem. exec. com. United Fund L.I., 1965-68; mem. bd. ethics Nassau County, 1967—; trustee Hofstra U. Recipient Met. award Yeshiva U., 1966; Citizen of Year award Dowling Coll.; Tree of Life award Boys' Town, 1968. Fellow Phi Beta Kappa Assos.; mem. Am., N.Y.C., Nassau County bar assns., Bankers Club Am., County Lawyers Assn., Phi Beta Kappa, Order of Coif. Editor: Yale Law Jour., 1930-31. Home: 15 Wensley Dr Great Neck NY 11021 Office: Nat Bank North Am 44 Wall St New York City NY 10005

FRIEDMAN, SIDNEY N., luggage co. exec.; b. Detroit, Sept. 26, 1918; s. Julius and Anna (Rabin) F.; A.B., U. Mich., 1940, M.B.A., 1947; m. Ada Goldman, Dec. 6, 1942; children—Joel Philip, Alan Jay. Cost accountant Shwayder Bros., Inc., Detroit, 1940-47, purchasing agt., controller, 1948-60, asst. to v.p., gen. mgr. div., 1960-62; v.p. finance Samsonite Corp., Denver, 1963—, sec., 1968—. Lectr., U. Mich., 1948-61, Am. Mgmt. Assn., 1962—. Bd. dirs. Colo. Pub. Expenditure Council, Colo. Travelers Aid Soc. Served to lt. USNR, 1942-46. Mem. Financial Execs. Inst., Nat. Assn. Accountants, Beta Gamma Sigma, Phi Kappa Phi. Jewish religion (bd. dirs. temple). Club: Green Gables Country (Denver). Home: 3175 South St Paul St Denver CO 80210 Office: 11200 E 45th Av Denver CO 80217

FRIEDMAN, STANLEY B., sec. Borman's Inc. Address: 12300 Mark Twain Av Detroit MI 48227

FRIEDMAN, THEODORE, rabbi; b. Stamford, Conn., Jan. 5, 1908; s. Harry and Anna (Kapit) F.; B.A., Coll. City N.Y., 1929; rabbi, M. Hebrew Lit., Jewish Theol. Sem. of Am., 1931, D.D., (hon.),' 1964; M.A., Columbia, 1931, Ph.D., 1952; m. Ruth Braunhut, Dec. 27, 1931; children—Hillel, Naomi Meyer, Judy Spritzer. Ordained rabbi, 1931; rabbi in Jackson Heights, L.I., N.Y., 1943-54, Congregation Beth El of the Oranges and Maplewood, N.J., 1954—. mng. editor Judaism, 1952-61; vis. prof. homilectics Jewish Theological Seminary, 1954-55. Mem. Rabbinical Assembly Am. (chmn. com. Jewish law and standards 1954-55, pres. 1962- 64), Nat. Acad. Adult Jewish Studies, Am. Acad. Jewish Research. Co- editor; Jewish Life in America, 1955. Auditor: Judgement and Destiny, 1965; Letter to Jewish College Students, 1966; Judgment and Destiny, 1966. Contbr. encys. weeklies. profl. jours. Home: 225 Grove Rd South Orange NJ 07079 Office: 222 Irvington Av South Orange NJ 07079

FRIEDMAN, WILBUR HARVEY, lawyer; b. N.Y.C., May 2, 1907; s. Isador Peter and Zara (Sloat) F.; A.B., Columbia, 1927, LL.B., 1930; m. Frances Margolis, May 21, 1943; children—Joan Sara, Roy Ronald. Admitted to N.Y. bar, 1931; law sec. U.S. Supreme Ct. Justice Harlan F. Stone, 1930-31; atty. office U.S. solicitor gen., 1931-32; mem. firm Proskauer, Rose, Goetz, & Mendelsohn, N.Y.C., 1932-40, partner, 1940-70, sr. partner, 1955—; dir., sec. The Charter Corp. Lectr. N.Y. U. insts. on fed. taxation, 1943-65, N.Y. U. Sch. Gen. Edn., 1955-60. Bd. dirs., sec. Lawrence M. Gelb Found.; bd. dirs., v.p. Erwin S. Wolfson Found. Mem. N.Y. County Lawyers Assn. (v.p. dir. 1969-70, chmn. com. on group ins. 1960-70), Am., N.Y. (exec. com. sect. taxation 1968-70), N.Y.C. bar assns., Phi Beta Kappa, Tau Delta Phi. Clubs: Lotos, Columbia U. (N.Y.C.). Contbr. articles to profl. jours. Home: 1016 Fifth Av New York City NY 10028 Office: 300 Park Av New York City NY 10022

FRIEDMAN, WILLIAM J., lawyer; b. Chgo., Oct. 5, 1903; s. Oscar J. and Clara (Schlesinger) F.; Ph.B., U. Chgo., 1923; LL.B., Harvard, 1926; m. Irene Jones Beville, Nov. 16, 1940; children—Judith Irene (Mrs. R.L.J. Gillispie III), Katharine Lester (Mrs. Jay Musselman). Admitted to Ill. bar, 1926; asso. Levinson, Becker, Frank, Glenn & Barnes, 1926-30, Gottlieb & Schwartz, 1930; partner Gettlieb & Schwartz. Gottlieb, Schwartz & Friedman, 1931- 50; now partner Friedman, Koven, Shapiro, Salzman, Koenigsberg, Specks & Homer; former ltd. partner Bear, Stearns & Co.; former corp. counsel Hilton Hotels Corp.; dir. Maritime Fruit Carier Co., Ltd., DPA, Inc., Erie-Lackawanna Ry., Unicare Health Service, Mid- Continental Realty Corp., Hyatt Internat., Inc., Atlass Communications, Inc., Univ. Properties, Inc., Spector Industries, others. Bd. govs. Menninger Found. Mem. Am. Judicature Soc., Am. Ill., Chgo. bar assns., Phi Beta Kappa. Clubs: Marco Polo, Standard, Lake Shore Country, Mid-America, La Quinta Country. Home: 55 Sycamore Pl Highland Park IL 60035 Office: 208 S LaSalle St Chicago IL 60604

FRIEDMANN, GEORGES PHILIPPE, educator, writer; b. Paris, France, May 13, 1902; s. Adolphe and Elisabeth (Nathan) F.; Agrégé de l'Université, Sorbonne, Paris, France, 1926, Docteur ès Lettres, 1947; m. 2d, Marcelle Remond, Dec. 22, 1960; 1 dau. by previous marriage, Liliane (Mrs. Laurent B. Gibod). Asst., Ecole Normale Superieure 1932-35; gen. insp. tech. teaching Ecole Pratique des Hautes Etudes, Sorbonne, 1945, dir. studies, 1947—. Served as lt. French Army, 1932-40. Decorated officer Legion of Homor, Medal of Resistance. Mem. Internat. Sociol. Assn. (pres. 1956-59), Latin Am. Faculty Social Scis. (pres. 1958-64). Author: Industrial Society, 1955; The Anatomy of Work. 1957; The End of the Jewish People? 1967; Le Puissence et le Sagesse, 1970. Address: 11 Rue Francois-Ponsard Paris 16e France

FRIEDMANN, HERBERT, educator, ornithologist; b. Bklyn., Apr. 22, 1900; s. Uriah M. and Mary (Behrmann) F.; B.Sc., Coll. City N.Y., 1920; Ph.D., Cornell U., 1923; m. Karen Juul Vejlö, 1937; 1 dau., Karen Alice (Mrs. J.N. Beall). Instr. in zoology Cornell U., summer, 1922, U. Va., summer 1923; NRC research fellow in zoology Harvard, 1923-26; instr. biology Brown U., 1926-27, Amherst Coll., 1927-29; curator of birds, U.S. Nat. Museum, 1929-57, head curator zoology, 1957-61; dir. Los Angeles County Mus. Natural History, 1961-70; asst. prof. exptl. embryology Grad. Sch., Howard, 1931-33; Lida Scott Brown lectr. U. Cal., 1957; adj. prof. biology U. So. Cal., 1962—; research asso. zoology U. Cal. at Los Angeles, 1962, prof. in residence zoology, 1963-70. Guggenheim research fellow 1950-51; recipient Leidy medal Acad. Nat. Sci. Phila., 1955, Elliot medal Nat. Acad. Sci., 1959; Brewster medal Am. Ornith. Union, 1964. Fellow A.A.A.S. (sect. pres. 1939), Am. Ornithologists Union (pres. 1937-39); mem. Am. Soc. Zoologists, Am. Soc. Naturalists, Washington Acad. Sci. (hon. diploma in biology 1940, v.p. 1957), Biol. Soc. Washington (pres. 1957-58), Cooper Ornith. Soc. (div. pres.), Nat. Acad. Sci., Paleobiological Soc. Washington (pres. 1938). Participated in expdns. to Argentina, the Mexican border, S. and E. Africa. Author books including: Birds of North and Middle America, Part IX 1941, Part X, 1946, Part XI, 1950; the Parasitic Cuckoos of Africa, 1948; The Symbolic Goldfinch, 1946; Birds of Mexico, Part I, 1950. Part II 1957; The Honeyguides, 1955; The Parasitic Weaverbirds, 1960; Host Relations of Parasitic Cowbirds, 1963. Contbr. on sci. and art subjects. Home: 350 S Fuller Av Los Angeles CA 90036 ☆

FRIEDMANN, NORMAN ERNEST, computing co. exec.; b. Los Angeles, Mar. 18, 1929; s. Joseph and Estelle (Jonas) F.; B.S., U. Cal. at Los Angeles, 1950, M.S., 1952, Ph.D., 1957; m. Sarelle R. Riave, June 22, 1952; children—Marc, Lance, Keyla. Vice pres. ITT Fed. Labs., San Fernando, Cal., 1962-64; pres. ITT Data and Information Systems div. Paramus, N.J., 1964-65; chmn. bd., pres. Computing and Software, Inc., Los Angeles, 1965—. Recipient award Cal. Scholastic Fedn. Author papers in field. Home: 5327 Andasol Av Encino CA 91316 Office: 1900 Building Century City Los Angeles CA 90067

FRIEDMANN, WOLFGANG GASTON, educator; b. Berlin, Germany, Jan. 25, 1907; s. Leonhard and Anna (Kapferer) F.; LL.D., U. London, 1947; Dr. jur., U. Berlin, 1930; LL.M., U. Melbourne, 1948; Barrister-at-law, Middle Temple, London, 1944; m. May Lewis, Jan. 9, 1937; children—Anthony, John Peter, Martin. Reader in law U. London, 1938-47; prof. pub. law U. Melbourne, 1947-50; prof. law U. Toronto, 1950-55; prof. internat. law, dir. internat. legal research Columbia, 1935—. Vis. prof. U. Paris (France), 1968-69, gen. course pub. internat. law Hague Acad. Internat. Law, 1969—; Fagore law prof., Calcutta, 1970; cons. FAO, 1971. Mem. Am. Acad. Arts and Scis., Am. Soc. Internat. Law (bd. editors), Modern Law Rev. (bd. dirs.). Author: Crisis of National State 1943; Allied Military Government of Germany, 1947; Australian Administrative Law, 2d edit., 1962; (with D.G. Benjafield) Law and Social Change in Contemporary Britain, 1951; Legal Theory, 5th edit., 1967; Introduction to World Politics, 5th edit., 1965; Law in a Changing Society, 1959, 2d edit., 1971; The Changing Structure of International Law, 1964; Recht und Sozialev Wandel, 1969; De l'Efficacité des Institutions Internationales, 1970; (with Béguin) Joint International Business Ventures With Developing Countries, 1971. Editor: The Pub. Corp., 1954—, Matrimonial Property, 1955, Anti-trust Laws, 1956, (with R.C. Pugh) Legal Aspects of Foreign Investment, 1959; (with Kalmanoff) Joint International Business Ventures, 1961; (with Kalmanoff and Meagher) International Financial Aid, 1966; (with Garner) Government Enterprises, 1970. 1969. Home: Hawley Rd North Salem NY 10560

FRIEDNER, RELNARD WALTER, ins. co. exec.; b. Chgo., June 24, 1911; s. Frank and Ellen (Anderson) F.; student Northwestern U., 1938-31; m. Marian A. Nelson, Aug. 11, 1934; children—Barbara (Mrs. Robert M. Stevens), Marilyn L. (Mrs. Richard P. Amundsen). Pres., dir. Washington Nat. Ins. Co., Evanston, Ill.; vice chmn. Washington Nat. Corp. Mem. Ill., Evanston chambers commerce. Mason, Rotarian. Home: 740 Chilton Lane Wilmette IL 60091 Office: 1630 Chicago Av Evanston IL 60201

FRIEDRICH, CARL JOACHIM, prof. govt.; b. Leipzig, Saxony, Germany, June 5, 1901; s. Paul Leopold and Charlotte (Baroness von Buelow) F.; student univs. of Marburg, Frankfurt, Vienna; Ph.D., U. Heidelberg, 1925, U.J.D. (hon.), 1951; A.M. (hon.), Harvard, 1941; LL.D., Grinnell Coll., 1952, Duke, 1963; L.H.D., Columbia, 1954, Colby Coll.; Dr. rer. pol. U. Cologne, U. Padua; m. Lenore Pelham, Oct. 6, 1924; children—Paul William, Otto Alva, Elizabeth Charlotte (dec.), Matilda Cornwall, Dorothea Amanda. Came to U.S., 1922, naturalized, 1938. Lectr. in govt. Harvard, 1926-27, asst. prof., 1927-31, asso. prof., 1931-36, prof. govt., 1936—, Eaton prof. sci. of govt. 1955- -; mem. faculty Grad. Sch. Pub. Adminstrn., Harvard, 1938—, dir. Sch. of Overseas Adminstrn., 1943-46; prof. polit. sci. Juristiche Fakultät, U. Heidelberg, 1956-66; vis. prof. Sorbonne, spring 1971; govtl. affairs adviser to Mil. Gov., Germany, 1946-49. Recipient First prize $5,000, Greater Boston Contest. Decorated knight comdr.'s cross with star German Order of Merit, Officier de L'Ordre de Leopold (Belgium); A.V. Humboldt Gold medal. Mem. Am. Polit. Sci. Assn. (pres. 1962), Internat. Polit. Sci. Assn. (pres. 1967-70), Inst. Internat. de Philosophie Politique (pres.), Hist. Assn., Am. Acad. Arts and Scis., Am. Soc. Polit. Legal Philosophy, Phi Beta Kappa (hon.). Episcopalian. Clubs: The Athenaeum (London); Harvard (N.Y.C.). Author Books including: Constitutional Government and Democracy, 1940, 4th rev. edit., 1968; The Age of the Baroque, 1952, rev. edit., 1962; (with Brzezinski) Totalitarian Dictatorship and Autocracy, 1956, rev., 1965; The Philosophy of Law in Historical Perspective, 1957, rev. edit., 1965; Constitutional Reason of State, 1958; Man and His Government, 1963; Transcendant Justice, 1964; An Introduction to Political Theory, 1967; Trends in Federalism, 1968; Europe: An Emergent Nation?, 1969. Editor: Public Policy, 1940-63; Studies in Federalism, 1954; American Experiences in Military Government in World War II, 1947; NomosYearbook of American Society Political and Legal Philosophy, 1958-66. Home: 14 Hawthorn St Cambridge MA 02138 ☆

FRIEDRICH, GERHARD G., coll. dean; b. Graudenz, Germany, Feb. 4, 1916; naturalized U.S. citizen; B.A. summa cum laude, Guilford Coll., 1942; M.A. (Thomas Wistar Brown fellow), Haverford Coll., 1957; Ph.D., U. Minn.; m.; 1 son. Instr. English, Pa. State U., 1947-51; asst. prof. English, Haverford Coll., 1951-58; from asso. prof. to prof. English, head dept. Cedar Crest Coll., 1958-61; prof. English, chmn. dept., also humanities div. Cal. State Coll., Fullerton, 1961-64; asso. dean, dean acad. planning Cal. State Colls., Los Angeles, 1964—. Chmn. advanced placement program, lit. and English composition com. Coll. Entrance Exam. Bd., 1958; mem. advanced placement com., mem. English adv. com. Nat. Survey Undergrad. Programs, 1964-69; mem.-at-large Commn. Higher Edn., 1968-69; asso. chmn. State Accreditation Com., 1970—. Mem. Nat. (bd. dirs. 1962—, chmn. com. on comparative and world lit. 1970—), Cal. (pres. 1963-64) councils tchrs. English, English Council Cal. State Colls. (pres. 1962-64). Author: A Course in Advanced Placement English, 2 vols., 1964, 65; also numerous articles. Address: Cal State Colls 5670 Wilshire Blvd Los Angeles CA 90036

FRIEDRICH, JACK A., assn. exec.; b. Danville, Ill., Dec. 1, 1930; s. Stanley Maxwell and Ruth (Popejoy) F.; student U. Cal. at Berkeley, Formerly sales mgr. Patterson Glass Co., Leesburg, Fla., office mgr. So. Athletic Co., Leesburg, community devel. mgr. Fla. Jr. C. of C., Lakeland; now internal affairs mgr., exec. v.p. U.S. Jr. C. of C., Tulsa. Pres. Leesburg Jr. C. of C., 1959-60; hon. dir 1967; now exec. vice pres. Leesburg (Fla.) C. of C. Trustee, sec.-treas. U. S. Jr. C. of C. since 1967—. Trustee, sec.- treas. U.S. Jr. C. of C. War Meml. Fund, U.S. Jr. C. of C. Mental Health and Mental Retardation Fund; mem. at large Nat. council Boy Scouts Am. Served with USNR, World War II. Mem. Am. Inst. Parliamentarians, Am. Soc. Assn. Execs., Fla. C. of C. Execs., Fla. Retail Fedn., U.S. C. of C. Execs., So. Assn. C. of C. Execs., Internat. Platform Assn., inst. for Advancement Sailing. Elk. Home: PO Box 854 Leesburg FL 32748 Office: PO Box 269 Leesburg FL 32748

FRIEDRICH, LAWRENCE WILLIAM, educator; b. Parkston, S.D., Dec. 15, 1912; s. Henry and Anna (Thury) F.; A.B., St. Louis U., 1939, Ph.L., 1941, M.S. in Physics, 1942, Ph.D. in Physics, 1953; S.T.L., St. Mary's Coll., 1948; postgrad. U. Ill., summer 1953. Joined Soc. of Jesus, 1934; ordained priest Roman Catholic Ch., 1947; faculty Marquette U., 1953-68, chmn. dept. physics, 1955-65, dean Grad. Sch., 1960-68, asst. prof. physics, 1955-62, asso. prof., 1962-68; edn. specialist, grad. programs Bur. Higher Edn., U.S. Office Edn., 1967-68, asst. chief grad. acad. programs br., 1968—. Mem. Am. Phys. Soc., A.A.A.S., Sigma Xi (pres. Marquette U. chpt. 1962). Club: Milw. Physics (past pres.). Editor: The Nature of Physical Knowledge, 1960. Home: 1111 University Blvd W Silver Spring MD 20902 Office: Div Univ Programs US Office Edn Washington DC 20202

FRIEDRICH, OTTO ALVA, editor, writer; b. Boston, Feb. 3, 1929; s. Carl Joachim and Lenore (Pelham) F.; A.B. magna cum laude, Harvard, 1948; m. Priscilla Boughton, Apr. 13, 1950; children—Elizabeth Charlotte, Margaret Emily, Nicholas Max, Amelia Anne, Charles Anthony. Mem. copy desk Stars & Stripes, 1950- 52; with United Press in Paris and London, 1952-54; with telegraph desk N.Y. Daily News, 1954-57; mem. fgn. dept. Newsweek, 1957-62, asst. fgn. editor, 1959-62; fgn. editor Sat. Eve. Post, 1962-63, asst. mng. editor, 1963-65, mng. editor, 1965-69; free lance writer, 1969—. Author: (novels) The Poor in Spirit, 1952, The Loner, 1964; (history) Decline and Fall, 1970 (winner George Polk Meml. award); (juveniles with wife) The Easter Bunny That Overslept, 1957, Clean Clarence, 1959, Sir Alva and the Wicked Wizard, 1960, The Marshmallow Ghosts, 1960, The Wishing Well in the Woods, 1961, Noah Shark's Ark, 1961, The Christmas Star, 1962, The April Umbrella, 1963; The League of Unusual Animals, 1965; also numerous articles and short stories. Home: 569 Bayville Rd Locust Valley NY 11560

FRIEDRICHS, GEORGE SHELBY, investment banker; b. New Orleans, Aug. 23, 1911; s. Camille Jerome and Marguerite (Shelby) F.; B.B.A., Tulane U., 1933; m. Virginia Gore, Oct. 8, 1935; children—Mary Virginia Gore (Mrs. Peter G. Burke), George Shelby, Joseph Maybin Gore. With Woolfolk, Huggins & Shober, New Orleans, 1933-46, partner, 1942-46; with SEC, 1935-36; partner Howard, Weil, Labouisse, Friedrichs & Co., New Orleans, 1946-71; pres., chief exec. officer Howard, Weil, Labouisse, Friedrichs, Inc., New Orleans, 1971—. Chmn. Nat. Assn. Securities Dealers 1965—; gov. Assn. Stock Exchange Firms, 1963-70. Bd. dirs. Met. area com. Bur. Govtl. Research, New Orleans. Trustee Tulane U., U.S. Internat. Sailing Assn. Home: 204 Mulberry Dr Metairie LA 70005 Office: 211 Carondelet St New Orleans LA 70130

FRIEDRICHS, KURT OTTO, mathematician, educator; b. Kiel, Germany, Sept. 28, 1901; s. Karl and Elisabeth (Entel) F.; Ph.D., U. Göttingen, 1925; Sc.D., U. Aachen, 1971; m. Nellie Bruell, Aug. 11, 1937; children—Walter, Elisabeth, David, Christopher, Martin. Came to U.S., 1937, naturalized, 1944. Privadozent Technische Hochschule Aachen, U. Göttingen, 1929; prof. math. Technische Hochschule Braunschweig, 1930-37; vis. prof. N.Y.U., 1937-39, asso. prof., 1939-43, prof. applied math., 1943—, Distinguished prof. applied math., 1964, asso. dir. Courant Inst., 1966, dir., 1966-67. Fellow A.A.A.S.; mem. Nat. Acad. Scis. Author: (with Richard Courant) Supersonic Flow and Shock Waves, 1948; Mathematical Aspects of the Quantum Theory of Fields; From Pythagoras to Einstein; Perbutations of Spectra in Hilbert Space; also articles in profl. jours. Home: 24 Lester Pl New Rochelle NY 10804

FRIEDRICHS, ROBERT WINSLOW, educator; b. Bath, Me., Feb. 16, 1923; s. Hans William and Gladys (Donnelly) F.; student Antioch Coll., 1941-43; B.A., Oberlin Coll., 1946; M.A., U. Wis., 1952, Ph.D., 1957; postdoctoral studies, Oxford U., 1964, Princeton, 1970, Cambridge U., 1970, London Sch. Econs., 1971; m. Pauline E. Carlson, June 16, 1951; children—Robin, Paul, Carl. Instr. Ming Hsien Middle Sch. and Coll., China, 1946-48; instr. sociology Columbia, 1953-54; asst. prof., chmn. sociology dept. Elmira Coll., 1954-57; vis. prof. grad. program in sociology Bklyn. Coll., 1967; prof., chmn. dept. sociology Drew U., 1957-70; prof. sociology Williams Coll., 1971—; cons. Victoria Found., Newark Bd. Edn. Vice chmn. Madison-Florham Park A.R.C., 1959-60; chmn. human relations com. Morris County Community Chest and Council, 1958-59. Co-chmn. Citizens for Kennedy and Johnson, Morris County, 1960. Named man of year Morris County Urban League, 1959. Fellow Am. Sociol. Assn., Soc. Religion in Higher Edn.; mem. Am. Assn. Univ. Profs., A.A.A.S., Eastern Sociol. Soc., Soc. Sci. Study Religion, Soc. Psychol. Study Social Issues, Soc. Study Social Problems, Danforth Assos. Author: A Sociology of Sociology, 1970. Contbr. articles profl. jours. Address; Williams College Williamstown MA 01267

FRIEL, BRIAN, author; b. Omagh, County Tyrone. North Ireland, Jan. 9, 1929; s. Patrick and Christina (MacLoone) F.; student St. Joseph's Tng. Coll., Belfast, Ireland, 1959-60; m. Anne Morrison, Dec. 27, 1955; children—Paddy, Mary, Judy, Sally, David. Came to U.S., 1963. Tchr. various schs., 1950-60; writer, 1960—; with Tyrone Guthrie Theatre, Mpls., 1963. Macauley fellow Irish Arts Council, 1963; Author: (short stories) A Saucer of Larks, 1964; The Gold in the Sea, 1966; (play) Philadelphia, Here I Come!, 1966; (play) The Loves of Cass McGuire, 1966; (play) Lovers, 1967; (play) Crystal and Fox, 1968; (play) The Mundy Scheme, 1969. Contbr. short stories to New Yorker. Address: Muff Lifford County Donegal Ireland

FRIELE, BERENT, corp. exec.; b. Norway, Mar. 29, 1895 s. Berent and Dagny (Beyer) F.; ed. Bergen Katedralskole; m. Jenny Muller Camps, Dec. 29, 1920; children—Berent Edward, Anita Dagny. Came to U.S., 1924, naturalized, 1938. Vice pres., gen. mgr. Am. Coffee Corp., N.Y.C., 1924-29; pres., dir., 1929-46; dir. Great A & P Tea Co., N.Y.C., 1931-46; spl. rep. Brazil Office of Coordinator Inter-Am. Affairs, advisor to Am. ambassador, 1941-44; sr. v.p., dir. Internat. Basic Economy Corp., 1946-62, cons., 1962—; sr. v.p., dir. Am. Internat. Assn., N.Y.C., 1946-69; dir. Scandinavian Airlines System, Inc. Mem. Pan Am. Soc. U.S. (dir.), Brazilian-Am. C. of C. (dir.), Nat. Fgn. Trade Council (dir.), Council Fgn. Relations. Home: 6 Brooklands Bronxville NY 10708 Office: 30 Rockefeller Plaza New York City NY 10020

FRIEMAN, EDWARD ALLAN, physicist, educator; b. N.Y.C., Jan. 19, 1926; s. Joseph and Belle (Davidson) F.; B.S., Columbia, 1945; M.S., Poly. Inst. Bklyn., 1948, Ph.D., 1951; m. Ruth Rodman, June 19, 1949 (dec. May 1966); children—Jonathan Paul and Michael Rodman (twins), Joshua Adam; m. 2d, Joy Fields, Sept. 17, 1967. Research asso. Poly Inst. Bklyn., 1947-49, instr., 1949-51; research asso. Project Matterhorn (B), Princeton 1952-53, head theoretical div. of project, 1953-64, dir. plasma physics program, 1959—, lectr. physics, 1959-60, prof. astronomy, 1961—, asso. dir. Plasma Physics Lab., 1964—; cons. Inst. Def. Analyses, Los Alamos Sci. Lab.; cons., bd. dirs. Aero. Research Assos. Princeton; sci. adv. com. Gen. Precision Instruments Co. Deep-sea diving officer Bikini tests, 1945-46; mem. research adv. com. nuclear processes NASA, 1959-60; mem. Watson com. Weapons Systems Evaluation Group, 1961—. Dir Trans-East Airlines. Trustee, Jersey City State Coll., 1968—. John Simon Guggenheim Meml. Found. fellow. Fellow Am. Phys. Soc.; mem. Am. Astron. Soc., Am. Assn. U. Profs., A.A.A.S., Sigma Xi. Author articles plasma physics, hydromagnetics, statis. mechanics. Bd. editors Physics of Fluids, 1964-66. Am. Phys. Soc., 1965, Phys. Rev., 1966-67. Home: 70 Heather Lane Princeton NJ 08540

FRIEND, ALBERT WILEY, cons. engr., physicist; b. Morgantown, W.Va., Jan. 24, 1910; s. Lemuel Ellsworth and Louisa Gertrude (Michael) F.; B.S. in Elec. Engring., W.Va. U., 1932, M.S., 1936; S.D., Harvard 1948; m. Evelyn Augusta Hall, Aug. 6, 1931; children—Albert Wiley, Evelyn Joyce (Mrs. William C. Everett), John Robert. Engr., Ohio Power Co., 1933-34; from instr. to asst. prof. physics W.Va. U., 1934- 44; instr., research fellow, instr. Harvard (on leave W.Va. U.), 1939- 42, 46-47; research asso., staff Radiation Lab., Radar Sch., tech. dir. Heat Research Lab., Mass. Inst. Tech., 1941-44; research staff RCA, 1944- 51; dir. engring. Daystrom, Inc., 1951; dir. engring. Magnetic Metals Co., 1951-53; cons. engr., physicist, 1953—; pres. Amicon Corp., Acoustex, Inc., 1968—, A.W. Friend Engrs. Lectr., U. Pa., 1965. Cons. controls, electromagnetic isolation, tropoopheric radio echo phenomena; research and devel. electronic color TV system and equipment, also radar, guided missiles, telemetering, electronic computer components, magnetic materials and components, weather radar, lunar exploration communications, satellite communications systems, noise abatement, archtl. acoustics, vibration etc. Recipient award for outstanding research RCA Labs., 1950; award for contbns. to advancement electronic art Nat. Electronics Conf., 1955. Fellow I.E.E.E. (chmn. tech. com. recording and reproducing), A.A.A.S., Am. Phys. Soc.; mem. Acoustical Soc. Am., Am. Geophys. Union, Air Force Assn., Am. Inst. Physics, Am. Meteorol. Soc., Am. Ordnance Assn., Harvard Engrs. Soc., Am. Ordnance Assn., Harvard Engrs. Soc. N.Y., Electrochem. Soc., Franklin Inst., Nat., Pa. socs. profl. engrs., Tau Beta Pi, Sigma Xi, Sigma Pi Sigma. Clubs: Engineers (Phila.); Cosmos (Washington). Author numerous tech. papers and reports. Contbg. author: Magnetic Recording in Science and Industry. Holder U.S., fgn. patents. Home: 6816 Newbold Dr Bethesda MD 20015 Office: PO Box 34420 W Bethesda Br (Md) Washington DC 20034

FRIEND, IRWIN, educator; b. Schenectady, July 10, 1915; s. Solomon and Dina (Ryzowy) F.; B.S., Coll. City N.Y., 1935; Ph.D., Am. U., 1953; m. Corinne Vernon, Nov. 5, 1941; children—Peter Sayre, Leslie Andrea. Asst. dir. trading and exchange div. SEC, 1937-47; chief bus. structure div. Dept. Commerce, 1947-53; Richard K. Mellon prof. finance U. Pa., Phila., 1953—. Vis. Frederick R. Kappel Prof. govt. and bus. U. Minn., 1970; cons. U.S. govt. agys., Congl. coms., India, Greece, Argentina, and bus. orgns.; mem. exec. com. Conf. on Income and Wealth, 1960-63; dir. Rodney L. White Center for Financial Research. Recipient research fellowship, research grants Ford Found. and NSF. Fellow Am. Statis. Assn.; mem. Am. Econ. Assn., Am. Finance Assn., Am. Statis. Assn. (chmn. bus. and econ. statis. sect. 1961-62, bd. editors jour. 1968—). Author: Study of the Savings and Loan Industry, 1970; Mutual Funds and Other Institutional Investors: A New Perspective, 1970; Investment Banking and The New Issues Market, 1967; Private Capital Markets, 1964; A Study of Mutual Funds, 1962; Comsumption and Saving, 1960; The Over-The-Counter Securities Market, 1958; Consumer Expenditures, Inc. and Savings, 1957; Individual Savings: Volume and Composition, 1954. Editorial bd. Am. Econ. Rev., 1968—. Home: 706 Argyle Rd Wynnewood PA 19096 Office: Wharton Sch Finance and Commerce Philadelphia PA 19104

FRIEND, JAMES A., mfg. co. exec.; b. Milw., 1894; ed. Cornell U., 1916. Chmn. bd., sec. with Nordberg Mfg. Co., Milw. Home: Chenequa Hartland WI 53029 Office: 3073 S Chase Av Milwaukee WI 53207

FRIEND, THEODORE WOOD, III, educator; b. Wilkinsburg, Pa., Aug. 27, 1931; s. Theodore Wood and Jessica (Holton) F.; grad. St. Paul's Sch., 1949; B.A., Williams Coll., 1953; Ph.D., Yale, 1958; m. Elizabeth Groesbeck Pierson, Feb. 20, 1960; children—Theodore Porter, Pierson, Elizabeth Robinson. Asst. instr. Yale, 1955-57; mem. faculty State U. N.Y. at Bufalo, 1959—, prof. history, 1966—, faculty advisor to pres., 1968-69, exec. asst. to pres., 1969-70. Fulbright grantee in Philippines, 1957-59; Rockefeller Found. fellow internat. relations, 1961-62; Nat. Def. Fgn. Lang. postdoctoral fellow, 1966-67; Guggenheim Found. fellow, Indonesia, Philippines, Japan, 1967-68; recipient Bancroft prize in Am. History, 1966. Mem. Am. Hist. Assn., Assn. Asian Studies, Soc. Historians of Am. Fgn. Relations, N.A.A.C.P., Phi Beta Kappa. Presbyterian. Clubs: Pundit, Buffalo Tennis and Squash (Buffalo). Author: Between Two Empires; The Ordeal of the Philippines, 1929-46, 1965; also articles. Editor: The Philippine Polity, A Japanese View, 1968. Home: 103 Highland Av Buffalo NY 14222

FRIEND, WALTER WILLIAM, Jr., investment banker; b. Allenhurst, N.J., June 25, 1920; s. Walter William and Helen E. (Butcher) F.; grad. Polytech. Prep. Country Day Sch., 1938; B.A., Dartmouth, 1942; postgrad. in Law, Yale, 1942, 46; m. Doris Eleanor Schwanhausser, Dec. 20, 1947; children-Walter William III, Eleanor Provost. With Pressprich Corp., N.Y.C., 1948—, partner, 1962- 68, exec. v.p., 1968-69, pres., 1969—; trustee Greater N.Y. Savings Bank. Trustee Low-Haywood Sch., Stamford, Conn. Served to 1st lt. AUS, 1942-46. Mem. Municipal Finance Officers Assn. U.S., Can., Municipal Forum N.Y., Municipal Analysts N.Y. (pres. 1950-53). Home: Valley Rd Wilson Point South Norwalk CT 06854 Office: 80 Pine St New York NY 10005

FRIENDLY, ALFRED, corr.; b. Salt Lake City, Dec. 30, 1911; s. Edward Rosenbaum and Harriet Friendly; graduate Amherst (Mass.) Coll., 1933, L.H.D. (hon.), 1958; m. Jean Ulman, July 23, 1937; children—Alfred, Jonathan, Lucinda, Nicholas, Victoria. Reporter Washington Daily News, 1936-39; reporter Washington Post, 1939-52, assistant mng. editor, 1952-55, mng. editor, 1955-66, corr., 1965—; Washington corr. London Financial Times 1949-52. Asst. to trustee for reorgn. Asso. Gas & Electric Corp., 1940. Dir. overseas information ECA, 1948-49. Served as maj. USAAF, 1942-45. Decorated Legion of Merit. Recipient Pulitzer prize, foreign correspondence, 1967, internat. reporting, 1968. Mem. Phi Beta Kappa. Clubs: Garrick, Royal Air Force, Fgn. Affairs (London); Overseas Writers, Gridiron (Washington). Author: The Guys on the Ground, 1944; co-author Crime and Publicity, 1967. Home: 17 Westmoreland Terrace London SW1 England Office: 80 Haymarket St London SW 1 England

FRIENDLY, FRED W., educator, journalist; b. N.Y.C.; student Cheshire Acad., Nichols Jr. Coll., Providence Bus. Coll.; L.H.D., Grinnell U., Brown U.; m. Ruth W. Mark; children (by previous marriage)—Andrew, Lisa, David; stepchildren—Jon Mark, Michael Mark, Richard Mark. Began career in radio 1938; wrote, produced and narrated radio series Footprints in the Sands of Time, later at NBC, Who Said That (quiz based on quotations of famous people); collaborated with Edward R. Murrow in presenting aural history of 1932-45 (recorded by Columbia Records under title I Can Hear It Now); collaborated with Walter Cronkite, Vol. IV, I Can Hear It Now-The Sixties; formerly with CBS radio series Hear It Now, also CBS TV Series See It Now; past exec. producer CBS TV show CBS Reports, also producer Face The Nation debates; pres. CBS News, N.Y.C., 1964-66; Edward R. Murrow prof. broadcast journalism Columbia U.; adviser on TV, Ford Found. Recipient George Peabody award for TV prodn. of The Population Explosion, 1960. Served with AUS, 1941- 45; CBI. Decorated Legion of Merit and 4 battle stars. Mem. Am. Assn. U. Profs., Assn. for Edn. in Journalism. Author: Due to Circumstances Beyond Our Control, 1967. Home: Riverdale NY Office: Columbia U Grad Sch Journalism New York City NY 10027 also Ford Found 320 E 43d St New York City NY 10017

FRIENDLY, HENRY JACOB, judge; b. Elmira, N.Y., July 3, 1903; s. Myer H. Leah (Hallo) F.; A.B., Harvard, 1923, LL.B., 1927; D.H.L., Hebrew Union Coll.; LL.D., Syracuse U., Bklyn. Law Sch., Jewish Theol. Sem., Western Res. U., Brandeis U., U. Cin., U. Chgo., Harvard; m. Sophie M. Stern, Sept. 4, 1930; children—David, Joan, Ellen. Admitted to N.Y. bar, 1928, D.C. bar, 1947; law clerk to Mr. Justice Brandeis, Washington, 1927-28; asso. law firm Root, Clark, Buckner & Ballantine, N.Y.C., 1928-36, partner, 1937-45; own firm of Cleary, Gottlieb, Friendly & Hamilton, 1946-59; dir. v.p., gen. counsel Pan Am. World Airways System, 1946-59; U.S. judge Ct. Appeals, 2d Circuit, 1959—, chief judge, 1970—. Overseer Harvard U., 1964-69, chmn. overseers long range study com., 1969. Mem. Am., N.Y. State, N.Y.C. bar assns., Am. Law Inst. (council, mem. exec. com.), Harvard Alumni Assn. (pres. 1960-61). Clubs: Harvard, Harmonie, Century. Author: The Federal Administrative Agencies; The Need for Better Definition of Standards, 1962; Benchmarks, 1967. Contbr. articles to law periodicals. Home: 1088 Park Av New York City NY 10028 Office: US Courthouse New York City NY 20014

FRIENDLY, OSCAR NATHAN, mining engr.; b. Corvallis, Ore., Aug. 24, 1884; s. Max and Adolphina (Simon) F.; B.S., U. Cal., 1907; m. Carrie Sappington, Aug. 29, 1923. Mine engr. and geologist, Daly Judge Mining Co., 1909-13; engr. in charge Snake Creek Mining & Tunnel Co., 1909-18; gen. supt. Daly Judge Mining Co., 1913-17, Judge Mining and Smelting Co., 1917-22, Daly West Mining Co., 1918-22; gen. mgr. Park City Mining and Smelting Co., 1922- 25; chief engr. and asst. gen. mgr. and treas. Park Utah Consol. Mines Co., 1925-34; cons. mining, v.p., gen. mgr., 1934-46, v.p., cons. engr., 1946-52; pres. Park City Utah Mines Co. Gov. Utah chpt. Am. Mining Congress, 1936-37, chmn. bd. govs. Western div., 1937. Dir. Childrens Service Soc. of Utah. Mason (32). Club: Alta. Home: 2540 E Haven Lane Salt Lake City UT 84117

FRIERSON, JOHN BURTON, Jr., textile processing exec.; b. Shelbyville, Tenn., Aug. 26, 1903; s. John Burton and Lissie Mai (Ransom) R.; grad. Sewanee (Tenn.) Mil. Acad. 1919; student U. South, Sewanee, 1919-21; m. Rowena Kruesi, June 9, 1934; children—John Burton, III, Paul Kruesi, Thomas Cartter, Daniel Kennedy, James William. With First Nat. Bank Chattanooga, 1922-28; treas. Dixie Mercerizing Co. (now Dixie Yarns, Inc.), 1928-33, v.p., 1933-47, pres., 1947-63, chmn., 1963—, also dir.; pres. Durene Assn. Am., N.Y.C., 1934, 43; dir., exec. com. Am. Nat. Bank and Trust Co., Chattanooga, Vol. State Life Ins. Co., Chattanooga, Monumental Corp., Balt. Vice pres. Nat. Cotton Council, 1969, 70. Chmn. sch. bd., Lookout Mountain, Tenn., 1944-52, mayor, 1952-56. Trustee, exec. com. U. Chattanooga; trustee Baylor Sch. for Boys; bd. dirs. Louisville Presbyn. Theol. Sem. Mem. Am. Textile Mfrs. Inst. (pres. 1966), Tenn. Mfrs. Assn. (bd. dirs.), Tenn. Taxpayer Assn. (bd. dirs.), Phi Delta Theta. Presbyn. (elder). Clubs: Mountain City, Fairyland (Lookout Mountain). Home: 515 E Brow Rd Lookout Mountain, TN 37350 Office: Dixie Yarns Inc Chattanooga TN 37401

FRIES, ROBERT FRANCIS, univ. prof.; b. LaCrosse, Wis., Dec. 16, 1911; s. William James and Laura Merlinda (Olsen) F.; B.E., LaCrosse State Tchrs. Coll., 1933; Ph.M., U. Wis., 1936, Ph.D., 1939; m. Frances Katherine Clements, Jan. 2, 1936; children—Mary Ann, Margaret Frances. Social sci. teacher Cashton (Wis.) High Sch., 1933-35; asst. in history U. Wis., 1936-38; asst. prof. history De Paul U., Chgo., 1939-43, asso. prof., 1943-45, prof. history, 1945—, chmn. dept. 1945-56, 67—, dean univ. coll., 1955—. Fellow in history U. Wis., 1938-39. Mem. Am. Assn. U. Profs. (chapter sec. 1947-48), Am. Hist. Assn., Orgn. Am. Historians, Wis. Hist. Soc. Contbr. to hist. jours. Author: Empire in Pine, the Story of Lumbering in Wisconsin, 1951; Crown and Parliament in Tudor-Stuart England, 1959; European Civilization: Basic Historical Documents, 1965. Editor: Readings in European Civilization 1956. Home: 2817 Wilmette Av Wilmette IL 60091 Office: 25 E Jackson Blvd Chicago IL 60604

FRIES, VOLLMER WALTER, mfg. exec.; b. Pleasant Valley, N.Y., July 17, 1902; s. William Christian and Lona A. (Vollmer) F.; E.E., Rensselaer Poly. Inst., 1924; D.Eng., Fenn Coll., 1965; m. Ruth Dudley Wick, July 17, 1928; children—William Vollmer, Carole Wick. With The White Motor Co., Cleve., 1924-56, v.p., dir., then exec. v.p., dir. 1944-55; chmn. bd. White Consol. Industries, Inc. (formerly White Sewing Machine Corp.), Cleve., 1955-69, chmn. exec. com., 1969-70, dir., 1954—. With conservation div. WPB, 1940-41; mem. W. Averell Harriman mission, Am. embassy, London, 1942-43. Trustee Fenn Ednl. Found., Rensselaer Poly. Inst., Troy, N.Y. Clubs: Union, Country; Mid Day, Fifty (Cleve.); Engineers (N.Y.C.); Coral Reef Yacht (Coconut Grove, Fla.); Ocean Reef (Key Largo, Fla.); Country (Coral Gables). Home: 3441 Alhambra Circle Coral Gables FL 33134 Office: 11770 Berea Rd Cleveland OH 44111

FRIESEN, ERNEST CLARE, Jr., govt. ofcl.; b. Hutchingson, Kan. Oct. 11, 1928; s. Ernest C. and Clara (Mitchell) F.; A.B., U. Kan., 1950; LL.B., Columbia, 1955; m. Corleta Mary Gibson, July 12, 1952; children—Peter Gibson, Carol Marjorie, Daniel Ernest Anne Clare. Admitted to N.Y. bar, 1955-56; atty. tax div. Dept. Justice, 1956-58; asst. prof. law U. Cin., 1958-61; dir. Joint Com. Effective Justice, 1961-64; dean Nat. Coll. State Trial Judges, 1964- 65; asst. dep. atty. gen. U.S., 1965-66, asst. atty gen for adminstrn., 1966-68; formerly dir. adminsrv. office U.S. Cts. Served to 1st lt. USMCR, 1950-52, Ford Founds. Fellow, 1959, Mem. Nat. Inst. Pub. Adminstrn. Brookings Conf. Pub. Service, Am. Law Inst., Am. Bar. Assn. (member house of delegates), Nat. Acad. of Public Adminstrn., Inst. Jud. Adminstrn., Am. Judicature Soc., Delta Sigma Rho (pres. Kan. U. chpt. 1949), Omicron Delta Kappa (pres. Kan. U. chpt. 1949),Delta Upsilon. Christian Scientist. Home: 6423 Cavalier Corridor Falls Church VA 22044 Office: Supreme Ct Bldg Washington DC 20543

FRIESEN, GORDON ARTHUR, health care cons.; b. Rosthern, Sask., Can. Jan. 21, 1909; s. Abraham James and Eliza (Friesen) F.; LL.D., George Washington U.; m. Jane Helen Fuller, July 25, 1947; children—Mary Jane, Sarah Elizabeth. Came to U.S., 1951, naturalized, 1962. Bus. mgr. Saskatoon City Hosp., 1929- 37; adminstr. Belleville (Ont., Can.) Gen. Hosp., 1937-41; prin. cons. sr. hosp. adminstr. United Mine Workers Hosps. in Appalachia, 1952-54; propr. Gordon A. Friesen Internat., Inc., Washington, 1954—; lectr. St. Louis U. Grad. Sch., Columbia Grad. Sch. Hosp. Adminstrn.,

Cornell U. Sch. Hotel Adminstrn. and Grad. Sch. Bus. and Pub. Adminstrn., George Washington U. Grad. Sch., U.S. Army Med. Field Service Sch., U.S. Naval Sch. Hosp. Adminstrn., Nat. Naval Center; preceptor program George Washington U., 1963—; cons. surgeon gen. U.S. Navy. Mem. adv. council Xavier U., Cin. Served with RCAF, 1941- 46. Recipient numerous Modern Hosp. of Month awards. Fellow Am. Coll. Hosp. Adminstrs., Royal Soc. Health; hon. mem. Costa Rican Hosp. Assn. (hon. pres.); mem. Internat. Hosp. Fedn., Am. Assn. Hosp. Planning, Am. Assn. Hosp. Cons. (exec. com., chmn. ad hoc research center com.), Am. Hosp. Assn., Am. Pub. Health Assn., Cath. Hosp. Assn., Am. Assn. Contamination Control, Luther Rice Soc. Club: Internat. Contbr. articles to profl. jours. Home: 10904 Burbank Dr Potomac, MD 20854. Office: 1250 Connecticut Av NW Washington DC 20036

FRIESS, HORACE LELAND, educator; b. N.Y.C., Mar. 4, 1900; s. Louis G. and Louise S. (Jagle) F.; A.B., Columbia, 1918, Ph.D., 1926; Cutting Travelling fellow, Heidelberg U., 1924-25; m. Ruth Adler, June 25, 1923; 1 dau., Anne. Instr. philosophy Columbia, 1921-26, asst. prof., 1926; asso. prof. 1936-46, prof. philosophy, 1946—, now Joseph L. Buttenwieser prof. emeritus human relations; exec. officer, dept. of religion, Barnard Coll., 1940-47, chmn. dept. of religion, Columbia, 1962-65. Guggenheim fellow, 1942-43. Bd. leaders N.Y. Soc. for Ethical Culture, 1950—. Mem. Am. Philos. Assn., Am. Ethical Union, Phi Beta Kappa. Ethical Culture religion. Author books including: Our part in this world (edited selections from Felix Adler), 1946. Editor The Review of Religion, 1942-58. Contbr. articles. Home: 460 Riverside Dr New York City NY 10027

FRILEN, HERBERT, mfr., corp. exec.; b. Springfield, Mass., Jan. 18, 1904; s. Carl A. and Matilda (Sandall) F.; M. Helen Neal, July 17, 1922; children—Robert H. (M.D.), Barbara Helen (Mrs. Richard S. Veres). With Am. News Co., 1924—, mgr. N.Y.C. br., 1954-55, became v.p. 1955, also dir.; now exec. v.p.; with Am. Match Co. div. Am News Co., 1956—, became v.p., dir., 1958, now exec. v.p.; v.p. American News Co., Ltd., 1956—, also dir.; dir. Union News Co. Home: 765 N Broadway Hastings-on-Hudson NY 10706 Office: 131 Varick St New York City NY 10013

FRIME, NORMAN E., coll. dean; b. Toronto; grad. Ill. Inst. Tech.; rabbi Hebrew Theol. Coll., Chgo.; D. Hebrew Lit. Yeshiva U., 1953. Formerly met. dir. B'nai B'rth Hillel Founds. and Hillel dir. Bklyn. Coll; now dean Stern Coll. for Women, Yeshiva U. Address: 1253 Lexington Av New York City NY 10016*

FRIML, RUDOLF, composer, pianist; b. Praha, Czechoslovakia, Dec. 7, 1879; s. Frantisek and Maria (Kremenak) F.; came to U.S. 1904, naturalized, 1925; studied piano with Josef Jiranek, composition with Antonin Dvorak at Conservatory of Music, Praha, 1896-99; m. Kay Ling, Apr. 16, 1952. Composed many compositions for piano, violin and cello; (operettas) Firefly, 1912; High Jinks, 1913; The Peasant Girl, 1914; You're in Love, 1916; Katinka, 1916; Sweet Kitty Darling, 1917; Glriana, 1918; Sometime, 1918; Tumble In 1919; Little Whopper, 1919; June Love, 1920; Blue Kitten, 1922; Cinders, 1923; Dew Drop Inn, 1923; Rose Marie, 1923; Ziegfeld Follies, 1921, 23, 24, and 25; Vagabond King, 1925; The Wild Rose, 1926; Palm Beach Girl, 1926; No Foolin', 1926; White Eagle 1927; Three Musketeers, 1928; Bird of Paradise, 1930; The Lottery Bride, 1930; Annina, 1934; (2-piano concerto) Round The World Symphony. Mem. Am. Soc. Composer, Authors and Pubs. Home: 8782 Appian Way Hollywood CA 90046

FRINGS, KETTL, author; b. Columbus, O.; d. Guy H. and Pauline (Sparks) Hartley; student Principia Coll.; m. Kurt Frings, Mar. 18, 1938; children—Kathie, Peter. Author: (novels) Hold Back the Dawn, 1942, God's Front Porch, 1945; (plays) Mr. Sycamore, 1943, Look Homeward, Angel, 1957; The Long Dream, 1960; (screen plays) Come Back Little Sheba, 1952, About Mr. Leslie 1954, Fox Fire, The Shrike, 1955. Recipient Pulitzer prize for best play, Look Homeward, Angel, N.Y. Dramra Critics Circle award, 1957. Address: 1 W 72d St New York City NY 10023

FRISARD, EMILE LOUIS, advt. exec.; b. Quiney, Ill., Feb. 19, 1918; s. Emile Louis and Lena Fern (Condit) F.; A.B., Miami U., Oxford, O., 1940; m. Louise Marguerite Draeger, Nov. 22, 1947 (dec. Nov. 25, 1965); children—Louise, Steven and John. Assistant purchasing agent Hotel Gibson, Cin., 1940-41; plant superintendent, salesman, asst. sales mgr. Davis Container Co., Dayton, O., 1942-43; research analyst Young & Rubicam Inc., N.Y.C., 1943-45; copywriter Ted Bates & Co., Inc., N.Y.C., 1945-49; copy group head Biow Co., Inc. (name later changed to Biow-Beirn-Toigo, Inc.), N.Y.C., 1949-56; copy group head Grey Advt. Agy., N.Y.C., 1956-57; v.p., creative dir. Compton Advt., Inc., N.Y.C., 1957-59; with Lennen & Newell, Inc., N.Y.C., 1959-64, sr. v.p., asso. creative dir., 1962-64 v.p., dir. creative services Parkson Advt. Agy., Inc., 1964-65; asso. creative dir. Cunningham & Walsh, 1965; creative group head J. Walter Thompson, 1965-67; copy dir. W. M. Zemp & Assos., Inc., St. Petersburg, Fla., 1968—. Home: 1119 Eden Isle Dr N E St Petersburg FL 33704. Office: 1213 16th St N St Petersburg FL 33705

FRISBEE, DON CALVIN, utilities exec.; b. San Francisco, Dec. 13, 1923; s. Ira Nobles and Helen (Sheets) F.; B.A., Pomona Coll., 1947; M.B.A., Harvard, 1949; m. Emilie Ford, Feb. 5, 1947; children—Ann, Robert, Peter, Dean. Sr. investment analyst, asst. cashier investment analysis dept. 1st Nat. Bank Ore., Portland, 1949-52; with Pacific Power & Light Co., Portland, 1953—, treas., 1958-60, then v.p., exec. v.p., pres., 1966—; dir. 1st Nat. Bank of Ore., Lucky Stores, Inc., San Leandro, Cal. Trustee, Whitman Coll. Served to 1st lt., AUS, 1943-46. Clubs: Arlington, University, Multnomah Athletic. Home: 01546 SW Military Rd Portland OR 97219 Office: Public Service Bldg Portland OR 97204

FRISCH, ARTHUR WALN, educator; b. Chisholm, Minn., Mar. 3, 1910; s. Louis and Sadie (Wain) F.; B.S., U. Wis., 1930, M.A., 1933, Ph.D., 1935, M.D., 1937; m. Miriam Ferber, Dec. 14, 1940; children—Lawrence E., Paul R. Instr. bacteriology and clin. pathology Wayne U. Coll. Medicine, 1939-40, asst. prof., 1940- 46; asst. prof. bacteriology U. Ore. Med. Sch., 1946-48, asso. prof., 1948-54, prof., 1954—, head dept., 1956—; cons. VA Hosp., Portland, Ore.; cons. virology USPHS; active evaluation studies Salk Vaccine program. Served with M.C., AUS, 1942-46. Mem. Soc. Am. Bacteriologists, Am. Soc. Clin. Research, Western Assn. Physicians. Am. Soc. Immunologists. Author articles microbiology. Home: 6841 SW 3d St Portland OR 97219

FRISCH, MAX, writer, architect; b. 1911; ed. Zurich (Switzerland) U. and Tech. High Sch.; diploma in architecture, 1941. Formerly fgn. corr. newspapers throughout Europe and Near East; archtl. designs include Zurich Recreation Park; engaged as writer, 1955—. Rockefeller grantee for drama, 1951; recipient prize Germany Acad., 1958, also Jerusalem prize. Author: (plays) Nun singen sie wieder, 1945, Die chinesische Mauer, 1946, Graf Oederland, 1950, Don Juan, oder die Liebe zur Geometrie, 1952, Biedermann und die Brandstifer, 1958. Adorra (trans. 11 langs.), 1961; Biografy: a gamel Comedy, 1967; (novels) Tagebuch 1945-1949, 1950, Stiller (trans. 10 langs.), 1954, Homo Faber (trans. 7 lang.), 1957. Mein Name sei Gantenbein, 1964. Address: care Suhrkamp-Verlag Frankfurt/Main Federal Republic of Germany*

FRISCH, RAGNAR ANTON KITTIL, economist; b. Oslo, Mar. 2, 1895; s. Anton and Ragna Fredrikke (Kittilsen) F.; M.A. in Econs., U. Oslo, 1919, Ph.D., 1926; Dr. honoris causa, Handelshögskolan i Stockholm, 1959, Kbenhavns Universitet, 1959, Stockholms Universitet, 1966; D.Sc. (honoris causa), U. Cambridge Queen's Coll., 1967; m. Marie Smedal, Apr. 28, 1920; 1 dau., Ragna. Formerly Jeweller-journeyman; mem. faculty U. Oslo, 1925—, prof. econs. and statistics, 1931—, dir. research U. Inst. Econs. Found., 1932—; vis. prof. Yale, 1930, Sorbonne, Paris, 1933. Chmn. UN Econ. and Employment Commn., 1947; mem. various govt. money and banking coms. Co-recipient Nobel prize in econ. sci., 1969. Fellow Econometric Soc., Inst. Math. Statistics, Royal Statis. Soc. (hon.); corr. fellow British Acad.; hon. mem. Am. Econ. Assn., Am. Acad. Arts and Scis.; corr. mem. Royal Econ. Soc.; mem. Internat. Statis. Inst., Am. Philos. Soc. (fgn.), Det Norske Videnskapakademi i Oslo, Kungl. Humanistiska Vetnkappamfundet i Lund, Kungl, Svenska Vetenskapakademien. Author: New Methods of Measuring Marginal Utility, 1932; Statitical Confluence Analysis by Means of Complete Regression Systems, 1934; Noen Trekk av Konjunkturlderen, 1947. Editor Econometrica, 1933—. Contbr. papers memoranda and compendia. Researcher regarding nat. income conputations and as result constructed a system describing the econ. circulation, the esocirc system. Interested in genetics, particularly breeding of bees. Address: Vinderen Oslo Norway

FRISCHE, CARL ALFRED, electronics co. exec.; b. Freeport, Kan., Aug. 13, 1906; s. Ernst and Julie (Kordarning) F.; student Park Coll., Parkville, Mo., 1923-25; A.B., Miami U., Oxford, O., 1928, D.Sc., 1955; M.S., U. Ia., 1931, Ph.D., 1932; D.Sc., L.I. U., 1964; m. Harriet Catherine Ross, June 2, 1930; children—Richard, Gretchen (Mrs. Charles H. Gillespie), Eric. Physicist, research fellow Columbia, 1932-33; with Sperry Gyroscope Co., 1933-68, chief research dir., 1943-45, v.p. engring., 1945-54, v.p. operations, 1954-57; exec. v.p. Sperry Gyroscope div. Sperry Rand Corp., 1957-58, pres., 1958-68, cons. corp., 1968-71; adv. bd. dir. Human Resources, Abilities, Inc. Mem. N.Y. State Joint Legislative Com. Sch. Financing, 1960-63. Bd. dirs., mem. exec. com. United Fund L.I., 1965-70, pres., 1967-68. Sci. adv. bd. Chief Staff USAF, 1956-59. Fellow I.E.E.E., Am. Inst. Aeros. and Astronautics; mem. A.A.A.S., Am. Inst. Physics, Aircraft Industry Assn. (gov. 1967-68), Phi Beta Kappa, Sigma Xi, Beta Theta Pi, Gamma Alpha. Episcopalian. Clubs: Deepdale Golf, University, Lake Placid, Paradise Valley Country, Desert Forest Golf. Patentee airplane soundproofing, electronic controls, gyroscopic instruments. Contbr. articles profl. publs. Home: 114 Wheatley Rd Brookville Glen Head NY 11545 also 6642 Praying Monk Rd Scottsdale AZ 85253

FRIST, THOMAS FEARN, Jr., hosp. co. exec.; b. Nashville, Aug. 12, 1938; s. Thomas Fearn and Dorothy A. (Cate) F.; B.A., Vanderbilt U., 1961; M.D., Washington U., 1965; m. Patricia Gayle Champion, Dec. 22, 1961; children—Patricia Champion, Thomas Fearn III, William Robert. Surg. intern Vanderbilt U. Hosp., 1965-66; founder Hosp. Corp. Am., Nashville, 1968, exec. v.p., mem. exec. com., dir., 1968—. Served as flight surgeon USAF, 1966-68. Mem. A.M.A., Tenn. Med. Assn., Nashville Acad. Medicine, Fedn. Am. Hosps. (dir.), Nashville Cancer Soc. (dir.), Phi Delta Theta. Republican. Presbyn. Home: 508 Belle Meade Blvd Nashville TN 37205 Office: 242 25th Av N Nashville TN 37203

FRITCHEY, CLAYTON, columnist; b. Bellonfontaine, O.; s. Franklin W. and Elizabeth (Shurr) F.; m. Naomi Williamson (dec. 1942); 1 dau., Phyllis. Editor, New Orleans Item, 1944-50; asst. to Sec. of Defense and dir. Office of Pub. Information, Dept. of Def., 1950-52; asst. to Pres. U.S., 1952; dep. chmn. Democratic Com., 1953-57, also editor Democratic Digest; chmn. No. Va. Sun, Arlington, 1957-61; spl. asst. to U.S. Ambassador to UN, 1961-65; syndicated columnist. Address: 2100 Massachusetts Av NW Washington DC 20008

FRITCHMAN, HARRY VERNON, coal co. exec.; b. McDonald, Pa., Nov. 27, 1907; s. Frank Markle and Margaret (Crilley) F.; A.B., Pa. State U., 1929; postgrad. U. Pa. Law Sch., 1929-30; LL.B., U. Pitts., 1932; m. Ethel Rendleman, Oct. 14, 1933; 1 son, Vernon N. Admitted to Pa. bar, 1933; practice in Indiana, Pa., 1933-37; with Rochester & Pitts. Coal Co., Indiana, 1937—, gen. counsel, 1948—, exec. v.p., 1959-70, pres., dir., 1970—; sec., dir. United Eastern Coal Sales Corp.; pres., dir. Helvetia Coal Co.; dir. Rochester & Pitts. Coal Co. (Can.), Ltd. Mem. Nat. Coal Assn. (dir.), Beta Theta Pi, Phi Delta Phi, Pi Lambda Sigma. Presbyn. Elk, Mason. Clubs: Laurel Valley (Ligionier, Pa.); Hare Law (U. Pa.); Oakmont Country (Pitts.); Indian Country. Home: 549 Chestnut St Indiana PA 15701 Office: 655 Church St Indiana PA 15701

FRITCHMAN, STEPHEN HOLE, clergyman; b. Cleve., May 12, 1902; s. Addison Hutton and Esther (Hole) F.; student U. Pa., 1921-22; B.A., Ohio Wesleyan U., 1924; B.D., Union Theol. Sem., 1927; M.A., N.Y. U., 1929; postgrad. Harvard Grad. Sch., 1930-32; L.H.D., Starr King Sch. Ministry, Berkeley, Cal., 1967; m. Frances Putnam, Sept. 8, 1928. Instr. English Bible, Ohio Wesleyan U., 1924-25, N.Y. U., 1925-28; asso. prof. English, Boston U., 1929-32; religious news editor, N.Y. Herald Tribune, 1925-27; asso. editor, Ch. Sch. Jour. (Meth.), 1928-29; pastor lst Parish Unitarian, Petersham, Mass., 1930- 32, Unitarian Ch., Bangor, Me., 1932-38; exec. dir. Unitarian Youth Activities, Am. Unitarian Assn., Boston; editor The Christian Register (Unitarian), 1943-48; minister First Unitarian Ch. of Los Angeles, 1948-69, Coachella Valley Unitarian Fellowship, Palm Springs, 1969—. Pres. Com. Protection Fgn. Born. Mem. Pacific S.W. Unitarian Ministers Assn. (pres. 1958-59, 70-71), Unitarian Universalist Ministers Assn. (mem. executing com. 1963-65), Phi Mu Delta. Democrat. Author books including: Men of Liberty, 1944, reissued 1969; Unitarianism Today, 1950; Politics and The Pulpit, 1963, Editor: Together We Advance, 1946. Contbr. chpts. in Toward A Socialist America, 1958, Public Ownership in The U.S.A., 1961. Home: 604 Cavanagh Rd Glendale CA 91207 ☆

FRITH, JAMES ROBERT, educator; b. Galeton, Pa., Aug. 24, 1917; s. Ward Kilbourne and Mabel (Krebs) F.; B.A., M.A., Bucknell U., 1939; Ph.D., Cornell U., 1950; m. Catherine Roddey Jones, Oct. 10, 1942; children—Catherine, Eleanor, Martha, Jane, Nancy, Rebecca, James, Robert. Lang. tchr. high sch., Danville, Pa., 1939-41; instr. French, Cornell U., 1948-50, acting asst. prof., 1950-51; adviser Air Force Lang. Program, 1951-53, supr., chief lang. tng. br. Air Force Inst. Tech., 1953-57; adviser lang. tng. Dept. Def., 1953-57; mem. Inter-Agy. Coordinating Com. on Govt. Lang. Tng., 1955-57; mem. evaluation team Middle States Accrediting Commn., 1956; fgn. service officer, dir., Dept. State French Lang. Sch., Nice, France, 1957-59, lang. tng. supr. for North Africa, 1958-59, asst. dean Sch. Langs., Fgn. Service Inst., dir. overseas lang. tng. for Fgn. Service, 1959-62, asso. dean School Langs., 1962-66, dean, 1966—. Served to lt. comdr. USNR, 1941-47. Decorated DFC; recipient Meritorious Civilian Service award, 1956. Mem. Linguistic Soc. Am., Phi Beta Kappa, Sigma Alpha Epsilon. Methodist. Author articles on lang. learning. Home: 4919 N 14th St Arlington VA 22205 Office: Foreign Service Inst State Dept Washington DC 20521

FRITH, LESLIE ORVAL, railroad ofcl.; b. Thayer, Mo., Mar. 1, 1905; s. Ulysses Simpson and Hattie Ellen (Whitten) F.; ed. pub. schs., Mo.; m. Emma Dahlem, Aug. 14, 1926 (dec. Feb. 1949); m. 2d, Erna Haggart, Apr. 24, 1957. With K.C.S. Ry., Kansas City, Mo., 1923—, v.p., exec. asst., 1952-61, exec. v.p. 1961—; exec. v.p., dir. La. & Ark. Ry. Co., 1961—; exec. v.p. Kansas City So. Industries, 1962—, dir. Chmn. railroad div. Kansas City (Mo.) United Fund, 1960; met. dir. Nat. Alliance Businessmen, Kansas City, 1968-69, chmn., 1969; mem. Mid-Continent Regional Manpower Com., 1969- 70. Mem. Christian Ch. Club: Kansas City (Mo.). Home: 809 W 87th St Kansas City MO 64114 Office: 114 W 11th St Kansas City MO 64105

FRITSCH, CHARLES THEODORE, educator, clergyman; b. Allentown, Pa., Apr. 5, 1912; s. Robert R. and Carrie (Fehr) F.; A.B., Muhlenberg Coll., 1932; Th.B., Princeton Theol. Sem., 1935; Ph.D., Princeton, 1940; m. Eleanor Melville Anderson, May 18, 1946; children—Susan A., Charles Theodore. With Princeton Theol. Sem., 1937—, successively instr., asst. prof., asso. prof., 1937-57, prof. O.T., 1957—; ordained to ministry Presbyn. Ch., 1941; vis. lectr. New Brunswick Theol. Sem., 1938-39, Temple Sch. Theology, 1945-46, Am. Sch. Oriental Research, Jerusalem, 1954, Westminster Choir Coll., 1956-59; adj. prof. religion Temple U., 1962-63; dir. Negev Archael. Seminar, Israel, digging at Tel Najila, 1963, Tel Arad, 1964. Chief field archeologist Link Underwater Expdn. to Holy Land, 1960; spl. lectr. Hankuk Sem., Seoul, Korea and in Japan, 1965; adj. prof. Greek, Dropsie U., 1969—; ednl. dir. joint archaeol. expdn. to Khirbet Shema, under Am. Schs. Oriental Research, 1970. Trustee Westminster Found. Princeton U., N.J. Synod. Mem. Am. Oriental Soc., Am. Schs. of Oriental Research, Nat. Assn. Profs. of Hebrew, World Union Jewish Studies, Archaeol. Soc., Soc. Bibl. Lit. and Exegesis. Author: Anti- Anthromorphisms in Greek Pentateuch, 1943; The Qumran Community, Its History and Scrolls, 1956; Lexical Handbook of the Hebrew Bible (Genesis), 1957; also articles. Contbr. commentary on Proverbs Interpreters Bible, 1955; commentary on Genesis, Layman's Bible Commentary, 1959; 3 major articles Interpreters Bible Dictionary; commentary on I and II Chronicles, Ezra, Nehemiah, I Esdras, article on the Prophetic Literature, Interpreter's One-Vol. Commentary on Bible, 1971. Home: 80 Mercer St Princeton NJ 08540

FRITSCHE, ERNEST GARFIELD, developer, builder; b. Westerville, O., Aug. 5, 1916; s. Garfield Helmuth and Clara (Dickey) F.; student Otterbein Coll., 1934-36, LL.D. 1965; student Franklin U., eves. 1938-41; m. Neva Clyde Lilly, Dec. 1, 1945; children—Nevalyn Anne, Roberta Kay, William Carl. Real estate salesman George W. Fritsche & Co., Columbus, O., 1946-49; organizer, 1949, since pres. Ernest G. Fritsche & Co., comml. and residential builders, Columbus, O. Trustee Nat. Housing Center, Washington, 1962-65, Bldg. Research Adv. Bd., Washington, 1969—; mem. U.S. housing study delegation to USSR, 1956. Pres. Citizens Research, Inc., Columbus, 1959-62; chmn. Columbus United Appeals, 1964, Columbus YMCA, 1962-63; trustee Devel. Com. Greater Columbus, 1950—; 1st v.p. Big Bros. Am., 1963-66; pres. United Appeal of Columbus, 1969, 70. Mem. bd. Otterbein Coll., 1958—; bd. dirs. Nat. Bldg. Research Adv. Bd., Washington, 1969—. Served to lt. col., C.E., AUS, 1941-46. Mem. Nat. Assn. Home Builders (life mem. bd. dirs. 1952—), Nat. Assn. Real Estate Bds., Urban Land Inst., Columbus C. of C., Columbus Symphony Orch. Home: 5800 Clover Lane Westerville OH 43081 Office: 144 E State St Columbus OH 43215

FRITSCHEL, ARTHUR LAWRENCE, coll. dean; b. Mpls., Sept. 27, 1919; s. Theo L. and Elsie (Huth) F.; A.B., Colo. State Coll., 1940; M.A., Northwestern U., 1944; Ed.D., U. Colo., 1952; m. Betty June Reader, June 6, 1943; children-Larry Edwin, Allen Edward, Ann Louise, Barbara Lynn. Prof., chmn. dept. edn. Western Ill. U., Macomb, 1946-67; dean instrn. N.E. Mo. State Coll., Kirksville, 1967-70; dean Coll. Profl. Studies, Wis. State U.-Stevens Point, 1970—. Chmn. Macomb March of Dimes, 1954-57. Bd. dirs. Kirksville YMCA; bd. dirs., exec. com. Augustana Coll., Rock Island, Ill. Mem. Am. Assn. Colls. Tchr. Edn., Nat. Council Accrediation Tchr. Edn. (chmn. central evaluation bd.), Soc. Acad. Achievement (charter, bd. dirs. 1958-70), N.E.A., Phi Delta Kappa, Kappa Delta Pi, Phi Alpha Theta. Democrat. Lutheran. Rotarian. Home: 3233 Dan's Dr Stevens Point WI 54481

FRITTS, HARRY WASHINGTON, Jr., educator, physician; b. Rockwood, Tenn., Oct. 4, 1921; s. Harry Washington and Hyder (Smith) F.; student Vanderbilt U., 1941; B.S., Mass. Inst. Tech., 1943; M.D., Boston U., 1951; m. Helen Dyer Goodwin, Aug. 25, 1949; children—John Goodwin, Benjamin Carroll, Patricia Louise. Mem. research staff Mass. Inst. Tech., 1946-47; intern, then resident Univ. Hosp., Boston, 1951-53; vis. fellow Columbia Coll. Physicians and Surgeons, 1953-56, mem. faculty, 1956—, prof. medicine, 1967—; vis. physician Bellevue Hosp., 1957-68, Presbyn. Hosp., N.Y.C., 1961—; vis. physician, cons. Manhattan VA Hosp., 1957-68. Bd. dirs., adv. council research N.Y. Heart Assn.; mem. physiology study sect., mem. cardiovascular tng. com. USPHS. Served to lt. (j.g.) USNR, 1943-46. Guggenheim fellow, 1959-60. Diplomate Am. Bd. Internal Medicine. Fellow A.C.P.; mem. Am. Physiol. Soc., Am. Soc. Clin. Investigation, Assn. Am. Physicians, Am. Clin. and Climatological Soc., Alpha Omega Alpha. Contbr. profl. jours. Asso. editor Jour. Clin. Investigation; editorial bd. Medicine Thoracalis, Am. Rev. Respiratory Diseases. Home: 27 Brook Rd Tenafly NJ 07670 Office: Columbia Coll Physicians and Surgeons 630 W 168th St New York City NY 10032

FRITZ, CARL RIVERS, fgn. service officer; b. Tiffin, O., Sept. 26, 1923; s. Gottleb and Mary Ellen (Price) F.; A.B., Heidelberg Coll., 1948; M. Internat. Affairs, Columbia, 1951; postgrad. Inst. Internat. Devel. Johns Hopkins, 1962, Fgn. Service Inst. Precention, 1966-67; Nat. Interdepartmental Seminar, 1966, Fgn. Service Inst. Vietnam Tng., 1968-69; m. Barbara Jeanne Fricker, June 19, 1948; children—Judith E., Carl Edward, Lauren P., Cynthia J. Jr. program analyst ECA, Washington, 1951; program asst. Tech. Coop. Mission, New Delhi, India, 1951-53, program officer, 1953-56; with Operations Mission, Colombo, Ceylon, 1956-59, acting program officer, 1956-59, program officer, 1959; tech assistance study officer ICA, Washington 1960-61; with AID, 1961—, mem. task force research, 1961, dep. coordinator for Latin Am., dep. coordinator Africa, 1962-63, mem. implementation project, 1962-63; East Africa regional activities officer, Nairobi, Kenya, 1963-66; dep. dir. North African Affairs, 1967; Eastern and So. African Affairs, 1967-68, asst. dep. civil operations and revolutionary devel. support III Marine Amphibious Force, Da Nang, South Vietnam, 1969-70; asst. dep. CORDS XXIV Corps, Da Nang, 1970; asst. fir. program USOM, Bangkok, Thailand, 1970—. Served with USAAF, 1943-46. Decorated Medal for Revolutionary Devel. 1st class (Vietnam); recipient certificate appreciation Nat. Rehat. Inst., Vietnam, 1970. Princeton fellow, 1966-67. Mem. Soc. Internat. Devel., Am. Fgn. Service Assn. Bus. editor Jour. Internat. Affairs, 1950-51. Contbr. articles profl. jours. Home: 131 Soi 65 Sukhumvit Bangkok Thailand Office: AD/P USOM APO San Francisco CA 96346

FRITZ, CHARLES ANDREW, Jr., educator; b. Columbus O., Apr. 12, 1917; s. Charles A. and Ethel (Scherer) F.; A.B., Columbia, 1939, Ph.D., 1950; M.A., Brown U., 1940; m. Anita E. Dunlevy, May 12, 1942; children—Charles Andrew III, Barbara J. Instr. philosophy

Columbia, 1946-47; mem. faculty U. Conn., Storrs, 1947—, instr. 1947-51, asst. prof., 1951-62, asso. prof., 1962- 66, prof., 1966—, chmn. dept. philosophy, 1961-71. Served with USAAF, 1942-46. Mem. Am. Philos. Assn., Phi Beta Kappa. Author: Bertrand Russell's Construction of the External World, 1952; Bertrand Russell: On the Philosophy of Science, 1965. Contbr. papers to philos. jours. Home: 3 Storrs Heights Rd Storrs CT 06268

FRITZ, HAROLD WILLIAM, corp. exec.; b. Chgo., Jan. 14, 1927; s. Andrew and Susan (Fritch) F.; B.S., U. Ill., 1952; m. Betty Joanne Morris, Aug. 30, 1952; children—William, Michael, Carol Ann. Audit mgr. Arthur Andersen & Co., Chgo., 1952-65; with Richardson Co., Chgo., 1965-70, treas., 1967-70; treas. Services Corp. Am., 1970—. Treas. DuPage County council Girl Scouts Am., 1963-65; area chmn. United Fund, Glen Ellyn, 1964-66, Central DuPage Hosp. Assn., Glen Ellyn, 1965. Served with AUS, 1945-48, USAF, 1952-56. C.P.A., Ill. Mem. Am. Inst. C.P.A.'s, Ill. Soc. C.P.A.'s, Am. Accounting Assn., Financial Execs. Inst., Sigma Phi Epsilon. Methodist. Home: 196 Crest Rd Glen Ellyn IL 60137 Office: 2700 Lake St Melrose Park IL 60160

FRITZ, ROGER JAY, univ. pres.; b. Browntown, Wis., July 18, 1928; s. Delmar M. and Ruth M. (Sandley) F.; B.A. in Polit. Sci., Monmouth (Ill.) Coll., 1950; M.S. in Speech, U. Wis., 1952, Ph.D. in Ednl. Counseling, 1956; m. Kathryn Louise Goodard, Oct. 13, 1951; children—Nancy Goddard, Susan Marie. Asst. dean men, asst. prof. Purdue U., 1953-56; mgr. pub. relations Cummins Engine Co., also sec. Cummins Engine Found., 1956-59; sec. John Deere Found., also mem. pub. relations staff Deere & Co., 1959-65; dir. mgmt. devel. and personnel research Deere & Co., 1965-69, also dir. John Deere Found. and dir. mgmt. devel. and personnel research; pres. Willamette U., 1969—. Mem. edn. com. Taxpayers' Fedn. Ill., 1962-69; mem. bd. edn. Central Ill. conf. Meth. Ch., 1962-67; co-chmn. finance com. Econ. Edn. Workshop, Augustana Coll., Rock Island, Ill., 1965-67; mem. Midwest Coll. Placement Assn., 1965-69; mem. com. preparation coll. tchrs. Ill. Bd. Higher Edn., 1965-67, mem. com. med. edn., 1967-68; edn. com. N.A.M., 1967-69; founder Quad-Cities Council Grad. Edn., 1967-69; mem. Ia.-Ill. Indsl. Devel. Group, 1964-69; council contbr. Nat. Indsl. Conf. Bd., 1960-65, council devel., edn. and tng., 1966-69; adv. com. solicitations Nat. Better Bus. Bur., 1964-69; v.p. Ore. Ind. Colls. Assn., 1969—; mem. Pres.'s Citizens Adv. Bd. on Youth Opportunity, 1968-69. Trustee Monmouth Coll. (chmn. 1961-69). Mem. Phi Eta Sigma, Omicron Delta Kappa, Tau Kappa Epsilon, Phi Alpha Theta, Sigma Tau Delta, Pi Kappa Delta. Republican. Methodist. Clubs: University, Arlington (Portland, Ore.); Rotary; Illahe Hills Country. Author: A Handbook for Resident Counselors, 1952; The Argumentation of William Jennings Bryan and Clarence Darrow in the Tennessee Evolution Trial, 1952; A Comparison of Attitude Differences and Changes of College Freshmen Men Living in Various Types of Housing, 1956; also articles, papers. Home: 325 Lincoln St S Salem OR 97302

FRITZEMEYER, JOE RODNEY, assn. exec.; b. Hutchinson, Kan., Mar. 8, 1934; s. Ben and Gertrude Louise (Shaft) F.; B.B.A., Baylor U., 1956; M.B.A., Ind. U., 1957, D.B.A., 1960; m. Sharon Lee White, Dec. 26, 1958; children—Lee Ann, Thomas Joe. Teaching asso., instr. Ind. U., 1956-60; research asst. Am. Inst. C.P.A.'s, summer 1960; mem. faculty U. Ia., 1960-68, asso. prof. accounting, 1964-67, chmn. dept., 1964-67, prof. accounting, 1968; asst. to exec. v.p. Am. Inst. C.P.A.'s, N.Y.C., 1968-69, dir. tech. services div., 1969—. C.P.A., Tex. Mem. Am. Inst. C.P.A.'s, Am. Accounting Assn. (sec.-treas. 1964-67), Ia. Soc. C.P.A.'s, Beta Alpha Psi, Beta Gamma Sigma, Alpha Kappa Psi. Home: 351 Sylvan Av Leonia NJ 07605 Office: American Inst of CPAs 666 Fifth Av New York City NY 10019

FRITZLAN, ANDREW DAVID, fgn. service officer; b. Poona, India, June 20, 1914; s. Andrew David and Daisy (Skinner) F.; student Bishop Cotton Coll., Simla, India, 1931- 32; A.B., Northwest Nazarene Coll., 1934; M.A., U. Ky., 1936; postgrad. Fletcher Sch. Law and Diplomacy, 1937-38; m. Cynthia M. Helyar, Sept. 3, 1946; children—Simon A. Helyar, Charles David. Appointed fgn. service officer, diplomatic sec., vice consul, 1938; vice consul, Naples, Italy, 1938-39; 3d sec., vice consul Baghdad, Iraq, 1940, Tehran, Iran, 1940-42; vice consul, Basra, Iraq, 1942-44; 3d sec., Tangier, Morocco, 1944-45; vice consul, 1944-48, 2d sec., 1945-48; Arabic lang., area study Dept. State, Princeton, 1948-49; charge d'affaires, Amman, Jordan, 1949-50, consul, 1st sec. 1950; polit. adviser U.S. delegation 6th, and 7th UN Gen. Assemblies, Dept. of State, 1953-55; Army War Coll., 1955-56; counselor Am. embassy, Baghdad, Iraq, 1956-59; Am. consul gen., Barcelona, Spain, 1959-64, Alexandria, Egypt (UAR), 1964-67; polit. adviser U.S. delegation 20th UN Gen. Assembly, 1967; mem. spl. state-def. study group, Washington, 1968—; Am. consul gen., Thessaloniki, Greece, 1970—. Mem. Middle East Inst., Royal Central Asian Soc. Club: Oriental (London). Address: 3277 Prospect St NW Washington DC 20520

FRITZSCHE, HELLMUT, educator, physicist; b. Berlin, Germany, Feb. 20, 1927; s. Carl Hellmut and Anna (Jordan) F.; diploma, U. Göttingen (Germany), 1952; Ph.D., Purdue U., 1954; m. Sybille Charlotte Lauffer, July 5, 1952; chldren— Peter Andreas, Thomas Alexander, Susanne Charlotte, Katharina Sabine. Came to U.S., 1952, naturalized, 1966. Instr., then asst. prof. physics Purdue, 1954-56; mem. faculty U. Chgo., 1957—, prof. physics, 1963—. Fellow Am. Phys. Soc. Home: 5801 Blackstone Av Chicago IL 60637

FRIZELLE, ERWIN PARKE, banker; b. Mpls., June 25, 1911; s. S. Parke and Eleanor (Adams) F.; student U. Minn., 1931, Am. Inst. Banking, 1934; m. Dorothy Dryer, Feb. 20, 1936; children—E. Parke, Susan Jo (Mrs. Wayne A. Veenman), Scott D. With First Nat. Bank Mpls., 1929-34, First Bank Stock Corp., Mpls., 1934- 38; asst. v.p. Midland Nat. Bank, Billings, Mont., 1938-46; pres. First Metals Bank & Trust Co., Butte, 1946—; dir. Butte, Anaconda & Pacific Ry. Co., Intermountain Transp. Co. Home: Country Club Manor Butte MT 59701 Office: PO Box 548 Butte MT 59701

FRIZOL, SYLVESTER M., educator; b. Peru, Ill., June 26, 1906; s. Emil John and Dorothy (Hildebrandt) F.; B.S. in Commerce, Loyola U., Chgo., 1931, A.M., 1933; Ph.D., U. So. Cal., 1941; m. Carolyn Miller, Dec. 24, 1934. Asst. prof. Loyola U., Los Angeles, 1934-42; adminstrv. asst. Douglas Aircraft Corp., 1942-45; lectr., then asst. prof. U. So. Cal., 1945-50; prof. Loyola U., Chgo., 1950—, chmn. dept. finance, 1965; cons. in econs., 1962—. Mem. Am., Midwest econ. assns., Am., Midwest Finance assns., Investment Analyst Soc. Chgo., Pub. Utilities Securities Club Chgo., Chartered Financial Analysts, Blue Key, Artus, Beta Alpha Psi, Delta Sigma Pi, Phi Kappa Phi, Pi Epsilon Theta, Pi Gamma Mu, Beta Gamma Sigma. Home: 6608 N Central Av Chicago IL 60646

FRIZZELL, DONALD LESLIE, educator; b. Bellingham, Wash., Oct. 19, 1906; s. Thomas Fisher and Bessie Pearl (Knapp) F.; B.S., U. Wash., 1930, M.S., 1931; Ph.D., Stanford, 1936; m. Harriet Idola Exline, Aug. 29, 1938 (dec. Feb. 1968). Paleontologist Shell Oil Co., Houston, 1936; paleontologist, geologist Internat. Petroleum Co., Peru and Ecuador, 1937-44; asso. prof. geology U. Tex., Austin, 1945-48; asso. prof. geology U. Mo., Rolla., 1948-52, prof., 1952—. Mem. Geol. Soc. Am., Am. Assn. Petroleum Geologists, Paleontol. Soc., Soc. Econ. Paleontologists and Mineralogists, Soc. Systematic Zoology, Am. Soc. Ichthyologists and Herpetologists. Soc. Vertebrate Paleontology, Sociedad Geologica del Peru (corr.). Research on classification fossil fish otoliths, holothurians, foraminifera and mollusks. Home: 6 Rolla Gardens Rolla MO 65401

FRIZZELL, KENT, lawyer; b. Wichita, Kan., Feb. 11, 1929; s. Elton Sanderson and Irma A. (Hays) F.; B.A., Friends U., 1953; J.D., Washburn U., 1955. Admitted to Kan. bar, 1955; pvt. practice, Wichita, 1955-63; partner firm McCarter, Frizzell & Wettig, 1963-68; mem. Kan. Senate, 1965-69; atty. gen. Kan., 1969-71. Pres., Bd. of Edn., Wichita, 1959-65; mem. Kan. Municipal Accounting Bd., 1960-65. Precinct committeeman County Republican Central Com., Kan., 1951-66. Served with USMCR, 1948-50. Mem. Am. Bar Assn., Am. Legion, Phi Alpha Delta, Phi Kappa Psi. Home: 8937 NW Rochester Rd Topeka KS 66617

FRIZZELL, WILLIAM KENNETH, architect; b. Knox City, Tex., Dec. 10, 1928; s. Thomas Paul and Kelphia (Williams) F.; B.A. magna cum laude in Architecture, Princeton, 1950; M.A., U. Okla., 1954; m. Patricia Callender, Dec. 24, 1959; children—Jane, John Callender. Individual practice architecture, N.Y.C., brs. in Rome, Washington; works this country, abroad. Served to lt. (j.g.) USNR. Mem. A.I.A. Club: Racquet and Tennis (N.Y.C.). Works include Camelback Inn, Scottsdale, Ariz, Sheraton Hammamet Hotel, Tunisia, Yves St Laurent Boutique, N.Y.C. Home: "No Gain" 7121 Brookville Rd Chevy Chase MD 20015 Office: Ahrens Di Grazia Frizzell Architects and Engrs Viale America 11 Rome Italy also 3518 Thornapple St Chevy Chase MD 20015

FRODIN, REUBEN, educator; b. Chgo., July 10, 1912; s. Rube S. and Gladys (Gamman) F.; student Dartmouth, 1929-30; Ph.B., U. Chgo., 1933, J.D., 1941; m. Rebecca Durand Hayward, June 15, 1937; children—David Gamman, Joanna Hayward. Admitted to Ill. bar, 1941; staff writer A.P., 1933-36; writer Time mag., 1936-38, contbg. editor, 1937-38; Pacific Coast editorial rep. Time, Life, Fortune mags., San Francisco, 1937-38; with U. Chgo., 1938-51, mng. editor alumni pub., 1939-41, adminstrv. asst. to pres. and v.p., 1941-48, asst. dean of Coll., 1943-46, adviser spl. projects in central adminstrn., 1948-51, lectr. polit. sci., 1943-51; sec. Midwest Inter-Library Corp., 1949-54; cons. State U. N.Y., 1950-51, exec. dean, 1951-57; sr. Fulbright lectr. law and govt. New South Wales U., Sydney, Australia, 1957; cons., program specialist overseas devel. Ford Found., 1958-67, program adviser in edn., research 1967—; cons. Inter-Am. Devel. Bank, 1966; vis. prof. polit. sci. U. Cal. at Los Angeles, 1959-60; staff Am. Univs. Field Staff, West Africa, 1961-62; dean Coll. Liberal Arts and Sci., prof. polit. sci. Coll. City N.Y., 1964-67. Mem. Phi Beta Kappa. Club: Century Assn. (N.Y.C.). Author: (with others) The Idea and Practice of General Education, 1950; Some Recent Growth Trends in Private Universities and Colleges, 1968. Editor Jour. Gen. Edn., 1949-54. Home: 15 W 72d St New York City NY 10023 also Thetford Center VT 05075 Office: 320 E 43d St New York City NY 10017

FROEHLKE, ROBERT FREDERICK, govt. ofcl.; b. Neenah, Wis., Oct. 15, 1922; s. Herbert O. and Lillian (Porath) F.; LL.B., U. Wis., 1949; m. Nancy Jean Barnes, Nov. 9, 1946; children—Bruce, Jane, Anne, Scott. Admitted to Wis. bar, 1949; with firm McDonald & MacDonald, Madison, 1949-50; mem. faculty U. Wis. Law Sch., 1950-51; with Sentry Ins. Co., 1951-69, resident v.p., Boston, 1968-69; asst. sec. def. for adminstrn., 1969—. Treas., mem. bd. Laird Youth Leadership Found., 1968. Chmn., treas. Laird for Congress Club, 1952-68. Mem. bd. St. Michael's Hosp., Stevens Point, Wis., Wis. Regional Med. Program. Served to capt. AUS, 1943-46. Mem. Am., Wis. bar assns., Order of Coif, Psi Upsilon. Republican. Presbyn. Home: 5440 Jordan Rd Washington DC 20016 Office: The Pentagon Washington DC 20301

FROESSEL, CHARLES WILLIAM, judge, educator; b. Bklyn., Nov. 8, 1892; s. Theodore and Barbara (Hoffman) F.; LL.B., N.Y. Law Sch., 1913, LL.M., 1914, LL.D., 1955; LL.D., Adelphi Coll., 1954, Pace Coll., 1968; m. Elsie Stier, June 1, 1927 (dec.). Librarian, N.Y. Law Sch., 1913-14; admitted to N.Y. bar, 1915; counsel to sheriff Queens County, 1916-20, asst. dist. atty. in charge of appeals, 1924-26, sr. trial asst., 1926-30; spl. asst. U.S. atty. gen. in charge slum clearance projects, N.Y., 1935-37; justice City of N.Y., Queens Co., 1937, of Supreme Ct., 2d jud. dist. N.Y., 1937-49; asso. judge Ct. Appeals of N.Y. State, 1950-62; dean N.Y. Law Sch., 1968-69, prof., 1969—, also chmn. bd. trustees; trustee Ridgewood (N.Y.) Savs. Bank. Vice pres. Queensborough C. of C., 1934-37; dir. Ridgewood C. Of C. 1932—; pres. Queens council Boy Scouts Am., 1930-49, also mem. exec. bd. for N.Y. City, regional chmn., 1951-56, exec. bd., nat. council; del. N.Y. State Constl. Conv., 1967. Sponsor, Queens Fedn. Chs.; mem. adv. bd. Big Brother movement; exec. com. N.Y. World's Fair Corp. Served with USNRF, World War I. Recipient Silver Buffalo award Boy Scouts of Am.; Distinguished Achievement award Grand Lodge of Masons, N.Y.; award Nat. Conf. Christians and Jews, 1955; Spl. Social Services award, 1954; God and Country award St. George's Assn. Mem. Am., N.Y. State (chmn. jud. sect. 1945-46), Queens County (pres.) bar assns., Am. Legion, Ret. Officers Assn. Presbyn. (hon. pres. bd. trustees, elder). Mason (past grand master, N.Y., chmn. conf. grand masters U.S. 1946-47), Elk. Clubs: Brooklyn, Fort Orange. Home: Whitman Hotel Jamaica NY 11432

FROGGATT, ALBERT MAURICE, communications co. exec.; b. Nottingham, Eng., 1906; s. Albert and Lois (Norman) F.; brought to U.S., 1913, naturalized, 1919; B.S. in Engring. Physics, U. Ill., 1931; m. Charlotte R. Baumann, Sept. 22, 1933; 1 son, James R. Various engring positions Ill. Bell Telephone Co., 1929-50; with Am. Tel. & Tel. Co., 1950—, successively engr., plant extension engr., asso. dir. engring. econs., asst. chief engr., 1950-65, v.p. charge bus. relations, 1965-66, v.p. charge engring. econs. dept., 1966- 70, v.p. charge service costs dept., 1970—; dir. Mountain States Tel. & Tel. Co. Mem. Phi Sigma Phi, Pi Mu Epsilon. Conglist. Home: 27 Delwick Lane Short Hills NJ 07078. Office: 195 Broadway New York City NY 10007

FROHLICH, LUDWIG WILLIAM, advt. exec.; b. Germany, July 30, 1913; s. Ludwig and Elsie (Oppein) F.; B.S., Johann W. Goethe U., Frankfurt, Germany, 1931; student Ecole Dierot, also Inst. des Beaux Arts, France. Came to U.S., 1931, naturalized, 1938. Creative advt., corporate counsel promotional field to 1939; founder L. W. Frohlich & Co., 1939, L. W. Frohlich & Co., Inc., 1943, now chmn.; chmn. IMS Internat. Dir. Royal Soc. Medicine Found., London; trustee Nat. Found., Med. Congress, Ltd.; trustee, chmn. Alumni Council of Internat. House; trustee, vice chmn. Coll. Pharm. Scis., Columbia U. Mem. Young Pres.' Orgn. Clubs: Pharmaceutical Advertising, Art Directors, N.Y. Athletic (N.Y.C.); Maidstone, Devon Yacht (East Hampton, N.Y.). Home: 150 E 63d St New York City NY 10021 Office: 34 E 51st St New York City NY 10022

FROHLICH, MOSES MICHAEL, psychiatrist, educator; b. Peczenizyn, Austria, Oct. 18, 1902; s. Gerson and Mina (Zweig) F.; student City Coll. N.Y., 1921-23; A.B., U. Mich., 1928, M.D., 1932; postgrad. Detroit Psychoanalytical Inst., 1946-53; m. Dorothy Francis Wick, Apr. 5, 1946; children—Mickel Wick, Thomas Gerson. Came to U.S., 1920, naturalized, 1926. Resident. instr. internal medicine Univ. Hosp., Ann Arbor, Mich., 1933-35; instr. psychiatry U. Mich. Sch. Medicine, 1936-42, asst. prof., 1945-47, asso. prof., 1947- 51, prof., 1951—, clin. dir. neuropsychiat. inst. U. Med. Center; cons. psychiatrist VA, Social Security Adminstrn., Dept. Def., Mich. Dept. Mental Health. Served to lt. col., M.C., AUS, 1942-46. Mem. A.M.A., Am. Psychiat. Assn., Am., Mich. psychoanalytical assns., Group for Advancement Psychiatry, Am. Geriatric Assn., Phi Beta Kappa, Phi Kappa Phi. Home: 817 Berkshire Rd Ann Arbor, MI 48104

FROHMAN, CHARLES EUGENE, paper co. exec.; b. Sandusky, O., Aug. 9, 1901; s. Daniel and Helen (Wagner) F.; B.S., in Econs., U. Pa., 1923; LL.B., Yale, 1926; Ph.D. in Bus. Adminstrn., Bowling Green U., 1958; m. Ruth Elisabeth Dunsmore, June 10, 1933; children—David James, Daniel Charles, Asso. mem. law firm, King Ramsey & Flynn, Sandusky, O., 1926-32, King Flynn & Frohman, 1932-36, Flynn, Frohman, Buckingham, Py and Kruse, 1936-46; gen. counsel Hinde & Dauch Paper Co., Sandusky, 1932-48, v.p., dir., 1941-49, pres., dir., mem. exec. com., 1949-58; vice chmn., dir. Hinde & Dauch Paper Co. Can., Ltd., 1940-59; dir. 3d Nat. Bank, 1938—, v.p., 1953—; dir. v.p. O.P. Craft Co., 1935-70, Trustee R.B. Hayes Found. Mem. Ohio, Sandusky chambers commerce, Ohio Soc. N.Y., Ohio Hist. Soc. (trustee 1956—; pres. 1961-63), Philomathean, Am. Bar Assn., Acacia, Theta Alpha Phi, Beta Gamma Sigma, Delta Theta Phi. Episcopalian. Mason (32, K.T.). Elk. Clubs: Yale (N.Y.); Yacht (Sandusky); Rotary, Rockwell Trout. Author: History of Sandusky, 1965; Rebels on Lake Erie, 1965; Sandusky's Yesterdays, 1968; Cedar Point Yesterdays, 1969; Put-in-Bay, 1971; Sandusky's Third Dimensions, 1971. Bd. editors Yale Law Jour., 1925-26. Address: 1313 Cedar Point Rd Sandusky OH 44870

FROHMAN, PHILIP HUBERT, architect; b. N.Y.C., Nov. 16, 1887; s. Gustave and Marie (Hubert) F.; ed. Throop Poly. Inst., Pasadena, Cal., 1899-1903, Throop Coll. Engring. (now Cal. Inst. Tech.), specializing in art, archtl. engring. and civil engring., 1903-07; m. Olivia Avery, July 15, 1922 (dec. Apr. 1955); children—Mary, Alice; m. 2d, Mary Ann Evans, Feb. 27, 1957 (dec. Mar. 1970). Began practice as architect at Pasadena, Cal., 1908; mem. Frohman & Martin, 1909-17; opened office in Boston, 1919; mem. Frohman, Robb & Little, 1920-34; pvt. practice 1934—; opened office in Washington, 1924, continuing assn. with former partners in Boston and Cal. on certain projects; specializes in church architecture; architects of Nat. Episcopal Cathedral, Washington, Md. Cathedral, Balt., Trinity Coll. Chapel, Hartford, Conn., Catholic Cathedral, Los Angeles, and other monumental churches; cons. architect Kent Sch. Chapel, also various chs.; cons. architect cathedral projects. Served with U.S. Army, 1917-19; assigned to Ordnance Constrn. Sect. and Supply Div.; designed bldgs. at Rock Island Arsenal and Aberdeen Proving Grounds. Decorated Medal Pro Ecclesia et Pontifix (Pope John). Fellow A.I.A. (mem. Washington chpt.); mem. Nat. Cathedral Assn., Guild Religious Architecture, Liturgical Art Soc., The Restorers of Mount Carmel in Md., Am. Ord. Assn. (life). Republican. Catholic. Club: Gibson Island. Specialist in structural engring. as applied to cathedrals, etc. Regarded as an authority on Romanesque and Gothic architecture, stained glass, and also on design and voicing of ch. organs and in field of sci. of mus. sounds. Inventor electric organs and various apparatus for elec. reporduction of mus. sounds. Writer on ecclesiastical art and architecture. Home: 3514 Macomb St NW Washington DC 20016 Office: Washington Cathedral Hearst Hall Mount St Alban Washington DC 20014

FROHOCK, WILBUR MERRILL, educator; b. South Thomaston, Me., June 20, 1908; s. Horatio Wilbur and Sarah (Merrill) F.; Ph.B., Brown U., 1930, M. A., 1931, Ph.D., 1935; m. Natalie Barrington, Aug. 16, 1938; children—Natalie, Sarah. Instr. French, Brown U., 1935-37; instr. French, Columbia, 1937-42, asst. prof., 1945-48, asso. prof., 1948-53; prof. romance langs. Wesleyan U., 1953-56; prof. romance langs. and gen. edn. Harvard, 1956-59, prof. romance langs., 1959; Bacon Exchange prof., Lille, 1959. Author: The Novel of Violence in America, 1950; Andre Malraux and the Tragic Imagination, 1952; Strangers to This Ground, 1962; Rimbaud's Poetic Practice, 1963; Style and Temper, 1967. Home: 10 Shady Hill Sq Cambridge MA 02138

FROHRING, PAUL ROBERT, chem. mfr.; b. Cleve., Aug. 2, 1903; s. William E. and Martha L. (Bliss) F.; student Ohio State U., 1921-22; B.S., Case Inst., 1926; m. Maxine A. Prince, Mar. 7, 1941; children—Martha Louise, Paula Christine. With research labs. S.M.A. Corp., 1926-34, v.p., 1942-44; pres. Eff Labs., Inc., 1934-40; pres., gen. mgr. Gen. Biochems., Inc., Chagrin Falls, O., 1940-61; gen. mgr. Emdee Labs., 1942-44; pres. Life Products, Inc., 1942-45; dir. Cleve. Machine Controls, Inc., Irving & Co., Shaker Heights, O., Alco Standard, Inc., Phila., Am. Home Products Corp., N.Y.C., Newbury Industries, Inc. (O.), Curtis Mfg. Co., St. Louis. Mem. pharm. mfrs. adv. com. WPB, 1942; del. President's Conf. Indsl. Safety, 1954. Trustee Cleve. Health Museum, Hiram (O.) Coll.; overseer Case Western Res. U. Fellow N.Y. Acad. Scis.; mem. Ohio Acad. Sci., Am. Chem. Soc., Am. Dairy Sci. Assn., Am. Oil Chemist Soc., A.A.A.S., Navy League (life), Ohio Soc. (N.Y.), Alpha Chi Sigma. Clubs: Chagrin Valley Hunt (Gates Mills, O.); Hillbrook (Russell, O.); Union (Cleve.); Key Biscayne (Fla.) Yacht. Home: 7630 Chagrin Rd Chagrin Falls OH 44022 Office: Box 428 Chagrin Falls OH 44022

FROISTAD, VERNON D., battery co. exec.; b. Newman Grove, Neb., 1925; ed. U. Minn., 1956; LL.B., William Mitchell Coll. Law, 1952. Sec. Gould Nat. Batteries, Inc., Wilkening Mfg. Co.; asst. sec. Gould-Nat. Can. Ltd. Mason. Home: 2140 E Nebraska Av St Paul MN 55119 Office: First Nat Bank Bldg St Paul MN 55101*

FROLIK, ELVIN FRANK, coll. dean; b. DeWitt, Neb., June 9, 1909; s. Anton and Fannie (Kolarik) F.; B.Sc., U. Neb., 1930, M.Sc., 1932; student Cornell U., 1940; Ph.D., U. Minn., 1948; research fellow, Cal. Inst. Tech., 1947-48; m. Rita Haley, Aug. 11, 1938; children—Thomas E., M. Maureen, Lawrence A. County agrl. agt. Nemaha County, Neb., 1933-34; farm mgr. Bankers Life Ins. Co. Neb., Omaha, 1934-35; faculty U. Neb., 1936—, prof. agronomy, 1951—, chmn. dept. 1952-55, asso. dir. agrl. expt. sta., 1955-60, dean Coll. Agr., 1960—; cons. Molinos de Puerto Rico, 1959-60. Vice chmn. ESCOP. Maj., U.S. Army Res. (ret.). Fellow Am. Soc. of Agronomy; mem. A.A.A.S., Internat. Corp. Improvement Assn. (pres. 1945-47), Soil Conservation Soc. Am., Am. Dehydrator's Assn. (past research council), U. Neb. Innocents Soc. (hon.), Farm House Frat., Sigma Xi (past pres. Neb.), Gamma Sigma Delta (past pres. Neb.), Alpha Zeta. Home: 1225 N 38th St Lincoln NB 68503

FROMAN, DAROL KENNETH, physicist; b. Harrington, Wash., Oct. 23, 1906; s. James Henderson and Eva (Wallace) F.; B.S., U. Alta., 1926, M.S., 1927, LL.D., 1964; Ph.D., U. Chgo., 1930; m. Ethel Norris, June 10, 1931; children—Kay Joyce (Mrs. Ralph P. Johnson, Jr.), Eva May (Mrs. Edwin K. Tucker). Lectr., U. Alta., 1930-31; lectr., asst. prof. Macdonald Coll., 1931-39; asst. prof. McGill U., 1939-41; prof. U. Denver, 1941-42; group leader USN Radio and Sound Lab., San Diego, 1942; research asso. Metall. Lab., U. Chgo., 1942; group leader, div. leader, asst. dir. Los Alamos Sci. Lab., 1943-51, tech. asso. dir., 1951-62, cons., 1963—; sci. dir. Operation Sandstone, Einewetok, Marshall Islands, 1948; cons. prof. physics U. N.M., 1952-62; mem. sci. adv. com. on ballistics missiles to sec. defense, 1955-61; sci. adv. council McDonnell-Douglas Corp., St. Louis, Mo., 1963-69; mem. gen. adv. com. AEC, Washington,

1964-66; dir. development Espanola (N.M.) Hosp., 1967-69. Chmn. bd. organizers Los Alamos Nat. Bank; chmn. bd. First Nat. Bank Rio Arriba, Espanola, N.M. Recipient certificate commendation Sec. Navy, 1960. Fellow Am. Phys. Soc., Am. Nuclear Soc.; mem. Sigma Xi, Gamma Alpha. Contbr. articles profl. jours. Patentee electronics, nuclear reactors. Home and office: Box 428 Route 1 Espanola NM 87532

FROMAN, LEWIS A., educator; b. Plattsburg, Mo., Aug. 17, 1906; student Mo. Wesleyan Coll., 1923-25; A.B., U. Mo., 1927; Ph.D., Cornell U., 1931; LL.D., Union Coll., 1966; L.H.D., Russell Sage Coll., 1970; m. Nadine Nichols, July 3, 1927; children—James, Lewis A., Francelia. Instr. U. Mo., 1927-28, Cornell U., 1928-31, U. Buffalo, 1931-35; dean Millard Fillmore Coll., 1935-48; prof. finance U. Buffalo, 1939-48; pres. Russell Sage Coll., 1948-70; vis. prof. U. Cal. at Los Angeles, summer 1939, U. So. Cal., summers, 1941, 46, 47, 48, 51, 60, 68, U. Hawaii, summer 1955; vis. prof. econs. St. John's U., Jamaica, N.Y., 1970—; dir. Troy Savs. Bank, 1948—, chmn. bd., 1968-70. Trustee Emma Willard Sch., 1950-65; trustee Troy Public Library, 1951-70, pres., 1958-68, 69-70; trustee Albany Acad., 1968-70. Named Man of Year, Greater Troy C. of C., 1968. Mem. Assn. Evening Colls. (pres. 1945), Am. Finance Assn. (pres. 1947). Author: Money and Banking (with Tippetts), 1935; Principles of Economics, 2 vol., 1940 (rev. 1946); Industrial Supervision (with Mason), 1942; Introduction to Business, 1948. Home: 6700 192d St Flushing NY 11365

FROMBERG, GERALD, artist, educator; b. Bklyn., July 19, 1925; s. Charles and Anna (Feldman) F.; B.A., Bklyn. Coll., 1946; M.A., U. N.M., 1951; postgrad. Bklyn. Mus. Sch. Art, 1949, New Sch. Social Research, 1947; m. LaVerne Ray, Sept. 13, 1952; children—Paul, Robert Matthew, Steven. Instr. art U. Wash., 1952-53, Dillard U., 1953-55; instr. art Bradley U., 1955-58, asst. prof. Sch. Art, 1958-64, asso. prof., 1964—; tchr.-mem. Peoria (Ill.) Art Center; comml. artist Metro Asso Services, 1946-47, Fromberg and Charles, 1947-49, Marwell Advt., 1949, Advt. Aides, 1951; filmmaker Burdon Advt., Peoria, Ill., 1969—; group exhbns.: Momentum Midcontinental, Chgo., 1954, Northwest Ann., Seattle, 1952, Contemporary Arts Gallery, N.Y.C., 1952, 53, New Orleans Art Assn. Ann., 1954, 55, Audubon Artists Ann., 1956, 57, Denver Ann. Western Artists, 1958, 62, Butler Inst., 1958, New Horizons in Sculpture, Chgo., 1967, N. Mississippi Valley Artists Invitational, 1968, 69, Ill. Arts Council Traveling Exhibit, 1969-70, Artists Who Teach Exhibit, Springfield, Ill., 1969, Md. Film Festival, Balt., 1969; one man shows N.M. Mus., 1951, U. N.M., 1951, Henry Gallery, Seattle, 1953, Bradley U., 1962, 64, Smolin Gallery, N.Y., 1964, Lakeview Center, Peoria, Ill., 1966, Bradley U., 1967, Ill. Wesleyan U., 1969, Springfield (Ill.) Art Mus., 1969; 2 man shows (with wife) Dillard U., 1954, 55, 331 Gallery, New Orleans, 1955, Contemporary Artists Gallery, Peoria, 1956, 60, Barone Gallery, N.Y.C., 1957, Bradley U., 1961, Contemporary Gallery, Dallas, 1968, Fulton Gallery, N.Y.C., 1969, S.E. Ark. Arts & Sci. Center, Pine Bluff, 1969, Bibo Gallery, Peoria, 1971. Recipient lst prize oil painting Pacific Northwest Arts Fair, 1952, 53, 54; medal of honor Audubon Artists Exhbn., 1957; 2d prize Peoria Art Center mems. show, 1957; 2d prize abstract painting Heart of Ill. Fair, 1958, 62; 2d prize water color Ill. State Fair, 1962; 2d prize Nat. Exhbn. Small Paintings, 1962; lst prize Peoria Art Center mems. Show, 1963, Central Ill. Exhbn. Painting, 1963; 1st prize and Purchase award Lakeview Center Ann. Area Show, Peoria, 1965; Putnam award for excellence in teaching Bradley U., 1968. Mem. Artists Equity (dir. Seattle 1953), Coll. Art Assn., Univ. Film Assn., Delta Phi Delta, Phi Kappa Phi. Home: 1205 N Glenwood Av Peoria IL 61606

FROMENT, FRANK LIVINGSTON, sugar exec.; b. N.Y.C., Jan. 5, 1909; s. Eugene McKibbin and Edith Hoyt (Smith) F.; grad. Hotchkiss Sch., 1927; A.B., Princeton, 1931; m. Elizabeth Cauldwell McAlpin, Oct. 27, 1934; children—Elizabeth (Mrs. J.M. Brown), Jeanne (Mrs. B.L. Tiedmann). Pres. Schrock & Squires Steel Corp., 1938-43; with Guantanamo Sugar Co., N.Y.C., 1947-58, pres., dir., 1955-58; v.p., dir. N.Am. Sugar Industries, Inc., 1958—. Served with AUS, 1943-45. Mem. Assn. Ex-mems. Squadron A (gov.). Club: Princeton (N.Y.C.). Home: Treadwell Av Convent NJ 07961 Office: 500 Fifth Av New York City NY 10036

FROMER, JULIAN PHILIP, fgn. service officer; b. Bklyn., May 26, 1915; s. Joseph Henry and Mary (Shapiro) F.; B.A., U. Wis., 1935, student Law Sch., 1935-36; grad. Mgmt. Program for Execs., U. Pitts., 1958; m. Pauline Norman, Apr. 13, 1966. Newspaperman, writer Lit. Digest, Buffalo Times, Columbia Pictures, PM, 1936-41; staff OWI, N.Y.C., Trinidad, N. Africa, Italy, 1941-45; pub. affairs officer Dept. State, Palermo, Florence, Bologna and Milan, Italy, 1946-51; fgn. service officer, 1951—; consul, Bilbao, Spain, 1951-55; chief Spanish service Voice Am., USIA, 1955-56; desk officer for Haiti and Dominican Republic, Office Caribbean Affairs, Bur. Inter-Am. Affairs, 1956-57, Office Spl. Asst. for Pub. Affairs, Bur. Inter-Am. Affairs, 1957-59; 1st sec. Am. embassy, Vientiane, Laos, 1959-61; mem. U.S. delegation Internat. Conf. on Laos at Geneva, 1961-62; 1st sec. Am. embassy, Rome, 1962-64; assigned to NATO Def. Coll., 1964-65; with Office Dept. Undersec. for Adminstrn., Dept. State, Washington, 1965-68; charge d'affairs Am. embassy, Port Louis, 1968-70; State Dept. rep. Armed Forces Staff Coll., Norfolk, Va., 1970—. Mem. Am. Fgn. Service Assn., Sigma Delta Chi, Phi Kappa Phi, Alpha Epsilon Pi. Address: care Fgn Service Mail Room Dept State Washington DC 20025

FROMM, ALFRED, distbg. co. exec.; b. Kitzingen, Germany, Feb. 23, 1905; s. Max and Mathilda (Maier) F.; student Viticultural Acad., 1920; m. Hanna Gruenbaum, July 5, 1936; children—David George, Carolynn Anne. Came to U.S., 1938, naturalized, 1943. Export dir. N. Fromm, Bingen, Germany, 1924-33; v.p. Picker-Lintz Importers, Inc., N.Y.C., 1937-44; exec. v.p. Fromm & Sichel, Inc., N.Y.C., also San Francisco, 1944-65, pres., 1965—; dir. Joseph E. Seagram & Sons, Inc. Vice chmn. Cal. Med. Clinic for Psychotherapy, San Francisco, 1964—. Mem. nat. council Eleanor Roosevelt Meml. Found., N.Y.C.; v.p., trustee San Francisco Conservatory Music; regent St. Mary's Coll., Moraga; v.p. Jewish Nat. Fund. Clubs: Concordia, Commonwealth (San Francisco). Contbr. articles profl. jours. Home: 850 El Camino del Mar San Francisco CA 94121 Office: 1255 Post St San Francisco CA 94109

FROMM, ERICH, psychoanalyst; b. Frankfurt, Germany, Mar. 23, 1900; s. Naphtali and Rosa (Krause), F.; Ph.D., U. Heidelberg, 1922; postgrad. U. Munich, 1922-26; student Psychoanalytic Inst., Berlin; m. Frieda Reichmann, June 16, 1926 (div.); m. 2d, Henny Gurland, July 24, 1944 (dec. 1952); m. 3d, Annis Freeman, Dec. 18, 1953. Lectr., Psychoanalytic Inst., Frankfurt, and Inst. for Social Research, U. Frankfurt, 1929-32; Internat. Inst. Social Research, N.Y.C., 1934-39; guest lectr., Columbia, 1940-41; lectr., Am. Inst. Psycholanalysis 1941-42; Terry lectr. Yale, 1949; faculty Bennington (Vt.) Coll., 1941-50; fellow faculty William Alanson White Inst. Psychiatry, N.Y.C.; prof. Nat. U. Mexico, 1951—, Mich. State U., 1957-61; adj. prof. N.Y. U., 1962—. Diplomate in clin. psychology Am. Psychol. Assn. Fellow N.Y. Acad. Sci.; mem. Washington Psychoanalytic Soc., Mexican Nat. Acad. Medicine (hon.). Author book including: Psychoanalysis and Religion, 1950; The Forgotten Language, 1951; The Sane Society, 1955; Sigmund Freud's Mission, 1958; The Dogma of Christ and Other Essays on Religion, Psychology and Culture, 1962; The Heart of Man, 1964; The Crisis of Psychoanalysis, 1970. Contbr. to jours. Addresses: 180 Riverside Dr New York City NY 10024 also Patricio Sanz 748-5 Mexico City 12 Mexico

FROMM, HENRY GORDON, bus. exec.; b. Burlington, Ia., June 10, 1911; s. Henry Carl and Lillian (Lohmann) F.; B.S. in Chem. Engring., Ia. State U., 1933; M.S. in Bus. Adminstrn. (Sloan Fellow), Mass. Inst. Tech., 1950; m. Elizabeth H. Orthner, July 15, 1936; children—Dan G., Allan P., Martha E., Mark H., Eric C., Lynne M. Gen. plant mgr. Manhattan Soap Co., Bristol, Pa., 1937-44; prodn. mgr. Johnson & Johnson, 1944-55; v.p. operations Intenat. Latex Corp., 1955-61; v.p., gen. mgr. operations Sun Chem. Corp., N.Y.C., 1961-63; gen. mgr. Crown Cork & Seal Co., Phila., 1963-64; v.p. operations Marathon Electric Co., Wausau, Wis., 1964-69; pres. Bell & Howell Communications Co., Waltham, Mass., 1969, Bell & Howell Electronics & Instruments Group, Pasadena, Cal., 1969—. Mem. gen. council Am. Baptist Conv. Mem. Dover (Del.) City Council, 1958-62; chmn. Dover City Planning Commn., 1960-62. Mem. Am. Mgmt. Assn. (v.p.), Am. Inst. Chem. Engrs. Clubs: Engineers, Canadian (N.Y.C.). Home: 1435 Edgecliff Lane Pasadena CA 91107 Office: Bell & Howell Electronics & Instruments Group 360 Sierra Madre Villa Pasadena CA 91109

FROMM, PAUL, found. exec.; b. Kitzingen, Germany, Sept. 28, 1906; s. Max and Matilde (Maier) F.; ed. high sch.; Dr. Music, New Eng. Conservatory Music, Boston, Mass.; m. Erika Oppenheimer, July 2O, 1938; 1 dau., Joan. Came to U.S., 1938, naturalized, 1944. Established, 1939, since pres. Geeting & Fromm, Inc., wine importers, Chgo.; founder, 1952, since pres. Fromm Music Found., Chgo. Mem. citizens com. U. Ill.; mem. bd. Inst. Psychoanalysis, Chgo., Jewish Childrens Bur.; adv. council Princeton; vis. com. humanities U. Chgo.; vis. com. music dept. Harvard U.; bd. overseers Boston Symphony Orch.; bd. dirs. Orchestral Assn., Erikson Inst. Early Childhood Edn.; bd. govs., sec. Ill. Arts Council; pres. Family Inst. Chgo. Home: 5715 S Kenwood Av Chicago IL 60637 Office: 1028 W Van Buren St Chicago IL 60607

FROMME, ALEX M., judge; b. Hoxie, Kan., Mar. 11, 1915; s. Joseph H. and Frances (Morgan) F.; A.B., LL.B., Washburn U; m. Ruth Marie 1939, and practiced in Hoxie; partner with brother, 1949-66; justice Kansas Supreme Ct., Topeka, 1966—; county atty. Sheridan County, 1941-48. Institutional representative local council Boy Scouts Am., 1948-49; home service chmn. Sheridan County chpt. A.R.C., 1941-47; pres. Sheridan County Community Fund, 1964-65. Mem. Am., Kan. (exec. council 1949-58, pres. 1961- 62), Northwest Kan. (past council) bar assns., Nat. Conf. Bar Pres. Rotarian (pres. Hoxie 1946). Author articles legal jours. Home: 5108 Shunga Dr Topeka KS 66614. Office: Statehouse Topeka KS 66612

FROMMELT, HENRY JULLUS, chain store exec.; b. N.Y.C., May 18, 1911; s. Alfred J. and Martha (Schoenewerk) F.; student U. Minn., 1933; m. Inez V. Okins, Feb. 15, 1936; children—Roger, Jeffrey, Christine. With Gamble Skogmo, Inc., Mpls., 1934—, dir. pub. relations, asst. to exec. v.p., 1952-61, v.p. pub. relations, 1961—; dir. Gambles Holiday Travel Service. Bd. dirs. Mpls. Goodwill Industries, 1955—, pres., 1965-67, chmn. bd., 1967—; bd. dirs. Better Bus. Bur. Mpls., 1968—, Jr. Achievement Greater Mpls., 1963—. Mem. Mpls. C. of C. (chmn. marketing com. 1958), Mpls. (pres. 1958-59, chmn. adv. com. 1959-60), Nat. (bd. dirs. 1960-61) sales execs. clubs: Mpls. Ad Club. Presbyn. Clubs: Minn. Press. Interlachen Country (Mpls.). Home: 5034 Gladstone Av Minneapolis MN 55419. Office: 5100 Gamble Dr Minneapolis MN 55416

FROMMEYER, WALTER BENEDICT, Jr., educator, physician; b. Cin., Nov. 23, 1916; s. Walter Benedict and Alma (Donahue) F.; A.B., U. Cin., 1939, M.D. (Peter T. Kilgour award 1942), 1942; m. Elizabeth Ann Lee, Jan. 8, 1944; children—Elizabeth Lee, Virginia. Intern Cin. Gen. Hosp., 1942-43, jr. asst. resident, sr. asst. resident, 1946-48; research fellow medicine Thorndike Meml. Lab., also asst. medicine Harvard Med. Sch., 1948-49; dir. Tumor Clinic, U. Hosp. and Hillman Clinic, chief med. service Birmingham VA Hosp., 1953-54; mem. faculty U. Ala. Sch. Medicine, 1949—, asso. dean, 1954-57, prof. medicine, 1957—, Distinguished prof. U. Ala., 1968—, chmn. dept., 1957-68; physician-in-chief Univ. Hosp., 1957-68, chief staff, 1963-64, 65-66; chmn. dean's com. Birmingham VA Hosp., 1954-59. Mem. exec. com. Jefferson County Coordinating Council Health Services, 1955. Served from 1st lt. to maj., M.C., AUS, 1943-46. Decorated Bronze Star with oak leaf cluster, Purple Heart; recipient Gold Heart award Am. Heart Assn., 1971. Diplomate Pan Am. Med. Assn., Am. Bd. Internal Medicine (dir. 1962-68, vice chmn. 1967-68; emeritus mem. 1968—). Fellow A.C.P. (bd. govs. 1960-66, bd. regents 1967—, v.p. 1969-70, exec. com. bd. regents 1968—, chmn. annual sci. session com. 1967-70, chmn. com. ednl. activities 1970—, chmn. com. postgrad. courses), Am. Coll. Cardiology; mem. So. Med. Assn. (past sec. sect. medicine), So. Soc. Clin. Investigation, Vis. Nurses Assn. (past mem. exec. com., trustee), Am. (pres. 1968-69, dir., dir. at large, chmn. com. med. edn.; hon. fellow council cardiology), Ala. (trustee, past pres., chmn. bd.; Distinguished Service award) heart assns., Assn. Am. Physicians, A.A.A.S., A.M.A., Med. Assn. Ala., Am. Fedn. Clin. Research, Sigma Xi, Alpha Omega Alpha, Pi Kappa Epsilon. Clubs: Mountain Brook; Ponte Vedra (Fla.). Contbr. articles med. jours. Home: 2920 Cherokee Rd Birmingham AL 35223

FRONCKIEWICZ, ROBERT LAWRENCE, retail store exec.; b. St. Louis, Mo., Oct. 4, 1936; s. Al Joseph and Genevieve (Wojcicki) F.; B.S., Christian Bros. Coll., St. Louis, 1954; student St. Louis U., Washington U., St. Louis, 1954-60; m. Susan E. Spieldoch, Nov. 29, 1969; children—Jeannine Marie, Craig Robert. With Wohl Shoe Co., 1960—, treas., 1968—. Served with AUS, 1959-60. Mem. Nat. Retail Merchants Assn., Greater St. Louis Retail Controller Group. Home: 217 Laduemont Dr St Louis MO 63141 Office: 8350 Maryland Av St Louis MO 63105

FRONDEL, CLIFFORD, mineralogist; b. N.Y.C., Jan. 8, 1907; s. George and Martha (Kindermann) F.; B.S. in Geol. Engring., Colo. Sch. Mines, 1929; M.A., Columbia, 1936; Ph.D., Mass. Inst. Tech., 1939; m. Eleanor Travis, Sept. 9, 1941; 1 dau., Dana L.; m. 2d, Judith Weiss, Nov. 26, 1949; 1 dau., Barbara. Teaching fellow crystallography Mass. Inst. Tech., 1937-39; research asso. Harvard, 1939-42; sr. civilian physicist War Dept., 1942-43; dir. research Reeves Sound Labs., 1943-45; asso. prof. mineralogy Harvard, 1946-54, prof., 1954—, chmn. dept. geol. scis., 1965—, also curator mineralogical museum. Recipient Roebling medal Mineral. Soc. Am., 1964; Distinguished Achievement medal Colo. Sch. Mines, 1964; Boricky medal Charles U., Prague, 1968. Fellow Am. Acad. Arts and Scis., Mineral Soc. Am., Geol. Soc. Am.; mem. Am. Crystallographic Assn., Great Britain, Germany, France, Italy mineral socs.; corr. mem. Natural History Museum of Vienna, Am. Mus. of Natural History, Deutsche Akademie der Naturforscher; fgn. mem. Austrian Acad. Sci., Accademia dei Lincei Rome. Author: Dana's System of Mineralogy (With C. Palache and H. Berman), 7th edition 1951. Contbr. profl. jours. Home: 20 Beatrice Circle Belmont MA 02173

FROSCH, AARON R., lawyer; b. N.Y.C., July 9, 1924; B.A., Bklyn. Coll., 1944; LL.B., Bklyn. Law Sch., 1947; m. Marjorie MacMillan, Jan. 17, 1955; children-Juliana, Phoebe, Suzanna. Admitted to N.Y. bar, 1948; sr. partner Weissberger & Frosch, N.Y.C.; gen. counsel, dir. Marilyn Monroe Prodns., 1962—, Elizabeth Taylor Prodns., 1964—, Harkness Found., 1962-69. Chmn. Mayor's com. for N.Y. Shakespeare Festival, 1967—, Trustee N.Y. Shakespeare Festival, 1963—; founder Hardecker Lab. and Children's Clinic, Nassua, Bahamas. Mem. Am., N.Y. State, N.Y.C. bar assns., N.Y. County Lawyers Assn. Home: 300 Central Park W New York NY 10024 Office: 120 E 56th St New York NY 10022

FROSCH, ROBERT ALAN, govt. ofcl., physicist; b. N.Y.C., May 22, 1928; s. Herman Louis and Rose (Bernfeld) F.; A.B., Columbia, 1947, A.M., 1949, Ph.D., 1952; m. Jessica Rachael Denerstein, Dec. 22, 1957; children—Elizabeth Ann, Margery Ellen. Scientist, Hudson Labs. Columbia, 1951-53, asst. dir. theoretical div., 1953-54, asso. dir., 1954-56, dir. 1956-63; dir. nuclear test detection Advanced Research Projects Agy., Office Sec. Def., 1963-65, dep. dir. Advanced Research Projects Agy., 1965-66; asst. sec. navy for research and devel., Washington, 1966-67; chmn. Inter-agy. Com. on Marine Research, Edn. and Facilities, 1967-69; Dept. Def. mem. com. for policy rev. Nat. Council on Marine Resources and Engring. Devel., 1969—; chmn. U.S. Delegation to Intergovtl. Oceanographic Commn. meetings UNESCO, Paris, 1967, 70. Recipient Arthur S. Flemming award, 1966. Fellow A.A.A.S., Acoustical Soc. Am., I.E.E.E.; mem. Am. Geophys. Union, Seismol. Soc. Am., Soc. Exploration Geophysicists, Marine Tech. Soc. Research and publs. numerous sci. and tech. articles. Home: 10105 Hurst St Bethesda MD 20014 Office: Pentagon Dept of Navy Washington DC 20350

FROST, ARTHUR ATWATER, chemist, educator; b. Onarga, Ill., Aug. 3, 1909; s. Henry Hoag and Mary (Tuttle) F.; B.S., U. Cal. at Berkeley, 1931; Ph.D., Princeton, 1934; m. Faye Hibbard, Sept. 14, 1934; children—Barbara Joan, Sylvia Jean, Linda June. Research fellow Harvard, 1934-36; faculty Northwestern U., 1936—, beginning as instr. chemistry, successively asst. prof., asso. prof., 1936-54, prof., 1954—, chmn. dept. chemistry, 1957-62. Mem. Am. Chem. Soc., Am. Phys. Soc., A.A.A.S., Phi Beta Kappa, Sigma Xi. Home: 606 Juniper Rd Glenview IL 60025 Office: Technological Inst Northwestern University Evanston IL 60201

FROST, BENJAMIN BURT, constrn. co. exec.; b. Chehalis, Wash., July 25, 1908; s. Edgar A. and Annie Grey (Millett) F.; A.B. in Engring., Stanford, 1930, M.E., 1933; m. Harriett Odin Noyes, June 26, 1940; children—Heidi, Suzanne (Mrs. Terry Burt), Anne Grey. Metallurgist, Inland Steel Co., 1934-36; with Arthur G. McKee and Co., Cleve., 1936—, v.p. iron and steel div., 1962-65, sr. v.p., 1965—, group v.p., 1967—, dir., 1968—. Dir. Am. Petroleum Inst., 1970. Recipient Joseph E. Johnson, Jr. award Am. Inst. Mining and Metall. Engrs., 1948. Mem. Am. Iron and Steel Inst., Am. Inst. Mining Engrs., Nat. Constructors Assn. (pres. 1971), Eastern States Blast Furnace and Coke Oven Assn. Club: Duquesne (Pitts.) Home: 21249 Claythorne Rd Shaker Heights OH 44122 Office: 6200 Oak Tree Blvd Independence OH 44131

FROST, DAVID (Paradine), author, producer, columnist; b. Apr. 7, 1939; s. W.J. Paradine Frost; M.A., Gonnville and Caius Coll., U. Cambridge (Eng.). TV appearances include That Was the Week That Was, 1962-63, Not So Much a Programme, More a Way of Life, 1964-65, The Frost Report 196667, Frost Over England, 1967, David Frost at the Phonograph, 1966, The Frost Programme, 1966-68, David Frost's Night Out in London, 1966-67; now star The Frost Programme, Frost on Friday David Frost Show; theatrical appearances include An Evening with David Frost, 1966; joint founder London Weekend TV; chmn., mng. dir. David Paradine Prodns. Recipient Golden Rose, Montreaux, 1967; Roy, TV Soc. silver medal, 1967. Richard Dimbleday award, 1967. Author: That Was the Week that Was, 1963; How to Live Under Labour, 1964; Talking with Frost, 1967; To England with Love, 1967; The Presidential Debate, 1968. Address: 46 Egerton Crescent London SW 3 England*

FROST, DEE LLOYD, banker; b. Centralia, Ill., Dec. 2, 1921; s. Cleon F. and Pearl (Boyle) F.; B.A., Ill. Coll., 1943; J.D., Drake U., 1948; grad. Stonier Grad. Sch. Banking, Rutgers U., 1954; m. Rosemary Rice, Sept. 23, 1943; children—Gregory Dee, Deborah Sue. Admitted to Ia. bar, 1948; with Ia.-Des Moines Nat. Bank, 1948—, sr. v.p. charge trust div., 1967—. Mem. bd. counselors Drake U. Law Sch., 1958—; treas., mem. exec. com. Polk County Soc. Crippled Children and Adults, 1968-69; adv. bd. Salvation Army Booth Meml. Hosp., 1970—. Served with USNR, 1943-46. Mem. Am., Ia., Polk County bar assns., Ia. Trust Assn. (exec. com. 1969-70), Am. Bankers Assn. (trust legislative council), Nat. Adv. Council Taxes and Estates, Drake U. Law Sch. Alumni Assn. (pres. 1966-67), Greater Des Moines C. of C., Order of Coif. 3131 Fleur Dr Des Moines IA 50315 Office: Ia-Des Moines Nat Bank 6th and Walnut Sts Des Moines IA 50304

FROST, DOUGLAS VAN ANDEN, nutritionist; b. Pitts., Oct. 31, 1910; s. Donald Karne and Amy (Craig) F.; B.A. in Chemistry, U. Ill., 1933; M.A. in Biochemistry, U. Wis., 1938, Ph.D., 1940; m. Muriel Louise Newkirk, Aug. 10, 1940; children—Nancy Newkirk (Mrs. James Kroening), Melodie Louise (Mrs. Peter Cooey), Roy Craig, Constance Manning. Analytical and research chemist Chappel Bros. Co., Pacini Labs., also Rival Packing Co., 1936; grad. asst. U. Wis., 1936- 39, research and teaching asst., 1938-40; with Abbott Labs., 1940-66, head nutrition research, 1946-59, research specialist nutrition, 1959-66; research asso. Dartmouth Med. Sch. Trace Element Lab. at Brattleboro Hosp., 1966-69; cons. Selenium-Tellurium Devel. Assn. Mem. com. on seleniumin nutrition Nat. Acad. Sci.-NRC, 1968—; chmn. Animal Nutrition Research Council, 1960; mem. amino acids adv. com. U.S. Pharmacopeia XIV, 1950; cons. USPHS Drinking Water Standards Com., also Industry Task Force Agrl. Arsenical Pesticides. Fellow N.Y. Acad. Scis., A.A.A.S.; mem. Assn. Vitamin Chemists (pres. 1953), Am. Inst. Nutrition (treas. 1962-65), Agrl. Research Inst. (v.p. 1965-66), Metric Assn. (pres. 1969-70), Poultry Sci. Assn., Soc. Animal Sci., Am. Feed Mfg. Assn. (nutrition council), Sigma Xi, Gamma Alpha, Phi Eta Sigma, Alpha Chi Sigma, Delta Tau Delta, Presbyn. (elder). Spl. research vitamin role nicotinic acid; devel. first i.v. fibrin hydrolysate, vitamin K source for poultry; anti-cancer role of selenium and arsenic. Home: 48 High St Brattleboro VT 05301

FROST, EARLE WESLEY, lawyer; b. Blue Rapids, Kan. July 11, 1899; s. John and Myrtle Mary (Pulleine) F.; B.S., Kan. State Coll., 1920; LL.B., Columbia U., 1923; m. Esther C. Houston, June 24, 1930; children—Earle W., Jr., Sylvia Elaine. Admitted to Mo. bar, 1923; asst. pros. atty. Jackson County, Mo., 1926; spl. asst. solicitor U.S. Dept. Agr., 1930-33; judge Municipal Ct., Kansas City, Mo., 1940-67; practice law, Kansas City, Mo. Bd. dirs. Helping Hand Inst. of Kansas City, Mo., Santa Claus Club, Inc. Chmn. traffic ct. div. Nat. Safety Council, 1942-43, 54-55; mem. enforcement com. Pres.'s Highway Safety Confs., 1946-67. Mem. Inst. Judicial Adminstrn., Inc. Mem. Cosmopolitan Internat. (pres. Kansas City club, 1941; internat. pres., 1946-47), Lawyers Assn. Kansas City (Mo.), Kansas City, Mo., Am. (chmn. com. on improvement in traffic cts. 1943-47; mem.

council sect. jud. adminstrn. 1947-52, vice chmn. 1952) bar assns., Am. Judicature Soc., Phi Delta Phi, Pi Kappa Delta, Sigma Phi Epsilon (nat. pres., 1945-46). Contbr. articles to legal jours. Home: 501 East 54th St Kansas City MO 64110 Office: 1006 Grand Av Kansas City MO 64106

FROST, FREDERICK GEORGE, Jr., architect; b. N.Y.C., June 10, 1907; s. Frederick G. and Bessie (Wilcox) F.; A.B., Princeton, 1930, M.F.A., 1932; postgrad. Yale, 1930-31; m. Gwendolyn B. Corwin, May 13, 1933; children—Arthur Corwin, Claudia Elizabeth (Mrs. Jeremy H. Dole), Frederick George III. Partner firm Frederick G. Frost, 1936-55, Frederick G. Frost, Jr. and Assos., N.Y.C., 1955-68; partner with A. Corwin Frost in Frost Assos., 1968—. Mem. N.Y. State Bd. Examiners of Architects, 1961-64; rep. Union Internationale des Architects to UN, 1964—; archtl. cons. rewriting N.Y.C. Bldg. Code, 1962-66. Dir. Citizens Housing and Planning Council N.Y., 1950—, v.p., 1954-56, 60- 65, pres., 1965-68. Trustee N.Y. Sch. for Deaf; bd. govs. Lawrence Hosp., Bronxville, 1947-58, pres., 1954-55; mem. architecture vis. com. R.I. Sch. Design. Fellow A.I.A. (1st v.p. and mem. exec. com. N.Y. chpt. 1970-71, pres. 1971-72); mem. Nat. Inst. Archtl. Edn., N.Y. Soc. Architects, N.Y. Bldg. Congress (dir.). Clubs: Century Assn. (N.Y.C.); Bronxville (N.Y.) Field (pres. bd. govs. 1952); Shenorock Shore (Rye, N.Y.); Princeton of N.Y. Home: 39 Elm Lane Bronxville NY 10708 also Dorset VT 05251 also Governors Harbour Eleuthera Bahamas Office: 30 E 42d St New York City NY 10017

FROST, FREDERICK WILLIAM, advt. exec.; b. San Francisco, Nov. 21, 1911; s. Frederick W. and Bertha (Arnett) F.; B.A., Union Coll., 1937; m. Joan Alice Matthews, May 19, 1946; children—Christopher, Jeremy. Copywriter Gen. Electric Co., Schenectady, N.Y., 1937-40; free lance writer, Mexico, 1940-42; copy group head, TV prodn. McCann Erickson, Inc., N.Y.C., 1950-53; copywriter Young & Rubicam, Inc., N.Y.C., 1946-50, v.p., adminstr. creative depts., mgr. TV prodn., 1953—. Chmn. Com. Use Minority Talent in TV, 1968—; mem. pub. relations com. Manhattan Eye and Ear Hosp., 1946-50, Eye Bank for Sight Restoration, 1946-50. Served with CIC, AUS, 1942-46. Mem. Wilton Library Assn. (pres. 1966-69), Union Coll. Alumni Assn. (alumni rep., 1957-67), Am. Assn. Advt. Agencies, Mohawk Valley Hunting Soc., Kappa Alpha. Episcopalian (vestryman, financial officer). Club: Wilton Riding. Home: Over the Brook 41 Nod Hill Rd Wilton CT 06897 Office: Young & Rubicam Inc 285 Madison Av New York City NY 10017

FROST, GEORGE ALEXANDER, marketing exec.; b. Montclair, N.J., July 16, 1918; s. Georg0 Walter and Elizabeth (Brabender) F.; grad. Montclair Acad., 1936; A.B., Williams College, 1940; m. Dorothy Hanau, Mar. 21, 1942; children—George A., Peter Douglas, William Kenneth. With George Fry & Assos., 1946-49; asst. to sales mgr. Cannon Mills, Inc., N.Y.C., 1949- 50, sales promotion mgr., 1950-52, asst. sales mgr., 1952-53, adv. mgr., 1953-58, v.p. marketing, 1958-62; v.p., gen. mgr. Chadbourn-Gotham, Inc., 1965-68; marketing coordinator, cotton div. J. P. Stevens Co., 1969—. Served from 2d lt. to col., USMCR, World War II. Home: 154 Hampshire Rd Wellesley MA 02181

FROST, HAROLD MAURICE, physician; b. Boston, May 21, 1921; s. Harold M. and Lucy (Church) F.; B.A., Dartmouth, 1943; M.D., Northwestern U., 1945; m. Elsa Claudius, Oct. 21, 1956; children—Harold Maurice III, Mary Jean, Michael, Patricia, Robert, Eric. Intern Mary Hitchcock Meml. Hosp., Hanover, N.H.; resident Worcester (Mass.) City Hosp., 1948-50. Buffalo Gen. Hosp., 1950-52, Buffalo Children's Hosp., 1952-53; clin. instr. orthopaedic surgery Buffalo U. Med. Sch., 1953-55; asst. prof. orthopaedic surgery Yale U. Sch. Medicine, 1955-57; asso. orthopaedic surgeon Henry Ford Hosp., Detroit, 1957—, dir. orthopedic research lab., 1957—, chmn. dept. orthopedic surgery, 1966—. Served to lt. (j.g.), M.C., USNR, 1946-48. Mem. A.M.A. (Hektoen gold medal award basic research 1963), Am. Acad. Orthopaedic Surgeons, Orthopaedics Research Soc., Am. Geriatric Soc., Am. Gerontol. Soc., Am. Rheumatism Soc., Detroit Physiol. Soc., Detroit Surg. Soc., Detroit Acad. Orthopaedic Surgery, Assn. of Bone and Joint Surgeons, also Mich. Orthopaedic Soc., Sigma Xi. Author: Clinical Fundamentals of Orthopaedic Surgery, 1953; Bone Remodeling Dynamics, 1963; Mathematical Elements of Bone Remodeling, 1964; Laws of Bone Structure, 1964; Bone Biodynamics, 1964; Dynamics in Osteonorosis and Osteomalacia, 1966: Interduction to Biomechanics, published 1966. Contributor articles to profl. jours. Asso. editor Clin. Orthopaedics. Spl. research biomechanics bone physiology and cell dynamics. Home: 922 Dowling St Bloomfield Hills MI 48013 Office: Henry Ford Hosp Detroit MI 48202

FROST, JACK, oil and cattle exec.; b. Greenville, Tex., May 26, 1900; s. E. Luther and Bernice (Caradine) F.; student Simmons Coll., So. Meth. U.; m. Lucy Adele Patterson, Nov. 12, 1948. With various cos., 1919-30; v.p. Byrd- Frost, Inc., 1930-54; pres. Frost Oil Corp., 1948—; chmn. bd. Toreador Royalty Co., 1952—; v.p. Leon Land & Cattle Co., 1958—; cattle rancher, Hudspeth, Edwards, Kinney and Nolan counties, Tex. Mem. Am. Assn. Petroleum Geologists, Am. Petroleum Inst., Soc. Independent Earth Scientists, South Tex., West Tex. geol. socs. Clubs: Brook Hollow Country, Dallas Athletic, Terpsichorean (Dallas); Argyle, Menger Patio, Fiesta San Antonio Commn., Permian Basin Pioneers (San Antonio). Home: 112 E Lynwood Av San Antonio TX 78212 Office: National Bank of Commerce Bldg San Antonio TX 78205

FROST, JAMES ARTHUR, univ. ofcl.; b. Manchester, Eng., May 15, 1918; s. Harry Arthur and Janet (Wilson) F.; brought to U.S., 1926, naturalized, 1942; B.A., Columbia, 1940, M.A., 1941, Ph.D., 1949; m. Elsie Mae Lorenz, Sept. 14, 1942; children—Roger Arthur, Janet, Elise. Tchr. Am. history high sch., Nutley, N.J., 1946-47; instr. State U. Coll. Oneonta, N.Y., 1947-49, asst. to pres., 1949-52, dean State U. Coll. at Oneonta, N.Y., 1952-64; asso. provost acad. planning State U. N.Y., Albany, 1964-65, exec. dean for four year colls., 1965-68, vice chancellor for univ. colls., 1968—, mem. editorial bd. State U. N.Y. Press; instr. Am. history Columbia, summers, 1947-48; Smith-Mundt prof. Am. hist. U. Ceylon, 1959-60. Mem. com. on research and devel. Coll. Entrance Exam. Bd.; mem. commn. on higher edn. Middle States Assn. Colls. and Secondary Schs. Served from pvt. to maj., AUS, 1941-46; Rockefeller grantee, 1959. Fellow N.Y. State Hist. Assn.; mem. Am. Hist. Assn. Presbyn. (elder). Author: Life on the Upper Susquehanna, 1783-1860, 1951; (with David M. Ellis, Harold Syrett, Harry J. Carman) A Short History of New York State, 1957, 2d edit., 1967; (with David M. Ellis and William B. Fink) New York: The Empire State, 1961, 3d edit., 1969; (with R. A. Brown, D. M. Ellis, William B. Fink) A History of the United States: The Evolution of A Free People, 1967, 2d edit., 1969. Contbr. articles on history, edn. to mags. Home: 42 Old Ox Rd Delmar NY 12054 Office: State U NY 8 Thurlow Terrace Albany NY 12203

FROST, LEON JOHN, food co. exec.; b. Mpls., Jan 19, 1922; s. Edward William and Mary (Daun) F.; student St. John's U., 1939-41; B.B.A. in Accounting, U. Minn., 1943; grad. Internat. Accountants Soc., 1946; m. Mary Shannon Frank, Nov. 27, 1943; children—Mark E., Richard P., Stephen G., Mary E., Christine A. With Green Giant Co., Le Sueur, Minn., 1946—, controller, 1968-71, v.p., controller, 1971—. Scoutmaster local Boy Scouts Am., 1946-47, mem. scouter's com., 1948—; finance chmn. bldg. fund for St. Anne's Sch. and Convent 1956—. Served to lt. USNR 1943-46. Mem. Le Sueur C. of C. (bd. dirs.), Planning Execs. Inst. (regional dir. 1966- 69), Delta Tau Delta. Roman Cath. (trustee). K.C. (4). Author article. Home: 302 Elmwood St Le Sueur MN 56058 Office: 1100 N 4th St Le Sueur MN 56058

FROST, LESLIE MISCAMPBELL, former prime minister Province of Ontario, Canada; b. Orillia, Ont., Can., Sept. 20, 1895; s. William Sword and Margaret Jane (Barker) F.; ed. Orillia Collegiate Inst., U. Toronto, Osgoode Hall; LL.D. Queen's U., Kingston, Ont., 1946, Ottawa U., 1948, McMaster U., 1951, U. Toronto, 1952, Assumption Coll. 1954, Royal Mil. Coll., 1960, Laurentian Univ., 1961; D.C.L., U. Western Ont., 1950; m. Gertrude Jane Carew, June 2, 1926. Admitted to Ont. bar, 1921; created King's Counsel, 1933; mem. Queen's Privy Council for Can., 1961—. Elected mem. Ont. Legislature, 1937, 43, 45, 48, 51, 55, 59; became treas. Ont. and minister of mines, 1943, pres. Provincial Mines Ministers Assn. of Can., 1944; became leader Progressive Conservative Party Ont., 1949-61; prime minister Prov. Ont., and pres. of the Council, 1949-61, treas., 1949-55; mem. law firm Frost, Inrig & Gorwill. Vice pres., dir. Victoria & Grey Trust Co., Bank of Montreal; dir. Can. Life Assurance Co., Massey-Ferguson, Ltd., Radio Station CKLV, and other firms. Chancellor of Trent U., Peterborough. Served from asst. adj. to co. comdr. Simcoe Regt., 1914- 18, with 20th Canadian Inf. Bn., France and Belgium, 1917-18. Mem. Canadian Legion (Sir Sam Hughes br. past zone rep.), Bencher Law Soc. Upper Can. (hon.), Phi Delta Phi (hon.). Mem. Progressive Conservative Party. Mem. United Ch. Can. (chmn. mgmt. bd. Lindsay). Mason (Shriner, 33). Clubs: Rotary (past pres.), Lindsay Curling, Albany, Twenty. Garrison, Royal Canadian Mil. Inst., National, Granite. Author: Fighting Men. Home: 17 Sussex St N Lindsay Ontario Canada Office: Temple Bldg 169 Kent St W Lindsay Ontario Canada

FROST, MORRIS MCCAMPBELL, former cement co. exec.; b. Nashville, July 10, 1898; s. Louis O. and Sarah (Faris) F.; student pub. schs.; m. Mary Wallace Lambright, Feb. 9, 1939; 1 step-dau., Caroline Rebecca (Mrs. Armin H. Smith Jr.); 1 son, Jack Harris. Sales exec. Fla. Portland Cement Co., Tampa, Fla., 1927-41; v.p., asst. to pres. Eastern Air Lines, N.Y.C., 1945-49, v.p. charge traffic and sales, 1950-54, v.p., exec. asst. chmn. bd., 1954-61; v.p. Fla. div. Gen. Portland Cement Co., Tampa, until 1968; dir. Midway Bank of Tampa, First Fla. Bancorp., Tampa; past pres., dir. Liberty Fed. Savs. & Loan Assn., Tampa. Pres., dir. Asso. Industries of Fla., 1963-64, chmn. bd. dirs., 1964-65; past sec., treas., vice chmn. Tampa Port Authority; bd. dirs. Greater Tampa Citizens Safety Council. Mem. Fla. Legislature, 1933, 35; Fla. Commerce and Industry Council, 1949-55. Served as col. USAAF, 1942-45. Decorated Legion of Merit, Officer Commendation Ribbon with 3 stars. Pres. Jr. C. of C., Jacksonville, Fla., 1932, Fla. State Jr. C. of C., 1937-42. Mem. Nat. Aero. Assn. (pres. Tampa chpt. 1939-41; regional v.p.), Fla. (dir., state aviation com. 1937-42), Tampa (v.p., chmn. aviation com. 1939-41, chmn. mil. affairs com.) chambers commerce, Hillsborough County Taxpayers Assn. (pres. dir.), Ye Mystic Krewe of Gasparilla, Mil. Order World Wars, Am. Legion. Elk, Mason (Shriner, Jester), Rotarian. Clubs: University, Palma Ceia Golf and Country, Tampa Yacht and Country (dir.) (Tampa); Seminole (Jacksonville); Wings (past dir.) (N.Y.C.). Home: 2401 S Dundee Tampa FL 33609

FROST, NORMAN BURKE, lawyer; b. Montgomery County, Md., Oct. 4, 1897; s. Edward Halleck and Elizabeth (Burke) F.; LL.B., Georgetown U., 1921; m. Mary Demova King, Apr. 27, 1918; children—Betty Demova, Norma. Admitted to D.C. bar, 1921; law clk. Supreme Ct. U.S., 1921-22; asso. counsel Landreau Arbitration, U.S.-Peru at London, 1922-23; mem. Frost & Towers, 1923-33, 48—, Frost, Myers & Towers, 1933-48; pres. Gen. Hydraulic Co., 1935-41, The Rennert Corp., Balt.; counsel Nat. Bank Wash.; dir. Financial Gen. Bankshares, Inc., Nat. Mortgage & Investment Co., Financial Securities Corp. Chmn. U.S. Air Force Price Adjustment Bd., 1944-45. Trustee James F. Mitchell Found.; chmn. bd. trustees James M. Johnston Trust for Charitable and Ednl. Purposes. With AEF, 1918-19; attached to staff Hon. Henry White Peace Commn., Paris, 1919. Recipient Exceptional Civilian Service award, 1945. Mem. Internat. Ins. Counsel, Am. Bar Assn., Bar Assn. D.C. Episcopalian. Clubs: Barristers, University, Columbia Country, Burning Tree, Chevy Chase (Washington); Everglades, Seminole (Palm Beach, Fla.). Home: 3523 Hamlet Pl Chevy Chase MD 20015 Office: Southern Bldg Washington DC 20005

FROST, ROBERT CLINTON, electronics co. exec.; b. Riverside, Ia., Nov. 13, 1921; s. Alan Ott and Arleigh (Buchwalter) F.; B.S., State U. Ia., 1943, J.D., 1952; m. Mary Lou Borg, Aug. 13, 1949; children—Alan Borg, Scot Joseph. Admitted to Ia. bar, 1952; with internat. operations dept. Collins Radio Co., Cedar Rapids, Ia., 1952-60, internat. counsel, Dallas, 1960—, asst. v.p., 1963-69. v.p., sec., 1969—; dir. various Collins subsidiaries. Served to lt. (j.g.) USNR, 1943-46. Mem. Confrerie des Chevaliers du Tastevin, Order of Coif. Office: Collins Radio Co Dallas TX 75207

FROST, STANLEY BRICE, clergyman, educator; b. London, Eng., Feb. 17, 1913; s. Henry George and Rosa (Goodbody) F.; B.D., London U., 1936, M.Th., 1943; Dr.Phil., Marburg U., 1938; D.D., Victoria U., Toronto, Ont., Canada, 1963, Montreal Presbyn. Coll., 1968; D.Litt., Meml. U., Newfoundland, 1967; m. Margaret Florence Bradshaw, July 29, 1939; children—David Brice, Valerie Margaret. Came to Can., 1956, citizen, 1961. Ordained to ministry Brit. Methodist Conf., 1939; pastor, London, 1939-42, Staffordshire, 1942-49; prof. O.T. studies Didsbury Coll., 1949- 56; spl. lectr. Hebrew, Bristol U., 1952-56; prof. O.T. lang. and lit. McGill U., 1956—, dean divinity, 1957-63, dean grad. studies and research, 1963-69, vice prin. adminstrn. and profl. faculties, 1969—. Mem. Canadian Bible Soc. (pres. 1960-61), Am. Assn. Theol. Schs. (pres. 1962-64), Canadian Assn. Grad. Schs. (pres. 1964). Author: The Pattern of Methodism, 1948; Old Testament Apocalyptic, 1952; The Beginning of the Promise-Eight Lectures in Genesis, 1960; Patriarchs and Prophets, 1963; Standing and Understanding; A Reappraisal of the Christian Faith, 1969. Home: 5 Granville Rd Hampstead Quebec Canada Office: McGill U Montreal Quebec Canada

FROST, THOMAS C., banker; b. San Antonio, Tex., Dec. 22, 1903; s. Thomas C. and Lillie C. (Beall) F.; student San Antonio Acad., U. Tex.; m. Ilse Herff, Aug. 3, 1925; children—Thomas C., Ilse Herff. With Frost Nat. Bank, San Antonio, 1924—, now chmn. bd.; sec. and dir. Elsinore Cattle Co. Trustee Marion Koogler McNay Art Inst. Episcopalian. Home: 105 Wyckham Rise San Antonio TX 78209 Office: Post Office Box 1600 San Antonio TX 78206

FROTHINGHAM, A. MICHAEL, advt. exec.; b. London, Eng., Oct. 4, 1921; s. Robert and Elinor (Shiff) F.; A.B., Dartmouth Coll., 1943; LL.B., Yale, 1948; m. Sara Struthers, July 31, 1948; children—Christen, Andrew, Victoria, Eric. Admitted to N.Y. bar, Conn. bar; asso. firm Coudert Bros., N.Y.C., 1948- 58; v.p., sec., gen. counsel Ted Bates & Co., Inc., N.Y.C., 1958-68, sr. v.p., sec., dir., 1968—. Served to lt. USNR, 1943-46. Mem. Am., N.Y. State bar assns., Assn. Bar City N.Y., Phi Beta Kappa. Home: Rye NY 10580 Office: 666 Fifth Av New York City NY 10019

FRUDAKIS, EVANGELOS WILLIAM, sculptor; b. Rains, Utah, May 13, 1921; s. William and Christina (Legerakis) F.; student Greenwich Work Shop, N.Y.C., 1935-39, Beaux Arts Inst. Design, N.Y.C., 1940-41, Pa. Acad. Fine Arts, 1941-42, 45-49, Am. Acad. in Rome, 1950-52; m. Virginia L. Parker, Nov. 12, 1949; children—Anthony, Jennifer. Asst. to sculptors Paul Manship and Jo Davidson, 1942-45; one man shows include Atlantic City Art Center, 1956, 61, Woodmere Art Gallery, 1957, 62, Phila. Art Alliance, 1958, Pa. Acad. Fine Arts, 1962; numerous group shows, 1940—, including Pa. Acad. Fine Arts anns., N.A.D. anns., Am. Acad. in Rome, Audubon Artists, Phila. Mus. Art, Allied Artists Am., Nat. Arts Club; rep. permanent collections Pa. Acad. Fine Arts, Lehigh Valley Art Alliance, Woodmere Art Gallery, also pvt. collections; tchr., demonstrator sculpture Nat. Acad. Fine Art, N.Y.C., 1941—; sculptor John F. Kennedy meml. monument Atlantic City Conv. Hall 1964; portrait works Brian Brewer Blades, 1969, Melvin R. Laird, 1970, Barnes Woodhall, 1971; coins and medals: Ted Shawn and Ruth St. Denis medal, Jacobs Pillow, Mass.; Gemini Space Flights Nat. Commemorative Soc., 1966; Dacron medallion Dupont, Wilmington, Del.; Capt. James Cook medal Hawaii Festival; Dolly Madison coin medal Sociéte Commemorative de Femmes Celebres, 1967; Joseph Brant coin Internat. Fraternal Commemorat Soc., 1968; Paul Lawrence Dunbar medal Am. Negro Commemorative Soc., 1969; St. Damasus I medal Cath. Commemorative Soc.; Life of Christ series 12 coin medals, 1968-70; Alfred the Great medal Britannia Commemorative Soc., 1970; Prince of Peace medal Cath. Commemorative Soc.; Scapular medal Cath. Art Guild, 1970; St. John the 4th Apostle 12 Apostle series Cath. Commemorative Medal Soc., 1970; John Quincy Adams and Lillian Wald medals Hall of Fame for Great Ams., 1971; Brian Brewer Blades award medal Statesmen in Medicine, 1970. Mem. Art Commn., Atlantic City, N.J. Served with AUS, World War II; ETO. Recipient 2 1st prizes Greenwich Work Shop, 1939, Beaux Art Inst., 1941; lst Julian B. Slevin prize Pa. Acad. Fine Arts, 1941, Stimson prize, 1947, Stewardson prize, 1947, Cresson European scholarship, 1947, spl. citation achievement, 1948, 1st hon. mention fellowship, 1948, Fellowship gold medal, 1949, 55, 56, Henry Scheidt Meml. scholarship, 1949; lst hon. mention Prix de Rome, 1942; Prix de Rome, 1950, 51; Helen Foster Barnett prize N.A.D. 1948, Thomas R. Proctor prize, 1957; Eben Demarest Trust Fund prize, 1949; Louis Comfort Tiffany scholarship, 1949; Da Vinci Alliance silver medal, 1955; hon. mention sculpture Woodmere Art Gallery, 1955; lst prize sculpture profl. class Regional Council Community Art Centers, 1955; Sculpture House award Allied Artists Am., 1959; best portrait sculpture award Nat. Sculpture Soc.-Nat. Art Club, 1961; John Gregory award Nat. Sculpture Soc., 1963; Nat. Fountain Competition award Little Rock, 1965; Elizabeth N. Watrous gold medal N.A.D., N.Y.C., 1968; Dessie Greer prize N.A.D., N.Y.C., 1970. N.A. Fellow Pa. Acad. Fine Arts (bd. mgrs.), Am. Acad. in Rome, Nat. Sculpture Soc. (council); mem. Phila. Art Alliance (sculpture com.), Allied Artists Am.; hon. mem. Am. Inst. Commemorative Art. Address: 10 S Oxford Av Ventnor NJ 08406

FRUGE, AUGUST, univ. press exec.; b. Weiser, Ida., Dec. 5, 1909; s. August and Orion (Kirkpatrick) F.; A.B., Stanford, 1933; library certificate, U. Cal. at Berkeley, 1937, M.A., 1949; m. Grete Wiese, Dec. 31, 1938 (div. Jan. 1958); 1 son, John; m. 2d, Susan J. Haverstick, Jan. 25, 1959. With U. Cal. Library, Berkeley, 1936-39; head order librarian Cal. State Library, 1939-44; asst. mgr. U. Cal. Press, 1944-47, asso. mgr., 1947- 50, mgr., 1950-58, dir., 1958—; dir. IBEG, Ltd., London. Bd. dirs. Centro Interamericano de Libros Academicos, Mexico City, 1964—. Mem. Assn. Am. U. Presses (pres. 1957-59). Democrat. Club: Sierra (editor bull. 1954-59, chmn. editorial bd. 1960—, bd. dirs. 1969—). Home: 683 Oberlin Av Berkeley CA 94708. Office: U Cal Press 2223 Fulton St Berkeley CA 94720

FRUHBECK-DE BURGOS, RAFAEL, condr., music dir.; b. Burgos, Spain, Sept. 15, 1933; s. Wilhelm and Stefanie (Ochs) F.; student law U. Madrid (Spain), 1950-53, conservatoire Bilbao and Madrid, 1950-53; grad. cum laude Acad. Music Munich (Germany), 1958; m. Maria Carmen Martinez, Dec. 21, 1959; children—Rafael, Gemma. Prin. condr. orch., Bilbao, Spain, 1958-62; music dir. Nat. Orch. Madrid (Spain), 1962—; also music dir. Düsseldorf Symphoniker, Germany, 1966—. Decorated Gran Cruz Al Merito Civil, encomienda con placa de la Orden de Isabel La Catolica. encomienda con placa de la Orden de Alfonso X (Spain). Home: 20 Reyes Magos Madrid 7 Spain

FRUMKIN, PAUL, TV producer; b. Omaha, Aug. 20, 1914; s. Louis and Anna (Dubnoff) F.; student Omaha U., 1932-34. Advt. mgr. M.L. Rothschild, Chgo., 1936-42; v.p. W.H. Altice Advt. Agy., 1947-51; producer Mike Douglas Hi Ladies, WGN-TV, 1952-55; producer-writer At Random, Susie's Show, CBS-TV, Chgo., 1956-62; producer Kup's Show, ABC-TV, Chgo., 1962-68; producer Kup's Show, NBC-TV, Chgo., 1968—. Mem. Chgo. Unltd., 1960—, Council Fgn. Relations, 1958—. Served with AUS, 1942-46; ETO. Recipient Emmy award for best producer, 1966. Mem. Acad. TV Arts and Scis. (pres. Chgo.), Sigma Delta Chi. Home: 235 W Eugenie St Chicago, IL 60614. Office: NBC-TV Merchandise Mart Chicago IL 60654

FRUTON, JOSEPH STEWART, biochemist; b. Czestochowa, Poland, May 14, 1912; s. Charles and Ella (Eisenstadt) F.; B.A., Columbia, 1931, Ph.D., 1934; M.A. (hon.), Yale, 1950; m. Sofia Simmonds, Jan. 29, 1936. Asst. in chemistry Rockefeller Inst. for Med. Research, 1934-38, asso., 1938-45; with Yale, 1945—, successively asso. prof. physiol. chemistry, prof. biochemistry, 1951-57, Eugene Higgins prof. biochemistry, 1957—, chmn. dept. biochemistry, 1951-67, dir. div. sci., 1959- 62; spl. fellow Rockefeller Found., 1948, Commonwealth Fund, 1962-63. Mem. div. chemistry and chem. tech. Nat. Research Council, 1950-52, chem. biol. coordination center, 1946-51, fellowship bd., 1951-53, 55- 58, panel on enzymes, chmn. com. on growth, 1946-49, exec. com., div. med. scis., 1961-64; sci. advisor NIH, 1951-52, Anna Fuller Fund, 1951—; vis. prof. Rockefeller U., 1969. Recipient Lilly Award in biol. chemistry, 1944; Benjamin Franklin fellow Royal Soc. Arts. Fellow A.A.A.S.; mem. Internat. Commn. Biochem. Nomenclature, Am. Soc. of Biol. Chems., Am. Chem. Soc., Chem. Soc. Gt. Britain, Biochem. Soc. (Gt. Britain), Harvey Soc., N.Y. Acad. Sci., History Sci. Soc. (mem. council 1951-54), Am. Philos. Soc., Nat. Acad. Sci., Am. Acad. Arts and Sci., Sigma Xi, Phi Beta Kappa. Co-author: General Biochemistry (with S. Simmonds), 1953, 2d edit., 1958. Mem. editorial bd. Jour. Biol. Chemistry, 1948-58, Biochemistry, 1962—. Home: 123 York St New Haven CT 06511

FRY, ARTHUR JAMES, educator; b. Dodson, Mont., Mar. 10, 1921; s. Sidney Wilbert and May Lenora (Brown) F.; B.S. in Chemistry, Mont. State Coll., 1943; Ph.D. U. Cal. at Berkeley, 1951; m. Lois Marie Gunning, Nov. 16, 1947; children—Gene Richard, Brian Douglas, Marian Gail. Asso. chemist Oak Ridge Nat. Lab., 1946-48; faculty U. Ark., Fayetteville, 1951—, prof., 1959—, chmn. dept., 1956-57, 64-67. With Coll. Chemistry Cons. Service, 1967—; evaluation panelist various NSF programs; vis. prof. U. Auckland, New Zealand, 1969-70, U. Adelaide, Australia, 1970. Active various local sch. and civic coms. Served with USNR, 1944-46. Recipient Faculty research award Ark. Alumni Assn., 1969. Fellow A.A.A.S.; mem. Am. Chem. Soc. (pres. local sect., nat. councilor), Chem. Soc. London, Ark. Acad. Sci. (past pres.), Am. Assn. U. Profs., Sigma Xi,

Alpha Chi Sigma, Phi Kappa Phi, Phi Eta Sigma. Kiwanian. Contbr. articles to profl. jours., textbooks. Home: 1508 Wedington Dr Fayetteville AR 72701

FRY, CHRISTOPHER, dramatist; b. Bristol, Eng., Dec. 18, 1907; s. Charles John Harris and Marguerite Hammond Fry; student Beford Modern Sch.; m. Phyllis Marjorie Hart, 1936. Writer: The Boy with a Cart, 1939 (prod. 1950): The First Born. 1945 (prod. 1952); A Phoenix Too Frequent, 1946 (prod. 1946); The Lady's Not for Burning, 1949 (prod. 1948, 1949); Venus Observed, 1950 (prod. 1950); Ring Round the Moon, 1950 (prod. 1950); A Sleep of Prisoners, 1951 (prod. 1951); The Dark is Light Enough, 1954 (prod. 1954); Curtmantle (prod. Holland, 1961); A Yard of Sun, 1970; one of the film script- writers The Bible, 1966. Author film commentary for The Queen is Crowned (coronation film), 1953. Translator: The Lark, 1955: Tiger at the Gates, 1955: Duel of Angels, 1957; Barabbas, 1962; author: Heat of the Day, A Summer Comedy, 1970; Peer Gynt, 1970. Fellow Royal Soc. Lit. Recipient Queen's Gold medal for poetry, 1962. Home: 37 Blomfield Rd London W 9 England

FRY, EDWARD EWART, can co. exec.; b. Montreal, Que., Can., Aug. 9, 1916; s. Ewart Gladstone and Ida Marion (Munro) F.; mgmt. tng. course, U. Western Ont., 1955; m. Caroline Melva Smith, Oct. 5, 1944; children—Gary, Gail. With Continental Can Co. Can. Ltd., 1936—, v.p. metal div., exec. v.p., 1964- 66, pres., chief exec. officer, 1966—, also dir. Mem. Board Trade Met. Toronto. Mem. Canadian C. of C., Canadian Mfrs. Assn. (council), Canadian Pulp and Paper Assn. (mem. exec. bd.). Mem. United Ch. Can. Clubs: Mt. Stephen (Montreal): Granite, National, Rosedale Golf (Toronto): Canadian (N.Y.C.): Briars Golf and Country (Keswick). Home: 11 Killarney Rd Toronto 7 Ontario Canada Office: 790 Bay St Toronto Ontario Canada

FRY, EDWARD IRAD, educator; b. Long Branch, N.J., Jan. 7, 1924; s. Wallace Cordiner and Abigail Elizabeth (Hidden) F.; B.A., U. Tex., 1949, M.A., 1950; Ph.D., Harvard, 1958; m. Peggy June Crooke, Dec. 23, 1950. Cons. to U.S. Air Force, also asst. prof. Antioch Coll., 1955-56; asso. prof. U. Neb., Lincoln, 1956-66; prof. anthropology So. Meth. U., Dallas, 1966—. Served with USAAF, 1942-45. Fulbright fellow New Zealand and South Pacific, 1953-54; Hong Kong U., 1963-64. Mem. A.A.A.S., N.Y. Acad. Scis., Soc. for Study Human Biology, Am. Assn. Phys. Anthropologists (exec. com. 1967-69) sec.-treas. 1969—), Sigma Xi. Research on child growth and human biology especially skeletal aging. Home: 7139 Edgerton Dr Dallas TX 75231

FRY, EDWIN MAXWELL, architect; b. Cheshire, Eng., Aug. 2, 1899; s. Ambrose and Lydia (Thompson) F.; student Liverpool Inst., 1910-17, Liverpool U. Sch. Arch., 1918-22; m. Ethel Speakman, 1927 (marriage dissolved); 1 dau., Ann (Mrs. Robert Collin); m. 2d Jane B. Doew, Apr. 25, 1942. Partner firm Gropius & Fry, 1934-36, London, Maxwell Fry and Jane Drew, London, 1945-50, Fry, Drew, Drake & Lasdun, London, 1951-58, Fry Drew & Partners, London, 1958—; cons. planner Hatfield New Town; prof. arch. Royal Acad. Arts; town planning adv. resident minister for West Africa, 1943-45; sr. architect to new Capital Chandigarh, Punjab, 1951-54. Served with Royal Engrs., 1939-44. Fellow A.I.A., Royal Inst. Brit. Architects. Home: 63 Gloucester Pl London WIH 4DJ England Office: 63 Gloucester Pl London WIH 4DJ England

FRY, F. E. J., educator; b. Woking Surrey, Eng., Apr. 17, 1908: s. Ernest and Mabel- (Holmes) F.; B.A., U. Toronto, 1933, M.A., 1935, Ph.D., 1936; D.Sc., U. Man., 1970; m. Irene Stewart. Oct. 19, 1935; children—John Ernest, James William, Frederick Joseph. Faculty U. Toronto, Ont., Can., 1936—, prof. zoology, 1956—. Served to squadron leader RCAF, 1941-45. Decorated Order Brit. Empire. Fellow Royal Soc. Can. Home: 10 Riverlea Rd Weston Ontario Canada Office: U Toronto Toronto Ontario Canada

FRY, GEORGE ARTHUR, mgmt. cons.; b. Swayzee, Ind., Oct. 20, 1901; s. Arthur West and Anna (Moulder) F.; B.S., Northwestern U., 1924; m. Geraldine Brode, June 17, 1926; children—Janet Elizabeth (Mrs. Janet F. Kuney), Willard Arthur. Asst. dir. personnel Northwestern U., 1924-25; with Edwin G. Booz Surveys, 1925-36; partner Booz, Fry, Allen & Hamilton, 1936-42; sr. partner Fry, Lawson & Co., Chgo., 1942-46, founder, successor firm George Fry & Assos., Inc. (now Fry Consultants, Inc.); dir., chmn. finance com. Hurletron, Inc. Chmn. Citizens for Eisenhower and Nixon Com., 1952. Mem. Northwestern U. Assos., Am. Mgmt. Assn., S.A.R., Sigma Nu. Republican. Methodist. Clubs: Chicago, Commonwealth (Chgo.); Glen View (Golf, Ill.); Riomar Country, Riomar Bay Yacht (Vero Beach, Fla.). Home: Glen View Club Golf IL 60029 (winter) Porpoise Point Vero Beach FL 32960 Office: 231 S LaSalle St Chicago IL 60606

FRY, GLENN ANSEL, educator, optometrist; b. Wellford, S.C., Sept. 10, 1908; s. Sebastian R. and Amy (Brown) F.; A.B., Davidson Coll., 1929; M.A., Duke, 1931, Ph.D., 1932; D.O.S. (hon.), No. Ill. Coll. Optometry, 1939; m. Martha Cooper Ray, Sept. 20, 1935; children—Roger Ansel, Amelia Ray, Randall Gregory, NRC fellow Washington U., 1932-34, research asst. ophthalmology, 1934-35; asst. prof. physiol. optics Ohio State U., 1935- 42, asso. prof., 1942-46, prof. physiol. optics, dir. Sch. Optometry, 1946-66, regents prof., 1966—, co-director Inst. Research in Vision, 1949-56; lectr. Brit. Optical Assn., 1955. Mem. U.S. nat. committee of the Internat. Commn. Illumination; mem. Armed Forces- NRC Vision Com.; asso. editor Jour. Optical Soc. Am.; editorial board Am. Jour. Optometry. Fellow Am. Acad. Optometry, Illuminating Engring. Soc.; mem. Psychonomic Soc., Am. Optometric Assn., Optical Soc. Am., Brit. Optical Assn., Inter-Soc. Color Council, A.A.A.S. Home: 200 Arden Rd Columbus, OH 43214.

FRY, GUY, artist; b. Milton, Pa., Aug. 5, 1903; s. William H. and Sarah (Mauger) F.; student Phila. Coll. Art, 1922-26. Free lance artist, 1926—; exhibited one man show Phila. Art Alliance; exhibited group shows Pa. Acad. Fine Arts, Phila. Art Alliance, Nat. Acad. Design, Am. Watercolor Soc. Past chmn. bd. Phila. Coll. Art; past trustee Phila. Mus. Art. Recipient Zimmerman award Phila. Water Color Club, 1959, Dana award Phila. Water Color Club, 1960, Albert Dorne award Nat. Acad. Design, 1970, Silver medal Art Dirs. Club Phila., 1971. Mem. Phila. Art Dirs. Club (past pres.), Nat. Soc. Art Dirs. (past pres.). Address: 750 Old Lancaster Rd Berwyn PA 19312

FRY, J. PATRICK, corp. exec.; b. Weatherford, Tex., 1900. Formerly sr. v.p., treas., now cons., dir. Thorofare Markets, Inc., also mem. exec. com.; dir., mem. exec. com. Pitts. Brewing Co. Home: PO Box 44 Murrysvile PA 15668 Office: PO Box 237 Pittsburgh PA 15230

FRY, JOHN HAYDEN, univ. athletic dir.; b. Eastland, Tex., Feb. 28, 1929; s. John Hayden and Cora (Hodge) F.; B.A., Baylor U., 1951; m. Hue Leita Zachry, Dec. 29, 1951; children—Hayden Randolph, Zachry Hodge, John Kelly, Adrian Warren, Robin Elaine. High sch. counselor, backfield coach, Odessa, Tex., 1951, tchr., head coach football, 1955-59; defensive football coach Baylor U., 1959, 60; offensive backfield caoch U. Ark., 1961; head football coach So. Meth. U., 1962—, athletic dir., 1964—. Adv. bd. Wilson Sporting Goods Co. Bd. dirs. Fellowship Christian Athletes, Pop Warner's Little League. Served to capt. USMCR, 1952-55. Named Sir. Coll. Coach of the Year Tex. Sports Writers Assn., 1962; Southwest Football Coach of Year, Coach and Athlete, 1962; Coach of Year, S.W. Conf., 1966. Mem. Tex. High Sch. Coaches Assn., Am. Football Coaches Assn. Methodist. Home: 4409 Goodfellow St Dallas TX 75229.

FRY, LESLIE MCGEE, lawyer; b. Louisiana, Mo., Mar. 13, 1913; s. Octa McGee and Sally (Wilcoxen) F.; student U. Mo., 1930-35; LL.B., U. Louisville, 1939; m. Jean Sauer, May 2, 1936; children—Leslie Mack, Maralyne (Mrs. John Mallott), Sally Catherine, Robert James, Stanley Preston. Admitted to Ky. bar, 1938, Nev. bar. 1946, also U.S. Supreme Ct. bar; partner firm Fry & Catinna, Hartford, Ky., 1939-41; practice in Reno, 1946—; partner firm Fry & Fry, 1965—. Pres. Future Farmers Am., 1930-31; pres. Nev. area council Boy Scouts Am., 1953-58, regional rep., 1953—, nat. rep., 1953—. Chmn. Washoe County Republican Com., 1956-58, 64-66; mem. Am. Battle Monuments Commn., 1970. Served to maj. F.A., AUS, 1941-45; PTO. Decorated Bronze Star; recipient Silver Beaver award Boy Scouts Am., 1947, Silver Antelope award, 1968. Mem. Am., Nev. bar assns., Kappa Alpha (pres. 1934). Presbyn. Mason (Shriner), Lion. Home: 991 Whitaker Dr Reno NV 89503. Office: 105 N Sierra St Reno NV 89505

FRY, MALCOLM CRAIG, clergyman; b. Detroit, June 6, 1928; s. Dwight Malcolm and Josephine (Craig) F.; student Bible Bapt. Sem., 1950; Th.B., Am. Div. Sch., Chgo., 1959; student McNeese State Coll., Lake Charles, La., 1958-61; B.S., Austin Peay State Coll., 1962; M.Ed., U. Ariz., 1969; m. Myrtle Mae Downing, June 5, 1948; children—Pamela (Mrs. Ralph Edward Flanary, Jr.), Malcolm Craig, Rebecca Dawn, Matthew Dwight. Asst. jewelery store mgr. Sonne Bros., Norwich, N.Y., 1948-50; ordained to ministry Free Will Bapt. Ch., 1953; pastor in Lake Charles, La., 1955-58, 59-61, Bryan, Tex., 1958-59, Ashland City, Tenn., 1961-62; asst. pastor in Royal Oak, Mich., 1962-64; pastor First Free Will Bapt. Ch., Tucson, 1964-71; dir. curriculum and research Bd. Ch. Tng. Service, Nat. Assn. Free Will Baptists, Nashville, 1971—. Program writer adult tng. mag. Nat. Assn. Free Will Baptists, 1963-68, clk., 1965-67, chmn. stewardship commn., 1962-67. Sec.-treas. Tucson chpt. Nat. Assn. Evangelicals, 1965-68, mem. stewardship commn., 1962—; moderator Ariz. Assn. Free Will Baptists, 1965-67, 69-71. Served with AUS, 1946-48, with USAF, 1951-57; Korea. Author: Total Involvement, 1964; Why Worry?, 1967; Sunday School Evangelism, 1969. Home: 3727 Valley Ridge Dr Nashville TN 37211 Office: 1134 Murfreesboro Rd Nashville TN 37217

FRY, MORTON HARRISON, banker; b. Ephrata, Pa., Jan. 27, 1888; s. Jacob Martin and Margaret (Ruth) F.; prep. edn., Franklin and Marshall Acad., Lancaster, Pa. A.B., Princeton, 1909; m. Julia Gladys Angell, June 22, 1909; children—Morton Allan Harrison, George Thomas Clark. Partner Scholle Bros., bankers, N.Y. City, 1923-42, Riter & Co., investment bankers, 1942—; pres. Overseas Securities Co.; dir. and mem. exec. com. Alabama Great Southern Railroad; pres., dir. Overseas Securities Co., Inc.; pres., trustee Rembrandt Corp.; dir. Northwest Airlines, Inc. Trustee Hun School, Princeton, New Jersey; trustee of Athens Coll., Greece. Mem. Am. Acad. Political Sci. Phi Beta Kappa. Democrat. Clubs: University, Princeton, Tiger Inn (Princeton U.), Down Town Assn. Author: Bank Acceptances as an Investment; contbr. numerous articles on financial subjects. Address: 40 Wall St New York City NY 10005 Deceased.

FRY, SAMUEL ROEDER, banker, fabric co. exec.; b. Reading, Pa., Nov. 10, 1901; s. Howard Morton and Ella Amanda (Roeder) F.; student N.Y. Mil. Acad., U. Pa.; m. Margaret Thun, June 26, 1924; children—Barbara Ann, Thomas Morton, Howard Morton II, Margaret Victoria. Office mgr., asst. sec. Narrow Fabric Co., Reading, Pa., 1923, v.p., dir., 1931-48, pres., chmn. bd., 1948—; chmn. bd. Reading Trust Co., 1955—; treas., dir. Wyomissing Fed. Savs. & Loan Assn., 1933—. Chmn. supervisory bd. Berks County Boys' Home, 1946—; trustee St. Joseph's Hosp., Reading, Pennsylvania. Mem. Theta Delta Chi. Clubs: Union League (N.Y.C.); Radnor Hunt, Racquet (Phila.); Rolling Rock (Ligonier, Pa.); Bath and Tennis (Palm Beach, Fla.). Home: Museum Rd Wyomissing PA 19610 Office: Wyomissing Corp 7th and Reading Av West Reading PA 19610

FRY, SHERRY EDMUNDSON, sculptor; b. Creston, Ia., Sept. 29, 1879; s. John Wesley and Ellen (Green) F.; Art. Inst. Chgo., 1900; Academie Julian, Paris, 1902; Ecole des Beaux Arts, Paris, 1903; Florence, Italy, 1904; pupil of Frederick MacMonnies, Barrias, Verlet, and Lorado Taft; unmarried. Traveled and studied in Italy, Greece and Germany, 1908-11; hon. mention, Salon, Paris, 1906, gold medal, 1907; Nat. Roman prize, 1908 (held for 3 yrs.); silver medal, Panama P.I. Expn., San Francisco, 1915; Elizabeth Watrous gold medal, N.A. exhbn., 1917; William M. R. French gold medal, Art Inst., Chgo., 1923. Prin. works; reliefs on Grant Memorial, Washington, D.C.; fountains for William A. Clark, Jr., and Walter B. James; pediments. Frick House (N.Y.C.), mausoleum (Los Angeles); pediment for Labor and Interstate Commerce Bldg.; statues, Ira Allen. U. of Vt.; Capt. Abbey, , Enfield, Conn.; Indian Chief, Oskaloosa, Ia.; pediment, Labor & Commerce Bldg., Washington, 1936; etc. N.A., 1931; mem. Nat. Sculpture Soc. Enlisted as pvt. U.S. Army, Sept. 5, 1917; served in Camouflage Corps; 1 yr. as liaison officer, camouflage sect., French Army. Club: Century. Home-Studio: Mt Algo Kent CT 06757

FRY, THOMAS ALBERT, Jr., clergyman; b. Cleve., Apr. 23, 1919; s. Thomas Albert and Bertha (Wiggs) F.; B.A., Davidson Coll., 1940; B.D., Union Theol. Sem., Richmond, Va., 1943, Th.M., 1949; D.D., King Coll., 1952; m. Louise Sullivan, May 15, 1942; children—Thomas Albert III, Charles Sullivan. Ordained to ministry Presbyn. Ch., 1943; pastor in Blackstone, Va., 1943-46, Red Springs, N.C., 1946-50, Bristol, Tenn., 1950-56, Atlanta, 1956-59, Dallas, 1959- -; pastor on radio programs. Bd. dirs. Children's Med. Center, Dallas, Presbyn. Village, Dallas, Gen. Council Presbyn. Ch. U.S. Recipient Freedom Found. award, 1960. Mem. UN Assn. (pres. Dallas 1970-71). Author: Get Off the Fence-Morals for Moderns, 1964; Doing What Comes Supernaturally, 1966; Change, Chaos and Christianity, 1967; They Dared To Dream, 1972. Home: 7317 Baxtershire St Dallas TX 75230 Office: 408 Park St Dallas TX 75201

FRY, THORNTON CARL, mathematician; b. Findley, O., Jan. 7, 1892; s. William Watson and Elizabeth Hanna (Dingle) F.; A.B., Findlay Coll., 1912, D.Sc., 1958; A.M., U. Wis., 1913, Ph.D., 1920. Instr., U. Wis., 1912-16; mathematician Western Electric Co., 1916-24; mathematician Bell Telephone Labs., 1924-56, dir. math. research, 1940-44, dir. switching research, 1944-47, dir. switching research and engring., 1947-49, asst. to exec. v.p., 1949-51, asst. to pres., 1951-56, now ret.; communications cons. Internat. Tel. & Tel. Co., 1956-57; sr. cons. Univac div. Sperry-Rand Corp., 1956-57, v.p., dir. Univac engring. Remington Rand div., 1957-60, v.p. research and engring., 1960-61; cons. to dir. Nat. Center for Atmospheric Research, 1961-67; cons., dir. Granville-Phillips Co., 1964—; sci. cons. Boeing Sci. Research Labs., 1964-70; lectr. elec. engring. Mass. Inst. Tech., 1927; lectr. math. Princeton, 1929-30. Mem. div. 7, Nat. Def. Research Com., 1940-44, chief sect. 7.2, 1942-44, dep. chief applied math. panel, 1942-45. Recipient Presdl. Certificate of Merit for Nat. Def. Research Com. achievements, 1948. Fellow Am. Phys. Soc., A.A.A.S., Inst. of Math. Statistics, I.E.E.E.; mem. Am. Math. Soc., Math. Assn. Am., Am. Astron. Soc., Soc. for Promotion Engring. Edn., Econometric Soc., Sigma Xi. Author: Elementary Differential Equations, 1929; Probability and Its Engineering Uses, 1928. Contbr. profl. jours. Home: 500 Mohawk Dr Boulder CO

FRY, WILLIAM FREDERICK, educator; b. Carlisle, Ia., Dec. 16, 1921; s. William C. and Flossie (Parsons) F.; B.S. in Elec. Engring., Ia. State Coll., 1943, Ph.D. in Physics, 1951; m. Virgie Eastburn, June 14, 1943; children—David A., Diane E. AEC postdoctoral fellow U. Chgo., 1951-52; faculty U. Wis., 1952—, prof. physics, 1956—. Served with USNR, 1944-45. Fulbright lectr., Italy, 1956-57; Guggenheim fellow, 1956-57. Research in high-energy physics, acoustics of musical instruments. Home: 626 Langdon St Madison WI 53706

FRY, WILLIAM H., lawyer; b. Cin., Oct. 20, 1905; A.B. cum laude, Ohio State U., 1927; LL.B., Xavier U., 1933. Admitted to Ohio bar, 1933; now partner firm Rendigs, Fry, Kiely & Dennis, Cin. Served to lt. col. AUS, 1942-45. Fellow Am. Coll. Trial Lawyers; mem. Am., Ohio State, Cin. bar assns., Internat. Assn. Ins. Counsel. Office: Central Trust Tower Cincinnati OH 45202*

FRYBURGER, VERNON RAY, Jr., educator; b. Cin., June 9, 1918; s. Vernon Ray and Florence Rose (Steding) F.; B.S. in Bus. Adminstrn., Miami U., Oxford, O., 1939; Ph.D. in Econs., U. Ill., 1950; m. Marjorie Anne Clarke, June 19, 1948; 1 dau., Candace. Salesman, U.S. Printing & Lithograph Co., 1940-41; instr. marketing Miami U., 1941-43; asso. research dir. Nat. Assn. Broadcasters, 1946; asst. prof. journalism U. Ill., 1947-53; faculty Northwestern U., 1953—, prof. advt. and marketing, chmn. dept. advt., 1959—; vis. prof. marketing U. Hawaii, 1965—. Ednl. dir. Inst. Advanced Advt. Studies, 1963—; nat. asso. dean Am. Acad. Advt., 1964-65, nat. dean, 1965-66, chmn. bd.; cons. to bus., 1954—. Bd. dirs. Lake Forest Library. Served to lt., submarines, USNR, 1943-46; PTO. Mem. Am. Marketing Assn., Assn. Edn. Journalism, Beta Gamma Sigma, Kappa Tau Alpha, Delta Tau Delta, Delta Sigma Pi, Artus. Presbyn. Author: (with C. H. Sandage) Advertising Theory and Practice, 1963; (with Boyd and Westfall) Cases in Advertising Management, 1964. Editor: (with C. H. Sandage) The Role of Advertising, 1960. Home: Shoreacres Rd PO Box 62 Lake Bluff IL 60044 Office: Northwestern Univ Evanston IL 60201

FRYCHIUS, SVEN, Swedish diplomat; b. Fryksande, Sweden, Mar. 27, 1907; s. Gustaf and Karolina (Erikson) Svenson; student U. Uppsala (Sweden), 1926-28, U. Lund (Sweden), 1930-32, also U. Stockholm (Sweden); m. Valborg Elisabeth Anderson, Aug. 30, 1955. Reporter, provincial dailies, 1928-30, 32-35; reporter, daily Svenska Morgonbladet, Stockholm, 1935-40; head polit. press dept. Swedish Info. Bd., 1940-45; head press sect. Fgn. Ministry, 1945-55; press attache, Oslo, Norway, 1955-62; press counsellor, Washington, 1962—. Adviser Govt. Com. on Psychol. Def., 1949-55. Decorated knight Swedish Order Vasa, Swedish Order No. Star, knight comdr. Norwegian Order St. Olaf. Mem. Publicistklubben Stockholm. Clubs: Nat. Press, Capital Press (Washington). Contbr. profl. jours. Home: 3117 N Nelson St Arlington VA 22207 Office: 600 Watergate Washington DC 20037

FRYE, GLENN MCKINLEY, Jr., physicist, educator; b. Ithaca, Mich., Apr. 20, 1926; s. Glenn McKinley and Margaret (Woodruff) F.; student Albion Coll., 1943-44; B.S., U. Mich., 1946, M.S., 1947, Ph.D., 1950; postgrad. U. Glasgow (Scotland), 1950-51; m. Ruth Lowson, June 1, 1948; children—Douglas Alan, Stephen Andrew, Thomas Jeffrey. Staff mem. physics div. Los Alamos Sci. Lab., 1951-58; physicist research div. U.S. AEC, Washington, 1959-60; asso. prof. physics Case Inst. Tech., Cleve., 1960-66, prof., 1966—. Served to ensign USNR, 1944-46. Fulbright fellow, 1950. Mem. Am. Phys. Soc., Am. Astronautical Soc., A.A.A.S., Phi Beta Kappa, Sigma Xi, Tau Beta Pi, Sigma Nu. Home: 14817 Drexmore St Shaker Heights OH 44120 Office: 10900 Euclid Av Cleveland OH 44106

FRYE, JOHN CHAPMAN, geologist; b. Marietta, O., July 25, 1912; s. Harley Edgar and Maude Vesta (Chapman) F.; A.B., Marietta Coll., 1934, D.Sc., 1955; Ohio State U., 1935; M.S., U. Ia., 1937, Ph.D., 1938; m. Ruth L. Heizer, Aug. 29, 1936; children—Sally Jean, John Douglas, Terri Ruth. Grad. asst., research asst. U. Ia., 1935-38; geologist U.S. Geol. Survey, 1938-42; asst. dir. Kan. State Geol. Survey, 1942-45, exec. dir., 1945-54; asst. state geologist, 1942-45, state geologist 1952-54; asst. prof. U. Kan., 1942-45, asso. prof., 1945-52, prof. geology, 1952-54; chief Ill. State Geol. Survey, 1954—; prof. geology U. Ill., 1963—; spl. research geologist Bur. Econ. Geology, U. Tex., summer 1955-64. Adv. com. to sec. interior for U.S. Geol. Survey, 1960-66; sci. adv. council to gov. Ill., 1964—; adv. com. health physics Oak Ridge Nat. Lab., 1959—; del. to 19th Internat. Geol. Congress, Algiers, 1952; mem. div. earth scis. NRC, 1958-70, mem. div. exec. com., 1961-64, mem. com. geologic aspects radioactive waste disposal, 1955-64, chmn., 1962-64; chmn. adv. com. on earth resources remote sensing to U.S. Geol. Survey, 1966-69; mem. com. on mineral sci. and tech., adv. to U.S. Bur. Mines, 1966-70; chmn. com. on Radioactive Waste Mgmt., 1970—; mem. U.S. Nat. Commn. UNESCO, 1967—, exec. com., 1968—; mem. Sci. Manpower Commn., 1956-58; mem. exec. com. Ill. Water Resources Center, 1963—; mem. nat. adv. bd. Desert Research Inst., U. Nev., 1970—; mem. exec. adv. com. future oil prospects Nat. Petroleum Council, 1968-70. Fellow Geol. Soc. Am. (councilor 1958-61, bd. asso. editors 1962—), A.A.A.S.; mem. Ill. Geol. Soc., Am. Inst. Mining. Metall. and Petroleum Engrs., Am. Assn. Petroleum Geologists (chmn. fed., state and local agys. adv. com. 1968- -), Soc. Econ. Geologists, Ill. Acad. Sci. (pres. 1962-63), Soc. Econ. Paleontologists and Mineralogists (v.p. 1965-66), Am. Geol. Inst. (pres. 1966), Assn. Am. State Geologists (editor 1956-57, sec.-treas. 1957-58, pres. 1960), Am. Inst. Profl. Geologists (pres. Ill. 1967-68, exec. com. 1969-69), Am. Geophys. Union, Ill. Mining Inst., Sigma Xi, Sigma Gamma Epsilon, Alpha Sigma Phi. Mason, Rotarian. Club: Cosmos (Washington). Contbr. sci. articles profl. jours. Home: 708 W Vermont St Urbana IL 61801 Office: State Geol Survey U Ill Campus Urbana IL 61801

FRYE, NORTHROP, educator, author; b. Sherbrooke, Que., Can., July 14, 1912; s. Herman and Catharine (Howard) F.; B.A., U. Toronto, 1933; M.A., Oxford U., 1940; also 21 hon. degrees; m. Helen Kemp, Aug. 24, 1937. Lectr. English, Victoria Coll., U. Toronto, 1939-47, prof., 1947—, prin. col., 1959-67; prof. U. Toronto, 1967—; editor Canadian Forum, 1948-52. Ordained to ministry United Ch. Can., 1936; adviser curricular planning and English teaching Can. and U.S.; mem. adv. com. Am. Council Learned Socs., 1965; adv. mem. Can. Radio and TV Commn. Mem. Mod. Lang. Assn. (exec. council 1958-61). Author: Fearful Symmetry, 1947; Anatomy of Criticism, 1957; also 12 other books. Home: 127 Clifton Rd Toronto 7 Ontario Canada

FRYE, RICHARD NELSON, orientalist; b. Birmingham, Ala., Jan. 10, 1920; s. Nels and Lillie (Hagman) F.; A.B., U. Ill., 1939; M.A., Harvard, 1940, Ph.D., 1946, jr. fellow Soc. Fellows, 1946-48; m. Barbara York, May 29, 1948; children—Jeffrey, Rebecca, Robert. Staff Nr. East sect. research and analysis OSS, 1942-45, East European sect., 1946; travel Central Deserts of Iran and Baluchistan, 1951-52, Soviet Central Asia, 1955; adv. editor Indo-Iranica; mem. editorial bd. Central Asia Jour., The Hague, Holland; founder Nat.

Assn. Armenian Studies and Research, Boston; Aga Khan prof. Iranian, Harvard, 1957—. Pres. Asia Inst., Pahlavi U., Shiraz, Iran, also editor bull. of inst. Mem. Am. Oriental Soc., German Oriental Soc., Indo-Iranian Soc. Calcutta. Author: History of Bukhara, 1954; Iran, 1954; others. Editor: The Near East and The Great Powers, 1950; Islam and the West, 1957, The Heritage of Persia, 1963, Persia, 1968, others. Home: 25 Cabot St Winchester MA 01890 Office: Widener Library Cambridge MA 02138

FRYE, ROYAL MERRILL, coll. chancellor; b. Milford, N.H., May 27, 1890; s. Frank Barton and Elsie Wiletta (Merrill) F.; A.B., Boston U., 1911, A.M., 1912, Ph.D., 1934; student New Eng. Conservatory Music, 1906-08, Harvard Grad. Sch., 1912-13, Mass. Inst. Tech., part-time 1916-27, Am. Inst. Normal Methods, 1928; Sc.D. (hon.), Belknap Coll., 1968; m. Louise Alexander, June 11, 1915 (dec. Apr. 1969); m. 2d, Virginia May Brigham, May 7, 1970. Instr. physics Boston U. 1913-14, chemistry, 1914-16; instr. physics Mass. Inst. Tech., 1915-31, Worcester Poly. Inst., 1926-27; instr. physics Lincoln Inst., Boston, 1930-46, 52-61; mem. staff grad. div. Coll. Engring., Northeastern U., 1951-60; instr. physics Boston U., 1931-36, asst. prof., 1936-42 prof., and chmn. dept. physics, Grad. Sch., 1942-50; prof. physics, head dept. Simmons Coll., 1950-59; prof. physics, dean Coll. Advanced Sci., Canaan, N.H., 1959-63; pres. Belknap Coll., Center Harbor, N.H., 1963-69, chancellor, 1969—; pres. Wood Products Chem. Co., Inc., 1970—. Sci. cons., Operation Crossroads, Bikini, 1946; cons. AAF, AMC, Watson Labs., C.F.S. in connection with V-2 firing, 1946. Pres. Coop. Service, Inc., 1944-49, Boston Center Adult Edn., 1950-53. Bd. aldermen, Waltham, Mass., 1916-17. Mem. Am. Phys. Soc., A.A.A.S., Am. Assn. Physics Tchrs., Am. Assn. U. Profs. (nat. councillor 1950-53), Boston U. Alumni Assn. (v.p. 1954-56), Phi Beta Kappa. Club: Torch (Boston). Author: Practical Physics (with Robert E. Hodgdon), 1935; Graphical Mathematics, 1941; Graphical Introduction to the Harmon (with Esther W. Tipple), 1942; Essentials of Applied Physics, 1947. Contbr. Torch mag., also numerous sci. jours. Address: Belknap Coll Center Harbor NH 03226

FRYE, THEODORE RAYMOND, found. exec.; b. Wellsville, O., Aug. 21, 1921; s. Leroy B. and Edys (Culnon) F.; student Ohio U., Athens, 1941-43; A.B., Oberlin Coll., 1947; postgrad. George Washington U., 1954-57; M.B.A., N.Y.U., 1967; m. Martha Elizabeth Kissane, June 28, 1947; children-Michael E., Susan M., Margaret R., Dorothy, Raymond. With Dept. State and Fgn. Service, 1947- 63, assignments in India, 1950-53, Israel, 1958-62, Washington, 1947-50, 54-58, 62-63; asst. treas. Rockefeller Found., N.Y.C., 1963-67, treas., 1967—, coordinator Workshop in Bus. Opportunities, 1968-70. Chmn. bd. Am. Internat. Sch., Tel Aviv, Israel, 1960-62; treas. Scarsdale Fair Housing Group, 1962-68. Served with AUS, 1943-46. Mem. N.Y. Soc. Security Analysts, Phi Beta Kappa. Home: 174 Webster Rd Scarsdale NY 10583 Office: 111 W 50th St New York NY 10020

FRYE, THOMAS CARLTON, banker; b. Ontario, Ore., June 1, 1919; s. Leonard B. and Emma E. (Fiser) F.; ed. pub. schs.; m. Marguerite F. McCormick, July 30, 1950; children—Rebecca, Frances, Kate, Thomas Brooks. With Ida. First Nat. Bank, Boise, 1937—, pres., 1970—, also dir. Served to capt., F.A., AUS, 1941-46. Rotarian. Club: Arid (Boise). Home: 700 McMullen Rd Boise ID 83705 Office: PO Box 7009 Boise ID 83705

FRYE, WILLIAM RUGGLES, journalist; b. Detroit, Dec. 15, 1918; s. William Caleb and Anna Mildred (Ruggles) F.; B.S. cum laude, Harvard, 1940; m. Joan Bogert Ripperger, June 6, 1953; children—John Randall, Nancy Bogert. Local reporter Christian Sci. Monitor, Boston, 1941-42, copy reader, asst. to fgn. editor, 1946-50, UN corr., 1950-63; dir., editor World in Focus, newspaper syndicate, 1957—; self-syndicated, diplomatic corr., 1963—; lectr. world affairs, 1948—. Served with AUS, 1942-46; mem. staff Stars and Stripes. Co-recipient Deadline Club N.Y.C. UN award, 1963; recipient citation Overseas Press Club, 1955. Mem. Council Fgn. Relations, UN Corr. Assn. Mem. Christian Sci. Ch. Author: In Whitest Africa, 1968; A United Nations Peace Force, 1957. Contbr.: Arms Control, Disarmament and National Security, 1961. Home: 2 Tudor City Pl New York City NY 10017 Office: UN New York City NY 10017

FRYE, WILLIAM WESLEY, physician, educator; b. North English, Ia., July 26, 1903; s. Cyrus Alexander and Martha E. (Sheetz) F.; B.S., Ia. Wesleyan Coll., 1926; M.S., Ia. State Coll., 1927, Ph.D., 1931; M.D., Vanderbilt Univ., 1939; Sc.D., Iowa Wesleyan Coll., 1957; m. Lillian Emily Brown, Apr. 5, 1929; children—William Wesley, Emily Ann, Cynthia Brown, Martha Lois, Jane Ellen. Instr. zoology, entomology Ia. State Coll., 1928-31; research asst. dept. preventive medicine, pub. health Vanderbilt U., 1931-37, instr., 1937, intern pediatrics Commonwealth Fund fellowship, 1939-40, asst. prof. dept. preventive medicine, pub. health, asst. clin. medicine, 1940-42, asso. prof., asst. clinical obstet., 1942-45, prof., head dept. preventive medicine, pub. health, 1945-48, dir. Sch. Pub. Health, 1946-48; asst. dean, dir. div. grad. medicine, prof. tropical medicine, pub. health, Tulane U., 1948-49; dean, prof. tropical medicine, pub. health, La. State U., 1949-59 v.p., dean School of Medicine, 1959-65, chancellor La. State U. Medical Center, 1965-69, chancellor emeritus, 1969—; spl. cons. Tex. Tech. U. Sch. Medicine, Lubbock, 1970—; field trip tropical diseases Central Am., 1943; mem. Cholera Commn. China, 1945; spl. cons. USPHS, 1946—, chmn. tropical disease study sect., research grants div., 1951-56, chmn. advisory com. Epidemiology and Biometry, 1956—; chmn. combined deans com. VA Hosp., New Orleans, 1949- -; dep. dir. commn. enteric infections Armed Forces Epidemiol. Bd., 1950- 56; nat. adv. allergy and infectious diseases council of Nat. Insts. Health, Bethesda, Md., 1958—. Awarded Ben Witt Key prize by Vanderbilt U., 1939. Diplomate Am. Bd. Preventive Medicine and Public Health. Fellow A.M.A., Am. Pub. Health Assn., Am. Coll. Physicians, 1951; mem. Am. Soc. Tropical Medicine and Hygiene (pres. 1960-61), So. Medical Assn., Louisiana State, Orleans Parish medical societies, Louisiana State Public Health Assn., Am. Gastroenterological. Assn., New Orleans Acad. Internal Medicine, New Orleans Grad. Med. Assembly, Am. Cancer Soc. (mem. adv. com. Institutional Grants 1958-60). Am. Soc. of Parasitologists, Louisiana Mental Health Assn. (pres. 1957-59), Am. Acad. Preventive Medicine, Omicron Delta Kappa, Delta Omega, Sigma Xi, Phi Kappa Phi, Alpha Omega Alpha. Author articles on med. subjects in profl. jours. Co-author tropical medicine manual. Home: 1617 27th St Altura Towers Lubbock TX 79405 Office: Tex Tech U Sch Medicine PO Box 4390 Lubbock TX 79409

FRYER, FREDERICK LEAR, architect; b. Washington, Apr. 29, 1910; s. Ross Lauder and Martha (Lear) F.; B.Arch., Cornell U., 1942; m. Eleanor Fitch Moise, June 21, 1947; children—Eleanor Diane, Edith Bolton. Architect, Faulkner, Kingsbury & Stenhouse, architects, Washington, 1946-52, asso., 1952-58, jr. partner, 1959-65; partner Faulkner, Stenhouse, Fryer & Faulkner, 1965-68, Faulkner, Fryer & Vanderpool, 1968—. Chmn. for assns. Nat. Symphony Orch. sustaining fund, Washington, 1960. Served with USNR, 1942-46. Recipient 1st prize Chgo. Tribune Better Rooms Competition, 1947, diploma of merit for Bethesda (Md.) Library, Washington-Met. chpt. A.I.A., 1954, Potomac Valley chpt. A.I.A. award for Watkins Art Bldg., Washington, 1962, Washington Bd. Trade award and Modern Hosp. of Year award for Providence Hosp., Washington, 1956, also for Holy Cross Hosp., Silver Spring, Md., 1963, Modern Hosp. of Month award for St. Agnes Hosp., Balt., 1963. Mem. A.I.A., Am. Hosp. Assn., Sigma Alpha Epsilon. Republican. Episcopalian. Clubs: Chevy Chase; Cosmos (Washington). Home: 5609 Pioneer Lane Sumner MO 20016 Office: Faulkner Fryer & Vanderpool 2000 L St NW Washington DC 20036

FRYER, HOLLY CLAIRE, educator; b. Carlton, Ore., Dec. 6, 1908; s. Lewis E. and Daisy (Nichols) F.; B.S., U. Ore., 1931; M.S., Ore. State U., 1933; Ph.D., Ia. State U., 1940; m. Elsie Beth Alsup, Dec. 27, 1966; children by previous marriage—Gaye (Mrs. Roger W. Badeker), Claire (Mrs. James D. Farris). Faculty Kan. State U., 1940—, prof. statistics, 1945—, head dept. statistics and computer sci., 1959—; asso. mathematician Nat. Def. Research Council, Columbia, 1944-45. City commr., Manhattan, 1962-66, mayor, 1965-66. Fellow Am. Statis. Assn., Royal Statis. Soc.; mem. Biometrics Soc., Inst. Math. Statistics, Assn. Computing Machinery. Republican. Author: Elements of Statistics, 1954; Concepts and Methods of Experimental Statistics, 1966. Home: Rural Rt 4 Lakeview Manhattan KS 66502

FRYER, MALCOLM FORREST, Jr., c. of c. exec.; b. Melrose, Mass., Apr. 3, 1934; s. Malcolm Forrest and Lillian Augusta (Anderson) F.; student Wabash Coll., 1951-53; B.A., U. N.H., 1959; m. Judith Anne Young, Aug. 24, 1963; children—Stephen Forrest, Eric John. Staff exec. Indpls. C. of C., 1959-60; chief exec. Brunswick (Me.) C. of C., 1960-61, Rutland, Vt., 1961-63, Northampton, Mass., 1963-66; devel. exec. Hartford (Conn.) exec. C. of C., 1966-67; exec. v.p. Lowell (Mass.) C. of C., 1967-69, Cambridge, Mass., 1969—. Corporator Cambridge Savs. Bank. Adviser Inst. Orgn. Mgmt., Nat. Chamber at Syracuse U. Bd. dirs. Model Cities Community Services, Welfare Adv. Com., Cambridge. Pres. Kappa Sigma Chpt. Housing Corp., Lowell, Mass. Served with AUS, 1955-57. Mem. Mass. (treas.), Vt. (past pres.), New England assns. c. of c. execs., Am. C. of C. Execs. Rotarian, Mason. Club: Vesper Country (Tyngsboro, Mass.). Home: 200 Proctor Rd Chelmsford MA 01824 Office: 69 Rogers St Cambridge MA 02142

FRYER, MINOT PACKER, surgeon; b. Willimantic, Conn., Mar. 16, 1915; s. Minot Samuel and Mary (Packer) F.; A.B., Brown U., 1936; M.D., Johns Hopkins, 1940; D.Sc. (hon.), Brown U., 1971; children—Edwin Samuel, Minot Packer; m. Nancy Niedringhaus Mills, 1966. Intern Johns Hopkins Hosp., 1940-41; resident Barnes Hosp., St. Louis, 1941-44, fellow in plastic surgery, 1946-48, asst. surgeon, 1948- 67; asso. prof. clin. surgery Washington U. Med. Sch., St. Louis, 1957- 67, prof. clin. surgery, 1967—, asso. prof. clin. maxilo-facial surgery, Dental Sch., 1957-67, prof. clin. maxilo-facial surgery, 1967- -; asso. surgeon St. Louis Children's Hosp., Barnes Hosp.; active staff DePaul Hosp., 1948—, chief surgery, 1962-64; cons. surgeon plastic surgery St. Louis City Hosp., Homer G. Phillips Hosp.; cons. plastic surgery VA Hosp., Shriners Hosp. for Crippled Children. Served to lt., M.C., USNR, 1944-46. Diplomate Am. Bd. Surgery, Am. Bd. Plastic Surgery (mem. 1962-68, sec.-treas. 1963-67, vice chmn. 1967- 68). Fellow A.C.S. (past chmn. council plastic surgery), Am. Assn. Surgery Trauma; mem. A.M.A., Am. Surg. Assn., St. Louis Med. Soc., Assn. Mil. Surgeons, Am. Soc. Plastic and Reconstructive Surgery, Am. Assn. Plastic Surgeons (pres. 1967-68), Central Surg. Assn., Am. Assn. Surgery Trauma, Soc. Head and Neck Surgeons, Western Surg. Assn., Halsted Soc. Author: (with J. Brown) Surgery of Face, Mouth and Jaws, 1954; Postmortem Homografs, 1960. Cons. editor: Surgery, Gynecology and Obstetrics, 1960-65. Contbr. articles to sci. jours. Home: 665 S Skinner St Louis MO 63105 Office: 4989 Barnes Hosp Plaza St Louis MO 63110

FRYER, ROBERT SHERWOOD, theatrical producer; b. Washington, Nov. 18, 1920; s. Harold and Ruth (Reade) F.; B.A., Western Res. U., 1943. Asst. to mng. dir. Theatre Inc., 1946, casting dir., 1946-48; asst. to exec. CBS., 1949-51, casting dir., 1951-52; Broadway co-producer A Tree Grows in Brooklyn, 1951, By the Beautiful Sea, 1954; producer Wonderful Town, 1953, The Desk Set, Shangri-La, Auntie Mame, Redhead, There Was a Little Girl, Advise and Consent, A Passage To India, Hot Spot, Roar Like a Dove, Sweet Charity, Mame, 1966; producer films The Boston Strangler, The Prime of Miss Jean Brodie, Myra Breckenridge, Ace Eli and Rodger of The Skies, Travels with My Aunt, Mame; now v.p. Fryer, Carr & Harris, Inc., N.Y.C.; mng. dir. Ahmanson Theatre, Center Theatre, 135 N. Grand Av. Group, Los Angeles. Served as capt. AUS, 1941-46; maj. Res. Decorated Legion of Merit. Rockefeller Found. fellow. Mem. Episcopal Actors Guild (v.p.), League of N.Y. Theatres (bd. govs.). Author: Professional Theatrical Management New York City, 1947. Home: 8800 Thrasher Av Los Angeles CA 90069 Office: 20th Century Fox Films Box 900 Beverly Hills CA 90213

FRYLING, GEORGE PERCY, II, electronic components co. exec.; b. St. Mary's, Pa., Jan. 15, 1929; s. G. Richard and Florence (McCauley) F.; B.S. in Bus. Adminstrn., Allegheny Coll., 1951; M.S. in Indsl. Mgmt., Mass. Inst. Tech., 1964; m. Jane Walker, June 6, 1956; children—G. Richard II, Susan, Linda, William S., Robert D. With Erie Tech. Products, Inc. (Pa.), 1959—, exec. v.p., 1964-66, pres., dir., 1966—. Bd. dirs. Northwest Pa. Heart Fund, 1964- -, United Fund Erie County, 1967—. Served with USAF, 1951-55. Mem. Greater Erie C. of C. (bd. dirs. 1965—). Episcopalian. Home: 111 Columbia Circle Erie PA 16505 Office: 644 W 12th St Erie PA 16512

FRYLING, GEORGE RICHARD, mfg. exec.; b. St. Marys, Pa., Mar. 24, 1901; s. George Percy and Emma Elisabeth (Spratt) F.; student Mercersburg Acad., 1917-18, Rensselaer Poly. Inst., 1918-23; LL.D., Gannon Coll., 1957; m. Florence K. McCauley, Sept. 22, 1927; children—Florence Elisabeth, George Percy II, Richard McCauley, Mary Patricia. Salesman Speer Carbon Co., St. Marys, Pa., 1923-26; v.p., gen. mgr. Elk Graphite Milling Co., St. Marys, 1926- 32; pres. Erie Technol. Products, Inc. (formerly known as Erie Resistor Corp.) (Pa.), 1928-62, chmn. bd., treas., 1962-64, chmn. bd., pres., 1964- -; chmn., chief exec. officer Erie Technol. Products, Inc., 1966-70, chmn. bd., 1970—; chmn. Fryling Mfg., Inc., Electron Research, Inc., Tech. Materials Div., Erie Technol. Products Can., Ltd., Erie Technol. Products, Ltd., London; dir. Security Peoples Trust Co., Keithley Instruments, Inc. (Cleve.), Pa. Mfrs. Casualty& Fire Ins. Co. Mem. Pa. Planning Bd., 1948-55. Bd. mgrs. Hamot Hosp., Erie; mem. bd. Gannon Coll., 1960—. Mem. Pa. Mfrs. Assn. (dir.), N.A.M. (dir.), Mfrs. Assn. Erie (dir., past pres.), Pa. C. of C. (dir., pres. 1957-59), Theta Chi. Republican. Episcopalian. Clubs: Erie (dir., past pres.), Kahkwa Country (Erie). Home: 1950 S Shore Dr Erie PA 16505 Office: 644 W 12th St Erie PA 18501

FRYMOYER, WILLARD WEBSTER, indsl. instrument co. exec.; b. Mt. Carmel, Pa., May 14, 1899; s. William K. and Elizabeth (Brosius) F.; student Carnegie Inst. Tech., 1917-19; B.S. in Mech. Engring., Mass. Inst. Tech., 1921; m. Elizabeth Whitney Kimball, June 2, 1928; children—Mary (Mrs. Fred A. Brown, Jr.), William, John Willard. Asso. engr. aero. instrument devel. Nat. Bur. Standards, 1921-26; with Foxboro Co. (Mass.), 1926—, various positions, 1926-54, v.p. mfg. and engring., 1954-57, exec. v.p., 1962-65, sr. v.p., dir. corporate planning, dir. exec. com., 1965-70, exec. v.p. emeritus, dir., mem. exec. com., cons. on mgmt. and engring., 1970—. Conglist. (deacon). Home: 43 Granite St Foxboro MA 02035 Office: Foxboro Co Foxboro MA 02035

FRYOU, THEODORE W., electric co. exec.; b. Portland, Ore., 1905; student Northwestern U., U. Ore.; married. With Portland Gen. Electric Co., 1928—, treas., controller, 1951—. Home: 10190 SW Crestwood Ct Beaverton OR 97005 Office: 621 SW Adler St Portland OR 47205*

FRYXELL, FRITIOF MELVIN, educator; b. Moline, Ill., Apr. 27, 1900; s. John and Anna Sophia (Olson) F.; A.B., Augustana Coll., 1922; A.M., U. Ill., 1923; Ph.D., U. Chgo., 1929; postgrad. U. Colo., U. Ia.; D.Sc. (hon.), Wittenberg U., Upsala Coll., 1960; m. Regina Christina Holmen, June 22, 1928; children—John Birger (dec.), Roald Hilding, Thomas Walcott. Tchr., Augustana Coll., 1923, prof. geology, 1929—, chmn. sci., 1946-52; instr. U. Chgo., 1927-28; geologist Nat. Park Service, at intervals, 1929-39; sr. geologist Philippine Commonwealth, 1939-40; U.S. Geol. Survey with Mil. Geol. Unit., 1942- 46; asst. chief 1944; lit. exec. of late François E. Matthes, 1948-65; Guggenheim fellow, 1954- 55. Del. 18th Internat. Geol. Congress, London; Internat. Council Museums, Paris, 1948; hon. fellow Am. Scandinavian Found. with travel in Scandinavia, 1948. Trustee Davenport (Ia.) Public Mus., 1942—; bd. dirs. Augustana Research Found., 1947—, Am. Geol. Inst., 1950-51, Fryxell Geology Mus., 1968- -; cons. on Western history U. Wyo., 1968—. Recipient Neil Miner award Assn. Geology Tchrs., 1953. Augustana Coll. Meritorious Service award, 1958; research grant Laura Spelman Rockefeller Found., U. Chgo., 1926, Geol. Soc. Am., 1941, NSF, 1959-60, 60-61; Distinguished Service citation U.S. Geol. Survey, 1966. Fellow A.A.A.S., Am. Geog. Soc., Geol. Soc. Am.; mem. Ill. Acad. Sci. (life mem., pres. 1942- 43), Appalachian Mountain Club (corr.), Assn. Coll. Geology Tchrs. (pres. 1938-39), Phi Beta Kappa, Sigma Xi. Lutheran. Clubs: Sierra of Cal. (life); Am. Alpine, Explorers (N.Y.). Author editor, books and articles on sci. mountaineering, and nat. parks. Contbr. to Ency. Brit. Address: Augustana College Rock Island IL 61201 ☆

FUBINI, EUGENE GHIRON, bus. cons.; b. Turin, Italy, Apr. 19, 1913; s. Guido and Anna (Ghiron) F.; student Polytech. Turin. 1929-31; D. Physics summa cum laude, U. Rome, 1933; D.Sc., Rensselaer Poly. Inst.; D.Eng., Pratt Inst., 1967, Bklyn. Poly. Inst., 1968; m. Jane Elizabeth Machmer, May 5, 1945; children—Sylvia, Sandra, Carol, Laurie, David, Susan. Naturalized U.S. citizen, 1945. Research asso. Nat. Inst. Electrotechnics, Rome, 1935-38; engr. charge microwave and internat. broadcasting CBS, 1938-42; research asso. devel. electronic countermeasures, radio research lab. Harvard, 1942-44; intelligence reconnaissance and radar countermeasure missions U.S. Army, U.S. Navy, USAAF, 1944; radar countermeasures 8th Air Force, Eng., 1944-45; attached War Dept., 1945; with Airborne Instruments Lab., 1945-61, div. head to v.p., 1960-61; with Office Sec. Def., 1961-65, asst. sec. def., dep. dir. def. research and engring.; v.p., group exec. IBM, N.Y., 1965-69, cons., 1969—; dir., officer of bd. Tex. Instruments, Inc., 1969—. Cons. President's Sci. Adv. Com., 1957-61, 69—; mem. USAF Sci. Adv. Bd., 1958-61, 65-69, Adv. Council Advancement Sci. Research and Devel. N.Y. State 1958—; mem. panel sci. adv. bd. Nat. Security Agy., 1958-61; chmn. electromagnetic warfare adv. group Air Research and Devel. Command, 1958-61; adv. group spl. projects Dept. Def., 1958-61; mem. Pres.'s Commn. Law Enforcement, 1965-67; mem. sci. adv. com. Def. Intelligence Agy., 1965—, chmn., 1965-70; mem. Def. Sci. Bd. 1966-69; mem. sci. adv. com. Am. Newspaper Pubs. Assn., 1969—, Def. Communications Planning Group, 1970—; lectr. Harvard, 1956. Trustee Urban Inst.; bd. dirs. Vols. for Internat. Tech. Assistance, Inc.; mem. vis. com. Harvard U. Computing Center, Stanford Sch. Engring., George Washington U. Sch. Engring. Recipient Presdl. certificate of Merit, 1946; Def. medal for distinguished service, 1966; Exceptional Service medal Def. Intelligence Agy., 1970. Fellow I.E.E.E.; mem. Nat. Acad. Engring. (mem. exec. com.), N.Y. Acad. Scis. Club: Cosmos (Washington). Author, patentee in field. Home: 2300 Hunter Mill Rd Vienna VA 22180 Office: 1411 Jefferson Davis Hwy One Jefferson Plaza Arlington VA 22202

FUCHS, BERNARD, dept. store exec.; b. N.Y.C., 1926; ed. Pace Coll. Exec. v.p., dir. S. Klein Dept. Stores, Inc., N.Y.C. Home: Rock Lane Harrison NY 10528 Office: 6 Union Sq New York City NY 10003*

FUCHS, FRITZ, physician, educator: b. Denmark Nov. 27, 1918; s. Josef and Sofie (Petersen) F.; M.D., U. Copenhagen, 1944, D. Med. Scis., 1957; m. Seere Anna-Rita Olsson, May 19, 1948; children—Anneli, Martin, Peter Erik, Lars Frederik. Came to U.S., 1964. Postgrad. tng. obstetrics and gynecology, also surgery in Danish and Swedish hosps., 1945-58; gynecologist-in-chief Kommunehospital, Copenhagen, 1958-65; obstetrician, gynecologist-in-chief N.Y. Hosp., 1965—; Given Found. prof., chmn. dept. obstetrics and gynecology Cornell U. Med. Coll., 1965—; cons. Rockefeller U., 1968—. Served with Danish Brigade, 1945. Author articles, chpts. in books. Home: 630 Wolf's Lane Pelham Manor NY 10803. Office: 530 E 70th St New York City NY 10021

FUCHS, HANNO, advt. exec.; b. Karlsruhe, Germany, Dec. 23, 1928; s. William Werner and Marianne (Hirsch) F.; came to U.S., 1941, naturalized, 1950; B.S. in Journalism, Syracuse U., 1949; student Columbia Grad. Sch. Bus. Adminstrn., 1950, N.Y.U., Coll. Law, 1961; m. Carol Runyan, Dec. 15, 1962; children-Andrew W., Jessica M., Daniel R., Michael J. With Young & Rubicam, Inc., 1952-69, creative exec., v.p., 1961-69; exec. v.p. Richard K. Manoff, Inc., N.Y.C., 1969-70; Pres., 1970. Served with AUS, 1951-53. Mem. Alpha Delta Sigma, Beta Gamma Sigma. Democrat. Jewish religion. Home: 18 Hartford Lane White Plains NY 10603 Office: 845 3d Av New York NY 10022

FUCHS, JAMES EMMANUEL, communications exec.; b. Chgo., Dec. 6, 1927; s. Richard and Violette (Fenton) F.; B.A., Yale, 1950; m. Barrington King, Jan. 14, 1956; children—Bettina Barrington, Barrington King, Holly Armstrong, Sharon Victoria, Kimberley Corbin. Sales exec. trainee Bigelow Sanford Carpet Co., N.Y.C., 1950-51; exec. trainee NBC, N.Y.C., 1951-52, film program salesman, mgr. nat. and regional sales, account exec. spl. program sales television network, 1952-62; asst. to pres., gen. corp. exec. Curtis Pub. Co., N.Y.C., 1962, v.p., dir. Eastern div., 1963-64; v.p. Curtis Circulation Co., 1964-66; gen. partner C-F Film Distbg. Co., 1966—; v.p. marketing and communications, dir. MBS, 1966-68; pres., dir. Mut. Sports, Inc., 1967-68; exec. v.p., treas. Culligan Communications Corp., 1968-70, also dir.; pres., pub., treas. Culligan Mid-Fairfield Pub. Co., Inc., 1969-70, also dir.; sr. v.p. Thinc Career Planning Corp., 1971—. Mem. People to People Sports Com. Bd.; mem. President's Council on Phys. Fitness; co-chmn. N.Y. Mayor's Committee for Olympic Fund Raising: mem. N.Y. Mayor's Sports Com. for Youth. Trustee Campfire Girls, Inc., Hugh O'Brien Found. Recipient U.S. Olympic Team medalist for shot putting, 1948, 52. Mem. St. Elmo Soc., Yale Track Assn. (pres.). U.S. Olympic Assn. Clubs: Yale, New York Athletic (N.Y.C.); Yale (dir.) (Darien, Conn.); University

(N.Y.); Apawamis (Rye, N.Y.); Yale (Greenwich); Belle Haven Beach. Home: 78 Mayo Av Greenwich CT 06830 Office: 1345 Av Americas New York City NY 10019

FUCHS, JOSEPH PHILIP, violinist; b. N.Y.C., Apr. 26, 1900; s. Philip and Kate (Weiss) F.; diploma Inst. Mus. Art (now Juilliard Sch. Music), 1918, artist's diploma, 1920; m., 1 dau. Debut at Aeolian Hall, N.Y.C., 1920; concertmaster Cleve. Orch., 1926-40, also leader Cleve. String Quartet; ofcl. debut as virtuoso Town Hall, N.Y.C., 1943; soloist N.Y. Philharmonic, 1944, since has performed in concerts throughout U.S. and with most maj. Am. orchs.; several European tours, 1954—, S. Am. tour, 1957; active in encouragement contemporary composers, premiered Walter Piston's 2d Violin Concerto with Pitts. Symphony Orch., 1960; presented recitals with Arthur Balsam on Sonata program, WBGH-TV, Boston, 1957-60; prof. violin Juilliard Sch. Music, 1946—; soloist Prades Festival, 1953, 54; tour USSR, 1965, Japan, 1967; recording artist for Decca, Everest, Columbia records. Co-founder Musicians Guild. Recipient Morris Loeb Meml. Prize, Isaac Newton Seligman prize. Ford Found. grantee, 1959. Address: care Herbert Barrett Management Inc 250 W 57th St New York City NY 10009*

FUCHS, LAWRENCE HOWARD, educator; b. N.Y.C., Jan. 29, 1927; s. Alfred F. and Frances S. (Scheiber) F.; B.A., N.Y. U., 1950; Ph.D., Harvard, 1955; m. Betty Corcoran, Sept. 12, 1970; children by previous marriage—Janet Pearl, Frances Sarah, Naomi Ruth. Teaching fellow Harvard, 1950-51; faculty Brandeis U., 1951—, chmn. dept. politics, 1959-60, dean faculty, 1960-61, prof. Am. civilization and politics, 1963—, chmn. dept. Am. Studies, 1970—; on leave as dir. Peace Corps, Philippines, 1961-63; part-time radio-TV news commentator for stas. WCRB and WGBH, Boston, 1951-59. Mem. nat. adv. bd. commn. law and social action Am. Jewish Congress; nat. adv. bd. United World Federalists; adv. bd. Mass. Congress Racial Equality; 1st chmn. Commonwealth Service Corps Commn.; chmn. exec. com. social studies curriculum program Edn. Devel. Center, Inc.; pres. Human Devel. Found.; founding pres. Self-Devel. Group, Inc. Social Sci. Research Council Sr. grantee Am. Govt. processes, 1958-59. Served with USNR, 1945-47. Mem. Am., New Eng. polit. sci. assns., Civil Liberties Union, N.A.A.C.P., Phi Beta Kappa. Democrat. Jewish religion. Author: The Political Behavior of American Jews, 1955; Hawaii Pono; A Social History, 1961; John F. Kennedy and American Catholicism, 1967; "Those Peculiar Americans". The Peace Corps and American National Character, 1967; American Ethnic Politics, 1968. Contbr. profl. journals. Home: 127 Bay State Rd Weston MA 02193 Office: Brandeis U Waltham MA 02154

FUCHS, ROLAND JOHN, educator; b. Yonkers, N.Y., Jan. 15, 1933; s. Alois L. and Elizabeth (Weigand) F.; B.A., Columbia, 1954, postgrad., 1956-57; postgrad. Moscow State U., 1960-61; M.A., Clark U., 1957, Ph.D., 1959; m. Gaynell Ruth McAuliffe, June 15, 1957; children—Peter K., Christopher K., Andrew K. Asst. prof. to prof. U. Hawaii, Honolulu, 1958—, chmn. dept. geography, 1964—, asst. dean to asso. dean Coll. Arts and Scis., 1965-67, dir. Asian Studies Lang. and Area Center, 1965-67. Vis. prof. Clark U., 1963-64; asst. editor Econ. Geography, 1963-64; mem. editorial adv. com. Soviet Geography; Review and Translation, 1966—. Mem. U.S. nat. commn. for Internat. Geog. Union, 1969—. Ford Found. fellow, 1956-57; Fulbright Research scholar, 1966-67. Mem. Am. Assn. Geographers, Am. Geog. Soc., Regional Sci. Assn., A.A.A.S., Am. Assn. Advancement Slavic Studies, Assn. for Asian Studies. Home: 5136 Maunalani Circle Honolulu HI 96816

FUCHS, THEODORE, educator; b. Bklyn., Jan. 28, 1904; s. Theodore and Clara (Heller) F.; B.S., Poly. Inst. Bklyn., 1923; M.A., Northwestern U., 1937; m. Elinor Rice, Aug. 18, 1934. Editor and cons., Drama League of Am., 1924-28; stage lighting specialist, Gen. Electric Co., 1923-26; pvt. practice as archtl., mech. and elec. cons. in design of numerous theatre bldgs., 1926—; prodn. mgr. Goodman Theatre, Chgo., 1932-33; with Northwestern U. 1934—, chmn. theatre dept., dir. Northwestern U. Theatre, 1939-51, prof. dramatic prodn., 1947—. Recipient New Eng. Theatre Conf. spl. award, 1967; award of merit for distinguished service to the ednl. theatre Am. Ednl. Theatre Assn., 1970. Registered profl. engr. Ill. Mem. U.S. Inst. for Theatre Tech., Soc. Motion Picture and Television Engrs., Illuminating Engring. Soc., Nat. Theatre Conf., Am. Ednl. Theatre Assn., ANTA. Author: Stage Lighting, 1929, 64; Lighting Equipment for the Small Stage, 1939; Course Outline in Theatre Management, 1967; Functional Planning of Educational Theatre Facilities, 1968. Contbr. articles profl. jours. Home: 1426 Chicago Av Evanston IL 60201

FUCHS, SIR VIVIAN, geologist; b. Isle of Wight, Feb. 11, 1908; s. Ernest and Violet (Watson) F.; student Brighton Coll., 1922-26; M.A., Cambridge U., 1932, Ph.D., 1936, D.Sc., 1959; LL.D., Edinburgh U., 1958; D.Sc., Durham U., 1958; m. Joyce Connell, 1933; children—Hilary (Mrs. Howard Brooks), Peter E. K. Geologist, Cambridge East Greenland Expdn., 1929, East Africa Expdn. 1930-32; leader Lake Rudolf Rift Valley Expdn. 1934, Lake Rukwa Expdn., 1938, Falkland Islands Dependencies Survey, 1947-50; dir. Brit. Antarctic Survey, 1950—; leader Trans-Antarctic Expdn., 1955-58. Recipient founders medal Royal Geog. Soc., 1951, spl. gold medal, 1958; gold medal Royal Scottish Geog. Soc., 1958, Paris Gold medal, 1958; silver medal Royal Soc. Arts, 1952, Polar medal, 1953, 58; gold Richthofen medal Berlin Geog. Soc., 1958; gold Kirchenpauer medal Hamburg Geog. Soc., 1958; gold Plancius medal Amsterdam Geog. Soc., 1958; Hubbard medal Nat. Geog. Soc., 1959; gold medal Chgo. Geog. Soc., 1959; gold medal N.Y. Explorers Club, 1959; Hans Egede silver medal Copenhagen Geol. Soc., 1959; Prestwich medal Geol. Soc. London, 1960. Fellow Royal Geog. Soc., Geol. Soc. London. Club: Atheneaum (London). Author: Crossing of Antarctica, 1959. Author geog., geol. papers. Home: 78 Barton Rd Cambridge England Office: care Brit Antarctic Survey 30 Gillingham St London England

FUCHS, WOLFGANG HEINRICH, educator; b. Munich, Germany, May 19, 1915; s. Martin Erich and Alice (Manasse) F.; B.A., St. John's Coll. Cambridge U. 1936, Ph.D., 1941; m. Dorothee J. Rausch von Traubenberg, Sept. 25, 1943; children-Ann, John, Claudia. Came to U.S., 1950, naturalized, 1958. Tchr. univs., Gt. Britain, 1940-49; asso. prof. maths. Cornell U., 1950-58, prof., 1958—. Mem. Am. Math. Soc. Democrat. Home: 1105 Trumansburg Rd Ithaca NY 14850

FUCILLA, JOSEPH GUERIN, educator; b. Chgo., Dec. 14, 1897; s. John and Marie Frances (De Marco) F.; B.A., U. Wis., 1921, M.A., 1922; Ph.D., U. Chgo., 1927; m. Reba Ann South, May 9, 1925; children—Jasper South, Van South. Instr. Romance langs. Ia. State Coll., 1921-23; asst. prof. Butler U., 1923-28; vis. asst. prof. U. Chgo., spring 1927, summer 1929, prof., summers 1949, 50; asst. prof. Romance lang. Northwestern U., 1928-32, asso. prof., 1932-36, prof., 1936-66, emeritus, 1966—; vis. prof. U. Wis., 1966-67, U. Colo., 1967, U. Cal. Santa Barbara, 1967-69. Fulbright grantee, Italy, 1952-53. Recipient Nat. Fgn. Lang. Achievement award Nat. Fedn. Modern Lang. Tchrs. Assns.; Distinguished Achievement medal, Dante Soc. Am. Mem. Modern Lang. Assn., Am. Assn. U. Profs., Am. Assn. Tchrs. Italian (hon. pres.), Am. Assn. Tchrs. Spanish, Dante Soc., Renaissance Soc., Am. Name Soc., Phi Beta Kappa, Phi Kappa Phi; fgn. mem. Arcadian Acad. (Rome, Italy); hon. mem. Accademia Cosetia; corr. mem. Hispanic Soc. Am., Real Academia Sevillana de Buenas Letras. Commendatore al merito della Repubblica Italiana. Author: Forgotten Danteiana, 1939; Universal Author Repertoire of Italian Essay Literature, 1941; The Follett Spanish Dictionary, 1943; Our Italian Surnames, 1949; Studies and Notes (Literary and Historical), 1953; Relaciones Hispanoitalianas, 1953: Saggistica Letteraria Italiana: 1938- 1953, 1956; Estudios sobre el Petrarquismo en Espaa, 1960; Superbi colli e altri saggi, 1963; The Teaching of Italian in the United States, 1967. Co-author: Bibliografia Analitica Tassiana, 1935; D'Annunzio Abroad (two volumes), 1935, 1937; Italian Criticism of Russian Literature, 1937; A. Bibliographical Guide to the Romance Languages and Literatures, 8th edit., 1971. Editor: Grazia Deledda, Il Vecchio della Montagna, 1932; Carlo Goldoni, La Locandiera (with E. Hocking), 1939; Pedro Antonio de Alarcón; Novelas Cortas, 1952; Cuentos Hispano-americanos de Ayer y de Hoy (with F. D. Maurino), 1956. Editor of Italica, 1943-68; adv. bd. Philol. Quar. Translator and annotator of Count Ciano's manuscript diary in draft form for Chicago Daily News (with A. Borselli and A. B. Fallico). Translator Metastasio, Pietro: Dido Forsakeñ, 1952. Contbr. articles to various lit., philological and linguistic publs. Home: 1862 Sherman Av Evanston IL 60201

FUCILLO, EDWARD A., finance co. exec.; b. N.Y.C., Oct. 21, 1924; s. Joseph B. and Evelyn (Endom) F.; B.A., Georgetown U.; LL.B., St. John's U.; m. Margaret Dineen, Dec. 26, 1949; children—Kathleen, Mary Anne, Edward J., John, Margaret Mary, Sharon, Carolyn. Admitted to N.Y. bar; with tax dept. U.S. Rubber Co., 1951-53; corp. sec., mgr. tax dept. Gen. Motors Acceptance Corp., 1953—. Home: 10 Donna Dr Upper Brookville NY 11771. Office: 767 Fifth Av New York City NY 10022

FUDENBERG, HUGH, hematologist; b. N.Y.C., Oct. 24, 1928; s. Nathan and Frances (Chachowitz) F.; A.B., U. Cal. at Los Angeles, 1949; M.D., U. Chgo., 1953; m. Betty Sams Roof, Nov. 23, 1955; children—Drew Douglas, Brooks Roberts, David Melton, Hugh Haskell. Intern, U. Utah, 1953-54; fellow hematology Tufts U., 1954-56; asst. resident medicine Mt. Sinai Hosp., N.Y.C., 1956-57, Peter Bent Brigham Hosp., Boston, 1957-58; research asso. Rockefeller Inst. for Med. Research, 1958-60; asst. prof. medicine U. Cal. Sch. Medicine, San Francisco, 1960-62, asso. prof. medicine, 1962-66, prof., 1966—, dir. hematology unit, 1962—; prof. bacteriology and immunology U. Cal. at Berkeley, 1966—. Mem. expert adv. panel on immunology WHO. Recipient Pasteur Medal Inst. Pasteur, Paris, 1962, Robert A. Cooke Meml. medal Am. Acad. Allergy, 1967. Fellow A.A.A.S.; mem. Am., Brit. assns. immunologists, Am. Soc. for Human Genetics, Am. Soc. for Clin. Investigation, Am. Assn. Physicians, Internat. Soc. Blood Transfusion (exec. council), Western Assn. Physicians, Internat., Am. (past pres. elect subdiv. immunohematology and immunogenetics) socs. hematology. Editorial bd. Blood, Vox Sang., Biochem. Genetics, Clin. and Exptl. Immunology, Jour. Immunology, Immunochemistry, Am. Jour. Human Genetics, Transfusion. Home: 4 Heather Way Mill Valley CA 94941 Office: Dept Medicine U Cal San Francisco CA 94122

FUECHSLIN, HOWARD R., business exec. Comptroller, A. Epstein & Sons, Inc., Chgo. Office: 2011 W Pershing Rd Chicago IL 60609*

FUENTES, CARLOS, author; b. 1928; ed. U. Mexico, also Institut des Hautes Etudes Internationales, Geneva. Mem. Mexican delegation ILO, Geneva, 1950-52; asst. head press sect. Ministry Fgn. Affairs, Mexico, 1954; asst. dir. cultural dissemination U. Mex., 1955-56; head dept. cultural relations Ministry Fgn. Affairs. Editor: Revista Mexicana de Literatura, 1954-58, Siempre and Politica, 1960—; co-editor: El Espectador, 1959-61. Author: Los dias enmascarados, 1954; La region mas transparente, 1958; Las buenas conciencias, 1959; Aura, 1962; The Death of Artemio Crũz, 1962; Whither Latin America, 1963. Address: 2a Cerrada de Fontera 14 San Angel Mexico D F Mexico *

FUERBRINGER, ALFRED OTTOMAR, clergyman, educator; b. St. Louis, Aug. 11, 1903; s. Ludwig Ernst and Anna (Zucker) F.; student Concordia Coll., Ft. Wayne, Ind., 1918-21; B.D., Concordia Sem., St. Louis, 1925, S.T.M. 1927, D.D., 1953; L.H.D. Valparaiso U., 1959; Litt.D., Concordia Tchrs. Coll., Seward, Neb., 1969; m. Carolyn Kuhlman, June 1, 1934; children—Kenneth Paul, Max Robert, Marian Ruth, Jane Carolyn. Ordained to ministry Luth. Ch., 1927; pastor Trinity Luth. Ch., Norman, Okla., 1927-34, Trinity Luth. Ch., Okmulgee, Okla., 1934-37, St. Paul's Luth. Ch., Leavenworth, Kan., 1937-41; pres. Concordia Tchrs. Coll., Seward, Neb., 1941-53, Concordia Sem., St. Louis, 1953-69, prof., 1969—, dir. continuing edn., 1969—. Commr. Luth. Church-Mo. Synod, Europe, 1948, 57, 58, 63, 66, Australia, Asia, 1957- 58, Latin Am., 1957, 59, 61; mem. commn. on theology and ch. relations, 1950-69. Pres. Found. for Reformation Research, 1957-64, exec. dir., 1965-66, bd. dirs., 1967-69; v.p. Nat. Luth. Edn. Conf., 1963, pres., 1964. Trustee, Clayton Pub. Library, 1960-70. Mem. Am. Mgmt. Assn. (theologians adv. council), Hist. Soc. Mo. (trustee 1953- -). Editorial bd. Concordial Theol. Monthly. Home: 16 Seminary Terrace St Louis (Clayton) MO 63105

FUERBRINGER, OTTO, journalist; b. St. Louis, Sept. 27, 1910; s. Ludwig and Anna (Zucker) F.; A.B., Harvard, 1932; L.H.D., Wagner Coll., 1966; m. Winona Gunn, Sept. 11, 1939; children—Peter, Alexis Jonathan, Juliana. Reporter St. Louis Post-Dispatch, 1932-42; writer Time, N.Y.C., 1942-46, sr. editor, 1946-51, asst. mng. editor, 1951-60. mng. editor, 1960-68; v.p. Time, Inc., 1968—. Trustee Wagner Coll. Mem. Council Fgn. Relations, Found. Reformation Research Lutheran. Clubs: Harvard, Knickerbocker (N.Y.); Round Hill (Greenwich, Conn.). Home: Round Hill Rd Greenwich CT 06830 Office: Time and Life Bldg New York City NY 10020

FUESS, JOHN CUSHING, fgn. service officer; b. Andover, Mass., Apr. 13, 1912; s. Claude Moore and Elizabeth (Goodhue) F.; grad. Phillips Acad., Andover, Mass., 1931; B.A., Harvard, 1935, M.A., 1936; m. Cora Frances Henry, Jan. 6, 1943; children—James Henry, David Cushing. Tchr., Brooks Sch., N. Andover, Mass., 1937-39; fgn. service officer, vice consul, Mexico City, 1939-40; assigned Dept. State, 1940-41, Belfast, N. Ireland, 1942-43; consul, prin. officer, Auckland, N.Z., 1944-46; consul, Capetown, S. Africa, 1947- 49, Milan, Italy, 1949-50; European area specialist Office Internat. Labor Affairs, Dept. Labor, 1951-54; labor attache, 1st sec. Am. embassy, Santiago, Chile, 1955-57, Rome, Italy, 1957-62; dep. dir. Office Internat. Confs., Dept. State, 1962-65; consul gen., Trieste, Italy, 1965—. Decorated commendatore Ordine al Merito della Repubblica Italiana. Mem. Am. Fedn. Govt. Employees, Soc. Colonial Wars. Mason. Clubs: D.U. (Harvard); Internat. (Washington); Monterey Peninsula Country. Home: Singing Pines Carmel CA 93921 Office: American Consulate Trieste Italy

FUGASSI, JAMES PAUL, educator; b. Trafford City, Pa., Feb. 1, 1909; B.S., Carnegie Inst. Tech., 1930, fellow, 1930-33, M.S., 1931; Coffin fellow, U. Wis., 1931- 33, univ. fellow, 1933-34, Ph.D., 1934, Asst. in chemistry Carnegie- Mellon Univ., 1930-31, instr., 1935-38, asst. prof., 1938-44; asso. prof., 1944-49, prof., 1949—, now also Silliman prof. chemistry; research asst. U. Wis., 1934-35. With OSRD, AUS, 1944. Fellow N.Y. Acad. Sci.; mem. Am. Chem. Soc., Electrochem. Soc., Faraday Soc. Office: Carnegie-Mellon Univ Pittsburgh PA 15213*

FUGATE, JOSEPHINE BRAUCHER, educator; b. Kansas City, Mo., Nov. 26, 1903; d. Joseph and Jane Campbell (McKeever) Braucher; A.B., U. Kan., 1924, M.A., 1929; postgrad. Columbia, 1929; m. Justus H. Fugate, Jan. 25, 1931; children—Brauch, Justus, Jane. Tchr., Hutchinson, Kan., 1924-27, U. Kan., 1927-31, Plainview (Kan.) High Sch., 1948-54; dean of women U. Wichita, 1955-70, coordinator student services, 1958-70; prof. mathematics Wichita State U., 1970—. Speaker radio and TV. Mem. bd. regents U. Wichita, 1940-55. Mem. Am. Assn. U. Women (pres. Kan. 1940-42), Sigma Xi, Pi Lambda Theta (nat. v.p. 1946- 47), Pi Mu Epsilon, Alpha Omicron Pi. Democrat. Mem. Disciples of Christ Ch. Contbr. articles to profl. jours. Home: 1340 N Yale Wichita KS 67208

FUGAZY, WILLIAM DENIS, travel co. exec.; b. Wyndham, N.Y., Aug. 17, 1924; s. Itio and Irene (Cronin) F.; student Fordham U., Cornell U.; m. Joan Boggiano, May 24, 1947; children—Denise, William Denis, John, Daria, Roy. Pres., Diners/Fugazy Travel and Incentive, Inc., chmn., dir. Gen. Leisure Corp. Chmn., All-Am. Collegiate Golf Dinner; tournament dir. Tony Lema Meml. Golf Tournament for Coll. Scholarships. Chmn. bd. John V. Mara Meml. Fund Cancer Research; bd. dirs. Nat. Cath. Youth Orgn., St. Vincent's Hosp., N.Y.C., Discover America. Served with USNR, World War II. Named knight Equestrian Order Holy Sepulchre, knight Grand Cross, 1963. Mem. Hotel Sales Mgmt. Assn., Sales Execs. Club N.Y.C. Clubs: Westchester Country; Winged Foot Golf. Home: Sunnyridge Rd Harrison NY 10528 Office: 10 Columbus Circle New York City NY 10019

FUHLRODT, NORMAN THEODORE, ins. co. exec.; b. Wisner, Neb., Apr. 24, 1910; s. Albert F. and Lena (Schafersman) F.; student Midland Coll., 1926-28; A.B., U. Neb., 1930; M.A., U. Mich., 1936; m. Clarice W. Livermore, Aug. 23, 1933; 1 son, Douglas B. Tchr., athletic coach high schs. in Sargent, Neb., 1930-32, West Point, Neb., 1932-35; with Central Life Assurance Co., Des Moines, 1936—, pres., chief exec. officer, 1964—, also dir.; dir. Ia.-Des Moines Nat. Bank. Named Monroe St. Jour. Alumnus of Month, U. Mich. Grad Sch. Bus. Adminstrn. Gen. chmn. Greater Des Moines United campaign United Community Service, 1969-70. Bd. dirs. Des Moines Center Sci. and Industry, Greater Des Moines C. of Fellow Soc. Actuaries. Home: 3926 River Oaks Dr Des Moines IA 50312 Office: 611 5th Av PO Box 1555 Des Moines IA 50306

FUHR, SAMUEL E., educator; b. Oklahoma County, Okla., Aug. 23, 1918; s. Antoine H. and Riva (Abram) F.; B.Sc., Langston U., 1939; M.Sc., Okla. State U., 1952, grad. student, 1960-61; m. Willie Ella Sams, Dec. 27, 1939; children—Sandra Loise (Mrs. Willis G. Tilford), William Edward. Sci. tchr. Rosenwald High Sch., Henryetta, Okla., 1939-41; vocational agr. tchr. Dunbar High Sch. in Henneseey, Okla., 1941-43, in Okmulgee, Okla., 1943-48; state supr. instl. farm tng. Okla. State U., 1948-51; agrl. edn. specialist USOM, Iran, 1953-57, vocational ednl. adviser, 1957-58, dep. chief edn. adviser, 1958-59; dep. chief edn. div. USAID, Nigeria, 1961-64, chief edn. div., 1964-68; dep. chief edn. div. Africa Bur., AID, 1968—. Served with AUS, 1944-46. Recipient Commendation award USOM, 1956, USAID, 1963. Mem. N.E.A., Okla. Tchrs. Assn., Am. Rifleman Assn., Am. Legion, Alpha Phi Alpha, Phi Kappa Phi. Home: 536 N 10th St Muskogee OK 74401. Office: Africa Bureau AID Dept of State Washington DC 20525

FUHRMAN, CHARLES ANDREW, lawyer; b. Milw., June 14, 1933; s. Harry H. and Gertrude (Wynn) F.; B.S., U. Wis., 1955, LL.B., 1957; m. Rosann Lois Aronoff, Aug. 22, 1954; children—Anthony Andres, Nicolas Andrew. Admitted to Wis. bar, 1957, Ohio bar, 1958, Mich. bar, 1964; pvt. practice, Toledo, 1958-62; partner Fuhrman, Gertner, Britz & Barkan, 1963—. Mng. Partner Varsity Sq. Apts. Co., Alexian Co., Dundee Post Office Co. Served to 2d lt., Transp. Corps, U.S. Army, 1958. Mem. Am., Wis., Mich., Ohio, Toledo bar assns., Lucas County Sheriffs Posse, Phi Delta Phi, Pi Lambda Phi. Republican. Jewish Religion. Home: 4778 Springbrook Dr Toledo OH 43615 Office: Spitzer Bldg Toledo OH 43604

FUHRMAN, FREDERICK ALEXANDER, educator; b. Coquille, Ore., Aug. 13, 1915; s. Cyrus Jacob and Josie (Lyons) F.; B.S., Ore. State Coll., 1937, M.S., 1939; postgrad. Universität Freiburg im Breisgau, 1937-38, U. Wash., 1939-41; Ph.D., Stanford, 1943; m. Geraldine Jackson, Nov. 12, 1942. Univ. fellow in pharmacology U. Wash., 1939-41; research asso. in physiology Stanford, 1941-45, instr., 1945-49, asst. prof., 1949-52, asso. prof., 1952-57, prof. physiology, 1957-61, dir. basic med. scis. labs. Med. Sch., 1959—, prof. exptl. medicine, 1961—, dir. Max C. Fleischmann Labs. of the Med. Scis., 1961-70. Active in med. research OSRD, World War II. Guggenheim fellow, labor of zoophysiology U. Copenhagen, 1951-52; sr. postdoctoral fellow NSF, Inst. Biol. Chemistry, U. Copenhagen and Donner Lab., U. Cal., 1958-59; Commonwealth Fund fellow, 1966-67. Fellow A.A.A.S., N.Y. Acad. Scis.; mem. Am. Physiol. Soc., Am. Soc. Pharmacology and Exptl. Therapeutics, Sigma Xi, Phi Kappa Phi. Author: Multidiscipline Laboratories for Teaching the Medical Sciences. Asso. editor: Ann. Review of Physiology, 1954-62. Contbr. articles profl. jours. Home: PO Box 313 Pebble Beach CA 93953

FUHRMAN, RALPH EDWARD, civil and environmental engr.; b. Kansas City, Kan., Sept. 6, 1909; s. Ralph William and Olga (Woinova) F.; B.S. in Civil Engring., U. Kan., 1930; M.S. in San. Engring., Harvard, 1937; D.Eng., Johns Hopkins, 1954; m. Josephine Ackerman, Jan. 1, 1935; children—William Edward, Ann Louise. Asst. pub. health engr. Mo. Dept. of Health, 1931, 37; city san. engr., Springfield, Mo., 1931-36; asst. supt. D.C. Water Pollution Control Plant, 1937-42, supt., 1942-53; dep. dir. san. engring. D.C. Govt., 1953- 55; exec. sec. Water Pollution Control Fedn. 1955-69, pres., 1950-51; asst. dir. Nat. Water Commn., 1969—; lectr. civil engring. George Washington U., 1941-60. Fellow Am. Pub. Health Assn., Am. Soc. C.E. (chmn. exec. com. san. engring. div. 1954-55), Inst. Water Pollution Control (Brit., hon.), Instn. Pub. Health Engrs. (Brit., hon.); mem. Chesapeake Water Pollution Control Assn., Am. Water Works Assn., Am. Acad. Environmental Engrs. Episcopalian. Club: Cosmos (Washington). Home: 2917 39th St N W Washington DC 20016 Office: 800 N Quincy St Arlington VA 22203

FUJII, SHINZO, industrialist; b. Hiroshima Prefecture, Japan; grad. Tokyo U., 1918. Pres., Shin Mitsubishi Heavy Industries, Ltd., 1950-59, 62-64, chmn. bd., 1959-62; pres. Mitsubishi Heavy Industries, Ltd., 1964-65, chmn. bd., 1965—. Dir. Japan Employers' Fedn. Home: 12-18 7-chome Koyama Shinagawaku Tokyo Japan Office: 10 2-chome Marunouchi Chiyodaku Tokyo Japan

FUJINAGA, KAKUMIN, clergyman, religious assn. ofcl.; b. Shigaken, Japan, Aug. 8, 1911; s. Eiju and Fuiie (Emura) F.; came to U.S. 1936; grad. Kyoto Ryukoku Buddhist U., 1934; m. Florence Iseki, June 21, 1952; children—Karen, Calvin, Rodger. Ordained to Buddhist ministry, 1934; head minister Fresno (Cal.) Buddhist Ch., 1945-47, Parlier Ch., 1948-53, Lodi Ch., 1954-59; exec. sec. Buddhist

Chs. Am. Nat. Hdqrs., San Francisco, 1960- -; chmn. Buddhist Chs. Am. Sunday Sch. Material, San Francisco, 1947—. Home: 361-3 N Grant St San Mateo CA 94401 Office: 1710 Octavia St San Francisco CA 94109

FUKUSHIMA, KAZUO, composer; b. Tokyo, Japan, 1930. Lectr. on no plays and relationship to Japanese music in Darmstadt, 1961; spent year at Cambridge, Eng. Composer; Hi-Kyo (for flute, piano, strings and percussion). Address: Deutsche Grammophon Gesellschaft Rothenbaumstausee 2 Hamburg 13 Federal Republic of Germany*

FULBRIGHT, FREEMAN, pub. relations counsel; b. Atlanta, Apr. 26, 1925; s. Ernest Alexander and Lessie (Freeman) F.; student Ohio State U.; m. Jane Meese, Aug. 4, 1947; children—Carolyn Frances, Charles Cary. Reporter, Durham (N.C.) Morning Herald, 1941-43, Cin. Post, 1943-45; legislative corr. I.N.S., Columbus, O., 1945-46, news editor, Chgo., 1947-50, Washington corr., 1951-52; night mng. editor, N.Y.C., 1952-55; v.p., gen. mgr. Walker & Crenshaw, Inc., pub. relations, 1955-57; gen. editor Newsweek, 1957-61; exec. editor N.Y. Herald Tribune, 1961-62; exec. v.p. Selvage & Lee, Inc., 1962-68; sr. v.p. Hill and Knowlton, Inc., 1969—; cons. in field, 1943—. Mem. Sigma Delta Chi. Presbyn. (trustee). Clubs: Overseas Press, (N.Y.C.); Nat. Press (Washington); Downtown (Richmond, Va.). Home: 277 West End Av New York City NY 10023. Office: 150 E 42d St New York City NY 10017

FULBRIGHT, JAMES WILLIAM, U.S. Senator; b. Sumner, Mo., Apr. 9, 1905; s. Jay and Roberta (Waugh) F.; A.B., U. Ark., 1925; B.A., Oxford U., Eng., 1928, M.A., 1931; LL.B., George Washington U., 1934; m. Elizabeth Williams, June 15, 1932; children—Elizabeth (Mrs. John Winnacker), Roberta (Mrs. Edward Thaddeus Foote II). Admitted to D.C. bar, 1934; spl. atty. Anti-Trust Div. U.S. Dept. of Justice, 1934-35; instr. in law, George Washington U., 1935-36; lectr. in law, U. Ark., 1936-39, pres., 1939-41. Mem. 78th Congress (1943-45), 3d Dist., Ark. U.S. Senator January 1945—, mem. com. on finance, chmn. com. on fgn. relations. Del. 9th Gen. Assembly UN, 1954. Mem. Sigma Chi, Order of Coif. Democrat. Mem. Disciples of Christ Ch. Rotarian. Home: Fayetteville AR 72701 Office: Senate Office Bldg Washington DC 20510

FULD, EDWIN BERNARD, finance co. exec.; b. Balt., Jan. 8, 1895; s. Manes Edwin and Bertha (Cahn) F.; A.B., U. Cal. at Berkeley, 1916; m. Georgea Catts, June 18, 1927. With Crown Zellerbach Corp., 1916-23; with Valley Morris Plan, Stockton, Cal., 1924-64, chmn. bd., 1960-64; asst. chmn. bd. Morris Plan Co. of Cal., 1964-69; ret. Pres. Stockton Community Chest, 1952. Served with USNR, 1917-19. Home: 1030 Bristol Av Stockton CA 95204

FULD, LEONHARD FELIX, lawyer; b. N.Y., Aug. 12, 1883; s. Bernhard and Helen E. (Schwab) F.; A.B., Columbia, 1903, A.M., 1904, LL.B., 1905, LL.M., 1906, Ph.D., 1909; hon. diploma, Am. Acad. Phys. Edn., 1913; LL.D., Hahnemann Med Coll., Phila., 1963. Admitted to N.Y. State bar, 1905, U.S. Supreme Ct., 1952; practice of law, 1905—. Editor for Carnegie Instn., Sabin's Dictionary Am. Bibliography, 1905-07; examiner Municipal Civil Service Commn., N.Y., 1907-14, asst. chief examiner, 1914-19; expert U.S. Bur. Edn. 1915- 19; examiner civilian personnel War Dept., 1917-19; editor Corpus Juris, 1919-21; ednl. dir. Henry L. Doherty & Co., 1919-23; lectr. investment Coll. City N.Y., 1910-45. Dir. Med. Center, Jersey City, 1923-47; pres. Helene Fuld Sch. Nursing N.J., Trenton, Helene Fuld Health Found.; cons. student nurse health Helene Fuld schs. nursing, Balt., N.Y.C., Camden, N.J., Trenton, N.J., Helen Fuld Nursing Preparatory School, Helene Fuld Geriatric Nursing School, N.Y.C. Fellow Am. Geriatric Soc. Am. Public Health Assn., A.A.A.S.; mem. Internat. Assn. Chiefs Police, Phi Beta Kappa. Author books. Editor Journal Helene Fuld Health Found. Home: 93 Fuld St Trenton NJ 08638 Office: Helene Fuld Hospital Trenton NJ 08638

FULD, STANLEY H., judge; b. N.Y.C., Aug. 23, 1903; s. Emanuel I. and Hermine (Frisch) F.; A.B., Coll. City N.Y., 1923; LL.B., Columbia, 1926, LL.D., 1959; LL.D., Hamilton Coll., 1949, Union Coll., 1961, Yeshiva U., 1962, N.Y. Law Sch., 1962, N.Y. U., 1963, Jewish Theol. Sem. Am., 1964, Syracuse U., 1967, St. John's U., 1970; m. Florence Geringer, May 29, 1930; children—Hermine (Mrs. Maurice N. Nessen), Judith (Mrs. Frank Miller). Admitted to N.Y. bar, 1926; pvt. practice N.Y.C., 1926-35, 1944-46; asst. dist. atty. N.Y. County, 1935-44; spl. asst. atty. gen., liaison counsel, state investigations N.Y. State, 1944-45; apptd. asso. judge Ct. of Appeals, 1946; elected for full term beginning 1947, 61; chief judge State of N.Y. and Ct. of Appeals, 1967—. Chmn. adminstrv. bd. Jud. Conf. State N.Y., 1967—; chmn. N.Y. Fair Trial-Free Press Conf., 1968—. Commr. Nat. Hillel Commn., 1947-56; mem. bd. visitors Columbia Law Sch. Chmn. bd. dirs. Jewish Theol. Sem. Am., Inst. for Advanced Studies in Humanities; bd. dirs. Bath Israel Hosp. trustee Sara Delano Roosevelt House, Hillel Found. (chmn. met. adv. council 1947-51). Recipient Joseph M. Proskauer medal, lawyers div. Fedn. Jewish Philanthropies, 1960; Cardozo award Knights of Pythias; Harlan Fiske Stone award Assn. Trial Lawyers City N.Y., 1966; medal for excellence Columbia Law Sch. Alumni Assn., 1967; Gold medal for distinguished service N.Y. State Bar Assn., 1971; John Peter Zanger award N.Y. Soc. Newspaper Editors, 1970; Gold medallion for distinguished service Nassau County Bar Assn., 1971. Mem. Bar Assn. City N.Y., N.Y. County Lawyers' Assn., N.Y. State, Am. bar assns., Coll. City N.Y. Alumni Assn. (v.p., Finley medal 1971), Columbia Law Alumni Assn. (dir.), Am. Law Inst., Acad. Am. Arts and Scis., Phi Beta Kappa, Phi Beta Kappa Assos. (dir.), Columbia Law Rev. Assn. (dir.). Republican. Jewish religion (trustee synagogue). Club: University of Albany. Home: 30 Park Av New York City NY 10016 Office: 36 W 44th St New York City NY 10036

FULDA, CARL HERMAN, educator; b. Berlin, Germany, Aug. 22, 1909; s. Ludwig and Helen (Hermann) F.; Dr. Law, U. Freiburg (Germany), 1931; student U. Geneva (Switzerland), 1927, U. Berlin, 1928-30; LL.B., Yale, 1938; m. Gaby Gros, Feb. 28, 1935; children—Thomas Richard, John Anthony. Came to U.S., 1936, naturalized, 1941. Law clk., Berlin, Germany, 1931-33; with Victoria Ins. Co., Paris, France, 1934-35; research asst. N.Y. State Law Revision Commn., 1938-41, cons., 1949, 52, 55; atty. Treasury Dept., 1942, OPA, 1942-46; from asst. to prof. law Rutgers U., New Brunswick, N.J. 1946-54; prof. law Ohio State U., Columbus, 1954-64; prof. law U. Tex., Austin, 1964—, Hugh Lamar Stone prof. law, 1965—. Vis. prof. Columbia Law Sch., 1952, La. State U. Law Sch., 1962, U. Frankfurt (Germany), 1962, U. Tübingen (Germany), 1964, 70, orientation program Am. law Princeton, 1965, Salzburg Seminar Am. Law, 1960, Osgoode Hall Law Sch., York U., Toronto, Ont., Can., 1970; vis. lectr. U. Trieste (Italy), 1964, 65; mem. White House Task Force on Antitrust Policy, 1968; pub. mem. gov. N.J. Com. Pub. Utilities Labor Disputes Legislation, 1954; cons. AID, 1967. Mem. Am. Bar. Assn. mem. commn. to study Fed. Trade (commn. 1969); chmn. subcom. fgn. antitrust laws, sect. antitrust law 1968-70), Am. Soc. Study Comparative Law (bd. dirs.), Tex. State Bar, Am. Soc. Internat. Law, Am. Fgn. Law Assn., Am. Assn. U. Profs., Am. Civil Liberties Union. Author: Competition in Regulated Industries; Transporation, 1961; (with Warren F. Schwartz) Cases and Materials on the Regulation of International Trade and Investment, 1970; Introduction to American Law (in German), 1966; also numerous articles. Bd. editors Am. Jour. Comparative Law; editorial adv. bd. Jour. Air Law and Commerce, Transp. Law Jour. Home: 3410 Shinoak Dr Austin TX 78731

FULGHAM, CECIL EVERETT, bus. dir.; b. Mineola, Tex., Nov. 13, 1913; s. James Edward and Hattie (Hanks) F.; B.A., Washington U., St. Louis, 1935; m. Helen Jones, July 12, 1939; children—Carolyn (Mrs. Preston Butcher), Edward Everett. Sec.- treas. Community Ice & Produce Co., Dallas, 1935-39; dist. mgr. So. Ice & Utilities Co., Arkadelphia, Ark., 1939-41; owner-mgr. Superior Ice Co., Texarkana, Tex., 1941-46; founder, 1946, Steel Built Products Co., Lubbock, Tex., partner, 1946-53; organizer Western Royalty Corp., Lubbock, 1953, pres., 1953-58, dir., sec. state Tex., 1954-55; Tex. commr. on Canadian River Compact Commn., 1955-63; exec. v.p. First Nat. Bank, Lubbock, Tex., 1955-64, dir., 1952—; exec. v.p. First City Nat. Bank, Houston, 1964-67; dir. bus. affairs for Winthrop Rockefeller Little Rock, Ark., 1967—; dir. 1st Nat. Bank, Floydada, Tex.; mem. Tex. Securities Bd., 1963—. Chmn. Tex. Indsl. Commn., 1953-54. Chmn. United Fund campaign, Lubbock, 1955, Lubbock chpt. A.R.C. campaign, 1956; v.p., mem. bd. Lubbock YMCA, 1962-63. Mem. bd. devel. So. Methodist U.; bd. dirs. Houston Jr. Achievement. Mem. A.I.M., Little Rock C. of C. (sec.- treas., dir.). Methodist (past steward). Mason (Shriner), Rotarian (v.p., dir. Lubbock 1952-53). Clubs: Lubbock Country (pres. 1952-53); Ramada (Houston). Home: 3700 Cantrell Little Rock AR 72202 Office: Tower Bldg Little Rock AR 72201

FULGHAM, JOHN RAWLES, Jr., banker; b. Windsor, Va., July 29, 1927; s. John Rawles and Gypsie (Matthews) F.; B.A., Va. Mil. Inst., B.B.A. in Money and Banking, So. Methodist U.; m. Betty Berger, Dec. 2, 1950; children—Emily Ann, Janie Rawles, John Rawles III. With First Nat. Bank, Dallas, 1954—, sr. v.p., 1963—, controller, 1965—, head adminstrv. services, 1966—, now exec. v.p. and chmn. trust com.; dir. Vancouver Plywood Co., Inc.; mem. faculty Southwestern Grad. Sch. Banking, lectr. Am. Inst. Banking, Fed. Savs. & Loan Inst. Leader fund raising campaigns Wadley Research Inst., Dallas Goodwill Industries, United Fund Dallas, Presbyn. Hosp., Dallas. Trustee Tex. Presbyn. Found. Served to capt. USMCR, 1950-53. Mem. Dallas Salesmanship Club, Financial Execs. Inst., Va. Mil. Inst. Alumni Assn. (pres. N. Tex. chpt. 1959), Kappa Alpha. Presbyn. (deacon). Clubs: Dallas Country (bd. govs.), Dallas Petroleum. Home: 4414 Lorraine Av Dallas TX 75205 Office: 1401 Elm St Dallas TX 75222

FULGINITI, VINCENT ANTHONY, physician, educator; b. Phila., Aug. 8, 1931; s. John and Rose (Perry) F.; A.B., Temple U., 1953, M.D., 1957, M.S., 1961; m. Shirley Lee Van Gorden, June 28, 1958; children—John, Jeffrey, Laura, Paul. Intern, Phila. Gen. Hosp., 1957-58; resident pediatrics St. Christopher's Hosp., Phila., 1958-60, chief pediatric research, 1960-61; cons. Fitzsimons Gen., Children's, Gen. Rose, Nat. Jewish hosps., all Denver, 1966—; asst. in pediatrics St. Christopher's Hosp., Phila., 1960-61; fellow in virology U. Colo. Med. Center, Denver, 1961-62, instr. pediatrics, 1962-64, asst. prof., 1964-67, asso. prof., 1967-69; prof., head dept. pediatrics U. Ariz., Tucson, 1969—. Markle Acad. scholar in medicine, 1964. Mem. Western Soc. for Pediatric Research (recipient Ross Research award, 1965), Rocky Mountain Pediatric Soc., Phila. Pediatric Soc., Infectious Disease Soc. Am., A.A.A.S., Am. Acad. Pediatrics, A.M.A., Soc. Pediatric Research, Am. Soc. Microbiology. Contbr. articles profl. jours. Home: 5101 Camino Esplendora Tucson AZ 85718

FULHAM, GERARD AQUINAS, corp. exec.; b. Winthrop, Mass., Mar. 7, 1920; s. John N. and Mary E. (Maloney) F.; A.B., Harvard, 1942; m. Barbara Ann McGoldrick, Feb. 22, 1944; children—John Bernard, Trudy Deane, Gerarda Marie, Gerard Aquinas, Barbara Ann, Maura Jude. With Estabrook & Co., Boston, 1946-47; pres., treas. Fulham Bros., Inc., Boston, 1947-57; financial v.p. Cleve. Pneumatic Industries, 1958-61; sr. v.p., dir. Pneumo Dynamics Corp., Cleve., 1961-69, chmn. bd., chief exec. officer, 1969—; pres. LaTouraine Coffee Co., Boston, 1961—, chmn. bd. dirs., 1963—. Served to lt. (s.g.) USNR, 1942-46. Clubs: Union (Cleve.); Shaker (Shaker Heights, O.); Oyster Harbors (Osterville, Mass.). Home: 24 Carisbrooke Rd Wellesley Hills MA 02181 Office: 64 State St Cambridge MA 12139

FULHAM, THOMAS ANTHONY, univ. pres.; b. Winthrop, Mass., July 18, 1915; A.B., Coll. Holy Cross, 1937; D.C.S. (hon.), Suffolk U., 1963; m. Annette M. Healy, July 23, 1942; children—Annette, Mary, Ellen, Christina, Thomas, Deborah, Nicholas, Gretchen, Gregory. Chmn. bd. Fulham Bros., Inc., 1948-62; pres. Boston Fish Market Corp., 1962-70; now pres. Suffolk U.; pres. Boston Fishing Boat Co., Inc., 1962-70. Chmn. Mass. Bd. Natural Resources, 1955—; U.S. commr. Internat. Commn. for Northwest Atlantic, 1957—; fishery adviser State Dept., 1950—; mem. nat. adv. com. Nat. Oceanographic and Atmospheric Agy., 1971—. Trustee Suffolk U., New Eng. Aquarium; asso. trustee Holy Cross Coll.; corporator Provident Instn. for Savs.; bd. dirs. Assn. for Better Housing, Boston. Served to maj. AUS, 1941-46. Home: 7 Arlington Rd Wellesley Hills MA 02181 Office: 41 Temple St Boston MA 02114

FULK, ROSCOE NEAL, accountant; b. Lebo, Kan., June 23, 1916; s. Roscoe Lloyd and Maude (Calvert) F.; B.S., U. Ill., 1940; m. Marie Therese Rabbitt, June 15, 1946; children—Thomas, Janet, David, Robert, Kenneth, Howard. With Ernst & Ernst, C.P.A.'s, Chgo., 1940—, partner, 1957—. Treas., Winnetka (Ill.) Caucus Com., 1956, vice chmn., 1962, chmn. accountants group United Republican Fund Ill., 1958, Met. Crusade of Mercy, 1970; pres. Civic Fedn. Chgo., 1968-70. Pres., New Trier Twp. Citizens League, 1961- 65, now mem. bd.; mem. Ill. Commn. on Urban Area Govt., Gov.'s Adv. Council; mem. adv. com. to Coll. Commerce and Bus. Administrn., U. Ill.; pres., dir. Juvenile Protective Assn.; v.p., bd. govs. Chgo. Met. Housing and Planning Council; chmn. Winnetka Zoning Bd. Appeals, 1968-71; mem. Parking Adv. Council Chgo.; mem. grand council Am. Indian Center; chmn. pres.'s council bus. assos. Elmhurst Coll., 1969-70. Bd. dirs. State Equity Council. Served to lt. USNR, 1942-46. Mem. Am. Inst. C.P.A.'s (mem. council), Ill. Soc. C.P.A.'s (dir. 1963-64, pres. 1969-70), Newcomen Soc. N.Am. Clubs: Sunset Ridge Country (dir. 1961-65, treas. 1965-66) (Winnetka); Executives, Mid-Am., Economic (dir.), Mid-Day (Chgo.); Newton (Ia.) Country. Home: 227 Church Rd Winnetka IL 60093 Office: 231 S LaSalle St Chicago IL 60604

FULLAGAR, WILLIAM ALFRED, educator; b. Western Springs, Ill., Nov. 28, 1915; s. George Payne and Maude Madeline (Humphreys) F.; A.B., N.Y. State Coll. Tchrs., Albany, 1936, A.M., 1940; Ed.D., Columbia, 1951; m. Evelyn Louise Hoyt, 1938; children—Paul David, Joan Linda, Lois Gayle, Neil Scott; m. 2d, Roberta A. E. Johnson, 1958. High sch. sci. tchr., Schaghticoke, N.Y., 1936-38, Hudson Falls, 1938-40; chmn. sci. dept. Bethlehem Central High Sch., Delmar, N.Y., 1940-42; sci. supr. N.Y. State Coll. Tchrs., Albany, 1942- 46; asso. prof. edn. U. Fla., 1948-56; part-time lectr. Queens Coll., N.Y.C., 1951; vis. prof. Mont. State U., 1954, Denver U., 1956; prof. edn., chmn. div. edn. U. Rochester, 1956-58, dean Coll. Edn., 1958-68, Earl B. Taylor prof. edn., 1968—. Ex officio mem. Regents Adv. Council Tchr. Edn. Bd. dirs., treas. Eastern Regional Ednl. Lab.; bd. dirs. Rochester Sch. for Deaf. Served from ensign to lt. USNR, 1943-57; navigator. Mem. N.E.A., N.Y. State Tchrs. Assn., Am. Assn. Higher Edn., Nat. Soc. Study Edn., Rochester Assn. UN, Phi Delta Kappa, Kappa Delta Pi. Sr. editor: Readings for Educational Psychology, 1956, 2d edit., 1964. Home: Box 40 Mendon NY 14506

FULLAGAR, WILLIAM WATTS, lawyer; b. Chgo., July 3, 1914; s. William Watts and Grace (Wilson) F.; B.S., Northwestern U., 1937; LL.B., Chgo. Kent Coll., 1942; m. Doris Virginia Olson, Feb. 11, 1956. With loan dept. First Nat. Bank & Trust Co., Evanston, Ill., 1938-43; admitted to Ill. bar, 1942; partner firm Hackbert, Rooks, Pitts, Fullagar & Poust, Chgo., and predecessors, 1943—; instr. comml. law Am. Inst. Banking, Chgo., 1947-51. Trustee, gen. counsel Union League Found. for Boys' Clubs. Mem. Am., Ill., Chgo. (chmn. com. on fed. legislation 1957-59) bar assns., Alpha Delta Phi. Republican. Presbyn. Club: Union League (sec. 1966-68) (Chgo.). Home: 2320 Isabella St Evanston IL 60201 Office: 208 S La Salle St Chicago IL 60604

FULLAM, JOHN P., U.S. judge; b. Gardenville, Pa., Dec. 10, 1921; s. Thomas L. and Mary (Nolan) F.; B.S. in Edn., Villanova U., 1942; LL.B., Harvard, 1948; m. Alice Hilliar Freiheit, Apr. 15, 1950; children—Nancy, Sally, Thomas, Jeffrey. Admitted to Pa. bar, 1949; with firm Easthurn, Begley & Fullam, Bristol, Pa., 1948-60; judge Ct. Common Pleas, Bucks County, Pa., 1960-66; judge U.S. Dist. Ct. Eastern Dist. Pa., 1966—. Mem. Del. River Joint Toll Bridge Commn., 1955-60, chmn., 1958. Dem. candidate for Congress, 1954-56. Trustee Bucks County Community Coll., 1964—, 1st chmn., 1964-67; v.p., bd. dirs. Welcome House, Doylestown, Pa., 1965—. Home: Wrightstown PA 18940 Office: US Court House Philadelphia PA 19107

FULLBRIGHT, WILBUR DALE, educator, musician; b. Spearman, Tex., Jan. 19, 1926; s. Ralph Robert and Myrtle Ella (Files) F.; B.A., Okla. State U., 1950; M.F.A., Bob Jones U., 1953; Ph.D., Boston U., 1960; m. Lorraine Barker, Jan. 2, 1947; children—Glen Arthur, Karl Robert, Dale Norman. Mem. faculty Bob Jones U., 1953-56; registrar, asst. prof. music Boston U., 1957-59, asst. dean, asso. prof. music, 1959-65, prof. music, chmn. div., 1966—. Nat. pres. Pi Kappa Lambda, 1966-70, regent, 1970—; province gov. Phi Mu Alpha Sinfonia, 1964-66; dir. Contemporary Music Project in Boston, 1970—, Fedn. Music Clubs, 1969—, New Eng. Regional Opera, 1969—, Greater Boston Youth Symphony Orch., 1965—; mem. com. Mass. Arts Scholastic Awards, Greater Boston Council Arts in Higher Edn., Mason and Hamlin Scholarship, Opera Co. Boston Consortium. Served with USN, 1944-46. Mem. Am. Musicol. Soc., Coll. Music Soc., Music Educators Nat. Conf., Music Tchrs. Nat. Assn., (dir.), Mass. Music Tchrs. Assn. (dir.). Home: 24 Euston St Brookline MA 02146 Office: 855 Commonwealth Av Boston MA 02215

FULLER, ALFRED CARL, brush mfr.; b. Weisford, Kings County, N.S., Jan. 13, 1885; s. Leander Joseph and Phebe Jane (Collins) F.; ed. common sch.; M.A., Trinity Coll.; A.F.D., Hartt Coll. Music, 1952; D.C.L., Acadia U., Wolfeville, N.S., 1958; D.C.L. Bates Coll., 1963; m. Evelyn W. Ells, Apr. 8, 1908; children—Alfred Howard, Avard Ells; m. 2d, Mary Primrose Pelton, Oct. 21, 1932. Naturalized citizen, 1918. Established Fuller Brush Co., Somerville, Mass., 1906, since pres. and chmn. bd.; now ret. Trustee U. Conn.; chmn. bd. trustee Hartt Coll. of Music; life trustee Kingswood Sch.; bd. regents U. Hartford. Recipient Horatio Alger award, 1959. Mem. Conn. Mfrs. Assn. (pres. 1942- 46). Republican. Christian Scientist. Mason (32, K.T., Shriner). Clubs: Hartford, Hartford Golf. Home: 32 Colony Road West Hartford CT 06007 Office: Hartford CT 06101

FULLER, AVARD E., mfg. exec.; b. Hartford, Conn., 1918. Formerly v.p., pres., now chmn. Fuller Brush Co. Home: 49 Blue Ridge Lane West Hartford CT 06007 Office: 3580 Main St Hartford CT 06002*

FULLER, CLYDE DALE, orgn. exec.; b. Iroquois, S.D., Sept. 24, 1915; s. Clyde DeVere and Hattie Pearl (Stoner) F.; B.A., U. Denver, 1937, M.A., 1939; certificate Russian Inst., Columbia, 1949; m. Ethelyn Goldberg, Dec. 16, 1953; children—Diana Kim, Laurel Jan, Claire Ellen. Instr. social studies Webster (S.D.) High Sch., 1937-38; faculty U. Denver, 1938-42, 46, 53-59, dir. social sci. found., chmn. dept. internat. relations, 1953- 59; exec. v.p. Fgn. Policy Assn., N.Y.C., 1959—; dir. Russian project Nat. Assn. Edn. Broadcasters, 1951-52; mgr. research br. information and reference dept., Radio Free Europe, 1952. Analyst, Journeys Behind the News, weekly radio series, 1938-42, 46; moderator Focus, weekly TV series, 1953-59; narrator 20th Century Revolutions in World Affairs, TV series, 1959. Served with AUS, 1942-46. Mem. Am. Polit. Sci. Assn., Council on Fgn. Relations, Adult Edn. Assn. Author: Training of Specialists in International Relations, 1957; also articles. Home: 20 Clinton St Mount Vernon NY 10552 Office: 345 E 46th St New York City NY 10017

FULLER, CURTIS G., editor, publisher; b. Necedah, Wis., Mar. 2, 1912; s. Clarence Curtis and Lyda (Gross) F.; A.B., U. Wis., 1933; M.S., Northwestern, 1937; m. Mary Margaret Stiehm, Sept. 24, 1938; children—Nancy Abigail, Michael Curtis. Newspaper work, 1933-37; asst. journalism Northwestern, 1936-37; asso. editor Nat. Almanac and Year Book, 1937-38; information dir. State Wis., 1938-39; asso. editor Better Roads Mag., 1939-43; asst. mng. editor, later mng. editor Flying Mag., 1943-48, editor, 1948-51; editorial dir. Pubs. Devel. Corp., 1951-53; pres. Clark Pub. Co., 1952—; editor Advt. Publs., Inc., 1953-55; mng. dir. Modern Castings Mag., 1955-56; v.p. Greenleaf Pub. Co., 1956-57; pres. Oak Ridge Atom Industries Sales Corp., 1960-62, Woodall Pub. Co., 1965—; pub. Woodall's Trailer Travel, Woodall's Directories, Fate Mag., Better Camping Mag. Winner 1st place indsl. marketing competition for conceiving and executing best bus. mag. promotion of yr., 1941. Mem. Ill. Soc. for Psychic Research (pres. 1961-64), Spiritual Frontiers Fellowship (treas. 1962-69, v.p. 1970—), Sigma Delta Chi, Theta Delta Chi, Phi Kappa Phi. Home: 301 S Ridge Rd Lake Forest, IL 60045. Office: 500 Hyacinth Pl Highland Park IL 60035

FULLER, DEREK JOSEPH HAGGARD, educator, mathematician; b. London, Eng., June 17, 1917; s. Brian Maitland and Olive (Haggard) F.; B.S. in Engring., U. Witwatersrand, Johannesburg, S. Africa, 1950; M.Sc., U. S.Africa, 1960; A.M., Ph.D., U. Cal. at Los Angeles, 1963. Came to U.S., 1965. Lectr., Pius XII Coll., Basutoland, Africa, 1950-59; sr. lectr. U. Basutoland, 1963-65; prof. math. Creighton U., 1965—. Served with RAF, 1941-46. Mem. Am. Math. Soc., Math. Assn. Am., Vatican Philatelic Soc. Home: 561 S 26th Av Omaha NB 68105

FULLER, DOUGLAS RAYMOND, banker; b. Campo Seco., Cal., May 8, 1909; s. Raymond August and Edith May (Fairfield) F.; A.B., Stanford, 1928, M.B.A., 1930; Ph.D., George Washington U., 1947; m. Ruth Vivian Cook, June 2, 1934; children—Thomas, Anne (Mrs. James C. Wall), William Raymond. With N.Am. Investment Corp., San Francisco, 1930-42, v.p., 1937-42; economist Dept. Commerce, 1942; cons. faculty mem. Grad. Sch. Bus., Stanford, 1937-46; with No. Trust Co., Chgo., 1946, sr. v.p., 1962-63, pres., 1963—. Bd. dirs. Cradle Soc., Community Fund Chgo.; mem. adv. council Stanford Grad. Sch. Bus., Northwestern U. Grad. Sch. Bus.; mem. citizens bd. U. Chgo.; mem. adv. bd. Salvation Army, Chgo. Served to lt. comdr.

USNR, 1942-46. Mem. Assn. Res. City Bankers, British-N.Am. Com., Phi Beta Kappa. Clubs: University, Chicago, Comml., Economic, Bankers, Execs., Casino, Mid-America (Chgo.); Old Elm; Barrington Hills Country. Author: (with Dowrie and Calkins) Investments, 3d edit., 1961; Government Financing of Private Enterprise, 1948. Home: PO Box 726 Barrington IL 60010 Office: 50 S LaSalle St Chicago IL 60690

FULLER, DUDLEY DEAN, engring. educator; b. Woodhaven, N.Y., Feb. 8, 1913; s. Elbridge George and Estelle (Wilson) F.; B.Mech. Engring., Coll. City N.Y., 1941; M.S., Columbia, 1945; m. Helen Dorothy Garbe, Oct. 13, 1945; 1 son, Dean Dudley. Faculty Columbia, 1943—, prof. mech. engring., 1954—, chmn. dept., 1964-70; prin. engr. part-time Franklin Inst., 1954—. Mem. bearing panel Nat. Acad. Scis., 1958-59, Inst. Def. Analysis, 1962; bearing panel project forecast USAF, 1963; chmn. 1st Internat. Symposium Gas Lubricated Bearings, 1959, also editor proc.; mem. mech. failure prevention group Office Naval Research, 1968—. Recipient citation on 10th anniversary gas-lubricated bearing research program for Chief Naval Research, Dept. Navy, 1967. Franklin Inst. fellow, 1968. Registered profl. engr., N.Y. Fellow Am. Soc. M.E. (Pi Tau Sigma Richards Meml. award 1962, Mayo D. Hersey award 1971); mem. Am. Soc. Lubrication Engrs. (Nat. award 1957, bd. dirs. 1957-60), Soc. Automotive Engrs., Instn. Mech. Engrs., Sigma Xi, Tau Beta Pi, Pi Tau Sigma. Author: A Survey of Journal Bearing Literature, 1958; (with others) A Manual for the Design of Gas-Lubricated, Tilting-Pad, Journal and Thrust Bearings with Special Reference to High-Speed Rotors, 1965; also articles in field. Home: 139 Gramatan Dr Yonkers NY 10701 also Lake Hill NY 12448 Office: Columbia Univ New York City NY 10027

FULLER, EDGAR, educator; b. La Crosse, Wis., Mar. 23, 1904; s. Ernest Edgar and Mary (Wise) F.; A.B., Brigham Young U., 1927; J.D., U. Chgo., 1932; Ed.D., Harvard, 1940; m. Alta Pamela Call, Sept. 10, 1926; children—Mary Margaret, Kathryn Jean (Mrs. L.S. Reid, Jr.), Carol Yvonne (Mrs. John H. Hinrichs, Jr.). Laborer in timber woods and mills, 1919-23; mucker and miner, 1923-27; supt. schs., Virden, N.M., 1929-31, 32-33; pres. Gila Jr. Coll., Thatcher, Ariz., 1933-39; lectr. on ednl. adminstrn. Harvard, 1940-42; prin. educationist and acting chief aviation edn. div. U.S. CAA, Washington, 1942-46; commr. edn. State of N.H., 1946-48; exec. sec. Council Chief State Sch. Officers, 1948-69, exec. sec. emeritus, 1969—. Mem. Pres.' Nat. Com. for Devel. Scientists and Engrs.; mem. various ednl. bds. and commns. Recipient Brewer trophy Nat. Aeros. Assn. for outstanding contbn. to air youth edn. Mem. N.E.A., Am. Assn. Sch. Adminstrs., Nat. Joint Com. Ednl. TV, Horace Mann League (pres. 1959); chmn. com. constnl. law 1962- -). Unitarian. Author numerous articles on pub. law, ednl. finance and adminstrn. and aviation edn. in Harvard Law Rev., Harvard Ednl. Rev., Am. Sch. Bd. Jour., Nat. Aeros., and similar periodicals; also bulls. and pamphlets on these subjects, 1932-. Home: 11700 Old Columbia Pike Silver Spring MD 20904

FULLER, EDWARD C., educator, chemist; b. Helena, Mont., Aug. 8, 1907; s. George N. and Claudia E. (Tinker) F.; B.S., Mont. State Coll., 1928; Ph.D., Columbia, 1941; m. Dorothy B. Edsall, June 26, 1937; children—David Edsall, Carol Margaret. Asst. in chem. engring. Mont. State Coll., 1928-31; asst. in chemistry Columbia, 1931-34; univ. fellow, 1934-35; instr., asst. prof., asso. prof., prof. chemistry, Bard Coll., 1935-43, pres., 1946-50; prof. chemistry, dir. area natural scis. and mathematics State U. of N.Y., Champlain Coll., 1950-53; prof. chemistry, chmn. dept. Beloit Coll., 1953—. Served as adminstrv. aide, Manhattan project, U.S. Army Engr. Corps. 1944-45. Fellow A.A.A.S., Am. Inst. Chemists; mem. Am. Chem. Soc. (div. chem. edn.; chmn. div. chem. edn. 1963), Am. Assn. U. Profs., Sigma Xi, Phi Lambda Upsilon, Alpha Chi Sigma, Phi Kappa Phi. Author: Discussion Guide and Laboratory Manual for Basic Natural Science. Contbr. chpt. and papers to publs. Home: 2648 Riverside Dr Beloit WI 53511

FULLER, EDWARD LATEN, railroad exec.; b. Scranton, Pa., Nov. 23, 1904; s. Mortimer Bartine and Kathryn I. (Steell) F.; student Lawrenceville (N.J.) Sch., 1920-25, Princeton, 1925-27; m. Laura Rice Green, Aug. 28, 1929; children—Kathryn Emelene (Mrs. Michael Spitzer), Susanne Steell (Mrs. Thomas O. Ryan), Edward Laton, III, James Mortimer. Joined Internat. Salt Co., 1927, v.p., 1929-31, pres., 1931-68, chmn. bd., chief exec. officer, 1968-69; pres. Genesee and Wyoming R.R. Co., 1931—; dir. Northeastern Pa. Nat. Bank & Trust Co., Sprague Henwood Co., Marine Midland Bank N.Y.C., Akzona, Inc., Asheville, N.C.; mem supervisory bd. AKZO, N.V., Arnhem, Netherlands. Republican. Presbyn. Clubs: Essex (Conn.) Yacht; Scranton Country (Scranton); Union League (New York); Cap and Gown (Princeton); Waverly Country (Waverly, Pa.); Princeton of N.J. Home: Dalton PA 18414 Office: Clarks Summit PA 18411

FULLER, EDWIN KEITH, newspaperman; b. Arlington, Kan., Jan. 10, 1923; s. Daniel Eugene and Sylvia (Glasgow) F.; student Lamar Coll., Beaumont, Tex., 1940-41, So. Methodist U., 1945-47; m. Mattisue Scott, Aug. 10, 1946; children—Barbara Jean, Geoffrey Scott, Andrew Clayton. Reporter, Dallas Morning News, 1947-49; with A.P., 1949—, chief bur., Denver, 1959-64, asst. gen. mgr., N.Y.C., 1964—; asst. gen. mgr., asst. sec., v.p. Wide World Photos, Inc. Served to capt. USAAF, World War II; prisoner of war in Germany. Decorated Air medal. Mem. Phi Delta Theta. Republican. Episcopalian. Supr. editor: The Torch is Passed, 1964. Home: 17 Orsini Dr Larchmont NY 10538 Office: 50 Rockefeller Plaza New York City NY 10020

FULLER, FRANCIS BROCK, educator; b. Eugene, Ore., July 8, 1927; s. Lon Luvois and Florence Gail (Thompson) F.; A.B., Princeton, 1949, M.A., 1950, Ph.D., 1952; m. Alison Clark, July 4, 1957; 1 dau., Lynn Dorcas. Instr., Princeton, 1951-52; mem. faculty Cal. Inst. Tech., Pasadena, 1952—, prof. math., 1966—. Fulbright research fellow, France, 1967-68. Mem. Am. Math. Soc., Sigma Xi, Phi Beta Kappa. Author articles in field. Home: 1959 Meadowbrook Rd Altadena CA 91001 Office: Math Dept Cal Inst Tech Pasadena CA 91109

FULLER, FRED ELLSWORTH, lawyer; b. Bedford, Ia., Sept. 26, 1901; s. Ren Herman and Bess M. (Smith) F.; A.B. cum laude, Ohio Wesleyan U., 1923; J.D. magna cum laude, Ohio State U., 1926; m. Mary Isabelle Beetham, Sept. 1, 1923; children—Anne (Mrs. Alan C. Boyd), Fred Ellsworth, Bess (Mrs. Robert D. Brownell), Margaret (Mrs. Trygve J. Sandberg). Admitted to Ohio bar, 1926, since practiced in Toledo; now partner law firm Fuller, Seney, Henry & Hodge; gen. counsel Glass Container Mfrs. Inst. Dir. Toledo Edison Co. Corp. trustee from alumni Ohio Wesleyan U., 1953-63, trustee-at-large, 1964-70. Ohio Wesleyan Assos. (1st chmn.). Fellow Am. Coll. Trial Lawyers, Ohio Bar Found. (life), Am. Bar Found. (life mem.; mem. U.S. Atty. Gen.'s nat. com. to study anti-trust laws); mem. Am. (former chmn. anti-trust sect., mem. com. on restrictive trade practices fgn. 1966- 67), Ohio (former chmn. com. antitrust law), N.Y., Toledo, Inter-Am., Internat., Fed. bar assns., Assn. Bar N.Y.C., Am. Judicature Soc., Internat. Assn. Ins. Counsel (def. research inst. liaison com.), Ohio Hist. Soc. (trustee, mem. exec. com.), Newcomen Soc. N. Am., Ohio Soc. N.Y., Am. Law Inst., Order of Coif, Chi Phi, Phi Delta Phi, Delta Sigma Rho. Republican. Methodist. Clubs: Toledo, Toledo Country; Inverness, Rotary, Skytop (Skytop, Pa.); Home: 3721 Sulphur Springs Rd Toledo OH 43606 Office: Edison Plaza 300 Madison Av Toledo OH 43604

FULLER, HELEN, editor; b. Cullman, Ala.; d. Arthur Wright and Lela E. (Thompson) Fuller; A.B., U. Ala., 1933, M.A., 1934, student law sch., 1935. Spl. atty. U.S. Dept. of Justice, 1935-39; asst. to adminstr. Nat. Youth Adminstrn., 1939-41; joined New Republic, 1941, asst. editor, 1944-46, Washington editor, 1946-48, polit. editor, 1948-51, mng. editor, 1952—. Mem. bd. MEDICO, Inc.; bd. dirs. Pub. Welfare Found. Mem. Am. Polit. Sci. Assn., Phi Beta Kappa. Author: Year of Trial, 1962. Home: 3242 Woodland Dr N W Washington DC 20037. Office: 1244 19th St N W Washington DC 20036

FULLER, JACK GLENDON, Jr., plastics engr.; b. Ft. Lewis, Wash., Feb. 25, 1923; s. Jack Glendon and Matilda Margaret (Kindschi) F.; B.S., Dickinson Coll., 1947; postgrad. high polymer chemistry U. Del., 1947-48; m. Nancy Dorr Tatnall, May 14, 1945; children—Jack Glendon III, Margaret Tatnall, Pamela Dorr, Joellen Swift, Charlotte Mahaffy. Prodn. engr. Master Plastics, Wilmington, Del., 1946-48; research chemist Hercules Powder Co., Parlin, N.J., sr. tech. rep., Boston and Wilmington, Del., mgr. plastics sales, Los Angeles, 1948-58; v.p. sales and gen. mgr. Chemtrol div. Rexall Drug & Chem. Co., 1958-60; nat. sales mgr. Ankerwerk Internat., 1960-62; pres. Polymer Machinery Corp., Berlin, Conn., 1962—; exec. v.p., dir. Old Harbor Marina Co., Inc., Clinton, Conn., 1966—; pres., dir. Wilmington Terminal Co., Inc., Wilmington, Del., 1967—; exec. v.p., dir. Molding Systems, Inc., Berlin, 1968—. Trustee Stevens Inst. Tech.; vice chmn. bd. dirs. Plastics Edn. Found. Served from 2d lt. to 1st lt. AUS, 1943-46. Mem. Soc. Plastics Engrs. (nat. council 1959, 60, treas. 1962, internat. pres. 1963), Soc. Plastics Industry. Author numerous tech. papers. Home: 115 Vine St New Britain CT 06052 Office: 68 Woodlawn Rd Berlin CT 06037

FULLER, JAMES OSBORN, geologist, univ. pres.; b. Chaumont, N.Y., Aug. 14, 1912; s. Merton Otis and Ethel Rose (Osborn) F.; A.B., Lehigh U., 1934; Ph.D., Columbia, 1941; m. Marjorie Crossette Hall, July 1, 1931; children—Richard Osborn, Christine Gaylord, Jonathan Alden. Asst., U.S. Geol. Survey, summer 1936, asst. geologist, 1944-45; asst. Columbia, 1936-39; asst. geologist Newfoundland Geol. Survey, summer 1937; asst. prof. Mt. Union Coll., 1939-41; geologist Geol. Survey of Ohio, 1941—; instr. Ohio State U., 1941-43, asso. prof., 1946-48, prof., 1948-49, prof., asst. dean, 1949- 51, prof., acting dean, 1951-52, prof., asso. dean, 1952-55, prof., asso. dean., exec. sec. Univ. Adv. Research Council, 1955-57, prof., dean Coll. of Arts and Scis., 1957-67, pres. univ., 1967-68; pres. Fairleigh Dickinson U., 1968—; asst. prof. W.Va. U., 1943-44, 45-46; cons. geologist on oil, gas, non-metallic minerals, Ohio geology. Mem. Geol. Soc. Am., Ohio Acad. Sci., Am. Assn. Petroleum Geologists, Assn. Geology Tchrs., Phi Beta Kappa, Sigma Xi. Author articles on stratigraphy, econ. geology, also bulletins. Home: 130 Mill Rd Hohokus NJ 07423 Office: Fairleigh Dickinson U Rutherford NJ 07073

FULLER, JENNINGS BRYAN, govt. ofcl., veterinarian; b. York, Neb., Sept. 25, 1897; s. James Martin and Flora (Robertson) F.; D.V.M., Colo. State U., 1924; m. Ida Marie Feeser, July 18, 1922; children—James Henry, Margaret Ann (Mrs. Kenneth Kennedy). Veterinarian, Torrington, Wyo., also engaged in cattle feeding and farming. Mem. Wyo. Prodn. Credit Assn., 1934-62, Dist. Farm Credit Bd. Omaha, 1949-62; mem. Fed. Farm Credit Bd., 1962—, chmn., 1967—. Served with U.S. Army, World War I. Mem. Am., Wyo. vet. med. assns. Methodist. Mason. Home: 3043 Alta Vista Torrington WY 82240

FULLER, JOHN A., business exec.; b. Montreal, Que., Mar. 4, 1903; s. Henry J. and Nancy (Archibald) F.; student Hotchkiss Sch., Lakeville, Conn.; A.B., Princeton, 1924; m. Katharine Boyd, 1924; children—John A., Helen B. (Mrs. A. P. Bisset), Nancy B. (Mrs. T. A. Reaper), William H. With Security Savs. & Trust Co., Portland, Ore., 1924-26; sec., later v.p. Aldred & Co., 1926-36; sec. Shawinigan Chemicals, Ltd., 1937-40, sec.- treas., 1940-45, dir., 1940—, v.p., 1945-57, chmn. bd.; officer, dir. Shawinigan Water & Power Co., 1945-63, chmn., chief exec. officer, 1961-63; exec. com., dir. Bell Telephone Co. Can.; dir. Sherwin Williams Co. of Can. Ltd., U.S. Steel Corp., Gen. Reins. Corp., N.Y.C., Royal Bank of Can., Montreal, Rolls-Royce Holdings Can., Ltd., Montreal Sun Life Assurance Co. of Can., Boston Common Stock Fund. Mem. bd. Royal Edward Laurentian Hosp.; bd. govs. Welfare Fedn. Montreal. Mem. Royal Canadian (past pres.), Canadian Senior's (bd. govs.) golf assns. Presbyn. Clubs: St. James', Royal Montreal Golf. Home: 47 N Ridge Rd Ile Bizard Quebec Canada Office: 620 Dorchester Blvd W Montreal 101 Quebec Canada

FULLER, JOHN GARSED CAMPBELL, food and drug co. exec.; b. Phila., Dec. 16, 1930; s. William Duncan and Katherine Harper (Campbell) F.; A.B., Harvard, 1952, M.B.A., 1958; m. Elizabeth Ann Dobbins, Nov. 29, 1969. Engaged in marketing and distbn. Acme Markets, Inc., Phila., 1958-66, asst. treas., 1966-69, treas., 1969—. Chief adminstr. officer Acme Markets Found., Inc. Republican. Episcopalian. Clubs: Harvard, Cricket (Phila.). Home: 4000 Gypsy Lane Philadelphia PA 19144 Office: 124 N 15th St Philadelphia PA 19101

FULLER, JOHN GRANT, author, columnist, documentary film producer; b. Phila., Nov. 30, 1913; s. John Grant and Alice (Jenkins) F.; A.B., Lafayette Coll., 1936; m. Nora Wheatley, Feb. 8, 1960 (div. 1969); 1 son, Judd Wheatley; children by previous marriage—John Grant III, Geoffrey Tousley. Engaged in pub. and industry, 1936-49; sales promotion mgr. NBC, 1949-53; producer TV series Road to Reality, 1960- 61; writer, dir. Twentieth Century, 1958-59, Conquest, 1957, du Pont Show of the Week, 1962; writer Home Show, 1953-55, Garry Moore Show, 1956; others; producer Gt. Am. Dream Machine, Nat. Ednl. TV, 1971; columnist Trade Winds in Sat. Rev., 1957-67; also documentary film producer and dir.; producer, writer, dir. documentaries for USIA NBC-TV, Nat. Ednl. TV. Recipient award Nat. Assn. Improvement Mental Health, 1961, Nat. Assn. Womens Clubs for Road to Reality, 1961; Sigma Delta Chi award for Light Across the Shadow (TV documentary), 1966. Mem. Delta Kappa Epsilon, Pi Delta Epsilon. Democrat. Mem. Soc. of Friends. Author: (plays) The Pink Elephant, 1953, Love Me Little, 1959; (books) Gentlemen Conspirators, 1962; The Money Changers, 1962; Incident at Exeter, 1966; Interrupted Journey, 1966; Games for Insomniacs, 1966; The Day of St. Anthony's Fire, 1968; Aliens in The Skies, 1969; The Great Soul Trial, 1969. Home: Box 116 Saugatuck P O Westport CT 06880

FULLER, JOHN LANGWORTHY, psychobiologist; b. Brandon, Vt., July 22, 1910; s. John H. and Joyce (Langworthy) F.; B.S., Bates Coll., 1931; Ph.D., Mass. Inst. Tech., 1935; m. Ruth I. Parsons, Sept. 2, 1933; children—Mary Jean (Mrs. Richard C. Farrington), Sarah Ann. Instr. biology Sarah Lawrence Coll., 1935-36, Clark U., 1936-37; instr. zoology U. Me., 1937-41, asst. prof., 1941-45, asso. prof., 1945-47; staff scientist Jackson Lab., Bar Harbor, Me., 1947-58, sr. staff scientist, 1958-70, asst. dir. tng., 1958-63, asso. dir., 1963-70; prof. psychology State U. N.Y. at Binghamton, 1970—; vis. lectr. Harvard, 1965-65, AID-NSF India Program, 1968. Guggenheim fellow, 1955-56. Fellow Am. Psychol. Assn.; mem. Genetics Soc., Phi Beta Kappa, Sigma Xi. Democrat. Episcopalian. Author: (with W.R. Thompson) Behavior Genetics, 1960; Nature and Nurture, 1954; Motivation, 1962; (with J. P. Scott) Genetics and Social Behavior of the Dog, 1965. Contbr. sci. articles to profl. jours. Home: 633 Harvard St Vestal NY 13850 Office: State U NY at Binghamton Binghamton NY 13850

FULLER, LAWRENCE JOSEPH, army officer, lawyer; b. Everett, Wash., Dec. 20, 1914; s. Harry J. and Lila (Lawrence) F.; A.A., Grand Rapids (Mich.) Jr. Coll., 1935; B.S., U.S. Mil. Acad., 1940; J.D., U. Mich., 1951; M.A., Stanford, 1957; student Soochow U. Law Sh., 1958-59, Nat. War Coll., 1959-60; LL.M., George Washington U., 1962; m. Mary Elizabeth Matthews, Aug. 27, 1944; children—Patricia (Mrs. Harry C. Brundick), Victoria (Mrs. James V. Kelly, Jr.), Laureen, Mariel. Admitted to Mich. bar, 1951; also U.S. Supreme Ct.; commd. 2d lt. C.E., U.S. Army, 1940, advanced through grades to maj. gen., 1967; co. officer 3d Engr. Regt., Schofield Barracks, Hawaii, 1940-42; comdg. officer 52d Engr. Bn., Camp Abbott, Ore., 1943; comdg. officer 183d Engr. Combat Bn., Europe, 1944-45; instr. Command and Gen. Staff Coll., Ft. Leavenworth, Kan., 1945-48; with Office Judge Adv. Gen., 1951-55, 60-63; student Chinese lang. and Chinese law, Taiwan, 1955-59; staff judge adv. UN Command, U.S. Forces Korea and U.S. 8th Army, 1963-64; asst. judge adv. gen. for civil law, 1963-67; dep. judge adv. gen., 1967—. Mem. Presdl. Econ. Mission to Republic of Korea, 1952. Decorated Legion of Merit, Army Commendation medal. Mem. Am., Fed., Inter-Am. bar assns., Am. Soc. Internat. Law, Inst. Jud. Adminstrn., Washington Fgn. Law Soc., Internat. Legal Soc. Korea, Royal Asiatic Soc., Judge Advs. Assn., Assn. U.S. Army, Order of Coif. Author: Country Law Study of China, 1959; Criminal Code of the Republic of China, 1960; Code of Criminal Procedure of the Republic of China, 1960; Police Law of the Republic of China, 1960; Examination of the Judicial System of Okinawa, 1961; Country Law Study of Thailand, 1962. Home: 7213 Thrasher Rd McLean VA 22101 Office: Dept of Army Pentagon Washington DC 20310

FULLER, LON LUVOIS, educator; b. Hereford, Tex., June 15, 1902; s. Francis Bartow and Mary Salome (Moore) F.; student U. Cal., 1919-20; A.B., Stanford U., 1924, J.D., 1926; m. Florence Gail Thompson, Aug. 11, 1926 (dec. 1960); children—Francis Brock, Cornelia; m. 2d, Marjorie D. Chapple, Nov. 5, 1960. Instr. law, U. Oregon Law School, 1926-28, U. Ill. Coll. of Law, 1928-31; prof. of law, Duke U., 1931-40; vis. prof. of law, Harvard, 1939-40; prof. of law, Harvard, 1940-48; Carter prof. jurisprudence, 1948—. Mem. Mass. bar; asso. in practice of law with Ropes, Gray, Best, Coolidge and Rugg, Boston, Mass., 1942-45; lecturer summer schools, U. Chgo., 1930-33, U. of Wash., 1931, Univ. of N.C., 1934, U. of Southern Calif., 1937. Received Phillips award from Am. Philos. Soc. for essay on Am. Legal Realism, 1935. Mem. Am. Acad. Arts and Sciences, Delta Chi, Phi Delta Phi, Phi Beta Kappa, Order of Coif. Democrat. Author: The Law in Quest of Itself, 1940; The Morality of Law, 1964; Legal Fictions, 1967; Anatomy of the Law, 1968. Home: 16 Traill St Cambridge MA 02138

FULLER, MARGARET HARTWELL, (Mrs. Francis A. Fuller), librarian; b. Providence, July 19, 1904; d. William Burgess and Lucy (Hartwell) Peck; B.A., Wheaton Coll., Norton, Mass., 1925; library tng. Columbia, 1939-43; m. Francis Albert Fuller, July 12, 1946. With Moodys Investors Service, 1925-27; research Western Electric Co., 1927- 32, 35-38; library asst. Am. Tel. and Tel. Co., 1938-43; librarian George S. Armstrong & Co., Inc., 1943-49, Am. Iron & Steel Inst., 1949-69, editorial asst. Steelways mag., 1949-69. Capt., Girl Scouts Am., 1925- 38. Mem. Am. Woman's Assn. (dir. 1945-47), Spl. Libraries Assn. (pres. N.Y. chpt. 1952-53, chmn. metals div. 1954-55, 1st v.p. 1957-58, pres. 1958-59). Club: Wheaton of N.Y. (dir. 1953-55). Home: Maplelm Phillips ME 04966 Retired

FULLER, MAURICE DE LANO, lawyer; b. Eveleth, Minn., Oct. 3, 1898; s. Maurice De Lano and Mary A. (Shufflebotham) F.; A.B., U. Cal. at Berkeley, 1921, J.D., 1923; m. Marie Elizabeth Haub, June 21, 1929; children—Maurice De Lano, Charles Edwin, Marie Elizabeth, Richard Lee. Admitted to Cal. bar, 1923, practiced in San Francisco; mem. firm Pillsbury, Madison & Sutro, San Francisco, 1940—. Bd. dirs. Paul Masson, Inc. Mem. Am., San Francisco bar assns., Cal. State Bar. Clubs: Bohemian, Commonwealth (San Francisco). Home: 117 Lunado Way San Francisco CA 94127 Office: 225 Bush St San Francisco CA 94104

FULLER, MELVIN STUART, educator; b. Livermore Falls, Me., May 5, 1931; s. George Raymond and Hilda Gordon (Pike) F.; B.S., U. Me., 1953; M.S., U. Neb., 1955; Ph.D., U. Cal., 1959; Master's ad eundum, Brown U., 1963; m. Barbara Paul Newman, Apr. 2, 1955; children—Erica Ann, Scott Eliot, Amy Elizabeth. Instr. Brown U., 1959, asst. prof., 1960-63, asso. prof., 1963-64; asst. prof. U. Cal., 1964-65, asso. prof., 1965-68; prof., head dept. botany U. Ga., 1968—; mem. editorial bd. for publs. in biology McGraw Hill. Mem. Bot. Soc. Am., Mycol. Soc. Am. (counselor 1966-68, 70-72), Soc. Study of Growth and Devel. Author: The Science of Botany, 1962. Research on growth and devel. aquatic fungi. ultrastructure. Home: 195 Pioneer Ct RR 3 Athens GA 30601

FULLER, MORRIS GREENLEAF, ins. exec.; b. Gallipolis, O., Feb. 24, 1892; s. William Burtt and Ada (Morris) F.; student Kenyon Mil. Acad.; m. Octavia Carr, June 19, 1917 (dec. 1960); children—Myra (Mrs. Charles A. Harper), Caroll W., Douglas G.; m. 2d, Alice Warren, Feb. 24, 1961. Employed as actuarial clk. and statistician Am. Central Life, 1912-17; various positions as agt., agy. mgr., agy. supt., ins. firms, 1919-29; with State Farm Life, Bloomington, 1929—, successively v.p., exec. v.p., pres., 1952-61, vice chmn. bd. dirs., 1961—; dir. State Farm Mut. Auto, 1953—. Served as 1st lt. 143d Inf., N.G. U.S., World War I; capt. 92d Engrs., AUS, World War II. Home: 3981 East River Dr Ft Myers FL 33901 Office: 112 E Washington St Bloomington IL 61701

FULLER, MORTIMER BARTINE, Jr., salt co. exec.; b. Scranton, Pa., July 23, 1907; s. Mortimer Bartin and Kathryn (Steell) F.; grad. Lawrenceville Sch., 1928; grad. Princeton 1932; m. Frances Marion Acker, Feb. 20, 1932; children—Patricia A. (Mrs. Peter R. Mott), Frances W. (Mrs. John M. Hallstead), Mortimer Bartine III. Dir. Internat. Salt Co., 1936—, treas., 1942-64, v.p., 1956-61, exec. v.p., 1961-68, pres., 1968—; pres., dir. Central State Bank, Dalton, Pa., 1931-65; treas., dir. Genesee & Wyoming R.R. Co., 1936—; dir. First Nat. Bank of Carbondale (Pa.). Del., Republican Nat. Conv., 1956, 60. Bd. dirs. Hahnemann Hosp., Scranton, 1936-62, pres., 1952-62. Mem. Lackawanna County Mfrs. Assn. (pres. 1956—). Home: Lily Lake Rd Dalton PA 18414 Office: International Salt Co Clarks Summit PA 18411

FULLER, PARRISH, lumber mfr.; b. Madison, Wis., May 21, 1892; s. William Wilson and Minnie Lora (Parrish) F.; student Wabash Coll., 1910-11, M.A., 1949, LL.D. (hon.), 1954; m. Miss Hester Porter, Oct. 18, 1919; children—Mary Margaret (Mrs. Jas. D. Voorhees), William Porter. Gen. mgr. J.O. Parrish Lumber Co., Shelbyville, Ind., 1914-18; asst. to pres. Hillyer Deautsch Edwards Inc., Oakdale, La., 1919-20, v.p., gen. mgr., 1920—; v.p. Hillyer Edwards Fuller, Inc., Glenmora,

La., 1923-40; gen. partner King-Edwards-Fuller & Co., St. Francisville, La., 1940-47, Avoyelles Timber Co., Bordelonville, La., 1940-64; v.p. King Lumber Industries, Canton, Miss., 1946-50, Canton & Carthage R.R. Co., 1946-53, Porter Steel Specialties, Inc., Shelbyville, Ind., 1946- 51; gen. partner Heflands Timber Co.; dir., chmn. forest lands and products Celotex Corp., 1946-66; gen. partner Fuller Farms, Shelbyville, Ind., Edwards & Fuller, Oakdale, La.; dir. Nat. Bank Commerce, New Orleans, South Shore Oil and Devel. Co., New Orleans & Lower Coast R.R.; pres. J.O. Parrish Lumber Co., Shelbyville, Ind. Salvage chmn. La., 1942-45; chmn. United War Fund, 1943-45, La. Citizens Adv. Com. Education, 1964; Pres. Pub. Affairs Research Council La., 1958; mem. coordinating council La. State Colls. and La. State U., 1948-52; mem. La. Bd. Edn., 1929-52, pres., 1952; Served as 2d lt., aviation sect., O.R.C., 1919. Recipient Citizenship citation La. div. V.F.W.; pub. service citations So. U., 1952, La. Council Coll. Pres., 1953. Bd. visitors Tulane U., 1953; 1955-56; bd. govs. Ochsner Med. Found., New Orleans; trustee Wabash Coll. Mem. Sigma Chi. Presbyn. Clubs: The Chicago; Boston, Internat. House (New Orleans). Address: Box 60 Oakdale LA 71463

FULLER, PERRY LUCIAN, lawyer; b. Central City, Neb., Oct. 26, 1922; s. Perry L. and Ruth (Howorth) F.; A.B., U. Neb., 1947, J.D., 1949; student U. Chgo. Law Sch., 1946-47; m. Alice Moorman, Mar. 6, 1948; 1 dau., Leslie Ann. Admitted to Ill. bar, 1950; mem. staff Chgo. Crime Commn., 1949; sr. partner firm Hinshaw, Culbertson, Moelmann, Hoban & Fuller, and predecessors, Chgo., 1956—. lectr. in law U. Chgo. Law Sch.; vice chmn. exec. com. Law in Am. Soc., 1966, chmn., 1967-69; pres. Law In Am. Soc. Found. Chmn. Cook County Civil Service Commn., 1967-69. Bd. dirs. Winnetka Community Chest, 1966-69. Served to capt. USMCR, 1944-46, 52-53. Decorated Air medal. Fellow Am. Coll. Trial Lawyers; mem. Am. (chmn. pub. relations com. 1968-69), Ill., Chgo. (bd. mgrs. 1967-69) bar assns., Soc. Trial Lawyers (bd.. dirs. 1963, 67-68), Am. Judicature Soc., Internat. Assn. Ins. Counsel, Fedn. Ins. Counsel (v.p. 1961-62), Def. Research Inst. (vice chmn. indsl. relations com.), Scribes. Republican. Clubs: Executives, Legal Law, Trial Lawyers (Chgo.). Home: 255 Poplar St Winnetka IL 60093 Office: 1 N LaSalle St Chicago IL 60602

FULLER, PETER DAVENPORT, automobile dealership exec.; b. Boston, Mar. 22, 1923; s. Alvan T. and Viola (Davenport) F.; grad. Milton Acad., 1942; B.A., Harvard, 1946; LL.D., Bates Coll., 1969; m. Joan Beth Marcotte, June 30, 1951; children—Miranda Elizabeth, Sandra Anne, Suzanne Marie, Peter D., Abigail Joan, Jessica Lee, Charlotte Irene, Michelle Marcotte. Pres. Cadillac Automobile Co., Boston, 1949—, Fuller Industries, Inc., Fort Myers, Fla., 1960—. Treas. The Fuller Found., Boston, 1958—; mem. corp. Mass. Gen. Hosp., Boston, 1966—; mem. Council of 100 Fla., 1965—. Bd. dirs. The Jimmy Fund Cancer Research, Am. Cancer Soc., Inc.; mem. Civic Edn. Found. Lincoln Filene Center of Tufts U.; Served with USMCR, 1942-44. Mem. Thoroughbred Owners and Breeders Assn. (trustee). Owner Dancer's Image, 1968 Ky. Derby winner. Home: 285 Dudley St Brookline MA 02146 Office: 808 Commonwealth Av Boston MA 02215

FULLER, REGINALD HORACE, clergyman, educator; b. Horsham, Eng., Mar. 24, 1915; s. Horace and Cora L. (Heath) F.; B.A. with 1st class honours in Classics and Theology, Peterhouse, Cambridge U., 1937, M.A., 1942; S.T.D., Gen. Theol. Sem., N.Y.C., 1960, Phila. Div. Sch., 1962; m. Ilse Barda, June 17, 1942; children—Caroline (Mrs. Robert E. Sloat), Rosemary (Mrs. John G. Bazuzi), Sarah. Came to U.S., 1955. Ordained deacon Ch. of Eng., 1940, priest, 1941; curate in Derbys, Eng., 1940-43, Ashbourne-w-Mapleton, Eng., 1943-46, Birmingham, Eng., 1946-50; lectr. theology Queen's Coll., Birmingham, 1946-50; prof. theology St. David's Coll., Lampeter, Wales, 1950-55; examining chaplain to Bishop of Monmouth, 1950-55; prof. N.T. lit. and langs. Seabury- Western Theol. Sem., Evanston, Ill, 1955-66; Baldwin prof. sacred lit. (N.T.) Union Theol. Sem., N.Y.C., 1966—; adj. prof. Columbia, 1969—; canon theologian of Brit. Honduras, also Bishop's commissary for U.S.A., 1968—. Mem. study commn. World Council Chs., 1957—; Mem. Episcopal-Lutheran Conversations, 1969—, Anglican-Lutheran Conversations, 1970—. Recipient Schofield prize and Crosse studentship, 1938; fellow Am. Assn. Theol. Schs., 1961-62. Mem. Studiorum Novi Testamenti Societas (mem. com. 1969—), Chgo. Soc. Bibl. Research, Soc. Bibl. Research. Author: (with R. Hanson) The Church of Rome, A Dissuasive, 1948; The Mission and Achievement of Jesus, 1954; (with G. Ernest Wright) The Book of Acts of God, 1957; What is Liturgical Preaching?, 1957; Luke's Witness to Jesus Christ, 1958; The New Testament in Current Study, 1962; Interpreting the Miracles, 1963; The Foundations of New Testament Christology, 1965; A Critical Introduction to the New Testament, 1966; (with B. Rice) Christianity and Affluence, 1966; Lent with the Liturgy, 1969; The Formation of the Resurrection Narratives, 1970. Contbr. books, encys. Translator; (D. Bonhoeffer) The Cost of Discipleship, 1948, Prisoner for God, 1954; (H. W. Bartsch, editor) Kerygma and Myth I, 1953; (R. Bultmann) Primitive Christianity, 1956; (J. Jeremias) Unknown Sayings of Jesus, 1957; (W. von Loewenich) Modern Catholicism, 1959; Kerygma and Myth II, 1962; (H. Flender) St. Luke Theologian of Redemptive History, 1967; (J. Moltmann and J. Weissbach) Two Studies in the Theology of Bonnoeher, 1967; (A. Schweitzer) Reverence for Life, 1969. Home: 99 Claremont Av New York City NY 10027

FULLER, RICHARD BUCKMINSTER, archtl. engr., educator; b. Milton, Mass., July 12, 1895; s. Richard Buckminster and Caroline Wolcott (Andrews) F.; student Milton (Mass.) Acad., 1904-13, Harvard, 1913-15, U.S. Naval Acad., 1917; Dr. Design, N.C. State U., 1954; Dr. Arts, Mich. U., 1955; D.Sc., Washington U., 1957, U. Colo., 1964, Bates Coll., 1969; Dr. Fine Arts, So. Ill. U., 1959, U. N.M., 1964, Cal. Coll. Arts and Crafts, 1966, Ripon Coll., 1968, Boston Coll., 1969, Mpls. Sch. Art, 1970; H.H.D., Rollins Coll., 1960, Monmouth Coll., 1965, Cal. State Coll., 1966, L.I. U., 1966, Dartmouth, 1968, U. R.I., 1968, New Eng. State Coll., 1968, Brandeis U., 1970, Columbia Coll., 1970; Litt.D., Clemson U., 1964; D.Eng., Clarkson Coll., 1967; D.Archtl. Engring., U. Wis., 1969; LL.D., Park Coll., 1970; D.Sc. and Humane Letters, Wilberforce U., 1970; fellow St. Peter's Coll., Oxford (Eng.) U., 1970; m. Ann Hewlett, July 12, 1917; children—Alexandra Willets (dec.), Allegra (Mrs. Robert Snyder). Apprentice machine fitter Richards, Atkinson & Haserick, cotton mill machinery importers, Boston, 1914; in various apprentice positions Armour & Co., N.Y.C., 1915-17, asst. export mgr., 1919-21; nat. account sales mgr. Kelly-Springfield Truck Co., 1922; pres. Stockade Bldg. System, 1922-27; founder 4-D Co., Chgo., 1927, pres., 1927-32; asst. dir. research Pierce Found.-Am. Radiator-Standard San. Mfg. Co., 1930; founder Dymaxion Corp., Bridgeport, Conn., 1932, dir., chief engr., 1932-35; asst. to dir. research and devel. Phelps Dodge Corp., 1936-38; tech. cons. Fortune Mag., 1938-40; v.p., chief engr. Dymaxion Co., Inc., Del., 1941-42; chief mech. engring. sect. Bd. Econ. Warfare, 1942-44; spl. asst. to dir. Fgn. Econ. Adminstrn., 1942-44; chmn. bd. adminstrv. engr. Dymaxion Dwelling Machines, 1944-46; chmn. bd. trustees Fuller Research Found., Wichita, Kan., 1946—; pres. Geodesics, Inc., Raleigh, N.C., 1954—, Plydomes, Inc., Des Moines, 1957—; chmn. bd. Tetrahelix Corp., Hamilton, O., Buckminster Fuller Inst., Carbondale; cons. Ford Found., Calcutta (India) Planning Orgn., 1961—; cons. space age devel. to gov. N.C., 1962—; Distinguished Univ. prof., prof. generalized design sci. exploration So. Ill. U., Carbondale, 1959—; Charles Eliot Norton prof. Harvard, 1961-62; vis. prof., lectr., critic Cornell U., Yale, Mich. U., Mass. Inst. Tech., Princeton, U. Minn., Washington U., U. Cal. at Berkeley, U. Ill., others; Hamilton lectr. Oberlin Coll., 1953; Trowbridge lectr. Yale, 1955; Hill Found. lectr. St. Olafs Coll., 1957; Lorado Taft lectr. U. Ill., 1960; vis. lectr. U. Witwatersrand, Johannesburg, U. Pretoria, Cape Town U., U. Natal, Durban (all South Africa 1958); guest lectr. archtl. socs. Japan, Hong Kong, U. Burma, archtl. and engring. socs. India, Pakistan, Keyna (all 1958); delivered "Annual Discourse" for Royal Inst. Brit. Architects, London, 1958; guest speaker Royal Coll. Art, London, archtl. and engring. depts. Cambridge U., archtl. dept. U. Liverpool, Inst. Contemporary Arts, London (all Eng. 1958); guest speaker Royal Coll. Arts, The Hague, Holland, also W. German Archtl. Soc., Düsseldorf, 1958; condr. 4 day seminar Die Hoch Schule von Gestaltung at Ulm, also Museo Della Scienca et Della Technica, il Collegio Degli Architetti et Assoc. Azone per il Disegno Industriale, Milan, Italy, 1958; Ullman lectr. Brandeis U., 1962; vis. scientist lectures Yomiuri Shimbun-NTV network, Japan, 1961; also guest lectr., India, W. Germany, U.K., Sweden, 1961, 62, Greece, Austria, Scotland, 1963; speaker many fgn. countries, including Ghana, Nigeria, Uganda, Kenya, Egypt, Australia, Ireland, 1964. Mem. U.S. presdl. sci. advisers com. on human resources to consider new ednl. strategies, Yale 1958; U.S. rep. Am. Russian Protocol Exchange, USSR, 1959; mem. U.S.A. team 4th Soviet-Am. Citizens Conf., Leningrad, 1964. Bd. dirs. Oceanographic Soc.; trustee N.Y. Cancer Research Inst. Served from ensign to lt. USN, World War I. Recipient award of merit N.Y. chpt. A.I.A., 1952, USMC, 1954; Gran Premio, Trienniale de Milano, 1954, 57 (Italy); Centennial award Mich. State U., 1955; Gold medal scarab Nat. Archtl. Soc., 1958; Gold medal Phila. chpt. A.I.A., 1960; Frank P. Brown medal Franklin Inst., 1960; Allied Professions Gold medal A.I.A., 1963; honored with Buckminster Fuller Recognition Day, U. Colo., 1963; Benjamin Franklin life fellow Royal Soc. Arts, 1960 (Eng.); Plomado de Oro award Soc. Mexican Architecture, 1963; gold medal Royal Inst. Brit. Architects, 1968; gold medal of architecture Nat. Inst. Arts and Letters, 1968; honor award, U.S. pavillion at Expo 67, A.I.A., 1968; Gold medal A.I.A., 1970. Life fellow A.A.A.S.; fellow Royal Inst. Brit. Architects (hon.), Building Research Inst. of Nat. Acad. Scis., Inst. Gen. Semantics (hon. trustee), World Acad. Art and Sci., Lincoln Acad. Ill., Inst. for Advanced Philosophic Research; mem. N.A.D., A.I.A. (hon. life), Nat. Inst. Arts and Letters (life mem.), Harvard Engring. Soc., Am. Soc. Profl. Geographers, Archtl. League N.Y., Am. Assn. U. Profs., Soc. Archtl. Historians, Phi Beta Kappa (hon.), Alpha Rho Chi (life). Clubs: Somerset (Boston); Century Assn., Coffee House (N.Y.C.); Authors (London, Eng.). Author: Nine Chains to the Moon, 1938; No More Second Hand God, 1962; Education Automation, 1962; (poetry) Unfinished Epic of Industrialization, 1963; Charles Eliot Norton 1961- 62; Lectures at Harvard University, 1963; Ideas and Integrities, 1963; Operating Manual for Spaceship Earth, 1968; Utopia or Oblivion, 1970; (co-author) New Worlds in Engineering, 1940. Author, editor Notes on the Future column in Saturday Rev. mag., 1964—. Editor of Convoy mag., 1918-19; editor, pub. Shelter mag., 1931-32. Inventor Dymaxion House, Chgo., 1927, Dymaxion 3 wheeled automobile, 1932-35; designer Dymaxion Deployment Unit steel igloo in conjunction with Butler Mfg. Co., Kansas City, 1940; patentee Dymaxion World Map (pub. by Life mag. as portfolio), 1943; designer geodesic structure for Ford Motor Co. Rotunda Dome, Dearborn, Mich., USMC advance base shelters, Dept. Commerce Internat. Trade Fair Dome Pavillions, 1956—, all D.E.W. Line Radomes, USN Geodesic Storage Domes, Antarctica, 1956, Union Tank Car repair shop domes, Baton Rouge, La., also Wood River, Ill., 1958-59; designer Kaiser aluminum domes, Hawaii, 1957, Virginia Beach, 1958, Oklahoma City, Borger, Tex., Abilene, Kan., Okla. Bank, 1959; designer Golden Dome for Am. exhibit, Moscow, USSR, 1959, Geodesic Dome nat. hdqrs. Am. Soc. Metals, Climatron for Mo. Bot. Gardens, St. Louis, 1960; domes for U.S. Sci. Halls, Boeing Co. Spaceorama Dome, Ford Motor Dome, Ency. Brit. Dome (all at Seattle World's Fair 1962), Sports Palace, Paris, France, 1960, Cinerama Theatre, Hollywood, 1963, Yomiuri Star dome, Tokyo, 1964, also dome for N.Y. World's Fair Pavilion, 1964. Exhibited in Form Givers of 20th Century Exhibit of Am. Fedn. Arts, Corcoran Gallery, Washington, 1959, Met. Mus. Art, N.Y.C., 1959, Carnegie Inst., Pitts., 1959, Richmond Mus. Art, 1960, Art Inst. Chgo., 1960; one man shows; Mus. Modern Art, N.Y.C., 1959-60, Walker Art Center, Minn., 1960, Am. embassy, London, 1962, Harvard (1962), U. Colo., Pratt Inst., A.I.A. Conv., also in Vienna (all 1963). Inventor-discoverer energatic-synergetic geometry, geodesic structures, tensegrity structures. Address: 407 Forest St Carbondale IL 62901

FULLER, RICHARD EUGENE, museum pres., dir.; b. N.Y.C., June 1, 1897; s. Eugene and Margaret Elizabeth Mactavish) F.; Ph.B., Yale 1918; B.S., U. Wash., 1924, M.S., 1925, Ph.D., 1930; LL.D., Wash. State Coll., 1944; m. Mrs. Elizabeth Morrison Emory, Oct. 9, 1951; 1 dau., Elizabeth (Mrs. John E. Friday, Jr.). Asst. prof. U. Wash., 1930-34, research appointment, asso. prof., 1934-40, research prof., 1940—; dir. Barkon Tube Lighting Corp., 1933-35, chmn., 1935-37, pres., 1937-39; dir. Cornucopia Gold Mines, Seattle, 1935-36, v.p., treas., 1935-38, pres., 1938-41; dir. Northwestern Glass Co., 1940-48, chmn., 1948-68. Served with Am. Field Service, France, 1917; lt. 42d C.A.C., A.E.F., 1918-19; maj. Army Specialist Corps, 1942-43. Pres. Art Inst. Seattle, 1930-33; pres. Western Assn. Mus. Dirs., 1935-37; pres., dir. Seattle Art Mus. (donor with his mother), 1933—. Pres. Seattle Found., 1946-50; chmn. Pacific Northwest div. Inst. Pacific Relations, 1950-51; dir. Nat. Bank of Commerce of Seattle. Co- chmn. Northwest regional audition bd. Met. Opera, 1957-61, regional chmn. nat. council, 1962. Incorporator Pacific Sci. Ct. Found., 1962-67. Treas., trustee Seattle C. of C. (chmn. arts and edn. com. 1946-48). Recipient award Seattle Real Estate Bd. for outstanding civic service, 1940, King's medal (Gt. Britain) for service in the cause of freedom, 1946; Raymond W. Huff award Seattle World Affairs Council, 1960; asso. officer Am. Soc. Order of Hosp. St. John of Jerusalem (Brit.), 1964, asso. commr., 1969. Dir. Seattle War Chest, 1942-44, Brit.-Am. War Relief, 1941-44, Russian War Relief, 1941- 45; chmn. Seattle Com., 1943-45; chmn. U.S. Com. for Study Particutin (Mexican volcano), div. geology NRC, 1944-50. Fellow Geol. Soc. Am., Mineral. Soc. Am., A.A.A.S.; mem. Am. Geophys. Union (pres. volcanology sect. 1944-47), Am. Assn. Museums (council 1954- 61), Internat. Council Museums (mem. U.S. nat. com. 1958-62), Japan Soc. Seattle (pres. 1957-58), A.I.D. (hon.), Assn. Art Mus. Dirs. (pres. 1962- 63), A.I.A. (hon.), Phi Beta Kappa, Sigma Xi. Clubs: Rainier, University, Rotary (Seattle); Yale, Century (N.Y.C.). Contbr. articles on geology to sci. jours. Home: 3801 E Prospect Seattle WA 98102 Office: Seattle Art Museum Seattle WA 98102

FULLER, ROBERT FERREY, pub. co. exec., lawyer; b. St. Paul, Aug. 11, 1929; s. Robert Garfield and Gwendolen (Ferrey) F.; grad. Deerfield Acad., 1946; A.B. magna cum laude, Harvard, 1950, LL.B., 1953; m. Marcelle McIntosh, June 6, 1953; children—Julie, Gordon McIntosh. Admitted to N.Y. bar, 1956; practiced in N.Y.C. with firm Patterson, Belknap & Webb, 1955-66; sec., gen. counsel Reuben H. Donnelley Corp., 1966-68, account exec., 1968-70; chmn., mng. dir. R.H. Donnelley Internat. Ltd., 1970—. Served to lt. (j.g.) USCGR, 1953-55. Mem. Am. N.Y. State bar assns., Assn. Bar City N.Y., Downtown Assn. Republican. Presbyn. (deacon) Clubs: Harvard (N.Y.C.), Shenorock Shore (Rye, N.Y.); Oxford and Cambridge University (London); St. George's Hill Tennis (Weybridge). Home: Ridgemount South Ridge St George's Hill Weybridge Surrey England Office: 26 Clifton St London EC2 England

FULLER, ROBERT LEROY, mfg. co. exec.; b. New Brunswick, N.J., Oct. 20, 1925; s. Leroy MacMillan and Adelaide (Krieger) F.; B.S. in Accounting, Rider Coll., 1951; C.P.A., Pa., 1952; m. Carol Annette Jones, June 9, 1951; children—Jeffrey, Deborah, Cynthia, Douglas. With Johnson & Johnson, New Brunswick, 1956—, v.p. finance, mem. mgmt. bd., 1963-68, v.p., dir. planning and finance, 1968-71; v.p. planning, asst. to pres., 1971—. Active local chpts. Am. Cancer Soc., United Cerebral Palsy Assn.; pres. Middlesex council Boy Scouts Am., 1965; mem. devel. council Rider Coll. Mem. Nat. Indsl. Conf. Bd. Presbyn. Club: Treasurers. Home: 23 Hardscrabble Rd Basking Ridge NJ 07920 Office: 501 George St New Brunswick NJ 08901

FULLER, ROBERT WORKS, coll. pres.; b. Summit, N.J., Oct. 26, 1936; s. Calvin Souther and Willmine (Works) F.; student Oberlin Coll., 1952-55, Princeton, 1955-57, Ecole Normale Superieure, Paris, 1957-58, U. Chgo., 1958-59; M.A., Princeton, 1959, Ph.D., 1961; m. Ann Ellen Lackritz, Oct. 18, 1959; children—Karen Lackritz, Benjamin Calvin. Instr. physics Columbia, 1961- 63; asst. prof. physics Columbia, 1963-66, Barnard Coll., 1963-65; fellow Center Advanced Studies, Wesleyan U., Middletown, Conn., 1966-67, Battelle Seattle Research Center, 1967-68; dean faculty, coll. prof. Trinity Coll., Hartford, Conn., 1968-70; pres. Oberlin (O.) Coll., 1970—. Mem. commn. sci. edn. A.A.A.S. French Govt. fellow, 1957-58. Author: (with F. W. Byron, Jr.) Mathematics of Classical and Quantum Physics, Vol. I, 1969, Vol. II, 1970. Home: 154 Forest St Oberlin OH 44074

FULLER, RUFUS CLINTON, educator, scientist; b. Providence, Mar. 5, 1925; s. Rufus Clinton and Alice (Anthony) F.; B.A., Brown U., 1945; M.A., Amherst Coll., 1949; Ph.D., Stanford, 1952; A.M. (hon.), Dartmouth, 1961; m. Carol June Seager, Sept. 14, 1946; children—David Cushman, Katheline Ann, Marilyn Gail, Jonathan Ames. Teaching fellow Brown U., Amherst Coll., Stanford, 1946-52; research microbiologist Lawrence Radiation Lab., U. Cal. at Berkeley, 1952-55; asso. plant physiologist Brookhaven Nat. Lab., 1955- 57, plant biochemist, 1957-59; NSF sr. Postdoctoral fellow Oxford (Eng.) U., 1959-60; prof. microbiology Dartmouth Med. Sch., 1960-66, chmn. dept., 1960-65; vis. prof. life sci. U. Cal. at Riverside, 1966; dir. U. Tenn.-Oak Ridge Grad. Sch. Biomed. Scis., 1966—. Mem. med. scientist tng. com. Nat. Inst. Gen. Med. Scis., 1962-65; mem. cell biology study sect., div. research grants NIH, 1965-69. Served with USNR, 1943-45. Mem. Am. Soc. Biol. Chemists, Am. Soc. Microbiology, Soc. Gen. Physiologists, A.A.A.S., Am. Soc. Plant Physiologists, Am. Assn. U. Profs., Am. Soc. Cell Biology, Sigma Xi. Author articles in field. Home: 105 Wiltshire Dr Oak Ridge, TN 37830.

FULLER, SAMUEL ASHBY, lawyer; b. Indpls., Sept. 2, 1924; s. John L.H. and Mary (Ashby) F.; B.S. in Gen. Engring., U. Cin., 1946, LL.B., 1947; m. Betty Winn Hamilton, June 10, 1948; children-Mary Cheryl, Karen E., Deborah R. Admitted to Ohio bar, 1948, Ind. bar, 1951; Cleve. claims rep. Mfrs. and Mchts. Indemnity Co., 1947-48; claims supr. Indemnity Ins. Co. N.Am., 1948-50; with firm Stewart, Irwin, Gilliom, Fuller & Meyer (formerly Murray, Mannon, Fairchild & Stewart), Indpls., 1950—, Pres., dir. Irsugo Consol. Mines, Ltd.; v.p., dir. Key Investments, Inc., Nat. Heritage Life Ins. Co.; dir. Midland Electric Coal Corp., Ind. Pub. Helth Found., Inc.; staff instr. Purdue U. Life Ins. and Marketing Insr., 1954-61; instr. Am. Coll. Life Underwriters, Indpls., 1964—. Bd. dirs. Southwest Social Centre, Inc. Mem. Am., Ind. State, Indpls. (treas. 1961-62) bar assns., Am. Coll. Probate Counsel, Estate Planning Council Indpls. (pres. 1966), Internat. Assn. Ins. Counsel, Research Inst., Mil. Order Loyal Legion U.S. (recorder 1970), Ind. Pioneer Soc., Central Ind. Bridge Assn., Inc. (pres. 1969), Beta Theta Pi, Phi Delta Phi. Republican. Mem. Disciples of Christ. Mason. Clubs: Indianapolis Athletic; Crooked Stick Country, Woodland Country (pres. 1958), Riviera (Indpls.). Home: 8403 Spring Mill Ct Indianapolis IN 46260 Office: Mchts Bank Bldg Indianapolis IN 46204

FULLER, SAMUEL SPENCER, banker; b. Suffield, Conn., July 12, 1923; s. William S. and Amy (Street) F.; student Phillips Andover Acad., 1938-42, Williams Coll., 1942-47; m. Jane Purtill, June 17, 1950; children-Thomas, James, Benjamin, Abigail. Treas., Fuller-Griffin Tobacco Co., E. Windsor Hill, Conn., 1947-56; with Hartford (Conn.) Nat. Bank, 1956—, sr. v.p., 1967- 68, exec. v.p., 1968—; dir. DeBell & Richardson, Inc., Ensign-Bickford Co. Pres. Ray Sch. Corp., Coordinating Council for Founds.; treas. Conn. Hist. Soc., Knox Found.; trustee Wadsworth Atheneum, Kent Meml. Library, Hartford Sem. Found.; bd. mgrs. Conn. Conv. Am. Bapt. Chs. Home: 555 N Main St Suffield CT 06078 Office: 777 Main St Hartford CT 06115

FULLER, S.B., cosmetic mfg.; b. Monroe, La., 1905. Chmn., pres., treas., dir. Fuller Products Co., Chgo.; pres., treas., dir. Boyer Internat. Labs., Inc.; sec., dir. Rose Meta Beauty Products Co., N.Y.C. Home: 13526 S Kedzie Av Robbins IL 60472 Office: 50 E 26th St Chicago IL 60616*

FULLER, STEPHEN DOW, investment banker; b. N.Y.C., May 10, 1908; s. Ernest M. and Miriam (Dow) F.; grad. Phillips Exeter Acad., 1926; A.B., Harvard 1930, postgrad. Law Sch., 1930-31; m. Emily Clarkson Harry, Aug. 2, 1940; children—Emily Rutgers (Mrs. C. John Kingston), Ann Brewster (Mrs. John S. F. Daly), Stephen Washington. Salesman, F. Eberstadt & Co., 1933, asst. sales mgr., 1935-40; sr. partner, founder S.D. Fuller Co., investment bankers, N.Y.C., 1940- 68, pres. S.D. Fuller & Co. Inc., 1968—; dir. Graphic Scis., Inc., Hidoc Internat., Inc. (both Danbury, Conn.), Nease Chem. Co., Inc., State Coll., Pa., Telefile Computer Corp., Irwin, Cal., Paradise Fruit Co., Inc., Plant City, Fla., Cybertek, Inc., N.Y.C., Ranch House Am., Inc., Ft. Lauderdale, Fla., Datatype Corp., Miami, Fla. Mem. zoning bd. Village of Laurel Hollow, N.Y., 1958-62. Mem. Soc. Cincinnati, Soc. Colonial Wars, Soc. Mayflower Descs., English Speaking Union. Clubs: Downtown Assn., Racquet and Tennis (N.Y.C.); Seawanhaka Corinthian Yacht (Oyster Bay, L.I., N.Y.); Piping Rock (Locust Valley, N.Y.). Home: Moores Hill Rd Oyster Bay NY 11771 Office: 26 Broadway New York City NY 10004

FULLER, STEPHEN HERBERT, educator; b. Columbus, O., Feb. 4, 1920; s. Josiah Allen and Mary Ellen (Quinn) F.; A.B., Ohio U., 1941; student Harvard Law Sch., 1941-42, I.A., Harvard, 1943, M.B.A., 1947, D.C.S., 1958; Ph.D. (hon.) in Humanities, Ateneo De Manila U.; m. Frances Gertrude Mulhearn, June 23, 1951; children—Teofilo M. (adopted), Mark Benton, Joseph Barry. Instr. econs. and labor relations at Ohio U., 1947; with Harvard, 1947—, successively research asst. Grad. Sch. Bus. Administrn. instr. Bus. Sch., asst. prof. asso. prof., 1947-61, prof., 1961—, dir. internat. Tchrs. program, 1959-60, asso. dean external affairs, 1964—. Mem. faculty

Advanced Mgmt. Program of Far East, P.I., summers 1956, 57, 59, 63, Pakistan, summers 1962, 63; faculty Keio U., Tokyo, Japan, summer 1957; faculty Mgmt. Devel. Inst., Lausanne, Switzerland, 1960-61. Dir., Chgo. Musical Instrument Co. Pub. trustee New Eng. bd. Amalgamated Clothing Workers Ins. Fund, 1954-60. Served to capt. AUS, 1943-46. Mem. Am. Arbitration Assn., Nat. Mgmt. Assn., Phi Beta Kappa, Phi Eta Sigma, Omicron Delta Kappa, Delta Tau Delta. Author: (with others) Problems in Labor Relations, rev. edit., 1958; contbg. author: Case Method of Teaching Human Relations and Administration, 1951. Editorial bd. Harvard Bus. Review, 1957-61. Home: 136 Fletcher Rd Belmont, MA 02178 Office: Harvard Business Sch Soldiers Field Boston MA 02163

FULLER, WALLACE HAMILTON, educator; b. Old Hamilton, Alaska, Apr. 15, 1915; s. Henry Ray and Bessie (Gaines) F.; B.S., Wash. State U., 1937, M.S., 1939; Ph.D., Ia. State U., 1942; m. Winifred Elizabeth Dow, Dec. 23, 1939; 1 dau., Pamela Elizabeth. Research asst. Wash. State U., Pullman, 1937-39; soil surveyor U.S. Dept. Agr., Lancaster, Wis., Neosho, Mo., 1939-40, bacteriologist, Beltsville, Md., 1945-47, soil scientist, 1947-48; research asso. Ia. State U., Ames, 1940-45; asso. prof., biochemist U. Ariz., Tucson, 1948-56, prof., biochemist, head dept. agrl. chemistry and soils, 1956—; cons. Fellow Am. Soc. Agronomy and Soil Sci., A.A.A.S., N.Y. Acad. Sci.; mem. Am. Chem. Soc., Am. Soc. Biol. Sci., Am. Soc. Plant Physiologists, Sigma Xi, Phi Kappa Phi, Phi Lambda Upsilon, Gamma Sigma Delta, Alpha Zeta. Presbyn. Home: 740 Mescal Pl Tucson AZ 85718

FULLER, WARREN GRAHAM, orgn. exec.; b. Bangkok, Thailand, July 30, 1920 (parents Am. citizens); s. Graham and Geraldine (Emerson) Fuller; grad. Mt. Hermon Sch. for Boys, 1938; student Princeton, 1938-40; B.A., U. Ill., 1942; m. Edith McKlarty Barbee, Sept. 10, 1949; children—Emerson Graham, Elizabeth Lyle. With displaced persons operations UNRRA, Germany, 1945-47; with Internat. Refugee Orgn. in Germany, 1947-48, dep. dir., dir. resettlement hdqrs., Geneva, 1949-52; dep. chief operations Intergovtl. Com. for European Migration, Geneva, 1952-55, chief of mission, Brazil and Paraguay, Rio de Janeiro, 1955-59, Rome, Italy, 1959-62; dep. dir. Latin Am. programs Peace Corps, Washington, 1962-64, dir. for Brazil, Rio de Janeiro, 1964-67; asst. sec. gen. Internat. Secretariat for Vol. Service, Washington, 1967-70; dir. financial devel. Internat. Planned Parenthood Fedn., London, 1970—. Served with Am. Field Service with Brit. forces in Middle East, N. Africa, ETO, 1942-45. Decorated Brit. campaign medals; Medaglia Ricordo (Italy), 1958; cross with crown Order of Merit (Sovereign Order Malta), 1961; recipient Honor certificate for service to Hungarian refugees Brazilian Red Cross, 1958. Clubs: Princeton (Washington); American (v.p. Rome 1961-62); International (Rio de Janeiro). Home: 3107 Garfield St N W Washington DC 20008 Office: 18-20 Lower Regent St London SW1 England

FULLER, WILLIAM PARMER, III, glass mfr.; b. San Francisco, Jan. 6, 1913; s. William Parmer and Adaline (Wright) F.; A.B., Stanford, 1934; LL.B., Harvard, 1937; m. Marylee Harlan, June 29, 1935; children—William Parmer IV, Joan, Richard Harlan. Admitted to Cal. bar, 1937; v.p. Pitts. Plate Glass Co.; dir. Wells Fargo Bank, Western Pacific R.R. (both San Francisco), Yosemite Park & Curry Co. (Cal.). Pres. bd. trustees Stanford. Mem. San Francisco C. of C. (pres. 1952), Alpha Delta Phi. Clubs: Bohemian, Pacific Union, San Francisco Golf. (San Francisco). Home: 900 Black Mountain Rd Hillsborough CA 94010 Office: 405 Montgomery St San Francisco CA 94104

FULLER, WILLIAM SIDNEY, lawyer; b. Auburn, Ala., Aug. 9, 1931; s. William Melton and Ernestine (Tolbert) F.; A.B., Auburn U., 1953; LL.B., U. Ala., 1956; m. Joyce Jeffrey, Nov. 5, 1953; children—Jeffrey Melton, Barbara Rush. Student asst. to dean U. Ala. Law Sch., 1952-53; admitted to Ala. bar, 1956; law clk. to U.S. dist. judge, Montgomery, Ala., 1956-57; practice law, Andalusia, 1957—; mem. firm Tipler, Fuller and Melton, 1957—; lectr. Southwestern Trial Inst. Mem. grievance com. Ala. State Bar. Mem. Am., Ala., Covington County bar assns., Am. Trial Lawyers Assn., Ala. Plaintiff Lawyers Assn., Ala. Trial Lawyers Assn. (pres. 1968), Phi Delta Phi, Kappa Alpha, Alpha Phi Omega. Presbyn (deacon, trustee, past chmn. bd., Sunday sch. tchr.). Club: Andalusia (dir., v.p.). Author: Personal Injury Treatises. Home: 100 South Ridge Rd Andalusia AL 36420 Office: Tipler Bldg Andalusia AL 36420

FULLERTON, BUSHNELL, corp. exec.; b. Evanston, Ill., June 4, 1922; s. Charles Bushnell and Charlotte (Hand) F.; A.B., Bucknell U., 1947; LL.B., Duke, 1950; m. Lois Miller, June 19, 1948; children—Katherine E., David H., Sally A. Admitted to Ill. bar, 1950; practice in Chgo., 1950-52; asst. sec., atty. Am. Hosp. Supply Corp., Evanston, 1952-66; sec., gen. counsel Old Ben Coal Corp., Chgo., 1966-69; sec., corporate counsel Hammond Corp., Deerfield, Ill., 1969—. Mem. Bd. Edn., Park Ridge, Ill., 1963-69, pres., 1966-69. Served to lt. (j.g.) USNR, 1943-46. Mem. Am. Soc. Corporate Secs., Am., Ill., Chgo. bar assns., Am. Arbitration Assn., Chgo. Tax Club, Phi Alpha Delta, Phi Kappa Psi. Republican. Methodist. Home: 820 Courtland Av Park Ridge IL 60068 Office: 100 Wilmot Rd Deerfield IL 60015

FULLERTON, JAMES DAVIS, mutual fund exec.; b. St. Louis, Jan. 17, 1917; s. Robert and Ora (Davis) F.; A.B., Stanford, 1939; M.B.A., Harvard, 1941; m. Harriet Anson Price, Feb. 19, 1943; children—Katherine Alexa, James Price, Victoria Chandler. Security analyst Lester & Co. (later Lester, Ryons & Co.), Los Angeles, 1941-42; free lance journalist, 1946-49; ins. broker Ingham, Coates & Payne, Pasadena, Cal., 1950-57; sr. v.p., dir. Capital Research & Mgmt. Co., Los Angeles; v.p. Am. Mut. Fund, Inc., Los Angeles, 1962-68, sr. v.p., 1968—; v.p. Internat. Resources Fund, Los Angeles, 1962-65, also dir.; pres. AMCAP Fund, Inc., Los Angeles, 1966-68, chmn. bd., chief exec. officer, 1968—; sr. v.p., dir. Capital Group, Inc., Phoenix, 1968—; sr. v.p. Investment Co. Am., 1968—; v.p. Investment Co. Am., Los Angeles, 1962—; v.p., dir. Greenwich Mgmt. Co., Greenwich, Conn., 1970—; dir. Capital Guardian Trust Co., Los Angeles, Capital Mgmt. Services, Los Angeles. Gov., chmn. pub. information com., mem. exec. com. The Investment Co. Insts. Bd. dirs., Family Service Pasadena, 1955- 57; vice chmn. Pasadena Citizens Com. for Good Govt., 1955; trustee Polytech. Sch., Pasadena, 1955-65. Served to maj. AUS, 1942- 46. Decorated Bronze Star. Mem. Beta Theta Pi. Republican. Episcopalian. Clubs: Annandale Golf, Valley Hunt (Pasadena); California (Los Angeles); Valley of Montecito. Home: 1550 Hillcrest Av Pasadena CA 91106 Office: 611 W 6th St Los Angeles CA 90017

FULLERTON, RICHARD COCHRAN, utility exec.; b. Economy, Pa., July 14, 1904; s. Boyd Van Doren and Anna (Cochran) F.; LL.B., Cumberland U., 1929; m. Mary Hampton, Feb. 12, 1926, 1 son, Richard. With Fla. Light & Power Co., 1930—, v.p. personnel and customer service, 1950-61, exec. v.p., 1961-68, v.p. and gen. mgr., 1968-69, pres. and chief exec. officer, 1969—, chmn. bd., 1971—, also dir. Trustee Dade County United Fund, 1961-64; bd. dirs. Jr. Achievement, 1958-59. Econ. Opportunity Program Dade County, 1964- 66. Mem. Miami Jr. C. of C., Sigma Alpha Epsilon. Presbyn. Rotarian (past bd. dirs.). Home: 1025 S Alhambra Circle Coral Gables FL 33146 Office: 4200 W Flagler St Miami FL 33101

FULLRIEDE, WILLIAM H., banker. Sr. v.p. in charge operations LaSalle Nat. Bank, Chgo. Office: 135 S LaSalle St Chicago IL 60690*

FULMER, DANIEL WEATHERBEE, govt. ofcl.; b. N.Y.C., Nov. 23, 1932; s. Robert Archibald and Ireneaus (Getchell) F.; A.B., Hamilton Coll., 1954; LL.B., Harvard, 1962; m. Janet Cegledy, Dec. 29, 1958; children—Dana, Robert Anthony, Michael. Jr. account exec. Roy S. Durstine, Inc., advt., N.Y.C., 1954-55; admitted to D.C. bar, 1962; legal asst. Office Atty. Gen., N.Y. State, 1961; dep. dir. Office Legislative Liaison, Office Sec. Def., 1963; staff atty. com. govt. operations U.S. Ho. of Reps., 1964-65; exec. sec. Peace Corps, 1966-67; dir. spl. projects Nat. Hwy. Safety Bur., U.S. Dept. Transp., Washington, 1967-70, exec. sec. Nat. Hwy. Traffic Safety Adminstrn., 1970—, dir. consumer and pub. affairs, 1971—. Dir., sec. Lafayette Fed. Credit Union, 1966-67. Mem. planning com. Mt. Vernon Council Civic Assns., 1966. Bd. dirs. Alexandria Council Human Relations, 1964—. Served to lt. (j.g.) USNR, 1956-59. Mem. Fed. Bar Assn., Am. Polit. Sci. Assn. (Congl. fellow 1963-64), Alpha Delta Phi. Unitarian. Home: 7121 Devonshire Rd Alexandria VA 22307 Office: Nassit Bldg 7th and D St SW Washington DC 20024

FULMER, HUGH SCOTT, educator, physician; b. Syracuse, N.Y., June 18, 1928; s. Herbert C. and Emily (Price) F.; A.B., Syracuse U., 1948; M.D., State U. N.Y. at Syracuse, 1951; M.P.H., Harvard, 1961; m. Zola M. Jones, July 12, 1952; children—James, Kim, Scott. Intern R.I. Hosp., 1951-52; resident internal medicine State U. N.Y. at Syracuse, 1954-57; asst. dir., research asso. Navajo-Cornell Field Health Research Project, 1958-60; asst. prof. community medicine U. Ky. Coll. Medicine, 1960-64; asso. prof., 1964-66, prof., 1966-68; tech. cons. health Peace Corps, Malaysia, 1968-69; prof., chmn. dept. community medicine U. Mass. Med. Sch., 1969—. Served with M.C., USAF, 1952-54. Mem. Worcester Dist. Med. Soc., Mass. Med. Soc., A.M.A., Am. Pub. Health Assn. Independent. Presbyn. Research on chronic disease, med. care research, med. edn. Home: 61 Cherlyn Dr Northboro MA 01532 Office: 419 Belmont St Worcester MA 01604

FULMER, LEMOS LEROY, educator; b. Homer, La., May 22, 1914; s. Leroy Patrick and Gertrude (Honeycutt) F.; B.A., La. State U., 1936, M.A., 1938, Ph.D., 1950; postgrad. George Peabody Coll., 1946; m. Zulma Marie Haydel, Jan. 20, 1934; children—Delmar Claire (Mrs. Jasper S. Brock III), Carol Ann (Mrs. James E. Mire), Lemos Leroy. Tchr., athletic coach Covington (La.) High Sch., 1936; supr. Lab. Sch., La. State U., 1937-41; head dept. tchr. edn. Southeastern La. Coll., 1946-50; asso. prof. edn. La. State U., 1950-58, head dept. edn., asso. dean Coll. Edn., 1958-64, dean Coll. Edn., 1964—. Chmn., Joint N.E.A.-Am. Textbook Pubs. Inst., 1967. Served to lt. col. USAAF, 1941-45; PTO. Mem. N.E.A., Am. Legion, V.F.W., La. Tchrs. Assn. (pres. 1958), Phi Delta Kappa, Kappa Delta Pi, Phi Kappa Phi. Omicron Delta Kappa. Kiwanian. Contbr. numerous articles to mil. and profl. jours. Home: 1263 Lee Dr Baton Rouge LA 70808

FULMER, VINCENT ANTHONY, ednl. administr.; b. Alliance, O., Oct. 23, 1927; s. Anthony and Catherine (Long) F.; A.B. cum laude, Miami U., Oxford, O., 1949; postgrad. Harvard, 1950; S.M., Mass. Inst. Tech., 1963; LL.D., Suffolk U., 1971; m. Mary Alma Pineau, Dec. 27, 1950; children—Kevan, Kristine, David, Amy, Charles, Alma Leigh. Mem. staff Mass. Inst. Tech., 1951—, exec. asst. office chmn., 1960-63, v.p., sec. inst., 1963—; instr. econs. Williams Coll., 1952. Mem. financial devel. adv. council Urban Coalition; adviser planning office for urban affairs Archdiocese Boston. Trustee Inst Social Tech. P.R. Served with USNR, 1944- 46. Mem. Am. Econ. Assn., Operations Research Soc. Am., Inst. Mgmt. Scis., Phi Beta Kappa, Sigma Chi, Omicron Delta Kappa. Contbr. chpts. to books. Home: 26 Kimball Rd Arlington, MA 02174 Office: 77 Massachusetts Av Cambridge MA 02139

FULOP, IRWIN MARTIN, lawyer; b. Salt Lake City, July 9, 1904; s. David Louis and Rebecca (Boukofsky) F.; A.B., U. Cal. at Berkeley, 1925; J.D., Harvard, 1928; m. Clara S. Sherman, July 15, 1938. Admitted to Ore. bar, 1928, Cal. bar, 1931; practice in Portland, 1928-31, Los Angeles, 1931-50, Beverly Hills, 1950—; partner Herzog, Fulop & Keuin, 1929-31; asso. Mark M. Cohen, 1931-50; pvt. practice, 1950-60; partner Fulop & Rolston, 1960- 62; partner Fulop, Rolston & Burns, 1962-70; pres. Fulop, Rolston, Burns & McKittrick, profl. corp., Beverly Hills, 1970—. Bd. dirs. Brandeis (Cal.) Camp Inst.; mem. exec. bd. Los Angeles chpt. Am. Jewish Com. Served to 1st lt. Cal. State Guard, 1940-45. Mem. Am., Los Angeles, Beverly Hills bar assns., Zeta Beta Tau, Pi Delta Epsilon. Home: 518 N Crescent Dr Beverly Hills CA 90210 Office: 9601 Wilshire Blvd Beverly Hills CA 90210

FULTON, CHARLES B., judge U.S. Ct. So. Dist. Fla. Address: Federal Bldg Miami FL 33130*

FULTON, CONRAD HOBART, lawyer; b. Little Rock, Aug. 1, 1925; s. Hobart C. and Elizabeth (Norris) F.; A.B., U. Ala., 1950, LL.B., 1951; grad. Judge Adv. Gen. Sch., U. Va., 1952; m. Dorothy Curry, July 21, 1945; 1 dau., Frances Curry. Admitted to Ala. bar, 19—; practice in Tuscaloosa, 1953—; partner Jones, McEachin, Ormond & Fulton, 1953—. Pres., dir. Alpha Phi Zeta House Corp. of Lambda Chi Alpha. Pres. Tuscaloosa chpt. A.R.C., Tuscaloosa County Tb. Assn. Served to capt. AUS, 1944-46, U.S. Army, 1951-53. Recipient Outstanding Alumnus award Alpha Phi Zeta, 1967. Mem. Am., Ala., Tuscaloosa County (past pres.) bar assns., Ala. Def. Lawyers Assn., Farrah Law Soc., Am. Arbitration Assn., S.A.R. (past chpt. pres.), Tuscaloosa Jr. C. of C. (past pres.), Phi Delta Phi. Presbyn. (elder). Clubs: Indian Hills Country (Tuscaloosa), Tuscaloosa Exchange (pres. elect). Home: 3 Buena Vista Tuscaloosa AL 35401 Office: First Nat Bank Bldg Tuscaloosa AL 34501

FULTON, DAVID GRAY, broadcasting co. exec.; b. Winston-Salem, N.C., July 30, 1925; s. Thomas Pinkney and Nannie (Martin) F.; A.B., U. N.C., 1945; M.B.A., Columbia, 1950; m. Mildred Elizabeth Kinghorn, Dec. 10, 1965. Staff asst. Price, Waterhouse & Co., N.Y.C., 1950-55; financial analyst, budget dir., div. controller ACF Industries, Inc., N.Y.C., N.Y., 1955-59; dep. asst. comptroller Int. Tel. & Tel. Corp., N.Y.C., 1959-61; dir. budgets, asst. to comptroller N.Am. Philips Corp., N.Y.C., 1962-66; treas. Digitronics Corp., Albertson, L.I., N.Y., 1966-69; mgr. planning, comptroller ABC, Inc., N.Y.C., 1970—. Served with USNR, 1943-46. C.P.A., N.Y. Mem. Am. Inst. C.P.A.'s, N.Y. State Soc. C.P.A.'s. Home: 30 W 89th St New York City NY 10024 Office: 1330 Av of Americas New York City NY 10019

FULTON, EDMUND DAVIE, lawyer; b. Kamloops, B.C., Can., Mar. 10, 1916; s. Frederick J. and Winifred M. (Davie) F.; B.A., U. B.C., 1936, (Rhodes scholar), St. John's Coll., Oxford U., 1937-39; LL.D., U. Ottawa, 1960, Queen's U., 1963; m. Patricia M. Macrae, Sept. 7, 1946; children—Catherine M., Patricia, Cynthia A. Called to bar, 1940; partner firm Fulton, Cumming, Bird, Richards; mem. Can. House of Commons, 1945- 63, 65-68; minister justice, atty. gen., 1957-62; acting minister citizenship and immigration, 1957-58; minister of pub. works, 1962-63; Queen's counsel, 1957. Chmn. Canadian delegation Can.-U.S.A. Columbia River Treaty, Wash., 1961. Pres., Young Progressive Conservatives of Can., 1946-49, leader Progressive Conservative Party B.C., 1963-66; chmn. Law Reform Commn. B.C., 1969—. Dir. Eddy Match Co., Ltd., Toronto, Crestwood Kitchens Ltd., Vancouver, EDP Industries Ltd., Vancouver. Mem. senate U. B.C., 1948-57, 69—. Hon. mem. Fellows Am. Bar Found. Roman Catholic. Clubs: Vancouver; Shaughnessy Golf and Country. Home: 1965 Matthews St Vancouver British Columbia Canada Office: 900 W Hastings St Vancouver British Columbia Canada

FULTON, GEORGE PEARMAN, Jr., educator; b. Milton, Mass., June 3, 1914; s. George P. and Lottie (Fulton) F.; B.S., Boston U., 1936, M.A., 1938, Ph.D., 1941; m. Miriam Alice Hunt, Aug. 1942 (div. 1964); children—Margaret, Susan, Peter Herrick, George Pearman III; m. 2d, Mary D. Shanks, Mar. 1970. Instr. biology Boston U., 1941-42; indsl. physiologist Arthur D. Little, Inc., Boston, 1946-47; asst. prof. biology Boston U., 1947-49, asso. prof., 1949-53, prof., 1953—, chmn. dept., 1956—, chmn. Biol. Grad. Sch., 1956—, Shields Warren prof., 1959—; staff mem. Children's Cancer Research Found., 1964—; vis prof. Stanford Med. Sch., 1958. Cons. div. nursing Pub. Health Services; mem. sci. adv. bd. New Eng. Aquarium; mem. adv. bd. on marine sci. and oceanography Mass. Bd. Higher Edn.; mem. sci. adv. bd. Sea Farms, Inc. Served from 2d lt. to capt. USAAF, 1942-46; lt. col. USAF Res. Fellow Am. Acad. Arts and Scis., Am. Coll. Angiology, Gerontology Soc.; mem. Am. Physiol. Soc., Soc. Exptl. Biology and Medicine, Am. Assn. Anatomists, Am. Soc. Zoologists, Radiation Research Soc., Microcirculatory Soc., Sigma Xi, Phi Beta Kappa. Founding editor Microvascular Research. Author numerous papers on vascular physiology, also motion picture films. Home: 69 Bay State Rd Boston MA 02215 Office: 2 Cummington St Boston MA 02215

FULTON, JAMES GROVE, congressman; b. Allegheny County, Pa., Mar. 1, 1903; s. James Ernest and Emilie (Fetterman) F.; A.B., Pa. State U., 1924; LL.B., Harvard, 1927; student Carnegie Inst. Tech. 2 years. Admitted to Pa. bar, 1928; gen. practice law, Pitts., 1928-42; solicitor for Dormont Borough, 1942; mem. Pa. Senate, 1939- 40; mem. 79th-82d congresses, 31st Pa. Dist., mem. 83d-91st congresses, 27th Dist. Pa., mem. fgn. affairs com., chmn. sub-com. for Europe, chmn. spl. sub-com to investigate Displaced Persons and Internat. Refugee Orgn., mem. sci. and astronautics com., mem. vets. affairs com. 87th; U.S. del. UN Internat. Trade Orgn. Conf., Havana, 1947-48, U.S., del. 14th Gen. Assembly UN, 1959. Co-author: Definitive study on Internat. Trade Orgn.; owner Mt. Lebanon (Pa.) News, The Boro News and The News (Allegheny County), Chartiers Valley Times Progress, The Tribune, also The News Progress, Dormont News (both Pitts.). Served as lt. USNR, 1942-45; service Pacific combat area; ret. capt. Mem. bd. dirs. Pittsburgh Playhouse, Pitts. Opera Bd. Mem. Allegheny Bd. Law Examiners, 1934-42. Rep. for President U.S. at Uruguay inauguration, 1964. Decorated by Republic of Italy, 1956. Mem. Am., Pa., Allegheny County bar assns., V.F.W., Am. Legion, Phi Delta Theta. Republican. Elk, Eagle. Clubs: Civic of Allegheny County, Harvard of Western Pennsylvania, Harvard-Yale-Princeton, Duquesne, St. Clair Country, Chartiers Country, Law (Pitts.) Home: 2850 Epsy Av Dormont Pittsburgh PA 15216 also Golden Pheasant Farm East Shady Dr Mt Lebanon PA 15228 Office: Federal Bldg Pittsburgh PA 15222 also 2886 W Liberty Av Dormont Pittsburgh PA 15216 also Rayburn House Office Bldg Washington DC 20515

FULTON, JAMES MURDOCK, lawyer; b. Cin., Jan. 2, 1914; s. Herbert F. and Marie Louise (Murdock) F.; B.S. with honors, Yale, 1935; LL.B., 1938; m. Anne Hall O'Connor, Feb. 23, 1943; children—Pattison, Judith Hood, Millicent Barnard, Joan Murdock, James Murdock. Admitted to Ohio bar, 1939, N.Y. bar, 1940; asso. Tompkins, Boal & Tompkins, N.Y.C., 1939-41, 45-51; asso. gen. atty. Merck & Co., Inc., Rahway, N.J. 1951-53, gen. atty., 1953-55; counsel Merck Sharpe & Dohme Internat., 1955-61, gen. counsel, 1961—, sec., 1970—; dir. Patent Trader, Inc., Mt. Kisco, N.Y. Trustee The Gill Sch., Bernardsville, N.J., Glen Kirk Sch., Morristown, N.J. Mem. Am., N.Y. State bar assns., Assn. Bar City N.Y. Clubs: Vineyard Haven Yacht; Essex Hunt; Somerset Lake, Roxiticus Golf; Down Town Assn. (N.Y.C.). Home: Roxiticus Rd Far Hills NJ 07931 Office: Merck & Co Inc 126 E Lincoln Av Rahway NJ 07065

FULTON, JAMES STREET, educator; b. Columbia, Tenn., Aug. 29, 1904; s. Henry Osgood and Lucile (Street) F.; B.A., Vanderbilt U., 1925, M.A., 1929; postgrad. Gottingen U., 1927-28; Ph.D., Cornell U., 1934; m. Edythe King, Sept. 19, 1932; children—Asa King, Cynthia. Lectr., asst. prof McGill U., 1934-43; asst. prof. Shrivenham Am. U., 1945, Yale, 1946; asst. prof. Rice U., 1946-49, asso. prof., 1949-53, prof., 1953—, chmn. dept. philosophy and psychology, edn., 1956-63, chmn. dept. philosophy and edn., 1963-64, chmn. dept. philosophy, 1964-68, dean humanities, 1964, master Will Rice Coll., 1957- 69. Served as lt. Royal Canadian Navy Vol. Res., 1943-45. Mem. Am. Philos. Assn., Southwestern Philos. Soc. (past pres.), So. Soc. Philosophy and Psychology, Husserl Circle, Phi Beta Kappa, Sigma Chi. Author: Science and Man's Hope, 1955. Contbr. articles to profl. jours. Home: 5203 Grand Lake St Bellaire TX 77401

FULTON, MARSHALL NAIRNE, physician; b. Koekuk, Ia., Mar. 10, 1899; s. William and Jessie Macqueen (Fisher) F.; Ph.B., Brown U., 1920, Sc.D., 1960; B.A. with honors in physiology (Rhodes Scholar), Oxford U., Eng., 1923: M.D., Johns Hopkins, 1925; m. Mary Howe De Wolf, June 22, 1940; children—Edith Weeks, Harriet Fisher, Winthrop DeW., Frank T. II, Mary, Nancy, Katherine, Holly. Intern, asst. resident Peter Bent Brigham Hosp., Boston, 1927-29, resident, 1929-31, vis. physician on staff, 1931-46; asst. Harvard Med. Sch., 1929-32, instr., 1932-36, asso. in medicine, 1936-46; practice internal medicine 1946—; physician in chief R.I. Hosp. 1948-63; prof. medicine emeritus Brown U. at R.I. Hosp.; cons. physician Providence Lying-In, Westerly, Roger Williams, Pawtucket Meml., Miriam, Lady of Fatima hosps. Served with rank of major in charge dept. cardiovascular disease, and asst. chief of med. service, Walter Reed Hosp., Washington, 1942; chief med. service, with rank of lt. col., Valley Forge Gen. Hosp., 1942-45; chief med. serv. Ashford Gen. Hosp., White Sulphur Springs, 1945-46; promoted col., 1945. Mem. Joint Commn. Accreditation of Hosps., 1963—. Awarded Legion of Merit. Fellow A.M.A., A.C.P. (gov. R.I., chmn. bd. govs., 1959-62, 1st v.p. 1962-63, regent 1963-69, Alfred Stenge medal 1971); mem. Am. Soc. Clin. Investigation, Assn. Am. Physicians, Providence Med. Assn., R.I. Med. Soc., Am., N.E. (v.p. 1948-49), R.I. (pres. 1956) heart assns., Am. Clin. and Climatol. Assn. (sec. treas. 1950-58; pres. 1959-60), Alpha Delta Phi, Phi Beta Kappa, Sigma Xi, Alpha Omega Alpha. Republican Episcopalian. Clubs: Hope, Agawam Hunt (Providence). Address: 284 President Av Providence RI 02906

FULTON, RICHARD ALSINA, lawyer; b. N.Y.C., Feb. 27, 1926; s. Robert B. and Consuelo (Alsina) F.; A.B., U. Fla., 1949; J.D., Tulane U., 1957. Admitted to La. bar, 1957; practiced in Baton Rouge, 1957-60; asst. gen. counsel La. Dept. Hwys., 1957-58, La. Dept. Revenue, 1959-60; asst. to U.S. Senator Allen J. Ellender, 1961; exec. dir., gen. counsel United Bus. Schs. Assn., 1962—; gen. counsel Accrediting Commn. for Bus. Schs.; project dir. Manpower Devel. and Tng. Act, Research and Demonstration Project for Health, Edn. and Welfare-U.S. Office Edn.; cons. fed. relations Nat. Fedn. Licensed Practical Nurses. Trustee, Nat. Licensed Practical Nurse Edn. Found. Served with U.S. Mcht. Marine, World War II, Korea. Mem. Am., Fed., La. bar assns., D.C. Tuland Alumni Assn. (past pres., treas.),

Sigma Chi, Phi Delta Phi. Democrat. Episcopalian. Mason. Clubs: University, National Lawyers, Potomac Boat (Washington). Author: You Career as a Secretary, 1963; Accounting for Your Future, 1966. Editor in chief The Compass, 1962—. Contbg. editor Ency. Ednl. Research, 1969, Nat. Bus. Edn. Yearbook, 1969. Contbr. articles profl. jours. Home: 1533 Foxhall Rd NW Washington DC 20007 Office: 1730 M St NW Washington DC 20036

FULTON, RICHARD HARMON, congressman; b. Nashville, Jan. 27, 1927; s. Lyle Houston and Labina (Plummer) F.; student U. Tenn., 1946-47; m. Jewel Simpson, Dec. 23, 1945; children—Richard, Michael, Barry, Donna, Linda. Real estate broker, Fulton & Riddle Realty Co., Nashville; mem. Tenn. Senate, 1959-60; mem. 88th-92d Congresses, 5th Tenn. Dist. Served with USNR, 1945-46. Democrat. Methodist. Mason (Shriner). Home: 911 Preston Dr Nashville TN 37206 Office: House Office Bldg Washington DC 20515

FULTON, ROBERT B, v.p. Newmont Mining Corp. Address: 300 Park Ave New York City NY 10022*

FULTON, ROBERT BURWELL, educator, navy officer; b. Burlington, Vt., Dec. 22, 1910; s. William Lawrence and Mary (Haley) F.; B.S., U.S. Naval Acad., 1932; student U.S. Naval Postgrad. Sch., 1938-40; M.S., Mass. Inst. Tech., 1940; grad. Advanced Mgmt. Program, Harvard, 1945; m. Laura Frances McCarley, Oct. 3, 1936; children—William Lawrence II, Frances Anne Commd. ensign U.S. Navy, 1932, advanced through grades to rear adm., 1961; served in ships and staff U.S. Fleet, 1932-38; survived sinking U.S.S. Houston, 1942; Japanese prisoner of war, 1942-45; various engring. assignments, 1946- 58; comdr. Phila. Naval Shipyard, 1959-61; asst. chief tech. engring. Bur. Ships, U.S. Navy, 1961-66; dep. comdr. for engring. Naval Ship Systems Command, U.S. Navy, Washington, also comdr. Naval Ship Engring. Center, 1966-68; head engring. technols. div. State Tech. Inst. at Memphis, 1968—. Decorated D.S.M., Bronze Star, Purple Heart. Registered profl. engr. Mem. Am. Soc. Naval Engrs., Am. Soc. for Engring. Edn., Nat. Soc. Profl. Engrs. Presbyn. Home: 571 N Mendenhall Rd Memphis TN 38122 Office: 5983 Macon Cove Memphis TN 38128

FULTON, ROBERT DAVID, mem. Democratic Nat. Com., lawyer; b. Waterloo, Ia., May 13, 1929; s. Lester Charles and Fern F. (Ryan) F.; student Ia. State Tchrs. Coll., 1947-49; B.S., State U. Ia., 1952, J.D., 1958; m. Rachel Marie Breault, Sept. 10, 1955; children—Susan, Mary, John, James. Admitted to Ia. bar, 1958, since practiced in Waterloo; mem. firm Fulton, Frerichs & Nutting, 1960—; atty. Legal Aid Soc., Waterloo, 1960-62; mem. Ia. Ho. of Reps. from Blackhawk County, 1959-61, Ia. Senate, 1963-65; lt. gov. Ia., 1965-69. Chmn. Blackhawk County United Services Drive, 1960. Mem. Democratic Nat. Com for Ia., 1968—. Served with USAF, 1953-55. Mem. Am. Legion, AMVETS. Democrat. Home: 141 Hillcrest Rd Waterloo IA 50701 Office: 616 Lafayette St Waterloo IA 50703

FULTON, ROBERT LESTER, educator; b. Toronto, Can., Nov. 30, 1926; s. Edgar John and Mary Grace (Ouderkirk) F.; A.B. cum laude, U. Ill., 1951; M.A., U. Toronto, 1953; Ph.D., Wayne State U., 1959; m. Julie Ann Rockman, June 13, 1964; children—David, Richard, Regan. Instr., U. Wis., 1957-58; from asst. prof. to prof. sociology Cal. State Coll., Los Angeles, 1958-66; prof. sociology U. Minn., Mpls., 1966—, dir. Center for Death Edn. and Research, 1969—; vis. prof. U. Minn., 1963, 65, U. Osmania (India), 1967. Served with Royal Canadian Navy, 1944. Fellow Am. Sociol. Assn.; mem. Am. Assn. U. Profs., Acad. Psychosomatic Medicine, Societe de Thanatologie de Langue Francaise. Author: Death and Identity, 1965; Education and Social Crisis, 1967. Asso. editor Omega, 1970—. Home: 25 E Minnehaha Pkwy Minneapolis MN 55419

FULTON, THOMAS, educator; b. Budapest, Hungary, Nov. 19, 1927; s. Michael and Irene (Weisz) F.; came to U.S., 1941, naturalized, 1949; B.A. summa cum laude, Harvard, 1950, M.A., 1951, Ph.D., 1954; m. Babette Pilzer, June 14, 1952; children—Ruth Carol, Judith Pamela. Asst. prof. Johns Hopkins, Balt., 1956-59, asso. prof., 1959-64, prof. physics, 1964—. Cons. Brookhaven Lab., Upton, L.I., N.Y., 1954, 62, U. Cal. at Berkeley, 1959, Argonne (Ill.) Nat. Labs., 1968, Brandeis Inst., 1962, Aspen (Colo.) Inst., 1963, 66, 67, Aspen Center Physics, 1968, U. Vienna, 1964-65, Stanford Linear Accelerator Center, 1967; vis. scientist CERN, Geneva, 1969-70. Served with AUS, 1946-47. Jewett fellow, 1954-55; NSF fellow, 1956-59; Fulbright Sr. Research scholar, 1964-65; Guggenheim fellow, 1964-65. Fellow Am. Phys. Soc.; mem. Archeol. Inst. Am., Am. Assn. U. Profs., Fedn. Am. Scientists, Phi Beta Kappa, Sigma Xi. Home: 5600 Roxbury Pl Baltimore MD 21209

FULTON, THOMAS BENJAMIN, clergyman; b. St. Catharines, Ont., Can., Jan. 13, 1918; s. Thomas Francis and Mary Catharine (Jones) F.; student St. Augustines Sem., Toronto, 1935-41; D. Canon Law, Cath. U. Am., 1948. Ordained priest Roman Catholic Ch., 1941; asst. pastor in Toronto, 1941-51; sec. Toronto Tribunal, 1948-51; chancellor Archdiocese Toronto, 1952-69, aux. bishop, 1969—; nat. sec. Soc. Propagation Faith, 1952—. Author: The Prenuptial Investigation, 1948. Home: 200 Church St Toronto 2 Ontario Canada Office: 55 Gould St Toronto 2 Ontario Canada

FULTON, WILLIAM JOHN, Jr., newspaper corr.; b. Sycamore, Ill., Feb. 12, 1907; s. William John and Laura (Busey) F.; grad. Exeter (N.H.) Acad., 1925; A.B., U. Ill., 1939; m. Joan Eileen Twelftree; children—Jill Mary, Sally Ann, Elizabeth, William Scott. Newspaper reporter Aurora (Ill.) Beacon-News, 1928, Rockford Republic, 1929-30, Chgo. Am., 1930; with Chgo. Tribune, 1931—, chief London bur., 1946-49, Eastern corr. 1949—, UN corr., news columnist, 1954—; covered peace conf. Paris, France, 1946; fgn. ministers confs., London, Moscow, N.Y.C. Recipient Chgo. Tribune ann. Bech award, 1954. Served with USAAF, 1944-45. Mem. UN Corrs. Assn., Phi Delta Theta. Republican, Conglist. Club: Overseas Press (N.Y.C.). Home: 74 River Rd Cos Cob CT 06807 Office: care Chicago Tribune Chicago IL 60611

FULTON, WILLIAM YOST, investment banker; b. Chgo., Mar. 7, 1903; s. William H. and Mary Brank (Yost) F.; A.B., Wabash Coll., 1923; m. Florence Bunn, Nov. 29, 1948 (dec.); children—Edward, James, Marylou, Stewart. Employed as salesman, Maynard H. Murch & Co., Cleve., 1924, partner, 1943-50, partner successor firm Fulton, Reid & Co., 1950-56; pres., dir. Fulton Reid & Co., Inc., 1956-63, chmn. bd., dir., 1963-67; chmn. bd., dir. Fulton, Reid & Staples, Inc., 1967-71; pres., dir. Clariden Corp.; dir. Data Mark, Inc., Fairport Devel. Corp., Dasher Rubber & Chem. Co., Summit Nat. Holding Co., Barton Brands Inc., Keithley Instruments, Inc., Roadway Express, Inc., Pultrusions Corp., Lauren Mfg. Co., TopRoc Precast Corp., Transam. Investment Group, Rand Devel. Co., Oxford Products. Treas. Cleve. Humane Soc. Treas. Fulton Reid & Staples Fund, Inc. Mem. Phi Gamma Delta. Presbyn. Clubs: Rockwell Springs Trout; Union, Clevelander (Cleve.); India House (N.Y.C.); Union League (Chgo.). Home: 2419 Derbyshire Rd Cleveland Heights OH 44106

FULTS, LEON A., auto supply co. exec.; b. Center, Tex., May 14, 1912; s. Ernest C. and Neta (Taylor) F.; student Stephen F. Austin U., 1931-33; m. Doris Badders, Nov. 14, 1937; children-Suzanne, Jeffry. With Western Auto Supply Co., Kansas City, Mo., 1935—, regional mgr., 1961-66, corporate v.p., 1966-70, pres., 1970—. Home: 4902 W 96th Terrace Overland Park KS 66207 Office: 2107 Grand Av Kansas City MO 64108

FULTZ, CLAIR ERVIN, banker; b. nr. Jeffersonville, O., Nov. 23, 1911; s. Roy Bertis and Addis (Ervin) F.; B.S., Ohio State U., 1934; grad. Rutgers U. Grad Sch. Banking, 1946; m. Isabelle Eichelberger, Aug. 18, 1935; children—Robert Edward, Karen Lynn, Pamela Jane. With Huntington Nat. Bank, Columbus, O., 1934—, v.p., 1953-57, dir., 1956—, pres., 1958-67, chmn., chief exec. officer, 1967—; pres. Huntington Bancshares, Inc., 1966—; dir. Midland Mut. Life Ins. Co.; trustee Greenlawn Cemetery Assn. (all Columbus). Chmn., trustee Battelle Meml. Inst.; trustee, past pres. Children's Hosp. Past chmn. Devel. Com. Greater Columbus. Mem. Assn. Res. City Bankers, Ohio Bankers Assn. (past pres.), S.A.R., Ohio State Med. Assn. (hon. mem.), Beta Gamma Sigma, Alpha Kappa Psi, Phi Alpha Kappa. Clubs: Scioto Country, Columbus, Faculty, Ohio Society N.Y. Home: 2575 Haverford Rd Columbus OH 43220 Office: 17 S High St Columbus OH 43216

FULTZ, DAVE, educator, meteorologist; b. Chgo., Aug. 12, 1921; s. Harry T. and Ora L. (Voyles) F.; B.S., U. Chgo., 1941, certificate meteorology, 1942, Ph.D., 1947; m. Jean Laura McEldowney, Apr. 6, 1946; children—Martha M., David L., Katherine E. Emergency asst. U.S. Weather Bur., Chgo., 1942; research asst. U. Chgo. and U.S. Weather Bur., 1942-43; research asst., instr. U. P.R., 1943; research asst. U. Chgo., 1943-44, faculty, 1945-46, prof. meteorology, 1960—, dir. hydrodynamics lab., 1946—. Cons. USAF Sci. Adv. Bd., 1959-64; mem. nat. com. fluid mechanics films Ednl. Services, Inc., Newton, Mass., 1962—; research grants adv. com. Nat. Air Pollution Control Adminstrn., 1969. Served with USAAF, 1945. Guggenheim fellow, 1950-51; NSF sr. postdoctoral fellow, 1957-58; recipient Golden Plate award, Am. Acad. Achievement, 1968. Fellow Am. Meteorol. Soc. (Meisinger award 1951, C. G. Rossby Research medal 1967), Am. Geophys. Union; mem. Am. Astron. Soc., A.A.A.S., Phi Beta Kappa, Sigma Xi (sec., treas. Chgo chpt. 1946). Contbr. profl. jours. Home: 5516 S Kenwood Ave Chicago IL 60637

FULWIDER, ROBERT W., patent lawyer; b. Los Angeles, July 14, 1903; s. David Earl and Alice (Wirthlin) F.; B.S., Cal. Inst. Tech., 1925; LL.B., U. Cal., 1932; m. Helen Sara Ferguson, Feb. 24, 1940. Admitted to Cal. bar, 1932; practice of patent law, 1932—, sr. partner Fulwider, Patton, Rieber, Lee & Utecht, Los Angeles. Mem. Am., Los Angeles, San Diego bar assns., Instrument Soc. Am., Soc. Motion Picture and TV Engrs. Home: 1351 N Spaulding Av Los Angeles CA 90046 Office: 5225 Wilshire Blvd Los Angeles CA 90036

FULWILER, ROBERT A., Jr., sec. Hercules Inc., ret. 1968. Address: 910 Market St Wilmington DE 19899

FUMICH, GEORGE, govt. ofcl.; b. Clamady, Pa., Dec. 8, 1917; s. George and Madeline (Sekeres) F.; A.B., W.Va., U., 1941, LL.B., 1948; m. Marie R. Romano, June 13, 1959; children—George, Paul, Sheila, Frank. Admitted W.Va. bar., 1948; atty. Christopher Coal Co., Osage, W.Va., 1948-61; dir. Office Minerals Exploration, Dept. Interior, 1961-63, dir. Office Coal Research, 1963—. Served with inf. AUS, 1941-45; Italy. Decorated Silver Star, Bronze Star. Mem. W.Va., Monongalia County, Fed. bar assns. Elk. Home: 510 N Montana St Arlington VA 22203 Office: Dept Interior Bldg Washington DC 20240

FUNARI, JOHN H., fdn. exec.; b. Connellsville, Pa., Apr. 6, 1929; s. Fred Joseph and Anna (Dowling) F.; B.A., U. Va., 1950; postgrad. Princeton, 1950-51, Queen's Coll., Oxford U., 1951-54, U. Pitts., 1957-59; m. Barbara J. Burriss, Apr. 4, 1959; children—Tracey Anne, Jonathan Daniel, Victoria Celeste. Exec. asst. to chancellor U. Pitts., 1958-62; exec. asst. to adminstr. AID, Dept. of State, 1962-63, coordinator legislative presentation, 1963-65, dir. Office Nr. Eastern Affairs, 1965-67, dir. AID Mission in Jordan, 1967-68, dep. and acting dir. AID Mission in India, 1968-70; Ford Found. rep., Mexico, 1970—. Served to lt. USNR, 1954-57. Rhodes scholar, 1951-54. Mem. Raven Soc., Phi Beta Kappa. Democrat. Clubs: Serpentine (Charlottesville, Va.); Gymkhana (New Delhi). Home: Calderon de la Barca 14 Mexico 5 DF Mexico Office: Reforma 243 7th Floor Mexico 5 DF Mexico

FUNARI, MARIO R., corp. exec.; b. Trenton, Aug. 16, 1920; s. Robert U. and Nancy Funari; B.S. in Commerce magna cum laude, Rider Coll., 1941; postgrad. Carnegie Inst. Tech., 1949; m. Virginia A. Founds, Oct. 13, 1945; children—Robert Glen, Patricia Ann. Cost accountant U.S. Rubber Co., 1941-42; supr. cost accounting Blaw-Knox Co., 1942-49; supt. plant accounting Rockwell Mfg. Co. 1949-53; v.p. controller Weatherhead Co., Cleve., 1953—; adminstrv. v.p. Fastener Group, Lamson & Sessions Co., 1971—; lectr. cost accounting Cleve. Engring. Soc. Mem. Ft. Wayne (Ind.) Sch. Bd., 1958-59. Trustee, Brentwood Hosp., Cleve. Mem. Financial Execs. Inst., Nat. Assn. Accountants (Man of Year Award Cleve. chpt. 1963). Clubs: Tanglewood Country, Forest Hill (v.p. 1967-68) (Cleve.). Contbg. author handbook; author articles in field. Home: 2892 Alvord Pl Pepper Pike OH 44124 Office: 5000 Tiedeman Rd Cleveland OH 44144

FUNG, YUAN-CHENG BERTRAM, educator, author; b. Yuhong, Kiangsu, China, Sept. 15, 1919; s. Chung- Kwang and Lien (Hu) F.; came to U.S. 1945, naturalized, 1957; B.S., Nat. Central U., Chungking, China, 1941, M.S., 1943; Ph.D., Cal. Inst. Tech., 1948; m. Luna Hsien-Shih Yu, Dec. 22, 1949; children—Conrad Antung, Brenda Pingsi. Research fellow Bur. Aero. Research China, 1943-45; research asst., then research fellow Cal. Inst. Tech., 1946-51, mem. faculty, 1951-66, prof. aero., 1959-66; prof. bioengring. and applied mechanics U. Cal. at San Diego, 1966—; cons. aerospace indsl. firms, 1949—. Recipient Achievement award Chinese Inst. Engrs., 1965; Guggenheim fellow, 1958-59. Fellow Am. Inst. Aeros. and Astronautics; mem. Am. Soc. M.E., Soc. Engring. Sci., Microcirculatory Soc., Am. Physiol. Soc., Nat. Heart Assn., Basic Sci. Council, Sigma Xi. Author: The Theory of Aeroelasticity, 1956; Foundations of Solid Mechanics, 1965; A First Course in Continuum Mechanics, 1969; also papers. Home: 2660 Greentree Lane La Jolla CA 92037

FUNK, CARL WILLIAM, lawyer; b. Phila., Aug. 9, 1900; s. C. William and Helen (Hoopes) F.; B.S. in Econs., Wharton Sch., U. Pa., 1922, J.D., 1925; m. Madeleine E. Hawkes, Aug. 8, 1945; children—Elizabeth, Sarah T. Gowen fellow U. Pa. 1925-26; admitted to Pa. bar, 1925, since practiced in Phila.; partner firm Drinker, Biddle & Reath, 1936-41, 46-71, counsel, 1971—. Mem. Rev. Com. Permanent Editorial Bd., Am. Law Inst. and Commrs. Uniform State Law, 1966-71, counsel Permanent Edn. Bd. 1971—; mem. Pa. Banking Law Commn., 1964-67; mem. legal div. WPB, 1941-42. Vice pres. Soc. P.E. Ch. Advancement Christianity in Pa., 1965—. Served with U.S. Army, 1918; to capt. USNR, 1942-46. Decorated sec. navy commendation. Mem. Am. Law Inst., Am., Pa., Phila. bar assns., Assn. Bar City N.Y. Author: Pennsylvania Banks and Uniform Commercial Code, 1954; Banks and the Uniform Commercial Code, 1962; also articles. Home: 3127 Queen Lane Philadelphia PA 19129 Office: Phila Nat Bank Bldg Philadelphia PA 19107

FUNK, CASIMIR, biochemist; b. Warsaw, Poland, Feb. 23, 1884; s. Jacques and Gustawa (Zysan) F.; student Gymnasium, Warsaw, 1894-1900, U. of Geneva, 1900-01, Ph.D., U. of Berne, 1901-04; post grad. work Inst. Pasteur, Paris, 1904- 06, Univ. of Berlin, 1906-07; U. of London, D.Sc., 1913; m. Alix Denise Schneidesch, June 19, 1914; children—Ian Casimir, Doriane Jacqueline. Biochemist Wiesbaden Municipal Hosp., 1907-08, biochemist, Huntington Cancer Research Fund, Cornell Med. Sch., 1915-16; research head, Metz & Co., N.Y.C., 1917-23; asso. in biochemistry, Coll. Phys. and Surgs., Columbia, 1921-23; head biochem. dept., Warsaw Sch. of Hygiene, Rockefeller Found. 1923-27, Rueil Research Lab., France, 1928-39; cons. U.S. Vitamin Corp., N.Y.C., 1936—. Pres. Funk Found. for Med. Research. Mem. British Biochem. and physiol. Socs., French Biochem. Soc., Am. Chem. Soc., Soc. for Exptl. Biology and Medicine, Am. Soc. Biol. Chemists. Author books. Home: 186 Riverside Dr New York City, NY 10024. Office: US Vitamin Corp 800 2d Av New York City NY 10017 ☆

FUNK, HELEN BEATRICE, educator, microbiologist; b. Waverly, Ia., May 23, 1913; d. Joseph Oliver and Maude (Stover) Funk; B.A., Ia. State Tchrs. Coll., 1935; M.S., U. Ia., 1936; Ph.D., U. Wis., 1955. Tchr. biology Washington (Ill.) High Sch., 1936-42; instr. bacteriology and zoology Milw.-Downer Coll., 1943-46; teaching fellow bacteriology U. Wis., 1946- 48, 49; asst. prof. botany Barnard Coll., also Grad. Faculty Columbia, 1950-56; faculty Goucher Coll., 1956—, prof. microbiology, 1961—, chmn. dept. biol. scis., 1958-61; Fulbright lectr. U. Tehran (Iran), 1961-62. Mem. steering com. for sci. seminars for gifted children, Balt. and Baltimore County, 1959-67. Univ. fellow U. Ia., 1942-43; fellow bacteriology U. Wis., 1948-49; Helen Dodson Prince fellow Goucher Coll. 1965. Mem. Am. Soc. Microbiology (pres. Md. br. 1965-66), Sigma Xi, Sigma Delta Epsilon. Author: (with Ann M. Lacy) From One Cell to Many, 1966; also articles. Office: Goucher Coll Baltimore MD 21204

FUNK, PAUL EUGENE, advt. and marketing exec.; b. Coshocton, O., Mar. 13, 1920; s. Abraham Bantam and Helen (Kaiser) F.; certificate Graphic Reprodn. Arts, Sorbonne, Paris, France, 1945; m. Betty Jane Walter, Sept. 28, 1940 (div. July 1951); 1 son, Karl E.; m. 2d, Joan Anna Cornish, Dec., 1964 (div. July 1969); stepchildren—Douglas Cornish, Joyce Cornish. Mgr., sign and decal div. Dura-Products Mfg. Co., Canton, O., 1938-41; dir. advt. and pub. relations Maguire Industries Canton, 1945-47; dir. pub. relations Norman Malone Assos., Akron, O., 1947-49; account exec. Fuller & Smith & Ross, Inc., Cleve., 1949-54; account supr. McCann-Erickson, Inc., N.Y.C., 1954-66, v.p., 1957-66, exec. v.p., gen. mgr. indsl., tech. and sci. marketing div., 1962-66; pres. McCann/ITSM, Inc., 1967-68; chmn., chief exec. officer Pritchard Wood Assos., Inc., N.Y.C., 1968-70; chmn. Scenario Resources, Inc., 1970—; dir. King- Casey, Inc. Faculty creative workshop Advt. Age, 1963, 69, 70. Bd. dirs. Epilepsy Found., Epilepsy Assn. Am.; 1st v.p. Epilepsy Found., 1964-68, pres., 1969—70, exec. v.p., 1970—. Served with AUS, 1941-45. Mem. Internat. Advt. Assn., Internat. Execs. Assn., Pub. Relations Soc. Am., A.I.M. (pres.'s council), Assn. Indsl. Advertisers, Am. Marketing Assn. Clubs: Athletic, Marco Polo (N.Y.C.); Lone Palm Golf (Lakeland, Fla.). Mem. editorial adv. bd. Indsl. Marketing mag. Home: 1659 32d St NW Washington DC 20007 Office: 733 15th St NW Washington DC 20005

FUNK, RALPH HAMILTON, librarian; b. Holdenville, Okla., May 7, 1931; s. Ralph-Ernest and Alpha Lenore (Hamilton) F.; B.A., U. Okla., 1954, M.L.S., 1958. Tchr., Marshall (Okla.) High Sch., 1955-56; reference asst. U. Kan. Libraries, Lawrence, 1958-59, asst. head, acquisitions dept., 1959-60; legislative reference librarian Okla. State Library, 1960-67; dir. Okla. Dept. Libraries, Oklahoma City, 1968—. Instr., U. Okla. Sch. Library Sci., 1965-67, adj. asso. prof. library systems mgmt. program Sch. Indsl. Engring., 1971—. Sec. Okla. Arts and Humanities Council, 1968—; state archivist Okla., 1968—; state records adminstr., 1968—. Exec. sec. Bibliog. Center for Research, Inc., Denver, 1970. Mem. A.L.A. (adult services div. bd. 1967-70), Soc. Am. Archivists. Editor, contbr. articles profl. publs. Home: 807 Carey Dr Norman OK 73069 Office: 109 State Capitol Oklahoma City OK 73105

FUNK, ROBERT NORRIS, coll. dean; b. Yakima, Wash., Nov. 10, 1930; s. Edgar Norris and Ione (Anderson) F.; B.A., U. Ore., 1952, LL.B., 1955; Ph.D., Stanford, 1967. Admitted to Ore. bar, 1956; pvt. practice, Pendleton, 1958-62; mem. adminstrn. Stanford, 1962-70, asst. dean undergrad. edn., 1965-66, asst. dean Sch. Edn., 1966-70, also lectr. edn.; dean faculty Stephens Coll., Columbia, Mo., 1970—. Served with Judge Advocate Gen.'s Corps, AUS, 1955-58. Mem. Ore. Bar. Assn., Am. Judicature Soc., Phi Delta Phi, Phi Delta Kappa, Tau Kappa Epsilon. Republican. Episcopalian. Contbr. profl. jours. Home: 1411 E Broadway St Columbia MO 65201

FUNK, ROBERT WALTER, educator; b. Evansville, Ind., July 18, 1926; s. Robert J. and Ada (Adams) F.; A.B., Butler U., 1947, B.D., 1950, M.A., 1951; Ph.D. (Hillel fellow), Vanderbilt U., 1953; m. Inabelle McKee, Aug. 20, 1950; children—Andrea Elizabeth, Stephanie Alyson. Lectr. in Bible, Butler U., 1947-49, Vanderbilt U., 1951-53, prof. N.T., Div. Sch., 1966-69, chmn. grad. dept. religion, 1967-69; asst. prof. religion Tex. Christian U., 1953-56; instr. Harvard Div. Sch., 1956-57; asst. prof. bibl. theology Emory U., 1958-59; asso. prof. N.T., Drew U., 1959-66; prof. religious studies U. Mont., Missoula, 1969—. Ann. prof. Am. Sch. Oriental Research, Jerusalem, 1957-58; Fulbright sr. scholar U. Tubingen (Germany), 1965-66. Guggenheim fellow, 1965-66. Fellow Soc. for Religion in Higher Edn.; mem. Am. Acad. Religion (dir., com. chmn.), Soc. Bibl. Lit. (exec. sec., com. chmn., mem. exec. com.), Am. Schs. Oriental Research, Studiorum Novi Testamenti Societas, New Testament Colloquim (past chmn. exec. com., sec.), Cath. Bibl. Assn., Assn. Disciples for Theol. Discussion, Soc. for Sci. Study Religion, Am. Assn. U. Profs., Am. Council Learned Socs. (mem. Conf. Secs., exec. com.). Editor, chmn. editorial bd. Jour. for Theology and the Church, 1964—. Editorial bd. Hermeneia; A Critical Historical Commentary on the New Testament, 1964—, Jour. Am. Acad. Religion, 1970—. Contbr. articles profl. jours. Home: 12 Martha's Ct Missoula MT 59801

FUNKE, LEWIS, drama editor; b. Bronx, N.Y., Jan. 25, 1912; s. Joseph and Rose (Keimowitz) F.; A.B., N.Y. U., 1932; m. Blanche Bier, July 3, 1938; children—Phyllis Ellen, Michael Jeffrey. Free-lance writer, sports dept. N.Y. Times, 1928-36, staff sports writer, 1932-44, gen. news staff, movie dept., 1944, drama editor, 1944—. Club: Dutch Treat. Author articles various nat. mags. Co-author: Actors Talk About Acting, 1962; Max Gordon Presents, 1963; A Gift of Joy, 1965; author: The Curtain Rises, 1971. Address: care New York Times Editorial Dept 229 W 43d St New York City NY 10036

FUNKHOUSER, A. PAUL, railroad ofcl.; b. Roanoke, Va., Mar. 8, 1923; s. Samuel King and Jane Harwood (Cocke) F.; grad. Woodberry Forest (Va.) Sch., 1941; B.A., Princeton, 1945; LL.B., U. Va., 1950; m. Eleanor Rosalie Gamble, Feb. 4, 1950; children—John Paul, Eleanor Kent. Admitted to Va. bar 1951; with firm Hunton, Williams, Anderson, Gav and Moore, Richmond, 1950-51; with N.&W. Ry., 1952-63, asst. gen. counsel, 1960-63; asst. v.p. Pa. R.R., 1963-65, v.p. coal and ore traffic, 1965-68; v.p. coal and ore traffic Penn Central

Transp. Co., 1968-70, v.p. pub. affairs, 1970—; dir. Philadelphia Housing Development Corp., Bd. mgrs. Childrens Hosp. Phila.; pres. Roanoke Valley United Fund, 1956-57. Trustee Hollins Coll. Served to 2d lt. AUS, 1943-46. Mem. Phi Beta Kappa, Order of Coif, Omicron Delta Kappa, Delta Psi, Phi Delta Phi. Episcopalian. Clubs: Gulph Mills Golf, Racquet (Phila.); Princeton (N.Y.C.); Merion Cricket (Haverford); Shenandoah (Roanoke); Metropolitan (Washington). Home: 328 Grays Lane Haverford PA 19041 Office: Transportation Center Philadelphia PA 19104

FUNKHOUSER, ELMER NEWTON, Jr., metal co. exec.; b. Hagerstown, Md., Nov. 23, 1916; s. Elmer Newton and Nellie Evelyn (Spielman) F.; B.S., Otterbein Coll., 1938, LL.D., 1963; M.B.A., Harvard, 1941; m. Gladys Elizabeth McFeeley, Apr. 8, 1940; children—Elmer Newton III, Richard Nelson II, Susan Lynn, Lois Erica, David Kirsten. With Dewey and Almy Chem. Corp., 1940-54, gen. mgr. cryovac div., 1950-54; with W.R. Grace & Co., 1954-62, exec. v.p. Cryovac div., 1956-62; exec. v.p., dir. Am. Metal Climax, Inc., N.Y.C., 1962-66; now sr. v.p. Am. Can Co.; dir. Arkwright-Boston Mfrs. Mut. Ins. Co., Waltham, Mass., Martin Veneer Co., Hagerstown, Md. Trustee Otterbein Coll., Emerson Hosp., Concord, Mass. Mem. Am. Inst. Mining, Metall. and Petroleum Engrs. Clubs: Milwood Hunt (Farmingham, Mass.); Concord Country; River (N.Y.C.). Home: 435 E 52d St New York City NY 10022 also October Farm Monument St Concord MA 01742 Office: American Lane Greenwich CT 06830

FUNKHOUSER, RICHARD, fgn. service officer; b. Trenton, N.J., Sept. 10, 1917; s. Edgar Bright and Evelyn (Hayes) F.; B.A. summa cum laude, Princeton, 1939; grad. Nat. War Coll., 1954; m. Phyllis Parkin, Mar. 4, 1944; children—Phillip (dec.), Bruce Bedford, Blaine. Cons., Bethlehem Steel Co., 1939, Shell Union Oil Co., 1939, Standard Oil Co. Venezuela, 1940-42; joined U.S. fgn. service, 1945; assigned Am. embassies in Paris, Bern, Brussels and Luxembourg, 1945-47; regional petroleum attache Am. embassies in Cairo, Jidda, Baghdad, Damascus, Beirut and Teheran, 1947-49; officer charge Iraq, Syria and Lebanon affairs State Dept., Washington, 1950-52; polit. officer, dep. chief mission, charge d'affaires Am. legation, Bucharest, Rumania, 1954-55; chief polit. and econ. sects. Am. embassy, Damascus, Syria, 1957-58; spl. asst. to asst. sec. of state, Washington, 1959-60; counselor econ. affairs Am. embassy, Moscow, USSR, 1961-64; counselor polit. affairs Am. embassy, Paris, France, 1965-68; ambassador E. and P. to Gabon, 1969-70; assigned to AID, 1970—. Served to 1st lt. USAAF, 1943-45. Decorated D.F.C. with 3 oak leaf clusters, Air medal with 4 oak leaf clusters. Mem. Phi Beta Kappa. Presbyn. Club: Princeton (Wash. and N.Y.); Racing, Automobile (Paris). Home: 3319 N St N W Washington DC 20007

FUNKHOUSER, RICHARD NELSON, tennis mfg. co. exec.; b. Hagerstown, Md., Dec. 3, 1917; s. Elmer N. and Nellie E. (Spielman) F.; grad. Mercersburg (Pa.) Acad., 1936; A.B., Dartmouth, 1940; m. Janet A. Kunkel, Jan. 26, 1946; children—Richard Nelson, Marsha Jill, Linda Jane. Vice pres. Funkhouser Co., Hagerstown, 1946-58; v.p., gen. mgr. roofing granule div. Ruberoid Co., 1959-67; pres., dir. Har-Tru Corp., mfrs. tennis courts, 1956—; dir. Martin Veneer Corp., Prudential Equities Corp. Vice pres. Goodwill Industries Hagerstown. Regent Mercersburg Acad. Served to maj. USAAF, 1941-46. Mem. Advt. Club N.Y.C., Quiet Birdmen, Sigma Alpha Epsilon. Methodist. Clubs: Winged Foot Golf (Mamaroneck, N.Y.); Canadian (N.Y.C.); Beaver Creek Country, Fountain Head Country (Hagerstown); West Side Tennis (Forest Hills, N.Y.); Sea View Country (Absecon, N.J.); Ocean Reef (North Key Largo, Fla.). Home: 1880 Fountain Head Rd Hagerstown MD 21740 also 200 E 64th St New York City NY 10021

FUNSTON, GEORGE KEITH, business exec.; b. Waterloo, Ia., Oct. 12, 1910; s. George Edwin and Genevieve (Keith) F.; A.B., Trinity Coll., Hartford, Conn., 1932; M.B.A., Harvard, 1934, LL.D.; also hon. doctorates from numerous colls. and univs.; m. Elizabeth Kennedy, Sept. 25, 1939; children—Marquerite, Elizabeth, George K. Mem. research staff Harvard Bus. Sch., Boston, 1934-35; with Am. Radiator & Standard Sanitary Corp., N.Y.C., then Sylvania Electric Products, Inc., N.Y.C., 1935-40, spl. asst. to chmn. War Prodn. Bd., Washington, 1941-44; pres. Trinity Coll., Hartford, Conn., 1944-51, on leave of absence for duration of World War II; pres. N.Y. Stock Exchange, 1951-67; chmn. bd. Olin Mathieson Chem. Corp., 1967—; dir. Ill. Central Industries, Inc., Chem. Bank, Chem. N.Y. Corp., I.B.M., Met. Life Ins. Co., Hartford Steam Boiler Inspection & Ins. Co., Nat. Aviation Corp., Putnam Trust Co., Republic Steel Corp., Avco Corp., Winn-Dixie Stores, Inc. Mem. Bus. Council, Pres. Conn. Council Higher Edn., 1948-49; mem. State Hwy. Commn., 1947-53, Commn. on Orgn. State Govt., 1949-51; chmn. Greater N.Y. Fund Campaign, 1953; mem. nat. adv. council Jr. Achievement; com. consultants on cancer U.S. Senate Com. on Labor and Pub. Welfare; mem. Canadian council Conf. Bd. Trustee Trinity Coll., Seabury House, Westover Sch., Logistics Mgmt. Inst.; bd. dirs. Episcopal Ch. Found., Am. Cancer Soc., Seabury House, Internat. Exec. Service Corps, Bus. Com. for Arts. Served as lt. comdr. USNR, 1944-46, asst. dir. indsl. readjustment br. Navy Dept. Mem. N.Y. C. of C. (v.p.), Internat. C. of C. (conf. bd.), Pilgrims of U.S., Phi Beta Kappa, Alpha Delta Phi, Pi Gamma Mu, Kappa Beta Pi, Republican. Episcopalian (vestryman). Clubs: Round Hill Country (Greenwich); University, Century Assn., Links (N.Y.C.) Home: Vineyard Lane Greenwich CT 06830 Office: 460 Park Av New York City NY 10022

FUNT, ALLEN, TV performer; b. Bklyn., Sept. 16, 1914; ed. Cornell U., Columbia; m. Evelyn Kessler; children—Peter, Pat, John; m. 2d, Marilyn Laron, 1965; children—Juliet, William. Originator and host Candid Camera television program. Producer films for United Artist What Do You Say To A Naked Lady?, 1970; It's Only Money. Home: Croton-on-Hudson NY 10520 Office: Allen Funt Productions 60 W 55th St New York City NY 10019

FUOSS, RAYMOND MATTHEW chemist, educator; b. Bellwood, Pa., Sept. 28, 1905; s. Jacob Zachariah and Bertha May (Zimmerman) F.; Sc.B., Harvard, 1925; Ph.D., Brown, 1932; M.A. (Hon.), Yale, 1945; m. Rose E. Harrington, July 25, 1926; 1 dau., Patricia Rose; m. 2d, Ann M. Stein, Mar. 1, 1947. Sheldon research fellow, Munich, 1925-26; Austin teaching fellow, Harvard, 1926-27; cons. Skinner, Sherman & Esselen, Boston, 1927-30; student with C.A. Kraus, Brown U., 1930-32; research instr., Brown U., 1932-33, asst. prof., 1933-36; Internat. research fellow (on leave from Brown U.), Leipzig, Jena and Cambridge univs., 1934-35; research chemist, Gen. Electric Co., Schenectady, 1936-45; Sterling prof. chemistry, Yale, 1945—; cons. in chemistry 1945—. Priestley lectr. Pa. State Co., 1948. Mem. Am. Chem. Soc. (award in pure chemistry 1935), Nat. Acad. Scis., N.Y., Conn. acads. sci., Am. Acad. Arts and Scis., Sigma Xi, Alpha Chi Sigma, Phi Beta Kappa. Contbr. articles on electrolytes, polymers and dielectrics in various sci. jours. Home: 57 Mill Rock Rd New Haven CT 06511

FUOSS, ROBERT, dept. store exec.; b. Saline, Mich., Dec. 16, 1912; s. Martin and Edith Eliza (Mattison) F.; A.B., U. Mich., 1933; m. Mary Holton Leckner, Aug. 30, 1936; 1 dau., Mary Marshall (Mrs. Kenneth E. Claus, Jr.). Mng. editor Saturday Evening Post, 1942-45, exec. editor, 1956-61, editor-in-chief, 1961-62; v.p. pub. relations Federated Dept. Stores, Inc., 1962-64, exec. v.p., 1965—; sr. editor Reader's Digest, 1964-65; Bd. dirs. Presbyn. Life trustee Dickinson Coll. Recipient Distinguished Service award Overseas Press Club, 1961. Mem. Theta Chi, Sigma Delta Chi. Home: 6700 Shawnee Ridge Lane Cincinnati OH 45243 Office: 222 W 7th St Cincinnati OH 45202

FUQUA, DON, congressman; b. Jacksonville, Fla., Aug. 20, 1933; s. J. D. and Lucille (Langford) F.; B.S. in Agrl. Econs., U. Fla., 1957; m. Doris Akidakis, Dec. 20, 1955; children—Laura, John Eric. Mem. Fla. Ho. of Reps. from Calhoun County, 1958-62; mem. 88th-92d Congresses, 2d Dist. Fla. Trustee Fla. Sheriffs Boys Ranch, Rodeheaver Boys Ranch. Served with AUS. Named one of five outstanding young men in Fla., Fla. Jr. C. of C., 1963. Mem. Future Farmers Am. (pres. Fla., 1950-51), Jr. C. of C., Red Cross Constantine, Am. Legion, Fla. Blue Key, Fla. Gold Key, Alpha Gamma Rho. Presbyn. (elder). Elk, Woodman of the World, Mason (32, Shriner, Jester), Rotarian (sec. Blountstown, Fla.). Home: Altha FL 32421 Office: Cannon House Office Bldg Washington DC 20515

FUQUA, HERBERT B, banker; b. Duncan, Okla., 1895. Chmn. bd. Ft. Worth Nat. Bank Home: 709 Alta Dr Ft Worth TX 76107 Office: Ft Worth Nat Bank Bldg Ft Worth TX 76102

FUQUA, JOHN BROOKS, indsl. exec.; b. Prince Edward County, Va., June 26, 1918; ed. pub. schs.; m. Dorothy Chapman, Feb. 10, 1945; children—Rex, Alan (dec.). Owner, Royal Crown Bottling Co., Augusta, Ga., 1945-48, Fuqua Nat., Inc., Augusta, 1949—, Rentavision of Brunswick, Inc. (Ga.), 1965—, Claussens, Augusta, 1963—; chmn. bd., pres., chief exec. officer Fuqua Industries, Inc.; dir. Ga. & Fla. Ry. Co. Mem. Augusta Aviation Commn., 1945—; finance chmn. Augusta Hosp. Authority, 1948-52. Mem. Ga. Ho. of Reps., 1957-63, Senate, 1963-64; chmn. Democratic Exec. Com. Ga., 1962-66. Named Broadcaster-Citizen of Year, Ga. Assn. Broadcasters, 1963, Boss of Year, Augusta Jr. C. of C., 1960. Mem. Augusta C. of C. (pres. 1962), Young Pres.' Orgn. Home: 3574 Tuxedo Rd NW Atlanta GA 30305 Office: Fuqua Industries Inc 1st Nat Bank Bldg Atlanta GA 30303

FURBACHER, STEPHEN, aluminum co. exec.; b. St. Louis, July 16, 1920; s. Henry and Theresa (Hora) F.; B.S. in Bus. Administrn., U. Mo., 1944; M.B.A., U. Chgo., 1955; m. Hildegard Ann Salzmann, Jan. 6, 1945; children—Ann Elizabeth, Stephen Arthur, Richard John, Susan Margaret. Sales engr. Corning Glass Works (N.Y.), 1944-48; with Am. Metal Climax, Inc., Niles, Mich., 1948-71, exec. v.p. Kawneer Co. div., 1961-63, pres., 1963-65, exec. v.p. AMAX Aluminum Co. div., 1965-66, pres., 1966-71, v.p. parent co., 1966-71, also dir.; pres., chief exec. officer Neptune Meter Co., N.Y.C. 1971—. Home: 38 Coach Lamp Lane Greenwich CT Office: 630 Fifth Av New York City NY 10020

FURBAY, JOHN HARVEY, educator, author; b. Mt. Gilead, O., Sept. 23, 1903; s. William LeRoy and Caroline Talbott (Wood) F.; student Otterbein Coll., Ky., 1924; student Ohio State U., 1925-26; M.A., 1921-23, LL.D., 1959; B.S., Asbury Coll., Wilmore, N.Y. U., 1927; Ph.D., Yale, 1931; student Sorbonne, Paris, summer 1930, U. Chgo., summer 1934; studies of colonial edn. U. London, 1935; Ed.D., Hillsdale Coll., 1966; m. Elizabeth Jane Dearmin, Dec. 19, 1928 (dec. 1946); children—John Talmadge, Judith Alison; m. 2d, Mauri Helda, Sept. 29, 1951. Prof. biology and edn. Taylor U., Upland, Ind., 1927-29, 31- 33; prof. edn. and biology Coll. of Emporia, Kan, 1933-35; pres. Coll. West Africa, Monrovia, Liberia, 1935-38; lectr. on Liberia and other African subjects, 1939-40; asso. prof. edn. Mills Coll., 1939-44, dir. Summer Session and Casa Pan-Americana, 1942, 43; specialist in edn. in Latin Am., U.S. Office Edn., 1943-45; U.S. del. UNESCO, Mexico City, 1947, Beirut, 1948, Paris, 1949, Florence, Italy, 1950; ednl. mission to various countries 1948—, latest being India, Siam, Formosa, 1953-54, Iran, Iraq, Lebanon, 1955, Ethiopia and Kenya, 1956, Viet Nam, 1964, aviation mission to Russia, 1962; trade mission to Outer Mongolia, 1963; dir. cultural and ednl. service Trans World Airlines, Inc., 1945-70, cons. cultural affairs, 1970—; also ednl. cons. Gen. Motors, 1957—; pres. John Furbay Assos., Inc., 1970—; staff lectr. Def. Intelligence Sch., 1960—. Mem. collecting staff Am. Mus. Natural History, Field Mus. Col. Civil Air Patrol. Recipient Brewer aviation trophy, 1955. Fellow A.A.A.S., Nat., Royal Geog. socs., Royal Anthrop. Soc.; mem. N.E.A., Phi Kappa Phi. Republican. Mem. Soc. of Friends. Author numerous books, latest being: World Without Strangers, 1955; Aviation and the Cold War, 1955; Shifting Sands in Arab Lands, 1956; The Shape of Things to Come, 1961; Spotlight on Africa, 1960; Why Study Abroad, 1964. Contbg. editor several books, latest being: Facing the Iron Curtain, 1952; Education in a Divided World, 1952. Feature writer Phila. Public Ledger, also mags.; creator syndicated features, The Debunker, Know Thyself; syndicated radio program Holiday World, 1970—. Five recorded albums. Home: La Jolla 5346 N 20th St Phoenix AZ 85016 Office: 605 3d Av New York City NY 10016 ☆

FURBEE, DICK WAITMAN, food co. exec.; b. Marietta, O., May 8, 1930; s. Fred and Mary (Scott) F.; student Kenyon Coll., 1947-49; B.Sc. in Commerce, U. Pa., 1951; m. Sue Ann Emmons, Apr. 30, 1962; children—Linda, Craig, Scott, Ruthanne. Accountant United Carbon Co., Charleston, W.Va., 1955-57, budget dir., 1957-60; with Standard Fruit & S.S. Co., 1960—, mgr. financial analysis, Le Ceiba, Honduras, 1960-63, controller, 1963-67, v.p., controller, New Orleans, 1967—; dir. Cerveceria Hondurena, Belize Brewing Co. Served with USAF, 1951-55. Mem. Internat. House. Clubs: Plimsoll, Alpine (New Orleans). Home: 5120 Purdue Dr Metairie LA 70003 Office: 2 Canal St New Orleans LA 70130

FURBER, PERCIVAL ELVERTON, business exec.; b. Paris, France, May 16, 1906; s. Percy Norman and Cornelia Chamberlain (Chapman) F.; student Princeton, 1927; m. Dorothy Adele McMillan, Feb. 26, 1931; 1 dau., Audrey Furber (Mrs. Donohue). Student Equitable Trust Co., brokerage firm, 18 mos.; joined Trans-Lux Corp., rental projection equipment and operation theatres, 1931, now chmn. bd., chmn. subsidiaries; dir. Episcopalian. Clubs: Racquet and Tennis, Princeton, Union (N.Y.C.); Wee Burn (Darien, Conn.). Home: Tokeneke Darien CT 06820 Office: 625 Madison Av New York City NY 10022

FURCHTGOTT, ERNEST, educator, psychologist; b. Zlate Moravce, Czechoslovakia, Nov. 2, 1922; s. Adelbert and Sara (Schor) F.; came to U.S., 1938, naturalized, 1944; A.B., U. Cal. at Los Angeles, 1946, M.A., 1948, Ph.D., 1950; m. Mary A. Wilkes, July 23, 1953; children—Margaret A., David G., Harold W. Asst. prof. psychology U. Tenn., 1949-53, asso. prof., 1953-59, prof., 1959-69; prof., head dept. psychology U. S.C., 1969—. Cons. VA, 1953, Nat. Acad. Sci.-Nat. Research Council, 1963-65, 70-72; mem. U.S. delegation to UN Sci. Com. Atomic Radiation, 1967-69; mem. psychopharmacology study sect. Nat. Insts. Health, 1965-67, neurology study sect., 1968-72; Phi Kappa Phi lectr. U. Tenn., 1970. Served with AUS, 1943. Mem. A.A.A.S., Am. Assn. Univ. Profs., Gerontol. Soc., Radiation Research Soc., Internat. Soc. Developmental Psychgiology (dir. 1970), Am., Southeastern (exec. com. 1966-69), Tenn. (pres. 1969), S.C. psychol. assns., Sigma Xi. Jewish religion. Home: 4600 Perry Ct Columbia SC 29206

FURCRON, AURELIUS SYDNEY, geologist, state govt. ofcl.; b. The Plains, Va., Apr. 3, 1899; s. Aurelius Wyckliffe and May Louise (Heiskell) F.; B.A., U. Va., 1923; M.A., 1923; Ph.D., U. Ia., 1931. Asst. geologist, Va., 1918-23, Ia., 1923-25; instr. Western Res. U., 1925-36; geologist Va. Geol. Survey, summers, 1925-36; with Ga. Div. Mines, Mining and Geology, 1937—, chief geologist, 1951-65, dir., 1965-69, hon. state geologist and dir. dept., 1969—. Fellow A.A.A.S., Geol. Soc. Am., Ga. Acad. Sci. (pres. 1955); mem. Am. Assn. State Geologists (hon.), Ga. Mineral Soc., Ga. Geol. Soc., Sigma Xi, Gamma Alpha, Sigma Gamma Epsilon. Democrat. Episcopalian. Contbr. profl. jours. Home: 23 Walker Terrace N E Atlanta GA 30309 Office: 19 Hunter St SW Atlanta GA 30334

FUREY, FRANCIS JAMES, bishop; b. Summit Hill, Pa., Feb. 22, 1905; s. John and Anna (O'Donnell) F.; student St. Charles Sem., Overbrook, Pa., 1920-24; Ph.D., Pontificio Seminario Romano, Rome, 1926, S.T.D., 1930; LL.D., La Salle Coll., Phila., 1944, St. John's U., Bklyn., 1946, Villanova U., 1947, St. Joseph's Coll., Phila., 1949. Ordained priest Roman Catholic Ch., 1930; pvt. sec. to Cardinal Dougherty, 1930-36; pres. Immaculata (Pa.) Coll., 1936-46; rector St. Charles Sem., 1946-58, St. Helena's Parish, Phila., 1958-63; consecrated bishop, 1960; aux. bishop Phila., titular bishop Temnus, 1960-63; bishop of San Diego, 1963-69; archbishop of San Antonio, 1969—. Dir. Cath. Charities Appeal, Phila., 1958. Bd. dirs. Misericordia Hosp., Phila., St. Joseph Hosp., Phila., Ravenhill Acad., Germantown, Pa.; trustee Roman Cath. High Sch., Phila. Named Domestic Prelate by Pope Pius XII, 1947; knight comdr. Legion Cedars Lebanon. Mem. Nat., Pa. Cath. ednl. assns., Assn. Coll. Presidents Pa., John Henry Newman Soc. Home: 2600 W Woodlawn San Antonio TX 78228 Office: 9123 Lorene Lane San Antonio TX 78213

FUREY, W. RANKIN, ret. ins. co. exec.; b. Pitts., July 8, 1902; s. William M. and Jessie Benton (Rankin) F.; A.B., Princeton, 1922; C.L.U., Am. Coll. Life Underwriters, 1928; m. Martha Riecks, Jan. 12, 1924; children—William M. II, Martha (Mrs. John Kittredge) (dec.). With Berkshire Life Ins. Co., Pittsfield, Mass., 1922-67, beginning as mem. staff home office, successively agt. N.Y. office, then Pitts. office, partner, Pittsfield, dir. agys., v.p., dir., exec. v.p., 1922-54, pres., 1954-67, mem. bd. finance, adv. coms. until 1970; dir. Agrl. Nat. Bank Pittsfield. Past pres. United Community Services, Pittsfield; past pres. Urban Coalition, Pittsfield. hon. dir., past pres. Boys Club Pittsfield. Mem. Million Dollar Round Table, Life Ins. Agy. Mgmt. Assn. (past dir.), Nat. C.L.U.'s (past dir.), Nat. Assn. Life Underwriters (past trustee), Nat. Gen. Agts. and Mgrs. Assn. (past chmn.), Accident and Health Assn. (past dir.), Life Ins. Assn. Ams. Conglist. Mason. Club: Country of Pittsfield (past pres.). Home: 11 W View Circle Pittsfield MA 01201 Office: 700 South St Pittsfield MA 01201

FURGASON, ROBERT ROY, educator; b. Spokane, Wash., Aug. 2, 1935; s. Roy Elliott and Margaret (O'Halloran) F.; B.S., U. Ida., 1956, M.S., 1957; Ph.D., Northwestern U., 1961; m. Gloria L. Althouse, June 14, 1964; children—Steven Scott, Brian Alan. Successively instr., asst. prof., asso. prof., prof. U. Ida., Moscow, 1957—, acting head dept. chem. engring., 1964-65, head. dept., 1965—; engr. Phillips Petroleum Co., Bartlesville, Okla., 1957; research engr. Martin-Marietta Co., Denver, 1958; cons. J. R. Simplot Co., Minute Maid Corp., Ida. Potato Processors Assn., TRW. Profl. cons. B.F. Goodrich Chem. Co. Devel. Center, Avon Lake, O., 1969-70. Recipient Outstanding Tchr. award U. Ida., 1966, Ida.'s Outstanding Young Engr. award, 1967. Registered profl. engr., Ida. Mem. Am. Inst. Chem. Engrs., Am. Chem. Soc., Am. Soc. Engring. Edn., Nat., Ida. socs. profl. engrs., Sigma Xi, Phi Kappa Phi, Phi Eta Sigma, Sigma Tau, Kappa Sigma. Lion, Elk. Home: 1443 Sunnyside St Moscow ID 83843

FURGESON, HARRY EDWARD veterinarian; b. Kansas City, Mo., June 26, 1915; s. Harry Edward and Delma (Saunders) F.; D.V.M., Colo. State U., 1941; postgrad. N.Y. U., 1957, Oak Ridge Inst. Nuclear Studies, 1958; m. Dorothy Rita Stefanich, Oct. 30, 1950; children—Judith Ann (Mrs. Larry Stramel), Harry Edward, Dorothy Ann. Dep. veterinarian State of Mont., Bozeman, 1941-45, 46- 53; chief veterinarian UNRRA China Office, Shanghai, 1945-46; veterinarian City of Butte (Mont.), also pvt. practice, Butte, 1946-53; vet. cons. Anaconda Co. and subsidiaries, 1953—; pres., mgr. Mt. Haggin Livestock, Inc., cattle and sheep ranch, Anaconda, Mont., 1956—. U.S. del. UN S.W. Pacific Area Vet. Congress, Sydney, Australia, 1945; animal health and marketing specialist Nat. Acad. Scis.-NRC, studying animal disease control in W. African countries for AID, 1964; vice chmn. adv. bd. Vet. Research Lab., Mont. State U., 1960—. Mem. Am. (ho. of dels. 1963-65, pres. 1966-67), Mont. (past pres.) vet. med. assns., Am. Coll. Vet. Toxicologists (dir., past pres.), U.S. Targhee Sheep Assn. (v.p., dir.), Am. Hampshire Sheep Assn. (dir.), Mont. Wool Growers Assn., Nat. Woolgrowers Assn., Mont. Stockgrowers Assn., Nat. Cattlemen's Assn., Mont., Nat. reclamation assns., Order Ky. Cols. Mason (Shriner), Elk, Kiwanian. Contbg. editor Western Livestock Reporter, Sheep Breeder Mag. Contbr. articles to various publs. Address: Willow Glen Box 640 Anaconda MT 59711

FURGURSON, ERNEST BAKER, Jr., journalist; b. Danville, Va., Aug. 29, 1929; s. Ernest Baker and Passie Durham (Ferguson) F.; student Averett Coll., 1948-50; A.B., Columbia, 1952, M.S., 1953; postgrad. Georgetown U., 1961; m. Mary Louise Stallings, Apr. 6, 1954; children—Ernest Baker III, Elisabeth Glyn. Reporter, Danville Comml. Appeal, 1948-51; sports editor radio sta. WDVA, 1949-50; reporter Roanoke (Va.) World-News, 1952; reporter Richmond (Va.) News Leader, 1955-56; reporter, Washington corr. Balt. Sun, 1956-61, chief Moscow bur., 1961-64, White House corr., nat. polit. corr., Saigon corr., nat. affairs columnist, 1964—; syndicated by Los Angeles Times Syndicate, 1970—. Served to 1st lt. USMCR, 1953-55. Author: Westmoreland, The Inevitable General, 1968. Home: 3706 Williams Lane Chevy Chase MD 20015 Office: Nat Press Bldg Washington DC 20004

FURIE, SIDNEY J., film dir., writer, producer; b. Toronto, Can., 1933. Canadian films include Dangerous Age; A Cool Sound from Hell; dir. Hudson Bay TV series To England, 1960; U.S. films include Dr. Blood's Coffin; During One Night; Brester's Millions; The Young Ones; The Boys; The Leather Boys; Wonderful Life; The Ipcress File; South to Sonora; The Naked Runned; The Appaloosa; The Lawyer; exec. dir. Galaworldfilm Prodns., Ltd., 1961.*

FURLAUD, RICHARD MORTIMER, diversified pharm. corp. exec., lawyer; b. N.Y.C., Apr. 15, 1923; s. Maxime Hubert and Eleanor (Mortimer) F.; student Institut Sillig, Villars, Switzerland; A.B., Princeton, 1943; LL.B., Harvard, 1947; m. Elspeth Banks, Sept. 11, 1948 (div. Mar. 1967); children—Richard Mortimer, Eleanor Jay, Elizabeth Tamsin; m. 2d, Lisa Auchincloss, Aug. 1967. Admitted to N.Y. bar, 1949; asso. Root, Ballantine, Harlan, Bushby & Palmer, 1947-51; legal dept. Olin Mathieson Chem. Corp., 1955-56, asst. to exec. v.p. for finance, 1956-57, asst. pres., 1957-59, v.p., 1959-64, gen. counsel, 1957-60, gen. mgr., v.p. internat. div., 1960-64, exec. v.p., 1964-66, now dir.; pres., dir. E. R. Squibb & Sons, Inc., 1966-68; pres., chief exec., dir. Squibb Beech-Nut, Inc., 1968— (renamed Squibb Corp. 1971); dir. Mut. Benefit Life Ins. Co.; mem. trust bd. First Nat. City Bank. Mem. profl. staff Ho. of Reps. Com. Ways and Means, 1954. Trustee Barnard Coll.; mem. adv. council Sch. Advanced Internat. Studies, Johns Hopkins. Served as 1st lt., Judge Adv. Gen. Corps, U.S. Army, 1951-53. Mem. Assn. Bar City N.Y., Pharm. Mfrs.

Assn. (dir. 1965—). Clubs: Fifth Avenue, River, Racquet and Tennis (N.Y.C.). Home: 620 Park Av New York City NY 10021 Office: 460 Park Av New York City NY 10022

FURLEY, DAVID JOHN, educator; b. Nottingham, Eng., Feb. 24, 1922; s. Athelstane Willis and Dorothy (Bee) F.; B.A., Jesus Coll., Cambridge (Eng.) U., 1943; M.A., 1947; m. Diana Dill Armstrong, Aug. 28, 1948; children—Athelstane John Dill, William David; m. 2d. Phyllis Mary Huntley, Sept. 11, 1967. Came to U.S., 1966. Successively asst. lectr., lectr., reader Greek and Latin, Univ. Coll., London, Eng., 1947-66; prof. Classics, Princeton, 1966—; vis. lectr. U. Minn., 1960-61; mem. Inst. Advanced Study, Princeton, 1964. Served to capt. Royal Arty., 1942-45; CBI. Author: Aristotle: of the Cosmos, 1955; Two Studies in the Greek Atomists, 1967; also articles. Home: 76 Alexander St Princeton NJ 08540

FURLONG, CLAIR WILLITS, banker; b. Weaver, W.Va., Oct. 31, 1905; s. John C. and Emma (Willits) F.; LL.B., Chgo.-Kent Coll. Law., 1926; m. Elizabeth Angela Tamblyn, Oct. 12, 1927 (dec.); 1 dau., Jean Ann (Mrs. Robert Russell Foster); m. 2d, Janet Calender Buffington. Admitted to Ill. bar, 1927; practiced in Chgo., 1927-28; with Continental Ill. Bank & Trust Co., Chgo., 1929—, asst. sec., 1937-41, trust officer, 1941-44, 2d v.p., 1944-47, v.p., 1947-65, sr. v.p., 1965-70; now mem. pension com. Weil-McLain Co.; dir. Blackfoot Coal & Land Corp. Treas., trustee Chgo. Bar Assn. Found., 1959-66; adv. bd. Ill. Masonic Hosp.; exec. com. estate planning program Loyola U.; trustee, v.p., Ill. Childrens Home and Aid Soc.; v.p., trustee Chgo.-Kent Coll. Law, 1953-70; dir. United Charities Chgo.; mem. Northwestern U. Assos.; mem. citizens bd. U. Chgo.; sec., treas. A.C. Buehler Found. Mem. Am. (chmn. com. on banking instns. and regulated investment cos. of taxation sect. 1957-59), Ill., Chgo. (treas., ex-officio mem. bd. mgrs. 1957-59) bar assns., Corp. Fiduciaries Assn. Chgo. (pres. 1957-58), Ill. Bankers Assn. (pres. exec. com. trust div. 1961-62), Newcomen Soc., Chgo. Council Fgn. Relations, Chgo. Assn. Commerce and Industry. Clubs: Law, Legal, Bankers, Union League, Economic, Commercial, Tavern Chicago (Chgo.); Exmoor Country (Highland Park, Ill.) Home: 219 E Lake Shore Dr Chicago IL 60611 Office: 231 S LaSalle St Chicago IL 60604

FURLONG, EDWARD COLSON, Jr., educator; b. Morgantown, W.Va., May 31, 1913; s. Edward Colson and Mary Jane (Edgar) F.; student W. Va. U., 1931-33, Potomac State Coll., Keyser, W.Va., 1934-36; B.S., John B. Stetson U., DeLand, Fla., 1938, A.M., 1940; m. Charlotte D. Werwage, July 27, 1942; children—Edward C., James Joseph, Jane Vesta, William Robert, Elsbeth Charlotte. Mem. faculty John B. Stetson U., 1938—, asso. prof. econs., 1946-47, dean Sch. Bus., 1947—, prof. bus. administrn., 1947—, bus. mgr., 1957-63. City commr., DeLand, Fla. 1949-53, mayor, 1953-56; mem., incorporator Valusia County Indsl. Bd.; chmn. DeLand Housing Authority. Regent Fla. Episcopal Coll.; trustee Diocese South Fla., Episcopal Ch., 1963-68. Served to capt., inf., AUS, 1942-46. Received Army Commendation ribbon, 1945. Awarded grant Carnegie Found. for Advancement of Teaching, 1949. Mem. Am. Acad. Polit. and Social Sci., Am., So. econ. assns., Am. Bus. Law Assn., So. Intercollegiate Athletic Assn. (v.p.), N.E.A., DeLand C. of C. (pres. 1963), United Bus. Edn. Assn., DeLand Meml. Hosp. Bd. (pres.), Sigma Phi Epsilon, Episcopalian. Elk. Editor: Stetson Survey (a method of measuring the effectiveness of radio advertising), 1948. Home: 201 W Pennsylvania Av DeLand FL 32720

FURLONG, JOSEPH FRANCIS, utility co. exec.; b. N.Y.C., Jan. 9, 1921; s. Joseph Francis and Velma (Crum) F.; B.S. in Elec. Engring., Union Coll., Schenectady, 1942; M.B.A., Harvard, 1948; m. Elizabeth Graham, Sept. 27, 1947; children—Joseph Francis III, Michael Graham, Kevin Patrick, Cathleen Anne, Patricia Elizabeth. Asst. engr. Western Electric Co., 1942-44; with Central Hudson Gas & Electric Corp., 1948—, sec., 1955—, treas., 1966—; dir. Phoenix Devel. Co., Inc., Cruger Devel. Corp., Green Point Devel. Corp. Chmn. Dutchess County Youth Bd., 1967—. Bd. dirs., pres. Family Service Assn., Poughkeepsie, 1955-62; bd. dirs., chmn. finance com. Dutchess County council Boy Scouts Am., 1957-63; treas. Hudson Valley Philharmonic Soc., 1961-67; mem. ind. adminstrn. adv. council Union Coll., 1964—, mem. alumni council, 1968—. Served to lt. (j.g.) USNR, 1944-46. Mem. I.E.E.E., Am. Soc. Corp. Secs., Tau Beta Pi. Home: 19 Hornbeck Ridge Poughkeepsie NY 12603 Office: 284 South Av Poughkeepsie NY 12603

FURLONG, PHILIP JOSEPH, bishop; b. N.Y.C., Dec. 8, 1892; s. Peter A. and Marie E. (Cosgrove) F.; A.B., Cathedral Coll., 1914; grad. St. Joseph's Sem., 1918; Ph.D., Fordham U., 1922, LL.D., 1956; LL.D., Manhattan Coll., 1946, Iona Coll., 1956. Ordained priest, R.C. Ch., 1918; curate St. Dennis Ch., Yonkers, 1918-20; prof. history, dean, pres. Cathedral Coll., 1920-41; prin. Cardinal Hayes High Sch., N.Y.C., 1941-45; sec. edn. Archdiocese of N. Y., 1945-46; 1st pastor St. Thomas More Ch., N.Y.C., 1950—; auxiliary bishop Mil. Ordinariate, 1955—. Nat. Cath. chaplain Girl Scouts Am., 1948-55. Decorated Al Merito, Republic of Peru, Republic of Ecuador. Mem. Am., Am. Cath. hist. assns., U.S. Cath. Hist. Soc., Am. Acad. Polit. and Social Sci., N.Y. Acad. Pub. Edn. Home: 65 E 89th St New York City NY 10028 Office: 30 E 51st St New York City NY 10022

FURLONG, THOMAS RAPHAEL, journalist, trust adminstr.; b. Sault Ste. Marie, Mich., Dec. 27, 1905; s. Patrick Manning and Anna (McCann) F.; student U. Mich., 1924-26; m. Winifred Castle, Apr. 3, 1943; children—James Castle, Robert McCann, Thomas Castle. Reporter, City News Bur. Chgo., 1926-28; gen. news and bus. news reporter, Chgo. Tribune, 1928-32, asst. financial editor, 1932-39, financial editor, 1939-52; mng. editor Times-Herald, Washington, 1952-54; city editor Chgo. Tribune, 1954-61, asst. mng. editor, 1961-67, mng. editor features, 1967-69, exec. editor, 1969-70; exec. dir. Robert R. McCormick Charitable Trust; v.p., dir. Postrib Tribune Press Corp. until 1970, Chgo. Tribune Press Service, Inc.; dir. Chgo. Tribune-New York News Syndicate, Inc., Chgo. Am. Pub. Co. Clubs: Press, Tavern (Chgo.); Westmoreland Country (Wilmette, Ill.). Author pamphlets; Taxes That Destroy, 1945; Who Owns U.S. Wealth, 1946. Home: 930 Hinman Av Evanston IL 60202 Office: Tribune Tower Chicago IL 60611

FURLONG, WILLIAM REA, ret. naval officer; b. Washington County, Pa., 1881; s. William Allen and Ethel A. (Grant) F.; Ed.M.E., Tchrs. Coll., California, Pa., 1898; B.S., U.S. Naval Acad., 1905; M.A., Columbia, 1914; Naval War Coll., 1933; m. Cora Glover, 1910; 1 son, William Rea Jr.; m. 2d, Lula McKie Stephens, Nov. 26, 1969. Ensign U.S. Navy, 1907, and advanced through grades to rear adm., 1937; on staff of Adm. Fletcher after landing at Vera Cruz, 1914; gunnery officer U.S.S. South Carolina, 1916, and U.S.S. Nevada, 1917; attached to Brit. battleship Ramailles, 1918; during World War I served as gunnery officer Atlantic Fleet and as gunnery observer in Grand Fleet of Brit. Navy in North Sea, at Scapa Flow and Firth of Forth; also on staff of Adm. Sims at London hdqrs.; in charge design and procurement navy fire control, 1919-20; sent to Germany to investigate German ordnance materials and methods; introduced into U.S. Navy, Synchronous fire control system and remote control of guns by power; fleet gunnery officer U.S. Pacific Fleet, 1921-23; in charge of Island Govts. under the Navy, 1923-26; comdg. officer of Chicago (cruiser), Nechez (oil tanker), div. destroyers; comd. Marblehead, 1932-33, Naval Proving Ground, 1934-35; captain West Virginia (flagship), 1936; on staff comdr.-in-chief U.S. Fleet, Adm. Hepburn, 1937; rear adm. and chief Bur. of Ordnance, Washington, Aug. 1937-Feb. 1941; comdr. Minecraft Battle Force, Apr. 1941; engaged in def. of Pearl Harbor, Dec. 7, 1941, when his flagship, U.S.S. Oglala, was sunk by Japanese torpedo; comdt. Navy Yard and Pearl Harbor Operating Base, Dec. 1941-45, in charge salvage operations on ships sunk during Japanese attack, also of repairs on ships of Pacific Fleet engaged in North and South Pacific actions. Decorated Legion of Merit and gold star; recipient Freedoms Found. award, 1950. Mem. Am. Legion, V.F.W., S.A.R., Mil. Order of World Wars (nat. comdr. 1949). Clubs: Army and Navy, Chevy Chase. Author articles on history and origin of U.S. Flag. Home: 3611 Lowell St N W Washington DC 20016

FURLOW, MACK VERNON, Jr., pipe mfg. co. exec.; b. Summit, Miss., Aug. 20, 1931; s. Mack Vernon and Trudie Dena (Ratcliff) F.; B.S., La. State U., 1953; grad. advanced mgmt. program Harvard, 1968; m. Barbara Elaine Rolfs, Mar. 20, 1954; children—David Wayne, Kevin Rolfs. Financial and systems analyst Humble Oil & Refining Co., Baton Rouge, 1957-61; asst. controller Skyland Internat. Corp., Chattanooga, 1961-65; v.p., corporate controller Blount, Inc., Montgomery, Ala., 1965-71; pres. Pipeco. Steel Co., Inc., Wilmington, Del., 1971—, also dir.; dir. Security Mut. Casualty Co., Chgo. Asst. treas. 54th Advanced Mgmt. Program class Harvrd Bus. Sch., 1968—. Served to 1st lt. AUS, 1953-57. Mem. La. State U. Alumni Assn. (mem. adv. com. Montgomery chpt. 1967-71), Nat. Assn. Accountants. Republican. Lutheran. Home: 700 Burnley Rd Wilmington DE 19803 Office: 501 E 2d St Wilmington DE 19899

FURMAN, DAVID DICKSON, judge; b. N.Y.C., Nov. 22, 1917; s. Walter F. and Gertrude (Workman) F.; grad. Phillips Exeter Acad., 1935; A.B. Harvard, 1939; LL.B., N.Y.U., 1950; m. Alice McDowell, Mar. 5, 1942. Admitted to N.J. bar, 1951; legal sec. to Judge Nathan L. Jacobs, 1950-51; asso. firm Stryker, Tams & Horner, Newark, 1951-54; dep. atty. gen. N.J., 1954-58, atty. gen., 1958-62; judge Superior Ct. of N.J., 1962—; instr. Rutgers U. Sch. Law, 1952-53, N.Y. U. Sch. Law, 1956-68. Mem. Nat. Assn. Attys. Gen (past pres.). Democrat. Home: Far Hills NJ 07931 Office: Middlesex County Ct House New Brunswick NJ 08901

FURMAN, JOHN ROCKWELL, lumber co. exec.; b. Wellsville, N.Y., June 25, 1917; s. Harry Brennan and Helen (Rockwell) F.; B.A., Cornell U., 1939; m. Mary Hale Sutton, Aug. 2, 1941; children—John Rockwell II, Margery, Harry. New Eng. mgr. Dant & Russell, Inc., Portland, Ore., 1948-56; founder, pres. Furman Lumber, Inc., Boston, 1956—. Alternate mem. Am. Lumber Standards Com. for Lumber Wholesalers, 1964—. Trustee Tilton (N.H.) Sch. Served with USNR, 1941-46. Mem. Nat. Am. Wholesale Lumber Assn. (dir. 1967—), Sigma Nu. Home: 21 Deerfield Rd Wellesley Hills MA 02181 Office: 108 Massachusetts Av Boston MA 02115

FURNAS, HOWARD EARL, govt. ofcl.; b. Battle Creek, Mich., Jan. 29, 1919; s. Howard Earl and Dorothy Anna (Collings) F.; A.B., Hillsdale (Mich.) Coll., 1940; student Harvard, 1945-47; m. Gail Abbott, May 14, 1942; children—Howard Earl III, Paul, Abbott, Christopher Collings. Joined State Dept., 1947; assigned embassy New Delhi, India, 1948-49; asst. to spl. asst. to sec. state for intelligence, 1949-52, 54-57; assigned U.S. mission to NATO, Paris, France, 1952-54; mem. policy planning staff, also alternate. State Dept. rep. Nat. Security Council Planning Bd., 1957-61; dep. spl. asst. to sec. state for atomic energy and outer space, 1961-62; dept. exec. sec. State Dept., 1962-63; del. 2d Nat. Conf. Peaceful Uses Space, Seattle, 1962; dep. spl. asst. to sec. state for multilateral force negotiations, 1963-64, spl. asst. to sec. state, 1964-65, mem. sr. seminar in fgn. policy, 1965-66, assigned Office Undersec. State Polit. Affairs, 1966-69; spl. asst. to dir. U.S. Arms Control & Disarmament Agy., 1969—. Spl. advisor to chmn. gen. adv. com. on Arms Control and Disarmament. Mem. bd. Montgomery County (Md.) Scholarship Fund, 1954-60. Served to maj. USAAF, 1942-45; ETO. Recipient Alumni Achievement award Hillsdale Coll., 1957. Mem. Delta Tau Delta. Episcopalian. Clubs: Edgemoor Club (Bethesda, Md.), Kenwood Golf and Country (Washington); Linden Hill (Bethesda, Md.). Author articles. Home: 6005 Dellwood Pl Bethesda MD 20034 (summer) McGregor Bay Ontario Canada Office: Dept of State Washington DC 20451

FURNAS, JOSEPH CHAMBERLAIN, writer; b. Indpls., Nov. 24, 1905; s. Isaiah George and Elizabeth (Chamberlain) F.; A.B., Harvard, 1927. Mem. Phi Beta Kappa. Clubs: Harvard, Century Assn. Author: The Prophet's Chamber, 1937; Many People Prize It, 1938; So You're Going to Stop Smoking, 1939; Anatomy of Paradise, 1948 (won 1948 Anisfield-Wolff non-fiction award); Voyage to Windward; The Life of Robert Louis Stevenson, 1951. Collaborator; Sudden Death and How to Avoid It (with Ernest M. Smith), 1935; How America Lives (with editorial staff of Ladies' Home Jour.), 1941; author Goodbye to Uncle Tom, 1956; The Road to Harpers Ferry, 1959; The Devil's Rainbow, 1962; The Life and Times of the Late Demon Rum, 1965; Lightfoot Island, 1968; The Americans, 1969. Address: care Brandt & Brandt 101 Park Av New York City NY 10017

FURNESS, BETTY, state ofcl., actress, television personality; b. N.Y.C., Jan. 3, 1916; d. George Choate and Florence (Sturtevant) Furness; student Brearly Sch., N.Y.C., Bennett Sch., Millbrook, N.Y., m. John Waldo Green, Nov. 27, 1937 (div. Aug. 1943); 1 dau. Barbara Sturtevant; m. 2d, Hugh B. Ernst, Jr., Jan 3, 1945 (dec. Apr. 1950); m. 3d, Leslie Midgeley, Aug. 15, 1967. Movie actress, 1932-37; appeared stage plays Golden Boy, My Sister Eileen, Doughgirls; commls. for Westinghouse Corp., 1949-60; own shows include Penthouse Party, 1951, Success Story, 1951, Meet Betty Furness, 1953, At Your Beck & Call, 1961, Dimension of a Woman's World (radio), Answering Service (TV), Ask Betty Furness (radio); spl. asst. to Pres. U.S. for consumer affairs, 1967-69; chmn. Pres.'s Com. Consumer Interests, 1967-69; exec. sec. Consumer Adv. Council, 1967—; columnist McCall Mag., 1969-70; chmn., exec. dir. N.Y. State Consumer Protection Bd., 1970—. Address: Exec Office Bldg Pennsylvania Av and 17th St Washington DC 20006

FURNISH, WILLIAM M., educator; b. Tipton, Ia., Aug. 17, 1912; s. William Madison and Jean Minto (Swartzlender) F.; B.A., State U. Ia., 1934, M.S., 1935, Ph.D., 1938; m. Eula B. Beck, Aug. 28, 1938; children—Dale, Ann, Jean, James, Joseph. Petroleum geologist, E. Tex. and Miss., 1941-46, Creole Petroleum, Venezuela, 1946-49, Arabian-Am. Oil Co., Saudi Arabia, 1949- 53; prof. geology U. Ia., 1953—. Del. 20th and 21st internat. geol. congresses. Fellow Geol. Soc. Am.; mem. Soc. Econ. Paleontologists and Mineralogists (editor, council mem. 1955-58, pres. 1960), Am. Assn. Petroleum Geologists (dist. rep. 1957-60), Am. Assn. Geology Tchrs. Author articles fossil cephalopods and conodonts. Home: Route 3 Iowa City IA 52240

FURNISS, WARREN TODD, ednl. adminstr.; b. Pelham, N.Y., June 5, 1921; s. Henry Dawson and Ruth Kellogg (Pine) F.; B.A., Yale, 1942, M.A., 1948, Ph.D. (Lewis-Porter fellow 1948-49), 1952; m. Barbara Ann Ripley, June 11, 1949; children—Patricia Kellogg, Abigail Anne. Instr. English, Wesleyan U., Middletown, Conn. 1946; instr. English, Yale, 1946-47, Mt. Holyoke Coll., 1949-51; faculty Ohio State U., 1952-63, asso. prof. English, 1959-63, asso. dean Coll. Arts and Scis., 1960-63, dean Coll. Arts and Scis.; prof. English, U. Hawaii, 1964-69; dir. commn. on acad. affairs Am. Council on Edn., 1969—. Pres., Council Colls. Arts and Scis., 1967. Carnegie Corp. travel grantee, 1962-63. Served to capt. USAAF, 1942-46. Mem. Modern Lang. Assn., Am. Assn. U. Profs., Am. Ornithol. Union. Author: Ben Jonson's Masques, 1958. Editor, contbr.: Higher Education For Everybody?, Issues and Implications, 1971. Home: 3422 Dent Pl N W Washington DC 20007 Office: 1 Dupont Circle Washington DC 20036

FURNIVAL, A.S., advt. agy. exec. Exec. v.p., dir. operations Vickens & Benson Ltd., Toronto, Ont., Can. Office: 980 Yorge St Toronto 5 Ontario Canada*

FURNIVAL, GEORGE MASON, educator; b. Johnson City, Tenn., May 1, 1925; s. George Mason and Phyllis (Lott) F.; B.S. in Forestry, U. Ga., 1949; M. Forestry, Duke, 1951, D. Forestry, 1957; M.A. (hon.) Yale, 1966; m. Gloria Madeline Hays, Aug. 24, 1946; children—Bernard Hays, Lawrence Richard. Research forester Miss. Agrl. Expt. Sta., 1948-50; research forester U.S. Forest Service, 1952-57; faculty Yale Sch. Forestry, 1955—, prof., 1966- ; dir. Yale Computer Center, 1969-70; dir. biometrical studies U.S. Forest Service, 1964-66; vis. scientist, lectr., cons. Served with AUS, 1943-45. Mem. Soc. Am. Foresters, Am. Statis. Assn., Technometric Soc., Sigma Xi. Home: 11 Trumbull Pl North Haven CT 22070 Office: 360 Prospect St New Haven CT 06511

FURR, ROY, chain grocery exec.; b. McKinney, Tex., Sept. 18, 1904; s. Crone W. and Annie Furr; student Clarendon Jr. Coll., U. Okla.; L.H.D., McMurry Coll., 1962; m. Lela Close, Dec. 27, 1923; children—Don G., Shelly Rose (Mrs. Jack Hall), Roy K. With Furr Food Stores, Amarillo, Tex., 1927, then mgr. 6 stores, Lubbock, Tex.; now pres. Furr's Super Markets, Inc., 70 stores in 3 states, Lubbock; chmn. bd. Furr's Cafeterias, Inc., Lubbock Packing Co.; dir. Southwestern Bell Telephone Co., 1st Nat. Bank of Lubbock. Bd. dirs. Tex. Technol. Coll., Methodist Hosp., Lubbock, Boys Ranch, Amarillo, McMurray Coll. Mem. Lubbock C. of C., Phi Delta Theta. Methodist (steward). Rotarian Home: 3120 20th St Lubbock TX 79410 Office: Box 1650 Lubbock TX 79408

FURRY, WENDELL HINKLE, physicist, educator; b. Prairieton, Ind., Feb. 18, 1907; s. John Henry and Effie (Hinkle) F.; A.B., DePauw U., 1928; A.M., U. Ill., 1930, Ph.D. (fellow in physics), 1932; A.M. (hon.), Harvard, 1941; m. Elizabeth Josephine Sawdey, Dec. 27, 1931; children—Ellen Jane (Mrs. William F. Brewer, Jr.), Mary Susan. Asst. physics U. Ill., 1928-31; instr. physics Harvard U., 1934-37, asst. prof., 1937-40, asso. prof., 1940-62, prof., 1962—; research asso. radiation lab., Mass. Inst. Tech., 1943-45; research in relativistic quantum theory, cosmic rays, kinetic theory, quantum theory of measurement. NRC fellow U. Cal., Cal. Inst. Tech., 1932-34; Guggenheim fellow, Copenhagen, Denmark, 1950. Fellow Am. Phys. Soc., A.A.A.S., Am. Acad. Arts and Scis.; mem. Sigma Xi, Phi Beta Kappa. Author: Physics for Science and Engineering Students (with E. M. Purcell and J. C. Street), 1952; also articles sci. jours. Home: 17 Frost Rd Belmont MA 02178 Office: Dept of Physics Harvard Univ Cambridge MA 02138

FURSHPAN, EDWIN JEAN, educator; b. Hartford, Conn., Apr. 18, 1928; B.A., U. Conn., 1950; Ph.D. in Animal Physiology, Cal. Inst. Tech., 1955; married; 3 children. Fellow, hon. asst. Univ. Coll., London, Eng., 1955-58; instr. neurophysiology Med. Sch., Johns Hopkins U., 1958-59; asso. in neurophysiology and neuropharmacology Harvard Med. Sch., 1959-62, asst. prof., 1962-68, prof. neurobiology, 1968—. Served with AUS, 1946-48. Office: Harvard Med Sch 25 Shattuck St Boston MA 02115*

FURST, ARTHUR, medical educator; b. Mpls., Dec. 25, 1914; s. Samuel and Doris (Kolochinsky) F.; A.A., Los Angeles City Coll., 1935; A.B., U. Cal. at Los Angeles, 1937, A.M., 1940; Ph.D., Stanford, 1948; m. Florence Wolovitch, May 24, 1940; children—Carolyn, Adriane, David Michael, Timothy Daniel. Tchr. sci. and math. Pacific Mil. Acad., Culver City, Cal., 1939-40; mem. faculty, dept. chemistry San Francisco City Coll., 1940-47; asst. prof. chemistry U. San Francisco, 1947-49, asso. prof. chemistry, 1949-52; asso. prof. medicinal chemistry Stanford Sch. Medicine, 1952-57, prof., 1957-61; with U. Cal. War Tng., 1943-45, San Francisco State Coll., 1945; research asso. Mt. Zion Hosp., 1952—; clin. prof. pathology Columbia Coll. Phys. and Surg., 1969-70; dir. Inst. Chem. Biology, prof. chemistry U. San Francisco, 1961—. Fellow A.A.A.S., N.Y. Acad. Scis.; mem. Am. Soc. Pharmacology and Exptl. Therapeutics, Am. Chem. Soc., Am. Assn. Cancer Research, Japanese Pharm. Assn., Soc. Toxicology, Sigma Xi, Phi Lambda Upsilon. Contbr. profl. and ednl. jours. Research activities on organic synthesis, chemotherapy Tb and viruses. Home: 3736 La Calle Ct Palo Alto CA 94306 Office: U San Francisco Inst Chem Biology San Francisco CA 94117

FURST, MILTON, educator, physicist; b. N.Y.C., Sept. 10, 1921; s. Louis and Fannie (Smith) F.; B.S., Coll. City N.Y., 1942; M.S., N.Y.U., 1948, Ph.D., 1952; m. Edna Hedy Gordon, June 9, 1945; children—David Arthur, Mitchell Leslie. Physicist, N.Y. Naval Shipyard, 1947-50; from research asst. to research scientist N.Y.U., 1950-67; mem. faculty Hunter Coll., 1955—, prof. physics, 1967—; cons. in field. Served with USAAF, 1942-46. Mem. Am. Phys. Soc., A.A.A.S., Am. Civil Liberties Union, Sigma Xi, Sigma Pi Sigma. Jewish. Author, patentee in field. Home: 2625 Grand Concourse Bronx NY 10468 Office: 695 Park Av New York City NY 10021

FURTH, ALAN COWAN, railroad ofcl., lawyer; b. Oakland, Cal., Sept. 16, 1922; s. Victor L. and Valance (Cowan) F.; A.B., U. Cal. at Berkeley, 1944, LL.B., 1949; grad. Advanced Mgmt. Program, Harvard, 1959; m. Virginia Robinson, Aug. 18, 1946; children—Andrew Robinson, Alison Anne. Admitted to Cal. bar, U.S. Supreme Ct. bar; with S.P. Co., 1949—, gen. counsel, 1963—, v.p. 1966—; dir., mem. exec. com. St. Louis Southwestern Rwy. Co.; gen. counsel Pacific Motor Trucking Co., So. Pacific Land Co., So. Pacific Pipe Lines, Inc. Trustee Anna Head Sch., Pomona Coll., Human Resources Research Orgn. Served to capt. USMCR, 1944-46, 51-52. Mem. Am. (council pub. utilities sect.), San Francisco bar assns., State Bar Cal., Assn. ICC Practitioners, San Francisco C. of C. (bd. dirs. 1967-69). Clubs: Family, World Trade San Francisco); Orinda (Cal.) Country; Metropolitan, Burning Tree (Washington). Home: 54 Sotelo Av Piedmont CA 94611 Office: 1 Market St San Francisco CA 94105

FURTH, GEORGE, actor, playwright; b. Chgo., Dec. 14, 1932; s. George R. and Evelyn (Tuerk) Schweinfurth; B.S.in Sch. Speech, Northwestern U., 1954; postgrad., Sch. Dramatic Arts, Columbia, 1955. Actor both off and on Broadway, N.Y.C., 1956—; appeared in approximately 20 feature films, 3 TV series, also all major TV shows; writer Broadway musical Company, 1970 (Antoinette Perry (Tony) award 1971, N.Y. Drama Critics Circle award 1970, Drama Desk award 1970, Outer Critics Circle award 1970). Served with USNR, 1958-62. Mem. Actors Studio, Motion Picture Acad. Arts and Scis. Address: 3030 Durand Dr Hollywood CA 90068

FURTH, HANS GERHARD, psychologist; b. Vienna, Austria, Dec. 2, 1920; s. Hugo and Julia (Schindler) F.; L.R.A.M. in Piano, Royal Acad. Music, London, 1940; B.A. in Philosophy, Charterhouse,

Sussex, Eng., 1950; M.A. in Clin. Psychology, U. Ottawa (Ont. Can.), 1954; Ph.D. in Exptl. Psychology, U. Portland, 1960; m. Madeleine B. Steen, May 22, 1954; children—Sonia, Peter, Julia, Daniel, David, Paul, Catherine. Came to U.S., 1955, naturalized, 1961. Research psychologist mental health project for deaf N.Y. State Psychiat. Inst., N.Y.C., 1955-57; sch. psychologist Ore. State Sch. for Deaf, Salem, 1958-60; asst. to prof. dept. psychology Cath. U. Am., Washington, 1960—, dir. Center for Research in Thinking and Lang., 1964—, chmn. dept. psychology, 1967—. Research asso. Children's Hearing and Speech Center, Washington, 1960-66. Mem. Am. Psychol. Assn., Am. Assn. U. Profs. Author: Thinking without Language, 1966; Piaget and Knowledge, 1969; Piaget for Teachers, 1970. Research and publs. on intellectual processes, particularly of deaf persons with edn. implications; concluded that language is not necessary or intrinsic to intellectual devel. Home: 3224 Northampton St N W Washington DC 20015

FURTH, HAROLD PAUL, physicist, educator; b. Vienna, Austria, Jan. 1930; s. Otto and Gertrude (Harteck) F.; came to U.S., 1941, naturalized, 1947; grad. Hill Sch., 1947; A.B., Harvard, 1951, Ph.D., 1960; postgrad. Cornell U., 1951-52; m. Alice May Lander, June 19, 1959; 1 son, John Frederick. Physicist, U., Cal. Lawrence Radiation Lab., Livermore, 1956-65, group leader, 1965- 67; prof. astrophys. scis., co-head exptl. div. Plasma Physics Lab., Princeton 1967—; cons. Advanced Kinetics, Inc., Costa Mesa, Cal., 1961- -. Recipient award Am. Acad. Achievement, 1968. Fellow Am. Phys. Soc. Bd. editors Physics of Fluids, 1965-68, Nuclear Fusion, 1965—. Contbr. articles to profl. jours. Patentee in field. Home: 55 Locust Lane Princeton NJ 08540.

FURTH, JACOB, physician; b. Miskolc, Hungary, Sept. 20, 1896; s. Jonas and Henrietta (Sussman) F.; M.D., German U., Prague, 1921; D.Sc. (hon.), U. Pa., 1968; m. Olga Berthauer, Aug. 1, 1924; children— John J. and Eugene D. (twins). Came to U.S., 1924, naturalized, 1930. Asst. bacteriology and hygiene German U., Prague, 1921-22; clin. asst. 2 med. Clinic Charité Hosp. Berlin Germany, 1923; asst., then asso. Henry Phipps Inst., U. Pa., 1924-26, 28-32; asst. Rockefeller Inst., 1926-28; asst. pathologist N.Y. Hosp.; instr. to prof. pathology Cornell U., 1923-47; chief pathologist VA, Dallas, 1947-49; sect. chief biology Oak Ridge Nat. Lab., 1949-53; asso. dir. Children's Cancer Research Found., Boston, 1954-59; clin. prof. pathology Harvard, 1958- 59; head exptl. pathology dept. Roswell Meml. Research Inst., Buffalo, 1959-61; prof. exptl. pathology, 1959-61; prof. pathology Columbia U., N.Y.C., 1961-66, emeritus prof. pathology, spl. lectr., 1966—, acting dir. Inst. Cancer Research, 1968-69, dir. labs. F. Delafield Hosp. div., 1961-67. Mem. vis. com. Asso. U.; mem. Surgeon Gen's Adv. Com. Smoking and Health. Diplomate in pathologic anatomy Am. Bd. Pathology. Fellow A.A.A.S.; mem. Am. Assn. Cancer Research (pres. 1957-58), Am. Assn. Pathologists and Bacteriologists, Am. Soc. Exptl. Pathology (pres. 1956-60), Soc. Exptl. Biology and Medicine, Am. Acad. Arts and Scis., Endocrine Soc., Harvey Soc., A.C.P., Sigma Xi. Home: 128 Ft Washington Av New York City NY 10032 Office: F Delafield Hosp Columbia U New York City NY 10032

FURTSEVA, EKATERINA ALEXEYEVNA, USSR ofcl.; b. 1909 d. Alexei Furtseva; grad. Chem. Engring., Moscow Tech. Inst.; m. Nikolai P. Firyubin; 2 children. Admitted to Communist Youth Orgn. 1924, party membership, 1930; various party posts, 1930-40, second sec. Moscow City Com., 1950; dept. to Supreme Soviet, 1950; 1st sec. City Com., 1954; alternate mem. Supreme Exec. Com. USSR, 1956; past mem. Presidium Communist Party, Soviet Union, formerly sec. Central Com. of the Party; also now USSR minister of culture. Address: Embassy of USSR Washington DC 20521

FUSEE, FREDERICK GEORGE, corp. exec.; b. Winchester, Ont., Can., Oct. 7, 1917; s. George Maynard and Lucinda (Jackson) F.; B.S.A., U. Toronto 1941; m. Marjorie Christina Campbell, Dec. 18, 1941; children—Murray Campbell, Frederick George, Nina Christine. Came to U.S., 1956, naturalized 1963. With Avon Products Can., Ltd., 1945-56, asst. gen. mgr., 1949-56, dir., 1965—; with Avon Products, Inc., 1956—, now pres. and dir., sr. v.p., dir. Avon Overseas Capital Corp. Mem. Avon Products Found. Mason. Clubs: N.Y. Yacht; Apple Ridge Country (Mahwah, N.J.). Home: 60 Timberlane Rd Upper Saddle River NJ 07458 Office: 30 Rockefeller Plaza New York City NY 10020

FUSON, JACK CARTER, army officer; b. St. Joseph, Mo., Nov. 23, 1920; s. L.H. and Nell (Warren) F.; B.S., U. Md., 1964; m. Georgia Zelna Bahnsen, Dec. 27, 1941; children—J. Warren, Nell M., Jack Carter, Jr., Peter B., Jennie C. Commd. 2d lt. U.S. Army, 1942, advanced through grades to maj. gen., 1969; comdr. Saigon Port, 1966, Vietnam, 1967; dep. chief of staff U.S. Army, Pacific, 1970—. Decorated Legion of Merit with four oak leaf clusters, Bronze Star medal, Commendation medal, Purple Heart. Mem. Nat. Def. Transp. Assn. (past hon. pres.). Home: 8 Palm Circle Fort Shafter HI 96558 Office: Hdqrs US Army Pacific APO San Francisco CA 96558

FUSSELMAN, ROSWELL THOMAS, investment corp. exec.; b. Berkeley, Cal., Dec. 7, 1923; s. Roswell Troxell and Marjorie (Cummins) F.; student Long Beach City Coll., 1940, U. Cal. at Los Angeles, 1947-48; m. Helen Bolton, Oct. 29, 1945; children—John, Pamela, Christian. Asst. v.p. Morris Plan Co. Los Angeles, Cal., 1948-57; exec. v.p. Investors Thrift Co., Fresno, Cal., 1957-69; pres., chmn. bd. Surety Savings & Loan Co., Burbank, Cal., 1969—; pres. 1st Surety Corp., Burbank, 1969—. Served to lt. (s.g.) USNR, 1941-47. Decorated Air medal with two stars. Episcopalian. Mason. Home: 401 Meadowview La Canada CA 91011 Office: 237 E Olive Burbank CA 91503

FUSSLER, HERMAN HOWE, librarian, educator; b. Phila., May 15, 1914; s. Karl Hartley and Irene Graham (Howe) F.; A.B., U. N.C., 1935, A.B. in L.S., 1936; A.M., U. Chgo., 1941, Ph.D., 1948; m. Gladys Foster Otten, Jan. 7, 1937; 1 dau., Barbara Lynn (Mrs. Boyd). Asst. sci. and tech. div. N.Y. Pub. Library, 1936; head dept. photog. reproduction U. Chgo. Library, 1936-46, sci. librarian, 1943-47, asst. dir. 1947, asso. dir., 1947-48, dir., 1948—; instr. Grad. Library Sch., U. Chgo., 1942-44, asst. prof., 1944-48, prof. l.s., 1948—, acting dean Grad. Library Sch., 1961-63; asst. dir. information div. and librarian Manhattan Project, Chgo., 1942-45. Head demonstration of microphotog. Paris Internat. Expn., 1937; del. to World Documentation Congress, Paris, 1937; 14th Internat. Conf. on Documentation, Oxford and London, Eng., 1938; 1st Japan-U.S. Conf. on Libraries in Higher Edn., Tokyo, 1969. Bd. dirs. Center for Research Libraries, 1950-67, vice chmn., 1954- 55, 59-60, chmn. bd. dirs., 1960-61; cons. Ford Found., Paris 1960, 63, Brazil, 1961, mem. bd. regents Nat. Library Medicine, 1963-67; bd. dirs. Assn. Research Libraries, 1961-64, 70-71; mem. Nat. Adv. Commn. on Libraries, 1966- 67; mem. library; vis. com. Duke, Mass. Inst. Tech., Princeton. Mem. Am. Council Learned Socs. (Com. on Research Libraries, 1970-70), Am. Soc. for Information Sci., A.L.A. (former mem. council; Melvil Dewey medal, 1954; chmn. com. civil rights 1960- 61), Assn. Coll. Research Libraries. Methodist. Clubs: Quadrangle, Caxton. Author: Photographic Reproduction for Libraries, 1942; Characteristics of the Research Literature Used by Chemists and Physicists in the U.S., 1949. Co-author: Patterns in the Use of Books in Large Research Libraries, 1961, rev. edition, 1969. Editor: Library Buildings for Library Service, 1947; The Function of the Library in the Modern College, 1954. The Research Library in Transition, 1957. Asso. editor Library Quar., 1949—. Home: 5844 Stony Island Av Chicago IL 60637

FUTCH, OLIVIA, educator; b. Alachua, Fla., July 21, 1906; d. Oliver Mitchell and Clara Belle (Godbey) Futch; A.B., Fla. State Coll. for Women, 1927, M.A., 1927; Ph.D., Bryn Mawr Coll., 1934; student U. Chgo., U. N.C., U. Fla. Tchr. secondary sch., La Belle, Fla., 1927-28, demonstration sch. Fla. State Coll. for Women, 1928-29, Alachua, 1931-32; head dept. edn. St. Mary Coll., Leavenworth, Kan., 1935-38; asst. prof. Furman U., 1938-44, asso. prof., 1944-48, prof., 1948—, head dept. edn., 1945-50, dean Woman's Coll., 1950-65; part-time psychologist Greenville City Schs., 1942-50. Mem. S.C. Com. on Fulbright Scholarships; mem. state adv. council adult edn.; steering com. State Conf. Edn.; state com. on tchr. certification requirements State Adv. Council Tchr. Edn. NSF grantee, 1964. Mem. Am. Assn. U. Women (pres. S.C. div. 1953-55, mem. fellowship awards com., 1957-59, state leadership chmn. 1961-63), S.C. Assn. Women Deans and Counselors (pres. 1964), S.C. Conf. Status Women (pres. 1964-66, Woman of Year 1968), Nat. Soc. Study Edn., Nat. Assn. Deans Women, N.E.A., Phi Kappa Phi, Kappa Delta Pi, Eta Sigma Phi. Baptist. Club: Business and Professional Women. Contbr. articles profl. jours. Home: Regent Dr Route 7 Greenville SC 29609

FUTORIAN, MORRIS, mfg. co. exec. Pres., Futorian Mfg. Corp. subsidiary Mohasco Ind. Inc., Chgo. Office: 666 N Lake Shore Dr Chicago IL 60611*

FUTRELL, JEAN H., educator; b. Dry Prong, La., Oct. 20, 1933; s. H.E. and Catherine (Padgitt) F.; B.S., La. Poly. Inst., 1955; Ph.D., U. Cal., 1958; m. Lula Earlene Welch, June 3, 1955; children—Craig Forrest, Alison Renee. Research chemist Humble Oil & Refining Co., 1958-59; group leader high energy kinetics Aerospace Research Labs., Wright-Patterson Air Force Base, O., 1961-67; asso. prof. chemistry U. Utah, 1967-68, prof., 1968—; cons. chemist. Mem. sci. adv. panel U.S. Senate Com. Pub. Works, 1969—, chmn. sub-panel environmental research policy, 1971—. Served as 1st lt., USAF, 1959-61. Alfred P. Sloan fellow, 1968-72; recipient career devel. award, Nat. Insts. Health, 1968-73. Mem. Am. Chem. Soc., Am. Phys. Soc., Faraday Soc., Am. Soc. Mass Spectrometry, A.A.A.S., Sigma Xi. Democrat. Presbyn. (ruling elder). Author: Ion Molecule Reactions, 1971. Contbr. articles profl. jours. Patentee in field. Home: 875 Northcrest Dr Salt Lake City UT 84103

FYE, PAUL MCDONALD, oceanographer; b. Johnstown, Pa., Aug. 6, 1912; s. Orlando G. and Jennie (McDonald) F.; B.S., Albright Coll., 1935, Sc.D., 1955; Ph.D. in Phys. Chemistry, Columbia, 1939; m. Ruth Elizabeth Heym, Apr. 26, 1942; children—Kenneth Paul, Elizabeth Ruth. Asst. prof. Hofstra Coll., 1939- 41; research asso. Carnegie Inst. Tech., 1941-42; research supr., research dir. underwater explosives research lab. Woods Hole Oceanographic Instn., 1942-47; asso. prof. chemistry U. Tenn., 1947-48; div. chief, then chief explosives research dept. U.S. Naval Ordnance Lab., 1948-56, asso. dir. research, 1956-58; dir. Woods Hole Oceanographic Instn., 1958—, pres., 1961—. Mem. Polaris steering task group, 1956-58, Polaris ad hoc group long range research and devel., 1960-65, Undersea Warfare Research and Devel. Planning Council, 1959—; mem. com. oceanography Nat. Acad. Scis., 1961—; trustee Bermuda Biol. Sta. for Research, 1960—, State Coll. Mass., 1966—; mem. corp. Marine Biol. Lab., 1958—; trustee State Colls. Mass., 1966. Recipient Devel. award Bur. Ordnance, 1946; Presdl. Certificate of Merit, 1948; Meritorious award U.S. Navy, 1961; certificate of commendation Sec. Navy, 1960, 66; Distinguished Alumni award Albright Coll., 1951. Mem. Am. Chem. Soc., Am. Geophys. Union, Am. Phys. Soc., Am. Soc. Limnology and Oceanography, A.A.A.S., Marine Tech. Soc., Sigma Xi, Phi Lambda Upsilon, Epsilon Chi, Pi Tau Beta. Clubs: Cosmos (Washington); Edgartown (Mass.) Yacht. Home: 21 Challanger Dr Woods Hole, MA 02543 Office: Woods Hole Oceanographic Instn Woods Hole MA 02543

FYLER, WOLFGANG, magazine art dir.; b. Pforzheim, Germany, Jan. 18, 1905; s. Karl Julius and Elsa (Geiges) F. Student Acad. Karlsruhe, Baden, Germany, 1920-22, Kunstgewerbeschule, Munich, Germany, 1923-24, Art Sch., Berlin, Germany, 1924-26; m. Dorothy Elizabeth Calvert, June 8, 1945; children—Peter Calvert, Michael Calvert. Came to U.S., 1926, naturalized, 1931. Artist, Berlin, 1924-26, N.Y.C., 1926-31; art dir. advt. and promotion Conde Nast Publs., N.Y.C., 1931-42; art editor House & Garden Mag., 1942-62, art. dir., 1962—. Lutheran. Home: Hidden Brook 781 Pinesbridge Rd Ossining NY 10562 Office: Conde Nast Publs 420 Lexington Av New York City NY 10017

GAAL, STEVEN ALEXANDER, educator; b. Budapest, Hungary, Feb. 22, 1924; s. Istvan and Aranka (Gaspar) G.; Ph.D., U. Budapest, 1947; m. Isle Lisl Novak, Aug. 24, 1952; children—Barbara Sandra, Dorothy Janet. Came to U.S., 1950, naturalized, 1963. Asst., Inst. Tech. Budapest, 1947; attache de recherches U. Paris, 1948-50; mem. Inst. Advanced Study, Princeton, 1950-52; asst. prof. Cornell U., 1952-58; research asso. Yale, 1958-60; prof. math. U. Minn., Mpls., 1960—. Chief investigator Army Research Office, 1959; dir. research project NSF, 1963-70; research asso. Office Naval Research, 1958; adviser AID, India, 1966. Mem. Am., London math. socs., Math. Assn. Am. Soc. Mathematique de France. Research point set topology. Home: 51 Barton Av Minneapolis MN 55414

GABBARD, EARNEST GLENDON, educator; b. Berea, Ky., Nov. 1, 1919; s. Ernest Edward and Allie (Blanton) G.; A.B., Berea Coll., 1941; postgrad. La. State U., 1941-42; M.A., State U. Ia., 1947, Ph.D., 1954; postgrad. U. Ill., summers 1950, 51; m. Lucina Mildred Paquet; children—Krin Ernest, Glen Owens. Faculty, Eastern Ill. U., Charleston, 1947—, prof. speech and theatre arts, 1958—, dir. plays, 1947—, head dept. theatre arts, 1964—. Tchr., dir. State U. Ia., summer 1957. Mem. Civil War Observance Com., 1960-61; mem. performing arts com. Ill. Sesquicentennial Commn., 1967-68. Served with USNR, 1942-45. Mem. Phi Kappa Phi, Alpha Psi Omega, Theta Alpha Phi, Tau Delta Tau, Purple Masque. Home: 4 Orchard Dr Charleston IL 61920

GABBERT, HOWARD MARKLAND, former govt. ofcl.; b. Oxnard, Cal., Nov. 16, 1906; s. Myron Howard and Mabel (Jones) G.; A.B. in Geology, Stanford, 1932; m. Marjorie Caroline Gosnell, May 24, 1929, children—Howard Markland II, Thomas Gosnell, James Jeffry, John Stephen. Agrl. prodn., Ventura, Cal., 1932- 34; regional technician, soil scientist Soil Conservation Service, Dept. Agr., 1934-37, charge preliminary watershed surveys region 10, 1937-40, project leader inter-bur. flood control investigations, 1940-41, tech. cons. Bur. Agrl. Econs., 1940-42, asst. chief project plans div. Soil Conservation Service, 1942-43; sr. soil scientist Inst. Inter-Am. Affairs, San Salvador, El Salvador, 1943-44, sr. soil scientist, asst. chief field party, Asuncion, Paraguay, 1944-47, chief field party div. agr. and natural resources, dir. Servico Tecnicto Interamericano de Cooperacion Agricola, San Jose, Costa Rica, 1947-51, chief mission to Costa Rica, 1951-52; dir. U.S. Operations Mission, FOA, Costa Rica, 1952- 54; pvt. agr., Ventura, Cal., 1954-56; cons. Ventura, State Dept., Washington, 1956-57, asst. chief commodities div., charge agrl. surplus commodities disposal, 1957-63; chief food resources Food for Peace div. AID, 1963-66, dep. div. dir. operations, 1966-68, dep. dir. Food for Freedom Service, 1968; asso. coordinator Food for Peace, 1969, ret., 1969, part-time cons., 1970—; sec.-treas. Rice Jour., Washington, 1971—. Mem. Delta Tau Delta. Home: 1981 Upshur St NW Washington DC 20011

GABETTI, GIANLUIGI, mfg. co. exec.; b. Torino, Italy, Aug. 29, 1924; s. Ottavio and Elena (Davicini) G.; degree in law magna cum laude, U. Torino, 1946; m. Bettina Sichel, Mar. 4, 1961; children—Christina, Alessandro. Came to U.S., 1959. Dep. mgr. Torino br. Banca Commerciale Italiana, 1946-58; asst. to v.p. finance C. Olivetti & Co., Ivrea, Italy, 1958-59; v.p., treas. Underwood Corp. (now Olivetti Corp. of Am.), N.Y.C. 1960-63, exec. v.p., treas., 1963-65, pres., 1965—, also dir. Trustee, mem. bus com. for arts Mus. Modern Art; bd. dirs. Philharmonic Symphony Soc. N.Y., Inc. Decorated comdr. Order of Republic of Italy. Mem. A.I.M. (pres., council), Assn. Internationale des Etudiants en Sciences Economiques et Commerciales (dir.), Italy Am. C. of C. (dir.). Home: 770 Park Av New York City NY 10021 Office: Olivetti Corp Am 500 Park Av New York City NY 10022

GABHART, HERBERT CONWAY, coll. pres.; b. Morganfield, Ky., Aug, 19, 1914; s Riley C. and Betty (Conway) G.; B.S., Carson-Newman Coll., 1934; Th.M., So. Bapt. Theol. Sem., 1940, Th.D., 1943; m. Helen Ashburn, Aug. 7, 1942; children—Diana Ruth, Betty Fay, Jo Ellen. Bus. mgr. Bapt. Messenger, 1935-37; ordained to ministry Baptist Ch., 1938; pastor in Williamsburg, Ky., 1943-51, Memphis, 1951-59; pres. Belmont Coll., Nashville, 1959—. Mem. Assn. So. Bapt. Colls., Affiliated Independent Colls. Tenn. Kiwanian. Author: Thinking With Youth, 1947; Introduction to a Study of the Bible and Its Central Figure, Jesus Christ, 1958. Home: 2425 Bear Rd Nashville TN 37215

GABIANELLI, VINCENT JAMES, found. dir.; b. Bridgeport, Conn., July 8, 1932; s. Joseph Charles and Emily (Gabianelli) G.; A.B. in Zoology, U. Vt., 1954; M.Ed., U. Miami, 1959; m. Allene Jane Caise, Aug. 14, 1954; children—Mary Emily, Kathy Ann, Vincent James, Laura Ann. Sci. tchr., Norwalk, Conn., 1955-57; curator edn. Mus. Sci., Miami, Fla., 1957-60, dir., 1960-66; dir. Mus. Sci. and Space Transit Planetarium, Miami, 1966-68; chmn. interpretation dept. Fla. State Mus., Gainesville, 1968-69; dir. Ocean Space Center, Internat. Oceanographic Found., Miami, 1969—. Bd. govs. Fla. Zool. Soc., Tropical Audubon Soc. Mem. Southeastern Museums' Conf. Named Man of Year Miami Jr. C. of C., 1966. Fellow A.A.A.S.; mem. Am. Assn. Museums. K.C. Conducted spl. tng. program in STP instrument for Spitz Labs. Home: 8811 SW 52d St Miami FL 33165 Office: Ocean Space Center 10 Rickenbacher Causeway Miami FL 33149

GABIN, JEAN, (Alexis Jean Montcorgel), motion picture actor; b. Paris, France, May 17, 1904; ed. in Paris; m. 3d, Dominique Fournier, 1949; 1 son, 2 daus. Formerly mason, unskilled laborer, shopkeeper; extra at Folies-Bergères; singer, 1923-30; film actor since advent of talkies; sometimes stage actor. Decorated Medaillie Militaire, Croix de Guerre, officer, Legion of Honor; recipient Venice prizes, 1951, 54, Prix Populiste, 1956. Motion pictures include Pépé le Moko; Bandera; Belle Equipe; Bete humaine; Bas Fonds; Grande Illusion; French Can-can; Port of Shadows; Jour se léve; Gueule d'amour Remorques; marie du port; Au dela des prilles; Minute de Verite; Touchez pas au Grisbi; La Nuit est mon royaume; Crime and Punishment; Chnouf; En cas de Malheur; The Case of Doctor Laurent; Maigret Tond Un Piege; La Clochard; UN Singe en Hiver; co-producer L'Age Ingrat, 1964. Address: care Andre Bernheim 1 rue Francoise ler Paris France*

GABLE, CHARLES JAY, Jr., banker; b. Lansford, Pa., Mar. 2, 1907; s. Charles Jay and M. Dorothy (Kostenbader) G.; A.B., Princeton, 1929; m. Linda Virginia Fowler, Sept. 23, 1933; children—Virginia (Mrs Roderick Vitty), Susan (Mrs. Edwin Zerrer), Charles Jay III, Linda (Mrs. James Carmine, Jr.), Peter. Statistician, Halsey, Stuart and Co., investment bankers, 1929-31; formerly v.p. First Nat. Bank Phila.; with merged bank First Nat. Pa. Banking and Trust Co., Phila., now exec. v.p.; asst. to sec. treasury, 1958-59; dir. C. Schmidt and Sons, Inc., Jomac, Inc. Mem. bd. pensions Lutheran Ch. Am., also bd. common investing fund; active local Community Chest, A.R.C., YMCA and YWCA. Mem. Am., Pa. (sec., treas. group 1, 1950-51, chmn. fed. res. relations com. 1960-61) bankers assns. Home: 1820 Valley Rd Meadowbrook PA 19046 Office: First Pennsylvania Banking and Trust Co 15th and Chestnut Sts Philadelphia PA 19101

GABLE, G. ELLIS, lawyer; b. Kerens, Tex., Mar. 7, 1905; s. George Warren and Sue Ethel (Collins) G.; life tchrs. certificate Northeastern State Coll., Tahlequah, Okla., 1922; J.D., Okla U., 1926; m. Frances Doyle, Dec. 30, 1933; children—Richard Warren, Thomas Doyle. Admitted to Okla. bar, 1926, since practiced in Tulsa; now mem. Gable, Gotwals, Hays, Rubin and Fox: judge pro-tem Tulsa County, 1938-39. Past mem. Tulsa Bd. Edn., pres. 1956-57; vice chmn. Okla. State Regents for Higher Edn.; trustee Memorial Park Cemetery. Mem. Am. (mem. Fellows), Okla. (pres. 1954), Tulsa County (pres. 1949) bar assns., Phi Delta Phi. Methodist. Mason (Shriner, Jester). Clubs: Summit, Rotary (pres. 1961-62), Cedar Ridge Country. Assisted on Kleinschmidt and Highley's Oklahoma Form Book, 6th and 7th edits. Home: 2004 E 38th St Tulsa OK 74105 Office: Fourth National Bank Bldg Tulsa OK 74119

GABLE, RICHARD WALTER, educator; b. Joliet, Ill., Nov. 16, 1920; s. Walter Emmanuel and Matilda (Endres) G.; B.S., Bradley U., 1942; M.A., U. Chgo., 1948, Ph.D., 1950; m. Myra Ann Kagen, June 16, 1946; children—Cyrel Lee, Richard Siroos, Carl Walter. Mem. faculty Ohio State U., 1948-50, Stanford, 1950-53, U. So. Cal., 1954-66; mem. faculty U. Cal. at Davis, 1966—, chmn. dept. polit. sci., 1969—; vis. faculty U. Tehran, ICA/U. So. Cal. contract, 1955-57, U. Panjab, AID/ U. So. Cal. contract, 1962-63. Mem. Gov. Cal.'s Intergovernmental Relations Council, 1971; mem. AID/Ralph M. Parsons contract team, India, 1969. Served with AUS, 1942-46. Haynes Found. grantee, 1967-68; S.E. Asia Devel. Adv. Group grantee, 1969-71. Mem. Am. Soc. Pub. Adminstrn. (pres. Sacramento chpt. 1967-68), Am., Western polit. sci. assns., Soc. Internat. Devel., Am. Assn. U. Profs., Pub. Personnel Assn. Author: (with H. Koontz) Public Control of Economic Enterprise, 1955; (with F.P. Sherwood) The California System of Governments, 1967. Editor (with J. Finkle) Political Development and Social Change, 1971; contbr. profl. jours. Home: 1210 Colby Dr Davis CA 95616

GABLER, ROBERT EARL, educator; b. Lodi, O., Nov. 22, 1927; s. Earl Raymond and Carrie (Geisinger) G.; B.S. with honors, Ohio U., 1949; M.S., Pa. State U., 1951; Ed.D., Columbia, 1957; m. Mary Ellen Johnston, Aug. 19, 1950; children—Robert Allen, Janet Ann, Mary Elizabeth. Social studies tchr. Canton (O.) pub. schs., 1950-55; lectr. geography Hunter Coll., N.Y.C., 1955-57; mem. faculty Western Ill. U., Macomb, 1957—, prof. geography, chmn. dept. geography, 1965—. Dir. Nat. Def. Edn. Act Title XI Insts. Geography, 1965-67, Geography-History, 1968. Served with C.E., AUS, 1946-47. Mem. Assn. Am. Geographers, Am. Assn. U. Profs., Nat. Council Geog. Edn. (dir. coordinators, exec. bd. 1963—), Phi Kappa Tau, Gamma Theta Upsilon, Phi Sigma Epsilon. Author: (with others) Follett Intermediate Social Studies Textbook Series, 1970. Editor: Bull. Ill.

Geog. Soc., 1958-65; Handbook for Geography Tchrs. 1966; mem. editorial bd. Jour. Developing Areas, 1965—. Home: 711 E Piper St Macomb IL 61455

GABO, NAUM, sculptor; b. Briansk, Russia, Aug. 5, 1890; s. Boris and Fannie (Osersky) Pevsner; student Munich U., 1910-14; hon. doctorate Royal Coll. Art, London, 1967; m. Miriam Israels, Oct. 13, 1936; 1 dau., Nina Serafima. Came to U.S., 1946, naturalized, 1952. Exhibited, Oslo, 1916, Moscow, 1920, Germany, 1922, Paris, 1925; chief designer ballet La Chatte, for Diaghileff, 1926; first Am. exhbn., 1926, Chgo., 1933, London, 1937, Mus. Modern Art, N.Y.C., 1948; works represented European Museums, Mus. Modern Art, Mus. Non-Objective Art, N.Y.C., Providence Mus., Wadsworth Atheneum, Phillips Coll., Washington, Yale U., also pvt. colls.; 80 ft. sculpture unveiled in Rotterdam, Netherlands, 1957. Mem. Nat. Inst. Arts and Letters, Royal Acad. of Sweden (foreign mem.). Author: Gabo, 1957; of Divers Arts, 1962. Editor: Circle (London, Eng.), 1937. Address: Breakneck Hill Middlebury CT 06762

GABRIEL, ASTRIK LADISLAS, educator, scholar; b. Pecs (Funfkirchen), Hungary, Dec. 10, 1907; s. Alois and Mary (Boross) G.; student Hautes Etudes, Paris, 1932-34, Ecole des Chartes, Paris, 1935-36; Ph.D., U. Budapest (Hungary), 1936, privat- dozent, 1941; Dr. honoris causa, Ambrosiana Library, Milan, 1967. Came to U.S., 1948, naturalized, 1953. Dir., French Coll., Hungary, 1938-47; privat-dozent prof. U. Budapest, 1941-47; guest prof. Pontifical Inst. Mediaeval Studies, Toronto, Can., 1947-48; mem. Inst. Advanced Study, Princeton, N.J., 1950-51; prof. U. Notre Dame, 1948—, dir. Medieval Inst., 1953—; Charles Chauncey Stillman guest prof. Harvard, 1963-64. Recipient Prix Thorlet, French Academie des Inscriptions, 1956; Prix Dourlans, 1965; Legion of Honor; Fulbright scholar and lectr., Luxembourg 1959. Fellow Internat. Acad. Arts and Letters (Paris), Societe de l'Histoire de France (Paris) Royal Hist. Soc. (London), Mediaeval Acad. Am.; corr. fellow Inst. de France; mem. Am. Catholic Hist. Assn. (2d v.p.), Modern Lang. Assn., Hist. Com. on Canons of Premontre, Internat. Com. Hist. Scis. (v.p. internat. commn. for history of univs. 1961—). Author: Index Romain et Literature Francaise a l'Epoque Romantique, Tongerloo, 1936; Les Rapports Dynastiques Franco-Hongrois au Moyen-Age, 1944; Die Heilige Margarethe von Ungarn, 1944; English Masters and Students in Paris during the XIIth Century, 1949; Student Life in Ave Maria College, Mediaeval Paris History and Chartulary of the College (Mediaeval Studies 14) 1955; The Educational Ideas of Vincent of Beauvais (History of Mediaeval Education No. IV), 1956; Skara House at the Mediaeval University of Paris (History of Mediaeval Education No. IX), 1960; Auctarium Chartularii universitatis paris, 1964; catalogue of Microfilms of One Thousand Manuscripts in the Ambrosiana, 1968; The Mediavel Universities of Pécs and Pozsong, 1969; Garlandiu; Studies in the History of Mediaevel Universities, 1969; also numerous articles, chpts. on mediaeval subjects. Home: Box 578 U Notre Dame IN 46556

GABRIEL, MORDECAI LIONEL, educator, b. N.Y.C., Mar. 18, 1918; s. Joseph and Bertha (Fram) G.; A.B., Yesiva U., 1938; M.A., Columbia, 1938, Ph.D., 1944; m. Elinor Rosenstein, Nov. 11, 1945; children—Alisa, Jessica. Instr. genetics U. Conn., 1943-45; mem. faculty Bklyn. Coll., 1945—, prof. biology, 1963- -, chmn. dept., 1965—. Vis., prof. Columbia, 1956; Fulbright lectr., vis. prof. U. Tel Aviv, 1959-60; Mem. staff Marine Biol. Lab., Woods Hole, Mass., 1950—. Ford Found. faculty fellow, 1955-56. Fellow A.A.A.S.; mem. Am. Soc. Zoologists, Am. Assn. Anatomists, Soc. Study Evolution, Vertebrate Paleont. Soc., Am. Assn. U. Profs. (pres. Bklyn. Coll. chpt. 1964-66), Sigma Xi. Author: (with S. Fogel) Great Experiments in Biology, 1956. Home: 120 Old Mill Rd Great Neck NY 11023 Office: Biology Dept Brooklyn Coll Brooklyn NY 11210

GABRIEL, ROMAN, profl. football player; b. Wilmington, N.C., Aug. 5, 1940; ed. N.C. State Coll.; m. Suzanne; children—Roman III, Ram Alan, Rory Jan. Profl. football player Los Angeles Rams, 1962—; named Most Valuable Player, U.P.I., A.P., Sporting News, Columbus Touchdown Club, 1969; holder; career record passing yardage. Recipient Jim Thorpe trophy and many others. Address: Los Angeles Rams 10271 W Pico Blvd Los Angeles CA 90064*

GABRIELSON, GUY GEORGE, lawyer; b. Sioux Rapids, Ia., May 22, 1891; s. Frank August and Ida (Jansen) G.; B.A., U. La., 1914; J.D., Harvard, 1917; LL.D. (hon.), Upsala Coll., 1932, Colby Coll., 1953; m. Cora M. Speer, Feb. 5, 1918; children—Guy George, Nancy G. Owens. Admitted to N.J. bar, 1919, since in private practice, N.J.; also practice in N.Y.C., 1931—; chmn., dir. Nicolet Industries, Inc.; dir. Somerset Hills Nat. Bank, Bernardsville, N.J. Trustee Colby Coll., Waterville, Me., Drew U., Madison, N.J. Mem. N.J. Ho. of Assembly, 1926-30, majority leader, 1928, speaker, 1929; Republican nat. committeeman for N.J.; chmn. Rep. Nat. Com., 1949-52. Served as 2d lt. Air Service, Aircraft Prodn., World War I. Mem. N.J. Bar Assn., N.Y. County Lawyers Assn., Am. Legion, S.A.R. Republican. Methodist. Mason. Clubs: Union League, Downtown Assn. (N.Y.C.); Essex (Newark); Nat. Press (Washington). Home: Bernardsville NJ 07924 Office: 70 Pine St New York City NY 10005

GABRIELSON, IRA NOEL, biologist; b. Sioux Rapids, Ia., Sept. 27, 1889; s. Frank August and Ida (Jansen) G.; B.A., Morningside Coll., 1912, LL.D., 1941; postgrad. Lakeside Lab. of State U. of Ia., Lake Okoboji, 1911, 13, D.Sc., Ore. State Coll., 1936; D.Sc. (hon.), Middlebury Coll., 1959, Colby Coll., 1969; m. Clara Speer, Aug. 7, 1912; children—Clara June, Iris V. (dec), Dorothy Jean, Grace Gail. Tchr. biology Marshaltown (Ia.) High Sch., 1912-15; with Bur. Biol. Survey, USDA, 1915-46, asst. in econ. ornithology, 1915; food habits research, 1918, rodent control in N.D., S.D., Ia. and Ore., 1918-30, Pacific Coast regional supr. rodent and predatory control, 1930-34, game mgmt. dir., 1934-35, asst. chief div. wild life research, 1935, chief bur., 1935-40, dir. U.S. Fish and Wildlife Service (formed by consolidation of Bur. Biol. Survey and Bur. Fisheries), 1940-46; pres. Wildlife Mgmt. Inst., Washington, 1946-70. Pres. World Wildlife Fund; chmn., No. Va. Regional Park Authority; vice chmn. Va. Commn. on Outdoor Recreation. Recipient Audubon Conservation award; Dept. of Interior distinguished service award; Leopold medal The Wildlife Soc.; Hugh Bennett award; Distinguished Service award Am. Forestry Assn., 1962. Mem. Soc. Systematic Zoology, Am. Ornithologists Union, Wilson Ornithologist Club, Cooper Ornithol. Club, Pacific N.W. Bird and Mammal Club, Ecol. Soc. Am., Wash. Biologists Field Club, Ore. Audubon Soc., Izaak Walton League, Washington Acad. Sci. Methodist. Club: Cosmos. Author: Western American Alpines, 1932; Birds of Oregon (with S.G. Jewett), 1940; Wildlife Conservation, 1941; Wildlife Refugees, 1943; Wildlife Management, 1951; The Birds of Alaska (with F.C. Lincoln), 1958; also many articles on birds, mammals and plants. Editor: The Fisherman's Encyclopedia, 1950. Home: 2500 Leeds Rd Oakton VA 22124

GABRILOVE, JACQUES LESTER, physician; b. N.Y.C., Sept 21, 1917; s. Benjamin and Pauline (Levine) G.; B.S. magna cum laude, Coll. City N.Y., 1936; M.D. (Alpha Omega Alpha prize), N.Y.U., 1940; m. Hilda R. Weiss, May 19, 1946; children—Sandra Leslie, Janice Lynn. Intern Mt. Sinai Hosp., N.Y.C., 1940-41, rotating intern, 1941-43, vol. radiology, 1943, resident medicine, 1943-44, Blumenthal fellow medicine, 1946-48, research asst. medicine, 1949-51, asst. attending physician, 1952-60, asso. attending physician, 1960-68, attending physician, 1969—, cons. endocrinology, 1953—, also clin. prof. medicine Mt. Sinai Sch. Medicine, 1969—; Libman fellow medicine Yale, 1945; clin. asst. prof. medicine State U. N.Y. Coll. Medicine N.Y.C., 1957-59, clin. asso. prof., 1959-66, clin. prof., 1966—; cons. endocrinology VA Hosp., East Orange, N.J., 1958-66, Elizabeth A. Horton Hosp., Middletown, N.Y., 1961—, VA Hosp., Bronx, N.Y., 1969—. Mem. panel on metabolic and rheumatoid diseases U.S. Pharmacopeia, 1956—. Diplomate Am. Bd. Internal Medicine. Fellow A.C.P., N.Y. Acad. Medicine; mem. N.Y. County Med. Soc., A.M.A., N.Y. Acad. Sci., A.A.A.S., N.Y. Diabetes Assn., Endocrine Soc., Am. Diabetes Assn., Harvey Soc., Royal Soc. Medicine, Peruvian Endocrine Soc. (hon.), Pan Am. Med. Assn. (v.p. N.Am. endocrinology), Phi Beta Kappa, Alpha Omega Alpha. Club: Lotos. Author, contbr. bks. in field, also articles in med. jours. Editorial bd. jour. Mt. Sinai Hosp. Home: 25 E 86th St New York City NY 10028 Office: 79 E 79th St New York City NY 10021

GABRO, JAROSLAV, bishop; b. Chgo., July 31, 1919; s. John and Katherine (Tymusz) G.; student St. Procopius Coll., Lisle, Ill., 1937-39, St. Charles Coll., Catonsville, Md., 1939-40; student St. Basil's Coll., Stamford, Conn., 1940-42; B.A., Cath. U., 1945. Ordained priest Ukrainian Catholic Ch., 1945; bishop St. Nicholas Ukrainian Cath. Diocese, Chgo., 1961—. Home: 1101 N Elmwood Av Oak Park IL 60302 Office: 2238 W Rice St Chicago IL 60622

GABURO, KENNETH LOUIS, composer, educator; b. Sommerville, N.J., July 5, 1926; Mus.B., Mus.M., Eastman Sch. Music; ed. Conservatory Santa Cecelia, Rome; Mus.D., U. Ill., also pvt. study. Former mem. faculty Kent State U., McNeese Coll.; asso. prof. music U. Ill., Urbana, 1956; now with music dept. U. Cal. at San Diego, La Jolla. Recipient numerous awards for compositions. Fulbright fellow. Composer: 2 Shorts and a Long (piano); 3 String Interludes; The Snow Queen (opera); On a Quiet Theme (Gershwin Meml. award); Music for 5 Instruments; Elegy; Line Studies; Two; The Window (opera) Viola Concerto, Hydrogen Jukebox Music; Ideas and Transformations No. 1; The Night Is Still; 3 Dedications to Lorca (Eastman Alumni Assn. choral award); Mass for Tenors, Basses (World Library Sacred Music award); Ad Te Domine. Address: 6417 La Jolla Scenic Dr S CA 92037

GABUZDA, GEORGE JOSEPH Jr., physician, educator; b. Freeland, Pa., Jan. 26, 1920; s. George Joseph and Anna Mary (Silvasi) G.; B.A. magna cum laude, Lehigh U., 1941; M.D. cum laude, Harvard, 1944; m. Marion E. Jarvis, Apr. 2, 1946; children—Anne T., George Joseph III, Denise C. Intern, Pa. Hosp., Phila., 1944-45; resident medicine Mary Fletcher Hosp., Burlington, Vt., 1945-46; mem. dept. medicine Thorndike Meml. Lab., Boston City Hosp., from instr. to asso. medicine Harvard Med. Sch., 1948-54; faculty Case Western Res. U. Med. Sch., Cleve., 1954—, prof. medicine, 1964—; asso. dir. dept. medicine Cleve. Met. Gen. Hosp., 1966—; cons. Cleve. VA, Luth. hosps. Sec. sci. adv. com. Cleve. Diabetes Fund, 1965-70; sec. adv. com. liver Office Surgeon Gen., 1955-65; mem. sci. adv. com. United Health Founds,. 1964-66. Served to capt. M.C., AUS, 1946-48. Mem. Am. Soc. Clin. Investigation, Central Soc. Clin. Research, Am. Assn. Study Liver Diseases (pres. 1960-61), Soc. Exptl. Biology and Medicine, Am. Fedn. Clin. Research, A.A.A.S., Am. Inst. Nutrition, Am. Soc. Clin. Nutrition, Internat. Assn. Study Liver. Contbr. papers on metabolic abnormalities in liver disease with spl. reference to hepatic coma, ascrites, renal functio, nutrition in man to profl. jours. Clin. Nutrition. Home: 1854 Langerdale Blvd South Euclid OH 44121 Office: 3395 Scranton Rd Cleveland OH 44109

GACCIONE, ANTHONY SALVATORE, paper mill exec.; b. Cosenza, Italy, May 13, 1898; s. Angelo and Christina (Pignataro) G.; student Cornell U., 1917-20; m. Helen Frances Adams, Aug. 30, 1921 (dec. Apr. 1956); m. 2d, Marion Bunnell, May 4, 1957. Partner Gaccione Bros. and Co., Inc., N.Y.C., 1921-26; mgr. paper stock dept. Box Board and Lining Co., N.Y.C., 1926-31; mgr. Charles A. Mastronardi & Co., N.Y.C., 1931-36; pres. Toga Paper Stock Co., Inc., 1936-63; pres. Toga Paper Stock Co., Inc. div. Fed. Paper Board Co., Inc., Montvale, N.J., 1963-69, cons., 1969—; pres. of Kingsland Paper Corp., 1937-63, Seaboard Mill Supply, Inc., 1948-63 (all N.Y.C.). Mem. Cornell U. Council 1954—; adminstry. bd. Casa Italiana, Columbia, 1958—. Decorated chevalier Ancient Order of St. Hubert (Europe); recipient Columbia U. Casa Italiana award, 1962. Mem. N.Y. Assn. Dealers in Paper Mills Supplies (pres. 1951-54), Nat. Assn. Waste Material Dealers (dir. 1952-55), Italian Hist. Soc. Am. (hon.), Cornell Alumni Assn. (pres. N.Y.C. 1955). Clubs: Saints and Sinners (hon. life; exec. dir.), Cornell (life mem., bd. govs., exec. com., treas. 1969—), Lambs (N.Y.C.). Home: 14 Sutton Pl S New York City NY 10022 Office: 120 Wall St New York City NY 10005

GADBERRY, GEORGE ROBERT, banker; b. Carthage, Mo., Aug. 10, 1918; s. William Arthur and Ethel (Clark) G.; B.S., Kan. State Coll., 1940, m. Grace Brutonne Hood, Aug. 2, 1941; children—Marcia Lynne (Mrs. Robert Wayne Shideler), Barbara Diane (Mrs. John L. Fielder). Announcer radio sta. KOAM, Pittsburg, Kan., 1938-41; sports dir. radio sta. KFBI, Wichita, Kan., 1941-42; news and sports dir. Armed Forces Radio Service, C.Z., 1942-45; news dir. KFBI-KFH, Wichita, 1946-52; v.p. pub. relations, advt., estate planning, community relations, marketing Fourth Nat. Bank, Wichita, 1952—. Tchr. community relations Bank Pub. Relations and Marketing Sch., Northwestern U. Kans. chmn. March of Dimes, 1956-59, Radio Free Europe, 1962-64, Cancer Crusade, 1968-69. Kans. chmn. Bo Dole for Senate Com., 1968. Bd. govs. Nat. A.R.C.; pres. bd. trustees Wesley Med. Center. Served with USAAF, 1942-43. Kiwanian. Home: 6519 Jacqueline St Wichita KS 67206 Office: PO Box 1090 Wichita KS 67201

GADDAFI, MOAMAR AL-; prime minster Libya; b. Misurata, Libya, 1938; ed. U. Libya, Benghazi. With Libyan Army, 1965—; chmn. Revolutionary Council, comdr. in chief Armed Forces, 1969—; prime minster and minister def., 1970—. Address: Tripoli Libya*

GADDIS, WILLIAM, writer; b. N.Y.C., 1922. Author: The Recognitions, 2d edit., 1962. Address: care Russell and Volkening 551 Fifth Av New York City NY 10017

GADDY, ROBERT JOSEPH, banker; b. St. Joseph Mo., Aug. 10, 1924; s. Joseph Vernon and Austa (Gibson) G.; student Westminster Coll., Fulton, Mo., 1946-47; LL.B., Washington U., St. Louis, 1950; m. Martha Dunbar, Sept. 16, 1949; children—Virginia Hess, Helen Gibson. Admitted to Mo. bar, 1950; partner firm Dunbar and Gaddy, St. Louis, 1953-58; v.p., gen. counsel Tower Grove Bank and Trust Co., St. Louis, 1958-60, now pres., and dir. Pres., St. Louis Clearing House. Mem. bd. trustees Bethesda Gen. Hosp.; bd. advisers South Side YMCA; trustee Drury Coll. Served to 1st lt. USAAF, 1943-45. Recipient alumni achievement award Westminster Coll., Mo., 1960. Mem. Am., Mo., St. Louis bar assns., Am., Mo. (v.p.) bankers assns., Financial Pub. Relations Assn., Young Presidents Orgn. (treas., St. Louis chpt.), Am. Inst. Banking (chmn. adv. bd. St. Louis chpt.), Asso. Bankers St. Louis and St. Louis Co. (pres.) Home: 500 Oak Valley Dr St Louis MO 63131 Office: 3134 S Grand Av St Louis MO 63118

GADEN, ELMER LEWIS, Jr., educator; b. Bklyn., Sept. 26, 1923; s. Elmer Lewis and Gertrude Estelle (McClellan) G.; B.S., Columbia, 1944, M.S., 1947, Ph.D., 1949; m. 2d, Jennifer Marie Soley, Mar. 28, 1964; 1 dau. by previous marriage, Barbara Joan; 1 son, David Andrew. Research engr. Charles Pfizer and Co., 1948-49; mem. faculty Columbia, 1949-, prof. chem. engring., 1958—, chmn. dept., 1960-69, 71—; tech. dir. Biochem. Processes, Inc., 1969—. Served with USNR, 1943-46. Mem. Am. Chem. Soc., Am. Inst. Chem. Engrs., Am. Soc. Microbiology. Editor Jour. Biotech. and Bioengring., 1959—. Home: 100 Ocean Av Islip NY 11751 Office: Dept Chem Engring Columbia Univ New York City NY 10028

GADES, ANTONIO, Spanish dancer; b. Madrid, 1936. Debut with Circo Price; performer, student co. of Pilar Lopez; collaborator with Anton Dolin on Ravel's Bolero, Rome Opera House; dancer, co-choreographer Pavane for a Dead Infanta and Teatrino di Cristobal, Festival of Two Worlds, Spoleto, 1962; guest dancer Teatro alla Scala, Milan, also choreographer and tchr. Spanish dance; appeared in Los Tarantos, Spain, 1963; formed own co., appeared at N.Y. World's Fair, 1964.*

GADSBY, EDWARD NORTHUP, lawyer; b. North Adams, Mass., Apr. 11, 1900; s. Herbert H. and Sigma Mirta (Northup) G.; A.B., Amherst Coll., 1923, M.A. (hon.), 1958; J.D., N.Y.U., 1929; m. Isabella E. Halsey, Dec. 29, 1934; children—Edward Northup, Susan Elizabeth. Admitted to N.Y. bar, 1929, Mass. bar, 1937; with firm Rushmore, Bisbee & Stern, N.Y.C. 1929-37; pvt. practice, N. Adams, Mass., 1937- 47; with firm Sullivan and Worcester, Boston, 1956-57; commr. Mass. Dept. Pub. Utilities, 1947-52, chmn., 1947-49, counsel, 1952-56; mem. chmn. SEC, 1957-61; partner Gadsby and Hannah, Boston and Washington, 1961—. Mem. Am., Fed. bar assns., Phi Beta Kappa, Chi Phi. Author: 11A Business Organizations, Federal Security Exchange Act. Home: 39A Lee St Cambridge MA 02139 Office: 75 Federal St Boston MA also 1700 Pennsylvania Av N W Washington DC 20006

GADSDEN, HENRY WHITE, chem. co. exec.; b. N.Y.C., Apr. 16, 1911; s. Philip Henry and Estelle (White) G., B.S., Yale, 1933; m. Patricia Parker, July 31, 1943; children—Christopher H., Thomas P., William F., Robert W. With Banker Trust Co., N.Y.C., 1933-34; sales engr. R.A. Lasley, Inc., N.Y.C., 1934- 37; asst. to exec. v.p. Sharpe and Dohme, Inc., Phila., 1937-42; dir. prodn., engring., 1946-49, v.p., 1949-55, dir., 1952-55; exec. v.p., dir. Merck & Co., Inc., Rahway, N.J., 1955-65, pres., chief exec. officer, 1965—, also dir. dir. Ford Motor Co., N.J. Bell Telephone Co., Campbell Soup Co. Trustee The Seeing Eye, Nat. Safety Council. Served from 1st lt. to lt. col. AUS, 1942-46; dist. chief Phila. Ordnance Dist., U.S. Army, 1948-55. Mem. Pharm. Mfrs. Assn. (chmn. elect, dir.), Bus. Council. Clubs: Cotton Bay (Bahamas); Baltusrol Golf, Short Hills; Yale, Sky (N.Y.C.). Home: 30 Lake Rd Short Hills NJ 07078 Office: Merck & Co Inc Rahway NJ 07065

GAEBELEIN, FRANK ELY educator; b. Mt. Vernon, N.Y., Mar. 31, 1899; s. Arno Clemens and Emma Fredericka (Grimm) G.; B.A., N.Y. U., 1920; A.M., Harvard, 1921; Litt.D., Wheaton (Ill.) Coll., 1931; D.D., Ref. Episcopal Theol. Sem., 1951; LL.D., Houghton (N.Y.) Coll., 1960; m. Dorothy Laura Medd, Dec. 8, 1923; children—Dorothy Laura (Mrs. Clyde R. Hampton), Donn Medd, Gretchen Elizabeth (Mrs. Philip G. Hull). Organizer Stony Brook Sch., 1921, headmaster, 1922-63, headmaster emeritus, 1963—, also trustee; co-editor Christianity Today, 1963-66. Commd. 2d lt. inf., U.S. Army, 1918. Deacon R.E. Ch., 1940, Presby., 1941; mem. pub. com. Am. Tract Soc.; chmn. bd. Evang. Books; Mem. commn. on edn. Nat. Assn. Evangelicals. Mem. Headmasters Assn., Am. Acad. Religion, Phi Beta Kappa, Kappa Sigma. Republican. Clubs: Harvard, Andiron, Am. Alpine, Alpine of Can., Cosmos. Author: Down Through the Ages, 1924; A Brief Survey of Scripture, 1929; Exploring the Bible, 1929; The Hollow Queen, 1933; Facing the Fact of Inspiration, 1934; From a Headmaster's Study, 1935; Philemon, the Gospel of Emancipation, 1939; Looking Unto Him, 1941; The Christian Use of the Bible, 1946; The Servant and the Dove, 1946; Christian Education in a Democracy, 1951; The Pattern of God's Truth, 1954, The Practical Epistle of James, 1955; A Varied Harvest, 1967; Four Minor Prophets: Their Message for Today, 1970. Editor: A Christianity Today Reader, 1967. Griffith Thomas Memorial lecturer Dallas Theol. Sem., 1944, 52; Bauman lectr. Grace Theol. Sem. and Coll., 1962; Lilly lectr. Eastern Bapt. Coll., 1969; dir. faculty seminar on faith and learning Wheaton (Ill.) Coll., 1969—; Bible conf. speaker and guest preacher in chs., colls., and univs. Home: 3816 Lorcum Lane Arlington VA 22207

GAEHDE, JOACHIM E., educator. Prof. fine arts Brandeis U. Office: Dept Fine Arts Brandeis U Waltham MA 02154*

GAER, JOSEPH, author; b. Russia, Mar. 16, 1897; s. Solomon and Naomi (Shkolnik) Fishman; student pub. schs. and colls. U.S., Can.; m. Fay Ratner, Mar. 14, 1923; children—Elsa Gay Luce, Paul Joseph. Came to U.S., 1917, naturalized, 1926. Pres., Gaer Assos. Pub. Co. (formerly Boni and Gaer), N.Y.C., 1946-49; founder, dir. Pamphlet Press. div. Reynal and Hitchcock, 1945-46; publicity dir. polit. action com. C.I.O., 1943-45, also dir. Pamphlet-of-the-Month; spl. asst. to sec. of treasury Treasury Dept., 1941-43; cons. to adminstr. Farm Security Adminstn., 1939-41; editor-in-chief, chief field supr. Fed. Writers Project, W.P.A., 1935- 39; tchr. U. Cal., 1930-35; cons. to producer of Bibl. films. Exec. dir. Jewish Heritage Found.; editor Recall: A Quar. Mem. Am. Jewish com. Commn. on Jewish Affairs; mem. bd. Nat. Jewish Music Council; mem. corp. Found. for Arts, Religion and Culture. Recipient citation Nat. Conf. Christians and Jews. Fellow Internat. Inst. Arts and Letters; mem. Screen Writers Guild. Author many books, most recent being: The Fables of India, 1955; The Wisdom of the Living Religions, 1956; The Bible for Family Reading (with Chester C. McCown), 1956; Our Jewish Heritage (with Rabbi Albert Wolf), 1957; The Jewish Bible for Family Reading, 1957; The Legend of the Wandering Jew, 1958; What the Great Religions Believe, 1963; (with Ben Siegel) The Puritan Heritage, 1964; Upton Sinclair: Bibliography and Biographical Data, 1969. Editor: Our Lives, 1948; Washington; City and Capitol, 1937; The Federal Government and How it Functions, 1938; New England Guides-Mass., Me., N.H., and others. Contbr. to periodicals including The Bookman, The Dial, Sat. Rev. of Lit., Southwest Rev., New Republic; Schaff-Herzog Ency. of Religious Knowledge, 1952; Book of Knowledge, 1963. Home: 201 San Vincente Blvd Santa Monica CA 90402

GAERTNER, JOHANNES ALEXANDER, educator; b. Berlin-Lichterfelde, Germany, Apr. 26, 1912; s. Carl Eugen and Fanny (Horwitz) G.; student U. Berlin, 1930-33; Th.D., U. Heidelberg, 1936; m. Gerda Meyer, May 31, 1941; 1 dau., Susanna Barbara. Came to U.S., 1945, naturalized, 1952. Asst. mgr. Libreria Internacional del Peru, Lima, 1939-45; researcher, editor Frederick Ungar Pub. Co., N.Y.C., 1945-47; instr. Lafayette Coll., Easton, Pa., 1947-48, asst. prof., 1948-58, asso. prof., 1958-66, prof. art history, head dept. art and music, 1966—. Mem. Medieval Acad., Classical Assn., Coll. Art Assn., Am. Soc. Aesthetics, Archeol. Inst., Modern Lang. Assn., Am. Assn. U. Profs. Republican. Author: Vox Humana, 1954; Prisma der Demokratie, 1961; Diapason, 1961; Cantus Firmus,

1966; Zur Deutung des Junius-Bassus-Sarkophages in Jahrbuch des Deutschen Archaeol. Instituts, 1968. Contbr. articles profl. jours. Home: 2 E Campus Dr Easton PA 18042

GAERTTNER, ERWIN RUDOLF, educator, research scientist; b. Denver, Feb. 27, 1911; s. Rudolf and Pauline Karoline (Groezinger) G.; B.S. in Elec. Engring., U. Denver, 1932; Ph.D. in Physics, U. Mich., 1937; m. Dorothy Mary Polcar, Dec. 21, 1940; children—Robert E., Martin R. NRC fellow physics Cal. Inst. Tech., 1937- 38, Horace H. Rackham fellow physics, 1938-39; from instr. to asst. prof. physics Ohio State U., 1939-46; on leave to radiation lab. Mass. Inst. Tech., 1942-46; research asso. research lab. Gen. Electric Co., 1946-51, Knolls Atomic Power Lab., 1951-58; prof. physics Rensselaer Poly. Inst., Troy, N.Y., 1958-60, dir. Linear Accelerator Lab., 1958—, prof. nuclear engring. and sci., head dept., 1960—. Fellow Am. Phys. Soc., Am. Nuclear Soc.; mem. Phi Beta Kappa, Sigma Xi. Presbyn. Home: 10 Kenworth Av Troy NY 12180 Office: Linear Accelerator Lab Troy NY 12180

GAETH, JOHN HENRY, audiologist, educator; b. Fremont, Neb., Sept. 19, 1913; s. Henry J. and Lydia (Stuermer) G.; B.A., U. Neb., 1940, M.A., 1942; Ph.D., Northwestern U., 1948; m. Donna M. Hart, Feb. 15, 1939; children-Gary J., Julie Anna. Asso. prof. audiology Denver U., 1948-49; asst. prof., asso. prof. Northwestern U., 1949-56; prof. audiology Wayne State U., 1957—, chmn. dept. audiology, 1965—, also prof. speech. Cons. VA, Tenn. Sch. for Deaf. Served with USNR, 1944-46. Mem. Am. Speech and Hearing Assn., Am. Psychol. Assn., Acoustical Soc. Am., Am. Statis. Assn. Contbr. articles to profl. jours. Home: 1907 Houstonia Av Royal Oak MI 48073 Office: 261 Mack Blvd Detroit MI 48201

GAFFIGAN, MICHAEL AMBROSE, banker; b. Springfield, Ill., Jan. 21, 1936; s. Joseph P. and Cecilia (Gardiner) G.; B.A., Georgetown U., 1957; M.B.A., N.Y.U., 1961; m. Marcia Mitchell, May 18, 1956; children—Catherine, Pamela, Michael, Richard, Joseph, James. Analyst, Chase Manhattan Bank N.A., N.Y.C., 1957-63, asst. treas., 1963-65; 2d v.p. Central Nat. Bank, Chgo., 1965-67, v.p., 1967-69, sr. v.p., 1969—; dir. Curtis Electro Corp., Dallas, Nationwide Industries, Inc., Chgo. Mem. Am. Inst. Banking. Clubs: University, Economic (Chgo.), Barrington Hills Country; Sangamo (Springfield). Home: 101 Pine Rd Barrington IL 60010 Office: 120 S LaSalle St Chicago IL 60606

GAFFNEY, MERRILL MASON, educator, economist; b. White Plains, N.Y., Oct. 18, 1923; s. Matthew Page and Laura (Clarke) G.; student Harvard, 1941-42; B.A., Reed Coll., 1948; Ph.D., U. Cal. at Berkeley, 1956; m. Estelle Pao An Lau, Mar. 8, 1952; children—Bradford Clarke, Ann Reed, Stuart Morgan. Asst. prof. econs. N.C. State Coll., Raleigh, 1954-58; asso. prof., then prof. agrl. econs. U. Mo., 1958-62; prof. econs. U. Wis.-Milw., 1962—. Vis. prof. U. Cal. at Los Angeles, 1967; vis. scholar Resources for Future, Washington, 1969-71; cons. speaker in field, 1959—; mem. steering com. Taxation, Resources and Econ. Devel., 1961—. Served to 1st lt. USAAF. 1943-46. Ford fellow, 1957-58; co-recipient Jesse Neal award bus. journalism Asso. Bus. Publs., 1960. Mem. Am. Econ. Assn., Am. Farm Econ. Assn., Nat. Tax Assn., Regional Sci. Assn. Author: Land Rent, Taxation and Public Policy, 1968; Urban Expansion, 1958; Diseconomies in Western Water Law, 1960; Containment Policies for Urban Sprawl, 1964; Extractive Resources and Taxation, 1967. Home: 2070 Belmont Rd NW Washington DC 20009

GAFFNEY, PETER CHARLES, wood and paper products exec.; b. New Orleans, Nov. 7, 1912; s. Peter Charles and Jane (Kingsmill) G.; m. Marjorie Bertoniere, May 1, 1940 (dec. Mar. 1941); m. 2d, Mary Jane Ballina, Apr. 17, 1948; children—Peter Charles, Patrick Michael, Jane Ellen, Elizabeth Ann, Mary Ann. With So. Pine Assn., New Orleans, 1927-53, asst. sec.-mgr., also mgr. labor information com., 1946-53; asst. sec. So. Pine Industry Com., New Orleans, 1946-53; exec. v.p. S.W. Forest Industries, Inc., Phoenix, 1953—. Mem. Ariz. State Retirement Bd. Served to maj. USAAF, 1942-46. Mem. S.W. (pres. 1960), Western pine assns., Nat. Lumber Mfrs. Assn., Phoenix C. of C. (pres., dir. 1963-64), Phoenix Better Bus. Bur. dir. treas.), Ariz. Mfrs. (dirs., pres. 1969-70). Club: Phoenix Executives (pres. 1968-69). Home: 5701 N 3d St Phoenix AZ 85012 Office: 3443 N Central Av Phoenix AZ 85012

GAFFNEY, THOMAS, banker; b. San Francisco, Sept. 22, 1915; s. John and Hannah (Doherty) G.; certificate Am. Inst. Banking, 1940; m. Claire Bastian, Dec. 15, 1945; children—Bruce Edward, Bryan Keith. Bank insp. Bank of Am., 1935- 50, Transamerica Corp., San Francisco, 1953-55; asst. cashier First Nat. Trust and Savs. Assn., Santa Barbara, Cal., 1950-51; asst. cashier, asst sec. Oakland Central Bank (Cal.), 1951-53; v.p., auditor First Western Bank, San Francisco, 1955-61, New First Western Bank, Los Angeles, 1961—. Pres. Golden Gate chpt. Bank Adminstrn Inst., San Francisco, 1961, nat. bd. dirs., 1965-67, gen. chmn. conv., Los Angeles, 1967, speaker conv., Portland, Ore., 1966. Elk (bd. dirs. Locker Room 67 club San Francisco 1960). Club: Los Angeles Athletic. Home: 813 N. Vail Av Montebello, CA 90640 Office: 548 S Spring St Los Angeles CA 90013

GAFFNEY, THOMAS EDWARD, educator, physician; b. East St. Louis, Ill., Nov. 5, 1930; s. John V. and Leola (Heisner) G.; A.B., U. Mo., 1951, M.S., 1953; M.D., U. Cin., 1957; m. Edith Ann Heitholt, June 12, 1954; children—John, David, Michael. Intern, Harvard Med. Service of Boston City Hosp., 1957-58; resident medicine Mass. Gen. Hosp., 1958-59; instr. pharmacology, asst. medicine U. Cin., 1959-60; clin. asso. Nat. Heart Inst., 1960-62; asso. prof. pharmacology U. Cin., 1962-67, asst. prof. medicine, 1962-65, dir. div. clin. pharmacology, 1962—, prof. pharmacology, 1967—, prof. medicine, 1969—; attending physician Cin. Gen. Hosp.; vis. scientist Karolinska Inst., Stockholm, 1969-70. Mem. cadiovascular panel Nat. Acad. Scis. Drug Efficacy Study, 1967-70; mem. pharmacology and exptl. therapeutics study sect. Nat. Heart Inst., 1967-69; mem. med. adv. bd. Council High Blood Pressure Research, mem. Council on Basic Scis. of Am. Heart Assn., 1969—; mem. program rev. com. pharmacology and toxicology Nat. Inst. Gen. Med. Scis., 1971-75; mem. hypertension center rev. com. Nat. Heart and Lung Inst., 1971. Served with USPHS, 1960-62. Recipient research career devel. award Nat. Heart Inst., 1962. Mem. Am. Fedn. Clin. Research, Am. Soc. Pharmacology and Exptl. Therapeutics, Central Soc. Clin. Research, Am. Soc. Clin. Investigation, Alpha Omega Alpha. Mem. editorial bd. Jour. Pharmacology and Exptl. Therapeutics, 1965—. Contbr. articles to profl. jours. Home: 269 Compton St Cincinnati OH 45215

GAFFORD, FRANK HALL, univ. dean; b. Afton, Okla., Jan 11, 1903; s. Benjamin Ford and Elizabeth Newman (Payne) G.; B.A., U. Tex., 1925. M. A., 1927, Ph.D., 1940; m. Anita Marguerite Engerrand, Dec. 28, 1926; children—Eleanor Marguerite (Mrs. Ernest Owen Bransford, Jr.), Frank Hall, Jeanne Engerrand. Instr. history U. Miss., 1927-29, asst. prof., 1929-31; asst. prof. history Coll. Charleston (S.C.), 1931-32, asso. prof., 1932-41, prof., 1941-49; asso. prof. history N. Tex. State U., Denton, 1949-51, prof., 1951—, chmn. dept., 1951-52, dir., 1952-65, dean Coll. Arts and Scis., 1953—; summer instr. U. of South, 1944, Tulane U., 1949. Mem. Am. Hist. Assn., Am. Assn. U. Profs., Phi Alpha Theta, Pi Sigma Alpha, Pi Kappa Alpha. Home: 2520 Royal Lane Denton TX 76201

GAFFRON, HANS, educator, biochemist; b. Lima, Peru, May 17, 1902; s. Eduard and Hedwig (von Gevekot) G.; Ph.D., U. Berlin, 1925; m. Clara Ostendorf, Aug. 31, 1932; 1 son, Peter. Came to U.S. 1937, naturalized, 1945. Asst., Kaiser Wilhelm Inst. of Biologie, 1925-31, biochemistry, 1932-37; instr. U. Chgo., 1939- 41, asst. prof., 1941-46, asso. prof. biochemistry, 1946-52, prof. biochemistry, 1952-60; research prof. biochemistry, plant physiology Inst. of Molecular Biophysics, Fla. State U., Tallahasse, 1960—. Recipient award for excellence in field of photosynthesis Am. Soc. Plant Physiologists, 1965. Mem. A.A.A.S., Am. Soc. Biol. Chemistry, Bot. Soc. Am., Soc. Gen. Physiologists, Am. Soc. Plant Physiologists, Biophysical Soc., Sigma Xi. Contbr. sci. articles and papers to jours. Home: 312 E Georgia St Tallahassee FL 32301.

GAGARIN, ANDREW, mfg. exec.; b. Russia, Dec. 6, 1914; s. Serge A. and Catherine (Shouhoff) G.; brought to U.S., 1925, naturalized, 1930; grad. St. Paul's Sch., 1933; B.A., Yale, 1937; m. Jamie Porter, July 22, 1939; children—Jamie, Michael, Peter Nicholas. With Morgan Stanley and Co., N.Y.C., 1937-41; with Torin Corp., Torrington, Conn., 1945—, asst. to pres., 1947-50, v.p., 1950-53, pres., dir., 1953-69, chmn. bd., 1970—; dir. Scovill Mfg. Co., Waterbury, Conn., Mut. Ins. Co. of Hartford (Conn). Vice pres., trustee Conn. Jr. Republic, Litchfield; gov. Charlotte Hungerford Hosp., Torrington. Served from ensign to lt. comdr. USNR, 1941-45. Clubs: Links, River (N.Y.C.); Litchfield Country. Home: Gallows Lane Litchfield CT 06759 Office: Kennedy Dr Torrington CT 06790

GAGE, CHARLES A., banker. Sr. v.p., exec. officer Northwestern Nat. Bank Mpls. Office: 7th and Marquette Sts Minneapolis MN 55440*

GAGE, ELBERT MAUNEY, investment banker; b. El Paso, Tex., Feb. 19, 1912; s. Fred Mauney and Louise (Delauze) G.; B.S. in Mech. and Indsl. Engring., U. Mich., 1933; m. Jean C. Clarke, Sept. 2, 1939; children—John C., William D. Engaged in ins. and real estate bus., 1933-41; with Sparton Co., 1942; pres. Teer. Wickwire Co., auto parts mfrs., Jackson, Mich., 1942-57; with Pacific Industries, Inc., San Francisco, 1958—, exec. v.p., 1961—; partner McIntyre and Gage, San Francisco, 1964-70; mgr. corporate finance dept. Hambrecht & Quist, investment bankers, San Francisco, 1970—. Clubs: World Trade, Bankers (San Francisco). Home: 51 Upper N Terrace Tiburon CA 94920 Office: 235 Montgomery St San Francisco CA 94104

GAGE, EVERETT LYLE, neurosurgeon; b. Whitehall, Wis., Oct. 22, 1901; s. Charles Quincey and Rosalinda (Wing) G.; student U. Wis., 1921-26, B.A., 1964; M.D., U. Pa., 1928; M.S., McGill U., 1931; postgrad. neurosurgery Royal Victoria Hosp., Neurol. Inst., Montreal, Can., 1930-34; Mary Isabella Sloatman, Oct. 12, 1934; children—Everett Lyle, Grace Caroline, Barbara Murel, Charles Quincey, John Sloatman. Intern U. Pa. Hosp., Phila., 1928-30; chief resident Montreal (Can.) Neurol. Inst., 1934; asso. surgeon Brit. Am. Hosp., Lima, Peru, 1934-39; chief of staff chief of surgery Bluefield Sanitarium and Asso. Hosps.; cons. neurosurgery Beckley Hosp., Miner's Meml. Hosp. (both Beckley, W.Va.). Chmn. Bluefield Community Chest, 1949; pres. Bluefield Symphony Orchestra, 1955-56; bd. dirs. Bluefield Area Devel. Corp., Bluefield Sanitarium, Inc. Served from lt. comdr. to comdr., M.C., USNR, 1942-46; chief surgery Naval Hosp., Bainbridge, Md. Diplomate Am. Bd. Surgery, Am. Bd. Neurosurgery. Fellow A.C.S.; mem. Am. Assn. Neuropathologists, Harvey Cushing Soc., So. Neurosurg. Soc., Interurban Neurosurg. Soc., Mercer County Med. Soc. (past pres.), W.Va. State Med. Assn. (past pres., chmn. council). Republican. Episcopalian (vestry). Editorial bd. W.Va. Med. Assn. Jour. Home: 216 Oakhurst Av Bluefield VA 24605 Office: 525 Bland St Bluefield VA 24605

GAGE, ROBERT, banker; b. Chester, S.C., July 18, 1885; s. George Williams and Janie (Gaston) G.; prep. edn. Kings Mountain Mil. Acad., York, S.C.; student Wofford Coll., Spartanburg, S.C., 1901-03; m. Mary Smith, Dec. 18, 1906; 1 dau., Mrs. Alice Gage Davidson. Began with Comml. Bank, Chester, 1903, v.p. and cashier 1906—, pres., 1941—; pres. Chester Bldg. & Loan Assn.; mem. bd. dirs. Fed. Res. Bank of Richmond, Charlotte (N.C.) br. Fed. Res. Bank of Richmond, Va.; fed. receiver Peoples State Bank of S.C.; chmn. bd. dirs. Aragon-Baldwin Mills, Whitmire, S.C.; mem. adv. council Charlotte Loan Ag., Reconstrn. Finance Corp. Mem. City Council, Chester, 1914-17, 1922—; mem. Chester Co. Hwy. Commn., 1917-20 (bd. of 3 expanding $500, 000 on roads); chmn. Pub. Works Dept. of Chester, bldrs. of modern water system; mem. S.C. State Bd. of Bank Control. Chmn. Alien Enemy Hearing Bd. for Western Dist. of S.C., chmn. Chester Co. War Finance Com. of Fifth Fed. Res. Dist. Pres. S.C. Bankers Assn., 1937. Mem. bd. of dirs. J. P. Stevens Co., Inc., N.Y. Pres. Meth Coll. Found S. C. Recipient alumni citation Wofford Coll.; citation for distinguished service to ch. and state, Columbia Coll. Mem. Chi Psi. Methodist. Rotarian. Address: 108 York St Chester SC 29706

GAGEN, FRANKLIN CONRAD, mfg. co. exec.; b. Marion, O., June 26, 1916; s. Franklin Conrad and Josephine (Anderson) G.; A.B., Ohio Wesleyan U., 1938; LL.B., Yale, 1941; m. Marian F. Stone, Feb. 15, 1947; children—Stephen C., Deborah B., David S. Admitted to Ill. bar, 1941; practiced in Chgo., 1941-49; with Chgo. and Western Ind. R.R. Co., also Belt Rt. Co. Chgo., 1949-63, gen. counsel, 1954-63; sec., gen. atty. Allied Mills, Inc., Chgo., 1964— Mem. Evanston Dist. 65 Sch. Bd. Served with AUS, 1942-46. Mem. Phi Beta Kappa, Phi Delta Theta. Presbyn. Address: 82 Salem Lane Evanston IL 60203 †

GAGGE, ADOLF PHARO, educator; b. Columbus, O., Jan. 11, 1908; s. Axel Christian Pharo and Edith (Smith) G.; B.A., U. Va., 1929, M.A. in Physics, 1930; Ph.D. in Physics, Yale, 1933; m. Edwina Winter Mead, Dec. 23, 1936; children—Peter Mead, Eleanor (Mrs. James St. John Martin), John Pharo, Ann (Mrs. Gerry H. Vogt). Biophysicist Lab. Hygiene, John B. Pierce Found., New Haven, 1933-41, fellow, 1963—, dep. dir., 1970—; mem. faculty Yale, 1933-41, 63—, prof. environmental physiology, 1969—; chief biophysics, dir. research Aeromed. Lab., Wright Field, 1941-50; with Research and Devel. Hdqrs. USAF, Washington, 1950-55, Air Force Office Sci. Research, 1955-60, Office Sec. Def. Advanced Research Projects Agy., 1960-63. Chmn. com. hearing, bioacoustics and biomechanics Nat. Acad. Scis.-NRC, 1967-68, mem. council, 1965-69. Served to col. USAAF, 1941-63. Decorated Legion of Merit with oak leaf cluster, Army Commendation ribbon, Def. Commendation ribbon. Fellow Aerospace Med. Assn., A.A.A.S., Am. Physo. Soc., Am. Physiol. Soc.; mem. Am. Soc. Heating, Ventilation, Refrigeration and Air-Conditioning Engrs. (chmn. tech. com. physiology and human comfort 1968-71). Home: 57 Island View Av Branford CT 06405 Office: 290 Congress Av New Haven CT 06519

GAGNARD, FRANK LEWIS, journalist; b. Kerrville, Tex., Nov. 8, 1929; s. Frank and Leona Jo (Bevins) G.; B.A., N. Tex. State U., 1951. Mem. amusements staff Dallas Morning News, 1951-57; critic, fine arts editor New Orleans Item, 1957- 58; critic, amusements editor New Orleans Times-Picayune, 1959—. Home: 538 Madison St New Orleans LA 70116 Office: 3800 Howard Av New Orleans LA 70140

GAGNE, JEAN, lawyer; b. Valleyfield, Que., Can., Dec. 18, 1921; s. Thomas and Josephine (Lalonde) G.; Bachelor es-arts, U. Montreal, 1943; Licence in Law, Laval U., 1947, degree in Social Scis.; grad. student Harvard, 1950; m. Rita Bisonnette, Sept. 21, 1948; children—Maud Ann, Paule, Jean M., Martin, Vincent, Rita, Joan. Prof. indsl. and labour law Laval U., 1948-50, sec. dept. indsl. relations, 1948-51; admitted to Que bar, 1948, created Queen's counsel, 1957; practice law, Quebec, 1951—; sr. partner Gagne, Trotier, Letarte, LaRue & Royer, 1955—. Dir. Compagnie d'Assurance du Club Automobile de Quebec, Opemiska Copper Mines (Que.) Ltd., La Nationale Compagnie d'Assurances incendies et risques divers, Vailancourt, Inc., Paquet Inc. Bd. dirs. H87opital Christ-Roi, Quebec. Mem. Quebec C. of C., Canadian, Que. bar assns., Laval U. Alumnae, Montreal U. Alumnae, Internat. Assn. Jurists, Canadian Inst. Mining and Metallurgy. Roman Catholic. Clubs: Quebec Garrison, University (Quebec); Engineers' (Montreal). Home: 1640 des Rocs Av St Foy Quebec Canada Office: 2 Chauveau Av Quebec Quebec Canada

GAGNE, ROBERT MILLS, educator; b. North Andover, Mass., Aug. 21, 1916; s. Alphonse F. and Alice E. (Mills) G.; A.B., Yale, 1937; Ph.D., Brown U., 1940; m. Harriet N. Towle, Nov. 26, 1942; children—Samuel T., Ellen D. Instr. psychology Conn. Coll., for Women. 1940-41, asst., then asso. prof. psychology, 1946-49; asst. prof. psychology Pa. State Coll., 1945-46; research dir. perceptual and motor skills lab. Air Force Personnel and Tng. Research Center, Air Research and Devel. Command, 1949-53, tech. dir. maintenance lab., 1953-58; prof psychology Princeton, 1958-62; cons. Dept. Def., 1958-61; dir. research Am. Inst. Research, Pitts., 1962-65; prof. ednl. psychology U. Cal., Berkeley, 1966-69; prof. dept. ednl. psychology Fla. State U., Tallahassee, 1969—. Served from pvt. to 1st lt., USAAF, 1941-45. Mem. A.A.A.S., Am. Psychol. Assn. (fellow div. 3,15 and 19), Am. Ednl. Research Assn. Author: (with E.A. Fleishman) Psychology and Human Performance, 1959; The Conditions of Learning, 1965, 2d edit., 1970. Editor: Psychological Principles in System Development, 1962; Learning and Individual Differences, 1966; (with W.P. Gephart) Learning Research and School Learning, 1968. Home: 417 E Call St Tallahassee FL 32301

GAGNEBIN, ALBERT PAUL, mining exec.; b. Torrington, Conn., Jan. 23, 1909; s. Charles A. and Marguerite E. (Huguenin) G.; B.S. in Mech. Engring., Yale, 1930, M.S., 1932; m. Genevieve Hope, October 26, 1935; children—Anne (Mrs. John. D. Coffin), and Joan (Mrs. David O. Wicks). With Internat. Nickel Co., 1932, successively staff research lab., research ferrous metallurgy, devel. ductile iron, staff devel. and research div., 1932-55, mgr. nickel sales dept., 1956-61, v.p., 1958-64, exec. v.p. 1964-66, pres., 1967—; v.p. Internat. Nickel Co. Can., Ltd., 1960-64, exec. v.p., 1964-67, pres., 1967—, mem. exec. com., dir., 1965—; v.p., dir. Tokyo Nickel Co., Ltd.; trustee Atlantic Mut. Ins. Co., Bank of N.Y.; dir. Toronto-Dominion Bank, Abex Corp., Centennial Ins. Co., Ill. Central Industries. Bd. dirs. Am. Com. for Inst. Advanced Study-Europe, Inc., Sterling Forest (N.Y.) Bd. of Design, Albert Gallatin Assos. of N.Y.U., Internat. Copper Research Assn., Canadian Export Assn. Recipient ann. award Ductile Iron Soc., 1965; Grande Medaille d'Honneur, L'Association Technique de Fonderie, 1967. Mem. Am. Soc. M.E., Am. Inst. Mining and Metall. Engrs., Am. Soc. Metals, American Foundrymens Soc. (hon. life, Peter L. Simpson gold medal award 1952). Pan Am. Soc. U.S., Am. Soc. for Friendship with Switzerland, Woods Hole Oceanographic Inst., French C. of C. in U.S. (councillor), Mining and Metall. Soc. Am., Yale Engring. Assn. (dir). Sigma Xi. Clubs: Seabright (N.J.) Beach; Economic; Down Town Assn., Yale (N.Y.C.). Duquesne (Pitts.), Corinthians, Mining of N.Y., City Midday, Rumson Country. Author: The Fundamentals of Iron and Steel Castings. Co- inventor ductile iron. Home: 143 Grange Av Fair Haven, NJ 17701 Office: 67 Wall St New York City NY 10005

GAGNON, ALFRED JOSEPH, former mgmt. cons.; b. Waterbury, Conn., Sept. 9, 1914; s. John and Amelia (L'Heureux) G.; B.S., Yale, 1936; m. Mary Perry, Dec. 9, 1939; children—Marianne (Mrs. F.W. Palmer), Susanne (Mrs. Douglas Campbell), Thom, Joanne (Mrs. P.C. Janca). With Booz, Allen and Hamilton, San Francisco, 1945-70, formerly exec. v.p. charge Central and Western regions, also dir.; pres. Booz, Allen and Hamilton Can., Ltd., PAR Tech. Inc. Mem. Sigma Xi, Tau Beta Pi, Phi Gamma Delta. Clubs: San Francisco Golf, Stock Exchange (San Francisco); Pine Valley Golf (Clementon, N.J.); Stanwich (Greenwich, Conn.); California (Los Angeles). Home: 745 Chiltern Rd Hillsborough CA 94010

GAGNON, ANDRE, lawyer; b. Quebec City, Que., Can., June 11, 1921; B.Social Sci., Laval U., 1942, L.L.L., 1943; M.A., Oxford U. (Eng.), 1947. Admitted to Que. bar, 1943; now partner firm Gagnon, de Billy, Cantin & Dionne, Quebec City. Mem. Canadian, Que. bar assns. Office: 100 d'Youville St Quebec City 4 Quebec Canada*

GAGNON, CLAUDE BERNARD, lawyer; b. Quebec, Que., Can., May 8, 1922; s. Onesime G. and Cecile (Desautels) G.; B.A., Jesuits' Coll., Quebec, 1940; B.Social Sci. magna cum laude, Laval U., 1942, LL.L cum laude, 1943; M.A. in Jurisprudence (Rhodes scholar), Oxford (Eng.) U., 1947; m. Lucie Langlais, Sept. 24, 1949; children—Pierre, Marc, Paule. Called to bar, 1943; created Queen's counsel, 1956; practice law, D'Youville, Que., 1947—; mem. firm Gagnon, de BiBilly, Cantin, Dionne & Martin, 1947—. Pres. Bar of Province of Que., 1969-70; lectr. constl. law Faculty Commerce, Laval U., 1949-60. Mem. Bd. Broadcast Govs., 1962-68; sec. Que. region Canadian Mental Health Assn., 1968; mem. Oxford U. Found. Can., 1960—. Vice pres. Que Progressive Conservative Assn., 1961-62. Served to lt. Canadian Army, 1943-45. Recipient Centennial medal Can., 1967; Service medal Order Can., 1970. Mem. Que. Bar, Canadian Bar Assn., Canadian Assn. Rhodes Scholars (pres. 1967-69), Cercle Universitaire. Clubs: Cap Rouge (Que.) Golf; Que. Automobile (v.p., dir. University (Quebec). Home: 1121 Ploermel Quebec 6 Quebec Canada Office: 100 D'Youville Quebec 4 Quebec Canada

GAGNON, JOHN HENRY, sociologist, educator; b. Fall River, Mass., Nov. 22, 1931; s. George and Mary (Murphy) G.; B.A., U. Chgo., 1955, Ph.D., 1969; m. Patricia A. Orlikoff, Mar. 20, 1955; children—Andrée Giselle, Christopher Hans. Adminstrv. asst. to sheriff Cook County (Ill.), 1955-58; clin. asst. dept. neurology and psychiatry Northwestern U. Med. Sch., Chgo., 1958-59; lectr. Ind. U., Bloomington, 1959-67, trustee Inst. for Sex Research, 1959-68, sr. research sociologist, 1959- 68; asso. prof. State U. N.Y., Stony Brook, 1968-70, prof., 1970—, dir. lab. for social relations, 1968-70, dir. Center for Continuing Edn., 1970—. Mem. Am. Sociol. Assn., A.A.A.S., Soc. for Study Social Problems, Sex Information and Edn. Council U.S. (dir. 1967-70, mem. steering com. biol. scis. curriculum study 1969—). Author: Sex Offenders: An Analysis of Types, 1965; Sexual Deviance, 1967; The Sexual Scene, 1970; Sexuelle Aussenseiter, 1970. Research in urban studies, environmental, human sexual behavior. Home: 33 Blinkerlight Rd Stony Brook NY 11790

GAGNON, PAUL ADELARD, educator; b. Springfield, Mass., Jan. 6, 1925; s. Joseph E. and Alice (Tougas) G.; B.A., U. Mass., 1950; postgrad. U. Paris, 1951-52; M.A., Harvard, 1951, Ph.D., 1960; m. Mona Ann Harrington, May 21, 1960; children—Eliza, Benjamin, Thomas. Instr. history U. Mass., Amherst 1952-60, asst. prof., 1960-64, asso. prof., 1964-65; chmn. social sci. div. U. Mass., Boston, 1965-66, dean of faculty, prof. history, 1966—. Mem. Amherst Democratic Town Com., 1952-56. Served with USNR, 1942-46. Fulbright scholar, 1951-52. Mem. Am. Hist. Soc., Soc. French Hist. Studies, Societe d'Histoire Moderne, Council Basic Edn., Am. Assn. Univ. Profs., Mass. Alumni Assn. (dir. 1958-64), Phi Beta Kappa, Phi Kappa Phi. Author: France Since 1789, 1964. Founder, mem. editorial bd. of Mass. Review, 1959-63. Research on modern France, higher edn. Home: 12 St Charles St Boston MA 02116

GAHMAN, FLOYD, artist; b. Elida, O., Oct. 14, 1899; s. William Henry and Nancy (Brenneman) G.; tchrs. certificate Valparaiso U., 1916; B.S., Columbia U., 1924, M.A., 1939; studied art with Hobart Nichols, Henry Varnum Poor Dong Kingman; m. Ruth Louise Leyse; 1 dau., Phyllis. Asst. prof. art Pa. State U., 1948-60. Landscape painter: exhibited nationally; represented in permanent collections Pa. State U., Ind. U. Served as 2d lt., combat pilot, U.S. Army Air Forces, World War I, in U.S. and France; 1st lt., Res U.S. Army, 1919-24; capt. USAAF, 1943-46. Recipient prizes, Scarsdale (N.Y.) Art Assn., 1936-37, Salmagundi Club, 1938, 39, 42, 61, Allied Artists Am., 1943, Kirk prize Ogunquit Art Center; Gold medal Am. Artists Profl. League, 1962; landscape prize Acad. Artists, 1966, Salmagundi Club, 1970, Allied Artists Am., 1970, Hudson Valley Art Assn., 1970. Mem. N.A.D., Allied Artist Am., Audubon Artists, Ind. Art Assn., Phi Delta Kappa. Club Salmagundi. Home: 90 La Salle St New York City NY 10027 Studio: Morrisville VT 05661

GAIENNIE, LOUIS RENE, corp. executive; b. Kansas City, Mo., Oct. 24, 1912; s. L. Rene and Alice Mae (Greene) G.; A.B., Washington U., 1936, Ph.D., 1940; postgrad U. Ia., 1936-37; M.S., U. Wis., 1938; M.B.A., U. Chgo., 1950; m. Beatrice Clark, Apr. 18, 1942; children—Clark Rene, William (dec.). Dir. personnel Am. Investment Co., 1940-42; cons. Stevenson, Jordan and Harrison, Chgo., 1945-47; asst. v.p. Richardson Co., 1947-48; dir. personnel Fairbanks, Morse & Co., Chgo., 1948-55, v.p. in charge personnel, 1955- 57; v.p. indsl. and pub. relations ACF Industries, N.Y.C., 1957-59; v.p. adminstrn. The Canadian Fairbanks-Morse Company, Ltd., Montreal, 1959- 60, sr. v.p., 1960-62; pres., gen. mgr. Howe Richardson Scale Co., Clifton, N.J., 1962-68; dir. corporate analysis The Singer Co., N.Y.C., 1968—. Served as lt. comdr. USNR, World War II. Decorated Order Brit. Empire. Fellow Am. Psychol. Assn.; mem. Indsl. Psychol. Assn., Phi Beta Kappa, Sigma Xi, Beta Theta Pi, Omicron Delta Kappa. Episcopalian. Clubs: Union League, Economic, Executive (Chgo.); University (N.Y.C.); St. James (Montreal); Seigniory (Que.); Pennington (Passiac, N.J.); Montclair (N.J.) Golf. Author tech. articles. Home: 10 Belleclaire Pl Verona NJ 07094 Office: 30 Rockefeller Plaza New York City NY 10020

GAIGE, WILLIAM CLEMENT, state ofcl.; b. Warren, Pa., June 30, 1901; s. Frederick Hughes and Florence Mabel (Jenks) G.; A.B., Oberlin Coll., 1932; A.M., U. Chgo., 1935; Ed.D., Harvard, 1955; Sc. D., R.I. Coll. Pharmacy and Allied Scis., 1955; LL.D., Brown U., 1958; Providence Coll., 1959; Litt. D., Bryant Coll., 1962; Pd.D., U. R.I., 1963; m. Beatrice Emily Farrell, Aug. 25, 1934; children—Frederick Hughes, Lucille Ann, Linda Jean. Tchr., North Quincy (Mass.) High Sch., 1932-38; prin. Pembroke (Mass.) High Sch., 1938-41, Wellesley (Mass.) Sr. High Sch., 1941-48; supt. schs., Claremont, Cal., 1948-52; pres. R.I. Coll. (formerly R.I. Coll. Edn.), Providence, 1952-66; dir. research Adv. Council on Edn. in Mass., 1966- -; asso. in edn. Harvard, 1968—. Mem. Mass. Edn. Compact Council, 1968- -; mem. Narragansett council Boy Scouts Am. Mem. corp. Butler Hosp., Providence Instn. Savs.; dir. Research and Design Inst., 1964-66. Chmn., Mayor's Com. Urban Renewal, 1963-66. Trustee Roger Williams Jr. Coll., 1959-65; bd. dirs. R.I. Higher Edn. Assistance Corp., 1962-66, World Affairs Council R.I. (hon.), Providence Youth Progress Bd., 1965- 66; mem. corp. Miriam Hosp., Providence, Blue Cross and Physicians Service; hon. v.p. R.I. Audubon Soc. Served to lt. USNR, 1944- 46. Mem. Nat., R.I. edn. assns., Am. Assn. Sch. Adminstrs., New England Assn. Colls. and Secondary Schs. (commn. on instns. higher learning 1964-68), Assn. State Colls. and Univs. (sec.- treas. 1966), Am. Assn. Colls. for Tchr. Edn. (com. on relations with Nat. Council Accreditation Tchr. Edn. 1963-65), Assn. Higher Edn. Clubs: University (hon.) (Providence); Barnard (pres. 1963-64). Home: 20 Elm St Wellesley Hills MA 02181

GAILEY, FRANKLIN BRYAN, educator; b. Atlanta, Oct. 18, 1918; s. James Herbert and Edna (Bryan) G.; B.S. in Chemistry, Ga. Inst. Tech., 1940; M.S., U. Wis., 1942, Ph.D. in Biochemistry, 1946; m. Sara Helen Clark, July 31, 1948; children—David Clark, Carol Bryan, Patricia Lowe, Mark Alan. Instr. biology, chemistry Lees Jr. Coll., Jackson, Ky., 1946-48; mem. faculty Berea (Ky.) Coll., 1948—, prof. biology, chmn. dept., 1957—. Research participant Oak Ridge Inst. Nuclear Studies, summers 1954, 55, U. Ill., summer 1966, U. Ky., 1966-67. Fellow A.A.A.S.; mem. Am. Chem. Soc., Am. Inst. Biol. Scientists, Sigma Xi, Phi Kappa Phi. Mem. Ch. of Christ, Union. Home: 112 Van Winkle Grove CPO 2312 Berea KY 40403

GAILLARD, EDWARD MCCRADY, former banker; b. Phila., June 12, 1896; s. Samuel Gourdin and Esther Lynch (McCrady) G.; A.B., Yale, 1919; m. Virginia Ticknor, Oct. 14, 1922; children—Edward (dec.), Benjamin T., Virginia T. With Bankers Trust Co., N.Y.C., 1920-23; asst. to pres. Union and New Haven Trust Co., New Haven, 1923-28, v.p., 1928-42, dir., 1940-68, exec. v.p. 1942, pres., 1943-62, chmn. bd., 1963-68; trustee Conn. Savs. Bank; hon. dir. United Illuminating Co., Gaylord Farm Assn., Wallingford, Conn. Mem. Huguenot Soc. S.C., S.C. Hist. Soc., Sachem's Head Property Owners Assn. Clubs: Lawn, Quinnipiac (New Haven); Yale (N.Y.C.); Sachem's Head Yacht. Home: Sachem's Head Guilford CT 06437 Office: 205 Church St New Haven CT 06510

GAILLARD, JOHN PALMER, Jr., city ofcl.; b. Charleston, S.C., Apr. 4, 1920; s. John Palmer and Eleanor Ball (Lucas) G.; m. Lucy Huguenin Foster, July 15, 1944; children—John Palmer III, William Foster, Thomas Huguenin. Alderman, Charleston, S.C., 1951-59, mayor, 1959—. Pres. Municipal Assn. S.C., 1964-65. Served to lt., USNR, 1941-45. Mem. C. of C., St. Andrews Soc., U.S. Conf. Mayors (adv. bd. 1969—). Episcopalian. Elk. Clubs: Carolina Yacht, Hibernian, Charleston. Office: City Hall Charleston SC 29401

GAILLARD, WILLIAM DAWSON, lawyer; b. N.Y.C., Aug. 29, 1906; s. William Dawson and Marie (Planten) G.; grad. Hotchkiss Sch., 1922; A.B., Princeton, 1926; LL.B., Harvard, 1929; Katharine Miller, Sept. 6, 1930; children—William Dawson, Peter Saxton, Katharine Saxton (Mrs. John E. Strong). Admitted to N.Y. bar, 1929; partner Milbank, Tweed, Hadley and McCloy, N.Y.C., 1938—. Clubs: Fishers Island (N.Y.) Country; Princeton (N.Y.C.); St. Andrews Golf (Hastings-on-Hudson, N.Y.). Home: 4 Wayside Lane Scarsdale NY 10583 Office: 1 Chase Manhattan Plaza New York City NY 10007

GAIN, HOWARD F., lawyer; b. Lethbridge, Alta., Can., 1920; B.A., LL.B., U. Alta. Admitted to Alta. bar, 1948; now partner firm Saucier, Jones, Peacock, Black, Gain, Stratton & Laycraft, Calgary. Mem. Canadian, Calgary (pres. 1962) bar assns., Law Soc. Alta. Office: 444 7th Av SW Calgary 2 Alberta Canada*

GAINES, ALEXANDER PENDLETON, lawyer; b. Atlanta, May 27, 1910; s. Lewis M. and Virginia Ethel (Alexander) G.; A.B., U. Ga., 1932; LL.B., Emory U., 1935; m. Mary Delia Upchurch, Oct. 2, 1937; children—Mary (Mrs. William F. Ford), Alexander Pendleton, Delia. Admitted Ga. bar, 1935; asso Jones, Fuller and Clapp, 1935-41; asst. regional counsel OPA, 1942; partner Clapp and Gaines, 1945-50, Gaines and deGive, 1951-53, Hurt, Gaines and Baird, 1954-62; mem. firm Alston, Miller and Gaines, Atlanta, 1962—; sec., dir. George Muse Clothing Co., 1947—; dir. Genuine Parts Co., 1950—. Trustee, J.M. Tull Found., Agnes Scott Coll., Berry Schs., John Bulow Campbell Found., Charles Loridans Found., Vassar Wooley Found. Served with USAAF, 1942-45. Fellow Am. Coll. Probate Counsel; mem. Am., Ga., Atlanta bar assns., Atlanta C. of C., Phi Delta Theta, Phi Delta Phi. Presbyn. (elder). Clubs: Commerce, Atlanta Lawyers, Piedmont Driving. Home: 2832 Dover Rd NW Atlanta GA 30327 Office: C and S Nat Bank Bldg Atlanta GA 30303

GAINES, ERVIN JAMES, librarian; b. N.Y.C., Dec. 8, 1916; s. Ervin J. and Helen (Hennessy) G.; B.S., Columbia, 1942, A.M., 1947, Ph.D., 1952; m. Martha Zirbel, Feb. 11, 1938; children—Colleen Joy (Mrs. John Clark), Sanford Ervin. Instr., Columbia, 1946-53; chief tng. Radio Liberation, 1953-56, Teleregister Corp., 1956-57; free-lance cons., 1957-58; asst. dir. Boston Pub. Library, 1958-64; dir. Mpls. Pub. Library, 1964—. Mem. A.L.A., Am., Minn. (dir.) civil liberties unions. Home: 400 Groveland Av Minneapolis MN 55403 Office: 300 Nicollet Mall Minneapolis MN 55401

GAINES, FRANCIS PENDLETON Jr., univ. dean; b. State College, Miss., Sept. 7, 1918; s. Francis Pendleton and Sadie (Robert) G.; grad. Woodberry Forest Prep. Sch., 1935; student Washington and Lee U., 1935-37; A.B., U. Ariz., 1942; M.A., U. Va., 1946, Ph.D. (DuPont fellow), 1950; L.H.D., Coll. Artesia, 1968; m. Dorothy Ruth Bloomhardt, Oct. 10, 1942; children— Francis Pendleton III, Paul Randolph, Sallie du Vergne. Engr. on Miss. River, War Dept., 1937-39; dean of mem. asst. to pres. Birmingham So Coll., 1946-48; supt. Gulf Coast Mil. Acad., 1948; dir. pub. relations and devel. U. Houston, 1950; dean of students So. Meth. U., 1951-52; pres. Woffoed Coll. 1952- 57; v.p. Piedmont Nat. Bank, Spartanburg, S.C. 1957-58; dir. research study Fund for Advancement Edn., 1958-59; dean continuing edn. and summer session U. Ariz., Tucson, 1959—; sec. Assn. Summer Session Deans and Dirs., 1961-62. Pres. Conf. Ch.-related Colls. South, 1956-57; ofcl. del. to jurisdictional, gen. and world-confs. of Meth. Ch., 1956; mem. Council for Basic Edn,; mem. Woodrow Wilson Regional Selection com.; treas. S.C. Found. Ind. Colls.; citizens adv. council U.S. Senate Com. to P.O. and Civil Service; mem. Ariz. Civil War Centennial Commn. Served as capt. AUS, War Dept., Gen. Staff, M.I., 1942-45. Named S.C. Young Man of the Year, Jr. C. of C., 1954. Mem. U. Ariz. Alumni Assn. (dir. 1967—), Newcomen Soc., Phi Beta Kappa, Omicron Delta Kappa, Phi Kappa Phi, Pi Delta Epsilon, Phi Kappa Sigma, Raven Soc. Methodist (mem adminstrv. bd.). Clubs: Old Pueblo (Tucson), Davis-Monthan Officers'. Editorialist Spartanburg Herald-Jour. Contbr. profl. publs. Former holder regional tennis championships. Home: 3919 E Cooper St Tucson AZ 85711

GAINES, RALPH DEWAR, Jr., lawyer; b. Cartersville, Ga., July 10, 1925; s. Ralph Dewar and Bessie (Shaw) G.; B.B.A., Tulane U., 1946; LL.B., U. Ala., 1949; m. Mary Sue Pafford, July 21, 1951; children—Ralph Dewar III, Charlie P., Mary Susannah, Priscilla Shaw, Lucius Shaw. Admitted to Ala. bar, 1949, since practiced in Talladega. Dist. chmn. Boy Scouts Am., 1968-70; pres. United Givers Fund, 1963; chmn. Talladega Bd. Edn., 1966—. Trustee Ala.. Inst. for Deaf and Blind. Served with USNR, 1943-46. Named Talladega Young Man of Year, 1960. Mem. Am., Ala., Talladega County bar assns., Ala. Law Inst. (mem. council), Ala. Def. Lawyers Assn. (exec. v.p.), Talladega C. of C. (past pres.), Phi Alpha Delta, Pi Kappa Alpha. Baptist (deacon). Kiwanian. Home: New Shocco Rd Talladega AL 35160 Office: 127 North St Talladega AL 35160

GAINES, TILFORD CRAIG, banker; b. Spokane, Wash., Oct. 12, 1920; s. Grover and Lillian (Allen) G.; A.B., M.A., Washington U., St. Louis, 1946; Ph.D., Columbia, 1959; m. Ruth Burkhalter, Dec. 27, 1940 (div. Oct. 1964); 1 dau., Pamela Dolores; m. 2d, Regina Oddone, Dec. 12, 1964; 1 dau., Carla E. Instr., Fla. State U., 1950-51; economist Fed. Res. Bank N.Y., 1951-60; v.p. charge govt. bond operations First Nat. Bank Chgo., 1961-67; v.p., economist Hanover Trust Co., 1967—. Served with USAAF, 1944-46. Mem. Am. Econ. Assn., Am. Finance Assn., Am. Statis. Assn., Chgo. Assn. Commerce and Industry, Internat. C. of C. (chmn. monetary relations com.), Nat. Assn. Bus. Economists. Clubs: University, Economics (Chgo.). Home: 1467 Conway Lake Forest IL 60045

GAINEY, DANIEL CHARLES, bus. exec.; b. Winona, Minn, Nov. 28, 1897; s. Daniel and Ella (Leach) G.; A.B., Hamline U., St. Paul, 1921, D.B.A. 1948; m. Harriette Swearingen, July 17, 1924; 1 son, Daniel James; m. Elaine L. Frock, 1962. College sports writer Mpls. and St. Paul papers; athletic coach, Hancock, Minn., 1921-22, with Josten's Owatonna, Minn., 1922—, pres. 1933-59, chmn. bd., chief exec. officer, 1933-68, chmn. board emeritus, 1968—; pres. Charles Rochester Co, Am. Yearbook Co., Owatonna, 1950-59; now pres. Arabian Horse Club Registry Am.; pres. Danco Fund. Inc.; dir. First Trust Co. of St. Paul; rancher, Scottsdale, Ariz. and Santa Ynez, Cal. Trustee of Hamline U; bd. dirs. Am. Inst. for Fgn. Trade, Phoenix; officer Gainey Found. Mem. bd. regents U. Minn.; bd. trustees Minn. Community Research Council, Inc. Del. Rep. Nat. Conv., 1948, 52, 56, 60, 64; Stassen Floor leader Rep. Conv., 1952; past nat. treas. Republican Party; mem. nat. com. Citizens for Eisenhower, 1956; nat. finance cmn. Goldwater campaign, 1964; nat. co- chmn, finance com. Nixon campaign, 1968. Mem. Ednl. Jewelry Mfrs. Assn. (past pres. and dir.), N.A.M., State Employers Assn. (dir.), C. of C., Delta Sigma Phi. Republican. Clubs; Minneapolis, Minikahda Country (Owantonna); Metropolitan (Washington); Paradise Valley Country (Scottsdale Ariz.). Home: Route 2 Owatonna MN 55060 Office: 154 E Broadway Owatonna MN 55060

GAINEY, DANIEL JAMES, bus. exec.; b. Owatonna, Minn., Oct. 19, 1925; s. Daniel Charles and Harriette E. (Swearingen) G.; B.S., Carleton Coll., 1949; M.S., U. Minn., 1952; m. Catherine L. Holland, Apr. 11, 1953; children— Catherine, Melinda, Martha, Daniel Holland. With Hosten's, Owatonna, Minn., 1954—, asst. gen. mgr., 1956-59, v.p., vice chmn. bd., 1959, pres., 1960- -, chief exec. officer, 1967—, now chmn. bd. dirs. Bd. trustees Shattuck Sch., Faribault, Minn. Served with USNR, 1952-54. Mem. Young Pres.'s Orgn. Office: 148 E Broadway Owatonna MN 55060

GAINSBRUGH, MARTIN REUBEN, economist; b. Rochester, N.Y., Feb. 12, 1908; s. Jocob and Rachel (Isaacs) G.; A.B., U. Rochester, 1928; postgrad. Columbia, 1929-32; LL.D., Grove City Coll.; m. Elizabeth J. Augsbury, July 4, 1935; children—Susan Rachel, Jonathan Jo, Glenn Martin. Econ. analyst Trade-Ways, Inc., 1933-38; chief economist Nat. Indsl. Conf. Bd. 1939—, v.p., 1962-65, sr. v.p., 1966—; cons. panel Comptroller-Gen. U.S., 1967—; lectr. econs., N.Y.U., 1944-48, adj. asso. prof. econs., 1949-50, adj. prof. econs., 1951—. Chmn. Bus. Research Adv. Council. Bur. Labor Statistics, 1955-57; mem. bus. adv. com. Council Econ. Advisers, 1947-57; cons. Council for Advancement Secondary Edn., 1955-57; bd. advisers Indsl. Coll. Armed Forces, 1958-66; mem. econ. adv. com. Council for Econ. Growth and Security, Inc., 1960—; mem. Pres.'s Com. to Appraise Employment and Unemployment Statistics, 1961- 62; mem. Adv. Group on Research Program of Social Security Administrn., 1961-64; chmn. nat. quota com. Nat. Budget and Consultation Com., 1963; adv. com. on mgmt. automatic data processing Exec. Office Pres., 1963-64; mem. cons. panel U.S. comptroller gen., 1967-68; mem. pvt. sector task force Nat. Adv. Com. on Civil Disorders, 1967. Recipient merit award Citizens Com. for Hoover Report, 1952, citation Freedom Found., 1953, certificate of award U.S. Dept. of Labor, 1957. Fellow A.A.A.S., Am. Statis. Assn. (council, chmn. program com. 1955, v.p. 1956-58, pres. 1961); mem. Royal Statis. Soc., Met. Econ. Assn. Conf. Bus. Economists (chmn. 1955), Soc. Bus. Adv. Professions (pres. 1957), Am. Econ. Assn., Am. Finance Assn. Phi Beta Kappa. Contbr., author, editor publs. and books. Home: 230 E 50th St New York City NY 10022 Office: 845 3d Av New York City NY 10022

GAINZA PAZ, ALBERTO, journalist; b. Buenos Aires, Argentina, Mar. 16, 1899; s. Alberto and Zelmira (Paz) Gainza; student Colegio Nat. Domingo F. Sarmiento, 1915; law degree, U. Buenos Aires, 1922; Dr. Journalism (hon.), Northwestern U., 1951; LL.D., Columbia, 1951; m. Elvira Castro, June 17, 1922. Editor La Prensa, Buenos Aires, 1921-51, 55—. Recipient Freedom House award, 1951, Theodore Brent award, 1956. Sigma Delta Chi fellow, 1952. Mem. Inter Am. Press Assn. (hon. chmn. bd.). Clubs: Circulo de Armas, Jockey (Buenos Aires); Metropolitan, Overseas Press (hon.) (N.Y.) Home: 1324 Villanueva Buenos Aires Argentina

GAIRDNER, JOHN SMITH, investment dealer; b. Toronto, Ont., Can., July 25, 1925; s. James A. and Norma Ecclestone (Smith) G.; grad. Appleby Coll., Oakville, Ont., 1942; student U. Toronto, 1942-43; m. Ivy Jane Brothwell, Nov. 30, 1946; children—John Lewis, Robert Donald, Brenda Leigh. Clk., Gairdner & Co., Ltd., Toronto, 1945-48, dir., 1948-55, v.p., dir., 1955-58, pres., 1958-66, chmn. bd., dir., 1965—; pres. Glengair Group, Ltd., 1966-70, chmn., 1970—; dir. Canadian Security Mgmt., Ltd., 1963-66, 70—, chmn., 1971—; dir. Atlantic Sugar Refineries Co., Ltd., Montreal, 1956-68, 70—, chmn., 1968-70; chmn. bd., dir. Gairdner, Son & Co., Ltd.; pres., dir. pres., dir. Gairdner Internat., Ltd.; dir. Gairdner & Co., Inc., N.Y.C.; v.p., dir. Canadian Gas & Energy Fund, Ltd., Canadian Security Growth Fund, Ltd., Trafalgar Investments Co., Ltd.; dir. Allanson & Redi-Set Corp., Ltd., Atlantic Sugar Refineries Co. Ltd., Bridge & Tank Co. of Can., Ltd., Hamilton, Can. Brick Co., Ltd., Streetsville, Ont., Mineral Resources Internat. Ltd., CSM Japan Fund Ltd., Toronto, No. Tar, Chem. & Wood, Ltd., Thunder Bay, Ont., Orangeroof Can., Ltd., Glentech Instruments Ltd., Tamco Ltd., Windsor, Tancord Industries, Ltd., Venpower Ltd., Toronto. Bd. govs. Appleby Coll. Served with RCAF, 1943-45. Mem. Zeta Psi. Home: 1502 Lakeshore Rd E Oakville Ontario Canada Office: Box 53 Toronto Dominion Centre Toronto 111 Ontario Canada

GAISMAN, HENRY JACQUES, inventor; b. Memphis, Dec. 5, 1869; s. Jaques and Sarah (Kaufman) G.; ed. pub. schs. Cin.; hon. M.E., Stevens Inst. Tech., 1932; m. Catherine A. Vance, Apr. 18, 1952. Founder, pres., chmn. bd. Auto- Strop Safety Razor Co., 1906-30; chmn. bd. Gillette Safety Razor Co., 1930-38; inventor of many articles, especially relating to photography, cutlery and machines to produce same. Founder of Inventors Found., Inc., non-profit orgn. for furthering edn. and guidance of students interested in inventions and to prepare courses for promoting inventions in tech. schs.; founder Gaisman Found., charitable orgn. Mem. bd. N.Y. State Reformatories, 1911-19. Served as expert with chief of Bur. of Research of the Gen. Staff, with Port of N.Y. War Bd., also chmn. safety razor div. War Industries Bd., during World War. Clubs: Lotos (N.Y.C.); Westchester Country (Rye, N.Y.). Home: Hartsdale NY 10530

GAITAN, EDUARDO, diplomat; b. Cucuta, Colombia, Oct. 14, 1927; s. Emilio and Delina (Duran) G.; B.S. in C.E., U. Miss., 1952; m. Doris Elizabeth Mills, Nov. 29, 1952; children—Maria Delina, Liza Consuelo, Victoria Carolina. Engr., N.Y.C. R.R., Chgo., 1952-54, partner, mgr. Perez & Gaitan Constrn. Co., Cucuta, 1954-63; sec. pub. works North Santander, Colombia, 1963-64; congressman to the Colombian Parliament, 1964-67; pres. Antex Oil & Gas Co., Barranquilla, 1967-68; minister plenipotentiary Colombian embassy, Washington, 1968—. Dir. Antares Ltda., Bogota, Colombia. Mem. Liberal Party State Com., adviser to nat. com., 1964-68. Mem. Colombian Soc. C.E., Sociedad Economica de Amigos del Pais, Pi Kappa Phi. Clubs: International Washington; del Comercio (Cucuta, Colombia). Sponsor gas tax revenue bill, urban reform bill, 1964-66. Home: 3701 Upton St NW Washington DC 20016 Office: 2118 LeRoy Pl NW Washington DC 20008

GAITER, LEWIS LEON, Jr., banker; b. Fort Leavenworth, Kan., Sept. 27, 1933; s. Lewis Leon and Ethel (Marks) G.; B.S. in Bus. Adminstrn., U. Denver, 1963, J.D., 1970; m. Sandra Mae Ashford, Dec. 21, 1958; children—Lewis III, Byron James, Kimberli Sanislea. Nat. bank examiner, 1963-66; loan operations officer United Bank Denver, 1966-70; chmn. interim bd., then pres. Skyline Nat. Bank, Denver, 1971—; chmn. bd., pres. United Assos., Inc., Denver, 1970—; pres. Skyline Towers, Inc., Denver, 1971—. Campaign mgr. Jerome Rose for Colo. Legislature, 1968, 70. Bd. dirs. United Way, A.R.C., Am. Cancer Soc., Central YMCA, and others, all Denver; chmn. bd. govs. Metro Housing Center. Served with USNR, 1951-55. Mem. Kappa Alpha Psi, Democrat. Home: 531 E Caley Dr Littleton CO 80121 Office: University Bldg 910 16th St Denver CO 80202

GAITHER, ROBERT BARKER, educator; b. N. Bay, Ont., Can., Aug., 12, 1929 (parents Am. citizens); s. Edwin Hampton and Loyola (Barker) G.; B. Mech. Engring., Auburn U., 1951; M.S. in Mech. Engring., U. Ill., 1957, Ph.D., 1962; m. Renate- Konstanze Zielke, Dec. 11, 1954; children—Patricia, Vivienne, Francesca, Instr., U. Ill., 1957-62; mem. faculty U. Fla., Gainesville, 1962—, prof. mech. engring., 1965—, also chmn. dept.; cons. in field, 1956—. Treas. Fla. Found. Future Scientists, 1966—. Served to lt. USNR, 1951-54. Ford Found. fellow, 1959-62. Mem. Am. Soc. M.E. (vice chmn. mech. engring. dept. heads 1970), Am. Soc. Engring. Edn., Sigma Xi, Tau Beta Pi, Pi Mu Epsilon, Pi Tau Sigma. Research in electron gas in plasma flow systems. Home: 2100 NW 63d Terrace Gainesville FL 32601

GAJRAJ, RAHMAN BACCUS, diplomat; b. Georgetown, Guyana, S.Am., May 11, 1910; s. Husain Baksh and Lateefan (Bacchus) G.; student Queen's Coll., Guyana, 1921-26; A.B., McKinley-Roosevelt U. Coll., Chgo., 1937; m. Hazrah Rohoman, Nov. 6, 1933; children—Shamyoon Moseda (Mrs. Ramcharran Kachan), Roshenara (Mrs. Derek Jagan), Raphiq Baksh, Gulshenara (Mrs. Neville Anthony Moonsawmy), Badrudin Iqbal. With H.B. Gajraj, Ltd., 1937-70, mng. dir., 1943-63, governing dir., 1963-70; dir. Hand-in-Hand Mut. Fire Ins., Ltd., 1956-70, Hand-in-Hand Fire Ins. Co., Ltd., 1966-70, Sterling Products, Ltd., 1963-70; councillor Corp.

of City of Georgetown, 1944-70; mayor, City of Georgetown, 1951, 52, 65, lord mayor, 1966; A.E. and P., Washington, 1970—. Chmn. Rice Marketing Bd., 1956-61, Rice Devel. Co., Ltd., 1962-63. Mem. Legislative Council, 1951, 54-57, 57-64; mem. State Council, 1953; speaker Legislative Assembly, 1961-64; speaker Nat. Assembly, 1968-70. Chmn. bd. govs. Bishops High Sch., 1955-69; hon. treas., bd. govs. U. Guyana, 1965-69; trustee Mariners Club, 1956-65. Decorated comdr. Order Brit. Empire, Justice of Peace. Mem. Brit. Inst. Mgmt. Home: 6911 Bradley Blvd Bethesda MD 20034 Office: 2490 Tracy Pl NW Washington DC 20008

GALAGAN, DONALD JOSEPH, dentist, educator; b. Buffalo Center, Ia., Apr. 27, 1914; s. Clement Henry and Laura (Agnew) G.; D.D.S., State U. Ia., 1937; M.P.H., U. Cal. at Berkeley, 1950; m. Dorothea Streib, Oct. 19, 1939; children—Patricia Ann, Sheila Mary, Christopher William. Joined USPHS, 1937, advanced through ranks to asst. surgeon gen., 1962; intern USPHS Hosp., San Francisco, 1937-38; participated devel. community dental treatment programs, preventive dental programs, especially topical flouride and water flouridation programs; chief div. dental pub. health and resources Dept. Health, Edn. and Welfare, 1960-66; dean Coll. Dentistry, U. Ia. 1966—. Mem. Internat. Assn. Dental Research, A.A.A.S., Am. Coll. of Dentistry, Fed. Dentistry Internat., Am. Dental Assn., Am. Pub Health Assn., Am. Assn. Pub. Health Dentists, Am. Bd. Dental Pub. Health, Delta Omega. Bd. editors Pub. Health Reports, 1960- -; editorial bd. Oral Research and Abstracts. Home: 611 River St Iowa City IA 52240

GALAMBOS, ROBERT, educator; b. Lorain, O., Apr. 20, 1914; s. John and Julia (Petti) G.; A.B., Oberlin Coll., 1935, M.A., 1936, A.M., Harvard, 1938, Ph.D., 1941; M.D., U. Rochester, 1946; m. Jeannette Wright, Dec. 30, 1939; children—Joan B., Katherine W., Ann J. Instr. physiology Harvard, 1942- 43; jr. investigator OSRD, 1942-43, tutor biochemistry, 1941-42, 47- 48; asst prof. anatomy Emory U. Med. Sch., 1946-47; research fellow psycho-acoustic lab. Harvard, 1947-51; chief dept. neurophysiology Walter Reed Army Research Inst., 1951-62; prof. psychology, physiology Yale U., 1962-68; prof. neuroscis. Sch. Medicine, U. Cal. at San Diego, 1968—. Mem. Am. Physiol. Soc., Acoustical Soc. Am., Nat., Am. acads. sci. Editorial bd. Am. Jour. Physiology, Jour. Applied Physiology, 1956-59, Jour. Neurophysiology, 1958-59. Spl. research hearing and learning in nervous system. Home: 2722 Glenwick Pl La Jolla CA 92037

GALAMBOS, THEODORE VICTOR, educator; b. Budapest, Hungary, Apr. 17, 1929; s. Paul and Magdalen (Potzner) G.; brought to U.S., 1948, naturalized, 1954; B.S., U. N.D., 1953, M.S., 1954; Ph.D., Lehigh U., 1959; m. Barbara A. Asp, June 25, 1957; children—Paul, Ruth, Ronald, John. Asst. prof. civil engring. Lehigh U., 1959-62, asso. prof., 1962-65; prof. civil engring. Washington U., St. Louis, 1965—, chmn. dept., 1970—; cons. engr. Steel Joint Inst., 1965—. Chmn. Column Research Council, Engrs. Joint Council, 1970—. Served with C.E., AUS, 1954-56. Mem. Am. Soc. Engring. Edn., Am. Soc. C.E. (Huber Research prize, 1964, Moiseieff award 1968), Internat. Assn. Bridge and Structural Engrs. Author: (with others) Structural Steel Design, 1964; Structural Members and Frames, 1968. Contbr. profl. jours. Home: 505 N Bemiston St St Louis MO 63130

GALAMIAN, IVAN ALEXANDER, musician, educator; b. Tabriz, Persia, Jan, 23, 1903; s. Alexander J. and Sarah (Khounoutz) G.; grad. Philharmonic Sch., Moscow, USSR, 1923; Mus. D., Curtis Inst., 1954, Cleve. Inst. Music, 1968; hon. degree Oberlin Coll., 1966; m. Judith Johnson, Nov 22, 1941. Came to U.S., 1937, naturalized, 1944. Mem. violin faculty Russian Conservatory, Paris, France, 1925-39, Ecole Normale de Masique, Paris, 1936-39, Curtis Inst. Music, 1944—, Julliard Sch. Music, N.Y.C., 1946—; dir. Meadowmount Sch. Music, Westport, N.Y., 1952—. Pres. Soc. for Strings, Inc., 1952. Hon. mem. Royal Acad. Music. Author: Principles of Violin Playing and Teaching, 1962. Address: 170 W 73d St New York City NY 10023

GALAND, RENE MARIE, educator; b. Chateauneuf-du-Faou, France, Jan. 27, 1923; s. Pierre and Anne (Nédélec) G.; Licence ès Lettres U. Rennes (France), 1944; grad. Ecole Spéciale Militaire de Saint-Cyr, 1945; Ph. D., Yale, 1952; m. Francoise Texier, Dec. 23, 1959; children—Joel, Caroline. Came to U.S., 1947; naturalized, 1953. Instr. French, Yale, 1949-51; mem. faculty Wellesley Coll., 1951, prof. French, 1963, chmn. dept. French, 1968—. Served with French Army, 1944-46. Decorated chevalier Ordre des Palmes Académiques. Mem. Modern Lang. Assn., Soc. des Profs. Francais en Am., Am. Assn. Tchrs. French, Author: L'Ame celtique de Renan; Baudelaire: póetiques et poésie, 1969. Co-author: Baudelaire as a Love Poet and other Essays. Contbr. articles, revs. to publs. Home: 8 Leighton Rd Wellesley MA 02181

GALANOS, JAMES, designer; b. Phila., Sept. 20, 1924; s. Gregory D. and Helen (Gorgoliatos) G.; with Hattie Carnegie, 1944; asst. to designer Columbia Pictures Corp., Hollywood, Cal., 1946-47; trainee Robert Piguet, Paris, France, 1947-48; founder, designer Galanos Originals, Beverly Hills, 1951—. Recipient award for distinguished service in field of fashion Neiman-Marcus, 1954, Am. Fashion. Critics award Met. Mus. Art Costume Inst., 1954, 56, Creativity award Internat. Achievements Fair, 1956, Filene's Young Talent design award, Boston, 1958, Cotton Fashion award, 1958. Home: 1316 Sunset Plaza Dr Los Angeles CA 90069 Office: 2254 S Sepulveda Blvd Los Angeles CA 90064

GALANTER, EUGENE, educator, psychologist; b. Phila., Oct. 27, 1924; s. Max and Sarah (Honigman) G.; A.B., Swarthmore Coll., 1950; A.M., U. Pa., 1951, Ph.D., 1953; m. Patricia Anderson, Dec. 22, 1962; children—Alicia, Gabrielle. From instr. to prof. psychology U. Pa., 1952-62; research fellow Harvard, 1955-56; Center Advanced Study Behavioral Scis., 1958-59; chmn. dept. psychology U. Wash., 1962-64, prof., 1964-66; Joseph Klingenstein vis. prof. social psychology Columbia, N.Y.C., 1966-67, prof. psychology, 1967—. Cons. NIH, NSF, also to industry; mem. Council for Biology in Human Affairs, chmn. commn. on biology, learning and behavior Salk Inst. Served with AUS, 1942-46. Fellow A.A.A.S.; mem. Eastern Psychol. Assn., Accoustical Soc. Am., N.Y. Acad. Scis., Assn. Aviation Psychologists (pres. 1970-71). Author: Plans and Structure of Behavior, 1960; New Directions in Psychology, 1962; Textbook of Elementary Psychology, 1966. Editor: Handbook of Mathematical Psychology, 3 vols., 1963-64; Readings in Mathematical Psychology, 2 vols., 1963-65. Home: 460 Riverside Dr New York City NY 10027

GALANTI, MARINUS CHARLES, educator; b. Lodi, N.J. Oct. 25, 1903; s. Paul and Rosalie (Martinico) G.; Ph.B., Brown U., 1927; M.A., Columbia, 1933; LL.D., Fairleigh Dickinson U., 1965; m. Silvia Guarino Feb 27, 1927; children—Silvia (Mrs. Philip Chopalis), Frances (Mrs. Herbert Hummler), Garry. Tchr., Lodi (N.J.) Jr. High Sch., 1927-31; vice prin. Teaneck (N.J.) High Sch., 1931-34; prin. Lodi High Sch., 1934-45; personnel mgr. United Piece Dye Co., Lodi, 1945-57; dean Evening Coll., Fairleigh Dickinson U., 1957-60, dean Teaneck campus, 1960-69, dir. Wroxton Coll. (Eng.), 1969—. Mem. N.J. Scholarship Commn., 1967—. Pres. Bergen County Federated Bds. Edn., 1955-56. Bd. dirs. Lodi Boys Club, 1955, Group Health Ins. N.J., 1965, Lodi Library, 1952-57, YMCA Greater Bergen County, 1965—; trustee Englewood (N.J.) Hosp., 1962. Mem. N.J. Mfrs. Assn., N.J. Edn. Assn. (exec. com. 1942-46), Kappa Alpha Phi. Rotarian (pres. Lodi 1948-49; dist. sec. 1944-45). Home: 817-B Cedar Lane Teaneck, NJ 07666.

GALANTIERE, LEWIS, writer, cons. internat. relations; b. Chgo., Oct. 10, 1895; m. Nancy N. Davis, 1938. With Internat. C. of C., Paris, France, 1920-27, Fed. Res. Bank of N.Y., 1928-40; dir. French operations OWI, U.S., London and Paris, 1942-45; counsellor Free Europe Com., 1952-64. Organizer, mem. Am. Round Table of Advt. Council, 1951-52; mem. Fulbright Selection Com. for France, 1951-53; subcom. books abroad Nat. Book Com., 1953-55; mem. study groups Democratic leadership, Germany, U.S. and European Capitalism, France, East Europe, of Council Fgn. Relations, 1957-65; pres. P.E.N. Am. Center, 1965-67. Pres 34th Internat. P.E.N. Congress, N.Y.C., 1966. Bd. dirs. Am. Civil Liberties Union, 1951-66, mem. editing com. report on Am. Democracy, Rockefeller Bros. Fund, 1959. Guggenheim fellow, 1941. Mem. Acad. Polit. Sci., Mediaeval Soc. Am., Authors League Am. (council 1966—), Am. Translators Assn. (dir. 1962- 65). Clubs: Century Assn., Coffee House (N.Y.C.). Publs: France is Full of Frenchmen; America Today; America and the Mind of Europe; (plays) And Be My Love, Lamachus; Goncourt Journals 1851-70; Portable Maupassant (with G. de Poncins) Kabloona. Translator numerous works; contbr. polit. and lit. mags. Address: 7 W 43d St New York City NY 10036 ☆

GALANTIN, IGNATIUS JOSEPH, former naval officer; b. N.Y.C., Sept. 24, 1910; s. Ignatius Peter and Mary Elizabeth (Binder) G.; B.S., U.S. Naval Acad., 1933; grad. Nat. War Coll., 1955; m. Virginia Elizabeth Jaeckel, June 14, 1935; children—Mary Joy (Mrs. S.E. Veazey), Vivien Elizabeth (Mrs. Philip D. Creelman), Linda. Commd. ensign U.S. Navy, 1933, advanced through grades to adm., 1967; stationed battleship New York, 1933-35; comdr. submarines R-11 and Halibut, World War II; submarine liaison officer ComNav-Group, China, 1945; comdr. Submarine Div. 51, 1949, Submarine Squadron 7, 1953- 54; comdr. fleet oiler Navasota, Korean War; assigned Office Chief Naval Operations, 1955-57; mem. NATO staff of CinCSouth, Naples, Italy, 1957- 59; comdr. task group Cruiser Div. 2 of 6th Fleet, 1960; dir. submarine and anti-submarine warfare Navy Dept., 1961, dir. Spl. Projects Office charge devel. and prodn. Polaris weapon system, Navy Dept., 1962-65, chief naval materiel, 1965-70; U.S. project officer implementaton U.S.-U.K. Polaris Sales Agreement, 1963-65; ret., 1970. Decorated D.S.M., Navy Cross, Silver Star (3), Commendation medal. Home: Watergate East Washington DC 20037

GALASSO, ANTHONY, banker. Adminstrv. v.p., also cashier U.S. Nat. Bank. Office: U S Nat Bank 190 Broadway PO Box 1550 San Diego CA 92112*

GALATZAN, MORRIS A., lawyer; b. El Paso, Tex., Jan. 21, 1911; s. Benjamin and Elka (Snider) G.; B.A., U. Tex., 1934; m. Irene Asbach, June 19, 1947; children—Judith, Sandra, David. Admitted to Tex. bar, 1934; judge 65th Jud. Dist. Tex., 1950-57; partner firm Hardie, Grambling, Sims & Galatzan, El Paso, 1957—. Pres. El. Paso Jr. C. of C., 1939; v.p. Tex. Jr. C. of C., 1941. Served to capt. AUS, 1942-46. Decorated Bronze Star. Recipient Legion of Honor, Internat. Supreme council Order of DeMolay, Kansas City, Mo., 1955. Mem. El Paso Bar Assn. (pres. 1955), El Paso C. of C. (dir. 1969). Democrat. Jewish religion. Lion (dir. 1961); mem. B'nai B'rith (past pres. lodge). Home: 1220 Baltimore St El Paso TX 79902 Office: El Paso Natural Gas Co Bldg El Paso TX 79901

GALBRAITH, ALEX MCNICOL, communications co. exec.; b. Chgo., June 29, 1929; s. Victor A. and Maxine M. (MacHatton) G.; B.A. magna cum laude, Amherst Coll., 1950; M.A., Harvard, 1951; M.B.A., U. Pa. Wharton Sch., 1956; m. Mary Ann Smucker, May 3, 1957; children—Janet Elisabeth, John Alexander, Anne Ruth. Mgr. profit planning and investment control Trans Union Corp., Chgo., 1956-57; mgr. financial analysis Meredith Corp., Des Moines, 1967-68, treas., 1968—. Served with AUS, 1951-53. Decorated Bronze Star medal. Mem. Nat. Assn. Accountants, Phi Beta Kappa, Beta Gamma Sigma. Club: Des Moines Golf and Country. Home: 7014 Jefferson St Des Moines IA 50322 Office: 1716 Locust St Des Moines IA 50303

GALBRAITH, FRANCIS JOSEPH, fgn. service officer; b. Timber Lake, S.D., Dec. 9, 1913; s. Fred J. and Clara Belle (Stearns) G.; B.A., Coll. Puget Sound, 1939; B.A., U. Wash., 1940; postgrad. Yale, 1948-49; m. Martha Townsley Fisher, July 18, 1948; children—Susan Kathleen, Kelly Francis. Reference librarian U. Wash., 1940-41, with U.S. Dept. of State, 1946—, vice counsul, Hamburg, Germany, 1946-48; Indonesian lang. and area tng. at Yale, 1948-49, polit. officer Am. Embassy, Djakarta, Indonesia, 1949-51, 1956-58, Indonesian desk officer, 1951-55, consul, Medan, Sumatra, 1955; 1st sec., polit. officer, Gt. Britain, 1958-62; counselor, dep. chief of mission Am. Embassy, Djakarta, Indonesia, 1963-65; fgn. service inspector, 1965; ambassador to Singapore, 1965-69; ambassador to Indonesia, 1969—. Served as captain F.A, AUS, 1941-46. Mem. Am. Fgn. Service Assn., Dacor, Sigma Zeta Epsilon. Clubs: Circumnavigators, Am. Assn. Singapore, Singapore Island Country, American (Singapore). Home: 2242 Decatur Pl N W Washington, DC 20008. Office: Am Embassy Singapore

GALBRAITH, J. KENNETH, economist; b. Iona Station, Ont., Can., Oct. 15, 1908; s. William Archibald and Catherine (Kendall) G.; B.S., U. Toronto, 1931; M.S., U. Cal., 1933, Ph.D., 1934; student Cambridge U., Eng., 1937-38; LL.D., Bard Coll., 1958, Miami U., 1959, U. Mass., 1963, Brandeis U., 1963, U. Toronto, 1963, U. Guelph, 1965, U. Sask., 1965, U. Mich. 1966, R. I. Coll., 1966, Boston Coll. 1967, Hobart and William Smith Colls., 1967, Albion Coll., 1968; L.H.D., Tufts U., H.H.D., Adelphi Stuffolk Coll.; m. Catherine Atwater, Sept. 17, 1937; children—Alan, Peter, James. Research fellow, U. Calif., 1931-34; instr. and tutor, Harvard, 1934-39; asst. prof. econs. Princeton, 1939-42; econ. adviser, Nat. Defense Adv. Commn., 1940-41; asst. adminstr. in charge price division OPA, 1941-42, dep. adminstr., 1942-43; mem. bd. of editors, Fortune Mag., 1943-48; lectr. Harvard, 1948-49, prof. econs., 1969—, Paul M. Warburg prof. econs., 1959-60, 63- -; A.E. and P., India 1961-63. Dir. U.S. Strategic Bombing Survey, 1945; dir. Office of Econ. Security Policy, State Dept., 1946. Fellow Social Sci. Research Council, 1937-38. Trustee of Twentieth Century Fund. Fellow Am. Acad. Arts and Scis.; mem. Nat. Inst. of Arts and Letters, Am. Econ. Assn., Am. Farm Econs. Assn., Ams. for Democratic Action (chmn. 1967—). Awarded Medal Freedom, 1946. Clubs: Century (N.Y.), Federal City (Washington). Author: several books, latest being American Capitalism, 1952; A Theory of Price Control, 1952; The Great Crash, 1955; The Affluent Society, 1958; The Liberal Hour, 1960; Economic Development, 1963; The Scotch, 1964; The New Industrial State, 1967; Indian Painting, 1968; The Triumph, 1968. Contbr. to econ. and sci. jours. Home: 30 Francis Av Cambridge MA 02138 ☆

GALBRAITH, JAMES GARBER, physician, educator; b. Anniston, Ala., May 28, 1914; s. Samuel L. and Sarah (Garber) G.; student U. Notre Dame, 1930-32; B.S., St. Louis U., 1936, M.D., 1938; m. Marguerite Stabler, June 6, 1942; children—Ann, Jane, Mary Kay, Laura. Intern, Loyd Noland Hosp., Fairfield, Ala., 1938- 39, resident gen. surgery, 1939-40; resident neurol. surgery Neurol. Inst., Columbia Presbyn. Med. Center, N.Y.C., 1940-43, instr. neurology, 1942-43; practice medicine, specializing in neurol. surgery, Birmingham, Ala., 1946—; asso. prof. surgery Med. Coll. Ala., 1946-54, prof. surgery, 1954—, prof., chmn. div. neurosurgery, 1965. Mem. lay bd. advisers St. Bernard Coll. Served to lt., M.C., USNR, 1943-46. Diplomate Am. Bd Neurol. Surgery. Fellow A.C.S.; mem. A.M.A., So., (pres., past chmn. council), Ala. (counsellor) med. assns., Jefferson County Med. Soc. (past pres.), So. Neurol. Soc. (past pres.), Harvey Cushing Soc., Soc. Neurol. Surgeons, Assn. Research Mental and Nervous Disorders, Birmingham C. of C. (past dir.). Home: 4227 Altamont Rd Birmingham AL 35213 Office: 1919 7th Av S Birmingham AL 35233

GALBRAITH, JOHN SEMPLE, educator; b. Glasgow, Scotland, Nov. 10, 1916; s. James M. and Mary (Marshall) G.; came to U.S., 1925, naturalized, 1931; B.A., Miami U., Oxford, O., 1938; M.A., U. Ia., 1939, Ph.D., 1943; LL.D., Mount Union Coll., 1968; m. Laura Huddleston, Aug. 20, 1940; children—James M., John H., Mary P. Asst. prof. Ohio U., 1947-48; prof. Brit. Empire history U. Cal. at Los Angeles, 1948-64, chmn. dept., 1954-58; chancellor U. Cal. at San Diego, 1964-68; Smuts vis. fellow Cambridge (Eng.) U., 1968-69; prof. history U. Cal. at Los Angeles, 1969—. Served as officer AUS, 1943-46. Mem. Royal Hist. Soc., Am. (pres. Pacific Coast br. 1965), Canadian hist. assns., Soc. Am. Historians, African Studies Assn., Am. Assn. U. Profs., Phi Beta Kappa. Author: The Establishment of Canadian Diplomatic Status in Washington, 1951; The Hudson's Bay Company as an Imperial Factor, 1957; Reluctant Empire, 1963. Home: 654 Thayer Av Los Angeles CA 90024

GALBRAITH, RALPH ARTHUR, coll. dean; b. Ash Grove, Mo., Aug. 1, 1911; s. Arthur and Almira (Chandler) G.; student Drury Coll., 1929-30; B.S. U. Mo. 1934; Ph.D., Yale, 1937; m. Ruth R. Gorton, Aug. 21, 1944; children—David L., Susan C. Research engr. Detroit Edison Co., 1937-38; instr. elec. engring. U. Mo., 1938-39; asst. prof. U. Tex. 1941-43, asso. prof. 1943-44; radar sch. staff Mass. Inst. Tech., 1944-45; prof. elec. engring Ga. Inst. Tech. 1946; chmn. elec. engring. dept. Syracuse U., 1946-50, dean Coll. Engring., 1951—; also exec. v.p. Syracuse U. Research Corp. Mem. Am. Soc. Engring. Edn., Am. Inst. E.E., Inst. Radio Engrs., A.A.A.S., Am. Assn. U. Profs., Sigma Xi, Tau Beta Pi, Kappa Alpha, Eta Kappa Nu. Author: Fundamentals of Electrical Engineering, 1954. Contbr. to Principles of Radar, 1946. Home: 225 Redfield Av Fayetteville NY 13066 Office: Syracuse University Syracuse NY 13202

GALBRAITH, VIRGINIA LEE, educator; b. Boise, Ida.; d. Eugene Robert and Ione (Atkinson) Galbraith; A.B., U. Cal. at Berkeley, 1941, Ph.D., 1954. Instr., Vassar Coll., 1945-47, U. Cal. at Berkeley, 1949-50; prof. econs. Mt. Holyoke Coll., 1950—. Vis prof. U. Minn., summers 1959, 61. Mem. Consumer Council Mass., 1958-63. Mem. Am. Econ. Assn. Democrat. Author: World Trade in Transition, 1965. Contbr. articles profl. jours. Home: 7 Greenwood Lane South Hadley MA 01075

GALE, CHARLES COUNSEL, pharm. co. exec.; b. Ypsilanti, Mich., Sept. 18, 1914; s. Grover J. and Ethel Ann (Bergin) G.; Ph.B., U. Detroit, 1937, LL.B., 1939; m. Harriet Thomas Mellen, Mar. 8, 1941; children—William Charles, Diane Lynn. Admitted to Mich bar, 1939; auditor Butterfield Theatres, Detroit, 1939- 41; with govt., property control div. Vickers, Inc., Detroit, 1941-43, 46-47; with Parke, Davis & Co., Detroit, 1947—, asst. treas., 1964- 66, treas., 1966—. Treas., dir. Neighborhood Service Orgn., Detroit, 1964—; mem. financial Policy com. Detroit Symphony Orch., 1966—; mem. finance com., bd. dirs. Jr. Achievement of Southeastern Mich., Inc. Served as officer USNR, 1943-46. Mem. Mich. Bar Assn., Downtown Detroit Mgmt. Club (pres. 1954), Pharm. Mfrs. Assn. (chmn. financial sect. 1968-69). Club: Detroit Athletic. Home: 5482 Red Fox Rd Brighton MI 48116 Office: Parke Davis & Co Joseph Campau at the River Detroit MI 48207

GALE, DAVID, educator, mathematician; b. N.Y.C., Dec. 13, 1921; s. Henry and Therese (Strauss) G.; A.B., Swarthmore Coll., 1943; M.A. in Math., U. Mich., 1947; Ph.D. in Math., Princeton, 1949; m. JulieBirgitte Skeby, Apr. 2, 1954; children—Kirsten, Karen, Katharine. Mem. staff radiation lab. Mass. Inst. Tech., 1943-45; Henry B. Fine instr. math. Princeton, 1949- 50; mem. faculty Brown U., 1950-65; chmn. dept. math., 1960-65, prof. math., 1961-65; vis. prof. U. Cal. at Berkeley, 1965-66, prof. math. and engring sci., 1966—. Fulbright research scholar U. Copenhagen (Denmark), 1953-54; cons. RAND Corp., 1957-58; vis. prof. U. Osaka (Tokyo), 1962-63; spl. research math. econs., theory of games, geometry convex sets. Guggenheim fellow, 1962-63; NSF sr. postdoctoral fellow 1968-69. Fellow Econometric Soc.; mem. Am. Math. Soc., Math. Assn. Am., Phi Beta Kappa, Sigma Xi. Author: The Theory of Linear Economic Models, 1960; also articles. Home: 791 Hilldale Av Berkeley CA 94708

GALE, GEORGE ALEXANDER, Canadian chief justice; b. Quebec, Can., June 24, 1906; s. Robert Henry and Elma Gertrude (Read) G.; B.A., U. Toronto, 1929; grad. Osgoode Hall Law Sch., Toronto, 1932; LL.D. (hon.), McMaster U., 1968, York U., 1969; m. Hilda Georgina Daly, Dec. 29, 1934; children—Robert, Peter, David. Read law with firm Mason, White and Foulds, Toronto, 1929; called to Ont. bar, 1932, created King's counsel, 1945; partner firm Mason, Foulds, Davidson and Gale, Toronto, 1944-46; justice Supreme Ct. Ont., 1946—, justice Ct. of Appeal Ont., 1963-64; chief justice High Ct. Justice Ont., 1964-67; chief justice Ont., 1967—. Hon. lectr. Osgoode Law Sch., also faculty medicine U. Toronto; chmn. Com. Rules of Practice for Ont., 1941; chmn. Jud. Council Provincial Judges, 1968—; mem. adv. com. Met. Toronto Courthouse, 1958—; chmn. council Canadian Jud. Conf., 1968—. Bd. govs. Wycliffe Coll., U. Toronto, Upper Can. Coll., Toronto. Mem. Canadian Bar Assn. (council), Bar of Ga. (hon.), Delta Kappa Epsilon (pres. local chpt. 1932, internat. sec. 1932), Phi Delta Phi. Mem. Anglican Ch. Clubs: Lawyers (pres. 1940, hon. pres. 1968), University (v.p. 1959); Curling (pres. 1956), York (Toronto); Saugeen Golf, Chippewa County (Southampton, Ont.). Co- editor: Practice and Procedure in Ontario. Home: 2 Brookfield Rd Willowdale Ontario Canada Office: Osgoode Hall Toronto 1 Ontario Canada

GALE, HERBERT MORRISON, educator; b. Macon, Mo., Mar, 28, 1907; s. Edward Justus and Anna (Morrison) G.; A.B., State U. Ia., 1929; M.A., Boston U., 1931, S.T.B., 1932, Ph.D., 1939; student U. Berlin (Germany), 1932-33; m. Winifred Florence Rannells, June 5, 1932; children—Herbert Morrison, Winifred (Mrs. Robert W. Crawford, Jr.), Edward Rannels. Ordained to ministry Meth. Ch., 1931; minister, Carrollton, Mo., 1933-35, Pelham, N.H., 1935-38, Westboro, Mo., 1938-39; tchr. Bible, Northfield Sch. Girls, E. Northfield, Mass., 1939-44, head dept., 1940-44; mem. faculty Wellesley (Mass.) Coll., 1944—, prof. Bible, 1958—; dir. music First Congl. Ch., Lowell, Mass., 1937-38, Greenwood (Mass.) Union Ch., 1945—. Fulbright Research Grantee, Germany, 1953-54. Mem. Studiorum Novi Testamenti Societas, Soc. Bib. Lit. and Exegesis, Am. Acad. Religion, Phi Beta Kappa. Author: A Study of the Old Testament, 2d edits., 1958; The Use of Analogy in the Letters of Paul, 1964. Home: 9 Upland Rd Wellesley MA 02181

GALE, JOSEPH WASSON, educator, surgeon; b. Milton, Ia., Jan. 21, 1900; s. William (M.D.) and Mary (Rhoades) G.; A.B., U. Mo., 1921, A.M., 1922; M.D., Washington U., 1924; m. Marion Sutherland Read, Oct. 20, 1928; children— Christina May, Margaret Read. Intern, Barnes Hospital, St. Louis, 1924-25, asst. resident surgeon, 1925-26, resident surgeon, 1926-27; asst. prof. surgery, U. Wis., 1927-30, asso. prof. 1930-41, prof. surgery, 1941—. Served to col. AUS. Diplomate Am. Bd. Surgery. Fellow Am. Coll. Surgeons; mem. Am. Board Thoracic Surgery (founding mem.), A.M.A., Am. Surg. Assn., Western Surg. Assn., Wis. Surg. Soc., Central Surg. Soc., Internat. Surg. Soc., Soc. Univ. Surgeons, Am. Soc. for Thoracic Surgery, Nat. Tb Assn., Wis., Dane County med. socs., Scabbard and Blade, Sigma Xi, Nu Sigma Nu, Kappa Sigma. Mason (32 Shriner). Contbr. in field of thoracic and gen. surgery to profl. jours. Home: 126 Marinette Trail Madison WI 53705

GALE, WALTER JOHN, ednl. adminstr., b. Phila., July 14, 1914; s. Walter E. and Kathryn Gertrude (Ryan) G.; B.S., N.J. State Coll., Glassboro, 1936; M.Ed., Duke, 1946, Ph.D., 1950; m. Mary E. De Mauro, Oct. 27, 1944 (div.); children—Geraldine M., Cynthia K., Gregory W., Karen L.; m. 2d, Barbara Ann Ransel, Oct. 25, 1969. Instr. ednl. psychology Duke, 1946-48; prin Broughton High Sch., Raleigh, N.C., 1948- 52; prof. ednl. psychology Woman's Coll. of U. N.C., 1952-55; vis. lectr. U. N.C., 1955-56; pres. Pembroke (N.C.) State Coll., 1956-63; dean West Chester (Pa.) State Coll., 1963-65; dir. Nat. Def. Student Loan Program, U.S. Office of Edn., Washington, 1965—. Bd. dirs. N.C. Soc. Crippled Children and Adults, N.C. Symphony Soc. Served with USNR, 1941-45. Mem. Am. Sociol. Soc., N.E.A., Am. Soc. Curriculum Devel. Home: 4005 Mill Creek Dr Annandale VA 22003

GALENSON, WALTER, educator, economist; b. N.Y.C., Dec. 5, 1914; s. Louis Peter and Libby (Mishell) G.; A.B., Columbia, 1934, Ph.D., 1940; m. Marjorie Spector, June 25, 1940; children—Emily, Alice, David. Prin. economist OSS, 1942- 44, U.S. Fgn. Service, 1944-46; asst. prof. econs. Harvard, 1946-51; prof. econs. U. Cal. at Berkeley, 1951-66, Cornell U., Ithaca, N.Y., 1966—; Pitt prof. Cambridge U., 1970-71. Mem. Am. Econs. Assn., Indsl. Relations Research Assn. Author: Rival Unionism in the United States, 1940; Labor in Norway, 1944; The Danish System of Labor Relations, 1952; Labor Productivity in Soviet and American Industry, 1955; The CIO— Challenge to the AFL, 1960; The Quality of Labor, 1964; A Primer on Employment and Wages, 1966; The Chinese Economy Under Communism, 1968. Address: Sch Indsl Relations Cornell Univ Ithaca NY 14850

GALES, ROBERT SYDNEY, physicist; b. Boston, Dec. 12, 1914; s. Robert Joseph and Grace Risley (Moore) G.; A.B., U. Cal. at Los Angeles, 1938, M.A., 1942; m. Dorothea Frances Yocum, Aug. 29, 1942; children—Robert Timothy, Patricia Frances, Michael Jeffery. Asso. physicist U. Cal. Div. War Research, San Diego, 1942-45; physicist Navy Electronics Lab., San Diego, 1946-69; supervisory physicist Naval Undersea Research and Devel. Center, San Diego, 1969—. Acoustical cons. Fellow Acoustical Soc. Am. (councilman 1967, v.p. elect 1971); mem. Fed. Profl. Assn. (chmn. San Diego chpt. 1963, 65). Presbyn. (elder). Clubs: Alamitos Bay Yacht (commodore Long Beach, Cal. 1942); Mission Bay Yacht (commodore San Diego 1948). Contbr. to books, also articles to profl. jours. Patentee in field. Home: 1645 Los Altos Rd San Diego CA 92109 Office: Naval Undersea Research and Devel Center San Diego CA 92132

GALIFIANAKIS, NICK, U.S. congressman; b. Durham, N.C., July 22, 1928; s. Mike and Sophia (Kastranakis) G.; A.B., Duke, 1951, LL.B., 1953; m. Louise Cheatham, Apr. 5, 1963; children—Stephenie, Katherine, Jon Mark. Admitted to N.C. bar, 1956, since practiced in Durham; partner Upchurch & Galifianakis, 1956- -; rep. N.C. Gen. Assemblies from Durham County, 1961, 63, 65; atty.- staff instr. Duke Law Sch. Legal Aid Clinic, 1956-59, asst. prof. bus. law, 1959-67; mem. 90th Congress 5th Dist. N.C., 91st-92d congresses 4th Dist. N.C. Mem. N.C. Com. Mental Instns., 1961-64, chmn., 1965—; mem. N.C. Bd. Sci. and Tech., 1965—. Bd. dirs. March of Dimes, Am. Cancer Soc., United Fund, Cerebral Palsy, Durham County Mental Health Assn; bd. advisers ALSEC. Served with USMCR, 1953-56. Recipient Distinguised Service award Durham County Jr. C. of C., 1963, N.C. Jr. C. of C. Outstanding Young Man of Year award, 1963. Mem. Am., N.C., Durham County, 14th Jud. Dist. bar assns., Am. Assn. U. Profs., Am. Hellenic Ednl. Progressive Assn., Durham Young Lawyers Club (pres.). Democrat. Mem. Greek Orthodox Ch. (trustee). Kiwanian. Home: 2648 University Dr Durham NC 27707 Office: House Office Bldg Washington DC 20515

GALIHER, RICHARD WILKINSON, lawyer; b. Washington, Apr. 25, 1913; s. Claude and Anne May (Quackenbush) G.; A.B., Cath. U. Am., LL.B., 1935; m. Phyllis A. Sullivan, Oct. 26, 1940; children—Richard Wilkinson, Phyllis, Patricia, Kathleen. Admitted to D.C. bar, 1935; gen. practice law, 1936—; mem. firm Galiher, Steward & Clarke, Washington, 1951—. Fellow Am. Coll. Trial Lawyers, Am. Bar Found., Internat. Acad. Trial Lawyers; mem. Bar Assn. D.C. (pres. 1960-61), Am. Bar. Assn. (Ho. of Dels., past chmn. sect. ins. negligence and compensation law), Internat. Assn. Ins. Counsel (pres. 1963-64). Home: 5816 Highland Dr Kenwood MD 21212 Office: 1215 19th St NW Washington DC 20036

GALIMIR, FELIX, violinist; b. Vienna, Austria, May 20, 1910; s. Mosco and Elsa (Russo) G.; diploma Vienna Conservatory Music, 1928; student Carl Flesch in Berlin and Baden-Baden, 1929-30; m. Suzanne Hirsch, Feb. 18, 1945. Came to U.S., 1938, naturalized, 1943. Founder Galimir String Quartet, Vienna, 1929; travelled, concertized throughout Europe and Near East, 1929-36; reorganized Galimir String Quartet in N.Y.C., 1938—; with NBC Symphony Orch., 1939-53; mem. faculty Juillard Sch. Music, 1962—, Coll., City N.Y., 1953—, Marlboro Music Sch. and Marlboro Music Festival, 1953—; recording artist for Columbia, Decca, Period Records. Address: 225 E 74th St New York City NY 10021

GALIN, MILES A., physician; b. N.Y.C., Jan. 6, 1932; s. Albert and Freda (Simkowitz) G.; A.B cum laude, N.Y. U., 1951, M.D., 1955; m. Glenda Goldenberg, June 27, 1953; children—Amy, Elizabeth, Scott, Jonathan. Intern Mt. Sinai Hosp., 1955-56; resident surgery N.Y. Hosp., N.Y.C., 1956-58, resident surgeon, 1958-59, surgeon to out-patients, 1959-61, asst. attending surgeon, 1961- 64, asso. attending surgeon, 1964-66; practice medicine, specializing in ophthalmology, N.Y.C., 1959—; cons. ophthalmology Meml. Hosp., 1960-66; attending ophthalmologist Flower and Fifth Av. Hosp., Met. Hosp., Bird S. Coler Hosp., Blythedale childrens Hosp., N.Y.; asst. in surgery ophthalmology Cornell U. Med. Coll., N.Y.C., 1956-58, instr. surgery, 1958-61; clin. asst. prof., 1961-63, asst. prof., 1963-66; prof., chmn. dept. ophthalmology N.Y. Med. Coll., 1966—, exchange scientist to USSR, U.S.-Soviet Health Exchange, 1969—; cons. FAA, Nat. Multiple Sclerosis Found.; tech. cons. Regional Med. Program; mem. med. adv. com. Quality Vision Care; tech. adv. com. ophthalmology Bur. for Handicapped Children. Prin. investigator and coinvestigator Nat. Soc. for Prevention Blindness, Cornell U., 1959-66, N.Y. Med. Coll., 1966-67, Nat. Council to Combat Blindness, Cornell U., 1955-66, N.Y. Med. Coll., 1966-67, USPHS, Cornell U. Med. Coll., 1959-66, N.Y. Med. Coll., 1966—, NIAID, N.Y. Med. Coll., 1968—; career scientist Health Research Council, N.Y.C., 1963-66. Recipient Borden award N.Y. U., 1955; William Warner Hoppin award N.Y. Acad. Medicine, 1959; award of merit Am. Acad. Ophthalmology and Otolaryngology, 1967; Dr. Henry Balconi Meml. lectr., Rochester, N.Y., 1967; Culler Meml. lectr., Columbus, O., 1967. Diplomate Nat. Bd. Med. Examiners, Am. Bd. Ophthalmology. Mem. Am. Acad. Ophthalmology and Otolaryngology, A.A.A.S., Am. Inst. Ultrasound in Medicine, Am. Soc. Microbiology, N.Y. Acad. Medicine, N.Y. Acad. Scis., N.Y. Soc. for Clin. Ophthalmology, Royal Soc. Health, Royal Soc. Medicine, Surg. Soc. N.Y. Med. Coll., A.M.A., Assn. Career Scientists N.Y.C., Assn. U. Profs. Ophthalmology, Assn. for Research in Vision and Ophthalomology, Internat. Strabismological Assn., French, Israel ophthalmol. socs., Instituto Barraquer, N.Y. State Soc. Med. Research, Ophthalmol. Soc. U.K., Oxford Congress, Pan Am. Assn. Ophthalmology (hon.), Argentine, Peruvian assns. ophthalmolgoy, Colo. Ophthalmol. Soc., Ga. Soc. Ophthalmology and Otolaryngology, Oklahoma City Clin. Soc., Pacific Coast Oto-Ophthalmology Soc., Pa. Acad. Opthalmology and Otalaryngy, Phi Beta Kappa, Alpha Omega Alpha. U.S. editor: Annali de Ottalmologia, 1967—; mem. editorial bd. Annals of Opthalmology. Contbr. articles profl. jours. Home: 180 East End Av New York City NY 10028 Office: 1249 Fifth Av New York City NY 10029

GALINA, ANNA, prima ballerina. Address: Le Theatre d'Art du Ballet care Paul Szilard Prodns 250 W 57th St New York City NY 10019*

GALINDO POHL, REYNALDO, diplomat of El Salvador; b. Sonsonate, El Salvadore, Oct. 18, 1918; s. Hector Galindo and Lilian Pohl; Doctor Juris, U. El Salvador; m. Esperanza Velez, Aug. 10, 1954; 1 son, Francisco Humberto. With El Salvador Ministry Edn., 1950-56; chief bur. mem. states UNESCO, 1957-59; mem. commn. interam. de derechos humanos OEA, 1960-64; ambassador to UN, 1967—; prof. theory of state and philosophy of law U. El Salvador, 1959- 67; pres. Asamblea Nacional Constituyente, 1950. Decorated Legion of Honor (France). Corr. mem. de la Real Acad. Espanola; mem. del Inst. Interam. de Estudios Juridicos Internat., Assn. del. Inst. Hispano-Luso- Am. de Derecho Internat. Author: Notes de Filosofia, 1950; Guion Historico de la Ciencia del Derecho, 1969. Home: 10 Park Av New York City, NY 10016. Office: 211 43rd St New York City NY 10017

GALITZ, HAROLD LUVERN, banker; b. Fedora, S.D., Mar. 22, 1919; s. Herman William Frederick and Fanny (Newmarch) G.; student Cornell Coll., 1939; m. Dorothy Homrighausen, Apr. 11, 1941; children—Steve, Scott, Jan. With Coast Fed. Savs. & Loan Assn., Los Angeles, 1946-56, v.p., mgr. loan dept., 1953-56; exec. v.p., asst. mgr. World Savs. & Loan Assn., Lynwood, Cal., 1956—, also dir.; vice chmn. bd. Loyalty Savs. & Loan Assn., Sacramento; dir., v.p., sec. Trans-World Financial Co., Beverly Hills, Cal., 1959—. Served with USAAF, 1942-46. Mem. Cal. Savs. & Loan League (bd. dirs.), Nat. League Insured Savs. & Loan Assns. (gov. Cal.), U.S. Savs. and Loan League (mem. com. capital stock assns.). Republican. Methodist. Home: 11703 E Norino Dr Whittier CA 90601 Office: 11170 Long Beach Blvd Lynwood CA 90262

GALKIN, ELLIOTT WASHINGTON, educator, musician; b. Bklyn., Feb. 22, 1921; s. Samuel and Ethel (Heifetz) G.; B.A., Bklyn. Coll., 1943; diplome de Direction d'Orchestra, Conservatoire Nat. de Paris (France), 1948; certificate Equivalentà la Licence de Concert, L'Ecole-Normale de Musique de Paris, 1948; M.A., Cornell U., 1955, Ph.D., 1960; m. Jean R. Dubois, Jan 2, 1958. Asso. condr. L'Orch. Philharmonique internat., 1949; instr. music Saranac Lake Rehab. Guild, 1949-52; apprentice condr. Vienna (Austria) Staatsoper, 1955-56; faculty Goucher Coll., 1956—, chmn. dept. music, 1960, prof., 1964—; faculty Peabody Conservatory, 1957—, condr. orch., 1957-64, chmn. music history and lit. dept., 1964—; dir. mus. activities, prof. Johns Hopkins U., Balt., 1968—; guest condr. Balt. Symphony Orch., 1965-68; dir. Rockefeller Found.-Balt. Symphony Orch. Am. Composers Project at Goucher Coll., 1965, 66, 67; condr. Balt. Chamber Orch., 1960—; music editor, critic Balt. Sun, 1962- -; vis. lectr. Tanglewood Music Festival, 1965, 66, chmn. music critics project, 1968, dir. Fromm Found. fellowship program in music criticism, 1968, 69. Mem. Md. Adv. Council Arts, 1966—. Served with USAAF, 1943-46. Mem. Internat., Am. musicol. socs., Coll. Music Soc., Am. Fedn. Musicians, Music Critics Assn., Am. Newspaper Guild, Phi Beta Kappa. Contbr. articles profl. jours. Home: 2211 Midridge Rd Timonium MD 21093 Office: Goucher Coll Towson Baltimore MD 21204

GALL, EDWARD ALFRED, ednl. adminstr., physician: b. N.Y.C., June 10, 1906; s. Julius and Eva (Fleischl) G.; student Coll. City N.Y., 1923-27; M.D., Tulane U., 1931; m. Phyllis H. Rivard, Sept. 17, 1933; children—Eric Papineau, Thomas Monroe. Intern Sydenham Hosp., N.Y.C., 1931-33; dist. physician Boston Dispensary, 1933-35; resident, asst. pathologist Mass. Gen. Hosp., 1935- 40; dir. labs. Bethesda Hosp., Cin., 1941-48, Cin. Gen. Hosp., 1948—; asst. medicine, instr. pathology Tufts Med. Sch., 1933-40; instr. pathology Harvard Med. Sch., 1940-41; asst. and asso. prof. pathology U. Cin., 1941-48, Mary M. Emery prof. pathology, 1948—, acting v.p. Med. Center. Cons. Armed Forces Inst. Pathology, VA, Daniel Drake, Dunham, Children's hosps. Decorated grand officer Order Daniel Carrion (Peru); recipient Townsend Harris medal Coll. City N.Y., 1968. Mem. Am. Assn. Pathologists and Bacteriologists (pres. 1963-64), Sociedad Peruana de Anatomia Patalogica (hon.), Internat. Acad. Pathology (exec. council 1962-65, pres. 1969-70), Am. Soc. Exptl. Pathology, Soc. Exptl. Biology and Medicine, Am. Soc. Clin. Pathologists (bd. dirs. 1962-68), Japanese Am. Soc. Pathologists Tokyo (hon.), Am. Assn. for Cancer Edn. (pres. elect 1970-71), Am. Assn. Univ. Profs., Am. Assn. Study Liver Disorders, Central Soc. Clin. Research, Sigma Xi, Alpha Omega Alpha. Asso. editor Am. Jour. Clin. Pathology, 1949-57; editor-in-chief Am. Jour. Pathology, 1957-66. Home: 101 Lafayette Circle Cincinnati OH 45220

GALL, EDWARD B., physician, surgeon; b. Cleve., Aug. 24, 1905; s. Edward and Emma (Schmidt) G.; A.B., Ohio State U., 1933, M.D., 1933; m. Janet M. Laudick, Sept. 16, 1935; 1 dau., Penny Lee. Intern, Meml. Hosp., Lima, O., 1933-35; resident Louisville City Hosp., 1938-40; asst. chief surgery Brown Hosp., Dayton, O., 1946-49, chief thoracic surgery, 1949- 52; pvt. practice, Dayton, 1952—; thoracic surgery staff Good Samaritan Hosp., St. Elizabeth Hosp., Miami Valley Hosp., Kettering Meml. Hosp.; cons. thoracic surgery Stillwater Sanatorium, Wright Patterson AFB, Va; instr. thoracic surgery Coll. Medicine, Ohio State U., 1954—. Served surg. staff USPHS, USCG, USN, 1941-46. Diplomate Am. Bd. Surgery, Am. Bd. Thoracic Surgery. Fellow A.C.S. Home: 515 Sweetwood Lane Dayton OH 45419 Office: 1810 Grant Deneau Tower Dayton OH 45402

GALL, JOSEPH GRAFTON, biologist, educator; b. Washington, Apr. 14, 1928; s. John Christian and Elsie (Rosenberger) G.; B.S., Yale, 1949, Ph.D., 1952; m. Dolores Marie Hogge, Sept. 17, 1955; children—Lawrence, Barbara. Faculty, U. Minn., 1952-63, prof., 1963; prof. biology and molecular biophysics Yale, 1963- -. Mem. cell biology study sec. NIH, 1963-67. Mem. A.A.A.S., Am. Soc. Cell Biology (past pres.), Genetics Soc. Am., Am. Soc. Zoologists. Contbr. articles profl. jours. Home: 3 Crestview Dr North Haven CT 06473 Office: Yale Kline Biology Tower 219 Prospect St New Haven CT 06520

GALL, LAWRENCE HOWARD, lawyer, pipeline co. exec.; b. Leesville, S.C., Dec. 17, 1917; s. John J. and Bertha (Smyer) G.; A.B., U. S.C., 1939, LL.B., 1941; m. Winifred Belle Nelson, Dec. 18, 1948; children—Sally Patricia, Linda, Constance. Admitted to S.C. bar, 1941, D.C. bar, 1948, Tex. bar, 1966, U.S. Supreme Ct. bar; mem. legal dept. E.I. duPont de Nemours & Co., Inc.; asst. to gen. counsel Remington Arms Co., Bridgeport, Conn., 1941-43; asso., then partner firm Disney & Gall, Washington, 1946-52; research dir., gen. counsel Ind. Natural Gas Assn. Am., Washington, 1952-61, exec. dir., 1961-65; v.p., gen. counsel Transcontinental Gas Pipe Line Corp., 1965—. Served to lt. (s.g.) USNR, 1943-46. Mem. Am., Fed. Power, Houston bar assns., State Bar Tex. Clubs: Petroleum (Houston); Congressional Country (Washington). Home: 643 Shartle Circle Houston TX 77024 Office: 3100 Travis St Houston TX 77006

GALL, WILLIAM RAY, banker; b. Kansas City, Mo., Oct. 15, 1927; s. Albert Ray and Adeline Glenara (Oakley) G.; B.S., U. Mo., 1951; M.B.A., U. Tulsa, 1960; grad. exec. program bus. adminstrn. Columbia, 1970; m. Laura Hudson Woods, May 23, 1953; children—Catherine, Caren. Dir. tng. and devel. Tex. Instruments, 1964-65; exec. dir. devel. So. Meth. U., 1965-67; with Republic Nat. Bank, Dallas, 1967—, sr. v.p., trust officer, mem. exec. com., 1970—; dir. Mary Kay Cosmetics, Inc. Bd. govs. Dallas Estate Council. Served with USMCR, 1945-46, 51-53. Mem. Acad. Mgmt., Bank Marketing Assn., Sigma Chi, Alpha Kappa Psi. Republican. Methodist. Clubs: Dallas, Lakewood Country (Dallas). Contbr. articles to profl. jours. Home: 11409 Snow White Dr Dallas TX 75229 Office: PO Box 5961 Dallas TX 75222

GALLACCI, ROBERT JOHN, banker; b. Port Angeles, Wash., Apr. 5, 1928; s. James John and Gladys Marie (Long) G.; student U. Wash., 1947-50; grad. U. Wis., 1966; m. Amelia E. Catania, May 27, 1960; children—Deborah, Jeffrey, Larry, Richard, Lynn. With Pacific Nat. Bank, Seattle, 1950—, asst. auditor, 1959-64, auditor, 1964-70, v.p., sr. auditor, 1970—. Served with USMCR, 1945-47, 50-52. Mem. Bank Adminstrn. Inst. (pres. Puget Sound chpt. 1963-64). Home: 1648 180th St NE Bellevue WA 98008 Office: 900 2d Av Seattle WA 98111

GALLAGAN, WILLIAM F., Jr., exec. v.p. Buckingham Corp. Address: 620 Fifth Av New York City, NY 10020*

GALLAGER, DONALD ALEXANDER, lawyer; b. Phila., Oct. 2, 1911; s. Harold M. and Elizabeth (Naugle) G.; A.B., Franklin and Marshall Coll., 1933; LL.B., U. Pa., 1936; m. Sara Jane Grundy, Mar. 10, 1951; children—D. Frederick, Stephen J., David A. Admitted to Pa. bar, 1938; partner firm Waters, Fleer, Cooper & Gallager, Norristown and Jenkintown, Pa., 1949—. Trustee, past pres. Hist. Found Montgomery Co.; trustee Asso. David Library Am. Revolution; trustee, past pres. Abington Library Soc. Served to capt. AUS, World War II. Mem. Am., Pa., Montgomery County (pres. 1967) bar. assns., Pa. Fedn. Hist. Socs. (past pres.), Hist. Soc. Montgomery Co. (trustee, past pres.), Old York Rd. Hist. Soc. (mem. exec. com., past pres.). Author, speaker hist. subjects.‡

GALLAGHER, BERNARD EDWARD, utilities exec.; b. Parsons, Pa., Mar. 27, 1908; s. John Francis and Mary (McGowan) G.; B.S., State Tchrs. Coll., Bloomsburg, Pa., 1929; M.A., Columbia, 1934; m. Louise Gabrielli, June 14, 1936; children—Marianne, Paul, David. Tchr. schs., Wilkes Barre (Pa.) Twp., 1929-30; with Consol. Edison Co. of N.Y., Inc., 1930—, asst. to chmn., 1950-56, asst. v.p., 1956-58, v.p., 1958-68, sr. v.p., 1968—. Pres. Civic Assn. of Lake Success; trustee Village of Lake Success. Home: 30 W Woods Rd Lake Success NY 11040 Office: 4 Irving Pl New York City NY 10003

GALLAGHER, BERNARD PATRICK, editor, pub.; b. N.Y.C., Feb. 25, 1910; s. Bernard A. and Mary Helen (Fitzsimmons) G.; student Columbia, 1928-29, Akron U., 1941-44; m. Harriet Denning, Oct. 17, 1942; children—Joan, Jill. Dist. mgr. Nat. Circulating Co., 1928-32; single-copy sales mgr. Crowell Pub. Co., 1932- 34; sales mgr. charge sales tng. Stenotype Co., Inc., Chgo., 1934-39; pres. Stenotype Co. Ohio, Inc., Cleve., 1939-44, World Wide Publs., Inc., N.Y.C., 1945—, Bernard P. Gallagher & Co., Inc., 1950—; editor, pub. The Gallagher Report, 1952—, The Gallagher Presidents' Report, 1965—. Mem. activities com. N.Y. Infirmary. Served with AUS, 1944-45. Mem. Nat. Better Bus. Bur., Central Registry Mag. Pubs. Assn., U.S. C. of C., Cath. Press Assn. Home: 325 E 41st St New York City, NY 10017. Office: 230 Park Av New York City NY 10017

GALLAGHER, BUELL GORDON, educator; b. Rankin, Ill., Feb. 4, 1904; s. Elmer David and Elma Maryel (Poole) G.; B.A., Carleton Coll., 1925, LL.D., 1959; B.D., Union Theol. Sem., 1929; student London Sch. Econs., 1929-30; Ph.D., Columbia, 1939, LL.D., 1954; D.D., Oberlin Coll., 1943; LL.D., Doane Coll., 1953, Lincoln U., 1954, Brandeis U., 1959, Hebrew Union U., 1961, Tuskegee Inst., 1963; Litt.D., U. Cin., 1957; L.H.D., Wagner Coll. 1954, Moravian Coll., 1958, Adelphi Coll., 1966, Alfred U., 1967, Iona Coll., 1967; D.L., U. Cin., 1967; m. June Lucille Sampson, Sept. 1, 1927; children—Helen Maryel (Mrs. Sidney S. Herman), Barbara Lucille (Mrs. F. Tomasson Jannuzi). instr., Doane Coll., 1925-26; ordained to ministry Conglist. Ch., 1929; sec. Intersem. Movement, 1930-31; pastor, Passaic, N.J., 1931-33; pres. Talladega Coll., 1933-43; prof. Christian ethics Pacific Sch. Religion, 1944-49; cons. Fed. Security Adminstrn., 1949; asst. commnr. U.S. Office Edn., 1950-52; pres. Coll. City N.Y., 1952-61, 62-69; chancellor Cal. State Colls., 1961-62. Chmn. U.S. gen. com. World Univ. Service, 1953- 57, chmn. internat. assembly, 1962-66; mem. Permanent Panel Ednl. and Corp. Relations, 1956—; commn. religion and race Nat. Council Chs., 1962—. Bd dirs. N.A.A.C.P., Knickerbocker Hosp., Youth Aid, Inc., Manhattanville Community Centers, Herman Muehlstein Found. Democratic nominee for U.S. Congress, 1948. Decorated chevalier Legion of Honor; recipient Outstanding Civilian Service medal U.S. Army, 1961; medal City N.Y., 1961; John H. Finley medal City Coll. N.Y. Alumni Assn., 1962; gold medal San Francisco Chronicle, 1961, also recipient Amistad medal, 1968. Mem. Phi Beta Kappa, Delta Sigma Rho. Author: American Caste and the Negro College, 1939; Color and Conscience, 1946; Portrait of a Pilgrim, 1946. Home: 65 Central Park W New York City NY 10023 Office: 555 Madison Av New York City NY 10022

GALLAGHER, CHARLES E., editor; b. Lowell, Mass., Oct. 29, 1898; s. Patrick Joseph and Elizabeth (Slattery) G.; student Boston U., 1917-18, Northeastern U., 1918-19; m. Irene F. Donnelly, June 29, 1925; children—Charles Edward (dec.), Andrea Farrington, Walter. Reporter, 1917-22; night editor Lowell Courier- Citizen (Mass.), 1922-33, mng. editor Lowell Leader, 1933-41; editor Lowell Jour., 1941; exec. editor Lynn Item (Mass.), 1967—. Mem. Lowell Municipal Centennial Com., 1936; chmn. Community Council, Greater Lynn United Fund; chmn. North Area div. Mass. United Community Services; pres. Neighborhood Legal Services, Lynn. Mem. Am. (bull. adv. com.), N.E. (pres. 1964) socs. newspaper editors, N.E. Asso. Press News Execs. Assn., Acad. New Eng. Journalists. Democrat. Catholic. Contbr. mags. Home: 17 Mohawk Rd Marblehead MA 01945 Office: 38 Exchange St Lynn MA 01901

GALLAGHER, CHARLES P., banker. Vice pres., also trust officer Central Bank and Trust Co. Office: 15th and Arapahoe Sts Denver CO 80217*

GALLAGHER, CORNELIUS EDWARD, congressman; b. Bayonne, N.J., Mar. 2, 1921; s. Cornelius E. and Anne (Murphy) G.; grad. John Marshall Coll., 1941; LL.B. with honors, John Marshall Law Sch., 1947; postgrad. N.Y. U., 1950; m. Claire Richter, Oct. 16, 1943; children—Diane, Christine, Patrice, Briget. Amitted to N.J. bar, 1948; practice law, Gallagher, Bayonne; mem. 86th-92d Congresses, 13th dist. N.J., mem. fgn. affairs and govt. operations coms., chmn. spl. com. on invasion of privacy; chmn. Canadian-U.S. Interparliamentary Group. Del. Disarmament Conv., Geneva, 1963-70; mem. Woodrow Wilson Commn.; mem. privacy panel Nat. Acad. Scis.; congl. adviser to Standing Com. on Peaceful Uses Seabed. Former member Faculty Rutgers University. Dir., counsel Broadway Nat. Bank. Mem. Hudson County Bd. Freeholders, 1953; commr. N.J. Turnpike Authority, 1955, vice chmn., 1956, 58. Mem. Hudson County Democratic Exec. Com., 1950—; del. Dem. Nat. Conv., 1952-68. Served from sgt. to capt., inf. AUS, World War II, Korean War. Decorated Bronze Star medal with oak leaf cluster, Purple Heart with 2 oak leaf clusters, Combat Inf. Badge, Presdl. citation. Mem. Am., N.J., Hudson County bar assns., Am. Legion, Am. Tunnel and Bridge Soc. K.C., Elk. Lectr., author articles on toll highways, individual privacy and fgn. affairs. Home: 102 W 5th St Bayonne NJ 07002 Office: House Office Bldg Washington DC 20515

GALLAGHER, D. NORA, librarian; b. N.Y.C.; d. Anthony Augustus and Helen (Branigan) Gallagher A.B., Hunter Coll., 1941; B.L.S., Columbia, 1943, postgrad. 1946-48, 49-50. Clk. Queens Borough Pub. Library, Bayside W., 1936-37; library asst. Hunter Coll. Library, N.Y.C., 1943-44; circulation librarian Adelphi U., Garden City, N.Y., 1944-45, acting librarian, 1945-46, librarian 1946—, asso. prof., 1950—. Chmn. Com. State Aid for Libraries, 1951—. Mem. Nassau County Library Assn. (chmn. program com., 1948-50, publicity com., 1950-51, 1st v.p. 1950—), A.L.A. (mem. recruitment com. 1951—), N.Y. Library Assn., Spl. Libraries Assn., Library Public Relations Council. Club: Library (N.Y.C.). Home: 1893 Andrews Av New York City NY 10453 Office: Adelphi U Garden City NY 11530

GALLAGHER, DONALD ARTHUR, educator, author; b. Union City, N.J., Nov. 9, 1914; s. John Joseph and Abigail (Whitehouse) G.; student Fordham U., 1933-34; A.B., St. Louis U., 1936, M.A., 1939; Ph.D., Marquette U., 1944; Fulbright postdoctoral fellow. U. Louvain (Belgium), 1952-53; student Cambridge (Eng.) U., 1953, U. Paris (France), 1953-54; m. Idella Smith, June 29, 1938; children—Paul, Maria Noel. Asso. editor St. Louis Catholic, 1936-40; mem. faculty Marquette U., 1939-58, asso. prof. philosophy, 1951-58; prof. philosophy, vice chmn. Villanova U., 1958-62; prof. philosophy Boston Coll., 1962—. Co-founder Cardijn Center Cath. Action, Milw., 1949. Vice pres., dir. De Rance Found., Milw., 1949—. Named Ky. col., 1962. Mem. Am. Cath. Philos. Assn. (life) exec. council 1957-60, 61-64, v.p. 1961-62, pres. 1962-63), Am. Philos. Assn., New Eng. Philosophy Edn. Soc., Am. Assn. U. Profs., Metaphys. Soc. Am., Am. Studies Assn., Assn. for Realistic Philosophy (pres., 1965—), Internat. Platform Assn., Soc. Study Ancient Philosophy, Alpha Sigma Nu, Phi Alpha Theta, Delta Epsilon Sigma, Eta Sigma Phi. Club: Fullerton (sec. 1959-62) (Phila.). Author: (with wife) The Achievement of Jacques and Raissa Maritain, a bibliography, 1962. Editor: Some Philosophers on Education, 1956; (with wife) The Education of Man: the Educational Philosophy of Jacques Maritain, 1962. Translator: (H. Bordeaux) (with wife) Edith Stein: Thoughts on Her Life and Times, 1959. Editor series Christian Culture and Philosophy, 1956—; asso. editor The New Scholasticism, 1965. Contbr. articles profl. jours., chpts. to books, encys. Home: 18 Nashoba Rd Sudbury MA 01776 Office: Boston Coll Chestnut Hill MA 02167

GALLAGHER, EDWARD GEORGE, advt. exec.; b. Lancaster, Pa., Aug. 15, 1922; s. John L. and Louise (Rohr) G.; grad. Lancaster Catholic High Sch., 1939; m. Rosa Hamaker Heckel, Dec. 27, 1945; children—Brian, Bruce, Daniel David. Retail clk. Kirk Johnson & Co., Lancaster, 1940-42; advt. mgr. Steinman Hardware Co., Lancaster, 1945-50; with CBS-TV, 1953-54; with N. W. Ayer & Son, Inc., Phila., 1951-53, 55—, exec. v.p. creative services, 1967—, also dir. Served with AUS, 1942-45. Home: 82 S Rolling Rd Springfield, PA 19064. Office: 1271 Av Americas New York City NY 10020 also NW Ayer & Son W Washington Sq Philadelphia PA 19106

GALLAGHER, EDWARD JOHN, lodging and restaurant co. exec.; b. Providence, Oct. 24, 1936; s. Farrell J. and Mary B. (Smith) G.; B.B.A., Fairfield U., 1958; m. Sarah Ann Morrison, May 2, 1964; children—Fred, Helen, Raymond. With Montgomery Ward Co., Chgo., 1958-70, asst. corporate budget mgr., 1965-67, controller Balt. catalog ty., 1967-70; dir. budgets and analyses Howard Johnson Co., Braintree, Mass., 1970, corporate controller, 1970—. Served with AUS, 1960. Home: 20 Village Green Norfolk MA 02056 Office: 250 Granite St Braintree MA 02184

GALLAGHER, EDWARD JOSEPH, oil co. exec.; b. Erie, Pa., Aug. 22, 1906; s. Alexander and Margaret (McCullough) G.; B.Sc. in Petroleum Engring., U. Pitts., 1930; m. Mary Eleanor Carnahan, Feb. 8, 1928; children—Colleen Anne (Mrs. Dennis R. Dennehy), Edward Joseph. With Gulf Oil Co., 1930-56. mgr. prodn. Canadian Gulf Oil, Calgary, Alta., 1952-56; with British Am. Oil Co., Ltd., 1956-68, gen. mgr. prodn., Calgary, 1958-64, v.p., 1964-68; v.p. Gulf Oil Can., Ltd., 1969—; pres., dir. Gulf Alberta Pipe Line Co., Ltd., Gulf Sask. Pipe Line Ltd., Rimbey Pipe Line Co. Ltd., Glen Park Gas Pipe Line Co. Ltd. Bd. dirs. local United Fund. Mem. Am. Petroleum Inst., Canadian Gas Assn., Canadian Petroleum Assn. Clubs: Petroleum, Calgary Golf and Country, Ranchmen's (Calgary). Home: 1405 Premier Way Calgary Alberta Canada Office: 707 7th Av S W Calgary 2 Alberta 23 Canada

GALLAGHER, EDWARD MICHAEL, advt. exec.; b. Rockville Center, N.Y., June 11, 1929; s. Edward M. and Louise (Jordan) G.; B.S. in Econs., Canisius Coll., 1951; M.B.A., Harvard, 1953; m. Gretchen Shirey Diehl, Apr. 18, 1959; children—Edward Michael III, Elizabeth Diehl. Sr. v.p., asst. to pres., dir. Compton Advt., Inc., 1953-66; with McCann-Erickson, Inc., 1966—, exec. v.p., dir., 1968—; pres. Marketing Pragmatics, Inc., 1968—. Democrat. Roman Cath. Clubs: Westhampton Country (Westhampton Beach, N.Y.); N.Y. Athletic. Home: 35 E 85th St New York City NY 10028 Office: 485 Lexington Av New York City NY 10017

GALLAGHER, EUGENE BERNARD, clergyman, educator; b. Perth Amboy, N.J., Dec. 12, 1910; s. Frank J. and Anna (O'Donnell) G.; student Fordham U., 1927-28, Xavier U., Cin., 1928-31; A.B., Woodstock (Md.) Coll., 1933, M.A. 1934, S.T.L., 1941, postgrad; 1953-58. Ordained priest Roman Cath. Ch., 1940; instr. English, Canisius Coll., Buffalo, 1934-37; chmn. depts. religion, Georgetown U., 1944-58, dir. pub. relations, faculty adviser student publs., 1943-48, dir. coll. debating, 1948-53; prof. theology Scranton (Pa.) U., 1959—, chmn. dept. theology, 1961-67. Lectr., Inst. Social and Religious Studies, Jewish Theol. Sem., 1951-52; chaplain Washington Council K. C., the Alhambra, Alcantara Caravan, 1955-58. Mem. Cath. Theol. Soc., Am. Mariological Soc., Am. Conf. Sci., Philosophy and Religion, N.E. Pa. Ednl. TV Assn. (incorporator, gov., exec. com. Editor Proc. National Jesuit Inst. on Coll. Religion, 1951. Contbr. articles religious publs. Office: U Scranton Scranton PA 18510

GALLAGHER, FRANCIS JOSEPH, lawyer; b. Joliet, Ill., May 28, 1901; s. Anthony J. and Catherine (Rutledge) G.; A.B., Campion Coll., 1923; J.D., U. Mich., 1926; m. Dorothy Dell Shadle, Dec. 29, 1934; children-Francis A., Loretta M. (Mrs. Donald J. Wenger), Charles P., Terrence J., Michael J., Kevin J. Admitted to Ohio bar, 1926 also Fed. Dist. Ct., U.S. Ct. of Appeals, U.S. Supreme Ct.; gen. practice law, Toledo, 1926—. Mem. Am., Ohio, Toledo (past pres.) bar assns., Am. Judicature Soc. Democrat. Roman Catholic. Lion. Clubs: Sierra Internat. (Chgo.); North Cape Yacht (LaSalle, Mich.); Toledo. Home: 2165 Evansdale Av Toledo OH 43607 Office: Libbey-Owens-Ford Bldg 811 Madison Av Toledo OH 43624

GALLAGHER, FRANK ARTHUR, lawyer; b. Lexington, Mo., Aug. 20, 1907; s. Arthur C. and Lilla (Fell) G.; B.A., U. Mont., 1934, J.D., 1934; m. Katherine M. Kelley, Dec. 10, 1936; children—James N., Richard F., Carol Ann (Mrs. Terrence Helseth). Admitted to Mont. bar, 1934; dep. county atty. Missoula, Mont., 1934-39; atty. Dept. Agr., 1939-53, atty Midwest region, 1945-53; partner firm Crowley, Kilbourne, Haughey, Hanson & Gallagher, Billings, Mont., 1953- -. Dir. Small Bus. Improvement Co., 1959—; sec. Central Park, Inc., 1965—, First Land Co., 1968—, Western Film Service Corp., 1958—. Pres., Midland Empire chpt. A.R.C., 1962-65. Alternate mem. Bd. Forest Appeals, Dept. Agr., 1966-70. Mem. Am., Mont., Yellowstone County (pres. 1969-70) bar assns., Am. Judicature Soc. Lutheran (councilman 1954-55). Home: 2611 Terrace Dr Billings MT 59102 Office: 500 Electric Bldg Billings MT 59101

GALLAGHER, HAROLD JOHN, lawyer; b. Clinton, Ia., Dec. 29, 1894; s. James A. and Ella (Walsh) G.; LL.B., Ia. State U., 1916; postgrad., Harvard, 1916-17; LL.D., St. John's U., 1954; m. Alicia Schnoebelen, Sept. 26, 1917; children—Alicia Ellen, Harold John (dec.), Katherine E. (Mrs. W. Voelker, dec.), Mary L. (Mrs. James Cremins). Admitted to Ia. bar, 1916, to N.Y. bar, 1919, since practiced in N.Y.C.; entered office of Hornblower, Miller and Garrison, 1917, became mem. firm, 1925, later firm of Willkie Farr Gallagher Walton and FitzGibbon; formerly gen. counsel S.A.L. Ry. Past pres. Am. Bar Assn. Endowment. Fellow Am. Bar Found. (dir.), Am. Coll. Trial Lawyers; mem. Am. Bar Assn. (chmn. standing com. pub. utility sect., 1934- 35, chmn. standing com. commerce, 1935-38, 48-49, mem. N.Y. State Council, 1931-36, former mem. bankruptcy com., mem. ways and means com., chmn. public utility sect., 1938-39, chmn. com. on resolutions, 1946, N.Y. State del. 1948-49, pres. 1949-50), N.Y. State Bar Assn., Assn. Bar City of New York, N.Y. Co. Lawyers' Assn., Am. Law Inst., Am. Judicature Soc., Order of Coif. Republican. Roman Catholic. Clubs: University, Recess, Blind Brook, American Yacht, Siwanoy, Wall Street. Home: 5 Elm Rock Rd Bronxville NY 10708 Office: 1 Chase Manhattan Plaza New York City NY 10005

GALLAGHER, HELEN, actress, singer, dancer; b. Bklyn., 1926; student Am. Ballet Sch.; m. Frank Wise, Oct. 14, 1956. Debut in Seven Lively Arts, N.Y.C., 1947; appeared in plays Mr. Strauss Goes to Boston, 1945, Billion Dollar Baby, 1945, Brigadoon, 1947, High Button Shoes, 1947, Tough and Go, 1949, Make a Wish, 1951, Pal Joey, 1952, Hazel Flagg, 1953, Annie Get Your Gun, 1954, Guys and Dolls, 1955, Finian's Rainbow, 1955, Pajama Game, 1954, Brigadoon, 1957, Portofino, 1958, Oklahoma!, 1958, Guys and Dolls, 1958; toured with Bus Stop, 1956; appeared on TV in Shangri-La, Hallmark Hall of Fame, 1960, Colgate Comedy Hour, Ed Sullivan Show, Kraft Television Theatre; performed at nightclubs including Thunderbird, Las Vegas, 1951, Mocambo, Hollywood, Cal., 1951, Persian Room, Plaza Hotel, N.Y.C., 1954, revue Too Good for the Average Man, Camelot, N.Y.C., 1960. Recipient Tony award as best actress in musical for No, No Nannette, 1970. Address: 46th St Theatre 228 W 46th St New York City NY 10036*

GALLAGHER, HERBERT KEMP, architect; b. Vancouver, B.C., Can., Nov. 10, 1926; s. Walter Manuel and Irma (Kemp) G.; came to U.S., 1950, naturalized, 1960; student U. B.C., 1944-45; B.Arch., U. Wash., 1949; postgrad. Pa. State U., 1953; m. Christina Hamilton, May 15, 1950; children—Lauren Beth, Bruce Hamilton, Jeffrey David. Practiced in Vancouver, 1950-52; lectr. archtl. design U. B.C., 1950-52; research on bldg. problems Nat. Research Council Can. for Pacific Coast region, 1952-53, on bldg. materials and thermal characteristics of materials Engring. Research Sta., Pa. State U., 1953-54; with Architects Collaborative, Cambridge, Mass., 1954—, v.p., 1967- -, also dir.; founder, 1968, since dir. Instructional Game Materials, Inc.; prin. in charge Tufts New Eng. Med. Center, Boston, 1964—; prin. works include innovative ednl. instns. Chmn. planning bd., Stow, Mass., 1963-64. Mem. Am. Inst. Architects, Boston Soc. Architects, Royal Archtl. Inst. Can. Home: 56 Orchard Lane Wayland MA 01778 Office: 46 Brattle St Cambridge MA 02138

GALLAGHER, HUBERT R., govtl. cons.; b. Salida, Colo., Jan. 8, 1907; s. Hugh and Margaret (Dinsmore) G.; A.B., Stanford U., 1929; M.S., Syracuse U., 1930; m. Luthera Wakefield, July 29, 1930; children—Hugh, Janet. Instr., Syracuse (N.Y.) U., 1930; asst. prof. Stanford U., 1932; research cons., later asso. dir., council of state govts., 1933-50; asso. dir. state div. Nat. Def. Commn., 1940-41; chmn. Internat. Bd. of Inquiry for Great Lakes Fisheries, 1940; office dir. OCDM and Office Emergency Planning, exec. office of Pres., 1950-69; spl. cons. Nat. Gov.'s Conf. and Council State Govts., 1969—. Mem. Am. Soc. Pub. Adminstrn. (past pres. Washington), Delta Tau Delta; hon. scholastic frats. Presbyn. Author: Crime Prevention (Syracuse U., 1930); Report of International Board of Inquiry for the Great Lakes Fisheries (U.S. Govt., Dept. of State, 1943). Editor: The Book of the States (Council of State Govts., 1943). Contbr. articles in profl. mags. Home: 5416 Burling Rd Bethesda MD 20014 Office: 1735 De Sales St Washington DC 20036

GALLAGHER, J. WES, journalist; b. San Francisco, Oct. 6, 1911; s. James and Chispa (Howard) G.; student U. San Francisco, 1929, 1931; B.A., La. State U., 1935; m. Betty L. Kelley, June 1, 1946; children—Brian, Jane, Christine. Reporter Baton Rouge State Times, 1935, Rochester (N.Y.) Democrat and Chronicle, 1935-36; with A.P., 1937—), editor, Buffalo, 1937-39, Albany, N.Y., 1939, N.Y.C., 1939, became fgn. corr., 1940, chief of mil. staff for African Invasion 1942, chief invasion staff for France, 1944, acting chief Paris bur., 1945, chief bur. in Germany, 1945-51, gen. exec., N.Y.C., 1951- 54, asst. gen. mgr., 1954-62, gen. mgr., 1962—; chmn. The Asso. Press, Ltd.; pres. Press Assn., Inc., La Prensa Asociada, City News Assn., The Asso. Press Can., World Wide Photos, Inc.; shareholder The Asso. Press Norway, The Asso. Press Belgium. Selected one of the outstanding young men in the U.S., U.S. C. of C., 1945; recipient William Allan White award, 1967; John Peter Zenger award U. Ariz., 1968; Carvan Anda award Ohio U., 1969; George Polk award L.I. U., 1969. Fellow Sigma Delta Chi. Clubs: Apawamis (Rye, N.Y.); Overseas Press. Author: Back Door to Berlin, 1943. Home: 4 Hook Rd Rye NY 10580 Office: 50 Rockefeller Plaza New York City NY 10020

GALLAGHER, JAMES J., educator; B.S., U. Pitts., 1948; M.S., Pa. State U., 1950, Ph.D. in Clin. and Child Psychology, 1951. Chief psychologist Dayton (O.) Hosp. Disturbed Children, 1951-52; asst. prof. Mich. State U., also asst. dir. Psychol. Center, 1952-54; prof. edn., asso. dir. Inst. Research Exceptional Children, U. Ill. at Urbana, 1954-66, dir. Acad. Year Inst. for Gifted, 1963-64; U.S. asso. commr. edn.; chief bur. edn. for handicapped U.S. Office Edn., 1967-70; Kenan prof. edn., dir. Frank Porter Graham Child Devel. Center, 1970—. Chmn. adv. council on gifted for Ill.; mem. Ill. Com. Emotionally Disturbed; adv. com. div. handicapped children and youth U.S. Office Edn., also mem. project rev. bd. Mem. Council Exceptional Children (chmn. publs. com.), Am. Psychol. Assn., Ill. Council Exceptional Children, Am. Ednl. Research Assn., Am. Soc. Curriculum Devel. Author: Analysis of Research on the Education of Gifted Children, 1960; Tutoring of Brain-Injured Mentally Retarded Children, 1960; Teaching the Gifted Child, 1964; also chpts. in books, monographs, articles, revs. Editor: Teaching the Gifted Child: A Book of Readings, 1964. Asso. editor Exceptional Children. Home: 9415 Linden Av Bethesda MD 20014 Office: US Office Edn Washington DC 20203

GALLAGHER, JAMES JOSEPH, Jr., educator, lawyer; b. Bryn Mawr, Pa., Nov. 6, 1926; s. James Joseph and Grace (McCarthy) G.; B.A., Albright Coll., Reading, Pa., 1950; LL.B., U. Pa., 1953; m. Mary Diane Bechtel, Feb. 14, 1953; children—Kevin, Sean, Kerry. Admitted to Pa. bar, 1954; asst. prof. Wharton Sch. Finance and Commerce, U. Pa., 1952-62; asst. to dir., joint com. continuing legal edn. Am. Law Inst. and Am. Bar Assn., 1962-63; v.p. Pub. Fidelity Life Ins. Co., 1963-65; prof., head law dept. Drexel U., Phila., 1965—; cons. in field, 1954—. Mem. Lynnewood Park Civic Assn. Served with AUS, 1945-46. Recipient Distinguished Tchr. award U. Pa., 1959; scroll of appreciation Am. Coll. Life Underwriters, 1965; Outstanding Edn. award Beta Nu, Drexel U., 1966-67; Pedagogue award Commerce and Engring. Sch., Drexel U., 1968; Outstanding Achievement award Sr. Class, Drexel U., 1968; Pre-Jr. Class Appreciation award Drexel U., 1969. Mem. Am Contract Bridge League (life master), Sigma Tau Delta, Pi Gamma Mu. Democrat. Roman Catholic. Clubs: Lawyers (Phila.); Drexelbrook (Drexelhill, Pa.). Home: 1739 Tyson Rd Havertown, PA 19083. Office: Drexel U Philadelphia PA 19104

GALLAGHER, JAMES ROSWELL, physician; b. New Haven, May 7, 1903; s. John Currier and Bessie (Radigan) G.; B.A., Yale, 1925, M.D., 1930; m. Constance R. Dann, July 12, 1926; 1 son, John Currier. Intern med. sevice New Haven Hosp., 1929- 31; chief med. resident Pa. Hosp., Phila., 1931-32; instr. cardiology Grad. Sch. Medicine, U. Pa., 1932-34; sch. physician Hill Sch., Pottstown, Pa., 1932-34. Phillips Acad., Andover, Mass., 1934-50; cons. medicine Children's Hosp., Boston, 1948-51, chief adolescents' unit, 1951-67, chief emeritus, 1968—; college physician Wesleyan U., Middletown, Conn., 1950-51; mem. faculty Harvard Med. Sch., 1953-67, clin. prof. pediatrics, 1965-67; cons. Jewish Hosp., Bklyn., 1963—, clin. prof. pediatrics Yale Med. Sch., 1967—. Mem. nat. health and safety com. Boy Scouts Am., 1945—; liaison rep. Am. Acad. Pediatrics, 1959—. Bd. overseers Boys Club Boston, 1956-68. Mem. A.M.A. (mem. com. exercise and fitness 1964—), A.C.P., Am. Acad. Pediatrics, Am., New Eng. pediatric socs., Am. Pub. Health Assn., Mass. Med. Soc., Soc. for Irish, Medicine (pres. 1968-70), Irish Am. pediatric socs. Clubs: Harvard, Yale (N.Y.C.); Graduates (New Haven). Author: Understanding Your Son's Adolescence, 1951; (with H. I. Harris) Emotional Problems of Adolescents, 1958; Medical Care of the Adolescent, 1961; (with Hallock and Goldberger) Health for Life, 1961. Home: 67 Mill Rock Rd New Haven, CT 06511.

GALLAGHER, JAMES WES, press exec.; b. San Francisco, Oct. 6, 1911; s. James and Chispa (Howard) G.; B.A., U. San Francisco, 1931; postgrad. La. State U., 1935; m. Betty L. Kelley, June 1, 1946; children—Brian, Jane, Christine. Reporter, Baton Rouge State Times, 1935; reporter Rochester (N.Y.) Democrat and Chronicle, 1935-36; with A.P., 1937—, editor, Buffalo, 1937-39, Albany, 1939, N.Y.C., 1939, became fgn. corr., 1940, chief mil. staff African invasion, 1942, chief invasion staff for France, 1944, acting chief Paris Bur., 1945, chief bur. in Germany, 1945-51, gen. exec. A.P., N.Y.C., 1951-54, asst. gen. mgr., 1954-62, gen. mgr., 1962- -. Chmn. A.P., Ltd.; pres. Press Assn., Inc., La Prensa Asociada, City News Assn., A.P. Can., World Wide Photos, Inc.; dir. A.P. Norway, A.P. Belgium. Recipient William Allan White award, 1967; George Polk award L.I. U., 1969; Carr Van Anda award Ohio U., 1969; Peter Zenger award Ariz. U., 1969; named One of Outstanding Young Men in U.S., U.S. C. of C., 1945. Fellow Sigma Delta Chi. Clubs: Apawamis (Rye, N.Y.); Burning Tree (Bethesda, Md.). Author: Back Door to Berlin, 1943. Home: 4 Hook Rd Rye NY 10580 Office: 50 Rockefeller Plaza New York City NY 10020

GALLAGHER, JESSE LEROY, labor union ofcl.; b. Cleve., Feb. 27, 1909; s. John and Caroline (Williams) G.; ed. pub. schs.; m. Geraldine Audrey Knight, Nov. 24, 1933; children—John William, Patricia (Mrs. Robert Thinschmidt). Bus. rep., then internat. rep. Laundry Workers Internat. Union, 1933-37; organizer A.F.L., 1937-48, regional dir. for Ohio, 1948-54, Ky. and Ohio, A.F.L.-C.I.O., 1953-56, Ohio, Ky., and W.Va., 1956—. Mem. labor adv. com. Cleve. United Appeal, 1960—; adv. council Am. Arbitration Assn., 1965—; mem. appeals bd. No. Ohio dist. SSS, 1966—. Adv. bd. Sch. Applied Social Sci., Western Res. U., 1945- 50, St. John Coll. Adult Edn., 1954—; trustee Cleve. Welfare Fedn., 1950-59, Cleve. Ch. Fedn., 1945-55. Mem. U.S. Power Squadron. Republican. Episcopalian. Mason. Home: 20609 Hilliard Rd Rocky River OH 44116 Office: Leader Bldg Cleveland OH 44114

GALLAGHER, JOHN BENTLEY, banker; b. St. Paul, Nov. 9, 1894; s. Michael William and Julia (Bentley) G.; LL.B., St. Paul Coll., 1916; m. Anastasia Murphy, June 1, 1921. Practiced law, St. Paul, 1916-17; engaged in banking, 1917-18, 1919-22; in U.S. Navy, 1918-19; with War Finance Corp., Washington, 1922-25; practiced law, Mpls., 1925-28; became pres. Chgo. Joint Stock Land Bank, agrl. loans, 1928; chmn. exec. com. Western Power And Gas Co.; dir. Central Life Ins. Co., Mpls. Gas Co., Brinks, Inc., C. M., St. P. & P.R.R.; mem. adv. com. Chgo. Dist. Reconstrn. Finance Corp. Trustee Chgo., N. Shore and Milw. R.R. Dir. Arlington Park Jockey Club. Republican. Roman Catholic. Clubs: Attic, Tavern (Chgo.); Everglades (Palm Beach, Fla.). Home: 1448 Lake Shore Dr Chicago IL 60611 Office: 120 S LaSalle St Chicago IL 60603

GALLAGHER, JOHN FRANCIS, Jr., merchandising exec.; b. Middleton, Wis., Oct. 15, 1918; s. John Francis and Katherine Elliott (Morris) G.; Ph.B., U. Wis., 1940; m. Claire Kathryn Vaughn, Dec. 16, 1942; children—Susan Marie, Michael John, Gregory Vaughn. With Sears, Roebuck and Co., 1940—, beginning as salesman, Beloit, Wis., successively staff asst. personnel dept., Chgo., personnel recruitment for Sears expansion into Latin Am., mgr. fgn. adminstrn., 1940-55, pres. Sears-Venezuelan subsidiary, 1955-60, v.p. internat. operations, 1960—; dir. Simpson-Sears, Globe Union, Brascan, Ltd. Vice chairman Council of Americas; mem. Nat. Export Expansion Council;

mem. Gov.'s Adv. Council for State of Ill. Trustee Milton Coll., Pan Am. Devel. Found.; mem. U. Wis. Found.; bd. dirs. Mid-Am. Com. for Internat. Bus. and Govt. Cooperation. Served to maj. AUS, 1942-46. Mem. U.S. C. of C. (mem. Mexican-U.S. com.), Council Fgn. Relations, Sao Paulo Ill. Partners Alliance. Nat. Planning Assn. (mem. Canadian-Am. com.), Am. C. of C. in Venezuela (past pres.), N. Am. Assn. Venezuela (past dir.). Clubs: North Shore Country; Internat. Trade of Chicago. Home: 841 Appletree Lane Glenview IL 60025 Office: 7401 Skokie Blvd Skokie IL 60076

GALLAGHER, JOHN PATRICK, oil co. exec.; b. Winnipeg, Man., Can., July 16, 1916; s. James and Constance Mary (Burdett) G.; B.Sc. in Geology, U. Man., 1937; grad. Advanced Mgmt. Program, Harvard, 1948; m. Kathleen Marjorie Stewart, Aug. 20, 1949; children—James Stewart, Thomas Patrick, Frederic Michael. Mem. Canadian Geol. Survey, 1936-37; with Shell Oil Co., 1938, Standard Oil Co. N.J., 1939-48, Imperial Oil Ltd., Calgary, Alta., 1950-52, pres., 1953—, also dir. Mem. Am. Assn. Petroleum Geologists. Home: 4315 Britannia Dr Calgary Alberta Canada Office: 706 7th Av S W Calgary 2 Alberta Canada

GALLAGHER, JOHN PIRIE, corp. exec.; b. Chgo., Oct. 12, 1916; s. Edward and Elsie (Pirie) G.; student Northwestern U., 1934-40; M.B.A., U. Chgo., 1947; m. Penny Boyer, Sept. 13, 1940; children—David A., Kathe L., Laurie S. (Mrs. Michael Stone), Steven R. With Commonwealth Edison Co., Chgo., 1934-46; partner, v.p. Booz, Allen and Hamilton, Inc., Chgo., 1946-63; dir. McKinsey and Co., Chgo., 1963-68; pres., chmn. Chemetron Corp., Chgo., 1968—, also dir., mem. exec. com.; dir. AMSTED Industries, Midwest Carbide Corp. Bd. dirs. Community Renewal Soc. Chgo., 1961—, pres., 1965-68. Mem. council Grad. Sch. Bus., U. Chgo., 1960—; trustee Ill. Inst. Tech.; bd. advisers Lake Forest Coll. Mem. Beta Gamma Sigma. Mem. Hinsdale Union Ch. (trustee). Home: 420 E 3d St Hinsdale IL 60521 Office: 840 N Michigan Av Chicago IL 60611

GALLAGHER, RAYMOND JOSEPH, bishop; b. Cleve., Nov. 19, 1912; s. Hugh and Ella (Reedy) G.; B.A. John Carroll U., Cleve., 1934; student St. Mary's Sem., Cleve., 1939; M.S.W., Loyola U., Chgo., 1948. Ordained priest Roman Catholic Ch., 1939; asst. pastor St. Colman Ch., Cleve., 1939-44; dir. Cath. Youth Service Bur., Cleve., 1948-55; dir. St. Anthony's Home For Boys, Cleve., 1949- 61; sec. Nat. Conf. Cath. Charities, Washington, 1961-65; bishop of Lafayette (Ind.), 1965—. Founder Cath. Big Brothers, Cleve., 1951, Cath. Child Guidance Clinic, Cleve., 1953, Don Bosco Sch. For Boys, Cleve., 1957; vice chmn. White House Conf. Children and Youth, 1960; mem. exec. planning com. White House Conf. Aging, 1961; vice chmn., mem. nat. exec. com. Citizens Crusade Against Poverty. Bd. dirs. Nat. Council Aging, United Community Funds and Councils Am., Nat. Social Welfare Assembly, Nat. Housing Conf.; trustee Nat. Council Crime and Delinquency. Served to lt. USNR. 1944-46. Recipient Alumni award Loyola U., Chgo., 1960. Mem. Nat. Cath. Edn. Assn. (pres.-gen. 1968—), Alpha Sigma Nu. Address: 610 Lingle Av Lafayette, IN 47902.

GALLAGHER, THOMAS, judge; b. Faribault, Minn., Nov. 24, 1897; s. Patrick James and Helena (McCall) G.; ed. St. Thomas Acad., St. Paul, 1912-14; A.B., U. Minn., 1918, LL.B., 1921; m. Elizabeth Jane Gillum, Aug. 19, 1931; children—Sharon E. (Walsh), Thomas Patrick, Michael John, Robert Brian. Admitted to Minn. bar, 1921, practiced in Mpls., 1921-43; asso. justice Supreme Ct. Minn., 1943—. Referee, Nat. R.R. Adjustment Bd., 1945, 47, 50; mem. Presdl. Emergency Bd. G. T. Ry. and Nat. Maritime Union, 1948, T. & P. Ry. and Brotherhood Locomotive Engrs., 1950, Atlantic & E. Carolina Ry. Co and sixteen r.r. labor orgns., 1950. Dem. nominee for gov. of Minn., 1938. Served as 2d lt. F.A., U.S. Army, 1918. Mem. Minn., Hennepin County bar assns., Minn. Safety Council (pres. 1961- 63), U. Minn. Law Sch. Alumni Assn. (pres. 1959-60), Alpha Sigma Phi, Phi Delta Phi. Scabbard and Blade, Am. Legion, Forty and Eight, Home: 2200 Newton Av S Minneapolis MN 55405 Address: Supreme Court Chambers St Paul MN 55101

GALLAGHER, THOMAS FRANCIS, biochemist; b. Chgo., Dec. 29, 1905; s. Thomas Francis and Catherine Margaret (Regan) G.; A.B., Fordham, 1927; Ph.D., U. Chgo., 1931; m. Beatrice Marie Sheehan, July 21, 1930; children—Thomas Francis, Brian Boru, Michael Jerome. Successively research asso., asst. prof. and asso. prof. biochemistry U. Chgo., 1930-47; chief divs. steroid bio-chemistry, steroid metabolism Sloan-Kettering Inst., N.Y.C., 1947-63; chief Inst. Steroid Research, Montefiore Hosp., N.Y.C., 1963—. Gen. Edn. Bd. fellow Free City of Danzig and Berlin, Germany, 1936-37. Mem. Am. Soc. Biol. Chemists, Am. Chem. Soc., Am. Assn. Cancer Research, Soc. Exptl. Biology and Medicine. Author articles in profl. jours. Home: 136 E 64th St New York City NY 10021 Office: Inst Steroid Research Montefiore Hosp 111 E 210th St New York City NY 10034

GALLAGHER, VERNON FRANCIS, assn. exec.; b. Pitts., Sept. 26, 1914; s. Francis J. and Bertha (Noe) G.; A.B., B.D., Holy Ghost Sem., Norwalk, Conn., 1940: M.A., U. Pa., 1942. Ph.D., 1952. Ordained priest Roman Cath. Ch., 1939; faculty St. Joseph's High Sch., Phila., 1939-43; asst. prof. English, Duquesne U., Pitts., 1943-45, asst. dean coll. arts and sci., 1945-46, coll. dean, 1946-50. univ. v.p., 1946-50, pres., 1950-59, chmn. bd., 1959-67, now mem. bd. Asso. dir. Pontifical Assn. Holy Childhood, 1969—; chmn. edn. study commn. Diocese of Pitts., 1968—. Mem. Modern Langs. Assn. K.C. Address: 800 Allegheny Av Pittsburgh, PA 15212.

GALLAHGER, MATTHEW PETER, Jr., financial exec.; b. Bklyn., Aug. 21, 1928; s. Matthew Peter and Veronica (Powers) G.; B.S., Seton Hall U., 1950; m. Mary Louise Shields, Nov. 13, 1954; children—Maureen, Christine, Matthew Peter III, Sheila. Plant accountant Daystrom, Inc., Elizabeth, N.J., 1950-53; cost accountant Lanston, Inc., Phila., 1953-54; auditor Peat, Marwick, Mitchell & Co., Phila., 1954-61; audit supr. CIT Financial Corp., N.Y.C., 1961-65; with Diners Club, Inc., N.Y.C., 1965—, controller, 1966—, treas., 1967—, v.p., 1968—. C.P.A. Mem. Am. Inst. C.P.A.'s, Nat. Assn. Accountants. Home: 132 Cottage Pl Ridgewood NJ 07450 Office: 10 Columbus Circle New York City NY 10019

GALLAHUE, DUDLEY RICHARD, retired bus. exec.; b. Richmond, Ind., Feb. 24, 1898; s. Philip M. and Pearl Marie (Teague) G. Ins. examiner Ind., 1918-19; with bro. E. F. Gallahue organized Am. States Ins. Co., 1929, chmn. bd., treas., 1947- 63; past dir. Mchts. Nat. Bank & Trust Co., Pub. Service Co. Ind.; chmn. bd., treas. Am. Economy Life Ins. Co., 1959-63, Am. States Life Ins. Co., 1957-63; retired from ins., 1963; now engaged in investments. Hon. bd. dirs. Boys Club Indpls.; hon. mem. Girl Scouts Am. Recipient Wisdom award. Mem. Indpls. Bd. Trade, C. of C., Children's Mus., Art Assn. Indpls., S.A.R., Ind. Soc. Chgo., Council of Sagamores of Wabash, Newcomen Soc. N.Am. Mason (32, Shriner). Clubs: University, Indpls. Athletic, Columbia, Dramatic Players, Lambs, Woodstock (Indpls.); Athenaeum; Traders Point Hunt. Home: 4404 N Meridian St Indianapolis, IN 46208.

GALLAHUE, EDWARD FRANCIS, former ins. exec.; b. Indpls., May 12, 1902; s. Philip M. and Pearl Marie (Teague) G.; ed. pub. schs., Indpls.; L.H.D., Boston U., 1956, Earlham Coll., 1957; LL.D., De Pauw U., 1961; m. Dorothy V. Fitzpartick, Oct. 31, 1943; 1 dau., Gloria Ann. Organized with Dudley Richard Gallahue, Am. States Ins. Co., Indpls., 1929, pres., 1947-63; pres. Am. States Life Ins. Co., Am. Economy Ins. Co., until 1963. Trustee, chmn. gifts and bequests com. Butler U.; pres. Indpls. Hosp. Devel. Assn., 1950-61, dir., mem. exec. com., 1950—; pres. Ind. Assn. Mental Health, 1948-50; bd. dirs. Yokefellow Assos., 1954-61; trustee Meth. Hosp., Ind. Found. of Meth. Ch., Menninger Found., Topeka; sponsor Edward Gallahue Confs. on Religion and Psychiatry at Menninger Found., Edward F. Gallahue World Religions Conf. at Princeton Theol. Sem. Recipient citations Ind. Assn. Mental Health, Indpls. Med. Soc., Indpls. Hosp. Devel. Assn.; Ind. U. Hall Fame in philanthropy. Mem. S.A.R., Soc. Cincinnati. Methodist. Mason (32). Clubs: Indianapolis Athletic, Columbia, University, Dramatic, Lambs, Woodstock, Meridian Hills Country, Traders Point Hunt, Crooked Stick Country. Author: Edward's Odyssey (autobiography), 1970. Home: 200 Forest Blvd Indianapolis IN 46240 (winter) Boca Raton FL 33432 Office: 1010 E 86th St Indianapolis IN 46240

GALLALEE, JACK CAULKINS, lawyer; b. Lookout Mountain, Tenn., Aug. 13, 1918; s. John Morin and Lua (Caulkins) G.; A.B., U. Ala. 1939. LL.B., 1941; m. Jeppie Blacksher Adams, Mar. 17, 1951; children—Margaret Vaughn, John Adams. Admitted to Ala. bar, 1941, since practiced in Mobile; mem. firm Gallalee Denniston & Edington, and predecessors, 1947—. Pres., Acreage Devel., Inc., Gen. Securities, Inc., Mem. exec. com. Estate Planning Council Mobile, 1966-67, 70; mem. Mobile County Sch. Bd. Commnrs., 1961-66, pres., 1964-66; pres. Mobile Tb Assn., 1956. Bd. dirs. Ala. Tb Assn. Mem. Ala. Ho. of Reps., 1950-54. Served with AUS, 1941-46, 50- 51. Mem. Historic Mobile Preservation Soc., Mobile County Wildlife and Conservation Assn., Am., Ala., Mobile County (pres. 1966) bar assns., Newcomen Soc., Ala. Hist. Assn., U. Ala. Alumni Assn., Mobile C. of C., Phi Beta Kappa, Omicron Delta Kappa, Delta Kappa Epsilon. Clubs: Mobile Country, Athelstan. Home: 143 Myrtlewood Lane Mobile AL 36608 Office: 50 Emanuel St Mobile AL 36602

GALLAN, GORDON JENNINGS, publisher; b. Boston, July 13, 1905 s. Frank Agustus and Elizabeth (Jennings) G.; m. Dorothy Estelle Young, Oct. 3, 1931; children—Bruce Floyd, Diane Joan, Cheryl Lee. Chmn. exec. com. G. & C. Merriam Co., Springfield, Mass., 1952-69, pres., 1953-69, dir., 1952—, also cons.; trustee Springfield 5 Savs. Bank; dir. First Bank and Trust Co., Springfield. Cons. Ency. Brit. Episcopalian. Mason. Home: 125 Pleasantview Av Longmeadow MA 01106 Office: 47 Federal St Springfield MA 01105

GALLAND, GEORGE FREEMAN, lawyer; b. Wilkes-Barre, Pa., Nov. 8, 1910; s. Abram Strauss and Martha (Freeman) G.; A.B., Cornell U., 1931; LL.B., Harvard, 1934; m. Marion Isabel Gibbs, Nov. 11, 1938; children—Anne (Mrs. Carlos Chacon, Jr.), George Freeman. Admitted to N.Y. bar, 1936, D.C. bar, 1951; practice in N.Y.C., 1936-41, Washington, 1941—; with firm Chadbourne, Stanchfield & Levy, 1936-41; divisional counsel OPA, 1941-43; with Office of Solicitor, U.S. Maritime Commn., 1946-51; partner Becker, Maguire & Galland, 1951-55, Galland, Kharasch, Calkins & Brown, 1955—. Served to lt. USNR, 1943-46. Mem. Maritime Adminstrv. Bar Assn. Washington (past pres.). Clubs: Jefferson Islands (past pres.), Army-Navy (Washington); Whitehall (N.Y.C.). Home: 1403 Bishop Lane Alexandria VA 22302 Office: Canal Sq 1054 31st St NW Washington DC 20007

GALLAND, RICHARD I., oil co. exec., lawyer; b. Denver, Oct. 13, 1916; s. Raymond F. and Mabel (Wilson) G.; A.B., Yale, 1937, LL.B., 1940; m. Alice Halstead, July 21, 1941; children—Richard I., Holley, John H. Admitted to N.Y. bar, 1940, asso. Cravath, deGersdorff, Swaine and Wood, N.Y.C., 1940-43, Cravath, Swaine & Moore, 1946-50; chief counsel Mathieson Chem. Corp., 1950-55; v.p., gen. counsel Colo. Oil and Gas Corp., 1955-58; pres. Am. Petrofina Co. of Tex., 1958—; pres. Am. Petrofina, Inc., 1969- -. Served as lt. (j.g.) USNR, 1943-46. Home: 4647 Miron Rd Dallas, TX 75220. Office: PO Box 2159 Dallas TX 75221

GALLAS, JACK ALBERT, banker; b. Chgo., Dec. 19, 1926; s. Albert John and Anna (Nelson) G.; B.S.L., Northwestern U., 1950, J.D., 1952; m. Barbara A. Barringer, May 23, 1953; 1 dau., Anne Reed. Admitted to Ill. bar, 1952; atty. Office Gen. Counsel, Dept. Agr., Chgo., 1955-59; with LaSalle Nat. Bank, Chgo., 1952-55, 59—, v.p., 1966-69, sr. v.p., 1969—; mem. faculty Nat. Trust Sch., Am. Bankers Assn., 1962-69. Served with U.S. 1945-46. Mem. Delta Upsilon, Phi Delta Phi. Clubs: University, Economic (Chgo.). Home: 2633 Broadway Av Evanston IL 60201 Office: 135 S LaSalle St Chicago IL 60603

GALLAWAY, ROBERT DRAPER, airline exec.; b. N.Y.C., Dec. 31, 1933; s. Robert W. and Grace (Draper) G.; grad. Hotchkiss Sch., 1951; B.A., Yale, 1955; M.B.A., Harvard, 1961; m. Gay Williams, Dec. 26, 1955; 1 dau., Robin. Financial analyst Litton Industries, 1962; controller transp. div. Trans World Airlines, 1963-68; v.p. aquisitions Gen. Host Corp., 1968; gen. mgr. Brit. W. Indian Airways, 1968-69; exec. v.p., system gen. mgr. Frontier Airlines, 1969—. Mem. metro transp. steering com. Denver C. of C. Mem. adv. com. Children's Hosp., Denver. Served to capt. USMCR, 1955-59. Clubs: Harvard Business (Denver); Yale (N.Y.C.). Home: 4061 S Cherry St Englewood CO 80110 Office: 5900 E 39th Av Denver CO 80207

GALLEN, JOHN JAMES, coll. dean; b. Phila., Nov. 21, 1905; s. Harry S. and Kathryn M. (Stewart) G.; B.S. in Civil Engring., Villanova U., 1927, C.E., 1929, Dr. Engring., 1968; M.S. in Civil Engring., U. Pa., 1947; m. Frances L. Fitzgerald, May 1, 1937; children—John J., Robert M., Frances L., Kevin P., Kathyn M., Raymond J., Elaine A. Constrn. engr. Pa. R.R., 1927-32; instr. math. Roman Cath. High Sch., Phila., 1932-35; sr. engr. WPA, 1936; maintenance supr., purchasing agt. to supt. schs., Diocese Phila., 1936-40; mem. faculty Villanova (Pa.) U., 1940- -, prof. civil engring., 1949—, dean Coll. Engring., 1961—. Cons. engr., Phila., 1946-60. Exec. sec. John McKee Scholarship Com., 1957—; chmn. United Fund drive Villanova U., 1963. Recipient Lindbach Distinguished Teaching award Villanova U., 1961. Registered profl. engr., Pa. Fellow Am. Soc. C.E. (pres. Phila. 1961-62); mem. Franklin Inst., Engrs. Club Phila., Am. Soc. Engring. Edn., Nat., Pa. (Engr. of Year, Delaware County 1968) socs. profl. engrs. Home: 643 Lawson Av Havertown PA 19083 Office: Villanova Univ Villanova PA 19085

GALLER, SIDNEY ROLAND, govt. ofcl.; b. Balt., Nov. 9, 1922; s. Samuel D. and Ann (Brownstone) G.; grad. Balt City Coll., 1940; Ph.D., U. Md., 1948. Cons. ecology Office Naval Research, 1948-50, head biology br., 1950-65; asst. sec. sci. Smithsonian Instn., 1965-70; dep. asst. sec. commerce for sci. and tech. (environmental affairs), Dept. Commerce, Washington, 1970—. Recipient Navy Civilian Service award, 1963, Distinguished Civilian Service award Sec. Navy, 1965. Fellow A.A.A.S., Marine Tech. Soc., Md. Acad. Scis.; mem. Am. Soc. Limnology and Oceanography, Research Soc. Am., Natural History Soc. Md., Am. Inst. Biol. Scis., Sigma Xi. Club: Cosmos (Washington). Contbr. articles profl. jours. Designer oceanographic research ships, center for short-lived phenomena, orbitting satellite animal tracking systems. Home: 6242 Woodcrest Av Baltimore, MD 21209. Office: Dept of Commerce Washington DC 20230

GALLETTI, PIERRE MARIE, physiologist; b. Monthey, Switzerland, June 11, 1927; s. Henri and Yvonne (Chamorel) G.; M.D., U. Lausanne (Switzerland), 1951, Ph.D., 1954; m. Sonia Aidan, Dec. 31, 1959; 1 son, Marc Henri. Research fellow Inst. for Med. Research Cedars of Lebanon Hosp., Los Angeles, 1957-58; mem. faculty Emory U., Atlanta, 1958-67, prof. physiology, 1962-67; prof., chmn. div. med. sci. Brown U., Providence, 1967—. E. Roosevelt fellow Internat. Union Against Cancer, U. Palermo, Italy, 1964-65. Fellow Am. Coll. Cardiology (gov. R.I. 1968-71); mem. Am. Physiol. Soc., A.A.A.S., Swiss Physiol. and Pharmacological Soc., Biomed. Engring. Soc., Am. Heart Assn., I.E.E.E., Am. Soc. Artificial Internal Organs (pres. 1969- 70). Author: (with G.A. Brecher) Heart-Lung Bypass: Principles and Techniques of Extra-corporeal Circulation, 1962; also numerous articles. Research on design, devel., technique of application artificial hearts, lungs, kidneys, placentas; enhancement of drug action. Home: 36 Taber Av Providence RI 02906

GALLICO, PAUL WILLIAM, writer; b. N.Y.C., July 26, 1897; s. Paolo and Hortense (Erlich) G.; B.S., Columbia, 1921; m. Alva Thoits Taylor, Sept. 5, 1921 (div. 1934); children—William Taylor, Robert Leston; m. 2d, Elaine St. Johns, Apr. 12, 1935 (div. 1936); m. 3d, Baroness Pauline Gariboldi, 1939 (div.); m. 4th, Baroness von Falz-Fein, July 19, 1963. Movie critic N.Y. Daily News, 1922-23, sports writer, 1923-24, sports editor, columnist, 1924-36; free lance fiction writer, 1936—; war corr. Cosmopolitan mag., 1944. Served as seaman gunner R.F., U.S.N., 1918. Clubs: Fencer's, Quiet Birdman (N.Y.C.); Bucks, EPEE' (London). Author: Farewell to Sport, 1938; Adventures of Hiram Holliday, 1939 (London, 1939); The Secret Front, 1940; The Snow Goose, 1941; Golf Is a Friendly Game, 1942; Confessions of a Story Writer 1946; The Lonely (London) 1947; The Abandoned, 1950; Jennie (London), 1950; Trial by Terror, 1950: The Foolish Immortal, 1953: Love of Seven Dolls, 1954: Snowflake, 1957; Thomasina, 1958: The Steadfast Man. 1958; Mrs. 'Arris Goes to Paris, 1958; Ludmila, 1959; Too Many Ghosts, 1959: The Hurricane Story. 1960: Mrs. Harris Goes to New York. 1960; Further Confessions of a Story Writer 1961; Coronation, 1962: Scruffy, 1962; Love, Let Me Not Hunger, 1963: The Hand of Mary Constable, 1964; The Silent Miaow, 1964; Mrs. 'Arris Goes to Parliament, 1965; The Golden People. 1965; The Man Who Was Magic, 1966; The Story of Silent Night, 1967; The Revealing Eye, 1967; Manxmouse, 1968; The Poseidon Adventure, 1969; Mathilda, 1970. Contbr. fiction Sat. Eve. Post, Good Housekeeping, Esquire. Office: care H Ober 40 E 49th St New York City NY 10017

GALLIGAN, CLARENCE JOSEPH. publishing co. exec.; b. N.Y.C., Jan. 16, 1920; s. Clarence Joseph and Kathleen Marie (O'Mara) G.; student N.Y. U., 1937-40; grad. Command and Gen. Staff Coll., 1945; B.S., U. N.C., 1949; M.B.A., Harvard, 1953; m. Florence Marie Riordan, June 9, 1945; 1 son, Michael William. Grad. flight tng., 1941, commd. 2d lt. USAAF, 1941, advanced through grades to brig. gen. USAF, 1963: comdr. air combat group Europe and N. Africa, World War II; financial and data mgmt. logistical elements USAF, 1949- 60; dep. chief, then chief Army and Air Force Exchange Service, 1960-66; dep. comdr. Sacramento Air Material Area, 1966-68; ret., 1968: dir. internat. planning Lorillard Corp., N.Y.C., 1968-69; v.p. Crowell, Collier and Macmillan, Inc., N.Y.C., 1969—. Legion of Merit with 2 oak leaf clusters, D.F.C., Air medal with oak leaf cluster; Croix de Guerre (France); Order Brit. Empire. Mem. Harvard Bus. Sch. Assn., Air Force Assn., Def. Supply Assn. Club: Harvard (N.Y.C.). Home: Pound Ridge Box 1496 FDR Station NY 10022 Office: CCM Inc 866 3d Av New York City NY 10022

GALLIGAN, PATRICK T., lawyer; b. 1930; B.A., St. Patrick's Coll., 1952; LL.B., Osgoode Hall Law Sch. Admitted to Ont. bar, 1956; now partner firm Soloway, Wright, Houston, Galligan & McKimm, Ottawa; part-time lectr. Ottawa U., 1963—. Mem. Canadian Bar Assn., County of Carleton Law Assn. Office: 170 Metcalfe St Ottawa 4 Ontario Canada*

GALLIGAN, THOMAS JOSEPH, Jr., utility co. exec.; b. Watertown, Mass., Sept. 13, 1919; s. Thomas Joseph and Winifred C. (McKeon) G.; A.B., Boston Coll., 1941; M.B.A., Harvard, 1943; m. Lauretta E. Durkin, Feb. 9, 1944; children—Thomas, John, Christopher, Martin, Peter. With Lybrand, Ross Bros. and Montgomery, C.P.A.'s, Boston, 1946-53; dir. stores and service Boston Edison Co., 1953-57, asst. to pres., 1957-58, v.p., 1958-60, exec. v.p., 1960-67, pres., 1967—, also dir.; trustee, mem. auditing com. Union Warren Savs. Bank; dir. Cramer Electronics, Inc., First Nat. Bank of Boston, First Nat. Boston Corp., Pub. Utilities Reports, Inc. Chmn. finance com., mem. steering com. Electric Companies Pub. Information Program; v.p., dir. Electric Council New Eng. Chmn. Mass. Com. Catholics, Protestants and Jews; chmn. Boston Citizens Seminar Planning Com.; vice chmn. adv. com. Positive Program for Boston. Bd. dirs. Mass. Bay United Fund, Mass. Higher Edn. Assistance Corp., Internat. Center New Eng.; trustee Plimoth Plantation, Newton-Wellesley Hosp.; mem. president's council Boston Coll.; dir. Family Counseling, Guidance Centers, Inc.; dir., treas. Med. Found., Inc. Served as officer USNR, 1943-46. C.P.A., Mass. Mem. Mass. Soc. C.P.A.'s, Nat. Assn. Accountants, Greater Boston C. of C. (v.p.), Mass Electric and Gas Assn. (treas., dir.), Edison Electric Inst. (mem. exec. com. pub. employee and investor relations div.), Electric Heating Assn. (dir.), Am. Inst. C.P.A.'s. Home: 1806 Beacon St Waban, MA 02168. Office: 800 Boylston St Boston MA 02199

GALLIN-DOUATHE, MICHEL, diplomat Central African Republic, Ambassador to U.S., 1960; permanent rep. UN, 1960, mem. Permanent Mission of Central African Republic to UN. Address: 386 Park Av S New York City NY 10022

GALLINGTON, RALPH ORA, educator; b. Dennison, Ill., Nov. 18, 1908; s. Ora Albert and Nora Belle (Crockett) G.; B.S., Ind. State U., 1931; M.A., Columbia, 1937; Ed.D., George Washington U., 1947; m. Mary Katherine Roales, Aug. 30, 1931; children—Roger Wayne, Daniel Jay. Tchr., Towson (Md.) High Sch., 1931-38; asst. prof. indsl. edn. U. Md., 1938-43; asso. prof. indsl. arts Eastern Ill. State U., Charleston, 1947-48; prof. indsl. edn. Pa. State U., 1948-55, mem. univ. senate, 1952-55; prof. indsl. edn., chmn. dept. So. Ill. U., Carbondale, 1955-68, acting dean Sch. Tech., 1960-62; prof., dir. vocational edn. Fla. State U., Tallahassee, 1968—; chief engr. Bowen Instrument Co., Bethesda, Md., 1943-44; prodn. design engr. Flight Tng. Research Assn., Washington, 1944-46; plant supt. Lofstrand Mfg. Co., Rockville, Md., 1946-47; asso. mech. engring. George Washington U., 1946. Pres. Md. Vocational Assn., 1942-43; dir. research vocational edn. Ill. Revenue Commn., 1962-63; cons. Bur. Research, U.S. Office Edn., Dept. Health, Edn. and Welfare, 1965-68. Mem. Am. Council Indsl. Arts Tchr. Educators (pres. 1962-64), N.E.A., Am. Indsl. Arts Assn., Am. Vocational Assn., Nat. Assn. Indsl.-Tech. Tchr. Educators (trustee 1969—, Am. Tech. Edn. Assn., Phi Delta Kappa (pres. Alpha Tau chpt. 1952-53), Iota Lambda Sigma (pres. Grand chpt. 1943-44), Epsilon Pi Tau. Mason (32), Rotarian. Author: (with J.W. Giachino) Course Construction in Industrial Arts, Vocational Education and Technical Education, 3d edit., 1967; Industrial Arts for Disadvantaged Youth, 1970. Home: 2314 Clare Dr Killearn Tallahassee FL 32303

GALLION, ARTHUR BANTA, educator, architect; b. Chgo., June 30, 1902; s. Charles Horace and Lucille (Banta) G.; B.S. in Architecture, U. Ill., 1924; student Ecole des Beaux Arts. Paris, 1928; m. Pearle Nesbitt, Oct. 2, 1926; children—Alan L., Janne. Planner, housing div., PWA, Washington, 1934-36; pvt. archtl. practice, Oakland-Berkeley, Cal., 1936-38; regional project planner, U.S. Housing Authority, Western Region, San Francisco, 1938-42; dir. for devel. Fed. Pub. Housing Authority, Calif., Ariz., Nev. T.H., 1942-45; dean Sch. of Architecture U. So. Cal., Los Angeles, 1945-60; planner Harland, Bartholomew & Assos., Honolulu, 1960-63; faculty Cal. State Poly. Coll., 1963—. Chmn. sect. on regional planning and devel. Town Hall, Los Angeles, 1946-48; commnr. Housing Authority of Los Angeles Co., 1950-53. Registered architect Ill. Cal., Hawaii. Awarded Steedman fellowship, 1927-28. Fellow American Am. Inst. Architects; mem. Am. Inst. Planners, Scarab, Daubers, Alpha Rho Chi, Chi. Psi, Delta Phi Delta, Tau Sigma Delta. Author: The Urban Pattern. Home: San Luis Obispo CA 93401

GALLION, MACDONALD, state ofcl.; b. Montgomery, Ala., Apr. 5, 1913; s. Dr. Thomas Travis and Varina Ann (George) G.; LL.B., U. Ala., 1937; m. Velma Lee Biddy, July 10, 1942: children—Thomas Travis III, Frances Mallory. Addmitted to Ala. bar. 1937; practiced in Birmingham, 1937-42, Montgomery, 1950-54; asst. atty. gen. Ala., 1945-50, chief asst. atty. gen., 1955-57, atty. gen., 1959-63, 67—; spl. counsel for Ala., Phenix City crime cleanup, 1954; sr. partner law firm Gallion, Hare & Anderson, Montgomery, 1963-67. Chmn., So. Attys. Gen. Conf., 1961-62. Served from pvt. to 1st lt. USMCR, 1942-45; PTO. Mem. Am. Legion, V.F.W., S.C.V., Nat. Assn. Pros. Attys., Am., Ala. (past asso. editor The Ala. Lawyer), Montgomery bar assns., Am. Judicature Soc., Ala. Sheriffs and Peace Officers Assn., Montgomery C. of C., Alpha Tau Omega. Democrat. Presbyn. Elk, Moose, Mason, Woodmen of World (nat. dir., past state pres.). Home: 806 E Edgemont Av Montgomery AL 36111 Office: State Capitol Montgomery AL 36104

GALLMAN, WALDEMAR JOHN, former fgn. service officer; b. Wellsville, N.Y., Apr. 27, 1909; s. John and Henrietta (Engelder) G.; A.B., Cornell U., 1917-21; student Georgetown Law Sch., 1923-24; m. Marjorie Gerry, July 29, 1925; children—John Gerry, Philip Gerry. Instr. English, Cornell U., Ithaca, N.Y., 1921-22; became sec. Am. embassy, 1922; assigned to Habana, State Dept., 1923, Am. legation, San Jose, Costa Rica, 1925, Quito, Ecuador, 1926, Riga, Latvia, 1930, Am. embassy, Warsaw, Poland, 1934; apptd. consul Free City of Danzig, 1934; asst. chief div. European affairs State Dept., 1941; 1st sec., London, Eng., 1942; counselor, London, 1944; minister, London, 1945; became ambassador to Poland, 1948; dep. for Fgn. Affairs, Nat. War Coll., 1950-51; ambassador Union South Africa, 1951, Iraq, 1954; dir. gen. Fgn. Service, 1959-61; mem. faculty grad. sch. George Washington U., 1961—; adviser Fgn. Service Tng. Inst., Korean Ministry Fgn. Affairs, Seoul, 1963-65, Fgn. Service Tng. Center, South Viet Nam Ministry Fgn. Affairs, 1966- 67. Mem. S.A.T.C., Cornell, 1918. Author: Iraq Under General Nuri-My: Recollections of Nuri-Al-Said, 1954-58. Address: 3312 Woodley Rd N W Washington, DC 20008

GALLO, FRANK, sculptor; b. Toledo, Jan. 13, 1933; B.F.A., Toledo Mus. Sch. Art; M.F.A., U. Ia. Presently asso. prof. sculpture U. Ill.; exhbns. include AIC, 1964, Whitney Mus. Art, 1964, 65, Ravinia Festival Art, 1964, also Kennedy Meml. Exhbn.; rep. permanent collections Mus. Modern Art, Whitney Mus. Art, AIC, Los Angeles Mus. Art; commd. for Commemorative Medal civil engring. U. Ill. Recipient prize Interior Valley competition, Cin., 1961. Address: 804 W Nevada St Urbana, IL 61801 *

GALLO, WILLIAM VICTOR, cartoonist; b. N.Y.C., Dec. 28, 1922; s. Francisco and Henrietta (Caballero) G.; ed. Columbia Extension, Cartoonists and Illustrators; m. Dolores Rodriguez, Mar. 13, 1950; children—Gregory, William. With N.Y. Daily News, 1941—, sports cartoonist, 1960—; works rep. permanent collection Baseball Hall of Fame (Cooperstown, N.Y.). Served with USMC, 1942-45. Recipient 3 Page One awards N.Y. Newspaper Guild, 1965, 68, 69; named best sports cartoonist, Nat. Cartoonist Soc., 1969, 70, 71. Home: 1 Mayflower Dr Yonkers NY 10710 Office: 220 E 42d St New York City NY 10017

GALLOP, MYER ROBERT, lawyer; b. N.Y.C., Aug. 1, 1908; s. Morris and Bessie (Aranow) G.; B.S., Coll. City N.Y., 1928; student Fordham U. Sch. Law, 1929; J.D., N.Y.U., 1931; m. Sally Subin, July 2, 1933; children—Richard Charles, Barbara Ann. Admitted to N.Y. bar. 1931, since practiced in N.Y.C.; counsel to firm Shea, Gallop. Climenko and Gould, 1964—. Sr. v.p., gen. counsel United Brands Co.; dir. Acme Hamilton Rubber Corp., Morrell (John) & Co. Chmn. lawyers div. N.Y.C. chpt. Am. Cancer Soc., 1960—, N.Y.C. chpt. Multiple Sclerosis Soc., 1960—; founder Brotherhood-in-Action, 1962, dir., 1962—. Trustee Beth Israel Med. Center. Mem. N.Y. County Lawyers Assn. Home: 150 E 69th St New York City NY 10021; also Old StoneHill Rd Pound Ridge NY Office: 330 Madison Av New York City NY 10017

GALLOWAY, ALEXANDER HENDERSON, corp. exec.; b. Winston-Salem, N.C., Dec. 27, 1907; s. Alexander H. and Mamie (Gray) G.; student Woodbery Forest Sch., Orange, Va., 1921-25; A.B., U. N.C., 1929; m. Martha Erckman, May 10, 1930; children—Alexander Henderson, Robert, James G. With R.J. Reynolds Tobacco Co., 1929—, asst. treas., 1937-51, treas., 1951-55, dir., 1955—, v.p., treas., 1955-59, exec. v.p., 1959-60, pres., 1960-70, chmn. bd., 1969-70, also chief exec. officer, 1967-70, chmn. exec. com., 1962-70; chmn. bd., chief exec. officer R.J. Reynolds Industries, Inc., 1970—; dir. Am. Independent Oil Co., Inc., McLean Industries, Inc., Wachovia Bank and Trust Co., N.A., Piedmont Aviation, Inc. Mem. Bus. Council, Washington; founding mem. Bus. Com. for Arts, N.Y.; mem. Nat. Indsl. Pollution Control Council, U.S. Dept. Commerce; mem. N.C. Adv. Com. on Pub. Edn. Bd. dirs. N.C. Bus, Found., Grocery Mfrs. Am. Mem. Soc. of Cincinnati, Phi Beta Kappa, Beta Theta Pi. Democrat. Episcopalian. Clubs: Rotary, Twin City, Old Town, Country of N.C.; Augusta Nat. Home: 1048 Arbor Rd Winston-Salem NC 27104 Office: RJ Reynolds Industries Inc Winston-Salem NC 27101

GALLOWAY, GEORGE HAROLD, petroleum co. exec.; b. Palmyra, Neb., Apr. 18, 1916; s. Harold S. and Hazel (Smith) G.; B.Sc. in Civil Engring. and Geology, U. Neb., 1939; grad. Advanced Mgmt. Program, Harvard, 1956; m. Pearl Anne Stuhr, June 23, 1940; children—John, Betsy, Mark, Tracey. With Pan Am Petroleum Corp., 1939—, v.p. exploration, 1959-64, exec. v.p., 1964—, also dir.; dir. Southeastern State Bank, Tulsa, First Nat. Bank and Trust Co., Tulsa. Bd. dirs. Tulsa Port Authority. Trustee Tulsa U., Hillcrest Med. Center, Tulsa, Childrens Med. Center, Tulsa. Mem. Am. Petroleum Inst. (chmn. exploration and devel. statistics div. 1966—), Am. Assn. Petroleum Geologists. Mid-Continent Oil and Gas Assn., Tulsa C. of C. (dir.). Home: 2455 E 27th Pl Tulsa, OK 74114. Office: Pan American South Bldg Tulsa OK 74102

GALLOWAY, JAMES HARRISON, oil co. exec.; b. Sour Lake, Tex., May 11, 1908; s. James Harrison and Katherine (Williams) G.; B.S., Tex. A. and M. Coll., 1930; grad. Advanced Mgmt. Program, Harvard, 1954; m. Marie Muenster, Jan. 20, 1934. With Humble Oil & Refining Co., Houston, 1930—, asst. mgr. prodn. dept., 1954, dir., 1958, v.p. Central region, 1962—, dir., Houston, 1963, v.p., dir., 1967—. Served to capt. C.E., AUS, 1942-45. Decorated Bronze Star with oak leaf cluster. Registered engr., Tex. Mem. Am. Petroleum Inst., Am. Inst. Mining, Metall. and Petroleum Engrs., Mid-Continent Oil and Gas Assn., Tex. Soc. Profl. Engrs., Houston Engring. and Sci. Soc. Episcopalian. Clubs: Houston, Houston Country, Petroleum (Houston). Home: 327 Westminster Dr Houston, TX 77024. Office: PO Box 2180 Houston TX 77001 also 800 Bell Av Houston TX 77002

GALLOWAY, JAMES VANCE, army officer; b. Lake Tokaway, N.C., Aug. 10, 1919; s. Ransom C. and Lillie (Wood) G.; B.S., Ohio U., 1940; grad. Armed Forces Information Sch., 1948, Armor Advanced Course, 1954, Command and Gen. Staff Coll., 1957, Army War Coll., 1961; M.A., George Washington U., 1961; Faculty fellow, Harvard, 1966-67; m. Eve Blackshear Graham, June 7, 1952; children—James Vance, Eve Ellisa, Graham Wood, Thomas Roderick. Commd. 2d lt. U.S. Army, 1940, advanced through grades to maj. gen., 1971; mil. asst. to asst. sec. army, 1957-60; comdr. 14th Armored Cav. Regt., Germany, 1961-63; with G-3, V Corps, Germany, 1963-64, J-3, Office Joint Chiefs of Staff, 1964-66, MACV, Vietnam, 1967-68; asst. div. comdr. Americal Div., 1968, MACV, 1969; asst. comdt. Armor Sch., Ft. Knox, Ky., 1969-71; comdr. 1st Armored Div., Göppingen, Germany, 1971—. Decorated D.S.M., Silver Star, Legion of Merit with two oak leaf clusters, Bronze Star, Air medal with eight oak leaf clusters, Nat. Order 4th and 5th class, Air Force Distinguished Service Order 1st class, Navy Distinguished Service Order 1st class, Cross of Gallantry with palm, Medal of Honor (Vietnam); Nat. Order Merit Wha Rang (Korea). Mem. Assn. U.S. Army, Armor Assn., Army War Coll. Assn., Phi Kappa Tau. Episcopalian. Mason. Home: Quarters 1 Goeppingen Germany Hdqrs 1st Armored Div APO New York City NY 09326

GALLOWAY, MITCHELL OLIN, airline exec.; b. Hosford, Fla., June 28, 1928; s. Jesse Olin and Velma (Mitchell) G.; B.B.A. cum laude, Ga. State U., 1958; m. Doris M. Pollard, Mar. 23, 1958; children—David Alan, Mitchell Glen. With Delta Air Lines, Inc., Atlanta, 1945—, dir. financial analysis and control, 1963-67, asst. v.p., comptroller, 1967-69, v.p., comptroller, 1969—; dir. Bank of Fulton County, East Point, Ga. Served with Finance Corps, AUS, 1950-52. Mem. Financial Execs. Inst., Airline Finance and Accounting Conf., East Point (past dir.), South Fulton chambers commerce. Baptist (deacon). Club: Washington Colonies Civic (past v.p.) (East Point, Ga.). Home: 3646 Charles Dr East Point GA 30344 Office: Delta Air Lines Inc Gen Offices Atlanta Airport Atlanta GA 30320

GALLOWAY, PAUL VERNON, bishop; b. Mountain Home, Ark., Apr. 5, 1904; s. James Jesse and Ella (Burkhead) G.; student Hendrix Coll., 1921-22, D.D., 1951; A.B., Henderson-Brown Coll., 1926; postgrad. So. Meth. U., 1926-27, L.D. (hon.), 1964; B.D., Yale, 1929; student U. Chgo., 1933; LL.D., Ark. A. and M. Coll., 1947; L.H.D., Oklahoma City U., 1960; Litt.D., McMurray Coll.; m. Elizabeth Boney, June 14, 1932; 1 son, Paul Vernon. Ordained to ministry Meth. Ch., 1929, consecrated bishop, 1960; pastor in Ark., 1925-50, Okla., 1950-60; bishop San Antonio-N. W. Tex. area. 1960-64; bishop Arkansas area, Little Rock, 1964—. Vistor mission fields abroad, 1947, 54, 58, 59, 61, 65; chmn. conf. hosp. and homes Meth. Ch., 1939-48, chmn. commn. world service and finance, 1952-60, program chmn., also chmn. commn. entertainment, 1952-60; Episcopal adviser, 1960; mem., v.p. nat. div. Bd. Missions, 1960-64, chmn. home sect., 1964—, chmn. com. on Spanish speaking work. Mem. gov. Ark. Com. to Study Vocational Tng., 1939; rep. Ark. A. and M. Coll. on Ednl. Com. Colls. and Higher Edn., 1936-50. Trustee Meth. Hosp., Memphis, Meth. Childrens Home, Little Rock; bd. dirs. So. Meth. U., Lydia Patterson Inst., El Paso, McMurry Coll., Southwestern U., Ark. A. and M. Coll., Hendrix Coll.; bd. mgrs. Ark. Indsl. Schs. Mem. Delta Chi, Pi Kappa Delta (pres. 1925-26; Diamond key 1926). Mason (32, grand chaplain Ark.). Address: 3909 S Lookout St Little Rock AR 72205

GALLUN, EDWIN ALFRED, tannery exec.; b. Milw., Oct. 14, 1898; s. Albert Frederick and Hedwig (Mann) G.; student U. Wis., 1915-18, Columbia, 1920, Colo. Coll., 1922; m. Jane F. Washburn, Apr. 12, 1928; children—Lorna (Mrs. James S. Schelble), Edwin Alfred, Douglas A., Arthur B.; m. 2d Evelyn Johnson, June 18, 1959. With A. F. Gallun And Sons Corp., Milw., 1918—, v.p., 1931-33, pres., 1933-57, chmn. bd., 1958—; pres., treas., dir. Argola Corp.; dir., chmn. bd. Perfex Corp. (Milw.), Ozite Corp. (Chgo.); dir. Marshall & Ilsley Bank, (Milw.), Sta-Rite Industries, Inc. (Delavan, Wis.) Pres., bd. dirs. Milw. YMCA, 1952-57. Served with U.S. Army, 1918. Home: Route 3 Hartland WI 53029 Office: 1818 N Water St Milwaukee WI 53201

GALLUP, DONALD CLIFFORD, educator; b. Sterling, Conn., May 12, 1913; s. Carl Daniel and Lottie Elizabeth (Stanton) G.; A.B., Yale, 1934, Ph.D., 1939. Instr. English, So. Meth. U., Dallas, 1937-40, 41-42; cataloguer library Yale, 1940-41, asst. prof. bibliography, curator collection Am. lit., editor Library Gazette, fellow Jonathan Edwards Coll., 1947—. Guggenheim fellow, 1961, 68. Served as lt. col. AUS, 1941-46. Mem. Bibl. Soc. Am. Clubs: Elizabethan, Grolier, Yale (N.Y.C.). Author: Ezra Pound Bibliography, 1963; T. S. Eliot Bibliography, 1969; T. S. Eliot & Ezra Pound, 1970; On Contemporary Bibliography, 1970. Editor: The Flowers of Friendship, 1953; Eugene O'Neill, Inscriptions, 1960; Eugene O'Neill, More Stately Mansions, 1964. Home: 472 Whitney Av New Haven CT 06511

GALLUP, GEORGE HORACE, pub. opinion statistician; b. Jefferson, Ia., Nov. 18, 1901; s. George Henry and Nettie (Davenport) G.; B.A., State U. Ia., 1923, M.A., 1925, Ph.D., 1928, LL.D., 1967; LL.D., Northwestern U., Drake U., Boston U., Chattanooga U.; D.Sc., Tufts Coll.; H.H.D., Colgate U.; D.C.L., Rider Coll., 1966; m. Ophelia Smith Miller, Dec. 27, 1925; children—Alec Miller, George Horace, Jr., Julia (Laughlin). Head dept. journalism Drake U., 1929-31; prof. journalism and advt. Northwestern U., 1931-32; dir. research Young & Rubicam Advt. Agy., N.Y.C., 1932-47; prof. Pulitzer Sch. Journalism, Columbia U., 1935-37; pres. Market Research Council, 1934, 35; pres. Nat. Municipal League, 1954-56, Internat. Insts. Pub. Opinion, 1947—. Chmn. emeritus Gallup and Robinson, Inc., advt. and marketing research; chmn. bd. Gallup Orgn., Inc., marketing and attitude research. Made editorial surveys of many newspapers, and also many editorial and advt., surveys of Liberty, Saturday Evening Post, Ladies Home Jour. and Colliers'. Mem. Am. Assn. Pub. Opinion Research (pres. 1954-55), Council Fgn. Relations, Sigma Alpha Epsilon, Sigma Delta Chi, Sigma Xi. Club: Nat. Press (Washington). Recipient award for distinguished achievement Syracuse U., 1950; Distinguished Citizen award Nat. Municipal League, 1962; Parlin award Am. Marketing Assn., 1965; Christopher Columbus Internat. prize for outstanding achievement in communications, 1968. Founder Am. Inst., 1935, Brit. Inst. Pub. Opinion, 1936; founder and pres. Audience Research Inst., Inc., 1939; founder Quill and Scroll (internat. honor soc. for high sch. journalists), now chmn. bd. trustees. Originator of method to measure comparative interest of readers in news features and advertising in newspapers and mags., also a method for measuring radio audiences of individual radio programs. Episcopalian. Author: The Pulse of Democracy, A New Technique for Measuring Reader Interest: Guide to Public Opinion Polls; The Miracle Ahead; also numerous articles on pub. opinion. Home: The Great Rd Princeton NJ 08540

GALLUZZI, NICHOLAS JOSEPH, hosp. adminstr.; b. Bklyn., Mar. 18, 1923; s. Charles F. and Gertrude (Santora) G.; B.S., U. Mich., 1944; M.D., U. Chgo., 1948; m. Eileen M. McGlone, Sept. 22, 1945; children—Katherine, Margaret, Patricia. Research asst. U. Chgo. Med. Sch., 1948-49; rotating intern USPHS Hosp., S.I., N.Y., 1949-50, resident internal medicine, 1950-53; with USPHS, 1953—, dir. USPHS Hosp. S.I., 1967—; asso. clin. prof. medicine N.J. Coll. Medicine, 1966—. Served with AUS. 1943-46. Recipient Meritorious Service medal USPHS, 1966. Diplomate Am. Bd. Internal Medicine. Fellow A.C.P.; mem. Alpha Omega Alpha. Address: USPHS Hosp Staten Island, NY 10304.

GALOVIC, MILUTIN PETAR, Yugoslav diplomat; b. Dragalic, Yugoslavia, Dec. 17, 1932; s. Peter Jovan and Milka Pavle (Kresojevic) G.; diploma Ek. Fakultet, U. Zagreb (Yugoslavia), 1957; m. Gordana Ilic, Jan 28, 1970. Chief investment office, sugar factory, Zupanja, 1957-60; comml. attache embassy, Rome, 1961-66; desk officer for Italy, State Secretariat Fgn. Affairs, Beograd, 1966-70; 1st sec. econs., Washington, 1970—. Home: 11801 Rockville Pike Rockville MD 20852 Office: 2410 California St NW Washington DC 20008

GALPHIN, BRUCE MAXWELL, writer; b. Tallahassee, Aug. 11, 1932; s. Lawrence Tatum and Helen (Hoskins) G.; A.B., Fla. State U., 1954. With Atlanta Congtn., 1954-69, editorial asso., 1963-69; Atlanta bur. chief Washington Post, 1969-70; freelance writer; 1970—. Nieman fellow Harvard, 1962-63; named Outstanding Young Man in Proffessions, Atlanta Jr. C. of C., 1967. Club:Atlanta Press (pres. 1968). Author: The Riddle of Lester Maddox, 1968; also articles. Address: 217 Westminster Dr NE Atlanta GA 30309

GALSTON, ARTHUR WILLIAM, biologist; b. N.Y.C., Apr. 21, 1920; s. Hyman and Freda (Saks) G.; B.S., Cornell U., Ithaca, N.Y., 1940; M.S., U. Ill., 1942, Ph.D., 1943; m. Dale Judith Kuntz, June 27, 1941; children—William Arthur, Beth Dale. Research plant physiologist emergency rubber project Cal. Inst. Tech., 1943-44, sr. research fellow, 1947-50, asso. prof. biology, 1951-55; instr. Yale, New Haven, 1946-47, prof. plant physiology, 1955-65, prof. biology, 1965—, dir. div. biol. med. scis., 1965-66, chmn. dept. botany, 1961-62. Cons. central research dept. E. I. DuPont de Nemours & Co.; mem. div. biology and agr. NRC, 1963-66, Guggenheim fellow, Stockholm, Paris, Sheffield, Eng., 1950-51; Fulbright fellow, Canberra, Australia, 1960-61; Sci. Faculty fellow NSF, 1967-68. Served as ensign USNR, 1944-46; mil. govt., Okinawa. Fellow A.A.A.S. (chmn. com. on meetings 1956-59); mem. Am. Soc. Plant Physiologists (sec. 1955-57, v.p. 1957-58, pres. 1963- 64), Internat. Assn. Plant Physiology (sec.-treas. 1961-67), Bot. Soc. Am. (editorial bd. 1959-61, pres. 1967-68), Growth Soc. (exec. bd. 1959), Am. Soc. Biol. Chemists, Soc. Gen. Physiologists, Scandinavian Soc. Plant Physiologists. Author: Life of the Green Plant, 1961, 2d edit., 1964; (with James Bonner) Principles of Plant Physiology, 1952; (with Peter J. Davies) Control Mechanisms in Plant Development, 1970; also sci. articles. Home: 307 Manley Heights Orange CT 06477 Office: Yale University New Haven CT 06520

GALSTON, CLARENCE ELKUS, lawyer, ins. co. exec.; b. Cedarhurst, N.Y., June 5, 1909; s. Clarence G. and Estelle (Elkus) G.; A.B. magna cum laude, Harvard, 1930. LL.B., 1933; m. Constance Matthiessen, May 18, 1937 (div. 1952); children—Virginia (Mrs. John J. Walsh, Jr.), John Wood, Linda Jane (Mrs. Richard J. Fates); m. 2d, Nina Moore Shields. Feb. 17, 1955; 1 stepson, William Shields III. Admitted to N.Y. bar. 1933; asso., then mem. firm Spence, Hotchkiss, Parker & Durvee, N.Y.C., 1933-42, 45- 47; pres., chief exec. officer Motor Haulage Co., N.Y.C., 1947-55; v.p. U.S. Trucking Corp., N.Y.C., 1955-59; trustee Welfare and Pension Funds of N.Y.C. Trucking Industry, Local 807, 1948-63; v.p., gen. counsel Tchrs. Ins. & Annuity Assn. Am., also Coll. Retirement Equities Fund, N.Y.C., 1960, now exec. v.p., gen. counsel, sec. Served from 1st lt. to col., USAAF, 1942-45. Decorated Legion of Merit. Fellow Am. Bar Found.: mem. Am., N.Y. State bar assns., Bar Assn. City N.Y., Assn. Life Ins. Counsel, Nat. Assn. Coll. and U. Attys. Republican. Clubs: Cold Spring Harbor Beach; Harvard (N.Y.C.): Pining Rock; Huntington Country: Metropolitan (Washington). Home: 338 Woodbury Rd. Huntington, NY 11743. Office: 730 3d Av New York City NY 10017

GALT, ERROL FAY, former banker; b. Myrtle, Minn., Oct. 2, 1889; s. William Wylie and Emma Retta (Robinson) G.; grad. So. Minn. Normal Coll., 1906; m. Florence E. Johnson, Aug. 28, 1916; children—Fay, Edna Ann, William Wylie, Gwen, Jack Patricia. Office boy Eclipse Lumber Co., Belle Plaine, Ia., 1907; various positions with lumber cos., Toeterville, Ia., 1908-09, hardware bus., Stanford, Mont., 1910-16; organizer First Nat. Bank, Geyser, Mont., 1916-32; asst. to pres. First Nat. Bank of Great Falls (Mont.), 1932, v.p., 1934, pres., 1946-54, chmn. bd., 1954-68. Montana State Senator from Judith Bosin County, 1930-34. Mem. bd. regents Coll. Great Falls. Clubs: Meadow Lark Country (Gt. Falls); Montana. Home: 2925 4th Av N Great Falls MT 59401 Office: First National Bank Great Falls MT 59401

GALT, W. T., mng. editor Vancouver Sun. Address: 2250 Granville St Vancouver 9 British Columbia Canada*

GALVEZ-BARNES, ROBERTO, Honduran diplomat; b. Puerto Cörtes, Honduras, May 18, 1925; s. Juan Manuel and Laura (Barnes) Galvez; ed. La. State U., Mass. Inst. Tech.; m. Lucia Cristina Montes, 1948; 2 sons, 3 daus. Capt. in charge Ground Sch. for Pilots, Honduran Air Force, 1949-50; dir.-gen. civil aeros., 1950-55; mgr. Honduran Cotton Co-operative and Honduras Indsl. S.R.L., 1955-56; minister communications and pub. works, 1956; mem. Mil. Junta, 1956-57; mgr. Honduras Indsl. S.R.L., 1957-58; v.p., gen. mgr. TAN Airlines, 1958-70; ambassador to U.S., Washington, 1970—. Decorated Medal of Merit, First Class, Order of Morazán (Honduras); Order of Vasco Naez de Balboa (Panama); Order of Propitious Cloud (China). Office: 4715 16th St NW Washington DC 20011*

GALVIN, ALOYSIUS CARROLL, univ. pres.; b. Balt., Jan. 15, 1925; s. John Thomas, Jr. and Agnes Mercedes (Smith) G.; A.B., Loyola Coll., Balt., 1948; M.A., Ph.L., Bellarmine Coll., 1953; S.T.L., Woodstock Coll., 1958. Joined Soc. of Jesus, 1948, ordained priest Roman Cath. Ch., 1957; instr. St. Joseph's Prep. Sch., Phila., 1953-54; tchr. theology St. Joseph's Coll., Phila., 1958; dean studies Loyola Coll., Balt., 1959-65; pres. U. Scranton (Pa.), 1965—. Incorporator Lackawanna Indsl. Fund Enterprises; bd. dirs. Northeastern Pa. Ednl. TV Assn. Served as ensign USNR, 1943-46. Address: U Scranton Scranton, PA 18510.

GALVIN, CHARLES O'NEILL, law sch. dean; b. Wilmington, N.C., Sept. 29, 1919; s. George Patrick and Marie (O'Neill) G.; B.S., So. Meth. U., 1940: M.B.A., Northwestern U., 1941, J.D., 1947; S.J.D., Harvard, 1961; m. Margaret Edna Gillespie, June 29, 1946; children—Katherine Marie, George Patrick, Paul Edward, Charles

O'Neill, Elizabeth Genevieve. Admitted to Ill. bar, 1947, Tex. bar, 1948; practice law, Dallas, 1947-52; asso. prof. So. Meth. U., Dallas, 1952-55, prof., 1955—, dean Sch. Law, 1963—. Served to lt. comdr. USNR, 1942-46. C.P.A., Tex. Mem. Am., Tex., Dallas bar assns., Am. Law Inst., Am., Tex. bar founds., Am. Judicature Soc., Tex. Soc. C.P.A.'s, Am. Inst. C.P.A.'s, Phi Delta Theta, Beta Gamma Sigma. Home: 5404 Park Lane Dallas TX 75220

GALVIN, EDWARD J., lead co. exec.; b. N.Y.C., Nov. 5, 1926; s. Michael J. and Margaret (O'Shea) G.; B.B.A., St. John's U.; m. Margaret McGuire, June 6, 1959; children—Dennis, Kathleen, Michael. Audit mgr. Arthur Young and Co., C.P.A.'s, N.Y.C.; asst. controller Am.-Standard Co.; controller Nat. Lead Co., N.Y.C., 1968—. C.P.A. Mem. Am. Inst. C.P.A.'s, N.Y. State Soc. C.P.A.'s Home: 114 Hendrickson Av Rockville Center, NY 11570. Office: 111 Broadway New York City NY 10006

GALVIN, HOYT REES, library cons.; b. Pleasantville, Ia., Feb. 26, 1911; s. Guy Gordon and Grace (Rees) G.; A.B., Simpson Coll., 1932; B.S. in Library Sci., U. Ill., 1933; certificate Brookings Inst. Center for Advanced Studies, 1967; m. Mary Elizabeth Sayre, May 25, 1935; children—Douglas Gordon, Jane Ann. Student asst. Simpson Coll. Library, Indianola, Ia., 1928-32; circulation asst. U. Ill. Library, 1933-34; reference and acquisition librarian TVA Tech. Library, Knoxville, Tenn., 1934-35; dir. Tri-County Regional Library Service, Huntsville, Ala., 1936-40; dir. Pub. Library of Charlotte (N.C.) and Mecklenburg County, 1940-71; head librarian U. N.C. at Charlotte, 1967-68; library cons., 1971—. Chmn. Ala. Library Bd., 1939-40; mem. pres.' Adv. Com. Library Research and Tng. Projects, 1965-70. Recipient Young Man of Yr. award Charlotte Jr. C. of C., 1942; Outstanding Pub. Librarian award Southeastern Library Assn., 1970. Mem. A.L.A. (pres. library adminstrn. div. 1965-66, 2d v.p. of assn. 1969-70), Ala. (pres. 1939-40), S.E. (pres. 1962-64), N.C. (pres. 1942-43) library assns., N.C. Adult Edn. Assn. (pres. 1957-58). Unitarian. Rotarian (pres. 1949-50). Author: Films in Public Libraries, 1947; also co-author monograph. Editor: Planning a Library, 1955. Contbr. library periodicals, also numerous library cons. reports. Address: 2259 Vernon Dr Charlotte NC 28211

GALVIN, JAMES PATRICK, clergyman, educator; b. Indpls., July 23, 1914; s. James F. and Mary H. (Moran) G.; B.A., St. Meinrad Sem., 1938; Ph.D. in Edn., Cath. U. Am., 1950. Ordained priest Roman Cath. Ch., 1938; asst. pastor, Richmond, Ind., 1938-42; asst. dean of men. Cath. U. Am., 1949-50; supt. Cath. High Sch., Indpls., 1940-54, Indpls. Archdiocesan Schs., 1954-63; now exec. sec. Archdiocesan Sch. Bd.; dir. Archdiocesan Pre-Marriage Confs., 1954—. Mem. exec. com. Ind. Youth Council; del. White House Conf. Edn., 1956. Served as chaplain AUS, 1942-46; ETO. Mem. N.E.A., Nat. Cath. Edn. Assn., Religious Edn. Assn. K.C. Author: A Comparative Study of Personality Patterns in Boys of Different Ages, 1950. Papal Chamberiain, Very Rev. Monsignor, 1959. Home: 5692 Central Av Indianapolis IN 46220 Office: 144 W Georgia St Indianapolis IN 46225

GALVIN, JOHN E., steel co. founder; b. Chattanooga, Jan. 9, 1878; s. John William and Elizabeth (Murray) G.; student Wittenberg U., 1900; m. Florence Cole Fetter, May 10, 1905; children—Robert F., Virginia Cole (Mrs. John L. Crouse). Founder, Ohio Steel Foundry Co., Lima, Springfield. O., 1907, chmn. bd. until recently; dir. Fed. Res. Bank of Cleve., 1930-40. Vice chmn. Ohio Republican Finance Com., 1940-50. Mem. Steel Founders' Soc. Am. (past pres.). Home: 2217 W Market St Lima OH 45805 Office: Teledyne Ohio Steel W 4th St Lima OH 45802

GALVIN, JOHN MICHAEL, banker; b. Buffalo, Oct. 30, 1905; s. John Francis and Margaret Gertrude (Donahue) G.; student U. Buffalo, 1925-28, Am. Inst. Banking, 1925-33; LL.D., Canisius Coll., 1959; m. Grace Kleinbauer, Oct. 23, 1936; children—John Michael, Grace Ann, Richard James. With Marine Trust Co. Western N.Y., Buffalo, 1921—, sr. v.p., 1958-61, exec. v.p., 1961-62, chmn. exec. com., chief exec. officer, 1962—, now vice chmn. bd. dirs., also dir.; dir. Buffalo br. Fed. Res. Bank N.Y., S. Buffalo Ry. Co., Conax Corp., Marine Midland Corp., Niagara Frontier Transit Corp., Seiberling Rubber Co.; chmn. bd., dir. Kissing Bridge Ski Corp., Golden, N.Y. Mem. disaster loan adv. com. Buffalo area Small Bus. Adminstrn., 1963—. Bd. dirs., trustee United Fund Buffalo and Erie Co., United Health Found. Western N.Y.; bd. dirs. Buffalo and Erie Co. Planning Assn., Greater Buffalo Devel. Found., Main St. Assn., Buffalo Area Conv. and Visitor's Bur., Buffalo Philharmonic Orch. Soc., Better Bus. Bur. Western N.Y., Buffalo Civic Auto Ramps; trustee Western N.Y. Ednl. TV Assn., U. Buffalo Found., Catholic Charities Buffalo; adv. bd. Canisius Coll., Rosary Hill Coll., Brothers of Mercy, St. Mary of the Angels (all Buffalo). Named Good Fellow of Year, Buffalo Courier-Express, 1958; recipient Silver Beaver award Boy Scouts Am., 1960, Spl. Service citation Buffalo chpt. Nat. Conf. Christians and Jews, 1961; named 1 of 10 outstanding citizens Buffalo Evening News, 1961; named knight of Malta, 1962; recipient citation for devoted leadership ednl. devel. Niagara Frontier, Judge John D. Hillery Meml. Scholarship Found., 1963; named Man of Year, Greater Buffalo Advt. Club, 1963, Distinguished Citizens Achievement award Canisius Coll. Bd. of Regents, 1967. Mem. Buffalo Area C. of C. (pres. 1966-67). K.C. (4). Clubs: Buffalo Athletic, Buffalo, Automobile, Mid-Day, Country of Buffalo, Frontier Press (Buffalo). Home: 25 Woodbury Dr Snyder, NY 14226. Office: 241 Main St Buffalo NY 14205

GALVIN, ROBERT FETTER, steel co. exec.; b. Cin., Apr. 13, 1915; s. John E. and Florence (Fetter) G.; grad. Culver Mil. Acad., 1933, Lawrenceville (N.J.) Sch., 1934; B.S. in Mech. Engring., Princeton, 1939; m. Jeanne Marie Latson, Apr. 26, 1941; children—Suzanne (Mrs. Tom Van Sickle), John L., Joanne. With Ohio Steel Foundry Co. (co. name changed to Teledyne Ohio Steel), 1940—, pres., 1949-66, chmn. bd., 1966—; vice chmn. bd. Ohio Steel of Belgium, 1964—. Mem. regioanl exec. com. Boy Scouts Am., 1964—, trustee Shawnee council, 1962—; chmn. Lima (O.) Jr. Achievement, 1964—; chmn. finance com., mem. adv. com. Lima Community Chest, 1954—; bd. govs. Ohio Devel. Commn., 1964—. Mem. exec. com. Ohio Republican Finance Com., 1956—. Trustee Lima YMCA. Mem. Ohio Mfrs. Assn. (bd. dirs.), Am. Iron and Steel Inst., Am. Soc. M.E., Am. Soc. Metals. Presbyn. Mason (Shriner). Clubs: Princeton (N.Y.C.); Union (Cleve.); Shawnee Country (Lima); Presidents (Ohio State U.). Office: Teledyne Ohio Steel W 4th St Lima OH 45802

GALVIN, ROBERT W., mfg. exec.; b. Marshfield, Wis., Oct. 9, 1922; student U. Notre Dame, U. Chgo.; LL.D. (hon.), Quincy Coll., St. Ambrose Coll. With Motorola, Inc., Chgo., 1940—, now chmn. bd., dir., chief exec. officer; dir. Harris Trust & Savs. Bank, Chgo. Mem. Pres.'s Commn. on Internat. Trade and Investment. Mem. 12 fellows U. Notre Dame; trustee Ill. Inst. Tech.; dir. Jr. Achievement Chgo. Served Signal Corps, AUS, World War II. Mem. Electronic Industries Assn. (pres. 1966, dir., Medal of Honor 1970). Office: 9401 W Grand Av Franklin Park IL 60131

GAM, RITA ELENORE, actress; b. Pitts., 1929; d. Ben and Belle (Faley) Gam; student Columbia, 1948-54; m. Sidney Lumet, 1954 (div.); m. 2d, Thomas Guinzburg, 1956 (div.); children—Kate, Michael. Appeared in Broadway plays A Flag is Born, 1948, Monserrat, 1949, The Insect Comedy, The Young and the Fair, 1950, Theres a Girl in My Soup, 1967; appeared in Hollywood films The Thief, 1952, Saadia, 1953, Night People, 1954, Mohawk, 1955, Attila the Hun, 1955, Hannible, 1953, Magic Fire, 1956, No Exit (winner Berlin Best Actress Silver Bear award), 1962, Clut, 1971, Shootout, 1971, Such Good Friends; played opening year at Tyrone Guthrie Theatre, Minn., 1964, played Masha in Three Sisters. Mem. Actors Studio. Author: The Beautiful Woman, 1969. Home: 1095 Park Av New York City NY 10028

GAMACHE, GEORGE, life ins. co. exec.; b. Bronx, N.Y., July 12, 1911; C.E., Cooper Union, 1935; m. Josephine Tobiassen, June 26, 1936; children—Gale R. (Mrs. C. Ralph Beamon), Elise A. (Mrs. Robert T. Staten). Vice pres., sec. Home Life Ins. Co. N.Y.C. Home: 96 Kenmore Pl Glen Rock, NJ 07452. Office: 253 Broadway New York City NY 10007

GAMACHE, GEORGE PAUL, air force officer; b. Fall River, Mass., Sept. 26, 1929; s. Louis Philippe and Rose (Montplaisir) G.; student Assumption Coll., Worcester, Mass., 1947-49; B.S., Okla. State U., 1962, M.S., 1963; m. Pauline Alice Masse, June 4, 1955; children—Monique Marie, Janine Renée, Murielle Ellen, Daniel Charles. Commd. 2d lt. USAF, 1952, advanced through grades to maj., 1964; navigator B-29 and RB-47 in Okinawa, N. Africa, Ohio, 1952-60; student Air Force Inst. Tech., 1960-63; electronics engr., system analysis div. Hdqrs. Air Force Eastern Test Range, Patrick AFB, Fla., 1963-65; prof. aerospace studies, head dept. Mass. Inst. Tech., 1965-69; chief, sensor monitor control Task Force Alpha, Thailand, 1969-70. Decorated Air Force Commendation medal. Registered profl. engr., Fla. Mem. I.E.E.E., Phi Kappa Phi, Eta Kappa Nu. Roman Catholic. Home: 3220 Ramey Circle McCoy AFB FL 32812 Office: McCoy AFB FL 32812

GAMBILL, EARL EDWARD, physician; b. Blaine, Ky., Mar. 11, 1907; s. Hugh Chilton and Minnie (Pigg) G.; A.B., Berea Coll., 1930; student U. Louisville Med. Sch., 1930-32; M.D., U. Pa., 1935; student U. Ky., summer 1935; M.S. in Medicine, Mayo Grad. Sch., U. Minn, 1942; m. Alleen Louise Maupin, Aug. 23, 1934; children—Edward Lee, John Douglas, David Earl, Margaret Alleen. With rural pub. health service in Ky., 1935-38; intern Passavant Meml. Hosp., Chgo., 1938-39; first asst. Mayo Clinic, 1942-44, cons. medicine and gastroenterology, 1944—; prof. medicine Mayo Grad. Sch. Medicine, 1963—; spl. research chronic relapsing pancreatitis. Mem. A.M.A., A.C.P., Am. Gastroent. Assn., Central Soc. Clin. Research, Sigma Xi. Republican. Presbyn. (elder). Author articles in field. Home: Oak Crest 12th Av N E Rochester, MN 55901. Office: 200 First St SW Rochester MN 55901

GAMBILL, JOHN RANDOLPH, physician, mental health adminstr.; b. Harrisonburg, Va., Apr. 21, 1918; s. John Randolph and Alice (Filler) G.; B.A., Bridgewater Coll., 1940; Th.B., So. Bapt. Theol. Sem., Louisville, 1943; M.D., U. Louisville, 1946; LL.B., Blackstone Sch. Law, Chgo., 1958; m. Wilmer Peters, Apr. 26, 1946; children—John David, Sarah Frances, Martha Sue, Paul William, Intern Louisville Gen. Hosp., 1946-47; sr. physician, chief female service Taunton (Mass.) Hosp., 1948-51; clin. dir., dir. tng. Norwich (Conn.) State Hosp., 1951-59; clin. dir., dir. tng. and research Madison (Ind.) State Hosp., 1959-62; dep. commr. Ind. Dept. Mental Health. Indpls., 1962-67, acting commr., 1966-67; supt. Mental Health Inst., Clarinda, Ia., 1967—; clin. instr. psychiatry Yale Med. Sch., 1957-59; asst. prof. psychiatry Med. Center Ind. U., 1962-67. Served with USPHS, 1947- 48. Named Sagamore of the Wabash. Diplomate Am. Bd. Psychiatry and Neurology. Fellow Am. Psychiat. Assn., Am. Geriatrics Soc.; mem. A.M.A., A.A.A.S., Assn. Mil. Surgeons U.S. Baptist (deacon). Mason, Rotarian. Club: Sycamores (past bd. dirs.), Indianapolis. Address: Mental Health Inst Clarinda, IA 51632.

GAMBLE, BERTIN CLYDE, corp. exec.; b. Chgo., Mar. 1, 1898; s. William Clyde and Florence Mae (Moody) G.; ed. pub. schs. and high sch.; LL.D., U. N.D., 1965; m. Gladys Lucille Pearson, Nov. 24, 1927; children—Jerry (dec.), Karen Rae. Began as partner automobile bus., 1920; opened first Gamble Store, St. Cloud, Minn., 1925; organized Gamble Stores, Inc., owners 55 stores, 1928, now chmn. bd.; established Solar Corp., 1933; acquired Nasco, Inc., finance co. Fargo, N.D., 1935, Macleod's, Ltd., 1945 (all merged with Gamble-Skogmo, Inc. 1946); acquired Gen. Outdoor Advt. Co., Inc., 1963, merged into Gamble-Skogmo, subsequently sold advt. plants, retaining Canadian subsidiary, Claude Neon Advt., Ltd.; acquired Aldens, Inc., retail, mail order merchandising co., Chgo., 1964, merged into Gamble-Skogmo, 1964; organized Founders, Inc., 1925, subsequently became operators Rasco, Mode O'Day and Cussins & Fearn Stores, merged into Gamble-Skogmo, 1966; dir. Northwestern Nat. Bank. Aldens, Inc., Cussins & Fearn Co., Inc., Gambles Can. Ltd., Red Owl Stores, Inc. Mem. men's adv. com. Northwestern Hosp.; dir. Nat. Boys' Clubs Am.; trustee United Hosp. Fund, Ripon (Wis.) Coll.; patron Mpls. Soc. Fine Arts. Methodist. Clubs: Minneapolis, Minikahda, Minneapolis Athletic (Mpls.); Woodhill Country (Wayzata, Minn.); Eldorado (Palm Desert, Cal.). Home: Route 3 Cedarhurst Dr Wayzata MN 55391 Office: 5100 Gamble Dr Minneapolis MN 55416

GAMBLE, CLINTON, architect; b. Newark, Mar. 15, 1910; s. George W. and Reine (Mackey) G.; B.Arch., U. Miami, 1931; m. Virginia Day Ralston, Aug. 31, 1935 (div.); children—Robert C., Nancy V.; m. 2d, Marion Gill, 1966. Draftsman, Russell T. Pancoast, architect, 1931-35, asso., 1935-42; asso. Albert Kahn, architect, 1942-43; sr. partner Gamble, Pownall & Gilroy, Ft. Lauderdale, Fla., 1946-65; partner Gamble & Gilroy, 1965—. Served to lt. comdr. USNR, 1943-46. Fellow A.I.A. (past nat. sec., past regional dir.); mem. Fla. Assn. Architects (past pres.), Ft. Lauderdale C. of C. (dir.). Club: Lauderdale Yacht (past comdr.). Home: 1731 S E 13th St Ft Lauderdale FL 33305 Office: 1628 N Federal St Ft Lauderdale FL 33305

GAMBLE, DAVID GIBBS, lawyer; b. Cin., Dec. 26, 1915; s. Cecil Huggins and Louise (Gibbs) G.; A.B., Princeton, 1937; LL.B., Yale, 1940; m. Priscilla Reed, Aug. 4, 1942; children—David Gibbs, Priscilla, Foster Reed, Hathway Louise, Polly Reed. Admitted to Ohio bar, 1940, since practiced in Cin.; partner Taft, Stettinius and Hollister, 1953—; dir. Procter and Gamble Co., Cin. Reds, Inc., Cin. Bengals, Inc., Continental Mfg. Co. Trustee, Berea College, Children's Home of Cin.; bd. dirs. Cemetery of Spring Grove, Cin. Served as lt. USNR, 1942-46. Clubs: Camargo, Racquet (Cin.). Home: 8221 Spooky Hollow Rd Cincinnati OH 45242 Office: Dixie Terminal Bldg Cincinnati OH 45202

GAMBLE, DAVID S., banker; b. New Haven, 1909; grad. Yale, 1932. Sr. v.p. Bank N.Y., N.Y.C. Dir. Callahan Mining Corp., Trans Air Freight Systems Inc. Home: Deer Park Greenwich CT 06830 Office: 48 Wall St New York City NY 10015*

GAMBLE, KATHRYN ELIZABETH, museum dir.; b. Van Wert, O., Aug. 19, 1915; d. Verne Gorham and May (Cassel) Gamble; A.B., Oberlin Coll., 1937; certificate Newark Mus. Tng. Course, 1941; M.A., N.Y. U., 1948. With Montclair (N.J.) Art Mus., 1944—, now dir. Mem Am. Assn. Museums, Museums Council N.J., N.E. Museums Conf., Internat. Conf. Museums. Home: 15 Francis Pl Caldwell NJ 07006 Office: 3 S Mountain Av Montclair NJ 07042

GAMBLE, PHILIP LYLE, economist; b. Amesbury, Mass., Sept. 25, 1905; s. Fred Keightley and Sarah Olive (Lord) G.; B.S. cum laude, Wesleyan U., 1928; A.M. (Rich fellow in econs.), 1929; Ph.D., (N.Y. State Tax Commn. fellow), Cornell U., 1935; m. Elizabeth Davis Scales, Aug. 7, 1939; children—Ruth Scales, Philip Lyle, Richard Andrew. Instr. in econs. Cornell U., 1929-32, Wesleyan U., 1932-35, Mt. Holyoke Coll. (vis.), 1934-36; asst. prof. econs. Mass. State Coll., 1935-42, asso. prof. Tulane U., summer 1939; vis. prof. Amherst Coll., 1942, Clark U., 1960, 61; prof., head dept. econs., govt., U. Mass., 1942-50, acting chmn. dept. bus. administrn., 1947, acting dean sch. bus. adminstrn., 1947-52, prof. econs., 1942-71, head dept., 1942-64; Theodore Roosevelt prof. econs. Naval War Coll., 1969-70, 71—. Fulbright lectr. Tungai U. China, 1964, 65. Pub. panel mem. War Labor Bd., 1943-44; mem. consumers council Atty.-Gen.'s Office. Mem. Consumers Union (mem. nat. ednl. adv. council), Am. Arbitration Assn., Am. Assn. U. Prof., Pioneer Valley Assn. (pres. 1962-64), Am. Econ. Assn., Tax Research Found., Phi Kappa Phi, Sigma Chi. Author: The Taxation of Insurance Companies, 1937. State corr. and contbr. to The Municipal Yearbook, 1937-40, 43-50. Home: 2 Mary Jane Lane Newport RI 02840

GAMBLE, WILLIAM BLAINE, utilities exec.; b. McKeesport, Pa., May 30, 1910; s. W. Blaine and Margaret (Gleason) G.; student Robert Morris Sch. Bus., 1928-30; B.S., Grove City (Pa.) Coll., 1934; m. Kathryn Linderman, June 15, 1936; children—Susan (Mrs. Eugene P. Feinour), Betsey (Mrs. Thomas K. Ward). Mgr., Price Waterhouse & Co., C.P.A.'s, Pitts., 1935-55; v.p., dir. Am. Water Works, Inc., Phila., 1955—; dir. Am. Commonwealth Co., Westfay Co., Am. Land Developers, Inc., Greenwich Water System, Inc., New Eng. Water Service Corp., So. Conn. Real Estate Co., N. Pa. Gas Co., also 23 water cos. Bd. dirs. Am. Water Works Found., Nat. Water Co. Conf. C.P.A., Pa. Mem. Financial Execs. Inst., Am. Inst. C.P.A.'s, Am. Water Works Assn. Republican, Presbyn. Clubs: Merion (Pa.) Golf; Urban, Union League (Phila.). Home: 312 Pine Tree Rd Radnor PA 19087 Office: 3 Penn Center Plaza Philadelphia PA 19102

GAMBRELL, BARMORE PEPPER, lawyer; b. Belton, S.C., Jan. 27, 1894; s. Enoch Pepper and Macie (Latimer) G.; A.B., Furman U., 1915; student Washington and Lee U., 1916; LL.B., Georgetown U., 1918. Admitted to D.C. bar, 1919, Ga. bar, 1920; clk. office of sec. U.S. Senate, 1917-18; practicing lawyer, Atlanta, 1920—; mem. Arnold & Gambrell and predecessors, 1930-57, now in individual practice. Mem. adv. council to bd. trustees Furman U. Served as chief petty officer, USN, World War I. Recipient Distinguished Alumnus award Furman U., 1968. Fellow Am. Coll. Trial Lawyers, Am. Bar Found.; mem. Am., Atlanta bar assns., State Bar Ga., Am. Judicature Soc., Am. Legion (comdr. Atlanta post 1922-23). Democrat. Baptist. Clubs: Capital City, Piedmont Driving, Lawyers, Commerce (Atlanta). Home: 2025 Peachtree Rd N E Atlanta GA 30309 Office: Nat Bank of Ga Bldg Atlanta GA 30303

GAMBRELL, CHARLES GLENN, former banker; b. Belton, S.C., Sept. 27, 1902; s. Enoch Pepper and Macie Amanda (Latimer) G.; student U. S.C., 1918-19; A.B.,Furman U., 1922; M.B.A., Harvard, 1925; LL.D., Presby. Coll., 1962; m. Sarah Walkup Belk, Nov. 21, 1952; 1 dau., Sarah. Clk., Wilmington (N.C.) Saving and Trust Co., 1923, Irving Trust Co., N.Y.C., 1925-29, asst. sec., 1929-34, asst.. v.p., 1934-46, v.p., 1946-67; now chmn. com. on finance, chmn. pension fund com. Belk Stores, Charlotte, N.C. Treas., dir. 580 Park Av. Corp., N.Y.C.; bd. visitors St. Andrews Coll., Laurinburg, N.C.; mem. devel. com. Princeton (N.J.) Theol. Sem.; trustee Converse Coll.; chmn. exec. com., bd. dirs. Presbyterian Progress Found. Served to lt. col., USAAF, 1942-45. Mem. Harvard Bus. Sch. Alumni Assn. N.Y. (past pres.), N.Y. So. Soc. (mem. exec. com.), Sigma Alpha Epsilon. Presbyn. Clubs: Union, University, Harvard (N.Y.C.); Apawamis (Rye, N.Y.); Charlotte City, Charlotte Country (Charlotte, N.C.). Home: 580 Park Av New York City NY 10021 Office: 308 E 5th St Charlotte NC 28202

GAMBRELL, DAVID HENRY, lawyer; b. Atlanta, Dec. 20, 1929; s. E. Smythe and Kathleen (Hagood) G.; B.S., Davidson Coll., 1949; LL.B. cum laude, Harvard, 1952; m. Luck Coleman Flanders, Oct. 16, 1953; children—Luck Coleman, David Henry, Alice Kathleen Hagood, Mary Latimer. Admitted to Ga. bar, 1951; pvt. practice, Atlanta, 1952-54, 56—; teaching fellow Harvard Law Sch., 1954-55; partner firm Gambrell & Mobley, 1963—. Gen. counsel Atlanta Crime Commn., 1970. Bd. dirs. Ga. YMCA, 1965—, v.p., 1965-66; trustee Met. Atlanta Commn. Crime and Juvenile Delinquency, 1966-68; bd. dirs. Nat. Legal Aid and Defender Assn., 1965—. Chmn. Democratic Party State of Ga., 1970. Mem. Am., Atlanta (pres. 1965-66) bar assns., State Bar Ga. (bd. govs. 1964-66, pres. 1967-68), Lawyers Club Atlanta, N.C. Soc. Cinc., Sigma Alpha Epsilon, Omicron Delta Kappa. Democrat. Presbyn. Kiwanian. Clubs: Piedmont Driving, Atlanta Country, Capital City (Atlanta). Bd. editors Am. Bar Assn. Jour., 1969-70. Home: 3820 Castlegate Dr N W Atlanta GA 30327 Office: First National Bank Bldg Atlanta GA 30303

GAMBRELL, ENOCH SMYTHE, lawyer; b. Belton, S.C., Jan. 29, 1896; s. Enoch Pepper and Macie Amanda (Latimer) G.; A.B., U. S.C., 1915, LL.D., 1953; LL.B., Harvard, 1922; LL.D., So. Meth. U., 1956, U. Montreal, 1956, Emory U., 1964; m. Kathleen Hagood, Feb. 24, 1927 (dec. 1932); children—Robert (dec.), David. Prin. pub. sch., Bannockburn, S.C., 1915-16; supt. schs., Pelzer, S.C., 1916-18; admitted to Ga. bar, 1922, since practiced in Atlanta; partner inlaw firm Gambrell, Russell, Killorin, Wade & Forbes; counsel, dir. numerous indsl., ins., transp. and other companies; prof. law Emory U., 1922-40. Trustee U.S.C. Ednl. Found., chmn. Chair Endowment Club U. S.C. 1960-70. Served with Machine Gun Co., 324th Inf., 81st Div., A.E.F., 1918-19; was instr. A.E.F. Univ., Beaune, France, Pres. Atlanta Legal Aid Soc., 1924-41 (organizer); mem. Ga. State Council YMCA, 1931—. Recipient Am. Bar Assn. medal for conspicuous service to cause of Am. jurisprudence, 1958. Fellow Am. Coll. Trial Lawyers; mem. Atlanta Lawyers Found. (chmn. bd. 1958-69, trustee), Ga. C. of C. (pres. 1952-54), gen. counsel 1954—), Am. (pres. 1955-56, bd. govs. 1955-57), Ga. (v.p. 1934), Atlanta bar assns., Assn. Bar City of N.Y., Internat. Assn. Ins. Counsel, Am. Law Inst., Am. Judicature Soc. (v.p. 1956-58), Acad. Polit. Sci., Lawyers Club Atlanta (pres. 194-49), Harvard Law Sch. Assn. (mem. council 1956—), Am. Bar Found. (pres. 1955-56, chmn. fellows 1956-57), Order of Coif, Phi Beta Kappa, Phi Delta Phi, Sigma Alpha Epsilon. Baptist. Clubs: Capital City, Harvard, Piedmont Driving, Commerce. Contbr. articles to legal publs. Home: 1327 Peachtree St Atlanta GA 30303 Office: First Nat Bank Tower Atlanta GA 30303

GAMBRELL, MARY LATIMER, educator; b. Belton, S.C., Jan. 14, 1898; d. Enoch Pepper and Macie (Latimer) Gambrell; A.B., Greenville Woman's Coll. (now Furman U.), 1917, Litt. D., 1951; A.M., Columbia, 1931, Ph.D., 1937; L.H.D., Queens Coll., 1958. Instr. history New Haven State Tchrs. Coll., 1932-37; lectr. dept. edn. extension state of Conn., 1934; instr. history Hunter Coll., N.Y.C., 1937-43, asst. prof., 1944-48, asso. prof., 1949-53, prof., 1953—, chmn. dept. history, 1948-62, dean faculties, 1961-66, acting pres.,

1965, 66, pres., 1967, pres. emeritus, 1968—. Mem. legislative conf. City Colls., 1946-48. Mem. Am. Hist. Assn., Am. Assn. U. Women (named Woman of Year, N.Y.C. chpt. 1967), Berkshire Hist. Conf. (pres. 1946- 49), English-Speaking Union, Phi Beta Kappa Assos., Phi Beta Kappa. Presby. Club: Cosmopolitan. Author: Ministerial Training in Eighteenth Century New England, 1937. Contbr. to profl. jours. Home: 70 E 96th St New York City NY 10028 Office: 695 Park Av New York City NY 10021

GAMELIN, FRANCIS CLIFFORD, assn. exec., educator; b. South St. Paul, Sept. 13, 1917; s. Francis W. and Elsie (Oesterreich) G.; B.A., Gustavus Adolphus Coll., 1938; M.A., U. Minn., 1946, Ph.D., 1953; L.H.D., Gettysburg Coll., 1966; m. Ruth Vikner, Oct. 8, 1938; children—Theodore, Daniel, Timothy, Steven, Quentin, Lili Marie. Instr., Luther Coll., Decorah, Ia., 1938-40; instr. Gustavus Adolphus Coll., 1940-43, registrar, 1943-47; instr. U. Minn., 1947-50, sr. student personnel worker, 1953-55; acting dir. mental health services Minn. Dept. Health, 1951-52; co-ordinator psychol. services Austin (Minn.) Pub. Schs., 1955-58; asst. dist. supt. pub. schs., Robbinsdale, Minn., 1958-62; sec. coll. edn. Luth. Ch. in Am., N.Y.C., 1962-64, exec. sec. Bd. Coll. Edn., 1964-67; v.p., dean faculty Augustana Coll., 1967-69; exec. dir. Central States Coll. Assn., Rock Island, Ill., 1969—. Mem. dist. sch. bd. Robbinsdale, 1954-55; mem. Minn. Adv. Bd. Exceptional Children, 1959-62; pres. Minn. Council Gifted, 1960-61; sec. nat. council Assns. for Internat. Studies, N.Y. Bd. dirs. Youth Research Center, Mpls., Endicott Coll., Beverly, Mass., Luth. Ch. in Am. Bd. Parish Edn., Phila. Served with USNR, 1945. Home: 2359 29th St Rock Island IL Office: 1308 20th St Rock Island IL 61201

GAMER, SAUL RICHARD, lawyer; b. New Haven, Mar. 27, 1906; s. Samuel and Bertha (Resnik) G.; Ph.B., Yale, 1927, LL.B., 1929; m. Ethel Huchberger, June 28, 1934; children—Janet G. (Mrs. T.S.L. Perlman), Susan J. (Mrs. William B. Blacklow). Admitted to Conn. bar, 1929, N.Y. bar, 1931, D.C. bar, 1939, U.S. Supreme Ct., 1935; faculty research asst. Yale Law Sch., 1929-30; charge investigations for Report Nat. Commn. on Law Observance and Enforcement (Wickersham Commn.), on Lawlessness in Law Enforcement, 1930-31; pvt. practice law, N.Y.C.; asso. Engelhard, Pollak, Pitcher & Stern, 1931- 34; atty. NRA, Dept. Agr., Rural Electrification Adminstrn., 1934-37; practice law, New Haven, 1938; supervisory loan atty. Rural Electrification Adminstrn., chief court claims sect., civil div. Dept. Justice, 1939-58; commr. U.S. Ct. Claims, Washington, 1958—. Recipient merit citation Nat. Civil Service League, 1958. Mem. Am., Fed. bar assns., Phi Beta Kappa. Bd. editors Yale Law Jour., 1928-29. Contbr. legal periodicals. Home: 2818 Kanawha St N W Washington DC 20015 Office: Court of Claims Washington DC 20005

GAMET, DONALD MAX, accountant; b. Mapleton, Kan., Feb. 21, 1916; s. Carl Adolph and Pearl (McClanahan) G.; B.S., Ft. Hays (Kan.) State Coll., 1938; M.B.A., U. Kan., 1939, LL.B., 1942; m. L. Pauline Fleming, Apr. 14, 1938; children—Merilyn Kay, Carleton Lenoir, Kathy Lynn. With Arthur Andersen & Co., C.P.A.'s, 1942—, partner, 1954—, partner charge Kansas City office, 1956-70, mng. partner taxes, Chgo., 1970—, also dir. Chmn. spl. gifts div. United Fund campaign, 1963. Pres., bd. dirs. Estate Planning Council Kansas City; bd. dirs. Heart of Am. United Funds, chmn. 1967, pres. campaign, 1968; bd. dirs., exec. com., treas. Civic Council Greater Kansas City, 1967-68; bd. dirs. Kansas City Indsl. Found., Jr. Achievement Kan. Mem. Kansas City C. of C. (econ. devel. estate planning council, past vice chmn. indsl. com., 1st v.p. 1969, pres. 1970), Am. Inst. C.P.A.'s, Mo. Soc. C.P.A.'s. Presbyn. Kiwanian. Club: Kansas City (past dir.). Home: 19 W 064 Av Normandy S Oak Brook IL 60521 Office: 69 W Washington St Chicago IL 60602

GAMLEM, THORALF ERNST, aircraft co. exec.; b. Mpls., June 19, 1908; s. Ingvald Thomas and Marie (Mikkelsen) G.; student U. Wash., 1926-27; m. Gladys Elizabeth Delaware, June 5, 1931. With Boeing Airplane Co. (now The Boeing Co.), 1929—, chief engr. Wichita (Kan.) div., 1956-58, asst. gen. mgr. transport div., 1958-60, v.p. co., 1960—, v.p., gen. mgr. fabrication and service div. of comml. airplane group, Auburn, Wash., 1966—; v.p., dir. Boeing of Can. Ltd., 1969—. Asso. fellow Am. Inst. Aeros. and Astronautics. Home: Route 3 Box 63 Snohomish WA 98290 Office: The Boeing Co Comml Airplane Group Fabrication and Service Division Auburn WA 98002

GAMMELL, NOBLE FREDERICK, electronic co. exec.; b. Lineville, Ia., Aug. 26, 1920; s. Frederick Wayne and Myrie (Noble) W.; student Cummings Sch. Art, 1939-40, Ia. State U. Extension, 1940; m. Shirley Larson, Mar. 14, 1942; children—Stephen, Rebecca, Timothy, Janet. With J. C. Penney Co., 1941; artist Meredith Pub. Co., 1941-51; art editor Better Homes and Gardens mag., 1951-61, editor art prodn., 1961-70; editor art prodn. Successful Farming mag., 1961-70; art dir. GC Electronics, Rockford, Ill., 1970—. Served with Signal Corps, AUS, 1943-45. Office: 400 S Wyman St Rockford IL 61101

GAMMIE, GEORGE, clay products mfg. exec.; b. Glasgow, Scotland, Nov. 2, 1898; s. James Alexander; and Jane (Leslie) G.; m. Rena Anys. June 8, 1923; children—Donald, James, Jane (Mrs. William G. Barnard). Mgr. Hydraulic Press Brick Co., 1936-40; sales mgr. Ill. Brick Co., 1940-47, v.p., gen. sales mgr., 1947-60, pres., dir., 1960—; pres., dir. Poston-Herron Brick Co., Attica, Ind.; treas., dir. Structural Clay Products Inst., Washington. Rotarian. Clubs: Builders (Chgo.); La Grange Country. Home: 408 S Kensington Av La Grange IL 60525 Office: 228 N LaSalle St Chicago IL 60601

GAMMILL, HOMER LEE, educator; b. Charleston, Ill., Feb. 21, 1905; s. Finis I. and Loura (Milholland) G.; A.B., U. No. Colo., 1926; M.A., U. Neb., 1938; Ph.D., 1952; m. Rose M. Hoffmann, June 13, 1935; children—Robert Charles, Jean Ann (Mrs. Phillip M. Shelton). Tchr., Whittier Jr. High Sch., Lincoln, Neb., 1926-43; instr. Ark. A. and M. Coll., Monticello, 1943; tng. dir. Victor Div. RCA Victor, Bloomington, Ind., 1944-45; mgr. personnel Gardner-Denver Co., Quincy, Ill., 1945-46; mem. faculty dept. indsl. psychology U. Ill. at Urbana, 1946—, prof., 1959—; cons. to industry. Mem. Am. Psychol. Assn., Am. Mgmt. Assn., Phi Delta Kappa. Home: 1201 E Florida Av Urbana IL 61801

GAMMON, LANDON HAYNES, lawyer; b. Saltville, Va., Sept. 28, 1896; s. Landon Haynes and Rosa Cabell (Miller) G.; A.B., U. Va., 1918; LL.B., Harvard, 1922; m. Katherine C. Conn, June 30, 1926. Admitted to Tenn. bar, 1922, since practiced law, Chattanooga; mem. Goins, Gammon, Baker & Robinson and predecessor firms, 1925—; spl. judge Ct. Appeals, Tenn., 1959-60. Trustee Chattanooga Pub. Library. Served in U.S. Army, World War I; mem. Selective Service Bd., World War II. Mem. Am., Tenn., Chattanooga bar assns., Selden Soc., Am. Legion. Democrat. Presbyn. Contbr. articles law jour. Home: 705 Battery Pl Chattanooga TN 37403 Office: Maclellan Bldg Chattanooga TN 37402

GAMMON, ROLAND IRVINE, author, lectr., pub. relations exec.; b. Caribou, Me., Nov. 18, 1916; s. Charles G. and Fern (Irvine) G.; B.A., Colby Coll., 1937; postgrad. Oxford (Eng.) U., 1938. Reporter, Portland (Me.) Press Herald, 1938-41, Life Mag., 1941-48; asso. editor Pageant mag., 1948-50; mng. editor See mag., 1950-54; pres. Roland Gammon Assos., N.Y.C., 1955-58; v.p. Peed, Gammon & Co., N.Y.C., 1959-63; pres. Comminicorp Pub. Relations, N.Y.C., 1963-64, also Editorial Communications. Inc., N.Y.C., 1964—; religion editor NANA Syndicate and author syndicated column Faith is a Star, 1965—. Mem. Nat. Religious Pub. Relations Council. Served as 2d lt. USAAF, 1941-45. Mem. Nat. Assn. Universalist Men (pres. 1956-59), World Parliament of Religions (v.p. 1950). Unitarian Universalist Assn., Am Vets. Com., Soc. Am. Mag. Writers, Laymen's Movements, Internat. Christian Leadership, Fellowship in Prayer (v.p.), Phi Beta Kappa. Club: Overseas Press (N.Y.C.). Universalist-Unitarian (pres. ch.). Author: (with H.J. Forman) Truth Is One, 1955; Faith is a Star, 1963; A God for Modern Man, 1967; All Believers are Brothers, 1969. Lectr. on religion and culture. Home: 114 E 72d St New York City NY 10021 Office: 555 Madison Av New York City NY 10022

GAMSER, HOWARD G., lawyer; b. N.Y.C.; s. Gustave and Rose (Harris) G.; B.S.S., Coll. City N.Y., 1940; M.A., Columbia, 1941; J.D., N.Y.U., 1952; m. Doris P. Gold, Oct. 5, 1952; children—Matthew Simon, Diana Marion. Admitted to N.Y. and D.C. bars; with NLRB, 1946-52, Wage Stblzn. Bd., 1952-53, N.Y. Mediation Bd., lectr. labor law Columbia, 1957- 61; pvt. practice law and arbitration, N.Y.C., 1952-61; lectr. N.Y. SSILR, Cornell U., 1947-61, London Sch. Econs., 1953-54; chief counsel com. edn. and labor U.S. Ho. of Reps., 1961-63; chmn., mem. Nat. Mediation Bd., 1964-69; atty.-arbitrator, Washington, 1969—; counsel commn. non rules Democratic Nat. Com., 1969—; adj. prof. law Georgetown U., 1965—. Served to capt. AUS, 1941-46. Mem. Indsl. and Labor Relations Assn., Am. Econ. Assn., N.Y., D.C., Feb. bar assns., Nat. Acad. Arbitrators (dir.), Phi Beta Kappa. Democrat. Contbr. articles to various legal and econ. periodicals. Home: New York City NY also 3022 Cambridge Pl NW Washington DC 20007 Office: 1225 19th St Washington DC 20036

GAMSO, RAFAEL ROBERT, med. adminstr., physician; b. N.Y.C., Apr. 21, 1911; s. Nathan Michael and Mary R. (Shubert) G.; B.S., N.Y. U., 1932; M.D., Baylor U., 1936; m. Rose Raher, Apr. 3, 1955. Intern, Cumberland Hosp., Bklyn., 1936-38; pvt. practice, Bklyn., 1938-41, 46-48; dir. out patient dept. Kings County Hosp., Bklyn., 1948-50, asst. hosp. adminstr, charge psychiat. div., 1950-53; med. supt. Riverside Hosp., N. Brothers Island, N.Y., 1953-61; adminstr. Harlem Hosp., N.Y.C., 1961-65, Goldwater Meml. Hosp., N.Y.C., 1965-68; dir. med. services N.Y. State Narcotic Addiction Control Commn., N.Y.C., 1968—. Served to maj. M.C., AUS, World War II; PTO. Decorated Silver Star medal. Mem. A.M.A., Med. Assn. N.Y., Med. Soc. County N.Y., Assn. Mil. Surgeons U.S., A.A.A.S., Profl. Assn. Pub. Execs. City N.Y. and Met. Area, Hosp. Adminstrs. Assn. N.Y.C., Phi Delta Epsilon. Jewish religion. Author articles in field. Spl. research devel., operation treatment young drug addicts. Home: 35 Crescent Dr Searington NY 11507 Office: 1855 Broadway New York City NY 10023

GANDHI, INDIRA, prime minister of India; b. Allahabad, India, Nov. 19, 1917; d. Jawaharlal and Kamala (Koul) Nehru; student schs. Switzerland, Shantiniketan Univ., India; Somerville Coll., Oxford (Eng.) U.; D.Litt. (hon.), Andrha U., 1963; m. Feroze Gandhi, 1942 (dec.); children—Rajiv, Sanjay. Disciple of Gandhi; formed children's orgn. to help Indian Nat. Congress during non-cooperation movement; worked among untouchables popularizing hand-spun cloth and Indian made goods; active student movement India, Eng.; mem. Indian Nat. Congress, 1938—, mem. working com., central election com., central parliamentary bd., 1955—, pres. Congress, 1959; minister of information and broadcasting Govt. of India; prime minister of India, 1966—. Ofcl. hostess Prime Minister Nehru, 1947. Hon. pres. Adv. Council of Edn. Centre for Southeast Asia Internat. Coop. Alliance; chmn. Citizens' Central Council, 1962; exec. com. Nat. Def. Fund, 1962; sec. Jawaharal Nehru Meml., 1964. Pres. Indian Council Child Welfare; v.p. Internat. Union Child Welfare. Mem. Indian Delegation, UNESCO, 1960, mem. exec. bd. UNESCO, mem. central adv. bd. edn. Chmn. Nat. Integration Com., Indian Nat. Congress, Nat. Inst. Women, Kamala Nehru Vidayalaya, Bal Bhavan, Bal Sahyog; also with several other social welfare orgns. Mem. governing body Himalayan Mountaineering Inst., Tibetan Homes Found. Recipient Mother's award, U.S.A., 1953; Yale U. Howland Meml. prize, 1960. Mem. Fed. Film Socs. India (v.p.). Address: 1 Safdarjang Rd New Delhi India

GANDIN, JOHN LIVINGSTON, Jr., mfg. co. exec.; b. Boston, Jan. 22, 1910; s. John Livingston and Isabel (McCurdy) G.; B.S., Harvard, 1932, M.B.A., 1934; m. Susanne Preston Wilson, Aug. 24, 1940; childrenJohn Livingston III, Edward W., Preston B. Trustee J.L. Grandin, 1934-41, 46-48; asst. sec. Gillette Co., Boston, 1948, now sec.; dir. Boston Safe Deposit & Trust Co., The Boston Co., Inc., Constn. Exchange Fund. Vice pres., exec. com. Franklin Sq. Ho.; corp. mem. Mass. Meml. Hosp., Northeastern U., Mus. Sci., Boston; chmn. bd. trustees Northfield and Mount Hermon Schs. Served to lt. comdr. USNR, 1942-46. Clubs: Commercial, Merchants (Boston); Country (Brookline, Mass.). Home: 169 Chestnut Hill Rd Chestnut Hill MA 02167 Office: Gillette Co Gillette Park Boston MA 02199

GANDY, EDYTHE EVELYN, state ofcl.; b. Hattiesburg, Miss., Sept. 4, 1922; d. Kearney C. and Abbie (Whigham) Gandy; student U. So. Miss., 1939-40; LL.B., U. Miss., 1944. Admitted to Miss. bar, 1944; practiced in Hattiesburg, 1948-56; atty. Miss. Dept. Pub. Welfare, 1954-58; asst. atty. gen. Miss., 1959; treas. Miss., 1960-64, 68—; commr. pub. welfare, 1964-67. Mem. Miss. Econ. Council, 1968—, Miss. Mental Health Commn., 1964-67, Miss. Cabinet Women in Pub. Affairs, 1948—; mem. Gov.'s Commn. on Status of Women, 1964—. Mem. Miss. Ho. of Reps., 1948-52. Bd. dirs. Miss. Hosp. and Med. Service. Mem. Miss. Fedn. Bus. and Profl. Womens Clubs (past pres.), Miss. Bar Assn., Am. Pub. Welfare Assn., (life) Miss. Congress P.T.A., Miss. Ofcl. Womens Club. Democrat. Baptist. Club: Altrusa (Jackson, Miss.). Home: 727 Arlington St Jackson MS 39202 Office: New Capitol Bldg Jackson MS 39205

GANDY, JOSEPH EDWARD, former lawyer; b. Spokane, Wash., Oct. 9, 1904; s. Lloyd E. and Helen D. (George) G.; B.A., U. Mich., 1926; LL.B., U. Wash., 1929; m. Laurene Tatlow, Aug. 11, 1937; 1 dau., Marilyn L. Admitted to Wash. bar, 1929; practiced law, Seattle, 1929-71; mem. LeSourd, Patton, Fleming & Hartung, 1968-71. Chief, dep. regional dir. WPB, 1942-46; automobile dealer Smith-Gandy, Inc., 1946-71; consul of Ceylon, 1967-71. Chmn. bd. United Good Neighbors, 1953; bd. dirs., v.p. Seattle Urban League, 1954-57, Seattle Art Mus. Vice pres. Seattle Municipal League, 1958; pres. Seattle Symphony Orch. Assn., 1948-50, Seattle World's Fair 1959-62; Neptune Rex X of Seattle Seafair, 1959; v.p. Arboretum Found., 1958-60. Mem. Seattle C. of C. (past pres.), Central Assn. Seattle (past pres.), Nat., Wash. (dir.), Seattle (dir.) auto dealers assns., Phi Gamma Delta, Phi Delta Phi, Phi Kappa Psi. Episcopalian. Clubs: Rainier, Tennis (Seattle). Home: 1509 Shenandoah Dr E Seattle WA 98102 Office: Northern Life Tower Seattle WA 98101 Died June 13, 1971

GANE, JOHN FREDERICK, architect; b. Phila., Oct. 8, 1908; s. Frederick and Martha M. (Smith) G.; B.A., Williams Coll., 1931; B.F.A., Sch. Architecture, Yale U., 1936; m. Ann Katherine Paxson, Feb. 22, 1941 (dec. Sept. 1956). Partner, Wigham & Tilden, architects, 1950-56, Wright, Andrade, Amenta & Gane, architects, 1960-63, Wright & Gane, architects, Phila., 1963-69; architect, editor Am. Architects, Directory, Phila., 1969—; instr. U. Pa., 1943-47. Mem. A.I.A. Home: 2135 Naudain St Philadelphia PA 19146

GANEY, J. CULLEN, judge; b. Bethlehem, Pa., Apr. 22, 1899; s. Thomas and Catherine (Cullen) G.; A.B., Lehigh U., 1920, LL.D., 1960; LL.B., Harvard, 1923; LL.D., St. Joseph's Coll., 1952; m. Evelyn Gorman, Nov. 19, 1933; 1 dau., Jean Mary. Admitted to Pa. bar, 1923, and practiced in Bethehem; U.S. atty. eastern dist. Pa., 1937-40; fed. judge eastern dist. Pa., 1940-61, chief judge, 1958-61; judge U.S. Ct. Appeals 3d Circuit, Phila., 1961-66, sr. U.S. circuit judge, 1966—. Rep., Dist. Judges N.J., Pa.; del. Jud. Conf. U.S. Mem. Am., Pa. bar assns. Democrat. Home: Philadelphia PA 19101 Address: Fed Ct Bldg 9th and Chestnut Sts Philadelphia PA 19107

GANGE, JOHN FREDERIC, educator; Lindsay, Cal., May 30, 1910; s. Charles Frederick and Luri (Theone) G.; A.B., Stanford, 1932, A.M., 1934, postgrad., 1934-36; m. Martha Eugenia Arnold, June 11, 1937; children—Jared Jefferson, Julie Beryl. Mem. faculty Eastern Wash. Coll. of Edn., Princeton, Stanford, 1936-41; with Brookings Instn. Survey of Dominican Republic, 1941, 47, 48; U.S. exec. sec. Anglo-Am. Caribbean Commn. and exec. sec. Central Secretariat, Office U.S. Sec. of State, 1941-47; exec. sec. Central Secretariat, ECA, 1948-49; dir. Woodrow Wilson Sch. Fgn. Affairs, U. Va., 1949-56; dir. research tng. Social Sci. Research Council, N.Y.C., 1957; Fulbright vis. prof. U. Heidelberg (Germany), 1956-57, cons. U.S. Dept. Def. and U.S. Psychol. Strategy Bd., 1952; exec. dir. Am. Polit. Sci. Assn., 1953-54; faculty fellow Fund for Advancement Edn., 1955-56; dir. rev. and devel. Asia Found.; resident rep. The Asia Found., Hong Kong, B.C.C., 1957-60; dir. Inst. Internat. Studies and Overseas Adminstrn., U. Ore., 1961—, prof. polit. sci., 1961—; participant 1st Asian- Am. Assembly, Malaya, 1963; Ford Found. grant for research, Greece and Turkey, 1967. Mem. U.S. Nat. Commn. for UNESCO, 1968-70, Com. on Internat. Exchange of Persons, Conf. Bd. of Asso. Research Councils, 1968—, U.S. Dept. State Am. Specialist Program, Spain, 1969. Adv. trustee Social Sci. Found., 1955-59. Mem. Am. Polit. Sci. Assn., Internat. Studies Assn. (pres. 1964-66), Soc. Internat. Devel., Phi Beta Kappa, Pi Sigma Alpha. Co-author: Refugee Settlement in the Dominican Republic, 1942; Major Problems of U.S. Foreign Policy, 1947. Author: The Secretariat Function, 1953; University Research in International Affairs, 1958; American Foreign Relations, 1959. Home: 2421 Washington St Eugene OR 97405

GANGE, JOSEPH GEORGE, bus. exec.; b. Woburn, Mass., Oct. 8, 1905; s. Anthony and Rose (Zita) G.; grad. Bentley Coll. Accounting and Finance, 1924; m. Edith G. Farnsworth, June 4, 1929; 1 son, Joseph George, Jr. With U.S. Smelting Refining & Mining Co., 1925—, comptroller, 1948-53, v.p., comptroller, 1953-54, administrv. v.p., 1954-60, sr. v.p., 1960—, also sec., treas., dir., mem. exec. com.; v.p., dir. Hanover Bessemer Iron & Copper Co., U.S. Lead Refinery. Inc., Usram Exploration Co., v.p. U.S. Fuel Co.; v.p., dir. Richmond-Eureka Mining Co., Washington Mining Co., Mueller Brass Co.; dir. Ruby Hill Mining Co. Trustee Bentley Coll. Accounting and Finance. C.P.A., Utah. Mem. Am. Inst. C.P.A.'s, Mass. Soc. C.P.A.'s. Home: 67 Lawrence Pkwy Tenafly NJ 07670 Office: 235 E 42d St New York City NY 10017

GANGER, ROBERT MONDELL, former bus. exec.; b. Greenville, O., June 20, 1903; s. Ora Lynn and Della (Cox) G.; A.B., Ohio State U., 1926; m. Jean Wyvle Ward, Dec. 25, 1933; 1 son, Robert Ward. Vice pres. Geyer, Cornell, Newell, Inc., N.Y.C., 1933- 45; partner Geyer, Newell & Ganger, Inc., 1945-50; exec. v.p. P. Lorillard & Co., 1950-52, pres., 1952-53, dir., mem. exec. com., 1950-53; chmn. bd., exec. com. D'Arcy Co., 1953-69. Bd. dirs., mem. exec. com. United Service Orgn., Advt. Council; bd. dirs. Advt. Research Found. Mem. Am. Assn. Advt. Agys. (past chmn. bd.), Ohio Soc. N.Y. Republican. Mem. Ref. Ch. Clubs: Siwanoy, University, National Golf Links, Country of Florida; Mid Ocean Country (Bermuda); Gulf Stream Golf, Gulf Stream Bath and Tennis. Home: 1443 N Ocean Blvd Delray Beach FL 33444

GANGWERE, GEORGE HENRY, Jr., lawyer; b. Pitts., July 5, 1917; s. George Henry and Pauline (Brown) G.; student Youngstown (O.) Coll., 1937; A.B., U. Mich., 1940, LL.B., 1949; m. Blanche M. Gregory, June 30, 1946; children—George Henry III, Margaret, Robert. Admitted to Mo. bar, 1948, since practiced in Kansas City; partner firm Swanson, Midgley, Jones, Eager & Gangwere, and predecessors, 1952—; lectr. estate planning, 1960—. Pres. Estate Planning Council Kansas City. Mo., 1966. Served to capt. AUS, 1941-46; ETO. Decorated Bronze Star medal. Mem. Lawyers Assn. Kansas City (sec. 1964-66, treas. 1960), Am., Mo. (bd. govs. 1970—) bar assns., U. Mich. Alumni Assn. (dir. 1962-64), Am. Legion (past post comdr.), V.F.W., Kansas City (Mo.) C. of C., Kansas City Real Estate Bd., Alpha Sigma Phi. Mason (Shriner). Clubs: University of Michigan (pres. 1955), Blue Hills Country (pres. 1969), Kansas City. Home: 6940 Edgevale Rd Kansas City MO 64113 Office: Commerce Bank Bldg Kansas City MO 64106

GANLEY, OSWALD HAROLD, govt. ofcl.; b. Amsterdam, Holland, Jan. 28, 1929; s. Eric Harold and Emily (Auerbach) G.; came to U.S., 1947, naturalized, 1952; A.B., Hope Coll., 1950; M.S., Ph.D., U. Mich., 1953; M.P.A., Harvard, 1965; m. Gladys Dickens, Sept. 3, 1950; children—Robert C., Delia A. Research asst. Walter Reed Inst., 1953-55; research asso. Merck Inst. Therapeutic Research, Rahway, N.J., 1955-60; asst. dir. internat. relations Merck, Sharp and Dohme Research Labs., Rahway, 1960-64; head tech. div. Bur. Internat. Sci. and Tech. Affairs, State Dept., 1965-66, head European affairs, 1966-69; sci. attaché Am. embassy, Rome and Bucharest, 1969—. Dir. Jaycees, 1958-60; dir. pub. relations Civil Def., Plainfield, N.J., 1962-64. Served with AUS, 1953-55. Sci. and Public Policy fellow Harvard, 1964-65. Fellow Am. Acad. Microbiology; mem. Am. Physiol. Soc., Am. Soc. Microbiology, Sigma Xi. Presbyn. Club: Circolo Catoniere Tevereremo (Rome). Contbr. articles sci. jours. Home: Via Archimede 106 Roma Italy Office: Am Embassy APO New York City NY 09794

GANN, ERNEST KELLOGG, author; b. Lincoln, Neb., Oct. 13, 1910; s. George Kellogg and Caroline (Kupper) G.; student Culver Mil. Acad., Yale U. Sch. Fine Arts; m. Eleanor Michaud, Sept. 18, 1933 (div.); children—George Kellogg, Steven Anthony, Polly Wing; m. 2d Dodie Post, May 20, 1966. Author: Island In the Sky, Blaze of Noon, Fiddler's Green, Benjamin Lawless, The High and the Mighty, Soldier of Fortune, Twilight for the Gods, Trouble with Lazy Ethel, Fate Is the Hunter, Of Good and Evil, In the Company of Eagles, Song of the Sirens, also many short stories. Served as capt. Air Transport Command, AUS, 1942-46, Decorated Distinguished Flying award. Home: Friday Harbor San Juan Island WA 98250

GANN, GENE E., steel mfg. co. exec.; b. New Castle, Ind., Mar. 5, 1917; s. John C. and Lilah (Gary) G.; grad. high sch.; m. Jessie C. Torrence, Aug. 7, 1936; 1 dau., Patricia (Mrs. Clinton Sampson). Supr., Ford Motor Co., Dearborn, Mich., 1940-44; v.p., gen. mgr. Gaylord Mfg. Co., Gaylord, Mich., 1946-54; exec. v.p. McLouth Steel Corp., Detroit, 1954—; pres., dir. Ashland Mining Corp., 1968—; v.p., dir. Empire Mining Co., 1963—; dir. McLouth Steel Corp. Served with USMCR, 1944-46. Clubs: Detroit Athletic, Recess, Oakland

Hills Country (Detroit); Otsego Ski (Gaylord, Mich.). Home: 18575 Saratoga Lathrup Village MI 48075 Office: 300 S Livernois Detroit MI 48017

GANNER, THOMAS ALAN, accountant; b. N.Y.C., Mar. 9, 1921; s. Russon Giddings and Claire M. (Whelan) G.; student N.Y. U., 1938-41; B.S. summa cum laude, Ohio State U., 1947; m. Donna Marie Daron, May 26, 1950; children—Thomas Alan, William Russon. With Price Waterhouse & Co., C.P.A.'s, N.Y.C., 1947—, gen. partner, 1958—, mem. policy com., 1965—. Bd. dirs. Lower Downtown-Manhattan Assn. Served to 1st lt. AUS, 1941-45. C.P.A., N.Y. Mem. Am. Inst. C.P.A.'s, N.Y. C. of C., Commerce and Industry Assn. N.Y., Beta Gamma Sigma, Beta Alpha Psi. Clubs: Recess, Union League, Metropolitan (N.Y.C.); Duquesne (Pitts.); Canoe Brook Country (Summit). Home: 69 Portland Rd Summit NJ 07901 Office: 60 Broad St New York City NY 10004

GANNETT, MICHAEL ROSS, govt. ofcl.; b. Neuilly-sur-Seine, France, July 13, 1919; s. Lewis Stiles and Mary Elizabeth (Ross) G.; came to U.S., 1919; B.S., Harvard, 1941; student Nat. War Coll., 1961-62; m. Bernice Catherine Axford, Mar. 12, 1942; 1 son, Michael Ross; m. 2d, Charlotte Elizabeth Peeler, June 14, 1951; children—Lewis Alan, Frederick Walker, William Peeler, Margaret Anne. Fgn. service officer U.S. Dept. State, Chile, Dominican Republic, Austria, Washington, Iran, Italy, 1942-61, Rome, Italy, 1962-65, Washington, 1965-69, Bonn, Germany, 1969-71, Washington, 1971—. Served with inf. AUS, 1944-45. Home: 7310 Meadow Lane Chevy Chase MD 20015 Office: State Dept Washington DC 20520

GANNETT, THOMAS B., bus. exec.; b. Hopedale, Mass., 1912; grad. Harvard 1935; m. Ann Cole, Apr. 18, 1936; children—Thomas B., Ann W. (Mrs. Robert S. Hurlbut, Jr.), Benjamin H., Deborah, Peter C. Trustee Boston Five Cent Savs. Bank; partner Hornblower & Weeks, Hemphill, Noyes, Boston. Trustee Milton Acad.; bd. dirs. Robert Breck Brigham Hosp. Home: Mainstone Farm Wayland MA 01778 Office: 160 Franklin St Boston MA 02110

GANNON, SISTER ANN IDA, coll. pres.; b. Chgo., 1915; d. George and Hanna (Murphy) Gannon; A.B., Clarke Coll., 1941; A.M., Loyola U., Chgo., 1948; Ph.D., St. Louis U., 1952. Mem. Sisters of Charity; tchr. English, St. Mary's High Sch., Chgo., 1941-47; residence, study abroad, 1951; chmn. philosophy dept. Mundelein Coll., 1951-57, pres. coll., 1957- -. Mem. edn. com. Gov.'s Commn. on Status of Women. Mem. Am. Cath. Philos. Assn. (exec. council 1953-56), Assn. Am. Colls. (dir. 1965—, chmn. 1969-70), Religious Edn. Assn. Am. (v.p.), Am. Assn. Sch. Administrs., Fedn. Ill. Colls., Nat. Cath. Edn. Assn., Am. Assn. U. Women, Metaphys. Soc. Am. Contbr. articles philos. jours. Address: 6363 Sheridan Rd Chicago IL 60626

GANNON, DONALD ALBERT, grocery co. exec.; b. Richmond, Vt., June 9, 1903; s. Edmond Bernard and Katherine (O'Donnell) G.; B.S., U. Vt., 1925, LL.D., 1961; m. Dorothy Julia Ellis, July 23, 1927; children—John Gregory, Susan Catherine. Head buyer A & P Food Stores, Kansas City, Kan., 1938-40, sales mgr. northside unit, Chgo., 1940-41, head buyer Chgo. unit, 1941-44; dir. grocery buying and sales Stop & Shop, Inc., Boston, 1944-53, dir. co. sales and buying, 1953-56, v.p. charge retailing, 1956-61, exec. v.p., 1961-65, pres., 1965—, also dir.; chmn. regional merchandising com. Eastern region of Supermarket Inst., 1958-59. Bd. dirs. Wellesley chpt. A.R.C., chmn. West div. drive, 1951; chmn. fund drives food sect., industry div. Community Fund, Boston; bd. dirs., v.p. Medical Found., Inc., 1967—. Trustee U. Vt., chmn. bd., 1950. Mem. Newcomen Society North America. Club: Wellesley Country (2d v.p., bd. govs.). Home: 120 Hampshire Rd Wellesley Hills MA 02181 Office: 393 D St Boston MA 02210

GANNON, JOHN DEANE, govt. ofcl.; b. Madison, Wis., Mar. 2, 1907; s. Thomas C. and Anna (Welsh) G.; A.B., U. Wis., 1930; m. Doretha V. Schoman, Aug. 29, 1936; children—James T., John D. Spl. agt. Aetna Life Ins. Co., 1931-33; bank examiner Wis. State Banking Dept., Madison, 1933-38, securities examiner, 1938-39, supr. credit union div., 1939-53; dir. bd. fed. credit unions U.S. Dept. Health, Edn. and Welfare, 1953-70; dep. adminstr. Nat. Credit Union Adminstrn., Washington, 1970—. Staff mem. Pres.'s Com. on Financial Instns., 1963. Recipient Presdl. citation, 1964. Club: Exchequer (chancellor 1969-70) (Washington). Home: 4806 Dover Rd Washington DC 20016 Office: 1325 K St SW Washington DC 20456

GANNON, RICHARD D., business exec. Controller, Younker Bros., Inc., Des Moines. Office: 7th and Walnut Sts Des Moines IA 50306*

GANOE, CHARLES STRATFORD, banker; b. Abington, Pa., July 16, 1929; s. Robert L. and Leonette (Rehfuss) G.; B.A., Princeton, 1951; M.B.A., U. Pa., 1952; postgrad. Am. Inst. Banking 1952-53, Pa. Bankers Assn. Summer Sch., 1953—; m. Frances- Sue Williams, Apr. 2, 1960; children-F. Hemsley, Alice N. With Fidelity- Phila. Trust Co. (name now changed to Fidelity Bank), 1952—, v.p., 1961- 66, sr. v.p., 1966-69, exec. v.p. charge internat. dept., 1969—; v.p. Co. for Investing Abroad (name now changed to Fidelity Internat. Corp.), 1963-65, pres., dir., 1965—; chmn. dir. Fidelity Internat. Corp. (Bahamas), Ltd., Nassau; dir., mem. exec. com. Am. Internat. Bank, N.Y.C.; mem. exec. com. Am. Internat. Bank, N.Y.C.; mem. exec. com., acting dir. Banque Europeenne de Financement, Paris, France; dir. Balthex Internat., Inc. Class agt. Class of 1951 Princeton, 1954-56, treas., 1956-61; chmn. pvt. edn. div. Phila. United Fund, 1958-62; dir. Phila. Council for Internat. Visitors, 1963-69, chmn., 1969—; mem. Phila. Export Expanision Council, 1966—. Past treas., bd. dirs. Arthritis and Rheumatism Found. Phila.; sec., mem. exec. com. Phila. Com. on Fgn. Relations; bd. dirs. Pa. Export Corps; bd. dirs., mem. exec. com. World Affairs Council Phila.; mem. adv. bd. Fgn. Credit Interchange Bur. Recipient Duning Meml. awards Robert Morris Assos., 1962, 65, 68. Mem. Fgn.. Traders Assn. Phila. (past gov.), Bankers Assn. for Fgn. Trade (dir., com. chmn.), Internat. Econ. Council, English Speaking Union, Port of Phila. Maritime Soc.,Pan Am. Soc., Am. Acad. Polit. and Social Scis., Robert Morris Assos. (past Am. Soc., Am. Acad. Polit. and Social Scis., Robert Morris Assos. (past pres. Phila. chpt.), Am. Inst. Banking, Atlantic Council of U.S., Greater Phila. C. of C. (treas., past sec.), Wharton Grad. Sch. Alumni Assn. (past pres.), Delta Psi. Clubs: Racquet, St. Anthonys (past v.p., gov.), Princeton (Phila.); Merion Cricket (Haverford, Pa.); Princeton (N.Y.C.); Princeton (N.J.) Elm; Ausable (St. Huberts, N.Y.). Contbr. articles profl. jours. Home: 213 Orchard Way Wayne PA 19087 Office: Broad and Walnut Sts Philadelphia PA 19109

GANS, HERBERT JULIUS, educator, sociologist; b. Cologne, Germany, May 7, 1927; s. Carl M. and Elise (Plaut) G.; came to U.S., 1940, naturalized, 1945; Ph.B., U. Chgo., 1947, M.A., 1950; Ph.D., U. Pa., 1957; m. Louise Gruner, Mar. 19, 1967; 1 son, David. Planner pvt. and pub. housing agys., Chgo. and Washington, 1950-53; from lectr. to asso. prof. urban studies and planning U. Pa., 1953-64; from asso. prof. to adj. prof. sociology Columbia, also sr. staff scientist Center Urban Edn., 1964-69, prof. sociology, 1971—; prof. sociology and planning Mass. Inst. Tech., also Mass. Inst. Tech.-Harvard Joint Center for Urban Studies, 1969-71; cons. Ford Found., U.S. Dept. Health, Edn. and Welfare, Nat. Adv. Commn. Civil Disorders; dir. Trans-action, Inc. Dir. League Indsl. Democracy, 1964-69, Ams. Dem. Action, 1969—; sponsor Am. Friends of Danilo Dolci, 1970—. Served with AUS, 1945-46. Fellow Am. Sociol. Assn. (exec. council); mem. Soc. Study of Social Problems (exec. com.), Eastern Sociol. Soc. (pres.-elect), Soc. Applied Anthropology. Author: The Urban Villagers, 1962; The Levittowners, 1967; People and Plans, 1968. Adv. editor Library Urban Affairs, 1965—, Jour. Am. Inst. Planners, 1965—, Urban Life and Culture, 1971—. Home: 460 Riverside Dr New York City NY 10027

GANS, HIRAM SELIG, lawyer; b. N.Y.C., July 13, 1905; s. Joseph and Delia (London) G.; B.S., Harvard, 1926; J.D., N.Y.U., 1929; m. Ethelyne P. Holzman. Admitted to N.Y. bar, 1929; mng. clk Root, Clark, Buckner & Ballantine, N.Y.C., 1928-31; mem. firm Amen, Gans, Weisman & Butler, N.Y.C. and Amen, Gans, Weisman, Butler & Hardy, Washinggton, 1948-58; dir. trustee, gen. counsel Spanish-Am. Bd. of Trade, Inc.; counsel for Protective Com. Mortgage Bonds, Hudson & Manhattan R.R. Co., Third Av. Transit System in reorgn. N.Y., Westchester & Boston Ry., N.Y., N.H. & H. reorgn., Fonda, Johnstown & Gloversville Ry., Nat. Rys. of Mexico, Philippine Ry., Brockway Motors, Army and Navy Investment Trust Co. (Eng.). Bankers Investment Trust Co. (Eng.); reorgn. mgr. Eastern Paper & Pulp Co., spl. counsel U.S. Atty. Gen. for enemy alien corps taken over by Office Alien Property, U.S. Dept. Justice; treas., dir. Sixth St. Investing Corp. Trustee Children's Cancer Research Found. Dir., sec., counsel Just One Break, Inc.; pres. bd. edn. Tuxedo (N.Y.) Pub. Sch. Dist. Chmn. planning com. mil. govt. finance U.S. Zone, Germany, 1945; chief fgn. exchange controls br. SHAEF. Served U.S. Army, 1942-46, with Signal Corps, 3d Inf. Div., N. Africa and Sicily, instr. Am. Sch. Center, Shrivenham, Eng., chief Financial Instns. br. G-55 S.H.E. A.F., dep. dir. Div. Investigation of Cartels, U.S. Group Control Council for Germany; editor Finance and Property Control Tech. Manual for Mil. Govt. in Germany; U.S. mem. quadripartite coms. on central banking, financial instns., fgn. exchange in Allied Control Council for Germany, 1945. Decorated Bronze Star medal, Invasion Arrowhead, Expert Combat Inf. badge. Mem. Mil. Govt. Assn. (pres., chmn. exec. com. and bd. dirs.), Assn. Bar City of N.Y., N.Y. Co. Lawyers Assn., Am. Bar Assn. (sects. internat. law and banking, corps, and reorgn.), Federal Bar Assn., A.I.M. (pres. council), N.Y. State, Internat. bar assns, Am. Judicature Soc., Am. Soc. Internat. Law. Clubs: Harvard, City Midday, Harvard Varsity, City, Lotos (N.Y.C.): United Hunts (London, Eng.); Nat. Lawyers (Washington). Home: Tuxedo Park NY 10017 Office: Chrysler Bldg 405 Lexington Av New York City NY 10017

GANT, KENNETH A., educator; b. Aura, N.J., May 16, 1919; s. George and Mary (Murphy) G.; B.S., Glassboro State Coll., 1943; M.Ed., Rutgers U., 1949; Ed.D., Temple U., 1962; m. Patricia Jane Walklett, Apr. 21, 1951; 1 dau., Melinda Ellen. Tchr. Franklin Sch., Bergenfield, N.J., 1946-47; tchr., prin. Willard Gibbs Sch., Clementon, 1947-51; prof. State U. N.Y. Coll. at Potsdam, 1951-57, dir. lab. sch., 1957-63, dir. grad. studies, 1963-69, dean grad. studies, 1969—. Served with AUS, 1943-46. Mem. N.E.A., Am. Assn. Sch. Adminstrs., N. Country, N.Y. Adminstrs. Council, N.Y. State Tchrs. Assn., Faculty Assn. State U. Colls., Phi Delta Kappa. Episcopalian (vestryman). Club: Saint Lawrence County Torch (v.p. 1965-66). Home: 11 Hillcrest Dr Potsdam NY 13676

GANTNER, GEORGE EUGENE, Jr., pathologist; b. St. Louis, June 7, 1927; s. George Eugene and Dorothy (Andrews) G.; B.S., St. Louis U., 1949, M.D., 1953; m. Genevieve Timm, June 16, 1951; children—George Eugene III, Christine, Jeanne Marie, Thomas, Robert, Michael, Stephen. Intern in surgery St. Mary's Group of Hosps., St. Louis, 1953-54; fellow pathology St. Louis U. Sch. Medicine, 1954-57; practice medicine, specializing in pathology, St. Louis, 1957—; asst. pathologist St. Mary's Group Hosps., 1957-58; patholoist, dir. labs. St. Louis U. Hosps., 1958—; asso. prof. pathology St. Louis U. Sch. Medicine, 1962—, acting chmn. dept. pathology, 1965-66, prof., 1969—; coroner's pathologist, St. Louis County, 1958-68, chief med. examiner, 1969—. Served with USNR, 1945-46. Diplomate Am. Bd. Pathology. Fellow Am. Acad. Forensic Scis., Am. Soc. Clin. Pathologists, Coll. Am. Pathologists; mem. A.M.A., Mo. State Med. Assn., St. Louis Med. Soc., Mo. Soc. Pathologists, St. Louis Path. Soc. (pres. 1962), Am. Rheumatism Assn., St. Louis Rheumatism Soc., A.A.A.S., Drug Information Assn., Internat. Soc. for Cybernetic Medicine, Internat. Acad. Pathology, Internat. Assn. Coroners and Med. Examiners, Nat. Assn. Med. Examiners. Author: (with Mary Jean Rutherford and Katharyn Schwartz) A Practical Manual of Clinical Chemistry, vols. 1-6, 1966; Data Processing Methods for Diagnostic Codes: Systemized Nomenclature of Pathology, 1969; also articles. Home: 233 Woodbourne Dr St Louis MO 63105 Office: 1325 S Grand Av St Louis MO 63104

GANTT, FRED, Jr., educator; b. Foreman, Ark., Nov. 12, 1922; s. Fred and Bettie (Taaffe) G.; A.A., So. State Coll. of Ark., 1941; B.A., So. Meth. U., 1943, M.A., 1948; Ph.D., U. Tex., 1962. Instr. polit. sci. So. Meth. U., 1947-51; adminstrv. asst. to personnel dir. Lone Star Ordnance Plant, Texarkana, Tex., 1952-55; instr. social scis. Texarkana Coll., 1955-58; teaching fellow U. Tex., 1959-69, vis. prof. govt., 1968; instr. polit. sci. Tex. A. and M. Coll., 1961-62; asst. prof. polit. sci. North Tex. State U., 1962-64, asso. prof., 1964-66, prof., 1966—, chmn. dept., 1969—; cons. Nat. Gov.'s Conf., 1968, Tex. Constnl. Revision Commn., 1967-68. Del. Democratic State Conv., 1964. Served with AUS, 1944-46. Named outstanding prof., North Tex. State U., 1970. Mem. Am., So., Midwest, Western, Southwestern (pres. 1970-71) polit. sci. assns., Am. Soc. Pub. Adminstrn., Pi Sigma Alpha, Phi Theta Kappa, Psi Chi. Methodist. Author: The Chief Executive in Texas: a Study in Gubernatorial Leadership, 1964. Editor: (with others) Governing Texas: Readings and Documents, 2d edit., 1970. Contbr. articles to profl. jours. Home: 1900 Westminster Dr Denton TX 76201

GANTT, JOHN WING, banker; b. Atlanta, Jan. 10, 1925; s. Benjamin Jones and Ruth (Wing) G.; A.B., Harvard, 1947; postgrad. Dartmouth, 1957; m. Helen Conroy, July 7, 1947; children—John Wing, Sarah Graham. Dist. sales mgr. Reynolds Aluminum Corp., Cin., 1947-54; asst. v.p. First Nat. Bank of Cin., 1955-59, v.p., 1959-68, exec. v.p., 1968—, also dir.; dir. Frank F. Taylor Co., Frankfort, Ky., Robert A. Cline Co., Cin. Gen. chmn., bd. dirs. United Fine Arts Fund, 1965. Bd. dirs. YMCA, Community Improvement Corp. Greater Cin.; treas., trustee United Appeal; trustee Asheville (N.C.) Sch. Mem. Assn. Res. City Bankers, Bankers Club (bd. govs.). Mem. Ch. of Redeemer. Rotarian. Clubs: Cin. Country (treas., bd. govs.), Queen City (bd. govs., chmn. finance com.), Commonwealth, Harvard, Camargo (Cin.). Home: 5895 Mohican Lane Cincinnati OH 45243 Office: 111 E 4th St Cincinnati OH 45202

GANTT, NICHOLAS JOURDAN, Jr., lawyer; b. Magnolia, Ark., July 13, 1879; s. Nicholas John and Laura (Browning) G.; B.A., Hendrix Coll., Conway, Ark., 1898; M.A., Vanderbilt U., 1901, LL.B. (now J.D.), 1903; m. Clara McRae, Apr. 28, 1915. Admitted to Ark. bar, 1903, since practiced in Pine Bluff; mem. firm Coleman, Gantt, Ramsay & Cox and predecessor firms, 1904—. Pres., dir. Nat. Credit Corp., Reliable Abstract & Title Co., Coca-Cola Bottling Co. of S.W. Ark.; v.p., dir. First Fed. Savs. & Loan Assn.; sec., dir. Ark. Oak Flooring Co., S. Ark. Livestock Corp., Ark.-Ga. Co. Mem. Jefferson County Bd. Health, 1925—; city atty., Pine Bluff, 1929-32. Recipient Outstanding Lawyer awards Ark. Bar Assn. and Ark. Bar Found., 1961. Mem. Ark. Bar Assn. (pres. 1940, chmn. past presidents), Sigma Alpha Epsilon. Democrat. Methodist (trustee). Mason (Shriner, 33, K.T.). Home: 402 Martin Av Pine Bluff AR 71601 Office: Simmons Nat Bldg 501 Main St Pine Bluff AR 71601

GANTT, PAUL HAWKINS, lawyer, govt. ofcl.; b. Vienna, Austria, Mar. 26, 1907; s. Henry and Olga (Otte) Gans; J.U.D., U. Vienna, 1931; J.D., Coll. William and Mary, 1942; m. Hilda E. Delaney, June 26, 1948. Admitted to Va. bar, 1942, D.C. bar, 1950; practiced law in Vienna, Austria, 1935-38; atty. Arthur T. Vanderbilt, Newark, 1943-44, Nat. Housing Authority, 1944-45, U.S. Bur. Mines, 1945-46; trial atty., chief counsel War Crimes, Nuernberg, Germany, 1946-49, dir. spl. projects div., 1947-49; atty. Bur. Reclamation, Denver, 1950-52; atty.-adviser office solicitor Dept. Interior, 1952-58, procurement counsel, 1958-59, chmn. bd. contract appeals, 1959-64; chmn. bd. contract appeals AEC, Washington, 1964—. Mem. D.C. Civil War Centennial Commn., 1962-65. Served with inf. AUS, 1942-43. Mem. Am., Fed. (past pres.), Va. bar assns., United League Lawyers (pres. U.S. sect.), Nat. Lawyers Club (past dir.), Am. Legion (past post comdr.), D.C. Lincoln Group (past pres.), The Westerners (past sheriff). Author: The Case of Alfred Packer, the Man-Eater, 1952; (with Irvin M. Gottlieb) Uncle Sam as a Landlord Under the Federal Tort Act, 1967. Home: 5825 Bradley Blvd Bethesda MD 20014 Office: Atomic Energy Commn Washington DC 20545

GANTZ, DAVID MARTIN, motor freight co. exec.; b. Wilkes-Barre, Pa., Nov. 29, 1907; s. Louis and Anna (Katz) G.; B.A., U. Wis., 1929; m. Lila Tashman, Sept. 15, 1951; children—Laura Ann, Joseph S., Harry M. Partner, Joseph M. Gantz Agy., Cin., 1929—; chmn. bd., pres. Wilson Freight Co., 1939—. Served to lt. col. Motor Transport Service, AUS, World War II; CBI. Elected to Hall of Honor, Ohio Trucking Assn., 1968. Mem. Common Carrier Conf. (bd. govs.), Am. Trucking Assn., Eastern Central Motor Carriers Assn. (trustee), Greater Cin. C. of C. (trustee), Ohio Soc. N.Y., Pi Sigma Alpha. Clubs: Kenwood Country, Logantiville Country, Bankers (Cin.). Home: 3981 Rose Hill Av Cincinnati OH 45229 Office: Follett Av Cincinnati OH 45223

GANTZ, HALLIE GEORGE, univ. pres.; b. Durham, Okla., May 13, 1910; s. John Gottfred and Letatia Paine (Thomas) G.; A.A., Randolph Jr. Coll., Cisco, Tex., 1929; B.A., Phillips U., Enid. Okla., 1931, M.A., 1932, B.D., 1933, L.H.D., 1956; B.D., Yale, 1937; D.D. (hon.), Tex. Christian U., 1946; m. Sylvia Lee Baker, Nov. 7, 1933; children—Charles Baker, Gwendolyn (Martin), Kaye (Gates). Ordained to ministry Christian Ch., 1933; minister in Ft. Worth, 1933-36, Ft. Trumbull, Conn., 1936-37, Lubbock, Tex., 1938-48, Tulsa, 1948-61; pres. Phillips U., 1961—. Pres. Tex. Conv. Christian Chs., 1945-46, Tulsa Council Chs., 1950; chmn. com. ministry Disciples of Christ Ch., 1950; chmn. program and arrangements com. St. Louis Assembly Internat. Conv. Christian Chs., 1958. Pres. trustees Okla. Christian Missionary Soc., 1954-55; bd. dirs. Nat. Benevolent Assn. Disciples of Christ, 1952-56; trustee United Christian Missionary Soc., 1957-60, Hillcrest Med. Center, Tulsa, 1956-61; mem. commn. restructure of Christian Ch., mem. commn. Christian Unity Christian Ch., Disciples of Christ, chmn. bd. higher edn., 1968—; trustee Christian Board of Pub., 1967—. Recipient Pawnee Dist. Conservationist award, 1954, Okla. Lay Conservationist award, 1955. Mason (Shriner). Rotarian. Home: 2602 E Maine St Enid OK 73701

GANUS, CLIFTON LOYD, Jr., clergyman, coll. pres.; b. Hillsboro, Tex., Apr. 7, 1922; s. Clifton Loyd and Martha Jewel (Bearden) G.; B.A., Harding Coll., 1943; M.A., Tulane U., 1946, Ph.D., 1953; profl. diploma Tchrs. Coll., Columbia, 1956; m. Louise Nicholas, May 27, 1943; children—Clifton Loyd III, Deborah Lynn, Charles Austin. Ordained ministry Ch. of Christ, 1943; minister, Charleston, Miss., 1943-45; asso. prof. history Harding Coll., Searcy, Ark., 1946—, dean Sch. Am. Studies, 1952-65, v.p., 1956- 65, pres., 1965—. Dir. Finest Foods, Inc., New Orleans, First Security Bank, Searcy, Ark. Treas., bd. dirs. Johnnie Donaghey Wallace Found.; pres. Ark. Found. Asso. Colls.; bd. dirs. Quapaw Area council Boy Scouts Am. Recipient medals Freedoms Found., 1955, 56, 57, 58, 59, 67. Mem. Am. Studies Assn., So. Hist. Assn., Ark. Acad. Scis., Phi Alpha Theta, Psi Delta Sigma, Sigma Chi. Lion. Author: History of the Freedmans Bureau in Mississippi, 1953. Home: 208 S Cross St Searcy AR 72143

GANZ, PETER FELIX, coll. dean, musician; b. Basel, Switzerland, Jan. 23, 1922; s. Paul J. and Beatrice C. (Kern) G.; profl. diploma in piano, Musikakademie Basel, 1945; student U. Basel; M.Mus., Chgo. Mus. Coll., 1948; Ph.D., Northwestern U., 1960. Instr. piano Chgo. Mus. Coll., 1947-54, dir. prep. div., 1950, dir. conservatory, 1953; asst. prof. piano and mus. literature Roosevelt U., 1954-61, asso. prof., 1961-70, prof., 1970—, dean Chgo. Mus. Coll. of Roosevelt U., 1970—; adviser Contemporary Concerts (Chgo.); judge music competitions; lectr.; mem. bd. Midwest Piano Award. Mem. exec. bd. Auditorium Theatre Council. Served as 1st lt., Swiss Army, 1942-46. Mem. Soc. Am. Musicians, Am. Musicol. Soc., Music Educators Nat. Conf., Music Tchrs. Nat. Assn., Internat. Soc. Contemporary Music, Am. Assn. Univ. Profs., Swiss Heraldic Soc., Swiss Musicians League, Arts Club (Chgo.), Cliff Dwellers (Chgo.). Contbr. articles profl. jours. Pianist, performing solo, ensemble and lecture recitals U.S. and abroad. Office: 430 S Michigan Av Chicago IL 60605

GANZ, RUDOLPH pianist, condr.; b. Zurich, Switzerland, Feb. 24, 1877; s. Rudolph and Sophia (Bartenfeld) G.; studied conservatories of Music, Zurich, Lausanne and Strassburg, later with Busoni, Berlin; composition with Blanchet, Lausanne, and Urban, Berlin; D.Mus. (hon.), U. Rochester, Grinnell Coll., De Paul U., Cin. Conservatory Music; D.N.L., Roosevelt U.; m. Mary Forrest, July 12, 1900 (dec. 1956); 1 son, Anton Roy; m. 2d, Esther La Berge Dec. 23, 1959; 1 dau., Jeanne Colette. Debut at age 12, Zurich; later made extended concert tours in Europe; came to U.S., 1900; music tchr., Chgo., 1901-05; played with leading orchs., mus. orgns. U.S., Can., 1905-21; condr. St. Louis Symphony Orch., 1921-27; pres. Chgo. Mus. Coll. Roosevelt U., 1933-54, now pres. emeritus. Apptd. condr. N.Y. Philharmonic and San Francisco Young People's concerts, 1939- 49; condr. children concerts Chgo. Symphony Orch. Composer of symphony, concerto for piano and orch., symphonic sketches, variations on a theme by Brahms, many other pieces for piano, over 200 songs. Named officer French Legion of Honor; chevalier French Order of Arts and Letters; recipient Northwestern U. Centennial award; award for performing arts Lincoln Acad. Ill., 1965. Corr. mem. Royal Acad. in Florence. Clubs: Arts, Tavern. Home: 1550 Lake Shore Dr Chicago IL 60610 Office: 430 S Michigan Av Chicago IL 60605

GANZ, SAMUEL, service orgn. exec.; b. Bklyn., Nov. 12, 1911; s. Emanuel and Dora (Zahalsky) G.; B.S., Coll. City N.Y., 1932, M.S., 1932; postgrad. N.Y. U., 1941-43; m. Helen Lichtig, June 26, 1938; children—Edward, Jeffrey. Exec. in men's clothing industry, 1932-36; with N.Y. State Dept. Labor, 1936-40, U.S. Dept. Labor, Washington, 1940-66, asst. adminstr. wage and hour and pub. contracts div., 1953-62, asst. dir. manpower and automation research Office Manpower, Automation and Tng., 1962-64, exec. officer manpower adminstrn., 1964-65, dep. manpower adminstr. Manpower Adminstrn., 1965-66; commr. for manpower and career devel. agy.

City of N.Y., 1966-68; pres. Econ. & Manpower Corp., N.Y.C., 1968—; mem. faculty New Sch. for Social Research; adj. prof. Pace Coll., N.Y.C., 1971—. Mem. research sub-com. Nat. Manpower Adv. Com. to Secs. of Labor, and Health, Edn. and Welfare, 1966-69; mem. N.Y. Gov.'s Com. on Manpower, Com. on Youth and Work. Recipient Distinguished Service award U.S. Dept. Labor, 1962, 66. Mem. Indsl. Relations Research Assn., Am. Soc. for Pub. Adminstrn., Am. Vocational Assn., N.Y. C. of C. (mem. spl. com. on environment 1971, mem. manpower com., urban affairs com.), Commerce and Industry Assn. N.Y. (manpower com., welfare com.). Jewish religion. Contbr. articles profl. publs. Home: 6700 192d St Fresh Meadows NY 11365 Office: 119 W 57th St New York City NY 10019

GANZI, RICHARD LOUIS, cons. mgmt. engr.; b. N.Y.C., Jan. 24, 1923; s. Louis and Mary (Genarro) G.; B.B.A., Manhattan Coll., 1948; M.B.A., N.Y. U., 1950; children—Alicia Marie, Denise Irene. Mgr., indsl. engr. Alexander Smith, Inc., Yonkers, N.Y., 1948-53; sr. cons. Paul B. Mulligan & Co., Inc., Scarsdale, N.Y., 1953-57, pres., 1958, also dir.; dir. Venetian Constrn. Co., Inc., N.Y.C. Served with USMCR, 1942-45; PTO. Mem. Assn. Cons. Mgmt. Engrs., Nat. Assn. Cost Accountants, Office Execs. Assn., Am. Inst. Indsl. Engrs., Am. Mgmt. Assn., Nat. Office Mgmt. Assn. Author: How to Gain and Maintain Control of Office Costs, 1963. Home: 260 Garth Rd Scarsdale NY 10583 Office: 2 Overhill Rd Scarsdale NY 10583

GAPOSHKIN, SIRGAY ILLARIONOVICH, astronomer; b. Yevpatoria, Russia, July 10, 1898; s. Illarion Mihailovich and Iekaterina Kuzminochna (Zolotuhina) G.; Ph.D. in Lit., Russian U., Berlin, Germany, 1928; Ph.D. in Astronomy, Berlin U., 1932; m. Cecelia Helena Payne, Mar. 5, 1934; children—Edward, Michael, Katherine, Leonora, Peter John Arthur. Came to U.S., 1933, naturalized, 1939. Various occupations, 1917-22; traveler in Asia Minor, 1922-24; astronomer, Berlin, 1931-33, Harvard, 1933; research MacDonald Obs., Tex., Mt. Wilson and Mt. Palomar Obs. in Cal., Mt. Stromlo Obs., Australia. Mem. Am. Astron. Soc., Astron. Soc. Pacific. Author numerous publs. on astronomy, history of sci., painting, poetry, athletics and gardening. Developed methods for study of variability in single and double stars; numerous stellar observations including relationship between Milky Way and Magellanic Clouds, 1969-70. Home: 55 Farmcrest Av Lexington MA 02173 Office: Harvard Observatory Cambridge MA 02138

GARAAS, JOHN OSCAR, lawyer; b. Wheelock N.D., Sept. 1, 1922; s. Halfdan and Jennie (Thorsdal) G.; student St. Olaf Coll., 1940-43; B.A., U. N.D., 1948, LL.B., 1949; m. Barbara Ann Thomson, June 13, 1947; children—Jonathan, David, Barry, Susan. Admitted to N.D. bar, 1949, practiced Watford City, 1949-61; city atty. Watford City, 1949-54, 56-61; state's atty. McKenzie County, 1950-57; state senator for McKenzie County, 1956-60; U.S. atty. N.D. dist., 1961-68; practice law, Fargo, N.D., 1968—; state's atty. Cass County, N.D., 1971—. Served with AUS, 1943-46. Mem. Am. Legion. Lutheran. Elk. Home: Fargo ND Office: 10 1/2 Broadway Fargo ND 58102

GARABEDIAN, HAROLD ARSEN, educator; b. Boston, Feb. 8, 1898; s. Samuel A. and Hannah (Lindquist) G.; B.S., Tufts Coll., 1919; m. Doris Eaton, Oct. 21, 1922; children— Frieda (Mrs. Edward L. Bjornson), Janet (Mrs. Robert Hohman). With John Hancock Mut. Life Ins. Co., Boston, 1919-63, actuarial clk., asst. actuary, asso. actuary, 2d v.p., v.p., 1919-56, v.p. and actuary, 1956-61, v.p., acturial cons., 1961-63; prof. actuarial sci. Northeastern U., 1964. Dir. Financial Pub. Co. Boston. Fellow Soc. Actuaries; mem. Boston Actuaries Club, Harvard Mus. Assn., Phi Beta Kappa. Home: 33 Royal Crest Dr North Andover MA 01845 Office: 360 Huntington Av Boston MA 02115

GARABEDIAN, HENRY LESLIE, math. physicist; b. Dorchester, Mass., Nov. 22, 1901; s. Samuel A. and Hannah (Lindquist) G.; B.S., Tufts U., 1922; M.A., Harvard, 1923; Ph.D., Princeton, 1930; m. R. Geraldine Sawyer, Mar. 15, 1947; 1 dau., Nancy Ellen (Mrs. John L. Senter). Mem. faculties Harvard, U. Rochester, Princeton, Northwestern U., 1924-46; prin. physicist Oak Ridge Nat. Lab., 1946-48, chief research reactors sect. AEC, 1948-49; cons. physicist Bettis Atomic Power div. Westinghouse Electric Corp., 1949-56; head math. dept., research labs. Gen. Motors Corp., 1956-66; prof. math. and energy engring. U. Ill. at Chgo. Circle, 1966-70. Fellow Nuclear Soc.; mem. Am. Math Soc., Phi Beta Kappa, Sigma Xi. Club: Harvard (Boston). Editor: Approximation of Functions, 1965. Contbr. articles to profl. jours. Home: 2394 1 E Via Mariposa W Laguna Hills CA 92653

GARAGIOLA, JOE, radio-TV personality; b. St. Louis, Feb. 12, 1926; s. John and Angelina (Garavaglia) G.; ed. pub. schs.; m. Audrie Dianne Ross, Nov. 5, 1949; children—Joseph, Stephen, Gina. Profl. baseball player with St. Louis Cardinals, Pitts. Pirates, Chgo. Cubs and N.Y. Giants, 1946-54; engaged in radio-TV, St. Louis, 1955—; broadcaster All Star Baseball games and World Series, Game of The Week, N.Y. Yankee games; appeared on Johnny Carson show, Jack Paar show; regular mem. cast Today Show; host for Monitor programs; own radio show, 1963—. Served with AUS, World War II. Author: Baseball is a Funny Game. 1960. Address: care NBC 30 Rockefeller Plaza New York City NY 10020

GARAVAGLIA, BROTHER ABDON LEWIS, ednl. adminstr.; b. Detroit, Dec. 16, 1915; s. Amadeo and Rose (Ray) Garavaglia; B.A., Cath. U. Am., 1942; M.A. in French Lit., Manhattan Coll., 1947; postgrad. St. John's U., 1947-50, Columbia, 1952-55; Litt.D., Coll. Mt. St. Vincent, 1970. Joined Brothers of Christian Schs., 1936; prof. world lit. and theology Manhattan Coll., Bronx, N.Y., 1950-62, dean Sch. Arts and Scis., 1962-70, dir. grad. div., 1970—. Asso. univ. seminar higher edn. Columbia, 1962; spl. research Japanese culture and civilization. Trustee, Manhattan Coll., 1965-68. Ford Found. fellow Harvard, 1951-52. Mem. Cath. Renascene Soc. Am. (adv. bd. 1955-63), Am. Council Edn., Assn. Am. Colls., Assn. Higher Edn., Am. Conf. Acad. Deans, Modern Lang, Assn., Renaissance Soc. Am., Nat. Cath. Edn. Assn., Eastern Assn. Deans, Phi Beta Kappa. Contbr. articles profl. jours. Address: Manhattan Coll Riverdale NY 10471

GARBARINI, EDGAR JOSEPH, civil engr., constrn. co. exec.; b. Jackson, Cal., Aug. 1, 1910; s. Henry Casamero and Elvira (Gardella) G.; B.S., U. Cal. at Berkeley, 1933; m. Lillian Rosemarie Arata, Nov. 14, 1936; children—Paul Henry, Ann Elisabeth. Jr. research engr. U. Cal. at Berkeley, 1933-34, research engr., 1934-38; field engr. W.A. Bechtel & Six Cos. Cal., San Francisco, 1934; civil engr. Cal. Commn., Golden Gate Internat. Expn., 1938-39, Dewell & Earl, cons. engrs., San Francisco, 1939, Pacific Gas & Electric Co., San Francisco, 1939-40; with Bechtel Corp., San Francisco, 1940—, v.p., now sr. v.p., also mining and metals div. mgr., 1966—, also dir.; dir. Canadian Bechtel Ltd., Bechtel Nuclear Corp. Registered profl. engr., Cal. Fellow Am. Soc. C.E.; mem. Structural Engrs. Assn. No. Cal., Assn. of U.S. Army, Order of Golden Bear, U. Cal. Alumni Assn., Sigma Xi, Tau Beta Pi, Chi Epsilon. Clubs: Cal. (Los Angeles); World Trade, Stock Exchange, Engineers (San Francisco); Meadow (Fairfax, Cal.). Office: 50 Beale St San Francisco CA 94119

GARBARINI, ROBERT FRANK, corp. exec., mech. engr.; b. Woodside, N.Y., Dec. 31, 1918; s. Anthony M. and Adeline (Regalia) G.; M.E. with distinction, Stevens Inst. Tech., 1940, M.S., 1945; m. Mary Eileen Driscoll, June 15, 1946; children— Laura Marie, Frances Mary, Virginia Ann, Helen Marita, John Michael. Dep. asso. adminstr. space sci. and applications Office Space Sci. and Applications, NASA, 1963-67; engring. mgmt. space sci. and applications, comstime tech. cons. Dept. Def.; adviser sci. adv. bd. USAF, 1960-67; chmn. bd. to conduct rev. obs.-class Earth satellites NASA, 1966; group v.p. exchange services Western Union Telegraph Co., N.Y.C., 1967—. Recipient Exceptional Service medal NASA, 1967, 69. Mem. I.E.E.E. Patentee in field. Home: Harbor Rd Harbor Acres Port Washington NY 11050 Office: 60 Hudson St New York City NY 10013

GARBE, RICHARD W., clothing mfg. co. exec.; b. Aurora, Ill., 1907; ed. Columbia. Sec.-treas., v.p. Hart Schaffner & Marx. Home: 805 S Cumberland Av Park Ridge IL 60068 Office: 36 S Franklin St Chicago IL 60606 *

GARBEE, EUGENE EMMETT, former univ. pres.; b. Billings, Mo., May 29, 1907; s. John Richard and Mary Etta (Schmidt) G.; B.S., S.W. Mo. State Coll., 1931; M.A., George Peabody Coll., 1933; Ed.D., N.Y.U., 1949; L.H.D., Upper Ia. U., 1969; m. Mildred Everts, July 12, 1930; children—Mary Jean, Everett Lee. Prof. Appalachian State Tchrs. Coll., 1933-46, U. Ga., Savannah, 1946-48; instr. phys. edn. N.Y. U., 1948-49; asso. prof. edn. Drake U., 1949-52; pres. Upper Ia. U., 1952-70, emeritus, 1970—. Pres. Wapsipinicon area council Boy Scouts Am., 1959-61, mem. exec. bd. Region Eight, 1967—, Silver Beaver award. Mem. Gov.'s Commn. Human Rights, 1957, 1963, 1964. President Ia. Coll. Found., 1966-67. Served as lt. comdr. USNR, World War II. Mem. Internat. Platform Assn., Newcomen Soc. N.Am., Am. Legion, N.E.A., Am. Assn. Sch. Adminstrs., A.A.H.P.E.R., Am. Camping Assn., Assn. Ia. Coll. Presidents (pres. 1961-62). Mason (past master, Shriner), Rotarian (pres., West Union, Ia., dist. gov. 1963-64). Author: Dr. Garbee's Wild Game Dinners, 1965. Home: 3152 W Glenwood Springfield MO 65804

GARBER, ALEX, educator; b. Chgo., Apr. 20, 1912; s. Edward and Bella (Dolinky) G.; A.B. in Sociology, U. Chgo., 1942, A.M. in Social Sci., 1946; Ph.D. in Sociology, U. Cal. at Berkeley, 1958; m. Joan Carole Shields, July 24, 1967. Ednl. tng. specialist VA, Oakland, Cal., 1946-49; adminstrn. Flight Sch. Transocean Airlines, Oakland, 1949-51; asst. prof. sociology U. Colo., 1956-64; asst. prof. sociology Sacramento State Coll., 1964-66, asso. prof., 1966-68, prof., chmn. dept., 1968—. Mem. Nat. adv. Bd. World Without War Council, 1966-68. Mem. nat. com. Socialist Party U.S., 1962—. Served with USAAF, 1942-45. Named Prof. of Year U. Colo., 1957-58. Mem. Am., Pacific sociol. assns., Far Western Slavic Assn. Home: 1101 Teneighth Way Sacramento CA 95818

GARBER, EDWARD DAVID, educator; b. N.Y.C., Mar. 22, 1918; s. Harry and Ada (Gordon) G.; B.S., Cornell U., Ithaca, N.Y., 1940; M.S., U. Minn., 1942; Ph.D., U. Cal. at Berkeley, 1949; m. Rosalie E. Kirshtein, July 31, 1943; children—Joel Lee, Martha Ann, Jane Bernadette. Asst. research geneticist Naval Biol. Lab., Oakland, Cal., 1949-53; mem. faculty U. Chgo., 1953—, prof. biology, 1961—. Served to 1st lt. AUS, 1942-46. Mem. Genetics Soc. Am., Bot. Soc. Am., Am. Soc. Microbiology, Soc. Gen. Microbiology, A.A.A.S., Sigma Xi, Gamma Alpha. Discoverer antibiotic effective against human fungal pathogens. Home: 5707 S Maryland Av Chicago IL 60637

GARBER, LAWRENCE LOWELL, mfg. exec.; b. Ashland, Pa., Feb. 18, 1909; s. Tillman E. and Laura (Boyer) G.; B.S., Carnegie Inst. Tech., 1932; m. Elinor Smith, July 31, 1937; children—Susan S. (Mrs. Richard B. Elste), Lawrence Lowell. Vice pres. H.K. Porter Co., Inc., 1950-58; v.p., group Electric Auto-Lite Co., 1958—; v.p., dir. Eltra Corp., 1963—; pres. Prestolite Co. Mem. S.A.R., Beta Theta Pi. Presbyn. Mason. Home: 6 Clovelly Rd Pittsburgh PA 15202 Office: 511 Hamilton St Toledo OH 43602

GARBER, PAUL EDWARD, mus. curator; b. Atlantic City, N.J., Aug. 31, 1899; s. Paul Greenwood and Margaret (Sithens) G.; student McKinley Tech.. Sch., Washington, 1917, U. Md., 1918; student aero. engring. Research U., Washington, 1920-21, nat. Aviation Sch., Washington, 1927-28, U.S. Grad. Sch., 1939-40, 47-48, 52; m. Irene Tusch Reece, May 10, 1952; children (by previous marriage)—Paul James, Edward Williams, Barbara Jane. Joined Postal Aviation Service, 1918; with Smithsonian Instn., 1920; served as asso. curator div. engring., curator nat. Air, Mus., Washington, 1946, head curator, 1952-65, asst. director aeros., 1965. Served as sgt. U.S. Army, World War I; comdr., spl. devices div. Br. Aero., USNR, World War II. Recipient Washington Air Derby Assn. trophy, 1954, Air Line Traffic Assn. citation, 1955; Frank G. Brewer Trophy, for air-youth edn., 1959, Elder Statesman of Aviation award, 1964, Crocciero Atlantica medal (Italy), 1964, Santos Dumont medal of Merit, Brzzil, 1967. Mem. Nat. Aero Assn., Air Mail Pioneers, Early Birds Aviation (archivist, historian). Episcopalian. Clubs: National Rocket (governor), OX-5. Author: Building and Flying Model Aircraft, 1928; Kites, 1931; The National Aeronautical Collections, 1956; also handbooks, pamphlets, ency. and mag. articles on aeros. Home: 310 N Jackson St Arlington VA 22201 Office: National Air and Space Museum 10th and Independence Av Washington DC 20003

GARBER, PAUL NEFF, bishop; b. New Market, Va., July 27, 1899; s. Samuel and Ida Alice (Neff) G.; A.B., Bridgewater (Va.) Coll., 1919; student Crozer Theol. Sem., Chester, Pa., 1919-21; A.M., U. Pa., 1921, Harrison fellow, 1922-23, Ph.D., 1923; L.H.D., Simpson Coll.; D.D., Duke, Emory U.; LL.D., Randolph-Macon Coll., Bridgewater Coll.; Litt. D., Lycoming Coll., 1965; m. Orina Winifred Kidd, Aug. 21, 1927 (dec. July 1959); m. 2d, Nina Fontana, Apr. 27, 1963. Asst. instr. history U. Pa., 1921-22; instr. in history Brown U., 1923-24; asst. prof. history Duke, 1924-26, prof. ch. history Div. Sch., 1926—, registrar of sch., 1928-41, dean, 1941-44; dir. Junaluska Summer Sch. (affiliated with Duke), 1934-40. Thirkield lectr. Gammon Theol. Sch., 1941; Southwestern lectr. Southwestern U., 1948; Jarrell lectr. Emory U., 1951; Brown lectr. Randolph-Macon Coll., 1955; chmn. Meth. Commn. on Higher Edn., Meth. Commn. on Camp Activites; v.p. Meth. Bd. Edn., Meth. Commn. of Chaplains; chmn. Bd. Edn., Meth. Ch., 1960- 64, mem. Commn. on Promotion and Cultivation, 1960-68, chmn. Bicentennial Hist. Commn., 1965-66; mem. World Meth. Council; Lamar lectures Wesleyan Coll., 1962. Ordained to the ministry Meth. Episcopal Ch., South, 1926; bishop of The Meth. Ch., 1944, assigned to Geneva (Switzerland) Area, 1944-52, Richmond area 1952-64, Raleigh 1964-68; active orgnl. affairs ch., confs., mem. coms. and commns. on internal orgn. and interdenominational relations; mem. Meth. Commn. on Chaplains; pres. Assn. of Meth. hist. socs., 1940-42; Pres. Internat. Meth. Hist. Soc. Trustee Randolph-Macon Coll., Randolph-Macon Women's Coll.; High Point Coll., Westminster Theol. Sem., Pfeiffer Coll., Louisburg Coll., Ferrum Jr. Coll., Randolph-Macon Acad., Am. U., Wesley Theol. Seminary. Member Am. Soc. Ch. History, Am. Hist. Assn., Wesley Hist. Society, Phi Beta Kappa, Delta Sigma Phi, Tau Kappa Alpha, Theta Pi. Author several books, latest being: The Methodists of Continental Europe, 1949. Contbr. to Dict. Am. Biography. Home: 1 Rue du Colombier Geneva Switzerland

GARBER, STANLEY THOMAS, physician; b. Cin., May 19, 1908; s. Frederick W. and Alice (Woodward) G.; B.S., Princeton, 1930; M.D., Harvard, 1934; m. Frances Davis, 1935; children—Frances, Thomas, David, Helen. Intern Christ Hosp., Cin., 1934- 35; resident obstetrics Cin. Gen. Hosp., 1935-37; house surgeon gynecology Free Hosp. for Women, Boston, 1938-39; practice of medicine specializing obstetrics and gynecology, Cin., 1938—; faculty U. Cin., 1938—, prof. obstetrics, 1947-66, prof. obstetrics and gynecology, 1966—; dir. obstetrics Cin. Gen. Hosp., 1947-65. Diplomate American Bd. Obstetrics and Gynecology. Mem. Assn. Am. Med. Colls., Pan-Pacific Surg. Assn., N.Y. Acad. Scis., Am. Soc. Sterility, Am. Coll. Obstetricians and Gynecologists (charter), Am. Assn. Profs. Obstetrics and Gynecology. (charter). Editor: Stedman's Med. Dictionary, 1942-49, other obstet.-gynecol. publs. Home: 1206 Hayward Av Cincinnati OH 45226 Office: 104 William H Taft Rd Cincinnati OH 45219

GARBO, GRETA, actress; b. Stockholm, Sweden, Sept. 18, 1905; d. Sven and Louvisa Gustaffson; ed. Royal Dramatic Acad., Stockholm. Won her first film recognition in "Goesta Berling, 5 through work in Royal Acad.; came to U.S. and appeared in "The Temptress". "The Torrent", "Love", "Flesh and the Devil", and other films; more recent successes gained in "Anna Christie", "Susan Lenox", "Mata Hari". "Grand Hotel". "As You Desire Me", "Queen Christina", "The Painted Veil", "Anna Karenina", "Camille", "Conquest", "Ninotchka", "Two Faced Woman", 1941.*

GARBO, NORMAN, author, artist, lectr.; b. N.Y.C., Feb. 15, 1919; s. Max W. and Fannie (Deitz) G.; student Coll. City N.Y., 1935-36; B.F.A., Acad. Fine Art, N.Y.C., 1940; m. Rhoda Ivy, Apr. 15, 1942; 1 son, Mickey. Author syndicated art column Chgo.-Tribune-N.Y. News Syndicate, 1954-61; lectr. throughout U.S., 1956—; portraits exhibited in galleries throughout U.S., also Met. Mus., Phila. Art Mus. Author: Pull Up An Easel, 1955; (with H. Goodkind) Confrontation, 1966; The Movement, 1969; also short stories. Address: 6 Crown Top Rd Manhasset NY 11030

GARBOUSOVA, RAYA, concert cellist; b. Tiflis, Russia, d. of Boris and Vera (Kaminiar) Garbousoff; student under Pablo Casals; m. Dr. Kurt Biss, Chicago, 1948. Concert cellist, having appeared throughout the U.S., Europe and Palestine with major orchs.; considers her greatest achievement appearance with Barcelona Symphony Orch. under condr. Pablo Casals. Performed world premiere of Samuel Barber Concerto with the Boston Symphony Orch., Serge Koussevitsky conducting. Home: 524 W Lincoln Highway DeKalb IL 60115 Office: care Mildred Shagal Inc 119 W 57th St New York City NY 10019

GARCEAU, GEORGE JOSEPH, physician; b. Anoka County, Minn., May 24, 1896; M.D., Northwestern U., 1925; m. Julia Davidson, June 2, 1927; children—Mary Dolores (Mrs. Charles Pickerell), Diana Ruth (Mrs. W.W. Scamman). Intern, Meth. Episcopal Hosp., 1924-25, St. Francis Hosp., Miami Beach, Fla., 1925-26; resident Shriners' Hosp. for Crippled Children, Chgo., 1926-27; mem. attending staff Meth. Episcopal, St. Francis and St. Vincent's hosps.; chief orthopaedic surgeon Ind. Hosps.; chief orthopaedic surgeon and chief resident James Whitcomb Riley Hosp. for Children, 1928-33. Distinguished Service prof. emeritus dept. orthopedic surgery Ind. U. Med. Center. Fellow A.M.A., Internat. Coll. Surgeons, Internat. Soc. Orthopedic Surgery and Traumatology; mem. Am. Acad. Orthopaedic Surgeons, Clin. Orthopaedic Soc., Am. Orthopaedic Assn. Home: 1164 Ivy Lane Indianapolis IN 46220 Office: 23 E Ohio St Indianapolis IN 46204

GARCEAU, OLIVER, educator; b. Boston, Nov. 22, 1911; s. Dr. Edgar and Sally Holmes (Morse) G.; A.B., Harvard, 1933, M.B.A., 1935, A.M., 1939, Ph.D., 1940; student Oxford (Eng.) U., 1933, U. Chgo., 1943-44; m. Iris Virginia Thistle, Aug. 18, 1934; 1 son, Laurence. Instr., asst. prof. Harvard, 1935-41, 45-46; asso. prof. U. Me., 1946-47; staff asso. Social Sci. Research Council, 1947-48; prof. govt. Bennington (Vt.) Coll., 1948-59; research prof. govt. Harvard, 1959-60, research cons. polit. economy and polit. behavior, 1960—; exec. asso., cons. Ford Found., 1955-58; exec. bd. Inter-univ. Case Program, 1952-58. Mem. Gov.'s Task Force on State Govt. Reorgn., 1967-69. Served to lt. comdr. USNR, 1941- 45. Fellow Social Sci. Research Council (mem. com. on polit. behavior 1950- 64); mem. Am. Polit. Sci. Assn. (exec. council 1951-53), Phi Beta Kappa. Author: Political Life of American Medical Association, 1941; Public Library in the Political Process, 1949. Author, editor: Political Research and Political Theory, 1968. Asso. editor Human Organization, 1956-66. Home: Box 8 Sedgwick ME 04676

GARCIA, CELSO-RAMON, educator, physician; b. N.Y.C., Oct. 31, 1921; s. Celso Ondina and Oliva Menendez (del Valle) G.; B.S., Queens Coll., 1942; M.D., State U. N.Y. Downstate Med. Center, 1945; m. Shirley Jean Stoddard, Oct. 14, 1950; children—Celso-Ramón, Sarita Stoddard. Intern, Norwegian Hosp., Bklyn., 1945-46; resident Cumberland Hosp., Bklyn., 1948-53; asst. prof. obstetrics and gynecology U. P.R., San Juan, 1953-55; co-dir. Rock Reproductive Study Center, asst. obstetrician and gynecologist Boston Lying-In Hosp., asso. surgeon Free Hosp. for Women, Brookline, Mass., 1955-65; sr. scientist, dir. tng. program in physiology reprodn. Worcester Found. for Exptl. Biology, Shrewsbury, Mass., 1960-62; asst. surgeon, chief Infertility Clinic, Mass. Gen. Hosp., clin. asso. obstetrics and gynecology Harvard Med. Sch., 1962-65; prof. obstetrics and gynecology U. Pa., Phila., 1965—, William Shippen, Jr. prof. human reprodn., 1970—. Mem. sci. adv. bd. Inst. Human Reprodn. and Fetal Devel., U. Tel Aviv Med. Sch., 1970; rapporteur com. of experts on clin. aspects oral gestogens WHO, Geneva, Switzerland, 1965; mem. ad hoc adv. com. Nat. Inst. Child Health and Devel., 1971. Co-chmn. exec. com., nat. med. adv. com. Planned Parenthood World Population, 1971. Bd. dirs. Am. Fertility Soc. Served with AUS, 1946-48. Recipient Carl G. Hartman award Am. Soc. Study Sterility, 1961. Sidney Graves fellow in gynecology Harvard Med. Sch., 1955. Mem. Am. Physiol. Soc., Am. Coll. Obstetricians and Gynecologists, A.M.A., A.C.S., Coll. Physicians Phila., Boston, Phila. obstet. socs., Alpha Epsilon Delta. Republican. Presbyn. Mason. Mem. original team developing application of progestagen-estrogen combinations for oral contraception (the Pill); developer, dir. 1st formal tng. program in physiology of reprodn. in U.S. Home: 109 Merion Rd Merion PA 19066 Office: 3400 Spruce St Philadelphia PA 19104

GARCIA-GODOY, HECTOR diplomat of Dominican Republic; b. Moca, Dominican Republic, Jan. 11, 1921; s. Emilio and Ana (Caceres) Garcia-G.; Doctor Law, U. Santo Domingo, 1944; m. Matilde Pastoriza Espaillat, Aug. 26, 1944; children— Ana Matilde, Guillermo. Second sec. Dominica embassy San Jose, Costa Rica, 1944-45, 1st sec. charge d'affaires, Managua, Nicaragua, 1945-47; head consular div. Dominica Ministry Fgn. Affairs, 1947-48; sec. bd. dirs. Res. Bank, 1948-54, supt. gen. banks, 1954-55, vice-gov. Central Bank Dominican Republic, 1955-56; minister counsellor Dominican embassy, London, Eng., also permanent del. internat. sugar council, 1956-63; ambassador Belgium, 1957-59, to Great Britain, 1959-63; minister fgn. relations Dominican Republic, 1963; resigned upon overthrow of constl. govt., 1963; v.p. Compañia Anonima Tabacalera, tobacco co., Santiago, 1964-65; upon solution of revolution selected pres. Dominican Republic, 1965-66; ambassador to U.S., and OAS, 1966—. Decorated Grand Cross Order Duarte, Sanchezy mella; Grand Cordon de l'Ordre de la Couronne (Belgium). Home: 2930 Edgevale Terrace Washington DC 20008 Office: 1715 22d St Washington DC 20008

GARCIA-ROBLES, ALFONSO, Mexican rep. to UN; b. Zamora, Mexico, Mar. 20, 1911; LL.D. magna cum laude, U. Paris, 1936; diploma Acad. Internat. Law, The Hague, 1938; married. Mem. Mexican Fgn. Service, 1939—, on leave as dir. gen. polit. div. UN Secretariat, 1946-57; undersec. fgn. affairs, Mexico, 1964-70; permanent rep. of Mexico to UN. Sec. internat. affairs Nat. Commn. Peace Planning, 1944—; chmn. preparatory commn. Denuclearization of Latin Am., 1964-67; chmn. Mexican delegation to Com. on Disarmament, to Conf. of Non-Nuclear Weapon States, Geneva, 1968; lectr. Decorated by 10 Latin Am., European, African and Asian countries. Mem. Internat. Studies Assn. Paris U. (hon. chmn.), Nat. Acad. History and Geography, Nat. Athenaeum Arts and Scis., Mexican Bar Assn., Mexican Acad. Internat. Law, Hispanic-Portuguese-Am. Inst. Internat. Law, Indian Soc. Internat. Law. Author: Le Panamericanisme et la Politique de Bon Voisinage, 1938; Premier Congres d'Etudes Internationales, 1938; La Question du Petrole au Mexique et le Droit International, 1939; La Clausula Calvo ante el Dreecho Internacional, 1939; El Panamericanismo y la Politica del Buen Vecino, 1940; La Sorbona Ayer y Hoy, 1943; Mexico en la Postquerra; Marco Mundial y Continental de la Paz, 1944; La Conferencia de San Francisco y su Obra, 1946; L'Universite de Paris a travers les Siecles, 1946; Politica Internacional de Mexico, 1946; Ecos del Viejo Mundo, 1946; El Mundo de La Postquerra, 2 vols., 1946; La Conferencia de Ginebra y la Anchura del Mar Territorial, 1959; La Anchura del Mar Territorial, 1966; La Desnuclearizacion de la America Latina, 1966; The Denuclearization of Latin America, 1967; El Tratado de Tlatelolco—Genesis, Alcance y Propositos de la Proscripcion de las Armas Nucleares en la America Latina, 1967; Mexico en las Naciones Unidas, 2 vols., 1970. Contbr. articles profl. jours. Office: Permanent Mission of Mexico to the United Nations 8 E 41st St New York City NY 10017

GARD, ROBERT EDWARD, educator, author; b. Iola, Kan., July 3, 1910; s. Samuel Arnold and Louisa Maria (Ireland) G.; B.A., U. Kan., 1934; M.A., Cornell U., 1938; m. Maryo Kimball, June 7, 1939; children—Maryo Gwendolyn, Eleanor Copeland. Instr., U. Kan., 1934-37, Cornell U., 1940-43; dir. Alta. (Can.) Folklore and Local History Project, 1943-45; dir. Wis. Idea Theatre, U. Wis., 1945—, prof. agr. and extension edn., 1955—, also prof. drama; Fulbright prof. U. Helsinki (Finland), 1959-60, vis. prof., 1963. Pres. Wis. House, pubs., 1969—. Survey of Cultural Arts Gt. Britain, 1953; U.S. del. World Theatre Congress, Vienna, Austria, 1961. Trustee nat. Theatre Conf., 1958-62, Found. Integrated Edn., 1961—. Recipient Gold medal honor Finnish nat. Theatre, 1961, distinguished service award Internat. Inst., Milw., 1964, service award department of speech U. Kan., 1958, Gov.'s award for creativity, 1967. Mem. Wis. Arts Found. and Council (pres. 1957-59). Wis. Regional Writers Assn. (pres., 1961-64), Am. Ednl. Theatre Assn., ANTA. Author: Johnny Chinnook 1945; Lake Guns of Seneca and Cayuga, 1940; (with Drummond) Cardiff Giant, 1948; Wisconsin is my Doorstep, 1948; Grassroots Theatre, 1955; Community Theatre, 1959; Winconsin Lore, 1962; Error of Sexton Jones, 1964; (Am. history-mystery series) Midnight, 1952; Horse named Joe, 1955; Devil Red, 1962; (with Balch and Temkin) Theatre in America, 1968; (with Sorden) Romance of Wisconsin Place Names, 1968. Home: 3507 Sunset Dr Madison WI 53705

GARD, SPENCER AGASSIZ, former judge; b. Iola, Kan., June 24, 1898; s. Samuel Arnold and Louisa (Ireland) G.; LL.B., U. Kan., 1922; m. Marjoie P. Garlinghouse, Sept. 27, 1924; 1 dau., Amy Lou (Mrs. Jack Brazil). Admitted to Mo. bar, 1922, Kan. bar, 1942; practiced in Kansas City, 1922-42, Iola, 1942-50; judge 37th Kan. Jud. Dist., Iola, 1950-69; county atty. Allen County (Kan.), 1943-47; faculty Nat. Coll. State Trial Judges U. Colo., 1964. Vice pres. Kansas City Area council Boy Scouts Am., 1941; mem. Nat. Conf. Commrs. on Uniform State Laws, 1947-62; chmn. spl. com. which drafted Kan. Code Civil Procedure, 1963. Mem. Kan. Ho. of reps., 1947; mem. Kan. Senate, 1949; nominated for Kan. Supreme Ct., 1964. Recipient Distinguished Alumnus citation from U. Kan. Sch. Law, 1968. Mem. Am. Bar. Assn., Order of Coif, Scribes. Methodist (trustee). Rotarian. Author: Jones on Evidence, 1958; Illinois Evidence Manual and Kansas Code of Civil Procedure Annotated, 1964; Florida Evidence Manual, 1967. Contbr. profl. jours. Home: RR 3 Iola KS 66749 Office: 20 N Washington St Iola KS 66749

GARDINER, GEORGE RYERSON, stock broker, orgn. ofcl.; b. Toronto, Ont., Can., Apr. 25, 1917; s. Percy Ryerson and Gertrude (Corcoran) G.; B. Commerce, U. Toronto, 1939; M.B.A., Harvard, 1941; m. Anne Dumstrey, June 20, 1942; children— Judith, Michael, Cindy. Pres., dir. Gardiner, Watson Ltd., mems. Toronto Stock Exchange, Toronto, 1955—, Gardiner, Watson, Edmonds Ltd., Toronto, 1955—; pres. Scott's Restaurants Ltd., Toronto, 1948-65, chmn. bd., 1965—; chmn. bd. dirs. Colonial Homes Ltd., Westhill, Ont., 1961—, Beatty Bros. Ltd., Fergus, Ont., 1961—; Skyway Hotels. Ltd., London, Eng., 1961—, Miami Springs Villa, Miami, Fla., 1962—; dir. Maple Leaf Gardens Ltd., Zenith Electric Supply Ltd., Gen. Steel Wares Ltd. Trustee, Toronto Gen. Hosp., Ont. Crippled Children Centre; bd. govs. York U. Home: 259 Dunvegan Rd Toronto Ontario Canada Office: 335 Bay St Toronto Ontario Canada

GARDINER, GERALD AUSTIN, lord chancellor Gt. Britain; b. London, Eng., May 30, 1900; s. Robert and Alice Marie (von Zeigesar) G.; student Harrow Sch.; M.A., Magdalen Coll., Oxford; m. Miss Trounson, Dec. 1925 (dec. 1966); 1 dau., Carol Susan. Called to bar, 1925, created Queen's Counsel, 1948; mem. Com. on Supreme Ct. Practice and Procedure, 1947-53; mem. Lord Chancellor's Law Reform Com., 1952-63; chmn. Gen. Council of the Bar, 1958, 59; Lord Chancellor of Gt. Britain. Co-chmn. Nat. Campaign for Abolition of Capital Punishment. Served as 2d lt. Coldstream Guards, 1918; mem. Friends Ambulance Unit, 1943-45. Master of the bench Inter Temple, 1955. Club: Garrick. Author: Capital Punishment as a Deterrent, 1956. Co-editor: Law Reform Now, 1963. Address: Lord Chancellor's Residence House of Lords London SW 1 England

GARDINER, HENRY GILBERT, museum dir.; b. Boston, Aug. 27, 1927; s. Robert Hallowell and Elizabeth (Denny) G.; B.A., Harvard, 1950, M.A., 1959. With J.P. Morgan & Co., 1951-57; asst. to curator Wadsworth Atheneum, Hartford, Conn., 1959; curatorial asst. to dir. Addison Gallery Am. Art, Andover, Mass., 1959-60, asst. curator painting and sculpture Phila. Mus. Art, 1960-69; dir. Fine Arts Gallery San Diego, 1969—. Sec.-treas. San Diego Inter-Mus. Council. Trustee N.Y. Studio Sch., Roland Gibson Found. Served with USNR, 1945-46. Mem. Am. Assn. Mus. Dirs. Author mus. bulls. and catalogues. Home: 2909 1st Av San Diego CA 92103 Office: PO Box 2107 San Diego CA 92112

GARDINER, ROBERT HALLOWELL, banker; b. Needham, Mass., Sept. 29, 1914; s. Robert Hallowell and Elizabeth (Denny) G.; grad. Groton Sch., 1933; A.B., Harvard, 1937, LL.B., 1940; m. Frances Weld, June 7, 1941; children—Alison, Robert Hallowell, Holly, Nathaniel S., Phyllis. With Fiduciary Trust Co., Boston, 1946—, pres., 1957—, dir., 1948—; dir Scudder Stevens & Clark Funds, Putnam Investors, Putnam Income Fund; trustee Consol. Investment Trust, Gardiner Savs. Instn., Putnam Growth Fund, George Putnam Fund. Bd. dirs. Mass. Bay United Fund, New Eng. Forestry Found.; bd. dirs., treas. Action for Boston Community Devel., Inc.; trustee, v.p. Boston Symphony Orch.; treas., trustee Radcliffe Coll.; pres. bd. trustees Groton Sch. Served to lt. USNR, 1941-45. Club: Tavern (Boston). Home: Oaklands Gardiner ME 04345 Office: 10 Post Office Sq Boston MA 02109

GARDINER, ROBERT KWEKU ATTA, UN ofcl.; b. Kumasi, Ghana, Sept. 29, 1914; s. Philip H.D. and Nancy T. (Ferguson) G.; B.A. with honours, Cambridge (Eng.) U., 1941; grad. student Oxford (Eng.) and London (Eng.) univs.; B.Sc. in Econs. (hon.), D.C.L. (hon.), U. E. Anglia, 1966; LL.D., U. Bristol, 1966; Ph.D. (hon.), U. Uppsala (Sweden); m. Linda Charlotte Edwards, July 24, 1943; children—Charlotte, George, Roberta. Lectr. econs. Fourah Bay Coll., Sierra Leone, 1943-46; mem. trusteeship dept. UN, 1947- 49; dir. extra-mural stdies Univ. Coll., Ibadan, Nigeria, 1949-53; dir. dept. social welfare and community devel. Gold Coast (now Ghana) 1953-55, permanent sec. Ministry Housing, 1955-57, head civil service, 1957- 59; dep. exec. sec. Econ. Commn. Africa, UN, 1959-60; mem. UN mission to Congo, 1961; dir. pub. affairs div. UN dept. econ. and social affairs, 1961-62; exec. sec. Econ. Commn. Africa, UN, 1962—, officer-charge UN operations in Congo, 1962-63. Hon. fellow Selwyn Coll., Cambridge U., U. Ibadan. Author: (with H. O. Judd) The Development of Social Administration, 2d edit., 1959; A World of Peoples, 1965. Address: UNECA Post Office Box 3001 Addis Abada Ethiopia

GARDINER, ROBERT MCPHERSON, investment banker; b. Denver, Nov. 17, 1922; s. Clement E. and Margaret (McPherson) G.; student Princeton, 1940-43; m. Janet Eaton, Dec. 6, 1947; children—Margaret M., Peter E., Susan N., Thomas B. Analyst. A.M. Kidder & Co., N.Y.C., 1946-51; partner, syndicate mgr. Reynolds & Co., N.Y.C., 1951-57, mng. partner, 1957—. Gov., Am. Stock Exchange, 1956- 57. Mem. Nat. Assn. Securites Dealers (chmn.), Investment Bankers Assn. Am. (pres. N.Y. group 1967). Clubs: Bankers, Links, Bond (sec.); (N.Y.C.); Somerset Hills Golf (Bernardsville, N.J.); Morristown (N.J.); Ekwanok Country (Manchester, Vt.). Home: Glen Apline Rd New Vernon NJ 07976 Office: 120 Broadway New York City NY 10005

GARDINER, SPRAGUE HEMAN, physician, educator; b. Toledo, Oct. 20, 1910; s. John P. and Antonette (Sprague) G.; A.B., U. Mich., 1930, M.D., 1934, M.S., 1937; m. Mary Sherret Biggers, Oct. 22, 1941; children—John Biggers, William Sprague, Thomas Kelsey, Ann Sherret. Intern dept. obstetrics and gynecology U. Mich. Hosp. and Sch. Medicine, Ann Arbor, 1934-35, resident, 1935-38, instr., 1938-39; Rockefeller fellow in psychiatry Johns Hopkins Hosp. and Sch. Medicine, Balt., 1939-41, instr. obstetrics, asst. psychiatrist, 1941-42; asst. prof. obstetrics and gynecology Ind. U. Sch. Medicine, Indpls., 1947-53, asso. prof., 1953- 57, prof., 1957—; cons. obstetrics and gynecology Marion County Gen., Methodist, St. Vincent's, Community hosps. Pres. bd. trustees Orchard Country Day Sch., 1954-58, pres. bd. govs., 1962-66; pres. bd. mgrs. Marion County Home, 1969—. Served to maj. M.C., AUS, 1942-46. Diplomate Am. Bd. Obstetrics and Gynecology, Am. Bd. Psychiatry and Neurology. Mem. A.M.A. (chmn. com. on maternal and child care), Am. Coll. Obstetricians and Gynecologists (asst. sec. 1959-65, treas. 1965—), Am. Gynecol. Soc., Am., Central (mem. council 1964-66) assns. obstetricians and gynecologists, Continental Gynecol. Soc. (pres. 1962), Ind. Obstet. and Gynecol. Soc., Ind. Med. Assn., Marion County Med. Soc., Psi Upsilon, Nu Sigma Nu. Mem. editorial bd. Jour. Obstetrics and GynecologV, 1964-66. Research and publs. on gynecologic pathology and surgery, psychosomatic studies in obstetrics and gynecology. Home: 330 W 62d St Indianapolis IN 46260

GARDNER, ALFRED, ret. lawyer; b. N.Y.C., Nov. 8, 1896; s. Alfred Augustus and Katharine Taber (Willets) G.; A.B., Harvard, 1918, LL.B., 1822; m. Rena Holmes Harris, Sept. 2, 1919; 1 dau., Patricia (Mrs. Floyd H. Lander); m. 2d, Ruth Bodwell Sherman, June 15, 1929; 1 dau., Ann (Mrs. Paul F. New). Admitted to Mass. bar, 1922, since practiced in Boston; former partner firm Palmer & Dodge. Pres. Boston Legal Aid Soc., 1951-62; chmn. Mass. Adv. Com. Corrections, 1955-57; chmn. Mass. Crime Commn., 1962-65. Mem. Mass., Boston (pres. 1955-57) bar assns., Am. Law Inst. Clubs: Eastern Yacht (Marblehead); White Mt. Ski Runners (past pres.) (Boston). Home: 34 Gregory St Marblehead MA 01945

GARDNER, ALVIN FREDERICK, oral pathologist, govt. ofcl.; b. Chgo., Mar. 22, 1920; s. Leon William and Sarah (Kanter) G.; A.A., U. Fla., 1940; D.D.S., Emory U., 1943; postgrad. certificate U. Kansas City, 1946; postgrad. (NIH fellow) State U. Ia., 1954-55; M.S. (NIH fellow), U. Ill., 1957; Ph.D. (NIH fellow), Georgetown U., 1959; m. Esther Vita Shochet, June 11, 1942; 1 dau., Ava Lee. Staff dentist AEC, Richland, Wash., 1944-45; chief dental staff Stockton (Cal.) State Hosp., 1945-46; pvt. practice dentistry, 1946-54; resident in oral pathology, mem. dental staff Armed Forces Inst. Pathology, Walter Reed Army Med. Center, Washington, 1957- 59, mem. research staff, 1954—; asso. prof. pathology U. Md., Balt., 1959-63; dental officer Bur. of Medicine, FDA, Dept. Health, Edn. and Welfare, 1963—. Vis. scientist Nat. Bur. Standards, 1957-59; cons. in oral pathology Stedmans Med. Dict., USPHS, VA. Served to capt., Dental Corps, AUS Res., 1942-51. Grantee U.S. Army Research and Devel. Command, Surg. Gen.'s Office, 1962-63, NIH, USPHS, 1961-64, Sigma Xi, New Haven, 1962-63, Md. div. Am. Cancer Soc., 1962-63; recipient 3d prize Am. Soc. Oral Surgeons, 1962, Schering essay award, 1957. Diplomate Internat. Bd. Applied Nutrition. Fellow A.A.A.S., Internat. Assn. Anesthesiologists, Internat. Coll. Applied Nutrition, Am. Soc. Advancement Gen. Anesthesia in Dentistry, Am. Pub. Health Assn., Am. Med. Writer's Assn.; mem. A.M.A. (asso.), Am., Md., Conn. dental assns., So. Md. Dental Soc., Am. Assn. Dental Editors, Am. Acad. Oral Pathology, Am. Acad. Dental Medicine, Internat. Assn. Dental Research, Fedn. Dentaire Internationale, Am. Nutrition Soc., Am. Assn. Endodontists, Royal Soc. Health (Eng.), Am. Soc. Cytology, N.Y. Acad. Arts and Scis., Georgetown U., U. Ill., Emory U. alumni assns., Sigma Xi. Author: Oral Pathology, Oral Roentgenology and Periodontics, 1963; Pathology in Dentistry, 1968; Differential Oral'Diagnosis in Systemic Disease, 1970; Pathology of Oral Manifestations of Systemic Diseases, 1971; also monographs, numerous articles in profl. jours. Editor: American Lectures in Dentistry, 1968; corr. editor El Salvador Dental Jour.; sci. editor Jour. of Conn. Dental Assn. Home: 9039 Sligo Greek Pkwy Silver Spring MD 20901 Office: Bur Medicine FDA Dept Health Education and Welfare Washington DC 20201

GARDNER, ANDREW LEROY, educator, physicist; b. Ogden, Utah, Feb. 6, 1919; s. Ivin Estelvin and Eunice (Iverson) G.; B.S., Utah State Agrl. Coll., 1940; Ph.D., U. Cal. at Berkeley, 1955; m. Myrtle May Izatt, Oct. 10, 1941; children—Kayleen (Mrs. Dennis Mack Silver), Keith Leroy, Lynn Andrew, David Lloyd, Janis Karen. Communication asst. Ida. Nat. Forest, summer 1941; radio engr. Office Chief Signal Officer, War Dept., Washington, 1942-44; staff mem. Mass. Inst. Tech. Radiation Lab., 1944-45; asst. research engr. U. Cal. Inst. Engring. Research, Berkeley, 1946-54; physicist U. Cal. Lawrence Radiation Lab., Livermore, 1954-64, cons., 1968—; asso. prof. physics Brigham Young U., Provo, Utah, 1964-66, prof., 1966—. Tech. adviser U.S. Delegation 2d Internat. Atoms for Peace Conf., Geneva, Switzerland, 1958; cons. Japan Inst. Plasma Physics, 1962. Fellow Am. Phys. Soc.; mem. Sigma Xi, Phi Kappa Phi. Mem. Ch. of Jesus Christ of Latter-day Saints (bishop). Patentee in field. Home: 555 East 2950 North Provo UT 84601

GARDNER AUSTIN THAYER, elec. utility exec.; b. Chgo., Oct. 7, 1908; s. George Albert and Charlotte May (Thayer) G.; Ph.B., U. Chgo., 1930; m. Mary N. Miller, Sept. 2d, 1933; children—Diane G. (Mrs. Padgett), George T. With Utilities Power & Light Corp., Chgo., 1930-37, Asso. Electric Co., N.Y., 1937-43; sec., comptroller Delmarva Power & Light Co., Wilmington, Del., 1943-46, v.p., sec., 1946-60, pres., dir., 1960, chief exec. officer, 1966-69, chmn. bd., 1969—; dir., mem. exec. com. Del. Trust Co., Wilmington. Bd. dirs., pres. Greater Wilmington Devel. Council; bd. dirs., past treas. Del. chpt. A.R.C.; bd. dirs. Del. Safety Council, Health Planning Council, Wilmington Symphony Orch., Better Bus. Bur.; trustee Blue Cross and Blue Shield, Bradywine Jr. Coll. Mem. Am. Gas Assn. (past chmn. accounting sect.), Sigma Alpha Epsilon. Clubs: Wilmington Country (dir., mem. finance com.), University and Whist, Lions (past pres.). Home: 215 Peirce Rd Wilmington DE 19803 Office: 600 Market St Wilmington DE 19801

GARDNER, AVA, motion picture actress; b. Smithfield, N.C., Dec. 24, d. Jonas B. and Mary Elizabeth Gardner; student Atlantic Christian Coll.; m. Mickey Rooney, Jan. 10, 1942; m. 2d, Artie Shaw, 1945; m. 3d, Frank Sinatra, 1951 (div.). Motion picture debut in We Were Dancing, 1942; other motion pictures include Lost Angel, Three Men in White, Maisie Goes to Reno, Whistle Stop, The Hucksters, Singapore, One Touch of Venus, Great Sinner, East Side West Side, My Forbidden Past, Show Boat, Pandora and the Flying Dutchman, Lone Star, Snows of Killmanjaro, Ride Vaquero, Mogambo, Knights of The Roundtable, The Barefoot Contessa, Bhowani Junction, The Little Hut, The Sun Also Rises, Naked Maja, On the Beach, 55 Days to Peking, Night of the Iguana, The Bible, Mayerling, Tam-Lin. Address: care A Morgan Maree Jr & Assos 6363 Wilshire Blvd Los Angeles CA 90048

GARDNER, BURLEIGH BRADFORD, consumer research co. exec.; b. Galveston, Tex., Dec. 4, 1902; s. William A. and Mary (Bradford) G.; B.A., M.A. in Anthropology, U. Tex., 1930; Ph.D. in Social Anthropology, Harvard, 1936; m. Mary Ruby, July 1, 1933; children—Andrew, Stephen, Thomas. Charge social. survey of N.M. for Soil Conservation Service, 1936-37; research and devel. personnel counseling Western Electric Co., 1937-42; past prof. Sch. Bus., U. Chgo., also exec. sec. com. on human relations in industry of univ., 1942-46; pres. Social Research, Inc., Chgo., 1946—, Social Research Internat., Ltd., 1957—; sec.-treas. Inst. for Social and Psychol. Studies, 1960—; Active Winnetka (Ill.) village caucus, Winnetka schs. Bd. dirs. Duncan Med. Center, YMCA. Mem. Am. Marketing Assn. (chmn. publs. policy and rev. bd.), Soc. Applied Anthropology, N.Y. Acad. Scis. Author: (with D.G. Moore) Human Relations in Industry, 1955; (with A. Davis and Mary R. Gardner) Deep South-a Social Anthropological Study of Caste and Class, 1941. Home: 857 Burr Av Winnetka IL 60093 Office: 740 N Rush St Chicago IL 60611

GARDNER, CLIFFORD SPEER, educator; b. Ft. Smith, Ark., Jan. 14, 1924; s. John Carnall and Caroline (Klingensmith) G.; grad. Phillips Acad., 1940; B.A., Harvard, 1944; Ph.D., N.Y. U., 1952; m. Marilyn Rose Martinez, July 19, 1967; stepchildren—David Jackson, Jeffrey Jackson. Physicist, NACA, Langley Field, Va., 1944-46, U. Cal. Radiation Lab., 1953-55, N.Y. U., 1955-60; vis. scientist U.K. Atomic Energy Authority, Harwell, 1960; physicist Plasma Physics Lab., Princeton, 1963-67; prof. math. U. Tex., Austin, 1967—. Mem. Am. Math. Soc., Math. Assn. Am. Home: 3415 Shinoak Dr Austin TX 78731

GARDNER, DAVID BRUCE, educator, psychologist; b. Salt Lake City, Dec. 7, 1924; s. Joseph A. and Martha (Blunck) G.; B.S., U. Utah, 1948, M.S., 1949; Ph.D., Cornell U., 1952; m. Ila Mary Christensen, Mar. 31, 1945; children—Don B., Christine, Anita. From asst. prof. to asso. prof. child devel. and psychology, head dept. child devel. Utah State U., 1951-55; prof. child devel. and psychology, head dept. child devel. Ia State U., 1955-67; prof. psychology, chmn. dept. U. Denver, 1967-70; prof., chmn. child devel. Colo. State U., Fort Collins, 1970. John R. Emens Distinguished prof. Ball State U., Muncie, Ind., 1971-72; cons. in field. Pres., Midwestern Assn. Edn. Young Children, 1966-67. Served to 1st lt. USAAF, 1943-46. Mem. Am., Rocky Mountain psychol. assns., Soc. Research Child Devel., Nat. Assn. Edn. Young Children (editorial bd. 1969—). Author: Development in Early Childhood: The Preschool Years, 1964. Home: 1820 Yorktown Fort Collins CO 80521

GARDNER, DAVID LEE, pub. utility exec.; b. St. Louis, Aug. 26, 1925; s. Russell E. and Enid (Simpkins) G.; grad. Phillips Acad., Andover, Mass., 1943; B.S., U.S. Naval Acad., 1946; m. Anne Stanard McCandless, Dec. 4, 1951; children—Anne McCandless, Eleanor Stanard, David Lee, Robert Ridgely, Allan Thacher. Commd. ensign U.S. navy, 1946, advanced through grades to lt. (s.g.), 1953, ret., 1953; with Laclede Gas Co., St. Louis, 1949—, sec., 1962-70, asst. treas., 1966-70, v.p. corporate devel., 1970—; v.p. Laclede Devel., Laclede Investment, Laclede Gas Family Services; sec. Midwest Mo. Gas, St. Charles Gas, Laclede Pipeline Co. Bd. dirs. St. Louis chpt. A.R.C., 1963—, chmn., 1967, mem. Midwest Area council, 1965-67; bd. dirs. St. Louis Symphony Soc., 1965—, also treas.; bd. dirs. St. Louis Arts and Edn. Council, 1966—, v.p., 1968; bd. dirs. Cardinal Ritter Institute, 1965—, also pres.; bd. dirs. St. Louis YMCA, 1964-66, Municipal Theatre Assn., 1969—, Mary Inst., 1969— , Mo. Amateur Ice Hockey Assn. Mem. Am. Soc. Corporate Secs. (v.p. dir.), Am. Soc. Ins. Mgmt., Am. Soc. Financial Analysts, Am. Gas Assn., St. Louis Met. C. of C. (bd. dirs. 1967-68). Home: 3 Mayfair Rd St Louis MO 63124 Office: 720 Olive St St Louis MO 63101

GARDNER, DONALD LAVERE, bldg. products mfg. co. exec.; b. Winfield, Kan., Aug. 1, 1930; s. Lindell L. and Eva (Robinson) G.; B.S., U. Kan., 1952; M.B.A., U. Chgo., 1956; m. Dolores E. Willson, Dec. 27, 1952; children—Theresa L., Michelle M., Blake R. Div. asst. No. Trust Co., Chgo., 1954; v.p. Security Pacific Nat. Bank, Riverside, Cal., 1957-63; pres., gen. mgr., G.T. Wolfe Mobile Homes, Inc., Corona, Cal., 1963-66; exec. v.p. Evans Products Co., Corona, 1966—. Instr., Valley Coll., San Bernardino, Cal., 1959-63, Riverside (Cal.) City Coll., 1960-64. Active United Fund. Corona water commr., 1965. Served with arty. AUS, 1952-54. Named Citizen of Year, City of Riverside, 1960. Mem. Corona C. of C. (bd. dirs.), Beta Gamma Sigma. Rotarian (pres. 1964). Home: 621 Lancer Lane Corona CA 91720 Office: 1346 Railroad St Corona CA 91720

GARDNER, EDWARD JAMES, advt. co. exec.; b. Jersey City, Sept. 7, 1924; s. Charles and Katherine (Schmiegel) G.; B.S. in Engring., U.S. Mcht. Marine Acad., 1944; B.A. cum laude in English Lit., Tufts U., 1949; m. Marion Inge Ritter, June 8, 1958. Advt. and sales trainee Vick Chem. Co., 1949-50; copywriter Young & Rubicam, N.Y.C., 1950-54; account supr. Ogilvy, Benson & Mather, N.Y.C., 1954-57; v.p., dir., creative head McKim Advt. Ltd.(Can.), 1957-59; exec. v.p., dir. Robert Conahay, Inc., N.Y.C., 1959- 64; advt. dir. Crowell Collier

Pub. Co., N.Y.C., 1961-63; v.p. account supr. Doherty, Clifford, Steers & Shenfield, advt., N.Y.C., 1964-65; exec. v.p. Ross Roy of N.Y., Inc., N.Y.C., 1966—. Instr. advt. City Coll. N.Y., 1954-57. Bd. dirs. King Cove Assn. Served to lt. (j.g.) USNR, 1943-46. Mem. Pubs. Advt. Club. Club: N.Y. Tufts (chmn. spl. gifts com. N.Y.C.). Home: 80 Park Av New York City NY 10016 Office: 555 Fifth Av New York City NY 10017

GARDNER, ELDON JOHN, univ. dean; b. Logan, Utah, June 5, 1909; s. John William and Cynthia (Hill) G.; B.S., Utah State U., 1934, M.S., 1935; Ph.D., U. Cal. at Berkeley, 1939; m. Helen Richards, Aug. 21, 1939; children—Patricia (Mrs. Jerome L. Mahrt), Donald Eldon, Betty (Mrs. George T. Morrison), Cynthia (Mrs. Stephen R. Pulley), Alice, Mary Jane. Instr., dean Salinas (Cal.) Jr. Coll., 1939-46; geneticist spl. guayule project Bur. Plant Industry, Salinas, 1943-46; asso. prof. U. Utah, 1946-49; prof. Utah State U., Logan, 1949—, dean Coll. Sci., 1962-67, dean Sch. Grad. Studies, 1967—, faculty honor lectr., 1953. Mem. Utah Acad. Sci. Arts and Letters (pres. 1968-69, Distinguished Service award 1957), Genetics Soc. Am., Am. Soc. Human Genetics (sec. 1955-58, v.p. 1960-61), A.A.A.S., Am. Eugenics Soc., Am. Soc. Naturalists, Sigma Xi, Phi Kappa Phi. Mem. Ch. of Jesus Christ of Latter-day Saints. Author: History of Biology, 2d edit., 1965; Principles of Genetics, 3d edit., 1968. Home: 369 N 5th East Logan UT 84321

GARDNER, ELLIS BENJAMIN, Jr., shipbldg. exec.; b. Little Rock, Feb. 29, 1920; s. Ellis Benjamin and Rose (Hooker) G.; A.B., Columbia, 1940; m. Mary Elizabeth List, May 23, 1942; children—Kathryn (Mrs. Sommers), Ellis Benjamin III, Sara. Asso. with Gen. Electric Co., 1940-46; with Hewitt- Robins, Inc. div. Litton Industries, Stamford, Conn., 1946-66, exec. v.p., 1959-66, pres. Ingalls Shipbldg. Corp. div., 1966—, v.p. parent co., 1966-67, sir. v.p., group exec. parent co., 1967—. Bd. dirs. Shipbuilders Council Am.; mem. Am. Bur. Shipping: mem. adv. council on naval affairs Comdt. 6th Naval Dist.; mem. industry adv. com. Comdr. Naval Ship Systems Command; mem. Maritime Transp. Research Bd. Mem. Soc. Naval Architects and Engrs., Soc. Naval Engrs., S.R., Phi Beta Kappa, Sigma Alpha Epsilon. Clubs: Columbia University (N.Y.C.); Wee Burn Country (Darien, Conn.); Hickory Hill Country (Gautier, Miss.); Boston (New Orleans). Home: Long Neck Point Darien CT 06820 Office: PO Box 149 Pascagoula MS 39567

GARDNER, ERIC FREEMAN, educator; b. Brooklyn, N.S., Can., Mar. 16, 1913; s. Clayton E. and Elizabeth E. (Taylor) G.; A.B., Harvard, 1935, Ed.D., 1947; M.Ed., Boston Tchrs. Coll., 1936; certificate naval architecture, U. Mich., 1944; m. Catherine Smalley-Smith, June 24, 1939; 1 dau., Elizabeth Holdsworth. Came to U.S., 1913, naturalized, 1917. Tchr. math. pub. and pvt. schs., Mass., R.I., Vt., 1936-41; instr. Harvard, 1946-47; faculty Syracuse U., 1947—, prof. psychology and edn., 1952—, dir. grad. studies Sch. Edn., 1952-60, chmn. psychology dept., 1960—, dir. Psychol. Services and Research Center, 1960—, now Margaret O. Slocum prof. edn. and psychology; chmn. bd. trustees Test Research Service, Inc., 1960-68; adv. com. exptl. programs N.Y. State Edn. Dept., also adv. com. coll. proficiency exams. Trustee Manlius-Pebble Hill Sch. Served to lt. USNR, 1942-46. Fellow Am. Psychol. Assn.; mem. Am. Statis. Assn., Inst. Math. Statistics, Psychometrics Soc., Biometrics Soc., Am. Assn. U. Profs. Author: Tomorrow's Graduate School of Education, 1958. Co-author: Stanford Achievement Test, rev. edit., 1964; Syracuse Scales of Social Relations, 1959; Educational Psychology, 1959; Social Relations and Moral in Small Groups, 1956; Stanford High School Achievement Tests, 1966; Stanford Diagnostic Reading Tests, 1968; Stanford Diagnostic Arithmetic Tests, 1968; Adult Basic Learning Examinations, 1968; Stanford Modern mathematics Concepts Test, 1967; Classification and Placement Examination, 1966. Content editor: Library of Education, 100 vols., 1962. Home: 103 Draycott St Fayetteville NY 13066 Office: Psychology Dept Huntington Hall 157 Marshall St Syracuse NY 13210

GARDNER, FREDERICK CALKIN, ins. co. exec.; b. Pawling, N.Y., Aug. 1, 1910; s. John C. and Elizabeth (Calkin) G.; A.B., Columbia, 1932, LL.B., 1934; m. Nancy Lewis, Dec. 29, 1949. Charge legal dept. Gt. Am. Indemnity Co., 1937-42; with Office Gen. Counsel USN, 1946-47; sec. Chubb Corp., N.Y.C., 1967—; v.p., sec. Chubb & Son, Inc., 1965—; v.p., sec. Fed. Ins. Co., N.Y.C., 1960- -; sec. Vigilant Ins. Co., 1960—; dir. Am. Sea Ins. Co. Served with AUS, 1941-42, 44-45. Decorated Bronze Star medal. Clubs: India House, Metropolitan (N.Y.C.). Home: Pecksland Rd Greenwich CT 06830 Office: 90 John St New York City NY 10038

GARDNER, FREDERICK WILLIAM, investment banker; b. Gallion, O., July 14, 1893; s. Russell E. and Annie (Cathey) G.; Litt.B., Princeton, 1914; m. Margaret Watkins, Mar. 18, 1931. Vice pres. Chevrolet Motor Co., St. Louis, 1915-18, Gardner Motor Co., St. Louis, 1922-30; gen. partner Reinholdt & Gardner, St. Louis, 1931—. Chief cork-asbestos br., dir. gen. indsl. equipment div. WPB, Washington, 1941-44; adviser Dept. State, Washington, 1945. Bd. dirs. St. Louis Bi State chpt. A.R.C. Served as lt. USNRF, 1917. Clubs: ST. Louis Country, Noonday (St. Louis). Home: 320 N Union Blvd St Louis MO 63108 Office: 506 Olive St St Louis MO 63108

GARDNER, GEORGE EDWARD, psychiatrist; b. West Bridgewater, Mass., Aug. 12, 1903; s. Charles Edward and Lulu Bernice (Penpraese) G.; A.B., Dartmouth, 1925; Ed.M., Harvard, 1926; Ph.D., 1930, M.D., 1937; m. Beatrice Reside Kershaw, June 10, 1935; children—Ruth Isabella, Mary Edith. Psychologist McLean Hosp., Belmont, 1928-36, psychiatrist, 1939; research fellow in pediatrics Mass. Gen. Hosp., Boston, 1937, house physician, 1937-38, resident physician, 1938-39; psychiatrist Juvenile Ct., Boston, 1936-43; Commonwealth fellow Judge Baker Children's Psychiat. Clinic, 1939- 40, staff psychiatrist, 1940-41, dir., 1941—; asst. in psychology, Harvard, 1929-31, lectr. clin. psychology, 1946—; asst. pediatrics Harvard Med. Sch., 1941, clin. prof. psychiatry, 1953- 65, prof. psychiatry, 1965—; psychiatrist-in-chief Children's Hosp., Boston, 1953-70; lectr. Boston Coll. Sch. Social Work, 1942, prof. child psychiatry, 1943-50; asso. prof. psychiatry Boston U. Med. Sch., 1946-53; cons. psychiatry Children's Hosp. Med. Center, 1947-53. Pres., Am. Assn. Psychiat. Clinics for Children, 1951-53; mem. mental health study sect. NIH, 1953—. Trustee Dennison House (Boston), Mass. Speech Inst.; bd. dirs. So. Edn. Found., Washington. Served from lt. comdr. to comdr. M.C., USNR, 1943-46. Recipient Agnes P. McGavin award for contrbns. in field of child psychiatry, 1968. Diplomate Nat. Bd. Med. Examiners. Mem. Am. Acad. Child Psychiatry (pres. 1953- 55), Am. Orthopsychiat. Assn., Am. Psychiat. Assn., Mass. Med. Soc., Am. Psychoanalytic Assn., Phi Beta Kappa, Sigma Xi. Author: (with Arthur D. Wright) Hall's Lectures on School-Keeping, 1925; also many tech. papers. Home: 29 Louise Rd Belmont MA 02115 Office: 295 Longwood Av Boston MA 02115 ☆

GARDNER, GEORGE PEABODY, found exec.; b. Boston, Mass., Jan. 28, 1888; s. George Peabody and Esther (Burnett) G.; grad. St. Mark's Sch., Southboro, Mass., 1906; A.B. cum laude, Harvard, 1910; m. Rose Phinney Grosvenor, Jan. 28, 1913; children—Katharine Peabody (Mrs. James V. Coleman), Isabella Stewart (Mrs. Isabella Tate), George Peabody, John Lowell, Rose Phinney (Mrs. Philip Cutler), Robert Grosvenor. Sec. Harvard Corp., 1911-14; hon. chmn. Gardner Assos., Inc.; chmn. bd. trustees Shareholders Trust, Boston, Chase Fund of Boston; dir. mass. Hosp. Life Ins. Co., Income & Capital Shares, Inc. Vice pres., trustee Childrens Hosp.; v.p. Humane Soc. Commonwealth Mass.; trustee Mus. Fine Arts, Boston, Children's Cancer Research, Diocesan Investment Trust; pres. Isabella Stewart Gardner Mus. Commd. capt. O.R.C., 1917, q.m. USNR, 1918, ensign Naval Aux. Res., 1918. Mem. Phi Beta Kappa. Republican. Episcopalian. Clubs: Somerset, Tavern, Harvard (Boston); Harvard, Links (N.Y.C.). Author: Chiefly the Orient, 1912; Ready About, 1959; Turkish Delight, 1964. Home: 135 Warren St Brookline MA Office: 225 Franklin St Boston MA

GARDNER, GEORGE PEABODY, Jr., investment banker; b. Newton, Mass., Sept. 22, 1917; s. George Peabody and Rose (Grosvenor) G.; grad. St. Mark's Sch., 1935; A.B., Harvard, 1939; m. Tatiana Stepanova, June 21, 1947; children—George Peabody 3d, Alexandra, Tatiana Expdn. to Peru, Mus. Comparative Zoology, 1939-40; with advt. dept. Boston Herald Traveler, 1947-48; account exec. Batton, Barton, Durstine & Osborn, advt., 1948-51; with Paine, Webber, Jackson & Curtis, Boston, 1952—, partner, 1955—; dir., mem. exec. com. United Brands; dir. Stanely Home Products, Inc., Barry Wright Corp., W.R. Grace & Co., Instron Corp., Ritz Carlton Hotel Co. Boston. Life mem. corp. Mass. Inst. Tech.; trustee Boston Mus. Sci., John F. Kennedy Library, Inst. Def. Analyses, Children's Hosp. Med. Center, Escuela Agricola Panamericana (Honduras). Served from ensign to lt. comdr. USNR, 1940-46; PTO. Fellow Am. Acad. Arts and Scis. Clubs: A.D. (Cambridge, Mass.); Tavern (Boston); Links (N.Y.). Home: 130 Warren St Brookline MA 02146 Office: 24 Federal St Boston MA 02101

GARDNER, GEORGE THOMAS, mfg. exec. b. Grifton, N.C., July 24, 1912; s. G. Thomas and Johnnie (Coward) G.; B.S., N.C. State Coll., 1934; m. Martha Brown Hunter, Mar. 27, 1959. Mgmt. apprentice Cramerton (N.C.) Mills (div. Burlington Mills Corp. 1946—), 1934-35, asst. to gen. mgr., 1936-38, asst. supt. in charge finishing, 1939-42, supt. in charge finishing, weaving, 1946-47; asst. div. mgr. Burlington Mills Corp., 1948, div. mgr., 1949-51, area mfg. exec. Cramerton, Decorative Fabrics, Cotton Spinning, Ribbon divs., 1951-53, mgr. man-made fibers spinning and weaving divs., 1953, mgr. spinning, weaving man-made and natural fibers, 1954, v.p., 1954-55; exec. v.p., dir., mem. exec. com. Riegel Textile Corp., 1955—, vice chmn. bd., 1969—. Chmn. tech. adv. com. So. Garment Mfg. Assn., 1960—. Trustee Textile Research Inst. Served from 2d lt. to maj. AUS, 1943-46. Mem. Q.M. Assn., Am. Soc. Textile Colorists and Chemists. Methodist. Mason. Club: Poinsett. Home: MG Ranch Route 3 Box 29 Gray Court SC 29645 Office: Riegel Textile Corp Greenville SC 29607

GARDNER, HENRY, supt. schs.; b. Kansas City, Kan., Sept. 20, 1920; s. Jesse F. and Julia (Henry) G.; A.B., St. Benedict's Coll., Atchison, Kan., 1942; student Kenrick Sem., St. Louis, 1945; M.A., Cath. U. Am., 1953. Ordained priest Roman Cath. Ch., 1945; tchr., athletic coach, Hayden High Sch., Topeka, 1945-52; supt. schs. Archdiocese Kansas City, Kan., 1953—; tchr. Donnelly Coll., Kansas City, Kan., 1954-58; tchr. grad. summer sch. St. Mary Coll., Leavenworth, Kan. Vice pres. Community Action Program, Kansas City, Kan., 1966—; advancement chmn. Kan. council Boy Scouts Am., 1963—; pres. Cancer Assn. Wyandotte County, Kan., 1967—. Mem. Nat. Cath. Edn. Assn. (mem. exec. bd., past pres. secondary dept.). Kiwanian. Home: 801 Vermont St Kansas City KS 66101 Office: 2220 Central St Kansas City KS 66102

GARDNER, HY, columnist, TV-radio performer, writer, producer; b. N.Y.C., Dec. 2, 1908; s. John Jacob and Sarah (Guilden) G.; student Columbia U. Sch. Journalism; m. 3d, Marilyn Boshnick, Apr., 1958; 1 son, Jeffrey Scot; 1 son (by previous marriage), Ralph Richard. With Fed. and Herald Advt. agys., 1924; writer Broadway column N.Y. Herald Tribune, 1950-67, currently distributed coast to coast, editor TV mag.; conducts Broadway and Hollywood Hy Gardner's Celebrity Party, radio series, Miami Beach, Fla.; producer, performer Miami TV-WCIX, nat. syndicate; formerly on TV series and panelist To Tell the Truth, Hy Gardner Calling. Served as capt., AUS, 1942-45; ret. maj. Res. Recipient Freedoms Found. award in Journalism. Cast, produced "Hi-Yank" soldier entertainment mus.; made movie The Girl Hunters. Author: Champagne Before Breakfast; So What Else is New, 1960; Tales Out of Night School; Off-Beat Guide to New York; also articles nat mags. Home: 2121 N Bayshore Dr Miami FL 33137 Office: 1111 Brickell Av Miami FL 33131

GARDNER, ISABELLA STEWART, poet; b. Newton, Mass., Sept. 7, 1915; s. Goege Peabody and Rose (Grosvenor) Gardner; student Foxcroft Sch., Middleburg, Va., 1931-33, Embassy Sch., Acting, London, Eng., 1937; m. Harold Van Virk, 1939; 1 dau., Rose; m. 2d, Robert H. McCormick, Jr., 1943; m. 3d, Maurice Seymour, 1949; 1 son, Daniel Seymour; m. 4th Allen Tate. Asso. editor Poetry mag., 1951-56. Nominee Nat. Book award (twice). Mem. N.A.A.C.P. (life), Congress of Racial Equality. Author: Birthdays From the Ocean, 1954; The Looking Glass, 1959; West of Childhood, 1965. Address: Chelsea Hotel 222 W 23d St New York City NY 10011

GARDNER, JOHN HALE, physicist; b. Logan, Aug. 24, 1922; s. Willard and Rebecca Viola (Hale) G.; B.S. with honors, Utah State U., 1943; A.M., Harvard, 1947, Ph.D., 1950; m. Olga Dotson, July 23, 1943; children—Helen, John, Kristin, Rebecca, Robert, Eric, Ann, Margaret. Mem. staff Mass. Inst. Tech. Radiation Lab., 1943-46; teaching fellow Harvard, 1946-49; asst. prof. physics Brigham Young U., 1949-52, asso. prof., 1952-58, prof., 1958—, chmn. dept., 1961—; tech. staff Ramo-Wooldridge Corp., 1955-57; cons. Space Tech. Labs., 1957—, mem. tech. staff, 1963-64. Fellow Phys. Soc. London; mem. Am. Phys. Soc., Am. Assn. Physics Tchrs., Am. Assn. U. Profs., A.A.A.S., Utah Acad. Sci., Arts and Letters (v.p. 1966-67, pres. 1967-68, mem. council, 1968-69), Sigma Xi (chpt. pres. 1961-62), Phi Kappa Phi (chpt. pres. 1958- 59). Republican. Mem. Ch. of Jesus Christ of Latter-day Saints. Contbr. articles to profl. jours. Holder 3 patents on microwave antennas. Home: 1140 Aspen Av Provo UT 84601

GARDNER, JOHN RIDGELY, investment banker; b. St. Louis, Mar. 16, 1920; s. Russell E. and Enid (Simpkins) G.; grad. St. Paul's Sch., 1938; grad. Princeton, 1943; m. Virginia Shell, Dec. 31, 1959; children—John Ridgely, William Edmund Scripps, Elizabeth, Katherine, Russell Eugene II, Enid Ridgely. Account exec. St. Louis Union Trust Co., 1946-49; partner Reinholdt & Gardner, St. Louis, 1950—. Mem. Chgo. Bd. Trade; bd. govs. Am. Stock Exchange, 1967-70. Served with USNR, World War II. Republican. Episcopalian. Clubs: Cottage (Princeton, N.J.); Links (N.Y.C.); St. Louis Country, Noonday (St. Louis). Home: 6 Upper Ladue Rd St Louis MO 63124 Office: 506 Olive St St Louis MO 63101

GARDNER, JOHN WILLIAM, writer, cons.; b. Los Angeles, Oct. 8, 1912; s. William and Marie (Flora) G.; A.B., Stanford, 1935, A.M., 1936; Ph.D., U. Cal., 1938, LL.D., 1959; hon. degrees from various colls, and univs.; hon. fellow Stanford, 1959; m. Aida Marroquin, Aug. 18, 1934; children—Stephanie (Mrs. Phillip Trimble), Francesca (Mrs. John R. Reese). Teaching asst. in psychology U. Cal., 1936- 38; instr. psychology Conn. Coll., 1938-40; asst. prof. psychology Mt. Holyoke Coll., 1940-42; head Latin-Am. sect. FCC, 1942-43; staff mem. Carnegie Corp. of N.Y., 1946-47, exec. asso., 1947-49, v.p., 1949-55, pres., 1955-65, cons., 1968-70; pres. Carnegie Found. Advancement of Teaching, 1955-65; sec. Dept. Health Edn. and Welfare, 1965-68; chmn. Urban Coalition, 1968-70; chmn. Common Cause, 1970—; vis. prof. Mass. Inst. Tech., 1968-69; fellow Kennedy Inst. Politics, Harvard, 1968-69. Chmn. social scis. panel Sci. Adv. Bd. USAF, 1951-55; adv. com. social scis. NSF, 1959-62; chmn. U.S. Adv. Commn. Internat. Ednl. and Cultural Affairs, 1962-64; chmn. White House Conf. Edn., 1965. Trustee N.Y. Sch. Social Work 1949-55; bd. dirs. Woodrow Wilson Found., 1960-63; trustee Met. Mus. Art, 1957-65. Served from 1st lt. to capt., USMCR, 1943-46, assigned OSS, MTO, ETO, 1944-45. Recipient USAF Exceptional Services award, 1956; Presdl. Medal of Freedom, 1964; Herbert H. Lehman Ethics medal Jewish Theol. Sem., 1970. Fellow Am. Psychol. Assn., Am. Acad. Arts and Scis.; mem. Council on Fgn. Relations, A.A.A.S. (past dir.), Pilgrims U.S., Sigma Xi, Kappa Delta Pi. Clubs: Bohemian (San Francisco); Century Assn., Coffee House, Stanford (N.Y.C.); Cosmos (Washington); Dutch Treat. Author: Excellence: Self-Renewal; No Easy Victories, 1968; Recovery of Confidence, 1970. Editor: To Turn the Tide. Home: 5325 Kenwood Av Chevy Chase MD 20015 Office: 2100 M St NW Washington DC 20037

GARDNER, KARL EDRICK, coll. dean; b. Chgo., Feb. 11, 1913; s. Charles Anson and Clara (Carlton) G.; B.S., Purdue U., 1936; M.S., Cornell U., 1939, Ph.D., 1940; m. June Ellen Hackleman, Aug. 14, 1938; children—James Andrew, Nancy Ellen, Deborah Ann. Grad. asst. Cornell U., Ithaca, N.Y., 1936-40; faculty U. Ill., Urbana, 1940-43, 46—, prof. dairy sci., 1953—, asso. dean, dir. resident instrn. Coll. Agr., 1959—. Chief of party U.S. AID-U Ill., Njala U. Coll., Sierra Leone, 1963-64; adviser dean agr. J. Nehru Agr. U., Jabaipur, India, 1967; spl. cons. in nutrition interdepartmental com. nutrition nat. def. NIH, 1956—; dept. dir. nutrition survey teams to Turkey, 1957, W. Indies, 1961; chmn. resident instrn. sect. div. agr. Nat. Assn. State Univs. and Land Grant Colls., 1970-71. Mayor, Village Tolono, Ill., 1952-60. Served to capt. San. Corps, AUS, 1943-46. Mem. Am. Inst. Nutrition, Am. Dairy Sci. Assn., Am. Soc. Animal Prodn., Am. Assn. U. Profs., Sigma Xi, Alpha Zeta, Gamma Sigma Delta, Alpha Tau Alpha, Alpha Gamma Rho. Presbyn. (trustee). Lion. Home: Tolono IL 61880 Office: Mumford Hall Univ Illinois Urbana IL 61801

GARDNER, KEITH, editor; b. Des Moines, Nov. 8, 1930; s. Arthur E. and Edith D. (McConnell) G.; student Coll. City San Francisco, 1948-50; A.B. in Journalism, San Jose (Cal.) State Coll., 1952. Reporter, Daly City (Cal.) Record, 1952-53; with Ford Motor Motor Co., Long Beach, Cal., 1955-56; copy boy N.Y. Mirror, 1956-57; messenger Benton & Bowles, advt., N.Y.C., 1957; staff Travel mag., 1957—. asso. editor, 1958-69; editor Fishing World mag., 1969—. Served with AUS, 1953-55. Home: 124 Remsen St Brooklyn NY 11201 Office: 51 Atlantic Av Floral Park NY

GARDNER, KIRTLAND CUTTER, Jr., mfg. exec.; b. Pitts., Apr. 5, 1909; s. Kirtland Cutter and Myrta (Neubauer) G.; A.B., Williams Coll., 1930; B.S., Lehigh U., 1932; m. Elizabeth B. Miller, June 29, 1932; children—Kirtland Cutter III, Helen Campbell (Mrs. Charles Heide), Elizabeth Miller (Mrs. Gilbert N. Riley). With United Engring. & Foundry Co., 1933—, successively engr., proposal dept. supr., asst. supt. Youngstown plant, asst. gen. mgr., v.p. charge operations, 1933-52, dir., mem. exec. com., 1951—, exec. v.p., 1952-59, exec. v.p., treas., 1959-64, pres., 1964—; exec. v.p., dir. Wean United, Inc.; dir. Wean Industries, Inc., Woodings-Verona Tool Works, Pitts. Testing Lab., Adamson-United Co. Mem. Pi Tau Sigma, Phi Sigma Kappa. Clubs: Duquesne, Allegheny Country, Edgeworth. Home: 12 Woodland Rd Edgeworth PA 15232 Office: 948 Ft Duquesne Blvd Pittsburgh PA 15222

GARDNER, LUCIEN DUNBIBBIN, Jr., lawyer; b. Troy, Ala., Mar. 1, 1903; s. Lucien Dunbibbin and Henrietta (Wiley) G.; B.A., U. Ala., 1922; LL.B., Harvard, 1925; m. Amy Cothran Young, Jan. 11, 1930; 1 son, William Fenwick. Admitted to Ala. bar, 1925; practice in Birmingham, 1925-42, 46—; mem. firm Cabaniss, Johnston, Gardner & Clark, 1946—; v.p., trust officer First Nat. Bank Montgomery, Ala., 1945-46; gen. counsel, dir. Protective Life Ins. Co., Birmingham, 1958—. Trustee Children's Hosp., Birmingham, 1952—; past asso. mem. Neighborhood House, Birmingham. Served to lt. col. USAAF, 1942-45. Fellow Am. Coll. Trial Lawyers; mem. Am., Ala., Birmingham (pres. 1959) bar assns., Newcomen Soc., Assn. Life Ins. Counsel, Am. Life Conv. (legal sect.), S.R., Sigma Nu. Episcopalian (vestry). Clubs: Mountain Brook (bd. govs., pres. 1960), Redstone (past bd. govs.), Club, Relay House (Birmingham). Home: 34 Fairway Dr Birmingham AL 35213 Office: First Nat Bldg Birmingham AL 35203

GARDNER, MARK FRANKLIN, utility co. exec.; b. Harvard, Neb., Sept. 4, 1920; s. Harry Charles and Florence (Weaver) G.; B.S. in Elec. Engring., U. Neb., 1948; m. Mildred Mary Pogue, June 7, 1948; children—Margaret Mary, John Mark. With Toledo Edison Co., 1948-52; with Ia. Pub. Service Co., Sioux City, 1952—, exec. v.p., dir., 1970—. Chmn. adv. bd. Sioux City Salvation Army; bd. dirs. Morningside Coll., Sioux City Concert Course, St. Luke's Med. Center, Sioux City. Served to capt. AUS, 1943-46. Decorated Bronze Star. Mem. I.E.E.E. (past chmn. Siouxland sect.), N. Central Electric Assn. (adv. com.), Am. Guild Organists. Republican. Methodist (trustee). Home: 720 S Newton St Sioux City IA 51106 Office: Orpheum Electric Bldg Sioux City IA 51102

GARDNER, MARSHALL C. govt. ofcl.; b. Logansport, Ind., June 11, 1918; s. Harry Marshall and Alice (Closson) G.; B.S., George Washington U., 1943, M.S., 1950, J.D. with distinction, 1955; m. June Archer Haller, Jan. 5, 1946; children—David Marshall, Debra June. Biologist, U.S. Fish and Wildlife Service, 1942-55; admitted to D.C. bar, 1955, also U. S. Supreme Ct.; sr. trial atty. antitrust div. Dept. Justice, Washington, 1955—; editorial notes editor, sec. George Washington U. Law Sch., 1954-55. Dir. Fed. Bar Bldg. Corp. Pres. N. Four Corners (Md.) Citizens Assn., 1954-55. Sec., dir. Fed. Bar Found. Served to lt. USNR, 1943-46, 50-53. Recipient Outstanding Law Student award George Washington U. Law Sch., 1955. Mem. Am. (del. 1967-70), Fed. (pres. 1965-66, gen. editor jour. 1956—), D.C. bar assns., Washington Acad. Scis., Am. Legion (comdr. D.C. 1968-69, judge adv. D.C., 1969—), Order of Coif, Sigma Xi (asso.), Omicron Delta Kappa, Tau Kappa Epsilon, Delta Theta Phi. Clubs: National Lawyers, Biologists Field, National Aviation (Washington). Home: 12118 Long Ridge Lane Bowie MD 20715 Office: Antitrust Div Justice Dept Washington DC 20530

GARDNER, PAUL VICKERS, mus. curator; b. Savona, N.Y.; s. George Augustus and Anja (Vickers) G.; B.S. in Ceramic Art, Alfred U., 1930; student Geneseo (N.Y.) State Tchrs. Coll., summer 1928, U. Miami, 1947. Designer, Steuben Glass, Corning, N.Y., 1929-32; asst. to art dir. Corning Glass Works, 1933-43; curator Nat. Collection of Fine Arts, Smithsonian Instn., Washington, 1948-57, curator charge div. ceramics and glass Mus. Hist. and Tech., 1957—. Cons. on ceramics and glass White House, 1956, Dept. State, 1960- 64, other govt. agys.; lectr. Corning Mus. Glass, Sandwich Mus. Glass, Chgo. Art Inst., Washington Antique Show, Sulgrave Club, Washington. Trustee Alfred U.; bd. govs. Wedgwood Internat. Seminar. Served with USNR, 1942-46. Mem. Am. Ceramic Soc., Am. Guild Organists, Washington Kiln Club (hon.), Lambda Chi Alpha. Methodist. Mason.

Contbr. articles to Ency. Britannica, also profl. publs. Home: 312 Massachusetts Av NW Washington DC 20007 Office: Smithsonian Instn Washington DC 20560

GARDNER, PETER D., univ. dean; b. Salt Lake City, Jan. 17, 1927; s. Pete D. and Margaret (Rasmason) G.; B.S., U. Utah, 1949, M.S., 1950, Ph.D., 1953; m. Arlene Thomas, Aug. 6, 1950; children—Mark S., Connie J., Stephen P. Chemist, Merck & Co., Rahway, N.J., 1951-52; mem. faculty U. Tex. at Austin, 1953- 65, prof. chemistry, 1962-65; prof. chemistry U. Utah, 1965—, dean sci., 1970—. Served with AUS, 1945. Home: 2200 S 2300 E Salt Lake City UT 84112

GARDNER, R. H. (Rufus Hallette III), drama and film critic; b. Mayfield, Ky., July 25, 1918; s. Rufus Hallette and Kathleen (Moorman) G.; A.B., Tex. Christian U., 1941. Aircraft engr. Glenn L. Martin Co., 1941-49; reporter, feature writer Balt. Sun, 1951-54, drama and film critic, 1954—. Guest lectr. Goucher Coll., 1968. Author: (play) I.O.U. Jeremiah, 1950; (book) The Splintered Stage: The Decline of the American Theatre, 1965. Office: Sunpapers Baltimore MD 21203

GARDNER, RANDOLPH SCOTT, univ. dean; b. West View, Va., Aug. 19, 1915; s. William Brown and Bessie Clarice (Hudlow) G.; A.B., Hampden-Sydney Coll., 1935; M.A., Columbia Tchrs. Coll., 1941; Ed.D., Columbia, 1947; m. Mdeleine Hayes, Apr. 11, 1943; children—Randolph Scott, Madeleine, Patricia Hayes. Tchr. math. pub. schs., Staunton, Va., 1936-41, Am. Sch. in Japan, Tokyo, 1939-40; prof. math. edn. State U. N.Y. at Albany, 1947-62, dean Sch. Edn., 1962—. Fulbright lectr. Karchi (Pakistan) U., 1953-54, Makerere Coll., U. E. Africa, Kampala, Uganda, 1960-61. Served as aviator USNR, World War II; comdr. Res. Mem. Nat. Council Tchrs. Math., Assn. Math. Tchrs. N.Y. State (pres. 1956-57), Phi Delta Kappa, Lambda Chi Alpha, Tau Kappa Alpha, Chi Beta Phi, Kappa Phi Kappa. Author: Instruments for Enrichment of Secondary School Mathematics, 1951; Applied General Mathematics, 1960; also articles. Home: Box 87 Slingerlands NY 12159 Office: School of Education State Univ NY Albany NY 12203

GARDNER, REECE ALEXANDER, lawyer; b. Columbia, Mo., Oct. 6, 1911; s. Glenn Warner and Hazel (Straight) G.; A.B., Harvard, 1933, J.D., 1936; m. Jean Clare McKeen, July 15, 1939; 1 dau., Ann Morton. Admitted to Mo. bar, 1936, Kan. bar, 1941; partner firm Stinson, Mag, Thomson, McEvers & Fizzell, Kansas City, Mo., 1939—; dir. C.M. Buettner Cos., Mojaba Corp., Security Benefit Life Ins. Co. City clk., Mission Hills, Kan., 1959-70. Pres., Andrew Drumm Inst., 1955—; trustee Mag Found., Park Found., H.O. Peet Found., Stinson, Mag, Thomson, McEvers & Fizzell Found., Kansas City Art Inst.; hon. bd. dirs. Rockhurst Coll. Served to capt. AUS, 1942-46. Mem. Am., Fed., Kansas City bar assns., Am. Law Inst., Am. Judicature Soc., Judge Advocates Assn., Lawyers Assn. Kansas City, Mil. Order World Wars. Republican. Episcopalian. Clubs: Mission Hills Country (Kan.); Nat. Lawyers (Washington); University (Kansas City). Lectr., author in field. Home: 5049 Wornall Rd Kansas City MO 64112 Office: 2100 Ten Main Center Kansas City MO 64105

GARDNER, RICHARD NEWTON, educator; b. N.Y.C., July 9, 1927; s. Samuel I. and Ethel (Elias) G.; A.B. magna cum laude, Harvard, 1948; LL.B., Yale, 1951; Ph.D. (Rhodes scholar 1951-53), Oxford (Eng.) U., 1954; m. Danielle Luzzatto, June 10, 1956; children—Nina Jessica, Anthony Laurence. Corr., United Press., 1946-47, A.P., 1948; admitted to N.Y. bar, 1952; teaching fellow internat. legal studies Harvard Law Sch., 1953-54; with Coudert Bros., N.Y.C., 1954-57; asso. prof. law Columbia, 1957- 60, prof., 1960-61, 65-66, prof. law and internat. relations, 1966—, now Henry L. Moses prof. law and internat. orgn.; dept asst. sec. state internat. orgns., State Dept., 1961-65; vis. prof. U. Istanbul, 1958, U. Rome, 1967-68; dep. U.S. rep. UN Com. on the Peaceful Uses of Outer Space, 1962-65, U.S. alternate del. 19th UN Gen Assembly; sr. adviser to U.S. ambassador to UN, 1965—; sr. adviser U.S. delegation to 20th and 21st UN Gen. Assemblies; adv. editor, trade dept. McGraw Hill, 1966—. Dir. Freedom House, Planned Parenthood Fedn. Am. Served with AUS, 1945-46. Harvard Club scholar, N.Y.C., 1944; recipient Detur prize for distinguished scholarship Harvard, 1948, Arthur S. Flemming award, 1963. Mem. American, N.Y. State bar assns., UN Assn. (dir.), Fgn. Policy Assn. (dir.), Assn. Bar City of N.Y., Council Fgn. Relations, Am. Econ. Assn., Royal Econ. Soc., Phi Beta Kappa, Order of Coif. Club: Century Assn. (N.Y.C.); Metropolitan (Washington). Author: Sterling-Dollar Diplomacy, 1956; New Directions in U.S. Foreign Economic Policy, 1959; In Pursuit of World Order, 1964; Blueprint for Peace, 1966; (with Max F. Millikan) The Global Partnership: International Agencies and Economic Development, 1968. Note editor Yale Law Jours., 1950-51. Home: 1150 Fifth Av New York City NY 10028 Office: Columbia Law Sch New York City NY 10027

GARDNER, SAMUEL NEWTON, beverage co. exec.; b. Reynolds, Ga., July 1, 1907; s. Emmett Emerson and Celeste (Thompson) G.; A.B., U. Ga., 1929, M.A. in Exptl. Psychology, 1932; m. Edwina Arnold, Oct. 14, 1932; 1 dau., Lynn Arnold (Mrs. Philip Swingle). Tchr. pub. schs. Ga., 1927-37; prin. Griffin (Ga.) High Sch., 1937-38, supt. schs., 1938-42; with Coca-Cola Co., 1946—, mgr. bottler sales promotion, 1956-65, v.p. 1962—, staff v.p. of plans, 1965-67, spl. asst. to pres., 1967—. Served to lt. comdr. USNR, 1942-45. Mem. Am. Legion, Phi Beta Kappa, Phi Kappa Phi. Methodist. Clubs: Commerce; Univ. Yacht, Confrerie de la Chaine des Rotisseurs. Home: 455 Riverside Pkwy NW Atlanta GA 30328 Office: 310 North Av Atlanta GA 30313

GARDNER, STEPHEN S., pres. Girard Trust Bank, 1966—. Address: Girard Trust Bank Broad and Chestnut Sts Philadelphia PA 19101

GARDNER, WALTER, artist; b. Liverpool, Eng., May 7, 1902; s. Herman G. and Lily (Cuddy) G.; elementary edn. Eng.; student Pa. Acad. Fine Arts, 1921-25; m. Emilie Roland, Nov. 1, 1937 (dec. June 1947); m. 2d, Jane Beckwith, Aug. 1948. Exhibited at Whitney Mus., N.Y.C., Artists for Victory Show, Met. Mus., N.Y.C., Corcoran Gallery, Washington, Chgo. Art Inst., Detroit Inst. Art, Va. Mus. Fine Arts, Richmond, Pa. Acad., Phila. Cresson Traveling scholar, 1924; recipient purchase prize Wanamaker Regional Art Exhibit, 1934; fellow Pa. Acad., 1938. Murals: post offices at Honesdale, Pa., Phila. (Sta. O), Berne, Ind.; new Municipal Ct. Phila. Home: 221 Winona Av Germantown Philadelphia PA 19144

GARDNER, WARNER WINSLOW, lawyer; b. Richmond, Ind., Sept. 25, 1909; s. Frank Karl and Camilla (Winslow) G.; A.B., Swarthmore Coll., 1930; M.A., Rutgers U., 1931; LL.B., Columbia, 1934; m. Henrietta Gertrude Tucker, Sept. 10, 1940; children—Hannah Winslow, William Tucker, Richard Randolph, Frances Winslow. Law clk. Justice Stone, U.S. Supreme Ct., 1934-35; atty. and spl. asst. to atty. gen., office Solicitor Gen., Dept. Justice, 1935-41; solicitor U.S. Dept. Labor, 1941- 42, U.S. Dept. Interior, 1942-46, asst. sec., 1946-47; mem. firm Shea & Gardner, Washington, 1947—. Spl. counsel Fed. Maritime Bd., 1957; pub. mem. Adminstrn. Conf. U.S., 1968—. Served with AUS, 1943-45. Decorated Legion of Merit; Croix de Guerre. Mem. Phi Beta Kappa. Mem. Soc. of Friends. Club: Metropolitan. Author: Building and Loan Liquidity, 1931; Taxation of Government Bondholders and Employees, 1938. Contbr. articles to mags. Home: 6903 Armat Dr Bethesda MD 20034 Office: 734 15th St NW Washington DC 20005

GARDNER, WARREN HENRY, educator; b. Ottumwa, La., Mar. 23, 1895; s. Alvah Thomas and Laura Jeannette (Klinker) G.; A.B., Harvard, 1918; Ph.D., State U. Ia., 1936; m. Dorothy D. Chase, June 12, 1942; children—Donald Hunt, Mary Ellen (adopted wife's children). Import-export bus., N.Y.C., 1918-22; hearing and vision cons., Ore. State Bd. Health, 1940-42; hearing conservation specialist Cal. State Bd. Health, 1942-45; prof. hearing and speech therapy Western Res. U., 1945-54; chief hearing and speech div. Cleve. Hearing and Speech center, 1945-54; chief audiology and speech pathology dept. otolaryngology Cleve. Clinic, 1954-65; prof. audiology and speech pathology Cleve. Clinic Ednl. Inst., 1955-65; pvt. practice, 1965—; lectr. Am. Acad. Ophthalmology and Otolaryngology, 1957, 58, summer sch. U. So. Cal., 1943-45, U. Cal., Los Angeles, 1943, San Francisco State Coll., 1943-45; inst. lectr. colls. edn., Cal. and Ore. Served as ensign U.S. Navy, 1917-18, mem. U.S.N.R., 1917-22. Fellow Am. Speech and hearing Assn.; mem. Internat. Council Exceptional Children, Am. Hearing Soc. (dir. 1940-46, pres. 1942-45, chmn. com. conservation of hearing, 1938-53), Speech Assn. Am., Central States Speech Assn., Am. Assn. Instrs. of Deaf, Volta Assn., Ohio Assn. Speech and Hearing Therapy (pres. 1950-51), Internat. Assn. Laryngectomees (founder, bd. dirs. 1952-56, 65—, chmn. nat. adv. com. 1956-65, dir. admissions, lectr., voice inst., 1960-64). Author: Left Handed Writing Manual, Text-Manual for Remedial Writing, Laryngectomee Speech and Rehabilitation. Contbr. articles, papers. Home: 776 Woodview Rd Cleveland Heights OH 44121 ☆

GARDNER, WILLIAM HENRY, retired newspaper editor; b. Austin Tex., Oct. 30, 1907; s. William Henry and Elizabeth (Jagual) G.; student U. Tex., 1924-28; m. Mildred Louise McMinn, June 22, 1938; children—Elizabeth (Mrs. William P. Jones) (dec.), Terry Gardner, Stephen. Reporter, Galveston (Tex.) Tribune, 1928-29, Houston Press, 1929-30; reporter Galveston News, 1930-32, city editor, 1932-34; with Internat. News Service, 1935; telegraph editor Tyler (Tex.) Courier-Times, 1935; reporter, city editor, mag. editor, Austin bur. chief Houston Post, 1935-63, mng. editor, 1963-65, polit. affairs editor, 1965-69, editor editorial pages, Houston, 1969-70; retired, 1971; adminstrv. asst. to Gov. Allan Shivers, Austin, 1952. Editor news and information service U. Tex., 1946. Mem. Tex. Library and Hist. Commn. Served to capt. USAAF, 1942-45. Mem. Am. Assn. Newspaper Editors, Internat. Press Inst., Sigma Delta Chi. Mem. Disciples of Christ Ch. Clubs: Headliners, Forty Acres (Austin). Author: The Texas Citizen, 1955. Home: 303 Moore Blvd Austin TX 78705

GARDNER, WILLIAM ULLMAN, educator; b. Kinbrae, Minn., Nov. 11, 1907; s. James Arthur and Josephine (Ullman) G.; B.S., S.D. State Coll., 1930, D.Sc., 1960; A.M., U. Mo., 1931, Ph.D., 1933; A.M. (hon.), Yale, 1943; Dr. Medicine and Surgery, U. Perugia, 1969; m. Katherine Homsley, July 15, 1934. NRC fellow dept. anatomy Yale, 1933-35, research asst., instr., 1935-36, research asst., asst. prof., 1936-38, research asso., asso. prof., 1938-41, asso. prof., 1941-43, prof., chmn. dept. anatomy, 1943-58, K.K. Hunt prof. anatomy, 1958—. Sci. adv. bd. J. Coffin Childs Meml. Fund, 1953—; v.p. Internat. Union Against Cancer, 1948-50, chmn. fellowship com., 1960—, pres., 1970—; mem. bd. sci. consultants Nat. Cancer Inst., 1961—; sec., treas. Am. Assn. Cancer Research, 1942-45, pres., 1945-46; mem. Med. Fellowship Bd. NRC; Nat. Adv. Cancer Council, 1948-54; med. adviser Anna Fuller Fund. Mem. Am. Cancer Soc. (dir. 1970—), Am. Assn. Anatomists (pres. elect 1971-72), Am. Assn. Study Internal Secretions, Soc. Exptl. Biology and Med., Soc. for Study Devel. and Growth, N.Y. Acad. Scis. Clubs: Faculty, Kiwanis, Yale (New Haven). Asso. editor Cancer Research, 1931-59, Anatomical Record, 1940-60, Execerpta Medici, 1950—. Home: 985 Orange Center Rd Orange CT 06477 Office: 333 Cedar St New Haven CT 06510

GARDNER, WOFFORD GORDON, educator; b. Winfield, Kan., Mar. 29, 1914; s. Nelson Samuel and Abbye (Matson) G.; A.B magna cum laude, Southwestern Coll., Winfield, 1935; M.A., Northwestern U., 1941, Ph.D., 1952; m. Virginia Rose Moore, Aug. 16, 1936; children—Beverly Jane (Mrs. James Abbott), Kathleen Rose (Mrs. Brantley Alexander), Stephen Gordon. Tchr. high schs., Garfield, Kan., 1935-37, Wellington, Kan., 1937-39, Hutchinson, Kan., 1939-46; with U. Me., 1946—, prof., head dept. speech, 1953—. Served as cpl. AUS, 1944-45. Mem. Am. (sec. treas. 1960-62, nat. council 1954-56, 60-62), Eastern (pres. 1954-56) forensic assns., N.E. Forensic Conf. (pres. 1952-53, 56-57), Speech Assns. Am. (legislative assembly 1957-59, 62-64, 66-68), Eastern States (v.p. 1963-64, pres. 1964-65), N.E. (v.p. 1957-58, pres. 1958-59), Me. speech assns., Am. Assn. U. Profs., Pi Kappa Delta, Phi Kappa Phi, Pi Gamma Mu. Methodist. Kiwanian. Home: 13 Park St Orono ME 04473

GARDNER, BYRON EUGENE, aviation exec.; b. San Angelo, Tex., Nov. 25, 1927; s. Byron and Octa (Cole) G.; B.S. with honors, U. Tex., 1949; m. Veronika S. Stancuis, Nov. 11, 1958; children-Pamela Anne, Mark Kevin. Engr. Tex. Power & Light Co., Dallas, 1949; pres. Spartan Aviation, Inc., Tulsa, 1953-68; exec. v.p. Aerodex, Inc., API Corp., ACI Corp, Miami, Fla., 1969—. Nat. adviser to Civil Air Patrol; mem. of govs. Air Edn. Com. State of Okla. Served with AUS, World War II. Mem. (Tulsa) C. of C. (twice chmn.), Sigma Iota Epsilon, Beta Gamma Sigma, Phi Kappa Sigma. Republican. Unitarian. Home: 19000 Bob O Link Dr Hialeah FL 33015 Office: 4000 NW 28th St Miami FL 33142

GAREK, MORRIS DANIEL, dept. store exec.; b. Columbus, O., Jan. 25, 1913; s. Louis and Ida (Bloom) G.; grad. high sch.; m. Rose Lee Cohen, June 17, 1934; children—Lois (Mrs. David Madison), Robert, Diane (Mrs. Ronald Clowson). With F. & R. Lazarus Co., Columbus, 1935—, exec. v.p., 1966-70, vice chmn. bd., 1970—. Bd. dirs. Goodwill Industries, Inc., Heritage House. Mem. Better Bus. Bur. (trustee), Associated Merchandising Corp. (chmn. gen. mdse. mgrs. 1966-68). Jewish religion. Club: Winding Hollow Country. Home: 2721 Bryden Rd Columbus OH 43209 Office: Lazarus Town & High Sts Columbus OH 43215

GARETS, WALLACE EARL, educator; b. Grangeville, Ida., Aug. 10, 1916; s. Herbert William and Josephine (Miller) G.; B.S., U. Ida., 1938, M.S., 1947; postgrad. Coll. City N.Y., 1942-43; m. Helen Meredith Moffatt, Sept. 21, 1939; children— Michael Kent, Jane Moffatt; m. 2d, Vivian Geraldine Johnson, July 34, 1946; children—David Earl, Stephen Brent, Paul Jeffrey. Editorial staff Am. mag., N.Y.C., 1940; editorial staff nat. Cyclopedia Am. Biography, N.Y.C., 1941-46; instr. journalism and sociology So. br. U. Ida., Pocatello, 1946-47; founder dept. journalism Ida. State Coll., Pocatello, 1947, asst. prof., dir., 1947-54, asso. prof., dir., 1954-56; reporter, feature writer, wire editor Ida. State Jour., Pocatello, summers 1954-56; asso prof. Tex. Technol. Coll., 1956-57, prof., head dept. journalism, 1957-70; prof. dept. journalism L.I. U., 1970—. Sec.-treas., mgr. Ida. Allied Dailies, Inc., 1953-56; bus. mgr. journalism Educator, 1958-60, editor, 1960-61. Mem. Am. Council on Edn. for Journalism, 1966—, accrediting com., 1971—. Mem. Ida. (founder, exec. sec.), West Tex. (founder, exec. sec.) high sch. press assns., Am. Soc. Journalism Sch. Adminstrs. (pres. 1962-63), Assn. Edn. Journalism (exec. com. 1962-63), Am. Assn. U. Profs., Alpha Delta Sigma, Phi Mu Alpha, Phi Delta Theta, Sigma Delta Chi. Episcopalian (vestryman, lay reader). Co-author: Modern Journalism. Home: 191 Willoughby St Brooklyn NY 11201

GARFIELD, BRIAN WYNNE, author; b. N.Y.C., Jan. 26, 1939; s. George and Frances (O'Brien) G.; B.A., U. Ariz., 1959, M.A., 1963; m. Veve Sein, 1962 (div. 1965); m. Shan Willson Botley, 1969. Mem. dance band The Casuals, 1958-59, dance band The Palisades, 1959-60; instr. English, U. Ariz., 1962-63. Served with AUS, 1957. Mem. Western Writers Am., Tucson Fedn. Musicians, Authors Guild, Authors League, Dramatists Guild, Writers Guild Am. (West), Mystery Writers Am. Author: Range Justice, 1960; The Arizonans, 1961; (under name Frank Wynne) Massacre Basin, 1961; Justice at Spanish Flat, 1961; (under name Frank Wayne) The Big Snow, 1962; (under name Frank O'Brien) The Rimfire Murders, 1962; (under name Bennett Garland) Seven Brave Men, 1962; The Lawbringers, 1962; Trail Drive, 1962; (under name Frank Wynne) Arizona Rider, 1962, Rio Concho, 1963, Lynch-Law Canyon, 1964, Call Me Hazard, 1964, Lynch-Law Canyon, 1965, The Lusty Breed, 1966, The Wolf Pack, 1967, Dragoon Pass, 1963; (under name Brian Wynne) Mr. Sivgun, 1965, The Night It Rained Bullets, 1966, The Bravos, 1967, The Proud Riders, 1967, Brand Of The Gun, 1968, A Badge For A Badman, 1969, Big Country, Big Men, 1970; Sliphammer, 1970; Valley Of The Shadow, 1970; The Hit, 1970; The Villiers Touch, 1970; numerous others. Home: 105 W 13th St New York City NY 10011

GARFIELD, DAVID CROSBY, machinery mfg. co. exec.; b. Ames, Ia., June 28, 1927; s. Theodore Greenlief and Carolyn (Crosby) G.; B.S., Ia. State U., 1950; postgrad. (Rotary Found. fellow) McGill U., 1950-51; m. Lynette Joan Fuert, Feb. 16, 1953; children—Sharyll, David Crosby, Craig Lindsey, Kathleen. With export dept. Ingersoll-Rand Co., N.Y.C., 1952, spl. rep., Tokyo, Japan, 1953-59, spl. rep. Ingersoll-Rand Co. Ltd., London, Eng., 1959-60, gen. mgr. Internat. div., N.Y.C., 1960-61, v.p., 1961-68, exec. v.p., 1968—, dir., 1964—. Mem. Phi Kappa Phi, Phi Kappa Psi. Episcopalian. Clubs: Downtown Athletic (N.Y.C.); Plainfield, (N.J.) Country. Home: 2106 Arrowood Dr Westfield, NJ 07090. Office: 11 Broadway New York City NY 10004

GARFIELD, THEODORE GREENLIEF, former judge; b. Humboldt, Ia., Nov. 12, 1894; s. George Selwyn and Mary Ellen (White) G.; A.B., U. Ia., 1915, LL.B., 1917; m. Louise Keith, Apr. 1, 1918; m. 2d, Carolyn Crosby, June 30, 1924; children—Theodore Greenlief, David Crosby, John Clement, Carol. Admitted to Ia. bar, 1916; practiced at Ames; mem. firm Lee & Garfield, 1917-27; judge 11th Jud. Dist. Ia., 1927-41; justice Ia. Supreme Ct., 1941- 61, chief justice, 1961-69. Chmn., Conf. Chief Justices, 1965-66. Served as 1st lt. F.A., U.S. Army, World War I. Recipient Ann. award merit Ia. Bar Assn., 1970. Mem. U. Ia. Alumni Assn. (pres. 1948-51), Order of Coif, Phi Beta Kappa, Phi Kappa Psi, Phi Delta Phi, Delta Sigma Rho. Republican. Unitarian. Home: 1109 Ridgewood Av Ames IA 50010 Office: 240 1/2 Main St Ames IA 50010

GARFIN, ALVIN, publisher; b. Bronx, N.Y., July 27, 1931; s. George David and Miriam (Weiner) G.; B.B.A., Coll. City N.Y., 1952; . Dale Etzler, Sept. 8, 1956; children—Susan Michele, Jeffrey David. Circulation mgr. Surg. Bus. mag. and Nursing Home Adminstr., 1955-57; circulation dir. Cantor Publns., 1957-61; with Art News mag., N.Y.C., 1961—, publisher, 1968—. Served with USCGR, 1953-55. Home: 13-39 Lyle Terrace Fair Lawn NJ 07410 Office: 444 Madison Av New York City NY 10022

GARFIN, LOUIS, actuary; b. Mason City, Ia., June 7, 1917; s. Sam and Etta (Larner) G.; student Mason City Jr. Coll., 1934-36; B.A., State U. Ia., 1938, M.S., 1939, Ph.D., 1942; m. Clarice Fagen, Apr. 11, 1943; children— Eugene Arthur, Erica. Instr. USAAF, Scott Field, Ill., 1942-43; instr. math. Ill. Inst. Tech., Chgo., 1943, U. Minn., 1943-44; actuary Ore. Ins. Dept., Salem, 1946-52; asso. actuary Pacific Mut. Life Ins. Co., Los Angeles, 1952-62, actuary, 1962-64, v.p., chief actuary, 1964—; dir. Computer Communications, Inc. Mem. Young Musicians Found., 1962—; pres. Mr. & Mrs. chpt. City of Hope, 1960-61. Served from ensign to lt. (j.g.), USNR, 1944-46. Fellow Soc. Actuaries; mem. Am. Acad. Actuaries (dir.), Internat. Congress Actuaries, Actuarial Club Pacific States (pres. 1967-68), Los Angeles Actuarial Club (past pres.), Am. Math. Soc., Am. Risk and Ins. Assn., Town Hall Cal., Phi Beta Kappa, Sigma Xi. Home: 1364 Stradella Rd Los Angeles CA 90024 Office: 523 W 6th St Los Angeles CA 90054

GARFINKEL, BERNARD MAX, editor, writer; b. Bklyn., May 3, 1929; s. Max and Ida (Konwiser) G.; B.A., U. Mo., 1951, M.A., 1953. Copy writer at Batten, Barton, Durstine and Osborn, advt., N.Y.C., 1957-58; editor Mag. Mgmt Co., N.Y.C., 1958-64, mng. editor Male and Men mags., 1959-64; editor-in-chief Platt & Munk Co., Inc., N.Y.C., 1965-69; spl. projects editor Simon & Schuster Inc., N.Y., 1969-70; pres. Paladin Assos., pub. cons., 1970—; Mem. Phi Beta Kappa. Club: Columbia University. Author children's books. Home: 300 E 57th St New York City NY 10022 Office: 143 E 49th St New York City NY 10017

GARFINKEL, HERBERT, univ. dean; b. N.Y.C., June 16, 1920; s. Julius Louis and Gertrude (Goldstone) G.; M.A., U. Chgo., 1950, Ph.D., 1956; m. Evelyn Epstein, Sept. 3, 1940; children—Laura, Paul. Instr. polit. sci. Ill. Inst. Tech., 1948-51; research asst. Nat. Opinion Research Center, U. Chgo., 1950-51; instr. Mich. State U., 1951-53; asst. prof. Dartmouth, 1953-59; faculty Mich. State U., East Lansing, 1959—, prof. polit. sci., 1964—, dean James Madison Coll., 1966—. NATO prof. Inst. Social Studies, The Hague, Netherlands, 1965-66. Served as officer U.S. Mcht. Marine, 1943-45. Center for Advanced Study Behavioral Scis. fellow, 1958-59; research fellow Social Sci. Research Council, 1960-61. Mem. Am. Polit. Sci. Assn. Author: When Negroes March, 1959; The Democratic Republic, 2d edit., 1970; (co-author) The Constitution and The Legislature, 1961. Contbr. articles to profl. jours. Home: 1009 Chesterfield Pky East Lansing MI 48823

GARFINKEL, MARVIN, lawyer; b. Phila., Mar. 23, 1929; s. Simon L. and Theresa (Brier) G.; B.A., Pomona Coll., 1951; LL.B. magna cum laude, U. Pa., 1954; LL. M. in Taxation, N.Y.U., 1962; m. Marian Schwartz, Apr. 6, 1963; 1 son, Simson Leon. Admitted to Pa. bar, 1955; law clk. to Curtis Bok, Gerald F. Flood, and Louis E. Levinthal, Phila., 1954-55, W.H. Kirkpatrick, Phila., 1957-58; dept. atty. gen. Pa., 1955-57; partner firm Goodis, Greenfield, Narin and Mann, and predecessors, Phila., 1956—. Nat. exec. com. Am. Jewish Congress. Mem. Am., Fed., Phila., Pa. bar assns., Am. Soc. Internat. Law, Lawyers Club, Internat. Law Assn., Phila. C. of C. (tax com.), Order of Coif. Club: Locust (Phila.). Home: 15 Merion Rd Merion Station, PA 19066. Office: 1315 Walnut St Philadelphia PA 19107

GARFINKLE, HENRY, corp. exec.; b. 1903; married. With Union News Co., 1924-26; propr. Garfinkle News Co., 1926-34; pres. Garfield News Co. Inc., N.Y.C., 1935 55; pres., treas. Manhattan News Co. Inc., N.Y.C., 1947-55; formerly pres., dir. Greater Boston Distbrs. Inc., Greater Boston Financial Corp., Distbn. Services Co.

Inc.; Formerly pres., treas. 627 W. 42d St. Corp.; pres., dir. Am. News Co., (name changed to Ancorp Nat. Services, Inc.), 1955—, chmn. bd., chief exec. officer, 1969—, also dir.; pres., dir., chief stockholder Garfield News Co. Can. Ltd. Address: 131 Varick St New York City NY 10013

GARFUNKEL, ART, singer, mem. team Simon and Garfunkel; recordings include: The Sounds of Silence, Dangling Conversation, Homeward Bound, I Am a Rock, 7 O'Clock News, Silent Night. Address: care Columbia Recording Co 51 W 52d St New York City NY 10019

GARGAN, EDWARD THOMAS, educator; b. N.Y.C., Feb. 25, 1922; s. Thomas and Elizabeth (McAuliffe) G.; B.A., Bklyn. Coll., 1945; M.A., Cath. U. Am., 1947, Ph.D., 1955; M.A. (hon.), Wesleyan U., Middletown, Conn., 1964; m. Louise Quesnel, Apr. 29, 1949 (dec. Sept. 1956); children—Edward A., Christopher; m. 2d, Bernadette Agnes Praetz, Aug. 24, 1957. Instr. history Boston Coll., 1949-52; dir. Sheil Sch. Social Studies, Chgo., 1952-53; from asst. prof. to prof. history Loyola U., Chgo., 1953-63; prof. history Wesleyan U., 1963-66, chmn. dept., 1965-66; prof. history U. Wis., Madison, 1966—. Grantee Am. Council Learned Socs., 1961, Am. Philos. Soc., 1962; decorated Palmes Académiques (France), 1962; Guggenheim fellow, 1966-67. Mem. Am., Am. Cath. (1st v.p. 1969, pres. 1970) hist. assns., Soc. French Hist. Studies, Soc. d'Histoire Moderne, Am. Acad. Polit. and Social Sci. Author: Alexis de Tocqueville The Critical Years, 1955; De Tocqueville, 1965. Editor: The Intent of Toynbee's History, 1961; Leo XIII and the Modern World, 1961. Home: 722 Miami Pass Madison WI 53711

GARI, GIULIO, opera and concert singer; b. Medians, Rumania, Sept. 9, 1912; s. Jacob Samu and Amalia (Klein) G.; student Verdi Conservatory, Milan, 1934-37; married; children—Gail A., Glen. Came to U.S., 1938, naturalized, 1942. Operatic debut in The Barber of Seville, Rome's Theatre Reale dell' Opera, 1938; Am. debut in Flying Dutchman, 1945; leading tenor N.Y.C. Opera Co., 1945-52; leading tenor Met. Opera Assn., N.Y.C., 1952-64; head voice and opera dept. L.I. Inst. Music, Flushing, N.Y.; made concert tour, appeared with St. Louis, San Francisco, Pitts. and Cin. Opera cos. Served as pvt., AUS, 1942-44. Address: LI Inst Music Flushing NY 11352

GARIN, VASCO VIEIRA, Portuguese diplomat; b. Lisbon, Portugal, June 23, 1907; s. Marcos and Ernestine (Vieira) G.; Licentiate in Econs. and Finance, U. Lisbon, 1929; m. Phyllis Harrison, June 2, 1939. Career diplomat Portuguese Ministry Fgn. Affairs, 1931—, 2d sec., London, Eng., 1934-39; 1st sec., counsellor, charge d'affaires, Washington, 1941-46; chief Bur. Polit. Affairs, Ministry Fgn. Affairs, 1946; consul gen., Montreal, Que., Can., 1947; minister to India, 1948-55, Thailand and Ceylon, hdqrs. in New Delhi, India, 1952-53; ambassador to Can., Ottawa, Ont., 1956-59; permanent Portuguese rep. UN, 1956-64; ambassador to U.S., 1964—. Portuguese rep. Conf. for Establishment Internat. Agy. for Atomic Energy, 1956. Decorated by govts. of Portugal, Spain, Denmark, Gt. Britain, Brazil. Address: Embassy of Portugal 2125 Kalorama Rd NW Washington, DC 20008

GARINGER, LOUIS DANIEL, journalist; b. Johnson City, Tenn.; s. Merrion X. and Hilda (Gasteiger) G.; A.B., U. Tenn., 1947, LL.B., 1949; M.A. in Govt., Harvard, 1957; m. Joanne Mazna, June 21, 1958. Staff writer Christian Sci. Monitor Youth Forums, Boston, 1949-51; teaching fellow, tutor govt. Harvard, 1955-58; asso. dir. Salzburg Seminar in Am. Studies, 1958-60; editorial writer Christian Sci. Monitor, 1965-67, religious affairs editor, 1965—. Served with AUS, 1952-53. Recipient Religious Pub. Relations Council merit award, 1969. Mem. Religion Newswriters Assn., Scarabbean, Pi Kappa Phi, Phi Kappa Phi, Phi Eta Sigma, Sigma Delta Pi. Christian Scientist. Contbr. articles to profl. jours. Home: 254 Westfield St Dedham MA 02026 Office: 1 Norway St Boston MA 02115

GARIS, ROGER, author; b. Newark, Sept. 10, 1901; s. Howard R. and Lilian C. (Mcnamara) G.; Princeton, 1920-23, N.Y.U., 1924-26; LL.B., N.J. Law Sch., 1927; m. Mabel Robinson Burns, Nov. 1, 1941; children—Leslie Ann, Roger Brooks, Howard, John. Writer, 1919—; staff mem. Newark Evening News, 1930-35; author mag. stories in Redbook, Collier's, Saturday Evening Post, others; staff N.Y. Times Mag.; author TV dramas. Head publn. editor OWI, World War II. Recipient Pulitzer award for reporting, 1939. Mem. Writers Guild Am. Author: Never Take Candy from a Stranger, 1960; My Father Was Uncle Wiggily, 1966; also 60 children's books under own and pen names. Playwright: The Pony Cart, 1959. Home and office: RD 3 Amherst MA 01002

GARLAND, CARL WESLEY, educator, chemist; b. Bangor, Me., Oct. 1, 1929; s. Cecil G. and Blandena (Couillard) G.; B.S., U. Rochester, 1950; Ph.D., U. Cal. at Berkeley, 1953; m. Joan A. Donaghy, July 30, 1955; children—Leslie J., Andrew E. Instr. chemistry U. Cal. at Berkeley, 1953; faculty Mass. Inst. Tech., 1953—, asso. prof. chemistry, 1959-68, prof. chemistry, 1968—. Fellow Am. Acad. Arts and Sci., N.Y. Acad. Scis.; mem. Am. Chem. Soc., Am. Phys. Soc. Author: (with D.P. Shoemaker) Experiments in Physical Chemistry, 2d edit., 1967. Editor: Optics and Spectroscopy, 1960—. Research, publs. on infrared spectra of chemisorbed molecules to characterize structure and bonding in such species, low temperature elastic constants measured to provide information for lattice dynamical calculations of properties of solids, ultrasonic studies on order-disorder phenomena and critical points. Home: 4 Edward St Belmont MA 02178 Office: Mass Inst Tech Dept Chemistry Cambridge MA 02139

GARLAND, CECIL RAYMOND, foundry exec.; b. Orient, Pa., Dec. 6, 1907; s. Cecil B. and Elizabeth O. (Walters) G.; A.B. in Accounting, Washington and Jefferson Coll., 1929; m. Ruby Gene Haught, Mar. 3, 1929; children—Cecil W., Wibur L. Accountant, Uniontown, Pa., 1929-40, Bender Body Co., Cleve., 1940-41, Welsh & Beard, C.P.A.'s, Cleve., 1941-42; with W.O. Larson Foundry Co., Grafton, O., 1942—, sec., 1945—, treas., 1960—, v.p., 1961—; v.p., treas., dir. subsidiary co.; asst. sec. subsidiary Larson Steel Castings, Inc. Treas. Gray Iron Founders Soc., 1957-60, v.p., 1960-61, bd. dirs., 1960—, pres., 1961-62. Mem. Nat. Assn. Accountants, Am. Foundrymens Soc., Nat. Castings Council. Mason (Jester). Club: Cleveland Athletic. Home: 129 Penny Lane Elyria OH 44035 Office: 1080 Cleveland St Grafton OH 44044

GARLAND, CHARLES RALEIGH, educator; b. Potter, Neb., June 10, 1917; s. Charles R. and Pearl (Finchum) G.; student Carson-Newman Coll., 1935; B.S., U. Ky., 1939; student Eastman Sch. Music, 1939-40; M.A., U. Ia., 1942, Ph.D., 1945; postdoctoral studies U. Ind., 1951; m. Shirley Winifred White, Sept. 9, 1945; 1 dau., Susan. Tchr. Morningside Coll., 1945-51, U. Mo., 1951-62; mem. faculty Roosevelt U., 1962—, now prof. music. Mem. Am. Assn. Univ. Profs., Music Tchrs. Nat. Assn., Coll. Music Soc. Club: Cliff Dwellers (Chgo.). Composer opera, songs, sonata. Home: 828 W George St Chicago IL 60657

GARLAND, CLYNE FREDERICK, educator; b. Elizabeth, Colo., Mar. 14, 1903; s. Charles F. and Ivy (Bowen) G.; B.S., U. Colo., 1923; M.S., Yale 1920; m. Alice E. Jenne, Aug. 1, 1927 (dec. 1956); children—Fred Richmond, Bruce Douglas, Marilyn Doris; m. 2d, Edith Poole, 1957. Jr. engr. Westinghouse Electric Corp., 1923-24; instr. mech. engring. U. Colo., 1925-29; teaching asst. Yale, 1929-30; asst. prof. U. Cal. at Berkeley 1930-40, asso. prof., 1940-49, chmn. div. engring. design, 1947-56, prof. engring. design, 1949-58, asst. dean coll. engring, 1956-58, prof., 1958- 62, chmn. dept. mech. engring., 1958-60, asso. dean Coll. Engring., 1958-62; prof. mech. engring., asso. dean Coll. Engring., U. of Cal., at Davis, 1962-69, prof. emeritus mech. engring., 1970—, Served as lt. comdr. USNR, 1941-45, capt., 1956—. Mem. Am. Soc. M.E., Am. Soc. Engring. Edn., Sigma Xi, Tau Beta Pi, Pi Tau Sigma. Home: 1133 Skycrest Dr Walnut Creek CA 94595

GARLAND, FRED MCKEE, chemist; b. Corsicana, Tex., Mar. 16, 1912; s. Walter and Alice (McKee) G.; B.S., Trinity Univ., 1934; M.S., Tex. Tech. Coll., 1936; Ph.D., U. Tex., 1939; m. Josephine Stockard, Sept. 3, 1939; children— Gail, Luther Stockard. Instr. in chemistry, U. Tex., 1936-39; asso. prof. chemistry, Trinity U., Waxahachie, Tex., 1939-41; research chemist Armour & Co., Chgo., 1941-43, Union Oil Co. of Cal., Wilmington, summer 1938; prof. chemistry Tex. Coll. Arts and Industries, 1946—, chmn. dept. 1950—. Served to capt. Signal Corps, AUS, 1943-46. U.S. Army, 1943; served as exec. officer, 314th Gen. Hosp., Philippines, Mem. Am. Chem. Soc., Am. Assn. U. Profs., Phi Lambda Upsilon. Democrat. Presbyn. Contbr. to sci. lit. in field of fatty acids and their derivatives and in study of nitrogen bases found in petroleum. Home: 826 Leslie St Kingsville TX 78363

GARLAND, GILBERT CLAYTON, univ. dean; b. Concord, N.H., Sept. 10, 1912; s. Charles Clayton and Mildred Anna (Emerson) G.; B.S., Springfield (Mass.) Coll., 1935; M.Ed., 1942; postgrad. Harvard, 1938; Ed.D., Columbia, 1952; m. Katherine Louise Rice, Oct. 11, 1941; children—Nancy Emerson, Gail Katherine, Andrea Louise. High sch. prin., Porter, Me., 1935-37; mem. English dept., coach basketball Plymouth (Mass.) High Sch., 1937-40; asst. dir. admissions, instr. speech and journalism Springfield Coll., 1940-42; head English dept. Vt. Coll., 1942-44; dean, prof. psychology Nichols Coll., Dudley, Mass., 1946-48; dir. tng. Westinghouse Electric Corp., 1950-52; dean, dir. admissions Northeastern U., 1952—; frequent lectr. Chmn. Weston (Mass.) Citizens Edn. Com., 1959-60; pres. Weston P.T.A., 1954-55; moderator Congl. Ch., Weston, 1960-61, also rep. to and nat. confs. Served with AUS, 1944-46. Named hon. alumnus, Northeastern U., 1960. Mem. Soc. Advancement Edn., N.E.A., Coll. Entrance Exam. Bd., Nat. Assn. Collegiate Registrars and Admission Officers, Greater Boston Vocational Guidance Assn., Assn. Coll. Admissions Officers. Author articles. Home: Chestnut St Duxbury MA 02332 1922-48; staff Mass. Office: 360 Huntington Av Boston MA 02115

GARLAND, JOHN HENRY, educator; b. Kirkland, Ill., Feb. 2, 1904; s. Walter Harrison and Bertha (Gritzbaugh) G.; student No. Ill. State Tchrs. Coll., 1923-25; Ph.B., U. Chgo., 1928, M.S., 1929, Ph.D., 1940; m. Dorothy Merritt Hutchison, Aug. 22, 1931; children—Dorothy (Mrs. Charles P. Davis), John Middleton. Tchr. Kirkland Pub. Schs., 1925-26; instr. Ohio State U., 1929-30, 31-39, Wash. State Coll., 1930-31; asst. prof. Western Res. U., 1939-43; asst. prof. geography U. Ill., 1943-45, asso. prof., 1945-50, prof., 1950—. Fellow Am. Geog. Soc.; mem. Assn. Am. Geographers, Nat. Council Geog. Edn., A.A.A.S., Sigma Xi. Republican. Presbyn. Mason. Club: Exchange (Urbana). Author: The North American Midwest, 1955; Water for Industrial and Domestic Purposes—Conservation of Our Natural Resources, 1970. Home: 1308 Eliot Dr Urbana IL 61801

GARLAND, JOSEPH, physician, author; b. Gloucester, Mass., Jan. 1, 1893; s. Joseph E. and Sarah M. (Rogers) G.; A.B., Harvard, 1915, M.D., 1919; D.Sc. (hon.), Boston U., 1955, Tufts U., 1955; m. Mira W. Crowell, Sept. 20, 1921; children—Joseph E., Anne Kimball. Instr., Harvard Med. Sch., 1922-47; practice medicine, specializing in pediatrics, Boston, 1922-48; staff Mass. Gen. Hosp., 1923—. Pres. bd. Boston Med. Library. Hon. fellow Royal Soc. Medicine; mem. Mass. Med. Soc. (sec. 1947), Am. Acad. Arts and Scis., A.M.A., N.E. Pediatric Soc., Am. Acad. Pediatrics, Aesculapian. Club: St. Botolph (Boston). Author: The Story of Medicine, 1949; All Creatures Here Below, 1954. Editor N.E. Jour. Medicine, 1947-67, editor emeritus, 1967—; editor The Physician and His Practice, 1954, Harvard Med. Alumni Bull., 1967—; cons. editor in U.S. for The Practitioner, 1953-68. Home: 150 Fairway Rd Chestnut Hill MA 02167 Office: 25 Shattuck St Boston MA 02115 ☆

GARLAND, WILLIAM M., (Red), jazz pianist; b. Dallas, May 13, 1923. Mem. Miles Davis group, 1955-57, 58; formed own trio, 1959, toured U.S.; has performed at Memory Lane, It Club; pres. Jazzl. Address: Riverside Phono Records 235 W 46th St New York City NY*

GARLINGHOUSE, F. MARK, lawyer, telephone co. exec.; b. Topeka, Dec. 4, 1914; s. Lewis F. and Katherine (Fogwell) G.; Ph.B., Washburn Coll., 1936, LL.B., 1939; m. Marjorie Beard, Nov. 18, 1939; children—Kent, Webb, Whitney. Admitted to Kan. bar, 1939, N.Y. bar, 1941, Mo. bar, 1950; practiced in Kan., 1939-40; atty Am. Tel. & Tel. Co., N.Y.C., 1940-48, N.J. Bell Telephone Co., 1948-50; v.p., gen. counsel Southwestern Bell Telephone Co., St. Louis, 1950-65; v.p. Am. Tel. & Tel. Co., 1965—; chmn. M-C Industries, Inc., Bellville, Kan., L.F. Garlinghouse Co., Inc., Topeka; dir. Ohio Bell Telephone Co., Cleve. Trustee Washburn U., Topeka. Mem. Am. Bar Assn. Home: 25 Hemlock Rd Short Hills NJ 07078 Office: 195 Broadway New York City NY 10007

GARMAN, WILFORD OLDEN HIGGETT, clergyman; b. Phila., Aug. 15, 1899; s. Samuel and Bertha Rodgers (Plant) G.; grad. Phila. Sch. Bible, 1922; Th.B., Pitts. Theol. Sem., 1925; D.D., Burton Coll., 1953; Th.M., Bible Baptist Sem., 1955; D.D., Bob Jones U., 1970; m. Josephine Pearl Hill, June 26, 1931; children—Joyce Esther, Paul Wilford, Linda Ruth. Ordained to ministry, United Presbyn. Ch., 1925, independent, 1939—; pastor Indiana Co., Pa., 1925-29, Altoona, 1929-39, Callender Meml. Ch., Wilkinsburg, Pa., 1939; organizer, dean, Altoona Sch. Bible, 1933-40; pres. Immanuel Coll. Bible, 1953-59; instr. Christian Crusade's Anti-Communist U., Manitou Springs, Colo.; asso. tour dir. Christian Crusades yearly Holy Land Tours, 1965-69. Past pres. Fundamental Chs. Am.; tours of Europe, 1947, Germany, 1948, Far East, 1953 at invitation of fed. govt.; attended lst Plenary congress, Internat. Council Christian Chs., Amsterdam, Holland, 1947, 2d plenary congress, Geneva, 1950, regional congress, Scotland, 1952; engaged world missionary tour, 1949; visited S. Africa, Rhodesia and Greece, 1967; chmn. Wilkinsburg Citizens for law and Order, 1968—; mem. Aux. Allegheny County Mounted Police, 1967—. Mem. adv. group to chief Air Force Chaplains. Dir. Christian Youth Crusade Camp. Recipient citation, chief of staff USAF, 1956; Congress of Freedom award, 1959, 68, 70. Fellow Royal Geog. Soc.; mem. Asso. Gospel Chs. (chmn. commn. chaplains 1958-59), pres., Am. Assn. Christian Schs. Higher Learning (pres. 1967—), Am. Ordnance Assn., U.S. Navy League, Mil. Chaplains Assn., Am. Council Christian Chs. (past pres., chmn. commn. edn., mem. exec. com.). Author: The Life and Teachings of Christ; Communist Infiltration In The Churches, 3d edit.; numerous religious pamphlets. Editor A.G.C. Reporter. Address: 1919 Beach St Pittsburgh PA 15221

GARMAN, WILLARD HERSHEL, assn. exec.; b. Indiana County, Pa., Oct. 21, 1912; s. Warren H. and Effie (Berringer) G.; B.S., Pa. State U., 1933, M.S., 1934, Ph.D., 1939; m. Edna Webb, Aug. 25, 1938; children—Shirley Garman Clark, Warren Webb. Asst., then asso. prof. agronomy U. Ga., 1939-42; soil scientist S.C. Agrl. Expt. Sta., Clemson, 1942-47; head dept. agronomy U. Ark., 1947-49; prin. soil scientist Expt. Stas. div. USDA, Washington, 1949-54; chief agriculturist Nat. Plant Food Inst., Washington, 1954-64; v.p., The Fertilizer Inst., Washington, 1964- -. Served to lt. (s.g.) USNR, 1944-46. Fellow A.A.A.S., Am. Soc. Agronomy (pres. So. br. 1952-53, bd. dirs. 1953-54, 58-59, pres. N.E. br. 1964-65); mem. Soil Sci. Soc. Am. (div. chmn. 1957-58), Nat. Soil Research Com. (chmn. 1952-54), Am. Soc. Hort. Sci., Am. Soc. Plant Physiologists, Soil Sci. Soc. Am., Internat. Soil Sci. Soc., Soil Conservation Soc., Am. Inst. Biol. Scis., Am. Chem. Soc., Sigma Xi, Gamma Sigma Delta, Delta Theta Sigma. Clubs: Cosmos, Internat. (Washington); Belle Haven Country (Alexandria, Va.). Contbr. articles soil chemistry and the environment to sci. jours., popular mags. Home: 3423 Woodside Rd Alexandria, VA 22310 Office: 1015 18th Street NW Washington DC 20036

GARMATZ, EDWARD ALEXANDER, congressman; b. Balt., Feb. 7, 1903; s. Herman Frederick and Marie (Doering) G.; student Poly. Inst., 1916-17; m. Ruth Burchard, Mar. 20, 1937. Engaged in elec. work, 1920-46; asso. with Md. State Racing Commn., 1941-44; police magistrate, 1944-47; mem. 80th-92d Congresses, from 3d Md. Dist. Democrat. Lutheran. Home: 2210 Lake Av Baltimore MD 21213 Office: Rayburn Bldg Washington DC 20515

GARMHAUSEN, ERWIN JOHN, lawyer; b. Washington, Oct. 13, 1913; s. Erwin John and Hazel (Karshner) G.; LL.B., Ohio State U., 1937; m. Marjorie Marshall Best, Dec. 23, 1938; children—Linda (Mrs. Thomas J. Orlow), John Marshall. Admitted to Ohio bar, 1937; with firm Spencer, Hardman & Fehr, Dayton, 1937-38; practice in Sidney, 1938—; partner firm Garmhausen, Kerrigan & Elsass, 1960—. Sec., dir. Am. Budget Co., Caravanner Ins., Inc., Everyday Mfg. Co., Airstream, Inc., Peerless Bread Machine Co.; dir., v.p. Scott Port-A-Fold, Inc., asst. sec. Sidney Pattern Works Co.; dir. Sidney Electric Co., First Nat. Bank, New Bremen, O., Piqua Engring., Inc., Port Clinton News Herald Pub. Co.; pres., dir. Coldway Food Express, Inc.; partner C J Investment Co. Solicitor, City of Sidney, 1941-48. Trustee, sec. Sidney Community Found. Served to lt. USNR, 1944-46. Mem. Am., Ohio Shelby County bar assns. Home: 841 Port Jefferson Rd Sidney OH 45365 Office: Ohio Bldg Sidney OH 45365

GARNER, ALTO LUTHER, univ. dean; b. Dothan, Ala., Dec. 10, 1916; s. Albert Early and Martha (DeBardeleben) G.; student Howard Coll., 1940-43; A.B., U. Ala., 1944; postgrad. So. Bapt. Theol. Sem., 1944-45, U. Tex. at Austin, 1947; M.A., N.Y.U., 1947; Ed.D., U. Ky., 1954; m. Katie Mae Sanders, Oct. 5, 1945; 1 son, Robert Edward Lee. Ordained to ministry Bapt. Ch., 1942; instr. history and polit. sci. Georgetown Coll., 1947- 49, asst. prof., 1949-53; asso. prof. edn. Howard Coll., 1953-54; prof. edn. Samford U., Birmingham, Ala., 1954—, chmn. div. tchr. edn., head dept. edn., 1964-66, dean Sch. Edn. and Psychology, 1966—. Ala. regional ednl. cons. State Farm Ins. Cos., 1955—. Served with AUS, 1941. Mem. Kappa Phi Kappa, Kappa Delta Pi, Phi Alpha Theta. Home: 3325 Misty Lane Birmingham AL 35243 Office: 800 Lakeshore Dr Birmingham AL 35209

GARNER, CLIFFORD SYMES, educator, chemist; b. Newark, Oct. 4, 1912; s. Albert J. and Dorothy (Weiss) G.; B.S., Cal. Inst. Tech., 1935, Ph.D., 1938; m. Ellen Louise Sanderhoff, Aug. 7, 1937. Noyes research fellow Cal. Inst. Tech., Pasadena, 1938-39; faculty U. Tex., Austin, 1939-46, asst. prof., 1941-46; reseearch asso. plutonium project U. Cal., Berkeley, 1942-43; group leader chemistry and metallurgy div. Manhattan Project, Los Alamos Sci. Lab., 1943-46; faculty U. Cal., Los Angeles, 1946—, prof. chemistry, 1953—. Cons. in phys. inorganic and nuclear chemistry to various indsl. corps. John Simon Guggenheim Meml. fellow, 1959. Mem. Am. Chem. Soc., Am. Phys. Soc., Am. Inst. Physics, A.A.A.S., Sigma Xi, Phi Lambda Upsilon. Author: (with others) The Rare-Earth Elements and Their Compounds, 1949; (with others) Radioactivity Applied to Chemistry, 1951; (with others) Modern Chemistry for the Engineer and Scientist, 1957; (with others) Transition Metal Chemistry. Contbr. articles profl. jours. Patentee in field. Office: Chemistry Bldg U Cal Los Angeles CA 90024

GARNER, DONALD PAUL educator; b. Kennett, Mo., Nov. 5, 1929; s. Robert Lee and Alverta (Stephens) G.; B.A., Harding Coll., Searcy, Ark., 1951; M.A., Kent State U., 1953; Ph.D., Wayne State U., 1964; m. Suellyn Lindsey, June 12, 1966; children—Josh Adam, Dirk Andrew. Dir. studio theatre Kent State U., 1951-52, dir. exptl. theatre Ohio State U., 1952; dir. theatre David Lipscomb Coll., Nashville, 1952-58; asst. debate coach Wayne State U., 1958, dir. extemporary speaking, 1959; lectr. U. Md., 1960-61; prof. speech, head dept. Eastern Ill. U., Charleston, 1963—; dir. Community Theatre, Charleston, Ill., 1963—. Served with AUS, 1956-57. Mem. Speech Assn. Am., Central States, Ill. speech assns., Am. Ednl. Theatre Assn., Alpha Psi Omega (editor Playbill 1967—), Pi Kappa Delta. Editor: Delta Psi Omega Playbill, 1967—; CallBoard, 1957. Home: 770 12th St Charleston, IL 61920

GARNER, ERROLL, (Louis), jazz pianist; b. Pitts., June 15, 1923; s. Ernest and Estella Garner; ed. pub. schs., Pitts. Profl. piano debut, 1930; with radio program ensemble Candy Kids, KDKA, Pitts.; accompanist dance orch., Pitts.; appeared Strand Theatre, N.Y.C., 1946; jazz recordings Columbia Records; now recording for Octave Record Co.; jazz musician Festival in Paris, 1948; solo recital jazz Music Hall in Cleve., 1950, concert Town Hall, N.Y.C., 1950, Cleve. Symphony, 1956; on tour U.S., 1958-59; Carnegie Hall concert debut, 1959; tours; composer for motion pictures; composer numerous compositions, including song, Misty; main themes for film A New Kind of Love, 1963. Recipient French Prix du Disque for jazz recording, Paris, 1957; award album Concert by the Sea (Brazil), 1957; chosen best pianist Internat. Jazz Critics Poll, Downbeat mag., 1957; Man of Year award Variety Club, Pitts., 1966; album That's My Kick chosen as best piano album Internat. Critics Poll, Jazz and Pop Mag., 1967. Mem. A.S.C.A.P. Roman Catholic. Home: 520 Fifth Av New York City, NY 10036

GARNER, HARRY HYMAN, physician, educator; b. Chgo., Jan. 19, 1910; s. Louis and Clara (Barasch) G.; B.S., U. Ill., 1932, M.D., 1934; m. Eleanor Hetherington, Apr. 5, 1940; children—Larry, Edward. Intern, Cook County Hosp., Chgo., 1935- 36; resident Chgo. State Hosp., 1936-39, clin. dir., 1939-41; cons. neurologist and psychiatrist Oak Forest Infirmary, Chgo., 1945—; supt. Community Clinics Ill., 1945-47; attending neurologist Cook County Hosp., Chgo., 1946-52, attending psychiatrist, 1956—; chief neuropsychiat. service br. 7, VA, 1947-48; attending psychiatrist, chmn. dept. psychiatry and neurology Mt. Sinai Hosp., Chgo., 1952-70, chmn. dept. psychiatry and behavioral scis. Med. Center, 1970—; attending physician in psychiatry, cons. psychiatrist Hines (Ill.) VA Hosp., 1970—; asst. prof. psychiatry U. Ill., 1945-48; prof., chmn. dept. psychiatry and neurology Chgo. Med. Sch., 1948-70, prof., chmn. dept. psychiatry and behavioral scis., 1970—. Mem. Gov. Ill. Psychiat. Adv. Council, 1950—. Served to lt. col. M.C., AUS, 1941- 46. Decorated Bronze

Star medal with cluster; co-recipient St. Guthiel -Von Domarus award. Diplomate Am. Bd. Psychiatry, Am. Bd. Neurology. Fellow Am. Psychiat. Soc.; mem. Acad. Psychoanalysis, Central Neuropsychiat. Assn., Chgo. Neurol. Soc., Acad. Neurology, A.M.A., Assn. Advancement Psychotherapy. Author: Psychosomatic Management of Patient with Malignancy; Psychotherapy and a Confrontation Problem-Solving Technique; also articles, sects. in books. Home: 433 Roscoe St Chicago, IL 60613. Office: 6 N Michigan Av Chicago IL 60602

GARNER, HARVEY LOUIS, elec. engr.; b. Lake, Colo., Dec. 23, 1926; s. Homa and Violet (Thuelin) G.; B.S., U. Denver, 1949, M.S., 1951; Ph.D., U. Mich., 1958; m. Yvonne Lillian King, Aug. 7, 1949; children-Susan Ann, Harvey Thomas. Engr. with devel. computers U. Mich., 1951-55, instr. elec. engring., 1955-58, asst. prof., 1958-60, asso. prof., 1960-63, prof., 1963-70, dir. Information Systems Lab., 1960-64, dir. Systems Engring. Lab., 1964-66, acting chmn. dept. communications scis., 1965-67, prof. computer and communications scis., 1967-70; prof. elec. engring., dir. Moore Sch. Elec. Engring.1970—; cons. in field; appt. nat. lectr. Assn. Computing Machinery, 1965. Served with USNR, 1945-46. Mem. I.E.E.E., Am. Soc. Engring. Edn., Assn. Computing Machinery A.A.A.S., Sigma Xi, Eta Kappa Nu, Sigma Pi Sigma. Contbr. articles profl. jours. Home: 719 King of Prussia Rd Radnor PA 19087 Office: Moore Sch Elec Engring U Pa Philadelphia PA 19104

GARNER, HENRY THOMAS, coll. dean; b. Gilliam, La., Jan. 2, 1925; s. Henry Thomas and Inda (Barnett) G.; B.S., Northwestern State Coll. (Natchitoches, La.), 1948; M.S., U. Ark., 1952, Ed.D., 1962; m. Cindy Moore, Nov. 20, 1954; children—Ginger, Kimberly. Tchr. pub. schs. Vivan, La., 1948-51, prin. jr. high sch., 1955-67; prin. elementary sch. Hosston, La., 1952-55; dean Coll. Edn., Northeast La. U., Monroe, 1967—. Vis. lectr. summers various univs., 1962-67. Served with USAAF, 1943-46. Mem. Am. Assn. Sch. Adminstrs., N.E.A., La. Tchrs. Assn., Assn. Supervision and Curriculum Devel., Am. Ednl. Research Assn., Am. Assn. Colls. Tchrs. Edn., Phi Delta Kappa, Phi Kappa Phi, Kappa Delta Pi, Lambda Zeta. Kiwanian, Mason. Contbr. profl. jours. Home: 907 Eason Pl Monroe LA 71201

GARNER, JAMES, (James Baumgardner), actor; b. Norman, Okla., Apr. 7, 1928; student N.Y. Berghof Sch., m. Lois; children—Kim, Greta. Worked as traveling salesman, oil field worker, carpet layer, bathing suit model; toured with road cos.; appeared on TV in Cheyenne; assumed lead in Maverick, 1957; motion picture debut in Toward the Unknown; other films include Shoot-out at Medicine Bend, Darby's Rangers, Sayonara, Up Periscope, Americanization of Emily, 36 Hours, The Art of Love, A Man Could Get Killed, Duel at Diablo, Mister Buddwig, Grand Prix, Hour of the Gun, Support Your Local Sheriff. Joined U.S. Mcht. Marine, 1944; served with AUS, Korea. 11492 Thurston Circle Los Angeles CA 90049*

GARNER, LESLIE W., stock broker; b. Butler, Pa., 1908; A.B., Stanford, 1929; M.B.A., Harvard, 1931; married. With Arthur Anderson & Co., 1933-37, 40-44; with Am. Ice Corp., 1937-40; controller T.J. Baker subsidiary Richardson-Merrell Inc., 1944-54, v.p., controller, 1954-59, controller parent co., 1959—. C.P.A., N.Y. Home: 670 Belvidere Rd Phillipsburg NJ 08865 Office: 122 E 42d St New York City NY 10017*

GARNER, MARVIN PERKINS, educator; b. Humphrey, Ky., Jan. 29, 1916; s. George P. and Myrtle (Hatter) G.; B.A., Transylvania Coll., 1936; M.A., Columbia, 1947, Ed.D., 1952; student Cranbrook Acad. Art, 1955, New Sch. Social Research, 1946-47; m. Margaret Stratton Toliver, May 29, 1941; 1 dau., Margaret Sallee. Asst. to hdqrs. auditor Atlantic Commn. Co., 1937-43; mem. Faculty N.Y. State U. Coll., Potsdam, 1947—, prof. art, chmn. dept., 1948—. Served with USAAF, 1943-46. Mem. Coll. Art Assn., Am. Craftsmen Council. Home: 23 Hillcrest Dr., Potsdam NY 13676.

GARNER, MILDRED MAXINE, educator; b. nr. Liberty, N.C., Mar. 15, 1919; d. Robert Monroe and Maize (Kimrey) Garner; B.A., U. N.C. at Greensboro, 1939; M.A., Union Theol. Sem., N.Y.C., 1946; Ph.D., U. Aberdeen (Scotland), 1952. Tchr. English, history, journalism, Roanoke Rapids, N.C., 1939, 41-42; asst. editor Biblical Recorder, Raleigh, N.C., 1940; dir. religious activities Woman's Coll., U N.C. at Greensboro, 1942-50; asso. prof. religion Meredith Coll., Raleigh, 1952-58; prof. religion Sweet Briar (Va.) Coll., 1958—, Wallace Eugene Rollins prof. religion, 1969—, chmn. dept., 1961-62, 63—. Fellow summer seminar history and culture India, U. Va., 1964, summer seminar history and culture China, 1965, summer inst. S. Asia, Duke, 1966; Fulbright scholar U. Aberdeen, 1950-51, 51-52; fellow program advanced religious studies Union Theol. Sem., 1955-56; fellow Am. Inst. Indian Studies, Poona, India, 1962-63. Mem. Phi Beta Kappa. Home: 123 N Asheboro St Liberty NC 27298 Office: Sweet Briar Coll Sweet Briar VA 24595

GARNER, OSCAR GEORGE, indsl. exec.; b. Vienna, Austria, Apr. 3, 1915; s. Abraham and Gisela R. (Grobtuch) G.; grad. Vienna Tech. Inst.; m. Deborah Garner, Feb. 12, 1939; children—Vivenne Eve (now Mrs. Eichholz) Carrol Marie (now Mrs. Suttles), Elizabeth Debora. Engr. Gen. Cable Co., Perth Amboy, N.J., 1940, plant engr., 1943, corp. maintenance engr., 1946, chief engr., 1948, v.p. mfg. and engring., 1949-53, v.p. research, engring., 1953-66, sr. v.p. mfg., research, engring., 1966—, dir., 1952—. Home: Cedar Cliff Rd Greenwich, CT Office: 730 3d Av New York City NY 10017

GARNER, ROBERT LIVINGSTON, former internat. banker; b. Bolton, Miss. Aug. 7, 1894; s. Robert V. and Lillian (Hardgrave) G.; B.S., Vanderbilt U., 1916; student Columbia U. Sch. Journalism, 1916-17; m. Ellen Wright, Sept. 4, 1926 (dec.); children—Robert W. (dec.), Joan F. (Mrs. Stanley Reid McCampbell). With ednl. dept. Guaranty Trust Co. of N.Y., 1919, transferred to Guaranty Co., 1920; with financial dept. Continental Ins. Co., 1925-26; asst. treas. Guaranty Trust Co. of N.Y., 1926-28, treas., 1928-29, v.p. and treas., 1929-43; financial v.p., dir., Gen. Foods Corp., 1943-47; v.p. Internat. Bank for Reconstrn. and Devel., 1947-56; pres. Internat. Finance Corp., 1956-61; dir. Am. Security and Trust Co., Washington, Hewlett-Packard Co., Palo Alto, Cal. Trustee, Vanderbilt U. Served as capt. 305th Inf., 77th Div., World War I. Clubs: University, The Links (N.Y.C.); Metropolitan (Md.); Chevy Chase (Md.); Metropolitan (Washington). Home: 2101 Connecticut Av NW Washington, DC 20009. Office: 730 15th St NW Washington DC 20005

GARNER, SAMUEL PAUL, univ. dean, accountant; b. Yadkinville N.C., Aug. 15, 1910; s. Samuel W. and Ila Jane (Hoots) G.; A.B., Duke, 1932, A.M., 1934; postgrad. Columbia, 1936; Ph.D., U. Tex., 1940; D.Ec. (hon.), Pusan Nat. U., 1966; LL.D., U. Ala., 1971; m. Ruth Bailey, Aug. 24, 1935; children—Thad Barclay, Walter Samuel, Sarah Jane. Faculty, Duke, 1934-35, Miss. State Coll., 1935-37, U. Tex., 1937-39; asso. prof. accounting U. Ala., University, 1939-43, prof., 1943—, head dept. accounting 1949-55, dean Sch. Bus. Adminstrn., 1954-71. Mem. Knight & Garner, C.P.A.'s, University, 1942-49; dir. First Fed. Savs. & Loan Assn., Hardins Bakery, Inc., O. Bowers Co., Tuscaloosa, Ala., Ames Bag Corp., Marion, Ala. Cons. edn. to comptroller gen. U.S., 1955-61; cons. grad. edn. U.S. Office Edn., 1965-70; cons. mgmt. edn. U.S. Dept. Def., 1965-70; Comer lectr. U. Ga., 1957, Price Waterhouse Found. lectr. Ga. State Coll., 1964; Distinguished Faculty lectr. Tex. Western Coll., 1963, U. S.D., 1963, East Carolina Coll., 1965, Va. Poly. Inst., 1966. U.S. del. internat. mgmt. and accounting congresses, 1957—; condr. spl. ednl. assignments U.S. State Dept. and other agys. in Turkey, 1958, Far East, 1960, 66, 68, 69, Europe, 1957, 60, 61, 63-70, S.Am., 1962, 65, Africa, 1964; adv. bd. Internat. U. Contact for Mgmt., Holland; U.S. Council Internat. Exchange Commerce Students. C.P.A., Tex., Ala. Mem. Am. Accounting Assn. (life, pres. 1951, exec. com. 1948, 51-54, chmn. com. internat. relations 1966-67), Am. Inst. C.P.A.'s (chmn. com. profl. statistics 1960-62), Nat. Assn. C.P.A. Examiners (chmn. com. accounting edn. 1960-61), Am. Coll. C.L.U.'s (council ednl. advisers 1961-69), U.S. Council Internat. Progress in Mgmt. (nat. bd. dirs.), Assn. Edn. Internat. Bus., Fed. Govt. Accountants Assn. (adv. com. relations with univs.), Financial Execs. Inst. (nat. com. edn. 1956-70), Am. Assn. Collegiate Schs. Bus. (pres. 1964-65), Soc. Expert Accountants France, Nat. Assn. Accountants, Ala. Soc. C.P.A.'s (sec.-treas. 1949-58), Sigma Alpha Epsilon, Phi Beta Kappa, Beta Gamma Sigma (nat. exec. com. 1961-66), Beta Alpha Psi, Omicron Delta Kappa, Pi Tau Chi, Omicron Delta Epsilon, Alpha Kappa Psi (trustee found.; Found. award 1962), Pi Gamma Mu. Baptist. Club: University. Author: (with G. H. Newlove) Elementary Cost Accounting, 1941, rev. edit., 1949, Spanish edit., 1952; Advanced Accounting, vol. I, 1951, vol.II, 1950; Advanced Accounting Problems, Book I, 1951, Book II, 1950; Handbook of Modern Accounting Theory, 1955; Education for the Professions, 1955. Readings in Cost Accounting, Budgeting and Control, 1955, rev. edit., 1960; Evolution of Cost Accounting to 1925, 1954, Japanese edit., 1956; co-author others. Co-editor: Readings in Accounting Theory, 1966; editorial adv. bd. Mgmt. Internat. mag., 1964-70; editorial bd. Accounting Rev., Essays in International Business (annual). Contbr. articles to profl. jours. Home: 1016 Indian Hills Dr Tuscaloosa AL 35401 Office: Box J University AL 35486

GARNER, SOUIL W., ins. co. exec. Treas., Md. Casualty Co., Balt. Office: 701 W 40th St Baltimore MD 21211*

GARNER, WENDELL RICHARD, educator; b. Buffalo, Jan. 21, 1921; s. Richard Charles and Lena Belle (Cole) G.; A.B., Franklin and Marshall Coll., 1942; A.M., Harvard, 1943, Ph.D., 1946; m. Barbara Chipman Ward, Feb. 18, 1944; children—Deborah Ann, Peter Ward, Elinor. Teaching fellow Harvard, 1942- 43, research asso., 1943-46; instr. Johns Hopkins, 1946, asst. prof., 1947-51, asso. prof., 1951-55, prof., 1955-67, dir. Psychol. Lab. Inst. Coop. Research, 1949-55, chmn. dept. psychology, 1954-64; James Rowland Angell prof. psychology Yale, 1967—. Recipient Distinguished Sci. Contbn. award Am. Psychol. Assn., 1964. Fellow Am. Psychol. Assn., A.A.A.S. (v.p. psychology 1967—), Acoustical Soc. Am.; mem. Soc. Exptl. Psychologists (chmn. 1959), Am. Assn. U. Profs., Md. (pres. 1961-62), Eastern psychol. assns., Nat. Acad. Scis., Sigma Xi. Author: Uncertainty and Structure as Psychological Concepts, 1962. Home: 48 Yowago Av Branford CT 06405 Office: Yale U New Haven CT 06520

GARNER, WILLIAM CHADWICK, educator; b. Belmont, Mass., Sept. 10, 1912; s. William and Ada (Chadwick) G.; B.S., Tufts Coll., 1936; Edn.M., 1938; m. Edith Harris, Nov. 12, 1938; childrenEdwin Chadwick, Nathan Conant, James Rockwell, Jean Elizabeth, Timothy Fielding. Tchr. Brandford (Vt.) Acad., 1938-40; prin. Shoreham (Vt.) High Sch., 1940-42; guidance dir. Spaulding High Sch., Barre, Vt., 1942-43; prin. Woodstock (Vt.) High Sch., 1943-44; pres. Dean Acad. and Jr. Coll. 1946—. Served as lt., USNR, 1944-46. Mem. school com. Town of Franklin, Mass.; dir. Ray Library Assn.; mem. corp. Bouvé-Boston Sch. Mem. Am. Guidance and Personnel Assn. Episcopalian. Mason, Rotarian. Home: 144 School St Franklin MA 02038

GARNETT, DAVID, author; b. Brighton, Sussex, Eng., Mar. 9, 1892; s. Edward and Constance (Black) G.; student U. Coll. Sch., London; A.R.C.Sc., Imperial Coll. Sci. and Tech., London, 1913, D.I.C., 1915, fellow 1956; m. Rachel Alice Marshall, Mar. 1921 (dec. 1940); children—Richard Duncan Carey, William Tomlin Kasper; m. 2d, Angelica Vanessa Bell, May 1942; childrenAmaryllis Virginia, Henrietta Catherine Vanessa, Frances Olivia, Nerissa Stephen. Bookseller with Francis Birrell, 1920; author, writer, 1919—; author: Lady Into Fox, 1922 (Hawthornden prize, James Tait Black prize 1923); A Man in the Zoo, 1923; The Sailor's Return, 1924; Go She Must, 1927; No Love, 1929; The Grasshoppers Come, 1931; A Rabbit in the Air, 1932; Pocahontas, 1933; Beaney-Eye, 1935; War in the Air, 1941; The Golden Echo, 1953; Flowers of the Forest, 1955; Aspects of Love, 1955; A Shot in the Dark, 1958; A Net for Venus, 1959; The Familiar Faces, 1962; Two By Two, 1963; Ulterior Motives, 1967. Served as flight lt. RAF, 1939-40; with Dept. of Foreign Office, 1941-46. Decorated Comdr. Order Brit. Empire. Fellow Royal Soc. Lit., Imperial Coll. Sci. and Tech. Home: Hilton Hall Huntington, England Office: care Harcourt Brace and World Books Inc 757 3d Av New York City NY 10017

GARNETT, RICHARD LEE, lawyer; b. Glasgow, Ky., Nov. 19, 1895; s. Richard E. and Mattie (Wilson) G.; student Campbellsburg Coll., U. Va., 1916-17, Bowling Green B.U., 1919-20; A.B., Ohio State U., 1927, LL.B., 1929, J.D., 1967; m. to Zeba Nuckols, Dec. 26, 1936; children—Geraldine, Ruth Annett. Admitted to Ohio and Ky. bars, 1928; dir. Bur. Govtl. Research, 1924-28; gen. practice of law, Columbus, O., 1928-31, Glasgow, 1931—; state senator, Ky., 1960. Mem. Ohio Legislative Com. to Redraft Tax Laws of Ohio, 1928-30; city atty., Glasgow; commonwealth atty., 10th and 43d dists. of Ky. Vice pres. Mammouth Cave Nat. Park Assn. Served as sgt. USMC, 1917-19; maj. USAAF, 1941-45. Recipient Outstanding Citizen medal City of Glasgow and Am. Legion, 1958; Distinguished award City of Glasgow, 1960. Mem. Am. Legion (dist. comdr.), Glasgow C. of C. (pres.), Am., Ky. (pres. 1958) bar assns., V.F.W., Phi Delta Gamma, Gamma Etta Gamma. Mason, K.P. Clubs: Country; Rotary (pres.). Home: Glasgow KY 42141

GARNEVICUS, FRANK P., bank exec.; b. Bloomfield, N.J., 1925; grad. Pace Coll., 1956. Comptroller, Nat. Newark & Essex Bank. Home: 14 Mountain View Dr Clifton NJ 07013 Office: 744 Broad St Newark NJ 07101*

GARNIEZ, BERNARD, educator; A.B., U. Utah, 1950; A.M., N.Y.U., 1952, Ph.D., 1960. Prof. French, chmn. dept. Romance langs. and lit. N.Y.U. Office: Dept Romance Langs and Lit NYU Bronx NY 10453*

GARNSEY, LEON LESLIE, metal products co. exec.; b. Brewster, N.Y., Feb. 16, 1924; s. Leon and Anna M. (O'Hara) G.; student U. So. Cal., 1955; m. Margaret Bradbury, Jan. 17, 1942; 1 dau., Lesley (Mrs. Frederick R. McCarty). With Heat-X, Inc., Brewster, N.Y., 1947-53; gen. mgr. Dunham-Bush, Inc., West Hartford, Conn., 1953-57, asst. treas., 1957-64, treas., 1964—, v.p., 1969—, sec., dir., 1968—; dir. Dunham-Bush of Can., Ltd., 1968—. Served with USAAF, 1943-45. Home: 67 Reverknolls St Avon CT 06001 Office: 175 South St West Hartford CT 06110

GARNSEY, MORRIS EUGENE, educator; b. Aurora, Mo., Oct. 12, 1906; s. Harry F. and Laura E. (Pallardy) G.; A.B., Drury Coll., 1928; M.A., Clark U., 1929; Ph.D., Harvard, 1937; student Louvain U., 1933-34, U. Paris, 1929-30; m. Colleen M. Kenney, June 28, 1929; 1 dau., Laura K. Instr. econs. Brown U., 1931-35, Harvard, 1935-37; With U. Colo., 1937—, prof., 1960—, chmn. dept. 1960-63; spl. cons. Colo. gov. on natural resources study, 1957; cons. regional Resources Planning Bd., 1941-43; pub. mem. regional bd. Wage Stblzn. Bd., 1950-53. Fellow Am. Field Service, 1929-30, Belgian- Am. Ednl. Found., 1933-34, Guggenheim Meml. Found., 1947-48; faculty research fellow Ford Found., 1957-58. Mem. Am. Econ. Assn. Author: America's New Frontier: The Mountain West, 1950; also articles. Editor: (with James R. Hibbs) Social Sciences and the Environment 1968. Home: 1505 Bluebell Av Boulder CO 80302

GARRAHY, JOHN JOSEPH, lt. gov. R.I.; b. Providence, Nov. 26, 1930; s. John and Margaret (Neylon) G.; student U. Buffalo, 1952, U. R.I., 1953; m. Margherite DePietro, 1956; children—Colleen, John, Maribeth, Sheila, Seanna. Mem. R.I. Senate, 1962-68, dep. majority leader, 1963-68, also mem. Senate finance com., judiciary com., joint com. on water resources; mem. R.I. Commn. to Study Juvenile Delinquency, Commn. to Study Drug Addiction, Commn. to Study Entire Field of Edn., Commn. on Econ. Devel., R.I. Commn. to Study Reorgn. Dept. Social Welfare; lt. gov. R.I., 1968—. Chmn. Gov.'s Council on Youth Opportunities, 1969—; chmn. screening com. Small Bus. Devel. Center, 1965-66; gen. chmn. Heart Fund Drive, 1970; chmn. Cerebral Palsy Drive, Providence, 1954-55; mem. New Eng. adv. com. Northeast Regional Kidney Program, 1970. Chmn. Democratic State Com., 1967. Bd. dirs. Nat. Council Vocational Rehab. Served with USAF, 1953-55. Author: Rhode Island in the Year 1975, 1969. Home: 31 Elmcrest Av Providence RI 02908 Office: State House Providence RI 02903

GARRARD, DON, opera singer; b. Vancouver, B.C., Can.; ed. Brentwood Coll., Royal Conservatory Music, Toronto, Music Acad. of West, Santa Barbara, Cal., Opera Sch., Milan, Italy; m. Margaret Gale; 1 dau. Prin. soloist Canadian Opera Co., Sadler's Wells, 1961; appearances in Britain include Anna Bolena, Jeptha, Il Trovatore, Eugne Onegin; solo appearance with Scottish Opera and Welsh Nat. Opera; recs. include Rake's Progress, Bruckner's Te Deum, Roberto Devereax, also appearances TV, motion pictures. Address: 85 Morden Hill London SE 13 England*

GARRARD, RALPH H., beverage mfg. exec.; b. Dothan, Ala.; ed. bus. schs., Atlanta; m. Anne Garrard; 1 son, Ralph H. With Coca-Cola Co., 1933—, mem. fountain sales dept., spl. rep. N.Y. World's Fair, 1940; mgr. fountain sales dist., Richmond, Va., 1940-43, various exec. positions, 1943-56, mem. nat. sales dept., 1956-60, mgr. nat. sales, 1960-63, v.p., gen. mgr. nat. sales dept., 1963—. Clubs: Peachtree Golf, Capital City, Atlanta Country. Home: 90 Polo Dr NE Atlanta GA 30309 Office: Coca-Cola Co Box 1734 Atlanta GA 30301

GARRATT, GEORGE ALFRED ednl. cons.; b. Bklyn., May 7, 1898; s. Henry Masters and Rebecca (Kerr) G.; B.S., Mich. State U., East Lansing, 1920; M.F., Yale, 1923, Ph.D., 1933; D.Sc., U. of South, 1957; m. Barbara Julia Lillie, July 28, 1922; children—Stephen Masters, Rowland Masters. Instr. forestry Mich. State Coll., 1920- 22; prof. forestry and engring. U. of South, Sewanee, Tenn., 1923- 25; asst. prof. forest products Yale, 1925-31, asso. prof., 1931-39, Mfrs. Assn. prof. lumbering, 1939-55, asst. dean Sch. Forestry, 1936-39, dean, 1945-65, dean emeritus, 1965—, Pinchot prof. forestry, 1955- 66, emeritus, 1966—, part-time leave to serve as chief div. tech. service tng. U.S. Forest Products Lab., Madison, Wis., 1942- 1945; dir. Canadian Forestry Edn. Study, 1965-71. Mem. Conn. State Park and Forest Commn., 1949-71, chmn., 1951-71; mem. Conn. Council Agr. and Natural Resources, 1959-71, chmn., 1961-64. Fellow Soc. Am. Foresters (v.p. 1956-57, pres. 1958-59); mem. Soc. Wood Sci. and Tech., Forest Products Research Soc. (v.p. 1947, pres. 1948), Forest History Soc. (dir. 1965—, pres. 1970-72), Am. Forestry Assn. (dir. 1970—), Sigma Xi, Xi Sigma Pi. Author: The Mechanical Properties of Wood, 1931; Wood Preservation (with Geo. M. Hunt), 1938, rev. edit., 1967; Forestry Education in Canada, 1971. Home: 421 Ridge Rd Hamden CT 06517

GARRATY, JOHN ARTHUR, educator, historian; b. Bklyn., July 4, 1920; s. Arthur J. and Helen (Tobias) G.; B.A., Bklyn. Coll., 1941; M.A., Columbia, 1942, Ph.D., 1949; L.H.D., Mich. State U., 1969; m. Gail Nielson, May 17, 1965; children—Katharine, John, Sarah. Mem. faculty Mich. State U., 1947-59; mem. faculty Columbia, 1959—, prof. history, 1961—. Ford fellow, 1953-54; Guggenheim fellow, 1965-66; Social Sci. Research Council fellow, 1955-57; fellow Centre Advanced Study Behavioral Scis., 1962-63. Mem. Soc. Am. Historians (pres. 1969—), Am. Hist. Assn., Orgn. Am. Historians, Am. Assn. U. Profs. Author: Henry Cabot Lodge, 1953; Woodrow Wilson, 1956; Nature of Biography, 1957; Right-Hand Man, 1960; American Nation, 1966; The New Commonwealth, 1968; Interpreting American History, 1970; (with Walter Adams) From Main Street to the Left Bank, 1959; (with Walter Adams) Is The World Our Campus?, 1960; (with Walter Adams) Guide to Study Abroad, 2d edit., 1969. Home: 310 W 102d St New York City, NY 10025.

GARRE, WALTER JOHN, psychiatrist; b. Vienna, Austria, July 5, 1907; s. Filip M. and Hedwig (Litchtenstein) Goldner; med. edn. U. Vienna, 1938; M.D., Loyola U., Chgo., 1941; div.; children—John M., June P. Came to U.S., 1939, naturalized, 1942. Cons. No. State Hosp., Sedro Wooley, Wash., 1958-59; chief psychiatry VA Hosp., San Francisco, 1962; sr. psychiatrist Camarillo (Cal.) State Hosp., 1962; supt. Peoria (Ill.) State Hosp., 1963-64; pvt. practice, Chgo., 1964—; asst. clin. prof. Chgo. Med. Sch., 1963—; attending psychiatrist Hines (Ill.) VA Hosp.; mem. staff, cons. psychiatrist River Edge, St. Francis, Blue Island Mercy, Mt. Sinai, Little Company of Mary, Christ Community, Ridgeway hosps. (all Chgo.). Served with AUS, 1943. Diplomate Am. Bd. Psychiatry and Neurology. Mem. A.M.A., Am. Psychiat. Assn., Ill., Chgo. med. socs., Acad. Psychosomatic Medicine. Author: Basic Anxiety, 1962; also articles. Home: 9546 Flamingo Terrace Hickory Hills IL 60457 Office: 3900 W 95th St Evergreen Park IL 60642

GARRELS, JOHN CARLYLE, chem. co. exec.; b. Detroit, Mar. 5, 1914; s. John Carlyle and Margaret (Gibney) G.; B.S. in Chem. Engring., U. Mich., 1935; AM.P., Harvard Bus. Sch., 1955; m. Valerie Smith, May 7, 1938; children—John Carlyle III, Molly (Mrs. Sürgen Wolfgang Brendel), Anne L. Supr. prodn. Pa. Salt Mfg. Co., Wyandotte, Mich., 1936-42, Monsanto Co., Trenton, Mich., 1942; with Monsanto Chem. Co., various locations, 1942, 46—, dir. prodn., Springfield, Mass., 1955-56, asst. div. mgr., Springfield, 1956-61; dep. mng. dir. Monsanto Chems. Ltd., London, Eng., 1961-62; mng. dir., 1962-68; chmn. bd. Monsanto Textiles Ltd., London, 1968—; dir. Forth Chems. Ltd., Monsanto Australia Ltd., British Saccharin Sales Ltd. Mem. Chem. Industries Assn. (U.K.), Nat. Econ. Devel. Council (U.K.), British Plastics Fedn. (pres.), C. of C. of Am. in London (bd. dirs.). Home: Brockendale North Dr Wentworth Surrey England Office: 10-18 Victoria St London SW1 England

GARRELS, ROBERT MINARD, educator; b. Detroit, Aug. 24, 1916; s. John C. and Margaret A. (Gibney) G.; B.S., U. Mich., 1937; M.S., Northwestern U., 1939, Ph.D., 1941; M.A. (hon.), Harvard, 1955; Sc.D. (hon.), U. Brussels, 1969; m. Jane M. Tinen, Dec. 21, 1940 (div. 1969); children—Joan F., James C., Katherine G.; m. 2d, Cynthia A. Hunt, 1970. From instr. to asso. prof. geology Northwestern U., 1941-52; geologist U.S. Geol. Survey, 1952-55; asso. prof. geology Harvard, 1955-57, prof., 1957-65, chmn. dept. geol. scis., 1963-65; Henri Speciael prof. sci. U. of Brussels (Belgium), 1962-63; prof. geology Northwestern U., Evanston, Ill., 1965—. Trustee Bermuda Biol. Sta. Recipient of Arthur L. Day medal Geol. Soc. Am., 1966. Fellow A.A.A.S., Geol. Soc. Am., Mineral. Soc. Am.; mem. Geochem. Soc. (pres. 1962), Nat. Acad. Scis., Soc. Econ. Geologists, Am. Acad. Arts and Sci., Am. Chem. Soc., Sigma Xi. Author: Textbook of Geology, 1951; Mineral Equilibria, 1959; (with C.L. Christ) Minerals, Solutions, and Equilibria, 1965. Office: Scripps Instn Oceanography U Cal at San Diego La Jolla CA 92037

GARRELTS, JEWELL MILAN, univ. dean; b. McPherson, Kan., Oct. 25, 1903; s. Arthur J. and Mabel N. (Cramer) G.; B.S. in C.E., Valparaiso U., 1925; M.S., Columbia, 1933; m. Esther S. Strickland, Sept. 6, 1925; children—Lois Joy, Robert Jewell, William Arthur. Draftsman for power houses Ill. Steel Co., Ind., 1924-25; instr. in structural engring. Cornell U., 1925-27; asso. in mechanics Columbia, 1927-36, asso. in civil engring. and mechanics, 1936-37, asst. prof. civil engring., 1937-39, asso. prof., 1939-46, prof., chmn. civil engring., 1946—, asso. dean, 1957—; asst. engr. Am. Bridge Co., N.Y.C., 1930-32, 34-35; engr. Waddell & Hardesty, 1936-51; cons. engr., 1952—. Mem. Am. Soc. C.E., Am. Soc. for Engring. Edn., Columbia U. Alumni Assn., A.A.A.S., Internat. Assn. Bridge and Structural Engrs., Sigma Xi, Tau Beta Pi. Club: Faculty of Columbia. Contbr. articles to profl. jours. Home: 15 Brook Rd Tenafly NJ 07670 Office: SW Mudd Bldg Columbia U New York City NY 10028 Community Devel. Corp. (all St. Paul). Trustee

GARREN, HENRY WILBURN, educator; b. Hendersonville, N.C., Apr. 2, 1925; s. Morris King and Christina (Barnwell) G.; A.B., U. N.C., 1947; B.S., N.C. State U., 1948; M.S., U. Md., 1951, Ph.D., 1953; m. Martha Elizabeth Johnson, Dec. 28, 1946; children—Deborah Faye, Nathan Morris. Physiologist, Med. Labs. Army Chem. Center, Edgewood, Md., 1952-53; asst. prof. poultry sci. N.C. State U., Raleigh, 1953-54, asso. prof., 1954-60, prof., head dept., 1960-68; dean, coordinator U. Ga. Coll. Agr., Athens, 1968—. Dir. C & S Bank, Atlanta. Served with USNR, 1943-46. Mem. Poultry Sci. Assn. (Poultry Sci. Research award 1953), Am. Physiol. Soc., Soc. Exptl. Biology and Medicine, Exchange Club (pres. N.C. dist. clubs 1967-68), Sigma Xi, Alpha Zeta, Phi Kappa Phi, Gamma Sigma Delta, A Aghon. Contbr. articles to sci. jours. Home: 225 Pine Valley Dr Athens GA 30601

GARRETSON, ALBERT HENRY, educator, lawyer; b. Tacoma, Mar. 30, 1910; s. Max H. and Anna (Hammond) G.; B.A., Whitman Coll., 1931; M.A., Am. U., 1932; B.A. (Rhodes scholar), Oxford (Eng.) U., 1934; J.D., Syracuse U., 1942; m. Agnes P. Ernst, July 22, 1935; children—David P., Deborah A., Peter P. Admitted to N.Y. bar, 1942, U.S. Supreme Ct. bar; asst. prof. Colgate U., 1936- 42; practice in N.Y.C., 1946-47, 57—, Ethiopia, 1947-57; sr. atty. Dept. Justice, 1942; chief sect. econ. warfare div. Am. embassy, London, Eng., 1943; chief econs. sect. G-2, SHAEF,1944; asst. legal adviser State Dept., 1945; legal adviser Ethiopian Govt., 1947-57; dir. Inst. Internat. Law, N.Y. U., 1961—, prof. law, 1946-47, 57—; hon. prof. Kings Coll., U. London, 1963. Mem. UNESCO Commn. Nigerian Univ., 1961, UNESCO Commn. Internat. Hydrologic Devel., 1962. Trustee Walter E. Meyer Found.; bd. dirs. Internat. Sch. Services, Grace Ch. Sch. Carnegie fellow internat. law, 1935-36. Mem. Internat. Law Assn., Council Fgn. Relations, Am. Bar Assn. (chmn. diplomatic and consular law com. 1964-69). Episcopalian (vestryman). Editor, Jour. Maritime Law, 1969—. Home: 1 Lexington Av New York City NY 10010

GARRETSON, DONALD EVERETT, mfg. co. exec.; b. Elizabeth, N.J., Nov. 22, 1921; s. James W. and Helen (Crane) G.; A.B. in Commerce, Washington and Lee U., 1943; M.B.A., Harvard, 1947; student Northwestern U., 1942, 48; m. Adele F. Anderson, Sept. 17, 1949; children—James Robert, Katherine Crane, Donald Everett, Peter Andrew, Andrea Drew. With Arthur Andersen & Co., C.P.A.'s, Chgo., 1947-50; with Minn. Mining & Mfg. Co., St. Paul, 1950—, asst. treas., 1963- 67, treas., 1967—; dir. First Mchts. State Bank, Liberty Plaza Corp., Community Devel. Corp. (all St. Paul). Trustee, treas. Macalester Coll., St. Paul; bd. dirs. Greater St. Paul United Fund, 1966—, chmn. budget com., 1965-69. Served to lt. USNR, 1943-46. Presbyn. (elder). Club: St Paul Pool and Tennis (dir.). Home: 709 Linwood Av St Paul, MN 55105. Office: 3 M Center St Paul MN 55101

GARRETSON, FRANK EDMUND, retired marine corps officer; b. Salem, Ia., Feb. 27, 1918; s. Herman John and Marion Scott (Becker) G.; B.A., U. Wash., 1940; M.A., George Washington U., 1964; student Inf. Sch., 1946-47, Command and Gen. Staff Coll. Kan., 1957-58, Nat. War Coll., 1963-64; m. Cecily Fleetwood Forbes, Aug. 2, 1941; children—John Forbes, Cecily Fleetwood, Sarah Jane. Joined USMC, 1940, commd. 2d lt., 1941, advanced through grades to brig. gen., 1966; troop comdr., 1941-45; instr. USMC Sch., Quantico, Va., 1947-50, 59-61; sec. gen. Staff USMC, Washington, 1961-63; comdg. officer 9th Marines, Vietnam, 1965; liaison officer to chief naval operations, Washington, 1965-66; dir. information hdqrs., 1966-68; task force comdg. gen. 3d Marine Div., 1968-69; asst. base comdr. Camp Pendleton, Cal., 1969-70; retired, 1970; v.p. Garretson Mortgage Co., Los Angeles, 1970—. Decorated Navy Cross, D.S.M., Legion of Merit with V and 2 gold stars, Bronze Star, Purple Heart, Presdl. Unit Citation with 3 bronze stars; Order Nat. Rep. Vietnam, Vietnamese Cross Gallantry. Mem. Marine Corps Assn., Phi Gamma Delta. Club: Nat. Press (Washington). Home: 6171 Tamilynn St San Diego CA 92122 Office: 900 Wilshire Blvd Los Angeles CA 90017

GARRETSON, RICHARD C., banker; b. Cleve., 1923; grad. Yale, 1947. Sr. v.p. Society Nat. Bank Cleve.; sr. v.p. Society Corp. Home: 2861 Broxton Rd Shaker Heights OH 44120 Office: 127 Public Sq Cleveland OH 44114*

GARRETSON, ROBERT HEWIT, mfg. co. exec.; b. Ritzville, Wash., Sept. 1, 1915; s. Robert Ketchum and Frances Rogers Hewit) G.; B.A., Stanford, 1938; m. Alta Marie Paquette, Oct. 15, 1939; children—Robert Hewit, Roger R., David L. Sales mgmt., corporate mgmt. positions IBM, N.Y.C., 1938-57; pres., bd. dirs. Stationers Corp., Los Angeles, 1957-59; group v.p., exec. v.p., then pres. Consol. Electrodynamics Corp., 1959-67 (became subsidiary Bell & Howell Co. 1960); exec. v.p., dir. Bell & Howell Co., Chgo., 1961-67, exec. v.p., dir., pres. bus. equipment group, 1967-68; dir. Josten's, Inc., Owatonna, Minn., 1967—, chmn. bd., chief exec. officer, 1968-69, dir., mem. exec. com., 1968—; pres. RHG Corp., El Monte, Cal., 1969—; dir. O.K. Earl Corp., Pasadena, Cal. Served to col. AUS, 1942-47. Decorated Bronze Star medal; Croix de Guerre (France). Clubs: California (Los Angeles); Annandale Country (Pasadena); Army-Navy (Washington). Home: 1365 Woodstock Rd San Marino CA 91108 dir. McLachlen Nat. Bank, 1937—, gen. counsel, 1951-68. Atty. in Office: 9640 Telstar Av El Monte CA 91731

GARRETT, ALFRED BENJAMIN, educator; b. Glencoe, O., June 28, 1906; s. Robert E. and Margaret (McMaster) G.; B.S., Muskingum Coll., 1928, Sc.D. (hon.), 1960; M.S., Ohio State U., 1931, Ph.D., 1932; Sc.D., Ohio Wesleyan U., 1962, Denison U., Granville, O., 1966; m. Jessie Campbell, Sept. 1, 1934; children—Carol Lynn, John Calvin, Lois Nancy. Tchr. math. Harding High Sch., Aliquippa, Pa., 1928-29; teaching asst. Ohio State U., 1929-32; asst. prof. chemistry Kent State U., 1932-35; faculty Ohio State U., 1935—, prof. chemistry, 1944—, head div. gen. chemistry, 1942-59, chmn. dept. chemistry, 1960-62, v.p. for research, 1962-69, prof. chemistry, 1969—; vis. lectr. chemistry Nat. Sci. Found., 1957-66. Adv. com. ednl. services div. NASA, 1966—; chmn. adv. com. Prodn. High Sch. Chemistry Courses on Films, 1957-58. Trustee Muskingum Coll., Denison U. Research Found. Recipient Honored Tchr. award Coll. Arts and Scis., Ohio State U., 1958; Gov.'s award State Ohio, 1964; Sci. Apparatus Makers Award in Chem. Edn., Am. Chem. Soc., 1964; Ohioana Citation, 1970. Fellow A.A.A.S., Royal Soc. Arts; mem. Am. Chem. Soc. (chmn. div. chem. edn. 1955, counselor div. 1958-61, Nat. Sci. Tchrs. Assn. (pres. 1969-70), Land Grant Coll. Assn. (mem. exec. com. 1968), Sigma Xi, Phi Lambda Upsilon, Sigma Pi Sigma. Presbyn. (elder). Club: Torch. Author eight books and labs. manuals, also numerous articles profl. jours. Home: 162 Erie Rd Columbus OH 43214

GARRETT, BERNARD ROBERT, electronic co. exec.; b. N.Y.C., Feb. 23, 1926; s. Max and Gussie (Pachter) G.; B.S., N.Y. Coll. Engring., 1948; student Princeton, 1942-43; m. Rita Blumberg, Jan. 15, 1950; children—Mitchel Owen, Lisa Karen. Project engr. Reeves Instrument, N.Y.C., 1948-53; v.p. engring. Sterling Precision, N.Y.C., 1953-55; program mgr. Am. Bosch Arma Corp., N.Y.C., 1955-57; v.p. engring. Loral Corp., N.Y.C., 1957-64; exec. v.p. Instrument Systems, Jericho, N.Y., 1964—. Served with AUS, 1943-45. Mem. N.Y. Acad. Scis., I.E.E.E., French C. of C. (bd. dirs.). Developed multiplexing communication systems for entertainment and passenger service on jumbo jets, 1970, anti-submarine and electronic warfare systems, 1964. Home: 66 Hummingbird Dr East Hills NY 11576 Office: 410 Jericho Turnpike Jericho NY 11753

GARRETT, CAROL JOY, violist; b. Denver, Mar. 28, 1940; d. Lawrence and Marjorie (Creswell) Garrett; B.A. magna cum laude, Smith Coll., 1961; postgrad. Paris Conservatory Music, 1961-63. Asst. prin. violist San Antonio Symphony, 1963-67; prin. violist Santa Fe Opera, 1964—; with Houston Symphony, 1967-69, San Francisco Opera and Symphony, 1970—; with Aspen Festival Orch., 1963. Tchr. viola San Francisco Conservatory of Music. Fondation des Etats Unis grantee, Paris. Home: 141 Buena Vista Av E San Francisco CA 94117

GARRETT, CLYDE D, lawyer, ins. exec. banker; b. Washington, Oct. 25, 1887; s. John P. and Emma (Caywood) G.; LL.B., George Washington U., 1910; m. Verda Jones, Nov. 14, 1911 (dec. Aug. 1942); 1 son, Marshall Jones; m. 2d, Belle Hoagland, Sept. 13, 1941. Admitted to D.C. bar, 1911, also U.S. Supreme Ct. bar; dir. Equitable Life Ins. Co., 1933—, gen. counsel, 1944-68, v.p., 1961-68, legal cons., 1968—; dir. McLachlen Nat. Bank, 1937—, gen. counsel, 1951-68. Atty. in SSS, World War I, govt. appeal agt., World War II. Mem. Republican Nat. Com., D.C., 1948-60. Mem. Met. Washington Bd. Trade, Am. Bar Assn., Bar Assn. D.C., Theta Delta Chi. Episcopalian. Mason. Clubs: University, Capitol Hill (Washington); Columbia Country (Chevy Chase, Md.); Farmington Country (Charlottesville, Va.). Home: 3300 Rittenhouse St NW Washington DC 20015 Office: 3900 Wisconsin Av NW Washington DC 20016

GARRETT, DONALD WALLACE, banker; b. New Braunfels, Tex., Nov. 6, 1928; s. William W. and Thelma (Crossley) G.; B.A., Tex. A. and M. U. 1950; postgrad. Northwestern U., 1960, So. Meth. U., 1967; m. Ilse Frost, Dec. 27, 1949; children—Ilse Frost, Kathleen Crossley. With Lone Star Brewing Co., San Antonio, 1950- 57; asst. v.p. Frost Nat. Bank, San Antonio, 1957-59, v.p., 1959-65, mem. exec. com., 1962—, sr. v.p., 1965-68, exec. v.p., 1968—, also dir.; v.p. Frost Realty Co., 1969—. Past pres., bd. dirs. United Fund San Antonio, also campaign chmn., 1969; past pres., bd. dirs. Fiesta San Antonio Commn.; bd. dirs. Jersig Speech and Hearing Center, 1965-68, Downtown, Inc., 1966-69, Tex. Cavaliers, 1966-70; adv. trustee S.W. Found. for Research and Edn.; trustee San Antonio Acad. Tex.; bd. dirs., v.p. Former Students Assn. Tex. A and M U.; mem. Council of Presidents. Served with U.S. Army, 1953-55. Home: 305 Castano St San Antonio, TX 78209. Office: 101 Main Plaza San Antonio TX 78205

GARRETT, EDWARD ROBERT, educator, chemist; b. N.Y.C., Apr. 9, 1920; s. Murray and Stella (Abrams) G.; B.S., Mich. State U., 1941, M.S., 1948, Ph.D. (Hinman fellow 1949-50), 1950; m. Irene Brewer, July 31, 1941; children—Jan Edward, Terry Lee, Kurt Lane. Asst. foreman Gen. Chem. Co., Claymont, Del., 1941-42; supt. TNT prodn. Keystone Ordnance Works, Meadville, Pa., 1942-43; chem. process engr. synthetic rubber Gen. Tire & Rubber Co., Baytown, Tex., 1943-45; asst. plant mgr. sulfuric acid prodn. Stauffer Chem. Co., Hammond, Ind., 1945-46; grad. asst. Mich. State U., 1946-49; sr. research scientist, group leader Upjohn Co., 1950-61; grad. research prof. Coll. Pharmacy, U. Fla., Gainesville, 1961—, chmn. grad. studies. Vis. prof. U. Wis., 1958, U. Buenos Aires, 1965; cons. Smith Kline & French Labs., 1963—; vis. scientist U. Cal. at San Francisco, 1964; pres. symposium indsl. pharmacy and biochemistry Latin Am. Congress Chemistry, Buenos Aires, 1962. Recipient Lawson Essay prize Mich. State U., 1938; Upjohn award Upjohn Co., 1959; Ebert prize Am. Pharm. Assn., 1962. Hon. mem. Argentine, Chilean socs. indsl. pharmacy and biochemistry; mem. N.Y. Acad. Scis., Am. Chem. Soc., Am. Pharm. Assn. (research achievement award phys. chem. in pharm. scis. 1963, research achievement award in drug standards and assay 1969), A.A.A.S., Am. Soc. Microbiology, Sigma Xi, Pi Mu Epsilon, Sigma Pi Sigma, Rho Chi, Rho Pi Phi, Alpha Chi Sigma. Democrat. Unitarian. Contbr. numerous articles in field. Editor Internat. Jour. Clin. Pharmacology, 1967—; editorial bd. Jour. Pharm. Scis., 1966—. Co-editor: Fundamentals of Clinical Pharmacology. Home: 1826 NW 26th Way Gainesville, FL 32601

GARRETT, ETHEL SHIELDS, civic worker; b. Pitts., May 7, 1896; d. Peter and Cora (Lewis) Shields; grad. Miss Spence Sch., N.Y.C., 1915; m. Harry Darlington, Jr., Jan. 31, 1917 (dec. Jan. 1931); children—Harry III, McCullough, Elaine Darlington (Mrs. Andrew Fowler); m. 2d, George Angus Garrett, Apr. 11, 1935. Trustee John F. Kennedy Center Performing Arts, Urban America Inc.; women's com. Nat. Symphony Orch. Assn.; nat. council Met. Opera; mem.-at-large Garden Club Am.; mem. Washington com. ANTA, Nat. Trust Historic Preservation. Episcopalian. Home: 2030 24th St NW Washington, DC 20008.

GARRETT, GEORGE PALMER, Jr., educator, writer; b. Orlando, Fla., June 11, 1929; s. George Palmer and Rosalie (Toomer) G.; grad. Hill Sch., 1947; A.B., Princeton, 1952, M.A., 1956; m. Susan Parrish Jackson, June 14, 1952; children—William, George, Rosalie. Asst. prof. English, Wesleyan U.; writer-in-residence, resident fellow in creative writing Princeton, 1964-65; former asso. prof. U. Va.; prof. English, Hollins Coll. Va., 1967-71, prof. U. S.C., Columbia, 1971—. Recipient Rome prize Am. Acad. Arts and Letters, 1958-59, Sewanee Rev. fellow poetry, 1958-59. Served in occupation of Trieste, Austria and Germany. Ford Found. grantee in drama, 1960; Nat. Found. of Arts grantee, 1966. Fellow Am. Acad. in Rome; mem. Modern Lang. Assn., Author's League. Democrat. Episcopalian. Author: The Reverend Ghost: Poems (Poets of Today IV), 1957; King of the Mountain, 1958; The Sleeping Gypsy and Other Poems, 1958; The Finished Man, 1959; Which Ones Are the Enemy, 1961; Abraham's Knife (poems), 1961; In the Briar Patch, 1961; Sir Slob and the Princess (play), 1962; Cold Ground Was My Bed Last Night, 1964; (screenplay) The Young Lovers, 1964; Do, Lord, Remember Me, 1965; For a Bitter Season, 1967; A Wreath for Garibaldi, 1969; Death of the Fox, 1971. Editor: The Girl in The Black Raincoat, 1966. Home: 3600 Chateau Dr Columbia SC 29204

GARRETT, GEORGE WILLIAM, assn. exec.; b. DuBois, Pa., Mar. 19, 1921; s. George Anthony and Kathryn Rose (Gargin) G.; B.B.A., St. Bonaventure U., 1950; M.B.A., U. Me., 1968; m. Betty Jane Ayers, Apr. 5, 1942; children—Mary Ellen, George Michael. Exec. sec. Salamanco Bd. Trade (N.Y.), 1949-51; mgr. Oswego (N.Y.) C. of C., 1951-53; exec. v.p. C. of C. of The Tonawandas, North Tonawanda, N.Y., 1953-60; exec. v.p. Greater Portland (Me.) C. of C., 1960—; dir. Esco Research Corp., Portland. Dir. Me. chpt. Am. Cancer Soc., 1969-71. Served to 2d lt. USAAF, 1945. Mem. Am. C. of C. Execs. (dir.), New Eng. (pres.), Me. (past pres.) assns. C. of C. execs. Rotarian. Home: 80 Oakhurst Rd Cape Elizabeth ME 04107 Office: 142 Free St Portland ME 04101

GARRETT, HARRISON, investment banker; b. Balt., Apr. 27, 1911; s. Robert and Katharine Barker (Johnson) G.; B.A., Princeton, 1933; m. Grace Dodge Rea, June 20, 1936; children—Robert II, Thomas Harrison, James Rea, Julia. With Bankers Trust Co., N.Y.C., also London, 1933-41; gen. partner Robert Garrett & Sons, Inc., Balt., mems. N.Y. Stock Exchange, 1947—, now chmn. bd.; dir. A.S. Abell Co., Murray Corp., Pharma- Plastics, Inc. Trustee Evergreen House Found., Calvert Sch., Robert Farrett Fund for Surg. Treatment of Children, Inc., Johns Hopkins Hosp., Hosp. for Consumptives of Md., Children's Hospital. Served to lt. col. F.A., AUS, 1941-45. Episcopalian (trustee ch. pension fund N.Y., standing com. Diocese of Md., vestryman). Clubs: Maryland, Merchants (Balt.); Princeton (N.Y.C.); Cap and Gown, Nassau (Princeton). Home: Brooklandville PO Baltimore County MD 21022 Office: Robert Garrett & Sons Inc Baltimore MD 21203

GARRETT, J. EARL, bus. exec.; b. Nephi, Utah, 1907; ed. Brigham Young U. Vice chmn., chief exec. officer, dir. Arden-Mayfair, Inc., Los Angeles, until 1967; organizer, chmn. bd., chief exec. officer Kings Drug Center, Rosemead, Cal., 1967—. Home: 635 Georgian Rd La Canada CA 91011 Office: 8225 Garvey Av Rosemead CA 91770

GARRETT, JAMES BRENSON, coll. dean; b. Centralia, Ill., Apr. 15, 1940; s. Silas Grifton and Thelma (Jackson) G.; B.A., So. Ill. U., 1967; student law, Howard U., 1968-69; m. Helen Elizabeth Scott, Sept. 27, 1969; 1 stepdau., Lisa Marie Morgan. System engr. trainee IBM Corp., Oklahoma City, 1967; acting program dir. CNA, Chgo., 1968; adminstrv. aide Ill. Atty. Gen.'s Office, 1969; dean black students Lake Forest (Ill.) Coll., 1969—; cons. Black Conf. Edn., Waukegan, Ill. Served with USNR, 1958-62. Mem. Black Am. Law Student Assn. (regional dir. Mid-East, chmn. Howard U. chpt.), Afro-Am. Adminstrs. Higher Edn. Home: 241 Washington Rd Lake Forest IL 60045

GARRETT, JAMES W., lawyer; b. Tallassee, Ala., 1913; grad. U. Ala., LL.B., 1940. Admitted to Ala. bar, 1940; now mem. firm Rushton, Stakely, Johnston & Garrett, Montgomery. Fellow Am. Coll. Trial Lawyers; mem. Am., Montgomery County (pres. 1954) bar assns., Ala. State Bar, Internat. Assn. Ins. Counsel, Phi Alpha Delta. Office: Bell Bldg Montgomery AL 36101*

GARRETT, JOHNSON, fgn service officer; b. Balt., Oct. 26, 1912; s. Robert and Katharine Barker (Johnson) G.; student Princeton, 1931-35; m. Margaret Dodge, Aug. 5, 1936. With Safe Deposit & Trust Co., Balt., 1935-41; sta. mgr. Pan Am. World Airways, Damascus, Syria, 1946-48; with Nat. City Bank of N.Y., 1949-60, mgr. Paris br., 1952-60; asst. sec.-gen. for prodn., logistics and infrastructure NATO, Paris, 1960-65; indsl. devel. attaché Am. embassy, Paris, France, 1966—. Bd. govs. Am. Hosp. of Paris. Served from 1st lt. to lt. col., AUS, 1941-45. Clubs: Brook (N.Y.C.); Travellers, American (pres. 1957-59) (Paris); Metropolitan (Washington); Princeton of N.Y. Home: 18 Quai d'Orleans Paris 4, France. Office: Am Embassy 2 Av Gabriel Paris 8 France

GARRETT, PAUL, pub. relations counsel; b. Lincoln, Kan., Nov. 27, 1891; s. Sidney L. and Ida I. (Holcomb) G.; B.S., Whitman Coll., 1913, LL.D., 1947; A.M. (Gilder fellow polit. sci. 1913-14), Columbia, 1914; m. Mrs. Lillian Riggs, July 19, 1939. With Bur. Municipal Research, N.Y.C., 1915, bur. state research N.J. C. of C., 1916-17, War Industries Bd., Washington, 1918-19, Am. Internat. Corp., N.Y.C., 1919-20; financial columnist The Investor, N.Y. Evening Post, 1920-25, financial editor, 1925-31; dir. pub. relations Gen. Motors Corp., 1931-56, v.p., 1940-56; now dir., mem. exec. com. TelePrompter Corp.; dir., chmn. finance com. Nylok Corp.; dir. G.T. Schieldahl Co., Celebrity Register, Ltd., Unimed, Inc.; pub. relations counsel Xerox Corp. Chmn. pub. relations com. Automobile Mfrs. Assn., 1938-48; chmn. bd. Advt. Fedn. Am., 1940-41. Bd. dirs. Nat. Indsl. Conf. Bd., 1947-56, Automotive Safety Found., 1937-46; bd. overseers Whitman Coll. Recipient 1944 Ann. award Nat. Assn. Pub. Relations Counsel; citation extraordinary N.Y. chpt. Pub. Relations Soc. Am., 1957. Mem. Phi Beta Kappa, Phi Delta Theta. Republican. Clubs: Everglades, Bath and Tennis (Palm Beach, Fla.); University (N.Y.C.); Recess, Detroit Athletic; Surf (Miami Beach, Fla.); Nat. Press (Washington); Bel-Air Country (Beverly Hills, Cal.). Author numerous monographs, 1917—, latest being: If I Had Your Chance, 1947; A New Dimension for Public Relations, 1956. Home: 580 Park Av New York City NY 10021 Office: 630 Fifth Av New York City NY 10036 ☆

GARRETT, PEARSON BEVERLY, banker; b. Brenham, Tex., Aug. 22, 1895; s. William Beverly and Elizabeth Overton (Pearson) G.; LL.B., U. Tex., 1915; m. Ruth Evens, 1919; children—Pearson Beverly, Richard Gordon. Admitted to Tex. bar, 1915; partner Garrett & Garrett, 1915-17; partner, Breg, Garrett & Co., investment bankers, 1919-24; owner Garrett & Co., investment bankers 1924-45; pres. Texas Bank & Trust Co. of Dallas, 1945-58, vice chmn. bd., 1958—; dir. Shovel Supply Co. Pres. Assn. of State Chartered Banks Texas, Inc. 1962-63. Served from 1st lt. to capt., Air Service, U. S. Army, 1917-19; AEF. Mem. Am. Bankers Assn. (chmn. econ. edn. com.), Tex. Council on Econ. Edn. (pres.). Home: 3131 Maple Av Dallas, TX 75205. Office: 1 Main Pl Dallas TX 75226

GARRETT, ROBERT AUSTIN, physician, educator; b. Indpls., Jan. 25, 1919; s. John Dempsey and Mary Susan (Pierson) G.; A.B., Miami U., 1940; M.D., Ind. U., 1943; m. Elizabeth Ramge Steiner, Feb. 13, 1946; children—Mary Alice, Robert Austin, Susan Elizabeth, John Dempsey II. Intern Cin. Gen. Hosp., 1943, surg. res., 1944-46; genito-urinary surgery Ind. U. Med. Center, 1947- 48; instr. urology Ind. U. Med. Sch., 1949-50, asst. prof. urology, 1951-52, asso. prof., 1953, prof., chmn. dept., 1954—. Served with AUS, 1946. Diplomate Am. Bd. Urology. Mem. A.M.A., Am. Urologic Assn.,

Mont Reid Surg. Soc., Am. Urologic Assn. North Central Sect., Am. Assn. Genito-Urinary Surgeons, A.C.S., Am. Acad. Pediatrics, Soc. for Pediatric Urology (pres.), Phi Beta Kappa, Alpha Omega Alpha, Omicron Delta Kappa, Sigma Chi. Episcopalian. Club: Meridian Hills. Home: 95 Wellington Rd Indianapolis IN 46260 Office: 1100 W Michigan St Indianapolis IN 46202

GARRETT, ROBERT EDWIN, mfg. exec.; b. Saginaw, Ala., Dec. 13, 1908; s. John Allen and Lena Jane (Naish) G.; student U. Ala., 1926-27; m. Annie Cole Smith, Aug. 8, 1931; children—Robert Michael, Joan Elizabeth. Office boy Sloss-Sheffield Steel & Iron Co., 1929, exec. asst., 1945-52, asst. to pres., 1952; v.p. U.S. Pipe & Foundry Co., Birmingham, Ala., 1952-59, exec. v.p., 1959-60, pres., 1960-70, chmn. bd., 1964—, dir., mem. exec. com., 1954—; dir. Jim Walter Corp., First Nat. Bank of Birmingham, Jefferson Fed. Savs. & Loan Assn., Birmingham. Ordnance Association, Cast Iron Pipe Research Assn., Ala. (dir.), Methodist. Clubs: Vestavia Country, Downtown, Country (Birmingham). Home: 204 Vestavia Circle Birmingham AL 35216 Office: 3300 1st Av N Birmingham AL 35202

GARRETT, ROBERT NORVAL, former coll. adminstr.; b. Kennard, Ind., Feb. 15, 1904; s. Norval Freemont and Grace Opal (Bussear) G.; A.B., Ball State Tchrs. Coll., 1928; M.S., Ind. U., 1934, Ed.D., 1944; m. Dorothy Louise Wilson, June 17, 1930; children—Joy Ellen, Robert Norval. High sch. tchr., Walkerton, Ind., 1928-30; faculty Southeastern La. Coll., Hammond, 1930-70, prof. head dept. bus. adminstrn., 1930-70, dean div. applied scis., 1967-70. Mem. United, So., La. (past pres.), Nat. bus. edn. assns., La. Edn. Assn., Phi Delta Kappa. Methodist. Kiwanian (charter). Author textbook. Home: 511 Sanders Av Hammond LA 70401

GARRETT, ROBERT YOUNG, Jr., banker; b. Balt., May 24, 1903; s. Robert Young and Anne (Hanson) G.; student Am. Inst. Banking; grad. Rutgers U. Grad. Sch. Banking, 1945; m. Margaret S. Ruff, Oct. 24, 1925; 1 son, Robert Young III. With Central Nat. Bank Phila., 1921-35, Farmers Bank and Trust Co., Lancaster, Pa., 1935-63, pres., 1961-63; pres. merged bank Lancaster County Farmers Nat. Bank, 1963-70; vice chmn. Nat. Central Bank, Lancaster, Pa., 1970—; dir. Watt & Shand, Lancaster, Donegal Mut. Ins. Co., Marietta, Pa. Mem. adv. com. banking policies and practices 3d Nat. Bank Region, 1965-68. Treas. Lancaster Gen. Hosp., 1952-; pres. bd. Lancaster br. Pa. Assn. for Blind, 1963—, N. Milton Woods Home for Ret. Presbyn. Ministers of Donegal Presbytery, 1958—; mem. bd. nat. missions Presbyn. Ch. U.S.A., 1955-61. Mem. Pa. Soc., Lancaster C. of C. Presbyn. (elder). Lion (pres. Lancaster 1949-50). Clubs: Lancaster (Pa.) Country, Hamilton, University (Lancaster). Home: Williamson Apts 1111 Wheatland Av Lancaster PA 17603 Office: 23 E King St Lancaster PA 17604

GARRETT, SYLVESTER, arbitrator; b. Elkins Park, Pa., Dec. 15, 1911; s. Sylvester S. and Mary (Thompson) G.; A.B., Swarthmore Coll., 1933; LL.B., U. Pa., 1936; m. Mary Alexander Yard, Aug. 30, 1938; children—Joan Hickcox, James Yard, John Sharpless. Chmn. Regional War Labor Bd., Phila., 1942-45; vice chmn. Nat. Wage Stabilization Bd., Washington, 1946; coordinator labor relations Libbey-Owens-Ford Glass Co., Toledo, and Pittsburgh Plate Glass Co., 1946-49; prof. law Stanford, 1949-51; chmn. bd. arbitration U.S. Steel Co. and United Steelworkers 1951—. Mem. citizens assembly Health and Welfare Assn. Allegheny Co. Mem. National Acad. Arbitrators (gov. 1956-58, pres. 1963, exec. com. 1964-65, chmn. com. on ethics and grievances), Am. Bar Assn. Indsl. Relations Research Assn. (counsel 1953-57), Am. Arbitration Assn. (panel arbitrators), Nat. Planning Assn. (nat. council). Author: (with Dr. L. Reed Tripp), Management Management Problems Implicit in Multi-Employer Bargaining, 1950. Home: Box 158 Stahlston PA 15687 Office: Grant Bldg Pittsburgh PA 15219

GARRETT, WILBUR EUGENE, editor; b. Kansas City, Mo., Sept. 4, 1930; s. Clay Dean and Cecil Zora (Melton) G.; B.J., U. Mo., 1954; m. Lucille Hall, Dec. 26, 1950; children—Michael Dean, Kenneth Lewis. Photographer, Hallmark Greeting Card Co., 1948-50; picture editor, then asst. illustrating editor, asso. illustrating editor, now sr. asst. editor Nat. Geog. Soc., 1954—; mem. faculty photojournalism mag. color workshop U. Mo., 1963, 64, 69, 70; designer photog. exhbn. People-to-People lounge U.S. Pavilion, N.Y. World's Fair, 1965; designer-producer Nat. Geog. Soc. exhbns. 23d, 24th, 25th Picture of Year Competition; contbr. Smithsonian's Nehru Photog. Exhibit. 1965, Smithsonian-Charles Eames's Photography and City Exhibit, 1968; mem. 38th Joint Civilian Orientation Conf.; hon. cons. XIX Olympiad Cultural Com., Mexico City; lectr. univs. Alaska, Boston, Md., Miami, Minn., Mo., N.C., So. Ill.; photog. judge Eastman-Kodak Snapshot Contest, 1965, 25th Ann. Pictures of the Year Competition, 1967. Served with USNR, 1950-52. Recipient Newhouse citation U. Syracuse, 1963; 14 awards Pictures of Year competition, including Mag. Photographer of Year, 1969. Mem. Nat. Press Photographers Assn., White House News Photographers Assn. Clubs: University, Cosmos (Washington). Home: 209 Seneca Rd Herndon VA 22070 Office: Nat Geog Soc 17th and M Sts Washington DC 20036

GARRETT, WILBUR RAY, educator; b. Connersville, Ind., Apr. 10, 1908; s. Ray P. and Maude E. (Silvers) G.; B.S., U. So. Calif., 1932, M.B.A., 1933, M.A., 1934, Ph.D., 1941. Instr. in bus. adminstrn. and econs. Loyola U. of Los Angeles 1935-38, asst. prof., 1938-41, asso. prof., 1941-45, prof. accounting and finance, 1945-67, dean of Coll. Bus. Adminstrn., 1946-66, prof. accounting, 1967—. Mem. Am. Accounting Assn., Phi Beta Kappa, Phi Kappa Phi, Beta Alpha Psi, Beta Gamma Sigma, Order of Artus.

GARRETT, WILLIAM ADELOR, journalist; b. Troy, N.Y., Sept. 23, 1910; s. Joseph Adelor and Delia Rose (Fassett) G.; student Trinity Coll., Hartford, Conn.; m. Calista C. McEnany; children—Evelyn (Mrs. Victor H. Long, Jr.), William J., Mary L. (Mrs. Mark U.P. Zolly), Margaret (Mrs. Verner Hugh King, Jr.). Reporter, New Britain (Conn.) Herald, 1929-35, Hartford Times, 1935-41, 47-49; editor weekly, Bristol, Conn.; asst. pub. relations dir., news mag. writer, editor New Departure div. Gen. Motors, Bristol, 1942-47; Washington corr. Gannett Newspapers, 1949—; broadcast interviewer congl. members. Founder, past pres., sec. Eastern Profl. Basketball League. Mem. bd. edn., Bristol, also justice of peace, mem. Housing Authority. Trustee St. Vincent de Paul Soc. Camp St. Florence. Recipent several citations for journalistic achievement. Mem. Bus. Editors South New Eng. (past pres.), White House Corrs. Assn., Senate and House Press Galleries, Sigma Delta Chi. Roman Catholic. K.C. Clubs: Crocodile (Conn.); Nat. Press (Washington); Bristol Exchange (past pres.), Press (past pres.) (Bristol); Nat. Exchange (past dist. gov.). Author: The Frank Wheaton Story. Co-editor: Passionist mag.; Retreat Forward, 1948-49. Home: 11310 Galt Av Wheaton MD 20902 Office: Nat Press Bldg Washington DC 20004

GARRICK, ISADORE EDWARD, aero research scientist; b. Chgo., Mar. 3, 1910; s. Rubin and Ida (Leavitt) G.; B.S., U. Chgo., 1930; m. Cicely Berlin, Feb. 14, 1937; children—Michael, Linda, Danielle. Physicist aero. research Langley Aero. Lab. NACA, 1930—, chief dynamic loads div., 1949—, chief math. scientist, 1970—, now Langley Research Center, NASA; adj. prof. George Washington U.; Jerome Clarke Hunsaker prof. Mass. Inst. Tech., 1956-57. Mem. applied math. adv. council Nat. Bur. Standards, 1947-50; NASA rep. to div. math. scis. Nat. Acad. Scis.-NRC, 1968—. Recipient Exceptional Service award NASA, 1964. Fellow Am. Inst. Aeros. and Astronautics; mem. Am. Phys. Soc., Soc. for Indsl. and Applied Math. Author numerous sci. papers; contbr. tech. articles profl. publs. Home: 2208 Crescent Dr Hampton VA 23361 Office: Langley Research Center Hampton VA 23365

GARRICK, NATHAN HENRY, Jr., asset mgmt. exec.; b. Boston, Mar. 18, 1920; s. Nathan Henry and Rose (Devaney) G.; B.S., Harvard, 1942; m. Velda M. Poeton, July 20, 1942; 1 dau., Patience. With Quincy Savs. Bank (Mass.), 1946-47; Boston Safe Deposit and Trust Co., 1947—, exec. v.p., 1966—, also dir., mem. exec. com.; with Boston Co., 1964—, exec. v.p., 1967—, also dir., mem. exec. com.; dir. Douglas T. Johnston Co., Inc., Johnston Mut. Fund. Rinfret-Boston Assos., Inc.; trustee Eastern Utilities Assos. Mem. corp. Boston Soc. Natural History; mem. vis. com. Harvard Med. Sch. and Sch. Dental Medicine. Served to capt. AUS, 1942-46. Mem. Boston C. of C., Bank Officers Assn., Boston Soc. Security Analysts, Newcomen Soc. Mason. Clubs: Harvard (Boston and N.Y.C.); Cohasset (Mass.) Golf: Union (Boston). Home: 21 Deep Run Cohasset MA 02025 Office: 1 Boston Pl Boston MA 02106 Office: 100 Franklin St Boston, MA 02106

GARRIGUE, JEAN, poet; b. Evansville, Ind., Dec. 8, 1914; s. Allan Colfax and Gertude Louise (Heath) G.; B.A., U. Chgo., 1937; M.A., U. Ia., 1943. Free-lance writer and editor, 1938—; intermittent instr. U. Ia., Bard Coll., Queens Coll., New Sch., U. Colo., U. Conn.; lectr. poetry Smith Coll., 1965-66. Rockefeller fellow, 1954; Hudson River fellow poetry, 1957; Guggenheim fellow, 1960; recipient grant in lit. Nat. Acad. Arts and Letters, 1952; Radcliffe Inst. fellowship, 1967-68. Mem. P.E.N. Democrat. Author: Thirty-Six Peoms and a Few Songs (in Five Young American Poets), 1944; The Ego and the Centaur, 1947; The Monument Rose, 1953; A Water Walk by Villa d'Este, 1959; Country Without Maps, 1964; New and Selected Poems, 1967.; also short stories, essays, revs. Address: 4 Jones St New York City, NY 10014

GARRIGUS, WESLEY PATTERSON, educator; b. Storrs, Conn., June 16, 1909; s. Harry Lucian and Bertha May (Patterson) G.; B.S., U. Conn., 1931; M.S., U. Ill., 1933, Ph.D., 1935; m. Helen Peabody Robbins, Aug. 18, 1933; children—Robert Robbins, Elizabeth Ann, James Patterson. Grad. asst. animal husbandry dept. U. Ill., 1931-36; agronomist U.S. Dept. Agr., 1936-37; instr. U. Ky., Lexington, 1937-39, asst. prof. animal husbandry, 1939-40, 1939-40, asso. prof., 1940-41, prof., 1941—, chmn. animal industry group, 1941-61; asso. dir. Ky. Agr. Exptl. Sta., 1951-62, chmn. dept. animal scis., 1966—. Mem. Am. Soc. Animal Prodn. (pres. 1959), Sigma Xi, Gamma Sigma Delta, Phi Kappa Phi, Alpha Gamma Rho, Lambda Gamma Delta, Omicron Delta Kappa, Alpha Zeta. Presbyn. (elder). Clubs: Rotary Internat., Black and Bridle. Author: Introductory Animal Science, 1951; also expt. sta. bulls., articles profl. jours. Home: 227 Shady Lane Lexington KY 40503

GARRISON, CHARLES WILLIAM, Jr., mcht.; b. Garnett, Kan., May 27, 1909; s. Charles W. and Myrtle (Dye) G.; B.S., U. Kan., 1930; M.B.A., U. Pa., 1931; m. Rosemary Haas, Aug. 27, 1931; children—Hillary, Charls W. III. Mgmt. positions Macy Corp., 1931-47; v.p., dir. Lasalle & Koch, Toledo, 1947-59; sr. v.p., dir. Bamberger's, Newark, 1959—. Co-chmn. Bus. and Indsl. Coordinating Council, Newark, 1963-65; trustee N.J. Community Action Tng. Inst., 1959; bd. dirs. Essex (N.J.) chpt. A.R.C., 1968—, YM-YWCA of Newark and vicinity; exec. com., trustee United Community Corp., Newark, 1964-71. Served as 1st lt. USNR, World War II. Mason (Shriner), Rotarian. Clubs: Morris County Golf (Convent Station, N.J.); Down Town (Newark). Home: 45 West Rd Short Hills NJ 07078 Office: 131 Market St Newark NJ 07101

GARRISON, CLAYTON, univ. dean; b. Independence, Kan., Dec. 27, 1921; s. Emery and Blanche (Cook) G.; B.A., U. So. Cal., 1947; Ph.D., Stanford, 1956; m. Lillian Gleason, June 20, 1947; children—Jacqueline, Michele, Mark, Suzanne. Prof. drama Palos Verdes Coll., 1949-58, Cal. State Coll. at Long Beach, 1955-60; chmn. drama dept. U. Cal. at Riverside, 1960-64; dean Sch. Fine Arts, U. Cal. at Irvine, 1964—, dir. plays, musicals, operas, 1966—. Cons. Nat. Found. Arts and Humanities, 1966—, Arts and Humanities Inst., 1967—. Chmn. bd. Laguna Beach Chamber Music Soc.; bd. dirs. Laguna Beach Sch. Arts and Design, Council Arts Orange County Coastal Area. Served with USAAF, 1943-46. Mem. Internat. Council Fine Arts Deans, Shakespeare Assn. Am., Am. Ednl. Theatre Assn., Am. Soc. Theatre Research. Contbr. profl. jours. Home: 554 Diamond St Laguna Beach, CA 92651. Office: Sch Fine Arts Univ Cal Irvine CA 92664

GARRISON, GARNET R., educator, TV producer; b. Warrick County, Ind., Dec. 30, 1911; s. Ray V. and Girtha M. (Billups) G.; A.B., Wayne U., 1933; A.M., U. Mich., 1936; m. Isabelle M. Schelbe, Sept. 22, 1934; 1 dau., Patricia. Announcer, dir. radio stas., Detroit, Lansing, Mich., 1931-36; instr. speech, dir. radio Wayne U., 1936-42, asst. prof., 1942; prodn. dir. NBC, N.Y.C., 1942-47; lectr. Columbia, 1945-47; lectr. speech U. Mich., 1947-58, asso. prof., 1948-50, prof., dir. TV, 1950—, dir. broadcasting, 1958—. Mem. Am. Assn. U. Profs., Radio Dirs. Guild N.Y., Speech Assn. Am. (exec. council 1950-53), Pi Kappa Delta, Delta Sigma Rho, Phi Delta Kappa. Co-author: Radio and Television, 1950, rev. 1956, 63, 71; Television and Radio. Home: 1201 Arborview Blvd Ann Arbor MI 48103

GARRISON, GEORGE NELVIN, educator; b. Walhonding, O., Sept. 11, 1905; s. Frank Orlin and Gladys Adeline (Young) G.; B.S., Denison U., 1927; M.A., Ohio State U., 1929; Ph.D. in Math., Princeton, 1939; m. Mildred Louise Koch, Aug. 25, 1934; 1 dau., Helen Marguerite. Instr. math. Case Inst. Tech., 1929-31; tchr. DeWitt Clinton High Sch., N.Y.C., 1934-47; mem. faculty City Coll. N.Y., 1937-46, 48-64, prof. math., 1957-64, chmn. dept., 1952-64; asso. dir. grad. summer sch., lectr. math. Wesleyan U., Middletown, Conn., 1964—; asst. prof., then asso. prof. math. Lehigh U., 1946-48. Mem. Am. Math. Soc., Math. Assn. Am., Phi Beta Kappa, Sigma Xi. Home: 174 Lincoln St Middletown CT 06457

GARRISON, GUY GRADY, librarian; b. Akron, O., Dec. 17, 1927; s. Grady and Emma (Dodson) G.; B.A., Baldwin-Wallace Coll., 1950; M.S., Columbia, 1954; Ph.D., U. Ill., 1960; m. Joanne Ruth Sergeant, Mar. 22, 1964; 1 dau., Anne Olivia. Mem. staff Oak Park (Ill.) Pub. Library, 1954-58; head reader services Kansas City (Mo.) Pub. Library, 1960-62; prof., dir. library research center Grad. Sch. Library Sci., U. Ill., 1962-68; prof., dean Grad. Sch. Library Sci., Drexel U., 1968—. Served with AUS, 1950-52. Mem. A.L.A., Am. Soc. Information Sci., Assn. Am. Library Schs., Beta Phi Mu. Contbr. articles profl. jours. Home: 2280 N 52d St Philadelphia PA 19131

GARRISON, HARRELL EDMOND, former coll. pres.; b. Hugo, Okla., Nov. 4, 1908; s. James Henry and Cynthia (Adams) G.; A.B., Bethany-Peniel Coll., 1932; M.S., Northwestern U., 1936; Ph.D., Geroge Peabody Coll., 1949; m. Virginia Clarice Taylor, Mar. 5, 1933; children—Linda Clarice, Sandra Sue. Tchr. pub. schs., Swink, Ft. Towson and Durant, Okla., 1932-45; diagnostician child study George Peabody Coll., 1945-48; dir. Demonstration Sch., North Tex. Tchrs. Tchrs. Tchrs. Coll., 1949, U. Okla., 1950-51; pres. Northeastern State Coll., Tahlequah, Okla., 1951-70, pres. emeritus, 1970—. Past exec. com. Okla. Congress P.T.A. Mem. Nat., Okla. edn. assns., Am. Assn. U. Profs., Phi Delta Kappa, Kappa Delta Pi. Kiwanian (past dist. lt. gov.). Co-author: Phonetic Keys to Reading. Home: Riverview Farm Rt 3 Tahlequah OK 74464

GARRISON, JIM, lawyer; b. Dennison, Ia., Nov. 20, 1921; s. Earling R. and Jane Ann (Robinson) G.; LL.B., Tulane U., 1949, LL.M., 1951; m. Leah Elizabeth Ziegler, Sept. 20, 1957; children—Jim, Virginia, Lyon, Elizabeth Eberhard. Admitted to La. bar, 1949, since practiced in New Orleans; mem. firm Deutsch, Kerrigan & Stiles, 1952-54; asst. dist. atty. City of New Orleans, 1954-58, dist. atty. Orleans Parish, 1962—; individual practice law, 1958-62. Served with F.A., AUS, 1941-46; ETO. Decorated Air medal. Democrat. Home: 4600 Owens Blvd New Orleans LA 70122 Office: Criminal Cts Bldg Tulane and Broad Sts New Orleans LA 70119

GARRISON, JOHN DORSEY, lawyer; b. N.Y.C., Aug. 12, 1909; s. Elsiha Ely and Helen (Hotchkiss) G.; grad. Taft Sch., 1927; B.A., Yale, 1931, LL.B., 1934; m. Edith Hooe, Apr. 2, 1932; children—Jean (Mrs. Charles O. Thompson), John Dorsey, Admitted to N.Y. bar, 1936; with firm Lord, Day & Lord, N.Y.C., 1934—, mem., 1943—. Dir. Crane Co., 1961—, Research Corp., 1962—, Served to lt. USMCR, 1944-45. Mem. Internat. Am., N.Y. bar assns., Assn. Bar City N.Y., Maritime Law Assn., Am. Judicature Soc., Marine Corps Res. Officers Assn., Wolfshead Soc. Clubs: Down Town Assn., Yale, Links (N.Y.C.); Round Hill (Greenwich, Conn.); Mid Ocean (Bermuda). Home: 555 Park Av New York City NY 10021 Office: 25 Broadway New York City NY 10004

GARRISON, LEMUEL ALONZO, ednl. adminstr.; b. Pella, Ia., Oct. 1, 1903; s. Lemuel Addison and Mary Canyon, Aria., 1970—; asst. supt. Glacier and Grand Canyon nat. Canyon, Ariz., 1970—; asst. supt. Glacier and Grand Canyon nat. (Firth) G.; A.B., Stanford, 1926; m. Inger Wilhelmine Larsen, Mar. 21, 1930; children—Lars A., Erik (dec.), Mary Karen (Mrs. Eldon Reyer). Sch. tchr., also with U.S. Forest Service, Alaska, 1929-31; seasonal ranger, ranger Sequoia and Yosemite Nat. Park, 1932-39; supt. Hopewell Village Nat. Historic Site, 1939-41; asst. chief information Nat. Park Service, Washington, 1941-42, chief conservation and protection, 1955-56, regional dir. Midwest region, Omaha, 1964-66, Northeast region, Phila., 1966-70; dir. Horace M. Albright Tng. Acad., Grand Canyon, Ariz., 1970—; asst. supt. Glacier and Grand Canyon nat. parks, 1942-53; supt. Big Bend Nat. Park, 1953-55, Yellowstone Nat. Park, 1955-63; free lance writer, 1935—; adj. prof. Tex. A. and M. U. Chmn. steering com. Nat. Park Service Mission 66 study, devel. program, Washington, 1955-56; del. Vatican-Italian Govt. Conf. on Spiritual Values in Tourism, 1967; spl. park study, site of ancient Olympic Games, Govt. of Greece, 1969. Recipient Distinguished Service award Dept. Interior, 1962; Pugsley award (gold), 1969. Mem. Soc. Am. Foresters, Nat. Recreation and Park Assn., Nat. Conf. on State Parks (1st v.p.), Western History Assn., Internat. Union Conservation Nature, Wilderness Soc., Izaak Walton League, Sierra Club, Ducks Unlimited, Trout Unlimited, Dude Ranchers, Nat. Geog. Soc., Outdoor Writers Am. Mason (32, Shriner), Rotarian. Home: Box 487 Grand Canyon AZ 86023 Office: Horace M Albright Training Acad Box 477 Grand Canyon AZ 86023 Nat Park Service Northeast Region 143 S 3d St Philadelpia, PA

GARRISON, LLOYD KIRKHAM, lawyer; b. N.Y.C., Nov. 19, 1897; s. Lloyd McKim and Alice (Kirkham) G.; A.B., Harvard, 1919, LL.G., 1922; LL.D., Lawrence Coll., 1942, U. Wis., 1964, Howard U., 1970; m. Ellen Jay, June 22, 1921; children—Clarinda Kirkham, Ellen Shaw, Lloyd McKim. Admitted to N.Y. bar, 1923, began practice in N.Y.C.; with Root, Clark, Buckner and Howland, 1922-26, Parker & Garrison, 1926-32; dean U. Wis. Law Sch. and prof. law, 1932-45; gen. counsel, exec. dir. Nat. War Labor Bd., 1942-43; pub. mem., 1944, chmn. 1945; mem. Paul Weiss, Rifkind, Wharton & Garrison, 1946—. Chmn., NLRB, 1934; mem. Pres.'s Commn. on Labor Relations in Great Britain and Sweden, 1938; Assn., 1947-; labor adv. com. AEC, 1946-48; legal adv. com. NSRB, 1948- co-author with Solicitor Gen. Thacher of report to the president on the Bankruptcy Act and its adminstrn. in U.S. cts., 1931; (1931), (with Willard Hurst) The Legal Profession; referee Nat. R.R. Adjustment Bd., intermittently, 1936-64; mem. Internat. Bd. Arbit. of Am. Newspaper Pubs. Assn. and Internat. Printing Pressmen and Assistant Union N.A., 1940-50; mem. arbitration bd. under agreement between TVA and Tenn Valley Trades and Labor vice chmn. Nat. com. Am. Civil Liberties Union, 1937-67; treas. Nat. Urban League, 1926-32, pres., 1947-52, dir., 1947—; exec. com. Nat. Lawyers Com. on Civil Rights, 1965—. Mem. Bd. Edn., N.Y.C., 1961-68, pres., 1965-67. Bd. dirs. Field Found., 1950—; trustee Inst. for Advanced Study, 1952—; trustee trustee Sarah Lawrence Coll., 1946-60, chmn., 1956-60; trustee, treas. New York City NY 10021 Potomac Inst., 1953—; trustee, v.p. Taconic Found., 1953—. Served in USN, 1917-19. Mem. Assn. Bar City N.Y. (exec. com., 1952-55). Democrat (mem. N.Y. state com. 1951-57, N.Y. county com. 1951-61). Home: 116 E 66th St New York City NY 10021 Office: 345 Park Av New York City NY 10022 575 Madison Av New York City 33, NY

GARRISON, LLOYD LEE, educator; b. Shelby County, Mo., Mar. 24, 1920; s. Homer Austin and Ona Lee (Harland) G.; B.S., State Tchrs. Coll., Kirksville, Mo., 1940; M.Ed., U. Mo., 1942, Ed.D., 1951; m. Irene Joy Nelson, June 16, 1946; 1 dau., Jill Kay. Tchr. bus. high schs., Brashear and Shelbina, Mo., 1940-41, 46-47; mem. staff Mo. Valley Coll., Marshall, 1947-49, chmn. div. econs. and bus. adminstrn., 1948-49; mem. faculty Okla. State U., Stillwater, 1951—, prof. bus. edn., 1960—, asso. dean Coll. Bus., 1962-66, head dept. adminstrv. services and bus. edn., 1966—. Vis. prof. U. Colo., U. Denver, U. N.M., Kan. State Coll. cons. Okla. Com. Improvement Instrn. Bus. Edn., 1960-62; curriculum coordinator econ. edn. workshops. Recipient Outstanding Tchr. award Okla. State U. Coll. Bus., 1961, Univ. Outstanding Service award, 1963. Mem. Nat. (exec. bd. 1963-66, treas. 1964-66), Mountain-Plains (exec. bd. 1953-56, 1959-65, pres. 1967-68), Okla. (pres. 1955-56) bus. edn. assns., Am. Accounting Assn., Phi Kappa Phi, Delta Pi Epsilon, Phi Delta Kappa, Lion. Co-author: A Teacher's Guide to Economics in the Business Education Curriculum, 1963. Author articles, chpts. in books. Gen. services editor Bus. Edn. Forum, 1960-61. Home: 2010 W 3d Stillwater OK 74074

GARRISON, LLOYD MCKIM, journalist; b. N.Y.C., May 26, 1931; s. Lloyd Kirkham and Ellen (Jav) G.; grad. Milton Acad., 1950; student Am. U. Beirut (Lebanon), 1950-51; B.A., Harvard, 1954; m. Sarah Crocker, June 18, 1960; children—John Lloyd, Benjamin Hallowell. Newswriter, NBC News, N.Y.C., 1954; editor Nightbeat, Dumont TV Network, N.Y.C., 1956-57; writer NBC-TV spl. projects, N.Y.C., 1957-58; mng. editor Radio Press Internat., N.Y.C., 1958-60; free-lance writer, Africa, 1960; asso. editor Newsweek mag., 1960-61; staff corr. N.Y. Times, N.Y.C., Washington, UN, also Leopoldville and Lagos, Africa, 1961-64, sr. corr. for Africa, Lagos, 1964—; editorial adviser Crossroads Africa, 1960. Served with AUS, 1954- 56. Mem. Episcopal Soc. Cultural and Racial Unity. Democrat. Clubs:

Owl (Harvard); Overseas Press (N.Y.C.). Contbr. nat. mags. Home: 5 Maduike St Lagos Nigeria Office: New York Times New York City NY 10036

GARRISON, MORTIMER, Jr., educator; b. Bridgeton, N.J., Nov. 5, 1920; s. Mortimer Garrison and Emma (Pepper) G.; A.B., Washington Coll., Chestertown, Md., 1942; M.A., Columbia, 1947, Ph.D., 1948; m. Jean Wood, Feb. 3, 1945; children—Penelope J. (Mrs. Joseph J. Haber, Jr.), Jeffrey Wood, Janice Denne, Christopher Pepper. Chief psychologist The Tng. Sch., Vineland, N.J., 1954-57; research cons. U.S. Children's Bur., 1957-59; research dir. Woods Schs., Langhorne, Pa., 1959-67; prof. ednl. psychology Temple U., 1967—, chmn. dept. spl. edn., 1970—; cons. U.S. Children's Bur., also President's Com. Mental Retardation, 1964-68. Mem. adv. bd. Phila. Mental Health and Mental Retardation, 1969—. Mem. Bucks County Library Bd., 1965-66. Served with USNR, 1942-46. Mem. Am., Eastern, Pa. psychol. assns., Am. Assn. Mental Deficiency (past chmn. mid-eastern region; councillor 1965-67), Soc. Research Child Devel., Sigma Xi. Contbr. profl. jours. Home: 551 Lenape Circle Langhorne PA 19047 Office: Coll Edn Temple Univ Philadelphia PA 19122

GARRISON, OLEN BRANFORD, scientist, educator, b. Columbia S.C., May 31, 1910; s. Thomas Branford and Fairey Belle (Birt) G.; B.S., Clemson Coll., 1933; M.S., La. State U., 1934; Ph.D., Cornell U., 1939; m. Dorothy McKissock, Jan. 27, 1939; children—Doralynn Elizabeth, Margaret Ann, Jean Faye. Grad. asst. La. State U., 1933-34, teaching asst., 1934-35; asst. to dean of agr. Clemson Coll., 1935-36; asst. horticulturist Edisto Expt. Sta., Blackville, S.C., 1939-42; asso. prof. horticulture and asso. horticulturist Clemson Agrl. Coll., 1943-49, prof. and horticulturist, 1949-53, dir. S.C. Agr. Expt. Sta., 1953—. Mem. adv. bd. YMCA. Mem. S.C. Tech. Action Panel, Com. on Agr.; sec. agr. com. Am.-German Coop. Agrl. Research. Served from lt. to maj., AUS, 1942-45. Decorated Am. Soc. Hort. Sci., S.C. Acad. Sci., S.C. Agrl. Com., S.C. Seedsmen's Assn. (adv. com.), S.C. Plant Food Ednl. Soc. (adv. com.), Clemson Fellowship, Blue Key, Sigma Xi, Alpha Zeta, Gamma Sigma Delta. Rotarian. Contbr. to profl. jours. Home: 111 Folger St Clemson SC 29631

GARRISON, WALTER R., engring. exec.; b. St. Louis, July 7, 1926; s. Walter Raymond and Esther (Kohlhepp) G.; student Washburn U., 1944-46; B.S., U. Kan., 1948, M.S., 1950; m. Rose Faye Wilson, Aug. 10, 1946; children—Bruce Robert, Susan Kay, Mark Raymond, Pamela Ann, Charles Jeffrey. Instr. U. Kan., 1948-50; structures engr. Boeing Airplane Co., Seattle, 1950-53; pres., dir. Pa. Inst. Tech., Upper Darby, 1953—; staff engr. Comprehensive Designers, Inc., Phila., 1956-58, v.p., dir., 1958-61, pres., chmn. bd., 1961—; pres., chmn. bd. Comprehensive Designers Internat. Ltd., London, Aerospace Research Labs., Washington, Deltec Corp.; chmn. bd. dirs. Sass Widders Corp. (Cal.), V.I.P. Engring. Co., Inc. (Cal.), Unispace Engring. Corp. (Cal.); dir. Islelease Equipment Co., Ltd. (London), Tampa Bay Engring. Co. (Fla.), Kennedy House, Modern Engring. Co. (Mich.), Laminated Materials Corp., Comp Data Services Corp., Computer Professions, Inc. (Washington), Lincoln & Lee (Mass.), PMI Corp. (Cal.), M & T Co., Stubbs, Overbeck & Assos., Inc. (Tex.). Mem. State Bd. Pvt. Schs., 1965-71. Served with USNR, 1944-46. Registered profl. engr., Pa. Mem. Nat. Tech. Services Assn. (pres. 1968-69, dir. 1966-70), Pa. Soc. Profl. Engrs., Young Pres.'s Orgn., Phila. Engrs. Club, Sigma Tau, Tau Beta Phi. Home: 501 Gainesboro Rd Drexel Hill PA 19026 Office: 5 Penn Center Plaza Philadelphia PA 19103

GARRISON, WELDON STRONG, hotel exec.; b. Lansing, Mich., Apr. 8, 1924; s. Ross W. and Anna (Sabrosky) G.; B.A., Mich. State U., 1946, M.A., 1960; m. Audrey Howard, Dec. 29, 1953; children—Beth, Julie, Linda. Mgr., Kellogg Center, Mich. State U., 1948-56; gen. mgr. Shawnee Inn, Shawnee-on-Delaware, Pa., 1956-60; v.p. gen. mgr. Cavalier Hotel, Virginia Beach, Va., 1960-62; hotel mgr. Sheraton Corp., 1962-, gen. mgr. Sheraton-Elms, Excelsior Springs, Mo., 1962-64, Sheraton-Kingston, Jamacia, 1964-66, Sheraton-Okla., Oklahoma City, 1966—; lectr. U. N.H., Pa. State U., Okla. State U. Mem. Hotel Sales Mgmt. Assn. (chmn. Speakers Bur.). Am., Okla. (pres.) Oklahoma City (pres.) hotel and motel assns., Okla. C. of C. Kiwanian. Club: Twin Hills Golf and Country (Oklahoma City). Home: 228 W Sheridan St Oklahoma City, OK 73101

GARRISON, WILLIAM CARL, former state ofcl.; b. Alfalfa County, Okla., Jan. 8, 1910; s. William and Mary (Lasswell) G.; B.A., U. Okla., 1932; grad. Arty. Sch., 1941, Army War Coll., 1953, Command and Gen Staff Coll., 1947, Armed Forces Staff Coll., 1947; m. Jessie L. Dunham, June 4, 1933; children—Sharon (Mrs. Thomas L. Lias), Mary Nell (Mrs. Francis J. Stewart), Linda Carol (Mrs. William D. Clifford). Commd. 2d lt. Okla. N.G., 1935, capt. U.S. Army, 1946, advanced through grades to maj. gen., 1963; instr. Arty. Sch., 1942-43; comdr. arty. bn., then arty. group, also asst. corps arty. officer 3d Army, Europe, 1944-45; mem. faculty Engrs. Sch., 1946-48; personnel officer U.S. Army, Caribbean, 1948-52; assigned gen. staff Dept. Army, also mil. asst. to undersec. army, 1953-57; adviser V Korean Corps, 1958; comdr. 2d Missile Command, 1959-60; dep. G-3, Continental Army Command, 1960-61; comdg. gen. 24th Div. Arty., also VII Corps Arty., Europe, 1961-63, X U.S. Corps, 1964-65; dep. insp. gen. Dept. Army, 1965-66; insp. gen., 1966-68; fed.-state coordinator Oklahoma Governor's Office Oklahoma City, 1968-70. Mem. Am. Battle Monuments Commn., 1969—. Decorated Legion of Merit, Bronze Star with V device and cluster, Army Commendation medal with cluster, D.S.M.; Croix de Guerre with palm (France); War for Fatherland medal (Russia). Home: 3117 NW 61st Terrace Oklahoma City, OK 73112

GARRITY, DEVIN ADAIR, editor, publisher; b. S.I., N.Y., Nov. 26, 1905; s. Henry and Cecil (Engleheart) G.; B.S., Princeton, 1928; m. Joan Tucker Holt, Sept. 26, 1936; children—Page, Sheila, Adair, Norah, Devin Adair, Joan. With Farmers Loan & Trust Co., N.Y.C., 1928-31, R.H. Macy Co., N.Y.C., 1931- 34; with Devin Adair Co., N.Y.C., 1935—, v.p., 1937, pres., 1939—. Bd. govs. Nature Conservancy, Washington, 1955-66, Natural Food Assos. of Tex.; panelist Answers for Americans, Station WOR-radio-TV, 1953-56; v.p. Ind. Citizens Research Found., N.Y.C. Mem. 101st Cav., N.Y. N.G., 1930-42. Mem. Linaean Soc. N.Y., Ex-Mems. Squadron A. Clubs: Dutch Treat, University, Explorers (N.Y.C.); Manursing Island (Rye). Editor: New Irish Poets, 1948; 44 Irish Short Stories, 1955; The Irish Genius, 1958; Mentor Book of Irish Poetry, 1965. Home: 682 Forest Av Rye NY 10580 Office: 1 Park Av Old Greenwich CT 06870

GARRITY, W. ARTHUR, Jr., dist. judge; b. Worcester, Mass., June 20, 1920; s. W. Arthur and Mary B. (Kennedy) G.; A.B., Holy Cross Coll., 1941; LL.B., Harvard, 1946; m. Barbara A. Mullins, May 24, 1952; children—W. Arthur III, Charles, Anne, Jean. Admitted to Mass. bar, 1946; asst. U.S. atty. for Mass., 1948-50; U.S. atty. for Mass., 1961-66; judge U.S. Dist. Ct. for Mass., 1966—. Home: 40 Radcliffe Rd Wellesley MA 02181 Office: Office US Dist Court for Mass Boston MA 02108

GARROU, ALBERT FRANCIS, textile co. exec.; b. Praly, Italy, July 22, 1893; s. John and Marie (Pons) G.; student pub. schs., N.C.; m. Louise Victoria Holloway, June 22, 1918 (dec. Nov. 1955); children—Alba Louse (Mrs. J.G. Johnson), Leith Holloway, Jane Gardner (Mrs. Eddie Lane), Mary Frances (Mrs. Parks Sherrill), Louis William, Albert Francis; m. 2d, Hilda Yoder, Nov. 3, 1956. Mgr., Waldensian Hosiery Mills, Valdese, N.C., 1928-48; chmn. bd. Alba-Waldensian, Inc., 1962—; chmn. bd. dirs. Valdese Mfg. Co., 1956—; dir. Morgantown br. Wachovia Bank & Trust Co., N.A., Colonial Theaters, Valdese Savs. & Loan Co. Trustee, Grace Hosp., Morganton, Valdese Gen. Hosp. Served with U.S. Army, 1917-19. Mem. Newcomen Soc. Presbyn. Mason (Shriner, Jester). Club: Lenoir (N.C.) Country. Address: PO Box 9 Valdese NC 28690

GARROU, LOUIS WILLIAM, textile co. exec.; b. Morganton, N.C., Apr. 6, 1920: s. Albert F. and Louise (Holloway) G.; grad. Darlington Sch., Rome, Ga., 1937; student Davidson Coll., 1937-39, Lenoir Rhyne Coll., Hickory, N.C., 1939-40, U. N.C., 1959-60; m. Dora Elizabeth Bowles, Sept. 16, 1939; children—John L.W., Elizabeth Louise, Albert Leith. With Waldensian Hosiery Mills, Inc., Valdese, N.C., 1947-62, exec. v.p., 1957-62; exec. v.p. Alba Hosiery Mills, Inc., Valdese, 1959-62; pres. Alba-Waldensian, Valdese, N.C., 1962—, bd. Redesco, S.A., Paris, France, 1966—. Bd. dirs. Valdese Gen. Hosp., 1958—; trustee Lees-McRae Coll., Banner Alk, N.C. Served with AUS, 1943-45. Mem. Nat. Assn. Hosiery Mfrs. (bd. dirs.). Presbyn. Rotarian (pres. Valdese 1951-52). Home: 405 Louise Rd Valdese, NC 28690. Office: 408 Armaud St Valdese NC 28690

GARROWAY, DAVE, TV personality; b. Schenectady. Emcee Dave Garroway Show, NBC radio network, 1947-49, TV program Garroway at Large, 1949-51, Pontiac TV Show, 1953-54; narrator Wide Wide World, 1955-59; segment on NBC (radio) Monitor; star Dave Garroway Today Show, NBC-TV Network, 1952-61; star Exploring the Universe, Nat. Ednl. TV, 1961-62, Garroway AM and PM, CBS, 1964-65; star Tempo-Boston TV Show, 1969—; asso. with USIA, 1961. Bd. dirs. Fed. Union. Served as ensign USNR, 1942-45. Mem. Nat. Acad. Television Arts and Scis. (gov. 1968). Office: care Al Bruno Assos 9777 Wilshire Blvd Beverly Hills CA 90012 care Al Bruno Assos 9777 Wilshire Blvd Beverly Hills CA 90012 90028

GARRY, CHARLES L., bank exec. Auditor, Am. Nat. Bank & Trust Co. Chgo. Office: LaSalle St at Washington St Chicago IL 60690*

GARSIDE, BETTIS ALSTON, educator, relief exec.; b. Stringtown, Okla., Nov. 22, 1894; s. Joseph and Sarah Emeline (Alston) G.; A.B., U. Okla., 1913; student Kennedy Sch. Missions, 1916-17, N. China Union Lang. Sch., 1922-23; M.A., Columbia, 1922; L.H.D., Coll. Ozarks, 1935; m. Margaret Helen Cameron, Sept. 10, 1921; 1 dau., Jean Alston (Mrs. Irving V.E. Barth, Jr.). Prin. high sch., Pittsburg, Okla., 1913-16. Stringtown, 1920-21; tchr. high sch., Jersey City, 1922; missionary to China, Presbyn. Bd. U.S.A., 1922- 26; middle sch. tchr., Weihsien, China, 1923; asso. prof. edn. Cheeloo U., Tsinan, China, 1923-26; sec. China Union Univs. Central Office, N.Y.C., 1927-32; exec. sec. Asso. Bds. Christian Colls. China, N.Y.C., 1932-41; exec. dir. United China Relief, Inc., N.Y.C., 1941-42, v.p., sec., 1942-45; exec. v.p., sec. United Services to China, Inc., N.Y.C., 1946-67; dir., 1950-67; exec. dir. Am. Bur. Med. Aid to China, N.Y.C., 1950-68, exec. dir. for adminstrn. and promotion, 1968—; exec. dir. Aid Refugee Chinese Intellectuals, Inc., 1952- 70, Free China Fund, 1954-60; exec. vice chmn. Am. Emergency Com. Tibetan Refugees, 1959-70; dir. Tibetan Found., 1970—. Vice chmn. Am. Com. Non Participation in Janapese Aggression, 1938-41; treas. com. One Million Against Admission of Communist China to UN, 1962-70; treas. Am.- Asian Ednl. Exchange, 1957—. Served as seaman to warrant officer U.S. Navy, 1917- 19. Decorated Order of Auspicious Star (China). Mem. Phi Gamma Delta. Mem. Riverside Ch. Mason. Club: Tiffin (pres. 1942-43), (Shanghai). Author: One Increasing Purpose, the Life of Henry Winters Luce, 1948; articles, stories ednl. jours. Home: 635 Riverside Dr New York City NY 10031 Office: 1790 Broadway New York City NY 10019

GARSIDE, LEONARD JAMES, univ. dean; b. Stringtown, Okla., Jan. 23, 1922; s. Alex H. and Maudie (Thompson) G.; B.S., U. Okla., 1949, M.S., 1950; Ph.D., U. Wis., 1959; m. Klella Gabbart, Mar. 6, 1943; children—Virginia (Mrs. Charles Davis), Leonard James, Robert Earl. Tchr. sci., math. U. Okla. Campus Sch., Norman, 1949-50; supr. sci., math. Wis. State Coll., Platteville, 1950- 56, chmn. edn., psychology dept., 1959-63, dean Grad. Sch., 1964—; research asso. physics project U. Wis., Madison, 1957-59. Vis. prof. U. Hawaii, summer 1960; mem. Platteville High Sch. Parents Council, 1965; mem. Wis. Sci. Curriculum Com., 1966. Served with M.C., AUS, 1940- 45; ETO. Named Tchr. of Year, Wis. State U., 1965. Mem. N.E.A., Wis. Edn. Assn., Phi Eta Sigma, Phi Delta Kappa, Kappa Delta Pi. Kiwanian. Home: 200 Preston Dr Platteville WI 53818

GARSON, BARBARA, playwright satirist, b. 1942; ed. U. Ca.; married. Author: (play) MacBird, 1966, performed at Village Gate, N.Y.C., 1967. Address: c/o Grove Press Inc 80 University Pl New York City, NY 10003

GARSON, GREER, actress; b. County Down, Ireland; d. George and Nina (Greer) Garson; student London U.; B.A. cum laude, Grenoble U.; hon. doctorate Rollins Coll.; m. 3d, E.E. Fogelson. Stage plays include Golden Arrow, Vintage Wine, Accent on Youth, Butterfly on the Wheel, Page from a Diary, The Visitor, Mademoiselle, Twelfth Night, School for Scandal, Auntie Mame, Captain Brassbound's Conversion. Motion pictures include Goodbye, Mr. Chips, Remember, Pride and Prejudice, Blossoms in the Dust, When Ladies Meet, Mrs. Miniver, Random Harvest, Madame Curie, Mrs. Parkington, Adventure, That Forsyte Woman, The Miniver Story, The Law and the Lady, Scandal at Scourie, Strange Lady in Town. Her Twelve Men, Sunrise at Campobello, The Singing Nun. Chmn. N.M. state campaign Tb, Cancer Assns. Life gov. Women's Hosp., Melbourne, Australia; bd. dirs. Dallas Symphony Orch., Dallas Theater Center; bd. trustees Dallas Fine Arts Mus. Recipient Acad. award for performance in Mrs. Miniver, 1943; in Julius Caesar, 1953. Home: 680 Stone Canyon Los Angeles CA 90024 and 3525 Turtle Creek Dallas TX 75219 also Forked Lightening Ranch Pecos NM 87552 Office: Republic Bank Bldg Dallas TX 75201

GARSON, H. NEIL, govt. ofcl.; b. Romania, Dec. 2, 1921; s. Harry and Milly (Zeichick) G.; A.B., U. Ga., 1947; J.D., Georgetown U., 1949; m. Helen Sylvia Perlman, May 26, 1944; children—Wendy Carlin, Eliot Bruce, Lisa Jill. Asso. gen. counsel ICC, 1962-65, sec., 1965—; instr. law Am. U. Law Sch. Pres. Georgetown Village Civic Assn., 1952-54. Served with AUS, World War II; lt. col. Res. Mem. Am., Va., Fed. (chmn. council transp. law 1960—, mem. nat. council) bar assns., Phi Beta Kappa. Contbr. articles. Office: Interstate Commerce Commn 12th and Constitution Av Washington DC 20423 Office: Interstate Commerce Commn 12th and Consitution Av Washington, DC 20423

GARST, DELMOND, union ofcl. Dir. Region 15 Dept. Orgn. AFL-CIO. Office: 1215 Paul Brown Bldg 818 Olive St St Louis MO 63101*

GARST, JONATHAN, agrl. cons., author; b. Rockford, Ill., Dec. 4, 1893; s. Edward and Bertha (Goodwin) G.; student Ia. State U. Sci. and Tech., 1911-12; B.S., U. Wis., 1915; student U. Edinburgh (Scotland), 1919, Ph.D. in Geography, Geography, 1930; postgrad. U. 1930; postgrad. U. Grenoble (France), 1936; m. Aida Gilchriste, Feb. 19, 1926 (dec. 1959); 1 son, Perry; m. 2d, Gertrude Flint Jones, Nov. 23, 1960 (dec. Feb. 1969). engaged in farming, Coon Rapids, Ia., 1915- 17, Man., Can., 1919-23; with E.G. Clark Seed Co., Salinas, Cal., 1926- 27; tchr. geography U. Cal. at Los Angeles, 1927-29; with Macauley Inst. Soil Sci. and Scottish Dept. Agr., 1930-33; consumers counsel Dept. Agr., Washington, 1934, regional dir. FSA, 1935, regional dir. Surplus Marketing Adminstrn., 1938-40; with WPB, Alaska, 1940, Office Coordinator Inter-Am. Affairs, N.E. Brazil, 1941; raised, processed hybrid seed corn, Sacramento Valley, 1942-60; cons. disposal surplus Army ammonia plants to fertilizer companies, Washington, 1947; spl. asst. to sec. agr. to expand fertilizer prodn., 1951; adviser to fertilizer industires, Rumania, USSR, Poland, 1960, U.S. Food for Peace Program, Brazil, 1961; with Fgn. Agrl. Service, Dept. Agr. in Caribbean and Central Am., 1962; cons. establishment fertilizer factories, Iran, Pakistan and India, 1964. Served with inf. U.S. Army, 1917-19; AEF; France. Author: No Need for Hunger, 1964. Patentee mech. beet topper. Address: 5017 Swingle Dr Davis CA 95616

GARSTECKI, JOHN MICHAEL, hosp. adminstr.; b. Green Bay, Wis., Nov. 8, 1923; s. Michael John and Mary (Faltynski) G.; B.Ed., Whitewater (Wis.) State U., 1945; postgrad. U. Wis., 1948, 60, 62-63; grad. Inst. Hosp. Adminstrs., Am. Coll. Hosp. Adminstrs., 1955; m. Phyllis Ann Plucker, June 5, 1948; children—Linda Louise, Juel Marie, Michael John, David James, Paul Thomas. Dir. comml. edn. Rochester (Wis.) High Sch., 1945- 50; asst. supt. So. Wis. Colony and Tng. Sch., Union Grove, 1951- 55, supt., 1956—, mem. 20 Year Club, 1970—. Guest lectr. U. Wis., 1953, Marquette U. Med. Sch., 1956; participant London (Eng.) Conf. Sci. Aspects Mental Deficiency, 1960; mem. task force commn., adv. bd., also bd. dirs. field mental health and mental retardation. Pres. Racine-Kenosha (Wis.) Tchrs. Coll. P.T.A., 1960-63, Union Grove (Wis.) High Sch. P.T.A., 1966-68; chmn. adv. com. vocational edn. Union Grove High Sch., 1965-68. Bd. dirs. Racine County Assn. Retarded Children, 1968-69. Recipient Distinguished Service award Whitewater State U., 1970. Fellow Am. Assn. Mental Deficiency; mem. Nat., Wis. assns. retarded children, United Assn. Retarded Children, Children, Union Grove C. of C. (sec. 1956-58). Contbr. profl. jours. Address: So Wisconsin Colony and Tng Sch Union Grove, WI 53182.

GART, MURRAY JOSEPH, journalist; b. Boston, Nov. 9, 1924; s. John and Frieda (Fisher) G.; B.A. in Econs., Northeastern U., 1949; m. Jeanne Brooks, Feb. 26, 1950; children—Mitchell Brooks, Marcia Anne. Reporter, Honolulu Star-Bull., 1949-50; editor Weekly Ind. Record, Cape May County (N.J.), 1950-51; reporter, ciy editor Wichita Beacon, 1951-53; reporter, news editor Wichita Eagle, 1953-55; bur. chief Time-Life mag. News Service, Toronto, Can., 1955-57, Boston, 1957-59, chief Midwest corr. Time mag., 1959-61, bur. chief, Chgo., 1961-64, London, 1964-66; asst. mng. editor Fortune mag., N.Y.C., 1966-69; chief Time-Life News Service, 1969—. Served with AUS, 1943-46. Club: The Garrick (London). Home: 180 E 79th St New York City NY 10021 Office: Time and Life Bldg Rockefeller Center New York City NY 10020

GARTENHAUS, SOLOMON, educator, physicist; b. Kassel, Germany, Jan. 3, 1929; s. Leopolt and Hanna (Brandler) G.; came to U.S., 1937, naturalized, 1943; B.S., U. Pa., 1951; M.S., U. Ill., 1953, Ph.D., 1955; m. Johanna Lore Weisz, Aug. 30, 1953; children—Michael M., Kevin M. Instr., Stanford, 1955-58; faculty physics Purdue U., Lafayette, Ind., 1958—, prof., 1963—. Cons. Lockheed, summers 1958-60; officer, dir. Advanced Research Corp., 1961-65. Fellow Am. Phys. Soc.; mem. Am. Assn. Physics Tchrs., Phi Beta Kappa, Sigma Xi. Author: Elements of Plasma Physics, 1964; also articles. Theoretical research in nuclear physics, plasma physics, many-particle systems, nuclear interactions based on meson fields and condensation phenomena at low temperatures. Home: 444 Littleton St West Lafayette IN 47906 Office: Dept Physics Purdue U Lafayette IN 47907

GARTHOFF, RAYMOND LEONARD, fgn. service officer; b. Cairo, Egypt, Mar. 26, 1929; s. Arnold Alexander and Margaret Louise (Frank) G.; A.B., Princeton, 1948; M.A., Yale, 1949, Ph.D., 1951; m. Vera Alexandrovna Vasilieva, Sept. 16, 1950; 1 son, Alexander Raymond. Research specialist Soviet Affairs Rand Corp., Washington, 1950-57; fgn. affairs adviser Dept. Army, 1957-61; spl. asst. Soviet bloc politico-mil. affairs Dept. of State, 1961-68; counselor for polit.-mil. affairs U.S. Mission NATO, Brussels, Belgium, 1968—; escort officer with Vice Pres. Nixon, USSR, Poland, 1959; escort interpreter with chmn. McCone, USSR, 1959; mem. U.S. delegations to 18 Nation Disarmament Conf., Geneva, Switzerland, 1962, 64, NATO Ministerial Conf., Athens, Greece. 1962; professorial lectr. polit. sci. Inst. Sino-Soviet Studies, Geo., Washington U., 1962- 64; lectr. U.S. Nat., Army and Air War colls., Foreign Service Inst., National Defense Coll. (Can.), Sch. for Advanced Internat. Studies, Johns Hopkins, 1964-67. Mem. Council Foreign Relations Am. Mil. Inst., Am. Assn. Advancement Slavic Studies, Inst. Strategic Studies (London). Clubs: Princeton, Yale (Washington). Milford Yacht. Author: Soviet Military Doctrine, 1953; Soviet Strategy in the Nuclear Age, 1958; Soviet Military Policy, 1966; Sino-Soviet Military Relations, 1966. Co-author; Transformation of Russian Society, 1861-1961, 1962; Russian Foreign Policy, 1963; Communism and Revolution, 1964; Sino-Soviet Military Relations, 1966; others. Translator, editor: Science and Tech. in Contemporary War, 1959; Soviet Military Strategy, 1963. Contbr. profl. publs., Ency. Britannica. Home: 256 Av Baron D'Huart Crainhem Belgium Av Milford CT 06460 also 2128 Bancroft Pl NW Washington DC 20008 55 Governor's Av Milford CT 06460 Office: USNATO Brussels Belgium

GARTLEY, HAROLD MCKINLEY, pub. relations exec.; b. Newark, Jan. 19, 1899; s. William Henry and Violet (Sendell) G.; M.B.A., N.Y.U., 1920; m. Jeanette Kaye, Aug. 1, 1952. Propr., H.M. Gartley, Inc., 1934-42; with Gartley and Mathieu, Inc. (formerly Gartley & Assos. Inc., N.Y.C., 1942—). now chmn. bd.; dir. Nat. Securities & Research Corp. Served with U.S. Army, 1917-20. Mem. Pub. Relations Soc. Am. (past nat. treas.). N.Y. Soc. Security Analysts, Lawyers Club. Republican. Mason. Author: Profits in The Stock Market, 1934. Home: 192 Evergreen Rd Menlo Park, NJ 08837. Office: 84 William St New York City NY 10038

GARTNER, ARTHUR EDWARD. utility exec.; b. Jersey City, May 10, 1910; s. Edward George and Edith (Tayler) G.; B.C.S. cum laude, N.Y.U., 1935, student Grad. Sch. Bus. Adminstrn., 1940; m. Elise Catherine Rehrer, June 15, 1940; children—Arthur Edward, Richard, James, Lynn Ann. Accountant Standard Oil Co. (N.J.). 1927-43; with Consol. Natural Gas Co., N.Y.C, 1943—, chief accountant, 1947-51, asst. treas., 1951-56, controller, 1956—. Mem. Am. Gas Assn., Am. Mgmt. Assn., Controllers Inst. Am. Club: Economic (N.Y.). Home: 71 Pine St Garden City NY 11530 Office: 30 Rockefeller Plaza New York City NY 10020

GARTNER, BERTIL EDGAR, educator, clergyman; b. Gothenburg, Sweden, Dec. 13, 1924; s. Edgar D. and Karin (Bolander) G.; theol. lic., Uppsala (Sweden) U., 1951, theol. dr., 1955; m. Margit H. E. Hultin, Aug. 13, 1949; children—S. Christer, Martin E., Jonas B., Elisabeth M. Came to U.S., 1965. Ordained to minister Ch. of Sweden, 1948; student pastor Uppsala U., 1951-52, docent, 1955; asst.

prof. N.T., 1961, asst. prof. O.T., 1964; prof. Princeton Theol. Sem., 1965—. Asso. univ. seminar studies N.T., Columbia, 1965. Served with Swedish Army, 1944-45. Mem. Nathan Soederblom Soc., Am. Soc. Study Religion. Home: 31 Alexander St Princeton NJ 08540

GARTNER, MURRAY, lawyer; b. N.Y.C., Sept. 23, 1922; s. Leo and Celia (Orner) G.; A.B., N.Y. U., 1942; LL.B., Harvard, 1945; m. Anne Ellis Thompson, June 9, 1961; children—Marion Moreau, Thomas Murry. Admitted to N.Y. bar, 1946, Cal. bar, 1948; law clk. U.S. Supreme Ct. Justice Robert H. Jackson, 1945-47; asso. firm Pillsbury, Madison & Sutro, San Francisco, 1947-51; lectr. law Hastings Coll. Law, San Francisco, 1948; asst. to gen. counsel, U.S. rep. in Paris, ECA-Mut. Security Adminstrn., 1951-53; asso. firm Roosevelt, Freidin & Littauer, N.Y.C., 1953-59; partner firm Poletti, Freidin, Prashker, Feldman & Gartner, and predecessors, N.Y.C., 1959—. Trustee Children's Aid Soc. Home: 520 E 86th St New York City NY 10028 Office: 777 3d Av New York City NY 10017

GARVAN, ANTHONY NICHOLAS BRADY, educator, curator; b. Raquette Lake, N.Y., Oct. 4, 1917; s. Francis P. and Mabel (Brady) G.; grad. Hotckiss Sch., 1935; B.A., Yale, 1939. M.A., 1932. Ph.D., 1948; m. Jane M. Nicodemus; children—Mary Jane, Kathleen Anne, Virginia Brady, Frances Courtney, Anthony Nicholas Brady, Nicohola, Christine, Margaret Blacke. Chief Yale br. research and analysis div. OSS, 1943-44; instr., then asst. prof. history Bard Coll., 1946-49; fellow Am. civilization U. Pa., 1950-51, asst. prof., then asso. prof. Am. civilization, 1951-60, prof. chmn. dept., 1960—; lectr. Henry F. duPont Winterthur Mus., 1953-57; head curator civil history Smithsonian Instn., 1957-60, curator growth of U.S. exhbn. hall, 1957—. Mem. Montgomery Co. Democratic Com., 1955-57. Bd. dirs. Library Co. of Phila. Served with USNR, 1944-46. Rockefeller fellow, 1949- 50; Guggenheim fellow, 1954-55. Mem. Soc. Archtl. Historians (medal 1951, dir. 1960—). Roman Catholic. Clubs: Cricket, Aviation (Phila.); Meadowbrook (L.I.). Author: Architecture and Town Planning in Colonial Connecticut 1951; Index of Americian Cultures, 1953—; also articles. Editor: Am. Quar., 1951-57. Home: Penllyn Pike Spring House PA 19477 Office: Dept of Am Civilization Univ of Pa Philadelphia PA 19104

GARVER, CHAUNCEY BREWSTER, lawyer; b. N.Y.C., Apr. 4, 1886; s. John A. and Rebecca (Brewster) G.; grad. Phillips Acad., Andover, Mass., 1904; A.B., Yale, 1908; LL.B., Harvard, 1911; m. Alice Pine, June 27, 1917; children—Edith P. (Mrs. F. Y. Larkin), Allison (Mrs. H.A. Caesar II); m. 2d, Virginia Rook, May 7, 1938; children—Joan B., Maud D. (Mrs. Donald Greer), John A. Admitted to N.Y. bar, 1911, since practiced in N.Y.C.; asso. Sherman & Sterling, 1911-17, partner, 1917—; dir. Stora Kopparberg Corp., N.Y.C. Mayor of Village of Oyster Bay Cove, 1948-59. Bd. dirs. Legal Aid Society of N.Y.; bd. trustees Miriam Osborn Meml. Home, Harrison, N.Y.; hon. trustee, St. Luke's Hosp., N.Y.C. Served as 2d lt., Signal Corps, U.S. Army, 1917-19. Mem. Am., N.Y. State bar assns., Assn. Bar City N.Y. (treas. 1944-52). Clubs: Century Assn., University, Down Town Assn. (N.Y.C.); Capital Hill (Washington). Home: Sandy Hill Rd Oyster Bay NY 11771 Office: 20 Exchange Pl New York City NY 10005

GARVER, GEORGE P., former utilities co. exec.; b. Topeka, Kan., Nov. 30, 1905; s. Robert D. and Charlotte (Parkhurst) G.; B.A., U. Kan., 1926; LL.B., U. Mich., 1928; m. Sue Wright, June 24, 1931 (dec.); 1 son, Robert; m. 2d, L. Catherine Barrett, Apr. 22, 1967. Admitted to Mo. bar, 1928; atty. legal dept. Nat. Gas Pipeline Co. Am., 1931-45, sec.-treas., 1946-49, v.p., sec.- treas. 1949-57, pres., 1957-69; vice chmn. Peoples Gas Co. and Natural Gas Pipeline Co. of Am., 1969-70; dir. Peoples Gas Light & Coke Co., Peoples Gas Co. Mem. Chgo. Com. Served as lt. USNR, 1942-45. Mem. Am. Gas Assn., Ill. C. of C., Chgo. Assn. Commerce and Industry, Tex. Mid-Continent Oil and Gas Assn., Ind. Natural Gas Assn. Am., Phi Kappa Psi, Phi Delta Phi. Clubs: Economic, Athletic, Chicago (Chgo.). Home: 1300 Lake Shore Dr Chicago, IL 60610

GARVER, HOWARD MARLYN, mfg. co. exec.; b. Decatur, Ill., June 14, 1910; s. William Sherman and Alice G. (Schultz) G.; A.B., Murray (Ky.) State Coll, 1933; grad. student U. Ill., 1942-43; m. Mary Eloise Gann, Aug. 19, 1935. Sales mgr. Continental Coffee Co., Chgo. and Washington, 1935-40; labor relations mgr. Minn. Mining & Mfg. Co., Chgo., 1942-45; asst. gen. mgr. Dryden Rubber Co., Chgo., 1945-57; asst. gen. mgr. indsl. products div. Gen. Tire & Rubber Co., Wabash, Ind., 1957-64, v.p., 1964-69; cons. Nixon Newspapers, Inc., Wabash, 1970—; dir. Thrush & Co., Peru, Ind. Instr., Ind. U., Ft. Wayne. Pres. Wabash Valley Music Assn., 1963—; dist. rep. Gov. Ind. Commn. Arts, 1964-68; commr. Pub. Housing Authority, Wabash. Recipient Distinguished Citizen award, Wabash. Mem. Wabash C. of C., Ind. Mfrs. Assn., Welfare Adv. Bd., Indiana Soc. Chgo. Presbyn. Kiwanian. Club: Wabash Country (pres. 1964—). Home: 110 Highland Dr Wabash IN 46992 Office: 313 S Wabash St Wabash IN 46992

GARVERICK, LOWELL BENNETT, lawyer; b. Mt. Gilead, O., Jan. 3, 1932; s. Bennett H. and Henrietta (McPeek) G.; B.S., Ohio State U., 1953, J.D., 1959; m. Dolores M. Logsdon, Sept. 16, 1961; children—Debra, Dawn, Grant. Admitted to Ohio bar, 1959; practice in Columbus, 1959-65, Galion, 1966—; asst. atty. gen. State of Ohio, Columbus, 1959-62; atty. legal dept. Grange Mut. Casualty Co., 1962-66; atty. Petri, Hottenroth & Garverick, 1966—. Served to 1st lt. USAF, 1954-56. Mem. Ohio, Crawford County (pres.) bar assns., Phi Delta Phi. Home: 500 S State Circle Galion OH 44833 Office: 125 N Columbus St Galion OH 44833

GARVEY, RICHARD CONRAD, newspaper editor; b. Northampton, Mass., May 23, 1932; s. Michael Edward and Lucy (Bradford) G.; student U. Mass., 1941-42; m. Anne Elizabeth Vanasse, May 18, 1957; children—Philip Michael, John Bradford, Mary Agnes, Margaret Anne. Reporter, Daily Hampshire Gazette, Northampton, 1943-44; reporter Springfield (Mass.) Daily News, 1944-51, asst. mng. editor, 1951-66, mng. editor, 1966-69, editor, 1969—; corporator Springfield Instn. for Savs., 1967—, trustee, 1970—; dir. Springfield Area Devel. Corp. Pres. Our Lady of Providence Childrens Center; bd. dirs. Springfield Goodwill Industries; trustee Springfield Coll., Mercy Hosp., Wesson Womens Hosp. Mem. Am., New Eng. (v.p. 1970—, past bd. govs.) socs. newspaper editors, Am. Cath. Hist. Soc., Am. Soc. Ch. History. Home: 90 Macomber Av Springfield MA 01119 Office: 1860 Main St Springfield MA 01101

GARVEY, ROBERT ROBEY, Jr., orgn. adminstr.; b. Elkin, N.C., Feb. 16, 1921; s. Robert Robey and Rose Edna (Brown) G.; student Davidson Coll., 1938-41; m. Nancy Douglas Maclay, June 15, 1945; children—Robert Michael, Jean Maclay, Lee Beasley, William Sinclair. Gen. mgr. Dennis, Inc., Winston-Salem, N.C., 1945-54; exec. dir. Old Salem, Inc., Winston-Salem, 1955-60, Nat. Trust for Historic Preservation, Washington, 1960-67; exec. sec. Adv. Council on Historic Preservation, Dept. Interior, 1967—; asst. sec. Nat. Park Found., 1968—; Nat. Park Service liaison officer Am. Revolution Bicentennial Commn., 1968- -. Mem. internat. com. Nat. Assn. Housing and Redevel. Ofcls., 1963—; v.p. Internat. Council of Monuments and Sites; cons. on cultural property UNESCO; mem. council arts and scis. George Washington U. Served to maj. USMCR., 1942-45. Decorated D.F.C. Club: Old Capital (hon. life) (Monterey, Cal.). Address: 1722 S Arlington Ridge Rd Arlington VA 22202

GARVEY, WILLIAM D., educator, psychologist; b. Richmond, Va., Jan. 17, 1923; s. John Wycliff and Birdie (Bigue) G.; B.A., U. Richmond, 1947; M.A., U. Va., 1949, Ph.D., 1951; m. Catherine Jane Jones, Dec. 31, 1957; 1 dau., Stephanie Kate. Head engring. psychology research sect. Naval Research Lab., 1951- 61; dir. communication project Am. Psychol. Assn., Washington, 1961-66; prof. psychology, dir. Center Research Sci. Communication, Johns Hopkins, Balt., 1966—. Served with USNR, 1943-46. Fellow Am. Psychol. Assn.; mem. Sigma Xi. Reserach in flow of sci. information. Home: 6031 Hollins Av Baltimore, MD 21210.

GARVIN, CLIFTON CANTER, Jr., chem. co. exec.; b. Portsmouth, Va., Dec. 22, 1921; s. Clifton Cnater and Esther (Ames) G.; B.S. in Chem. Engring., Va. Poly. Inst., 1943, M.S., 1947; m. Themla E. Volland, Mar. 15, 1943; children—James C., Carol Ann, Sandra Louise, Patricia Lynn. With Esso Standard Oil Co., Baton Rouge, 1947-59; with Humble Oil & Refining Co., 1960-64, v.p. central region, 1963-64; exec. asst. to pres. Standard Oil Co. (N.J.), 1964-65, v.p., 1968, exec. v.p., 1968—, also dir.; pres. Enjay Chem. Co., N.Y.C., 1965, Esso Chem. Co. Inc., N.Y.C., 1965-68. Mem. Am. Chem. Soc., Am. Inst. Chem. Engrs., Am. Petroleum Inst., Mfg. Chemists Assn. Methodist. Home: 34 Byfield Lane Greenwich CT 06830 Office: 30 Rockefeller Plaza New York City NY 10020

GARVIN, GEORGE KINNE, broker; b. Monroe, N.Y., July 28, 1897; s. George Kinne and Ella (Conkling) G.; student N.Y.U.; m. Ruth Miller Mitchell, June 26, 1950; children—Margaret Ella (Mrs. John K. Clarke, Jr.), George Kinne, Muriel Alice (Mrs. Harold G. Williams, Jr.). Partner Farber, Garvin & Co., mems. N.Y. Stock Exchange, 1922-31, Garvin, Bantel & Co., mems. N.Y. and other stock exchanges, 1931—. Served with Am. Field Service, World War I. Office: 120 Broadway New York City NY 10005

GARVIN, JOHN SAMUEL, Neurologist, educator; b. Windsor, Ill., Feb. 23, 1921; s. Bruce and Ora (Stivers) G.; A.B., U. Ill., 1942, B.S., 1943, M.D., 1944; m. Elizabeth Harding Stone, Apr. 7, 1951; children-Mary Grigsby, Bruce Peters, Elizabeth Randall. Intern, Ill. Research and Ednl. Hosps., 1944-45; resident neurology Ill. Neuropsychiatric Inst., 1945-46, research electroencephalographer, 1948-49; asst. in neurology U. Ill., 1945-46, instr. neurology, 1951-53, asst. prof., 1953-58, clin. asso. prof. neurology, 1958-62, prof., 1962—; clin. clk, in neurology Nat. Hosp. for Nervous and Mental Diseases. Queen's Sq., London, 1949- 50; dir. electroencephalography Presbyn.-St. Lukes Hosp., 1954-64, sr. attending neurologist, 1962—; sr. attending neurologist U. Ill. Hosps., 1962—; cons. neurologist Sherman Hosp., 1962—; cons. neurologist Sherman Hosp., Elgin, Ill., 1959—, Mercy Hosp., 1966—, St. Francis Hosp., Evanston, Ill., 1966—. Served to capt., M.C., AUS, 1946-48

GARVIN, LUCIUS, ednl. adminstr.; b. Cumberland, R.I., Feb. 2, 1908; s. Lucius Fayette Clark and Sarah Emma (Tomlinson) G.; A.B., Brown U., 1928, A.M., 1929, Ph.D., 1933; m. Evelyn Eaton Walmsley, June 8, 1933; 1 son, Eliot Wayne. Instr. philosophy Ind., U., 1933-35, Oberlin Coll., 1935-38, asst. prof., 1939-46, asso. prof., 1946-84, prof., 1948-52; prof. and head dept. philosophy U. Md., 1952-61; dean Macalester Coll., St. Paul, 1961-65, v.p. for acad. affairs, 1965- 66, exec. v.p., provost, 1966—. Mem. Am. Philos. Assn., Am. Soc. for Aesthetics, Phi Beta Kappa, Sigma Phi Sigma. Author: A Modern Introduction to Ethics, 1953; The Free Man in a Free Society, 1959. Contbr. articles to Jour. Philosophy, Analysis, Philosophy and Phenomenological Research, Philos. Review Ethics, also contbr. discussions and revs. Address: Macalester Coll St Paul, MN 55105

GARWOOD, JOHN DELVERT, coll. dean; b. Carroll, Neb., Mar. 20, 1915; s. Harvey and Forrest (Hill) G.; A.B., Wayne (Nev.) State Coll., 1936; Ph.M., U. Wis., 1940; postgrad. U. La., 1940-41, U. So. Cal., 1947; Ph.D. in Econs., U. Colo., 1951; m. Kathleen Marie Schnoor, Aug. 6, 1943; children—Jan Dierks, Shelley Hill. Supt. schs., Lindsay, Neb., 1936-38; teaching fellow U. La., 1940-41, U. Colo., 1949-51; instr. Moringside Coll., Sioux City, 1941- 42; prof. econs. Ft. Hays (Kan.) State Coll., 1947- 49, 51-62, dean faculty, 1962—. Mem. exec. com. Kan. Council Econ. Edn., 1961—, Danforth Asso., 1957—. Served with AUS, 1942-46. Mem. N.E.A., Kan. Tchrs. Assn. (pres. elect), Am. Econ. Assn., Hays C. of C., Phi Kappa Phi, Sigma Phi Sigma, Pi Gamma Mu, Phi Delta Kappa, Lambda Delta Lambda, Kappa Mu Epsilon. Lutheran (pres.). Rotarian. Contbr. articles profl. jours. Home: 332 W 24th St Hays KS 67601

GARWOOD, VICTOR PAUL, educator; b. Detroit, Sept. 13, 1917; s. Paul J. and Helen (Garwood) Schultz; B.A., U. Mich., 1939, M.S., 1948, Ph.D., 1952; m. Dorothy Ann Olson, Mar. 13, 1942; children—Don P., Martha Hill. Teaching fellow, head exam. div. Speech-Hearing Clinic, U. Mich., 1946-50; instr., asst. prof., asso. prof., prof. dept. speech U. So. Cal., Los Angeles, 1950-67, prof., chmn. grad. program in communication disorders, 1967—; cons. audiology Childrens Hosp., Los Angeles, Los Angeles County-U. So. Cal. Med. Center, Providence Speech and Hearing Clinic; cons. audiology and speech pathology Med. Services div. Dept. Health Care Services, State of Cal., 1970—. Mem. profl. adv. com. on speech and hearing Welfare Planning Council Los Angeles, 1966-68. Postdoctoral fellow NIH, 1957-58, Spl. Research fellow NIH, 1960-63. Fellow Am. Speech and Hearing Assn.; mem. Am., Western psychol. assns., Psychonomic Soc., Acoustical Soc. Am., Am. Pub. Health Assn., Cal. Speech and Hearing Assn., Am. Assn. U. Profs., Sigma. Xi. Contbr. articles profl. jours. Home: 1240 Chautauqua Blvd Pacific Palisades CA 90272 Office: 734 W Adams Blvd Los Angeles CA 90007

GARWOOD, WILMER ST. JOHN, lawyer; b. Bastrop, Tex., Dec. 15, 1896; s. Hiram M. and Hettie (Page) G.; A.B., Georgetown U., 1917; postgrad. U. Tex., 1919; LL.B., Harvard, 1922; m. Ellen Clayton, July 11, 1927; children—Wilmer St. John, William Lockhart. Admitted to Tex. bar, 1919, N.Y. bar, 1923; atty. legal dept. Texas Co., N.Y.C., 1922-23, Baker, Boots, Parker & Garwood, Houston, 1924-28; resident Am. counsel Standard Oil Co. (N.J.), Buenos Aires, 1929-33; mem. law firm Andrews, Kelley, Kurth & Campbell, Houston, 1934- 41; pvt. practice, Houston, 1945-47; vice chmn. Houston Civil Service Commn., 1945-46; apptd. to Supreme Ct. of Tex., 1948, asso. justice, 1948-58; counsel law firm Graves, Dougherty & Gee, Austin, 1958—. Prof. law U. Tex., 1961. Dir. Austin Nat. Bank, Houston Prodn. Co. Mem. U.S. delegation to Atlantic Congress, London, 1959; pres. Tex. Civil Jud. Council. A founder St. John's Sch., Houston, 1945; trustee Houston- Tillotson Coll., Austin, U. Tex. Law Sch. Found., Tex. League Women Voters Edn. Fund. Served as 1st lt. Cav., Tex. N.G., 1918-23; from lt. to lt. comdr., naval intelligence USNR, 1942-45. Decorated Orden al Merito (Chile); hon. consul Poland for Tex., 1937-39. Fellow Am. Bar Found. Mem. Am., Inter-Am. bar assns., Am. Law Inst., Austin C. of C., Philos. Soc. Tex. (pres. 1960), English Speaking Union U.S. (nat. dir.), Am. Soc. Internat. Law, Am. Judicature Soc. (dir. 1963-68), Fed. Union (dir.), Order of Coif, Phi Delta Phi. Democrat. Episcopalian (vestryman). Clubs: Headliners, Austin Country, 40 Acres, Westwood Country, Kiwanis (Austin); Bayou (Houston). Home: 1802 San Gabriel St Austin TX 78701 Office: Austin Nat Bank Bldg Austin TX 78701

GARY, FRANK B., lawyer; b. Abbeville, S.C., Sept. 29, 1900; s. Frank Boyd and Marie Lee (Evans) G.; B.S., U.S. Naval Acad., 1922; LL.B., U. S.C., 1928; m. Patricia Thompson, Mar. 17, 1945; 1 son, Frank Boyd III. Admitted to S.C. bar, 1928; practice in Spartanburg, 1928-29, Columbia, 1929-33; with Gen. Chem. Co., N.Y.C., 1934-36; practice in Columbia, 1936-41; mem. firm Cooper, Gary, Nexsen & Pruet, and predecessor, Columbia, 1946- -. Dir. Cosmos Broadcasting Co., Am. Sentinel Life Ins. Co.; mem. S.C. adv. bd. Westinghouse Electric Corp. Pres. Columbia Town Theatre, 1949-59, Columbia United Fund, 1955; chmn. Columbia Red Feather drive, 1947; mem. Gov. S.C. Com. Higher Edn., 1955- 56, 61-62, S.C. Commn. Higher Edn., 1962-63; chmn. Mayor Columbia Finance Adv. Com., 1960-62. Alternate del. Democratic Nat. Conv., 1956. Served to capt. USNR, 1941-46. Decorated Navy Commendation ribbon; chevalier Legion of Honor, Croix de Guerre (France); Order of Phoenix (Greece). Mem. Am. (ho. dels. 1954-60, state del. 1965—, chmn. com. mil. justice 1959-60, chmn. standing com. lawyers and legal service in def. establishment 1961-62, 64-68), S. C. (chmn. exec. com. 1952-53, pres. 1963-64), Richland County (pres. 1950-51) bar assns., Am. Law Inst., Fedn. Ins. Counsel, Am. Bar Found., Am. Coll. Probate Counsel, Assn. Bar City N.Y. Episcopalina (past vestryman). Clubs: Forest Lake, Pine Tree Hunt, Palmetto (Columbia); Army-Navy (Washington); Farmington Country (Charlottesville, Va.). Home: 1 Lake Point Columbia, SC 29206. Office: Security Fed Bldg Columbia SC 29201

GARY, J. VAUGHAN, former congressman; b. Richmond, Va., Feb. 25, 1892; s. T. Jack and Mary Harris (Vaughan) G.; B.A., U. Richmond, 1912, LL.B., 1915, LL.D., 1954; m. Eunice Croswell, Nov. 23, 1918; children—Carolyn (Mrs. Laurence V. Hugo), J. Vaughan. Tchr. Blackstone (Va.) Acad. for Boys, 1912-13; asst. counsel Va. Tax Bd., 1916-18, sec. Nat. Agrl. Adv. Com., Washington, 1918; claims examiner Va. Indsl. Commn., Jan.-July 1919; exec. sec. Nat. Com. on Inheritance Taxation, 1925-26; mem. Va. House of Dels. (rep. City of Richmond), 1926-33; mem. 79th-88th Congresses, from 3d Va. Dist. Served in U.S. Army World War I. Pres. Richmond Stadium. Dir. State Dem. Speakers Bur. Presidential Compaigns, 1936, 1944; Va. Democratic presidential elector, 1968. Mem. Va. World War II History Commn.; chmn. Va. Post-war Employment Com., 1943-45, War Bond Com., 1941-43. Bd. dirs. Va. Coop. Ednl. Assn.; bd. trustees U. Richmond, Fork Union Mil. Acad.; chmn. mayor's com. Richmond Juvenile and Domestic Relations Ct., 1943. Recipient Distinguished Service award U.S. Treasury Dept., 1964. Mem. Va. State of C. of C. (pres. 1944-45), Va. Tb Assn. (pres. 1938-40), Am., Richmond (pres. 1941), Va. (chmn. exec. com. 1941-42) bar assns., Am. Legion, Phi Beta Kappa, Sigma Phi Epsilon, Delta Theta Phi, Omicron Delta Kappa. Democrat. Baptist. Mason (33, Shriner). Home: 18 Maxwell Rd Richmond VA 23226 Office: 10 S 10th St Richmond VA 23219

GARY, JAMES HUBERT, chem. engr., educator; b. Victoria, Va., Nov. 18, 1921; s. James Edward and Jessie (DuPriest) G.; B.S., Va. Poly. Inst., 1942, M.S., 1946; Ph.D., U. Fla., 1951; m. Jane Zerbee, July 18, 1945; children—Jane Lynne, Sue Ellen, Robert James, John Stephen. From jr. engr. to group engr., tech. service div. Standard Oil Co., Ohio, 1946-52; asst. prof. chem. engring. U. Va., Charlottesville, 1952-56, research dir. engring. expt. sta., 1952-56; asso. prof. U. Ala., 1956-59, prof., 1959-60; chem. engr. So. Research Lab., U.S. Bur. Mines, 1957-60; prof., head chem. and petroleum-refining engring. dept. Colo. Sch. Mines, Golden, 1960—, chem. engr. research inst., 1960—, dir., trustee, 1970—. Mem. tech. adv. com. Regional Air Pollution Control Adminstrn., Denver, 1967—. Served to maj. CAC, AUS, 1942-46. Decorated Bronze Star. Mem. Am. Inst. Chem. Engrs. (sect. vice- chmn. 1962, chmn. 1963), Am. Chem. Soc., Am. Soc. for Engring. Edn., Am. Inst. Mining Engring., Sigma Xi, Tau Beta Pi. Contbr. articles to profl. jours. Patentee in field. Home: 1021 18th St Golden CO 80401

GARY, JOHN, singer; b. Watertown, N.Y., Nov. 29, 1932; ed. pub. schs., N.Y.C. and Cal.; m. Muriel Stafford (div.); 1 son, John; m. 2d, Lois McDonnell; 1 son, John Andrew; three step-children. Concert tours with U.S.O., World War II; motion picture appearance in The Time of Your Life, 1948; solo soprano TV revue series Blackouts, 1948-49; engaged as folk singer after Marine service, then appeared at TV stas. WNBF, Binghamton, N.Y., WDSU, New Orleans; guest appearances on Lawrence Welk and Jack Parr TV shows; seriously engaged in skin diving and made skin diving endurance test in New Orleans, also then working for USAF in fresh water skin diving; returned to nightclub field, then appeared on Don McNeil's Breakfast Club, 1961-62; singer at pvt. parties, N.Y.C., 1963; recording artist for RCA Victor Records, 1963—; numerous nightclub appearances, 1963—; guest appearances on TV shows of Danny Kaye, Tennessee Ernie Ford, Johnny Carson; summer replacement for Danny Kaye, 1966; concert appearance at Carnegie Hall, 1967; appeared on his own syndicated TV show 1968. Served with USMCR; Korean War. Address: care Jacob Csida Enterprises Inc 33 E 48th St New York City, NY 10017 *

GARY, MILTON ELLIS, meat packing co. exec.; b. Kenedy, Tex., Dec. 11, 1914; s. Charles Lester and Zora (Coward) G.; student Draughon's Bus. Coll., San Antonio, 1930-33; m. Laura Lois Rogers, Aug. 10, 1935; children—Milton Ellis, Lawrence D. Accountant, Rath Packing Co., Dallas, 1933-35, plant supt., 1936-39, asst. br. mgr., 1939-43, br. mgr., Des Moines, 1943-46, nat. br. house operations, Waterloo, Ia., 1946-62, gen. sales mgr., 1962-64, v.p. sales, 1964-69, sr. v.p., 1969—; with retail food store, Green, Tex., 1935-36; dir. Century Enterprises, Inc., Waterloo. Mem. Am. Meat Inst. (25 Year award 1959), Nat. Mgmt. Assn., Waterloo C. of C. Baptist. Mason. Home: 121 Hillcrest Rd Waterloo IA 50701 Office: Rath Packing Co Elm and Sycamore Sts Waterloo IA 50703

GARY, ROMAIN, author; b. Wilno, USSR, May 8, 1914; s. Lejba and Minna (Josel) Kacew; student U. Aix-en-Provence; Degree in Law, U. Paris; diploma Slavic langs., U. Warsaw; m. Lesley Blanch; m. 2d, Jean Seberg, Oct. 16, 1963. Sec., French embassy, Sofia, 1945-49, Bern, Switzerland, 1949-52; 1st sec., spokesman French delegation to UN, N.Y.C., 1952-55; sec. French embassy, London, 1955; consul gen. of France, Los Angeles, 1956-60. Pilot French Air Force, 1937- 40, capt. 1940-46; mem. Lorraine Bombing Squadron of Free French, Abyssinia, Libya, Syria, 1940-43. Decorated Croix de la Liberation, Croix de Guerre, Chevalier Legion of Honor (France). Author: Education Europeenne, 1945; Company of Men, 1951; Colors of the Day, 1952; The Roots of Heaven, 1956; The Ski Bum, 1965; Dance of Genghis Cohn; Lady L., 1959; Guilty Head; White Dog. Address: care Editions Gallimard 5 rue Sébastien-Buttin Paris 7 France*

GARY, THEODORE SAUVINET, communications exec.; b. Kansas City, Mo., Dec. 23, 1912; s. Hunter L. and Lamora (Sauvinet) G.; student Yale, 1932-33, Northwestern Bus. Sch., 1933-34; m. Laura Avritt Brown, July 23, 1934 (dec.); children—Theodore Sauvient, Laura Castleman (Mrs. Edwin Thorne, Jr.); m. 2d, Patricia Murrill Du Vivier, Aug. 22, 1958; children—Jerome S., Tracy DuVivier. Asst. to chmn. bd. Automatic Electric Co., 1934-36, v.p., 1936-45, vice chmn. bd., 1955, dir., 1955-57; pres., dir. Automatic Electric Sales Corp.,

1945, dir., 1956-57; pres., dir. Theodore Gary & Co., 1955; co. merged into Gen. Telephone Corp., 1955; v.p., dir. Gen. Telephone & Electronics Corp. (formerly Gen. Telephone Corp.), until 1966, vice chmn. bd., 1966—; v.p., dir. Gen. Telephone Services Corp., 1955—; chmn. bd., pres. Gary Industries, Inc.; chmn. exec. com., pres. Acco Products (div. Gary Industries, Inc.); chmn. bd. Acco Canadian Co., Ltd., 1955, dir., 1955-57; v.p., dir. Asso. Tel. & Tel. Co., Cie Dominicana de Telefonas C. por A., Continental Telephone Co., Community Telephone Co., Inland Telephone Co., Ill. Telephone Co., Ia. Continental Telephone Co., Mo. Telephone Co., Neb. Continental Telephone Co., Ohio Consol. Telephone Co., So. Continental Telephone Co. (Tex.), Union Telephone Co., Anglo-Canadian Telephone Co.; pres. Madeline Island Golf Links, Inc., Madeline Isalnd Marina, Inc., Madeline Island Corp. (all La Pointe, Wis.); dir. B.C. Telephone Co. Trustee Northland Coll., Ashland, Wis., N.Y. Boys Club. Mem. Armed Forces, Communications Assn. (exec. com., past pres.). Clubs: Chicago, Racquet, Mid-America (Chgo.); Brook, River, Racquet (N.Y.C.); Tuxedo (Tuxedo Park, N.Y.); Key Largo Anglers, Coral Reef Yacht (Miami, Fla.); Country of Fla. (Delray Beach); Coral Habour Yacht (Bahamas); Woodhill Country (Wayzata, Minn.); Minneapolis; Surf, Bath, Indian Creek Country (Miami Beach, Fla.). Home: 8 Indian Creek Island Miami Beach FL 33154 also 1 Sutton Pl S New York City NY 10022 also 426 S Ferndale Rd Wayzata MN 55391; also Madeline Island LaPointe WI 54850 Office: 730 3d Av New York City NY 10017 also 332 S Michigan Av Chicago IL 60604

GARY, WYNDHAM LEWIS, textile co. exec.; b. N.Y.C., Feb. 29, 1916; s. Irving Curtis and Marguerite (Case) G.; B.A., Yale, 1938, LL.B., 1941; m. Shirley Davis Spaulding, Aug. 6, 1948; 1 son, Wyndham Bradford. Admitted to N.Y. bar, 1941, asso. mem. firm Breed, Abbott & Morgan, 1941-42, 46-50; with alien enemy control unit Dept. Justice, Washington, 1942-43; asst. gen. counsel J.P. Stevens & Co., Inc., 1961-64, asst. treas., 1965-68, treas., 1969—; adv. bd. Mfrs. Hanover Trust Co., N.Y.C. Mem. Rumson (N.J.) Boro Council, 1956-58; chmn. design com. Middletown (N.J.) Planning Bd., 1960-65; dir., treas. J.P. Stevens & Co. Found. Served to capt. AUS, 1943-46. Mem. Am. Bar assn., Delta Kappa Epsilon, Phi Delta Phi. Episcopalian (sr. warden). Clubs: Rumson (N.J.) Country; Seabright (N.J.) Beach (bd. govs.); Princeton, Weavers (N.Y.C.). Home: Box 256 Navesink NJ 07752 Office: 1185 Av of the Americas New York City NY 10036

GARZA, REYNALDO G., judge; b. Brownsville, Tex., July 7, 1915; s. Ygnacio and Zoila (Guerra) G.; B.A., LL.B., U. Tex.; LL.D. (hon.), U. St. Edwards, Austin, Tex., 1965; m. Bertha Champion, June 9, 1943; children—Reynaldo G., David C., Ygnacio Daniel, Bertha Victoria, Monica Bernadette. Admitted to Tex. bar, 1939; pvt. practice, 1939-42, 46-50; partner firm Sharpe, Cunningham & Garza, 1950-60, Cunningham, Garza & Yznaga, 1960-61; U.S. dist. judge So. dist. Tex., Brownsville, 1961—. Treas. Cameron County Child Welfare Bd., 1950-52; mem. Tex. Good Neighbor Commn., 1957-61. Commr., City Brownsville, 1947-49. Trustee Brownsville Ind. Sch. Dist., 1941-42. Served with USAAF, 1942-45. Recipient Pro Ecclesia et Pontifica medal Pope Pius XII, 1952; decorated knight Order St. Gregory the Great, Pope Pius XII, 1954. Mem. Am., Cameron County bar assns., State Bar Tex. Home: 234 Calle Retama Brownsville TX 78520 Office: Post Office Bldg Brownsville TX 78520

GASCH, OLIVER, judge; b. Washington, May 4, 1906; s. Herman E. and Marie (Manning) G.; A.B., Princeton, 1928; LL.B., George Washington U., 1932; m. Sylvia Meyer, Oct. 17, 1942; 1 son, Michael Barrett. Admitted to D.C. bar, 1931; asst. corp. counsel for D.C., 1937-53; prin. asst. U.S. atty. for D.C., 1953-56; U.S. atty. for D.C., Washington, 1956-61; partner Craighill Aiello, Gasch & Craighill, 1961-65; judge U.S. Dist. Ct. for D.C., 1965—; gen counsel Interstate Commn. on Potomac River Basin, 1940-60; chmn. Council on D.C. Law Enforcement, 1958-62; mem. Jud. Conf. D.C. Circuit; co-chmn. Commrs. Crime Council, 1962-63. Mem. dean's council Georgetown U. Law Center, 1960-65. Served as lt. col. Judge Adv. Gen. Dept., AUS, 1942-46; PTO; U.S. Army Res. ret. Fellow Am. Coll. Trial Lawyers, Am. Bar Found.; mem. Fed. (chmn. of com. of gen. counsel of fed. govt. 1960-61), Am., D.C. (dir. 1961-63, pres. 1964-65) bar assns., Am. Law Inst., Barristers of Washington (pres. 1962-63), Res. Officers Assn. (past pres. D.C. dept.), Inst. Mil. Law, Judge Adv.'s Assn., Mil. Order Fgn. Wars (comdr. D.C. 1956), Law Alumni George Washington U. (pres.), Selden Soc. (London, Eng.), Phi Delta Phi. Republican. Episcopalian (vestryman, chancellor, v.p. exec. council diocese of Washington 1961-64, dep. to gen. conv. 1961, 64). Clubs: University, Lawyers, Princeton (Washington); Counsellors; Princeton (N.Y.C.); Chevy Chase. Home: 3673 Upton St Washington DC 20008 Office: US Courthouse Washington DC 20001

GASIOROWICZ, STEPHEN GEORGE, educator; b. Gdansk, Poland, May 10, 1928; s. Alexander A. and Maria K. (Landau) G.; B.A., U. Cal. at Los Angeles, 1948, M.A., 1949, Ph.D., 1952; postgrad. U. Delhi, 1945-46; m. Hilda E. Fromm, Apr. 4, 1953; children—Nina E., Catherine A., Mara E. Came to U.S., 1946, naturalized, 1952. Physicist, Lawrence Radiation Lab., U. Cal. at Berkeley, 1952-60; asso. prof. physics U. Minn., 1960-63, prof., 1963—; vis. scientist Max Planck Inst. Physics and Astrophysics, Munich, Germany, 1959-60, Deutsches Elektronen Synchrotron, Hamburg, Germany, 1968-69; cons. Argonne Nat. Lab., 1961-70. NSF fellow, 1957-58. Fellow Am. Phys. Soc. Author: Elementary Particle Physics, 1966. Home: 2786 Dean Blvd Minneapolis MN 55416

GASIOROWSKA, XENIA, educator; b. Kiev, Russia; d. Grzegorz and Magdalena (Olszewska) Zytomirksi; came to U.S., 1945, naturalized, 1964; Ph.D. in Slavic Langs. and Lit., U. Cal. at Berkeley, 1949; m. Zygmunt J. Gasiorowski, Mar. 3, 1949. Mem. faculty U. Wis., Madison, 1949—, prof. Slavic lit., 1965—. Vis. asso. prof. Wellesley Coll., 1958-59. Mem. Am. Assn. U. Profs., Modern Lang. Assn. Am., Am. Assn. Tchrs. Slavic and E. European Langs., Polish Acad. Scis. in Am., Internat. Fedn. Modern Lang. and Lit. Author: Women in Soviet Fiction: 1917-1964, 1968; also 3 vols. verse and a novel in Polish. Office: Slavic Dept Univ Wis Madison WI 53706

GASKELL, JAMES SHIELDS, Jr., banker; b. Evergreen, Ala., Nov. 12, 1921; s. James Shields and Annie Lois (Wiggins) G.; B.S., U. Ala., 1943; postgrad. La. State U., 1956; m. Dorothy Dale, Sept. 6, 1947; children—Dale, Barbara Anne, Lauri. Exec. v.p., dir. First Nat. Bank, Montgomery, Ala., 1966—. Am. Inst. Banking instr., guest lectr. La. State U., 1964-68. Campaign chmn. Montgomery United Appeal, 1962-63; pres. bd. Montgomery Tb Sanitorium, 1965-66. Served to lt. col. AUS, World War II, Korean War. Decorated Silver Star, Bronze Star. Mem. Montgomery Sales and Marketing Execs. Club (treas.). Baptist. Optimist (past pres.). Home: 3508 Landsdown Dr Montgomery AL 36111 Office: PO Box 511 Montgomery AL 36111

GASKELL, ROBERT EUGENE, educator, mathematician; b. Grelton, O., Jan. 18, 1912; s. Eugene R. and Effie (Fish) G.; A.B., Albion Coll., 1933; Ph.D., U. Mich., 1940; m. Jane Ardith Weyand, Aug. 22, 1940; children—Ellen (Mrs. Nathaniel W. Alcock), Robert Weyand. Instr. math. U. Ala., 1940-42; research asso. Brown U., 1942-46; asst. prof., then asso. prof. math. Ia. State U., 1947-51; supr. math. services unit Boeing Airplane Co., 1951-59; prof. math. Ore. State U., 1959-66; prof. math., chmn. dept. Naval Postgrad. Sch., Monterey, Cal., 1966—; cons. in field, 1944—, Fellow A.A.A.S.; mem. Am. Soc. Engrng. Edn. (chmn. math. div. 1966), Soc. Indsl. and Applied Math. (council 1959-63), Math. Assn. Am. (chmn. vis. lectrs. com. 1963-67), Am. Math. Soc., Phi Beta Kappa, Sigma Xi. Research and publns. in application of math. to heat conduction, structural vibrations, calendering of plastic materials, ground water flow. Author: Engineering Mathematics, 1958. Home: 1207 Sylvan Rd Monterey CA 93940

GASKELL, THOMAS FROHOCK, petroleum co. exec.; b. Bolton, Eng., Jan. 26, 1916; s. Harold and Dorothy May (Frohock) B.; M.A. (Sr. scholar 1934) with 1st class honours in Natural Scis., Trinity Coll., Cambridge U., 1937, Ph.D., 1940; m. Joyce Winifred Kenyon, Mar. 28, 1952; children—Anthony Horatio, Joanna Mary. Chief petroleum physicist Anglo-Iranian Oil Co., Iran, 1946-49; chief scientist oceanographic expdn. on H.M.S. Challenger, 1949-52; mem. exploration dept. British Petroleum Co. Ltd., 1952-62, sci. adviser information dept., 1962—; cons., lectr. in field. Served with British Navy, 1939-46. Fellow Royal Soc. Arts (Silver medal 1964), Inst. Arbitrators; mem. Royal Astron. Soc. (geophys. sec. 1965—), Inst. Petroleum (council 1960—), Royal Inst. (mgr. 1962-65), Japan Soc. London. Club: Athenaeum (London). Author: Under the Deep Oceans, 1960; World Beneath the Oceans, 1964; (with Bryan Cooper) North Sea Oil-The Great Gamble, 1966; also articles. Home: 96 Belle Hill Bexhill-on-Sea Sussex Englnd Office: Britannic House Moor Lane London EC2 England

GASKILL, HAROLD VINCENT, banker, scientist; b. Fayette County, O., Feb. 3, 1905; s. Ralph Pern and Elta (Scott) G.; B.A., Ohio State U., 1926, M.A., 1927, Ph.D., 1930; m. Pauline Ellen Pinnick, July 21, 1926; children—Harold Vincent, Ellen Jane, Charles Shreve. Asst. dept. psychology Ohio State U., Columbus, 1925-27, instr., 1927-30; asst. prof. Ia. State U., 1930-31, asso. prof., 1931-35, prof. psychology, 1935—, dean sci., 1938—, dir. Indsl. Sci. Research Inst., Ia. State U., 1938—, also dir. war research, 1941—; chief scientist U.S. Army, dep. chief research and devel., Pentagon; v.p. planning Collins Radio Co., Cedar Rapids, 1956-62; v.p. Financial Gen. Corp., 1962—; v.p. planning Internat. Bank Washington, 1962—; Mem. NRC; chmn. NAS-NRC Com. Hwy. Safety Research. Fellow A.A.A.S., Ia. Acad. Sci., Am. Assn. Applied Psychology (charter mem.); mem. Am., Midwestern psychology assns., Am. Council on Edn. (liaison officer coop. study, gen. edn.), A.L.A. (psychology com.), I.R.E., Am. Statis. Assn., Ia. Hist. Soc., Sigma Xi, Kappa Sigma, Alpha Psi Delta, Phi Kappa Phi, Phi Delta Kappa (Cardinal Key). Episcopalian (vestryman). Mason (32, Scottish Rite), Rotarian. Club: Des Moines (Ia.) Author: Personality, 1936; collaborator and contbr. Handbook of Chemistry and Physics, 1930-55; contbr. psychol. and ednl. jours. Home: Del Ray Beach FL 33444 Office: 1701 Pennsylvania Av Washington DC 20006

GASKILL, HERBERT STOCKTON, physician, educator; b. Phila., Jan. 31, 1909; s. Herbert M. and Willa M. (Troth) G.; A.B., Haverford Coll., 1932; M.D., U. Pa., 1937; m. Evelyn Waring Remington, Aug. 13, 1938; children—Elizabeth B., Herbert Stockton, Evelyn W., Daniel W. Intern, Pa. Hosp., Phila., 1937-39, fellow psychiatry, 1941-42; resident neurology Jefferson Med. Coll. Hosp., 1939- 40, fellow neuropathology, 1940-41; postgrad. Chgo. Inst. Psychoanalysis, 1950-57; pvt. practice, Phila., 1946-49, Indpls., 1949-53, Denver, 1953—; asst. prof. psychiatry U. Pa., 1946-49; prof., chmn. dept. psychiatry Ind. U., 1949-53; prof., head dept. psychiatry U. Colo., 1953—. Mem. tng. com. USPHS, 1954-57; mem. council, exec. com. Western Inst. Higher Edn., 1957—; mem. research career award com. Nat. Inst. Mental Health, 1960-64, mem. continuing edn. com., 1967—, chmn., 1967-68. Served to maj. AUS, 1942-46. Diplomate Am. Bd. Psychiatry and Neurology. Mem. Am. Psychiat. Assn. (council 1955-58, v.p. 1970—), A.M.A. (mem. residency rev. com. for neurology and psychiatry, 1969—), Am. Psychosomatic Soc., Central, Colo. neuropsychiat. socs., Chgo. Psychoanalytic Soc. Home: 480 S Marion Pkwy Denver CO 80209 Office: 4200 E 9th Av Denver CO 80220

GASKILL, WILLIAM JOHN, pub. relations counsel; b. Trenton, N.J., June 5, 1910; s. William Richard and Jane (McCarran) G.; A.B., Rutgers U., 1937; postgrad. Pa. State U., 1938-42; m. Mary Alice Duggan, June 5, 1936; children—Patricia, Jo-ann. Reporter Trenton State Gazette, 1934-38; instr. Pa. State U., 1938-42; editor Am. Inst. Pub. Opinion (Gallup Poll), 1942-47; exec. v.p. Hawaiian Econ. Found., Honolulu, 1947-49; dir. pub. relations Hawaiian Pineapple Co., Honolulu, 1949-54; partner Ivy Lee & T.J. Ross, N.Y.C., 1954-62; exec. v.p. T.J. Ross & Assos., Inc., N.Y.C., 1962-65, pres., 1965-71, chmn. bd., 1971—. Faculty asso. Grad. Sch. Bus., Ind. U., 1963-66. Trustee Rutgers U.; bd. dirs. Roper Research Center, Williams Coll., Willamstown, Mass. Mem. Am. Sociol. Soc., Am. Assn. Pub. Opinion Research, Pub. Relations Soc. Am. (treas., dir. 1966-67, mem. accreditation bd. 1965—, chmn. 1968-70), Phi Beta Kappa, Delta Kappa Epsilon. Clubs: Cloud (bd. govs.), Yale (N.Y.C.); Westchester Country (Rye, N.Y.). Home: 17 Briarwood Lane Pleasantville NY 10570 Office: 405 Lexington Av New York City NY 10017

GASPER, THOMAS A., banker. Comptroller, First Trenton Nat. Bank. Office: 1 W State St Trenton NJ 08608*

GASS, CLINTON BURKE, educator; b. Lake Wilson, Minn., Jan. 9, 1920; s. Frederick G. and Elvira A. (Burke) G.; A.B. magna cum laude, Gustavus Adolphus Coll., 1941; M.A., U. Neb., 1943, Ph.D., 1954; m. Myrtle Brewer, Oct. 18, 1941; children—Frederick S., Kenneth B., Glenn C. Instr. math. U. Neb., 1942- 43; asso. prof. math. Neb. Wesleyan U., 1943-46, prof., 1946-47, 53-54, prof., dean of men, 1947-53; asso. prof. math. DePauw U., Greencastle, Ind., 1954-56, prof., 1956-64, John T. and Margaret Deal prof. math., 1964—, head dept. math. and astronomy, 1960—. Asso. program dir., tchr. edn. sect. NSF, 1965-66; cons. Dept. Def. Overseas Schs. in Europe, 1969-70. Served with AUS, 1944-46. Decorated knight York Cross of Honour; cited for heroism by Nat. Ct. of Honor of Boy Scouts Am. Mem. Am. Math. Soc., Math. Assn. Am. (chmn. Neb. 1949-50), Ind. 1957-58), Am. Assn. U. Profs., Sigma Xi, Phi Kappa Phi, Pi Mu Epsilon, Sigma Pi Sigma. Mason. Home: 707 Highridge Av Greencastle IN 46135

GASS, MANUS M., accountant; b. Montreal, Que., Can., June 28, 1928; s. Maurice and Bertha (Silverberg) G.; student McGill U., 1945-48; B.B.A. cum laude, Coll. City N.Y., 1953; m. Estelle Lea Lefkowitz, Oct. 8, 1950; children—Thomas Evan, Winifred. Came to U.S., 1948, naturalized, 1953. Comptroller, Delca Fish Preservators, Bklyn., 1948-51; comptroller Allied Molding Corp., Corona, L.I., N.Y., 1951-52; staff mem. Brach, Gosswein & Lane, C.P.A.'s, N.Y.C., 1953-56; asso. Schorr, Katz & Co., N.Y.C., 1956-66; treas., controller Buitoni Food Corp., South Hackensack, N.J., 1966—; dir. Your Fabric Shop, Inc., Cango, Inc. (both Red Bank, N.J.). Accountant, Am. Jewish Tercentenary Com., 1953-54. Chmn. River Edge-Oradell United Jewish Appeal, 1964-65, 67-71. C.P.A., N.Y. Mem. Am. Inst. C.P.A.'s, N.Y. State Soc. C.P.A.'s. Jewish religion (treas. temple 1964, trustee temple brotherhood). Home: 184 Woodland Av River Edge NJ 07661

GASS, SYLVESTER F., clergyman; b. Milw., Dec. 31, 1911; s. Jacob and Julia (Weninger) G.; B.A., St. Francis Sem., Milw., 1937, M.A., 1939; J.C.D., 1942. Ordained priest Roman Catholic Ch., 1939; clergy counsellor St. Michael Hosp. Family Clinic, 1948—, spiritual dir., 1961—; speakers staff Archdiocese Cath. Family Life Program, 1949—; archiepiscopal vicar Dominican Sisters, 1956—; Cath. vicar gen. Archdiocese of Milw. Mem. Canon Law Soc. Am. (Pres. 1960-61), Canadian Canon Law Soc. Address: 2000 W Wisconsin Av Milwaukee WI 54803 *

GASS, WILLIAM H., author, educator; b. 1924; A.B., Kenyon Coll., 1947; Ph.D., Cornell U., 1953. Prof. philosophy Purdue U., also Washington U., St. Louis. Author: Omensetter's Luck, 1966; In the Heart of the Heart of the Country and Other Stories, 1968; Willie Masters' Lonesome Wife, 1968; Fiction and the Figures of Life, 1970. Address: Washington U St Louis MO 63130

GASSAWAY, FRANKLIN DRENNAN, physician; b. San Francisco, Sept. 5, 1918; s. Franklin Eugene and Ruth (Richardson) G.; B.S., U. Md., 1941, M.D., 1944; M.S. in Surgery, U. Pa., 1949; m. Ruth M. Michaels, June 23, 1944; children—Michael, Jean. Intern S. Balt. Gen. Hosp., 1944- 45, resident 1945-46; resident U. Pa. Grad. Sch., 1948-49, Western Pa. Hosp., 1949-52; med. dir., chief surgeon Gulf Oil Corp., also pvt. practice surgery, Pitts., 1952—; sr. surgeon Western Pa. Hosp., 1958—; clin. asso. prof. U. Pitts. Med. Sch., 1962—; mem. teaching staff U. Tex. Med. Sch., 1953; spl. research lymphosarcoma intestinal tract. Trustee Internat. Found.; bd. dirs. Indsl. Hygiene Found. Am., St. Joseph's House. Served to lt. USNR, 1946-48; col. Res., 1961. Recipient award of merit Community Chest Allegheny Co., 1954. Diplomate Am. Bd. Surgery, Internat. Coll. Surgeons. Fellow Am., Internat. colls. surgeons, Indsl. Med. Assn.; mem. Pa., Allegheny Co. med. socs., A.M.A., Pitts. Surg. Soc., Pitts Acad. Medicine, Acad. Occupational Medicine, World Med. Assn., N.Y. Acad. Scis. , Phi Delta Chi, Nu Sigma Nu. Clubs: Duquesne, Longue Vue. Author articles in field. Home: 550 Grant St Pittsburgh PA 15219 Office: Gulf Bldg Pittsburgh PA 15230

GASSENHEIMER, EARL CADDEN, printing co. exec., b. Montgomery, Ala., June 5, 1911; s. Leo and Ray (Cadden) G.; B.S., U. Pa., 1931; m. Rose Cohn, Feb. 10, 1935; children—Earl Harold, David. Controller, Schenley Industries, Inc., 1952- 54; v.p., treas., dir. Am. Sinteel Corp., 1955-58; controller Rust Craft Greeting Cards, Inc. (formerly United Printers and Pubs., Inc.), 1958-62, dir., 1962-65, treas., 1962—. Mem. Am. Contract Bridge League. Mem. B'nai B'rith. Home: 150 Prince St West Newton MA 02165 Office: Rust Craft Greeting Cards Inc Rustcraft Park Dedham MA 02026

GASSER, HENRY MARTIN, artist; b. Newark, Oct. 31, 1909; s. William Henry and Mary Teresa (Jansus) G.; student Fawcett Art Sch., 1924-25, Newark Sch. Fine and Indsl. Art, 1928-34, Grand Central Art Sch., 1935, Art Students League, 1938-41; m. Joane Rone, May 27, 1930. Dir. Newark Sch. Fine and Indsl. Art, 1946-54; past. pres. N.J. Art Council, lectr. Am. Water Color Soc., Nat. Acad. Audubon Artists, Allied Artists Am., Mobile Art League, Shreveport Art Club, Art Assn. Guild New Orleans. Has exhibited in most well known museums and art galleries throughout U.S.; represented in collections of numerous museums and galleries, including Met., Phila., Boston, Newark museums; recipient many honors and awards, among the most recent, Am. Watercolor Soc., 1967, Nat. Art Club, 1969. Served with inf. AUS, 1944-45. Mem. N.A.D., Nat. Arts Club (life); Am. (past v.p.), N.J. (past pres.), Cal. water color socs., Allied Artists Am., Conn. Acad., Audubon Artists, Artists and Craftsmen Asso., Acad. Artists Assn., Am. Artists Profl. League, Royal Soc. Art London. Clubs: Philadelphia Water Color; Baltimore Water Color; New Haven Paint and Clay. Author: Casein Painting Methods and Demonstrations; Oil Painting Methods and Demonstrations; Watercolor-How To Do It; Techniques of Painting; Techniques of Painting the Waterfront; Techniques of Picture Making, 1962; How to Draw and Paint; Exploring Casein (motion picture), 1962. Address: 654 Varsity Rd South Orange NJ 07079 ☆

GASSER, ROBERT CARPENTER, banker; b. Marquette, Mich., Nov. 8, 1925; s. Wilbert W. and Mildred M. (Carpenter) G.; B.S. in Engring., Northwestern U., 1947; m. Barbara L. Mayne, June 18, 1949; children—Tom, David, Leigh Ann, Sally. With Gary Nat. Bank (Ind.), 1947—, pres., 1964—, also dir.; with Continental Ill. Nat. Bank, Chgo., 1949-50; dir. Chgo., S. Shore & S. Bend R.R. Co. Served as officer USNR, World War II. Mem. Am., Ind. bankers assns. Rotarian. Home: Box 533 Ogden Dunes Portage IN 46368 Office: 504 Broadway Gary IN 46402

GASSER, WILBERT, Jr., banker; b. Marquette, Mich., Apr. 5, 1923; s. Wilbert Warner and Mildred (Carpenter) G.; student Purdue U., 1941-42; B.S. in Bus., Ind. U., 1948; m. Mary C. Kratz, Dec. 6, 1952; 1 son, Wilbert Warner III. With Gary Nat. Bank (Ind.), 1948—, v.p., 1953-63, chmn. bd., 1964—; dir. 1st United Life Ins. Co., Gary Hotel. Pres. Gary YMCA, 1960-62; treas. Gary Urban League, 1960-65, now dir.; treas. N.W. Ind. Heart Assn., 1958-65; mem. bd. dirs., treas. Methodist Hosp., Gary. Served with USAAF, 1943-46. Mem. Gary C. of C. (v.p. 1961). Presbyn. (elder). Kiwanian (treas. Gary 1963—). Home: 638 Ogden Dunes Portage, IN 46368 Office: 504 Broadway Gary IN 46401

GASSER, WILLIAM DANIEL, educator; b. Rochester, N.Y., Aug. 13, 1913; s. Alfred and Anna (Schmitt) G.; student St. Michael's Coll., Toronto, Ont., Can. 1932-33; B.B.A. cum laude, Niagara U., 1937; m. Catherine Mowle, Sept. 2, 1939; children—William D., Marilyn Ann. Various positions Miller, Franklin, McLeod & Co., C.P.A.'s (merged with Haskins & Sells, Rochester, 1958), Rochester, 1937-47, gen. partner, 1947-57, sr. partner, 1957-58, gen. partner, 1958-60, partner charge Rochester office, 1960- 67; asso. prof. Sch. Bus., asst. dir. Extended Service div. Rochester Inst. Tech., 1967—; dir. Heany Industries, Scottsville. Bd. examiners Am. Inst. C.P.A.'s, 1965; former mem. N.Y. State Bd. C.P.A. Examiners; adv. council Rochester Inst. Tech. Recipient Golden Key award Acad. Sacred Heart, 1962; named Outstanding Kiwanian of Year, 1962; Boss of Year, Flower City chpt. Nat. Secs. Assn., 1965. Mem. Am. Inst. C.P.A.'s (council 1955-58), A.I.M. (pres.'s council), Assn. C.P.A. Examiners (treas. 1961-65, v.p. 1965—), N.Y. (v.p. 1957-58, past dir.), Cal. socs. C.P.A.'s, Am. Accounting Assn., Accountants Club Am., Nat. Assn. Accountants, Niagara U. Alumni Assn., Rochester C. of C., Am. Assn. Hosp. Accountants, Rochester Soc. Investment Analysts, Delta Mu Delta, Beta Alpha Psi. K.C. (4). Clubs: Kiwanis, University, City (Rochester). Author: Routine Auditing Procedures for Interdepartmental Auditors, Model City, U.S.A. Home: 66 Pinecrest Dr Rochester, NY 14617. Office: 800 Midtown Tower Rochester NY 14604

GASSERT, ROBERT GEORGE, coll. dean; b. Milw., July 6, 1921; s. Joseph C. and Emily (Bier) G.; B.A., St. Louis U., 1945, M.A., 1948, Ph.L., 1948; S.T.L., St. Mary's (Kan.) Coll., 1955; S.T.D., Gregorian U., Rome, Italy, 1958. Joined Soc. of Jesus, 1941, ordained priest Roman Catholic Ch., 1954; tchr. Campion High Sch., Prairie du Chien, Wis., 1949-51; mem. faculty Marquette U., 1958-62, dean Coll. Liberal Arts, 1963—, asso. prof. theology, 1966—. Theol. fellow Menninger Found., 1962-63. Mem. Assn. Higher Edn., Assn. Am.

Colls., Jesuit, Nat. Cath. edn. assns., N. Central Assn. Author: (with Bernard H. Hall) Psychiatry and Religious Faith. Home: 1131 W Wisconsin Av Milwaukee, WI 53233.

GASSMAN, VITTORIO, actor; b. Genova, Italy, Sept. 1, 1922; s. Henry and Luisa (Ambron) G.; student Liceo Tasso, Rome; student, U. of Law, Rome; div.; children—Paola, Vittoria. Began career Acad. Dramatic Art, Rome, 1943; actor numerous plays, also dir. plays, including Shakespeare's Hamlet, Othello, Romeo and Juliet, Aeschylus' Persians, Ibsen's Ghosts, Manzoni's Adelchi; founder, dir. Teatro Poplare Italiano, 1960-63; actor motion picture films, including Bitter Rice, Big Deal on Madonna Street, The Great War, Love and Larceny, Easy Life, The Monsters, The Dirty Game. Recipient awards in Italy: Sangenesio (twice), Olimpo; (motion picture awards) Nastro d'Argento, 2 Davide di Donatello; best actor award Buenos Aires Festival, 1964. Home: 32 Piazzo S Alessio Rome Italy.

GAST, AARON EDWARD, clergyman; b. Baroda, Mich., July 22, 1927; s. Edward F. and Oral (Arend) G.; A.B., Wheaton Coll., 1950; B.D. Princeton Theol. Sem., 1953; postgrad., Cambridge (Eng.), U., 1954; Ph.D., Edinburgh (Scotland) U., 1955; m. Beverly Shaffer, June 16, 1950; children—Gregory, Lisa, Brian. Ordained to ministry Presbyn. Ch., 1953; asst. to minister, Narbeth, Pa., 1950-52; minister in Phila., 1955-60; lectr. Temple U., 1960—; prof. Conwell Sch. Theology, Phila., 1960-67, dean, 1960-67, vis. prof., 1968—; lectr. Eastern Baptist Coll., St. Davids, Pa., 1968—; sr. minister First Presbyn. Ch., Germantown, Phila. Vice pres. Baroda Hardware Co., Inc., 1959—. Bd. dirs. Nat. Conf. Christians and Jews; pres. bd. trustees, chmn. ch. relations com. Phila. Presbytery; bd. dirs. Phila. Presbytery Found.; bd. corporators Presbyn. Ministers Fund. Served with USNR, 1944-46. Rotarian. Clubs: Princeton Symposium; Canterbury, Adelphoi Cleric (Phila.). Author profl. articles. Contbr. Upper Room Disciplines, 1962- 66; columnist Christian Herald; adv. council Who's Who in Am. Home: 2823 Belmont Av Ardmore PA 19003. Office: 35 W Chelten Av Philadelphia PA 19144

GAST, FREDERICK CHARLES, wholesale grocery co. exec; b. Benton Harbor, Mich., Aug. 9, 1916; s. Frederick William and Edna Mae (Bassett) G.; grad. pub. schs.; m. Rosalind Paulina Ferris, Feb. 20, 1937; children—Frederick Charles II, Stefan Paul. Service bur. mgr. IBM, San Francisco, 1934-39; data processing mgr. Ore. Unemployment Compensation Commn., 1939-43; asst. commnr., comptroller Ore. Indsl. Accident Commn., 1943-51; office mgr., asst. mgr. United Grocers Inc., Milwaukie, Ore., 1951-68, exec. v.p., gen. mgr., 1968—; pres. United Supermarket Investment Co. Portland; v.p. U.G. Ins. Inc.; pres. Buttercup Bakery Inc., Gresham, Ore.; dir. First State Bank of Ore. Sec.-trustee Warehousemems Employers Health & Welfare Trust, Portland; bd. dirs. Sunshine div. Portland Police Dept. Mem. Financial Exec. Inst. Am., Cooperative Food Distbrs. Am. (chmn. trade relations com. 1970-71), Portland Freight Traffic Assn. Mason. Home: 2818 Beuhla Vista Terr Portland OR 97210 Office: 6433 SE Lake Rd Milwaukie OR 97222

GAST, HAROLD N., lawyer, oil co. exec.; b. Carteret, N.J., Dec. 14, 1908; s. Max and Frieda (Hollander) G.; A.B., Cornell U., 1930; LL.B., Yale, 1933; m. Diana Sobo Levitow, Jan. 29, 1954; children—David, Barbara, Sara. Admitted to N.J. bar, 1933; practice in Perth Amboy, 1934-46; asso. firm David T. Wilentz, 1934-46; v.p., gen. counsel Hess Oil & Chem. Corp., Perth Amboy, N.Y.C., 1951-62, sr. v.p., gen. counsel Hess Oil & Chem. div. Amerada Hess Corp., 1962—. Mem. Am. Bar Assn., Am. Petroleum Inst. Club: Yale. Home: 721 Scotch Plains Av Westfield NJ 07090 Office: 1 Hess Plaza Woodbridge NJ 07095

GAST, PAUL FREDERICK, physicist; b. St. Paul, May 29, 1916; s. Gustav Carl and Alma May (Young) G.; student Capital U., Columbus, 1933-35; A.B., Ohio State U., 1937; Ph.D., U. Wash., 1941; m. Virginia Holt, June 15, 1941; children—Barbara Lee, Cynthia Ann. Physicist research lab. Remington Arms Co., Bridgeport, Conn., 1941-43; engaged in tech. liaison and devel. work in connection with design of nuclear reactors, for DuPont Co., Hanford Works of Manhatten Project, 1943-44; chief of physics sect. Hanford Works, for Gen. Electric Co., Richland, 1946-56, mgr. physics and instrument research and devel., 1956-64; faculty Gen. Electric Sch. Nuclear Engring.; sr. scientist Argonne (Ill.) Nat. Lab., 1964-66, asso. dir. liquid metal fast breeder reactor program office, 1966—. Mem. reactor physics planning group AEC, mem. U.S. delegation Internat. Conf., Switzerland, 1955, mem. tech. mission to U.K., 1956. Mem. Am. Nuclear Soc. (dir. 1964-67), Am. Phys. Soc., Am. Inst. Physics. A.A.A.S., Phi Beta Kappa. Contbr. articles to Phys. Rev. on cosmic rays and on nuclear fission. Mem. editorial bd. Reactor Handbook for AEC com. on reactor reclassification. Home: 3706 Madison St Oak Brook IL 60521 Office: Argonne Nat Lab 9700 S Cass Av Argonne IL 60439

GASTER, THEODOR HERZL, educator; b. London, Eng., July 21, 1906; s. Moses and Lucy (Friedlaender) B.; B.A., Hons. in Classics, U. London, 1928, M.A. in Archeology, 1936; Ph.D., Columbia, 1943; D.D., U. Vt., 1965; m. Lotta Schmitz; 1 dau., Corinna Michal. Came to U.S., 1939, naturalized, 1944. Curator Near Eastern antiquities Wellcome Mus., London, 1928-32, 36-38; prof. comparative religion Dropsie Coll., Phila., 1944-59; prof. ancient civilizations and history of religions Fairleigh Dickinson U., 1959-66; prof. religion Barnard Coll., N.Y.C., 1966—. Lectr., O.T. and Semitic civilizations N.Y. U., 1946-50; chief Hebraic sect. Library of Congress, 1944-48; Guggenheim fellow, 1954, 59; Fulbright prof. U. Rome (Italy), 1951, U. Melbourne (Australia), 1961; Burton prof. U. Leeds (Eng.), 1959, 63. Mem. Soc. Sci. Study Religion, Am. Acad. Religion, Am. Oriental Soc., Archaeol. Inst. Am., Asia Soc., Soc., Bibl. Lit., Soc. O.T. Study, N.Y. Oriental Soc., Am. Classical Assn. Author: Thespis, 1950; The Dead Sea Scriptures, 1956; The New Golden Bough, 1959; The Oldest Stories in the World, 1952; The Holy and the Profane, Evolution of Jewish Folkways, 1955; Myth, Legend and Custom in the Old Testament, 1969; also numerous articles. Home: 390 Riverside Dr New York City NY 10027

GASTIL, RUSSELL GORDON, educator, geologist; b. San Diego, June 25, 1938; s. Russell Chester and Frances (Duncan) G.; A.B,, U. Cal. at Berkeley, 1950, Ph.D., 1954; m. Emily Janet Manly, Sept. 13. 1958; children—Garth Manly, Mary Margaret, George Christopher, John Wheeler. With Shell Oil Co., 1954, Canadian Javelin Co., 1956-58; lectr. U. Cal. at Los Angeles, 1958-69; mem. faculty San Diego State Coll., 1959—, prof. geology, 1965—, chmn. dept., 1969—. Fellow Geol. Soc. Am. (vice chmn. cordilleran sect. 1967); mem. A.A.A.S., Soc. Econ. Mineralogists and Paleontologists, Nat. Assn. Geology Tchrs. Author papers in field. Home: 9435 Alto Dr La Mesa CA 92041 Office: San Diego State Coll San Diego CA 92115

GASTON, DAVID AIKEN, lawyer; b. Waynesville, N.C., Aug. 21, 1903; s. Arthur Lee and Virginia Carolina (Aiken) G.; A.B., U. S.C., 1924, M.A., 1926, LL.B., 1926; student Columbia; m. Reubie Holliday, May 9, 1931; children—Virginia Aiken (Mrs. Julian Hennig), Arthur Lee. Admitted to S.C. bar, 1926, since practiced in Chester; partner firm Gaston & Gaston, 1948—; dir. Comml. Bank Chester; v.p., dir. Chester Bldg. & Loan Assn. Mem. S.C. Hwy. Commn., 1956-60, chmn., 1959-60; chmn. Chester dist. Boy Scouts Am., 1955, mem. exec. bd. Palmetto area council, 1955—; pres. Chester Area United Fund, 1957-58. Mem. S.C. Ho. of Reps. from Chester Co., 1941-44; del. Democratic Nat. Conv., 1960. Trustee U. S.C., 1955-56. Mem. Am., S.C. (pres. 1961-62), Chester Co. (pres. 1955-57) bar assns., S. Caroliniana Soc., Chester Co. Hist. Soc., Chester Co. C. of C. (pres. 1937-38), Kappa Alpha. Presbyn. (chmn. deacons 1948-49, 60-61). Rotarian (pres. Chester Co., 1953-54). Author: Chester County Economic and Social, 1924. Home: Pinckney Rd Chester SC 29706 Office: Commerical Bank Bldg Chester SC 29706

GASTON, EVERETT THAYER, educator; b. Woodward, Okla., July 4, 1901; s. Bentley Larn and Jennie Smith (Clyde) G.; A.B., Sterling Coll., 1923, B.M., 1935; A.M., U. Kan., 1938, Ph.D., 1940; grad. study Bethany Coll., 1925, Colo. State Coll., 1935; m. Ardis May Waite, Aug. 11, 1924; 1 son, Dr. Lamont Waite. Tchr. music pub. schs., 1923-34; asst. prof., music edn. U. Kan., 1940-43, asso. prof., 1943-45, prof., chmn. dept. music edn., 1945-62, prof. music education, director music therapy, 1962—, University professor, since 1968—, first class music therapy, 1946, 1st grad. deg. course, 1948; lectr. music therapy, influence of music on behavior; cons. music therapy Topeka V.A. Hosp. since 1948. Topeka State Hosp., 1951—, Menninger Clinic, 1953-65, Osawatomie St. Hospital, Parsons St. Hospital and Training School. Recipient 1st grant authorized by National Inst. Mental Health in discipline of music therapy. Fellow of A.A.A.S.; member National Association of Music Therapy (president, 1952, research, edn. coms., liaison appointee A.M.A., hon. life mem.), Am. Psychol. Assn., Music Tchrs. Nat. Assn. Music Educators Nat. Conference, National Federation of Music Clubs, also Pi Kappa Lambda, Phi Delta Kappa, Phi Mu Alpha. Author: Mjsic in Therapy, published 1968; also articles profl. publications. Editor: Music Therapy, 1954, 55, 56, 57; Music in Therapy, 1968. Home: 602 Country Club Terrace Lawrence KS

GASTON, W.M., yarn co. exec. Vice pres., also gen. mgr. Am. Enka Corp. Office: Am Enka Corp Enka NC 28728*

GATCH, MILTON M., banker; b. Milford, O., 1905; ed. Miami U. Sr. v.p., dir. Fifth Third Bank, Cin., 1966—, v.p., dir. First Milford Savs. Assn.; dir. J.R. Greeno Co. Trustee, v.p. Elizabeth Gamble Deaconess Home Assn., Christ Hosp. Served to comdr. USNR, World War II. Mem. Am., Ohio bankers assns., Delta Kappa Epsilon. Clubs: Queen City, Bankers (Cin.). Home: Box 11 Route 1 Milford OH 45150 Office: Fountain Sq Plaza 4th and Walnut Sts Cincinnati OH 45201

GATCHELL, WILLIAM HENRY, banker; b. Memphis, Mar. 20, 1910; s. Harry Lavender and Hannah May (Ellis) G.; student Memphis Univ. Sch., 1926-28, Am. Inst. Banking, 1929- 35; m. Janice A. Northrup, Sept. 19, 1931; 1 dau., Barbara Ellen (Mrs. A. Douglas Salmon). With Union Planters Nat. Bank, Memphis, 1929—, sr. v.p. charge nat. accounts div., 1967—. Past treas. local U.S.O., Boy's Town, Muscular Dystrophy Assn. Bd. dirs. Duration Sch., 1966—, treas., 1967-68; chmn. adv. bd. Memphis Salvation Army, 1948, bd. dirs., 1968—. Mem. Memphis Execs. Club (pres. 1957), Memphis C. of C. (life, past chmn. welcome com.), Memphis Secret Soc. (treas.), Memphis Cotton Carnival Assn. (past asst. treas.). Mem. Christian Ch. (vice chmn. bd. elders 1968—). Lion (past v.p., dir.). Club: Chickasaw Country (past v.p., treas.) (Memphis). Home: 36 Wynchewood Dr Memphis TN 38117 Office: 67 Madison Av PO Box 387 Memphis TN 38101

GATELY, JAMES HAYES, mcht.; b. Chgo., Nov. 12, 1882; s. William and Alice (Hayes) G.; student pub. schs., Orr Bus. Coll.; m. Gertrude A. Crane, June 11, 1912; children—John, Dorothy Squyres, Alice Ryan, Rita Kelly. Pres. Peoples Store, Chgo., 1917-55, chmn., 1955—, also treas. Chmn. Bd. of Zoning Appeals, Chgo., 1935-45; pres. Chgo. Park Dist., 1945—. Clubs: South Shore Country, Chicago Athletic (Chgo.). Home: 10655 S Hoyne Av Chicago IL 60643 Office: 11201 S Michigan Av Chicago IL 60628

GATENBY, ANDREW B., hardware chain exec. Sec., also atty. Ace Hardware Corp. Office: Ace Hardware Corp 6501 W 65th St Chicago IL 60638*

GATES, CASSIUS EMERSON, lawyer; b. Alma City, Minn., Apr. 26, 1886; s. Emerson and Emma Jane (Grey) G.; LL.B., U. Minn., 1908; m. Clara M. Shaughnessy, Feb. 25, 1911 (dec.); m. 2nd, Mabel Rankin June 29, 1918 (dec.); m. 3d, Rosella M. Paulsen, Jan. 14, 1939; 1 adopted son, Robert Emerson; stepchildren—Chester R. Paulson, Kathryn Paulson (Mrs. Floyd K. McCroskey). Admitted to Minn. bar, 1908; practiced in Mankato, 1909, in Seattle, 1909—; mem. Bogle, Bogle & Gates (firm now Bogle, Gates, Dobrin, Wakefield and Long), 1926—; chmn. bd., dir. Citizens Fed. Savs. & Loan Assn., KXA, Inc. Trustee, v.p. Pacific N.W. Research Found.; past trustee Seattle Symphony Orch., former trustee Automobile Club of Wash. Asso. mem. Assn. Bar City of New York; mem. Seattle C. of C. (chmn. mem. council 1923- 24, pres. 1933-34), Am. (v.p. 9th circuit, 1935-36; mem. gen. council 1932-35), Internat., Wash. Seattle bar assns., Internat. Assn. Ins. Council (v.p., 1936), Am. Soc. Internat. Law, Am. Judicature Soc., Am. Bar Found., Seattle Hist. Soc. (trustee), World Affairs Council (trustee), English-Speaking Union (past trustee), Am. Coll. Probate Counsel, Nat. Fraternal Congress Am., Delta Theta Phi. Clubs: Seattle Press, Ranier (past pres.), Seattle Golf and Country, Broadmoor Golf and Country, Rotary (pres. 1953-54) (Seattle); Bohemian (San Francisco); Lawyers (N.Y.C.). Home: 2017 Parkside Dr Seattle WA 98102 Office: Norton Bldg Seattle WA 98104

GATES, CRAWFORD MARION, condr., composer; b. San Francisco, Dec. 29, 1921; s. Gilbert Marion and Leila (Adair) G.; B.A., San Jose State Coll., 1944; M.A., Brigham Young U., 1948; Ph.D., Eastman Sch. Music, 1954; m. Georgia Lauper, Dec. 19, 1952; children—Stephen Randall, Kathryn, Elizabeth, David Wendell Orchestrator radio sta. KSL, Salt Lake City, 1946-47; grad. asst. music theory Eastman Sch. Music, 1948-50; faculty Brigham Young U., 1950- 66, prof. music, chmn. dept., 1960-66; artist-in-residence Beloit (Wis.) Coll., 1966—; music dir., condr. Beloit Symphony Orch., 1963-64, 66—; music dir. Quincy Symphony Orch., 1969-70, Rockford Symphony Orch., 1970—; asst. to music dir. Broadway prodn., Redhead, 1958; owner Pacific Publs., music pubs., Provo, Beloit, 1948—; free-lance orchestrator, 1946—; guest condr. Utah Symphony, 1948—. Mem. gen. bd. Mut. Improvement Assn., Ch. Jesus Christ of Latter-day Saints, 1949-66, mem. gen. music com., 1960—. Served with USNR, World War II; PTO. Recipient Max Wald Meml. Fund award N.Y.C., 1955; A.S.C.A.P., standard award annually, 1965-70. Mem. Nat. Fedn. Music Clubs (nat. choral chmn. 1951-55, 1969—), A.S.C.A.P. Club: Timpanogos (Salt Lake City). Composer Utah Centennial mus. play, Promised Valley, 1947, Hill Cumorah Pageant, Palmyra, 1959, also commns. for religious ednl. films and Utah Symphony, U. Utah. Author: Catalog of Published American Choral Music, rev. edit. Home: 911 Park Av Beloit WI 53511 Office: Beloit Symphony Orch Box 185 Beloit WI 53511

GATES, EDWARD DWIGHT, coll. pres.; b. Wauwatosa, Wis., Mar. 26, 1921; s. Perez Dickinson and Delia (Dousman) G.; B.A., Beloit Coll., 1943; student U. Chgo., 1943; B.D., Pacific Sch. Religion, 1945; Ph.D., Bradley U., 1953; LL.D., Hiram Scott Coll., 1969; m. June Elizabeth Rowell, Sept. 10, 1944; children—Pamela, Geoffrey, James. Ordained to ministry, 1945; asst. minister to First Presbyn. Ch., Peoria, Ill., 1947-48, minister, 1948-54; ministerial staff First Congl. Ch., Los Angeles, 1954- 56; gen. sec. Macalester Coll., St. Paul, 1956-60; pres. Beaver Coll., Glenside, Pa., 1960—. Sec., bd. visitors Freedom Center of Freedoms Found., Valley Forge, Pa.; co-chmn. 1964 nat. and sch. awards jury Freedoms Found. at Valley Forge; bd. Christian edn. U.P. Ch. U.S.A., 1968—. Served as chaplain USNR, 1944-47. First place winner sermon category Freedoms Found. award, 1950, 2d place, 1951, 52, others, 53, 54, 55. Mem. Council Protestant Colls. and Univs. (chmn. bd. dirs. 1965-66), Presbyn. Coll. Union (exec. com.), Assn. Am. Colls. (mem. commn. on coll. adminstrn. 1964-67), Beta Theta Pi, Delta Sigma Rho, Phi Kappa Delta. Mason. Rotarian. Home: 1273 Butler Pike Blue Bell PA 19422

GATES, EDWIN WILDER, physician; b. Nashua, N.H., May 18, 1900; s. Edwin Lewis and Alice (Wilder) G. ; B.S., Colby Coll., 1922, D.Sc. (hon.), 1968; M.D., Harvard, 1926; m. Agnes Jessie Cameron, Dec. 22, 1922; 1 son, Edwin Wilder. Intern U.S. Marine Hosp., Staten Is., N.Y., 1926-27, resident, 1927-29; chief medicine Mt. St. Mary's Hosp., 1947-50, chief staff, 1950- 54, hon. cons. diabetes, 1966—; chief medicine Niagara Falls (N.Y.) Meml. Hosp., 1950-67, head div. diabetes 1959-69, hon. chief medicine, 1967—; dir. Katherine Nye Bartlett Diabetic Teaching Unit, 1966—; instr. medicine Niagara U. Sch. Nursing, 1947-50. Established Niagara Falls Diabetes Assn., 1954, continuous gen. med. audit Niagara Falls Meml. Hosp., 1955, pub. med. forums Niagara Falls Meml. Hosp. and Mt. St. Mary's Hosp., 1957, div. diabetes Niagara Falls Meml. Hosp., 1959, Dr. Charles H. Best Birthplace Trust, Inc., 1959. Treas. Niagara Falls Community Chest, 1946-49. Bd. dirs. Children's Aid Soc., 1933-35, Niagara Falls YMCA, 1933-39. Served with U.S. Army, 1918. Recipient Colby Coll. gavel Colby Coll. Alumni Assn., 1968. Fellow A.C.P.; mem. Am. Diabetes Assn. (bd. dirs. 1955-69, pres. 1967-68; Banting medal 1968), A.M.A., Buffalo Acad. Medicine, Niagara County, N.Y. State (chmn. subcom. diabetes 1951) med. socs., Am., Western N.Y. socs. internal medicine, Phi Beta Kappa. Author: (with others) Diabetes Mellitus: Diagnosis and Treatment, 1964; also articles. Home: 509 College Av Niagara Falls NY 14305 Office: 625 6th St Niagara Falls NY 14301

GATES, HOWARD PERRY, Jr., cons. electronics engr.; b. Los Angeles, Aug. 10, 1917; s. Howard Perry and Nina (Williams) G.; student U. Cal. at Los Angeles, 1935-37, B.S. in Elec. Engring., U. Cal. at Berkeley, 1939; m. Patricia Bonnell, June 18, 1945; children—Ann-Louise, Carol, Douglas, Teresa, Guilbert. Electronics engr. Bur. Ships, Navy Dept., 1940-45; head communications and nav. sect. U.S. Navy Electronics Lab., San Diego, 1945-50; with Hughes Aircraft Co., 1950-54; with Litton Industries, 1954-60, program mgr., 1958-60; v.p. Teledyne Inc., Hawthorne, Cal., 1961-64; asst. for electronics to asst. sec. army for research and devel., 1964-67; dep. asst. sec. army (research and devel.) S.E. Asia matters, 1968-69; cons., 1969—; ionospheric progagation and diversity system research, design and devel. satellite communication and nav. systems, also mil. communication and data processing systems. Cons., Army Sci. Adv. Panel, 1971—; chmn. vortac improvement spl. com. Radio Tech. Commn. for Aeros., 1970—; mem. Electronics and Aerospace Conv. Com., 1969—, chmn., 1971. Recipient Civilian Service awards Dept. of Army, 1966, 69. Registered profl. engr., D.C. Mem. I.E.E.E., Am. Geophys. Union, Armed Forces Communications Electronics Assn. (honor award 1966), Am. Inst. Aeros. and Astronautics, Am. Arbitration Assn. (panel arbitrators). Home: 6500 Waterway Dr Falls Church VA 22044

GATES, JAMES EDWARD, univ. prof., economist; b. Louisville, Ky., Nov. 21, 1908; s. George Demorrier and Ellen Theresa (Bullock) G.; B.S., U. Ky., 1929; grad. student, U. Chgo., 1930-31; Ph.D., U. Va., 1935; m. Mary Ann Chester; children (by previous marriage)—Patricia Lee, Jeffrey Read. Price investigator NRA, 1933-35; utility rate investigator Fed. Power Commn., 1935-37; prof. econs. and govt., Clemson Agrl. Coll., S.C., 1937-40; asst. prof. marketing, Ind. U., 1940- 41; economist and materials officer, WPB, 1941-45; economist Container Corp. of Am., 1945-47; economist Bur. Pub. Adminstrn., U. Va., 1947; prof. econs., dean Coll. Bus. Adminstrn., U. Ga., 1948-62, prof. econs., 1962—, also dir. exec. devel. program; econ. cons. to paperboard and paperboard container fields, 1947—. Chmn., chief exec. officer Lee House, 1969—. Mem. creative leadership council, Creative Edn. Found. Fellow A.I.M.; mem. Am. Econ. Assn., So. Econ. Assn., Acad. Mgmt., So. Inst. Mgmt. (ednl. counselor), Alpha Phi Omega, Beta Gamma Sigma, Omicron Delta Kappa, Delta Sigma Pi, Pi Sigma Alpha, Pi Sigma Epsilon. Democrat. Methodist. Mason, Elk. Clubs: Athens Country, Gridiron. Author: (with R. A. Egger) Municipal Ownership of Electric Undertakings in Virginia, 1937; (with Harold Miller) Personal Adjustment to Business, 1958. Home: 497 Milledge Terrace Athens GA 30601

GATES, JAY RAYMOND, coll. pres.; b. Steubenville, O., Feb. 23, 1892; s. James M. and Katherine Elizabeth (Koontz) G.; A.B., Washington and Jefferson Coll., 1913; J.D., Case Western Res. U., 1922; m. Gertrude Slater, June 10, 1914; children—Jayne (Mrs. Homer A. Forsythe), Kathryn (Mrs. William H. Kavanaugh); m. 2d, Gertrude Hollmer, Nov. 20, 1931; 1 son, Jay Hollmer. Admitted to Ohio bar, 1922; practiced in Cleve. until 1937; pres. Dyke Coll. (formerly Dyke and Spencerian Coll.), Cleve., 1935—. Mem. Nat. Bus. Tchrs. Assn. (past pres.), Ohio Bus. Schs. Assn. (past pres.), Bus. Edn. Research Assos. (trustee), Cleve. C. of C., Cleve. Advt. Club, Order of Coif, Delta Tau Delta, Phi Delta Phi. Rotarian, Mason (32, Shriner). Club: Cleveland Executives. Author: Gates' Ohio Corporation Law, 2d edit., 1932. Asso. editor: Throckmorton's Ohio Code, 1924; Baldwin's Ohio Code Service, 1926; Bates' Ohio Digest, 1926. Home: 12900 Lake Av Lakewood OH 44107 Office: 1375 E 6th St Cleveland OH 44114

GATES, JOHN MONTEITH, ret. architect; b. Elyria, O., June 25, 1905; s. William Nahum and Ada Laura (Cook) G.; student Milton (Mass.) Acad., 1918-23, Harvard, 1923-26; B.Arch., Columbia, 1929; m. Ellen Crenshaw, Dec. 27, 1927 (div. 1939); children—John, Ellen Gates (Mrs. R.G. Doench, Jr.,), Peter; m. 2d, Evelyn Byrd Dows, Sept. 28, 1940; children—Evelyn, Ada, Jonathan. With archtl. office, N.Y.C., 1931-33; v.p., dir. design Steuben Glass, N.Y.C., 1933-70; dir. design Corning Glass Works, 1959-70. Lt. comdr., USNR (inactive) since 1945; June 1942- Oct. 1945 field group comdr. under G-2, SHAEF, Eng., France, Luxemburg, Holland. Decorated Croix de Guerre with silver star, Croix de Guerre (Luxemburg); Officer Order of the Oak Crown (Luxemburg); Bronze Star (U.S.). Recipient spl. award. Phelps-Stokes Housing competition, 1932; co-winner 1st prize, Internat. Competition for Replanning of Stockholm, Sweden, 1933. Steuben glass designs exhibited internationally and in permanent collections in many museums. Registered architect, N.Y. Mem. Indsl. Designer Soc. Am., Royal Soc. Arts London (life; Benjamin Franklin fellow), A.I.A. Episcopalian. Water color painter. Home: 131 E 66th St New York City NY 10021

GATES, MAHLON EUGENE, army officer; b. Tyrone, Pa., Aug. 21, 1919; s. Samuel Clayton and Elsie (Nieweg) G.; B.S., U.S. Mil. Acad., 1942; M.S., U. Ill., 1948; postgrad. Command and Gen. Staff Coll., 1957, Army War Coll., 1962, Harvard, 1965; m. Patricia Ann

Lawrence, Dec. 19, 1942; children—Pamela Townley, Lawrence Alan. Commd. 2d lt. U.S. Army, 1942, advanced through grades to brig. gen., 1966; area engr. Iran, Gulf Dist., 1960-61; chief, engr. br., officer Personnel Directorate, Dept. Army, 1963-64; gen. staff Dept. Army, 1964-66; comdg. gen. Cam Ranh Bay, Vietnam, 1966-67; dir. constrn., Vietnam, 1967; dir. research, devel. and engring. Army Materiel Command, Washington, 1971. Mem. Dept. Army Bd. to Rev. Army Officer Schs., 1965-66. Decorated D.S.M., Bronze Star, Air medal; Army Distinguished Service Order 1st class Govt. Vietnam, Meritorious Service award. Mem. Soc. Am. Mil. Engrs., SHAPE Officers Assn., Brussels. Clubs: Internat., Harvard Bus. Sch., Army-Navy Country (Washington). Home: 1200 N Nash St Arlington VA 22209 Office: Hdqrs Army Materiel Command Washington DC 20315

GATES, MARSHALL DEMOTTE, Jr., chemist, editor; b. Boyne City, Mich., Sept. 25, 1915; s. Marshall DeMotte and Virginia (Orton) G.; B.S., Rice Inst., 1936, M.S., 1938; Ph.D., Harvard, 1941; D.Sc. (hon., MacMurray Coll., 1963; m. Martha Louise Meyer, Sept. 9, 1941; children—Christopher David, Catharine Louise, Marshall DeMotte III, Virginia Alice. Asst. prof. chemistry Bryn Mawr Coll., 1941-43; asso. prof., 1947-49; tech. aid NDRC, 1943-46; lectr. chemistry U. Rochester, 1949-52, part-time prof., 1952-60, prof., 1960-68, Charles Frederick Houghton prof. chemistry, 1968—; Welch Found. lectr., 1960; Max Tishler lectr. Harvard, 1953. Mem. com. on drug addiction and narcotics, div. med. scis. NRC, also com. on organic nomenclature div. of chemistry; mem. Pres.'s Com. on Nat. Medal of Sci., 1968-70. Recipient Edward Peck Curtis award for excellence in undergraduate teaching, 1967. Fellow Am. Acad. Arts and Scis., N.Y. Acad. Scis.; mem. Am. Chem. Soc., Nat. Acad. Scis. Editor: Jour. Am. Chem. Soc., 1963-69. Home: 41 W Brook Rd Pittsford NY 14534 Office: Univ of Rochester Rochester NY 14627

GATES, OLIVE, educator, pathologist; b. Worcester, Mass., Nov. 3, 1900; A.B., Vassar Coll., 1925; M.D., Yale, 1929. Resident pathology Collis P. Huntington Meml. Hosp., Harvard Cancer Commn., 1931-32, asst. pathologist, 1934-40, asso. pathologist, 1940-41; instr. neuropathology Boston U. Med. Sch., 1932; asst. pathologist Palmer Meml. Hosp., Boston, 1933-34; asst. pathologist Harvard Cancer Commn., 1941; research asso. Harvard Med. Sch., 1942-58, now clin. prof. pathology; asst. vis. pathologist Pondville Hosp., 1936-48, vis. pathologist, 1948-50; pathologist N.E. Deaconess Hosp., 1943-56, cons. pathologist, 1957—; cons. pathologist Westfield State Sanatorium, 1947—; asst. pathologist tumor diagnosis service Commonwealth Mass., 1934-55, cons., 1955. Recipient Distinguished Service in Cancer Control award Am. Cancer Soc., 1958. Address: 1397 Beacon St Brookline MA 02147*

GATES, PAUL WALLACE, educator; b. Nashua, N.H. Dec. 4, 1901; s. Edwin Lewis and Alice Ella (Wilder) G.; B.S., Colby Coll., 1924, L.H.D., 1967; A.M., Clark U., 1925; postgrad. U. Wis., 1926-27; Ph.D., Harvard, 1930; LL.D., U. Me., 1968; m. Lillian Francis Cowdell, Aug. 7, 1929; children—Edward Wilder, Lillian Francis (Mrs. Richard Goodman), Annette (Mrs. Preston Shimer), Rosemary (Mrs. Joseph Campos). Tutor Harvard, 1929-30; asst., asso. prof., Bucknell U., 1930-36; agrl. economist, land policy sect., Agrl. Adjustment Adminstrn., 1934-35; asst. prof., asso. prof., prof., John Stambaugh prof., Cornell U., 1936-71, emeritus, 1971—, chmn. dept. of history, 1946-56; summers; lectr., Mo., 1930, Pa. State U., 1933, Western Res. U., 1937, Duke, 1940, U. Cal. at Los Angeles, 1950, Harvard, 1960, U. Utah, 1969; vis. prof. U. Wis., 1968-69, U. Kan., 1971-72; cons., expert appraiser Quapaw, Chippewa, Pottawatomie claims U.S. Dept. Justice; cons. expert on pub. land history Pub. Land Law Rev. Commn., 1966-69. Past dir., pres. Coop. Consumers Soc. Ithaca, N.Y. Trustee Econ. History Assn., 1942-46, v.p., 1956; mem. State Hist. Commn., Pa. (apptd. by govt.), 1936; cons. 2d, Hoover Commn. on organization of exec. br. of govt., 1954. Awarded David A. Wells prize, Harvard, 1933. Fellow Social Sci. Research Council, 1933-34, 63-64; Guggenheim fellow, 1949-50; Huntington Library fellow, 1956-57. Mem. Orgn. Am. Historians (chmn. program com. 1946, 54, exec. com. 1948-52, 61-66, pres. 1961-62), Am., So. Wis., N.Y. State, Kan. hist. assns., Agrl. History Soc. (pres. 1949-50). Author books including: The John Tipton Papers (introduction), 1942; Frontier Landlords and Pioneer Tenants, 1945; Fifty Million Acres, 1954; The Farmers' Age, 1960; The Wisconsin Pine Lands of Cornell University, 1965; Agriculture and the Civil War, 1965; California Ranchos and Farms, 1846-1862, 1967; History of Public Land Law Development, 1968. Home: Ellis Hollow Rd Ithaca NY 14850

GATES, ROBERT LAWRENCE, sports editor; b. Cleve., Nov. 20, 1934; s. Lawrence Berry and Elizabeth (Parsch) G.; B.A., Miami U., Oxford, O., 1956; postgrad. Columbia, 1967; m. Judy Jane Stivers, Jan.. 22, 1966; children—Tracy Jane, Clayton Garrett. Sportswriter, Christian Sci. Monitor, 1956-62, sports editor, 1962—. Bd. dirs. Periwinkle Sch., Marblehead, Mass. Served with AUS, 1957-59. Mem. Baseball Writers Assn. Am., Nat. Hockey League Writers Assn., U.S. Ski Writers Assn., Football Writers Assn. Am. Christian Scientist (mem. bd.). Home: 73 Pond Lane Marblehead MA 01945 Office: 1 Norway St Boston MA 02115

GATES, ROBERT MAYNARD, educator, geologist; b. Madison, Wis., June 26, 1918; s. Clarence William and Myrtle (Perry) G.; B.A., U. Wis., 1941, M.A., 1941, Ph.D., 1949; m. Lera Robling, Oct. 9, 1948 (div. 1968); children—Robin William, Thomas Maynard, Faculty U. Wis., 1949—, prof. geology, 1960—; cons. Conn. Geol. Survey, 1949-70; spl. research on geology of Western Conn. highlands. Served to maj. USAAF, 1942-46. Fellow Geol. Soc. Am., Mineral. Soc. Am.; mem. Am. Assn. U. Profs., Sigma Xi. Office: Science Hall Univ Wis Madison WI 53706

GATES, ROY LYNDON, gas co. exec.; b. Sikes, La., Oct. 10, 1928; s. Clinton F. and Lettie (Burnett) G.; B.S., La. State U., 1952; m. Betty Huxtable, Dec. 21, 1954; children—William H., Susan B. With Touche, Ross Bailey & Smart. Houston, St. Louis, Memphis, 1952-64; v.p., controller Coastal States Gas Producing Co., Corpus Christi, Tex., 1964-66, v.p., treas., 1966-69, sr. v.p., dir., 1969—. Served with AUS, 1946-49, 52-53. Mem. Am. Petroleum Inst., Am. Inst. C.P.A.'s, Tex. Soc. C.P.A.'s, Nat. Assn. Accountants. Home: 4917 Cherry Hills St Corpus Christi TX 78413 Office: PO Drawer 521 Corpus Christi TX 78403

GATES, SAMUEL EUGENE, lawyer; b. Lagro, Ind. Feb. 9, 1906; s. Eugene Franklin and Fannie (Miller) G.; A.B., U. So. Cal., 1926, M.A., 1929, LL.B., 1933; postgrad. Harvard, 1929-30; diplome U. Paris (France), L'Institut des Hautes Etudes Internationales, 1931; m. Philomene Asher, Apr. 26, 1941; children—Gilda (Mrs. Cecil Wray, Jr.), Sharon (Mrs. Richard B. Stearns, Jr.), Mary Kathe (Mrs. Edwin D. Williamson). Tchr. pub. schs., Long Beach, Cal., 1927-29; fellow Carnegie Found., 1930-31; admitted to Cal. bar, 1933, N.Y. bar, 1938; asso. atty. Haight, Trippet & Syvertson, Los Angeles, 1933-35; partner Gates & Inch, Los Angeles, 1936-38; internat. counsel CAB, Washington, 1938-42; partner Douglas, Proctor, MacIntyre & Gates, Washington, 1946- 48, Debevoise, Plimpton & McLean, N.Y.C., 1948-62, Debevoise, Plimpton, Lyons & Gates, 1962—. Mem. Comite Internat. Technique des Experts Juridiques Aerien (Am. sec.), 1939-46; mem. U.S. commn. Permanent Am. Aero. Commn., 1941-44; mem. Am. delegations U.S.-Can. Civil Aviation Confs., 1939-40; adviser Am. delegation Internat. Civil Aviation Conf., Chgo., 1944. Anglo-Am. Civil Aviation Conf., Bermuda, 1946, 1st Gen. Assembly Provisional Internat. Civil Aviation Orgn., Montreal, 1946, Internat. Civil Aviation Orgn. Montreal, 1947. Dir. Goodwill Industries N.Y. Served as col. Air Transport Command, USAAF, 1942-46. Decorated D.S.M. Mem. Am., N.Y. State bar assns., State Bar Cal., Bar Assn. N.Y.C., Am. Law Inst., Am. Coll. Trial Lawyers, Am. Judicature Soc., Am. Soc. Internat. Law. Clubs: University, Union (N.Y.C.); Metropolitan (Washington); Westhampton Country, Quantuck Beach (Westhampton Beach, N.Y.); Nat. Golf Links of Am. Home: 830 Park Av New York City NY 10021 Office: 320 Park Av New York City NY 10022

GATES, SAMUEL GERALD, ednl. adminstr.; b. Denver, Dec. 3, 1919; s. Con Leonard and Bessie (Davidson) G.; A.B., Colo. State Coll., 1945, M.A., 1947; student Social Sci. Found., U. Denver, summer 1946; Ed.D., Stanford, 1953; m. Mary Katherine Parker, Jan. 30, 1942; children—Samuel Bartlett, Kristie Marie. Permanent substitute tchr. Jr. high sch. sci., Greeley (Colo.) pub. schs., 1941-42; tchr. jr. high sch. sci., Canon City (Colo.) pub. schs., 1942; instr. social studies Lab. Sch., Colo. State Coll., 1946- 48, dir. coll. high sch. Lab. Sch., 1948-49, dir. Lab. Sch., 1949-55, dean grad. div. of coll., 1955-65; pres. Wis. State U. at LaCrosse, 1965-70; asso. dir. Wis. State Univs. System, 1971—. Pres. LaCrosse Citizens Planning Corp., Inc.; chmn. adv. bd. U.S. Army Staff and Gen. Command Coll., 1967-68, mem., 1968—; bd. visitors USAF Air U., 1968—. Bd. dirs. St. Francis Hosp., LaCrosse, Wis., 1968—. Served to capt., as pilot, USAAF, 1942-46; maj. Res. Mem. Colo. Ednl. Assn. (dir. 1957-60), N. Central Assn. Colls. and Secondary Schs. (commr. 1960—, dir.), Am. Assn. Colls. of Tchr. Edn. (dir. 1971—), LaCrosse C. of C. (dir.), Sch. Masters Club Colo., Am. Legion, Blue Key, Phi Alpha Theta, Lambda Sigma Tau, Phi Delta Kappa, Kappa Delta Pi. Conglist. Rotarian. Home: 2 Sumter Ct Madison WI 53705 Office: 142 E Gilman St Madison WI 53703

GATES, THEODORE ROSS, govt. ofcl.; b. Milw., May 22, 1918; s. W. Ross and Mary (Balcom) G.; A.B., Dartmouth, 1940; student Yale Sch. Law, 1940-41; M.A., Harvard, 1948; m. Dorothy P. Kaiser, Dec. 17, 1942; children—C. Parker, Mary M. Economist, Guaranty Trust Co., 1948-50; internat. economist Nat. Indsl. Conf. Bd., 1950-63; chief economist Office Spl. Rep. for Trade Negotiations, Exec. Office of Pres., 1963-67, asst. spl. rep., 1967—. Served with AUS, 1942-46. Mem. Phi Beta Kappa. Democrat. Author: Costs and Competition; other books, articles on econ. subjects. Home: 7827 Overhill Rd Bethesda MD 20014 Office: Exec Office Bldg Washington DC 20506

GATES, THOMAS SOVEREIGN, Jr., banker, former sec. of def.; b. Phila., Apr. 10, 1906; s. Thomas Sovereign and Marie (Rogers) G.; A.B., U. Pa., 1928; LL.D., U. Pa., Yale, Columbia; m. Millicent Anne Brengle, Sept. 29, 1928; children—Millicent Anne, Patricia S., Thomas S. (dec.), Katharine Curtin. Asso. with Drexel & Co., Phila., 1928, partner, 1940-53; pres., dir. Morgan Guaranty Trust Co., 1961-65, chmn. bd., chief exec. officer, 1965-70, chmn. exec. com. 1969—; dir. Gen. Electric Co., Scott Paper Co., Campbell Soup Co., Ins. Co. N.Am., Smith, Kline & French Labs., Cities Service Co., Bethlehem Steel Corp.; under sec. navy, 1953-57, sec. navy, 1957-59; dep. sec. def., 1959, sec. def. 1959-60. Mem. adv. council Sch. Advanced Internat. Studies, Johns Hopkins. Trustee Foxcroft Sch., life trustee U. Pa.; bd. dirs. Council for Financial Aid to Edn., Inc.; bd. consultants Nat. War Coll. Served as comdr. USNR, 1942-45; overseas. Mem. Acad. Polit. Sci. (trustee), Council Fgn. Relations, Navy League, Bus. Council, Pa. Soc., Colonial Soc. Pa., Phi Beta Kappa. Clubs: Philadelphia, Racquet (Phila.); Gulph Mills Golf, Metropolitan, Links (Washington); Economic (N.Y.C.). Home: Mill Race Farm Devon PA 19333 Office: 23 Wall St New York City NY 10005

GATES, WILLIAM BYRAM, Jr., educator, economist; b. Indpls., Oct. 18, 1917; s. William Byram and Margaret (Detrick) G.; student U. Geneva (Switzerland), 1935-36; A.B., Williams Coll., 1939; M.A., Ph.D., U. Chgo., 1947; m. Sylvia Clack, July 24, 1953; children—Barbara (by previous marriage), William Mark, Nicola. With tax research div. Treasury Dept., 1941-42; mem. faculty dept. econs. Williams Coll., 1947-50, 1954—, Herbert Lehman prof., 1960- -, chmn. dept., 1961—, exec. com. Williams Center Devel. Econs., 1960- -; economist Export-Import Bank, 1950-54; Brookings Nat. Research prof., Port-au-Prince, Haiti, 1957-58; dep. project mgr., chief devel. specialist Devel. Projects Cons. Service, Indonesia, 1962-63; project dir. Devel. Adv. Service, Malaysia, 1966-68; occasional cons. Ford Found., also State Dept. Served with USNR, 1942-46. Mem. Am. Econ. Assn., Econ. History Assn., Phi Beta Kappa. Author: Michigan Copper and Boston Dollars, 1951. Home: Sabin Dr Williamstown MA 02167

GATES, WILLIAM FRED, Jr., bishop; b. Lexington, Va., Mar. 29, 1912; s. William Fred and Edna (Brundige) G.; student Hobart Coll., 1931-32; A.B., U. Chattanooga, 1934; B.D., Va. Theol. Sem., 1937, D.D., 1967; D.D., U. of South, 1967; m. Jane Gregory Dillard, Apr. 25, 1938; children—Anne Gregory, Susan Wenrick. Ordained priest Episcopal Ch., 1938; asst. minister Calvary Episcopal Ch., Memphis, 1937-38; priest-in-charge St. John's Ch., Old Hickory, Tenn., 1938-42; rector St. Peter's Ch., Columbia, Tenn., 1943-66; suffragan bishop Episcopal Diocese Tenn., Memphis, 1966—, also mem. bishop and council, standing com., bd. examining chaplains. Chmn. Maury Co. chpt. A.R.C., 1947-49; pres. Maury Co. United Givers Fund, 1965-66. Mem. Kappa Alpha. Club: Memphis Country. Home: 5302 Southwood Dr Memphis, TN 38117. Office: 692 Poplar Av Memphis TN 38105

GATESON, MARJORIE, actress; b. Bklyn., Jan. 17, 1900; d. Daniel T. and Augusta V. (Smith) Gateson; student Packer Collegiate Inst., Bklyn. Conservatory Music. Debut in chorus The Dove of Peace, Damrosch operetta; appeared in The Little Cafe, Her Soldier Boy, Fancy Free, Little Miss Charity, The Rose Girl, Lady Butterfly, The Love Letter, For Goodness Sake, Strange Bedfellows, As Good As New, Sweethearts, Parthy Ann in Showboat; played Mother Barbour in One Man's Family (TV), 1949-52; currently Grace Tyrell in Secret Storm (TV); featured in about 100 films. Starred in Kiss and Tell, U.S.O., Italy, 1944-45. (Mem. Actors Equity Assn. (council 10 yrs.) Address: care Hotel Royalton 44 W 44th St New York City NY 10036

GATEWOOD, BUFORD ECHOLS, educator, aero. and astronautical engr.; b. Byhalia, Miss., Aug. 23, 1913; s. Robert P. and Irene (Echols) G.; B.S. in Mech. Engring., La. Poly. Inst., 1935; M.S., U. Wis., 1937, Ph.D., 1939; m. Margaret Murphy, June 28, 1939; 1 dau., Marianne. Faculty, La. Poly. Inst., 1939-42, Air Force Inst. Tech., 1947-60; with McDonnell Aircraft Corp., 1942-46, Beech Aircraft Corp., 1946-47; prof. aero. and astronautical engring. Ohio State U., Columbus, 1960—. Cons. on structural design and analysis, structural fatigue, problems in dynamics, thermal Problems to various cos., 1949—. Mem. Am. Inst. Aeros. and Astronautics, Soc. Exptl. Stress Analysis, Math. Assn. Am., Am. Soc. M.E., Am. Soc. Engring. Edn., Sigma Xi. Author: Thermal Stresses, 1957. Research, publs. on thermal stresses and inelastic structures for flight vehicle structures. Home: 2150 Waltham Rd Columbus OH 43221

GATHANY, VAN R., banker; b. Evanston, Ill., July 16, 1926; s. William Vandervoort and Isabel (Risser) G.; B.A., Swarthmore Coll., 1950; M.B.A., U. Chgo., 1953; m. Hilda Lang Denworth, Oct. 13, 1951; children—Virginia Lynn, Douglas Vandervoort, Robin Elizabeth. Vice pres. No. Trust Bank, Chgo., 1963-67, sr. v.p., 1967—; dir. Top Star, Inc., Lake Forest Book Store, Inc. Instr., Am. Inst. Banking, Lake Forest (Ill.) Coll. Indsl. Mgmt. Inst.; lectr. Nat. Trust Sch. Mem. Lake Forest Caucus, 1960-63; mem. Lake Forest Elementary Sch. Bd., 1963-70; bd. assos. Nat. Coll. Edn., Evanston; asst. treas. St. Luke's- Presbyn. Hosp., Chgo. Served with AC, USNR, 1944-46. Presbyn. (elder). Clubs: Lake Forest (past pres., dir.), University (Chgo.). Home: 786 Longwood Dr Lake Forest IL 60045 Office: 50 S LaSalle St Chicago IL 60690

GATHINGS, JAMES ANDERSON, ret. educator; b. Peachland, N.C., Sept. 10, 1900; s. William Daniel and Nora (Rivers) G.; A.B., Furman U., 1925; A.M., Duke, 1930; fellow polit. scis., U. Chgo., 1930-31; Ph.D., N.Y. U., 1937; m. Elizabeth Daniel, Aug. 6, 1931 (dec. Mar. 1962); 1 dau., Elizabeth Jane (Mrs. David S. Snook). Prin., Simpsonville (S.C.) High Sch., 1925-27, supt. schs., 1927-29; asst. prof. polit. sci. Tex. Christian U., 1931-32; faculty Bucknell U., 1932—, prof. polit. sci., 1946-71, emeritus, 1971—, chmn. dept., 1947-69; tech. adviser Pa. Unemployment Compensation Bd. Rev., 1938. Recipient Lindbach award inspirational teaching Bucknell U., 1962, Burma-Bucknell Bowl for contbn. to internat. understanding, Bucknell U., 1968. Mem. Am. Polit. Sci. Assn., Am. Soc. Internat. Law, Pa. Polit. Sci. and Pub. Adminstrn. Assn. (pres. 1948-50), Pi Sigma Alpha, Omicron Delta Kappa. Author: International Law and American Treatment of Alien Enemy Property, 1940; A Survey of Governments, 1950. Editor: Politics and The American Businessman, 1960. Home: 90 University Av Lewisburg PA 17837

GATHRIGHT, JOSEPH RADFORD, banker; b. Louisville, Mar. 23, 1911; s. Jesse N. and Lucy (Farmer) C.; A.B., Dartmouth, 1931; LL.B., U. Louisville, 1934; m. Jane Dobbins, Dec. 7, 1935; 1 son, Joseph Radford. Admitted to Ky. Bar, 1934; practiced in Louisville, 1934-38; asst. city atty., Louisville, 1935-38; with Ky. Trust Co., Louisville, 1938—, trust officer, 1945—, sr. v.p., 1961-67, exec. v.p. 1967-71, pres., 1971—, also dir.; dir. First Ky. Bank Louisville, First Ky. Co., W.E. Caldwell Co., Commonwealth Land Title Ins. Co. Phila.; Pres. Estate Planning Council, Louisville, 1948; Pres. Legal Aid Soc. Louisville, 1959. Mem. Am., Ky., Louisville bar assns. Presbyn. (deacon). Home: 180 West Wind Rd Louisville KY 40207 Office: 216 S 5th St Louisville KY 40201

GATI, LASZLO, symphony condr.; b. Timisoara, Rumania, Sept. 25, 1925; s. Ignatie and Veronica (Grosz) Osterreicher; diploma in Violin, Conservatory of Music, 1945; student Ferencz Liszt Acad. Music, Budapest, 1946-49; degree in Violin, Conducting, Nat. Conservatory Music, Budapest, 1949; diploma, Pan Am. Orch. Conductors Course, Mexico, 1958; diploma in Conducting, Academie Internationale D'Ete, Nice, 1969; m. Agnes Keresztesi, Nov. 10, 1951; children—Suzanne, Kathleen. Violinist, State Philharmonic Orch. (formerly Capital's Orch.), 1946-53; condr. choir and orch. U. Econs., 1950-56; prof. violin Mus. Sch. Budapest, 1953-54; condr. Nat. State Philharmonic, 1953-56; head symphonic and chamber music dept. and internat. music programe exchange dept. Hungarian Radio, 1954-56; asst. solo viola Montreal Symphony, 1957-64; acting asst. condr. Zubin Mehta, Montreal, 1960-64; condr. Philharmonia Orch. Montreal, 1958-61; founder, condr. Montreal Chamber Orch., 1959—; music dir., condr. Victoria Symphony Orch., 1967—; regular guest condr. with numerous Canadian, Mexican, European orchs. Sr. Art fellow Can. Council, 1964. Mem. Zoltan Kodaly Acad. (hon. mem.). Home: 591 Falkland Rd Victoria British Columbia Canada Office: 1960 Lansdowne Rd Victoria British Columbia Canada

GATLIN, CARL, ednl. adminstr.; b. Wichita Falls, Tex., July 9, 1924; s. Carl Napoleon and Lois (Looney) G.; B.Engring., U. So. Cal., 1951; M.S. in Petroleum Engring., U. Tulsa, 1955; Ph.D. in Petroleum Engring., Pa. State U., 1959; m. Lila Lee Krause, Sept. 3, 1947; children—Ameera Lee, Jefferson, Laura, Jennifer Gatlin. Started as petroleum engr. with Phillips Petroleum Co., Anderson-Prichard Oil Corp., Tex. Crude Oil Co., 1951-53; faculty U. Tulsa, 1953-57, asst. prof., 1956-57; faculty U. Tex., 1959-64, chmn. dept. petroleum engring., 1960-63; chmn. dept. mech. engring., 1963, prof., 1961-64; v.p. for research dir. grad. studies Drexel Inst. Tech., Phila., 1964-65, v.p. acad, affairs, 1965-69; pres. Stanislaus State Coll., Turlock, Cal., 1969—. Served to lt. (j.g.) USNR, 1943-46. Registered profl. engr., Tex., Okla. Mem. Soc. Petroleum Engrs. (chmn. edn. com. 1961-63), Am. Soc. M.E., Sigma Xi, Tau Beta Pi, Sigma Gamma Epsilon, Pi Epsilon Tau. Club: Del Rio Golf. Author: Petroleum Engineering-Drilling and Well Completions, 1960; also articles. Home: 3405 Weymouth Lane Modesto CA 95350 Office: Stanislaus State Coll Turlock CA 95380

GATOS, HARRY CONSTANTINE, educator; b. Greece, Dec. 27, 1921; s. Constantine B. and Paraskevi (Merinztos) G.; came to U.S., 1946, naturalized, 1955; diploma in chemistry U. Athens (Greece), 1945; M.A. in Chemistry, Ind. U., 1948; Ph.D., Mass. Inst. Tech., 1950; m. Dawn Spiropoulos, July 15, 1950; children—Pamela Dawn, Niki Ann, Constantine Harry. Instr., U. Athens, 1943-46; mem. research staff Mass. Inst. Tech., 1948-52; research engr. E.I. duPont de Nemours & Co., Inc., 1952-55, from sect. leader to div. head solid state div. Lincoln Lab., 1955-64, prof. metallurgy and elec. engring. Mass. Inst. Tech., Cambridge, 1962—; cons. to industry, 1962—. Trustee Longy Sch. Music, Cambridge, Mass. Mem. Electrochem. Soc. (pres. 1967-68), Am. Chem. Soc., Am. Phys. Soc., Am. Inst. Metall. Engrs., Am. Acad. Arts and Scis., Acad. Athens (corr.). Contbr. profl. jours. Editor-in-chief Surface Science. Home: 20 Indian Hill Rd Weston, MA 02193 Office: Mass Inst Tech Cambridge MA 02139

GATOV, ELIZABETH RUDEL, former U.S. treas.; b. Montreal, Que., Can., Apr. 27, 1911 (parents Am. citizens); d. Clarence M. and Anna M. (Ryder) Rudel; student Smith Coll., 1929-31; B.A., U. Mich., 1937; children by former marriage—Jane (Mrs. James Jackson), Daniel Upham Smith; m. Albert W. Gatov, June 22, 1962. Feature editor Ind.-Jour., San Rafael, Cal., 1948-50; staff mem. Coro Found., pub. affairs internship program, San Francisco, 1951-53; treas. U.S., 1961-62; asst. labor commr. State Cal., 1960; v.p. San Rafael Fed. Savs. & Loan Assn. Mem. exec. com. Planned Parenthood World Population. Chmn. Marin County Dem. Central Com., 1955-56; dir. Cal. Dem. Council, 1955-56; del. nat. conv., 1956, 60, 64, 68; Dem. nat. committeeman for Cal., 1956-65. Home: 21 Rancheria Rd Kentfield CA 94904 Office: 874 4th St San Rafael CA 94901

GATSKI, ROBERT LAWRENCE, physician; b. West Hazelton, Pa., May 27, 1919; s. Peter Paul and Estella (Schlacky) G.; student Bucknell U., 1942-44; M.D., Jefferson Med. Coll., 1948; m. Betty Eileen Carey, June 29, 1942; children—Robert Lawrence, Charles P., Marsha E., Mark. Intern St. Josephs Hosp., Lancaster, Pa., 1948-49; resident Danville (Pa.) State Hosp., 1949-53; acting clin. dir. Gov. Bacon Health Center, Delaware City, Del., 1954-55; clin. dir. Danville (Pa.) State Hosp., 1954-55, supt., adminstr., 1955—; acting supt. Retreat State Hosp., 1965-67; psychiat. cons. Geisinger Med. Center, Bloomsburg (Pa.) Hosp., Muncy (Pa.) State Indsl. Home, Eastern Fed. Penitentiary, Lewisburg, Pa. Diplomate Am. Bd.

Psychiatry, Nat. Bd. Med. Examiners. Mem. A.M.A., Am. Psychiat. Assn., Am. Acad. Neurology, Am. Coll. Hosp. Adminstrs. Editor Pa. Psychiat. Quar., 1959-63, cons. editor, 1963—. Research mental disorders. Address: Danville State Hosp Danville, PA 17821.

GATTS, ROBERT ROSWELL, educator, mech. engr.; b. Berlin Heights, O., Mar. 2, 1925; s. Christian Peter and Blanche (Derby) G.; student Kent State U., 1946-47; B.M.E., Ohio State U., 1950, M.Sc., 1951, Ph.D., 1959; m. Donna Ellen Wertman, May 14, 1949; children—Robert Kent, Gail Ann, Roslyn Ruth, Maryl Jan, Christian Peter. Engr. Visking Corp., Terre Haute, Ind., 1951-53; research asso. Ohio State U., 1953-58, asst. prof., 1958-59; engr. mechanics and materials Gen. Elec. Corp., Schenectady, N.Y., 1959-63; prof., chmn. dept. mech. engring. U. Kan., 1963—; reliability cons. John Deere Waterloo Tractor Works. Trustee U. Kan. Center Research, Inc., 1968—. Mem. Am. Soc. M.E., Am. Soc. Engring. Educators, Am. Soc. Testing and Materials, Soc. Automotive Engrs., Soc. Exptl. Stress Analysis, Soc. Mfg. Engrs., Newcomen Soc. Research on cumulative damage of materials due to cyclic fatigue. Home: RR 4 Lawrence KS 66044

GATY, T.E., III, business exec.; b. 1922; B.S., Rensselaer Poly. Inst., 1949; married. Dist. mgr. Line Material Industries div. McGraw-Edison Co., 1949-61; v.p. sales Standard Transformer Co., 1961-63, exec. v.p., gen. mgr., 1963-67, pres., 1967-70; exec. v.p. Am. Gage & Machine Co., 1967-70; exec. v.p. operations Kuhlman Corp., Birmingham, Mich., 1970—; dir. Am. Welding & Mfg. Co., Warren, O. Served to lt. col. USAF, 1940-65. Office: PO Box 288 Birmingham MI 48012*

GATZKE, HANS WILHELM, educator; b. Duelken, Germany, Dec. 10, 1915; s. Wilhelm and Else (Schwab) G.; student U. Munich, Germany, 1935, U. Bonn, 1936; A.B., Williams Coll., 1938; M.A., Harvard, 1939, Ph.D., 1947; M.A. (hon.), Yale, 1964. Came to U.S., 1937, naturalized, 1944. Teaching fellow, tutor history Harvard, 1939-41, 42-44, 46-47; Sheldon traveling fellow, 1941-42, asst. sr. tutor Eliot House, 1942-43; instr. history Williams Coll., 1942; asst. prof. history Johns Hopkins, 1947- 51, asso. prof., 1951-56, prof. history, 1956-64; prof. history Yale, 1964—, fellow Timothy Dwight Coll., 1964—; mem. Inst. Advanced Study, Princeton, 1951-52; Rockefeller grant, 1962-63. Served as 2d lt. AUS, 1944-46, psychol. warfare div. SHAEF. Recipient Herbert Baxter Adams prize Am. Hist. Assn., 1950; Guggenheim fellow, 1956-57. Mem. Am. Hist. Assn., Phi Beta Kappa, Delta Kappa Epsilon. Editor, translator: (Carl von Clausewitz) Principles of War, 1942; Germany's Drive to the West, 1950; Stresemann and the Rearmament of Germany, 1954; The Present in Perspective, 1957; The Course of Civilization, 1961. Editorial bd. Jour. Modern History, 1954-57, Current History; U.S. editor in chief Documents on German Foreign Policy, 1969—. Home: 56 Farrell Rd Weston CT 06880 Office: Dept History Yale U New Haven CT 06520

GAUD, WILLIAM STEEN, govt. ofcl.; b. N.Y.C., Aug. 9, 1907; s. William S. and Isabel Cleland (Williams) G.; B.A., Yale, 1929, LL.B., 1931; m. Eleanor Mason Smith, June 1, 1935; 1 dau., Anne Timothy. Instr. Yale Law Sch., 1931-33; practiced law, N.Y.C., 1933-35; asst. corp. counsel, N.Y.C., 1935-41; spl. asst. to sec. of war, 1945-46; mem. law firm Carter, Ledyard & Milburn, 1946-61; asst. adminstr. Bur. for Near East and South Asia, AID, Dept. State, 1961-64, dep. adminstr. AID, 1964-66, adminstr., 1966-69; exec. v.p. Internat. Finance Corp., 1969—. Served from capt. to col. AUS, 1942-45, 2 yrs. China, Burma and India. Decorated Legion of Merit with Oak Leaf Cluster, Order of British Empire. Home: 4926 Rockwood Pkwy NW Washington DC 20016

GAUDETTE, EDGAR ALLEN, mfg. co. exec.; b. Lowell, Mass., June 18, 1914; s. Albert William and Ethel (Barton) G.; A.B., Rutgers U., 1940; m. Ruth E. Crater, Sept. 10, 1937; children—Alan, Jeanne. Dir. purchasing Gen. Cable Corp., N.Y.C., 1945-51; treas. Permacel Tape Co., New Brunswick, N.J., 1953-57; v.p., treas. LePages, Inc., Gloucester, Mass., 1957-60; joined Neptune Meter Co., 1960, became exec. v.p., 1963, later pres., dir.; financial cons., 1958-62. Mem. Controllers Inst., Am. Mgmt. Assn., Nat. Indsl. Conf. Bd. Home: 772 Norgate St Westfield NJ 07090

GAUDIAN, MARTIN FERDINAND, trade assn. exec.; b. New Britain, Conn., Jan. 11, 1902; s. Martin Waldemar and Ann (Passig) G.; student Gettysburg Coll., 1919-20; B.S., Trinity Coll., 1923; M.A., Ohio State U., 1926, postgrad. 1926-28; grad. Nat. Inst. Trade Assn. Execs., 1950; m. Evelyn Gettings, June 19, 1937; children—Barbara Lee, Evelyn Augusta (Mrs. Robert Parks) Edythe Mae (Mrs. Hubert Kleinpeter III). Coach athletics, instr. Bainbridge (O.) High Sch., 1926-27; faculty U. Cin., Butler U., U. Colo., 1927-33; research Bur. Bus. Research, Ohio State U., 1926, also Akron C. of C., spl. taxation commn. State Ohio, 1926-27; asst. dir. field service U.S. Savs. & Loan League, 1933-37; exec. sec. N.C. Bldg. & Loan League, 1937-41; v.p. Citizens Fire Ins. Co., Newberry, S.C., 1941- 42; with the Producers Council, Trade Assn. Bldg. Supply Mfrs., 1944-45; sec., exec. v.p. Nat. Assn. Cemeteries (formerly Nat. Cemetery Assn.), Washington, 1945—. Staff OPA, War Labor Bd., World War II. Member Am. Soc. Trade Assn. Execs. (named charter assn. exec. 1961), English Speaking Union, Sigma Nu. Lutheran. Clubs: Arts (Washington); Fairfax Hunt; International; Communications. Author: The Operation of a Cemetery. Editor: Cemetery Selling, Cemetery Counselor Handbook, Cemetery Yearbook. Contbr. to trade jours. Home: Windswept Route 1 Box 215 B Ashburn VA 22011 Office: 1911 N Fort Myer Dr Arlington VA 22209

GAUDION, DONALD ALFRED, diversified mfg. exec.; b. Buffalo, July 10, 1913; s. William Thomas and Orpha (Gascoyne) G.; A.B. magna cum laude, U. Rochester, 1936; M.B.A. magna cum laude, Harvard, 1938; m. Gertrude Margaret McKie, Aug. 3, 1940; children—Sharon Margaret, Jacquelyn Elaine, Donald A. Asst. to v.p. charge sales and advt. Eastman Kodak Co., 1938-45; v.p. Kryptar Corp., 1945-48; chmn., chief exec. officer, dir. Sybron Corp., Rochester, 1948—; dir. Rochester Telephone Corp., Garlock, Inc., Palmyra, N.Y., Schlegel Mfg. Co., Rochester, N.Y., USM Corp., Boston, Security Trust Co. of Rochester, Security N.Y. Corp.; trustee Monroe County Savs. Bank, Rochester. Exec. com. Machinery and Allied Products Inst., Washington. Chmn. bd. trustees Rochester U.; trustee Rochester Bur. Center for Govtl. and Community Research. Mem. Rochester Soc. Investment Analysts, Rochester (past pres., bd. trustees) C. of C., Phi Beta Kappa. Methodist. Clubs: City (past pres.), University, Rochester Country (Rochester); Genessee Valley; Harvard (N.Y.C.); Harvard Business School (past pres.); Philosophers'. Home: 30 Golfside Pkwy Rochester NY 14610 Office: Midtown Tower Rochester NY 14604

GAUER, CHARLOTTE EDWINA, assn. exec.; b. Balt., Jan. 16, 1912; d. Charles E. and Lucinda D. (Smith) Gauer; B.S., U. Ill., 1932, LL.B., 1935. Admitted to Ill. bar, 1935; legal editor Commerce Clearing House, Chgo., 1935-42; legal staff Montgomery Ward & Co., 1942-50, Pub. Housing Adminstrn., 1951-54; exec. dir. Am. Patent Law Assn., Arlington, Va., 1954—. Nat. bd. Med. Coll. Pa., 1953—. Served with Am. Women's Vol. Services, 1942- 45. Mem. Women's Bar Assn. Ill. (pres. 1942-43), Nat. Assn. Women Lawyers (v.p. Ill. 1943-44, pres. 1947-49). Am. Bar Assn., Delta Delta Delta, Alpha Alpha Alpha, Kappa Beta Pi, Mortar Bd. Republican. Conglist. Home: 2111 Jefferson Davis Hwy Arlington VA 22202 Office: 2001 Jefferson Davis Hwy Arlington VA 22202

GAUGER, PAUL WILLIAM, educator; b. Milw., May 2, 1914; s. Paul Max and Alma (Kreblin) G.; Ph.D., U. Wis., 1951; m. Jennie Rosenthal, June 6, 1942. Tchr., Antigo (Wis.) High Sch., 1942-43; with N.Am. Aviation Co., Inglewood, Cal., 1943-44; faculty U. Wis., Madison, 1944-58; head dept. speech Wis. State U., Platteville, 1958—. Mem. Speech Communication Assn., Edn. Theatre Assn. Home: Route 4 Platteville WI 53818

GAULT, HARRY G., lawyer; b. Mt. Morris Twp., Genesee County, Mich., Jan. 25, 1892; s. William Henry and Nora (Ryan) G.; A.B., U. Mich., 1915, J.D., 1917, LL.D., 1959; m. Alice Margaret Wiard, June 30, 1917 (dec. 1949); children—Barbara, James Lane; m. 2d, Hilda Reava Draws, Sept. 16, 1950. Practiced at Flint, Mich., 1919—; admitted to practice before U.S. Supreme Court, Feb. 1932; pros. atty. Genesee Co., Mich., 1921-24; mem. Gault & Parker, 1925-28, Carton, Gault & Parker, 1929-31, Carton & Gault 1932-1934, Carton, Gault & Davison, 1935-47, Gault & Davison 1947-52, Gault, Davison & Bowers, 1952- -. Mem. and vice chmn. Charter Revision Commn., Flint, 1928-29; mem. Mich. State Crime Commn., 1929-43; mem. bd. commrs. Mich. State Bar, 1939-48, pres., 1947-48. Mem. bd. trustees Women's Hosp. Assn. Mem. Am. (mem. ho. of dels. 1948-54), Mich. State, Genesee Co. bar assns., Am. Judicature Soc. (dir. 1958-61), Order of Coif, Theta Chi, Phi Delta Phi Mason, Elk, Kiwanian. Clubs: Flint Golf, Flint City, Flint University; Detroit. Home: 2031 Hampden Rd Flint MI 48503 Office: Genesee Bank Bldg Flint MI 48502

GAULT, N.L., Jr., med. educator; b. Austin, Tex., Aug. 22, 1920; s. N.L. and Pauline (Johnson) G.; student Baylor U. Med. Sch., 1946-48; B.A., U. Tex., 1950; M.B., U. Minn., 1950, M.D., 1951, student Grad. Sch., 1951-54; m. Sarah Jane Dickie, Dec. 2, 1922; children—Elizabeth Jean, John Dickie, Paul Alan. Intern Mpls. Gen. Hosp., 1950-51; resident internal medicine Mpls. VA Hosp., 1951-52; chief resident internal medicine Ancker Hosp., St. Paul, 1952, U. Minn. Hosp., 1953-54; faculty U. Minn. Med. Sch., 1953-67, asso. prof. internal medicine, asso. dean, 1962-67; prof. medicine U. Hawaii, asso. dean med. sch., 1967—; chief adviser Seoul (Korea) Nat. U. Coll. Medicine, 1959-61; med. edn. cons. China Med. Board, N.Y.C., 1963, 71, AID, 1964-68; dir. postgrad. med. edn. program for Ryukyu Islands, 1967-69, cons. Mpls. VA Hosp., 1956-57. Sec.-treas. Minn. Med. Found., 1956-67. Served to capt. AUS and USAAF, 1942-46. Decorated Commendation medal; recipient Supreme award Japan Med. Assn., 1969. Mem. Am. Rheumatism Assn. Address: 3675 Kilauea Av Honolulu HI 96816

GAULT, THOMAS GOWER, educator; b. Cornersville, Tenn., Sept. 2, 1919; s. H. Wayman and Mary Arlene (Gower) G.; B.S., Middle Tenn. U., 1946; M.A., George Peabody Coll. Tchrs., 1949, Ed.D., 1959; m. Virginia Lee Garner, Sept. 8, 1942; 1 son, Richard Thomas. Tchr. coach Franklin County High Sch., Decherd, Tenn., 1946-47; prin., tchr. Christiana (Tenn.) Sch., 1947-50; prin., supt. Waverly (Tenn.) City Sch., 1950-52; asso. prof. social sci. Edinboro (Pa.) State Coll., 1952-55; prof., chmn. dept. geography Indiana (Pa.) U., 1956—; pres. Ind. Book and Record, Inc., 1970—. Sec. Nat. Council for Geog. Edn., 1965-67. Vice-chmn. Indiana Housing Authority, 1964-71. Pres., bd. dirs. Indiana Westminster Found., 1962-68. Served to lt. USAAF, 1941-45. Decorated Air medal with 9 oak leaf clusters. Mem. Am. Assn. U. Profs., Assn. Am. Geographers, Pa. Acad. Sci., Pa. Council Geog. Edn., Phi Delta Kappa, Kappa Delta Pi, Pi Gamma Mu, Gamma Theta Upsilon. Home: 295 Elm St Indiana PA 15701

GAULTNEY, JOHN ORTON, life ins. co. exec.; b. Pulaski, Tenn., Nov. 7, 1915; s. Bert Hood and Grace (Orton) G.; student Am. Inst. Banking, 1936; diploma Life Ins. Agy. Mgmt. Assn., 1948, Little Rock Jr. Coll., 1950; C.L.U., 1948, Mgmt. C.L.U Diploma, 1952; grad. sales mgmt. and marketing Rutgers U., 1957; m. Elizabethine Mullette, Mar. 30, 1941; children—Elizabethine (Mrs. Donald H. McClure), John Mullette, Walker Orton, Harlow Denny. With N.Y. Life Ins. Co., 1935—, regional v.p., Atlanta, 1956-64, v.p., N.Y.C., 1964-67, v.p. in charge group sales, 1967-68, v.p. marketing, 1969—. Chmn. Downtown YMCA, Atlanta, 1963-65; mem. pub. relations com. Nat. Council YMCAs, 1965—; mem. bd. Grand Central YMCA, N.Y.C., 1966—; mem. internat. world service com. YMCA, 1968—; vice chmn. Grand Central YMCA, 1969. Bd. dirs. Memphis YMCA, 1939-40, Little Rock YMCA, 1941-55, Atlanta YMCA, 1959-65; Served to capt. inf., AUS, 1942-45; Italy. Decorated Bronze Star with 3 clusters, Silver Star, Purple Heart with 2 clusters; recipient Devereux C. Josephs award N.Y. Life Ins. Co., 1954; named Ark. traveler, 1955, hon. citizen Tenn., 1956, Ky. col., 1963. Mem. Am., N.Y. socs. C.L.U.'s, Nat., N.Y. assns. life underwriters, N.Y. Gen. Agts. and Mgrs. Conf., Sales and Marketing Execs. Internat., N.Y. Sales Execs. Club, N.Y. Southern Soc. (trustee), 361st Infantry Assn. World War II (pres. 1967-70), S.A.R., Tenn. Soc. in N.Y., Am. Risk and Ins. Assn. Mem. Reformed Ch. (deacon). Rotarian. Clubs: Capital City (Atlanta); Siwanoy Bronxville, N.Y.); American Yacht (Rye, N.Y.). Home: 22 Oriole Av Bronxville, NY 10708 Office: 51 Madison Av New York City NY 10010

GAUMNITZ, ERWIN ALFRED, univ. adminstr.; b. St. Cloud, Minn., Feb. 24, 1907; s. August H. and Ada H. (McNeal) G.; B.B.A., U. Minn., 1929, M.A., 1934, Ph.D., 1935; m. Evelyn E. Kenney, Sept. 5, 1928; children—Jane (Mrs. Kieth F. Johnson), Roger K. Jack E., Thomas W. Prof., U. Minn., 1929-35, Coll. of St. Thomas, 1934-36; dir. research Minn. Unemployment Compensation Dept., also U.S. Bur. Labor Statistics, St. Paul, 1937-38; with U. Wis., 1938- -, beginning as asst. prof., successively asso. prof., 1941-45, prof. econs., 1945—, prof., asst. dean Sch. Commerce, 1946-50, prof., dean Sch. Commerce, 1955—, now dean Grad. Sch. Bus. Adminstrn. Economist OPA, 1942-44; regional price exec. OPS, 1951; cons. research, mgmt. for bus. firms; Arthur H. Eliott lectr., Gt. Britain, 1968; seminar lectr. U.S. Africa, 1971. Vice pres. Wis. Council of Chs., 1957-71, Madison YMCA, 1956- 69. Fellow Royal Econ. Soc. (Eng.); mem. Am. Statis. Assn. (life), Am. Econ. Assn., Am. Risk and Ins. Assn. (past pres.), Beta Alpha Psi, Beta Gamma Sigma, Phi Kappa Phi. Author: Social Security and Life Insurance, 1941; Life Insurance Mathematics, 1951; Futures Trading Seminar, 1966; Life Insurance Mathematics (Formosa), 1970; also articles. Home: 5114 Milward Dr Madison WI 53711

GAUMNITZ, WALTER HERBERT, rural edn. specialist; b. Rice, Minn., Oct. 10, 1891; s. Frederick Oscar and Louise (Meisner) G.; B.S., U. Minn., 1921, M.A., 1924; Ph.D., George Washington U., 1935; spl. diploma, Columbia, 1924-25; m. Agnes M. Cooper, Apr. 4, 1920; children—Gordon Arthur, Jean (Mrs. Robert H. Gruber), Walter Glen. Tchr., prin. Ottertail County, Minn., 1914-16; supt. schs., Lake Wilson, Minn., 1916-18; instr., U. Minn., 1920-22, high sch., Mpls., 1922-24; head social sci. dept., State Tchrs. Coll., Madison, S.D., 1925-27; specialist, rural high schs., U.S. Office Edn., 1927-31, sr. specialist, rural edn. problems, 1931-45, prin. specialist rural and small high schs., 1945-55; prin. specialist rural school research and statistics, 1956-62, chief edn. research and statistics, local schs., 1960-62; lectr. summer schs.; mem. survey staffs and ednl. confs. Served as sgt., U.S. Army, A.E.F., 1918-19. Awarded Purple Heart, Distinguished Service Award U. Minn., 1963. Chief U.S. rep., Internat. Conf. on Edn., Geneva, 1939; study guest of German Fed. Republic, 1952. Fellow A.A.A.S.; mem. N.E.A., Am. Schoolmen's Club, Nat. Com. Coordination in Secondary Edn., D.A.V., The Fossils, Pi Gamma Mu, Phi Delta Kappa. Conglist. Mason. Author numerous books and ofcl. reports, latest being: Survey of Education in 1200 Rural Counties, 1959; also articles ednl. jours. Home: 5720 Oregon Av NW Washington DC 20015 Office: Office of Education Washington DC 20202 ☆

GAUMOND, EDWARD JOSEPH, fgn. service officer; b. Chgo., Aug. 27, 1913; s. Hector J. and Emma (Marsolais) G.; student Loyola U., Chgo., 1936-38, Stanford, 1945, Sophia U., Tokyo, 1950, George Washington U., 1951; m. Kathleen Johnston, Apr. 30, 1949; children—Mark, Margaret, John. Comptroller transp. service Far East Command, Tokyo, 1946-48; budget analyst SCAP, Tokyo, 1948-49, Dept. of State, 1950-51, Dept. of Army, 1951-52; budget and fiscal officer Am. Embassy, New Delhi, India, 1953-54, Am. Embassy, Athens, Greece, 1955; dep. chief adminstrv. sect. Am. Embassy, Athens, 1956-57; supervisory budget office Dept. of State, 1957-59; adminstrv. officer Am. Embassy, Tunis, 1959-64; chief adminstrv. officer Am. Embassy, Tunis, 1959-64; chief adminstrv. officer U.S. Mission to UN, 1964-68; counselor for adminstrn. U.S. Mission to European Office, UN, 1968—. Served as maj. AUS, 1941-46. Roman Catholic. Home: Northbrook IL 60062 Office: 80 Rue de LaSaunne Geneva Switzerland

GAUNT, ROBERT, scientist; b. Macon, Mo., Apr. 13, 1907; s. Robert Earl and Mary Elizabeth (Summers) G.; A.B., U. Tulsa, 1929; A.M., Princeton, 1930, Ph.D., 1932; m. Josephine Howland, July 8, 1933; 1 son, Robert Howland. Asst. and fellow dept. biology Princeton, 1929-32; prof. biology, chmn. dept. Coll. of Charleston, 1932-35; asst. prof. biology Wash. Sq. Coll. N.Y. U., 1935-42, asso. prof., 1942-46; prof. zoology, chmn. dept., Syracuse U., 1946-51; dir. endocrine research CIBA Pharm. Co., Summit, N. J., 1951-57, dir. biol. research, 1958-66, dir. basic biol. sci., 1967—; vis. prof. physiology Ohio U., 1955. Guggenheim Meml. fellow, 1943. Fellow N.Y. Acad. Sci., A.A.A.S.; mem. Assn. Study Internal Secretions (council, 1943-47), Am. Assn. Anatomists, Am. Physiol. Soc., Am. Soc. Zoologists, Soc. Exptl. Biology and Medicine, Sigma Xi. Author: (with J. H. Birnie) Hormones and Body Water, 1951; also articles in various sci. jours., symposia and encyclopedia, on endocrinology, particularly adrenal gland. Editor: The Adrenal Cortex, pub. in Annals of N.Y. Acad. Home: Hilltop Terrace Chatham NJ 07928 Office: Research Labs CIBA Pharm Co Inc Summit NJ 07901

GAUSTER, WILHELM FRIEDRICH, sci., engring. cons.; b. Vienna, Austria, Jan. 6, 1901; s. Friedrich and Gabriele (Deltsch) G.; Dipl. Ing., U. Tech., Vienna, 1923, Dr. Techn., 1924, Dr. Habil., 1927; m. Marietta (Countess Belrupt- Tissac), Feb. 24, 1940; children—Wilhelm Belrupt, Christian Belrupt. Came to U.S., 1950, naturalized, 1954. Mgr., Elin Corp. for Elec. Industrie, Austria, 1924-41; research for German Navy, 1941-45; prof. U. Tech., Vienna, 1945-50; prof. N.C. State Coll., 1950-57; dir. magnet lab. Oak Ridge Nat. Lab., 1957-70, cons., 1971—. Hon. prof. U. Tech., Vienna. Recipient German KVK I and II medal merit; Great Silver Badge of Honor (Austria). Fellow I.E.E.E., Am. Phys. Soc.; mem. Austrian Soc. Elec. Engring., Austrian Acad. Scis. (corr.) Contbr. numerous sci. publs. Home: 104 Seymour Lane Oak Ridge TN 37830 Office: Oak Ridge Nat Lab PO Box Y Oak Ridge TN 37830

GAUTHIER, CLARENCE JOSEPH, utility exec.; b. Houghton, Mich., Mar. 16, 1922; s. Clarence A. and Muriel V. (Beesley) G.; B.S., in Mech. Engring., U. Ill., 1943; M.B.A., U. Chgo., 1960; m. Grayce N. Wicall, July 25, 1941; children—Joseph H., Nancy M. With Pub. Service Co., N. Ill., 1945-54; with No. Ill. Gas Co., 1954—, v.p. finance, 1960-62, v.p. operations, 1962-64, exec. v.p., 1965-69, pres., 1969, also chmn. chief exec. officer, 1971—, dir., 1965—; pres., dir. Midwest Nitrogen, Inc., 1968—; exec. v.p. Gt. River Gas Co., 1966-71, pres., 1971—, also dir.; v.p. NI Gas Supply, Inc., 1960-64, exec. v.p., 1970-71, pres., 1971—, also dir.; dir. Apple River Chem. Co., Bank of Yorktown, Lombard, Ill., Target, Inc., Naperville Nat. Bank & Trust Co. (Ill.), Gen. Am. Transp. Corp., Chemetron Corp. Mem. pres.' council bus. assos. Elmhurst (Ill.) Coll., 1965-69; mem. businessmen's adv. council Coll. Bus. Adminstrn., U. Ill., Chgo. Circle, 1971—; mem. council of 100 U. Chgo. Grad. Sch. Bus., 1960—. Trustee George Williams Coll., Downers Grove, Ill. Bd. dirs. Mid-Am. chpt. A.R.C.; trustee Met. Crusade of Mercy, Chgo.; mem. U. Ill. Found. Served to capt. C.E., AUS, World War II; PTO. Decorated Silver Star, Bronze Star with V. Registered profl. engr., Ill. Mem. Internat. Gas Union, Am. (dir. 1970—), Midwest (dir. 1964-67), So. (dir. 1966-69) gas assns., Inst. Gas Tech. (trustee 1964-70, 71—), A.A.A.S., Am. Finance Assn., Am. Mgmt. Assn., Western Soc. Engrs., Newcomen Soc. N.Am., U. Chgo. Grad. Sch. Bus. Alumni Assn. (pres. 1964-65) Ill. C. of C., Chgo. Assn. Commerce and Industry (dir.), Sigma Pi, Beta Gamma Sigma, Tau Nu Tau. Clubs: Chicago Commercial, Economic, Mid-America, Executives (Chgo.). Contbr. profl. jours. Home: 15 Lochinvar Lane Oak Brook IL 60521 Office: P O Box 190 Aurora IL 60507

GAUTHIER, JOSEPH DELPHIS, clergyman; b. Hartford, Conn., Aug. 23, 1909; s. Victor Adélard and Marie Alexandrine (Domingue) G.; B.S., Trinity Coll., Hartford, 1930; A.B., Weston Coll., 1940, A.M., 1941, S.T.L., 1945; D. ès L., U. Laval, 1948. Spl. agt. Hartford Accident & Indemnity Co., 1930-35; entered Soc. of Jesus, 1935, ordained priest Roman Cath. Ch., 1944; asst. prof., chmn. Romance lang. dept., Boston, Coll., 1948-52; chmn. dept., 1952-61, asso. prof. French lit., until 1966, prof., 1966—; editorial adviser, cons. Britannica World Lang. Dictionary, 1955. Mem. Mass. adv. com. fgn. lang. cons.; steering com. for Mass., Nat. Def. Edn. Act. Decorated Chevalier, Palmes Académiques, 1951, Officer, 1958. Mem. N.E. Modern Lang. Assn. (pres. 1958), Modern Lang. Assn., Renaissance Soc. Am., Cath. Commn. Cultural and Intellectual Affairs, Am. Assn. Tchrs. French, Franco-American Hist. Soc., Am. Assn. Tchrs. German, Am. Assn. Tchrs. Spanish and Portuguese, Am. Assn. Tchrs. Italian. Author: Le Canada français et le roman americain, 1948; Nouvelle Promenade littéraire, 1959; Variétés, 1960; (with Lewis A. Sumberg) Les Grands Ecrivains Francais, 1965; Douze voix Francaises, 1969; (with Vera G. Lee) La Vie des Lettres, 1970. Address: Boston Coll Chestnut Hill MA 02167

GAUTHIER, VICTOR ARTHUR, Jr., govt. ofcl.; b. Bklyn., May 21, 1917; s. Victor Arthur and Martha Louise (Cantrell) B.; B.A. cum laude, St. Lawrence U., 1939; grad. student Columbia, N.Y.U., Johns Hopkins, Am. U. Inst. Pub. Adminstrn., N.Y.C.; m. Mary Faison Richardson, Sept. 8, 1943; children—Robert Cantrell, Richard Faison, Mary Dixon, Frank Raymond. Prin. orgn. and planning analyst ECA, 1948-52; Far East industry adviser Mut. Security Adminstrn., 1953-55; chief Near East-S. Asia industry div. ICA, 1955-59; acting dep. sec. gen. econ. also tech. asst. adviser Central Treaty Orgn., Ankara, Turkey, 1959-62; with AID, 1962—, dir. Central Treaty Orgn. Affairs, Washington, 1962-64, dir. Greece-Cyprus CENTO Affairs, 1964-67, U.S. dep. econ. coordinator for CENTO affairs, Ankara, Turkey, 1967-68, econ. coordinator for CENTO affairs, 1968-69; program officer AID, Washington, 1969—. U.S. Del. CENTO Econ. Com., Karachi, 1963, CENTO Ministerial

Council, 1964. Served to capt. AUS, 1942-46. Mem. Soc. Internat. Devel., Soc. Pub. Adminstrn. Home: 2302 Tracy St Alexandria VA 22311

GAUTIER, AUGUSTO RAFAEL, architect; b. Santurce, P.R., Sept. 5, 1932; s. Aurelio R. and Carmen Luisa (Mayoral) G.; B.Arch., Rensselaer Poly. Inst., 1955; m. Carmen Margarita Lloveras, Oct. 16, 1955; children—Augusto Ramon, Carmen Margarita, Carlos Enrique, Luis Eduardo. Head bldg. design div. Dept. Pub. Works, Govt. P.R., Santurce, 1957-60; partner Llenza & Gautier, Architects, Santurce, 1960-67; owner Augusto R. Gautier, Santurce, 1968—. Fgn. evaluation com. Nat. Council Archtl. Registration Bds.; mem. Bd. Examiners Engrs., Architects and Surveyors P.R. Alternate del. Democratic Nat. Conv., 1964, del., 1968. Served as 1st lt. C.E., U.S. Army, 1955-57. Mem. Coll. Engring. Architects and Surveyors P.R., Inst. Architects P.R. (past pres.), Pan Am. Congress Architects (v.p.), A.I.A. (asso. editor P.R. chpt.), Pan Am. Fedn. Architects Assn. (pres.), Sigma Xi, Tau Beta Pi, Pi Kappa Phi. Home: DA-4 F P Hastings Garden Hills Bayamon PR 00619 Office: 1403 Georgetti St Santurce PR 00910

GAUTIER, REDMOND BUNN, Jr., lawyer; b. Miami, Fla., Apr. 3, 1909; s. Redmond Bunn and Ida (Miller) G.; student Riverside Mil. Acad., Washington and Lee U.; m. Frances Roe, Nov. 19, 1937; children—Gary Bunn, Vicki Frances. Admitted to Fla. bar; practice of law, 1932—; now mem. law firm Worley, Gautier & Patterson, Miami. Pres. Atlas Terminals of Fla., Inc.; dir. Greater Miami Fed. Savs. & Loan Assn., Mchts. Bank of Miami. Mem. Orange Bowl Com. Mem. Fla. Ho. of Reps., 1942-43, 47-48, Fla. Senate, 1948- 55. Trustee U. Miami. Served to Lt. USNR, 1943-46. Mem. Am. Legion, Miami-Dade County C. of C., Sigma Alpha Epsilon. Clubs: Kiwanis (Miami); Riviera Country (Coral Gables). Home: Island House Apts Key Biscayne FL 33152 Office: 200 SE 1st St Miami FL 33131

GAVAN, JAMES ANDERSON, anthropologist, educator; b. Ludington, Mich., July 17, 1916; s. James B. and Mary (Anderson) G.; B.A., U. Ariz., 1939; M.A., U. Chgo., 1949, Ph.D., 1953; m. Margaret Sheninger, Dec. 17, 1945; children-Margaret Jean, James Charles. Research staff Yerkes Labs. Primate Biology, Orange Park, Fla., 1950-53; asst. prof. anatomy Med. Coll. S.C., 1953-60, asso. prof., 1960-62; asso. prof. anatomy, anthropology U. Fla., 1962-67; prof. anthropology U. Mo., at Columbia, 1967—, chmn. dept. anthropology, 1968—. Fellow A.A.A.S., Am. Anthrop. Assn.; mem. Am. Soc. Human Genetics, Am. Assn. Phys. Anthropology, Sigma Xi. Editor: The Non- Human Primates and Human Evolution, 1955. Contbr. articles profl. jours. Home: 1503 Wilson Av Columbia MO 65201

GAVAZZENI, GIANANDREA, condr., composer, author; b. Bergamo, Italy, July 25, 1909; s. Giuseppe and Piera Monzini G.; diploma pianoforte and premio Durini, Conservatorio Verdi, Milan, Italy, 1930, diploma for composition, 1931; m. Maria Grazia Polli, May 19, 1932; children—Franco, Giuseppe. Condr., 1933—, appearing in Austria, Belgium, Germany, Scotland, Spain, Switzerland, U.S.; condr. La Scala, Milan, 1944—. Recipient commendatore Italian Republic; academician Saint Cecilia; gold medallist Ministry Pub. Instrn.; gold medallist Commune of Bergamo. Mem. Superior Council of Fine Arts, Pen Club. Composer: Preludio sinfonico, 1928; Three sonatas for piano, violin and cello, 1930; Concerto bergamasco, 1931; Paolo e Virginia (1 act opera), 1932; Panfila (ballet), 1933; Fantasia for cello and piano, 1934; Tre Episodi for orch., 1935; Concerto in la for cello, 1936. Author critical essays on Donizetti, Mussorgsky, others, also books of memoirs, jours. Home: Via Porta Dipinta 5 Bergamo Italy Office: La Scala Milan Italy

GAVAZZI, ALADINO A., hosp. adminstr.; b. Exeter, Pa., July 24, 1922; s. Guido and Ambrozina (Santoni-O'Brien) G.; B.S., Columbia, 1953, M.S., 1955; diploma, U. Chgo., 1959; m. Nancylee Ray, June 21, 1958; children—William A., Ann Marie, Lisa Kathryn, Alan Lee, Michael J. Adminstrv. officer VA br.- dist. office, N.Y.C., 1946-50; med. adminstrv. officer VA hosps., Bklyn., Bronx, N.Y., 1950-53; hosp. adminstrv. resident Bronx, Beth Israel and Presbyn. hosps., N.Y.C., 1953-54; hosp. adminstr. VA Hosps., Hampton, Va., 1955-57, Chgo. Research Hosp., 1957-59, Dwight, Ill., 1960- 62, Mt. Alto VA Hosp., Washington, 1963-64, asso. dir. hosp. constrn., Washington, 1964-65, center dir., Martinsburg, W.Va., 1965-68; exec. asst. to chief med. dir., Dept. Med. and Surgery, VA, 1968-70, exec. dir. for adminstrn. Dept. Medicine and Surgery, 1970-71; dir. VA Hosp., Washington, 1971—; professorial lectr. health care adminstrn. George Washington U. Guest lectr. hosp. adminstrn. Med. Coll. Va., Richmond, Northwestern U., Chgo., U. Fla., U. Ala., Duke, Cornell U., Columbia U., U. Sao Paulo (Brazil). Dist. chmn. Boy Scouts Am., W.Va., 1967-68; chmn. Combined Fed. Campaign for W.Va. for all fed. agys., 1966-68. Served to 1st lt. Armored Div., AUS, 1940- 45; lt. col. Res. Recipient Outstanding Performance awards VA, 1952, 56, 59, 63. Fellow Am. Coll. Hosp. Adminstrs. (mem. various commns.), Royal Soc. Health (London); mem. Am. Hosp. Assn. Home: 1541 Dahlia Ct McLean VA 22101

GAVELL, STEFAN FRANCIS, economist; b. Cracow, Poland, Dec. 3, 1915; s. Nicholas and Mary (Podsiadlo) G.; B.A., B.Litt., M.A., Oxford (Eng.) U., 1946; m. Mary P. Ladd, Jan. 11, 1953; children—Stefan Michael, Anthony Christopher. Came to U.S., 1947, naturalized, 1956. With FAO, 1947—, liaison officer World Food Program, 1970—. Served as officer with Polish, French and Brit. air forces, 1939-42. Author articles in field. Home: 88 Viale Dei Primati Sportivi Rome Italy Office: Food and Agr Orgn Rome Italy

GAVER, MARY VIRGINIA, librarian, ret. educator; b. Washington, Dec. 10, 1906; d. Clayton Daniel and Ruth L. (Clendening) Gaver; A.B., Randolph-Macon Woman's Coll., 1927; B.S. in L.S., Columbia, 1932, M.S. in L.S., 1938, postgrad. Tchrs. Coll., 1945-50; LL.D., L.I. U., 1967, Mt. Holyoke Coll., 1968. Librarian, George Washington High Sch., Danville, Va., 1927-37; tech. dir. library project WPA of Va., 1938-39; librarian Scarsdale (N.Y.) High Sch., 1939- 42, Trenton (N.J.) State Coll., 1942-54; asso. prof., prof. Grad. Sch. Library Service, Rutgers U., 1954-71, emeritus, 1971—; dir. library cons. services Bio-Dart Industries, Inc., 1971—; leader-specialist Dept. State U. Tehran, 1952-53. Carnegie fellow, 1937; recipient Good Teaching award Beta Phi Mu, 1965; Research Council award Rutgers U., 1963; Herbert Putnam Honor Fund award A.L.A., 1963. Mem. Am. (pres. 1966-67), N.J. (pres. 1954- 55) library assns., Am. Assn. Sch. Librarians (pres. 1959-60), Woman's Nat. Book Assn., N.E.A., Am. Assn. Univ. Profs., Phi Beta Kappa. Author: Effectiveness of Centralized Library Service in Elementary Schools, 3d edit., 1969; (with Gonzalo Valezquez) School Librairies of Puerto Rico, 1963; (with Lucyle Hook) The Research Manual, 4th edit., 1969. Home: 29 Baldwin St New Brunswick NJ 08901

GAVIN, AUSTIN, lawyer; b. Phila., Feb. 6, 1909; A.B., Ursinus Coll., 1930; LL.B., U. Pa., 1933; Helen A. Blaisdell; children—Austin III, Susan. Admitted to Pa. bar, 1933; jr. counsel Pa. Dept. Revenue, 1934-35; law clk. to justice Pa. Supreme Ct., 1935-36; with Pa. Power & Light Co., Allentown, 1936—, gen. counsel, 1958-60, v.p., gen. counsel, 1960-65, v.p. mgmt. services, 1965-69, exec. v.p., 1969—. Pres. bd. directors Minsi Trails council Boy Scouts Am. (pres. 1966—); trustee Allentown YMCA. Served as 1st sgt. AUS, World War II. Decorated Silver Star, Purple Heart. Mem. Am. Pa., Lehigh County bar assns., Am. Arbitration Assn. (nat. panel arbitrators). Home: R D 1 Macungie PA 18062 Office: 901 Hamilton St Allentown PA 18101

GAVIN, JAMES M., corp. exec.; b. N.Y.C., Mar. 22, 1907; s. Martin Thomas and Mary (Terrel) G.; B.S., U.S. Mil. Acad., 1929; grad. Inf. Sch., officers course, 1933; Command and Gen. Staff Sch. Parachute Sch.; m. 2d, Jean Emert Duncan, July 31, 1948; children—Caroline (Mrs. Richard K. O'Neill), Patricia, Aileen and Chloe; 1 dau. (by previous marriage), Barbara Margaret. Enlisted as pvt. U. S. Army, 1924; commd. 2d lt. inf., 1929, advanced through grades to lt. gen., 1944; service included World War II in ETO; ret. 1958; exec. v.p. of Arthur D. Little, Inc., 1958-60, pres., 1960-61, now chmn. bd., chief exec. officer; U.S. ambassador to France, 1961-62; dir. John Hancock Mut. Life Ins. Co., Am. Electric Power Co. Decorated grand officer Legion of Honor, Croix de Guerre with palm (France); D.S.C. with oak leaf cluster, Purple Heart, Silver Star (U.S.); Distinguished Service Order (Eng.). Author: Airborne Warfare, 1947; War and Peace in the Space Age, 1958; Crisis Now. Home: 85 Yarmouth Rd Chestnut Hill MA 02167 Office: 25 Acorn Park Cambridge MA 02140

GAVIN, JOHN, actor; b. Los Angeles, Apr. 8, 1932; s. Herald Ray and Delia Diana (Pablos) G.; B.A., Stanford, 1952; m. Cicely Jean Evans, Aug. 2, 1958; children—Christina Miles, Maria Delia. Actor, 1956—; films include A Time to Live, A Time to Die, 1957, Psycho, 1959, Midnight Lace, 1960, Backstreet, 1961, Thoroughly Modern Millie, 1966, Mad Woman of Chaillot, 1969. Spl. adviser to sec. gen. Orgn. Am. States, 1961-65. Bd. trustees Villanova Prep. Sch. Served from ensign to lt. USNR, 1952-55. Mem. Screen Actors Guild (1st v.p., dir.), Omicron Delta Kappa, Chi Psi. Catholic. Club: Jonathan (Los Angeles). Office: Box 961 Beverly Hills CA 90213

GAVIN, ROBERT LEE, lawyer; b. Roseboro, N.C., May 22, 1916; s. Edwin Lee and Mamie (Caudle) G.; A.B., U. N.C., 1945, LL.B., 1956; m. Grace McNeill Blue, Nov. 27, 1947; children—Edwin Lee II, Grace Blue, John David. Admitted to N.C. bar, 1946; practiced in Sanford, 1946-54; partner Gavin, Jackson & Gavin, 1946-54; asst. U.S. atty., Middle Dist. N.C., 1954, U.S. atty., 1957-58; city atty. Sanford, 1965—. Dir., So. Nat. Bank N.C., Sanford. Mem. N.C. State Constn. Study Commn., N.Y. State Zool. Adv. Bd. Del. Republican Nat. Conv., 1960, 64; Rep. candidate for gov. of N.C. 1960, 64; chmn. N.C. Rep. Exec. Com. Mem. Am., N.C. bar assns., N.C. State Bar, 4th Circuit Jud. Conf. (life mem.), Sanford C. of C. (dir., v.p.), Am. Legion, Phi Delta Phi. Baptist. Elk. Clubs: Tin Whistles, Pinehurst Country. Home: 227 N Vance St Sanford NC 27330 Office: 114 Wicker St Sanford NC 27330

GAXIOLA, FRANCISCO JAVIER, lawyer; b. Toluca, Mexico, Sept. 6, 1898; s. Francisco Javier and Blanca, (Zendejas) G.; legal degree, Escuela libre de Derecho, 1922; m. Clothilde Ochoa, June 28, 1924; 1 son, Francisco Javier. Admitted to Mexico bar, 1922, since practiced in Mexico City; pres., bd. dirs. several banks, ins. companies, financing instns. and indsl. companies. Fiscal rep. Mexico, 1919-20; sec. of Govt. in Baja, Cal., 1930; pres. Mexican Labor Ct., 1932; sec. to Pres. Republic Mexico, 1932-34; sec. nat. economy, 1940-44; pres. several gubernamental coms., World War II; mem. Bd. Properties and Concerns of Enemy, World War II; personal rep. of Pres. Mexico to Pres. Roosevelt, 1942. Decorated Orden de honor forense, Gran Cruz de la Dignidad Profesional. Mem. Colegio de Abogados, Internat. Bar Assn. (co-pres. 1963), Sociedad Mexicana de Geografia y Estadistica y Academia Mexicana de Geografia y Estadistica y Academia Mexicana de Jurisprudencia, Colegio de Abogados de Madrid (hon.). Author: El Juicio Constitucional por Invasion de Jurisdicciones, 1922; El Presidente Rodriquez, 1938; Algunos-problemas de la Economia Mexicana, 1940; Cuestiones pentientes entre Mexico y Estados Unidos, 1943; Sobre la Creacion de una Secretaria de Justicia, 1960; y Ciudadania y Regimen-Democratico, 1961; La Empresa Pública en México, 1971. Address: Paseo de la Reforma 284 Mexico City 6 Mexico

GAY, DONALD, Jr., ret. naval officer; b. Newport News, Va., Apr. 22, 1914; s. Donald and Martha Louise (Land) G.; B.S., U.S. Naval Acad., 1937; postgrad. Armed Forces Staff Coll., 1950, Naval War Coll., 1952; m. Milred C. Palmer, Apr. 19, 1941; children—Donald III, Priscilla, Tracy Treadwell. Commd. ensign U.S. Navy, 1937, advanced through grades to rear adm., 1964; dep. chief naval operations air detailer, 1944-47; comdr. Fighter Squadron 41, 1947-49; navigator U.S.S. Roosevelt, 1949-50; comdr. Jet Carrier Air Group 3, 1952-53; plans officer Naval Strike Force South Europe, Naples, 1953-55; dir. service test Naval Air Test Center, Patuxent River, Md., 1955-57; comdr. 7th Fleet Operations, 1957-59, U.S.S. Floyds Bay, 1959-60; comdg. officer U.S.S. Ranger, 1960-61; chief naval operations spl. studies and presentations, 1961-63, Carrier Div. 18, 1963-64; comdr.-in-chief Pacific staff for plans, 1964- 66; comdr. Fleet Air Wings Pacific, Fleet Air Moffett Field, Cal., 1966- -69; retired, 1969. Decorated D.F.C. with gold star, Bronze Star with combat V, Air medal with gold star, Legion of Merit (2). Mem. Soc. of the Cincinnati. Home: 170 Stone Pine Lane Menlo Park CA 94025

GAY, E. LAURENCE, diversified co. exec.; b. Bridgeport, Conn., Aug. 10, 1923; s. Emil D. and Helen (Mihalich) G.; B.S., Yale, 1947; J.D., Harvard, 1949; m. Harriet A. Ripley, Aug. 2, 1952; children-L. Noel, Peter C., Marguerite S., Georgette A. Admitted to N.Y. bar, 1950, Conn. bar, 1959; atty. Root, Ballantine, Harlan, Bushby & Palmer, N.Y.C., 1949-51; legal staff U.S. High Commr. for Germany, 1951-52; law sec., presiding justice appellate div. 1st dept. N.Y. Supreme Ct., 1952-53; atty. Debevoise, Plimpton & McLean, 1953-58; v.p., sec.-treas. Hewitt-Robins, Inc., Stamford, Conn., 1958-65; pres. Litton Gt. Lakes Corp., N.Y.C., 1965-67; sr. v.p. finance AMFAC, Inc., Honolulu, 1967—. Exec. com. Honolulu Symphony Soc., 1968—. Served to 2d lt. AUS, 1943-46. Mem. Phi Beta Kappa. Roman Catholic. Home: 1159 Maunawili Rd Kailua HI 96734 Office: PO Box 3230 Honolulu HI 96801

GAY, HAYWARD ANDREWS, pub. cons.; b. Swarthmore, Pa., Feb. 6, 1909; s. Carl Warren and Catherine (Andrews) G.; B.S. in Mech. Engring., Ohio State U., 1930; M.B.A., Harvard, 1932; m. Louise Hickox, Aug. 18, 1935; children—Marilyn Andrews (Mrs. Mason B. Jones, Jr.), Nancy Leigh, (Mrs. Anthony A. Tully), Charles Warren. With Cin. Milling Machine Co., 1932-64, successively prodn. engr., mgr. products div., 1932-57, mgr. machine tool div., 1957-62, v.p., 1951-64, group v.p., 1962-64; v.p., dir. Carlisle Chem. Works, Inc., 1948-64; pres. Pratt & Whitney, Inc. div. Colt Industries, Inc., until 1970; v.p., group exec. Colt Industries, Inc., until 1970; chmn. bd. Elox Corp. div. Colt Industries, Detroit, until 1970; chmn. editorial adv. bd. Hitchcock Pub. Co., Wheaton, Ill., 1971—. Trustee Hillsdale-Lotspeich Schs., 1953-58. Clubs: Commonwealth, Cincinnati Country (Cin.); Hartford, Hartford (Conn.) Golf; Eastward Ho Country (Chatham, Mass.); Skyline Country (Tucson). Home: 5142 Oakmont Dr Tucson AZ 85718 also Strong Island Rd Chatham MA 02633

GAY, HELEN, biologist; b. Pittsfield, Mass., Aug. 30, 1918; d. Ulrich and Alice (Gonnet) Gay; B.A., Mt. Holyoke Coll., 1940; M.A., Mills Coll., 1942; Ph.D. (Lalor fellow 1951-54), U. Pa., 1955. Research asst. dept. genetics Carnegie Instn., Cold Spring Harbor, L.I., N.Y., 1942, 43, 45- 51, asso. in research, 1954-60 asso. cytogeneticist, 1960-62, cytogeneticist, 1962—, charge Cytogenetics Lab., 1963—; lectr. cytology, biology dept. Adelphi Coll., Garden City, N.Y., 1959-62; jr. profl. asst. NIH, Bethesda, Md., 1943-45; prof. zoology U. Mich., 1962—. Fellow A.A.A.S.; mem. Am. Soc. Zoologists, Internat., Am. socs. cell biology, Genetics Soc. Am., Am. Soc. Naturalists, Soc. for Developmental Biology, Sigma Xi. Asso. editor cytology sect. Biol. Abstracts. Contbr. to sci. jours. Home: 2650 Heather Way Ann Arbor MI 48104

GAY, J. EDWIN, lawyer; b. Jacksonville, Fla., Nov. 19, 1909; s. Gracey David and Callie (Beard) G.; B.S. in Bus. Adminstrn., U. Fla., 1928-31, LL.B., J.D., 1951; m. Dorothy Dyrenforth, Apr. 25, 1946; 1 son, Rhodes Gay. Mgr. Credit Assn. No. Fla., 1931-33; asst. to pres. Am. Investment and Mortgage Co., 1935-41; plant supt., dist. salesman Sun Oil Co., 1933-35; div. mgr. N. Fla. div. Can. Dry Bottling Co. Fla., 1946-48; admitted to Fla. bar, 1951; with firm Bedell & Bedell, Jacksonville, 1951, 52; asst. U.S. dist. atty. So. Dist. Fla., Jacksonville div., 1951-53; adminstrv. asst. to Gov. LeRoy Collins, 1955-56; partner firm Rogers, Towers, Bailey, Jones & Gay, Jacksonville, 1962—; lectr. U. Fla., 1951—. Mem. Fla. Racing Commn., 1957-58; mem. com. parish coop. Episcopal High Sch., Jacksonville. Served to lt. comdr. 1941-46, USNR, World War II; rear adm. Res. ret. Mem. Jacksonville Bar Assn. (pres. 1967), Kappa Alpha, Phi Delta Phi (past pres.). Clubs: Steppers (past pres.), Bachelors (past pres.), Friars (past pres.), Fla. Yacht (past commodore), Meninak (Jacksonville). Home: 4804 Apache Av Jacksonville FL 32210 Office: Fla Title Bldg Jacksonville FL 32201

GAY, JAMES, lawyer; b. Seattle, Oct. 4, 1918; s. Charles Lloyd and Ethel (Cockcroft) G.; B.A., U. Wash., 1940, LL.B., 1943; m. Elizabeth Anne Rogers, June 19, 1948; children—James C., Carl L., Robert L., Stephen C., Carol A. Admitted to Wash. bar, 1943, since practiced in Seattle; asso. Weter, Roberts & Shefelman, 1943-50, partner, 1950-62; partner Roberts, Shefelman, Lawrence, Gay & Moch, 1962—; lectr. U. Wash. Law Sch., 1956- 58. Trustee Municipal League Seattle and King County, pres., 1968-70; treas., bd. dirs. Wash. Law Sch. Found. Mem. Am. (mem. council sect. local govt. law), Wash., Seattle-King County bar assns., U. Wash. Law Sch. Alumni Assn. (treas., dir.), Order of Coif, Phi Beta Kappa. Presbyn. Home: 4240 Crestwood Pl Mercer Island WA 98040 Office: 1818 IBM Bldg Seattle WA 98101

GAY, PETER, educator, author: b. Berlin, Germany, June 20, 1923; s. Morris Peter and Helga (Kohnke) G.; came to U.S., 1941, naturalized, 1946; B.A., U. Denver, 1946; M.A., Columbia, 1947, Ph.D., 1951; m. Ruth Slotkin, May 30, 1959; stepchildren—Sarah Glazer, Sophie Glazer, Elizabeth Glazer. Faculty Columbia, 1947-69, prof. history, 1962-69, William R. Shepherd prof. history, 1967-69; prof. comparative European intellectual history Yale, 1969—, Durfee prof. history, 1970—. Fellow Am. Council Learned Soc., 1959-60; fellow Center Advanced Study Behavioral Scis., 1963-64; Guggenheim fellow, 1967-68; Overseas fellow Churchill Coll., Cambridge, 1970-71; recipient Nat. Book award, 1967. Mem. Am., French hist. socs., Phi Beta Kappa. Author: The Dilemma of Democratic Socialism: Eduard Bernstein's Challenge to Marx, 1952; Voltaire's Politics: The Poet as Realist, 1959; The Party of Humanity: Essays in the French Enlightenment, 1964; A Loss of Mastery: Puritan Historians in Colonial America, 1966; The Enlightenment: An Interpretation, vol. I, The Rise of Modern Paganism, 1966 (Nat. Book award 1967, Melcher Book award 1967); Weimar Culture: The Outsider as Insider, 1968 (Ralph Waldo Emerson award Phi Beta Kappa 1969); The Enlightenment, vol. II, The Science of Freedom, 1969; The Bridge of Criticism: Dialogues on the Enlightenment, 1970. Home: 13 Tulip Tree Lane Woodbridge CT 06525

GAY, ROBERT A., banker; b. N.Y.C., 1910; s. Robert A. and Catherine V. (Dwyer) G.; ed. Manhattan Coll., Pace Coll.; m. Carolyn V. Strand, Oct. 3, 1936; children—Florence, Robert, Nancy, James, Carol. Formerly exec. v.p., now pres., trustee Emigrant Savs. Bank. Mem. Cardinal's Com. for Edn., Cath. Charities Diocese Rockville Centre, N.Y., mem. mgmt. and labor com. Archdiocese N.Y.; treas. Irish Emigrant Soc. Trustee Marymount Coll. Mem. Newcomen Soc., Knights of Malta, Am. Cancer Soc., Pace Coll. Alumni Soc., Friendly Sons St. Patrick, K.C. Club: Cloud (N.Y.C.). Home: 24 Ridge Dr W Flower Hill Roslyn NY 11576 Office: 5 E 42d St New York City NY 10017

GAY, ROGER CROWELL, coll. adminstr.; b. Metuchen, N.J., May 11, 1912; s. Peter Joseph and Lydia White (Crowell) G.; A.B., Harvard, 1935, Ed.M., 1937; postgrad. Advanced Sch. Edn., Teachers Coll., Columbia, 1949-50, M.A., Profl. Diploma, 1954; L.H.D., Hillyer Coll., 1956; LL.D., New Eng. Coll., 1956; Sc.D., Wilberforce U., 1960; Sc. Ed. D., Nasson, 1969; m. Cynthia L. Beck, Jan. 1, 1962; children by previous marriage—Peter Leighton, Nancy Crowell. Dir. guidance, instr. social studies, Suffield Acad., 1937-39; asst. to dean, registrar, instr. edn. psychology Bard Coll., Columbia, 1939-41; asst. dean N.Y. Med. Coll., Flower and Fifth Av. Hosps., 1941-50; lectr. and cons. in psychology Flower-Fifth Av. Sch. Nursing, 1942-50; pres. and prof. social sci. Nasson Coll., Springvale, Me., 1950-69, pres. emeritus, 1969—; adminstr. Coll. Arts and Scis., State U. N.Y. at Plattsburgh, 1969—. Ednl. cons. King Features Syndicate, N.Y.C., 1937-40; cons. Bur. Adult, Vocational and Tech. Edn., U.S. Office Edn., 1970—. Asst. dir. civil def. and pub. safety York Co., 1950-60. Deans com. U.S. V.A. Hosp. Kingsbridge, N.Y.C., 1946-50; mem. bd. dirs. and sec. Found. for Integrated Edn., 1947-58; pres. Me. Welfare Assn. 1953-55; sec., treas., council for Advancement Small Colls., 1956-62, sec. 1962-65; trustee Nasson Coll., 1956-69; adv. council, New England Coll., 1956; civilian expert cons. U.S. War Dept. for Higher Edn., 1943-44; chmn. citizens com. to determine aims and needs of pub. schs. Eastchester, N.Y., 1949-50; mem. nat. adv. bd. Coll. Housing Program for U.S. Housing and Home Finance Agy., 1958-61. Bd. dirs. Austro-Am. Inst., Vienna, Austria. Mem. New Eng. Council (sec.-treas. Me. div., 1961-62, dir., 1964-70), Am. Assn. Ind. Coll. and U. Presidents (dir. 1968-70), Phi Delta Kappa, Kappa Delta Pi. Episcopalian. Rotarian. Contbr. to ednl. jours. Lectr. on human relations. Home: Alpine Acres Rangeley ME 04970 Office: Plattsburgh State Univ Coll Plattsburgh NY 12901

GAY, THOMAS BENJAMIN, lawyer; b. Richmond, Va., May 22, 1885; s. Thomas Bolling and Mary Radcliffe (Ellett) G.; law student U. Va., 1904-06; m. Lenore Temple Skeen, June 10, 1916; 1 son, Thomas Benjamin; m. 2d, Mary Stuart Pattison, Nov. 25, 1921. Admitted to Va. bar, 1906, began practice in Richmond; mem. Hunton, Williams, Gay, Powell & Gibson, 1916—; former counsel So. Ry.; counsel Scott Protective Com. of Stockholders of C. & O. Ry. which defeated Van Sweringen plan of uniting C. & O. with Nickel Plate, 1924-25; rep. N.Y. Stock Exchange before Congl. coms. which drafted National Securities Exchange Act, 1934. Mem. bd. vis. U. Va., 1946-54. Recipient Fellows Am. Bar Found. Fifty- Year award, 1966. Mem. Bar Assn. of District of Columbia, Am. (chmn. ho. of dels., 1939-41), Va. (pres. 1946-47), Richmond (pres. 1936-37) bar assns., Assn. Bar City N.Y., Assn. Life Ins. Counsel, U. Va. Law Sch. Assn. (pres. 1944- 45), Am. Law Inst., American Judicature Society, Phi Beta Kappa, Raven Soc. Episcopalian. Clubs: Cosmos (Washington); Commonwealth, Country of Va., Deep Run Hunt, Masters of Foxhounds Assn. of America; Farmington Country. Home: Prestwould Apts Richmond VA 23220 Office: 700 Bldg Richmond VA 23219

GAY, WILLIAM SAMUEL, Sr., educator; b. Smithfield, Va., Mar. 8, 1900; s. Samuel Tilton and Roxanna Dinwiddie (Turner) G.; student Washington and Lee U., 1920-22; B.S., Va. Poly. Inst., 1928, M.S., 1931; m. Grace Irene Osborn, Sept. 7, 1929; children—William Samuel, Cynthia Todd. Salesman, Cooper Riddick Co., 1922-25, Am. Lumber Corp., 1928; faculty Va. Poly. Inst., 1929- 69, prof. accounting, 1947-69, head dept. Sch. Bus., 1961-66; partner Harrell and Gay, C.P.A., Blacksburg, 1939-58. Mem. Va. Bd. Accountancy, 1946-56, Va. Adv. Legislative Com. Accounting and Bookkeeping, 1960-61. Mem. exec. bd. Blue Ridge council Boy Scouts Am., 1952—, chmn. New River Dist., 1952-54; chmn. planning com. Blacksburg Dist. Recreation Center. Bd. dirs., treas. Blacksburg United Fund, 1963-65. Served to maj. AUS, 1941-45; PTO. C.P.A., Va. Mem. Am. Inst. C.P.A.'s, Va. Soc. C.P.A.'s (bd. dirs. 1961- 62, pres. S.W. chpt. 1940-45, chmn. accounting research com. 1953-54, ednl. com. 1964—), Am. Accounting Assn., Nat. Assn. Accounting, Assn. C.P.A. Examiners, Am. Mgmt. Assn., Am. Legion, S.A.R., Alpha Kappa Psi (accounting award com. of Found. 1961-62), Omicron Delta Kappa, Sigma Mu Sigma, Alpha Phi Omega, Beta Alpha Psi. Democrat. Presbyn. (past deacon, elder; trustee 1955-69, chmn. stewardship com. Montgomery Presbytery 1963—). Mason (Shriner), Lion (past pres. Blacksburg). Author articles in field. Home: 3319 Pasley Av Roanoke, VA 24015.

GAY, ZHENYA, artist, author; b. Norwood, Mass.; student Columbia, 1919-22, also Solon Borglum, N.Y.C.; pupil of Winold Reiss, N.Y.C., Gaston Dorfinant, Paris, France. Exhbt. paintings, drawings and lithographs Davis Galleries, Mexico City, 1927, Montross Gallery, N.Y.C., 1930, Dutton's, N.Y.C., 1931, H.H. de Young Meml. Mus., San Francisco, 1931, Am. Mus. Natural History, N.Y.C., 1935, Rains Galleries, N.Y.C., 1939; costumer, designer Brooks Theatrical Costumes; free-lance motion picture and advt. work. Recipient certificate N.Y. State Assn. Supervision and Curriculum Devel., 1961. Illustrator, author: (juveniles) The Dear Friends, 1959; Look!, 1961; Wonderful Things, 1954; Who Is It?, 1957; Small One, 1958; What's Your Name?, 1955; The Nicest Time of Year, 1960; I'm Tired of Lions, 1961; Who's Afraid?, 1965. Illustrator with lithographs: de Quincy's Confessions of an English Opium-Eater, 1930; Wilde's Ballad of Reading Gaol, 1937; illustrator with line drawings: Poems of Catullus, 1931. Address: RD 2 Box 189D Saugerties NY 12477

GAYDOS, JOSEPH MATTHEW, congressman; b. Braddock, Pa., July 3, 1926; s. John and Elona (Magella) G.; student Duquesne U.; LL.B., U. Notre Dame, 1951; m. Alice Ann Gray, Nov. 26, 1955; children—Joseph Matthew, Colleen, Kathleen, Kelly, Tammy. Admitted to Pa. bar, 1953; mem. Pa. Senate for 45th Dist., 1967-68; dep. atty. gen. Pa., 1955; asst. solicitor Allegheny County, Pa.; gen. counsel dist. 5, United Mine Workers Am., then legal counsel dist. 50; mem. 91st Congress, 20th Dist. Pa. Served with USNR, World War II; PTO. Mem. Allegheny County Bar Assn., Am. Legion, Cath. War Vets., V.F.W., Sons of Italy, McKeesport Am.-Slovak Club, Croatin Fraternal Union, Jednota, Polish Nat. Alliance, U. Notre Dame Alumni Soc. Democrat. Roman Cath. Home: 3000 Valley Ridge Rd McKeesport PA 15133 Office: Longworth House Office Bldg Washington DC 20515

GAYLE, GIBSON, Jr., lawyer; b. Waco, Tex., Oct. 15, 1926; s. Gibson and Elsie (Little) G.; A.B., LL.B., Baylor U., 1950; m. Martha Jane Wood, May 29, 1948; children—Sally Ann, Martha, Gibson III, Jane, Philip. Admitted to Tex. bar, 1950, since practiced in Houston; partner Fulbright, Crooker, Freeman, Bates & Jaworski; instructor U. Houston Law Sch., 1951-55. Bd. govs. Harris County Center for Retarded, 1956—; bd. dirs. Am. Bar Endowment. Served to 2d lt. F.A., AUS, 1945-47. Fellow Am. Bar Found., Tex. Bar Found. (chmn. 1968-69); mem. Am. (chmn. jr. bar conf. 1959-60, ho. of dels. 1960-62, 63—, sec. 1963-67), Houston bar assns., State Bar Tex. (dir. 1966-69) Internat. Assn. Ins. Counsel, Sigma Alpha Epsilon. Democrat. Bd. editors Am. Bar Assn. Jour. Home: 14 Inwood Oaks Dr Houston TX 77024 Office: Bank of Southwest Bldg Houston TX 77002

GAYLER, NOEL ARTHUR MEREDYTH, naval officer; b. Birmingham, Ala., Dec. 25, 1914; s. Ernest Rotteck and Anne (Roberts) G.; B.S., U.S. Naval Acad., 1935; m. Caroline Groves, Nov. 3, 1941; children—Caroline (Mrs. Archibald K. Maness), Ann Deborah, Alexander Groves, Christopher Noel. Commd. ensign U.S. Navy, 1935, advanced through grades to vice adm., 1967; carrier-based fighter pilot, test pilot, naval ship and task force comdr., research and devel. adminstr.; formerly dep. dir. Spl. Devices Center; head fighter design br. Bur. Aero.; flag capt. U.S. Middle East Forces; comdg. officer U.S.S. Ranger, then Carrier Div. 20; naval aide to sec. navy; attache to Great Britain; asst. chief naval operations for devel. Navy Dept., 1965; dep. dir. Joint Strategic Target Planning Staff, SAC, Offutt AFB, Neb. unit, 1969; dir. Nat. Security Agy. Office: Nat Security Agy Ft Meade FL 33841

GAYLIN, GEORGE ROBERT, newspaperman; b. Cleve., Jan. 21, 1910; s. Philip and Ida (Loppelman) G.; student pub. schs. Cleve.; m. Ida Polay, Mar. 25, 1934; children—Barbara Lou, Harvey Stuart. Joined NEA-Acme (now U.P.I. Newspictures), 1927, Washington photo bur. mgr., 1938—, covered Korean war, also in Japan, 1950-51. Mem. Nat. Press Photographers Assn., White House News Photographers Assn. (v.p. 1952, pres. 1953). Club: Nat. Press (Washington). Home: 1436 Primrose Rd Washington DC 20012 Office: 1013 13th St Washington DC 20005

GAYLOR, DONALD HUGHES, naval med. officer; b. Bklyn., Apr. 17, 1926; s. Norman Hunter and Frances (Hughes) G.; student Queen's Coll., 1943; A.B., U. Rochester, 1946, M.D., 1949; m. Joan Winifred Power, Apr. 3, 1948; children—David, Christopher, Steven, Susan, Timothy. Commd. lt. (j.g.) USN, 1949, advanced through grades to capt. Med. Corps, U.S. Navy, 1966; intern U.S. Naval Hosp., Phila., 1949-50; student flight surgeon Sch. Aviation Medicine, Pensacola, Fla., 1950-51; flight surgeon U.S. Naval Sta., Trinidad, B.W.I., 1951-53; resident gen. surgery U.S. Naval Hosp., St. Albans, N.Y., 1953-57; postgrad. fellow surgery Royal Victoria Hosp., Montreal, Can., 1957; resident thoracic surgery U.S. Naval Hosp., St. Albans, 1957-59; resident cardiovascular surgery St. Francis Hosp., Roslyn, L.I., N.Y., 1958; staff thoracic surgeon U.S. Naval Hosp., Portsmouth, Va., 1959-64; surgeon U.S.S. Enterprise, 1964; staff thoracic surgeon U.S. Naval Hosp., Nat. Naval Med. Center, Bethesda, Md., 1964-65, chief thoracic and cardiovascular surgery, 1965-68; chief surgery, exec. officer U.S.S. Repose, 1968-69; exec. officer Naval Med. Sch., Nat. Naval Med. Center, Bethesda, Md., 1969—. Diplomate Am. Bd. Surgery, Am. Bd. Thoracic Surgery. Mem. A.M.A., Am. Thoracic Soc., Soc. Thoracic Surgeons (a founder), Md. Thoracic Soc. Roman Catholic. Author articles in field. Home: 11531 Cushman Rd Rockville, MD 20852 Office: Naval Med Sch Nat Naval Med Center Bethesda MD 20014

GAYLORD, CHARLES NELSON, engr.; b. Sharon, Pa., s. Edwin Henry and Lettie (Jones) G.; B.S., Ohio U., 1930; M.S.E., U. Mich., 1936; m. Dorothy Schuh, Aug. 29, 1931; children—Nelson, David, Frederick. Instr. and design engr., Hampton Inst., 1930-39; instr. civil engring., Clemson Coll., 1939-40; asst. project engr. Charleston Naval Ammunition Depot, 1940; asst. prof. engring. mechanics, N.C. State Coll., 1940-42; stress cons. Goodyear Aircraft Corp., 1942; structures research engr. Bell Aircraft Corp., 1943; prof. structural engring. and asst. dean, coll. engring., U. Ala., 1945; chmn. dept. civil engring. and dir. hwy. research U. Del., 1949-52; chmn. dept. civil engring. U. Va., asst. dean Sch. Engring., 1952—, also prof. of civil engring. Mem. Hwy. research bd., Am. Concrete Inst. Fellow Am. Soc. C.E.; mem. Soc. Engring. Edn., Sigma Xi, Beta Theta Pi, Tau Beta Pi, Theta Tau. Presbyn. Rotarian. Researcher in indeterminate structures stressed beyond proportional limit. Co-author: Design of Steel Structures with Application in Aluminum; Structural Engineering Handbook. Home: 1531 Westwood Road Charlottesville VA 22901

GAYLORD, CHARLES REID, oil and gas co. exec.; b. Berkeley, Cal., Mar. 26, 1922; s. Charles Edward and Jeanette (Reid) G.; ed. pub. schs.; m. Virginia Huck, Feb. 9, 1946; children—Charlotte Reid, Jeanette Reid. Builder, real estate investor, 1940-41; constrn. foreman C.E., U.S. Army, Anchorage, Alaska, 1941; realtor, bldg. contractor, San Diego, 1946-49; realtor, oil investor, gen. contractor, owner office bldgs., Midland, Tex., 1949-56; pres. Gaylord Properties Corp., Long Beach, Cal., 1957—, Gaylord Devel. Corp., Long Beach, 1957—, Gaylord Land Corp., Long Beach, 1957—; v.p. Signal Oil and Gas Co., Los Angeles, 1959, sr. v.p., 1959- 62, cons., 1962-67, aldo dir.; sr. v.p., dir. Signal Cos., Los Angeles, 1968—; pres., dir. Signal Investment Co., 1968—; v.p., trustee Signal Cos. Found. Adminstr. Will J. Reid Estate, 1956—, pres., trustee Will J. Reid Found.; bd. dirs. Long Beach chpt. Boy Scouts Am. Served with AUS, 1942-46; ETO. Decorated Purple Heart, Bronze Star. Mem. Nat. Assn. Rainbow Div. Vets., V.F.W., Am. Legion, Ducks Unltd. Presbyn. (deacon, trustee). Elk. Office: 1010 Wilshire Blvd Los Angeles CA 90017

GAYLORD, CLAYTON R., milling machine co. exec.; b. Rockford, Ill., Jan. 18, 1919; s. Robert March and Mildred (Ingersoll) G.; grad. Phillips Exeter Acad., 1937; B.A., Princeton, 1941; m. Gail Gartz, Aug. 8, 1942; children—Jenny (Mrs. Charles B. Lorch), Holly, March, Russell. With Ingersoll Milling Machine Co., Rockford, 1954—, pres., 1958-71, now chmn. bd.; dir. Ill. Bank & Trust Co., chmn. Winnebago United Republican Fund, 1958—. Trustee Rockford Meml. Hosp., pres., 1955; trustee Keith Country Day Sch., chmn., 1957-61; bd. dirs. Tax Found., Inland Lake Yachting Assn. Home: 2310 Spring Creed Rd Rockford IL 61107 Office: 707 Fulton Av Rockford IL 61101

GAYLORD, EDSON INGERSOLL, machine tool co. exec.; b. Rockford, Ill., Feb. 18, 1922; s. Robert M. and Mildred (Ingersoll) G.; grad. Phillips Exeter Acad., 1941; B.A., Princeton, 1945; m. Jane Wanzer, May 22, 1952; children—William Bradley, Susan Starr, Charles Ingersoll, John Wanzer, Mary March. With Ingersoll Machine Co., 1947—, pres., 1967-70, chmn., chief. exec. officer, 1970—. Served to capt. F.A., AUS, World War II. Home: 2811 Country Club Terrace Rockford IL 61103 Office: 707 Fulton Av Rockford IL 61101

GAYLORD, EDWARD KING, editor; b. Muscotah, Kan., Mar. 5, 1873; s. George Lewis and Eunice M. (Edwards) G.; grad. Cutler Acad., Colorado Springs, Colo., 1892; student Colo. Coll., 1894-97, LL.D., 1936; studied law at Colorado Springs, 1900-02; m. Inez Kinney, Dec. 29, 1914; children—Edith Kinney, Edward Lewis, Virginia Elizabeth. Clerk Dist. Ct., Colorado Springs and Cripple Creek, 1897-1900; telegraph editor and editorial writer Colorado Springs Telegraph, 1901; bus. mgr. St. Joseph Gazette, 1902; gen. mgr. Daily Oklahoman, Oklahoma City Times and Oklahoma Farmer-Stockman 1903—; pres. Okla. Pub. Co., 1918—, Mistletoe Express Co.; chmn. bd. WKY Television, Systems, Inc.; dir. Southland Paper Mills, Inc., Lufkin, Tex. Mem. commn. in charge constrn. Okla. State Capitol, 1918. Bd. dirs. Oklahoma City YMCA; trustee Midwest Research Inst., Kansas City, Mo., Southwest Research Inst., San Antonio. Mem. Asso. Press, Am. Newspaper Pubs. Assn., Southern Newspaper Pubs. Assn. Okla. City C. of C. (pres. 1915). Democrat. Conglist. Mason. Home: 6907 Avondale Av Oklahoma City OK 73116 Office: 500 N Broadway Oklahoma City OK 73102

GAYLORD, EDWARD LEWIS, publishing co. exec.; b. Denver, May 28, 1919; s. Edward King and Inez (Kinney) G.; A.B., Stanford, 1941; LL.D., Oklahoma City U., Okla. Christian Coll.; m. Thelma Feragen,. Aug. 30, 1950; children—Christine Elizabeth, Mary Inez, Edward King II, Thelma Louise. Pres., treas., dir. WKY Television System, Inc.; sec.-treas., dir. Mistletoe Express Service; exec. v.p., asst. gen. mgr., treas., dir. Okla. Pub. Co.; owner Publishers Petroleum, Colorgraphics, Nat. Packaging Co. Chmn., trustee Okla. Industries Authority; pres., dir. Okla. State Fair, 1961—; past v.p. United Fund. Chmn. president's council Okla. Christian Coll.; past trustee, mem. exec. com. Oklahoma City U.; trustee Casady Sch. Served with AUS, 1942-46. Recipient Brotherhood award Nat. Conf. Christians and Jews. Mem. Oklahoma City C. of C. (dir., treas., past pres.), So. Newspaper Publishers Assn. (past pres.). Conglist. Home: 1506 Dorchester Dr Oklahoma City OK 73120 Office: PO Box 25125 Oklahoma City OK 73125

GAYLORD, EDWIN HENRY, Jr., ret. educator, civil engr.; b. Youngstown, O., Jan. 16, 1903; s. Edwin Henry and Lettie (Jones) G.; A.B. Wittenberg U., 1924, D.Sc. (hon.), 1959; B.S., Case Western Reserve U., 1926; M.S., U. Mich., 1936; fellow human relations, Harvard Bus. Sch., 1948; m. Margaret R. Ball, Dec. 31, 1930; 1 dau., Marjorie Ann (Mrs. William A. Bardeen). With Mount Vernon Bridge Co., 1926-27; faculty Ohio U., 1927-44, 45- 56, prof., chmn. dept. civil engring., 1945-56; cons. stress analysis Goodyear Aircraft Corp., 1944-45; prof. civil engring. U. Ill., 1956-71, prof. emeritus, 1971—. Mem. specification com. Am. Inst. Steel Constrn. Mem. Am. Soc. C.E. (chmn. engring. edn. com. 1955), Am. Soc. Engring. Edn. (chmn. civil engring. div. 1951, mem. gen. council 1952-54), Column Research Council (chmn. 1962-66), Research Council on Riveted and Bolted Structural Joints, Sigma Xi, Tau Beta Pi, Beta Theta Pi. Club: University (Urbana). Author: (with Charles N. Gaylord) Design of Steel Structures, 1957. Editor: Structural Engineering Handbook, 1968. Home: 27 G H Baker Dr Urbana IL 61801

GAYLORD, HARVEY, aviation exec.; b. Buffalo, July 1, 1904; grad. Princeton, 1927; m. Ann Flershem, 1934; children—Nancy (Mrs. Robert F. Thompson Jr.), Susan. With Bell Aircraft Corp., 1941-60, dir., 1956-60, pres., 1959-60; pres. treas., dir. Bell Aerospace Corp., 1960—; pres. Bell Helicopter Corp., 1957- 60; exec. v.p. Textron, Inc., 1963-70; pres., chief exec. officer Nat. Aviation Corp., 1970—. Mem. adv. bd. dirs. Assn. U.S. Army; trustee Grad. Research & Devel. Center, So. Meth. U. Mem. Am. Helicopter Soc., Newcomen Soc. Clubs: Saturn (Buffalo): Chevy Chase Country (Washington); Black Hall (Old Lyme, Conn.). Office: One Rockefeller Plaza New York City NY 10020

GAYLORD, MARY FLETCHER WARDWELL, mem. Republican Nat. Com.; b. Detroit, June 2, 1915; d. Harold F. and Helen (Russell) Wardwell; B.A., Bennington Coll., 1936; M.S. Simmons Sch. Social Work, 1937; m. Dr. Henry Swan II, June 25, 1936 (div.); children—Edith, Henry III, Helen, Gretchen; m. 2d, Charles Gaylord, June 23, 1967. Republican precinct committeewoman, 1944-48, dist. capt., 1948-52, Colo. finance vice chmn., 1952-56, mem. exec. com. Rep. Nat. Com., 1956—. Mem. mayor's commn. on human relations; health planning com. Denver Area Welfare Council; mem. Denver Library Commn., 1959—. Trustee Bennington Coll., Denver Symphony Soc., Denver Art Mus., Winter Park Recreational Assn.; treas. Colo. Mental Health Assn., Mem. Colo. Fedn. Rep. Women (pres. 1952-54), Vis. Nurse Assn. Home: 410 Marion Street Denver, CO 80218.

GAYLORD, RALPH ELLISON, food co. exec.; b. Ogden, Utah, Apr. 11, 1908; s. George Ellison and Catherine (Yeager) G.; m. Annetta Dorothy Tennant, Aug. 24, 1925; children—Beverlee Helen (Mrs. C. Eugene McCraney), Carol Ann (Mrs. James E. Bertram). With Gen. Mills, Inc., 1921—, v.p., 1964—. Home: 6223 France Av S Edina MN 55410 Office: 9200 Wayzata Blvd Minneapolis MN 55440

GAYLORD, ROBERT EDMUND, orthodontist; b. Geneva, Ill., May 12, 1914; s. William P. and Lulu (Ercanbrack) G.; student Mich. State U., 1930-33; D.D.S., Northwestern U., 1937, M.S.D., 1939; m. Martha Conway Maryman, Nov. 7, 1962; children—William Gaylord, Robert E., Martha Conway, Alison Louise. Pvt. practice orthodontics, Dallas, 1941—; prof., chmn. dept. grad. orthodontics Baylor U. Coll. Dentistry, 1965—. Served to maj. AUS, 1947-49. Recipient diploma de Merito, U. Havana, 1959. Diplomate Am. Bd. Orthodontics. Fellow Am. Coll. Dentists; mem. Am. Assn. Orthodontists (pres. elect 1971), Tweed Orthodontic Group (past pres.), S.W. Angle Soc. Orthodontics (past pres.), Omicron Kappa Upsilon; hon. mem. Colegio de Odontologos de Venezuela. Home: 5241 Meaders Lane Dallas TX 75229 Office: 25 1/2 Highland Park Dallas TX 75205

GAYLORD, ROBERT MARCH, corp. exec.; b. Mpls., Oct. 11, 1888; s. Edson Starr and Louise (March) G.; B.A., U. Minn., 1911; m. Mildred Ingersoll, Oct. 30, 1915 (dec.); children—Robert March, Clayton Russell, Edson Ingersoll, Helen (Mrs. David G. Townsend); m. 2d, Elma Morlan Birch, May 18, 1949. With Mpls. Steel & Machinery Co., 1911-12, with Emerson Brantingham Co., Rockford, 1912-14; v.p. Gray tractor Co., Mpls., 1914-17; v.p. The Ingersoll Milling Machine Co., Rockford, 1917-28, pres., 1928-58, chmn. bd., 1958-68, chmn. exec. com., 1968—. Trustee Found. Econ. Edn., Ducks Unlimited Found., N. Am. Wildlife Found.; bd. dirs. World Wildlife Fund. Mem. Machinery and Allied Products Inst. (v.p. 1937-44), Ill. Mfrs. Assn. (pres. 1941), Nat. Assn. Mfrs. (pres. 1944), Nat. Machine Tool Builders Assn. (pres. 1932), Ducks Unltd. (pres. 1953-54), Rancheros Visitadores, Chi Psi, Republican. Episcopalian. Clubs: Country (Rockford); Tavern, Chicago, University (Chgo.): Oglethorpe (Savannah, Ga.); Mid-Day (Rockford). Home: 2425 Clinton Rd Rockford IL 61103 Office: 707 Fulton Av Rockford IL 61103

GAYLORD, WILLIAM N., banker. Vice pres., also auditor Conn. Nat. Bank. Office: Conn Nat Bank 888 Main St Bridgeport CT 06602*

GAYMON, WILLIAM EDWARD, govt. ofcl.; b. Bryn Mawr, Pa., Nov. 11, 1929; s. Fred and Victoria (Brown) G.; B.S., Howard U., 1951, M.S., 1956; Ph.D., Temple U., 1964; m. Estelle Smith, Aug. 18, 1956; children—William Victor, Nicole Gabrielle. Human engring specialist USAF, 1953-55; research psychologist Naval Research Lab., 1956-58, Pittman-Dunn Research Lab., 1959-60; asso. prof. psychology Lincoln U., 1961-65; with Peace Corps, 1965—, chief field assessment, 1965-66, regional dir. selection, 1966-67, dir., Liberia, 1967-69, Niger, 1969—; prof. psychology Continuing Center Edn., Pa. State U. at Swarthmore, 1963-65. Bd. commrs. Civil Rights Commn. Chester County, Pa., 1965, Montgomery County, Md., 1967. Doctoral research grantee Temple U., 1961-62. Mem. Am. Psychological assn. Home: 1 Elkdale Rd Lincoln University PA 19352

GAYN, MARK, journalist; b. China, 1909; grad. magna cum laude, Pomona Coll.; grad. Columbia Grad. Sch. Journalism. Corr. in China for Washington Post, then news editor and editorial writer China Press, Shanghai; mem. staff St. Louis Post-Dispatch, Newsweek, also Time mag. during World War II; chief Tokyo bur. Chgo. Sun, 1945-47; roving corr. Toronto Star, 1948- 53, fgn. corr., 1953—, now also Communist affairs analyst and editorial writer; reports distributed in U.S. through Chgo. Daily News Fgn. Service. Mem. Phi Beta Kappa. Author: Japan Dairy, 1947. Address: Repulse Towers 119 A Repulse Bay Rd Hong Kong

GAYNOR, ARTHUR FRANCIS, lawyer; b. N.Y.C., Apr. 17, 1910; s. Joseph Henry and Mary (Kennedy) G.; A.B., St. Joseph's Coll., 1931; LL.B., St. John's U., 1934; m. Anna C. Stines, July 16, 1938; children—Ann (Mrs. Joseph P. Starke), Margaret (Mrs. Eddi Haslam), Mary, Elizabeth, Constance. Admitted to N.Y. bar, 1934; practice in Bklyn., 1934-35, Mt. Vernon, 1935-36, White Plains, 1936—; law sec. to presiding justice, appellate div. N.Y. Supreme Ct., 1942-43. Mem. title adv. bd. Security Title & Guaranty Co. Chmn. Hartsdale (N.Y.) Pub. Parking Dist., 1962—. Bd. dirs. Westchester Sect. Nat. Conf. Christians and Jews; adv. bd. Westchester County Youth Services. Served to lt. USNR, 1943-46. Mem. N.Y. State, Westchester County, White Plains (pres. 1958) bar assns., Am. Soc. Internat. Law, Bklyn. and Manhattan Trial Counsel Assn. Home: 125 Yale Rd Hartsdale NY 10530 Office: 175 Main St White Plains NY 10601

GAYNOR, JAMES KENNETH, lawyer; b. Greensburg, Ind., Aug. 11, 1912; s. Silas Oliver and Nelle (Haymond) G.; B.S., Ind. U., 1946, J.D., 1950; LL.M., George Washington U., 1953, S.J.D., 1957; m. Phyllis Inez Vint, Nov. 12, 1939; children—Mary Eileen (Mrs. William H. Patterson, Jr.), James Kenneth. Profl. baseball umpire, 1934-38, 40, 46; constable Decatur County, Ind., 1934-38; city editor Bloomington (Ind.) Star Courier, 1945-47; commd. 1st lt. U.S. Army, 1947, advanced through grades to col., 1962; served in Judge Advocate Gen.'s office, 1950-54; mem. Staff Judge Advocate, Okinawa, 1954-57, Fort Knox, 1961-63, 1st Army 1966-67; legislative counsel, 1957-60; mem. bd. rev., 1960-61; legal adviser European Command, 1963-66; retired, 1967; admitted to Ind. bar, 1950, Ohio bar, 1967; asso. prof. Cleve. Marshall Law Sch., 1967, prof., dean, 1968-69; dean, prof. Coll. Law, Cleve. State U., 1969-71; prof. Chase Coll. Law, Cin., 1971—. Served with AUS, 1941-45. Decorated Legion of Merit, Bronze Star with cluster (U.S.), Croix de Guerre (France); Mil. Cross (Czechoslovakia). Mem. Am., Ind., Fed., Ohio, bar assns., Judge Advocates Assn., Am. Legion, Sigma Pi, Phi Delta Phi. Roman Catholic. K.C. (4). Editor: Military Jurisprudence, Cases and Materials, 1951. Office: Chase Law Sch 1105 Elm St Cincinnati OH 45210

GAYNOR, MITZI, actress; m. Jack Bean. Dancer Los Angeles Light Opera Co.; acting role The Great Waltz, South Pacific; motion pictures include My Blue Heaven, Anything Goes, The Joker, Les Girls, South Pacific, Happy Anniversary, Surprise Package, Anniversary Waltz, Birds and the Bees, There's No Business Like Show Business, Bloodhounds of Broadway, Take Care of My Little Girl, Golden Girl, The I Don't Care Girl, We're Not Married, For Love or Money. Address: care Twentieth Century-Fox 444 W 56th St New York City NY 10019*

GAYNOR, PAUL, Sr., advt. pub. relations exec.; b. Battan, Conn., Oct. 13, 1920; s. Harry and Estelle (Seale) G.; student N.Y.U., 1938-39; m. Jean Watters, Dec. 19, 1941; children—Anne, Paul. Account exec. Marschalk & Pratt Co., advt., 1948-50; v.p. CBS-Columbia, 1950-51, Buchanan & Co., Inc., 1951-53; pres., chmn. bd. Gaynor & Co., Inc., 1953—, Gaynor & Ducas, Inc., N.Y.C., 1955—, PR Assos., Inc.; pres. Columbia Devel. Corp., 1958—. Cons. to sec. def., 1950-52, Exec. Office Pres., 1952, sec. air force, 1953; coordinator Nat. Blood program, 1952-53. Served to col. USAAF, 1941- 48. Decorated Air Medal, Bronze Star. Mem. Pub. Relations Soc. Am. Clubs: Wings, N.Y. Athletic (N.Y.C.); Army-Navy, Nat. Press, Nat. Aviation (Washington). Home: 133 80th St New York City NY 10021 Office: 575 Madison Av New York City NY 10022

GAZIN, CHARLES LEWIS, geologist; b. Colorado Springs, Colo., June 18, 1904; s. Charles Edward and Janie Frances (Nicklaus) G.; B.S., Cal. Inst. Tech., 1927, M.S., 1928, Ph.D., 1930; m. Alice Van Deusen, Jan. 29, 1927 (div. Oct. 1942); children—Margaret A. (Mrs. H. T. Schellhous), Chester L., Barbara J. (Mrs. H. G. Neubauer); m. 2d, Elisabeth Parker Hobbs, May 11, 1943. Asst. and teaching fellow Cal. Inst. Tech., 1927-30, also geol. and paleontol. field work in Cal., Ore., Nev. and Ariz.; jr. geologist U.S. Geol. Survey, 1930-32 (assisted in geol. studies in Mont., Ida., Cal.); asst. curator vertebrate paleontology, Smithsonian Instn., U.S. Nat. Mus. 1932-42, asso. curator 1942-46, curator, 1946-67, mus. geologist, 1956-62, supervisory mus. geologist, 1962-67, sr. scientist (paleobiology), 1967-70, paleobiologist emeritus, 1970— (also led various expdns. to the western states and Central Am. for exploration and collection of fossil vertebrates); mem. div. earth scis. NRC, 1948-51, 57-60; incorporator, Am. Geol. Inst. rep. Soc. Vertebrate Paleontology, 1947, dir., 1956-58. Served as maj., A.C., AUS, World War II; assigned to Hdqrs. USAAF, AC/AS-2 (intelligence). Decorated Legion of Merit, 1946. Recipient Geol. Soc. Am. (Cordilleran Sect.) prize, 1930. Fellow Geol. Soc. Am. (editorial bd. 1946-48), Paleontol. Soc.; mem. Soc. Vertebrate Paleontology (pres. 1949), Am. Soc. Mamalogists, Washington Acad. Sci. (editor 1938-40, sec. 1947-48), Geol. Soc. Washington, Am. Soc. Zoologists, Soc. for Study of Evolution, Associacion Paleontológica, Argentina, Sigma Xi, Tau Beta Pi, Pi Alpha Tau. Clubs: Explorers (N.Y.C.); Cosmos (Washington). Author various sci. papers on vertebrate paleontology and geology. Home: 6420 Broad St Brookmont MD 20016 Office: US National Museum Washington DC 20560

GAZZANIGA, MICHAEL SAUNDERS, educator, psychologist; b. Los Angeles, Dec. 12, 1939; s. Dante Achilles and Alice (Griffth) G.; A.B., Dartmouth, 1961; Ph.D., Cal. Inst. Tech., 1964; m. Linda Jean Rea, Sept. 7, 1963; children—Marin Ann, Anne Lee, Kate Michel. Research fellow Cal. Inst. Tech., 1964-66; internat. USPHS research fellow U. Pisa (Italy), 1966; from asst. prof. to asso. prof. and chmn. dept. psychology U. Cal. at Santa Barbara, 1968-69; asso. prof. grad. psychology N.Y. U., 1969. Mem. Am. Psychol. Soc., Am. Acad. Neurology, Am. Physiol. Soc., N.Y. Acad. Sci. Author: The Bisected Brain, 1970. Home: 21 November Trail Weston CT 06880

GAZZARA, BEN, actor; b. N.Y.C., Aug. 28, 1930; s. Antonio and Angelina (Cusumano) G.; student Coll. City N.Y., 1948-50. actor, appearing in End As a Man, 1953, Cat on a Hot Tin Roof, 1955, Hatful of Rain, 1955; starring role in film version End As A Man, 1956; The Night Circus, 1959; motion picture Anatomy of Murder, 1959; Joy of Laughter, 1960; The Young Doctors, 1961, Convicts Four, 1961; Husbands, 1969; stage play Strange Interlude, 1963; Broadway play, Traveller Without Luggage, 1964; TV series, Arrest and Trial, 1963-64; motion picture A Rage to Live, 1964; TV series Run for Your Life, 1965-68. Recipient Drama Critics award for role in End As a Man, 1953; Theatre World award, 1953. Home: 67 Riverside Dr New York City NY 10024 Office: care CMA 600 Madison Av New York City NY 10022

GAZZARD, ALBERT EDWARD, mining co. exec.; b. Sydney, New S. Wales, Australia, Oct. 8, 1910; s. Albert Carrington and Georgina (Brand) G.; student Sydney Tech. Coll., 1926-30; m. Alice Enid Hallam, May 2, 1933; 1 dau., Judith Anne (Mrs. William Boucock). With Placer Devel. Ltd., Vancouver, B.C., Can., 1937-41, 45-49, 55—, exec. v.p., 1969-70, sr. v.p., 1970—, also dir.; gen. mgr. Yeomans Pty. Ltd., Sydney 1949-55; chmn., mng. dir. Placer Exploration Ltd., 1965—; dir. Commonwealth-New Guinea Timbers Ltd., Territory Fisheries (Pty.) Ltd., Karlander New Guinea Line Ltd., Canadian Exploration Ltd., Gibraltar Mines Ltd. (NPL). Served with New Guinea Vol. Rifles, 1941-45. Clubs: Royal Vancouver Yacht, Capilano Golf and Country (Vancouver); Papua (Territory Papua and New Guinea); Australian Golf, American Nat. (Sydney). Home: 1501 845 Chilco St Vancouver 5 British Columbia Canada Office: 1030 W Georgia St Vancouver 5 British Columbia Canada

GAZZELLONI, SEVERINO, flute soloist; b. Roccasecca, Frosinone, Jan. 5, 1919; s. Giuseppi Tailor and Amalia Pascarella; diploma for flute studies. Prof. at Pesaro Rossini Conservatory; title of Flute Internat. Chair, for Contemporary Music, Darmstadt Conservatory; soloist Symphonic Orch., Rome RAI-TV; recordings classic, also modern music. Address: 4 Via Simeto Rome Italy*

GAZZOLO, DOROTHY HAVEN, mag. editor; b. Ft. Wayne, Ind., Apr. 28, 1911; d. Frank R. and Sue (Bolster) Haven; student Ind. U., U. Chgo.; m. Louis J. Gazzolo, Dec. 30, 1940 (dec. Sept. 1958). With Nat. Assn. Housing and Redevel. Ofcls., Chgo., 1939—, dep. exec. dir. nat. orgn., adminstr Chgo. office, 1950- 61, editor publ. Jour. of Housing, 1944—. Mem. Nat. Housing Conf., Internat. Fedn. Housing and Planning, Met. Washington Housing and Planning Assn. (dir.), Nat. Conf. on Social Welfare, Pub. Housing Assn. Chgo. (dir.). Club: Kenwood Golf and Country. Contbr. housing articles to Municipal Yearbook, Book of the States. Home: 4000 Massachusetts Av NW Washington DC 20016 Office: 2600 Virginia Av NW Washington DC 20037

GEANAKOPLOS, DENO JOHN, educator; b. Mpls., Aug. 11, 1916; s. John Christ and Helen (Economou) G.; diploma in violin, Juilliard Sch. Music, 1939; B.A., U. Minn., 1941, M.A., 1946; Litt. D., U. Pisa (Italy), 1946; Ph.D. Harvard, 1953; M.A., Yale, 1967; m. Effie Vranos, Aug. 23, 1953; children—John, Constance. Violinist, Mpls. Symphony Orch., 1939-42, 46; teaching fellow Harvard, 1951-53; fellow Dumbarton Oaks, Washington, 1949-50; instr. history Brandeis U., 1953-54; prof. Greek Theol. Sch., Boston, 1953-54; from asst. prof. to prof. Western medieval and Renaissance history U. Ill., Urbana, 1954-67; prof. depts. history and religious studies Yale and Yale Div. sch., teaching Byzantine and Renaissance history and history Eastern Orthodox Ch., 1967—; lectr. univs. Athens (Greece), 1961, Paris (France), 1964, Salonika (Greece), 1964, Rome (Italy), 1964, Oxford (Eng.), 1967, U. Ill., Chgo., 1967, Cini Found., Venice, Italy, 1962-68; lectr. on Orthodoxy, Rosary Coll., Chgo., 1959. Attended Vatican I Council, 1962, Council of Chalcedon conf. World Council Chs., Geneva, 1969; mem. campus commn. Standing Conf. Am. Orthodox Bishops; mem. U.S. Com. Byzantine Studies. Served to capt. Q.M.C., AUS, 1942-46. Recipient awards Am. Council Learned Socs., 1960, 61, 68; decorated gold cross Order King George (Greece), 1966, Order St. Andrew by Patriarch Constantinople, 1970; Fulbright scholar, 1960-61, Guggenheim fellow, 1964; grantee Am. Philos. Soc., 1962, 66. Mem. Am. Hist. Assn., Medieval Acad., Ch. History Soc., Renaissance Soc. Am. Assn. Advancement Slavic Studies, Cretan Hist. Soc., Soc. Byzantine Studies (Athens), Soc. for Macedonian Studies (Salonika), G. Palamas Soc. (Milan), Orthodox Theol. Soc. Am. Author: Emperor Michael Palaeologus and the West, 1959; Erasmus and the Aldine Academy, 1960; Greek Scholars in Venice in the Renaissance, 1962; Byzantine East and Latin West, 1966; Bisanzio e il Rinascimento, 1967; (with others) Western Civilization, 1968. Editor Jour. Greek, Roman Byzantine Studies; editorial bd. Greek Orthodox Theol. Rev., Studies in Medieval and Renaissance History. Contbr. articles, revs. profl. jours. Office: History Dept Hall Grad Studies Yale U New Haven CT 06520

GEAR, HARRY SUTHERLAND, educator; b. Germiston, Transvaal South Africa, July 31, 1903; s. John and Joann (Sutherland) G.; student St. John's Coll., Johannesburg, 1920; M.B., B.Ch., U. Witwatersrand, 1928, M.D., 1935; D.P.H., U. London, 1931; m. Joyce Leishman, July 21, 1932; children—Michael, Peter, Adrian. Med. officer British Colonial Med. Service, Rhodesia, 1929-30, Lester Inst. Med. Research, Shanghai, 1932-35; first asst., then dep. chief med. officer, S. Africa, 1935-51; asst. dir. gen., also cons. WHO, 1951-59; sec. gen. World Med. Assn., also Conf. Med. Edn., 1961-66; prof. internat. health U. Toronto, 1966—, chmn. dept. preventive medicine, 1967—. Mem. gov.-gen. commn. med. services Fedn. Rhodesias and Nyasaland, 1959. Recipient Duncan medal London Sch. Tropical Medicine. Hon. life mem. Australian Austrialian med. assns.; fellow Royal Statis. Soc., Royal Health Soc., Royal Soc. Tropical Medicine; mem. British, S. African (Gold medal 1962) med. assns. Author: World Medical Research, 1959; Modern Health, 1966. Address: Faculty Medicine Univ Toronto Toronto 5 Ontario Canada

GEARHART, LESTER ROY, accountant; b. Mainville, Pa., May 2, 1909; s. Levin Samuel and Emma (Nuss) G.: A.A., N.E. Kan. Jr. Coll., Highland, 1932; spl. accounting studies, LaSalle Extension U., 1938-42; m. Lorene Elizabeth Focke, Nov. 19, 1938; children—Carol Elizabeth, Stephen Samuel. Mgr. retail yard Foster Lumber Co., Kansas City, Mo., 1935-38; asst. purchasing agt. E. C. Robinson Lumber Co., St. Louis, 1938-41; with Ernst & Ernst, C.P.A.'s, St. Louis, 1941-54, mgr., Memphis, 1956-59, partner, 1959—. Mem. Tenn. Bd. Accountancy, 1960-63. Pres. Jr. Achievement Memphis, 1963; bd. dirs., treas. Mid-South Dist., Lutheran Ch.-Mo. Synod. Bd. dirs. Shelby United Neighbors, 1965—; bd. dirs. United Cerebral Palsy Assn. Memphis and Shelby County, 1963—, sec., 1963—. Served with AUS, 1943-45, C.P.A., Tenn., 7 other states. Mem. Am. Inst. C.P.A.'s, Tenn. Soc. C.P.A.'s (pres. Memphis 1960), Nat. Assn. Accountants, Am. Accounting Assn. Club: Chickasaw Country (mem. bd., treas. 1969). Home: 327 Chuckwood Rd Memphis TN 38117 Office: Sterick Bldg Memphis TN 38103

GEARHEART, DON HUGH, corp. exec.; b. Dallas, Dec. 8, 1904; s. Willis Robert Dowell and Naomi M. (Wilson) G.; A.B., Butler U., 1928; m. Caro Shaw Austin, Feb. 4, 1966; children—Elizabeth (Mrs. Gilbert M. Richmond), Susan. Sales mgr. Cleve. Coop. Stove Co., 1935-38; exec. v.p. Warren Refining & Chem. Co., 1938-42; v.p. Globe Machine & Stamping Co., 1942-44; v.p. Hupp Corp., 1944-55, dir., 1944-68, pres., 1955-67, chmn., 1964-68 (all Cleve.). Mem. Am. Ordnance Assn., Soc. Automotive Engrs., Assn. U.S. Army. Mason. Clubs: Union, Buckeye Retriever (Cleve.); University (N.Y.C). Home: Cedar Point Royal Oak MD 21662 Office: 11770 Berea Rd Cleveland OH 44111

GEARHEART, ERNEST THEODORE, lawyer; b. Salem, Va., Mar. 6, 1915; s. Ernest Tilvern and Atha A. (Coleman) G.; B.A., U. Richmond, 1936; J.D., George Washington U., 1949; m. Dorothy P. Bates, June 8, 1940; children—John Coleman, Robert Ernest. Admitted to Va. bar, 1937; practiced in Arlington, 1938—; mem. firm Phillips Kendrick, Gearheart & Aylor: lectr. tech. subjects Va. State Bar Continuing Legal Edn. Seminars. Served with AUS, World War II. Mem. Am., Va., Arlington Co. bar assns., Phi Beta Kappa. Baptist. Home: 6230 N 19th St Arlington VA 22205 Office: 2009 14th St Arlington VA 22216

GEARIEN, JAMES EDWARD, chemist, educator; b. Peoria, Ill., Aug. 27, 1919; s. Grover C. and Anna (Sperry) G.; B.S., U. Ill., 1941; M.S., U. Mich., 1942, Ph.D., 1950; m. Helen G. Gray, Feb. 14, 1948; children—James Edward, Anne J. Mem. faculty U. Ill. Med. Center, Chgo., 1948—, prof., head chemistry dept., 1958—. Mem. Ill. Bd. Pharmacy, 1963-68. Mem. Am. Chem. Soc. (chmn. div. medicinal chemistry), Am. Pharm. Assn. Contbr. articles profl. jours. Home: 1606 Courtland St Park Ridge IL 60068 Office: 833 S Wood St Chicago IL 60612

GEARY, DONALD D., Jr., mining co. exec.; b. N.Y.C., May 13, 1924; s. Donald D. and Pauline H. (Stevens) G.; grad. Deerfield Acad., 1942; B.A., Yale, 1948, LL.B., 1951; m. Ann H. Tuttle, June 10, 1950; children—Laura S., Pamela D., Martha W. Admitted to N.Y. bar, 1951; with firm Chadbourne, Parke, Whiteside & Wolff, N.Y.C. 1951-58; with Anaconda Co., 1958—, gen. counsel, 1964-66, v.p. gen. counsel, 1966—, also officer and dir. various subsidiaries. Vice chmn. Yale Law Sch. Fund, 1960. Served with AUS, 1944-46; ETO. Mem. Assn. Gen. Counsel, Assn. Bar City N.Y., Am. Bar Assn., Am. Inst. Mining, Metall. and Petroleum Engrs., N.A.M. (chmn. subcom. mining and mineral resources), Phi Beta Kappa, Beta Theta Pi, Phi Delta Phi. Clubs: Lawyers, Mining, University Glee (dir., sec. 1959-64); Larchmont Yacht, University (Larchmont).
‡

GEBALLE, RONALD, educator, physicist; b. Redding, Cal., Feb. 7, 1918; s. Oscar and Alice (Glaser) G.; B.S., U. Cal. at Berkeley, 1938, M.S. 1940, Ph.D., 1943; m. Marjorie Louise Cohn, Oct. 31, 1940; children—Margaret F., Thomas R., Leslie A., Daniel T., Robert O., Jonathan L., Emily R., Anthony J. Teaching asst. physics U. Cal. at Berkeley, 1938-42, physicist radiation lab., 1943; physicist Applied Physics Lab., U. Wash., 1943-46; mem. faculty U. Wash., 1946—, prof., chmn. dept. physics, 1959—; guest scientist Lab. for Atomic and Molecular Physics, Amsterdam, 1964- 65. Cons. NSF, Army Research Office: mem. research adv. com. electro- physics NASA, 1962-64; Internat. Conf. on Physics Electronic and Atomic Collisions, 1967—; mem. adv. com. grants Research Corp., 1967—; mem. Commn. on Coll. Physics, 1966-71. Mem. citizens committee edn. Wash. State Legislature, 1960. Fellow Am. Phys. Soc. (chmn. div. electron and atomic physics 1968); mem. Am. Assn. U. Profs., Am. Assn. Physics Tchrs. (pres. 1969-70), A.A.A.S., Fedn. Am. Scientists, Am. Civil Liberties Union, Pacific N.W. Assn. Coll. Physics (chmn. bd. dir. 1965-70), Am. Inst. Physics (mem. governing bd., exec. com.), Phi Beta Kappa, Sigma Xi. Home: 4201 N E 92d St Seattle WA 98115.

GEBALLE, THEODORE HENRY, educator; b. San Francisco, Jan. 20, 1920; s. Oscar and Alice (Glaser) G.; B.S. in Chemistry, U. Cal. at Berkeley, 1941, Ph.D. in Phys. Chemistry, 1949; m. Frances C. Koshland, Oct. 19, 1941; children—Gordon, Alison, Adam, Monica Ruth. Research asso. Low Temperature Lab., U. Cal. at Berkeley, 1949-51; mem. staff Bell Telephone Lab., Murray Hill, N.J., 1952—, head low temperature physics dept., 1958-67, research cons., 1967—; prof. applied physics Stanford, 1967—. Served to capt. AUS, 1941-46. Fellow Am. Phys. Soc.; mem. Am. Chem. Soc., Phi Beta Kappa, Sigma Xi. Recipient Oliver E. Buckley solid state physics prize Am. Phys. Soc., 1970. Home: 259 Kings Mountain Rd Woodside CA 94062 Office: Dept Applied Physics Stanford Univ Stanford CA 94305

GEBER, STEPHEN EDWIN, musician; b. Los Angeles, Aug. 17, 1942; s. Edwin Martin and Gretchen Hildegarde (Kuehny) G.; Mus.B. with Honors, performers certificate, Eastman Sch. Music, 1965; m. Judith Ann Ryder, June 19, 1964; children—Pamela Elise, Kristin Ann. Cellist, Rochester (N.Y.) Philharmonic and Eastman-Rochester Symphony, 1961-65; mem. Boston Symphony Orch., 1965—; artist, tchr. New Eng. Conservatory of Music, Boston, 1967—; solo and chamber music performances on East and West coasts. Home: 248 Summit Av Brookline MA 02146

GEBHARD, BRUNO FREDERIC, health cons.; b. Rostock, Germany, Feb. 1, 1901; s. Frederic William and Meta Louise Mary (Ross) G.; ed. Abiturium, Realgymnasium, Rostock, 1919; M.D., U. Rostock, 1924; student U. Munich, 1921-22, U. Berlin, 1922-23; m. Gertrude Juliane Adolph, April 8, 1927; children—Suzanna Elizabeth (Mrs. Alvin Goodman), Christine (Mrs. Bernard McCabe), Ruth (Mrs. Raymond Fink). Came to U.S., 1937, naturlized 1944. Resident physician Children's Hosp., Dortmund, 1926; curator German Hygiene Museum, Dresden, 1927-37; sci. dir. Office Expns., Berlin, 1932-37; dir. exhbn. "Woman" 1933, "Wonder of Life" 1935; cons. for Med. and Pub. Health Exhibits, N.Y. World's Fair, 1937-40; dir. Cleve. Health Museum, 1940-65; asso. in health edn., Western Res. U., 1940-65; cons. Army Med. Mus., Washington, 1951; del. Internat. Council of Museums, UNESCO, Paris, 1948. Recipient Austrian Red Cross award, 1930, Olympic Games award, 1936; Elisabeth S. Prentiss award, 1965; Outstanding Service award Cleve. Welfare Fedn., 1965; Golden Door award Nationality Services Center, 1968. Diplomate American Bd. Preventive Medicine and Pub. Health. Fellow A.M.A., Am. Public Health Assn.; hon. fellow, Rochester Museum Arts and Scis.; hon. mem. Internat. Coll. Dentists, U.S. Sect.; hon. life mem. Markle Research Found.; mem. Am. Assn. History Medicine, Cleve. Acad. Medicine (distinguished mem.), Am. Assn. Museums, C. of C., Midwest Museums Assn. (v.p.), German Soc. History Medicine. Clubs: Rowfant, Rotary. Author: From Medicine Show to Health Museum, 1947; editor. Home: 3276 Braemer Rd Shaker Heights OH 44120 ☆

GEBHARD, DAVID, mus. dir.; b. Cannon Falls, Minn., July 21, 1927; s. Walter J. and Ann (Olson) G.; B.A., U. Minn., 1949, M.A., 1951. Ph.D., 1957; m. Patricia Peeke, July 7, 1954; 1 dau., Ellen Jean. Curator, instr. art U. N.M. 1953-55; dir. Roswell (N.M.) Mus., 1955-61; prof. art, dir. art galleries U. Cal., Santa Barbara, 1961—; field research in archeology, summers 1949-57; Fulbright prof. Tech. U. Istanbul, Turkey, 1960-61. Pres. Citizens Planning Assn. Santa Barbara, 1970—. Dir. Western Found., Inc.; trustee N.M. Archaeol. Soc. Served to cpl., AUS, 1945-47. Recipient research grants NSF and Nat. Park Service; Ford found. grant study Turkish architecture, 1965. Mem. A.I.A., Soc. Am. Archaeology, Am. Anthrop. Assn., Coll. Art Assn., Soc. Archtl. Historians (dir.). Author: Prehistoric Cave Paintings of the Diablo Region of Texas, 1960; A Guide to the Architecture of Purcell and Elmslie, 1960; A Guide to Architecture in Southern California, 1964; R.M. Schindler: Architect; Architecture in California, 1868-1968, 1968; Kem Weber and the Moderene, 1969; The Richfield Building 1928-1968, 1969; Charles F.A. Voysey, Architect, 1970. Contbr. articles to profl. jours. Home: 895 E Mountain Dr Santa Barbara CA 93103 Office: Art Gallery U Cal Santa Barbara CA 93106

GEBHARD, LOUIS AUGUST, scientist; b. Buffalo, June 11, 1896; s. August and Caroline (Deuter) G.; J.D., Georgetown U., 1924; B.S. in Elec. Engring., George Washington U., 1930; m. Marguerite A. Strauss, Aug. 6, 1931; children—Katharine (Mrs. Harlan Q. Stevenson), Paul. With U.S. Naval Research Lab., Washington, 1923—, successively head radio transmitter sect. radio div., supt. radio engring. div., supt. aircraft div., asst. supt. radio div., asst. supt. charge devel., 1923-45; supt. radio div., 1945-68, cons. for electronics, 1968—. Recipient Presdl. Certificate of Merit for achievements in radar, 1946. Fellow I.E.E.E., Am. Phys. Soc., A.A.A.S.; mem. Research Soc. Am., Am. Inst. Physics, Armed Forces Communication and Electronics Assn., U.S. Naval Inst. Patentee electronics and radio. Home: 2142 Branch Av SE Washington DC 20020 Office: US Naval Research Lab Washington DC 20014

GEBHARD, PAUL HENRY, anthropologist, educator; b. Rocky Ford, Colo., July 3, 1917; s. Paul Adam and Eva (Baker) G.; B.S. cum laude, Harvard, 1940, M.A., 1942, Ph.D., 1947; m. Agnes E. West, May 19, 1939; children—Mark West, Jan Cynthia, Karla Lynn. Asso., Inst. for Sex Research, Ind. U., Bloomington, 1946-55, exec. dir., 1956—, , instr. dept. anthrolology, 1947-52, asst. prof., 1953-60, asso. prof., 1961-66, prof., 1967- -. Fellow Am. Anthrop. Assn., Am. Sociol. Assn., Ind. Acad. Sci.; mem. Soc. Am Archaeology, Soc. Study Social Problems. Author: (with A. Kinsey) Sexual Behavior in the Human Female, 1953; sr. author Pregnancy, Birth and Abortion, 1958, Sex Offenders, 1965. Home: Route 1 Box 135 Nashville IN 47448

GEBHARDT, LOUIS PHILIPP, Jr., educator; b. Jackson, Cal., Dec. 20, 1905; s. Judge Louis Philipp and Ellen Harriett (Merkel) G.; A.B., Stanford, 1929, A.M., 1934, Ph.D., 1937, M.D., 1942; m. Johann Else Burket, Sept. 11, 1938; children—Laurence Philbert, Michael John, Karl Anson. Research asst. in bacteriology and exptl. pathology Stanford U., 1929-36; research asso., 1937-39, acting asst. prof., 1941-42, asso. prof. bacteriology and pathology, sch. medicine U. Utah, 1942-43, prof. microbiology, 1943—, head dept., 1943-70. Dir. div. bacteriology, Salt Lake Gen. Hosp., 1943-57. Cons. and examiner Utah State Merit Council, 1943-50; dir. Spl. Weapons Def. State Utah, 1951-61; expert civilian cons. to War Dept., 1944; cons. USPHS, 1957-62, ecology research, microbiology, Dugway Proving Grounds, 1955-69; attending pathologist VA Hosp., 1953—. Pres. Utah Pub. Health Assn., 1948-49; v.p. Western br. Am. Pub. Health Assn. 1948-49. Mem. N.Y. Acad. Sci., Am. Soc. Microbiology, Am. Public Health Assn., Utah Pub. Health Assn. (bd. dirs.), Soc. Exptl. Biology and Medicine (chmn. Rocky Mountain sect. 1945-46), Am. Assn. Immunologists, Sigma Xi, Alpha Omega Alpha. Club: Exchange (Salt Lake City). Contbr. sci. papers to publs. Home: 2194 S 19th St E Salt Lake City, UT 84106.

GEBHARDT, RICHARD GEORGE, transp. co. exec.; b. Cleve., May 14, 1924; s. Eugene W. and Rose (Adolph) G.; B.S. in Mech. Engring., Case Inst. Tech., 1949; m. Milma J. Fagan, Sept. 3, 1949; children—Jean Louise, Elizabeth Ann, Robert William. Machine design engr. Nat. Machinery Co., Tiffin, O., 1949-52; service engr. White Motor Co., Cleve., 1952; asst. v.p. maintenance Roadway Express Inc., Akron, O., 1953-65; v.p. maintenance Greyhound Lines Inc., Chgo., 1965—. Named Ky. col., 1963. Mem. Soc. Automotive Engrs. Home: 576 Clavey Ct Highland Park IL 60035. Office: 140 S Dearborn St Chicago IL 60603

GECKLER, RICHARD DELPH, corp. cons.; b. Toledo, Nov. 4, 1918; s. Maurice T. and Edith (Payne) G.; A.B., DePauw U., 1939; m. Elaine Mary Campbell, June 27, 1965; 1 dau. by previous marriage, Carole Faye (Mrs. Jon Countryman). Chem. engr. Standard Oil Co. (Ind.), 1939-45; with Aerojet-Gen. Corp., 1945-68, v.p., mgr. solid rocket plant, Sacramento, 1956-63, corp. v.p., El Monte, Cal.,

1963-68; chmn. bd., chief exec. Aerojet Delft Corp., 1968-69; exec. v.p. Anellux Systems Corp., El Segundo, Cal., 1970-71; asst. dir. strategic weapons Office Sec. Def. 1964-66. Recipient Meritorious Pub. Service Citation, Navy Dept., 1961. Fellow Am. Inst. Aero. and Astronautics; mem. Am. Chem. Soc., Am. Math. Soc., Phi Beta Kappa. Club: Internat. (Washington). Home: 135 Belday Rd Pasadena CA 91105

GEDDA, NICOLAI, opera singer; b. Stockholm, Sweden, July 11, 1925; s. Michaeil Ustinoff and Olga Gedda; grad. Swedish Coll., Södra Latin Stockholm 1945; div., 1956; 1 dau., Tatiana; m. 2d, Anastasia Caraviotis, Feb. 21, 1965. Debut, Stockholm Opera, 1952; appeared La Scala, Milan, 1953, Paris Opera, 1953, Covent Garden, London, 1954; concert appearances, Vienna, Germany, France, Italy, Rome Opera, Monte Carlo Opera, Bordeaux Opera, Switzerland; tenor summer festivals Aix-en-Provence, Salzburg, Lucerne, Edinburgh, Holland, 1961, Vienna, 1962; tour U.S. and Can., 1957; debut Met. Opera Co., 1957; recordings Angel Records, Master's Voice. Address: care Lies Askonas 190 Air St London W1 England

GEDDES, BARBARA BEL, actress; b. N.Y.C., Oct. 31, 1922; d. Norman and Belle (Sneider) Geddes; student Buxton Sch., Putney; Andrebrook; m. Carl Schreuer, Jan. 24, 1944 (div. 1951); 1 dau., Susan; m. 2d. Windsor Lewis, Apr. 15, 1951; 1 dau., Betsy. First stage role in School for Scandal, Clinton (Conn.) Playhouse, 1939; made Broadway debut in Out of The Frying Pan, 1940; appeared in Little Darling, 1942; Nine Girls, 1943; Mrs. January and Mr. X., 1944; Deep Are the Roots, 1945; The Moon Is Blue, 1952; The Living Room, 1954; Cat on a Hot Tin Roof, 1955; The Sleeping Prince, 1956; Silent Night, Lonely Night, 1959; Mary, Mary, 1961; The Porcelain Year, 1965; Everything in the Garden, 1967; entered motion pictures, 1946. Home: Putnam Valley NY 10579

GEDDES, DAVID DARWIN, univ. dean; b. Haines, Ore., May 17, 1922; s. Archie Waldo and Lula (Speelman) G.; B.S., Willamette U., 1948; M.S., Brigham Young U., 1952; Ph.D., U. So. Cal., 1959; m. Marise Alder, Apr. 17, 1946; children—Lee Anne, David Gordon. Physiologist, USPHS, Los Angeles, 1953-56; asso. clin. prof. medicinee Cal. Coll. Medicine, 1955-56; chmn. dept. health scis. Brigham Young U., 1956-59, chmn. dept. phys. edn. men, 1961-67, prof. edn., 1968-69; adviser Iran Ministry Edn., U.S. Overseas Mission, 1959-61; postdoctoral fellow Center for Study Higher Edn., U. Mich., 1967-68; dean Coll. Scis. and Arts, Mich. Tech. U., Houghton, 1969—; cons. campus planning, 1964—. Mem. Steering Com. for City Status, Houghton, 1969. Pres. Copper Country Arts Council. Served with AUS, 1942- 46; PTO. Decorated Eftekar and service medals Shah of Iran, 1961. Fellow Am. Coll. Sports Medicine, Am. Acad. Phys. Edn., Am. Assn. Higher Am. Council Edn. Mem. Ch. of Jesus Christ of Latter-day Saints. Author: Our Word of Wisdom, 1964. Contbr. articles profl. jours. Home: 1201 7th Av Houghton MI 49931

GEDDES, EUGENE MAXWELL, investment banker, broker; b. Bklyn., Mar. 20, 1908; s. Donald Grant and Grace (Maxwell) G.; student St. Paul's Sch., Concord, N.H., 1921-27; m. Lydia Ahles, Aug. 31, 1932; children—Eugene M., Robert A. Asso. with Brown Bros. Harriman & Co., bankers, N.Y.C., 1928-30, with Clark, Dodge & Co., 1930-32; mem. N.Y. Stock Exchange as ind. broker, 1932-34; gen. partner firm Clark, Dodge & Co., 1934-60; pres. dir. Clark, Dodge & Co., Inc., 1960-66, chmn. bd., chmn. exec. com., 1966- -; dir., mem. exec. com. Western Union Telegraph Co., 1939—. Served from lt. to comdr., USNR, 1941-45; on active naval reserve duty 3d naval dist. and Washington. Mem. Nat. Soc. Prevention of Blindness (bd. dirs.), N.Y. Stock Exchange. Episcopalian. Clubs: Racquet and Tennis (N.Y.) Piping Rock (Locust Valley, L.I.) Home: Horse Shoe Rd Millneck NY 11765 Office: 140 Broadway New York City NY 10005

GEDDES, ROBERT LOUIS, architect; b. Phila., Dec. 7, 1923; s. Louis J. and Kay (Malmed) G.; student Yale, 1941-46; M.Arch., Harvard, 1950; m. Evelyn Basse, June 15, 1947; children—David, Annie. Sr. partner Geddes-Brecher Qualls Cunningham, architects, Phila., 1954—; faculty U. Pa., 1951-65, prof. architecture and civic design, 1961-65; prof. architecture, dean Sch. Architecture and Urban Planning, Princeton, 1965, William Kenan prof., 1968—; prin. works include Penn's Landing Phila., 1959-65, Rockville (Md.) Town Center, 1965—; Moore Sch. Elec. Engring., U. Pa., 1958, Police Hdqrs., Phila., 1962, Northeast Regional Library, Phila., 1963, resident hall groups U. Del., 1966, Moore Sch. Grad. Research Center, U. Pa., 1967, master plan and urban renewal plan Univ. City Sci. Center, Phila., 1963, low-rent pub. housing projects, Westchester, Pa., also Phila. and Coatesville, Pa., 1966, sci. bldg. Beaver Coll., 1971, Inst. for Advanced Study, Princeton, 1971, master plan and bldgs. So. Ill. U., 1968-71, also Stockton State Coll., 1971. Dir., Johns-Manville Corp. Chmn. adv. bd. design Redevel. Authority Phila., 1959-66; mem. com. 2d regional plan Regional Plan Assn. N.Y., 1966; bd. dirs. Citizens Council City Planning, Phila., 1961-63; mem. Charles Center design bd., Balt., 1971—. Bd. dirs. Urban America, Inc. Served with AUS, 1942-45. Appleton Traveling fellow Harvard, 1950-51; recipient Design awards Progressive Architecture, 1954, 55, 56, 58, 60, First Design award, 1958; 2d prize Nat. Opera House, Sydney, Australia, 1958; first prize Internat. Town Planning Competition for Expansion of Vienna (Austria), 1971. Fellow A.I.A. (dir. edn. research project 1965-67; Harvard Sch. medal 1950, First Honor award 1960, Gold medal Phila. chpt. 1960, 63, 68, Silver medal Pa. Soc. 1960, 63, 68); mem. Harvard Grad. Sch. Design Alumni Assn. (past pres.). Club: Nassau (Princeton). Home: 229 Mercer St Princeton NJ 08540

GEDDES, WILLIAM WORTH, banker; b. Scarsdale, N.Y., Feb. 14, 1920; s. F. Bramwell and Alice (Worth) G.; diploma The Hotchkiss Sch., 1935-37; B.A., Swarthmore Coll., 1941; m. Jean McCullough, June 18, 1943; children—William Worth, James McCullough. With Wilmington Trust Co., Wilmington, (Del.), 1941—, exec. v.p., 1968-70, pres., 1970- -. Bd. dirs. Wilmington Med. Center Children's Bureau. Served to lt. comdr., USNR, 1942-46. Clubs: Bidermann Golf (dir. 1968—), Vicmead Hunt (Greenville); Wilmington, Wilmington Country. Home: West Farm Rd Greenville DE 19807 Office: Wilmington Trust Co 10th and Market Sts Wilmington DE 19899

GEDEON, CHARLES G., chmn. Publitec Publns. Address: Andalusia Bldg Gouraud St Beirut, Lebanon.*

GEDIMAN, HENRY JAMES, newspaper exec.; b. Boston, Apr. 30, 1904; s. Lewis Mansfield and Mollie (Brenner) G.; student Boston U., 1922-23, Tufts Coll., 1925-26; m. Pauline Shayevitz, June 17, 1928; children—Ruth Claire, Lewis Mark. Reporter, East Boston Free Press, 1922; house organ editor, advt. copy writer, 1922-24; advt. salesman Boston Herald-Traveler, 1924-26; promotion mgr. Boston Morning Record Eve. Am. Sunday Advertiser, 1927- 30; mgr. plans dept. Rodney E. Boone Orgn., pub. reps., 1930-36; nat. advt. mgr. N.Y. Jour. Am. 1936-43; regional mgr. Hearst Advt. Service (name Key Market Advt. Reps., Inc. 1966), pub. reps., 1943-51, exec. v.p., 1955-64, pres., 1965—; exec. v.p. Am. Weekly, also Puck the Comic Weekly, 1951-55; past pres., dir. Cannon Point North. Mem. Am. Assn. Newspaper Reps. (pres. N.Y. 1950-51, dir. 1956), Am. Newspaper Pubs. Assn. (chmn. plans com. Bur. Advt. 1964-67), Internat. Newspaper Advt. Execs. (hon. life dir. 1961- 63), Alpha Epsilon Pi (life). Contbr. bus., profl. publs. Home: 25 Sutton Pl S New York City NY 10022 Office: 235 E 45th St New York City NY 10017

GEDNEY, EDWIN KEMBLE, clergyman, educator; b. N.Y.C., June 22, 1904; s. Orison and Jennie Grant (Kemble) G.; Ph.B., Brown U., 1926, Sc. M., 1928; M.A., Harvard, 1937, student Grad. Sch. Edn., 1946-49; LL.D., Gordon Coll., 1962; m. Dorris Mae Clough, June 10, 1930; children—Barbara Lois (Mrs. Dale R. Schaeffner), Priscilla Marie (Mrs. Clinton E. Taber), Donald Clough, Robert Edwin, Cynthia Elsie. Dir. exploration and research Ventures, Ltd., 1930-34; ordained to ministry Advent Christian Ch., 1935; pastor in Somerville, Mass., 1935-40, Melrose, Mass., 1941-61; faculty Gordon Coll., Beverly Farms, Mass., 1934—, prof. edn., 1950—, chmn. of div., 1955—, dean of Coll., 1964-68. Pres., Advent Christian Gen. Conf., 1958-64. Dir. Christian Mut. Life Ins. Co., Concord, N.H. Chmn. regents Berkshire Christian Coll., Lenox, Mass. Mem. Mass. Council Tchr. Edn., Am. Coll. Personnel Assn., Am. Sci. Affiliation, Am. Personnel and Guidance Assn., Nat. Vocational Guidance Assn., Assn. Acad. Deans, N.E.A., Nat. Council Geog. Edn., Phi Delta Kappa, Phi Alpha Chi. Co-author: Modern Science and Christian Faith, 2d edit., 1954; also articles. Home: 114 North St Stoneham MA 02180 Office: Gordon Coll Beverly Farms MA 01915

GEE, EDWARD FOWLKES, banker; b. Victoria, Va., May 28, 1910; s. Edward Lewis and Ruth Naomi (Gary) G.; student U. Richmond, 1928-29; honor grad. Am. Inst. Banking, 1933; grad. accounting and bus. adminstrn. Va. Mechanics Inst., 1939; grad. Rutgers U. Grad. Sch. Banking, 1940; m. Margaret Osborne Williams; 1 dau., Ruth Ann (Mrs. B. Franklin Skinner IV). With State-Planters Bank of Commerce and Trusts (now United Va. Bank State Planters), Richmond, Va., 1929—, v.p., sec., 1952-61, exec. v.p. comml., mem. adv. bd., 1961- 63, pres., dir., 1963-71, chmn. bd., 1971—; vice chmn. United Va. Bankshares Inc., 1971—; dir., past chmn. bd. Va. Indsl. Devel. Corp.; dir. Lawyers Title Ins. Corp., Victoria Hardware & Furniture Co., Inc., Mut. Assurance Soc. Va., Overnite Transp. Co. Past instr. U. Richmond Evening Sch. Bus. Adminstrn., Va. Mechanics Inst., also numerous bankers confs. Sr. mission officer to N. Africa for Lend-Lease Adminstrn. World War II. C.P.A., Va. Mem. Robert Morris Assos. (past pres.), Am. Inst. Banking (past pres. Richmond), Richmond Assn. Credit Men (past pres.), Am. Inst. C.P.A.'s, Newcomen Soc., Va., Richmond (past pres.) chambers commerce. Clubs: Commonwealth, Forum, Country of Virginia (Richmond). Author: The Evaluation of Receivables and Inventories, 1943; Co-author: Analyzing Financial Statements, 1948. Contbr. articles in field. Home: 305 Greenway Lane Richmond VA 23226 Office: 900 E Main St Richmond VA 23219

GEE, RONALD CALLAWAY, educator; b. Barron, Wis., July 6, 1920; s. Robert Harold and Clara (Callaway) G.; B.S. in Edn., Wis State U., Platteville, 1942; M.S., U. Wis., 1951; Ph.D., 1958; m. Rita M. Vaughn, July 11, 1942; children—Barbara Joan (Mrs. James Radcliffe), Mary Zoe (Mrs. Dennis Moon), Martha Vaughn (Mrs. John Metropulos), Deborah Clair. Tchr., Delavan (Wis.) High Sch. 1946-48; instr. Wis. Idea Theatre. U. Wis. extension div., 1951-55; instr., then asst. prof. State U. Ia., 1955-59; prof. communication arts and scis., chmn. dept. Western Ill. U. Macomb, 1959—. Exec. sec. Wis. Idea Theatre Conf., 1951-55; founder, 1958, 1st exec. sec. Ia. Community Theatre Assn. Served with USAAF, 1942- 45. Mem. Speech Communication Assn., Ill. Speech and Theatre Assn. Home: 910 Memorial Dr Macomb IL 61455

GEE, SAMUEL EDWARD, army officer; b. Kenbridge, Va., July 17, 1908; s. Frank Asbury and Anna Rives (Inge) G.; B.S., U.S. Mil. Acad., 1933; grad. Inf. Sch., 1937, Chem. Warfare Sch., 1938, army War Coll., 1953; student personnel adminstrn., U. N.C., 1946-47; m. Gladys Finks Clarke, Sept. 2, 1933; children—Kathryn Ann (Mrs. James M. Bowers), Jane Clarke (Mrs. Donald B. Smith, Jr.). Commd. 2d lt. U.S. Army, 1933, advanced through grades to maj. gen., 1962; co. officer 1st Inf. Div., 1933-39; mil. police officer, provost marshal 25th Inf. Div., 1939-42; mem. Americal Div., 1942-46, comdr. 164th Inf. Regt., 1944; mem. faculty Inf. Sch., 1946; mem. gen. staff War Dept., 1947-49; dir. mil. psychology and leadership U.S. Mil. Acad., 1949-52; chief staff 1st Inf. Div., then comdr. 16th Inf. Regt., Germany, 1953-55; chief combat devels. div. Continental Army Command, Ft. Monroe, Va., 1956-57; asst. div. comdr. 7th Inf. Div., Korea, 1957-58; assigned gen. staff Dept. Army, 1958-63, dir. army programs, Office Chief Staff, 1962-63; chief staff, combined mil. planning staff CENTO, Turkey, 1963-65; dep. U.S. rep. to mil. com./standing group NATO, 1965-67; comdg. gen. U.S. Army Phys. Disability Agy., 1967—. Rep. army chief staff Nat. Bd. Promotion Rifle Practice, 1959-63. Decorated Silver Star, Bronze medal with 2 oak leaf clusters, Army Commendation ribbon, Combat Inf. badge, numerous service and area ribbons; Order Ulchi (Republic Korea); D.S.M. Life mem. West Point Alumni Found. (pres. class 1933, 59-60); mem. Nat. Rifle Assn., Assn. Grads. U.S. Mil. Acad. (v.p.), S.A.R. (chpt. charter mem.). Contbr. to Ency. Americana. Home: Kenbridge VA Office: US Army Phys Disability Agy Washington DC 20012

GEEHAN, ROBERT WILLIAM, govt. ofcl.; b. Yakima, Wash., Dec. 12, 1909; s. Michael and Susan (Stratton) G.; E.M., U. Minn., 1932; student Am. U., 1954, U. Colo., 1959; m. Iria Alanne, June 11, 1932; children—Roberta (Mrs. Robert Horton), David, Patrick. Mining engr. Winston Bros. Co., Helena, Mont., 1932-34, Cripple Creek Mining Co., Folger and Anchorage, Alaska, 1934- 39; designing engr. Alaska R.R., Anchorage, 1939-42; with U.S. Bur. Mines, 1942—, successively mining engr., Nev. and Va., commodity specialist tungsten and molybdenum, Washington, asst. chief ferrous metals and alloys br., asst. chief div. minerals, chief div. mineral tech., Rolla, Mo., 1956-59, chief div. resources, Denver, 1959, regional dir., 1960-63, area dir., then program mgr., 1964—; U.S. rep. for tungsten and molybdenum Internat. Materials Conf., Washington, 1952- 53; mem. manganese ore com. Am. Standards Assn.-Internat. Standards Orgn., meetings in Leningrad, USSR, 1954, 56; cons. tungsten and molybdenum, NATO, Paris, 1954; mem. tungsten raw materials panel Nat. Acad. Scis.-NCR, 1958-60. Mem. Am. Inst. Mining and Metall. Engrs., Wyo. Mining Assn., Rocky Mountain Coal Mining Assn., Denver Mining Club, Sigma Xi, Tau Beta Pi. Mem. Methodist Ch. Club: Teknik (Denver) Contbr. articles to profl. jours., bulls. Home: 1201 S Scott St Arlington VA 22204 Office: Interior Bldg Washington DC 20242

GEELHOOD, STEWART STEVEN, furniture co. exec.; b. Byron Center, Mich., June 11, 1917; s. Orie and Nellie (Dreyer) G.; A.B., Calvin Coll., 1938; M.B.A., U. Mich., 1940; m. Florence Ornee, Apr. 17, 1942; children—Bruce D., Elaine J., Janice K. Auditor, Gen. Motors Corp., Grand Rapids, Mich., 1940-41, War Dept., Lansing, Mich., 1942; accountant, asst. treas. Kalamazoo Veg. Parchment Co., 1946-59; asst. v.p., asst. treas. KVP Sutherland Paper Co., 1960- 62, treas., 1962-66; v.p., treas. Brown Co., 1966-68; v.p., treas., dir. Chgo. Paper Co., 1968-71; sec.-treas. Am. Seating Co., Grand Rapids, Mich., 1971—. Trustee Calvin Coll., Grand Rapids. Served to lt. USNR, 1943-45. Mem. Tax Execs. Inst. Home: 2460 Okemos Dr Grand Rapids MI 49506 Office: 901 Broadway Av NW Grand Rapids MI 49504

GEEN, ELIZABETH, educator; b. Dallas, Jan. 8, 1903; d. Robert S. and Elanora (Hillhouse) Geen; A.B., U. Cal. 1925, A.M. 1927; Ph.D., U. Ia. 1940; LL.D. (hon.), Alfred U., 1953; L.H.D. (hon.), Coll. Notre Dame, Md., 1968; D.L.H. (hon.), Goncher Coll., 1969. Tchr. Sonora (Cal.) Union High Sch., 1930-34; instr., Mills Coll., Oakland, 1935-38, asst. prof. English, 1940-42; dean of women, asso. prof. English, Alfred (N.Y.) U., 1946-50; became dean Goucher Coll., Balt., 1950, now dean and v.p. emeritus; adminstrv. asst. to dean and pres. Mt. St. Agnes Coll., Balt., 1968-70, pres. coll., 1970—; staff asso. commn. on instructions and higher edn. Middle States Assn., 1960-68; adminstrv. asst. to dean and pres. Mt. St. Agnes Coll., Balt. Mem. mayor's Task Force Civil Rights. Served as lt. comdr. USNR, 1942- 46. Mem. Nat. Assn. Acad. Deans, Am. Assn. U. Profs., Am. Assn. U. Women, Modern Lang. Assn., Phi Beta Kappa, Delta Kappa Gamma. Co-editor: Man and the Modern City, 1962. Home: 6303 Pinehurst Rd Baltimore MD 21212

GEER, JACK CHARLES, medical educator; b. Galesburg, Ill., Sept. 19, 1927; s. John Charles and Ruth (McGee) G.; B.S. in Chemistry, La. State U., 1950, M.D., 1956; m. Sarah Kathleen Williamson, Feb. 16, 1951; children—Charles, Richard, John, Cynthia, Michael. With La. State U., New Orleans, 1954—, prof. pathology, 1965-66; prof. pathology U. Tex. S. Tex. Med. Sch., 1966-67; prof., chmn. dept. pathology Ohio State U. Med. Sch., 1967—; vis. investigator Rockefeller Inst., 1960-61. Recipient Outstanding Sr. award Omicron D, Delta Kappa-Mortar Bd., 1956; J.A. Majors award for scholastic achievement in pathology, 1956, George W. McCoy award La. State U., 1956, USPHS Research Career Devel. award, 1959-66. Mem. Am. Heart Assn., Soc. Exptl. Pathology and Bacteriology, A.A.A.S., Internat. Acad. Pathology, Am. Soc. Clin. Pathologists, Council Arteriosclerosis. Contbg. author: Atherosclerosis and its Origin, 1963; (with McGill) Evolution of the Atherosclerotic Plague, 1963; (with Freeman) Cellular Fine Structure, Student Atlas, 1964; also numerous articles. Research on morphology atherosclerosis, chem. changes with atherosclerosis, pulmonary vascular changes with hypertension. Home: 4391 Mumford Dr Columbus OH 43220

GEER, WILLIAM DUDLEY, univ. dean; b. Augusta, Ga., Dec. 25, 1922; s. William Fred and Ida (Fuller) G.; B.S., Stetson U., 1948, M.A., 1950; D.Bus. Adminstrn., Ind. U., 1963; m. Elizabeth Durner, Dec. 18, 1949; children—John William, Deborah Elizabeth, Margaret Ruth. Instr., Mars Hill (N.C.) Coll., 1950-52; asso. prof. Miss. Coll., Clinton, 1953-56; asst. prof. Stetson U., Deland Fla., 1956-59; prof. bus. adminstrn. Samford U., Birmingham, Ala., 1959-66, dean Sch. Bus., 1966—; faculty Sch. Banking of South, La. State U.; cons. to bus. Bd. mgrs. Five Point YMCA. Served with Signal Corps, AUS, 1943-45. Mem. Ala. Acad. Sci. (v.p.), So. Bus. Adminstrn. Assn. (v.p.), Am. Econ. Assn., Am. Finance Assn., Am. Risk and Ins. Assn., Am. Soc. C.L.U.'s, Alpha Kappa Psi, Beta Gamma Sigma, Phi Alpha Theta. Baptist (deacon). Rotarian. Contbr. articles to profl. jours. Home: 3021 Lakeland Trail Birmingham AL 35216

GEERDES, JAMES, (Divine), chem. co. exec.; b. Davenport, N.D., Apr. 13, 1924; s. William A. and Martha (Buchholz) G.; B.S., N.D. State U., 1949, M.S., 1950; Ph.D., U. Minn., 1953; m. Patricia Seney, July 6, 1968; children—Andrew, John, Laura, Margaret. Instr. biochemistry U. Minn., 1950-53; research chemist E.I. duPont de Nemours & Co., Inc., Richmond, Va. and Seaford, Del., 1954-58, group supr., 1958-60, tech. supr., 1960-62, research asso., 1962-64; dir. research Entoleter, Inc., Hamden, Conn., 1964-65, exec. v.p., 1965- 66, pres., 1966-67; asst. to v.p. fibers div. Allied Chem. Corp., N.Y.C., 1967, asst. to pres., 1967-68, exec. v.p., 1968, pres., 1968-71; pres., dir. Alrac Corp., Stamford, Conn., 1971—; dir. Action Concepts Tech., Inc., Rochester, N.Y. Served to 1st lt. C.E., AUS, 1943-46. Mem. Del. Acad. Sci., Am. Chem. Soc., A.A.A.S., Nanticoke (Del.) Rocket Soc. (dir.), Sigma Xi, Phi Kappa Phi, Gamma Sigma Delta, Gamma Alpha. Contbr. articles to profl. jours. Patentee in field. Home: Trinity Keep Fanton Hill Rd Weston CT 06880 Office: Alrac Corp Stamford CT 06907

GEERLINGS, GERALD KENNETH, architect, etcher, indsl. designer; b. Milw., Apr. 18, 1897; s. Jacob and Cattalina G.; B.A. in Architecture, U. Pa., 1921, M.A., 1922; studied at Saint John's Coll. (Cambridge U.), Eng., Royal Coll. Art, London; m. Elizabeth Filby Edmunds, Sept. 2, 1924; children—Barbara Filby (Mrs. John F. Collins), Gillian (Mrs. David D. Brown III). Employed as a newspaper reporter, Milw.; 3 yrs. a head designer York & Sawyer, also Starrett & Van Vleck, architects, N.Y.; own archtl. practice in N.Y., 1926—. Etchings exhibited in Europe, also in Am. collection entitled "Contemporary Etching" frequently since 1929, and in "Fine Prints of the Year," London; etchings in permanent collection of Victoria and Albert Mus., London, Congl. Library, Met. Mus., N.Y.C., Nat. Collection Fine Arts, Washington, Bklyn. Mus., Chgo. Art Inst., Boston Pub. Library, Phila. Mus. Art. Awards include 1st prize for best etching Chicago Century of Progress, 1933; etc. Served to 2d lt., F.A., A.E.F., World War I; served from capt. to col., USAAF, World War II; spl. civilian cons. USAF, 1949-55. Awarded Legion of Merit with Oak Leaf Clusters; five battles stars for Air Offensive over Europe, Sicilian Campaign, Battle of Ploesti, Italian Campaign and Campaign against Japan; Army Commendation medal. Mem. A.I.A. Archtl. League N.Y., Am. Soc. Graphic Artists, Theta Xi, Tau Sigma Delta. Author several books. Contbr. articles to mags.; also Ency. Brittanica. Home: 26 Gower Rd New Canaan CT 06840 ☆

GEESAMAN, EDGAR R., lawyer; b. Omaha, Aug. 2, 1921; A.B. cum laude, U. Neb., 1942; LL.B., Harvard, 1950. Admitted to Neb. bar, 1950; mem. firm Fitzgerald, Brown, Leahy, McGill and Strom, Omaha. Mem. Am., Omaha, Neb. State bar assns., Phi Beta Kappa. Office: 1000 Woodmen Tower Omaha NB 68102*

GEFFEN, MAXWELL MYLES, editor, publisher; b. Bklyn., May 31, 1896; s. Abraham D. and Anna (Levit) G.; Litt.B., Columbia, 1916; m. Pauline Felix, 1916; children—Roger, Joan; m. 2d, Helen Catherine Dowling, 1936; 1 dau., Melinda; m. 3d, Florence Kalander, 1951; 1 son, Peter. Reporter, N.Y. American, 1916; pres. Select Printing Co., 1919-42; pub. N.Y. Med. Week, 1922-41, This Week in N.Y., 1930- 40, Med. World News, 1960-68, Family Health Mag., 1969—; pub., editor Omnibook, Book-Mag., 1938-57; chmn. bd. Arrow Press, Inc., 1957-63; chmn. bd. David McKay Pub. Co., Morgan-Grampian, Inc., N.Y.; dir. Lemmon Pharmacal Co., Morgan-Grampian Ltd., London. Clubs: Deepdale Golf (Manhasset, N.Y.); Breakers Golf (Palm Beach, Fla.). Editor: Treasury of Modern Best Sellers (with Victor W. Knauth), 1944. Office: 1271 Av of Americas New York City NY 10020

GEFFS, GEORGE STRICKLETT, lawyer; b. nr. Casey, Ill., Jan. 5, 1894; s. John and Mary (Stricklett) G.; student U. N.D., 1916-18, U. Wis., 1919-20; m. Marguerite Haverson, Aug. 22, 1922 (dec.); 1 son, Robert H.; m. 2d, Esther Munro, Aug. 16, 1958. Admitted to Wis. bar, 1920, since practiced in Janesville; sr. partner firm Geffs, Geffs, Block & Geffs, until 1969; dist. atty., Rock County, 1925-29. Dir. Rock County Nat. Bank, Rock County Savs. & Trust Co., Janesville Improvement Co., Rock County Bank Bldgs. Corp., Main Street Realty Co. Inc.; dir., sec. Cedar Crest, Inc. Mem. fire and police commn., Janesville, 1936-70. Served with U.S. Army, World War I. Fellow Am. Bar Found. (bd. dirs. 1957-59, bd. govs. 1956-59), Am. Coll. Probate Counsel; mem. Am. (ho. of dels. 1949-59, gov. 1956-59, state del. 1962- 65), Wis. (chmn. finance commn. Wis. Bar Bldg., dir. real estate sect.), Rock County bar assns., Am. Legion, Vets. World War I, Rock County Hist. Soc., Nat. Legal Aid and Defenders Assn. (past mem. bd. dirs.), Phi Alpha Delta. Mason (32, Shriner). Club: Janesville Country. Home: 2506 Linden Av Janesville WI 53545 Office: 1 S Main Janesville WI 53545

GEFKE, HENRY JEROME, lawyer; b. Milw., Aug. 4, 1930; s. Jerome Henry and Frances (Daley) G.; B.S., Marquette U., 1952, LL.B., 1954; postgrad. Ohio State U., 1955- 56; m. Caroline Ann Lawrence, June 25, 1955 (div. Jan. 1968); children—Brian Lawrence, David Jerome. Admitted to Wis. bar, 1954, Tax Ct. U.S., 1969; accountant-auditor John G. Conley & Co., C.P.A.'s, Milw., 1956-59; with J.I. Case Co., Racine, Wis., 1959-68, corp. sec., asst. gen. counsel, 1965-68; asso. Maier & Mulcahy, S.C., Milw., 1968-69; prin. Mulcahy & Gefke, S.C., Milw., 1969—. Bd. dirs. Racine County Mental Health Assn., 1963-67; pres., dir. Big Bros. Greater Racine, 1965-67; trustee Racine County Instns., 1960-63. Served with AUS, 1954-56. C.P.A., Wis. Mem. Am., Wis., Milw. bar assns., Wis. Soc. C.P.A.'s, Delta Sigma Pi, Delta Theta Phi. Home: 1570 N Prospect Av Milwaukee WI 53202 Office: 811 E Wisconsin Av Milwaukee WI 53202

GEFTER, WILLIAM IRVIN, educator, physician; b. Phila., Jan. 29, 1915; s. Samuel and Pauline (Bulmash) G.; A.B., U. Pa., 1935, M.D., 1939; m. Winnie Neiman, June 17, 1939; children—Sharon (Mrs. William Greene), Ellen, Warren, Gail. Intern, then resident medicine Phila. Gen. Hosp., 1939-43; mem. faculty Woman's Med. Coll. Pa., 1943-66, Mullen prof. medicine, 1959-66; mem. faculty Temple U. Sch. Medicine, 1966—, prof. medicine, 1966—; chief medicine Phila. Gen. Hosp., 1959-66; dir. dept. medicine Episcopal Hosp., Phila., 1966—, pres. med. bd., 1970-72, also mem. bd. mgrs., exec. com. Served to capt., M.C., USAAF, 1943-46. Recipient Distinguished Service citation Woman's Med. Coll. Pa., 1966, Phila. Gen. Hosp., 1964. Diplomate Am. Bd. Internal Medicine. Fellow A.C.P., Coll. Physicians Phila., Am. Coll. Cardiology; mem. Am., Pa., Phila. med. assns. Author: Synopsis of Cardiology, 1965; also numerous articles. Home: 366 Penn Rd Wynnewood PA 19096 Office: Episcopal Hosp Philadelphia PA 19125

GEHLHOFF, WALTER, German ambassador to U.N.; b. Berlin, May 6, 1922; s. Kurt and Elsbeth (Legies) G.; student U. Berlin, 1946-47, U. Frankfurt, 1947-49; M.D., U. Heidelberg, 1952; m. Eva Biegel, Oct. 1, 1949; children—Judith, Beatrix, Georg. Joined Fed. Republic of Germany fgn. service, 1951; dir. Middle East and N. African Affairs, Fgn. Office, Bonn, 1966-69; dep. asst. sec. of state, 1969-70, asst. sec. of state, 1970—, ambassador to U.N. Mem. German Fgn. Policy Assn., German Soc. Ornithology. Home: 119 E 65th St New York City NY 10021 Office: 600 Third Av New York City NY 10016

GEHMAN, HARRY MERRILL, mathematician; b. Norristown, Pa., Jan. 15, 1898; s. Abner Haring and Barbara Bergey (Clemens) G.; A.B., U. Pa., 1919, A.M., 1920, Ph.D., 1925; m. Marian Barr, Sept. 2, 1922; children—Margery Barr (Mrs. Horace E. Dodge III), Jean Virginia (Mrs. Floyd E. Adamson), Harry Merrill. Instr. math. U. Pa., 1920-25; Nat. Research Council fellow, U. Tex., 1925-26; instr. Yale, 1926-27, asst. prof. math., 1927-29; prof., head math. dept. U. Buffalo, 1929-62; prof. mathematics State U. N.Y., Buffalo, 1962-68, prof. emeritus, 1968—. Served as head math. dept. Shrivenham, Eng. U. U.S. Army, 1945. Fellow A.A.A.S.; mem. Math. Association Am. (treas., emeritus exec. dir., award, 1966) Am. Math. Soc., Canadian Math. Congress, Am. Soc. Engring. Edn. (chmn. math. div. 1951-52), Phi Beta Kappa, Sigma Xi, Pi Kappa Alpha. Republican. Presbyn. Home: 163 Winspear Av Buffalo NY 14215

GEHRET, ANDREW MARTIN, physician; b. Reading, Pa., 1902; M.D., Jefferson Med. Coll., 1929; grad. study obstetrics and gynecology U. Pa., 1945-46; intern Jefferson Med. Coll. Hosp., 1929-32; personal asst. to Dr. E.H. Lenderman, Wilmington, Del., 1932-39; asst. resident Margaret Hague Maternity Hosp., 1946-47; dir. obstetrics and gynecology Del. Hosp., Wilmington. Mem. Adv. Bd. Med. Specialties, Inc. Diplomate Am. Bd. Obstertrics and Gynecology, 1950. Fellow A.C.S. Address: 1007 Park Pl Wilmington DE 19806*

GEHRIG, LEO JOSEPH, physician; b. Mapleton, Minn., Apr. 25, 1918; s. Paul P. and Marcella (Hund) G.; B.S., U. Minn., 1942, B.Medicine, 1944, M.D., 1945; m. Marilyn May Nelson, June 10, 1944; children—Gregory Paul, Mark Nelson. Intern, Salt Lake County Gen. Hosp., Salt Lake City, 1944-45; resident New Eng. Deaconness Hosp., Boston, 1947-50; with USPHS 1950—; chief chest surgery unit, S.I. N.Y., 1950-52, resident, 1952-55, chief surgery, Seattle, 1955-57; asst. chief div. hosps., Washington, 1957-59, dep. chief, 1959-60, program officer bur. med. services, Washington, 1960-61, med. dir. Peace Corps, 1961-62, asst. surgeon gen., dep. chief Bur. Med. Services, 1962- 64, chief bur., 1964-65, dep. surgeon gen., 1965-68; dir. office internat. health Dept. Health, Edn. and Welfare, 1968-70; asso. dir. Washington service bur. Am. Hosp. Assn., 1970—. Diplomate Am. Bd. of Surgery, Am. Bd. Thoracic Surgery. Fellow A.C.S.; mem. A.M.A., Assn. Mil. Surgeons, USPHS Clin. Soc., Am. Pub. Health Assn., Alpha Omega Alpha. Home: 4535 Alton Pl NW Washington DC 20016 Office: 1 Farragut Sq S Washington DC 20006

GEHRIG, LEONARD FREDERICK, bus. forms mfg. co. exec.; b. Omaha, Sept. 10, 1912; s. Jacob and Francis (Buller) G.; student U. Omaha, 1930-31, Creighton U., 1933-36; m. Frances Reeves, Aug. 12, 1960; children—Jeffrey, Jessica and Jennifer (twins). Personal asst. to Gwin A. Whitney, Merrit-Chapman & Scott Corp., N.Y.C., 1937-39; sec., asst. treas. Whitney Corp., Duluth, Minn., 1939-40; sr. staff accountant Peat, Marwick, Mitchell & Co., Dallas, 1947-50; pres., chief exec. officer, dir. Ennis Bus. Forms, Inc. (Tex.), 1941-46, 51—; v.p., treas., dir. Ennis Brandon Computer Services, Inc., Dallas; dir. Citizens Nat. Bank Ennis. Mem. steering com. Ennis Polka Festival, 1967-68. Mayor, Ennis, 1957-60. Mem. adv. bd. Tex. Pvt. Jr. Coll. Found., Houston. C.P.A., Tex. Mem. Tex. Mfrs. Assn., Tag and Label Mfrs. Inst. (past pres.), Assn. Bus. Forms Mfrs. (v.p.), Ennis C. of C. (past pres.), Internat. Bus. Forms Industries (past v.p.). Methodist. Kiwanian. Clubs: Sokol, Lakeside Country (Ennis). Home: 1408 Hillcrest St Ennis TX 75119 Office: 214 W Knox St Ennis TX 75119

GEHRING, BENJAMIN ROBERT, mgmt. cons.; b. Chillicothe, O., Feb. 26, 1915; s. Louis C. and Jennie (Rector) G.; student Ohio State U., 1936; m. Ellen R. Payne, Nov. 6, 1937; children—Julie, Barbara Lee, Susan Jane. With Kent & Rector, 1940-49; pres. Andre Wood Products, Inc., 1949-59; pres., dir., Kilgore, Inc., Westerville, O., 1951-56; pres. Am. Gen. Corp.; dir., sec., Timmons Metal Products Co., Stardust Lanes, Inc., Eastern Enterprises Corp., Columbus, O., Zip Lock Co.; mgmt. cons. C.P.A., O. Mem. Am. Inst. C.P.A.'s, Am. Accounting Assn., Am. Mgmt. Assn., Ohio Soc. C.P.A.'s. Mason. Clubs: Rotary, Scroto Country, Athletic. Home: 2500 Johnston Rd Columbus OH 43221 Office: 3280 Riverside Dr Columbus OH 43221

GEHRING, MARY LOUISE, coll. dean; b. Oakdale, La., Mar. 21, 1922; d. Francis and Voss (Kersh) Gehring; B.A., Baylor U., 1943; M.A., La. State U., 1949, Ph.D., 1952. With RCA Victor Co., Camden, N.J., 1943-44, U.S. Civil Service, Japan, 1946-47; instr. speech Auburn U., 1949-50; vis. instr. Baylor U., 1949 summer; asso. prof. Miss. So. Coll., 1952-56; vis. lectr. U. Wis., 1962-63; prof. Stetson U., 1956-62, 63-65; dean Westhampton Coll. of U. Richmond, 1965—. Mem. Women's Com. Richmond Symphony, 1968—. Served to ensign Women's Res., USCGR, 1944-46. Mem. Speech Communication Assn. (legislative assembly 1956-63, 65-68), So. Speech Communication Assn. (exec. sec. 1958-61), Am. Assn. U. Women, Am. Assn. U. Profs. (pres.). Democrat. Baptist (bd. adminstrn.). Author: (with Waldo W. Braden) Speech Practices, 1958. Address: U Richmond Richmond VA 23173

GEHRKE, HANS, Jr., banker; b. Detroit, July 23, 1912; s. Hans and Ella Marie (Gorenflo) G.; ed. U. Mich., 1934; m. Annamay Muer, May 2, 1942; children—Susan (Mrs. Peter O'Rourke), William, John. Appraiser, mortgage dept. 1st Fed. Savs., Detroit, 1937-43, asst. v.p., 1943-46, v.p., 1946-52, exec. v.p., 1952-56, dir., 1953—, pres., 1956-64, pres., chief exec. officer, 1964-69, chmn. bd., chief exec. officer, 1969—; dir. Nat. Corp. for Housing Partnerships, Washington. Bd. dirs. Grace Hosp., Detroit. Mem. Mortgage Bankers Assn. Mich. (pres. former Detroit Mortgage Bankers Assn. 1950), U.S. (pres. 1968), Mich. (pres. 1957-58) savs. and loan leagues, Detroit Real Estate Bd. (pres. 1958), Fed. Home Loan Bank Bd. (adv. council, Washington, 1969,70,71), Greater Detroit C. of C. (chmn. 1967-68), Central Bus. Dist. Assn. Detroit (pres. 1969,70). Clubs: Detroit, Athletic, Country (Detroit); Lost Tree (North Palm Beach, Fla.). Home: 45 N Deeplands Grosse Pointe Shores MI 48236 Office: 1001 Woodward Av Detroit MI 48226

GEHRKE, LELAND B., mfg. co. exec. Treas., controller Nat. Advt. Co., Chgo., 1949-55; with parent company Minn. Mining & Mfg. Co., 1957—, asst. treas., 1959-63, treas., 1963-67; mng. dir. Minn. Mining & Mfg. Co., Ltd., London, Eng., 1967—. care Minn Mining & Mfg Co 2501 Hudson Rd St Paul MO 63366

GEHRON, WILLIAM JULES, fgn. service officer; b. N.Y.C., Aug. 5, 1924; s. William and Grace P. (McDermott) G.; B.A., Williams Coll., 1950; m. Patricia Coleman, Dec. 20, 1950; children—William C., Michael M., Anne P. Dir. pub. relations Carnegie Endowment Internat. Peace, 1952-56; coordinator pub. affairs White House Disarmament Staff, 1956-58; with Office Spl. Asst. to Sec. State Atomic Energy and Disarmament, State Dept., 1958-60; dep. pub. affairs adviser U.S. Arms Control and Disarmament Agy., 1960-64; adviser U.S. delegation UN Gen. Assembly, 1958, U.S. delegation 18 Nation Disarmament Conf., Geneva, Switzerland, 1964-66; pub. affairs adviser European Bur., Dept. State, 1966—; joined U.S. Fgn. Service, 1964. Served with AUS, 1943-46, 50-52. Clubs: Nat. Press, Internat. (Washington). Home: 2112 Belle Haven Rd Alexandria VA 22307 Office: Dept State Washington DC 20525

GEIDUSCHEK, ERNEST PETER, biophysicist, educator; b. Vienna, Austria, Apr. 11, 1928; s. Sigmund and Frieda (Tauber) G.; B.A., Columbia, 1948; A.M., Harvard, 1950, Ph.D. 1952; m. Joyce Barbara Brous; 2 children. Came to U.S. 1945, naturalized, 1946. Instr. chemistry Yale, 1952-53, 55-57; asst. prof. chemistry U. Mich., 1957-59; asst. prof. biophysics U. Chgo., 1959-62, asso. prof., 1962-64, prof., 1964-70; prof. biology U. Cal. at San Diego, LaJolla, 1970—. Cons., USPHS, 1963-69. Served with AUS, 1953-55. Recipient Research award Am. Postgrad. Med. Assn., 1962, Research Career Devel. award USPHS, 1962; Guggenheim Found. fellow, 1964-65. Mem. Am. Chem. Soc., Am. Soc. Biol. Chemists, Biophys. Soc. (council 1964-66), A.A.A.S. Editorial bd. Biophys. Jour., 1967-69, Ann. Revs. Biophysics and Bioengring., 1971—. Research in biophys. chemistry, molecular biology, chem. genetics. Home: 8460 Cliffridge Lane La Jolla CA 92037

GEIER, FREDERICK V., machinery co. exec.; b. Cin., Sept. 5, 1893; s. Fred A. and Amanda Virginia (Mayer) G.; B.A., Williams Coll., 1916; LL.D., U. Cin., 1956, Williams Coll., 1963; m. Amey Massey Develin, Feb. 9, 1918; children—Mary Alice (Mrs. Albert C. Turner), Amey Acheson (Mrs. John M. Garber), Frederick Virginius, James Avlward Develin. Employed Cin. Milacron, Inc., 1916, pres., 1934-58, chmn., 1958-63, chmn. exec. com., 1963—; also dir.; dir. McCurdy Co., Little Miami R.R. Co. Trustee Heritage Found., Deerfield, Mass., Herman Schneider Found. (pres. 1942-47). Com. for Econ. Devel., 1946-48, Children's Home; hon. trustee Berkshire Sch., Sheffield; chmn. bd. trustees Cin. Mus. Natural History, 1957-63. Past vice chmn. Bus. Adv. Council, Dept. Commerce; dir. Cin. Post. Am. Ordnance Assn., 1930-63 (pres. 1944-45); dir. Ohio Mechanics Inst. 1934-49; mem. Indsl. adv. com. ECA, 1948. Mem. exec. com. Machinery and Allied Products Inst., 1936-39; chmn. Cin. Com. Econ. Devel., 1943-46; cons. to Fgn. Econ. Adminstrn., 1945; asst. chief Cin. Ordnance Dist., 1938-40. Recipient Outstanding Citizenship award Cin. Real Estate Bd., 1963; Harrison medal Cin. chpt. Am. Ordnance Assn., 1966; Silver Beaver award Dan Beard Council Boy Scouts Am., 1967; 50th Anniversary Gold medal Am. Ordnance Assn., 1968; Great Living Cincinnatian award Greater Cin. C. of C., 1969. Mem. Nat. Machine Tool Builders Assn. (pres. 1941, v.p. 1939-40, treas. 1930), Cincinnatus Assn. (pres. 1931, hon. life mem.). Engring. Soc. Cin., Am. Soc. M.E. (asso.), Comml. Club of Cin. (pres. 1945, v.p., 1943, sec. 1938-39), Zeta Psi, Phi Beta Kappa, Omicron Delta Kappa. Newcomen Soc. Eng. Clubs: William (N.Y.C.); Camargo, Queen City, Cincinnati Country (Cin.); Bay Head (N.J.) Yacht; Mantoloking (N.J.) Yacht. Home: 8880 Old Indian Hill Rd Indian Hill Cincinnati OH 45243 Office: 4701 Marburg Av Cincinnati OH 45209 ☆

GEIER, JAMES AYLWARD DEVELIN, mfg. co. exec.; b. Cin., Dec. 29, 1925; s. Frederick V. and Amey (Develin) G.; student Williams Coll., 1947-50, U. Cin., 1950-52; m. Anne Whittier, July 22, 1950; children—Deborah Anne, James Develin, Aylward Whittier. With Cin. Milacron Inc., 1951—, pres., 1970—; dir. Clar Equipment Co., Buchanan, Mich. Pres. Cin. Museum Natural History, 1964—; trustee Cin. Zoo, 1968—, Tools for Freedom, 1964-69. Served with USAAF, 1944-46. Mem. Nat. Machine Tool Builders Assn. Clubs: Queen City, Camargo (Cin.). Home: 9100 Kugler Mill Rd Cincinnati OH 45243 Office: 4701 Marburg Av Cincinnati OH 45209

GEIER, PHILIP OTTO, Jr., mfg. co. exec.; b. Cin., Aug. 9, 1915; s. Philip Otto and Gladys M. (Jones) G.; A.B., Williams Coll., 1937; M.B.A., Harvard, 1939; LL.D., Xavier U., 1970; D.C.S., U. Cin., 1971; m. Susanne Ernst, Mar. 22, 1946; children—Philip Otto III, Susanne, Richard Ernst, Edward Simpson. With Cin. Milacron, Inc., 1939—, v.p., gen. mgr., 1961-63, pres., 1963-70, chmn., 1970—, also dir.; dir. Hobart Mfg. Co., Cin. Bell, Inc., Procter and Gamble Co., Goodyear Tire and Rubber Co., Armco Steel Co. Mem. Bus. Council; mem. bd. area council Boy Scouts Am., Boys Club Cin., United Appeal Cin., Community Chest Greater Cin., Family Service Cin. Served to lt. USNR, 1942-46. Decorated Bronze Star. Mem. Engring. Soc. Cin., Nat. Machine Tool Builders Assn., Machinery and Allied Products Inst. (exec. com.), Cincinnatus Assn. (past pres.), Nat. Indsl. Conf. Bd. (dir.), Am. Ordnance Assn. (pres. Cincinnati), Zeta Psi. Clubs: Cincinnati Country, Camargo, Queen City, Commonwealth (past pres.), Commerical (v.p.) Gyro (Cin.). Home: 6000 Redbirdhollow Lane Cincinnati OH 45243 Office: 4701 Marburg Av Cincinnati OH 45209

GEIGER, GEORGE, hotel exec.; b. Nyiregyaza, Hungary, May 1, 1905; s. Bela and Ilona (Geiger) G.; doctorate, U. Budapest (Hungary), 1926; m. Ella Spelman, Aug. 1, 1948; 1 dau., Peggy Ann (Mrs. Mark Jeffrey Ellis). Came to U.S., 1948, naturalized, 1956. Dir. Ungarische Algemeine Sparcasse, Hungary, 1930-45; pres. Paramount Hotel, N.Y.C., 1958-60, Abbey Hotel, N.Y.C., 1959-65, Flamboyan Apts., Inc., (P.R.), also Flamboyan Hotel Corp. (P.R.), 1963—, Dorado Hilton Hotel Corp. P.R., 1964—, Victoria-Abbey Corp., 1965—. Mem. Internat. Hotel Assn., Hotel Assn. N.Y.C., Hotel Assn. N.Y. State, Am. Hotel/Motel Assn., Am. Soc. Travel Agts., West Side Assn. Commerce, N.Y. Conv. and Visitors Bur. Home: 30 E 65th St New York City NY 10021 Office: 781 7th Av New York City NY 10019

GEIGER, GEORGE RAYMOND, educator; b. N.Y.C., May 8, 1903; s. Oscar Harold and Nina Cecelia (Daly) G.; A.B., Columbia, 1924, B. Lit., 1925, M.S., 1926, Ph.D., 1931; m. Julia Louise Jarratt, Dec. 25, 1934. Asst. prof. philosophy Bradley Poly. Inst., Peoria, Ill., 1928-30, 35-37; asso. prof. philosophy U. N.D., 1930-34, U. Ill., 1934-35; prof. philosophy Antioch Coll., Yellow Springs, O., 1937-68, John Dewey prof. in humanities, 1968—; vis. prof. philosophy U. Wis., 1947-48, U. Cal. at Santa Barbara, 1963. Mem. Am. Philos. Assn. (sec. treas. Western div. 1944-47, nat. sec., treas., 1947-53), Phi Beta Kappa. Author several books, 1933—, latest being: Philosophy and the Social Order, 1947; John Dewey in Perspective, 1958; Science Folklore and Philosophy, 1966; also contbr. to The Philosophy of John Dewey, 1939; Value: A Cooperative Inquiry, 1949; The Cleavage in Our Culture, 1952; Modern Philosophies and Education, 1955. Mem. bd. editors Antioch Rev., Am. Jour. Econ. and Sociology. Home: 131 W Center College St Yellow Springs OH 45387

GEIGER, HOMER KENT, educator; b. Bluffton, O., June 23, 1922; s. Homer Harvey and Flora Alberta (Gottshall) G.; A.B., Princeton, 1947; A.M., Harvard, 1950, Ph.D., 1955; m. Mildred Sharpe Shade, Aug. 17, 1950 (div.); children—Martha Ellen, Daniel William; m. 2d, Elinor C. Schick, Jan. 23, 1970. Teaching and research in sociology Tufts U., 1954-61, Ohio State U., 1961-63, U. Cal. at Berkeley, 1963-64; prof. sociology U. Wis., Madison, 1964—; research fellow Russian Research Center, Harvard, 1954-55, 58-59; research asso. New Eng. Bd. Higher Edn., 1957-58. Served with AUS, 1943-46. Mem. Am. Sociol. Assn., Internat. Studies Assn. Author: The Family in Soviet Russia, 1968; National Development 1776-1966, 1969. Home: 2725 Chamberlain Av Madison WI 53705

GEIGER, LAWTON DELANY, govt. ofcl.; b. Stuart, Fla., May 21, 1918; s. Lawton F. and Irene (McPherson) G.; B.S. in Archtl. Engring., Ga. Inst. Tech., 1939. Constrn. worker, 1939-41; mgr. Ia. area office AEC, Ames, 1946-48, mgr. Pitts. area office 1948-58, Pitts. Naval Reactors Operations Office, 1958—. Served from 2d lt. to maj., C.E. AUS, 1941-46. Recipient outstanding service award AEC, 1956. Home: 60 Dover Dr Pittsburgh PA 15230 Office: Box 1105 Pittsburgh PA 15230

GEIGER, LOUIS GEORGE, educator; b. Boonville, Mo., Mar. 21, 1913; s. George Victor and Dorothea Elizabeth (Hoflander) G.; student Elmhurst Coll., 1929-30; B.S., Central Mo. State Coll., 1934; M.A., U. Mo., 1940, Ph.D., 1948; m. Helen Margery Watson, Dec. 20, 1946; 1 son, Mark Watson. Tchr. pub. sch., Mo., 1930-31, 34-39; grad. asst., instr. U. Mo., 1939-42; asst. prof. history U. N.D., 1946-55, asso. prof., 1955-58, prof., 1958-60; prof. history, chmn. dept. Colo. Coll., 1960-70; vis. prof. U. Mo., 1960, Jadavpur U., 1963-64, Miami U., Ohio, 1967, Ariz. State U., 1970-71. Chmn. N.D. Com. Social Sci. Curricular Revision, 1959-60. Served to 1st lt. AUS, 1942-46. Fellow Fund Advancement Edn., Harvard and Stanford, 1953-54; Fulbright lectr. U. Helsinki, 1954-55; recipient research award Social Sci. Research Council, 1963. Mem. Rocky Mountain (v.p. 1965-66, 68-69), N.D. (pres. 1959-60) social sci. assns., Am. Assn. U. Profs., Am. Hist. Assn., Am. Studies Assn., History Edn. Soc., Agrl. History Soc., Orgn. Am. Historians. Clubs: Saturday (Calcutta); Winter Night (Colorado Springs). Author: From Appennines to Po, 1948; Joseph W. Folk of Missouri, 1953; University of the Northern Plains, 1958; Higher Education in a Maturing Democracy, 1963; Voluntary Accreditation: History of North Central Association, 1970. Contbr. Muckrakers and American Society, 1968. Home: 975 Terrace Circle Colorado Springs CO 80904

GEIGER, ROBERT, newspaper man. Sports editor Newark News. Office: Evening News Pub Co 215-221 Market St Newark NJ 07101*

GEIGLE, FRANCIS R., educator; b. Trevorton, Pa., Nov. 7, 1906; s. Charles W. and Daisy May (Swinehart) G.; student Lycoming Coll., 1924-26, L.H.D., 1960; student Bucknell U., 1926-27, Ind. State Coll., 1927-30, Bloomsburg State Coll., 1931; B.S., Susquehanna U., 1933; M.A., N.Y.U., 1936, Ed.D., 1941; postgrad. Harvard, 1934; m. Helen Dickert, Nov. 27, 1935. Tchr. bus. Trevorton (Pa.) High Sch., 1926-29; head dept. bus. adminstrn. Lycoming Coll., 1929- 35; head dept. bus. edn. Montclair State Coll., 1935-45; asst. v.p. Montclair (N.J.) 1st Nat. Bank & Trust Co., 1945-51; mem. faculty No. Ill. U., 1951-70, head, organizer Dept. Bus. Edn., 1951-53, adminstrv. asst. to pres., 1953- 57, v.p., 1957-59, exec. v.p., 1959-63, exec. v.p., provost, 1963-69, exec. v.p., 1969-70; acting pres. Ill. State U., Normal, 1970—. Mem. Am. Assn. Sch. Adminstrs., Chgo. Planetarium Soc., N.E.A., Am. Philatelic Soc., Nat. Audubon Soc., Am. Assn. Colls. for Tchr. Edn. (mem. team for Northeast Mo. State Coll. and Whitewater State Coll.). Presbyn. (bd. session, bd. trustees). Rotarian (past pres.). Home: 607 N Main St Normal IL 61761

GEILFUSS, JOHN CRITTENDEN, banker; b. Milw., Mar. 9, 1906; s. Carl F. and Florence (Crittenden) G.; B.A. cum laude, Williams Coll., 1935; LL.B., Harvard, 1938; m. Mary E. Balding, Apr. 1, 1950; children—Thomas S., C. Frederick II, Mary C. Admitted to Wis. bar, 1938, Mass. bar, 1946; practiced in Milw., 1938- 41; spl. asst. to under sec. navy, 1945-46; mem. law firm Herrick, Smith Donald Farley & Ketchum, Boston, 1946-47; asst. v.p. Marine Nat. Exchange Bank, Milw., 1948-52, v.p., 1953-57, then sr. v.p., dir., now pres.; sec., dir. The Marine Corp., Milw., 1957—; dir. Universal Foods Corp., Interstate Drop Forge Co., Will Ross, Inc., Thilmany Pulp & Paper Corp., Kaukauna, Wis. Bd. dirs. United Community Services, Milw., 1960—, pres., 1962-63, chmn. bd., 1963—; bd. dirs. Milw. Country Day Sch., 1951-62, pres., 1953-55; bd. dirs. Vis. Nurse Assn. Milw., 1950-58, treas. 1950-56; bd. dirs. Wis. Heart Assn., 1956-62, treas., 1957-59; treas., trustee Milw. Downer Coll., 1955. Mem. Am., Wis., Milw. bar assns,. Am. Inst. Banking, Wis. Hist. Soc. (curator, 1957—, pres., 1963), Phi Beta Kappa, Chi Psi. Episcopalian. Home: 1025 W Green Tree Rd Milwaukee, WI 53217. Office: 1 Marine Plaza Milwaukee WI 53201

GEIRINGER, KARL, educator, musician; b. Vienna, Austria, Apr. 26, 1899; s. Ludwig and Martha (Wertheimer) G.; student U. Berlin, 1920-21; Ph.D., U. Vienna, 1922; m. Irene Steckel, Apr. 19, 1928; children—Martin Frederick, George Karl. Came to U.S., 1940; naturalized, 1945. Curator archives Soc. of Friends of Music, Vienna, 1930-38; vis. prof. Royal Coll. Music, London, 1939-40, Hamilton Coll., Clinton, N.Y., 1940-41; prof. music Boston U. Sch. Fine Arts, chmn. dept. history and theory of music. and dir. grad. studies, 1952-62; prof. music charge grad. studies in music U. Cal., Santa Barbara, 1962-70, prof. emeritus, 1971—. Recipient Austrian Cross of

Honor 1st Class, 1969; Studies in 18th Century Music, a tribute to Karl Geiringer on his 70th birthday, edited by H.C.R. Landon and R. Chapman, 1970. Fellow Am. Acad. Arts and Scis.; mem. Am. (pres. 1955-56; exec. bd. 1954, 57-58, 64, 68-69, hon. mem.), Internat. musicol. socs., Coll. Music Soc. (exec. bd. 1965-67), Music Library Assn. Methodist. Author: Musical Instruments, 1943; Haydn, 1946, 3d edit., 1968; Brahms, rev. edit., 1947; Bach Family, 1954; Music of the Bach Family, 1955; Symbolism in the Music of Bach, 1956; The Small Sacred Works by Haydn; The Structure of Beethoven's Diabelli Variations, 1964; Johann Sebastian Bach, 1966. Editor: J. Haydn: 100 Scottish Songs, 1961, J. Haydn: Orlando Paladino (opera), 1971, Chr. W. Gluck: Telemaco (opera), 1971. Gen. editor: Univ. of Cal. Santa Barbara Series of Early Music, 1970—. Contbr. to Grove's Dictionary Music and Musicians. Home: 1823 Mira Visa Av Santa Barbara CA 93103

GEIS, BERNARD, book pub.; b. Chgo., Aug. 30, 1909; s. Harry M. and Bessie (Gesas) G.; B.A., Northwestern U., 1931; m. Darlene Stern, Mar. 28, 1940; children—Peter, Stephen. Newspaper reporter, contbr. mags., 1931-33; editor Apparel Arts mag., 1933-38; asst. editor Esquire mag., 1938-45; editor Coronet mag., 1930-45; war corr., ETO for Coronet and Esquire mags., 1942-43; editor-in-chief Grosset & Dunlap Pub. Co., 1945-53, v.p., 1949-53, editor Prentice-Hall Pub. Co., 1954-57; editor, dir. Bernard Geis Assos., N.Y.C., 1958—; pres. subsidiary Ampersand Press Inc., 1963- -. Chmn. publishers group N.Y.C. Salvation Army ann. appeal, 1960-66, N.Y. Heart Assn. Campaign, 1966—. Bd. dirs. Ams. Democratic Action, mem. exec. com., 1965—. Home: 1385 York Av New York City NY 10021 Office: 128 E 56th St New York City NY 10022

GEIS, DUANE VIRGIL, investment banker; b. Okeene, Okla., Apr. 16, 1923; s. Harry H. and Margareth (Tieman) G.; B.A., Okla. State U., 1947; m. Lois Blakey, Mar. 13, 1944; children—Duane Gregory, Paul Geoffrey. Accounting machine salesman IBM Corp., 1948-54; with Rotan Mosle Dallas Union, Inc., Houston, 1954-70, 1st sr. v.p., 1966-70, also dir.; partner Paine, Webber, Jackson & Curtis, 1970—. Bd. dirs. Star of Hope Mission, 1963—; vice chmn. Houston Ednl. Found., 1967—; trustee annuity bd. So. Baptist Conv., 1970—. Mem. Houston C. of C. (life), Financial Analysts Soc., Phi Kappa Phi, Phi Eta Sigma (pres. 1942-43), Beta Alpha Psi (pres. 1946-47), Kappa Sigma, Blue Key (v.p. 1946-47). Republican. Baptist. Clubs: Houston Country, Coronado (Houston). Home: 522 Shadywood St Houston, TX 77027. Office: Tenneco Bldg Houston TX 77002

GEIS, GILBERT LAWRENCE, educator; b. Bklyn., Jan. 10, 1925; s. Joseph and Ida (List) G.; A.B., Colgate U., 1947; student U. Stockholm, 1947; M.S., Brigham Young U., 1949; Ph.D., U. Wis., 1953; m. Ruth Steinberg, Apr. 4, 1948; children—Ellen Dagney, Jean Marit; m. 2d, Robley Huston, Dec. 17, 1966. Instr., then asst. prof. sociology U. Okla., 1952-57; faculty Cal. State Coll. at Los Angeles, 1957—, prof. sociology, 1963—; fellow law and sociology Harvard Law Sch., 1964-65; vis. prof. criminal justice State U. N.Y. at Albany 1969-70; vis. prof. social ecology U. Cal. at Irvine, 1971-72. Adviser, Pres.'s Com. on Narcotic and Drug Abuse, 1963-64; cons. Pres.'s Commn. on Law Enforcement and Adminstrn. Justice, 1966-67, Joint Commn. on Correctional Manpower and Tng., 1967-69, Nat. Commn. on Causes and Prevention Violence, 1968-70; mem. narcotic addition and drug abuse rev. com. Nat. Inst. Mental Health, 1970—. Served with USNR, 1943-46. Fulbright and Social Sci. Research Council fellow, Oslo, 1952-53. Mem. Am. (chmn. sect. criminology 1970-71), Pacific sociol. socs., Soc. Study Social Problems (chmn. criminal and delinquency sect. 1964-66). Author: (with H. Bloch) Man, Crime and Society, 1962, 2d edit., 1970; (with W. Bittle) Longest Way Home, 1964; Juvenile Gangs, 1966. Editor: White Collar Criminal, 1968. Home: 500 Crane Blvd Los Angeles CA 90065

GEIS, LAWRENCE RAYMOND, naval officer; b. Salina, Kan., July 14, 1916; s. John Raymond and Rara (Benn) G.; student Wesleyan Coll., Salina, 1934; B.S., U.S. Naval Acad., 1939; grad. Nat. War Coll., 1959, Advanced Mgmt. Program, Harvard, 1961; m. Jane Hamilton Brown Brashears, Aug. 3, 1946; 1 dau. Eleanor Owings; 1 stepson, Thomas Fort Williamson. Commd. ensign U.S. Navy, 1939, advanced through grades to rear adm., 1965; asst. gunnery officer U.S.S. Maryland, 1939-40; gunnery officer, U.S.S. Mahan, 1940- 42; designated naval aviator, 1943; exec. officer Patrol Bombing Squadron 54, 1944-45; assigned aviation plans div. Office Chief Naval Operations, 1945-47; comdg. officer Fighting Squadron 3, 1947-49; adminstrv. aide to dep. chief naval operations (air), 1949-51; comdr. Carrier Air Group 4, 1951-52; operations officer staff comdr. Fleet Air, Jacksonville, 1953-54; asst. dir. test div., then exec. officer Naval Air Sta., Naval Air Test Center, Patuxent River, Md., 1954-56; exec. officer U.S.S. Lake Champlain, 1956-57; comdg. officer Fighter Air Devel. Squadron 3, Atlantic Fleet, 1957-58; exec. asst., sr. aide to chief naval operations, 1959-61; comdg. officer U.S.S. Duxbury Bay, 1961- 62; comdr. U.S.S. Forrestal, 1962-63; mem. net evaluation subcom. Office Sec. Def., 1963-65; chief U.S. Naval Mission to Brazil, also chief navy sect. Mil. Assistance Adv. Group, Brazil, 1965-66; chief U.S. navy sect. Mil. Assistance Adv. Group, Brazil, 1966-67; comdr. Carrier Div. 4, 1967- 68; chief information Navy Dept., 1968—. Decorated Legion of Merit, Air medal, numerous area and campaign ribbons. Home: 1600 S Eads St Arlington, VA 22202. Office: Office Chief Information Navy Dept Washington DC 20305

GEIS, NORMAN WINER, lawyer; b. St. Paul, July 13, 1925; s. Alexander and Shirley (Magid) Winer; A.B. with honors,, U. Chgo., 1947, J.D., 1951; m. Dorothy Bockman, Oct. 17, 1954; children-Deborah, Nancy, Carolyn, Sarah. Mng. editor U. Chgo. Law Review, 1949-50; admitted to Ill. bar, 1950; practice in Chgo., 1951—; mem. firm Aaron, Aaron, Schimberg & Hess, 1965—; lectr. Univ. Coll., U. Chgo., 1959-60. Served with inf., AUS, 1943-45. Decorated Purple Heart, Bronze Star medal. Mem. Am., Ill., Chgo. (chmn. real property law com. 1970-71) bar assns., Pi Lambda Phi. Prin. draftsman Ill. Residential Real Estate Protection Act, 1969. Home: 396 Carol Ct Highland Park IL 60035 Office: 1 First Nat Plaza Chicago IL 60670

GEISEL, THEODOR SEUSS, (Dr. Seuss), cartoonist, publicist; b. Springfield, Mass., Mar. 2, 1904; s. Theodor Robert and Henrietta (Seuss) G.; grad. Dartmouth Coll., 1925; postgrad. Lincoln Coll., Oxford U., 1925-26; L.H.D. (hon.), Dartmouth Coll., 1955; L.H.D. (hon.), Am. Internat. Coll., 1968; m. Helen Marion Palmer, Nov. 29, 1927 (dec. Oct. 23, 1967); m. 2d, Audrey Stone Dimond, Aug. 6, 1968. Began career as humorist, illustrator for publs. including Life, Judge, Vanity Fair, Liberty mags.; advt. illustrator (12 yrs. creator of humorous adv. campaigns for Standard Oil of N.J., such as "Quick Henry the Flit! "series), mural painter, author and illustrator of children's books; editorial cartoonist PM (newspaper), N.Y.C.; mag. and newspaper writer on post-war Japanese edn.; pres. pub. Beginner Books, Inc.; pub. Bright and Early Books; pres. Beginner Books div. Random House, Inc.; designer of Dr. Seuss-Mattel Toy Line; designer children's furniture for Sears Roebuck. Asso. in war publicization work with numerous U.S. Govt. agys., including Treasury Dept. Served as maj. I. and E. Div., AUS; lt. col., Res. Awarded Legion of Merit for war film work. Mem. Authors League of Am., Sigma Phi Epsilon. Clubs: Century (N.Y.C.); Beach and Tennis (La Jolla, Cal.). Author numerous books, including: Gerald McBoing-Boing (Academy award best motion picture cartoon of 1950); Scrambled Eggs Super, 1953; Horton Hears a Who, 1954; On Beyond Zebra, 1955; If I Ran the Circus, 1956; How the Grinch Stole Christmas, 1957; The Cat in the Hat, 1957; The Cat in the Hat Comes Back, 1958; Yertle the Turtle, 1958; Happy Birthday, 1959; One Fish Two Fish Red Fish Blue Fish, 1960; Green Eggs and Ham, 1960; The Sneetches and Other Stories, 1961; Dr. Seuss's Sleep Book, 1962; Hop on Pop, 1963; Dr. Seuss's ABC Book, 1963; Fox in Socks, 1965; I had Trouble in Getting to Solla Sellew, 1965; The Cat in the Hat Songbook, 1967; The Foot Book, 1968; I Can Lick 30 Tigers Today and Other Stories, 1969; My Book About Me, 1969; I Can Draw It Myself, 1970; Mr. Brown Can Moo! Can You?, 1970. Co-author (with wife) of 1947 Acad. Award documentary film, Design for Death (the history of Japan). Producer animated cartoons for TV: How the Grinch Stole Christmas, Horton Hears a Who, The Cat in the Hat. Home: La Jolla CA ☆

GEISER, AUGUSTE, Swiss diplomat; b. Paris, France, May 6, 1916; Licencie en Droit, U. Paris, 1939; m. Lilli Weber, 1944; 1 son, Martin. With Fed. Dept. Pub. Economy, Berne, Switzerland, 1941-44; with Fed. Polit. Dept., 1945—; sec. to Swiss embassy, Ottawa, Can., 1952-58; sec. to Swiss legation, Prague, Czechoslavakia, 1958-61, charge d'affaires, 1960-61; dep. chief Finance and Econ. Sect., Berne, 1961-65; chief Swiss delegation Neutral Nations Supervisory Commn., Panmunjom, Korea, 1964; sect. chief div. commerce Dept. Pub. Economy, Berne, 1966-67; counselor Swiss embassy, Washington, 1968—. Del. 8th session Internat. Civil Aviation Orgn., Montreal, Can., 1954; mem. Swiss delegation Kennedy Round GATT, 1966-67. Office: 2900 Cathedral Av NW Washington DC 20008

GEISER, KARL FREDERICK, lawyer; b. New Hampton, Ia., June 6, 1903; s. Mathias Edgar and Belle (Rowe) G.; student Oberlin Coll., 1921-22; A.B., State U. Ia., 1925, J.D., 1927; m. Jane Schoentgen, June 6, 1928; children—Karl Frederick, Gretel (Mrs. George E. Stephens, Jr.). Admitted to Ia. bar, 1927, Cal. bar, 1946; partner firm Geiser, Donohue & Geiser, New Hampton, 1927-29; exec. v.p. E.H. Lougee, Inc., 1929-30; partner firm Tinley, Mitchell, Rosa, Everest & Geiser, Council Bluffs, Ia. 1930-42; pvt. practice, Beverly Hills, Cal., 1945—. Served to comdr. USNR, 1942-45. Mem. Am., Fed., Ia., Cal. bar assns., Businessmens Art Inst, Order of Coif, Phi Delta Phi, Sigma Alpha Epsilon. Republican. Home: 51 Malibu Colony Dr Malibu CA 90265 Office: 424 S Beverly Dr Beverly Hills CA 90212

GEISER, THEODORE WILLIAM, lawyer; b. Newark, June 1, 1925; s. Alwyn E. and Christine (Eadie) G.; student Montclair State Tchrs. Coll., 1942, Northeastern U., 1943, Seton Hall U., 1947; J.D. Rutgers U., 1969; m. Mary Catherine Wander, Aug. 8, 1948; 1 son, Theodore William. Admitted to N.J. bar, 1950; practiced in Newark, 1958—; gen. atty. N.J. Hwy. Authority, 1953-58; mem. firm Hughes, McElroy, Connell, Foley & Geiser, 1958—; instr. Rutgers Law Sch., 1953-55. Served with AUS, 1943-46; ETO. Decorated Bronze Star medal, Combat Inf. badge. Fellow Am. Coll. Trial Lawyers; mem. Am., N.J. bar assns. Home: 76 Gooseneck Point Rd Oceanport NJ 07757 Office: 24 Commerce St Newark NJ 07102

GEISERT, WAYNE FREDERICK, coll. pres.; b. Elmo, Kan., Dec. 20, 1921; s. Frederick Jacob and Martha E. (Lauer) G.; A.B., McPherson (Kan.) Coll., 1944; Ph.D. in econs., Northwestern U., 1951; m. Ellen Maurine Gish, July 2, 1944; children—Gregory Wayne, Bradley Kent, Todd Wilfred. Instr., Hamilton (Kan.) High Sch., 1946-48; part-time instr. Kendall Coll., Evanston, Ill., 1948-50; grad. asst. Northwestern U., 1950-51; asso prof., later prof. and head dept. econs. and bus. Manchester Coll., N. Manchester, Ind., 1951-57; dean coll. McPherson Coll., 1957-64; pres. Bridgewater (Va.) Coll., 1964—; cons. in field. Dir., Planters Bank Bridgewater. Pres. Assn. Va. Colls., 1970-71. Served with USNR, 1944-46; PTO. Mem. Am. Econ. Assn., Pi Kappa Delta, Alpha Psi Omega. Mem. Ch. of Brethren. Rotarian. Home: 409 E College St Bridgewater VA 22812

GEISMAR, MAXWELL DAVID, writer; b. N.Y.C., Aug. 1, 1909; s. Leon and Mary (Feinberg) G.; B.A., Columbia, 1931, M.A. (Moncreif Proudfit fellow letters), 1932; teaching fellow, Harvard, 1932-33; m. Anne Rosenberg, Sept. 11, 1932; children—Katherine (Mrs. Lawrence Seiden), Peter, Elizabeth. Mem. dept. lit. Sarah Lawrence Coll., 1933-44; free-lance writer, historian, critic, lectr., 1945—; contbg. editor The Nation, 1945-50. Guggenheim fellow 1943-44; fellow Boston U. Libraries, 1966-67; recipient award lit. work Nat. Acad. Arts and Letters, 1952. Author: Writers in Crisis, 1942; The Last of the Provincials, 1947; Rebels and Ancestors, 1952; American Moderns, 1958; Henry James and the Jacobites, 1963; Mark Twain: an American Prophet, 1970. Editor: Thomas Wolfe Portable, 1944; Walt Whitman Reader, 1955; Short Stories of Sherwood Anderson, 1962; Ring Lardner Reader, 1963. Sr. editor Ramparts magazine; founding editor Scanlan's Monthly. Contributor to the N.Y. Times Bookrev., Herald Tribune Books, Am. Scholar, Sat. Rev., Yale Rev., Va. Quar., Ency. Britannica, Compton's Ency. Address: Winfield Harrison NY 10528

GEISMAR, RICHARD LEE, communications co. exec. cons.; b. Paterson, N.J., Aug. 22, 1927; s. Sylvan and Marjorie (Leeser) G.; B.Mgmt. Engring., Rensselaer Poly. Inst., 1949; M.B.A., Harvard, 1951; m. Patricia Willard, Nov. 27, 1954; children—John, Elisabeth, Nancy. With DuMont TV Network, 1951-55; with Metromedia, Inc. and predecessors, N.Y.C., 1955-69, treas., 1958-68, v.p., 1961-68, also dir.; pres., dir. Reeves Telecom Corp., 1969-70; communications cons. BGW Assos., Inc., 1970—; chmn. Broad St. Communications Corp., 1971—. Active local Boy scouts Am., Community Chest. Served with USNR, 1945-46. Republican. Conglist. Clubs: Riverside Yacht; Canadian (N.Y.C.); Internat. (Washington). Home: Tower Rd Riverside CT 06878 Office: Box 151 Riverside CT 06878

GEISMER, ALAN STEARN, lawyer; b. Cleve., May 17, 1917; s. Eugene L. and Mollie (Stearn) G.; A.B. magna cum laude, Harvard, 1938; LL.B., 1941; m. Barbara Peck, Aug. 2, 1942; children—Alan Stearn, Martha England, Mollie Rose. Admitted to Ohio bar, 1941; clk. to justice Supreme Ct. Ohio, 1941- 42; with firm of Hahn, Loeser, Freedheim, Dean & Wellman (formerly Hahn, Loeser, Keough, Freedheim & Dean), Cleve. 1946-51, 52—, partner, 1955- -. Sec., dir. Child Welfare League Am., 1954-62; trustee past pres. Jewish Childrens Bur. Cleve. and Bellefaire, O.; mem. Shaker Heights (O.) Bd. Edn., 1957-64, pres., 1964-66; trustee, past sec. Musical Arts Assn., operating Cleve. Symphony Orch.; past trustee Cleve. Welfare Fedn.; past trustee, v.p. Cleve. Guidance Center. Served to capt., Counter Intelligence Corps, AUS, 1942-46, 51-52. Mem. Am., Ohio, Cleve. bar assns., Phi Beta Kappa. Club: Rowfant (Cleve.). Home: 14620 Shaker Blvd Shaker Heights OH 44120 Office: National City-E 6th Bldg Cleveland OH 44114

GEISSER, SEYMOUR, educator; b. Bronx, N.Y., Oct. 5, 1929; s. Leon and Rose (Kielmanowicz) G.; B.A., Coll. City N.Y., 1950; M.A., U. N.C., 1952, Ph.D., 1955; m. Mary Lee George, Jan. 30, 1955; children—Mindy Sharon, Dan Levi, Georgia Lynn, Adam Dov. Mathematician, Nat. Inst. Mental Health, Bethesda, Md., 1955-61; chief biometry sect. Nat. Inst. Arthritis and Metabolic Diseases, Bethesda, 1961-65; prof. statistics State U. N.Y. at Buffalo, 1965-71, chmn., 1965-70; prof., dir. Sch. Statistics, U. Minn., 1971—; professorial lectr. George Washington U., 1960-65; vis. asso. prof. Ia. State U., Ames, 1960; vis. prof. U. Wis., Madison, 1964, U. Tel-Aviv (Israel), 1971. Fellow Inst. Math. Statistics, Royal Statis. Soc., Am. Statis. Assn. (bd. dirs. 1964-65); mem. Biometric Soc., Math. Assn. Am., Internat. Assn. Statistics in Phys. Scis., Sigma Xi. Home: 1884 Summit Av St Paul MN 55105 Office: Sch Statistics U Minn Minneapolis MN 55455

GEISSINGER, JOHN BLANK, supt. schs., assn. exec.; b. Bethlehem, Pa., Aug. 27, 1906; s. John Benner and Sadie (Blank) G.; A.B., Muhlenberg Coll., 1927; M.A., U. Pa., 1929, Ph.D., 1945; m. Amy Helen Findon, June 21, 1928; children—Amy Diane, John Brent. Tchr. Jenkintown (Pa.) High Sch., 1927-30; prin. high sch., supervising prin., Springfield Twp., Bucks County, Pa., 1930-40; supervising prin., North Wales, Pa., 1940-46; supt. schs., Palmyra, N.J., 1946-52, Somerville, N.J., 1952-58, Tenafly, N.J., 1958—; instr., lectr. Pa. State Coll., 1949—, U. Del., 1950-51, Lehigh U., 1952-58; Temple U., 1957-58; mem. N.J. Scholarship Commn., 1961-68. Adv. bd. Channel 13 Ednl. TV. Mem. adv. com. N.J. Tercentary, 1961-64. Trustee Center Urban Edn., N.Y.C., Englewood (N.J.) Hosp. and Sch. of Nursing Com. Mem. Am. Assn. Sch. Adminstrs. (mem. exec. com. 1965—, pres. 1971-72), N.J. Sch. Supts. Assn. (pres. 1958-59), Nat. Council Accreditation Tchr. Edn. (appeal bd.), Alpha Tau Omega, Phi Delta Kappa, Kappa Phi Kappa. Republican. Lutheran. Mason (Shriner). Contbr. articles to profl. jours. Home: 83 Woodland Park Dr Tenafly NJ 07670

GEISSMAN, THEODORE ALBERT, educator; b. Chgo., June 17, 1908; s. Theodore Kenneth and Lina (Herold) G.; B.S., U. Wis., 1930; Ph.D., U. Minn., 1937; m. Loraine Skinner, Dec. 31, 1936; children-James Roger, Anne Elizabeth. With Standard Oil Co. (Ind.), 1930-34; postdoctoral research asso. U. Ill., 1937-39; instr. U. Cal. at Los Angeles, 1939-48, prof. chemistry, 1948—; cons. USPHS adv. panels, Walter Reed Army Research Inst. Fulbright research scholar, 1957- 58, Guggenheim fellow, 1949-50, 64-65. Mem. Am., Mexican (hon.) chem. socs., Chem. Soc. (London), Phytochemical Soc. N.Am., Soc. Econ. Botany. Author: Principles of Organic Chemistry, 1968; (with D.H.G. Crout) Organic Chemistry of Secondary Plant Metabolism, 1970. Editor: Chemistry of Flavonoid Compounds, 1962. Contbr. articles profl jours. Patentee in field. Home: 425 24th St Santa Monica CA 90402 Office: Dept Chemistry U Cal Los Angeles CA 90024

GEIST, HARRY, business exec.; b. 1900; B.S., N.Y.U., 1921, LL.B., 1924; married. Admitted to N.Y. bar, practice in N.Y.C.; v.p., gen. counsel Chock Full O'Nuts Corp., N.Y.C., 1960-69, pres., dir., 1969—. C.P.A., N.Y. Office: 425 Lexington Av New York City NY 10017*

GELATT, CHARLES DANIEL, mfg. exec.; b. LaCrosse, Wis., Jan. 4, 1918; s. Philo Madison and Clara (Johnson) G.; B.A., M.A., U. Wis., 1939; m. Jane Leicht, Mar. 6, 1942; children—Sarah Jane, Charles D., Philip Madison. Vice pres. No. Engraving & Mfg. Co (name changed to Gelatt Corp. 1965), La Crosse, Wis., 1940-52, gen. mgr., 1941—, chmn., 1945-56, pres., 1952—; pres. Neco Ordnance Corp., 1951-59; pres. Microcard Corp., 1956-66, chmn., 1966-67; pres. No. Engraving Co., 1958-67, chmn., 1967—; trustee Northwestern Mut. Life Ins. Co., Milw., also mem. exec. com., 1961—. Regent U. Wis., 1947—, pres., 1955-57, chmn. com. to appoint pres. of univ., 1957- 58, v.p. bd. regents, 1964-68, pres., 1968-69; mem. Wis. Coordinating Com. for Higher Edn., 1955-59, 64-69, chmn., 1956; chmn.-elect Assn. Governing Bds. Univs. and Colls., Washington, 1970-71. Mem. Phi Beta Kappa. Home: 1326 Cass St LaCrosse WI 54601 Office: Box 869 LaCrosse WI 54601

GELATT, ROLAND, mag. editor; b. Kansas City, Mo., July 24, 1920; s. Arthur Alvin and Leah (Kaufman) G.; A.B., Swarthmore Coll., 1941; m. Esther Frishkoff, May 26, 1948; 1 son, Timothy Arthur. Asso. editor Musical Digest mag., 1946-47; feature editor Saturday Rev., 1948-54; music editor High Fidelity mag., 1954-58, editor-in-chief, 1958-67, editor, asso. pub., 1967-68; mng. editor Saturday Rev., 1969—. Founder Montreux (Switzerland) Internat. Record Award. Served to lt. (j.g.) USNR, 1942-45. Author: Music Makers, 1952; The Fabulous Phonograph, 1955, revised edition, 1965; also numerous articles and revs. Home: 155 E 76th St New York City, NY 10021. Office: 380 Madison Av New York City NY 10017

GELB, ARTHUR, journalist; b. N.Y.C., Feb. 3, 1924; s. Daniel and Fanny (Gherig) G.; B.A., N.Y. U., 1946; m. Barbara Stone, June 2, 1946; children—Michael, Peter. Mem. staff N.Y. Times 1944—, met. editor, 1967—; lectr. on theatre, also Eugene O'Neill, 1961—. Author: (with Mrs. Gelb) O'Neill, 1962; (with Dr. Salvatore Cutolo) Bellevue is My Home, 1956; (with A.M. Rosenthal) One More Victim, 1967. Editor: (with A.M. Rosenthal) The Pope's Journey to the United States, 1965; The Night the Lights Went Out, 1965. Address: care NY Times 229 W 43d St New York City NY 10036

GELB, BRUCE S., cosmetic co. exec.; b. N.Y.C., Feb. 24, 1927; s. Lawrence M. and Joan Driedman (Hewett) G.; student Phillips Acad., Andover, Mass., 1943; Choate Sch., Wallingford, Conn., 1943-45; B.A., Yale, 1950; M.B.A., Harvard, 1953; m. Leuza Denise Thirkield, June 6, 1953; children—John T., Joan H., Richard E., Mary C. With Clairol Inc., 1950-51, 58—, exec. v.p., 1961-65, pres., 1965—; brand mgr. Procter & Gamble, 1953-57; v.p., dir. Charter Corp.; now sr. v.p. Bristol Myers Co. Bd. dirs. Madison Sq. Boys Club; trustee St. Bernard's Sch., Choate Sch. Home: 1060 Fifth Av New York City NY 10028 Office: 345 Park Av New York City NY 10019

GELB, IGNACE JAY, univ. prof.; b. Tarnow, Poland, Oct. 14, 1907; s. Salo and Regina (Issler) G.; student Univs. of Florence and Rome, Italy, 1925-29; Ph.D., U. Rome (Italy), 1929; m. Hester Mokstad, May 13, 1938; children—Walter Alexander, John Vincent. Came to U.S., 1929, naturalized, 1939. Travelling fellow to research asso., U. Chgo., 1929-41, asst. prof. Assyriology, 1941-43, asso. prof., 1943-47, prof., 1947-65, Frank P. Hixon distinguished service prof., 1965—; vis. prof. U. Mich., 1954, 67. Mem. archaeol. expdns. to Near East, 1932, 35, 47, 65, 66. Served with AUS, 1943-45. Fellow Am. Acad. Arts and Scis.; hon. mem. Societe Asiatique (Paris), Finnish Oriental Soc. (Helsinki); mem. Am. Oriental Soc. (br. pres. 1959-60, nat. pres. 1965-66), Am. Schs. Oriental Research, Linguistic Soc. Am., Linguistic Circle N.Y., Am. Name Soc. (pres. 1963-64), Archaeol. Inst. Am., Societe Hittite (Paris), Inst. Asian Studies (hon. mem. Hyderabad, India). Clubs: Quadrangle, Philological, Near East (pres., 1942-43) (Chicago). Scientific collaborator of Polish Acad. Scis. (Cracow); fgn. mem. Accademia Nazionale dei Lincei, Italy. Author several books 1931—; latest publs.: Hurrians and Subarians, 1944; Study of Writing 1952; Sargonic Texts from the Diyala Region, 1952; Old Akkadian Writing and Grammar, 1952; Glossary of Old Akkadian, 1955; Sequential Reconstruction of Proto-Akkadian, 1968. Editor: Chicago Assyrian Dictionary, 1947—. Contbr. articles. Home: 5454 Woodlawn Av Chicago IL 60615 ☆

GELB, RICHARD LEE, corp. exec.; b. N.Y.C., June 8, 1924; s. Lawrence M. and Joan F. (Bove) G.; student Phillips Acad., 1938-41; B.A., Yale, 1945; M.B.A., Harvard, 1950; m. Phyllis L. Nason, May 5, 1951; children—Lawrence N., Lucy G., Jane E., James M. Joined Clairol, Inc., N.Y.C., 1950, pres., 1959-64; exec. v.p. Bristol-Myers Co., 1965-67, pres., 1967—; dir. Charter Corp., Bankers Trust Co.,

Bankers Trust N.Y. Corp. Mem. N.Y. Urban Coalition; mem. Com. on 2d Regional Plan; vice chmn. Criminal Coordinating Council N.Y.C. Trustee Mt. Sinai Hosp., Com. Econ. Devel.; bd. trustees and treas. Nat. Council Crime and Delinquency; bd. dirs. Lincoln Center for Performing Arts. Author: Your Future in Beauty Culture. Home: 1060 Fifth Av New York City NY 10028 Office: 345 Park Av New York City NY 10022

GELBACH, JOHN A., banker; b. Ellwood City, Pa., Oct. 22, 1917; s. Loring Lusk and Stella (Fisher) G.; A.B., George Washington U., 1938; M.B.A., Harvard, 1940; m. Marion Soerens, Oct. 16, 1941; children—John Loring, Robert Walter. Clk., 1st Wis. Nat. Bank, Milw., 1940-41; v.p., treas. Stock Equipment Co., Cleve., 1941-56; with Central Nat. Bank, Cleve., 1956—, sr. v.p., then pres., chief exec. officer, dir.; v.p., dir. Sherman Corp. Trustee, treas. Tb League Cuyahoga County; trustee Cleve. Council World Affairs, Health Fund, Greater Cleve. Growth Corp., Greater Cleve. Growth Assn., United Appeal Greater Cleve., Cleve. Found.; treas. A.R.C. Mem. Newcomen Soc., Assn. Res. City Bankers. Clubs: Country, Union, Pepper Pike, The 50, Bluecoats, Inc., Harvard Business School of Cleveland (trustee). Home: 31615 Creekside Dr Cleveland OH 44124 Office: 800 Superior Av Cleveland OH 44114

GELBACH, MYRON SCHENCK, Jr., corp. exec.; b. Ellwood City, Pa., June 14, 1921; s. Myron Schenck and Gretta (Coleman) G.; B.A., Marietta (O.) Coll., 1943; M.B.A., Harvard, 1947; m. Loretta Morrissey, Feb. 1, 1947; 1 son, Thomas Myron. Sec.-treas. T.H. Jones & Co., 1948-56; v.p., treas. Rainbow Prodn. Corp., 1954-56; sec., treas., dir. Alco Chem. Corp., 1956-65; with Alco Standard Corp., 1965—, pres., 1969—, also dir.; dir. FML Growth Fund, Inc., FML Equity Income Fund, Inc. Served with USNR, 1943-46, 51-54. Mem. S.A.R., Geneal. Soc. Pa., Pa. Soc., S.R., Hist. Soc. Pa. Republican. Presbyn. Clubs: Union (Cleve.); Whitmarsh Valley Country (Phila.). Home: 6029 Joshua Rd Fort Washington PA 19034 Office: Alco Standard Corp Valley Forge PA 19481

GELBART, ABE, educator; b. Paterson, N.J., Dec. 22, 1911; s. Wolf and Pauline (Landau) G.; B.Sc., Dalhousie U., 1938; Ph.D. in Math., Mass. Inst. Tech., 1940; m. Sara Goodman, July 2, 1939; children—Carol Marie (Mrs. Ivan P. Auer), Judith Sylvia (dec.), William Michael, Stephen Samuel. Asst., Mass. Inst. Tech., 1939-40; instr. math. N.C. State Coll., 1940-42; research asso. Brown U., 1942; asso. physicist NACA, Langley Field, Va., 1942-43; asst. prof. to prof. math. Syracuse U., 1943-58; dir. Inst. Math., Yeshiva U., 1958-59, dean Belfer Grad. Sch. Sci., 1959-70, dean emeritus, 1970—, distinguished univ. prof. math., 1968—. Mem. Inst. Advanced Study, Princeton, 1947-48; Fulbright lectr., Norway, 1951-52. Mem. directorate math. scis. USAF Office Sci. Research. Mem. Am. Math. Soc., Math. Assn. Am. editor Scripta Mathematica, 1957—. Co-developer theory of pseudo-analytic functions. Home: 140 West End Av New York City NY 10023

GELBART, LARRY, writer; b. Chgo., Feb. 25, 1928; s. Harry and Frieda (Sturner) G.; m. Pat Marshall, Nov. 25, 1956; children—Cathy, Gary, Paul, Adam, Becky. Writer for radio; Duffy's Tavern, 1945-48, Jack Paar, 1947—, Jack Carson, 1947- 48, Bob Hope, 1947-51; for TV.: Bob Hope, 1949-51, Red Buttons, 1951-52, Sid Caesar, 1953-55, Art Carney, 1960; for theatre: My L.A., 1950, The Conquering Hero, 1960, A Funny Thing Happened on the Way to the Forum, 1961; for films; The Notorious Landlady, 1960, (Also co-producer) the Wrong Box, 1966, Not With My Wife You Don't, 1966; for films Little Me, 1968, The Ecstacy Business, 1968. Served with AUS, 1945-46. Recipient Sylvania award, 1960, Emmy award, 1960, Antoinette Perry award, 1962. Mem. Dramatists Guild, Writers Guild Am., A.S.C.A.P., Writers Guild Gt. Britain. Home: RD 1 Ghent NY 12075 Office: Redstacks Compton Av London N 6 England

GELBAUM, BERNARD RUSSELL, univ. adminstr., mathematician; b. N.Y.C., Feb. 26, 1922; s. Harry and Regina (Kratka) G.; A.B., Columbia, 1943; M.A., Princeton, 1947, Ph.D. (NRC Predoctoral fellow), 1948; m. Beatrice Lerner, Nov. 14, 1942; children—Daniel, David, Martin, Ethan. Instr., Princeton, 1947; mem. faculty U. Minn., Mpls., 1948-64, prof., 1957-64; prof., chmn. dept. math. U. Cal. at Irvine, 1964-68, asso. dean Coll. Phys. Scis., 1968-71; v.p. acad. affairs state U. N.Y. at Buffalo, 1971—; vis. mem. Inst. Advanced Study, Princeton, 1960; cons. Inst. Def. Analyses, Washington, 1962-67; cons. editor W. B. Saunders Co., Phila., 1964-68. Pulitzer scholar, 1939; NSF research grantee, 1959—. Mem. Am. Math. Soc., Math. Assn. Am., Am. Assn. U. Profs., Am. Civil Liberties Union, Phi Beta Kappa, Sigma Xi. Author: (with J.M.H. Olmsted) Counterexamples in Analysis, 1964; (with J.G. March) Mathematics for the Social and Behavioral Sciences, 1969. Editor: Functional Analysis, 1967. Contbns. to functional analysis, study of topological groups, theory of games. Home: 127 Ruskin Rd Amherst NY 14226 Office: Hayes Hall State Univ New York Buffalo NY 14214

GELBER, JACK, writer; b. Chgo., Apr. 12, 1932; s. Harold and Molly (Singer) G.; B.S. in Journalism, U. Ill., 1953; m. Carol Westenberg, Dec. 23, 1957; children—Jed, Amy. Author: (plays) The Connection, 1959; The Apple, 1961, Square in the Eye, 1965, The Cuban thing, 1968; (novel) On Ice, 1964. Recipient of the Best Play award for The Connection, Village Voice, 1959-60; Vernon Rice award for outstanding contbn. to Off-Broadway, 1959-60; Guggenheim fellow for creative writing for theatre, 1963-64, 66-67; adj. asso. prof. Columbia, N.Y.C., 1967- -. Home: 697 West End Av New York City NY 10025 Office: care Ronald Konecky 555 Madison Av New York City NY 10022

GELBOIN, HARRY VICTOR, biochemist; b. Chgo., Dec. 21, 1929; s. Herman and Eva (Jurkowsky) G.; A.B., U. Ill., 1951; M.S., U. Wis., 1956, Ph.D., 1958; m. Marlena Maisels, Apr. 1, 1962; children—Michele Ida, Lisa Rebecca, Sharon Anna, Tamara Rachel. Devel. chemist U.S. Rubber Co., 1952-54; research asst. McArdle Meml. Lab. Cancer Research, U. Wis., 1954-58; biochemist Nat. Inst. Mental Health, 1958-61; supervisory biochemist Nat. Cancer Inst., 1962-64, head chemistry sect., 1964-66, chief chemistry br., etiology, 1966—; adj. prof. chemistry Mt. Vernon Jr. Coll., Washington, 1959—. Predoctoral fellow Nat. Cancer Inst., 1957-58; travel grantee 8th Internat. Cancer Congress, 1962, 9th, 1966; keynote speaker Gordon Research Conf. Cancer, 1965; prin. lectr. Internat. Symposium Molecular Carcinogenesis, Dunedin, New Zealand, 1966. Recipient Claude Bernard award U. Montreal, 1970. Mem. A.A.A.S., Am. Assn. Cancer Research Am., Soc. Biol. Chemists, Am. Soc. Pharmacology and Exptl. Therapeutics. Jewish religion. Author articles, chpts. in books. Asso. editor Cancer Research, Archives Biochemistry and Biophysics. Home: 2806 Abilene Dr Chevy Chase MD 20015 Office: Nat Insts Health Bethesda MD 20014

GELDARD, FRANK ARTHUR, psychologist; b. Worcester, Mass., May 20, 1904; s. Arthur and Margaret Hardy (Gordon) G.; A.B., Clark Univ., 1925, A.M., 1926, Ph.D., 1928; Sc.D., Washington and Lee U., 1969; m. Jeannette Manchester, June 20, 1928; 1 dau., Deborah Rea. Asso. prof. psychology U. Va., 1928-37, prof. psychology, dir. psychol. lab., 1937-60, chmn. dept., 1946-60, dean Grad. Sch. Arts and Scis., 1960-62; Stuart prof. psychology Princeton, 1962—. Served as col. U.S. Army Air Corps, chief field service and liaison sect., psychol. br., Office of Air Surgeon, hdqrs. Army Air Forces, 1942; chief psychol. sect. Office of Surgeon, hdqrs. Army Forces Tng. Command, 1942-45; comdg. officer, psychol. mission to P.I. and Japan, 1945; col. USAF Res., 1946-57. Cons. research and devel. bd. Nat. Mil. and Office of Naval Research, U.S. Navy Dept., 1947-58; research chief human resources div., research and devel. directorate Hdqrs. USAF, 1949-50; chmn. human resources com. Office Sec. of Def., 1950-56, Sci. liaison officer, Office Naval Research, London br., 1956-57. Awarded Legion of Merit. Chmn. NATO Adv. Group on Human Factors, 1959-65; chmn. Mil. Psychology Comm., mem. Committee Internat. Relations in Psychology NRC Vision Com., com. on biol., med. scis. NSF, 1953-59. Fellow Am. Psychol. Assn. (past pres. div. exptl. psychology and div. mil. psychology), Royal Soc. Medicine (Gt. Brit.), A.A.A.S. (v.p. sect. I, 1957-58); mem. Am. Assn. U. Profs., Optical Soc. Am., Soc. Exptl. Psychologists, So. Soc. for Philosophy and Psychology (past pres.), Internat. Brain Research Orgn., UNESCO, Eastern Psychol. Assn., Am. Inst. Physics, Va. Acad. Sci., Phi Beta Kappa, Sigma Xi, Raven, Gryphon, Phi Sigma, Kappa Phi, Omicron Delta Kappa. Dem. Clubs: Colonnade, Nassau (Princeton); Cosmos (Washington). Author: The Human Senses, 1953; Fundamentals of Psychology, 1962. Contbr. numerous articles to psychol. and ednl. jours. Cons. editor: Jour. Psychology, Jour. Comparative and Physiological Psychology, Perception and Psychophysics, Jour. Exptl. Psychology, Jour. Gen. Psychology, Contemporary Psychology. Home: 551 Lake Dr Princeton NJ 08540 ☆

GELDART, LLOYD PHILIP, educator, geophysicist; b. Can., Oct. 20, 1914; s. Oscar David and Edith (Waterbury) G.; B.A. summa cum laude, Mt. Allison U., 1937; M.A., U. Toronto, 1941; Ph.D. in Physics, McGill U., 1941. Geophys. Engr., Cal. Inst. Tech., 1949; m. Helena Marie Burridge, Sept. 4, 1940; 1 son, David Philip. Head physics dept. Acadia U., 1942-47; with Standard Oil Co. Cal., 1948-60, chief geophysicist subsidiary Cal. Exploration Co., 1956-60; Webster prof. geophysics McGill U., 1960-69; mgr. project for strengthening teaching basic scis. U. Bahia, UNESCO, 1968—; cons. in field, 1962-68. Mem. Soc. Exploration Geophysicists, Am. Geophys. Union, European Assn. Exploration Geophysicists, A.A.A.S. Author articles. Home: Ed Maria Izabel 1004 Av Princesa Isabel 118 Barra Salvador Bahia Brazil Office: Reitoria UFBA Salvador Brazil

GELDMACHER, ROBERT CARL, educator; b. Elgin, Ill., Apr. 22, 1917; s. Walter Carl and Emma (Goers) G.; B.E., No. Ill. U., 1942; M.S., Purdue U., 1946; Ph.D., Northwestern U., 1959; m. Theresa Julia Swanberg, Sept. 27, 1941; children—Ann Marie (Mrs. Peter A. Alicandri), Cecily Louise, Mary Ellen. Tchr. physics and math., Chadwick (Ill.) High Sch., 1942-43; instr. Naval Tng. Sch., Purdue U., 1943-45, research asst., 1945-47, from asst. prof. to asso. prof. engrng. sci., 1947-60; prof. engrng. sci., asso. dean sch. Engrng. and Sci., N.Y. U., 1960-66; Anson Wood Burchard prof., head dept. elec. engrng. Stevens Inst. Tech., 1966—; cons. to govt., 1952—. Dir. Inter Poly Corp. Mem. Am. Soc. Engrng. Edn., Am. Phys. Soc., A.A.A.S., I.E.E.E., Math. Assn. Am., Soc. Indsl. and Applied Math., Am. Assn. U. Profs., Sigma Xi, Tau Beta Pi. Research in magneto elasto dynamics, graph theory. Home: 1004 Troy Towers Mt Rd Union City NJ 07087 Office: Burchard Hall Steves Inst Tech Hoboken NJ 07030

GELERMAN, BENJAMIN E., ins. co. exec.; b. Cambridge, Mass., Apr. 19, 1923; A.B., J.D., Harvard. Admitted to Mass. bar, N.Y. bar, U.S. Supreme Ct. bar; with Consol. Mut. Ins. Co., Bklyn., 1949—, now exec. v.p., sec., also dir. Trustee Bklyn. Psychiat. Centers Mem. Am. Bar Assn., New York County Lawyers Assn., Am. Mgmt. Assn., Am. Mut. Ins. Alliance, Paralyzed Vets. Assn. (v.p., dir.), N.Y. Property Ins. Underwriting Assn., N.Y. State Mut. Ins. Assn. Club: Harvard. Home: 2 Farmers Rd Kings Point NY 11024 Office: 345 Adams St Brooklyn NY 11201

GELFAND, MORRIS ARTHUR, librarian; b. Bayonne, N.J.. June 1, 1908; s. Joseph Samuel and Sadie (Schneider) G.; B.S., N.Y. U., 1933, M.A., 1939, Ph.D., 1960; B.S. in library service, Columbia, 1934; m. Beatrice Margaret Traube, February 1, 1948; children—James Munn, Lisa Jay. Supr. res. reading room Washington Sq. Library, N.Y. U., 1931-37; library asst. Queens Coll. Library, 1937-41, asst. librarian, 1941-42, librarian, 1946- 59, prof. librarian, 1959-70; chmn. dept. library sci. Queens Coll., 1970—. Fulbright lectr., cons. U. Rangoon, Burma, 1958-59; spl. examiner library positions N.Y. State Civil Service Dept., 1946-47; mem. visitation coms., commn. instns. higher edn. Middle States Assn. Colls. and Secondary Schs., 1949—; cons., Yeshiva Univ. (library survey), 1956; library cons. Seton Hall U., 1962; UNESCO library expert, Thailand, 1962; vis. prof. U. Delhi (India), 1966; library cons. Ford Found., Brazil, 1964, 66, 67, 69. Pres. Roslyn chpt. Am. Field Service, 1964-65; trustee Council on Research in Bibliography, Inc., Bryant Library, Roslyn, N.Y., N.Y. Met. Reference and Research Agy., Inc. Served as private, U.S. Army, 1942; 2d lt. to maj., A.C., 1942-45; statis. officer, adj. E.T.O.; library officer, U.S. Army Forces, Pacific, 1945- 46. Recipient Army Commendation Ribbon. Mem. Am. Assn. U. Profs. (pres. Queens Coll., 1952-53), A.L.A. (rep. to United Nations Orgn., 1962-65, Association Coll. and Reference Libraries (chmn. program com., coll. sec. 1949-50), Bibliog. Soc. Am., N.Y. Library Club (pres. 1947-48), Steering Com. on Library Cooperation in Met. N.Y. (sec. 1949), Sigma Society of N.Y. U. (pres. 1928), Phi Delta Kappa, Alpha Lambda Phi. Clubs: Archons of Colophon, Grolier (N.Y.C.). Author: University Libraries for Developing Countries, 1968. Editor New York Library Club Bulletin, 1940- 41, 51-52. Contbr. to library publs. Home: The Stone House Post Dr Roslyn Harbor NY 11576 Office: Dept Library Sci Queens Coll Flushing NY 11367

GELLER, BRUCE, writer, producer, dir.; b. N.Y.C., Oct. 13, 1930; s. Abraham N. and Dorothy (Friedlander) G.; B.A., Yale, 1952; m. Jeannette Marx, Sept. 7, 1953; children—Catherine, Lisa. Author, Man on a White Horse for Kaiser Aluminum Hour, 1956; author books and lyrics for musical Livin' the Life, N.Y.C., 1957, musical comedy All in Love, N.Y.C., 1961-62, London, Eng., 1964; author, dir. duPont Show, Shirley Temple Show, Dr. Kildare, Zane Grey Theatre, The Westerner, 1959-62; author screenplay Sail a Crooked Ship, 1962; author, producer Dick Powell Show, 1963, Rawhide, 1964; created series, author, producer Mission Impossible, 1965, exec. producer, 1966—; devel. series, author, producer Mannix, 1966, exec. producer, 1967—. Recipient Silver Gavel award Am. Bar Assn., 1963, Western Heritage award, 1964 (2), Emmy award (2), 1966, Golden Globe award, 1967, Image award N.A.A.C.P., 1967. Home: 707 N Arden Dr Beverly Hills CA 90210 Office: care Paramount Pictures Hollywood CA 90028

GELLER, HENRY, lawyer; b. Springfield, Mass., Feb. 14, 1924; s. Samuel and Sadie (Kramer) G.; B.S., U. Mich., 1943; J.D., Northwestern U., 1949; m. Judith Foelak, Oct. 14, 1955; children—Kathryn Ann, Peter R. Admitted to Ill. and Mich. bars, 1949; law clk. Ill. Supreme Ct. Justice Schaefer, 1951-52; atty. NLRB, 1950-51; with antitrust div. Dept. Justice, 1957- 61; dep. gen. counsel FCC, 1961-64, became gen. counsel, 1964. Mem. Order of Coif. Home: 2104 Pickwick Lane Alexandria VA 22307

GELLER, MAX A., bus. exec.; b. N.Y.C., 1899; Ph.D., N.Y.U.: m. Ida Wachstien; children—Jack, Marjorie, Harriet, Genevieve. Pres., Yoo Hoo Chocolate Beverage Corp.; chmn. bd. Weiss & Geller Inc., Nedick's N.Y. Bottling Co. Author: Advertising at Crossroads. Home: 168 Bon Air Av New York City NY Office: 880 3d Av New York City NY 10022

GELLER, WILLIAM SPENCE, librarian; b. Los Angeles, Mar. 31, 1914; s. Raymond Nelson and Alicia (Spence) G.; A.B., U. So. Cal., 1936, M.S. in Pub. Adminstrn., 1937; B.S. in L.S., U. Cal. at Berkeley, 1953; m. Helen Hamilton, Nov. 19, 1938; 1 dau., Penelope. With Co. Los Angeles, 1937-48, dept. adminstrv. research, 1937-38, adminstrv. and sr. adminstrv. asst. health dept. and dept. charities, 1938-45, adminstrv. analyst, chief adminstrv. office, 1945-48; mem. staff Los Angeles Co. Library, 1948—, asst. co. librarian, 1963—. Mem. Cal. Pub. Library Devel. Bd., 1967—. Cons. library bldgs. Western Govt. Research Assn.; mem. hist. landmarks com. Los Angeles Co. Mem. Am. (chmn. equipment com. library adminstrn. div. 1961-64), Cal. (pres. so. dist. 1966, chmn. finance com. 1964-65, constl. revision com. 1955, exhibits com. 1954, pres. elect, also v.p. (1969-70) library assns., Pub. Libraries Execs. Assn. So. Cal. (pres. 1959-60), Alumni Assn. U. Cal. at Berkeley Sch. Librarianship (pres. 1961), Speechcrafters, Pi Sigma Alpha, Scapa Praetors. Contbr. articles to profl. jours. Home: 624 Knight Way La Cañada CA 91011 Office: 320 W Temple St Los Angeles CA 90012

GELLERT, EVERETT, publisher; b. Bklyn., Nov. 17, 1907; s. Abraham and Kathryn (Frankel) G.; student pub. schs.; m. Beatrice Maisel, Sept. 15, 1930; children—Nan (Mrs. Elliott Silverman), Paul Anthony. Chmn. bd. Gellert Pub. Co., N.Y.C., Mura Corp., Jericho, N.Y. Club: Old Westbury Golf (L.I.). Home: 14 Pasture Lane Roslyn Heights NY 11577 Office: 33 W 60th St New York City NY 10023

GELLES, ROBERT W., broadcasting exec.; b. Anchorage, Alaska, 1923; B.S., U. Ill., 1948; J.D., St. Johns U., 1954; married. Admitted to N.Y. bar; with successively Arthur Andersen & Co., R.G. Rankin & Co., Stewart, Watts & Bollong, Price Waterhouse & Co., 1948-56; sec., asst. treas., treas. Pepsi-Cola United Bottlers Inc., 1956-60; ins. mgr., asso. corporate counsel Hudson Pulp & Paper Corp., 1961-63; asst. sec., asst. treas., comptroller Capital Cities Broadcasting Corp., N.Y.C., 1963-68, comptroller, 1968—. Bd. dirs. Inst. Broadcast Financial Mgmt. Home: 39 W 46th St New York City NY 10036 Office: 245 E 51st St New York City NY 10022*

GELLHORN, ALFRED, physician, educator; b. St. Louis, June 4, 1913; s. George and Edna (Fischel) G.; student Amherst Coll., 1930-32; M.D., Washington U., 1937; D. Sc., Amherst Coll., 1969; m. Olga Frederick, Aug. 4, 1939; children—Martha, Anne, Christina, Maria, Edna. Gen. surg. tng. Barnes Hosp., St. Louis, 1937-39; gynecology tng. Passavant Meml. Hosp., Chgo., 1939-40; fellow Carnegie Instn. of Washington, Balt., 1940-43; instr., later asst. prof. physiology, Coll. Phys. and Surg., Columbia, 1943-45, asst., asso. prof. pharmacology, 1945-48, asso. prof. clin. cancer research, dept. medicine 1948-52, asso. prof. medicine, 1952-58, prof. internal medicine, 1958-68; prof. medicine, prof. pharmacology, dean Sch. Medicine, also dir. Med. Center, U. Pa., 1968—; asst. physician Vanderbilt Clinic, Presbyn. Hosp. 1945-68; vis. physician Francis Delafield Hosp., N.Y.C., 1949-52, and chief of Medical Service, 1952-68; vis. prof. of medicine, Albert Einstein Med. Sch. Dir. Inst. Cancer Research, Columbia, bd. regents Nat. Library Medicine. Diplomate Am. Bd. Internal Med. Mem. Soc. for Clin. Investigation, Philadelphia Co. Med. Soc., Am. Assn. Cancer Research (pres. 1962-63), Am. Soc. Pharm. and Exptl. Therapeutics, Soc. Exptl. Biology and Medicine, Am. Soc. Biol. Chemists, Assn. Am. Physicians, Internat. Orgns. Med. Scis. (pres. council 1970—). Home: 2225 Delancey St Philadelphia PA 19103

GELLHORN, MARTHA, author, foreign corr.; b. St. Louis; d. George and Edna (Fischel) G.; student John Burroughs Sch., St. Louis, and Bryn Mawr Coll.; 1 son, George Alexander. War corr. for Collier's Weekly in Spain, 1937- 38, Finland, 1939, China, 1940-41, England, Italy, France and Germany, 1943-45, Java, 1946; war corr. for The Guardian, London, Eng., in Vietnam, 1966, and in Israel, 1967. Author: The Trouble I've Seen, 1936; A Stricken Field, 1940; The Heart of Another, 1941; Liana, 1943; Wine of Astonishment, The Honeyed Peace, 1954; Two by Two, 1958; The Face of War, 1959; His Own Man, 1961; Pretty Tales for Tired People, 1965; The Lowest Trees Have Tops, 1967. Contbr. to mags. Address: care Morgan Guaranty Trust Co 31 Berkeley Sq London W 1 England.

GELLHORN, WALTER, educator; b. St. Louis, Sept. 18, 1906; s. George and Edna (Fischel) G.; A.B., Amherst, 1927, L.H.D., 1952; LL.B., Columbia, 1931; LL.D., U. Pa., 1963, U. Akron, 1968, Boston U., 1971; m. Kitty Minus, June 1, 1932; children—Ellis, Gay. Law sec. to U.S. Surpeme Ct. Justice Harlan F. Stone, 1931; admitted to N.Y. bar, 1932; atty., Office of Solicitor Gen., U.S. Dept. Justice, 1932-33; mem. faculty law Columbia U., 1933—, also faculty of polit. sci., 1937—, Betts prof. law, 1957—. Regional atty. U.S. Social Security Bd., 1936-38; dir. atty. gen.'s. com. on adminstrv. procedure, 1939-41; asst. gen. counsel and regional atty. OPA, 1942-43; spl. asst. to sec. of interior, 1943-44; vice chmn. Nat. War Labor Bd., 2d Region, 1944-45, chmn., 1945; vis. prof. U. Manchester, Eng., 1951, Tokyo U., 1958. Awarded Henderson Meml. Prize, 1946 (co-winner), Goldsmith award, 1951, Hillman award, 1957; Columbia Law Alumni medal for excellence, 1971. James Schouler lectr. Johns Hopkins U., 1941; Edward Douglass White lectr. La. State U., 1956; Oliver Wendell Holmes lectr. Harvard, 1966. Mem. council Adminstrv. Conf. U.S., 1961-62, 68—. Fellow Am. Acad. Arts and Scis.; mem. Am. Philos. Soc. (council 1970—), Assn. of Am. Law Schs. (pres. 1963), Nat. Acad. Arbitrators, Nat. Acad. Pub. Adminstrn., Alpha Delta Phi (pres. 1955-58), Phi Beta Kappa, Phi Delta Phi. Author: Administrative Law-Cases and Comments, 1940, 5th edit., 1970; Federal Administrative Proceedings 1941; Security, Loyalty, and Science, 1950; Children and Families in the Courts, 1954; Individual Freedom and Governmental Restraints, 1956; Kihonteki Jinken (in Japanese), 1959; American Rights, 1960; When Americans Complain, 1966; Ombudsmen and Others, 1966; (with others) Civil Liberties Under Attack, 1951, The States and Subversion, 1952, The Freedom to Read, 1956; The Sectarian College and the Public Purse, 1970. Home: 54 Morningside Dr New York City NY 10025

GELLING, J. BURK, corp. exec.; b. 1927; student Marshall Coll., also U. Tex.; married. With Montgomery Ward & Co., 1949-66; with Federal's Inc., 1966—, now pres., chmn. bd., chief exec. officer, dir. Address: 1200 E McNichols Rd Detroit, MI 48203.*

GELLIS, IKE, journalist; b. N.Y.C., Jan. 5, 1908; s. Sam Emanuel and Sarah (Marder) G.; student pub. schs.; m. Kathaleen Dwyer, Mar. 19, 1938; children—Harry Paul, Dorothy and Nancy (twins). With N.Y. Post., N.Y.C., 1926—, sports editor, 1949—. Home: 147-58 77th Av Flushing NY 11367 Office: 75 West St New York City NY 10006

GELLIS, SYDNEY SAUL, educator, physician; b. Claremont, N.H., Mar. 6, 1914; s. Morris Aaron and Minna (Bernstein) G.; A.B., magna cum laude, Harvard, 1934, M.D., 1938; m. Matilda Lichter, Mar. 7, 1939; children—Beth Louise, Stephen. Intern pediatrics Yale Med. Sch., 1938-39; resident pediatrics Children's Hosp., Cin., 1939-41;

chief resident pediatrics Johns Hopkins Hosp., 1941-42; instr. pediatrics John Hopkins Med. Sch., 1942-46, Harvard Med. Sch., 1946-56; faculty Boston U. Sch. Medicine, 1956- 65, prof. pediatrics, chmn. dept., 1956-65, acting dean, 1962-64; dir. pediatrics Boston City Hosp., 1956-65; prof., chmn. dept. pediatrics Tufts U., 1965—. Mem. Army Epidemiological Bd., 1943-46; cons. sec. War on infectious diseases, 1943-46; mem. Gov. Mass. Legislative Com. Mental Retardation,1963—. Trustee Mass. Fund for Children and Youth, 1966—. Served to captain, M.C., AUS, 1944-46. Fellow Am. Acad. Pediatrics; mem. Am. Pediatric Soc., Soc. Pediatric Research (sec. 1951-58, pres. 1959- 60), French Pediatric Soc. (corr.), New Zealand Pediatric Soc. (hon.), Phi Beta Kappa, Sigma Xi, Alpha Omega Alpha. Editor Year Book of Pediatrics, 1952—; asso. editor American Journal of Diseases of Children, 1958—. Co-author: Current Pediatric Therapy, 1962. Contbr. Ency. Britannica. Home: 77 Alderwood Rd Newton MA 02159 Office: 20 Ash St Boston MA 02111

GELL-MANN, MURRAY, theoretical physicist; b. N.Y.C., Sept. 15, 1929; s. Arthur and Pauline (Reichstein) Gell-M.; B.S., Yale, 1948; Ph.D., Mass. Inst. Tech., 1951; m. J. Margaret Dow, Apr. 19, 1955; children—Elizabeth, Nicholas. Mem. Inst. for Advanced Study, 1951; instr. U. Chgo., 1952-53, asst. prof., 1953-54, asso. prof., 1954, research dispersion relations, developed strangeness theory; asso. prof. Cal. Inst. Tech., Pasadena, 1955-56, prof., 1956—, now R.A. Millikan prof. physics, research theory of weak interactions, developed eightfold way theory and Quark scheme. NSF post doctoral fellow, vis. prof. Coll. de France and U. Paris, 1959-60. Recipient Dannie Heineman prize Am. Phys. Soc., 1959; E.O. Lawrence Meml. award AEC, 1966; Franklin medal, 1967; Carty medal Nat. Acad. Scis., 1968; Research Corp. award, 1969; Nobel prize in physics, 1969. Fellow Am. Phys. Soc.; mem. Nat. Acad. Scis., Am. Acad. Arts and Scis. Club: Cosmos. Author: (with Y. Ne'eman) Eightfold Way. Home: 1024 Armada Dr Pasadena CA 91103

GELLY, GEORGE BALFOUR, mgmt. cons.; b. Cornwall, N.Y., June 8, 1900; s. Thomas B. and Margaret (Ireland) G.; student Lehigh U., 1918-19; B.S. in Engring., U.S. Coast Guard Acad., 1924; m. Margaret G. Vaughan, June 30, 1925; children—George V., Margaret (Mrs. E. C. Waller III). Commd. ensign USCG, 1924, advanced through grades to capt., 1944; comdr. Nike, 1934-36; chief pub. relations, 1936-40; chief staff 14th Coast Guard Dist., Honolulu, 1940-42; comdr. Taney, 1942-43; capt. Port of Los Angeles, 1943-46; ret., 1946; Washington rep. asst. sec. Douglas Aircraft Co., Santa Monica, Cal., 1947-55, corporate sec., 1955-57; indsl. def. coordinator, 1956-57; v.p. marketing Hoffman Electric Corp., Lab. div., 1958—; pres. G.B. Gelly Assos. Decorated Commendation Ribbon. Mem. Sigma Phi Epsilon. Clubs: Nat. Press, Army and Navy (Washington). Home: 104 Medio Dr Los Angeles CA 90049

GELMAN, DAVID GRAHAM, editor; b. Bklyn., Nov. 1, 1926; s. George and Rose (Shulman) G.; student Bklyn. Coll., 1947-55; m. Elaine Edith Rodkinson, Apr. 6, 1952; children-Eric Adam, Andrew Seth, Amy Miriam. Reporter, writer N.Y. Post, 1943-62; dir. spl. projects Peace Corps, Washington, 1962-66; asso. editor nat. affairs and spl. projects Newsweek, N.Y.C., 1966-68; v.p. for edn. U.S. Research & Devel., N.Y.C., 1968-69; editorial page editor, nat. editor Newsday, Garden City, N.Y., 1969—. Served with USNR, 1944- 46. Home: 205 West End Av New York City NY 10023 Office: 550 Stewart Av Garden City NY 11530

GELMAN, FRANK HERMAN, lawyer; b. Phila., May 11, 1912; s. Samuel and Fannie (Perchin) G.; A.B., Temple U., 1932; J.D., U. Pa., 1935; m. Rivie Perlmutter, Mar. 17, 1940; children—Norris E., Marcia. Admitted to Pa. bar, 1935, since practiced in Phila.; mem. firm Mesirov, Gelman, Jaffe & Levin, 1959—; lectr. Am., Pa. law insts., also legal edn. program Pa. Bar. Assn.; counsel, chief negotiator Phila. Sch. Bd. in collective bargaining, 1966-69; pub. employer collective bargaining cons. to Colonial and Haverford Sch. Dists. Served with USNR, 1943-46. Mem. Am., Pa., Phila. bar assns. Club: Philadelphia Lawyers. Author: (course materials) Pennsylvania Mortgages and Their Enforcement, 1965; The Real Estate Transaction, 1964. Home: 1418 Ashbourne Rd Wyncote PA 19095 Office: Fidelity Bldg Philadelphia PA 03109

GELMIS, JOSEPH STEPHAN, film critic, author; b. Brooklyn., Sept. 28, 1935; s. Steve Andrew and Tillie (De Pietro) G.; B.A., Bklyn. Coll., 1956; M.S. in Journalism, Columbia, 1960; divorced; children—Steven Keith, Susan Valerie. With Newsday, 1960—, film critic, 1964—; syndicated columnist, 1971—; host radio and TV shows; coll. lectr. Served with USAF, 1956-59. Recipient Polk award for journalism, 1961. Mem. N.Y. Film Critics Circle (chmn. 1970). Author: The Film Director as Superstar, 1970. Office: 230 W 41st St New York City NY 10036

GELTZ, CHARLES GOTTLIEB, forester, educator; b. McKeesport, Pa., Feb. 21, 1896; s. William and Mary (Ditter) G; B.S., Pa. State Forest Sch., 1924; M.S.F., U. Cal., 1927; m. Mildred Harry Julin, Aug. 18, 1930; children—Charles Gottlieb, Betty Anne (Mrs. Joel D. Swanson); stepchildren—Helen Julin (Mrs. Ralph L. Reiley), Jane Julin (Mrs. William T. Keenen, Jr.). Forester, Ala. Commn. of Forestry, 1924-25; instr. forestry, registrar, N.Y. State Forest Ranger Sch., Coll. of Forestry, State U. of N.Y., Wanakena, 1925-26; research asst., div. forestry U. Cal., 1926-27; jr. forester U.S. Forest Service, 1927-29; instr. forestry State Forest Sch., Pa. U., 1929-30; asst. prof. Purdue U., 1930-34, asso. prof., 1934-46; dir. Purdue Forestry Summer Camp, 1930-42; prof. silviculture Sch. Forestry, U. Fla., 1946-70, prof. silviculture emeritus, 1970—; so. regional counsel for Nat. Sch. Forestry and Conservation, Wolf Springs Forest, Minong, Wis.; operator, owner, also chief forester Charles G. Geltz Assos., forestry, conservation, edn. cons. Cons. Forest Recreation and Family Camping, Fla. Family Camping Assns.; outdoor recreation cons. to dir. resources programs Dept. Interior, 1961-63; mem. Fla. Gov.'s Resource Use Edn. Com. Neighborhood commr. Boy Scouts Am. Served with 13th U.S. Cav., Mex. Border Campaign and World War I, to Sept. 1919, U.S. Cav. Res., 1922-42; with Adj. Gen.'s Corps, 1942-46; now maj. U.S. Army Res. (ret.). Recipient unit citation award and plaque, commendation ribbon; Silver Beaver award Boy Scouts Am., 1951; Wisdom Honor award Wisdom Soc., 1970. Registered forester, Ga., Fla. Fellow Am. Geog. Soc.; mem. Soc. Am. Foresters (Outstanding Forester award Fla. sect. 1966), Am., Fla. (hon. life; dir. exec. bd.) forestry assns., Fla. C. of C., Forest Farmers Assn., Fla. Forestry Council (sec.), Fla. Forestry Council, Ret. Officers Assn., Xi Sigma Phi, Phi Sigma, Phi Delta Kappa, Kappa Delta Pi, Scabbard and Blade, Alpha Phi Omega (hon.). Episcopalian (lay reader). Mason (32, Shriner). Home: 1521 NW 7th Av Gainesville FL 32601

GELVIN, LYLE MILLARD, mfg. co. exec.; b. Marshalltown, Ia., Apr. 14, 1928; s. L.M. and Grace E. (Elder) G.; A.B. cum laude, Harvard, 1950, M.B.A., 1952; m. Kathleen M. Burton, June 14, 1950; children—Linda Gay, Grant Millard, Scott Burton, Ann Louise. With Gulf Oil Corp., 1952-56; gen. mgr. operations B.F. Whitehill Co., Tulsa, 1956-59; with Sunray DX Oil Co., 1959-62; exec. v.p., dir. Fisher Governor Co., Marshalltown, 1962-69; owner, pres. Joor Mfg. Co., 1968—, Lyle Corp., Escondido, Cal., Lyco Mfg., Inc., Escondido. Mem. Am. Petroleum Inst., Instrument Soc. Am., Am. Inst. Mining, Metall. and Petroleum Engrs. Home: 2562 Mountain View Dr Escondido CA 92025 Office: 1189 Industrial Av Escondido CA 92025

GEMEINHARDT, LAURENCE EDWIN, educator; b. Pawtucket, R.I., Apr. 7, 1907; s. John Laurence and Lydia (Patt) G.; A.B., Brown U., 1929; M.A., Columbia, 1931; Ph.D., Yale, 1940; M.A. (hon.), Wesleyan U., 1952; m. Ruth Evelyn Johnston, Mar. 31, 1934; 1 dau., Susan Anne (Mrs. Clifford C. Carlson). Faculty Wesleyan U. Middletown, Conn., 1931—, prof. German, 1952—, counselor fgn. students, also Fulbright program adviser, 1947—. Mem. Conn. Fulbright- Hays Com., 1951—. Adv. com. Middlesex Hosp. Sch. Nursing, 1965—. Recipient German Govt. Travel award, 1956; Fulbright research scholar, Germany, 1957-58. Mem. Modern Lang. Assn. Am., Am. Assn. Tchrs. German, New Eng. Modern Lang. Assn., Goethe Soc. New Eng., Nat. Assn. Fgn. Student Affairs (bd. dirs. 1953-57), Phi Beta Kappa. Author articles, revs. Editor: Ein Tag aus dem Schulleben Hanno Buddenbrooks, 1948; Reinecke Fuchs, 1945. Home: Arawana Newfield St Middletown CT 06457

GEMMECKE, RICHARD HAROLD, educator; b. Terre Haute, Ind., June 8, 1907; s. Charles L. and Grace (Nation) G.; B.S., Ind. State Tchrs. Coll., 1929; M.A., Ind. U., 1936, Ph.D., 1955; m. Margaret K. Hoare, May 21, 1933. High sch. tchr., Martinsville, Ind., 1929-38, chmn. dept. social studies, 1936-38; tchr. Elkhart (Ind.) High Sch., 1938-48, chmn. dept. social studies, 1941-48; chmn. social studies Elkhart city schs., 1941-48; faculty Ind. State U., 1948—, prof. history, 1954—, dean Coll. Arts and Sci., 1962-71, asso. to v.p. for acad. affairs, univ. research prof., 1971—. Mem. Ind. Sesquicentennial Commn., 1960-67, sec., 1960-67. Mem. Ind. Classroom Tchrs. Assn. (pres. 1947-48), Ind. Acad. Social Sci., Ind. Hist. Soc., Orgn. Am. Historians, N.E.A., Phi Alpha Theta. Mem. United Ch. Christ. Mason. Home: 607 Gardendale Rd Terre Haute IN 47803

GEMMELL, HORTENSIA TYLER, librarian; b. Pulaski, Va., Nov. 4, 1904; d. Andrew Hamilton and Annette (Leache) G.; A.B., Randolph-Macon Woman's Coll., 1926; B.S., Columbia Sch. Library Service, 1931, M.S., 1940. Asst. librarian Randolph-Macon Woman's Coll., Lynchburg, Va., 1926-38; asst. cataloger Vassar Coll. Library, Poughkeepsie, N.Y., 1939-45; head cataloger N.J. Coll. for Women Library, New Brunswick, 1945-47; head Librarian Mary Helen Cochran Library, Sweet Briar Coll., 1947-69; vis. cataloger Washington and Lee U., 1969—; vis. prof. George Peabody Coll. for Tchrs. Grad. Library Sch., Nashville, summers 1949, 58, 59, Trenton (N.J.) State Tchrs. Coll., summers 1950-52, 54. Fulbright lectr., Mandalay, Burma, 1955-56; lectr., cons. U.S.-India Women's Coll. Exchange Program, in India, 1966-67. Member Am., Southeastern, Va. library assns., Am. Assn. U. Profs., Bibliog. Soc. U. Va., Phi Beta Kappa. Episcopalian. Address: 108 W Preston St Lexington VA 24450

GEMMELL, JAMES, coll. pres.; b. Glasgow, Scotland, Oct. 13, 1914; s. James and Martha (Clunie) G.; B.S. in Commerce, U. Wyo., 1938; M.S., State U. N.Y., 1943; D.Ed., N.Y. U., 1946; m. Mary Elizabeth Robbins, June 26, 1940; children—Kathleen Suzanne, James Christopher, Ted K. Instr. commerce State U. N.Y., 1942-45; faculty Pa. State U., 1945-60, prof. econs. and edn., 1945-60, chmn. div. bus. edn., 1947-60; pres. Clarion (Pa.) State Coll., 1960—. Exec. dir. Commn. Econs. Tchr. Edn., 1954; program coordinator Nat. Com. Edn. Family Finance, 1959-60; cons. U.S. Office Edn., 1947-48, Joint Council Econ. Edn., 1955; adv. council Asso. Orgns. Tchr. Edn., 1960; chmn. adv. com. econ. edn. Invest-in-Am. Nat. Council, Inc., 1964-67; Fulbright lectr., Finland, 1957; mem. council Eastern Regional Inst. for Edn., 1967—; advisor Pa. Bd. Edn., 1969—; mem. cultural affairs com. Am. Assn. State Colls. and Univs.; bd. advisers Regional Council on Internat. Edn. Mem. Delta Pi Epsilon, Sigma Chi, Phi Delta Kappa, Kappa Delta Pi. Author: Business Organization and Management, 1949; Principles of Economics, 1953. Home: 840 Wood St Clarion PA 16214

GEMMELL, JOSEPH P., banker; b. Bklyn., July 23, 1935; s. Joseph and Rose (McCarrol) G.; B.B.A. in Finance, Pace Coll., 1967; m. Diane Kormanik, Sept. 7, 1957; children—Joseph, Donald, Dennis, Barbara. With First Nat. City Bank, N.Y.C., 1953-57; auditor Fed. Res. Bank N.Y., 1957-64; auditing officer S.I. Savs. Bank, 1964-69, Savs. Bank Trust Co., also Instl. Securities Corp., N.Y.C., 1969—. Treas. Mariners Family Home, 1968-69; mem. Bay Terrace Civic Assn., 1964—. Served with AUS, 1958-60. Mem. Savs. Banks Auditors-Controllers N.Y. State, Bank Adminstrn. Inst. Club: Great Kills Yacht (Staten Island). Home: 103 Bay Terrace Staten Island NY 10306 Office: 200 Park Av New York City NY 10017

GEMMILL, CHALMERS LAUGHLIN, pharmacologist; b. Cresson, Pa., Nov. 24, 1901; s. Benjamin McKee and Clara Marie (Genso) G.; student William Penn Charter Sch., Phila., 1914- 18; B.S., Lafayette Coll., 1922; grad. study, U. Chgo., 1923; M.D., Johns Hopkins, 1926; grad. study, Kaiser Wilhelm Inst., Heidelberg, Germany, 1931, Physiological Inst., Lund, Sweden, 1933, Biochemical Inst., Cambridge, Eng., 1934; m. Vivienne Angeline Warry, Jan. 10, 1938; 1 dau., Daphne De Jersey. Asst. in physiology, Johns Hopkins Med. Sch., 1926-27, instr., 1927-28, asst. prof., 1928-41, asso. prof., 1941-45; prof. pharmacology, U. Va. Med. Sch., 1945—. Lt. comdr., M.C., U.S.N.R., on active duty, 1941-45, capt. since 1945; Naval Air Station, Pensacola, Fla., 1941-45; Bur. Medicine and Surgery, Washington, 1945. Commonwealth Fund fellowship history of medicine, London, 1965. Mem. Am. Physiol. Soc., Consultants Armed Forces of U.S., Am. Soc. Biol. Chemists, Am. Soc. Pharm. Exptl. Therapy, Biochem. Soc. (Eng.), Va. Acad. Sci., Endocrine Soc., Phi Beta Kappa, Sigma Xi, Alpha Omega Alpha, Nu Sigma Nu. Democrat. Presbyn. Author: Physiology in Aviation, 1943. Contbr. numerous articles. Address: 19 Farmington Dr Charlottesville VA 22901 ☆

GEMMILL, HENRY, editor; b. Toledo, June 11, 1917; s. Robert Bringhurst and Mary (Mehaffie) G.; A.B., Yale, 1939; m. Ann-Mari Andersson, Feb. 11, 1940; children—Elisabeth (Mrs. Steven Izenour), John, Ann-Mari. Reporter Washington Evening Star, 1939-42; reporter Washington bur. Wall St. Jour., 1942-46, news editor, 1946-50, 1954-59, mng. editor, 1950-54, chief of corrs., London, 1959-60, Washington News Bur. chief, 1960-68, asso. editor, Washington office, 1968-70; editor The Nat. Observer, Silver Spring, Md., 1971—. Clubs: Federal City, Press, Gridiron (Washington). Home: 638 G St SE Washington DC 20003 Office: 11501 Columbia Pike Silver Spring MD 20904

GEMMILL, KENNETH WILFRED, lawyer; b. Ivyland, Pa., Feb. 16, 1910; s. Benjamin M. and Clara (Genso) G.; grad. Mercersburg Acad., 1928; A.B., Princeton, 1932; LL.B., U. Pa., 1935; m. Helen Hartman, July 19, 1941; children—John Kenneth, Elizabeth Hartman, Catharine Clare, William Kenneth. Admitted to N.Y. bar, 1936, Pa. bar, 1942; partner, Dechert, Price & Rhoads, attys., Phila., 1942—; asst. to Sec. Treasury, 1953-54, acting chief counsel Internal Revenue Service, 1953. Dir. Am. Water Works, Inc., United Utilities Co., Watt and Shand. Lectr. N.Y. U. tax inst., Pa. State Coll. tax inst., Practicing Law Inst. Mem. Am., Pa., Phila., N.Y.C. bar assns. Author various articles in law revs. Home: Jamison PA 18929 Office: 3 Penn Center Philadelphia PA 19102

GEMMILL, ROBERT ANDREW, lawyer; b. Marion, Ind., Sept. 12, 1911; s. Willard B. and Florence (Jones) G.; A.B., Ind. U., 1932, J.D., 1934; m. Lottie Wine Lugar, Apr. 25, 1970. Admitted to Ind. bar, 1934, since practiced in Marion; sr. partner firm Gemmill Browne Torrance, Sisson & Morin and predecessors, 1935—. Mem. bd. law examiners Ind. Supreme Ct., 1956-60, pres., 1958-59; mem. Gov. Ind. Probate Study Commn., 1956-64; vis. com. Ind. U. Sch. Law, 1964—; bd. dirs. Ind. Bar Found., 1961—, pres., 1965-66. Served to lt. comdr. USNR, 1942-45; comdr. Res. Decorated Navy Commendation medal. Fellow Am. Bar Found.; mem. Am. (ho. dels. 1962-64), Ind. (bd. mgrs. 1954-56, 61-65, 69-70, pres. 1963-64, chmn. ho. of dels. 1969-70), Grant County (pres. 1951-52), Fifth Dist. (pres. 1935-36), Indpls. bar assns., Nat. Conf. Bar Pres. (council 1964-65), Am. Judicature Soc. (dir. 1967-71), Am. Legion, Delta Upsilon, Phi Delta Phi. Republican. Episcopalian. Mason (33, Shriner). Clubs: Mecca, Meshingomesia Country (Marion); Columbia (Indpls.). Home: Shadeville Farm 5760 S Strawtown Pike PO Box 927 Marion IN 46952 Office: 122 E 4th St Marion IN 46952

GEMZELL, CARL-AXEL, educator; b. Motala, Sweden, Jan. 4, 1910; s. Charles and Eva (Sandberg) G.; M.D., Karolinska Inst., Stockholm, Sweden, 1940, Ph.D., 1948, Docent in expl. endocrinology, 1953, Obstetrics and Gynecology, 1955; m. Lisa Langerquist, Mar. 11, 1936. Asso. prof. obstetrics, gynecology Karolinska Inst., 1953-60; prof., chmn. dept. obstetrics, gynecology U. Uppsala, Sweden, 1960—. Mem. Endocrine Soc. Am., Svenska Lakarsallskapet. Pioneer induction of ovulation in human with human gonadotropins extracted from pituitaries which led to great number of multiple births. Research, publs. exptl., clin. endocrinology, obstetrics, gynecology. Home: 2 A Stigbergsgatan Uppsala Sweden Office: Akademiska Sjukhuset Uppsala Sweden

GENAUER, EMILY, art critic, editor, writer; b. N.Y.C.; d. Joseph and Rose (Milch) G.; Hunter Coll., N.Y. City; B.Lit., Columbia Sch. Journalism, 1930; m. Frederick Gash, 1935; 1 dau., Constance Lee. Staff writer, art feature writer, New York World, 1929-31; art critic, editor, New York World-Telegram, 1932-49; art critic N.Y. Herald Tribune, 1949-66; art critic, editor N.Y. World Jour. Tribune, N.Y.C., 1966-67; art commentator ednl. TV, Channel 13, N.Y.C., 1967—; arts critic- columnist for the Newsday Syndicate, 1967—. Exec. bd. Conn. Coll. Sch. Dance; bd. Martha Graham Sch. Contemporary Dance; adv. bd. Columbia U. Sch. Journalism; mem. Nat. Council Humanities. Recipient N.Y. Newspaper Women's Club ann. award for outstanding writing in specialized field, 1937, for outstanding column in any field, 1949, 56, 58, 60, 69; Columbia U.'s Journalism alumni award, 1960. Author: Best of Art, 1947; Monograph on Toulouse-Lautrec for Met. Mus. of Art, 1953; Biography of Chagall, 1957; Hommage a l' Ecole de Paris, 1962; Biography of Tamayo, 1971; Chagall at the Met, 1971. Home: 243 E 49th St New York City NY 10017 ☆

GENCH, W.L., ins. co. exec.; b. Rich Hill, Mo., 1909; ed. Northwestern U., 1931. sec., dir. Western Casualty & Surety Co., Fort Scott, Kan.; sec., dir. Western Fire Ins. Co., Western Indemnity Co., Western Ins. Securities Co. Mason. Home: 420 Rosemary Lane Fort Scott KS 66701 Office: 14 E 1st St Fort Scott KS 66701

GENDEBIEN, ALBERT WILLIAM, educator; b. Phila., Mar. 15, 1913; s. Peter William and Emily (Moritz) G.; B.S., Lafayette Coll., 1934, M.A., 1935; Ph.D., Am. U., 1951; m. Frieda Funk, Dec. 19, 1950. With personnel adminstrn. U.S. War Dept., 1939-48; prof. history Lafayette Coll., 1948—, head dept., 1967—. Active Family Counseling Service. Served from pvt. to capt., USAAF, 1943-46. Mem. Am. Hist. Assn., Am. Assn. Univ. Profs., Fgn. Policy Assn., Phi Alpha Theta, Theta Chi. Home: 511 Parsons St Easton PA 18042

GENDRON, MAURICE, cellist; b. Nizza, France, Dec. 26, 1920; s. Maurice and Jeanne (Lemarchand) G.; grad. Nice, Paris conservatories; m. Monique Nerot, Aug. 30, 1947; children—Caroline, Francois-Eric. Began to play cello at age 5; appeared with London Philharmonic in premier performance Prokofiev Cello Concerto, 1945, later capital cities of Europe, North Africa; has concertized in France, Germany, Austria, Italy, Switzerland, Eng., Scotland, Ireland, Holland, Spain, Portugal, Denmark, Sweden, Belgium, North and South Africa, Israel, Angola, Mozambique, Canary Islands; appeared U.S., 1958—, performing with N.Y. Philharmonic, other orchs.; participated festivals Aix-en-Provence, Toulouse, Divonne, Besancon, Monaco, Vienna Festwochem, Lugano, Aldeburgh, Gstaad; appears TV shows, France and Germany; tchr. master classes Am. Cons., Fontainebleau, France; prof. State Music Sch., Saarbruecken, Germany; title role in film Maurice Gendron, Metamorphose of the Cello; solo cello recs. Epic Recs., also recs. with Pablo Casals conducting Lamoureux Orch. Paris. Recipient Grand prix Paris Conservatory. Home: 5 Bd Magenta Fontainebleau (SM) France Office: care Eleanor Morrison 327 Central Park W New York City NY 10025

GENEEN, HAROLD SYDNEY, mfg. exec.; b. Bournemouth, Eng., Jan. 22, 1910; s. S. Alexander and Aida (DeCruciani) G.; brought to U.S., 1911, naturalized (derivative), 1918; B.S., N.Y. U., 1934; grad. Advanced Mgmt. Program Harvard; LL.D. (hon.), Lafayette Coll., PMC Colleges; m. June Elizabeth Hjelm, Dec. 1949. Accountant and analyst Mayflower Assos., 1932-34; sr. accountant Lybrand, Ross Bros. & Montgomery, 1934-42; chief accountant Am. Can Co., 1942-46; dir., v.p., controller Bell & Howell Co., Chgo., 1946-50; v.p., controller Jones & Laughlin Steel Corp., Pitts., 1950-56; exec. v.p., dir. Raytheon Mfg. Co., Waltham, Mass., 1956-59; pres., chief officer, dir. Internat. Tel. and Tel. Corp., 1959—, chmn. bd., 1964—, also mem. exec. com.; dir. fgn. subsidiaries, affiliated cos.; dir. Nat. Shawmut Bank. Regional leader Nat. Alliance of Businessmen. Pres. Internat. Mgmt. Edn. Found. Decorated grand officer Order of Merit (Peru); commander Order of the Crown (Belgium); Grand Cross of Civil Merit, Grand Cross of Isabella Cath. Mothers of the Americas (Spain). C.P.A., N.Y., Ill. Mem. Am. Inst. C.P.A.'s, Financial Execs. Inst., Soc. C.P.A.'s N.Y. Episcopalian. Clubs: Duquesne (Pitts.); Saint Bartholomew Community House, Oakmont Country, Braeburn Country, Oyster Harbours, Union League (N.Y.C.); Harvard (Boston). Office: 320 Park Av New York City NY 10022

GENERALES, CONSTANTINE DEMOSTHENES JOHN, physician; b. Athens, Greece, Nov. 10, 1908 (parents Am. citizens); s. Demosthences John and Urania (Tselepis) G.; student Harvard, 1925-28, med. sch. univs. Heidelberg, Zurich, Athens, Paris, Berlin, 1929-36; M.D., U. Berlin (Germany), 1936, D.Phil., 1937; postgrad. nuclear physics Columbia U.; m. Johanna Schellekens, Dec. 10, 1938. Asst. U. Women's Clinic, Charité, Berlin, 1934-36; research asst. Inst. Genetics and Animal Breeding, Berlin-Dahlem, 1936-37; faculty N.Y. Med. Coll., 1939-62, asst. prof. space medicine, coordinator space med. program, 1960-62; practice medicine, specializing in internal medicine, chest diseases and space medicine, N.Y.C., 1939—; asso. with N.Y. Cancer Inst., Bellevue Hosp., 1939-42, Met. Hosp., Flower Fifth Av. Hosp., 1939-62, Bird S. Coler Hosp., 1947-62, French Hosp., 1965-69; attending physician, research asso. Mt. Sinai Hosp., 1952—; cons. on space medicine David Sarnoff Research Center, RCA, 1961. Pres. Council for Hellenic Affairs. Bd. dirs. Council on Hosp. Automation. Served with USAAF, 1942-46. Recipient award for original research space medicine and space scis. Hellenic Astron.

Soc., 1961; Am. Bill of Rights award for distinguished service in space medicine, 1963; gold medallion City Thessalonika, 1965; Photenos prize Acad. Athens, 1969; Wisdom award of Honor, 1970; certificate of merit London, 1970; cited in Congl. Record, 1962. Fellow Brit. Interplanetary Soc., Inst. World Affairs, N.Y. Acad. Medicine (co-founder adv. bd. sect. on biomed. engring. 1969—), N.Y. Med. and Surg. Soc., Royal Soc. Health (London), Am. Geriatrics Soc., Hellenic Astronautical Soc. (hon.), Hermann Oberth Gesellschaft (hon.), N.Y. Acad. Scis., A.C.P., Am. Coll. Chest Physicians, N.Y. Cardiol. Soc. (pres. 1967-68), Am. Coll. Angiology, Am. Heart Assn.; mem. A.M.A., Med. Soc. State N.Y. (founder, chmn. sect. on space medicine 1960—), Aerospace Med. Assn., Am. Assn. for History Medicine, Am. Heart Assn., Am. Inst. Aeros. and Astronautics (sr.), I.E.E.E. (sr.), Instrument Soc. Am. (sr.), Société Internationale d'Histoire de la Medicine, Am. Astron. Soc. (sr.), A.A.A.S., Am. Geol. Soc., Am. Geophys. Union, Soc. Biol. Rhythm (Sweden), Am. Fedn. for Clin. Research, Am. Numis. Soc., Marine Tech. Soc. Club: Explorers (N.Y.C.). Author: (with H. Stiasny) Hereditary Disease and Fertility (German), 1937; New Biometric Studies on Human Spermatozoa and Fertility (German), 1938; also numerous articles on space medicine. Asso. editor Jour. Astronautical Scis. Inventor surg. aspiration syringe, Paris, 1932; discovered pathol. spermatozoa morphology in hereditary diseased men, Berlin, 1937; pioneer research (with Wernher von Braun) in space medicine, 1931-32; inventor Biocyclothanation (world's 1st multi- disciplinary subterranean cosmic vehicle simulator for advanced biomed. research), 1960. Home: 2211 Broadway New York City NY 10024 Office: 115 Central Park W New York City NY 10023 ☆

GENERES, LOUIS F., supt. schs.; b. New Orleans, Nov. 20, 1927; s. Louis F., Jr. and Pauline A. (Toujan) G.; B.S. in Elec. Engring., La. State U., 1948, B.S. in Secondary Edn., 1949, M.Ed., 1952; postgrad. Cath. U. Am., 1950-52, Notre Dame Sem., New Orleans, 1952-56. Ordained priest Roman Cath. Ch., 1956; asst. pastor various ch. parishes, 1956-63; asst. supt. sch. Archdiocese New Orleans, 1961-63; chaplain Ursuline Acad., 1963-64; prin. St. John Vianney Prep. Sch., New Orleans, 1964-68; supt. schs. Archdiocese New Orleans, 1968—. Mem. Total Community, Inc., Young Audiences Inc., Tb Assn. Greater New Orleans, WYES-TV Greater New Orleans, Ednl. TV Found., C. of C. New Orleans Area, La. Arts and Sci. Center Adv. Com., La. Adv. Com. Tchr. Edn. and Certification, Jr. Achievement Greater New Orleans; mem. adv. council vocational edn. La. Bd. Edn. Home: 2705 State St New Orleans LA 70118 Office: 7887 Walmsley Av New Orleans LA 70125

GENET, JEAN, playwright; b. Paris, France, Dec. 19, 1910; s. Gabrielle Genet; abandoned as a child; pardoned from life sentence for theft because of his artistic achievement, 1948. Author plays including The Maids, 1947, Deathwatch, 1949, The Balcony, 1956, The Blacks, 1959, The Screens, 1961; novels include Our Lady of the Flowers, 1942, The Thief's Journal, 1949, The Miracle of the Rose, 1966, Querelle of Brest, 1966; also poems and prose poems. Address: care Editions Gallimard 5 rue Sebastien-Bottin Paris 7 France Office: care Rosica Colin 4 Hereford Sq London SW 7 England*

GENG, EDWARD JOSEPH, govt. ofcl.; b. Queens, N.Y., Feb. 9, 1931; s. William and Vera (Scanlan) G.; student Manhattan Coll., 1948-49, Fordham U., 1949-51; B.B.A., St. Johns U., 1957; M.B.A., N.Y. U., 1962; grad. Stonier Grad. Sch. Banking, 1966; m. Arlene Fuchs, Sept. 7, 1957; children—Alan Edward, Glenn William, Scott Matthew. With Gt. A & P Tea Co., N.Y.C., 1949-57 with Fed. Res. Bank of N.Y., 1957-69, asst. sec., 1966-67, asst. v.p. open market operations, 1968-69, 70—; spl. asst. to sec. for debt mgmt. Treasury Dept., Washington, 1969-70. Served with AUS, 1951-53. Recipient Money Marketeers award for U.S. Treasury bills N.Y. U., 1962. Home: 1632 Demott Ct North Merrick NY 11566 Office: Fed Res Bank NY New York City NY 10045

GENGE, WILLIAM HARRISON, advt. exec., writer; b. Warren, Pa., May 7, 1923; s. Valleau Francis and Beatrice (Badger) G.; B.A., U. Pitts., 1948; grad. Internat. Marketing Inst., Harvard, 1967; m. Beverly Ann Milway, June 23, 1945; children—Deborah Ann, William Dean. Writer, Bull. Index, Pitts., 1947- 48; editor Gulf Oil Corp., 1948-53; with Ketchum, MacLeod & Grove, Inc., 1953—, sr. v.p., 1965-68, exec. v.p., 1968-70, pres., 1970—, also dir.; dir. Botsford-Ketchum, Inc. Div. chmn. Allegheny County United Fund, 1968—. Bd. dirs. Pitts. Plan for Art, Pitts. Symphony Soc., Planned Parenthood Assn. Served to 1st lt. USAAF, 1942-46; prisoner of war, 1944-45. Decorated Purple Heart, D.F.C. with oak leaf cluster. Mem. Phi Gamma Delta. Republican. Presbyn. (elder). Clubs: Duquesne, University (Pitts.). Home: 489 Old Clairton Rd Pittsburgh PA 15236 Office: 4 Gateway Center Pittsburgh PA 15222

GENGERELLI, JOSEPH ANTHONY, psychologist, educator; b. Glouster, O., Feb. 2, 1905; s. Nugent and Filomena (Leonetti) G.; A.B., Ohio U., 1925; M.A., U. Wis., 1927; Ph.D., U. Pa., 1928; m. Carmen Noguero y Cierco, Aug. 27, 1942; 1 dau., Carmen Anna Maria. Research fellow Nat. Research Council, Yale, 1928-29; instr. U. Cal., Los Angeles, 1929-32, asst. prof. psychology, 1932-42, asso. prof., 1942-49, prof. 1949—, chmn. dept., 1950-55, devel., dir. constrn. miniature transmitter for radio broadcasting of brain waves; designer method for stimulation brain of waking animal while in process of learning in order to study learning process. Served with planning staff O.S.S., Washington, 1942-44; chief psychol. warfare br., Naples, Italy, 1944-45; chief intelligence officer U.S. Information Service, Am. Zone, Austria, 1945. Mem. Am. Psychol. Assn., Soc. Exptl. Biology and Medicine, N.Y. Acad. Scis., Sigma Xi. Research areas physiol. psychology, exptl. psychology, psychometries, learning theory. Home: 2001 Linda Flora Dr Los Angeles CA 90024 Office: U Cal Los Angeles CA 90024

GENGLER, DOROTHY JEANNE, hosp. adminstr.; b. Mackville, Wis., Feb. 10, 1912; d. Jacob Joseph and Jeannette (Mullen) G.; R.N., Marquette U., 1937, B.S. in Pub. Health, 1957. Staff nurse St. Anthony Hosp., St. Louis, 1937-40; supr. nursing St. Mary Hosp., Racine, Wis., 1940-50, also ednl. dir. A.R.C. aids; nursing service, personnel dir., Waterloo, Ia., 1950-54, also coordinator disaster program; dir. out-patient comprehensive family clinic St. Michael Hosp., Milw., 1953-58, adminstr., 1958-64, dir., 1958—; pres., dir. St. Joseph Hosp., Milw., 1965—; Dir. hosp. bldg. project Milw. Hosp. Council, constrn. program coordinator St. Joseph's Hosp., 1965-68. Mem. United Community Service Greater Milw., 1954—, Area Planning Bd., 1965—. Bd. dirs. Wis. Cath. Conf. Fellow Am. Coll. Hosp. Adminstrs.; mem. Wis. Hosp. Assn. (bd. dirs. 1970—), Mental Health Assn., Coll. Hosp. Adminstrs. Developer psychiat. in-patient unit St. Michael Hosp., 1958, re-organizer out-patient clinic, 1958. Address: 5000 W Chambers Milwaukee WI 53210

GENGRAS, E. CLAYTON, ins. co. exec.; b. W. Hartford, Conn., Aug. 21, 1908; s. Alfred J. and Elizabeth (Doyle) G.; ed. pub. schs.; m. Elizabeth Hutchins, Feb. 11, 1936; children—Elizabeth (Mrs. Peter O Kilbourn), Judith (Mrs. E. Merritt McDonough), Merrily, E. Clayton, Guy, John, Richard, Mark, James, Joel. Pres. Gengras Motors, Inc., Hartford, Conn., 1949—; pres., then chmn. bd., treas. Security-Conn. Ins. Group, New Haven, 1957—; pres. Fire & Casualty Inc. Co., Hartford, 1950-57, chmn. bd., 1957—; chmn. bd., chief exec. officer New Amsterdam Casualty Co., Balt.; dir. Newton Co., Manchester, Conn. Past mem. parole bd. Conn. State Prison, now dir., chmn. bldg. com.; adv. bd. Hartford Girl Scouts Am., Greater Hartford Community Chest; adv. bd., chmn. fund and planning com. St. Joseph Coll., also chmn. spl. gifts com. St. Joseph Cathedral Bldg. Fund; corporator Inst. of Living; bd. dirs. St. Francis Hosp.; chmn. Jesuit Shadowbrook Bldg. Fund; pres. Gengras Found., Inc.; hon. mem. Hartford Assn. Help of Retarded Children. Clubs: Hartford Golf (dir.), Hartford; Wampanoag Country; Carlouel Yacht (Clearwater, Fla.). Home: 1093 Prospect Av West Hartford CT 06007 Office: 175 Whitney Av New Haven CT 06511

GENN, LEO, actor, lawyer; b. London, Eng., Aug. 9, 1905; s. William and Ray (Asserson) G.; M.A., St. Catharine's Coll., Cambridge U., 1927; m. Marquerite van Praag, May 14, 1933. Called to bar, 1928; practice of law, full-time, London, 1928-31, part-time, 1931—. Dir. Bonnar Prodns., Ltd. Distinguished vis. prof. theatre arts Pa. State U., 1968; vis. prof. drama U. Utah, 1969. Motion picture appearances include: Henry V, Green for Danger, Mourning Becomes Electra, Snake Pit, Quo Vadis, Moby Dick, Lady Chatterley's Lover (in French), I Accuse, No Time To Die, The Longest Day, others; N.Y. stage appearances in The Flashing Stream, 1939, Another Part of The Forest, 1946, Small War on Murray Hill, 1957, The Only Game in Town, 1968; title role the Devils Advocate, 1961, others. Councillor, Arts Ednl. Trust, London, Eng.; gov. Mermaid Theatre, London: trustee, bd. mgmt. Yvonne Arnaud Theatre, Guildford, Eng. Served from 2d lt. to lt. col. Royal Arty., 1940-45; comdg. officer cadet tng. unit, 1943-44, No. 1 War Crimes Investigation Team; charge Belsen concentration camp investigation, asst. pros. at trial, 1945. Decorated Croix de Guerre (France); recipient Acad. Award nomination for Quo Vadis, 1952. Home: Locketts Farm Itchingfield Sussex England Office: care AFA Inc 1301 Av of Americas New York City NY 10019

GENNARO, PETER, dancer, choreographer; b. Metairie, La.; s. Charles and Conchetta (Sabella) G.; ed. pub. schs.; student Am. Theatre Wing; m. Jean Kinsella, Jan. 24, 1948; children—Michael, Liza. Danced professionally at San Carlo Opera, 1949, in Broadway prodns. Make Mine Manhattan, 1949, Subway Circuit, 1949, Kiss Me Kate, 1950, Guys and Dolls, 1950, Arms and the Girls, 1950, Pajama Game, 1954, Bells Are Ringing, 1956; choreographer Broadways prodns. Seventh Heaven, 1955, Fiorello, 1959, Mr. President, 1963, Bajour, 1964, film Unsinkable Molly Brown, 1960; co-choreographer Broadway prodn. West Side Story, 1957; TV choreographer, performer Polly Bergen Show, 1958, Andy Williams Show, 1960, Bob Crosby Show, 1960, Perry Como Show, 1961-63, Judy Garland Show, 1964, Bing Crosby Show, 1964, 1965 Acad. Awards, Ed Sullivan Show, 1966, 67, 68; various TV spls., 1967—, Ed Sullivan's Tribute to Irving Berlin, 1968, Recipient Dance Educators Am. award, 1957, Ann. Dance Mag. award, 1965, Boston Dance Assn. award, 1963; nominated for Emmy award for Brigadoon spl., choreography. Address: 228 Alpine Dr Paramus NJ 07652

GENNIS, JOSEPH, physician; b. N.Y.C., Feb. 1, 1912; s. Louis and Ladi (Hammer) G.; B.S. magna cum laude, N.Y.U., 1932, M.D., 1936; m. Sylvia Levine, June 25, 1942; children—Robert Bennett, Paul Richard, Mark Alan, Jean Barbara. Intern N.Y.U. Bellevue Med. Sch. 1936-38; resident Seaview Hosp., S.I., N.Y., 1939; asst. chief med. service VA Hosp., N.Y.C., 1940-54; attending physician Montefiore Hosp., 1954-56; pres. Labs. for Therapeutic Research, Bklyn. Coll. Pharmacy, L.I. U., 1958-70; exec. v.p., exec. editor Med. Tribune, Inc., 1964-70, cons., 1970—. Served as Maj., M.C., AUS, 1944. Albert Gallatin fellow N.Y.U. Diplomate Am. Bd. Internal medicine. Fellow A.C.P., N.Y. Acad. Medicine; mem. A.M.A., N.Y. County Med. Soc., Phi Beta Kappa. Home: 25 Cortlandt Av New Rochelle NY 10801

GENOVESE, EUGENE DOMINICK, educator, historian; b. Bklyn., May 19, 1930; s. Dominick F. and Lena (Chimenti) G.; B.A., Bklyn. Coll., 1953; M.A., Columbia, 1955, Ph.D. (Richard Watson Gilder fellow 1957-58), 1959. Asst. prof. Poly. Inst. Bklyn., 1958-63; asso. prof. Rutgers U., 1963-67; prof. history Sir George Williams U., Montreal, Can., 1967-69; Social Sci. research fellow 1968-69; prof. history U. Rochester, 1969—; vis. prof. Columbia, 1967, Yale, 1969. Served with AUS, 1953-54. Author: The Political Economy of Slavery, 1965; The World the Shareholders Made, 1969; In Red and Black, 1971; also articles, revs. Mem. editorial bd. Jour. Social History. Office: U Rochester Rochester NY 14627

GENOVESE, PASQUALE DANTE, educator, cardiologist; b. N.Y.C., Oct. 19, 1907; s. Anthony and Erminia (Cardieri) G.; B.S., U. Va., 1929; M.D., L.I. Coll. Medicine, 1934; m. Rosita Elena Carlotti, Sept. 26, 1936; children—Pat, Richard, Eleanor (Mrs. Robert Lockman). Intern Flushing Hosp., N.Y.C., 1934-35, resident, 1935-36; asst. cardiologist VA Hosp., Hines, Ill., 1941-42; cardiologist VA Hosp., Wichita, Kan., 1942-43; asst. chief med. service VA Hosp., Indpls., 1946—; instr. medicine Ind. U. Sch. Medicine, 1950-55, asst. prof., 1955-60, asso. prof., 1960-64, prof., 1964—; attending physician, cardiologist Marion County Gen. Hosp., Indpls., 1947—. Served with USNR, 1943-46. Named Outstanding Clinician of Year sr. class Ind. U. Sch. Medicine, 1970. Fellow Am. Coll. Chest Physicians, Am. Coll. Physicians, Am. Coll. Cardiology; mem. Am. Fedn. Clin. Research, Alpha Omega Alpha. Home: 556 N Central Ct Indianapolis IN 46205

GENSAMER, MAXWELL, metallurgist; b. Bradford, Pa., June 3, 1902; s. Francis Xavier and Louise (McCafferty) G.; B.S., Carnegie Inst. Tech., 1924, D.Sc., 1933; m. Betsy Lauze, Dec. 1, 1928 (dec. Oct. 17, 1947) m. 2d, Evelyn Heigley, June 3, 1950. Metallurgist, Am. Chain and Cable Co., Monessen, Pa., 1924-29; research metallurgist, Carnegie Inst. Tech., 1929-35, asst. prof., asso. prof. and prof., 1935-45; prof. metallurgy and head Dept. Mineral Tech., Pa. State Coll., 1945-47; asst. to dir. research, Carnegie Ill. Steel Corp., Pitts., 1947- 50; prof. metallurgy, Columbia U., 1950-39, Howe prof. metallurgy, 1959—; mem. numerous coms. on application of metals; cons. A.E.C., Brookhaven Nat. Lab., Esso. Research & Engring. Co., U.S. Steel Corp. Recipient Howe medal, 1932, Albert E. White Distinguished Tchr. award, 1968 (both from Am. Soc. for Metals). Registered profl. engr., Pa. Mem. Am. Soc. Metals, Am. Inst. Mining and Metall. Engrs. (chmn. Inst. Metals, 1950-51, Howe Meml. lectr. 1958), British Inst. Metals, British Iron and Steel Inst., Am. Soc. for Testing Materials, Tau Beta Pi, Sigma Tau, Phi Kappa Phi, Sigma Xi. Republican. Author: Strength of Metals Under Combined Stresses, 1941. Contbr. numerous articles on metals to profl. and tech. jours. and publs. Delivered Campbell Meml. lecture for Am. Soc. Metals, 1945, Sauveur Meml. lecture, 1945; Andrew Carnegie Meml. lectr., 1962, Zay Jeffries lectr., 1965. Home: 39 Claremont Av New York City NY 10027 also Florence Dr South Chatham MA Office: School of Mines Columbia New York City NY 10027

GENSCHMER, FRED, educator; b. Chgo., Dec. 30, 1906; s. Fred and Alvina (Mueller) G.; B.A., Lake Forest Coll., 1928; M.A., U. Wis., 1929; Ph.D., U. Ill., 1935; m. Eunice V. Teele, June 7, 1935. Instr. German and English, U. Ark., 1929-30; teaching asst. German, U. Ill., 1931-34; head dept. modern langs. Rose Poly Inst., 1934-45; asst. prof. German, U. Minn., 1945-47; prof., chmn. dept. modern langs. N.D. State U., 1947-53; prof., head dept. modern langs. Carnegie-Mellon U., 1953-68, professor of modern languages, 1953—. Fellow for study Inst. Internat. Edn., U. Köln, Germany, 1930-31. Mem. Modern Lang. Assn. Am., Am. Assn. Tchrs. German, Am. Assn. U. Profs. Contbr. articles scholarly jours. Home: 7008 Penn Av Pittsburgh PA 15208

GENTELE, C. GORAN H.A., opera dir.; b. Stockholm, Sweden, Sept. 20, 1917; s. Marit Bergson. With Dramatic Theatre Tng. Sch., Stockholm, 1941-44; actor Dramatic Theatre, 1944-46, stage mgr., 1946-52; staff Royal Theater, 1952—, dir., 1963—; now gen. mgr. Met. Opera Co., Stockholm; vis. stage mgr., Brussels, Belgium, London, Eng.; film writer and producer. Address: Royal Opera House Stockholm Sweden

GENTILE, GEORGE MARVIN, govt. ofcl.; b. Sioux Falls, S.D., Mar. 23, 1922; s. Henry Philip and Mona Susan (Carson) G.; B.S., Northwestern U., 1946; grad. Indsl. Coll. Armed Forces, 1963-64; M.A., George Washington Univ., Washington, 1966; m. Barbara Ellen Foster, Oct. 16, 1948; children—Bruce Foster, Lisabeth Morgan, Ellen Louise. With FBI, 1941-44, 46-52; with CIA, 1952-64; dep. asst. sec. for security State Dept., 1964—. Served with USNR, 1944-46. Mem. Soc. Former Spl. Agts. FBI, Northwestern U. Alumni Assn. Home: 14808 Claude Lane Silver Spring MD 20904 Office: Dept of State Washington DC 20525

GENTNER, WILLIAM ELLIS, Jr., cons., ret. naval officer; b. Douglas, Ariz., July 18, 1907; s. William Ellis and Eva Laura (Simpson) G.; B.S., U.S. Naval Acad., 1930; student U.S. Naval Postgrad. Sch. 1937-39; M.S. in Aero. Engring., Cal. Inst. Tech., 1940; grad. Naval Air Flight Tng. Sch., 1934, Nat. War Coll., 1952; m. Katherine J. La France, Nov. 28, 1935; children—William Ellis III, Barbara J. Commd. ensign U.S. Navy, 1930, advanced through grades to vice adm., 1963; designated naval aviator, 1934; comdg. officer Bombing Squadron 127, 1942-43; operations officer Fleet Air Wing 16, 1943-44; exec. officer carrier U.S.S. Mission Bay, 1944-45; dir. tng. staff comdr. Naval Air Operational Tng., 1945-48; chief staff for operations on staff comdr. Air Force, Pacific Fleet, 1948-50; chief staff comdr. Fleet Air Japan, also liaison officer Gen. Van Fleet, Korea, 1950-51; comdg. officer U.S.S. Rendova, 1953-54, U.S.S. Coral Sea, 1955-56. Carrier Div. 7, Pacific Fleet, 1959-60; dir. strategic plans div. Office Chief Naval Operations, Navy Dept., 1960-63; comdr. U.S. Sixth Fleet, 1963-64; comdr. Taiwan Def. Command on Nationalist Chinese Formosa, 1964- 67; sr. mem. Bd. Decorations and Medals, Navy Dept., 1967-69; retired, 1969; cons. Sperry Rand Corp., 1969—. Decorated D.S.C., Legion of Merit and V, Meritorious Service medal, Bronze Star with gold star, Air medal with gold star, Commendation ribbon D.S.M.; Cruzero Do Sul (Brazil); Cloud and Banner (China). Mem. Naval Acad. Athletic Assn., U.S. Naval, Cal. Inst. Tech. Tech. alumni assns. Home: 2111 Jefferson-Davis Hwy Arlington VA 22202 Office: Sperry Rand Corp Cafritz Bldg Washington DC 20006

GENTRY, BOBBIE, singer, songwriter; b. Chickasaw County, Miss.; student music Los Angeles Conservatory, U. Cal. at Los Angeles. Singer, performer night clubs, TV, concerts; songwriter Ode to Billie Joe, others. Address: care Dir Pub Relations Capitol Records 1750 N Vine St Hollywood CA 90028

GENTRY, BYRON BURK, lawyer, assn. ofcl.; b. Coulee City, Wash., Oct. 20, 1913; s. James J. and Evelena (Burke) G.; A.B., U. So. Cal., 1936; J.D., Southwestern U., 1942; m. Ruth Genevieve Jensen, Sept. 10, 1949; children—Kathleen, Sharon. Admitted to Cal. bar, 1948, U.S. Supreme Ct., 1958; dep. city atty., Los Angeles, 1948; asst. city pros., Pasadena, 1948-50, city pros., 1950—; pvt. civil law practice. Mem. V.F.W., 1949—, mem. Cal. com. 1956-57, mem. nat. council adminstrn., 1957-59, judge adv. gen., 1959-60, nat. jr. vice comdr.-in-chief, 1960-61, nat. sr. vice comdr.-in-chief, 1961-62, nat. comdr.-in-chief, 1962-63. Instr. Cal. Peace Officers Traffic Inst., 1959-62; co-founder, past pres. Pasadena Com. Edn. on Alcoholism, Pasadena Com. Narcotics Edn.; mem. Los Angeles County Com. Aging; bd. dirs. Los Angeles County Com. Aging Assos., Inc., 1963—; mem. Cal. Vets. Bd., 1957-69, chmn., 1960. Bd. dirs. Am. Gold Star Mothers Home, Pasadena Com. Employment Physically Handicapped, Los Angeles Vets. Service Center; bd. visitors Freedoms Found. at Valley Forge. Served to capt. AUS, 1942-46. Decorated Presdl. citation, combat and area ribbons; Fourragere (Belgium); Combat Cross (France), USAF Exceptional Service medal, Freedoms Found. Distinguished Service award, V.F.W. Distinguished Service medal, French Combat Medal of Merit; recipient Distinguished Vet. award Am. Legion, 1963; Merit award U. So. Cal. Gen. Alumni Assn., 1965; Wisdom Honor award, 1970. Mem. U.S. Supreme Ct., Cal., Pasadena bar assns., Internat. Platform Assn., Phi Alpha Delta, Phi Kappa Tau. Author: (verse) Voices of the Airways, 1962; (prose, essays) The Way the Ball Bounces, 1962; other poems, numerous mag. articles. Home: Route 1 Box 189 Paso Robles CA 93446 Office: 142 N Arroyo Pkwy Pasadena CA 91101

GENTRY, GRANT CLAYBOURNE, retail exec., lawyer; b. Chgo., June 5, 1924; s. Grant Claybourne and Helen (Cooley) G.; J.D., DePaul U., 1949; m. Doris Lorraine Helsten, Sept. 8, 1943; children—Grant Claybourne III, Scott Wesley. Admitted to Ill. bar, 1949; asso. firm McKnight, McLaughlin & Dunn, Chgo., 1949-53; tax atty. Internat. Harvester Co., 1953-57; asst. sec., corp. atty. Jewel Cos., Inc., Chgo., 1957-64, v.p., sec., gen. counsel, 1964-70, exec. v.p. adminstrn., gen. counsel, 1970—, also dir.; adv. bd. Arkwright-Boston Ins. Co.; dir. Midco, S.A. Mem. Gov.'s Revenue Study Com., 1968-69; bd. dirs. Nat. Assn. Food Chains. Mem. bd. lay trustees Loyola U., Chgo. Served with 11th Airborne Div., AUS, World War II. Decorated Purple Heart. Mem. Am. Soc. Corporate Secs., Econ. Club Chgo., Phi Alpha Delta, Phi Kappa Delta. Clubs: Glen View; Union League (Chgo.). Home 524 S Patton Av Arlington Heights IL 60005 Office: 5725 E River Rd Chicago IL 60631

GENTRY, JOHN TILMON, physician, educator; b. St. Louis, Dec. 31, 1921; s. John Tilmon and Ethel Marie (Hambley) G.; A.B., Washington U., St. Louis, 1944, B.S., M.D., 1948; M.P.H., Harvard, 1951; m. Geraldine Evelyn Heyne, Feb. 5, 1949; children—John A., Kristine A., David T., Laurie J., Glenn S. Intern U. Chgo. Clinics, 1948-49; resident pub. health N.Y. State Dept. Health, 1949-50; asst. to chief epidemiology br. Communicable Disease Center, USPHS, Atlanta, 1951-52; health officer, Anchorage, Alaska, 1952- 53; dist. health officer N.Y. State Dept. Health, Syracuse, 1954-57, regional dir., Syracuse, 1957-64; clin. asst. prof. preventive medicine State U. N.Y., Upstate Med. Center, Syracuse, 1955-63, asso. prof., 1963- 64; prof., dir. program in med. care and health services adminstrn. U. N.C. Sch. Pub. Health, 1964—; adj. prof. hosp. adminstrn. Duke U., Durham, N.C., 1970—; cons. div. radiol. health USPHS, 1959-62; chief med. edn. br., dept. chief health div. AID mission to India, New Delhi, 1961-63, acting chief health div., 1961-62. Mem. vital statistics com. USPHS, 1960-61; chmn. regional planning com. health White House Conf. Children and Youth, 1960, mem. regional planning com. 1961 Conf. Aged; exec. com. N.Y. Regional Hosp. Planning Council, 1957-61, trustee, 1963-64; chmn. maternal and child health com. N.Y. State Conf. City, County and Dist. Health Officers, 1956; vice chmn. Syracuse regional N.Y. State Regional Mental Health Planning Com., 1963-64, N.Y. State Regional Interdepartmental Rehab. Com., 1963-64; mem. population panel White House Conf. Internat. Coop., 1965. Bd. dirs. Onondaga County unit Am. Cancer Soc., 1954-60, Onondaga County United Cerebral Palsy Assn., 1954-58, Onondaga

Health Assn., 1954-64, Cayuga Health Assn., 1954-58; bd. dirs. council aging Council Social Agencies Onondaga County, 1954- 60, legislative committee, 1955-64, chmn. planning com. health and hosp. div., 1955-60; self-study cons. Nat. Commn. on Community Health Services, Charleston, S.C., 1964-65; cons. Forsyth County Citizens Planning Council, 1964-65; instl. rep., mem. exec. com. N.C. State Adv. Com. Devel. Regional Med. Complex, 1965-68. Diplomate Am. Bd. Preventive Medicine. Fellow Am. Coll. Preventive Medicine (charter), Am. Pub. Health Assn.; mem. A.A.A.S., N.Y. Acad. Scis., Am. Thoracic Soc., A.M.A., Population Assn. Am. N.C. Acad. Preventive Medicine and Public Health, N.C. State Public Health Association, New York Acad. Preventive Medicine (charter), N.Y. State Pub. Health Assn., Phi Beta Kappa, Delta Omega. Contbr. articles profl. jours. Home: 2018 N Lake Shore Dr Chapel Hill NC 27514

GENTRY, REED OVERTON, lawyer; b. Kansas City, Mo., June 23, 1917; s. Reed Gilbert and Georgia (Lawrence) G.; student Jr. Coll. Kansas City, 1933-35; A.A., U. Mo., 1937; LL.B., U. Mo. at Kansas City, 1940; m. Dorothy E. Foerschler, Mar. 15, 1942; children—Dorothy (Mrs. John J. Schmersey), Nicholas R. Admitted to Mo. bar, 1940, since practiced in Kansas City; partner Rogers, Field, Gentry, Benjamin & Robertson. Dir. Mercantile Bank & Trust Co. Chmn. Citizens Assn., 1966-67. Mem. Kansas City City Council, 1948-57. Served to capt., AUS, 1942-46. Fellow Am. Coll. Trial Lawyers; mem. Am., Mo., Kansas City bar assns., Am. Judicature Soc., Lawyers Assn. Kansas City. Home: 11906 Washington St Kansas City MO 64114 Office: 600 E 11th St Kansas City MO 64106

GENTRY, RICHARD HOMER, educator; b. Lookeba, Okla., Sept. 29, 1929; s. Jason Homer and Hattie Emmaline (Holland) G.; B.A. in Journalism, U. Tulsa, 1951; M.A., Stanford, 1954; Ph.D. in Communications, U. Ill., 1960; m. Diane Kay Koos, June 8, 1966. Reporter, copyreader Tulsa World, 1948-52; acting instr. Stanford, 1952-53; teaching asst. journalism U. Ill., 1953-56; instr. Rutgers U., 1956-59; asst. prof., then asso. prof. Ohio U. Sch. Journalism, 1959-68; Lozano prof., chmn. journalism Trinity U., San Antonio, 1968—. Dir. Bexar County Election Bur. Mem Sierra Club (treas. S. Tex. chpt. 1971), Sigma Delta Chi (pres. San Antonio chpt. 1971), Kappa Tau Alpha, Alpha Delta Sigma. Home: 105 End Gate Lane San Antonio TX 78231

GENTZLER, WALDO EMERSON, cons.; b. York, Pa., July 3, 1903; s. Milton J. and Elizabeth Thomas (Schriver) G.; B.S., Gettysburg Coll., 1925; A.M., Columbia, 1927; m. Helen Loftus Duck, Apr. 4, 1940; Tchr. math. Vermont Acad., Saxtons River, 1925-26; asst. math. Columbia, 1927-28, instr., 1928- 30, asst. dir. univ. extension, 1928-30, sec. appointments, 1930-35, bursar of univ., 1935-49, bus. mgr., 1949-50, asst. provost, dir. students interests, 1950-56; trustee Empire City Savs. Bank, N.Y.C., 1938-67, exec. v.p., 1956-57, pres., 1957-67; chmn. bd. Empire Savs. Bank (merger Empire City Savs. Bank and Excelsior Savs. Bank), 1967-68, trustee, 1967—; dir. M.S.B. Fund. Bd. dirs. Operation-Crossroads Africa, treas., 1957-67; trustee Knickerbocker Hosp., N.Y.C., 1937-69, treas., 1945-47, pres., 1948-50; dir. Manhattanville Community Centers, 1948-69, pres., 1957-60; dir. Asso. Hosp. Service of N.Y., 1948-59; bd. publs. United Luth. Ch. in Am., 1960-62; mem. bd. pensions Luth. Ch. in Am., 1962—, v.p., 1966-68, pres., 1968—; treas. Luth. Council in U.S.A., 1966; trustee Gettysburg Coll., 1952-58. Mem. U.S., N.Y. (chmn. com. edn. 1960-62, chmn. com. city affairs 1965-67; chmn. adv. com. vocational edn. 1966-68) chambers commerce, Phi Beta Kappa, Phi Delta Theta, Kappa Phi Kappa. Lutheran. Clubs: University (N.Y.); Country (York, Pa.), Home: 203 Chadwick Rd Teaneck NJ 07666 Office: 830 3d Av New York City NY 10022

GENZ, LEONARD FRANCIS, corp. ofcl., lawyer; b. Elizabeth, N.J., Nov. 26, 1908; s. Alexander and Catherine (O'Brien) G.; Ph.B., Yale, 1930; J.D., St. John's U., 1941; m. Martha Virginia Tidwell, Apr. 27, 1946; 1 son, Michael Andrew. With Elizabethtown Gas Co., 1931-33; sales supr. Bklyn. Union Gas Co., 1934-41, asst. sec., 1946- 49; admitted to N.Y. bar, 1946, Tex. bar, 1950, U.S. Supreme Ct. bar, 1950; practiced in Tex., 1950; with RCA Victor, Rio de Janeiro, Brazil, 1951-52; exec. dir. Am. Soc. Corporate Secs., 1952-54; asst. sec. Gen. Foods Corp., 1954, sec., 1955- -, v.p., 1967—; pres. and trustee Gen. Foods Fund. Inc. Trustee, U.S. Naval Aviation Mus., U.S. Naval Acad. Found.; bd. dirs. Marjorie Merriweather Post Found., Winston Churchill Meml. Found. Served with USNR, 1941-46, asst. naval attache, Chile, 1942-43, on staff of Comdr. S. Pacific, 1943-44, liaison officer Brit. Admiralty London, 1945-46; capt. USNR ret. Cited by Sec. of Navy, 1964, 68; recipient N.Y. State Conspicuous Service Cross, 1965. Mem. Tex., N.Y. State bar assns., Am. Soc. Corporate Secs., Am. Arbitration Assn. (nat. panel), Navy League, U.S. Lawn Tennis Umpires Assn., Am. Polar Soc., Soc. South Pole, Delta Kappa Epsilon, Phi Delta Phi. Roman Catholic. Clubs: Yale (N.Y.C.); Westchester Country, Milbrook; Explorers. Home: 1 Putnam Park Greenwich CT 06830 Office: 250 North St White Plains NY 10602

GEOFFREY, JAWAID IQBAL, artist; b. Chiniot, Pakistan, Jan. 1, 1939; s. Syed Iqbal Hussian and Shahzadi (Mumtazjehan) Shah; B.A., Panjab U., 1957; LL.B. summa cum laude, 1959, D.F.A., 1962; LL.M., Harvard, 1966; A.M.B.I.M., London, 1969; m. Regina Wai-Ling Cheng, 1967; 1 son, Syed. Prin. one man shows include Hull U., New Vision Center, London, Arts Council No. Ireland, Belfast, Queens U., Belfast, 1962, Swetzoff Gallery, Boston, Los Angeles Municipal Art Gallery, Grand Central Moderns, N.Y.C., Kaiser Center Art Mus., Oakland, Cal., 1963, Radcliffe Coll., Arts Council Pakistan, Lahore, Henri Gallery, Alexandria, Miami Mus. Modern Art, 1964, Ward-Nasse Gallery, Boston, Greenross, N.Y.C., Kovler Gallery, Chgo., Seton Hall U., Theodore Lyman Wright Art Center, Beloit, Wis., 1965; (on tour Nihonbashi Gallery, Tokyo, Mexico Nat. Mus. Modern Art, Ward-Nasse Gallery, Boston, Santa Barbara Mus. Art, Am. Friends Middle East, 1966; participant collective exhbns. 20th Century art in Europe, U.S. and Japan, including Paris Biennial, 1963, 65, Sao Paulo Biennial, 1963, 65, Tokyo and Ljubljana Biennials, 1965; rep. permanent collections Boston Mus. Fine Arts, Phillips Collection, Washington, Phoenix Mus. Art, Tate Gallery, Arts Council Gt. Britain, Brit. Mus., London, Brit. Govt., Chase Manhattan Bank. Sr. partner Geoffrey & Khitran, 1961-66; human rights officer UN, 1966-67; vis. prof. fine arts St. Mary's Coll., Notre Dame, Ind., 1967-68; pres. Mus. Modern Art, Lahore, Pakistan, 1969- -. Recipient hon. mention Paris Biennial, 1965; Huntington Hartford Found. fellowship, 1962; Fay B. Kent fellowship, Alpha Chi Omega, 1963; JDR 3d fellowship, 1964. Fellow Royal Soc. Art; mem. Assn. Indsl. Comml. Exec. Accountants. Author: Qose-Qizah, 1957; A Critical Study of Moral Dilemmas, Iconographical Confusions and Complicated Politics of XX Century, 1967. Contbr. articles profl. publs. Grad. editor Harvard Art Rev., 1965-66. Home: Sul Sabeel Shahra-e-Iqbal Gulberg 3 Lahore Pakistan Office: Dept Fine Arts St Mary's Coll Notre Dame IN 46556

GEOFFRION, CHRISTOPHE ANTOINE, lawyer; b. Montreal, Can., Mar. 14, 1916; s. Aime and Rita (Thibeaudeau) B.; LL.B., U. Montreal, 1937; m. Madeleine Amyot, Sept. 9, 1944; children—Anne-Claude, Christine. Called to Que. bar, 1937, created Queen's counsel, 1960; with firm Geoffrion & Prud'homme, Montreal, 1937- -, sr. partner, 1962—. Dir. Royal Trust Co., Abitibi Paper Co., Can. Steamship Lines Ltd., Great-West Life Assurance Co., Investors Growth Fund Can. Ltd., Investors Mut. Can. Ltd., Melchers Distilleries Ltd., Viau Ltd., Canadian Merrill Ltd., Quebecair Inc., MonDev Corp., Ltd. With Dept. Munitions and Supply, also Wartime Shipping Bd., Ottawa, 1941-44. Bd. dirs Canadian Council Christians and Jews. Mem. Canadian Bar Assn., Internat. Law Assn., Canadian Tax Found. Roman Cath. Home: 26 Sunnyside Av Westmount 217 Quebec Canada Office: 500 Place d'Armes Montreal 126 Quebec Canada

GEOFFROY, CHARLES HENRY, advt. agy. exec.; b. Longford, Ireland, Sept. 24, 1926; s. Francis Louis and Kathleen Elizabeth (Fetherston) G.; came to U.S., 1927, naturalized, 1945; B.A., Haverford Coll., 1949; postgrad. U. Pa., 1950; m. Alida Baird McClenahan, Apr. 24, 1954; children—Evan Lloyd, Mark Lee, Douglas Baird. Ins. adjuster Gen. Motors Ins. Corp., Phila., 1950-51; mgr. research dept. Ward Wheelock Co., Phila., 1951-54; asso. research dir., account exec. Lennen & Newell, Inc., N.Y.C., 1954-59; account exec. Young & Rubicam, Inc., N.Y.C., 1959-64, v.p., Los Angeles, 1965-67; pres., mng. dir. Young & Rubicam, Ltd., Toronto, Ont., Can., 1968—, also dir.; dir. Bur. Indsl. Services, Ltd. Served with AUS, 1945-46. Clubs: Riverside (Conn.) Yacht; Oakville (Ont.); National (Toronto). Home: 277 Dalewood Dr Oakville Ontario Canada Office: 250 University Av Toronto Ontario Canada

GEOGHAN, WILLIAM F.X., Jr., lawyer; b. Bklyn., Jan. 25, 1918; A.B., Georgetown U., 1939; LL.B., Fordham U., 1947. Admitted to N.Y. bar, 1947; mem. firm Speiser, Shumate, Geoghan, Krause and Rheingold, N.Y.C.; lectr. trial tactics Practising Law Inst., 1959—; guest lectr. trial tactics Fordham Law Sch., 1955—, St. John's Law Sch., 1958—, Syracuse U. Law Sch., 1959, Bklyn. Law Sch., 1959-62, U. Tenn. Law Sch., 1961; guest lectr. med.-legal problems A.M.A., 1961, Am. Heart Assn., 1961. Fellow Internat. Acad. Trial Lawyers; mem. Bd. Edn. Manhasset, N.Y., 1959-65. Mem. Assn. Bar City N.Y. (mem. com. on cts. of superior jurisdiction 1957-60), Nassau County, Queens County, N.Y. State (mem. com. on aviation law 1961-63), Am. bar assns., Met. Trial Lawyers Assn. (v.p. 1961-63, pres. 1963-65), N.Y. County Lawyers Assn. (mem. com. on aero. law 1968—), N.Y. State Assn. Trial Lawyers (dir. 1964—), Am. Trial Lawyers Assn. (bd. govs. 1967—). Office: Pan Am Bldg 200 Park Av New York City NY 10017*

GEOGHEGAN, JOHN JOSEPH, publisher; b. Phila., Mar. 14, 1917; s. John Joseph and Kathryn Genevieve (Landers) G.; student Columbia Extension Sch., 1942. U.S. Air Force Sch. Engring. and Operations, 1943; m. Margaret Anna Chittick, June, 1940; children—Michael, Peter, Margaret Kathryn, John Joseph II. Publishers rep. J.B. Lippincott Co., 1945-48; pub. rep. Doubleday & Co., 1948-53, trade advt. mgr., 1953-55, West Coast editorial rep., dist. sales mgr., 1955-58; v.p., mgr. trade dept. Coward-McCann and Geoghegan, Inc., N.Y.C., 1959, editor-in-chief, 1959-60, pres., 1960—; dir. G.P. Putnam's Sons, Berkeley Pub. Co. N.Y. Served with USAAF, 1942-45; China. Clubs: Aspetuck Country (Weston); Editors Lunch, Players (N.Y.C.); Publishers Lunch. Author short stories. Home: Lilac Lane Weston CT 06880 Office: 210 Madison Av New York City NY 10016

GEOGHEGAN, PHILMORE WOODLAND, banker; b. Cambridge, Md., Jan. 24, 1911; s. Howard Philmore and Martha (Johnson) G.; B.S. in Econs., Johns Hopkins, 1931; m. Marion A. Sibbet, June 25, 1938; children—William Howard, John Sibbet. With comptrollers dept. Nat. City Bank N.Y., 1931-38; with Md. Nat. Bank, Balt., 1938—, v.p., 1959—, cashier, 1964—. Trustee, asst. treas. Roland Park Country Sch., Balt., 1966—; sec., mem. exec. com. Md. Gen. Hosp., Balt., 1958—; trustee, treas. Balt. Conf. Pensions Fund, 1952—; trustee Md. Bible Soc., 1960—. Mem. Kappa Alpha. Clubs: Merchants, Johns Hopkins (Balt.). 708 Regester Av Baltimore MD 21212

GEOGHEGAN, WILLIAM ALOYSIUS, lawyer, former govt. ofcl.; b. Cin., Jan. 3, 1925; s. Thomas M. and Stella (Griffin) G.; student Xavier U., 1942-43, U. Fla., 1943-44; B.A., U. Cin., 1951; LL.B., Harvard, 1949; m. Margaret Brown, Sept. 24, 1955; children—Kathy, Beth, Ann, Mary. Admitted to Ohio bar, 1949; asso. Geoghegan, Levy & Daly, Cin., 1949-55; with Dinsmore, Shohl, Barrett, Coates & Deupree, and predecessors, Cin., 1955-61, partner, 1958-61; asst. dep. atty. gen. Dept. Justice, 1961-65; partner Pierson, Ball & Dowd, Washington, 1965—. Active United Appeal, Red Cross fund-raising drives. Pres. Cin. bur. Govtl. Research, Inc.; bd. govs. Alumni Xavier U.; dir. Cin. chpt. Nat. Conf. Christians and Jews. Served with inf. AUS, 1943-45. Home; 9612 Acord Dr Potamac MD 20854 Office: Ring Bldg Washington DC 20036

GEOGHEGAN, WILLIAM DAVIDSON, educator and clergyman; b. Wilmington, Del., July 16, 1922; s. Presley Downs and Mildred (Davidson) G.; B.A., Yale, 1943; student Harvard Div. Sch., 1943-44; B.D., Drew Theol. Sem., 1945; Ph.D., Columbia-Union Theol. Sem., 1951; m. Sarah Elizabeth Phelps, Oct. 5, 1946; children—Grace Elizabeth, Andrew Phelps, Emily Bernice, William Davidson II. Ordained to ministry Methodist Ch., 1947; pastor in Christiana, Del., 1944-47; tchr. jr. high sch., New Castle, Del., 1945- 56; chaplain, asst. prof. religion U. Rochester, 1950-54; prof. religion, chmn. dept. Bowdoin Coll., 1954—. Mem. Am. Acad. Religion, Am. Assn. U. Profs., Soc. Sci. Study Religion, Phi Beta Kappa, Zeta Psi. Republican. Author: Platonism in Recent Religious Thought, 1958. Home: 40 Federal St Brunswick ME 04011 also PO Box 336 Wolfeboro NH 03894

GEORG, ANDERS, Danish diplomat; b. Copenhagen, Denmark, Feb. 10, 1919; s. Carl and Kirsten (Friis) G.; ed. Sortedam Gymnasium, 1936; m. Annette Knuth, Feb. 16, 1952; 1 dau., Susanne. Journalist, provincial papers; 1937-40; fgn. corr. Politiken, Stockholm, Sweden, 1945, London, Eng., 1946-50; press. attache hosp. ship Jutlandia, Korea, 1951-53; corr. Berlingske Tidende, Washington, 1957-67; editorial writer, 1967-70; press counselor Danish embassy, Washington, 1970—. Recipient Jutlandia medal, 1952, UN Service medal, 1952; decorated knight Order Solomon's Seal (Ethiopia). Mem. Publicistklubben (Copenhagen). Clubs: Nat. Press, Federal City (Washington). Author: Under Three Flags, 1951; Along the Bamboo Curtain, 1953; Decision in Vietnam, 1962; After Lyndon Johnson, 1968 (all in Danish). Home: 4867 Glenbrook Rd NW Washington DC 20015 Office: Danish Embassy 3200 Whitehaven St NW Washington DC 20008

GEORGE, BEAUFORD JAMES, Jr., educator; b. Kansas City, Mo., Oct. 16, 1925; s. Beauford James and Elizabeth (Pope) G.; B.A., U. Mich., 1949, J.D., 1951; m. Grace Isabella Loucks, June 17, 1950; children—Paul, Andrew, Nancy. Asst. prof. law U. Mich., Ann Arbor, 1952-55, asso. prof., 1955-58, prof., 1958-68; lectr. law Kyoto U., 1956-57; lectr. fgn. law Tokyo U., 1962-63; asso. dir. Practicing Law Inst., N.Y.C., 1968-71; adj. prof. law N.Y. U., 1968-71; prof. law, dir. Center for Adminstrn. Justice, Wayne State U., Detroit, 1971—. Mem. Gov. Mich. Commn. on Crime, Delinquency and Criminal Adminstrn., 1966-68. Served with inf. AUS, 1943-46. Mem. Am. Law Inst., Am. Bar Assn., State Bar Mich., Internat. Penal Law Assn. (past pres. Am. chpt.), Order of Coif. Baptist. Editor-in-chief Am. Jour. of Comparative Law, 1966-68. Home: 1030 Spruce Dr Ann Arbor MI 48104 Office: Wayne State Univ Law School Detroit MI 48202

GEORGE, CHARLES, corp. exec.; b. Williamsport, Pa., Mar. 17, 1919; s. George and Helen (Mitchell) G.; B.S. in Metall. Engring., Columbia, 1943; M.B.A., N.Y. U., 1945; m. Martha Allen Hardy, Apr. 18, 1964; children—Charles, Christopher Corey. Former chmn. bd., pres. Telerad Mfg. Corp., Flemington, N.J., 1948-61, dir., 1948-62; pres. govt. support div. Lionel Corp., Hillside, N.J., 1961-62; chmn. bd., pres. Oral Books, Inc., N.Y.C., 1961—, also dir.; chmn. bd., chief exec. officer, dir. Internat. Breweries, Inc., Buffalo, 1965; chmn. Lee Myles Corp.; pres. Lee Myles Assos. Corp., TPM Corp.; dir. Mardon Realty, Hunterdon Finance Co.; cons. Lionel Corp., Servo Corp. Am. Named Ky. col., 1965. Mem. Young Pres. Orgn. (co-chmn. Eastern area conf. 1967), Am. Soc. Metals, I.E.E.E. Episcopalian. Club: Capri Yacht (Manorhaven). Home: 35 South Dr Gt Neck Estates NY 11021 Office: 59-24 Maurice Av Maspeth NY 11378

GEORGE, CLARKE MARANVILLE, fgn. service officer; b. Santa Barbara, Cal., May 24, 1911; s. Frank John and Josephine Ellen (Maranville) G.; A.B., Santa Barbara State Coll., 1933; postgrad. U. Cal., 1939-40, Am. U., 1942-43, Blackstone Coll. Law, Chgo., 1948-49; m. Edna Fern Hollister, Dec. 18, 1937; children—Eugene Owen, Donald Clark, Guy Hollister, m. 2d, Chung Hee Kim, Apr. 4, 1958; children—Leland Kim, Audrey Ellen. Free lance reporter, Santa Barbara, 1934-37; reporter San Luis Obispo (Cal.) Telegram-Tribune, 1937; clk. U.S. Customs Service, San Francisco, 1937-42; shipfitter trainee Kaiser Richmond Shipyard, 1942; jr. economist U.S. Tariff Commn., Washington, 1942-44; econ. analyst SCAP, Nagoya, Japan, 1946-47; econ. officer Dept. Army, Tokai-Hokuriku Region, Japan, 1947-51, internat. economist, Korea, 1951; adviser UN Civil Assistance Command to Rep. of Korea, 1952-56; program operations officer ICA, Seoul, Korea, 1952-56; asst. program officer, Mogadiscio, Somalia, Republic, 1958-60; program officer ICA/AID, Freetown, Sierra Leone, 1961-64, affairs officer, 1965; asst. dir. program AID, Dar es Salaam, Tanzania, 1966-69, Mogadiscio, 1969—. Oboe, English horn player civic orchs. Served to lt. USNR, 1944-46. Mem. Am. Fgn. Service Assn., Am. Econ. Assn., Acad. Polit. and Social Sci., Nat. Planning Assn. Home: 2047 Mountain Av Santa Barbara CA 93101 Office: Mogadiscio (ID) Dept State Washington DC 20521

GEORGE, CLAUDE SWANSON, Jr., univ. dean; b. Danville, Va., June 4, 1920; s. Claude Swanson and Myrtle Ann (Dillard) G.; B.S., U. N.C., 1942, M.S., 1951; Ph.D., State U. Ia., 1953; m. Eleanor Anthony, Dec. 22, 1960. Mem. mgmt. staff Western Electric Co., 1946-50; instr. State U. Ia., 1951-53; asso. prof. magmt. U. Tex., 1953-54; prof. indsl. mgmt. U. N.C., 1954—, asso. dean Sch. Bus. Adminstrn., 1958—. Fellow Acad. Mgmt.; mem. Soc. Advanced Mgmt., So. Mgmt. Assn., Phi Beta Kappa, Beta Gamma Sigma, Order Artus, Sigma Iota Epsilon, Delta Sigma Pi. Author: Management in Industry, 2d edit., 1964; The History of Management Thought, 1968; Management for Business and Industry, 1970. Home: Coker Dr Chapel Hill NC 27514

GEORGE, COLLINS CRUSOR, music critic; b. Washington, June 30, 1909; s. John S. and Margaret (Crusor) G.; A.B., Howard U., 1929; M.A. in Anthropology, Harvard, 1932; A.M. in French, U. So. Cal., 1939. Tchr. English, A. and T. Coll., Greensboro, N.C., 1932-33; tchr. French and German, Langston (Okla.) U., 1933-35, Lemoyne Coll., Memphis, 1935-42; with Pitts. Courier, 1944-53, mng. editor Detroit edit., 1946-53; with Detroit Free Press, 1953—, music critic, 1960—; conductor classical music program, radio sta. WQRS- FM; music columnist Birmingham (Mich.) Eccentric, 1968—. Mem. Am. Newspaper Guild, Music Critics Assn., Detroit Hist. Soc., Sigma Delta Chi, Omega Psi Phi. Club: Detroit Press. Home: 1525 Cherboneau St Detroit MI 48207 Office: 321 W Lafayette St Detroit MI 48226

GEORGE, EDWIN ORDELL, utility exec.; b. Petoskey, Mich., Feb. 9, 1905; s. Edward Daley and Ethel (Brott) G.; student Alma Coll., 1925; A.B., Knox Coll., 1928; M.A. U. Ill., 1929; postgrad. Wayne U., 1938; LL.D., No. Mich. U., 1966; m. Florence E. Watchpocket, June 6, 1931; 1 dau., Julie Ann (Mrs. Glenn Pope, Jr.). With Detroit Edison Co., 1929—, comml. office clk., supr. tng., asst. supr. comml. office div., supr. comml. office div., asst. comml. mgr., comml. mgr., mgr. sales, 1929-56, v.p., 1956-65, sr. v.p., 1965-67, exec. v.p. for marketing, 1967, pres., 1967-70, dir., 1967—; dir. Reddy Kilowatt, Inc., First Fed. Savs. Detroit, Panax Corp. Chmn. bldg. and grounds com. Meadow Brook Music Festival; mem. adv. bd. Salvation Army; dir., past pres. Detroit Ednl. TV Found.; pres. Traffic Improvement Assn. Oakland County; v.p. Detroit Adventure. Bd. dirs. Grand Opera Assn., Seven Ponds Nature Center; bd. dirs., past pres. Detroit Area council Boy Scouts Am.; trustee Detroit Sci. Center, Detroit Renaissance '70's, Detroit Area Council World Affairs, Oakland U. Found., Grace Hosp., Detroit Country Day Sch.; trustee, mem. exec. com. Alma Coll.; chmn. bd. trustees Merrill-Palmer Inst., trustee, adv. council Detroit Renaissance, mem. bd. control, past chmn. No. Mich. U.; mem. exec. bd., past pres. Greater Mich. Found. Mem. Nat. Alliance Businessmen (former met. chmn.), World Soc. for Ekistics, Newcomen Soc. N.Am., Pi Kappa Delta, Pi Gamma Nu. Presbyn. (trustee). Clubs: Rotary (past pres.), Detroit Athletic (past pres., dir.), Detroit (Detroit); Circumnavigators (past pres. Mich. br.); Oakland Hills Country. Home: 352 Barden Rd Bloomfield Hills MI 48013 Office: 1132 Washington Blvd Detroit MI 48226

GEORGE, HAROLD LEE, ret. air force officer; b. Somerville, Mass., July 19, 1893; s. Horace and Susan Elizabeth (Lee) G.; LL.B., George Washington U., 1920; grad. Air Corps Tactical Sch., 1932, Command and Gen. Staff Sch., 1937; D.Aero. Scis., Pa. Mil. Coll., 1943; rated command pilot, combat and aircraft observer; m. Violette A. Houghlan, May 26, 1929; children—Mary Suzanne, Sidney Regina, Loretta Adrian. Commd. 2d lt. U.S. Army Air Force, 1917; advanced through grades to lieut. gen. 1944, ret., 1947; comdg. officer 2d Bombardment Group, 1939; dir. dept. tactics and strategy Air Corps Tactical Sch., 1932-35; asst. chief of staff for war plans, 1941; comdg. gen. Air Transport Command, Army Air Forces, 1942-46; chmn. bd., pres. Peruvian Airways, Lima, Peru, 1947- 48; past v.p. Hughes Tool Co.; gen. mgr. Hughes Aircraft Co., Culver City, 1948-53; ret. v.p. Thompson-Ramo-Wooldridge Corp., Los Angeles, 1960. Mem. city council, mayor, Beverly Hills, Cal., 1952-60. Decorated D.F.C., Air medal, D.S.M., Legion of Merit; knight comdr. Order Brit. Empire; Order of Cloud-Banner, China; comdr. Legion of Honor, France; Distinguished Flying Cross, Peru. Mem. Order of Daedalians, Omicron Delta. Mason. Clubs: Army and Navy (Washington), Nacional (Lima, Peru), Jonathan (Los Angeles), Los Angeles Country; Fort Worth (Tex.). Home: 10101 Wilshire Blvd Los Angeles CA 90024

GEORGE, JOHN DEMOSTHENES, steel co. exec.; b. Phila., May 11, 1926; s. John Kyriakos and Catherine (Balson) G.; B.S., Temple U., 1956, M.B.A., 1967; m. Mary Thomas Vassos, Nov. 8, 1959; children— Katherine Joanne, Athanasius D. Chief accountant Kellett Aircraft Corp., Horsham, Pa., 1951-65; controller Spitz Labs., Inc., Chadds Ford, Pa., 1965-70; corporate controller Phoenix Steel Corp., Claymont, Del., 1970—. Vice pres. Phila. chpt. Greek Orthodox

Youth of Am. Mem. Nat. Assn. Accountants, Am. Accounting Assn. Republican. Greek Orthodox (sec., dir.). Club: Hellenic University (past dir., treas.) (Wilmington). Home: 3122 Wilmont Dr Wilmington DE 19810 Office: Phoenix Steel Corp Claymont DE

GEORGE, JOSEPH JOHNSON, meteorologist; b. West Plains, Mo., June 20, 1909; s. William and Bess (Johnson) G.; student U. Cal. at Los Angeles, 1926-29, Cal. Inst. Tech., 1933-34; m. Mary Beale Sasscer, Oct. 16, 1937; children—Mary B., Margaret Lynn, Penelope, Joseph Sasscer. Weather and dispatch dept. Western Air Express, Los Angeles, 1929-34; supt. meteorology Eastern Airlines, Atlanta, 1934-41, 46-64, dir. meteorology, 1964—. Chmn. adv. com. on weather services Dept. Commerce, 1953—; mem. President's Adv. Com. on Weather Control, 1953; mem. NACA sub com. Meterorol. Problems, 1946-56; mem. tech. adv. bd. to adminstr. FAA; mem. Pres.'s Adv. Com. on Oceans and Atmosphere, 1971. Served from capt. to col., weather service USAF, 1942-46. Recipient Meisinger award for aero. research Am. Meteorol. Soc., 1941; Losey award Inst. Aero. Scis., 1944; Am. Meteorol. Soc. award, applied meteorology, 1955. Fellow Am. Meteorol. Soc. (v.p. 1950-52); mem. Nat. Acad. Scis. (mem. panel on rivers and weather services, 1968- 69). Author: Weather Forecasting for Aeronautics; also numerous papers on weather forecasting. Home: 2521 N Greenway Dr Coral Gables FL 33134 Office: Eastern Airlines Miami Internat Airport Miami FL 33148

GEORGE, MARCUS B., newspaper exec. Exec. editor Ark. Democrat. Office: Capitol Av and South St Little Rock AK 72203*

GEORGE, NEWELL A., lawyer; born Kansas City, Mo., Sept. 24, 1904; s. Adolphus K. and Ida (Scobee) G.; student Park Coll., Parksville, Mo., Kansas City U.; LL.B., Nat. U., 1934, M.P.L., LL.M., 1935; m. Jean Hannan, Apr. 16, 1934. Mem. staff U.S. Senator George McGill of Kan., 1933; admitted to D.C. bar, 1935, Kan. bar, 1943; regional atty. Bur. Employment Security, also FSA, 1935-52; chief legal counsel War Manpower Commn., 1942-44; pvt. practice law, Kansas City, Kan., 1943—; 1st asst. atty. Wyandotte County Kan., 1952-58; mem. 86th Congress, 2d Dist. Kan.; U.S. attorney for Kansas, 1961-68; practice of law, Kansas City, Kansas, 1968—. Mem. Gov.'s Com. on Criminal Adminstrn., Interstate Oil Compact Commn. President Kansas Assn. Hi-12 Clubs; bd. dirs. for Kan., Nat. Multiple Sclerosis Soc. Mem. Am., Kan., Wyandotte County bar assns., Am. Judicature Soc., Am. Acad. Polit. and Social Sci., Kansas City (Kan.) C. of C., Delta Theta Phi. Democrat. Presbyn. Mason (Shriner). Clubs: Optimist, Hi-12 (past pres.), Top O'the Morning (Kansas City, Kan.). Author articles Kan. Law Rev. Home: 1831 New Jersey Av Kansas City KS 66102 Office: Huron Bldg Kansas City KS 66101

GEORGE, NICHOLAS APOSTOLOS, mfg. co. exec.; b. Decatur, Ill., Oct. 10, 1908; s. Apostolos Nicholas and Helen (Kastanas) G.; student Wash. U., 1925-27, University of Minnesota, 1944, U. Michigan, 1949-50; m. Jacoba K. Benton, June 8, 1963. Muskegon director in industrial relations of the Brunswick-Balke- Collender Company, 1941-49, The Murray Corp. Am., 1949-54; v.p., Ohio Boxboard Co., Rittman, O., 1954-59, Brunswick Corp., Chgo., 1959-64; pres., dir. Muskegon Paper Box Co., 1964—. Mem. Muskegon Area Devel. Council. Vice pres. Brunswick Found., 1960-64. Mem. A.I.M., Am. Mgmt. Association, National Paper Box Association, Folding Paper Box Association of America. Mason (32, Shriner). Clubs: Chicago Athletic Assn.; Muskegon Country, Muskegon Century, Muskegon Yacht. Home: 1565 Davis St Muskegon MI 49442 Office: 1801 Keating Muskegon MI 49442

GEORGE, PHILIP, biophys. chemist, educator; b. Maidstone, Kent, Eng., Jan. 30, 1920; s. Walter and Frances Alice (Brook) G.; B.A., Christ's Coll., Cambridge, Eng., 1941, M.A., 1944, Ph.D., 1945; m. Kathleen Margaret Hoff, Sept. 37, 1946; children—Francis, Sarah, Emma, Simon, Hannah, Edwin. Came to U.S., 1955. Research Molteno Inst. for Parasitology, Cambridge, 1945-47; lectr. phys. chemistry Leeds (Eng.) U., 1947-49; asst. dir. research dept. colloid sci. Cambridge U., 1949-55; prof. biophys. chemistry U. Pa., 1955—, chmn. group com. in molecular biology, dir. tng. program, 1960-61, dir. gen. honors program, 1961-63, chmn. dept. history and philosophy of sci. Grad. Sch. Arts and Sci., 1964—. Cons. Hartford Found. project Presbyn. Hosp., Phila., 1960—; mem. biophys. scis. study sect. Nat. Inst. Gen. Med. Scis., 1963-66. Mem. Am. Chem. Soc., Soc. Biol. Chemists, Biophys. Soc., Am. History Sci. Soc., A.A.A.S., Franklin Inst., Renaissance Soc., Chem. Soc. (Eng.), Biochem. Soc. (Eng.), Faraday Soc. (Eng.), Brit. Soc. for Hist. Sci., Phi Beta Kappa, Sigma Xi. Contbr. profl. jours. Home; 4 Herford Pl Lansdowne PA 19050 Office: Dept of Chemistry University Pa Philadelphia PA 19104

GEORGE, RAYMOND L., cosmetic co. exec.; b. Bklyn., Mar. 17, 1918; s. Clinton Henry and Florence (Kreuscher) G.; student Syracuse U., 1937-38; m. Doris H. Aschoff, Sept. 21, 1941; children—Raymond L., Carol Ann, Garrett. Sr. v.p. Lanvin Parfums; pres. Jacqueline Cochran Cosmetic Co.; exec. v.p. cosmetic and toiletry div. Shulton Inc. Bd. dirs. U.S.O., N.Y. Served with USAF Me. Militia Assn. N.Y. (Pres. 1958-59), Assn. Ex-Mems. Squadron A. Club: Huntington Country. Home: Mallard Drive-Lolyd Neck Huntington NY 11721 Office: 630 Fifth Av New York City NY 10020

GEORGE, ROBERT JONAS, banker; b. New Tripoli, Pa., May 29, 1909; s. Oliver J. and Elenora (Rex) G.; student Allentown Bus. Coll., 1927, Am. Inst. Banking, 1939; m. Erma A. Deibert, June 6, 1935; 1 son, Robert O. Sr. v.p. Continental Bank, Norristown, Pa., 1961—; dir.. Montgomery County Indsl. Devel. Corp., Norristown Convertible Leverage Fund, Abington, Pa. Served with AUS, 1944-46. Mason. Club: Plymouth Country (Norristown). Home: 1203 Vilsmeier Rd Lansdale PA 19446 Office: Continental Bank Main and Swede Sts Norristown PA 19404

GEORGE, ROWLAND HERBERT, banker; b. Detroit, Mar. 11, 1895; s. Harry and Carrie E. (Rowland) G.; Ph.B., U. Chgo., 1916; m. Alexandra Markoff, Jan. 11, 1937; 1 son, Mihail M. With Halsey, Stuart & Co., Chgo., 1916-17, George W. Goethals & Co., N.Y.C., 1919-21; joined Wood, Struthers & Co., N.Y.C., 1921, partner, 1929-63; partner Wood, Struther & Winthrop, 1963—; pres., dir. Wood, Struthers & Co., Inc., 1963—; chmn. bd., Pan Holding Co.; dir. Consol. Securities Corp.; organizer, 1st pres. United Med. Service (Blue Shield Plan) of N.Y., 1941-49; gov. N.Y. Stock Exchange, 1953-56. Vice chmn. bd. dirs. Athens Coll. in Greece; trustee Tolstoy Found. Served as lt. A.A.C., 1917-19. Mem. Delta Kappa Epsilon. Home: 1 E 66th St New York City, NY 10021. Office: 20 Exchange Pl New York City NY 10005

GEORGE, WALTER EUGENE, Jr., architect; b. Wichita Falls, Tex., Oct. 28, 1922; s. Walter Eugene and Mamie Alta (Evans) G.; B.Arch., U. Tex., 1949; M.Arch., Harvard, 1950; m. Virginia Pauline Stullken, Sept. 8, 1954; children—Susan Elizabeth, Carol Ann, Barbara Jane. Draftsman, Gieseke, Kuehne and Brooks, architects, Austin, Tex., 1948; designer Wiltshire and Fisher architects, Dallas, 1950-51; designer Richard Colley, architect, Corpus Christi, Tex., 1952; partner Pendley, George and Bowman, architects and engrs., Austin, 1952-57; asst., then asso. prof. architecture U. Tex., 1956-62; prof. architecture, chmn. dept. U. Kansas, 1962-67; dean Coll. Architecture, Univ. Houston, 1967-69; practice of architecture, Austin, 1969—. Served as pilot USAAF, 1943- 46, ETO. Decorated Air medal with oak leaf cluster, Purple Heart; recipient Mont San Michele and chartres award A.I.A., 1949; 2d award 1st annual Southwestern furniture competition Dallas Mus. Fine Arts. Mem. A.I.A., Archaeol. Inst. Am., Soc. Archtl. Historians, Tau Sigma Delta. Presbyn. Home: PO Box 5459 Austin TX 78703

GEORGE, WILLIAM ARTHUR, educator, dentist; b. Pitts., Jan. 29 1910; s. Arthur G. and Edith E. (Hall) G.; B.S., U. Pitts., 1932, D.D.S., 1932; m. Wilma M. Mackey, Aug. 29, 1936; children—Ruth Ann, William Arthur, Richard Allan. Gen. practice dentistry, Pitts., 1932-43, 46-58; dentist for Sewickley (Pa.) Child Health Assn., 1938-39; part-timer instr. then asst. prof. Sch. Dentistry U. Pitts., 1947-58, prof., head dept. prosthodontics, 1958—, chmn. postgrad. edn., 1958—, mem. exec. and curriculum coms., 1958—, asst. dean Sch. Dentistry, 1965-68, associate dean, 1968—, director graduate education; consultant VA Central Office; cons. dentistry VA Hosp., Pitts.; cons. Vietnam edn. project Am. Dental Assn., 1970—. President bd. health O'Hara Township, Allegheny County, Pa., 1958-63. Served from lieutenant (j.g.) to lt. (s.g.), USNR, 1943-46; capt. Res. Recipient letters of commendation from U.S. Navy, 1955; Plaque award E. Liberty YMCA, Pitts., 1956. Fellow Am. College Dentists; mem. Internat. Assn. Dental Research, Am. Dental Assn. (chmn. council on dental research 1965-67), Pa. Acad. Gen. Dentistry (pres. elect 1969—), East End Dental Soc. (past pres.), Pennsylvania Dental Assn. (pres. elect 1970-71), Chgo. Dental Soc. Chgo. (asso.), Odontological Soc. Western Pa. (pres. 1963, delegate), Pa. Dental Association (trustee), Allied Dental Assn. Vietnam, American Prosthodontic Society (executive com.), International College Dentists, U. Pitts. Dental Alumni Assn. (past pres.), Res. Officers Assn., Sigma Xi, Pi Kappa Alpha, Psi Omega, Omicron Kappa Upsilon, Omicron Delta Kappa. Presbyn. (elder). Mason (32, Shriner). Home: 110 N Oak Hill Rd Pittsburgh PA 15238

GEORGE, WILLIAM HENRY KROME, aluminum co. exec.; b. St. Louis, Mar. 27, 1918; s. Robert J. and Anne (Krome) G.; S.B., Mass. Inst. Tech., 1940; m. Jean Murphy, May 4, 1946; children—Krome Doyle, Robert Charles, Peter Gillham. With Aluminum Co. Am., 1942—, v.p. charge econ. exec. v.p., 1967-70, pres., 1970—, also dir. Presbyn. Home: 642 Grove St Sewickley PA 15143 Office: Alcoa Bldg Pittsburgh PA 15219

GEORGES, PAUL, painter; b. Portland, Ore., 1923; student U. Ore.; pupil of Leger and Hans Hofmann; married; children—Paulett, Yvette. Exhibitions include Whitney Museum in 1962, 63-64, Pa. Acad. Fine Arts, 1964, Corcoran Gallery Art, 1954, Mus. Modern Art, 1964, Boston U., 1964, Sch. Visual Arts, N.Y.C., 1965, New Sch. Social Research, 1965; rep. permanent collections Longview Found., Newark Mus. Art, Mass. Inst. Tech., Reed Coll., N.Y.U., Mus. Modern Art, Whitney, N.Y.; artist-in- residence Dartmouth, 1964, La. State U., Baton Rouge; leader seminar art Yale, 1964; instr. painting U. Colo., 1960; mem. staff Yale Sch. Art, 1964—, Longview fellow; recipient Hallmark purchase award, 1961; Carol Beck gold medal Pa. Acad. Fine Arts, 1964. Contbr. Art News. Address: 85 Walker St New York City NY 10013 also: Sagaponack NY

GEORGI, CARL EDUARD, educator; b. Milw., Feb. 18, 1906; s. Herman Emil and Ottilie (Memmler) G.; B.S., U. Wis., 1930, M.S., 1932, Ph.D., 1934; Fulbright scholar U. Paris (France), 1951-52; student Inst. Nuclear Studies, Oak Ridge, summer 1950, Cornell U., summer 1960; m. Marjorie Clare Womelsdorff, Aug. 20, 1936; children—Liesl Andrea (Mrs. Benjamin Vrana), Todd Anthony. Chemist, Pfister & Vogel Leather Co., Milw., 1924-26; asst. instr. chemistry U. Wis., 1934-35; mem. faculty U. Neb., 1935—, prof. bacteriology, 1947—, chmn. dept., 1953—, Murray Longworth prof. microbiology, 1964—, mem., staff dept. biochemistry, nutrition; research microbiologist Neb. Agrl. Expt. Sta., 1949- -; spl. research biochemistry, physiology and anatomy of microbial cells, microbial utilization agrl. products. Trustee Lincoln Gen. Hosp., 1962—. Recipient Seaman award N.Y. Acad. Medicine, 1951. Diplomate Am. Bd. Microbiology. Charter fellow Am. Acad. Microbiology; fellow A.A.A.S.; mem. Am. Inst. Biol. Scis. (vis. coll. lectr. 1960—), Am. Soc. Microbiology (pres. Mo. Valley br. 1942-43; chmn. div. gen. microbiology 1966), Neb. Acad. Sci. (past pres.), Electron Microscope Soc. Am., Am. Soc. Cell Biology, Soc. Exptl. Biology and Med., Soc. Gen. Microbiology, Soc. Indsl. Microbiology, Am. Soc. Biol. Chemists, Sigma Xi (pres. Neb. 1948-49), Alpha Chi Sigma, Phi Lambda Upsilon, Gamma Alpha, Phi Beta Kappa (hon.). Episcopalian. Author: (with G.L. Peltier and L.F. Lindgren) Laboratory Manual for General Microbiology, 5th edit., 1959. Editorial bd. Applied Microbiology, 1953- 58. Contbr. articles to profl. jours. Home: 3033 Georgian Ct Lincoln NB 68502

GEPHARDT, THOMAS STEUBER, editor; b. Anderson, Ind., May 23, 1927; s. Ralph Andrew and Clara Charlotte (Steuber) G.; student U. Chgo., 1947-49; A.B., George Washington U., 1950; M.S. in Journalism, Columbia, 1951; m. Deborah Ann Rotruck, Oct. 15, 1960; children—Andrew David Ellis, Clare Deborah Rotruck. Editor Anderson Herald, 1951-60; editorial writer Cin. Enquirer, 1960, editor editorial page, 1960—. Served with AUS, 1945-47. Mem. Am. Soc. Newspaper Editors, Nat. Conf. Editorial Writers, Sigma Chi. Republican. Catholic. Home: 851 Clifton Hills Terrace Cincinnati OH 45220 Office: 617 Vine St Cincinnati OH 45202

GEPSON, JOHN MORGAN, telephone co. exec.; b. Omaha, Feb. 13, 1913; s. Edward D. and Mae (Morgan) G.; A.B., U. Neb., 1934; LL.B. cum laude, Creighton U., 1937; m. Elizabeth Shearer, Oct. 26, 1938; children—John Edward, Mary Elizabeth. Atty. Northwestern Bell Telephone Co., 1939-43, Am. Tel. & Tel. Co., 1946-51; with New Eng. Tel. & Tel. Co., 1951—, v.p., gen. counsel, 1956- -. Served to lt. USNR, World War II. Mem. Am., Boston bar assns. Clubs: Union (Boston); Dedham (Mass.) Country and Polo. Home: 14 Old Town Rd Wellesley MA 02181 Office: 185 Franklin St Boston MA 02107

GERACE, FELIX JOHN, corp. exec.; b. Turin, Italy, Mar. 12, 1918; s. Salvatore and Catherina (Bordiga) G.; B.S., U.S. Mil. Acad., 1941; M.B.A., Stanford, 1948; postgrad. Indsl. Coll. Armed Forces, 1958; m. Doris Elisabeth McGahan, Sept. 27, 1941; children—Susanne (Mrs. Brian Anthony Flatley), John Wheeler, William Laston, Elisabeth, Melissa. Commd. 2d lt. U.S. Army, 1941, advanced through grades to maj. gen., 1969; group comdr. ETO, World War II; exec. officer Post Q.M., U.S. Mil Acad., 1948-51; asst. chief plans and tng. br. QM Div., Hdqrs. U.S. Army Europe, 1951-52; chief orgns., tng. and doctrine br. Mil. Personnel and Tng. Div., Office Q.M. Gen., Washington, 1955-56, spl. adviser for airborne matters, 1956-57; staff officer, br. and div. chief Mil. Personnel and Tng. Div., ODCSLOG, DA, 1958-60; chief logistics br. U.S.A. Element MAAG, Vientane, Laos, 1961, chief G-4 Div., 1961-62; comdt. U.S. Army Logistics Mgmt. Center, Ft. Lee, Va., 1962-65; exec. officer Office Asst. Sec. Army installations and logistics), Washington, 1965-66; asst. chief staff G-4 Hdqrs. 8th U.S. Army, USARPAC, Korea, 1966-68; comdg. gen. U.S. Natick Labs. and U.S. Army Materials and Mechanics Research Center, Watertown, Mass., 1968-69; comdg. gen. U.S. Army Natick Labs., 1969; dir. requirements and procurement Hdqrs. U.S. Army Material Command, Washington, 1969-70; ret., 1970; asst. to v.p. forward planning Northrop Corp., Los Angeles, 1970—. Decorated D.S.M., Legion of Merit with 2 oak leaf clusters, Bronze Star, Army Commendation medal. Home: 1957 Linda Flora Dr Los Angeles CA 90024 Office: 1800 Century Park E Los Angeles CA 90067

GERAGHTY, HELEN TIEKEN (Mrs. Maurice P. Geraghty), theatrical prod., dir.; b. Chgo., Nov. 16, 1902; d. Theodore and Bessie (Chapman) Tieken; B.S., U. Chgo., 1924, M.A., 1928; student Sorbonne, 1926, Goodman Theatre, 1927, Oxford U. (Eng.), summer 1926; m. Maurice Patrick Geraghty, Apr. 15, 1933; children—Betsy (Mrs. David Fryberger), Helen (Mrs. Stephen Weissman), Molly (Mrs. Eric Teicholz). Producer, dir. Wings of a Century, Chgo., 1933-34; dir. dramatics Francis W. Parker Sch., Chgo., 1943-57; producer, dir. Wheels-a Rolling, Chgo. R.R. Fair, 1948-49, Mile Posts, C., B. & Q. R.R. Centennial, 1949, Frontiers of Freedom, Chgo. R.R. Fair, 1950, Song of Mid-Am., I.C. R.R. Centennial, 1951, Adam to Atom, Mus. Sci. and Industry Centennial of Engring., 1952, numerous other indsl. shows, 1951- 59; dir. Seventeenth Star, symphonic drama Ohio State Sesquicentennial, Columbus, 1953, entertainment Chicagoland Fair, 1957, cultural activities and entertainment Chgo. Internat. Fair, 1958-60, Galavante Chgo. Lyric Opera Co., 1959; prod., dir. Galerie Vivante, Ravinia Park Festival, 1957; gen. mgr. Ravinia Festival, 1963-64; chief arts program Ill. Sesquicentennial Commn., 1966-69; cons. Chgo. chpt. Am. Inst. Architects. Tech. dir. Passavant Hosp. Cotillion, 1950-70, St. Luke's Fashion Show, 1948-60, Chgo. Jr. League Children's Theater, 1930-32, Hull House Theatre, 1937-40; prod., dir. Rotary Internat. Anniversary Album, 1955, Banner High for 75th Anniversary A.R.C., 1956. Women's bd. dirs. Art Inst. Chgo., Presbyn.-St. Luke's Hosp., U. Chgo., Field Mus. Natural History. Mem. Arts Club Chgo., Chgo. Jr. League, Phi Beta Kappa. Home: 2236 Lincoln Park W Chicago, IL 60614.

GERAGHTY, JAMES, art editor; b. Spokane, Wash., Apr. 22, 1905; s. James Michael and Nora (Toolen) G.; student Gonzaga U., 1924-27; m. Eva Elizabeth Carr, Oct. 3, 1931; children—James Michael, Sarah Ann. Radio writer, 1930-38; art editor New Yorker mag., 1939—. Clubs: Century Assn., Grolier (N.Y.C.). Home: 98 Old Redding Rd Weston CT 06880 Office: 25 W 43rd St New York City NY 10036

GERAGHTY, JOHN JAMES, lawyer; b. Weehawken Heights, N.J., Feb. 12, 1908; s. James and Martha (Andrews) G.; A.B., Columbia, 1933, LL.B., 1935; m. Ruby Tyson, July 23, 1945. Admitted to N.Y. and North Carolina bars; with firm Duke and Landis, New York City, 1937-42, 46-51, Poyner, Geraghty, Hartsfield and Townsend, Raleigh, North Carolina, 1951—; lectr. law New York U. Sch. Finance, 1946-51. Served to maj. AUS, 1941-46. Decorated Legion of Merit. Home: 1003 James Pl Raleigh NC 27605 Office: 615 Oberlin Rd Raleigh NC 27605

GERALD, JAMES EDWARD, univ. prof.; b. Evant, Coryell County, Tex., May 6, 1906; s. James Edward, Sr., and Martha Alice (Hunter) G.; A.B., West Texas State Teachers Coll., 1927; B.J., U. of Mo., 1928, A.M., 1932; Ph.D., U. of Minn., 1946; m. Opal Dutton, June 7, 1930; children—James Edward III, Patricia Ellen (Mrs. William C. Bourne, Jr.). Engaged as editor of the Canyon (Tex.) Prairie, 1925-27; staff corr. United Press Assn., Denver, 1928; editor Canyon (Tex.) News, 1929; mem. staff Sch. of Journalism. U. of Mo., 1929-46 (part time while holding additional appointments, 1937- 41), instr., 1929-30, asst. prof., 1930-35, asso. prof., 1935-46, acting dean, 1941-42, (on sabbatical leave, copy reader St. Louis Star-Times, 1936-37); mgr. Mo. Press Assn., Inc., 1937-41; prof. Sch. of Journalism, U. of Minn., 1946—, in research work; dir. Mpls. Star program of Information on World Affairs for secondary schs., 1949-52; fellow Guggenheim Meml. Found., 1953-54; cons. Brookings Instn., mass media coverage govtl. processes, 1964. Mem. Assn. for Edn. in Journalism (pres. 1952), Am. Civil Liberties Union, Am. Polit. Sci. Assn., Sigma Delta Chi (nat. distinguished research award 1948). Kappa Tau Alpha, Alpha Delta Sigma. Author: The Press and the Constitution, 1931-47, 1948; British Press Under Government Economic Controls, 1956; Social Responsibility of the Press, 1963; articles in profl. and trade jours. Home: 2530 Ulysses St NE Minneapolis MN 55418

GERARD, RALPH WALDO, educator; b. Harvey, Ill., Oct. 7, 1900; s. Maurice and Eva (Teitelbaum) G.; B.S., U. Chgo., 1919, Ph.D., 1921; M.D., Rush Med. Coll., 1924; D.Sc., U. Md., 1952; LL.D., U. St Andrews (Scotland), 1964; Litt.D., Brown U., 1964; D.Sc., McGill University, Montreal, Que., Can.; M.D. (hon.), U. Leiden, 1962; m. Margaret Wilson, June 15, 1922 (dec. Jan., 1954); 1 son, James; m. 2d, Leona Bachrach Chalkley, Jan. 1, 1955. Prof. physiology, S.D. U., 1921-22; nat. research fellow, Europe, 1925-27; asst. prof. physiology U. Chgo., 1927-29, asso. prof. 1929-41, prof., 1941-52, prof. behavioral sci., 1954-55; prof. neurophysiology and physiology, coll. med. U. Ill., 1952-55; prof. neurophysiology, Mental Health Research Inst., U. Mich., 1955-64, cons. sr. scientist, 1964—; director special studies, prof. biol. scis., dean grad. div. U. Cal. at Irvine, 1964—, special adviser academic affairs, until 1970. Praelector U. St. Andrews. Lowell lectr., 1958, Robert Johnson, Jr. meml. lectr., 1958, Lakeside lectr., 1960, Stanley R. Dean lectr., 1964. Dir. spl. war research; chmn. physiol. adv. panel, Office Naval Research, 1947-53; chmn. VA com. on problems aging, 1955-60; mem. exec. com., div. biology and agr. NRC, 1960—. Awarded medal Charles U. (Prague), Order White Lion (4th class), Czech govt.; Fellow Ford Found., 1954-55. Mem. Nat. Acad. Scis. (editor Proc.), Am. Acad. Arts and Scis., Am. Psychiat. Assn. (hon.), Physiol. Soc. (pres. 1951-52), Assn. for Research in Nervous and Mental Disease, Chgo. Inst. Medicine, Brit. Physiol. Soc., Biochem. Soc., Am. Neurol. Assn., Am. Naturalists, A.A.A.S., Pan Hellenic Med. Assn. (hon.), Am. Assn. U. Profs., Soc. Exptl. Biol. and Medicine, Soc. Gen. Physiol., Nat. Soc. Med. Research (sec. treas. 1955-57), Soc. Electroencephalography. Internat. Brain Research Orgn. (council 1962- 64), Acad. Psychoanalysis, Acad. Neurology, Soc. Biol. Psychiatry (pres. 1966), Operations Research Soc. Am., Phi Beta Kappa, Sigma Xi, Alpha Omega Alpha. Clubs: Cosmos, Quadrangle, Chicago Literary. Author: Unresting Cells, 1940; The Body Functions, 1941; Food for Life, 1952; Mirror to Physiology; A Self-Survey of Physiological Science, 1958; Computers and Education, 1967. Editor: Methods in Medical Research, 1950; Concept of Biology, 1958; (with Cole) Psychopharmacology, Problems in Evaluation, 1959; (with Duyff) Information Processing in the Nervous System, 1964. Contbr. jours. Editor Behavioral Sci., Jour. Electroencephalography. Home: 1007 Goldenrod Av Corona del Mar CA 92014 Office: Univ of Cal Irvine CA 92664

GERARDIA, HELEN, artist, educator; b. Ekaterinislov, Russia, Dec. 25, 1903; d. Jacob and Sophie (Lipshitz) Goldberg; student N.Y. Tng. Sch. for Tchrs., Art Students League, Hans Hoffman, Bklyn. Mus. Art Sch. Tchr., N.Y. Tng. Sch. Tchrs., 1921-23; tchr. pub. schs., N.Y.C., 1924—; artist in oil, watercolor, casein, lithography, etching, drawing media; one man shows include Research Studio Art Center, Maitland, Fla., 1953, 57, Rudolph Galleries, Woodstock, N.Y., 1953, 55, Albany Inst. History and Art, 1955, U. Me., Orono, 1957, (oils) Bodly Gallery, N.Y.C., 1957, 59, 61, 63, 65, 68, Fairleigh Dickinson U., 1960, Fordham U., 1967, Ga. Mus., Athens, Ga., 1968, Carver Mus., 1969; exhibited in group shows Art U.S.A., 1958,59, Corcoran Gallery, 1959, 60, Provincetown Art Assn., 1958, 59, Soc. Am.

Graphic Artists, 1959, print retrospective at Marist College, 1968, also France, Holland, Belgium, Italy, Lithuania, Africa, Japan, Greece, Switzerland, Yugoslavia, oil painting in Athens, Greece, 1957; many traveling shows in U.S. and abroad; one man traveling show of caseins in U.S., 1957—, of graphics in U.S., 1957—, paintings and graphics, 1969; represented in collections N.Y.U., Fogg Mus., Cin. Mus., Butler Art Inst., Met. Mus., Bklyn. Mus., Dartmouth, Lincoln Centre, N.Y.C., Tampa Art Centre, other colleges and univs. Demonstrator casein technique 64th and 65th ann. Nat. Assn. Woman Artists. Adv. bd. Marquis Biog. Library Soc., 1969—. Recipient purchase prize award Boston Soc. Independents, 1951, 56, Abraham Lincoln Graphics Exhbn. fellowship Research Studio Art Center, 1952, 53, Yaddo, Saratoga Springs, 1955, Maganini award for an oil Silvermine Guild 8th N.E. Ann., 1957, award Painters and Sculptors Soc. N.J., 1961, Joel Landres prize oil Bklyn. Soc. Artists, 1957, 2d Grumbacher award Nat. Soc. Painters in Casein, 1960, award, 1963, 66, Lempert award N.J. Painters and Sculptors, 1960; also Robert Boardman prize, 1968; Paris Meml. prize Am. Soc. Contemporary Artists, 1968; Dr. Holzman Meml. award Nat. Assn. Women Artists 1969. Mem. Nat. Soc. Painters in Casein (v.p. 1968-69, award juror 1968 Ann.), Soc. Am. Graphic Artists (corr. sec. 1966—, mem. executive bd. 1968-69, del. and/or observer Internat. Assn. Art 1962—), Blkyn. Soc. Artists (past bd. govs., juror in all mediums), League of Present Day Artists (past chmn.), Vectors, Am. Soc. Contemporary Artists (award 1963-66; president 1965-66, executive board 1967, vice president 1968—), Silvermine Guild Artists, Artists Equity (corr. sec. 1964—, executive board), National Association Woman Artists (treasurer 1968—, medal of Honor, Markell prize 1961, 64, award 1962, 63, Berne Meml. prize 1966), Woodstock Artists Assn. (bd. govs., past chmn.). Creative Assos., Soc. Young Am. Artists, Print Club, Color Print Soc., Audubon Artists Inc. (pub. relations chmn. 1964-68; juror selection Ann. in Graphics 1968, treas. 1969—). Home: 490 West End Av New York City NY 10024 Office: 246 W 80th St New York City NY 10024

GERATHY, CARROLL, insurance co. exec.; b. Long Island City, N.Y., June 25, 1915; s. Joseph Hewson and Emma E. (Donady) G; M.B.A., U. Chgo., 1962; m. Julia F. Gill, Sept. 7, 1942; children—Nancy, John. With McKesson & Robbins, Inc., 1933- 48; with Prudential Ins. Co. Am., 1948—, sr. v.p., 1964—. C.L.U. Mem. N.J. C. of C. Clubs: Maplewood (N.J.) Country; Mid-America, Executives (Chgo.). Home: 42 Knob Hill Dr Summit NJ 07901 Office: Prudential Plaza Newark NJ 07101

GERBER, DANIEL F., business exec.; b. Fremont, Mich., May 6, 1898; s. Frank and Dora Pauline (Platt) G.; student St. Johns Mil. Acad., Delafield, Wisconsin, (co-author) Pharmacy, 1913-16, Babson Institute, Wellesley Hills, Mass., 1919-20; married Dorothy Marion Scott, January 18, 1923; children—Dorothy S. (Mrs. Ralph K. Merrill, Jr.), Sally Scott (Mrs. R.H. Phinny), Paula P. (Mrs. David Warm), Arabella G. (Mrs. H.M. Cummings), Daniel F. Entire career with Gerber Products Company (formerly Fremont Canning Company), Fremont, Michigan, salesman, 1920-21, dir., 1926-28, asst. gen. mgr., 1926-28, 1st vice president, 1928-45, pres., dir., 1945, president, 1945-64, now chairman board, chief executive officer; dir. Old State Bank of Fremont. Served in United States Army 1917-19; served as head fruit and vegetable sect. food price div., Office Price Adminstrn., 1942-43. Awarded Cross of War (France), 1918. Mem. Mich. Canners Assn. (past pres.), Grocery Association of Am. Member of Babson Inst. Republican. Mem. Christian Science Ch. Home: 6120 W 56th St Fremont MI 49412 Office: Gerber Products Co Fremont MI 49412 Gerber Products Co Fremont MI

GERBER, ELLA, theatre dir., actress; b. N.Y.C., Aug. 25, 1916; d. Isadore and Esther (Treisman) Gerber; student Columbia, 1943, Am. Theatre Wing, 1948-49, U. Birmingham (Eng.), 1955, Actors Studio, 1960-61, N.Y. U., 1963; m. Sam Kasakoff, May 29, 1943. Appeared in plays Pins and Needles on Broadway and U.S. and Can. tours, 1938-41, Inside Emily Payne, 1959, The Laundry, 1963; with Army Spl. Services, Hawaii, Japan, Korea, 1946-47; appeared in film Barabbas, 1961; dir. Broadway show Design for a Stained Glass Window, 1950, Off Broadway plays Homecoming, 1950, Tiger Rag, 1961; dir. for Equity Theatre, Dark of the Moon, 1949, Primrose Path, 1950, All God's Chillun, 1952, Flight Into Egypt, 1958, Dial M for Murder, 1958, Lost in the Stars, 1968; dir. Dark of the Moon, Rome, Italy, 1961, Porgy and Bess in New Zealand, 1965, Australia, 1965-66, Israel, 1966, Carousel in Johannesburg, S.Africa, 1968; dir. mus. theatres in Tex., N.J., Pa., Ohio. Can., Fla., Mo., Conn., R.I., Md, N.Y., Mass, 1958-67; dir. summer stock, 1949-57; dir. Porgy and Bess in Eastern U.S. and Can., 1958, 65, colls. univs., 1966-67, S.C. Tri-Centennial Celebration, 1970; mem. faculty Studio of the Theatre, Hollywood, Cal., 1947-48, Am. Acad. Dramatic Arts, N.Y.C., 1957-59, 66-67, Am. Mus. and Dramatic Acad., N.Y.C., 1967-68; guest faculty London (Eng.) Opera Center, 1968; artistic dir. Youngstown (O.) Playhouse, 1964-65, dir.-tchr. for arts Six Theatre Program Mass., 1969—. Bd. dirs. Found. for Extension and Devel. of Am. Profl. Theatre, 1968. MacDowell Colony fellow, 1966-67. Mem. Soc. Stage Dirs. and Choreographers (past mem. exec. bd.), Actors Equity Assn., A.F.T.R.A. Address: 329 E 58th St New York City NY 10022

GERBER, JOHN CHRISTIAN, educator; b. New Waterford, O., Jan. 31, 1908; s. Christian G. and Leonora (Hauptmann) G.; A.B., U. Pitts., 1929, M.A., 1932; Ph.D., U. Chgo., 1941; m. Margaret E. Wilbourn, Sept. 3, 1941; children—Barbara Page, Ann Wilbourn. Instr. English, U. Pitts., 1931-36; instr. English, U. Chgo., 1938-42, pre-meteorology, 1942-44; asst. prof. English, U. Ia., 1944-47. asso. prof., 1947-49, prof., 1949—, chmn. dept. English, 1961—, director School of Letters, 1967—; visiting associate professor English, U. So. Cal., summer 1949; vis. prof. U. N.M., summers 1952, 57, Trinity Coll., summers 1960, 63, U. Cal. at Berkeley, 1960-61, University of Colorado, summer 1965, Am. U. at Cairo, 1970. Consultant on English, U.S. Office of Education, 1964-65. Member National Council Teachers English (recipient Hatfield award 1964, trustee of research found. 1962-65; pres. 1955), Conf. Coll. Composition and Communication (chmn. 1950), Modern Lang. Assn. (chairman of American literature section 1969), Midwest Modern Lang. Assn. (pres. 1966), Am. Assn. U. Profs., Am. Studies Assn., Assn. Depts. English (chairman 1964). Author: (with Walter Blair) Factual Prose, 1945; Literature, 1948; Writers Resource Book, 1953; (with Fleece and Wylder) Toward Better Writing, 1958; (with Arnold, Ehninger) Speakers Resource Book; Repertory, 1960; Twentieth Century Interpretations of the Scarlet Letter, 1968; Studies in Huckleberry Finn, 1971; also chpts. in Toward General Education, 1948. Mem. editorial bd. College English, 1947-48, 65-71, Am. Quar., 1963-68; editorial adviser Philol. Quar., 1951-57; editorial adv. bd. Resources for American Literary Study, 1971—; general editor Iowa-California Editor of the Works of Mark Twain; editor Teaching Coll. English, 1965, Scott-Foresman Key Edits. Contbr. articles to profl. jours.; author introductions several books. Home: 359 Magowan Av Iowa City IA 52240

GERBER, JOHN JAY, public relations; born Morton, Ill., Nov. 26, 1914; s. John E. and Anna (Mosiman) G.; A.B., U. Utah, 1935; student Northwestern, 1937-39; m. Gladys Eittreim, Sept. 20, 1941; children—Jay T., Julia Ann, Stephen E. Salesman Keystone Steel & Wire Co., Peoria, Ill., 1935-37; pub. relations dept., Northwestern U., 1937-42, 46-52, dir., 1947, v.p. pub. relations, 1949-52; partner firm Gonser-Gerber-Tinker-Stuhr, Chgo., 1952—; spl. agt. FBI, 1942-46; v.p., dir. Bank of Westmont (Ill.), Bank of Naperville (Illinois); director Bank of Hinsdale (Illinois), Bank Lisle (Ill.), Bank Glen Ellyn (Ill.), Bank of Lockport (Ill.). Past alumni regent Northwestern Universtiy. Recipient Alumni Service award Northwestern University, 1961. Member Public Relations Society America, American College Public Relations Association, Phi Beta Kappa, Beta Gamma Sigma. Republican. Conglist. Clubs: University, Economic. Author: (with Thomas A. Gonser) Gonser and Gerber on College Development, 1961. Home: 25 W 8th Av Naperville IL 60540 Office: 105 W Madison St Chicago IL 60602

GERBER, JOSEPH NEWTON, coll. dean; b. Bloomington, Ill., Jan. 1, 1910; s. Elmer Joseph and Mary Edna (Hilton) G.; B.A., Illinois State U., 1934; M.S., U. Ill., 1935; Ph.D., George Peabody Coll., 1941; m. Gertrude Palmer, Aug. 9, 1942; children—John (dec.), Barbara Hilton. High sch. tchr. and prin., Witt, Ill., 1935-39; coordinator workshop activities George Peabody Coll., summer 1951; dir. student personnel Northwestern State Coll., Natchitoches, La., 1941-50; dean jr. div. Stephen F. Austin State Coll., Nacogdoches, Tex., 1950-55, dean of coll., 1955-59, dean of coll., dean Grad. Sch., 1959-67, dean Grad. Sch., director research, 1967—; workshop cons. U. Fla., also Fla. State U., summers 1948-49. Mem. Tex. Commn. on Guidance; bd. So. Bd. Tchr. Edn. Bd. dirs. Nacogdoches County United Fund, Nacogdoches Community Hotel Corp.; exec. com. Attoyac area council Boy Scouts Am. Served to lt. comdr. USNR, 1942-45; comdr. Res. Mem. Assn. Tex. Colls. and Universities (chmn. commn. standards and classification 1965-68, v.p. 1968-69), Am. Psychol. Assn., A.A.A.S., Am. Assn. Sch. Adminstrs., Am. Coll. Personnel Assn., Nacogdoches C. of C. (dir.), Phi Delta Kappa, Kappa Delta Pi, Kappa Phi Kappa, Gamma Theta Upsilon. Methodist (steward). Rotarian (past pres. Nacogdoches, Tex.). Contbr. articles profl. jours. Home: 3307 N Raguet St Nacogdoches TX 75961

GERBER, MORRIS, lawyer; b. Phila., Nov. 29, 1908; B.S. in Econs., U. Pa., 1929, LL.B., 1932. Admitted to Pa. bar, 1932; mem. firm Wisler, Pearlstine, Talone and Gerber, Norristown, Pa.; judge Ct. of Common Pleas, 1957-60; chief counsel Auditor Gen. Pa., 1961-65; counsel State Treas., 1965-69. Mem. Am., Pa., Phila. Montgomery County (dir. 1943-45) bar assns. Office: 515 Swede St Norristown PA 19401*

GERBER, PHILIP LESLIE, educator; b. Aberdeen, S.D., Dec. 4, 1923; s. Henry Philip and Agnes (Egan) G.; B.A., U. Ia., 1946, M.A., 1948, Ph.D., 1952; m. Eugenia Nelidov, June 3, 1953; children—Gaylen Leslie, Vivien Elaine, Glenn Philip. Instr. English, U. Ia., 1950-52; prof. English, Pan Am. Coll., Edinburg, Tex., 1952-57; dir. freshman English, U. Utah, 1957-62; prof. English, chmn. dept. English and speech Cal. State Polytech. Coll., San Luis Obispo, 1962-65; chmn. dept. English, U. S.D., 1965-66, N.Y. State U., Brockport, 1966—. Mem. Am. Studies Association, Nat. Council Tchrs. English, Conf. Coll. Composition and Communication, Coll. English Assn., Modern Lang. Assn. Author: Effective English, 1959; Theodore Dreiser, 1964; Singer English Handbooks, 1965; Robert Frost, 1966; Lessons in Language, 1968. Home: 79 Hollybrook Rd Brockport NY 14420

GERBER, THOMAS WILLIAM, newspaper editor; b. Portland, Ore., May 2, 1921; s. Thomas W. and Mary Anne (Smith) G.; A.B., Dartmouth, 1948; m. Gail L. Graham, Jan. 20, 1951; children—Cheryl Ann, Linda Lee. Reporter, U.P.I., Boston, 1948-51, mgr. Providence bur., 1952-53; rewriteman, spl. assignment reporter Boston Herald and Traveler, 1953-56, chief Washington bur., 1956-61; gen. mgr. Concord (N.H.) Monitor, 1961-67, editor, asst. pub., 1967—; dir., sec. Monitor Pub. Co., 1962—; dir. TeleCable, Inc., Concord, 1968—, Concord br. Bank, N.H., 1962—. Mem. adv. com. N.H. Tech. Inst., 1966- 70; chmn. dir. quality com. N.H. Environmental Council 1970; mem. Citizens Task Force, 1969. Bd. dirs. Concord YMCA, N.H. Council World Affairs, N.H. Council Better Schs., Concord Hosp.; pres. bd. Bishop Brady High Sch., Concord, 1969—. Served with AUS, 1942-53, USAAF, 1942- 45, USAF, 1951-52. Decorated Air medal with two oak leaf clusters; recipient Heywood Broun award Am. Newspaper Guild 1955. Mem. New Eng. Daily Newspaper Assn., New Eng. Soc. Newspaper Editors (pres. 1967), Sigma Delta Chi. Home: 181 Loudon Rd Concord NH 03301 Office: 3 N State St Concord NH 03301

GERBER, WILLIAM, writer, cons.; b. Phila., July 12, 1908; s. Samuel and Fanny (Kramer) G.; B.A. with honors, U. Pa., 1929; M.A., George Washington U., 1932; student Johns Hopkins, 1932-33, 35-37; Ph.D., Columbia, 1945; m. Sylvia R. Wigdor, Aug. 6, 1933; 1 son, Louis M.W. Tchr. secondary sch., 1929- 30; staff Office Hist. Adviser, Div. Research and Publ., Hist. div. Dept. State, 1930-57, fgn. service officer, 1957-60, staff div. fgn. labor conditions Dept. Labor, 1958-65, dep. chief, 1965- 68; cons. Harvard U. Program on Technology and Society, 1968-69; fgn. affairs writer Editorial Research Reports, Washington, 1968—; instr. philosophy and world literature Washington Hall Jr. Coll., 1955-57, acting dir. humanities div., 1956-57; lectr. philosophy U. Md., 1959-60, 63—, Am. U., 1962. Program participant Internat. Congress Philosophy, Mexico City, 1963, Vienna, 1968, Inter-Am. Congress Philosophy, Washington, 1957. Mem. Am. Philos. Assn., Phi Beta Kappa, Eta Sigma Phi (editor nat. jour. 1928-29). Jewish religion. Author: The Department of State of the United States, 1942; The Domain of Reality, 1946; (with Letitia A. Lewis) Freedom of Information in American Policy and Practice, 1948; (with Edwin S. Costrell) The Department of State, 1930-55, 1955; The Mind of India, 1967. Contbr. American, British periodicals. Home: 4307 38th St NW Washington DC 20016 Office: Editorial Research Reports 1735 K St Washington DC 20006

GERBERMANN, HUGO MARK, bishop; b. Nada, Tex., Sept. 11, 1913; s. John Jerome and Matilda (Hiltpold) G.; Ph.D., St. John's Sem., San Antonio, 1939; postgrad. Maryknoll, N.Y.C., 1943; D.D., Vatican, 1962. Ordained priest Roman Catholic Ch., 1943; missionary in Ecuador, 1943-48, Guatemala, 1948-62; bishop of Huehuetenango, Guatemala, 1962—. Recipient Hermano Pedro award, 1959. Home: Box 12 Huehuetenango Guatemala

GERBINO, JOHN, art director; b. N.Y.C., Mar. 28, 1941; s. John and Pauline (Valenti) G.; student N.Y. Community Coll., 1959; student design Sch. Visual Arts, 1963-66; m. JoAnna LoPresti, Jan. 20, 1962; one son, John Paul. Designer Lashe and Driscoll Studio, N.Y.C., 1959-61, Dell Pub. Co., N.Y.C., 1961-64; asst. art dir. Harper's Bazaar mag., 1964-66; art dir. New York mag. and Book Week mag. of World Jour. Tribune Co., 1966-67; asst. to editorial dir. Condé Nast Publs., 1967-69; art dir., designer U.S. Mag.; art dir. Essence Mag., 1969, New Woman Mag., 1969—; designed, illustrated 1st edit. Nixon Poems; freelance book jacket designer, 1962—; cons. art dir. to mags., 1964—; work rep. Art Dirs. Show, 1966. Mem. N.Y. N.G., 1966-70. Recipient 2 awards Sch. Visual arts Show, 1965, Certificate of Merit, Art Dirs. Show, 1966. Contbr. New York local mag. Home: 616 Isle of Palms Fort Lauderdale FL 33301 Office: New Woman Magazine 2900 NE 12 Terrace Fort Lauderdale FL 33304

GERBINO, ROSARIO URBINO, artist; b. Castellamare, Sicily, Nov. 23, 1905; s. Francesco and Camilla (Mione) G.; student N.A.D., 1922-25. Tchr., Leonardo da Vinci Art Sch., 1938, Ednl. Alliance, 1942; tchr., dir. own art sch., N.Y.C., 1936; paintings represented in Westmore, Salter Hansen, Forestal, other collections, also Meml. Library, Georgetown U., Capricorn Galleries, Bethesda, Md. Recipient Allied Artists prize for best painting, 1948, 1st hon. mention, 1945, AAA prize for figure painting in oil, 1951; 1st hon. mention for self portrait Salmagundi Club, 1949; 1st hon. mention for painting Ogunquit Art Center, 1950, 51; certificate award Worlds Overseas Exhbn., 1952, Grand Central Art Galleries, 1953-55; Allied Artists Am. award Council Am. Artists Socs. 1968. Mem. Am. Fedn. Artists, Audubon Artists, Allied Artists Am., Italian Art Assn. Club: Salmagundi. Address: 155 E 96th St New York City NY 10019

GERBNER, GEORGE, educator; b. Budapest, Hungary, Aug. 8, 1919; s. Arpad and Margaret (Muranyi) G.; came to U.S., 1939; naturalized, 1944; student U. Budapest, 1937-38, U. Cal. at Los Angeles, 1940-41; B.A., U. Cal. at Berkeley, 1943; M.S., U. So. Cal., 1951, Ph.D., 1955; m. Ilona Kutas, Oct. 8, 1946; children—John C., Thomas J. Reporter, asst. financial editor The Chronicle, San Francisco, 1942-43; engaged in free-lance publicity, 1947-48; instr. Pasadena (Cal.) Jr. Coll., 1948-51, El Camino Coll., Los Angeles, 1951-56; asst. prof., then asso. prof. U. Ill. at Urbana, 1956-64; prof. communications, dean Annenberg Sch. Communications, U. Pa., 1964—. Served to 1st lt. inf. AUS, 1943-46; ETO. Decorated Bronze Star; grantee U.S. Office Edn., 1959, NSF, 1962, Nat. Inst. Mental Health, 1958, Internat. Sociol. Assn., 1963, UNESCO, 1963, Nat. Commn. Causes and Prevention Violence, 1969, Surgeon Gen.'s Sci. Adv. Com., 1970. Mem. Am. Acad. Polit. and Social Sci., Nat. Soc. Study Communications, N.E.A., Am. Sociol. Assn., Internat. Assn. Mass Communication Research, Soc. Study Social Problems, Assn. Edn. Journalism. Author numerous articles in field. Home: 234 Golf View Rd Armore PA 19003 Office: Annenberg Sch Communications Univ Pennsylvania Philadelphia PA 19104

GERBOSI, WILLIAM A., bus. cons.; b. Chgo., Feb. 6, 1909; s. Paul and Mary (Palermo) G.; Ph.C., U. Ill., 1928; m. Celia Gambardella, July 13, 1929; 1 dau., Maryann. With Jewel Tea Co., Inc., 1930—, v.p., gen. mgr. routes dept. 1945-55, dir., 1948—, exec. com., 1951-55; cons., 1955-59; asst. to pres. Salerno Megowen Biscuit Co., 1959-65; v.p. Boden Products, Inc., 1962—; v.p., dir. Safeway Trucking Co., 1962-67; v.p., chmn. exec. com. Ramo, Inc., unitl 1967; v.p., dir. Foto Audio Visual, 1965—; chmn. exec. com., dir. Jet X Corp., 1970—; dir. Resco, Inc., 1st Nat. Bank of Barrington, Navjo Freight Lines. Trustee Village of Arlington Heights, 1952-54. Decorated Star of Solidarity (Italy). Mem. Nat. Retail Tea and Coffee Mchts. Assn. (past pres., dir.). Club: Hiwan Country. Home: Rural Route 1 Evergreen CO 80439

GERDEN, PAUL, lawyer, pharm. exec.; b. Chgo., May 26, 1914; s. John Oscar and Christine (Nelson) G.; B.S., U. Ill., 1937; J.D., Northwestern U., 1940; m. Mary E. Pente, Aug. 15, 1942; children—Marilyn, Pamela, Paula. Admitted to Ill. bar, 1940; pvt. practice law, Chgo., 1940-41, 47-49; legal dept. Abbott Labs., North Chicago, 1949-61, asst. sec., 1951-55, gen. counsel, 1954-61, sec., 1955-61, v.p. adminstrn., 1961-66, exec. v.p. adminstrn., 1966—, also dir.; dir. Abbott Labs., Ltd., Can.; mng. dir. Abbott Finance Co. S.a.r.l., Switzerland. Mem. Chgo. Crime Commn. Treas., bd. dirs. Hosp. Planning Council for Met. Chgo.; pres., bd. dirs. Abbott Labs. Fund; bd. dirs., pres. Abbott Found.; chmn. bd. dirs. Evanston Hosp.; bd. dirs. Northwestern U. - McGaw Med. Center. Served as capt. Signal Corps, AUS, 1942-46. Mem. Internat., Am., Ill., N.Y. State, Chgo. bar assns., Am. Judicature Soc., Theta Chi, Phi Delta Phi. Mason. Clubs: Glen View (Golf, Ill.); University, Attic (Chgo.). Home: 770 Bryant Av Winnetka IL 60093 Office: 135 S LaSalle St Chicago IL 60603

GERDES, LOUIS GEORGE, editor; b. Hamlin, Ia., Jan. 14, 1919; s. Louis George and Mable (Hunt) G.; B.J., U. Mo., 1941; m. Helen M. Swank, July 9, 1941; 1 son, Stephen Lee. Sports editor Grand Island (Neb.) Herald, 1937; reporter Grand Island Bull., summers 1938, 39; editor Jefferson County (Wis.) Union, 1941; sports copy writer Omaha World-Herald, 1941-43, govtl. and polit reporter, 1943-51, city editor, 1951-66, exec. editor, 1966—, v.p., 1969—; dir. World Pub. Co. Bd. dirs. Neb. Crippled Childrens Soc., Omaha Found. Pub. Giving. Mem. Am. Philatelic Soc., Am. Soc. Newspaper Editors, Omaha Tennis Assn. (bd. dirs.). Mem. United Ch. Christ (deacon). Club: Omaha. Author booklets on municipal govt., parking. Home: 1326 S 91st Av Omaha NB 68124 Office: Omaha World Herald 14th and Dodge Sts Omaha NB 68102

GERDINE, LEIGH, coll. pres.; b. Sheyenne, N.D., June 22, 1917; s. O. E. and Margaret E. (Mattson) G.; A.B., U. N.D., 1938; Mus. B. (Rhodes scholar), Oxford U. (Eng.), 1941, postgrad., 1946-48; Ph.D., U. Ia., 1941; m. Alice Strauch Meyer, Nov. 21, 1961. Asst. prof. music Miss. State Coll. for Women, Columbus, 1941-42; asso. prof. music, exec. sec. dept. music Miami U., 1948-50; prof., chmn. dept. music Washington U., St. Louis, 1950-70; pres. Webster Coll., St. Louis, 1970—. Chmn. bd. Block Partnership, Inc., 1967-70. Program annotator St. Louis Symphony Orch., 1950-66, acting mgr., 1965-67; chmn. music com. Mo. Council Arts, 1965-70; bd. dirs. Greater St. Louis Arts and Edn. Council, St. Louis Symphony Soc. Served with USAAF, 1942-46; ETO. Decorated Bronze Star medal; Croix de Guerre (France). Mem. Blue Key, Phi Beta Kappa, Omicron Delta Kappa, Phi Mu Alpha. Home: 6244 Forsyth Blvd St Louis MO 63105

GERE, BREWSTER HUNTINGTON, mathematician, educator; b. Syracuse, N.Y., Dec. 5, 1910; s. William Peck and Gertrude (Gardner) G.; B.A., Yale, 1930; M.A. (grad. scholar 1933-34), Syracuse U., 1934; Ph.D., Mass. Inst. Tech., 1938; m. Margaret Jewitt Chamberlain, July 31, 1937; children—Judith Chamberlain, Brewster Huntington, Margaret Lynn. Grad. asst. Syracuse U., 1934-35; instr. Mass. Inst. Tech., 1936-39, Herzl Jr. Coll., Chgo., 1939-42; asst. prof. math. and mechanics U.S. Naval Postgrad. Sch., 1946-47, vis. prof. mathematics and mechanics, 1962-63; mem. faculty Hamilton Coll., 1947—, prof. math., 1953—, chmn. dept., 1950-69, dir. summer Insts., 1959-62, 64, 67—, now also Samuel F. Pratt prof.; vis. prof. dept. statistics U. N.C., 1970-71. Served to lt. comdr. USNR, 1942-46; comdr. Ret. Res. Mem. Am. Math. Soc., Math. Assn. Am. (dir. Programed Learning Project com. on ednl. media 1965-68), Nat. Council Tchrs. Math., Am. Assn. U. Profs. Home: 11 Stryker Lane Clinton NY 13323

GERE, JAMES MONROE, educator; b. Syracuse, N.Y., June 14, 1925; s. William S. and Carol (Hixson) G.; B.S., Rensselaer Poly. Inst., 1949, M.S. 1951; Ph.D., Stanford, 1954; m. Janice M. Platt, June 1, 1946; children—Susan M., William P., David S. Instr., Rensselaer Poly. Inst., 1949-51; faculty Stanford, 1954—, prof. civl engring., 1962—, asso. dean Sch. Engring., 1960-67, exec. head dept. civil engring., 1967—. Cons. in field, 1954—. Served with USAAF, 1943-46; ETO. Mem. Am. Soc. C.E., Am. Soc. Engring. Edn., Sigma Xi, Tau Beta Pi. Author textbooks in field, also tech. papers. Cons. editor D. Van Nostrand Co., Inc., 1965—. Home: 932 Valdez Pl Stanford CA 94305

GEREN, PRESTON MURDOCH, Jr., architect, engr.; b. Ft. Worth, Dec. 16, 1923; s. Preston Murdoch and Linda (Giesecke) G.; student Tex. A. and M. U., 1941-43; B.S., Ga. Inst. Tech., 1947; m. Eva Colleen Edwards, May 2, 1952; children—Charles Lupton, Preston

Murdoch III, Eva Colleen, Chandra E. Archtl. draftsman Austin Co., 1941; designer, engr. Preston M. Geren, Ft. Worth, 1947-51, partner, 1951-69, sr. partner, 1969—; dir. Cassco Land Co., Equitable Savs. Assn.; works include 1st Nat. Bank of Ft. Worth, Oceanography and Meterology Bldg. of Tex. A. and M. U., Lee High Sch. (Midland, Tex.). Vice pres. Ft. Worth Progress, Inc. Mem. exec. com. Trinity River Authority. Dir. Ft. Worth Children's Hosp. Served as 1st lt., AUS, 1943-46; ETO. Decorated Silver Star, Purple Heart. Recipient design awards, Tex. Soc. Architects, Am. Assn. Sch. Adminstrs. Mem. Tex. Soc. Architects (pres.). Episcopalian (vestryman). Clubs: Rotary (dir.), Exchange (pres.), Ft. Worth (dir.), River Crest Country (dir.), Shady Oaks Country (Ft. Worth). Home: 32 Valley Ridge Ft Worth TX 76107 Office: Ft Worth National Bank Bldg Ft Worth TX 76102

GERETY, PETER LEO, bishop; b. Shelton, Conn., July 19, 1912; s. Peter Leo and Charlotte (Daly) G.; student St. Thomas Sem., Bloomfield, Conn., 1934, Seminaire St. Sulpice, Paris, France, 1939. Ordained priest Roman Cath. Ch., 1939; asst. pastor, New Haven, 1939-42; dir. Blessed Martin de Porres Interracial Center, 1942-56; pastor, New Haven, 1956-66; coadjutor bishop, Portland, Me., 1966—; apostolic adminstr., Portland, 1967—; bishop Portland, 1969—. Address: 510 Ocean Av Portland ME 04103

GERETY, PIERCE JOSEPH, lawyer, bus. exec.; b. Shelton, Conn., Mar. 6, 1914; s. Peter Leo and Charlotte U. (Daly) G.; LL.B. cum laude, Fordham U., 1942; m. Helen Martin, June 8, 1940; children—Pierce, Peter Leo, Thomas Richard, Miles Stephen. Admitted to N.Y. bar, 1942, Conn. bar, 1942, D.C. Investment Policy, 1970-71; adv. com. UN Trade and Devel. Bd.; adviser Com. Econ. bar, 1958; asso. Wilkie, Owen, Otis, Farr, Gallagher and Walton, N.Y.C., 1942-43, 44-47; partner Curtis, Trevethan and Gerety, Bridgeport, Conn., 1947-57; gen. counsel U.S. Civil Service Commn. and legal adviser to the Pres.'s asst. on personnel, Washington, 1954-55; dep. adminstr. Refugee Relief Program, Dept. of State, 1955-57; gen. counsel Fed. Housing Adminstrn., 1957-58; N.Y. partner Wolf, Bloch, Schorr and Solis-Cohen, Phila., 1959-61; partner Wolf and Gerety, N.Y.C., 1961-63, Royall, Koegel and Rogers, N.Y.C., 1963-66; v.p., counsel Ogden Corp., N.Y.C., 1966-68; chmn. bd., dir. Gould, Cargill & Co., Inc., 1968—. Town counsel, Fairfield, Conn., 1945-55. Chmn., Am. Immigration and Citizenship Conf., 1964-65. Mem. Rep. State Central Com. Conn., 1948-54. Mem. Am., Fed., Conn., Bridgeport bar assn. Home: 1133 Cedar Rd Southport CT 06490 Office: 245 Park Av New York City NY 10017

GERGEN, JOHN L., educator; b. Hastings, Minn., Sept. 23, 1927; s. Albert Nicholas and Frances (Lindley) G.; B.S., U. Minn., 1952, M.S., 1956, Ph.D., 1960; m. Candace E. Halloff, June 1, 1960. Asst. prof. physics U. Minn., Duluth, 1960-64, asso. prof., 1964-68, prof., 1968—, acting dir. Computer Center, 1965-70, dir., 1970—. Cons. USAF, 1960-61. Served with USAAF, 1944-47. Research in atmospheric physics, real-time computer operating systems. Home: 910 W Tischer Rd Duluth MN 55803

GERHARD, GERHARD RUSSELL, lawyer; b. Eureka Springs, Ark., Aug. 12, 1906; s. Albert W. Rhein and Emme C. Gerhard; A.B., Amherst Coll., 1927; J.D., Harvard, 1930; m. Jean Anne Opdyke, Apr. 7, 1947; children—Geoffrey, Gina. Admitted to Mo. bar, 1930, N.Y. bar, 1931, N.H. bar, 1969; practiced in N.Y.C., 1931-68; of counsel Appleton, Rice & Perrin, 1969—. Past dir. Cin. Chem. Works. Served to lt. comdr. USNR, 1942-45. Mem. Am., N.H. bar assns., Assn. Bar City N.Y., Phi Beta Kappa, Beta Theta Pi. Clubs: Harvard (N.Y.C.); Manhasset Bay (N.Y.) Yacht (past trustee). Home: Shaker Rd North Sutton NH 03260 Office: 63 Wall St New York City NY 10005

GERHARDSEN, EINAR HENRY, mem. parliament Norway; b. Oslo, Norway, May 10, 1897; s. Gerhard and Emma (Hansen) Olsen; ed. pub. sch., tech. sch. and socialist day sch.; Conrad Mohr scholar studying labor movement in Germany and Austria, 1929- 30; m. Werna Christie, Oct. 11, 1932; children—Torgunn, Truls, Rune. Road laborer, Oslo, 1914-22; sec. Norwegian Municipal Working Men's Assn., 1922-23, Norwegian Labor Party, 1923-25, Oslo Labor Party, 1925- 36; mem. Oslo City Council since 1932, dep. mayor of Oslo, 1940 and 1945; sec. Norwegian Labor Party, 1936-39; imprisoned by Germans, 1941- 45; prime minister of Norway under coalition govt., June 1945, under labor govt., Nov. 1945-Nov. 1951; mem. Storting, pres., 1945-55; leader of Labor Party, 1945-65; prime minister under labor govt., 1955-65; mem. parliament, 1965—. Author: The Delegate, A Handbook for Practical Organization Work, 1931. Home: Sofienberggt 61 Oslo Norway Office: Akersgaten 42 Oslo Norway Akersgaten 42 Oslo, Norway.

GERHARDT, HARRISON ALAN, corp. exec.; b. Bklyn., Jan. 9, 1909; s. Jacob Herman and Rose (Schneider) G.; B.S., U.S. Mil. Acad., 1932; M.A., Columbia, 1942; grad. Command and Gen. Staff Sch., 1943, Armed Forces Staff Coll., 1947, Nat. War Coll., 1952; m. Eleanor Mason, June 21, 1949. Commd. 2d lt., C.A.C., U.S. Army, 1932, advanced through grades to maj. gen., 1961; assigned C.A. Sch., 1938-39, U.S. Mil. Acad., 1939-43, War Dept. Gen. Staff, 1943; exec. officer Office Asst. Sec. War, 1943-45; U.S. sec. Allied Control Council, Berlin, 1945-48; assigned Dept. Army Gen. Staff, 1948- 49; spl. asst. to U.S. High Commnr., Germany, 1949-51; div. dir. Dept. Def., 1952-54; comdg. officer 19th ARAD Group, 1954-55; faculty Nat. War Coll., 1955-56; comdg. gen. 31st Arty. Brigade, Tacoma, 1957-58; chief staff I Corps, Korea, 1958-59; dep. chief legislative liaison Dept. Army, 1959-61, chief, 1961-62; comdg. gen. So. European Task Force, Italy, 1962-64, 1st ARAD COM Region, 1964-67; project dir. UN Assn., N.Y.C., 1967-69; pres. Norala, Inc. Military adviser Council of Foreign Ministers, 1947, 49, 50, 54, 3d Gen. Assembly UN, 1948, NATO Ministerial Council, 1952, 53, 54. Decorated D.S.M. with cluster, Commendation ribbon; Order White Lion, Distinguished Mil. Medal Merit (Czechoslovakia); Order Ulchi (Korea); Knight Officer (Italy); hon. citizen Wash. State. Mem. Am. Mil. Inst., Royal Arcanum, Polit. Sci. Acad., Assn. U.S. Army, Council Fgn. Relations, UN Assn. U.S.A. Club: N.Y. Athletic. Home: 5142 Worthington Dr Westgate MD 20016 Office: United Nations Assn 345 E 46th St NYC10017

GERHARDT, PHILIPP, educator, microbiologist; b. Milw., Dec. 30, 1921; s. Philipp W. and Agnes (Daigh) G.; Ph.B. with honors, U. Wis., 1943, M.S., 1947, Ph.D., 1949; m. Vera Mary Armstrong, Feb. 24, 1945; children—Ellen Daigh, Stephen Philipp, Doris Mary. Asst. prof. microbiology Ore. State U., 1949-51; faculty microbiology U. Mich. Med. Sch., 1953-65; prof., chmn. dept. microbiology and pub. health Colls. Natural Sci., Human Medicine and Vet. Medicine and Agr. Expt. Sta., Mich. State U., 1965—. Cons. U.S. Army Biol. Labs., NRC. Served with AUS, 1943-46, 51-52. Wis. Alumni Research Found. fellow, 1946-47; NIH research fellow, 1947-49. Mem. Am. Soc. Microbiology (sec. 1961-67), Am. Acad. Microbiology (charter fellow, bd. govs. 1970—), Brit. Soc. Gen. Microbiology, A.A.A.S., Phi Beta Kappa, Sigma Xi. Contbr. articles to profl. jours. Home: 529 Woodland Dr East Lansing MI 48823

GERHART, PAUL, pharm. co. exec.; B.S., Columbia, 1948; married. Jr. accountant Arthur Young & Co., N.Y.C., 1948-55, sr. accountant, Caracas, Venezuela, 1949-51, N.Y.C., 1951-53; individual practice accounting, 1953-56; auditor, systems gen. accountant Warner-Lambert Co., Morris Plains, N.J., 1956, controller, profl. products group, 1956-69, controller, 1969—. Served with AUS, 1943-46. C.P.A., N.Y. Office: 201 Tabor Rd Morris Plains NJ 07950*

GERHOLD, PAUL E. J., assn. exec.; b. Hamilton, O., Oct. 24, 1916; s. George S. and Amanda (Block) G.; B.S.C. with highest distinction, Northwestern U., 1936, M.B.A., 1938; m. Corinne Krusemark, Jan. 6, 1942; children—Paul E. J., Timothy, Mark, Philip. Sr. asso. Stewart Dougall & Assos.; mgr. market research dept. Dancer, Fitzgerald & Sample, N.Y.C., 1954; v.p. charge media and research Foote, Cone & Belding, N.Y.C., 1954-64, director media and research, 1959-64; vice president, director research, devel. and planning J. Walter Thompson Co., 1964-69; pres. Advt. Research Found., 1969—. Past pres. Market Research Council, Copy Research Council. Served to capt. AUS, 1940-46. Mem. Am. Marketing Assn. Author: How Advertising Works. Home: 24 Crescent Rd Larchmont NY 10538 Office: 3 E 54th St New York City NY 10022

GERHOLZ, ROBERT PAUL, home builder; b. Merrill, Wis., June 25, 1896; s. Robert and Bertha (Degener) G.; grad. Ferris Inst., Big Rapids, Mich., 1916, LL.D., 1957; student U. Wis., 1919-21; m. Freda Clark, Sept. 15, 1923; children—Robert Charles, Barbara Lee, Janyce Allyn. Organizer, Robert P. Gerholz Co., homebuilders, realtors, 1922; pres. Gerholz Ins. Service 1940-59, Gerholz Community Homes, Inc., 1947—, Gerholz Supply Co., 1949- -, Robert P. Gerholz Orgn., 1952—, Gerholz Agy., Inc., 1959-68; treas. Gerholz-Healy Co., 1941-47, Bassett Park Homes, Inc., 1943-47; dir. Mich. Nat. Bank of Flint, central bd. Mich. Nat. Bank, Lansing, Mack Trucks, Inc., The Wickes Corp. Active YMCA, Boy Scouts; mem. Mich. Gov.'s Exec. Com. State Unemployment Compensation, 1932; mem. Civil Service Commn., 1944-49; mem. industry adv. com. FHA, 1957-61. Sec.-treas. Genesee County Real Estate Bd., 1927, pres., 1928, now mem.; pres. Citizens Civic League, 1929; treas. Flint Light Opera Co., 1944; dir. Am. Real Property Fedn., 1956; mem. adv. com. U. Wis. Sch. Bus., 1966-68; mem. bd. control Ferris State Coll., 1967—, vice chmn., 1969—; mem. exec. com. Religious Heritage Am., 1969—. Served to lt. F.A., U.S. Army, 1917-19. Named Flint Realtor of Year, 1966, Mich. Realtor of Year, 1966. Mem. Mich. Real Estate Assn. (pres. 1931), Nat. Assn. Home Builders (pres. 1944, chmn. Research Inst. 1961; dir.), U.S. C. of C. (dir.-at-large 1960-65); chmn. Can.-U.S. com. U.S. sect. 1963-64; pres. 1965-66, chmn. bd. 1966- 67, chmn. exec. com. 1967-68, F. Stuart Fitzpatrick Meml. award 1968), Mich. C. of C. (dir. 1968—), Urban Land Inst. Am. (trustee 1966—, 1st v.p. 1953-54), Nat. Assn. Real Estate Bds. library sci., (dir.; pres. 1950), Flint Fedn. Chs. (pres. 1932), Beta Gamma Sigma (hon. Alpha chpt.). Presbyn. (elder). Mason, Elk, Rotarian (pres. 1932). Home: 1704 Crescent Dr Flint, MI 48503 Office: 4020 Hammerberg Rd Flint MI 48507

GERICKE, OTTO LUKE, hosp. med. dir., psychiatrist; b. San Francisco, July 16, 1907; s. Julius Philip and Therese H. (Correia) G.; A.B., U. Cal. at Berkeley, 1929; M.D., U. Cal. Med. Sch., 1933; certificate psychiatry, U. Pa., 1939; m. Catherine Rose Levi, Mar. 31, 1934; children—Philip Otto, Douglas Neil, Robert James, Kathleen T. Intern San Francisco Hosp., 1932- 33; asst. resident St. Joseph's Hosp., San Francisco, 1933-34, resident, 1934-35; pvt. practice gen. medicine, Daly City, Cal., 1935-36; asst. dist. surgeon Ft. Douglas Civilian Conservation Corps Dist., 1936; physician, psychiatrist Mendocino State Hosp., Talmage, Cal., 1939-42; asst. supt. Stockton (Cal.) State Hosp., 1945-46; supt., med. dir. Patton (Cal.) State Hosp., 1946—; asso. clin. prof. psychiatry Loma Linda U., 1958-67, clin. prof. psychiatry, 1967—; med. examiner criminal cases and lunacy cases, 1951—. Served to lt. col., M.C., AUS, 1942-45; col. Res. ret. Diplomate Am. Bd. Psychiatry and Neurology. Life fellow Am. Psychiat. Assn. Address: Patton State Hosp Patton CA 92369

GERICKE, PAUL WILLIAM, librarian, educator; b. St. Louis, Apr. 8, 1924; s. Orville Herman and Irma Rose (Reinhart) G.; B.S. in Elec. Engring., Washington U., St. Louis, 1949; B.D., So. Bapt. Theol. Sem., 1960; Th.D., New Orleans Bapt. Theol. Sem., 1964; postgrad. La. State U., 1970-71; m. Jean Fisher, Feb. 18, 1953; 1 son, Michael Paul. Instr. electronics USAF, 1949; calibration engr. Emerson Electric Co., St. Louis, 1950; asst. pastor Calvary Bapt. Ch., St. Louis, 1951-53; ordained to ministry Bapt. Ch., 1952; pastor First Bapt. Ch., Marceline, Mo., 1954-56, New Hope Bapt. Ch., St. Louis, 1957, Summit Park Bapt. Chapel, Louisville, 1959-60, Logtown (Miss.) Bapt. Ch., 1960-64; asst. prof., dir. library services New Orleans Bapt. Theol. Sem., 1965—. Served with AC, USNR, 1942-46. Mem. Am. Theol. Library Assn., Creation Research Soc., Theta Xi. Author: The Preaching of Robert G. Lee, 1967; The Ministers Filing System, 1971. Home: 4309 Seminary Pl New Orleans LA 70126 Office: 3939 Gentilly Blvd New Orleans LA 70126

GERIG, JARED FRANKLIN, clergyman, educator; b. Allen County, Ind., June 29, 1907; s. Jonas F. and Clara Mae (Miller) G.; diploma Fort Wayne (Ind.) Bible Coll., 1929; Th.B., Malone Coll., Canton O., 1938; A.B., Cleve. State U., 1941; M.A., Ariz. State U., 1946; D.D., Wheaton Coll., 1958; postgrad. Ind. U., U. Cal. at Los Angeles; m. Mildred Grace Eicher, Dec. 22, 1928; children—Wesley Lee, Gwendolyn Grace (Mrs. Arthur Riewald), William Dean. Ordained to ministry Missionary Ch., 1931; minister in Ind., Ohio, Ariz., 1929-45; dean Ft. Wayne Bible Coll., 1945-50, Azusa (Cal.) Coll., 1950-52; pres. Missionary Ch., Ft. Wayne, 1952-58; pres. Ft. Wayne Bible Coll., 1958-71, chancellor, 1971—. Vis. prof. Am. Inst. Holy Land Studies, Jerusalem, Israel, fall 1964, mem. bd., 1962—. Pres., Nat. Assn. Evangelicals, 1964-66, also chmn. bd. adminstrn. and exec. com.; mem. exec. com. Accrediting Assn. Bible Colls., 1959-60, 62—, pres., 1970—; mem. gen. bd. Missionary Ch., 1948-50, 52-68; mem. bd. Winona Lake (Ind.) Christian Assembly, 1962-67. Mem. Delta Epsilon Chi. Co-author: The Missionary Church Association, Its Origin and Development, 1950. Home: 2121 Engle Rd Fort Wayne IN 46809

GERITY, JAMES, Jr., corp. exec.; b. Toledo, Jan. 5, 1904; s. James and Mary (Kelley) G.; student Toledo U., 1921-23; m. Virginia Boland, Aug. 11, 1927. Pres. Gerity-Whitaker Co., 1930-37, Gerity Adrian Mfg. Corp., 1937-45; pres., gen. mgr., dir. Gerity Mich. Corp., Adrian, since 1938, chmn. bd. 1946-56, chmn. bd. Gerity Mich. Die Casting Co., 1945-46, pres., 1946- 47; owner, pres. Gerity Broadcasting Co., Gerity Pub. Co., Bay City, Mich., Lee Travel Bur., Bay City, Saginaw and Flint, Mich., Gerity Products, Inc., Toledo; a founder Schultz Die Casting Co., Toledo (became Gerity-Schultz Corp. 1963), chmn. bd., maj. stockholder. Dir. Heart Inst. Miami Beach; chmn. adv. council Coll. Commerce, U. Notre Dame; on bd. Toledo Clinic Found., St. Francis Hosp. (Miami Beach). President's Com. 100, Miami Beach, Fla. Hon. del. Mich. State Med. Soc. Recipient Air Force Exceptional Service award, 1963; decorated Knight Comdr. Equestrian Order Holy Sepulchre Jerusalem. Mem. Am. Legion. Lion, Elk. Clubs: Golf, Athletic, Recess, Detroit (Detroit); Warwick Hills Country (Flint, Mich.); Seaview (Absecon, N.J.); Key Largo (Fla.); Coral Harbor (Nassau); Bath, La Gorce Country, Surf (pres.) (Miami Beach); Indian Creek Country (Miami); Chicago Press, Chicago Athletic Assn. (Chgo.); Detroit (Mich.) Press; Iverness, Toledo, Adrian (Toledo); Bloomfields Country (Detroit); Metropolitan, Advertising, Canadian (N.Y.); New York Athletic; Nat. Press, Broadcasters (Washington). Home: Deer Park Adrian MI (winter): Surf Club Surfside FL Office: 121 W Maumee St Adrian MI 49221 also: Pick-Durant Hotel Flint MI 48501

GERKEN, WALTER BLAND, ins. co. exec.; b. N.Y.C., Aug. 14, 1922; s. Walter Adam and Virginia (Bland) G.; B.A., Wesleyan U., 1948; M. Pub. Adminstrn., Maxwell Sch. Citizenship and Pub. Affairs, Syracuse, 1958; m. Darlene Stolt, Sept. 6, 1952; children—Walter C., Ellen M., Beth L., Daniel J., Andrew P., David A. Supr. budget and adminstrv. analysis Wis., Madison, 1950-54; mgr. investments Northwestern Mut. Life Ins. Co., Milw., 1954-67; v.p. finance Pacific Mut. Life Ins. Co., Los Angeles, 1967-69, exec. v.p., 1969—, also dir.; dir. A.C.S.C. Mgmt. Services. Bd. dirs. Los Angeles Jr. Achievement, Asso. Cal. Inst. Tech., Los Angeles World Affairs Council, Cal. Taxpayers Assn., Childrens Hosp.; trustee Occidental Coll., Wesleyan U., Middletown, Conn. Served to capt. USAAF, 1942-46. Decorated D.F.C., Air medal. Clubs: Town (Milw.); California (Los Angeles). Home: 1340 E California Blvd Pasadena CA 91006 Office: Pacific Mut Bldg Los Angeles CA 90054

GERLACH, ARCH C. geographer; b. Tacoma, May 12, 1911; s. William Henry and Kate Alice (Cooper) G.; A.B., San Diego State Coll., 1933; M.A., U. Cal. at Los Angeles, 1935; Ph.D., U. Wash., 1943; m. Arlene M. Schmiedeman, 1935. Geographer, Los Angeles City Coll., 1939-42; acting chief map div. Dept. State, 1945-46; asso. prof. geography U. Wis., 1946-50; chief geography and map div., incumbent chair of geography Library of Congress, Washington, 1950-67; U.S. rep. directing council Pan-Am. Inst. Geography and History, 1958-69, v.p., 1965-69, pres., 1969—. Vis. prof. geography U. Mich., 1957-58; chief Nat. Atlas project U.S. Geol. Survey, 1962-63, staff geographer, 1963- 67, chief geographer U.S. Geol. Survey, 1967—. U.S. mem. commn. on nat. atlases Internat. Geog. Union, 1964—, v.p., 1964-68; chmn. NRC adv. com. geography Dept. State, 1956-62. Served as lt., cartographer and map intelligence officer OSS, USNR, 1942-45. Recipient Distinguished Service award Interior Dept., 1971. Hon. fellow Am. Geog. Soc.; mem. Am. Congress on Surveying and Mapping, Assn. Am. Geographers (pres. 1962-63), Nat. Council Geography Tchrs., Spl. Libraries Assn. (nat. chmn. geog. and map div. 1953-55, mem. exec. bd. 1956-59), Am. Soc. Photogrammetry, Pan Am. Inst. Geography and History (pres. 1969—). Editor: Profl. Geographer, 1951-54. Home: 5615 Newington Rd Washington DC 20016 Office: US Geol Survey Washington DC 20242

GERLACH, JOHN B., glass and rubber co. exec.; b. Columbus, O., Jan. 28, 1927; s. John Joseph and Pauline (Pollitt) G.; student Ohio State U., 1945-47, Ohio U., 1947-49; m. Dareth Axene, Sept. 30, 1949; children—John B., David P., Susan. Partner, John Gerlach & Co., Columbus, 1949—; pres., dir. Lancaster Glass Corp. (Ohio), 1958—, Ind. Glass Co., Dunkirk, 1952—, Lancaster Colony Corp., 1963—; sec.-treas., dir. Pretty Products, Inc., Coshocton, O., Nat. Glove, Inc., Coshocton; dir. Columbus Dental Mfg. Co., Bush Woolen Mills, Inc., Columbus, Jackson Corp. (Ohio). Clubs: University, Columbus, Sciotto Country; Coshocton Country; Lancaster Country. Home: 2320 Onandaga Dr Columbus OH 43215 Office: 37 Broad St Columbus OH 43215

GERLACH, SISTER MARY CANISIA, hosp. adminstr.; b. Germany, Aug. 29, 1914; d. Joseph and Maria Anna (Balzer) Gerlach; came to U.S., 1935, naturalized, 1941; R.N., St. Francis Sch. Nursing, Peoria, Ill., 1937-40, certified registered nurse anesthetist, 1941; B.S., Creighton U., 1951; M.A. in Hosp. Adminstrn., U. St. Louis, 1960. Joined Sisters Third Order St. Francis, 1935; instr. St. Francis Sch. Anesthesia, 1944, 51-54, dir. sch., 1954-58, instr. Sch. Nursing, 1946-48; floor supr. St. Joseph's Hosp., Keokuk, Ia., 1940- 43; floor supr. St. Francis Hosp., 1945, adminstr., 1960—. Bd. mgrs. Sisters Third Order St. Francis, 1960-66. Pres. St. Francis Community Clinic, Peoria, 1967—; mem. adv. council for health agys. Ill. Central Coll., Peoria. Fellow Am. Coll. Hosp. Adminstrs.; mem. Am., Cath., Ill. hosp. assns. Address: St Francis Hosp Peoria IL 61603

GERLI, FRANCIS M., business exec.; b. Bronxville, N.Y., Jan. 28, 1914; s. Paolino and Pearl (Egan) G.; A.B., Georgetown U., 1934; LL.B., Fordham U., 1937; Doctor of Economics, Assumption College, 1967; m. Madeline Maher, June 18, 1945; children—Jennifer, Antonia, Madeline Marie, Nina. Admitted to N.Y. bar, 1938; pres., dir. Gerli & Co., Inc.; v.p., dir. Cheney Bros., Inc.; dir. Bank of Tokyo Trust Co. Hon. trustee Fordham U.; trustee Assumption Coll., Manhattan Coll. Served as comdr. USNR, 1940-45. Clubs: University (N.Y.C.); Greenwich Country, Ekwanok Country; Farmington Country. Home: Field Point Park Greenwich CT 06830 Office: 155 E 44th St New York City NY 10017

GERLI, PAOLINO, silk mcht.; b. Milan, Italy, Oct. 20, 1890; student Dr. Schmidt's Sch., St. Gaul, Switzerland, Leo XIII Coll., Milan, Italy; LL.D., Manhattan Coll.; Dr. Textile Industries, Clemson Coll.; m. Pearl Kingston Egan, 1910 (dec.); children—Francis, Pauline. Gerli & Co., Inc., N.Y.C., Cheney Bros., Inc.; pres., dir. Cheney Bros.-So., Inc.; v.p., dir. Commodity Exchange; chmn., dir. Julius Kayser & Co., Belding Heminway Co.; chmn. bd. Gerli & Co., Inc.; dir. Interstate Dept. Stores, Brit. & Fgn. Ins. Co.; hon. dir. Mfrs. Hanover Trust Co.; trustee Emigrant Indsl. Savs. Bank. Dir. Am. Italy Soc., Inc., Japan Soc., N.Y. Conv. Bur. Trustee Manhattan Coll., St. Vincent's Hosp. Served with OSS, World War II. Decorated Knight Comdr. Orders Holy Sepulchre, Sacred Treasure (Japan), Italian Crown; Knight Malta; recipient Emanuel d'Alzon medal. Mem. Nat. Fedn. Textiles (pres.), Internat. Silk Assn. (hon. chmn.), Nat. Raw Silk Exchange (pres.). Clubs: Greenwich (Conn.) Country; Manhattan, Metropolitan (N.Y.C.). Home: Field Point Park Greenwich CT 06830 Office: 155 E 44th St New York City NY 10017

GERLOFF, GERALD CARL, educator; b. Aurora, Neb., Jan. 26, 1920; s. Kay T. and Meta (Nielsen) Gjerloff; B.S., U. Neb., 1941; Ph.D., U. Wis., 1948; m. Mary Ellen Varney, Jan. 22, 1949; children—Barbara, Robert. Chemist, Hercules Powder Co., 1942-45; grad. research asst. soils dept. U. Wis., 1941-42, 45-48, project asso. botany dept., 1948-49, mem. faculty, 1949—, prof. botany, 1959—, dir. Inst. Plant Devel., 1966—; on leave with Kearney Found. Soil Sci., U. Cal. at Berkeley, 1956-57. Mem. Am. Soc. Plant Physiologists, Soil Sci. Soc. Am., Scandinavian Soc. Plant Physiology, A.A.A.S., Sigma Xi. Home: 5 Montauk Pl Madison WI 53711

GERLOUGH, DANIEL LAUDER, educator; b. San Diego, May 31, 1916; s. Ludwig Sherman and Margaret E. (Lauder) G.; B.S. in Engring., Cal. Inst. Tech., 1937; M.S. in Elec. Engring., U. Cal. at Berkeley, 1948; Ph.D. in Engring., U. Cal. at Los Angeles, 1955; m. Jean Claire Shearer, Aug. 3, 1939; 1 dau., Constance Claire (Mrs. David H. Boyd); 1 foster dau., Liv Johnsen (Mrs. Willard R. Stevens, Jr.). Chief geophys. field party Mott-Smith Corp., Houston, 1937- 40; research analyst, methods analyst N.Am. Aviation, Inc., Los Angeles, 1940-42; research engr., quality control engr. Plomb Tool Co., Los Angeles, 1942-44; quality control engr. Pettit Engring. Co., Los Angeles, 1944-45; research engr. Menasco Mfg. Co., Burbank, Cal., 1945- 47; mem. faculty U. Cal. at Los Angeles, 1948-59, asso. prof. engring., asso. research engr. Inst. Transp and Traffic Engring., 1956-59; head traffic systems sect. Thompson Ramo Wooldridge Inc., R-W Div., Canoga Park, Cal., 1959-63; mgr. traffic systems sect.

Planning Research Corp., Los Angeles, 1963-67; prof. transp. engring. U. Minn., 1967—; cons. in field, 1956—. Mem. Inst. Traffic Engrs., I.E.E.E., Operations Research Soc. Am., Am. Soc. Engring. Edn., Sigma Xi. Contbr. profl. jours. Patentee in field. Home: 1432 W Idaho Av St Paul, MN 55108. Office: Dept Civil Engring Univ Minn Minneapolis MN 55455

GERMAN, EDWARD CECIL, lawyer, b. Phila., Dec. 28, 1922; s. S. Edward and Reba L. (Trimble) G.; LL.B., Temple U., 1950; m. Jane L. Harlos, Sept. 2, 1950; 1 son, Jeffrey Neal. Admitted to Pa. bar, 1951; practice in Phila., 1951—; partner firm LaBrum and Doak. 1955—. Dist. dir. United Fund campaign, 1960; solicitor-counsel Civic Assns. Delaware County, 1955-60; sec. Haven Beach Assn., 1962-63, v.p. 1963-64; lectr. Practicing Law Inst. Bd. dirs. Def. Research Inst., 1962—; hon. trustee Pop Warners Little Scholars, 1966-67. Served with USAAF, 1942-46, with USAF, 1950-51. Mem. Am. (vice chmn. trial tactics com., 1966—), Pa., Phila. (mem. Pa. rules of civil procedure com. 1963—, unathorized practice law com. 1965—, common pleas court com. 1964—), bar assns., Fedn. Ins. Counsel (bd. govs, 1960-62, v.p. 1962-63, sec.-treas. 1963-65, exec. v.p. 1965-66, pres. 1966-67, chmn. bd. 1967-68), Am. Legion, 40 and 8, Internat. Assn. Ins. Counsel (def. research com.), Internat. Assn. Humble Humbugs, Pa. U.S. sec. state ednl. and cultural affairs, 1965-67; host C. of C., Phila. Def. Counsel Assn., Scribes, Phi Delta Phi. Presbyn. (treas. 1946-54). Mason (Shriner). Clubs: Union League, Down Town, Maxwell Memorial Football (Phila.); Beach Haven (N.J.) Yacht: Spray Beach (N.J.) Yacht; Seaview Country (Absecon, N.J.). Contbr. articles and monographs to legal lit. Home: 1208 Ormond Av Drexel Hill PA 19026 Office: 1500 Seven Penn Center Plaza Philadelphia PA 19103

GERMAN, LESLIE, educator; b. Dayton Ky., May 10, 1904; s. Orland and Etta (Underwood) G.; B.S., Centre Coll., Danville, Ky., 1926; M.S., Lafayette Coll., 1927; Ph.D., U. Cin., 1933; m. Mary Elizabeth Scales, Aug. 23, 1944; 1 son, Leslie Meriwether. Instr. chemistry Va. Mil. Inst., 1928-30, asst. prof., 1935-40, asso. prof., 1940, prof. chemistry, head dept., 1941-68; research chemist Sinclair Refining Co., East Chicago, Indiana, 1933-35; prof. chemistry Brevard (N.C.) Coll., 1968—. Mem. A.A.A.S., Am. Chem. Soc., Va. Acad. Sci. Democrat. Episcopalian. Address: 534 E Main St Brevard NC 28712

GERMANI, GINO, educator, sociologist; b. Rome, Italy, Feb. 4, 1911; s. Louis and Lina (Catalini) G.; student faculty econ. scis., U. Rome, 1930-34; Licenciado in Philosophy, U. Buenos Aires (Argentina), 1943; M.A. (hon.), Harvard, 1965; m. Celia Carpi, Nov. 12, 1954; children—Louis, Anna. Came to U.S., 1966. Research asso. Inst. Sociology, U. Buenos Aires, 1941-45; prof. sociology Colegio Libre de Estudios Superiores, Buenos Aires and Rosario, Argentina, 1946-55; prof. sociology U. Buenos Aires, 1955-65; dir. research Inst. sociology, 1955-65; prof. sociology Harvard, 1966—; vis. prof. U. Chgo., 1959, U. Cal. at Berkeley, 1961-62, Columbia, 1964- 65, U. Montevideo (Uruguay), 1958, 59, 63. Mem. Internat. Social Sci. Council, 1962-67; pres. Asociacion Sociologica Argentina, 1962-66. Mem. Internat. Sociol. Assn. (v.p. 1962-66), Consejo Latino Americano de Cencias Sociales (member of executive committee 1967—); fgn. hon. mem. Am. Acad. Arts and Scis. Author: Estructura Social de la Argentina, 1965; La Sociologia Cientifica, 1956; Politica y Sociedad, 1962; Politica Massa, 1960; La Sociologia en America Latina, 1964; Estudios de Sociologia y Psicologia Social, 1966; Sociologia de la modernization, 1969. Co-editor: Argentina Sociedad de Masas, 1965; also articles. Home: 201 Highland St West Newton, MA 02165 Office: William James Hall Kirkland St Harvard Univ Cambridge MA 02138

GERMANO, FRANK J., educator; b. Pittsfield, Mass., Apr. 24, 1910; s. Achille and Ernesta Germano; C.E., Rensselaer Polytech. Inst., 1931, M.C.E., 1932, D.C.E., 1934; m. Alma O'Connor, Sept. 7, 1937; children—Andrea, Carolyn, Charles. Head dept. engring. mechanics La. State U., 1948-52, prof., head dept. civil engring., 1953—, lectr. Politecnico di Milano, Italy, 1952-53. Mem. Am. Soc. C.E., Am. Soc. Engring. Edn., La. Engring. Soc., Sigma Xi, Tau Beta Pi, Phi Kappa Phi. Author: (with Cox) Fluid Mechanics; also (with Cox and Bateman) Strength of Materials. Home: 492 Stanford Av Baton Rouge LA 70808

GERMANY, ARCHIE HERMAN, educator; b. Dixon, Miss., Nov. 18, 1917; s. Willis H. and Virgie (White) G.; B.A., Miss. Coll., 1939; Ph.D., U. N.C., 1943; student Tufts U., 1959, U. S.W. La., 1966, N.W. La. Coll., 1968; m. Margaret Longino, May 30, 1943; children—Jean (Mrs. Michael L. Mosley), Betty (Mrs. Daniel Baugh, Jr.), Alice. Teaching fellow U. N.C., 1942, Ethyl Dow fellow, 1943; research asso. metall. lab. U. Chgo., 1943; chemist Clinton Labs., Oak Ridge, 1944-46; mem. faculty Miss. Coll., 1946—, prof. chemistry, 1949—, chmn. div. sci. and math., 1962—. Mem. Am. Chem. Soc., A.A.A.S., Miss. Acad. Scis. (pres. 1961), Sigma Xi. Kiwanian (pres. Clinton 1961). Home: 803 E Leake St Clinton MS 39056

GERMANY, EUGENE BENJAMIN, petroleum producer; b. Sweetwater, Tex., Sept. 18, 1892; s. John Wesley and Arona (Lea) G.; student Southwestern U., Georgetown, Tex., 1910-12, LL.D., 1947; student So. Meth. U., Dallas, 1915; m. Maggie Lee Wilson, June 8, 1915; children—Eugene Wilson, Annette Myra (Mrs. Jack S. Wilkes), Norman Garvin. Tchr. Grand Saline (Tex.) High Sch., 1915-20; cons. geologist, 1921-27; sr. partner E. B. Germany and Sons, 1927—; past chmn. Preston Bank, Dallas; pres. Lone Star Steel Co., 1947-62, chmn. bd. 1962-63. Columnist The Way I See It. Pres. Dallas Co. Park Cities Water Control and Development; mayor, Highland Park, 1934-42. Pres. Tex. State Parks Development Assn., 1957; chmn. Texas Indsl. Commn., 1958-65. Exec. com. Meth. Hosp., Dallas; mem. bd. Scottish Rite Crippled Children's Hosp., Dallas, Sabine River Development Board; mem. bd. trustees Southwestern U.; trustee Tex. Found. Voluntarily Supported Colls. and Univs. Mem. Tex. Employers' Ins. Assn. (bd.), Red River Valley Assn. (v.p. Tex. 1953), East Tex., Dallas chambers commerce, Philosophical Soc. of Texas (pres. 1962), Y.M.C.A. (bd.), Tex. Police Assn., Tex. Alcoholics Anonymous Assn., Petroleum Inst., Am. Foundrymen's Soc., Am. Assn. Petroleum Geologists, Am. Iron and steel Inst. (mem. of bd. of dirs.) Am. Inst. Mining and Metallugical Engrs., Tex. Acad. Sci., Nat. Assn. Mfrs., Nat. Indsl. Conf. Bd., Nat. Assn. Churches. Democrat (chmn. state exec. com. 1938-41). Methodist. Mason (past potentate), Elk. Clubs: Petroleum, Country (Dallas). Author: Pioneer of the Future, 1938; And Passing Through the Valley of Bacca He Made it a Well, 1941; Birds of a Feather, 1943; Honesty and Integrity in Methodist Church Politics, 1943; Democracy in Acting, 1944; Integrity As I Have Seen It, 1958. Home: Route 2 Caney Creek Rd Grand Saline TX 75140 Office: PO Box 12226 Dallas TX 75225

GERMER, LESTER HALBERT, physicist; b. Chgo., Oct. 10, 1896; s. Dr. Hermann G. and Marcia (Halbert) G.; A.B., Cornell U., 1917; M.A., Columbia, 1922, Ph.D., 1927; m. Ruth Woodard, Oct. 2, 1919; children—Emily (Mrs. V. W. Samms), John Halbert G. Engring. dept. Western Electric Co., 1917-25, research physicist, 1925-53: tech. staff. research physicist Bell Telephone Laboratories, 1925-61, Cornell University, New York, 1961—. Served as second lt. 139th aero squadron, A.E.F., 1918. Received Elliot Cresson medal, 1931. Fellow A.A.A.S., N.Y. Acad. Sci., Am. Phys. Soc. (chmn. N.Y. sect. 1944); mem. Soc. X-Ray and Electron Diffraction (v.p. 1943, president 1944), American Crystallographic Society, also Sigma Xi. Republican. Club: Appalachian Mountain of Boston (chmn. N.Y. chpt. 1951-52). Author sci. articles. Discoverer (with Dr. C.J. Davisson) of diffraction of electrons by crystals. 1927. Home: Long Hill Rd Millington NJ 07946 Office: Clark Hall Cornell U Ithaca NY 14850

GERMESHAUSEN, KENNETH JOSEPH, electronic research and devel. exec.; b. Woodland, Cal., May 12, 1907; s. of William and Florence (Bomberg) G.; student Poly. Coll. Engring., 1927-29; B.S., Mass. Inst. Tech., 1931; m. Pauline Seltzer, 1934; 1 dau., Nancy. Research asso. elec. engring. Mass. Inst. Tech., 1932—; staff mem. radiation lab., 1941-45; partner firm Edgerton, Germeshausen State U. of N.Y., 1970—; Nat. exec. com. bd. mem., & Grier, 1934-58; v.p., treas., Edgerton, Germeshausen & Grier, Inc. (co. name changed to EG&G, Inc. 1966), Bedford, Mass., 1947-54, president, 1954-65, chmn. bd. dirs., director research, 1965—. Mem. corp. Boston Mus. Sci.; mem. vis. com., standing com. on devel. Mass. Inst. Tech. Fellow I.E.E.E., Am. Acad. Arts and Sciences; member Am. Mgmt. Assn., Boston Research Dirs. Club, Soc. of Profl. Engrs. Alumni Assn. Mass. Inst. Tech. (v.p.). Inventor strobotron and hydrogen-thyraton. Patentee in field. Home: 240 Highland St Weston, MA 02193. Office: Crosby Dr Bedford MA 01730

GERMOND, STEPHEN D., banker. Sr. v.p., cashier 1st Nat. Bank Passaic County, Totowa, N.J. Office: 515 Union Blvd Borough of Totowa NJ 07511*

GERMUTH, FREDERICK GEORGE, Jr., physician, pathologist; b. Balt., Sept. 28, 1921; s. Frederick G. and Elizabeth (Brown) G.; A.B., Johns Hopkins, 1943, M.D., 1945; m. Felix Creighton, Apr. 14, 1964; children—Frederick Germu III, Michael Allen, Mary Allen, Robin Rebacca, Peter Allen, Felix Creighton. Immunologist, NIH, 1948-51; asst. prof. pathology Harvard Med. Sch., 1953-54; asso. prof. Johns Hopkins Sch. Medicine, 1955-58; prof., chmn. dept. pathology St. Louis Sch. Medicine, 1966-68, clin. prof. pathology, 1968—; dir. dept. lab. medicine St. John's Mercy Hosp., 1968; cons. surgeon gen. USPHS. Served with USPHS, 1948-51. Mem. Am. Assn. Pathologists and Bacteriologists, Am. Assn. Immunologists, Soc. Exptl. Pathology, Coll. Am. Pathologists, Phi Beta Kappa, Sigma Xi, Alpha Omega Alpha. Contbr. profl. jours. Home: Route 1 PO Box 229 Chesterfield, MO 63017. Office: 615 S New Ballas Rd St Louis MO 63141

GERNREICH, RUDI, designer, b. Vienna, Austria, Aug. 8, 1922; s. Siegmund and Elisabeth (Mueller) G.; came to U.S., 1938, nautralized, 1943; student Los Angeles City Coll., 1938-41, Los Angeles Art Center Sch., 1941-42. Modern dancer Lester Horton Dance Theatre, 1942-48; free-lance designer, N.Y.C., Los Angeles, 1948-51; designer Walter Bass, Inc., Beverly Hills, Cal., 1951- 59; swimwear designer Westwood Knitting Mills, Los Angeles, 1953-59; shoe designer Genesco Corp., 1958-60; founder, pres. GR Designs, Inc. (name changed to Rudi Gernreich, Inc. 1964), Los Angeles, 1960—; knitwear, swimwear designer Harmon Knitwear, Marinette, Wis., 1960—; mem. internat. designer adv. council Montgomery Ward, 1967—. Recipient Designer of Year award Sports Illustrated mag., 1956; Sporting Look award, 1963; spl. award for swimming design Coty Am. Fashion Critics, 1960, Winnie award, 1963; award for creative achievement women's knitwear industry Wool Knit Assos., 1960, 62; Am. Fortnight trophy Nieman-Marcus Co., 1961; London Sunday Times Internat. Spl. award, 1965; Filene's Design award, 1966; Coty Am. Fashion Critics Return award, 1966; named to Hall of Fame, 1967. Office: 8460 Santa Monica Blvd Los Angeles CA 90069 also 530 7th Av New York City NY 10018

GERNSBACK, MARCELLUS HARVEY, editor, publisher; b. N.Y.C., May 31, 1912; s. Hugo and Rose (Harvey) G.; B.A., Columbia, 1935; m. Elizabeth Ann Sandt, Sept. 25, 1943 (div. Jan. 1970); children—Mark, Wendy; m. 2d, Carol Ann Roth, Nov. 7, 1970. Asso. editor Short Wave and TV mag., 1938-40; cons. editor Radio-Electronics mag., 1946—, editor, 1961—, editor, pub., 1967—, editor-in-chief, pub., 1970—; pres. Gernsback Pub., Inc., N.Y.C., 1954—, Sexology Corp., N.Y.C., 1967—, Luz Mag., Inc., N.Y.C., 1967—; pub. Sexology, also Luz mag., 1967—, editor in chief, pub., 1970—. Served to maj. AUS, 1941-45. Office: 200 Park Av S New York City NY 10003

GEROLD, NICOLAS JOHN, educator; b. N.Y.C., Jan. 1, 1919; s. Nicolas Jean and Cecilia (Schwarz) G.; B.A., Brown U., 1942, M.A., 1948; Ph.D., Cornell U., 1951; m. Patricia Kenyon, June 25, 1949; children—Nicolas John, Alison Louise. Asst. prof. biology Hamilton Coll., Clinton, N.Y., 1951-58, asso. prof., 1958-64, prof., 1964—, chmn. dept. biology, 1966—. Served with AUS, 1942-46. Mem. Am. Inst. Biol. Scis., Am. Soc. Zoologists, A.A.A.S., Nat. Assn. Biol. Tchrs., Am. Assn. Med. Colls., Sigma Xi. Research histochemistry of cell division. Home: 13 Griffin Rd Clinton NY 13323

GEROW, RICHARD OLIVER, bishop; b. Mobile, Ala., May 3, 1885; s. Warren Rosencranz and Annie A. (Skehan) G.; prep. edn., McGill Inst., Mobile; A.B., Mt. St. Mary's Coll., Emmitsburg, Md., 1904, A.M., 1906, LL.D., 1957; S.T.D., North Am. Coll., Rome, 1909. Ordained priest R.C. Ch., 1909; asst. Cathedral, Mobile, vice chancellor and chancellor, 1909-20, rector, 1920-24; bishop of Natchez, 1924-57; bishop of Natchez-Jackson, 1957-66. Home: 814 N Congress St Jackson, MS 39202. Office: 237 E Amite St Jackson MS 39205

GERRARD, ROBERT WILKIN, banker; b. Houston, Sept. 4, 1927; s. Oswald and Marie Cage (Hickman) G.; student Tex. A. and M. Coll., 1944-45, U. Houston, 1948-50; B.B.A., U. Tex., 1951; m. Myrtle Watkins, June 14, 1952; children—Celia Gail, Jann Marie, Robert Wilkin, Sheri Lynn. With Nat. Bank Commerce, Houston, 1952—, v.p., 1961-66; sr. v.p. Tex. Nat. Bank of Commerce (merger Nat. Bank Commerce and Tex. Nat.) 1966-68, exec. v.p., 1968—; dep. chmn. Burston and Tex. Commerce Bank, London, 1968—; instr. Am. Inst. Banking, 1960-65. Trustee Wilkin Found., Tex. Inst. Rehab. and Research. Served with USNR, 1945-48. Mem. Am. Inst. Banking, Robert Morris Assos., Chi Phi. Mem. Ch. of Christ. Clubs: Houston, Houston Yacht. Home: 1 Blalock Circle Houston TX 77024 Office: PO Box 2558 Houston TX 77001

GERRAUGHTY, ROBERT JOSEPH, educator; b. Newton, Mass., Aug. 30, 1928; s. John Joseph and Dorothy (Moran) G.; B.S., Mass. Coll. Pharmacy, 1950, M.S., 1952; Ph.D., U. Conn., 1958; m. G. June Wheatley, Sept. 18, 1953; children—David R., Andrew M., Susan J. Matthew E., Samuel W. Asst. prof. pharmacy, Rutgers U., 1958-60; prof., chmn. dept. pharmacy U. R.I., 1960-72, dir. tng. course drug inspectors, 1964-72; dean sch. Pharmacy Creighton U., Omaha, 1972—; cons. pharm. cos. Chmn. Heart Fund Narragansett, R.I., 1966. Chmn. Democratic Party Narragansett, 1969. Served to capt. USAF, 1952-55. Mem. Am., R.I. pharm. assns., Sigma Xi, Rho Chi, Phi Lambda Upsilon, Phi Sigma, Kappa Psi. Author: Pharmacy Examination Review Book, 1964—. Office: Creighton U Omaha NB 68102

GERRIETTS, JOHN SEBASTIAN, educator; b. Chgo., May 11, 1912; s. John Dietrich and Mary Caroline (Graber) G.; A.B. cum laude, Loyola U., Chgo., 1934, M.A., 1937, Ph.D., 1954. Mem. faculty Loyola U., Chgo., 1937—, prof. English, 1960—, dir. univ. honors program, 1949-58, chmn. dept. English, 1958—. Mem. Am. Assn. U. Profs., Coll. English Assn., Conf. Coll. Composition and Communication, Modern Lang. Assn., Nat. Council Tchrs. English. Home: 1447 Highland Av Chicago IL 60626

GERRISH, BRIAN ALBERT, educator; b. London, Eng., Aug. 14, 1931; s. Albert and Doris (King) G.; B.A., Queens' Coll., Cambridge, Eng., 1952, M.A., 1956; certificate Westminister Coll., Cambridge, 1955; S.T.M., Union Theol. Sem., N.Y.C., 1956; Ph.D., Columbia, 1958; m. Millicent June Warburton, June 25, 1955; children—Carolyn, Paul. Asst. pastor West End Presbyn. Ch., N.Y.C., 1956-58; tutor philosophy of religion Union Theol. Sem., N.Y.C., 1957-58; instr. ch. history McCormick Theol. Sem., Chgo., 1958-59, asst. prof., 1959-63, asso. prof., 1963-65; asso. prof. hist. theology U. Chgo., 1965-68, prof., 1968—. Am. Assn. Theol. Schs. faculty fellow, 1961; Guggenheim fellow, 1970. Mem. Mind Assn., Am. Soc. Ch. History, Am. Soc. for Reformation Research, Renaissance Soc. Author: Grace and Reason: A Study in the Theology of Luther, 1962. Editor: The Faith of Christendom: A Source Book of Creeds and Confessions, 1963; Reformers in Profile, 1967. Contbr. articles to profl. jours. Home: 18541 Klimm Homewood IL 60430 Office: Swift Hall U Chgo IL 60637

GERRITY, EDWARD JOSEPH, Jr., communications co. exec.; b. Scranton, Pa., Jan. 3, 1924; s. Edward Joseph and Helen T. (Walton) G.; B.S., U. Scranton, 1946; M.S., Columbia, 1948; m. Katharine Casey, Sept. 22, 1956; children—Katharine, Edward J. III. With Internat. Tel. & Tel. Corp., 1958—, v.p., 1961-64, sr. v.p., dir. corporate relations and advt., 1964—; dir. Am. Cable & Radio Corp., ITT World Communications, Inc., Inc., Howard W. Sams & Co., Inc., ITT World Directories, Inc. Lay mem. bd. trustees Trinity Coll. Served with AUS, 1942-45; ETO. Decorated Silver Star, Bronze Star with cluster. Mem. Pub. Relations Soc. Am., Internat. Pub. Relations Assn., Internat. Econ. Policy Assn. (dir.), Internat. Advt. Assn. (dir.), Assn. Nat. Advertisers (board of directors), Sigma Delta Chi. Clubs: Overseas Press (New York City, N.Y.); Metropolitan, Federal City, and National Press (Washington); Westchester County (Rye, N.Y.); International Golf (dir.). Home: 18 Mohegan Rd Larchmont NY 10538 Office: 320 Park Av New York City NY 10022

GERRITZ, ELLSWORTH MELVIN, univ. dean; b. Little Falls, Minn., Sept. 13, 1913; s. George John and Ellen M. (Johnson) G.; B.E., St. Cloud State Coll., 1938; M.S., U. Minn., 1949, Ph.D., 1951; m. Grace Luella Lundblad, Sept. 26, 1936; children—Ellsworth Keith, Catherine M. (Mrs. Charles Hays), George Allen, Grace L. (Mrs. James Wilson). Tchr. pub. schs., Minn., 1932-43; asst. prin., Rochester, Minn., 1943-46; dir. admissions U. Minn., 1948-54; dean admissions and records Kan. State U., Manhattan, 1954—. Asso., N. Central Assn. Colls. and Univs., 1963—; mem. bd. Am. Coll. Testing Program, 1959-69, chmn., 1965—. Kiwanian. Home: 2030 Thackery Rd Manhattan KS 66502

GERRY, ELBRIDGE THOMAS, banker; b. N.Y.C., Nov. 22, 1908; s. Robert L. and Cornelia (Harriman) G.; student Aiken Prep. Sch., St. Paul's Sch.; A.B., Harvard, 1931; m. Marjorie Kane, May 21, 1932; children—Elbridge T., Peter G., Majorie K. with Hanover Bank, 1931-36; with Brown Brothers Harriman & Co., N.Y.C., 1936—, partner, 1956—; chmn. exec. com. Union Pacific Corp.; dir. Doubleday & Co., Inc., Biltmore Co. Mem. Am. Stock Exchange. Pres., dir. N.Y. Soc. for Prevention Cruelty to Children. Trustee, treas. Am. Mus. Natural History. Home: Delhi NY 13753 90012 Office: 59 Wall St New York City NY 10005

GERSCHEFSKI, EDWIN, educator, composer; b. Meriden, Conn., June 10, 1909; s. Otto J. and Josephine (Sturmer) G.; Ph.B., Mus.B., Yale, 1931 (1st recipient $2000 Charles Ditson fellowship for year's study abroad); diploma (Jeffrey Reynolds scholar), Matthay Pianoforte Sch. London), 1932; postgrad. study piano with Artur Schnabel; m. Ina Magnuson, June 18, 1931; children—Jo Ellen, Peter, Martha, Michael, John. Mem. piano faculty Yorkville Music Sch., N.Y.C., 1933-37, Turtle Bay Music Sch., N.Y.C., 1937-40; dir. music dept. Home Thrift Assn., N.Y.C., 1938-40; tchr. piano, theory and composition Converse Coll., Spartanburg, S.C., 1940—, dir. Summer Sch. Music, 1942-45, dean Sch. Music, 1945-59; tchr. piano and composition Cummington Sch., summer 1943; guest faculty Appalachian State Tchrs. Coll., Boone, N.C., summer 1956; composer, radio performer, recs. and motion picture scores; chmn. dept. music U. N.M., 1959-60, U. Ga., Athens 1960—. Mem. bd. New Music Recs. 1938- 43; judge Young Artists contest Nat. Fedn. Music Clubs, 1954, 1961; mem. founders bd. Southeastern Composers League, 1952—; mem. scholarship com. Presser Found; participant Danforth Found. Workshop, Sarah Lawrence Coll., summer 1957. Recipient invitation to spend 2 summers Yaddo Found., Saratoga Springs, N.Y., 1936-37; award radio commn. League Composers, 1937; winner band music competition N.Y. World's Fair, 1939; Carnegie grantee, 1947, Fund for Advancement Edn. grantee, 1952; gold medal Arnold Bax Soc. for musicial composition in Harriet Cohen Internat. awards, 1963. Mem. Nat. Assn. Schs. Music (regional v.p. 1953-55, examiner 1955—, chmn. library com. 1962-65), Music Tchrs. Nat. Assn., Ga. Composers (pres. 1961-63), Ga. Music Council (pres. 1962-64), Phi Beta Kappa, Phi Kappa Phi, Pi Kappa Lambda, Phi Mu Alpha, Sinfonia. Contbr. articles to publs. Composer: Classic Symphony, 1944; Half Moon Mountain (women's chorus, baritone), 1948; Song of the Mountains (for piano), 1957; Saugatuck Suite (orch.), 1958; Salutation of the Dawn (mixed chorus), 1964; 100th Psalm (mixed chorus), 1965; also numerous manuscripts. Regional editor Jour. Music Theory, 1957—. Home: 765 Riverhill Dr Athens GA 30601

GERSCHENKRON, ALEXANDER, economist, educator; b. Russia, Oct. 1, 1904; s. Paul and Sophie (Kardow) G.; Dr. Rerum Politicarum, U. Vienna, 1928; m. Erica Matschnigg, 1928; children—Helga-Suzanna, Maria-Renate. Came to U.S., 1938, naturalized, 1945. Research asso. Austrian Inst. for Bus. Cycle Research, 1937-38, dept. econs. U. Cal., 1938-42, lectr., 1942-44; staff mem. Bd. Govs. Fed. Res. System, 1944-48, chief fgn. areas sect. 1946—; asso. prof. econs. Harvard, 1948-51, prof., 1951-55, Walter S. Barker prof. econs., 1955—, Frank W. Taussig research prof. econs., 1961-62, dir. econ. history workshop, 1959—. Dir. econ. projects Russian Research Center 1949-56; Ford Research prof. U. Cal., Berkeley, 1958; vis. fellow St. Catherine's Coll., Oxford, Eng. Guggenheim fellow, 1954-55. Corr. fellow Brit. Acad.; mem. Am. Statis. Assn., Am. Hist. Assn., Am. Philos. Soc., Am. Econ. Assn. (Distinguished fellow 1969), Econ. History Assn. (pres. 1966-68), Phi Beta Kappa (hon.). Author: Bread and Democracy in Germany, 1943; Economic Relations with the U.S.S.R., 1945; A Dollar Index of Soviet Machinery Output, 1951; Economic Backwardness in Historical Perspective, 1962; Continuity in History and Other Essays, 1968; Europe in the Russian Mirror, 1970. Contbr. articles to profl. jours. Home: Mather House Harvard Cambridge MA 02138

GERSHAW, FRED WILLIAM, Canadian senator; b. Emerson, Man., Can., Apr. 11, 1883; M.D., C.M., ed. U. Man.; m. Harriet Grace Robinson, 1912; children—Margaret (Mrs. H.M. Roche), Edith (Mrs. R.E. Sullivan), Norman (Mrs. G.M. Blackstone), Lorraine (Mrs. E.C. Harrison). Mem. Medicine Hat Sch. Bd. 12 years; elected to Ho. of Commons, 1925, 26, 30, 40; defeated, 1921, 35; mem. Canadian Senate, 1945—. Fellow A.C.S.; mem. Royal Coll. Physicians and Surgeons Can. Mem. Liberal Party. Mem. United Ch. Can. Address: Medicine Alberta Canada*

GERSHENFELD, LOUIS, bacteriologist; b. Phila., Dec. 25, 1895; s. George and Jennie (Stupe) G.; B.Sc., Phila. Coll. Pharmacy and Sci., 1917, Ph.M., 1920, D.Sc., 1940; spl. student Jefferson Med. Coll., U. Pa; m. Bertha Miller, Nov. 17, 1918; children—George, Marvin A. With Phila. Coll. Pharmacy and Sci., 1917—, dir. Gershenfeld Lab., 1919-70, prof. emeritus, dir. emeritus dept. bacteriology, 1968—, also hon. chmn. faculty council. Chemist, bacteriologist Upper Darby Twp. Dept. Health, 1930-66; sci. cons., past sec., mem. bd. govs. Dropsie U. Mem. sterile adv. bd. U.S. Pharmacopoeia XII, XIII, XIV; chmn. bacteriological and serological com. Pharm. Syllabus; exec. finance com., v.p. Nat. Biol. Stain Com.; chmn. com. clin. lab. preparations Nat. Formulary VII; mem. com. antisepticity tests, com. ingredients bacteriological media; biol. products and diagnostic tests com., past chmn. com. bacteriology and immunology Nat. Council Pharm. Research. Fellow A.A.A.S., Am. Pub. Health Assn.; mem. Am. Pharm. Assn., Am. Soc. Microbiologists, Am. Acad. Polit. and Social Sci., N.Y. Acad. Scis. Author hand books, monographs, articles. Asso. editor U.S. Dispensatory, XXII, XXIII, Remington's Practice of Pharmacy (9th, 10th edit.), Ficarra's Emergency Surgery, Reddish's Antiseptics and Disinfectants, Disinfection, Sterilization and Preservation (Lawrence, Block), others Home: 1101 N 63d St Philadelphia PA 19151

GERSHENSON, HARRY, lawyer; b. St. Louis, July 8, 1902; LL.B., Benton Coll. Law, 1924; m. Dorothy Rose Lupfer; children—Harry, Dorothy (Mrs. Ralph Clock). Admitted to Mo. bar, 1923; pvt. practice law, St. Louis, 1923—, sr. partner Gershenson & Gershenson. Lectr. law St. Louis U., 1948-57. Fellow Am. Coll. Probate Counsel (v.p. bd. regents, pres. 1965-66); mem. Fed. Bar Assn., Am. Bar Found., Scribes Law Writers Assn. (past pres.), Bar Assn. St. Louis (pres. 1946-47, past mem. exec. com.), Practicing Law Inst. (dir.), Mo. State Bar (pres. 1957-58, bd. govs., Pres.'s Distinguished Service award 1966), C. of C. Met. St. Louis, Am. Bar Assn. (ho. of dels. 1948-66, bd. govs. 1962-64, com. on ethics, Lawyers Title Guaranty Fund), Am. Judicature Soc. (dir.), Mo. Bar Found. (pres.), Am. Trial Lawyers Assn., Phi Alpha Delta. Mason (33, grand orator, grand lodge 1963-64). Club: Square St. Louis. Home: 542 Warder Av University City MO 63130 Office: 611 Olive St St Louis MO 63101

GERSHINOWITZ, HAROLD, chemist; b. Bklyn., Aug. 31, 1910; s. Louis and Mamie (Leibowitz) G.; B.S., Coll. City N.Y., 1931; A.M., Harvard, 1932, Ph.D., 1934; m. Mary Piesman, June 14, 1935. Research asso. Columbia, 1935-36, Harvard, 1936-38; research technologist Shell Oil Co., 1938-40, dir. mfg. research, 1940-45, dir. exploration, prodn. research div., 1945-50, v.p. in charge exploration, prodn. tech. div., 1950-52, cons. to pres., 1965-66; pres., dir. Shell Devel. Co., 1953-62; research coordinator, chmn. research council, dir. Royal Dutch Shell Group of Cos., 1962-65; cons. Orgn. for Econ. Cooperation and Devel., 1966-70, Chmn. environmental studies bd. Nat. Acad. Scis-Nat. Acad. Engring., 1967-70; affiliate mem. faculty Rockefeller U., 1967—. Fellow A.A.A.S.; mem. N.Y. Acad. Sci., Am. Chem. Soc., Phi Beta Kappa, Sigma Xi. Clubs: Cosmos (Washington); Harvard of New York; Harvard of Boston. Address: 25 Sutton Pl S New York City NY 10022

GERSHON-COHEN, JACOB, radiologist, educator; b. Phila., Jan. 9, 1899; s. Abraham and Dora (Starkman) Cohen; M.D., U. Pa., 1924, D. Sc. in medicine, 1936; m. Sara Eskin, Mar. 26, 1921. Intern Jewish Hosp., Phila., 1924-25; resident X- ray dept. U. Pa. Hosp., 1926-28; practice medicine specializing in radiology, Phila., 1929—; asst. prof. radiology U. Pa. Grad. Med. Sch., 1941-68; dir. div. radiology Albert Einstein Med. Center, Phila., 1949- 65; prof. radiology Hahnemann Med. Coll., 1952-59; prof. research radiology Temple U. Med. Sch., 1965—; cons. various area hosps., 1929- -. Served to comdr., M.C., USNR, 1942-46. Recipient Alvarenga prize Coll. Physicians of Phila., 1934; gold medal award Internat. Coll. Radiology, 1937; Clement Cleveland award Am. Cancer Soc., 1967. Diplomate Am. Bd. Radiology. Fellow Am. Coll. Radiology, Gerontol. Soc.; mem. Am. Roentgen Ray Soc., Radiol. Soc. N.Am., Inter-Am. Coll. Radiology, Soc. Nuclear Medicine, Fedn. Am. Socs. Exptl. Biology, A.M.A., Med. Soc. Pa., Am. Cancer Soc., N.Y. Acad. Sci., Coll. Physicians Phila., Phila. County Med. Soc., Laennec Soc., Pa. Radiol. Soc., Phila. Roentgen Ray Soc. (v.p. 1964-65, pres. 1965- 66). Author numerous articles in field. Home: 2401 Pennsylvania Av Philadelphia PA 19130 Office: 255 S 17th St Philadelphia PA 19103

GERSHOY, LEO, historian, educator; b. Krivoi Rog, Russia, Sept. 27, 1897; s. Morris and Miriam (Lioubarski) G.; came to U.S., 1903, naturalized, 1913; A.B., Cornell, 1919, A.M., 1920, Ph.D., 1925; m. Ida Elizabeth Prigohzy, Sept. 24, 1924. Social Science Research Council fellow, 1927-28; asst. prof. history L.I. U., 1929-30, asso. prof., 1930-38; mem. social sci. dept. Sarah Lawrence Coll., 1938-46; prof. N.Y. U. 1946—. Vis. prof. Columbia, 1947-48, 51-52, U. Cal., 1953-55, summer 1966, summers U. Chgo., 1938, Cornell U., 1932-34, 1936. U. Cal., 1948; fellow Center Advanced Study Behavioral Scis., 1963-64. Cons. OSS, 1942, prin. analyst Fgn. Broadcast Intelligence Service, 1943-44; chief regional specialist for France overseas br. OWI, Washington, 1944-45. Fulbright grantee for research, France, 1952-53; Guggenheim Found. fellow, 1936-37, 39, 46, 59. Fellow Am. Acad. Arts and Scis.; mem. Am. Hist. Assn., P.E.N., Société des Etudes Robespierristes (com. dir.), Societe d'histoire Moderne, Soc. French Hist. Studies, Am. Soc. Eighteenth-Century Studies, Phi Beta Kappa. Author: The French Revolution, 1789-99, 1932; The French Revolution and Napoleon, 1933; From Despotism to Revolution, 1763-1789, 1944; The Era of the French Revolution, 1789-1799, Ten Years That Shook the World, 1957; Bertrand Barère: A Reluctant Terrorist, 1962. Bd. editors Am. Hist. Rev., 1959-63. Contbr. articles to profl., other jours. Office: NY U New York City NY 10003

GERSHWIN, IRA, lyricist; b. N.Y.C., Dec. 6, 1896; s. Morris and Rose (Bruskin) G.; student Townsend Harris Hall, 1910-14; Coll. City of N.Y., 1914-16; Columbia U. Extension, 1918; D.F.A., U. Md., 1966; m. Leonore Strunsky, Sept. 14, 1926. Wrote lyrics for music written by his brother George Gershwin: (stage plays) A Dangerous Maid, 1921; Lady, Be Good, 1924; Primrose (with Desmond Carter), 1924; Tell Me More (with B. G. DeSylva), 1925; Tip Toes, 1925; Oh, Kay, 1926; Funny Face, 1927; Rosalie (with P. G. Wodehouse), 1927; Treasure Girl, 1928; Strike Up The Band, 1929; Show Girl (with Gus Kahn), 1929; Girl Crazy, 1930; Of Thee I Sing (won Pulitzer prize), 1932; Pardon My English, 1932; Let 'Em Eat Cake, 1933; Porgy and Bess (with DuBose Heyward), 1935; (motion pictures) Delicious, 1930; Shall We Dance?, 1936; A Damsel in Distress, 1937; Goldwyn Follies, 1937. Also wrote lyrics for Two Little Girls in Blue (music by Youmans and Lannin), 1921; Be Yourself (with Kaufman and Connelly; music by Gensler and Schwartzwald), 1924; That's a Good Girl (music by Charig and Meyer), 1928; Life Begins at 8:40 (with Harburg and Arlen), 1934; Ziegfeld Follies (music by Duke), 1936; Lady in the Dark (music by Weill), 1940; North Star (music by Copland), 1943; Cover Girl (music by Kern), 1943; Where Do We Go From Here? (music by Weill), 1944; Firebrand of Florence (music by Weill), 1945; Park Avenue (music by Schwartz), 1946; The Shocking Miss Pilgrim (posthumous music, George Gershwin), 1946; The Barkleys of Broadway (music by Warren) 1948; An American in Paris (music by Gershwin), 1952; Give A Girl A Break (music by Lane), 1952; A Star Is Born (music by Arlen), 1954; The Country Girl (music by Arlen), 1954; Kiss Me, Stupid! (posthumous music Gershwin), 1964. Awarded Coll. City N.Y. Townsend Harris Medal, 1952. Mem. A.S.C.A.P., Dramatists Guild. Author: Lyrics on Several Occasions, 1959. Address: 1021 N Roxbury Dr Beverly Hills CA 90210

GERSON, LOUIS LIEB, educator; b. Tomaszow, Lubelski, Poland, Nov. 10, 1921; s. Morris and Ann (Berger) G.; came to U.S., 1938, naturalized, 1942; B.A. with high distinction, U. Conn., 1948; M.A., Yale, 1950, Ph.., 1952; m. Elizabeth Shanley, June 24, 1950; children—Elliot, William, Ann. Mem. faculty U. Conn., 1950—, prof. polit. sci., 1963—, head dept., 1967—; research fellow Yale, 1953-54; research asso. Inst. War and Peace, Columbia, 1964-66; Fulbright vis. prof. U. Bombay (India), 1966-67. Vice chmn. Center Environment and Man; mem. adv. bd. John Foster Dulles Oral History Project, Princeton. Chmn. Democratic Town Com., Mansfield, Conn., 1969—. Trustee Inst. Meditteranean Studies, 1957—. Rockefeller fellow, 1963-64; Ford fellow, 1952-53; Guggenheim fellow, 1956-57. Mem. Am. Hist. Assn., Am. Polit. Sci. Assn., Phi Beta Kappa, Pi Sigma Alpha, Phi Alpha Theta, Phi Kappa Phi. Author: Woodrow Wilson and the Rebirth of Poland, 1953; The Hyphenate in Recent American Politics and Diplomacy, 1964; John Foster Dulles, 1967. Home: Ball Hill Rd Stoors CT 06268

GERSON, NATHANIEL CHARLES, research physicist; b. Boston, Oct. 15, 1915; s. Benjamin Kolman and Julia (Blumenthal) G.; B.S. magna cum laude. U. P.R., 1943; M.S., N.Y. U., 1948; m. Sareen Ruth Epstein, Aug. 26, 1945. children—Donald Franklin, Stanton Laurence, Richard Kelvin, Martha Blythe, Stephanie Dr Topeka KS 66606 Lynn. Meteorol. observer Weather Bur., 1938-43, asst. chief tech. investigations sect., 1944-46; asst. radio propagation LF Loran, Watsons Labs., USAF, 1946-48, chief ionospheric physics lab. Geophysics Research Directorate, 1948-56; with AVCO Advanced Research Devel. Lab. Boston, 1956—; tech. staff Mitre Corp., 1966-68; cons., 1968-69; cons. Lincoln Lab., Mass. Inst. Tech., 1958-59, Advanced Research Projects Agy., 1961-66, Syracuse U. Research Corp., 1966-68. Sec., Nat. Com. for IGY, 1953-57, sec. exec. com., vice chmn. arctic com.; U.S. del. Internat. Sci. Radio Union, The Hague, 1954, del. spl. com. Internat. Geophys. Year, Rome, 1954, Brussels, 1955. Mem. A.A.A.S., Am. Geophys. Union, Am. Meteorol. Soc., Arctic Circle, Arctic Inst. N.Am., Canadian Assn. Physicists, Research Soc. Am. Jewish religion. Mason. Clubs: Cosmos. Co-author: Theory of Electromagnetic Waves; Geophysics in the IGY; Advances in Geophysics, vols. 1-5; Reports on Progress in Physics, vol. 10: Arctic Communications; Radio Waves at Frequencies below 300kc/s. Editor: Conference on Mesospherie Physics; Radio Wave Absorption in the Ionosphere. Co-editor: Conference on Auroral Physics. Contbr. sci. articles to Brit., German, Italian, French, Argentinian, Am. publs. Home: Trapelo Rd Lincoln MA 01773

GERSON, NOEL BERTRAM, author; b. Chgo., Nov. 6, 1914; s. Samuel Philip and Rosa Anna (Noel) G.; A.B., U. Chgo., 1934, M.A., 1935; 1 dau., Noel Anne (Mrs. Brennan); m. 2d, Marilyn A. Hammond; stepchildren—Michele, Margot, Paul. Reporter rewriteman Chgo. Herald-Examiner, 1931-36; exec. radio sta. WGN, Chgo., 1936-41; radio and TV scriptwriter over 10,000 scripts for nat. networks, 1936-51. Fellow Internat. Inst. Arts and Letters; mem. Authors Guild Am., Am., Miss. Valley hist. assns., Am. Acad. Polit. and Social Sci., Centro Studi E Scambi Internat., Phi Beta Kappa, Kappa Alpha. Clubs: Players (N.Y.C.); Liguanea (Jamaica, W.I.). Author 98 fiction and non-fiction books under own name and various pseudonyms; books include: The Golden Lyre, 1961; The Land is Bright, 1961; The Naked Maja, 1962; Queen of Caprice, 1963; The Slender Reed, 1964; Old Hickory, 1963; Sex and the Mature Man, 1964; Kit Carson, 1964; Lady of France, 1965; Yankee Doodle Dandy, 1965; Give Me Liberty, 1966; Sex and the Adult Woman, 1965; Light-Horse Harry Lee, 1966; The Swamp Fox, The Anthem, 1967; Sam Houston, 1968; Jefferson Square, 1968; The Golden Ghetto, 1969; P.J., My Friend, 1969; TR, 1969; Mirror, Mirror, 1970; Warhead, 1970; The Divine Mistress, 1970; The Jersey Lily, 1971; Paradise, 1971; Vitor Hugo, 1971; Hugh M. Hefner, 1971; also numerous articles. countries. Books pub. in 17 Home: 63 Pratt Av Clinton CT 06413

GERSON, ROBERT, educator; b. N.Y.C., Dec. 5, 1923; s. Ephraim and Claire (Millman) G.; B. Ch.E., Coll. City N.Y., 1943; Ph.D., N.Y. U., 1953; m. Charlotte Wyle, June 27, 1948; children—Janet, Carolyn, Marianne. Physicist, Erie Resistor Corp. (Pa.), 1953-56; physicist Clevite Corp., Cleve., 1956-62; prof. physics U. Mo., Rolla, 1962—; studies Centre D'Etudes Nucleaires, Grenoble, France, 1969. Served with AUS, 1943-46. AEC grantee, 1964-70; USAF research grantee, 1970—. Mem. A.A.A.S., Am. Assn. U. Profs., Am. Phys. Soc., Sigma Xi, Tau Beta Pi. Contbr. articles to profl. jours. Home: 27 McFarland Dr Rolla MO 65401

GERST, IRVING, educator, applied mathematician; b. N.Y.C., May 30, 1912; s. Nathan and Jeny (Jacobs) G.; B.S., Coll. City N.Y., 1931; M.A., Columbia, 1932, Ph.D., 1947; m. Gussie Siegal, Feb. 14, 1937; children—Cynthia Harriet, Adrienne Sari. Tchr. math. high sch., N.Y.C., 1937-41; instr. USAAF, Miss., 1942-44; cons. Transp. Corps, U.S. Army, N.Y.C., 1944-46; research mathematician, head applied analysis group Burroughs Corp., N.Y.C., 1946-58; head network group RCA, N.Y.C., 1958-61; prof. math., chmn. dept. applied analysis State U. N.Y. at Stony Brook, 1961-70, prof. math., chmn. dept. applied math., statistics, 1970—. Lectr., City U., N.Y.C., 1958-61; cons. Sperry Rand Corp., 1961-63; Mem. Am. Math. Soc., Math. Assn. Am., Am. Assn. U. Profs., Phi Beta Kappa, Sigma Xi. Contbr. articles to profl. jours. Asso. editor SIAM (jour. applied math.), 1959—, SIAM Rev., 1959—. Address: State U NY Stony Brook NY 11790.

GERSTACKER, CARL ALLAN, chem. co. exec.; b. Cleve., Aug. 6, 1916; s. Rollin Michael and Eda (Uninck) G.; B.S., U. Mich., 1938; LL.D., Central Mich. Coll. Edn., 1957; m. Jayne Harris, Oct. 22, 1950 (div.); children—Bette Mignon, Lisa Jayne. Accounting dept. Dowell, Inc., 1938-40; chem. engr. Dow Chem. Co., 1946- 48, dir., 1948—, treas., 1949-59, v.p., 1955-60, mem. exec. com., 1957—, chmn. finance com., 1959—, chmn. bd. dirs., 1960—; dir. Dow Chem. A.G., Zurich, Dow Corning Corp., Chem. Bank & Trust Co., Midland, Mich., Nat. City Bank, Cleve., Dundee Cement Co., Eaton Corp.; Carrier Corp.; mem. internat. adv. com. Chase Manhattan Bank. Chmn. export expansion council U.S. Dept. Commerce, Bd. dirs. Rollin M. Gerstacker Found., U.P. Found., Elsa U. Pardee Found.; trustee Albion Coll., Starr Commonwealth for Boys; Northwood Inst. Recipient Ohio Gov.'s award, 1966; U.S. Pres.'s E award, 1971. Mem. Synthetic Organic Chem. Mfrs. Assn. (pres. 1960-61), Mfg. Chemists Assn. (chmn. 1968-69), Theta Xi, Beta Alpha Psi, Sigma Iota Epsilon. Presbyn. Mason (32), Rotarian. Clubs: Exchange, Midland Country, Fifth Avenue. Home: Box 226 Midland MI 48640 Office: Dow Chem Co Midland MI 48640

GERSTEIN, MELVIN, educator, scientist; b. Chgo., May 8, 1922; s. Israel and Fanny (Greenstein) G.; A.A., Wright Jr. Coll., 1940; B.S. in Chemistry, U. Chgo., 1942, Ph.D. in Chemistry, 1945; 1 son, Norman Jeffrey; m. 2d, Ralphleen Mazzotti, Dec. 22, 1962; stepchildren— Melanie, Marissa. Instr., Army Special Tng. Program, U. Chgo., 1942-44, research asso.,, 1944-46, jr. chemist Manhattan Project, 1944; aero. research chemist NACA-Lewis Research Center (name later changed to NASA-Lewis Research Center), Cleve., 1946-49, head combustion fundamentals sect., 1949-54, chief chemistry br., 1954-57, asst. chief propulsion div., 1957-59; chief phys. sci. div. Jet Propulsion Lab., Cal. Inst. Tech., 1959-60; v.p., tech. dir. Dynamic Sci. Corp., South Pasadena, Cal., 1960-64, pres., Monrovia, Cal., 1964-66; prof., chmn. mech. engring. dept. U. So. Cal. at Los Angeles, 1966—; asso. dean engring., 1969—; lectr. Fenn Coll., Cleve., 1949-54; sr. lectr. Cal. Inst. Tech. at Pasadena, 1962-64; cons. to industry. Sci. rep. AGARD, NATO, Rome, Italy, 1952, Cambridge, Eng., 1953, mem. combustion panel, 1954-57, combustion and propulsion panel, 1957-64. Served with USNR, 1945-46. Recipient Outstanding Achievement award Cleve. Tech. Societies Council, 1957; Mary Strong Sheldon fellow U. Chgo., 1942-43; Eli Lilly fellow, 1943-44; U.S. Naval Research Lab. hon. fellow U. Wis., 1950. Mem. Combustion Inst. (chmn. program western states sect. 1960-69, chmn. elect 1969-71, chmn. 1971—), Am. Chem. Soc. (editor Cleve. sect. mag. Isotopics 1955-58), Am. Soc. M.E., Sigma Xi, Pi Tau Sigma. Home: 1661 E Mendocino St Altadena CA 91001

GERSTEL, DAN ULRICH, educator; b. Berlin, Germany, Oct. 23, 1914; s. Alfred and Else (Flato) G.; B.S. with highest honors, U. Cal. at Cal. at Davis, 1940; M.S., U. Cal. at Berkeley, 1942, Ph.D., 1945; m. Eva Krojanker, Feb. 13, 1938; children—David Ury, Naomi Ruth. Came to U.S., 1938, naturalized, 1945. Asso. genetics U. Cal. at Berkeley, 1944-46; asso. geneticist Stanford Research Inst., 1947; with Natural Rubber Research Sta. Dept. Agr., Salinas, Cal., 1947-49; asst. prof. crop sci. and genetics N.C. State U., 1950-53, asst. prof., 1953-56, asso. prof., 1956-59, prof., 1959-64, William Neil Reynolds prof., 1964—. Vis. prof. Weizmann Inst., Rehovoth, Israel, 1961-62. Gosney research fellow Cal. Inst. Tech., 1949-50; NSF grantee, 1954—. Mem. Genetics Soc. Am., Am. Soc. Botany, Am. Soc. Naturalists. Jewish religion. Home: 1314 Crabapple Lane Raleigh NC 27607

GERSTELL, RICHARD, state ofcl.; b. Ardmore, Pa., July 30, 1910; s. Arnold and Rebecca (Daily) G.; A.B., Dartmouth, 1933; Ph.D., U. Mich., 1942; m. Vivian Southworth, May 29, 1936; children—Richard III, Arnold T. Chief, div. research Pa. Game Commn., 1933-42; dir. research Animal Trap Co. Am., 1946-48; radiol. def. cons. Office of Sec. Def., 1948-49; radiol. and biol. def. cons. Fed. Civil Def Adminstrn., 1949-51; dir. civil def. Commonwealth of Pa., Harrisburg, 1951—. Served to lt. comdr. radiol. safety sect. Operation Crossroads, USNR, World War II. Mem. Am. Soc. Mammalogists, Am. Ornithol. Union, Wildlife Soc. Am. Home: 1046 Buchanan Av Lancaster PA 17603 Office: Transp and Safety Bldg Harrisburg PA 17123

GERSTELY, WILLIAM, II, investment broker; b. Atlantic City, N.J., July 26, 1910; s. Isaac and Lotti (Greil) G.; grad. Swarthmore Prep. Sch., 1928; B.A., Dartmouth, 1932; m. Carol Kaffenburgh, Apr. 5, 1938; children—William III, Virginia May, David Greil. With Gerstly, Sunstein, investment brokers, Phila., 1934—, partner, 1941—; dir. Blue Ridge Mutual Fund., N.Y.C.; bd. govs. Phila.-Balt. Stock Exchange; treas., gov. Stock Clearing Corp. of Phila. Dir. Fedn. Jewish Agencies of Phila.; trustee Louis N. Cassett Charitable Found. Served as maj. USAAF, 1943-46. Decorated Bronze Star Medal. Mem. Dartmouth Alumni Soc. Club: Philmont Country (pres.). Home: 947 Frog Hollow Terrace Rydal PA 19046 Office: 211 S Broad St Philadelphia PA 19107

GERSTENBERG, RICHARD CHARLES, automotive exec.; b. Little Falls, N.Y., Nov. 24, 1909; s. Richard Paul and Mary Julia (Booth) G.; A.B., U. Mich., 1931; m. Evelyn Josephine Hitchingham, Dec. 29, 1934; children—Barry Thomas, Mary Christine. Asst. comptroller Gen. Motors Corp., Detroit, 1949-55, treas., 1956-60, v.p. charge of financial staff, 1960-67, exec. v.p. finance, 1967-70, vice chmn., 1970—, also dir. Clubs: Links, University (N.Y.C.); Detroit, Detroit Athletic, Recess (Detroit); Bloomfield Hills Country; Mohawk (N.Y.) Fish and Game. Home: 1000 Stratford Lane Bloomfield Hills MI 48013 Office: 3044 W Grand Blvd Detroit MI 48202

GERSTENMAIER, EUGEN, German politician; b. Kirchheim-Teck, Württemberg, Germany, Aug. 25, 1906; s. Albrecht and Albertine (Lauffer) G.; student univs. Tübingen, Rostock, Zurich; Dr. theol. habil., U. Münster, Wittenberg U.; m. Brigitte von Schmidt; children—Cornelia, Albrecht, York. Mem. Bundestag, 1949—, pres., 1954—. Head welfare orgn. Evang. chs., Germany, 1945; pres. Evang. Siedlungswerk (housing project), 1952—, German Africa Soc., 1956—. Author: Reden und Aufsatze; New Nationalism? Home: Oberwinter Federal Republic of Germany Office: Bundeshaus Bonn Federal Republic of Germany

GERSTENZANG, NATHANIEL M., newspaper editor; b. Bklyn., Oct. 10, 1907; s. Leon and Rose (Glassberg) G.; B.S., N.Y.U., 1929, J.D., 1931; m. Miriam L. Rosenbaum, Nov. 30, 1934; children—Nina Lee (Mrs. Chaitn), James Ross. Sports reporter, asst. sports editor New York Post, 1927-34; with New York Times, 1934-70, asst. fgn. news editor, 1948-68, asst. news editor, 1969-70; former adj. asso. prof. Grad. Sch. Journalism, Columbia. Recipient George L. Polk Meml. award, 1960. Home: 45 Parker Av Maplewood NJ 07040

GERSTLEY, JAMES MACK, indsl. exec.; b. London, Eng., Nov. 11, 1907; s. James and Adele (Mack) G.; student Cheltenham Coll., Gloucester, Eng., 1919-24, Cambridge U., Eng., 1926-28; studied with Mr. Weber, Bonn, Germany, 1924-25, Mme. de la Rive, St. Avertin, France, 1925-26; m. Elizabeth Lilienthal, Sept. 7, 1934; children—James Gordon, Ann. L. (Mrs. G. R. Pieper). Became naturalized U.S. citizen, 1939. With Gt. Western Electro Chemical Co. (now Great Western div. Dow Chem. Co.), 1930-33; with Pacific Coast Borax Co. div. Borax Consol., Ld. (becme U.S. Borax & Chem. Corporation 1956), 1930—, president, 1950-61, vice chairman board, 1961- -, also director; pres. Death Valley Hotel Co., Inc. Vice chmn. Com. Asian Art and Culture, San Francisco; vice chmn., treas. Asian Art Found. San Francisco. Trustee Pomona Coll. Mem. Cheltonian Soc., Peterhouse Soc., Museum Assn. Los Angeles County, Am. Forestry Assn., Save the Redwoods League, Brandeis U. Assos. Home: 160 Farm Rd Woodside CA 94062 Office: 3075 Wilshire Blvd Los Angeles CA 90005

GERSTNECKER, WILLIAM ROBERT, r.r. ofcl.; b. Phila., May 4, 1914; s. William Bennett and Helen Rebecca (Bozoarth) G.; student Wharton Sch., U. Pa., 1938; grad. Advanced Mgmt. Program, Harvard, 1951; m. Dorothy Jordan, Jan. 27, 1940 (dec.); children—Robert William, Lynn Jordan. Staff financial dept. Pa. R.R., 1932-48, asst. to treas., 1948-51, asst. treas., 1951-55, treas., 1955- -, also treas. subsidiary and affiliated firms; treas., dir. Great Southwest Corp.; treas. John Edgar Thomson Found.; sec. and trustee Estate of J. Edgar Thomson; v.p. Pa. R.R.; dir. Madison Sq. Garden Center, Inc., Provident Tradesmens Bank & Trust Co. Episcopalian. Mason. Clubs: Harvard Business School, Harvard, Racquet (Phila.); Manufacturers Golf and Country (Oreland, Pa.). Home: 738 Wolcott Dr C-1 Philadelphia PA 19118 Office: 6 Penn Center Plaza Philadelpia PA 19103*

GERSTNER, ROBERT WILLIAM, educator; b. Chgo., Nov. 10, 1934; s. Robert Berty and Martha (Tuchelt) G.; B.S., Northwestern U., 1956, M.S., 1957, Ph.D., 1960; m. Elizabeth Willard, Feb. 8, 1958; children—Charles Willard, William Mark. Instr., Northwestern U., Evanston, Ill., 1957-59, research fellow, 1959-60; asst. prof. U. Ill., Chgo., 1960-63, asso. prof., 1963-69, prof. structural engring., architecture, 1969—; structural engr. cons., 1959—. Registered structural engr., Ill. Mem. Am. Soc. C.E., Am. Concrete Inst., Am. Soc. for Engring. Edn., A.A.A.S., Am. Assn. U. Profs., Am. Civil Liberties Union. Contbr. articles profl. jours. Home: 2628 Agatite Av Chicago IL 60625

GERTH, HANS HEINRICH, educator; b. Kassel, Germany, Apr. 24, 1908; s. Karl Jonas and Anna (Schmidt) G.; Ph.D., U. Frankfurt am Main (Germany), 1933; m. 2d, Nobuko Yabuno, June 27, 1957; children—Anne K. (Mrs. Thomas H. Logan), Julia C., Richard J. Research asst. Kiel (Germany) U., 1932-33; journalist, Berlin, Germany, 1934-37; vis. asst. prof. U. Mich., 1938-39, U. Ill., 1939-40; asst. prof. U. Wis., Madison, 1940-47, now professor sociology; vis. prof. U. Frankfurt am Main, U. Tokyo (Japan). Author: (with C. Wright Mills) Character and Social Structure, 1953; (translation with C. Wright Mills) From Max Weber, Essays in Sociology, 2d edit., 1958. Home: 10 S Blackhawk Av Madison WI 53705

GERTSCH, WILLIS JOHN, biologist; b. Montpelier, Ida., Oct. 4, 1906; s. Paul and Louise (Sarbach) G.; B.A., U. Utah, 1928, M.A., 1930; Ph.D., U. Minn., 1935; Colbert and grad. study Columbia; m. Jean Elizabeth Moore, Aug. 20, 1932; children—Louise Ruth (Mrs. Corey), John Willis, Mary Alice (Mrs. J. Smallhouse). Curator arachnids Am. Mus. Natural History, N.Y.C., 1932- 68, mem. N.Y. Entomol. Soc., Entomol. Soc. Am., N.Y. Zool. Soc., Soc. Systematic Zoology, Evolution Soc., Lepidopterists Soc., Sigma Xi, Phi Kappa Phi, Gamma Alpha. Author: American Spiders, 1949; also papers on systematics and biologies of spiders and other arachnids. Home: Box 157 Portal AZ 85632

GERTY, FRANCIS JOSEPH physician; b. Chgo., Nov. 17, 1892; s. Frank K. and Josephine (Vincent) G.; grad. Chgo. Tchrs. Coll., 1912; B.S., Loyola U., 1920; M.D., 1921, D.Sc. (hon.) 1957; m. Ursula Mitchell, Dec. 21, 1922 (dec. 1968); children—John Mitchell, Josephine (dec.), Mary Frances (Mrs. William C. Taylor, Jr.), Helen Joan (Mrs. Brian Owens), Frank J. Tchr. pub. schs., Chgo., 1912-16; intern, resident physician Cook County Hosp., 1920-22; supt. Cook County Psychopathic Hosp. and county physician, 1922- 41; attending neurologist Cook County Hosp., 1932-41; asst. and asso. prof. nervous and mental diseases Loyola U. Med. Sch., 1923-30, prof., head dept., 1931-41; prof. psychiatry, head dept. U. Ill. Coll. Medicine, 1941-61, now prof. emeritus; dir. psychiat. div. Ill. Neurophychiat. Inst., 1941-61; attending specialist in neuropsychiatry Edward Hines Jr. Hosp. 1940-61, 63—; chmn. neuropsychiatry dept. Presbyn. St. Luke's Hosp., 1958-60; dir. Dept. Pub. Welfare, State of Ill., 1961, Dept. Mental Health, State of Ill. 1961-63; psychiatrist-in-chief Riveredge Hosp., Forest Park, Ill. Mem. psychiat. adv. council State Ill., 1933-61, mem. psychiat. tng. and research authority, 1957- 63; mem. adv. council in neuropsychiatry U.S. Vets. Bur., 1955-61; mem. profl. adv. com. Nat. Assn. Mental Health, 1956-65; mem. Nat. Mental Health Inst., 1951-55; chmn. deans com. for psychiatry VA Hosp., Hines, Ill., 1946-60; mem. Med. Center Commn. Chgo., 1961-67; chmn. profl. adv. com. Ill. Assn. for Mental Health, 1965—; chmn. constrn. grants commn. Ill. Dept. Mental Health, 1965—. Served as pvt. Med. R.C., 1917-18, lt. comdr. USNR, 1933-51, Decorated knight St. Gregory; recipient George Howell Coleman award Inst. Medicine Chgo., 1961; Stritch medal Stritch Sch. Medicine, 1964. Diplomate Am. Bd. Psychiatry and Neurology (pres. 1959). Fellow Am. Coll. Psychiatrists (Bowis award 1968); mem. A.M.A. (chmn. sect. on nervous and mental diseases 1948, mem. council on mental health 1954-57). Ill., Chgo. med. socs., Chgo. Neurol. Soc., Am. Psychiat. Assn. (council 1952-55, chmn. com. on med. edn. 1951-52. pres. 1958-59), Soc. Biol. Psychiatry, Inst. Medicine Chgo., Central Neuro-Psychiat. Assn. (pres. 1956), Am. Psychopath. Assn., Ill. Psychiat. Soc. Blue Key, Phi Chi, Sigma Xi, Alpha Omega Alpha. Roman Catholic. Contbr. articles to profl. jours. Address: 1150 Laurie Lane Hinsdale IL 60521

GERTZ, ELMER, lawyer, author; b. Chgo., Sept. 14, 1906; s. Morris and Grace (Grossman) G.; Ph.B., U. Chgo., 1928, J.D., 1930; m. Ceretta Samuels, Aug. 16, 1931 (dec.); children—Theodore, Margery Ann; m. 2d, Mamie L. Friedman, June 21, 1959; 1 son, Jack M. Friedman. Admitted to Ill. bar, 1930, since practiced in Chgo.; asso. McInerney, Epstein & Arvey, Chgo.; asst. to masters in chancery Jacob M. Arvey, Samuel B. Epstein, 1930-41; atty. for Nathan Leopold in successful parole procs., 1957-58; atty. various censorship litigations, 1961—; atty. for Jack Ruby in setting aside death sentence; counsel commn. to investigate disorders in Chgo. during spring, summer 1968. Dir. pub. relations Ill. Police Assn., 1934; mem. exec. com. Ill. Com. Equal Job Opportunity; mem. nat., Chgo. adv. bd. commn. on law and local action Am. Jewish Congress; chmn. soldier vote com. Profl. and Bus. People, 1944; mem. law and order com. Commn. on Human Relations, 1945—; v.p. Ill. Freedom to Read Com.; chmn. Vets. Housing Com., 1945-47; mem. Mayor's Housing Com., 1946-48, legal chmn., 1946-47; mem. Chgo. Com. on Housing Action, 1947-49; adv. com. Chief Justice Municipal Ct. Chgo., 1950-51; pres. Greater Chgo. Council Am. Jewish Congress, 1959-63; del. 6th Ill. Constl. Conv., 1969, chmn. conv. Bill of Rights com., 1969-70. Bd. dirs. Jackson Park Hosp.; trustee Belefaire; nat. bd. trustees City Hope (Golden Key award 1966). Recipient awards Ill. div. Am. Civil Liberties Union, 1963, U. Chgo. Alumni Assn., 1959, others. Mem. Pub. Housing Assn. (founder, counsel, pres. 1943-49). Civil War Round Table (founder, exec. com., pres., hon. life), Adult Edn. Council Chgo. (sec., pres.), Am. Friends of Hebrew U., Shaw Soc. (founder, pres., exhibit chmn. Centennial 1956, Darrow Centennial 1957), Am., Fed., Chgo. (chmn. legal edn. com. 1970-71) bar assns., Bar Assn. 7th Circuit, Chgo. Hist. Soc., Decalogue Soc. Lawyers (mgr., pres.), Soc. Midland Authors (award 1969), Authors Guild Appellate Lawyers Assn. Ill. Clubs: Chicago Literary (v.p. 1968-69), Cliff Dwellers, Caxton, Boswell, City. Author: (with A.I. Tobin) Frank Harris: A Study in Black and White, 1931: The People vs. The Chicago Tribune, 1942: (play) Mrs. Bixby Gets a Letter, 1942: Joe Medill's War, 1946; American Ghettos, 1946: A Handful of Clients, 1965; Moment of MadnessThe People vs. Jack Ruby, 1968; foreward The Tropic of Cancer Litigation, 1968; others. Contbr. to Henry Miller and the Critics, 1963, Mass Media and the Law, 1969; Far the First Hours of Tomorrow, 1971; also articles in various periodicals. Selected for Chicagoland honor roll Chgo. Council Against Discrimination, 1946, 47. Home: 6249 N Albany Av Chicago IL 60645 Office: 120 S LaSalle St Chicago IL 60603

GERVAN, ROBERT BRUCE, indsl. exec.; b. Buffalo, Dec. 18, 1907; s. John Simpson and Bertha (Conrad) G.; grad. high sch.; m. Roberta Mickler, Apr. 30, 1932; children-Robert Dennis, Marian Nancy (Mrs. Leslie Tarr). Printing bus., Buffalo, Ithaca, N.Y., 1924-34; writer, account exec. Agrl. Advt. Research, Ithaca, 1934-38; advt. mgr. Coop. GLF Exchange, Ithaca, 1938- 47, dir. pub. relations, 1949-57, sec., 1958-64; gen. mgr. Rural Radio Network, 1947-49; v.p., sec., dir. planning Agway, Inc., Syracuse, N.Y., 1964—; dir. Lincoln Nat. Bank & Trust Co. Central N.Y., Am. Agriculturist, Texas City Refining, Inc. Chmn. Tompkins County United Fund,, 1956; mem. exec. com. Nat. Farm-City Council Mem. Syracuse C. of C. (v.p., dir.). Episcopalian (dir. Found. for Diocese Central N.Y.). Club: Century (Syracuse). Home: Bittersweet and Leverett Lane Fayetteville NY 13066 Office: Box 1333 Syracuse NY 13201

GERVASI, FRANK, artist, painter; b. Palermo, Italy, Oct. 5, 1895; s. Angelo and Elizabeth (Bottone) G.; brought to U.S., 1908, naturalized, 1919; student N.Y. Sch. Indsl. Design, Art Students League of N.Y.; m. Leonilda Isabella Sansone, Dec. 23, 1933. Works exhibited nat. exhbns., Nat. Acad. Design, Allied Artists Am., Audubon Artists, American Watercolor Soc., Albany Inst. History and Art, Balt. Watercolor Club, So. Vt. Artists; works in collections Brueckner Mus., Albion, Mich., Mus. of Lubbock (Tex.), Okla. Mus. Art, Oklahoma City, also pvt. collections. Served with U.S. Army, World War I. Recipient bronze medal for painting Allied Artists Am., 1st prize for painting Salmagundi Club Hudson Valley Art Assn., Balt. Water Color Club. Mem. Allied Artists Am. (past pres.), Audubon Artists (past v.p.), Am. Watercolor Soc., N.A.D., Art Students League N.Y. Clubs: Baltimore Watercolor; Salmagundi (N.Y.C.). Home: PO Box 415 Marfa TX 79843

GERWICK, BEN CLIFFORD, Jr., constrn. engr., educator; b. Berkeley, Cal., Feb. 22, 1919; s. Ben Clifford and Bernice (Coultrap) G.; B.S., U. Cal., 1940; m. Martelle Louise Beverly, July 28, 1941; children—Beverly (Mrs. Robert A. Brian), Virginia, Ben Clifford III, William. With Ben C. Gerwick, Inc., San Francisco, 1939-70, pres., 1952-70; exec. v.p. Santa Fe-Pomeroy, Inc., 1968-71; prof. civil engring. U. Cal. at Berkeley, 1971—; sponsoring mgr. Richmond-San Rafael Bridge substructure, 1953-56, San Mateo-Hayward bridge, 1964-66; lectr. constrn. engring. Stanford U.; cons. maj. bridge and marine constrn. projects. Dir. Stiles Hall YMCA. Served with USNR, 1940-46; comdr. Res. ret. Fellow Am. Soc. C.E.; mem. Federation Internationale de la Precontrainte (dep. gen. v.p. 1970—), Moles and Beavers, Prestressed Concrete Inst. (pres. 1957-58), Deutscher Beton Verein (hon.), Phi Beta Kappa, Tau Beta Pi, Sigma Xi, Chi Epsilon, Kappa Sigma. Republican. Conglist. Club: Bohemian (San Francisco). Author: (with Peter U. Peters) Russian-English Dictionary of Prestressed Concrete and Concrete Construction, 1966; Construction of Prestressed Concrete Structures, 1971. Contbr. articles to profl. jours. Home: 5874 Margarido Dr Oakland CA 94618 Office: 217 McLaughlin Hall U Cal Berkeley CA 94720

GESCHICKTER, CHARLES FREEBORN, physician, educator; b. Washington, Jan. 8, 1901; s. Leo and Rose (Zirkin) G.; B.A., George Washington U., 1920, M.A., 1922; M.D., Johns Hopkins, 1927; m. Mildred Clark, May 21, 1927; children—Charles Freeborn, Edmund Harrison, Jacqueline. Intern medicine Balt. City Hosp., 1927-28; fellow surgery Mayo Clinic, 1928; dir. surg. path. lab. Johns Hopkins, 1929-40, also asso. surgery, dir. cancer research lab.; dir. research lab. Johns Hopkins Med. Sch., 1929-40, dir. Garvan Cancer Research Fund, 1940-46; spl. cons. pathology NIH, 1946—; prof. pathology Georgetown U. Med. Sch., 1946—, chmn. dept. pathology, 1946- 62, chmn. dept. research pathology 1962—, chmn. com. devel. and planning, 1960—; cons. Dept. Health, Edn. and Welfare, Social Security Administrn., 1961—; spl. cons. Walter Reed Army Med. Hosp., 1962—. Spl. research pathology cancer and neoplastic diseases, relationship endorines to diseases of breast, chemotherapy treatment cancer. Served to comdr. USNR, 1942-46. Decorated Legion of Merit. Diplomate Am. Bd. Pathology. Mem. Am. Geriatrics Soc., A.M.A., Coll. Am. Pathologists, Am. Soc. Clin. Pathologists, A.A.A.S. Clubs: Army-Navy (Washington); Johns Hopkins Univ. (Balt.). Author: (With M.M. Copeland) Tumors of The Bone, 3d edit., 1949; Diseases of the Breast, 3d edit., 1948; (with N.J. White) Diagnosis in Daily Practice, 1947; also numerous articles, chpts. in books. Editor: Color Atlas of Pathology, vols. I and II, 1954-56, vol. I rev., 1959. Home: 10800 Harley Rd Lorton VA 22079 Office: Gorman Bldg Georgetown U Med Center Washington DC 20007

GESCHWIND, NORMAN, physician, educator; b. N.Y.C., Jan. 8, 1926; s. Morris and Anna (Blau) G.; B.A., Harvard, 1946, M.D., 1951; m. Patricia Dougan, Sept. 8, 1956; children—Naomi, David, Claudia. Moseley Travelling fellow Nat. Hosp., London, Eng., 1952-53, USPHS Research fellow, 1953-55; research fellow Mass. Inst. Tech., 1956-58; staff neurologist Boston VA Hosp., 1958-62, chief neurology service, 1962-66; asso. prof. neurology Boston U., 1962- 66, prof., chmn. dept., 1966-68; James Jackson Putnam prof. neurology Harvard Med. Sch., 1969—. Fellow Am. Acad. Neurology; mem. Acad. Aphasia, Am. Neurol. Assn. Research, publs. on anat. basis higher functions nervous system, explanation disturbances higher function on basis damage to pattern cortico-cortical connections in animals and man. Office: 818 Harrison Av Boston MA 02118*

GESELL, GERHARD ALDEN, judge; b. Los Angeles, June 16, 1910; s. Arnold Lucius and Beatrice (Chandler) G.; grad. Phillips Andover Acad., 1928; A.B., Yale, 1932, LL.B., 1935; m. Marion Holliday Pike, Sept. 19, 1936; children—Peter Gerhard, Patricia Pike. Admitted to Conn. bar, 1935, D.C. bar, 1941; with Securities and Exchange Commn., Washington, 1935-40, tech. advisor to chmn., 1940-41; acted for Commn. as spl. counsel Temporary Nat. Economic Committee, study legal res. life insurance companies; member Covington & Burling, Washington, 1941-67; judge U.S. District Court, D.C., 1968—; chief asst. counsel Joint Congressional Com. on Investigation Pearl Harbor Attack, 1945-46. Chairman of the President's Committee on Equal Opportunity in the Armed Forces, 1962-64; chmn. com. on adminstrn. of justice D.C. Jud. Council, 1965-67. Dir. Fed. Jud. Center. Mem. Am. Bar Assn., Bar Assn. D.C., Am. Law Inst., Am. Coll. Trial Lawyers, Phi Delta Phi, Zeta Psi. Clubs: Lawyers, Metropolitan (Washington); Casino (N. Haven, Me.), Co-author: Study of Legal Reserve Life Insurance Cos., 1940; Families and Their Life Insurance, 1940. Home: 3304 N St Washington DC 20007 Office: US Courthouse Washington DC 20001

GESMER, HENRY, lawyer; b. Quincy, Mass., Apr. 1, 1912; s. Abraham Meyer and Esther (Zide) G.; grad. Thayer Acad., 1929; B.S., Harvard, 1933, LL.B., 1936; m. Bessie Nathanson, Nov. 24, 1940; children—Linda, Gabriel M., Ellen F. Admitted to Mass. bar, 1936, since practiced in Boston; partner firm Brown, Rudnick, Freed & Gesmer, and predecessors, 1960—. Sec., City Bank & Trust Co., Boston, 1957—; dir., clk. Marrud, Inc., and subsidiaries, 1960-67, Beta Instrument Corp., 1968—. Past pres. Jewish Family and Children's Service Boston, Jewish Centers Assn. Greater Boston. Mem. Mass. Bar Assn., Mass. Trial Lawyers Assn. Jewish religion. Club: Harvard (Boston). Home: 111 Dane Hill Rd Newton Highlands MA 02161 Office: 85 Devonshire St Boston MA 02109

GESNER, CONRAD HERBERT, clergyman; b. Detroit Lakes, Minn., Aug. 30, 1901; s. Anthon Temple and Blanche Louise (Pinniger) G.; A.B., Trinity Coll., Hartford, Conn., 1923; postgrad. Gen. Theol. Sem., N.Y.C., 1924-27, D.S.T. (hon.); fellow Coll. Preachers, Washington, 1939; D.D. (hon.) Trinity Coll. 1946; m. Betty Magee Merrell, June 23, 1927 (dec. Mar. 1968); children—John Edward (dec.), Joan Merrell, Rosalind Browell, Nancy Dickinson; m. 2d, Claudia Catherine Dorland, June 10, 1970. Ordained to ministry P.E. Ch., 1927; canon missionary Calvary Cathedral, Sioux Falls, S.D., 1927-29; rector Trinity Ch., Pierre, S.D., 1929-33, St. John the Evangelist, St. Paul, 1933-45; bishop-coadjutor S.D., 1945-54; bishop S.D., 1954-70. Pres., Province of Northwest, 1953-56. Mem. Soc. Mayflower Descs., Alpha Delta Phi. Home: 186 Longmeadow St Longmeadow MA 01106

GESSLER, ALBERT EDWARD, chemist; b. Metzingen, Wurtt, Germany, May 8, 1885 s. Edward Albert and Marie Louise (Leuze) G.; B.S., U. of Stuttgart, 1905; Ph.D., U. of Berlin, 1907; m. Mildred B. Murray, Feb. 2, 1915; childrenIsolde (Mrs. mgn. tech., 1958-69, head of math. computing and systems, 1969—, Mem. daughter Sally (Mrs. F. G. Appleton). Came to United States, 1908, became naturalized, 1922. Chemist, G. Siegle Co., Rosebank, N.Y., 1908, vice pres. and mem. bd., 1914-18; partner and vice pres. Utro Chem. Corp., 1918, firm consol. with Zinsser & Co., 1926; chief chemist, mem. bd. and exec. com. Zinsser & Co., 1926-34; dir. research Inter- chem. Corp., N.Y. City, 1934-44, vice pres. and dir. research, 1944-52. director emeritus of research since 1952; now engaged in private practice as chemical cons. Recipient certificate awarded for effective (ofcl. bd.). Home: 1900 Washington St Houston TX 77007 effective service in work on camouflage organized through Nat. Defense Research Council. Mar. 1, 1945; recipient grant for cancer research from Lillia Babbitt Hyde Found., 1944-53: Ault Award, National Assn. Printing Ink Makers. Fellow N.Y. Acad. Sci.; mem. Am. Chem. Soc. (councillor), Am. Assn. Cancer Research, A.A.A.S., Electron Microscope Society. Assn. Research Dirs. Rep. Luth. Club; University (Winter Park, Florida), Contributor of papers to chemical and to medical publications. Holder chemical patents. Full family nameGessler von Braunegg with hereditary rank of Knight decreed by Emperor Charles VI of Austria. 1726. Address: 100 Sands Point Rd Sarasota FL 33577

GESSLEY, NORMAN, telephone co. exec.; b. Topeka, Kan., Mar. 19, 1921; s. Royal N. and Gladys V. (Houk) G.; student Westminster Coll., Fulton, Mo., 1939, Purdue U., 1941, Columbia, 1960; m. Annabel S. Teeter, Oct. 12, 1940; children—Daniel I., Bruce C., Glen R. Exchange service engr. Am. Tel. & Tel. Co., 1951-53; asst. v.p. operations Southwestern Bell Telephone Co., 1961; v.p., dir. Pacific Northwest Bell Telephone Co., 1962-63; v.p. N.Y. Telephone Co., 1964—; adv. bd. Chem. Bank N.Y.; exec. bd., exec. com. Commerce Labor & Industry Corp. of Kings County Trust Co. Mem. exec. bd. Greater N.Y. Council Boy Scouts Am., pres. Bklyn. council; recipient Silver Beaver award. Trustee, commr. police, Laurel Hollow, N.Y. Adv. bd. United Hosp. Fund Bklyn.; bd. dirs. Downtown Bklyn. Assn. Served with AUS, 1943-46; ETO. Mem. N.Y.C., Bklyn. (bd. dirs.), Queensboro chambers commerce.

GESSNER, HAROLD BERNARD, shoe mfg. co. exec.; b. Escanaba, Mich., Nov. 18, 1903; s. Herman and Anna (Silverman) G.; grad. St. John's Mil. Acad., 1920; B.A., U. Mich., 1924; m. Shirley M. Cohen, Oct. 2, 1942; children—Harold Milton, Deborah. With Ozite Corp., 1925-31, European advt. mgr., 1928-31; with Fair Store, Escanaba, 1931-41, now sec.; with Oomphies, Inc., N.Y.C., 1942—, pres., 1968—, also dir.; v.p. La Marquise Footwear, Inc., Lawrence, Mass., 1942—; dir. Fgn. Footwear Corp., N.Y.C. Industry adv. com. WPB, 1943-46. Trustee Hosp. Joint Diseases, N.Y.C.; trustee Children's Blood Found., 1962, treas., 1963. Member Met. Shoe Mfg. Assn. (pres. 1943-48), Nat. Shoe Mfrs. Assn. (dir. 1948—), Nat. Shoe Inst. (trustee 1956, chmn. 1960), Am. Footwear Inst. (chmn. 1970-71), Am. Footwear Mfrs. Assn. (chmn. elect 1970-71), Phi Sigma Delta. Clubs: Fairview Country (pres. 1962-63, gov.) (Elmsford, N.Y.); City Athletic (N.Y.C.). Home: 880 Fifth Av New York City NY 10021 Office: 350 Fifth Av New York City NY 10001

GETIS, ARTHUR, educator; b. Phila., July 6, 1934; s. Samuel J. and Sophie (Zeitzew) G.; B.S., Pa. State U., 1956, M.S., 1958; Ph.D., U. Wash., 1961; m. Judith M. Marckwardt, July 23, 1961; children—Hilary Hope, Victoria Lynn, Anne Patterson. Asst. instr. geography U. Wash., 1960-61; asst. prof. Mich. State U., 1961-63; faculty Rutgers U., New Brunswick, N.J., 1963—, prof. geography, 1969—, dir. grad. programs in geography, 1970—. Vis. lectr. Bristol U. (Eng.), 1966-67, U. Cal. at Los Angeles, summer 1968, U. B.C., summer 1969; vis. prof. Princeton, 1971. Mem. Regional Sci. Research Group, Harvard, 1970. Rutgers U. faculty fellow, 1970. Mem. Assn. Am. Geographers (grantee 1964-65, vis. scientist 1970—), Am. Geog. Soc., Regional Sci. Assn., Inst. Brit. Geographers. Contbr. monographs, articles to profl. lit. Contbg. editor Jour. Geography. Home: 92 Moore St Princeton NJ 08540 Office: Dept Geography Rutgers Univ New Brunswick NJ 08903

GETLEIN, FRANK, author, art critic; b. Ansonia, Conn., Mar. 6, 1921; s. Frank and Katherine (Sheehan) G.; B.S., Coll. Holy Cross; M.A., Catholic U., Am.; m. Dorothy Woollen, May 26, 1943; children—Christine, Steve, Mary, Bill, Karl. Art critic New Republic, Washington, 1957—; art critic, editorial writer Washington Star, 1961—; Washington corr. Art in Am., Burlington Mag. Served with AUS, 1942-45; MTO. Roman Catholic. Club: Nat. Press (Washington). Author: (with wife) Christianity in Art, 1959, Christianity in Modern Art, 1961, The Bite of the Print, 1964, Georges Rouault's Miserere, 1964; A Modern Demonology, 1961; (with wife and Anne Peck) Wings of an Eagle, 1963; Trouble with Catholics, 1964. Editor: Ten French Impressionists, 1966. Contbr. to Country Beautiful, Horizon, Commonweal, Jubliee, Sign, Am. Scholar, Time, also others. Address: 2007 Citadel Pl Vienna VA *

GETMAN, BURRILL MYERS, former mfg. co. exec.; b. Ilion, N.Y., May 29, 1905; s. George Burrill and Bertha (Myers) G.; B.S., U. Pa., 1927; m. Virginia Birdsong, June 30, 1930; children—Burrill Myers, Richard Birdsong. With Gorham div. Textron, Inc., and predecessor, 1927-70, v.p. sales, 1945-59, dir. marketing, 1959-61, pres., 1963-68, chmn., 1968-70; dir. Indsl. Nat. Bank, Indsl. Nat. Corp., Dieges & Clust, Providence, New Eng. Electric System, Boston. Clubs: Warwick (R. I.) Country; Hope (Providence); Dunes (Narragansett, R.I.). Home: 55 Pegwin Dr East Greenwich RI 02818

GETSONS, WILLIAM TIMOTHY chemist, educator; b. Chicago, 1928; B.S in Physics, Yale, 1950; Ph.D. in Chemistry, Harvard, 1956; m. Sally Ann Jones, July 5, 1957; children--Kenneth J., Nancy A. Chemist, Acme Chem. Co., Blue Island, Ill., 1950-51; director of Research Lab., Indsl. Chemicals Corp., Cambrige, Mass., 1956-60; project coordinator environmental sect. Steinmetz Assos., Chgo., 1960-61; v.p. for research Bauer Bros. Chem. Co., Inc., Memphis, 1961-64; asst. prof. chemistry Washington U., St. Louis, 1964-66, asso. prof., 1966-70, prof., 1970--, head of chemistry dept., 1970-71. Vis. prof. So. Ill. U., summer 1967, U. of Ore., 1969. Bd. dirs. Rest Haven Home for Elderly, 1960-61; trustee of the Lutheran Hosp., 1965-71. Served from lt. to capt., AUS, 1951-53. Mem. Am. Chem. Soc., Sci. Research Soc. Am. (chpt. treas. 1967), Sigma Xi. Author:

(with others) Basic Inorganic Chemistry, 1971. Home: Fairfax Apts 7291 Windermere Dr University City MO 63105 Office: Dept Chemistry Washington University St Louis MO 63130

GETTE, WARREN ANDREWS, physician, former hosp. adminstr.; b. Phillipsburg, Pa., Apr. 17, 1910; s. Claude Anthony and Anna Margaret (Hamer) G.; A.B., U. Pa., 1932, M.D., 1943; m. Doris Fitzgibbon, July 8, 1944; 1 dau., Gladys Ruth. Intern U. Pa. Hosp., 1944; resident Dixon Hosp., South Mountain, Pa., 1944-45, Tb physician, 1945-51, chief med. staff, 1951-59, became med. dir., 1959; clin. dir. unitl 1970. Pres. corp. South Mountain Ch. of God, 1960—. Fellow Am. Coll. Chest Physicians; mem. A.M.A., Franklin County (pres. 1962), Pa. med. socs., Pa. Assn. Chest Physicians, Am. Thoracic Soc., Am. Assn. Tb Physicians. Lutheran. Address: 19 Oller Ct Waynesboro PA 17268

GETTELL, RICHARD GLENN, economist, pres.; b. Hartford, Conn., Mar. 3, 1912; s. Raymond G. and Nelene G. (Knapp) G.; A.B., Amherst Coll., 1933, LL.D., 1957; Ph.D., U. Cal. at Berkeley, 1940; L.H.D., U. Mass., 1962; LL.D., Mount Holyoke Coll., 1970; m. Landonia B. Richards, June 9, 1948. Asst. to dir. bur. fgn. and domestic commerce U.S. Dept. Commerce, 1933-34; spl. asst. com. price policy U.S. Cabinet, 1934-35; teaching fellow, head teaching fellow, univ. fellow econs. U. Cal., Berkeley, 1935-37; instr., tutor econs. Harvard, instr. econs. Wellesley Coll., 1938; instr. to asst. prof. econs. Yale, 1937-46; asst. to pub. Fortune mag., 1945-50; chief staff economist Time, Inc., 1950-53; chief fgn. economist Tex. Co., 1953-57; pres. Mount Holyoke Coll., South Hadley, Mass., 1957-68. Chief silk and rayon unit, asso. price exec. textiles, chief apparel rationing, dir. miscellaneous products rationing OPA, 1941-43; operations research 8th Air Force, dep. chief operations analysis 20th Air Force, USAAF, 1943-45; cons. operations analysis Hdqrs. USAF, 1945-60, White House, 1953, DDM, 1954-56; lectr. econs. Columbia, 1947-48. Financial v.p. Phoebe Waterman Found., 1969-70; overseer Coll. V.I. Mem. Am. Econ. Assn., Am. Marketing Assn. Am. Statis. Assn. Delta Sigma Rho, Pi Sigma Alpha, Alpha Delta Phi. Home: 4 Berenda Way Menlo Park CA 94025

GETTELMAN, THOMAS R., business exec. Chmn. exec. com. Froedtert Malt Corp., Milw. Office: PO Box 712 Milwaukee WI 53215*

GETTEMY, JAMES NOAH, clergyman, seminary exec.; b. Greensburg, Pa., Oct. 19, 1919; s. Shaffer S. and Emma Jeannette (Wilson) G.; A.B., Allegheny Coll., 1941, D.D., 1956; B.D., Union Theol. Sem., 1944; L.H.D., Adelphi Coll., 1956; m. Helen Catherine McCartney, Aug. 4, 1945; children—Kathleen Ann, Christine E., Jessica J., Sara Beth. Ordained to ministry Presbyn. Ch., 1944; faculty dept. philosophy and religion Adelphi Coll., 1945-55; minister Garden City (N.Y.) Community Ch. 1944-58; pres. Hartford Sem. Found., 1958—. Program bd., div. overseas ministries Nat. Council Chs.; mem. council on higher edn. United Ch. Christ. Bd. mem. Japan Internat. Christian U. Found., Inc., N.Y.C. Mem. Phi Beta Kappa. Home: Talcott Notch Rd Farmington CT 06032 Office: 55 Elizabeth St Hartford CT 06105

GETTING, IVAN ALEXANDER, corp. exec.; b. N.Y.C., Jan. 18, 1912; s. Milan Alexander and Hermina (Almasy) G.; B.S., Mass. Inst. Tech., 1933; D. Phil., Oxford U., Eng., 1935; D.Sc., (hon.), Northeastern U.; m. Dorothea Louise Gracy, Oct. 2, 1937; children—Nancy Louise, Ivan Craig, Peter Alexander. Edison scholar, Mass. Inst. Tech., 1929-33; Rhodes scholar, Oxford U., 1933-35; Soc. Fellows, Harvard, 1935-40; with radiation lab. Mass. Inst. Tech., 1940-45, asso. prof., 1945-46, prof. elec. engring., 1946-51; on leave, 1950-51, to serve USAF, asst. for devel. planning Dep. Chief of Staff, Devel.; v.p. research and engring. Raytheon Co., 1951-60; pres. Aerospace Corp., El Segundo, Cal., 1960—. Decorated Medal for Merit, D.S.M. (USAF); recipient Naval Ordnance award. Fellow Am. Phys. Soc., I.E.E.E., Am. Acad. Arts and Sciences; mem. Am. Assn. Rhodes Scholars. Club: Cosmos. Author sci. articles, chiefly in publs. of Am. Phys. Soc. Home: 605 Tigertail Rd Los Angeles CA 90049 Office: 2350 E El Segundo Blvd Los Angeles CA 90045

GETTING, VLADO ANDREW, educator, physician; b. Pitts., July 20, 1910; s. Milan and Hariet (Almasy) G.; A.B., Johns Hopkins, 1931; M.D., Harvard, 1935, M.P.H. magna cum laude, 1939, D.Pub. Health cum laude, 1940; m. Rose M. Klaus, Dec. 2, 1937; children—Andrew Vlado. Linda. Dist. health officer 1941-42, commr. Worcester (Mass.) Dept. Pub. Health, 1942-43; Mass. commr. pub. health, Boston, 1943- 53; asst. in epidemiology and preventive medicine Harvard Med. Sch., Harvard Sch. Pub. Health, 1939-43, lectr. pub. health practice Harvard Sch. Pub. Health 1943-54; prof. pub. health administrn. U. Mich. Sch. Pub. Health, Ann Arbor, 1953—, chmn. dept. community health services. Cons. Ill. Dept. Pub. Health; v.p. pub. health Am. Coll. Preventive Medicine. Diplomate Am. Bd. Preventive Medicine. Fellow Am. Pub. Health Assn., A.M.A.; mem. Assn. State and Territorial Health Officers, A.A.A.S., Mich. State Med. Soc., Mich. Assn. for Tb and Respiratory Diseases, Mich. Health Officers Assn. Tchrs. Preventive Med., Washtenaw County Med. Soc., Mich. Pub. Health Assn., Phi Beta Kappa, Delta Omega. Contbr. numerous articles to med. jours. Home: 1200 Arlington Blvd Ann Arbor MI 48104

GETTS, CLARK H., pub. relations counsel; b. Whitehall, Wis., Aug. 5, 1893; s. Edmund Cyrus and Pearl (Sherwood) G.; A.B., U. Wis., 1914; LL.B., Columbia, 1916; m. Osa Johnson, Feb. 3, 1941 (dec.); m. 2d, Dorothy Raphun Jones, Dec. 30, 1955. Rep. Am. and Brit newspapers, China, 1920-26; writer for mags., lectr. on China and Manchuria, 1927-30; with NBC, promoting tours for Paderewski, Rachmaninoff and others, 1930-32: established ind. lecture and radio prodn. bur., 1933; inc. as Clark H. Getts, Inc., 1937: inc. pub. relations bus., 1940; asso. in prodn. radio shows, including Heinz Mag. of the Air, 1937, Army-Navy-Red Cross show, 1944, John T. Flynn's Behind the Headlines, 1947, John Tasker Howard's Our American Music, 1950; TV programs, Crime Report, Chronoscope (both received Freedoms Found. and TV gold medal awards), 1951, Men and Ideas, 1952, and others. Mgr. and condr. Johnson expdn. to Africa, making Stanley and Livingstone feature film for 20th Century-Fox; arranged nat. tours for numerous artists, speakers, internat. figures, including, Harold Stassen. C. J. Hambro, Esequiel Padilla, Grand Duchess Marie, Alexander Wollcott, Eleanor Roosevelt, William Lyon Phelps, Rajan Nehru, Mme V. L. Pandit, Maj. Alexander P. de Seversky, Gen. Leslie R. Groves, Gen. Robert L. Eichelberger, Adm. Blandy, Marquis of Donegal, Gen. George C. Kenney, Prince Peter and Princess Irene of Greece; concert prodns. including, Nat. Tipica Orchestra of Mexico, Chinese Cultural Theatre, Mia Slavenska and her Ballet, Dublin Players, Gay Tyroliers, Fiesta Mexicana, London Players. Pres. Clark H. Getts Assos., Transat Inc. Pres. Am. Inst. for Civic Edn. Methodist. Mason (Shriner). Club: Dutch Treat. Office: 663 Fifth Av New York City NY 10022

GETTY, GEORGE FRANKLIN, II, bus. exec.; b. Los Angeles, July 9, 1924; s. J. Paul and Jeannette (Demont) G.; student Princeton, 1942; m. Gloria Alice Gordon, June 29, 1951 (div.); children—Anne, Claire, Caroline. Ind. oil operator, Cal., Tex., 1947-48, discovered South Crane oil field, W. Tex., 1948; mgr. Saudi Arabian div., Pacific Western Oil Corp., 1949-50, mgr. Mid- Continent div., 1951-53; v.p., dir., Spartan Aircraft Co., Tulsa, 1953- 55; pres. Minnehoma Ins. Co., Minnehoma Financial Co., 1953-56; exec. v.p., Pacific Western Oil Corp. (the Getty Oil Co.), 1955-56; v. p., gen. mgr. eastern div., dir., Tidewater Oil Co., 1956-58, pres., 1958- 67; exec. v.p., chief operating officer, dir. Getty Oil Co., 1967—; dir. Bank of Am. N.T. & S.A., Mission Corp. Mem. 1st U.S. petroleum industry exchange delegation inspecting Soviet oil industry, 1960. Trustee Council for Econ. Devel., Los Angeles World Affairs Council, So. Cal. Symphony-Hollywood Bowl Assn. Served as 1st lt. AUS, 1942-47, PTO. Recipient gold medal of merit V.F.W., 1964. Mem. Am. Petroleum Inst. (dir., mem. exec. com.), Nat. Petroleum Council (dir.). Clubs: Los Angeles (dir. 1963—, pres. 1964-65), California. Office: 3810 Wilshire Blvd Los Angeles CA 90010

GETTY, J. RONALD, oil exec.; b. Berlin, Germany, Dec. 19, 1929; s. J. Paul and Fini (Helmle) G.; student Zurich U., Switzerland, 1950-51, Heidelberg U., Germany, 1952; B.A., U. So. Cal., 1953; m. Karin Seibl, 1964; children—Christopher Ronald, Stefanie Marie, Cecile Karin Margarita. Asst. rep. Tidewater Oil Co., Europe, 1953, asst. rep., Europe, North Africa, Middle East, 1954, asst. mng. dir. subsidiary Veedol Corp., 1954, spl. rep. Tidewater Oil Co., Europe, Africa, Middle East, 1955, adminstrv. v.p. for marketing Tidewater Oil Co., 1957—; pres., chmn. bd. Veedol Petroleum Internat. A.G., Zug, Switzerland, 1961—, Huiles Veedol France S.A., Paris; dir. Veedol (U.K.) Ltd., Veedol GMBH (Hamburg, Germany), Gerry Oil Hamburg; chmn. bd., chief exec. officer, cons. Getty Oil Co., Los Angeles, 1970—; chmn. bd., chief exec. officer Fromkess Picture Corp., Los Angeles. Home: Veedol GmbH Hamburg 36 Jungfernstieg 51 Germany Office: Veedol Internat Höhenweg 9 Zug Switzerland

GETTY, JEAN PAUL, business exec.; b. Minneapolis, Dec. 15, 1892; s. George Franklin and Sarah McPherson (Risher) G.; student U. Cal. at Los Angeles, U. Cal. at Berkeley; grad. in economics and polit. sci. Oxford U., Eng.; LL.D. (hon.), Ohio No. U., 1966; m. Jeannette Demont, 1923 (div.); 1 son, George Franklin H; m. 2d, Allene Ashby, 1926 (div.); m. 3d, Fini Helmle, 1928 (div.); 1 son, Jean Ronald; m. 4th, Ann Rork, 1932 (div.); children—Jean Paul, Gordon Peter; m. 5th, Louise Dudley Lynch, Nov. 14, 1939 (div.); 1 son, Timothy Christopher (dec.). Ind. oil producer, 1914—; pres., gen. mgr. George F. Getty, Inc., 1930-33; dir. Petroleum Corp., 1932-34; dir. Tidewater Asso. Oil Co., 1932-36; pres., gen. mgr. Minnehoma Financial Corp. (formerly Spartan Aircraft Co.), 1942-61, prin. owner, 1942—; pres. Mission Corp.; pres., prin. owner Getty Oil Co., 1956—, Mem. N.Y., Cal. chambers commerce. Clubs: Explorers (N.Y.); Beach (Santa Monica, Cal.); Los Angeles Athletic; Nouveau Cercle (Paris). Author: History of the Oil Business of George Franklin and J. Paul Getty, 1903-39, 1941; Europe in the 18th Century, 1947; Collector's Choice (with Ethel LeVane), 1956; My Life and Fortunes, 1963; The Joys of Collecting, 1965; How to be Rich, 1966; The Golden Age, 1968. Home: 17985 Pacific Coast Hwy Malibu CA 90265 Office: 3810 Wilshire Blvd Los Angeles CA 90010

GETTY, ROBERT, educator; b. Cin., Nov. 10, 1916; s. Robert and Elsa (Muehe) G.; D.V.M., Ohio State U., 1940; M.S., Ia. State U., 1945, Ph.D., 1949; m. Roberta B. Musgrave, Dec. 28, 1944; children-Rita Ann (Mrs. Charles Hammerberg), Rikel Kent. Practice vet. medicine, Norwood, O., 1940-41; instr. vet. anatomy Ia. State U., 1941-42, asst. prof. vet. bacteriolgy, 1943-45, asst. prof. vet. anatomy, 1943-49, asso. prof. vet. anatomy, 1949-51, prof., head vet. anatomy, 1951—, mem. com. biomed. electronics, 1957—, chmn. 1963-65. Mem. vet. medicine rev. com. N.I.H., 1970—; exec. bd. Council on Med. TV, 1969—; exec. bd. Audiovisual Conf. Med. and Allied Scis., 1962—, co-chmn., 1962-63, v.p., 1963-67, pres., 1967-69. Mem. governing com. Ia. State U. Research Found., 1962—, trustee, 1964—, v.p., 1964-66, pres., 1966-68. Recipient Distinguished Alumnus award Ohio State U., 1970, Distinguished prof. vet. medicine award Ia. State U., 1970. Fellow Gerontol. Soc., A.A.A.S.; mem. N.Y. Acad. Scis., Assn. for Advancement Aging Research (council advisers), World Assn. Vet. Anatomists (v.p. 1960-63, mem. internat. vet. anat. nomenclature com. 1959—, chmn. sect. organa Sensuum 1959-68),Am. Vet. Med. Assn. (Sec. nat. research council 1952-56, chmn. 1956-59), Am. Assn. Vet. Anatomists (pres. 1961-62), Am. Assn. Human Anatomists, Am. Pub. Health Assn. Ia. State U. Alumni Assn. (faculty citation 1968), Sigma Xi, Phi Zeta, Phi Kappa Psi, Gamma Sigma Delta, Alpha Zeta. Author: Veterinary Anatomy, 1962; Veterinary Histology and Embroyology, 1964; Atlas for Applied Veterinary Anatomy, 1964; Atlas and Dissection Guide for the Study of the Anatomy of Domestic Animals, 1960; rev. and updated edit. Sisson and Grossman's Anatomy of Domestic Animals, 1971; also numerous articles, chpts. in books vet. anat. films. Home: 1002 Jarret Ct Ames IA 50010

GETTY, WILLIAM PATTON, steel co. dir.; b. Pitts., Mar. 26, 1910; s. William Fleming and Bertha A. (Keefe) G.; B.S., U. Pitts., 1932; m. Betty Ann Cochran, Nov. 23, 1938; children—Judith Ann (Mrs. John Walter Treadwell), William Patton III. With Weirton Steel Co., 1933-36; with Jones & Laughlin Steel Corp., 1936—, asst. v.p. prodn., 1953-63, v.p. prodn., 1963-67, exec. vice president, 1967-69, president, 1969-70, now dir.; v.p., dir. Gateway Coal Co.; dir. Mesaba Cliffs Mining Co., Marquette Iron Mining Co., Bristol Que. Mining Co., Ltd. Chmn. trustees Winchester-Thurston Sch., 1961-65; mem. exec. council Allegheny council Boy Scouts Am., 1959—. Mem. A.A.A.S., Bituminous Coal Operators Assn. (director), Newcomen Society of North America, American (chairman mfg. problems com. 1966- 68), British iron and steel insts., Am. Soc. Metals, Am. Welding Soc., Soc. Automotive Engrs., Coal Mining Inst. Am., Eastern States Blast Furnace and Coke Oven Assn. Clubs: Pitts. Athletic, Duquesne, Long Vue Country (Pitts.); Laurel Valley (Ligonier, Pa.). Home: 107 Hawthorne Rd Fox Chapel Pittsburgh PA 15238 Office: 3 Gateway Center Pittsburgh PA 15230

GETTYS, CHARLES MARTIN, army officer; b. Charlotte, N.C., Jan. 1, 1915; s. Thomas Roddy and Missouri (Martin) G.; B.S., Clemson Coll., 1936; postgrad U. Mich., 1946; grad. Command and Gen. Staff Coll., 1949, Army War Coll., 1956; m. Blossom Millbrook, Dec. 22, 1942; 1 son, Mark Martin. Commd. 2d lt. U.S. Army, 1936, advanced through grades to maj. gen., 1968; company comdr., bn. comdr. ETO, World War II; staff officer NATO Hdqrs., Naples, Italy, 1952-54; staff officer UN Command, U.S. Armed Forces, Korea, 1958-59; chief war plans div. Dept. of Army, Washington, 1959-63; chief of staff 8th Inf. Div., Europe, 1963-65, asst. div. comdr., 1965-66; dep. dir. operations to dep. spl. asst. strategic mobility Office Joint Chiefs of Staff, Washington, 1966-68; comdg. gen. Americal Div., Vietnam, 1968-69; dir. individual tng. Dept. of Army, 1969-70; chief of staff U.S. Army Vietnam, 1970-71; comdg. gen. U.S. Army, Alaska, 1971—. Decorated D.S.M. with oak leaf cluster, Silver Star with oak leaf cluster, Legion of Merit with 2 oak leaf clusters, Bronze Star with valor device (U.S.); Croix de Guerre (France); Abdon Calderon Primera Clase (Ecuador); Gallantry Cross with palm (Vietnam). Mem. Assn. U.S. Army. Home: 4421 48th St NW Washington DC 20016 Office: Hdqrs US Army Alaska APO Seattle WA 98749

GETTYS, LOYD BRYANT, numismatist; b. Lincoln, Neb., Oct. 19, 1893; s. James Robert and Cora E. (Scofield) G.; A.B., Neb. Wesleyan Univ., 1916; m. Eloine Crosthwaite, June 27, 1917; 1 son, Robert Loyd. With Mut. Life Ins. Co. of N.Y., 1915, mgr. agency, Sioux City, Ia., 1925-36, Davenport, Ia., 1936-50, ret. 1950; now profl. numismatist. Served with 350th Machine Gun Co., France, 1917-18, World War 1. Awarded Medaille de Verdun; Medal of Merit, Gold medal Am. Numis. Assn. Mem. U.S. 1953 Assay Commn. Mem. Davenport Life Underwriters Assn. (past pres.), Nat. Assn. Life Underwriters, Gen. Agts. and Mgrs. Assn. (past pres.), Am. Numis. Assn. (past pres.), Am. Legion, V.F.W., Zeta Psi. Republican. Methodist. Mason (Shriner), Rotarian. Lectr. on U.S. paper money. Home: 483 10th St David City NB 68632 Office: PO Box 378 David City NB 68632

GETTYS, THOMAS SMITHWICK, congressman; b. Rock Hill, S.C., June 19, 1912; s. John E. and Maud (Martin) G.; student Clemson Coll., 1929-30; A.B., Erskine Coll., 1933; grad. student Duke, Winthrop Coll.; m. Mary Phillips White, Dec. 9, 1947; children—Julia Martin, Sara Elizabeth. Tchr., coach Rock Hill High Sch., 1933-35; prin. Central Sch., Rock Hill, 1935-41; sec. to Congressman Richards 1941-51, postmaster, Rock Hill, 1951-54; admitted to S.C. bar, 1953; practice in Rock Hill, 1954-64; mem. firm Gettys, McFadden and Wilkerson; mem. 88th-92d Congresses 5th Dist. S.C., mem. banking and currency com. Pres. Rock Hill YMCA, 1960; chmn. Rock Hill United Fund campaign, 1955; chmn. trustees Rock Hill Sch. Dist. 3. Served with USNR, World War II; PTO. Mem. Am., S.C., York County bar assns., Am. Legion, V.F.W., Rock Hill C. of C. (past pres.). Democrat. Mem. Asso. Reformed Presbyn. Ch. (elder). Elk, Rotarian (past pres. Rock Hill). Home: Rock Hill SC 29730 Office: House Office Bldg Washington DC 20515

GETZ, GEORGE FULMER, Jr., business exec.; b Chgo., Jan. 4, 1908; s. George Fulmer and Susan Daniel (Rankin) G.; student Choate Sch.; m. Olive Cox Atwater, Jan. 17, 1933; children—George Fulmer, III (dec.), Bert Atwater. With Eureka Coal & Dock Co.; pres., dir. Globe Corp.; chmn. bd. Getz Coal Co., 1939-48, pres., 1948-53; dir. Upper Av. Nat. Bank, Chgo., Nat. League Ball Club: exec. com., dir. A.T. & S.F. ry., Sante Fe Industries, Inc. Mem. United Republican Fund Ill. Mem. citizens' bd. U. Chgo.; bd. dirs. Jr. Achievement Chgo., 1939—, v.p., 1947-49; bd. dirs. Getz Found., Ind. U. Found.; pres., dir. Arthur R. Metz Found.; hon. trustee Chgo. Zool. Soc.; past v.p. finance, treas. Nat. Safety Council; mem. Northwestern U. Assos., v.p. Geneva Lake Water Safety Com., Inc., 1956-66; mem. Ill. State Com. Crusade for Freedom, Inc., 1957, 58. Dir. Ch. of Holy Communion Foundation; pres., dir. Nat. Hist. Fire Found.; pres. Ariz. Zool. Soc. (dir.). Mem. Chgo. Assn. Commerce and Industry (com. mem. govtl. affairs council). Episcopalian. Clubs: Executives Kiva (Phoenix); Chicago, Mid-America, Tavern, Chicago Yacht (Chgo.), Lake Geneva Yacht, Lake Geneva Country (Wis.); Glen View (Golf, Ill.); Economic; Los Rancheros Visitadores (Santa Barbara, Cal.); Kingman Country (Ariz.); Mountain Shadows Country (Scottsdale); Paradise Valley Country (Ariz.); Valley Field Riding and Polo (Ariz.). Home: 175 E Delaware Pl Chicago IL 60611 61 N Lake Shore Dr Lake Geneva WI 53147 120 Mountain Shadows W Scottsdale AZ 85252 Office: Globe Corp Wrigley Bldg 400 N Michigan Av Chicago IL 60611

GETZ, GEORGE W., physician. Supt., Larned (Kan.) State Hosp. Office: Box 89 Larned KS 67550*

GETZ, LOWELL LEE, educator; b. Chersterfield, Ill., sept. 21, 1931; s. Carl C. and Evelyn (Dowland) G.; B.S., U Ill., 1953; M.S., U. Mich., 1959, Ph.D., 1960; m. Mary Ruth Clardy, July 5, 1953; children-Colleen Marie, Allison Lynn. Reserach asso. U.Mich., 1959-61; asst. prof., then asso. prof. zoology U. Conn., 1961-69; prof. zoology U. Ill. at Urbana, 1969—; hon. fellow zoology U. Wis.-Madison, 1967-68. Served to 1st lt. AUS, 1953-55. Mem. Am. Soc. Mammalogists, Ecol. Soc. Am., Brit. Ecol. Soc., Animal Behavior Soc., Phi Beta Kappa, Sigma Xi, Phi Eta Sigma, Phi Kappa Phi, Phi Sigma (editor Biologist 1967—). Author papers in field. Home: 2113 Lynwood Dr Champaign IL 61820

GETZ, OSCAR, distilling co. exec.; b. Chgo., Nov. 20, 1897; s. Meyer Philip and Jennie (Mann) G.; student Northwestern U. Sch. Commerce, 1918-19; m. Emma Dorothy Abelson, Jan. 9, 1923; children—Constance Joy (Mrs. Otto Bresky, Jr.), William Murray. With William D. McJunkin Advt. Agy., Chgo., 1920-23; owner Radio Doctors, Inc., Chgo., 1924-27; pres. Steinite Radio Corp., Chgo., 1927-30; with Arlington Time Labs., Fluorescent Lighting Co., 1930-33; chmn. bd. Barton Brands, Inc., Chgo., 1933—, also dir.; v.p., dir. Barton Western Distilling Co., Barton Internat. Corp., Barton Distillers Import Corp.; chmn. bd., dir. Barton Distilling (Can.) Ltd. Founder Barton Mus. Whiskey History, Bardstown, Ky.; gen. chmn. Lyric Opera Fund campaign, 1955; co-chmn. Auditorium Theatre Restoration Council, Chgo. Mem. Mayor Chgo. All Citizens Com., 1958. Bd. dirs. World Rehab. Fund, Inc., N.Y.C.; fellow Brandeis U., Waltham, Mass.; dir. Jewish Welfare Fund. Mem. Chgo. Hist. Soc., Manuscript Soc. Clubs: Standard, Executives, Caxton (Chgo.); Briarwood Country (Deerfield, Ill.). Home: 1550 N Lake Shore Dr Chicago IL 60611 Office: 200 S Michigan Av Chicago IL 60604

GETZ, STAN, saxophonist; b. Phila., Feb. 2, 1927. Bass, then bassoon player, N.Y.C.; with All City Orchestra, Bronx, then with Dick Rogers; with bands Jack Teagarden, Dale Jones, Bob Chester, Stan Kenton, Jimmy Dorsey, Benny Goodman, others; formed trio, appeared at Swing Club, Hollywood, 1947; with Woody Herman Band, 1947-49; leader quartet with Al Haig, pianist; on tour, Scandinavia, 1951; studio musician NBC, N.Y.C., 1952; leader quintet, jazz clubs and concerts; on tour with Jazz at the Philharmonic, 1957-58. Recipient poll award Metronome mag., 1950-55, Down Beat mag., 1950-54, critics poll award Down Beat, 1953-54. Recordings include Jam Session, Concert at the Shrine, Getz Meets Mulligan in Hi-Fi, Lestorian Mode, Stan Getz and the Cool Sounds, Stan Getz in Stockholm.

GETZELS, JACOB WARREN, educator, psychologist; b. Bialystok, Poland, Feb. 7, 1912; s. Hirsch and Frieda (Solon) G.; came to U.S., 1921, naturalized, 1933; B.A., Bklyn. Coll., 1936; M.A., Columbia, 1939; Ph.D., Harvard, 1951; m. Judith Nelson, Dec. 24, 1949; children—Katharine, Peter, Julia, instr. ednl. psychology U. Chgo., 1951, asst. prof. edn., psychology, 1952-54, asso. prof., 1955-57, prof., 1957-, now R. Wendell Harrison Distinguished Service prof. Vis. prof. phychology U. P.R., summer 1962, Stanford, summer 1963; mem. U.S. Office Edn. Mission to Soviet Russia, 1960; mem. research adv. council U.S. Office Edn., 1964. Trustee Morgan Park Acad.; mem. vis. com. Sch. Edn. Cornell U.; bd. dirs. Spencer Found. Served with OSS, AUS, 1942-46. Recipient Research award Am. Personnel and Guidance Assn., 1959. Livingston fellow Harvard, 1949-50; fellow Center For Advanced Study Behavioral Scis., 1960-61, center for Policy study, U. Chgo., 1967—. Mem. Nat. Acad. Edn., Am. Psychol. Assn., Am. Sociol. Assn., Am. Ednl. Research Assn. Author: (with A. Coladarci) The Use of Theory in Educational Administration, 1955; (with P.W. Jackson) Creativity and Intelligence: Explorations with Gifted Students, 1962; (with J. M. Lipham, R.F. Campbell) Educational Adminstration as a Social Process, 1968. Mem. nat. adv. bd. editors Trans-action, 1966. Dontbr. articles to profl. jours. Home: 5704 S Dorchester Av Chicago IL 60637 Office: 5835 S Kimbark Av Chicago IL 60637

GEUPEL, JOHN C., constrn. co. exec.; b. Indpls., 1927; grad. Yale, 1949. Chmn. bd. Carl M. Geupel Constrn. Co., Indpls. Home: 4766 Riverside Dr Columbus OH 43212 Office: 1919 N Meridian St Indianapolis IN 46204*

GEURINK, BOB, journalist. Motion picture-theatrical editor Atlanta Constitution. Office: 10 Forsyth St Atlanta GA 30302*

GEUVARA-ARZE, WALTER, diplomat of Bolivia; b. Cochambamba, Bolivia, Mar. 11, 1912; s. Walter and Victoria (Arze) Guevara-A.; D. Law and Polit. Sci., U. La Paz, 1938; postgrad. student sociology, U. Chgo., 1944; m. Rosa Elena Rodriquez. Nov. 10, 1951; children—Walter, Ramino, Carlos. Mem. Bolivian Ho. of Reps., 1938-39; minister sec. gen., 1943-44; minister fgn. affairs, 1952-56; ambassador to France, 1956-58; minister of interior, 1959-60; ambassador, permanent rep. Bolivia to UN, 1968—; prof. civil law Sch. Econs., U. La Paz, 1944-45. Candidate for presidency Bolivia, 1960. Decorated grand cross France, Germany, Brazil, Peru, Argentina, numerous others. Mem. Nat. Assn. Attys. Law Chief Authentic Revolutionary Party Roman Cath. Author: Theory, Means and Ends of National Revolution, 1944; Foreign Policy of Bolivia, 1953; Economic Policy of the National Revolution, 1955. Home: 154 Puritan Av Forest Hills NY 11375 Office: 211 E 43d St New York City NY 10017

GEUZE, EMMERICUS CAREL WILLEM ADRIANN, educator, civil engr.; b. Dordrecht, Netherlands, Mar. 27, 1906; s. Peter Jan and Catharina (Krafft) G.; Civiel Ingenieur, Delft (Netherlands) Technol. U., 1931; m. Melanie Nancy Veenstra, May 3, 1934; 1 son, Pieter Jan Willem. Came to U.S., 1960. Mem. faculty Delft Technol. U., 1931-60, dir. research lab. soil mechanics, 1948-60, prof. soil mechanics, 1951-60; prof. soil mechanics, internat. course hydraulic engring. Netherlands U. Found. for Internat. Cooperation, 1957- 60; prof. soil mechanics and found. engring. Rensselaer Poly. Inst., Troy, N.Y., 1960—, chmn. dept. civil engring., 1961-66, William Weightman Walker prof. civil engring., 1966—; spl. lectr. schs., including Technion, Haifa, Israel, 1951, U. Madrid (Spain), 1952, U. Glasgow (Scotland), 1952, 1956, U. Birmingham (Eng.), 1954, Free U. Brussels (Belgium), 1955, U. Karlsruhe (Germany), 1960. Adviser to Govt. Israel, UN Tech. Assistance Assn., 1951-59; adviser com. on runway constrn. NATO, 1955; Netherlands Govt. adviser to Govt. Japan, 1957-59; mem. NRC adv. com. to U.S. Army Research Office, 1960—; mem. rev. panel, div. math., phys. and engring. scis. NSF, 1960—; cons. Raymond Internat., Inc., N.Y.C., 1961—, Gen. Electric Co., Schenectady, 1962-, Mech. Technology, Inc., Latham, N.Y., 1962—, U.S. Geol. Survey, Washington, 1962—, N.Y. State Dept. Pub. Works, 1966—; mem. com. rock and soil mechanics Hwy. Research Bd., 1964—; participant numerous internat. congresses and symposiums in field. Mem. Royal Netherlands Soc. Engrs., German Soc. Soil Mechanics and Found. Engring., Am. Soc. C.E. (rev. panel, div. soil mechanics and founds. 1960-), brit. Soc. Rhedogy, Am. Soc. for Testing and Materials, Internat. Soc. Terrain Vehicle Systems (hon.), Am. Soc. Engring. Edn., Sigma Xi, Chi Epsilon. Research and publs. in field. Home: 2 Ledgestone Rd Troy, NY 12180.

GEVANTMAN, LEWIS HERMAN, chemist, govt. ofcl.; b. N.Y.C., Sept. 12, 1921; s. Benjamin and Ida (Goldberg) G.; B.Engring., Johns Hopkins, 1942; Ph.D. in Phys. Chemistry, U. Notre Dame, 1951; m. Leatrice Black, Aug. 22, 1948; children—Sandra Cay, Janis Mara. Chem. operator Johns Hopkins, Bethlehem Steel Co., 1942-43; research chemist Clinton Labs., Manhattan Project, 1943-46; supervisory research chemist U.S. Naval Radiol. Def. Lab., San Francisco, 1951-56, acting head allied research br., 1956-59, head radiation chemistry br., 1959-61, sci. research adminstr., head chem. tech. div., 1961-64; sr. sci. adviser U.S. mission Internat. Atomic Energy Agy., 1964-67; program mgr. Office Standard Reference Data, coordinator nuclear material safeguard program U.S. Dept. Commerce, 1967—; AEC-Nat. Bur. Standards coordinator, 1970—. Cons. Nuclear Sci. & Engring. Corp., 1956-59; mem. Bd. Civil Service Examiners, 1958-61; mem. Nat. Com. on Civil Def. and Disaster, 1970—. Mem. Am. Chem. Soc. (chmn. civil def. com. No. Cal. sect. 1961-64), Am. Soc. Testing Materials (ad hoc com. dosimetry), A.A.A.S., Radiation Research Soc., N.Y. Acad. Scis., Sigma Xi. Contbr. articles to profl. jours. Patentee in field. Address: Nat Bur Standards Washington DC 20234

GEWIN, WALTER PETTUS, judge; b. Nanafalia, Ala., Dec. 9, 1908; s. John Walker and Julia (Crenshaw) G.; A.B. cum laude, Birmingham So. Coll., 1930; B.A. in Library Sci., Emory U., 1932; LL.B., U. Ala., 1935; m. Anna Fidelia Sledge, Dec. 5, 1936; children—Walter Pettus, James William, Margaret Juliette. Admitted to Ala. bar, 1935, practiced in Birmingham, 1935, Greensboro, 1936-51, Tuscaloosa, 1951-61; judge U.S. Ct. Appeals, 5th circuit, 1961—; state pros., Hale County, Ala., 1943-51. Mem. Code Com. of Ala., 1940. Mem. Ala. Ho. of Reps., 1939-43; mem. Ala. Democratic Exec. Com., 1943-47. Bd. dirs. Ala. Law Sch. Found. Served as sgt., judge adv. gen. dept., AUS, 1944-45. Mem. Am., Ala. (pres.), Tuscaloosa bar assns., Am. Coll. Trial Lawyers, Am. Law Inst. Presbyn. (elder). Mason (Shriner), Kiwanian. Home: 35 The Downs Tuscaloosa AL 35401 Office: U S Courthouse and Fed Bldg Tuscaloosa AL 35401

GEWIRTH, ALAN, philosopher, educator; b. Union City, N.J., Nov. 28, 1912; s. Hyman and Rose (Lees) G.; B.A. with honors in Philosophy, Columbia, 1934, Ph.D. (Rockefeller Found. fellow), 1947; postgrad. (Sage fellow in philosophy) Cornell U., 1936-37; m. Marcella Tilton, Mar. 18, 1956; children—James, Susan (by former marriage), Andrew Alan, Daniel Tilton, Letitia Rose. Teaching, research asst. philosophy U. Chgo., 1937-41, faculty, 1947—, prof., 1960—; instr. Ill. Inst. Tech., 1942. Vis. prof. Harvard, 1957, U. Mich., 1959-60, Johns Hopkins, 1966- 67; lectr. Humanities Conf., Ohio State U., 1958; Cooper Found. lectr. Swarthmore Coll., 1961; Niebuhr lectr. Elmhurst Coll., 1969; Distinguished guest lectr. Ia. Philos. Soc., 1969. Served from pvt. to capt. AUS, 1942-46. Recipient Woodbridge prize Columbia, 1948. Rockefeller Found. fellow, 1957-58. Mem. Am. Philos. Assn. (chmn. program com. 1953-54, 70-71), Am. Soc. for Polit. and Legal Philosophy, Am. Polit. Sci. Assn., Institut International de Philosophi Politique, Am. Civil Liberties Union, Phi Beta Kappa. Author: Marsilius of Padua and Medieval Political Philosophy, 1951. Co-author: Social Justice, 1962; The Forward Movement of the Fourteenth Century, 1961. Editor: Political Philosophy, 1965. Translator: Marsilius of Padua: Defensor Pacis, 1956. Mem. adv. bd. editors Nomos. Home: 1365 E Park Pl Chicago IL 60637

GEX, RICHARD STANLEY, coll. dean; b. Graham, Mo., Jan. 29, 1912; s. William Burris and Mary Lodema (Anderson) G.; B.S., N.W. Mo. State Coll., 1935; postgrad. U. Wyo., summer 1937; M.A., U. Mo., 1941, Ed.D., 1948; m. Mary Kathryn Brady, Oct. 7, 1938; children—Jeannie Louise (Mrs. Russell Utz), Karen Lee (Mrs. Mohamed Asfour), Nancy Elizabeth. Tchr. rural schs., high schs., Mo., 1930-42; instr. math., asst. prof. edn. U. Mo., 1946- 48; asst. prof. edn., asso. prof. edn. U. Cin., 1948-54; head dept. edn. Eastern Mich. U., Ypsilanti, 1954-57, dean Coll. Edn., 1957-67, dean internat. studies, 1967—, chief party tchr. edn. contract team, 1963-65. Vis. summer prof. Johns Hopkins, 1952, Bradley U., 1953, So. Ill. U., 1957. Mem. subcom. student teaching N. Central Assn. Colls. and Secondary Schs., 1957-69, Mich. Curriculum Planning Com., 1958-62; rep. Am. Assn. Colls. Tchr. Edn. on adv. council Asso. Orgns. Tchr. Edn., 1958-62; chmn. and or mem. vis. teams instns. higher edn. Nat. Council Accreditation Tchr. Edn.; mem. ednl. survey team Somali Republic, 1961. Mem. Ypsilanti City Charter Commn., 1971. Served to lt. (j.g.) USNR, 1943-46. Mem. Nat., Mich. edn. assns., Nat. Assn. Secondary Sch. Prins., Assn. Student Teaching, Am. Ednl. Research Assn., Phi Delta Kappa, Kappa Delta Pi. Unitarian (trustee, pres. 1968-70). Rotarian. Club: Forum (Ypsilanti). Author book revs. Contbr. articles to profl. jours. Home: 620 Collegewood Ypsilanti MI 48197

GEYELIN, PHILIP LAUSSAT, journalist; b. Devon, Pa., Feb. 27, 1923; s. Emile Camille and Cecily (Barnes) G.; grad. Episcopal Acad., Overbrook, Pa., 1940; B.A., Yale, 1944; m. Cecilia Sherman Parker, Jan. 28, 1950; children—Mary Sherman, Emile Camille, Philip Laussat, Cecily, Parker. With Washington bur. A.P., 1946-47; mem. staff Wall St. Jour. 1947-66, diplomatic corr., 1960-67; mem. editorial staff Washington Post, 1967—, editor editorial page, 1968—. Bd. dirs. Alliance Francaise, Washington, 1964—, Served to 1st lt. USMCR, 1943-46. Fellow Inst. Politics, Harvard Sch. Govt., 1967; recipient Pulitzer prize for editorial writing, 1969. Clubs: Gridiron, Metropolitan, Overseas Writers, Federal City (Washington). Author: Lyndon B. Johnson and the World, 1966. Home: 4511 Cathedral Av NW Washington DC 20016 Office: 1515 L St Washington DC 20005

GEYER, ALAN, clergyman, editor; b. Dover, N.J., Aug. 3, 1931; s. Curtis Bayley and Ada (Wehrly) G.; B.A., Ohio Wesleyan U., 1952, Litt.D. (hon.), 1970; S.T.B., Boston U., 1955, Ph.D., 1961; m. Joanne Shirley Goodnow, Mar. 28, 1953; children—Nancy, Peter, David, Philip. Probation officer, Delaware, O., 1952; ordained to ministry Methodist Ch., 1954; pastor in Cambridge, Mass., 1954-55; asst. prof. polit. sci. and sociology Lycoming Coll., Williamsport, Pa., 1957-58; pastor in Newark, 1958-60; mem. faculty Mary Baldwin Coll., 1960-65, asso. prof. polit. sci., 1963- 65, chmn. dept., 1960-65; dir. internat. relations United Ch. Christ, 1965-68; editor The Christian Century, pres. Christian Century Found., 1968—; lectr. U. Va., 1962-64; vis. prof. Grad. Theol. Union, Berkeley, Cal., 1970; scholar-in-residence Gammon Theol. Sem., 1970. Dir. YM-YWCA Washington Seminar, 1965; cons. assemblies Nat. Council Chs., 1966, 69; dir. Eastern Europe Seminar, 1967; adviser 4th assembly World Council Chs., Uppsala, Sweden, 1968; cons. United Meth. Structure Commn., 1969- 70; v.p. Newark Council Chs., 1958-60; chmn. bd. social relations Newark Conf. Meth. Ch., 1960; mem. internat. affairs com. Nat. Council Chs., 1965—, mem. China panel, 1966-68; mem. Nat. Com. U.S.-China Relations, 1967—; exec. com. Nat. Com. Polit. Settlement in Vietnam, 1966-68; chmn. Am. Com. for Conf. Christian Approaches to Def. and Disarmament, 1965—; chmn. Chgo. Interreligious Com. Peace, 1969—. Bd. dirs. Lycoming County (Pa.) Council Community Services, 1957-58, Center for Study Power and Peace, 1970—; trustee Council Religion and Internat. Affairs, 1969—, Ohio Wesleyan U., 1970—. Recipient Community Service award Newark YM-YWCA, 1959; Frontiers of Am. Human Relations award, 1960; Wilton Park fellow Brit. Fgn. Office, 1966; Distinguished Alumnus award Boston U., 1969. Fellow Am. Sociol. Assn., Soc. Religion in Higher Edn. (bd. dirs. 1965—); mem. Am. Polit. Sci. Assn., Inst. Strategic Studies, Am. Soc. Christian Ethics (bd. dirs. 1967-71), Soc. Internat. Devel., Christian Peace Conf., So. Christian Leadership Conf., Am. Civil Liberties Union, Asso. Ch. Press, Phi Beta Kappa, Omicron Delta Kappa, Delta Sigma Rho, Alpha Kappa Delta, Beta Sigma Tau (pres. 1954-56). Democrat. Author: Piety and Politics, 1963; The Maze of Peace, 1969. Home: 303 N Ashland Av Park Ridge IL 60068 Office: 407 S Dearborn St Chicago IL 60605

GEYER, CHARLES JAMES, Jr., corp. exec.; b. Richmond, Va., Nov. 13, 1915; s. Charles James and Frances (Bennett) G.; B.S. in Chemistry, Hampden-Sydney Coll., 1937; Ph.D. in Chemistry, U. Va., 1941; m. Harriet Rogers, June 2, 1945; children—Charles James III, Pleas Blair Rogers, Harriet Frances, Ruth Ann, Thomas Joseph, Helen Claire. With Am. Viscose Corp. (now Am. Viscose div. FMC Corp.), 1941—, mfg. and tech. dir. fibers div., 1961- 62, v.p. fibers div., 1962-65, gen. mgr. fiber operations Am. Viscose div., 1965—, gen. mgr. Am. Viscose div., 1969—; dir. Ketchikan Pulp Co., Tyrex, Inc., Viscosa de Chihuahua S.A. Bd. dirs. Hampden Sydney Coll. Mem. Sigma Xi, Alpha Chi Sigma, Kappa Sigma. Presbyn. Clubs: Urban (Phila.); St. Davids (Pa.) Golf; Country of N.C.; Seaview Country (Absecon, N.J.); Empire State, Weavers (N.Y.C.). Home: 1224 Lancaster Av Berwyn PA 19312 Office: 1617 J F Kennedy Blvd Philadelphia PA 19103

GEYER, GEORGIE ANNE, journalist; b. Chgo., Apr. 2, 1935; d. Robert George and Georgie Hazel (Gervens) Geyer; B.S., Northwestern U., 1956; postgrad. (Fulbright scholar), U. Vienna (Austria), 1956-57. Reporter, Southtown Economist, Chgo., 1958; soc. reporter Chgo. Daily News, 1959-60, gen. assignment reporter, 1960-64, Latin Am. corr., 1964—, now roving fgn. corr. Active Orgn. for S.W. Community Chgo., 1960-64. Recipient 1st prize Am. Newspaper Guild, 1962, 2d prize Ill. Press Editors Assn., 1962; award for best writing on Latin Am., Overseas Press Club, 1966; Alumni award Northwestern U., 1967; Nat. Headliner award Theta Sigma Phi, 1968. Mem. Mortar Bd., Theta Sigma Chi, Sigma Delta Chi. Contbr. articles Atlantic mag. Sat. Rev., Look mag., The Nation, Nat. Observer, The Progressive, New Republic, others. Home: 339 W Barry Av Chicago IL 60657 Office: 401 N Wabash Av Chicago IL 60611

GEYER, HAROLD CAR, artist, author; b. Cold Spring, N.Y., Aug. 16, 1905; s. Harold Carl and Mary Brinsmade (deCamp) G.; A.B., Yale, 1926, B.F.A., 1930; m. Ina Helen Doane, July 29, 1944. Exhibited Soc. Am. Etchers, Nat. Acad.; rep. in permanent collections of Library of Congress, Mus. of Troyes, France, Bibliotheque Nationale. Awarded 3d purchase prize Joseph Pennell exhbn. Library of Congress, 1945, Asso. Nat. Acad.; mem. Soc. Am. Graphic Artists. Author and illustrator; All Men Have Lived Thee, a song of France, 1941; The Long Way Home, a song of France, 1949. Lectr. Home: Powerville Rd R F D 1 Boonton NJ 07005

GEYER, JOHN CHARLES, educator, engr.; b. Neosho, Mo., Aug. 11, 1906; s. Harold G. and Nina (Dorman) G.; student Drury Coll., 1925-27, D.Sci., 1969; B.S. in C.E., U. Mich., 1931; M.S., Harvard, 1933; D.Engring., Johns Hopkins, 1942; m. Dorothy Anderson, July 19, 1933; 1 dau., Joellen (Mrs. Randolph Reed). Asst. prof. san. engring. N.C. U., 1934-37; faculty Johns Hopkins, 1937—, asst. dept. civil engring., 1937-42, on leave as asst. chief engr., health and sanitation div. Office Inter-Am. Affairs, Washington, 1942- 43, asso. prof. san. engring., 1946-48, prof., 1948—, chmn. dept. san. engring. and water resources, 1957-70, prin. investigator AEC waste disposal projects, 1948-65. Cons. WHO, U. Chile Sch. Pub. Health, Santiago, Chile, 1955-56; commr. Md. Geol. Survey 1956—. Dir. survey Textile Found., Washington, 1935-36; mem. adv. com. Spl. Weapons Def., 1951-55; mem. com. on ednl. objectives NRC, 1957—; dir. Low-Flow Augmentation for Stream Pollution Abatement, 1958-63, Residential Water Use Project, 1959-66; dir. san. sewage research project FHA, 1959-66; dir. cooling water research Edison Electric Inst., 1961—; mem. adv. com. on reactor safeguards AEC, 1961-64; mem. environmental pollution panel PSAC, 1964—; mem. study sect. san. engring. and occupational health NIH, 1959-63. Cons. Md. State Planning Commn., 1949—, Bur. Water Supply, Balt., 1952—, Balt. Regional Planning Council, 1958-59, Phila. Electric Co., 1959—, Interstate Commn. on Potomac River Basin, 1956-57. Served from lt. to lt. comdr. USNR, 1943- 46. Recipient Harrison Prescott Eddy medal, 1952. Fellow A.A.A.S., Am. Pub. Health Assn., Am. Soc. C.E.; mem. Am. Water Works Assn. (utilities com. Cheseapeake sect. 1958—), Fedn. Sewage Works Assns., Am. Geophys. Union, Md.-Del. Water and Sewerage Assn., Am. Acad. Environmental Engrs., Nat. Acad. Engring., Phi Beta Kappa, Sigma Xi, Tau Beta Pi, Phi Kappa Phi, Delta Omega. Author: (latest book) Ground Water in Baltimore Industrial Area. 1944; co-author: Water Supply and Waste-Water Disposal, 1954; Water and Wastewater Engineering, vol. 1, Water Supply and Waste water Removal, 1966, vol. 2, Water Purification and Wastewater Treatment and Disposal 1968, Elements of Water Supply and Waste water Disposal, 1971. Home: 710 Bosley Rd Cockeysville MD 21030 Office: Johns Hopkins U Baltimore MD 21218

GEYER, RICHARD ADAM, educator; b. N.Y.C., Oct. 27, 1914; s. Hugo A. and Hedwig (Bernet) G.; B.S., N.Y.U., 1937, M.S., 1940; M.A., Princeton, 1950, Ph.D., 1951; m. Anna M. Thomson, May 13, 1940; children—Sandra Anne (Mrs. Dudley Youman III), Richard Adam. Head oceanography sect. Humble Oil Co., Houston, 1947-54; mgr. gravity magnetics dept. Geophys. Service Inc., Dallas, 1954-61; tech. dir. oceanography Tex. Instruments, Inc., 1961-66; prof. oceanography, head dept. Tex. A. and M. Univ., 1966—, Vice chmn. President's Commn. Marine Sci. and Engring. Resources, 1966—; mem. ocean wide surveys panel, com. oceanography Nat. Acad. Scis., 1961—; chmn. adv. panel to NSF for Internat. Decade of Oceanic Exploration, 1969—; mem. ho. of reps. Tex. Com. on Oceanography, 1969—. Mem. Am. Soc. Oceanography (bd. dirs.), Nat. Oceanography Assn. (dir.), Soc. Exploration Geophysicists, Marine Tech. Soc., Am. Geophys. Union, Nat. Security Indsl. Assn., Dallas Geophys. Soc. (pres. 1965), Sigma Xi. Republican. Editor Geophysics, 1949-51. Contbr. to Ency. Brit. Home: 300 Greenway Dr Bryan, TX 77801. Office: Dept Oceanography Tex A and M Univ College Station TX 77843

GEYER, RICHARD BENNETT, educator; b. Urbana, O., Oct. 24, 1919; s. Miller Ray and Henrietta (Hurlburt) G.; A.B., Miami U., Oxford, O., 1941, M.A., 1947; postgrad. U. Aberdeen (Scotland), 1945; Ph.D., Northwestern U., 1951; m. Elizabeth Jane Geyer; children—Paul Bennett, David Seymour, Christopher Locke. Grad. asst. Miami U., 1946-47, Northwestern U., 1947-50; prof. English, head dept. U. Dubuque, 1950-54; faculty Gettysburg (Pa.) Coll., 1954—, prof. English, chmn. dept., 1955- -. Served with AUS, 1942-46; ETO. Decorated Combat Inf. badge. Mem. Modern Lang. Assn., Nat. Council Tchrs. English, Coll. English Assn., Phi Delta Theta. Home: RD 3 Gettysburg PA 17325

GEZORK, HERBERT, clergyman, educator; b. Insterburg, Germany, June 15, 1900; s. Friedrich and Anna (Schirrmann) G.; student Bapt. Div. Sch., Hamburg, Germany, 1921-24, U. Berlin, 1925-28; Ph.D., So. Bapt. Theol. Sem., 1930; D.D., Colby Coll., 1942, Bucknell U., 1956, Colgate U., 1957, Brown U., 1964; LL.D., Emerson Coll., 1956, Anderson-Broaddus Coll., 1968; D.S.O., Curry Coll., 1970; m. Ellen Markus, May 22, 1937; children—Herbert Peter, Thomas Edward, James William, Janet Ellen. Came to U.S., 1936, naturalized, 1943. Ordained to ministry Bapt., Ch., 1927; asso. pastor First Bapt. Ch., Berlin, Germany, 1925-28; gen. sec. German Bapt. Youth Movement, 1931-34; asst. prof. religion Furman U. 1937-38; interim pastor First Bapt. Ch., Clarksburg, W.Va., 1939; asst. prof. Bibl. history Wellesley Coll., 1939-43, lectr. social ethics, 1943-50; prof. social ethics, Christian world relations Andover Newton Theol. Sch., 1939-50, pres. sch., 1950-65, pres. emeritus, 1964—; vis. lectr. Brown U., 1965-66; vis. prof. Harvard Div. Sch., 1965-68, Assumption Coll., 1968, Kanto Gakuin U., Japan, 1968-69; dir. dept. religion Chautauqua Instn., 1968—. Mem. U.S. Strategic Bombing Survey in Germany, 1945; chief Protestant affairs U.S. Mil. Govt. for Germany, 1946-48; cons. U.S. high commr. in Germany, 1950. Mem. Mass. Council Chs., chmn. com. on legislation, 1948-49; mem. com. on internat. justice and goodwill Nat. Council Chs., del. World Conf. on Faith and Order, Lund, Sweden, 1952, Montreal, 1963; v.p. Am. Bapt. Conv., 1954- 55, pres., 1959-60; mem. Christian Deputation to Russia, 1956; del. World Council Chs., Evanston, 1954, New Delhi, 1961. Mem. bd. preachers Harvard. Trustee Wheaton Coll. Recipient Am. Legion Outstanding Fgn. Born Citizen award, 1969. Fellow Am. Acad. Arts and Scis. Mason. Author: Die Gottlosenbewegung, 1932; So Sah Ich Die Welt (in Finnish, Dutch), 1933. Contbr. articles, essays to various publs. Home: 18 Sherwood Rd Natick MA 01760

GHANDHI, SORAB KHUSHRO, educator; b. Allahabad, India, Jan. 1, 1928; s. Khushro S. and Dina (Amroliwalla) G.; came to U.S., 1947, naturalized, 1960; B.Sc. in Elec. and Mech. Engring., Benares (India) Hindu U., 1947; M.S., U. Ill., 1948, Ph.D., 1951; m. Madonna Inez Stahl, July 1, 1950; children—Khushro, Rustom, Behram. Mem. electronics lab. Gen. Electric Co., 1951-60; mgr. electronic components and functions lab., research div. Philco Corp., 1960-63; prof. elec. engring. Rensselaer Poly. Inst., Troy, N.Y., 1963—, chmn. electrophysics div., 1968—. Cons. to industry, 1963—. J.N. Tata fellow, 1947-50. Fellow I.E.E.E.; mem. Am. Standards Assn., Sigma Xi, Eta Kappa Nu, Pi Mu Epsilon, Phi Kappa Pi. Author: (with R. F. Shea editor) Principles of Transistor Circuits, 1953, Transistor Circuit Engineering, 1957, Amplifier Handbook, 1966; The Theory and Practice of Microelectronics, 1968. Home: 7 Linda La Schenectady NY 12309 Office: Rensselaer Poly Inst Troy NY 12181

GHAZNAVI, COUROS, educator; b. Teheran, Iran, Mar. 21, 1927; s. Hassan and Sedighe (Ghaemaghami) G.; diploma Elec. Engring., Ecole Poly. de L'université de Lausanne (Switzerland), 1951; diploma Power Engring., Ecole Supérieure d'Electricité de Paris (France), 1953: D.Engring. with highest honors, U. Paris, 1955; m. Parvin Omidvaran, Apr. 18, 1953; 1 dau., Ina. Came to U.S., 1956, naturalized, 1963. Engr., Electricite de France, Paris, 1953- 54; research engr. Brown-Bovery Co., Baden, Switzerland, 1955-56; project engr. Curtiss-Wright Corp., 1957-58; prof. elec. engring. Pratt Inst., 1958-68; Dibner prof. elec. engring. U. Bridgeport (Conn.), 1968- -. Cons. to industry, 1958—. Mem. Am. Soc. Engring. Edn., I.E.E.E., Eta Kappa Nu. Author: (textbook) Electronic Circuit Analysis, 1972. Contbr. articles to profl. jours. Home: 103 Stoneleigh Rd Trumbull CT 06611 Office: U Bridgeport Bridgeport CT 06604

GHENTS, JOHN HENRY, oil co. exec.; b. Bklyn., May 7, 1916; s. Frederick Michael and Mary Cecillia (O'Malley) G.; B.B.A., St. John's U., Bklyn., 1942; m. Ruth Heig, Jan. 10, 1943; children—Pamela May (Mrs. Bulkley), Bonnie Ruth (Mrs. Flaherty), Michelle Ann. With Asiatic Petroleum Corp., N.Y.C., 1936—, asst. treas., 1954-62, controller, 1962-63, treas., 1963- 65, v.p., dir., 1965-; dir. Shell Funding Corp., Shell and Commonwealth Chems., Inc., Shell Venezuelan Oil Concessions Ltd. Bd. dirs. Nat. Hemophilia Found. Mem. Econ. Club N.Y.C., Am. Petroleum Inst., Am. Mgmt. Assn., Tax Inst., Newcomen Soc. Clubs: Internat. (Washington); New Canaan Field. Home: 309 Main St New Canaan CT 06840 Office: 1 Rockefeller Plaza New York City NY 10020

GHERIANI, VICTOR, hotel exec.; b. Cairo, Egypt, May 30, 1919; s. Elie V. and Mary (Yanni) G.; B.Commerce, Brothers Sch., Cairo, 1937; m. Juliette Morabia, Aug. 31, 1942; children-Elie, Andrew, Mireille, Roger. With Banco Italo Egiziano, Cairo, 1938-40; with Egyptian Hotels, Ltd. (Sheapheard's Hotel), 1940-48; gen. mgr. Upper Egyptian Hotels, Luxor Var., 1949-61; tech. adviser Tourism-Adminstrn., Tunis, 1961-62; exec. asst. mgr. Hilton Internat., Cavalier-Hilton, Rome, 1962-65; gen. mgr. Fontainebleau Motel, Montreal, 1965-66; Port Royal bldg. mgr., 1966-67; gen. mgr. Sonesta Hotel, Montreal, 1967-68; gen. mgr. LeChateau Champlain, Montreal, 1968—. Decorated Order of Merit of Yugoslavia, 1958. Mem. Montreal Hotel Assn., Provincial Hotel Assn. Que., Montreal Conv. and Visitor Bur., Hotel Sales Mgmt. Assn. Club: Skal (Montreal). Home: 416 70th Av Chomedey Laval Quebec Can Office: Le Chateau Champlain Place du Canada Montreal 101 Quebec Can

GHIARDI, JOHN FELIX LINUS, govt. ofcl.; b. Negaunee, Mich., Mar. 6, 1918; s. Martin and Catherine (Chiabotto) G.; B.A., Sacred Head Sem., Detroit, 1939; M.A. in Econs., Cath. U. Am., 1942, doctoral student, 1946-48; m. Lucille Torreano, Apr. 7, 1947; children—Christopher, Giancarlo. Economist, VA, 1946-48: with Treasury Dept., 1948-66, sr. rep. Am. embassy, Italy, 1953-66; dir. Office Developing Nations, 1966; dep. asst. sec. state for internat. monetary affairs, State Dept., 1966-68; adviser internat. finance to bd. govs. Fed. Res. System, 1968—, Served to 2d lt. AUS, 1942-46. Decorated Bronze Star, Purple Heart. Mem. Am. Econ. Assn. Roman Cath. Home: 12 Park Overlook Ct Bethesda MD 20034 Office: Bd Governors Fed Reserve System Washington DC 20551

GHIAUROV, NICOLAI GEORGIEV, bass; b. Velingrad, Bulgaria, Sept. 13, 1932; s. George and Marianne (Michailova) G.; ed. Moscow Music Conservatory; m. Zlatina Christova Mishakova, July 11, 1955; children—Vladimir, Elena. Leading roles as bass in opera houses throughout world, including La Scala, Met. Opera, also Salzburg. Recipient Grand Prix of Paris, 1955, Gold Medal of Warsaw, 1955; named Nat. Artist of Bulgaria. Address: La Scalla Milan Italy

GHIGLIONE, ANGELO FRANCESCO SKINNER, engr., former govt. ofcl; b. Seattle, May 29, 1909; s. August Joseph and Estelle (Skinner) G.; B.S., U. Wash., 1931; S.M., Mass Inst. Tech., 1932; m. Alice Genevieve Palmer, June 2, 1939; children—Ann Palmer, Kay Estelle, Susan Maria. Engr., U.S. Engr. Dept., Alaska, summers 1929-33; engr. to dist. supt. Alaska Rd. Commn., 1933-41, dist. supt. to asst. chief engr., 1945-48, chief engr., 1948-50, commr. rds., Alaska charge activities 1951-57; chief fgn. program, Bur. Pub. Rds., 1957-58, regional engr., 1958-59, dep. asst. commr., 1959-62, dep. dir. operations, 1962-70; cons. Fed. Hwy. Adminstrn., 1970—. Served from lt. (j.g.) to comdr. C.E. Corps, USNR, 1941-45. Mem. Alaska Bd. Architects and Engrs. Examiners, Am. Soc. C.E. (chmn. joint com. snow ice and permafrost 1951- 56, past pres. Alaska sect.), Arctic Inst. N.Am., C. of C. (pres. 1956), Sigma Xi, Phi Beta Kappa, Tau Beta Pi. Rotarian, Toastmaster. Club: Cosmos. Home: 5518 Ann Arbor NE Seattle WA 98105 Office: 1717 H St NW Washington DC 20006

GHISELIN, BREWSTER, educator; b. Webster Groves, Mo., June 13, 1903; s. Horace and Eleanor (Weeks) G.; A.B., U. Cal. at Los Angeles, 1927, M.A. at Berkeley, 1928, student, 1931-33; student Oxford U. (Eng.), 1928-29; m. Olive F. Franks, June 7, 1929; children—Jon Brewster, Michael Tenant. Asst. in English, U. Cal. at Berkeley, 1931-33; instr. English, U. Utah, 1929-31, 34-38, lectr., 1938-39, asst. prof., 1939-46, asso. prof., 1946-50, prof., 1950—, Distinguished Research prof., 1967-68, dir. Writers' Conf., 1947-66; poetry editor Rocky Mt. Rev., 1937-46; asso. editor Western Rev., 1946-49; lectr. creativity, cons. Inst. Personality Assessment and Research, U. Cal. at Berkeley, 1957-58; cons. Hercules Powder Co.; editorial adv. bd. Concerning Poetry, 1968—. Ford Found. fellow, 1952-53; recipient award Nat. Inst. Arts and Letters, 1970. Mem. Am. Assn. U. Profs., Modern Lang. Assn., Utah Acad. Scis., Arts and Letters, Phi Beta Kappa, Phi Kappa Phi. Author: Against the Circle, 1946; The Creative Process, 1952; The Nets, 1955; Writing, 1959; Country of the Minotaur, 1970. Home: 1747 Princeton Av Salt Lake City UT 84108 Office: U Utah Salt Lake City UT 84112

GHISELLI, EDWIN ERNEST, educator; b. San Francisco, June 28, 1907; s. Ernest J. and Emma (Barron) G.; A.B., U. Cal., 1930, M.A., 1933, Ph.D., 1936; m. Louisa Hickox, Aug. 13, 1938; children—William, John, David. Research asst. Harvard, 1936-37; asst., Cornell U., 1937; instr. U. Md., 1937-39; professor psychology University of California at Berkeley, 1939—, chairman of psychology dept., 1955-57; visiting prof. U. Bologna. Italy, 1957-58. Served from capt. to lt. col, USAAF, 1942-45. Mem. Am. Psychol. Assn. (pres. div. 14 1954-55). Author: Personnel and Industrial Psycholoby (with C. W. Brown), 1948: Scientific Method in Psychology (with C. W. brown), 1955; Theory of Psychological Measurements, 1964; The Validity of Occupational Aptitude Tests, 1966; Explorations in Managerial Talent, 1971. Home: 427 Boynton Av Berkeley CA 94707

GHORMLEY, WILLIAM KERR, former army officer, assn. exec.; b. Hutchinson, Kan., Sept. 29, 1905; s. Davis Wilbert and Sarah Lansing (Dales) G.; student Coll. Emporia (Kan.), 1923-24; B.S., U.S. Mil. Acad., 1929; m. Margaretta Elizabeth Clark, Aug. 31, 1929. Commd. 2d lt. U.S. Army, 1929, advanced through grades to maj. gen., 1959: chief tank, vehicle sect. Office Chief Ordnance, Detroit, 1942-43; staff ordnance officer Western Base, Channel Base Sects. ETO, 1944-45, acting chief staff OISE Sect. Communications Zone, 1945-46, Continental Base Sect., 1946-47: chief service br. logistics group N.G. Bur., 1947-49; comdg. officer Phila. Ordnance Dist., 1950-52; chief automotive br., indsl. operations Indsl. div. Office Chief Ordnance, 1952-53, dep. chief indsl. div., 1954; asst. staff dir. purchasing, contracting policies Office Sec. Defense, 1954-55, staff dir., 1956-57; comdg. gen. U.S. Army Ordnance Weapons Command, Rock Island, Ill., 1957-59, U.S. Army Ordnance Spl. Weapons-Ammunition Command, Dover, N.J., 1959-61, U.S. Army Munitions Command, Dover, 1962; ret., 1962; asst. to exec. v.p. Am. Ordnance Assn., Washington, 1963, exec. v.p., 1964-. Decorated D.S.M., Bronze Star medal; Croix de Guerre with palm (France); Belgian Order de Couronne. Mem. West Point Assn., Assn. U.S. Army, Nat. Rifle Assn. Club: Army and Navy. Home: 3604 Massachusetts Av NW Washington DC 20007 Office: Union Trust Bldg Washington DC 20005

GHORRA, EDWARD, Lebanese diplomat; b. 1913; ed. U. de St-Joseph, Beirut. Consul gen., N.Y.C., 1945, Sydney, Australia, 1950; dir. UN dept. Ministry Fgn. Affairs, 1956-59; ambassador to USSR, 1959-63; dir. dept. Lebanese overseas Ministry Fgn. Affairs, 1963-65; ambassador to Czechoslovakia, 1965-68; permanent rep. of Lebanon to UN, 1968—. Address: 866 UN Plaza NY 10017*

GIACOMANTONIO, ARCHIMEDES ARISTIDES MICHAEL, sculptor; b. Jersey City, Jan. 17, 1906; s. Gaetano and Rosina (Fanelli) G.; student Leonardo da Vinci Art Sch., N.Y.C.; grad. Royal Acad. Art, Rome, Italy, 1929; pvt. student Onorio Ruotolo and Vincenzo Gemito; m. Muriel Rose Ruoff, Aug. 10, 1935. Prin. works; bust Shah Iran, Mohammed Riza Pahlevi; heroic size bronze Christopher Columbus; granite fountain Journal Sq., Jersey City; Columbus monument, Hazelton, Pa.; bronze bust Dr. Harry A. Sprague, Sprague Library, Montclair (N.J.) State Coll.; bust Harry S. Truman and bronze statuette Woodrow Wilson for Truman Library, Independence, Mo.; bust Robert Kinter; bust Gen. Eisenhower for West Point Acad., Leonard Goldenson; bust Martin Luther King, Jr., Dr. King Sch., Jersey City; Madonna of Assumption Shrine, North Arlington, N.J.; designed Ann. Spirit medal Cath. Poetry Soc. Am. Trustee Mus. Jersey City, Internat. Inst. Jersey City. Recipient 1st prize 6th Ann. N.J. Exhbn., Montclair Mus., 1936; Maynard prize N.A.D., 1940. Technician Med. Corps. with 42d Div. (Rainbow), overseas. Mem. Nat. Sculpture Soc., Nat. Acad. TV Arts and Scis., Allied Artists Am. Roman Catholic. Clubs: Lotos (N.Y.C.); Carteret (Jersey City); Kiwanis. Home: Glen Lake Sparta NJ 07871 Office: 42 W 67th St New York City NY 10027

GIAIMO, ROBERT NICHOLAS congressman; b. New Haven, Oct. 15, 1919; s. Rosario and Rose (Scarpulla) G.; A.B., Fordham Coll., 1941; LL.B., U. Conn., 1943; m. Marion Schuenemann, May 17, 1945; 1 dau., Barbara Lee. Admitted to Conn. bar, 1946, practiced in New Haven 1946—; asso. Sachs, Sachs, Giaimo & Sachs. Mem. 86th-92d Congresses 3d Dist. of Conn., mem. house appropbrations com., subcoms. HUD-Space-Sci., D.C., joint commn. on coinage. Past. chmn. personnel appeals bd. state Conn. Served as 1st AUS, World War II; capt. Judge Adv. Gen. Corps, Res. Democrat. Home: 139 Washington Av North Haven CT 06473 Office: Rayburn Office Bldg Ho of Reps Washington DC 20515

GIAMATTI, VALENTINE, educator; b. New Haven, Feb. 9, 1911; s. Angelo and Mary (Lavorgna) G.; A.B., Yale, 1932; Ph.D., Harvard, 1940; Litt.D., U. Florence (Italy), 1947; m. Mary Walton, July 3, 1937; children—A. Bartlett, Elena Maria, Dino Walton. Mem. faculty Vt. Coll., 1936-39; mem. faculty Mt. Holyoke Coll., 1940—, prof. Italian lit., 1949, chmn. dept. Italian lang. and lit., 1940—. Overseer Williston Acad.; mem. Pestalozzi Found. Decorated commendatore Ordine dello Concordia (Italy), 1950. Mem. Modern Lang. Assn., Medieval Soc., Am. Assn. U. Profs., Phi Beta Kappa. Author: Panoramic view of Dante's Inferno, 1943; Panoramic View of Dante's Purgatory, 1944; Panoramic View of Dante's Paradise, 1945; Basic Italian Grammar, 1947; also articles, translations. Home: 29 Silver St South Hadley MA 01075

GIANELLY, ANTHONY ALFRED, educator; b. Boston, Aug. 19, 1936; s. Eugene and Pasquelena (Carideo) G.; A.B., Harvard, 1957, D.M.D., 1961; Ph.D., Boston U., 1967; orthodontic certificate, 1963; m. Ernestine Painter, May 27, 1960; children—Lisa Lawrence, Anthony Todd. Research fellow orthodontics Harvard Sch. Dental Medicine, 1961-63; research fellow Nat. Inst. Dental Research, Boston U., 1964-67, prof. orthodontics, chmn. dept. Sch. Grad. Dentistry, 1967—, research prof. biochemistry, 1968—, head orthodontic sect. Univ. Hosp., 1967—. Mem. Adv. council Mass. Med. Assistance Program, 1970—. Named One of Outstanding Educators in Am., 1970. Mem. Am. Assn. Orthodontics, Am. Dental Assn., Angle Orthodontic Soc., Tweed Found. Orthodontic Research, Mass. Dental Soc. (chmn. continuing edn. sect.), Sigma Xi. Author: Biologic Basis of Orthodontics, 1971. Home: 43 Palmer Rd Waban MA 02168 Office: 100 E Newton St Boston MA 02118

GIANNINI, GABRIEL MARIA, industrialist, physicist; b. Rome, Italy, Oct. 21, 1905; s. Torquato and Maria (Laccetti) G.; D.Physics, U. Rome, 1929; m. Luisa Casazza, July 18, 1931; children—Maria Laura (Mrs. Gerald F. Madigan), Valerio; m. 2d, Olga Harrington, Sept. 27, 1964; 1 dau., Gabriella-Caria. Came to U.S. 1930, naturalized, 1938. Research in acoustics RCA, Curtis Inst. Music, Phila., 1931-35; research in acoustics and telephony Transducer Corp., N.Y.C., 1936-40; engring. mgmt. Lockheed Aircraft Co., 1941-44; founder Giannini Controls Corp., Pasadena, Cal. 1945, pres. 1945-57; pres. Giannini Inst., 1957—. Asso., Cal. Inst. Tech. Fellow Am. Inst. Aeros. and Astronautics (asso.), Royal Aero. Soc.; mem. I.E.E.E. (sr.), Società Italiana Di Fisica, Instrument Soc. Am., Am. Phys. Soc., Am. Optical Soc., Acoustical Soc., Am. Soc. M.E., Soc. Automotive Engrs., Assn. Computing Machinery, Solar Energy Soc., Marine Tech. Soc., Brit. Interplanetary Soc., U.S. Naval Inst. Clubs: California (Los Angeles), Brook (N.Y.C.); Cruising America; Sewanhaka Corinthian Yacht (Oyster Bay, N.Y.); Circolo della Vela (Rome); Parkinson Transatlantic Trophy. Home: Valmaria Ranch Indio CA 92201 also Lungo Tevere Mellini 24 Rome Italy

GIAP, VO NGUYEN, Vietnamese army officer; b. 1912; ed. French lycee in Hue, also law studies U. Hanoi. History tchr. Thang Long Sch., Hanoi; joined Vietnam Community Party, 1930; fled to China, 1939; helped organize Vietminh Front in Vietnam, 1941; minister of interior, 1945; comdr. in chief Vietminh Army, 1946; defeated French at Dien Bien Phu, 1954; now dep. prime minister, minister of def. and comdr. in chief N. Vietnam. Mem. Politburo Lao-Dong party. Author: People's War; People's Army; Big Victory; Great Test, 1968. Address: care Ministry of Def Hanoi Democratic Republic Vietnam*

GIARDINO, ALFRED A., lawyer; b. Bklyn., May 1, 1913; s. Joseph and Lucy (Tasca) G.; A.B., Bklyn. Coll., 1934; LL.B., Columbia, 1937; student Inst. Internat. Affairs, Geneva, Switzerland, 1946; m. Lucie Veulliez, 2 children. Admitted to N.Y. bar, 1937; trial atty., exec. sec. N.Y. State Labor Relations Bd., 1937-48; mem. firm Lorenz, Finn & Giardino, N.Y.C., 1948—. Arbitrator panels Fed. Mediation and Conciliation Service, N.Y. State Mediation Bd., Am. Arbitration Assn.; former tchr. Bklyn. Coll., Columbia, N.Y. U. Grad. Sch., Cornell U. Extension; dir. research Gov. N.Y. Spl. Commn. Illegitimacy, 1936-47. pub. mem. Internat. Commn. Labor Experts to Bolivia, 1943; spl. rep. State Dept. and Labor Dept. in Brazil, Chile, Argentina, and Uruguay, 1942-43; mem. com. character and fitness Jud. Dept., 1st Dept. N.Y., 1961—; mem. N.Y.C. Bd. Edn., 1964—, pres., 1967-68. Served as officer AUS, World War II. Mem. Am. Bar Assn., Assn. Bar City N.Y., Internat. Soc. Labor and Social Legislation. Home: 4600 Fieldston Rd New York City NY 10471 Office: 21 West St New York City NY 10006

GIAUQUE, WILLIAM FRANCIS, educator; b. Niagara Falls, Ont., Can., May 12, 1895; s. William Tecumseh Sherman and Isabella Jane (Duncan) G. (parents U.S. citizens); B.S., U. Cal., 1920, Ph.D., 1922, LL.D. 1963; D.Sc. (hon.), Columbia, 1936; m. Muriel Frances Ashley, July 19, 1932; children—William Francis Ashley, Robert David Ashley. Instr. chemistry U. Cal., 1922-27, asst. prof. 1927-30, asso. prof., 1930-34, prof. chemistry, 1934—, Berkeley fellow (hon.). Recipient prize for discovery (with H.L. Johnston) oxygen isotopes Pacific div. A.A.A.S., 1929; Chandler medal Columbia, 1936; Elliott Cresson medal Franklin Inst., 1937; Nobel Prize for Chemistry, 1949; G.N. Lewis medal, 1956. Fellow Am. Phys. Soc., Am. Acad. Arts and Scis.; mem. Am. Chem. Soc. (Gibbs medal 1951), Am. Assn. U. Profs., Nat. Acad. Scis., Am. Philos. Soc., Sigma Xi, Phi Lambda Upsilon (hon.). Club: Faculty (Berkeley). Home: 2643 Benvenue Av Berkeley CA 94704

GIBBARD, HAROLD ALLAN, educator, sociologist; b. Mission City, B.C., Can., Jan. 25, 1912; s. George and Clara Gertrude (Cox) G.; B.A., U. B.C., 1932; M.A., McGill U., 1934; Ph.D., U. Mich., 1938; m. Eleanor E. Reid, Sept. 8, 1937; children—Allan Fletcher, Sarah Eleanor. Came to U.S., 1934, naturalized, 1944. Instr. sociology, research asst. Mich. State U., 1937-38; instr. to asst. prof. Brown U., 1938-46; asst. prof. U. Kan., 1946-48; vis. asso. prof. U. Mo., summer 1947; prof. sociology W.Va. U., Morgantown, 1948—, chmn. dept., 1948-69, acting dean Coll. Arts and Scis., 1969-70, asst. to provost, 1970—. Research asso. Makere Inst. Social Research and Faculty Agr., Makere U. Coll., Kampala Uganda, East Africa, 1968. Mem. Am. Sociol. Assn., Ohio Valley Sociol. Soc. (pres. 1960-61), Am. Assn. U. Profs. Co-author: Fundamentals of Sociology, A Situational Analysis, 1950; The Southern Appalachian Region: A Survey, 1962; Poverty Amid Affluence, 1966; Retraining the Unemployed, 1968. Home: 741 Augusta Av Morgantown WV 26505 Greensboro Travelers Aid Soc. (pres. 1937-43), Fed., Internat. (chmn. sect. on real property, probate Phi. Mem. Soc. of Friends. Clubs: Greensboro Barristers (pres. 1928), Greensboro Merchants and Manufacturers (pres. 1929, 33) Greensboro Review, 1922. Home: 620 Woodland Dr Greensboro NC 27482

GIBBERD, FREDERICK, architect; b. Jan. 7, 1908; ed. King Henry VIII Sch., Coventry, Eng. Architect London, Eng., 1930—, Harlow New Town, 1956—; former prin. Archtl. Assn. Sch. Architecture; architect-planner Harlow New Town, 1947- -; planning cons. Nuneaton, 1948—, Doncaster, Hull, 1954—, Leamington Spa, Swindon, 1957— (all Eng.), Santa Teresa, Venezuela, 1959—. Named comdr. Brit. Empire; winner competitions for Met. Roman Cath. Cathedral, Liverpool, Eng., 1960, monastery Douai Abbey, 1961. Fellow Royal Inst. Brit. Architects, Soc. Indsl. Artists; mem. Royal Acad. (asso.), Town Planning Inst., Royal Fine Arts Commn. Prin. works include Scunthrope steel works, tech. colls. at Hull, Kidderminster, Stourbridge (all Eng.), also numerous schs., London Airport, Belfast (Ireland) Hosp., Nat. Dock Labour Bd. offices, London, civic centers Doncaster, Edmonton, Hull, St. Albans (all Eng.). Home: 49 Downshire Hill London N W 3 England Office: 8 Percy St London W1 England*

GIBBON, JOHN HEYSHAM, Jr., surgeon; b. Phila., Sept. 29, 1903; s. John Heysham and Marjorie (Young) G.; A.B., Princeton, 1923; M.D., Jefferson Med. Coll., 1927, Ph.D.; fellow surgery Harvard, 1930-31, 33-34; fellow surg. research U. Pa., 1936-42; Sc.D., U. Buffalo, Princeton, Dickinson Coll.; m. Mary Hopkinson, Mar. 14, 1931; children—Mary, John, Alice, Marjorie. Intern, Pa. Hosp., 1927-29, cons. surgeon, 1950—; chief surg. service Mayo Gen. Hosp., 1945; asst. prof. surgery U. Pa., 1945-46; prof. surgery, dir. surg. research Jefferson Med. Coll., 1946-56, Samuel D. Gross prof., head dept. surgery, 1956-67, emeritus prof. surgery, 1967- -. Served as lt. col. M.C., AUS, 1943-46. Recipient Albert Lasker Med. Research award, 1968. Diplomate Am. Bd. Surgery, Am. Bd. Thoracic Surgery. Fellow A.C.S., Royal Coll. Surgeons (Eng.); mem. Am. Surg. Assn. (past pres.), Am. Assn. Thoracic Surgery (past pres.), Soc. Clin. Surgery (past pres.), Phila. Acad. Surgery (past pres.), Heart Assn. Southeastern Pa. (past pres.), Coll. Physicians Phila. (past pres.), Soc. Vascular Surgery (past pres.), A.M.A. Democrat. Contbr. articles to surg. jours. Home: Lynfield Farm 2103 N Providence Rd Media PA 19063

GIBBON, ROBERT OUTHWAITE, educator; b. Tonganoxie, Kan., Jan. 14, 1923; s. W. O. and Nadine (Rankin) G.; A.B., Kan. U., 1944, M.A., 1945; Ph.D., U. Minn., 1954; student U. Edinburgh (Scotland), 1948-49; m. Joan Burch, Dec. 18, 1949. Asst., then asso. prof. polit. sci. Ill. Wesleyan U., 1947-55; asst., then asso. prof. polit. sci. Okla. State U., 1955-59; mem. faculty Wis. State U. at Eau Claire, 1959—, prof. polit. scis., chmn. dept., 1960—, dean Sch. Arts and Scis., 1964-66. Mem. Midwest Conf. Polit. Scientists, Phi Beta Kappa. Co-author: European Government and Politics, 1960. Home: 1705 Badger Av Eau Claire WI 54701

GIBBONEY, RICHARD ALLEN, educator; b. Altoona, Pa., Feb. 6, 1927; s. James W. and Marguerite (Keen) G.; B.S. in Clin. Speech and Edn., Pa. State U., 1950; M.Ed. in Case Work and Psychology, Wayne State U., 1955; Ed.D. in Curriculum and Humanities, George Peabody Grad. Sch., 1957; m. Roberta Henderson, June 20, 1953; children—Richard, Diane. Tchr. elementary and secondary schs., Mich., 1950-55, Peabody Coll., 1956-57; with Pa. Dept. Pub. Instrn., 1957-65, dep. supt. research and devel., 1962-65; commr. edn. Vt., 1965- -; vis. prof. edn. Grad. Sch. Edn., U. Pa., Phila., 1967-68, asso. prof. edn., 1968—. Lectr. edn. various univs.; mem. grad. faculty Kent State U., summer 1965, Lehigh U., summer 1966. Chief staff Gov. Pa. Com. on Task Force Curriculum; mem. curriculum devel. com. Eastern TV Network; com. religion and pub. edn. Pa. Council Chs., 1964; mem. com. ch. and pub. edn. Presbyn. Ch. Served with USNR, 1945-56. John Hay fellow, summer 1962; recipient Distinguished Service award Pa. Library Assn., 1965, Linback award U. Pa., 1969. mem. Assn. Supervision and Curriculum Devel. (dir.), John Dewey Soc. (mem. Distinguished Service Awards com.), Am. Edn. Research Assn., Nat., Pa. edn. assns., New Eng. Commrs. Assn., Phi Delta Kappa, Pi Gamma Mu. Author chpts. in books, contbr. revs. Editor, contbr.: The School Instructional Materials Center and the Curriculum, 1962. Home: 687 Malin Rd Newton Square PA 19073 Office: U Pa Philadelphia PA 19104

GIBBONS, ARTHUR S., lawyer; b. Tampa, Fla., Nov. 21, 1908; J.D., U. Fla., 1932. Admitted to Fla. bar, 1932; now mem. firm Gibbons, Tucker, McEwen, Smith, Cofer & Taub, Tampa. Mem. Am., Tampa, Hillsborough County (pres. 1947-48) bar assns., Fla. Bar (gov. 1951-58), Blue Key, Phi Delta Phi. Office: 606 Madison St Tampa FL 33602*

GIBBONS, DON CARY, educator, author; b. Newport, Wash., June 6, 1926; s. George and Mildred (Snow) G.; B.A., U. Wash., 1950, M.A., 1953, Ph.D., 1956; m. Carmen L. Baker, Sept. 1, 1951; children—Michael, Diane. Faculty, U. B.C., 1956-57, San Francisco State Coll., 1957-69; prof. sociology Portland (Ore.) State U., 1969—. Served with USNR, 1944-46. Mem. Am. Sociol. Assn., Pacific Sociol. Soc., Soc. Study Social Problems, Law and Soc. Assn. Author: Changing the Lawbreaker, 1965; Society, Crime and Criminal Careers, 1968; Delinquent Behavior, 1970; Becoming Delinquent, 1970. Home: 1100 SW Hillcroft Dr Portland OR 97225

GIBBONS, DONALD FRANK, educator; b. Birmingham, Eng., July 23, 1926; s. Frank Oliver and Leah (Faulkner) G.; B.Sc., U. Birmingham, 1947, Ph.D., 1950; m. June Esme Rosbrook, June 7, 1950; children—Kathryn Ann, Peter Brook. Came to U.S., 1950. Research asso. Inst. Study Metals, U. Chgo., 1950-52; D.R.B. fellow, instr. Royal Mil. Coll. Can., Kingston, Ont., 1952-54; mem. tech. staff, metallurgy div. Bell Telephone Labs., 1954-62; prof. metallurgy, dir. Center Study Materials, Case Inst. Tech., 1962—; vis. prof. theoretical metallurgy U. Birmingham, 1960; vis. prof. solid state applied physics Yale, 1961. Mem. A.A.A.S., Am. Inst. Physics, Am. Mining and Metall. Engrs., Sigma Xi. Author papers in field. Home: 3196 Warrington Rd Shaker Heights OH 44120 Office: Case Western Res Univ Univ Circle Cleveland OH 44102

GIBBONS, EDWARD FRANCIS, food co. exec.; b. Boston, Sept. 1, 1919; s. Patrick J. and Frances (Hearne) G.; B.S.A., Bentley Coll., Boston, 1948; student Mass. Inst. Tech., 1960; C.P.A., 1950; m. Elizabeth Ann Ring, May 22, 1948; children—Vincent, Edward Francis, John, Peter, Mary. Staff accountant Lybrand Ross Bros. & Montgomery, C.P.A.'s, 1946-51, 56-58, controller overseas chem. div. W. R. Grace & Co., 1951-56, 58-63; asso. prof. Bentley Coll., 1963-65; controller United Fruit Co., 1966—. Served with USCGR and USNR,

1942-46. Mem. Am. Inst. C.P.A.'s Home: 25 Glendale Rd Marblehead, MA 01947. Office: United Fruit Co Prudential Center Boston MA 02199

GIBBONS, FRANCIS JOSEPH, corp. exec.; b. Canton, Mass., Apr. 26, 1909; s. Michael and Delia M. (Lynch) G.; B.S., Boston U., 1931, M.C.S., 1935; m. Helen C. Hanlon, Aug. 6, 1938; m. 2d, Bernice Lee Sargent, Dec. 23, 1970. With Calumet & Hecla, Inc., 1945—, controller, 1953-57, treas., 1957-62, v.p. of finance, 1962—, also dir.; dir. Hayward Marum Knitting Mills, Inc. Mem. Financial Execs. Inst., N.A.M., Am. Mgmt. Assn. Home: 1235 Asbury Av Winnetka IL 60093 Office 800 E Northwest Hwy Palatine IL 60067

GIBBONS, FRANKLIN A., banker; b. Washington. Sr. v.p., comptroller Riggs Nat. Bank, Washington. Home: 4848 N 28th St Arlington VA 22207 Office: 1503 Pennsylvania Av NW Washington DC 20013*

GIBBONS, JAMES JOSEPH, army officer; b. Lawrence, Mass., Dec. 14, 1919; s. James Joseph and Lillian (MacCormack) G.; A.B., Harvard, 1941; grad. Nat. War Coll., 1960; M.Sc., George Washinton U., 1966; m. Dorothy James Cain, Sept. 18, 1943; children—Patricia, James, Robert, Susan. Commd. 2d lt. U.S. Army, 1941, advanced through grades to maj. gen. 1964; served in S.W. Pacific, World War II, Japan, 1945-48, Germany, 1952-55, 66-68, Vietnam, 1963-64; dep. J3, Joint Chiefs of Staff, 1968-70; dep. comdr. U.S. Mil. Assistance, Command, Thailand, 1970—. Active Boy Scouts Am. Decorated Legion of Merit with oak leaf cluster, Bronze Star, Army Commendation medal. Mem. Assn. U.S. Army. Mem. Order St. Sylvester. Address: Box 71 Military Assistance Command Thailand APO San Francisco CA 96346

GIBBONS, JOHN JOSEPH, judge; b. Newark, Dec. 8, 1924; s. Daniel Lehane and Julia (Murray) G.; B.S., Holy Cross Coll., 1947; LL.B. cum laude, Harvard, 1950; m. Mary Jeanne Boyle, Apr. 19,1952; children-Daniel J., Mary E., Nora F., Richard G., Deirdre E., Maude A. Admitted to N.J. bar, 1950; partner Crummy, Gibbons & O'Neill, Newakrk, 1953—; judge 3d Circuit Ct. Appeals, 1970—. Mem. N.J. Bd. Bar Examiners, Trenton, 1959-64, chmn., 1963-64; mem. Gov's Select Commn. on Civil Disorders, 1968, N.J. Council Against Crime, 1968-69. Asso. trustee Holy Cross Coll., 1970—. Served to lt. (j.g.) USNR, 1943-46. Mem. Am. (Ho. of Dels. 1968), N.J. (pres. 1967-68), Essex County (trustee 1961-64) bar assns., Holy Cross Coll. Gen. Alumni Assn. (v.p.). Home: 50 Grosevenor Rd Short Hills NJ Office: US Court House Newark NJ 07102

GIBBONS, JOHN JOSEPH, Jr., educator, physicist; b. Chgo., Apr. 8, 1906; s. John Joseph and Geneva (Kennard) G.; B.A., U. Ill., 1928, M.S., 1930, Ph.D., 1933; m. Muriel Mullins, July 10, 1935; children—Julie Catherine (Mrs. Marvin Redditt), John Joseph III, Hugh Vincent Kennard. Faculty, Pa. State U., 1937- -, prof. physics, 1954—, acting chmn. dept., 1962-64. Spl. research theoretical physics, ionospheric research. Mem. commn. III Union Radio Sci. Internat. Mem. Phi Beta Kappa, Sigma Xi. Home: 210 Outer Dr State College PA 16801 Office: Physics Dept Pa State U University Park PA 16802

GIBBONS, JOHN LYON, banker; b. N.Y.C., 1903; s. John Lyon and Sarah (Ryan) G.; spl. student Bklyn. Law Sch., 1937; grad. Sch. Banking, Rutgers U., 1941; m. Margaret Antoinette Francis, Aug. 17, 1935; children—Sarah Ann (Mrs. Kenneth Ward), John B., Margaret R. (Mrs. Richard Carroll). With Chem. Bank N.Y. Trust Co. (formerly Chem. Corn Exchange Bank), N.Y.C., 1929—, asst. trust officer, trust officer, v.p., 1929-56, exec. v.p., 1956, chmn. trust com., dir., 1963, also mem. exec. com., ret., 1968, now adviser fiduciary div., mem. adv. com. bd. dirs.; dir., mem. exec. com. Avnet, Inc., City Investing Co.; dir. Chock Full O'Nuts Corp., N.Am. Life Assurance Co., Toronto, Greater N.Y. Fund, Inc.; trustee Central Savs. Bank; trustee, mem. exec. com. City Investing Mortgage Group; dir., mem. finance com. First Realty Investment Corp. Mem. N.Y. State Tchrs. Retirement Bd. Chmn., pres., dir., chmn. exec. com. Epilepsy Assn. Am., trustee, chmn., finance com. Emergency Shelter. Mem. Assn. Res. City Bankers. Clubs: Pilgrims, Brook, Economic. Home: 20 Zukor Rd New York City NY 10966 Office: 20 Pine St New York City NY 10015

GIBBONS, JOSEPH JOHN, builders supply co. exec.; b. Wheatland, Wyo., Mar. 18, 1906; s. Michael and Edith (D'Arcy) G.; Ph.B., U. Chgo., 1930; student Northwestern U., 1931-33, DePaul U. Law Sch., 1933-35; m. Hazel M. Bisson, Jan. 1, 1930; children—Betty Louise (Mrs. Donald G. Smith), Albert J., Robert J. Office mgr. George Hardin Constrn. Co., Chgo., 1927-35; exam. agt. Internal Revenue Service, 1935-40; sr. tax accountant Arthur Andersen and Co., C.P.A.'s, Chgo., 1941; tax supr. U.S. Steel Corp., Duluth, Minn. and Pitts., 1941-50; mgr. tax and ins. dept. Mine Safety Appliances Co., 1950-52; with Blaw-Knox Co., 1952-69, treas., 1967-68, v.p. finance, 1968-69; pres. Corde Co., 1967-69; treas. Blaw Knox Can. Ltd., 1967- 69; controller Cleve. Builders Supply Co., 1969—. Mem. Allegheny Trails council Boy Scouts Am. C.P.A., Ill. Mem. Am. Inst. C.P.A.'s, Tau Kappa Epsilon, Alpha Kappa Psi. Presbyn. (elder). Club: Edgewood Country (Pitts.). Home: 12520 Edgewater Dr Lakewood OH 44107 Office: 2100 W 3d Cleveland OH 44113

GIBBONS, MYLES F., lawyer; b. Scranton, Pa., Nov. 27, 1910; s. Patrick Francis and Mary Christine (Madden) G.; A.B., Georgetown U., 1932; LL.B. Harvard, 1935; m. Margaret Mack Chandler, Sept. 5, 1942; children—Patrick Chandler, James Henry, Helen. Admitted to N.Y. bar, 1936, Pa. bar, 1939, Ill. bar, 1956; with Root, Clark, Buckner & Ballantine, N.Y.C., 1935-37, Donovan Leisure, Newton & Lumbard, N.Y.C., 1937-38, Comml. Credit Co., N.Y.C., 1938; atty. R.R. Retirement Bd., 1939-42, gen. counsel, 1944—. Served as lt. USNR, 1942-44. Home: 707 Forest Av Wilmette IL 60091 Office: 844 Rush St Chicago IL 60611

GIBBONS, SAM MELVILLE, congressman; b. Tampa, Fla., Jan. 20, 1920; s. Gunby and Jessie Kirk (Cralle) G.; LL.B., U. Fla., 1947; m. Martha Hanley, Sept. 14, 1946; children—Clifford, Mark, Timothy. Admitted to Fla. bar, 1947; mem. firm Gibbons, Tucker, McEwen, Smith & Cofer, Tampa, 1947—; mem. Fla. Ho. of Reps. from Hillsborough County, 1952-58, Fla. Senate, 1958-62; mem. 88th-92d Congresses, 6th Dist. Fla., 1962—, mem. ways and means com. Founder, 1st pres. U.S. Fla. Found., 1958. Served to maj. AUS, 1941-45; ETO. Decorated Bronze Star; named Outstanding Young Man, Tampa Jr. C. of C., 1954; recipient President's award Tampa C. of C., 1955. Mem. Tampa (dir.), Hillsborough (dir.) bar assns., Greater Tampa C. of C. (dir.). Democrat. Presbyn. (deacon). Home: 940 S Sterling Av Tampa FL 33609 Office: House Office Bldg Washington DC 20515

GIBBONS, WALTER BERNARD, lawyer; b. Coatsville, Pa., Dec. 19, 1894; s. Patrick Henry and Mary Jane (Bowen) G.; LL.B., Temple U., 1917, LL.D., 1945, J.D., 1968; spl. course U. Pa., St. Joseph Coll.; LL.D., Villanova U., 1960; m. Helen Eustace, Dec. 26, 1918; 1 son, Walter Bernard (dec.). Admitted to Pa. bar 1917, since practiced in Phila.; propr. Donoghue & Gibbons, 1939—(now Gibbons & Obert). Spl. counsel Pa. Turnpike Commn. 1941-51 Chmn., pub. interest dir. Fed. Home Loan Bank Pitts., 1941-65. Chmn. bd. mgrs. House of Detention, 1938-58; mem. Phila. Councilmanic Commn. Commitments and Detentions; commonwealth mem. Southeastern Pa. Transp. Authority, 1964-67; chief standing master bd. governance Supreme Ct. Pa.; permanent mem. Conf. 3d Jud. Dist. U.S. Mem. bd. dirs. Nazareth Hosp., Mercy Catholic Med. Center, Sacred Heart Free Home for Incurable Cancer; trustee Holy Family Coll., Phila. Served as ensign, U.S. Navy, World War I. Mem. Am. Law Inst., Mil. Order Fgn. Wars, Am. Legion, Am. (ho. dels. 1942-44, spl. com. on legal assistance to armed forces 1943-51), Pa., Phila., N.Y. bar assns., Phi Delta Phi. Republican. Roman Catholic. Clubs: Lawyers, Midday, Catholic Philopatrian Literary Inst., Overbrook Farms (past pres.). Author articles legal publs. Home: 6400 Church Rd Overbrook Philadelphia PA 19151 Office: Fidelity-Philadelphia Trust Bldg 123 S Broad St Philadelphia PA 19109

GIBBS, CAREY A., clergyman; b. Madison, Fla., Mar. 20, 1892; s. Jack and Lila (Davis) G.; ed. Edward Waters Coll., 1917; B.D., Payne Theol. Sem., 1923; student Wilberforce U.; m. Pennie Simmons; m. 2d, Alithia B. Frazier, Feb. 12, 1962. Ordained to ministry African Meth. Episcopal Ch., 1923; pastor in Fla., 1924-30; pres. Edward Waters Coll., 1930-32; pastor, 1932-48; bishop, 1948—, serving at various times in West Africa, Miss., La., Fla., Ala., West Indies, S. Am., S.C.; now bishop 13th Ky.-Tenn. Episcopal Dist. Former chmn. bd. edn. A.M.E. Ch., now mem. bd. incorporators. Former chmn. bd. trustees Edward Waters Coll., Allen U., Campbell Coll., Daniel Payne Coll. Mem. World Meth. Council, Nat. Council Chs. Mason, Elk. Home: 1011 W 8th St Jacksonville FL 32209

GIBBS, CHARLES HASKELL, lawyer; b. Charleston, S.C., Dec. 22, 1915; s. John Ernest and Anne (Ball) G.; A.B., Coll. Charleston, 1936; LL.B., Duke U. Law Sch., 1939; m. Wilmot K. Welch, Jan. 19, 1942; children—Charles Haskell, Jr., Benjamin S. Admitted to S.C. bar, 1939; mem. firm Sinkler, Gibbs, Simons & Guerard, Charleston, 1947—; county atty. Charleston County, 1949-55; spl. judge S.C. Ct. Common Pleas, 1957. Chmn. Charleston County Planning Bd., 1965-68; mem. Charleston City Council, 1947-50. Trustee Coll. Charleston. Served with USNR, 1941-45. Mem. Charleston, S.C., Am. bar assns., Maritime Law Assn. U.S., Assn. Ins. Attys., S.C. Defense Attys. Assn., Southeastern Admiralty Law Inst., Hibernian Soc., Phi Delta Phi. Episcopalian. Clubs: Propeller; Carolina Yacht. Home: 309 Stono Dr Charleston SC 29407 Office: 2 Prioleau St Charleston SC 29402

GIBBS, DAVID GEORGE, food mfg. co. exec.; b. Vancouver, B.C., Can., May 5, 1925; s. Albert Edward and Florence (Bedford) G.; grad. high sch.; m. Lenore Joyce De Geer, Oct. 7, 1949; 1 dau., Susan Caroline. Audit clk. Price Waterhouse, chartered accountants, 1943-46; with Kelly Douglas Co. Ltd., Vancouver, 1946—, controller, 1965—. Named Ky. col., 1968. C.P.A., Can. Mem. Financial Execs. Inst. (v.p. systems and procedures). Mason. Home: 956 Belgroave St North Vancouver British Columbia Canada Office: PO Box 2039 Vancouver British Columbia Canada

GIBBS, DAVID PARKER, army officer; b. Ft. Leavenworth, Kan., Mar. 11, 1911; s. George Sabin and Ruth (Hobby) G.; B.S., U.S. Mil. Acad., 1933; postgrad. Air War Coll., 1948, Nat. War Coll., 1953; grad. Advanced Mgmt. program, Harvard, 1958—: m. Elizabeth Coyle Goodrich, June 17, 1933; children-Patricia Ann (Mrs. William S. Carpenter), David Parker, Paul Goodrich. Commd. 2d lt. U.S. Army, 1933, advanced through grades to maj. gen. 1962; chief communications br. Far East Command, Tokyo, Japan, 1954- 55; comdg. gen. Signal Tng. Center, Ft. Gordon, Ga., 1957-60; dep. chief of staff J-6, NORAD, Colorado Springs, Colo., 1960-61; asst., dep. then chief signal officer U.S. Army, 1962-66; cons. Gen. Instrument Corp., Burroughs Corp., 1966-68, Vitro Labs., 1969-70; initiated Mallard Project and participated in engring. design, 1963—. Decorated D.S.M., Legion of Merit, Bronze Star medal with two oak leaf clusters, Army Commendation medal, French Croix de Guerre. Mem. Armed Forces Communications and Electronics Assn. (past nat. v.p.), Assn. U.S. Army, Assn. of Old Crows. Episcopalian. Home: PO Box 283 Monument CO 80132

GIBBS, DELBRIDGE LINDLEY, lawyer; b. Jacksonville, Fla., Jan. 13, 1917; s. Elbridge Lindley and Myrtle Josephine (King) G.; B.S. in Bus. Adminstrn., U. Fla., 1939, LL.B., 1940; m. Jane Phillips Reese, Nov. 23, 1947; children—Elizabeth, Joanne, Delbridge Lindley. Admitted to Fla. bar, 1940; practice in Jacksonville, 1946—; partner firm Marks, Gray, Conroy & Gibbs, 1957—. Served with AUS, 1941-46; col. Res. ret. Fellow Am. Bar Found.; mem. Am. (ho. dels. 1964-68), Fed., Jacksonville (pres. 1956) bar assns., Fla. Bar (pres. 1963-64), Duval County Legal Aid Assn. (pres. 1952), Am. Judicature Soc. Judge Adv. Assn., Assn. Ins. Attys., Newcomen Soc. Rotarian. Clubs: River, Timuquana Country (Jacksonville); Ponte Vedra (Ponte Vedra Beach, Fla.). Home: 4101 Venetia Blvd Jacksonville FL 32210 Office: PO Box 447 Jacksonville FL 32201

GIBBS, FREDERIC ANDREWS, neurophysiologist, electroencephalographer, epileptologist; b. Balt., Feb. 9 1903; s. Rufus Macqueen and Cornelia (Andrews) G.; A.B., Yale, 1925; M.D., Johns Hopkins, 1929; m. Erna Leonhardt, 1930; children—Erich Leonhardt, Frederic Andrews. Asst. neuropathology Harvard Med. Sch., 1929; research fellow Johnson Found., 1939, research fellow in neuropathology, 1933, in physiology, 1934, in neurology, 1935, instr. neurology, 1937, instr. neurophysiology, 1937-42; asso. prof. psychiatry U. Ill., 1944-51, prof. neurology; research dir. Ill. Consultation Clinic for Epilepsy, 1945—. Recipient Mead-Johnson award, 1938; co-winner of the Lasker award, 1951, St. Valentine's award, 1971. Mem. Am. Physiol. Soc., Am. Neurol. Soc., Am. Acad. Cerebral Palsy, Am. Acad. Neurology, Brain Research Found., Internat. League Against Epilepsy. Author: Atlas of Electroencephalography, 1941, rev. Vol. I, 1950. Vol. II, 1952, Vol. III, 1964; Epilepsy Handbook, rev. edit., 1971; Medical Electroencephalography, 1967; Electroencephalography for Surgeons and Anesthesiologists, 1967. Home: 1427 Astor St Chicago IL 60610 Office: 720 N Michigan Av Chicago IL 60611 also 912 S Wood St Chicago IL 60612

GIBBS, GORDON, former educator; b. Providence, Jan. 17, 1900; s. William and Katharine Marie (Ryan) G.; student Columbia Extension, 1918-19, Columbia, 1919-22; m. Blanche Lorraine, Dec. 18, 1934; children—Lorraine Marie, Valerie. Promotion mgr. Katharine Gibbs Sch., N.Y.C., 1922-26, v.p., 1926-34, pres. Katharine Gibbs Sch., Boston, Montclair, N.Y.C., Providence, 1934-65, chmn. bd., 1965-68. Served with U.S. Army Ambulance Service, 1917-18, A.E.F. base comdr. C.A.P., Coastal patrol, 1942-43. Decorated Medale Militare (Italy); Croix de Guerre (France). Clubs: St. Botolph (Boston); Beverly Yacht (Marion, Mass); Cruising Club of Am. Home: Lewis St Marion MA 02738

GIBBS, HENRY, writer, artist; b. Salisbury, Wiltshire, Eng., June 28, 1909; s. Henry John and Beatrice (Rumbold) G.; ed. Marlborough and pvt. tutors; studied art Bromley Sch. Art and Beckenham Sch. Art. Royal Coll. Art. also in Paris, Venice and Berlin. Portrait painter, London, Eng., 1928-31; exhibited portraits, London and Paris, 1931; toured Europe, Africa and Middle East while painting and writing, 1932-34; reporter various news agencies, reported phases of Abyssinian and Spanish wars, 1933-38. Served with Royal Corps of Signals, 1940-41, as instr. fire and rescue with London Civil Def., 1941-45. Mem. Crime Writers Assn. Nat. Geographic Soc., Mystery Writers Am., Brit. Soc. Authors, P.E.N., The Paternosters, South African Inst. Racial Relations. Independent Conservative. Author: At a Farthing's Rate, 1942; (polit.-travel books) Twilight in South Africa, 1950 (Anisfield-Wolf Award, 1950), Crescent in Shadow, 1952, Italy on Borrowed Time, 1953; The Masks of Spain, 1955; (novels) Children''s Overture, 1948, Pawns in Ice, 1948, Cream and Cider, 1952; (history) Theatre Tapestry, 1950, Africa on a Tightrope, Background to Bitterness, 1954; (biography) Affectionately Yours, Fanny, 1948; a tetralogy of South African hist. novels: The Splendour and the Dust, 1955, The Winds of Time, 1956, Thunder at Dawn, 1957, The Tumult and the Shouting, 1958; A series of adventures, under pen name Simon Harvester with Asian settings, 1955-61; The Hills of India, 1960; The Bamboo Prison, 1963; Crimson Gate, 1963; Warlords, 1966; Shadows in a Hidden Land, 1966; Treacherous Road, 1967. Reported from Asia, 1956-57, North Africa and Middle East, 1958. Office: Hutchinson Ltd 178-202 Great Portland St London W1 England also Walker and Co 10 W 56th St New York City NY 10019

GIBBS, HUBERT SMITH, educator; b. La Crosse, Wis., Oct. 7, 1917; s. Elmer Eugene and Lark Estelle (Smith) G.; student Wis. State Coll., 1935-37; B.A., U. Ia., 1939; M.A., U. Minn., 1940; Ph.D., Johns Hopkins, 1952; m. Lorna June Staley, Apr. 22, 1938; children—Margaret, Christopher, Cynthia. Mem. faculty Emmetsburg (Ia.) Jr. Coll., 1941-43; instr. history Allegheny Coll., 1943-44; asst. prof. history Hastings Coll., 1946-48; asst. instr. polit. sci. Johns Hopkins, 1948-50; faculty Boston U., 1950—, prof. govt., 1958—, chmn. dept., 1956-69, dean Met. Coll., 1969—, dir. overseas programs, 1967—. Served to lt. (s.g.) USNR, 1944-46. Mem. Am. Polit. Sci. Assn., Phi Beta Kappa. Co-author: Problems in International Relations, rev. edit., 1970. Home: Nebo St Medfield MA 02052 Office: 236 Bay State Rd Boston MA 02215

GIBBS, JULIAN HOWARD, educator, phys. chemist; b. Greenfield, Mass., June 24, 1924; s. Howard Brown and Judith Martha Bassett (Hemenway) G.; B.A., Amherst Coll., 1947; M.A., Princeton, 1949, Ph.D., 1950; m. Cora Lee Gethman, July 27, 1946; children—James Hemenway, Judith Maxwell, Jeffrey Stephen, Jonathan Myles. Instr. phys. chemistry U. Minn., 1951-52; with research lab. Gen. Electric Co., 1952-55, Am. Viscose Corp., 1955-60; mem. faculty Brown U., 1960—, prof. chemistry, 1963—, chmn. dept., 1964—. Served with USNR, 1944-46, Fulbright fellow Cambridge (Eng.) U., 1950-51; Guggenheim fellow, 1967-68; Fulbright research scholar Max Planck Inst. for Phys. Chemistry, 1967-68. Trustee Roger Williams Hosp. Fellow Am. Phys. Soc. (chmn. high polymer physics 1963, exec. com. div. 1963—, High Polymer Physics prize 1967), Am. Chem. Soc., Phi Beta Kappa, Sigma Xi, Theta Delta Chi. Mem. adv. bd. Biopolymers. Author articles in field. Home: White Birch Lane Barrington RI 02806 Office: Brown Univ Providence RI 02912

GIBBS, MARTIN, educator, biologist; b. Phila., Nov. 11, 1922; s. Samuel and Rose (Sugarman) G.; B.S., Phila. Coll. Pharmacy, 1943; Ph.D., U. Ill., 1947; m. Svanhild Karen Kvale, Oct. 11, 1950; children—Janet Helene, Laura Jean, Steven Joseph, Michael Seland, Robert Kvale. Scientist, Brookhaven Nat. Lab., 1947-56; prof. biochemistry Cornell U., 1957-64; prof. biology, chmn. dept. Brandeis U., Waltham, Mass., 1965—. Cons. NSF, 1961-64, NIH, 1966—; Sigma Xi; RESA lectr., 1969; NATO cons. fellowship bd., 1968—. Mem. Am. Assn. U. Profs., Am., Japanese socs. plant physiologists, Biochem. Soc. Eng., Am. Soc. Biol. Chemists, Sigma Xi. Editor-in-chief Plant Physiology, 1963—; asso. editor Physiologie Vegetale, 1966—, Ann. Rev. Plant Physiology, 1966—. Home: 32 Slocum Rd Lexington MA 02173 Office: Brandeis Univ Waltham MA 02154

GIBBS, PETER GODBE, educator, physicist; b. Salt Lake City, Dec. 7, 1924; s. Lauren Worthen and Mary (Godbe) G.; student Berea Coll., 1943-44, U. Mich., 1944-45; B.S., U. Utah, 1947, M.S.,, 1949, Ph.D., 1951; m. Miriam Starling Kvetensky, July 12, 1953; children—Laurence Kay (Doon), Victoria Emmeline, Nicholas, Peter. Research asso. U. Ill., Urbana, 1951-52, instr., 1952-54; Fulbright lectr. theoretical physics U. Ceylon, Colombo, 1954-55; faculty U. Utah, Salt Lake City, 1956—, prof. physics, 1962—, chmn. dept. physics, 1967—. Fulbright lectr. solid state physics Sao Carlos Engring. Sch., U. Sao Paulo (Brazil), 1963. Recipient Ross Coffin Purdy prize Am. Ceramic Soc., 1962. Fellow A.A.A.S.; mem. Am. Phys. Soc., Am. Assn. Physics Tchrs., Utah Acad. Sci., Arts and Letters, Sigma Xi. Contbg. author: Physical Chem-An Advanced Treatise, 1967. Contbr. articles profl. jours. Home: 79 Laurel St Salt Lake City UT 84103

GIBBS, RICHARD BURPEE, clergyman; b. Arlington, Mass., Feb. 18, 1907; s. Richard and Emily E. (White) G.; A.B., Tufts U., 1937, S.T.B., 1939; student Suffolk Law Sch., 1930-34; m. Mildred D. Williamson, Mar. 4, 1940; 1 dau., Brenda E. Ordained to ministry Unitarian Ch., 1940; pastor in Smithton Pa., 1936, Washington, Vt., 1938, Stoneham, Mass., 1938-39, Brockton, Mass., 1940- 45, Memphis, 1945-54; regional dir. Southwestern Unitarian Conf., Memphis, 1949-54; dir. extension dept. Unitarian Universalist Assn., Boston, 1954-67; minister Unitarian Ch., Ellsworth, Me., 1968—. Home: 21 Pine St Ellsworth ME 04605

GIBERT, HUGH WARING, lawyer; b. North Augusta S.C., Nov. 5, 1929; s. Paul Carrington and Helen (Burns) G.; A.B., U. S.C., 1951; LL.B., Emory U., 1957; LL.M., Yale, 1959; m. Mary Evelyn Wellons, July 19, 1954; children—Arthur Littleton, Kenneth Hamilton, John Carrington, James Waring. Admitted to Ga. bar, 1957; asst. atty. gen. Ga., 1957-58; asst. prof. law U. Ala. Law Sch., 1959-61; asso. prof. law U. Tex. Law Sch., 1961-62; instr. tax law Emory U. Law Sch., 1962-64; partner firm Gibert, Walling & Hubert, Atlanta, 1962-64; firm Haas, Holland, Freeman, Levison & Gibert, Atlanta, 1964—. Served o lt. (j.g.) USNR, 1951-55. Mem. Am., Ga., Atlanta bar assns., Am. Judicature Soc., Lawyers Club Atlanta, Am. Civil Liberties Union (Ga. pres. 1963-65, past nat. bd. dirs.). Home: 3521 Ivy Rd NE Atlanta GA 30342 Office: 1st Nat Bank Tower Atlanta GA 30303

GIBIAN, THOMAS GEORGE, chem. co. exec.; b. Prague, Czechoslovakia, Mar. 20, 1922; s. Richard and Vera (Sindelar) G.; B.S., U. N.C., 1942; Ph.D., Carnegie Inst. Tech., 1948; m. Laura Cynthia Sutherland, Feb. 19, 1949; children—Barbara Mary, Janet Cynthia, Thomas Richard, David George. Came to U.S., 1941, naturalized, 1951. Research chemist Atlantic Refining Co., 1948-51; with W.R. Grace & Co., 1951—, devel. engr. Dewey & Almy Chem. div., plant mgr., gen. mgr. battery separators, v.p., gen. mgr. organic chems. div., now v.p., dir. Bd. dirs. Sandy Spring Friends Sch.; mem. vis. com. chemistry dept. Carnegie- Mellon U. Served with RAF, 1942-46. Mem. Am. Chem. Soc., Am. Inst. Chem. Engrs., Indsl. Research Inst., Am. Inst. Chemists. Clubs: Cosmos (Washington); Chemist (N.Y.C.). Home: Box 127 Sandy Spring MD 20860 Office: 3 Hanover Sq New York City NY 10004

GIBLIN, EDMUND BURKE, pharm. exec.; b. Bklyn., Dec. 23, 1913; s. Joseph and Elizabeth (Burke) G.; B.A. in History and Econs., St John's U., 1935; M.B.A., Harvard, 1937; LL.B., Boston U., 1950; m. Katharine Bukay, May 5, 1946; children—Carol, Edmund Burke, Jean Marie, Stephen Joseph, Gregory Mark, Joseph John, David Richard. With Haskins & Sells, C.P.A.'s, N.Y.C., 1937- 42; with Gen.

Foods Corp., 1946-, operations mgr. Walter Baker div., 1955-57, operations mgr. Jell-O div., 1957-59, gen. mgr. Jell-O div., 1959-64, v.p. corp., 1960-64, v.p., group operations exec., 1964- 65, sr. v.p., dir., 1965-66, exec. v.p., dir., 1966-68; pres., dir., mem. exec. com. Warner-Lambert Pharm. Co., 1968—; dir. Fidelity Union Trust Co. Trustee Morriston Meml. Hosp.; bd. overseers Cranwell Sch. Served to lt. USNR, 1942-46. C.P.A., N.Y.; admitted to Mass. bar, 1951. Mem. Chocolate Mfrs. Assn. (pres. 1959), Am. Cocoa Research Inst. (chmn. 1959), Am. Inst. C.P.A.'s, N.Y. Soc. C.P.A.'s, Mass., Boston bar assns., Am. Judicature Soc. Clubs: Presidents, Economic of New York, Boston Harvard. Home: 201 Tabor Rd Morris Plains NJ 07950

GIBLIN, EDWARD, corp. exec.; b. 1917; B.A., Fordham U.; M.B.A., N.Y. U.; married. With Peat, Marwick, Mitchell & Co., C.P.A.'s, prior to 1953; with Ex-Cell-O Corp., 1953—, v.p., treas., 1968—. Address: 1200 Oakman Blvd Detroit MI 48238

GIBNEY, LAURENCE VINCENT, architect; b. N.Y.C., July 26, 1914; s. Terrence Vincent and Laura (King) G.; B.S. in Architecture, Manhattan Coll., 1936; Certificate Mgmt. Devel. , U. Tenn., 1960; m. Katherine Elizabeth McGuire, Sept. 6, 1941 (dec. May 1965); children—Laurence Vincent, Katherine Elizabeth, Thomas Denis. With TVA, Knoxville, Tenn., 1938—, adminstrv. asst. to br. chief, 1961-71, asst. chief architect, 1971—. Mem. A.I.A. (sec. E.Tenn. 1967, bd. dirs. 1968), Tenn. Soc. Architects. K.C. (4). Home: 2956 Kenilworth Lane North Hills Knoxville TN 37917 Office: Home Fed Bldg Knoxville TN 37902

GIBRAN, KAHLIL, sculptor; b. Boston, Nov. 29, 1922; s. Nicholas and Rose (Gibran) G.; student Boston Mus. Sch., 1940-43; m. Jean English, July 1, 1957; children—Timothy (by previous marriage), Nicole. Exhibited widely as painter, 1949-52; life sized steel sculpture, 1953—; rep. permanent collections Pa. Acad., Tenn. Fine Arts Center, Norfolk (Va.) Mus., Chrysler Mus., William Rockhill Gallery, Swope Gallery, Brockton Fine Arts Center. Recipient George Widener award Pa. Acad., 1958; Guggenheim fellow, 1959-61; award Nat. Inst. Arts and Letters, 1961; Grand prize Boston Arts Festival, 1964; John Gregory award sculpture, 1965; Gold medal Internat. Sacred Art Show, Trieste, Italy, 1966. Author: Sculpture—Kahlil Gibran, 1970. Address: 160 W Canton St Boston MA 02118

GIBSON, ALTHEA, tennis player, golfer; b. Silver, S.C., Aug. 25, 1927; d. Daniel and Annie B. (Washington) Gibson; B.S., Fla. A. and M. Coll., 1953; m. William A. Darben, Oct. 17, 1965. Amateur tennis player in U.S., Europe and S.Am., 1941-58; made profl. tennis tour with Harlem Globetrotters, 1959; won world profl. tennis championship, 1960; became community relations rep. Ward Baking Co., 1959; joined Ladies Profl. Golf Assn. as profl. golfer, 1963; apptd. to N.Y. State Recreation Council, 1964. Asst. instr. dept. health and phys. edn. Lincoln U., Jefferson City, Mo., 1953-55. Named Woman Athlete of Year, AP Poll, 1957-58. Mem. Alpha Kappa Alpha. Author: I Always Wanted to Be Somebody, 1958. Home: 275 Prospect St East Orange NJ 07017

GIBSON, ARRELL MORGAN, educator; b. Pleasanton, Kan., Dec. 1, 1921; s. Arrell Morgan and Vina Lorene (Davis) G.; B.A., U. Okla., 1947, M.A., 1948, Ph.D., 1954; m. Dorothy Deitz, Dec. 24, 1942 (div. Apr. 1971); children—Patricia Gibson, Michael Morgan, Kathleen Camille. Prof. history Phillips U., Enid, 1949-57; prof. history U. Okla., Norman, 1957—, chmn. dept. 1964, 70—; curator history Stovall Mus., U. Okla., 1959—. Mem. adv. bd. Mus. Gt. Plains, Lawton, Okla., 1962—. Served with USNR, 1942-45. Recipient Rockefeller Found. U. Okla. Press award, 1961; Am. Philos. Soc. Research grantee, 1963, 69; Duke Found. Research grantee, 1968, 69; U. Okla. Faculty Research grantee, 1957-71. Mem. Am. Hist. Assn., Southern, Western history assns., Orgn. Am. Historians, Southwestern Social Sci. Assn., Okla. Hist. Soc. (bd. dirs.), Phi Beta Kappa, Phi Alpha Theta. Author: The Kickapoos, 1963; Life and Death of Colonel Albert Jennings Fountain, 1965; Oklahoma: A History of Five Centuries, 1965; Fort Smith: Little Gibraltar on the Arkansas, 1969; The Chickasaws, 1971. Office: Home: Route 2 Noble OK 73068

GIBSON, BYRON HALL, educator; b. Cullman, Ala., Mar. 13, 1908; s. Joseph Sylvanus and Mary Elizabeth (Gurley) G.; A.B. summa cum laude, Birmingham So. Coll., 1928; A.M., U. Ill., 1929, Ph.D., 1931; m. Alberta Moore Lotspeich, Mar. 16, 1934; children—John Sevier, Mary Ruth, Richard Joseph, James Byron. Prin., Cold Springs (Ala.) Sch., 1929; instr. U. Ill., 1931-32; head dept. langs. Union (Ky.) Coll., 1932-46; prof. English, John B. Stetson U., DeLand, Fla., 1946—, chmn. div. humanities, 1948-56, head dept. English, 1948—. Trustee scholar, fellow U. Ill., 1929-31. Mem. Modern Lang. Assn. Democrat. Baptist. Kiwanian. Author: Word Power: A Short Guide to Vocabulary and Spelling, 1966. Researcher: Anglo-Saxon survivals in U.S. Home: 811 N Florida DeLand FL 32720

GIBSON, CHARLES ARNOLD, textile co. exec.; b. Hanover, Mass., Mar. 8, 1906; s. George and Lenora G.; grad. Dartmouth, 1927; m. Mary Alice, June 1, 1932; children—Ellen, Meredith, William. Exec., Burlington Industries; dir. S.C. Nat. Bank; trustee Textile Hall Corp. Trustee Sirrine Found., Greenville County Found., S.C. Assn. Ind. Colls.; adv. bd. trustees Furman U., Presbyn. Coll. Mem. S.C. C. of C., Greater Greenville C. of C. (pres.), S.C. Textile Mfrs. Assn. (pres. 1952-53), Am. Textile Mfrs. Inst. (past dir.). Presbyn. Rotarian. Clubs: Poinsett, Tarantella, Cotillion, Green Valley Country. Home: 300 Woodland Way Greenville SC 29607 Office: Burlington Industries Daniel Bldg Greenville SC 29602

GIBSON, CHARLES COLMERY, rubber mfg. exec.; b. Edwards, Miss., Sept. 12, 1914; s. William Bayne and Anna (Colmery) G.; A.B., Harvard, 1937, grad. Advanced Mgmt. Program, 1953; m. Margaret Eaton, Nov. 4, 1939; children—William Bayne II, John Clark. With Goodyear Tire & Rubber Co., Akron, O., 1937—, v.p., 1956—. Served from ensign to lt. comdr. USNR, World War II. Home: 855 Mayfair Rd Akron OH 44303 Office: Goodyear Tire & Rubber Co Akron OH 44316

GIBSON, COUNT DILLON, Jr., physician, educator; b. Covington, Ga., July 10, 1921; s. Count Dillon and Julia (Thompson) G.; B.S., Emory U., 1942, M.D., 1944; m. Katherine Vislocky, June 10, 1950; children—Gabriella, Thomas, Alexis, George. Intern, Columbia-Presbyn. Med. Center, 1944-45, asst. resident medicine, 1947- 50, med. resident, 1950-51; asst. prof., asso. prof. medicine Med. Coll. Va., 1951-57; prof. preventive medicine, chmn. dept. Tufts U. Sch. Medicine, Boston, 1958-69; physician-in-chief Home Med. Service; attending physician New Eng. Med. Center Hosps.; gen. dir. Tufts-Columbia Point Health Center; vis. physician Boston City Hosp., to 1969; prof., chmn. dept. community and preventive medicine, asso. dean community health programs Stanford U., Stanford, 1969—. Served from 1st lt. to capt., M.C., AUS, 1945-47. Diplomate Am. Bd. Internal Medicine. Mem. A.M.A., A.C.P., Am. Fedn. Clin. Research, Mass. Med. Soc. Roman Catholic. Contbr. articles to profl. jours. Home: 200 Valencia Dr Los Altos CA 94022 Office: Stanford U Med Center Stanford CA 94305

GIBSON, DANIEL PARKE, author, business cons.; b. Seattle, Oct. 8, 1930; s. Everett Brooks and Emma (Parker) G.; student Coll. City N.Y., 1955. Partner Laws-Gibson Assos., Inc., Phila., 1952-54; advt. rep. Interstate United Newspapers, N.Y.C., 1954-56; a dvt. rep. Ebony Mag., 1956-57; promotion mgr., 1957-59; promotion dir. Chgo. Daily Defender, 1959; pres. Gibson Assos., N.Y.C., 1960—; dir. Intramerica Life Ins. Co.; sr. cons. D. Parke Gibson Assos., Inc. bd. dirs. Interracial Council Bus. Opportunity, 1970-72. United Service Orgns., 1970-72. Served with USAF, 1948-52. Mem. Pub. Relations Soc. Am. Author: The Billion Negro, 1969. Home: 2185 5th Av New York City NY 10037 Office: 475 Fifth Av New York City NY 10017

GIBSON, DANIEL ZACHARY, former coll. pres.; b. Middlesboro, Ky., Jan. 26, 1908; s. Daniel Z. and Mellie (Rice) G.; A.B., Ky. Wesleyan Coll., 1929, LL.D., 1956; A.M., U. Cin., 1931, Ph.D., 1939; L.H.D., Washington Coll., 1970; m. Helen Katharine Schaefer, Aug. 12, 1936; children—Linda (Mrs. Thomas Haag), Daniel Douglas, Mary Laurent, Helen Clark. Instr. English, Cin. Conservatory Music, 1931- 40; Taft teaching fellow U. Cin., 1934-35; asst. prof. English, The Citadel, 1940-43; asso. prof. English, Franklin and Marshall Coll., Lancaster, Pa., 1946-50, dean coll., 1946-50; pres. Washington Coll., Chestertown, Md., 1950-70. Mem. Md. State Scholarship Bd.; mem. exec. com. Middle States Assn. Colls., Md. Fulbright com.; community council Wye Inst.; chmn. Rhodes Scholarship Com. for Md., D.C., 1965-68. Served as lt. USNR, 1943-46. Mem. Am. Council for Pharm. Edn. (bd. grants), Phi Mu Alpha, Omicron Delta Kappa. Episcopalian. Home: 1004 Camden Av Salisbury MD 21801

GIBSON, DAVID MARK, educator, biochemist; b. Kokomo, Ind., Aug. 7, 1923; s. Carl Banta and Marie (Loop) G.; A.B., Wabash Coll., 1944; M.D., Harvard, 1948; m. Margaret Lockhart, June 2, 1951; children—Carl L., John L., Shauna M., Heather R., Mark C. Intern Northwestern U. Med. Sch., 1948-49; research asso. biochemistry U. Ill. at Urbana, 1950-53; asst. prof., research asso. Inst. Enzyme Research, U. Wis., 1953-55, 55-58; mem. faculty Ind. U. Sch. Medicine, 1958—, prof. biochemistry, 1961—, chmn., 1967- -; established investigator Am. Heart Assn., 1957-61). Mem. A.A.A.S., Am. Soc. Biol. Chemists, Am. Chem. Soc., Am. Diabetes Assn., Sigma Xi. Research biochem. mechanisms and control fatty acid synthesis and oxidation. Home: 3436 Brisbane Rd Indianapolis IN 46208

GIBSON, EDWARD GEORGE, astronaut; b. Buffalo, Nov. 8, 1936; s. Calder Alexander and Geraldine (Shannon) G.; B.S., U. Rochester, 1959; M.S., Cal. Inst. Tech., 1960, Ph.D. in Engring. and Physics, 1964; m. Julie Anne Volk, Aug. 22, 1959; children—Mannet Lynn, John Edward, Julie Ann. With Aronutronic research lab. Philco Corp., Newport Beach, Cal., 1964-65; astronaut Manned Spacecraft Center, Houston, 1965—. Solar physics Subcom. NASA. Mem. Am. Astron. Soc., Am. Inst. Physics, Am. Inst. Aeros. and Astronautics, Sigma Xi, Tau Beta Pi, Theta Chi. Home: 18611 Martinique Dr Nassau Bay Houston TX 77058 Office: Code (CB) Manned Spacecraft Center Houston TX 77058

GIBSON, ELMER JOHN, retired army officer; b. Shenandoah, Pa., Dec. 21, 1910; s. Harry and Caroline Anna (Hechler) G.; student Bucknell U., 1929; B.S. in Engring., U.S. Mil. Acad., 1935; grad. F.A. Sch., 1939-40, Ordnance Sch., 1940, Command and Gen. Staff Coll., 1945, Indsl. Coll. Armed Forces, 1948; m. Mary Elizabeth Murray, Oct. 3, 1936; 1 son, William McCampbell. Commd. 2d lt. U.S. Army, 1935, advanced through grades to maj. gen., 1963; various assignments in U.S., 1935-44; ordnance mem. Army Ground Force Bd., New Guinea, 1944; asst. ordnance officer Hdqrs. 4th Army, Ft. Sam Houston, Tex., 1944-45; exec. officer ordnance sect. Hdqrs. 10th Army, Okinawa, 1945, Oahu Ordnance Service, Hawaii, 1946-47; staff officer prodn. planning br., procurement div. Office Asst. Chief Staff, G-4, War Dept., 1948-50, chief indsl. facilities sect., 1951-52, exec. and asst. chief, 1952-54; purchasing and contracting officer, dep. comdr. and comdr. Ordnance Procurement Center, U.S. Army Europe, 1954-57; chief procurement div. Office Dept. Chief Staff Logistics, 1957-59; asst. chief staff G-4, Hdqrs. 8th Army, Korea, 1959-60; comdg. gen. U.S. Army Ordnance Weapons Command, Rock Island (Ill.) Arsenal, 1961-62; dir. procurement and prodn. Hdqrs. Army Material Command, 1962-64; asst. dep. chief staff logistics Dept. Army, 1964-67; dep. chief staff logistics U.S. Continental Army Command, 1967-70; retired, 1970. Decorated Legion of Merit, D.S.M. with oak leaf cluster, Bronze Star, Army Commendation ribbon with oak leaf cluster. Mem. Assn. U.S. Army, Am. Ordnance Assn., Nat. Rifle Assn. Mason (32 Shriner). Home: Goliad TX 77963

GIBSON, EVERETT G., labor union exec.; b. Wallingford, Conn., Dec. 28, 1903; s. George Gluster and Clara (Stearns) G.; student pub. schs. Huntington, N.Y.; m. Katherine Lewis, June 10, 1928; 1 son, Everett Howard. Joined Nat. Fedn. Post Office Motor Vehicle Employees, AFL, 1925, pres., 1945—. Pres. Bklyn. Sunday Sch. Union. Mem. Post Office St. George Assn., Post Office Sq. Club of N.Y. No. 278. Republican. Ref. Episcopalian. Mason. Home: 147-33 20th Rd Whitestone NY 11357 Office: 412 5th St SW Washington DC 20001

GIBSON, FLOYD ROBERT, U.S. judge; b. Prescott, Ariz., Mar. 3, 1910; s. Van Robert and Katheryn Ida (Weitzel) G.; A.B., U. Mo., 1931, LL.B., 1933; m. Gertrude Lee Walker, Apr. 23, 1935; children—Charles R., John M., Catherine L. Admitted to Mo. bar, 1933; practiced in Independence, 1933-37, Kansas City, 1937-61; mem. firm Johnson, Lucas, Bush & Gibson, and predecessor, 1954-61; county counselor Jackson County, 1943-44; chief judge U.S. Dist. Ct., Western Dist. Mo., until 1965; U.S. circuit judge Ct. Appeals, 8th circuit, Kansas City, Mo., 1965—; former chmn. bd. Mfrs. & Mechanics Bank, Kansas City, Mo., Blue Valley Fed. Savs. & Loan Assn.; sec., dir. Midland Food Labs., Inc., 1949-61, Syko Engring. Corp., 1950-61, Bestex Corp., 1954-61, Latimer Motors Ltd., 1943-61. Commr. Nat. Conf. Commrs. Uniform State Laws, 1957—; bd. mgrs. Council State Govts., 1960-61; pres. Nat. Legislative Conf., 1960. Mem. Mo. Gen. Assembly from 7th Dist., 1940-46; mem. Mo. Senate, 1946-61, majority floor leader, 1952-56, pres. pro tem, 1956-60; del. Nat. Democratic Conv., 1956, 60. Bd. dirs. Greater Kansas City Mental Health Found.; trustee Kansas City Philharmonic Assn. Mem. Mo. N.G. Named 2d most valuable mem. Mo. Legislature, Globe Democrat, 1958, most valuable, 1960; recipient Faculty- Alumni award U. Mo., 1968. Mem. Am. (adv. bd. editors Jour.), Mo., Kansas City bar assns., Lawyers Assn. Kansas City (past v.p.), Mo. Law Sch. Found. (life), Phi Delta Phi, Phi Kappa Psi. Clubs: University, Carriage, Mercury (Kansas City, Mo.). Home: 11521 Winner Rd Independence MO 64052 Office: US Ct House Kansas City MO 64106

GIBSON, FOYE GOODNER, clergyman, gerontologist; b. Bristol, Tenn., Oct. 5, 1903; s. Blair T. and Virginia (Leftwich) G.; student King Coll., Bristol, 1922-23; A.B., Emory and Henry Coll., 1927, L.H.D., 1960; postgrad. Vanderbilt U., 1927, 29-30; D.D., Randolph-Macon Coll., 1944; m. Doris Aldrich, Apr. 19, 1925; children—Marita (Mrs. Fred N. Sesler), Helen (Mrs. Robert O. Duncan), Eleanor (Mrs. David L. Via). Mem. Holston Conf. Meth. Ch.; ordained elder, 1931; apptd. to White Pine, Tenn., 1928-29, English Congregation, Warszawa, Poland, 1930, Instl. Ch., Katowice, Poland, 1931-32; pastor, Lake City, Tenn., 1933; finance dir. Central Ch., Knoxville, Tenn., 1934-37; pastor First Ch., Pulaski, Va., 1937-41; pres. Emory and Henry Coll., 1941-56, Scarritt Coll., Nashville, 1956-59; adminstr. Asbury Acres, Holston Meth. Home for Ret., Maryville, Tenn., 1959—. Sec., Polish Meth. Mission, 1931-33; del. Meth. Gen. Conf., Jackson, Miss., 1934; mem. Gen. Council on World Service and Finance Meth. Ch., 1944-56, exec. com., 1952-56, 64—, bd. Evangelism, 1956-60; del. Meth. S.E. Jurisdictional Conf., Columbia, S.C., 1948. Former mem. Va. Adv. Com. on Schs. and Colls.; chmn. Ch. Related Colls. of South, 1953; pres. Tenn. Assn. Homes for Aging, 1961- 66. Recipient DeFriece award for Service to Humanity, 1967. Mem. Gerontological Soc., Tau Kappa Alpha, Kappa Phi Kappa, Theta Phi, Blue Key. Rotarian. Address: Asbury Acres Maryville TN 37801

GIBSON, FRANK EVERETT, librarian; b. Des Moines, May 30, 1913; s. Frank Wesley and Maude Elizabeth (Trotter) G.; B.A., Drake U., 1948; B.S. in L.S., U. Minn., 1949, M.A., 1952; m. Bette J. Beckett, Dec. 15, 1935; 1 dau., Marianne. With Ia. Power & Light, Des Moines, 1932-42; asso. librarian U. Omaha, 1952-53; staff Omaha Pub. Library, 1953—, librarian, 1957—. Served with AUS, 1942-46. Recipient Lura Hutchison award in library sci. U. Minn., 1949. Mem. A.L.A., Neb. Library Assn. (pres. 1956-57), Phi Beta Kappa. Contbr. articles to profl. publs. Home: 6802 N 41st St Omaha NB 68112 Office: 1823 Harney St Omaha NB 68102

GIBSON, GEORGE, educator, chemist; b. Yonkers, N.Y., Mar. 20, 1909; s. John and Louisa (Sutherland) G.; B.S. in Chemistry, Bklyn. Poly. Inst., 1932, M.S., 1935, Ph.D., 1942; m. Victorine Robinson, Aug. 17, 1940; children—Janet (Mrs. William Teagardin), David George. Chemist, Chemco Photoproducts Co., Inc., 1932-33, Charles Pfizer Co., 1936-37; substitute tchr. N.Y.C. High Sch., 1934-36; research chemist E.I. duPont de Nemours & Co., Inc., 1937-42; from asst. prof. to prof. chemistry Ill. Inst. Tech., 1942-60; prof. chemistry Bklyn. Coll. of City U. N.Y., 1960—, chmn. dept., 1962- -. Asso. chemist Argonne Nat. Labs., 1949-50. Mem. N.Y. Acad. Sci., Am. Chem. Soc., Sigma Xi, Phi Lambda Upsilon. Contbr. articles to profl. jours. Home: 636 Baldwin Av Baldwin NY 11510 Office: Bklyn Coll Bedford Av and Av H Brooklyn NY 11210

GIBSON, GEORGE, artist; b. Edinburgh, Scotland, Oct. 16, 1904; s. George and Elizabeth L. (Gilchrist) G.; student Edinburgh Sch. Art, Glasgow Sch. Art, Chouinard Art Inst., Los Angeles; pupil William E. Glover, F. Tolles Chamberlain; m. Alice C. Milligan, June 4, 1937; 1 dau., Jean. Came to U.S., 1930, naturalized, 1938. Scenic art dir., head scenic art dept. Metro-Goldwyn-Mayer Studios, 1934-69. One-man shows include: Chabot Galleries, Los Angeles, 1950, Long Beach, Cal., 1950, Laguna Beach (Cal.). Art Assn., 1951, Santa Barbara Mus. Art, 1952, Santa Monica Library Art Gallery, 1958, St. Mary's Coll., 1958; exhibited Am. Watercolor Soc. anns., 1945—, Cal. Watercolor Soc. anns. and travelling shows, also galleries, museums in U.S.; represented in permanent collections San Diego Mus., Newport Union High Sch., Los Angeles County Mus., Santa Paula C. of C., Laguna Beach Art Gallery. Recipient 1st prize Santa Paula Ann., 1946, City Los Angeles Ann., 1947, 49, Santa Cruz Ann., 1948, 50, Ariz. State Fair, 1948, Montgomery (Ala.) Exhbn., 1949, Westwood Art Assn. Ann., 1951, Cal. Watercolor Soc. 32d Ann., 1953, Newport Beach 6th Ann., 1953; also numerous 2d and 3d prizes, hon. mentions. Served with USMCR, World War II. Asso. N.A.D.; mem. Am., Cal. (pres. 1950-51) watercolor socs., Acad. Motion Picture Arts and Scis. Home: 12157 Leven Lane Los Angeles CA 90049 Office: MGM Studios Culver City CA 90230

GIBSON, GEORGE DANDRIDGE, lawyer; b. Richmond, Va., May 8, 1904; s. George Armistead and Alice (McClung) G.; B.A., U. Va., 1924; A.M., Harvard, 1925, LL.B., 1928; m. Edith Ludlow Sedgwick, Feb. 23, 1935 (div. 1966); children—Pamela (Mrs. John T. Farrar), Alice (Mrs. Malcolm W. Stothers); m. 2d, Roberta Pearson Grymes, Aug. 26, 1966. Admitted to Va. bar, 1928, since practiced in Richmond; asso. firm now known as Hunton, Williams, Gay, Powell and Gibson, 1931—, partner, 1934—; gen. counsel Va. Electric & Power Co., Richmond, 1958—. Dir. Richmond Hotels, Inc. Spl. counsel Va. Code Commn. on Corp. Law, 1955-56. Mem. Va. Commn. Arts and Humanities, 1968—. Trustee Va. Mus. Fine Arts, 1952-63. Fellow Am. Bar Found. (chmn. com. model bus. corp. acts 1965—, mem. adv. com. corporate debt financing); mem. Acad. Polit. Sci., Richmond, Va. (chmn. com. portraits justices 1957-61), Am. (chmn. sect. corp., banking and bus. law 1959-60, chmn. com. corporate laws 1962-65, chmn. com. sect. projects 1965-70, editor The Business Lawyer 1957-58) bar assns. Am. Law Inst., Am. Judicature Soc., Assn. Bar City N.Y., Bar Assn. D.C., Edison Electric Inst. (chmn. legal com. 1965-67), Soc. Colonial Wars, S.R., Va. Hist. Soc. (exec. com. 1965—), Richmond, Va. chambers Commerce, English Speaking Union (nat. dir. 1964-71), Phi Beta Kappa, Phi Kappa Sigma. Episcopalian. Clubs: Forum (past pres.), German, Commonwealth, Country, Westwood, Downtown (Richmond); Metropolitan (Washington); Knickerbocker, Century, Brook, Coffee House (N.Y.C.); Buck's (London). Contbr. legal jours. Home: 9 River Rd Richmond VA 23226 Office: 7th and Main Sts Richmond VA 23212

GIBSON, GLENN VENNING, govt. ofcl.; b. Youngstown, O., May 26, 1913; s. Clair Ellis and Bessie Katherine (Blair) G.; B.S., U. Ala., 1938; M.S. (Alfred P. Sloan fellow), U. Denver, 1941; m. Helen Marie Frederick, Sept. 3, 1938; children—Donald Wade, Carol Virginia, June Pauline. Asst. to maintenance officer Fleet Air Base, Pearl Harbor, 1931-35; asst. dean men U. Ala., 1938; research asst. Chgo. Civic Fedn. and Bur. Pub. Efficiency, 1941; asst. to dep. dir. gen. for field operations WPB, 1942; dir. program analysis div. Office Naval Fiscal Dir., 1946, chief budget estimates div. Navy Dept., 1947-49; asst. budget dir. Dept. Def., 1950-54, dep. comptroller, budget dir., 1954-55, spl. asst. sec. def., 1956, dir. planning and requirements policy Office Asst. Sec. Def., Supply and Logistics, 1957-60, prin. dep. asst. sec. def. (installations and logistics), 1961—. Guest lectr. Maxwell Sch., U. Syracuse Grad. Sch. Bus. Adminstrn., 1958-63, George Washington U., 1958-61. Dir. Vets. Coop. Housing Assn., 1948-54, pres., chmn., 1949-51; expert exam. budget adminstrs. U.S. Civil Service Commn., 1949. Served from ensign to lt. USNR, 1943-46; lt. comdr. Res. Recipient Distinguished Service award, 1961. Mem. Am. Soc. Pub. Adminstrn. (sr. adviser Washington 1958-60), Phi Eta Sigma, Beta Gamma Sigma. Presbyn. (deacon 1952—, elder). Club: International (Washington). Author: (with M.A. Leonard) Aspects of Financial Management, City of Chicago, 1941. Contbr. financial mgmt. chpt. Report on Chicago Government, 1954. Home: 9322 W Parkhill Dr Bethesda MD 20014 Office: The Pentagon Washington DC 20301

GIBSON, HENRY, actor; b. Germantown, Pa., Sept. 21, 1935; s. Edmund Albert and Dorothy (Cassidy) Bateman; B.A. in Drama cum laude, Cath. U. Am., 1957; observer Royal Acad. Dramatic Arts, London, 1961; m. Lois Jean Geiger, Apr. 6, 1966; children—Jonathan David, Charles Alexander, James Bateman. Appeared as child actor Mae Desmond Theatre Co., Phila., other East coast stock cos., 1943-57; made Broadway debut in Lillian Hellmann's My Mother, My Father and Me, 1962; appeared on stage, film and television, 1962-68; co-star television show Laugh-In, 1968—. Adviser, Keep Am. Beautiful, 1967-69, Nat. Teach-In, 1970, Actors Fund, 1970—.

Served to 1st lt. USAF, 1957-60. Mem. Nat. Acad. Television Arts and Scis., Nat. Acad. Rec. Arts and Scis., UN Assn., World Federalists, Common Cause, Am. Civil Liberties Union, Center for Study Dem. Instns., Audubon Soc., Sierra Club, Nat. Wildlife Fedn., Friends of the Earth, League Conservation Voters, John Muir Inst., Zero Population Growth, Planning and Conservation League, Conservation Found., Defenders Wildlife, Izaak Walton League, Nat. Trust for Historic Preservation, Save the Redwoods League, Environmental Def. Dund, Wilderness Soc., Cal. Tomorrow, World Wildlife Fund. Author: A Flower Child's Garden of Verses, 1970; Carnival of the Animals, 1971. Contbr. articles to various mags., including Reader's Digest, Nat. Wildlife, Audubon, The Progressive, Common Cause. Address: Malibu CA 90265

GIBSON, HERBERT RICHARD, mcht.; b. Berryville, Ark., Sept. 16, 1901; s. William Thomas and Flora (Bell) G.; student pub. schs.; m. Belva Grace Acklin, 1932; children—Pauline (Mrs. Pepper), Frances (Mrs. Greer), Herbert Richard, Richard Herbert, Gerald Patrick. Past pres. Gibson Products Co., Dallas; chmn. bd. Gibson Discount Centers, Dallas, 1958—. Mem. Ch. of Christ. Home: 1358 Bar Harbor Dr Dallas TX 75232 Office: 519 Gibson St Seagoville TX 75159.

GIBSON, J. CORDNER, coll. dean; b. Templeton, Cal., Dec. 17, 1912; s. John H. and Hilda (Anderson) G.; B.S., U. Cal. at Berkeley, 1937; M.S. in Edn., U. So. Cal., 1957; m. Betty Ann Earll, July 12, 1940; children—David Earl, John C. Tchr. agr. Downey and Whittier (Cal.) high schs., 1938-43; supr. agrl. edn. Cal. Dept. Edn., 1946-49; mem. faculty Cal. State Poly. Coll., 1949—, dean Sch. Agr. and Natural Resources, 1967—; chief party survey teams to Argentina, Tanzania, Guatemala. Mem. San Dimas (Cal.) Water Bd., 1954-57. Served with AUS, 1943-46; ETO. Decorated Bronze Star. Mem. Cal. Agrl. Tchrs. Assn., San Dimas (Cal.) C. of C., Alpha Zeta. Republican. Presbyn. Elk, Kiwanian (local pres. 1955). Home: 538 Princeton Pl San Luis Obispo CA 93401

GIBSON, J. DOUGLAS, match co. exec.; b. Toronto, Ont., Can., Sept. 3, 1909; s. Albert Ralph and Hannah (Black) G.; B.A. in Polit. Sci. and Econs., U. Toronto, 1931; m. Mary Margaret Renfrew, Mar. 31, 1934 (dec. June 1958); 2 sons; m. 2d, Lila Elizabeth McPhedran, May 28, 1959; 2 sons, 1 dau. Chmn. bd. Eddy Match Co., Ltd., Toronto. Mem. Ont. Econ. Council. Trustee Queen's U. Decorated Order Brit. Empire. Mem. Canadian C. of C. (chmn. nat. exec. com. 1957-61), Canadian Polit. Sci. Assn. (pres. 1955-56). Contbr. articles to profl. jours. Clubs: Toronto, Nat., Toronto Golf, University (Toronto). Home: 406 Glenayr Rd Toronto Ontario Canada Office: 7 King St E Toronto Ontario Canada*

GIBSON, JAMES, ct. appeals judge; b. Salem, N.Y., Jan. 21, 1902; s. James and Caroline H. (MacCartee) G.; A.B., Princeton, 1923; LL.B., Albany Law Sch., 1926; LL.D., Union Coll., 1970; m. Judith Angell, June 11, 1929 (dec. Mar. 1956); children—Caroline (Mrs. Paul Fordham Nugent, Jr.), Judith (Mrs. James A. Kendall). Admitted to N.Y. bar, 1926, since practiced in Hudson Falls; asso. Rogers & Sawyer, 1926-29; partner Sawyer & Gibson, 1929-36; pvt. practice, 1936-53; dist. atty. Washington County, N.Y., 1936-53; justice Supreme Ct. N.Y. 1953-69, designated appellate div., 1956, presiding justice appellate div., 1964-69; judge et appeals N.Y., Albany, 1969—. Mem. adminstrv. bd. Jud. Conf. State of N.Y. 1964-69. Trustee Albany Law Sch., Union U. Served with AUS, 1943-45; ETO. Mem. Am., N.Y. State (chmn. jud. sect. 1970—, mem. exec com. 1970—), Washington County bar assns. Clubs: Fort Orange, University, Hudson River (Albany); Glens Falls Country; Princeton (N.Y.C.). Home: 93 Pearl St Hudson Falls NY 12839 Office: Ct Appeals Hall Albany NY 12207

GIBSON, JAMES J., educator, psychologist; b. McConnelsville, O., Jan. 27, 1904; s. Thomas Benton and Mary Gertrude (Stanbery) G.; B.S., Princeton, 1925, A.M., 1926, Ph.D., 1928; m. Eleanor Grier Jack, Sept. 17, 1932; children—James Jerome, Jean Grier. Instr. to asso. prof. psychology Smith Coll., 1928-49; research asso. Yale, 1935-36; prof. psychology, Cornell U., Ithaca, N.Y., 1949—, chmn. dept., 1961-64. Vis. prof. U. Cal., Berkeley, 1954- 55; sr. Fulbright research scholar U. Oxford, 1955-56; mem. Inst. Advanced Study, 1958-59; fellow Center for Advanced Study in Social Scis., Stanford, Cal., 1963-64; dir. research unit AAF Aviation Psychology Program, 1942-46. Served from capt. to lt. col. USAAF, 1942-46. Recipient Howard Crosby Warren medal, 1952; NIH Career Devel. award, 1964—. Fellow Am. Psychol. Assn. (Sci. Contbn. award 1961, pres. div. III 1954- 55, pres. div. X 1958-59); mem. Soc. Exptl. Psychologists, Soc. for Psychol. Study Social Issues, Am. Assn. U. Profs., Nat. Acad. Scis., Eastern Psychol. Assn. (pres. 1959-60), Sigma Xi. Author: The Perception of the Visual World, 1950; The Senses Considered as Perceptual Systems, 1966. Editor-author: Motion Picture Testing and Research (Aviation Psychology Research Report 7), 1947. Contbr. articles, revs. to profl. jours. Home: 111 Oak Hill Rd Ithaca NY 14850

GIBSON, JAMES K., physician. Supt., Cambridge (O.) State Hosp. Office: Route 21 N Cambridge OH 43725*

GIBSON, JAMES OLIVER, rural and urban cons.; b. Atlanta, Apr. 1, 1934; s. Calvin Harrison and Julia (Richardson) G.; A.B., Duquesne U., 1956; student U. Atlanta, 1959- 60, Temple U., 1960-61; m. Flora Kathryn DeFrantz, July 18, 1964; 1 dau., Julia Louise; legal guardian Clifford H. Carle, Judith C. Carle, Tanya M. Carle. Reporter columnist Atlanta Inquirer, 1960-61; exec. sec. N.A.A.C.P., Atlanta, 1961-63; program dir. Flanner House, Indpls., 1963- 64; dir. neighborhood devel. program United Planning Orgn., 1964-66; exec. asso. Potomac Inst., Washington, 1966—; cons. in field, 1963—. Bd. dirs. Washington Housing and Planning Assn., Greater Washington chpt. Americans for Democratic Action, New Sch., Afro-Am. Thought, New Thing Art and Architecture Center, Met. Washington Coalation for Clean Air; mem. President's Nat. Adv. Commn. Rural Proverty, 1967-68, Nat. Capital Planning Commn., 1968-69. Served with AUS, 1956-59. Mem. N.A.A.C.P., Nat. Assn. Intergroup Relations Ofcls., Sigma Tau Delta. Contbr. profl. jours. Home: 3462 Macomb St NW Washington DC 20016 Office: 1501 18th St NW Washington DC 20036

GIBSON, JAMES THOMAS, Jr., chem. co. exec.; b. Bessemer, Mich., Nov. 22, 1921; s. James Thomas and Bernice (Roberts) G.; Ph.B., U. Chgo., 1948, J.D., 1952. Admitted to Ill. bar, 1952; practiced in Chgo., 1952-61, Skokie, 1961—; atty. Schradzke, Gould & Ratner, 1953-60; atty., asst. treas., treas. Internat. Minerals and Chem. Corp., 1960—; v.p. asst. sec. Universal Bulk Shipping Corp.; pres. dir. Carnforth Ltd., Bermuda; treas. IMC Corp., Amino Products, Co., Internat. Mineral & Chem. Corp. (Can.), Ltd., IMC Phosphate Terminal Co., Miami Fertilizer Co., Overseas Marine Services, Ltd., Thomson Phosphate Co., Aristo Corp., Frederick A. Stresen-Reuter, Inc.; treas., dir. Consol. Feldspar Corp., Eastern Clay Products, Inc., Internat. Minerals and Chems. (Bahamas), Ltd., MSG Trading Co., Inc.; asst. treas. Internat. Minerals & Chem. S.A.; dir. Coromandel Fertilisers, Ltd., IMC Italia S.p.A.; mem. finance com. Compagnie Senegalaise des Phosphates de Taiba. Served with AUS, 1943-46. Mem. Chgo. Bar Assn. Home: 3 W Burton Pl Chicago IL 60610 Office: 5401 Old Orchard Rd Skokie IL 60076

GIBSON, JERRY LEIGH, med. supply co. exec.; b. El Dorado, Ark., Jan. 24, 1930; s. Oscar Edward and Ruth (Coleman) G.; B.B.A. with honors, N. Tex. State U., 1951; M.B.A., So. Meth. U., 1956; m. Almo Gail Peoples, Apr. 11, 1953; children—Sallie Gail, Gregory Leigh. With Mobil Oil Corp., 1952-59, 60-62, asst. to asst. comptroller, 1961-62; mgmt. cons. Peat, Marwick, Mitchell and Co., C.P.A.'s, 1959; with Standard Oil Co. (N.J.), 1962-66, asst. controller Esso Internat. div., 1965-66; v.p., sec., treas. Riviana Foods Inc., Houston, 1966-69; pres., chief exec. officer Intermedco Inc., Houston, 1969—; tchr. accounting, So. Meth. U., 1956-57. Served with USAF, 1950-52. Mem. Am. Mgmt. Assn. Am. Inst. C.P.A.'s, Financial Execs. Inst. Home: 14223 Kellywood Lane Houston TX 77024 Office: 3322 Richmond Av Houston TX 77006

GIBSON, JOHN WALTER, mfg. co. exec.; b. Huntingtown, Md., Nov. 12, 1926; s. Walter C. and Helen V. (Buckmaster) G.; B.S., Johns Hopkins, 1948, M.S., 1949, Ph.D., 1952; m. Katherine Pauline Simmons, June 11, 1949; children—John Scott, Elizabeth Stewart. With IBM Corp., 1953—, gen. mgr. components div., 1961-63, v.p., group exec. 1963-67, pres. components div., 1967—, corp. v.p., 1968—. Spl. asst. sci. and tech. to Pres. U.S., 1959- 60. Served with USNR, 1944-46. Mem. Sigma Xi, Tau Beta Pi. Club: University (N.Y.C.); Campfire of America (Chappaqua). Home: RD I Box 364 Mount Kisco NY 10549 Office: IBM Corp Armonk NY 10504

GIBSON, JONATHAN CATLETT, lawyer; b. Culpeper, Va., July 26, 1897; s. Edwin H. and Janie A. (Grigg) G.; LL.B., George Washington U., 1923; m. Maude Lucile Allen, Dec. 24, 1929. Examiner, Interstate Commerce Commn., 1923-30; jr. partner Olcott, Holmes, Glass, Paul & Havens and Olcott, Paul & Havens, N.Y. and Wash., 1930-34; gen. atty. Atchison, Topeka and Santa Fe Ry. Co., Chgo., and Los Angeles, 1934-46, gen. solicitor, 1946-47, v.p., gen. counsel, Chgo., 1948-62, v.p. law, Chgo., 1962-67, dir., 1956—; dir. Santa Fe Industries, Inc.; mem. firm Welsh and Gibson, San Diego, 1967—. Served as 2d lt., Va. Inf., Mexican Border Service, 1916-17; capt. 116th Inf., 29th Division, 1917-19. Mem. Am., Cal., San Diego bar assns., Assn. ICC Practitioners. Clubs: Chicago, Olympia Fields Country, Union League, Racquet (Chgo.); Cuyamaca, Rancho Santa Fe Country (San Diego); University, Burning Tree (Washington). Home: PO Box 1272 Rancho Santa Fe CA 92067 Office: 707 Broadway San Diego CA 92101

GIBSON, KENNETH ALLEN, mayor; b. Enterprise, Ala., May 15, 1932; s. Willie Foy and Daisy (Lee) G.; B.S., Newark Coll. Engring., 1960; m. Muriel Cooke, July 1960; children—Cheryl, JoAnn, Engr., N.J. Hwy. Dept., 1950-60; chief engr. Newark Housing Authority, 1960-66; chief structural engr. City of Newark, 1966-70; mayor of Newark, 1970—. Co-chmn. Bus. and Indsl. Coordinating Council. Bd. dirs. Newark Urban Coalition, Newark YM-YWCA. Served with C.E., U.S. Army, 1956-58. Named Jaycee's Man of Year, Newark, 1964. Mem. Am. Soc. C.E., Frontiers Internat. Office: City Hall Broad St Newark NJ

GIBSON, MOSES CARL, educator; b. St. Thomas, Nev., May 31, 1919; s. Robert Orson and Edith Alice (Hinton) G.; B.A., Brigham Young U., 1947, M.A., 1949; Ph.D., U. Ore., 1960; m. Irma Burdette, Dec. 6, 1944; children-Tanya, Randy, Marla, Steven, Brent. Missionary, Ch. of Jesus Christ of Latter Day Saints, Brazil, 1941-43; mem. faculty Brigham Young U., 1949-56, 58—, prof. langs., 1949—, dir. resident program, Madrid, 1961, Mexico City, 1962; mem. faculty U. Ore., 1956-58. Served with USAAF, 1943-45. Mem. Modern Lang. Assn., Am. Assn. Tchrs. Spanish and Portuguese, Rocky Mountain Lang. Assn. Author articles. Mem. Ch. of Jesus Christ of Latter Day Saints (bishop 1958-63, pres. stake 1963—). Home: 410 S 1350 E Provo UT 84601

GIBSON, PATRICK ARMISTEAD, lawyer; b. Richmond, Va., July 7, 1907; s. George Armistead and Alice (McClung) G.; B.A., U. Va., 1928; LL.B., Harvard, 1931; B.A. (Rhodes scholar), U. Oxford, 1933; m. Roxane Frederique Mathieu, Aug. 21, 1939; 1 dau. Clare Meade (Mrs. Jack Lewis Powell). Admitted to Va. bar, 1930; practice in Richmond, 1933—; asso. Page & Leary, 1933-41; spl. asst. to atty. gen. Antitrust div. Dept. Justice, N.Y.C., 1941-43, Washington, 1943-45; asso. Hunton, Williams, Gay, Powell & Gibson, 1945-47, partner, 1948—. Mem. Am., Va., Richmond bar assns., Fed. Power Bar Assn., World Peace Through Law, Nat. Lawyers Club Washington, Phi Beta Kappa. Episcopalian. Clubs: Fishing Bay Yacht (past commodore); Country of Virginia; Bull and Bear. Home: 4 Tappan Rd Richmond VA 23226 Office: PO Box 1535 Richmond VA 23212

GIBSON, RALPH EDWARD, educator, phys. chemist; b. Kings Lynn, Norfolk, Eng., Mar. 30, 1901; s. John and Jane (Ferry) G.; student George Watson's Boys' Coll., Edinburgh, 1914-19; B.S., U. Edinburgh, 1922; Ph.D. (Carnegie Research scholar), 1924; m. Elizabeth Burnham Derby, Apr. 4, 1927; children—John D. Southmayd, Anne K. (Mrs. W. Kumm), Ronald Malcolm Eustace. Came to U.S., 1924, naturalized, 1940. Mem. staff Geophys. Lab., Carnegie Instn. Washington, 1924-46; lectr. in chemistry George Washington U., 1929-39, adj. prof., 1932-45; vice chmn. section H div. 3 NDRC, 1941-44; dir. research Allegany Ballistics Lab., 1944-46; mem. Applied Physics Lab., Johns Hopkins, 1946—, acting dir., 1947-48, dir., 1948- 69, dir. emeritus, 1969—, prof. biomed. engring., 1969—. Recipient Crum Brown chem. medal, 1920, Hope prize in chemistry, 1921, Hillebrand prize Chem. Soc. Washington, 1939, Pres.'s certificate of Merit, 1948; Navy Distinguished Pub. Service award, 1958; Capt. David Dexter Conrad award, 1960; Dept. Def. Distinguished Pub. Service medal, 1969; decorated hon comdr. Most Excellent Order Brit. Empire; Edward Orton Jr. fellow lectr. Am. Ceramic Soc., Fellow Am. Inst. Aeros. and Astronautics; mem. Am. Ordnance Assn., Am. Geophys. Union, Am. Chem. Soc. (chmn. Chem. Soc. Washington 1931, councilor 1932, 33, 35-36, 38-41, chmn. div. phys. and inorganic chemistry 1942-43, councilor 1942-43), Am. Phys. Soc., Washington Acad. Scis. (pres. 1956), Armed Forces Chem. Assn. (v.p. 1953-56), Philos. Soc. Washington (pres. 1940), Sigma Xi (hon.), Sigma Tau (hon.). Episcopalian (organist, choir dir. 1935—). Club: Cosmos (pres. 1956, Washington). Home: 3607 Dunlop St Chevy Chase MD 20015 Office: Applied Physics Lab Johns Hopkins Silver Spring MD 20907

GIBSON, RANKIN MACDOUGAL, lawyer; b. Unionville, Mo., Oct. 9, 1916; s. Alexander R. and Murle L. (Fletcher) G.; student N.E. Mo. State Tchrs. Coll., 1934- 36; LL.B., U. Mo., 1939; B.S. in Law, St. Paul Coll. Law, 1948; LL.M., George Washington U., 1950; m. Eloise M. Corns, Sept. 13, 1941; children—Phillip, Barbara. Admitted to Mo. bar, 1939, Ohio bar, 1954, Supreme Ct. U.S.; gen. practice law, Unionville, 1939-40; atty. T.H. Mastin & Co., St. Louis, 1940-42, VA, Des Moines, St. Paul, Washington, 1945-51; enforcement and litigation atty. Nat. Wage Stblzn. Bd., 1951; asso. prof. law U. Toledo Coll. Law, 1951-56; mem. firm DiSalle, Green, Haddad & Lynch, Toledo, 1956-59; asst. to gov. Ohio, 1959-61; dir. Ohio Dept. Commerce, 1961-62; mem. Pub. Utilities Commn. Ohio, 1962-63; judge Supreme Ct. Ohio, 1963-65; now partner firm Lucas, Prendergast, Albright, Gibson, Brown & Newman, Columbus, O. Tchr. adminstrv. law Franklin U. Sch. Law, 1960. Mem. Nat. Enforcement Commn. Econ. Stblzn. Agy., 1952-53; chmn. labor law round table council Assn. Am. Law Schs., 1952-53; labor arbitrator panels Am. Arbitration Assn., Fed. Mediation and Conciliation Service, Toledo Labor-Mgmt. Citizens Com., 1952-53; rep. Ohio on interstate Coop. Com., chmn. Gov. Ohio Com. Pub. Information, 1959-61; mem. Ohio Water Pollution Bd., Civil War Centennial Commn., Ohio Housing Bd., Ohio rep. on Interstate Oil Compact Commn. and Nat. Rivers and Harbors Congress, 1961-62. Democratic nominee for rep. Mo. Gen. Assembly, 1940. Served to 2d lt. AUS, 1942-45. Mem. Fed. (pres. Columbus chpt. 1967-68), Ohio, Columbus (sec.-treas.) bar assns., Indsl. Relations Research Assn. (pres. central Ohio chpt. 1966-68). Contbr. articles to profl. jours. Home: 2690 Fishinger Rd Columbus OH 43221 Office: 42 E Gay St Columbus OH 43215

GIBSON, RAYMOND EUGENE, clergyman; b. Shelbyville, Ky., Mar. 10, 1924; s. Wallace and Laura Belle (Lee) G.; A.B. in Philosophy and History, Berea Coll., 1944; B.D., Union Theol. Sem., N.Y.C., 1947; Ph.D., Columbia, 1963; m. Susan Cochran, June 29, 1945; children—Cyrus Noel, Mark Scott, Christopher Watt, Laurence Kristin, Jonathan Geoffrey. Ordained to ministry Congl. Ch., 1947; adminstrv. asst. Inst. Religious and Social Studies, N.Y.C., 1947-48; pastor in New Lebanon, N.Y., 1948-49, Pittsfield, Mass., 1950- 61, Center Congl. Ch., Providence, 1961—. Mem. com. evangelism and devotional life R.I. Congl. Conf., 1962-65, dir., 1965—; exec. com. R.I. br. Acad. Religion and Mental Health, 1962. Chmn. R.I. adv. com. U.S. Commn. Civil Rights; mem. mayor's com. to end de facto segregation in Providence pub. schs. Bd. dirs. R.I. Group Health Assn., Inc.; trustee Berea Coll., 1963—. Recipient Howard prize for citizenship Berea Acad., 1941; named Man of Year in Pittsfield Area, 1959; recipient Distinguished Service award Pittsfield Jr. C. of C., 1959; named one of four outstanding young men in state Mass. Jr. C. of C., 1959. Mem. Nat. Acad. Religion and Mental Health, Nat. Geog. Soc., R.I. State Council Churches (dir.). Author: God, Man and Time, 1966. Editor: Conversations with God: The Devotional Journals of Myrtie L. Elmer, 1962. Asso. editor Minister's Quar., 1958—. Home: 283 Wayland Av Providence RI 02906 Office: Central Congl Church Angell and Diman Pl Providence RI 02906

GIBSON, RICHARD CUSHING, educator; b. Cambridge, Mass., Dec. 31, 1919; s. Alec Cushing and Ethel (Howe) G.; S.B., Mass. Inst. Tech., 1942, S.M., 1946, Sc.D., 1953; m. Olive Rae White, May 29, 1942; children—Richard Cushing, Virginia Rae, Anne Christine, Elizabeth Jane. Commd. 2d lt. U.S. Army, 1942, advanced through grades to col. USAF, 1953; radar and communications officer, 1942-45; asst. prof. elec. engring. USAF Inst. Tech., 1946-51; project dir. Air Force Systems Command, 1953-59; prof. astronautics USAF Acad., 1960-65; vice comdr. Nat. Range Div., 1965-67; ret., 1967; prof. elec. engring., head dept. U. Me., Orono, 1967—. Lectr., U. Conn., 1960 -66; mem. USAF Sci. Adv. Bd., 1970—. Decorated Legion of Merit. Mem. A.A.A.S., Am. Soc. Engring. Edn., I.E.E.E., Mass. Inst. Alumni Assn. (regional chmn. 1967—), Sigma Xi, Tau Beta Pi, Phi Kappa Phi. Home: 3 Cedarwood St Orono ME 04473

GIBSON, ROBERT, athlete; b. Omaha, Nov. 9, 1935; ed. Creighton U.; m. Charline Johnson, Apr. 14, 1957. Played with Omaha, 1957-59, Columbus, 1957, Rochester, 1958, 60, St. Louis, 1959—; 35 strikeouts, 1968 season; pitcher St. Louis Cardinals, World Series, 1964, 67. Established record for most strikeouts in World Series, 1964; recipient Gold Glove award as outstanding Nat. League pitcher, 1965-66, 67, 68. Address: care St Louis Cardinals 250 Stadium Plaza St Louis MO 63102

GIBSON, ROBERT DESMOND, univ. dean; b. Utica, Kan., July 2, 1922; s. Carl Alfred and Nina Louise (Workman) G.; B.S., U. Kan., 1948, M.S., 1950; Ph.D., Purdue U., 1954; m. Lois Marie Jamison, Dec. 28, 1947; children—Nancy Kay, Richard Desmond, Gretta Louise. Asst. instr. pharmacy U. Kan., 1948-50, instr., 1950-51; asso. prof., chmn. dept. pharmacology Southwestern State Coll., 1954-57; asso. prof., chmn. dept. pharmacy U. Neb., Lincoln, 1957-61, prof., dean Coll. Pharmacy, 1961—. Research pharmacologist Dorsey Lab., 1959, research cons., 1959-62. Served with USNR, 1942-46, 51-52. Fellow Am. Found. Pharm. Edn., A.A.A.S.; mem. Am., Neb. pharm. assns., N.Y., Neb. acads. scis., Sigma Xi, Phi Lambda Upsilon, Rho Chi. Mem. Christian Ch. Home: 4109 Prescott St Lincoln NB 68506

GIBSON, ROBERT FISHER, bishop; b. Williamsport, Pa., Nov. 22, 1906; s. Robert F. and Harriet (McKenney) G.; A.B., Trinity Coll., Hartford, Conn., 1928; A.M., U. Va., 1932; B.D., Va. Theol. Sem., 1940, D.D., 1948; m. Alison Morice, June 1, 1935; children—Robert Fisher III, John V.M., Margaret Alison, Peter McKenney. Ordained priest Protestant Episcopal Ch., 1940; bus. and teaching positions, P.I., Dutch East Indies, Balt., N.Y.C., 1928-38; asso. prof. church history Va. Theol. Sem., 1940-46; liaison officer P.E. Ch. in Mexico, 1946-49; dean Sch. Theology, U. of South, 1947-49; suffragan bishop P.E. Ch., Diocese of Va., 1949-54, bishop coadjutor, 1954-61, diocesan bishop, 1961—. Chmn. Joint Commn. on Ecumenical Relations. Home: 8737 River Rd Richmond VA 23229 Office: 110 W Franklin St Richmond VA 23220

GIBSON, ROBERT LEE, Jr., food co. exec., b. Anaheim, Cal., Feb. 14, 1919; s. Robert Lee and Dorothy (Morrison) G.; B.S., U. Cal., 1940; M.S., Mass. Inst. Tech., 1955; m. Charlotte Lowe, June 1, 1940; children—Anne, Carol, Robert, Ellen, Thomas. With Libby, McNeill & Libby, 1940-67, v.p., gen. mgr. West Coast div., San Francisco, 1958-62, dir. 1961-67, pres., Chgo., 1962-67; pres. Cal. Canners and Growers Coop., 1967—. Trustee Nutrition Found., Golden Gate Coll., San Francisco. Served as 2d lt., CIC, AUS, World War II. Mem. Soc. Sloan Fellows, Theta Delta Chi. Home: 428 El Centro Rd Hillsborough CA 94010 Office: Ferry Bldg San Francisco CA 94106

GIBSON, ROBERT LESLIE, educator; b. Washington, Feb. 15, 1904; s. Cornelius T. and Frances T. (Carter) G.; A.B., Park Coll., Mo., 1925; m. Margaret Anna Stone, May 26, 1934; children—Charles T., George C. With Gen. Electric Co., 1925—, v.p., gen. mgr. chem., metall. div., Pittsfield, Mass., 1954-59, v.p., gen. mgr. transformer div., 1959-64, v.p., gen. mgr. power distbn. div., 1964-67; faculty bus. adminstrn. Berkshire Community Coll., Pittsfield, 1967—; dir. 1st Agrl. Nat. Bank, Pittsfield, Loctite Corp., Hartford, Conn., Rogers Corp. (Conn.). Trustee Park Coll., Parkville, Mo.; bd. dirs. Berkshire Med. Center; v.p., bd. dirs. United Community Services, Pittsfield; bd. dirs. Boys' Club Pittsfield; bd. mgrs. Lenox (Mass.) Library. Republican. Conglist. Rotarian. Clubs: University (N.Y.C.); Country (Pittsfield). Home: 44 Kenilworth St Pittsfield MA 01201

GIBSON, ROBERT MCKENZIE, food chain exec.; b. Montclair, N.J., Mar. 11, 1916; s. Samuel and Ida (Hornsby) G.; grad. Phillips Acad., 1934; B.A., Yale, 1938; J.D., Harvard, 1941; m. Ruth-Elizabeth Hall, July 22, 1950; children—Diana Hall, Samuel Hornsby. Admitted to N.Y. bar, 1942; pvt. practice law, N.Y.C., 1941-42, Hartford, Conn., 1946-47; atty. United Shoe Machinery Corp., Boston, 1947-53; pvt. law practice Portland, Ore., 1953-55; counsel Sayford Corp., Bklyn. and Litchfield, Conn., 1955-64; atty. Am. Overseas Petroleum Ltd., N.Y.C., 1964-69, Gen. Foods Corp., White Plains, N.Y., 1969-70; v.p., counsel Burger Chef Systems, Inc., Indpls., 1970—. Served to maj. AUS, World War II. Mem. Am. Bar

Assn., Assn. Bar City N.Y. Conglist (trustee). Club: Yale (N.Y.C.). Home: 44 E 73d St Indianapolis IN 46240 Office: 1348 W 16th St Indianapolis IN 46202

GIBSON, ROBERT WALTER, newspaperman; b. Cin., July 21, 1928; s. Robert R. and Ethelyn (Johnson) G.; B.A., Stanford, 1950, M.A. (Melville Jacoby fellow Asian studies), 1956; m. Carol Veronica Brazie, Sept. 25, 1954; children—Christopher, Paula, Valerie. Staff corr. U.P.I., 1950-53, A.P., 1953-57; news editor McGraw-Hill, London, Eng., 1957-58, bur. chief, Moscow, USSR, 1958-60; asst. fgn. editor Bus. Week mag., 1960-63; sr. editorial writer Los Angeles Times, 1963-64, fgn. editor, 1964—. Sr. lectr. U. So. Cal., 1967—, bd. councilors Sch. Politics and Internat. Relations, 1970—. Served with AUS, 1953-55. Mem. Los Angeles Com. Fgn. Relations, Phi Kappa Sigma. Club: Overseas press (N.Y.C.). Home: 4344 Fairlawn Dr La Canada CA 91011 Office: Times Mirror Sq Los Angeles CA 90052

GIBSON, RUSSELL COLE, mfg. co. exec.; b. Elgin, Ill., Aug. 6, 1907; s. William A. and Jessie (Russell) G.; B.S., U. Ill., 1929; m. Irva J. Rankin, Sept. 3, 1930; children—Peter R., Judith G. (Mrs. Louis W. Fisher). With J.L. Clark Mfg. Co., Rockford, Ill., 1938—, dir., 1958, v.p. operations, 1959-64, exec. v.p., 1964-67, pres., chief exec. officer, 1967—; dir. First Nat. Bank & Trust Co., Rockford. Bd. dirs. Rockford United Fund; trustee Rockford Coll., Rockford Community Trust. Mem. Ill. (dir., past v.p.), Rockford (past pres.) chambers commerce, Alpha Kappa Lambda. Conglist. Mason (Shriner), Kiwanian. Club: Rockford Country. Home: 2322 Rock Terrace Rockford IL 61103 Office: 2300 6th St Rockford IL 61101

GIBSON, SAM THOMPSON, physician; b. Covington, Ga., Jan. 1, 1916; s. Count Dillon and Julia (Thompson) G.; B.S. in Chemistry, Ga. Inst. Tech., 1936; M.D., Emory U., 1940; m. Alice Chase, Oct. 31, 1942; children—Gail S., Stephen C., Judith T., Lucy F. Med. house officer Peter Bent Brigham Hosp., Boston, 1940-41, asst. resident medicine, 1946-47, asst. medicine, 1947-49; research fellow medicine Harvard Med. Sch., 1941-42, spl. research asso., 1943, Milton fellow medicine, 1947-49; asso. medicine George Washington U. Med. Sch., also George Washington U. Hosp., 1949-63, asst. clin. prof. medicine, 1963—; asst. med. dir. A.R.C. Blood Program, 1949-50, asso. med. dir., 1950-52, asso. dir., 1952-56, dir., 1956-66; sr. med. officer A.R.C., 1957-67; asst. dir. div. biologics standards NIH, 1967—; cons. blood Naval Med. Sch., Nat. Naval Med. enter, Bethesda, Med., 1950-63; mem. med. adv. bd. CARE- Medico, 1962-70. Chmn. U.S. com. for tranfusion equipment for med. use Am. Standards Assn., 1954-66; adviser orgn. blood transfusion services League Red Cross Socs., 1955-66. Served from lt. (j.g.) to comdr. M.C., USNR, 1941-46; capt. Res. Diplomate Am. Bd. Internal Medicine. Mem. A.M.A., A.A.A.S., Am. Soc. Hematology, Nat. Health Council (dir. 1957-60, 61-64), Internat. Soc. Blood Transfusion (regional counselor 1962-66), Am. Pub. Health Assn., Am. Fedn. Clin. Research, Delta Tau Delta, Alpha Kappa Kapppa, Alpha Chi Sigma, Tau Beta Pi, Phi Kappa Phi, Omicron Delta Kappa, Alpha Omega Alpha. Contbg. editor Vox Sanguines Jour. Blood Transfusion, 1956-65, mem. adv. bd., 1965—. Home: 5801 Rossmore Dr Bethesda, MD 20014. Office: Division of Biologics Standards National Institutes of Health Bethesda MD 20014

GIBSON, THOMAS ESSINGTON, physician; b. Ojai, Cal., Sept. 16, 1896; s. Charles Edson and Anna Jane (Thompson) G.; A.B., U. Cal., Berkeley, 1918, M.D., 1922, M.A., 1923; m. Jeannette Marie Furrer, Aug. 23, 1952. Intern, resident urology U. Cal., Berkeley, 1922-26, asst. clin. prof. urology, 1962-70; practice medicine, specializing in urology, San Francisco, 1926-71; ret., 1971; urologist in chief St. Josephs Hosp., So. Pacific R.R. Hosp., 1932-68; civilian cons. urology U.S. Army Letterman Gen. Hosp., 1945-71. Served with USNRF, World War I. Diplomate Am. Bd. Urology (pres. 1970-71). Fellow A.C.S., A.M.A., Am. Assn. Genito-Urinary Surgeons, Cal. Med. Assn.; mem. Am. Urol. Assn. (pres. Western sect. 1953), Internat. Soc. Urology, Am. Med. Soc. of Vienna, San Francisco County Med. Soc. (hon. life). Clubs: Bohemian (San Francisco); Menlo Country. Contbr. articles profl. jours. Home: 1941 Skycrest Dr Walnut Creek CA 94595

GIBSON, TRUMAN K., Jr., lawyer, corp. exec.; b. Atlanta, Jan. 22, 1912; s. Truman Kella and Alberta (Dickerson) G.; Ph.B., U. Chgo., 1932, J.D., 1935; m. Isabelle Carson, Feb. 9, 1939; 1 dau., Karen Isabelle. Practice of law, Chgo., 1935-40; entered War Dept., as asst. to civilian aide to the sec. of war, 1940-43, acting civilian aide, Feb.-Sept. 1943, civilian aide Sept. 22, 1942-Dec. 19, 1945. In practice of law, Chgo., 1946—; mem. firm Gibson & Gibson; gen. counsel Tuesday Publs., Inc.; dir., mem. exec. com. Supreme Life Ins. Co.; dir. Parkway Hotel Mgmt., Inc. Former mem. sec. Chgo. Land Clearance Commn. Awarded Medal for Merit by Sec. of War Henry L. Stimson, Sept. 1945. Apptd. mem. Pres.' Adv. Com. on Universal Mil. Tng., Dec. 1946; apptd. mem. Pres.' Com. on Morals, Character Devel. and Religion in Armed Services, 1948. Mem. Kappa Alpha Psi, Sigma Pi Phi. Home: 601 E 32d St Chicago IL 60616 Office: 471 E 31st St Chicago IL 60616 and 1840 W Madison St Chicago IL 60603

GIBSON, TRUMAN KELLA, life ins. co. exec.; b. Macon, Ga., Aug. 5, 1882; A.B., Atlanta U.; A.B., Harvard; D.Bus. Adminstrn. (hon.), Central State Coll.; L.H.D., Atlanta U.; m. Alberta Dickerson (dec.); children—Truman Kella, Harry H.C., Alberta Marshall. Organizer Fireside Mut. of Ohio, Supreme Life & Casualty of Ohio; now hon. chmn. bd. Supreme Life Ins. Co. Am., Chgo.; ins. cons. Pres. Moton Meml. Found., Gloucester, Va. Recipient Harmon award. Mem. Chgo. Assn. Commerce and Industry, Sigma Pi Phi, Alpha Phi Alpha. Club: City (Chgo.). Home: 601 E 32d St Chicago IL 60616 Office: 3501 South Pkwy Chicago IL 60655

GIBSON, WELDON BAILEY, research exec.; b. Eldorado, Tex., Apr. 23, 1917; s. Oscar and Susie (Bailey) G.; A.B., Wash. State Coll., 1938; M.B.A., Stanford, 1940, Ph.D.; 1950, m. Helen Mears, Mar. 1, 1941; children—Arthur (dec.), David Mears. Staff asst. Standard Oil Co. Cal., San Francisco, 1939; salesman Burroughs Adding Machine Co., San Francisco, 1940; asst. dir. Air Force Inst. Tech., Dayton, O., 1946-47; dir. economics research, chmn. internat. research Stanford Research Inst., Menlo Park, Cal., 1947-56, asso. dir., 1956-59, v.p., 1950-60, exec. v.p., 1960—; pres. SRI-Internat., 1966—; lectr. Grad. Sch. Bus., Stanford, 1948-53. Cons. Bur. Budget, Nat. Security Resources Bd., 1949-53; co-dir. Internat. Indsl. Conf., 1957—; dir. Pacific Indsl. Conf., 1967, N. Atlantic Indsl. Conf., 1967; exec. com. Pacific Basin Econ. Coop. Council, 1968—. Mem. Soc. Internat. Devel., Am. Econ. Assn., Am. Geog. Assn., Beta Theta Pi, Alpha Kappa Psi. Mason (Shriner). Author: (with assos.) Global Geography, 1944; (with Renner, Durand, White) Economic Geography, 1951, others. Home: 593 Gerona Rd Stanford CA 94305 Office: Stanford Research Inst Menlo Park CA 94025

GIBSON, WILLIAM, author; b. N.Y.C., Nov. 13, 1914; s. George Irving and Florence (Doré) G.; student Coll. City N.Y.; m. Margaret Brenman, Sept. 6, 1940; children—Thomas, Daniel. Author: (play) I Lay in Zion, 1947; (poems) Winter Crook, 1948; (play) Dinny and The Witches, 1950; (novel) The Cobweb, 1954; (play) Two for the Seesaw, 1958; (theatre chronicle) The Seesaw Log, 1958; (play) The Miracle Worker, 1960; (musical) Golden Boy, 1964; (family chronicle) A Mass for the Dead, 1968. Address: Stockbridge MA 01262

GIBSON, WILLIAM WILLARD, lawyer; b. Collin County, Tex., Aug. 15, 1897; s. Isaac Harrison and Florence (Boles) G.; student West Tex. State Coll., 1915-18; LL.B., U. Tex., 1922; m. Genelle Works, May 28, 1925; children—Mary Nell (Mrs. F. Blair Reeves), Joan (Mrs. Mark A. Taylor), William Willard. Admitted to Tex. bar, 1922, since practiced in Amarillo; mem. firm Gibson, Ochsner, Adkins, Harlan & Hankins, and predecessor firms, 1923—. Research fellow Southwestern Legal Found. Fellow Am. Bar Found.; mem. Am. Counsel Assn. (pres. 1957- 59), Internat. Assn. Ins. Counsel, Am., Amarillo (past pres.) bar assns., State Bar Tex. Methodist (trustee, steward). Clubs: Lions (past pres.). Hole-in-One, Knife and Fork (past pres. Amarillo). Home: 2808 Bowie St Amarillo TX 79109 Office: Fisk Bldg Amarillo TX 79101

GIBSON BARBOZA, MARIO, diplomat of Brazil; b. Olinda, Brazil, Mar. 13, 1918; s. Oscar Alves and Evangelina Gibson Barboza; LL.B., Law Sch., Recife, Brazil, 1937; grad. superior war course, Superior War Coll., 1951; m. Yolanda Jordao. Joined Brazil Diplomatic Service, 1940; assigned successively Houston, Washington, Brazil, Buenos Aires and N.Y.C; permanent rep. Brazil to UN; A.E. and P., Vienna, Asuncion; under sec.-gen. fgn. policy, 1967-68, sec. gen., 1968; now ambassador to U.S.; chief and/or mem. numerous Brazilian delegations internat. confs. Decorated grand cross Order Rio Branco, grand officer Order Mil. Merit (Brazil); grand cross Aztec Eagle (Mexico), Order Merit (Chile), Order Merit May (Argentina), Order Merit (Austria), Order Flag (Yugoslavia), Order Merit (Tunisia,) Order Merit (Paraguay); grand officer Order San Martin (Argentina), Order Sun (Peru); comdr. Order Christ (Portugal), Order Hussein Alahouite (Morocco); officer Order Leopold (Belgium). Clubs: Jockey (Brazil); Internat., Metropolitan (Washington). Home: 3000 Massachusetts Av NW Washington DC 20008 Office: 3007 Whitehaven St NW Washington DC 20008

GICOVATE, BERNARD, educator; b. Santos, Brazil, Apr. 21, 1922; s. Jose and Clara Gicovate; came to U.S. 1944, naturalized, 1952; Dr. en Filosofia Letras, U. Buenos Aires, 1943; B.A., Bowdoin Coll., 1945; M.A., U. N.C., 1946; Ph.D., Harvard, 1952; m. Alice Echeverz, July 4, 1944; 1 son, Henry S. Asst. prof. Spanish, U. Ore., 1949-55; prof. Tulane U., 1955-65; prof. Spanish, Stanford, 1965—, also chmn. dept. Spanish and Portuguese. Mem. Modern Lang. Assn., Am. Assn. Tchrs. Spanish and Portugese, Inst. Internat. Literatura Iberoamericano. Author: Julio Herrera y Reissig and the Symbolists, 1957; La poesia de Juan Ramon Jiménez, Asomante, 1959; Conceptos fundamentales de literatura comparada, A somante, 1962; Ensayos sobre poesia Hispánica, 1967; Saint John of the Cross, 1971. Home: 1001 Pine St San Francisco CA 94109

GIDDENS, KENNETH RABB, govt. ofcl., broadcaster; b. Pineapple, Ala., Sept. 10, 1908; s. Lovick Pierce and Addie (Rabb) G.; B.Arch., Ala. Polytech. Inst., 1931; LL.D. (hon.) Westminster Coll., 1970; m. Zelma Kirk, May 19, 1934; children-Zelma Ansley (Mrs. Thomas H. Buce, Jr.), Theresa Elaine (Mrs. Toulmin Greer), Sara Kay. Practice architecture, Mobile, 1931-39; gen. contractor, Mobile, 1939-43; partner Giddens & Rester Radio, Mobile, 1946-52; pres. WKRG-TV (AM-FM-TV), Mobile, 1952-69; partner Giddens & Rester Theaters, Mobile, 1943—; asst. dir. USIA, dir. Voice of Am., 1969—; dir. New Orleans Br. Fed. Res. Bank Atlanta, 1961-67, chmn. 1963- 66; dir. First Nat. Bank Mobile, 1968—, Dahlgren Mfg. Co. Trustee Mobile Infirmary, Am. Jr. Miss Pageant Scholarship Found. Served with USNR, 1943-45. Mem. Nat. (bd. dirs.), Ala. (pres. 1962-62) assns. broadcasters, Sigma Chi, Sigma Delta Chi. Home: 2555 N Delwood Dr Mobile AL Office: Voice of America 330 Independence Av SW Washington DC 20547

GIDDENS, PAUL HENRY, former coll. pres.; b. Bellflower, Mo., Feb. 1, 1903; s. Jackson and Bertha A. (Patterson) G.; A.B., Simpson Coll., 1924, LL.D., 1953; A.M., Harvard, 1926; postgrad. (fellow in history) U. Ia., 1927-28, Ph.D., 1930; Guggenheim fellow, 1945-46; m. Marie Jeanette Robins, Mar. 18, 1927; children—Jackson Alfred, Thomas Robins, Judith Ann. Instr. history U. Kan., 1926; instr. history, govt. La. State Coll., 1926-28; asst. prof. history Ore. State Coll., 1930-31; asst. prof. history and polit. sci. Allegheny Coll., 1931-37, asso. prof., 1937-38, prof., head dept., 1938-53; pres. Hamline U., St. Paul, 1953-68, emeritus, 1968—. Summer session faculties Simpson Coll., Indianola, Ia., 1926, U. Ia., 1929-31, Tchrs. Coll., Terre Haute, Ind., 1933; hist. cons. Standard Oil Co. (Ind.), Chgo., 1968-70; dir. Am. Nat. Bank, St. Paul. Curator, Drake Well Meml. Park, Titusville, Pa., 1943-53; pres. Friends of Pub. Library, 1962- 64, Assn. Minn. Colls., 1960-61. Mem. Am., Mississippi Valley hist. assns., Am. Assn. U. Profs., Newcomen Soc., Alpha Tau Omega, Pi Kappa Delta, Pi Gamma Mu, Phi Alpha Theta. Methodist. Author several books including Standard Oil of Indiana: Oil Pioneer of the Middle West, 1956. Contbr. articles to profl. jours. Home: 258 Jefferson St Meadville PA 16335

GIDDENS, WILLARD A., machinery and equipment mfg. exec; b. Childress, Tex., July 31, 1910; s. Charlie L. and Sallie (Wilson) G.; B. B.A. with honors, U. Tex., 1931; m. Elizabeth Ann McDonnel, Dec. 23, 1932; children—Warren W., Jean Anne (Mrs. A.J. Cass, Jr.), Paul J. Engaged as pub. accountant, San Antonio, Corpus Christi, Tex., 1931-34; spl. agt. FBI, 1934-42; asst. controller Oil Well Supply Co., subsidiary U.S. Steel Corp., Cleve., 1943-47; sr. v.p., treas., dir., chmn. finance com., mem. exec. com. Hupp Corp. (merged into White Consol. Industries 1967), 1947-67, v.p. finance, treas. White Consol. Industries, 1967—; v.p., treas. Kelvinator, Inc.; dir. Blaw Knox Co., Hupp Inc., Bullard Co., Hupp Credit Corp. C.P.A. Mem. Am. Inst. Accountants, Financial Execs. Inst., Beta Alpha Psi. Clubs: Treasurers, Cleveland Athletic, Canterbury Golf. Home: 2557 Fairmount Blvd Cleveland Heights OH 44106 Office: 11770 Berea Rd Cleveland OH 44111

GIDDINGS, HORACE ALPHEUS, educator; b. Chocorua, N.H., Jan. 16, 1902; s. Robert A. and Sarah (Webster) G.; B.S., U. N.H., 1923; Ph.D., Mass. Inst. Tech., 1934; m. Marion Bonyman, Sept. 13, 1924; 1 son, Horace A. Instr. mathematics U. Vt., 1924-30, Mass. Inst. Tech., 1930-36; asst. prof. math. Ill. Inst. Tech., 1936-42; asso. prof. math. U. N.H., 1942-49; prof., chmn. dept. math. N.Y. U. Engring. Coll., 1949-59; dir. N.Y. U. Grad. Center, Bell Telephone Labs., Murray Hill, N.J., 1959-66, prof. math. N.Y. U., 1966—. Mem. Am. Math. Soc., Am. Soc. Engring. Edn. (gen. council 1959-61), N.H. Acad. Scis., Alpha Chi Sigma, Phi Kappa Phi, Alpha Sigma Phi. Home: Laurel Ridge Tuxedo Park NY 10987 Office: Math Dept NY U University Heights New York City NY 10453

GIDDINGS, SPOFFORD, utility exec.; b. 1905; B.S., U. Me., 1926; married. With Central Me. Power Co., Augusta, 1928—, mgr. no. div., 1946-62, v.p., mgr. div. operations, 1962-66, exec. v.p., 1966—, also dir. Office: 9 Green St Augusta ME 04330*

GIDEON, FRANCIS CLARE, air force officer; b. Payne, O., Feb. 18, 1917; s. Glenn G. and Floy (Lyon) G.; student Miami U., Oxford, O., 1934-36; B.S., U.S. Mil. Acad., 1940; grad. Air War Coll., 1952, Advanced Mgmt. Program, Harvard, 1960; m. Josephine West, Jan. 19, 1942; children—Francis Clare, Anna Huntington, William, Glenn. Commd. 2d lt. AUS, 1940, advanced through grades to maj. gen. USAF, 1961; combat pilot 5th Air Force, S.W. Pacific, also dir. operations Far East Air Forces, World War II; mem. air staff War Dept. Gen. Staff, also mem. strategic plans staff Joint Chiefs Staff, 1946-51; dir. operations Mil. Air Transp. Service, 1952- 54; comdr. 1607th Air Transp. Wing, 1954-58; civil engr., dir. transp., also dir. data systems Air Force Logistics Command, 1958-62; dir. logistics services Def. Supply Agy., 1962-64, dep. dir. agy., 1964-66; comdr. Warner Robins Air Materiel Area, 1966-68; comdr. 13th Air Force, Clark Air Base, P.I., 1968—. Decorated Distinguished Service medal, Legion of Merit, Bronze Star medal. Presbyn. (ruling elder). Home: Quarters 2050 APO San Francisco CA 96274 Office: Hdqrs 13th Air Force (C) APO San Francisco CA 96274

GIDEON, MIRIAM, composer; b. Greeley, Colo., Oct. 23, 1906; d. Abram and Henrietta (Shoninger) Gideon; B.A., Boston U., 1926; M.A., Columbia, 1946; D.Sacred Music, Jewish Theol. Sem., 1970; m. Frederic Ewen, 1949. Music faculty Bklyn. Coll., 1944-54, Coll. City N.Y., 1947-55, Cantors Inst., Jewish Theol. Sem., 1955—, Manhattan Sch. Music, N.Y.C., 1967—. Works performed in Europe, U.S. and S.Am. by Internat. Soc. Contemporary Music, League Composers, London, Tokyo, Zurich symphony orchs. Recipient Bloch prize for choral work, 1948; Nat. Fedn. Music Clubs and A.S.C.A.P. award for symphonic music, 1968. Mem. Am. Composers Alliance (bd. govs.), Internat. Soc. Contemporary Music (gov.). Composer: Fortunato (opera); Symphonia Brevis, Lyric Piece for Strings; String Quartet; Wood-wind Quartet; Viola Sonata; chamber settings of Hound of Heaven, Shakespeare Sonnets, Millay Sonnets; Biblical Masks; Cello Sonata; Songs of Voyage; The Condemned Playground; Questions on Nature; The Habitable Earth (cantata); Spiritual Madrigals; Rhymes from the Hill; Seasons of Time; Sacred Service. Orchestral, chamber, choral works recorded Westminster, Paradox, Composers Recs., Inc., RCA Victor Records, Desto Records. Home: 410 Central Park W New York City NY 10025

GIDEONSE, HARRY DAVID, univ. chancellor; b. Rotterdam, Netherlands, May 17, 1901; s. Martin Cornelius and Johanna Jacoba Helena Magdalena (de Lange) G.; came to U.S., 1904; B.S., Columbia, 1923, M.A., 1924; Diplomé des Hautes Etudes Internationales, U. Geneva, 1928; LL.D. Bklyn. Law Sch., St. Lawrence U., 1943, Western Res. U., 1946, Columbia, 1954, Lake Forest U., 1962; L.H.D., Hebrew Union Coll., 1953, U. Hawaii, 1955, Bklyn. Coll., 1966; Litt.D., L.I. U., 1966, Denison U., 1967; m. Edmee Koch, June 15, 1926; children—Hendrick, Martin. Chem. research Eastman Kodak Co., 1919-21; lectr. econs. Barnard, Columbia, 1924-26; dir. internat. students' work, Geneva, Switzerland, 1926-28; asst. prof. econs. Rutgers U., 1928-30; asso. prof. econs. U. Chgo., 1930-38; prof. econs. Columbia, chmn. dept. econs. and sociology Barnard Coll., 1938-39; pres. Bklyn. Coll., U. N.Y., 1939-66; chancellor New Sch. Social Research, N.Y.C., 1966—. Mem. exec. com. Chgo. Council Fgn. Relations, 1936; mem. N.Y. Council Fgn. Relations; exec. v.p. Economist's Nat. Com. on Monetary Policy, 1937- 46; pres. U. Chgo. chpt. Am. Assn. U. Profs., 1936-38; chmn. youth div. com. Nat. Social Welfare Assembly, 1946-48; mem. Nat. Commn. Ednl., Sci. and Cultural Co-operation, 1946; chmn. Commn. of Inquiry into Forced Labor, 1948-50. Bd. dirs. Woodrow Wilson Found.; chmn. bd. dirs. Freedom House, 1942—. Decorated King Christian X Order of Liberation (Denmark); knight comdr. Order of Orange-Nassau (Netherlands); chevalier Legion of Honor (France). Mem. Am. Econ. Assn., Phi Beta Kappa, Kappa Delta Pi. Author: Transfert des Reparations et Plan Dawes, 1928; The International Bank, 1930; The Higher Learning in a Democracy, 1937; The Economic Foreign Policy of the United States, 1953; Against the Running Tide, 1967. Editor Pub. Policy Pamphlets (U. Chgo.), 1932-42. Office: 66 W 12th St New York City NY 10011

GIDEONSE, MAX, educator; b. Rotterdam, Netherlands, Apr. 24, 1904; s. Martin Cornelius and Johanna Jacoba Helena Magdalena (DeLange) G.; came to U.S., 1904; A.B., U. Rochester, 1925, A.M., 1926; Ph.D., Harvard, 1932; m. Isabel Edmond Alexander, Aug. 19, 1931; children—Hendrik Alexander, Louise Baird. Amherst Meml. fellow, 1929-30; asst. prof. Rutgers U., 1930-40, asso. prof., 1940-45, prof. econs., 1945-69, chmn. dept. econs., acting dir. Bur. Econ. Research, 1950-60; vis. prof. econs. Rider Coll., 1969-71. With U.S. Dept. State, 1943-46; asst. chief and adviser Office Spl. Polit. Affairs, 1945-46, sec. Econ. and Social Com., UN San Francisco Conf., 1945. Impartial arbitrator N.J. Mediation Service. Mem. Am. Econ. Assn., Acad. Polit. Sci., Econ. History Assn., Alpha Delta Phi. Contbr. articles to profl. jours. Home: 15 Cliff Ct Highland Park NJ 08904 Office: Rutgers U New Brunswick NJ 08903

GIDNEY, DEAN ROBERT, chem. mfg. exec.; b. Washington, Sept. 15, 1915; s. Ray M. and Jean (Brock) G.; A.B., Dartmouth, 1936; M.B.A., N.Y. U., 1940; m. Olive Milbrandt, July 28, 1941. With U.S. Trust Co., 1936-37; v.p., sales mgr. U.S. Potash Co., 1937, v.p., gen. mgr., dir. U.S. Borax & Chem. Corp., 1956-59; v.p. sales Potash Co. Am. div. Ideal Basic Industries, Inc., N.Y.C., 1960—. Served as lt. comdr. USNR, 1941-46. Mem. Phi Beta Kappa. Clubs: St. Andrews Golf; Bridgehampton; Shinnecock Hills Golf. Home: 40 Fifth Av New York City NY 10011 Office: 630 Fifth Av New York City NY 10020

GIDNEY, RAY MILLARD, banker; b. Santa Barbara, Cal., Jan. 17, 1887; s. Charles Montville and Clara Maude (Jones) G.; B.S., U. Cal., 1912, LL.D., 1962; LL.D., Western Res. U., 1953, Rutgers, 1961; m. Jean Ellison Brock, Sept. 6, 1913 (dec.); children—James Brock, Dean Robert, John Archibald; m. 2d, Rose Haworth Tenney, June 5, 1965. Clk., Comml. Bank Santa Barbara, 1903-08, First Nat. Bank Bakersfield, Cal., 1912- 14; sec. to mem., dep. settling agt., Fed. Res. examiner Fed. Res. Bd., Washington, 1914-17; asst. to Fed. Res. agt., asst. Fed. Res. agt., mgr. Buffalo br. controller-at-large Fed. Res. Bank N.Y., 1917-23, controller-at-large, controller loans, asst. dep. gov., dep. gov., asst. Fed. Res. agt., v.p., 1924-44; v.p., dir. Citizens Trust Co., Buffalo, 1923; v.p. Marine Trust Co., Buffalo, 1923-24; pres. Fed. Res. Bank Cleve., 1944-53; comptroller currency Treasury Dept., 1953-61; chmn. bd. Fla. Nat. Bank of Jacksonville, 1962—. Former pres. Robert Morris Assn.; treas. Cleve. Community Fund, 1947-51, pres., 1952. Recipient Alexander Hamilton award U.S. Treasury Dept., 1961. Mem. Phi Beta Kappa, Phi Beta Kappa Assos. Rotarian. Clubs: Rowfant (Cleve.); Cosmos, Burning Tree, University, Capitol Hill (Washington); Florida Yacht, San Jose Country, River, Seminole, University (all Jacksonville). Home: 3946 St Johns Av Jacksonville FL 32205 Office: Fla Nat Bank of Jacksonville West Bay Annex Jacksonville FL 32203

GIDWITZ, GERALD, business exec.; b. Memphis, 1906; grad. U. Chgo., 1927; married; 5 children. Chmn. bd., chmn. exec. com., chief exec. officer Helene Curtis Industries, Inc.; chmn. bd., pres., chief exec. officer Continental Materials Corp.; vice chmn. bd. Consol. Packaging Corp.; pres. Eurovest. Trustee Highland Park Hosp. Found., Roosevelt U. Home: 970 Sheridan Rd Highland Park IL 60035 Office: 4401 W North Av Chicago IL 60639

GIDWITZ, JOSEPH LEON, paper box co. exec.; b. Memphis, Jan. 16, 1905; s. Jacob and Rose (Wolff) G.; Ph.B., U. Chgo., 1928; m. Emily Rose Klein, Sept. 11, 1930; children—Alan Klein, Ralph Wolff, Betsy Rose. With Lanzit Corrugated Box Co., Chgo., 1928-63, v.p.,

1941-48, pres., 1948-63, merged into Consol. Paper Co., 1963; dir. John Strange Paper Co., Menasha, Wis., 1945—, v.p., 1945-55, pres., 1955-56, chmn. bd., 1956—; pres., dir. Crandon Paper Mills, Inc., Chgo., 1957-63, merged into Consol. Paper Co., 1963; chmn., dir. Consol. Paper Co. (now named Consol. Packaging Co.), Monroe, Mich., 1963—, pres., 1964-68; mem. exec. com. Helene Curtis Industries; vice chmn. bd. Continental Materials, Inc.; trustee Federated Mortgage Investors; dir. Harmony Co. Mem. industry labor adv. com. WPB, 1944-45; founder Container Indsl. Conf., chmn., dir., 1948-53. Chmn., Jewish Fedn.-Central Coordinating and Planning Orgn., 1970—; del. White House Conf. on Aging, 1971. Bd. dirs. Jewish Children's Bur., Chgo., 1934-52, pres., 1949-52; pres., bd. dirs. Div. Fund Chgo., 1943-67; bd. dirs. Jewish Fedn. Chgo., 1952-67, pres., 1962-64; chmn. Jewish Fedn.-Gerontological Council, 1968-70; bd. dirs. Combined Jewish Appeal Chgo., 1959-65, v.p., 1962-64; bd. dirs. Council Jewish Fedns. and Welfare funds N.Y., 1963-67, v.p., 1964-67; trustee Cancer Research Found., U. Chgo., 1956-66; adv. council U. Mo. Sch. Forestry, 1959-64. Recipient Julius Rosenwald Meml. award, 1969. Mem. Fibre Box Assn., Chgo. Council on Fgn. Relations (Chgo. com. 1967—), A.I.M. (pres. council), N.A.M., Ill. C. of C., Chgo. Assn. Commerce and Industry, Nat. Paperboard Assn. (dir.). Jewish religion. Clubs: Harmonie (N.Y.C.); Standard (Chgo.). Home: 175 E Delaware Pl Chicago IL 60611 Office: 72 W Adams St Chicago IL 60603

GIEBEL, AGNES, soprano; b. Heerlen, 1921; ed. Folkwang Acad. Music, Essen; m. Herbert Kanders; 1 son, 2 daus. First concert appearances, 1940; weekly broadcasts Radio RIAS, Berlin, 1950; concerts in Rome, Berlin, London, Paris, Vienna, Zürich, others, 1950—; appearance at many festivals. Address: 5 Klolin-Lindenthal Bachemer Strasse 84 Federal Republic of Germany*

GIEGERICH, CARL RICHARD, advt. exec.; b. N.Y.C., May 4, 1910; s. Charles Joseph and Catherine Dolores (Wolf) G.; B.S., Lehigh U., 1932; m. Elizabeth Eckerson, Apr. 18, 1936; children—Gail, Lynn, Jill. Salesman Johns Manville, 1932-34; copywriter Newell-Emmett Co. (became Cunningham & Walsh), 1934-41, 1948, v.p., 1949, dir., 1950—, sr. v.p., 1950—, creative head agy., 1956—, chmn. exec. com., 1958—, chmn. plans bd., 1961—; pres., dir. Jack Wyatt Co., Dallas, N.Y.C., 1963—; account exec., writer, v.p. Cecil & Presbey, 1946-48; v.p. spl. projects, chmn. creative review bd. Fuller & Smith & Ross, Inc. 1963-65, exec. v.p. 1965—. Served from 2d lt. to maj., USAAF, 1941-46, chief programs and promotions Army Information Service. Mem. Am. Assn. Advt. Agencies, Alpha Tau Omega, Pi Delta Epsilon, Alpha Kappa Psi, Omicron Delta Kappa, Scabbard and Blade. Clubs: Mount Kisco (N.Y.) Country; Wings (N.Y.C.); Yacht (St. Thomas, V.I.). Home: Tower Rd Brookfield Center CT 06805 Office: 666 Fifth Av New York City NY 10019

GIELGUD, SIR ARTHUR JOHN, actor, dir.; b. London, Eng., Apr. 14, 1904; s. Frank and Kate (Terry-Lewis) G.; student Hillside Godalming, 1913-18, Westminster Sch., 1918-20, Royal Acad., 1922-23; LL.D., U. St. Andrews, 1950; Litt.D., Oxford, 1953; studied Lady Benson, 1920-21. Appeared in Hamlet, 1929, 30, 34, 36, 37, 39, 44, Richard II, 1929, 38; appeared as Hotspur in Henry IV, 1930; Macbeth, 1929, 42; Mark Anthony in Julius Caesar, 1929; achieved 1st London triumph as Lewis Dodd in The Constant Nymph, 1926; Malvolio in Twelfth Night, 1930; The Good Companions, 1930, movie of latter play, 1931; Musical Chairs, 1931; Richard of Bordeaux, 1932; School for Scandal, 1938; appeared as Shylock in The Merchant of Venice, 1938 (Queen's Theatre), Dear Octopus, 1939; The Importance of Being Earnest, 1939-40, 47; The Duchess of Malfi, 1944; dir. Lady Windermere's Fan, 1946; played in movies including The Prime Minister, Secret Agent, Diary for Timothy (documentary); established repertory theatre in London, 1938 and again during World War II; appeared in Love For Love during war in Eng. and in Am., 1947. Played in Crime and Punishment, Medea (Am.), 1947-48, The Return of the Prodigal, Nov. 1948. Producer, The Glass Menagerie, starring Helen Hayes, 1948; Medea, Aug. 1948; The Heiress, Feb. 1949; Stratford-on-Avon Festival played in Measure for Measure, Julius Caesar, Much Ado About Nothing, King Lear, 1950; played in Winters Tale, 1950; dir. Much Ado About Nothing, 1952; in M.G.M. film Julius Caesar, 1952; dir., actor A Day By the Sea, 1953; dir. The Cherry Orchard, 1954; appeared in Much Ado About Nothing, King Lear, with Stratford-on-Avon Co. on tour, in London, 1955; dir., actor Sebastian, Nude with a Violin, 1956; Prospero in The Tempest, 1957; Cardinal Wolsey in Henry VIII; Broadway recital Ages of Man, 1959; dir., actor Much Ado About Nothing, N.Y.C., Boston, 1959; appeared as Julian in Tiny Alice, N.Y.C., 1964-65. Recipient Antoinette Perry award Ages of Man, 1958; producer Britten's A Midsummer Nights Dream, Royal Opera House, Convent, London, 1961; dir. Big Fish Little Fish, N.Y.C. (Tony award), 1961; dir. Dazzling Prospect, 1961, Sch. for Scandal, Haymarket, 1962; played Othello, Stratford-on-Avon, 1961, Gaer in Cherry Orchard, Stratford-on-Avon, 1961, Aldwych, London, 1962; dir., actor Joseph Surface in Sch. for Scandal, U.S., 1963, Ages of Man, Lyceum Theater, N.Y.C., 1963, Australia, New Zealand, 1963-64, Finland, Scandinavia, Poland, USSR, 1964, U.S.A., Eng., 1965-66; dir. Hamlet, Can., Boston, N.Y.C., 1964; film The Loved One, 1964, Chimes at Midnight, 1966, Mister Sebastian, 1967, The Charge of the Light Brigade, 1967; played in Tartuffe, Oedipus, Nat. Theatre, 1967-68, in films Shoes of the Fisherman, Oh! What a Lovely War, 1967-68, Eagle in a Cage, 1969; dir. Halfway Up a Tree; appeared in Forty Years On, London stage, 1968, Battle of Shrivings, 1969-70, Home, 1970, N.Y.C., 1971. Mem. Ch. of Eng. Club: Players (N.Y.C.). Author: Early Stages (autobiography), 1938; Stage Directions, 1964. Home: 16 Cowley St SW1 London England Office: care Internat Famous Agy 11-12 Hanover St London W1 England

GIELOW, FREDERICK CHRISTOPHER, lawyer; b. Detroit, Apr. 30, 1902; s. Frederick C. and Auguste (Kolodsick) G.; A.B., U. Mich., 1922, J.D., 1924; m. Ruth Canfield, Feb. 2, 1928 (dec. 1964); children—James Canfield, Frederick Christopher. Admitted to Mich. bar, 1924; partner firm Lewis & Watkins, Detroit, 1936-67, Dahlberg, Mallender & Gawme, Detroit, 1967—. Mem. Am., Mich., Detroit bar assns. Home: 14140 Abington Rd Detroit MI 48227 Office: Ford Bldg Detroit MI 48226

GIES, THOMAS GEORGE, educator; b. Detroit, Jan. 12, 1921; s. Charles G. and Jane E. (Sturman) G.; A.B., U. Mich., 1946, M.A., 1948, Ph.D., 1952; m. Thelma Irene Young, Sept. 6, 1941; children—Laurie Hollis, Thomas Michael, Joseph Christopher. Instr. econs. U. Mich., 1948-51; financial economist Fed. Res. Bank Kansas City, Mo., 1951-57; lectr. econs. U. Colo., 1955, 57, 70; lectr. finance U. Kansas City (Mo.), 1956-57; faculty U. Mich., Ann Arbor, 1957—, prof. finance, 1960—. Lectr. Netherlands Sch. Econs., 1964; cons. in field, 1957—; dir. Huron Valley Nat. Bank, Ann Arbor Chmn., Gov. Mich. Com. Revision Financial Code, 1964-65; mem. Gov. Mich. Com. Econ. Growth, 1959-60, 61-62; vice chmn. Gov. Mich. Council Financial Advisers, 1965-69. Served with USAAF, 1941-46. Mem. Am. Econ. Assn., Midwest (pres. 1971-72), Am. finance assns., Phi Kappa Phi. Author: Consumer Installment Credit, 1957; Portfolio Policies and Regulations of Private Financial Institutions, 1962; Consumer Finance Companies in Michigan, 1960; Public Utility Regulations: New Directions in Theory and Policy, 1966; Legislating for Economic Expansion, 1970; Banking Markets and Financial Institutions, 197l. Contbr. articles to profl. jours. Home: 2980 Devonshire Rd Ann Arbor MI 48104

GIESE, HENRY, agrl. engring. educator; b. Danville, Ia., Dec. 23, 1890; s. George Frederic and Ella Elvira (Catlin) G.; B.S. in Archtl. Engring., Ia. State Coll., 1919, M.S. in Agrl. Engring., 1927, Archtl. Engr., 1930; m. Dollie Frances Kelly, June 7, 1913; children—Barbara Ruth (Mrs. Douglas F. Graves), William Henry, Mary Joan (Mrs. James F. Herber). Instr., Howe's Acad., Mount Pleasant, Ia., 1911-12; dir. manual tng. Ames (Ia.) Pub. Schs., 1912-16; tng. of manual tng. tchrs. Ia. State Coll., summers, 1914-18, in charge, 1917- 18; with engring. extension service Ia. State Coll., 1916-19; with U.S. Vets. Bur., 1919-22; instr in engring. math. Ia. State Coll., 1923; with agrl. engring. dept. Ia. State U., 1923—, on leave to direct Farm Structures Research Survey for U.S. Dept. Agr. (sr. engr.), 1929-30. Served with U.S. Army, 1918. Recipient Cyrus Hall McCormick gold medal for exceptional and meritorious engr. achievement in agr., 1947; faculty citation Ia. State Coll. Alumni Assn., 1957, Merit award, 1958. Registered profl. engr. Mem. Fire Prevention Edn. Com. of President Truman's Conf. on Fire Prevention. Fellow Ia. Acad. Sci., Am. Soc. Agrl. Engrs. (life); mem. Nat. Assn. Mut. Ins. Cos. (hon.), Ia. Engring. Soc., Sigma Xi, Phi Kappa Phi, Tau Beta Pi, Gamma Sigma Delta, Phi Mu Alpha, Pi Kappa Phi. Republican. Presbyn. (elder). Mason (32, Shriner). Author: 200 books, fed. and state bulletins, tech. and popular jour. articles, latest book being: Of Mutuals and Men. Home: 3507 Oakland St Ames IA 50010 Office: Iowa State U Agrl Engring Dept Ames IA 50010

GIESECKE, GUSTAV ERNST, educator: b. Marble Falls, Tex., Sept. 13, 1908; s. Walter C. and Ulrika (Matern) G.; A.B., Stanford, 1931, A.M., 1934, Ph.D., 1938; LL.D., U. Toledo, 1962; m. Louise Helene Bittner, Sept. 17, 1943; children—Mark, Helene. Teaching asst. German, Stanford, 1932-37; instr. and asso. in German, counselor student personnel bur., U. Ill., 1937-42, supr. counseling in residence halls, 1946, asst. dean liberal arts sch., asst. prof. German, 1946, asst. dean Galesburg (Ill.) undergrad. div., asst. prof. German, 1946-49; dean sch. applied arts and scis. N.D. State U., Fargo, 1949-53; v.p. Tex. Tech. Coll., Lubbock, 1953-59; prof. higher edn., asso. dean Grad. Sch. Edn., U. Chgo., 1959-65; univ. prof., provost U. Toledo, 1965-70; prof. humanities, acting v.p. acad. affairs Sangamon State U., Springfield, Ill., 1970—; founder N.D. Inst. for Regional Studies, 1950, exec. sec., 1950-53, dir. summer session, 1950-53. Mem. Southwest adv. com. Inst. Internat. Edn., 1958-59; mem. visitation and appraisal com. Nat. Council Accreditation Tchr. Edn., 1963-66; cons., examiner N. Central Assn. Colls. and Secondary Schs., 1960—; chmn., dir. Midwest Fulbright Terminal Conf., 1964. Chmn. Mayor's com. on the Young Citizen and the Ballot, 1956-58; mem. Tex. adv. com. conservation edn., 1956-59; chmn. Lubbock Internat. Affairs Cóm., 1954-59; mem. research adv. com. Tex. Commn. Higher Edn., 1956-59; chmn. Mental Health Week in Lubbock, 1958. Trustee Toledo Ednl. Television Found., 1967-70. Served as lt. USNR, 1942-46. Fellow Inst. Internat. Edn., Germany, 1931-32. Mem. Am. Ednl. Research Assn. (mem. com. 1967—), W. Tex. C. of C. (bd. dirs. 1957-58). Made study tour, guest Fed. German Republic, 1958. Author: N.D. Inst. for Regional Studies, Fargo, 1952. Contbr. articles to profl. publs. Home: 1628 Dennison Dr Springfield IL 62704

GIESECKE, RAYMOND HENRY, elec. mfg. co. exec.; b. Chgo., 1906; s. Henry F. and Emma G.; B.S., U. Ill., 1927; m. Marie Walther Keese, Apr. 24, 1937; children—John, Nancy (Mrs. Stuart Greene), Sally (Mrs. William Giese). With Arthur Andersen & Co., 1927-49; with McGraw-Edison Co., Elgin, Ill., 1949—, treas., 1956—, asst. to pres., 1956-60, exec. v.p., 1960-67, pres., 1967—. Past pres. P.T.A.; chmn. Council Profit Sharing Industries. Trustee Elmhurst Coll., Bensenville Home. C.P.A., Ill. Mem. Delta Chi, Beta Gamma Sigma, Beta Alpha Psi. Clubs: Dunham Woods Riding; Fin and Feather; St. Charles Country; University (Chgo.); Executives. Home: Wayne IL 60184 Office: 333 W River Rd Elgin IL 60120

GIESEN, RICHARD ALLYN, pub. co. exec.; b. Evanston, Ill., Oct. 7, 1929; s. Elmer J. and Ethyl (Lillig) G.; B.S., Northwestern U., 1951; m. Jeannine St. Bernard, Jan. 31, 1953; children—Richard Allyn, Laurie J., Mark S. Research analyst new bus. and research depts. Glore, Forgan & Co., Chgo., 1951-57; asst. to pres. Gen. Dynamics Corp., N.Y.C., 1957-60, asst. treas., 1960-61, asst. v.p. operations and contracts, 1961-63; financial cons. IBM Corp., 1963, exec. asst. to sr. v.p. 1964-65; treas. subsidiary Sci. Research Assos., Inc., Chgo., 1965-66, v.p. finance and adminstrn., 1966-67, exec. v.p., chief operating officer, 1967-68, pres., chief exec. officer, 1968—, also dir.; dir. Sci. Research Assos. (Can.), Ltd., Sci. Research Assos., Ltd. (U.K.), Sci. Research Assos. (Pty.), Ltd. (Australia). Bd. dirs. Am. Ednl. Pubs. Inst., N.Y.C. Mem. bus. adv. council Chgo. Urban League. Mem. Investment Analysts Soc. Chgo., Alpha Tau Omega, Beta Gamma Sigma. Clubs: Chicago, University (N.Y.C.). Home: 126 Hazel Av Glencoe IL 60022 Office: 259 E Erie St Chicago IL 60611

GIESLER, HERBERT CARL, mfg. co. exec.; b. N.Y.C., Nov. 9, 1921; s. Wilhelm and Anna (Knupfer) G.; B.B.A., Pace Coll., 1951; m. Edna Reighling, Sept. 25, 1943; 1 dau., Jean. Asst. treas. Knapp Mills, N.Y.C., 1946-47; sr. accountant Price Waterhouse & Co., C.P.A.'s, N.Y.C., 1947-51; chief accountant Landers, Frary and Clark Corp., New Britain, Conn., 1951-56; mgr. budgetary control Mergenthaler-Linotype Co., N.Y.C., 1956-59; with Curtiss-Wright Corp., 1959-70, exec. dir. finance, controller 1966-70, also subsidiaries; v.p. finance Diversified Industries, Inc., St. Louis, 1970—; Mem. Financial Execs. Inst., Aerospace Industries Assn. Author articles. Office 7701 Forsyth Blvd Clayton MO 63105

GIETZ, ARNOLD W., banker; b. Toronto, Ont., Can., Nov. 14, 1919; s. Lewis Ernest and Florence (Bell) G.; B.A., U. Rochester, 1947; M.B.A., U. Mich., 1948; m. Elizabeth Jean Heise, Dec. 24, 1942; children—William A., Clifford A. Vice pres. Nat. Bank Detroit, 1948-63; exec. v.p. Elgin Nat. Watch Co., 1963-65; sr. v.p. 1st Western Bank and Trust Co., Los Angeles, 1965-68; pres., dir. Beverly Hills Nat. Bank (Cal.), 1970—; exec. v.p., dir. Beverly Hills Bancorp., 1970—. Home: 2400 Palos Verdes Dr W Palos Verdes Estates CA 90274

GIFFIN, JAMES FRANCIS, univ. dean; b. nr. Casey, Ill., Feb. 2, 1919; s. George Erson and Elsie (Beck) G.; B.S., Eastern Ill. U., 1946; M.C.S., Ind. U. 1947; Ph.D., Northwestern U., 1953; m. June Eloise Bubeck, Aug. 29, 1948; children—Jon William, Gina Sue. Instr., Eastern Ill. U., Charleston, 1947-49, asst. prof., 1949-53, asso. prof., 1953-59, prof., head dept., 1959-62, dean Sch. Bus., 1962—. Drive chmn. Eastern Coles United Fund, 1968, bd. dirs., 1967-69, pres., 1968-69. Served to lt. (j.g.) USNR, 1941-46. Mem. Am. Econ. Assn., Acad. Mgmt., N.E.A., Ill., Nat. Bus. edn. assns., Am. Vocational Assn., Charleston C. of C. (past pres., dir.). Methodist (pres. bd.). Home: 1800 10th St Charleston IL 61920

GIFFORD, ALLAN THURSTON, coll. adminstr.; b. Fall River, Mass., Sept. 6, 1906; s. Frank J. and Gertrude (Piercy) G.; S.B., Mass. Inst. Tech., 1927, S.M., 1946; m. Harriett Holmes, Oct. 11, 1934; children—Rachel (Mrs. Willard E. Spearin), Constance (Mrs. Warren R. Jones), Susan Torrey (Mrs. Kenneth T. Alcorn). Field engr. Met. Dist. Water Supply Commn., Enfield, Mass., 1927-28, office engr., Hardwick, Mass., 1928-31, asst. to resident engr., 1931-34, concrete technician, Ware, Mass., 1934-35; asso. san. engr. TVA, Norris, Tenn., 1935-37; instr. civil engring. Mass. Inst. Tech., 1937-40, asst. prof. hydraulic engring., 1940-44, asso. prof., 1944-53; asst. chief operations div. Richland (Wash.) Operations Office, AEC, 1953-56, dir. prodn. div., 1956-66; prof., head dept. civil engring. Lowell (Mass.) Technol. Inst., 1966-68, chmn. div. engring. sci., 1968—; cons. City of Lowell; weather forecasting research USAAF, 1942-44. Dir. Garden Hose Spray Co. Treas. Columbia Basin Girl Scout Council Richland, 1958-65, mem. finance com. Merrimack River Council, 1967—. Fellow Am. Soc. C.E.; mem. Boston Soc. C.E., New Eng. Water Works Assn., Am. Geophys. Union, Am. Soc. for Engring. Edn., Chi Epsilon, Tau Beta Pi. Home: 69 Amble Rd Chelmsford MA 01824 Office: 1 Textile Av Lowell MA 01854

GIFFORD, CHESTER GLEN, business exec.; b. Pierre, S.D., Apr. 23, 1906; s. Ebenezer Franklin and Ethel (Myers) G.; student U. S.D., 1924-25, U. Cal. at Los Angeles, 1925-27, U. Cal., 1934; m. Loretta O'Connell, Dec. 20, 1939; 1 dau., Patricia Josephine. Sales mgr. McGraw Electric Co., 1936-40; v.p., dir. Swank, Inc., 1948-50; regional sales mgr. Schick, Inc., 1940-48, exec. v.p., 1950-52, pres., dir., 1952-54; pres. Crosley div., v.p. Avco Mfg. Corp., 1954-58; chmn. bd., dir. Schick, Inc., Lancaster, Pa., 1958-60; pres., dir. Simoniz Co., Chgo., 1960-65; chmn. bd., chief exec. officer Schick Electric, Inc., Lancaster, 1965-68; v.p. passenger div. Matson Nav. Co., San Francisco, 1968—. Served with Signal Corps, AUS, 1943-45; ETO. Mem. Beta Theta Pi. Home: 1221 W Coast Hwy Newport Beach CA 92660 Office: 100 Mission St San Francisco CA 94105

GIFFORD, CLARENCE HAMILTON, Jr., banker; b. Elizabethtown, Ky., Mar. 6, 1913; s. Clarence Hamilton and Vera Lee (Bailey) G.; B.A., Brown U., 1936; m. Priscilla Marshall Kilvert, Oct. 29, 1937; children—Kilvert Dun, John Francis, Charles Kilvert, Priscilla Marshall. Treas. C. H. Gifford & Co., Inc., N.Y.C., 1936-42; with G. H. Walker & Co., investments, Providence, 1946-48; v.p. Phenix Nat. Bank, Providence, 1948-53; v.p. Rhode Island Hosp. Trust Co., Providence, 1953-63, pres., 1963—, also dir.; dir. Allen & Reed Co., Almacs, Inc., Blackstone Mut. Ins. Co., Cherry & Webb Co., Fall River Stas., Inc., Fram Corp., Gifford Enterprises (N.Y.), Kilburn Glass Industries, Inc., Osceola Operating Corp., Pacific Nat. Bank (Nantucket, Mass.), Roger Williams Savs. and Loan Assn., Stamps, Inc., Title Guarantee Co. R.I. Clubs: Agawam Hunt, Brown, Hope (Providence); Nantucket Yacht (past commodore), Sankaty Head Golf (Nantucket); Ocean Reef Yacht (N. Key Largo, Fla.). Home: 5 Charles Field St Providence RI 02906 Office: 15 Westminster St Providence RI 02903

GIFFORD, DON CREIGHTON, educator; b. Schenectady, Feb. 27, 1919; s. Henry R.L. and Edna (North) G.; B.A., Principia Coll., Elsah, Ill., 1940; student Harvard, 1940-42; m. Honora Kammerer, Oct. 5, 1963; children by previous marriage—Marin Gifford (Mrs. David O. Haythe), Nina. Instr. English, Mills Coll. Edn., 1947-51, Williams Coll., 1951-58; cons. Arthur D. Little, Cambridge, Mass., 1958-59; prof. English, Williams Coll., 1959—. Mem. Am. Field Service, 1942-44; served with AUS, 1944-46. Democrat. Author: The Literature of Architecture, 1966; Notes for Joyce, 1967. Home: Bryant St Williamstown MA 01267

GIFFORD, HAROLD, Jr., physician, educator; b. Omaha, 1906; M.D., U. Neb., 1931. Intern, Passavant Meml. Hosp., Chgo., 1931-32; intern Mass. Eye and Ear Infirmary, Boston, 1932-34, spl. resident, 1932-34; trainee Northwestern U., Chgo., 1935; practice medicine, specializing in ophthalmology, Omaha, 1936—; mem. staff Neb. Methodist Episcopal Hosp., Deaconess Home, U. Neb. Hosp., prof. ophthalmology U. Neb., Omaha, also chmn. dept. Diplomate Am. Bd. Opthalmology. Mem. A.M.A., Am. Assn. Ophthalmologists and Otolaryngologists, Am. Ophthal. Soc. Office: Coll Medicine U Neb Omaha NB 68102

GIFFORD, HARRY C. F., physician. Exec. v.p., dir. Springfield (Mass.) Med. Center. Office: 759 Chestnut St Springfield MA 01107*

GIFFORD, JOHN ARCHER, lawyer; b. Newark, Dec. 6, 1900: s. Charles Alling and Helen (Conyngham) G.; grad. Hill Sch., Pottstown, Pa., 1918; B.A., Yale, 1922; LL.B., Harvard, 1925; m. Barbara Prosser, June 20, 1928; 1 son, Prosser. Admitted to N.Y. bar, 1926, since practiced in N.Y.C.; partner firm White & Case, 1937—; trustee N.Y. Bank Savs. Hon. dir. Commonwealth Fund; trustee, sec. Presbyn. Hosp., N.Y.C. Served to lt. comdr. USNR, 1943-45. Mem. Am., N.Y. State bar assns., Bar Assn. City N.Y. Home: 117 E 72d St New York City NY 10021 Office: 14 Wall St New York City NY 10005

GIFFORD, PORTER WILLIAM, mfr. constrn. materials; b. Dallas, Dec. 14, 1918; s. Porter William and Evelyn Victoria (Bonorden) G.; B.S. in Mech. Engring., Cornell U., 1941; m. Elizabeth Butte, Jan. 19, 1946; children—Porter William III, Sharon (Mrs. Richard P. Chandler), Geoffrey Butte. With Gifford-Hill & Co., Inc., Dallas, 1948—, pres., 1958-59, chmn. bd., 1969—; pres. Gifco Properties, Inc., 1969—; dir. First Nat. Bank Dallas, Graniterock Co., Watsonville, Ca., Coastal Plains, Inc., Dallas. Mem. Dallas Citizens Council. Bd. dirs. Dallas County unit Am. Cancer Soc.; trustee Found. Econ. Edn.; trustee, chmn. bd. devel. Bishop Coll. Served to maj. AUS, 1941-45. Decorated Bronze Star. Mem. Nat. Sand and Gravel Assn. (dir., treas., mem. exec. com.), Tex. Aggregates Assn. (pres. 1967-68), Dallas Salesmanship Club, Tau Beta Pi, Delta Kappa Epsilon. Club: Northwood Country (Dallas). Home: 9107 Devonshire Dr Dallas TX 75209 Office: 2949 Stemmons Freeway PO Box 47127 Dallas TX 75247

GIFFORD, PROSSER, coll. dean; b. N.Y.C., May 16, 1929; s. John Archer and Barbara (Prosser) G.; B.A., Yale, 1951, Ph.D., 1964; B.A., Oxford (Eng.) U., 1953, M.A., 1958; LL.B., Harvard, 1956; M.A., Amherst Coll., 1969; m. Shirley Mireille O'Sullivan, June 26, 1954; children—Barbara, Paula, Heidi. Admitted to D.C. bar, 1957; asst. to pres. Swarthmore Coll., 1956-58; asst. prof. history Yale, 1964-66; dir. 5 yr. B.A. program, 1965-66; dean faculty Amherst Coll. , 1967—, asso. prof. history, 1967-69, prof. history, 1969—. Trustee Hotchkiss Sch. Rhodes scholar, 1951-53; Fgn. Area fellow No. Rhodesia, 1963-64. Clubs: Century; Elizabethan (Yale); Woods Hole (Mass.) Yacht. Co-editor, contbr.: Britain and Germany in Africa, 1967. Home: 97 Spring St Amherst MA 01002

GIFFORD, STACEY HARRY, food co. exec.; b. Alberdeen, S.D., Mar. 27, 1902; s. H.W. and May (Van Epps) G.; LL.B., St. Paul Coll. Law, 1924; m. Marian Drisko, Aug. 12, 1925. Admitted to Minn. bar, 1924, Ill. bar, 1925; asso. firm Orr Stark & Kidder, St. Paul, 1924; house atty. Reid, Murdock and Co., Chgo., 1924- 38, asst. sec., counsel, 1938-45, sec., gen. counsel, 1945-46; asst. sec. Consol. Grocers Corp., 1946-52; sec. Consol. Foods Corp., 1953-67, v.p., 1955-67, dir., 1963—; cons. and atty., 1967—; dir. Kitchens of Sara Lee, Inc., Kitchens of Sara Lee (Can.) Ltd., Bak-Kraft Corp., Cardinal Food Stores, Inc., Coastal Foods, Inc., Golden Dairy Co., Happy Baker Products, Inc., Lawson Milk Co., Monarch Finer Foods, Inc., Ocoma Foods Co., River Grove Warehouse Corp., U.S.P. Corp., Van Wagenberg- Festens NV (Holland). Chmn. wholesale grocers group

A.R.C. campaigns, 1947, 49. Bd. dirs. Nathan Cummings Consol. Foods Scholarship Fund, Inc.; bd. dirs., charter mem. Agribusiness Council, N.Y.C. Mem. Ill., Chgo. bar assns., Food Law Inst., Ill. Mfrs. Assn., U.S. C. of C., Nat. Wholesale Grocers Assn., Chgo. Assn. Commerce and Industry, Nat. Canners Assn., Food-Law Inst. Mem. United Ch. Christ. Mason. Clubs: Attic, Chicago Athletic (Chgo.); Pistakee Yacht (Commodore) (McHenry, Ill.). Editor Consol. Foods Monthly Mgmt. News Letter. Home: 940 Beaver Lane Glenview IL 60025 Office: 135 S LaSalle St Chicago IL 60603

GIGLIO, WILLIAM PETER, pub. co. exec.; b. Tampa, Fla., Apr. 11, 1929; s. William T. and Carrie (Lopez) G.; B.A. in Govt., George Washington U., 1953; m. Sept. 21, 1952 (div.); children—Dionne, William James. Dir. travel dept. Aircraft Owners and Pilots Assn., Washington, 1955-57; with Nat. Bus. Publs., Washington, 1957-64, mng. dir., 1963-64; exec. v.p. Am. Bus. Press. Inc., 1964-66; dir. pub. services McGraw-Hill Publs., N.Y.C., 1966-68, dir. pub. affairs, 1968-70, v.p. adminstrn., 1970—. Publicity chmn. Waynewood Citizens Assn., Alexandria, Va., 1963-64. Served with USMCR, 1953-55. Mem. Assn. Indsl. Advertisers, Pi Delta Epsilon, Omicron Delta Kappa, Sigma Alpha Epsilon. Club: National Communications (Washington). Home: 26 Remsen St Brooklyn Heights NY 11212 Office: 330 W 42d St New York City NY 10036

GIGLIOTTI, FRANK BRUNO, clergyman; b. Italy, Oct. 15, 1896; s. Carmen and Mary (Guzzo-Pane) G.; came to U.S., 1900; student Bibl. Sem., N.Y.C.; postgrad., U. Rome, 1925-28; D.D., S.T.D., Monet-Mario Coll., Rome, 1928; Dr. Humanities, Palmer Coll. Chiropractic, 1945; m. Mabelle Esther Pirazzini, 1922; children—Agide Pirazzini, Mary, John David. Licensed minister Presbyn. Ch., 1914, ordained, 1921; pastor Italian Presbyn. Ch., Schenectady, 1921-24, Terry (Mont.) Community Presbyn. Ch., 1928-30, First Presbyn. Ch., Baker, Ore., 1930-33; moderator Presbytery of Yellowstone, 1929-30, of Grande-Ronde, 1930-33; pastor counselor for Ore., Soc. Christian Endeavor, 1930-32; hon. retired ministry, 1933; chaplain Cal. Assembly, 1934-35. Mem. Cal. Bd. Social Welfare; chief cons. Italian sect. OSS, 1941-45; chmn. com. social welfare and relief Tax Reduction Conf., 1936; mem. Cal. Relief Commn., 1937-39; chmn. San Diego County com. Governor's Com. Employment Handicapped, 1953-56; pres. San Diego County Taxpayers Assn., 1953-55, 59, 62; chmn. Cal. Citizens Com. Morality and Integrity in Govt., 1958; pres. San Diego Race Relations Soc., 1958-63, San Diego County Better Govt. League, 1950-53; chmn. delegation from Italy to nat. conv. Am. Legion, 1926, alternate delegate St. Louis, 1935, sec. Paris conv., 1927; sec. Am. Com. Italian Relief and Italian Democracy, 1943-45; mem. commn. religious and civil rights. Nat. Assn. Evangelical Chs. U.S.; del. Internat. Assn. Evangelicals, 1950; del. Italy for study rehab. and relief Italian Protestant Chs., 1947; active community orgns., vets. orgns., organizer Am. Legion in Italy, 1925 (dept. commdr.'s medal 1927); nat. comdr. Regular Vets. Assn. U.S. 1951-52; pres. Calif. Civic Fedn., 1938-39; nat. Adv. Rehab. Council, U.S. Office Rehab., 1941-46; chmn. Gov.'s Adv. Vets. Com., 1959-62; mem. Gov.'s Com. Children and Youth, 1960-64. Del. Mont. Republican Conv., 1928. Served with U.S. Army World War I; AEF. Decorated Croix de Guerre with palm (France); recipient Alfaro medal Alfaro Found., 1950; Knight comdr. Order Merit Republic Italy, 1970 Knight comdr. Mil. Order St. Mary of Bethlehem, 1970; gold medal City and Region Trieste, 1970. Mem. Nat. Assn. Italian Vets. (hon. life, Roma Gold medal 1927), Men's Republican League San Diego (pres. 1958-61), Sons Columbus (hon. nat. pres.). Life mem. Internat. Supreme Council, Order of DeMolay, 1959; Mason (33; hon. grad master for life Grand Orient of Italy; mem. emeritus Supreme Council, Scottish Rite of Italy; recipient nine gold medals for work done in Italy for Masonry also silver medal 1970 (life mem. Nat. Grand Orient of Italy). Author: Religious Liberty in Italy. Home: 3785 Gigliotti Dr Lemon Grove CA 92045

GIGNOUX, EDWARD THAXTER, U.S. dist. judge; b. Portland, Me., June 28, 1916; s. Frederick Evelyn and Katherine (Denison) G.; A.B. cum laude, Harvard, 1937, LL.B. magna cum laude, 1940; LL.D., Bowdoin Coll., 1962, U. Me., 1966; m. Hildegarde Schuyler Thaxter, June 30, 1938; children—Marie Andrée (Mrs. James F. Grisé), Edward Thaxter. Admitted to D.C. bar, 1941, Me. bar, 1946; asso. Slee, O'Brian, Hellings & Ulsh, Buffalo, 1940-41, Covington, Burling, Rublee, Acheson & Shorb, Washington, 1941-42; partner Verrill, Dana, Walker, Philbrick & Whitehouse, Portland, 1946-57; U.S. dist. judge, Portland, 1957—. Former corporator Me. Savs. Bank; council mem. Harvard Law School; past mem. adv. panel internat. law U.S. State Dept. Asst. corp. counsel City of Portland, 1947- 48, mem. city council, 1949-55, chmn., 1952. Pres., bd. dirs. Greater Portland Community Chest, 1955-56, United Fund, 1956-57; corporator, trustee Me. Med. Center; trustee Me. Eye and Ear Infirmary, Portland Symphony Orch., Portland Pub. Library. Served as maj. AUS, 1942-46. Decorated Bronze Star, Legion of Merit. Mem. Am. com. on jud. adminstrn., other coms.), Me., Cumberland County bar assns., Inst. Jud. Adminstrn., Jud. Conf. U.S., Am. Judicature Soc., Am. Law Inst. (council). Episcopalian. Rotarian. Clubs: Harvard (pres. Me. 1957 Boston, N.Y.C.); Portland Country Editor Harvard Law Rev., 1939-40 (now overseer). Home: Starboard Lane Cumberland Foreside Portland ME 04110 Office: 156 Federal St Portland ME 04112

GIKOW, RUTH, artist; b. Ukraine; d. Boris and Lena (Pohoriles) Gikow; came to U.S., 1922, naturalized, 1928; student Cooper Union Art Sch., 1932-35; m. Jack Levine, Oct. 4, 1946; 1 dau., Susanna. One-man shows Weyhe Gallery, 1946, Grand Central Moderns, 1948, 50, Ganso Gallery, 1952, 53, 54, Rehn Gallery, 1956-58, Nordness Gallery, 1961, Forum Gallery, 1967, 70; group shows at Whitney Gallery, Corcoran Gallery, Washington, others; represented in permanent collections Colby Coll., Springfield Mus., Nat. Acad. Arts and Letters, Brandeis U., Nat. Gallery Fine Arts, Smithsonian Instn., Whitney Mus.; print collections Met. Mus. Art, Mus. Modern Art, Phila. Art Mus., others. Former tchr. New Sch. Social Research. Illustrator: Crime and Punishment, History of Jews in America. Author: Ruth Gikow-Paintings, Prints and Drawings, 1970. Nat. Inst. Arts and Letters grantee, 1959. Address: 231 W 11th St New York City NY 10014

GIL, FEDERICO GUILLERMO, educator; b. Havana, Cuba, Feb. 10, 1915; s. Adolfe J. and Elena (Izquierdo) G.; LL.D., U. Havana, 1940, Dr. Polit. and Social Sci., 1941, licentiate diplomatic and consular law, 1942. Came to U.S., 1942, naturalized, 1951. Instr. polit. sci. La. State U., 1942-44; instr. U.N.C., 1943-45, asst. prof., 1945-49, asso. prof., 1949-55, prof., 1955-66, Kenan Prof. polit. sci., 1966—; via. lectr. Duke, summer 1944; vis. prof. Middlebury Coll., summer 1947; dir. Inst. Latin Am. Studies. Trustee Latin Am. Scholarship program Am. Univs. Hon. prof. U. Chiles decorated Order Bernardo O'Higgins (Chile); Rockefeller Found. fellow, 1944-45, 55-57, 63; Ford Found. fellow, 1958. Mem. Nat. Acad. Law and Social Scis. Argentina, Am. So. polit. sci. assns., Latin Am. Studies Assn., (pres. 1971), Latin Am. Assn. Sociology, Southeastern Conf. Latin Am. Studies (pres. 1962), Order Golden Fleece, Delta Psi. Democrat. Roman Catholic. Author: Governments of Latin America, 1957; The Political System of Chile, 1966; Instituciones y desarrollo político de América Latina, 1966; El sistema político de Chile, 1969; Latin American-United States Relations, 1971. Contbg. author anthologies. Contbr. articles profl. jours. Home: 5 Mount Bolus Rd Chapel Hill NC 27514

GIL, FRANCISCO ANDRES, Jr., U.S. dist. atty.; b. Aibonito, P.R., Nov. 30, 1910; s. Francisco Andres and Antonia (Rivera) G.; B.A. in Econs., U. P.R., 1934; LL.B., U. Richmond (Va.), 1941; m. Nilda Rivera, June 3, 1944; children—Carmen Nilda, Francisco Andres III, Maria Victoria. Admitted to P.R. bar; with legal div. VA, San Juan, 1945-50; atty. Dept. of Labor, 1950-55; adjudicator VA, San Juan, 1955-56; asst. U.S. dist. atty. P.R., 1955-58, dist. atty., 1958—. Served with AUS, World War II. Mem. Am., Fed., Va. bar assns., Am. Soc. Pub. Adminstrn., Navy League, Colegio de Abogados de P.R. Elk. Club: Villa Caparra (P.R.). Home: 37 J St Villa Caparra PR 00922 Office: Box 2856 San Juan PR 00903

GILBANE, JEAN ANN, (Mrs. Thomas F.), constrn. co. exec.; b. Providence, Aug. 22, 1923; d. Vincent Thaddeus and Edna (Leary) Murphy; student Elmhurst Acad., 1941, Coll. New Rochelle, 1945; m. Thomas F. Gilbane, Sept. 12, 1946; children—Thomas, Robert, Richard, Jean, John, James. Sec. Gilbane Bldg. Co., Providence, 1950—. Active Boy Scouts Am.; corresponding sec. Butler Hosp., Providence, R.I., 1969—. Catholic. Home: 151 Grotto Av Providence RI 02906 Office: 90 Calverly St Providence RI 02908

GILBANE, THOMAS FREEMAN, bldg. co. exec.; b. Providence, Nov. 4, 1911; s. William Henry and Frances Virginia (Freeman) G.; Ph.B., Brown U., 1933, M.A., 1958; m. Jean Ann Murphy, Sept. 12, 1946; children—Thomas Freeman, Robert V., Richard T., Jean Marie, John D., James. Sec. Gilbane Bldg. Co., Providence, 1933, supt., 1933-36, pres., treas., 1939—; treas. B.T. Equipment Co., Providence, 1943—; pres. Calverley Realty Co., Providence, 1953—. Varsity football coach Westminster Coll., 1935; head coach freshman football Brown U., 1936-40. Bd. dirs. R.I. Community Chest, Inc.; trustee Brown U. Mem. Asso. Gen. Contractors R.I. (past pres.). Roman Catholic, Knight of Malta, Knight of Holy Sepulchre. Clubs: University, Turks Head, Engineers, Brown University (past pres.). Home: 151 Grotto Av Providence RI 02906 Office: 90 Calverley St Providence RI 02904

GILBARG, DAVID, educator; b. Bklyn., Sept. 17, 1918; s. Simon and Bella (Kaufmann) G.; B.S., City Coll. N.Y., 1938; Ph.D., Ind. U., 1941; m. Shirley Deskin, Oct. 19, 1941; 1 son, Daniel. Physicist, Nat. Bur. Standards, 1941-42; physicist Naval Ordnance Lab., 1942-46, head theoretical mechanics subdiv., 1945-46; faculty Ind. U., 1946-57, asso. prof. math., 1950-57; faculty Stanford, 1957—, prof. math., 1957—, head dept., 1959—; spl. research partial differential equations, theoretical fluid dynamics. Served as ensign USNR, 1944-45. Mem. Am. Math. Soc., Math. Assn. of Am., Soc. Applied Math. and Mechanics (Germany), Am. Assn. U. Profs. Editor Pacific Jour. Math., 1958-60; editorial bd. Jour. Math. and Mechanics, 1952—. Home: 209 Creekside Dr Palo Alto CA 94306 Office: Mathematics Dept Stanford U Stanford CA 94305

GILBART, ARTHUR WILLIAM, business exec.; b. Bklyn., Aug. 18, 1914; s. Arthur W. and Helen (Folk) G.; B.S., Mass. Inst. Tech., 1935; M.B.A., Harvard, 1937; m. Stella Chung, June 12, 1948. Security analyst Equitable Life Assurance Soc. U.S., N.Y.C., 1937-42, asst. mgr. indsl. securities, 1946-51, 2d v.p., 1953-56, v.p., 1956-57; spl. asst. to pres. Freeport Sulphur Co., N.Y.C., 1951-53, 57-58, asst. to chmn. bd., 1958-61, v.p., 1961—. Served from 2d lt. to maj. USAAF, 1942-46. Mem. N.Y. Soc. Security Analysts, Theta Delta Chi. Clubs: Harvard, Wings. Home: 114 Llewellyn Dr New Canaan CT 06840 Office: 161 E 42d St New York City NY 10017

GILBAUGH, JOHN WESLEY, educator; b. Fort Morgan, Colo., July 23, 1918; s. Newell Ivan and Celia Loraine (Bay) G.; B.S., Kan. State Coll., Pittsburg, 1947, M.S., 1948; postgrad. U. Colo., summers 1948-50; Ed.D., U. Kan., 1953; m. Doris Faye Wilder, Dec. 31, 1941; children—Bruce Lee, Susan, Jane Ellen, Nancy, Carol. Elementary sch. tchr.-prin., Mound Valley, Kan., 1940-42, Manhattan, Kan., 1947-48; supt. schs., Winona, Kan., 1948-50, Humboldt, Kan., 1950-53; asst. prof. edn. Kan. State U., Manhattan, 1954-56; asso. prof. edn. San Jose (Cal.) State Coll., 1956-59, prof. edn., asst. to pres., 1959-60, dean coll., 1959-66, prof. edn., 1966—. Newspaper columnist, inventor. Served with AUS, 1942-46. Mem. N.E.A., Nat. Writers Club, Cal. Tchrs. Assn. Mason. Author: (novel) The Bull with Golden Horns, 1958; The School Board Policy Guide, 1956; A Plea for Sanity in the Public Colleges and Universities, 1966. Contbr. articles to profl. jours. Editor: Social Studies and Science Resource Units for Grades Kindergarten through Eight (9 pamphlets), 1955-58. Home: 19396 Monte Vista Dr Saratoga CA 95070

GILBERT, ALBERT M., lawyer; b. N.Y.C., 1907; A.B., Coll. City N.Y., 1926; J.D., Columbia, 1929. Admitted to N.Y. bar, 1929; mem. firm Davis, Gilbert, Levine and Schwartz, N.Y.C. Mem. Assn. Bar City N.Y., Am., Inter-Am., N.Y. State bar assns. Office: 500 Fifth Av New York City NY 10036*

GILBERT, ALLAN H., educator; b. Rushford, N.Y., Mar. 18, 1888; s. Eddy Clifton and Helen Josephine (White) G.; A.B., Cornell U., 1909, Ph.D., 1912; A.M., Yale, 1910; m. Katharine Everett, Aug. 1, 1913 (dec. 1952); children—Everett Eddy, Creighton Eddy; m. 2d, Mary Moss Wellborn, 1953. Instr. English, Cornell U., 1912-19, Rice Inst., 1919-20; prof. English, U. Tenn., 1920-21; prof. English, Duke U., 1921-57, emeritus, 1957—; vis. prof. lit. Drew U., 1963—; lectr. U. Florence, 1948; Fulbright research fellow in Italy. 1955- 56; vis. lectr. Wayne U., 1957, U. Pa., 1959-60; Arensberg vis. prof. U. So. Cal., 1958; vis. prof. U. Ore., 1958-59, Wayne State U., 1960; Berg prof. N.Y. U., 1961; adj. prof. English lit. Columbia U., 1962-63; prof. English lit. City U. N.Y., 1962-63. Decorated Cavaliere dell' Ordine al Merito della (Italy). Fellow Southeastern Mediaeval and Renaissance Inst. (sr.); mem. Milton Soc. Am., Modern Lang. Assn. Am. (v.p. 1955-56), Am. Assn. Tchrs. Italian (v.p. 1957-58), South Eastern Renaissance Soc. (pres. 1956), Dante Soc. (council asso.), Modern Humanities Research Assn., S. Atlantic Modern Lang. Assn. (pres. 1946-47), Phi Beta Kappa, Erasmus. Author: A Geographical Dictionary of Milton, 1919; Dante's Conception of Justice, 1925; Machiavelli's Prince and Its Forerunners, 1938; Historical and Mythological Characters in Ben Jonson's Masques, 1947; On the Composition of Paradise Lost, 1947. Translator and editor: John Milton's Ars Logica, 1935; Literary Criticism from Plato to Dryden, 1940; Machiavelli, The Prince and Other Works, 1941; Translation of Ariosto's Orlando Furioso, 1954; The Principles and Practice of Criticism: Othello, The Merry Wives of Windsor, Hamlet, 1959; Machiavelli, The Prince, 1959; Machiavelli's Familiar Letters, 1960; Dante and His Comedy, 1963; Machiavelli, Works Translated (3 vols.), 1964; Dante's Inferno, a New Translation, 1968. Editor Renaissance Studies, 1954-56. Editorial bd. Rivista di letterature moderne e comparate. Contbr. to profl. jours. Home: 69 W 9th St New York City NY 10011 (summer) 503 Compton Pl Durham NC 27701

GILBERT, BEN WILLIAM, editor; b. N.Y.C., Feb. 10, 1918; s. Harry and Tessie (Goldberg) G.; B.S.S., Coll. City N.Y., 1937; A.M., U. Mo., 1939; m. Maurine Coffee, Mar. 11, 1941; children—Ian Richard, Amy Jean Mann. Grad. asst. journalism U. Mo., 1938-39, city hall reporter St. Louis Star-Times, 1940-41, asst. Washington corr., 1941; reporter Washington Post, 1941-45, city editor, 1945-64, dep. mng. editor, 1964-69, asso. editor, 1969-70; editor newsroom WETA-TV, Washington, 1970—. Lectr. journalism Am. U., 1950-51; John H. Finley lectr. Coll. City N.Y., 1959; mass media lectr. Seminar in Am. Studies, Salzburg, Austria, 1963. Del., Press Congress of World, Columbia, Mo., 1959. Information specialist Nat. War Labor Bd., 1942. Recipient Emmy award for program and editor Washington chpt. Television Soc. Arts and Scis., 1970. Mem. Phi Beta Kappa, Kappa Tau Alpha. Author, editor: Ten Blocks from the White House, the Anatomy of the Washington Riots of 1968 (Silver Gavel award Am. Bar Assn. 1969). Home: 4537 Grant Rd NW Washington DC 20016 Office: 2600 4th St NW Washington DC 20001

GILBERT, BERNARD L., corp. exec.; b. N.Y.C., 1909; ed. Columbia, also Coll. City N.Y.; LL.B., Harvard, 1934. Vice pres., sec., gen. counsel, dir. Diana Stores Corp.; sec., mem. mgmt. bd. com. Diana Profit Sharing Fund. Home: 201 E 79th St New York City NY 10021 Office: 7801 Tonneville Av North Bergen NJ 07047*

GILBERT, CASS, Jr., architect; b. St. Paul, May 10, 1894; s. Cass and Julia (Finch) G.; grad. Hill Sch., 1913; grad. Yale, 1918; postgrad. Columbia; m. Elizabeth Jarres Wyeth, Dec. 1917; children—Jarvis, Francis (Mrs. John S. Nichols), Cass III, Farnham, Steve Goodrich; m. 2d, Louise Guion, Nov. 1941. Partner, Office of Cass Gilbert, N.Y.C., 1920-36, owner, 1936- -; dir., sr. asso. Theodore J. Richters & Assoc., cons. engrs., Teaneck, N.J., 1942—. Served to 2d lt., arty., U.S. Army, 1917-18; AEF in France. Decorated grand cross Legion of Honor (France). Fellow N.A.D. Mem. Soc. of Cin. Republican. Christian Scientist. Mason. Club: Yale (N.Y.C.). Prin. works include: W.Va. State Capitol, U.S. Ct. House, N.Y.C., U.S. Supreme Ct., Washington, U.S. legation, Ottawa, Ont., Can., Detroit Pub. Libary. Home: Old Sleepy Hollow Rd Pleasantville NY 10570 Office: 342 Madison Av New York City NY 10017

GILBERT, CHARLES, fgn. service officer; b. Bklyn., June 23, 1907; s. Adolph and Bertha (Gelber) G.; certificate in fgn. trade N.Y. U., 1928; m. Mercedes Peypoch de la Riva, Mar. 28, 1945; 1 dau., Mercedes Isabel. Office staff, later export mgr. Chgo. Rawhide Mfg. Co., N.Y.C., 1928-30; pres. Bertgil Corp., N.Y.C., 1940-45. Joined U.S. Fgn. Service, 1930; assigned Asuncion, Paraguay, Rio de Janeiro, St. Jean de Luz, France, Madrid, Valencia and Barcelona, Spain, temporary assignments, Marseille, France, Le Havre, St. Jean de Luz, France, also Seville, San Sebastian and Madrid, Spain, 1930-41; vice counsul, attache, Madrid, 1941-45, sec. embassy, 1945; vice counsul, Amsterdam, 1945, Rotterdam, 1945-48; 2d sec., vice counsul embassy, Belgrade, 1948; counsul Am. consulate Zagreb, Yugoslavia, 1948-50; fgn. affairs officer, mgmt. specialist Dept. State, Washington, 1950-53; 2d sec., counsul embassy, Lisbon, Portugal, 1953-57; counsul Am. consulate, Medellin, Colombia, 1957-58, Cochabamba, Bolivia, 1958-60; 1st sec., consul embassy, London, Eng., 1960-64, consul gen., 1964-67; counsul gen., consular liaison officer Am. embassy, Paris, France, 1967-68. U.S. del. spl. conf. Gold and Assets Commn. of Allied Control Council, London, 1956. Recipient Medal of Freedom, USAF, 1947; Commendable Service award Dept. of State, 1952, Superior Honor award medal, 1966. Clubs: Rotary (Lisbon); Lions (Medellin, Colombia; Cochabamba, Bolivia); American (London, Madrid and Paris). Home: Neustra Senora de Lujan 17 Madrid Spain Office: US Embassy Madrid Spain

GILBERT, CHARLES EDWARD, educator; b. Albany, N.Y., May 29, 1927; s. Edward Strong and Genevieve (Hunt) G.; B.A., Haverford Coll., 1950; student London (Eng.) Sch. Econs., 1950-51; Ph.D., Northwestern U., 1955; m. Annalee Schendorf, Nov. 27, 1954; children—Susan Elizabeth, Jonathan Hunt. Asst. to U.S. Senator Humphrey, 1954; instr. Oberlin Coll., 1955; mem. faculty Swarthmore Coll., 1955—, asso. prof. polit. sci., 1962-67, prof., 1967—, chmn. commn. ednl. policy, 1967, provost, 1969—; cons. Pa. Dept. Pub. Welfare, Com. Econ. Devel.; guest scholar Brookings Inst., 1964-65, 68-69, sr. fellow, 1968-69, 69—. Past chmn., now mem. bd. Delaware County (Pa.) Health and Welfare Council. Served with the USNR, 1945-46. Research fellow Social Sci. Research Council, 1952-53, 59-60; fellow Rockefeller Found., 1964-65. Mem. Am. Polit. Sci. Assn. (council 1959-61, exec. com. 1959-60), Am. Soc. Pub. Adminstrn. Democrat. Author: (with W.H. Brown) Planning Municipal Investment, 1961; Governing the Suburbs, 1967; also articles. Home: 406 Walnut Lane Swarthmore PA 19081

GILBERT, CHARLES MERWIN, geologist; b. Washington, May 22, 1910; s. Walter M. and Leila (Fraser) G.; A.B., Cornell U., 1933; Ph.D., U. Cal. at Berkeley, 1938; m. Lora Hall, 1964; children—Jane, David, Douglas, Stephen. Instr., asst. prof. geology U. Cal. at Berkeley, 1938-43, asso. prof., then prof., 1946—, chmn. dept., 1959; geologist U.S. Geol. Survey, 1943-46. Mem. Geol. Soc. Am., Am. Assn. Petroleum Geologists, Am. Geophys. Union. Home: 1077 Cragmont Av Berkeley CA 94708

GILBERT, CREIGHTON EDDY, art historian; b. Durham, N.C., June 6, 1924; s. Allan H. and Katharine (Everett) G.; student Duke, Columbia, Johns Hopkins; B.A., N.Y. U., 1942, Ph.D., 1955. Chmn. editorial bd. Marsyas, 1945-46; instr. history of art Emory U., 1946-47; instr., asst. prof. U. Louisville, 1947-56; asst. prof. Ind. U., 1956-58; curator Ringling Mus. Art, Sarasota, Fla., 1959-61; asso. prof. fine arts Brandeis U., 1961-65, Sidney and Ellen Wien prof. history of art, 1965-69, chmn. dept., 1963-66, 68-69; prof., chmn. Queens Coll. City U. N.Y., 1969—. Vis. prof. Harvard, summer 1964; Fulbright vis. lectr. U. Rome, 1951-52; vis. lectr. N.Y. U., summer 1956, U. Cal. at Berkeley, summer 1959; Kress fellow Harvard Center for Italian Renaissance Studies, Florence, Italy, 1967-68. Past pres. Ky. Fedn. Tchrs. Recipient Mather award Coll. Art Assn., 1964. Fellow Am. Acad. Arts and Scis.; mem. Inst. Fine Arts Alumni Assn. (nat. v.p. 1956-57, chmn. bd. dirs. 1970—), Coll. Art Assn., Renaissance Soc. Am. (council 1964-65), Am. Assn. U. Profs. Author: 17th Century Paintings from the Low Countries, 1966; Michelangelo, 1967; change in Piero della Francesca, 1968. Editor: Renaissance Art: Contemporary Essays, 1970. Translator: Complete Poems and Selected Letters of Michelangelo, 1963, 2d rev. edit., 1965; articles in encys. Contbg. editor Arts mag. until 1965. Contbr. research studies on Italian Renaissance art jours. U.S., Britain, France, Italy. Office: Queens Coll City U NY Flushing NY 11367

GILBERT, DATON, actuary; b. Warsaw, N.Y., Jan. 28, 1909; s. Ellis and Lora Jane (Mills) G.; A.B., Colgate U., 1931; postgrad. Brown U., 1931-32; m. Barbara E. Walker, July 21, 1934; children—Stephen Daton, Patricia Spaulding. Actuarial staff Prudential Life Ins. Co., 1932-36; research staff Life Ins. Agy. Mgmt. Assn. (formerly Life Ins. Sales Research Bur.), 1936-42; asst. actuary Conn. Mut. Life Ins. Co., 1942-50, asso. actuary, 1950-51, actuary, 1951—, 2d v.p., 1953-62, v.p., 1962-69, sr. v.p., 1969—. Fellow Soc. Actuaries; mem. Nat. Assn. Accountants, Soc. Advancement Mgmt., Am. Pension Conf., Phi Beta Kappa. Republican. Clubs: University, Actuaries of Hartford. Home: 10 Thomson Rd West Hartford CT 06107 Office: 140 Garden St Hartford CT 06105

GILBERT, DEWITT, editor, govt. ofcl.; b. Eugene, Ore., June 19, 1896; s. William Sylvester and Florence Ritta (Davisson) G.; B.A., U. Ore., 1919; postgrad. Sorbonne, Paris, France, U. Grenoble, France, 1919, Columbia, 1920; m. Olive Ann Risley, Nov. 19, 1920; children—William S., John R. City editor Astoria (Ore.) Budget, 1920-28; asso. editor Pacific Fisherman, Seattle, 1928-39, editor, 1942-66, editorial dir., 1966—; editor Mining World, Seattle, 1939-42, Ocean Fisheries, Seattle, 1964-67; cons. editor Nat.

Fisherman, 1967—, Fishing News Internat., London, 1968—; editor Future of the Fishing Industry of the U.S., U. Washington Coll. Fisheries, 1968. Adviser, Am. sect. Internat. N. Pacific Fisheries Commn., 1955-67; U.S. mem. Internat. Pacific Salmon Fisheries Commn., 1957—; mem. U.S. Dept. State Fisheries Adv. Com., 1960-68. Mem. Phi Gamma Delta, Sigma Delta Chi. Home: 2852 44th Av W Seattle WA 98199 Office: 71 Columbia St Seattle WA 98104

GILBERT, ELIZABETH ANN DINWIDDIE, coll. librarian; b. nr. Berea, Ky., Apr. 15, 1907; d. Joseph C. and Laminia Walker (Armstrong) Gilbert; B.A., Berea Coll., 1930; B.S., Western Res. U., 1938; postgrad. Columbia, Western Res. U. Library supr. circulation Berea Coll., 1930-44, librarian, chmn. dept. library sci., 1944—. prof. library sci., 1965—. Mem. Ky. Librarian's Certification Bd., 1957—. Mem. A.L.A. (Ky. rep. coll. and reference libraries div.), Southeastern (Ky. rep. 1966-70), Ky. (pres. 1945-46) library assns., Am. assn. U. Profs., Am. Assn. U. Women, Kappa Delta Pi, Phi Kappa Phi. Club: Progress. Contbr.: Libraries in the Southeast, 1949. Home: RFD 1 Berea KY 40403

GILBERT, ERNEST H., lawyer; b. Morgantown, W.Va., 1907; LL.B., W.Va. U., 1928. Admitted to W.Va. bar, 1928; now partner firm Campbell, Love, Woodroe & Kizer, Charleston. Served to lt. comdr. USNR, 1942-46. Mem. Am., W.Va., Kanawha County bar assns., W.Va. State Bar, Phi Alpha Delta. Office: Charleston Nat Plaza Charleston WV 25301*

GILBERT, FELIX, historian; b. Baden-Baden, Germany, May 21, 1905; s. William Henry and Cecile Mendelssohn (Bartholdy) G.; Ph.D., U. Berlin, 1931; m. Mary Raymond, Apr. 21, 1956. Came to U.S., 1936, naturalized, 1943. Research analyst OSS, 1943-45, State Dept., 1945-46; prof. history Bryn Mawr Coll., 1946-62; prof. Sch. Hist. Studies, Inst. Advanced Study, Princeton, N.J., 1962—. Fellow Am. Acad. Arts and Scis.; mem. Am. Philos. Soc., Soc. Italian Hist. Studies (pres. 1970), Am. Hist. Assn., Renaissance Soc. Am. Author: To The Farewell Address, 1961 (Bancroft prize 1962); Machiavelli and Guicciardini, 1965; The End of the European Era, 1970. Co-author: History, 1965. Editor: Hitler Directs His War, 1950. Co-editor: Makers of Modern Strategy, 1943; The Diplomats, 1953. Home: 266 Mercer St Princeton NJ 08540

GILBERT, FREDERICK AUGUSTUS, chem. exec.; b. Buffalo, May 2, 1912; s. Lester F. and Josephine (Hoyt) G.; grad. Taft Sch., Phillip Exeter Acad.; A.B., Harvard, 1934; m. Nancy Porter, June 17, 1937; children—Charles R., Samuel L., Nancy P. With Buffalo Electro-Chem. Co., Inc., 1935-52 (merged with Food Machinery & Chem. Corp. 1952), div. mgr., 1956-58, v.p., 1958-62 (co. now known as FMC Corp.), v.p., gen. mgr., 1962—. Mem. Am. Chem. Soc., Am. Inst. Chem. Engrs., Soc. Chem. Industries, Chem. Inst. Can. Club: Union League (N.Y.C.). Home: 19 Searles Rd Darien CT 06820 Office: 633 3d Av New York City NY 10017

GILBERT, GUSTAVE MARK, psychologist, educator; b. N.Y.C., Sept. 30, 1911; s. Mark and Ethel (Nierenberg) G.; B.A., Coll. City N.Y., 1932; M.A., Columbia, 1936, Ph.D., 1939; m. Matilda Safran, June 15, 1941; children—Robert, John, Charles. Instr., Conn. Coll. for Women, 1939-40, Bard Coll., 1940-42; prison psychologist Internat. Mil. Tribunal, Nuremberg, Germany, 1945-46; asso. prof. Princeton, 1947-50; chief psychologist VA Hosp., Northport, L.I., 1950-51; asso. prof. Mich. State U., 1951-59; prof. psychology, chmn. dept. L.I. U., Bklyn., 1959—, pres. univ. faculty senate, 1967-68. Cons. VA, Mich. Dept. Correction, 1952-58; cons., witness Eichmann trial, Jerusalem, 1961; cons. Peace Corps, 1963—. Served with AUS, 1942-45. Mem. Am., Eastern, N.Y. State psychol. assns., Inter- Am. Soc. Psychology (pres. 1959-61), Sigma Xi. Author: Nuremberg Diary, 1947; The Psychology of Dictatorship (Bernays award 1950), 1950; Personality Dynamics: a Biosocial Approach, 1970. Home: 6 Crystal Dr Great Neck NY 11021 Office: Long Island U Brooklyn NY 11201

GILBERT, HARRY GEORGE, carpet mfg. co. exec.; b. Chgo., May 25, 1910; s. Thomas Jefferson and Anna (Hacking) G.; Ph.B., U. Chgo., 1931; m. Aileen Hilja Kahil, Dec. 23, 1933; children-James Henry, Robert Thomas. Divisional controller Montgomery Ward & Co., N.Y.C., 1947-50; controller Frank G. Shattuck Co., N.Y.C., 1951; asst. controller gen. Bigelow-Sanford, Inc., N.Y.C., 1952-61, controller, 1961—. Served to lt. USNR, 1942-45. Mem. Financial Execs. Inst., Advt. Club N.Y.‡ Mailing Address:

GILBERT, HELEN HOMANS, coll. trustee; b. Quincy, Mass., Oct. 29, 1913; d. Robert and Abigail (Adams) Homans; grad. Westover Sch., 1931; A.B., Radcliffe Coll., 1936; m. Carl J. Gilbert, June 27, 1936; 1 son, Thomas T. Chmn. bd. trustees Radcliffe Coll.; bd. overseers Harvard. Address: Strawberry Hill St Dover MA 02030 also 1308 29th St NW Washington DC 20007

GILBERT, HENRY E., labor union ofcl.; b. Ethel, Mo., Oct. 5, 1906; s. Henry H. and Irene R. (Windle) G.; student Cleveland Coll., 1943; m. Alice Marie Iman, Dec. 26, 1925; 1 dau., Norma Gwen (Mrs. J.C. Soneeton). With Brotherhood of Locomotive Firemen and Enginemen, 1927—, successively local chmn., sec., treas. Alton gen. grievances com., legislative rep., mem. exec. bd., Ill. legislative bd., asst. in pres. office, bd. dirs., v.p., pres., 1953—; asst. pres. United Transp. Union, 1969—. Presbyn. Mason (Shriner). Home: 22449 Blossom Dr Rocky River OH 44116 Office: 15401 Detroit Cleveland OH 44107

GILBERT, HORACE DURHAM, bearings mfr.; b. Lake Forest, Ill., Aug. 22, 1910; B.S., Yale, 1933, LL.B., 1936; m. Katharine de Pierrefeu, Aug. 31, 1935; children—Stephen de Pierrefeu, Anne Tudor, Frederic Sargent, Katharine; m. 2d, Helene Mohl, Apr. 9, 1966. Advt. mgr. Yankee mag., 1937; asst. to pres. F.B. Oldham Co., Buffalo, 1938-40; engr. Package & Container Corp., N.Y.C., 1940-41; pres., dir. MPB Corp. Keene, N.H., 1941- -, now also chmn. bd. Past dir. Anti-Friction Bearing Mfrs. Assn. Mem. Am. Ordnance Assn., Rocket Soc. Republican, Unitarian. Home: Feld Rt Keene NH 03431 Office: Precision Park Keene NH 03431

GILBERT, JACOB H., congressman; b. Bronx, N.Y., June 17, 1920; s. Isidore and Rose (Miller) G.; LL.B., St. John's U., 1943; m. Irma Steuer, June 7, 1949; children—Miriam Sharon, Sandra, Samuel Stephen. Admitted to N.Y. bar, 1944, since practiced in N.Y.C.; asst. corp. counsel N.Y.C., 1949-50; mem. N.Y. State Assembly, 1951-54, N.Y. State Senate, 1955-60; mem. 86th- 91st congresses 22d Dist. N.Y. State, mem. ways and means com. Mem. South Bronx Community Council; adv. bd. community center Pub. Sch. 65. Mem. Bronx County Bar Assn., Fed. Bar Assn. N.Y., N.J., Conn., Plaintiffs Trial Law Assn., Bronx Bd. Trade, Am. Jewish Congress, A.F.L.-C.I.O., Bronx C. of C. Democrat. Lion, Elk; mem. B'nai B'rith. Home: 1160 Evergreen Av New York City NY 10472 Office: House Office Bldg Washington DC 20515

GILBERT, JAMES FREEMAN, educator, geophysicist; b. Vincennes, Ind., Aug. 9, 1931; s. James Freeman and Gladys (Paugh) G.; B.S., Mass. Inst. Tech., 1953, Ph.D., 1956; NSF postdoctoral fellow, U. Cambridge (Eng.), 1956-57; m. Sally Bonney, June 19, 1959; children—Cynthia, Sarah, James Sherwood. Research asso. Mass. Inst. Tech., 1956-57; successively asst. research geophysicist, asst. prof., asso. prof. U. Cal. at Los Angeles, 1957-59; sr. research geophysicist Tex. Inst., Dallas, 1959-61; prof. geophysics U. Cal. at San Diego, 1961—, chmn. dept. earth scis., 1963-64. Guggenheim fellow, 1964-65. Fellow Am. Acad. Arts and Scis., Am. Geophys. Union; mem. Am. Phys. Soc., Am. Math. Soc., Seismological Soc., N.Y. Acad. Scis. Home: 650 Rimini Rd Del Mar CA 92014 Office: PO Box 109 La Jolla CA 92037

GILBERT, JAMES RALPH, baking co. exec.; b. N.Y.C., Oct. 13, 1921; s. Wilmer R. and Gladys (O'Connell) G.; B.S., N.Y. U., 1947; m. Betty L. Rogers, May 20, 1950; children—James Ralph, Richard Rogers, John Philip, Christine Louise. Asst. chief auditor Richardson Merrell Co., 1947-50; controller Nestle Co., Inc., 1950-68; v.p. finance Keebler Co., Elmhurst, Ill., 1968—. Served with USAAF, 1942-46. Mem. Nat. Assn. Accountants. Home: 1650 Waldorth Ct Wheaton IL 60187 Office: 677 Larch Av Elmhurst IL 60126

GILBERT, JOHN BAPTISTE, paper co. exec.; b. San Rafael, Cal., Mar. 26, 1915; s. Louis Jules and Willa (Sale) G.; A.B., U. Cal., 1937; grad. Advanced Mgmt. Program, Harvard, 1956; m. Lavinia Cresap, June 21, 1942; children—John Baptiste IV, Lavinia Grace, Joan Willa, Thomas C. Various positions Zellerbach Paper Co., 1937-41, exec. sales supr., gen. mgr., 1946-55, v.p., dir., 1955—, gen. mgr., 1959-61; v.p. marketing Crown Zellerbach Corp., 1961-63, sr. v.p. marketing, 1963—, also dir.; dir. Morris Plan Co. Cal., Morlan Pacific Corp., Yosemite Ins. Co. Served from 2d lt. to maj., inf., AUS, 1941-45. Mem. Am. Acad. Advancement Sci., C. of C. Episcopalian. Rotarian. Clubs: Orinda Country; Stock Exchange; Richmond Yacht. Office: 1 Bush St San Francisco CA 94119

GILBERT, JOSEPH, assn. exec.; b. Cleve., Dec. 18, 1920; s. Morris and Yetta (Schwedock) G.; B.C.E., Coll. City N.Y., 1942; M.S. in Indsl. Engring., Columbia, 1950; m. Doris Chaiken, June 20, 1943; children—Jeffrey A., Karen Sue. Mem. staff Soc. Automotive Engrs., 1946—, asst. gen. mgr., 1957-60, sec., gen. mgr., 1960—; group leader Man Marketing Clinic, 1947-59. Served to 1st lt. USAAF, 1942-46. Sr. mem. Am. Soc. Tool and Mfg. Engrs.; mem. Council Engring. and Sci. Soc. Secs. (sec. 1961-62, pres. 1963-64), Soc. Automotive Engrs., Am. Soc. M.E., Am. Inst. Aeros. and Astronautics, Engring. Soc. Detroit, Am. Rocket Soc., Am. Soc. Testing Materials, Am. Soc. Metals, Instn. Automotive and Aero. Engrs. (Australia), Instn. Mech. Engrs. (Eng.), Société des Ingenieurs de l'Automobile (France), Associazione Tecnica Automobile (Italy), Soc. Automotive Engrs. (Japan). Home: 864 Troy St Elmont NY 11003 Office: 2 Pennsylvania Plaza New York City NY 10001

GILBERT, LAWRENCE IRWIN, educator, biologist; b. N.Y.C., Jan. 24, 1929; s. Charles and Matilda (Bronznick) G.; B.S., L.I. U., 1950; M.S., N.Y.U., 1955; Ph.D., Cornell U., 1958; m. Doris Paule Millstein, Oct. 26, 1952; children—Scott David, Daniel Todd, Joanne Robin. Mem. faculty Northwestern U., 1958—, prof. biol. scis., chmn. dept., 1965-70, also sec.-treas. div. comparative endocrinology, chmn. div. comparative endocrinology. NSF Sr. fellow Universitat Bern (Switzerland), 1964-65; vis. prof. U. Nijmegan (Netherlands), 1971-72. Mem. Soc. Developmental Biology, Soc. Exptl. Biology, Am. Soc. Zoologists, Am. Soc. Cell Biology, Entomol, Soc. Am., Soc. Gen. Physiologist, Phi Beta Kappa. Editor: Metamorphosis: A Problem in Developmental Biology, 1968. Editorial bd. Gen. and Comparative Endocrinology, Physiol. Chemistry and Physics, Insect Biochemistry. Contbr. articles to profl. jours. Home: 937 Sutton Dr Northbrook IL 60062 Office: Northwestern U Dept Biology Hogan Lab Evanston IL 60201

GILBERT, LEWIS, film dir., writer, actor; b. London, Eng., Mar. 6, 1920. Asso. with various motion picture companies, including London Films, Brit., Mayflower, RKO-Radio firms, G.B.I., Gainsborough Pictures, Argyle Prodns., Nettefold Films, Ltd.; pictures include: Under One Roof, I Want to Get Married, Haunting Melody, Once a Sinner, Scarlet Thread, There Is Another Sun, Time Gentlemen Please, Emergency Call, Johnny on the Run, The Good Die Young, The Sea Shall Not Have Them, Reach for the Sky, Cast a Dark Shadow, The Admirable Crichton, Carve Her Name with Pride, A Cry from the Street, Ferry to Hong Kong, Sink the Bismarck, Light Up the Sky, The Greengage Summer, H.M.S. Defiant, The Patriots, Spare the Rod, The Seventh Dawn, Alfie, You Only Live Twice, The Adventurers. Served with RAF, World War II. Address: care United Artists Corp 729 7th Av New York City NY 10019*

GILBERT, LEWIS DUSENBERY, investor, economist; b. Palo Alto, Cal., Nov. 27, 1907; s. Caston J. and Minnie (Dusenberry) G.; student pvt. schs. Pvt. investor, rep. ind. stockholders at corporate ann. meetings 1934—. Served with AUS, 1942-45. Democrat. Clubs: City (trustee), Overseas Press, Nat. Arts (N.Y.C.). Author: Dividends and Democracy, 1956. Pub. ann. report stockholder activities at corp. meetings. Address: 1165 Park Av New York City NY 10028

GILBERT, LOU, actor; b. Sycamore, Ill., Aug. 1, 1909; s. Morris and Rose (Chosid) Gitlitz; ed. pub. schs., Cleve.; m. Martha Lou Hawkins, May 5, 1951; children—Nicholas David, Frances E. Appeared with Cleve. Play House, 1925, Chgo. Repertory Group, 1933, Arena Theatre, Washington, D.C., 1967- 68; Broadway appearances have included Beggars Are Coming to Town, 1944, Detective Story, 1948-49, Enemy of the People, 1951, Diary of Ann Frank, 1957-58, The Great White Hope; appearances in various motion pictures have included Viva Zapata, 1950, Juliet of the Spirits, 1965, Goldstein, 1964, Across the River, 1959, Requiem for a Heavyweight, 1963, Middle of the Night, 1959. Recipient Derwent award Actors Equity, 1949, Yale award, 1965. Mem. Actors Studio. Office: 432 W 44th St New York City NY 10036

GILBERT, LUCYLLE SMITH (Luci Puci) (Mrs. Walter T. Gilbert), milinery designer; b. Chgo., Aug. 17, 1907; d. Walter E. J. and Maude (Fuhl) Smith; student pub. schs., Chgo.; m. Walter T. Gilbert, May 6, 1932. Designer, Lemington, Inc., Chgo., 1928—; v.p. Mark III, Ltd., Suzi "B" Hats; designer Lemington, Luci Puci, Miss Luci, Sam Budwig, Ronnie, Lucylle Smith, Gilbert, Junior B, Luci Junior, Mark III, Suzi B. and Mademoiselle hats. Named Best Dressed Career Woman, Chgo. Fashion Group, 1960. Mem. Chgo. Fashion Group, Inc. Office: Lemington Inc 200 W Adams St Chicago IL 60606

GILBERT, MARTHA SMITH, former educator; A.B., A.M., Mt. Holyoke Coll.; Ph.D., U. Wis.; m. Frederic Don Huntington Gilbert; children—Charles Bixby, Elizabeth Sisson. Research asst. Harvard Med. Sch., Boston City Hosp., 1931- 32; faculty Woman's Coll., U. N.C., 1937-41, Mt. Holyoke Coll., 1932-34, 41-46; vis. scholar Columbia, 1961-62; faculty Sarah Lawrence Coll., Bronxville, N.Y., 1962-69, ret. prof. chemistry. Home: 33 Sleepy Hollow Rd Briarcliff Manor NY 10510

GILBERT, PHIL EDWARD, Jr., lawyer; b. Chgo., Jan. 31, 1915; s. Phil Edward and Florence (Miller) G.; student Phillips Andover Acad., 1931-32; A.B., Dartmouth, 1936; LL.B., Harvard, 1939; m. Nancy Thompson Merrick, June 24, 1939 (div., 1967); children—Mary Randolph, John Sale, Clinton Merrick; m. 2d, Joan Stulman, Oct. 6, 1968. Admitted to N.Y. bar, 1941, since practiced in N.Y.C.; atty. Donovan, Leisure, Newton & Lumbard, 1939-41; atty. Debevoise, Stevenson, Plimpton & Page, 1941; partner Gilbert, Segall & Young and predecessor firm, 1946—. Pres. Rolls-Royce, Inc., N.Y.C.; dep. chmn. Magnesium Elektron, Inc.; dir. Rolls-Royce Aero Engines, Inc., Sanger-Funnell, Inc. Vice-chmn. Westchester County Democratic Com., 1960—; Dem. candidate for U.S. Ho. of Reps. 26th N.Y. Congl. Dist., 1958, 60. Trustee, gov. Nat. Conf. Christians and Jews. Served to maj., inf., AUS, 1941-46; ETO. Decorated Bronze Star medal, Croix de Guerre. Mem. Am., Fed., Westchester bar assns., Bar Assn. City N.Y., Phi Beta Kappa. Baptist. Home: The Croft Spring Valley Rd Ossining NY 10562 Office: 405 Park Av New York NY 10022

GILBERT, RICHARD GEOFFREY, savs. and loan assn. exec.; b. Chgo., Apr. 7, 1920; s. George and Marie (Bensley) G.; commerce diploma Northwestern U., 1943, B.S. in Bus. Adminstrn., 1947, grad. student, 1947; grad. Ind. U. Grad. Sch. Savs. and Loan, 1954; m. Wynifred I. Shull, Nov. 11, 1961; children by previous marriage—Pamela, Rene, Jeffrey, Dana. With Fed. Res. Bank Chgo., 1938, Cleve. Trust Co., 1939-41; asst. investment fund mgr., instr. Northwestern U., 1945-47; with Citizens Savs. Assn., Canton, O., 1947—, pres., 1963—, also dir.; pres. Ohio Financial Service Corp., Columbus; instr. Grad. Sch. Savs. and Loan, 1960—, Malone Coll., Canton, 1962—. Mem. adv. com. govt. securities Treasury Dept., 1963—; mem. adv. com. truth in lending Fed. Reserve Bd.; mem. Akron-Canton Airport Authority. Pres. Central Canton Devel. Assn., 1959—. Served with USNR, 1941-45. Mem. U.S. (chmn. blue ribbon com. 1969), Ohio (exec. com. 1966—, 2d v.p.) savs. and loan leagues. Home: 3420 Parkridge Circle NW Canton OH 44718 Office: 100 Central Plaza S Canton OH 44702

GILBERT, ROBERT PERTSCH, educator, mathematician; b. N.Y.C., Jan. 8, 1932; s. Ralph H. and Ruth (Pertsch) G.; B.S., Bklyn. Coll., 1952; M.S. in Physics, Carnegie-Mellon U., 1955, M.S. in Math., 1955, Ph.D. in Math., 1958; m. E. Eileen Manton, Oct. 28, 1955. Faculty, U. Pitts., 1957-60, Mich. State U., 1960-63; research asst. prof. Inst. for Fluid Dynamics and Applied Math., U. Md., 1961-64, research asso. prof., 1964-65; prof. dept. math. Georgetown U., Washington, 1965-66; prof. math. Ind. U., Bloomington, 1966—; cons. spl. coal research div. U.S. Bur. Mines, 1958-60, Naval Ordnance Lab., 1961-64. Mem. Am. Inst. Physics, Am. Math. Soc., Soc. for Indsl. and Applied Math. (asso. editor jour.), Washington Acad. Scis., Sigma Xi, Pi Mu Epsilon. Author: Function Theoretic Methods in Partial Differential Equations, 1969. Co-editor: Analytics Methods in Mathematical Physics, 1970. Editor-in-chief Applicable Analysis: an internat. jour. Research and publs. on analysis, especially harmonic functions, boundary value problems, math. physics, partial differential equations, numerical analysis. Home: 2201 Queens Way Bloomington IN 47401

GILBERT, VEDDER MORRIS, educator; b. Amsterdam, N.Y., May 12, 1914; s. Dr. Archibald M. and Anna E. (Morris) G.; A.B., Union Coll., N.Y., 1936; postgrad. Montpellier U. (France). 1936-37; M.A., Cornell U., 1938, Ph.D., 1952; m. Gertrude Gile Hosford, Feb. 12, 1944; children—Lindley Anne, Abigail Morris. Instr., U. Mo., 1938-44; grad. asst. Cornell U., 1944-46; asst. prof. U. Toledo, 1946-51; asst. prof. U. Mont., Missoula, 1952-55, Danforth asso., 1954-59, asso. prof., 1955-58, prof., 1958—, chmn. dept. English, 1957-62, fgn. student adviser, 1957—, coordinator humanities, 1966-67. Actor, summer stock, 1958—. Participant, Nat. Assn. Fgn. Student Affairs Seminar, France, 1964; active Pease Corps liaison, 1960-65; co-founder Glastonbury Assn.; del. Missoula County Ednl. Council, 1957-60. Past pres. P.T.A. unit. Pres. bd. dirs. Missoula-Mineral County chpt. A.R.C. Mem. Rocky Mountain Modern Lang. Assn. (past pres.), Mont. English Council, Modern Lang. Assn., Council Tchrs. English, Coll. English Assn., Buckinghamshire Archaeol. Soc., Johnson Soc. N.W., Psi Upsilon, Phi Delta Phi (asso. charter). Episcopalian (vestryman). Kiwanian. Contbr. articles to profl. jours. Home: 1330 Gerald Av Missoula MT 59801

GILBERT, WALTER, scientist, molecular biologist; b. Boston, Mar. 21, 1932; s. Richard V. and Emma (Cohen) G.; B.A., Harvard, 1953, A.M., 1954; Dr. Phil., Cambridge U. (Eng.), 1957; m. Celia Stone, Dec. 29, 1953; children—John Richard, Kate. NSF postdoctoral fellow Harvard, 1957-58, lectr. physics, 1958-59, asst. prof. physics, 1959-64, asso. prof. biophysics, 1964-68, prof. molecular biology, 1968—. Recipient U.S. Steel Found. award Nat. Acad. Sci., 1968; Guggenheim fellow, 1968-69; Ledlie prize Harvard, 1969. Mem. Am. Phys. Soc., Am. Soc. Biol. Chemists, Am. Acad. Arts and Scis. Home: 107 Upland Rd Cambridge MA 02140

GILBERT, WILLIAM JAMES, educator; b. Shelton, Wash., Feb. 10, 1916; s. Cyrus Lloyd and Bessie Mae (Carr) G.; B.S., U. Wash., 1938; M.S., U. Mich., 1939, Ph.D. in Botany, 1942; m. Ruth Elizabeth Willoughby, June 27, 1942; children—Paul William, Bruce David, Mark Allen, Lee Ralph. Research biologist Comml. Solvents Corp., Terre Haute, Ind., 1944-46; faculty Albion (Mich.) Coll., 1946—, prof. biology, chmn. dept., 1957—, chmn. div. Sci. and Math., 1962-66. Faculty dir., sec. Mich. Intercollegiate Athletic Assn., 1947-57; coordinator Mich. Jr. Acad. Sci., Arts and Lettres, 1949- 51. Mem. Mich. Acad. Sci., Arts and Letters (life, chmn. botany sect. 1950, exec. com. 1968—), Am. Inst. for Biol. Scis., A.A.A.S., Phycological Soc. Am., Internat. Phycological Soc., Am. Assn. U. Profs., Phi Beta Kappa, Sigma Xi, Phi Sigma. Presbyn. (elder). Contbr. articles to profl. jours. Home: 616 E Erie St Albion MI 49224

GILBERTO, ASTRUD, singer; b. Bahia, Brazil, 1940. Singer with Stan Getz Combo; recorded song (with Joao Giberto) The Girl From Ipanema, others. Address: care Dir Pub Relations Verve Records 1540 Broadway New York City NY 10036*

GILBERTS, ROBERT DUBOIS, univ. dean; b. Sand Creek, Wis., June 27, 1924; s. Arnold and Adina (Ellefson) G.; B.S., Wis. State Coll., 1950; M.S., U. Wis., 1955, Ph.D., 1961; m. Marjorie Jean Fosterling, Mar. 29, 1947; children—Bethel Lynn, Deborah Ann, James Robert. Tchr.-prin., Wausau, Wis., 1950-52; adminstrv. asst. to pres. Wis. State Coll., Superior, 1952-53; supervising prin., Shell Lake, Wis., 1953-56; supt. schs., Oconomowoc, Wis., 1956-62, Madison, Wis., 1963-67, Denver, 1967-70; dean U. Ore. Coll. Edn., Eugene, 1970—. Mem. Mayor's Adv. Com., Madison, 1963-67; v.p. Denver United Fund; exec. bd. Council Econ. Edn., Denver council Boy Scouts Am. Bd. dirs. Denver Met. Mus., Colo. Safety Council. Served with USAAF, 1942- 45; ETO. Mem. Nat. Council for Econ. Edn. (trustee), Am. Assn. Sch. Adminstrs. (adv. bd.), Sales and Marketing Execs. Internat., Am. Vocational Assn., Nat. Soc. for Study Edn. Lutheran. Mason, Rotarian. Home: 2145 Rocky Lane Eugene OR

GILBERTSON, LYLE ITHIEL, educator, chemist; b. Beloit, Wis., July 10, 1903; s. George Herman and Minnie (Stordock) G.; A.B., Augustana Coll., 1925; M.A. in Chemistry, U. Wis., 1926; Ph.D., Ind. U., 1937; m. Ruth Schlund, Aug. 23, 1930; children—Barbara (Mrs. Grover H. Emrich), Lyle, Jeanne (Mrs. O. Manning Sexton). Instr. chemistry Carleton Coll., 1926-27; asst. prof. chemistry Wash. State U., 1927-46; research supr. dept. war research Columbia, 1942-46; research supr. Air Reduction Co., Inc., 1946- 48, coordinator research and engring. dept., 1948-49, adminstrv. mgr., 1949-53, dir. Murray

Hill (N.J.) Labs., 1953-58, adminstrv. dir. Central Research Labs., 1958-62, mgmt. cons., 1962-65; pres. Gilbertson Assos., Inc., 1964-66; prof. chemistry S.D. Sch. Mines and Tech., Rapid City, 1966—, head dept., 1966-69. Cons. chemist, 1962—. Fellow N.Y. Acad. Sci., Am. Inst. Chemists; mem. Electro- chem. Soc. (past pres.), Research Soc. Am., Am. Chem. Soc., C. of C., Sigma Xi, Alpha Chi Sigma, Phi Lambda Upsilon, Delta Sigma Rho, Pi Kappa Delta. Lutheran. Home: 1215 St Andrew St Rapid City SD 57701

GILBRETH, FRANK BUNKER, Jr., writer, newspaperman; b. Plainfield, N.J., Mar. 17, 1911; s. Frank Bunker and Lillian Evelyn (Moller) G.; student St. John's Coll., Md., 1928-29; B.A., U. Mich., 1933; m. Elizabeth Cauthen, Sept. 29, 1934 (dec. 1954); 1 dau., Betsy; m. 2d, Mary Manigault, June 4, 1955; children—Edward, Rebecca Motte. Reporter N.Y. Herald Tribune, 1933-34; corr. A.P., Raleigh, N.C., 1938-42, cable editor, 1945-47; editorial writer News & Courier, Charleston, S.C., 1947-50, asso. editor, 1951-57, asst. pub., v.p. News & Courier and Charleston Evening Post, 1957-; v.p. Packet Motor Lines, Charleston, 1958—, Beaufort (S.C.) Gazette, 1962—, Aiken (S.C.) Communications, Inc., Aiken Cablevision, Inc., Buenos Aires Herald. Served from lt. (j.g.) to lt. comdr. USNR, 1942-45. Decorated Air medal, Bronze Star. Mem. Alpha Delta Phi. Author: (with Ernestine Gilbreth Carey) Cheaper by the Dozen, 1949, Belles on Their Toes, 1950; (with John Held, Jr.) Held's Angels, 1952; I'm a Lucky Guy, 1951; Innside Nantucket, 1955; Of Whales and Women, 1957; How to Be a Father, 1958; Loblolly, 1959; He's My Boy, 1962; Time Out for Happiness, 1971. Home: 430 Maybank Hwy Charleston SC 29407 also The Shoe Hulbert Av Nantucket MA 02554 Office: The News and Courier and The Charleston Evening Post Charleston SC 29402

GILBRETH, LILLIAN MOLLER, cons. engr.; b. Oakland, Cal., May 24, 1878; d. William and Annie (Delger) Moller; B.Litt., U. Cal., 1900, M.Litt., 1902, LL.D., 1933; Ph.D., Brown U., 1915, Sc.D., 1931; M. Engring., U. Mich., 1928; D. Engring., Rutgers Coll., 1929, Stevens Inst. Tech., 1950, Syracuse U., 1952; Sc.D., Russell Sage Coll., 1931, Colby Coll., 1951, Lafayette Coll., 1952; LL.D., Smith Coll., 1945, Mills Coll., 1952; L.H.D., Temple U., 1949, Alfred U., 1948; Dr. Indsl. Psychol., Purdue U., 1948; hon. degrees from Milw. Downer Coll., Washington U., Princeton, Skidmore Coll., U. Wis., Pratt Inst., U. Mass., Western Coll. Women; LL.D., Ariz. State U., 1964; m. Frank Bunker Gilbreth, Oct. 19, 1904; children—Anne Moller (Mrs. Robert E. Barney), Mary Elizabeth (dec.), Ernestine Moller (Mrs. Charles E. Carey), Martha Bunker (dec.; Mrs. Richard E. Tallman), Frank Bunker, William Moller, Lillian Moller (Mrs. Donald D. Johnson), Frederick Moller, Daniel Bunker, John Moller, Robert Moller, Jane Moller (Mrs. G. Paul Heppes, Jr.). Pres. Gilbreth, Inc., cons. engrs. in mgmt., Montclair, N.J., 1924—; dir. courses in motion study, 1925-32; prof. mgmt. Purdue U., 1935-48; chmn. dept. personnel relations Newark Coll. Engring., 1941-43; univ. teaching P.I., Formosa, 1953-54; prof. mgmt. U. Wis., 1955; lectr. tech. and human relations problems in mgmt. in Asia, Australia, Can., Europe, Mexico, U.S.A., 1955—. Mem. U.S. Govt. coms. on civil def., also state and local coms. Mem. Essex County Vocational Bd. Trustee Montclair Library, 1944-54. Recipient Henry Lawrence Gantt medal (with Frank Gilbreth) Nat. Inst. Social Scis.; Wallace Clark Internat. award; gold medal Comite Internat. de l'Orgn. Scientifique; Washington award; Allan R. Cullimore medal, 1959; Hoover medal Am. Soc. C.E., 1966. Hon. mem. mgmt. socs. in U.S.A. and fgn. countries. Mem. Nat. Acad. Engring., Internat. Acad. Mgmt. Author: (with Frank B. Gilbreth) Fatigue Study, 1911, Applied Motion Study, 1917, Motion Study for the Handicapped, 1919; The Psychology of Management, 1921; Living with Our Children, 1928; Normal Lives for the Disabled (with Edna Yost), 1945; The Foreman and Manpower Management (with Alice Rice Cook), 1947; Management in the Home (with O. M. Thomas, Eleanor C. Clymer), 1954, 59. Contbr. Indsl. Engring. Handbook. Home: 215 Fernwood Av Upper Montclair NJ 07043

GILBRIDE, JOHN THOMAS, shipyard exec.; b. Bklyn., May 29, 1916; s. Francis Joseph and Mary (Figueira) G.; B.A., U. Pa., 1938; postgrad. Bklyn. Poly. Inst., Pratt Inst.; m. Rosemary Shelare, Sept. 7, 1940; children—Francis Joseph, John Thomas, Gary G. With Bklyn. div. Todd Shipyards Corp., 1932- 46, asst. gen. mgr. Los Angeles div., 1946, gen. mgr., 1946-58, pres., dir., 1958—; chmn. Lester Engring. Co., Designers & Planners, Inc., mem. downtown Manhattan adv. com. Chase Manhattan Bank. Mem. sub-council nat. indsl. pollution control Dept. Commerce; mem. industry adv. council Dept. Def.; adv. bd. Georgetown U. Center for Strategic and Internat. Studies. Trustee United Seaman's Service. Mem. U.S. Naval Inst. (asso.), Am. Bur. Shipping (bd. mgrs., pension and classification coms.), Shipbuilders Council Am. (dir., chmn. shipbuilding com., mem. exec. finance com.), Soc. Naval Architects and Marine Engrs. (hon. v.p., mem. exec. com., finance and audit com.), Am. Soc. Naval Engrs., Maritime Assn. Port of N.Y. (dir.), A.I.M. (asso.), Am. Shipping Soc., Am. Welding Soc., Nat. Def. Transp. Assn., Navy League U.S. (N.Y. council), N.E. Coast Instn. Engrs. and Shipbuilders (Eng.), Propeller Club U.S.A. (nat. exec. com.), Webb Inst. Naval Architecture vice chmn., trustee, mem. devel. com. Center for Maritime Studies), Newcomen Soc. N.Am., Gen. Alumni Soc. U. Pa., Phi Sigma Kappa. Roman Catholic. Elk. Clubs: Downtown Athletic, New York Athletic, Whitehall Luncheon (bd. govs.), Produce Exchange Luncheon, India House (bd. govs.), Chiselers, University of Pennsylvania, New York Yacht (N.Y.C.); Greenwich (Conn.) Country; Oslo Golf Klub. Home: Cedarwood Dr Greenwich CT 06830 Office: 1 Broadway New York City NY 10004

GILCHRIST, GUY GEORGE, utilities exec.; b. Randolph, Ia., Feb. 19, 1918; s. George G. and Sue (Wright) G.; B.S., Ia. State U., 1940; J.D., Georgetown U., 1948; m. Catherine Raymond, Jan. 25, 1943; children—George G., Lee Brien, Kevin Paul, Joan Patrice. Admitted to Ia. bar, 1948; pvt. practice, Bedford, 1948-49; research-legislative dir. Ia. Farm Bur., Des Moines, 1949-57; real estate supr. Ia. Power & Light Co., Des Moines 1957-61, sec., mgr. legal dept., 1961—. Dir., Des Moines Community Playhouse, 1970—; troop com. chmn. Boy Scouts Am., Des Moines Area, 1958-69; exec. com. Des Moines Playhouse. Served to maj. USAAF, 1940-46. Mem. Am., Ia. bar assns., Ia. Taxpayers Assn. (mem. exec. com.), Edison Electric Inst., Am. Right of Way Assn. (nat. dir., past Ia.-Neb. chpt. pres.), Am. Soc. Corporate Secs., Greater Des Moines C. of C., Ia., Mfrs. Assn., Des Moines Real Estate Bd., Ia. Assn. Tax Reps., Midwest Econ. Assn. Republican. Roman Catholic. Home: 1640 66th St Des Moines IA 50322 Office: 823 Walnut St Des Moines IA 50303

GILCHRIST, JOHN RAYMOND, former air force officer, financial mgmt. exec.; b. Woonsocket, R.I., May 18, 1906; s. John S. and Alice (Talbot) G.; B.S., U.S. Mil. Acad., 1928; grad. Indsl. Coll. Armed Forces, 1948; m. Mabel Moran, Nov. 7, 1930; children—Carole Jean (Mrs. Kimbrough S. Bassett), John Raymond, Robert Michael. Commd. 2d lt. U.S. Army, 1928, advanced through grades to maj. gen., 1952; chief operations Office Chief Finance, 1941-42; chief fgn. fiscal affairs War Dept., 1942-43; chief finance div. German country unit Hdqrs. SHAEF, 1944; dep. dir. econs. div. U.S. Group Control Coun. for Germany, 1944-45; alternate U.S. mem. econ. div. Allied Control Council for Germany, 1945; rep. Sec. War, Reparations Mission to Japan, 1945; chief econs. and supply br. Civil Affairs Div., War Dept. Spl. staff, 1945-47; chief projects Logistics Div., Army Gen. Staff, 1948; dep. dir. finance USAF, 1948-52; comdg. gen. AF Finance Center, 1950-52; dir. finance USAF, 1952-56, asst. comptroller USAF, comdg. gen. Air Force Finance Center, Denver, 1957, ret.; adminstrv. v.p. for orgn. planning and devel. Tidewater Oil Co., 1957-58; adminstrv. v.p., dir. Financial Indsl. Fund Mgmt. Corp., Denver 1958—, FIF Assos., Inc.; exec. v.p., dir. Financial Programs, Inc.; dir. Financial Assurance, Inc., Financial Trust Co.; v.p. Financial Indsl. Fund, Financial Indsl. Income Fund, Financial Dynamics Fund, Financial Venture Fund. Decorated D.S.M., Legion of Merit. Clubs: Army and Navy Country (Washington); Denver; Columbine Country (Littleton, Colo.). Home: 10 Niblick Lane Littleton CO 80120 Office: 900 Grant St Denver CO 80203

GILCHRIST, MALCOLM DANIEL, oil co. exec.; b. McNair, Miss., Dec. 16, 1905; s. Daniel Holland and Mollie (Stephens) G.; student Miss. State Coll., Miss. Coll., La. State U., DePaul U.; m. Angela Mary Colussi, Mar. 4, 1933; 1 dau., Mary Ann. With Universal Oil Products Co., Des Plaines, Ill., 1929—, v.p., 1952, now vice chmn. bd., also dir.; chmn. bd., chief exec. officer, dir. Procon, Inc., Compania Procon Iberica, S.A., Procon (Gt. Britain), Ltd., Procon Internat., Pacific Procon Ltd., Thai Indsl. Constructors, Procon Pty. Ltd. Mem. Am. Petroleum Inst., Am. Ordnance Assn. Home: 555 Somerset Lane Northfield IL 60093 Office: 1111 Mt Prospect Rd Des Plaines IL 60018

GILCHRIST, RICHARD KENNEDY, surgeon; b. Canadian, Tex., Jan. 20, 1904; s. Charles E. and Mabel E. (Boyle) G.; B.S., U. Chgo., 1926; M.D., Rush Med. Coll., 1930; m. Madeline Wenger; children—Kennedy W., Lynn E. Attending surgeon Cook County Hosp., Chgo., 1946-58, Presbyn. Hosp., 1950—; clin. prof. surgery U. Ill., 1948—; asso. attending surgeon Ravenswood Hosp. Trustee Rush-Presbyn.-St. Luke's Med. Center, Rush Med. Coll. Diplomate Am. Bd. Surgery. Fellow A.C.S. (treas. 1955—); mem. A.M.A., Internat., Am. (Sec. 1953-57), Central (recorder 1947-51, pres. 1952-53), So., Western surg. assns., Soc. Clin. Surgery (sec. 1948-52, pres. 1954-56), Chgo. Surg. Soc. (pres. 1961-62), Soc. for Surgery Alimentary Tract (v.p. 1968-69). Clubs: University, Glenview Golf, Commercial, Billings Medical (Chgo.). Contbr. articles to profl. jours. Home: 2430 Lakeview Chicago IL 60614 Office: 122 S Michigan Av Chicago IL 60603

GILCHRIST, ROBERT, business exec.; b. 1917; B.A., Cornell U., 1940; M.B.A., U. Chgo., 1965; married. With Fed. Sign and Signal Corp., Chgo., 1943—, v.p., 1963-66, exec. v.p., 1966, pres., 1966—, chief exec. officer, 1967—, chmn. bd., 1968—, also dir.; chmn., pres. Western Industries, Inc. Served with AUS. Home: 424 Woodside Av Hinsdale IL 60521 Office: 120 S Riverside Plaza Chicago IL 60606*

GILDART, LEE WILLIAM, educator; b. Albion, Mich., Oct. 24, 1910; s. Emerson Osborn and Estelle (Cross) G.; B.S., U. Mich., 1936, M.S., 1938; Ph.D., Northwestern U., 1950; m. Marcella Faulds Markland, Feb. 22, 1941; children—Laura (Mrs. Nicholas Peck), Martha, Rebecca, Sarah. Physicist Dow Chem. Co., Midland, Mich., 1939-42; instr. U. Mich., 1942-44; physicist Beckman Instruments, Pasadena, Cal., 1945; instr. Northwestern U., 1946-50; asst. prof. U. N.C., 1950-54; asso. prof. U. Ky., 1955-60, 63-64; lab. dir. Inst. Tech., Bandung, Indonesia, 1960-63; prof. physics Fairleigh Dickinson U., 1965—; chmn. dept., 1969—. Mem. Am. Phys. Soc., A.A.A.S., Am. Assn. Univ. Profs., Am. Fedn. Tchrs. Patentee in field. Home: 722 Booth Av Englewood NJ 07631 Office: 1000 River Rd Teaneck NJ 07666

GILDEA, ARTHUR PHILIP, labor union exec.; b. Boston, Dec. 4, 1911; s. Hugh J. and Catherine (Ward) G.; extension student Mass. U.; student Boston Cath. Labor Sch.; m. Marie T. Jewell, Feb. 22, 1941; children—Arthur P., William T., Thomas J., Hugh G., Joseph M., Kevin. Bus. rep. Internat. Union Brewery Workers, Boston, 1946-53, exec. sec., Mass., 1947-53, mem. internat. gen. exec. bd., 1949-53, internat. sec.-treas., 1953—; mem. exec. bd. Mass. CIO, 1947-53; v.p. union label and service trades dept. AFL-CIO, 1957—. Chmn., Mass. CIO-COPE, 1948; labor rep. Nat. Safety Council; labor chmn. Boston Labor Com. to Combat Intolerance. Active fund raising Boston Children's Hosp.; blood donor com. Boston chpt. A.R.C. Chmn. Democratic Ward Com., Boston; treas. Boston Dem. Com. Mem. Ancient Order Hibernians. K.C. Home: 274 Glenfield Ct Cincinnati OH 45238 Office: 2347 Vine St Cincinnati OH 45219

GILDEA, EDWIN FRANCIS, psychiatrist; b. Colorado Springs, Colo., May 7, 1898; s. Patrick Frederick and Mary Francis (O'Brien) G.; A.B., Colorado Coll., 1920; M.D., Harvard, 1924; m. Margaret Crane-Lille, May 12, 1934. Interne in medicine, Boston City Hosp., 1924-26; interne, Boston Psychopathic Hosp., 1926-27, resident, 1927-28; resident in neurology, Boston City Hosp., 1928, jr. vis. neurologist, 1928-29; asst. in neuropathology, Harvard Med. Sch., 1928-29; instr. psychiatry and mental hygiene, Sch. of Medicine, Yale, 1930-32, asst. prof., 1932-37, asso. prof., 1937-42; asso. psychiatrist, New Haven Hosp. and New Haven Dispensary, 1930-42; prof. psychiatry and head dept. psychiatry, neurology, Sch. Medicine, Washington U., St. Louis, Mo., 1942-63, Wallace Renard prof. psychiatry, 1963—; psychiatrist in chief, Barnes, Renard and allied hosps., St. Louis, 1942-63, emeritus, 1963—; cons. psychiatrist, St. Louis City Hosps. Served with S.A.T.C., 1917-18. Mem. Am. Psychiatric Assn., Am. Neurol. Assn., Am. Soc. Clin. Investigation, A.M.A., A.A.A.S., Am. Psychosomatic Soc., Nat. Epilepsy League, Am. League Against Epilepsy, Research in Nervous and Mental Diseases, Interurban Clin. Club, Mo. Assn. Mental Hygiene, Mo. Assn. Social Welfare, Soc. Exptl. Biology and Medicine, Alpha Omega Alpha, Sigma Xi. Contbr. to sci. and med. jours. Home: 6 Westmoreland Pl St Louis MO 63108 Office: Barnes and Renard Hospitals 4940 Audubon Av St Louis MO 63110

GILDEA, JOSEPH JAMES, educator; b. Lawrence, Mass., July 26, 1913; s. James Edward and Mary Jane (Fitzgerald) G.; A.B., Villanova U., 1936; postgrad. Augustinian Coll., 1936-39; M.A., Cath. U. Am., 1940; Ph.D., U. Pa., 1946; LL.D., Merrimack Coll., 1960. Joined Order St. Augustine, 1931, ordained priest Roman Cath. Ch., 1939; instr. modern langs. Villanova U., 1940-47, v.p. acad. affairs, 1959-64; prof., dean, v.p. Merrimack Coll., 1947-59. Mem. Modern Lang. Assn., Internat. Arthurian Soc., Société des anciens textes francais, Modern Humanities Research Assn. Editor: Durmart le Galois, vol. 1, 1965, vol. 2, 1966; Partonopeu de Blois, vol. 1, 1967, vol. 2, 1968-70. Address: The Monastery Villanova PA 19085

GILDER, ROSAMOND, writer, dramatic critic; b. Marion, Mass.; d. Richard Watson and Helena (deKay) G.; ed. pub. schs.; L.H.D., U. Denver, 1969. Writer, 1916—; editorial sec. Nat. Theatre Conf., 1932-35; dir. Playwrights' Bur., Fed. Theatre, 1935-36; dramatic critic, asso. editor, editor-in-chief Theatre Arts, 1938-48; bd. mem. ANTA, 1945-69; pres. Internat. Theatre Inst.; dir. U.S. Center, 1948—; lectr. Barnard Coll., 1948-55. Chmn., U.S. delegation 1st World Conf. on Theatre, Bombay, India, 1956, U.S. delegations Internat. Theatre Congresses, 1948—. Served with A.R.C., France, 1917-19, Children's Bur., A.R.C., 1917-20. Decorated médaille d'Epidemie, médaille de Reconnaissance (France); officer l'Ordre des Arts et des Lettres (France); recipient Fulbright award, Paris, 1955-56. Club: Cosmopolitan (N.Y.C.). Author books including: Biography of Richard Watson Gilder, 1916; John Gielgud's Hamlet, 1937; Enter the Actress, 1960. Translator: My Life (Emma Calvé), 1922. Contbr. articles to profl. jours. Home: 24 Gramercy Park New York City NY 10003

GILDERSLEEVE, THOMAS ARTHUR, hotel exec.; b. Seattle, Oct. 26, 1903; s. Maro Davis and Eva L. (Dodds) G.; student pub. schs. corr. courses; m. Anne Clarice Walken, Mar. 16, 1929; 1 dau., Lynn Marie. Dir. Olympic, Inc., Am. Underwriters Corp.; asso. with Leopold Hotel, Bellingham, Wash., Mt. Baker Lodge, Wash., New Washington Hotel, Benjamin Franklin Hotel, Seattle, 1925-30; mgr. Roosevelt Hotel, 1930-43; mng. dir. Davenport Hotel, Tennis, Broadmoor Country, Washington Athletic, Spokane, Robert Treat Hotel, Newark, 1945-47; v.p., gen. mgr. Olympic Hotel, 1943-57, gen. mgr., 1957- 60, mng. dir., 1960—; v.p. Seattle Olympic Hotel Co., 1960-64, pres., 1964-68; now with William Lockwood Saunders, Corporate Counsel, Seattle; dir. Franklin Savs. & Loan Assn. Bd. dirs. Wash. State Internat. Trade Fair, Broadmoor Maintenance Commn.; bd. dirs., mem. exec. com. Greater Seattle. Mem. Am., Wash. State hotel assns., Seattle C. of C. (trustee), Navy League U.S. (sec. Seattle council), Urban League (dir.). Rotarian. Clubs: Rainier (trustee), Seattle Tennis, Broadmoor Country, Washington Athletic (sec., mem. exec. com.). Home: 1121 Parkside Dr E Seattle WA 98102 Office: White Henry Stuart Bldg 416 Seneca St Seattle WA 98101

GILE, DAVID EMERY, banker; b. Boston June 7, 1922; s. Clement M. and Anne (Ryce) G.; A.B., Yale, 1944; LL.B., U. Pitts., 1949; m. Patricia Rogers Schoen, Oct. 22, 1949; children—Nancy Rogers, David Emery, Lawrence Macalester. Admitted to Pa. bar, 1949; with firm Burgwin, Ruffin & Hazlett, Pitts., 1949-51; trust officer Union Nat. Bank, Pitts., 1951-57; v.p. comml. banking Pitts. Nat. Bank, 1957-64; with Marine Midland Bank, N.Y.C., 1964—, sr. v.p., 1968—; dir. Macrodyne-Chatillon Corp. Chmn. Rye (N.Y.) Recreation Commn. Trustee, treas. United Hosp., Port Chester, N.Y.; bd. dirs. Rye YMCA, Rye United Fund. Served to lt. USNR, 1943-46. Clubs: City Midday, Yale (N.Y.C.); Apawamis, Manursing Island, Am. Yacht (Rye); Pitts. Golf. Home: 129 Grandview Av Rye NY 10580 Office: 140 Broadway New York City NY 10015

GILELS, EMIL, pianist; b. Odessa, Russia, Oct. 19, 1916; s. Grigory and Esphir (Zamoshina) G.; grad. Odessa Conservatory, 1935, Sch. of Mastership of Moscow Conservatory, 1938; m. Farizet Hucistova, Jan. 19, 1947; 1 dau., Elena. First concert, Odessa 1929; has given concerts throughout U.S.S.R., 1933—, Europe, 1945—, U.S.A., 1955, 58, 60, 62, 64, 66, Mex., 1955, Japan, 1957, Can., 1958, 60, 62, 64; debut in N.Y. at Carnegie Hall, 1969; prof. Moscow Conservatory, 1954—. Recipient 1st prize All Union Contest Musicians, Moscow, 1933, 2d prize Vienna Contest, 1936, 1st prize Internat. Contest Pianists, Brussels, 1938; State prize, 1946; Lenin prize, 1962; decorated Order Labor Red Banner, Order of Lenin, 1961, 2d Order of Lenin, 1966; Order de Commandeur Mérite Culturel et Artistique de Paris, 1967; Comdr. Order Leopold I, Brussels, Belgium, 1968. Médaille de Vermeil de la Ville de Paris, 1967. Mem. Central House of Art Workers, Royal Acad. Music London (hon.). Address: State Conservatory Hertzen St 13 Moscow USSR

GILES, FREDERIC THOMAS, coll. dean; b. Sprague, Wash., July 11, 1916; s. Elvin and Flora (Milsap) G.; B.A., Eastern Wash. Coll., 1937; M.A., Wash. State Coll., 1946; Ed.D., Wash. State U., 1961; m. Dorothy Pence, Nov. 22, 1940; children—Barbara, Catherine, Robert. Coach phys. edn., Albion, Wash., 1937-39; coach, instr. pub. schs., Pullman, Wash., 1939-40, Kelso, Wash., 1940-42; asst. supt. schs., Sunnyside, Wash., 1942-49; dir. personnel Everett Jr. Coll., 1949-53, pres., 1953-61; prof. edn., coordinator jr. coll. relations U. Wash., 1961—, dean Coll. Edn., 1967—. Mem. Am. Assn. Jr. Colls. (bd. dirs.), Phi Delta Kappa, Kappa Delta Pi. Mason, Rotarian. Home: 3391 46th Av NE Seattle WA 98105

GILES, H. HARRY, educator; b. Oberlin, O., Oct. 6, 1901; s. Harry Edmund and Florence (Cherry) G.; A.B., Amherst Coll., 1923; A.M., U. Wis., 1937; Ph.D., Ohio State U., 1912; m. Edna Taylor; m. 2d, Mary Albright, Sept. 3, 1935; children—Laurence, Patricia, Gordon, Ann, David. Dir. Holyoke Jr. Achievement Found., 1923-24; mem. English dept., dir. dramatics, athletic coach E. Ill. State Tchrs. Coll., 1924-30; dir. Boys' Club, Hull House, 1929-30; staff English dept. U. Wis., 1930-33; asst. prof. Ohio State U., 1933-37, research asso., cons. 8-year study secondary edn., 1937-41; dir. community work W. Ga. Coll., cons. Julius Rosenwald Found., 1942-44, Am. Council Race Relations, 1944; exec. dir. Bur. Intercultural Edn., 1944-48, adminstrn. adviser, 1948-49; prof. edn., founder, dir. Center for Human Relations Studies, N.Y. U., 1947-56; cons. Action Research Assn., Nat. YMCA, N.Y. State U.; curriculum and community cons. chmn. Ann. Conf. Current Ednl. Issues, 1945- 63; Distinguished cons. humanies Springfield (Mass.) Coll., 1970—; exec. sec. Fund for Research and Edn. Past pres., bd. dirs. Englewood Urban League; past vice chmn. bd. trustees Goddard Coll.; past chmn. bd. Stockbridge Sch.; chief adviser Program Human Devel. and Social Relations, N.Y. U. Mem. Am. Civil Liberties Union, Am. Assn. U. Profs. (past chpt. pres.), Am. Psychol. Assn., Am. Sociol. Assn., N.E.A., Soc. for Psychol. Study Social Issues. Author: Teacher-Pupil Planning, 1941; (with S.P. McCutchon, A.N. Zechiel) Exploring the Curriculum, 1942 (with Robert Cadigan) Playwrights Present, 1942; Human Dynamics, 1954, Education and Human Motivation, 1956; The Integrated Classroom, 1959; Understanding Begins at Home. Contbr. articles to ednl. jours. Office: NY U New York City NY 10003

GILES, JAMES PAUL, Jr., cement co. exec.; b. Texarkana, Tex., Nov. 24, 1919; s. James Paul and Mabel (Legg) G.; B.S., Tex. A. and M. Coll., 1941; M.B.A. with high distinction, Harvard, 1948; m. Joan Epperson, June 24, 1946; children—Christopher, William, Allison. Chem. analyst E.I. duPont de Nemours & Co., 1941, prodn. supr., 1946-47; plant mgr. Dewey & Almy Chem. Co., 1949-51; asst. to pres. Hercules Cement Corp., 1951-54, asst. gen. mgr., 1954, gen. mgr., 1955, v.p., gen. mgr., 1956-58, pres., 1958- 60; pres., chief exec. officer, chmn. exec. com., 1961—; chmn. bd., dir. Hawaiian Cement Corp.; dir. Union Bank. Mem. exec. bd. Tex. A. and M. Served to lt. col., AUS, 1941-46. Decorated Legion of Merit; Mil. Valor Cross (Italy). Mem. Los Angeles C. of C. (dir.), Portland Cement Assn. (dir.), Am. Mining Congress. Clubs: California, Annandale, Los Angeles (Los Angeles); Lincoln; Racquet (Phila.). Home: 1265 Old Mill Rd San Marino CA 91108 Office: 2404 Wilshire Blvd Los Angeles CA 90057

GILES, NORMAN HENRY, educator, geneticist; b. Atlanta, Aug. 6, 1915; s. Norman Henry and Alice (Guerard) G.; A.B., Emory U., 1937; M.A., Harvard, 1938, Ph.D., 1940; M.A. (hon.), Yale, 1951; m. Dorothy Lunsford, Aug. 26, 1939 (dec. Jan. 1967); children—Annette Guerard, David Lunsford; m. 2d, Doris Vos Weaver, Aug. 1, 1969; stepchildren—Gayle Weaver (dec.), Alix Weaver. Instr. botany 1941-45, asst. prof., 1945-46, asso. prof., 1946-51, prof., 1951-61, Eugene Higgins prof. genetics, 1961—; prin. biologist Oak Ridge Nat. Lab., 1947-50; cons. AEC, 1954-64. Mem. genetics study sect. NIH, 1960-64, mem. genetics tng. com., 1966—. Parker fellow Harvard, 1940-41; Fulbright and Guggenheim fellow U. Genetics Inst., Copenhagen, 1959-60; Guggenheim fellow Australian Nat. U., Canberra, 1966. Fellow Am. Acad. Arts and Scis., A.A.A.S.; mem. Nat. Acad. Scis., Genetics Soc. Am. (treas. 1954-56, pres. 1970), Bot. Am., Am. Soc. Naturalists, Radiation Research Soc., Am.

Ornithologists Union, Phi Beta Kappa, Sigma Xi, Editorial bd. Radiation Research, 1953-58, Am. Naturalist, 1961-64. Home: 85 Jackson Rd Hamden CT 06517 Office: Dept Biology Kline Biology Tower Yale U New Haven CT 06520

GILES, PHILIP RANDALL, clergyman, church ofcl.; b. Haverhill, Mass., Jan. 23, 1917; s. Nelson Randall and Ina Belle (Butler) G.; A.B., Tufts Coll., 1938, S.T.B., 1942, S.T.D., 1958; grad. student sociology U. N.H., 1946-47; D.D., St. Lawrence U., 1960; m. Aurelie L. Proctor, June 17, 1941; children—Aurelie Lee, Susan. Ordained to ministry Universalist Ch., 1942; minister Universalist chs., Vt., Mass., N.H.; staff Universalist Ch. Am., 1949-51, 1953-61, gen. supt., 1957-61; v.p. field relations Unitarian Universalist Assn., 1961-64; exec. sec. Joseph Priestley dist. Unitarian Universalist Socs., 1964—. Served from 1st lt. to capt., Chaplains Corps, USAAF, 1942-46; maj. USAF, 1951-53. Home: Towson MD 21204 Office: 200 Washington Av Towson MD 21204

GILES, RICHARD ALDEN, educator, biologist; b. Cummington, Mass., Dec. 12, 1917; s. Arthur L. and Ruth (Stevens) G.; B.S., Mass. State Coll., 1939; M.S., Mich. State Coll., 1941; Ph.D., Mich. State U., 1955; m. Elizabeth Van Maren, June 21, 1941; children—William R., Robert A., Mary E. Mgr., Stanley Works, Ashfield, Mass., 1941-47; mem. faculty Eastern Mich. U., 1947—, prof. biology, 1955—, head dept., 1966—; NSF staff mem. Inst. Elementary Tchr. Biology and Earth Sci., 1960-66. NSF fellow Inst. Botany Cornell U., 1957, Mem. A.A.A.S., Am. Inst. Biol. Scis., Bot. Soc. Am., Mich. Assn. Conservation Ecologists, Mich. Natural Areas Council, Nat. Assn. Biology Tchrs., Mich. Acad. Arts and Letters (chmn. bot. sect. 1962), Mich. Bot. Club (pres. 1959-61), Sigma Xi, Sigma Alpha Epsilon (pres. local chpt. 1938-39). Mem. United Ch. Christ (moderator). Author: (with others) Laboratory Manual for Biology, 1958; The Cell, 1965; The Microscope, 1965; also articles. Editorial bd. Mich. Botantist, 1962- 64. Home: 118 Linden Ct Ypsilanti MI 48197

GILES, ROBERT EDWARD, ins. corp. exec.; b. Spartanburg County, S.C., June 11, 1924; s. James Henry and Lillie Mae (Wilson) G.; B.S. in Commerce, U. N.C., 1949, J.D., 1952; m. Alice Garnett Ryland, Aug. 25, 1948; children—Martha, David, Lewis, Nancy. Admitted to N.C. bar, 1952, D.C. bar, 1969, U.S. Supreme Ct.; pvt. practice, Charlotte, 1952-53; asst. prof. pub. law and govt. U. N.C. Inst. Govt., 1953-55; asst. atty. gen. N.C., 1955-57; adminstrv. asst. to gov. N.C., 1957-61; gen. Counsel U.S. Dept. Commerce, Washington, 1961-67; v.p., gen. counsel Pharm. Mfrs. Assn., 1967-69; v.p. N.C. Blue Cross & Blue Shield, Inc., Durham, 1969—. Mem. Am., Fed., N.C. bar assns., Order of Coif, Phi Beta Kappa, Beta Gamma Sigma. Home: 4216 Oak Park Rd Raleigh NC 27609 Office: 800 S Duke St Durham NC 27702

GILES, ROBERT HARTMANN, editor; b. Cleve., June 6, 1933; s. Robert Hamilton and Grace (Hartmann) G.; B.A, DePauw U., 1955; M.S., Columbia, 1956; m. Nancy May Morgan, Feb. 6, 1960; children—David Morgan, Megan Elizabeth, Robert Hamilton II. Reporter, Newport News Daily Press, 1957-58; report Akron (O.) Beacon Jour., 1958-63, editorial writer, 1963-65, city editor, 1966-68, met. editor, 1968-69, mng. editor, 1969—. Trustee United Fund, Summit County; bd. govs. Blossom Music Center. Served with AUS, 1956-58. Nieman fellow Harvard, 1965-66; co-recipient Pulitzer prize for local reporting, 1971. Mem. Alpha Tau Omega, Sigma Delta Chi. Home: 1327 Merriman Rd Akron OH 44313 Office: 44 E Exchange St Akron OH 44309

GILES, WARREN CRANDALL, baseball exec.; b. Tiskilwa, Ill., May 28, 1896; s. William Francis and Isabelle (Slattery) G.; student Jubilee Coll., Oak Hill, Ill., 1912-13, Staunton (Va.) Mil. Acad., 1914-16; m. Mabel Jane Skinner, Oct. 29, 1932 (dec. July 10, 1943); 1 son, William Yale. Pres. Rochester (N.Y.) Baseball Club, 1928-36; v.p. Cincinnati Baseball Club, 1937-47, pres. since 1948. Pres. Internat. League, 1936; pres. Nat. League Profl. Baseball Clubs, 1951-70, mem. Major League Exec. Council, 1948-69. Mem. Am. Legion, Disabled Am. Vets., Ohio Philos. and Hist. Soc. Republican. Episcopalian. Elk. Clubs: Variety, Cuvier Press, Queen City (Cin). Home: 4878 LeBlond Av Cincinnati OH 45226

GILES, WILLIAM ELMER, pub. exec.; b. Somerville, N.J., July 5, 1927; s. Elmer and Mary Jane (Reed) G.; A.B. in Government, Columbia, 1950, M.S. in Journalism, 1951; m. Gloria Mastrangelo, June 4, 1949; children—William J., Michael E., Richard H. and Paul L. (twins), Joseph R. Reporter, Plainfield (N.J.) Courier-News, 1946-47; copyreader, reporter Wall St. Jour., 1951- 58, mng. editor Southwest edit., Dallas, 1958-61, news editor Washington bur., 1961; an organizer nat. weekly newspaper, Nat. Observer, 1961, editor, 1962-71; asst. gen. mgr. Dow Jones & Co., Inc., pub. Wall Street Jour. and Nat. Observer, 1971—. Mem. White House Corr. Assn., N.Y. Financial Writers Assn., Sigma Delta Chi. Club: Nat. Press (Washington). Home: 1901 Kimberly Rd Silver Spring MD 20903 Office: 11501 Columbia Pike Silver Spring MD 20910

GILES, WILLIAM LINCOLN, univ. pres.; b. Oklahoma City, July 5, 1911; s. William L. and Katherine M. (Hill) G.; B.S.A., U. Ark., 1934, M.S., 1935, LL.D., 1967; Ph.D., U. Mo., 1949; m. Jean Presson, July 11, 1946; children—Ginger K., Richard W., John P. Agronomist, Dept. Agr., 1937-52; supt. Delta br. Expt. Sta., 1952-61; v.p. Miss. State U., 1961-66, pres., 1966—. Dir. Memphis br. Fed. Res. Bank St. Louis. Bd. dir. So. Regional Edn. Bd., 1966—, mem. council grad. edn. agrl. scis., 1965—, chmn., 1967; co-chmn. agrl. research policy adv. com. Dept. Agr. and Nat. Assn. State Univs. and Land Grant Colls., 1969—. Named Man of Year in Agr., Progressive Farmer, 1960, Conservationist of Year, Am. Soc. Soil Conservation, 1963; recipient Distinguished Service award Miss. Farm Bur. Fedn., 1966; Hall of Distinction award Ark. Tech. Alumni Assn., 1968. Fellow A.A.A.S.; mem. Assn. So. Agrl. Workers (pres. 1964), Am. Soc. Agronomy (pres. Miss. sect. 1952), Am. Soc. Agronomy, Soil Conservation Soc. Am., Miss. Entomol. Assn., Sigma Xi, Farm House Frat, Alpha Zeta, Alpha Kappa Psi, Phi Kappa Phi, Gamma Sigma Delta, Omicron Delta Kappa (hon.), Phi Chi Theta (hon.), Blue Key (hon.). Methodist. Rotarian. Home: Drawer J State College MS 39762

GILFILLEN, GEORGE C., Jr., corp. exec.; b. Dayton, O., Oct. 31, 1919; ed. Cornell U.; m. Betty Wright; children—George C. III, Mary Kimbrough. Chmn. bd. E.F. MacDonald Co., Dayton, also dir. subsidiaries; dir. Super Food Services. Bd. dirs. Miami Valley council Boy Scouts Am., United Fund Montgomery and Greene Counties. Mem. Newcomen Soc., Montgomery County Hist. Soc. Mason (32). Clubs: Dayton Country, Bicycle, Dayton Y Athletic, City, Dayton Athletic, Antioch Shrine One Hundred, Miami Valley Skeet, Foreman's (Dayton); N.Y. Athletic; Detroit Athletic; Executive Golf Assn. (dir.). Home: 1215 Runnymede Rd Dayton OH 45419 Office: 129 S Ludlow St Dayton OH 45402

GILFILLEN, WILLIAM WARREN, architect; b. Sidney, O., Nov. 17, 1918; s. Cleon Warren and Helen Edna (Burhardt) G.; B.Arch., Ohio State U., 1949; m. Amy Knoop Stalter, Dec. 18, 1945; children—Statler Warren, Lorie Knoop, Lisa Kingsman. Pvt. practice architecture, 1954; with Wright & Gilfillen, 1955-63, Wright, Gilfillen, Keske, 1963-70; partner Wright-Gilfillen-Keske, Inc., Columbus, O., 1970—; works include United Christian Center, Goodwill Industries Sales Service Bldg., Bethany Luth. Ch. (all Columbus), St. John's Luth. Ch. (Celina, O.). Served with USAAF, 1941-45. Recipient award, Prestressed Concrete Assn., 1967, Columbus Plans award, 1966, award, Nat. Ch. Archtl. Guild, 1962, award, U.S. Steel Co., 1967. Mem. A.I.A., Architects Soc. Ohio, Beta Theta Pi. Presbyn. (elder). Mason. Club: University (Columbus). Home: 710 Carruthers Dr Worthington OH 43085 Office: 1375 Dublin Rd Columbus OH 42315

GILFORD, DOROTHY MORROW, govt. ofcl.; b. Ottumwa, Ia., Feb. 19, 1919; d. Frank Bliss and Mabel Irene (Coate) Morrow; B.S. in Math. magna cum laude, U. Wash., 1940, M.S. in Math., 1942; grad. student Bryn Mawr Coll., also Columbia; m. Leon Gilford, Mar. 31, 1950. Teaching fellow U. Wash., 1940-42; instr. math. Seattle Coll., 1942; lectr. statistics Bryn Mawr Coll., 1944-45; asst. prof. math. George Washington U., 1945-48, lectr., 1948-50; biometrician CAA, 1948-51; sampling expert FTC, 1951-55; head math. statistics br. Office Naval Research, 1955-58, head logistics and math. statistics br., 1959-61, dir. math. sci. div., 1962-68; asst. commr. U.S. Office of Edn., 1968—. Mem. adv. panel math. scis. NSF, 1958-59; mem. Presdl. Study Group Careers for Women, 1966—. Recipient Fed. Woman's award, 1965. Fellow A.A.A.S., Assn. Ednl. Data Systems, Inst. Math. Statistics (rep. conf. bd. math. societies 1963—, program sec. 1960-65), Am. Statis. Assn. (bd. dirs. 1961-63), Royal Statis. Soc.; mem. Inst. Mgmt. Scis., Internat. Statis. Inst. Editor: Naval Research Logistics Quar., 1959—; (with Scarf and Shelley) Multistage Inventory Models and Techniques, 1963; Monograph Series on Mathematical Methods in Logistics, 1963—; (with others) Research Program Effectiveness, 1966. Home: 6602 Rivercrest Ct NW Washington DC 20016 Office: US Office of Edn 400 Maryland Av SW Washington DC 20202

GILHOOLEY, JOHN J., business exec.; b. Bklyn.; Oct. 9, 1921; s. Francis Girard and Ann (Flynn) G.; B.B.A., St. John's Coll., 1942; student N.Y.U., 1942, Harvard, 1942- 43; LL.B., Cornell U., 1949; m. Jo Ann Bergin, Sept. 17, 1949; children—John J., Paul Girard, Mark, Thad, David, James. Admitted to N.Y. bar; asso. firm Lowenstein, Pitcher, Spence, Hotchkiss, Amann & Parr, Esqs., N.Y.C., 1949-53; exec. asst. sec. labor, Washington, 1953-54, spl. asst., 1954-57, asst. sec. labor, 1957-61; partner firm Lowenstein, Pitcher, Hotchkiss, Amann and Parr, 1961-62; commr. N.Y.C. Transit Authority, 1962-68; chmn. Urban Industries, Inc.; dir. Nat. Rail Passenger Corp. Served lt. USNR, 1943-46; communications officer U.S.S. Texas. Mem. Am. Bar Assn., N.Y. State Bar Assn., Assn. Bar City N.Y., Phi Delta Phi, Delta Psi Upsilon. Roman Catholic. Contbr. articles to profl. publs. Home: 35 Prospect Park W Brooklyn NY 11215 Office: 280 Park Av New York City NY 10017

GILIBERTY, FRANK RALPH, hosp. supt.; b. N.Y.C., July 14, 1909; s. Pasquale and Angela (Lavecchia) G.; Civil Engr., Bklyn. Poly. Inst., 1931; M.S., Yale, 1932; certificate N.Y. Sch. Social Work, 1940; m. Bernice E. Kelley, Apr. 3, 1942; children—Patricia E. (Mrs. Paul Poirier), Jean E. (Mrs. A. Krulic). Tchr., Conn. Sch. Boys, Meriden, 1932-33, social worker, 1933-41; mem. staff Southbury (Conn.) Tng. Sch., 1941—, dir. cottage life, 1956-59, supt., 1959—. Vice pres. Am. Assn. Mental Deficiency, 1960, sec.- treas., 1969—. Served with USNR, 1942-45. Decorated Legion of Honor, Bronze Star. Mem. Nat. Assn. Social Workers. Address: Southbury Training Sch Southbury CT 06488

GILINSKY, STANLEY ELLIS, dept. store exec.; b. Trenton, N.J., Aug. 7, 1918; s. Charles Edgar and Rose (Kohn) G.; B.S., Lehigh U., 1940; LL.B., U. Pa., 1944; m. Gerry Braslove, Nov. 25, 1945; children—Michael, Ellen. Admitted to Pa. bar, 1944; law sec. Justice Horace Stern, Supreme Ct., Phila., 1944-45; asso. firm Wolf, Block, Schor & Solis-Cohen, Phila., 1944-46; asst. budget dir. L. Bamberger & Co., Newark, 1946-50; research, planning dir. Gimbels, Phila., 1950-58, asst. dir. corporate expansion, devel. Gimbel Bros., Inc., N.Y.C., 1958-64, dir., 1964-68, corporate v.p., sec., 1968- -, also v.p. charge expansion, planning, devel. for Gimbels and Saks Fifth Ave., a subsidiary, 1964—. Mem. Teaneck (N.J.) Polit. Assembly, 1962—, Teaneck Redevel. Authority, 1970—. Mem. Am. Marketing Assn., Phi Beta Kappa, Pi Lambda Phi. Home: 32 Grayson Pl Teaneck NJ 07666 Office: Gimbel Bros Inc 1275 Broadway New York City NY 10001

GILKERSON, YANCEY SHERARD, editor; b. Laurens, S.C., Mar. 5, 1919; s. Yancey S. and Harriet (Bentz) G.; student Furman U., 1936-38; m. Vashti Keys, July 29, 1941; 1 son, Richard B. City editor The Greenville (S.C.) Piedmont, 1946-48, San Diego Jour., 1949; asst. city editor New Orleans Item, 1950-54; bur. chief Fairchild Publs., Greenville, S.C., 1954-58; editor Women's Wear Daily, N.Y.C., 1958-61; exec. v.p. Textile Hall Corp., 1961-66, pres., treas., 1966—. Home. 112 Lanneau Dr Greenville SC 29605 Office: Exposition Av PO Box 5823 Greenville SC 29606

GILKES, JOHN MILTON, copper co. exec.; b. N.Y.C., Apr. 16, 1915; s. Raymond and Clara (Friend) G.; ed. pub. schs., N.Y.C.; m. Margaret Ruckert, Aug. 22, 1942; 1 son, Craig Milton. With Phelps Dodge Corp., 1941—, asst. comptroller, 1958-66, comptroller, 1966—; also comptroller, dir. numerous subsidiaries. Mem. Financial Execs. Inst., Am. Accounting Assn., Nat. Assn. Accountants, Am. Inst. Mining, Metall. and Petroleum Engrs. Clubs: Manhattan (bd. mgrs. 1968—) (N.Y.C.); Bonnie Briar Country (Larchmont, N.Y.). Home: 39 Birchwood Lane Hartsdale NY 10530 Office: 300 Park Av New York City NY 10022

GILKESON, FILLMORE BOLLING, naval officer; b. Bluefield, W.Va., Oct. 27, 1915; s. William Eskridge and Elizabeth (Jones) G.; B.S., U.S. Naval Acad., 1937; Aero Engr., Cal. Inst. Tech., 1949; m. Elizabeth Jeannette Graham, Feb. 17, 1942; children—Ellen (Mrs. Arvil Lee Cook), Patricia Graham (Mrs. John F. Munger). Commd. ensign USN, 1937, advanced through grades to rear adm., 1965; comdr. Caloosahatchee (AO-98) and Shangri-La (CVA-38), 1959-61; comdr. Anti- Submarine Warfare Group 3 and U.S. Naval Base, Subic Bay, P.R., 1965-68; dir. logistic planning Office of Chief Naval Operations, Washington, 1968-70; U.S. def. attache, U.K., 1970—. Decorated Silver Star medal, Legion of Merit with gold star, D.F.C., Air medal with four gold stars, Purple Heart, Viet Nam Gallantry Cross with palm. Mem. Soc. Exptl. Test Pilots, Naval Order U.S. Episcopalian. Clubs: Army- Navy Country (Arlington, Va.); Royal Wimbledon (London); Sunningdale (Surrey). Home: 9 Hyde Park Crescent London W2 England Office: US Defense Attache US Embassy London W1 England

GILKESON, ROBERT FAIRBAIRN, utility exec.; b. Phila., June 26, 1917; s. Fairbairn and Helen (Geiger) G.; E.E., Cornell U., 1939; m. Marie L. Whitwell, Apr. 26, 1941; children—Katharine, Richard, Thomas, David, Elizabeth. Cadet engr. Phila. Electric Co., 1939-40, successively sta. operating dept., staff Westinghouse Atomic Power div., asst. to supt. generating stas., supt. Eddystone sta., mgr. engring. and research dept., v.p. engring. and research dept., 1946-62, exec. v.p., 1962-65, pres., 1966—, dir., 1962—; pres. dir. Phila. Elec. Power Co., Susquehanna Elec. Co.; v.p., dir. Susquehanna Power Co.; dir. First Pa. Banking and Trust Co., Penn Mut. Life Ins. Co. Trustee Williamson Free Sch. Mech. Trades. Served to capt. AUS, 1940-45. Registered profl. engr., Pa. Mem. I.E.E.E., Pa. Soc. Profl. Engrs., Soc. Am. Mil. Engrs., Franklin Inst., Sigma Alpha Epsilon. Mason. Clubs: Union League, Seaview, Philadelphia Country, Midday, Engineers (Phila.). Home: 1084 Broadview Rd Wayne PA 19087 Office: 1000 Chestnut St Philadelphia PA 19105

GILKEY, GORDON WAVERLY, univ. dean, artist; b. Albany, Ore., Mar. 10, 1912; s. Leonard Ernest and Edna Isabel (Smith) G.; B.S., Albany Coll., 1933; M.F.A., U. of Ore., 1936; Arts D. (honorary, Lewis and Clark College, 1957; m. Vivian Malone, Oct. 17, 1938; 1 son, Gordon Spencer. Ofcl. etcher, New York World's Fair, 1939, 1937-39; etcher Nat. Broadcasting Co., Radio City, 1937-39; mem. art staff, Stephens Coll., Mo., 1939-42; prof. of art and head of dept., Oregon State U., 1947-64, dean Sch. Humanities and Social Sciences, 1963—. Major works in permanent collections: Met. Mus. of Art, etc.; director Internat. Exchange Print Exhibits, 1956—; U.S. advisor IV Bordighera Biennale (Italy), 1957. Chmn., Gov.'s Planning Council for Arts and Humanities in Ore., 1965-67; cons. Ore. Arts Commn., 1967—; chmn. exec. bd. Ore. French Study Center, Ore. German Study Center, Ore. Japan Study Center. Entered Army United States, active duty July 1942 combat intelligence officer; 1946-47, head of War Dept. spl. staff art projects in Europe and chief of Joint-Chiefs-of-Staff Study in Europe of German Psychol. Warfare; collected War Dept. Hist. Properties collection of Nazi and German war art; disch. to Res. as major, Air Force, Oct. 1947. Recipient A.I.A., Carnegie Corp. fellowship, summers, 1930, 32. Officier d'Academie, France, with decoration Palmes Academiques; Order of Merit, Officer's Cross (W. Germany), Star of Solidarity (Italy); Comdr.'s Cross Order of Merit (W. Germany); comdr. Order of Merit (Italy); officer Order Acad. Palms (France); Mem. Am. Soc. Aesthetics, Portland Art Assn., Soc. Am. Graphic Artists, Am. Assn. Museums, Coll. Art Assn., Phi Kappa Phi, Kappa Pi. Artist- author: Etchings: New York World's Fair, 1939. Author articles on art. Home: 350 NW 35th St Corvallis OR 97330 ☆

GILKEY, HERBERT JAMES, educator, engr.; b. Montesano, Wash., Jan. 2, 1890; s. Herbert Luville and Mary Olive (Karr) G.; ed. pub. schs., Medford and Grants Pass, Ore.; B.S., Ore. State Coll., 1911; S.B., Mass. Inst. Tech., 1916; B.S., Harvard, 1916; M.S., U. Ill., 1923; Sc.D. (hon.), Buena Vista Coll., 1939; m. Mildred Virginia Talbot, Aug. 18, 1923 (dec. Dec. 1969); children—Herbert Talbot, Arthur Karr (dec.). Civil engr. various pub. constrn. projects, 1911-14, pvt. projects, 1916-21; mem. faculty U. Ill., 1921-23, U. Colo., 1923-31; prof., head dept. theoretical and applied mechanics Ia. State U., 1931-55, prof., 1955—. Mem. various research and adv. coms. concrete constrn.; cons. Hoover Dam, 1931-33. With Am. Relief Adminstrn., Paris, 1919. Served from 1st lt. to capt., Engr. Res., U.S. Army, 1917-19; AEF. Recipient Wason medal, 1939, Am. Concrete Inst., Henry C. Turner gold medal, 1958; Distinguished Service plaque Ia. Engring. Soc., 1960. Fellow A.A.A.S.; mem. Am. Soc. C.E., Am. Soc. Testing Materials (hon.), Am. Concrete Inst. (pres. 1949; hon. mem.), Soc. Am. Mil. Engrs. (charter), Western Soc. Engrs., Am. Soc. Engring. Edn. (v.p. 1943), Sigma Xi, Tau Beta Pi, Phi Kappa Phi, Chi Epsilon. Club: Osborn Research. Author or co-author books, hand-books and portions of publs. Home: 2328 Donald St Ames IA 50010 ☆

GILKEY, LANGDON, educator, theologian; b. Chgo., Feb. 9, 1919; s. Charles Whitney and Geraldine Gunsaulus (Brown) G.; grad. Asheville (N.C.) Sch., 1936; A.B. magna cum laude, Harvard, 1940; Ph.D. in Religion, Columbia, 1954; m. Dorothy Evelyn Bottom, June 25, 1949 (div.); 1 son, Mark Whitney; m. 2d, Sonja Weber, Jan. 26, 1963; children—Amos Welcome, Frouwkje Tjakien Rachel. Instr. English, Yenching U., Peking, China, 1940- 41; instr. theology Union Theol. Sem., N.Y.C., 1949-50; lectr. religion Vassar Coll., 1951-54; asso. prof. theology Vanderbilt U. Div. Sch., 1954-55, prof., 1955-63; prof. theology U. Chgo. Div. Sch., 1963—. Fellow Nat. Council Religion and Higher Edn., 1948, Am. Council Learned Socs., 1947-49; Fulbright scholar in Eng., 1950-51; Guggenheim fellow in Germany, 1960-61. Mem. Nat. Council Religion Higher Edn., Am. Council Learned Socs., Am. Ch. History Soc., Soc. Theol. Discussion, Phi Beta Kappa. Author: Maker of Heaven and Earth, 1959: How The Church Can Minister to the World Without Losing Itself, 1964; Shantung Compund, 1966; Naming the Whirlwind: The Renewal of God-Language, 1969; Religion and the Scientific Future, 1970. Address: U Chgo Div Sch Chicago IL 60637

GILL, ARDIAN C., actuary; b. Griswold, Conn., Oct. 9, 1929; s. Lewis A. and Sarah (Geer) G.; B.A. with honors in Math., U. Conn., 1951; m. Jill Freeman, May 29, 1954; children—Tracy, Claudia, John Freeman. With Travelers Ins. Co., 1951-54; with Mut. Life Ins. Co. N.Y., 1954—, 2d v.p., actuary, 1965-66, v.p., actuary, 1966-70, sr. v.p., chief actuary, 1970—. Fellow Soc. Actuaries; mem. Acad. Actuaries. Home: 152 E 89 St New York City NY 10028 Office: 1740 Broadway New York City NY 10019

GILL, ARTHUR, electronics co. exec.; b. N.Y.C., Feb. 4, 1931; s. Max and Estelle Gill; B.B.A., City Coll. N.Y., 1952; grad. work law and accounting, N.Y. U. Sch. Law, 1952-53; m. Helen Klein, Dec. 24, 1952; children—Susan Ellyn, Barbara Caryn. With Miller Donaldson and Co., C.P.A.'s, N.Y.C., 1955; asst. accounts mgr. KLM Royal Dutch Airlines, N.Y.C., 1955-56; partner S. Neufeld and Co., C.P.A.'s, N.Y.C., 1956-59; controller, asst. dir. operations Transitube Inc., N.Y.C., 1959-67; treas. Ceco Communications Inc., N.Y.C., 1967-68; pres. Avco Communications Ltd., 1968—; dir. Big Bromley Inc., Manchester, Vt. Treas. Bronxville-Eastchester United Community Fund, 1968—, bd. dirs., 1966—; mem. finance com., budget chmn. United Fund Westchester, 1967—; merit badge counselor Boy Scouts Am,., 1963—; pres. Am. Youth Hostels, Inc., 1968—, mem. exec., finance, nominating and devel. coms., 1959—, pres. Met. N.Y. council, 1957-62; ofcl. U.S. del. Internat. Youth Hostel Fedn. Conf., Duisberg, Germany, 1959; Served with AUS, 1953-55. Mem. Am. Inst. Accountants, Electronics Distbrs. Assn., Community TV Credit Assn. (treas.), Alpha Phi Omega. Home: 19 Tudor Lane Scarsdale NY 10583 Office: 55 W 16 St New York City NY 10011

GILL, ATTICUS JAMES, physician, educator; b. Okmulgee, Okla., June 8, 1914; s. X.R. and Martha (Trotter) G.; M.D., Duke, 1938; m. Lucille Hodge, Nov. 8, 1941; children—Frank Harrison, Mary, James Hodge. Intern, residency tng. pathology Duke Hosp. and St. Pauls Hosp., Dallas, 1938-41; instr. pathology U. Tenn., 1941-42, asst. prof., 1942-43; asst. prof. pathology Southwestern Med. Sch., 1943-46, asso. prof., 1947-49, prof., 1950—, asso. dean, 1950-51, asst. dean, 1952-55, dean, 1955-67; staff Parkland Meml. Hosp.; cons. staff Baylor Hospital, Presbyterian Hospital, St. Paul's Hospital, Dallas. Diplomate Am. Bd. Pathology. Fellow Am. Soc. Clinical Pathologists, College Am. Pathologists, American College of Physicians; member of A.M.A., So., Tex. med. assns., Tex. Soc. Pathologists, Dallas So. Clin. Soc., Dallas County Med. Soc. (dir. 1956- 58), Alpha Omega Alpha, Sigma Phi Epsilon, Phi Chi. Home: 7103 Lakewood Blvd Dallas TX 75214

GILL, BERNARD IVES, librarian; b. Rockford, Ill., May 16, 1921; s. Richard Hackett and Floss Adeline (Campbell) G.; student Beloit Coll., 1939, 42; B.A., U. Ill., 1943, M.S., 1949; grad. student U. Minn., 1962, 63-64; m. Dorothy Marie Hovde, Aug. 24, 1949; 1 son, Brian

Hovde. Tchr., Bensenville, Ill., 1946- 47; librarian Moorhead (Minn.) State Coll., 1950—. Served with USNR, 1943-46. Mem. N.E.A., A.L.A., Am. Assn. U. Profs., Am. Studies Assn. Methodist (local preacher). Home: 1010 16th St Moorhead MN 56560

GILL, BRENDAN, writer; b. Hartford, Conn., Oct. 4, 1914; s. Michael Henry Richard and Elizabeth (Duffy) G.; A.B., Yale, 1936; m. Anne Barnard, June 20, 1936; children—Brenda, Michael, Holly, Madelaine, Rosemary, Kate, Charles. Contbr. New Yorker, 1936—, film critic, 1960-67, drama critic, 1968—. Pres. Municipal Art Soc., N.Y.C.; bd. dirs. Film Soc. Lincoln Center. Mem. Victorian Society America (v.p.). Clubs: Grolier, Coffee House, Century Assn. (N.Y.C.). Author: The Trouble of One House, 1950; The Day The Money Stopped (adapted play with Maxwell Anderson, 1958), 1957; Fat Girl, 1971. Home: Bronxville NY 10708 also Norfolk CT 06058 Office: 25 W 43d St New York City NY 10036

GILL, EDWIN MAURICE, state ofcl.; b. Laurinburg, N.C., July 20, 1899; s. Thomas Jeffries and Mamie (North) G.; student Trinity Coll., 1922-24; LL.D., Duke, 1959. Admitted to N.C. bar, 1924; mem. firm Gibson and Gill, Laurinburg, N.C., 1924-31, Gardner, Morrison & Rogers, Washington, 1949-50; pvt. sec. to gov. of N.C., 1931-33; commr. paroles State of N.C., 1933-42; commr. revenue, 1942-49; collector, dir. internal revenue, Greensboro, N.C., 1950-53; treas. State of N.C., Raleigh, 1953—. Bd. commrs. Law Enforcement Officers' Benefit and Retirement Fund; mem., investment officer Local Govt. Employees' Retirement System; mem. N.C. Bd. Edn.; former mem. N.C. Probation Commn., N.C. Art Commn. Mem. N.C. Ho. of Reps., 1929, 31. Trustee, N.C. Art Mus. Mem. Am. Legion, Nat. Tax Assn., Nat. Assn. Tax Adminstrs., Sigma Nu Phi, Omicron Delta Kappa, Beta Gamma Sigma. Democrat. Methodist. Address: State Capitol Bldg Raleigh NC 27601

GILL, ERNEST CLARK, ins. exec.; b. Kingston, Ont., Can., Apr. 5, 1903; s. William and Mary (Spankie) G.; B.A., Queen's U., 1923, LL.D. (hon.), Queen's U., 1957; m. Mercedes Rae, Oct. 26, 1929; 1 dau., Mary Rae. Joined Can. Life Assurance Co., 1923, asst. actuary, 1927-30, asst. treas., 1930-38, treas., 1938-39, asst. gen. mgr. and treas., 1939-46, gen. mgr., 1946- 47, v.p., gen. mgr., 1947-51, pres., 1951-64, vice chmn. bd., 1964—, dir., 1946—; v.p., dir. Canadian Imperial Bank of Commerce; dir. Nat. Trust Co., Ltd. Recipient Gold Medal, Queen's U., 1923. Fellow Canadian Inst. Actuaries, Soc. Actuaries, Am. Life Conv. (exec. com. Chgo.; v.p. Ont.). Presbyn. Clubs: Toronto, Granite, Eastbourne, York. Home: 77 Hillholm Rd Toronto 7 Ontario Canada Office: 330 University Av Toronto 1 Ontario Canada

GILL, GEORGE NORMAN, newspaper editor; b. Indpls., Aug. 11, 1934; s. George E. and Urith (Dailey) G.; A.B., Ind. U., 1957; m. Kay Baldwin, Dec. 28, 1957; children—Norman A., George B. Reporter, Richmond (Va.) News Leader, 1957- 60; copy editor, reporter, acting Sunday editor, city editor, mng. editor Courier-Jour., Louisville, 1960—. Served with USNR, 1954-56. Recipient Picture Editors award Nat. Press Photographers Assn., 1965. Mem. Am. Soc. Newspaper Editors, Asso. Press Mng. Editors, Louisville Com. on Foreign Relations, Alpha Tau Omega, Sigma Delta Chi. Mason. Home: 308 Rebel Dr Pewee Valley KY 40056 Office: 525 W Broadway Louisville KY 40202

GILL, GRAYSON WOODWARD, architect, engr.; b. Port Clinton, O., Nov. 7, 1893; s. Elmer Ellsworth and Sarah (Woodward) G.; student Ohio State U., 1911-14; B.S., U. Mich., 1921; m. Cornelia Wade Douglas, June 16, 1927; 1 son, Grayson Douglas. Draftsman Mills Rhines, Bellman & Nordhoff, 1914-16, Am. Bridge Co., 1924-25; engr. Herbert M. Greene Co., 1925-34; pvt. practice architecture and engring., 1934-58; pres. Grayson Gill, Inc., Dallas, 1959—. Mem. Dallas City Plan Commn., 1939-48; chmn. Dallas Bldg. Code Com., 1946-47; mem. Greater Dallas Planning Council-Dallas Fire Council, 1966—; mem. Bldg. Tex. Commn. Code Com., 1968; chmn. Regional Bldg. Code Study Com., North Central Tex. Council Govts. Served as 1st lt., U.S. Army, 1916-19. Recipient award for meritorious design, Tex. Soc. Architects. Fellow A.I.A., Am. Soc. C.E.; mem. Bldg. Research Inst., Am. Concrete Inst., Constrn. Specifications Inst. Home: 4000 Rock Creek Dr Dallas TX 75204 Office: 1913 San Jacinto St Dallas TX 75201

GILL, JAMES FRANCIS, artist; b. Tahoka, Tex., Dec. 10, 1934; s. Francis Edward and Elizabeth (Crie) G.; painting scholarship, U. Tex., 1960-61; m. Antoinette Bower, Nov. 21, 1963; 1 son by previous marriage, Kevin Crie. One man shows include Alan Gallery, N.Y.C., 1962, 64, Felix Landau Gallery, Los Angeles, 1963; rep. permanent collections Mus. Modern Art, Chgo. Art Inst.; group shows include Mus. Modern Art. Recipient Watson F. Blair purchase prize Chgo. Art Inst., 1964. Served with USMC, 1953-56. ‡

GILL, JAMES M., petroleum co. exec.; b. Ruston, La., 1922; B.S., La. Poly. Inst., 1943; M.S., La. State U., 1948; married. With Armour & Co., 1943-44; with Ethyl Corp., N.Y.C., 1948—, gen. mgr. indsl. chem. div., 1963-66, v.p. chem. group, 1966-69, sr. v.p., 1969—, also dir. Home: 3178 McCarrol Dr Baton Rouge LA 70809 Office: 100 Park Av New York City NY 10017*

GILL, JOCELYN RUTH, astronomer; b. Flagstaff, Ariz., Oct. 29, 1916; d. Thomas B. and Sarah (Bailey) Gill; A.B. in Math., Wellesley Coll., 1938; S.M. in Astronomy and Astrophysics, U. Chgo., 1941; Ph.D. in Astronomy, Yale, 1959. Lab. asst., instr. astronomy Mt. Holyoke Coll., 1940-42; staff mem. radiation lab. Mass. Inst. Tech., 1942-45; from instr. to asst. prof. astronomy Smith Coll., 1945-52; grad. work, teaching asst. U. Cal. at Berkeley, 1946-48; asst. prof., then acting chmn. dept. astronomy Mt. Holyoke Coll., 1952-57; asso. prof. astronomy and math. Ariz. State Coll., 1959- 60; vis. lectr. Wellesley Coll., 1960-61; staff scientist Office Astronomy and Solar Physics, Office Space Sci., NASA, Washington, 1961- 63, with manned space sci. div., 1963-66, chief in-flight scis., 1963-66, staff scientist Manned Flight Experiments Office, 1966-67, program scientist for manned flight experiments, physics and astronomy Office of Space Science and Applications, 1967—; made solar eclipse flight in 1963. Recipient of the Fed. Woman's award, 1966; Multiple Sclerosis Woman of the Year award, 1966; Alumnus Achievement award Proviso E. High Sch., Maywood, Ill., 1969. Fellow A.A.A.S.; mem. Am. Astron. Soc., Nantucket Maria Mitchell Assn., Am. Assn. Variable Star Observers, Washington Philos. Soc., Sigma Xi. Presbyn. Club: Zonta. Home: 560 N St SW Washington DC 20024 Office: Hdqrs NASA Washington DC 20546

GILL, JOHN GEORGE, steel co. exec.; b. Rotherham, Eng., Dec. 16, 1916; s. John and Rose Gill; M.S., Coll. Tech., Rotherham; student Kingston Coll. Tech.; m. Barbara Bath, June 22, 1940; children—Margaret, Richard, Robert, Penelope. Asst. engr. Steel, Peech & Tozer, Sheffield, Eng., 1937-39; tech. officer Ministry Aircraft Prodn., 1940-45; engr. E. Ramsay Green, London, 1945-46; engr., mgr. Steel, Peech & Tozer, 1946-49; pvt. practice cons. engr., Can., 1949-53; v.p. Canadian Steel Improvement Co., Toronto, Can., 1953-58; joined Crucible Steel Co. Am., Pitts., 1959, became v.p. prodn.; now pres. Pa. Engring. Corp., New Castle. Mem. Bd. Beaver County chpt. Pa. Economy League, Rochester (Pa.) Gen. Hosp., Beaver County chpt. Health and Welfare Assn. Registered profl. engr., Ont. Mem. Profl. Engrs. Ont., Engring. Inst. Can., Canadian Mfrs. Assn. (mem. bd.), Inst. Mech. Engrs., Royal Aero. Soc., Inst. Prodn. Engrs., Am. Iron and Steel Inst., Am. Soc. Metals, Soc. Small Craft Designers. Home: Mantoloking NJ 08738 Office: Pa Engring Corp New Castle PA 16101

GILL, JOHN GLANVILLE, educator; b. Louisville, Nov. 22, 1909; s. John Glanville and Helen Chenoweth (Stites) G.; student Harvard, 1928-30, Ph.D., 1947; A.B. with honors, U. Wis., 1936; S.T.B., Union Theol. Sem., N.Y.C., 1940; m. Evalyn Ruth Pierpoint, Nov. 10, 1943; children—Susan Pierpoint, Mary Louise. Ordained to ministry Unitarian Ch., 1940; minister in Grafton, Mass., 1940-41, Alton, Ill., 1944-50, Tacoma, 1951-55; asst. prof. philosophy U. Alaska, 1960-63; asso. prof. Ft. Lewis Colo., Durango, Colo., 1965-66; prof. philosophy Central Mich. U., 1966—, chmn. dept., 1966-68. Participated in organizing civil liberties group challenging sch. segregation, Alton, 1950; chmn. Am. Civil Liberties Union, Tacoma, 1954. Fellow Am. Council Learned Socs., 1942. Mem. Am. Philos. Assn., A.A.A.S., Philosophy Sci. Assn., Am. Assn. Value Inquiry, Assn. Symbolic Logic, Unitarian Mininsterial Assn. (nat. exec. 1947-51, exec. bd. Pacific Coast council 1952-55), Fellowship Religious Humanists (exec. bd.), Detroit Philos. Soc. (exec. bd.), Wash. Mountineers. Author: Tide Without Turning, 1958; also articles and poems. Home: 3790 Stockman Rd Mount Pleasant MI 48858

GILL, JOHN KERMODE, Jr., mfg. co. exec.; b. Cleve., July 22, 1930; s. John Kermode and Elizabeth (McIntyre) G.; grad. Episcopal High Sch., Alexandria, Va., 1950; B.S., Va. Poly. Inst., 1957; part-time student Case Western Res. U., 1968; m. Barbara T. Houchins, Aug. 21, 1951; children—John M., Jane T., James P. With Clevite Corp., Cleve., 1957-69, sec., 1968-69, treas., 1969; sec., Gould Inc, 1969—; dir. Body Bros. Inc. Pres. Travelers Aid Cleve., 1968-69. Mem. Am. Soc. Corporate Secs., Ohio Soc. C.P.A.'s, Tax Execs. Inst., Tax Club Cleve. Episcopalian (treas.). Clubs: Mayfield Country, Union (Cleve.). Home: 1470 Pheasant Trail Inverness IL 60067 Office: 8550 W Bryn Mawr Av Chicago IL 60631

GILL, JOHN PAUL, educator; b. Warrior-Run, Pa., Jan. 7, 1910; s. John and Hedwig (Ryto) G.; student Pa. State Coll., 1929-31; A.B., U. Ala., 1932, M.A., 1934; Ph.D., U. Tex., 1950; m. Bernice Victoria Alman, May 24, 1932; 1 son, John Paul. Asst. instr. Sch. Bus. Adminstrn., U. Ala., 1932-34, instr. comml. math., 1934-42, instr. bus. statistics, statistician Bur. Bus. Research, 1942-43, asst. prof., 1945-46; head math. dept. John E. Brown Coll., summers 1934-35; research statistician dept. research Fed. Res. Bank, Dallas, 1943-45; chief research and progress analysis div. Houston regional office War Assets Adminstrn., 1946-47; instr. U. Tex., 1947- 49; asst. prof. Fla. State U., 1949-51; prof. econ. statistics, dir. div. research, also editor Atlanta Econ. Rev., Sch. Bus. Adminstrn., Atlanta div. U. Ga., 1951-54, prof. econs., dir. Bur. Bus. Research, coordinator grad. studies, also editor Ga. Bus., U. Ga. Coll. Bus. Adminstrn., 1954-60; prof., head dept. bus. statistics Sch. Commerce and Bus. Adminstrn., U. Ala., 1960—. Mem. Am. Assn. U. Profs., Am. Statis. Assn. (past chpt. pres.), So. Econs. Assn., Pi Mu Epsilon, Alpha Kappa Psi, Beta Gamma Sigma (nat. exec. com. 1958-61). Author booklet on indexes of retail sales, also chpt. 1953-54 Credit Mgmt. Year-Book; numerous articles in field. Editor: Southeastern Resources Handbook, vols. I, II, III. Home: 10 C Northwood St Northport AL 35476

GILL, LEWIS MERRITT, arbitrator; b. Grand Rapids, Mich., Feb. 4, 1912; s. Irving Leo and Mary E. (Whitney) G.; A.B., Swarthmore Coll., 1933; LL.B., U. Pa., 1936; m. Mary M. Lutz, Dec. 5, 1936; children—Lewis Merritt, Mary G. (Mrs. Donald Hoffman). Admitted to D.C. bar, 1936; atty. NLRB, 1937-41; staff mediator, pub. mem. Nat. War Labor Bd., 1941-45; dir. Labor Standards Assn., Phila., 1946-67; arbitrator, Merion, Pa., 1950—. Mem. Presidential Bd.-Aerospace, Airlines, Rys., 1962-64; chmn. Presidential Emergency Bd.-R.R. Dispute, 1970. Mem. Nat. Acad. Arbitrators (pres. 1971), Indsl. Relations Research Assn. Address: 527 Baird Rd Merion PA 19066

GILL, RICHARD THOMAS, educator; b. Long Branch, N.J., Nov. 30, 1927; s. Thomas Grant and Myrtle (Sickles) G.; A.B., Harvard, 1948, Ph.D., 1956; student Oxford (Eng.) U., 1948-49; m. Betty Bjornson, Jan. 6, 1950; children—Thomas Grandon, Peter Severin, Geoffrey Karl. Asst. dean Harvard, 1949-52, Allston Burr sr. tutor, 1955-63, asst. prof. econs., 1958-63, master Leverett House, also lectr. econs., 1963—. Trustee, Choate Sch.; bd. dirs. Harvard Cooperative Soc. Served with AUS, 1946-47. Recipient Atlantic First Short Story prize, 1954. Mem. Harvard Signet Soc. (pres. 1965-66). Author: Economic Development: Past and Present, 1963; Evolution of Modern Economics, 1967; Economics and the Public Interest, 1968. Home: Leverett House 25 DeWolfe St Cambridge MA 02138

GILL, STANLEY JENSEN, educator; b. Salt Lake City, Aug. 21, 1929; s. Stanley Hewitt and Frances (Jensen) G.; student Occidental Coll., 1947; A.B. magna cum laude, Harvard, 1951; Ph.D. in Chemistry, U. Ill., 1954; m. Jane C. Pittenger, June 7, 1952; children—Elizabeth J., Stanley C. Research and teaching asst. U. Ill., 1951-53; research asso. Cornell U., 1954; faculty U. Colo., Boulder, 1956—, prof. chemistry, 1964—. Cons. NIH, 1966-69. Served with AUS, 1954-56. Mem. Am., Brit. chem. socs., Sigma Xi, Phi Lambda Upsilon, Alpha Chi Sigma. Research properties macromolecules biophys. chemistry. Home: 2665 Dartmouth Av Boulder CO 80303

GILL, THOMAS HARVEY, author, found. exec.; b. Phila., Jan. 21, 1891; s. John Alexander and Clara (Lex) G.; B.A., U. Pa., 1913; M.F., Yale, 1915; Dr. honoris causa, U. Andes, Venezuela, 1953; m. Vivian Perry, Dec. 31, 1918. Asst. instr. forest mensuration Yale Forest Sch., 1914; timber estimator Kaul Lumber Co., 1915; asst. ranger U.S. Forest Service, 1915, forest ranger, 1916-17, dep. forest supr., 1920-21, forest supr., 1922, in charge forest service ednl. activities, 1922- 25; asso. editor Am. Forests and Forest Life Mag., 1925; exec. dir. Charles Lathrop Pack Forestry Found., 1952-60, sec. Forestry Found., 1926- 60; adviser on forest policy for Philippines, 1959. U.S. del., mem. organizing com. 5th World Forestry Congress, Seattle, 1960, del. 6th Congress, Madrid, 1966 (vice chmn. U.S. nat. com.); mem. U.S. nat. com. 7th Congress, Buenos Aires, 1972; mem. Timber Conservation Bd. (adv. com.); fellow Oberlaender Trust, 1936; mem. Wm. Alanson White Psychiat. Found., 1937-45; mem. publs. com. for psychiatry Jour. Biology and Pathology of Interpersonal Relations, 1937-45; mem. interim com. mgrs. Washington Sch. Psychiatry, 1937-45; spl. adviser on forestry UN Com. on Food and Agr., Copenhagen, Denmark, 1946, adviser Am. delegation, Washington, 1948-49, Rome, 1955; adviser on forest policy for Japan, 1951, Formosa, 1952, 56; del. U.S. Govt. 3d World Forestry Congress, Helsinki, 1949, Inter- Am. Conservation Conf., Denver, 1948; exec. dir. Internat. Union Socs. Foresters, 1966-70; chmn. FAO Com. Unexploited Forests, 1947—, chmn. Am. delegation FAO Conf. Land Utilization Far East, 1951, Far East Forestry Commn. meeting, 1952; chmn. FAO com. on forestry devel. in tropics, 1967-69; mem. Nat. Acad. Scis. adv. com. on research to Nat. Park Service, 1962- 65. Made 1st forest survey, party aerial, tropical forests in Carribean region, penetrating undiscovered sects.; 1st mosaic aerial map U.S., 1919. Served as 1st lt. AS, U.S. Army, World War I. Decorated D.S.C., Germany; Merito Civico Forestal (Mexico), chevalier Merite Agricole (France); Recipient diploma honor Mexican Inst. Renewable Resources, 1966; Fernow award Am. Forestry Assn. and German Forestry Soc., 1967. Fellow Soc. Am. Foresters (Schlich medal 1954) mem. Pacific Sci. Assn. (sec. for com. 1948), Soc. Filipino Foresters (hon.), Internat. Soc. Tropical Foresters (pres.), Am. Forestry Assn. (past v.p.), Soc. Mexican Foresters (hon.), Yale Forest Sch. Alumni Assn. (past v.p.), Nat. Acad. Scis. (chmn. internat. com. tropical forestry), La Sociedad Mexicana de Historia Natural (hon.), La Asociacion Mexicana de Proteccion a la Naturaleza (hon.). Clubs: Explorers (N.Y.C.); Army-Navy, Cosmos, International (Washington). Author books including: Land Hunger in Mexico, 1951; Tropical Forests of the Carribean, 1955; compiler (with E.C. Dowling) The Forestry Directory, 1943, 49. Contbr. articles to publs. Home: 2800 Jenifer St NW Washington DC 20015 Office: 1500 Massachusetts Av NW Washington DC 20005

GILL, THOMAS PONCE, lt. gov. Hawaii; b. Honolulu, Apr. 21, 1922; s. Thomas and Lorin (Tarr) G.; student U. Hawaii, 1940-41; B.A., U. Cal. at Berkeley, 1948, LL.B., 1951; m. Lois Hanawalt, Aug. 25, 1947; children—Thomas Anthony, Andrea Tiare, Eric William, Ivan Ponce, Timothy Michael, Gary Lorin. Admitted to Hawaii bar, 1951; partner firm Gill, Doi, Naito, Shim & McClung, Honolulu, 1951-62; atty. for Senate, T.H., 1955; adminstrv. asst. to speaker of House, T.H., 1957; mem. 30th Territorial and 1st State Legislature from 15th Dist., 1958-62; majority floor leader Ho. of Reps., 1959-62; mem. 88th Congress at large from Hawaii; adminstr. of Office Econ. Opportunity, Hawaii, 1965-66; lt. gov., State Hawaii, 1966—. Chmn. Oahu Dem. County Com., 1954-58; campaign chmn. Oahu County, 1952, 54; del. Dem. Nat. Conv., 1960, 64. Bd. dirs. Honolulu Community Chest. Served with inf. AUS, 1942-45; PTO. Decorated Bronze Star, Purple Heart. Mem. Am. Legion, John Howard Assn., Nat. Conf. State Legislative Leaders, U. Hawaii Alumni Assn. Home: 4104 Round Top Dr Honolulu HI 96822 Office: Iolani Palace Honolulu HI 96813

GILL, WILLIAM ALBERT, Jr., labor union ofcl.; b. Charleston, W.Va., Oct. 26, 1924; s. William Albert and Lucille (Groves) G.; student U. Mo., 1942, U. Minn., 1948-49; m. Bonita Gladys Ward, Jan. 20, 1944; children—Patricia (Mrs David G. Sneddon), William Ward, Robert Arthur. Mechanic, insp. Capital Airlines, 1946-52; flight engr. Pan Am. World Airways, 1952-63; mem. Flight Engrs. Internat. Assn., 1952—, v.p. Pan Am. World Airways chpt., 1957-63, master exec. bd. del., 1957-63, internat. pres. 1963—; pres. Internat. Tech. Inst. Flight Engrs., 1964—; mem. gen. bd. AFL-CIO, 1963—. Served with USAAF, 1942-46. Mem. Phi Gamma Delta. Home: 2311 Belair Dr Bowie MD 20715 Office: 905 16th St NW Washington DC 20006

GILL, WILLIAM NELSON, univ. provost; b. N.Y.C., Sept. 13, 1928; s. William Nelson and Frances (Murphy) G.; B.Chem. Engring., Syracuse U., 1951, M.A., 1955, Ph.D., 1960; m. Marie Louise Reichen, Jan. 23, 1954; children—Alison Louise, Christine Marie, Douglas Max, Max William. Field engr. Am. Blower Corp., 1951-55; mem. faculty Syracuse U., 1957-65, asso. prof., 1963-65; prof. chem. engring., chmn. dept. Clarkson Coll. Tech., 1965-71; provost engring. and applied sci. State U. N.Y. at Buffalo, 1971—; cons. in field Mem. Am. Inst. Chem. Engrs., A.A.A.S., Am. Chem. Soc., Am. Soc. Engring. Edn., Am. Assn. U. Profs., N.Y. Acad. Sci., Sigma Xi. Author numerous articles in field. Home: 19 Ruskin Rd Eggertsville NY 14226

GILLAM, BASIL EARLY, educator; b. Wellsville, Mo., Oct. 24, 1913; s. Charles Everett and Saloma (Tucker) G.; student Central Coll., 1931-34; A.B., U. Mo., 1935, M.A., 1936, Ph.D., 1940; m. Cleo Bryson, Aug. 19, 1939; children—Barbara Earlene, Boyd Edward. Asst. instr. math. U. Mo., 1936-40, instr., 1940- 44; asso. prof. Drake U., 1944-46, prof., head dept. math. since 1946. Mem. Am. Math. Soc., Math. Assn. Am., Ia. Acad. Sci., Pi Mu Epsilon, Kappa Mu Epsilon. Home: 1230 41st St Des Moines IA 50311

GILLARD, WILLIAM ANTHONY, librarian; b. Scranton, Pa., Oct. 22, 1904; s. Anthony W. and Mary (Clark) G.; student St. Thomas High Sch., Scranton; A.B., St. Thomas Coll. (now U. Scranton), 1925; J.D., St. John's U., 1932; B.S., Columbia, 1936, grad. student, 1940-41; student U. Chgo., 1945; m. Katherine E. McCann, Oct. 17, 1931; children—Robert W., William Anthony, Peter McCann. Tchr. St. Thomas High Sch., 1925-27; reference librarian St. Thomas Coll., 1927-29; tchr. St. John's U., 1929-36, asst. librarian, asst. dir. libraries, 1936-42, dir. libraries, 1942—, prof. library sci. 1949-66. Mem. N.Y., Cath. (pres. 1963-65) library assns., A.L.A. Roman Catholic. K.C. Home: 9005 210th Pl Bellaire NY 11428 Office: Grand Central and Utopia Pkwys Jamaica NY 11432

GILLELAND, BRADY BLACKFORD, educator; b. Wheeling, W.Va., July 12, 1922; s. Andrew J. and Catherine (Blackford) G.; A.B., Washington and Jefferson Coll., 1944; M.A., U. Okla., 1949; Ph.D., U. N.C., 1953; m. Doris Warrick, June 4, 1945; children—Elizabeth Ann, Margaret Dale. Instr., U. Tenn., 1953; asst. prof. Beloit (Wis.) Coll., 1954-57; mem. faculty U. Vt., 1958—, prof. Classics, 1960—, chmn. dept., 1968—. Served with USMCR, 1943-45. Mem. Classical Assn. New Eng., Vergilian Soc., Am. Philol. Assn., Am. Acad. Rome (adv. council). Editor: (with Evan T. Sage) Petronius: The Satiricon, rev. edit., 1969; also articles. Home: 87 Robinson Pkwy Burlington VT 05401

GILLEM, ALVAN CULLOM, II, air force officer; b. Nogales, Ariz., Apr. 20, 1917; s. Alvan Cullom, Jr. and Virginia (Harrison) G.; B.S., U.S. Mil. Acad., 1940; grad. Flying Sch., 1941, Command and Staff Coll., 1948, Air War Coll., 1954; m. Elizabeth Knight, July 31, 1940; children—Nancy (Mrs. Richard Ogden), Alvan Cullom IV, Jennings Frederick II. Enlisted in U.S. Army, 1935, commd. 2d lt., 1940, advanced through grades to lt. gen. USAF, 1968; served with Mediterranean Allied Air Forces, Algiers, Tunis, 1943-44; comdr. 307th Fighter Squadron, 31st Fighter Group, 1944; with plans staff USAAF, 1944-46, SAC, 1946-47, CIA, 1948-50; dep. comdt. 31st Fighter Wing, 1950-51; comdr. 108th Fighter-Bomber Wing, 1951; base comdr. RAF Sta., Upper Heyford, Eng., 1952-53; dep. comdt., later comdt. Command and Staff Sch., 1954-57; comdr. 380th Bomb Wing, SAC, 1957-61, 820th Air Div., 1961, 57th Air Div., 1961-62, 823d Air Div., 1963-64; dep. dir. operations SAC, 1964-65, dir. operations, 1965-66, dep. chief staff operations, 1966-68, comdr. 3d Air Div. Strategic Air Command, 1968-69. Decorated Legion of Merit, D.F.C. with oak leaf cluster, Air medal with 13 oak leaf clusters, D.S.M. Home: Ocean Reef FL 33140 Office: Comdr 3d Air Division SAC APO San Francisco CA 96334

GILLEN, ALBERT JOHN, broadcasting exec.; b. Queens, N.Y., Dec. 11, 1919; s. Henry Charles and Clara Vivien (Selig) G.; B.S. magna cum laude, Syracuse U., 1948; m. Doris Vivien Bossi, Mar. 5, 1944; children—Jeffrey Dana, Douglas John. With merchandising dept. Compton Advt., N.Y.C., 1940-42; sales mgr. WSYR-TV, Syracuse, N.Y., 1949-52; dir. sales WHAS-TV, Louisville, 1952-57; v.p., dir. sales WAPI-AM-FM-TV, 1957-60; gen. sales mgr. WPRI-TV, Providence, 1960-64; exec. v.p., gen. mgr. WJRT-TV, Poole Broadcasting, Flint, Mich., 1964-69, pres., 1969—; dir. Television Bur. Advt., N.Y.C., Mich. Nat. Bank, Flint. Co-chmn. radio and TV com. United Fund, 1967; chmn. Barrington Heart Fund, Providence, 1962. Trustee St. Joseph Hosp., Flint. Mem. exec. com.

Urban Coalition Greater Flint. Served with USCGR, 1942-44. Mem. Flint C. of C., Internat. Radio and Television Soc., Broadcast Pioneers, Mich. Assn. Broadcasters, Alpha Delta Sigma (pres. 1946), Beta Gamma Sigma. Rotarian. Clubs: Flint Golf, University (Flint); Marco Island Golf (Fla.); Murmuring Pines Fishing and Hunting. Contbr. to book TV Station Management, 1964. Home: 6490 Carriage Hill Dr Grand Blanc MI 48439 Office: 2302 Lapeer Rd Flint MI 48503

GILLEN, JAMES FREDERICK JOHN, educator; b. Winnepeg, Man., Can., May 6, 1915; s. Charles Frederick and Maud (Chisholm) G.; B.A., U. Wis., 1935, Oxford (Eng.) U., 1938; M.A., Harvard, 1938, Oxford U., 1962; Ph.D. Harvard, 1942; m. Sheila Cunningham Engert, Dec. 21, 1956; children—Isobel, Sara, Frederick. Instr., Bowdoin Coll., 1946, Princeton, 1946-47; historian Army Dept., 1948-59; Historian State Dept., 1950-53, cons., 1954-55, sr. research asso. human relations area files, 1955-58; asst. prof. Wabash Coll., 1958-60, asso. prof., 1958-62; prof., chmn. dept. history Cedar Crest Coll., 1962-68; prof. history State U. N.Y., Geneseo, 1968—. Served to lt. comdr., USNR, 1942-46. Mem. Am. Histo. Assn., Am. Polit. Sci. Assn., Soc. for French Hist. Studies, Am. Assn. Rhodes Scholars, Assn. Am. U. Profs. Author: Labor Problems in West Germany, 1952; State and Local Government in West Germany, 1953. Home: 19 Tuscarora Av Geneseo NY 14454

GILLEN, JOHN STEWART, newspaper editor; b. Bklyn., Jan. 29, 1914; s. Edward T. and Sara (O'Donnell) G.; m. Mary Kathryn Crouser, Jan. 22, 1937; 1 dau., Patricia. With Phila. Inquirer, 1937—, mng. editor, 1954—. Home: 930 Remington Rd Wynnewood PA 19096 Office: 400 Broad St Philadelphia PA 19130

GILLEN, STANLEY JAMES, automotive exec.; b. Toledo, Aug. 10, 1911; s. Bernard J. and Johanna P. (Spillane) G.; B.Sc., U. Detroit, 1933; m. Mary Elizabeth Marks, Aug. 10, 1935; children—Elizabeth C. (Mrs. William R. Doyle), Mary M. (Mrs. Douglas G. O'Kieffe), Catherine A. (Mrs. Michael D.M. Ann). Financial analyst Fisher Body div. Gen. Motors Corp., 1933-47; contract adminstr. def. products Ford U.S.A., 1947-48, cntroller steel div., 1948-55, controller tractor and implement div., 1955-56; asst. gen. mgr. steel div. Ford Motor Co., 1956-60, gen. mgr., 1960-61, gen. mgr. parts div., 1961-65; chmn. Autolite Products, Ltd., of Eng., 1962-65; dir. Ford Credit Co., Ltd., London, 1965-67; mng. dir., chief exec. officer Ford of Britain, 1965-67; v.p. mfg. Ford of Europe, Inc., Eng., 1967-69, chmn., chief exec. officer, 1969—; v.p. Ford Motor Co. U.S.A.; dir. Ford of Europe, Inc., Ford of Britain, Ford Werke A/G (Koln, Germany). Mem. nat. adv. council Motor Mfg. Industry London, 1966-67; mem. Brit. mfrs. exec. com. Soc. Motor Mfrs. and Traders, Ltd., 1965-67. Mem. Am. C. of C. (U.K.). Clubs: American, Annabels (London); Sunningdale Golf (Bucks, Eng.); White Lake (Mich.) Golf, White Lake Yacht; Thorndon Golf (Essex, Eng.). Home: St Leonards Ingatestone Essex England Office: Ford of Europe Inc Warley near Brentwood Essex England

GILLEN, WILLIAM ALBERT, lawyer; b. Sanford, Fla., May 26, 1914; s. William D. and Marie (Holt) G.; student U. Tampa, 1932-33; J.D., U. Florida, 1936; m. Lillian Thornton, Aug. 19, 1939; children—William Albert, Susan Marie. Admitted to Fla. bar, 1936, since practiced in Tampa; asso. Cody Fowler, Esq., 1936-43, Fowler & White, 1943-46; partner Fowler, White, Gillen, Yancey & Humkey, 1946-59, Fowler, White, Gillen, Humkey & Trenam, 1959-66, Fowler, White, Collins, Gillen, Humkey & Trenam, 1966-69, Fowler, White, Gillen, Humkey & Kinney, 1970, Fowler, White, Gillen, Humkey, Kinney & Boggs, 1971—. Pres. Gulf Ridge council Boy Scouts Am., 1959; mem. Hillsborough County Home Rule Charter Commn., 1969-70; dir. United Fund of Tampa, 1956-64, Greater Tampa Citizens Safety Council, 1966-69; bd. dirs. Univ. South Florida Foundation, 1965-68, president, 1967-68. Served from 1st lieutenant to major, infantry AUS, 1942-46. Fellow Am. Coll. Trial Lawyers, Am. Bar Found.; mem. Fla. Bar (bd. govs. 1951-57), Bar Assn. Tampa and Hillsborough County (pres. 1953), Fedn. Ins. Counsel (pres. 1960-61; chmn. bd. govs. 1961-62), Internat. Assn. Ins. Counsel, Def. Research Inst. (v.p. 1961-62, dir. 1962-64), Maritime Law Assn., U.S., Gasparilla Krewe (dir. 1961-67, 68-70, capt. 1966-68, King LVII 1970-71), Am. Bar Assn., Com. of 100, Nat. Assn. R.R. Trial Counsel, Atlanta Claims Assn., Tampa C. of C. (bd. govs. 1961-64, 67-70, pres. 1968-69), Am. Legion, Phi Delta Phi, Sigma Alpha Epsilon. Democrat. Episcopalian. Mason. Clubs: Rotary (pres. 1959-60), Tampa Yacht and Country (dir. 1962-64), University, Merrymakers, Propeller (Tampa); Palma Ceia Golf and Country. Asso. editor American Maritime Cases. Home: 3109 Sunset Dr Tampa FL 33609 Office: First Federal Bldg Tampa FL 33602

GILLENSON, LEWIS WILLIAM, author, pub.; b. Bklyn., Feb. 18, 1918; s. Sol and Nellie (Marder) G.; B.A., Washington Sq. Coll. N.Y.U., 1939, grad. student sch. edn., 1940; m. Bernice Zaconick Gillenson, Feb. 3, 1946; children—Wendy Fay, Joshua R., Amy Jo. Asso. editor Look Magazine, 1946-52; writer Am. Magazine, Harper's Bazaar, Sports Life, McCall's, Redbook, Esquire, Woman's Home Companion, Family Circle, others; mng. editor Cosmopolitan, 1952-54; editor-in-chief Coronet, 1955-61; editor, publisher Esquire Books, 1961- 66; v.p. editorial Grosset & Dunlap, Inc., N.Y.C., 1966—. Commd. 2d lt. AUS, 1943, advanced through grades to maj., 1946; editor Camp Pickett (Va.) News, 1943; exec. officer Yank, Australia, New Guinea, Japan, 1943- 45, comdg. officer, 1945. Decorated Bronze Star Medal, 1945; recipient Freedom Found. lit. award, 1950. Mem. U.S. Newspaper Guild, 1946-52. Club: Friars. Author: Billy Graham, The Man and His Message; Fabulous Yesterday, 1961; Billy Graham and Seven Who Were Saved, 1967. Editor and producer Pursuit of Equality. Contbr. articles Saturday Rev., Good Housekeeping. Home: 235 Lindenmere Dr Merrick NY 11566 Office: 51 Madison Av New York City NY 10010

GILLENWATER, JAY YOUNG, physician, educator; b. Kingsport, Tenn., July 27, 1933; s. Jay King and Anne (Young) G.; student Furman U., 1951-53; B.S., U. Tenn., 1954, M.D., 1957; m. Shirley Brockman, June 22, 1955; children—Linda, Ann, Jay. Intern, Grad. Hosp. U. Pa., 1958-59. medicine resident, 1959-60, urology resident, 1962-65; practice medicine specializing in urology, Charlottesville, Va., 1965—; asst. prof. dept. urology U. Va. Med. Sch., 1965-67, prof., chmn. dept. urology, 1967—. Served to capt. AUS, Army, 1960-62. Fellow A.C.S.; mem. A.M.A., Am. Urol. Assn., Univ. Urologists, Sigma Alpha Epsilon, Phi Rho Sigma. Editorial bd. Investigative Urology. Contbr. articles to profl. jours. Home: 1647 Brandywine Dr Charlottesville VA 22901

GILLENWATER, VIRGIL WAYNE, coll. pres.; b. Sciota, Ill., Feb. 26, 1915; s. Earl E. and Della E. (Warrington) G.; B.E. cum laude, Western Ill. State Coll., 1941, M.S., 1947; Ed.M., U. Ill., 1949, Ed.D., 1952; m. Clarine E. Boehm, Nov. 20, 1942; children—William V., Elizabeth Ann. Prin., Ray (Ill.) Pub. Sch., 1934-40; asst. edn. Western Ill. State Coll., Macomb, 1946-47; asst. edn. U. Ill., 1947-48, instr. edn. and counselor univ. council on tchr. edn., 1948-50; asst. prof. edn., dir. student tchrs. Ariz. State Coll., Flagstaff, 1950-52, prof. edn. and psychology, head dept., 1952- 57, exec. dean, 1957-65; exec. v.p. No. Ariz. U., 1965-66; pres. Trenton (N.J.) State Coll., 1966-68; exec. v.p., provost No. Ariz. U., Flagstaff, 1968—. Mem. N.E.A., N.J. Edn. Assn., Nat. Soc. for Study Edn., Kappa Delta Pi, Phi Delta Kappa, Phi Kappa Phi, Sigma Pi. Presbyn. Home: 911 W Anderson St Flagstaff, AZ

GILLER, EDWARD BONFOY, air force officer; b. Jacksonville, Ill., July 8, 1918; s. Edward Bonfoy and Ruth (Davis) G.; B.S. in Chem. Engring., U. Ill., 1940, M.S., 1948, Ph.D., 1950; m. Mildred Florana Schmidt, July 2, 1943; children—Susan Ann, Carol Elaine, Bruce Carleton, Penny Marie, Paul Benjamin. Jr. engr. Sinclair Oil Co., 1940-41; commd. 2d lt. USAAF, 1941, advanced through grades to maj. gen. USAF, 1968; pilot, 1941-46; chief radiation br. Armed Forces Spl. Weapons Project, Washington, 1950-54; dir. research directorate Air Force Spl. Weapons Center, Albuquerque, 1954-59; spl. asst. to comdr. Office Aerospace Research, Washington, 1959-64; dir. sci. and tech. Hdqrs. USAF, 1964-67; asst. gen. mgr. for mil. applications U.S. AEC, 1967—. Decorated Silver Star, Legion of Merit, D.F.C., Air medal, Purple Heart; Croix de Guerre (France). Fellow Am. Inst. Chemists; mem. Am. Chem. Soc., A.A.A.S., Am. Inst. Chem. Engrs., Sigma Xi, Alpha Tau Omega. Episcopalian. Home: 723 Lawton St McLean VA 22101 Office: AEC Washington DC 20545

GILLER, NORMAN MYER, architect, banker; b. Jacksonville, Fla., Feb. 14, 1918; s. Morris and Esther (Seltzer) G.; B.Arch., U. Fla., 1945; student Ga. Inst. Tech., 1943-44; m. Frances Schwartz, June 30, 1946; children—Ira, Anita, Brian. Pvt. archtl. practice, Miami Beach, Fla., 1944—; pres., chmn. bd. dirs. InterAm. Nat. Bank, 1964-68; pres., vice chmn. bd. dirs. Jefferson Nat. Bank, at Sunny Isles, 1968—; asst. sec., dir. Jefferson Bancorp.; dir. Jefferson Nat. Bank of Miami Beach; lectr. U. Fla., Ohio State U.; instr. U. Fla.; cons. U.S. Dept. State, Govts. of Panama, Brazil, Colombia, El Salvador, Nicaragua; archtl. works include Diplomat Hotel and Golf Course, Carillon Hotel, Miami Gardens Sch., Aguadulce Hosp., USAF housing. Vice chmn. Interama Authority; mem. Metro Planning Adv. Bd., Bay Harbor Planning and Zoning Bd.; mem. nat. council, pres. S. Fla. council Boy Scouts Am.; chmn. architects div. United Fund; active United Jewish Appeal. Dir. Parkinson Fund.; life dir. Douglas Gardens Home for Aged. Served with USNR, 1942-46. Recipient award for best design Am. Assn. Sch. Adminstrs., 1969, for excellence in specifications Constrn. Specifications Inst., 1964. Registered architect 15 states plus D.C., P.R., C.Z., Israel. Mem. Archtl. Guild, Interama Area C. of C. (pres.), Greater Miami C. of C., A.I.A. (dir. S. Fla.), Archtl. Soc. (pres.), Am., Fla., Dade County bankers assns., Bankers Adminstrn. Inst. Jewish religion. Mason (Shriner), Elk. Clubs: Exchange (dir.), Tiger Bay (Miami Beach.). Home: 4500 Prairie Av Miami Beach FL 33140 Office: 975 Arthur Godfrey Rd Miami Beach FL 33140

GILLES, NICHOLAS CHESTER, TV exec.; b. Worcester, Mass., May 27, 1924; s. Nicholas Chester and Ethel (Grady) G.; A.B., Harvard, 1945, M.B.A., 1949; m. Jean Diane Keilly, May 30, 1959; 1 dau., Kelly Diane. With NBC, 1949—, dir. bus. affairs TV Network, 1960-61, v.p., 1962-69, v.p. financial planning and treasury operations, 1970—, v.p. NBC Prodns., Inc., 1961—. Served to lt. (j.g.) USNR, 1943-46. Mem. Acad. TV Arts and Scis. Club: Harvard Business School of New York. Home: 160 E 84th St New York City NY 10028 Office: 30 Rockefeller Plaza New York City NY 10020

GILLESPIE, ALEXANDER JOSEPH, Jr., corp. exec., lawyer; b. N.Y.C., Sept. 2, 1923; s. Alexander Joseph and Catharine (Allen) G.; A.B. magna cum laude, Dartmouth, 1943; J.D., Fordham U., 1957; m. Elizabeth Margaret Roth, Dec. 4, 1944; children—Robert Daniel, James Edward, William Gerard, Patricia Elise, Anne Marie. Credit mgr. cosmetic div. Vick Chem. Co., 1946-50; dist. sales mgr. Avco Mfg. Co., 1950-54; asso. atty. Breed Abbot & Morgan, 1957-60; asst. gen. counsel Am. Smelting & Refining Co., N.Y.C., 1960-68, sec., 1968-69, sec., gen. counsel, 1969—. Bd. dirs. Brunswick Sch., Greenwich, Conn. Served to lt. (j.g.) USNR, 1943-46; PTO. Mem. Am., N.Y., Conn. bar assns., Assn. Bar City N.Y., N.Y. County Lawyers Assn., N.Y. C. of C., Bankers Club Am., Mining Club, Phi Beta Kappa, Delta Upsilon, Gamma Eta Gamma. Episcopalian. Club: Dartmouth Coll. (N.Y.C.). Home: 30 Will Merry Lane Greenwich CT 06830 Office: 120 Broadway New York City NY 10005

GILLESPIE, CHARLES WESLEY, cons. engr.; b. Phila., June 21, 1917; s. Charles Wesley and Edna (Wheeler) G.; M.E., Stevens Inst. Tech., 1939. Time study engr. Simmons Co., 1939-40; from prodn. control to supt. time standards dept. Chance- Vought Aircraft Co., 1940-45; from indsl engr. to dept. gen. foreman and prodn. mgr. Johnson & Johnson, 1945-48; indsl. engr. Gen. Foods Corp., 1949-50; with Coverdale & Colpitts, cons. engrs., N.Y.C., 1950—, partner, 1962- -; spl. work indsl. field, also traffic and revenue studies. Asso. mem. Am. So. M.E. Clubs: Engineers, Wall Street (N.Y.C.); Upper Montclair Country (Montclair, N.J.). Home: Country Club Towers 140 Hepburn Rd Clifton NJ 07012 Office: 120 Wall St New York City NY 10005

GILLESPIE, DAVID JOSEPH, advt. agy. exec.; b. N.Y.C., Mar. 9, 1915; s. David Joseph and Catherine (Mitchell) G.; B.A., Manhattan Coll., 1936; m. Jane Louise Reynolds, Sept. 5, 1949; 1 dau., Patricia Jane. With Kenyon & Eckhardt Advt., Inc., 1936—, v.p., 1954-57, dir., 1957—, mgmt. supr., head Detroit Office, 1966—. Mem. spl. gifts com. Detroit Round Table Nat. Conf. Christians and Jews, 1956—; adv. mem. Nat. Cath. Office for Radio and TV, 1961—; chmn. advt. adv. com. Northwood Inst., 1968—. Served with AUS, 1942-46. Decorated Bronze Star medal. Mem. Am. Assn. Advt. Agys. (past gov. Mich. region), Adcraft Club Detroit (dir.). Clubs: Detroit Athletic, Grosse Pointe Yacht, Grosse Pointe Hunt. Home: 61 Lochmoor Blvd Grosse Pointe Shores MI 48236 Office: 211 W Fort St Detroit MI 48226

GILLESPIE, HAROLD STANLEY, hosp. adminstr.; b. Rochester, Minn., Nov. 11, 1920; s. William H. and Vivian (Akers) G.; B.S. in Commerce, State U. Ia., 1957; M.H.A., Baylor U., 1962; m. C. Anne Waterbury, Aug. 10, 1946; children—Lynn (Mrs. W. Dean Neitzke), Scott W., Mary Anne Akers. Commd., U.S. Army, 1948, advanced through grades to maj., 1961; instr. Adj. Gen. Sch., 1949-51; procedures analyst Adj. Gen. Office, 1951-53; with med. operations office IV Armored Corps, Ft. Hoods, Tex., 1953-56; comptroller U.S. Army Hosp., Wurzburg, Germany, 1957-60, 3d Army Surgeon's Office, Ft. McPherson, Ga., 1962-64; retired, 1965. Asst. supt. Evansville (Ind.) State Hosp., 1965-69, supt., 1969; adminstr. Fairbault (Minn.) State Hosp., 1969—; tchr. corporate finance U. Evansville, 1966-68. Treas. Real Estate Devel. Corp., 1970—. Mem. Denver Hosp. Council, 1961, Evansville Community Council Rehab., 1966-67. Mem. Am. Coll. Hosp. Adminstrs., Assn. Mental Health Adminstrn., Am., Minn. hosp. assns., Am. Assn. Mental Deficiency, Soc. Preservation and Encouragement Barbershop Quar. Singing Am. (pres. 1968-69, bd. dirs. 1969-70). Episcopalian (vestry). Mason. Home: 1907 NW 16th St Faribault MN 55021 Office: Faribault State Hosp Faribault MN 55021

GILLESPIE, JAMES MACKINNON, educator; b. Andover, Mass., June 2, 1919; s. James and Lulu (MacKinnon) G.; A.B., Harvard, 1947, A.M., 1949, Ph.D., 1960. Asst. prof. psychology Colby Coll., Waterville, Me., 1951-61, asso. prof., 1961-69, prof., 1969—, chmn. dept. psychology, 1961—. Served with AUS, 1940-46. Mem. Am. Psychol. Assn., Am. Sociol. Assn. Author: (with G.W. Allport) Youth's Outlook on the Future, 1955. Home: 46 Mayflower Hill Dr Waterville ME 04901

GILLESPIE, JOHN BIRKS, (Dizzy), musician; b. Cheraw, S.C., Oct. 21, 1917; s. James and Lottie (Poe) G.; grad. Laurinburg (N.C.) Inst.; m. Lorraine Willis, May 9, 1940. Jazz trumpet player, 1930—. Rep. U.S. Dept. State on culture tour to Iran, Pakistan, Lebanon, Syria, Turkey, Yugoslavia, Greece, S.A. Mason. Home: 477 N Woodland Englewood NJ 07631 Office: care ABC 445 Park Av New York City NY 10019

GILLESPIE, JOHN THOMAS, journalist; b. N.Y.C., June 4, 1941; s. Kenrick S. and Emma (Cuddihy) G.; grad. Taft Sch., 1959; B.A. in History, Yale, 1963; m. Constance M. Faulk, May 17, 1969; 1 dau., Catharine Emma. Research asst. to minority counsel Joint Econ. Com., U.S. Congress, 1964-65; staff writer Congl. Quar. Inc., Washington, 1965-66; edn. reporter Phila. Evening & Sunday Bull., 1966—. Roman Catholic. Co-founder Yale Polit. Jour., 1962, editor, 1962-63. Home: 226 W Rittenhouse Sq Philadelphia PA 19103 Office: 30th and Market Sts Philadelphia PA 19101

GILLESPIE, KINGSLEY, publisher; b. Stamford, Conn., Aug. 15, 1895; s. Richard H. and Sarah E. (Scofield) G.; S.B. in Chem. Engring., Mass. Inst. Tech., 1917; m. Doris Kenyon, June 2, 1928; children—Kenyon, Joan (dec.). Tech. mgr. and dir. research Stamford Rubber Supply Co., 1919-41; pub. Stamford Advocate, 1942—; treas. Gillespie Bros., Inc., 1942—, v.p., 1922-49, pres., 1949—; pres., exec. dir. Western Conn. Broadcasting Co., 1946—; v.p. Stamford Rubber Supply Co., 1925-52, pres., 1952- 67; v.p., dir Fidelity Title & Trust Co.; pub Greenwich Time, 1958—; pres., treas. Fairview Enterprises, Inc., 1958—, Greenwich Pub. Co., 1958—; dir. Stamford Sav. Bank. Sec. Ferguson Library, 1942-66; sec. Stamford Zoning Commn., 1937-49; mem. Conn. Aero. Commn. 1960—. Registered chem. engr., Conn. Mem. Am. Inst. Chem. Engrs., Am. Chem. Soc. Republican. Presbyn. Clubs: Rotary, Stamford Yacht. Home: 91 Rogers Rd Stamford CT 06902 Office: Stamford Advocate 258 Atlantic St Stamford CT 06901

GILLESPIE, LOUIS FRANK, lawyer; b. Vienna, Ill., Jan. 20, 1900; s. George B. and Mary (Oliver) G.; student Cornell U., 1918-21; Ph.B., U. Chgo., 1922, J.D., 1924; m. Frances McGregor, Dec. 31, 1927; children—George B. II, Mary Ellis, Robert E. Admitted to Ill. bar, 1924, mem. Gillespie, Burke & Gillespie 1925—; gen. counsel Franklin Life Ins. Co., Springfield, 1944-65, sr. counsel, 1965—, chmn. bd., 1953-70, also dir. Mem. exec. com. Meml. Hosp., Springfield, Ill., 1960-69. Fellow Am. Coll. Trial Lawyers; mem. Soc. Trial Lawyers, Am. Bar Assn., Assn. Life Ins. Counsel, Phi Delta Phi, Delta Kappa Epsilon. Clubs: Sangamo, Illini Country (Springfield); University (Chgo.). Home 718 S 7th St Springfield IL 62703 Office: 217 S 7th St Springfield IL 62701

GILLESPIE, MCDONALD, television exec.; b. Bradley Beach, N.J., Aug. 25, 1911; s. John Thomas and Eleanor (Samson) G.; grad. Taft Sch., 1930; B.A., Yale, 1934; m. Peggy Adams, June 7, 1935; children—Lynda Hall, Laurie McDonald, Jeanie Adams. Account exec. J. Walter Thompson Co., N.Y.C., 1935-39, Pedlar & Ryan, Inc., N.Y.C., 1939-44; with Batten, Barton, Dustine & Osborn, Inc., N.Y.C. 1944-70, account supr., 1956-59, mgmt. supr., 1959-70, exec. v.p., 1964-70, also dir., mem. exec. com.; pres. Batten, Barton, Durstine & Osborn Internat., Inc., 1967-70; founder cable 10, North Canton, Conn., 1970—. Mem. Darien Rep. Town Meeting, 1954-57, Darien Town Govt. Study Com., 1956. Pres., Darien Fund, 1953, bd. dirs., 1952-56. Mem. N.Y. State N.G., 1939-43. Home: Cherry Brook Rd North Canton CT 06059

GILLESPIE, ROBERT GILL, judge; b. Madison, Ala., Sept. 17, 1903; s. Philander M. and Flora (Gill) G.; student Huntsville Jr. Coll., 1923-24, U. Ala., 1924-26; m. Margaret Griffith, June 30, 1930; children—Robert Gill, Virgil Griffith. Admitted to Miss. bar. 1927; practiced in Meridian, 1927-33; spl. agt. FBI, 1934-35; partner Bailey & Gillespie, 1939-43, Gillespie & Minniece, 1945-48, Gillespie, Huff & Williams, 1948-54; chancellor 2d Chancery Ct. Dist. Miss., 1939; justice Miss. Supreme Ct., Jackson, 1954-65, presiding justice, 1966-71, chief justice, 1970—. Mem. Miss. Council State Govts., 1944-48; mem awards jury Freedoms Found., 1959. Bd. dirs. Southwestern Coll., Memphis. Mem. Am., Miss. bar assns., Am. Judicature Soc., Delta Tau Delta. Presbyn. Home: 432 Dunbar St Jackson MS 39216 Office: Miss State Supreme Ct Jackson MS 39201

GILLET, R.E., artist; b. Paris, 1924; student Boulle Sch., 1938, Sch. Decorative Arts, 1944. Prof. Julian Acad., Paris, 1946-48; participant Salon de Mai, 1955- ; numerous one-man exhbns., Paris including Craven, Ariel galleries and Galerie de France, also Lefebe Gallery, N.Y.C., 1061. Recipient Feneon prize, 1954, Catherwood prize, 1955. Address: 3 rue du Faubourg St Honore Paris 8e France*

GILLETT, ALLEN LEWIS, savs. and loan assn. exec.; b. Auburn, N.Y., June 23, 1898; s. Francis and Frances Cornelia (West) G.; student N.Y. State Coll. for Tchrs., 1915-17; B.C.S., N.Y. U., 1924, M.C.S., 1925; m. Kathryn May Cole, Jan. 11, 1919; children—Kathryn Marian (Mrs. Wulff), Gertrude Elizabeth (Mrs. William Hernstadt). With Nat. City Bank N.Y., 1919-26; bank examiner State N.Y., 1926-30; mgr. fed. intermediate Credit Bank Springfield (Mass.), 1930-32, pres., 1933-44; chmn. bd., gen. agt. Farm Credit Adminstrn. Springfield, 1944-46; pub. accountant, Hartford, Conn., 1947-48; sec. Pioneer Bldg.-Loan and Savs. Assn. Troy (N.Y.), 1949, exec. v.p., dir., 1949, pres., 1951—, chmn. bd., 1967—; cons. Farm Credit Adminstrn., Washington, 1933. Mem. Nat. Budget Com. Bd. dirs. Rensselaer County chpt. A.R.C.; v.p. budget com., bd. dirs., chmn. Troy Community Chest; adv. bd. St. Mary's Hosp., Troy. Served with med. dept. U.S. Army, 1917-19. Named Man of Yr., Troy Real Estate Bd., 1954. Mem. Savs. Assn. League N.Y. (chmn., dir.), Capital Dist. Savs. and Loan League (pres., dir.), S.R. (regent William Floyd chpt., dir.), Soc. Descs. Colonial Clergy (treas. gen.), Greater Troy C. of C., N.Y. Hist. Assn., Huguenot Soc. N.Y., Order Founders and Patriots Am., Delta Mu Delta. Mason, Rotarian. Club: University (Albany, N.Y.). Home: 30 Farmingdale Rd Newtonville NY 12128 Office: 21 Second St Troy NY 12181

GILLETT, CHARLES, travel exec.; b. Newport, Ky., Sept. 9, 1915; s. Louis B. and Sarah (Maller) G.; B.A., U. Cin., 1938; m. Virginia Margaret Littmann, June 11, 1949; children—Valerie, David, Brian Paul, Peter Guy. Pub. relations dir. Netherland Plaza Hotel, Cin., 1938-39; account exec. Swafford & Koehl Advt. Agy., N.Y.C., 1939-40; advt. and sales promotion dir. Hotel Gibson, Cin., 1940-41; promotion and pub. relations dir. N.Y. Conv. and visitors Bur., N.Y.C., 1946-62, v.p., 1962-65, exec. v.p., 1966—. Mem. travel adv. com. U.S. Dept. Commerce, 1963-65, nat. adv. com. on hwy. beautification, 1965-66; del. White House Conf. Natural Beauty, 1965; spl. adviser to Discover Am. Travel Orgns., 1967-68, dir., 1968—. Mem. pub. affairs com. U.S. Air Force Acad., 1968-71. Served from pvt. to maj. AUS, 1941-45. Decorated Bronze Star. Recipient Most Original Travel Idea award Midwest Travel Writers Assn., 1964. Mem. Nat. Assn. Travel Orgns. (dir. 1960-62, pres. 1963-65, chmn. bd. 1965-67, award of merit 1966), Internat. Festivals

Assn. (dir. 1957-59, sec. 1959-61, sec.-treas. 1966-67), Am. Soc. Travel Agts., Soc. Am. Travel Writers, N.Y. State Travel Council, Nat. Tour Brokers Assn., Hotel Sales Mgrs. Assn., Nat. Indsl. Recreation Assn., Pub. Relations Soc. Am., Sales Promotion Execs. Assn., Internat. Assn. Conv. Burs. (dir. 1968-71). Club: Overseas Press (N.Y.C.). Editor: The Bridge, 1946. Writer, lectr. on travel bus. subjects. Home: 8 Ridge Dr E Great Neck NY 11021 Office: 90 E 42d St New York City NY 10017

GILLETT, RICHARD M., banker; b. Grand Rapids, Mich., 1923; grad. U. Mich., 1944. Pres., dir. Old Kent Bank & Trust Co., Grand Rapids; dir. W. Mich. Telecasters, Inc., A. May & Sons, Blink Lumber Co., Grand Hotel, Consumers Power Co.; partner Breton Co. Trustee Blodgett Meml. Hosp. Home: 2359 Breton Rd SE Grand Rapids MI 49506 Office: Old Kent Bldg Grand Rapids MI 49502*

GILLETTE, HYDE, investment banker; b. Chgo., June 23, 1906; s. Edwin and Mabel (Hyde) G.; grad. Exeter Acad., 1924; A.B. cum laude, Princeton, 1928; M.B.A. with distinction, Harvard, 1930; m. Marie Clarke Smith, Sept. 7, 1932; 1 dau., Marie Clarke Gerald. With Glore, Forgan & Co., 1930-53, partner, 1950-53; dep. asst. sec. USAF, 1953-57; asst. postmaster gen., bur. finance U.S. P.O., Washington, 1957-61; partner Auchincloss Parker & Redpath, 1961-70; regional v.p. children—Susan & McKinnon Auchincloss, Inc., Washington, 1970—. Exec. bd. Chgo. Area Project, 1936-53, chmn., 1948-53; bd., v.p. Nat. Capital area council Boy Scouts Am.; dir., vice chmn. budget com. Community Fund of Chgo., 1942; chmn. exec. com. Chgo. Opera Theatre, 1947; adv. bd. Dept. Pub. Welfare. Ill., 1949- 53; pres. Barrington Country Day Sch., 1941; v.p. Washington Heart Assn., 1961; bd. Am. Heart Assn., 1960-63. Served as lt. comdr. USNR, 1943-46. Recipient Exceptional Civilian Service award USAF, 1956. Mem. Mayflower Descs., Soc. Colonial Wars, Barrington Countryside Assn. (pres. 1949-50), Chevalier Tastevin, Phi Beta Kappa. Presbyn. Clubs: Barrington Hills Country; Quadrangle (Princeton); Fox River Valley Hunt, Commonwealth (Chgo.); Chevy Chase, Metropolitan (Washington); Princeton, India House (N.Y.C.); West River Sailing. Home: 4915 Glenbrook Rd NW Washington DC 20016 Office: 1705 H St NW Washington DC 20016

GILLETTE, NORMAN CAMPBELL, Jr., naval officer; b. Nov. 14, 1915. Commd. ensign U.S. Navy, 1936, advanced through grades to rear adm., 1964. Address: care Bur Personnel Navy Dept Washington DC 20025*

GILLETTE, ROBERT STONE, business exec; b. Cortland, N.Y., July 7, 1913; s. Harold Ralph and Ada Fleming (Stone) G.; B.S., Mass. Inst. Tech., 1936; m. Janet French, Oct. 19, 1939; children— Deborah G. Law, Edward French. Chief planning engr. Jones & Lamson Machine Co., Springfield, Vt., 1936-44; prodn. mgr. Submarine Signal Co., Fall River, Mass., 1944-46; research United Shoe Machinery Corp., Boston, 1947-49; asst. gen. mgr. Rock of Ages Corp., 1949-52, exec. v.p., dir., 1952-54, pres., chmn., dir., 1954—; chmn. bd. Nat. Life Ins. Co.; dir. Union Mut. Fire Ins. Co., Central Vt. Ry., Fellows Corp. Vice pres. Cardigan Mountain Sch., 1969—. Trustee children—Mary Pub. Library, Central Vt. Med. Center. Club: Quissett (Mass.) Yacht; Algonquin (Boston). Home: 51 Perry St Barre VT 05641 Office: Rock of Ages Corp Barre VT 05641

GILLETTE, STANLEY C., men's apparel co. exec.; b. N.Y.C., Aug. 12, 1915; m. Joan Gillette; children—Richard, Patricia. Vice pres., dir. Internat. Fashion Council, Amsterdam, Holland until 1947; with Phillips-Van Heusen Corp., 1947—, v.p. charge marketing, 1960-63, exec. v.p. charge men's div., 1963-64, exec. v.p., 1968—, pres. Van Heusen Co. div., 1964—, also dir. Industry chmn. Greater N.Y. Fund, Sister Kenny Fund, Heart Fund; an organizer bldg. N. Shore Hosp., L.I. Served to capt. AUS, World War II; CBI. Mem. Am. Apparel Mfrs. Assn. (co-chmn. marketing and econ. com.). Club: Yachting of Am. Office: 417 Fifth Av New York City NY 10016

GILLHAM, MARY MEWBORN, librarian; educator; b. Atlanta, July 12, 1899; d. Clarence Edwin and Salie Atha (Matthews) Mewborn; A.B., U. Toledo, 1927, A.M., 1931; A.B. in L.S., U. Mich., 1941 m. Richard E. Gilham, D.D.S., May 27, 1922. Librarian, U. Toledo 1921—, asso. prof. library sci., 1944- 50, prof., 1950—, chmn. dept. library sci. Coll. Edn., 1933-69. Exec. sec. Friends of U. Library, 1938-69, U. Toledo Ann. Endowment drives, 1943-47, chmn. library bldg. com., 1948-69. Mem. adv. bd. WPA projects City Toledo, 1938-41, mem. Ohio Sesquicentennial Commn., 1951-53; treas. Toledo Municipal League, 1957-69, also bd. dirs. Mem. U. Mich. Library Sci. Alumni (pres. 1943-45), A.L.A. (com. Friends of Libraries), Orgn. for Study of Peace (bibliog. com. 1943-45), Ohio Library Assn. (chmn. coll. and univ. div. 1957-60), Ohio Coll. Assn. (pres. library div. 1958-59), Am. Assn. U. Women (Toledo br.), Faculty Dames, Samagama, U. Toledo Alumni Assn. (mem. Tower Club 1965—), Women's Aux. Toledo Dental Soc., Toledo Mus. Art, Toledo Orch., Clements Library Assos., Alpha Omicron Pi (faculty alumni adviser Theta Psi chpt. 1940-51), Delta Kappa Gamma (chpt. pres. 1956-58), Phi Kappa Phi (pres. chpt. 1957-58), Beta Phi Mu, Chi Omega (chmn. Toledo alumnae chpt. recognition award com. 1954—, Recognition award 1967). Republican. Methodist. Clubs: University Women's (Toledo), Zonta (pres. 1953-54). Home: 618 Sylvania Av Toledo OH 43612

GILLIAM, JACKSON EARLE, bishop; b. Heppner, Ore., June 20, 1920; s. Edwin Earle and Mary (Perry) G.; A.B., Whitman Coll., 1942; B.D., Va. Theol. Sem., 1948, S.T.M., 1949, D.D., 1969; m. Margaret Kathleen Hindley, Aug. 11, 1943; children—Anne Meredith, Margaret Carol, John Howard. Ordained to ministry Episcopal Ch., 1948; rector in Hermiston, Ore., 1949-53; canon St. Mark's Cathedral, Mpls., 1953-55; rector Ch. Incarnation, Great Falls, Mont., 1955-68; bishop Episopal Diocese Mont., 1968—. Served to 1st lt. AUS, World War II. Rotarian. Home: 724 Harriston St Helena MT 59601 Office: Wheat Bldg Helena MT 59601

GILLIAM, JOHN CHARLES, coll. dean; b. Boulder, Colo., Sept. 19, 1927; s. Arthur Woodson and Marguerite (Hubbard) G.; B.A., Western State Coll. Colo., 1951; M.Bus.Ed., U. Colo., 1952; Ph.D., State U. Ia., 1959; m. Katherine Frances Mihevc, July 16, 1947; children—Bruce, Charles, Carol Ann. Instr. bus. Brush (Colo.) High Sch., 1952-55, State U. Ia., 1955-57; asst. prof. commerce U. Wyo., 1957-62, asso. prof., 1962; asso. prof. bus. edn. Tex. Tech. U., 1962-66, prof., 1966—, asso. dean Coll. Bus. Adminstrn., 1968—. Program specialist Ford Found., Amman, Jordan, 1966-68; cons. in edn. for bus. Ford Found.; vis. prof. several univs.; cons. bus. and econs. Served with USNR, 1945-47. Mem. Nat. Bus. Edn. Assn., Beta Gamma Sigma, Omicron Delta Epsilon, Alpha Kappa Psi, Delta Pi Epsilon, Pi Omega Pi. Episcopalian. Elk. Contbr. articles profl. jours. Home: 3608 57th St Lubbock TX 79413

GILLIAND, MERLE ELLSWORTH, banker; b. Pitcairn, Pa., Dec. 21, 1921; s. Walter M. and Elsie N. (Dean) G.; B.S. in Bus. Administrn. cum laude, Duquesne U., 1948; m. Olive Lee Henry, June 11, 1954; 1 son, Mark. With Albert A. Logan, C.P.A., 1948-53; instr. accounting Duquesne U., 1948-53; with Pitts. Nat. Bank, 1953—, exec. v.p., 1965-67, pres., 1967—, chief exec. officer, 1970—, also dir.; dir. Kissell Co., Pitts. Nat. Corp., Pitts. Urban Transit Council, Pitts. br. Fed. Res. Bank Cleve. Exec. com. Allegheny Conf. Community Devel.; adv. com. Robert Morris Coll. Bd. dirs. Pitts. Opera, United Fund Allegheny County, Blue Cross Western Pa.; trustee Duquesne U. Found., U. Pitts. children—Ronald with AUS, 1942-46. C.P.A., Pa. Mem. Bank Adminstrv. Inst. (past pres. Pitts. conf.), Allegheny Conf. Community Devel., Am. Bankers Assn. (exec. council), Duquesne U. Bus. Adminstrn. Alumni (treas. assn.), Pa. Inst. C.P.A.'s, Financial Execs. Inst., Assn. Res. City Bankers. Presbyn. (elder). Clubs: Duquesne (bd. dirs.), Allegheny, University, Churchill Valley Country, Fox Chapel Golf; Laurel Valley Golf (Ligonier, Pa.); Springfield (O.) Country. Home: 378 Fox Chapel Rd Pittsburgh PA 15238 Office: Pitts Nat Bank 1 Oliver Plaza Pittsburgh PA 15222

GILLIATT, NEAL, advt. exec.; b. Plainville, Ind., Dec. 24, 1917; s. Oliver Breden and Katherine Ann (Henderson) G.; B.S., Ind. U., 1939; M.B.A., Northwestern U., 1940; postgrad. Harvard Advanced Mgmt. program, 1960; m. Mary Rees, Feb. 6, 1943; children—David Rees, John Neal. Instr., Ind. U., 1940-42; chief food price div. OPA, Chgo., 1942-45; asso. dir. research McCann-Erickson, Inc., Chgo., 1945-46, account exec., 1946-50, v.p., account supr., 1950-55, v.p., account supr., N.Y.C., 1955-60, sr. v.p., mgmt. service dir., 1960-64, vice chmn., 1964-66; exec. v.p. Interpub., Inc., N.Y.C., 1964-67, chmn., 1967-68; group v.p., dir. Interpub. Group of Cos., Inc., N.Y.C., 1968-70, vice chmn., 1970—; dir. Chemed Corp. Recipient Broadcasting and Advt. Industries Human Relations award am. Jewish Com., 1969; Distinguished Alumni Service award Ind. U., 1970. Mem. Beta Gamma Sigma (recipient award 1963), Sigma Alpha Epsilon. Conglist. Clubs: Greenwich Country (Conn.); Piedmont Driving, Capital City (Atlanta); Fifth Avenue (N.Y.C.). Home: 266 Round Hill Rd Greenwich CT 06830 Office: 1271 Av of the Americas New York City NY 10020

GILLIATT, PENELOPE ANN DOUGLASS, author, film critic; b. London, Eng.; d. Cyril and Mary (Douglass) Conner; student Queen's Coll., London, Bennington Coll., Vt.; m. Prof. R.W. Gilliatt (div.); m. 2d, John Osborne (div.); 1 dau., Nolan. Film critic Observer (London), 1961-67, theatre critic, 1965; guest film critic New Yorker, 1967, regular film critic, 1968—; writer film scripts and play filmed for BBC-TV. Mem. Brit. Labour Party. Author: One by One, 1965; A State of Change, 1968; (short stories) Come Back If It Doesn't Get Better, 1970; Sunday, Bloody Sunday (original film script), 1971; Penguin Modern Stories, 1971. Office: New Yorker Mag 25 W 43d St New York City NY 10036

GILLICK, FREDERICK GEORGE, physician; b. Vallejo, Cal., May 14, 1911; s. John Chrysotom and Florence Louise (Fearon) G.; student U. Santa Clara, 1928-30; B.S., St. Louis U., 1933, M.D., 1935, Master Internal Medicine, 1939; M.P.H., Harvard, 1941; m. Elizabeth Ann Schiller, Oct. 24, 1939; children—Joseph George, John Schiller, Mary Beth, Michael F., Paul. Intern St. Marys' Group Hosp., St. Louis, 1935-36, resident fellow internal medicine, 1936-39; children—Patricia disease control officer City St. Louis, 1939-42, Herbert Arthur. With Nat. Comml. Bank & Trust Co., Albany, N.Y., 1924- devel. Electrokymograph, USPHS, Temple U., 1945-46; pvt. practice cardiovascular research U. Cal., 1946-49; chief heart disease control br. USPHS, Washington, 1949-50; from sr. asst. surgeon to sr. surgeon USPHS, 1942-51; mem. research br. Nat. Heart Inst., 1950-51; instr. internal medicine St. Louis U., 1940-47; lectr. Cath. U. Am., 1944-45; research asso. medicine U. Calif., 1946-49; adj. clin. prof. medicine Georgetown U., 1951; prof. preventive medicine, dean Sch. Medicine, Creighton U., 1951-59; chief staff Creighton Meml.-St. Jospeh's Hosp., 1955-59; dir. med. instns. County Santa Clara, Cal., 1959-62; engaged in pvt. practice internal medicine and cardiology; chmn. dean's com. Omaha VA Hosp.; med. dir. USPHS, 1956. Mem. bd. dirs. Omaha United Community Services, children—Margaret County Red Cross; chmn. bd. Cath. Social Service, Santa Clara County; vice chmn. San Francisco Archdiocesan Bd. Cath. Social Service; pres. bd. dirs. St. Elizabeth's Day Home, San Jose, Cal. Diplomate Am. Bd. Preventive Medicine and Pub. Health. Fellow Am. Coll. Preventive -. A.C.P., Am. Coll. Cardiology; mem. Am. Soc. Internal Medicine, Assn. Am. Med. Colls., Am., Neb. (pres.) heart assns., A.M.A., Alpha Omega Alpha. Alpha Sigma Nu. Roman Catholic. Author articles med subjects. Editor proc. Conf. Electrokymography, 1951. Home: 1861 University Dr San Jose CA 95126 Office: VA Hosp Palo Alto CA 94304

GILLICK, LAURANCE HENRY, heating co. exec.; b. Mpls., Aug. 25, 1898; s. James Thomas and Elizabeth (Feltus) G.; student Northwestern U., 1915; m. Dorothy Hart, Sept. 1, 1920; children—Dorothy (Mrs. John Drish), Dorice (Mrs. Dino Santoro). With Vapor Corp. and predecessor, Chgo., 1916-66, v.p., 1941- 63, vice chmn., 1963-66; pres. AAA Insulaire, Inc., Ft. Lauderdale, Fla., 1966-71. Mem. Am. Soc. M.E., Soc. Automotive Engrs., Soc. Naval Architects. Clubs: Coral Ridge Yacht, Chicago Athletic. Home: 328 Sheridan Rd Wilmette IL 60091 Office: 3537 NW 10th Av Ft Lauderdale FL 33309 Died Mar. 3, 1971.

GILLIES, BREWSTER ALLISON, aviation cons.; b. Haverstraw, N.Y., Nov. 15, 1905; s. John W. and Hannah B. (Allison) G.; B.S., Mass. Inst. Tech., 1927; m. Betty Huyler, Jan. 18, 1930; children—Peter Huyler, Patricia. Vice pres. Grover Loening Aircraft Co., N.Y., 1929-33, Grumman Aircraft Engring. Corp., Bethpage, N.Y., 1934-44, Ryan Aero Co., 1945; West Coast asso. Jones & Gillies, Inc., 1946-67; dir. exec. com. Pacific Airmotive Corp., 1955-66, Marquardt Corp., Van Nuys, Cal.; 1950-70; pres., dir. Cal. Minerals Corp.; chmn. bd. dirs. Spectral Dynamics Corp., San Diego; v.p., dir. Eason Enterprises, Inc., San Diego; dir. World Information Systems. Naval aviator 5th Fighting Squadron, U.S.S. Lexington, 1927-28. Mem. Nat. Aero. Assn., Nat. Pilots Assn., Soc. Exptl. Test Pilots, Am. Inst. Aeros. and Astroanutics, Quiet Birdmen. Republican. Methodist. Club: Aviation Country of California. Address: PO Box 625 Rancho Sante Fe CA 92067

GILLIES, MARY DAVIS, (Mrs. Joseph E. Johnston), writer; b. Partridge, Kan., May 1, 1900; d. Robert Abraham Lincoln and Lincoln and Harriet (Rehm) Davis; B.S., U. Wash., 1924, A.M., 1925; m. Robert Carlyle Gillies, May 5, 1930; m. 2d, Joseph E. Johnston, July 14, 1941. 14, 1941. Instr. in clothing and applied design U. Ore., 1926-27; with textile div. U.S. Bur. Home Econs., Dept. Agr., 1927-28; account exec. Gardner Advt. Agy., N.Y.C., 1928-29; interiors and archtl. editor McCall's mag., N.Y.C., 1929-67; interior designer, lectr., cons., 1968—. Recipient gold medal award Freedom's Found., 1949; Dorothy Dawes Furniture Industry award, 1954, 61. Mem. Am. Home Econs. Assn., Archtl. League, Fashion group, Design Design Writers Internat., Nat. Home Fashions League (pres. 1954-55), Chi Omega, Omicron Nu. Author books including: How to Keep House, rev. edit., 1968; McCall's Book of Modern Houses, rev. edit., 1959; McCall's Decorating Book, 1964. Home: PO Box 945 Sparta NY 07871

GILLIGAN, JOHN JOYCE, gov. of Ohio; b. Cin., Mar. 22, 1921; s. Harry J. and Blanche Joyce Gilligan; B.A., U. Notre Dame, 1943; M.A., U. Cin., 1947; m. Mary Kathryn Dixon, June 28, 1945; children—Donald, Kathleen, John, Ellen. Instr., Xavier U., 1948-53; mem. Cin. City Council, 1953-67; mem. U.S. Congress, 1964-66; partner Sauter-Gilligan & Assos., Ins., 1968—; gov. of Ohio, 1971—. Del.-at-large Democratic Nat. Conv., 1968. Served to lt. USNR, 1942-45; MTO, PTO. Decorated Silver Star; fellow John F. Kennedy Inst. Politics, Harvard, 1969, Adlai Stevenson Inst. Internat. Studies, U. Chgo., 1969. Address: 1875 William Howard Taft Blvd Cincinnati OH 45219*

GILLIHAN, WILLIAM J., advt. exec.; b. Pitts., Nov. 11, 1917; s. William J. and Eleanor (McWhinney) G.; Chem. Engr., Purdue U., 1939; m. Sara Wynn Parker, June 17, 1940; children William Allan III, John Vincent, Mary Eleanor. With Ketchum, MacLeod & Grove, Pitts., 1938—, sr. v.p., 1961-65, exec. v.p., 1965-69, vice chmn. bd., 1969—, also dir., mem. exec. com. and chmn. profit sharing trust com. Served to capt. USAAF, 1941-46. Mem. Am. Marketing Assn., Pitts. C. of C., Delta Tau Delta. Republican. Presbyn. Mason (Shriner). Clubs: Pittsburgh Athletic Assn., Duquesne, Chartiers Country (Pitts.) Home: 930 Osage Rd Pittsburgh PA 15216 Office: Gateway 4 Pittsburgh PA 15322 Bernard

GILLILAND, CHARLES EDWARD, Jr., coll. dean; b. Austin, Tex., Mar. 2, 1916; s. Charles Edward and Olive May (Wiley) G.; B.S., Harvard, 1938; M.S. in Bus. Adminstrn., Washington U., St. Louis, 1947, Ph.D., 1956; m. Flora Reller Smith, June 12, 1948; children—Thomas Lee, Susan Virginia. With budget div. treasurers office Goodyear Tire & Rubber Co., 1938-41, 45-46; asst. to dean Washington U. Sch. Bus. and Pub. Adminstrn., 1948-54; exec. sec. Am. Assn. Collegiate Schs. Bus., 1949-53; dean U. Kansas City (Mo.) Sch. Bus. Adminstrn., 1954-58; chief party Washington U. ICA project, Korea, 1958-60; prof. econs. Ariz State U., 1960; dean Temple U. Sch. Bus. Adminstrn., 1960- 65, prof. finance, 1960-68; dean Coll. Bus. Adminstrn., Fla. Tech. U., 1969—; U.S. aid Temple U., adviser Inst. Bus. Adminstrn., U. Karachi, 1965-66. sec.-treas. Council Profl. Edn. Bus., 1957-58; vice chmn. Nat. Council Devel. Small Bus. Mgmt. Tng., 1957-58. Served with USAAF, 1941-45. Mem. Am. Econ. Assn., Am. Finance Assn., Beta Gamma Sigma (nat. treas. 1963-65), Omicron Delta Epsilon, Beta Alpha Psi. Office: Fla Technological U PO Box 25000 Orlando FL 32816

GILLILAND, EDWIN R., educator, chem. engr.; b. El Reno, Okla., July 10, 1909; s. Owen Edwin and Elsie (Kelly) G.; B.Sc., U. Ill., 1930; M.Sc., Pa. State Coll., 1931; Sc.D., Mass. Inst. Tech., 1933; D.Engring., Northeastern U., 1948; m. Ann F. Miller, June 15, 1938; 1 dau., Gail Ann. Instr. chem. engring. Mass. Inst. Tech., 1934-36, asst. prof., 1936-39, asso. prof., 1939-44, prof., 1944, dep. dean engring., 1945-46, chmn. faculty, 1952-54, acting head dept., 1951-53, 55-56, 60, head dept., 1961-69, Warren K. Lewis prof. chem. engring., 1969—. Asst. rubber dir. charge research and devel. Office of Rubber, 1942-44; dep. chmn., mem. div. 11, NDRC, 1944-45; mem. Pres.' Sci. Adv. Com., 1960-65; cons. Office Sci. and Tech., 1965—. Chmn., dir. Ionics, Inc.; dir. Chromerics, Inc. Recipient Profl. Progress award, 1950, William H. Walker award, 1954, Baekland award Am. Chem. Soc., 1945, Indsl. and Engring. Chemistry award, 1959, Warren K. Lewis award chem. engring. edn., 1965—. Fellow Am. Inst. Chemists, A.A.A.S.; mem. Nat. Acad. of Engring., Am. Inst. Chem. Engrs. (dir. 1958-60), Am. Chem. Soc., Am. Soc. for Engring. Edn., Am. Acad. Arts and Scis., Sigma Xi, Tau Beta Pi. Republican. Presbyn. Joint author: 3d edit. Principles of Chemical Engineering; 4th edit. Elements of Fractional Distillation. Author articles on chem. engring. Office: Dept Chemical Engineering Mass Inst Tech Cambridge MA 02139

GILLILAND, JACK EDWARD, railroad ofcl.; b. Nacogdoches, Tex., Nov. 29, 1908; s. George E. and Mary (Hoben) G.; grad. Chgo. Coll. Commerce, 1927, Advanced Mgmt. Program, Harvard, 1950; m. Viola Schneidermeyer, Apr. 7, 1947. Successively office asst., traffic rep., spl. rep. M.P. R.R. Co., 1929- 42; trainmaster Terminal R.R. Assn. St. Louis, 1942-45; pres. Ala., Tenn. & No. R.R., 1946-49, now dir.; v.p. Frisco Transp. Co., 1949-50, dir., v.p. transp., 1950—; asst. to pres. Frisco Ry., 1950-54. asst. to v.p. traffic, 1954-55, v.p. traffic and indsl. devel., 1958-65, chmn. bd., pres., 1965—; past pres., now chmn. St. L.-S.F. R.R.; v.p., dir. Birmingham Belt R.R. Co., Frisco Ry., Clarkland, Inc., 906 Olive Corp.; v.p. Greater Tulsa, Inc.; dir. Clarkland Royalty, Inc., Trailer Train Co., Quanah, Acne & Pacific Ry. Mem. Nat. Def. Transp. Assn. (life), Nat. Freight Traffic Assn., Transp. Club Petroleum Industry, St. Louis, St. Louis County chambers commerce, Am. Soc. Traffic and Transp., Newcomen Soc. N.A., Delta Nu Alpha. Clubs: Harvard Business School, Missouri Athletic, Old Warson Country, Media, Noonday, Traffic (St. Louis); Union League, Traffic (Chgo.); Traffic (N.Y.C.). Home: 230 S Brentwood Blvd Clayton MO 63105 Office: 906 Olive St St Louis MO 63101

GILLILAND, JOHN LAWRENCE, Jr., cement co. exec.; b. Clearfield, Pa., Oct. 4, 1910; s. John Lawrence and Sophia Catherine (Fisher) G.; student U. Denver, 1927-29; B.S., U. Colo., 1933; m. Elsa Hildegard Moberg, Mar. 28, 1935; children—John Munro, Lawrence Jay, Joan Marie (Mrs. Attila Eroncel). Chem. engr. U.S. Bur. Reclamation Engring. Labs., Denver, 1933-41, head chem. and cement labs., 1941-51; gen. chemist Ideal Cement Co., Denver, 1951-64, dir. quality control, 1964-67, tech. dir., 1967—. Mem. Nat. Adv. Com. on Control Techniques (NAPCA-HEW). Registered profl. engr., Colo. Diplomate Am. Acad. Enivonmental Engrs. Fellow Am. Soc. Testing Materials (com. sec., award of merit 1971); mem. Air Pollution Control Assn. (dir.), Am. Chem. Soc., Am. Concrete Inst., Sigma Xi, Phi Delta Theta. Lutheran. Home: 1090 Lafayette St Denver CO 80218 Office: 821 17th St Denver CO 80202

GILLILAND, WILLIAM NATHAN, univ. adminstr., geologist; b. Portsmouth, O., May 23, 1919; s. Evan Russell and Elsie (Tipton) G.; B.A., Ohio State U., 1941, Ph.D., 1948; m. Paula Embree; children—Sherrie Ann, William Kimberly (both from previous marriage), Jane Elizabeth. With TVA, 1941, U.S. Geol. Survey, 1948-49; mem. faculty U. Neb., 1949-65, chmn. dept. geology, 1950-64; dean Coll. Arts and Scis., Rutgers U., Newark, 1965—; cons. to industry, 1950—; geol. cons. Neb. Boundary Commn., 1964—. Bd. dirs Kathol Petroleum, Inc. Served to 1st lt. USAAF, 1941-45. Mem. Am. Assn. Petroleum Geologists, Geol. Soc. Am., Neb. children—Cynthia Scis. Author: Geology of the Gunnison Quadrangle, Utah, 1951; also numerous articles, bulls.‡

GILLILLAND, WHITNEY, govt. ofcl.; b. Glenwood, Ia., Jan. 13, 1904; s. Shirley and Elsie children—Howard G.; student Ia. State Coll., 1921-22, U. Neb., 1923-26; m. Virginia Wegmann, Feb. 19, 1926; children—William S., Thomas M. Admitted to Ia. and Wis. bars. 1927; practice in Ia. 1927-53; judge 15th Jud. Dist., 1938-41; asst. to sec. agr., 1953; 1948—; War Claims Commn., 1953-54, Fgn. Claims Settlement Commn. U.S., 1954-59; mem. CAB, 1959— chmn., 1948—; vice chmn., 1969—; chmn. licencing com. Administrv. Conf. U.S., 1961-62, mem. personnel com., 1969—. Ia. Republican chmn., 1947-50; chmn. exec. com. Nat. Rep. Strategy Com., 1949. Mem. Am. (ho. del. 1962-63), Fed. (pres. 1959-60), Ia. bar assns., Washington Fgn. Law Soc. (pres. 1965-66). Conglist. Home: 4150 N 41st St Arlington VA 22207 Office: Civil Aeronautics Bd Washington DC 20428

GILLIM, MARION HAMILTON, educator, economist; b. Owensboro, Ky., Apr. 12, 1909; d. Parvin Douglas and Marion (Reid) Gillim; A.B., Mt. Holyoke Coll., 1930; M.A., Columbia, 1938, Ph.D., 1944. Instr. high sch., Owensboro, 1932-39; instr. econs. and sociology N.J. Coll. Women, 1941-42; from instr. to asso. prof. Mt.

Holyoke Coll., 1942-49; research Nat. Bur. Econ. Research, 1943; internat. cons. labor statistics Central and S. Am., Bur. Labor Statistics, 1949-52, 55-56; mem. faculty Barnard Coll., 1952—, prof. econs., 1962—, chmn. dept., 1955-63, 67-68; cons. in field; Brookings research prof., 1957-58. Mem. Am. Acad. Polit. Sci., Am. Assn. U. Profs., Am. Assn. U. Women, Am. Econ. Assn., Am. Statis. Assn., Internat. Fiscal Assn., Internat. Inst. Pub. Finance, Latin Am. Studies Assn., Met. Econ. Assn., Nat. Tax Assn., Tax Inst. Am., Phi Beta Kappa. Club: Cosmopolitan (N.Y.C.). Author: The Incidence of Excess Profits Mexico Taxation, 1945; also articles. Home: 1505 Griffith Av Owensboro KY 42301 Office: Barnard Coll New York City NY 10027

GILLINGBERG, ROBERT BRUCE diversified mfg. co. exec.; b. Cin., May 21, 1910; grad. Phillips Acad., Andover, Mass., 1927; B.S., Princeton, 1931; postgrad. Mass. Inst. Tech., 1931-33; m. Jean R. Holland, June 16, 1935; children--Lois A., Andrew M., James. Salesman, Brown Mfg. Co., Boston, 1932-33; jr. engr. Ball Metals Co., Carson City, Nev., 1933-36, engr., 1936-37, sr. engr., 1937-40; project engr. Kingston Engring. Co., Los Angeles, 1940-43; with dept. engring. City of Denver, 1946-50, dep. head, 1950-52; 2d v.p. Johnson Mfg. Co., Kansas City, Kansas, 1952-54, v.p. for engring., 1954-57; v.p. research Consol. Industries, Inc., South Bend, Ind., 1957-60, exec. v.p., 1960-65, pres., 1965-70, chmn. bd., chief exec. officer, 1970--, also dir.; dir. ABC Chem. Co., 2d Nat. Bank, Country Food Storage Co., Providence Indsl. Corp. Pres., Dewey High Sch., Kansas City, Mo., 1953-54; fund chmn. local div. Salvation Army, 1959-60. Mem. South Bend Republican Com., 1964-68. Bd. dirs. Ind. council Boy Scouts Am., 1969-71; trustee Lovell Found. Served to lt., Corps Engrs., AUS, 1943-45. Decorated Bronze Star medal. Member N.A.M., South Bend C. of C. (v.p. 1963-65, dir. 1965-70), Am. Mgmt. Assn., Ind. Engrs. Soc. (program com. 1961-63), Princeton Alumni Assn. Episcopalian. Home: 6823 Broad Terrace Av South Bend IN Instr., Ia. State U., 1946-47; asst. prof. biology Johns Hopkins, 1947-50, asso. prof., 1950-62, prof., 1962--, chmn. dept., 1963-69; vis. lectr. Stanford, 1970-71. Active Boy Scouts Am., 4-H Club. Served with AUS, 1940-46. Mem. Am. Soc. Biologists, Md. Soc. Cell Biologists, Am. Soc. Exptl. Biology, Internat. Union Biologists, A.A.A.S., Am. Acad. Arts and Scis., Phi Beta Kappa. Home: 48936 W Hancock Blvd Baltimore MD 20206

GILLINGHAM, WILLIAM JAMES, oil co. exec.; b. Wallasey, Eng., 1912; s. J.S. and Rose (Robus) G.; B.S., A.R.S.M., Royal Sch. Mines, U. London, 1933, D.I.C., 1934; m. Margaret Hadfield, July 22, 1937; children—Anne, Richard, Susan. Came to children—Kaylie, 1934. Asst. lectr. Royal Sch. Mines, 1933-34; with Schlumberger Well Surveying Corp., 1934—, successively engr., div. mgr., exec. v.p., 1951-57, pres., 1957-67, chmn., 1967—, dir., 1954—; v.p., gen. mgr. Schlumberger Surenco S.A., 1947-51; exec. v.p. Schlumberger, Ltd. Mem. Am. Inst. Mining, Metall. and Petroleum Engrs., Am. Assn. Petroleum Geologists, Am. Petroleum Inst. Episcopalian. Home: 4718 Hallmark St Houston TX 77027 Office: 277 Park Av New York City NY 10017

GILLIS, BERNARD THOMAS, univ. provost; b. Pierre, S.D., Mar. 7, 1931; s. Edward John and Evelyn (Lehrke) G.; B.S., Loras Coll., 1952; Ph.D., (Ethyl Corp. summer fellow, 1952) Wayne State U., 1956; postgrad. Mass. Inst. Tech., 1956-57; m. Arlene F. Hamilton, Aug. 22, 1953; children—Gregory H., Gwendolyn K., Kathryn J., Theresa A. Parke, Davis & Co. fellow Wayne State U., 1955-56, research asso., 1958; post-doctoral fellow Mass. Inst. Tech., 1956-67; asst. prof. Duquesne U., Pitts., 1957-60, asso. prof., 1960-64, prof. chemistry 1964, asso. chmn. chemistry dept., 1965-68, dean Grad. Sch., 1968-70; dean acad. affairs and faculty Indiana (Pa.) U., 1970-71, acad. v.p., provost, 1971—. Fellow A.A.A.S., Am. Inst. Chemists; mem. Am. Chem. Soc. (award coms. local sect. 1960-63, 65-67, chmn. mem. com. 1967—, nat. councillor 1970—), Chem. Soc. London, Am. Assn. U. Profs., Pa. Assn. Coll. Chemistry Tchrs., Internat. Soc. Heterocyclic Chemistry, Am. Ordnance Assn., Pitts. Chemists Club, Pa. Cath. Round Table Sci., Sigma Xi (research award 1955), Phi Lambda Upsilon, Phi Delta Kappa. Contbr. articles to profl. jours. Home: 52 S 9th St Indiana PA 15701

GILLIS, EVERETT ALDEN, educator, author; b. Cameron, Mo., Mar. 4, 1914; s. Earle Adrien and Pearle (Owens) G.; B.A., Tex. Christian U., 1936, M.A., 1939; Ph.D., U. Tex., 1948; m. Lizzie Mae Allen, Aug. 14, 1943. Asst. prof. English, Tex. Coll. Arts and Industries, Kingsville, 1947-49; prof. English, Tex. Tech. Coll., Lubbock, 1949—, chmn. dept., 1964-69. Served with AUS, 1942- 46. Fellow Ford Found., 1955-56. Mem. Modern Lang. Assn., Nat. Council Tchrs. English, Tex. Inst. Letters, Poetry Soc. Tex. (v.p. 1951) Am., Tex. (pres. 1961) folklore socs., Southwestern Am. Lit. Assn. (pres. 1970) Nat. Writers Club. Author: Sing Your America, 1954; A College Forum, 1963; (verse) Hello the House, 1944; Who Can Retreat, 1944; Sunrise in Texas, 1949; Angles of the Wind, 1954; Oliver La Farge, 1967; (music lyrics) Ballads for Texas Heroes, 1964; also articles. Home: 3209 26th St Lubbock, TX 79410.

GILLIS, JOHN LAMB, chem. co. exec.; b. Fargo, N.D., May 23, 1911; s. John Daniel and Mary (Lamb) G.; B.S., Washington U., 1933; m. Carol Randolph, June 18, 1938; children—John Lamb, Carol G. Manning, Ann Carter, Mary Barrett. Asst. export mgr. Monsanto Co., St. Louis, 1933-38, export mgr., 1938-41, asst. dir. fgn. dept., 1941-44, dir. fgn. dept., 1946-49, gen. mgr. Merrimac Div., Boston, 1949-51, gen. mgr. organic chems. div., children— also v.p. Monsanto Co., 1950-54, v.p. marketing, 1954-68, sr. v.p., 1968—, also dir.; dir. Am. Investment Co., Boatmen's Nat. Bank St. Louis. Mem. Culbertson Mission to N. Africa, Middle East, Italy, 1944. Pres.'s council St. Louis U. Trustee Govt. Research Inst., St. Louis, Marketing Sci. Inst.; bd. dirs., mem. exec. com. St. Louis Symphony Soc. Mem. U.S. C. of C. (policy com. 1950—, bd. dirs.), Am. Soc. Corporate Execs. (chmn.), Am. Chem. Soc. Clubs: Links (N.Y.C.); St. Louis Country (Clayton, Mo.); Racquet, Deer Creek Bogey (St. Louis). Home: 2 Colonial Hills Dr Creve Coeur MO 63141 Office: 800 N Lindbergh Blvd St Louis MO 63166

GILLIS, MARVIN BOB, chem. co. exec.; b. Treutlen County, Ga., Apr. 5, 1920; s. Bob Lee and Pearl (Gillis) G.; B.S.A., U. Ga., 1940; Ph.D., Cornell U., 1947; m. Helen Reed, Dec. 23, 1946; children—Margaret Susan, Marvin Reed, Kenneth Robert. Teaching asst. U. Ga., 1939-40; teaching fellow children—Quentin U., 1940-42, research fellow, 1945- 47, research asso., 1947-51; research chemist Internat. Minerals and Chem. Corp., 1947-50, supr. nutrition research, 1950-51, supr. biol. research, 1951-54, mgr. research organic and biol. scis., 1954-56, asst. dir. research, 1956-57, dir. research, 1957-64, dir. animal health and nutrition, 1964-66, div. v.p., 1966-70, corp. v.p., 1970—; dir. Continental Ore Co., IMC Devel. Corp. Sec. Agrl. Research Inst., Nat. Acad. Scis.-NRC, 1958-59, v.p., 1960-62, 1966—; pres., 1962-63, 68-69, mem. agrl. bd., 1962-67; mem. bus. adv. com. Ill. Jr. Acad. Scis., 1958- 61; bd. dirs. Animal Health Inst., 1966-69. Served to 1st lt. USAAF, 1942-45. Financial D.F.C. with oak leaf cluster, Air medal with 3 oak leaf clusters. Fellow Am. Inst. Chemists; mem. Am. Chem. Soc., Am. Inst. Nutrition, Poultry Sci. Assn. (Research prize 1948), Am. Soc. Animal Sci., Sigma Xi, Gamma Alpha, Alpha Zeta, Phi Kappa Phi. Baptist. Club: Chemists (N.Y.C.). Patentee in field. Author numerous papers in field. Editorial adv. com. Jour. Agrl. and Food Chemistry, 1962-65. Home: 2116 Larkdale Dr Glenview IL 60025 Office: 5401 Old Orchard Rd Skokie IL 60076

GILLIS, RICHARD SAMUEL, Jr., assn. exec.; b. Lawrenceville, Va., Sept. 10, 1915; s. Richard Samuel and Janie (Wilkins) G.; student U.S. Mil. Acad., 1935; B.A., Randolph-Macon Coll., 1940; m. Margaret Crawford Shelton, July 10, 1948; 1 dau., Margaret Kimbrough. News editor Herald Progress, Ashland, Va., 1940-41; adminstrv. asst. Randolph-Macon Coll., 1945-51; exec. dir. Va. C. of C., Richmond, 1951—; instr. U. Coll. Past Mem. mil. staff gov. Va.; mem. Va. Hosp. Bd., Gov. Va. Adv. Com. Travel; adv.council Va. Small Bus. Adminstrn. Trustee Jamestown Found., Common Glory Found; bd. dirs. Atlantic Rural Exposition. Served to capt. AUS, 1941-45. Recipient Distinguished Service awards Randolph-Macon Coll., 1960, Am. Cancer Soc., 1960. Mem. Richmond Pub. Relations Soc. (past pres.), Va. Assn. C. of C. Execs., S.A.R., Am. Legion (past comdr.), Export-Import Club (past pres.). Democrat, Methodist. Kiwanian. Home: 114 Snead St Ashland VA 23005 Office: 611 E Franklin St Richmond VA 23219

GILLISPIE, CHARLES COULSTON, educator; b. Harrisburg, Pa., Aug. 6, 1918; s. Raymond Livingston and Virginia Lambert (Coulston) G.; A.B., Wesleyan U., Middletown, Conn., 1940, M.A., 1942, D.Sc., 1971; student Mass. Inst. Tech., 1940-41; Ph.D., Harvard, 1949; m. Emily Ramsdell Clapp, Jan. 29, 1949. Teaching fellow, tutor history Harvard, 1946-47; faculty Princeton, 1947—, prof. history sci., 1959-67, Shelby Cullom Davis prof. European history, 1967—. Fellow Am. Council Learned Socs., 1951-52; Guggenheim fellow, 1954-55; Nat. Sci. Found. fellow, 1958-59, 62-63; fellow Center for Advanced Study in Behavioral Scis., 1970-71. Served to capt. C.W.S., AUS, 1942- 45. Mem. History Sci. Soc. (council 1952-55, 59-60, pres. 1964-66), Am. Acad. Arts and Scis., Académie Internationale d' Histoire des Sciences (v.p. 1965-68), Phi Beta Kappa. Clubs: Princeton (N.Y.C.); Nassau (Princeton, N.J.). Author: Genesis and Geology, 1951; A Diderot Pictorial Encyclopedia of Trades and Industry, 2 vols., 1959; The Edge of Objectivity: An essay in the History of Scientific Ideas, 1960; Lazare Carnot, Savant, 1971. Editor-in-chief: Dictionary of Scientific Biography. Home: 3 Morgan Pl Princeton NJ 08540 also 31 15th St Avalon NJ 08202

GILLMAN, CHARLES H., union ofcl. Dir. Region 6 Dept. Orgn. AFL-CIO. Office: 1026 Hurst Bldg Atlanta GA 30303*

GILLMAN, NATHANIEL mfg. exec.; b. Lima, O., Apr. 1, 1932; B.S., U. San Francisco, 1954; M.S., Stanford University, 1956; m. Rosemarie Lois Brown, May 15, 1955; 1 son, Anthony Robinson. Sales rep. Ames-Brockton Fabricated Products, Akron, O., 1956-58, sales mgr. Coshocton, Ohio, 1959-61, gen. manager plant, 1961-68, v.p. sales, 1968--. Instr. bus. Coshocton Jr. College, 1968-69. Secretary Coshocton YMCA, 1960-61; active Boy Scouts of America. Named Man of Year, Coshocton Junior Chamber of Commerce, 1968. Mem. Coshocton C. of C. (vice president 1967-68, pres. 1969-70), English Speaking Union, Coshocton Sertoma Club, Nat. Assn. Mfrs., Sales Executives Institute, Phi Beta Kappa, Sigma Chi, Phi Mu. Democrat. Mem. Christian Ch. (lay leader). Mason (32, Shriner). Clubs: Coshocton Country, Coshocton City, Running Deer Country. Home: 2d Av Coshocton OH Office: 3d Av Coshocton OH

GILLMAN, SIDNEY, profl. football coach; b. Mpls., Oct. 26, 1911; s. David J. and Sara (Dickerman) G.; B.A., Ohio State U., 1934; m. Esther Berg, Aug. 20, 1935; children—Lyle (Mrs. Jay Malkoff), Barbara (Mrs. Wallace Korbin), Terry Anne (Mrs. Lawrence Hill), Thomas Roger. Asst. football coach Denison U., 1935-38, asst. coach, 1940-41; asst. football coach Ohio State U., 1938-40; asst. coach Miami U., Oxford, O., 1942-44, head coach, 1945-47; assst. Coach West Point, 1948; head coach U. Cin., 1948-54, Los Angeles Rams, 1955-59; head coach, gen. mgr. San Diego Chargers, 1960—. Mem. Zeta Beta Tau. Mason (Shriner). Author: (with Alvin Roy) San Diego Chargers Strength Program In and Out of Season. Home: 9805 Summit Dr La Mesa CA 92041 Office: 2223 El Cajon Blvd San Diego CA 92104

GILLMOR, PAUL MARSHALL, trucking co. ofcl.; b. Fremont, O., Feb. 26, 1911; s. Clarence and Gladys (Speller) G.; student Ohio State U., 1929-30; m. Lucy Jeannette Fry, Jan. 20, 1934; children—Paul Eugene, Lucy Dianne (Mrs. Cubbage). Owner trucking business, 1931-56; v.p. Matlack, Inc., Lansdowne, Pa., 1956-67, chmn. bd. dirs., 1967—; pres. Old Fort Banking Co., Old Fort Telephone Co.; dir. Comml. Nat. Bank, Central Res. Life Ins. Co. Vice pres. exec. council Boy Scouts Am., 1970—; pres. Old Fort Fire Dept., 1942-64. Mem. Old Fort Sch. Bd., 1948-68, pres., 1962-68. Trustee N.W. Ohio Sch. Bds. Assn., 1964-68, Heidelberg Coll., 1970—. Methodist (trustee). Elk, Lion. Home: 240 Main St Old Fort OH 44861 Office: 2210 Oakdale St Oregon OH 43616

GILLON, JOHN WILLIAM, lawyer; b. Sherman, Tex., Apr. 24, 1900; s. John William and Lucie (Conner) G.; A.B., Miss. Coll.; LL.B. (Lafferty medal), U. Ky., 1925; m. Itzselle L. Cook, July 8, 1930; children—John William, Allen C., Edward J., Paul K., Harvey E., David C. Admitted to Ky., Ala. bars, 1925; asso. firm Coleman, Spain & Stewart, Birmingham, Ala., 1925-35; mem. firm Spain, Gillon & Young, Birmingham, 1935-66, Spain, Gillon, Riley, Tate & Ansley, 1966—. Dir., sec. Estes Lumber Co., 1939-64. Mem. Jefferson County Jud. Commn., 1953-58. Chmn., Med. Clinic Bd. City of Birmingham, 1966—; bd. mem. Estate Planning Council Birmingham. Served with SATC, 1918. Mem. Am., Ala. bar assns., Birmingham Bar (exec. com. 1955-57, pres. 1960, chmn. ednl. adv. com. 1966- 67), Birmingham C. of C., Miss. Coll. Alumni Assn. (bd.), Am. Life Conv. (legal sec.), Am. Law Inst., Farrah Law Soc., Order of Coif, Blue Goose, Phi Alpha Delta. Lions. Home: 1260 S 33d St Birmingham AL 35205 Office: First Nat Bldg Birmingham AL 35203

GILLOW, LOUIS STEPHEN, diversified mfg. co. exec.; b. West Chester, Pa., June 4, 1929; s. Louis and Julia (Matis) G.; B.S., U.S. Naval Acad., 1951; J.D., Temple U., 1957; postgrad. Harvard Sch. Bus. Adminstrn., 1965; m. Marlene Joann Madera, June 7, 1958; children—Marianne, Martin, Paul. Engring. and contracting officer Merck & Co., Phila., London, N.Y.C., 1956-69; v.p., gen. counsel, sec., dir. Worthington Corp., Mountainside, N.J., 1969—; admitted to D.C. bar, 1962; N.J. bar, 1968; dir. Worthington Pump & Machinery Corp., Worthington Ltd. Served to lt. (j.g.) USNR, 1951-54. Mem. Essex County, N.J. bar assns., Am. Soc. M.E. Author: The Salesman and the Law, 1970-71. Home: 23 Wellington Av Short Hills NJ 07078 Office: 270 Sheffield St Mountainside NJ 07092

GILLSTONE, ARCHIBALD chemist, educator; b. Chicago, 1928; B.S. in Physics, Yale, 1950; Ph.D. in Chemistry, Harvard, 1956; m. Sally Ann Jones, July 5, 1957; children--Kenneth J., Nancy A. Chemist, Acme Chem. Co., Blue Island, Ill., 1950-51; director of Research Lab., Indsl. Chemicals Corp., Cambridge, Mass., 1956-60; project coordinator environmental sect. Steinmetz Assos., Chgo., 1960-61; v.p. for research Bauer Bros. Chem. Co., Inc., Memphis, 1961-64; asst. prof. chemistry Washington U., St. Louis, 1964-66, asso. prof., 1966-70, prof., 1970--, head of chemistry dept., 1970-71. Vis. prof. So. Ill. U., summer 1967, U. of Ore., 1969. Scoutmaster, Boy Scouts America, University City, Mo., 1968-70. Bd. dirs. Rest Haven Home for Elderly, 1960-61; trustee of the Lutheran Hosp., 1965-71. Served from lt. to capt., AUS, 1951-53. Mem. Am. Chem. Soc., Sci. Research Soc. Am. (chpt. treas. 1967), Sigma Xi. Author: (with others) Basic Inorganic Chemistry, 1971. Home: Fairfax Apts 7291 Windermere Dr University City MO 63105 Office: Dept Chemistry Washington University St Louis MO 63130

GILMAN, AARON, food co. exec.; b. N.Y.C., Jan. 13, 1920; s. David E. and Celia (Guff) G.; student Hofstra Coll., 1937-39, N.Y. U. Law Sch., 1939-40; m. Betty Heller, Jan. 3, 1944; children—Lynda Marion, Mark Heller, William Eric. With Vita Food Products, N.Y.C., 1946—, exec.. v.p., 1956-60, pres., 1960- -, also dir.; v.p., dir. Oceanic Fisheries, Seattle, 1949—; Maywood Packing Co., Corning, Cal., 1948—, Ranier Boat Co., Seattle, 1951—. Former chmn. Nat. Fisheries Inst.; pres. Fish Smokers Trade Council, 1949—. Chmn. for fish industry in N.Y.C. for A.R.C., 1956. Mason (Shriner). Club: Sands Point (L.I.) Yacht. Home: 37 Gateway Dr Great children—Cynthia NY 11021 Office: 644 Greenwich St New York City NY 10014

GILMAN, ALFRED, educator, pharmacologist; b. Bridgeport, Conn., Feb. 5, 1908; s. Joseph and Frances (Zack) G.; B.S., Yale, 1928, Ph.D., 1931; m. Mabel J. Schmidt, Jan. 11, 1934; children—Joanna, Alfred Goodman. Research fellow biochemistry Yale, 1931-32, research asso., asst. prof. pharmacology, 1933-43; asso. prof. pharmacology Columbia, 1946-48, prof., 1948-55; prof. pharmacology, chmn. dept. Yeshiva U. Albert Einstein Coll. Medicine, 1956—, asso. dean grad. edn., 1964-69. Spl. cons. USPHS; mem. sci. and edn. council Am. Found. Allergic Disease; exec. com. med. div. NRC; mem. panel on chem. agts. Presdl. Sci. Adv. Com., 1970—; mem. drug research bd. NRC, chmn., 1971—. Served as maj. CWS, AUS, 1943-46. Fellow Am. Acad. Allergy (hon.), N.Y. Acad. sci.; mem. Am. Physiol. Soc., Am. Soc. Pharmacology and Exptl. Therapy (pres. 1960), Harvey Soc., Nat. Acad. Sci., Am. Acad. Arts and Scis., Soc. Exptl. Biology and Medicine, N.Y. Acad. Medicine (asso.), Sigma Xi, Alpha Omega Alpha. Author: (with L.S. Goodman) Pharmacological Basis of Therapeutics, 1941. Editorial bd. Am. Jour. Physiology, Jour. Applied Physiology, Pharmacol. Rev. Home: Garth Woods Apts Garth Rd Scarsdale NY 10583 Office: Albert Einstein Coll Medicine Eastchester Rd and Morris Pk Av Bronx NY 10061

GILMAN, ANDREW L., lawyer; b. Scottsburg, N.Y., Apr. 28, 1886; A.B., Cornell U., 1908; LL.B., Albany Law Sch., Union U., 1910. Admitted to N.Y. bar, 1911; mem. firm Oviatt, Gilman, Sturman and Clarke, Rochester, N.Y. Bd. dirs. Rochester Gen. Hosp., 1944-63, pres., 1947-50. Mem. Am., N.Y. State, Monroe County (pres. 1929) bar assns. Office: Central Trust Bldg 44 Exchange St Rochester NY 14614*

GILMAN, HARRISON WESTPHAL educator, biologist; b. Ames, Ia.; B.A., Ia. State U., 1936, M.A., 1937, Ph.D. with honors, 1940. Instr., Ia. State U., 1946-47; asst. prof. biology Johns Hopkins, 1947-50, asso. prof., 1950-62, prof., 1962--, chmn. dept., 1963-69; vis. lectr. Stanford, 1970-71. Active Boy Scouts Am., 4-H Club. Served with AUS, 1940-46. Mem. Am. Soc. Biologists, Md. Biologists, A.A.A.S., Am. Acad. Arts and Scis., Phi Beta Kappa.

GILMAN, HENRY, educator, organic chemist; b. Boston, May 9, 1893; s. David and Jane (Gordon) G.; B.S., Harvard, 1915, A.M., 1917, Ph.D., 1918; postgrad. postgrad. Zürich Polytechnikum and Oxford, 1916; m. Ruth V. Shaw, July 20, 1929; children—Jane Gordon, Henry Shaw. Instr. chemistry Harvard, 1918-19; asso. in chemistry U. Ill., 1919; prof. organic chemistry Ia. State U., 1919—. Cons. AEC; Air Force research dir.; plenary lectr. Internat. Symposia Organometallic and Organometalloidal Chemistry. Holder of various lectureships and mem. awards coms.; recipient Mid-West Gold medal, Ia. Am. Chem. Soc. medal award; Frederick Stanley Kipping award Am. Chem. Soc.; First Firestone Internat. Lectures award in organometallic chemistry; Distinguished Prof. in Sci. and Humanities, 1962. With CWS, World War I; Nat. Def. research work (Manhattan Project). Trustee Carver Research Found. Fellow A.A.A.S. v.p., chem. sect. chmn. 1930), Chem. Soc. London (hon.), Am. Chem. Soc. (councillor at large 1939-41, 42-44, chmn. organic div.), Nat. Acad. Scis. (ofcl. del., lectr. in Soviet Union 1963), Phi Beta Kappa, Sigma Xi, Phi Kappa Phi, Phi Lambda Upsilon (hon.), Author: (with C.J. West) Organomagnesium Compounds in Synthetic Chemistry, 1922; (with R.J. Jones) Organo-lithium Compounds in Organic Reactions; (with J.W. Morton Jr.) Metalation in Organic Reactions; (with D. Wittenberg) Silylmetallic Compounds; (with F.K. Cartledge) Characterization of Organometallics, 1968; More Than One-half Century of Organometallic Chemistry, 1968. Editor: Organic Syntheses, Vol VI, and Collective Vol. I; Organic Chemistry (2 vols.), 1943; Vols. III, IV Organic Chemistry: Organometallic Compounds in Encyclopedia of Chem. Tech. (with Benkeser); (with R.K. Ingham) Organopolymers of Silicon, Germanium, Tin, and Lead; (with W.H. Atwell and F.K. Cartledge) Catenated Organic Compounds of Group IV-B; (with G.L. Schwebke) Organic Substituted Cyclosilanes; (with H.J.S. Winkler) Organosilylmetallic chemistry. Mem. editorial bd. Advances in Organo-Metallic Chemistry, Current Contents-Chemical Sciences. Contbg. editor ann. Survey of Am. Chemistry, 1928, 1929-30, Organometallic Syntheses, Sci. Citation Index, Organometallic Reactions; asso. editor Chem. Revs., 1936, Jour. Organometallic Chemistry; editorial bd., exec. com. Jour. Organic Chemistry; asso. editor Jour. Am. Chem. Soc. Contbr. to ency.; also co-author monographs; contbr. articles in field to sci. periodicals, with current publs. particularly in area of polyhalo-organometallic chemistry. Home: 3221 Oakland St Ames IA 50010

GILMAN, HORTON PFEIL, wholesale food exec.; b. Sangerville, Me., Apr. 8, 1915; s. M. Elvin and Annally (Pfeil) G.; student pub. schs.; m. Mary Waterman Purkis, Aug. 29, 1942; children—Stephen Elvin, Lincoln Purkis, Michael Horton. With 1st Nat. Stores, Somerville, Mass., 1934-35; zone mgr. Milliken, Tomlinson Co., Portland, Me., 1935-42, div. mgr., Presque Isle, Me., 1946-58, v.p., Portland, Me., 1958-63; propr. Mister G Foodliner, Gorham, Me., 1963-67; v.p. retail operations, dir. J.H. Jones Co., Champaign, Ill., 1967-68, exec. v.p., 1968—. Chmn. Gorham (Me.) Rep. Com., 1966. Pres., trustee A. R. Gould Meml. Hosp., 1953-56. Served to capt., inf., AUS, World War II; ETO. Decorated Purple Heart. Home: 1113 Newbury Rd Champaign IL 61820 Office: 2611 N Lincoln Av Urbana IL 61801

GILMAN, IRVING, dept. store exec.; b. Hartford, Conn., 1922. Pres., dir. Ames Dept. Stores, Inc., Hartford. Home: 53 Juniper Lane West Hartford CT 06117 Office: 3363 Main St Hartford CT 06120*

GILMAN, JOHN S., lawyer; b. Rochester, N.Y., Nov. 30, 1918; A.B., Williams Coll., 1940; LL.B., Cornell U., 1949. Admitted to N.Y. bar, 1949; now mem. firm Woods, Oviatt, Gilman, Sturman & Clarke, Rochester. Bd. dirs. Rochester Gen. Hosp. Mem. Am., N.Y. State, Monroe County bar assns., Phi Beta Kappa. Office: Central Trust Bldg 44 Exchange St Rochester NY 14614*

GILMAN, MILTON, dept. store exec.; b. Hartford, Conn., 1918. Chmn. bd. Ames Dept. Stores, Inc., Hartford. Mason. Home: 127 Orchard Rd West Hartford CT 06117 Office: 3363 Main St Hartford CT 06120*

GILMAN, RICHARD, author, educator; b. N.Y.C., Apr. 30, 1925; s. Jacob and Marion (Wolinsky) G.; B.A., U. Wis., 1947, L.H.D., Grinnell Coll., 1967; 1 son, Nicholas; m. Lynn Nesbit; children—Priscilla, Claire. Free-lance writer, 1950-54; asso. editor Jubilee mag., 1954-57; drama critic, lit. editor Commonweal, 1961-64; asso. editor, drama critic Newsweek mag., 1964-67; lit. editor New Republic, 1968-70; prof. drama Yale, 1967—. Vis. lectr. English, Columbia, 1964- 65; vis. prof. drama Stanford, summer 1967. Served with USMCR, 1943-46. Author: The Confusion of Realms, 1970, Common and Uncommon Masks, 1971. Home: 33 Central Park W New York City NY 10025 Office: Sch Drama Yale New Haven CT 06520

GILMAN, RICHARD CARLETON, coll. pres.; b. Cambridge, Mass., July 28, 1923; s. George Phillips Brooks and Karen Elise (Theller) G.; B.A., Dartmouth, 1944; student New Coll., U. London (Eng.), 1947-48; Ph.D. Quebec Parker Bowne fellow philosophy, 1949-50), Boston U., 1952, L.H.D., 1969; LL.D., Pomona Coll., 1966, U. So. Cal., 1968, Coll. Ida., 1968; m. Lucille Young, Aug. 28, 1948; children—Marsha, Bradley Morris, Brian Potter, Blair Tucker. Teaching fellow religion Dartmouth, 1948; Mem. faculty Colby Coll., children—Gerald asso. prof. philosophy, 1955-56; exec. dir. Nat. Council Religion Higher Edn., New Haven, 1956-60; dean coll., prof. philosophy Carleton Coll., 1960-65; pres. Occidental Coll., 1965—. Pres. Assn. Ind. Cal. Colls. and Univs.; v.p. Ind. Colls. So. Cal.; bd. dirs. Assn. Am. Colls. Mem. acad. adv. com. Performing Arts Council of Music Center, Los Angeles. Trustee Westridge Sch.; hon. mem., bd. dirs. So. Cal. Symphony Assn.; bd. dirs. Los Angeles 1967—), Affairs Council. Served with USNR, 1944-46. Fellow Soc. Religion Higher Edn., Newcomen Soc., Cal. C. of C. (bd. dirs.). Presbyn. Clubs: University (N.Y.C. and Los Angeles); California (Los Angeles). Home: 1852 Campus Rd Los Angeles CA 90041

GILMAN, ROBBINS PAXSON, fgn. service officer; b. Mpls., Apr. 22, 1920; s. Robbins and Catheryne (Cooke) G.; student U. Minn., 1940-42; A.B., Williams Coll., 1947; M.A. Fletcher Sch. Law and Diplomacy, 1948; m. Dorothy Dewey, Dec. 20, 1947; children—Frances, Chandler Robbins, Catherine, Nicholas Paxson. Fgn. affairs officer Exec. Secretariat, Dept. State, 1948-53, acting chief com. secretariat staff, 1953, operations staff, 1953, acting chief reports and operations staff, 1954-55, chief, 1955-56; consul, sec. diplomatic service, Zurich, Switzerland, 1956-58; 1st sec. embassy, Bonn, Germany, 1958-60; polit. adviser to comdr.-in-chief U.S. Army Europe, 1960-63; spl. asst. to dir. Office European Regional Politico-Mil. Affairs, Dept. State, 1963-65, officer charge def. policy affairs, 1965- 66; student Nat. War Coll., 1966-67; chief polit. sect. U.S. Mission, Berlin, Germany, 1967—. Sec. delegation Four Power Fgn. Ministers Meeting, Paris, France, 1951, Berlin, Germany, 1954, asst. coordinator, Geneva, 1955; dep. coordinator U.K.-French Ministerial Talks, London, 1952. Served to 2d lt. AUS, 1942-45. Mem. Williams Coll., Fletcher Sch. alumni assns., Kappa Alpha. Clubs: Williams (N.Y.C.); Internat. (Washington). Home: Kleiststrasse 3 1 Berlin 37 Germany Office: USBER APO New York City NY 09742

GILMAN, STANLEY FRANCIS, filter co. exec.; b. Portland, Me., Mar. 31, 1921; s. Frank William and Elotia Ann (Noyes) G.; B.S. in Mech. Engring., U. Me., 1943; M.S., U. Ill., 1948, Ph.D., 1953; m. Jean Elizabeth Murphy, Feb. 4, 1943; children—Susan (Mrs. William B. Gentry), Michael, Kathleen, Steven, Christine. Co-owner Gilman Furnace Co., Portland, 1945-47; asst. prof. mech. engring. U. Ill., 1949-53; with Carrier Corp., 1953-70; v.p. engring. Climatrol Industries, Milw., 1970-71; mgr. environmental control planning Am. Air Filter Co., Louisville, 1971—. Served to lt. USNR, 1943-46. Registered profl. engr., N.Y. Mem. Am. Soc. Heating, Refrigerating and Air Conditioning Engrs. (dir., pres. 1971-72), Sigma Xi, Tau Beta Pi, Pi Tau Sigma, Sigma Alpha Epsilon. Republican. Roman Catholic. Contbr. articles to profl. jours. Home: 11101 Huntley Pl Middletown KY 40243 Office: Box 1100 Louisville KY 40201

GILMAN, STEPHEN, educator; b. Chgo., Aug. 26, 1917; s. Stephen and Martha Jane (Rogers) G.; B.A. summa cum laude, Princeton, 1940, Ph.D., 1943; M.A. (hon.), Harvard, 1955; m. Teresa Guillen, June 17, 1943; children—Antonio, Isabel Martha, Anna. Instr. Princeton, 1940-41, asst. prof., 1946-48; asso. prof. Ohio State U., 1948-50, prof., 1950-55; asso. prof. Harvard, 1955-57, prof. Romance langs., 1957—, acting chmn. dept., 1959. Served from pvt. to 1st lt. AUS, 1943-46. Guggenheim fellow, 1950; Ford travelling fellow, 1955. Mem. Modern Lang. Assn. Am., Am. Acad. Arts and Scis., Phi Beta Kappa. Author: Cervantes y Avellaneda, 1951; The Art of La Celestina, 1956; Tiempo y formas temporales en el Poema del Cid, 1961. Home: 15 Gray Gardens W Cambridge MA 02138

GILMAN, WILBUR ELWYN, educator; b. Amsterdam, N.Y., Nov. 7, 1902; s. Frank Alverson and Mary Lila (Sandford) G.; A.B., children—Michael 1923, Ph.D., 1937. Instr. English U. Mo., 1923-25, asst. prof., 1927-30, asso. prof., 1930-40, asso. prof. speech, 1940-46, chmn. dept., 1940-42; instr. pub. speaking Cornell, 1925-26; on leave at Queens Coll., N.Y.C., 1944-46, chmn. dept. speech, 1945-66, prof., 1955—; extension staff Columbia, 1944-46; vis. prof., summers City Coll., 1941, Bklyn. Coll., 1944, Cornell U., 1938, 47, U. Mich., 1951, Teachers Coll. Columbia, 1957, U. Ore., 1960, U. Hawaii, 1960; chmn. com. speech, dept. chmn. met. colls. and univs., N.Y.C., 1946-48; sec. sub-com. English and speech. high sch.-coll. articulation com. Bds. Edn. and Higher Edn. of N.Y.C., 1947-50. Served 2d lt. Inf. Res., 1923-27, 1st lt., 1927-37, Med. Replacement Tng. Corps, 1942-43. Mem. Mo. State Tchrs. Assn. (chmn. speech sect., 1935-39), Mo. Acad. Sci. (chmn. speech children—Frederick 1935-37), Speech Assn. Mo. (pres. 1935-39), Central States Speech Assn. (pres. 1940-41), Speech Assn. Am. (exec. council, 1940-41, 47-54, 63-65, chmn. com. publs., 1938-41, com. history speech edn. 1944-46, com. finance, 1962-65, policy com., 1952-57, legislative assembly, 1956-58, pres. 1951), Speech Assn. Eastern States (pres. 1948-49), N.E.A., N.Y. State Speech Assn. (pres. 1956- 57), Modern Lang. Assn. Am., Am. Assn. U. Profs. (pres. Queens chpt., 1949-50, 56-58, chmn. joint exec. com. 4 city colls. N.Y.C. 1956- 58), Phi Beta Kappa (pres. Queens chpt. 1959-62), Phi Mu Alpha. Author: A Course Book in Extemporaneous Speaking (with Aly), 1913; A Course Book in Public Speaking (with Aly and Reid), 1937-39; Speech Preparation (with Aly children—Peter Reid), 1946; The Fundamentals of Speaking (with Aly and Reid), 1951; Milton's Rhetoric, Studies in His Defense of Liberty, 1939; (with Aly and White) An Introduction to Speaking, 1962, rev., 1968, The Fundamentals of Speaking, 1964. Contbr. English Jour., Quar. Jour. of Speech (book rev. editor 1941, associate editor 1945-46); Historical Studies on Rhetoric and Rhetoricians, 1961; contbr. to The Communicative Arts and Sciences of Speech, 1967. Home: 57-53 Parsons Blvd Flushing NY 11365

GILMER, BEN SCREWS, former telephone exec.; b. Savannah, Ga., Mar. 5, 1905; s. Merriwether and Josephine (Screws) G.; B.S. Ala. Poly. Inst., 1926, D.Sc. 1958; m. Dorothy Cunningham, Oct. 14, 1939: 1 dau., Dorothy (Mrs. Penn Rooker). Various positions So. Bell Telephone Co., 1926-52; v.p. gen. mgr. Northwestern Bell Telephone Co., Mpls., 1952- 53; v.p. Cal. operations Pacific Tel.&Tel. Co., 1953-56; v.p. So. Bell Tel.&Tel. Co., 1956, pres., 1957-65; exec. v.p. Am. Tel.&Tel. Co., 1965-67, pres., dir., mem. exec. com., 1967-70. ret., 1970; dir. Rich's, Inc., U.S. Pipe & Foundry Co., N.J. Bell Telephone Co., So. Bell Telephone Co., Bell Telephone Labs., 195 Broadway Corp., Am. Tel.&Tel. Long Lines, Merck & Co., Mfrs. Hanover Trust Co. Regional exec. com. Boy Scouts Am. Trustee Agnes Scott Coll., Atlanta Art Alliance, Auburn U. Found., John Bulow Campbell Found. Served as 2d lt. F.A., U.S. Army Res., 1926-31; from maj. to lt. col. USAAF, 1942-45. Mem. Ga. Engring. Soc., I.E.E.E., Delta Sigma Pi (hon.), Kappa Sigma, Eta Kappa Nu. Presbyn. (elder). Clubs: Augusta National Golf, Capital City; Peachtree Golf; Piedmont Driving. Home: 3584 Rembrandt Rd NW Atlanta GA 30327 Office: First Nat Bank Tower Atlanta GA 30303

GILMER, BEVERLY VON HALLER, educator, psychologist; b. Draper, Va., June 15, 1909; s. Beverly Tucker and Willie Sue (Graham) G.; B.S., Kings Coll., 1930; M.S., U. Va., 1932, Ph.D., 1934; m. Ellen Conduff, Aug. 23, children—John 1 dau., Nancy Tucker. Instr. psychology King 1935—, Bristol, Tenn., 1934-36; asst. prof. psychology Carnegie Inst. Tech., 1936-42, prof. psychology, dept. head; asso. prof. psychology U. Va., 1946-47; now prof. psychology Carnegie -Mellon U.; adviser U.S. Office Edn., 1949-51; cons. USAF, 1950-51. Dir. Pitts. Child Guidance Center, Inc., 1952—, Mental Health Soc. Allegheny County, 1954- -. Served from 1st lt. to maj., USAAF, 1942-46. Fellow Am. (mem. edn. and tng. bd. 1955-57), Eastern psychol. assns.; mem. So. Soc. Philosophy and Psychology (pres. 1948), Pa. (dir. 1953-54), Pitts (dir. 1950-51) psychol. assns., Sigma Xi, Phi Kappa Phi, Phi Sigma Pi. Presbyn. Author 12 books on psychology; also numerous research publs. Home: 4601 Bayard St Pittsburgh PA 15213

GILMER, HOWARD CECIL, Jr., lawyer; b. Pulaski, Va., Dec. 27, 1906; s. Howard Cecil and Lila (Saul) children—Hannah A.B., Hampden-Sydney Coll., 1928; French studies, U. Poitiers (France), 1925; LL.B., U. Va., 1931; m. Mary Berkeley Cosby, July 28, 1931; children—Berekley (Mrs. R.W. MacAdoo), Sally Lou (Mrs. C.C. Hundley), Betsy (Mrs. W. L. Hartzman). Page Va. Senate, 1919; admitted to Va. bar, 1930, U.S. Supreme Ct. bar; practiced in Pulaski, 1930—, mem. firm Gilmer, Sadler, Ingram, Thomas, Sutherland & Hutton; asst. U.S. atty. for Western Dist. Va., 1934-46, acting U.S. atty., 1946-48, U.S. atty., 1948-53; dir. and counsel Va. Nat. Bank, First Fed. Savs. & Loan Assn., Va. Maid Hosiery Mills. Mem. jud. conf. U.S. Fourth Circuit. Vice chmn. Va. Council Higher Edn., 1956-66. Fellow Am. Coll. Trial Lawyers; mem. Am., Va. (pres. 1944-46), W.Va. (hon.), Pulaski County bar assns. Phi Beta Kappa, Pi Kappa Alpha, Omicron Delta Kappa. Democrat. Methodist. Elk (past exalted ruler, past dist. children—Jeffrey, grand exalted ruler), Mason. Home: 2311 Pleasant Hill Dr Pulaski VA 24301 Office: Va Nat Bank Bldg Pulaski VA 24301

GILMER, JOHN CAPILL, transp. co. exec.; b. Chester, Eng., Jan. 6, 1910; s. Victor Watters and Rose (Capill) G. Chartered Accountant, U. Man., 1934. With C.P. Ry., 1937-49, gen. auditor, 1947-49; with Canadian Pacific Air Lines, Ltd., 1949—, exec. v.p., 1963-65, pres., chief exec. officer, 1965—, also dir.; dir. The Investors Group. Gov., Pacific Nat. Exhbn. Bd. mgmt. St. Vincent's Hosp.; bd. dirs. B.C. Heart Found., Can.-Japan Soc. Vancouver. Mem. Canadian Inst. Chartered Accountants, Financial Execs. Inst. Clubs: Vancouver, Point Grey Golf and Country (Vancouver). Home: 1049 Chilco St Vancouver 5 British Columbia Canada Office: 1281 W Georgia St Vancouver 5 British Columbua Canada

GILMER, THOMAS EDWARD, educator; b. Draper, Va., Nov. 6, 1901; s. George Hudson and Margaret Louise (Painter) G.; B.S. Hampden-Sydney Coll., 1923; M.S., U. Va., 1926, Ph.D., 1937; postgrad. Cornell U., summers 1931, 33, 34, 36; D.Sc. (hon.), Med. Coll. Va., 1962; m. Betty Meredith Winston, Nov. 19, 1923; children—Thomas Edward, William N., Betty Winston (Mrs. M. Boyd Coyner, Jr.), Mary Frances (Mrs. E.A. Brandon), George H. Instr. math. and sci. Greenbrier Mil. Sch., Lewisburg, W.Va., 1923-27; faculty Hampden-Sydney (Va.) Coll., 1927—, prof. physics, 1952—. dept., 1934-61, acting dean, 1956-57, pres., 1961-63, prof. physics, 1964—. Vis. fellow in physics Princeton, 1963-64; instr. Pa. State Coll. Extension, summer 1941, Biarritz Am. Army U., 1945-46; acting prof. physics N.C. State Coll., summers 1946- 48; prof. physics U. Va., summer 1959, 60; chief radiol. monitor, Va., 1954-56. Mem. Am. Phys. Soc., Am. Assn. Physics Tchrs., Va. Acad Sci., Phi Beta Kappa, Sigma Xi, Omicron Delta Kappa, Pi Kappa Alpha. Presbyn. (elder). Address: Hampden-Sydney Coll Hampden-Sydney VA 23943

GILMORE, ALEXANDER JOHN, chemist, educator; b. Chicago, 1928; B.S. in Physics, Yale, 1950; Ph.D. in Chemistry, Harvard, 1956; m. Sally Ann Jones, July 5, 1957; children--Kenneth J., Nancy A. Chemist, Acme Chem. Co., Blue Island, Ill., 1950-51; director of Research Lab., Indsl. Chemicals Corp., Cambridge, Mass., 1956-60; project coordinator environmental sect. Steinmetz Assos., Chgo., 1960-61; v.p. for research Bauer Bros. Chem. Co., Inc., Memphis, 1961-64; asst. prof. chemistry Washington U., St. Louis, 1964-66, asso. prof., 1966-70, prof., 1970--, head of chemistry dept., 1970-71. Vis. prof. So. Ill. U., summer 1967, U. of Ore., 1969. Scoutmaster, Boy Scouts America, University City, Mo., 1968-70. Bd. dirs. Rest Haven Home for Elderly, 1960-61; trustee of the Lutheran Hosp., 1965-71. Served from lt. to capt., AUS, 1951-53. Mem. Am. Chem. Soc., Sci. Research Soc. Am. (chpt. treas. 1967), Sigma Xi. Author: (with others) Basic Inorganic Chemistry, 1971. Home: Fairfax Apts 7291 Windermere Dr University City MO 63105 Office: Dept Chemistry Washington University St Louis MO 63130

GILMORE, CHARLES W., newspaper editor; b. Williamsport, Pa., Apr. 16, 1917; s. Charles F. and Nora (Wurster) G.; A.B., U. N.C., 1938; postgrad. (Nieman fellow) Harvard, 1947-48; m. Margaret Merry Batsch, May 25th, 1956; children—Merry Theresa (Mrs. John L. Mann), Glynne, Kathleen Carol. Reporter, Atlanta Constn., 1938-40, A.P., 1941-42, 46-47; reporter Toledo Times, 1948-58, editor, 1959-70; asso. editor Monterey Peninsula- Herald, 1970—. Served to lt. USNR, 1942-46; PTO. Mem. Phi Delta Theta, Sigma Delta Chi. Episcopalian. Home: 50 Skyline Crest Monterey CA 93940 Office: Jefferson and Pacific Avs Monterey CA 93940

GILMORE, CLARENCE PERCY, writer, editor; b. Baton Rouge, Feb. 8, 1926; s. Clarence Percy and Clara (Cobb) G.; student La. State U., 1942-44, 46-48; m. Noel Dillard, Mar. 17, 1956; children—Robert Dillard, Patricia Anne. Reporter various radio, tv stas., 1948-56; free-lance mag. writer, 1956-67; sci. editor Metromedia TV, 1967-70; exec. editor Popular Sci. Pub. Co., N.Y.C., 1971—. Cons. in field. Served with USNR, 1944-46. Recipient Claude Bernard sci. journalism award Nat. Soc. Med. Research, 1969; Albert and Mary Lasker Found. award, 1969; Howard W. Blakeslee award Am. Heart Assn., 1969; Spl. commendation med. journalism A.M.A., 1969, 70; Sci. Writing award physics and astronomy Am. Inst. Physics, 1970. Mem. Soc. Mag. Writers (treas. 1968), Nat. Assn. Sci. Writers, A.A.A.S. Home: 22 Lounsbury Rd Croton-on-Hudson NY 10520 Office: 355 Lexington Av New York City NY 10017

GILMORE, DOUGLASS , mfg. exec.; b. Lima, O., Apr. 1, 1932; B.S., U. San Francisco, 1954; M.S., Stanford University, 1956; m. Rosemarie Lois Brown, May 15, 1955; 1 son, Anthony Robinson. Sales rep. Ames-Brockton Fabricated Products, Akron, O., 1956-58, sales mgr. Coshocton, Ohio, 1959-61, gen. manager plant, 1961-68, v.p. sales, 1968--. Instr. bus. Coshocton Jr. College, 1968-69. Secretary Coshocton YMCA, 1960-61; active Boy Scouts of America. Named Man of Year, Coshocton Junior Chamber of Commerce, 1968. Mem. Coshocton C. of C. (vice president 1967-68, pres. 1969-70), English Speaking Union, Coshocton Sertoma Club, Nat. Assn. Mfrs., Sales Executives Institute, Phi Beta Kappa, Sigma Chi, Phi Mu. Democrat. Mem. Christian Ch. (lay leader). Mason (32, Shriner). Clubs: Coshocton Country, Coshocton City, Running Deer Country. Home: 2d Av Coshocton OH Office: 3d Av Coshocton OH

GILMORE, DURWARD WILSON, lawyer, ins. co. exec.; b. East Prairie, Mo., Dec. 25, 1911; s. Ernest G. and Maude (Grissom) G.; student U.S. Naval Acad., 1931-32, U. Mo., 1934-37; LL.B. Washburn Coll., 1938; m. Dorothy Angeline DeField, Feb. 26, 1933; children—Theodore Eli, Patricia Jean (Mrs. John W. Blackemore), Thomas Ray, Webb Reilly, Robert Wilson. Admitted to Mo. bar, 1938, Kan. bar, 1938, also U.S. Supreme Ct.; pvt. practice law, 1938-51; circuit ct. judge, 1951-55; asso. counsel Kansas City Life Ins. Co. (Mo.), 1955-58, counsel, v.p., 1958-65, sr. v.p., gen. counsel, 1965—, also dir.; pres., dir. Oran State Bank (Mo.); v.p., dir. Glasgow Savs. Bank (Mo.); dir. Balt. Bank & Trust Co. (Kansas City, Mo.), Jefferson Bank & Trust Co., Delta Loan & Finance Co. (both St. Louis), Eureka Bank (Mo.). Pros. atty., 1947-48; mem. Mo. Senate, 1949-51; pres. Young Democratic Clubs Am., 1949-51. Served from ensign to lt. comdr., USNR, 1941-45. Mem. Am., Mo., Kansas City bar assns., Lawyers Assn. Kansas City. Mem. Christian Ch. Mason (Shriner, Jester). Home: 1250 W 61st Terrace Kansas City MO 64113 Office: 3520 Broadway Kansas City MO 64111

GILMORE, FRANKLIN BLACK, gas co. exec.; b. Emlenton, Pa., Mar. 19, 1907; s. Hugh Richmond and Margaret (Black) G.; B.S., Washington and Lee U., 1928; J.D. U. Mich., 1930; m. Doris J. Duhart, Nov. 11, 1932; 1 dau., Gay (Mrs. Kreiss). Admitted to Mich. bar, 1931; atty. legal dept. No. Penn Gas Co., Port Allegany, 1931-32, chief legal dept., 1932-53, sec., 1953-64, v.p., 1954, gen. counsel, 1953-64, exec. v.p., 1954-64, dir., 1954—, pres., 1964—. Pres., Port Allegany Sch. Bd. Fellow A.I.M.; mem. Am. Mgmt. Assn., Am., Pa. (bd. dirs.) gas assns., Am. Bar Assn., Nat. Lawyers' Club, Am. Forestry Assn., Wilderness Soc., Am. Horse Shows Assn., Eastern Saddle, (pres. 1970—), Md., Am. Saddlebred horse breeders assns., Pa. Soc., Horsemen's Meml. Hosp., 1947-67, Kansas City Conservatory of Music, 1951—; member Alpha Delta. Rotarian. Clubs: Duquesne; Cotillion; Airways, Oil City, Pennhills, Valley Hunt. Home: 211 Arnold Av Allegheny PA 15212 Office: 76 Mill St Port Allegany PA 15212

GILMORE, FRED W. bus. exec.; b. Williamsburg, Ia., June 1, 1907; s. Alexander and Sarah (Little) G.; student Omaha U.; m. Evelyn Mason, Aug. 7, 1937; children—Richard, William. Asst. cashier Farmers Savs. Bank, N. English, Ia., 1924-30; county treas. Marengo, Ia., 1931-33; successively tax mgr. Fed. Land Bank of Omaha, asst. to pres., v.p.; dep. gov., dir. land bank 54th Terrace Kansas City MO 64112 Co. of Omaha, Inc., 1961-69; dir. Stock Yards Nat. Bank, Guarantee Mut. Life Co., Omaha. Mason. Address: 5101 River Rd Washington DC 20016

GILMORE, GORDON LEONARD, airline exec.; b. Freeborn, Minn., Aug. 4, 1908; s. Ansel and Bertha Louisa (Scoville) G.; student Hamline U., 1926-28; children—Kellie Ethelmae Dawn Severson, July 31, 1928; children—Robert, James, Richard, Nancy (Mrs. Arthur A. Parks). Newspaperman, Mason City (Ia.) Globe Gazette, 1928-30, Omaha Bee-News, 1930, St. Paul Dispatch-Pioneer Press, 1930-46, exec. sports editor, 1944; mgr. N.Y. City news bur. Transcontinental & Western Air Inc. (now Trans World Airlines, Inc.), 1946, dir. pub. relations, 1948, v.p. pub. relations, 1951—. Cons. U.S. Dept. State, 1966—; chmn. Internat. Air Transp. Assn. PR Conf., The Hague, 1955. Bd. dirs. Travelers Aid Soc., N.Y.C. Served to lt. USNR, World War II. Mem. Soc. Am. Travel Writers, N.Y. Pub. Relations Soc., Pub. Relations Soc. Am., Aviation Writers Assn., Newcomen Soc. Eng. (N. Am. br.), Alpha Eta Rho, Pi Delta Epsilon. Episcopalian. Clubs: Wings, Overseas Press, Union League, Dutch Treat (N.Y.C.). Home: 360 E 72d St New York City NY 10021 Office: 605 3d Av New York City NY 10016

GILMORE, GRANT, educator; b. Boston, Apr. 8, 1910; s. Ernest Augustus and Louise (Beerbohm) G.; B.A., Yale, 1931, Ph.D., 1936, LL.B., 1942; m. Helen children—Daniel, Richter, Mar. 26, 1934; children—Nancy Hubbard, David Creighton. Admitted to N.Y. bar, 1943; with firm Milbank, Tweed & Hope, N.Y.C., 1942-44; instr. French, Lehigh U., 1936-37; instr. French, Yale, 1937-40, prof. law, 1946-65, William K. Townsend prof., 1957-65; prof. law U. Chgo., 1965- -, Harry E. Bigelow prof., 1967—; vis. prof. U. Chgo., 1949, 57, U. Cal., 1951, Columbia, 1953-54, Harvard, 1962-63. Served to lt. USNR, 1944-46. Mem. Am. Law Inst. Author: (with C.L. Black, Jr.) The Law of Admiralty, 1957; Security Interests in Personal Property, 2 vols., 1965 (Ames prize 1966, Coif award Assn. Am. Law Schs. 1967). Contbr. articles legal publs. Home: 49 E Elm St Chicago IL 60611

GILMORE, JAMES STANLEY, Jr., business exec.; b. Kalamazoo, June 14, 1926; s. James Stanley and Ruth (McNair) G.; student Culver Mil. Acad., Kalamazoo Coll., 1945; m. Diana Holdenreide Fell, May 21, 1949; children—Bethany, Sydney, James Stanley children—Peter, Elizabeth, Ruth. Pres. Jim Gilmore Enterprises, Kalamazoo, 1960—; pres., treas. Gilmore Broadcasting Corp.; pres. Jim Gilmore Cadillac-Pontiac, Inc., Wolverine Found., Gilmore Championship Racing Enterprises, Inc., Phoenix; v.p., dir. Continental Corp. Mich.; chmn. bd. Gilmore Advt., Inc.; dir. Shakespeare Co., Kalamazoo, First Nat. Bank & Trust Co., Kalamazoo, Mich. Carton Co., Battle Creek, Fabri-Kal, Mus., 1946—. Mem. N.Y. State Hist. Trust, N.Y. Nature and Islamorada, Fla. Mem. Mich. Water Resources Commn., 1961—; mem. pres.' adv. com. Western Mich. U.; mem. nat. adv. cancer council Dept. Health, Edn. and Welfare; pres. parents assn. Columbia (Mo.) Coll. Mem. Mich. Republican Finance Com., 1947- 49; pres. Kalamazoo County Young Rep. Club, 1947-49; mayor, Kalamazoo, 1959-61; past chmn. Kalamazoo County Rep. Party. Bd. dirs. Econ. Devel. Commn., Boys Clubs Am., Kalamazoo chpt. A.R.C.; chmn. bd. trustees, Nazareth Coll., trustee Greater Mich. Devel., Constance Brown Speech and Hearing Center. Kalamazoo Coll., Kalamazoo Nature Center, Inc., Childrens Home, Bronson Meth. Hosp., Mich. found. for Arts, Detroit, St. Margaret's Sch., Waterbury, Conn.; founder, mem. bd. Martin Luther King Meml. Fund; nat. sponsor Ducks Unlimited; bd. suprs. Kalamazoo County. Served with USAAF, 1943-46. Named Kalamazoo Young Man of 1960, One of Mich.'s 5 Young Men of 1960. Mem. Kalamazoo County (past pres., dir.; mem. exec. com. of indsl. devel. com.), Mich. (mem. law and order com.) chambers commerce. Clubs: Capitol Hill (Washington); Park (past dir.), Kalamazoo Country; Gull Lake Country; Mid-America (Chgo.); Otsego Ski (Gaylord, Mich.). Home: 1550 Long Rd Kalamazoo MI 49001 also Gull Lake MI Office: Jim Gilmore Enterprises Mich Bldg Kalamazoo MI 49006

GILMORE, JOSEPHUS JEFFREY chemist, educator; b. Chicago, 1928; B.S. in Physics, Yale, 1950; Ph.D. in Chemistry, Harvard, 1956; m. Sally Ann Jones, July 5, 1957; children--Kenneth J., Nancy A. Chemist, Acme Chem. Co., Blue Island, Ill., 1950-51; director of Research Lab., Indsl. Chemicals Corp., Cambrige, Mass., 1956-60; project coordinator environmental sect. Steinmetz Assos., Chgo., 1960-61; v.p. for research Bauer Bros. Chem. Co., Inc., Memphis, 1961-64; asst. prof. chemistry Washington U., St. Louis, 1964-66, asso. prof., 1966-70, prof., 1970--, head of chemistry dept., 1970-71. Vis. prof. So. Ill. U., summer 1967, U. of Ore., 1969. Bd. dirs. Rest Haven Home for Elderly, 1960-61; trustee of the Lutheran Hosp., 1965-71. Served from lt. to capt., AUS, 1951-53. Mem. Am. Chem. Soc., Sci. Research Soc. Am. (chpt. treas. 1967), Sigma Xi. Author: (with others) Basic Inorganic Chemistry, 1971. Home: Fairfax Apts 7291 Windermere Dr University City MO 63105 Office: Dept Chemistry Washington University St Louis MO 63130

GILMORE, JOSEPH PATRICK, educator; b. N.Y.C., Sept. 30, 1928; s. Thomas E. and Veronica (Burns) G.; B.S., St. John's Coll., Bklyn., 1950; M.S., St. John's U., Bklyn., 1952; Ph.D., George Washington U., 1963; m. Harriet E. Kuhlmann, July 6, 1950; children—Cathleen, JoAnne, Dennis, Gerard. Head dept. physiology Navy Med. Research Lab., Camp Lejeune, N.C., 1952-58; with lab. cardio-physiology NIH, Bethesda, Md., 1958-66; prof. physiology U. Va., Charlottesville, 1966-70; prof., chmn. dept. physiology U. Neb., Omaha, 1970—. Cons. Nat. Heart and Lung Inst. Recipient NIH Career Devel. award, 1967. Mem. Am. Physiol. Soc., Am. Soc. for Pharmacology and Exptl. Therapeutics, Am. Soc. Nephrology, Am. Heart Assn., Soc. for Exptl. Biology and Medicine, N.Y. Acad. Scis. Mem. editorial bd. Am. Jour. Physiology, 1966—, Jour. Applied Physiology, 1966—. Contbr. articles profl. jours. Home: 11715 Wakeley Plaza 117th and Dodge Omaha NB 68154

GILMORE, MYRON PIPER, educator, historian; b. Walpole, Mass., July 4, 1910; s. Charles Austin and Eunice Ethel (Piper) G.; A.B., Amherst Coll., 1932, L.H.D., 1962; A.M., Harvard, 1933, Ph.D., 1937; m. Sheila s. Apr. 2, 1938; children—Janet (Mrs. Christopher Greene), Diana Piper (Mrs. Lawrence Fane), Thomas North, John Allen Dehn. Instr. history Harvard, 1937-42, asso. prof., 1942-54, prof., 1954—, dir. Villa I Tatti, Center Italian Renaissance Studies, Florence, Italy, 1964- -. Served from lt. (j.g.) to lt. comdr., USNR, 1942-45. Mem. Am. Acad. Arts and Scis., Am. Hist. Assn., Medieval Acad. Am., Renaissance Soc. Am., Am. Soc. Reformation Research, Colonial Soc. Mass., Mass. Hist. Soc., Accademia Degli Intronati (Siena). Author: N.Y.C., from Roman Law in Polital Thought 1200-1600, 1941; The World of Humanism, 1952; Humanists and Jurists: Six Studies 1926—. the Renaissance, 1963. Home: Villa I Tatti Via di Vincigliata Florence, Italy.

GILMORE, VOIT, travel exec.; b. Winston-Salem, N.C., Oct. 13, 1918; s. John Merriman and Helen (Hensel) G.; B.J., U. N.C., 1939; grad. Nat. Inst. Pub. Affairs, Washington, 1940; m. Kathryn Kendrick, Jan. 21, 1945; children—Kathryn, Geraldine, Susan, Peter, David. Asst. to div. mgr. Pan Am. Airways, Miami, Fla., 1940-41; personnel mgr. Pan Am. Airways-Africa Ltd., Accra, Gold Coast, 1942-43; pub. relations dir. Pan Am. Airways, San Francisco, 1946-48; pres. Storey Corp. and affiliated cos., 1948-61, 64—; dir. U.S. Travel Service, Washington, 1961-64; dir. So. Nat. Bank of N.C. News corr. to Arctic, 1958, Antarctic 1958, 60, 61, 63. Mem. town council, mayor Southern Pines, N.C., 1953-57; mem. N.C. Senate, 1965- 69. Mem. N.C. Bd. Conservation and Devel., 1957-61; chmn. N.C. Commn. Edn. and Employment Women; Bd. dirs. N.C. Symphony; bd. advisers Nat. Trust for Historic Preservation. Mem. Explorer's Club N.Y.C., Am. (dir.), N.C. (v.p.) forestry assns. Club: Bohemian (San Francisco). Contbr. articles on polar exploration to newspapers, mags. Home: Indiana Av Southern Pines NC 28387 Office: PO Box 289 Southern Pines NC 28387

GILMOUR, LLOYD STRAUBE, investment banker; b. Fresno, Cal., Feb. 12, 1892; s. William E. and Laura (McGee) G.; A.B., U. Cal., 1915; m. Margery Blyth, Dec. 11, 1926; children—Lloyd S., Blyth. Asso. Blyth, Witter & Co., investment bankers, San Francisco, 1914-28; v.p., 1918-28, v.p., dir. Blyth & Co., Inc., N.Y.C. (successor children—Marshall 1929-35; formed group to acquire firm of Eastman Dillon Union Securities & Co., 1935, sr. partner to 1967, now ltd. partner; dir. Northwest Nitro-Chems., Ltd., Westcoast Transmission Co., Ltd., State Mut. Savs. & Loan Assn., Far 67—; Financial Corp. Chmn. of Upper Brookville, L.I., Planning Bd., 1946-52; trustee Village of Matinecock, Oyster Bay, N.Y. Trustee Zeta Psi Frat. of N.Am., 1930-33, Zeta Psi Ednl. Found., 1947—; vice chmn. bd. trustees N.Y. U. Mem. Investment Bankers Assn. (gov. 1941- 44, indsl. securities com. 1942, fed. legislation com. 1943). Clubs: Union, Brook, Recess, Bond (N.Y.C.); Piping Rock Country (L.I.); Pacific- Union (San Francisco); Connetquot River (Oakdale, L.I.); Creek (L.I.); Ekwanok Country (Manchester, Vt.); Everglades, Bath and Tennis (Palm Beach, Fla.); Gulf Stream (Fla.). Home: Duck Pond Rd Locust Valley NY 11560 Office: 1 Chase Manhattan Plaza New York City NY 10005

GILOT, FRANCOISE, painter; b. Neuilly-sur-Seine France, Nov. 26, 1921; d. Emile Armand and Madeleine (Renoult) G.; A.N., Sorbonne, Paris; student law and lit., 1939-41; student painting Endre Rozsda's Studio, Paris, 1941-42, drawing Souverbie Studio, Acad. Julian and Acad. Sect. d'Or., 1943-45; influenced by Picasso, 1943, 46-53, Matisse, 1946. m. Jonas E. Salk, 1970. Painter under contract Galerie Louise Leiris, Paris, 1951-56, Galerie Coard, Paris, 1958—, Galerie F. Mayor, London, Eng., 1958—, David Findlay Gallery, N.Y.C., 1965; one man exhbns. include 43 rue Boissy d'Anglas, Paris, 1943, Galerie La Hune, Paris, 1951, Galerie Louise Leiris, 1952, Galerie Folklore, Lyons, France, 1953, Galerie Coard, 1959, 61, 63, 66, 68, 70, Mayor Gallery, London, 1960, 62, Mrs. Herbert C. Morris gallery, Phila., 1962, David Findlay Gallery, 1965, Von der Hue Gallery, 1965, Galleria d'arte 32 Milano, 1965, Galleria Santo Stephano Venise, 1966, Chapman Kelly Atelier, Dallas, 1966-70; group exhbns. include Salon des Surindepdennts, Paris, 1945, Leicester Gallery, London, 1953, 68, Gallery Alex Vomel, Düsseldorf, Germany, 1954, Univ Paris/Bruxelles, 1957, Centre Culturel and Artisque de France-Amerique, 1957, Salon de Mai, Paris, 1951-56, Ecole de Paris, Gallerie Charpentier, 1956-60, Salon des Tuileries, Paris, 1959-62, Dalzell Hatfield Gallery, Los Angeles, 1969, 71; lithographer Asso. Am. Artists, N.Y.C., 1961—; designer scenery Janine Charrat, 1953, ballet Heracles, 1953, Theatre des Champs Elysees; rep. permanent collections Musleed'Art Moderne, Paris, Mus. Modern Art, N.Y.C., also pvt. collections. Author: Life with Picasso, 1964. Illustrator: Pages d'Amour (Andre Verdet), 1951; Pouvoir tout dire (Paul Eluard), 1952; Infus Amour (Andre Miguel), 1953; Vignettes pour les Vignerons (J. Prevert), 1953. Address: 19 Rue Jacques Dulud Neuilly-sur-Seine, France.

GILPATRIC, CHADBOURNE, found. exec., educator; b. N.Y.C., Nov. 25, 1914; s. Walter Hodges and Charlotte (Leavitt) G.; B.S. magna cum laude, Harvard, 1937, postgrad. 1940-41; Rhodes scholar, Balliol Coll., Oxford (Eng.) U., 1938-39; postgrad. Princeton, 1939-40; m. Marguerite Sentenac, Nov. 20, 1941 (div. May 1964); children—David L., Elisabeth C. Instr. philosophy Middlebury Coll., 1937-38; with Bd. Econ. Warfare, 1942, CIA, 1947-49; asst. dir. humanities Rockefeller Found., 1949-56, asso. dir., 1956-61, asso. dir. humanities and social scis., 1961—, adviser edn. and social sci. Indian program, 1967—; hon. Littauer fellow Harvard, 1963-64; vis. prof. U. Delhi (India), 1964-67. Mem. vis. com. philosophy Harvard, 1952-61. Served to capt. AUS, 1943-46; OSS. Mem. Council Fgn. Relations, Am. Philos. Assn., Assn. Asian Studies, Asia Soc., Phi Beta Kappa. Address: Rockefeller Found 17 Kautilya Marg New Delhi 21 India

GILPATRIC, CHARLES EDWARD diversified mfg. co. exec.; b. Cin., May 21, 1910; grad. Phillips Acad., Andover, Mass., 1927; B.S., Princeton, 1931; postgrad. Mass. Inst. Tech., 1931-33; m. Jean R. Holland, June 16, 1935; children--Lois A., Andrew M., James. Salesman, Brown Mfg. Co., Boston, 1932-33; jr. engr. Ball Metals Co., Carson City, Nev., 1933-36, engr., 1936-37, sr. engr., 1937-40; project engr. Kingston Engring. Co., Los Angeles, 1940-43; with dept. engring. City of Denver, 1946-50, dep. head, 1950-52; 2d v.p. Johnson Mfg. Co., Kansas City, Kansas, 1952-54, v.p. for engring., 1954-57; v.p. research Consol. Industries, Inc., South Bend, Ind., 1957-60, exec. v.p., 1960-65, pres. 1965-70, chmn. bd., chief exec. officer, 1970--, also dir.; dir. ABC Chem. Co., 2d Nat. Bank, Country Food Storage Co., Providence Indsl. Corp. (Ind.), Wilson Investment Co., Inc., Hammond Life Ins. Co., Inc. Pres., Dewey High Sch., Kansas City, Mo., 1953-54; fund chmn. local div. Salvation Army, 1959-60. Mem. South Bend Republican Com., 1964-68. Bd. dirs. Ind. council Boy Scouts Am., 1969-71; trustee Lovell Found. Served to lt., Corps Engrs., AUS, 1943-45. Decorated Bronze Star medal. Member N.A.M., South Bend C. of C. (v.p. 1963-65, dir. 1965-70), Am. Mgmt. Assn., Ind. Engrs. Soc. (program com. 1961-62), Princeton Alumni Assn. Episcopalian. Rotarian, Optimist. Clubs: South Bend Golf; Links (N.Y.C.). Home: 6823 Broad Terrace Av South Bend IL 46505 Office: PO Box 1019 South Bend IN 46501

GILPATRICK, ARTHUR ROBERT diversified mfg. co. exec.; b. Cin., May 21, 1910; grad. Phillips Acad., Andover, Mass., 1927; B.S., Princeton, 1931; postgrad. Mass. Inst. Tech., 1931-33; m. Jean R. Holland, June 16, 1935; children--Lois A., Andrew M., James. Salesman, Brown Mfg. Co., Boston, 1932-33; jr. engr. Ball Metals Co., Carson City, Nev., 1933-36, engr., 1936-37, sr. engr., 1937-40; project engr. Kingston Engring. Co., Los Angeles, 1940-43; with dept. engring. City of Denver, 1946-50, dep. head, 1950-52; 2d v.p. Johnson Mfg. Co., Kansas City, Kansas, 1952-54, v.p. for engring., 1954-57; v.p. research Consol. Industries, Inc., South Bend, Ind., 1957-60, exec. v.p., 1960-65, pres., 1965-70, chmn. bd., chief exec. officer, 1970--, also dir.; dir. ABC Chem. Co., 2d Nat. Bank, Country Food Storage Co., Providence Indsl. Corp. (Ind.), Wilson Investment Co., Inc., Hammond Life Ins. Co., Inc. (Ind.), Prudential Ins. Co., Haverford Mfg. Co., Leader Pub. Co. Pres., Dewey High Sch., Kansas City, Mo., 1953-54; fund chmn. local div. Salvation Army, 1959-60. Mem. South Bend Republican Com., 1964-68. Bd. dirs. Ind. council Boy Scouts Am., 1969-71; trustee Lovell Found. Served to lt., Corps Engrs., AUS, 1943-45. Decorated Bronze Star medal. Member N.A.M., South Bend C. of C. (v.p. 1963-65, dir. 1965-70), Am. Mgmt. Assn., Ind. Engrs. Soc. (program com. 1961-62), Princeton Alumni Assn. Episcopalian. Rotarian, Optimist. Clubs: South Bend Golf; Links (N.Y.C.). Home: 6823 Broad Terrace Av South Bend IN 46505 Office: PO Box 1019 South Bend IN 46501

GILPATRICK, GRANVILLE SHACKFORD, former corp. exec.; b. Old Orchard, Me., June 1, 1903; s. Howard and Jessie Maria (Shackford) G.; A.B., Bowdoin Coll., 1924; m. Evelyn Kristine Olsen, July 23, 1950; 1 dau., Susan. Pres., dir. Woodstock Corp., Boston, 1958-68, chmn., 1968-69; chmn. Woodstock Service Corp., 1968-69; v.p., dir. Big Sandy Co., Boston 1963—; v.p., sec., dir. Sunflower Petroleum Products Corp., Boston, Trustee Woodstock Trust, Sagamore Found. Mem. Delta Upsilon. Home: RFD 2 Brunswick ME 04011 Office: 70 Federal St Boston MA 02110

GILPIN, G. NOBLE, music educator; b. Sterling, Pa., Mar. 15, 1911; s. George I. and Grace (Noble) G.; B.Mus., Syracuse U., 1939, M.Mus., 1942; D.Sacred Music, Union Theol. Sem., N.Y.C., 1959. Supr. music Greene Dreher Community Sch., Sch., Newfoundland, Pa., 1936-42; Faculty Sweet Briar (Va.) Coll., 1946—, prof. music, 1959—, chmn. dept., 1960—. Served with AUS, 1942-46; ETO. Mem. Am. Guild Organists, Am. Assn. U. Profs., Phi Mu Alpha, Phi Kappa Phi. Address: Sweet Briar Coll Sweet Briar, VA 24595.

GILPIN, ROBERT GEORGE, Jr., educator; b. Burlington, Vt., July 2, 1930; s. Robert George and Beatrice (Sandspra) G.; B.A., U. Vt., 1952; M.S., Cornell U., 1954; Ph.D., U. Cal. at Berkeley, 1960; m. Jean Millis, Aug. 13, 1955; children—Linda, Elizabeth, Robert. Postdoctoral fellow Harvard, 1960-61; lectr. Columbia, 1961-62; mem. faculty Princeton, 1962—, prof. polit. sci., 1970—. Served with USNR, 1954-57. Congl. fellow, 1959-60; Guggenheim fellow, 1969. Author: American Scientists and Nuclear Weapons Policy, 1962; France in the Age of the Scientific State, 1968; co-author, co-editor: Scientists and National Policy Making, 1964. Home: 130 Moore St Princeton NJ 08540

GILREATH, ESMARCH SENN, educator; b. North Wilkesboro, N.C., Sept. 21, 1904; s. Frank Hackett and Mamie (Williams) G.; A.B., U. N.C., 1926, M.A., 1927, Ph.D., 1945; m. Sara Taylor, Oct. 17, 1936. Instr. chemistry Ga. Tech., 1927-29; high sch. chemistry tchr., 1933-42; instr. chemistry U. N.C., 1942-44, vis. prof. chemistry, summer 1949; research chemist Am. Enka Corp., 1945-46; asst. prof. chemistry Washington and Lee U., Lexington, Va., 1946-52, asso. prof., 1952- 54, prof., 1954—, head dept. chemistry, 1954-70. Vis. prof. chemistry summers U. Ore. 1957, U. B.C., 1959, Ore. State U., 1961. Mem. Am. Chem. Soc., A.A.A.S., Chem. Soc. Britain, Soc. Chem. Industry Britain, Va. Va. Acad Sci., Phi Beta Kappa, Sigma Xi, Alpha Chi Sigma, Alpha Epsilon Delta. Democrat Presbyn. Author: Qualitative Analysis, 1954; Inorganic Chemistry, 1958; Experimental Procedures in Elementary Analysis, 1968; Quantative Chemistry, 1969. Home: Honeysuckle Hill Lexington VA 24450

GILROY, FRANK DANIEL, playwright; b. N.Y.C., Oct. 13, 1925; s. Frank B. and Bettina (Vasti) G.; B.A. magna cum laude, Dartmouth, 1950; postgrad. Yale Sch. Drama; m. Ruth Dorothy Gaydos, Feb. 13, 1954; children—Anthony, John and Daniel (twins). Became tv writer, 1952, scripts produced on programs including U.S. Steel Hour, Omnibus, Kraft Theater, Studio One, Lux Video Theater, Playhouse 90; wrote play Who'll Save the Plowboy?, 1957, presented off-Broadway, 1962; completed play The Subject Was Roses, 1962, presented on Broadway, 1964; play presented on Broadway, That Summer-That Fall, 1967, The Only Game in Town, 1968; producer, dir. film Desperate Characters, 1970. Served with AUS, 1943-46; ETO. Recipient Obie award for best Am. play, 1962, Outer Circle award, 1964, Drama Critics Circle award, 1964, N.Y. Theatre Club award for 1964-65, Antoinette Perry award, 1965, Pulitzer prize for drama, 1965. Mem. Writers Guild Am., Dramatists Guild (pres. 1969-71), Dirs. Guild Am. Author: Private (novel), 1970. Address: care Blanche Gaines 350 W 57th St New York City NY 10019

GILSTRAP, SAMUEL PATRICK, univ. ofcl.; b. Chandler, Okla., May 1, 1907; s. Harry Benson and Harriet (Patrick) G.; grad. Devitt Prep. Sch., Washington, 1925; B.S., 136 Kooyong Rd Toorak Victoria Australia Office: 460 Bourke St Melbourne Victoria Australia Ronald E. Admitted to Okla. bar, 1932, P.R. bar, 1946; atty. Embry, Johnson, Crowe & Talbert, Oklahoma City, 1931-34; chief auditor Civilian Works Adminstrn., Oklahoma City, 1934-35; asst. dir. finance and accounts Works Progress Adminstrn., Washington, 1935-36; dir. finance and accounts Nat. Youth Adminstrn., Washington, 1936-39, children—Thomas, San Juan, P.R., Virgin Islands, 1939-42; exec. officer O.W.I., San Francisco, 1942-44; dir. OPA, San Juan, P.R., 1944-47; fgn. service officer, 1947—; attache, Cairo, 1947-50; dep. exec. sec. U.S. High Commr., Frankfurt, Germany, 1950-51; attache, Manila, P.I., 1951- 53, Mexico City, Mexico, 1953-55; counselor of Embassy, Teheran, Iran, 1955-56; exec. dir., bur. Far East affairs Dept. State, Washington, 1956- 58; counselor Embassy, dep. chief of Mission, Seoul, Korea, 1958-60; Am., 1968—; professorial lectr. Am. U., 1967—. Served with AUS, 1942- and minister, Singapore, 1961-64; A.E. and P. to Malawi, 1964-65; dep. asst. sec. of state, 1965-66; dep. chancellor for adminstrn. East-West Center, U. Hawaii, Honolulu, 1966—. Mem. Okla., P.R. bar assns., 10417 Service Assn., Kappa Sigma. Rotarian. Home: Office: 1125 15th St NW Washington DC 20006

GILSTROMMER, SAMUEL STAN educator, biologist; b. Ames, Ia.; B.A., Ia. State U., 1936, M.A., 1937, Ph.D. with honors, 1940; m. Ann Ross, Mar. 23, 1946; children--Edward, Thomas A., Mark. Instr., Ia. State U., 1946-47; asst. prof. biology Johns Hopkins, 1947-50, asso. prof., 1950-62, prof., 1962--, chmn. dept., 1963-69; vis. lectr. Stanford, 1970-71. Active Boy Scouts Am., 4-H Club. Served with AUS, 1940-46. Mem. Am. Soc. Biologists, Md. Soc. Cell Biologists, Am. Soc. Exptl. Biology, Internat. Union Biologists, A.A.A.S., Am. Acad. Arts and Scis., Phi Beta Kappa. Home: 48936 W Hancock Blvd Baltimore MD 20206

GIMBEL, SOPHIE HAAS, designer; m. Adam Long Gimbel; 1 son, Jay Rossbach. Mgr. women's modern dress div., designer Saks Fifth Av. Home: 166 E 64th St New York City NY 10021 Office: 611 Fifth Av New York City NY 10022

GIMBEL, STANLEY DICK, advt. exec.; b. Peoria, Ill., May 8, 1928; s. Clarence William and Marguerite Emily (Shaw) G.; A.B. in English, Ind. U., 1952; m. Joan Mary Hubbard, June 18, 1950; children—Cynthia Ellen, Claudia Shaw, Richard Hubbard. Account mgr. Gen. Electric Co., Schenectady, 1952-58; v.p. Marsteller Inc., Chgo., N.Y.C., 1958-68; pres. Fred Wittner Co., N.Y.C., 1968-71; pres. Gimbel, Hammond, Farrell & Walsh Inc., N.Y.C., 1971—. Served with AUS, 1946-48. Club: Whipperwill (Armonk, N.Y.). Home: 29 Helena Dr Chappaqua NY 10514 Office: 380 Madison Av New York City NY 10017

GIMLIN, ROBERT CHARLES, mfr. bldg. materials; b. Chgo., Jan. 11, 1921; s. Guy M. and Corinne M. (Koch) G.; B.S. in Mech. Engring., Purdue U., 1942; student mgmt. courses, Am. Mgmt. Assn. With U.S. Gypsum Co., Chgo., 1946-66, gen. mdse. mgr., 1962-63, v.p., 1963-66; sr. v.p. Abitibi Paper Co. Ltd., Toronto, 1966—; became exec. v.p. Abitibi Corp. Detroit, 1966, now pres. Served to lt. (s.g.) USNR, 1941-45. Clubs: Chicago Yacht; Royal Canadian Yacht. Home: 400 Walmer Rd Toronto Ontario Canada Office: 408 University Av Toronto 2 Ontario Canada

GIMMA, JOSEPH A., business exec.; b. Bari, Italy, 1907. Partner, Hornblower & Weeks- Hemphill, Noyes; chmn. N.Y. State Racing Commn.; dir. Lionel Corp. Past chmn. N.Y. Republican County Com. Mem. adv. bd. Marymount Coll.; trustee Marymount Manhattan Coll., N.Y.C., Saratoga Mus. Racing, Bagby Music Lovers Found. Decorated knight of Malta, knight Grand Cross Holy Sepulchre. Mem. Met. Opera Club. Home: 800 Park Av New York City NY 10021 Office: 8 Hanover St New York City NY 10004

GIMMILOUW, WILLIAM BRUCE, mfg. exec.; b. Lima, O., Apr. 1, 1932; B.S., U. San Francisco, 1954; M.S., Stanford University, 1956; m. Rosemarie Lois Brown, May 15, 1955; 1 son, Anthony Robinson. Sales rep. Ames-Brockton Fabricated Products, Akron, O., 1956-58, sales mgr. Coshocton, Ohio, 1959-61, gen. manager plant, 1961-68, v.p. sales, 1968--. Instr. bus. Coshocton Jr. College, 1968-69. Mem. Coshocton C. of C. (vice president 1967-68, pres. 1969-70), Sales Executives Institute, Phi Beta Kappa, Sigma Chi, Phi Mu. Democrat. Mem. Christian Ch. (lay leader). Mason (32, Shriner). Clubs: Coshocton Country, Coshocton City, Running Deer Country.

GINADER, GEORGE HALL, assn. exec.; b. Buffalo, Apr. 5, 1933; s. George Edward and Meredith (Hall) G.; B.A., Allegheny Coll., 1955; M.S.S., Drexel Inst. Tech., 1964. Asst. Buyer Lord & Taylor, N.Y.C., 1957-59; job analyst Ins. Co. N.Am., Phila., 1959-60; asst. buyer John Wanamaker, Phila., 1960-61; acting curator Thomas McKean Automobile Reference Collection, Free Library Phila., 1961-63; librarian N.Y. C. of C., N.Y.C., 1964-66; chief librarian N.Y. Stock Exchange, N.Y.C., 1966-67; exec. dir. Spl. Libraries Assn., N.Y.C., 1967—. Mem. Am., N.Y. socs. assn. execs., Council Nat. Library Assns., Nat. Assn. Exhibit Mgrs., N.Y. C. of C., S.A.R., Phi Delta Theta. Republican. Episcopalian. Home: 381 Broad St Newark NJ 07104 Office: 235 Park Av S New York City NY 10003

GINASCOL, FREDERICK HOMER, educator; B.A., Trinity Coll., San Antonio, Tex., 1948; M.A., U. Tex., 1950, Ph.D., 1952. Prof. philosophy and edn. U. Tex. at Austin. Office: Dept Philosophy U Tex Austin TX 78712*

GINASTERA, ALBERTO, composer; b. Buenos Aires, Argentina, Apr. 11, 1916; grad. Nat. Conservatory Music, Argentina, 1938. Pro., Nat. Conservatory Music, 1953. Guggenheim fellow, U.S., 1946-47. Composer: (ballets) Panambi, 1937, Estancia, 1941; Sinfonia elegiaca for orchestra, 1944; (motel) Lamentation for the Prophet Jeremiah, 1946; Pampeana No. 1 for violin and piano, 1947, No. 2 for cello and pianoforte, 1950, No. 3, a pastoral symphony, 1953; Variaciones Concertantes, 1953; also dances, songs, chamber music, overtures.*

GINGER, LEONARD GEORGE, lab. exec.; b. Chgo., 1918; B.S., Northwestern U., 1939, M.S., 1941; Ph.D., Yale, 1943; married. With Baxter Labs. Inc., Morton Grove, Ill., 1949—, v.p. research and devel., 1960-69, sr. v.p., 1969—; dir. 1st Nat. Bank Morton Grove. Office: 6301 Lincoln Av Morton Grove IL 60053*

GINGER, LYMAN VERNON, coll. dean; b. nr. Wickliffe, Ky., June 21, 1907; s. Grover Cleveland and Emma (Abell) G.; A.B., Ky. Wesleyan Coll., 1929; M.A., U. Ky., 1942, Ed.D., 1950; m. Elizabeth Gardner Sudduth, June 7, 1932; children—Leslie Thomas, William Wesley. Tchr., athletic coach Winchester High Sch., 1929- 39; prin. Owingsville Consol. Sch., 1939-42; prin. U. High Sch., Lexington, Ky., 1942-43, acting dir., 1943-46, dir., chmn. div. instrn. and placement, 1946-54; dean Coll. Adult and Extension Edn., U. Ky., 1954-56, became dean Coll. Edn., acting dean Coll. Adult and Extension Edn., 1956, now asso. dean tchr. edn. and certification. Mem. Ky. High Sch. Athletic Bd. Control, 1944-53, Nat. High Sch. Football Rules Com., 1945-52; chmn. Gov.'s Commn. Pub. Edn., 1960-61; mem. Ky. Council So. Regional Edn., 1954-60, Ky. White House Conf. Com., 1955-56. Dir. Lexington YMCA. Ky. col. Mem. Ky. High Sch. Athletic Assn. (pres. 1948- 53), Ky. Edn. Assn. (pres.

1952-54), N.E.A. (pres. 1957-58, treas. 1960- -), Phi Delta Kappa, Kappa Delta Pi. Presbyn. Mason. Home: 419 Queensway Dr Lexington KY 40502

GINGERICH, OWEN JAY, educator, astronomer; b. Washington, Ia., Mar. 24, 1930; B.A., Goshen Coll., 1951; M.A., Harvard, 1953, Ph.D. in Astronomy, 1962; m. 1954; 3 children. Dir. obs. Am. U., Beirut, 1955-58, instr., 1955-57, asst. prof., 1957-58; lectr. astronomy Wellesley Coll., 1958-59; astrophysicist Smithsonian Astrophys. Obs., 1961—; lectr. Harvard, 1960-68, asso. prof. astronomy and history of sci., 1968-69, prof., 1969—; Sigma Xi nat. lectr., 1971—. George Darwin lectr. Royal Astron. Soc., 1971. Mem. Harvard Obs. eclipse expdn. to Ceylon, 1955; mem. Harvard expdn. to observe occultation of Regulus by Venus, Beirut, 1959; astronomy cons. Harvard Project Physics, 1964-69; dir., central telegram bur. Internat. Astronomical Union, 1965-67, asso. dir., 1967—, pres. commn. history astronomy, 1970—. Research and publs. on model stellar atmospheres and in history of astronomy. Home: 100 Avon Hill Rd Cambridge MA 02140

GINGERY, DONALD EDWARD, city planner, contractor; b. Clearfield, Pa., Oct. 21, 1913; s. Don and Anna (Leavy) G.; LL.B., Columbus U., 1942; m. Mary Helen Robbins, Apr. 1937; children—Mary Anne, Michael Christian, Gregory William, Donald Edward, James Montgomery. Constrn. homes, office bldgs., apts., shopping centers, 1938—; pres. Donley Constrn. Co., Inc., Rockville, 1947—; v.p., dir. Dist., Lawyers and Washington Title Ins. Cons., 1961—; chmn. bd. Peter Hand Brewery Co., Chgo. Chmn. Nat. Capital Regional Planning Council; mem. Md. Nat. Capital Park and Planning Commn. Mem. Nat. Assn. Homebuilders U.S., Sigma Delta Kappa. Home: 9204 Jones Mill Rd Chevy Chase MD 20015 Office: 1001 Rockville Pike PO Box 446 Rockville MD 20852

GINGHER, PAUL R., lawyer, assn. ofcl.; grad. Ohio State U., LL.B., U. Cin.; LL.D., Capital U., Columbus, 1959; m.; children—Mrs. Richard Hutchinson, Richard H. Admitted to Ohio bar; now partner firm Gingher and Christensen, Columbus. Pres., chmn. bd. State Automobile Mut. Ins. Co. Mem. Am. Automobile Assn., 1925—, pres. Columbus Club, 1965; pres. Ohio Assn., 1956-58, nat. dir., 1959-63, sr. v.p., 1963-65, nat. pres., 1965—; participant devel. Columbus Traffic Code, Columbus Sch. Safety Patrol, also constrn. Columbus Airport. Formerly mem. Ohio Senate. Past pres. Griffith Meml. Found. Ins. Edn. Named Man of Year, Columbus Jr. C. of C., 1947; recipient medallion Boys' Club Am., 1959; named Outstanding Citizen, Central Ohio chpt. Pub. Relations Soc. Am., 1962; recipient Distinguished Service award Ohio Newspaper Assn., 1964. Mem. Am., Ohio, Columbus bar assns., Columbus Area C. of C. (past pres., chmn. trustees), Order of Coif. Address: 1725 Roxbury St Columbus OH 43212*

GINGOLD, HERMIONE FERDINANDA, actress; b. London, Eng.; d. Jame and Kate (Walter) Gingold; student pvt. schs., London, governesses in Paris; m. Michael Josef; children—Leslie, Stephen. Actress, Old Vic, Shakespeare at Stratford on Avon, also Paris; film appearances include Gigi, Naked Edge, Music Man, Gay Paree, Harvey Middleman-Fireman, I'd Rather Be Rich, Promise Her Anything, Rocket to the Moon; mem. cast Almanac, 1st Impressions, The Sleeping Prince, Fallen Angels, From A to Z, Milk and Honey, Oh Dad, Poor Dad, N.Y. City; made television appearance on Ed Sullivan Show, Omnibus, Matinee Theatre, The Importance of Being Ernest, Jack Paar, Alfred Hitchcock Presents, This is Your Life, Hallmark Hall of Fame, Merv Griffin Show, Girl Talk, The Girl from U.N.C.L.E. Recipient Donaldson award. Author: The World is Square: My Own Unaided Work; Sirens Should be Seen and Not Heard, 1963. Recordings: La Gingold, Life of the Party, Facade, Lysistrata. Home: 405 E 54th St New York City NY 10022

GINGRICH, ARNOLD, editor, author; b. Grand Rapids, Mich., Dec. 5, 1903; s. John Hembling and Clara Alice (Speare) G.; A.B., U. Mich., 1925; m. Helen Mary Rowe, Oct. 24, 1924 (dec. 1955); children—Rowe W., John A., Michael G.; m. 2d, Jane Kendall Abeli, Nov. 13, 1955. Advt. copy writer, 1925; editor Apparel Arts, Chgo., 1931-45, editor Esquire, 1933-45, Coronet, 1936-45; v.p. Esquire, Inc., 1933-45, pub., sr. v.p., 1952—; sr. v.p. charge publ. divs. Esquire, Gentleman's Quar. mag., 1961—; European editor Esquire and Coronet, 1945-49; v.p. Cowles Mag., Inc., also gen. mgr. Flair, 1949-51. Mem. Phi Beta Kappa, Phi Sigma Kappa. Clubs: Overseas Press, Lotos (N.Y.C.); Fario (Paris); Joe Jefferson (Saddle River). Author: Cast Down the Laurel, 1935; The Well- Tempered Angler, 1965; Toys of a Lifetime, 1966; Business and the Arts, 1969; A Thousand Mornings of Music, 1970; Nothing But People: The Early Days at Esquire, 1971. Home: 605 E Saddle River Rd Ridgewood NJ 07450 Office: 488 Madison Av New York City NY 10022

GINGRICH, KENNETH MERRILL, super-market exec.; b. McAlisterville, Pa., Jan. 24, 1926; s. Merill Haskings and Mabel (Secrist) G.; B.S. in Bus. Adminstrn., Elizabethtown Coll., 1950; m. Edna Marie Bohner, June 23, 1951; children—Barbara, Ann, Beth, Diane. Accountant, Main & Co., Harrisburg, Pa., 1951-55; office mgr. Wels Markets, Inc., Sunbury, Pa., 1955-66, controller, asst. sec., 1966—. Served with USAAF, 1944-46. Home: 301 Charles Av Selinsgrove PA 17801 Office: 1000 S 2d St Sunbury PA 17801

GINIGER, HENRY, newspaperman; b. Bklyn., Jan. 15, 1922; s. Abraham and Bertha (Wolf) G.; B.S. in Social Sci., City Coll. N.Y., 1942; M.S. in Journalism, Columbia, 1943; m. Janine Goldfeil, May 14, 1948; 1 dau., Marianne. Corr., Paris (France) bur., N.Y. Times, 1946-65, corr. for Mexico, Central America, and Caribbean, 1965-69, chief Paris corr., 1969—. Served with USMCR, 1943-46; PTO. Pulitzer Traveling fellow, 1946-47. Mem. Fgn. Corr. Assn. Mexico. Club: Overseas Press (award 1969 N.Y.C.). Home: Lamartine 144-201 Mexico 5 DF Mexico

GINIGER, KENNETH SEEMAN, publisher; b. N.Y.C., Feb. 18, 1919; s. Maurice Aaron and Pearl (Triester) G.; student U. Va., 1935-39, N.Y. Law Sch., 1940-41; m. Carol Virginia Wilkins, Sept. 27, 1952. Partner, Signet Press, 1939-40, asso. editor Arts and Decoration and The Spur, 1940-41; dir. pub. relations Prentice-Hall, Inc., 1946-49, editor-in-chief trade book div., 1949-52, v.p., gen. mgr. Hawthorn Books div., 1952-61; pres. Hawthorn Books, Inc., N.Y.C., 1961-65, K.S. Giniger Co., Inc., N.Y.C., 1965-69; pres. Consol. Book Pubs. div. Processing & Books, Inc., Chgo., 1969—; lectr. New Sch. Social Research, 1948-49. Sec. Com. Collective Security, 1952-65; nat. adv. bd. Found. Religious Action, 1956—; dir. Laymen's Nat. Bible Com., 1957—, pres., 1963-71. Served from pvt. to capt. AUS, 1941-45, 51-52. Decorated chevalier French Legion of Honor. Mem. Am. Inst. Graphic Arts (v.p. 1965-66), P.E.N., Phi Delta Phi. Republican. Clubs: Garrick, Authors (London, Eng.); Nat. Press, Army and Navy (Washington); Overseas Press, Players (N.Y.C.). Author: The Compact Treasury of Inspiration, 1955 (Nat. Conf. Christians and Jews Brotherhood Week citation); America, America, America, 1957; A Treasury of Golden Memories, 1958; What Is Protestantism?, 1965; A Little Treasury of Hope, A Little Treasury of Comfort, A Little Treasury of Healing, A Little Treasury of Christmas, The Sayings of Jesus (all 1968). Home: 219 E Lake Shore Dr Chicago IL 60611 Office: 1727 S Indiana Av Chicago IL 60616

GINKEL, WILLIAM LOUIS, govt. ofcl.; b. Rochester, N.Y., Aug. 14, 1920; s. Louis William and Hilda (Hurst) G.; B.S. in Chem. Engring., U. Rochester, 1942, B.A. in Bus. Adminstrn., 1942; m. Inez Browning Creech, June 30, 1945; children—Alan Ross, Robert Wayne. Devel. engr. Monsanto Chem. Co., 1943- 44; indsl. engr. Tenn. Eastman Corp., 1944-47; with AEC, 1950—, dep. mgr. Ida. operations office, 1962-64, mgr., 1964—. Bd. dirs. Sacred Heart Hosp., Idaho Falls, Community Chest, Idaho Falls. Mem. Am. Nuclear Soc., Fedn. Rocky Mountain States (bd. dirs.), Tau Beta Pi. Presbyn. Rotarian. Home: 2825 W Morningside Dr Idaho Falls ID 83401 Office: 550 2d St Idaho Falls ID 83401

GINN, RONN, architect; b. Jacksonville, Fla., Apr. 17, 1933; s. Angus Theodore and Joan Adelaide (Bailey) G.; A.A., U. Fla., 1957, B.Arch., 1960, B.Landscape Architecture, 1961; m. Valerie Jeanne Broderson, Mar. 15, 1969; 1 dau., Sharon Lee. Supervising architect, urban designer Roswell (N.M.) central bus. dist. redesign, 1964, Tucumari (N.M.) central bus. dist. redesign, 1967, St. Petersburg (Fla.) central bus. dist. redesign, 1971, Treasure Island (Fla.) civic center design, 1971; architect, urban designer, prin. Atrium One, Albuquerque, 1965-67; urban design specialist Model Cities Adminstrn., Dept. Housing and Urban Devel., Washington, 1967-68; practice architecture, urban planning, landscape architecture, St. Petersburg, Fla., 1968—; pres. Ginn Corp., 1967—, Atrium Corp., 1965—; urban design lectr. U. N.M., 1967—; planning cons. State Dept., 1967-68; design cons. Am. Revolution Bicentennial Commn., 1967-68. Mem. Albuquerque Fine Arts Commn., 1965-67, St. Petersburg Design Goals Com., 1971—; moderator radio program Design in Our Community WPKM, Tampa, Fla., 1971—; founder, bd. dirs. Catalyst, St. Petersburg. Recipient numerous archtl., landscape architecture, urban design awards. Mem. A.I.A. (mem. nat. com. on regional devel. 1969—), Am. Inst. Planners, Constrn. Specifications Inst., U.S. Power Squadron. Republican. Presbyn. Contbg. editor: Urban Affairs Symposia, 1965—. Important works include Albuquerque central bus. dist. redesign (nat. A.I.A. award 1966), new town, Major Center, Fla. (nat. Am. Soc. Landscape Architects award 1970). Address: 10355 Paradise Blvd Treasure Island FL 33706

GINN, ROSEMARY LUCAS (Mrs. Milton Stanley Ginn), mem. Republican Nat. Com.; b. Columbia, Mo., Aug. 28, 1912; d. Reuben E. and Mary (Bewick) Lucas; B.A., U. Mo., 1933, grad. student, 1933-34; m. Milton Stanley Ginn, June 21, 1934; children—Nancy Bewick (Mrs. Carl H. Almond), Sally Reuben (Mrs. Mike D. Hood). Bd. dirs. Mo. Stores Co., Columbia, 1939—. Mem. budget com. United Fund, Columbia, 1955-57, dir., 1957-59; mem. Columbia Bd. Health, 1956-59; bd. dirs. Boone County Hosp. Auxiliary, Friends of Arrow Rock; adviser Columbia Council Clubs, 1956-58. Pres. Lawrence County (Mo.) Women's Republican Club, 1937-38, Boone County (Mo.), 1948-49; mem. Mo. Rep. Speakers Bur., 1936, 38, 40, 46, 48, 50, 52, 54; dist. v.p. Mo. Young Rep. Club, 1948; del. county, dist. and state Rep. convs., 1948, 52, 56, alt. del.-at-large Mo. to Nat. Rep. Conv., 1956; permanent Sec. Mo. Republican Conv., 1956; mem. Rep. Nat. Com. for Mo., 1960—, mem. exec. com., 1962-64; pres. Fedn. Rep. Womens Clubs Mo., 1959-61. Dir. Delta Delta Delta Bldg. Corp.; trustee Nat. Mortar Bd. Found., 1956—. Mem. Assn. Coll. Honor Socs. (rep. Mortar Bd. 1949-57, exec. council 1953, pres. 1955-57, rep. nat. conf. on frats. and socs. 1956), Mortar Bd. (sect. dir. 1935-45; nat. dir. expansion 1945-48, nat. pres. 1948-55), Nat. Assn. Women Deans and Counselors, Am. Legion Auxiliary (counsellor Mo. Girls 1956—), League Women Voters, Kings Daus., Phi Beta Kappa, Alpha Kappa Delta, Delta Sigma Rho, Alpha Pi Zeta, Delta Delta Delta. Baptist. Clubs: Hawkeye Beagle, Orchid Soc. St. Louis, Tuesday, Columbia Country (Mo.); Womens City (Berkeley, Cal.). Address: 303 W Boulevard S Columbia MO 65201

GINNA, ROBERT EMMETT, utilities exec.; b. Bklyn., June 7, 1902; s. John J. and Emma (Flannigan) G.; pvt. tutoring; m. Margaret McCall, Sept. 5, 1923; children—Robert Emmett, Margretta Patricia. Jr. engr. Bklyn. Edison Co., 1921-26; cons. engr. E.J. Cheney Engrs., N.Y.C., 1926-34; dept. mgr. Rochester (N.Y.) Gas & Electric Corp., 1934-45, v.p., dir., 1945, exec. v.p., dir. 1950-56; pres., dir., mem. exec. com., 1956, chmn. bd., chief exec. officer, 1957-68, cons., 1968—; dir. Security Trust Co. Regent St. John Fisher Coll. Mem. Rochester Engring. Soc., Bur. Municipal Research (trustee). Clubs: The Rochester, Oak Hill Country, N.Y. Athletic, Gatineau Fish and Game of Canada; Capitol Hill, Metropolitan (Washington, D.C.); Rochester Ad. Author articles trade publs. Home: 12 San Rafael Dr Pittsford PA 16340 Office: 89 East Av Rochester NY 14604

GINNANE, ROBERT WILLIAM, govt. ofcl.; b. Addison, N.Y., Apr. 29, 1913; s. Edwin M. and Julia G. (McCarthy) G.; A.B cum laude, Syracuse U., 1934; LL.B., Cornell U., 1938; m. Katherine M. Hamilton, Dec. 3, 1938; 1 dau., Ellen H. Admitted to N.Y. bar, 1938; lawyer SEC, 1938-42, OPA, 1942-43, Solicitor Gen.'s Office, Dept. of Justice, 1947-55; gen. counsel ICC, 1955—. Mem. U.S. delegation Geneva Diplomatic Conf., 1949; mem. President's Conf. Adminstrv. Procedure, 1953-54. Served from ensign to lt. (j.g.), USNR. 1943-45; Southwest Pacific. Mem. Am. Bar Assn. Contbr. articles profl. jours. Home: 2860 Arizona Terrace NW Washington DC 20016 Office: Interstate Commerce Commn Washington DC 20423

GINOTT, HAIM G., psychologist, author; b. Aug. 5, 1922; B.S., Columbia Tchrs. Coll., 1948, M.A., 1949, Ed.D., 1952. Chief clin. psychologist Jacksonville (Fla.) Child Guidance Clinc, 195260; lectr. Jacksonville U., 1955-58; supr. tng. and research Fla. Council Tng. and Research Mental Health, 1956-59; group therapist Fla. Alcoholic Rehab. Program, 1958-60; sr. psychologist ICD, N.Y., 196061; tng. supr. L.I. Cons. Center, 1961; cons. group psychotherapist Adelphi U., 1960-63, guest lectr. Postgrad. Center Mental Health, 1961-63, cons. child psychotherapist Family Service Assn. Five Towns, Woodmere, 196263; cons. group counsellor Long Branch Bd. Edn., 1963-64; expert guidance and cons. UNESCO, Israeli Govt., 1965-66; group therapist N. Shore Child Guidance Center, Manhasset, L.I., 1960-61, chief psychologist, 1961-62, cons. child phychotherapist, 1962—; asso. clin. prof. postdoctoral program Adelphi U., 1966—; ind. cons. in field, 1960—. Author: Group Psychotherapy Children, 1961; Between Parent and Child, 1965; Between Parent and Teenager, 1969. Address: 350 E 30th St New York City NY 10016*

GINSBERG, ALLEN, poet; b. Newark, June 3, 1926; s. Louis and Naomi (Levy) G.; A.B., Columbia, 1948. with various cargo ships, 1945-56; market research cons., N.Y.C., San Francisco, 1951-53; read poetry aloud, art galleries, coffee shops, 1957-59, poetry readings Columbia, Harvard, Yale, U. Conception (Chile), Lima Mus., Oxford U., Calcutta U., Benares Hindu U., Havana, Prague, Moscow, Warsaw, London; addressed conf. Group Advancement Psychiatry, 1961; actor motion picture Pull My Daisy, 1961, Guns of the Trees, 1962, Wholly Communion, 1965, Chappaqua, 1966. Guggenheim fellow in poetry, 1965-66; grantee Am. Acad. Arts and Letters, 1969. Author: Howl and Other Poems, 1955; Empty Mirror, 1960; Kaddish and Other Poems, 1960; Reality Sandwiches, 1963; Planet News, poems 1961-1967, 1968; Indian Journals, 1970; various vols. published in several langs. Home: 416 E 34th St Paterson NJ 07504 Office: care City Lights 261 Columbus Av San Francisco CA 94133

GINSBERG, DONALD MAURICE, educator, physicist; b. Chgo., Nov. 19, 1933; s. Maurice J. and Zelda (Robbins) G.; B.A., U. Chgo., 1952, B.S., 1955, M.S., 1956; Ph.D., U. Cal. at Berkeley, 1960; m. Joli D. Lasker, June 10, 1957; children—Mark D., Dana L. Mem. faculty, U. Ill. at Urbana, 1959—, prof. physics, 1966—. Fellow Am. Phys. Soc.; mem. Am. Assn. Physics Tchrs., Phi Beta Kappa, Sigma Xi. Home: 1707 Parkhaven Dr Champaign IL 61820

GINSBERG, EDWARD, lawyer; b. N.Y.C., May 30, 1917; s. Charles and Rose G.; B.A. with honors, U. Mich., 1938; LL.B., Harvard, 1941; m. Rosalie Sinek, Aug. 11, 1941; children—William, Robert. Admitted to Ohio bar, 1941; partner law firm Gottfried, Ginsberg, Guren & Merritt, 1941—; dir. Sanitas Service Corp.; trustee, exec. v.p. U.S. Realty Investments; dir. First Israel Bank & Trust Co. N.Y. Gen. chmn. mem. exec. com., nat. campaign cabinet United Jewish Appeal, formerly nat. chmn; v.p. Jewish Telegraphic Agy.; vice chmn. Am. Joint Distbn. Com.; v.p. Hebrew Sheltering and Immigrant Aid Soc. Trustee United Israel Appeal, Jewish Community Fedn. Cleve., Mt. Sinai Hosp., Jewish Convalescent Home Cleve. Served with USAAF. Mem. Cleve., Ohio State bar assns., Phi Kappa Phi, Phi Sigma Delta. Jewish religion (pres. temple). Home: 18000 Shaker Blvd Shaker Heights OH 44120 Office: 650 Terminal Tower Cleveland OH 44113

GINSBERG, HAROLD LOUIS, educator; b. Montreal, Que., Can., Dec. 6, 1903; s. Mendel and Golda Anna (Levinson) G.; B.A., U. London (Eng.), 1927, Ph.D., 1930; auditor Hebrew U., Jerusalem, 1928-29; m. Anne Gelrud, Nov. 7, 1937 (dec.). Came to U.S., 1936, naturalized, 1942. Instr. Bible, Jewish Theol. Sem. Am., N.Y.C., 1936-40, Sabato Morais prof. Bibl. history and lit., 1941—. Vis. prof. Hebrew U., Jerusalem, 1957, 62, U. Pa., 1957-58, 68- 69, Yale, spring 1967; co-editor Jewish Publ. Soc. Bible Transl., 1956-62, editor-in-chief, 1962—, mem. publ. com., 1958—; non resident mem. Acad. Hebrew Lang., Jerusalem; officer World Union of Jewish Studies. Fellow Am. Acad. Jewish Research (v.p.); mem. Soc. Bibl. Lit. and Exegesis, Soc. Bibl. Lit. (hon. pres.), Am. Oriental Soc., Israel Exploration Soc., Am. Schs. Oriental Research (asso.). Author: The Ugarit Texts, 1936; The Legend of King Keret, 1946; Studies in Daniel, 1948; Studies in Koheleth, 1950; Commentary on Koheleth, 1961; The Five Megilloth and the Book of Jonah, 1969. Contbg. author: Ancient Near Eastern Texts relating to The Old Testament, 1950, 55, 69; Handbook of Aramaic, 1967. Editor: Texts and Studies of American Academy for Jewish Research, vol. I, 1941. Divisional editor for Bible, Ency. Judaica. Home: 280 Riverside Dr New York City NY 10025

GINSBERG, HAROLD SAMUEL, virologist, educator; b. Daytona Beach, Fla., May 27, 1917; s. Jacob and Anne (Kalb) G.; A.B., Duke, 1937; M.D., Tulane U., 1941; m. Marion Reibstein, Aug. 4, 1949; children—Benjamin Langer, Peter Robert, Ann Meredith, Jane Elizabeth. Resident Mallory Inst. Pathology, Boston, 1941-42; intern, asst. resident Boston City Hosp., 4th Med. Service, 1942-43; resident physician, asso. Rockefeller Inst., 1946-51; asso. prof. preventive medicine Western Res. U. Sch. Medicine, 1951-60; prof. microbiology, chmn. dept. U. Pa. Sch. Medicine, 1960—. Mem. commn. acute respiratory diseases Armed Forces Epidemiological Bd., 1959—; cons. NIH, 1959—, Army Chem. Corps, 1962—, NASA, 1969—; v.p. Internat. Com. on Nomenclature of Viruses, 1966—. Served to maj., M.C., AUS, 1943-46. Decorated Legion of Merit. Mem. Assn. Am. Physicians, Am. Acad. Microbiologists, Am. Society Clin. Investigation (councillor 1958-60), Am. Assn. Immunologists, Am. Soc. Microbiology (chmn. virology div. 1961-62), Soc. Exptl. Biology and Medicine, Harvey Soc., Central Soc. Clin. Research, Am. Soc. Biol. Chemists, Alpha Omega Alpha. Contbr. textbooks. Co-author: Microbiology, 1967. Editorial bds. Jour. Immunology, Jour. Exptl. Medicine, Jour. Virology and Bacteriological Reviews, Jour. Infectious Diseases. Editor Jour. Bacteriology. Home: 254 Forrest Rd Merion PA 19066 Office: Sch Medicine U Pa Philadelphia PA 19104

GINSBERG, PAUL, lawyer; b. Boston, Feb. 8, 1907; s. Louis and Frieda (Dinsfriend) G.; student Suffolk Coll., 1927; LL.B., Atlanta Law Sch., 1930; LL.D., Woodrow Wilson Coll. Law, 1942; m. Jean Cuba, June 5, 1928; children—Betty Sue (Mrs. Phillip Peskin), Marilyn Ginsberg. Admitted to Ga. bar, 1930, since practiced in Atlanta; asst. atty. gen. Ga., 1948; now asst. dist. atty. Atlanta Jud. Circuit. Mem. Atlanta Community Council, Atlanta Jewish Community Center Bd. dirs. Door of Hope. Served to capt. USAAF, 1942- 45; PTO. Decorated Bronze Star, Purple Heart with oak leaf cluster, Legion of Merit. Recipient Nat. award Anti-Nazi League in N.Y.C. for Americanism work, 1947; Distinguished Service award Am. Legion, 1944, 48, D.A.V., 1947; Testimonial plague Christian Friends of Ga., 1950; named Outstanding Vet. of Year, Ga. chpt. AMVETS, 1950; Brotherhood award for promotion Christian-Jewish relationship, 1948; Outstanding Leadership award Atlanta Jewish Community, 1950; named Outstanding Citizen of Year in Atlanta, 1963; numerous others. Mem. Am., Ga., Atlanta bar assns., Ga. State Bar, Lawyers Club Atlanta, Old War Horse Lawyers Club, Jewish War Vets. U.S. (nat. comdr. 1951-52), D.V.A. (nat. vice comdr. 1950). Jewish religion (bd. dirs. congregation). Mason (Shriner); mem. B'nai B'rith. Club: Progressive Country (v.p.). Author: Wake up America, 1952. Home: 786 W Wesley Rd NW Atlanta GA 30305 Office: 1765 S Pryor Rd SW Atlanta GA 30327

GINSBERG, REUBEN M., lawyer; b. Dallas, Aug. 16, 1922; s. Jacob B. and Hinda (Bernstein) G.; A.B., Am. U., 1943; summer student U. Mexico, 1942; LL.B., Columbia, 1949; grad. student taxation, So. Methodist U., 1951-53; m. Regine Silven, Aug. 17, 1947; children—Michael D., Debra S., Jacqueline B., Lisa A. Admitted to Tex. bar, 1949, Okla. bar, 1949; pvt. practice in Okla., 1949-50; practice in Dallas, 1950—; partner firm Clark, West, Keller, Saunders & Ginsberg and predecessors, 1965—; lectr., tax counselor. Chmn. speakers bur. Nat. Conf. Christians and Jews, 1956—; mem. adv. council Community Chest Trust, 1960—. Bd. dirs. Am. Jewish Com., Dallas chpt. Am. Civil Liberties Union; trustee Hexter Found.-Cripple Children's Endowment Fund. Served with AUS, 1942-46. Recipient citation Tex. Soc. Crippled Children. Mem. Home Builders Assn. Dallas Co. (chmn. legislative com.), Am., Tex., Dallas Co. bar assns. Jewish religion (dir. religious sch. com. 1961-64). Mason (32). Home: 7239 S Jan Mar St Dallas TX 75230 Office: First Nat Bank Bldg Dallas TX 75202

GINSBERG, STEWART THEODORE, physician, psychiatrist; b. St. Paul, Apr. 18, 1906; s. Jacob and Mollie (Balkind) G.; B.S., M.B., U. Minn., 1932, M.D., 1933; m. Ada Leah Leach, Aug. 31, 1930; children—Barbara Cecil (Mrs. Samuel Tisherman), Janet Mary (Mrs. Alvin Klein), Mark Bruce. Intern, St. Mary's Hosp., Duluth, Minn., 1932-33; practice medicine specializing in psychiatry VA hosps., St. Cloud, Minn., Augusta, Ga., Marion, Ind., 1936-53; mgr. VA Hosp. Pitts., 1953-55; chief psychiatry div., psychiatry and neurology service VA Central Office, Washington, 1955-57; Ind. commr. mental health, 1957-66; dir. VA Hosp., Lyons, N.J., 1966—; faculty psychiatry Ind. U. Sch. Medicine, 1948-53, asso. prof., 1957-61, prof., 1961-66; asso. clin. prof. psychiatry Georgetown U. Med. Sch., 1956-57; asst. examiner Am. Bd. Psychiatry and Neurology, 1950—. Cons. community services br. Nat. Inst. Mental Health, 1959-62, in-service tng. mental health tng. com., 1963-65; chmn. subcom. treatment, care and rehab. Conf. on Vol. Services to Psychiat. Patients, 1958; mem. exec. med. adv. com. Indpls. Hosp. Devel. Assn., 1964-66; Mem.

council legislation and pub. policy Nat. Assn. Mental Health, 1967—; cons. Task Force to Revise Standards Psychiat. Hosps. and Clinics, 1968-69. Pres., bd. dirs. Grant County (Ind). Council Social Agys.; v.p., bd. dirs. Family Service Soc., Marion; bds. dirs. Jewish Social Service, Indpls., Community Services Council Met. Indpls. Served from maj. to lt. col. M.C., AUS, 1944-46. Recipient Distinguished Service award Ind. Pub. Health Assn., 1964, award of merit Tri-State Hosp. Assembly, Chgo., 1964. Diplomate Am. Bd. Psychiatry. Hon. fellow Internat. Coll. Dentists; fellow Am. Psychiat. Assn. (past mem. council), Am. Coll. Psychiatrists, Am. Pub. Health Assn.; mem. Grant County Med. Soc. (past pres.), Ind. Rehab. Assn. (past pres.). Assn. Med. Supts. Mental Hosps. (council), N.J. Neuropsychiat. Assn. (mem. council), Am. Assn. Vol. Service Co- ordinators (adv. com. 1962—), A.M.A., Assn. Med. Rehab Dirs. and Co-ordinators (hon.). Contbr. articles to profl. jours. Address: VA Hosp Lyons NJ 07939

GINSBURG, ARNOLD LEWIS, investor; b. Boston, Oct. 26, 1927; s. Myer and Helen (Alberts) G.; grad. Lawrence Acad., Groton, Mass.; A.B., Brown U., 1950; m. Jane Martin, May 1, 1954; children—Martin, Donna, Lauren. Pres. Statler Tissue Corp., 1951-56, Bancroft Tissue Mills, 1951-56; treas. Windsor Industries, Inc., N.Y.C., 1956-60, pres., 1960-64; pres. Martinall Industries, Inc., 1960-66; past treas. Bates Mfg. Co., pres., 1964—, also chmn. With Oppenheimer & Co., investments, N.Y.C., 1956—; chmn. Va. Iron, Coal & Coke Co. Clubs: Fenway Country: Belmont Country; City Athletic; Brown. Office: Bates Mfg Co 1431 Broadway New York City NY 10018

GINSBURG, BENSON EARL, educator, geneticist; b. Detroit, July 16, 1918; s. Morris and Sonia (Udkowsky) G.; B.S., Wayne U., 1939, M.S., 1941; Ph.D., U. Chgo., 1943; m. Pearl Miner, Aug. 29, 1941; children—Judith Myra, Deborah Rose, Faye Diana. Instr. zoology U. Chgo., 1943-44, asst. prof. biology, 1946-49, asso. prof. natural scis., 1949-54, prof., 1954—, now William Rainey Harper prof. biology, also asso. dean of coll.; sci. asso. Jackson Lab., Bar Harbor, Me., 1946—. Fellow Center for Advanced Study Behavioral Scis., 1957-58. With Nat. Def. Research Com., 1944-46. Recipient award for excellence in under-grad. teaching, 1946. Mem. Genetics Soc. Am., Biometric Soc., Am. Soc. Human Genetics, Am. Soc. Naturalists, Am. Soc. Zoologists, Am. Assn. U. Profs., A.A.A.S., N.Y. Acad. Sci., Ill. Acad. Sci, Sigma Xi. Author sci. articles. Home: 8948 S Chappel St Chicago IL 60617

GINSBURG, CHARLES DAVID, lawyer; b. N.Y.C., Apr. 20, 1912; s. Nathan and Rae (Lewis) G.; A.B., W.Va. U., 1932; LL.B., Harvard, 1935; m. Christina Esslay; children—Jonathan, Susan, Mark. Atty. for pub. utilities div. and office of gen. counsel SEC, 1935-39; law sec. to Justice William O. Douglas, 1939; asst. to commr. SEC, 1939-40; legal adviser Price Stblzn. Div., Nat. Def. Adv. Com., 1940- 41; gen. counsel Office Price Adminstrn. and Civilian Supply, 1941-42, OPA, 1942-43; pvt. practice law, Washington, 1946—; partner firm Ginsburg, Feldman & Bress; adminstrv. asst. to Senator M. M. Neely (W.Va.), 1950; adj. prof. internat. law Georgetown U. Grad. Sch. Law, 1959-67. Dep. commr. U.S. delegation Austrian Treaty Commn., Vienna, 1947; adviser U.S. del. Council Fgn. Ministers, London, 1947. Mem. Presdl. Emergency Bd. 166 (Airlines), 1966. chmn. Presdl. Emergency Bd. 169 (Railroads), 1967; exec. dir. Nat. Adv. Commn. Civil Disorders, 1967. Board mem., chmn. exec. com. Nat. Symphony Orch. Assn., 1960-69; bd. govs. Weizmann Inst., 1965; mem. vis. com. Harvard-Mass. Inst. Tech. Joint Center on Urban Studies, 1969; trustee St. John's Coll., 1969. Served from pvt. to capt. AUS, 1943-46; dep. dir. econs. div. Office Mil. Govt., Germany, 1945-46. Decorated Bronze Star medal, Legion of Merit; recipient Presdl. Certificate of Merit. Mem. Phi Beta Kappa. Democrat. Clubs: Federal City, Army and Navy. Author: The Future of German Reparations. Contbr. to legal jours. Home: 1688 31st St Washington DC 20007 Office: 1700 Pennsylvania Av NW Washington DC 20006

GINSBURG, HERMAN, lawyer; b. Russia, June 12, 1903; s. David and Esther (Sudow) G.; came to U.S., 1906; LL.B. cum laude, U. Neb., 1925; m. Rebecca Rosenberg, Sept. 9, 1928; 1 son, Gerald M. Admitted to Neb. bar, 1925, since practiced in Lincoln. Spl. hearing officer conscientious objector cases Dept. Justice, 1942—; instr. U. Neb. Coll. Law, 1955—. Commr., Uniform State Laws, 1971—. Recipient Honor award Jewish Welfare Fedn. Lincoln, 1963. Mem. Am., Neb. (Pres.'s award 1971, chmn. ho. dels. 1960-63, pres. 1965-66), Lincoln (pres. 1958-59) bar assns. Democrat. Jewish religion (pres. congregation 1938- 48). Mem. B'nai B'rith. Home: 1601 S 20th St Lincoln NB 68502 Office: Stuart Bldg Lincoln NB 68508

GINSBURG, LESTER, corp. exec.; b. Boston, Dec. 17, 1906; s. Nathan and Anna R. (Berlow) G.; A.B., Harvard, 1926, M.B.A., 1929; m. Rosslyn Gorney, Jan. 16, 1932 (dec. June 1957); 1 dau., Paula Bess Terrel; m. 2d, Dorothy G. Lesser, Dec. 22, 1961. Instr. pub. utility mgmt. Harvard Sch. Bus. Adminstrn., 1929-30; mgr. Pittsfield Coal Gas Co. (Mass.), 1932-33; market research on pub. utility, 1933-37; spl. asst. to dir. gen. WPB, 1942-43; in charge studies air cargo potential Air Cargo, Inc., 1943-45; treas. Electric Bond & Share Co., N.Y.C., 1945-48, v.p., 1948-66, sr. v.p., 1966- 67; sr. v.p. Ogden Corp., N.Y.C., 1967-71; pres., dir. Ogden Food Products Corp., Tillie Lewis Foods, Inc., 1970—; dir. Lincoln Nat. Life Ins. Co. N.Y., Ogden Foods, ABC Consol. Bd. dirs. Jewish Family Service. Mem. N.Y. Assn. New Ams., Phi Beta Kappa. Clubs: Harmonie, Harvard, Recess (N.Y.C.); Sunningdale Country (Scarsdale, N.Y.). Home: 160 E 65th St New York City NY 10021 Office: 161 E 42d St New York City NY 10021

GINSBURG, MARCUS, lawyer; b. Marietta, O., Feb. 16, 1915; s. Louis and Dora (Brachman) G.; student Marietta Coll., 1932-33; A.B., U. Mich., 1936; LL.B., Harvard, 1939; m. Martine Heilbron, Feb. 23, 1949; children—Harold Heilbron, Robert L. Admitted to Tex. bar, 1939, since practiced in Ft. Worth; partner firm McDonald, Sanders, Wynn, Ginsburg, Phillips & Maddox, 1951- -. Dir. S.W. Nat. Bank, Ft. Worth; dir., exec. com. Pioneer Am. Ins. Co.; dir. Petrochems., Inc. Pres. United Fund and Community Services, Ft. Worth, 1962, Tarrant Council Community Council, 1966-67, Traveller's Aid Soc. Ft. Worth, 1953-54; vice chmn. city solicitations commn., Ft. Worth, 1963-67; past nat. v.p. Am. Jewish Congress; past v.p. Nat. Community Relations Adv. Council; mem. U.S. nat. commn. UNESCO, 1959-64, exec. com., 1963-64, steering com., 1964, chmn. pub. information com., 1962-64; past v.p., treas. Children's Mus. Ft. Worth; mem. Nat. Budget and Consultation Com., 1966—. Bd. dirs. Ft. Worth Art Assn. Served to 2d lt. USAAF, 1942-45. Decorated Army Commendation medal; recipient award excellency United Fund Ft. Worth; award Ft. Worth Traveller's Aid Soc., Ft. Worth Community Council. Mem. Harvard Law Sch. Assn. (pres. Tex. 1955-56, nat. v.p. 1956-57), Pi Lambda Phi. Jewish religion (v.p. temple). Clubs: Ft. Worth, Shady Oaks Country, Ridglea Country (Ft. Worth); Cipango (Dallas). Home: 3860 Bellaire Circle Fort Worth TX 76109 Office: Continental Nat Bank Bldg Fort Worth TX 76102

GINSBURG, NATHAN, educator, physicist; b. Casey, Ill., Aug. 25, 1910; s. Louis and Dora (Brachman) G.; student Marietta Coll., 1927-29; B.A., Ohio State U., 1931, M.A., 1932; Ph.D., U. Mich., 1935; m. Ruth Ostrow, Aug. 25, 1942; 1 dau., Susan Elsbeth. Engring. research fellow U. Mich., 1935-36; Johnston scholar Johns Hopkins, 1936-38, research asso., 1938-42; asst. prof. U. Tex., 1942-46; faculty Syracuse (N.Y.) U., 1946—, prof. physics, 1952—, chmn. dept., 1965—. Cons. Carrier Corp., 1963-65; dir. Inficon, Inc., Syracuse. Pres., Syracuse Friends of Chamber Music, 1962-63. Fellow Optical Soc. Am., Am. Phys. Soc.; mem. Sigma Xi (pres. Syracuse U. chpt. 1962-63). Contbr. articles to profl. jours. Home: 989 James St Syracuse NY 13203

GINSBURG, NORTON SYDNEY, educator; b. Chgo., Aug. 24, 1921; s. Morris and Sarah (Ginsberg) G.; B.A., U. Chgo., 1941, M.A., 1947, Ph.D., 1949. Geographer, U.S. Army Map Service, 1941-42; prof. geography U. Chgo., 1947—, asso. dean Coll., 1963-66, asso. dean social scis., 1967-69. Mem. UN missions to Japan, 1960, 62; cons. Office Naval Research, Social Sci. Research Council, Ency. Brit., Ford Found., Japanese Govt., UNESCO. Served to lt. USNR, 1942-46. Mem. Assn. Am. Geographers (pres. 1970-71). Co-author, editor: Pattern of Asia, 1958; co-author: Malaya, 1958; author: Atlas of Economic Development, 1961; Home: 1320 E Madison Park Chicago IL 60615

GINSBURG, ROBERT NATHAN, marine geologist, educator; b. Wichita Falls, Tex., Apr. 26, 1925; s. Joseph W. and Lillian (Fried) G.; A.B., U. Ill., 1948; M.A., U. Chgo., 1950, Ph.D., 1953; m. Helen Sloan, 1956. Research asst. Marine Lab., U. Miami (Fla.), 1950-54; with Shell Devel. Co., Coral Gables, Fla., 1954-65, sr. research geologist, 1960-65; joint prof. geology and oceanography Johns Hopkins 1965-70; prof. marine geology U. Miami (Fla.) Sch. Marine and Atmospheric Scis., 1970—. Trustee Bermuda Biol. Sta. Served with C.E., AUS, 1943-46. Fellow Geol. Soc. Am. (co-chmn. ann. meeting, 1964); mem. Soc. Econ. Paleontologists and Mineralogists (chmn. research com. 1960, pres. 1968-69), A.A.A.S., Am. Assn. Petroleum Geologists. Asso. editor Jour. Sedimentary Petrology, 1961-68, Marine Geology, 1967-70. Contbr. articles to profl. jours. Address: 251 SW 25th Rd Miami FL 33129

GINSBURGH, ROBERT NEVILLE, air force officer; b. Ft. Sill, Okla., Nov. 19, 1923; s. A. Robert and Elsie (Pinney) G.; grad. Phillips Andover Acad., 1940; B.S., U.S. Mil. Acad., 1944; M.P.A., Harvard, 1947, M.A., 1948; Ph.D., 1949; postgrad. Field Arty. Sch., 1944, Air Tactical Sch., 1950, Air Command and Staff Coll., 1953, Indsl. Coll., 1960, Air War Coll., 1961, Nat. War Coll., 1963); m. Nancy Brand, Dec. 28, 1948 (div. Feb. 1958); children—Robert Brand, Charles Lee; m. 2d, Gail H. Whitehead Winslow, Apr. 4, 1959; children—Carolyn, Anne, Neville; stepchildren—Alan F. Winslow III, William C. Winslow. Commd. 2d lt., F.A., 1944, advanced through grades to maj. gen USAF, 1971; asst. prof. social scis. U.S. Mil. Acad., 1948-51; with Air Force Legislative Liaison, 1951-55, Allied Air Forces So. Europe, Naples, 1955-58, Air Proving Ground Center, 1958, pub. affairs Dept. Def., 1959; asst. exec. air force chief of staff, 1959-62; research fellow Council Fgn. Relations, 1963-64; with Policy Planning Council, State Dept., 1964-66; staff group Office of Chmn. JCS, sr. staff mem. Nat. Security Council, 1966-69; comdr. Aerospace Studies Inst., Air U., Maxwell AFB, Ala., 1969-71. Office Air Force History, 1971—. Decorated Silver Star, Legion of Merit, Purple Heart, Joint Services, Army commendation medals. Mem. Council on Fgn. Relations. Clubs: Internat., Army Navy, Army Navy Country (Washington); Lotos (N.Y.C.). Author: US Military Strategy in the Sixties, 1965; US Military Strategy in the Seventies, 1970. Editor: Principles of Insurance, 1949-50. Contbr. to Economics of National Security, 1950; also articles profl. jours. Home: 5500 Newington Rd Washington DC 20016 Office: Forrestal Bldg Washington DC

GINSKY, MARVIN HERBERT, mfg. co. exec.; b. N.Y.C., Aug. 2, 1930; s. Jack and Edith (Yellen) G.; A.B., N.Y.U., 1952, LL.B. cum laude, 1955; m. Myrna Druvanoff, Mar. 24, 1951; children—Andrea, Mitchell. Admitted to N.Y. bar, 1955; mem. legal dept. Paramount Pictures Corp., 1955-59; asso. Mervin Rosenman, N.Y.C., 1959-60; asst. gen. counsel U.S. Plywood Corp. (co. name changed to U.S. Plywood-Champion Papers, Inc.), 1960—, sec., 1965-67, asso. counsel, asst. sec., 1967—. Mem. Am. Bar Assn., Am. Soc. Corp. Secs. Home: 189 Willow Dr Briarcliff Manor NY 10510 Office: 777 3d Av New York City NY 10017

GINZBERG, ELI, economist, educator, govt. cons.; b. N.Y.C., Apr. 30, 1911; s. Louis and Adele (Katzenstein) G.; student U. Heidelberg, U. Grenoble, 1928-29; A.B., Columbia, 1931, A.M., 1932, Ph.D., 1934; Litt.D., Jewish Theol. Sem., 1966; LL.D., Loyola U. Chgo., 1969; m. Ruth Szold, July 14, 1946; children—Abigail, Jeremy, Rachel. Dir. research econs., group behavior Columbia, 1939-42, 48-49, faculty, 1935—, now A. Barton Hepburn prof. econs., dir. conservation human resources project, 1950—. Hon. faculty mem. Indsl. Coll. Armed Forces. Spl. asst. to chief statistician U.S. War Dept., 1942-44, spl. asst. to dir. hosp. div. Surgeon Gen.'s Office, 1944, dir. resources analysis div., 1944-46; cons. Dept. Army, 1946-70, Dept. State, 1953, 56, 65-69, Dept. Labor, 1954—, Dept. Def., 1964—, Dept. Commerce, 1965-66, Exec. Office Pres., 1942; mem. med. adv. bd. to Sec. War, 1946-48; U.S. rep. 5 power Conf. Reparations for Non-Repatriable Refugees, 1946; dir. N.Y. State Hosp. Study, 1948-49; mem. Com. on Wartime Requirement for Sci. and Specialized Personnel, 1942; med. cons. Hoover Commn., 1952; adviser Commn. Chronic Illness, 1950-53; mem. adv. council Nat. Inst. Mental Health, 1959-63; chmn. com. on studies White House Conf. on Children and Youth, 1960; dir. staff studies Nat. Manpower Council, 1951-60; chmn. Nat. Manpower Adv. Com., 1962—; mem. Nat. Adv. Allied Health Council, 1968—; mem. sci. adv. bd. USAF, 1969—; chmn. taskforce manpower research Dept. Def., 1970-71. Dir. research United Jewish Appeal, 1941; gov. Hebrew U., Jerusalem, 1953-59. Fellow A.A.A.S.; mem. Am. Econ. Assn., Acad. Polit. Sci., Indsl. Relations Research Assn., Med. Consultants World War II (hon.), Phi Beta Kappa, Beta Gamma Sigma. Author: The House of Adam Smith, 1934; The Illusion of Economic Stability, 1939; Grass on the Slag Heaps: The Story of the Welsh Miners, 1942; The Unemployed, 1943; The Labor Leader, 1948; A Pattern for Hospital Care, 1949; Agenda for American Jews, 1950; Occupational Choice, 1951; The Uneducated, 1953; Psychiatry and Military Manpower Policy, 1953; What Makes an Executive, 1955; The Negro Potential, 1956; Effecting Change in Large Organizations, 1957; Human Resources, 1958; The Ineffective Soldier, 3 vols., 1959; The Nation's Children, 3 vols., 1960; Planning for Better Hosp. Care, 1961; The Optimistic Tradition and American Youth, 1962; The American Worker in the Twentieth Century, 1963; The Troublesome Presence, 1964; Talent and Performance, The Negro Challenge to the Business Community, 1964; The Pluralistic Economy, 1965; Keeper of the Law: Louis Ginzberg, 1966; Life Styles of Educated Women; Educated American Women-Self-Portraits, 1966; Manpower Strategy for Developing Nations, 1967; Manpower Strategy for the Metropolis, 1968; The Middle Class Negro in the White Man's World, 1967; Business Leadership and the Negro Crisis; 1968; Men, Money and Medicine, 1969; Urban Health Services-The Case of New York, 1971; Career Guidance, 1971, Manpower for Development, 1971. Home: 845 West End Av New York City NY 10025

GINZBURG, RALPH, editor; b. Bklyn., Oct. 29, 1929; s. Raymond and Rachel G. (Lipkin) G.; B.B.A., Coll. City N.Y., 1949; postgrad. Bklyn. Coll., 1950; diploma Henry George Sch. Econs., 1951; m. Shoshana Brown, Dec. 16, 1958; children—Bonnie, Shepherd, Lark. Copyboy, N.Y. Daily Compass, 1949-50; re-write man Washington Times-Herald, 1950-51; freelance writer, photographer, 1951-53; staff writer NBC, 1954-56; articles editor Esquire, 1956-58; editor Eros, 1962-63, Fact, 1964-68, Avant-Garde, 1969—, Moneysworth, 1971—. Served with AUS, 1950-51. Mem. Am. Civil Liberties Union, Sierra Club, Wilderness Soc., Friends of Earth, Urban Coalition, Fellowship of Reconciliation, War Resisters League, N.Y. Ramblers, Adirondack Mountain Club, Common Cause, Quaker Action Group, Scenic Hudson Preservation Soc., Am. Youth Hostels. Author: 100 Years of Lynching, 1961; An Unhurried View of Erotica, 1956; Eros on Trial, 1964. Office: 110 W 40th St New York City NY 10018

GINZTON, EDWARD LEONARD, corp. exec.; b. nr. Ekaterinoslavsk, Russia, Dec. 27, 1915; s. Leonard Louis and Natalie P. (Philipova) G.; came to U.S., 1929, derivative citizen; B.S., U. Cal., 1936, M.S., 1937; E.E., Stanford, 1938, Ph.D., 1940; m. Artemas A. McCann, July 12, 1939; children—Anne, Leonard, Nancy, David. Research engr. Sperry Gyroscope Co., N.Y.C., 1940-46; asst. prof. applied physics and elec. engineering Stanford, 1946-47, asso. prof., 1947-50, prof., 1951-68; dir., Microwave Lab., 1949- 59; dir. Varian Assos., 1948—, chmn. bd., chief exec. officer, 1959—, pres., 1964-68; dir. Stanford Bank, 1967—; expert cons. research and devel. bd. Nat. Mil. Establishment, 1947-50. Mem. commn. 1, U.S. Nat. Com. of Internat. Sci. Radio Union, 1960-68; dir. Stanford Project M, 1957-60; chmn. adv. bd. Sch. Engring., Stanford, 1968-70; co-chmn. Stanford Mid-PeniEsula Urban Coalition, 1968—. Recipient Morris Liebmann Meml. prize I.R.E., 1958. Fellow I.E.E.E. (bd. dirs.; medal of honor 1969); mem. Nat. Acad. Scis., Nat. Acad. Engring., Sigma Xi, Eta Kappa Nu, Tau Beta Pi. Author: Microwave Measurements, 1957. Contbr. articles to tech. jours. Patentee in field. Home: 28014 Natoma Rd Los Altos Hills CA 94022 Office: 611 Hansen Way Palo Alto CA 94303

GIOBBI, EDWARD GIACCHINO, artist; b. Waterbury, Conn., July 18, 1926; s. Achille and Teresa (Gasparetti) G.; student Whitney Sch. Art, New Haven, 1946-47, Vesper George Sch. Art, Boston, 1947-50, Cape Sch. Art, Provincetown, Mass., summer, 1949-50; Art Students League, N.Y.C., 1950-51, 55-56, Acad. Fine Arts, Florence, Italy, 1951-54; m. Elinor E. Turner, Feb. 14, 1959; children—Eugenia, Elizabeth, Chambless Martino. One man shows include Ward Eggleston Gallery, N.Y.C., 1951, Matatuck Mus., Conn., 1955, Artists Gallery, N.Y.C., 1956, Contempories Gallery, N.Y.C., 1956, 60- 61, 63, Heller Gallery, N.Y.C., 1957, 58, Brooks Meml. Art Gallery, Memphis, 1961, New Arts Center, London, Eng., 1964, 67, Bear Lane Gallery, Oxford, Eng., 1964, Queen Sq. Gallery, Leeds Gallery, 1964, Tirca Karlis Gallery, Provincetown, 1964-66, 67, Michelson Gallery, Washington, 1966, Alan Gallery, N.Y.C., 1966, Ark. Art Centre, Little Rock, 1966, Waddell Gallery, N.Y.C., 1967, Obelisk Gallery, Boston, 1968, Gertrude Kasle Gallery, Detroit, 1968; two-man shows include Galeries an der Reuss, Lucerne, Switzerland, 1953, Nexus Gallery, Boston, 1956; group exhbns. include Recent Drawings U.S.A., Mus. Modern Art, 1956, Am. Fedn. Arts Travelling Show, 1956, 58, 61, 63, Whitney Mus. Ann., 1957-61, 66, Corcoran Gallery, 1958, Pa. Acad. Fine Arts, 1961, Young Am., Whitney Mus., 1961, 40 painters under 40, Whitney Mus., 1962, Figure USA, Mus. Modern Art, 1962, Art in Progress, Finch Coll., N.Y.C., 1967; rep. permanent collections Tate Gallery, London, Eng., Magdalen Coll., Cambridge, Eng., St. Edmund Hall, Oxford, Eng., Poole Tech. Coll., Dorset, Eng., Whitney Mus., Balt. Mus. Art Inst. Chgo., Brooks Meml. Art Gallery, Marion Koogler McNay Art Inst., San Antonio, Boston Mus. Fine Arts, Spellman Coll., Atlanta, Allentown (Pa.) Mus., Wesleyan Coll., Macon, Ga., Syracuse U., Academia di Belle Arti, Florence, Memphis Acad. Arts, U. Mich., Leeds (Eng.) City Art Gallery, Bklyn. Mus., Finch Coll.; artist in residence Memphis Acad., 1960-61, Ford Found., Ark. Arts Centre, 1966. Recipient Emily Lowe award, 1951- 52. Served with inf. AUS, 1944-46. Decorated Combat Inf. Badge. Address: 161 Croton Lake Rd Katonah NY 10536

GIORDANO, ANTHONY BRUNO, inst. dean; b. N.Y.C., Feb. 1, 1915; s. Sabino and Natalina (Amata) G.; B.E.E., Poly. Inst. Bklyn., 1937, M.Elec. Engring., 1939, D.Elec. Engring., 1946; m. Peggy Cozzi, Dec. 23, 1939; 1 son, Clyde Anton. Faculty, Poly. Inst. Bklyn., 1939—, prof. elec. engring., 1953—, dean Grad. Sch., 1960—. Scientist, OSRD, 1942-45; research supr. Microwave Research Inst., Bklyn., 1945—; spl. research microwave waveguide attenuators. Chmn. engring. adv. com. Bd. Edn. City N.Y., 1958-60. Fellow I.R.E. (chmn. N.Y. sect. 1954-55, regional dir. 1960- 62, nat. dir. 1960-62), I.E.E.E. (chmn. basic scis. com. 1967-, chmn. 1967 internat. conv., rep. Engring Found. of United Engring. Trustees 1968—, sec. group on communication tech. 1965-71, numerous other coms.), mem. Am. Inst. E.E. (chmn. basic sci. div. 1955-56), A.A.A.S., Am. Soc. for Engring. Edn. (chmn. meetings com. Middle Atlantic States sect. 1969-71, chmn. sect. 1971-72), Internat. Sci. Radio Union, Sigma Xi, Tau Beta Pi, Eta Kappa Nu. Author: Network Theory, 1964; also articles in field. Asso. editor: Jour. Radio Sci., 1967—. Home: 35-46 74th St Jackson Heights 72 NY Office: 333 Jay St Brooklyn 1 NY

GIORDANO, HENRY LUKE, govt. ofcl.; b. San Francisco, June 10, 1914; s. Peter L. and Elisabeth M. (Dernbach) G.; Ph.G., U. Cal., 1934; m. Elaine Watson, June 11, 1939; children—Marjorie E., Anne Marie. Registered pharmacist, 1934-41; narcotic agt. Fed. Bur. Narcotics, 1941-43, Seattle, 1946-50, dist. supr., Mpls., 1950-54, Kansas City, Mo., 1954-55, field supr., 1956, asst. dep. commr., 1956-57, asst. to commr., 1957-58, dep. commr. narcotics, 1958-62, commr. narcotics, 1962—; chief investigator subcom. on narcotics House Ways and Means Com., 1955-56; adviser U.S. rep. 14th session UN Commn. on Narcotic Drugs, Geneva, Switzerland, also 18th session. Served with USCGR, 1943-46. Home: 9609 New Hampshire Av Silver Spring MD 20903 Office: 1300 E St NW Washington DC 20004

GIORDANO, SALVATORE, bus. exec.; b. N.Y.C., 1910. Pres., dir. Salvatore Giordano Found., Inc., N.Y.C., Giordano Found. Inc., N.Y.C.; chmn., pres., dir. Fedders Corp. Home: Bernardsville NJ 07924 Office: Edison NJ 08817

GIOVACCHINI, PETER LOUIS, psychoanalyst; b. N.Y.C., Apr. 12, 1922; s. Alex and Therese (Chicca) G.; B.S., U. Chgo., 1941, M.D., 1944; student Columbia, 1939; m. Louise Post, Sept. 29, 1945; children—Philip, Sandra, Daniel. Intern, Fordham Hosp., N.Y.C., 1944-45; resident U. Chgo. Clinics, 1945-46, resident and research fellow, 1948-50; candidate Chgo. Inst. Psychoanalysis, 1949-54, clin. asso., 1957—; clin. prof. U. Ill. Coll. Medicine, 1961—; pvt. practice, Chgo., 1950—; cons. Wilmette (Ill.) Family Service Bur. and United Charities. Served to capt. M.C., AUS, 1946-48. Diplomate Am. Bd. Psychiatry and Neurology. Fellow Am. Psychiat. Assn., Am. Orthopsychiat. Assn.; mem. Soc. Adolescent Psychiatry, Chgo. Psychoanalytic Soc., Am. Psychoanalytic Assn., Chgo. Soc. Adolescent Psychiatry (pres. 1966-67). Author: (with L.B. Boyer) Psychoanalytic Treatment of Schizophrenia and Characterological Disorders, 1967; Psychoanalytic Treatment, 1971; also articles. Co-editor Annals of Adolescent Psychiatry. Home: 270 Locust Rd Winnetka IL 60093 Office: 55 E Washington St Chicago IL 60602

GIOVANNETTI, ALBERT, diplomat of Holy See; b. Rome, Italy, July 20, 1913; s. Francesco and Vittoria (Aloisi) G.; D.D., J.C.D., Gregorian U., Rome, 1943; Dipl. Degree, Pontifical Acad.

Diplomacy, Rome, 1944. Ordained priest Roman Cath. Ch., 1935; editor Cath. Weekly, Teramo, Italy, 1936-40; joined Holy See Diplomatic Service, 1944; domestic prelate of His Holiness, 1960; permanent rep. of Holy See to UN, 1964—. Author: The Red Book of the Persecuted Church, 1957; We Have a Pope, 1958; The Vatican and the War, 1961; Rome Open City, 1963. Home: 315 E 47th St New York City NY 10017 Office: 323 E 47th St New York City NY 10017

GIOVANNITTI, LEN, writer; b. N.Y.C., Apr. 16, 1920; s. Arturo and Carrie (Zaikaner) G.; B.S., St. John's U., 1942; m. Sara Steinberg, Aug. 28, 1943; children—David, Nina. Labor journalist, 1946-58; free-lance writer, 1959- 61; tv documentary writer, 1961-62; writer, dir., producer NBC News, 1962-70; producer, writer, dir. NBC White Paper, The Decision of Japan to Surrender, 1965; producer, writer NBC TV documentaries The Hill Country: Lyndon Johnson's Texas, 1966, The Am. Alcoholic, 1968; asso. producer NBC White Paper programs The Death of Stalin, 1963, The Rise of Khrushchev, 1963, Cuba: The Bay of Pigs, 1964, Cuba: The Missile Crisis, 1964, The Decision to Drop the Bomb, 1965; writer ABC TV documentaries Winston Churchill: The Valiant Years, 1961, Walking Hard, 1962. Served with USAAF, 1942-45. Recipient Lasker Med. Journalism award, 1969, Ohio State U. award, 1969. Mem. Am. Acad. TV Arts and Scis., Writers Guild Am. East. Author: Sidney Hillman: Labor Statesman, 1948; The Prisoners of Combine D., 1957 (A.L.A. liberty and justice award 1958); The Decision to Drop the Bomb, 1965. Home: 239 Central Park W New York City NY 10024

GIRA, BERNARD FRANCIS, petroleum co. exec.; b. Custer, S.D., May 25, 1917; s. Bernard A. and Cassandra (Roy) G.; B.S., U. S.D., 1937; student U.S. Mil. Acad., 1939, Rankin Sch. Aeros., 1942; children by previous marriage—Robin W., Gail F., Teresa A., Bernard F.; m. 2d, Wanda A. Robertson, June 18, 1953; 1 dau., Gina Cassandra. Chief purchasing agt. Douglas Aircraft Co., 1940- 46; v.p. Indsl. Assos., Inc., 1946-48, now dir.; former pres. Topp Industries; pres. Bonner Machine Works, Inc., Los Angeles, 1948—, Ronland, Inc., Oil, Gas & Minerals Devel. Co., Master Oil and Gas Fund, Inc.; chmn. bd. MP Mgmt. Co.; pres., dir. Green Farms, Inc., United Indsl. Corp., WAG Investments, Inc., Rancho Engring., Inc.; dir. HRB, Inc., U.S. Semicondrs., Heli-Coil, Inc., Hayes Internat., Inc., Taylor Enterprises, Tremerton, Utah; mng. partner Resources Devel. Co. Mem. Ch. of Jesus Christ of Latter-day Saints (high priest, bishop). Clubs: Racquet (Palm Springs); Beverly Hills (Cal.), Cave De Roys. Home: 524 Skyline Rd Ventura CA 93003 Office: 16661 Ventura Blvd Encino CA 91316

GIRARD, ALEXANDER HAYDEN, architect; b. N.Y.C., May 24, 1907; s. Carlo Matteo and Lezlie (Cutler) C.; grad. Royal Inst. Brit. Architects, 1929, Royal Sch. Architecture, Rome, Italy, 1931, N.Y.U., 1935; m. Susan Needham, Mar. 1936; children—Sansi, Marshall. Worked archtl. offices, Florence, Rome, London, Paris, N.Y.C.; practice of architecture, Florence, 1930-32, N.Y.C., 1932-37, Detroit, 1937; works exhibited Barcelona, Florence, London, N.Y.C., Detroit, Walker Art Center, Rochester Mus., Cranbrook Acad.; Mus. Modern Art, Cooper Union, Mus. Internat. Folk Art, Santa Fe, Nelson Gallery, Atkins Mus., Kansas City, Mo.; outstanding works include part of Italian exhibit Internat. Exhbn., Barcelona, 1929, offices Ford Motor Co., Dearborn, Mich., 1943, cafeteria Lincoln Motor Co. Detroit, 1946, pvt. residences, Mich., 1962, L'Etoile Restaurant, N.Y.C. for Brody Corp.; color cons. San Francisco Civic Auditorium Rehab., 1963-64, Golden Gateway Redevel. Project, San Francisco, 1963-64; interiors and furnishings for St. John's College, Santa Fe, N.M., 1963; El Encanto de un Pueblo, Hemisphere '68, San Antonio; established Girard Found., 1961; dir. Modern Living exhbn. Detroit Inst. Arts, 1949; color cons. Gen. Motors Research Center, Detroit, 1951-52; now dir. fabric div. Herman Miller Furniture Co.; designer Design for Use traveling show, Mus. Modern Arts, 1950, Herman Miller Furniture Co. exhibit Furniture Mus., Grand Rapids, Mich., 1951, spl. fabric coll., catalog, 1952, Good Design exhbn., Mdse. Mart Chgo., 1952, 53; Herman Miller Showroom, San Francisco, 1958; La Fonda del Sol Restaurant N.Y.C., 1959-60; Herman Miller Textile and Objects Shop, N.Y.C.; other exhbns. in home furnishings, textile and ornamental arts Mus. Modern Art, 1954, 55, contbr. fabric designs to Am. Fabrics Exhbn., 1956; exhbn. table settings Georg Jensen, Inc., N.Y.C., 1955, 56, design and color project Main St. Rehab., Columbus, Ind., 1963, interiors Cummins Engine Co. offices, Columbus, Ind., 1964, 3-dimensional historic mural John Deere & Co.'s adminstrv. center, Moline, Ill., 1964, redesign visual aspects entire airport Braniff Airline, Dallas, 1965; cons. Internat. Exec. Service Corps, Mexico City, 1969. Juror Good Design exhibit Merchandise Mart, Chgo., 1950, Internat. Fabric Competition, Greensboro, N.C., 1952, Craftsman of N.M., 1962, Craft Guild, San Antonio, 1962, Own Your Own Exhibit, Denver Art Mus., 1963; The Magic of a People Exhbn., Hemisfair, 1968. Received Florence traveling scholarship Royal Inst. Br. Architects, Eng., 1929, gold medal Barcelona Exhibition, 1929, fabric competition Mus. Modern Art, N.Y.C., Trail Blazer award for Herman Miller Fabric Coll. Home Fashion League N.Y., 1952; Collaborative medal honor Archtl. League N.Y., 1965; Allied Professions medal A.I.A., 1966; Elsie de Wolfe award Am. Inst. Interior Designers, 1966; Hon. Distinction of Royal Designer for Industry diploma Royal Soc. Arts, London, Eng., 1966. Registered architect, N.Y., Mich., Conn., N.M. Benjamin Franklin fellow Royal Soc. Arts London; mem. A.I.A., Archtl. Assn. London, Eng. Club: Archtl. League (silver medal for design La Fonda del Sol Restaurant 1962) (N.Y.C.). Author: The Magic of a People, 1968. Contbr. articles trade publs. Address: PO Box 2168 Santa Fe NM 87501

GIRARD, CLARENCE HENRY, govt. ofcl.; b. Schenectady, Feb. 23, 1908; s. Hector Victor and Helen (Hines) G.; A.B., Union Coll., Schenectady, 1930; M.S., Syracuse U., 1931; LL.B. cum laude, Albany Law Sch., 1939; m. Mary Lydia Girard, Oct. 5, 1928; children—Diane Gayle (Mrs. Gaetano Anthony DeMattei), Robyn (Mrs. Wallace Morrison Graves), Bonnie Lynn, (Mrs. William H. Johnson), Karen Lee. Postal clk., Schenectady, 1928-39; admitted to N.Y. bar, 1939; practiced in Schenectady, 1939-41; trial atty. U.S. Dept. Agr., 1941-47, chief marketing div. Office Gen. Counsel, 1948-56, hearing examiner, 1956-61, dir. packers and stockyards div., 1961-62, dep. adminstr. Agrl. Marketing Service, 1962-65, dep. adminstr. consumer and marketing service, 1965—, mem. contract disputes bd., 1963—; vice chmn. Nat. Adv. Coms. Dairy and Dairy Products and Packers and Stockyards, 1963—. Pres., sec.-treas. Schenectady Postal Employees Credit Union, 1933-36. Served with AUS, 1944-45. Mem. Fed. Bar Assn., N.Y. State Fedn. Postal Clks. (past v.p.), Justinian Soc. (past pres.), Pi Gamma Mu, Club: Kenwood Country (Bethesda). Asso. editor Albany Law Rev., 1937-39. Home: 4325 Kentbury Dr Bethesda MD 20014 Office: US Dept Agr Washington DC 20515

GIRARD, LOUIS JOSEPH, ophthalmologist; b. Spokane, Mar. 29, 1919; s. Harry and Agnes (Cain) G.; B.A., Rice U., 1941; M.D., U. Tex., 1944; postgrad. N.Y. U. Postgrad. Med. Sch., 1947-48; m. Bonita Crossnay, Mar. 31, 1945; children—Hilaire Michelle (Mrs. Cliff Richey), Bryan Suzanne, Christina Ann, Michael Sanford, Hugh Ashley, Gabrielle Inez; m. 2d, Loraine McMurrey, June 30, 1967. Intern, Jersey City Med. Center, 1944-45; asso. to Dr. Conrad Berens, N.Y.C., 1947-49, 51-53; resident opthalmology N.Y. Eye and Ear Infirmary, 1949-51; asst. surgeon, 1951-53, dir. chronic infection project, 1949-52, asso. dir. dept. research, 1951-53; asst. attending St. Clare's Hosp., 1948-53, Willard Parker Hosp., 1949-53, N. Country Community Hosp., 1951-53, Nassau Hosp., 1951-53; cons. ophthalmologist Southside Hosp., 1951-53; attending opthalmologist Jefferson David Hosp., 1953-59, VA Hosp., Houston, 1954-58, Tex. Children's Hosp., 1954-57, St. Luke's Episcopal Hosp., 1954-61, Meth. Hosp., 1955-59; cons. Montgomery County Hosp., 1955—, Tex. Children's Hosp., 1957—, VA Hosp., Houston, 1958—, St. Luke's Episcopal Hosp., 1961—, St. Joseph's Hosp., 1965—; sr. attending Ben Taub Gen. Hosp., 1959—, Meth. Hosp., 1959—; coordinator grad. course ophthalmology N.Y. U. Postgrad. Med. Sch., 1948-49, instr., 1951- 53; clin. asst. prof. U. Tex. Postgrad. Sch. Medicine, 1953-57, lectr., 1957—; faculty Baylor U. Coll. Medicine, 1953—, prof. ophthalmology, chmn. dept., 1963-71. Asso. mng. dir. Ophthal. Found., 1951-55; cons. Ophthal. Found., 1957; exec. dir. Eyes of Tex. (sight Found.), 1960—; mem. Am. Orthoptic Council, 1962—; chmn. Internat. Eye Film Library, 1967-71; mem. med. adv. bd. Internat. Eye Bank, 1965—. Recipient Alfred H. Bond award for research in ophthalmology, 1950; Prof. Ignacio Barraquer Meml. award Smith, Miller & Patch, 1965; 2d prize Internat. Film Festival, 1966. Diplomate Am. Bd. Ophthalmology. Fellow A.C.S. (bd. govs. 1966—); mem. Am. Acad. Opthalmology and Otolaryngology (2d pl. award sci. . exhibits 1960), Pan Am. Assn. Ophthalmology (1st pl. award sci. exhibits 1960, 62, vis. prof. 1967), Assn. Research Ophthalmology, N.Y. Acad. Medicine, N.Y. Acad. Sci., Nassau, Houston opthal. socs., French Soc. Opthalmology, Houston Neurol. Soc., Jules Gonin Club, Tex. Opthal. Assn., Alumni Assn. N.Y. Eye and Ear Infirmary, Am. (certificate of merit sci. exhibit 1961), So. med. assns., Nat. Med. Found. Eye Care, Assn. Am. Physicians and Surgeons, Am. Assn. Ophthalmologists, Nat. Med. Found. Eye Care, Tex. Rehab. Assn., Harris County Med. Soc., Am. U. Profs. Ophthalmologists, Med. Research Found. Tex., Contact Lens Soc. Opthalmologists (Exceptional Merit award 1968), Inst. Horacio Ferrer (corr.). Contbr. numerous articles to profl. jours.; producer films. Editor: Corneal Contact Lenses, 1964; Corneal Scleral Contact Lenses, 1967. Mem. editorial bd. Ophthalmologia, 1965—, Annals of Ophthalmology, 1968—. Home: 3205 Del Monte St Houston TX 77019

GIRARD, RENE NOEL, educator, writer; b. Avignon, France, Dec. 25, 1923; s. Joseph and Therese (Fabre) G.; Archiviste-paleographe, Ecoles des chartes, Sorbonne, Paris, 1947; Ph.D., Ind U., 1950; m. Martha McCullough, June 18, 1951; children—Martin, Daniel, Mary. Came to U.S., 1947. Tchr. Romance langs. Ind. U., 1947-52, Duke, 1952-53, Bryn Mawr Coll., 1953-57; faculty Johns Hopkins, 1957-68, prof. French lit., 1961-68, chmn. dept. Romance langs., 1966-68; Faculty prof. arts and letters State U. N.Y. at Buffalo, 1968—. Guggenheim fellow, 1960, 67. Mem. Modern Lang. Assn. (exec. council 1969—). Author: Mensonge romantique et verite romanesque, 1961; Marcel Proust: A Collection of Critical Essays, 1962; Dostoievski: du doubleā l'unité, 1963; Deceit, Desire and the Novel, 1967. Contbr. articles to profl. jours. Gen. editor M.L.N., 1962-68. Home: 126 Kandahar Dr East Aurora NY 14052 Office: State U NY Buffalo NY 14214

GIRARD, ROBERT A., educator. Prof. law Stanford. Office: Annex 306 Stanford U Law Sch Stanford CA 94305*

GIRARD, STEPHEN A., Jr., corp. exec.; b. Hoquiam, Wash., Sept. 18, 1913; s. Stephen A. and Lena (Rogers) G.; student U. Wash.; m. Laurina Banks, Nov. 28, 1936; children—Julie (Mrs. Richard S. Miller), Caron (Mrs. Michael Cox), Stephanie (Mrs. George Le Boutillier), Stephen. Asso. Kaiser Corp., 1938- -, v.p., gen. mgr., Kaiser Jeep Corp., 1954-59, pres., 1959—; pres., dir. Kaiser Jeep Sales Corp., Kaiser Jeep Internat. Corp.; pres. bd. dirs. Kaiser Jeep Overseas S.A. (Switzerland); v.p. Kaiser Industries Corp.; dir. Kaiser Jeep of Can., Ltd., Kaiser-Ilin Industries, Ltd. (Israel), Willys Afrika (Pty.) Ltd. (South Africa), Turk-Willys Overland Fabrikalari A.O. (Turkey), Mahindra & Mahindra, Ltd. (Bombay, India), Willys-Overland do Brasil, S.A. (Sao Paulo), Industrias Kaiser Argentina, S.A. (Buenos Aires), Willys Motors (Australia) Pty., Ltd. Mem. A.I.M. (presidents council), Am. Mgmt. Assn., Automobile Mfg. Assn., Soc. Automotive Engrs., Sigma Nu. Clubs: Marco Polo (N.Y.C.); Orinda (Cal.) Country; Inverness, The Toledo (Toledo). Office: Kaiser Center Oakland CA 94612

GIRARDEAU, MARVIN DENHAM, educator; b. Lakewood, O., Oct. 3, 1930; s. Marvin Denham and Maude Irene (Miller) G.; B.S., Case Inst. Tech., 1952; M.S., U. Ill., 1954; Ph.D., Syracuse U., 1958; m. Susan Jessica Brown, June 30, 1956; children—Ellen, Catherine, Laura. NSF postdoctoral fellow Inst. Advanced Study, Princeton, 1958-59; research asso. Brandeis U., 1959-60; staff mem. Boeing Sci. Research Labs., 1960-61; research asso. Enrico Fermi Inst. Nuclear Studies, U. Chgo., 1961-63; asso. prof. physics, research asso. Inst. Theoretical Sci., U. Ore., Eugene, 1963-67, prof. physics, research asso., 1967—, dir., 1967-69. NSF research grantee, 1965-71. Mem. Am. Phys. Soc., Am. Assn. U. Profs. Contbr. articles to profl. jours. Research Quantum-mech. many-body problems, statis. mechanics. Home: 2398 Douglas Dr Eugene OR 97405

GIRAUD, RAYMOND DORNER, educator; b. N.Y.C., Aug. 26, 1920; s. Gabriel and Mabel (Dorner) G.; B.A., Coll. City N.Y., 1941; M.A., U. Chgo., 1949; Ph.D., Yale, 1954; m. Lise Kurzmann, Feb. 1, 1948. Instr. English and French, Ill. Inst. Tech., 1946-49; instr., then asst. prof. French, Yale, 1952-58; mem. faculty Stanford, 1958—, prof. French, 1962—, chmn. dept. French and Italian, 1968—. Served with AUS, 1942-45. Mem. Am. Assn. U. Profs., Modern Lang. Assn., Am. Assn. Tchrs. French. Author: The Unheroic Hero, 1957; Flaubert, A Collection of Critical Essays, 1964. Home: 2200 Byron St Palo Alto CA 94301 Office: Dept French and Italian Stanford Univ Stanford CA 94305

GIRAUDO, JOHN CHARLES, air force officer; b. Santa Barbara, Cal., Oct. 2, 1923; s. Joseph and Antoinette (Krier) G.; student U. Cal. at Santa Barbara, 1942; grad. Armed Forces Staff Coll., 1959, Nat. War Coll., 1964; m. Elizabeth Lucia Billo, Aug. 4, 1946; children—Jo Linda, Denise Antoinette. Commd. 2d lt. USAAF, 1942, advanced through grades to maj. gen. USAF, 1970; various jet fighter and all-weather interceptor assignments, 1946-52; comdr. 25th Fighter Squadron, 1952-53; prisoner-of-war, Korea, 1953; comdr. Fighter Weapons Sch., 1954-56; sr. adv. Hawaii ANG., 1956-59; operations staff officer Hdqrs. USAF and Joint Staff, 1959-63, vice comdr. Fighter Weapons Center, Libya, 1965; vice-comdr. 49th Tactical Fighter Wing, Germany, 1966, comdr., 1967; comdr. 355th Tactical Fighter Wing, Thailand, 1967-68; dep. dir. legislative liaison, 1968-70, dir., 1970—. Decorated Silver Star, D.F.C., Bronze Star, Air medal with 17 oak leaf clusters, Purple Heart with oak leaf cluster. Mem. Quiet Birdmen, Order Daedalians. Home: 1401 Juliana Pl Alexandria VA 22304 Office: SAFLL The Pentagon Washington DC 20330

GIRI, V. V., pres. of India; b. 1894. Formerly minister of labor; pres. of India, 1969—. Address: Office of the President Rashtrapati Bahran New Delhi 4 India*

GIROIR, CHARLES JOSEPH, Jr., lawyer; b. Pine Bluff, Ark., Feb. 13, 1939; s. Charles Joseph and Marcelline (Evans) G.; B.A., U. Ark., 1960, LL.B., 1962; LL.M., Georgetown U., 1965; m. Janinne Bare, Apr. 18, 1960; 1 dau., Janinne Ward. Admitted to ARK. bar, 1962; atty. Dept. Justice, 1962-63, SEC, 1963-65; with firm Rose, Barron, Nash, Williamson, Carroll & Clay, Little Rock, 1965—, partner, 1967—. Home: 45 Edgehill St Little Rock AR 72207 Office: 720 W 3d St Little Rock AR 72201

GIRONE, VITO ANTHONY, architect, educator; b. Orange, N.J., Feb. 12, 1910; s. Joseph and Rose (Pastore) G.; diploma Newark sch. Fine and Indsl. Arts, 1931; student (scholar) N.Y. U., 1932-35, (scholar) Harvard Grad. Sch. Design, 1935-36; diploma Fontainbleau Sch. Architecture, 1937; student New Sch. Social Research, 1937; diploma Nat. Inst. Archtl. Edn., 1937; pupil Eliel Saarinen (fellow) Cranbrook Acad. Art, 1939-40; m. Nancy Katherine Tenore, Sept. 6, 1945; children—Donald William, David Paul (dec.). Individual practice architecture, 1940—; design cons. Eastern nat. area., Ind., Ky.; prof. architecture U. Notre Dame, 1945-64, U. Ky., 1965—. Served with C.E., AUS, World War II. Recipient medals for design as student. Fellow Internat. Inst. Arts and Letters (Pres.'s medal 1964); mem. Am. Soc. Planning Ofcls., A.I.A. (pres. elect. chpt.), Tau Sigma Delta. Presbyn. (deacon). Contbr. articles to profl. jours. Home: 535 Woodbine Rd Lexington KY 40503 Office: U Ky Lexington KY 40506

GIROUX, ROBERT, editor; b. Jersey City, Apr. 8, 1914; S. Arthur J. and Katharine (Lyons) G.; A.B. with honors, Columbia, 1936; m. Carmen de Arango, Aug. 30, 1952 (div. 1969). Editor program book CBS, 1936-39; asst. editor Harcourt Brace & Co., 1940-47, editor-in-chief, 1948-55; v.p., editor-in-chief, dir. Farrar, Straus & Giroux, Inc., 1955—. Mem., bd. dirs. Nat. Bd. Rev. Motion Pictures 1935—. Served as lt. comdr. USNR, 1942-45. Mem. Phi Beta Kappa, Phi Beta Kappa Assos. Clubs: Metropolitan Opera, Players. Home: 219 E 66th St New York City NY 10021 Office: 19 Union Sq W New York City NY 10003

GIROUX, ROBERT J., coll. pres.; b. Burlington, Vt., Mar. 25, 1931; s. Abel A. and Aline R. (Choiniere) G.; A.B., M.A., St. Michael's Coll., Winooski, Vt.; Ph.D., U. Ottawa, Can., 1961; m. Anne E. McSheehy, Aug. 18, 1956; children—Robert Fix, Mary Elizabeth, Thomas More, John Fisher, Edmund Rich, Angela Grace, Anne Christine, Martine Avel. Tchr., Colchester (Vt.) Union Sch., 1954-55; tchr. West Av. Sch., Norwal, Conn., 1955-56; tchr. Locust Valley High Sch., N.Y.C., 1956-62; pres. St. Michaels Coll., Dubuque, Ia., 1961—; columnist Vt. Cath. Tribue, 1967—. Mem. N.E.A., Nat. Cath. Edn. Assn., Am. Ass. Ind. Colls. and Univ. Presidents. Home: 1105 Highland Pl Dubuque IA Office: 1550 Clarke Dr Dubuque IA 52001

GIRTON, RAYMOND ELWOOD, plant physiologist; b. Newton, Ia., Sept. 9, 1899; s. William Elwood and Marie M. (Reinmuth) G.; B.S., U. Cal., 1922, Ph.D., 1926, postgrad. 1939- 40; postgrad. U. Chgo., summer 1926, Cambridge U., 1926-27, summer 1963, Boyce Thompson Inst., 1927-28, Harvard, summer 1933, Oxford U., 1949-50, NRC fellow, 1926-28, Internat. Edn. Bd. fellow, 1926-27, Melbourne, Australia, 1959-60, Imperial Coll., London, Eng., spring 1960; m. Dorothea Emma Bannister, May 8, 1926; children—John Elwood, Barbara June, Judith Anne. Research asst. U. Cal., 1922-26, research asso., 1939-40; asst. prof. plant physiology Purdue U., 1928-34, asso. prof., 1934-37, prof., 1937-66, prof. emeritus, 1966—; research asso. U. Cal. at Berkeley, 1965—. Served with USNR, 1918-21. Fellow A.A.A.S., Ind. Acad. Sci. (pres. 1956); mem. Am. Soc. Plant Physiologists (nat. exec. com. mem., chmn. Purdue sect. 1930, 40, 46), Bot. Soc. Am., Am. Assn. U. Profs., Berkeley Fellowship of Unitarians, Sigma Xi. Club: Univ. California Faculty (Berkeley). Contbr. articles to sci. jours. Home: 908 Shevlin Dr El Cerrito CA 94530 Office: Dept Soils and Plant Nutrition U Cal Berkeley CA 94720

GIRTON, RICHARD ALEXANDER, constrn. co. exec.; b Sioux Falls, S.D., Feb. 1, 1914; s. William W. and Florence (Sullivan) G.; student U. Cal. at Los Angeles, 1935, Harvard, 1955; m. Dorothea Anderson, Feb. 1, 1941; children—Richard Alexander II, Heidi Ann. With Peat, Marwick, Mitchell & Co., C.P.A.'s, 1935; purchasing agt. Castle & Cooke, Ltd., 1936-44; sec.-treas. Merchandise Mart, Honolulu, 1945-48; v.p., mgr. Dillingham Bros. 1949-57; v.p., real estate broker Hawaiian Property Mgmt. Co., Honolulu, 1949-57; v.p., treas., dir. Oahu Ry. & Land Co., 1957-61; v.p., dir. Dillingham Corp., Honolulu, 1961—. Past v.p. Hawaii Employers Council. Bd. dirs. Jr. Achievement, Friends of East-West Center. Served with USNR, 1936-40. Mem. Beta Theta Pi, Alpha Kappa Psi. Club: Pacific (past sec., gov.). Home: 539 Hakaka Pl Honolulu HI 96815 Office: 1441 Kapiolani Blvd Honolulu HI 96801

GIRVETZ, HARRY KENNETH, educator, philosopher; b. Jeannette, Pa., Feb. 17, 1910; s. Jacob and Freda (Silver) S.; A.B., Stanford, 1931, M.A., 1933; Ph.D., U. Cal. at Berkeley, 1937; m. Bertha Wise, July 3, 1931; children—William Basil, Jon Eric. Faculty, U. Cal. at Santa Barbara, 1944—, prof. philosophy, 1952—, chmn. dept., 1958-64; research sec. to gov. Cal., 1959-60. Vice-pres. Santa Barbara County Citizens Planning Assn., 1961- -. Mem. Cal. Dem. Central Com., 1948, Santa Barbara County Dem. Central Com., 1939—. Mem. Am. Philos. Assn., Am. Assn. U. Profs., Am. Polit. Sci. Assn. Author: From Wealth to Welfare, 1950; Evolution of Liberalism, 1962. Editor: Contemporary Moral Issues, 1963; Literature and the Arts-The Moral Issues, 1971. Editor, contbr.: Science, Folklore and Philosophy, 1965; Democracy and Elitism, 1966. Home: 242 Las Alturas Rd Santa Barbara CA 93106

GIRVIN, EB CARL, educator; b. Georgetown, Tex., Dec. 27, 1917; s. Fitzhugh Bryson and Meta (Perlitz) G.; B.A., U. Tex., 1940, M.A., 1941, Ph.D., 1948; m. Virginia Lessor, Aug. 29, 1944; chilren—John Lessor, Eric Reed, Stacey Virginia. Prof. biology Millsaps Coll., 1948-53; prof. biology, head dept. Southwestern U., Georgetown, 1953—. Mem. Tex. Bd. Examiners Basic Sci., 1960—. Mem. div. coll. work Episcopal Diocese Tex., 1962- 65. Served to lt. comdr. USNR, 1941-45. Mem. Tex. Acad. Sci. (bd. dirs.), A.A.A.S., Sigma Xi. Contbr. articles to profl. jours. Home: 1256 Main St Georgetown TX 78626

GISCARD D'ESTAING, EDMOND, business exec.; b. Clermont-Ferrand, Puy-de-Dme, France, Mar. 29, 1894; s. Valéry and Louise (Monteil-Ansaldi) G. d'E.; ed. Faculté des lettres de Clermont-Ferrand, also Faculté de Droit de Paris; m. May Bardoux, Apr. 18, 1923; children—Sylvie (Contesse de Las Cases), Valéry Olivier, Isabelle (Comtesse de Lasteyrie du Saillant), Marie-Laure (Comtesse de Froissard de Broissia). Insp. of finances, 1919; French financial dir. Interallied High Commn. in Rhenish Territories, 1921; financial attaché to Germany, 1926; entered bus. career, 1929; pres. Société Financière pour la France et les Pays d'Outre-Mer; adminstr. Compagnie Thomson-Houston, Air France, Kleber Colombes, Compagnie Industrielle Maritime, Carbone Lorraine, others. Pres. d'Honneur Internat. C. of C., d'Honneur Secours Catholique. Mayor of Chanonat, Puy-de-Dme, 1935-46; dep. du Puy-de-Dme, ministre des Finances; dep. des. Alpes Maritimes. Served as lt., arty., French Army, 1914-18. Decorated grand officer Legion of Honor (France); comdr. Dannebrog, St. Grégoire le Grand, Crown of Belgium, officer Order Saints Maurice and Lazare (Italy), comdr. du Merite Italien, Croix de Guerre, chevalier de Malta; Orde d'Isabelle la Catholique (Spain). Author: Capitalisme, 1930; Essai de Pathologie Monétaire,

1933; Le Chemin de la Pauvreté, 1947; La France et l'Unification de l'Europe, 1953; Les Finances, Terre Inconnue, 1959. Mem. de l'Institut (Academie des Scis. Morales et Politiques). Home: 101 av Henri Martin Paris XVI France also Chteau de Varvasse Chanonat Puy-de-D#87ome France Office: 23 rue de l'Amiral d'Estaing Paris XVIe France

GISCHEL, CLYDE STOLL, mfg. co. exec.; b. Balt., Feb. 27, 1913; s. Frank William and Vera (Stoll) G.; student Johns Hopkins, 1930-31; B.S. in Elec. Engring., Carnegie Inst. Tech., 1935; m. Kathlyn M. McCaslin, May 15, 1937; children—Judith Stoll (Mrs. George Stanley, Jr.), Gary Caston. Tire sales mgr. Firestone Tire & Rubber Co., 1935-52; gen. consumer products mgr. Westinghouse Electric Supply Co., 1952-56; v.p. marketing Stanley Works, New Britain, Conn., 1956-64, v.p. constrn. components divs., 1964- -; dir. Rowland Products Co. Recipient certificate Appreciation, Council Internat. Progress Mgmt., 1961. Mem. Am. Mgmt. Assn., Sales Execs. Club, Delta Tau Delta. Home: White Oak Rd Farmington CT 06032 Office: 195 Lake St New Britain CT 06052

GISEL, WILLIAM GEORGE, corp. exec.; b. Jamestown, N.Y., Mar. 9, 1916; s. Otto E. and Emma (Koehl) G.; student U. Miami (Fla.), 1933-35; B.S., Miami U., Oxford, O., 1937; m. Katherine Lee, Nov. 25, 1944; children—Sarah L. (Mrs. William M. Green), Barbara K., William George. Salesman, Goodyear Tire & Rubber Co., Jamestown, 1937-39; with Bank of Jamestown (N.Y.), 1939-40; supr. payroll Bell Aircraft Corp., Buffalo, 1940-44, chief wage, salary control, 1944- 45, staff asst. to comptroller, 1945-48, chief accountant, 1948-52, chief accounting officer, 1952, comptroller, 1952-56, sec., 1954-57, treas., 1956-57, v.p., 1957-60, acting gen. mgr., 1959, gen. mgr., 1960- -; with Bell Aerosystems Co. (formerly Niagara Frontier div. Bell Aircraft Corp.), Wheatfield, N.Y., 1940—, pres., 1960—, (now Bell Aerospace Co. div. Textron Inc. 1970); dir. Marine Midland Trust Co. Western N.Y., Niagara Falls Gateway to Am. Corp.; trustee Western Savs. Bank Buffalo. Council mem. at large Boy Scouts Am.; adv. council Advancement Indsl. Research and Devel.; vice chmn. Niagara Frontier Transp. Authority. Bd. Dirs. Asso. Industries N.Y., Western N.Y. Nuclear Research Center, Western N.Y. Citizens Traffic Safety Council; adv. com. Children's Hosp., Buffalo Fine Arts Acad. Mem. Air Force Assn., Am. Mgmt. Assn., Assn. U.S. Army, Nat. Security Indsl. Assn., Am. Ordnance Assn., Nat. Aviation Club, Nat. Def. Transp. Assn., Buffalo Area, Niagara Falls chambers commerce, Navy League (adv. council), Nat. Aviation Hall Fame, U.S. Naval Inst., C. of C. Clubs: Aero (bd. dirs.) Country (pres.), Buffalo (Buffalo); National Space; Cherry Hill, Saturn; Buffalo Tennis and Squash; National Aviation; Port Colborne. Home: 58 Rumsey Rd Buffalo NY 14209 Office: Bell Aerospace Co PO Box 1 Buffalo NY 14240

GISH, LILLIAN, actress; b. Springfield, O.; d. James Lee and Mary (Robinson) G.; A.F.D., Rollins Coll.; H.H.D., Mt. Holyoke Coll. Debut on stage at 5; appeared in motion pictures 1914—, including: Birth of a Nation; Hearts of the World; Broken Blossoms; Way Down East; Orphans of the Storm; The White Sister; Romola; La Boheme; Scarlet Letter; Annie Laurie; The Wind; The Enemy; The Night of the Hunter; The Cobweb; Miss Susie Slagle's; Duel in the Sun; Portrait of Jennis; Orders to Kill; The Unforgiven, 1960; Follow Me Boys, 1966; The Comedians, 1967; in the theatre, 1930—, Uncle Vanja; Camille; 9 Pine Street; Within the Gates; Ophelia in Hamlet; Star Wagon; Life with Father; The Marquise; Legend of Leonora; Crime and Punishment, 1948; title role in Miss Mabel, 1950, The Curious Savage, 1950; The Trip to Bountiful; Portrait of a Madonna; The Wreck of the 5:25; The Family Reunion; (Pulitzer Prize play) All the Way Home, 1960-61; nurse in Romeo and Juliet, 1965; Anya, 1966; I Never Sang For My Father, 1967, 68; also many TV plays: Too True To Be Good, 1963; A Passage to India, 1963; Arsenic and Old Lace. Lectr. in Europe. Author: The Movies, Mr. Griffith and Me. Address: 430 E 57th St New York City NY 10022

GISH, NORMAN RICHARD, forest products exec.; b. Eckville, Alta., Can., Oct. 13, 1935; s. Robert Bruce and Lillian (Foster) G.; B.A., U. Alta., 1957; LL.B., U. B.C., 1960; m. Joan Ann Thompson, Sept. 5, 1959; children—David Cole, Carolyn Nancy, Graeme Christopher. Asst. trade commr. Fgn. Trade Service of Canadian Govt., Ottawa, 1961-62, Hong Kong, 1962-65; asst. to sec. B.C. Forest Products, Ltd., Vancouver, 1967, v.p., sec., 1967—. Mem. Law Soc. B.C., Canadian Bar Assn., Canadian Inst. Internat. Affairs. Clubs: Canadian, University (Vancouver). Home: 6769 Wiltshire St Vancouver British Columbia Canada Office: 1190 Melville St Vancouver British Columbia Canada

GISLASON, SIDNEY PAYSON, lawyer; b. Minnesota, Minn., May 22, 1908; s. Bjorn B. and Joan (Peterson) G.; LL.B., U. Minn., 1935; m. Marjorie L. Fleck, Sept. 17, 1938; children—James H., Daniel A., Marion F. Admitted to Minn. bar, 1935; asst. county atty. Brown Co., 1936-42, county atty., 1942; city atty., New Ulm. Minn., 1946-50; dist. judge 9th Minn. Dist., 1950-51; lectr. legal trial techniques. Govt. appeal agt. SSS, 1941—; chmn. 85th Dist. War Finance, 1946—; mem. faculty Law Sci. Inst.; chancellor Law-Sci. Found., 1957—. Chmn. Little Crow dist. Boy Scouts Am., 1950-54; mem. Minn. Coll. Bd., 1967—; mem. Minn. Higher Edn. Coordinating Com., 1969-. Mem. Am., (ho. delegates 1954- 57), Minn. (chmn. ct. rules com.; bd. govs. 1951-, v.p. 1953, pres. 1954-55) bar assns., Am. Coll. Trial Lawyers, Internat. Acad. Trial Lawyers (dir. 1956—, pres. 1959). Mason (Shriner). Home: 600 Summitt Av New Ulm MN 56073 Office: State and Center Sts New Ulm MN 56073

GIST, NOEL PITTS, educator, sociologist; b. Hermitage, Mo., June 17, 1899; s. Ruzan and Lucy Josephine (Pitts) G.; B.S., Kan. State Tchrs. Coll., 1923; A.M., U. Kan., 1929; Ph.D., Northwestern U., 1935; postgrad. U. Chgo., summer 1929, Geneva Sch. Internat. Studies, summer 1925; m. Mabel Wilks, Dec. 24, 1923; children—Ronald Ralph, Patricia Jane. Instr., asst. prof. sociology U. Kan., 1929-31, 32-37; successively asst. prof., asso. prof., prof. sociology U. Mo., Columbia, 1937-44, 45—. Vis. lectr. U. Wis., 1944-45; sometime vis. prof. various univ. and coll. summer schs.; research in sociology, India, with U.S. Ednl. Found., 1951-52; lectr. sociology Sociologische Instituut, Netherlands, 1958-59, U. Calcutta, U.S. Ednl. Found. in India, 1963-64; sr. specialist Inst. Advanced Projects, E.-W. Center, Honolulu, 1968-69. Served with USNRF, 1918-19. Mem. Am. (exec. com. 1945-48), Mid-West (pres. 1938-39) social. socs., Am. Assn. U. Profs., Alpha Pi Zeta, Alpha Kappa Delta, Kappa Delta Pi. Club: University (Columbia). Author: Secret Societies: A Cultural Study of Fraternalism in the United States, 1940; co-author: Urban Society, 1964; Selective Factors in Migration and Occupation, 1943. Home: 705 Crestland Rd Columbia MO 65201

GISVOLD, OLE, educator; b. Stanley, Wis., Sept. 24, 1904; s. John and Mary (Lee) G.; Ph.G., U. Wis., 1926, B.S., 1930, M.S., 1932, Ph.D., 1934; m. Evelyn L. Nelson, Feb. 14, 1929; children—Darrell Ivan, Roland Donald, Nancy Lou. Jr. biochemist Forest Products Lab., Madison, Wis., 1934-35; instr. pharm. chemistry U. Minn. Coll. Pharmacy, Mpls., 1935-38, asst. prof., 1938- 70, prof., 1940—, head dept. pharm. chemistry 1941—; prof. Ohio State U., 1940-41. Recipient Ebert Prize medal, 1942, 52; Outstanding Achievement award U. Wis., 1967. Mem. Am. (Research Achievement award 1962, chmn. com. pharm. research 1951-53, chmn. sci. sect. 1952-53), Minn. pharm. assns., Am. Chem. Soc., Am. Assn. U. Profs., A.A.A.S., Am. Assn. Colls. Pharmacy (chmn. sect. grad instrn.), Sigma Xi, Rho Chi, Phi Sigma, Phi Delta Chi. Lutheran (chmn. ch. bd. trustees). Author: The Chemistry of Plant Constituents (with C.H. Rogers, rev. edit.), 1943. Co-author, co-editor: Textbook of Organic Medicinal and Pharmaceutical Chemistry, 5th edit., 1966, 6th edit., 1971. Contbr. articles to profl. jours. Patentee prodn. drugs from plants, synthesis of drugs. Home: 2161 Dudley Av St Paul MN 55108 Office: U Minn Minneapolis MN 55455

GITHENS, JOHN HORACE, Jr., physician, educator; b Woodbury, N.J., Jan. 2, 1922; s. John Horace and Gladys (Jones) G.; B.A., Swarthmore Coll., 1944; M.D., Temple U., 1945; m. Virginia R. Freeman, Mar. 29, 1945; children—James S., Wendy M. Intern, Abington (Pa.) Meml. Hosp., 1945-46; resident pediatrics Phila. Children's Hosp., 1948-50, U. Colo. Med. Center, 1950-51; from instr. to asso. prof. pediatrics U. Colo., 1951-60; asso. dir. gen. med. clinic Denver Gen. Hosp., 1952-57; asst. dir. Rheumatic Fever Diagnostic Clinic, Denver, 1951-53; prof. pediatrics, chmn. dept. U. Ky. Med. Center, 1960-63; prof. pediatrics U. Colo. Med. Center, Denver, 1963—, asso. dean U. Colo. Sch. Medicine, 1964—. Served to lt. (j.g.) USNR, 1946-48. Diplomate Am. Bd. Pediatrics. Fellow Am. Acad. Pediatrics; mem. Soc. Pediatric Research, A.M.A., Western Soc. Pediatric Research (1st Ross award 1957), Soc. Cryobiology, Transplantation Soc., Am. Pediatric Soc., Am. Fedn. Clin. Research. Co- author: Teaching Comprehensive Medical Care: a Psychological Study of a Change in Medical Education, 1959. Contbr. articles to profl. jours. Home: 4200 E 9th Av Denver CO 80220

GITHENS, SHERWOOD, Jr., physicist; b. Phila., Oct. 31, 1908; s. Sherwood and Charlotte (Fretz) G.; A.B., Bucknell U., 1931; A.M., U. N.C., 1933, Ph.D., 1936; postgrad. Princeton, 1933-34; m. Nancy Elizabeth Coates, July 15, 1939 (dec. Dec. 1968); children—Sherwood, Nancy Lassiter (Mrs. Philip S. Washburn), Janet (Mrs. William K. Miller), John Dexter; m. 2d, Elizabeth Majors Smith, Sept. 3, 1969; stepchildren—Sarah (Mrs. Jimmy R. Randles), Ellen Cary Smith. Teaching fellow physics U. N.C., 1931-33, 1934-36; instr. Wake Forest Coll., 1936-37, asst. prof., 1937-41; instr. aircraft elec. systems Air Corps Tech. Sch., Chanute Field, Ill., 1941; asst. chief instr. Air Corps Tech. Sch., Sheppard Field, Tex., 1941-42; lectr. electronics Harvard, 1942-45, instr. communication engring., 1945-46; physicist Johns Hopkins Applied Physics Lab., Silver Spring, Md., 1946-49; chmn. dept. physics Baylor U., 1949-52; dir. phys. scis. div. U.S. Army Office Ordnance Research, Duke, Durham, N.C., 1952-58, dir. Internal Research div., 1958-59, dep. chief scientist, 1959-62, prof. sci. edn. Duke, 1962—. Spl. lectr. N.C. State, 1955, 56-57, NSF Summer Inst., Baylor U., 1957, Duke, 1958-59. Councilman, City Takoma Park, Md., 1947-49. Mem. Am. Phys. Soc., Am. Assn. Physics Tchrs., Sigma Xi, Pi Mu Epsilon, Tau Kappa Epsilon. Author: (with Cruft Electronics staff) Electronic Circuits and Tubes, 1947. Contbr. articles to physics jours. Home: 4427 Chapel Hill Rd Durham NC 27707

GITLER, ROBERT LAURENCE, librarian, educator; b. N.Y.C., May 1, 1909; s. Abraham and Frances Rita (Burnett) G.; A.B., U. Calif., 1930, grad. certificate in librarianship, Sch. Librarianship, 1931; M.S., Sch. of Library Service, Columbia, 1939; Ph.D., (hon.). Keio U., 1956. Asst., U. Cal. Library at Berkeley, 1927-30, teaching asst., dept. pub. speaking, 1930-31; circulation librarian San Jose (Cal.) State Coll., 1931-36, sr. librarian, instr. in librarianship, 1936-42; reference, research asst., Columbia U. Libraries, 1939, vis. prof. Sch. Library Service, summers, 1946-47; dir., asso. prof. U. Wash. Sch. Librarianship, 1946-53, on leave as dir. Japan Library Sch., Keio U., Tokyo, (Rockefeller Found. A.L.A.), 1951-56; exec. sec. library edn. div. sec. com. on accreditation, cons. Japan Library Sch., A.L.A., 1956-59, vis. prof., cons., 1961; dir. div. library edn. N.Y. State U. Coll., Geneseo, 1962-64; dir., prof. Peabody Library Sch., George Peabody Coll., Nashville, 1964-67; univ. librarian, prof. U. San Francisco, 1967—. Mem. library planning com. Internat. House Japan; library edn. standards com. Univ. Accrediting Assn. Japan. Vice-pres. Clarion Male Chorus, 1949; pres., 1949-51. Served to lt. comdr. USNR, 1942-46. Recipient Beta Phi Mu-A.L.A. award, 1961; Order of the Rising Sun, 4th award of Merit (Japan). Mem. A.L.A. (chmn. Jr. mems. round table 1942, pres. edn. div. 1971-72), Japan, Cal. (pres. Jr. mems. 1936, chmn. coll. and univ. sect. 1941, pres. Golden Gate dist. 1969), Pacific N.W. (mem. salaries, staff, tenure coms. 1947) library assns., Wash. State Certification Bd., Librarians Assn. Am. Library Schs. (exec. bd. 1947-49), Am. Assn. U. Profs., Assn. Coll. and Research Libraries, Spl. Libraries Assn. (chmn. recruiting com. Puget Sound 1948-49). Club: Roxburgh (San Francisco). Contbr. articles to coll., research libraries, Wilson Bull., A.L.A. bull., Japanese library periodicals. Home: 222 Willard N San Francisco CA 94118 Office: Gleeson Library U San Francisco San Francisco CA 94117

GITLIS, IVRY, violinist; b. Haifa, Palestine, 1922; ed. Nat. Conservatory, Paris; studied with Carl Flesch, Georges Enesco, also Jacques Thibaud; m. Paule Deglon. Performed numerous European countries, also Eng., appearing as soloist prin. symphony orchs.; performances include concertos, sonatas, modern and chamber music. Address: Recordings Div Dover Publications Inc 180 Varick St New York City NY 10014

GITLOW, ABRAHAM LEO, univ. dean; b. N.Y.C., Oct. 10, 1918; s. Samuel and Esther (Boolhack) G.; B.A., U. Pa., 1939; M.A., Columbia, 1940, Ph.D., 1947; m. Beatrice Alpert, Dec. 12, 1940; children—Allan Michael, Howard Seth. Substitute instr. Bklyn. Coll., 1946-47; instr. N.Y.U., N.Y.C., 1947-50, asst. prof., 1950-54, asso. prof., 1954-59; prof. econs., 1959—, acting dean Sch. Commerce, 1965-66, dean, 1966—. Vice pres. Servi-Clean Industries, Inc., Youngstown, O., 1970—; dir. J.W. Mays, Inc. Pres. bd. edn. Ramapo Central Sch. Dist. 2, 1963-66. Vice pres., sec. Samuel and Esther Gitlow Found., N.Y.C. Served to 1st lt. USAAF, 1943-46; PTO. Mem. Am. Arbitration Assn. (mem. nat. panel 1948—), Am. Econ. Assn., Royal Econ. Soc., Indsl. Relations Research Assn., Acad. Polit. Sci. Author: Economics, 1962; Labor and Manpower Economics, 1971. Co-editor: General Economics: A Book of Readings, 1963. Contbr. articles profl. jours. Home: 211 Old Nyack Turnpike Spring Valley NY 10977 Office: NYU Washington Sq Sch Commerce New York City NY 10003

GITT, CHARLES MOUL, editor; b. Hanover, Pa., Mar. 12, 1915; s. Josiah W. and Elizabeth (Moul) G.; grad. Gunnery Sch., 1934; A.B., Harvard, 1938; m. Laverne Garland, July 7, 1945; children—Cynthia, Peggy Ann, Stephen. With Gazette & Daily, York, Pa., 1938-70, pres., exec. editor, 1943-70, cons. York Daily Record, 1970—. Club: Lancaster (Pa.) Country. Home: 932 S Beaver St York PA 17403 Office: 31 E King St York PA 17405

GITT, JOSIAH WILLIAM ret. editor, pub.; b. Hanover, Pa., Mar. 28, 1884; s. Clinton Jacob and Emma (Koplin) G.; A.B., Franklin and Marshall Coll., 1904; postgrad. U. Pa., 1904- 05; m. Elizabeth Moul, June 12, 1913; children—Charles M., Eleanor (Mrs. George Taylor), Marian (Mrs. Michael B. Rebert), Susan Elizabeth (Mrs. Edmund Gordon). Admitted to Pa. bar, 1908, practiced in York, 1908-15; editor and pub. York (Pa.) Gazette and Daily, 1915-70. Democrat. Unitarian. Home: RD 5 Hanover PA 17331

GITTELSOHN, ROLAND BERTRAM, rabbi; b. Cleve., May 13, 1910; s. Reuben and Anna (Manheim) G.; B.A., Western Res. U., 1931; B.H., Hebrew Union Coll., 1934, D.D., 1961; Sc.D., Lowell Technol. Inst., 1961; m. Ruth Freyer, Sept. 25, 1932; children—Davd, Judith (Mrs. Richard A. Levine). Ordained rabbi, 1936; rabbi Central Synagogue Nassau County, 1936-53, Temple Israel, Boston, 1953—. Pres., Mass. Bd. Rabis, 1958-60, Jewish Community Council Met. Boston, 1961-63; mem. exec. bd. Central Conf. Am. Rabbis, 1949-51, chmn. placement com., 1949-52, chmn. Commn. on Justice and Peace, 1950-54, v.p., 1967-69, pres., 1969-71. Mem. Pres. Truman's Com. on Civil Rights, 1947; mem. Gov.'s Commn. to Survey Mass. Cts., 1955, Mass. Commn. on Abolition Death Penalty, 1957-58, Gov.'s Com. on Migratory Labor, 1960-62, Gov.'s Com. to Survey Operation Mass. Prisons, 1961-62. Served to lt. USNR, 1943-46. Mem. Union Am. Hebrew Congregations (trustee, chmn. Commn. Jewish Edn.), Phi Beta Kappa. Author: Modern Jewish Problems, 1943; Little Lower Than The Angels, 1954; Man's Best Hope, 1961; Consecrated Unto Me: A Jewish View of Love and Marriage, 1965; My Beloved Is Mine, 1969; Wings of the Morning, 1969; Fire in My Bones, 1969; The Meaning of Judaism, 1970. Home: Jamaicaway Tower Boston MA 02130 Office: Temple Israel Boston MA 02215

GITTENS, EDMUND DONALD, electronics industry exec.; b. Bklyn., Sept. 21, 1913; s. Edmund J. and Mae (Dunn) G.; B.S., Mass. Inst. Tech., 1935; grad. Harvard Advanced Mgmt. Program, 1963; m. Josephine W. Bokros, Sept. 9, 1939; children—Barbara, David. With Arma div. Am. Bosch Arma Corp., Garden City, N.Y., 1935—, v.p., div. mgr., 1957-62, v.p. govt. operations, exec. v.p. Am. Bosch Arma Corp., 1962-70, group v.p. AMBAC Industries, Inc., 1970—; pres. Mystic Oceanographic Co. Mem. L.I. Fund, 1959—; Mem. I.E.E.E., Nat. Security Indsl. Assn., Am. Ordnance Assn., Am. Mgmt. Assn., Am. Soc. Naval Engrs., Air Force Assn., L.I. Assn., Am. Inst. Aeros. and Astronautics, U.S. Naval Inst., Airline Avionics Inst. (dir.) Inst. Nav. Home: 10 The Spur Flower Hill Port Washington NY 11050 Office: 900 Old Country Rd Roosevelt Field Garden City NY 11530

GITTINGS, ROBERT WILLIAM VICTOR, author; b. Portsmouth, Eng., Feb. 1, 1911; s. Fred Claude Bromley and Dora (Brayshaw) G.; M.A., Jesus Coll., Cambridge (Eng.) U., 1936; m. Joan Grenville Manton, Jan. 8, 1948; children—Robert George Bromley, John. Clare St. Quentin. Research fellow, supr. history Jesus Coll., 1935-40; producer, scriptwriter BBC, London, 1940-63; ind. author, lectr., 1963—; vis. prof. English lit. Vanderbilt U., 1966, Boston U., 1970. Recipient Phoenix Trust award, 1963; Leverhulme Research award, 1964. Fellow Royal Soc. Lit.; mem. Keats-Shelley Meml. Assn. Gt. Britain. Author: John Keats: The Living Year, 1954; John Keats, 1968; also numerous others. Home: Dodds East Dean Chichester Sussex England

GITTINS, BERT STEVENS, advt. exec.; b. Griswold, Ia., June 6, 1905; s. Thomas and Beatrice Mary (Stevens) G.; B.S. in Agr., Ia. State Coll., 1926; m. Gretchen G. Steensen, June 18, 1938; 1 dau., Jane Agnes. Trainee, salesman Armour & Co., Chgo., 1926-28; research, publicity man Nat. Assn. Farm Equipment Mfrs., Chgo., 1928-29; copywriter Freeze-Vogel-Crawford, Inc., Milw., 1929-35; owner Bert S. Gittins, advt., Milw., 1935-55; pres. Bert S. Gittins Advt., Inc., Milw., 1955-62, Gittins Assos., Inc., Milw., 1962—; sec.-treas. Twin Pines Stock Farm, Inc., Griswold. Bd. dirs., mem. exec. com. Jr. Achievement S.E. Wis., 1955-62, nat. bd. dirs., 1960-63, recipient Raymond E. Brooks Meml. award S.E. Wis., 1961. Recipient Civic Service award Eagles, 1952. Mem. Advt. Fedn. Am. (v.p. 1954- 56), Milw. Advt. Club (pres. 1951-52), Milw. Farmers (pres. 1954- 55), Ia. State U. Coll. Alumni Assn. (Centennial award 1958, pres. Milw. 1941-42), Friends of Land (pres. S.E. Wis. 1950-51), Cardinal Key (Ia. State U.), Tau Kappa Epsilon, Phi Kappa Phi, Sigma Delta Chi, Alpha Zeta, Gamma Sigma Delta, Sigma Upsilon. Club: Milwaukee Athletic. Author: Lane of Plenty 1950. Contbr. articles to profl. jours. Address: 405 7th St Griswold IA 51535

GITTLER, JOSEPH BERTRAM, univ. dean; b. N.Y.C., Sept. 21, 1912; s. Morris and Toby (Rosenblatt) G.; B.S., U. Ga., 1934, M.A., 1936; Ph.D., U. Chgo., 1941; m. Lami Shapiro, June 28, 1934 (dec. 1966); 1 dau., Josephine; m. 2d, Susan Wolters, Sept. 15, 1968. From instr. to asso. prof. sociology U. Ga., 1936-43; research asso. Va. Planning Bd., 1942-43; research asso. U. Chgo., 1944; prof. sociology Ia. State U., 1945-54; prof. sociology, chmn. dept., dir. Center Study Group Operations, U. Rochester, 1954-61; dean faculty, prof. social scis. Queensborough Coll., City U. N.Y., 1961- 66; prof. sociology, dean Ferkauf Grad. Sch. Humnities and Social Scis., Yeshiva U., N.Y.C., 1966—. Cons. in field, 1940—. Mem. Rochester council N.Y. State Commn. Against Discrimination, 1955-60; chmn. regional selection com. Woodrow Wilson Fellowship Found., 1955-58; co-chmn. Brotherhood Week edn. com. Nat. Conf. Christians and Jews, 1950; council fellows Upland Inst., 1965—. Recipient Walter B. Hill prize philosophy U. Ga., 1934. Mem. Am. Sociol. Assn., N.Y. Acad. Scis., P.E.N., Eastern Sociol. Soc., Assn. for Higher Edn., Am. Assn. Acad. Deans, Phi Beta Kappa. Author: Social Thought Among the Early Greeks, 1940; Virginia's People, 1944; Social Dynamics, 1952; Review of Sociology, 1957; Understanding Minority Groups, 1964. Contbr. articles to profl. jours. Home: 55 Fifth Av New York City NY 10003

GITTLIN, A. SAM, industrialist, banker; b. Newark, Nov. 9, 1914; s. Benjamin and Ethel (Bernstein) G.; B.C.S., Rutgers U., 1938; m. Fay Lerner, Sept. 18, 1938; children—Carol (Mrs.. Alan H. Franklin), Regina (Mrs. Peter Gross), Bruce David, Steven Robert. Partner, Gittlin Bag Co., Newark, Charlotte, N.C., 1935-40, v.p., dir., 1954—, chmn. bd., 1963—; v.p., dir. Abbey Record Mfg. Co., West Newark, N.J., 1958-60; partner Benjamin Mission Co., Los Angeles, 1960-64; chief exec. officer Bishop Industries, Inc., chmn. Vida Bag Co., Glendale, Cal., 1969—; chmn. bd. of Barrington Industries, Inc., Covington Funding Co., Pines Shirt & Pajama Co., Inc., Aptex, Inc., Levin & Hecht, Inc., Barnes & Goldsmith, Brunswick Shirt Co. (all N.Y.C.), Berwirck (Pa.) Shirt Co., Fleetline Industries, Garland, N.C., also Wallco Imperial (Miami, Fla.), Pottsville (Pa.) Pines Shirt & Pajama Co., Inc., Packaging Products & Design Corp. (Newark), All State Auto Leasing & Rental Co., Beverly Hills; vice chmn. bd., chmn. exec. com. Peninsula Savs. & Loan Assn. (San Mateo, Cal.); past pres., dir. Falmouth Supply, Ltd. (Montreal, Can.), Ascher Trading Corp.; exec. v.p., dir., chmn. bd. Wallcoverings by Zins, Inc. (Milburn, N.J.), Zins Wallcoverings, Inc. (Newark); sec., chmn. exec. com., dir. First Peninsula Cal. Corp. (N.Y.C.); partner Benjamin Co. (N.Y.C.); investors cons., partner Mission Pak, Inc. (Los Angeles); dir., financial cons. Ramada Inns, Inc. (Phoenix), Realty Equities Corp. (N.Y.C.). N.C. chmn. Hillel Com. B'nai B'rith, 1940; treas. N.C. Fedn. B'nai B'rith Lodges, 1941-43, v.p., 1943- 44, pres., 1944-47; commr. N.J. Com. Efficiency and Economy in State Govt., 1964—. Trustee Benjamin Gittlin Charity Found., Newark, Hillel Found. at Rutgers U. Jewish religion (pres., trustee, chmn. bd. temples, Abraham, N.J., Charlotte). Club: Greenbrook Country (North Caldwell, N.J.). Home: 59 Glenview Rd South Orange NJ 07079 Office: 666 Fifth Av New York City NY 10022

GIUFFRE, JAMES PETER, (Jimmy Giuffre), saxophonist, clarinetist, arranger; b. Dallas, Apr. 26, 1921; Mus.B., No. Tex. State Tchrs. Coll., 1942; student U. So. Cal., 1946. Clarinetist, tenor saxophonist with Ofcl. Air Force Orch., 1944; tenor, Porgy and Bess,

Dallas Symphony, 1946; with Boyd Raeburn, then J. Dorsey, 1947, Buddy Rich, 1948, Woody Herman, 1949, Garwood Van and Spade Cooley, 1950. Lighthouse All Stars, 1951-52, Shorty Rogers' Giants; appeared in motion picture Glass Wall, also shorts with Buddy Rich, Woody Herman; organized trio with guitarist Jim Hall, bassist Ralph Pena, then Jim Atlas, 1956; night club, concert appearances, also Newport Jazz Festival; faculty Sch. of Jazz, Lenox, Mass., 1957; formed trio with trombonist Bob Brookmeyer, guitarist Hall, 1957, performing chamber music., Am. folk songs, jazz. Recordings include Jimmy Guiffre Clarinet, Jimmy Guiffre 3, Music Man, The Wild One, Private Hell 36, Best from the West.*

GIULIANO, VINCENT EDWARD, educator; b. Detroit, Nov. 17, 1929; s. Edward A. and Pearl (Quello) G.; A.B. with honors in Math., U. Mich., 1952, M.S., 1956; postgrad. U. Del., 1954-55; Ph.D., Harvard, 1959; m. Lilian C. Lindenfelser, Nov. 27, 1962; children—David, Michael, Vincent, Donald, Mark, Annie. Mathematician, Gen. Motors Engring. Staff, 1953-54, Aberdeen Proving Ground, U.S. Army, 1954-56; research asso. Wayne State U. Computation Lab., 1956; sr. research asso. Harvard Computation Lab., 1956-59; mem. sr. profl. staff Arthur D. Little Inc., Cambridge, Mass., 1959-67, 71—; prof. information and library studies State U. N.Y. at Buffalo, 1967-71, dean Sch. Information and Library Scis., 1967-69, dir. Center Information Research, 1969-71; adj. prof., 1971—; faculty Harvard, 1962-65. Participant NATO Inst., 1963; founding mem. Council Communications; mem. vis. com. Lehigh U. Served with AUS, 1953-54. Mem. I.E.E.E., Am. Assn. Humanistic Psychology, Operations Research Soc. Am., A.L.A., Soc. Information Sci., Sigma Chi. Contbr. papers to profl. lit. Home: 33 Hancock St Lexington MA 02140 Office: 35 Acorn Park Cambridge MA 02140

GIULINI, CARLO MARIA, conductor; b. May 9, 1914; ed. Accademia Santa Cecilia, Rome; married, 3 sons. Played viola, Santa Cecilia Orch.; debut as conductor, Rome, 1944; organized Orch. of Milan Radio, 1951; prin. conductor, La Scala, Milan, 1953-55; debut in Gt. Britain, Edinburgh Festival, conducting Verdi's Falstaff, 1955; appearances with Philharmonia Orch., Edinburgh, Lucerne, Vienna festivals; condr. revivals of Don Carlos and Il Barbiere di Siviglia, Covent Garden, also conducted U.S., Israel, Holland. Address: care Hurok Attractions Inc 730 Fifth Av New York City NY 10017*

GIUS, JULIUS, newspaper editor; b. Fairbanks, Alaska, Dec. 31, 1911; s. Julius and Mary (Sarja) G.; student U. Puget Sound, 1930-33; m. Elizabeth Gail Alexander, Aug. 24, 1940; children—Gary Alexander, Barbara Gail. Reporter, Tacoma (Wash.) Times, 1929-35; founding editor Bremerton (Wash.) Sun, 1935-60;; editor Ventura (Cal.) Star-Free Press, also editorial dir. John P. Scripps Newspapers, 1961—. Mem. Am. Soc. Newspaper Editors, Sigma Delta Chi. Elk, K.C., Rotarian. Home: 1274 Beachmont Ventura CA 93003 Office: 567 E Santa Clara St Ventura CA 93001

GIUSTI, GEORGE, artist, designer; b. Milano, Italy, Oct. 10, 1908; s. Emil and Edmeda (Giusti) Wuermli; student Reale Accademia Di Belle Arti Di Brera (Milano), 1923-27; m. Margot Louise Reiche Joachimsthal, July 11, 1936; 1 son, Robert George. Came to U.S., 1938, naturalized, 1946. Free-lance artist, cons. to industry, editorial and advt. designer, 1931- -; exhibited at maj. capitals of world; faculty Famous Artist's Schs., Inc., Westport, Conn., 1962—. Recipient Golden medals art dirs. clubs Chgo., 1951, 56, Phila., 1954, 58, N.Y.C., 1955, Milw., 1959, others; golden T. Square award; named Art Dir. of Year, 1958. Mem. Am. Inst. Graphic Arts, Alliance Graphique Internationale, Nat. Soc. Art Dirs. Club: Art Directors (N.Y.C.). Author: The Human Heart, 1961. Home: Chalburn Rd West Redding CT also 342 E 53d St New York City NY 10022; also Chiesa Vecchia Prunarolo Di Vergato Italy

GIVAN, THURMAN BOYD, physician; b. Alexandria, Tenn., Oct. 3, 1888; s. Henry Clay and Ellen (Luck) G.; A.B., Union U., Jackson, Tenn., 1910; M.D., Vanderbilt U., 1914; m. Dorothy Jagles, June 28, 1922; children—Joan (Mrs. Herbert Kritzler), Doris, Thurman Boyd; m. 2d, Marian Klein, July 14, 1951. Intern, St. Thomas Hosp., Nashville, 1914-16; resident pediatrics L.I. Coll., Hosp., 1919-20; practice medicine, Bklyn., 1920-69; lectr. pediatrics L.I. Coll. Hosp. and Med. Sch., 1919-23, asst. clin. prof., 1925-26, clin. prof., 1927-49; clin. prof. pediatrics Downstate Med. Sch., State U. N.Y., 1950-58, clin. prof. pediatrics emeritus, 1958—. Chmn. coordinating council Five County Med. Socs. of N.Y.C., 1949- 52; mem. Gov.'s Com. to End Poliomyelitis in N.Y. State, 1957-60. Served as 1st lt. M.C., U.S. Army, 1917-19. Mem. Med. Soc. State N.Y. (chmn. sect. pediatrics 1950, council 1951-58, pres. 1957-58), A.M.A. (council constn. and by-laws 1963—, chmn., 1970—, ho. of dels 1952-68), Bklyn. Pediatric Soc. (pres. 1925), Am. (N.Y. state chmn. 1947- 53), Bklyn. (pres., founder 1932) acads. pediatrics, Med. Soc. County of Kings (pres. 1946, chmn. bd. trustees 1961-67, now hon.), Am. Assn. Med. Milk Commns. (pres. 1950), Am. Legion, Sigma Alpha Epsilon, Alpha Kappa Kappa. Rotarian, Mason. Clubs: Medical, Brooklyn, Rembrandt, Ihpetonga (Bklyn.). 11 Green Wing Teal Hilton Head Island SC 29928

GIVAN, WALKER, govt. ofcl.; b. Los Angeles, Jan. 30, 1920; s. Hiram Luther and Mae Josephine (Walker) G.; B.A., Yale, 1940, M.A., 1942, Ph.D., 1951; m. Christine Lindblom Cadigan, June 18, 1941; children—Christopher, Margaret (Mrs. Nickerson Miles), Gail. Asst. instr. history Yale, 1946-47; instr. Duke, 1947-51; research specialist State Dept., Washington, 1951-55; joined Fgn. Service, 1955; dep. prin. officer, Trieste, 1956; polit. officer, Rome, 1959, Manila, 1961; internat. relations officer, 1963-66; personnel mgmt. specialist, 1966-68; polit. officer Mission to European office UN, other internat. orgns., Geneva, 1968—. Served with AUS, 1943-46; ETO. Mem.. Phi Beta Kappa. Address: 15 Eugene Pittard Geneva Switzerland

GIVEN, BERTRAM FRANCIS, machinery co. exec.; b El Paso, Tex., July 5, 1917; s. Samuel and Rena (Appel) G.; student U. Cal. at Los Angeles; m. Naomi Grossman, Aug. 20, 1939; children—Judith, Robert, John. Vice pres. Given Machinery Co., Los Angles, 1940—; pres. Waste King Corp., Los Angles, 1946—; dir. 1st Thrift of Los Angeles. First v.p. Los Angeles Psychiat. Service. Bd. govs. Cedars-Sinai Med. Center. Mem. Young Presidents Orgn. (past chmn. Los Angeles chpt.). Clubs: Stand (Chgo.); Del Rey Yacht; Brentwood Country. Home: 1715 Westridge Rd Los Angeles CA 90049 Office: 3300 E 50th St Los Angeles CA 90058

GIVENS, JAMES WALLACE, Jr., computer scientist; b Alberene, Va., Dec. 14, 1910; s. James Wallace and Mamie (Hughes) G.; B.S. cum laude, Lynchburg Coll., 1928, D.Sc., 1965; postgrad. U. Ky., 1928-29; M.S. (DuPont fellow), U. Va., 1931; Ph.D. (J.S.K. fellow), Princeton, 1936; m. Virginia Shelton, Sept. 16, 1937 (div. Mar. 1969); children—James Wallace III, Brian Hughes, Barry Shelton; m. 2d, Monique Pavel, Feb. 16, 1970. Part-time instr. Princeton, 1935- 36; asst. Inst. Advanced Study, Princeton, 1935-37; instr. Cornell U., 1937-41; instr. Northwestern U., 1941-42, asst. prof., 1942-46, prof. math., 1960—; asso. prof. Ill. Inst. Tech., 1946-47; prof. U. Tenn., 1947-56; prof., chmn. math. dept. Wayne State U., 1956-60; sr. mathematician applied math. div. Argonne Nat. Lab., 1962—, asso. dir., 1962-64, dir., 1964-70. Cons. math. and sci. univs., labs., mfg. firms. Mem. council Conf. Bd. Math. Scis., 1969-70. Mem. Am. Math. Soc. (council 1969—), Math. Assn. Am., Assn. Computing Machinery, Soc. Indsl. and Applied Math. (pres. 1969-70), A.A.A.S. (sec. sect. 1960-68, com. on meetings 1967-69). Contbr. articles to tech. publs. Home: 419 S Cass Av Westmont IL 60559 Office: Argonne Nat Lab Applied Math Div Argonne IL 60439

GIVENS, JOHNNIE ESTHER, librarian; b. Pleasant View, Tenn., Sept. 7, 1925; d. Claude Preston and Willie Lena (Brashear) Givens; B.S., Austin Peay State U., 1946; B.S. in L.S., George Peabody Coll., 1949; A.M., U. Chgo., 1960. Asst. librarian Austin Peay State U., 1946-58, head librarian, 1958—; order librarian George Peabody Coll. Library, summer 1947; library cons. coll. and spl. libraries, 1964—. Bd. dirs. Clarksville Community Concert Assn. Mem. Am., Tenn. library assns., Nat., Tenn. edn. assns. Am. Assn. U. Profs., Assn. Coll. and Research Libraries, Kappa Delta Pi, Delta Kappa Gamma, Beta Phi Mu. Democrat. Methodist. Contbr. profl. jours. Home: 413 Locust St Springfield TN 37172 Office: Austin Peay State Univ Clarksville TN 37040

GIVENS, JOSEPH EDWIN, farmer coop. exec.; b. Newport, Va., July 8, 1910; s. James Bittle and Mary (Spessard) G.; B.S., Va. Poly. Inst., 1931; m. Beatrice Gulnare Hyde, Dec. 28, 1937; 1 dau., Jane Hyde (Mrs. W.P. Jordan, Jr.). Tchr. vocational agr. Buchanan (Va.) High Sch., 1931-35; with So. States Coop., Inc., 1935—, exec. v.p. Coop. Mills, Inc., 1946-49, dir. community services, 1949-61, asst. gen. mgr., 1961—; cons. Office Edn. div. vocational and tech. edn. Dept. Health, Edn. and Welfare; chmn. Va. Commn. Industry of Agr., 1969—. Chmn. bd. Westminster Presbyn. Homes, Inc.; mem. exec. com. Big Bros. of Richmond, 1965-68; bd. visitors Va. Poly. Inst. and State U. Mem. Nat. Council Farmer Coops. (dir.), Am. Inst. Cooperation (trustee 1962-66, vice chmn. 1966-68, chmn. 1969—), Va., Richmond chambers commerce, Gamma Sigma Delta, Alpha Zeta. Clubs: Country of Virginia, Kiwanis, Downtown (Richmond). Home: 204 Ralston Rd Richmond VA 23229 Mailing: Office: 7th and Main Sts Richmond VA 23219

GIVENS, MEREDITH BRUNER, economist; b. Des Moines, Jan. 11, 1899; s. D. Findley and Celeste (Bruner) G.; A.B., Drake U., 1920; postgrad. U. Chgo., 1920-21; fellow econs. U. Wis., 1921-22, Ph.D., 1929; m. Ruth Wheelock Ayres, Oct. 6, 1929; 1 son, Richard Ayres. Teaching asst. U. Wis., 1922-24, research asst. labor, 1924-25; research staff Nat. Bur. Econ. Research, 1925-26, 28-30; labor cons. Am. Radiator Co., 1926-27; spl. agt. U.S. Bur. Labor Statistics, 1927-28; sec. for industry and trade Social Sci. Research Council, 1929-36; lectr. Wharton Sch. Finance and Commerce, U. Pa., 1930-32; mem. adv. com. Sec. of Labor, 1933-35; mem. tech. bd. occupational research U.S. Employment Service, 1933-46; mem. Central Statis. Bd., Washington, 1933-36; exec. sec. com. on Govt. Statistics and Information Services, Washington, 1933-36; cons. Pres.'s Com. on Econ. Security, 1934, Social Security Bd., 1935; dir. indsl. studies Research and Planning Bd., N.R.A., 1935; dir. research and statistics Employment div. Dept. Labor, N.Y., 1936-59; cons. labor statistics U.S. Bur. Budget, 1943-53; mem. tech. adv. com. econ. statistics Bur. Census, 1948-52; chmn. manpower panel, com. human resources Research and Development Bd., Dept. Def., 1949-53; vis. expert U.S. Mil. Govt. in Germany, 1949; cons. manpower NSRB, 1950-53; exec. dir. N.Y. State Interdept. Com. on Low Incomes, 1956-59; mem. com. on statis. programs, N.Y.C., 1955-59; Smith-Mundt tech. cons. Philippine Govt., 1951-52; prof. statistics U. Phillipines, 1954-55, also prin. UN adviser Statis. Center, Manila; adviser human resources Planning Commn., Govt. of Pakistan, 1959-61; sr. staff Inst. Pub. Adminstrn., N.Y.C., 1961; expert manpower ILO, Pakistan, 1962; dir. Office Research in Econs. and Sci., Dept. State, Washington, 1963-66; chief manpower and human resources planning Office Tech. Coop. and Research, AID, 1966-67; adviser manpower Govt. of Ghana, Ford. Found., 1968-70; econ. cons., 1971—. Recipient Certificate of Merit, Philippine Govt., 1952; Alumni Distinguished Service award Drake U., 1957. Fellow Am. Statis. Assn. (pres. N.Y. chpt. 1953-55), A.A.A.C.; mem. Philippine Statis. Assn. (founding), Am. Econ. Assn., Soc. for Internat. Devel. (chpt. pres. 1965—), Indsl. Soc. for Internat. Devel., Indsl. Relations Research Assn., Assn. Amateur Chamber Mus. Players, Phi Beta Kappa, Phi Delta Theta, Phi Mu Alpha, Lambda Alpha. Club: Cosmos. Author monographs, tech. articles. Home: 314 Hill Dr State College PA 16801

GIVENS, RANDOLPH SAMUEL mfg. exec.; b. Lima, O., Apr. 1, 1932; B.S., U. San Francisco, 1954; M.S., Stanford University, 1956; m. Rosemarie Lois Brown, May 15, 1955; 1 son, Anthony Robinson. Sales rep. Ames-Brockton Fabricated Products, Akron, O., 1956-58, sales mgr. Coshocton, Ohio, 1959-61, gen. manager plant, 1961-68, v.p. sales, 1968--. Instr. bus. Coshocton Jr. College, 1968-69. Mem. Coshocton C. of C. (vice president 1967-68, pres. 1969-70), Sales Executives Institute, Phi Beta Kappa, Sigma Chi, Phi Mu. Democrat. Mem. Christian Ch. (lay leader). Mason (32, Shriner). Clubs: Coshocton Country, Coshocton City, Running Deer Country. Home: 2d Av Coshocton OH Office: 3d Av Coshocton OH

GIVENS, STUART RAY, educator; b. Honolulu, Apr. 1, 1924; s. Willard Earl and Neva (Galbreath) G.; B.A., George Washington U., 1948; M.A., Stanford, 1949, Ph.D., 1956; m. Florence Annie Porter, May 23, 1947; children—Willard Porter, Martha Ellen, Bennet Stuart. Faculty, Bowling Green (O.) State U., 1952—, prof. history, 1965—, chmn. dept., 1965-69. Served with AUS, 1943-46. Mem. N.E.A., Am. Hist. Assn., Ohio Hist. Soc., Midwest Brit. Studies Assn., Phi Beta Kappa, Pi Gamma Mu, Phi Alpha Theta. Presbyn. Kiwanian. Home: 631 Haskins Rd Bowling Green OH 43402

GIVENS, THOMAS HENRY, govt. ofcl.; b. Childress, Tex., Aug. 6, 1918; s. Thomas Henry and Ethel (Payne) G.; student U. Omaha, 1941, George Washington U., 1946; m. Vivian Edith Fell, Apr. 24, 1945; children—Victoria Anne, Thomas Henry III. Tng. specialist VA, 1946-48; mgmt. specialist, placement officer Dept. State, 1948-55; exec. officer U.S. AID Mission, Amman, Jordan, 1956-58, Ankara, Turkey, 1958-62, Cairo, UAR, 1962-67; spl. asst. Office Mgmt. Operations AID, Dept. State, 1967-68; dep. dir. Office Vietnam mgmt. Bur. Vietnam Affairs, 1968—. Mem. Soc. Personnel Adminstrn., Am. Mgmt. Assn. Mason. Home: 820 Villa Ridge Rd Falls Church VA 22046 Office: AID Washington DC 20523

GIVENS, WILLIAM PHILLIP, banker; b. Indpls., Apr. 10, 1914; s. George M. and Sue (Ringo) G.; grad. Shortridge High Sch., Indpls., 1931; m. Madelyn May Rardon, July 12, 1936; children-William Phillip, Janice (Mrs. John Powers), Robert A., Jeanne M. (Mrs. Charles Jerden). Cashier, dir. First State Bank, Porter, Ind., 1935-46; v.p. First Bank & Trust Co., South Bend, Ind., 1946-56; exec. v.p. Merchants Nat. Bank, Muncie, Ind., 1956-58, pres., dir., 1958—; dir. Marsh Supermarkets, Inc., Maxon Premix Burner Co. Mem. Gov. Ind. Council Pvt. Action. Pres. Delaware County United Fund, 1966-67, Delaware County A.R.C., 1960-61, Community Services Council, 1967-68. Past bd. dirs. Delaware County council Boy Scouts Am.; mem. bd. Ind. Masonic Home Found. Named hon. Jaycee, 1966, Jaycee Boss of Year, 1969; recipient Silver Beaver award Boy Scouts Am., 1965. Mem. Am. (past bd. dirs.), Ind. (pres. 1962-63) bankers assns., Ind. (bd. dirs.), (pres. 1961-62) Chambers commerce, Ind. Bankers Assn. Am. (bd. dirs., exec. council), Sigma Alpha Epsilon. Presbyn. (ruling elder). Mason. Clubs: Delaware Country (v.p. 1962), Green Hills Country (Muncie). Home: 811 Beechwood Av Muncie IN 47303 Office: 122 S Mulberry St Muncie IN 47305

GIVLER, DONALD NEWTON, food co. exec.; b. Naperville, Ill., May 25, 1910; s. Rollo Newton and Alma Budd (Hamilton) G.; B.S., Northwestern U., 1932; m. Dorothy Slater, June 26, 1954; children—David Rollo, Michael Shannon (by former marriage), Donald Newton, Dorothy Grace. With Gen. Foods Corp., 1933-39; with Grocery Store Products Co., West Chester, Pa., 1939—, exec. v.p., 1949-63, pres., 1963—. Chmn. Chester Co. Devel. Council. Home: RD 2 Harmony Hill Downingtown PA 19335 Office: Grocery Store Products Co West Chester PA 19380

GIZERIAN, CHARLES J., advt. agy. exec.; b. N.Y.C., 1915; grad. Pace Coll., 1940. Sr. v.p., sec., treas., dir. Compton Advt. Inc., N.Y.C. Home: 653 3d Place Garden City NY 11530 Office: 625 Madison Av New York City NY 10022*

GJERDE, CLAYTON MORRIS, coll. dean; b. Amery, Wis., May 5, 1913; s. Mons P. and Christine (Dahlager) G.; B.A., Augsburg Coll., 1935; M.A., U. Minn., 1944, Ph.D., 1949; m. Esther Knudson, July 9, 1939; 1 dau., Kristine Ann (Mrs. Ronald J. Flynn). Pub. sch. tchr., Minn., 1935-40; counselor U. Minn. High Sch., 1940-46, U. Chgo. Lab. Sch., 1946-48; mem. faculty San Diego State Coll., 1948—, prof. ednl. psychology, 1948-65, dean ednl. services and summer sessions, 1965—; tchr. U. Minn., summer 1952. Mem. Am. Psychol. Assn., Am. Personnel and Guidance Assn. (life), Am. Ednl. Research Assn. Home: 5028 Art St San Diego CA 92115

GLAAB, CHARLES NELSON, educator, historian; b Williston, N.D., Dec. 19, 1927; s. Reuben and Betty (Nelson) G. B.Ph., U. N.D., 1951, M.A., 1952; Ph.D., U. Mo., 1958; m. Mary Ellen Anderson, Nov. 5, 1949; children—Martha Ann, John Reuben. Research asso. history Kansas City project U. Chgo., 1956-58; instr., asst. prof. history Kan. State U., 1958-60; asso. prof., prof. history U. Wis. at Milw., 1960-68; dir. urban history sect. Wis. Hist. Soc., 1960-63; prof. history U. Toledo, 1968—. Dir. Fox Valley research project Wis. Hist. Soc., 1963-64; mem. Milw. Landmarks Commn., 1965-68, Toledo Landmark Com., 1968—. Served with AUS, 1946-48. Mem. Am. Hist. Assn., Orgn. Am. Historians, Phi Beta Kappa. Author: Kansas City and the Railroads, 1962; The American City: A Documentary History, 1963; (with A.T. Brown) A. History of Urban America, 1967; (with L.H. Larsen) Factories in the Valley, 1969. Editor Urban History Group Newsletter, 1962-68, co-editor, 1968-70; bd. editors Urban Affairs Quar., 1966—. Home: 3021 Hopewell Pl Toledo OH 43606

GLADDERS, GLENN WARREN, oil co. exec.; b. Coal City, Ill., Aug. 1, 1914; s. Luke and Emily (Nicholson) G.; student U. Mich., 1934-35, 39, So. Ill. U., 1936-38; A.B., U. Ill., 1938; m. Jean Martin, Oct. 7, 1939; children—Thomas Luke, Emily Jean, Warren. Asst. sec.-treas. Martin Oil Co., St. Louis, 1939- 47, sec.-treas., 1947-71, pres., 1950—; pres. Gladders Towing Co., Inc.; chmn. Am. Waterways Operators, Inc., 1968-69; dir. First Nat. Bank, Carbondale, Ill., Merc. Trust Co. N.Am., St. Louis, Knapp- Monarch Co. Mem. exec. com. So. Ill. U. Found., 1956-65, pres., 1956-57. Served as lt. (j.g.) USNR, 1944-45; PTO. Mem. Nat. Def. Transp. Assn., Oil Men's Club (past pres.), Midwest Gasoline Marketers (past pres.), So. Ill. U. Alumni Assn. (past pres.). Clubs: Missouri Athletic (past pres. St. Louis). Home: 801 Cella Rd Ladue MO 63124 Office: 230 S Bemiston St Clayton MO 63105

GLADE, WILLIAM PATTON, Jr., educator; b. Wichita Falls, Tex., July 29, 1929; s. William Patton and Billie (Hatcher) G.; B.B.A., U. Tex., 1950, M.A., 1951, Ph.D., 1955; m. Marlene Louise Joseph, July 10, 1954; children—Anita, Mary, William, John. Instr., asst. prof. econs. U. Md., 1957-60; faculty U. Wis., Madison, 1960-71, prof. dept. econs. Grad. Sch. Bus., 1966-71; prof. econs. U. Tex., dir. Inst. Latin Am. Studies, Austin, 1971—. Mem. Am. Econ. Assn., Midwest Council Latin Am. Studies, Latin Am. Studies Assn., Assn. Evolutionary Econs. Author: Las empresas gubernamentales descentralizadas, 1959; The Political Economy of Mexico, 1963; The Latin American Economies, 1969; Marketing in a Developing Economy—the Case of Peru, 1970. Office: Inst Latin Am Studies U Tex Austin TX 78712

GLADEM, MARTIN DUANE, sugar co. exec.; b. Petersburg, Neb., June 19, 1923; s. John H. and Mabel (Score) G.; student Norfolk (Neb.) Sch. Bus., 1942; B.S., U. Denver, 1949; m. Irene T. Bygland, Sept. 16, 1951; children—DuAnn, James, David. Staff accountant Haskins & Sells, C.P.A.'s, Denver, 1950- 53; with Holly Sugar Corp., Colorado Springs, Colo., 1955—, controller, 1968—. Scoutmaster local Boy Scouts Am., 1967-69. Served with AUS, 1943- 45. C.P.A., Colo. Mem. Am. Inst. C.P.A.'s, Colo. Soc. C.P.A.'s, Nat. Accountants Assn., Data Processing Mgmt. Assn., Theta Chi. Home: 1316 Prairie Rd Colorado Springs CO 80909 Office: 100 Stone Center Colorado Springs CO 80902

GLADFELTER, MILLARD E., univ. chancellor; b. York County, Pa., Jan. 16, 1900; s. Phillip and Ida Jane (Shearer) G.; A.B., Gettysburg Coll., 1925, D.Sc., 1942; A.M., U. Wis., 1930; Ph.D., U. Pa., 1945; LL.D., Muhlenberg Coll., 1947; L.H.D. Lebanon Valley Coll., 1954, Dropsie Coll., 1960, St. Joseph's Coll., 1960; Litt.D., Ursinus Coll., 1956, Eastern Bapt. Coll., 1957, U. Pa., 1960, Drexel Inst. Tech., 1961, Albright Coll., 1964, Delaware Valley Coll. Agr., 1964; Ph.D., LaSalle Coll., 1963; D.C.L., Rider Coll., 1966; D.H.L., Hahnemann Med. Coll., 1967; m. Martha Louise Gaut, Dec. 29, 1931; children—Phillip, Bruce Gaut. Tchr. rural schs. Pa., 1918-22; prin., tchr. history West York High Sch., 1925-28; supervising prin. West York schs., 1928- 30; dir. Temple U. High Sch., 1930-31; registrar Temple U., 1931-41, v.p., 1941, provost, v.p., 1946-59, pres., 1959-67, chancellor, 1967—, also trustee. Dir. Continental Bank & Trust Co., Phila. Life Ins. Corp. Trustee Phila. Free Library, Ursinus, Gettysburg, Muhlenberg colls., United Fund Phila.; bd. dirs. Phila. Diagnostic and Relocation Center; pres., bd. dirs. North City Corp., Phila.; bd. corporators Presbyn. Ministers' Fund. Recipient Silver Beaver award Boy Scouts Am.; Grand Gold badge honor for merits Republic of Austria, 1964; Humanitarian award Phila. 32 Carat Club, 1964. Mem. Phila. C. of C. (bd. dirs.), Middle States Assn. Colls. and Secondary Schs. (pres. 1959), Pa. Assn. Coll. and Univs., Phi Beta Kappa, Kappa Phi Kappa, Phi Delta Kappa, Phi Delta Theta, Phi Beta Kappa Assos. Kiwanian. Contbr. articles to ednl. jours. Home: 342 Fisher Rd Jenkintown PA 19046

GLADIEUX, BERNARD LOUIS, mgmt., fiscal cons.; b. Toledo, Apr. 12, 1907; s. Victor Modest and Anna (Cook) G.; A.B., Oberlin Coll., 1930; student Zimmern Sch. Internat. Studies, Geneva, Switzerland, summer 1929; A.M. in Pub. Adminstrn., Syracuse U., 1943; m. Persis Skilliter, June 19, 1930; children—Bernard Louis, Russell Victor, Lawrence Edward, Jay Arthur. Tchr., prin., Am. Sch. in Japan, Tokyo, 1930-34; exec. sec. City Mgr. League, Toledo, 1935; adminstrv. cons. Pub. Adminstrn. Service, Chgo., 1936-39; mgmt. cons., chief war orgn. staff U.S. Bur. Budget, exec. office of pres., 1939-42; adminstrv. asst. to chmn. WPB, 1943-44; dep. chief operations and adminstrn. UNRRA, 1944; exec. asst. to sec. U.S. Dept. Commerce, 1945-50; asst. to pres. The Ford Found., 1950-54;

fiscal policy cons. Philippine Govt., 1955-56; cons. Com. Govt. Reorgn., 1952; lectr. dept. pub. law and govt. Columbia, 1953; pub. adminstrn. cons. Pakistan Govt., 1955; partner, v.p. Booz, Allen & Hamilton, Inc., 1957- 66; partner, dir. Knight & Gladieux, 1967-69, dir. Knight, Gladieux & Smith, 1969—. Spl. cons. Dept. State, 1968; Mem. nat. adv. council Hampshire Coll.; mem. com. Govt. Com. Econ. Devel., 1963—; mem. Com. Pub. Service, 1961—; corp. mem. Nat. Assembly Social Policy and Devel. Past v.p., mem. bd. of dirs. YMCA, of Greater N.Y.; past mem. nat. student com. Nat. Council of YMCA's; bd. mgrs. YMCA Schs. N.Y., 1951-55; adv. council dept. politics Princeton U., 1954-57; trustee Oberlin Coll., 1955-67; incorporator, bd. dirs. Tng. Resources for Youth, Inc., 1965-68. Mem. Govtl. Research Assn., Wilderness Soc., Sierra Club, Acad. Polit. Sci., Am. Soc. Pub. Adminstrn., Oberlin Alumni Bd. (treas. 1945-48; Alumni citation 1953), Nat. Civil Service League (chmn. bd. dirs. 1961- -), Nat. Social Welfare Assembly (exec. com. 1961-67), Group Health Assn. (past dir. Washington), Nat. Municipal League, Nat. Planning Assn., Nat. Acad. Pub. Adminstrn., Regional Plan Assn., Nat. Recreation and Park Assn., Inst. Mgmt. Consultants (a founder), Japan Soc., Phi Beta Kappa. Presbyn. Clubs: University, Town, Scarsdale (N.Y.) Golf; Army and Navy (Manila, P.I.); Potomac Appalachian Trail (Washington). Author articles in field. Home: 3 Walworth Av Scarsdale NY 10583 Office: 299 Park Av New York City NY 10017 ☆

GLADIEUX, VIRGIL A., food co. exec.; m. Beatrice Gladieux; children—Therese (Mrs. Thomas B. Geiger), Timothy. Pres. Ogden Foods, Inc., ABC Gladieux Corp. (founder), Holiday Houses, Inc., G & H Restaurants, Inc., Greenfield-Mills-Smiths Restaurant Co.; v.p. N. Shores Investment Co., Inc.; dir. Ohio Citizens Trust Co., Toledo, Toledo Edison Co. Mem. Hosp. Commn. and Hosp. Planning Assn. for steering com. Bond Issue, 1946; v.p., exec. com. Toledo Area Devel. Corp.; pres. Sports Arena, Inc., Toledo; chmn. 1959 financial campaign expansion Mercy Hosp., Toledo; chmn. Toledo citizens com. passage capital improvements proposals, 1961, co-chmn., 1962; co- chmn. financial campaign new wing St. Vincent Hosp., Toledo, 1963; chmn. bldg. fund drive Goodwill Industries, Toledo, 1966; mem. bldg. fund com. Little Sisters of Poor, 1967-68; mem. Toledo Civic Auditorium Study Com. Trustee Toledo Community Chest, City of Hosp. Los Angeles; bd. lay advisers Mary Manse Coll., Toledo; mem. president's adv. council St. John's High Sch., Toledo; adv. bd. St. Vincent Hosp.; trustee Boys Club Toledo; past pres. Toledo Zool. Soc.; bd. dirs. Catholic Charities Toledo, Cath. Club. Mem. Nat. Restaurant Assn. (bd. dirs.), Downtown Toledo Assos. (bd. dirs., past v.p.), Hosp. Planning Assn. Greater Toledo (past trustee), Toledo Small Bus. Assn. (past trustee), Arena Mgrs. Assn., Assn. Auditorium Mgrs., Internat. Assn. Amusement Parks, Internat. Bridge, Tunnel and Turnpike Assn., Toledo Orch. Assn., Toledo Conv. Bur., Toledo Mus. Art, Toledo Council World Affairs, Serra Club, U. Toledo Sch. Bus. Adminstrn. Alumni Assn. K.C., Elk. Clubs: North Cape Yacht; Exchange; President's Tower. Home: 2039 Mt Vernon Av Toledo OH 43607 Office: 2140 Ashland Av Toledo OH 43620

GLADING, BEN, conservationist; b. Washington, May 21, 1910; s. Harvey C. and Sarah (Baumgardner) G.; A.B., U. Mich., 1932; M.S., Kan. State Coll., Manhattan, 1933; student U. Cal. at Berkeley, 1933-36; m. Charlotte H. Hughson, May 26, 1934; children—Henry H., Arthur C., Sarah G. Teaching fellow Kan. State Coll., 1932-33, U. Cal. at Berkeley, 1933-36; jr. biologist U.S. Forest Service, 1936-40; with Cal. Dept. Fish and Game, 1940—, chief bur. game conservation, 1949—. Active local Boy Scouts Am. Mem. Pacific Flyway Council (pres. 1952, sec.-treas. 1952-65), Western Assn. State Game and Fish Commnrs. (sec.-treas. 1947—), Wildlife Soc. (pres. 1966-67), Sigma Xi. Club: Sierra. Home: 1413 El Tejon Way Sacramento CA 95825 Office: Resources Bldg 1416 9th St Sacramento CA 95814

GLADNEY, WILLIAM BECKETT, banker; b. Natchez, Miss., Jan. 30, 1898; s. Wallace Gardner and Mary Alice (Power) G.; A.B. magna cum laude, Wake Forest Coll., 1918; m. Ruth A. Washburn, Sept. 20, 1924; children—William W., Charles Wallace. Bookkeeper, Ouachita Nat. Bank, Monroe, La., 1917, asst. cashier, 1921- 26; teller, gen. bookkeeper Comml. Nat. Bank, Shreveport, La., summer 1918; asst. cashier Citizens Nat. Bank (now Ouachita Nat. Bank), 1918-21; v.p. Bastrop (La.) Bank & Trust Co. (now Bastrop Nat. Bank), 1926-38; exec. v.p. Fidelity Bank & Trust Co. (now Fidelity Nat. Bank of Baton Rouge), 1938-44, pres., 1944-54, dir., 1938—, vice chmn., 1954- 60, vice chmn. bd., chmn. exec. com., 1960—. Mem. State Adv. Bd. La., 1937—. Chmn. 2d War Loan drive, co-chmn. 3d drive; parish chmn. Baton Rouge Relief Fund, 1939; pres. Baton Rouge Community Chest, 1945; v.p. United Givers Fund Baton Rouge; chmn. Bastrop chpt. A.R.C.; pres. Jr. Achievement Baton Rouge, 1966-67. Served with U.S. Army, 1918. Recipient Silver Service award La. bankers, 1944. Mem. Am. Bankers Assn. (ins. and protective com. 1936, chmn. 1937-44, exec. council 1935-36, 44-47, mem. fed. legislative council and state legislative council, exec. com., nat. bank div. 1946-49, chmn. exec. com. 1947, pres. 1949-50, treas. 1951-53), First Regional Clearing House Assn. La. (an organizer 1927, pres. 1928), La. Bankers Assn. (exec. com. 1932-35, chmn. ins. com. 1936-42, chmn. legislative com. 1941-45, chmn. taxation com., v.p. 1934-35, pres. 1935-36), Bastrop C. of C. (past pres.), Baton Rouge C. of C. (past pres.), Baton Rouge Port Devel. Assn. (past treas., dir.). Methodist. Elk, Mason, Kiwanian. Clubs: City, Morehouse Country (an organizer, 1st pres.), Baton Rouge Country (past pres.); Boston (New Orleans). Home: 2589 E Lake Shore Dr Baton Rouge LA 70808 Office: Fidelity Nat Bank Baton Rouge LA 70802

GLADSTEIN, ROBERT DAVID, dancer, choreographer; b. Berkeley, Cal., Jan. 16, 1943; s. Morris and Wilda (Hetke) G.; student San Francisco State Coll., 1960-62; dance tng. San Francisco Ballet Sch.; m. Nancy Sharon Robinson, May 9, 1964; 1 son, Marcus Joseph. Mem. San Francisco Ballet Co., 1960-67, 70—, Am. Ballet Theatre, 1967-70; soloist San Francisco Opera, 1962, 63, 64, Dallas Opera Co., 1968; danced for Pres. Nixon, White House, 1969; TV credits include Ed Sullivan, 1965, Beauty and the Beast film, ABC-TV, 1968, Macy's Thanksgiving Parade, 1969; choreographer 15 ballets, 1962—. Home: 103 Buena Vista Terrace San Francisco CA 94117 Office: 378 18th Av San Francisco CA 94121

GLADSTONE, HERBERT JACK, mfg. co. exec.; b. N.Y.C., May 12, 1924; s. Joseph D. and Ella (Shabman) G.; student Hamilton Coll., 1944; Harvard, 1945; B.B.A., Coll. City N.Y., 1947; m. Sylvia Rosenberg, Dec. 28, 1946; children—Alan, Linda, Karen. Mem. staff Gershon & Strell, C.P.A.'s, N.Y.C., 1947-51; budget dir. F.M.C., N.Y.C., 1951-55; v.p., controller Condec Corp., Old Greenwich, Conn., 1955—; lectr. M.B.A. Program, U. Conn.; dir. Consol. Controls Corp., Hammond Valve Corp. Pres., P.T.A., 1956-57; asst. scoutmaster Yoquam council Boy Scouts Am., 1960-63. Served with USAAF, 1943-46. Mem. Financial Execs. Inst. (dir.), Am. Inst. C.P.A.'s, N.Y. State Soc. C.P.A.'s. Clubs: Roxbury Country (dir.), Roxbury Tennis and Swim (trustee). Home: 284 West Hill Rd Stamford CT 06902 Office: 1500 Post Rd Old Greenwich CT 06870

GLADSTONE, MILTON, publisher; b. N.Y.C., Nov. 11, 1914; s. Max H. and Rose (Ungar) G.; B.S., Coll. City N.Y., 1936; M.S., Columbia, 1937; M.E., U. Vt., 1942; m. Selma D. Lowitz, Sept. 12, 1942; children—Robert, William, Margaret, Thomas. Founder, Arco Pub. Co., Inc., N.Y.C., 1937, chief exec. officer, 1937—; co-founder Investors Planning Corp., N.Y.C. Bd. dirs. United Jewish Appeal, 1948-58; active fund raising Anti-Defamation League, 1947-55; mem. devel. fund Andover Acad.; trustee Hackley Sch. Served with Signal Corps, AUS, 1941-46; ETO. Mem. Am. Booksellers Assn., Am. Book Pubs. Assn., Book Pub. Council. Author: Gardner Encyclopedia, 1947. Home: 400 North St Greenwich CT 06830 Office: Arco Pub Co Inc 219 Park Av S New York City NY 10003

GLADWYN, LORD, (formerly Sir Gladwyn Jebb), diplomat; b. Firbeck Hall, Rotherham, Yorkshire, Eng., Apr. 25, 1900; s. Sydney Gladwyn and Rose (Chichester) J.; Eton Coll., Windsor, 1913- 18; Magdalen Coll., Oxford (1st class honors in history, 1922), 1919-22; D.C.L., Oxford U.; m. Cynthia Noble, Jan. 22, 1929; children—Miles Alvery Gladwyn, Vanessa Mary, Stella Candida. Entered diplomatic service, 1924; 3d sec., Tehran, 1924-27, 1st sec., Rome, 1931-35; pvt. sec. to Parliamentary Under Sec. of State, 1929-31, to Permanent Under-Sec. State, 1937-40; asst. Under-Sec. Ministry Economic Warfare, 1940; acting counselor in fgn. office, 1941, head Reconstrn. Dept., 1942, counselor, 1943, exec. sec. Prep. Commr., UN, 1945, acting sec.-gen., UN, Feb. 1946, asst. under-sec. of state and UN adviser, 1946-47, prin. adviser to Br. delegation UN, 1947-54, dep. Under Sec. of State, 1949, U.K. rep. to UN, 1950-54; Her Majesty's ambassador to France, 1954-60. Vice pres. Atlantic Treaty Assn.; chmn. Campaign for European Political Community; chmn. Britain in Europe; mem. Exec. Bur. European Movement. Dep. leader Liberal Party in Ho. of Lords. Decorated companion Order of the Bath, 1947; companion Order St. Michael and St. George, 1942, knight comdr., 1949; knight grand cross, 1954; knight grand cross Royal Victorian Order, 1957; Grand Croix de Legion d'Honneur, 1957. Author: The European Idea, 1966; Half-Way to 1948, 1967; DeGaulle's Europe, 1969. Home: Bramfield Hall Halesworth Suffolk England also 62 Whitehall Ct London SW 1 England Office: 23 Chapel St London SW 1 England

GLANCE, TIMOTHY JOHNSON mfg. exec.; b. Lima, O., Apr. 1, 1932; B.S., U. San Francisco, 1954; M.S., Stanford University, 1956; m. Rosemarie Lois Brown, May 15, 1955; 1 son, Anthony Robinson. Sales rep. Ames-Brockton Fabricated Products, Akron, O., 1956-58, sales mgr. Coshocton, Ohio, 1959-61, gen. manager plant, 1961-68, v.p. sales, 1968--. Instr. bus. Coshocton Jr. College, 1968-69. Named Man of Year, Coshocton Junior Chamber of Commerce, 1968. Mem. Coshocton C. of C. (vice president 1967-68, pres. 1969-70), English Speaking Union, Coshocton Sertoma Club, Nat. Assn. Mfrs., Sales Executives Institute, Phi Beta Kappa, Sigma Chi, Phi Mu. Democrat. Mem. Christian Ch. (lay leader). Mason (32, Shriner). Clubs: Coshocton Country, Coshocton City, Running Deer Country. Home: 2d Av Coshocton OH Office: 3d Av Coshocton OH

GLANCY, ALFRED ROBINSON, III, utility exec.; b. Detroit, Mar. 14, 1938; s. Alfred Robinson and Elizabeth (Tant) G.; grad. The Hill Sch., 1956; B.A., Princeton U., 1960; M.B.A., Harvard U., 1962; m. Ruth Mary Roby, Sept. 15, 1962; children—Joan Courts, Alfred Robinson IV. Mem. financial planning dept. Michigan Consolidated Gas Co., Detroit, 1962-64, supr. economic studies and rates, 1965-67, mgr. financial planning dept., 1967-69, treas., 1969—; dir. Community Nat. Bank of Pontiac. Mem. financial policy com. Detroit Symphony Orchestra Inc., 1969—. Republican precinct del., 1970—. Mem. Am. Gas Assn. (mem. rate com. 1967—), Economic Club Detroit, Clubs: Princeton Club of Mich. (dir. 1967—); Haroard Business School, University Club, Country (Detroit). Home: 235 Cloverly Rd Grosse Pointe Farms MI 48236 Office: 1 Woodward Av Detroit MI 48226

GLANDER, CHARLES EMORY, lawyer; b. W. Alexandria, O., Mar. 5, 1903; s. Charles Dietrich and Carrie Alice (Brower) G.; B.A., Ohio State U., 1925, J.D., 1930; student U. Mich., summers 1926-28; m. Frances Fay Chandler, Apr. 15, 1931; children—Charles Franklin, David Gordon. Debate coach Purdue U., 1925- 27, Ohio State U., 1927-43; admitted to Ohio bar, 1930; practice law, 1930-40, 51—; partner firm Wright, Harlor, Morris, Arnold & Glander, Columbus, O. 1953—; atty. Ohio Div. Securities, 1940; exec. sec. Gov. Ohio, 1941-45; tax commr. Ohio, 1945-51; lectr. Ohio State U. Coll. Law, 1948-64, adj. prof., 1965—. Pres. Council Social Agencies, Columbus and Franklin County, 1955-57, Ohio Citizens Council Health and Welfare, 1959-61; trustee, past chmn. bd., pres. Citizens Research Inc.; trustee, moderator, past pres. Columbus Town Meeting, weekly TV and radio forum. Mem. Nat. Assn. Tax Adminstrs. (pres. 1948-50), Ohio State U. Assn. (nat. pres. 1957-59), Ohio State U. Law Alumni Assn. (pres. 1952-53), Nat. Tax Assn. (pres. 1962-63), Am., Ohio (chmn. taxation com. 1960-63), Columbus bar assns., Am. Judicature Soc., Columbus Area C. of C. (past chmn. pub. finance com.), Kappa Sigma, Delta Sigma Rho, Phi Delta Phi. Conglist. Clubs: Kiwanis (pres. 1951), Kit-Kat, University (Columbus); Faculty (Ohio State U.). Contbr. articles law jour. Home: 4660 Haymarket Ct Columbus OH 43220 Office: Huntington Trust Bldg Columbus OH 43215

GLANTON, JOHN FLOYD, civil engr.; b. Mpls., Nov. 20, 1923; s. Herbert and Roselind (Griffen) G.; ed. Dunwoody Indsl. Inst., U. Minn.; m. Eunamae Pullie, Sept. 6, 1958; children—Joan, Beverly, John Floyd, Wayne Herbert, Callie Ann. Draftsman, Minn. Hwy. Dept., 1949-50, City of Mpls., 1950-68; engr. Glanton Engring., Mpls., 1968-69, pres., 1969—; v.p. Glanton Constrn. Co., Inc.; works include concrete plant, boat slip and asphalt plant for City of Mpls., Jordan Residential Paving Project, Warrington Residential Paving Project, 26th Av. N. Paving Project (all Mpls.). Served with C.E., AUS, 1943-46. Mem. Nat., Minn. socs. profl. engrs. Home: 3445 4th Av S Minneapolis MN 55408 Office: 1111 Nicollet Av Minneapolis MN 55403

GLANVILLE, ALBERT DOUGLAS, educator, psychologist; b. Auburn, N.Y., Jan. 5, 1906; s. Arthur and Annie (Dawson) G.; A.B., Cornell U., 1927, Ph.D., 1932; A.M., U. Ill., 1928; m. Blanche Sellers, Sept. 2, 1938; children—Alan Douglas, Bruce Dawson. Merriam research fellow. Cornell U., 1933; research fellow, Training Sch., Vineland, N.J., 1933-36; psychologist. Del. State Hosp. and Mental Hygiene Clinic, Farnhurst, Del., 1936-37; instr. to prof., dept. of psychology, U. Me., 1937—, formerly head dept. of psychology; clin. psychologist, 1936—. Mem. Bd. Examiners of Psychologists, Me., sec. 1955. Diplomate clin. psychology, Am. Bd. Examiners in Profl. Psychology, 1948. Asso. Am. Psychol. Assn.; mem. Am. Assn. U. Profs., Me. Psychol. Assn. (pres. 1951-52), Sigma Xi (pres., Maine chpt., 1949-51). Home: 45 Oak St Orono ME 04473

GLANVILLE-HICKS, PEGGY, composer, music critic; b. Melbourne, Australia; d. Ernest and Myrtle (Bailey) Glanville-Hicks; scholarship Royal Coll. Music, London, 1932- 36; Ecole Normale, Paris; pvt. study with Egon Wellesz; m. Stanley Bate, 1938 (dec.). Came to U.S., 1940, naturalized, 1948. With Dr. Carleton Sprague Smith, founded Internat. Music Fund to assist European artists; implemented Central Park concerts, League of Composers, N.Y.C.; music critic N.Y. Herald Tribune, 1948-58; dir. Composers Forum, prod. concert series for young composers Donnell Library Auditorium, Columbia, 1950- 60; with Chandler Cowles, prod. own opera Transposed Heads, 1958; prod. Lou Harrison's opera Rapunzel, under name of The Artists Co., N.Y.C., 1959; with Yehudi Menuhin, master of ceremonies for concerts of Indian music. Mus. Modern Art; commd. to compose ballet score Masque of the Wild Man for first Spoletto Festival, Italy, 1958, ballet Saul for CBS- TV, 1959, full-length opera Nausicaa, Athens Festival, 1961. Recipient award Am. Acad. Arts and Letters, 1953; Guggenheim fellow, 1956-57, 57-58; Rockefeller travel grant for research Middle East, 1960; Fulbright research grant for comparative study folk music of Greek Islands, 1961. Mem. League Composers, Contemporary Music Soc., Jr. Council of Mus. Modern Art. Composer: Sonata for Harp, Sonata for Piano and Percussion, Concert Romantico, Etruscan Concerto; Letters from Morocco; (operas) Transposed Heads, 1954; The Glittering Gate, 1959; 7 Havsikaa, Athens Festival, Greece, 1961, ballet scores for CBS-TV, film scores for UN. Contbr. articles popular mags., profl. periodicals.

GLARNER, FRITZ, artist; b. Zurich, Switzerland, July 20, 1899; s. Joseph and Donata (Ahignente) G.; student Regio Instituto di Belle Arti, Naples, Italy; m. Louise Powell, July 12, 1928. Came to U.S., 1936, naturalized, 1944. Exhibited abstract painting in Mus. Modern Art, N.Y.C., 1951, 1st biennial of Sao Paulo, Brazil, 1951, Carnegie Internat., Pitts., 1952, 58, 25th biennial Corcoran Gallery, Washington, 1957, also Tokyo, Japan, Kassel, Germany, Zurich, Switzerland, Venice, Italy; works represented in collections Yale U. Art Gallery, Phila. Mus. Art, Mus. Modern Art, N.Y.C., Balt. Mus. Fine Art, Whitney Mus. Am. Art, Walker Art Center, Mpls., others.; Mural Painting, main lobby Dag Hammerskjold Library, UN, N.Y.C., Time-Life Bldg., N.Y.C. Home: Round Swamp Rd Wheatley Hills NY 11101

GLASCO, JOSEPH, artist; b. Paul's Valley, Okla., Jan. 19, 1925; student U. Tex., 1941- 43; Jepson Art Inst., Los Angeles, Art Center Sch., Los Angeles, 1946-48; pvt. pupil of Rico Lebrun, 1946-48; student Escuela de Bellas Artes, San Miguel de Allende, Mexico, 1948, Art Students League, N.Y.C., 1949. One man exhbns. include Paris Galleries, 1950, Catherine Viviano Gallery, 1951-54, 56, 58, 61, 63, Arts Club Chgo., 1954-57; group exhbns. include Mus. Modern Art, Met. Mus., Whitney Mus., Corcoran Gallery, Bklyn. Mus., Chgo Art Inst., Dallas Mus. Fine Arts, Detroit Art Inst., Los Angeles Co. Mus. Art, U. Ill., U. Neb., Carnegie Inst., Pa. Acad. Fine Arts; rep. permanent collections Bklyn. Mus., Albright Mus., Buffalo, Mus. Modern Art, Met. Mus., Newark Mus., Princeton U. Mus., Whitney Mus., commnd. for mural by Amarillo (Tex.) Air Field. Served with USAAF, 1943-45, with AUS, 1945-46. Address: care Catherine Viviano Gallery 42 E 57th St New York City NY 10022

GLASE, JOHN T., banker; b. 1908; B.S., U. Ida., 1930; married. With Nat. Bank of Commerce of Seattle, 1930—, asst. trust officer, trust officer, asst. v.p., 1947-65, sr. v.p., mgr. trust dept., 1965—. Served with AUS. Office: Nat Bank of Commerce of Seattle 2d Av at Spring St Seattle WA 98124*

GLASER, ALBERT BERNARD, corp. exec.; b. Boston, July 13, 1926; s. Percy and Martha (Rosenberg) G.; student U. N.H., 1943-44, U. Chgo., 1945; LL.B. cum laude, Boston U., 1948; M.B.A. with distinction, Harvard, 1951; m. Esther Helen Hoffman, Oct. 31, 1948; children—William Philip, Frank Matthew, Charles Benjamin. Admitted to Mass. bar, 1948; practiced in Boston, 1948-49; with Fed. Dept. Stores, Inc., and divs., 1951—, asst. treas., 1958-64, treas., 1964—; treas. Fed. Acceptance Corp., 1959—, also dir.; treas., dir. Allmor Devel., Corp., 1967—; treas. Federated Dept. Stores Internat. Co., 1968—. Served with AUS, World War II. Mem. of Financial Execs. Inst. Club: Harvard Business School (Cin.). Mem. editorial bd. Boston U. Law Rev., 1947-48. Home: 3198 Esther Dr Cincinnati OH 45213 Office: 222 W 7th St Cincinnati OH 45202

GLASER, DANIEL, sociologist; b. N.Y.C., Dec. 23, 1918; s. Samuel Jacob and Lena (Solway) G.; A.B., U. Chgo., 1939, A.M., 1947, Ph.D., 1954; m. Pearl Bennett, Oct. 11, 1946; 1 dau., Lenore Meryl. Prisons officer U.S. Mil. Govt. Germany, 1946-49; sociologist-actuary Ill. Parole and Pardon Bd., Pontiac Prison, 1950-52, Joliet Prison, 1952-54; faculty U. Ill., 1954-68, prof. sociology, 1962-68, head dept., 1962-68; prof. Rutgers U., 1968-70, U. So. Cal., 1970—. Vis. asso. prof. U. Cal. at Los Angeles, summer 1961; vis. prof. Ariz. State U., 1963-64; cons. in field, 1956—. Mem. research council Nat. Council Crime and Delinquency; asso. commr. charge research div. N.Y. State Narcotic Control Commn., 1968-1970. Served with AUS, 1942-46. Mem. Ill. Acad. Criminology (pres. 1964-65), Am. Sociol. Assn. (chmn. criminology sect. 1965-66), Am. Correctional Assn., Soc. Study Social Problems, Am. Soc. Criminology. Author: The Effectiveness of a Prison and Parole System, 1964, rev., 1969; Crime in the City, 1969; Adult Crime and Social Policy, 1971; Social Deviance, 1971; also numerous articles, pamphlets, chpts. in books. Asso. editor Am. Jour. Sociology, 1965—, Social Problems, 1965-68, Jour. Research on Crime and Delinquency, 1968—, Fed. Probation, 1968—, Sociology and Social Research, 1970—. Contbr. to Ency. Brit., Internat. Ency. Social Scis. Home: 901 S Ogden Dr Los Angeles CA 90036

GLASER, DONALD A., physicist; b. Cleve., Sept. 21, 1926; s. William Joseph Glaser; B.S., Case Inst. Tech., 1946, Sc.D. (hon.), 1959; Ph.D., Cal. Inst. Tech., 1949; m. Ruth Louise Thompson, Nov. 28, 1961 (div. 1969); children—Louise, William. Prof. physics U. Mich., 1949-59; faculty U. Cal. at Berkeley, 1959-64, prof. physics and molecular biology, 1964—. NSF fellow, 1961; Guggenheim fellow, 1961-62. Recipient Henry Russel award U. Mich., 1955; Charles V. Boys prize Phys. Soc. London, 1958; Nobel prize in physics, 1960; Gold medal Case Inst. Tech., 1967; Alumni Distinguished Service award Cal. Inst. Tech., 1967. Fellow Am. Physics Soc. (prize 1959); mem. Nat. Acad. Sci., Sigma Xi, Tau Kappa Alpha, Theta Tau. Office: Molecular Biology Dept U Cal Berkeley CA 94720

GLASER, GILBERT HERBERT, educator, physician; b. N.Y.C., Nov. 10, 1920; s. Burnard Richard and Sidelle (Rogers) G.; A.B., Columbia, 1940, M.D., 1943, Med. Sc.D., 1951; M.A. (hon.), Yale, 1963; m. Morfydd Mai Pugh, Mar. 17, 1946; children—Gareth Evan, Sara Elizabeth. Intern, Mt. Sinai Hosp., N.Y.C., 1943-44; resident neurology N.Y. Neurol. Inst., 1944-46; from research asst. to asso. neurology Columbia Coll. Physicians and Surgeons, 1948-52; research scientist N.Y. Psychiat. Inst., 1948-50; head. sect. neurology Yale Sch. Medicine, 1952—, asst. prof. neurology, 1952-55, asso. prof., 1955-63, prof. neurology, 1963—; Commonwealth Fund vis. prof. neurology U. London (Eng.), 1965-66; cons. West Haven (Conn.) VA Hosp., 1955—. Mem. neurology research adv. com. USPHS, 1956-60, 68-72. Served as capt., M.C., AUS, 1946-48. Recipient Janeway prize Columbia, 1943, Bicentennial medal award, 1968. Diplomate Am. Bd. Psychiatry and Neurology. Mem. Am. Neurol. Assn., Am. Acad. Neurology (1st v.p. 1969-71), Am. Epilepsy Soc. (pres. 1963), Am. Electroencephalographic Soc. (council 1958-61, bd. qualifications), Eastern Assn. Electroencephalographers (pres. 1958), EEG Soc. (Gt. Britain), Royal Soc. Medicine, Epilepsy Found. Am. (med. adv. bd.), Myasthenia Gravis Foundation (med. adv. bd. chmn. 1964-65), Multiple Sclerosis Soc. (med. adv. bd.), Cerebral Palsy Found. (med. adv. bd.). Author: EEG and Behavior, 1963. Contbr. articles to profl. jours. Editor: Epilepsia, 1958—; mem. editorial bd. Archives of Neurology, Jour. Neurol. Sci., Jour. Nervous and Mental Diseases, Devel. Medicine and Child Neurology. Home: 205 Millbrook Rd Hamden CT 06518 Office: 333 Cedar St New Haven CT 06510

GLASER, JOHN FREDERIC, educator; b. Hamilton, O., Oct. 27, 1920; s. Carl Edward and Verna (Thoma) G.; A.B., Washington and Jefferson Coll., 1941; A.M., Harvard, 1942, Ph.D., 1949. Instr. history Washington Sq. Coll., N.Y. U., 1948- 52, 53-54; asst. prof., asso. prof. history Ripon (Wis.) Coll., 1954-63, prof., 1963—, chmn. dept. history, 1962-69. Served to 1st lt. AUS, 1942- 46. Am. Council Learned Socs. scholar, 1952-53. Mem. Am. Hist. Assn., Phi Beta Kappa, Phi Alpha Theta. Conglist. Home: 908 Newbury St Ripon WI 54971

GLASER, LEWIS HARRY, mfg. exec.; b. N.Y.C., Apr. 27, 1917; s. Charles and Cecelia (Isler) G.; radio engring. student Capitol Radio Engring. Inst., Washington, 1935; m. Royle Ebert; children—Kim, Leslie. Radio technician Radio Analysis Co., Beverly Hills, Cal., 1934-38; propr. Precision Radio Co., Los Angeles, 1938-42; propr. Precision Specialties, Los Angeles, 1942, partner 1943-45; pres. Precision Specialties, 1942, Revell, Inc., Venice, Cal., 1946—. Mem. Am. Technion Soc., Toy Mfrs. Assn. U.S., Soc. Plastics Industry, Cal. Toy Group, C. of C., Hobby Industry Assn. Am. (pres.), Young Presidents Orgn., Am. Mgmt. Assn. Home: 805 Nimes Pl Los Angeles CA 90024 Office: 4223 Glencoe Av Venice CA 90291

GLASER, MILTON, interior designer; b. Phila., Mar. 11, 1915; s. Sol and Helen (Rice) G.; B.F.A., U. Pa., 1936; m. Nancy Ward Goldbarth, Feb. 3, 1943; children—Elizabeth Lee, Nancy Ward. Interior architect Office of George Howe, 1936-38; asso. Walter M. Ballard Co., N.Y.C., 1938-40; with N.Y. Shipbldg. Corp., 1940-45; propr. Milton Glaser Assos., Richmond, Va., 1951—. Recipient numerous awards for interiors in non-residential field, including award Instns. mag., 1956, Interior of Year award S.M. Hexter Co., 1961. Fellow Am. Inst. Interior Designers (pres. Va. chpt. 1954, mem. nat. bd. 1956—, chmn. bd. 1959-60, nat. pres. 1961-63). Home: 304 Tarrytown Dr Richmond VA 23229 Office: 9 E Franklin St Richmond VA 23219

GLASER, ROBERT JOY, physician, found. exec.; b. St. Louis, Sept. 11, 1918; s. Joseph and Regina (Sonnenschein) G.; S.B., Harvard, 1940, M.D. magna cum laude, 1943; m. Helen Louise Hofsommer, Apr. 1, 1949; children—Sally Louise, Joseph II, Robert Joy. Med. intern Barnes Hosp., St. Louis, 1944, asst. resident physician, 1945-46, resident physician, 1946-47, asst. physician, 1949-57; asst. resident physician Peter Bent Brigham Hosp., Boston, 1944-45; NRC fellow med. scis. Wash. U. Med. Sch., 1947-49, instr. medicine, 1949-50, asst. prof., 1950-56, asso. prof., 1956-57, asst. dean, 1947, 53-55, asso. dean, 1955-57; dean, prof. medicine U. Colo. Med. Sch., 1957-63, v.p. for med. affairs, 1959-63; vis. physician Wash. U. Med. Service, St. Louis City Hosp., 1950, chief service, 1950-53, cons., 1953-57; attending physician Colo. Gen. Hosp., Denver, 1957-63; cons. medicine VA Hosp., Denver, 1957-63, Fitzsimons Army Hosp., Aurora, Colo., 1957-63; cons. Lowry AFB, Denver, 1957-63; prof. social medicine Harvard, Boston, 1963-65; pres. Affiliated Hosps. Center, Inc., 1963-65; v.p. med. affairs, dean Sch. Medicine, prof. medicine Stanford U., 1965-70, acting pres., 1968; attending physician Columbia-Presbyn. Med. Center, N.Y.C., 1971—, clin. prof. medicine, 1971—; mem. nat. adv. council USPHS; asso. mem. streptococcal commn. Armed Forces Epidemiologic Bd., 1958-61. Dir., Hewlett-Packard Co. Mem. Harvard Fund Council, 1953-56, Harvard Med. Alumni Council, 1956-59; mem. com. on med. affairs Yale U. Bd. dirs. Kaiser Found. Hosps., Kaiser Found. Health Plan, Henry J. Kaiser Family Found.; bd. dirs. Commonwealth Fund, v.p., 1970—; mem. vis. com. Harvard Med. Sch., 1968—, U. Pitts. Med. Sch.; trustee Inst. Ednl. Mgmt. Fellow A.A.A.S., Am. Acad. Arts and Scis. (mem. exec. bd.); mem. Am. Clin. and Climatological Assn., Am. Fedn. Clin. Research (chmn. midwestern sect. 1954-55), Central Soc. Clin. Research (councillor 1955-58), Am. Soc. Clin. Investigation, Assn. Am. Med. Colls. (asst. sec. 1956-59, chmn. com. edn. and research 1958-62, mem. exec. council 1959-62, v.p. 1962-63, chmn. exec. council and assembly 1968-69), Assn. Am. Physicians, Western Assn. Physicians (councillor 1960-63), Am. Soc. Exptl. Pathology, Soc. American Bacteriologists, Society Exptl. Biol. and Medicine, Am. Heart Assn., A.M.A., Nat. Inst. Allergy and Infectious Disease (tng. grant com. 1957-60), Inst. Medicine, Nat. Acad. Scis. (mem. exec. com. 1970—, chmn. membership com. 1970—, acting pres. 1971-72), Sigma Xi, Alpha Omega Alpha (bd. dirs.; editor Pharos 1962—). Clubs: Harvard (Boston, N.Y.C.); Century (N.Y.C.). Contbr. to sci. jours. Home: Bard Haven Apts 100 Haven Av New York City NY 10032 Office: Harkness House 1 E 75th St New York City NY 10021

GLASER, ROBERT LEONARD, TV exec.; b. Chgo., Jan. 9, 1929; s. Maurice L. and Sara (Ziegler) G.; B.A., U. Miami, 1950; m. Nancy L. Field, Jan. 4, 1959; children—Robert Leonard, Geoffrey L., Douglas L. Midwest mgr. Metromedia, 1960-64; Midwest sales mgr. Am. Broadcasting Co., 1964-66; v.p., gen. mgr. WOR-TV, N.Y.C., 1967—. Served to 1st lt. AUS, 1950-53. Mem. Internat. Radio and TV Soc., Nat. Acad. TV Arts and Scis. Club: Friars (N.Y.C.). Home: 88 Morningside Dr S Greens Farms CT 06436 Office: 1440 Broadway New York City NY 10018

GLASER, VERA ROMANS, (Mrs. Herbert R. Glaser), journalist; b. St. Louis; d. Aaron L. and Mollie Romans; student Washington U., St. Louis, George Washington, Am. Univs., Washington, 1937-40; m. Herbert R. Glaser, Apr. 16, 1939; 1 dau., Carol Jane (Mrs. R. Michael LeVesque). Reporter-writer Nat. Aero. mag., 1943-44; reporter Washington Times Herald, 1944-46; pub. relations specialist Great Lakes-St. Lawrence Assn., 1950- 51; promotion specialist, writer Congl. Quar. News Features, 1951-54; writer-commentator radio sta. WGMS, Washington, 1954-55; mem. Washington bur. N.Y. Herald Tribune, 1955-56; press officer U.S. Senator Charles E. Potter, 1956-59; dir. pub. relations, women's div. Rep. Nat. Com., 1959-62; press officer U.S. Senator Kenneth B. Keating, 1962- 63; Washington corr. N.Am. Newspaper Alliance, 1963-69, bur. chief, 1965- 69; contbg. editor Washingtonian mag., 1966-69; corr., columist Knight Newspapers, Inc., 1969—; free-lance writer nat. publs. Mem. Pres.'s Commn. on White House Fellows, Pres.'s Task Force on Women's Rights and Responsibilities. Mem. White House, State Dept. corrs. assns. Unitarian. Clubs: Women's National Press (Washington); Overseas Press (N.Y.C.). Home: 5000 Cathedral Av NW Washington DC 20016 Office: Nat Press Bldg Washington DC 20004

GLASGOW, JAMES, business exec. Pres., Glasgow, Inc. Office: 102 Willow Grove Av Glenside PA 19038*

GLASGOW, JAMES HERSMAN, univ. dean; b. Woodson, Ill., June 6, 1906; s. Samuel Arthur and Carrie (Hersman) G.; B.Ed., Ill. State Normal U., 1928; M.A., Clark U., 1929; Ph.D., U. Chgo., 1939; m. Ruth Ora Adams, July 27, 1929. Cartographer, McKnight Geog. Pub. Co., 1929-31; head dept. geography and geology Roosevelt Coll., 1932-36; asst. prof. geography Western Mich. U., 1936- 39; prof. geography, head dept. U. Hawaii, 1952-53; prof., head dept. geography and geology Eastern Mich. U., Ypsilanti, 1939-57, dean Grad. Sch., 1950—. Summer lectr. Eastern Ill. U., 1939, 48, Northwestern U., 1949; cons. Ill. Housing Bd., 1935-36, Chgo. Met. Housing Council, 1935-36. Mem. Am. Geog. Soc., Assn. Am. Geographers. Author: Shawneetown, Illinois: A Survey of Factors Relating to the Shawneetown Removal Project, 1936; Muskegon, Michigan: The Evolution of a Lake Port, 1939; Trends in the Population of the United States as Indicated by the Census of 1940, a series of seven maps, 1941; Geography of Michigan, 1947; The North American Midwest. A Regional Geography, 1952. Home: 116 Linden Pl Ypsilanti MI 48197

GLASGOW, JESSE EDWARD, newspaper editor; b. Monroe, N.C., Mar. 28, 1923; s. Jesse Edwin and Alma (Brown) G.; B.S., Wake Forest U., 1948; m. Beth BonDurant, June 25, 1949; children—Jeffrey David, Charles Christopher. Reporter, Kannapolis (N.C.) Ind., 1947-48, Durham (N.C.) Sun, 1948-49. Norfolk Virginian-Pilot, 1949-52; reporter Balt. Sun, 1953-59, financial editor, 1960—. Served with AUS, 1943-45. Democrat. Methodist. Home: 4904 Wilmslow Rd Baltimore MD 21210 Office: Balt Sun Calvert and Centre Sts Baltimore MD 21203

GLASGOW, LELAND ELBERT, airlines cons.; b. Monticello, Ill., Dec. 19, 1903; s. Elbert P. and Jessie L. (Garrett) G.; student U. Ill., 1923-25, Advanced Mgmt. Program, Harvard, 1953; m. Blanche A. Newbould, Feb. 6, 1926; children—Betty (Mrs. Roy Schaub), Gerald. Tchr., Monticello Pub. Schs., 1922-25; sr. accountant Utilities Power & Light Co., Chgo., 1926-29; mgr. Curtiss Flying Service, Indpls., 1929-31; officer mgr. Mgmt. & Engring. Corp., Chgo., 1932-36; v.p., controller Am. Airlines, Inc., N.Y.C., 1936-64; pres. Central Airlines, Inc., Ft. Worth, 1964-65; airline, gen. cons., 1966—. Mem. Harvard Advanced Mgmt. Assn., Harvard Bus. Sch. Assn. Clubs: Harvard (Westchester); Winged Foot Golf (Mamaroneck, N.Y.). Home: 2310 Las Vegas Blvd S Las Vegas NV 89105

GLASGOW, LOWELL ALAN, med. educator, physician; b. Cin., Aug. 28, 1932; s. Russell Lowell and Glenna (Wheeldon) G.; A.B., U. Rochester, 1954, M.S., 1958, M.D., 1958; m. Mary Ann Lewis, June 16, 1956; children—Russell, Lauren, Scott. Intern sch. medicine U. Rochester, N.Y., 1958-59, resident, 1959-60, mem. faculty, 1962-70, asst. prof. microbiology and pediatrics, 1965-67, asso. prof. microbiology and asst. prof. pediatrics, 1968-70, also asso. pediatrician, 1965-70 (all at U. Rochester); research asso. nat. inst. allergy and infectious disease NIH, Bethesda, Md., 1960-62; prof. and chmn. microbiology, prof. pediatrics Coll. Medicine, U. Utah, Salt Lake City, 1970—; asso. dir. clin. microbiology labs Strong Meml. Hosp., also Monroe Co. Health Dept., both Rochester, 1964-70; mem. staff U. Utah Med. Center. Cons. antiviral substances NIH, 1970—; editorial bd. Pediatric Research Jour., 1970. Recipient Mead Johnson Pediatric Research grant Am. Acad. Pediatrics, 1963-64; Townsend Found. Pediatrics Research award, 1970; student microbiology fellow U. Rochester, 1955-56, 57-58, Wyeth Pediatric fellow, 1959-61; spl. USPHS fellow, 1963-64. Diplomate Am. Bd. Pediatrics. Mem. Am. Soc. Microbiology, N.Y. Assn. Pub. Health Labs., Soc. Pediatric Research, Am. Soc. Pediatrics, Am. Assn. Immunology, Infectious Diseases Soc. Am., Sigma Xi, Alpha Omega Alpha. Contbr. numerous articles profl. jours. Speaker several sci. meetings. Home: 2200 Panorama Way Salt Lake City UT 84117

GLASHOW, SHELDON LEE, educator, physicist; b. N.Y.C., Dec. 5, 1932; s. Lewis and Bella (Rubin) G.; A.B., Cornell U., 1954; A.M., Harvard, 1955, Ph.D., 1958. NSF fellow U. Copenhagen (Denmark), 1958-60; research fellow Cal. Inst. Tech., 1960- 61; asst. prof. Stanford, 1961-62; asst. prof., asso. prof. U. Cal. at Berkeley, 1962-66; faculty Harvard, 1966—, prof. physics, 1967—. Cons. Brookhaven Nat. Lab. 1966—, NSF fellow, 1955-60; Sloan fellow, 1962-66; CERN vis. fellow, 1968; vis. prof. U. Marseille, 1971. Mem. Am. Phys. Soc. Contbr. articles to profl. jours. Home: 84 Prescott St Cambridge MA 02138

GLASOE, PAUL KIRKWOLD, educator, chemist; b. Northfield, Minn., Nov. 22, 1913; s. Paul Maurice and Gena Annette (Kirkwold) G.; A.B., St. Olaf Coll., 1934; Ph.D., U. Wis., 1938; m. Evelyn Virginia Gustuson, Sept. 3, 1935; children—Martha Dolores, Sigrid Muriel, Christina Karen. Instr. chemistry U. Ill., 1938- 40; research chemist Eastman Kodak Co., 1940-47; asso. prof. Wittenberg Coll., Springfield, O., 1947-51, prof., 1952—, chmn. chemistry dept., 1960-68; prof. chemistry Carthage Coll., 1951-52. NSF fellow Cornell U., 1958-59, King's Coll. U. London, 1968-69. Mem. Am. Chem. Soc., Am. Assn. U. Profs., Ohio Acad. Sci., Sigma Xi, Lutheran. Author: (with J. W. Barker) First Year College Chemistry, 1951; Laboratory Manual for First Year College Chemistry, 1951. Contbr. articles to profl. jours. Home: 1237 N Limestone St Springfield OH 45503

GLASS, BRYAN PETTIGREW, educator; b. Mandeville, La., Aug. 21, 1919; s. Wiley Blount and Jessie Ligon (Pettigrew) G.; A.B., Baylor U., 1940; M.S., Tex. A. and M. Coll., 1946; Ph.D., Okla. State U., 1952; m. Carolyn Elizabeth Smith, Aug. 24, 1946; children—Janis Elizabeth, Peggy Lee. Grad. asst. biology Tex. A. and M. Coll., 1940-42, 45-46; faculty Okla. State U., Stillwater, 1946—, prof. zoology, 1961—, dir. Okla. State U. Mus., 1966—. Research grantee for research on pub. health importance of bats in Okla., NIH, 1955-59; NSF grantee, 1962; NIH grantee, 1962—. Served with USAAF, 1942-45; Pacific, CBI. Mem. Am. Soc. Mammologists (life, exec. sec.-treas. 1957—), Am. Soc. Ichthyologists and Herpetologists (life), Southwestern Assn. Naturalists, Okla. Acad. Sci., Sigma Xi. Author: Key to the Skulls of North American Mammals, 1951. Home: 517 S Willis St Stillwater OK 74074

GLASS, EARDLEY WILLIAM, constrn. co. exec.; b. Conroy, Ia., Jan. 8, 1900; s. Homer John and Amy Mary Ann (Bell) G.; student Wash. State Coll., 1919-20; m. Bernice Pearl Doyle, June 2, 1930; children—Eardley William, Walton Conrad. With Grant Smith Constrn. Co., Spokane, 1924-27, Gen. Constrn. Co., Seattle, 1928- 33; with Morrison Knudsen Co., Inc., Boise, Ida., 1933-71, v.p., 1966-71, treas., 1945-68, v.p. finance, 1968-71, also dir., treas., dir. subsidiaries; chmn. bd. Transport Holding Co.; Inc., 1971—. Bd. dirs. Bench Sewer Dist.; bd. dirs. Blue Cross Ida., 1948-70, chmn. bd., 1967-70. Served with U.S. Army, 1918. Methodist. Elk, Mason (K.T.). Club: Hillcrest Country (Boise). Home: 4014 Hillcrest St Boise ID 83705

GLASS, FREDERICK MARION, corp. exec.; b. Miss., Aug. 15, 1913; s. Frederick Marion and Carolyn Woodson (Hunter) G.; B.A., U. Miss., 1934; J.D., Northwestern U., 1935. LL.M., 1936; m. Betsy Sunderland Keller, June 28, 1941; children—Frederick Marion, Barbara Richardson, William Keller. Chief atty. CAB, 1937-39; atty. Am. Airlines, Inc., 1939-42; v.p. Capital Airlines, pres. Air Cargo, Inc., 1945-49; dir. aviation Port of N.Y. Authority, 1949-55; vice chmn. bd., chief exec. officer Empire State Bldg., Corp., 1955-60, dir., 1955-61; exec. v.p. Hertz Corp., 1960- 62; also dir.; pres., dir. Nat. Car Rental System, Inc., 1962-65; chmn. Cosmos Am. Corp., 1965-70, also dir.; vice chmn. Cosmos Bank, Zurich, Switzerland, 1965—; pres. Cosmos Equities Corp., 1967-70, also dir.; pres., dir. Prudential Funds, Inc., 1970—; dir. Avemco Co., Gen. Services Life Ins. Co., Variable Annuity Life Ins. Co., Steadman Securities Corp., Prudential Resources Corp.; Compo Industries. Inc., Mechtron Corp., Producers Chem Corp.; Ventura Internat. Corp., Aberdeen Mgmt. Corp.; Steadman Am. Industry. Mem. Nat. Aviation Facilities Study Group, 1955, Com. Mil. Air Transport Policy, 1959; chmn. Task Force Nat. Aviation Goals, 1961, pres. Airport Operators Council, 1955. Bd. govs. Flight Safety Found.; trustee Acad. Aeros., N.Y.C. Served to col. USAAF, 1942-45; col. Res. Decorated Legion of Merit, Bronze Star. Mem. Am. Bar Assn., Inst. Aero. Scis., Am. Assn. Airport Execs., Phi Delta Theta, Phi Delta Phi Mason. Clubs: Wings (pres. 1953), Racquet and Tennis (N.Y.C.); Metropolitan, Nat. Aviation, Burning Tree, University, Army and Navy (Washington); Wee Burn (Darien); Coral Beach and Tennis (Bermuda). Home: Wildcat Rd Darien CT 06820 Office: 1 New York Plaza New York City NY 10004

GLASS, HENRY EDWARD, gov. ofcl.; b. East Orange, N.J., Apr. 14, 1914; s. Joseph and Sophie (Begum) G.; B.S. in Econs., N.Y.U., 1939, postgrad., 1939-41; postgrad. Am. U., 1942; m. Lilliam L. Silver, Aug. 31, 1941; children—Marcia Lynn, Laura Faye, David Vaughn. Asst. cons. Social Security Bd., 1941; asso. economist, div. research OPA, 1942-43; with Army Air Forces Material Command, 1943-44, chief labor utilization field survey teams, 1943-45; asst. chief indsl. planning sect. Army Air Forces Tech. Service Command, 1946-47; prof. econs., later bus. orgn. USAF Inst. Tech., 1947-51; program analyst for asst. for programming Hdqrs. USAF, 1951-53; comptroller Office Asst. Sec. Def., 1953-65; asst. to sec. and dep. sec. def. Dept. Def., 1965—. Served to 1st lt. USAAF, 1944-46. Recipient Commendation medal (2). Home: 2104 N Quintana St Arlington VA 22205 Office: The Pentagon Washington DC 20301

GLASS, HIRAM BENTLEY, biologist; b. Laichowfu (now Yehsein), Shantung, China, Jan. 17, 1906; (parents Am. citizens); s. Wiley B. and Eunice (Taylor) G.; student Decatur (Tex.) Bapt. Coll., 1923-25; A.B., Baylor U., 1926, M.A., 1929; LL.D., 1958; Ph.D., U. Tex., 1932; postgrad. (NRC fellow) U. Oslo, Norway, 1932-33, Kaiser-Whlhelm Inst. Biologie, Kaiser-Wilhelm Hirnforschung, Berlin, Germany, 1933, U. Mo., 1933-34; Sc.D., Washington Coll., 1957, Western Res. U., 1962, Cornell Coll., 1965, Western Md. Coll., 1966, Adelphi U., 1969, Alfred U., 1969; LL.D., Morgan State Coll., 1968; m. Suzanne G. Smith, Aug. 10, 1934; children—Lois Anne (Mrs. R.S. Edgar), Alan Bentley. Tchr. high sch., Timpson, Tex., 1926-28; teaching fellow Baylor U., 1928-29; instr. Stephens Coll., 1934-38; research asso. bur. ednl. research in sci. Columbia Tchrs. Coll., 1936-37; from asst. prof. biology to prof. Goucher Coll., Balt., 1938-47; asso. prof. biology John Hopkins, 1947-52, prof., 1952-65; acad. v.p., Distinguished prof. biology State U. N.Y. at Stony Brook, 1965—. Mem. Internat. Genetics Congress, 1932, 48, 53, 58, 63, 68; chmn. adv. com. biology and medicine AEC, 1962- 63, mem., 1956-63; mem. continuing com. Pugwash Confs. on Sci. and World Affairs, 1958-66; mem. Md. Gov.'s Adv. Com. on Nuclear Energy, 1959-65; ofcl. U.S. del. Internat. Union Biol. Socs., 1953, 55. Pres., Md. Br. Am. Civil Liberties Union, 1955-65; pres. Fund for Overseas Research Grants and Edn., 1966—; chmn. Biol. Sci. Curriculum Study, 1959-65. Trustee Biol. Abstracts, 1954-60, pres., 1958-60; trustee Cold Spring Harbor Lab. for Quantitative Biology, 1965- -, chmn., 1967—. Fellow Am. Acad. Arts and Scis.; mem. Am. Inst. Biol. Scis. (pres. 1954-56), Nat. (chmn. NASA life scis. rev. com. 1970, com. on genetic effect atomic radiation), Czechoslovakian acads. sci., Pacific Sci. Assn. (chmn. com. sci. edn. 1967- -), Am. Philos. Soc. (council 1966-69), A.A.A.S., acting editor Sci. and Sci. Monthly 1953, v.p. zoology 1956, pres. 1969, chmn. bd. 1970), 66), Am. Soc. Zoologists, Am. Soc. Naturalists (pres. 1965), Am. Genetic Assn. (council 1952-67), Genetics Soc. Am. (v.p. 1960), Soc. for Study Evolution, Am. Soc. Human Genetics (pres. 1967), Am. Soc. Phys. Anthropology, Nat. Assn. Biology Tchrs. (pres. 1971), Conf. Biol. Editors (chmn. 1957-59), History Sci. Soc., Eugenics Soc. (bd. dirs.), Am. Assn. U. Profs. (chmn. spl. com. on acad. freedom and tenure, pres. 1958-60), Phi Beta Kappa (senator 1963-66, pres. 1967-70), Sigma Xi. Author: Genes and the Man, 1943; Science and Liberal Education, 1959; Science and Ethical Values, 1965; The Timely and the Timeless, 1970. Editor: McCollum-Pratt Symposia vols. 1-9 (with W.D. McElroy), Forerunners of Darwin, 1959; Survey of Biological Progress, vol. 3-4 Editor: Quar. Rev. Biology; editorial bd. Human Biology; Isis. Home: Box 65 East Setauket New York City NY 11733 Office: State U NY at Stony Brook Stony Brook NY 11790

GLASS, MARVIN, toy designer; b. Chgo. Designer children's toys Marvin Glass & Assos., Chgo.; ann. exhibits Am. Toy Fair, N.Y.C. Holder numerous patents. Home: 1319 Forest Av Evanston IL 60201 Office: 815 N LaSalle St Chicago IL 60610

GLASS, MILTON, architect; b. N.Y.C., Jan. 30, 1900; s. Louis and Sarah B. (Hertzoff) G.; student Coll. City N.Y., 1925-28, 30-32, Columbia, 1925-30, N.Y.U., 1930-31, Beaux-Arts Inst. Design, 1925-31; m. Ruth M. Goodman, July 1, 1928 (dec. Sept. 1970); children—Joan Dorothy Cantor, Elliott Michael. Draftsman various archtl. offices, 1925-40; chief draftsman Mayer & Whittlesey, architects and town planners, 1940-45; partner Mayer, Whittlesey & Glass, 1945-60; sr. partner Glass & Glass, N.Y.C., 1960-67, 70—; instr. site planning Sch. Architecture, Cooper Union, 1961-62. Bd. dirs. Citizens Housing and Planning Council N.Y., 1955—, chmn. com. on community renewal and planning criteria, 1963; mem. Citizens Union N.Y. City Planning Com., 1962—; mem. Municipal Arts Soc. N.Y.; mem. architects adv. com. N.Y.C. Housing and Redevelopment Bd., 1966-67; mem. adv. com. N.Y. State Commr. Housing and Community Renewal, 1962-63; chmn. Bd. Standards and Appeals, City of New York, 1967-70. Mem. adv. com. Grad. div. Columbia U. Sch. Architecture, 1950. Recipient medal of honor N.Y. chpt. A.I.A., 1952, Apt. House medal N.Y. chpt. A.I.A., 1952, 1st Design award Progressive Archifecture, 1959, 60, certificate of merit Municipal Arts Soc. N.Y., 1961, 63, Bard award City Club N.Y., 1963, 1st Honor award for residential design FHA, 1963, award Merit Queens C. of C., 1965. Mem. A.I.A. (sec., chmn. com. on admissions N.Y. chpt. 1949-50, chmn. civic design com. 1961-62), N.Y. Soc. Architects (dir. 1950-62), Nat. Inst. Archtl. Edn. (trustee), N.Y. State Assn. Architects (jury on awards 1971). K.P. Important works include Master Plan City of Kitimat, B.C., Can., cons. Master Plan City of Ashdod, Israel, apt. houses Butterfield House and The Premier, N.Y.C., Forest Park Crescent, Queens, N.Y. Office: 31 Union Sq New York City NY 10003

GLASS, ROBERT RIGBY, mgmt. cons.; b. Me., Aug. 18, 1914; ed. Mil. Acad. Me.; B.S., U.S. Mil. Acad., 1935; grad. Command and Gen. Staff Sch., 1946, Armed Forces Staff Coll., 1950, Army War Coll., 1954; m. Phyllis Clarke Thompson; 5 children. Commd. 2d lt. U.S. Army, 1935, advanced through grades to maj. gen., 1965, ret., 1969; mgmt. cons. Planning Research Corp., McLean, Va., 1969—. Decorated Legion of Merit with 2 oak leaf clusters, D.S.M., Bronze Star, Air medal. Co-author: Intelligence Is for Commanders. Home: 2776 Ft Scott Dr Arlington VA 22202 Office: 7600 Old Springhouse Rd McLean VA 22101

GLASS, WILLIAM EVERETT, physician, hosp. supt.; b. Amarillo, Tex., May 14, 1906 s. William P. and Gertrude (Compton) G.; B.S., U. Ill., 1928, M.D., 1931; m. Margaret H. Quann, Nov. 21, 1931; children—William Lewis, Cynthia Anne. Staff physician Worcester (Mass.) State Hosp., 1931-36; city physician, Marlboro, Mass., 1936-37; asst. supt. Grafton (Mass.) State Hosp., 1938- 47; hosp. insp. Boston Dept. Mental Health, 1947-48; supt. Taunton (Mass.) State Hosp., 1948—; instr. psychiatry Tufts U. Med. Sch., 1939- 48; dir. clinics Bristol County Mental Health Inst., 1949-65; cons. psychiatry Sturdy Meml. Hosp., Attleboro, Mass., 1960—, Union, Truesdale hosps., Fall River, Mass., 1960—, Morton Hosp., Taunton, 1967—. Diplomate Am. Bd. Psychiatry and Neurology. Fellow A.M.A.; mem. Am. Psychiat. Assn., Mass. Med. Soc., Mass. Soc. Research

Psychiatry, New Eng. Soc. Psychiatry (past pres.), Am. Soc. Clin. Hypnosis. Rotarian. Home: Chambers Rd Taunton MA 02781 Office: Taunton State Hosp Taunton MA 02781

GLASSCO, JAMES BRINTON, aerospace research co. exec.; b. Fargo, N.D., June 23, 1913; s. Ray John and Clarabel (Brinton) G.; B.S. in M.E., Cal. Inst. Tech., 1940, postgrad., 1942-45; postgrad. U. Cal. at Los Angeles, 1941-42, 47-48, 53, U. So. Cal., 1943; m. Margaret Elizabeth Brinton, Dec. 20, 1941; children—John Edward, Vicki Ann. With McDonnell Douglas Corp. (formerly Douglas Aircraft Co.), 1940—, supr. structures, 1958-62, staff scientist research structures, 1962—. cons. engr. Glassco Instrument Co., 1955-63; dir. tng. courses profl. engrs. So. Cal. Profl. Engrs. Assn., 1955-58; tchr. grad. extension course structural design U. Cal. at Los Angeles, 1962, 63. Recipient Wright Bros. medal Soc. Automotive Engrs., 1964. Asso. fellow Am. Inst. Aeros. and Astronautics. Contbr. tech. papers, reports to profl. lit. Home: 5356 Encino Av Encino CA 91316 Office: 5301 Bolsa Av Huntington Beach CA 92647

GLASSCO, JOHN GRANT, pub. utility exec.; b. Los Angeles, Jan. 20, 1905; s. John Girdlestone and Esther Jane (Grant) G.; student Ridley Coll., St. Catherines, Ont., Can.; B. Commerce, McGill U., 1925; m. Willa Florence Blanche Price, June 9, 1928; 4 children. In pub. accounting McDonald Currie & Co., Montreal and Quebec, 1926-30; with Clarkson Gordon & Co., Toronto, 1931- 57, partner, 1935-57; exec. v.p. Brazilian Light & Power Co. Ltd., Toronto, 1957-63, pres., 1963-68, chmn. bd., 1968—, also dir.; pres. Transatlantic Fund, Inc., N.Y.; v.p. Canadian Imperial Bank of Commerce; dir. Southam Press, Ltd., McIntyre Porcupine Mines, Ltd., Canadian Corporate Mgmt. Co. Ltd., Nat. Trust Co. Ltd., Investors Syndicate, Ltd., Mfrs. Life Ins. Co., Consumers' Gas Co., Simpsons, Ltd., Simpsons-Sears, Ltd. Chmn. Royal Commn. Govt. Orgn., 1960-62. Mem. bd. trustees Hosp. for Sick Children, Toronto; a founder and past chmn. Canadian Tax Found.; past pres. Canadian Inst. Chartered Accountants. Served with Canadian Dept. Munitions and Supply, 1942-46. Officer Order of Brit. Empire. Fellow Royal Philatelic Soc. London. Clubs: York, Toronto (Toronto); Rideau (Ottawa); Mt. Royal (Montreal); Collectors (N.Y.C.). Mem. Anglican Ch. Home: 213B Popular Plains Rd Toronto 7 Ontario Canada also Cold Creek Farm Woodbridge Ontario Canada Office: 25 King St W Toronto Ontario Canada

GLASSELL, ALFRED CURRY, Jr., oil operator; b. Cuba Plantation, La., Mar. 31, 1914; s. Alfred Curry and Frances L. (Regan) G.; B.A., La. State U., 1934; m. Clare Attwell; children—Jean Curry, Alfred Curry. Inde. oil & gas operator, 1936- -; pres. Glassell Drilling Co., Glassell Producing Co., Inc., 1938—; dir. First City Nat. Bank, Transcontinental Gas Pipe Line Corp., Down Town Real Estate Co., El Paso Natural Gas Co. Bd. dirs. Houston Symphony Soc., Houston Mus. Natural Sci., Am. Oceanographic Found.; trustee Internat. Oceanographic Found. Mem. Am. Geog. Soc., Am. Mus. Natural History, Fine Arts Mus. of Houston. Clubs: Atlantic Tuna (Providence); Boston (New Orleans); Cabo Blanco Fishing (Peru); Cat Key (British West Indies) Texas Corinthian Yacht (Kemah); Bay of Islands Swordfish and Mako Shark (New Zealand); Sportsman's of America (Chgo.); Houston, Petroleum, Ramada, River Oaks Country, Houston Gun, Horse Show Assn., Houston Country (Houston); N.Y. Yacht; Coronado; Yale Fishing; Internat. Home: 3030 Inwood Dr Houston TX 77019 Office: First City Nat Bank Bldg Houston TX 77002

GLASSER, ARTHUR CHARLES, univ. ofcl.; b. Pitts., June 19, 1921; s. Herbert Glenn and Louise Marie (Lindner) G.; B.S., Duquesne, 1949; Ph.D., Ohio State 1953; m. Marjorie Ellen John, May 7, 1943; children—Stephan, Ellen, David. Asst., Ohio State U. Coll. Pharmacy, 1949-51; asso. prof. pharm. chemistry U. Ky., Lexington, 1953-58, prof. head dept., 1959-70, acting dean, 1964-67, asst. dean adminstrn. Coll. Pharmacy, 1967-70; dean U. Cin. Coll. Pharmacy, 1970—. Served with USNR, 1942-45. Am. Found. Pharm. Edn. fellow, 1951-53. Mem. Am. Pharm. Assn., Am. Chem. Soc., Sigma Xi. Home: 661 Allencrest Ct Cincinnati OH 45231

GLASSER, HAROLD LEWIS, apparel mfg. co. exec.; b. N.Y.C., Aug. 22, 1918; s. Herman and Etta (Gelenter) G.; A.B., N.Y.U., 1939; student Harvard Law Sch., 1939-41; LL.B., Columbia, 1942; LL.M., N.Y.U., 1949; m. Evelyn Liftin, Feb. 1, 1942; children—Farrell C., Kerry S. Admitted to N.Y. bar, 1942; gen. counsel Chester H. Roth, Inc., N.Y.C., 1945-49; pvt. practice, N.Y.C., 1949-58; v.p., sec., gen. counsel, dir. Kayser-Roth Corp., N.Y.C., 1958—; pres. Miss Universe, Inc., Pres. Great Neck (N.Y.) Village Ofcls. Assn., 1962; chmn. Anti-Defamation League Great Neck, 1964-65. Atty., Village Saddle Rock, N.Y., 1952- 53, mayor, 1953-62. Bd. dirs. Assn. Help Retarded Children, 1964—. Served as 1st lt. USAAF, 1943-45. Decorated D.F.C., Air medal with 3 oak leaf clusters; recipient Human Rights award Anti-Defamation League, 1966. Mem. N.Y. State Bar Assn., Bar Assn. N.Y.C., Am. Soc. Corp. Secs. (bd. dirs.), Mil. Order World Wars, Tau Delta Phi. Clubs: Harvard, City Athletic, Adventurers (N.Y.C.); Fresh Meadow Country (Great Neck). Author: The Corporation and The Professional Man-A Merger. Home: 860 United Nations Plaza New York City NY 10017 Office: 640 Fifth Av New York City NY 10019

GLASSER, MELVIN ALLAN, union exec.; b. N.Y.C. Sept. 6, 1915; s. David and Rae (Startz) G. student N.Y. U., 1932-33; B.S.S., Coll. City N.Y., 1935; postgrad. Grad. Sch. Jewish Social Work, N.Y. Sch. Social Work, 1939; LL.D., Adelphi Coll., 1951; m. Esther Kron, June 25, 1939; children—Stephen Andrew, Amy Helaine, Robin Ruth, Investigator, Dept. Welfare N.Y.C., 1936-37; caseworker Jewish Family Welfare Soc., Bklyn., 1937-40; asst. nat. dir., field supr., field dir. mil. and naval welfare service Am. Nat. Red Cross, 1940-44, asst. adminstr. internat. activities, 1944-49; exec. dir. Mid-Century White House Conf. Children and Youth, 1949-51; asso. chief U.S. Children's Bur., 1951-53; asst. to pres. Nat. Found. Infantile Paralysis, 1953-59; exec. v.p., 1959-61; dean univ. resources, vis. prof. social welfare Brandeis U., 1961-63; dir. social security dept. Internat. Union United Automobile, Aerospace and Agrl. Implement Workers, Detroit, 1963—. Past chmn. U.S. com. Internat. Conf. Social Work; dir., past chmn. exec. com. Nat. Health Council; mem. nat. com. White House Conf. Children and Youth, 1960; U.S. rep. health and welfare, Red Cross and govt. internat. confs., Europe, S.E. Asia, Latin Am., Japan; Vice chmn. bd. trustees Tuskegee Inst.; trustee Nat. Found.; Ga. Warm Springs Found., Salk Inst. for Exptl. Biology, Greater Detroit Hosp. Council, Com. for Nat. Health Ins.; bd. mem. Community Health Assn. Detroit, Met. Hosp. Detroit, Group Health Assn. Am. Decorated Order White Lion (Czechoslovakia); Order Orange-Nassau (Netherlands), govt. decorations Denmark, Argentina; Red Cross Award, Finland. Fellow Am. Pub. Health Assn. (governing council); mem. Nat. Assn. Social Workers, Nat. Conf. Social Welfare. Contbr. articles health and welfare to profl. jours. Home: 837 Moorland Dr Grosse Pointe MI 48236 Office: Solidarity House 8000 E Jefferson Av Detroit MI 48214

GLASSER, OTTO JOHN, air force officer; b. Wilkes-Barre, Pa., Oct. 2, 1918; s. Leo George and Lillian (Cave) G.; E.E., Cornell U., 1940; M.S. in Elec. Engring., Ohio State U., 1947; m. Norma Mayo, Sept. 11, 1943; children—Charlene Lee, Carole Jeanne. Test engr. Gen. Electric Co., 1940-41; commd. 2d lt. U.S. Army, 1941, advanced through grades to lt. gen. USAF, 1969; program dir. Atlas and Minuteman programs, 1954-59; asst. dep. chief staff research and devel. Hdqrs. USAF, Washington, 1966-69, dep. chief staff research and devel., 1969—. Decorated D.S.M. Legion of Merit, Air Force Commendation medal. Home: Quarters 28 Bolling AFB Washington DC 20332 Office: AFRDC Hdqrs USAF The Pentagon Washington DC 20330

GLASSER, WILLIAM, psychiatrist; b. Cleve., May 11, 1925; s. Ben and Betty (Silverberg) G.; B.S., Case Inst. Tech., 1945; M.A., Western Res. U., 1948, M.D., 1953; m. Naomi Judith Silver, Sept. 20, 1946; children—Joseph, Alice, Martin, Intern and resident VA Center, Los Angeles also U. Cal Med. Center, Los Angeles; psychiatrist Ventura (Cal.) Sch. Girls, Cal. Youth Authority, 1956-67, Orthopaedic Hosp., Los Angeles, 1957-66, adult narcotic program Cal., 1963-66, Sacramento, Palo Alto, Los Angeles City and County schs., 1960- -; founder Reality Therapy Inst., 1967. Served with AUS, 1946-47. Mem. A.M.A., Am. Psychiat. Assn. Author: Mental Health or Mental Illness?, 1961; Reality Therapy, 1965; Schools Without Failure, 1969. Office: 11633 San Vicente Blvd Los Angeles CA 90049

GLASSETT, ALFRED THOMAS, civil engr.; b. Boston, Jan. 17, 1900; s. Thomas S. and Anne L. (Stanton) G.; B.S., Mass. Inst. Tech., 1920; m. Esther Nowland Haberstroh; children—Mrs. Lillian Brown, John Haberstroh. With James H. Fuertes, Osgood Constrn. Co. and Stone & Webster Engring. Corp., Boston, 1920-24; estimator W. J. Barney Corp., N.Y.C., 1924- 29, chief estimator, 1929-36, v.p., treas., sec., dir., 1936-47. exec. v.p., 1947-51, pres. 1951—; pres. John William Contracting Co., N.Y.C., 1936-39; lectr. dept. architecture Columbia, 1936-46; dir. Townsend House Corp., N.Y.C., 1954—. Mem. corp. Mass. Inst. Tech., 1951-58; dir. N.Y. Bldg. Congress, 1952-53, v.p., 1957-61. Mem. Am. Soc. C.E. (life), Nat. Fire Protection Assn., Nat. Safety Council, Mass. Inst. Tech. Alumni Assn. (pres. 1951-52), N.Y. Engrs. Com. on Student Guidance (chmn. 1947-48), Am. Soc. Concrete Constructors (dir.). Clubs: Technology, Union League (gov. 1954, v.p.) (N.Y.C.); Scarsdale (N.Y.) Golf (gov. 1950-56, pres. 1955); St. Botolph (Boston). Home: 176 E 71st St New York City NY 10021 Office: 101 Park Av New York City NY 10017

GLASSFORD, JACK EDWARD, securities co. exec.; b. Pueblo, Colo., June 14, 1921; s. Emmanice Ulibarri; grad. high sch.; m. Gladys Overstreet, Sept. 28, 1941; children—David Jack, Steven Mathew, Jack Nathan. Pres., Internat. Securities Corp., Newport Beach, Cal., 1960—; pres. Coordinated Capital Cos., 1960—. Mem. Ont. Planning Commn., 1953-61. Served with USNR, World War II. Mem. Internat. Assn. Financial Counsellors (chmn. bd. govs.). Mason. Clubs: Los Angeles Athletic, Balboa Bay. Home: 30171 Silver Spur Rd San Juan Capistrano CA 92675 Office: 2121 San Joaquin Hills Rd Newport Beach CA 92660

GLASSGOLD, ALFRED EMANUEL, physicist, educator; b. Phila., July 20, 1929; s. Solomon S. and Anna (Blaukopf) G.; B.A., U. Pa., 1950; Ph.D., Mass. Inst. Tech., 1954; m. Irene Mihaly, Jan. 25, 1953; children—Judith, Eric. Research and teaching physics Oak Ridge Nat. Lab., 1954-55, U. Minn., 1955-57, U. Cal., 1957-63; mem. faculty N.Y.U., 1963—, prof., head dept. physics, 1969—; cons. Brookhaven, Los Alamos labs. Mem. Am. Phys. Soc., A.A.A.S., Phi Beta Kappa, Sigma Xi. Research on theoretical physics, nuclear structure, atomic collisions, statis. physics. Home: 3035 Palidade Av Bronx NY 10463 Office: 4 Washington Pl New York City NY 10003

GLASSIE, HENRY HAYWOOD, lawyer; b. Chevy Chase, Md., May 24, 1914; s. Henry Haywood and Gertrude (Caffery) G.; B.S., U. Va., 1935, LL.B., 1937; m. Adele Chichester Balderston, July 16, 1938 (div. 1959); children—Henry Haywood III, Julia A.; m. 2d, Jean Manning, Dec. 30, 1959, (div. 1969); 1 foster son, Steven Pate; m. 3d, Dorothy Dodson, Sept. 11, 1969. Admitted to N.Y. bar, 1940, D.C. bar, 1940, Md. bar, 1949; asso. firm Chadbourne, Wallace, Parke & Whiteside, N.Y.C., 1937-40; partner Barbour, Garnett, Pickett, Keith & Glassie, Washington, 1941-49, Glassie, Pewett, Beebe & Shanks; chief counsel subcom. procurement U.S. Ho. of Reps., 1948. Dir. D.C. Nat. Bank, A. Smith Bowman Distillery, Inc., Sunset Hills, Va., U.S. Axle Co., Pottstown, Pa. Exec. com U.S. Lawn Tennis Assn., 1964-66. Bd. dirs. Tchrs. Services Corp.; trustee Bowman Found. Served to lt. USNR, World War II. Mem. Am., Fed. (nat. council), D.C. bar assns., Nat. Lawyers Club (v.p., dir.), Middle Atlantic Lawn Tennis Assn. (pres. 1962-64, dir.), Columbia, N.Y. State, Montgomery County hist. assns., Soc. Archtl. Historians, Nat. Trust Hist. Preservation. Democrat. Clubs: Chevy Chase (Md.); Jefferson Islands (St. Marys County, Md.); Fairfax Hunt (Fairfax County, Va.). Home: 2883 Audubon Terrace Washington DC 20008 Office: 1819 H St NW Washington DC 20006

GLASSMAN, HERBERT HASKEL, architect; b. Boston, Mar. 29, 1919; s. Jacob and Jennie Rose (Levine) G.; student Ga. Inst. Tech., 1937-38; certificate in architecture (Spl. Student scholar) Mass. Inst. Tech., 1942, Boston Archtl. Center, 1941; student in structures Cath. U., 1942-43. George Washington U., 1942-43; m. Anne Shirley Resnick, June 20, 1948; children—Elsa Jan, Karin Melvey, Jack Ian. With Perley F. Gilbert Assos., Inc., Lowell, Mass., 1946—, partner in charge archtl. div., 1949-59, v.p., 1950-59, pres., 1959—. Critic in archtl. design Boston Archtl. Center Sch., 1947-59; vis. lectr. U. Mass. State Coll., Framingham, 1959—. Served with U.S. Coast and Geodetic Survey, 1942-43, USAAF, 1943-44. Fellow Internat. Inst. Arts and Letters, Kreuzlingen, Switzerland, 1960. Mem. Boston Soc. Architects, Mass. State Assn. Architects, A.I.A., Constrn. Specifications Inst., Internat. Inst. Fine Arts and Letters, Soc. Archtl. Historians, Architects-Engrs. Lodge. Jewish religion (v.p. temple 1966-68). Mem. B'nai B'rith. Important works include schs. in East Jaffrey, N.H., Springfield, Vt., Ayer, Mass., Attleboro, Mass., Portsmouth, N.H., Sterling (Mass.) High Sch., Brocton (Mass.) High Sch., Ayer (Mass.) Ednl. Park, Acton (Mass.) Ednl. Park, student Union, high rise dormitory Lowell Technol. Inst., Temple Isaiah, Lexington, Mass., Little Harbour Sch., Portsmouth, N.Y. Home: 19 Hancock St Lexington MA 02173

GLASSMAN, IRVIN, eductor; b. Balt., Sept. 19, 1923; s. Abraham and Bessie Mary (Snyder) G.; B. Engring., Johns Hopkins, 1943, D. Engring., 1950; m. Beverly Wolfe, June 21, 1951; children—Shari Lynn, Diane Joy, Barbara Ann. Chem. engring. research asso. Manhattan Project, 1943-46; mem. faculty Princeton, 1950—, prof. aerospace scis., 1964—; cons. to govt. and industry. Dep. chmn. propulsion and energetics com., adv. group aero. devel. and research NATO, 1964—; vis. prof. Inst. Aerodynamics, U. Naples (Italy), 1966-67. Trustee John F. Kennedy Am. Sch., Naples, 1966-67. NSF sr. postdoctoral fellow, 1966-67, Mem. Am. Inst. Aeros. and Astronautics (asso. editor jour. 1951-64), Am. Assn. U. Profs., Am. Soc. Engring. Edn., Am. Chem. Soc. (coop. lectr. 1959), A.A.A.S., Combustion Inst., N.Y. Acad. Scis., Sigma Xi. Co-author: Performance of Chemical Propellants. Editor: Recent Advances in Aerothermochemistry; Combustion Science and Technology (book series), 1969, co-editor: Heterogeneous Combustion, 1964; editor Combustion Sci. and Tech. Jour., 1969. Home: 27 Tyson Lane Princeton NJ 08540

GLASSMEYER, EDWARD, coll. pres.; b. Jersey City, Sept. 14, 1915; s. Edward and Claire (Stuckert) G.; B.A., Princeton, 1936; m. Elizabeth Fellows, Jan. 5, 1939; children—Marion (Mrs. Jack L. Treynor), Edward, Mary, Edith (Mrs. Colin Mathews). Statistician, Blyth & Co., Inc., N.Y.C., 1936-47, syndicate mgr., 1947-70, v.p., 1950-62, dir., 1950-70, exec. com., 1960-70, sr. v.p., 1962-70; pres. Athens (Greece) Coll., 1970; past dir., mem. exec. com. Emery Air Freight Corp.; past dir. Genesco, Inc., Foodco, Inc.; guest lectr. Princeton, other colls. Adv. bd. dept. Classics, Princeton; trustee, v.p., chmn. exec. com. Beekman Downtown Hosp., N.Y.C.,; trustee Athens Coll., Poly. Inst. Bklyn. Served as Sgt., OSS, AUS, 1945-46; Germany. Mem. Investment Bankers Assn. Am. (v.p., gov. 1958-60, chmn. N.Y. group 1959-60), Archeol. Inst. Am. (trustee). Republican. Presbyn. Clubs: Bond (pres. 1966-67), Down Town Assn., Links (N.Y.C.); Nassau (Princeton, N.J.); Country (New Canaan). Home: Weed St New Canaan CT 06840 Office: Box 175 Athens Greece

GLASSTONE, SAMUEL, cons.; b. London, Eng., Mar. 5, 1897; B.Sc., U. of London, 1916, M.Sc., 1920, Ph.D., 1922, D.Sc., 1926; m. Violette F. Collingwood, July 1929. Came to U.S., 1939, naturalized, 1944. Lectr. in phys. chemistry, U. London, 1919-21, Coll. of Southwest (Eng.), 1921-28, U. Sheffield (Eng.), 1929-39; research asso., Princeton, 1939-41, sci. editor U. Press, 1941-42; prof. chemistry U. Okla., 1942-43, Boston Coll., 1947- 48; cons. AEC 1948—, Armed Forces spl. Weapons Project, 1950-51, Los Alamos Sci. Lab., 1952—. Recipient Worcester Reed Warner medal Am. Soc. M.E., 1959. Mem. Chem. Soc. London, Am. Nuclear Soc. (Compton award 1968), Sigma Xi. Author numerous books, latest of which are: Elements of Physical Chemistry, 1946, rev., 1960; Thermodynamics for Chemists, 1947; Sourcebook on Atomic Energy, 1950, rev. edition, 1958; (with Edlund), Elements of Nuclear Reactor Theory 1952; Principles of Nuclear Reactor Engineering, 1955; (with R. H. Lovberg), Controlled Thermonuclear Reactions, 1960; (with A. Sesonske) Nuclear Reactor Engineering, 1963; Sourcebook on the Space Sciences, 1965, 3d edit., 1967; The Book of Mars, 1968. Co-editor: A Treatise on Physical Chemistry, 3d edit., 1942. Editor: Effects of Nuclear Weapons, 1957, rev. 1962. Exec. editor: The Effects of Atomic Weapons, 1950. Writer numerous papers in sci. mags. and jours. ☆

GLATFELTER, PHILIP HENRY, III, pulp and paper mfr.; b. Spring Grove, Pa., Mar. 17, 1916; s. Philip H. and Cassandra (McClellan) G.; grad. Hill Sch., 1934; A.B., Brown U., 1938; m. Anne C. Manifold, Nov. 15, 1940; children—Patricia Anne, Elizabeth M. With P.H. Glatfelter Co., Spring Grove, 1938—, pres., 1954—; staff asst. W.P.B., 1941-42; dir. Western Md. R.R., Phila. Fed. Res. Bd. York Bd. dirs. Welfare Fedn., 1952-54, Spring Grove Welfare Fedn., 1954- 55. Trustee U. Me. Pulp and Paper Found. Served with USNR, 1942-46. Mem. Printing Paper Mfrs. Assn. (chmn. 1961-62), Am. Paper Inst. (dir.), Am. Forest Inst. (dir.), Nat. Council Air and Stream Improvement (dir.), York C. of C. (dir. 1953-56). Mfg. Assn. York (pres. 1954). Home: Hickory Hill Spring Grove PA 17362 Office: Spring Grove PA 17362

GLATHART, JUSTIN LEON, educator; b. Findlay, O., Mar. 25, 1903 s. Harry Aaron and Clara Augusta (Landon) Ga; B.S., Case Inst. Tech., 1925; M.S., U. Mich., 1931; Ph.D., U. Chgo., 1939; m. Mary Jane Grabenstein, July 26, 1958; 1 dau., Deborah Lynn. Instr. physics Williams Coll., 1925-29, 31-35; prof. physics Shurtleff Coll., Alton, Ill., 1938-42; vis. prof. physics Kenyon Coll., 1942-44; research physicist Preston Labs., Butler, Pa., 1944-47; prof. physics Albion (Mich.) Coll., 1947-62, now prof. physics emeritus, chmn. dept., 1962—. Fellow A.A.A.S.; mem. Am. Assn. Physics Tchrs. (pres. Mich. 1962), Am. Phys. Soc., Am. Assn U. Profs., Sigma Xi, Sigma Zeta (nat. pres. 1940), Sigma Chi, Gamma Phi, Sigma Pi Sigma. Methodist. Rotarian. Author: Physics Laboratory Manual, 1933; College Physics, 1947. Home: 418 Darrow St Albion MI 49224

GLATZER, NAHUM NORBERT, educator, historian; b. Lemberg, Austria, Mar. 25, 1903; s. Daniel D. and Rose (Gottlieb) G.; student Talmudic Acad., Frankfort-Main, Germany, 1920-22; Ph.D., U. Frankfort, 1931; m. Anne Stiebel, Jan. 30, 1932; children—Daniel, Judith. Came to U.S., 1938, naturalized, 1944. Sr. lectr. Jewish philosophy U. Frankfort (Germany), 1932-33; instr. Hebrew lit. Betsefer Reali, Haifa, Palestine, 1933-38; with Coll. Jewish Studies, Chgo., 1938-43; prof. Hebrew Tchrs. Coll., Boston, 1943-47; prof. history Yeshiva U., 1947-51; asso. prof. Jewish history Brandeis U., Waltham, Mass., 1951-56, prof., 1956—, chmn. dept. Nr. Eastern and Judaic Studies, 1957- 69; Seminar asso. Columbia, 1959-62; vis. prof. history U. Cal., Los Angeles, 1967. Bd. dirs. Leo Baeck Inst. Guggenheim fellow, 1959-60. Fellow Internat. Inst. Arts and Letters; mem. Am. Hist. Soc., Assn. Jewish Studies (dir.), Jewish Publ. Soc., Franz Rosenzweig Soc. (v.p. 1958-69). Author numerous books, 1931—, including: In Time and Eternity, rev. edit., 1961; Language of Faith, rev. edit., 1967; A Midrash Reader, 1948; Franz Rosenzweig: His Life and Thought, rev. edit., 1961; Hillel the Elder, 1956, Spanish edit., 1964, German edit., 1966; Leopold Zunz, 2 vols., 1958, 64; Jerusalem and Rome 1960; The Rest is Commentary, 1961; Faith and knowledge, 1962; Dynamics of Emancipation, 1965; Beginnings of Judaism, 1966. Chief editor Schocken Books, 1954-64, sr. cons. editor, 1964—; editor Days of Awe, 1948; The Haggadah, 1953, rev. edit., 1969; editor Understanding the Sick and the Healthy, 1954; On Jewish Learning, 1955; A History of the Jews in the Time of Jesus, 1961; The Way of Response, 1966; Buber on Judaism, 1967; Buber on the Bible, 1968; The Dimensions of Job, 1969; contbg. editor: Judaism, Bitzaron also contbr. Ency. Brit. Home: 379 School St Watertown MA 02172 Office: Brandeis U Waltham MA 02154

GLAUBER, ROY JAY, educator, physicist; b. N.Y.C., Sept. 1, 1925; s. Emanuel B. and Felicia (Fox) G.; B.S summa cum laude, Harvard, 1946, M.A., 1947, Ph.D., 1949; mem. Inst. Advanced Study, 1949-51; research fellow, Swiss Fed. Poly. Inst., Zürich, 1950; m. Cynthia Marshall Rich, July 26, 1960; 1 son, Jeffrey Marshall. Mem. staff theoretical physics div. Los Alamos Sci. Lab., 1944-46; lectr. Cal. Inst. Tech., 1951-52; mem. faculty Harvard, 1952—, prof. physics, 1962—; vis. lectr. Ecole d'été de Physique Théorique, Les Houches, France, 1954, 64, U. Cal at Berkeley, 1955, 57, 63, U. Colo., 1958, 61, U. Wash. 1960, Brandeis U., 1961, U. Leningrad (USSR), 1964, dir. Enrico Fermi Internat. Sch. of Physics, 1967; Fulbright lectr., France, 1954; spl. research nuclear physics, quantum theory radiation, statis. mechanics, NRC predoctoral fellow, 1946-49; AEC postdoctoral fellow, 1949-50; Frank B. Jewett fellow, 1950- 51; Guggenheim fellow, 1959; NSF sr. postdoctoral fellow, 1966, 67. Mem. Am. Phys. Soc., Am. Acad. Arts and Scis., Phi Beta Kappa, Sigma Xi. Editor: Quantum Optics, 1969. Contbr. articles profl. jours. Bd. editors Jour. Math. Physics, 1961-63. Home: 221 Pleasant St Arlington MA 02174 Office: Lyman Lab Physics Harvard Univ Cambridge MA 02138

GLAUHMAN, MICHAEL JUDA, educator; b. Balt., Dec. 21, 1924; s. Mordecai Gimple and Rachel (Katz) G.; M.S., Hebrew U., 1947; postgrad. U. Chgo., 1948; Ph.D., U. Ill., 1953; m. Hilda Marjorie Dunn, May 30, 1961; children—David Jacob, Judith Anne, Jane Marjorie, Sarah Susannah. Research asst. Princeton, 1953-55, Columbia, 1955-56; sr. physicist Atomics Internat., Canoga Park, Cal., 1956-59; asst. prof. physics Northeastern U., Boston, 1959-61, asso. prof., 1961-69, prof., chmn. dept., 1969—. Mem. Am. Phys.

Soc., Am. Assn. Physics Tchrs., A.A.A.S. Home: 9 Blueberry Lane Lexington MA 02173 Office: Northeastern University Boston MA 02115

GLAUSER, ALFRED CHARLES, educator; b. St. Imier, Switzerland, Feb. 24, 1913; s. Alfred Louis and Berthe (Saurer) G.; Baccalauréat és lettres, Gymnase de La Chaux-de- Fonds, 1932; Licence-ès lettres, Université de Genève, 1935; student U. Pa., 1937-38; Ph.D., U. Wis., 1947. Came to U.S., 1937, naturalized, 1956. Tchr. pvt. schs. in Can., 1938-43; mem. faculty U. Man., 1943-46; mem. faculty U. Wis., Madison, 1947—, now prof. Decorated Palmes académiques; Guggenheim fellow, 1965-66. Author: Albert Thibaudet et la critique créatrice, 1951; Hugo et la poésie pure, 1957; Rabelais créateur, 1966; Le poeme-symbole, 1967; Montaigne Paradoxal, 1971. Home: 3104 Bluff St Madison WI 53705

GLAVAS, KOSMA JAMES, lawyer; b. Canton, O., June 28, 1930; s. James and Fay (Zaferakes) G.; B.A., Baldwin Wallace Coll., Berea, O., 1955; J.D., U. Notre Dame, 1959. Admitted to Ohio bar. 1959. since practiced in Elyria; asso. G.L. Severs, 1959-61; partner Severs & Glavas, 1961—. Vice pres. Beal Constrn. Co.; dir. Cove Investment Co., Inc. Law dir. City of Elyria, 1966-67, city solicitor, 1968—. Served to capt. USMCR Mem. Law Library Assn. (past trustee), Lorain County Bar Assn. (past mem. exec. com.). Kiwanian. Club: Elyria Memorial Hospital. Home: 1201 Park Av Elyria OH 44035 Office: Lorain County Bank Bldg Elyria OH 44035

GLAVIANO, VINCENT VALENTINO, educator, physiologist; b. Frankford, N.Y., July 19, 1920; s. Salvatore and Josephine (Manzo) G.; B.S., Coll. City N.Y., 1950; Ph.D., Columbia, 1954; m. Eleanor Spargimino, July 18, 1943; children—Joan J., Vincent S. Faculty, Columbia, 1951-53, fellow, 1954-56; instr. Hunter Coll., N.Y.C., 1952-54; asst. prof. physiology U. Ill. Coll. Medicine, Chgo., 1956-60; asso. prof. physiology Loyola U. Sch. Medicine, Chgo., 1960-64, prof., 1964-70; prof., chmn. Chgo. Med. Sch., 1970—; cons.. Cook County Hosp. Cardiopulmonary Lab., Abbot Labs. Postdoctoral research fellow N.Y. Heart Assn., 1954-56; travel awards Nat. Acad. Scis., 1962, 65. Mem. Am. Physiol. Soc., Soc. Exptl. Biology and Medicine, Am., Chgo. heart assns., Harvey Soc., N.Y. Acad. Sci., Sigma Xi. Research and publs. on heart function in hypotension, role of cardiac neuro-hormones in states of stress, mechanism of tranquilizer drugs on central nervous system, metabolism or heart. Home: 121 N Charles Av Villa Park IL 60817 Office: 2020 W Ogden Av Chicago IL 60621

GLAVIN, JOHN EDMUND, educator; b. South Bend, Ind., Apr. 22, 1911; s. John Edmund and Alice Priscilla (Montgomery) G.; B.A., U. Mich., 1932, J.D., 1935. Admitted to N.Y. bar, 1936, Mich. bar, 1937; practice in N.Y.C., 1935-36, Detroit, 1936-38; mem. faculty Wayne State U. Law Sch., 1938—, prof. law, 1947- -, asso. dean sch., 1956-68, acting dean, 1967-68, dir. grad. program, 1950—. Chmn. exec. com. Mich. Inst. Continuing Legal Edn., 1962-63; exec. com. Inst. Regional and Urban Studies, 1963-65. Served with USAAF, 1943-45; PTO. Mem. State Bar Mich. (chmn. com. on constnl. law 1966-67; 69-70), Am. Assn. U. Profs., Order of Coif, Phi Beta Kappa. Contbr. legal jours. Home: 1937 Byrd St Dearborn MI 48124 Office: Sch of Law Wayne State Univ Detroit MI 48202

GLAZER, DAVID, clarinet soloist; b. Milw., May 7, 1913; s. Benjamin and Clara (Glass) G.; B.E., Milw. State Tchrs. Coll., 1935; student Berkshire Music Center, summers 1940-42; m. Mia Helen Deutsch, Feb. 16, 1959. Bandleader, Plymouth (Wis.) High Sch., 1935-37; faculty Longy Music Sch., Cambridge, Mass., 1937-42; chamber music concerts, mem. WPA Symphony; mem. Cleve. Symphony Orch., 1946-51; mem. N.Y. Woodwind Quintet, 1951—, tour of S. Am. for U.S. State Dept., 1969; solo and chamber music concerts; appeared Casals Festival, Prades, France, 1953; ann. European tours, 1953—; faculty Mannes Coll. Music, N.Y., N.Y. Coll. Music, 1967; now lectr. music Harpur Coll. N.Y. State U.; faculty music dept. N.Y. State U. N.Y. at Binghamton and Stony Brook; on tour with Fine Arts String Quartet for Dept State, E. Asia; tchr. summer sessions U. Wis., Milw.; mem. jury Internat. Clarinet Competition, Munich, Germany, 1967; recordings Vox Records including Stamitz Concerto in B Flat, Brahms Sonatas, Beethoven and Brahms Trios with Frank Glazer, David Soyer; other recordings N.Y. Woodwind Quintet, Fine Arts Quartet. Served with AUS, 1942-46; with AAF Band, Bolling Field, Washington, 1944-46. Home: 270 W End Av New York City NY 10023

GLAZER, GULLFORD, constrn., bldg. co. exec.; b. Knoxville, Tenn., July 17, 1921; s. Aaron Oscar and Ida (Bressoff) G.; student George Washington U., 1938-39, U. Louisville, 1944-45; m. Francoise Wizenberg, Apr. 29, 1956 (div. 1964); children—Emerson Upton, Erika Jane; m. 2d, Diane Pregerson, Jan. 29, 1967. Organizer Glazer Steel Corp., Knoxville, 1945, Sun Constrn. Corp., gen. contractors, 1949, Shelbourne Towers, Inc., 1949, Colonial Village Corp., 1949, Champion, Inc., 1952, Glencoe, Inc., 1953, Mayfair Village Corp., 1949, Troy Constrn. Corp., 1950, Barbizon Terrace, Inc., 1953, Jerome Corp., 1952, G. & K. Machinery Corp., 1952, Allied Constrn. Corp., 1954, Builders Investment, Inc., 1954, Gen. Devel. Corp., 1954; builder Glencoe Homes, housing project, Oak Ridge, 1953-54; developer, builder, propr. comml. dist. Downtown Oak Ridge, 1955- -, Swifton Center, shopping center, Cin., 1956—; developer Park Shopping Center, Parkersburg, W.Va., 1956; now pres., chmn. Oak Ridge Properties, Inc., Tenn. Investment Corp., Downtown Mgmt. Corp.; organizer Tenn. Western Corp., Knoxville, 1959; organizer, pres. City Mgmt. Corp., 1964-68; v.p. Del Amo Properties Co. Active Great Smoky Mountain council Boy Scouts Am.; chmn. Knoxville Jewish Welfare, 1950; dir. Knoxville Community Chest, 1951, Jewish Community Center, 1952, Boys Club, 1952; organizer Aaron Glazer Charitable Found., 1953; bd. dirs. Inst. Cancer Research and Leukemia, Los Angeles. Served as warrant officer USNR, 1942- 45. Mem. Am. Legion, Jewish War Vets., Knoxville Symphony Soc. (past dir.), C. of C. (past dir.). Mason (32); mem. B'nai B'rith. Clubs: Deane Hill Country (dir.), Hillvale Country (Knoxville); Standard (Chgo.); Brentwood Country (Los Angeles); Oak Ridge (Tenn.) Country. Office: 1901 Av of Stars Los Angeles CA 90067

GLAZER, NATHAN, educator, sociologist; b. N.Y.C., Feb. 25, 1923; s. Louis and Tillie (Zacharevich) G.; B.S.S., Coll. City N.Y., 1944; M.A., U. Pa., 1944; Ph.D., Columbia, 1962; m. Ruth Slotkin, Sept. 26, 1943 (div. 1958); children—Sarah, Sophie, Elizabeth; m. 2d, Sulochana Raghavan, Oct. 4, 1962. Mem. editorial staff Commentary mag., 1945-53, Doubleday-Anchor Books, 1954-55; Walgreen lectr. U. Chgo., 1955; mem. staff Communism in Am. Life project Fund for Republic, 1956-57; vis. lectr U. Cal. at Berkeley, 1957-58; instr. Bennington Coll., 1958-59; vis. asso. prof. Smith Coll., 1959-60; fellow Joint Center Urban Studies, Harvard-Mass. Inst. Tech., 1960-61; study and travel in Japan, 1961-62; urban sociologist HHFA, Washington, 1962-63; prof. sociology U. Cal. at Berkeley, 1963-69; vis. prof. Grad. Sch. Edn., Harvard, 1968-69, prof. edn. and social structure, 1969—. Guggenheim fellow, 1954,66. Author: (with D. Riesman and R. Denney) The Lonely Crowd, 1950; (with D. Riesman) Faces in the Crowd, 1952; American Judaism, 1957; The Social Basis of American Communism, 1961; (with D. P. Moynihan) Beyond the Melting Pot (Anisfeld-Wolf award Sat. Rev. 1964), 1963, 2d edit., 1970; Remembering the Answers, 1970. Office: Grad Sch Edn Harvard Cambridge MA 02138

GLAZER, FRANK, pianist; b. Chester, Wis.; s. Benjamin and Clara (Glass) G.; pvt. piano instrn. with Artur Schnabel, 1932-33, 35; studied counterpoint with Arnold Schoenberg, 1933-34; M.A. (hon.), Spencerian Coll., 1955; m. Ruth Gevalt, Sept. 6, 1952. Debut, Town Hall, N.Y.C., 1936; orchestral debut with Boston Symphony Orch., 1939; debut Carnegie Hall, 1949; performed with maj. orchs. of world, including N.Y. Philharmonic, Chgo. Symphony Orch., Orchestre de la Suisse Romade; soloist with leading chamber music groups, including Fine Arts Quartet, N.Y. Woodwind Quintet; recording artist for Concert Disc and Vox; artist in residence Festival of Chamber Music, U. Wis., Milw., summers 1955-64, recipient award for distinguished service in performing arts, 1964; pianist-in-residence Bennett Coll., Millbrook, N.Y., 1960—; vis. prof. piano Eastman Sch. Music, U. Rochester, 1965—, prof. U., 1968—; mem. Eastman Quartet; mem. vis. com. in music Wheaton Coll., Norton, Mass., 1961—. Recipient Paderewski Centenary medal of London, 1966. Served with AUS, 1943-45; ETO. Mem. Nat. Honor Soc., The Bohemians. Office: Eastman Sch Music U Rochester Rochester NY 14627

GLAZIER, RICHARD LOWRY, life ins. co. exec.; b. Newport, Ky., Jan. 23, 1905; s. William L. and Florence D'Orsey (DeMoss) G.; B.S., Yale, 1927; m. Mary L. Lee, Nov. 24, 1937; children—Deborah, Richard. Asst. actuary Union Central Life Ins. Co., Cin., 1932-48; with Life Ins. Co. of Va., Richmond, 1948—, actuary, 1948-56, v.p., actuary, 1956-65, v.p., chief actuary, 1965—. Fellow Soc. Actuaries; mem. Internat. Congress Actuaries Club (past pres.). Home: 610 Mayfair Av Richmond VA 23226 Office: 914 Capitol St Richmond VA 23219

GLAZIER, ROBERT CARL, ednl. TV exec.; b. Brandsville, Mo., Mar. 26, 1927; s. Vernie A. and Mildred F. (Beu) G.; student Drury Coll., 1944-46; B.A., U. Wichita, 1949; m. Harriette Hubbard, June 5, 1949; children—Gregory Kent, Jeffrey Robert. Reporter Springfield (Mo.) Daily News, 1944-46; asst. city editor Wichita Eagle, 1946-49; journalism instr. U. Wichita, 1949-53; dir. pub. relations Springfield (Mo.) Pub. Schs., 1953-59; asso. dir. dept. radio and TV The Methodist Ch., Nashville, 1959-61; gen. mgr. WDCN-TV, Channel 2, Nashville, 1961-65; gen. mgr. KETC, Channel 9, St. Louis, 1965—; also exec. dir. St. Louis Ednl. TV Commn. Bd. dirs. Adult Edn. Council Greater St. Louis. Served with AUS, 1945-46. Mem. Nat. Sch. Pub. Relations Assn. (past regional dir.), Nat. Assn. Ednl. Broadcasters. Methodist. Rotarian. Home: 437 Gabriel Dr Kirkwood MO 63122 Office: 6996 Millbrook Blvd St Louis MO 63130

GLEASON, ANDREW MATTEI, educator; b. Fresno, Cal., Nov. 4, 1921; s. Henry Allan and Eleanor Theodalinda (Mattei) G.; B.S., Yale, 1942; jr. fellow Soc. Fellows, Harvard, 1946-50, M.A. (hon.), 1953; m. Jean Berko, Jan. 26, 1959; children—Katherine Anne, Pamela, Cynthia. Asst. prof. math. Harvard, 1950-53, asso. prof., 1953-57, prof., 1957—, Hollis prof. mathematics and natural philosophy, 1969—. Served from ensign to lt. (s.g.), USNR, 1942-46, lt. comdr., 1950-52. Recipient Newcomb Cleveland prize A.A.A.S., 1952. Mem. Am. Math. Soc., Math. Assn. Am., Societe Mathematique de France, Am. Acad. Arts and Scis., Nat. Acad. Scis. Club: Cosmos (Washington). Author: Fundamentals of Abstract Analysis, 1966. Home: 117 Larchwood Dr Cambridge MA 02138

GLEASON, DOUGLAS, telephone holding co. exec.; b. Mound City, Kan., Dec. 17, 1916; s. Ralph D. and Blanche (Douglas) G.; B.A., Wichita State U., 1939; LL.B., Washburn U., 1942; m. Billie Lone Lawrence, Mar. 5, 1963. Admitted to Kan. bar, 1942; asst. gen. counsel Kan. Corp. Commn., 1946-52; sr. partner firm Gleason, Gleason, Doty & Logan, Ottawa and Topeka, Kan., 1947-64; sec., counsel Kan. Telephone Assn., 1952-62; with United Utilities, Inc., Kansas City, Mo., 1964—, exec. v.p. finance, 1965—, also dir.; dir. Pension Equity Fund, Inc.; city atty., Ottawa, 195361. Chmn. Collegiate Young Republicans Kan., 1939-40. Chmn. trustees Franklin Mental Health Clinic, 1960-62; trustee, chmn. finance com. Baker U., 1968—. Served to capt. AUS. 1942-46; ETO. Decorated Bronze Star. Mem. Am., Franklin County (pres. 1962) bar assns., Bar Assn. Kan. Presbyn. Home: 1903 Romany Rd Mission Hill Shawnee Mission KS 66208 Office: PO Box 11315 Plaza Sta Kansas City MO 64112

GLEASON, ELIZA ATKINS, librarian, educator; b. Winston Salem, N.C., Dec. 15, 1909; d. Simon Green and Oleona (Pegram) Atkins; A.B., Fisk U., 1930; B.S., U. Ill., 1931; M.A., U. Cal. at Berkeley, 1936; Ph.D., U. Chgo., 1940; m. Maurice F. Gleason, Nov. 5, 1937; 1 dau., Joy Patricia. Asst. librarian Louisville Municipal Coll., 1931-32, librarian, 1932-36; head reference dept., asst. prof. Fisk U. Library, 1936-37; dir. libraries Talladega Coll., 1940-46; prof., dean Sch. Library Service Atlanta U., 1941-46; guest lectr. Grad. Library Sch., U. Chgo., 1953; head reference dept. Wilson Jr. Coll. Library, Chgo., 1953-54; asso. prof., head reference dept. Chgo. Tchrs. Coll. Library, 1954-63; asso. prof. library sci. Ill. Tchrs. Coll. Chgo. South, 1964-67; asst. librarian John Crerar Library, prof. library sci. Ill. Inst. Tech., 1967-70; asst. chief librarian charge regional centers Chgo. Pub. Library, 1970—. Mem. Hyde Park Kenwood Community Conf., 1950—. S.E. Chgo. Commn., 1952—, Ind. Voters Ill., 1952—; exec. com. Fisk U. Alumni Assn., 1969—; co- chmn. Fisk U. Centennial campaign, 1963-65; mem. bd. Chgo. Council Fgn. Relations, 1964—; mem. women's aux. Cook County Physicians Assn., 1940- -, women's aux. Meharry Med. Coll. Alumni Assn., 1940—, women's aux. Internat. Coll. Surgeons. Recipient Alumni award Fisk U., 1964. Mem. A.L.A. (council 1942-46; fellow 1938-40), Am. Assn. U. Profs. Author: History of the Fisk University Library, 1936; The Southern Negro and the Public Library, 1941; also articles. Home: 1025 E 50th St Chicago IL 60615

GLEASON, FRANK J., Jr., mfg. exec., b. Detroit, 1930; B.S., U. Notre Dame, 1956; m. With Ernst & Ernst, C.P.A.'s, 1956-58; with Copeland Refrigeration Corp., 1959—, pres. chief exec. officer, 1966—, also dir. Served with USAC, 1950-53. Home: 1716 N Broadway Sidney OH 45365 Office: Short Clinton St Sidney OH 45365*

GLEASON, GERALD THOMAS, educator; b. Iron Mountain, Mich., June 7, 1927; s. Howard J. and Olivine (Mongrain) G.; B.S., Milw. State Tchrs. Coll., 1949; M.S., Wis. State U., 1952; Ph.D., U. Wis., 1956; m. Betty J. Barbeaux, Aug. 13, 1949; children—Daniel, Brian. Tchr., Sheboygan, Wis. and Milw., 1949-53; mem. faculty U. Wis.-Milw., 1956—, prof. ednl. psychology, 1962—, chmn. dept., 1965-66, dir. research, 1966-68, spl. asst. to chancellor, 1968-70. Mem. bd. control, v.p. Coop. Edn. Research Lab., Inc. Exec. sec. Lakeshore Curriculum Study Council, 1959-68. Served with AUS, 1952- 54. Mem. Am. Psychol. Assn., Am., Wis. (pres. 1966-67) ednl. research assns., Phi Delta Kappa, Phi Kappa Phi. Home: 7001 N Bethmaur Lane Milwaukee WI 53209

GLEASON, HAROLD V., banker; b. N.Y.C., 1919; grad. Rutgers U. Sch. Banking, 1954; married. With Hamburg Savs. Bank N.Y., 1936-54. Savs. Bank Life Ins. Council, 1954-56; with Franklin Nat. Bank, 1956—, pres., chief exec. officer, 1968—, also dir. Chmn. bd. Nassau-Sufolk Econ. Devel. Council; bd. dirs. Tri-County L.I. Labor Mgmt. Inst.; mem. L.I.-New Eng. Bridge Study Com. Bd. mgrs. Meadowbrook Hosp.; bd. sponsors Mercy Hosp. Home: 94 Ocean Av Massapequa NY 11758 Office: 199 2d Av Mineola NY 11501*

GLEASON, JAMES ARTHUR, lawyer; b. Cleve., Feb. 20, 1905; s. M. James and Mary (O'Hare) G.; A.B., Georgetown U., 1928; LL.B., Western Res. U., 1931; m. Helen Mary Nightingale, Feb. 8, 1936 (dec. Apr. 1957); 1 son, Michael Robert; m. 2d, Elinor Ferguson, June 6, 1959; stepchildren—Mrs. Ed Harris, Mrs. Lawrence C. Phillips, Jeanie E. (Mrs. Jeffrey Hutzler). Admitted to Ohio bar, 1932; practiced in Cleve., specializing in probate, tax, corp. real estate, and ins. law, 1932-41, 46—; dir. Automatic Auto-Park, Inc., N.Y.C. Bd. govs., senate Georgetown U., Washington, 1953—. Pres. and comdg. brig. gen. emeritus Cleveland Grays; adv. bd. Marycrest Sch., Independence, O. Entered USAAF, 1941, assigned judge Adv.'s Dept., Hdqrs. 2d Air Force, Colorado Springs, Colo., 1943; in charge Kornberg jewel cases; trial judge adv. Watson Q.M.C. case, Col. Judge Adv. Gen. corps, Res. Decorated Bronze Star. Mem. Am. (state chmn. jr. bar conf. 1937-38, council mem. 6th dist. 1939-40, ho. dels. 1943—), Cleve., Ohio State (del. Internat. Bar Conf., Madrid, 1952; gen. chmn. 86th ann. conv. com. 1966), Internat. (del. conv. 1966), Inter-Am., Cuyahoga Co. (mem. fed. ct., probate ct., taxation com. 1966- 67) Fed. bar (pres. Cleve. chpt. 1961-62) assns., Judge Advs. Assn., Am. Soc. Internat. Law, Mil. Order World Wars (comdr. Cleve. 1961-62), Am. Legion (comdr. Shaker Heights post 1963-64), Res. Officers Assn., Assn. U.S. Army. Roman Catholic. Clubs: University (Washington); Grays, University, Georgetown, City, Playhouse (Cleve.); Mentor Harbor Yachting (O.). Home: 2525 Stratford Rd Cleveland Heights OH 44118 Office: 215 Euclid Av Cleveland OH 44114

GLEASON, JOHN MARTIN, community devel. cons.; b. N.Y.C., May 10, 1907; s. James S. and Letitia (Haydock) G.; student Columbia, 1927, N.E. Traffic Officers Tng. Sch., Harvard, 1936, Northwestern Traffic Safety Inst., 1936, Northwestern Exec. Officers Tng. Sch., 1938-41, Rutgers U., 1940, Yale, 1941, 43; grad. FBI Nat. Acad., 1944; m. Margaret Nicholson, Oct. 15, 1929; children—Nancy (Mrs. DeHart G. Scrantom, Jr.), John Martin. Cadet engr. Conn. Light & Power Co., 1927-30; with Greenwich (Conn.) Police Dept., 1930-56, beginning as patrolman, successively detective, sgt., lt., capt., chief of police, 1930-54, town chief adminstrv. officer, 1954-56; nat. dir. Boys' Clubs of Am., 1956-69, now mem. bd. dirs.; cons. community devel., Greenwich, 1969—. Instr., FBI Acad., Washington, 1945-55; guest lectr. Northeastern U., Northwestern U., Yale, Columbia; mem. adv. com. N.Y. U. Grad. Sch. Pub. Adminstrn. Chmn. state and local ofcls. Nat. Hwy. Safety Commn.; pub. safety specialist U.S. Army in Germany, 1949, Office U.S. High Commr. for Germany, Office Polit. Affairs, 1951; mem. Atty. Gen.'s Conf. Organized Crime, Washington; staff Pres.'s Hwy. Safety Conf.; gen. chmn. traffic sect., mem. exec. com. Nat. Safety Council, Chgo.; police cons. U.S. Office Civil Def.; nat. com. Uniform Traffic Laws and Ordnances, 1947—; mem. Citizens Adv. Com. on Fitness Am. Youth. Active Boy Scouts Am.; rep. non-govtl. orgn., UN, for Boys' Clubs of Am.; dir. A.R.C., Conn. Assn. Mental Health, Community Chest; pres. Greenwich Safety Council, 1965-70; mem. Pres.'s Task Force on Crime and Law Enforcement, 1969—. Recipient spl. honor diploma Cuban Soc. Police Sci. and Criminalistics, 1949; diploma of honor Bd. Traffic Control, Fed. Republic Germany, 1952. Mem. Internat. Assn. Chiefs Police (pres. 1950, life mem. exec. com.), N.E. Chiefs Police Assn. (dir.), Internat. Assn. Identification, Conn. Police Assn. (life mem.), Nat., Greenwich (v.p.) safety councils, Detective Endowment Assn., Nat. Law Enforcement Assns., Greenwich Taxpayers Assn., Jr. C. of C., Nat. Inst. Social Scis. K.C. Clubs: Kiwanis, Boat and Yacht (Greenwich); Union League (N.Y.C.); Harpoon. Home: 15 Overlook Dr Greenwich CT 06830 Office: Town Hall Greenwich CT 06830

GLEASON, JOHN SINON, Jr., banker; b. Chgo., Feb. 11, 1915; s. John Sylvester and Mary Ann (Maloney) G.; B.C.S., U. Notre Dame, 1936, LL.D., 1964; postgrad. Harvard, 1936-37; grad. U. Wis. Sch. Banking, 1951; Dr. Econs., Sophia U., Tokyo, Japan, 1963; LL.D., M.A., George Washington U.; D.Litt., Parsons Coll., 1966; m. Mary Jane Harrigan, Dec. 20, 1941; children—John Stephen III, Daniel, Richard C., Thomas L., David G., Martin J. With First Nat. Bank of Chgo., 1937—, v.p., 1956—; chmn. bd. Chgo. Helicopter Airways, Inc.; pres. dir. John. E. Maloney, Undertakers, Inc.; adminstr. vet. affairs, VA, Washington, 1961-65; v.p. 1st Nat. Bank of Chgo., 1965—. Nat. comdr. Am. Legion, 1957-58. Mem. Ill. Vets. Commn., 1949-61, chmn., 1965—; asst. treas. Chgo. council A.R.C.; chmn. Chgo. Girl Scout campaign, 1950; dir. Am. Boys Camp, 1950-53; mem. Nat. Housing Council, President's Council on Aging, President's Coms. on Employment Physically Handicapped, Equal Opportunity in Housing. Treas. Dem. Nat. Conv., 1952, exec. dir. vets. div., 1960. Vice pres., dir. Chgo. Youth Found., 1948-61; dir. United Cerebral Palsy Assn. Chgo., 1954-61. Served from pvt. to lt. col. AUS, 1940-46; maj. gen. comdg. 85th Inf. Div. Decorated Silver Star, Legion Merit, Bronze Star with clusters, Soldier's medal, Air medal; Knight of Malta, Knight Holy Sepulchre, French Legion Honor, Philippine Legion Honor, Distinguished Service medal Republic South Korea, Order of Merit, Republic Italy; recipient Club of Champions award Cath. Youth Orgn., 1950; Distinguished Vets. award, 1962; named Notre Dame Man of the Year, 1958. Mem. Am. Helicopter Soc., Res. Officers Assn., Nat. Guard Assn. U.S. K.C. Clubs: Irish Fellowship (past pres.). Chicago Athletic Assn., Bankers, North Shore Country (Chgo.); Army and Navy, Burning Tree (Washington). Office: 1 First Nat Plaza Chicago IL 60603

GLEASON, RALPH JOSEPH, journalist, critic; b. N.Y.C., Mar. 1, 1917; s. Ralph A. and Mary (Quinlisk) G.; student Columbia. 1934-38; m. Jean Rayburn, Oct. 12, 1940; children—Bridget, Stacy, Toby. Jazz and popular music critic San Francisco Chronicle, 1950—, also now daily columnist; former contbg. editor Down Beat, 1948-60. Hi/Fi Stereo Rev.; contbg. editor Scholastic Roto: writer numerous album liner notes for recording cos.; writer nationally syndicated jazz column; producer-host Jazz Casual, TV program, 1962—; lectr. in jazz U. Cal. Extension, 1960-63; lectr. music dept. Sonoma State Coll., 1965-67. Mem. adv. vis. bd. jazz Lenox Sch. Jazz, Inst. Jazz; adviser Stanford Jazz Jr., Stanford U., 1965, U. Cal. Jazz Festival, 1967-68. Served with OWI, 1942-44. Author: The Jefferson Airplane and the San Francisco Sound, 1969. Editor: Jam Session, Anthology of Jazz, 1957; Jazz. A Quar. of Am. Music, 1957-58. Contrbr. articles to publs. including New Statesman, Am. Scholar, Esquire, Show Bus. Illustrated, Saturday Rev.: cons. editor Rolling Stone; former mem. editorial bd. Ramparts. Home: 2835 Ashby Av Berkeley CA 94705 Office: San Francisco Chronicle 5th and Mission San Francisco CA 94119

GLEASON, RALPH NEWTON, govt. ofcl.; b. Townville, S.C., Jan. 5, 1922; s. Arthur Bryan and Clara Belle (McAdams) G.; B.S., Clemson Coll., 1942; M.S., Ohio State U., 1963; m. Marjorie Nelle Little, Apr. 4, 1942; children—Ralph Newton Jr., Delno Rex, Charles Stanley, Edward Dean, Cindy Ann. Statis. adviser to South Korean interim govt., 1947-48; food and econ. adviser ECA, Seoul, Korea, 1949-50; chief food and fertilizer div. Sine-Am. Joint Commn. Rural Reconstrn., Taipei, Taiwan, 1950-56; agrl. programs officer Near East South Asia, FOA, Washington, 1957-58; dep. chief agriculturist Tech. Cooperation Mission to India, New Delhi, 1958-62; chief food and agr. div. Econ. Mission to Turkey, 1963-68; dep. dir. Agr. and Rural Devel. Service Office War on Hunger, Washington, 1968-70; dep. asso. dir. food and agr. AID, South Vietnam, 1970—; mem. delegations UN Food and Agr. Agy. Confs. Bd. dirs., treas. Taipei Am. Sch., 1950-56. Served to maj. AUS, 1942-47; ETO, Korea. Decorated Silver Star, Bronze Star. Mem. Am. Fgn. Service Assn., Woodmen of the World, Phi Kappa Phi, Alpha Zeta. Mason. Clubs: New Delhi Golf; Saigon Golf. Home: 504 Blvd Anderson SC 29621 Office: AID/ADFA APO San Francisco CA 96243

GLEASON, SARELL EVERETT, govt. ofcl.; b. Bklyn., Mar. 14, 1905; s. Sarell Everett and Florence Agalia (Sellon) G.; A.B., Harvard, 1927, A.M., 1928, Ph.D., 1934; postgrad. U. Paris, Ecole des Chartes, Paris, 1931; m. Mary Eleanor Abbott, June 19, 1937; children—Abbott, Ellen Richmond. Instr. history Harvard, 1930-38; asst., asso. prof. history Amherst (Mass.) Coll., 1938-46; with OSS, Washington, 1943-45; with Dept. State, Washington, 1945, 1962—, historian, 1962—; historian Council Fgn. Relations, 1946-50; dep. exec. sec. NSC, Washington, 1950-59; cultural attaché Am. Embassy, London, 1959-61; Served as lt. Col., joint intelligence com., Joint Chief of Staff, AUS, 1943-45. Decorated Legion of Merit; recipient Bancroft Prize, 1954. Mem. Am. Hist. Assn. Mass. Hist. Soc., Council Fgn. Relations, Colonial Soc. Mass. Clubs: Athenaeum (London, Eng.); Century (N.Y.C.); Cosmos (Washington). Author: An Ecclesiastical Barony of the Middle Ages, 1937; (with W. L. Langer) The Challenge of Isolation, 1952, The Undeclared War, 1953; also articles, revs. profl. jours. Home: 1698 31st St Washington DC 20007 Office: Dept of State Washington DC 20525

GLEASON, THOMAS, head N.Y. local, pres. Atlantic dist., now also pres. Internat. Longshoremen's Assn. Address: 265 W 14th St New York City NY 10011*

GLEASON, WILLIAM THOMAS, retired army officer; b. Ely, Nev., June 30, 1917; s. William Thomas and V. Hazel (Woodcock) G.; B.S., U.S. Mil. Acad., 1941; student Command and Gen. Staff Sch., 1944; The Armed Forces Staff Coll., 1956; Indsl. Coll. Armed Forces, 1959; m. Karma Hill, June 12, 1941; children—Susan (Mrs. James P. Avett), Emilie (Mrs. Melvin A. Marini), Elizabeth Anne, William Thomas, Jr. Commd. 2d lt. U.S. Army, 1941, advanced through grades to brig. gen., 1967; dep. asst. chief staff logistics Material Assistance Command, Vietnam, 1967; asst. div. comdr. 25th Inf. Div., Vietnam, 1967-68, comdg. gen. U.S. Army Element, Allied Forces Central Europe, The Netherlands, 1968-71; chmn. Central Europe Pipeline Orgn.; retired, 1971; engr. Cavanagh Communities Corp., Miami Beach, Fla., 1971—. Chmn. Com. on Youth, 1970—. Decorated D.S.M., Silver Star, D.F.C., Bronze Star with oak leaf cluster. Mem. U.S. Armed Forces Mgmt. Assn., Assn. Grads. U.S. Mil. Acad., Netherlands Am. Inst. Lions. Office: 6820 Indian Creek Dr Miami Beach FL 33141

GLEATON, JONATHON AUSTIN mfg. exec.; b. Lima, O., Apr. 1, 1932; B.S., U. San Francisco, 1954; M.S., Stanford University, 1956; m. Rosemarie Lois Brown, May 15, 1955; 1 son, Anthony Robinson. Sales rep. Ames-Brockton Fabricated Products, Akron, O., 1956-58, sales mgr. Coshocton, Ohio, 1959-61, gen. manager plant, 1961-68, v.p. sales, 1968--. Instr. bus. Coshocton Jr. College, 1968-69. Mem. Coshocton C. of C. (vice president 1967-68, pres. 1969-70), English Speaking Union, Coshocton Sertoma Club, Nat. Assn. Mfrs., Sales Executives Institute, Phi Beta Kappa, Sigma Chi, Phi Mu. Democrat. Mem. Christian Ch. (lay reader). Mason (32, Shriner). Clubs: Coshocton Country, Coshocton City, Running Deer Country. Home: 2d Av Coshocton OH Office: 3d Av Coshocton OH

GLEAZER, EDMUND JOHN Jr., assn. exec.; b. Phila., Aug. 24, 1916; s. Edmund John and Jane Hunter (Laurie) G.; A.A., Graceland Coll., 1936; A.B., U. Cal. at Los Angeles, 1938; Ed.M., Temple U., 1943; Ed.D., Harvard, 1953; m. Charlene A. Allen, Apr. 14, 1940; children—Allen, Sandra Jo, John, Susan. Minister, Reorganized Ch. of Jesus Christ of Latter Day Saints, Phila., 1938-43, pres. So. Iowa dist., 1943-46; pres. Graceland Coll., Lamoni, Ia., 1946- 57; exec. dir. Am. Assn. Jr. Coll., Washington, 1958—. Mem. nat. adv. com. for asso. degree programs in nursing Nat. League Nursing; mem. U.S. Tech. Edn. Delegation to USSR, 1961, edn. survey team AID, Kenya, 1962; chmn. Def. Adv. Com. on Edn. in Armed Forces, 1962; mem. vis. com. Stanford U., Sch. Edn., 1962. Mem. North Central Jr. Colls. (pres. council 1954), North Central Assn. (commn. colls. and univs. 1955-57), Am. Assn. Jr. Colls. (pres. 1957), Am. Council on Edn. (sec.), Phi Delta Kappa. Clubs: Harvard, Rotary, Cosmos (Washington). Author: This is The Community College, 1968. Editor: American Junior Colleges, 1960, 63, 67. Home: 8208 Woodhaven Blvd Bethesda MD 20034 Office: 1 DuPont Circle Washington DC 20036

GLECKNER, ROBERT FRANCIS, educator; b. Rahway, N.J., Mar. 2, 1925; s. Adam F. and Frieda A. (Froehlich) G.; B.A., Williams Coll., 1948; Ph.D., Johns Hopkins, 1954; m. Glenda J. Karr, Feb. 7, 1946; children—Jeffrey M., Susan F. Jr. instr. English, Johns Hopkins, 1949-51; editor Research Studies Inst., Maxwell AFB, Ala., 1951-52; instr. English, U. Cin., 1952-54, U. Wis., 1954-57; asst., then asso. prof. Wayne State U., Detroit, 1957-62; prof. English, U. Cal. at Riverside, 1962—, chmn. dept., 1962-66, lectr. extension div., 1962-64, divisional dean of humanities, 1968-70, dean Coll. of Humanities, 1970—. Main speaker U. Cal. at Los Angeles extension conf. humanities, Lake Arrowhead, Cal., 1964. Manuscript reader jours., univ. presses; del. Am. Assn. Higher Edn. meeting, 1963, 69. Mem. adv. bd. dirs. Am. Blake Found., 1970—. Served to 1st lt. USAAF, 1943-45. Recipient Poetry Soc. Am. award 1959. Mem. Modern Lang. Assn., Phi Beta Kappa, Beta Theta Pi. Episcopalian. Author: The Piper and the Bard: A Study of William Blake, 1959; Byron and the Ruins of Paradise, 1967. Editor: (with G.E. Enscoe) Romanticism: Points of View, 1962, rev. edit. (sole editor), 1970; Selected Writings of William Blake, 1967, rev. edit., 1971. Contbr.: A James Joyce Miscellany, 3d Series, 1962; A Blake Bibliography, 1964; also contbr. Twelve and a Tilly: Essays on the 25th Anniversary of Finnegans Wake, 1966; William Blake; Essays for S. Foster Damon, 1969; A Concordance to the Writings of William Blake, 1967. Mem. editorial bd. Wayne State U. Press, 1960-62; asso. editor Criticism: A Jour. for Lit. and the Arts, 1960-62, adv. bd., 1962—, adv. editor Blake Studies, 1968- -. Author articles, contbr. to profl. jours., books. Home: 11879 Holly St Grand Terrace Colton CA 92324 Office: Coll Humanities Univ California Riverside CA 92502

GLECK, LEWIS EDWARD, Jr., ret. fgn. service officer; b. Lyon, Miss., Nov. 2, 1912; s. Lewis Edward and Eva (Davids) G.; B.A., Pomona Coll., 1935; postgrad. U. Chgo., 1935-38, Columbia 1949-50; m. Fira Svidler, July 11, 1954; 1 son. Lewis Alfred Research asst. William Alanson White Found., Washington, 1938-40; fgn. service officer State Dept., 1940-69, various positions, Can., 1940-41, Finland, 1941, 1942-43, Sweden, 1942, 1943-45, Austria, 1945-46, Iceland, 1946-48, Norway, 1948-49, office Eastern European Affairs, Dept. State, Washington, 1950- 51; with Internat. Broadcasting Service, 1951-53; 1st sec. of Embassy, Tokyo, Japan, 1953-55; consul in charge comml., econ. affairs, Osaka, Japan, 1955-57; assigned Army War Coll., 1957-58; officer in charge econ. affairs Office N.E. Asian Affairs, spl. asst. SEATO affairs, Washington, 1958-61; counselor, Karachi, Pakistan, 1961-62; consul gen., Manila, P.I., 1962-68. Mem. Phi Beta Kappa. Conglist. Home: Manila Philippines

GLEED, THOMAS F., business exec.; b. Glenwood, Wis., Sept. 5, 1900; student U. Wash., 1918- 22; m. Mary Elizabeth Balmer, Sept. 29, 1923; children—Betty Delanne, Thomas B. Service sta. salesman Standard Oil Cal., 1922-25; bond salesman Carstens & Earles, Inc., 1925-27; mgr. bond dept. Met. Nat. Bank, 1927; v.p. First Nat. Co. Seattle, 1929-46, dir., 1934, pres., 1946; became asst. v.p. Seattle-First Nat. Bank, 1934-37, v.p., 1937-45, dir., pres., 1945-51; pres. Simpson Timber Co., 1951-62, chmn. finance com., 1962-65; pres. Gleed & Co.; chmn. bd. Crows Nest Industries, Ltd.; dir., mem. exec., finance and investment, stock option coms. Safeco Corp.; dir. UAL Inc., United Air Lines, Puget Sound Nat. Bank, Western Internat. Hotels, Wash. Mut. Savs. Bank, Seattle, Seattle Times (presiding dir.), Eddy Investment Co., Port Blakely Mill Co.; mem. investment com. Am. Pres. Lines; dir., chmn. exec. com. Am. Mail Line; dir., mem. exec. com. Pacific Car & Foundry Co. Bd. dirs. Arboretum Found. Wash. Mem. Newcomen Soc., Internat. Order St. Hubert, Sigma Chi. Clubs: Vancouver (B.C., Can.); Twenty Nine, Turf and Field, Raffles (N.Y.C.); Thunderbird Golf (Palm Springs, Cal.); Bohemian, Pacific Union (San Francisco); University, Rainier, Seattle Golf, Yacht, 380, 487 (Seattle); Chicago; Takaro (Te Anau, New Zealand); Tacoma. Home: 3129 W Laurelhurst Dr NE Seattle WA 98105 Office: Washington Bldg Seattle WA 98101

GLEESON, FRANCIS DOYLE, bishop; b. Carrollton, Mo., Jan. 17, 1895; s. Charles and Mary Alice (Doyle) G.; A.B., Santa Clara U., 1917; A.M., Gonzaga U., 1920; theology student, St. Francis Xavier's Coll., Spain, 1923-27, Manresa Hall, Port Townsend, Wash., 1927-28; hon. Ph.D., Gregorian U., 1931. Ordained priest (S.J.) Roman Catholic Ch., 1926; instr., Seattle Coll. Prep. (Wash.), 1917-20, instr. Bellarmine High Sch., Tacoma, Wash., 1928-32, pres., 1933-39, pres. Jesuit Sem., Sheridan, Ore., 1939-42; consecrated bishop of Vicariate of Alaska, Apr. 5, 1948, installed as 1st bishop of Fairbanks, 1963. ret., 1968; now titular bishop of Cuicul (Numidia). Address: 1316 Peger Rd Fairbanks AL 99701

GLEESON, GEORGE WALTER, former educator; b. Granite, Ore., Mar. 1, 1905; s. Walter George and Lillian (Longmore) G.; B.S. in Chem. Engring., Ore. State Coll., 1928, M.S. in Mech. Engring., 1934, 1936; m. Barbara Rafferty, June 15, 1929; children—Frederick Walter, James Michael. Engring. expt. sta. fellow Ore. State Coll., Corvallis, 1928-29, instr. in mechanics and materials, 1929-32, asst. prof. chem. engring., 1932-36, asso. prof. in charge dept., 1936-37, prof., head dept., 1937-45, asst. dean engring., 1943-44, acting dean engring., 1944-45, dean, 1945-69, dir. Engring. Expt. Sta., 1953-69. Cons. various cos., NSF, 1952-56; mem. capitol planning commn. Oregon, 1947-68; adv. com. Selective Service Ore., 1956—; math. handbook com. Ore., 1953-57. Mem. Postwar Readjustment and Devel. Commn., 1946, China-Am. Council of Commerce and Industry, 1946. Registered profl. engr., Ore. Mem. Am. Chem. Soc., Am. Inst. Chem. Engrs. (mem. at large, chm. engr. edn. and accrediting commn. 1946), Am. Soc. Engring. Edn. (Lamme award com. 3 years, Northwest rep. chem. engring. sect. 1946), Profl. Engrs. Ore. (dir. 1946), Ore. Acad. Sci., Northwest Sci. Assn., Corvallis C. of C., A.A.A.S., Nat. Soc. Profl. Engrs., Sigma Xi, Phi Lambda Upsilon, Pi Tau Sigma, Sigma Tau, Tau Beta Pi, Phi Kappa Phi, Delta Kappa, Phi Eta Sigma. Republican. Contbr. tech. articles trade and profl. mags. Home: 112 N 29th St Corvallis OR 97330 ☆

GLEISSER, MARCUS DAVID, author, lawyer, editor; b. Buenos Aires, Argentina, Feb. 14, 1923 (parents Am. citizens): s. Ben and Riva (Kogan) G.; B.A. in Journalism, Case Western Res. U., 1945, M.A. in Econs., 1949; J.D., Cleve. State U., 1958; m. Helga Marianne Rothschild, Oct. 23, 1955; children—Brian Saul, Julia Lynne, Hannah Tanya, Ellyn Ruth. Police reporter Cleve. Press, 1942-44, copy editor, 1944-47; advt. copy writer McDonough-Lewy, Inc., 1947-50; copy editor Cleve. Plain Dealer, 1950-52, gen. assignment reporter, 1952-57, courthouse reporter, 1957-63, real estate editor, 1963—; admitted to Ohio bar, 1958, also U.S. Supreme Ct. bar. Trustee Cleve. Coll. Alumni Assn., 1968. Recipient Nat. bronze medal Am. Newspapers Pubs. Assn., 1944; Nat. Silver Gavel award Am. Bar Assn., 1958; Bronze medal Nat. Legal Aid and Defender Assn., 1963; Spl. Loeb award distinguished bus. and financial writing U. Conn., 1966; certificate of recognition Nat. Conf. Christian and Jews, 1967; Silver medal award consistently outstanding spl. feature columns Nat. Headliners Club, 1969; award Ohio Bar Assn., 1957, 58, 59, 60, 61, 62; award pub. service Cleve. Newspaper Guild, 1959; award Nat. Assn. Real Estate Editors, 1965, Nat. Assn. Real Estate Bds., 1966, 67, 68, 69, Nat. Assn. Home Builders, 1970; Bus.-Financial Writing award Press Club Cleve., 1969. Mem. Ohio Bar Assn., Am. Newspaper Guild, Nat. Assn. Real Estate Editors. Author: The World of Cyrus Eaton, 1965; Juries and Justice, 1968; also articles. Editor-in-chief Cleve.-Marshall Law Rev., 1956, 57. Home: 575 Hemlock Dr Euclid OH 44132 Office: 1801 Superior Av Cleveland OH 44114

GLEISSNER, HEINRICH, diplomat of Austria; b. Linz, Upper Austria, Dec. 12, 1927; exchange student Bowdoin Coll., Brunswick Me., 1948-49; LL.D., U. Vienna (Austria, 1950; student Coll. Europe, Bruges, Belgium, 1950-51. Joined Austrian Fgn. Service, 1951; successively assigned Paris, Strasbourg, London and Geneva; dep. consul gen. in N.Y.C., 1965-67, consul gen., 1967—. Address: 31 E 69th St New York City NY 10021

GLEITMAN, HENRY, educator, psychologist; b. Leipzig, Germany, Jan. 4, 1925; s. Abe and Eva (Stern) G.; B.S., City Coll. N.Y., 1946; Ph.D., U. Cal. at Berkeley, 1949; m. Lila Ruth Lichtenberg, June 15, 1958; children—Eleanor Beth, Claire Ella. Mem. faculty Swarthmore Coll., 1949-63, assoc. prof. psychology, 1957-63, acting chmn. dept., 1962-63; prof. psychology Cornell U., 1963-64; prof. psychology U. Pa., 1964—. Mem. Am., Eastern psychol. assns., Psychonomic Soc., A.A.A.S., Sigma Xi. Contbr. profl. jours. Home: 260 Sycamore Av Merion PA 19066 Office: Dept Psychology Univ Pa Philadelphia PA 19104

GLEKEL, NEWTON, food and book pub. co. exec.; b. Bklyn., Nov. 2, 1914; s. Israel and Pearl (Maxim) G.; A.B., Bklyn. Coll., 1935; LL.B., Columbia, 1938; L.H.D. (hon.), Marist Coll., 1969; m. Trudy Burr, Feb. 20, 1946; children—Jeffrey Ives, Laura Kay. Admitted to N.Y. bar, 1938; pres. Cork Insulation Co., N.Y.C., until 1954, Knickerbocker Printing Co., N.Y.C., until 1950, Wayne Works, Inc., until 1957, Divco-Wayne Corp., N.Y.C., 1957-68; chmn. bd. Hygrade Food Products Corp., 1969—; dir., chmn. acquisition com. Am. Book-Stratford Press. Founder Albert Einstein Coll. Medicine; v.p. Citizen's Union; exec. com. Emergency Gun Control. Bd. dirs. Beth Israel Hosp., N.Y.C., N.Y. Hall Sci.; exec. bd. Fedn. Jewish Philanthropies; trustee-at-large for all hosps. of fedn. Mem. N.Y. State Bar Assn. Home: 784 Park Av New York City NY 10021 Office: 680 Fifth Av New York City NY 10019

GLEN, ARTHUR RODERICK, credit union exec.; b. Ladysmith, B.C., Can., Oct. 24, 1918; s. Arthur Percy and Louise (Lewis) G.; m. Rita Eleanor Powell, Apr. 30, 1945; children—Adrienne Louise, Allison Rita. Engaged in newspaper work, 1938- 64; pres., chief exec. officer Nanaimo Dist. Savs. Credit Union (B.C.), 1964—; pres. Cuna Internat. Inc., 1966—, Creduco Ltd., 1963—; chmn. bd. Internat. Credit Union Services Corp., 1967—. Greater Nanaimo Water Dist., 1963—. Home: 446 4th St Nanaimo British Columbia Canada Office: 250 Albert St Nanaimo British Columbia Canada

GLEN, ROBERT ROBERT, entomologist; b. Paisley, Scotland, June 20, 1905; s. James Allison and Jeanie Blackwood (Barr) G.; B.Sc., U. Sask., 1929, M.Sc., 1931, LL.D., 1959; Ph.D., U. Minn., 1940; D.Sc., U. Ottawa, 1960; m. Margaret Helen Cameron, June 30, 1931; children—Robert Cameron, Ian Robert. Econ. entomologist Dominion Entomol. Lab., Saskatoon, Sask., 1928-45, charge wireworm investigations, Prairie Provinces, 1936-45; research coordinator, entomology div. Sci. Service, Can. Dept. Agr., Ottawa, Ont., 1945-50, chief entomology div., 1950-57, asso. dir. Sci. Service, 1957-59; dir.-gen. research br. Can. Dept. Agr., 1959-62, asst. dep. minister, 1962-68; sec. Commonwealth Sci. Com., 1968—. Mem. Entomol. research panel Def. Research Bd., 1947-55, chmn., 1955-59. Recipient Outstanding Achievement award U. Minn., 1960; Outstanding Achievement award Entomol. Soc. Can., 1964; certificate of merit Entomol. Soc. Am., 1964; Medal of Service of order of Can., 1967. Fellow Agriculture Inst. Can. (pres. Eastern Ont. br. 1950), Royal Soc. Can. (mem. council 1961-62); mem. Entomol Soc. Can. (pres. 1957), Entomol. Soc. Am. (pres. 1962), Entomol. Soc. Ont., Agrl. Econ. Research Council (v.p. governing bd. 1962-66), Canadian Seed Growers Assn. (hon. life), Ont. Soc. Profl. Agrologists, Profl. Inst. Can., Sigma Xi; fgn. asso Nat. Acad. Scis. Editorial bd. Ann. Rev. Entomologyy, 1955-60, Canadian Entomologist, 1959-62. Home: 20 Basil St London SW3, England. Office: Africa House Kingsway London WC2 England

GLENDINNING, C. DILLON, ret. economist, oil co. exec.; b. Centerville, Ia., June 15, 1916; s. James Alfred and Pauline (Payne) G.; A.B., Occidental Coll., 1939; M.A., Princeton, 1942; m. Jane Carol Travis, June 21, 1947; children—Bruce Gordon, Ann Elizabeth, James Travis. Instr. econs. Princeton, 1942-43; with Dept. State, 1947. Treasury Dept., 1943-46, 48-57, as sec. Nat. Adv. Council on Internat. Monetary and Financial Problems, 1948-57, dep. dir. Office Internat. Finance, 1950-57; with Socony Mobil Oil Co., 1957- -, asst. treas., 1959-70; adviser to Sec. of Treasury in financial negotiations U.S. and abroad. Recipient Alexander Hamilton award, 1957. Mem. Phi Beta Kappa. Methodist. Home: 19 Gault Park Dr Westport CT 06880

GLENDINNING, ROBERT MORTON, educator; b. Butte, Mont., Apr. 14, 1905; s. Lyle Robert and Bessie Morton (Billings) G.; A.B., U. Mich., 1927. A.M., 1930, Ph.D., 1933; m. Veda M. Blakeman, June 14, 1929; 1 dau., Bonnie Jean. Twp. supt. schs., Alger County, Mich., 1925-26; geography supr. Menominee (Mich.) High Sch., 1927-29; instr. U. Mich., 1929-34; asst. chief Isle Royale Survey, Lake Superior, 1930; asso. geographer T.V.A., 1934-36; successively asst. prof., asso. prof., prof. geography U. Cal. at Los Angeles, 1936—, chmn. dept., 1949-53, Mem. com. on land forms NRC, 1941-44, com. on geography adv. to Office Naval Research, 1949-52, mem. Fulbright awards, com. geography NRC, 1955-59. Fellow A.A.A.S.; mem. Geophys. Union, Asso. Am. Geographers (mem. council 1952-54), Am. Geog. Soc., Assn. Pacific Coast Geographers (v.p. 1951- 52), Internat. Geog. Union, Arctic Inst. N.Am., Sigma Xi, Phi Kappa Phi, Sigma Gamma Epsilon. Republican. Episcopalian. Author: Introduction to Geography, 1967; Introduction to Physical Geography, 1967; Your Country and the World, 1966; Eurasia, 1969; (with others) Eurasia, Africa, and Australia, 1966. Co-author: World Resources: Western Hemisphere, 1966, World Resources; Eastern Hemisphere, 1968; contbr. articles to geog. jours. Home: 11468 Thurston Circle Los Angeles CA 90049

GLENISTER, BRIAN FREDERICK, geologist, educator; b. Albany, Western Australia, Sept. 28, 1928; s. Frederick and Mabel (Frusher) G.; B.S., U. Western Australia, 1949; M.Sc., U. Melbourne, 1953; Ph.D., U. Ia., 1956; m. Anne Marie Treloar, Feb. 16, 1956; children—Alan Edward, Linda Marie, Kathryn Grace. Came to U.S., 1959, naturalized, 1967. Lectr., sr. lectr. geology U. Western Australia, Perth, 1956-59; asst. prof. U. Ia., Iowa City, 1959-62, asso. prof., 1962-66, prof., 1966-68, prof., chmn. geology dept., 1968—. Mem. Paleontol. Soc., Paleontol. Assn., Palaontologischen Gesellschaft, Soc. Econ. Paleontologists and Mineralogists, Geol. Soc. Am., A.A.A.S., Royal Soc. Western Australia, Sigma Xi. Home: 620 Whiting Av Iowa City IA 52240

GLENN, CHARLES, MELANCTHON, Jr., ins. co. exec.; b. Richmond, Va., Nov. 2, 1916; s. Charles Melancthon and Hazel (Cole) G.; student Va. Mil. Inst., 1935-36; U. Richmond, 1937-38; m. Virginia Technik, Nov. 23, 1953; children—Nancy Scott, Cynthia McLean. With Home Beneficial Life Ins. Co., Richmond, 1938—, asst.treas., 1947-60, corporate sec., 1960—. Served with Va. State Guard, 1943-45. Mem. Nat. Rifle Assn. (life), Co. Mil. Historians, Va. Hist. Soc. Club: Commonwealth (Richmond). Home: 300 Hollyport Rd Richmond VA 23229 Office: 3901 W Broad St Richmond VA 23230

GLENN, FRANK, surgeon; b. Marissa, Ill., August 7, 1901; s. Charles and Minnie (McMurdo) G.; M.D., Washington U., 1927; advanced study tching., surgery, Scotland, Eng., Germany, Austria, Orient, 1931-32; m. Esther Child, Jan. 15, 1938; children—Gardner, Prudence, Frank. Intern medicine Strong Meml. Hosp., Rochester, N.Y., 1927-28; first asst. resident surgeon N.Y. Hosp., 1932-33, surgeon-in-chief, 1947-67, cons. in surgery, 1967—; asst. surgery Cornell U. Med. Coll., 1932-33, asso. prof., 1941-47, prof. surgery, 1947-67, prof. emeritus, 1967—; adv. cons. surgeon VA, N.Y. Br., 1946-50; cons. gen. surgery VA 1946—; editorial cons. med. dept. Macmillan Co., N.Y.C. Served with M.C., AUS, 1942-46, as surg. cons. 6th Army, advancing from maj. to lt. col., also surg. cons. 6th Service Command, Chgo. Decorated Bronze star. Diplomate Am. Bd. Surgery (past vice chmn.). Fellow A.C.S. (pres.); mem. A.M.A., Am. Geriatrics Soc. (editor jour.), Am. Heart Assn. (exec. com.), Am. Soc. N.Y. Surg. Assns., N.Y. Soc. Thoracic Surgery N.Y. Med. Soc., N.Y. Acad. Medicine (pres. 1961—), Soc. U. Surgeons, Harvey Soc., Soc. Clin. Surgery, N.Y. Clin. Soc., N.Y. Gastroenterol. Assn., N.Y. Med., Surg. Soc., Soc. Exptl. Biology, Medicine, N.Y. Soc. Cardiovascular Surgery (pres.), Soc. U.S. Med. Consultants World War II, Alpha Omega Alpha. Republican. Club: University (N.Y.C.). Mem. editorial bd. Annals of Surgery; cons. editor Surgery, Gynecology and Obstetrics. Home: 200 E 66th St New York City NY 10021 Office: 525 E 68th St New York City NY 10021 ☆

GLENN, GARRARD WOOD, lawyer; b. Martinsburg, W.Va., Aug. 7, 1910; s. Garrard and Rosa Aubrey, (Wood) G.; A.B., Yale, 1933; LL.B., U. Va., 1936; grad. jr. course Naval War Coll., 1943; grad. gen. mgmt. course Am. Mgmt. Assn.; m. Priscilla Kent Roberts, Sept. 12, 1941; children—Susan F. (Mrs. William Armistead Christian, Jr.), Garrard L.; m. 2d, Avril Mullens Simpson, May 26, 1960. Admitted to N.Y. bar, 1937; asso. Cravath, de Gersdorff, Swaine & Wood, N.Y.C., 1936-42; asso. Lord, Day & Lord, N.Y.C., 1945-48, partner, 1948-54, 1958—; v.p. law N.Y. Central R.R., 1954-58. Served from lt. (j.g.) to lt. comdr. USNR, 1942-45. Decorated Purple Heart. Mem. Am. Law Inst., Am., N.Y. State bar assns., Assn Bar City N.Y., Commerce and Industry Assn. N.Y. (dir., treas.), Phi Beta Kappa, Phi

Delta Phi. Clubs: Downtown Assn., Century Assn. (N.Y.C.); Piping Rock (L.I.). Home: Cove Woods Rd Oyster Bay NY 11771 also 993 Park Av New York City NY 10028 Office: 25 Broadway New York City NY 10004

GLENN, HARRY DALE, rubber co. exec.; b. Pitts., Oct. 15, 1919; s. Floyd Marion and Marjorie Alice (Smith) G.; B.S., Westminster Coll., 1941; Ph.D. in Chemistry Purdue U., 1948; LL.D., Westminster Coll., 1966; m. Joan Van Alstyne, Aug. 24, 1946; children—David D., Peter V. With U.S. Rubber Co., 1948—, prodn. mgr., chem. div., 1962-64, v.p., gen. mgr. chem. div., 1964-66, group v.p. consumer, indsl. and plastic products divs., 1966—. Mem. Am. Chem. Soc., Mfg. Chemists Assn., Am. Mgmt. Assn., Newcomen Soc. N.Am., Sigma Phi Epsilon. Home: 240 Mine Hill Rd Fairfield CT 06430 Office: 1230 Av Americas New York City NY 10020

GLENN, HENRY ROBERTSON, lawyer, assn. exec.; b. Savannah, Ga., Oct. 31, 1904; s. Thomas L. and Ella Lou (Robertson) G.; LL.B., U. Ga., 1929; m. Ethel Harriet Bowen, Jan. 14, 1949; 1 son, Henry Robertson. Admitted to Ga. bar, 1929, N.Y. bar, 1932; with Life Ins. Assn. Am., N.Y.C., 1929—, asso. gen. counsel, 1948-57, gen. counsel, treas., sr. v.p. Served to capt. USAAF, World War II. Mem. Assn. Life Ins. Counsel, Assn. Bar City N.Y. Presbyn. (elder). Club: University (N.Y.C.). Home: 201 E 62d St New York City NY 10023 Office: 277 Park Av New York City NY 10017

GLENN, HORTENSE MCCLELLAN, univ. dean; b. Carthage, Tenn., May 25, 1909; d. Eugene W. and Vira (Donoho) McClellan; B.S., Tenn. Coll., 1928; postgrad. Duke, 1933-34; M.S., Fla. State U., 1950; Ph.D., 1958; m. Paul Mitchell Glenn, Jan. 20, 1940; children—Joan Marie, Paul Mitchell. Tchr., Carthage (Tenn.) High Sch., 1928-33; dietetic intern Duke Hosp., 1933-34; dietitian Univ. Hosps., Cleve., 1934-36, asst. dir. dietetics, 1937-42; instr. Frances Payne Bolton Sch. Nursing, Western Res. U., 1936-37; instr. home and family life Fla. State U., Tallahassee, 1946-58, dean Sch. Home Econs., 1958—. Mem. Am. Home Econs. Assn., Am. Dietetic Assn., Am. Sociol. Soc., Nat. Council Family Relations, Phi Kappa Phi, Omicron Nu. Methodist. Home: 2120 W Randolph Circle Tallahassee FL 32303

GLENN, JOHN HERSCHEL, Jr., astronaut; b. Cambridge, O., July 18, 1921; s. John Herschel and Clara (Sproat) G.; student Muskingum Coll., 1939, D.Sc., 1961; naval aviation cadet U. Ia., 1942; grad. flight sch. Naval Air Tng. Center, Corpus Christi, Tex., 1943, Navy Test Pilot Tng. School, Patuxent River, Md., 1954; m. Anna Margaret Castor, Apr. 1943; children—Carolyn Ann, John David. Commd. 2d lt. USMC, 1943, advanced through grades to lt. col.; assigned 4th Marine Aircraft Wing, Marshall Islands campaign, 1944, 9th Marine Aircraft Wing, 1945-46; with 1st Marine Aircraft Wing, North China Patrol, also Guam, 1947-48; flight instr. advanced flight tng., Corpus Christi, 1949-51; asst. G-2/G-3 Amphibious Warfare Sch., Quantico, Va., 1951; with Marine Fighter Squadron 311, exchange pilot 25th Fighter Squadron USAF, Korea, 1953; project officer fighter design br. Navy Bur. Eero., Washington, 1956-69; nonstop supersonic transcontinental Flight, July 16, 1957; astronaut Project Mercury, Manned Spacecraft Center NASA, 1959-64, pilot Mercury- Atlas 6, orbital space flight launched from Cape Canaveral, Fla., Feb., 1962. Vice pres. corporate devel. and dir. Royal Crown Cola Co. Decorated D.F.C. (five), Air medal (18), Astronaut medal USMC, Navy unit commendation; Korean Presidential unit citation; Distinguished Merit award Muskingum Coll.; Medal of Honor, N.Y.C. Mem. Soc. Exptl. Test Pilots, Internat. Acad. of Astronautics (hon.). Presbyn. Co-author: We Seven 1962. Author: P.S., I Listened to Your Heart Beat. Home: 203 Sleepy Hollow Ct Timbercove Seabrook TX 77586

GLENN, LAURENCE ALEXANDER, former bishop; b. Bellingham, Wash., Aug. 25, 1900; s. Thomas J. and Mary (Roche) G.; student St. John's U., Collegeville, Minn., 1919-21, St. Paul Sem., 1921-27; M.A., Cath. U., 1928. Ordained priest Roman Cath. Ch., 1927; sec. Bur. Cath. Charities, Duluth, Minn., 1928-48; pastor St. James Ch., Duluth, 1947-58; aux. bishop, Duluth, 1956-60; bishop, Crookston, Minn., 1960-70; ret. Home: 710 Beltrami Av Bemidji MN 56601

GLENN, MORTON BERNARD, physician; b. N.Y.C., Mar. 21, 1922; s. Harold and Mimi (Steinberg) G.; A.B., U. Pa., 1942; M.D., N.Y.U., 1946; m. Justine Manheim, July 21, 1963; children—Wendy Gail, Valerie Beth, John Allan. Intern, resident Bellevue Hosp., N.Y.C., 1946-47, 49-52, also asst. vis. physician; practice medicine, specializing in nutrition, N.Y.C., 1952—; med. cons. UN, 1954-56; chief Obesity Clinic, Knickerbocker Hosp.; asst. attending physician Univ. Hosp.; physician-in-charge Kips Bay Obesity Clinic, Morrisania Nutrition Clinic; instr., asst. prof. clin. medicine Coll. Medicine, N.Y.U.; vis. instr., then vis. asst. prof. preventive medicine Albert Einstein Coll. Medicine, 1958-70. Pres. Food and Nutrition Council Greater N.Y., 1962-64. Exec. bd. N.Y. chpt. Am. Jewish Com. Served to lt. (j.g.) USNR, 1943-45, 47-49. Recipient Travel award Am. Inst. Nutrition, 1963. Fellow Am. Coll. Nutrition (pres. 1966-68), Am. Pub. Health Assn., N.Y. Acad. Medicine; mem. A.M.A., N.Y. County Med. Soc., N.Y. Acad. Scis., Am., N.Y. diabetes assns., Am., N.Y. heart assns. Author: How To Get Thinner Once and For All, 1965; Home: 1070 Park Av New York City NY 10028 Office: 110 E 63d New York City NY 10021

GLENN, TERRELL LYLES, lawyer; b. Chester, S.C., June 3, 1930; s. John L., Jr., and Sarah (Terrell) G.; A.B., U. S.C., 1951, LL.B., 1953; m. Louise B. Owens, Oct. 25, 1955; children—John Lyles IV, Terrell Lyles, Rebecca, Louise O. Admitted to S.C. bar, 1953, also U.S. Supreme Ct., U.S. dist. cts.; practice law, Columbia, 1955—, partner firm Edens, Hammer & Glenn, 1955-61, Glenn, Porter & Sullivan, 1968—; U.S. dist. atty. Eastern Dist. S.C., 1961. Chmn. S.C. Arts Commn.; 1970—. Served to 1st lt., AUS, 1953-55. Mem. Am., S.C., Richland County bar assns., S.C. Plaintiffs Attys. Assn. (v.p. 1959-60), Columbia Jr. (pres. 1960), U.S. Jr. (internat. senator 1964) chambers of commerce, Phi Delta Phi, Omicron Delta Kappa. Democrat, Episcopalian. Home: 433 Saluda Av Columbia SC 29201 Office: Barringer Bldg Columbia SC 29201

GLENN, WAYNE EDWARD, oil co. exec.; b. Fort Worth, Nov. 3, 1915; s. Arthur E. and Lura M. (Hammon) G.; B.S. in Petroleum Engring., U. Okla., 1940; student Am. Mgmt. Sch., 1954; grad. Advanced Mgmt. Program, Harvard, 1957; Ph.D. in Engring., Mont. Sch. Mines, 1960; m. Barbara E. Gamble, July 13, 1941; children—Ellen Gail, Carvel Wayne, Lawrence Edward. With Continental Oil Co., 1936-62, asst. regional mgr. prodn. Rocky Mountain region, Denver, 1952- 58, gen. mgr. prodn. dept., Houston, 1958-61, v.p., 1961-62; pres., dir., gen. mgr. Hudson's Bay Oil & Gas Co. Ltd., Calgary, Atla., Can., 1962—; pres., dir. Mic Mac Oils, Ltd., 1963—; v.p., coordinator world- wide exploration and prodn. activities Continental Oil Co., 1965-67, exec. v.p., 1967-69, pres. Western Hemisphere Petroleum div., 1969—; also dir.; exec. v.p. N. Am. Petroleum Operations, 1968- -; 1st v.p., dir. Peace River Oil Pipe Line Co. Ltd.; dir. Security Freehold Petroleum Ltd.; voting trustee Trans-Can. Pipe Lines Ltd. Mem. Canadian Council Christians and Jews. Adv. com. engring. U. Alta. Bd. dirs. Jr. Achievement, United Engrs. Trustees Found. Served to capt. AUS, World War II. Mem. Am. Inst. Mining Metall. and Petroleum Engrs. (v.p.; pres. soc. petroleum engrs. 1960-61). Calgary (past chmn. petroleum and natural gas com.), Canadian, Houston (dir.) chambers of commerce, Canadian Petroleum Assn. (vice chmn., bd. govs. 1964-65; dir. Alta. div. 1962- 65), Internat. Oil and Gas Center, Canadian Businessmen's Aircraft Assn. (past dir.), Ind. Petroleum Assn., Mid-Continent Oil and Gas Assn. (dir.), Nat. Alliance Businessmen (met. chmn.), Am. Petroleum Inst. (past chmn. adv. com., dir.), Tex. Research League (dir.). Republican. Presbyn. (elder). Mason (32 Shriner). Club: Houston Petroleum, River Oaks Country. Home: 5025 Riverway Houston TX 77027 Office: PO Box 2197 Houston TX 77001

GLENN, WILBUR H., Beverage co. exec.; b. Enterprise, Ala., 1905; grad. U. Ala., 1928; m. Nell Gardiner, 1938; children—Eleanor S. Hardegil, Maragret W. Past pres., chmn. finance com., mem. bd. dirs. Royal Crown Cola Co., Columbus, Ga.; dir. First Nat. Bank. Pres., dir. Pickett & Hatcher Ednl. Fund, Inc. Home: 1641 Summit Dr Columbus GA 31906 Office: 1241 1st Av Columbus GA 31902

GLENN, WILLIAM WALLACE LUMPKIN, surgeon, educator; b. Asheville, N.C., Aug. 12, 1914; s. Eugene Byron and Elizabeth Elliot (Lumpkin) G.; B.S., U. S.C., 1934; M.D., Jefferson Med. Coll., 1938; M.A. (hon.), Yale, 1962; m. Amory Potter, May 15, 1943; children—William Amory Lumpkin, Elizabeth Amory. Intern, Pa. Hosp., Phila., 1938-40; surg. resident Mass. Gen. Hosp., Boston, 1940-42, 45- 46; asst. physiology Harvard Sch. Pub. Health, 1941-43; asso. surgery Jefferson Med. Coll., Phila., 1946-48; mem. faculty Yale Med. Sch., 1948—, prof. surgery, 1962—, chief cardiothoracic surgery Yale Med. Sch., 1948—; attending surgeon Grace-New Haven Hosp.; cons. VA, Griffin, Norwalk, Windham, Circle, Meridan hosps. Cons. Surgeon Gen. Com. Environmental Medicine, 1962-64; mem. com. cardiovascular systems NRC, 1955-56. Served to maj., M.C., AUS, World War II: ETO. Diplomate Am. Bd. Surgery, Am. Bd. Thoracic Surgery. Mem. Am. Heart Assn. (chmn. council cardiovascular surgery 1960-62, pres. 1970-71, award of merit 1966), Internat. Soc. Surgery (treas. 1968—), Internat. Surg. Group (pres. 1964), Am. Surg. Assn., A.C.S. (chmn. Conn. adv. com. 1963- -, gov. 1967-68), Soc. U. Surgeons, New Eng. Surg. Soc., Am. Assn. Thoracic Surgery, Vascular Surg. Soc., Halstead Soc., Alpha Omega Alpha, Sigma Xi. Episcopalian. Clubs: Morys' Assos., Lawn (New Haven). Co-author: Thoracic and Cardiovascular Surgery, 1962. Asso editor Surgery, 1967—. Contbr. profl. jours. Cons. editor: Cardiac Pacemakers, 1964. Home: 685 Forest Rd New Haven CT 06515

GLENNAN, THOMAS KEITH, govt. ofcl.; b. Enderlin, N.D., Sept. 8, 1905; s. Richard and Margart Laing (Pauline) G.; B.S., Yale, 1927, M.A. (hon.), 1961; D.Sc., Clarkson Coll., 1947, Oberlin Coll., 1950, John Carroll U., 1954, Akron U., 1959, Case Inst. Tech., 1960, U. Toledo, 1961, U. So. Cal., 1964, Lehigh U., 1966; Eng.D., Stevens Inst. Tech., 1951, Fenn Coll., 1953, Columbia, 1961, Muhlenberg Coll., 1961; LL.D., Tulane U., Miami (O.) U., Western Res. U., 1960, Ohio State U., 1967; m. Ruth Adams, June 20, 1931; children—Thomas, Catherine, Pauline, Sarah. With Elec. Research Products, Inc. subsidiary Western Elecric, 1927-35; operations, mgr. Paramount Pictures, Inc., Hollywood, Cal., 1935-39, studio mgr., 1939-41; studio mgr. Samuel Goldwyn Studios, 1941-42; dir. U.S. Navy Underwater Sound Lab. div. of war research, Columbia U., New London, Conn., 1942-45; exec. Ansco (General Aniline & Film Co.), Binghamton, N.Y., 1945-47; pres. Case Inst. Tech., Cleve., 1947-66, on leave as mem. AEC, 1950-52, as adminstr. NASA, Washington, 1958-61; pres. Asso. Univs., Inc., N.Y.C., 1965-68; asst. to chmn. The Urban Coalition, Washington, 1968-69; ambassador, U.S. rep. to IAEA, 1970—. Dir. Avco Corp., Republic Steel Corp., Air Products and Chems., Inc., Standard Oil Ohio; trustee Rand Corp. Trustee Case Western Res. U. Recipient U.S. Medal of Merit award for services at underwater sound lab., 1946; Distinguished Service medal NASA, 1967. Mem. Nat. Acad. Engring., Am. Acad. Arts and Scis., Nat. Acad. Pub. Adminstrn. Sigma Xi, Tau Beta Pi. Chi Phi. Clubs: Yale (N.Y.C.); Bohemian (San Francisco); Federal City, National Aviation (Washington). Address: 11483 Waterview Cluster Reston VA 22070

GLENNON, HARRISON RANDOLPH, Jr., shipping co. exec.; b. Port Gibson, Miss., Nov. 4, 1914; s. Harrison Randolph and May (Redus) G.; B.S., U.S. Naval Acad., 1937; m. Dickie Glen Bailey, Oct. 27, 1944; children—Harrison Randolph, Francis Whaley (dec.), Blair Bailey, Supr. ship repair and operation, engring. dept. Moore-McCormack Lines, Inc., N.Y.C., 1937-41, 46-53, supt. engr., 1953-57, v.p., head engring. div. 1959-62, exec. v.p. operations, dir., 1962-68, chmn. vessel replacement com. Am. S.S. Lines, 1962-64; pres. Comml. S.S. Co., Inc., 1968-71, Gt. Republics Transport, Inc., 1971—; pres. Container Terminals; dir. Portsmouth Terminals, Inc. Mem. N.Y. Shipping Labor Policy Com., 1962—; v.p., dir. N.Y. Shipping Assn., 1967-69. Served from ensign to comdr., USNR, 1941-46. Mem. Soc. Naval Architects and Marine Engrs. (v.p., mem. exec. com. and council), Am. Bur. Shipping (mem. classification and engring. com.), Am. Marine inst. (tng. and upgrading com.), Am. Inst. Mcht. Shipping (chmn. standard ship com.), Maritime Service Com. (sec. 1966-67). Episcopalian. Clubs: Riverside Yacht; Carolina Yacht; Harbor View. Home: Down Harbor Lane Riverside CT 06878 Office: 2 Broadway New York City NY 10004

GLESZER, ROLAND MERRILL, army officer; b. Brewer, Me., Mar. 18, 1915; s. Edward I. and Ada M. Gleszer; student U. Me., 1932-35, LL.D., 1967; B.S., U.S. Mil. Acad., 1940; grad. Army War Coll., 1968; m. Helen West Slee, Aug. 31, 1940; children—Peter Eaton, Susan Merrill (Mrs. Stephen J. Beaudry, Jr.). Commd. 2d lt. U.S. Army, 1940, advanced through grades to maj. gen., 1967; comdg. officer 3d Bn. 290th Inf., World War II, asst. chief of staff Joint Task Force 3 and 132 Enewetok Atoll, 1950-53; comdg. officer 21st Inf. Regt., 1958-59; comdg. gen. 5th Inf. Div. (mech.), 1968-69, Mil. Dist. Washington, 1969—. Decorated D.S.M. Home: Quarters 12 B Fort Myer VA 22211 Office: Hdqrs Mil Dist Washington Ft McNair Washington DC 20315

GLEYSTEEN, CULVER, fgn. service officer; b. Jenkintown, Pa., Mar. 21, 1924; s. William Henry and Theodora (Culver) G.; B.A., Yale, 1944, M.A., 1947; m. Elisabeth Katarina Mörner, Jan. 21, 1950; children—Peter, Nicholas, Jan, Marcus. Joined U.S. Fgn. Service, 1947; vice consul, Dairen, China, 1948- 49; 3d sec., then 2d sec. embassy, Moscow, USSR, 1950-52; polit. officer HICOG, Bonn, Germany, 1952-53; 2d sec. embassy, Djakarta, Indonesia, 1953- 55; assigned State Dept., 1956-60; 2d sec., then 1st sec. embassy, Moscow, 1960-62; assigned Naval War Coll., 1962-63; 1st sec. embassy, Paris, France, 1963-66; dep. asst. dir. internat. affairs Arms Control and Disarmament Agy., Washington, 1966-70; consul gen., Leningrad, USSR, 1970—. Served to lt. (j.g.) USNR, 1943-46. Episcopalian. Address: care American Embassy Moscow USSR

GLEYSTEEN, WILLIAM HENRY, Jr., fgn. service officer; b. Peking, China, May 8, 1926 (parents Am. citizens); s. William Henry and Theodora (Culver) G.; B.A., Yale, 1949, M.A., 1951; fellow Harvard Center Internat. Affairs, 1965-66; m. Zoe Marianna Clubb, Dec. 27, 1952; children—Thea, Guy, Michael. With Exec. Secretariat, Dept. of State, 1951-55; with Am. embassy, Taipei, Taiwan, 1956-58, dep. chief mission, 1971—; mem. staff Am. embassy, Tokyo, Japan, 1958-62; Am. consulate gen., Hong Kong, 1962-65; with Office UN Polit. Affairs, State Dept., 1966-69, dir. office research and analysis for East Asia, 1969-71. Served with USNR, 1944-46. Home: 5010 Worthington Dr Washington DC 20016 Office: care Dept of State Washington DC 20520

GLIBERT, JOSEPH FRANCIS, bank exec.; b. N.Y.C., Apr. 11, 1918; s. Joseph L. and Louise M. (Lozzero) G.; B.S., N.Y. U., 1949, M.B.A., 1953; m. Marguerite Pontier, Oct. 18, 1947; children—Jeffrey, Patricia. Investment counsellor, 1947-54; with Md. Casualty Co., Balt., 1954-66, v.p., 1959-63, exec. v.p., 1963-66; v.p. Bank of N.Y., N.Y.C., 1966—. Chmn. ins. div. Balt. United Appeal, 1963-64. Bd. dirs. Inst. Chartered Financial Analysts, Charlottesville, Va., 1964—. Served with AUS, 1942-45. Home: 131 Oak Ridge Rd Summit NJ 07901 Office: 48 Wall St New York City NY 10005

GLICK, DAVID, histochemist, educator; b. Homestead, Pa., May 3, 1908; s. Max and Anne (Lasday) G.; B.S., U. Pitts. (Phillips medal), 1929, Ph.D., 1932; student Columbia, summer 1930; m. Ruth Mueller, Sept. 16, 1929; children—David, Peter; m. 2d, Annette Zelzer, Aug. 9, 1941; m. 3d, Irene Ross, Sept. 2, 1945; children—Jonathon Michael, Jeffrey Alan. Fellow Mt. Sinai Hosp., N.Y.C., 1932-24, OSRD war research, 1942-43; chief chem. lab. Mt. Zion Hosp., San Francisco, 1934- 36; fellow Carlsberg Lab., Copenhagen, 1936-37, Rockefeller Found. fellow, 1937, advanced med. fellow Commonwealth Fund, 1939; head chem. lab. Beth Israel Hosp., Newark, 1937-42; head vitamin-enzyme research Russell Miller Milling Co., Mpls., 1943-46; cons. toxicity lab. U. Chgo., 1945-46; asso. prof. physiol. chemistry U. Minn., 1946-50, prof., 1950-61; prof. pathology, head div. histochemistry Stanford Med. Sch., 1961—. Cons., VA Hosp., Mpls., 1946-47, VA Hosp., Palo Alto, Cal., 1961—; Macfarlane prof. exptl. medicine U. Glasgow, 1970-71; advanced med. fellow Karolinska Inst. Stockholm, 1949, Commonwealth Fund, 1958-59. Recipient Career award USPH, 1962. Mem. Microchem. Soc., Internat., Am. socs. cell biology, Royal Micros. Soc., Gt. Britain, Royal Danish acads. sci. and letters, Histochem. Soc. (past pres.), Am. Soc. Biol. Chemists, Am. Chem. Soc., A.A.A.S., Soc Exptl. Biology and Medicine, Am. Assn. U. Profs., Sigma Xi, Phi Lambda Upsilon. Author: Black and White and other Poems, 1946; Techniques of Histo- and Cytochemistry, 1949; Quantitative Chemical Techniques of Histo- and Cytochemistry, Vol. 1, 1962, II, 63, Editor: Methods of Biochemical Analysis, 1953—. Asso. editor of Jour. Histo-and Cytochemistry, 1953-56, 65—. Contbr. articles sci. publs. Home: 680 Foothill Rd Stanford CA 94305

GLICK, FRANK ZIEGLER, former educator; b. Junction City, Kan., Dec. 22, 1905; s. Frank Lewis and Mae Malissa (Ziegler) G.; student Kan. State Agrl. Coll., 1924- 26; A.B., U. Kan., 1927; A.M., U. Chgo., 1930, Ph.D., 1939; m. Mary Bell Read, Sept. 20, 1932; children—Marian, Joseph. With Chgo. Council Social Agys., 1929-31; exec. sec. Ill. Bd. Pub. Welfare Commrs., 1931-32, asso. exec. sec. Ill. Emergency Relief Commn., 1932-36; prof. pub. welfare adminstrn., dir. Grad. Sch. Social Work, U. Neb., 1939-55; exec. dir. Unitarian Service Com., 1955-62; dir. Sch. Social Work, U. Ia., 1962-71. Mem. Nat. Assn. Social Workers. Author: The Illinois Emergency Relief Commission, 1940. Home: 840 Oakcrest St Iowa City IA 52240

GLICK, GARLAND WAYNE, coll. pres.; b. Bridgewater, Va., Jan. 27, 1921; s. John T. and Effie (Evers) G.; B.D., Bethany Bibl. Sem., Chgo., 1946; M.A. in N.T., U. Chgo., 1949, Ph.D. in Ch. History, 1957, LL.D., Bridgewater Coll., 1969; m. Barbara Roller Zigler, Jan. 1, 1943; children—Martha (Mrs. Howard Berthold), John, Mary. Ordained to ministry Ch. of Brethren, 1942; pastor, Lombard, Ill., 1945-48; instr., then asst. prof. Bibl. studies Juniata Coll., Huntingdon, Pa., 1948-53; mem. faculty Franklin and Marshall Coll., 1955-65, asso. prof. religion, 1958-65, prof., 1965, v.p., 1962-65, dir. research and long range planning, 1960, asst. to dean, 1960-61, dean coll., 1961-65; pres. Keuka Coll., Keuka Park, N.Y., 1966—. Vis. prof. Lancaster (Pa.) Theol. Sem., 1958-60, 64; coordinator of cons. Knox Seminars Ednl. Mgmt., 1963-65; seminar dir. Nat. Cath. Edn. Assn. Long-Range Planning Seminars, 1968. Bd. dirs., treas. Empire State Found. Ind. Liberal Arts Colls. Mem. Nat. Assn. Bibl. Instrs., Am. Soc. Ch. History, Am. Conf. Acad. Deans (treas. 1965-66), Societas Orphea, Pi Gamma Mu, Tau Kappa Alpha. Author: Maker of Modern Theology: Adolf von Harnack, 1967. Contbr. Ency. Britannica. Home: Keuka Park NY 14478 Office: Keuka Coll Keuka Park NY 14478

GLICK, JACOB EZRA, marine corps officer; b. Burlington, Ia., Feb. 12, 1920; s. Russell C. and Clara A. (Deputy) G.; B.S., U.S. Naval Acad., 1941; M.S. in Elec. Engring., Naval Postgrad. Sch., 1949; M.B.A., George Washington U., 1965; student Nat. War Coll., 1964-65; m. Marjorie L. Gardner, Dec. 7, 1951; children—Jeffrey Alan, Susan Goff, Thomas Bryan. Commd. 2d lt. USMC, 1942, advanced through grades to brg. gen., 1967; combat duty, World War II, Korea; asst. div. comdr., Vietnam; asst. dep. chief research and devel. USMC, 1962-64; chief operations directorate Joint Staff, Washington, 1968-71; exec. sec. Ret. Officers Assn., Washington, 1971—. instr., head dept. Marine Corps Schs., 1956-59; guest lectr. Nat. War Coll., 1963-70. Decorated D.S.M., Legion of Merit (3), Bronze Star, Navy Commendation Medal, Vietnamese Cross Gallantry with palm, Vietnamese Honor medal. Registered profl. engr., D.C. Mem. Marine Corps Assn., First Marine Div. Assn., U.S. Naval Acad. Alumni Assn., U.S. Naval Inst., 12th Def. Battalion Assn. Home: 407 Skyhill Rd Alexandria VA 22314 Office: 1625 Eye St NW Washington DC 20006

GLICK, MARY KATHRYN, educator; b. Columbus, Ind., Mar. 22, 1904; A.B., Franklin Coll., 1926; AM., U. Chgo., 1928, Ph.D., 1938. Instr. Latin and Greek, LaGrange Coll., 1927-28; asst. prof. Latin, Wilson Coll., 1929-35; asst. prof. Latin and Greek, Agnes Scott Coll., Decatur, Ga., 1938-43, asso. prof. classical langs. and lit., 1944-47, prof., 1947—, also chmn. dept. Mem. Am. Philol. Assn., Archaeol. Inst. Am., Classical Assn. Midwest and South. Research on poetic image in Lucretuis, Horace's use of volgus, colloquial exaggeration in Roman comedy. Address: Dept of Classical Langs and Lit Agnes Scott Coll Decatur GA 30030

GLICK, PHILIP MILTON, lawyer; b. Kiev, Russia, Dec. 9, 1905; s. David and Rebecca (Sussman) G.; derivative U.S. citizenship, from naturalization of father, 1924; student Crane Jr. Coll., 1924-26; Ph.B. cum laude, U. Chgo., 1928, J. D. cum laude, 1930; m. Rose Deborah Rosenfield, May 13, 1933. Gen. counsel fed. subsistence homesteads corp. U.S. Dept. Interior, 1933- 34; chief land policy div., asst. solicitor, office of solicitor USDA, 1934-42; solicitor War Relocation Authority, 1942-44, dep. dir., 1945-46; gen. counsel Fed. Pub. Housing Authority, 1946-48; gen. counsel The Inst. Inter-Am. Affairs, 1948-53, legal counsel Tech. Cooperation Adminstrn., Dept. State, 1951-53; vis. prof. econ. devel. and cultural change U. Chgo., 1953-55; mem. law firm Dorfman & Glick, 1955-67; asst. dir., legal adviser Fed. Water Resources Council, 1967-69; legal counsel Nat. Water Commn., 1969—. Served with USNR, 1944-45. Mem. Am. Bar Assn., Am. Polit. Sci. Assn., Soc. for Internat. Devel., Am. Soc. for Pub. Adminstrn., Internat. Inst. Adminstrv. Scis., Order of Coif, Phi Beta Kappa. Club: Cosmos (Washington). Author: The Administration of Technical Assistance, 1957. Contbr. profl. publs. Home: 116 E Melrose St Chevy Chase MD 20015 Office: 800 N Quincy St Arlington VA 22203

GLICK, ROBERT ADOLPH, retail furniture co. exec.; b. Columbus, O., Apr. 15, 1916; s. Frank A. and Julia (York) G.; B.S. in Bus. Adminstrn., Ohio State U., 1937; m. Ruth Rosenstock, July 18, 1943; children—Carole Joan, Marilyn, Marcia. With Kaufmann Furniture Co., Reading, Pa., 1937-38; floor covering buyer Glick's Furniture Co., Columbus, 1938-41, asst. gen. mgr., 1946-47, pres., 1947—; dir. Columbus Savs. & Loan Assn., Columbus Jets Baseball Team. Mem. budget com. United Appeal; pres. Friendship Settlement House, 1962-63; v.p. Community Camp. Bd. dirs. Columbus Urban Renewal Commn., Columbus Heart Fund, United Jewish Fund. Served to capt. AUS, 1941-45. Recipient award All Am. Mcht. Furniture Industry, 1955, award of merit Furniture World, 1955; named Brand Name Furniture Retailer of Year, 1961, Outstanding Mcht., Nat. Retail Furniture Assn., 1957. Mem. Nat. Retail Furniture Assn. (pres. 1966), Columbus Better Bus. Bur. (dir.), Zeta Beta Tau. Jewish religion. Club: Winding Hollow Country (Columbus). Home: 150 S Parkview St Columbus OH 43215 Office: 65 E Long St Columbus OH 43215

GLICKAUF, JOSEPH SIMON, Jr., accountant; b. Chgo., Jan. 15, 1912; s. Joseph Simon and Irene (Goldsmith) G.; m. Elizabeth Steele, Oct. 23, 1937; children—Carole (Mrs. Roy Fingerson), Peter. With IBM Corp., 1937-41; with Arthur Andersen & Co., C.P.A.'s, 1946—, partner charge adminstrv. services div., 1954—; guest lectr. U. Fla., Mass. Inst. Tech., Harvard Bus. Sch.; spl. research medico-electronics as grantee Michael Reese Hosp., Chgo. Mem. Chgo. Crime Commn. Bd. mgrs. Florence Crittenton Anchorage: bd. dirs. Midwest chpt. A.R.C. Served to lt. USNR, 1941-45. Clubs: University, Beverly Country (bd. govs., treas.), Union League, Attic (Chgo.). Contbr. profl. jours. Home: 1 E Schiller St Chicago IL 60610 Office: 69 W Washington St Chicago IL 60602

GLICKMAN, HAROLD JEROME, lawyer; b. Lorain, O., Aug. 10, 1908; s. Benjamin A. and Edith (Gordon) G.; A.B., Western Res. U., 1930, LL.B., 1932; m. Henrietta Blau, Sept. 23, 1934; children—Albert B., Amy (Mrs. Kenneth Rogat). Admitted to Ohio bar, 1932, since practiced in Cleve.; partner Ulmer, Berne, Laronge, Glickman & Curtis, 1943—; lectr. law fire ins. Ohio State U., Purdue U. Pres., trustee Free Loan Assn. Cleve. Mem. Jewish Community Council, Cleve., 1938-42; mem. del. assembly Cleve. Welfare Fedn., 1940-48; mem. Nat. Council United-Hias, 1947—; mem. attys. div. Cleve. United Appeal, 1938-55; mem. campaign cabinet Cleve. Jewish Welfare Fund, 1960-65. Past pres. trustees, now hon. trustee Jewish Convalescent Hosp. Cleve.; pres. Cleve. chpt. United World Federalists; v.p., trustee Family Service Assn. Cleve., ; past v.p., trustee Cleve. Jewish Communtiy Fedn.; bd. govs. Western Res. U. Law Sch. Mem. Am., Ohio, Cleve., Cuyahoga County bar assns., Am. Arbitration Assn. (arbitration panel), Def. Research Inst., Nat. Planning Assn. (nat. council), Phi Sigma Delta, Tau Epsilon Rho. Jewish religion (trustee temple). Clubs: Oakwood Country, Commerce, Cleveland City (past pres., trustee, dir.) (Cleve.). Home: 2 Bratenahl Pl Bratenahl OH 44108 Office: Keith Bldg Cleveland OH 44115

GLICKMAN, IRVING, educator, periodontist; b. N.Y.C., Jan. 17, 1914; s. Nathan and Rose (Gurland) G.; B.S., Bklyn. Coll., 1933; D.M.D., Tufts U., 1938, postgrad. dept. pathology Med. Sch., 1939-40; m. Violeta Arboleda, Mar. 13, 1954; children—Alan, Denise. Faculty, Tufts U. Sch. Dental Medicine, Boston, 1938—, prof. oral pathology, 1948—, research prof. oral pathology, 1960—, prof. periodontology, 1948—, chmn. dept., 1960—, dir. div. grad. and postgrad. studies, 1951-60. Mem. Army Med. Service Adv. Com. on Preventive Dentistry; mem. adv. group Cambridge (Mass.) Health Dept.; lectr. dental pathology Boston U. Sch. Medicine; cons. in periodontology Forsyth Dental Center, Boston, VA Hosp., Boston; cons. Armed Forces Inst. Pathology; dental cons. U.S. Naval Hosp., Chelsea, Mass.; asso. staff New Eng. Center Hosp.; staff Brookline Hosp.; cons. in oral pathology Grover Manor Hosp.; periodontist Boston City Hosp.; dir. Berkshire Conf. on Periodontology and Oral Pathology, 1950—. Chmn. alumni council Tufts U., 1963-64. Trustee, Combined Jewish Philanthropies, Boston. Recipient numerous awards including Samuel Charles Miller Meml. award in oral medicine, 1965, award for basic research in periodontology Internat. Assn. for Dental Research, 1966. Diplomate Am. Bd. Periodontology, Am. Bd. Oral Medicine, Am. Bd. Oral Pathology. Fellow Am. Acad. Dental Sci., A.A.A.S., Am., Internat. colls. dentists; mem. Am. Acad. Periodontology, Am. Acad. Dental Medicine, Am. Assn. Dental Schs., Am. Assn. Anatomists, New Eng. Soc. Pathologists, Internat. Assn. for Dental Research, Internat. Acad. Oral Pathology, Tissue Culture Assn., Am. Dental Assn., Mass. Dental Soc., Tufts U. Dental Alumni Assn. (pres. 1966-67), Sigma Xi, Omicron Kappa Upsilon; also hon. mem. fgn. socs. Jewish religion (trustee temple). Author: Clinical Periodontology, 4th edit., 1972; Periodonatal Disease, 1972. Contbr. numerous articles profl. jours., also chpts. to books. Home: 24 Manor House Rd Newton Center MA 02159 Office: Tufts U Dept Dental Medicine Medford MA 02111

GLICKMAN, LOUIS J., real estate investor, exec.; b. Feb. 22, 1905; s. Pincus and Sarah (Siegler) G.; student Brown U., 1924, U. Va., 1926; m. Helen Hauptmann, Aug. 16, 1931; children—Warren and Adam. Entered father's real estate and constrn. firm, 1928, partner, 1930; investment counsellor, 1940-42; founder Louis J. Glickman, realty investments, 1942; chmn., pres. Glickman Corp., N.Y.C., and affiliated corps., 1942—; real estate cons. N.Y., N.H. & H. R.R.; dir. Rogosin Industries of Israel. Chmn. City of Hope telethon campaign, 1959; active Cerebral Palsy, United Epilepsy assns. Founder Albert Einstein Sch. Medicine; v.p. Realty Found. N.Y.C.; trustee Karen Horney Clinic, Yeshiva U., Beth Israel Hosp., Lebanon Hosp., Brandeis U.; adv. com. Pace Coll. Named realty man of the year Real Estate Club, 1955. Mem. Nat. Urban League (v.p.). Mason. Club: Nat. Realty (gov.). Home: 936 Fifth Av New York City NY 10021

GLIDDEN, HARLEY FREMONT, educator; b. Lincoln, Neb., Nov. 29, 1905; s. Wilber John and Estella (Yelland) G.; B.S., Buena Vista Coll., Storm Lake, Ia., 1929; M.A., U. Ia., 1934; Ph.D., U. Neb., 1954; m. N. Joyce Cassen, June 4, 1933; 1 dau., Janet Joyce (Mrs. John K. Jerome). sch. sci. tchr., prin., Ia., 1929-36; jr. coll. chemistry tchr., also dean, Ia., 1936-40, 41-42; supr. natural sci. U. Neb. Tchrs. Coll., 1939-40; sci. supr., tchr. chemistry Colo. State Coll., Greeley 1942-43, tchr. coll. chemistry, 1946-55, chmn. div. scis., 1955-66, asso. dean sci. Sch. Arts and Sci., 1966—; guest prof. U. Guam, summer 1969. Mem. bd. Colo. Pub. Employees Retirement Assn., 1949-66, chmn., 1955-66; mem. Colo. Adv. Com. Conservation Edn., 1955-69. Bd. dirs. Greeley United Fund, 1957-59, chmn., 1957-58; bd. dirs., adv. bd. Greeley Salvation Army, 1959—. Served to lt. (s.g.) USNR, 1944-46. Mem. Colo.-Wyo. Acad. Sci. (pres. 1962-63), Nat. Assn. Research Sci. Teaching, Nat. Sci. Tchrs. Assn. (membership chmn. Colo. 1956), Greeley C. of C., Alpha Psi Omega, Alpha Delta Alpha, Phi Delta Kappa. Methodist. Kiwanian, Mason. Co-Author: Elements of Pre-Flight Aeronautics for High Schools, 1942. Contbr. articles to profl. Jours. Home: 1951 Montview Dr Greeley CO 80631

GLIDDEN, LLOYD SUMNER, Jr., ins. co. exec.; b. Wakefield. Mass., Aug. 11, 1922; s. Lloyd Sumner and Ida (Dow) G.; grad. Bentley Sch. Accounting, Boston, 1947; m. Lorraine Murphy, May 2, 1943; children—Debra Kent, Jeffrey DeRonde. With Liberty Mut. Ins. Co., Boston, 1939—, treas., 1959—, v.p., 1966—, also treas. affiliated cos.; trustee, mem., bd. investment Home Savs. Bank, Boston. Served with USCGR, 1942-46. Mem. Boston Security Analysts Soc., Boston Econ. Club. Home: 4 Cook's Farm Lane Lynnfield MA 01940 Office: 175 Berkeley St Boston MA 02117

GLIDDEN, ROBERT T., machinery mfg. co. exec.; b. Arlington, Mass., 1913; A.B., Dartmouth, 1935; A.M., Boston U., 1942; postgrad. Northwestern U., 1943-44; m. Ruth Mellisa Cooley, May 4, 1935; children—Mark, David. With Internat. Harvester Co., Chgo., 1938—, asst. sec., 1966—. Past mem. Batavia (Ill.) Pub. Sch. Bd. Mem. Farm and Indsl. Equipment Inst., Am. Marketing Assn., Am. Econ. Assn., Am. Statis. Assn., Am. Soc. Corp. Secs. Rotarian. Home: Batavia IL 60510 Office: 401 N Michigan Av Chicago IL 60611

GLIKBARG, ABNER SAMUEL, transp. exec.; b. Vallejo, Cal., Oct. 22, 1897; s. Abraham and Bertha (Logasa) G.; B.A., Stanford, 1919; LL.B., Harvard, 1922; m. Emilie Greenebaum, Sept. 17, 1925 (dec. 1930); children—Eleanor (Mrs. Arthur D. Sweet), Thomas S.; m. 2d, Clemence Jacob, Apr. 16, 1947; 1 dau., Janet. Admitted to Cal. bar, 1922, practiced in San Francisco, 1922-57; chmn. Pacific Intermountain Express Co.; pres. Intermountain Terminal Co.; chmn. bd. P.I.E. Leasing Co.; chief exec. officer Nat. Carloading Corp.; dir. Quinn River-Sonora Co., Pacific Cement & Aggregates, Inc., Pacific Industries, Inc. Clubs: Stock Exchange, Concordia-Argonaut (San Francisco). Home: 947 Green St San Francisco CA 94111 Office: 155 Sansome St San Francisco CA 94104

GLIMCHER, MELVIN JACOB, orthopedic surgeon; b. Brookline, Mass. June 12, 1925; s. Aaron and Clara (Fink) G.; student Duke, 1943-44; B.S. in Mech. Engring. with highest distinction, B.S. in Physics with highest distinction, Purdue U., 1946; M.D. magna cum laude, Harvard, 1950; postgrad. Mass. Inst. Tech., 1956-59; m. Geraldine Lee Bogolub, June 22, 1946; children—Susan Deborah, Laurie Hollis, Nancy Blair. Intern surgery Strong Meml. Hosp., Rochester, N.Y., 1950-51; 3d asst. resident surgery Mass. Gen. Hosp., Boston, 1951-52, 2d asst. resident, 1952-53, asst. resident orthopedic surgery, 1954-55, chief resident, 1956; asst. resident orthopedic surgery Children's Med. Center, Boston, 1953-54, jr. resident, 1955-56; mem. faculty Harvard Med. Sch., 1956—, Edith M. Ashley prof. orphopedic surgery, 1965-71, Harriet M. Peabody prof., 1971—, also chmn. dept.; chief orthopedic service Mass. Gen. Hosp., 1965-71, chmn. dept. orthopedic surgery, 1968-71. orthopedic surgeon-in-chief Children's Hosp. Med. Center, Boston, 1971—. Trustee Torsyth Dental Infirmary. Served with USMCR, World War II. Recipient Soma Weiss award Harvard Med. Sch., 1950, Borden Research award, 1950; Kappa Delta award, 1959; Internat. Assn. Dental Research award 1964. Fellow Am. Acad. Arts and Scis., Am. Acad. Orthopaedic Surgeons, Am. Orthopedic Assn. Home: 14 Channing Rd Brookline MA 02146 Office: Mass Gen Hosp Boston MA 02114

GLIMP, FRED LEE, coll. dean; b. Boise, Ida., Feb. 15, 1926; s. Fred Lee and Emily Massie (Turner) G.; student George Washington U., 1943-44; A.B., Harvard, 1950, postgrad., 1950-54, Ph.D., 1964; postgrad. Queens Coll., Cambridge, 1952- 53; m. Eleanor Croxon Foley, Dec. 22, 1951; children—Emily Ellen, Frederick Lee, Sarah Susan, Rebecca Jane. Asst. to the dean admission and financial aids Harvard, 1954-58, dir. freshman scholarships, 1958- 60, teaching fellow econs., 1956-59, dean admissions and financial aids, 1960-67, dean Harvard Coll., 1967-69; exec. dir. Com. Permanent Charity Fund, Boston, 1969—. Mem. Belmont Sch. Com., 1968- -. Trustee of Coll. Entrance Examination Bd., 1965—; chmn. Coll. Scholarship Service, 1965-66. Served to s/sgt. Army Air Corps, 1944-46. Member Assn. Coll. Admissions Counselors (exec. bd. 1963-65), Phi Beta Kappa. Home: 613 Pleasant St Belmont MA 02178

GLINSKY, VINCENT, sculptor; b. Russia, Dec. 18, 1895; s. Wolf and Sonia (Sherfman) G.; ed. pub. high schs., Syracuse, N.Y., Columbia U., Coll City N.Y., Beaux Arts Inst. Design; m. Cleo Hartwig, 1951; 1 son, Albert Vincent. Naturalized citizen of U.S. One-man show, Paris, 1929-30, N.Y.C., 1931, 56, 57; exhibited group shows including Expn. Artists Americans de Paris, 1932, Internat. Water Color Exhbn., Art Inst. Chgo., Contemporary Art, Golden Gate Expn., San Francisco, 1939, N.Y. World's Fair, 1939-40, Sculpture Internat., Phila. Museum Art, 1940, 1949, Am. Sculpture, Carnegie Inst., 1941, Contemporary Am. Art, London, 1941, First Annual Exhbn. Contemporary Am. Drawings; Nat. Acad., 1945, Met. Mus. Art, Bklyn. Mus., Whitney Mus. Am. Art, Mus. Modern Art, 150 Years of Am. Sculpture, Westbury Gardens, N.Y., 1960, World's Fair, 1964, Pa. Acad. Fine Arts, 1964, So. Vt. Art Center, 1964-70, also traveling shows; represented in collection Brookgreen Gardens Outdoor Mus., Norfolk (Va.) Mus., Wiltwyck Sch. for Boys, N.Y.C., Dept. Labor, Washington, Am. Cancer Found., N.Y.C., All Faiths Meml. Tower, Paramus, N.J., Bethesda, (Md.) Health Center, St. Paul's Coll., Washington, Nat. Commemorative Soc., N.Y. U. Hall Fame, USAF Acad.; Lenox Hill Hosp., N.Y.C.; represented in many pvt. collections; commd. execute sculptures for govt., pub., other bldgs., portrait Wilbur Wright N.Y. U. Hall Fame Great Ams., Theodore Roosevelt coin-medal Nat. Commemorative Soc. Recipient awards Arts and Letters Grant from Am. Acad. Arts and Letters and Nat. Inst. Arts and Letters, 1945; George D. Widener gold medal Pa. Acad. Fine Arts, 1935, Dr. Herbert M. Howe Meml. prize Pa. Acad. Fine Arts, 1948; First prize Adelphi Coll. Trophy Competition, 1956, Avery award Archtl. League N.Y., 1956, medal of hon. Nat. Arts Club, 1958; Silver Anniversary medal for sculpture Audubon Artists Ann., 1967; Gold Medal Nat. Sculpture Soc., 1967, C. Percival Dietsch prize Seventy-Fifth Annual Exhbn., 1968; P. Speyer prize N.A.D., 1970. Guggenheim fellow, 1930-31 . Engaged in war work with Diesel design sect. U.S.N., 1943-46. N.A. Fellow Nat. Sculpture Soc.; mem. Sculptors Guild (exec. sec. 1955-60), Audubon Artists, Archtl. League N.Y.C. (v.p. 1956-58). Instr. Beaux Arts Inst. Design, 1938-40, Bklyn. Coll., 1949-55, Columbia, 1957-61; adj. asst. prof. N.Y.U. Sch. Continuing Edn., 1950—. Home: 9 Patchin Pl New York City NY 10011 Studio: 5 W 16th St New York City NY 10011 ☆

GLITSCH, HANS CARL, petroleum mfr.; b. Commanche County, Tex., Nov. 5, 1905; s. Fritz W. and Frances M. (Haggard) G.; B.S. in Mech. Engring., Tex. A. and M. Coll., 1927, M.E., 1954; m. Dorothy L. Chamness, June 21, 1928; children—Michael C., Carol F. (Mrs. Carol G. Burnett). Engr., Gen. Electric Co., 1927-30; partner Glitsch Engring. Co., Dallas, 1936—; pres., mgr., engr., dir. Fritz W. Glitsch & Sons, Inc., Dallas, 1946—; pres., dir. Fritz W. Glitsch & Sons (Can.), Ltd., 1950—, Glitsch-Monterrey, S.A., Mexico, Glitsch Italiana, SPA, Aprilia, Italy. Mem. Dallas Citizens Council. Mem. Am. Petroleum Inst., Am. Soc. Tool Engrs., Tau Beta Pi. Mason. Clubs: Dallas Athletic, Engineers, City (Dallas). Patentee in field. Home: 3525 Turtle Creek Blvd Dallas TX 75219 Office: 4900 Singleton Blvd PO Box 6227 Dallas TX 75222

GLOCK, CHARLES YOUNG, sociologist, educator; b. N.Y.C., Oct. 17, 1919; s. Charles and Philippine (Young) G.; B.S., N.Y.U., 1940; M.B.A., Boston U., 1941; Ph.D., Columbia, 1952; m. Margaret Schleef, Sept. 12, 1950; children—Susan Young, James William. Research asst. Bur. Applied Social Research, Columbia, 1946-51, dir., 1951-58, lectr., then prof. sociology, 1954-58; prof. sociology U. Cal. at Berkeley, 1958—, chmn., 1967-68, 69-71, dir. Survey Research Center, 1958-67. Luther Weigle vis. prof. Yale U., 1968. Mem. bd. parish edn. Luth. Ch. Am., 1970—. Bd. dirs. Berkeley Found., Wright Inst., Cornerhouse Fund, Pacific Luth. Theol. Sem., Grad. Theol. Union, Fund Advancement Continuing Edn. Served from pvt. to capt., USAAF, 1942-46. Decorated Bronze Star medal, Legion Merit. Rockefeller fellow, 1941-42; fellow Center Advanced Study Behavioral Scis., 1957-58, Soc. for Religion in Higher Edn., 1968-69. Mem. Am. Assn. Pub. Opinion Research (v.p., pres.-elect 1962-64, pres. Pacific chpt. 1959-60), Soc. Sci. Study Religion (Western rep., pres. 1968-69), Am. Sociol. Assn., Religious Research Assn. Author: American Piety: Wayward Shepherds. Sr. author: Religion and Society in Tension: Christian Beliefs and Anti-Semitism: The Apathetic Majority; To Comfort and to Challenge: also numerous articles on social scis. Bd. editors Jour. Sci. Study of Religion; asso. editor Review Religious Research. Editor: Survey Research in the Social Sciences: Prejudice, U.S.A. Home: 40 Del Mar Av Berkeley CA 94708

GLOCK, JOHN WILLIAM, educator; b. Malmo, Neb., Dec. 27, 1915; s. William David and Sarah Mildred (Cook) G.; A.B., Neb. State Tchrs. Coll., 1940; M.A., U. Neb., 1948, Ed.D., 1955; m. Rhoda Rae Helvey, Oct. 10, 1942; children—JoAnn, John, Janice, James. Tchr. pub. sch., Staplehurst, Neb., 1940; tchr. Clay Center, Neb., 1946, supt., 1946-48; supt. Newman Grove, Neb., 1948-54; asst. prof. edn. Tex. Coll. Arts and Industries, 1955-58, chmn. dept. edn., 1958-59, dir. div. tchr. edn., 1959-66, dean of Sch. of Tchr. Edn., 1966—. Served with USNR, 1941-46. Mem. Nat. Sojourners, N.E.A., Tex. Tchrs. Assn., Phi Delta Kappa. Mason. Home: 804 W Lee St Kingsville TX 78363

GLOCK, MARVIN DAVID, educator; b. San Jose, Ill., Nov. 19, 1912; s. David William and Lydia (Gruensfelder) G.; student Blackburn Coll., 1930-32; A.B., U. Neb., 1934; M.S., U. Ill., 1935-38; Ph.D., State U. Ia., 1947; m. Elva Ruth Snell, Apr. 13, 1941; children—Carol Sue, Sandra Kay. Tchr., Edison (Neb.) High Sch., 1934-36; prin. Mason City (Ill.) Community High Sch., 1936-41; asst. prof. edn. Mich. State U., 1947-49; prof. ednl. psychology Cornell U., Ithaca, N.Y., 1949—. Served to lt. USNR, 1942-45. Fulbright fellow Ceylon, 1962-63. Fellow Am. Psychol. Assn.; mem. Am. Ednl. Research Assn., Internat. Reading Assn., Nat. Council Measurement in Edn., Nat. Soc. Study Edn., Sigma Xi, Phi Kappa Phi. Presbyn. Author: (with J.S. Ahmann and Helen Wardeberg) Evaluating Elementary School Pupils, 1960; (with J.S. Ahmann) Evaluating Pupil Growth: Principles of Tests and Measurements, 4th edit., 1971: The Improvement of College Reading, 2d edit., 1967; Readings in Educational Psychology, 1971. Home: 101 Homestead Terrace Ithaca NY 14850

GLOCK, WILLIAM, pianist, critic, radio dir.; b. London, Eng., 1908; student Christ's Hosp., Eng., 1919-26; B.A. in History, Caius Coll., Cambridge (Eng.) U., 1930; piano student with Artur Schnabel, Berlin, Germany, 1930-33; D.Music, Nottingham U., 1968. Asst. music critic London Daily Telegraph, 1934; asst. music critic The Observer, London, 1934-39, chief critic, 1939-45; writer Time and Tide, London critic The Scotsman, 1946-48; dir. Summer Sch. Music, Bryanston, Dorset, Eng., 1948-52, editor The Score mag., 1949-61; dir. Dartington (Eng.) Summer Sch., 1953—; critic New Statesman, 1958-59; controller of music BBC, 1959—. Examiner in music Bristol (Eng.) U., 1949; judge Canadian festivals, 1951. Bd. dirs. Royal Opera House, Covent Garden. Decorated Comdr. Brit. Empire. Author a life of Schubert, 1935. Address: 9 Clive House Connaught Pl London W 2 England

GLOCKNER, MAURICE, food service co. exec.; b. N.Y.C., July 20, 1906; s. Meyer and Anna (Wohl) G.; B.A., N.Y.U., 1929; postgrad. Columbia Tchrs. Coll., 1932- 33; m. Valentine Righthand, Feb. 10, 1928; children—Yolanda (Mrs. Harvey T. Lyon), Darrow M. With Automatic Canteen Co. Am. (name changed to Canteen Corp.) subsidiary I.T.T. Corp., Chgo., 1954—, v.p., 1955-67, group v.p., 1967, now sr. v.p. corporate devel. Mem. Phi Beta Kappa, Alpha Pi. Home: 1205 Crain St Evanston IL 60202 Office: Canteen Corp Merchandise Mart Chicago IL 60654

GLOGAU, RICHARD CLYDE, chem. corp. exec.; b. Denver, Nov. 20, 1916; s. Richard and Margaret L. (Sealbach) G.; B.S., Denver U., 1939; m. Charlotte McLagan, May 29, 1940; children—Richard Gordon, Charlotte Louise, Judith Ann. Tech. adminstr. DuPont Corp., Wilmington, Del., 1948-52, asst. plant mgr., Washington, 1952-53, lab. dir. Gibbstown, N.J., 1953-60, prodn. mgr. Wilmington, 1960-67; v.p. Engelhard Minerals & Chems. Corp., Newark, 1967-69, sr. v.p., dir., 1969—; v.p. Engelhard Industries, Newark, 1967-69, exec. v.p., 1969-70, pres., 1970—, dir. affiliated companies in Rome, Italy, London, Eng., Toronto, Can. and Tokyo, Japan; dir. Amerisil Inc., Hillside, N.J. Mem. Am. Chem. Soc., Sigma Phi Epsilon. Presbyn. (chmn. bd. trustees). Clubs: West Chester Golf and Country; Wilmington Country; Lake Placid, Bedens Brook (Princeton); Columbia (N.Y.C.). Home: 18 Woods Way Princeton NJ 08540 Office: 113 Astor St Newark NJ 07114

GLOMSET, DANIEL ANDERS, physician; b. Des Moines, Aug. 28, 1913; s. Daniel Johnson and Anna (Glerum) G.; B.S., U. Chgo., 1935, M.D., 1938; M.S., Mayo Clinic, U. Minn., 1943; m. Frances R. Morehouse, June 14, 1937; children—Martha Ann, Carol Anitra, Leif Morehouse. Intern Barnes Hosp., St. Louis, 1938- 40; fellow, 1st asst. Mayo Found., 1940-43; practice internal medicine, Des Moines, 1946—; treas. Internal Med. Clinic, 1947—; mem. staff Broadlawns Gen. Hosp., 1946-67. Served to capt., M.C., AUS, 1943-46. Mem. A.M.A., A.C.P., Am., Ia. (past pres.) socs. internal medicine, Des Moines Med. Library Club (past pres.), Ia. Clin. Med. Soc. (past pres.), Ia. Med. Soc.; asso. mem. Am. Gastro Enterol. Soc. Address: 2932 Ingersoll Av Des Moines IA 50312

GLOS, RAYMOND EUGENE, educator; b. Wayne, Ill., Feb. 5, 1903; s. Frederick A. and Flora (Mapes) G.; B.S., U. Ill., 1925, M.S., 1926; postgrad. Harvard, summer, 1931; Ph.D., Ohio State U., 1939; m. Dorothy Styan, July 9, 1927; children—Carol, Alan Styan. Asst. instr. dept. bus. orgn. U. Ill., 1925-26, asst. to dean of men, 1926-27; with Miami U., Oxford, O., 1927—, asst. prof. bus., 1927-30, asso. prof., 1930-37, asst. dean, School Bus. Adminstrn., 1931-37, acting dean, prof. business, 1937-39, dean, prof. accounting, 1939-47, dean, prof. bus., 1947-63, chmn. dept. bus., 1963-68, prof. business, 1963-69, dean, prof. bus. emeritus, 1969—. Dir. Citizens Bank, Hamilton, O. Trustee McCullough-Hyde Hosp., Blue Cross S.W. Ohio. C.P.A., Ill., Ohio. Mem. Am. Inst. C.P.A.'s, Am. Accounting Assn. (v.p. 1947), Am. Assn. Collegiate Schs. Bus. (pres. 1952), Ohio Soc. C.P.A., Alpha Sigma Phi (grand councilor 1956-58, nat. scholarship chmn. 1957-60, nat. pres. 1966-68), Beta Gamma Sigma (nat. v.p. 1954-57), Beta Alpha Psi, Phi Eta Sigma (nat. treas. 1937—), Delta Sigma Pi, Omicron Delta Kappa. Conglist. Kiwanian. Co-author: Introduction to Business, 7th edit., 1972. Home: 110 E Spring St Oxford OH 45056

GLOSSBRENNER, ALFRED STROUP, steel exec.; b. Indpls., June 6, 1901; s. Alfred M. and Minnie M. (Stroup) G.; student U. Wis., 1920-21, also several trade schs.; LL.D., Westminster (Pa.) Coll., 1959; m. Ramona Bertram, Sept. 19, 1923; children—Alfred Bertram, David Withers. Supt. father's printing plant, Indpls.; with Am. Sheet and Tin Plate Co., Gary, Ind., 1930-31; foreman South Chicago plant Ill. Steel, 1932- 35; asst. supt. Campbell hot strip mill Youngstown Sheet & Tube Co. (Ohio), 1935-36, supt., 1936-42, supt. Brier Hill works, 1942-43, gen. supt. Youngstown dist., 1943-47, asst. v.p., 1947-50, v.p. in charge operations, 1950-56, pres., 1956-65, chief exec. officer, 1960-66, chmn., 1965-67, mem. exec. com., 1960—, dir., 1953—; dir. Ohio Bell Tel. Co., Youngstown Steel Door Co. (Ohio), Dollar Savs. & Trust Co., Nat. City Bank Cleve. Bd. dirs. Mahoning chpt. A.R.C. Mem. Am. Iron and Steel Inst. (hon. v.p.), Newcomen Soc. N.Am., Assn. Iron and Steel Engrs. Clubs: Youngstown Country, Youngstown; Duquesne (Pitts.); Union (Cleve.); Laurel Valley Golf (Ligonier, Pa.); Hole-in-the-Wall Golf (Naples, Fla.). Home: 2782 Logan Rd Youngstown OH 44505 Office: Box 900 Youngstown OH 44501

GLOSSOP, PETER, baritone; b. July 6, 1928; ed. Sheffield, Eng.; m. Joyce Elizabeth Blackham, 1955. Joined Sadler's Wells Opera, 1952; with Covent Garden Opera Co., 1962-66; debut at La Scala, Milan, as Rigoletto, 1965. Recipient 1st prize, Gold medal First Internat. Competition for Young Opera Singers, Sofia, Bulgaria, 1961. Address: 11 The Bishop's Av London N 2 England

GLOSTER, HUGH MORRIS, coll. pres.; b. Brownsville, Tenn., May 11, 1911; s. John and Dora (Morris) G.; student LeMoyne Coll., 1927-29; B.A., Morehouse Coll., 1931; M.A. (Univ. fellow), Atlanta U., 1933; Ph.D. (Gen. Edn. Bd. fellow), N.Y. U., 1943; hon. doctorate U. Haiti, 1968; m. Louise Elizabeth Torrence, June 1, 1935 (div.); children—Alice Louise, Evelyn Elaine; m. 2d, Beulah Victoria Harold, Sept. 9, 1957; 1 son, Hugh Morris. Instr., asso. prof. English, LeMoyne Coll., 1933-41; prof. English, Morehouse Coll., 1941- 43; program dir. USO, Ft. Huachuca, Ariz., 1943-44, asso. regional exec., Atlanta, 1944-46; prof. English, chmn. dept. lang. and lit. Hampton Inst., 1946-67, dir. summer session, 1952-62, dean faculty, 1963-67; pres. Morehouse Coll., Atlanta, 1967—; prof. English, Atlanta U., summers 1942, 43; guest prof. English, N.Y. U., summers 1949, 62; Fulbright prof. English, Hiroshima U., Japan, 1953-55; lectr. Orientation Center Fgn. Grad. Students, Coll. William and Mary, summer 1955; vis. prof. Am. lit. U. Warsaw, Poland, 1961-62; lectr. tours, 1933-55, 56, 59; mem. summer faculty various univs. and colls. Mem. commn. on coll. adminstrn. Assn. Am. Colls.; mem. long range planning com. Nat. Collegiate Athletic Assn.; mem. pres.'s council Inst. European Studies; v.p. Assn. Pvt. Colls. and Univs. in Ga. Bd. dirs. Nat. Assn. for Equal Opportunity in Higher Edn., United Bd. for Coll. Devel., So. Fellowships Fund, Council Protestant Colls. and Univs.; bd. dirs., trustee United Negro Coll. Fund; trustee Atlanta U., Morehouse Coll., Interdenominational Theol. Center, Coll. Entrance Exam. Bd., Ednl. Testing Service. Recipient research grant Alpha Phi Alpha, summer 1940; research grant Carnegie Found., 1950-51; distinguished contbns. award Coll. Lang. Assn., 1958; Centennial medallion Hampton Inst., 1968; Alumnus of Year award LeMoyne Coll., 1967. Mem. Coll. Lang. Assn. (founder, pres. 1937-38, 48-50), Am. Assn. Higher Edn. (exec. com. 1967-69), Am. Assn. U. Adminstrs. (trustee), Phi Beta Kappa, Sigma Pi Phi Boule, Alpha Phi Alpha. Author: Negro Voices in American Fiction, 1948. Co-editor: The Brown Thrush: An Anthology of Verse by Negro College Students, 1935; My Life-My Country-My World: College Readings for Modern Living, 1952. Contbg. editor Phylon: The Atlanta U. Review of Race and Culture, 1948-53; adv. editor Coll. Lang. Assn. Jour., 1957—. Home: 900 Flamingo Dr SW Atlanta GA 30311

GLOTFELTY, JAMES SAMUEL, hosp. adminstr.; b. Batavia, Ia., June 15, 1905; s. Willis S. and Katherine (Hayden) G.; M.D., State U. Ia., 1934; m. Gertrude Alverson, May 19, 1923; 1 dau., Jean (Mrs. Victor Wacha). Intern, San Diego County Gen. Hosp., 1934-35; resident USPHS Narcotic Hosp., 1935-36; practice medicine, specializing in psychiatry, 1936-37; with VA, 1937—; med. dir. VA Center, Los Angeles, 1959-61; med. dir. Western Nine State Area, 1964-66; dir. VA Hosp., Long Beach, Cal., 1966—; instr. clin. psychiatry Washington U. Sch. Medicine, 1948-50; asst. prof. hosp. adminstrn. Duke Sch. Medicine, 1955-59, asso. prof. psychiatry, 1957-59; clin. prof. psychiatry and human behavior U. Cal. Coll. Medicine, Irvine, 1966; mem. Regional Med. Program Adv. Com. Cal. Area VIII, 1967—. Mem. Fed. Exec. Bd., San Francisco, 1961-66, Los Angeles, 1966—. Served from 1st lt. to maj., M.C., AUS, 1942-46. Fellow Am. Psychiat. Assn., A.C.P.; mem. A.M.A., Am. Hosp. Assn. Address: 5901 E 7th St Long Beach CA 90801

GLOTFELTY, PHILLIP RUTHERFORD, Jr., clergyman; b. Lebanon, Ill., May 14, 1906; s. Philip Rutherford and Annie Laurie (Burbank) G.; A.B., McKendree Coll., 1928; B.D., Garrett Bibl. Inst., 1932; m. Alma Henrietta Buess, June 13, 1928; children—Phyllis Ruth (Mrs. Richard Leroy Maxwell), Philip Rutherford III. Ordained to ministry, Meth. Ch., 1932; pastorates So. Ill. Conf., 1932-37; pastor, Battle Creek, Mich., 1940-44, Muskegon, 1944-48, Lakeside Ch., Lowell, Mich., 1948-55, Lawrence Av. Ch., Charlotte, Mich., 1955, Plainwell, Mich., 1961-64, Holt, Mich., 1964—. Trustee Northwestern U. 1956-60; dir. Mich. Temperance Found.; travel Europe, Middle East, Palestine, 1954, illus. lectr. Pilgrims in Bible Lands. Sec. minimum salary com., member conf. on youth publs., conf. bd. edn., treas. town and country commn., pres. rural fellowship Mich. Meth. Conf.; del. World Meth. Conf., London, Eng., 1966; dir. Mich. Council Chs.; bd. missions West Mich. Conf. United Meth. Chs. Bd. dirs. Mich. Council Alcohol Problems. Republican. Mason (Shriner, 32). Rotarian. Contbr. ch. periodicals. Home: 2205 Aurelius Rd Holt MI 48842 Office: Cedar St and Aurelius Rd Holt MI 48842

GLOVER, ALAN MARSH, electronics exec.; b. Rochester, N.Y., Sept. 26, 1909; s. Harry Mark Robinson and Elizabeth (Marsh) G.; B.A., U. Rochester, 1930, M.A., 1932, Ph.D., 1935; m. Janet M. Briggs, Feb. 5, 1949; children—Keith Terrott, John Carroll, Beth Marsh. Fellow physics U. Rochester, 1935; instr. physics Inst. Paper Chemistry, Lawrence Coll., 1935-36; devel. engr. phototubes, tube div. RCA, Harrison, N.J., 1936, mgr. gas tube and phototube engring., Harrison, 1941-43, Lancaster, 1943-50, gen. mgr. semiconductor div., Somerville, N.J., 1955-58, v.p., gen. mgr. semiconductor and materials div., 1958-63, div. v.p. tech. programs, electronic components and devices, Harrison, 1963—; adj. prof. physics Franklin and Marshall Coll., 1950. Mem. trustees council U. Rochester, 1966—, Univ. Alumni Council, 1968—. Fellow I.E.E.E.; mem. Am. Soc. Naval Engrs., Am. Phys. Soc., A.A.A.S. (chmn. Lancaster sect. 1953-54), Phi Beta Kappa, Sigma Xi, Theta Delta Chi. Unitarian. Home: 30 Oak Hill Rd Chatham NJ 07928 Office: Harrison NJ 07029

GLOVER, CHARLES CARROLL, III, lawyer; b. Washington, Apr. 9, 1918; s. Charles Carroll Jr. and Marion Everett (Wise) G.; A.B., Yale, 1940; LL.B., Harvard, 1943; m. Virginia Dougherty, July 29, 1944; children—Charles Carroll, Everett, Judith. Admitted to Mass. bar, 1944, D.C. bar, 1946; now partner Wilmer Cutler & Pickering. Dir. Riggs Nat. Bank of Washington. Sec. United Community Service of Washington, 1948-49, 1st v.p., 1949-52, pres., 1952-54; trustee Am. U.; bd. dirs. Eugene and Agnes E. Meyer Found.; bd. govs. Beauvoir Sch., Washington; mem. of chpt. Wash. Cathedral. Mil. intelligence service Office Chief of Staff, War Dept., 1943-46; staff Office Asst. Sec. Am. Rep. Affairs, Dept. State, 1945-46. Decorated Croix de Chevalier de L'ordre de la Couronne (Belgium). Mem. Phi Beta Kappa, Delta Kappa Epsilon. Clubs: Chevy Chase (Md.); Metropolitan (Washington). Home: 5235 Duvall Dr Westmoreland Hills MD 20016 Office: 900 17th St NW Washington DC 20006

GLOVER, CHARLES CARROLL, Jr., ret. banker; b. Washington, Jan. 1, 1888; s. Charles Carroll and Annie C. (Poor) G.; B.A., Yale, 1910. M.A., 1915; LL.B., George Washington U., 1912, LL.D., 1952; m. Marion Everett Wise, May 10, 1913; children—Marion Everett (dec.), Charles Carroll, Nancy Everett (Mrs. A. Lloyd Symington). Former partner Glover & Flather; pres. Washington Stock Exchange, 1927-28; hon. chmn. bd. Riggs Nat. Bank. Enlisted in navy, res. officers' course, Annapolis, 1918; asst. supply officer on U.S. transport Antigone; lt. comdr. USNRF, ret. Hon. trustee George Washington U., Corcoran Gallery Art (past pres.); counsellor Home for Incurables. D.C. rep. on Unemployment Relief Commn., 1931-32; mem. Bd. Pub. Welfare, D.C., 1929-32; past chmn. Asso. Charities; past vice chmn. Yale Alumni Adv. Bd.; mem. Washington Nat. Monument Soc.; past vice chmn., trustee D.C. Community Chest; mem. Com. of 100 on Fed. City; hon. trustee Washington Cathedral, Netherlands-Am. Found. (Washington chpt.). Decorated Order Orange-Nassau by Netherlands govt. State del. to Rep. Conv., 1940; recipient 1968 bowl Washington Yale Club. Mem. Soc. Colonial Wars, S.A.R., Columbia Hist. Soc., Alpha Delta Phi, Phi Delta Phi, Omicron Delta Kappa, Elihu. Clubs: Metropolitan (pres. 1939); Yale (pres. 1921); Chevy Chase, Alibi, Cosmos, Alfalfa, Nat. Press (Washington); Brook (N.Y.C.). Home: 3201 New Mexico Av NW Washington DC 20016 Office: 1503 Pennsylvania Av Washington DC 20013

GLOVER, CLIFFORD CLARKE, constrn. co. exec.; b. Newnan, Ga., May 15, 1913; s. Howard Clarke and Fannie Virginia (Jones) G.; B.S. in Civil Engring., U. N.C., 1934; m. Louis Liles, Jan. 16, 1937; children—Edmund Cook, Nancy Liles (Mrs. William T. Kennedy), Virginia Johnston (Mrs. R.H. Lee), Laura Clarke. With Batson-Cook Co., West Point, Ga., 1934—, now pres., chmn.; chief engrs. Contractors, Jacksonville, Fla., 1940-43; dir. First Nat. Bank West Point, Ga.-Ala. Supply Co. Mem. West Point Sch. Bd., 1951-69, chmn., 1964-68; chmn. West Point Planning Bd., 1964—. Trustee LaGrange Coll. Served with USNR, 1945-46. Methodist (ofcl. bd.). Rotarian. Clubs: Capital City (Atlanta); Riverside (West Point). Home: 103 Hillcrest St West Point GA 31833 Office: Box 151 West Point GA 31833

GLOVER, GLEASON, social worker; b. Newport News, Va., June 14, 1934; s. Joseph and Rachel (Robinson) G.; A.B., Norfolk div. State Coll. Va., 1961; M.A., Western Res. U., Cleve., 1963; m. Josephine Gladys Frazier, Apr. 11, 1964; children—Gleason Edward, Maury Todd. Spl. project dir. Urban League Cleve., 1965-66; dir. Cleve. Neighborhood Youth Corps, 1966-67; exec. dir. Mpls. Urban League, 1967—; sec. Nat. Urban League Exec. Council. Dir. First Plymouth Bank; instr. U. Minn. Sch. Sci. Commr. Civil Service Commn., 1968—; mem. admissions com. Sch. Social Work, U. Minn., 1969—; mem. Citizens Com. on Vocational Edn., Bd. Edn., Mpls., 1968-69; mem. Adv. Com. on Vocational Rehab. State of Minn. Bd. dirs. Outward Bound Program, Camp Fire Girls, Nat. Urban League Health Com., Group Health, Inc.; Served with USAF, 1955-59. Mem. Nat. Assn. Social Workers, Adminstrv. Mgmt. Soc., Mblzn. Econ. Resources (dir.). Kiwanian. Home: 2101 Washburn St N Minneapolis MN 55411 Office: 1016 Plymouth St N Minneapolis MN 55411

GLOVER, JOHN DESMOND, educator; b. Australia, Feb. 15, 1915; Ph.B., Brown U., 1936; M.B.A., Harvard, 1939, A.M., 1942, Ph.D., 1947; m. Ruth Eleanor Adams, Sept. 12, 1938; children—Elizabeth, Katherine, Margaret. Staff U.S. C. of C., 1936-37; instr. and tutor econs. dept. Harvard, 1939-42, faculty Grad. Sch. Bus. Adminstrn., 1942—, successively instr., asst. prof., asso. prof., 1949-54, prof. bus. adminstrn., 1954—; chmn. exec. com., dir. Cambridge Research Inst.; spl. cons. USAF, 1943-52; secretariat U.S. Strategic Bombing Survey, 1945, civilian rank of col.; bd. dirs. Alcon Labs., Inc., cons. Author: The Attack on Big Business, 1954; (with R.M. Hower) The Administrator, Cases on Human Relations in Business, 4th edit., 1963. Home: 400 Concord Rd Weston MA 02193 Office: Soldiers Field Boston MA 02163

GLOVER, ROBERT OGDEN, ret. naval officer; b. Norfolk, July 3, 1894; s. Henry Warburton Bibby and Edith Havre (Cleborne) G.; B.S., U.S. Naval Acad., 1915; M.S., Columbia, 1923; student Post Grad. Sch., U.S. Naval Acad., 1921-22, U.S. Naval War Coll., Newport, R.I., 1937-38; m. Rosalie Harwood, Apr. 18, 1938. Commd. ensign U.S.N., 1915, advanced through grades to rear adm., 1942; served in destroyer forces, Queenstown, Ireland, World War I; comdr. U.S.S. Massachusetts, South Pacific in support of Guadalcanal and New Georgia campaigns; comdr. Service Force 7th Fleet, 1944; served as hydrographer of Navy, 1946; ret. 1948; sr. v.p. Atlantic Rural Expn., Inc., Richmond. Bd. dirs. Community Chest, Richmond; dir., exec. com. A.R.C. Decorated D.S.M. Mem. Va. Hist. Soc., Am. Legion, Kappa Alpha So. Clubs: Army-Navy (Washington); Chevy Chase (Md.); Country of Va., Commonwealth (Richmond). Home: 4308 Cambridge Rd Richmond VA 23221

GLOVER, W. J., utility exec.; b. 1909; B.S.C., U. Louisville, 1967; married. With Louisville Gas & Electric Co., 1939—, v.p., sec., 1963—; C.P.A., Ky. Address: 311 W Chestnut St Louisville KY 40201*

GLOVER, WILLIAM, theatre critic; b. N.Y.C., May 6, 1911; s. William Harper and Lily P. (Freir) G.; Litt.B., Rutgers U., 1932; m. Isobel M. Cole, Oct. 26, 1936. City editor Asbury Park (N.J.) Press, 1935-39; news editor A.P. newsfeatures, 1941-53, theatre writer, 1953—, drama critic, 1960- -. Served to lt. (j.g.) U.S. Maritime Service, 1943-45. Mem. N.Y. Drama Critics Circle (pres.), N.Y. Drama Desk (v.p.), N.Y. Newspaper Reporters Assn., Phi Beta Kappa, Sigma Delta Chi. Clubs: The Players, Overseas Press (N.Y.C.). Contbr. periodicals. Home: 531 E 20th St New York City NY 10010 Office: Associated Press 50 Rockefeller Plaza New York City NY 10020

GLOVER, WILLIAM WAYNE, banker; b. Bedford, Ind., Dec. 31, 1901; s. Isaac Newton and Cornelia Jane (Ikerd) G.; student U. So. Cal., 1918-21; m. Gladys Gardner, Aug. 11, 1921; children—Jeanne Clair (Mrs. Joseph Othman Kilian, Jr.), Gladys Elaine (Mrs. Charles E. Kelly). With Citizens Nat. Trust & Savs. Bank, Los Angeles, 1921-23; asst. cashier Euclid Savs. Bank, Ontario, Cal., 1923-23; regional dir. Pacific Coast offices C.F. Childs & Co., 1924-30; municipal bond buyer Nat. City Co. of N.Y., San Francisco, 1930-34; v.p., dir. Shaw, Glover & Co., Los Angeles and San Francisco, 1935-37; Pacific Coast rep. N.Y. Stock Exchange firm Salomon Bros. & Hutzler, 1937-38; with Cal. Bank, Los Angeles, 1938—, v.p. charge investments, 1938-59, sr. v.p. 1959—; v.p. Western Bancorp., 1959-64, exec. v.p., 1965—, investment adviser, 1967—; exec. v.p. United Cal. Bank, 1964—. Mem. USCG Aux. Mem. U.S. Power Squadron, State Assn. County Treas., Cal., Los Angeles chambers commerce, Clubs: Stock Exchange, Bond (Los Angeles); Shark Island Yacht. Home: 1618 Ben Lomond Dr Glendale CA 91202 Office: 600 S Spring St Los Angeles CA 90054

GLOWER, DONALD DUANE, nuclear engr., educator; b. Shelby, O., July 29, 1926; s. Raymond W.W. and Irva (Scheerer) G.; B.S., U.S. Mcht. Marine Acad., 1946; B.S., Antioch Coll., 1953; M.S., Ia. State U., 1958, Ph.D. (NSF fellow), 1960; m. Betty Louise Stahl, June 18, 1953; children-Donald, Michel, Leilani, Jacob. Asst. engring. officer Grace Lines, Inc., San Francisco, 1947-49; research engr. Battelle Meml. Inst., Columbus, O., 1953-54; asst. prof. Coll. Engring., Ia. State U., 1954-58, 60-61; mem. research staff Sandia Corp., Albuquerque, 1961-63; head radiation effects dept. Gen. Motors Corp., Milw., 1963-64; prof., chmn. dept. mech. and nuclear engring. Ohio State U., 1964—. Cons. Mass. Inst. Tech., Battelle Meml., Martin Co., Gen. Motors Corp. Mem. I.E.E.E., Am. Nuclear Soc., Am. Phys. Soc., Am. Soc. Engring. Edn., A.A.A.S., Am. Assn. U. Profs., Ohio Acad. Sci., Argonne Univs. Assn., Ohio Atomic Energy Bd., Sigma Xi. Clubs: Faculty; Scioto Country. Author: Graphical Theory and Application, 1957; Basic Drawing and Projection, 1957, Working Drawings and Applied Graphics, 1957; Experimental Reactor Analysis and Radiation Measurements, 1965. Home: 2338 Kensington Dr Columbus OH 43221 Office: Robinson Lab 18th St Columbus OH 43210

GLOYN, CYRIL KENNARD, educator; b. Portland, Ore., June 6, 1906; s. John and Mary (Kennard) G.; B.A., Occidental Coll., 1927; B.D., Union Theol. Sem., 1930; postgrad. London Sch. Econs., 1930-31; M.A., Columbia, 1942, Ph.D., 1942; m. Frances Ryan, Aug. 14, 1930; children—Eleanor Anne (Mrs. Bernard Siegel), Robert Ward. Ordained to ministry United Ch. of Christ, 1939; prof. Pacific U., Ore., 1935-46, v.p., 1944-46; prof., chmn. dept. philosophy and religion Occidental Coll., Los Angeles, 1946-69, prof., chmn. dept. philosophy, 1969—; part-time teaching extension divs. U. Ore., 1938-46, U. Cal. at Los Angeles, 1947-68, Cal. Inst. Tech., 1948-49, Columbia, 1965. Chmn. social action com. Ore. Congl. Conf. Fogg traveling fellow Union Theol. Sem., 1930-31, Kent fellow Nat. Council on Religion in Higher Edn., 1930. Mem. Am. Assn. U. Profs., Am. Philos. Assn., Pacific Coast Theol. Discussion Group, Phi Beta Kappa. Democrat. Author: The Church in the Social Order, 1942. Contbr. articles profl. jours. Home: 1118 Stratford Av South Pasadena CA 91030 Office: Occidental Coll Los Angeles CA 90041

GLUCK, MAXWELL HENRY, store exec.; b. Commerce, Tex., Nov. 4, 1899; s. Adolph Wolf Gluck; m. Muriel Schlesinger, Oct. 1948. Founder, Darling Stores Corp., N.Y.C., 1929, now chmn. bd., pres.; chmn. bd. A.S. Beck Shoe Corp., Grayson-Robinson Stores, Inc., Willoughby's, Peerless Camera Stores; owner Elmendorf Farm, breeder thorobred race horses, Lexington, Ky.; U.S. ambassador to Ceylon, 1957-58. Mem. Western Harness Racing Assn. (pres., chmn. bd.). Clubs: Colombo, Havelock Country, Racquet, Turf & Field. Home: 930 Fifth Av New York City NY 10021

GLUCKIN, EDWIN W., apparel mfg. co. exec.; b. N.Y.C., 1915; Vice pres., dir. William Gluckin Co., Ltd., Hamilton, Bermuda; pres., dir. Pittston Apparel Co., Stephanie Co., Stage Play Foundations, Inc., Republic Mills Corp.; pres. William Gluckin Internat. Corp. Home: 66 Salem Rd Rockville Centre NY 11570 Office: 358 Fifth Av New York City NY 10001*

GLUCKSBERG, SAM, educator; b. Montreal, Que., Can., Feb. 6, 1933; s. Murray and Sonia (Afrin) G.; came to U.S., 1946, naturalized, 1954; B.S., Coll. City N.Y., 1956; Ph.D., N.Y. U., 1960; m. Trudy Hoenigswald, June 5, 1955; children—Matthew, Kenneth, Nadia. Mem. faculty Princeton, 1963—, prof. psychology, 1970—. Served to capt. AUS, 1958-63. Cons. editor Basic Books, Inc., N.Y.C., 1968—; asso. editor Am. Scientist, 1965-70. Contbr. profl. jours. Home: 14 Aiken Av Princeton NJ 08540

GLUCKSTERN, ROBERT LEONARD, educator, physicist; b. Atlantic City, July 31, 1924; s. Louis and Frieda (Dworkin) G.; B.E.E., Coll. City N.Y., 1944; Ph.D., Mass. Inst. Tech., 1948; m. Norma Block, Jan. 24, 1948; children—Steven Mark, Barbara Joy, Amy Sue. From research asso. to asso. prof. Yale, 1950-64; faculty U. Mass., 1964—, head dept. physics and astronomy, 1964-69, asso. provost, 1969-71, vice chancellor for acad. affairs and provost, 1971—. Vis. prof. U. Tokyo, 1969; cons. in field. Served with USNR, 1944-46. AEC fellow U. Cal. at Berkeley, 1948-49, Cornell U., 1949-50; Yale Faculty fellow CERN, 1961-62. Home: 100 Dana St Amherst MA 01002

GLUECK, BERNARD CHARLES, psychiatrist; b. Balt., Aug. 26, 1914; s. Bernard D. and Josephine (Stransky) G.; A.B., Columbia, 1934, certificate psychoanalytic medicine, 1951; M.D., Harvard, 1938; m. Marie Louise Howard, Sept. 19, 1936; children—Susan Howard, Charles David. Practice medicine, specializing in psychiatry, Mpls., 1955-60, Hartford, Conn., 1960—; prof., dir. research Med. Sch. U. Minn., 1955-60; dir. research Inst. Living, 1960—; lectr. psychiatry Sch. Medicine, Yale, 1965—. Harry Armstrong lectr. Aerospace Med. Assn., 1967. Fellow Am. Psychiat. Assn. (chmn. research com.); mem. Am. Psychopath. Assn. (pres.), Assn. For Psychoanalytic Medicine, Am. Coll. Neuropsychopharmacology, Sigma Xi, Alpha Omega Alpha. Research, numerous publs. in psychodynamics of sexual delinquency, devel. of quantitative personality assessments, application of computer techniques to psychiat. hosps. and psychiat. practice. Address: 34 Long View Rd West Hartford CT 06107

GLUECK, ELEANOR TOUROFF, (Mrs. Sheldon Glueck), criminologist; b. N.Y.C., Apr. 12, 1898; d. Bernard Leo and Anna (Wodzislawski) Touroff; A.B., Barnard Coll., 1920; diploma N.Y. Sch. Social Work, 1921; Ed.M., Harvard, 1923, Ed.D., 1925, Sc.D., 1958; m. Sheldon Glueck, Apr. 16, 1922; 1 dau., Mrs. Joyce Glueck Rosberg (dec.). Engaged in criminology research dept. social ethics Harvard U., 1925-28, research asst. Law Sch. Crime Survey, 1928-30, research asst. criminology Law Sch., 1930-53, research asso. criminology, 1953—, spl. studies in delinquency, co-dir. program research into the causes, treatment and prevention of juvenile delinquency, 1925—. Trustee, exec. com. Judge Baker Guidance Center. Recipient (with husband) August Vollmer award Am. Soc. Criminology, 1961; Beccaria Gold medal German Criminological Soc., 1924; Gold medal Inst. of Criminal Anthropology, U. Rome (Italy), 1964. Fellow Am. Acad. Arts and Scis., A.A.A.S.; mem. Am. Soc. Criminology, Nat. Assn. Social Workers, Mass. Conf. Social Welfare, Am. Assn. U. Women, Asso. Alumnae Barnard Coll. (Distinguished Alumna award 1969), Internat. Soc. Criminology, League Women Voters (Cambridge), Assn. N.Y. Sch. Social Work. Author: Community Use of Schools, 1927; Adventure in Japan, 1962; (with Sheldon Glueck) books including: One Thousand Juvenile Delinquents, 1934, After-Conduct of Discharged Offenders, 1945; Unraveling Juvenile Delinquency, 1950; Delinquents in the Making, 1952; Physique and Delinquency, 1956; Delinquents and Nondelinquents in Perspective, 1968. Co-editor: Preventing Crime, 1936; Predicting Delinquency and Crime, 1959; Family Environment and Delinquency, 1962; Ventures in Criminology, 1964; Delinquents and Nondelinquents in Perspective, 1968; Toward a Typology of Juvenile Offenders, 1970. Mem. editorial board Internat. Jour. Social Psychiatry; editorial cons. bd. jours. Office: Harvard Law Sch Langdell Hall Cambridge MA 02138 ☆

GLUECK, HELEN IGLAUER, educator, physician; b. Cin.; d. Samuel and Helen (Raneohoff) Iglauer; B.A., U. Wis., 1929; M.D., U. Cin., 1934; m. Nelson Glueck, Mar. 26, 1931; 1 son, Charles J. Intern, Cin. Gen. Hosp., 1934-35; asst. resident, 1935-36; externe Hadassah Rothschild U. Hosp., Jerusalem, Israel, 1936-38; research asso. May Inst. for Med. Research, Jewish Hosp., 1939-46, 49-55; dir. Student Health Service U. Cin. Coll. Medicine, 1945-59, research asso.

Cardiac Lab., 1946-47, faculty medicine, 1959—, prof., 1966—, dir. coagulation lab., asst. chief clinician outpatient dept., 1956—; attending physician Cin. Gen., Cin. VA, Christian R. Holmes hosps. Diplomate Am. Bd. Internal Medicine. Fellow A.C.P.; mem. Central Soc. Clin. Research, Am., Internat. scos. hematology, Cin. Acad. Medicine, Alpha Omega Alpha. Home: 162 Glenmary Av Cincinnati OH 45220

GLUECK, SHELDON, criminologist; b. Warsaw, Poland, Aug. 15, 1896; s. Charles and Anna (Steinhardt) G.; brought to U.S., 1903, naturalized, 1920; student Georgetown U. Law Sch., 1914, 15; A.B., George Washington U., 1920, S.S.D., 1963; LL.B., LL.M., Nat. Univ. Law Sch., 1920; student Harvard Law School, 1926; A.M., Harvard, 1922, Ph.D., 1924, Sc.D., 1958; LL.D., U. Thessaloniki (Greece), 1948; m. Eleanor Touroff, Apr. 16, 1922; 1 dau., Anitra Joyce Rosberg (dec.). Instr. criminology and penology, dept. social ethics Harvard, 1925-29, asst. prof. criminology Law Sch., 1929-31, prof., 1931-50. Lowell lectr., 1935, Roscoe Pound prof. law, 1950-63, emeritus, 1963--, dir. basic researches into causes, mgmt. and prevention of juvenile delinquency, 1925—. Bd. advisers Psychiatry and the Law Found. Ofcl. del. U.S. govt. to Internat. Prison Congress, Prague, 1930, Paris, 1950; mem. Adv. Com. on Rules of Criminal Proc., U.S. Supreme Ct., Am. Law Inst. for Youth Correction Authority and the Model Penal Code; adviser to Justice Robert H. Jackson on law governing War Crime Criminals. Bd. overseers Brandeis U. Center Study Violence. Served with A.E.F., World War I. Recipient Isaac Ray award Am. Psychiat. Assn., 1961; (with wife) August Vollmer award Am. Soc. Criminology, 1961; Gold medal Inst. of Criminal Anthropology, U. Rome (Italy), 1964; Beccaria Gold medal German Soc. Criminology, 1964. Fellow Am. Acad. Arts and Sci., A.A.A.S., Am. Psychiat. Assn. (hon.), Internat. Acad. Law and Sci.; mem. Am. Soc. Criminology (past v.p.), Am. Bar Assn. (juvenile delinquency com.), N.Y. State Bar. Club: Harvard Faculty. Author numerous books, 1925—, including: Mental Disorder and the Criminal Law, 1925; Crime and Justice, 1945; The Nuremberg Trial and Aggressive War, 1946; Crime and Correction: Selected Papers, 1952; Law and Psychiatry: Cold War on Entente Cordiale?, 1962; Roscoe Pound and Criminal Justice, 1965, (with Eleanor T. Glueck) books including: One Thousand juvenile Delinquents, 1934, After-conduct of Discharged Offenders, 1944, Unraveling Juvenile Delinquency, 1950, Delinquents in the Making, 1952, Physique and Delinquency, 1956, Predicting Delinquency and Crime, 1959, Family Environment and Delinquency, 1962, Ventures in Criminology, 1964; Delinquents and Non-Delinquents in Perspective, 1968, Toward a Typology of Juvenile Offenders: Implications for Therapy and Prevention, 1970. Editor publs. including: The Welfare State and The National Welfare, 1952; The Problem of Delinquency, 1958. Mem. editorial bd. Fed. Probation, Internat. Jour. Social Psychiatry; cons. editor Community Mental Health Jour. Contbr. to profl. jours. Office: Langdell Hall Harvard Law Sch Cambridge MA 02138 ☆

GLUHAREFF, MICHAEL E., aero. engr., designer; b. St. Petersburg, Russia, Sept. 17, 1892; s. Eugene and Iraida (Borisoff) G.; grad. (gen. scis.) Imperial Coll. Commerce, 1910, (mech. engring.) Poly. Inst. Tech., 1914, (mil. engr.) Imperial Mil. Engring. Coll., 1916, (mil. pilot) Mil. Aviation Sch., 1917; m. Antonina Gretzkoff, Apr. 21, 1915; children—Eugene, Alexander; m. 2d Anastasia Gartwig, Oct. 1947. Came to U.S., 1924, naturalized, 1937. Designer, builder, test pilot sailplanes of original types, Finland, 1920-24; designer 1st non-spinnable airplane, U.S., 1925; chief engr., Sikorsky Aviation Corp., 1925-35, in charge all models in regard to gen. structural aerodynamic and hydrodynamic design, developed wings known as G.S. airfoils with which all types of Sikorsky land planes, amphibions and flying boats were equipped; chief design, Vought-Sikorsky Aircraft, div. United Aircraft Corp., 1935-42, charge complete design of large flying boats which made 1st non-stop Pacific and Atlantic flights with Am. mail and passengers, inauguration of Pan- Am. Airways; also in charge design 1st successful helicopter, which set new world's records, 1942; chief engr. Sikorsky Aircraft div. United Aircraft Corp., in charge design research and devel. Sikorsky Helicopters, 1943-57, engring. mgr. Sikorsky Aircraft div., 1957-60, engring. cons. to div., 1960—. Mem. tech. adv. panel Office asst. sec. Def., 1954-58; mem. Army sci. adv. panel, 1959-61. Recipient certificate of merit Am. Helicopter Soc., 1948, Dr. Alex Klemin award, 1954; Chrysler Award as outstanding world designer, 1954; Elmer A. Sperry award for transp., 1964. Fellow Am. Inst. Aeros. and Astronautics, Soc. Automotive Engrs. (hon.), Royal Aero. Soc. (hon.), Am. Helicopter Soc. (hon.); mem. Soaring Soc. Am. Patentee first dartshaped airplane. Home: 2625 Park Av Bridgeport CT 06604 Office: N Main St Stratford CT 06497

GLUNTZ, MARVIN HENRY, ret. assn. exec.; b. Racine, Wis., July 5, 1906; s. Henry and Amelia (Sonnenberg) G.; B.S., U.S. Naval Acad., 1930; M.S., Mass. Inst. Tech., 1935; grad. Advanced Mgmt. Program, Harvard, 1948; m. Josephine Bunk, Aug. 23, 1933; children—Douglas M., Marilyn E., Thomas A. Commd. U.S. Navy, 1930, advanced through grades to capt., 1946; various assignments afloat and on shore, 1930-58; indsl. mgr. 9th Naval Dist., 1954-57, Bur. Ships, 1957-58; ret., 1958; exec. v.p., dir. H.C. Downer & Assos., Cleve., 1958-59; mem. staff soc. Naval Architects and Marine Engrs., 1959-69, sec., 1964-69. Treas. Harbour Green Civic Assn., Massapequa, N.Y., 1965- -. Mem. U.S. Naval Acad., Mass. Inst. Tech., Harvard alumni assns., Soc. Naval Architects and Marine Engrs., Soc. Naval Engrs. Author papers. Home: 40 Bay Dr Massapequa NY 11758

GLUSHIEN, MORRIS P., labor lawyer, arbitrator; b. Bklyn., Oct. 15, 1909; s. Isaac and Minnie (Hoffman) G.; A.B. with honors, Cornell U., 1929, LL.B. with honors, 1931; m. Anne Williams, Nov. 28, 1945; children—Minna, Ruth. Admitted to N.Y. bar, 1932, pvt. practice, Bklyn., 1932-38; mem. faculty Cornell Law Sch., 1938-39; chief U.S. Supreme Ct. sect., asso. gen. counsel NLRB, 1939-47; gen. counsel Internat. Ladies Garment Workers Union, A.F.L.-C.I.O., 1947—. Mem. N.Y. U. Conf. on Labor, mediation and arbitration panel N.Y. State Pub. Employment Relations Bd.; mem. N.Y. U. Conf. on Labor; mem. labor-bus. com. Am. Civil Liberties Union. Bd. dirs. Nat. Legal Aid and Defender Assn. Served with AUS, as cryptologist, 1942-45. Mem. N.Y. State (labor relations com.), Am. (chmn. labor law sect. 1962-63) bar assns., Am. Judicature Soc., Bar City N.Y. (past chmn. com. labor and social security legislation), Indsl. Relations Research Assn., Practicing Law Inst., Fed. Bar Council (labor relations com.), Am. Jewish Congress (com. law and social action), Ams. Dem. Action, Am. Arbitration Assn. (past vice chmn. arbitration law com., mem. nat. panel labor arbitrators), Phi Beta Kappa, Phi Kappa Phi, Curia. Editorial bd. Cornell Law Quar., 1931. Contbr. legal periodicals Home: 11 Station Rd Great Neck NY 11023 Office: 1710 Broadway New York City NY 10019

GLYNN, ARTHUR LAWRENCE, educator; b. Boston, Jan. 1, 1916; s. John Francis and Mary Ann (Johnson) G.; student Boston Coll., 1934-36, LL.B., 1939; M.B.A., Boston U., 1941; m. Fern Matthews, May 22, 1945; children—Kristin, Arthur Lawrence, John, Katharine, Steven, Karen. Admitted to Mass. bar, 1939; spl. agt. FBI, 1939-45; practice law, Boston, 1946—; with tax dept. Peat Marwick & Mitchell, C.P.A.'s, Boston, 1945-46; faculty Coll. Bus. Adminstrn., Boston Coll., 1946—, chmn. accounting dept., 1953—, prof. accounting, 1954—. Trustee 128 Trust, Yewelltide Trust; treas. Instrument Leasing Corp.; dir. Yewell Assos., Inc. Mem. Natick (Mass.) Indsl. Devel. Commn. C.P.A., Mass. Mem. Mass. Bar Assn., Am. Inst. C.P.A.'s, Financial Execs. Inst., Mass. Soc. C.P.A.'s, Nat. Assn. Accountants, Am. Accounting Assn., Soc. Former Agts. FBI, Beta Gamma Sigma (faculty adviser). Roman Catholic. Home: 31 Robinhood Rd Natick, MA 01762. Office: Boston College Chestnut Hill MA 02167

GLYNN, JOHN P., hotel co. exec.; b. 1930; B.B.A., Adelphi U., 1954; married. Mgr., Price Waterhouse & Co., 1954-68; controller Gen. Host Corp., N.Y.C., 1968-69, v.p., controller, 1969—. Office: 245 Park Av New York City NY 10017*

GLYNN, JOSEPH WILLIAM, ins. co. exec.; b. Chgo., Apr. 4, 1917; s. Thomas and Ellen (Gilmore) G.; student Am. Inst. Banking, 1936-38, Loyola U., Chgo., evenings 1945- 46, 50-51; m. Jeanette A. Newberg, May 17, 1941; children—Terrence M., Patricia A. With 1st Nat. Bank of Chgo., 1935-42; div. chief ins. VA, 1946-51; with Continental Assurance Co., Chgo., 1951—, comptroller, 1958-59, v.p., comptroller, 1959-66, sr. v.p., 1966—. Served with USAAF, 1942-45. Mem. Financial Execs. Inst. Clubs: Executives, Ridge Country, Chicago Athletic Assn. (Chgo.). Home: 10101 Kedvale Oak Lawn, IL 60453 Office: 310 S Michigan Av Chicago IL 60604

GLYNN, THOMAS JOSEPH, advt. exec.; b. Queens, N.Y., Jan. 18, 1927; s. Thomas A.J. and Irene W. (Shaw) G.; student Bklyn. Coll., 1947; B.B.A., St. John's U., 1950; m. Fairlie E. Fraser, Sept. 15, 1951; children—Barbara, Thomas, Nancy, Martha. In prodn. and research J. Walter Thompson Co., N.Y.C., 1950-53, media buyer, 1953-59, asso. media dir., 1959-67, media dir., Chgo., 1967—. Served with USAAF, 1945-46. Mem. Internat. Radio and TV Execs. Soc., Chgo. Advt. Club, Alpha Kappa Psi. Home: 117 Rose Terrace Barrington IL 60010 Office: 875 N Michigan Av Chicago IL 60611

GMEINER, HERMANN, social welfare exec.; b. Alberschwende, Austria, June 23, 1919; s. Hermann and Angelika (Eberle) G.; student medicine and psychology, U. Innsbruck (Austria), 1946-49, L.H.D. (hon.), Fordham U., 1963, LaSalle Coll., 1964; Founder SOS Children's Villages, family type homes for abandoned children, 1949, 70 such villages now in existence. Served to 1st lt. German Army, World War II; Russia. Decorated Grand Cross Pontificial Order Gregory the Gt., Most Noble Order of Crown Thailand, 1964. Recipient Silver Merit of Austrian Govt., 1956; Excellentis in Litteris, U. Innsbruck, 1957; medal Richard Meister U. Vienna, 1968. Mem. Austrian Acad. Scis. (hon.). Rotarian. Home: SOS Children's Village Imst/Tyrol Austria Office: Tuchlauben 7 Vienna 1 Austria

GNAGI, RUDOLF, govt. ofcl. Switzerland; b. Aug. 3, 1917; ed. Progymnasium and Gymnasium, Bienne, also U. Bern (Switzerland). Practice of law, 1943-46; sec. Farmers', Tradesmen and Burghers' Party Berne, also Peasants' Fedn. Berne, 1946; sec. Farmers', Tradesmen and Burgers' Party Switzerland, 1947; govt. councillor Canton of Berne, 1952; nat. councillor, 1953; Swiss fed. councillor, head Ministry Transp., Communications and Power, 1965-68; head War Ministry, 1968-71; pres. Swiss Confedn., 1971—. Address: Spiegel-Berne Steingrubenweg 8, Switzerland.*

GO, MATEO LIAN POA, educator; b. Amoy, Fukien, China, Sept. 17, 1918; s. Ramon Occo and Luy (Tan) G.; B.C.E. (Chi Epsilon, G.E., MacMillan scholar), Cornell U., 1942, Ph.D. in Structural Engring. (McGraw fellow), 1946; S.M.C.E. (M.I.T. scholar), Mass Inst. Tech., 1943; m. Jean Cheng, May 18, 1946; children—Genevieve, Mateo Jr., Marilyn. Came to U.S., 1956, naturalized, 1961. Constrn. engr. Mahony-Troast Constrn. Co., Passaic, N.J., 1942, 1946- 47; pres. Mateo L.P. Go Constrn. Co., Hamilton Furniture Co., Philippines, 1947-53; mgr. Go Occo & Co., Manila, 1954-56, tech. cons., 1949-54; structural designer R.C. Reese & Assos., Toledo, 1956; asst. prof. Syracuse U., 1957-59; asso. prof. U. Hawaii, 1959-63, prof. engring., 1963—, chmn. dept. civil engring., 1969-71, dir. nuclear defense design summer inst. for engring., archtl. faculty, 1965, 66, 68; tech. cons. archtl. and engring. devel. div. Office of Civil Defense, Washington, 1966-67. Dirs. Cebu Chinese High Sch., Philippines, 1951-53, Profl. Adv. Service Center, 1967—. Mem. Engring. Assos. (treas. 1969, pres. 1971), Hawaii Acad. Sci., Am. Soc. C.E., Am. Soc. E.E., Am. Concrete Inst., Sigma Xi, Chi Epsilon, Tau Beta Pi, Phi Kappa Phi, Rho Psi. Home: 2415 Ferdinand Av Honolulu HI 96822

GOBBEL, JAMES THOMAS, govt. ofcl.; b. Spencer, N.C., Mar. 20, 1909; s. James Thomas and Elizabeth Virginia (Mahaley) G.; student Duke, 1927-30; m. Isabel Pettigrew, Dec. 2, 1934; 1 son, James Thomas. In govt. service, 1934—, with Nat. Recovery Adminstrn., 1934-35, Resettlement Adminstrn., 1935- 36, Farm Security Adminstrn., 1936-42, Fed. Pub. Housing Adminstrn., 1942-43; community mgr., city mgr. federally built model housing community, Greenbelt, Md., 1943-48; mem. profl. staff govt. operations com. U.S. Ho. of Reps., 1949; dir. wartime civil disaster planning staff Gen. Services Adminstrn., 1950, sr. mem. bd. rev., Office Adminstr., 1951-62, mem. bd. contract appeals, Office Adminstr., 1962-69, mem. fed. procurement regulations staff, 1969—. Trustee Va. Meth. Childrens Home; v.p. No. Va. Bd. Missions and Ch. Extension; chmn. Builders Club for Ch. Extension; v.p. Va. Conf. Bd. Missions; mem. Va. Conf. Bd. Lay Activities. Served as 2d lt., F.A. Res., U.S. Army, 1933-34. Mem. Internat. City Mgrs. Assn. Methodist (chmn. ofcl. bd.). Home: 40 S Cambridge Rd Alexandria VA 22314 Office: Gen Services Adminstrn 18th and F Sts NW Washington DC 20006

GOBBI, TITO, singer; b. Bassano del Grappa, Oct. 24, 1915; s. Giovanni and Enrica (Weiss) G.; student Padua U.; m. Matilde de Rensis, Apr. 10, 1937; 1 dau., Cecilia. Singer all major opera houses U.S. and abroad, also radio and TV broadcasts, motion pictures and concerts; repertoire includes 99 operas; stage dir., 1965—. Patron, Verdi Soc., Liverpool, Eng. Clubs: Art (hon.) (London, Eng.); Warrington (Eng.) Opera; Lions (hon.). Home: Rome Via Asmara 10 Rome, Italy.

GOBEL, GEORGE, TV entertainer;. b. Chgo., May 20, 1919; s. Herman and Lillian (MacDonald) Goebel; student Chgo. pub. schs.; m. Alice Humecke, Dec. 13, 1942; children—Gregg, Georgia, Leslie Alice. Singer radio sta. WLS, Chgo., 1933-42; entertainer hotels and supper clubs, 1946-54; star George Gobel Show, NBC-TV, 1954-57; partner Gomalco Enterprises; v.p. Gomalco, Inc.; star of motion pictures The Birds and The Bees, 1956, I Married A Woman, 1957. Served as 1st lt., USAAF, 1942- 46. Recipient Emmy Award as personality of the year, Peabody Award for TV entertainment, Sylvania Award, Look Mag. award, Motion Picture Daily Poll, Radio-TV Daily Variety mag., and several others, all 1954-55; named AP Man of the Year, TV Personality of the Year, TV-Radio Life, all 1954-55. Clubs: Lakeside Golf (North Hollywood, Cal.); Bohemian (San Francisco); Indian Wells Golf (Palm Desert, Cal.).‡

GOBIN, LEO CALVIN, pub. co. exec.; b. Charlestown, Ind., Mar. 3, 1917; s. Estal Calvin and Alma (Spencer) G.; student Ind. U., 1935-40; m. Mildred L. Schuch, Nov. 4, 1939; children—Ronald, Daniel Joseph. Accountant, Citizens Gas & Coke Utility, Indpls., 1935-42; auditor War Dept. Contract Audit, 1942-43; asst. controller Consol. Vultee Aircraft, 1943-44; v.p., gen. mgr. Bobbs- Merill Co., Indpls., 1946-62, exec. v.p., 1963- 65, pres., 1965—; dir. Implement & Tractor, Inc., Sams Tech. Inst., Inc. Served to staff sgt. AUS, 1944-46. Mem. Nat. Assn. Accountants, Indpls. C. of C., Am. Mgmt. Assn., Am. Legion. Home: 4258 Westbourne Dr Indianapolis IN 46205 Office: 4300 W 62d St Indianapolis IN 46268

GOBLE, ALFRED THEODORE, educator; b. River Falls, Wis., Jan. 24, 1909; s. Lloyd and Carolyn (Green) G.; B.A., U. Wis., 1929, Ph.D., 1933; m. Ethel Thea Frank, July 31, 1935; children—Robert Lloyd, Louis Frank, Jonathan Charles. Instr., then asst. prof. physics U. Tulsa, 1934-37; asst. prof., then asso. prof. Alfred (N.Y.) U., 1937-44; vis. asst. prof. Princeton, 1942-43; research asso. Radio Research Lab., Harvard, 1944-45; mem. faculty Union Coll., Schenectady, 1945—, prof. physics, 1954—, chmn. dept., 1966-71; cons. to industry, 1949—. Mem. Am. Phys. Soc., Am. Assn. Physics Tchrs., Optical Soc. Am., Am. Assn. U. Profs., Sigma Xi. Unitarian. Author: (with D.K. Baker) Elements of Modern Physics, 1962. Home: 1366 McClellan St Schenectady NY 12309

GOBLE, GEORGE G., educator; b. Eagle, Ida., Sept. 11, 1929; s. William W. and Beatrice (Kolander) G.; B.S., U. Ida., 1951; M.S., U. Wash., 1957, Ph.D., 1961; postgrad. Stuttgart Technische Hochschule, 1957-58; m. Sabine Marianne Weber, Apr. 16, 1953; children—Tanya Bettina, Gregory George. Structural inspector Ore. Dept. Hwys., Roseburg, 1953-55; structural designer Marshall, Barr & Assos., Seattle, 1956-61; asst. prof. to prof. structures Case Western Res. U., 1961—; vis. prof. U. Cal., 1968-69; cons. structural design and analysis. Served to capt., USAF, 1951-53. Recipient Collingwood prize Am. Soc. C.E., 1965, profl. structural design award Lincoln Found., 1966. Mem. Am. Soc. C.E., Am. Concrete Inst., Prestressed Concrete Inst., Soc. Exptl. Stress Analysis, Kappa Sigma. Home: 18908 Lomond St Cleveland OH 44122

GOCKENBACH, HAROLD CONRAD, fed. savs. and loan exec.; b. Columbus, O., Feb. 11, 1923; s. Harold Conrad and Dorothy L. (Curran) B.; B.S., Ohio State U., 1944; m. Mary Jo Smith, May 31, 1944; children—Philip, JoAnn, Theresa, Michelle. Teller, Dollar Fed. Savs. & Loan Assn., Columbus, O., 1946-47, asst. treas., 1947-48, bd. dirs., 1948—, sec., 1948-50, exec. v.p., 1950-56, pres., chmn. bd., 1956—. Chmn., Franklin County Boys and Girls Fund, 1957, Christmas in Capitol Square, 1961-62, Downtown Area Com., 1961—, Geman Village Com., 1963-69, St. Agatha's Building Fund, 1953. Bd. dirs. Diocesan Child Guidance Center, Citizen's Research Inc., Convent of Good Shepard, Franklin County Soc. Crippled Children, Franklin County Chpt. Nat. Found., Pontifical Coll. Josephium. Served to lt. (j.g.) USNR, 1944-46. Recipient two George Washington medals Freedom Found., 1964-66; named Hon. Citizen Korea Navy League Columbus, 1964. Mem. Columbus Bd. Realtors, Am. Savs. and Loan Inst. (past pres.), Columbus Savs. and Loan League (past pres.), Navy League Columbus, Phi Gamma Delta, Beta Alpha. Republican. Roman Catholic. Lion. Clubs: Executive, Country, Columbus Maennerchor, Hundred, St. Agatha's Men's, University. Home: 141 Stanbery St Columbus OH 43209 Office: 1 E Gay St Columbus OH 43215

GODARD, JAMES MCFATE, ednl. orgn. exec.; b. Kankakee, Ill., Aug. 3, 1907; s. Gerald Darlington and Sarah (McFate) G.; A.B., Park Coll., 1929; A.M., Duke, 1930; LL.D., Tex. Christian U., 1952; Litt.D., Midwestern U., Tex., 1952; L.H.D., Lander Coll., 1957, St. Ambrose Coll., 1968; Pd.D., Belmont Abbey Coll., 1959; LL.D., Hobart and William Smith Colls., 1963, St. Ambrose Coll., 1969; m. Aura Holton, Dec. 21, 1930; children—Mary Grace, Gerald Holton, Elizabeth Holland. Instr., Park Coll., 1931-32, Duke, 1933-36; prof. edn., dean coll. Queen's Coll., N.C., 1936-49; exec. sec. commn. colls. and univs. So. Assn. Colls. and Secondary Schs., Atlanta, 1949-54; v.p., dean adminstrn. U. Miami (Fla.), 1954-56, exec. v.p., 1956-60; exec. dir. Council Protestant Colls. and Univs., 1960-66; dir. Inst. Higher Ednl. Opportunity, So. Regional Edn. Bd., Atlanta, 1966—; cons. Charlotte (N.C.) Mental Hygiene Clinic, 1937-47. Mem. So. Assn. Colls. Women, Am. Arbitration Assn., N.C. (bd. 1948-49), Charlotte (pres. 1949) mental hygiene socs., Kappa Delta Pi, Phi Kappa Pni. Presbyn. Clubs: Kiwanis, Executives (Charlotte). Author: Understanding Marriage and Family Relations, 1948; The Blue Light, 1964; co- author: Christian Bases of World Order. Home: 83 26th St NW Atlanta GA 30309 Office: 130 6th St NW Atlanta GA 30313

GODARD, JEAN LUC, motion picture dir.; b. Paris, France, Dec. 3, 1930; ed. Lycée Buffon, Paris; m. Anna Karina, Mar. 2, 1961. Journalist, film critic; prod. motion picture films, including Charlotte and Jules, The Little Soldier, The Carabiniers, A Bout de Souffle (recipient Prix Jean Vigo), New History of Lemmy Caution, Vivre sa Vie, Une Femme est une Femme. Recipient spl. prize Festival of Venice, 1962, Prix Pasinetti; Best Picture award Berlin Film Festival. Address: care les camiers du cinema 5 rue Clement-Marot Paris 8e France*

GODBOLD, JOHN COOPER, judge; b. Coy, Ala., Mar. 24, 1920; s. Edwin Condie and Elsie (Williamson) G.; B.S., Auburn U., 1940; J.D., Harvard, 1948; m. Elizabeth Showalter, July 18, 1942; children—Susan, Richard, John C., Cornelia, Sally. Admitted to Ala. bar, 1948; with firm Richard T. Rives, Montgomery, 1948-49; partner Godbold, Hobbs & Copeland, and predecessors, 1949-66; U.S. circuit judge Ct. Appeals 5th Circuit, Montgomery, 1966—. Served with F.A., AUS, 1941-46. Mem. Am., Ala., Montgomery County bar assns., Alpha Tau Omega, Omicron Delta Kappa, Phi Kappa Phi. Episcopalian. Kiwanian. Club: Montgomery Country. Home: 3590 Thomas Av Montgomery AL 36111 Office: Federal Bldg Montgomery AL 36102

GODCHAUX, FRANK AREA, III, food co. exec.; b. Nashville, Feb. 5, 1927; s. Frank Area, Jr. and Mary Lawrence (Ragland) G.; B.A. in Bus. Adminstrn., Vanderbilt U., 1949; m. Agnes Kirkpatrick, May 23, 1953; children—Katherine Area, Mary Lawrence, Leslie Kirkpatrick, Frank Kirkpatrick. Pres. Lastarmco Inc., Abbeville, La., 1964—, also dir., mem. exec. com.; chmn. bd., gen. mgr. internat. div. Riviana Foods Inc., Houston, 1965—; dir. New Orleans br. Fed. Res. Bank Atlanta, 1958-63, Self Service Restaurants, Inc., New Orleans, 1971—. Mem. nat. rice adv. com. Dept. Agr., 1964-66, 71-73. Mem. Evangeline area council Boy Scouts Am. Trustee Vanderbilt U., 1967-71; bd. dirs. U. Southwestern La. Found., 1955—. Served with USNR, 1945-46. Mem. Phi Delta Theta. Episcopalian. Home: 502 5th St Abbeville LA 70510 Office: PO Box 278 Abbeville LA 70510

GODCHAUX, FRANK AREA, Jr., rice milling exec.; b. Abbeville, La., Dec. 27, 1901; s. Frank Area and Agnes (Putnam) G.; grad. Woodbury Forest Sch., Orange, Va., 1920; civil engring. Vanderbilt U., class of 1924; m. Mary Lawrence Ragland, Dec. 21, 1925; children—Frank Area, III, Charles Ragland, Lawrence Putnam. Prodn. dept. La. State Rice Milling Co., Inc. (co. name changed to Lastarmco, Inc.), 1924-27, dir. 1927—, v.p., 1929-36, pres., 1936-67, chmn. bd., chmn. exec. com., 1967—; mem. firm Frank A. Godchaux & Son Live Oak Plantation, 1925—. Chmn. indsl. salvage com. WPB, 1942; mem. rice milling industry adv. com. to OPA, Prodn. and Marketing Adminstrn. and Dept. Agr., 1945-46; mem. adv. com. A.A.A., Nat. Indsl. Recovery Act. Dir. S.W. La. Midwinter Fair Assn.; mem. adv. com. La. Stock Show; mem. rice export adv. com. Dist. chmn. Evangeline area Boy Scouts Am., 1947-48, mem. exec. bd. 1948—.

Mem. C. of C. (past pres.), La. Cattlemen's Assn. (past v.p. and sec.), La. (past pres.), Nat. Aberdeen-Angus assns., La. Camellia Soc. (past v.p.), Phi Delta Theta. Home: Coulee Crest Abbeville LA 70510 Office: La State Rice Milling Co Inc Abbeville LA 70510

GODCHAUX, LEON, bus. exec.; b. New Orleans, 1917; s. Leon, Jr., and Hortense (Schlenker) G.; B.S., Yale, 1938; M.S., U. Ia., 1939; m. Marion Kahn, June 4, 1941; children—Bess, Leon. With Godchaux Sugars, Inc. 1938—, v.p., 1950, asst. to pres., 1950-53, pres., 1953-56; v.p., dir. Godchaux Clothing Co., 1956-67; exec. v.p., dir. Leon Godchaux Clothing Co., 1967—; pres., dir. Godchaux Clothing Co., Ltd., 1957—; dir. Nat. Blowpipe & Mfg. Co. Bd. dirs. United Fund, Council Social Agys. Home: 85 Audubon Blvd New Orleans LA 70118 Office: 828 Canal St New Orleans LA 70103

GODDARD, DAVID ROCKWELL, educator; b. Carmel, Cal., Jan. 3, 1908; s. Pliny Earle and Alice (Rockwell) G.; A.B., U. Cal., 1929, A.M., 1930, Ph.D., 1933; m. Doris Martin, Aug. 21, 1933 (dec.); children—Alison, Robert Martin; m. 2d, Katharine Evans, Feb. 2, 1952. NRC fellow, Rockefeller Inst. Med. Research, 1933-35; instr. to prof. U. Rochester, 1935-46, chmn. dept., 1938-46; prof. botany U. Pa., 1946-58, chmn. dept., 1952-57, dir. div. biology, 1957-61, provost, 1961-71, emeritus provost, 1971—, Gustave C. Kuemmerle prof. botany, 1958-64, prof. biology, 1964-71, univ. prof. sci. and pub. policy, 1971—; Walker-Ames prof. U. Wash., 1955; vis. prof. Rockefeller Inst., 1956- 64; Guggenheim fellow U. Chgo., 1942-43, U. Cambridge, 1950. Mem. nat. adv. council health research facilities, NIH, 1962-67, mem. health scis. advancement award rev. com., 1965-66, 67-70; cons. to President's spl. asst. for sci. and tech., cons. President's Sci. Adv. Com., 1961-63; chmn. ad hoc panel on drug abuse White House, 1962. Recipient Stephen Hales award Am. Soc. Plant Physiology, 1948. Fellow Am. Acad. Arts and Scis.; mem. Am. Philos. Soc., Nat. Acad. Sci. (chmn. com. on USSR and Eastern Europe 1964-68), A.A.A.S. (bd. dirs. 1963-68), Bot. Soc. Am., Am. Soc. Plant Physiology (pres. 1958), Soc. Study Growth and Devel. (pres. 1953), Soc. Gen. Physiologists (pres. 1948). Author: (with Höber) Physical Chemistry of Cells and Tissues, 1945; also articles sci. periodicals. Contbg. author: Treatise of Plant Physiology (Steward), Vol. 1A, 1960. Mem. editorial bd. Ann. Rev. Plant Physiology, 1948-54; asso. editor Quar. Rev. of Biology, 1950—; editor-in-chief Plant Physiology, 1953-57, asso. editor, 1958-63; bd. trustees Biol. Abstracts, 1950-56, pres. 1955-56. Home: 490 E Abington Av Philadelphia PA 19118 Office: Fels Center Govt U Pa Philadelphia PA 19104

GODDARD, EDWIN NEWELL, geologist, educator; b. Oshkosh, Wis., Oct. 22, 1904; s. Henry Newell and Mary Amber (Clemens) G.; A.B., U. Mich., 1927, M.S., 1928, Ph.D., 1936; m. Virginia E. Hobbs, June 30, 1928; children—Patricia Jane, Judy May, Barbara Jean. Jr. geologist to prin. geologist U.S. Geol. Survey, 1930-49, geologic map editor, 1944-49; instr. geology U. Mich., 1928-30, prof. geology, dir. geol. field work, 1949—, chmn. geology dept., 1952-56. Mem. field geology team Project Apollo, NASA. Fellow Geol. Soc. of Am. (chmn. publs. com. 1962, chmn. N.A. geologic map com.), Mineral Soc. Am.; mem. A.A.A.S., Geochem. Soc., Am. Assn. Petroleum Geologists, Am. Geophys. Union., Geol. Soc. Washington, Soc. Econ. geologists, Mich. Basin Geol. Soc., Seismol. Soc. Am., Société Geologique de France, Royal Nederlands Geol. and Mining Soc., Sigma Xi, Sigma Gamma Epsilon, Tau Kappa Epsilon. Rotarian. Chmn. com. Rock Color Chart, pub. NRC, 1948, Geologic Map Symbols, pub. U.S. Geol. Survey, 1948, author and co-author sci. papers. Home: 3091 Warwick Rd Ann Arbor MI 48104

GODDARD, FREDERICK PERCY, bishop; b. Seymour, Conn., Dec. 8, 1903; s. Frederick and Louisa (Marshall) G.; Ph.B., Yale. 1924; B.D., Berkeley Div. Sch., 1927, S.T.D., 1950; D.D., U. of South, 1954; m. May Selena Bennett, Sept. 8, 1928 (dec. Apr. 1965); children—Marie Louise (Mrs. John Bullard), Gladys Emily (Mrs. Roger Rishel); m. 2d, Hazel Bennett Falconer, Nov. 17, 1968. Ordained deacon Episcopal Ch., 1927, priest, 1928; rector St. John's Episcopal Ch., Marlin, Tex., 1927-55; suffragan bishop Diocese Tex., Tyler, 1955—, sec. Diocese Tex., 1939-46. Del. gen. conv. Episcopal Ch., 1934, 37, 43, 46, 49, 53; pres. standing com. Diocese Tex., 1950-55. Chmn. bd. dirs. A.R.C., Falls County, Tex., 1934-42, Community Welfare, Falls County, 1932-48. Trustee U. of South, Sem. of S.W. Recipient Silver Beaver award Boy Scouts Am. Mem. Tex. Archeol. Soc. Club: Yale Houston. Editor: Texas Churchman, 1930-39. Home: 2726 Tanglewood Dr Tyler, TX 75701.

GODDARD, GLORIA, writer; b. Phila., Pa., Feb. 18, 1897; d. William Beck and Agnes Gertrude (Knake) Goddard; grad. Central High Sch., Detroit, Mich., 1915; student Detroit Jr. Coll., 1915-17; m. Clement Wood, Apr. 2, 1926. Publicity writer for "Fatherless Children of France," 1919; statis. research writer, The Business Course, N.Y.C., 1919-20; adv. writer, Baton, Durstine & Osborne, Buffalo, 1920-21; librarian Henry L. Doherty & Co., 1921; free lance writer 1921—; co-dir. Bozenkill Sch. Creative Writing, 1947—. Mem. Poetry Soc. Am. (winner 1st gold prize, 1926); sec. Poetry Inst. Am., 1929. Mem. Soc. of Friends. Author books including: (with Clement Wood), A Dictionary of American Slang, 1926; Bargain Basement (novel), 1949; the Susan Merton series (under pen name Louise Logan). Asso. editor Unabridged Rhyming Dictionary, 1941; (with Clement Wood) The 1941 Quiz Book, 1941; (with Clement Wood) Complete Book of Games; Etiquette for Moderns, 1941; also 15 vols. in Haldeman-Julius Little Blue Book series; chief asso. editor World's Popular Ency. Contbg. editor Travel and The New Leader. Editor and pub. The Bozenkill Breeze. Author of 12 Susan Merton novels (pseudonym Louise Logan). Home: Bozenkill Delanson NY 12053 ☆

GODDARD, JAMES EDWARD, former glass mfg. co. exec.; b. Wellston, O., June 25, 1904; s. Robert Franklin and Zella (Davis) G.; A.B., Ohio U., 1926; M.B.A., Harvard, 1935; m. Jane Bagley, Nov. 29, 1928; 1 son, James Edward. Exec. dir. Zanesville (O.) C. of C., 1935-38, Zanesville Met. Housing Authority, 1938-43; with Anchor Hocking Glass Corp., 1943-71, plant mgr., Connellsville, Pa., 1950-61, v.p., gen. mgr. closure div., 1961-71; ret.; dir. Anchor Cap and Closure Corp., Ltd., Toronto. Chmn. Met. Authority, Connellsville, 1948-50. Bd. dirs., chmn. indsl. div. Connellsville C. of C., 1953-57; bd. dirs. Lancaster chpt. A.R.C., 1964—. Mem. Glass Container Mfrs. Inst. (chmn. com. closures 1964—), Harvard Bus. Sch. Alumni Assn., Am. Mgmt. Assn., Beta Theta Pi. Presbyn. (trustee). Mason (Shriner), Kiwanian (past dir. Connellsville), Elk (past local exalted ruler). Club: Lancaster Country. Home: 226 E Fair Av Lancaster OH 43130 Office: 109 N Broad St Lancaster OH 43130

GODDARD, JAMES LEE, physician; b. Alliance, O., Apr. 24, 1923; s. Frederick Oscar and Harriet Beryl (Calhoun) G.; student Mt. Union Coll., 1942-43, Washington and Lee U., 1943-44, Temple U., 1944; M.D., George Washington U., 1949; M.P.H. magna cum laude, Harvard, 1955; m. Mildred Mae Miller, May 20, 1945; children—Margaret L., Bruce E., Patricia Ann. Asst. surgeon gen. USPHS. Dept. Health, Edn. and Welfare, Washington, 1951-59, chief Communicable Disease Center, Atlanta, Ga., 1962-66; commr. FDA, Washington, 1966-68; v.p. health scis. EDP Tech., Inc., Atlanta, 1968—; civil air surgeon with FAA, Washington, 1959-62. Nat. adv. council Law-Medicine Research Inst.; sci. adv. council Consumers Union. Recipient John Jeffries award, 1962; award of merit George Washington U., 1966; Samuel Bronfman award, 1968. Fellow Am. Assn. Surgery of Trauma; mem. A.M.A., Am. Pub. Health Assn., Assn. Mil. Surgeons, Aerospace Med. Assn., Smith-Reed-Russell Honor Soc. George Washington U., Delta Omega. Contbr. articles profl. jours. Home: 1090 Churchill Downs Rd NE Atlanta GA 30319 Office: 3355 Lenox Rd NE Atlanta GA 30326

GODDARD, JOSEPH PAUL, educator; b. Harriman, Tenn., Feb. 6, 1920; s. Frank Louis and Julia (Evans) G.; B.S., U. Tenn., 1947, M.S., 1950, Ed.D., 1959; hon. degree in Human Engring., Ga. Inst. Tech., 1960; m. Martha Essex Duke, Aug. 24, 1946; children—Mary Ann (Mrs. Walter Armin Ganz, Jr.), Joseph Timberlake, Frank Moss. Adminstrv. asst. to dean Coll. Bus., U. Tenn., Knoxville, 1947-51, asst. dean students, 1951-55, dir. Univ. Evening Sch., 1960-67, asst. dean div. univ. extension, 1967-70, dean continuing edn., 1970—; personnel dir. Rich's, Knoxville, 1955-56; tech. personnel rep. Union Carbide Nuclear Co., Oak Ridge, 1956-60. Sec., Tenn. Indsl. Personnel Conf., 1967—; dep. comdr. Tenn. Wing, Civil Air Patrol, 1960- 69. Bd. dirs. Florence Crittenton Agy., Knoxville, 1969—. Served to capt. Q.M.C., AUS, 1942-45; PTO. Mem. Assn. U. Evening Colls. (pres., dir., program (chmn.), Nat. U. Extension Assn. (chmn. ednl. council 1971-72), Nat. Aerospace Edn. Council, Adult Edn. Assn., Tenn. Valley Personnel Assn. (past pres.), Scarabbean, Phi Kappa Phi, Beta Gamma Sigma, Phi Delta Kappa, Omicron Delta Kappa. Baptist. Home: 7000 Wellington Dr NW Knoxville TN 37919

GODDARD, RALPH F., banker. Sr. v.p., comptroller Eastchester Savs. Bank, Mount Vernon, N.Y. Office: 22 E 1st St Mt Vernon NY 10551*

GODDARD, ROBERT HALE IVES, investment mgr.; b. Providence, Dec. 9, 1909; s. Robert Hale Ives and Margaret (Hazard) G.; grad. St. Mark's Sch., 1928; B.A., Yale, 1932; M.B.A., Harvard, 1934; Dr. Humanitarian Service (hon.), Providence Coll., 1968; m. Hope Linton Drury, June 18, 1937; children—Margaret H. (Mrs. Robert Leeson, Jr.), Robert Hale Ives III, William Holland Drury, Thomas Poynton Ives, Moses Brown Ives. Mng. partner Lonsdale Co., Providence, 1940-43; mgr. machinery export dept. Anderson, Clayton & Co., 1946-50; trustee Providence Instn. for Savs., 1939- 66; dir. Mchts. Cold Storage & Warehouse Co., Inc.; dir. Providence Washington Ins. Co., 1942—, New Eng. Tel. & Tel. Co., 1962—, Providence Investors Co., 1952—; treas., dir. Warwick Land Co., 1932—, pres., 1960—. Bd. dirs. R.I. Hosp. Trust Co., 1938—, exec. com., 1959—, trust com., 1960—. Chmn. R.I. United Fund campaign, 1959; pres. Providence Athenaeum, 1966-70; v.p. Butler Health Center, Providence; trustee Brown & Ives, 1946—; pres. United Fund, 1964-67, Greater Providence YMCA, 1967-69. Served to 1st lt., Transp. Corps, AUS, 1944-46. Episcopalian (vestry). Clubs: Agawam Hunt, Hope (Providence); Dunes (Narragansett, R.I.). Author articles sailing vessels Am. Neptune mag. Home: 64 Angell St Providence RI 02906 Office: 50 S Main St Providence RI 02915

GODDARD, SAMUEL PEARSON, Jr., former gov. Ariz., lawyer; b. Clayton, Mo., Aug. 8, 1919; s. Samuel Pearson and Florence Hilton (Denham) G.; A.B., Harvard, 1941; LL.B., U. Ariz., 1949; m. Julia Hatch, July 1, 1944; children—Samuel Pearson III, Pascal Hatch, William Denham. Admitted to Ariz. bar, 1949; practice in Tucson, 1949- 64, Phoenix, 1964—; sr. partner Goddard, Sophy & L'Ecuyer, 1960—; gov. of Ariz., 1965-67. Campaign chmn. United Fund, 1959, pres., 1960-62; pres. Western Conf. United Funds, 1961-63; chmn. Tucson Youth Study Com., 1959; mem. White House Conf. Com. Children and Youth, 1959; mem. Tucson Hosp. Co-ordinating Com., 1964; an organizer Tucson Civic Chorus, Tucson Festival Soc., Tucson Watercolor Guild; pres. Leffingwell Forest Preserve, 1960-61; v.p. United Community Funds and Councils of Am., 1968-70. Chmn. task force exec. com. United Way of Am.; bd. dirs., chmn. nominating com. overseers and dirs. Asso. Harvard Alumni. Bd. dirs. Ariz. Acad., 1963-64, Catalina council Boy Scouts of Am., 1963-64. Served to maj. USAAF, 1941-46. Mem. Am., Ariz., Pima, Maricopa County bar assns., Am. Judicature Soc., Res. Officers Assn., V.F.W., Air Force Assn., Am. Legion, Phi Alpha Delta. Clubs: Harvard So. Ariz. (pres. 1957-58), Old Pueblo, Federal City. Home: 4724 E Camelback Canyon Dr Phoenix AZ 85018 Office: Ariz Title Bldg Phoenix AZ 85003 also SAB Financial Center Tucson AZ 85012

GODDARD, WESLEY RAWDON, educator; b. St. Louis, July 29, 1915; s. Charles Baldwin and Beatrice (Montgomery) G.; B.A., Swarthmore Coll., 1937; M.A., U. Cal. at Berkeley, 1939; Doctorat D'Universite, U. Paris (France), 1950: m. Shirley Beryl Tolin, Sept. 3, 1946; children—David Shandy, Christopher, Ghislaine. Mem. faculty San Jose (Cal.) State Coll., 1939—, prof. French, 1956—, chmn. dept. fgn. langs., 1958-69, resident dir. Cal. State Internat. Programs for France, 1964-65, for Italy, 1969-71; pres. Santa Clara Valley (Cal.) Verdi Festival. Author: (with Paul Roberts) Preface to Composition, rev. edit., 1955. Translator, editor: (Racine) Phedre, 1961. Home: 19140 Panorama Dr Saratoga CA 95070 Office: San Jose State Coll San Jose CA 95114

GODDEN, RUMER, author; b. Sussex, Eng., Dec. 10, 1907; d. Arthur Leigh and Katherine Norah G.; ed. Moira House, Eastbourne; m. Laurence S. Foster, Mar. 9, 1934; children—Jennifer Jane, Paula Mary; m. 2d, J.L. Haynes- Dixon, Nov. 26, 1949. Author books including: Black Narcissus, 1939; The River, 1946; A Candle for St. Jude, 1948; A Breath of Air, 1950; In Noah's Ark (poetry), 1950; Kingfishers Catch Fire, 1953; An Episode of Sparrows, 1955; The Greengage Summer, 1958; China Court, 1961; The Battle of the Villa Fiorita, 1964; Prayers From The Ark, 1964; The Feather Duster, 1964; (with Jon Godden) Two Under the Indian Sun, 1966; Prayers from the Ark (poetry); The Feather Duster (mus.); The Creatures Choir (poetry), 1966; In This House of Brede, 1969; also children's books. Home: Lamb House West St Rye Sussex England ☆

GODDING, GEORGE ARTHUR, army officer; b. Lawrence, Kan., July 12, 1920; s. Frank Eugene and Leota (House) G.; student U. Kan., 1938-40; B.S., Md. U., 1951; M.A., George Washington U., 1961; m. Mae Elizabeth Evans, June 20, 1945; children—Elizabeth Katherine (Mrs. Jay Willard Lytle), George Arthur Jr., Ruth Alta. Commd. 2d lt. U.S. Army, 1942, advanced through grades to brig. gen., 1967; dep. chief staff for intelligence, Pacific, 1969—. Active Boy Scouts Am. Decorated D.S.M., Silver Star, Legion of Merit with 2 oak leaf clusters, Bronze Star with oak leaf cluster, Air medal, Purple Heart. Mem. Assn. U.S. Army, Kappa Sigma. Mason (32). Home: Quarters 7 Palm Circle Fort Shafter Honolulu HI APO San Francisco CA 96558 Office: Dep Chief Staff for Intelligence HQ USARPAC APO San Francisco CA 96558

GODEL, KURT, educator; b. Bruenn, Czechoslovakia, Apr. 28, 1906; s. Rudolf and Marianne (Handschuh) G.; Ph.D., U. Vienna, 1930; Litt.D., Yale, 1951; Sc.D., Harvard, 1952, Amherst U., 1967; m. Adele Porkert, Sept. 20, 1938. Came to U.S., 1940, naturalized, 1948. Privatdozant U. Vienna, 1933-38; mem. Inst. Advanced Study, Princeton, 1933, 35, 38-53, prof., 1953—, research in math. and philosophy. Co-recipient Einstein award Lewis and Rosa Strauss Meml. Fund, 1951. Mem. Nat. Acad. Scis., Am. Acad. of Arts and Scis., Am. Philos. Soc., London Math. Soc. (hon.), Assn. of Symbolic Logic, Royal Soc. of London (U.K.). Author: Ueber formal unentscheidbare Saetze, 1931; The Consistency of the Continuum Hypothesis, 1940; Rotating Universes in General Relativity Theory, 1950. Address: Inst for Advanced Study Princeton NJ 08540

GODFREY, ARTHUR, radio and TV entertainer; b. N.Y.C., Aug. 31, 1903; s. Arthur H. and Kathryn (Morton) G.; ed. grammar school and 1 1/2 years high sch., Hasbrouck Heights, N.J.; various home study and correspondence courses; grad. Naval Radio Sch., Great Lakes, Ill., 1921; grad. Naval Radio Materiel Sch., Bellevue, D.C., 1929; m. Mary Bourke, Feb. 24, 1938; children—Richard, Michael, Patricia. Served in USN, 1920-24, USCG, 1927-30; commd. comdr., USNR, 1939, comdr., 1951; announcer and entertainer Sta. WFBR, Balt., Apr.-Nov. 1930, NBC Washington, 1930-34; free-lance radio entertainer, 1934—; artist Columbia records; nat. program, Arthur Godfrey Time, radio, 1960—, various TV programs. Appeared in The Glass Bottom Boat, 1966. Internat. trustee World Wildlife Fund. Past sec. Damon Runyon Meml. Fund. Mem. A.F.T.R.A., A.S.C.A.P., Musicians Protective Union. Clubs: N.Y. Yacht, QB'S. Home: Beacon Hill Paeonian Springs VA 22129 Office: care CBS New York City NY 10017

GODFREY, EDWARD SETTLE, III, univ. dean; b. Phoenix, July 21, 1913; s. Edward Settle and Alma (McDonald) G.; A.B., Harvard, 1934; LL.B., Columbia, 1939. Instr. English, Albany Acad., 1935-36; admitted to N.Y. bar, 1939; asst. atty. Fed. Home Loan Bank Bd., 1939-40; practiced law in Albany, 1946-48; prof. law Union U. Albany Law Sch., 1948-61; dean U. Me. Sch. Law, 1962—, provost univ., 1970. Cons. N.Y. Law Revision Commn., 1953-55, 59-60; exec. sec. bar exam. service com. Nat. Conf. Bar Examiners, 1953-61. Chmn. Senatorial Reapportionment Commn. Me., 1966-67; commr. Portland Renewal Authority, 1966-70. Served to maj. AUS, 1941-46. Decorated Bronze Star medal. Mem. Am. Law Inst., Am., Me., N.Y. State bar assns., Am. Soc. Internat. Law, Am. Judicature Soc., Acad. Polit. Sci. Contbr. articles to legal jours. Home: 68 High St Portland, ME 04101

GODFREY, EDWIN DREXEL, Jr., govt. ofcl.; b. N.Y.C., June 14, 1921; s. Edwin Drexel and Fanny Maatlack (Hoagland) G.; A.B., Williams Coll., 1944; M.A., Princeton, 1950, Ph.D., 1953; m. M. J. Hollingshead, June 14, 1942 (div. 1957); children—Edwin Drexel III, Kate Ludlam; m. 2d, Lois Shufro Tallman, Aug. 23, 1958; 1 dau., Susan Frances; stepchildren—Dan Allan Tallman, Peter Andrew Tallman. Instr. polit. sci. Williams Coll., 1946-47, asst. prof., 1951-57; asst. in instrn. politics Princeton, 1947-50; with CIA, 1957-70, office dir.; now cons. U.S. Dept. Justice. Chmn. bd. Burgundy Farm Country Day Sch., Alexandria, Va., 1961-63; chmn. Great Washington Area Unitarian-Universalist Coll. Centers Program, 1965. Served with AUS, 1942-45. Social Sci. Research fellow and Fulbright scholar, France, 1950-51. Mem. Am. Assn. U. Profs., Am. Polit. Sci. Assn., Am. Civil Liberties Union. Author: The Politics of the Non-Communist Left in Post War France, 1954; The Government of France, 3d edit., 1968. Home: 11446 Links Dr Reston, VA 22070. Office: Central Intelligence Agy Washington DC 20505

GODFREY, GARLAND ALONZO, coll. pres.; b. Booneville, Ark., Nov. 5, 1909; s. William Wylie and Lelar Clay (Courtney) G.; B.S., Okla. A. and M., 1933, M.A., 1936; Ed.D, Okla. State U., 1957; m. Merriam Jocille Morris, Nov. 4, 1933; children—Merriam Rose, Anna Lee, Joseph William, Jon Thomas. Tchr., Ark. rural schs., summers 1927-28, 28-29; tchr., prin. high schs., Kan., Okla., 1933-35, Pryor, Okla., 1935-39; supt. Pryor pub. schs., 1939-52; supt. schs., Durant, Okla., 1952-60; pres. Central State Coll., Edmond, Okla., 1960—. Vis. educator, Pakistan, 1964. Named to Hall Distinction Ark. Tech., Russeville, 1968; citations for outstanding ednl. leadership Durant Bd. Edn., 1960, Okla. Assn. Sch. Adminstrn., 1965. Mem. N.E.A., Okla. Edn. Assn. (pres. 1950-51, citation outstanding ednl. leadership 1958), Okla. Assn. Sch. Adminstrs. (pres. 1949-50), Phi Alpha Theta, Pi Kappa Delta. Baptist (deacon). Rotarian (pres. 1957-58). Home: 400 E Hurd St Edmond OK 73034

GODFREY, GEORGE DENTON, rubber mfg. co. exec.; b. New Rochelle, N.Y., Nov. 6, 1922; s. A. Merwin and Georgia (Denton) G.; A.B. in Bus. Adminstrn., Colby Coll., 1943; m. Elizabeth Vognild, Jan. 3, 1951; children—Leslee, Cheryl, Alan, Carolyn Sue. Textile broker, 1946-47; prodn. mgr. Southbridge Finishing Co. (Mass.), 1947-49; with W.J. Voit Rubber Corp., Santa Ana, Cal., 1949—, pres., 1960—, also dir.; dir. Whitley, Inc., Maywood, N.J., Athletic Inst., Chgo. Adv. bd. Orange Co. Empire council Boy Scouts Am. Served to lt. (j.g.) USNR, 1943-46. Decorated Silver Star, Purple Heart, Presdl. Letter of Commendation. Club: Balboa Bay. Home: 900 Zurich Circle Newport Beach CA 92663 Office: 3801 S Harbor Blvd Santa Ana CA 92704

GODFREY, HORACE DAVID, govt. ofcl.; b. Waxhaw, N.C., Aug. 22, 1915; s. Cloyd H. and Helen (Therrell) G.; certificate Charlotte (N.C.) Bus. Coll., 1934; student N.C. State Coll., 1937-41; m. Julia Orr, Mar. 17, 1943; children—Gloria Clair, Horace David, Douglas Michael. Engaged in farming, Waxhaw, until 1954; with AAA, Dept. Agr., 1934-43, P. and M.A., 1945-53, administrv. officer for N.C., 1949-61; with Commodity Stblzn. Service, Dept. Agr., (name changed to Agr. Stablzn. and Conservation Service), 1953—, adminstr., 1961—. Recipient Superior Service award Dept. Agr., 1957, Distinguished Service award, 1964; Career Service award Nat. Civil Service League, 1967. Served with USAAF, World War II. Mem. N.C. Farm Bur., N.C. Grange, Am. Legion. Office: Agr Stabilization and Conservation Service Dept of Agriculture Washington DC 20525

GODFREY, JAMES BROWN, lawyer; b. Everett, Mass., Sept. 19, 1909; s. Frederick E. and Ruth (Brown) G.; A.B., Dartmouth, 1931; J.D., Harvard, 1934; m. Barbara Leach, Oct. 6, 1934; children-James Brown, Anne K. (Mrs. Georg M. Feichtinger), Eugene L. Admitted to N.H. bar, 1934, since practiced in Concord; partner Sulloway, Hollis, Godfrey & Soden, 1939—. Dir. Concord Nat. Bank; trustee N.H. Savs. Bank. Trustee Holderness Sch. Fellow Am. Coll. Probate Counsel; mem. Am., N.H. bar assns., Phi Beta Kappa. Episcopalian (trustee). Home: 37 Ridge Rd Concord NH 03301 Office: 9 Capitol St Concord NH 03301

GODFREY, JAMES E., lawyer; b. Litchfield, Ill., Nov. 9, 1922; A.B., U. Notre Dame, 1943, LL.B., 1949. Admitted to Mo. bar, 1949, Ill. bar, 1949; formerly mem. Mo. Ho. of Reps., also speaker; now partner firm Thomas Busse, Weiss, Cullen & Godfrey, St. Louis. Mem. Am., Ill. bar assns., Bar Assn. Met. St. Louis, Mo. Bar, Lawyers Assn. St. Louis. Office: 418 Olive St St Louis MO 63102*

GODFREY, JAMES EDWIN, food co. exec.; b. Laurium, Mich., Dec. 2, 1906; s. James Dudley and Daisy (Danielson) G.; student U. Wis., 1928; m. Kathryne Schuette, Aug. 27, 1932; children— Nancy (Mrs. Henry B. Schacht), James D., Jane Asta. With Godfrey Co., Waukesha, Wis., 1927—, dir., 1941—, pres., 1950-69, chmn. bd., chief exec. officer, 1969—; dir. First Wis. Bankshares Corp., Milw. Bd. dirs. Better Bus. Bur. Greater Milw., Milw. Vol. Equal Employment Opportunity Council. Adv. bd. Salvation Army, Milw., Booth Meml. Hosp., Wauwatosa, Wis. Clubs: Blue Mound Golf and Country (Wauwatosa); University, Wisconsin (Milw.). Home: 2008 Wauwatosa Av Wauwatosa WI 53213 Office: 1200 W Sunset Dr Waukesha WI 53186

GODFREY, JAMES LOGAN, educator; b. Roanoke, Va., Aug. 31, 1907; s. James Thomas and Jean Rollins (Logan) G.; A.B., Roanoke Coll., 1931; A.M., U. N.C., 1933; Ph.D., U. Chgo., 1942; m. Eleanor Elsabeth Smith, June 17, 1937; children—Jean Lee, Eleanor Ann. Instr. dept. history U. N.C., Chapel Hill, 1936-41, asst. prof., 1941-44, asso. prof., 1944-47, prof. English history, 1947-64, Distinguished Univ. prof. English history, 1964—, chmn. faculty, 1956-57, dean of faculty, 1957-65, chmn. dept. history, 1965—, mem. bd. U. of N.C. Press, 1966—. Chmn. Ford Found. Coop. Program in Humanities, Duke U.-U. of N.C. President's fellow Brown U., 1951-52; trustee Roanoke Coll.; pres. So. Conf. on Brit. Studies, 1970—. Fellow Royal Hist. Soc.; mem. Am. Assn. U. Profs., Am., So. hist. socs., Sigma Chi. Democrat. Episcopalian. Author: (with C.H. Pegg and others) American Society and the Changing World, 1947; Europe since 1815 (with M.B. Garrett), 1947; Revolutionary Justice, 1951. Editor: The Graduate Sch.: Dissertations and Theses, 1947. Asso. editor: Jour. Brit. Studies, 1961- 68. Contbr. articles to jours. Home: Hillcrest Rd Chapel Hill NC 27514

GODFREY, PETER, film dir., author; b. Chiselhurst, Kent, Eng., Oct. 16, 1899; s. Frederick William and Elizabeth (Mabbett) G.; ed. Askes Sch., Hatcham, Surrey, Eng.; m. Renee Haal, Aug. 6, 1941; children—Barbara, Christina and Jill (twins). Came to U.S., 1937. Played vaudeville, 1914; circus in Ireland, 1915; appeared at London Pavillion, 1915-17; directed over 200 plays in West End, London, 1917-37; founder The Gate Theatre, London and Dublin, 1922-35; dir. Shadow and Substance (with Cedric Hardwick and Julie Hayden), N.Y., 1937; dir. films in Hollywood for Gaumont British, Columbia, R.K.O., Warners 1942—. Wrote and prod. in London; directed first modern dress prodns. of O'Neill, Ibsen, Kaiser, Wilde, Shakespeare; directed films for Warner Bros.; dir. TV films Disney Land, Four Star Theatre, Lux, Big Town, Readers Digest, Star and Story, Highways by Night, Forever and a Day, others. Clubs: Players, Masquers. Home: 909 Beverly Dr Beverly Hills CA 90210 Office: Warner Bros Studio Burbank CA 91503 ☆

GODFREY, WILFRED, investment co. exec.; b. Middlesbrough, Eng., Feb. 16, 1902; s. Charles and Anne E. (Wood) G.; m. Edythe Osgood Young, May 25, 1934; 1 dau., Anne Elizabeth. Came to U.S., 1931, naturalized, 1942. With Peat, Marwick, Mitchell & Co., Leeds and London, Eng., also N.Y.C., 1920-39; tax accountant United Fruit Co., Boston, 1940-43; dir. Keystone Custodian Funds, Inc., 1947—, chmn. 1963, 68, pres., 1965; chmn. bd. Constn. Exchange Fund, Inc., Keystone Internat. Fund, Inc., Investors Capital Exchange Fund, Inc., Keystone Provident Life Ins. Co. Mem. Am. Inst. Accountants, Financial Exec. Inst. (past chmn. fed. tax com.). Clubs: Wianno (Mass.); Oyster Harbors (Mass.); Weston (Mass.); Downtown, Commercial (Boston); Tin Whistles (Pinehurst, N.C.). Home: Smoke Valley Rd Po Box K Osterville, MA 02655 Office: 50 Congress St Boston MA 02109

GODFREY, WILLIAM SIMPSON, Jr., educator, anthropologist; b. Phila., Mar. 25, 1916; s. William Simpson and Marian Clifford (Angell) G.; grad. St. Mark's Sch., 1935; A.B., Harvard, 1939, A.M., 1951, Ph.D., 1952; m. Susan Henrotin, Aug. 11, 1945; children—William Simpson III, Isabel Angell, Asst. dir. Phila. U. Mus. expdn. to Piedras Negras, Guatemala, 1939; asst. treas. William Simpson, Sons & Co., Inc., textiles, 1940-43, sec., dir., 1945-47; dir. excavations Old Stone Mill, Newport, R.I., 1948-49; teaching fellow Harvard, 1949-50; teaching asst. U. Chgo., 1950-51; asst. prof. Beloit Coll., 1951-56, asso. prof., 1956- 62, prof., 1962—, asso. dir. Peabody-Beloit Expdn., 1953. Asso. dir. Logan Mus. Mexico Expdn., 1958, dir., 1960. Served to 2d lt., USAAF, 1943-45; CBI. Fellow Am. Anthrop. Assn., A.A.A.S.; mem. Soc. Am. Archeology, Am. Assn. Phys. Anthropologists, Wis., Ill. archeol. surveys, Wis. Acad. Scis., Arts and Letters. Home: 1229 Chapin St Beloit, WI 53511.

GODIN, EDGAR, clergyman; b. Negauc, N.B., Can., May 31, 1911; s. Joseph Albanie and Marguerite (Breau) G.; B.A., Bathurst Coll., 1935; License in Canon Law, Laval U., 1947; License in Canon Law, Gregorian U., Rome, Italy, 1948; Ph.D., U. Moncton; LL.D., St. Thomas U., 1970. Ordained priest Roman Catholic Ch., 1941; dir. Retreat House, Bathurst, N.B., Can., 1942-46; vice-chancellor Diocese of Bathurst, 1948-51, chancellor, 1951-69; bishop of Bathurst, 1969—. Mem. Can. Assn. Cath. Hosp. (pres. 1967-69). Author: Hospital Ethics, 1959. Address: Bishop's Residence 450 Murray Av Bathurst New Brunswick Canada

GODIN, GILLES, lawyer; b. Montreal, Que., Can., Feb. 5, 1928; s. Charles and V. (Mailhot) G.; B.A., Stanislas Coll., Paris, France; B.C.L., McGill U.; m. Huguette Legault, Apr. 19, 1960; children—Jean-Francois, Caroline, Catherine. Partner firm Deschenes, de Gradnpre, Colas, Godin & LaPointe, Montreal. Home: 800 Houde Blvd St Lambert Quebec Canada

GODING, HOWARD, pianist; b. Dedham, Mass., Apr. 28, 1893; s. George Page and Abbie F. (Gifford) G.; grad. New Eng. Conservatory Music, 1915. Soloist with Boston Symphony Orch., 1917; first Boston recital, 1919; other concerts include N.Y.C. and Chgo. recitals, also W. Coast appearances; tchr. piano New Eng. Conservatory Music, Boston, 1920—, also past chmn. dept. Recipient Mason and Hamilin prize New Eng. Conservatory Music, 1915. Home: 114 The Fenway Boston MA 02115

GODING, STOWELL COLLIDGE, educator; b. Dedham, Mass., June 17, 1904; s. Ira Coolidge and Viola Abby (Ross) G.; A.B., Dartmouth, 1925; M.A., Harvard, 1926; Ph.D., U. Wis., 1942; m. Nell Louise Rogers, Aug. 17, 1927 (dec. 1948); children—Ellen Louise (Mrs. Charles Culbertson), Elisabeth Ferol (Mrs. Klaus Flach); m. 2d Sandra Gulben, Sept. 2, 1950. Instr. French, Rice U., also extension U. Tex., 1926-27; mem. faculty U. Mass., 1927—, prof. French, 1949—, head dept. romance langs., 1954-63; summer vis. prof. Bowdoin Coll., 1947, 48. Mem. adv. council modern lang. project Mass. Council Pub. Schs., 1959—. Decorated Medaille d'Honneur aux Affaires Etrangeres, Officier dans L'Ordre des Palmes Academiques (France). Mem. Modern Lang. Assn. Am. (chmn. conf. tchr. tng. 1961), Am. Assn. Tchrs. French, New Eng. Modern Lang. Assn. (past pres.), N.E.A., Phi Beta Kappa, Phi Kappa Phi. Author: (with R. Y. Ellison) Seven French Plays for Stage and Study, 1957; Rhinoceros, 1961. Editor Bay State Fgn. Lang. Bull., 1956—. Home: Plumstree Rd Amherst MA 01002

GODLEY, GEORGE MCMURTRIE, fgn. service officer; b. N.Y.C., Aug. 23, 1917; s. Frederick Augustus and Anne Conyne Wood (Franchot) G.; grad. Hotchkiss Sch., 1935; A.B., Yale, 1939; postgrad. U. Chgo., 1940; m. Livia Paravicini, Jan. 4, 1946 (div.); m. 2d, Elizabeth McCray, 1966. Fgn. service officer, 1941—; vice consul, Marseilles, France, 1941; 3d sec., Bern, Switzerland, 1941-45; 2d sec., Brussels, Belgium, 1946-48; Dept. of State, 1948-52; 1st sec., Paris, France, 1952-55; counselor of Embassy, Phnom Penh, Cambodia, 1955-57; Dept. of State, 1957; counselor embassy, Leopoldville, Congo, 1961-62; dir. Office Central African Affairs, Dept. State, 1962-64; U.S. ambassador to Democratic Republic of the Congo, Leopoldville, 1964-66, career minister, 1966; fgn. service insp., 1967; dep. asst. sec. state for E. Asian and Pacific Affairs, 1968-69; U.S. ambassador to Laos, 1969—. Served as ensign USNR, 1939-40, as pvt. USMCR, 1945; liaison officer San Francisco Conf., 1945. Clubs: Metropolitan (Washington); The Brook (N.Y.C.); Chevy Chase. Home: Morris NY 13808 Office: care US Dept of State Washington DC 20525

GODMAN, JOHN FORBES, retired headmaster; b. Bridgeport, Conn., Mar. 20, 1908; s. Henry Clinton and Mabel Louise (Kabel) G.; Ph.B., Yale, 1930; grad. student edn., Harvard, 1935-36; LL.D. (hon.), Hahnemann Med. Coll., Phila., 1950. Tchr., Gunnery Sch., Washington, Conn., 1931-37, asst. headmaster, 1937-48; headmaster Germantown Acad., Phila., 1948-51, headmaster Berkshire Sch., Sheffield, Mass., 1951-70, also trustee, treas. Mem. Headmasters Assn., Alpha Delta Phi. Club: Yale (N.Y.C.). Home: Berkshire Sch Sheffield, MA

GODOLPHIN, FRANCIS RICHARD BORROUM, educator; b. Del Rio, Tex., Apr. 8, 1903; s. Francis Richard and Alma (Borroum) G.; A.B., Princeton, 1924, Ph.D., 1929; M.A., N.Y. U., 1926; m. Isabelle Simmons, July 25, 1925 (dec. Dec. 1964); children—Jeane, Thomas (dec.); m. 2d, Catherine V. Clark, June 19, 1965. Instr. in classics N.Y. U., 1924-26, N.J. Coll. for Women, 1926-27, Princeton, 1927-30, asst. prof., 1930-40, asso. prof., 1940-45, prof., 1946—, acting chmn., 1941- 42, chmn., 1942-45, dean coll., 1945-55; asst. editor Classical Weekly, 1937-39. Commd. lt., USMCR, 1942; promoted capt., 1944; inactive duty, Sept. 1945; service in Pacific with 4th Marine Div., Jan.-Sept. 1944, 1st Marine Air Wing, Sept. 1944-Apr. 1945. Decorated Bronze Star medal. Mem. Am. Philol. Assn., Classical Assn. of Atlantic States, Am. Assn. Univ. Profs. Democrat. Editor: The Greek Historians, 1942; The Latin Poets, 1949; Great Classical Myths, 1964. Contbr. to Am. Jour. Philology, Classical Philology. Home: 50 Broadripple Dr Princeton NJ 08540 Office: East Pyne Bldg Princeton U Princeton NJ 08540

GODOWSKY, LEOPOLD, Jr., musician, chemist; b. Chgo., May 27, 1900; s. Leopold and Freda (Saxe) G.; student Riverdale (N.Y.) Country Sch., U. Cal.; studied violin with O. Sevick, Vienna, Franz Kneisel and Rubin Goldmark, N.Y.C.; m. Frances Gershwin, 1930; children—Sandra, Leopold, Nadia, Georgia. Violinist; concerts given U.S., Europe; joined Eastman Kodak Co., 1930, for research color photography; co-inventor (with Leopold Mannes) of Kodachrome; participated in develop. Kodacolor, Ektachrome, allied processes. Recipient Edward Longstreet medal Franklin Inst., U.S. Camera achievement award, Modern Pioneer award, Progress medal Photog. Soc. Am., 1970. Hon. fellow Royal Photog. Soc. Gt. Britain; hon. mem. Soc. Photog. Scientists and Engrs. Home: 19 Stony Point Westport CT 06880

GODSELL, GEOFFREY T., journalist. Editorial writer Christian Sci. Pub. Soc. Office: 1 Norway St Boston MA 02115*

GODSHALK, ERNEST LUKENS, oil co. exec.; b. Charleston, S.C., Jan. 2, 1918; s. Ernest L. and Ada (Bean) G.; A.B., Coll. of Charleston, 1939; LL.B., Harvard, 1946, grad. Advanced Mgmt. Program, 1961; m. Gertrude Perkins, Nov. 21, 1942; children—Ernest Lukens III, Robert Earle, Cynthia Perkins. Admitted to N.Y. bar, 1947, Ill. bar, 1960; with firm Sullivan & Cromwell, N.Y.C., 1946-48; atty. Pan Am. Petroleum & Transp. Co., N.Y.C., 1948-54, Am. Oil Co., N.Y.C., 1954-59, gen. counsel, dir., Chgo., 1963—; atty. Standard Oil Co. (Ind.), Chgo, 1959-61, asst. gen. counsel, 1961-63. Served with AUS, 1941-46. Mem. Am., Ill., Chgo. bar assns., Assn. Bar City N.Y. Clubs: Chicago Athletic Assn.; Sheridan Shore Yacht (Wilmette). Home: 735 Glenview Rd Glenview IL 60025 Office: 910 S Michigan Av Chicago IL 60680

GODSOE, JOSEPH GERALD, textile co. exec.; b. Halifax, N.S., Can., Mar. 16, 1908; s. Walter M. and Nan G. Godsoe; student Collegiate Inst., Halifax; A.B., Dalhousie U., 1926, LL.B., 1928, LL.D., 1955; m. Margaret Graham Cowperthwaite, Aug. 6, 1932; children—Valerie, Peter, Gerald, Jane. Read law with Hon. J.A. Walker; called to bar N.S., 1928, Ont., 1936; asso. Burchell, Smith, Parker & Fogo, Halifax, 1928-30; pvt. sec. Cyrus S. Eaton, industrialist and financier, Cleve., 1930-31; joined Confederation Life Assn., Toronto, 1931, formed legal dept., 1931, asst. solicitor, 1934-36; exec. asst. and solicitor, 1936-39, asst. gen. mgr., 1939-45; v.p., dir. Brit. Am. Oil Co., Ltd., 1945-55, exec. v.p., 1955-58; pres., dir. Great Western Garment Co.; chmn., dir. Great Western Garment Co. (Eastern) Ltd., Dana Securities Ltd.; chmn. Newconex Holdings Ltd.; pres. Great Western Garment Co. (Man., Can.) Ltd.; dir. Copperfields Mining Corp., Ltd., Canatogs, Ltd., RCA Victor, Crown Life Ins. Co., Dominion & Anglo Investment Corp., Internat. Paints (Can.), Ltd., Canadian Alpha Lessors, Ltd., Citizens Research Inst. Can., Internat. Trust Co., Rocky Mountain Equipment Ltd., Vancouver Equipment Rentals Ltd., Vancouver Equipment Corporation Ltd. Mem. ct. referees under Dominion Unemployment Ins. Act; internat. adv. com. Boston Conf. on Distbn. Bd. dirs. Toronto Gen. Hosp.; past pres. Toronto Bd. Trade; v.p., dir. Ont. Safety League; bd. dirs. Community Chest Greater Toronto, Canadian Nat. Exhibition; mem. bd. Canadian Council Christians and Jews, Ont. Mental Health Found., Right Honourable C.D. Howe Found., Boys' Village. Decorated comdr. Order British Empire. Mem. Canadian C. of C. (v.p.), Canadian Mfrs. Assn. (vice chmn. edn. com.), Assn. Canadian Clubs (exec. com.), Canadian Inst. Internat. Affairs (exec. com. and co-opted mem. nat. council). Clubs: Canadian, Toronto (hon. sec. 1940-42, pres. 1942-43), National, York (Toronto); Rideau (Ottawa). Home: 120 Kilbarry Rd Toronto 7 Ontario Canada Office: Toronto-Dominion Centre Toronto 111 Ontario Canada

GODSON, JOSEPH, fgn. service officer; b. Poland, Jan. 15, 1913; s. Aaron and Clara (Drach) G.; B.S.S., Coll. City N.Y., 1937; LL.B., N.Y. U., 1940; m. Ruth Perlmann, Jan. 10, 1958; children—Roy, Carla, Dean. Pub. relations dir. labor, charity orgns., 1940-50; joined U.S. fgn. service; attache Am. embassy, Ottawa, 1950-52; labor attache Am. Embassy, London, 1953-59; 1st sec. Am. embassy, Belgrade, Yugoslavia, 1959-61; Am. consul. gen., Zagreb, Yugoslavia, 1962-64; labor, UN adviser European Bur. State Dept., 1964-68; Am. consul gen., Edinburgh, Scotland, 1968—. Club: Landsowne (London). Home: 88 Inverleith Place Edinburgh Scotland Office: 3 Regent Terrace Edinburgh Scotland

GODWARD, WILLIAM WARHURST, lawyer; b. New Rockford, N.D., July 14, 1913; s. William Alexander and Mattie (Young) G.; A.B., U. Cal. at Berkeley, 1934, LL.B., 1937; m. Ann Allison Chandler, Oct. 19, 1951; 1 dau., Jennifer. Admitted to Cal. bar, 1937; practiced in Santa Rosa, 1937-41, San Francisco, 1941—; partner firm Codey, Croley, Gaither, Godward, Castro & Huddleson, 1947—. Bd. dirs. San Francisco Chamber Music Soc., 1966—, Community Music Center, San Francisco, 1967—, San Francisco Spring Opera, 1968-70. Served with USNR, 1942-46. Mem. San Francisco Bar Assn. (bd. dirs. 1967-68), Boalt Hall Law Assn. (pres. 1968-70). Clubs: University, World Trade (San Francisco). Home: 2765 Vallejo St San Francisco CA 94123 Office: 1 Maritime Plaza San Francisco CA 94111

GODWIN, CHARLES WILLIAM, radio network exec.; b. McComb, Miss., Aug. 10, 1914; s. Alvah Wayne and Willie Beatrice (Smith) G.; student Oklahoma City U., 1931-33; m. Lorece M. Northcutt, Dec. 24, 1934; 1 dau., Patricia Gay (Mrs. Donald Housman). Announcer, salesman Radio Sta. WKY, Oklahoma City, 1931-34; announcer Radio Sta. WLW, Cin., 1934-36; presdl. announcer CBS, Washington, 1936; prodn. mgr. Newark offices, then asst. prodn. mgr., prodn. mgr., night mgr., asst. dir. sta. relations, dir. sta. relations WOR, MBS, N.Y.C., 1937-54, now sr. v.p. charge sta. relations, exec. com., dir.; v.p. charge advt. Sponsor mag., 1956-58. Bd. dirs. Broadcasters Found. Mem. Nat. Broadcast Pioneers (past v.p.), N.Y. Broadcast Pioneers, Radio & TV Execs. Soc., N.Y. Civil War Roundtable, Broadcast Pioneers (v.p. N.Y. chpt.). Home: 172 Wickham Rd Garden City NY 11530 Office: 135 W 50th St New York City NY 10020

GODWIN, MILLS EDWIN, Jr., lawyer; b. Nansemond County, Va., Nov. 19, 1914; s. Mills Edwin and Otelia (Darden) G.; LL.B., U. Va., 1938; LL.D. (hon.), Elon (N.C.) Coll., 1954, Coll. William and Mary, 1966, Roanoke Coll., 1969, Washington and Lee U., 1970; m. Katherine Beale, Oct. 26, 1940; 1 dau., Becky (dec.). Admitted to Va. bar 1937; practice in Suffolk, 1938-62, 70—; spl. agt. FBI, 1942-46; mem. Va. Ho. Dels. from Suffolk-Nansemond County, 1947-52, senate, 1952-61; lt. gov. Va., 1962-66; gov. Va., 1966-70; v.p., dir. Bank Whaleyville; dir. Va. Nat. Bank, N. & W. Ry., Standard Brands, Inc.; cons. Reynolds Metals Co. Chmn. So. Regional Edn. Bd., 1968-69; chmn. Appalachian Govs. Council, 1968- 69; vice chmn. So. Govs. Conf., 1968-69; exec. com. Nat. Govs. Conf., 1968-69. Trustee Elon Coll., Va. Wesleyan Coll. Named Suffolk and Nansemond County First Citizen, 1956, 59. Mem. Raven Soc., Omicron Delta Kappa, Phi Delta Phi. Democrat. Mem. Christian Ch. K.P., Mason (33, Shriner), Rotarian, Moose, Ruritan (nat. pres. 1952). Home: Cedar Point Crittenden VA 23342 Office: Nat Bank Bldg Suffolk VA 23434

GOEB, ROGER, composer; b. Cherokee, Ia., Oct. 9, 1914; s. Carl J. and Anna K. (Peters) G.; B.S.A., U. Wis., 1936; License de Contrepoint, Ecole Normale de Musique de Paris, 1939; Mus.M., Cleve. Inst. Music, 1942; Ph.D., State U. Ia., 1945; m. Janey Hoy Price, Feb. 15, 1941 (dec. Jan. 1967); children—John, Kathleen. Mem. faculty dept. music U. Okla., 1942-44, State U. Ia., 1944-45, Bard Coll., 1945-47, Juilliard Sch. Music, 1947- 50, Vt. Composers Conf., summers 1950-62, Columbia, 1952-53; former asst. prof. music Stanford. Guggenheim fellow music composition, 1950-52. Compositions include: Sonata for solo viola, 1942; Concerto for 2 sopranos and chamber orchestra, 1942; String Quartet No. 2, 1949; Piano Sonata No. 1, 1942; Miniatures for violin and viola, 1945; Suite in Folk Style, 1946; Suite for Woodwind Trio, 1946; Concertants III and IV, 1952; Fantasy for Oboe and Strings, 1947; Symphony No. 2, 1949; Symphony No. 3, 1952; American Dances for string orchestra, 1952; Fantasy for Oboe and String Orchestra, Romanza for String Orchestra, Prairie Songs for Small Orchestra, String Quartet No. 3, Quintet for Woodwinds I, II, Fuga Contraria, Symphony No. 4, Sinfonia No. 1 and 2 for orchestra, numerous others. Recipient award Nat. Acad. Arts and Letters, 1953. Mem. Am. Composers Alliance (treas. 1969—). Home: 11 Lakeside Dr Rockville Centre NY 11570

GOEBEL, CHARLES JAMES, physicist, educator; b. Chgo., Dec. 16, 1930; s. Harry Wilhelm and Gladys (Ibach) G.; Ph.B., U. Chgo., 1949, Ph.D., 1956; m. Belle C. Gorman, Oct. 27, 1951; children—George Harry, John Philip. Research asso. Lawrence Radiation Lab., Berkeley, Cal., 1954-56; mem. faculty U. Rochester, N.Y., 1956-61, asso. prof. physics, 1959-61; mem. faculty U. Wis., Madison, 1961—, prof. physics, 1964—; mem. staff Inst. Advanced Study, Princeton, 1960-61. Guggenheim fellow, 1967-68. Fellow Am. Phys. Soc. Home: 10 N Roby Rd Madison WI 53705

GOEBEL, EDMUND JOSEPH, former educator; b. Caledonia, Wis., Apr. 4, 1896; s. August and Rose Goebel; M.A., St. Francis Sem., Milw., 1924; postgrad. Marquette, Wis., McGill univs.; Ph.D., Cath. U. Am., 1937; LL.D., Marquette U., 1954. Ordained priest Roman Catholic Ch., 1924; vice rector Pio Nono Coll., Milw., 1925-29; prin. Messuer High Sch., Milw., 1929-34; former supt. Cath. schs., Archdiocese Milw., 1929-34, also from 1937. Organizer and founder Nat. Cath. Music Educators, 1942, mem. exec. com. 1942—; pres. secondary sch. dept. Nat. Cath. Edn. Assn.; mem. adv. com. Wis. Cath. Hosp. Assn., Nat. Cath. Music Assn. (pres.). Mem. Wis. State Bd. of Health, Milw. Safety Commn.; pres. Cath. Hosp. Assn. U.S.A. and Can., 1954-55. Trustee Am. Hosp. Assn., Wis. Hosp. Conf. (K.C.); bd. dirs. St. Francis Sem. Corp. Author: Pax Christi: A Workbook in Church History, 1936; Saints to Help the Sick and Dying, 1937; History of Catholic Secondary Education up to 1852, 1937; Our Civic Life, 1940; (with others) Living My Religion series, 1945-48; Catholic School History Series, 1951; Catholic Geography Series, 1958; Civics Review 1960; Church History, 1961. Home: 6700 N Teutonia Av Milwaukee WI 53209

GOEBEL, MAX THEODORE, chemist; b. Compton, Ill., Oct. 28, 1906; s. August and Louise (Brueckner) G.; A.B., U. Ill., 1928, Ph.D. in Organic Chemistry, 1934; m. Marguerite Kuehn, Feb. 6, 1932; children—Margaret, Richard. Research chemist Comml. Solvents Corp., Ind., 1928-30; asst. chemist U. Ill., 1930-32; research chemist exptl. sta. E. I. du Pont de Nemours & Co., Wilmington, Del., 1934-38, research group leader, 1938-41, asst. dir. exptl. lab., Cleve., 1941-44, dir., 1944-48, asst. dir. research div. indsl. and biochems. dept., Wilmington, 1948-50, now research dir. Vice pres. Agrl. Research Inst., NRC, 1958, chmn. budget and finance com., mem. governing bd., 1959. Mem. Am. Chem. Soc. Home: Route 1 Chadds Ford PA 19317 Office: Dupont Bldg Wilmington DE 19898

GOEBEL, WALTHER FREDERICK, biochemist; b. Palo Alto, Cal., Dec. 24, 1899; s. Julius and Kathryn (Vreeland) G.; A.B., U. Ill., 1920, A.M., 1921, Ph.D., 1923, scholar in chemistry, 1920-21, fellow, 1921-23; postgrad. U. Munich (Germany), 1923-24; D.Sc. (hon.), Middlebury (Vt.) Coll., 1959; m. Cornelia Van Rensselaer Robb, Oct. 23, 1930; children—Cornelia Van Rensselaer Bronson, Anne Kathryn Barkman. Research asst. Rockefeller U., 1924-27, asso., 1927-34, asso. mem., 1934-44, prof., 1957—. Mem. Nat. Acad. Scis., Am. Chem. Soc., Am. Soc. Biol. Chemists, Harvey Soc., Am. Assn. Immunologists, Am. Soc. Microbiology, Gesellschaft für Immunologie, Phi Beta Kappa, Sigma Xi, Phi Lambda Upsilon, Phi Eta. Contbr. monographs, reports and articles on chem. and immunological subjects sci. jours. Home: Vineyard Lane Greenwich CT 06830: also 333 E 68th St New York City NY 10021 Office: Rockefeller U New York City NY 10021

GOEBEL, WILLIAM MATHERS, lawyer; b. Jacksonville, Ill., Nov. 5, 1922; s. William George and Elizabeth (Mathers) G.; A.B., Ill. Coll., 1946; J.D., U. Mich., 1949; m. Barbara Leeper, Mar. 10, 1944; children—William Mathers, Helen Elizabeth. Admitted to Ill. bar, 1949; practice in Carmi, 1949-59, Bloomington, 1961—; partner Conger, Elliott, Goebel & Elliott, 1949-59; asst. gen. counsel Ill. Agrl. Assn. and affiliated cos., 1959-64; partner Dunn, Dunn, Brady, Goebel, Ulbrich & Hayes, 1964—; lectr. dept. edn. Ill. State U. Mem. Ill. Citizens Com. for Uniform Comml. Code, mem. Ill. Sch. Problems Commn., 1965-69. Bd. dirs Bloomington-Normal Symphony Soc.; trustee Brokaw Hosp., Normal, Ill.; sec. bd. trustees, mem. exec. com. Ill. Wesleyan U., Bloomington. Served with AUS, World War II. Mem. Am. Judicature Soc., Am., Ill. (past chmn. comml. banking and bankruptcy law sect. council), McLean County bar assns. Democrat. Presbyn. Rotarian. Contbr. to U. Ill. Law Forum, 1962. Home: 1311 E Washington St Bloomington IL 61701 Office: Peoples Bank Bldg Bloomington IL 61701

GOEDHARD, NEIL, city mgr.; b. Pasadena, Cal., June 24, 1925; s. Cornelis and Reiniera (Hatzmann) G.; A.A., Pasadena City Coll., 1947; B.A. in Polit. Sci., U. Cal. at Santa Barbara, 1949; M.S. in Pub. Adminstrn., U. So. Cal., 1954; m. Gloria Steers, July 12, 1950; children—Sheryl, Stacey, Shawna, Shayne. Mgmt. intern with U.S. Dept. State, Washington, 1949-50; U.S. resident officer, city and county of Hanau, Germany, Office of High Commr. for Germany, 1950-51; U.S. observer State of Northrhine- Westphalia, Germany, 1951, chief Trainee and Student Exchange Programs for Germany, 1951-53; cons. Air Pollution Found., 1954, city adminstr., Covina, Cal., 1954-68; city mgr. Fresno, Cal., 1968—. Lectr., U. So. Cal., 1957-64, Fresno State Coll., 1969—; asst. prof. Cal. State Coll., Los Angeles, 1964-68; 2d v.p. Covina Irrigation Co., 1959-63; 1st v.p., 1963-68, dir., 1956-68. Bd. dirs. Mt. San Antonio council Camp Fire Girls, United Way for San Gabriel Valley; dir. Covina-West Covina Recreation Dist., 1956-58; dir. area D. Civil Def., Los Angeles Co., 1956-68; pres. Covina area United Fund, 1961. Pres. bd. devel. Sch. Pub. Adminstrn., U. So. Cal., 1960. Served to q.m. 3d class USNR, 1943-45. Mem. Am. Soc. Pub. Adminstrn. (pres. 1959), Inter City Mgrs. Assn., Western Govtl. Research Assn., U. Cal. at Santa Barbara Alumni Assn. (pres. 1956-60), League Cal. Cities (dir. city mgrs. dept. 1962-64, 1st v.p. 1969), Pi Sigma Alpha. Clubs: Los Angeles Speakers (pres. 1967), Rotary (pres. Covina 1963, Dir.). Author: Organization and Administration of the Police in Germany, 1954; also articles in field. Home: 3870 Huntington Blvd Fresno CA 93702 Office: City Hall 2326 Fresno St Fresno CA 93721

GOEDSCHE, CURT RUDOLF, educator; b. Dresden, Germany, July 10, 1904; s. Georg and Frieda (Hering) G.; came to U.S., 1928, naturalized, 1933; A.B., Washington State Coll., 1930; A.M., Northwestern U., 1931, Ph.D., 1933; m. Terese Dorothy Kolander, June 6, 1933; 1 dau., Charlotte Louise. Part-time instr. in German, Northwestern U., 1931-34. instr., 1934-38, asst. prof., 1938-44, asso. prof., 1944-48, prof. 1948—, dir. lang. Civil Affairs Tng. Sch., 1943-45, chmn. German dept. 1945—. Mem. Modern Lang. Assn. Am., Linguistic Soc. Am., Am. Assn. Tchrs. German (past pres.), Phi Beta Kappa, Phi Beta Phi. Methodist. Author: Wie geht's, 1938; Sag's auf Deutsch, 1942; (with Brenes-Mesen) Conversamos, 1943; (with Flygt and Spann) A Modern Course in German, 1947; Graded Cultural Readers, 1953-65; (with Spann) Deutsche Denker und Forscher, 1955; (with Spann) Deutsch für Amerikaner, 1960; Patterns of German Conversation, 1958. Editor: Jugend und Reife, 1936; (with Leopold) Minna von Barnheim, 1937. Contbr. articles to Modern Lang. Jour., Germanic Rev. Home: 1312 Isabella St Evanston IL 60201

GOELMAN, ELAZAR, coll. pres.; b. Jedwabno, Poland, Dec. 15, 1913; s. Judah Laib and Raizl (Janushevsky) G.; B.A., Western Res. U., 1940; Ph.D., Dropsie Coll., Phila., 1953; m. Rose S. Belkin, Aug. 20, 1939; children—Don, Elana (Mrs. Avishai Ehrlich), Hillel. Lectr., U. Buffalo, 1957-59; exec. dir. Buffalo Bur. Jewish Edn., 1949-59; ednl. dir. Har Zion Temple, Phila., 1947-49; exec. dir. Intercollegiate Zionist Fedn. Am., 1946; registrar Hebrew Tchr. Sem., Cleve., 1935-46; dean Gratz Coll., Phila., 1959-70, pres., 1970—. Pres. Assn. Jewish Agy. Execs., 1966-69, Histadrut Ivrit, 1965-69, Cleve. Hebrew Tchrs. Assn., 1939-43, Nat. Council Jewish Edn., 1963-65, Assn. Hebrew Tchrs. Colls., 1970—. Recipient Vocational Service award B'nai B'rith, 1966; Phila. Jewish Library Assn. award, 1970. Mem. Inter-Faith Religious Edn. Com. Buffalo, Am. Assn. Profs. Hebrew, Dropsie Coll. Alumni Assn. (pres. 1965-70), Religious Edn. Assn., Nat. Conf. Jewish Communal Service, Nat. Conf. Christians and Jews. Editorial bd. Sheviley Hahinuch; Jewish Edn. Mag. Home: 622 W Mt Airy Av Philadelphia PA 19119 Office: Gratz Coll 10th St and Tabor Rd Philadelphia PA 19141

GOELZ, PAUL CORNELIUS, univ. dean; b. Bartelso, Ill., Oct. 7, 1914; s. Peter Paul and Clara (Bross) G.; certificate St. Louis U., 1939; B.B.A., U. Dayton, 1943, M.A., 1946; M.B.A., Northwestern U., 1951, Ph.D., 1954. Credit mgr. Adjustable Shoe Co., St. Louis, 1937-39; asst. comptroller Key Refinery Equipment Co., St. Louis, 1939-40; auditor Gen. Motors Acceptance Corp., St. Louis, 1940-41; instr. Southside High Sch., St. Louis, 1943-46; chmn. dept. marketing St. Mary's U., San Antonio, 1946-62, dean Sch. Bus. Adminstrn., 1962—. Vis. lectr. staff Army Mgmt. Engring. Tng. Agy. U.S. Dept. Def., Rock Island Arsenal; lectr. Exec. Devel. Insts. in U.S. and Mexico; cons. to bus. and govt. Chmn. spl. series of sessions at Internat. Conf. Am. Inst. Indsl. Engrs., 1963. Mem. Acad. Mgmt., Am. Marketing Assn., Sales and Marketing Execs. Internat., Am. Inst. Indsl. Engrs., San Antonio C. of C., Nat. Assn. Bus. Economists, South-Western Assn. Bus. Sch. Deans (pres. 1968-69), Adminstrv. Mgmt. Soc., Am. Assn. Collegiate Schs. Bus. (mem. planning com.), Delta Epsilon Sigma, Alpha Sigma Tau, Pi Sigma Epsilon. Contbr. articles profl. publs. Home: 2700 Cincinnati Av San Antonio TX 78284

GOERBING, ROSWELL CARL, bldg. products co. exec.; b. Buffalo, Sept. 27, 1916; s. Carl F. and Cora (Thuerk) G.; B.S. in Bus. Adminstrn., U. Buffalo, 1938; m. Elizabeth Alder, June 25, 1955; 1 son, Peter K. With Nat. Gypsum Co., 1946—, controller, 1966—. Served to capt. AUS, World War II; ETO. Mem. Buffalo C. of C. Home: 96 Tristan Lane Buffalo NY 14221 Office: 325 Delaware Av Buffalo NY 14221

GOERING, KENNETH JUSTIN, coll. adminstr.; b. San Francisco, Dec. 26, 1913; s. George Hans and Elsa (Toepper) G.; B.S., Mont. State Coll., 1936; M.S., Cal. Inst. Tech., 1939; Ph.D., Ia. State U., 1941; m. Marjory Gieseker, Aug. 14, 1936; children—Patricia DeBedout, John D., Kenneth Don. Research chemist Anheuser Busch Co., St. Louis, 1941-42; instr. Ia. State U., 1942-43; research chemist WPB, Lincoln, Neb., 1943-44; asst. chief chemist Omaha Alcohol Plant, 1944-45; v.p., gen. mgr. Mold Bran Ro and Enzymes, Inc., Eagle Grove, La., 1945-49; mem. faculty Mont. State U., Bozeman, 1949—, prof. biochemistry, 1960—, grad. dean, 1967—; cons. Kurth Malting Co., Sunburst Biochem. Co., Farm Bur., Ida. Potato Foods. Mem. Am. Chem. Soc., Am. Assn. Cereal Chemists, Sigma Xi (Mont. chpt. award 1961), Phi Kappa Phi. Asso. editor: Cereal Chemistry. Home: Route 2 Box 313 Bozeman MT 59715

GOERKE, LENOR STEPHEN, univ. dean; b. Hitchcock, Okla., Jan. 22, 1912; s. Leonard H. and Nellie (Bradon) G.; B.S., Southeastern State Tchrs. Coll., Okla., 1931; B.S., M.D., U. Okla., 1936; M.S. in Pub. Health, U. Cal. at Berkeley, 1938; m. Evelyn M. Foster, May 17, 1938; children—William S., Susan K. Intern, Good Samaritan Hosp., Portland, Ore., 1936-37; county health officer Astoria and McMinnville, Ore., 1938-39, Woodland, Cal., 1940; dir. med. bur., med. dir. also dir. dist. services Los Angeles City Health Dept. 1946-54; clin. asso. prof. preventive medicine and pub. health Coll. Med. Evangelists, 1947-50: asso. clin. prof. medicine U. So. Cal., 1951- 54; faculty U. Cal. at Los Angeles, 1950—, prof. pub. health Sch. Pub. Health, 1954-, dean Sch. Pub. Health, chmn. dept. preventive medicine and pub. health Sch. Medicine, 1956—. Mem. Cal. Bd. Health, Los Angeles City Bd. Health; chmn. So. Cal. adv. com. to SSS and Armed Forces, 1955—. Served to col., M.C., AUS, 1940-46; ETO. Mem. Am. Coll. Preventive Medicine (bd. regents 1955—), Am. (governing council 1955-58, pres. Western br. 1953), So. Cal. (pres. 1954) pub. health assns., Assn. of Schs. Pub. Health (pres.), Am., Cal. (chmn. pub. health sect. 1954-55, sec. 1953-54), Los Angeles County med. assns., Hollywood Acad. Medicine (exec. com. 1954-55), Cal. Acad. Preventive Medicine (pres. 1957). Editorial cons., contbr. The New Physician, 1958—. Home: 1262 Monaco Dr Pacific Palisades CA 90272 Office: Sch Pub Health U Cal at Los Angeles Los Angeles CA 90024

GOERS, MELVIN ARMAND, army officer; b. Sadorus, Ill., Aug. 29, 1918; s. Arthur Daniel and Marie (Schwerdtfeger) G.; B.S., U. Ill., 1940; grad. Cavalry Sch., 1941, Army Command and Gen. Staff Coll., 1946, Armed Forces Staff Coll., 1956, Indsl. Coll. Armed Forces, 1959; m. Kathryn Louise Lindsay, Nov. 20, 1941; children—Nancy Kay (Mrs. William Edwin Banta), Susan Jane (Mrs. Donald R. Briggs), Gayle Ann, Julie Lindsay. Commd. 2d lt. U.S. Army, 1940, advanced through grades to brig. gen., 1967; officer Cavalry Div. and Armored Div., U.S. and Europe, 1940-45; comptroller Exchange Service, Europe, 1946-47; staff officer Hdqrs. Far East and UN Command, 1950-53; comdr. RCN Bn., personnel dir. 1st Armored Div., 1953-55; exec. officer, comdr. sch. regt. Armor Sch., 1956-58; officer Gen. Staff and Orgn. Joint Chiefs of Staff, Washington, 1959-62; chief joint staff MAAG Rep. of China, Taiwan, 1962-64; dir. operations Hdqrs. 5th Army, Ft. Sheridan, Ill., 1964-67; sr. mil. advisor 1st ROK Army, Korea, 1967-68; dir. R.O.T.C., Hdqrs. CONARC, Ft. Monroe, Va., 1969—. Dir. Interservice Financial Assn., Ltd. (Hampton, Va.). Pres. bd. govs. Taiwan Am. Sch., 1963-64. Decorated Legion of Merit with 2 oak leaf clusters, Joint Service Commendation Medal, B.S.M. with oak leaf cluster (U.S.), Presdl. Medal of Merit (Czechoslovakia). Mem. Assn. U.S. Army, Armor Assn. Lutheran. Home: 147 Bernard Rd Ft Monroe VA 23351 Office: Dir ROTC ODSCIT Hdqrs CONARC Fort Monroe VA 23351

GOERTZ, RAYMOND C., engr.; b. Clearwater, Kan., Mar. 12, 1915; s. Norman E. and Flora (Saint) G.; B.S., Mont. State Col., 1940; grad. study, Poly. Institute of Brooklyn, 1942-46. Illinois Institute of Technology, 1947-49; m. Helen Boula, September 2, 1950; children—Alan, Jean, and Linda. Jr. engr., project engr. Servomechanisms Lab., Sperry Gyroscope Co., 1940- 47; formerly group leader Argonne Nat. Lab., Lemont, Ill., sr. engr. remote control engring. div. Mem. Am. Nuclear Soc., Research Soc. Am., Am. Inst. Chem. Engrs., I.E.E.E., Am. Nuclear Soc., Research Soc. Am. Home: 5510 Fairmont Av Downers Grove IL Office: 9700 S Cass Av Argonne IL

GOESS, FREDERICK V., former banker; b. Bklyn., Apr. 12, 1896; s. Andrew C. and Margaret (Kirchner) G.; student pub. schs.; Dr. Comml. Sci., St. John's U.; m. Helen E. Ochs., June 30, 1920; children—Helen E. Thran, Grace K. Donovan, Mary, Frederick, Doris Powers, Margaret Peguillan. With Mfrs. Trust Co., N.Y.C., 1912-41, v.p., 1932-41; receiver Harriman Nat. Bank & Trust Co.; became Pres. Prudential Savs. Bank, Bklyn., 1941, now trustee; pres. Fleetwood Enterprises, Inc., Fleetwood Parking, Inc. Bd. dirs. Bklyn. chpt. A.R.C., St. Catharine's Hosp.; mem. council adminstrn. St. John's U. Served as corpl., AEF, 1918-19. Decorated Knight of St. Gregory, Knight of Malta. Roman Catholic. K.C. Home: 85 Kilburn Rd Garden City NY 11530

GOETCHIUS, EUGENE VAN NESS, educator, clergyman; b. Augusta, Ga., Mar. 26, 1921; s. Eugene Foster and Agnes Louise (Stelling) G.; B.A., U. Va., 1941, M.S., 1947, M.A., 1948, Ph.D., 1949; B.D., Episcopal Theol. Sch., Cambridge, Mass., 1952; Th.D., Union Theol. Sem., N.Y.C., 1963; postgrad. U. Zurich (Switzerland), 1964, Mansfield Coll., Oxford, Eng., 1970-71; m. Ann Oliver Kirkpatrick, Dec. 17, 1955; children—Charles L.T., Nathaniel K., Edward V.N., John M. Master, Woodberry Forest Sch., 1947- 49; instr. math. Tufts U., 1950-52; instr. religion Trinity Coll., Hartford, Conn., 1952-54; fellow, tutor Gen. Theol. Sem., N.Y.C., 1954- 56; ordained to ministry Episcopal Ch., 1952; asst. Grace Ch., N.Y.C., 1954-55; asst. chaplain Columbia, 1955-56; head dept. math. Am. Acad. in Athens (Greece), 1957; asst. prof. N.T., Episcopal Theol. Sch., 1957-60, asso. prof., 1960-63, prof. Bibl. langs., 1963—; lectr. Hellenistic Greek, Harvard, 1957-58; dir. Inst. Bibl. Langs. and Linguistics, Vanderbilt U., summer 1968; vis. prof. Greek, Andover Newton Theol. Sch., 1968; vis. prof. Hebrew, Boston U., 1969. Mem. Studiorum Novi Testamenti Societas, Soc. Bibl. Lit., Linguistic Soc. Am., Swiss Am. Hist. Soc., Schweizerische Heraldische Gesellschaft, New Eng. Historic-Geneal. Soc. (chmn. com. heraldry), Phi Beta Kappa, Phi Epsilon Pi (asso.). Author: The Language of the New Testament, 1965; co-author: Teaching the Biblical Languages, 1967. Translator: Exegetical Method (by O. Kaiser and W. Kümmel). Home: 6 St John's Rd Cambridge MA 02138

GOETERS, HERMAN FRITZ PAT, architect; b. Bremen, Germany, Oct. 26, 1929 (parents U.S. citizens); s. Herman Fritz and Florence Elizabeth (Caroll) G.; student U. Toronto, 1948-50, Ill. Inst. Tech., 1952-53; B.S., B. Arch., U. Houston, 1955; M. Urban Studies, Yale, 1967; m. Georgia A. Hink, Sept. 4, 1954; children—Herman Fritz Pat, Frederick J., Carroll W., Edward S., B. Elizabeth, Burton W. With Donald Barthelme, 1955-57, Joseph Reynolds, 1957-58, Joseph Krakower, 1958-60; pvt. practice architecture, Houston, 1960-65, also faculty mem. U. Houston, 1960-65; spl. design cons. Perkins & Will Partnership, Washington, 1965; asso. prof. urban design U. Notre Dame, 1965-66; cons. Chgo. Com. Urban Opportunity, 1966; vis. critic dept. architecture Yale, 1966-67; cons. LKLP Community Action Agy., Whitesburg, Ky., 1967; asso. prof. archtl. design and city planning Yale, 1967—, also cons. Tech. Planning Assos., New Haven, 1968-69; cons. design review, cost analysis and gen. operations Mass. Housing Finance Agy., Boston, 1969-70, chief of operations, 1970—. Mem. Houston Council on Human Relations, 1962-65. Bd. dirs. Houston Contemporary Arts Mus., 1958—, chmn. bd., 1961; mem. Com. on social scis. Conn. Research Commn.; bd. dirs. Mountain Inst., Inc. Lexington, Ky. Mem. A.I.A., Boston Soc. Architects, Am. Inst. Planners (asso.). Contbr. articles profl. jours. Office: Old City Hall Boston MA 02108

GOETHALS, HENRY WEBB, journalist; b. Boston, Mar. 16, 1922; s. Thomas R. and Mary Addison (Webb) G.; B.A., Harvard, 1947; postgrad. Mexico City Coll., 1951- 53; m. Gabriela del Carmen Ramirez, Mar. 15, 1968. Corr. in Havanna, Cuba for McGraw Hill World News, ABC, also reporter Times of Havanna, 1956-60; corr. in Mexico and Central Am., Copley News Service, 1960-64, Washington, 1964-65; free-lance writer specializing Latin Am. affairs, 1965-68; Central Am. rep. Expansion mag., 1968—. Served to capt. AUS, 1943-46. Address: Edificio Biguria 12 Calle A 3-75 Zona 1 Guatemala City Guatemala

GOETHERT, BERNHARD HERMANN, educator, aero. engr.; b. Hannover, Germany, Oct. 20, 1907; s. Bernhard August and Elise (Rickmeyer) G.; B.S., Tech. U. Hannover, 1930; M.S., Tech. U. Danzig (Germany), 1934; Ph.D. cum laude, Tech. U. Berlin (Germany), 1938; m. Hertha Tod, Mar. 29, 1935; children—Hella (Mrs. D.A. Lacy), Winfried, Wolfhart, Reinhard. Came to U.S., 1945, naturalized, 1954. Research engr. DVL, German Research Inst. Aeros., Berlin, 1934-36, sci. staff engr., 1936-39, chief dept. high speed aerodynamics, 1939-45; cons. USAF Center Wright Field, Dayton, O., 1945-52; chief propulsion wind tunnel facility ARO, Inc., Tullahoma, Tenn., 1952-56, chief engine test facility, 1956-59, dir. engring., 1959-63, research v.p., chief scientist, 1963-64, dir., 1959-64; chief scientist USAF Systems Command, Andrews AFB, Washington, 1964-66; prof., dir. U. Tenn. Space Inst., Tullahoma, 1964—; prof. Tech. U., Aachen, Germany, 1961—. NASA research adv. com. fluid mechanics, 1963- 65; cons. Nat. Acad. of Sci., 1966-69, FAA, 1969- -; mem. panel fluid dynamics, adv. com. aeros. NATO, 1960-68. Recipient Spl. Appreciation plaque USAF Chief Staff, 1959; Meritorious Civilian Service award USAF, 1966. Fellow Am. Inst. Aeros. and Astronautics (chmn. tech. com. for ground testing 1960-62, mem. tech. activity com. 1967-69), N.Y. Acad. Sci. Lutheran. Author: Transonic Testing 1961; contbr. numerous articles in field. Home: 1703 Sycamore Circle Manchester TN 37355 Office: Dir U Tenn Space Inst Tullahoma TN 37388

GOETSCH, GERALD D., educator; b. Colby, Kan., Apr. 6, 1923; s. Herman G. and Myrtle (Murray) G.; D.V.M., Kan. State U., 1945; M.S., Purdue U., 1955, Ph.D., 1957; m. Barbara J. Garrett, May 27, 1947; children-Lynn L., Barbette S., Lisa Ann. With Ill. Dept. Agr., 1945; practice vet. medicine, Kankakee, Ill., 1945-47; asst. prof.. vet physiology U. Mo., 1948; asst. prof. Okla. State U., 1948-52; instr. Purdue U., 1952-57, asst. prof., 1958, prof., head dept. vet. physiology, 1959—. Served with AUS, 1943-45. Mem. Am. Vet. Med. Assn. (mem. commn. on pharmacy and vet. medicine 1969—), Am. Soc. Vet. Physiologists and Pharmacologists (prs. 1964), Ind. Vet. Med. Assn., Sigma Xi. Republican. Home: 328 Fernleaf Dr West Lafayette IN 47906

GOETT, EDWARD JOSEPH, indsl. exec.; b. Bronx, N.Y., Nov. 18, 1918; s. Harry and Mary (Falk) C.; grad. Fordham Prep. Sch., 1935; B.S., Fordham Coll., 1939; B.S., Columbia, 1942; m. Hazel Suess, Sept. 11, 1943; children—Barbara M., Edward Joseph, James M., Stephen J., Linda M., Mary C. Chem. engr., chem. exec., mem. bd. dirs. Chas. Pfizer & Co., Inc., Bklyn., 1942-54; dir. comml. devel. dept. Atlas Chem. Industries, Inc. (formerly Atlas Powder Co.), Wilmington, Del., 1954, v.p., 1954-57, dir., 1954—, sr. v.p., 1957, exec. v.p., 1958-66, pres., chief adminstrv. officer, 1966-68, pres., chief exec. officer, 1968—; dir. Bank of Del., Wilmington. Mem. U. Del. Research Found.; v.p., dir. United Fund and Council Del.; bd. dirs., mem. exec. com. Greater Wilmington Devel. Council. Mem. Am. Mgmt. Assn., A.I.M., Soc. Chem. Industry (Am. English groups), Am. Inst. Chem. Engrs., Am. Chem. Soc., Am. Inst. Chemists, A.A.A.S., Sigma Xi, Tau Beta Pi. Clubs: Wilmington, Wilmington Country (Wilmington); Pinnacle, Chemists (N.Y.C.). Home: 210 Country Club Dr Woodbrook Wilmington DE 19803 Office: Wilmington DE 19899

GOETT, HARRY JOSEPH, aero. engr.; b. N.Y.C., Nov. 14, 1910; B.S., Holy Cross Coll., 1931; Aero. Engr., N.Y.U., 1933. Chief full scale and flight research div. Ames Aero. Lab., NACA, Moffett Field, Cal., 1948-60; former dir. Goddard Space Flight Center, NASA, Greenbelt, Md., from 1960. Spl. work aircraft stability and control.*

GOETTE, JOHN, newspaper corr., author, lectr.; b. Phila., Dec. 3, 1896; s. Gustave and Irene (Jackson) G.; ed. Central High Sch., Law Sch., Temple U.; unmarried. Studying and writing in India and Peking, China, 1920; with China Famine Relief, A.R.C., 1921; corr. Assembly League of Nations, Geneva, 1926; mem. suite of Queen Marie of Rumania, Paris to N.Y., 1926; roving corr., U.S., Europe, Palestine, Egypt, Java, 1928-29; war corr. with Chinese Army, Manchuria-Russian crisis, 1929; with Japanese Army, Sino-Japanese Shanghai warfare, 1932, Manchukuo, 1932; with Chinese Army, Sino-Japanese fighting inside Great Wall, 1933; chief China corr. Internat. News Service, 1923-1941; corr. London Daily Express, 1927-39; with Japanese Army, N. China campaign, 1937-41; Japanese prisoner of war, Dec. 1941-June 1942, repatriated aboard S.S. Gripsholm, 1942; corr., Japan, Korea, China, Manchuria, 1946, Europe, 1951, 56, 60, 62-65, 66, Australia, 1954, Far East, 1959, S.Am., 1961; mem. editorial staff King Features Syndicate, 1949—. Testified for U.S. War Dept. at trial of Japanese war criminals, Tokyo, 1946. With USNR 1917-19; France and England, 1918-19. Recipient Chinese decoration, Chiao Ho. Mem. Am. Oriental Soc., Am. Platform Guild, Sigma Delta Chi. Clubs: Peking, Peking Golf; National Press; Overseas Press, Shanghai Tiffin; The Banshees. Specialist in Chinese jade. Author: Jade Lore, 1936; Japan Fights for Asia, 1943, London edit., 1945. Contbr. Am. periodicals. Book reviewer, radio commentator and lectr.; also war speaker for U.S. Treasury Dept. and United China Relief. Address: Edifico Maritimo Malaga Spain

GOETTELMANN, PAUL AUGUSTE, architect, educator; b. Bellevue, Ky., May 5, 1907; s. Fernand Camille and Germaine Helene (Schirr) G.; B.S. in Arch., Cath. U. Am., 1929, M.A. in Arch., 1930, Arch.D., 1933; diploma Beaux Arts Inst. Design, 1930; m. Emma Helene Laufenberg, June 20, 1933; children—Michael, Paula, Christine (Mrs. Franklin Calkins). Partner Locraft & Asso., 1954-64, Goettelmann & Xepapas, 1964— (both Washington); instr. Cath. U. Am., Washington, 1935-40, asst. prof., 1940-49, asso. prof., 1949-59, prof., 1959—, chmn. dept. arch., 1959-65, asso. dean, chmn. dept. arch., 1965-70, asso. dean, chmn. dept. arch. and planning, 1970—. Chmn. Urban Renewal Panel, Alexandria, Va., 1963-66; mem. archtl. cons. panel D.C. Hwy. Commn., 1964-66; pres. Bd. Registrars and Examiners for Architects, Washington, 1962-67; mem. Commn. Sacred Art, Archdiocese Washington, 1966—, D.C. Bldg. Code Adv. Com., 1970—. Trustee Fontainbleau (France) Sch. Fine Arts. Served to lt., USNR, World War II. Recipient Bene Merenti medal Pope Paul VI, 1964; Excellence in Design award Washington Bd. Trade, 1965, 66; award Cath. U. Am. Alumni Assn., 1966; Senator's Alumni award Cath. U. Am., 1967; Meritorious Pub. Service award D.C., 1967. Fellow A.I.A. (past pres. Washington Met. chpt.); mem. Soc. Archtl. Historians, Assn. Collegiate Schs. Architecture, Nat. Council Arch. Registration Bds. Kiwanian. Clubs: Cosmos (Washington). Prin. works include Our Lady Good Counsel Ch., Vienna, Va., 1971; Holy Spirit Ch., Forestville, Md., 1970; St. Catherine Greek Orthodox Ch., Northern, Va., 1969; Our Lady Sorrows, Takoma Park, Md., 1964; Chapel, Marine Corps, Quantico, Va., 1941, St. Anthony's Ch., 1940, St. Luke's Ch., 1960, Cath. U. Am. Hartke Theatre Social Center, 1970, Washington Permanent Bldg. and Loan Assn., 1960, Enterprise Fed. Bldg. and Loan Sch. of Linguistics, Georgetown U., 1958, Ambassador McClintock residence, 1968 (all Washington). Home: 201 Vierling Dr Silver Spring MD 20409 Office: Goettelmann & Xepapas 3612 12th St NE Washington DC 20017

GOETTING, M.L., educator; B.A., Rio Grande Coll.; M.A., Ph.D., Ohio State U. Prof. edn. Baylor U., Waco, Tex., also dean Sch. Edn. Office: Sch Edn Baylor U Waco TX 76706

GOETZ, BILLY EARL, educator; b. Chgo., Jan. 17, 1904; s. Albert and Cora (Maier) G.; Ph.B., U. Chgo., 1924, Ph.D., 1949; student Cornell U., 1926-28; m. Isabelle Reed, Sept. 1, 1928; children—Elizabeth C. (Mrs. Owen Hedden), Margaret L. (Mrs. Thomas Atkinson), Carolyn (Mrs. Richard Lindberg). Instr., U. Chgo., 1928-31, 36-39, U. Buffalo, 1931-32, Ill. Inst. Tech., Chgo., 1935-42; asst. prof. Am. U., 1942-43; sr. asso. Sessions Engring. Co., Chgo., 1935-45, 53-54; prof. bus. adminstrn. Antioch Coll., 1945- 53; prof. mgmt. Mass. Inst. Tech., 1954-69, emeritus prof. mgmt., 1969—; vis. prof. accounting Fla. Atlantic U., 1969—. Mem. Acad. Mgmt. (sec.-treas. 1953-56, pres. 1957-58), Soc. Advancement Mgmt. (pres. Chgo. chpt. 1940-42, Dayton (O.) chpt. 1951-52), Am. Soc. Engring. Edn. (chmn. engring. economy div. 1967-68). Author: Management

Planning and Control, 1949; Quantitative Methods, 1965; (with others) Accounting in Action, 1960. Home: 640 NE Golden Harbor Dr Boca Raton, FL 33432.

GOETZ, CHARLES ALBERT, educator, chemist; b. Lockwood, Mo., Jan. 7, 1908; s. Jacob George and Mary Elizabeth (Ripper) Getz; student U. Wis., 1926-31; B.S., U. Ill., 1932, M.S., 1934, Ph.D., 1938; m. Sidonia Helen Heck, Feb. 24, 1934; children—Charles Albert, Roger Melvin. Asst. agronomy U. Ill., 1933-34, teaching asst. chemistry, fellow, 1934-38; chief chemist Cardox Corp., Chgo., 1938-39, dir. research, 1939-43, v.p. charge research and devel., 1943-46; dir. engring. devel. Brunswick-Balke- Collander Co., 1947-48; mem. faculty Ia. State U., 1948—, prof., head chemistry dept., chief chem. div. Inst. Atomic Research and Ames Lab. AEC, 1950-65, prof. chemistry and sr. chemist Inst. Atomic Research and Ames Lab., 1965—. Chmn. bd., Ia. dist. West, Luth. Ch.- Mo. Synod, 1957-63, mem. commn. theology and ch. relations, 1962-67. Mem. Am. Chem. Soc., Electrochem. Soc. Patentee in field; inventor aerosol process. Home: 822 Ash Av Ames IA 50010

GOETZ, JAMES B., television exec.; b. Freeport, Ill., May 28, 1936; s. Thomas and Marian (Isley) G.; student U. Wis.; grad. Mid-Western Broadcasting Sch.; m. Ruth Elbert, June 16; children—James Jeffrey, Gregory Thomas. Successively radio announcer stas. WOHP, Bellafountaine, O., WSDR, Sterling, Ill., WDLB, Marshfield, Wis.; founder, pres. GEM Radio Stas., 1961, operating KAGE, Winona, Minn., 1961-71; pres. Gen. Television, Inc., Mpls., 1971—. Lt. gov. Minn., 1967-71; vice chmn. Nat. Conf. Lt. Govs., 1967-69. Republican party chmn. Winona County, then 1st Congl. dist. Chmn. bd. dirs. Paul Watkins Meml. Home, Winona. Served with AUS, 1958-59, 61-62. Named Young Man of Year, Winona C. of C., 1966; One of Ten Outstanding Young Men of Minn., 1966, of U.S., 1970. Mem. Nat. Assn. Broadcasters, Minn. (v.p. 1967), Daytime broadcasters' assns., Winona C. of C. Methodist. Mason, Lion. Home: Villa Seeblick Lakeland Shores MN 55043 Office: 17 Washington Av N Minneapolis MN 55401

GOETZ, JOHN FERDINAND, lawyer, chem. co. exec.; b. De Tour, Mich., Oct. 16, 1909; s. John Francis and Ann (McDonald) G.; LL.B., U. Detroit, 1933; m. Dolores Kinney, June 18, 1938 (dec.); children—Mary Ann, John Francis, Janet Elizabeth; m. 2d, Joan V. Glaza, June 30, 1960; 1 son, Michael Vincent. Admitted to Mich. bar, 1933, since practiced in Detroit; mem. Goetz & Goetz & Foley. Asst. sec. Reichhold Chemicals Inc., Detroit, 1948-55, became sec., 1955, dir., vice chmn. bd., 1959—; chmn. bd. Modiglass Fibers, Inc., 1960—; sec., dir. Golf Mart, Inc., Addis Co., Fork Truck Service, Inc., Equipco Co. Served to lt. USNR, 1944-46. Mem. Am., Mich., Detroit bar assns. K.C. Clubs: Detroit Athletic, Detroit Golf. Home: 17535 Oak St Detroit MI 48218 Office: Penobscott Bldg Detroit MI 48226

GOETZ, JOHN RICHARD, lawyer; b. Fond du Lac, Wis., Nov. 11, 1918; s. John Charles and Laura (Ruedebusch) G.; student Carleton Coll., 1935-37; B.A., U. Cal. at Berkeley, 1939; LL.B., Harvard, 1942; m. Margaret Youngquist, Nov. 21, 1942; children—John Charles, William Robertson. Admitted to Minn. bar, 1946; partner firm Lindquist & Vennum, and predecessors, Mpls., 1958-70. Bd. dirs. Minn. Civil Liberties Union; pres., chmn. bd. Guthrie Theatre Found., 1968-70. Served with AUS, 1942-45. Mem. Am., Minn. bar assns., Chi Psi. Club: Minneapolis. Home: 2028 Cedar Lake Blvd Minneapolis MN 55416

GOETZ, MAURUS T., mfg. co. exec. Pres., Teletype Corp. Office: 5555 Touhy Av Skokie IL 60076*

GOETZ, NORMAN S., lawyer; b. N.Y.C., Mar. 7, 1887; s. Samuel and Julia (Marx) G.; A.B. Columbia, 1906, LL.B., 1909; m. Mildred Blout, Feb. 12, 1925 (dec. 1953); m. 2d, Beatrice J. Lane, Jan. 12, 1956. Partner, Leventritt, Riegelman, Carns & Goetz, 1912-24, Proskauer, Rose, Goetz & Mendelsohn and predecessor firms, N.Y.C., 1925—. Dir. Greater N.Y. Fund, 1942-64, v.p., 1945-48, pres., 1956-59, chmn. bd., 1950-51, 55-56; pres. Fedn. Jewish Philanthropies N.Y., 1945-48, chmn. bd., 1961-63, trustee-at-large, 1940-48, hon. trustee, 1948—, chmn. lawyers div., 1937-38, chmn citywide campaign, 1942-43, chmn. com. communal planning, 1951-57, former chmn. legacy com.; bd. dirs. Hosp. Council Greater N.Y., 1944-64, pres., 1948-55; trustee State U. N.Y., 1948-58, chmn. com. on med. edn., 1952-57; bd. dirs., United Hosp. Fund, 1948-57, mem.- at-large, 1961-64; bd. dirs. N.Y. Adult Edn. Council, 1941-65, Hillside Hosp., 1941-48; former bd. dirs. Welfare Council City N.Y., Council Jewish Fedn. and Welfare Funds; former mem. exec., adminstrv. coms. Am. Jewish Com. Served to capt., non-flying AS, 1917-19. Mem. Assn. Bar City N.Y. (v.p. 1950-52, exec. com. 1943-47), N.Y. County Lawyers Assn. (past chmn. bankruptcy com.), Internat., Am., N.Y. bar assns. Democrat. Jewish religion. Club: Ocean Beach. Home: 480 Park Av New York City NY 10022 Office: 300 Park Av New York City NY 10022

GOETZ, RICHARD JOSEPH, lawyer; b. Tiffin, O., Feb. 21, 1933; s. Joseph Edward and Eulalie C. (Busam) G.; B.S. magna cum laude, John Carroll U., Cleve., 1955; postgrad. U. Detroit, 1955; LL.B., Cleve.-Marshall Sch. Law, 1961; m. Rhoda Ann Sullivan, Sept. 5, 1955; children—Timothy R., Philip C., Brian F., Andrea Marie. Credit analyst Union Commerce Bank, Cleve., 1956-61; admitted to Ohio bar, 1961; practice in Findlay, 1962—; mem. firm Drake, Phillips, Goetz & Kuenzli, 1962—, partner, 1964—; vis. instr. bus. law Findlay Coll., 1970. Pres. Findlay Investors, Ltd. Mem. Regional Planning Commn., 1968—, Bd. Tax Appeals Findlay, 1968—; pres. Sch. for Physically Handicapped Bd. Mem. Hancock County Republican Exec. Com., 1970—. Bd. dirs. A.R.C.; trustee Findlay Teen Center, Downtown Findlay Assos. Served to 1st lt. Transp. Corps, AUS, 1955-56. Recipient Freedoms Found. award, John Carroll U., 1955. Mem. Am., Ohio, Findlay, Northwestern (pres.) bar assns., Findlay Jr. C. of C. (legal counsel, sec.). Roman Catholic. Elk, Kiwanian. Contbr. articles to law jours. Home: 211 Glendale Av Findlay OH 45840 Office: Niles Bldg Findlay OH 45840

GOETZ, ROBERT LOUIS, architect; b. Berkeley, Cal., Nov. 17, 1925; s. Louis Albere and Adrienne Louise (Guittard) G.; A.B., U. Cal., 1949; m. Patricia Ann Way, Feb. 7, 1968; children—Paul Albere, Peter Greenwood, Robert Stephen. Pvt. archtl. practice, Oakland, Cal., 1952-55, 62-70; with Goetz & Hansen, Oakland, 1955-62; pres. Goetz, Hallenbeck & Goetze, Inc., Oakland, 1970—; pres. Robert Goetz, Inc. (San Francisco). Mem. Mayor's Com. on Rapid Transit, Oakland, 1968-70. Co-chmn. Dems for Finch Com., Oakland, 1964. Served as aviation cadet, 1943-45. Recipient numerous design awards. Mem. A.I.A. (chmn. Oakland chpt. 1967-68), Phi Gamma Delta. Clubs: Silverado Country, Orinda Country, Belvedere Tennis (Oakland). Home: 93 West Shore Rd Belvedere CA 94920 Office: 5758 Broadway Oakland CA 94618 also Pier 33 North San Francisco CA 94111

GOETZE, ALBERT F., Sr., business exec. Pres., Albert F. Goetze, Inc., Balt. Office: 2401 Sinclair Lane Baltimore MD 21213*

GOETZE, ALBRECHT, educator; b. Leipzig, Germany, Jan. 11, 1897; s. Rudolf and Elsa (Roemmler) G.; Ph.D., Heidelberg, 1920; A.M. (hon.). Yale, 1936; m. Frida Schirbel, Nov. 11, 1922; children—Dieter, Marianne (Mrs. Andrew Pfeiffer), Gabriele. Came to U.S. 1934, naturalized 1940. Docent, Heidelberg, 1923-30; prof. Marburg, 1930-33, dismissed by Hitler govt., 1933; vis. prof., Yale, 1934-46, William M. Laffan prof. Assyriology, 1936-56, Sterling prof., 1956-65, prof. emeritus, 1965—, chmn. dept. Near East langs., 1958-66; mem. Inst. for Comparative Research in Human Culture, Oslo, Norway; dir. Am. Sch. for Oriental Research, Baghdad, 1948-56. Mem. Am. Oriental Soc., Am. Schs. of Oriental Research, Linguistic Soc. of Am., Archaeol. Inst. Am., Soc. Bibl. Lit., Am. Philos. Soc. (life), Acad. des Inscriptions et Belles Lettres (corr.), Royal Danish Acad. (fgn.), Société Asiatique de Paris (hon. life), Inst. for Comparative Research in Human Culture (life), German Archaeol. Inst. (life). Author books including: Old Babylonian Omen Texts, 1947; Laws of Eshunna, 1956; Kulturegeschichte Kleinasiens, 2d edit., 1958. Contbr. articles to profl. jours. Home: 2 Maplewood Rd New Haven CT 06515 ☆

GOETZINGER, CHARLES STEPHEN, Jr., educator; b. Hammond, Ind., June 9, 1926; s. Charles Stephen and Violet (Coash) G.; B.S., Kent State U., 1950; M.S., Purdue U., 1952, Ph.D., 1954; divorced; children—Sarah, Jane, Anne. Teaching asst. Purdue U., 1950-54; asst. prof. speech, dir. forensics Kan. State U., 1954-59; asso. prof., dir. Bur. Communication Research, Inst. Behavioral Sci., U. Colo., 1959-64; prof. speech, Ore. State U., 1964-68; prof. speech, chmn. dept. speech communication State U. N.Y. at Geneseo, 1968—; cons., speaker in field, 1958—. Served with AUS, 1944-46. Mem. Am. Speech Assn., Am. Forensic Assn. (exec. council 1955-59), A.A.A.S., Internat. Communication Assn., Delta Sigma Rho, Tau Kappa Alpha, Pi Kappa Delta, Pi Delta Kappa. Author numerous articles in field. Home: PO Box 166 Perry NY 14530 Office: State Univ New York Geneseo NY 14454

GOETZMANN, WILLIAM HARRY, educator, author; b. Washington, July 20, 1930; s. Harry William and Viola (Nelson) G. B.A., Yale, 1952, Ph.D. in Am. Studies, 1957; LL.D., (hon.), St. Edward's U., Austin, Tex., 1967; m. Mewes Mary Mueller, Aug. 29, 1953; children—Will N., Anne S., Stephen R. From asst. in instrn. to asso. prof. Yale, 1955-64; mem. faculty U. Tex., 1964—, Stiles prof. Am. studies, prof. history, dir. Am. studies, 1967—, chmn. dept. history, 1968-69; Fulbright vis. lectr. Cambridge (Eng.) U., 1967-68; cons. in field. Vice pres. Great Games, Inc. Mem. president's adv. council St. Edwards U., 1967-69; mem. bd. Tex. Hist. Bldgs. Survey Commn.; editorial adviser Western Am. series Yale U. Press. Recipient John Addison Porter prize Yale, 1957; Joseph Pulitzer award history, 1967; Piper Teaching award, 1968; Golden Plate award Am. Acad. Achievement, 1968; Theta Sigma Phi award, 1967; Francis Parkman award, 1967; award Tex. Inst. Letters, 1967; Buffalo award N.Y. Westerners, 1960; asso. fellow Jonathan Edwards Coll., Yale. Fellow Royal Geog. Soc.; mem. Am. Hist. Assn., Orgn. Am. Historians, Soc. Am. Historians, Am. Studies Assn., N.Y. Westerners, Western History Assn., Tex. Inst. Letters, Tex. Hist. Assn., Brit. Am. Studies Assn., Soc. History of Discoveries, Collectors Inst., Phi Beta Kappa. Roman Cath. Club: Headliners (Austin). Author: Army Exploration in the American West, 1803- 1863, 1959; Exploration and Empire, 1966; When the Eagle Screamed; The Romantic Horizon in American Diplomacy, 1800-1865, 1966. Co-author: A Guide to Computer-Assisted Historical Research in American Education, 1970. Home: 4802 Timberline Dr Austin TX 78746

GOEWEY, GORDON IRA, univ. dean; b. Troy, N.Y., June 25, 1924; s. Ira A. and Flossie (Warger) G.; B.Mus., Boston U., 1948, Mus.A.D., 1969; M.A. in Teaching, Harvard, 1953; m. Marie Matteson Huening, May 30, 1968; children by previous marriage—Lynne Dee, Todd Ira. Mem. faculty State U. Coll. Arts and Sci., Geneseo, N.Y., 1949—, prof. music, 1963—, chmn. dept., 1952-69, dean grad. studies, 1969—, dir. summer session, 1969-71, chmn. faculty, 1963-64. Served with AUS, 1943-44. Mem. Music Educators Nat. Conf., N.Y. State Sch. Music Assn., Faculty Assn. State U. N.Y. (exec. com. 1964-67), Am. Assn. for Higher Edn., Am. Assn. U. Adminstrs., Phi Mu Alpha. Rotarian. Author: (with John Kucaba) Understanding Musical Form, 1962. Home: 18 Seminole Av Geneseo NY 14454

GOFF, ABE MCGREGOR, lawyer; b. Colfax, Wash., Dec. 21, 1899; s. Herbert William and Mary (Dorsey) G.; LL.B., U. Ida., 1924; m. Florence Richardson, Aug. 24, 1927; children—Timothy R., Annie McGregor. Admitted to Ida. bar 1924; since practiced in that state; pros. atty., Latah Co., Ida., 1926-34; solicitor, later gen. counsel Post Office Dept., 1954-58; mem. ICC, Washington, 1958-67, chmn., 1964. Mem. Ida. Bar Commn., 1938-41, Mem. Ida. Senate, 1940-42; mem. 80th U.S. Congress, 1st Dist. Ida.; candidate Republican nomination U.S. Senator, 1950; mem. Rep. steering com. Bd. dirs. Fed. Bar Found. Served as pvt. U.S. Army, World War I; from maj. to col., Judge Adv. Gen.'s Dept., AUS 1941-46. Decorated Legion of Merit. Mem. Fed., Ida. (pres. 1940-41), Am. (ho. dels. 1941) bar assns., Am. Soc. Internat. Law, Mil. Order Carabao, Beta Theta Pi, Scabbard and Blade. Episcopalian. Mason. Address: 503 E C St Moscow ID 83843

GOFF, CHARLES WEER, orthopedic surgeon; b. Rock Island, Ill., June 4, 1897; s. Edward L. and Cora (Weer) G.; student Augustana Coll., 1916; B.S., U. Ill., 1920, M.D., 1923; spl. orthopedic student European clinics, 1937-39; student anthropology Columbia, 1945-46, Yale, 1946-49, Harvard, 1949-51; m. Fern Harper, 1921; 1 son, Michael Harper; m. 2d, Mary Magdalen Lachkareff, Sept. 4, 1934; 1 stepson, George deHahn. Intern, Kings County Hosp., Bklyn., 1923-26; with traumatic clinic, South Manchester, 1926-28; surgeon, Hartford, Conn., 1928-30; asst. orthopedic surgeon St. Francis Hosp., Hartford, 1930-42, asso., 1943-48, vis., 1949-55, cons., 1956—; asst. orthopedic surgeon Newington (Conn.) Home and Hosp. for Crippled Children, 1931-42, attending orthopedic surgeon, 1943-63, cons., 1963—, chmn. med. staff, 1948-50; asst. clin. prof. orthopedic surgery Yale, 1948-55, asso. orthopedic surgeon, lectr. anatomy, 1956-65, emeritus, 1965—; anthropologist, adj. prof. anthropology U. Hartford, 1964—; cons. orthopedic surgeon div. crippled children State Conn., 1949-55, Bristol, Backus Meml., Manchester Meml., Day-Kimball, Bradley Meml. hosps.; orthopedic surgeon Nat. Found. Infantile Paralysis, Hartford; attending orthopedic surgeon Vets. Home and Hosp., 1950-55. Co- chmn. Rehab. Work Shop, 1948-58. Served as 2d lt. F.A., U.S. Army, 1917-19, pvt. 101st Cav., N.Y. N.G., 1923-25, capt. Conn. N.G., 1927-33. Recipient Kappa Delta award for orthopedic research, 1955. Diplomate Am. Bd. Orthopedic Surgery. Fellow A.C.S. (chmn. regional com. on trauma 1949-59, Med. Records award 1936), A.A.A.S., Am. Assn. Phys. Anthropology, Am. Assn. Anthropology, Am. Assn. Med. Writers, Am. Acad. Orthopedic Surgery (lectr.); mem. Assn. Bone and Joint Surgeons, Boston Orthopedic Club, Conn. Archeol. Soc. (past pres.), A.M.A., Hartford Med. Soc. (past sec.), Orthopedic Guild, Orthopaedic Research Soc., Soc. Internat. Surgery and Orthopaedics, Surg. and Orthopedic Soc. Guatemala, Archeol. Inst. Am. (chpt. pres.), Delta Kappa Epsilon, Nu Sigma Nu. Club: Golf (Hartford). Author: Legg-Calve-Perthes Syndrome, 1954; (with Phelps, Kiphuth) Diagnosis and Treatment Postural Defects, rev. edit., 1956; The Ruins of Zaculeu, Guatemala, 1954; Surgical Treatment of Unequal Extremities, 1960; Traumatic Cervical Syndrome and Whiplash, 1964. Asso. editor Clinical Orthopedics. Contbr. articles to profl. jours. Home: 1075 N Main St West Hartford CT 06109

GOFF, JOHN ALONZO, educator; b. Colorado City, Oct. 19, 1899; s. Joseph Randolph and Anna Bell (Cadwell) G.; student Colo. Agrl. Coll., 1917-19; B.S. in Mech. Engring., U. Ill., 1921, M.S., 1924, Ph.D., 1927; m. Virginia Brands Hanawalt, Jan. 27, 1933; children—John Randolph, Susan Virginia. Asst. mech. engring. U. Ill., 1921-23, instr., 1923-25, asso., 1925-27, asso. prof., 1930-35, prof. thermodynamics, 1935-38; geophysicist Sun Oil Co., Dallas, 1927-28; engr. Linde Air Products Co., N.Y.C., 1928-29; research engr. Westinghouse Research Labs., 1929-30; dean Towne Sci. Sch., dir. mech. engring., 1938-50; prof. mech. engring. U. Pa., 1950-70, prof. emeritus, 1970—. Cons. thermodynamics Westinghouse Electric & Mfg. Co., 1930-40, Div. 6, OSRD, 1942-44; dir. U. Pa. Thermodynamics Research Lab., 1945-51; cons. thermodynamics mech. systems sect. U.S. Nat. Bur. Standards, 1961-66. Fellow Am. Soc. M.E. (chmn. bd. honors 1964-65); mem. Am. Math. Soc., Tau Beta Pi, Gamma Alpha. Clubs: Horse-Shoe Trail (trails chmn. 1966—) University of Pennsylvana Faculty (incorporator, founding pres. 1958-1961). Author: Notes on Thermodynamics, 4th edit. 1946. Contbr. articles, revs. to profl. jours. Home: 623 Righters Mill Rd Narberth PA 19072 Office: U of Pa Philadelphia PA 19104

GOFF, ROBERT BURNSIDE, food co. exec.; b. Arcadia, La., Aug. 8, 1924; s. Carl and Ruth (Capers) G.; B.S., Rice U., 1947; m. Mary Jane Ellis, June 14, 1947; children—Gayle M., Robert B. Engr. Tex. Pipe Line Co., Tulsa, 1947-48; v.p., dir. Comet Rice Mills, Inc., Houston, 1948-58; sr. v.p. Riviana Foods, Inc., Houston, 1958—. Served to lt. (j.g.), USNR, 1942-46. Mem. Rice Council Market Devel. (dir.), Exec. Assos. Presbyn. Clubs: Houston Racquet, River Oaks Country (Houston). Home: 10829 Roaring Brook Houston TX 77024 Office: PO Box 2636 Houston TX 77001

GOFFIN, MARCEL, hotel exec.; b. Pont-a-Celles, Belgium, Apr. 1, 1907; s. Fernard and Flore (Vercauter) G.; grad. Hotel Sch., Grenoble, France, 1925; m. Marie Therese Peters, May 26, 1930; 1 dau., Jacqueline (Mrs. P. Dienst). With Metropole Hotel, Brussels, Belgium, 1928—, gen. mgr., 1957—. Served with Belgium Army, 1940. Decorated chevalier Order of Leopold II, chevalier Order de la Couronne (Belgium). Home: 58a av Leopold Rixensart Belgium Office: Hotel Metropole 31 pl de Brouckere Brussels Belgium

GOFFIO, FRANK LOUIS, relief agy. exec.; b. Bklyn., Jan. 22, 1916; s. Joseph Louis and Sarah Agnes (Vaccaccio) G.; LL.D., Kyung Hee U., Seoul, Korea; hon. LL.D., St. Michael's Coll., Winooski, Vt.; m. Evelyn M. Wilburger, Feb. 16, 1941; 1 dau., Christine Evelyn. With Abraham & Straus, retail mcht., Bklyn., 1935-47, packing mgr., 1945-47; with Coop. Am. Relief Everywhere, Inc., N.Y.C., 1947—, exec. dir., 1962—. Decorated Imperial Order of Merit of Red Lion and Sun Soc. (Iran); Cultural Order of Merit (Korea); Order of Commendatore (Italy); Golden medal for merit Yugoslav Red Cross; Order of Republic (Tunisia); Order of Quetzal (Guatemala); Sepas medal 1st class (Iran); Officers' Cross of Polish People's Republic. Home: 3 Sprain Valley Rd Scarsdale NY 10583 Office: CARE Inc 660 1st Av New York City NY 10016

GOFFMAN, ERVING, educator, sociologist; b. Manville, Alta., Can., June 11, 1922; A.B., U. Toronto (Ont., Can.) 1945; M.A., U. Chgo., 1949, Ph.D., 1953; m. Angelica Schuyler Choate, 1952 (dec. 1964); 1 son, Thomas Edward. Came to U.S., 1945. Mem. Shetland field research U. Edinburgh (Scotland), 1949-51; vis. scientist Nat. Inst. Mental Health, 1954-57; asst. prof. dept. sociology U. Cal. at Berkeley, 1958-59, asso. prof., 1959-62, prof., 1962-68; Benjamin Franklin prof. anthropology and sociology U. Pa., Phila., 1968—. Bd. dirs. Am. Assn. Abolition Involuntary Mental Hospitalization. Recipient MacIver award, 1961. Fellow Am. Acad. Arts and Scis. Author: Presentation of Self in Everyday Life, 1956; Encounters, 1961; Asylums, 1961; Behavior in Public Places, 1963; Stigma, 1964; Interaction Ritual, 1967; Strategic Interaction, 1969. Home: 259 S Fourth St Philadelphia PA 19106

GOFMAN, JOHN WILLIAM, research biophysicist; b. Cleve., Sept. 21, 1918; s. David and Sarah (Kaplan) G.; A.B., Oberlin Coll., 1939; Ph.D., U. Cal., 1943, M.D., 1946; m. Helen Fahl, Aug. 10, 1940; 1 son, John David. Nuclear chemistry research Manhattan Project, Berkeley, 1940-44, research large molecular phys. chemistry, especially ultracentrifugation of lipoproteins, U. Cal. Donner Lab., 1947—; intern Cal. U. Hosp., San Francisco, 1946-47; asso. prof. med. physics U. Cal., 1947, now prof. med. physics, dir. biomed. research div., asso. dir. Lawrence Radiation Lab., Livermore, 1963-69. Discoverer (with Glenn Seaborg) of Uranium 233, 1941; presence of certain blood lipoproteins asso. with form arteriosclerosis known as atherosclerosis, a major factor in coronary artery disease; research on chromosomes and cancer, discovery specific chromosome (E-16) asso. with human cancer, extensive research on radiation standards and biol. effects of radiation. Mem. Phi Beta Kappa, Sigma Xi. Author: (with A.V. Nichols and V. Dobbin) Dietary Prevention and Treatment of Heart Disease; What We Do Know About Heart Attacks; Coronary Heart Disease; (with Arthur Tamplin) Population Control Through Nuclear Pollution. Home: 1045 Clayton St San Francisco CA 94117

GOFORTH, FOY NELSON, banker; b. Rocky Mount, N.C., Jan. 18, 1921; s. Harrison Foy and Bertie May (Barnes) G.; A.B. in Phys. Sci., Atlantic Christian Coll., 1941; B.S. in Agronomy, Va. Poly. Inst., 1950, M.S. in Agronomy, 1951; postgrad. Ia. State U., 1951, Rutgers-State U. N.J., Stonier Grad. Sch. Banking, 1959-61; m. Joyce Nadine Parker, June 15, 1946; children—Foy Nelson, John Parker. With So. Dairies, Wilson, N.C., 1941-42, 46-47, T.W. Wood Seed Co., Richmond, Va., 1947-48; mem. staff Br. Banking & Trust Co., Wilson, 1952—, sr. v.p. charge credit div., 1968—. Active Boy Scouts Am.; chmn. A.R.C., Wilson, 1968. Mem. Wilson Civic Council, 1970—. Trustee Coll. Found., Inc. Served with USNR, 1942-46. Mem. Am. Inst. Banking, Assn. Agrl. Bankers (pres. 1963), N.C. Bankers Assn., Atlantic Christian Coll. Alumni Assn. (past pres.), Robert Morris Assos. (1st v.p. Carolina-Va. chpt.), Sales and Marketing Execs. (pres. 1965), N.C. Farm Mgrs. and Rural Appraisers, Newcomen Soc., Wilson, Wilson Jr. chambers commerce, Am. Legion, 40 and 8, Phi Sigma, Alpha Zeta. Baptist (deacon). Kiwanian (pres. Wilson 1970). Home: 903 W Nash St Wilson NC 27893 Office: Br Banking & Trust Co 223 W Nash St Wilson NC 27893

GOGERTY, HENRY L., architect; b. Zearing, Ia., Jan. 30, 1894; student Dubuque Coll., 1912- 13; B.Arch., U. Ill., 1917; spl. certificate U. So. Cal. Designer, draftsman various archtl., engring. firms, Tex., Cal., 1918-23; pvt. practice H.L. Gogerty, Los Angeles, 1924—; pres. H.L. Gogerty & Assos., architects-engrs., 1964—; prin. works include Susan Dorsey High Sch., Los Angeles, 1939, Naval Ordnance Test Sta., Invokern, 1944, Gardena High Sch., Antelope Valley Coll., Lancaster, 1962, South Hills High Sch., Covina, Cal., 1963. Chmn. bldg. commn. St. Annes Found., 1954-55. Registered architect, Cal. Fellow A.I.A.; mem. Am. Legion. Rotarian. Home: 5025 Maplewood Av Hollywood CA 90004

GOGGIN, MARGARET KNOX, (Mrs. John Mann Goggin), univ. dean, librarian; b. Nyack, N.Y., Feb. 24, 1919; d. Henry Julian and Eleanor (Green) Knox; A.B., Maryville Coll., 1940; B.S., Peabody Coll., 1942; M.S., U. Ill., 1948, Ph.D., 1957; m. John Mann Goggin, Nov. 22, 1962. Tchr., librarian Flintville (Tenn.) High Sch., 1940-42; reference asst. Joint U. Library, Nashville, 1942-43, acting reference librarian, 1943-45; vis. instr. Peabody Library Sch., Nashville, 1943-45; readers adviser Youngstown (O.) Pub. Library, 1945-46; bibliographer, reference librarian Office Tech. Services, Dept. Commerce, Washington, 1946-47; reference asst. U. Ill., 1948-49; asst. to dir. U. Fla. Libraries, asst. prof. library sci., 1949-50, head dept. reference and bibliography, asso. prof. library sci., 1950-62, asst. dir. Readers Services, asso. prof. library sci., 1965-66, asst. dir. libraries, prof. library sci., 1966, acting dir. libraries, 1967-68; vis. lectr. U. Okla. Library Sch., summer 1959; vis. lectr. Emory U. Sch. Librarianship, 1965; dean Grad. Sch. Librarianship, U. Denver, 1968—; cons. U.S. Office Edn. div. Library Programs, 1968-69. Haitian research, Haiti and Paris on Rockefeller Found. grants, 1958, 61-62. Mem. Am. (past div. pres.), Colo., Mountain Plains, Southeastern library assns., Am. Soc. for Information Sci., Nat. League Am. Pen Women, Delta Kappa Gamma, Beta Phi Mu (past dir.). Club: Altrusa (Denver). Home: 6151 S Kearney St Englewood CO 80110 Office: U Denver Grad Sch Librarianship Denver CO 80210

GOGGIN, WILLIAM CHARLES, chem. co. exec.; b. Alma, Mich., Aug. 26, 1911; s. Charles H. and Saran (Gee) G.; B.A., Alma Coll., 1933, D.Sc. (hon), 1954; B.S. in Elec. Engring., U. Mich., 1935, M.S., 1936; postgrad. Harvard; m. Flora Ahern, Aug. 5, 1939; children—Mary Lou (Mrs. Donald Oliver), Patrick Charles. Mgr. plastics dept. Dow Chem. Co., 1936-43, mgr. plastics, organizer plastics tech. service, 1943-59, gen. mgr. plastics dept., 1959-67; pres., dir. Dow Corning Corp., Midland, Mich., 1967—, chmn., 1971—, also mem. exec. com.; dir. First Nat. Bank & Trust Co., Midland, Midland Hosp. Assos.; tech. cons. O.M. Corps, Germany, 1945. Trustee Alma Coll. Mem. Mfg. Chemists Assn., Synthetic Organic Chemists Mfg. Assn. Author: (with others) German Plastics Practice, 1946. Home: 1204 Holyrood St Midland MI 48640 Office: Dow Corning Corp Midland MI 48640

GOGLIA, GENNARO LOUIS, educator; b. Hoboken, N.J., Jan. 15, 1921; s. Fred Goglia and Rose (Coppola) G.; B.S., U. Ill., 1942; M.S., Ohio State U., 1950; Ph.D., U. Mich., 1959; m. Lieselotte Pause, Oct. 4, 1942; children—Diann, Linda. Jr. engr. Rochester (N.Y.) Ordnance Dist., 1942- 44; devel. engr. Gen. Electric Co., 1945-47; tech. writer Detroit Edison Co., 1951-54; engring. cons. Overhead Heaters Co., Detroit, 1957-58; instr. Ohio State U., 1947-51; asst. prof. U. Detroit, 1951-59; asso. prof., acting head mech. engring. dept. N.C. State Coll., 1961-62; prof., head dept. mech. engring. U. Me., Orono, 1962-64; prof., head power and energy conversion Old Dominion Coll., Norfolk, Va., 1964, prof., chmn. dept. thermal engring., 1965-71, asst. dean engring., 1971—. Co-dir. Am. Soc. Engring. Edn.-NASA Langley Research Center Summer Faculty Insts., 1967- -; cons. NASA, 1966—; dir. research projects NSF. Recipient DuPont research grant, 1960; Am. Soc. Engring. Ed.-NASA post doctorate fellow, summers 1965-66. Registered profl. engr., Ohio, Mich. Mem. Am. Soc. M.E. (certificate award 1963, chmn. Norfolk group 1966-67), Am. Soc. Engring. Edn., Sigma Xi (chpt. pres. 1966-67), Tau Beta Pi, Pi Tau Sigma. Contbr. profl. jours. Home: 7416 Gardner Dr Norfolk VA 23518

GOGLIA, MARIO JOSEPH, educator; b. Hoboken, N.J., Mar. 30, 1916; s. Frederick Louis and Rosa (Coppola) G.; M.E., Stevens Inst. Tech., 1937, M.S., 1941; Ph.D., Purdue U., 1948; m. Juanita Dixon, June 8, 1940; children—David Dixon, Rozanne Teresa. Instr. mech. engring. Stevens Inst. Tech., 1937-38; asst. prof. mech. engring. U. Ill., 1938- 46; application engr. Republic Flow Meters Co., 1946-47; asst., asso. prof. mech. engring. Purdue U., 1947-48; prof. mech. engring. Ga. Inst. Tech., 1948-55, regents prof., 1955-58, asso. dean faculties, 1960-66, dean grad. div., 1961-66; dean U. Notre Dame Coll. Engring., 1958-60; vice chancellor research U. System Ga., Atlanta, 1966—. Recipient Naval Ordnance award, 1945. Fellow A.A.A.S.; mem. Am. Soc. M.E., Am. Soc. Engring. Edn. (dir.), Sigma Xi, Tau Beta Pi, Pi Tau Sigma, Pi Mu Epsilon, Phi Kappa Phi. Roman Catholic. Author: Thermodynamics, 1955. Contbr. articles to profl. jours. Home: 3066 Arden Rd NW Atlanta GA 30305 Office: 244 Washington St SW Atlanta GA 30334

GOGNIAT, GERARD JOSEPH, food products co. exec.; b. Switzerland; grad. Bus. Coll. City of Bienne, 1944. Pres., Nestle Co., Inc., White Plains, N.Y.; dir. Cain's Coffee Co., Manhattan Coffee Co., Gerber Cheese Co., Holland Food Corp. Home: 142 Foxwood Rd Stamford CT 06903 Office: 100 Bloomingdale Rd White Plains NY 10605

GOHDES, CLARENCE LOUIS FRANK, educator; b. San Antonio, July 2, 1901; s. Conrad and Clara (Heiser) G.; A.B., Capital U., 1921; M.A., Ohio State U., 1922, Harvard, 1928; Ph.D., Columbia, 1931; m. Celestine Marie Beamer, June 3, 1938; children—Eleanor Clara, Dorothy Mary. Asst. prof. English, So. Meth. Univ., 1926-27; instr. English, N.Y. U., 1929- 30; asst. asso. prof. and prof. English, Duke, Durham, N.C., 1930-61, James B. Duke prof., 1961—. Guggenheim fellow, 1962; vis. lectr. Grad. Sch., Columbia, 1932; vis. prof. summer schs. Harvard, Columbia, Pa. and Utah univs.; mng. editor Am. Lit., 1931-54, editor-in-chief, 1954-69. Mem. Modern Lang. Assn. Am., Am. Hist. Assn., Phi Beta Kappa, Phi Gamma Mu, Theta Alpha Phi. Author: The Periodicals of American Transcendentalism, 1931; American Literature in Nineteenth Century England, 1944; (with others) The Literature of the American People, 1951; Bibliographical Guide to the Study of the Literature of the U.S.A., 1959, 3d edit., 1970; Literature and Theater of the States and Regions of the U.S.A., 1967; Hunting in the Old South, 1967. Editor including: (with Rollo G. Silver) Faint Clews and Indirections by Walt Whitman, 1949; Russian Studies of American Literature, 1969. Contbr. scholarly mags. Home: 2737 Circle Dr Durham NC 27705 ☆

GOHEEN, JOHN DAVID, educator; b. Seattle, Dec. 4, 1906; s. Guy Maneford and Harriet Patton (Maclay) G.; A.B., Pomona Coll., 1929; M.A., Claremont Coll., 1930; student Sorbonne U., 1930-33; Ph.D., Harvard, 1935; m. Nancy Holden Reid, Sept. 22, 1932; children—Arthur Holden, Anne Elizabeth. Asst. in philosophy Harvard, 1935-37, instr., 1938-39, vis. lectr., summers 1941, 1946; instr. philosophy Wellesley Coll., 1937-38, 1938-39; chmn. dept. philosophy Queens Coll., 1940-50; chmn. dept. philosophy Stanford, 1950- 63, now prof. philosophy; dir. Stanford Center for Japanese Studies, Tokyo, 1961; lectr., Tokyo U., summer 1950, vis. prof. summer, 1950, 51, 53, 56; Rockefeller grant, research in philosophy, 1947-48; Fulbright lectr. philosophy Kyoto U., 1964-65. Decorated Order of Sacred Treasure (Japan). Mem. Am. Philos. Assn. (pres. Pacific div. 1957-58), Phi Beta Kappa. Club: Faculty (Stanford). Author: book. Contbr. to books and jours. Home: 536 Gerona Rd Stanford CA 94305

GOHEEN, ROBERT FRANCIS, univ. pres.; b. Vengurla, India, Aug. 15, 1919; s. Robert H.H. and Anne (Ewing) G.; B.A., Princeton, 1940, M.A. (Woodrow Wilson fellow), 1947, Ph.D. (Procter fellow), 1948; hon. LL.D., Litt.D., L.C.D., L.H.D. degrees from some 20 univs. and colls., including Madras, Harvard, N.C., Notre Dame, Yale; m. Margaret M. Skelly, June 21, 1941; children—Anne (Mrs. Thomas R. Crane, Jr.), Gertrude (Mrs. William M. Swain, Jr.), Stephen, Margaret, Elizabeth, Charles. Part-time tchr. classics Princeton, 1945- 48, instr. classics, 1948-50, asst. prof., 1950-57, prof., 1957, pres., 1957—, Arthur H. Scribner bicentennial preceptor, 1951-54; sr. fellow Classics Am. Acad. in Rome, 1952-53; dir. Nat. Woodrow Wilson Fellowship program, 1953-56. Mem. overseers' vis. com. to dept. classics Harvard; adv. com. Woodrow Wilson Internat. Center for Scholars; mem. Consultative Com. for Indian Colls., N.J. Higher Edn. Master Plan Commn. Mem. bd. Fund for Peace, Fund for Theol. Edn., Internat. Council for Ednl. Devel., Carnegie Found. Advancement Teaching (chmn. 1965-66), Rockefeller Found., Equitable Life Assurance Soc. U.S., Woodrow Wilson Found.; hon. trustee Inst. Internat. Edn. Served from pvt. to lt. col. AUS, 1941-45. Decorated Legion of Merit, Bronze Star. Mem. Am. Philol. Soc., Am. Archeol. Soc., Am. Council Edn. (chmn. 1961-62), Council Fgn. Relations, Am. Acad. Arts and Scis., Phi Beta Kappa. Clubs: University (N.Y.C. and Washington); Princeton, Century Assn. (N.Y.C.); Cosmos (Washington); Nassau (Princeton). Author: The Imagery of Sophocles' Antigone, 1951; The Human Nature of a University, 1969. Address: Princeton U Princeton NJ 08540

GOHEEN, ROLAND W., banker; b. Wyatt, Inc., 1899. Chmn. bd., pres. Nat. Bank & Trust Co. of South Bend (Ind.); Dir. Ben Feferman Motor Sales Inc., Martin Machine Co., Harry E. Berg, Inc., Mastic Corp., Marquette Lumber Co., H.J. Schrader Co., Nat. Autopark, Inc., South Bend Neon Co., Seaway, Inc., Nabankco, Inc., Nat-Lea Inc., Nat. Mortgage Marketing, Inc. Bd. dirs. Meml. Hosp. South Bend, Indsl. Found., Inc. Mason, Elk, K.T. Home: 1174 Ridgedale Rd South Bend IN 46614 Office: 112 W Jefferson Blvd South Bend IN 46601

GOIN, LAUREN JACKSON, govt. ofcl.; b. Mt. Vernon, Wash., Jan. 8, 1922; s. Irel Lauren and Ina Lorraine (Tittle) G.; B.A. in Tech. Criminology, U. Cal. at Berkeley, 1943, M.Criminology, 1948; m. Evelyn Winn, July 12, 1947; children—Susan Loreen (Mrs. Robert P. Henry), Thomas Richard, Peter Jackson. Chief microanalysis sect. Wis. Crime Lab., 1948-53; dir. Pitts. and Allegheny County Crime Lab., 1953- 55; pub. safety adviser criminalistics, Indonesia, 1955-57, Turkey, 1958- 60, Brazil, 1960-62; chief tech. services div. Office Pub. Safety, AID, Washington, 1963-64, chief operations div., 1964—. Fellow Am. Acad. Forensic Scis. (past chmn. criminalistics sect.); mem. Fed. Exec. Inst., Am. Chem. Soc., Soc. Internat. Devel. Home: 3532 Queen Anne Dr Fairfax VA 22030 Office: AID State Dept Washington DC 20523

GOING, ALLEN JOHNSTON, educator; b. Birmingham, Ala., Sept. 29, 1917; s. Clarence Johnston and Louise (Thornbury) G.; A.B., U. Ala., 1938, M.A., 1940; Ph.D., U. N.C., 1947; m. Dora Alice Henley, Aug. 21, 1954. From instr. to asso. prof. history U. Ala., 1942-57, asso. dean men, 1942-44; faculty U. Houston, 1957—, prof. history, 1958—, chmn. dept., 1959-67. Vis. asso. prof. U. N.C., 1954-55. Mem. Orgn. Am. Historians, Am., So. (mem. exec. council 1954-56, mem. bd. editors 1965-68) hist. assns., Am. Assn. U. Profs., Phi Beta Kappa, Omicron Delta Kappa, Phi Kappa Phi, Sigma Alpha Epsilon. Democrat. Presbyn. Author: Bourbon Democracy in Alabama. 1874-1890, 1951. Home: 9002 Latma Ct Houston TX 77025

GOING, WILLIAM THORNBURY, educator; b. Birmingham, Ala., June 3, 1915; s. Clarence Johnston and Louise (Thornbury) G.; A.B., U. Ala., 1936; M.A. (scholar, fellow English), Duke, 1938; Ed.D., U. Mich. 1954; m. Margaret Moorer, Dec. 15, 1951. Tchr. English, West End High Sch., Birmingham, Ala., 1938-39; asst. prof. edn. Howard Coll., Birmingham, summer 1939; instr. to asso. prof. English, U. Ala., 1939-57; teaching fellow U. Mich., 1952- 53; prof. English, So. Ill. U., Edwardsville, 1957—, dean instrn., 1958-63, dean acad. affairs, 1963-65. Mem. faculty com. Ill. Bd. Higher Edn. Mem. adv. bd. Alton Meml. Hosp. Nursing Sch. Mem. Midwest Modern Lang. Assn., Nat. Council Tchrs. English, N.E.A., Modern Lang. Assn. Am., Ill. Edn. Assn., Phi Beta Kappa, Phi Delta Kappa, Phi Eta Sigma, Sigma Alpha Epsilon. Democrat. Presbyn. Editor: 99 Fables by William March, 1960. Contbr. articles to profl. jours. Home: 1 Hickory Knoll Edwardsville IL 62025

GOINGS, RUSSELL L., Jr., investment co. exec.; b. Stamford, Conn., July 5, 1932; s. Russell L. and Rose (Pegues) G.; student Xavier U., 1955-59; m. Mattie M. Howell, June 23, 1955; children—Russell L., Rhodessa B. Investment exec. Jay W. Kaufman Co., N.Y.C., 1959-61, Van Alstyne Noel & Co., N.Y.C., 1961-62; with Bruns, Nordeman & Co., N.Y.C., 1962-68; mgr. Harlem br. Shearson, Hammill & Co., Harlem, N.Y., 1968—; pres. 1st Harlem Securities Corp.; dir. Essence mag., N.Y.C. Chmn. Better Bus. Bur. Harlem, Studio Museum Harlem. Trustee Rider Coll., Trenton, N.J. Mem. Alpha Sigma Nu. Mgr. of 1st basically black brokerage firm on N.Y. Stock Exchange. Home: 114-43 175th Place St Albans NY 11434 Office: 144 W 125th St New York City NY 10027

GOKHALE, NARAYAN RAMCHANDRA, educator, physicist; b. Bombay, India, Nov. 28, 1924; s. Ramchandra A. and Janakibai (Datye) G.; B.Sc. with honors in Chemistry, S.P. Coll., Poona, India, 1946, B.Sc. with honors in Physics, 1947; M.Sc. in Physics, U. Bombay, 1950, Ph.D., 1958; m. Sunanda Hirlekar, Feb. 7, 1953; children—Nivedita, Milind. Came to U.S., 1961. Teaching asst. physics S.P. Coll., 1948-52; tech. asst. Indian Ministry Transp., 1952-58; research asso. stormy weather research group McGill U., 1959-60; asst. prof. U. Windsor (Ont., Can.), 1960-61; mem. faculty State U. N.Y. at Albany, 1961—, prof. atmospheric scis., 1962—, chmn. dept. earth and atmospheric scis., 1963-68, project dir. NSF study on dynamic behavior of nuclei in ice formation, 1963-66. Mem. Am. Meteorol. Soc., Am. Geophys. Union, N.Y. Acad. Scis., Am. Assn. Physics Tchrs., Sigma Pi Sigma; fgn. mem. Royal, Japan meteorol. socs. Author articles, reports in cloud physics. Home: 16 Country Rd Albany NY 12203

GOLAND, LEONARD, engring. co. exec.; b. Bklyn., May 22, 1923; s. Herman and Josephine (Bloch) G.: B.S., Cornell U., 1944, M.S., 1948; Ph.D., U. Pa., 1962; m. Virginia Kasnetz, Aug. 6, 1950; children—Jay Howard, Eileen Lee. Research engr. Cornell Aero. Lab., 1948-50; head dept. Reaction Motors, Inc., 1950-52; asso. prof. Princeton, 1952-56; v.p. Kellett Aircraft Corp., Willow Grove, Pa., 1956-62; founder Dynasciences Corp., Los Angeles, 1962, pres., 1962-69, exec. v.p., 1969—; cons. USAF, U.S. Army, various indsl. cos. Served to 1st lt. AUS, 1942-46; ETO. Recipient Rotary Club Achievement award, 1955, Inst. Aero. Scis. award, 1949. Asso. fellow Royal Aero. Sci. Soc., Am. Helicopter Soc., Am. Inst. Aeros. and Astronautics, Phi Kappa Phi; mem. Sigma Xi. Contbr. articles profl. jours. Home: 16231 Dorilee Lane Encino CA 91316 Office: 11661 San Vicente Blvd Los Angeles CA 90049

GOLAND, MARTIN, research inst. exec.; b. N.Y.C., July 12, 1919, s. Herman and Josephine (Bloch) G.; M.E., Cornell U., 1940; LL.D. (hon.), St. Mary's U., San Antonio; m. Charlotte Nelson, Oct. 16, 1948; children—Claudia, Lawrence, Nelson. Instr. mech. engring. Cornell U., 1940-42; sect. head structures dept. research lab., airplane div. Curtiss-Wright Corp., Buffalo, 1942-46; chmn. div. engring. Midwest Research Inst., Kansas City, Mo., 1946-50, dir. for engring. scis., 1950-55; v.p. Southwest Research Inst., San Antonio, 1955-57, dir., 1957-59, pres., 1959—; prof. research (hon.) St. Mary's U., San Antonio. Chmn. subcom. vibration and flutter NACA, 1952-60; chmn. research adv. com. on aircraft structures NASA, 1960-68; sci. adv. com. Harry Diamond Labs., U.S. Amry Materiel Command, 1955—, Bell Aerospace Corp., 1967—; adv. panel com. sci. and astronautics Ho. of Reps., 1960—; mem. high speed ground transp. panel Dept. Commerce 1966-67, nat. invenors council, 1966-67, mem. State tech. Services evaluation com., 1967-69; mem. adv. bd. on undersea warfare Dept. Navy, 1968-70, chmn., 1970—; sci. adv. panel Dept. Army, 1966—; chmn. U.S. Army Weapons Command Adv. Group, 1966—; mem. materiels adv. bd. NRC, 1969—; mem. tech. adv. group Whirlpool Corp., 1970—. Dir., Nat. Bank Commerce, San Antonio. Dir. Engrs. Joint Council, 1966—; chmn. Citizens Adv. Commn. Municipal Employees, 1968; mem. Community Welfare Council Central Priorities Com., 1968. Bd. govs. St. Mary's U., San Antonio; research adv. com. coordinating bd. Tex. Coll. and Univ. System, 1966-68; pres. San Antonio Symphony, 1968-70, chmn. bd., 1970-71. Recipient Spirit of St. Louis jr. award Am. Soc. M.E., 1945, jr. award, 1946, Alfred E. Nobel prize Am. Soc. C.E., 1947. Fellow Am. Ordnance Assn., A.A.A.S., Am. Inst. Aeros. and Astronautics (pres. 1971); hon. mem. Am. Soc. M.E. (dir., mem. bd. tech., mem. tech. devel. com.; v.p. communications); mem. C. of C. (dir.), Nat. Acad. Engring. (mem. council), Research Soc. Am., Sigma Xi, Tau Beta Pi. Editor Applied Mechanics Review, 1952-59, editorial adviser, 1959—. Home: 211 Five Oaks St San Antonio TX 78209 Office: 8500 Culebra Rd San Antonio TX 78228

GOLAY, FRANK HINDMAN, educator, economist; b. Windsor, Mo., July 2, 1915; s. Frank Leslie and Alice (Hindman) G.; B.S. in Edn., Central Mo. State Coll., Warrensburg, 1936; M.A. in Econs., U. Chgo., 1948, Ph.D., 1951; LL.D., Ateneo de Manila Univ., P.I., 1966; m. Clara Ruth Wood, Oct. 23, 1945; children—Frank Hindman, John Wood, David Clark, Jane White. Economist internat. div. Fed. Res. System, 1950-52; mem. faculty Cornell U., Ithaca, N.Y., 1953—, prof. econs., 1962—, chmn. dept., 1963-67, asso. dir. Cornell Southeast Asia program, 1961-70, dir., 1970—. Vis. lectr. U. London Sch. Oriental and African Studies, 1965-66; dir. London-Cornell Project, 1968-70; dir. Cornell Philippines Project, 1967—. Served to lt. comdr. USNR, 1941-45. Decorated Silver Star medal with gold star, Bronze Star medal. Fulbright fellow, 1955-56; Guggenheim and Social Sci. Research Council fellow, 196-61. Mem. Philippines-Am. Soc. (bd. dirs. 1966—), Assn. Asian Studies, Asia Soc. (chmn. Philippines council 1964-67), Nat. Acad. Scis. (Pacific sci. bd. Philippines com.). Author: The Philippines; Public Policy and National Economic Development, 1961. Editor: The Santo Tomas Story (A.V.H. Hartendorp), 1964; editor, contbr. Am. Assembly, The U.S. and The Philippines, 1966. Co-author: Land and People in 1990: Philippine Rice Needs, Output and Input Requirements, 1967; Under development and Economic Nationalism in Southeast Asia, 1969. Home: 109 N Sunset Dr Ithaca NY 14850

GOLD, ALBERT, artist; b. Phila., Oct. 31, 1916; s. Rubin and Dora (Sklar) G.; grad. Pa. Mus. Sch. Indsl. Art, 1938; m. Aurora Mary Vanelli, Mar. 3, 1953; children—Madelaine, Robert. Exhibited at maj. ann. shows including: Pa. Acad. Fine Arts, Corcoran Gallery, Met. Mus., Art Inst., Chgo., Carnegie Inst., World's Fair, N.Y.C., 1939, Nat. Gallery, London, Eng., 1943, Musee Gallerie, Paris, France, La Tausca exhbn., Burlington Acad. Galleries, 1962, Phila. Coll. Art (Alumni grant), 1968; one-man shows at Pa. Acad. Fine Arts, Phila. Art Alliance; selected by War Dept. as one of 12 men in U.S. Army to make pictorial record of war, 1943, spent 3 yrs. in Eng., France and Germany on project; represented in collections Library of Congress, N.Y. Pub. Library, Phila. Mus. Art, War Dept., Pentagon Bldg., Pa. Acad. Fine Arts, Gimbel Pa. collection, numerous pvt. collections: tchr. pictoral expression Pa. Mus. Sch., Phila., 1945-48; dir. dept. illustration Phila. Mus. Coll. Arts; tchr. art centers, pvt. classes; commd. to paint various documentary series; illustrator various mags. Recipient John Gribbel Meml. prize Phila. Print Club, 1939; Prix de Rome, Am. Acad. in Rome, 1942; Tiffany Found. grant, 1947-48; Jennie Seaman Gold medal, 1950; Dorothy Kohl prize Phila. Art Alliance, 1953; Am. Artist citation Am. Water Color Soc., 1954; Am. Artists Guild award Am. Water Color Soc., 1955; Regional Water Color prize Phila. Art Alliance, 1955: Wm. W. Esty prize Am. Water Color Soc. Ann., 1961, award for series of illustrations Brandywine Ohio State U. Sch. Journalism; Woodmere Endowment Fund grant, 1968. Mem. Artists Equity (dir.). Illus. book The Commodore (by Robert L. Abrahams), 1954; This Was Our War (Frank Brookhouser), 1961; The Court Factor, 1964; The Captive Rabbi (Lillian S. Freehof). Mem. Am. Assn. U. Profs. Home: 6814 McCallum St Philadelphia PA 19119

GOLD, BELA, educator, economist; b. Kolozsvar, Hungary, Jan. 30, 1915; s. Leo and Esther (Ludwig) G.; came to U.S., 1920, naturalized, 1927; B.S. in Mech. Engring., N.Y.U., 1934; Ph.D. (Univ. fellow 1936-37), Columbia, 1948; m. Sonia Steinman, July 5, 1938; 1 son, Robert. Research cons. Life Ins. Sales Research Bur., Hartford, Conn., 1938-39; asst. head div. program surveys Bur. Agr. Econs., 1939-42; econ. cons. subcom. war mblzn. U.S. Senate, 1943-44; econ. adviser FEA, 1944-46; prof. indsl. econs. U. Pitts. Grad. Sch. Bus., 1947-66; Timken prof. indsl. econs., dir. research program indsl. econs., also chmn. dept. econs. Case Western Res. U., 1966—; vis. professorial fellow Nuffield Coll., Oxford (Eng.) U., 1964; vis. prof. Imperial Coll. Scis. and Tech., London, Eng., 1967; cons. to industry and ednl. instns., 1950—. Social Sci. Research Council fellow, 1937-38; Ford Found. fellow, 1961-62, 66-67. Mem. Am. Econ. Assn., Inst. Mgmt. Scis., Internat. Univ. Contact Mgmt. Edn., Nat. Assn. Bus. Economists, Acad. Mgmt. (bd. editors), Am. Assn. U. Profs., A.A.A.S. Author: Wartime Economic Planning in Agriculture, 2d edit., 1969; How is Higher Education Financed?, 1959; Foundations of Productivity Analysis, 1955; Long Term Iron and Steel Manufacturing Costs, 1956; Explorations in Managerial Economics, 1971; also numerous articles. Home: 2901 Litchfield Rd Shaker Heights OH 44120

GOLD, BILL, (William Emil), newspaper reporter; b. Bklyn., Aug. 9, 1912; s. Mayer and Miriam (Feldman) G.; B.S. in Journalism, Ohio State U., 1933; m. Bernice Radine Ellman, 1933; 1 son, Walter Leslie. Reporter, condr. Dist. Line column The Washington Post, 1947—. Mem. White House Corrs. Assn. Sigma Delta Chi. Club: Nat. Press. Home: 7036 Wilson Lane Bethesda MD 20034 Office: Washington Post Washington DC 20005

GOLD, HAROLD, lawyer; b. N.Y.C., Jan. 14, 1916; s. Samuel and Freida Swedlow) G.; B.S. in Accounting, U. Cal. at Los Angeles, 1938; LL.B., U. Minn., 1948; m. Ellen Facundus, June 18, 1946; children—Sandra L., Fred L. Admitted to Cal. bar, 1954, Minn. bar, 1948; with Renegotiation Bd., Los Angeles, 1951-57; partner Gold & Gold, Beverly Hills, Cal., 1957—. Mem. Am. (mem. council pub. contract sect. 1967—, sec. 1970—, chmn. com. renegotiation, termination and redeterminations, 1965, chmn. com. profit inceutives and controls 1966, chmn. region 7 1968—), Minn. bar assns., State Bar Cal., Am. Inst. C.P.A.'s, Cal., Minn. socs. C.P.A.'s, Los Angeles, Beverly Hills bar assns. Mason. Author: chpts. in books. Home: 806 Teakwood Rd Los Angeles CA Office: 144 S Beverly Dr Beverly Hills CA 90212

GOLD, HARRY, cardiologist; b. Russia, Dec. 25, 1899; s. Samuel and Naomi (Katz) G.; A.B., Cornell, 1919, M.D., 1922; m. Bertha Goldman, 1926; children—Naomi, Stanley, Muriel. Came to U.S., 1903, naturalized, 1910. Instr. pharmacology Cornell, Ithaca, N.Y., 1922-29, asst. prof., 1929-44, asso. prof., 1944-47, prof. clin. pharmacology, 1947-65, emeritus, 1965—; attending-in-charge cardiovascular research unit Beth Israel Hosp., 1931-65, cons. cardiology, 1965—; attending cardiologist, chmn. med. adv. bd. Hosp. Joint Diseases, 1933-65, cons. cardiologist, 1965—; mem. med. bd. Doctors Hosp., 1950-63, hon. mem. attending staff, 1963-68; cons. cardiologist at St. Vincent's Hosps. S.I., Army Med. Center Richmond Meml. Hosp., S.I.; civilian instr. and cons. U.S. Naval Hosp., St. Albans; lectr. therapeutics Post Grad. Extension div. Rutgers U. Mem. revision com. U.S. Pharmacopoeia, 1940-57. Fellow N.Y. Acad. Med.; mem. N.Y. Heart Assn. (bd. dirs.), Harvey Soc., Am. Coll. Clin. Pharmacology and Chemotheraphy (charter mem., bd. regents), Am. Pharm. Soc., A.A.A.S., A.M.A., N.Y. Acad. Scis., Am. Anesthesia Assn., Phi Beta Kappa, Alpha Omega Alpha; hon. mem. Argentine Med. Assn., Cardiological Soc. Brazil. Democrat. Jewish religion. Mng. editor Cornell Confs. on Therapy, 1949-55; asso. editor Am. Jour. Medicine, 1947-57, Am. Jour. Medical Sci., 1944-65. Contbr. sci. articles Am., European med. jours. Home: 7 E 82d St New York City NY 10028

GOLD, HERBERT, author; b. Cleve., Mar. 9, 1924; s. Samuel and Frieda (Frankel) G.; B.A., Columbia, 1948, M.A., 1949; postgrad. U. Paris (France), 1949-51; m. Edith Zubrin, Apr. 1, 1948 (div. 1956); children—Ann, Judy; m. 2d, Melissa Dilworth, Jan. 26, 1968; children—Nina, Ari, Ethan. Vis. prof. Cornell U., 1958, U. Cal. at Berkeley, 1963, Harvard, summer 1964, Stanford, 1967. Fulbright fellow, 1950-51; Hudson Rev. fellow, 1956; Guggenheim fellow, 1957; Ford Found. grantee, 1960. Recipient award Am. Inst. Arts and Letters, 1957; Longview award, 1959. Author: (novels) Birth of a Hero, 1951; The Prospect Before Us, 1954; The Man Who Was Not With It, 1956; The Optimist, 1958; Therefore Be Bold, 1961; Salt, 1963; Fathers, 1967; The Great American Jackpot, 1970; (short stories) Love and Like, 1960; The Magic Will, 1971; (essays) The Age of Happy Problems, 1962. Address: 1051-A Broadway San Francisco CA 94133

GOLD, IKE, union ofcl.; b. Russia, Apr. 25, 1912 (parents Am. citizens); s. Louis and Rose (Shainsky) G.; student U. Akron; m. Gertrude Glass, Aug. 1, 1937; children—Larry, Harvey. Propr. used-automobile firm until 1942; maintenance, constrn. welder Firestone Tire & Rubber Co., Akron, O., 1942; with United Rubber Workers Am., 1942—, successively union committeeman, divisional chmn., v.p., pres. local union, 1942-60, internat. sec.-treas., 1960, now internat. sec.-treas. United Rubber, Cork, Linoleum and Plastic Workers Am. Mem., sec.-treas., com. AFL-CIO; mem. operating com., adminstrv. com., com. polit. edn. COPE. Bd. dirs. U. Akron, Mental Retardation; v.p., trustee, labor operations com. United Found., trustee United Community Council; mem. exec. bd. Akron Area council Boy Scouts Am. Mem. N.A.A.C.P., Nat. Planning Assn. (mem. nat. council), Nat. Trade Union Council for Human Rights, Akron Jewish Center. Jewish religion. Mem. B'nai B'rith. Home: 350 Crestview Av Akron OH 44320 Office: 87 S High St Akron OH 44308

GOLD, JOSEPH, internat. ofcl.; b. London, Eng., July 12, 1912; LL.B., U. London, 1935, LL.M., 1936; S.J.D., Harvard, 1942; m. Ruth Schechter, Dec. 21, 1939; children—Julia, Joan, Richard. Lectr. law U. London (Eng.), 1937-39; mem. Brit. govt. mission to Washington, 1942-46; with Internat. Monetary Fund, Washington, 1946—, gen. counsel, dir. legal dept., 1960—. Author: Fund Agreement in the Courts, 1962; The Stand-By Arrangements of the International Monetary Fund, 1970; also pamphlets and articles on monetary law. Office: Internat Monetary Fund 19th and H Sts NW Washington DC 20431

GOLD, MILTON JACOB, coll. dean; b. Newark, Aug. 9, 1917; s. Samuel and Esther (Dunkelman) G.; B.A., Coll. City N.Y., 1937; M.A., Columbia, 1939, Ed.D., 1948; m. Esther Glicker, Aug. 25, 1945; children—Bonnie, Deborah, Janice Anne. Tchr., N.Y.C. schs., 1938-48; dir. curriculum Office State Supt. Pub. Instrn., Olympia, Wash., 1948-57; asso. prof. Hunter Coll., N.Y.C., 1957- 63, prof., 1963—, dir. tchr. edn., 1966-68, dean programs in edn., 1968—; instr. N.Y. U., 1946-48. Vis. lectr. Wash. State Coll., summer 1955, Columbia, 1957-59, Miami U. (O.), summer 1957. Served to 1st lt. AUS, 1942-46. Mem. Assn. Supervision and Curriculum Devel., N.E.A., Am. Assn. U. Profs., Met. Assn. for Study of Gifted (pres.). Author: Working to Learn, 1951; (with H. Schueler and H. Mitzel) Using Kinescopes for Improvement of Student Teaching, 1962; Education of the Intellectually Gifted, 1965. Home: 711 Amsterdam Av New York City NY 10025 Office: 695 Park Av New York City NY 10021

GOLD, NORMAN MYRON, lawyer; b. Chgo., May 21, 1930; s. Harry and Irene (Alpern) G.; B.B.A., U. Mich., 1951; J.D., Harvard, 1954; m. Barbara George, Sept. 8, 1962; children-Judith Ann, Walter Robert. Admitted to Ill. bar, 1954, since practiced in Chgo.; asso. Abbell & Abbell, 1954-57; asso., partner Altheimer, Gray, Naiburg, Strasburger & Lawton, 1957—. sec. Park Forest Savs. & Loan Assn.; dir. Peterson State Bank, Intercraft Industries Corp., Tech. Equipment Leasing Co. Trustee Coll. Jewish Studies. C.P.A., Ill Mem. Ill., Chgo. bar assns., Beta Gamma Sigma, Phi Kappa Phi, Alpha Kappa Psi. Club: Standard (Chgo.). Home: 2400 Lakeview St Chicago IL 60614 Office: 1 N LaSalle St Chicago IL 60602

GOLD, RAYMOND L., sociologist, educator; b. Chgo., Nov. 15, 1921; s. Samuel and Shirley (Katz) G.; student Wilson Jr. Coll., Chgo., 1946-47; M.A., U. Chgo., 1950, Ph.D., 1954; m. Marjorie Doris McClelland, Dec. 23, 1948; 1 dau., Karen Joan. Asst. prof. sociology U. Ala., 1953-57; from asst. prof. to prof. sociology U. Mont., 1957—, then research dir., now dir. Inst. Social Sci. Research of U. Mont., 1966—; sociol. cons. bus. and govt. Served with AUS, 1942-46. Fellow Am. Sociol. Assn. Unitarian-Universalist (pres. Missoula fellowship 1970-71). Contbr. articles profl. jours. and books. Home: 413 King St Missoula MT 59801

GOLD, THOMAS, educator, astronomer; b. Vienna, Austria, May 22, 1920; s. Max and Josephine (Martin) G.; B.A., Cambridge (Eng.) U., 1942, M.A., 1945, Sc.D., 1969, fellow Trinity Coll., Cambridge, 1947; M.A. (hon.), Harvard, 1957; m. Merle Eleanor Tuberg, June 21, 1947; children—Linda, Lucy, Tanya. Lectr. physics Cambridge (Eng.) U., 1948-52; chief asst. to Astronomer Royal, Gt. Britain, 1952-56; prof. astronomy Harvard, 1958, Robert Wheeler Willson prof., 1958-59; prof. astronomy, dir. Center Radio-physics and Space Research, Cornell U., 1959—, chmn. dept., 1959-68, asst. v.p. for research, 1970-71, John L. Wetherill prof., 1971—. Cons. mem. lunar and planetary missions bd. NASA; mem. space panel Pres.'s Sci. Adv. Com. Mem. Am. Acad. Arts and Scis., Royal Soc. London, Am. Astronautical Soc., Internat. Acad. Astronautics, Royal (past councillor), Am. astron. socs., Am. Geophys. Union, U.S. Nat. Acad. Sci. Contbr. articles to profl. jours. Address: Space Scis Bldg Cornell U Ithaca NY 14850

GOLDBERG, ABRAHAM ISAAC, retired newsman; b. Pitts., July 30, 1904; s. Nathan and Fannie (Schmidt) G.; student Ohio State U., 1923-24; m. Victoria Beebe, Nov. 20, 1933; children—Joel H.Z., Ethan. Reporter, Steubenville (O.) Gazette, 1922-25; news editor Steubenville Herald-Star, 1925-33; mem. staff A.P., 1933-70, chief Prague (Czechoslovakia) bur., 1947-49, mem. UN staff, 1949-56, mem. fgn. news desk, N.Y.C., 1956-59, mem. Moscow (USSR) bur., 1959-60, mem. UN bur., 1960-65, editor AP Log, 1965-69. Mem. Sigma Delta Chi. Mason. Club: Deadline. Address: Box 242 RD 1 Rhinebeck NY 12572

GOLDBERG, ALBERT LEVI, journalist, music critic; b. Shenandoah, Ia., June 2, 1898; s. A. W. and Minnie (Levi) G.; student U. Neb., 1915-16, Chgo. Mus. Coll., 1920-22; M.Mus., Gunn Sch. Music, 1923; also pvt. study. Faculty, Chgo. Mus. Coll., 1924-26, Gunn Sch. Music, 1926-35; music critic Chgo. Herald Exam., 1925-36 state dir. Fed. Music Project (WPA), 1936-43, co-conductor Ill. Symphony Orch., 1936-43; music critic Chgo. Tribune, 1943-47, Los Angeles Times, 1947-65, music staff writer, 1965—, critic emeritus, 1966—. Lectr. U. Cal. at Los Angeles, 1948-68. Contbr. articles to mus. periodicals. Office: Los Angeles Times Times Mirror Sq Los Angeles CA 90053

GOLDBERG, ARTHUR JOSEPH, lawyer, former U.S. rep. UN; b. Chgo., Aug. 8, 1908; s. Joseph and Rebecca (Perlstein) G.; B.S.L., Northwestern U., 1929, J.D., 1930; m. Dorothy Kurgans, July 18, 1931; children—Barbara L., Robert M. Admitted to Ill. bar, 1929, U.S. Supreme Ct. bar, 1937; practiced in Chgo., 1929-48; mem. firm Goldberg, Devoe, Shadur & Mikva, Chgo., 1945-61, Goldberg, Feller & Bredhoff, Washington, 1952-61; gen. counsel CIO, 1948-55, United Steelworkers Am., 1948-61, indsl. union dept. AFL-CIO, 1955-61, sec. labor, 1961-62; asso. justice U.S. Supreme Ct., Washington, 1962-65; U.S. rep. to UN, 1965-68. Past pres., now hon. pres. Am. Jewish Com. Served in OSS, 1942-43; from capt. to maj. AUS, 1942-44; ETO. Recipient Stephen Wise award, 1965. Author: AFL-CIO; Labor United, 1956; Defenses of Freedom, 1966. ‡

GOLDBERG, AVRAM JACOB, retailing co. exec.; b. Boston, Jan. 26, 1930; s. Lewis and Mildred (Levine) G.; A.B. magna cum laude, Harvard, 1951, J.D. cum laude, 1954; m. Carol Rabb, June 18, 1950; children—Deborah Beth, Joshua Rabb. Admitted to Mass. bar, 1954, U.S. Supreme Ct.; asso. firm Hill, Barlow, Goodale & Wiswall, Boston, 1954-55; with The Stop & Shop Cos., Inc., 1958—, exec. v.p., 1968-71, pres., 1971—; trustee New Eng. Aquarium Corp., Charlestown Savs. Bank. Sec., mem. class com. Harvard Class of 1951; past chmn. Brookline Redevel. Authority; exec. com. Mass. Com. Catholics, Protestants and Jews; vice chmn. bus. men's council Combined Jewish Philanthropies. Bd. dirs. Boston Coll., Hebrew Coll., Super Market Inst., Boston Coll.; trustee Beth Israel Hosp.; mem. visitors com. Freedom House; bd. govs. Am. Assn. Jewish Edn.; bd. dirs. Greater Boston chpt. Am. Friends Hebrew U.; trustee, exec. com. Combined Jewish Philanthropies. Served with USNR, 1955-58. Decorated chevalier de la Confrerie des Chevaliers du Tastevin. Jewish religion (temple). Home: 37 Hyslop Rd Brookline MA 02146 Office: 393 D St Boston MA 02210

GOLDBERG, BERNARD, corp. exec.; b. 1924; B.S., N.Y. U., 1947, M.A., 1950; married. With Schenley Industries Inc., 1947—, now pres., also dir. Address: 1290 Av Americas New York City NY 10019*

GOLDBERG, BERTRAND, architect; b. Chgo., July 17, 1913; s. Benjamin R. and Sadie (Getzhof) G.; student Harvard, 1930-32, Bauhaus, Berlin, Germany, 1932-33, Armour Inst. Tech., 1934; m. Nancy S. Florsheim, Dec. 4, 1946; children—Nan, Lisa, Jeffrey. Propr. archtl. and engring. office, Bertrand Goldberg Assos., Chgo., 1937—, Richmond, Va., 1940-45; archtl. engr. for plastic freight car, 1950; lectr. throughout U.S. and Can., 1958—; prin. works include Marina City, Chgo., 1963, Astor Tower Hotel, Chgo., 1963, Joseph Brennemann Pub. Sch., Chgo., 1962, Cinestage Theatre, Chgo., 1957, Elgin (Ill.) State Hosp., 1964, Affiliated Hosps. Center, Boston, 1964, Raymond Hilliard Housing Center, Chgo., 1966, Health Scis. Center State U. N.Y. at Stony Brook, Stanford Med. Center, Palo Alto, Cal., 1967, Chgo. Women's Hosp., 1968, St. Joseph's Hosp., Tacoma, Wash., 1968. Mem. exec. com. Chgo. Maternity Center; bd. dirs. Soc. Contemporary Music. Recipient award Archtl. Forum, 1952, Progressive Architecture, 1954, Hardware Assn., 1956, A.I.A.-C. of C., 1959; citation Assn. Sch. Adminstrs., 1962; Silver medal Archtl. League N.Y., 1965; Man of Yr. (field arch.), Chgo., 1965. Fellow A.I.A.; mem. Nat. Soc. Profl. Engrs., Ill. Soc. Architects, Am. Assn. Engrs., Am. Concrete Inst., Soc. Am. Mil. Engrs., Bldg. Research Inst. Clubs: Cliff Dwellers, Tavern, Arts (Chgo.); Harvard (Chgo. and Boston). Home: 1518 Astor St Chicago IL 60610 Office: Marina City Chicago IL 60610

GOLDBERG, CARNEY, architect; b. Chelsea, Mass., Apr. 6, 1907; B.S., Mass. Inst. Tech., 1928, M.Arch. (gold medal A.I.A., medal dept. architecture), 1929; Rotch traveling scholar, 1931-33. Draftsman, J.D. Leland & Co., 1928; designer Coolidge, Shepley, Bulfinch & Abbott, 1929- 31; pvt. practice as Carney Goldberg, 1933-46; founder, prin. Isidor Richmond & Carney Goldberg, Boston, 1946—; prin. works include County Courthouse, Hingham, Mass., 1936, U.S. Post Office, Brighton, Mass., 1937, South Brookline Community Center, Portland, Me., 1949-50. Chmn. Bd. Registration Architects Mass., 1969—. Recipient Harleson Parker gold medal Boston Soc. Architects, 1949. Fellow A.I.A. (award merit 1954). Address: 30 Newbury St Boston MA 11216

GOLDBERG, CHARLES L., lawyer; b. Milw., Dec. 21, 1902; Ph.B., U. Chgo., 1925; J.D. cum laude, Marquette U., 1928. Admitted to Wis. bar, 1928; gen. practice, Milw.; lectr. real estate law U. Wis-Milw., 1942—. Dir. Wis. Bar Found. Mem. Am. (bd. govs.), Milw. (pres. 1952) bar assns., State Bar Wis. (pres. 1958-59, bd. govs. 1947-51). Office: 735 N Water St Milwaukee WI 53202

GOLDBERG, DAVID ALAN, investment banker, lawyer; b. N.Y.C., Oct. 31, 1933; s. Joseph R. and Rose (Trutt) G.; A.B. magna cum laude, Harvard, 1954, J.D., 1957, postgrad. in bus. adminstrn., 1956-57; m. Victoria Liebson, July 7, 1957; children—Eric S., Jeremy P. Admitted to N.Y. bar, 1958; counsel firm R.W. Pressprich & Co., N.Y.C., 1958-64, gen. partner, 1965-68; exec. v.p. R.W. Pressprich & Co. Inc., 1968—, also chmn. exec. com.; dir. the F. & M. Schaefer Corp., Arnold Bakers, Inc. Served with AUS, 1957-58. Mem. Phi Beta Kappa. Club: Harvard (N.Y.C.). Home: 1225 Park Av New York City NY 10028 Office: 80 Pine St New York City NY 10005

GOLDBERG, EDWARD DAVID, educator, geochemist; b. Sacramento, Aug. 2, 1921; s. Edward Davidow and Lillian (Rothholz) G.; B.S., U. Cal. at Berkeley, 1942; Ph.D., U. Chgo., 1949; m. Betty Jean Anderson, Feb. 23, 1945; children—David Wilkes, Wendy Jean. Mem. faculty Scripps Instn. Oceanography, La Jolla, Cal., 1949—, prof. chemistry, 1960—; provost Revelle Coll., U. Cal. at San Diego, 1965-66. Guggenheim fellow, 1961; NATO fellow, 1970. Mem. Am. Geophys. Union, A.A.A.S., Geochem. Soc., Sigma Xi. Author: (with J. Geiss) Earth Sciences and Meteorities, 1964. Contbr. numerous articles profl. jours. Research, publs. primarily marine pollution, chem. composition sea water, sediments, marine organisms; radioactive dating techniques in marine environment and glaciers. Home: 2614 Ellentown Rd La Jolla CA 92037

GOLDBERG, HANNAH L., assn. exec.; b. Chelsea, Mass., d. Louis I. and Minna (Heifetz) G.; LL.B., Boston U. Admitted to Mass. bar, practiced in Boston; exec. sec. Jewish Reconstructionist Found., N.Y., 1944-53; exec. dir. Hadassah Women's Zionist Orgn. Am., 1953—. Home: 230 Central Park West New York City NY 10024 Office: 65 E 52d St New York City NY 10024

GOLDBERG, HAROLD, electronics co. exec.; b. Milw., Jan. 31, 1914; s. Esreal and Martha (Rabinowitz) G.; B.S. in Elec. Engring., U. Wis., 1935, M.S., 1936, Ph.D., 1937, Ph.D. in Physiology, 1941; m. Ruth Sweet, Dec. 23, 1936; children—Peter E., Nancy (Mrs. Jerald Goodstein). Postdoctoral fellow U. Wis., 1938-41; sr. engr. Stromberg-Carlson Co., 1941-45; prin. engr. Bendix Radio div. Bendix Co., 1945-47; chief ordnance electronics div. Nat. Bur. Standards, 1947-54; v.p. Emerson Radio and Phonograph Corp., 1954-61; exec. v.p., dir. Emertron, Inc., 1961-63; v.p. Raytheon Co., 1963-64; v.p. Ling Temco Vought, 1964-65; v.p., dir., gen. mgr. Garland div. LTV Electro Systems, Inc., 1965-69; exec. v.p., dir. Riker-Maxson Corp., Washington, 1969—. Recipient Distinguished Service award U. Wis., 1964; Exceptional Service award Commerce Dept., 1963. Fellow I.E.E.E.; mem. Am. Phys. Soc., Am. Inst. Aero. and Astronautics, Navy League. Author: (with others) Armament, Launching and Range Testing; Principles of Guided Missile Design, 1955; also articles. Patentee in field. Home: 5190 Linnean Terrace NW Washington DC 20008 Office: 1100 Connecticut Av NW Washington DC 20036

GOLDBERG, HAROLD SEYMOUR, elec. engr.; b. Bklyn., Jan. 22, 1925; s. David and Rose (Maslow) G.; B.E.E. (Schweinberg scholar), Cooper Union, 1944; M.E.E., Poly. Inst. Bklyn., 1949; student Columbia; m. Florence Meyerson, May 29, 1949; children—Lawrence, Irene. Engring. draftsman Cole Electric Products Co., 1944-45; radio engr. Press Wireless, Inc., 1945-47; asst. project engr. Radio Receptor Co., 1947-48; project engr. No. Radio Co., 1948-50; mgr. prodn. test, test equipment design sects. Allen B. DuMont Labs., Inc., 1950-56; mgr. engring. fabrication dept. Emerson Radio & Phonograph Corp., 1956-57; chief devel. engr. Consol. Avionics Corp., Westbury, N.Y., 1957-59; engring. mgr. data systems EPSCO, Inc., Cambridge, Mass., 1959-62; v.p. research Lexington Instruments Corp., Waltham, Mass., 1962- 66; prin. research engr. AVCO-Research div., Everett, Mass., 1966-68; operations mgr. Orion Research Inc., 1968-70; v.p. applications Analogic Corp., Wakefield, Mass., 1970-71. Operations mgr. Data Precision Co., Wakefield, 1971—. Served with AUS, 1945-47. N.Y. State Vets, scholar, 1957. Mem. I.E.E.E. (chmn. Boston group on medicine and biology 1965-66, mem. exec. com. Boston sect. 1967-69, vice chmn. Boston 1969-70, chmn. Boston 1970-71), Tau Beta Pi. Home: 10 Alcott Rd Lexington MA 02173 Office: Audubon Rd Wakefield MA 01880

GOLDBERG, HERMAN RAPHAEL, ednl. adminstr.; b. Bklyn. Nov. 20, 1915; s. Isidore Baruch and Rose (Saltser) G.; B.S., Bklyn. Coll., 1935; M.A., Columbia Tchrs. Coll., 1944; postgrad. N.Y.U., 1941-42, U. Rochester, 1956-57, LL.D., 1965; m. Harriette Balacaier, Jan. 23, 1943; children—Robert, Arnold. Tchr. spl. edn., English, social studies N.Y.C. pub. schs., 1939-48; cons. spl. edn. City Sch. Dist., Rochester, N.Y., 1948-49, dir. spl. edn., 1949-58, coordinator instructional services, 1958-63, supt. schs., 1963-70; U.S. asso. commr. edn. forelementary and secondary edn. U.S. Office Edn., Dept. Health, Edn. and Welfare, 1971—; lectr. edn. U. Rochester, 1949—, N.Y.U., 1943-48; Fulbright prof. U. Bologna (Italy), 1960-61; cons. Ministry Edn., Italy, Israel, 1960-61; N.Y. del. Edn. Commn. of States, 1966—. Mem. N.Y. State Council for Exceptional Children (charter pres.). Contbg. author: Otolaryngology, 1960; Education for the Exceptional, 1956; Educating for Tomorrow: The Role of Media, Career Development and Society, 1970. Editor: Rochester Occupational Reading Series, 1953-63. Inventor linguistics teaching machine. Home: 5101 River Rd Washington DC 20016 Office: 400 Maryland Av Washington DC 20028

GOLDBERG, ICCHOK IGNACY, educator; b. Warsaw, Poland, Mar. 6, 1916; s. Chaim and Ita (Majerczak) G.; Magister Philosophiae, U. Warsaw, 1938; M.A., Columbia, 1949, Ed.D., 1952; m. Diana R. Solarsh, Feb. 2, 1948; 1 dau., Vivian S. Came to U.S., 1948, naturalized, 1958. Tchr. secondary schs., Warsaw, 1937-39; press attache, information officer Polish consulate, Johannesburg, S. Africa, 1944-46; sales mgr. M. Golante, wholesale mcht., Johannesburg, 1946- 48; instr. depts. psychol. founds. and spl. edn. Columbia Tchrs. Coll., 1950-53, asst. dir. mental retardation project, 1957-61, asso. prof. edn., 1957-63, prof. edn., 1963—; dir. dept. rehab. Muscatatuck State Sch., Butlerville, Ind., 1953-56. Ednl. cons. Nat. Assn. Retarded Children, N.Y.C., 1956-57; lectr. Wis. State Coll., summer 1954, Ind. U., 1955-56, George Peabody Coll. For Tchrs., summer 1957, U. Kan., summer 1957; instr. Tex. Woman's U., summer 1960; vis. prof. U. Alaska, 1962; cons. spl. edn., vocational rehab. Woods Sch., Longhorne, Pa.; asst. examiner N.Y.C. Bd. Edn., 1961; chmn. sub-com. edn., recreation, vocational tng. in instns. President's Panel Mental Retardation, 1961; chmn. com. councils history Council For Exceptional Children, 1957-61; participant White House Conf. Edn., 1965. Bd. dirs. United Cerebral Palsy Assn.; adv. bd. N.Y. Assn. For Help Retarded Children, Nat. Assn. Retarded Children, Maimonides Inst., Shield of David, N.Y.C. Served with Polish Forces, 1941-44. Decorated Polish Cross Valor. Fellow A.A.A.S., Am. Assn. Mental Deficiency (past pres.); mem. Am. Assn. U. Profs., Council Exceptional Children (life, gov. at large 1950-64), Am. Ednl. Research Assn., Am. Psychol. Assn., N.E.A., Kappa Delta Pi, Phi Delta Kappa. Contbr. articles profl. jours. Home: 501 W 120th St New York City NY 10027

GOLDBERG, IRVING HYMAN, educator, pharmacologist, biochemist; b. Hartford, Conn., Sept. 2, 1926; s. Morris Wolfe and Rose (Krechevsky) G.; B.S., Trinity Coll., 1949; M.D., Yale, 1953; Ph.D., Rockefeller U., 1960; A.M., (hon.), Harvard, 1964; m. Margaret Field Ziskin, Apr. 15, 1956; children—Daniel Eliot, Nancy Elizabeth. Intern, Columbia-Presbyn. Med. Center, N.Y.C., 1953-54, asst. resident, chief resident, instr. medicine Coll. Phys. and Surgs., 1954- 57; practice medicine, specializing in endocrinology and metabolism, Chgo., 1960-64, Boston, 1964—; asst. prof. medicine, biochemistry U. Chgo., 1960-64, asso. prof., 1964; asso. prof. medicine Med. Sch. Harvard, 1964-68, prof. medicine, 1968—, chmn. div. med. scis. Faculty Arts and Scis., 1968-70, Gustavus Adolphus Pfeiffer prof. pharmacology, chmn. dept. pharmacology, 1972—. Chief endocrinology-metabolism unit Beth Israel Hosp., 1964-68, physician, 1964—. Served with USNR, 1945-46. Recipient Faculty Research award Am. Cancer Soc., 1960-64. Guggenheim fellow dept. genetics Oxford (Eng.) U., 1970-71. Mem. Am. Soc. Biol. Chemists, Am. Soc. Clin. Investigation, Endocrine Soc., Assn. of Am. Physicians, Am. Chem. Soc., Am. Assn. U. Profs., Phi Beta Kappa, Simga Xi, Alpha Omega Alpha. Mem. editorial bd. Endocrinology, 1964-68. Home: 61 Blake Rd Brookline MA 02146 Office: 25 Shattuck St Boston MA 02115

GOLDBERG, IRVING LOEB, judge; b. Port Arthur, Tex., June 29, 1906; s. Abraham and Elsa (Loeb) G.; B.A., U. Tex., 1926; LL.B., Harvard, 1929; m. Marian Jessel Melasky, Dec. 30, 1928; children—Nancy Paula (Mrs. Jay L. Todes), Julie Elsa (Mrs. Michael Lowenberg). Admitted to Tex. bar, 1929; partner Goldberg, Akin, Gump, Strauss & Hauer, Dallas, 1950-66; judge U.S. Ct. Appeals 5th Circuit, 1966—. Past vice chmn. Tex. adv. com. U.S. Commn. Civil Rights; past pres. Jewish Welfare Fedn. Dallas, Dallas Home and

Hosp. for Jewish Aged; past nat. v.p. Am. Jewish Com. Past bd. dirs. Dallas UN Assn., Dallas Council Social Agys., Nat. Conf. Christians and Jews, United HIAS Service, Council Jewish Fedns. and Welfare Funds. Served to lt. USNR, 1942-46. Recipient Brotherhood citation Nat. Conf. Christians and Jews, 1968. Mem. Am., Dallas bar assns. Clubs: Dallas, Columbian (Dallas). Home: 3701 Turtle Creek Dr Dallas TX 75219 Office: US Courthouse 1100 Commerce St Dallas TX 75202

GOLDBERG, IRWIN, dept. store exec.; b. 1918; B.S., Northwestern U., 1940; m. Treas., controller Goldblatt Bros., Inc. 1936—, v.p., 1968—. Served in World War II. Address: 333 S State St Chicago IL 60604*

GOLDBERG, JOHN JACOB, lawyer; b. Cambridge, Mass., Apr. 11, 1894; s. Benjamin and Ida (Bernstein) G.; student U. So. Cal., 1911-12; A.B., U. Cal. at Berkeley, 1915, J.D., 1917; m. Marjorie Lewin Fox, Mar. 19, 1954; children—Judith, John, Peter. Admitted to Cal. bar, 1917; spl. sec. Justices Supreme Ct. Cal., 1917; partner Henshaw, Black & Goldberg, San Francisco, 1918-20; asso. Jesse H. Steinhart, San Francisco, 1920-23; partner Steinhart, Goldberg, Feigenbaum & Ladar, 1924-69, counsel, 1969—. Mem. Cal. Commn. Jud. Qualifications, 1965-68; mem. Lawyers Committee on Civil Rights Under Law. Bd. dirs. Mervyn L. Brenner Found.; trustee Wollenberg Found. Fellow Am. Bar Found., Am. Coll. Trial Lawyers; mem. Bar Assn. San Francisco, Jewish Publs. Soc. Am. (trustee), State Bar Cal. (bd. govs. 1954-57, v.p., treas. 1956-57), Am. (ho. dels. 1958-64), Internat. bar assns., U. Cal. Law Sch. Assn. (pres. 1935-36), Order of Coif (hon.), Phi Delta Phi. Club: Concordia-Argonaut (pres. 1934-35). Home: 2205 Scott St San Francisco CA 94115 Office: Crocker Plaza San Francisco CA 94104

GOLDBERG, LEO, educator, astronomer; b. Bklyn., Jan. 26, 1913; s. Harry and Rose (Ambush) G.; S.B., Harvard, 1934, A.M., 1937; Ph.D., 1938; Sc.D., U. Mass., 1970; m. Charlotte B. Wyman, July 9, 1943; children—Suzanne, David Henry, Edward Wyman. Asst. dept. astronomy Harvard, 1934-37, Agassiz research fellow, 1937-38, spl. research fellow, 1938-41, research asso., 1941; research asso. McMath-Hulbert Obs., U. Mich., 1941-46, asst. prof. astronomy, 1945-46, asso. prof., chmn. dept. astronomy, and dir. obs., 1946-60, prof., 1948-60; Higgins prof. astronomy Harvard, 1960—, chmn. dept. astronomy, 1966-71, dir. Coll. Obs., 1966-71; dir. Kitt Peak Nat. Obs., Tucson, 1971—. Instr. astronomy, math. Wilson Coll., Chambersburg, Pa., 1939; staff mem. Smithsonian Astrophys. Obs., 1960-66. Chmn. Astronomy Missions Bd., 1967-71; mem. U.S. nat. com. Internat. Astron. Union, 1954-66, chmn., 1956-61, chmn. U.S. delegation to X Gen. Assembly. Moscow, 1958, v.p., 1958-64, pres. Commn. 12, 1958-61, pres. Commn. 44, 1961-67; mem. sci. adv. bd. USAF, 1959-62; mem. def. sci. bd. Dept. Def., 1962-66; mem. solar physics subcom. NASA, 1962-65, mem. sci. and tech. adv. com. manned space flight, 1964-70. Trustee Asso. Univs., Inc., 1957-66. Recipient Bowdoin Essay prize Harvard, 1938; USN award for exceptional service to naval ordnance devel. in connection with devel. fire control devices for navy and NDRC, 1946. Fellow Am. Acad. Arts and Scis.; mem. Nat. Acad. Scis. (mem. space sci. bd. 1958-63, dir. Benjamin Apthorp Gould Fund 1959), Internat. Acad. Astronautics, Internat. Astron. Union, Am. Philos. Soc., Optical Soc. Am., Am. Astron. Soc. (pres. 1964- 66), Assn. Univs. for Research in Astronomy, Inc. (dir. 1966-71), Royal Astron. Soc. (fgn. asso.), Société Royale des Sciences, de Liége. Author: Atoms, Stars and Nebulae (with L.H. Aller), 1943. Contbr. articles. Collaborating editor Astrophys. Jour., 1949-51, chmn. editorial board, 1954; editor Ann. Review Astronomy and Astrophysics, 1961—. Home: 3425 Via Guadalupe Tucson AZ 85716 Office: 950 N Cherry Av PO Box 4130 Tucson AZ 85717

GOLDBERG, MELVIN ARTHUR, communications exec.; b. N.Y.C., Feb. 5, 1923; s. Louis and Anna (Bergman) G.; B.S., Coll. City N.Y., 1942; A.M., Columbia, 1950; m. Norma N. Nertz, Oct. 18, 1956; children—Ronald, Richard, Joan Sandra. Staff, Bur. Applied Social Research, Columbia, 1946-47; news editor, research dir. TV mag., 1947-49; dir. sales planning and research DuMont TV Network, 1949-52; dep. dir. Office Research and Evaluation, U.S. Information Agy., 1952-53; exec. sec. Ultra-High Frequency TV Assn., 1953-54; cons., head research M-G Research, 1954-56; dir. research Westinghouse Broadcasting Co., 1956-62; v.p., dir. research Nat. Assn. Broadcasters, 1962-64; v.p. planning and research John Blair & Co., 1964; pres. Melvin A. Goldberg, Inc., N.Y.C., 1969—. Served as capt. USAAF, 1943-45. Decorated D.F.C., Air medal with clusters. Mem. Nat. Assn. Broadcasters, TV Bur. Advt. (chmn. research com.), Am. Assn. Pub. Opinion Research, Am. Marketing Assn., Radio-TV Research Council, Am. Sociol. Soc. Contbr. articles profl. publs. Home: 17 North Dr Kensington Great Neck NY 11021 Office: 347 Madison Av New York City NY 10017

GOLDBERG, MICHAEL, painter; b. N.Y.C., Dec. 24, 1924; s. Nathan and Henriette (Goldstein) G.; student Art Students League, N.Y.C., 1938-42, 46; pupil of Jose de Creeft, City Coll. N.Y., 1940-42, 46-47; student Hofmann Sch., 1941-42, 48-50; stepchildren—Lucas Matthiessen, Sarah Carey Matthiessen. Tchr., U. Cal. at Berkeley, 1961-62, Yale, 1967, U. Minn., 1968; one-man exhbns. include Tibor de Nagy Gallery, N.Y.C., 1953, Poindexter Gallery, N.Y.C., 1956, 58, Martha Jackson Gallery, N.Y.C., 1960, 62, 64, 66, Paul Kantor Gallery, Los Angeles, 1960, B.C. Holland Gallery, Chgo., 1961, Galerie Anderson-Mayer, Paris, 1963, Holland-Goldowsky Gallery, Chgo. (two-man), 1960, Bob Keene Gallery, 1963, Paley & Lowe Gallery, N.Y.C., 1971; group exhbns. include 9th St. Exhbn., N.Y.C., 1951, Stable Gallery anns., N.Y.C., 1952-57, Four Younger Americans, Sidney Janis Gallery, N.Y.C., 1956, Martha Jackson Gallery, 1958, 60, 61, 63, 64, 65, 67, Carnegie Mus., 1958, Whitney Mus., 1958, 65, 67 Gutai 9, Osaka, Japan, 1958, Turin (Italy) Art Festival, 1959, V Sao Paula (Brazil) Biennial, 1959, Documenta II, Kassel, Germany, 1959, Walker Gallery, Mpls., 1960, Am. Painters, 1960, Columbus (O.) Comtemporary Am. Painting, 1960, Hans Hofmann and His Students, Mus. Modern Art, 1963-64, Musee Cantonal des Beaux Arts, Lausanne, Switzerland, 1963, I Salon Internat. des Galeries Pilotes, 1963, Gallery Modern Art, N.Y.C., 1964, Am. Fedn. Arts, 1965, Am. Art Gallery, Copenhagen, 1965, Smithsonian Instn., 1966, Mus. Modern Art, N.Y.C., 1968, Corcoran Bienale, 1969, Rykert Gallery, N.Y.C., 1969, 70, Paula Cooper Gallery, N.Y.C., 1970, 71; represented in permanent collections Mus. Modern Art, Chgo. Art Inst., Dayton Art Inst., Corcoran Gallery Art, Nat. Gallery, Walker Art Center, Balt. Mus. Art, Albright-Knox Gallery, Buffalo, Cornell U., De Cordova Mus., Provincetown Chrysler Art Gallery, Guggenheim Mus., Smithsonian Instn., Mus. Modern Art, Israel, Mus. Modern Western Art, Tokyo. Served with AUS, World War II. Address: 222 Bowery Pl New York City NY 10012

GOLDBERG, MORTON WILLIAM, investment co. exec.; b. Washington, Dec. 11, 1916; s. Charles and Anna (Koresky) G.; LL.B., Boston U., 1938; m. Edna J. Cohen, Mar. 20, 1949; children—Lisa, Donna, Philip. Admitted to Mass. bar, 1938; practiced in Boston, 1938-48; chief exec. officer B.C. Morton Financial Corp., Boston, 1948-68, chmn. bd. First Instl. Corp. Trustee Combined Jewish Philanthropies Boston; pres. Asso. Jewish Community Centers Boston. Served with AUS, 1941-46. Mem. Am. Jewish Com. Mason (Shriner). Home: 35 Fisher Av Brookline MA 02146 Office: 140 Federal St Boston MA 02110

GOLDBERG, SAMUEL AURON, lawyer; b. Phila., June 2, 1898; s. Louis and Jennie (Gaber) G.; B.A., U. Pa., 1920, LL.B., 1923; m. Elizabeth Orowitz, Aug. 12, 1925; 1 dau., Leone Eve (Mrs. Malcolm L. Schoenberg). Admitted to Pa. bar, 1923, since practiced in Phila.; partner Wolf, Block, Schorr & Solis-Cohen, 1936-66; counsel Wolf, Block, Schorr and Solis-Cohen. Dir. emeritus Continental Bank & Trust Co., Phila. Lectr. for Bar and Title Assns. Past pres. Fedn. Jewish Charities, Jewish Family Service; former dir. United Fund; trustee Fedn. Jewish Agencies Greater Phila. Company comdr. Phila. Port Security Force, USCG, 1942-45. Mem. Am., Phila., Pa. bar assns., Am. Law Inst., Order of Coif. Author: Sales of Real Estate in Pennsylvania, 1958; Sales of Real Property, 1971; also monograph. Asso. editor: Law Notes. Mem. adv. com. that drafted Pa. Mechanics' Lein Law of 1963. Home: 2601 Parkway Philadelphia PA 19130 Office: Packard Bldg Philadelphia PA 19102

GOLDBERG, SEYMOUR, educator; b. Bklyn., Mar. 24, 1928; s. Benjamin and Florence (Cohen) G.; A.B., Hunter Coll., 1950; M.A., Ohio State U., 1952; Ph.D., U. Cal. at Los Angeles, 1958; m. Lillian E. Slominsky, Mar. 29, 1952; children—Florence Gail, Benjamin Frederick. Math. analyst Lockheed Aircraft Co., 1952-54; asst. prof. N.M. State U., 1959-62; faculty U. Md., College Park, 1962—, prof. math., 1966—. Cons. to industry. Served with AUS, 1945-47. Charles Brown fellow Hebrew U. of Jerusalem, 1958. Mem. Am. Math. Soc., Math. Assn. Am., Phi Beta Kappa. Author: Unbounded Linear Operators, 1966. Contbr. papers to profl. lit. Home: 1612 Peacock Lane Silver Spring MD 20904 Office: Math Dept Univ Md College Park MD 20742

GOLDBERG, SID, editor; b. N.Y.C., Mar. 1, 1931; s. Emanuel and Florence (Fischbein) G.; B.A., U. Mich., 1950, M.A., 1952; student N.Y. U., 1952-53; m. Lucianne S. Cummings, April 10, 1966; children—Joshua John, Jonah Jacob. editorial asst. Washington Post & Times Herald, 1955-56; fgn. affairs editor World Week mag., N.Y.C., 1955-57; asst. editor North Am. Newspaper Alliance, 1957-58, news editor, 1958-60, editor, 1960—, also gen. mgr., v.p., 1964—; editor Women's News Service, 1964—. Served with AUS, 1953-55. Mem. Sigma Delta Chi. Club: Overseas Press Am. (N.Y.C.). Home: 255 W 84th St New York City NY 10024 Office: 1501 Broadway New York City NY 10036

GOLDBERG, SZYMON, musician; b. Wloclawek, Poland, June 1, 1909; s. Israel N. and Gustava (Kamien) G.; pvt. studies violin with H. Czaplinski, 1915, M. Michalowicz, Warsaw, Poland, 1916, Carl Flesch, Berlin, Germany, 1917; music theory with A. Willner, Berlin; m. Maria Manasee, June 25, 1931. Came to U.S., 1934. First concert appearance, 1919; leader Dresden Philharmonic Orch., 1925, Berlin Philharmonic Orch., 1929; toured as violinist, Europe, U.S., Latin Am., Can., Australia, Japan, China, Israel, Africa, Far East; permanent trio with E. Feuerman, Paul Hindemith, 1930-34; permanent duo with Lili Kraus, 1935-40; concert violinist, 1955—; mus. dir., condr. Netherlannd Chamber Orch.; mem. Festival Quartet. Home: Amsterdam Holland Office: care Columbia Artists Mgmt 165 W 57th St New York City NY 10019

GOLDBERGER, ARTHUR STANLEY, educator; b. N.Y.C., Nov. 20, 1930; s. David M. and Martha (Greenwald) G.; B.S., N.Y.U., 1951; M.A., U. Mich., 1952, Ph.D., 1958; m. Iefke Engelsman, Aug. 19, 1957; children—Nina Judith, Nicholas Bernard. Acting asst. prof. econs. Stanford, 1956-59; asso. prof. econs. U. Wis., 1960- 63, prof., 1963-70, H.M. Groves prof., 1970—. Vis. prof. Center Planning and Econ. Research, Athens, Greece, 1964-65; Keynes vis. prof. U. Essex, 1968- 69. Fulbright fellow Netherlands Sch. Econs., 1955-56, 59-60; vis. prof. U. Hawaii, 1969, 71. Fellow Am. Statis. Assn., Econometric Soc.; mem. Am. Econ. Assn. Author: (with L. Klein) An Econometric Model of the United States, 1929-52, 1955; Impact Multipliers and Dynamic Properties, 1959; Econometric Theory, 1964; Topics in Regression Analysis, 1968. Bd. editors Am. Econ. Rev., 1964- 66. Home: 2828 Sylvan Av Madison WI 53705

GOLDBERGER, BERNARD JEROME, cigar co. exec.; b. Budapest, Hungary, Apr. 24, 1899; s. Moritz and Katie (Schiffblatt) B.; brought to U.S., 1906, naturalized; m. Olga Weisberg, June 15, 1921; 1 son, Alan J. Pvt. practice pub. accountancy, 1920—; sr. partner firm B.J. Goldberger & Co., N.Y.C.; chmn. exec. com. Bayuk Cigars Inc., Phila., 1959—, also dir. Sponsor N.Y.C. Center Theatre Drama and Ballet; asso. dir. Hebrew Home for Aged, Riverdale, N.Y. C.P.A. Mem. Am. Inst. C.P.A.'s, N.Y. State Soc. C.P.A.'s, Accountant's Sq. Club N.Y.C. Jewish religion. Mason; mem. B'nai B'rith. Home: 41 Park Av New York City NY 10016 Office: 424 Madison Av New York City NY 10017

GOLDBERGER, EDWARD, bus. exec.; b. Providence, Nov. 15, 1905; s. Samuel and Bertha (Steiner) G.; A.B., Brown U., 1927; LL.B., Harvard, 1931; m. Marjorie A. Lowenstein, Dec. 19, 1935; children—Ann Louise, Susan June. Admitted to R.I. bar, 1931, N.Y. bar, 1938; practiced with McGovern & Slattery, Providence, 1931-36; with M. Lowenstein & Sons, Inc., N.Y.C., 1936—, sec., 1936-70, treas., 1945—; vice chmn., 1970—. Mem. exec. com, textile sect. N.Y. Bd. Trade 1949—, chmn. 1951; mem. fgn. trade com. Am. Cotton Mfrs. Inst.; dir. Textile Distbrs. Assn., Am. Textile Mfrs. Inst.; mem. nat. commn., N.Y. exec. Anti-Defamation League, B'nai B'rith. Clubs; Metropolis Country (White Plains, N.Y.); Brown (N.Y.C.); City Athletic; Weavers. Home: 30 E 71st St New York City NY 10028 also 1367 Flagler Dr Mamaroneck NY 10543 Office: 1430 Broadway New York City NY 10018

GOLDBERGER, MARVIN L., educator, physicist; b. Chgo., Oct. 22, 1922; s. Joseph and Mildred (Sedwitz) G.; B.S., Carnegie Inst. Tech., 1943; Ph.D., U. Chgo., 1948; m. Mildred Ginsburg, Nov. 25, 1945; children—Samuel M., Joel S. Research asso. Radiation Lab., U. Cal., 1948-49, now cons.; research asso. Mass. Inst. Tech., 1949-50; asst. prof. U. Chgo., 1950-55, prof., 1955-57; Higgins prof. physics Princeton, 1953-54, 57—, chmn. dept., 1970—. Cons. Los Alamos Sci. Lab., Brookhaven Nat. Lab. Mem. Pres.'s Sci. Adv. Com., 1965-69. Fellow Am. Phys. Soc., Am. Acad. Arts and Scis.; mem. Nat. Acad. Scis. Home: 125 Fitz Randolph Rd Princeton NJ 08540

GOLDBLATT, JOEL, bus. exec.; b. Chgo., Aug. 12, 1907; s. Simon and Hannah (Diamond) Goldblatt; m. Lynne C. Walker, Dec. 31, 1948 (div. Nov. 1962); children—Jan Hannah, Jody Lou, Joel. Began as buyer, Goldblatt Bros., Inc., later in active mgmt. of co., v.p., operating dir., 1928-46, pres., 1945-64, became vice chmn., 1963, now dir.; pres., chief exec. officer Bell Industries, 1963—. Pres. State St. Council, 1948-49, chmn. bd. 1950-51, dir., 1952-53; mem. Chgo. Plan Commn. Co-chmn. Red Cross Drive, 1946; chmn. trades and industries div. Community Fund Drive, 1946. Trustee Goldblatt Brothers Found.; dir. Michael Reese Hosp. Served as maj. Q.M. Corps, AUS, World War II, disch. 1945. Office: 295 Fifth Av New York City NY 10010

GOLDBLATT, LOUIS, retail bus. exec.; b. Stashow, Poland, Dec. 25, 1903 (parents Am. citizens); s. Simon and Hannah (Diamond) G.; student pub. schs.; m. Roberta Marie Pernecky, Nov. 12, 1952; children—Gary, Stuart, David. With Goldblatt Bros., Inc., Chgo., 1918—, v.p., 1934, gen. advt. mgr., 1937, gen. merchandising mgr. for entire chain, 1939, exec. v.p., sec.-treas., 1945-64, pres., chief exec. officer, 1964—. Bd. dirs. State St. Council, Chgo. Better Bus. Bur., Gastro- Intestinal Research Found.; trustee Goldblatt Bros. Found. Pres., Heart Research Found. Served as 1st lt. AUS, World War II. Home: 15 E Linden Av Wilmette IL 60091 Office: Goldblatt Bros Inc 333 S State St Chicago IL 60604

GOLDBLATT, MAURICE, bus. exec.; b. Strashov, Poland, Dec. 17, 1893; s. Simon and Hannah (Diamond) G.; ed. pub. schs.; m. Sylvia Gottstein, June 22, 1924 (div 1935); children—Noel Lyman, Gloria Hope, m. 2d, Bernice Mendelson, Jan. 7, 1936; childrenMerle Ann, Stanford Jay. Salesman, E. Iverson & Co., 1912-14; pres. Goldblatt Bros., Inc., dept. stores, Chgo., 1914-45; chmn. bd. 1945—. Chmn. bd. trustees Goldblatt Bros. Found.; chmn. bd. U. Chgo. Cancer Research Found., Cancer Research Found., Inc., Heart Research Found., Inc.; past dir. Mt. Sinai Hosp., Chgo., La Rabida Jackson Park Sanitarium B'nai B'rith; hon. dir. Cancer Prevention Center of Chgo. Past pres. Marks Nathan Hall; former exec. dir. Am. Cancer Soc., past dir. Am. Heart Assn.; past mem. Nat. Adv. Cancer Council, USPHS. Mem. citizens bd. Loyola U., U. Chgo. Awarded Rosenberger medal, 1951. Mem. Chgo. Heart Assn. (dir.), Am. Hosp. Assn. (hon.). Mason, Elk. Clubs: Standard, Bryn Mawr Country (Chgo.). Home: 1040 Lake Shore Dr Chicago IL 60611 Office: 333 S State St Chicago IL 60604

GOLDBLITH, SAMUEL ABRAHAM, educator; b. Lawrence, Mass., May 5, 1919; s. Abraham and Fannie (Rubin) G.; S.B., Mass. Inst. Tech., 1940, S.M., 1947, Ph.D., 1949; m. Diana Greenberg, Apr. 27, 1941; children—Errol (dec.), Judith Ann, Jonathan Mark. Research, Arthur D. Little Co., Cambridge, Mass., 1940-41; faculty Mass. Inst. Tech., 1949—, prof. food tech., 1959—, acting head dept., 1959-61, exec. officer dept., 1961-66, dep. dept. head, 1967—. Mem. coms. radiation preservation and radionuclides in foods, chmn. com. radiation preservation of foods NRC-Nat. Acad. Scis. Dir. Gen. Econs. Corp., Mchts. Cold Storage and Warehouse Co., Providence, Cardinal Proteins, Ltd., Halifax, N.S. Served to capt. AUS, 1941-46. PTO. Named One of Ten Outstanding Young Men of Greater Boston, 1953; recipient Babcock-Hart award, 1969; Nicholas Appert medal, 1970. Mem. Inst. Food Technologists (chmn. N.E. sect. 1958; Monsanto Presentation award 1953;) Distinguished Food Scientist award N.Y. sect. 1969), Am. Chem. Soc., Radiation Research Soc., A.A.A.S., Sigma Xi, Phi Tau Sigma (pres. 1958). Mason. Clubs: Chemists (N.Y.C.); Cosmos (Washington); New Century (pres. 1962-63) (Boston). Author: An Introduction to Thermal Processing of Foods, 1961; Milestones in Nutrition, 1964. Home: 6 Meadowview Rd Melrose MA 02176 Office: Mass Inst Tech 77 Massachusetts Av Cambridge MA 02139

GOLDBLUM, NORMAN PENN, drug distbn. co. exec.; b. Phila., Mar. 26, 1924; s. Jacob G. and Rebecca (Mott) G.; student Temple U. Sch. Pharmacy, 1946; m. Simone Sheerr, Jan. 16, 1966; children by previous marriage—Joseph, Libby, Georganne. With West Wholesale Drug Co., Phila., 1947-71, exec. v.p., 1968-71; v.p. Spectro Industries, Jenkintown, Pa., 1968—. Bd. dirs. Phila. Drug Exchange. Served with USAAF, 1942-46. Mem. Nat. Wholesale Drug Assn. Jewish religion (pres. temple 1956-58). Clubs: Georgetown (Md.) Yacht (commodore 1967; Philmont Country; Chesapeake Bay Past Commodores. Home: 928 Frazier Rd Rydal PA 19046 Office: Jenkintown Plaza Jenkintown PA 19046

GOLDBLUM, STANLEY, corp. exec.; b. Pitts., Jan. 17, 1927; s. Victor and Eve (Zeisel) G.; student U. Ida., 1944-46; B.S., U. Cal. at Los Angeles, 1950; m. Marlene Becker, May 14, 1966; children—Corrine, Gary, Jolene, Wendi. Rep., Midland Mut. Life Ins. Co., Los Angeles, 1955-57; pres. Exec. Planning Corp., Los Angeles, 1957-59; pres., chmn. bd. dir. Equity Funding Corp. of Am., Beverly Hills, Cal., 1960—, pres. EFC Distbrs. Corp., Los Angeles, 1966—; chmn. bd. Equity Growth Fund Am., Inc., Fund of Am., Inc., Equity Progress Fund, Inc., Equity Funding Life Ins. Co., Inc. Served with AUS, 1946-48. Mem. A.I.M. (pres.'s council), Nat. Assn. Securities Dealers, Young Pres. Orgn. Home: 909 N Whittier Dr Beverly Hills CA 90210 Office: 1900 Av ot the Stars Los Angeles CA 90067

GOLDBURG, NORMAN MICHAEL, rabbi; b. St. Louis, Feb. 22, 1902; s. Burt and Julia (Posnanski) G.; A.B., U.Cin.,1927; B.H. and Rabbi, Hebrew Union Coll., 1929, D.D., 1955; LL.D., Augusta Coll., 1969; student U. Chgo., Harvard, Pacific Sch. Religion; m. Rose F. Colker, Aug. 18, 1929; children—Sally Ann, Jesse Bernard. Rabbi, Temple B'nai Israel, Sacramento, 1929-45, Temple Israel, Brockton, Mass., 1945- 48, Congregation Children of Israel, Augusta, Ga., 1948—; prof. dept. philosophy Augusta Coll.; prof. dept. religion Paine Coll., Augusta; lectr. Bibl. lit. U. Cal. Extensiion div., 1931, Cal. State Edn. Forum Series, 1937-40; tchr. pub. speaking Heald Coll., 1940- 41, chaplain Folsom Prison, Represa, Cal., 1929-41, Cal. State Legislature, 1931, VA hosps., Lenwood and Forest Hills; aux. chaplain Camp Gordon, Ga. Pres. bd. Augusta Library; pres. Bd. of Rabbis No. Cal., 1939, Sacramento Safety Council, 1936, Greek War Relief Campaign No. Cal., 1940-41, Council for Civic Unity, 1944-45; founder Sacramento Religious Fellowship, 1931; rep. S.E. area Jewish Chatauqua Soc.; mem. exec. bd. Community Chest; active YMCA, Goodwill Industries, Am. Sch. Safety Patrols, Tb Soc., Cancer Soc., A.R.C., Boy Scouts Am., Travelers Aid Soc., United Jewish Welfare, Nat. Conf. Christians and Jews. Served as chaplain U.S. Army, 1941-44. Mem. Vols. Am., Central Conf. Am. Rabbis (treas.), Alumni Assn. Hebrew Union Coll.-Jewish Inst. Religion (pres.). Mason, Rotarian. Clubs: Pacific Soc., Commonwealth, Ari- Man League, Augusta Country. Author: Assembly Prayers, 1932; Tell It To the Chaplain; Patrick J. McGillicuddy and the Chaplain (series). Originator program, Ramblings, Cal. Broadcasting System, 1930-41; feature speaker, Ramblings, radio sta. WGAC, Augusta. Home: 3006 Fox Springs Rd Augusta GA 30907 Office: Walton Way Temple Walton Way Extension Augusta GA 30907

GOLDEN, CHARLES FRANKLIN, bishop; b. Holly Springs, Miss., Aug. 24, 1912; s. J.W. and Mary P. (Tyson) G.; A.B., Clark Coll., Atlanta, 1936; B.D., Gammon Theol. Sem., 1937, D.D., 1958; S.T.M., Boston U., 1938, postgrad. 1946-47; LL.D., W.Va., Wesleyan Coll., 1964; m. Ida Elizabeth Smith, May 24, 1937. Ordained to deacon Meth. Ch., 1936, elder, 1938; pastor, Birmingham, Ala., Atlanta, Cooksville, Tenn., Clarkdale, Miss., 1935-41; dir. field service, dept. Negro work Meth. Bd. Missions, 1947-52, asso. sec. nat. div. Bd. Missions, 1952-56, dir. nat. div., 1956-60; bishop Nashville-Birmingham area Meth. Ch., 1960-64, Nashville-Carolina area, 1964-68; bishop Cal.-Nev. area 1968—; ofc. rep World Div. Bd. Missions to India Centennial, Lucknow, India, 1956; mem. gen. bd. missions Meth. Ch.; sec. Central Jurisdiction Coll. Bishops, pres., 1967; pres. Bd. Christian Social Concerns, United Meth. Ch., 1968—, vice chmn. Commn. on Religion and Race, 1968—) mem. program council, 1968—; chmn. div. peace and world order Bd. Christian Concerns of Meth. Ch., 1964-68; chmn. joint com. on missionary personnel Bd. Missions of Meth. Ch.; Meth. rep. to central com. World Council of Chs., Enugo, Nigeria, West Africa, 1965; chmn. dept. renewal, life and mission div. Nat. Council of Chs. of U.S.A.,

1967-68. Trustee Gammon Theol. Sem., Bennett Coll., 1964-70, Scarrit Coll., 1964-70, Morristown Coll., 1962-68, Pacific Sch. Religion, 1969—; regent U. of Pacific, 1969—; bd. mgrs. Bd. of Missions, 1960—. Served to capt., Chaplians Corps, AUS, 1942-46. Sec. Little Rock Interdenominational Ministers Alliance, 1939-42. Mem. Meth. Rural Fellowship (sec. 1952-56), Omega Psi Phi, Sigma Pi Phi. Contbr. articles to religious publs. Home: 1333 Gough St San Francisco CA 94109 Office: 330 Ellis St San Francisco CA 94102

GOLDEN, HAROLD, broadcasting exec.; b. Niagara Falls, N.Y., Aug. 4, 1924; s. Benjamin and Rose (Krasne) G.; student Biarritz Am. U., France, 1945-46, U. Buffalo, 1946-47; B.A., Syracuse U., 1949; m. Bernice N. Ginsberg, Nov. 7, 1953; children—Ricard, Margery, Donald. Radio, TV, theatre actor, 1949-53; v.p., dir. sales MCA-TV, N.Y.C., 1954-65; pres. ABC Films, N.Y.C., 1965-69; pres. Golden Prodns., 1969—. Mem. Syracuse U. Indsl. Adv. Council. Recipient Alumni award for significant achievement in TV, Syracuse U., 1965. Mem. Internat. Radio and TV Soc. Greater World Series of Tennis-TV. Home: 37 Dundee Rd Stamford CT 06903 Ofice: 1330 Av of Americas New York City NY 10019

GOLDEN, HARRY, editor, pub., writer; b. N.Y.C., May 6, 1902; s. Leib and Anna (Klein) Goldhirsch; student Coll. City N.Y., 1919-22; L.H.D., Belmont Abbey Coll., 1962, Johnson C. Smith Univ., Charlotte, N.C., 1965; Genevieve Gallagher, Apr. 20, 1926; children—Richard, Harry, William, Peter. Editor, pub. The Carolina Israelite, Charlotte, N.C., 1942—. Named Man of Year, Carver Coll., 1957, Johnson C. Smith Coll., 1958, Temple Emanu-El, N.Y.C., 1958. Mem. Am. Jewish Congress (mem. bd.), N.A.A.C.P. (life), Shakespeare Soc. Am., Cath. Interracial Council. Mem. B'nai B'rith. Author: Only in America, 1958; For 2 Cents, 1959; Enjoy, Enjoy! 1960; Carl Sandburg, 1961; You're Entitle', 1962; Forgotten Pioneer, 1963; Mr. Kennedy and the Negroes, 1964; So What Else is New, 1965; A Little Girl Is Dead, 1965; Eat, Eat, My Child, 1966; The Lynching of Leo Frank, 1966, The Right Time, 1968; So Long as You're Healthy, 1969; The Israelis, 1970. Home: 1316 Elizabeth Av Charlotte NC 28204

GOLDEN, HAWKINS, lawyer; b. Morton, Miss., June 24, 1905; s. John J. and Mary Elizabeth (Hawkins) G.; B.A., Vanderbilt U., 1926; M.A., Harvard, 1927; J.D., So. Methodist, U., 1930; m. Margaret Jackson, Feb. 25, 1939; children—Margaret, Hawkins. Aditted to Tex. bar, 1930, practiced in Dallas, 1930—; mem. firm Leake, Henry, Young & Golden, 1932-47, sr. partner Leake, Henry, Golden & Burrow, 1947-59, Leake, Henry, Golden, Burrow & Potts, 1959-66, Golden, Burrow, Potts & Boeckman, 1966—. Chmn. bd. Pig Stand Cos. Mem. Dallas Hosp. Found.; research fellow Southwestern Legal Found. Organizing dir. Dallas Crime Commn.; bd. rev. Judge Adv. Gen. Dept., World War II. Bd. devel. So. Meth. U. Mem. S.A.R., Am., Tex., Dallas (pres. 1950, chmn. 1952) bar assns., Phi Beta Kappa, Sigma Chi, Delta Theta Phi. Methodist (chmn. ofcl. bd. 1950). Mason (Shriner, Jester, 32). Clubs: Dallas Country, Salesmanship, Idlewild, Terpsichorean, Calyx, Rotary (pres. 1955-56), Knife and Fork (pres. 1958-60), Preston (Dallas). Home: 8931 Preston Rd Dallas TX 75225 Office: Republic Nat Bank Tower Dallas TX 75201

GOLDEN, JEROME BENJAMIN, lawyer, corp. exec.; b. N.Y.C., Nov. 26, 1917; s. Morris and Ida (Burke) G.; student Coll. City N.Y., 1938; LL.B., St. Lawrence U., Canton, N.Y., 1942; m. Rosamond Lukin, Sept. 7, 1947 (dec. Feb. 1965); children—Mark D., Dean P. Admitted to N.Y. bar, 1942; mem. legal dept. Paramount Pictures, Inc., 1942-50, United Paramount Theatres, Inc., 1950-53; with Am. Broadcasting-Paramount Theatres, Inc. (now Am. Broadcasting Cos., Inc.), N.Y.C., 1953—, sec., 1958—, v.p., 1959—. Home: 166 E 63d St New York City NY 10021 Office: 1330 Av Americas New York City NY 10019

GOLDEN, JOHN MATTHEW, mem. Dem. Nat. Com.; b. Old Saybrook, Conn., Nov. 4, 1895; s. Matthew J. and Alice P. (Strickland) G.; student pub. schs., Old Saybrook; m. Margaret J. Stumpf, Apr. 7, 1920; children—Margaret (Mrs. John A. Berges), Frances A. (Mrs. William Kresnisky). Supt., The Greist Mfg. Co., 1915-30; dir. pub. works City of New Haven, 1932-45; pres. Golden, O'Neill & Gebhardt, Inc., ins. agy., 1940; dir. Gen Bank & Trust Co. Winthrop Bank & Trust Co. Pres. Camp Palmer for Boys; dir. Catholic Diocesan Bur. Mem. of Democratic Nat. Com., 1952—. Trustee Hosp. St. Raphael, Albertus Magnus Coll., Amherst Coll., Woodstock, Conn., New Haven Found. Mem. Knights St. Patrick. Roman Catholic. K.C., Hibernian, Eagle. Clubs: Union League, Catholic of N.Y. Home: 110 Westwood Rd New Haven CT 06515 Office: 1 Columbus Plaza New Haven CT 06510

GOLDEN, LEON, educator; b. Jersey City, Dec. 25, 1930; s. Nathan and Regina (Okun) G.; B.A., U. Chgo., 1950, M.A., 1953, Ph.D., 1958. Instr. ancient langs. Coll. William and Mary, 1958-60, asst. prof. ancient langs., 1960- 65; asso. prof. classical langs. Fla. State U., 1965-68, prof., 1968—. Served with AUS, 1953-55. Fellow coop. program humanities U.N.C. and Duke, 1964-65, Soc. for Religion in Higher Edn., 1971-72. Mem. Am. Philol. Assn., Archeol. Inst. Am., Classical Assn. Middle West and South, Phi Beta Kappa. Author: In Praise of Prometheus: Humanism and Rationalism in Aeschylean Thought, 1966; Aristotle's Poetics, 1968. Office: Dept of Classics Florida State U Tallahassee FL 32306

GOLDEN, LOUIS B., vending machine co. exec.; b. 1904; student Adelbert Coll.; LL.B., John Marshall Law Sch., 1930; married. Pres., dir. Automatic Vending Corp., Cleve., 1933-70, chmn. bd., chief exec. officer, dir., 1970—. Office: 7501 Carnegie Av Cleveland OH 44103*

GOLDEN, MAX, lawyer, corp. exec.; b. Passaic, N.J., Feb. 18, 1913; s. Jacob and Pauline (Kitaeff) G.; student N.Y.U., 1931, Dana Coll., 1932; LL.B. magna cum laude, Rutgers U., 1935; m. Hannah G. Gleicher, Sept. 14, 1940; children—David, Jeffrey, Paul. Admitted to N.J. bar, 1936; practice of law, 1936-41; atty. legal div. office chief ordnance Dept. Army, 1941-48; asst., then asso. gen. counsel procurement office sec. USAF, 1948-51, dep. for procurement and material programs under sec., 1952, dep. to asst. sec. materiel, 1953-57, dep. asst. sec. materiel, 1957-58, gen. counsel Dept. Air Force, 1958-62; asst. to pres. Gen. Dynamics Corp., 1963-64, v.p., 1964—. Recipient exceptional civillan service award Dept. Air Force; Nat. Civil Service League award, 1961; Distinguished Civilian Service award Dept. Def., 1963. Mem. Fed. Bar Assn. Home: 200 S Brentwood Blvd St Louis MO 63105 Office: Pierre Laclede Center St Louis MO 63105

GOLDEN, ROSS, physician, educator; b. Iowa Center, Ia., Sept. 30, 1889; s. A. Lincoln and Jennie (Funk) G.; A.B., Cornell Coll., 1912, D.Sc. (hon.), 1947; M.D., Harvard, 1916; m. Hazel D. Smith, Oct. 29, 1923 (dec. Mar. 1957); children—Mary Jean Hamilton, Joann Limbacher; m. 2d, Frances L. Kraft, Dec. 30, 1961. Intern Peter Bent Brigham Hosp., Boston, 1916-17, asst. resident physician, 1920-22; resident physician, Roentgen ray dept. Mass. Gen. Hosp., Boston, 1920-21; asst. prof. medicine Columbia, 1922-29, asso. prof., 1929-34, prof. radiology, 1934-54, prof. emeritus, 1954—; vis. prof. radiology U. Cal. at Los Angeles, 1954-67; cons. Presbyn. Hosp., N.Y.C., 1954—. Chmn. Internat. Commn. Rules and Regulations of Internat. Congress Radiology, 1959—. Served with MC, U.S. Army, World War I, disch. as maj. Recipient gold medal Am. Coll. Radiology, 1958. Diplomate Am. Board Radiology. Hon. fellow Inter-Am. Coll. Radiology; hon. fellow faculty radiologists Royal Coll. Surgeons Ireland, mem. Am. Roentgen Ray Soc. (pres. 1945-46), Am. Coll. Radiology (pres. 1943-44), Radiol. Soc. N.A. (Carman lectr. 1940, Gold medal 1952), A.M.A., N.Y. Acad. of Medicine; hon. mem. Indian Radiol. Assn. (Sir Jagdish Bose Medal, 1956), Accademica Medica di Roma, Brit. Inst. Radiology, Deutsche Röntgen-Gesellschaft, Radiol. sect. Royal Soc. Medicine London, also six Latin Am. radiol. socs. Author: The Radiologic Examination of the Small Intestine, 1945; Roentgen-Ray Examination of the Digestive Tract, 1949; Roentgenology of the Abdomen, 1961; also 2 chpts. Golden's Diagnostic Radiology, 4 vols. Ross Golden lectureship established by Columbia U. and N.Y. Roentgen Soc., 1954. Home: 585B Av Majorca Laguna Hills CA 92653

GOLDEN, RUTH SULZBERGER, printing co. exec.; b. N.Y.C., Mar. 12, 1921; d. Arthur Hays and Iphigene (Ochs) Sulzberger; A.B., Smith Coll., 1943; m. Ben Hale Golden, June 1, 1946 (div. Mar. 1965); children—Stephen A.O., Michael D., Lynn Iphigene, Arthur Sulzberger. Reporter, N.Y. Times, summers 1939-45, dir. N.Y. Times Co., 1961—; music critic Chattanooga Times, 1946-57, dir. spl. activities, 1956—; asst. sec. Times Printing Co., 1950-60, v.p., 1956-65, pres., pub., 1965-70, chmn. bd., pub., 1970—; pres., pub. Chattanooga Post, 1964-69. Pres. bd. Chattanooga Symphony, 1959-61; bd. dirs. Chattanooga Ties Found., Inc.; trustee U. Chattanooga. Served with A.R.C., 1943-45; ETO. Sustaining mem. Jr. League. Home: 919 Scenic Hwy Lookout Mountain TN 37350 Office: 117 E 10th St Chattanooga TN 37401

GOLDEN, SIDNEY, educator, chemist; b. Boston, June 23, 1917; s. Harry and Fannie (Sher) G.; B.S., Coll. City N.Y., 1938; student Purdue U., 1940-42; Ph.D., Harvard, 1948; m. Muriel Nirenberg, Aug. 24, 1941; children—Harriet Rachel, Nancy Sue. Research supr. sect. H div. 3 Nat. Def. Research Com., George Washington U., 1942-46; phys. chemist Hydrocarbon Research, Inc., N.Y.C., 1948-51; adj. instr. Poly. Inst. Bklyn., 1949-50; mem. faculty Brandeis U., Waltham, Mass., 1951—, prof. chemistry, 1959—. Vis. prof. U. Cal. at Berkeley, 1963; vis. prof. Hebrew U., Jerusalem, 1967-68; cons. Nat. Bur. Standards, 1957-61. NRC predoctoral fellow, 1946-48; recipient Presdl. Certificate of Merit, 1948; Fulbright Sr. scholar Cambridge (Eng.) U., 1959-60; Guggenheim fellow, 1959-60. Fellow Am. Acad. Arts and Scis., Am. Phys. Soc., Am. Inst. Chemists; mem. Am. Chem. Soc. (vis. scientist 1963-68), Faraday Soc. Author: Introduction to Theoretical Physical Chemistry, 1961; Elements of Theory of Gases, 1964; Quantum Statistical Foundations of Chemical Kinetics, 1969; also articles. Home: 31 Winchester Dr Lexington MA 02173 Office: 415 South St Waltham MA 02154

GOLDEN, WILLIAM THEODORE, corporate dir. and trustee; b. N.Y.C., Oct. 25, 1909; s. S. Herbert and Rebecca (Harris) G.; A.B., U. Pa., 1930; postgrad. Harvard Grad. Sch. of Bus. Adminstrn., 1930-31; m. Sibyl Levy, May 2, 1938; children—Sibyl Rebecca, Pamela Prudence. Asst. to pres. Cornell, Linder & Co., indsl. and financial mgmt., N.Y.C., 1931-34; with Carl M. Loeb & Co. and Carl M. Loeb, Rhoades & Co., investment brokers and bankers, 1934-41; asst. to commr. AEC, 1946-50, cons. 1950-58; spl. sci. cons. to Pres. Truman, 1950-51 adviser on orgn. NSF to dir. Bur. Budget, 1950-51; mem. mil. procurement task force Commn. on Orgn. Exec. Br. Govt. (Hoover Commn.), 1954-55; mem. Dept. State Adv. Com. Pvt. Enterprise in Fgn. Aid, 1964-65. Chmn. bd. Federated Devel. Co.; dir. Crowell Collier and Macmillian, Inc., Verde Exploration, Ltd., Gen. Am. Investors Co., Inc., Block Drug Co.; chmn. trustees City Univ. Constrn. Fund; trustee Mitre Corp. Mem. Mayor's Commn. on Delivery Personal Health Services, 1966-68; vice chmn. com. to evaluate Health Research Council City N.Y., N.Y. Acad. Medicine com. social policy health care; mem. Mayor's Task Force on CATV and Telecommunications; adv. council Sch. Gen. Studies, Columbia, governing council Courant Inst. Math. Scis. (N.Y.U.); mem. vis. com. Princeton, Harvard. Trustee Mt. Sinai Hosp. and Med. Sch., N.Y. Found., Asso. Hosp. Service N.Y. (Blue Cross), Hebrew Free Loan Soc., Am. Mus. of Natural History, Marine Biol. Lab., Woods Hole, Mass., Inst. Ednl. Devel., Inst. for Future, Riverside Research Inst., Carnegie Inst. Washington, Center Advanced Study Behavioral Scis., Univ. Corp. Atmospheric Research, Hudson Inst. Served to lt. comdr. USNR, 1941-45. Recipient Letters of Commendations from sec. of navy, chief Bur. Ordnance for invention naval gunfire device. Benjamin Franklin fellow Royal Soc. Arts; mem. A.A.A.S. (treas., mem. exec. com.), Council on Fgn. Relations, Am. Psychosomatic Soc., Soc. Protozoologists. Clubs: Army and Navy, Cosmos (Washington); Century Association, City Midday (N.Y.C.). Home: 730 Park Av New York City NY 10021 also Olive Bridge NY 12461 Office: 40 Wall St New York City NY 10005

GOLDENBERG, LOUIS, art dealer; b. New Brunswick, N.J., May 16, 1913; s. Max and Sadie (Greif) G.; grad. Pace Inst.; m. Helen Domblatt, Aug. 20, 1944; children—Myra J., Barbara A. Accountant, Frederick William Greenfield Co., C.P.A.'s, N.Y.C., 1938-42; dir. govt. contracts Bulova Watch Co., N.Y.C., 1938-42, supr. internal accounting, 1942-46; partner Goldenberg & Goldenberg, C.P.A.'s, N.Y.C., 1946-65; with Wildenstein & Co., Inc., N.Y.C., art dealers, 1946—, v.p., 1958-68, pres., 1968—, also dir.; Treas., trustee Wildenstein Found. Mem. N.Y. Soc. C.P.A.'s, Am. Inst. Accountants, Anti-Defamation League B'nai B'rith (chmn. steering com. Westchester County, N.Y. intercultural affairs com., nat. program com.). Home: 247 Barnard Rd Larchmont NY 10538 Office: 19 E 64th St New York City NY 10021

GOLDENSON, LEONARD HARRY, motion picture, radio, TV exec.; b. Scottdale, Pa., Dec. 7, 1905; s. Lee and Esther (Broude) G.; Harvard Coll., 1927, Harvard Law Sch., 1930; m. Isabelle Weinstein, Oct. 10, 1939; children—Genise, Loreen, Maxine. Admitted to N.Y. bar, Pa. bar, 1930; practice in N.Y.C., 1930-33; asst. to Mr. Y. Frank Freeman in home office, in charge of theatre operations for Paramount Pictures, N.Y.C., 1937-38, in charge of theatre operations, 1941, v.p., Paramount Pictures, N.Y.C., 1942-50, dir. Paramount Pictures, Inc., 1944-50; pres. and dir. United Paramount Theatres, Inc., 1950-52; pres., dir. Am. Broadcasting-Paramount Theatres, Inc. (name changed to Am. Broadcasting Cos., Inc 1965), 1953—; mem. Uptown adv. group, 1953—, com. Bankers Trust Co. Founder, pres., dir. United Cerebral Palsy Assn., Inc., 1949-53, chmn. bd., 1954-60, vice chmn. bd., 1960—; bd. dirs. United Cerebral Palsy Research and Ednl. Found.; trustee Children's Cancer Research Found. of Children's Med. Center, Boston; adv. com. Nat. Cultural Center; trustee John F. Kennedy Center for the Performing Arts, Will Roges Meml. Hosp.; bd. dirs. Daus. of Jacob Geriatric Center, N.Y.C. Mem. Advt. Council (dir.), Internat. Radio and TV Soc. Club: Harvard (N.Y.C.). Home: 803 The Parkway Shore Acres Mamaroneck NY 10543 Office: 1330 Av Americas New York City NY 10019

GOLDENSON, ROBERT MYAR, psychologist; b. Albany, N.Y., Feb. 2, 1908; s. Dr. Samuel Harry and Claudia (Myar) G.; B.A. magna cum laude, Princeton, 1930; M.A., U. Pitts., 1932; Ph.D., Harvard, 1940; m. Irene Herz, June 25, 1940; children—Ronald, Daniel. Teaching fellow philosophy U. Pitts., 1931-32; instr. Black Mountain Coll., 1934-37; instr., asst. prof. psychology Hunter Coll., 1940-59; ednl. dir. Book-of-the-Month Club, 1960-68; writer, condr. vet. readjustment series When He Comes Home, radio sta. WMCA, N.Y.C., also Armed Forces Network, 1945-46; writer (with Dr. Luther Woodward) radio series Inquiring Parent, 1946-50; panel mem. It's a Problem, NBC-TV, 1951-52; mem. children's program review com., 1955; condr. TV series Keep Up to Date, NBC, later ABC, 1953-54. Mem. edn. commn. Internat. Congress Mental Health, 1949; del. U.S. Commn. UNESCO Conf., 1951; chmn. film com. New Rochelle Guidance Center, 1951-52. Mem. Tri-State Council Family Relations (pres. 1953), Am. Psychol. Assn. Phi Beta Kappa. Author: (with R. E. Hartley, L. K. Frank) Understanding Children's Play, 1952; Helping Your Child to Read Bettr, 1957; (with R.E. Hartley) The Complete Book of Children's Play, 1957, rev. edit., 1963; All About the Human Mind, 1963; Encyclopedia of Human Behavior 1969. Contbr. articles to family periodicals. Address: Sunny Ridge Rd Harrison NY 10528

GOLDENSTEIN, ERWIN HARMON, educator; b. Sterling, Neb., Jan. 11, 1921; s. Frank and Grace (Wehmer) G.: B.S., U. Neb., 1942, M.A., 1949, Ph.D., 1951; m. Valda Marie Panko, May 25, 1942 (dec. Feb. 1960); children—Diana, Ronald; m. 2d, Pearl Rosa Schaaf, Aug. 26, 1961; 1 son, Jeffrey. Tchr. secondary schs., supt. Neb., 1946-48; part-time instr. U. Neb., Lincoln, 1948-50, asst. prof. secondary edn., 1954-56, asso. prof. history and philosophy edn., 1956-59, prof., 1959—, chmn. dept., 1959-70; supr. secondary edn. Neb. Dept. Pub. Instrn., 1950-51, 52-54. Instr. field arty. gunnery and math. U.S. Army F.A. Sch., Fort Sill, Okla., 1951-52. Del. 4th Assembly World Council Chs., Sweden, 1968; pres. Luth. Student Found., Lincoln. Trustee Martin Luther Home and Sch., Beatrice, Neb.; regent Dana Coll., Blair, Neb. Served to capt. F.A., AUS, 1942-46. Mem. Am. Assn. U. Profs., Am. Ednl. Studies Assn., Comparative Edn. Soc., N.E.A., Philosophy Edn. Soc., Soc. Profs. Edn. (sec.-treas. 1964-68, pres. 1969), Phi Delta Kappa. Contbr. ednl. monographs, articles to periodicals. Home: 2201 N 61st St Lincoln NB 68505

GOLDFARB, JACOB A., clothing mfg. exec.; b. Warsaw, Russia, June 15, 1895; s. Aaron and Sarah (Fisher) G.; student Coll. City N.Y., 1909-10; fellow Brandeis U., 1953, L.H.D.; m. Bertha Leventhal, Sept. 14, 1930; children—Betty (Mrs. Robert Watson, Jr.), Miriam (Mrs. Landon K. Thorne, Jr.), Ruth Elaine (Mrs. William Lese), Robert Jack. Founder, chmn. Union Underwear Co.; Inc.; chmn. bd. CFC Corp., Fruit of Loom, Inc.; dir. Empire State Bank, Kansas City, Mo., Sterling Nat. Bank & Trust Co., N.Y.C., Imperial Reading Corp.; mem. adv. bd. Phila. & Reading Corp.; pres. Goldfarb Investing Corp. Trustee Grand St. Boys Found., 1954—; trustee, treas. Brandeis U.; v.p., trustee N.Y.U. Jewish Culture Found.; v.p., chmn. nat. finance com. Inst. Human Relations. Served with U.S. Army, World War I. Mem. Fedn. Jewish Charities (trustee- at-large), Am. Fair Trade Council (dir., treas. 1951), Underwear Inst. (exec. com. 1943). Mason; mem. B'nai B'rith. Clubs: Harmonie, Metropolis Country (N.Y.C.). Home: 895 Park Av New York City NY 10021 Office: 1290 Av Americas New York City NY 10019

GOLDFARB, RONALD LAWRENCE, lawyer; b. Jersey City, N.J., Oct. 16, 1933; s. Robert S. and Aida J. (Weintraub) G.; A.B., Syracuse U., 1954, LL.B., 1956; LL.M., Yale, 1960, J.S.D., 1962; m. Joanne Jacob, June 9, 1957; children—Jody, Nicholas, Maximilian Goldfarb. Admitted N.Y. bar, 1956, Cal. bar, 1959, D.C. bar, 1965, U.S. Supreme Ct.; practice law Washington, 1966—; spl. asst. to U.S. atty. gen. organized crime sect., 1961-64; partner Goldfarb & Singer, 1966—. Dir., Brookings Instn. program on cts. and adminstrn. Justice, 1966-67; mem. staff counsel com. on law and social action Am. Jewish Congress, 1960- 61; cons. Pres.'s Poverty Program, 1964, Riots Commn., 1967-68. Served to capt., Judge Adv. Gen. Corps, USAF, 1957-60. Recipient Fed. Bar Assn. award for book Ransom, 1966; Arthur Garfield Hays fellow N.Y.U., 1960- 61. Mem. Am., Fed., D.C., N.Y., Cal. bar assns., Am. Civil Liberties Union, Sigma Alpha Mu, Phi Delta Phi. Author: The Contempt Power, 1963; Ransom: A Critique of the American Bail System, 1965; (with Alfred Friendly) Crime and Publicity, 1967; (with Linda L. Singer) After Conviction—A New Review of the American Correction System, 1972. Contbr. articles profl. jours., popular mags. Home: 7312 Rippon Rd Alexandria VA 22307 Office: 1616 H St NW Washington DC 20006

GOLDFEDER, ANNA, cancer research; b. Poland, June 25, 1897; d. Harry and Tauba (Friedman) Goldfeder; D.Sc., Karl's U., Prague, Czechoslovakia, 1923; student medicine Masaryk U. Brno, Czechoslovakia, 3 years. Came to U.S., 1931, naturalized, 1940. Research asst. dept. exptl. pathology Masaryk U., 1923-25, then asso. in research dept. physiology, later dir. cancer and radio biol. lab.; fellow in cancer research, Vienna, 1928-29, Lenox Hill Hosp., N.Y.C., 1931; research dept. biol. chemistry Harvard Med. Coll., dept. bacteriology and immunology Columbia Coll. of Phys. and Surg., dept. biology N.Y. U.; apptd. research fellow cancer div. Dept. Hosps., N.Y.C., 1934, now prin. research scientist, dir. Cancer and Radio-Biol. Lab., Depts. Health and Hosps. City N.Y.; research work in assn. with N.Y. U., also prof. biology N.Y. U. Reported on exptl. results in developing immunity to cancer Fedn. Am. Socs. for Exptl. Biology, Boston. Recipient $5,000 award Damon Runyon Fund for Cancer Research. Fellow A.A.A.S., N.Y. Acad. Scis., N.Y. Acad. Medicine; mem. Royal Soc. Medicine, Harvey Soc., Am. Assn. for Cancer Research, Soc. for Exptl. Biology and Medicine, Radiol. Research Soc., Radiol. Soc. N.Am. (award). Contbr. numerous articles to profl. jours. Home: 920 Riverside Dr New York City NY 10032 Office: 99 Fort Washington Av New York City NY 10032

GOLDFELD, STEPHEN MICHAEL, educator; b. Bronx, N.Y., Aug. 9, 1940; s. Julius Morris and Ethel (Hammer) G.; A.B., Harvard, 1960; Ph.D., Mass. Inst. Tech., 1963; m. Laura Heend, July 1, 1962; children—Melanie, Keith. Asst. prof. Princeton, 1963-66, sr. economist Council Econ. Advisers, 1966-67, asso. prof., 1966-69, prof. econs., 1969—; vis. prof. Universite Catholique de Louvain, 1970-71; cons. Council Econ. Advisers, Nat. Indsl. Conf. Bd., Mathematica. Democratic campaign finance chmn., Princeton, 1969. Bd. dirs. N.J. Ednl. Computing Center, 1969-70. NSF sr. postdoctoral fellow, 1970-71. Mem. Am. Econ. Assn., Am. Statis. Assn., Am. Finance Assn., Econometric Soc. Author: Commercial Bank Behavior and Economic Activity, 1966; Precursors in Mathematical Economics, 1968. Contbr. articles profl. jours. Home: 40 Leabrook Lane Princeton NJ 08540

GOLDFIELD, EDWIN DAVID, govt. ofcl.; b. N.Y.C., Oct. 26, 1918; s. Maurice and Sarah (Spears) G.; B.S., City U. N.Y., 1939; M.A., Columbia, 1940; postgrad. Am. U., 1940-46. Research asso. dept. investigation, N.Y.C., 1938-39; statis. adviser Ct. Spl. Sessions, N.Y.C., 1939; with Bur. Census, Washington, 1940—, asst. dir., 1967—. Cons. in field, 1951—; staff dir. subcom. census and statistics Ho. of Reps., 1959-60, 67. Recipient Meritorious Service award Dept. Commerce, 1954. Fellow Am. Statis. Assn.; mem. Washington Statis. Soc. (past pres.), Am. Econ. Assn., Population Assn. Am., Conf. Research Income and Wealth, Phi Beta Kappa. Contbr. articles. Editor: Papers on Labor Force Statistics in the United States, 1952. Home: 4110 Suitland Rd Suitland MD 20023 Office: Bur of Census Washington DC 20233

GOLDFINE, WILLIAM, banker; b. Warsaw, Poland, Oct. 28, 1898; s. Morris and Helen (Hochzeit) G.; ed. high sch.; m. Pauline Berger, Dec. 8, 1929; children—Joyce L. (Mrs. Richard A. Walzer), Carol A. (Mrs. Bernard I. Fain). Treas., mgr. Bronx Credit Union, 1919-32, Underwriters Trust Co., 1932-34; asst. v.p. Nat. Safety Bank, 1934-44; v.p. Nat. Bronx Bank, 1944-49, Mfrs. Trust Co., 1949-51; exec. v.p. Royal Nat. Bank of N.Y., 1951-61, pres., chief exec. officer, 1961—, former chmn. bd., also dir.; dir. Dritch Crystal Dairies, Inc., Zion Kosher Products Corp., Security Mutual Ins. Co.; past chmn. bd. Royal Bus. Funds, Inc. Hon. chmn. Greater N.Y. Israel Bond Orgn. Pres. William Golfine found., Inc.; treas. Hebrew Home for Aged, New Bldg. Found. Fund; hon. pres. Hebrew Home for Aged at Riverdale; v.p. Bronx YM and YWCA, pres. of Pythian Camp. Mem. Am. Bankers Assn., Bronx Bd. Trade, Bronx C. of C., Bronx Real Estate Bd., Bldg. Industry League. K.P. (past grand chancellor N.Y.), Mason (past lodge master), mem. B'nai B'rith (past lodge pres.). Home: 40 E 84th St New York City NY 10028 Office: 1212 Av of Americas New York City NY 10036

GOLDFINGER, NATHANIEL, economist; b. N.Y.C., Aug. 20, 1916; s. Leo and Lena (Francis) G.; B.S., Coll. City N.Y., 1938; postgrad. New Sch. Social Research, 1941-42, Am. U., 1949-50; m. Elizabeth Claire Gordon, Mar. 5, 1954; children—Judith Susan, Ruth Irene. Dir. edn., research United Paperworkers Am., 1944-50; sec. CIO Com. Econ. Policy, 1950-53; asso. dir. research CIO, 1950-55; economist dept. research AFL-CIO, Washington, 1955-58, asst. dir. dept. research, 1958-60, dir., 1963—. Bd. dirs. Nat. Bur. Econ. Research; exec. com. Joint Council Econ. Edn., mem. adv. com. Export-Import Bank. Mem. Am. Econ. Assn., Indsl. Relations Research Assn. Home: 306 Hamilton Av Silver Springs MD 20901 Office: 815 16th St NW Washington DC 20006

GOLDFRANK, ESTHER S., anthropologist; b. N.Y.C., May 5, 1896; d. Herman J. and Matilda (Metzger) Schiff; grad. Ethical Culture Sch., N.Y.C., 1914; A.B., Barnard Coll., 1918; m. Walter S. Goldfrank, Dec. 8, 1922 (dec. 1935); 1 dau., Susan G. Lennhoff; m. 2d, Karl August Wittfogel, Mar. 8, 1940; step-children—Max, Alexander, Thomas. Field work on Am. Indian Pueblos in N.M., 1920-22, 24, among Blackfoot Indians of Alta., Can., 1939; staff anthropologist Chinese History project U. Wash., 1943—. Fellow N.Y. Acad. Scis., Am. Anthrop. Assn.; mem. Am. Ethnol. Soc. (sec.-treas. 1945-47, pres. 1948, editor 1952-56), Am. Folklore Soc., Soc. for Applied Anthropology. Author: The Artist of Isleta Paintings in Pueblo Society, 1967. Editor: Isleta Paintings with Notes and Commentary (Elsie Clews Parson), 1962. Home: 420 Riverside Dr New York City NY 10025 ☆

GOLDHABER, GERSON, physicist; b. Chemnitz, Germany, Feb. 20, 1924; s. Charles and Ethel (Frisch) G.; M.Sc., Hebrew U., Jerusalem, 1947; Ph.D., U. Wis., 1950; m. Judith Margoshes, May 30, 1969; 1 son, Amos Nathaniel. Came to U.S., 1948, naturalized, 1953. Instr. Columbia, 1950-53; acting asst. prof. physics U. Cal. at Berkeley, 1953-54, asst. prof., 1954-58, asso. prof., 1958-63, prof. physics, 1963—; group leader Lawrence Radiation Lab., Berkeley, 1962—; vis. prof. Math.-Sci. Inst., Madras, India, 1965; cons. Ford Found. Latin Am. Sch. Physics, Caracas, Venezuela, 1966; lectr. 2d Hawaii Topical Conf. Particle Physics, 1967. Ford Found fellow CERN, 1960-61. Fellow Am. Phys. Soc., Sigma Xi. Office: Lawrence Radiation Lab Univ of Cal Berkeley CA 94720

GOLDHABER, JACOB KOPEL, mathematician, educator; b. Bklyn., Apr. 12, 1924; s. Joseph and Shirley (Heller) G.; B.A., Bklyn. Coll., 1944; M.A., Harvard, 1945; Ph.D., U. Wis., 1950; m. Ruth Last, Dec. 25, 1951; children—Doreet, David, Aviva. Instr., U. Conn., Storrs, 1950-53; instr. Cornell U., Ithaca, N.Y., 1953- 54; asst. prof. Washington U., St. Louis, 1954-59, asso. prof., 1959- 61; asso. prof. U. Md., College Park, 1961-62, prof., 1962—, chmn. math. dept., 1968—. Vis. research asso. (NSF Sci. Faculty fellow) U. London (Eng.), 1966-67. Mem. A.A.A.S., Am. Assn. U. Profs., Am. Math. Soc., Math. Assn. Am., Sigma Xi. Author: (with Gertrude Ehrlich) Algebra, 1970. Contbr. papers to profl. jours. Home: 5517 39th St NW Washington DC 20015 Office: Dept Math U Md College Park MD 20742

GOLDHABER, MAURICE, physicist; b. Lemberg, Austria, Apr. 18, 1911; s. Charles and Ethel (Frisch) G.; Ph.D., Cambridge U., Eng., 1936; m. Gertrude Scharff, May 24, 1939; children—Alfred S., Michael H. Came to U.S., 1938, naturalized, 1944. Bye fellow Magdalene Coll., Cambridge, 1936-38; asst. prof. physics U. Ill., 1938-43, asso. prof., 1943-45, prof., 1945-50; sr. sci. Brookhaven Nat. Lab., 1950-60, chmn. dept. physics, 1960-61, dir., 1961—; cons. labs. AEC; Morris Loeb lectr, Harvard, 1955; adj. prof. physics State U. N.Y. at Stony Brook. Mem. nuclear sci. com. NRC. Mem. bd. govs. Weizmann Inst. Sci., Rehovoth, Israel, Tel Aviv U.; trustee Univs. Research Assn. Fellow Am. Phys. Soc., Am. Acad. of Arts and Scis.; mem. Nat. Acad. Sci. Asso. editor Phys. Review, 1951-53. Contbr. articles nuclear physics to sci. jours. Home: 91 S Gillette Av Bayport NY 11705 Office: Brookhaven Nat Laboratory Upton NY 11973

GOLDHAMMER, KEITH, univ. dean; b. Portland, Ore., July 26, 1917; s. Harry Jacob and Elizabeth (Herman) G.; B.A., Reed Coll., 1938; M.A., U. Ore., 1943, Ph.D., 1954; m. Helen Juhr, Oct. 7, 1939; children—Elizabeth (Mrs. Terry Kuhn), Carol Ann (Mrs. Richard Luplow), Harry John. Tchr., Salmon, Ia., 1940-42, Prineville, Ore., 1942-43; supt. schs., Gaston, Ore., 1943-48, Bandon, Ore., 1948-52; research asst. U. Ore., 1952-54, prof. edn., asso. dean, 1956-67; asst. prof. Stanford, 1943-56; dean Sch. Edn., Ore. State U., Corvallis, 1967—. Mem. Nat., Ore. edn. assns., Am. Assn. Sch. Adminstrs., Am. Ednl. Research Assn., Phi Delta Kappa. Author: The School Board, 1964; Issues and Problems in Contemporary Educational Administration, 1967; (with Farner) The Jackson County Story, 1964; (with Pellegrin) Jackson County Revisited, 1968; also articles, research studies. Home: 2929 NW Highland Dr Corvalis OR 97330

GOLDHAMMER, PAUL, educator, physicist; b. Portland, Ore., Nov. 10, 1929; s. Harry and Elizabeth (Herman) G.; B.A., Reed Coll., 1952; Ph.D., Washington U., 1956. Asst. prof. U. Neb., 1957-61, asso. prof., 1961-63, prof., 1963-64; prof. physics U. Kan., 1964—. Fellow Am. Phys. Soc. Research on structure of light nuclei. Home: 2412 Whitehall Manor Lawrence KS 66044

GOLDHAMMER, ROBERT FREDERICK, investment banker; b. N.Y.C., Feb. 9, 1931; s. Frederick and Helen (Thompson) G.; student Mich. State U., 1948-49; B.S. in Econs., Boston U., 1952; m. Joan Patricia Ditmars, Jan. 31, 1953; children—Susan, Robert, Richard. Registered rep. Kidder, Peabody & Co., 1956-63; v.p., dir. Kidder, Peabody & Co. Inc., 1964—; dir. Charles River Breeding Labs., Inc., Collaborative Research, Inc., Prelude Corp., Instrumentation Labs., Inc. Chmn. bd. govs. Boston Stock Exchange. Bd. visitors Coll. Bus. Adminstrn., Boston U., 1966—, chmn. 1967-68. Served to lt. USNR, 1952-55. Mem. Investment Bankers Assn. Am. (bd. govs. 1967- -, chmn. New Eng. group 1966-67). Clubs: Union (Boston); Winchester Country. Home: 1 Taft Dr Winchester MA 01890 Office: 75 Federal St Boston MA 02110

GOLDHOR, HERBERT, librarian, educator; b. Newark, Feb. 8, 1917; s. Adolph and Dora (Balshan) G.; B.A., Dana Coll., 1935; B.S. in Library Sci., Columbia, 1938; Ph.D., U. Chgo., 1942; m. Eleanor Payne Cheydleur, May 29, 1948; children—Jonathan Dana, Richard Scott, Elizabeth Payne, Barbara Ashley. Jr. asst. Newark Pub. Library, 1933-35, 36-37; asst. to librarian Ia. State Coll., Ames, 1938-39; asst. prof., asso. prof. U. Ill. Library Sch., Urbana, 1946-52, asso. dir. Grad. Sch. Library Sci., 1962-63, dir., 1963—; chief librarian Evansville (Ind.) Pub. Library, 1952-62. Served to 2d lt. AUS, 1944-46. Mem. Am., Ind., Ill. library assns., Phi Beta Kappa, Beta Phi Mu. Mem. Soc. Friends. Author: (with Joseph L. Wheeler) Practical Administration of Public Libraries. Contbr. articles to profl. jours. Home: 39 Maple Ct Lake Park Champaign IL 61820 Office: Library Bldg U of Illinois Urbana IL 61801

GOLDHURST, WILLIAM, author, educator; b. N.Y.C., Aug. 8, 1929; s. Harry Golden and Genevieve (Gallagher) G.; B.A., Kenyon Coll., 1953; M.A., Columbia, 1956; Ph.D., Tulane U., 1962; divorced; children—Barney, Rex; m. 2d, Ellen Eisemann Fleet. Asst. instr. English, Ohio State U., 1955-56; teaching fellow Tulane U. and Newcomb Coll., 1956-59; asso. prof. English, U. P.R., 1960-63; asso. prof. humanities U. Fla., 1964—; Fulbright prof. Am. lit. uunivs. Buenos Aires, and La Plata (Argentina), fall 1969; lectr. Am. lit. to Peace Corps, U. P.R., 1963. So. fellow, 1959-60; grantee Humanities Council and Faculty Devel., U. Fla., 1970-71. Mem. Am. Assn. U. Profs., Authors League Am. Author: F. Scott Fitzgerald and His Contemporaries, 1963; also articles, photo—stories in mags. Editor: Contours of Experience, 1967. Home: 1814 NW 10th St Gainesville FL 32601

GOLDIAMOND, ISRAEL, educator, exptl. psychologist; b. Ukraine, Nov. 1, 1919; s. Samuel and Clara (Rothenburg) G.; B.A., Bklyn. Coll., 1942; Ph.D., U. Chgo., 1955; m. Betty Ann Johnson, Feb. 28, 1946; children—Lisa Catherina (Mrs. Frederick Taylor), Joe David, Susannah. Adminstrv. asst. Inst. Design, Chgo., 1947-48; from research asst. to asso. U. Chgo., 1948-55; from asst. to asso. prof. psychology So. Ill. U., 1955-60; prof. psychology Ariz. State U., 1960-63; asso. to exec. dir. Inst. Behavioral Research, 1963-68; from asso. prof. to prof. psychiatry and behavioral sci. Johns Hopkins Med. Sch., 1965-68; prof. psychiatry and psychology U. Chgo., 1968—. Staff cons., div. neuropsychiatry Walter Reed Army Inst. Research, 1963-68. Served with AUS, 1942-45. Recipient Research Career Devel. award Nat. Inst. Mental Health, 1963-67. Fellow A.A.A.S., Am. Psychol. Assn. (v.p. div. exptl. analysis behavior 1967-70); mem. Am. Optical Soc., Am. Ecol. Soc., Am. Assn. U. Profs., Psychonomic Soc., Sigma Xi. Contbr. profl. jours. Editorial bds. Jour. Exptl. Analysis Behavior, 1963-68, Jour. Applied Behavior Analysis, 1968—, Jour. Abnormal Psychology, 1966—, Communications in Behavior Biology, 1968-71, Jour. Behaviorism, 1971—. Home: 5555 S Everett Av Chicago IL 60637

GOLDIN, JUDAH, educator; b. N.Y.C., Sept. 14, 1914; s. Gerson David and Rachel (Robkin) G.; B.S., Coll. City N.Y., 1934; diploma Sem. Coll., 1934; M.A., Columbia, 1938; M.H.L., Jewish Theol. Sem., 1938, D.H.L., 1943, H.L.D., 1968; M.A., Yale, 1958; m. Grace Avis Aaronson, June 21, 1938; children—Robin Elinor, David Lionel. Lectr., vis. asso. prof. Jewish lit. and history Duke, 1943-45; asso. prof. religion U. Ia., 1945-52; dean, asso. prof. Agada, Sem. Coll., Jewish Theol. Sem., 1952-58; adj. prof. religion Columbia, 1955-58; prof. Jewish studies Yale, 1958- 62, prof. classical Judaica, 1962—. Moderator summer round-table discussions Eternal Light, NBC, 1949-50. Am. Philos. Soc. grantee, 1957, 71; Guggenheim fellow, 1958; Fulbright fellow, 1958, 64-65. Fellow Am. Acad. Jewish Research; mem. Archeol. Inst. Am., Am. Schs. Oriental Research, Soc. Bibl. Lit., Phi Beta Kappa. Author: The Two Versions of Abot de Rabbi Nathan, 1945; Hillel the Elder, 1946; The Period of the Talmud, 1949; The Contemporary Jew and His Judaism, 1952; The First Chapter of Abot de Rabbi Nathan New York, 1953; The Fathers, 1955; The Living Talmud, 1957; The Three Pillars of Simeon the Righteous, 1958; A Philosophical Session in a Tannaite Academy, 1965; The End of Ecclesiastes, 1966; The Jewish Expression (ed.), 1970; The Song at the Sea, 1971. Home: 103 Millbrook Rd Hamden CT 06518 Office: Yale New Haven CT 06520

GOLDIN, LEON, artist; b. Chgo., Jan. 16, 1923; s. Joseph P. and Bertha (Metz) G.; B.F.A., Art Inst. Chgo., 1948; M.F.A., Ia. State U., 1950; m. Meta Solotaroff, July 30, 1949; children—Joshua, Daniel. Exhibited one man shows Oakland Art Mus., 1955, Felix Landau Gallery, Los Angeles, 1956, 57, 59, Galleria L'Attico, Rome, 1958, Kraushaar Galleries, N.Y.C., 1960, 64, 68; rep. permanent collections Bklyn. Mus., City Mus. St. Louis, Worcester Mus., Addison Gallery Am. Art, Pa. Acad. Fine Arts, Los Angeles County Mus., Santa Barbara Mus., Oakland Art Mus., Munson Proctor Inst., Va. Mus. Fine Arts, Portland (Me.) Mus., Everson Mus., Syracuse, N.Y., U. Ark., Okla. Art Center; asso. prof. Columbia, 1962—; former tchr. Cal. Coll. Arts and Crafts, Phila. Coll. Art, Queen's Coll., Cooper Union. Served with AUS, 1943-46. Recipient Tiffany grant, 1951, Prix de Rome, Am. Acad. Rome, 1955; Fulbright scholar to France, 1952; Guggenheim fellow, 1959; Jennie Sesnan gold medal Pa. Acad. Fine Arts, 1966; Sabbatical grant Nat. Endowment for Arts, 1967; grantee Nat. Inst. Arts and Letters, 1968. Home: 438 W 116th St New York City NY 10027

GOLDIN, MILTON, fund raising exec.; b. Cleve., Jan. 8, 1927; s. Hyman and Ida (Felsher) G.; B.A., N.Y. U., 1953, M.A., 1955; m. Aranka Nemcek, June 17, 1950; children—Karen, David. Mem. N.Y.C. Symphony, 1944-45, Denver Symphony Orch., 1949-51; adminstrv. dir. Am. Choral Found., 1955-61; asso. dir. devel. Brookdale Hosp. Center, 1963-66; fund raising campaign dir. Washington Sq. Coll. and Grade Sch. of Arts and Sci. of N.Y.U., 1966-67; v.p. Oram Assos., Inc., 1967—; mgr. Amor Artis Chorale and Orch., 1961—. Served with AUS, 1945-46. Recipient Deems Taylor award A.S.C.A.P., 1970. Mem. Nat. Soc. Fund Raisers, Phi Beta Kappa, Psi Chi, Mu Sigma. Author: The Music Merchants, 1969. Contbr. articles to periodicals. Home: 266 Crest Dr Tarrytown NY 10591 Office: 95 Madison Av New York City NY 10016

GOLDING, BRAGE, univ. pres.; b. Chgo., Apr. 28, 1920; s. Leon M. and Viola B. (Brage) G.; B.S., Purdue U., 1941, Ph.D., 1948; m. Hinda F. Wolf, Dec. 21, 1941; children— Brage, Susan, Julie. Asso. dir. research Lilly Varnish Co., Indpls.; also research asso. Purdue U., 1948-57; vis. prof. engring. Purdue U., dir. research Lilly Varnish Co., 1957-59; head Sch. Chem. Engring. Purdue U., 1959-66; v.p. Ohio State U. and Miami U., 1966-67; pres. Wright State U., Dayton, O., 1967—. Cons. to industry. Fellow A.A.A.S.; mem. Am. Chem Soc., Am. Inst. Chem. Engrs., Soc. Plastic Engrs., Am. Soc. Engring. Edn., Am. Assn. U. Profs., N.Y. Acad. Sci., Newcomen Soc. N.Am. Rotarian. Club: Engineers (Dayton). Author: Polymers and Resins, 1959. Contbr. articles to profl. jours. Home: Presidents House Wright State U Dayton OH 45431

GOLDING, ELIZABETH BASS, judge; b. N.Y.C., Apr. 12, 1902; d. William and Dora (Binkow) Bass; LL.B., N.Y. U. (scholarship 1921); postgrad. Wellesley Coll., Adelphi Coll.; m. Samuel Golding, Nov. 26, 1931. Admitted to N.Y. State bar, 1923, practiced in N.Y.C., 1923-40, in Hempstead, N.Y., 1940—; specialist in real estate law; dir. corps.; lectr. and community cons.; regional chmn. Office Civilian Def., 1942-45; vice chmn. U.S.O., Nassau County, 1943-46; chmn. Servicemans Legal Aid Com. for Mitchel Field., N.Y., 1942-46; legal adviser Wayside Home of Salvation Army, 1949-50; commr. of correction State of N.Y., 1961-63; family court judge for Nassau County, 1963—. Organized Nat. Woman's Forum, Inc. (founder 1946), Woman's Forum of Nassau County (founder-organizer 1944), Woman's Forum of Worcester County, Mass. (founder-organizer); pioneered in inter-group edn. of women's orgns. on the community level; organized Human Relations Workshop, 1948-50; pres. Hope for Youth, Inc., agency establishing group homes for homeless children, 1970—. Recipient Nassau County award for leadership and valuable contbn. in field of human relations and intergroup community activity, 1950. Mem. Nat. Council Jewish Women (dir. nat. bd. and exec. com., nat. chmn. social legislation 1938-44), Nat. Woman's Forum, Inc (pres. 1952), Internat. Assn. Women Lawyers (del. to UN Commn. on Human Rights 1959), United Hias Service, Inc. (exec. com., nat. bd.), Nat. Assn. Women Lawyers (chmn. labor relations; regional dir. 1959-61), Nassau County Bar Assn. chmn. community relations com., Woman's Bar Assn. Nassau County (pres., 1943-45). Author: The Health of the Nation, 1940; Don't Underestimate Woman Power; also pamphlets. Home: 312 East Shore Dr Massapequa NY 11758 Office: 266 Fulton Av Hempstead NY 11550

GOLDING, WILLIAM GERALD, author; b. Cornwall, Eng., Sept. 19, 1911; s. Alec Albert and Mildred Mary Agatha (Curnoe) G.; B.A., Brasenose Coll., Oxford U., 1935, M.A., 1960; m. Ann Brookfield, Sept. 30, 1939; children—David, Judith Diana. Tchr., Bishop Wordsworth Sch., Salisbury, Eng., 1945-60; writer in residence Hollins (Va.) Coll., 1961-62. Served with Brit. Navy, 1940- 45. Fellow Royal Soc. Lit. Author: Lord of the Flies, 1954; The Inheritors, 1955; Pincher Martin, 1956; Brass Butterfly, 1958; Free Fall, 1959; The Spire, 1964; The Hot Gates and Other Occasional Pieces, 1966; The Pyramid, 1967. Clubs: Savile (London); Royal Southampton Yacht. Address: Ebble Thatch Broadchalke 275 Wiltshire England

GOLDMAN, AARON, food service co. exec.; b. Washington, June 8, 1913; s. Hymen and Sadie (Cohen) G.; B.S., Georgetown U., 1934; m. Cecile A. Saloman, Nov. 26, 1939; children—Phyllis (Mrs. Philip Margolius), Michael D. With Macke Co., Washington, 1934—, pres., chmn. bd., 1946—; dir. First Nat. Bank Washington. Gen. chmn. Greater Washington Community Chest Campaign, 1954; chmn. Nat. Community Relations Adv. Council, 1964-67; pres. Jewish Community Council Greater Washington, 1953-56; chmn. D.C. Council Human Relations, 1958-63; vice chmn. Washington Center for Met. Studies. Served to lt. comdr. USNR, 1942-45. Recipient Nat. Brotherhood award Nat. Conf. Christians and Jews, 1958; Meritorious Pub. Service award Govt. of D.C., 1963; Stephen S . Wise Medallion award Am. Jewish Congress, 1964; John Carroll award Georgetown U., 1968. Fellow Brandeis U. Mem. Nat. Automatic Merchandising Assn. (pres. 1951-53, dir.), Am. Vets Com., Am. Jewish Congress. Clubs: Woodmont Country, Army- Navy (Washington). Home: 2801 New Mexico Av NW Washington DC 20007 Office: 1 Macke Circle Cheverly MD 20781

GOLDMAN, ALFRED, physician; s. Louis and Addie Goldman; B.A., Washington U., St. Louis, 1916, M.D., 1920, M.S. in Medicine, 1922; m. Miriam Londy, July 2, 1936; children—Alan, Roger, Thomas. Resident pathologist Barnes Hosp., 1920- 21, asst. resident medicine, 1922-24, resident medicine, 1922-24, now cons. chest diseases; dir. chest clinic Washington U. Med. Sch., 1930—, prof. emeritus clin. medicine; cons. chest diseases Jewish Hosp., Koch Hosp., Homer Phillips Hosp., VA Hosp., St. Louis; area cons. chest diseases area A, VA; sr. physician Jewish Hosp. Diplomate Am. Bd. Internal Medicine. Mem. Am., So., Mo. med. assns., St Louis Med. Soc., A.C.P., Central Soc. Clin. Research, Am. Coll. Chest Physicians (pres. 1964-65), St. Louis Soc. Internal Medicine (past pres.), Phi Beta Kappa, Sigma Xi. 1200 Hampton Park Dr St Louis MO 63117 Office: 8631 Delmar St St Louis MO 63124

GOLDMAN, ARTHUR SWORN, constrn. economist; b. St. Louis, Oct. 4, 1906; s. Louis and Edith (Leventhal) G.; A.B., Washington U., 1928; m. Ione Leon, Dec. 14, 1936; children—Laurel, Terry. Pres., Westland Constrn. Co., 1930-40; dir. marketing and research House & Home mag., 1940-62; pres. Arthur Sworn Goldman & Assos., Inc., 1963—; housing cons. Time, Inc., Am. Council to Improve Our Neighborhoods. Mem. subcom. on constrn., bus. research adv. com. Bur. Labor Statistics; mem. constrn. com. Bur. of Census. Mem. Am. Marketing Assn., Am. Statis. Assn., Phi Beta Kappa, Artus. Pioneered devel. of package and open-end mortgages. Home: Rayfield Rd Westport CT 06880 Office: 104 E 40th St New York City NY 10016

GOLDMAN, CHARLES REMINGTON, educator, scientist; b. Urbana, Ill., Nov. 9, 1930; s. Marcus Selden and Olive (Remington) G.; B.A., U. Ill., 1952, M.S., 1955; Ph.D., U. Mich., 1958; m. Shirley Ann Aldous, Apr. 4, 1953; children—Christopher Selden (dec.), Margaret Blanche, Olivia Remington, Ann Aldous. Asst. aquatic biologist Ill. Natural History Survey, 1954-55; teaching fellow fisheries U. Mich., 1955-58; fishery research biologist U.S. Fish and Wildlife Service, Alaska, 1957-58; mem. faculty U. Cal. at Davis, 1958—, prof. zoology, dir. Inst. Ecology, 1966-69, prof. environmental studies, 1971—; cons. water pollution to govt. and industry, 1959—. Mem. Cal. Assembly Sci. and Tech. Adv. Council, 1970-73. Served to capt. USAF, 1952-54. Guggenheim fellow, 1965; NSF sr. fellow, 1964; Goldman Glacier named in Antarctica, 1967; recipient Antartic Service medal, 1968. Fellow A.A.A.S.; mem. Am. Soc. Limnology and Oceanography (editorial bd. 1964-67; nat. pres. 1967-68, pres. Western sect. 1966-67), Ecol. Soc. Am. (editorial bd. 1966-68), Internat. Soc. Theoretical and Applied Limnology; hom. mem. Culver chpt. Cum Laude Soc. Author: Primary Productivity in Aquatic Environments, 1966. Discoverer trace element limiting factors in N. Am. and New Zealand lakes. Home: 1613 Holly Lane Davis CA 95616

GOLDMAN, ERIC FREDERICK, historian, writer; b. Washington, June 17, 1915; s. Harry Eric and Bessie (Chapman) G.; M.B., Johns Hopkins, 1935, Ph.D., 1938. Instr. history Johns Hopkins, 1938-41; writer Time Mag., 1941-43; asst. prof. history Princeton, 1943-47, asso. prof., 1947-55, prof., 1955-62, Rollins prof. of history, 1962—; spl. cons. to Pres. of U.S., 1963-66. Sr. fellow Council of humanities, 1955-56; Guggenheim fellow, 1956-57; Library of Congress fellow in Am. Civilization, 1947; McCosh fellow Princeton, 1963-64; State Department lectr. in Europe, 1953-54, in India, 1957; moderator NBC TV panel, The Open Mind, 1959— (Emmy award 1962, 66). Mem. Soc. Am. Historians (councilor 1955—; pres., 1961—, Phi Beta Kappa. Clubs: Players (N.Y.C.). Author: Charles J. Bonaparte, 1943; John Bach McMaster, 1943; (with Frederic Lane), The World's History, 1947; Rendezvous With Destiny, A History of Modern American Reform (awarded Bancroft prize for distinguished Am. history 1952), 1952; The Crucial Decade, America, 1945-55, pub. 1956; The Crucial Decade—And After, America, 1945-1960, 1961; contbr. popular and scholarly mags. Editor: Historiography and Urbanization, 1941.‡

GOLDMAN, HENRY MAURICE, educator; b. Boston, Dec. 9, 1911; s. Joseph and Rebecca (Levy) G., D.M.D., Harvard, 1935; m. Dorothy Alter, June 7, 1936; children—Richard, Gerald. Research fellow oral pathology Harvard, 1935-37, instr. oral pathology,

1938-46; chief stomatology and dental research, dir. Riesman Dental Clinic, Beth Israel Hosp., 1948; prof. peridontology, chmn. dept., Grad. Sch. Medicine U. Pa., 1955-64; prof., chmn. dept. stomatology Sch. Medicine, Boston U., 1958-64, prof., 1964—; dean, Grad. Sch. Dentistry, 1964—; also chief stomalogical service, bd. incorporators Univ. Hosp. Cons. dental and oral registry Army Inst. Pathology, Washington; sub-com. periodontia, com. dentistry NRC, 1948-51; cons. to surgeon gen. U.S. Army, 1969—. Served as capt., chief dental pathologic sect. AUS, 1943-45, pathologist dental registry Army Inst. Pathology. Recipient Gold medal Am. Acad. Periodontolgoy, 1968; Gies award, 1970. Diplomate Am. Bd. Periodontology (dir. 1953), Am. Bd. Oral Pathology (pres. 1954-55, dir. 1948-55). Fellow Am. Coll. Dentists, Royal Soc. Medicine, Internat. Coll. Dentists, A.A.A.S. (mem. Ivory Cross expdn. 1948), Am. Acad. Oral Pathology (pres. 1952-53); mem. Am. Soc. Perodontists (pres. 1963-64, editor jour.), M. Dental Assn. (council on dental research 1952-54), Acad. Periodontology, New Eng. Pathologic Soc., Internat. Assn. Dental Research, Brit. Periodontology Soc. (hon. mem.), Sigma Xi, Omicron Kappa Upsilon. Author: Periodontia, 4th rev. edit., 1959; Atlas of Dental and Oral Pathology, 3 rev. edit., 1944; co-author: Periodontal Therapy, 4th edit., 1968; Introduction to Periodontia, 1959, 4th edit., 1968; Oral Pathology, 1960. Editor Jour. Periodontology, 6th edit., Oral Pathology. Home: 176 Grant Av Newton Center MA 02159 Office: 1663 Beacon St Brookline MA 02146

GOLDMAN, IRVING, educator; b. N.Y.C., Sept. 2, 1911; s. Louis and Golda (Levine) G.; B.S., Bklyn. Coll., 1933; Ph.D., Columbia, 1941; m. Hannah Stern, June 13, 1934. Asst. in anthropology Columbia, 1936-37, lectr. 1938; tutor Bklyn. Coll., 1940-42; research analyst, Office Coordinator Inter-Am. Affairs, Washington, 1942-44; chief br. Latin Am. div. Office Research and Analysis, U.S. Dept. State, 1945-47; prof. anthropology Sarah Lawrence Coll., Bronxville, N.Y., 1947—. Served to 2d lt. OSS, AUS, 1944-45. Bollingen Found. fellow, 1960-62; Social Sci. Research Council fellow, 1969-70. Mem. A.A.A.S., Am. Anthrop. Assn., Am. Ethnol. Soc., Polynesian Soc. Author: The Cubeo Indians of the Northwest Amazon, 1963; Ancient Polynesian Society, 1970. Contbr. articles and essays profl. jours. Research in Carrier Indians B.C., 1935-36, Cubeo Indians Vaupes, Colombia, 1939-40, 68, 69-70. Home: 35 Pierrepont St Brooklyn NY 11201

GOLDMAN, JACOB E., machinery and equipment co. exec.; b. N.Y.C., July 18, 1921; s. Solomon and Sarah (Goldstein) G.; B.A., Yeshiva U., 1940, LL.D., 1961; M.A., U. Pa., 1943, Ph.D., 1943; m. 2d, Judith A. Mehler, Mar. 31, 1970; children by previous marriage—Melvin, Edith, Beth. Physicist, Westinghouse Research Labs., Pitts., 1943-50; mem. faculty Carnegie Inst. Tech., 1950-55; mgr. physics dept., sci. lab. Ford Motor Co., Dearborn, Mich., 1955-63, dir., 1962-68; sr. v.p. research and devel., dir. Xerox Corp., Stamford, Conn., 1968—; vis. scientist Brookhaven Nat. Lab., Upton, N.Y., 1952-54; vis. Edwin Webster prof. Mass. Inst. Tech., 1959; dir. United Brands Co. Mem. tech. adv. bd., chmn. panel on noise abatement Commerce Dept., 1966—; mem. statutory vis. com. Nat. Bur. Standards, 1969—. Bd. trustees Midwest Research Inst.; bd. overseers Bar-Ilan U., Israel. Mem. Am. Technion Soc. (dir.). Asso. editor Am. Jour. Physics, 1950-52, Jour. Applied Physics, 1959-61; editor: (The Science of Engineering Materials, 1957. Home: 41 Little Fox Lane Westport CT 06880 Office: Xerox Corp Stamford CT 06904

GOLDMAN, JAMES, playwright; b. Chgo. June 30, 1927; s. M. Clarence and Marian (Weil) G.; Ph.B., U. Chgo., 1947, M.A., 1950; postgrad. Columbia, 1950-52; m. Marie McKeon, Mar. 5, 1962; children—Julia, Matthew. Served with AUS, 1952-54. Mem. Dramatists Guild (council 1966—), Authors League Am. (council 1967—). Author: (plays) (with William Goldman) Blood, Sweat and Stanley Poole, 1961; (with William Goldman and John Kander) Family Affair, 1962; They Might Be Giants, 1961, The Lion in Winter (screenplay, Acad. award 1968), 1967; (novel) Waldorf, 1965; (screenplays) They Might Be Giants, 1970, Nicholas and Alexandra, 1971; Follies (music and lyrics by Stephen Sondheim-Broadway), 1971. Home: 52 W 11th St New York City NY 10011 Office: 137 Waverly Pl New York City NY 10011

GOLDMAN, JAY, educator; b. Norfolk, Va., Apr. 15, 1930; s. Louis H. and Rose (Oser) G.; B.S., Duke, 1950; M.S., Mich. State U., 1951; D.Sc., Washington U., St. Louis, 1955; m. Renitta Librach, Dec. 20, 1959. Acting chmn. human and orgn. factors area, asst. prof. engring., asst. prof. indsl. engring., lectr. indsl. engring. and indsl. mgmt. Washington U., 1952- 64; dir. indsl. engring. dept. Jewish Hosp., St. Louis, 1960-64; prof., grad. adminstr. dept. indsl. engring. N.C. State U., 1964-68; prof., chmn. dept. indsl. engring. U. Mo., Columbia, 1968—; mem. health care systems study sect. Nat. Center for Health Services Research and Devel., Dept. Health, Edn. and Welfare. Recipient R.H. Landes Methods Improvement award Indsl. Mgmt. Soc., 1953-54. Registered profl. engr., Mo. Mem. Am. Inst. Indsl. Engrs. (chpt. pres., nat. v.p., dir. hosp. and health services dir., nat. dir. research and devel., mem. editorial bd. publs.), Operations Research Soc. Am., Am. Soc. Engring. Edn., Mo. Acad. Sci., Sigma Xi, Alpha Pi Mu. Mem. B'nai B'rith. Contbr. articles profl. jours. Patentee in field. Home: 1111 Yuma Dr Columbia MO 65201

GOLDMAN, JEROME, lawyer, dept. store exec.; b. Cin., Jan. 2, 1910; s. Bernard and Gisela (Goldstein) G.; A.B., U. Cin., 1928, postgrad., 1928-29; LL.B., Harvard, 1932; m. Marjorie Louise Bergstein, Dec. 19, 1937; children—Jeffrey, Betsy (Mrs. Ronald Resler), Sally, Nancy (Mrs. Gregory C. Boyston), Steven, Michael. Admitted to Ohio bar, 1932, to practice before U.S. Supreme Ct.; mem. firm Goldman, Cole & Putnick, 1957—; sec. Interstate Folding Box Co., Middletown, O., 1948—; vice chmn. bd. dirs. Sucher Packing Co., Dayton, O., 1951—; chmn. bd. dirs., chief exec. officer Elder-Beerman Stores Corp., Dayton, 1970—. Dir. Charter Commn. Cin. and Hamilton County, 1953—, Jewish Fedn. Cin., 1957—, Hamilton County Good Govt. League, 1946—. Trustee, v.p. Beerman Found., Inc., 1951—. Served with USNR, 1943-45; Mem. Am. Judicature Soc. (dir.), Am., Ohio, Cin. bar assns., Phi Beta Kappa. Home: 230 Oliver Rd Wyoming Cincinnati OH 45215 Office: First National Bank Bldg Cincinnati OH 45202

GOLDMAN, JOSEPH BERNARD, lawyer; b. Washington, Jan. 29, 1917; s. Jacob and Sophie (Sures) G.; A.B. with distinction, George Washington U., 1937; LL.B. cum laude, Harvard, 1940; m. Loretta Irma Martone, July 20, 1948; children—Alan Richard, Bettie Ellen. Admitted to D.C. bar, 1940; atty. Bituminous Coal Consumers' Counsel, Washington, 1940-41; with OPA, 1941-44, Dept. Justice, 1944-47; spl. asst. to atty. gen., 1947-49; with CAB, 1947—, gen.counsel, 1966-70; partner Morrison, Murphy, Abrams & Haddock; adj. prof. law Georgetown U. Law Sch., 1967—; guest lectr. Am. U., Harvard, U. Mich.; U.S. del. numerous internat. confs. Home: 5250 Linnean Av NW Washington DC 20015 Office: 1776 K St NW Washington DC 20008

GOLDMAN, JOSEPH LAWRENCE, educator, otolaryngologist; b. N.Y.C., Jan. 16, 1904; s. Louis and Anna (Sapir) G.; A.B., Columbia, 1924; M.D., L.I. Coll. Hosp. Med. Sch., 1927; m. Florence A. Green, Nov. 16, 1941; children—Elizabeth Anne (Mrs. Richard M. Sevin), Barbara Jane (Mrs. Sheldon E. Steinbach), James Lawrence. Intern, Jewish Hosp., Bklyn., 1927-29; resident otolaryngology Mt. Sinai Hosp., N.Y.C., 1929-31, fellow bacteriology, 1931-32, mem. staff, 1933—, dir. dept. otolaryngology, 1954—; asst. surgeon otolaryngology, then asso. surgeon Bellevue Hosp., N.Y.C., 1935-54; pvt. practice medicine, specializing in otolaryngology, 1932—; from asst. clin. prof. to asso. prof. N.Y. U. Sch. Medicine, 1946-55; clin. prof. Columbia Coll. Phys. and Surg., 1955-67; prof. otolaryngology, chmn. dept. Mt. Sinai Sch. Medicine, 1966—. Prin. investigator research and tng. grants NIH, 1961—. Served to col., M.C., AUS, 1942-46. Diplomate Am. Bd. Otolaryngology. Mem. Am. Acad. Ophthalmology and Otolaryngology (v.p. 1964, Honor Key award and Certificate award 1959), Am. Laryngol., Rhinol. and Otol. Soc. (pres. 1969-70), Am. Broncho-esophagol. Assn., Am. Otol. Soc., Am. Laryngol. Assn., Am. Soc. Head and Neck Surgery, Am. Soc. Ophthal. and Otolaryngol. Allergy, Am. Acad. Facial Plastic and Reconstructive Surgery, N.Y. Acad. Medicine, A.M.A. (chmn. sect. laryngology, otology and rhinology 1963, Hektoen Bronze medal 1969), Soc. U. Otolaryngologists, Sigma Alpha Mu. Contbr. articles in field; contbr. chpts. books. Home: 1185 Park Av New York City NY 10028 Office: 1050 Park Av New York City NY 10028

GOLDMAN, LEON, educator, physician; b. Cin., Dec. 7, 1905; s. Abraham and Fannie (Friedman) G.; M.D., U. Cin., 1929; m. Belle Hurwitz, Aug. 23, 1930; children—John Steven, Carol (Mrs. Edward Schechter). Intern, resident internal medicine and dermatology clin. Gen. Hosp., 1929-37; research fellow Dermatologische Poliklinik, U. Zurich (Switzerland), 1932-33; mem. faculty U. Cin. Coll. Medicine, 1933—, prof. dermatology, 1948—, chmn. dept., 1948—; dir. dermatology Cin. Gen. Hosp., 1948—; dermatology Cin. Children's Hosp., 1948—, dir. Laser Labs., 1960—. Pres. Cin. Cancer Control Council; cons. USPHS. Mem. Cin. (pres. 1937, 63), Chgo. (pres. 1960) dermatol. socs., Cin. Soc. History Medicine (pres. 1966), Sigma Xi, Alpha Omega Alpha. Author: Laser Cancer Research, 1966; Introduction to Laser in Biology and Medicine, 1967; also articles. Co-author: Lasers in Medicine, 1969; Medicine and Science in Art, 1969.‡

GOLDMAN, LEON, surgeon; b. San Francisco, Feb. 14, 1904; s. Samuel and Lilly (Kalfin) G.; A.B., U. Cal. at Berkeley, 1926, M.D., 1930; M.S., Northwestern U., 1939; m. June 19, 1931; children—Dianne (Mrs. Bertram Feinstein), Yvonne (Mrs. Walter Banks), Lynn (Mrs. Bruce Kennedy). Intern surgery U. Cal. Hosp., San Francisco, 1929-30, asst. resident surgery Med. Center, 1930-33, resident, instr. surgery, 1933-35, prof. surgery, 1949—, chmn. dept., 1956-64, asso. dean, 1956-64; instr., exec. officer surgery San Francisco Hosp., 1935-37; asst. prof. surgery U. Cal. Med. Sch., 1937-43, asso. prof., 1943-49. Mem. A.C.S. (1st v.p. 1962-63), A.A.A.S., Am. Gastroent. Assn., Soc. Univ. Surgeons, Soc. Surgery Alimentary Tract, Internat. Soc. Surgeons, Am. (1st v.p. 1968-69), Pacific Coast (past pres.), Western surg. assns., Pan-Pacific Surg. Assn., Am. Thyroid Assn. Contbr. articles in field. Address: U Cal Med Center San Francisco CA 94122

GOLDMAN, MARSHALL IRWIN, educator, economist; b. Elgin, Ill., July 26, 1930; s. Sam and Bella (Silvian) G.; B.S., Wharton Sch. of U. Pa., 1952; M.A., Harvard, 1956, Ph.D., 1961; m. Merle Rosenblatt, June 14, 1953; children—Ethan Harris, Avra Lea, Karla Ann, Seth Abraham. Mem. faculty Wellesley Coll., 1958—, prof. econs. 1967—, chmn. dept., 1971—, asso. Russian Research Center, Harvard, 1957—; vis. asst. prof. Brandeis U., 1961-62; pres. Cambridge (Mass.) Econ. Research Group, 1967—; cons. in field. Dir. Century Bank and Trust Co., Somerville, Mass. Mem. Wellesley Clean Air. Com., 1969—, Wellesley Conservation Commn., 1971—. Mem. Wellesley Town Meeting, 1969—; mem. Wellesley Town Democratic Com., 1964—, sec., 1969. Served with AUS, 1953-55. Huber Found. study grantee, 1959; Brookings Instn. research prof., 1964. Mem. Council Fgn. Relations, Boston Com. Fgn. Relations, Am. Econ. Assn., N.Y. Acad. Scis., Assn. Comparative Econs. (exec. com. 1968-70). Author: Soviet Marketing: Distribution in a Controlled Economy, 1963; Comparative Economic Systems: A Reader, rev. edit., 1971; Soviet Foreign Aid, 1967- -; Controlling Pollution: The Economics of a Cleaner America, 1967; The Soviet Economy: Myth and Reality, 1968. Home: 17 Midland Rd Wellesley MA 02181

GOLDMAN, MORRIS H., lawyer; b. Phila., Mar. 30, 1906; s. Abraham and Annie (Doskow) G.; LL.B., Temple U.; Litt.D., Delaware Valley Coll.; m. Rose Ellman, June 26, 1932; children—Benjamin Donald, Andrew A. Admitted to Pa. bar, 1927, since practiced in Phila.; sr. partner Wolf, Block, Schorr and Solis-Cohen, 1955—. Chmn. trustees Delaware Valley Coll. Sci. and Agr.; trustee, sec. Fedn. Jewish Agys. Greater Phila.; trustee, chmn. exec. com. Pierce Jr. Coll. Served with AUS, 1943-45. Mem. Am., Pa., Phila. bar assns., Am. Judicature Soc. Home: 7937 Rolling Green Rd Cheltenham PA 19102 Office: Packard Bldg Philadelphia PA 19102

GOLDMAN, NATHAN, sociologist, educator; b. Bklyn., Dec. 9, 1907; s. Israel Isaac and Anna (Kladowski) G.; B.A., Clark U., 1929, M.A., 1930; Ph.D., U. Chgo., 1950; m. Elsa Reppin Weber, Apr. 5, 1940. Psychologist, Boston Psychopathic Hosp., 1932-35; psychologist Worcester State Hosp., 1935-37, Lyman Sch. for Boys, 1937-42; research sociologist Western Psychiat. Inst., Pitts., 1948-50; asso. prof. sociology Syracuse (N.Y.) U., 1950-68; prof. dept. sociology Ill. Inst. Tech., Chgo., 1968—, 1968-70. chmn., 1968-70. Served from lt. to comdr., USNR, 1942-46. Mem. Am. Sociol. Assn., Soc. For Study Social Problems, Nat. Council on Crime and Delinquency. Author: The Differential Selection of Juvenile Offenders for Court Appearance, 1963; A Sociopsychological Study of School Vandalism, 1959; also articles. Home: 9832 S Seeley Av Chicago IL 60643

GOLDMAN, OSCAR, educator; b. Bklyn., Feb. 2, 1925; s. Isaac and Esther (Schwartz) G.; B.S., Coll. City N.Y., 1944; A.M., Princeton, 1946, Ph.D., 1948; m. Madge Rosenbaum, Aug. 8, 1949. Benjamin Peirce instr. Harvard, 1948-51; mem. faculty Brandeis U., 1951-61, prof. math., 1961- 62, chmn. dept., 1956-61; prof. math. U. Pa., Phila., 1962—, chmn. dept., dept., 1962- 67, mem. Inst. for Advanced Study, 1960-62. Vis. scholar U. Cal. at Berkeley, 1967-68. Sci. faculty fellow NSF, 1960-61. Mem. Am. Math. Soc., Math. Assn. Am., Math. Soc. Japan, Sigma Xi. Author research papers algebra, theory numbers. Asso. editor Jour. Franklin Inst., 1963- 67; mem. editorial com. Mathmatical Revs., 1969—. Office: Math Dept U Pa Philadelphia PA 19104 Math Dept U Pa Philadelphia PA 19104

GOLDMAN, PETER EMANUEL, film director-producer; b. N.Y.C., June 5, 1939; s. Irving Isador and Gertrude (Jacobs) G.; A.B., Brown U.; m. Birgit Bogh Nielsen, Nov. 12, 1965; 1 son, Nepo Aram. Motion pictures include Echoes of Silence (named Best Film, Pesaro Film Festaval), Pestilent City, Wheel of Ashes (Venice Film Festival Selection 1968); Pres. Sahaja Films, Inc. Fulbright scholar, Paris, France. Mem. Phi Beta Kappa. Address: Filmmakers Distributing Center 175 Lexington Av New York City NY 10016 10016

GOLDMAN, RALPH, educator; b. N.Y.C., June 11, 1919; s. Henry and May (Hoffman) G.; A.B., U. Cal. at Berkeley, 1939; M.D., U. Cal. at San Francisco, 1942; m. Helen C. Wolfson, Jan. 15, 1941; children—Paul, Richard, Elizabeth. Intern, Los Angeles County Gen. Hosp., 1942-43, resident internal medicine, 1943-44; resident internal medicine VA Center Los Angeles, 1946-48, adminstrv. chief metabolic and renal disease sect., 1948-55; chief med. service VA Hosp., Sepulveda, Cal., 1955-58; prof. medicine U. Cal. at Los Angeles Med. Sch., 1958—. Served to lt., M.C., USNR 1944-46. Fellow A.C.P., Gerontol. Soc., Geriatrics Soc.; mem. Internat. Assn. Gerontology (chmn. Am. clin. sect.), Am. Geriatric Soc. (Willard O. Thompson award 1970), Am. Soc. Nephrology. Contbr. articles to profl. jours. Home: 10501 Wilshire Blvd Los Angeles CA 90024

GOLDMAN, RICHARD, clothing co. exec. With McGregor-Doniger, Inc., N.Y.C., 1962—, v.p., dir. merchandising knitwear B. Altmann div., 1966-69, v.p. knitwear, 1969-70, pres., 1970—, also dir. Office: 666 Fifth Av New York City NY 10019*

GOLDMAN, RICHARD FRANKO, educator, condr., composer, author; b. N.Y.C., Dec. 7, 1910; s. Edwin Franko and Adelaide (Maibrunn) G.; A.B. with honors, Columbia, 1930; D.H.L., Lehigh U., 1964; M.F.A. (hon.), U. Md., 1971; m. Alexandra Rienzi, June 8, 1934; 1 son, Daniel Franko. Fellow fine arts and archaeology Columbia, 1931; composer, author, music critic, 1931—; asso. condr. Goldman Band, 1937- 56, condr., 1956—; faculty Juilliard Sch. Music, 1947-60, chmn., dept. lit. and materials of music, 1953-60; faculty Princeton U., 1952- 56, Columbia U., 1961, N.Y. U., 1963; Guggenheim fellow, 1962; prin. N.Y. critic Musical Quar., 1948-68; editor Juilliard Rev., 1953-58, dir. Peabody Conservatory Music; pres. Peabody Inst., Balt., 1969- -. Pres., treas. Goldman Band Concerts, Inc.; lectr., guest condr. univs, communities U.S.; recs. with Goldman Band for Decca, Capitol. Chmn. Council Ind. Profl. Schs. Music, 1970—. Bd. dirs. Balt.Symphony Orch. Recipient commn. Nat. Fedn. Music Clubs, 1948, Nat. Band Assn., 1962; Juilliard Mus. Found. award, 1955, Little Orchestra Soc. award for opera libretto, 1960; Alice M. Ditson Conductor's award, 1961; Key to City of New Orleans, 1963, Distinguished Service in Music award Kappa Kappa Psi, 1971, Hall of Honor award Balt. Arts Council, 1971. Served with OSS, AUS, 1942-45. Mem. Music Library Assn., A.S.C.A.P., Am. Bandmasters Assn., League Composers (past exec. dir.). Phi Beta Kappa, Delta Omicron (nat. patron), Phi Mu Alpha (hon.), Phi Beta Mu, Kappa Kappa Psi, Kappa Delta Psi, Tau Beta Sigma. Composer numerous works for band, orch., chamber groups. Author: The Band's Music, 1938; The Concert Band, 1946; The Wind Band, 1961; Harmony in Western Music, 1965. Translator: The Mandarin and other stories (Eca de Queiroz), 1965. Contbr. to New Oxford History of Music, Musik in Geschichte und Gegenwart. Contbr. articles and fiction to numerous musical, scholarly and gen. publs. Address: Peabody Inst Baltimore MD 21202

GOLDMAN, ROBERT M., lawyer; b. Balt., Jan. 9, 1917; s. L. Edwin and Rita (Strauss) G.; A.B., The Johns Hopkins U., 1938; LL.B., U. Md., 1941; m. Louise Thunhouser, July 14, 1955; children—(by previous marriage) Elizabeth A. (Mrs. John W. Beckley, Richard C. Admitted to Md. bar; partner Nyburg, Goldman & Walter, Balt., 1945-66; partner Frank, Bernstein, Cungnay & Goldman. Balt., 1966—. Mem. Am., Md., Baltimore City bar assns., Order of Coif, Phi Beta Kappa. Editor Md. Law Rev., 1940-41. 3506 Old Court Rd Baltimore MD

GOLDMAN, ROBERT PHILIP, lawyer; b. Cin., May 17, 1890; s. Louis J. and Rose (Frohman) G.; A.B., Yale, 1911; LL.B., Harvard, 1914; student Université de Paris, Faculté de Droit, 1919; m. Therese Wolfstein, Oct. 16, 1921; children—David Wolfstein, Agnes Edna, Barbara Therese (Mrs. J.L. Cohen). Admitted to Ohio bar, 1914; asso. firm Paxton, Warrington & Seasongood, Cin., 1914-23, mem. firm, 1923-27; mem. Paxton & Seasongood, 1927-70; of counsel, 1971—. Pres. Proportional Representation League. Trustee Salinger A.B. Dolly and Ralph Cohen founds ., Hebrew Union Coll.- Jewish Inst. of Religion, chmn. bd., 1958-62, trustee City Charter Com., chmn. bd., 1955-58; former trustee, now hon. trustee Union Am. Hebrew Congregations, pres., 1937-43; chmn. Charter Revision Com., Cin., 1949; pres. Cin. Jewish Community Council, 1944-47. Served with 309th Supply Train, 84th Div., and with Sorbonne Detachment, U.S. Army, with A.E.F., 1918-19. Mem. Ohio Archaeol. and Hist. Soc. (trustee 1932-38), Am., Ohio (com. bnkg. and comml. law 1949-61, chmn.), Cin. (pres. 1954-55) bar assns., Am. Law Inst., Phi Beta Kappa. Clubs: University, Losantiville Country (Cin.); Yale (N.Y.C.). Author: (with Clyde M. Abbott) Anderson's Ohio Corporation Desk Book, 1951, 56, 66. Contbr. law revs. profl. jours. Home: 5300 Hamilton Av Cincinnati OH 45224 Office: Central Trust Tower Cincinnati OH 45202

GOLDMAN, WILLIAM, writer; b. Chgo., Aug. 12, 1931; s. M. Clarence and Marion (Weil) G.; B.A., Oberlin Coll., 1952; M.A., Columbia, 1956; m. Ilene Jones, Apr. 15, 1961; children—Jenny, Susanna. Recipient Acad. award best original screenplay Butch Cassidy and the Sundance Kid, 1970. Author: (novels) The Temple of Gold, 1957; Your Turn to Curtsy, My Turn to Bow, 1958; Soldier in the Rain, 1960; Boys and Girls Together, 1964; The Thing of It Is, 1967; (novel) (pseudonyn Harry Longbaugh) No Way to Treat A Lady, 1964; (play) (with James Goldman) Blood Sweat and Stanley Poole, 1961; (mus. comedy) (with James Goldman and John Kander) A Family Affair, 1962; (film) Harper, 1966; The Season: A Candid Look at Broadway, 1969; (film) Butch Cassidy and The Sundance Kid, 1969; (novel) Father's Day, 1971. Home: 815 Park Av New York City NY 10021

GOLDMANN, NAHUM, religious orgn. exec.; b. Wisznewo, Poland, July 10, 1895; s. Salomon and Rebecca (Kwint) G.; J.D., U. of Heidelberg, 1920; student U. of Marburg, 1914, U. of Berlin, 1915; m. Alice Gottschalk, Dec. 19, 1934; children—Michael, Guido. Came to U.S., 1940. Founder Eshkol Pub. Co., Berlin 1920; an editor Ency. Judaica, 1929; rep. Jewish Agy. for Palestine, League of Nations, Geneva, 1935, mem. exec. com., 1935, rep. in U.S. 1940-46, chmn. Am. sect., 1949—, chmn. exec. com., 1951—; former mem. adminstrv. com. World Jewish Congress, acting pres., 1949-53, former pres.; v.p. Jewish Restitution Successor Orgn., 1948—; pres. Conf. on Jewish Material Claims Against Germany, 1951—; chmn. com. for Jewish Claims on Austria, 1953—; pres. Palestine Found. Fund, 1951—, Meml. Found. Jewish Culture, 1965. Author: Reisebriefe von Erez Israel, 1913. Home: 16 Rue Crespin Geneva Switzerland Office: 515 Park Av New York City NY 10022 and PO Box 92 Jerasulem also 26 Route de Malagnou Geneva Switzerland

GOLDMANN, SIDNEY, judge; b. Trenton, N.J., Nov. 28, 1903; s. Samuel and Stella (Reich) G.; B.S. magna cum laude in Math., Harvard, 1924, LL.B., 1927; m. Beatrice Corosh, Nov. 20, 1938; 1 son, Donald Alan. Admitted to N.J. bar, 1928; city atty., acting city mgr., Trenton, 1935-39; exec. clk. Gov. Charles Edison, 1942-44; N.J. state librarian, 1944-47; head archives and history bur. Div. N.J. Library, 1947- 48; standing master N.J. Supreme Ct., 1949-51; became judge N.J. Superior Ct., 1951, now presiding and adminstrv. judge Appellate Div. Served 1947, N.J. Constl. Conv. as historian and archivist, and chmn. Gov.'s Commn. Preparatory Research. Bd. dirs. Trenton Jewish Community Center, Trenton Council of Human Relations, pres., 1949-51, Trenton Jewish Fedn., pres., 1936-40, life mem. Mem. Trenton Jewish Family Service (past pres.), Trenton Council Social Agys. (pres. 1951-53), Greater Trenton Symphony Assn., Am. Jewish Com. (life., gov.), Council Jewish Fedn. and Welfare Funds, Jewish Welfare Bd., Am.-Jewish Tercentenary Commn. Mem. Mercer

County (past pres.), N.J., Am. bar assns., Am. Law Inst., Am.-Jewish Hist. Soc., Trenton Hist. Soc. (past pres.), Trenton Jewish Hist. Soc. (pres.), Am. Judicature Soc., Inst. Jud. Adminstrn., N.J. Constl. Conv. Assn., Harvard Law Sch. Assn. of N.J. Democrat. Jewish religion (trustee temple). Club: Harvard of N.J. Author (with Thomas J. Graves) The Organization and Administration of the N.J. Highway Department, 1942. Contbr. to A History of Trenton, 1679-1929, 1929. Editor: Proc. N.J. Constnl. Conv. of 1947 (5 vols.). Home: 101 Renfrew Av Trenton NJ 08618 Office: State House Annex Trenton NJ 08625 ☆

GOLDMARK, PETER CARL, radio, TV exec.; b. Budapest, Hungary, Dec. 2, 1906; s. Alexander and Emmy G.; student U. Vienna, 1925-31, B.S., Ph.D.; D.Sc., Fairfield U., 1967; children—Peter Carl, Frances C., Christopher W., Andrew G., Jonathan, Susan. Came to the U.S., 1933, naturalized, 1937. TV engr. in charge dept. Pye Radio, Ltd., Cambridge, Eng. 1931-33; cons. engr. N.Y.C., 1934-35; chief engr. TV dept. CBS, N.Y.C., 1936- 44, dir. engring. research and devel., 1944-50, v.p. engring. research and devel. dept., 1950—, also pres. CBS Labs. div. CBS. War research part time Radio Research Lab. Harvard U.; vis. prof. med. electronics U. Pa. Med. Sch. Mem. Conn. Research Commn. Recipient Morris Liebman Meml. prize for electronic research, 1946; Vladimir K. Sworykin award for devel. and utilization electronic TV, 1961; George Washington award for contbns. to sci., 1967; Nat. Urban Service award for efforts war on poverty, 1967, Sarnoff Gold gold Medal award for pioneering contbrns. to communications, 1969; Elliott Cresson medal for devel. of LP record, color television broadcast system and electronic recording, 1969. Soc. Motion Picture and Television Engring. Soc. Progress medal , 1970. Fellow Am. Inst. Elec. Engrs., Inst. Radio Engrs., Soc. Motion Picture Engrs., TV Soc. (London); mem. Nat. Acad. Engring. Contbr. to profl. Jours. Patentee in field TV, radio Office: CBS Labs High Ridge Rd Stamford CT 06905

GOLDNER, JOSEPH LEONARD, educator, surgeon; b. Omaha, 1918; M.D., U. Neb., 1943. Intern, then asst. resident U. Neb. Hosp., 1942-44; asst. resident orthopedics, then resident Duke U. Hosp., Durham, N.C., 1946-49; orthopedic resident, then staff orthopedic surgery Ga. Warms Springs Found. 1947-48; mem. faculty Duke U. Med. Sch., 1950—, prof. orthopedic surgery, 1957—, chmn. div., 1967—. Research cons. physiology NIH, VA Hosp., Ft. Bragg (N.C.) Army Hosp.; surgeon N.C. Crippled Childrens Program and Vocational Rehab. Served to lt. (j.g.), M.C., USNR, 1944-46. Diplomate Am. Bd. Orthopedic Surgery. Mem. Am., So. (v.p. 1968, pres.-elect 1969, pres. 1970) med. assns., Am. Assn. Orthopedic Surgeons, Am. Soc. Surgery Hand (pres. 1969-70), Am. Orthopedic Assn., Am. Acad. Orthopaedic Surgeons, Am. Acad. Cerebral Palsy, Piedmont Orthopaedic Soc. (exec. sec. 1951—), Sigma Xi. Presbyn. (deacon 1965-67). Contbr. articles in field to med. jours. Home: 602 E Forest Hills Blvd Durham NC 27707 Office: Duke Univ Med Center Durham NC 27706

GOLDOVSKY, BORIS, musician; b. Moscow, Russia, June 7, 1908; s. Onesim and Lea (Luboshutz) G.; student Conservatory Music, Moscow, 1918-21, Acad. Music, Berlin, 1921-23; grad. Liszt Acad. Music, Budapest, 1930, Curtis Inst. Music, Phila., 1932; Mus.D., Bates Coll., 1956, Cleve. Inst., 1969; m. Margaret Codd, 1933; children—Michael, Marina. Came to U.S., 1930, naturalized, 1937. Debut as pianist Berlin Philharmonic, 1921; extensive tours in U.S., dir. opera dept. N.E. Conservatory Music, 1942—; head opera dept. Music Center, Berkshire Festival, Lenox, Mass., 1946-61; intermission commentator Met. Opera Co. broadcasts, 1946—; artistic dir. Goldovsky Opera Inst., Boston, 1963—; pianist, condr., lectr. Fellow Am. Acad. Arts and Scis. Author: Accents on Opera, 1953; Bringing Opera To Life, 1968. Home: 183 Clinton Rd Brookline MA 02146

GOLDREICH, PETER MARTIN, educator, astrophysicist; b. N.Y.C., July 14, 1939; s. Paul and Edith (Rosenfield) G.; B.Engring. Physics, Cornell U., 1960, Ph.D. in Physics, 1963; m. Susan Kroll, June 14, 1960; children—Eric, Daniel. Instr., Cornell U., 1963; postdoctoral fellow Cambridge (Eng.) U., 1963-64; asst. prof. astronomy and geophysics U. Cal. at Los Angeles, 1964-66; asso. prof. astronomy and planetary sci. Cal. Inst. Tech., 1966-69, prof., 1969—. Home: 2827 N Holliston Av Altadena CA 91001 Office: 1201 E California Blvd Pasadena CA 91109

GOLDRING, NORMAN MAX, advt. exec.; b. Chgo., June 22, 1937; s. Jack and Carolyn (Wolf) G.; B.S. in Bus., Miami (O.) U., 1959; M.B.A., U. Chgo., 1963; m. Cynthia Lois Garland, Dec. 20, 1959; children—Jay Marshall, Diane. Advt. account mgr. Edward H. Weiss & Co., Chgo., 1959-61; sr. v.p., dir. marketing services Stern, Walters & Simmons, Inc., Chgo., 1961-68; pres. Goldring & Co., Inc., mgmt. cons., Chgo., 1968—, CPM, Inc., advt., 1969—. Instr. marketing and advt. mgmt. Roosevelt U., 1965—. Commnr., Ridgeville Park Dist., Evanston, Ill., 1971—. Mem. Am. Marketing Assn. Home: 1212 Austin St Evanston IL 60202 Office: 919 N Michigan Av Chicago IL 60611

GOLDRING, WILLIAM, educator, physician; b. Anniston, Ala., May 8, 1898; s. Paul and Rebecca (Rosenfeld) G.; student St. John's Coll., Fordham U., 1916-18; B.S. in Medicine, N.Y.U., 1920, M.D., 1922; m. Helen Heffner, Sept. 4, 1928; 1 dau., Roberta (Mrs. Robert Coles). Intern Bellevue Hosp., N.Y.C., 1922- 24, resident 1924-26, mem. staff, 1926—, vis. physician, 1945—; mem. faculty N.Y.U. Sch. Medicine, 1926—, prof. medicine, 1960—; cons. physician Goldwater Meml. Hosp., Beth Israel Hosp., Manhattan VA Hosp.; attending physician N.Y.U. Hosp., 1949—, mem. exec. com. med. bd., 1950- 53. Mem. Macy Found. Confs. Hypertension, 1949-53; med. adv. bd. Ruth Papier Nephrosis Found., 1950—; cons. cardiovascular diseases WHO, 1951- 53. Recipient Alumni Sci. award N.Y.U. Sch. Medicine, 1961, Med. Sch. Alumni medallion, 1965. Diplomate Am. Bd. Internal Medicine (cardiovascular disease). Fellow A.C.P., N.Y. Acad. Medicine; mem. Harvey Soc., Am. Physiol. Soc., Soc. Exptl. Biology and Medicine, Am. (council high blood pressure research 1939-61, chmn. program com. peripheral vascular sect. 1939-40, exec. com. sci. council 1956-57, bd. dirs. 1956-57, mem. central com. 1957-58, chmn. council circulation 1957- 59), N.Y. (chmn. com. vocational guidance cardiacs 1928-35, mem. exec. com. 1943—, bd. dirs. 1945—, chmn. adv. council research 1946-47, 61- 63, pres., 1959-61, mem. med. adv. com. 1963—) heart assns. , Sigma Xi, Alpha Omega Alpha. Contbr. numerous articles profl. jours. Home: 25 E 79th St New York City NY 10021 Office: New York Univ Sch Medicine 550 1st Av New York City NY 10016

GOLDSBY, FREDERICK LEWIS, contracting co. exec.; b. Flora, Ill., June 6, 1903; s. Frank Ernest and Annie (Frederick) G.; student Bradley U., 1922-24; B.S. in Engring., U. Ill., 1927; m. Lillian Catherine Luther, May 18, 1929; children—Arthur Frederick, Marjorie Lou (Mrs. Jules A. Gilbert). With Chgo. Bridge & Iron Co., 1927-68, asst. to pres., 1957-59, gen. mgr. internat. div., 1959-65, v.p., dir., 1954-65, v.p. internat., 1965-68; ret.; cons. internat. licensing and operations, 1968—; past. pres., dir. Chgo. Bridge Panama S.A., Chgo. Bridge (Philippines) Inc., past dir. Chgo. Bridge Argentina SAIC, Chgo. Bridge Ltd., Chgo. Bridge (Proprietary) Ltd., S. Africa, C.B. Erectors, Ltd., London, Chgo. Bridge (Netherlands) N.V., Chgo. Bridge-Lennox Pty. Ltd., Australia. Vice chmn. internat. sect. N.Y. Bd. Trade, 1965—; pres. Acad. Water and Sanitation Dist. Colorado Springs, Colo. Mem. spl. gifts com. Westfield (N.J.) Community Fund, 1964—. Registered profl. engr., Ill. Mem. Western Soc. Engrs., Chgo. Engrs. Club, Am. Petroleum Inst., N.A.M., Hort. Arts Soc. Colorado Springs (pres. 1971), Rose Soc. Methodist (ofcl. bd.). Clubs: Nomads (N.Y.C.); men's Garden (pres. 1970, regional dir. 1971) (Colorado Springs). Contbr. articles profl. jours. Patentee in field. Address: 1185 Tari Lane Colorado Springs CO 80908

GOLDSCHMIDT, ARTHUR EDUARD, fgn. service ofcl.; b. San Antonio, Feb. 17, 1910; s. Herman M. and Gretchen (Rochs) G.; A.B., Columbia; m. Elizabeth Wickenden, May 27, 1933; children—Arthur Eduard, Ann (Mrs. Raymond Richardson), Jean (Mrs. James Murray Kempton). With Fed. Emergency Relief Adminstrn. and related agys., Washington, 1933-36; mem. staff U.S. Senate com. on interstate commerce, 1936-37; mem. staff consumers council Nat. Bituminious Coal Commn., 1938; with power div. PWA, 1938- 40, Dept. Interior, 1940-50, dir. power div., 1942-49; dir. tech. assistance, spl. fund operations UN, 1950-67, U.S. rep. to UN ECOSOC, 1967-69, sr. adviser, adminstr. devel. program UN, 1969—. Univ. fellow Columbia Seminars program, 1952—. Recipient Distinguished Service medal Dept. Interior, 1949. Mem. Soc. Internat. Devel., Delta Phi. Home: 544 E 86th St New York City NY 10028 Office: UN New York City NY 10017

GOLDSCHMIDT, BERTRAND LEOPOLD, scientist; b. Paris, France, Nov. 2, 1912; s. Paul and Marcelle (Dreyfus) G.; Engr., Ecole de Phsique et de Chimie, U. Paris, 1933, Ph.D. in Sci., 1939; m. Naomi Louisa Rothschild, Feb. 26, 1947; children—Paul, Emma. Asst. Curie Lab., Paris, 1935-40; sect. leader Anglo-Canadian Atomic Project, 1942-45, head chemistry div., 1946; head chemistry div. Commissariat a-l'Energie Atomique, 1946-59, head external relations div., 1953-59, head external relations and planning, 1959-70, head internat. relations, 1970—; gov. for France, Internat. Atomic Energy Agy., 1957—; prof. Inst. d'Etudes Politiques, 1960-65; exec. v.p. European Atomic Energy Soc., 1955-58; mem. sci. adv. com. to UN, 1955—. Decorated comdr. Legion of Honor; recipient Atoms for Peace award, 1967. Author L'Aventure Atomique, 1962; Les Rivalites Atomiques 1939-1966, 1967. Home: 11 blvd Flandrin Paris XVLe, France. Office: 29 rue de la Federation Paris XVe France

GOLDSCHMIDT, CAREL, tobacco mfr.; b. Amsterdam, Netherlands, Dec. 27, 1904; s. Adolf and Geertruida Sophia (Maylahn) G.; ed. Openbare Handelschool, Amsterdam also Lyceum Alpinum. Zuoz, Switzerland; m. Helena Woodruff Jelliffe, Dec. 30, 1925; children—Dolf Leeming, Smith Ely. Came to U.S., 1940, naturalized, 1944. Partner Gebing & Lieftinck, brokers Indonesian tobacco, Amsterdam, 1922-48, Goldschmidt & Jiskoot. importers Sumatra and Java leaf tobacco. N.Y.C., 1922-43; pres., dir. Imperial Agrl. Corp., Hartford, Conn., 1942-68, Am. Sumatra Tobacco Corp., N.Y.C., 1956-68, Imperial Commodities Corp., N.Y.C., 1943-68, Imperial Prodn. Corp., San Antonio, 1947-68., chmn. Jelliffe Corp., N.Y.C., Jelliffe Devel. Corp., N.Y.C. P.K. & H Devel. Corp. N.Y.C., 1968-70; dir. Anglo-Am. Corp. Ltd., Singapore, 1945-68, Corrie MacColl & Sons, Ltd., London, 1952-68, Commonwealth Tobacco Co., Richmond, Va., 1962-68; mem. mng. bd., exec. com. N.V. Deli-Maatschappij, Amsterdam, Netherlands, 1956-68. Mem. N.Y.C. Cancer Com., Soc. N.Y. Hosp.; pres., dir. Godlschmidt Found.; trustee Smith Ely Jelliffe Trust. Clubs: Recess, Wall Street, Netherlands (N.Y.C.); Lake George (Warren County, N.Y.). Home: 205 S Bedford Rd Mount Kisco NY 10549 also 110 E 57th St New York City NY 10022 Office: 110 Wall St New York City NY 10005

GOLDSCHMIDT, CHARLES, advt. exec.; b. N.Y.C., June 15, 1921; s. Harry and Adele (Safir) G.; B.A., N.Y.U., 1941; m. Patricia Nevins, Jan. 17, 1951; children—Richard Walter, Jane, Peter. Advt. copywriter Warner Bros. Pictures Co., 1946- 48, Buchanan & Co., N.Y.C., 1948-49, Ray Austrian Asso., N.Y.C., 1949- 52; a founder, partner Daniel & Charles, Inc., advt., N.Y.C., 1952, chmn. bd. 1959—; ltd. partner Sartorius & Co., N.Y.C.; dir. Adtel, Inc. Served to lt. (s.g.) USNR, 1941-46. Democrat. Club: Beach Point (Mamaroneck, N.Y.). Author fiction articles. Home: 48 Bradford Rd Scarsdale NY 10583 Office: 261 Madison Av New York City NY 10016

GOLDSCHMIDT, MAURE LEONARD, educator; b. Portland, Ore., Aug. 26, 1909; s. Sidney L. and Bessie (Golden) G.; B.A., Reed Coll., 1930, U. Oxford (Eng.), 1933, M.A., 1966; Ph.D., U. Chgo., 1941; m. Etha Louisa Smith, Aug. 2, 1946; children—David, Ann, Ellen. Instr. polit. sci. Reed Coll., 1935-37, mem. faculty, 1946—, prof. polit. sci., 1950—; instr. U. Chgo., 1938-41; instr. govt. Coll. City N.Y., 1941-42; economist OPA, 1942-44, anti-trust div. Dept. Justice, 1944; asst. prof. U. Chgo., 1944-46. Vis. asso. prof. U. Wash., summer 1949; vis. prof. U. Cal. at Berkeley, summer 1950, at Los Angeles, 1960-61, U. Wash., summer 1965; prof. govt., head dept. Univ Coll., Nairobi U., E. Africa, 1966-68; mem. field staff Rockefeller Found., 1966-68. Bd. dirs. Am. Civil Liberties Union Ore., 1960-66, Boys and Girls Aid Soc. Ore., 1962-66. Rhodes scholar, 1930-33; fellow Social Sci. Research Council, 1937-38, Fund Advancement Edn., Ford Found., 1952-53. Mem. Am. (v.p. 1961-62), Western (pres. 1965- 66), Pacific N.W. (pres. 1951-52) polit. sci. assns. Contbr. chpts. in books. Editor: (with Gertzel and Rothchild) Government and Politics in Kenya, 1968. Home: 3807 SE Harold St Portland OR 97202

GOLDSCHMIDT, WALTER R., educator, anthropologist; b. San Antonio, Feb. 24, 1913; s. Hermann and Gretchen (Rochs) G.; B.A., U. Tex., 1933, M.A., 1935; Ph.D., U. Cal. at Berkeley, 1942; m. Beatrice Lucia Gale, May 27, 1937; children—Karl Gale, Mark Stefan. Social scientist Bur. Agrl. Econs., 1940-46; mem. faculty U. Cal. at Los Angeles, 1946—, prof. anthropology, 1956—, chmn. dept., 1964-69, prof. anthropology and psychiatry, 1969—. Vis. lectr. Stanford, summer 1945, U. Cal. at Berkeley, 1949, Harvard, 1950; dir. radio program Ways of Mankind, 1951- 53, Culture and Ecology in E. Africa, 1960-68; spl. editor Aldine Pub. Co., 1966—; cons. Ginn & Co., 1964-69. Fulbright scholar, U.K., 1953; grantee Social Sci. Research Council, 1953, Wenner-Gren Found., 1953; NSF postdoctoral fellow, 1964-65; fellow Center Advanced Study Behavioral Scis., 1964-65, sr. sci. fellow Nat. Inst. Mental Health, 1970. Fellow Am. Anthrop. Assn., African Studies Assn. (founding, bd. dirs. 1957-60); mem. A.A.A.S., Soc Applied Anthropology, Southwestern Anthrop. Assn. (pres. 1950-51), Am. Ethnol. Soc. (pres. 1969-70), Internat. African Inst., Am. Assn. U. Profs., Phi Beta Kappa, Sigma Xi. Author: Small Business and the Community, 1946; As You Sow, 1947; Nomlaki Ethnography, 1951; Ways to Justice, 1953; Man's Way, 1959; Exploring the Ways of Mankind, 1960, 2d edit., 1971; Comparative Functionalism, 1966; Sebei Law, 1967; Kambuya's Cattle, The Legacy of an African Herdsman, 1968. On Being an Anthropologist, 1970. Editor: The U.S. and Africa, rev. 1963, French edit., 1965; The Anthropology of Franz Boas, 1959; (with H. Hosser) The Social Anthropology of Latin America, 1959. Editor Am. Anthropoligist, 1956-59. Home: 978 Norman Pl Los Angeles CA 90049

GOLDSMITH, ALEXANDER PHILLIP, clothing mfg.; b. London, Eng., Dec. 2, 1907; student Columbia; m. Sara Posemsky, Dec. 11, 1932; children—Ellyn Rhoda, Lynda Ann. Sales promotion women's hosiery industry, 1929—; former pres. Bates Mfg. Co., Lewiston, Me., now cons. in expansion program, dir.; pres. Goldsmith Enterprises, N.Y.C.; pres., dir. Venable Properties, Inc.; dir. Va. Iron Coal & Coke Co. Active United Jewish Appeal, other community and philanthropic orgns.; founding mem. Albert Einstein Sch. Medicine; chmn. Ramaz Sch., N.Y.C. Trustee, Yeshivah U. Home: 784 Park Av New York City NY 10021

GOLDSMITH, BERNARD MORTON, mfg. co. exec.; b. New Brunswick, N.J., Nov. 17, 1916; s. Morton and Fanny (Kramer) G.; B.S. in Elec. Engring., Rutgers U., 1937; postgrad. Stevens Inst. Tech., 1939; m. Ruth Adler, Apr. 9, 1936 (div. 1965); children—William, Bernard, Frances; m. 2d, Ellen de R. Bernard, 1965. Engr., Gen. Electric Co., 1937-38, Automatic Winding Co., 1939-40; chief engr. Essex Splty. Co., Hackettstown, N.J., 1940-43, pres., 1943-60; pres. Nytronics, Inc., Berkeley Heights, N.J., 1960-65, pres., chmn. bd., Alpha, N.J., 1965—; dir. Mallary Randall Corp. Mem. I.E.E.E., Alpha Chi Rho. Contbr. articles profl. jours. Patentee in field. Home: 39 Turkey Hill Rd S Westport CT 06880 Office: 10 Pelham Pky Pelham Manor NY 10803

GOLDSMITH, BERTRAM MELVIN, horticulturist; b. Newark, May 7, 1907; s. Nathan and Rosetta (Buckey) G.; B.A., Princeton, 1926; m. Fannie Newman, Jan. 25, 1934; children—Peter N., John H. With Ira Haupt & Co., mems. N.Y. Stock Exchange, 1932- 1963, partner, 1940-63, mng. partner, 1958-63; with Salomon Bros. and Hutzler, N.Y.C., 1963; partner L. F. Rothschild & Co., mem. N.Y. Stock Exchange, N.Y.C., 1964-69; nurseryman Watercress Farm, Annandale, N.Y., 1969—. Founder, Municipal Bond Investment Trust. Served to maj. AUS, 1943-45. Decorated Bronze Star medal; Croix de Guerre with oak leaf (France); Crown of Italy, Silver Combat medal (Italy). Mem. Municipal Bond Forum, Am. Inst. Mgmt. (presidents council), Am. Hort. Soc., Am. Orchid Soc., N.Y. Philharmonic Soc. Clubs: Princeton, New York Stock Exchange Luncheon (N.Y.C.). Author: Gold Letters, also articles on orchids. Home: Watercress Farm Annandale NJ 08801

GOLDSMITH, CLIFFORD HENRY, tobacco co. exec.; b. Leipzig, Germany, Sept. 6, 1919; s. Conrad and Elise (Stahl) G.; grad. Bradford (Eng.) Inst. Tech., 1939; m. Katherine W. Kaynis; children—Corine Elizabeth, Audrey Jane, Alexandra Eve. Came to U.S., 1940, naturalized, 1943. Technologist, Glenside Mills Corp., Skaneateles, N.Y., 1940-41; supt. Falls Yarn Mills, Woonsocket, R.I., 1941-42, Aldon Spinning Mills, Talcottville, Conn., 1942-43; with Benson & Hedges Co., 1943-53, plant mgr., 1945-53; with Philip Morris, Inc., 1954—, now v.p., dir.; exec. v.p. Philip Morris U.S.A.; dir. Milprint, Inc., Polymer Industries, Nicolet Paper Co., A.S.R. Products Co., Central Nat. Bank, Central Nat. Corp., Richmond, Va. Served with inf. AUS, 1943-45. Mem. Textile Inst., (Manchester, Eng., asso.). Clubs: Chemists (N.Y.C.); Downtown (Richmond). Home: 10 Park Av New York City NY 10016 Office: 100 Park Av New York City NY 10017

GOLDSMITH, GRACE ARABELL, physician; b. St. Paul, Apr. 8, 1904; d. Arthur William and Arabell Louise (Coleman) Goldsmith; B.S., U. Wis., 1925; M.D., Tulane U., 1932; M.S. in Medicine, U. Minn., 1936; D.Sc., Woman's Med. Coll., 1962. Intern Touro Infirmary, New Orleans, 1932-33, now cons. med. staff; fellow internal medicine Mayo Clinic, Rochester, Minn., 1933-36; instr. medicine Tulane U., New Orleans, 1936-39, asst. prof., 1939-43, asso. prof., 1943-49, prof. medicine, 1949-67, dean Sch. Pub. Health and Tropical Medicine, 1967—, prof. medicine and nutrition pub. health, 1967—, dir. div. nutrition, metabolism, 1946-67; cons. physician Charity Hosp., New Orleans. Mem. food and nutrition bd. NRC, 1948-69, chmn., 1958-68; mem. nutrition study sect. USPHS, 1959-63, mem. gastroenterology and nutrition tng. com., 1966-70; mem. panel world food supply Pres.'s Sci. Adv. Com., 1966-67; mem. food and nutrition research adv. com., agrl. research service USDA, 1951- 63; chmn., 1954-56; sci. adv. com. Nutrition Found., 1948-64; cons. La. Bd. Health, 1962- 67; panel chmn. advanced acad. teaching of nutrition White House Conf. on Food, Nutrition and Health, 1969; mem. nat. adv. arthritis and metabolic diseases council NIH, 1970. Mem. corp. vis. com., dept. nutrition and food sci. Mass. Inst. Tech., 1964-65; mem. Com. Etiology and Epidemiology Anemas-Internat. Union Nutritional Scis. 1967—; mem. tech. adv. com. Inst. Nutrition C. Am. and Panama, 1967. Recipient Outstanding Achievement award U. Minn., 1964; Goldberger award clin. nutrition A.M.A., 1965; Axson-Choppin award La. Pub. Health Assn., 1970; Seale-Harris award So. Med. Assn., 1970. Diplomate Am. Bd. Internal Medicine, Am. Bd. Nutrition (pres. 1966). Fellow A.C.P., Am. Pub. Health Assn. (mem. council food and nutrition sect. 1964-67, mem. governing council 1969—), A.A.A.S., N.Y. Acad. Sci.; mem. A.M.A. (mem. council foods and nutrition 1958-63, 65—, chmn. 1970), Assn. Am. Physicians, Am. Dietetic Assn. (hon.), Pan Am. Med. Assn., Am. Diabetes Assn., Am. Inst. Nutrition (Osborne and Mendel award 1959, pres. 1963), Fedn. Am. Socs. for Exptl. Biology (dir.; adv. com. 1962-65), Internat. Union Nutrition Scis. (U.S. nat. com. 1960-68), Am. Soc. Clin. Nutrition, Am. Soc. Clin. Investigation, Internat. Soc. Hematology, So. Med. Assn., So. Soc. Clin. Research, Soc. Exptl. Biology and Medicine, Sigma Xi, Alpha Omega Alpha, Delta Omega, Alpha Gamma Delta, Alpha Epsilon Iota. Episcopalian. Author: Nutritional Diagnosis, 1959; chpts. in books, articles profl. jours. Editorial bd. Am. Jour. Clin. Nutrition, 1952-63, Physiol. Revs., 1961-67, Jour. Atherosclerosis Research 1962-68, Archives Internal Medicine, 1966-69. Home: 1621 Peniston St New Orleans LA 70115 Office: 1430 Tulane Av New Orleans LA 70112 ☆

GOLDSMITH, JACK LANDMAN, former retail co. exec.; b. Memphis, Apr. 10, 1910; s. Fred and Aimee (Landman) G.; grad. Memphis Law Sch.; student Washington U., St. Louis; m. 2d, Dorothy Metzger, Feb. 9, 1960; children—Joan (Mrs. Stanley A. Marks), Jack Landman; stepchildren—Larry, Melvin. With Federated Dept. Stores, Inc., 1959—, v.p., 1961—; ret. chmn. bd., chmn. exec. com., Goldsmith's Dept. Store; dir. First Nat. Holding Co., Memphis. Mem. world trade adv. com. Dept. Commerce. Former trustee Brooks Art Gallery, Memphis; pres. Goldsmith Found.; bd. dirs. Bapt. Hosp., Memphis. Mem. Nat., Tenn. retail mchts. assns., Downtown Assn. (v.p.). Clubs: Rotary, One Hundred (Memphis). Home 601 Putting Green Lane Sarasota FL 33577 Office: Goldsmiths 123 S Main St Memphis TN 38103

GOLDSMITH, JOHN ALAN, journalist; b. Cin., Oct. 13, 1920; s. Alan G. and Mary (Boyd) G.; grad. Choate Sch., 1938; A.B. cum laude, Kenyon Coll., 1942; m. Rosemarie Mullany, Sept. 11, 1948; children—Alan, Gregory. Mem. staff Troy (N.Y.) Record, 1946-47; reporter U.P.I., 1947-68; writer (with Robert S. Allen) syndicated column Inside Washington, 1968—. Mem. Fairfax County (Va.) Sch. Bd., 1964—, vice chmn., 1966-69, chmn., 1969 —. Bd. dirs. Mellett Fund Free and Responsible Press, 1966, v.p., 1967. Served to lt. USNR, 1943-46. Mem. Wire Service Guild (charter mem., pres. 1960). Home: 4605 Franconia Rd Alexandria VA 22310 Office: Nat Press Bldg Washington DC 20004

GOLDSMITH, JULIAN ROYCE, educator, geochemist; b. Chgo., Feb. 26, 1918; s. Mitchel and Cecelia (Kallis) G.; S.B., U. Chgo., 1940, Ph.D., 1947; m. Ethel J. Frank, Sept. 4, 1940; children—Richard,

Susan (Mrs. Kent Wooldridge), John. Research chemist Corning Glass Works (N.Y.), 1942-46; mem. faculty U. Chgo., 1946 —, prof. geochemistry, 1958—, asso. dean div. phys. scis., 1960—, chmn. dept. geophys. scis., 1963—, Charles E. Merriam Distinguished Service prof., 1969—. Mem. earth-sci.-panel NSF, 1958-60, chmn. 1960, mem. nat. sci. bd. , 1964-70; cons. Lawrence Radiation Lab., U.S. Geol. Survey. Chmn. of gov. bd. Lab. Schs. U. Chgo., 1959-60. Fellow A.A.A.S., Mineral. Soc. Am. (counsellor 1960-62, award 1955, v.p. 1968-69, pres. 1970-71), Geol. Soc. America, (counsellor 1968—), Am. Acad. Arts and Scis.; mem. Geochem. Soc. (charter v.p. 1955, pres. 1964-66), Renaissance Soc. (pres. 1966- 68), Am. Chem. Soc., Am. Crystallographic Assn., Am. Ceramic Soc., Mineral. Soc. Gt. Brit., Am. Geophys. Union, Phi Beta Kappa, Sigma Xi. Author articles in field. Co-editor Jour. Geology, 1957-62; cons. editor Ency. Brit. Ency. Sci. and Tech. Home: 5631 Blackstone Av Chicago IL 60637

GOLDSMITH, JUSTIN J., diversified industry exec.; b. N.Y.C., 1919. Chmn. bd. All-Tech Industries, Miami Lakes, Fla. Mason. Home: 19740 NE 22d Av North Miami Beach FL 33160 Office: 1400 Northwest Ct Miami Lakes FL 33014*

GOLDSMITH, KARL ROBINSON, petroleum co. exec.; b. Pierre, S.D., Jan. 13, 1918; s. Karl and Kathryn (Robinson) G.; A.B., U. Minn., 1940; LL.B., Yale, 1948; m. Roberta D. Waldrep, Sept. 10, 1960; 1 son, Gilbert. Admitted to Okla. bar, 1948; with Amoco Production Co., Tulsa, 1948—, atty., 1948—, sec., 1953- -. Home: 4302 S Oswego St Tulsa OK 74135 Office: Amoco Bldg Tulsa OK 74103

GOLDSMITH, LEO, Jr., lawyer, city ofcl.; b. Newark, Apr. 2, 1912; s. Leo and Rebecca (Burnstine) G.; graduate Newark Acad., 1930; student U. Munich, 1932-33; B.A., Brown U., 1934; LL.B., Harvard, 1937; m. Beryl Kraus, Aug. 17, 1945; children—Margaret, Elizabeth, Patricia. Admitted to N.Y. bar, 1938, since practiced in N.Y.C.; partner Greenwald, Kovner and Goldsmith, 1940—. Chmn. bd. 1st Nat. Bank, Fleischmanns, N.Y. Acting mayor Larchmont, N.Y., 1962-66; mayor, 1966—, chmn. zoning bd. appeals, Larchmont. Served from pvt. to maj., AUS, 1942-45. Mem. Am. Ethical Union (pres.), Westchester Ethical Soc. (past pres.), N.Y. Co. Lawyers Assn., Harvard Law Sch. Assn., Am. Legion, N.Y. Soc. Mil. and Naval Officers of the World Wars, Air Force Assn., Aircraft Owners and Pilots Assn. Clubs: Brown University (N.Y.C.); Ocean Beach (Elberon, N.J.) (trustee, v.p.). Home: 14 Virginia Pl Larchmont NY 10543 Office: 170 Broadway New York City NY 10038

GOLDSMITH, MYRON, architect; b. Chgo., Sept. 15, 1918; s. Martin and Fannie (Fetman) G.; B.S. in Architecture, Armour Inst. Tech., Chgo., 1939; M.S., Ill. Inst. Tech., 1953; m. Robin W. Squier, July 29, 1962; children—Marc, Chandra. Architect, structural engr. firm Ludwig Mies van der Rohe, Chgo., 1946- 53; with Skidmore, Owings & Merrill, Chgo., 1955—, chief structural engr., San Francisco, 1955-58, asso. partner, sr. designer, Chgo., 1958-67, gen. partner, 1967—; prof. architecture Ill. Inst. Tech. Grad. Sch. Chgo., 1961—. Served with C.E., AUS, 1945-46. Mem. A.I.A., Am. Soc. C.E. Bldgs. designed include Norton Office Bldg., Seattle, 1959, United Air Lines hangers, San Francisco, 1959, Assn. Univs. for Research in Astronomy solar telescope, Kitt Peak, Ariz., 1962, Oakland (Cal.)- Alameda County Coliseum, 1966, United Air Lines Exec. Office Bldg. and Edn. and Tng. Center, Chgo., 1962, Home News Enterprises Daily Jour. Bldg., Franklin, Ind., 1963, The Brunswick Bldg., Chgo., 1965, Met. Structures, Dewitt-Chestnut Apts. Chgo., 1965, Inland Steel Co. research labs. East Chicago, Ind., 1969, Ill. Inst. Tech. Life Scis. Bldg., 1967, gymnasium, 1969, engring. bldg., 1968. Office: 30 W Monroe St Chicago IL 60603

GOLDSMITH, RAYMOND WILLIAM, educator, economist; b. Brussels, Belgium, Dec. 23, 1904; s. Alfred and Camilla (Marcus) G.; Ph.D., U. Berlin, 1927; m. Selma E. Fine, May 19, 1939 (dec. Apr. 1962); children—Jane, Donald, Paul. Came to U.S., 1930, naturalized 1939. Economist with SEC, WPB, Dept. State, 1934- 48; staff Nat. Bur. Econ. Research, 1952-70; prof. econs. N.Y. U., 1958- 59, Yale, 1960—; v.p. OECD Devel. Centre, Paris, 1963-64. Fellow Am. Statis. Assn. Author: Kapitalpolitik, 1933; The Changing Structure of American Banking, 1933; A Study of Saving in the United States, 1955; Financial Intermediaries in the American Economy, 1958; The National Wealth of the United States in the Postwar Period, 1962; Studies in the National Balance Sheet of the United States, 1963; Flow of Capital Funds in the Postwar Economy, 1965; Financial Structure and Development, 1969. Home: 111 Park St New Haven CT 06511

GOLDSMITH, SAMUEL LUNT, Jr., assn. exec.; b. N.Y.C., Sept. 25, 1916; s. Samuel Lunt and Margaret (Thurston) G.; B.A., Amherst Coll., 1939; postgrad. Columbia, N.Y.U.; m. Sybil Graham, Oct. 12, 1939 (div. 1966); children—Peter Lunt, John Graham; m. 2d, Beatrice A. Brennan, Dec. 1967. Salesman John H. Graham & Co. Inc., 1939-42, selection and tng. of employees, 1945-46, sales supr., 1946-49, treas., 1949-52; dir. econ. problems dept. N.A.M. , 1952-57; exec. dir. Sales and Marketing Exec.-Internat., 1957-64; exec. v.p. The Aluminum Assn., 1964—; bd. dirs. Internat. Social Service. Vice pres. Materials Disposal Research Council; bd. dirs. N.Y. chpt. Am. Soc. Assn. Execs. Served as lt. USNR, 1942-45; liaison officer Brit. Royal Navy. Mem. Pi Sigma Epsilon. Mem. Marine Hist. Assn., Catboat Assn. Club: Union League (N.Y.C.). Home: 3 Peter Cooper Rd New York City NY 10010 Office: 750 3d Av New York City NY 10017

GOLDSMITH, SIDNEY, physician, scientist, inventor; b. N.Y.C., Dec. 21, 1930; s. Max and Annie (Schneider) G.; B.Sc. cum laude, Coll. City N.Y., 1950; M.Sc., U. Geneva, Switzerland, 1952, M.D., 1956; m. Nancy Carrol Stinich, Apr. 2, 1966. Intern Hosp. for Joint Diseases, N.Y.C., 1957-58; resident internal medicine Bronx VA Hosp. and Columbia-Presbyn. Hosp., N.Y.C., 1958-61; fellow gastroenterology Temple U., 1961-62, instr. medicine, 1962-64, asso. prof., 1964; pvt. practice internal medicine specializing gastroenterology, Phila., 1963—; cons. medicine Merck & Co. (Rahway, N.J.); cons. gastroenterolgy Oxford Hosp.; book reviewer Am. Jour. Med. Scis. Served as capt. M.C., AUS, 1959-64. Recipient prize in immunology, Pasteur Inst., Paris, France, 1956, meritorious achievement award, Inventors Mfrs. Exchange, 1969. Diplomate Am. Bd. Internal Medicine. Fellow A.C.P.; mem. Am. Gastroenterol. Assn., Phila. Gastrointestinal Research Forum, N.Y. Acad. Scis., French Nat. Acad. Medicine. Inventor human tetanus antitoxin serum, multipurpose med. biopsy needle; discoverer new method of diagnosing silicosis; holder Russian patent on biopsy needle. Home: 929 Tyson Av Philadelphia PA 19111 Office: 3701 N Broad St Philadelphia PA 19140

GOLDSMITH, THOMAS TOLIVER, Jr., educator; b. Greensville, S.C., Jan. 9, 1910; s. Thomas T. and Charlotte B. (Manly) G.; B.S., Furman U., 1931, LL.D.; Ph.D., Cornell U., 1936; m. Helen Wilcox, 1938; children—Judson, Thomas III, Virginia Louise. Biophysics research, 1936; dir. research Allen B. DuMont Labs., Inc., 1936-53, v.p. research, 1953-56, v.p. engring. and research, 1956-60; dir. research Du Mont Labs. div. Clifton Fairchild Camera and Instrument Corp., 1960-66; pres. Du Mont TV & Electronics, Ltd., 1952-66; prof. of physics Furman U., 1966—; dir. Metromedia, Inc. Fellow I.E.E.E., Soc. Motion Picture and TV Engrs.; mem. Am. Phys. Soc., Montclair Soc. Engrs., Optical Soc. Am., Sigma Xi, Sigma Pi Sigma, Eta Kappa Nu. Baptist. Club: Cosmopolitan (Montclair). Contbr. tech. jours. Home: Route 2 Box 312 Travlers Rest SC 29690 Office: Furman U Greenville SC 29602

GOLDSMITH, ULRICH KARL, educator; b. Freiburg, Germany, Jan. 19, 1910; s. Hans Julius and Sophie Clara (Bickel) G.; Juristischer Referendar, Hamburg U., 1931; scholar London (Eng.) Sch. Econs., 1932-34; B.A., U. Toronto, 1942, M.A., 1946; Ph. D., U. Cal. at Berkeley, 1950; m. Helen Hart, 1951 (div. 1956); 1 dau., Sheila H.; m. 2d, Bobra Ballin, Dec. 19, 1966. Came to U.S., 1946, naturalized, 1955. Tchr., Wimbledon, Eng., 1934-40; tchr. German lang., German and comparative lit. U. Sask. (Can.), 1944-46, Princeton, 1947-50, U. Man. (Can.), 1950-51, U. Mass., 1951-55, Yale, 1955-57; mem. faculty U . Colo., Boulder, 1957—, chmn. dept. Germanic langs. and lit., 1961-65, prof. NO. OF RECORDS 00590 German, 1962—, chmn. comparative lit., 1965—. Vis. prof. dept. German, U. Cal., Berkeley, 1970. Mem. Internat. Comparative Lit. Assn., Am. Assn. Tchrs. German, Modern Lang. Assn. Am., Brecht Soc., Am. Civil Liberties Union. Author: Stefan George: A Study of His Early Work, 1959; Stefan George (Columbia Essays on Modern Writers), 1970. Home: 865 7th St Boulder CO 80302

GOLDSMITH, WILLIAM M., indsl. designer; b. Rochester, N.Y., Feb. 20, 1917; s. William M. and Florence (Hirsch) G.; B.A. in Indsl. Design, Carnegie Inst. Tech., 1939; m. Jean Ann Rosenbaum, June 30, 1943; children—Jan Ellen, Ted Grant; m. 2d, Ruth Epstein Saichek, Oct. 17, 1969; stepchildren—Daniel, Lisa, Gerald, Richard. With Dave Chapman, Goldsmith & Yamasaki, Inc. (formerly Dave Chapman, Inc.), indsl. design, Chgo., 1939-70, partner, v.p., 1951-55, exec. v.p., 1955-66, pres., 1966—; v.p. Design Research, Inc., 1955—, founder, pres. Goldsmith, Yamasaki, Specht & Anderson, Inc., indsl. design, Chgo., 1970—. Head U.S. tech. assistance team in Pakistan and Afghanistan, 1955-57. Served with AUS, 1942-46. Fellow Indsl. Designers Soc. Am. (pres. 1971—); mem. Package Designers Council (past dir.), Soc. Typographic Arts, Chgo. Council Fgn. Relations, Execs. Club Chgo. Jewish religion (past v.p. congregation). Home: 4 Timber Lane Northbrook IL 60062 Office: 75 E Wacker Dr Chicago IL 60601

GOLDSMITH, WILLIAM WALLCE, lawyer, coal corp. exec.; b. Newark, May 17, 1893; s. W. H. and Amelia (Hensley) G.; LL.B., U. Richmond, 1913; m. Mary Nan McGinnis, June 15, 1921; 1 dau., Beth (Mrs. J. P. Childers, Jr.). Admitted to Va. bar, 1914, W. Va. bar, 1920; practiced in Richmond, Va., 1914-20, Beckley, W. Va., 1920-37, Charleston, 1937—; chmn. bd. Elk Horn Coal Corp. Mem. Am., W. Va. bar assns. Club: Edgewood Country (Charleston). Home: 1105 Highland Rd Charleston WV 25302 Office: Union Bldg Charleston WV 25301

GOLDSTEIN, ABRAHAM SAMUEL, educator, lawyer; b. N.Y.C., July 27, 1925; s. Isidore and Yetta (Crystal) G.; B.B.A., Coll. City N.Y., 1946, LL.B., Yale, 1949, M.A., 1961; M.A., Cambridge (Eng.) U., 1964; m. Ruth Tessler, Aug. 31, 1947; children—William Ira, Marianne Susan. Admitted to D.C. bar, 1949; law clk. to judge U.S. Ct. Appeals, 1949-51; partner firm Donohue & Kaufmann, Washington, 1951-56; mem. faculty Yale Law Sch., 1956—, prof. law, 1961—, William Nelson Cromwell prof. law, 1967—, dean, 1970—, fellow Branford Coll., 1962—. Vis. prof. law Stanford Law Sch., summer 1963; vis. fellow Inst. Criminology, fellow Christ's Coll., Cambridge U., 1964- 65; faculty orientation program Am. law Princeton, 1968, faculty Salzburg Seminar in Am. Studies, 1969, Inst. on Social Sci. Methods in Legal Edn., U. Denver, 1970. Cons. Pres.'s Com. Law Enforcement; mem. Conn. Bd. of Parole; mem. Conn. Commn. Revise Criminal Code; mem. of the Conn. Planning Com. on Criminal Adminstrn. Served with AUS, 1943- 46. Guggenheim fellow, 1964-65. Mem. Am. Assn. U. Profs., Beta Gamma Sigma. Author: The Insanity Defense, 1967. Editorial adv. bd. Law and Soc. Rev. Contbr. profl. jours. Home: 545 Ellsworth Av New Haven CT 06511

GOLDSTEIN, AVRAM SHALOM, educator; b. N.Y.C., July 3, 1919; s. Israel and Bertha (Markowitz) G.; A.B., Harvard, 1940, M.D., 1943; m. Dora Benedict, Aug. 29, 1947; children—Margaret, Daniel, Joshua, Michael. Intern Mt. Sinai Hosp., N.Y.C., 1944; successively instr., asso., asst. prof. pharmacology Harvard, 1947-55; prof. dept. pharmacology, Stanford, 1955—, exec. head dept., 1955-70. Served from 1st lt. to capt., M.C., AUS, 1944-46. Mem. Am. Soc. Pharmacolology and Exptl. Therapeutics, A.A.A.S., Am. Soc. Biol. Chemists, Am. Assn. Cancer Research, Genetics Soc. Am. Home: 735 Dolores St Stanford CA 94305

GOLDSTEIN, BENJAMIN FRANKLIN, lawyer; b. St. Louis, June 16, 1895; s. Julius and Naomi (Goldstein) G.; A.B., Washington U., St. Louis, 1914; LL.B., Harvard, 1917; m. Wilda Carsten, Sept. 4, 1964. Admitted to Ill. bar, 1917, practiced in Peoria, 1917-20, Chgo., 1920—; mem. firm Haight, Goldstein & Hobbs, 1938-49, Haight, Goldstein & Haight, 1949-55; head own law firm, 1956-57, 60—; mem. firm Goldstein & Wahlen, 1958-60. Mem. bd. overseers vis. com. Harvard Law Sch., 1952-57; trustee Marquis Biog. Library Soc. Served with AEF, 1917-19. Mem. Am., Inter Am., Ill., Chgo. bar assns., Ill. Harvard Law Sch. Assn. (council 1958-62), Phi Beta Kappa, Delta Theta Phi. Clubs: Harvard, Economic. Author: Marketing-A Farmer's Problem, 1928. Address: Camelback Towers 4750 N Central Av Phoenix AZ 85012

GOLDSTEIN, DAVID HENRY, physician; b. New Orleans, Sept. 20, 1908; s. Gustav and Eva (Small) G.; B.A., Cornell U., 1928; M.D., N.Y. U., 1933, D.M.S., 1940; m. Joyce N. Benoit, Nov. 23, 1966; children—Paul, Janet. Med dir. N.Y. Times Co., N.Y.C., 1946—; prof. environmental medicine N.Y. U. Med Center, 1951—. Mem. exec. com. med. adv. bd. Hotel Trades, 1959—. Served to maj., M.C., AUS, World War II. Recipient N.Y. U. Meritorious Alumni Service medallion , 1969. Diplomate Am. Bd. Internal Medicine, Am. Bd. Preventive Medicine (Occupational Medicine). Fellow N.Y. Acad. Medicine, Am. Acad. Occupational Medicine, Indsl. Med. Assoc. (pres. 1968-69); mem. A.M.A. (editorial bd. Archives Environmental Health 1963-71), N.Y. U Sch. Medicine Alumni Assn. (pres. 1966-67), N.Y. U. Alumni Fedn. (v.p. 1967-70). Contbr. profl. jours. Home: 340 E 34th St New York City NY 10016 Office: 550 1st Av New York City NY 10016

GOLDSTEIN, E. ERNEST, lawyer; b. Pitts., Oct. 9, 1918; s. Nathan E. and Annie (Ginsberg) G.; A.B. cum laude, Amherst Coll., 1939; student U. Chgo. Law Sch., 1940-42; LL.B., Georgetown U., 1947; S.J.D., U. Wis., 1956; m. Peggy Janet Rosenfeld, June 22, 1941; children—Susan M. (Mrs. Ian I. Lipsitch), Daniel F. Admitted to D.C. bar, 1947, Tex. bar, 1958, also U.S. Supreme Ct.; pvt. practice, D.C., 1947; with Dept. Justice, also War Claims Commn., 1947-50; asso. counsel crime com. U.S. Senate, 1950-51; gen. counsel antitrust subcom. for com. jud. Ho. of Reps., 1951-52; restrictive trade practices specialist Office U.S. Spl. Rep., Paris, also U.S. rep. productivity and applied research com. Orgn. European Econ. Coop., 1952-53; prof. law U. Tex., 1955-65; counsel Coudert Freres, Paris, France, 1966-67, partner, 1969—; spl. asst. to Pres. U.S., 1967-69; lectr. Inst. Advanced European Studies. U. Nice (France), 1967, Free U. Brussels (Belgium), 1967, Europa Inst., Amsterdam, 1970; vis. prof. U. P. R. Law Sch., 1962; prof. Am. seminar Salzburg, Austria, 1963; internat. law cons. Naval War Coll., 1963. Chmn. S.W. regional adv. bd. Anti Defamation League, 1964-65; bd. dirs. Am. C. of C. in France, 1970—; treas. Democrats in France, 1970—. Served with AUS, 1942-46. Decorated Legion of Merit; Ford Found. Internat. Studies fellow, 1959-60. Mem. Am. Soc. Internat. Law, Order of Coif, Phi Delta Phi. Club: Travellers (Paris). Author: Cases and Materials on Patent, Trademark and Copyright Law, 1959; American Enterprise and Scandinavian Antitrust Law, 1962. Home: 6 Sq Emmanuel Chabrier Paris XVII France Office: 52 Champs Elysees Paris VIII France

GOLDSTEIN, GEORGE, real estate appraiser, cons.; b. N.Y.C., Dec. 17, 1901; s. Morris and Elizabeth (Rothman) G.; A.B., Columbia, 1922; m. Stella Levi, Aug. 13, 1933. Estimator The Stein Co., N.Y.C., 1923-25; broker Goldstein & Goldstein, Englewood, N.J., 1925-28; owner George Goldstein, real estate appraiser, cons., Newark, 1928—; dir. First Nat. State Bank of N.J. Mem. Adv. council zone I, War Assets Corp., 1947; rev. appraiser, cons. Navy Dept., 1941-47. Recipient Meritorious Civilian Service award Bur. of Yards and Docks, 1945; Distinguished Civilian Service award Navy Dept., 1945. Trustee, pres. Hosp. Center of Oranges; trustee Griffith Music Found.; trustee, v.p. Hosp. Service Plan N.J. Mem. Am. Soc. Real Estate Counselors (bd. govs.), Am. Inst. Real Estate Appraisers (pres. 1950, regional v.p., 1947-49). Clubs: Mountain Ridge Country (West Caldwell, N.J.) (pres.); Downtown (Newark); Economic (N.Y.C.). Contbr., lectr. on valuation of real estate. Home: Eagle Ridge Way West Orange NJ 07052 Office: 810 Broad St Newark NJ 07102

GOLDSTEIN, GERALD, dept. store exec.; b. N.Y.C., May 4, 1908; s. Samuel and Mary (Joseph) G.; grad. Coll. City N.Y., 1928; m. Pearl Einhorn, Sept. 23, 1934; children—Mary Elaine, Ellen Sue. Pub. accountant, N.Y.C., 1927-33; asso. R. H. Macy Co., N.Y.C., 1934—, with Bamberger's div., Newark, 1943—, controller, 1947-55, v.p., 1954-55, sr. v.p., sec., 1955-66, sr. v.p., sec., controller Macy's N.Y. div., 1966—, also dir., v.p. Macy Credit Corp. 1967—. Bd. dirs. N.Y.C. Council Econ. Edn. C.P.A. Mem. Am. Inst. C.P.A.'s, Financial Execs Inst., Am. Inst. Internal Auditors, Am. Arbitration Assn., Met. Controllers Assn. N.Y. (past pres.), Met. N.Y. Retail Mchts. Assn. (treas.). Home: One Lincoln Plaza New York City NY 10023 Office: 151 W 34th St New York City NY 10001

GOLDSTEIN, GERALD, fgn. service officer; b. N.Y.C., Aug. 2, 1921; s. Samuel and Rose (Greenberg) G.; B.A., Bklyn. Coll., 1944; M.A., U. Cal. at Berkeley, 1948. Econ. officer OPA, 1946; research asst. Bank Am., 1948; teaching asst. U. Cal. at Berkeley, 1948-50; fgn. service officer Dept. State, 1950; cons. economist, Munich, West Germany, 1950, Vancouver, B.C., Can., 1952-55; research analyst Dept. Intelligence, 1956-57; dep. prin. officer econs., Port of Spain, W.I., 1959-61; assigned State Dept., 1961-65, Nat. War Coll., 1965-66; supervising econ. officer, Bonn, West Germany, 1966, counselor for econ. affairs, 1969—. Address: Am Embassey Bonn Federal Republic Germany

GOLDSTEIN, HAROLD, univ. dean; b. Norfolk, Va., Oct. 3, 1917; s. Samuel and Jennie (Michelson) G.; B.S., U. Md., 1942; B.L.S., Coulmbia, 1947, M.A., 1948, Ed.D., 1949; m. Julia S. Deutsch, Nov. 4, 1943; children-William M., Richard H. Asst. librarian Enoch Pratt Free Library, Balt., 1938-42; asst. prof. U. Minn., 1949-51; dir. library services USIS, Ceylon, 1951- 53; dir. Davenport (Ia.) Pub. Library, 1955-59; prof. U. Ill., 1959-67; dean Sch. Library Sci., Fla. State U., Tallahassee, 1967—; cons. N.Y. State LIbrary, Md. State Library, Pa. STate Library, N.J. State Library, various community libraries. Served with USAAF, 1942-46. Mem. Am. Assn. U. Profs., Am., Fla., S.E. library assns., N.E.A., Nat. Conf. Audiovisual Uses in Library Edn. (editor 1963), Conf. Evaluation of Library Edn. (editor 1967). Home: 2352 Armistead Rd Tallahassee FL 32303

GOLDSTEIN, HERBERT, physicist, educator; b. N.Y.C., June 26, 1922; s. Harry and Betty (Gussow) G.; B.S., Coll. City N.Y., 1940; postgrad. Columbia, 1940-41; Ph.D., Mass. Inst. Tech., 1943; m. Channa G. Kleineramn, Nov. 20, 1960; children—Penina Perl, Aaron Meier, Shoshanna. Mem. Staff radiation lab. Mass. Inst. Tech., 1942-46, AEC postdoctoral fellow, 1949- 50; instr. physics Harvard, 1946-49; sr. physicist Nuclear Devel. Corp. Am., 1950-61; prof. nuclear sci. and engring. Columbia, 1961—. Sec. Tripartite Nuclear Cross Sect. Adv. Com., 1958-60; corr. sec. European- Am. Nuclear Data Com., 1962-66; chmn. nuclear cross sects. adv. group AEC, 1963-65. Bd. dirs. Union Orthodox Jewish Congregations Am. Recipient E. O. Lawrence Meml. award AEC, 1962. Fellow Am. Nuclear Soc. (chmn. shielding div. 1962-63, dir. 1963-66), Am. Phys. Soc., N.Y. Acad. Scis.; mem. Am. Assn. Physics Tchrs., Assn. Orthodox Jewish Scientists (pres. 1953-58, 61-62). Author: Classical Mechanics, 1950; Fundamental Aspects of Reactor Shielding, 1959. Address: Engring Terrace Bldg Columbia U New York City NY 10027

GOLDSTEIN, ISRAEL, rabbi; b. Phila., June 18, 1896; s. David L. and Fannie (Silver) G.; B.A., U. Pa., 1914; M.A., Columbia, 1917; rabbi, Jewish Theol. Sem. Am., 1918, D.H.L., 1927, D.D., 1945; L.H.D., Bandeis U., 1958; LL.D., N.Y. U., 1961; D.H.L., Chgo. Coll. Jewish Studies, 1961- 1961; m. Bertha Markowitz, July 21, 1918; children—Avram, Vivian Olum. Rabbi, Congregation B'nai Jeshurun, N.Y.C., 1918-60, rabbi emeritus, 1961- -. Pres. World Confedrn. Gen. Zionists, 1947-56, co-chmn., 1956—; pres. Jewish Conciliation Bd. Am., 1930-68, hon. pres., 1969—; v.p. Conf. Jewish Orgns. on Material Claims against Germany, Austria; lectr. homilectics Jewish Theol. Sem. Am., 1938; prof. Jewish history U. Judaism, 1954; honored by the establishment of the Israel Goldstein chair in practical theology, Jewish Theol. Sem., 1958; chair in history Zionism and modern Israel, Hebrew U., Jerusalem, 1967; Israel Goldstein Hebrew U. Synagogue, Jerusalem, 1967; Israel Goldstein Jerusalem Youth Village, 1950; served as leader in many Jewish orgns., pres. or chmn. of parent orgn. or of coms., including pres. Zionist Orgn. Am., 1943-45; chmn. World Jewish Congress, Western Hemisphere Exec. 1950-59; hon. v.p. World Jewish Congress, 1959—; pres. Am. Jewish Congress, 1951-58, now hon. pres.; mem. Jewish Agy. Exec., 1948—, treas., 1949-50; 1st chmn. Amidar Israel Nat. Housing Co., 1950; chmn. Israel's 10th Anniversary Celebration in U.S., 1958; del. World Zionist Congress, 1935-61; world chmn. Keren Hayesed United Israel Appeal, 1961—; chmn. council Jerusalem br. Israel-Am. Friendship League, 1969; mem. NLRB, 1935, Hon. vice chmn. Liberal Party N.Y., 1950- 60. Pres. Albert Einstein Found, Higher Learning, Inc., 1946; founder Brandeis, 1946; mem. bd. govs. Hebrew U. Jerusalem, Weizmann Inst. Sci., Rehovot, Israel, Haifa U.; chmn. Jerusalem Artists House, 1965-70, pres. World Assn. Hebrew Culture, 1963—. Mem. Am. Jewish Hist. Soc., Jewish Acad. Arts and Scis., Phi Beta Kappa. Author several books; contbr. Universal Jewish Ency., Ency. Hebraica, also articles and monographs. Office: Keren Hayesod Jerusalem Israel ☆

GOLDSTEIN, JACK STANLEY, educator; b. N.Y.C., May 10, 1925; s. Samuel S. and Lillian (Glantz) G.; B.S., Coll. City N.Y., 1947; M.S., U. Okla., 1948; Ph.D., Cornell U., Ithaca, N.Y., 1953; m. Nita Thorner, Sept. 5, 1948; children- -Philip, Sara, Naomi. With Cornell Aero. Lab., 1948-50, Inst. for Advanced Study, 1952- 53, Mass. Inst. Tech., 1953-54, Baird-Atomic, Inc., 1954-55; asst. prof. Brandeis U.,

Waltham, Mass., 1955-60, asso. prof., 1960-66, prof. astrophysics, 1966-69, dir. Astrophysics Inst., 1964—, chmn. physics dept., 1967-69. Spl. cons. UNESCO, 1971—. Chmn. steering com. African Primary Sci. Program; mem. steering com. African Math. Program. Served to lt. (j.g.) USNR; PTO. Fulbright research scholar Israel, 1960-61, Italy, 1966-67; Guggenheim fellow, 1966-67. Mem. Am. Phys. Soc., Am. Astron. Soc., N.Y. Acad. Scis., A.A.A.S., Sigma Xi. Home: 35 Grove St Auburndale MA 02166 Office: Brandeis U Physics Dept Waltham MA 02154

GOLDSTEIN, JACOB HERMAN, educator; b. Atlanta, Dec. 18, 1915; s. David and Jennie (Levine) G.; A.B., Emory U., 1942, M.S., 1944; A.M., Harvard, 1947, Ph.D., 1949; m. Audrey Jones, Dec. 26, 1952. Mem. faculty Emory U., 1949—, prof. chemistry, 1959—, Charles H. Candler prof., 1960—; spl. research molecular spectroscopy and structure, valence theory. NRC predoctoral fellow Harvard, 1946-49. Fellow Am. Phys. Soc.; mem. Am. Chem. Soc., Soc. Nuclear Medicine, Am. Assn. U. Profs., Phi Beta Kappa, Sigma Xi, Omicron Delta Kappa. Jewish religion.

GOLDSTEIN, JEROME, contract co. exec.; b. Chgo., Oct. 11, 1902; s. Asher and Mary (Adelsohn) G.; B.S., Armour Inst. Tech., Chgo., 1923; m. Mary Rose Greenstone, Jan. 7, 1931; children—Gerald N., Nancy Judith (Mrs. Alvin L. Gorman). An organizer Power Engring. Co., Chgo., 1926, partner, 1926-34; organizer, since pres. Power Constrn., Inc., engrs. and gen. contractors, Oak Park, Ill. 1935—, Manan Co., Real estate and bus. investment, Oak Park, 1958—. Co-chmn. bldg. div. Combined Jewish Appeal, Chgo., 1951-52, vice chmn., 1953. Trustee Ill. Inst. Tech., 1962—. Mem. Builders Assn. Chgo. Clubs: Standard (Chgo.); Briarwood Country (Deerfield, Ill.); Tamarisk Country (Palm Springs, Cal.). Home: 180 Greenbay Rd Highland Park IL 60035 Office: 851 Addison Av Elmhurst IL 60126

GOLDSTEIN, JOSEPH, educator; b. Springfield, Mass., May 7, 1923; s. Nathan E. and Anna (Ginsberg) G.; A.B., Dartmouth, 1943; Ph.D., London (Eng.) Sch. Econs., 1950; LL.B., Yale, 1952; grad. Western New Eng. Inst Psychoanalysis, 1968; m. Sonja Lambek, Aug. 3, 1947; children—Joshua, Anne, Jeremiah, Daniel. Admitted to Va. bar, 1953; law clk. to judge U.S. Ct. Appeals D.C., 1952-53; acting asst. prof. Stanford Law Sch., 1954-56; Russell Sage resident, vis. scholar Harvard Law Sch., 1955-56; asso. prof. Yale Law Sch., 1956-59, prof., 1959—, Justus S. Hotchkiss prof. law, 1968, Walton Hale Hamilton prof. law, sci. and social policy, 1970. Exec. sec., research dir. Gov. Conn. Prison Study Com., 1956-57; cons. devel. neighborhood legal service Community Progress, Inc., New Haven, 1963-64; mem. U.S. atty. gen. com. property and adminstrn. criminal justice, 1962-63; cons. Legal Assistance Assos., Inc., New Haven, 1964—; bd. dirs. Vera Inst. Justice, 1966—, Sigmund Freud Archives, 1968; mem. life scis. and social policy com. NRC, 1968, on legal services Office Econ. Opportunity, 1965, Council on Biology in Human Affairs, Salk Inst., 1969. Served with AUS, 1943-46. Fulbright scholar, 1949-50; law fellow U. Wis., 1958. Author: The Government of a British Trade Union, 2d edit., 1953; (with others) Criminal Law, 1962; The Family and the Law, 1965; Psychoanalysis, Psychiatry, and Law, 1967, Crime, Law and Society, 1971. Office: Yale U Law Sch New Haven CT 06520

GOLDSTEIN, KENNETH S., educator; b. Bklyn., Mar. 17, 1927; s. Irving M. and Tillie (Horowitz) G.; B.B.A., Coll. City N.Y., 1949, M.B.A., 1951; Ph.D., U. Pa., 1963; m. Rochelle Judith Korn, July 5, 1952; children—Rhoda Jean, Diane Ellen, Karl Stewart, Scott Douglas. Market research analyst Fairchild Publs., N.Y.C., 1949-56; asst. to pres. Abelard-Schulman Publs., N.Y.C., 1957; folk music editor Riverside Records, N.Y.C., 1958-59, Prestige Records, Bergenfield, N.J., 1959-62; pres., exec. editor Folklore Assos., Inc., Phila., 1961-69; asst. prof. folklore U. Pa., 1963-67, asso. prof., 1967-70, prof., 1971—, co-chmn. grad. group in folklore and folklife, 1968-70, co-chmn. dept., 1969-70, chmn., 1971—. Served with AUS, 1945-46, Fulbright fellow, 1959-60. Fellow Am. Anthrop. Assn., Am. Folklore Soc. (exec. sec., treas. 1965—, asso. editor jour. 1964-65); mem. Pa. Folklore Soc. (pres. 1964—), English Folk Song and Dance Soc., Folklore Soc. Gt. Britain (hon . mem.). Author: A Guide for Field Workers in Folklore, 1964; Two Penny Ballads and Four Dollar Whiskey, 1965; Thrice Told Tales, 1971. Home: 714 Vernon Rd Philadelphia PA 19119

GOLDSTEIN, LEWIS CHARLES, educator; b. Paterson, N.J., Dec. 31, 1917; s. Charles H. and Rose (Litchman) G.; student Columbia, 1934-35; B.S., U. Richmond, Va., 1938, M.S., 1940; Ph.D., U. Va., 1947. Instr., U. Va., 1946-47; asso. Coll. Upper N.Y., State U. N.Y., 1947-53; instr. U. Mass., 1953-54; vis. lectr. Smith Coll., 1953-55; asso. prof., chmn. dept. biology Richmond Profl. Inst. (now Va. Commonwealth U.), 1955-56, prof., chmn. dept., 1956—, asst. dean, 1968—. Served to lt. USNR, 1942-46. Mem. A.A.A.S., Am. Inst. Biol. Scientists, Am. Soc. Lodogists, N.Y., Va. acad. scis., Sigma Xi. Home: 1003E N Hamilton St Richmond VA 22221 Office: 901 W Franklin St Richmond VA 22220

GOLDSTEIN, MAX FULLMORE, lawyer; b. Birmingham, Ala., July 17, 1886; s. David and Sarah (Fullmore) G.; B.L., U. Ga., 1906; LL.B. cum laude, Yale, 1909; m. Sarah Ray London, Dec. 29, 1914; children—Elliott, Grace (Mrs. Burton Goldstein). Admitted to Ga. bar, 1906; mem. Powell, Goldstein, Frazer & Murphy, Atlanta, and predecessor, Little, Powell, Smith, Goldstein, 1913-39; pres. Nat. Albany Corp.; asst. sec. Sterling Pulp & Paper Co.; dir. Wellhouse Co. Mem. Am., Ga., Atlanta bar assns., Order of Coif. Jewish religion. Mason. Contbr. articles to various ins. and legal publs. Home: 1825 Clifton Rd NE Atlanta GA 30329 Office: Citizens and So Bank Bldg Atlanta GA 30303

GOLDSTEIN, MOISE HERBERT, architect; b. New Orleans, La., Sept. 17, 1882; s. Julius and Julie (Schwartz) G.; B.E., Tulane U., 1902; M.S., Mass. Inst. Tech., 1905; student Am. Acad. Rome, 1906-07; m. Lois Goetter, Aug. 27, 1924; children—Louis Allan, Moise Herbert, Jr., Nathalie (Mrs. Aaron Stern). Practiced as architect with firm Moise H. Goldstein & Assos., 1914-47, Goldstein, Parham & Labouisse, 1947-63, Moise H. Goldstein & Louis A. Goldstein, 1963—; prin. archtl. works include Civic Center, New Orleans, 1956-58, Moisant Internat. Airport, New Orleans, 1957-59, Dillard U., 1933-63. Mem. Nat. Archtl. Accrediting Bd., 1941-44. Fellow A.I.A. (bd. dirs. 1936-39). Home: 1309 Felicity St New Orleans LA 70130

GOLDSTEIN, MORRIS, investment broker; b. N.Y.C., May 6, 1914; s. Harry M. and Florence Viola (Aufsus) G.; B.S. in Bus. Adminstrn. with honors, Lehigh U., 1934; certificate N.Y. Stock Exchange Inst., 1936. Jr. statistician Granberry & Co., mems. N.Y. Stock Exchange, 1934-35, mgr. research dept., 1935-41; analyst Francis I. duPont & Co., mems. N.Y. Stock Exchange, 1941, mgr. research dept., 1941-49, dir. research, partner charge 1949-65, economist, parnter charge corporate dept., 1965-70; pres., chief exec. officer Francis I. du Pont, A.C. Allyn, Inc., 1970—; dir. Anebec Corp., Visual Electronics Corp., Hartfield-Zody, Inc., Nat. Chemsearch, Pak-Well Corp., Jacobson's Stores, Consol. Nat. Shoe Corp., R.G. Barry Corp., Jaclyn Inc., Jacobson Stores Inc., King Radio Corp., Nat. Silver Industries, Penn Engring. & Mfg., Sealectro Corp., Sunzin Electronics, Winklemans Stores Inc.; trustee Republic Mortgage Investors. Mem. adv. and screening com. of coop. tng. program of econs. and finance Bernard M. Baruch Sch. Bus., City Coll. N.Y.; mem. vis. com. of bd. trustees Lehigh U. Coll. Bus. and Econs. Trustee Mass. Merchandising Research Found. Mem. N.Y. Cotton Exchange, Chgo. Bd. Trade. Mem. Am. Statis. Assn., N.Y. Soc. Security Analysts, Assn. Customers Brokers, Acad. Polit. Sci., Alpha Kappa Psi (hon.), Sigma Alpha Mu. Clubs: Bond (N.Y.); Nat. Republican, Bankers of Am. Home: 1 Fifth Av New York City NY 10003 Office: 1 Wall St New York City NY 10005

GOLDSTEIN, MORTIMER DAVID, economist, govt. ofcl.; b. N.Y.C., Sept. 30, 1916; s. Herbert and Annette (Rodman) G.; B.S.S., Coll. City N.Y., 1935; student Columbia, 1936-38; m. Rita S. Miller, June 25, 1939; children—Judith E., Raymond E. Tchr. in N.Y. State, 1935-35; economist Railroad Retirement Bd., 1938-42, WPB, 1942-45, War Assets Adminstrn., 1945-46, Office Housing Expediter, 1946-47; with State Dept., 1947—, chief internat. finance div., 1961-64, dep. dir. Office Internat. Finance and Econ. Analysis, 1964-65, assigned to sr. seminar in fgn. policy Fgn. Service Inst., 1964-65, dep. dir. for Britain, Malta, Ireland, 1965-68, dir. for Britain, Malta, Ireland, 1968—. U.S. rep. to internat. confs., 1952, 55-64. Mem. Am. Econ. Assn., Am. Contract Bridge League, Am. Fgn. Service Assn. Author articles on econs. and contract bridge. Home: 405 Hinsdale Lane Silver Spring MD 20901 Office: Dept State Washington DC 20525

GOLDSTEIN, NATHANIEL LAWRENCE, former atty. gen. N.Y. State; b. N.Y.C., June 9, 1896; s. Max and Mollie (Marayna) G.; B.C.S., N.Y. U., 1915; J.D., N.Y. Law Sch., 1918, LL.D., 1957; LL.D., Syracuse U., 1949, Yeshiva U., 1952, Hobart and William Smith Colls., 1950, Hebrew U., 1968; D.C.L., Pace Coll., 1969; m. Etta May Brown, 1931; children—Lois Elaine (Mrs. Jerome Lowenstein), Stephen Martin. Admitted to N.Y. bar, 1918; C.P.A., 1919; pub. mem. Interboro Rapid Transit Depreciation Fund Bd., 1938-40; elected atty. gen. State of N.Y., 1942, 46, 50, ret. 1954; mem. firm Goldstein, Shames & Hyde. Vis. prof. forensic medicine Einstein Coll. Medicine. Asst. chief counsel Dir. Selective Service, N.Y., 1940-42; v.p., dir. Willkie Meml. of Freedom House; dir. Park Av. Synagogue; trustee Pace Coll., N.Y.C., N.Y. Law Sch.; chmn. emeritus bd. overseers Albert Einstein Coll. Medicine; bd. overseers Fletcher Sch. Law and Diplomacy; dep. chmn. bd. dirs. Hebrew U.; vice chmn. Gallatin Assos., N.Y.U. Mem. U.S. delegation to UN Narcotic Drug Control Commn. Mem. Am., Bklyn. bar assns., Am. Legion (past post comdr.), Sigma Omega Psi (nat. pres.), Alpha Epsilon Pi. Mason. Clubs: Harmonie (N.Y.C.); Capitol Hill (Washington). Contbr. to legal publs. Home: 737 Park Av New York City NY 10021 Office: 655 Madison Av New York City NY 10021

GOLDSTEIN, NORMAN PHILIP, neurologist; b. Bklyn., Mar. 31, 1921; s. Charles and Sadie (Fink) G.; B.A. magna cum laude, N.Y. U., 1941; M.A., George Washington U., 1942, M.D. with distinction, 1946; m. Gloria Silver, Nov. 14, 1943; children—Bette Karen, Carol Sue, Ellen Marie. Intern Mt. Sinai Hosp., N.Y.C., 1946-47; instr. biochemistry George Washington U., 1947-49; fellow Mayo Clinic, 1949-53; commd. officer USPHS, 1953-55; mem. staff Mayo Clinic, 1955—, head sect. neurology, 1966—; prof. neurology Mayo Grad. Sch. Medicine, U. Minn., 1967—; professorial lectr. George Washington U., 1967. Mem. Rochester Civic Theatre, Rochester Art Center. Diplomate Am. Bd. Psychiatry and Neurology. Fellow Am. Acad. Neurology; mem. Central Soc. Neurol. Research (pres. 1968-69), Am., Minn. med. assns., Am. Neurol. Assn., Am Psychiat. Assn., Assn. Research Nervous and Mental Diseases, Phi Beta Kappa, Sigma Xi, Alpha Omega Alpha. Author articles in field. Home: 821 10 1/2 St SW Rochester MN 55901

GOLDSTEIN, RICHARD JAY, educator; b. N.Y.C., Mar. 27, 1928; s. Henry and Rose (Steierman) G.; B.Mech. Engring., Cornell U., 1948; M.S. in Mech. Engring., U. Minn., 1950, M.S. in Physics, 1951, Ph.D., 1959; m. Anita Nancy Klein, Sept. 5, 1963; children—Arthur Sander, Jonathan Jacob, Benjamin Samuel. Instr., U. Minn., 1948-51, instr., research fellow, 1956-58, mem. faculty, 1961—, prof. mech. engring., 1965—; research engr. Oak Ridge Nat. Lab., 1951-54; asst. prof. Brown U., 1959-61; cons. in field, 1956—. Served to 1st lt. AUS, 1954-55. NATO fellow, Paris, 1960-61. Mem. Am. Assn. U. Profs., A.A.A.S., Am. Phys. Soc., Minn. Acad. Sci., Am. Soc. M.E., Sigma Xi, Tau Beta Pi, Pi Tau Sigma. Research publns. in thermodynamics, fluid mechanics, heat transfer, optical measuring techniques. Home: 520 Janalyn Circle Golden Valley MN 55416 Office: Dept Mech Engring Univ Minn Minneapolis MN 55455

GOLDSTEIN, SIDNEY, educator, sociologist; b. New London, Conn., Aug. 4, 1927; s. Max and Bella (Hoffman) G.; B.A., U. Conn., 1949, M.A., 1951; Ph.D. (Harrison fellow 1951-53), U. Pa., 1953; m. Alice Dreifuss, June 21, 1953; children—Beth Leah, David Louis, Brenda Ruth. Instr. sociology U. Pa., 1953-55; mem. faculty Brown U., Providence, 1955—, prof. sociology, 1960—, chmn. dept. sociology and anthropology, 1963—, dir. population studies and tng. center, 1965—. Demographic adviser Chulalongkorn U., Bangkok, Thailand, 1968-69; research fellow Inst. Contemporary Jewry, Hebrew U., Jerusalem, 1969—. Cons. Nat. Inst. Neurol. Diseases and Blindness, NIH, 1960—, Nat. center for Health Statistics, 1970—, R.I. Council Community Services, 1963—; mem. U.S. Bur. Census Adv. Com. Population Statistics; bd. dirs. Gen. Jewish Com. Greater Providence, 1964-68, Bur. Jewish Edn., Providence. Guggenheim fellow, 1961-62; Social Sci. Research Council fellow, 1961-62; Fulbright research scholar, Denmark, 1961-62. Recipient Distinguished Service medal Chulalongkorn U., 1969. Mem. Am. Sociol. Assn; Population Assn. Am. (dir.), Assn. Jewish Demography and Statistics (director), Am. Statis. Assn., Internat. Union Sci. Study Population, Gerontological Soc., Assn. for Asian Studies, European Center for Population Studies, Phi Beta Kappa. Author: Patterns of Mobility, 1910-1950, 1958; Consumption Patterns of the Aged, 1960; The Norristown Study: An Experiment in Interdisciplinary Research Training, 1961; The Jewish Population of Greater Providence, 1964; (with Kurt B. Mayer) The First Two Years: Problems of Small Business Growth and Survival, 1961; Migration and Economic Development in Rhode Island, 1958; People of Rhode Island, 1963; (with Calvin Goldscheider) Jewish-Americans. Contbr. profl. jours. Home: 95 Kiwanee Rd Warwick RI 02888 Office: Brown Univ Providence RI 02912

GOLDSTEIN, SIDNEY, lawyer; b. Bklyn., Oct. 13, 1906; s. Joseph and Esther (Mutchnick) G.; LL.B., St. John's Coll., 1930; m. Olga Stein, Jan. 7, 1945; 1 dau., Helena (Mrs. Peter Leslie). Admitted to N.Y. bar, 1931, since practiced in N.Y.C.; atty. Port of N.Y. Authority, 1934—, asst. gen. counsel, 1942-52, gen. counsel, 1952—. Pres. dir. 1172 Corp. Co-chmn. com. on airports World Peace Through Law Center, 1964—; panel mem. on noise abatement, commerce tech. adv. bd. Office Asst. Sec. Commerce, 1968—; mem. Municipal Forum, N.Y.C. Served with Signal Corps, AUS, World War II. Recipient Distinguished Pub. Service award Nat. Inst. Municipal Law Officers, 1956, Distinguished Service medal Port of N.Y. Authority, 1959, Distinguished Contbns. to Am. Aerospace Power award Met. Squadron Air Force Assn., 1961. Mem. Am. (com. chmn.), Internat., N.Y. State bar assns., Assn. Bar City N.Y., Internat. Law Assn., Fed. Bar Council (chmn. exec. com., trustee), N.Y. Co. Lawyers Assn. (dir., com. chmn.), Nat. Inst. Municipal Law Officers (past com. chmn.), Am. Assn. Port Authorities (gen. counsel, com. chmn.), N. Atlantic Ports Assn., Airport Operators Council Internat., Internat. Bridge, Tunnel and Turnpike Assn. (com. chmn.), Internat. Assn. Ports and Harbors, Am. Arbitration Assn., Am. Law Inst., Assn. ICC Practitioners. Contbr. articles profl. jours. Home: 1172 Park Av New York City NY 10028 Office: 111 8th Av New York City NY 10011

GOLDSTEIN, STANLEY PHILIP, educator; b. Bklyn., Feb. 3, 1923; s. Max and Rose (Ahrenstein) G.; B.S., U. Okla., 1949; M.S., N.Y. U., 1956; Ph.D., in Astronautics, Poly. Inst. Bklyn., 1969; m. Wanda Rouse, June 6, 1949; children—Bruce, Richard. Engr., Vapor Recovery Systems Corp., Compton, Cal., 1950-52; project engr. Alderson Research Labs., N.Y.C., 1952-54; mem. faculty Hofstra U., Hempstead, N.Y., 1954—, prof. engring., 1957—, chmn. engring. sci. dept., 1956-68, dir. acad. computer center, 1970—; cons. Alcorn Combustion Co., N.Y.C. Transit Authority. Served to 1st lt. USAAF, 1942-45. Decorated D.F.C., Air medal with 4 oak leaf clusters. Mem. Am. Soc. Engring. Edn., Assn. Computing Machinery, Am. Assn. U. Profs., Sigma Xi, Pi Sigma Pi. Home: 21 Harvard St Westbury NY 11590 Office: Hofstra U Hempstead NY 11550

GOLDSTEIN, SYDNEY, educator; b. Hull, Eng., Dec. 3, 1903; s. Abraham Joseph and Hilda (Jacobs) G.; B.A., St. Johns Coll., Cambridge U., 1925, M.A., Ph.D., 1928; D.Eng., Purdue U., 1967; D.Sc., Case Inst., 1967; m. Rosa Rachel Sass, Mar. 23, 1926; children—David John, Ruth Hilda. Rockefeller fellow U. Göttingen, 1928-29; lectr. applied math. U. Manchester, 1929-31, Beyer prof., 1945-50; fellow St. John's Coll., Cambridge U., 1929-32, 33-45, lectr. Cambridge U., 1931-45, Stokes lectr., 1938-45; Leverhulme research fellow Cal. Inst. Tech., 1938-39; aerodynamics div. Nat. Phys. Lab., 1939-45; Wright Brothers lectr. Inst. Aero. Scis., 1947; vis. prof. U. Mich., 1947, 50, Brown U., 1947, U. Md., 1950, U. Va., 1952, Harvard, 1952; prof. applied math., Israel Inst. Tech., Haifa, 1950-55, chmn. aero. engring., 1950-54, v.p., 1951- 54; vis. lectr. div. applied sci., Harvard, 1954, Gordon McKay prof. applied math., 1955-70, emeritus, 1970. Chmn. British Aero. Research Council, 1946- 49. Fellow Royal Soc., Royal Aero. Soc.; mem. Am. Acad. Arts, Scis.; foreign mem. Royal Netherlands Acad. Scis. Author: Lectures on Fluid Mechanics, 1960. Editor: Modern Developments in Fluid Mechanics, 1938. Address: 28 Elizabeth Rd Belmont MA 02178

GOLDSTINE, HERMAN HEINE, mathematician; b. Chgo., Sept. 13, 1913; s. Isaac Oscar and Bessie (Lipsey) G.; B.S., U. Chgo., 1933, M.S., 1934, Ph.D., 1936; m. Adele Katz, Sept. 15, 1941 (dec. 1964); children—Madlen, Jonathan; m. 2d, Ellen Watson, Jan. 8, 1966. Engaged as research asst. U. Chgo., 1936-37, instr., 1937-39; instr. U. Mich., 1939-42, asst. prof., 1942-45; asst. project dir., electronic computer project Inst. of Advanced Study, Princeton, 1946-55, acting project dir., 1954-57, permanent mem. Sch. Mathematics of Inst. Advanced Study; dir. sci. devel. IBM Data Processing Hdqrs., White Plains, N.Y.; now IBM fellow, cons. to dir. research IBM. Cons. various govt., mil. agys. Mem. adv. council math. dept. Princeton U.; adv. council biomath. dept. Cornell Med. Coll.; chmn. math. and phys. scis. com. NSF. Bd. dirs. Commn. Engring. Edn.; trustee Hampshire Coll. Served as lt. col. AUS, World War II. Mem. Am. Math. Soc., Math. Assn. Am., Phi Beta Kappa, Sigma Xi. Home: 18 Hayrake Lane Chappaqua NY 10514 Office: IBM TJ Watson Research Center PO Box 218 Yorktown Heights NY 10598

GOLDSTON, ELI, indsl. exec.; b. Akron, O., Mar. 8, 1920; s. Issachar Jacob and Gertrude (Robins) G.; A.B., Harvard, 1942, M.B.A., 1946, LL.B., 1949; LL.D. (hon.), Babson College, 1969, Bates Coll., 1970, Boston Coll., 1971; m. Elaine Friedman, Oct. 20, 1943; children—Dian Barbara, Robert James. Admitted to Ohio bar, 1949; with firm Hahn, Loeser, Keough, Freedheim & Dean, Cleve., 1949-62, partner, 1955-62; with Midland Enterprises Inc., Cin., 1954-62, pres., 1961-62; exec. v.p. Eastern Gas and Fuel Assos., Boston, 1962, pres., 1962—, chief exec. officer, 1963—, also trustee; dir., chmn. Ohio River Co., Boston Gas Co., Boston Tow Boat Co., Castner, Curran & Bullitt, Inc., Eastern Asso. Coal Corp., Eastern Asso. Properties Corp., Midland Enterprises Inc., Mystic Steamship Corp., Ohio River Corp., Orgulf Transport Co., Red Circle Transport Co.; dir. Arthur D. Little Inc., 1st Nat. Bank Boston, Raytheon Co., John Hancock Mutual Life Ins. Co., Algonquin Gas Transmission Co. Mem. White House Conf. Fulfill These Rights; chmn. Boston Kyoto Sister City Com. Trustee Hebrew Union Coll., Cin., Combined Jewish Philanthropies Greater Boston, New Eng. Aquarium, World Peace Found.; bd. dirs. Internat. Center New Eng.; chmn. Boston project Joint Center Urban Studies, Mass. Inst. Tech. and Harvard; chmn. Boston Winterfest, 1966, 67. Served with USNR. 1943-46. Mem. Am. Acad. Arts and Scis., Am., Ohio, Mass., Cleve. bar assns., C. of C. (dir. greater Boston), mem. Am. Law Inst. Clubs: Harvard, St. Botolph, Cambridge Boat. Contbr. Articles law revs. and other periodicals. Home: 7 Acacia St Cambridge MA 02138 Office: Prudential Tower Boston MA 02199

GOLDSTON, ROBERT CONROY, author; b. N.Y.C., July 9, 1927; s. Philip Henry and Josephine (Conroy) G.; student Columbia, 1946-48, Sch. Gen. Studies, 1948-51; m. Marguerite Garvey, Jan. 16, 1956; children—Rebecca, Gabrielle, Sarah, Francesca, Maximilian, Theresa. Guggenheim fellow, 1957-58. Author: (novels) The Eighth Day, 1956, The Catafalque, 1957, The Shore Dimly Seen, 1963, The Last of Lazarus, 1966, (juveniles) Tales of the Alhambra Retold, 1962, The Legend of the Cid, 1963, The Song of Roland, 1964, The Russian Revolution, 1966, The Civil War in Spain, 1966, The Life and Death of Nazi Germany, 1967, The Rise of Red China, 1967, The Negro Revolution, 1967; Great Depression; Negro Revolution; Soviets: A Pictorial History of Communist Russia; writer of TV documentary films The Bullfight, 1960, Bjorn's Inferno, 1964, Running away Backwards, 1965 (all for Canadian Broadcasting Co.). Home: Box 771 Manchester VT 05254 Office: care Willis Wing 24 E 38th St New York City NY 10022

GOLDSTONE, HARMON HENDRICKS, architect; b. N.Y.C., May 4, 1911; s. Lafayette A. and Aline (Lewis) G.; S.B. cum laude, Harvard, 1932, postgard Sch. Architecture, 1933-35; B.Arch., Columbia, 1936. Designer firm Harrison & Fouilhoux (later Harrison & Abramovitz), N.Y.C., 1936-41, 46-52; pvt. practice, N.Y.C., 1953-55; partner Golstone & Dearborn, N.Y.C., 1955-70, Goldstone, Dearborn & Hinz, 1970—. Mem. Planning Commn. N.Y.C., 1962-68; chmn. Landmarks Preservation Commn. N.Y.C., 1968—; pres. Municipal Art Soc., N.Y.C., 1960-61. Trustee N.Y. Hist. Soc., 1969—. Served with USAAF, 1942-46. Fellow A.I.A. (sec. N.Y. 1952, 54-56); asso. Nat. Acad. Design. Clubs: Harvard, Century Association (N.Y.C.). Home: 1172 Park Av New York City NY 10028 Office: 104 E 40th St New York City NY 10016

GOLDSTONE, MITCHELL EDWARD, mfg. co. exec.; b. N.Y.C., July 15, 1934; s. Abraham and Adelaide (Gottleib) G.; B.S., N.Y. U., 1955; m. Jill Leslie Turner, May 9, 1969. Sr. accountant Ernst & Ernst, N.Y.C., 1957-59, Fred Landau & Co., N.Y.C., 1959-61; mgr. J.K. Lasser & Co., N.Y.C., 1961-64; treas. Morning-star-Paisley, Inc., Clifton, N.J., 1964, Carnival Creations, Inc., Elizabeth, N.J., 1964-68; v.p. York Pala Records, Inc., Los Angeles, 1968-69; v.p., treas. Volt Information Scis., Inc., N.Y.C., 1969-71, also dir.; pres., dir.

Alphanumeric, Inc., 1971—. C.P.A., N.Y. Mem. Am. Inst. C.P.A.s, N.Y. Soc. C.P.A.s. Home: Longhill Rd W Briarcliff Manor NY 10510 Office: 640 W 40th St New York City NY 10018

GOLDSTONE, SANFORD, educator; b. N.Y.C., July 17, 1926; s. Albert and Anne (Steckel) G.; B.S., Coll. City N.Y., 1947; Ph.D., Duke, 1953; children—Susan Beth, Arthur Craig, Nancy Lynn; m. 2d, Lois Adams. Intern, Duke Sch. Medicine, 1949-51, chief clin. psychologist Psychiat. Out-Patient Clinic, 1951-54, lectr. psychology, 1953-54, asso. dept. psychiatry, 1953-54; asst. prof. to prof. psychiatry, chief psychologist, program dir. Baylor U. Coll. Medicine, 1955-67; prof., head div. psychology dept. psychiatry Cornell U. Med. Coll., 1967—, prof. psychology field neurobiology Grad. Sch. Med. Scis., 1969—. Cons. VA Hosps., Durham, N.C., 1953-54, Houston, 1959-67, Temple, Tex., 1964-67, Montrose, N.Y., 1968—; cons. criminal law sect. Am. Bar Assn., 1967-69, Westchester County Probation Dept., 1968-71, Community Service Bur., N.Y. State Tng. Schs., 1969—; head div. psychology Houston State Psychiat. Inst., 1958-67, acting bus. mgr., 1959-60, head div. crime and delinquency, 1966-67; clin. asso. prof. to clin. prof. U. Houston, 1958-67; dir. mental health services Harris County Probation Dept., Houston, 1963-67; psychologist-in-chief Payne Whitney Psychiat. Clinic, 1967—, Westchester div. N.Y. Hosp., 1967—; attending psychologist N.Y. Hosp., 1967—; head, community cons. services outpatient dept. Payne Whitney Psychiat. Clinic, 1970—. Served with USAAF, 1945. USPHS grantee, 1955-65. Mem. Am. Psychol. Assn., Am. Psychopath. Assn., Nat. Council Crime and Delinquency, N.Y. Acad. Scis., A.A.A.S., Sigma Xi. Contbr. numerous articles to profl. jours. Home: 214 Old Army Rd Scarsdale NY 10583 Office: 21 Bloomingdale Rd White Plains NY 10605

GOLDTHWAIT, DAVID ATWATER, educator; b. Providence, Nov. 7, 1921; s. Joel A. and Henrietta (Atwater) G.; student Harvard, 1939-42; M.D., Columbia, 1945; m. Priscilla Sprague, Apr. 16, 1949; children—Susan, Loren, Jan, David, Intern Presbyn. Hosp., N.Y.C.; prof. biochemistry, asso. prof. medicine Case Western Res. U., 1964—. Served with M.C., AUS, 1946-48. Mem. Am. Soc. Biol. Chemists, Am. Soc. Clin. Investgation. Home: 7 Pepper Ridge Rd Cleveland OH 44124

GOLDTHWAIT, JOHN TURNER, educator; b. Duluth, Minn., Mar. 31, 1921; s. Charles Francis and Isabel (Thatcher) G.; B.A., M.A., Oglethorpe U., 1944; Ph.D., Northwestern U., 1957; m. Elizabeth Virginia Benefield, Nov. 26, 1946; 1 son, Christopher Edgar. Faculty, Oglethorpe U., 1941-43, 46-50, Sacramento State Coll., 1952-55, U. Cal. at Davis, 1956-64; prof. philosophy State U. N.Y. at Plattsburgh, 1964—, chmn. div. humanities Coll. Arts and Sci., 1964-67, dean faculty humanities, 1967-69. Faculty, Pacific Philosophy Inst., U. Pacific, summer 1962; coordinator ednl. program for Diagnostic and Treatment Center Clinton Correctional Facility, Dannemora, N.Y., 1966- -. Mem. Lake Champlain Com., 1969—. Served to lt. USNR, 1943-46. Faculty summer research fellow U. Cal. at Davis, 1958. Mem. Am. Philos. Assn., Am. Soc. Aesthetics, Berkeley Aesthetics Seminar, Central Cal. Philos. Assn. (pres. 1959), Speech Assn. Am., Nat. Council Tchrs. English, Am. Translators Assn., Am. Assn. U. Profs. Translator, editor: (Kant) Observations on the Feeling of the Beautiful and Sublime, 1960; Contbr. articles to profl. jours. Home: PO Box 297 Plattsburgh NY 12901

GOLDTHWAIT, RICHARD PARKER, educator, geologist; b. Hanover, N.H., June 6, 1911; s. James Walter and Edith (Richards) G.; A.B., Dartmouth, 1933; M.A., Harvard, 1937, Ph.D., 1939; m. Katherine Davenport Burnham, June 12, 1937; children—Jane (Mrs. Robert W. Oldham), Susan (Mrs. Roy E. Carlson), Betsy (Mrs. Kenneth R. Sutherland), Thomas Burnham. Instr., Dartmouth, 1934-35; asst. prof. Brown U., 1939-43; mem. faculty Ohio State U., 1946—, prof. geology, 1948—, chmn. dept., 1965-69, dir. Inst. Polar Studies, 1960-65. Mem. Alaska earthquake com. Nat. Acad. Sci., 1964—. Recipient Commendation for Meritorious Civilian Service, USAAF, 1946; Antarctica Service medal, 1966. Fellow Geol. Soc. Am.; mem. A.A.A.S., Am. Geophys. Union, Am. Geog. Soc., Arctic Inst. N. Am. (past gov.), Ohio Acad. Sci. (pres. 1958- 59). Presbyn. (past elder). Author: (with J.W. and L. Goldthwait) Geology of New Hampshire, Vol. 1, Surficial, 1950; also numerous reports, articles. Editor: till, A Symposium, 1971. Home: 452 Colonial Av Worthington OH 43085 Office: 125 S Oval Dr Columbus OH 43210

GOLDTHWAITE, ALFRED WITHERSPOON, Republican state committeeman; b. Montgomery, Ala., Aug. 12, 1921; s. Archibald Campbell and Mary Goldthwaite (Arrington) G.; B.S., U. Ala., 1943, LL.B., 1948; m. Evelyn Adams, Dec. 12, 1958; children—Alfred Witherspoon, Mary Arrington. Admitted to Ala. bar, 1948; mem. Ala. Ho. of Reps., 1959-66; now chmn. Ala. Republican Com. Served with armed forces World War II, Korean War. Episcopalian. Address: 26 S Perry St Montgomery AL 36102 also 436 S Goldthwaite St Montgomery AL 36104*

GOLDTHWAITE, ROBERT, ret. naval officer; b. Montgomery, Ala., Sept. 20, 1903; s. Robert and Robert and Mary Phelan (Watt) G.; B.S., U.S. Naval Acad., 1924; student Naval War Coll., 1935-36, Nat. War Coll., 1947-48; m. Hathaway Crenshaw, Feb. 7, 1931; 1 dau., Hathaway (Mrs. Forrest P. Anderson). Commnd. ensign, U.S. Navy, 1924, advanced through grades to vice adm.; apptd. naval aviator, 1926; exec. officer U.S.S. Belleau Wood, 1943; chief staff Comdr. Fleet Air South Pacific, 1943-44; comdr. escort aircraft carrier Saginaw Bay, Okinawa campaign; comdr. aircraft carrier Coral Sea, 1949-50; chief staff Comdr. 2d Fleet, 1950-51; dir. fleet operations Navy Dept., 1951-53; comdr. Carrier Div. 17, 1953-54; chief staff Joint Task Force Seven, 1954-55; comdr. Carrier Div. 2, 1955- 56; dep. comdr.-in-chief U.S. Atlantic Fleet, 1956-57; chief Naval Air Tng. Command, 1957-61; comdr. Western Sea Frontier, also comdr. Pacific Res. Fleet, 1961-63, comdr. Fleet Air, Jacksonville, Fla., 1963-65; ret., 1965. Mem. Fla. Jud. Qualifications Commn. Bd. dirs. Pensacola Acad. Arts and Scis. Decorated D.S.M., Presdl. unit citation, Legion of Merit (3). Episcopalian. Home: 58 State Lake Dr Pensacola FL 32507

GOLDTHWAITE, WILBURN SCOTT, educator; b. Melrose, Mass., June 18, 1901; s. James Wilburn and Emma (Chandler) G.; Mus.B., Yale, 1926, Mus. M., 1938; studied with Nudia Boulanger, Paris, France, 1932; Ph.D., Harvard, 1956; m. Mildred Calvert Bryant, Aug. 4, 1936. Tchr., Kent (Conn.) Sch., 1926-27; asst. prof. then asso. prof. U. Mo., 1928-37; curator music library, asst. prof. U. Chgo., 1938-55; prof. music, chmn. grad. com. research and profl. curricula U. Ill.-Urbana, 1955-70, ret., 1970; vis. asso. prof. U. Cal. at Los Angeles, 1953. Mem. Am. Musicol. Soc., Music Library Assn. (pres. 1948-50), Coll. Music Soc. (treas. 1954), Internat. Music Library Assn., Pi Kappa Lambda. Contbr. articles. Home: 404 W Iowa St Urbana IL 60801

GOLDWASSER, EDWIN LEO, educator, physicist; b. N.Y.C., Mar. 9, 1919; s. Israel Edwin and Edith (Goldstein) G.; B.A., Harvard, 1940; student Columbia, 1941; Ph.D., U. Cal. at Berkeley, 1950; m. Elizabeth Weiss, Oct. 27, 1940; children—Michael, John, Katherine, David, Richard. Physicist, U.S. Navy Bur. Ordnance, 1941-45; sr. physicist 12th Naval Dist., also U.S. Navy Yard, Mare Is., Cal., 1943-45; teaching asst., research asst. U. Cal. at Berkeley, 1948-50, research asso., 1950-51; mem. faculty U. Ill., 1951— , prof. physics, 1959—, mem. phys. scis. study com., 1956-61; spl. research primary cosmic radiation, energy loss charged particles, photoprodn. of pi mesons, interactions of strange particles; dep. dir. Nat. Accelerator Lab., 1967—. Mem. physics survey com. NRC, 1964- -, vice chmn. div. phys. scis., 1961-66, chmn., 1966—; gen. adv. com. AEC, 1966—; mem. panel high energy accelerator physics gen. adv. com. AEC and Pres.'s Sci. Adv. Com., 1962-63. Bd. dirs. Midwest Univs. Research Assn., Asso. Midwest Univs.; trustee Univs. Research Assn., 1965—, Argonne Univs. Assn., 1965—. Westinghouse fellow, 1949-50; Fulbright fellow to Italy, 1957-58; Guggenheim fellow, 1957-58. Fellow Am. Phys. Society; mem. Fedn. Am. Scientists, Sigma Xi. Author: Optics, Waves, Atoms and Nuclei, 1965; also numerous articles, contbr. to books. Home: 520 Ellis Av Wheaton IL 60187 Office: Nat Accelerator Lab PO Box 500 Batavia IL 60510

GOLDWASSER, EUGENE, educator, biochemist; b. N.Y.C., Oct. 14, 1922; s. Herman and Anna (Ackerman) G.; B.S., U. Chgo., 1943, Ph.D., 1950; m. Florence Cohen, Dec. 22, 1949; children—Thomas Alan, Matthew Laurence, James Herman. Am. Cancer Soc. fellow U. Copenhagen (Denmark), 1950-52; research asso. U. Chgo., 1952-61, mem. faculty, 1962—, prof. biochemistry, 1963—, co-dir. Interdepartmental tng. program in developmental biology. Served with AUS, 1944-46. Guggenheim fellow U. Oxford (Eng.), 1966-67. Mem. Am. Soc. Biol. Chemists, Biochem. Soc., Am. Assn. U. Profs., A.A.A.S., Tissue Culture Assn., Internat. Soc. Developmental Biologists, Sigma Xi. Research biochemistry red blood cell formation. Home: 5727 Dorchester Av Chicago IL 60637

GOLDWATER, BARRY MORRIS, U.S. senator; b. Phoenix, Jan. 1, 1909; s. Baron and Josephine (Williams) G.; student Staunton Mil. Acad., U. Ariz., 1928; m. Margaret Johnson, Sept. 22, 1934; children—Joanne Goldwater (Mrs. Thomas H. Ross), Barry, Michael, Margaret (Mrs. Richard Holt). With Goldwater's, Inc., 1929—, pres., 1937-53, now chmn. bd.; U.S. senator (Ariz.), 1953-64, 68—, mem. Armed Services Com., Labor & Pub. Welfare Com. Councilman, Phoenix, 1949-52; mem. adv. com. Indian affairs Dept. Interior, 1948-50. Bd. dirs. Heard Mus., Mus. No. Ariz., St. Joseph's Hosp. Repub. candidate for President of the U.S., 1964. Served as pilot USAAF, 1941-45; col., chief staff Ariz. NG, 1945-52; maj. gen. Res. Recipient award U.S. Jr. C. of C., 1937; named Man of year, Phoenix, 1949. Mem. Royal Photog. Soc., Am. Assn. Indian Affairs (dir.), Am. Legion, V.F.W. Municipal League (v.p.), Am. Inst. Fgn. Trade (dir.), Eta Mu Pi, Sigma Chi. Mason (Shriner), Elk. Author: Arizona Portraits (2 vols.), 1940; Journey Down the River of Canyons, 1940; Speeches of Henry Ashurst; The Conscience of a Conservative, 1960; Why Not Victory?, 1962; Where I Stand, 1964; The Face of Arizona, 1964; People and Places, 1967; The Conscience of the Majority, 1970. Home: PO Box 1601 Scottsdale AZ 85252

GOLDWATER, LEONARD JOHN, educator; b. N.Y.C., Jan. 15, 1903; s. Abraham Lincoln and Belle (Delmar) G.; A.B., U. Mich., 1924; M.D., N.Y. U. 1928, D.M.S., 1936; M.S. in Pub. Health, Columbia, 1941; m. Charlotte von der Heyde, 1953. Intern and resident physician Bellevue Hosp., N.Y.C., 1929-32; instr. medicine N.Y. U. Coll. Medicine, 1932-36; sr. indsl. hygiene physicians N.Y. Dept. Labor, N.Y.C., 1936-38; instr. and asst. prof. preventive medicine, N.Y. U. Coll. Medicine, 1938-41, asso. prof., 1946; prof. indsl. hygiene Columbia U. Sch. Pub. Health, 1946-52, prof. occupational medicine, 1952-68, emeritus, 1969—, spl. lectr., 1969—, Cons., Office Vocational Rehab., Dept. Health, Edn. and Welfare, 1952-60, social and occupational health, WHO, 1951—, AEC, 1947-48; Harben lectr. Royal Inst. Pub. Health and Hygiene, London, 1964; cons. indsl. hygiene physician N.Y. Dept. Labor, 1954-68; corr. com. on occupational health and safety ILO; vis. scholar Duke U. Med. Center, 1967-69. Praelector St. Andrews U., Scotland, 1966. Trustee Village of Irvington (N.Y.), 1958 -60, 61-63. Served with M.C., USN, 1941-46; PTO. Diplomate Am. Bd. Internal Medicine, Am. Bd. Preventative Medicine. Fellow Indsl. Med. Assn., N.Y. Acad. Medicine, Am. Pub. Health Assn., Am. Acad. Occupational Medicine (pres. 1959), Royal Inst. Pub. Health and Hygiene (hon.); mem. A.M.A., Med. Soc. State N.Y., Am. Indsl. Hygiene Assn., Sigma Xi, Nu Sigma Nu, Alpha Omega Alpha. Contbr. articles indsl. medicine profl. jours. Home: Pleasant Hills Route 3 Chapel Hill NC 27514 Office: Box 2914 Duke U Med Center Durham NC 27706

GOLDWATER, RICHARD M., lawyer; b. Los Angeles, Dec. 10, 1904; A.B., Stanford, 1926, J.D., 1928; student Harvard Law Sch. Admitted to Cal. bar, 1928, mem. firm Wright, Rodi, Wright, Tolton & Van Zyl, Los Angeles. Mem. Am., Los Angeles bar assns., State Bar of Cal. Office: 458 S Spring St Los Angeles CA 90013

GOLDWATER, ROBERT, educator; b. N.Y.C., Nov. 23, 1907; s. S.S. and Clara (Aub) G.; B.A., Columbia, 1929; M.A., Harvard, 1931; Ph.D., N.Y.U., 1937; m. Louise Bourgeois, Sept. 12, 1938; children—Michel, Jean-Louis, Alain. Instr. fine arts N.Y.U., 1934-39; from asst. prof. art to prof. Queens Coll., 1939-57; prof. fine arts N.Y.U. Grad. Sch., 1957—; dir. Mus. Primitive Art, N.Y.C., 1957-63, chmn. admistrv. com., 1963—; editor Mag. of Art, 1947-53. Carnegie fellow, 1930-31; Guggenheim fellow, 1944-45; Fulbright scholar, 1950-51. Mem. Coll. Art Assn. (dir. 1956-59), Soc. Aesthetics, Internat. Assn. Art Critics. Author: Primitivism in Modern Painting, 1938; Rufino Tamayo, 1947; Modern Art in Your Life, 1949; Jacques Lipchitz, 1954; Gauguin, 1957; The Sculpture of the Bambara, 1960; Senufo Sculpture, 1964; Primitivism in Modern Art, 1967; Space and Dream, 1967; also articles. Editorial bd. Art Bull., 1954—. Home: 347 W 20th St New York City NY 10011 Office: 1 E 78th St New York City NY 10021

GOLDWATER, ROBERT WILLIAMS, dept. store exec.; b. Phoenix, July 4, 1910; Baron and Josephine (Williams) G.; student U. Ill., 1928-29, Stanford, 1930-31; m. Mary Johnston, May 28, 1936; children—Robert Williams, Lynne; m. 2d, Sally Harrington, Oct. 16, 1951; children—Sally Harrington, Don Harrington. with Goldwaters Stores, Phoenix, 1932-70, became pres., 1952, chmn. bd. to 1970; v.p. Asso. Dry Goods Corp., 1962—; chmn. Goldmar Inc., Phoenix, 1970—; dir. Valley Nat. Bank, Phoenix Home: 3811 E San Miguel Paradise Valley AZ 85253 Office: 3003 N Central Av Phoenix AZ 85012

GOLDWYN, SAMUEL, (surname adopted), motion picture producer; b. Warsaw, Poland, 1882; s. Abraham and Hannah Goldfish; came to U.S., 1896, naturalized, 1902; ed. night sch.; married. Organized Jesse Lasky Feature Photoplay Co., 1913, Goldwyn Pictures Corp., 1916, Eminent Authors Pictures, Inc., 1919, also Samuel Goldwyn, Inc., Famous Players-Lasky Corp.; dir. United Artists Corp. until 1940; chmn. bd. Samuel Goldwyn Prodn., Inc. A pioneer in inducing eminent authors to work actively in writing for motion pictures; introduced Vilma Banky, Eddie Cantor, Gary Cooper, Dana Andrews and Danny Kaye to the screen. Recipient Motion Picture Acad. award for prodn., The Best Years of Our Lives, 1947; Irving Tholberg Award for consistent high quality. Home: Beverly Hills CA 90213 Office: 1041 N Formosa Av Los Angeles CA 90046

GOLDY, DANIEL LOUIS, investment and engring. co. exec.; b. Butler, N.J., Aug. 17, 1915; s. Morris A. and Gussie (Silverman) G.; B.A. in Econs., U. Wis., 1936; grad. student U. Chgo., 1936-37; m. Genevieve B. Rustvold, Aug. 14, 1944; 1 son, Daniel Rustvold. Various positions with U.S. Govt., 1941-55; gen. partner Mountain Fir Lumber Co., Independence, Ore., 1955-61, 65-68; v.p. Internat. Systems & Control Corp., 1965-69, pres., 1969—, also dir.; pres., dir. Investors Counsel, Inc., 1969—, Capital Shares, Inc., 1969—; v.p. Pacific No. Lumber Co., 1959-61; dep. adminstr. Area Redevel. Adminstrn., Dept. Commerce, also adminstr. Bus. and Def. Services Adminstrn. and dep. asst. sec. commerce, 1962-63; Pres.'s Nat. export expansion coordinator, 1964-65; exec. dir. com. export expansion U.S. Cabinet, 1964-65; lectr. Northwestern U. Grad. Sch., 1938-41. Recipient John Lendrum Mitchell Meml. award U. Wis., 1936. Mem. Phi Beta Kappa, Phi Kappa Phi, Artus. Home: 2932 Albermarle St NW Washington DC 20008 also 2929 Buffalo Speedway Houston TX 77006 also Rural Rt 2 Box 1218 Bend OR 97701 Office: 2727 Allen Pky Houston TX 77019

GOLEMAN, D. LYLE, educator; b. nr. Charleston, Ill., Jan. 3, 1924; s. John Leslie and Viola (Bare) G.; B.S., Eastern Ill. State U., 1949; M.S., Ia. State U., 1952, Ph.D., 1954; m. Maurine Morgan, June 28, 1952; children—Kathy, Bill, Jane. Asso. entomologist Ia. State U., 1952-54; extension specialist entomology Ohio State U., Columbus, 1954-59, pesticide coordinator, 1965-68, chmn. dept. entomology, 1968—; sr. entomologist Am. Cyanamid Co., 1959-65. Served with AUS, 1945-46. Mem. Entomol. Soc. Am., A.A.A.S. Home: 2261 Pinebrook Rd Columbus OH 43220

GOLEMON, ALBERT SIDNEY, architect; b. Whistler, Ala., Sept. 19, 1904; s. James Oliver and Anna Ruth (Abbott) G.; B.S., Auburn U., 1924; M.Arch., Mass. Inst. Tech., 1925; diploma Ecole des Beaux Arts, Fontainebleau, France, 1927; m. Frances Elizabeth Perkins, May 4, 1930; 1 dau., Anabeth (Mrs. Robert C. Prendergast). Began career as chief draftsman F.W. & D.E. Steinman, 1928-31; partner Steinman & Golemon, 1931-42, Golemon & Rolfe, Houston, 1946—; outstanding works include new F.B.I. Acad., Quantico, Va., new Houston Intercontinental Airport, new VA Hosp., San Antonio, St. Frances Cabrini Hosp., Alexandria, La., Golemon & Rolfe Office Bldg., Houston, 1951, St. Vincent de Paul Ch., Houston, 1954, Bellaire High Sch., Houston, 1955, Dominican Coll. Bldgs, Houston, 1954-60, Galveston-Houston Diocese Chancery, 1963, U. Houston Engring. Bldg., 1966, Union Carbide Corp. Bldg., Houston, St. Joseph's Hosp., Houston, (with others) FAA Air Route Traffic Control Center, Houston, 1965, River Oaks Country Club, Houston; cons. architect Humble Oil Co. office bldg., Houston. Pres. Nat. Archtl. Accrediting Bd., 1962. Pres. Tex. Archtl. Found., 1956; mem. City Houston Appeals Bd., 1963—; participant Pres.'s White Conf. Natural Beauty, 1965; mem. Gen. Services Adminstrn. Archtl. Adv. Panel, 1966. Served as lt. col. C.E., AUS, 1943-45. Fellow A.I.A. (nat. dir. 1954-57); mem. Tex. Soc. Architects (pres. 1953), Phi Kappa Theta. Clubs: Petroleum, Houston, M.I.T. Alumni of South Tex., Auburn Alumni, River Oaks Country, Champions Golf, Fontainebleau Alumni; Eldorado Country (Cal.). Home: 2104 Chilton Rd Houston TX 77019 Office: 5100 Travis St Houston TX 77002

GOLENBOCK, JUSTIN MERTON, lawyer; b. N.Y.C., May 31, 1919; s. Philip Leo and Lillian (Barnett) G.; A.B. cum laude, N.Y.U., 1940; LL.B. cum laude, Yale, 1946; m. Hazel Bernice Taylor, Feb. 11, 1945; children—Susan Ann, Jeffrey Taylor, Douglas Taylor. Admitted to N.Y. bar, 1947; asso. firm Milbank, Tweed, Hope, Hadley & McCloy, N.Y.C., 1946-48; partner Lans, Goldstein, Golenbock & Abrams, N.Y.C., 1948-49, Goldstein & Golenbock, N.Y.C., 1949-51, Goldstein, Golenbock & Barell, N.Y.C., 1951-60, Golenbock & Barell, N.Y.C., 1960—. Dir. Fab Industries, Inc., Giffen Industries, Inc., Nat. Telefilm Assos., Inc., Tech-Ohm Electronics, Inc. Mem. Scarsdale (N.Y.) Non-Partisan Nominating Com. Bd. govs. Scarsdale Democratic Club. Bd. govs. Fox Meadow Assn., Scarsdale. Served to capt. USAAF, 1941-46. Mem. Assn. Bar City N.Y., Am., N.Y. State bar assns., Order of Coif, Phi Beta Kappa. Clubs: Yale (N.Y.C.); Beach Point Yacht and Tennis (bd. govs.) (Mamaroneck, N.J.); Town (Scarsdale). Editor: Yale Law Jour., 1942, comment editor, 1946. Home: 30 Cohawney Rd Scarsdale NY 10583 Office: 60 E 42d St New York City NY 10017

GOLFFING, FRANCIS, educator; b. Vienna, Austria, Nov. 20, 1910; s. Henry and Teresa (Mayer) G.; student U. Berlin, U. Goettingen, U. Basel, U. Grenoble; m. Barbara Gibbs, Feb. 1941. Came to U.S., 1940; naturalized, 1943. Asst. prof. Queens Coll., N.Y.C., 1945-46, Utah State U., 1946-48; prof. English, Bennington (Vt.) Coll., 1948-68; dir. Humanities, Franklin Pierce Coll., Rindge, N.H., 1968—; dir. Am. studies U. Berlin (Germany), 1953; vis. prof. comparative lit. U. Tuebingen (Germany), 1966-67. Served with AUS, 1943-46. Author: Selected Poems, 1961; (translation) Birth of Tragedy, 1962. Contbr. articles to profl. jours. Home: Middle Hancock Rd Peterborough NH 03458 Office: Franklin Pierce Coll Rindge NH 03461

GOLICK, PETER SAMUEL, advt. exec.; b. Montreal, Que., Can., Aug. 11, 1924; s. Louis L. and Jean (Bender) G.; B.A. with honors, Queen's U., (Kingston, Ont., Can.); m. Margaret S. Schwartz, July 7, 1951; children—Jonathan D.R., Jill A., Daniel J. With Ronalds Advt. Ltd., Montreal, 1947-59, v.p., 1954-56, mem. exec. com., 1956-59; founding pres. Grey Advt. Ltd., Montreal, Que., 1959—, also chmn. bd. Active various Catholic charities. Clubs: Amateur Athletic Assn., Lord Reading Yacht (Montreal). Home: 30 Oakland Av Westmount Quebec 217 Canada Office: 2055 Peel St 500 Montreal Quebec Canada

GOLIGHTLY, LENA MILLS, radio producer, composer; b. Horse Cave, Ky.; d. Julius C. and Lee (White) G.; student Ky. State Coll., 1936. Producer, interviewer radio programs WBEH, Edgewater Beach Hotel, 1966-68, WXFM-Radio, 1966—, WBEE- Radio, 1967— (all Chgo.). Active pub. relations Ada S. McKinley Community Service, 1967. Recipient Am. Friendship Club award. 1962-65, awards Chgo. No. Dist., Assn. Federated Clubs. 1966, WVON, 1965, WXFM, 1966, Carey Temple. 1966, Chgo. Music Assn., 1965. Mem. Chgo. Music Assn., N.A.A.C.P., Urban League. Democrat. Mem. A.M.E. Ch. Club: American Friendship (dir.) Composer: I Don't Worry, 1955; Sugarpie, Tears, Easy Now, 1955; Jack is Back, 1957; Mis Bronzeville, 1961; Eternal Flame, 1964. Author: Premonition of Last Christmas, 1947; Top of the Mountain, 1967; The Seventh Child, 1967. Address: 5333 S Michigan Av Chicago IL 60615

GOLIGHTLY, TRUEMAN HARLAN, banker; b. Metropolis, Ill., Feb. 25, 1897; s. Leander H. and May (Hanna) G.; grad. Sch. Commerce, Northwestern U., 1936; m. Gertrude MacDonald, Mar. 11, 1918 (dec. June 1955); 1 dau., Katherine Hanna (Mrs. Virgil A. Burks, Jr.); m. 2d, Hazel Bullock, Nov. 22, 1956. Gen. accountant, clk. Chgo. Savs. Bank & Trust Co., 1918-23; successively auditor, asst. v.p., v.p. Chgo. Trust Co., 1924-29; v.p. Nat. Bank of the Rep., Chgo., 1929-32; asst. gen. receiver Ill. state banks in liquidation, 1933-35; pres., chmn. bd. Nat. Bank of Commerce, Chgo., 1936-64, merged with Central Nat. Bank, 1964, vice chmn. bd., 1964-66, mem. dirs. adv. com., 1966-71. Mem. nat. council Boy Scouts Am., 1946-71. Pres., chmn. finance com. Trustees of Endowment Fund of Episcopal

Diocese of Chgo., 1968-71. Served with USN, World War I. Recipient citation Chgo. Financial Advertisers, 1967. Mem. Ill. Bankers Assn. (past pres. bd. govs.), Chgo. Financial Advertisers (pres. 1942), Robert Morris Assos. (life), Financial Pub. Relations Assn., Am. Legion, Tau Delta Kappa. Mason (Shriner). Clubs: Economic, Bankers, University, Chicago Yacht (Chgo.); Oak Park Country. Home: 376 Parkview St Elmhurst IL 60126 Office: 120 S La Salle St Chicago IL 60603

GOLINKIN, JOSEPH WEBSTER, painter, lithographer, ret. naval officer; b. Chgo., Sept. 10, 1896; s. Mathieu DeVos and Ellen (Webster) G.; student Art Inst. Chgo., Art Students League N.Y., navy schs.; m. Lucile Hunnewell, 1931; m. 2d, Ruth Forman Fowler, Dec. 16, 1949; 1 son, Webster Fowler. Has exhibited at Carnegie Internat., Chgo. Art Inst., Nat. Acad., Pa. Acad., Pan-Am. (S.A.), Am. Exhibit (Paris, 1924) Los Angeles, Buffalo, Corcoran museums, Am. Water Color Soc., N.Y. Water Color Club; 1-man shows at Museum City of N.Y. (group of pictures of N.Y.), MacBeth, Sporting Gallery, Ferargil Galleries, Gumps, San Francisco, Newport, Vander Straeten Gallery Contemporary Artists, N.Y.C., Raymond & Raymond Galleries, Beverly Hills, Cal. His work has appeared in N.Y. Times, Vanity Fair, Fortune, Coronet, Country Life and other mags, Am. Artists group series, Raymond & Raymond reprodns. Work included in anthologies of Am. art, such as Water Color Painting of Today (Adrian Bury), Eyes on American (Hall-Studio pub.), Incredible New York (Lloyd Morris), Life in America (Met. Museum, Davidson). Illustrator, co-author: New York Is Like This (text by H.I. Brock), 1929; The American Sporting Scene (text by John Kieran), 1941. Served in U.S. Navy, World Wars I, II; USNR and N.Y. Naval Militia, 1921-58, ret. with rank of rear adm. USN, 1958; rear adm. N.Y. Naval Militia. Awarded Bronze Star medal, Naval Res. medal with two stars, Victory Medal with clasp, Haitian medal, Am. Def. with star, Am. Area, European-African Area with two stars, Asiatic-Pacific Area with six stars, World War II Victory, Japan Occupation medal, Philippine Liberation medal with star, N.Y. Conspicuous Service, N.Y. Long Service; recipient 1st Gold Medal Internat. Exhbn. of Art in relation to sports, 1932 Olympiad; medal, 1936 Olympiad. Fellow Internat. Inst. Arts and Letters. Clubs: Century Assn., Seawanhaka-Corinthian Yacht, Corinthian Yacht (Phila.). Address: 210 E 68th St New York City NY 10021 also Yacht Club Rd Centre Island Oyster Bay NY 11771

GOLINO, CARLO LUIGI, univ. chancellor; b. Pescara, Italy, Jan. 6, 1913; s. Vittore and Elisabetta (Petrucciani) G.; B.A., Coll. City N.Y., 1936; M.A., Columbia, 1937; student U. Florence (Italy), 1937-39; Ph.D., U. Cal. at Berkeley, 1948; m. Anna Jean Martin, Dec. 14, 1940; children—Carlo M., Elizabeth, Bruce, Jean, Susan, Robert, Michael, Laura, John. Teaching asst. Italian, U. Cal. at Berkeley, 1939-42, 46-47; mem. faculty U. Cal. at Los Angeles, 1947-65, prof. Italian, 1960-65, chmn. dept. Italian, 1956-62, dean humanities, 1961-65; prof. Italian and dean Coll. Letters and Sci., U. Cal. at Riverside, 1965-69, vice chancellor univ., 1969—; editor Italian Quar., 1957—. Served to lt. (j.g.) USNR, 1942-46. Fulbright research scholar, Italy, 1960-61; recipient Star of Solidarieta (Italy), 1958. Mem. Modern Lang. Assn. Am., Am. Assn. Tchrs. Italian, Dante Soc. Am. Author: Contemporary Italian Poetry, 1962; Galileo Reappraised, 1966; also 2 vols. Italian Baroque lit., text books. Home: 2825 Rumsey Dr Riverside CA 92506

GOLLMAR, RICHARD JACOB, foundry co. exec.; b. Lorain, O., Dec. 23, 1908; s. William F. and Irma H. (Jacobs) G.; B.S.M.E., Purdue U., 1933; m. Jeanne Reid, Sept. 18, 1937. With Nat. Tube div. U.S. Steel Co., Lorain, 1934-35; prodn. mgr. Vulcan Mold & Iron Works, Latrobe, Pa., 1935-37; charge plant layout and maintenance Elyria Foundry (O.), 1937-42, prodn. mgr. Elyria Foundry div. Chromalloy Am. Corp., 1942-59, gen. mgr., 1959-60, v.p., gen. mgr., 1960-62, pres., 1962—, also v.p. Chromalloy Am. Corp., N.Y.C., 1961—; pres. Standard Foundry div. Chromalloy Am. Corp., Worcester, Mass., 1967—; dir., treas. Golf, Inc., Vermilion, O.; exec. dir. Lorain County Savs. & Trust Co., Elyria. Pres. Elyria YMCA, 1951. Mem. Gray and Ductile Iron Founders' Soc. (dir. 1968—, treas. 1970—), C. of C. Conglist. Club: Rotary (pres. Elyria 1957-58). Home: 177 Brentview Dr Grafton OH 44044 Office: 120 Filbert St Elyria OH 44035

GOLLONG, PAUL BERNHARD WERNER, engring. exec.; b. Berlin, Germany, May 24, 1916; s. Richard Julius and Margaret (Hietzig) G; Adminstrv. Engr., U. Cin., 1941; m. Mildred Brannan, May 13, 1944. Came to U.S., 1925, naturalized, 1938. Research engr. Celotex Corp., Chgo., 1942-43; project engr. Armstrong Cork Co., Lancaster, Pa., 1943-46; prin. asso. Griffenhagen & Assos., Chgo., 1947- 51; research engr. Armour Research Found., Chgo., 1951-52, chief Asia and Far East operations, 1952-54, mgr. internat. dept., 1954-58, dir. internat. div., 1958-62; internat. adminstr. Boeing Asso. Products, The Boeing Co., 1962-63. Spl. indsl. devel. adviser to UN, 1963-66; UN project mgr. Center Indsl. Research, Haifa, Israel, 1966—. Registered profl. engineer, Wash., Ohio, Pa., Ill. Mem. A.A.A.S., Am. Inst. Indsl. Engrs., Am. Mgmt. Assn., U.S. C. of C., Nat., N.Y., Ill. socs. profl. engrs., Chgo. Hist. Soc., Asia Soc., Soc. Internat. Devel., Library Internat. Relations. Author papers, lectr. on tech. devel. Asian, African and Latin Am. countries. Home: 50 Lafayette Pl Greenwich CT 06830 Office: UN New York City NY 10017

GOLMAN, LE ROY HARVEY, housing co. exec.; b. Chgo., Feb. 17, 1924; s. Jay and Rose (Rumberg) G.; student U. Mich., 1941-43, 46; B.S., Wayne State U., 1947; m. Anne Rose Goldman, June 12, 1949; children—Janet L., David S. Partner, Goldman & Golman, C.P.A.'s, Detroit, 1951-60; sec.-treas. Kaufman & Braod, Inc., Los Angeles, 1960-64, sr. v.p., sec.-treas., 1964-68, exec. v.p., 1968—, dir., 1960—. Committeeman, scoutmaster, Sea Scout skipper Boy Scouts Am., 1964-70. Trustee Edythe and Eli Broad Found., Donald B. Kaufman Found. Served to maj. AUS, 1943-46. Eagle Scout. Mem. Am. Inst. C.P.A.'s, Mich., Ariz. socs. C.P.A.'s, Sigma Alpha Mu. Home: 540 Warner Av Los Angeles CA 90024 Office: 10801 National Blvd Los Angeles CA 90064

GOLOB, EUGENE O., educator; B.A., M.A., Ph.D., Columbia. Prof. history Wesleyan U., Middletown, Conn. Office: Wesleyan U Middletown CT*

GOLODNER, JACK, labor union ofcl., cons.; b. N.Y.C., Nov. 2, 1931; s. Maurice S. and Regina (Gaber) G.; B.S., Cornell U., 1953; LL.B., Yale, 1958; m. Linda Louise Fowler, June 14, 1964; children-Dean Dovid, Daniel Dimmick, Jonathan Wilmot. Labor arbitrator, Washington, 1958-60; exec. asst. to U.S. Congressman Giaimo, 1960-62; cons. pub. affairs, 1962—; exec. sec. Council AFL-CIO Unions for Sci., Profl. and Cultural Employees, 1967—. Mem. arts adv. com. D.C. Recreation Dept., 1965-67; mem. com. specialized personnel Dept. Labor, 1968. Served to capt. USAF, 1953-55. Mem. Indsl. Relations Assn. (bd. dirs. D.C. chpt. 1970), A.L.A., Phi Kappa Phi. Home: 8800 Mansion Farm Pl Alexandria VA 22309 Office: 1225 19th St N W Washington DC 20046

GOLOMB, MICHAEL, mathematician, educator; b. Munich, Germany, May 3, 1909; s. Mortiz Isaac and Miriam (Margulies) G.; Ph.D. magna cum laude, U. Berlin, 1934; m. Dagmar Racic, Feb. 19, 1939; children-Miriam Wanda, Deborah. Came to U.S., 1939, naturalized, 1946. Lectr., U. Zagreb, Yugoslavia, 1934-38; research asso., instr. Cornell U., 1939-42; instr., asst. prof. Purdue U., Lafayette, Ind., 1942-44, asso. prof., 1946-50, prof. math. and engring., 1950—; chief analysis sect. Franklin Inst., Phila., 1944-46, also cons.; vis. prof. Math. Research Center, U. Wis., 1956-57, summers 1958, 67, 70; cons. Naval Ordnance Plant, Indpls., Argonne Nat. Lab., Chgo. Fellow A.A.A.S.; mem. Am. Math. Soc., Math. Assn. Am., Soc. for Indsl. and Applied Math., Soc. Natural Philosophy, Phi Beta Kappa (charter), Sigma Psi, Sigma Mu Epsilon. Author: Lectures on Theory of Approximations, 1962; (with M.E. Shanks) Elements of Differential Equations, 2d edit., 1965. Contbr. articles profl. jours. Home: 1407 Woodland Av West Lafayette IN 47906 Office: Div Math Scis Purdue U Lafayette IN 47907

GOLSCHMANN, VLADIMIR, mus. conductor; b. Paris, France, Dec. 16, 1893; s. Léon and Marie (Rasumny) G.; Mus. D. (hon.), Wesleyan U., Bloomington, Ill., Columbia U., Missouri, 1956; Litt. D. (hon.), Washington U., St. Louis; m. Odette le Cointe. Founder and conductor Concerts Golschmann, Paris, 1919-24; conductor Russian Ballet of Diaghilev, ballets of Anna Pavlova, Serge de Maré; mus. dir. Thetre Beriza, Paris; has conducted in Paris, all maj. cities France, London, Rome, Brussels, Liège, Madrid, Bilbao, Lisbon, Oslo; conductor of Scottish Orch., 1928-31; 1st appearance U.S. as guest condr. N.Y. Symphony, 1924; also guest conductor NBC Orch., N.Y. Philharmonic, Stokowski's Am. Orch., Tulsa, Atlanta, Louisville, Boston, Chgo., Phila., Mexico, Montreal, Rochester, Detroit, Cleve., Cin., Mpls., San Francisco., Balt., Los Angeles, Houston symphony orchs.; also conducted in Israel, Caracas, Rio de Janeiro, Sao Paulo, Montevideo, Montreux and Lucerne festivals; also summer appearances with the N.Y. Philharmonic at Lewisohn Stadium, Hollywood Bowl, Robin Hood Dell in Phila., Ravinia Park with Chgo. Orch.; condr. St. Louis Symphony Orch., 1931-57; condr. Denver Symphony Orch., now ret. Decorated Officer French Legion of Honor, comdr. French Order Arts and Letters. Address: 1615 California St Denver CO 80202

GOLSON, BENNY, tenor saxophonist, composer; b. Phila., Jan. 25, 1929; student of piano and saxophone; student Howard U. With Bull Moose Jackson band, 1951-53, Dameron's group, 1953, Lionel Hampton, 1953-54, Johnny Hodges, 1954, Bostic's band, 1954-56; with Dizzy Gillespie's band, 1956-58, touring S. Am., 1956; with Art Blakey, 1958-59; own quintet, 1959; combined with Art Farmer to co-lead The Jazztet, 1959. Composer: Stablemates; Whisper Not; I Remember Clifford. Address: 55 W 92d St New York City NY 10025*

GOLTER, ROBERT ANDREW, librarian; b. Chgo., Dec. 13, 1928; s. Samuel and Emily (Jakalski) G.; A.B., Wheaton Coll., 1954; M.S. in L.S., U. So. Cal., 1957; m. Joanna Weber, Dec. 15, 1951; children—Joanna, Stephen, David, Douglas, Susan, John, Glenn. Began career as librarian Wheaton Coll. Library, 1958, also asst. prof. library sci.; now librarian J. Henry Meyer Meml. Library, also asst. dir. univ. libraries Stanford, Cal.; cons. to industry for research information, 1958—. Adv. council Ill. State Library for Library Devel. Served with USAAF, 1946-49. Mem. A.L.A., Ill. Library Assn. (chmn. coll. research libraries sect.), Assn. Coll. and Research Libraries. Home: 914 Cottrell Stanford CA 94305

GOLTZ, GENE, newspaper reporter; b. Marquette, Ia., Apr. 30, 1930; s. Lawrence Walter and Lorene Cathryn (Breitbach) G.; student U. Kan., 1950-52, St. Louis U., 1953-55; m. Rosemary James, Jan. 30, 1960; children—Joseph, James, John. Reporter, Tama (Ia.) News-Herald, 1957-58, Decorah (Ia.) Newspapers, 1958-59; mem. staff Douglas (Ariz.) Dispatch, 1959-61, Phoenix Republic, 1960-61, Ariz. Jour., Phoenix, 1961-62; reporter Houston Post, 1962-66, Newsday, Garden City, N.Y., 1966-67, Detroit Free Press, 1967—. Served with USAF, 1947-50; PTO. Recipient Pulitzer prize local reporting, 1964, Heywood Broun award reporting, 1964; Nieman fellow Harvard, 1969-70. Mem. Am. Acad. Achievement. Co-author: Naked Came the Stranger. Home: 11027 Ingram Av Livonia MI 48150

GOLUB, LEON ALBERT, artist; b. Chgo., Jan. 23, 1922; s. Samuel and Sara (Sussman) G.; B.A., U. Chgo., 1942; B.F.A., Sch. Art Inst. Chgo., 1949, M.F.A., 1950; m. Nancy Spero, Dec. 15, 1951; children—Stephen S., Philip S., Paul S. Chmn., Exhbn. Momentum, Chgo., 1950; tchr. grad. painting Ind. U., 1957- 59; resided in Italy, 1956-57, Paris, 1959-64; now prof. art Livingston Coll., Rutgers U.; one man exhbns. include Hanover Gallery, London, Eng., 1962, Galerie Iris Clert, Paris, 1962, 64, Am. Cultural Center, Paris, 1960, Inst. Contemporary Arts, London, 1957, Pasadena (Cal.) Mus. Art, 1956, Pomona (Cal.) Coll., 1956, Ind. U., 1958, Purdue U., 1951, Gallery A, Melbourne, Australia, 1963, Temple U., 1964, U. Chgo., 1966, LoGiudice Gallery, Chgo., 1968, Mass. Inst. Tech., 1970, Nat. Gallery of Victoria, Melbourne, Australia, 1970-71, Galerie Darathea Speyer, Paris, 1971, Galerie Veranneman, Brussels, 1971; group exhbns. Internat. Exhbn. Modern Graphics, Austria, German, 1952, Exhbn. Momentum, Chgo., 1948-58, Carnegie Internat., 1955, 64, 67, anns. Am. Art at Whitney Mus., 1955, 56, Expressionism, 1900-1950 at Walker Art Center, 1956, Surrealist and Dadaist sculpture Chgo. Arts Club, 1958, Mus. Dirs. Choice at Balt. Mus., 1959, Young Am. Painters exhbn. Guggenheim Mus., 1954, also traveling exhbn., 1956, annual U. Ill., 1957, 61, 63, New Images of Man at Mus. Modern Art, 1959, 2d interam. biennial Acad. Fine Arts, Mexico (hon. mention), 1961, San Paolo Bienniale, 1962, 61st Am. Exhbn. at Chgo. Art Inst. (Florsheim Meml. prize 1961), 65th exhbn. (Watson F. Blair purchase prize 1962), Ann. Am. Art exhbn. Corcoran Mus., 1963, Realities Nouvelles, Paris, 1963, Forum Exhbn. Contemporary Art, Ghent, Belgium, 1963, Prix Marzotto, 1964-65, 67-68, Documenta III, Kassel, Germany, 1964, Dunn International Tate Gallery, 1964, Va. Mus., 1966, 70, Musee d'Art Moderne, Paris, 1967, Inst. Contemporary Art, London, 1968, II Bienial Internacional del Deporte en las Bellas Artes, Madrid, 1969, others; rep. permanent collections Mus. Modern Art, Art Inst. Chgo., La Jolla (Cal.) Art Center, Mus. Tel Aviv (Israel), Smithsonian Instn., Kansas City Mus., others. Grantee Ford Found., 1960, Cassandra Found., 1967, Guggenheim Found., 1968. Served with AUS, 1943-46. Home: 171 W 71st St New York City NY 10023 Office: 528 LaGuardia Pl New York City NY 10012

GOLUB, WILLIAM, food chain exec.; b. Schenectady, June 30, 1904; s. Lewis and Matilda (Gurkin) G.; student Union Coll., 1922-24; B.A., U. Mich., 1926; m. Estelle Dolores Ginsberg, Apr. 6, 1930; children—Paul David, Neil Mark, Meta Jill. With Lewis Golub, wholesale grocer, 1926-30; v.p. Grosberg-Golub Co., Inc., 1930-43; v.p. Central Markets, Inc., 1933-43, pres., 1943—, also dir.; v.p. Central Market Operating Co., Inc., 1937-43, pres., 1943—; v.p. The Golub Corp., Schenectady, 1943-68, pres., 1968—, also dir.; dir. and officer various subsidiary companies. Former mem. adv. bd. Pan-Am. Coffee Bur. Mem. adv. bd. Jr. Achievement, Schenectady; vice chmn. County Traffic Safety Commn., 1967—. Bd. dirs. Schenectady City Hosp.; bd. dirs., bd. govs. Jewish Community Center, Schenectady; bd. dirs. Sunnyview Hosp.; bd. dirs., treas. Schenectady Kiwania Found., 1967—; bd. dirs. Capitol Dist. and Daus. Sarah Jewish Home for Aged; mem. adv. bd. Schenectady Affiliated Hosp. Med. Edn. Program, 1969—. Named Hon. Patron City Schenectady, 1957; Man of Year, B'nai B'rith, 1962; presented Seal State Israel, 1967. Mem. Nat. Assn. Food Chains (past dir., 1st v.p. 1948), Schenectady C. of C. (dir. 1965-68), Tau Epsilon Rho. Jewish religion (trustee). Mem. B'nai B'rith. Kiwanian. Home: 1929 Union St Schenectady NY 12309 Office: 501 Duanesburg Rd Schenectady NY 12306

GOLZE, ALFRED RUDOLF, civil engr.; b. Washington, July 6, 1905; s. Rudolph Leon and Blanche (Wenderoth) G.; B.S., U. Pa., 1930, C.E., 1940; m. Gladys Louise Whitney; children—Gretchen Wenderoth, Peter Wenderoth. Engr. subways, Phila., 1925-27; valuation engr. ICC, Washington, 1930-33; designing engr. U.S. Bur. Reclamation, Denver, 1933-35; supervising engr. in charge Civilian Conservation Camps on reclamation projects Bur. Reclamation, Washington, 1936-43, asst. dir. operations and maintenance, 1945-47, dir. programs and finance, 1947-53, chief, program co-ordination and finance div., 1953-58, asst. commr., 1958-61; budget examiner public works Bur. Budget, San Francisco and Washington, 1943-45; chief engr. Cal. Dept. Water Resources, 1961-67, dep. dir., 1967-71; chief hydroelectric engr. Burns & Roe, 1971—. Cons., AID, Turkey, 1959, Pakistan, 1964. Mem. adv. council Sch. Engring., Stanford U. Recipient Distinguished Service award U.S. Dept. Interior, 1962; Toulmin medal Soc. Am. Mil. Engrs., 1964; Outstanding Service Engring. Profession award Engring. Council of Sacramento Valley, 1966; Director's Service award Cal. Dept. Water Resources, 1966. Fellow Am. Soc. C.E.s (pres. nat. capital sect. 1958-59, chmn. com. engring. edn. 1959-60, pres. Sacramento sect. 1968- 69); mem. Fed. Govt. Accountants Assn. (chpt. pres. 1960-61), Soc. Am. Mil. Engrs., Sigma Xi (asso.), Tau Beta Pi, Sigma Tau, Chi Epsilon (hon. U. Colo. chpt.), Theta Xi (pres. Washington alumni 1956-57). Clubs: Cosmos (Washington); Commonwealth of Cal.; Engineers (San Francisco); Sutter; Engineers (Sacramento). Contbr. to Applied Sedimentation, 1950. Author: Reclamation in the United States, 1952; Your Future in Civil Engineering, 1965. Contbr. numerous articles to profl. jours. Home: 404 San Vicente Blvd Santa Monica CA 90402 Office: Burns & Roe Inc 9800 S Sepulveda Blvd Los Angeles CA 90045

GOMBER, RAYMOND F., advt. exec.; b. N.Y.C., June 3, 1917; s. Francis C. and Lillian (Deaves) G.; student N.Y.U., 1936-38; m. Lillian D. Kuhfahl, Aug. 27, 1938; children—Barbara (Mrs. Robert Isham), Alan F., Marilyn E. (Mrs. Ronald Root), Douglas C. Employed as account exec. Basford, Inc., N.Y.C., 1936-42; sales promotion mgr., then indsl. advt. mgr. Westinghouse Electric Co., 1942-57; v.p. Compton Advt., Milw., 1957- 60; sr. v.p. KlauVan Pietersom-Dunlap, Milw., 1960-65, pres., 1965—, also dir. Mem. Wis. Devel. Authority; Milw. co-ordinator Pres.'s Youth Opportunity Program. Bd. dirs. Youth Opportunity Program. Mem. Assn. Indsl. Advertisers, Am. Advt. Fedn. (dir. Milw.). Clubs: Wisconsin; Westmoor Country. Home: 2320 Alta Louise Pkwy Brookfield WI 53005 Office: 111 E Wisconsin Av Milwaukee WI 53202

GOMBERG, HENRY JACOB, nuclear engr.; b. N.Y.C., Apr. 16, 1918; s. Alexander and Marie (Shuloff) G.; B.S.E., U. Mich., 1941, M.S.E., 1943, Ph.D. in Elec. Engring., 1951; Sc.D. (hon.), Albion Coll., 1968; m. Edna M. Cohen, Dec. 28, 1940 (dec. Nov. 1965); children—Richard, Robert; m. 2d, Edith S. Lisansky, June 24, 1967; stepchildren—Stephen, Judith, Eugene. Dir. Mich. Meml.-Phoenix Project, 1959-61; chmn. com. nuclear engring. U. Mich., 1955-58, chmn. dept. nuclear engring., 1958-61, prof. nuclear engring., 1958-61; dep. dir. P.R. Nuclear Center, Mayaquez, 1961-66, dir., 1966-71; pres. KMS Fusion, Inc., Ann Arbor, Mich., 1971—; Carnegie vis. prof. U. Hawaii, 1961; cons. Hawaiian Electric Co., Atomic Power Devel. Assos., Inc., Gen. Motors Corp., Lockheed Aircraft Co., Nuclear Products Co., Cook Research Labs., ICA, AEC, Nat. Acad. Scis. Chmn. com. research reactors NRC; del. Internat. Conf. Peaceful Uses Atomic Energy, 1955; U.S. rep. Nat. Acad. Sci. to USSR, 1957. Recipient Henry Russel award U. Mich., 1952. Fellow Am. Nuclear Soc.; mem. Am. Phys. Soc., Sigma Xi, Tau Beta Pi, Eta Kappa Nu, Phi Kappa Phi. Home: 430 Hillspur Rd Ann Arbor MI 48105 Office: KMS Fusion Inc 3941 Research Park Dr Ann Arbor MI 48104

GOMBERG, MORRIS, educator, musician; b. Chgo., Jan. 15, 1909; s. Samuel and Bella (Mitchell) G.; Mus.M., DePaul U., 1933; grad. Juilliard Sch. Music, 1930; m. Helen Winner, Dec. 5, 1937; children—David, Joel. Mem. faculty string instrument dept. DePaul U., Chgo., 1934-50; vis. prof. Ottumwa Coll., Ia., 1941; prof. violin Chgo. Musical Coll., Roosevelt U., 1951—, chmn. string instrument dept., 1951—; conductor Chgo. Chamber Players. Home: 2434 W Farwell Av Chicago IL 60645

GOMBERG, WILLIAM, educator; b. Bklyn., Sept. 6, 1911; s. Alexander and Marie (Shuloff) G.; B.S., Coll. City of N.Y., 1933; M.S., N.Y.U., 1941; Ph.D., Columbia, 1947; m. Adeline Wishengrad, Sept. 24, 1939; 1 dau., Paula. Dir. mgmt. engring. dept. Internat. Ladies Garment Workers Union, A.F. of L., N.Y.C., 1941-56; prof. indsl. engring. Washington U., St. Louis, 1956-58; vis. prof. Columbia, 1958-59, Stanford, 1958-65; prof. industry Wharton Sch., U. Pa., 1959—; cons. transp. labor sec. of commerce, Nat. Acad. Sci.; indsl. engring. cons. U.A.W.-C.I.O., Internat. Assn. Machinists, United Textile Workers, A.F. of L., Comml. Telegraphers Union, A.F. of L. Mem. adv. com. European Productivity. Recipient McKinsey award for article Cal. Mgmt. Rev., 1962. Mem. Nat. Acad. Arbitrators, Am. Soc. M.E., A.A.A.S., Am. Arbitration Assn., Am. Inst. Indsl. Engrs., Am. Econ. Assn. Author: Trade Union Analysis of Time Study, 1948; Labor Union Manual on Job Evaluation, 1948; (with Shostak) Blue Collar World, New Perspectives in Poverty, 1965; also articles tech. jours. Home: 392 Montgomery Av Wynnewood PA 19096

GOMER, ROBERT, scientist; b. Vienna, Austria, Mar. 24, 1924; B.A., Pomona Coll., 1944; Ph.D. in Chemistry, U. Rochester, 1949; AEC fellow chemistry, Harvard, 1949-50; m. Anne Olah, 1955; children—Richard, Maria. Naturalized citizen. Instr. chemistry Inst. Study Metals, U. Chgo., 1950-51, asst. prof., 1951-54, asso. prof., 1954-58, prof., 1958—; Sloan fellow, 1958-62; Bourke lectr., Eng., 1959. Served with AUS, 1944-46. Bd. dirs. and mem. editorial bd. Bull. of Atomic Scientists. Home: 4824 Kimbark Av Chicago, IL 60615. Office: 5640 Ellis Av Chicago IL 60637

GOMEZ, EDDIE (Edgar), musician; b. Santurce, P.R., Oct. 4, 1944; s. Julio and Aracelis (Delgado) G.; student Julliard Sch. Music, 1962-65; pupil of Fred Zimmerman, 1960-65; m. Amy Krusch, Sept. 19, 1963; 1 son, Scott David. Came to U.S., 1944. Bassist with Marian MacPartland, 1964, Gary MacFarland, 1965, Gerry Mulligan, 1966; mem. Bill Evans Trio, 1966—; occasional appearances with Miles Davis and Jeremy Steig, also occasional pvt. teaching. Trio recipient Grammy award, 1968; performed Montreux Jazz Festival, 1968; CBS scholarship, 1963. Recipient Downbeat Critics poll for talent deserving wider recognition, 1968. Mem. Nat. Acad. Recording Arts and Scis., Internat. Inst. String Bass. Address: 86-111 34th Av Jackson Heights NY 11372

GOMEZ, FORTINO, clergyman; b. Celaya, Gto, Mexico, Aug. 11, 1890; s. Felipe and Dolores (León) G.; student Coll. Pio Marieno of Querétaro, Sem. of Monterrey, Coll. Pio Latino Americano, Rome, Italy; Dr. Phil., 1910, Dr. Theology, 1914, Dr. Law, 1916. Ordained priest, Roman Catholic Ch., 1913; rector Sem. of Monterrey, 1934; gen. vicar Archdiocese of Monterrey, 1935, dean, 1937; archbishop of

Antequera (or Oaxaca), 1942-67, consecrated, Feb. 24, 1943; archbishop of Ceramo, 1967—; asst. pontifical throne, 1955. Home: Calle C Colon 206 Celaya Gto Mexico

GOMEZ, JOSE CARLOS, diversified enterprises exec.; b. Chgo., Dec. 18, 1933; s. Abraham and Leonor (Pena) G.; student U. Notre Dame, Roosevelt U., Loyola U.; m. Carmen Murguia, Nov. 17, 1956; children—Carman. Charles A., Rebecca. Asst. mgr. Cine Tampico Theatre, Chgo., 1952-54, gen. mgr., 1957—; mgr., sec.-treas. Plaza Theatre Corp., Chgo., 1954-56, gen. mgr., 1957- -; gen. mgr. Carta Blanca Dist., 1957—; pres. S. & C. Theatre Corp., San Juan Theatre Corp., Senate Theatre, A. & L. Gomez Bldgs., El Informador, Inc. Republican candidate for Cook County commnr., 1966. Bd. dirs. Pan Am. Assembly. Mem. 18th St. Businessmen's Assn., Puerto Rican C. of C., Latin Am. Rep. Orgn. K.C. Club: Lions (1st v.p. 1967). Home: 7238 W Main St Niles IL 60648 Office: 1510 W 18th St Chicago IL 60608

GOMEZ DE ESTAVILLO, GREGORIO, author, philologist, translator; b. Jimenex, Chichuahua, Mexico, Nov. 3, 1896; s. Gregorio Gomez Rueda and Florencia Estavillo; student English and French, Escuela Altos Estudios, Mexico City; Mexican Govt. student, Columbia, 1922; Tchr., 1919-20; translator for Mexican Govt., 1920-22; gen. practice as translator, 1922—. Roman Catholic. Author: Rexreacon Filologica; De Buen y Mal Humor; Readings in English; Mexican Proverbs: A Book for Linguists. Home: 16079 Norte Puebla Puebla Mexico

GOMEZ-IBANEZ, JOSE DANIEL, educator; b. Sarrion (Teruel), Spain, Oct. 9, 1911; s. Daniel Gomez Garcia and Emilia Ibanez Perez; licenciado en ciencias, U. Madrid, 1933; diploma Instituto Espanol de Oceanografia, 1934; A.M., Oberlin Coll., 1938; Ph.D., Cornell U., 1945; m. Lydia Ellen Ross, Sept. 7, 1939; children—Daniel A., J. Antonio, Michael A. Prof. auxiliar Instituto Velaquez, Madrid, 1934-36; from instr. to asso. prof. Wesleyan U., Middletown, Conn., 1942-54, prof. chemistry, 1955—. Beech prof., 1959—; vis. prof. Instituto de Quimica, Universidade de São Paulo, Brazil, 1971—. Mem. Am. Chem. Soc., Faraday Soc. London, History Sci. Soc., N.E. Assn. Chemistry Tchrs., Sigma Xi. Author: (with A. J. Scarlett) General College Chemistry, 1954. Dir. (editor): Revista Ibero-americana de Educacion Quimica, 1966—. Home: 28 Lawn Av Middletown CT 06457

GOMPERTZ, JOHN LANGDON, physician; b. San Francisco, Jan. 16, 1903; s. Charles William and Anita (Taggard) G.; A.B., U. Cal. at Berkeley, 1925; M.D., Jefferson Med. Coll., 1936; m. Margaret Bates, Aug. 16, 1933; children—Charles Bates, Margaret (Mrs. John B. Huntington), Joanne (Mrs. Peter Melvin). Intern, then resident Highland Gen. Hosp., Oakland, Cal., 1936-38; pvt. practice internal medicine, Oakland, 1938—; cons. VA Hosp., Livermore, Cal., 1946-50, Parks Air Force Hosp., 1951-55, U. Cal. at Berkeley, 1940-71. Pres. Alameda County Tb Assn., 1950, Tb and Health Assn. Cal., 1957, Cal. Thoracic Soc., 1967, Nat. Tb and Respiratory Disease Assn., 1968- 69. Served to maj., M.C., AUS, 1942-46. Diplomate Am. Bd. Internal Medicine. Fellow A.M.A., A.C.P., Am. Coll. Chest Physicians, Cal. Acad. Medicine; mem. Soc. Cal. Pioneers, Cal. Hist. Soc., Med. Friends of Wine (bd. govs. 1968), Sigma Nu. Alpha Kappa Kappa, Alpha Omega Alpha. Mason. Clubs: Claremont Country (Oakland); Commonwealth (San Francisco). Home: 5405 Broadway Terrace Oakland CA 94618 Office: 100 Bay Pl Oakland CA 94610

GOMPF, ARTHUR MILTON, mech. engr.; b. Pikesville, Md., Jan. 24, 1909; s. Henry and Anna May (Hartman) G.; student Balt. Coll. Commerce, 1925-29; B.E., Johns Hopkins, 1934, M. Liberal Arts, 1967; m. Margaret Jane Purdum, Aug. 24, 1940; children—Arthur Purdum, Henry Lewis. With Esso-Standard Oil Co. of N.J., Balt., 1934-38; sec.-treas. Egli & Gompf, Inc., Balt., 1938-50, pres., 1950—; dir. Progress Fed. Savs. & Loan Assn.; faculty Johns Hopkins, 1936-40. Pres., Bldg. Congress and Exchange of Balt., 1955; chmn. Air Quality Control Adv. Council Md., 1966-67. Vice pres., trustee McDonogh Sch.; treas., trustee Nat. Soc. Profl. Engrs. Ednl. Found.; bd. dirs. Florence Crittenton Home. Recipient Outstanding Service award Md. Soc. Profl. Engrs., 1961, Engring. Profession Meritorious Service award, 1968. Registered profl. engr., Md. Fellow Am. Soc. M.E. (com. chmn.); mem. I.E.E.E., Am. Soc. Heating, Refrigerating and Air Conditioning Engrs., Engrs. Club Balt. (pres. 1961), Nat. Soc. Profl. Engrs. (v.p. 1963-66, treas. 1966-70), Engring. Soc. Balt. Clubs: Johns Hopkins (v.p.), Civitan (pres. 1957), Center, Baltimore Country (Balt.). Contbr. articles to mags. Home: Jarrettsville MD 21084 Office: 1007 N Calvert St Baltimore MD 21202

GOMULKA, WLADYSLAW, Polish polit. ofcl.; b. Krosno. Lwów, Poland, Feb. 6, 1905; married; 1 son. Profl. organizer Communist party, promoter Polish working youth movement following World War I, also sec. several trade union orgns.; mem. underground resistance movement Polish Communists, 1941; sec. Warsaw group Polish Workers party, 1942, mem. central com., sec. Polish Workers party, 1943-49; prin. organizer Cominform (Communist Information Bur.), 1947; mem., 1st sec. Polish United Workers Party, 1956—; dep. premier Poland, 1944, minister recovered Western areas, 1945-49, vice minister Supreme Nat. Control Chamber, 1949-51; mem. Council of State, 1957—. Address: Office First Sec United Polish Workers Party Warsaw, Poland.

GONDA, THOMAS ANDREW, physician, educator; b. Vienna, Austria, Aug. 24, 1921; s. Victor E. and Ossy (Kopp) G.; student U. Chgo., 1939-40; A.B., Stanford, 1942, M.D., 1945; m. Elizabeth Marie Chandler, July 3, 1944; children—Paul Chandler, William Stuart, Lynn. Came to U.S., 1924, naturalized, 1929. Intern San Francisco Hosp., 1944-45; resident Langley Porter Clinic, San Francisco, 1948-51; clin. dir. psychiatry San Francisco Hosp., 1949-51; chief neurology and psychiatry VA Hosp., San Francisco, 1951-53; instr. psychiatry Stanford Sch. Medicine, 1954-55, asst. prof., 1955-58, asso. prof., 1958-65, prof., 1965—, acting exec., 1955-56, 58-61, asso. dean, 1967—; dir. Stanford Hosp., 1968—; vis. prof. Inst. Exptl. Psychology and spl. Nat. Inst. Mental Health research fellow Oxford U. (Eng.), 1961- 62; cons. VA, Cal. Dept. Mental Hygiene, 1956—; chmn. Nat. Psychiat. Residency Adv. Bd., 1968. Mem. profl. adv. bd. Found. Thanatology, 1968- -. Served to capt., M.C., AUS, 1946-48. Fellow Am. Psychiat. Assn., Am. Coll. Psychiatrists; mem. Am., Cal. med. assns., A.A.A.S. Home: 586 Foothill Rd Stanford CA 94305

GONDER, DOUGLAS VIVIAN, r.r. ofcl.; b. Pingyao, China, Jan. 4, 1908; s. Royal Kephart and Ruby (Dodds) G.; ed. schs., China and Can.; extension course U. Toronto, McGill U.; m. Doris Esther Poole, Oct. 28, 1933; children—John (Mrs. Jacques Daccord), Eleanor (Mrs. Jerry Eller), Dorothy (Mrs. Orville Messenger), Margaret (Mrs. Geoffrey Moore). With Royal Bank Can., 1924-25; with Canadian Nat. Rys., 1925-71, beginning as machinist apprentice, successively draughtsman, insp., foreman, locomotive foreman, supt. Montreal shops, gen. supt. motive power and car equipment at Moncton, gen. mgr. Winnipeg, 1925-50, asst. v.p. Montreal hdqrs., 1950-57, v.p., gen. mgr., Atlantic region, Moncton, 1957-60, v.p., 1960-62, v.p. Prairie region, Winnipeg, 1962-64, v.p. Great Lakes region, 1964-71; exec. dir. Canadian Keswick Conf., 1971—; dir. Canadian Premier Life Ins. Co. Decorated comdr. bro. St. John Jerusalem. Mem. Am. Soc. M.E., Toronto, Canadian ry. clubs, Gideons. Baptist. Clubs: Canadian (Toronto); Empire; York Downs Golf and Country; National. Home: 95 Thornecliffe Park Dr Toronto 17 Ontario Canada

GONDWE, VINCENT HORATIUS BONAR, diplomat of Malawi; b. Emanyaleni, Malawi, Mar. 29, 1931; s. Edward Kabifya and Grace (Shonga) G.; B.A., Rhodes U., S. Africa, 1954; certificate in edn., Bristol (Eng.) U., 1956; m. Mary Ngoma, Apr. 7, 1957; children—Kamuzu, Khataza, Donna Maria. Tchr., Zomba (Malawi) High Sch., 1957-58; sch. insp., Zomba and Chiradzulu, 1958-59; detained for polit. activity, 1959-60; dist. edn. officer Ft. Johnston and Kasupe, 1960-61; sec. scholarships com. Ministry Edn., Zomba, 1961-63; dep. regional edn. officer So. region, Blantyre, 1963; examinations officer Ministry Edn., 1963-64; Malawi high commnr. to Ghana, 1964-65; ambassador of Malawi to U.S., 1965-67, to Ethiopia and Israel, Nigeria, 1968-71; acting sec. edn. Ministry Edn., Limbe, 1967-68. Decorated Malawi Independence medal, 1964, Malawi Republic medal, 1966. Mem. Malawi Congress Party. Address: PO Box 616 Blantyre Malawi

GONYEA, WILFORD H., mfg. co. exec.; b. Tacoma, Nov. 26, 1911; s. Joseph Henry and Hilda (Anderson) G.; student U. Wash., 1929-30; m. Mildred R. Iverson, Nov. 12, 1964; children by previous marriage—Mary Ann (Mrs. Robert Stowell), Joyce (Mrs. Richard Davidson), Joseph Henry II, Douglas W., Lynn M. Owner W.H. Gonyea & Assos., Springfield, Ore.; pres. Yamhill Plywood Corp.; gen. partner Mich. Cal. Lumber Co., Placerville, Cal., Timber Products, Medford, Ore., Chgo. Mill & Lumber Co., Greenville, Miss.; dir. Drain Plywood Corp. Trustee, Lewis and Clark Coll., Portland, Ore. Clubs: Arlington, University (Portland, Ore.); Eugene (Ore.) Country; Racquet (Palm Springs, Cal.); LaQuinta Country (pres.) (Palm Desert). Home: Route 4 Box 77 Eugene OR 97405 Office: Box 269 Springfield OR 97477

GONZALES, BENNIE MONTAGUE, architect; b. Phoenix, June 11, 1924; s. Francisco M. and Guadalupe Montaque (Baca) G.; B.S., Ariz. State U., 1954, postgrad., 1955; postgrad. U. Mexico, 1954; m. Lupe Baca, Sept. 28, 1947; children—Barney James, Bianca. Practice various firms, Phoenix, 1954-59, individual archtl. practice, Phoenix, 1959—. Mem. Ariz. Bd. Tech. Registration, 1969—, Maricopa County (Ariz.) Adjustment Bd., 1958-59, Phoenix Adjustment Bd., 1962, Phoenix Bd. Housing Appeals, 1963. Bd. dirs. Archtl. Found. Ariz. State U., Good Shepherd Sch. for Girls. Served with USCGR, 1943-46. Recipient many citations, honors. Mem. A.I.A., Mexican C. of C. Ariz. (named Man of Year 1968). Works include libraries, med. bldgs., apts., schs., residences. Office: 4131 N 48th St Phoenix AZ 85018

GONZALES, BOYER, educator, artist; b. Galveston, Tex., Feb. 11, 1909; s. Boyer and Eleanor (Hertford) G.; B.S. in Arch., U. Va., 1931; student painting with McFee and Kuniyoshi; m. Elizabeth Cullyford Bole, Dec. 28, 1946. Tchr. art U. Tex., 1939-42, 46-54; prof., dir. Sch. Art, U. Wash., 1954-66, prof. Sch. Art, 1966—; rep. permanent collections Dallas Mus. Fine Arts, La Guna Gloria Gallery, Austin, Tex., Rochester (N.Y.) Gallery, Seattle Art Mus., Witte Meml. Mus., San Antonio; exhbns. include N.Y. and San Francisco world fairs, Corcoran Biennial, Pa. Acad. Annual, Santa Barbara (Cal.) Biennial, Denver Mus. Annual, Artists West of Miss., others. Past v.p., dir. Nat. Assn. Schs. Art. Mem. Seattle Municipal Art Commn., 1957-60. Served with USAAF, 1942-46. Mem. Scarab, Tau Sigma Delta. Home: 6525 51st Av NE Seattle WA 98115

GONZALES, CARLOTTA (Mrs. Richard Lahey), artist; b. Wilmington, N.C., Apr. 3, 1910; d. Anthony Manuel and Nettie Rivers (Van Tharp) Gonzales; student Pa. Acad. Fine Arts, N.A.D., Art Students League N.Y., Corcoran Sch. Art, Washington; m. Richard Lahey, Dec. 19, 1931. Tchr. children's classes Corcoran Sch. Art, 1935- 37, sculpture class Goucher Coll., 1935-37; staff artist Nat. Geog. Soc., Washington, 1941-47; exhibited Nat. Acad., N.Y.C., Corcoran Biennial, Washington, Goucher Coll., Towson Md., Montclair Museum Art. With husband commd. to design mural for war meml. edifice at Honolulu, dedicated 1966; with husband commd. to write Picasso, His Life and Art, 1968; Rembrandt, His Life and Art, 1968. Home: 9530 Clark Crossing Rd Vienna VA 22180 (summer) Box 412 Ogunquit ME 03907

GONZALES, RICHARD A. (Pancho), profl. tennis player; b. Los Angeles, May 9, 1928; s. Manuel A. and Carmen (Alire) G.; divorced; children—Richard, Michael, Danny, Christina, Mariessa, Andrea. Profl. tennis player; U.S. champion, 1948, 49; winner Davis Cup, 1949; participant profl. tennis championships, 1953-60; now tennis profl. Caesar's Palace, Las Vegas, Nev. Tournament chmn. Sports Celebrity Tennis Tournament for Dewar's Cup, 1971. Served with USNR, 1945-47. Home: Route 4 Box 126 Malibu CA 90265

GONZALEZ, DELFIN DE LEON, metals co. exec.; b. Manila, P.I., June 15, 1914; s. Juan Borja and Amalia Venturina (DeLeon) G.; LL.B., U. Philippines, 1938; m. Aurea Carballo, Dec. 9, 1941; children—Federico, Jaime, Jorge, Delfin De Leon, Ma. Regina. Admitted to Philippine bar, 1938; practiced in Manila, 1939-60; v.p., gen. counsel, sec., dir. Benguet Consol., Inc., Rizal, Philippines, 1960—. Mem. Philippine Gold Producers Assn. (pres.), Philippine Bar Assn. Home: 2279 Lamayan Sta Ana Manila Philippines Office: Pasong Tamo Extension Makati Rizal Philippines

GONZALEZ, EMILIO, educator, author; b. La Coruna, Spain, Nov. 13, 1903; s. Antonio and Carmen (Lopez) G.; B.A., Inst. Gen. y Tecnico, La Coruna, 1920; M. Social Scis. and Law summa cum laude, U. Madrid (Spain), 1926, Ph.D. summa cum laude, 1928; U. Madrid scholarum U. Munich (Germany), 1927-28; m. Maria Nunez, June 2, 1931. Came to U.S., 1939, naturalized, 1950. Adj. prof. U. Madrid (Spain), 1929-30; prof. U. La Laguna, Canary Islands, 1931- 32; dean Law and Social Scis. Sch., La Laguna, 1931-32; prof. U. Salamanca (Spain), 1932-36, U. Oviedo (Spain), 1936-37, U. Valencia (Spain), 1937, U. Barcelona (Spain), 1938; mem. faculty Hunter Coll., N.Y.C., 1940—, prof. Spainsh, 1959—, chmn. dept. Romance langs., 1964-67; exec. officer doctoral program in Spanish, City U. N.Y., 1967—. Vis. lectr. Middlebury (Vt.) Coll., 1947-63, dir. Spainsh Sch., 1963-70; lectr. history Spain, Columbia Grad. Sch., 1956- 63; vis. prof. N.Y. U. Grad. Sch., 1958-59, 61, Bklyn. Coll. Grad. Sch., 1960. Recipient Extraordinary prize for licenoisture U. Madrid, 1926, Extraordinary prize for doctorate, 1928. Mem. Royal Galician Acad. (corr.), La Coruna (corr.), Eucilides da Cunha Soc. (hon.) (Para, Brazil). Author: The Spirit of the University, 1930; The Principles of Justice, 1930; The Theory of Crime, 1931; Emilia Pardo Bazan, novelista de Galicia, 1944; Galicia, su alma y su cultura, 1954; Spanish Review Grammar, 2d edit., 1964; Historia de la civilizacion espanola, 2d edit., 1966; Grandeza y decadencia del reino de Galicia, 1957; La insumision gallega: martires y rebeldes, 1963; The Argentine Penal Code, 1963; Historia de la Literatura Espanola; La Edad Media y el Siglo de Oro, 1962; Historia de la Literatura española: la Edad Moderna, 1965; El arte dramatico de Valle-Inclan: Del decadentismo al expresionismo, 1967; Los politícos gallegos en la Corte de España y la convivencia europea; Galicia en los reinados de Felipe III y Felipe IV, 1969; Bajo la doble águila: Galicia en al reinado de Carlos V, 1970; also numerous articles, revs. Home: 425 W 57th St New York City, NY 10019.

GONZALEZ, HECTOR BLAS, Argentine diplomat; b. Coronel Pringles, Argentina, Nov. 29, 1924; s. Gregorio Gonzalez Vidal and Leandra (Febrero) G.; prof. in humanities, Nat. U. La Plata; m. Beatriz de Isasi, Sept. 9, 1961; children—Leanora Beatriz, Mariano Ramon Blas. Prof. U. of South, 1957; dir. Council Sci. and Tech. Investigations, 1959; mem. Argentine Commn. to UNESCO, 1959; dir. Sesquicentennial Library, 1961; dean U. La Plata, 1964; gen. dir. provinces, Argentina, 1957; gen. dir. of culture Argentina, 1959; press sec. to the President Argentina, 1966. Exec. dir. Found. of Stock Exchange of Buenos Aires, 1963; sec. Found. Obligado, 1963. Decorated Nat. Order Cruzeiro do Sul (Brazil); comdr. Order of Merit of Italian Republic, 1961 caballero Legion of Honor, 1964. Home: 1950 Charcas Buenos Aires, Argentina. also 175 E 80th St New York City NY 10021 Office: 12 W 56th St New York City NY 10019

GONZALEZ, HENRY B., congressman; b. San Antonio, May 3, 1916; s. Leonides and Genevieve (Barbosa) G.; grad. San Antonio Jr. Coll., St. Mary's U. Sch. Law; student U. Tex.; m. Bertha Cuellar, 1940; children—Henry B., Rosemary, Charles, Bertha, Stephen, Genevieve, Francis, Anna Marie. Formerly with father's translating company, pub. relations counselor for ins. co., San Antonio; chief probation officer Bexar Co., 1946; exec. sec. Jr. Deps. of Am. (predecessor Pan Am. Progressive Assn.); mem. San Antonio City Council, 1953-56, mayor pro-tem, 1955-56; state senator, 1956-61; mem. 87-92d congresses, 20th Dist. Tex. Civilian cable and radio censor Mil. and Naval Intelligence, World War II. Democrat. Home: 409 Kendall St San Antonio TX 78212 Office: New House Office Bldg Washington DC 20525

GONZALEZ, MICHAEL IBS, lawyer; b. San Diego, Cal., Oct. 4, 1915; s. Miguel and Ella (Ibs) G.; A.B., Stanford, 1937; LL.B., Harvard, 1940; m. Elizabeth Sibley, May 31, 1941; children—Elizabeth Farr, Victoria Harding, Georgiana Sibley, Michael Ibs, Cynthia Ella. Admitted to Cal. bar, 1940, since practiced in San Diego; partner Luce, Forward, Hamilton & Scripps. Pres. Fine Arts Soc. of San Diego, 1957-59; bd. dirs. Natural History Soc. of San Diego, YMCA; pres. Symphony Assn., 1967-68; chmn. Epis Community Services, 1969—; trustee La Jolla Country Day Sch., Bloy House Theol. Sem. Served to lt. USNR, 1942-45. Mem. San Diego County Bar Assn. (v.p.). Episcopalian (sr. warden). Home: 2174 Guy St San Diego, CA 92103. Office: Charter Oil Bldg San Diego CA 92101

GONZALEZ, RICHARD CHARLES, educator; b. San Antonio, Dec. 11, 1929; B.A., U. Tex., 1952, M.A., 1953; Ph.D., U. Md., 1957; married; 5 children. Asst. prof. psychology U. Md., 1957-59; USPHS fellow, vis. lectr. Bryn Mawr Coll., 1959-61, asst. prof., 1961-62, asso. prof., 1962-67, prof., 1968—. Recipient research career award Nat. Inst. Mental Health, 1963. Mem. Am. Psychol. Assn., Am. Psychonomic Soc. Office: Dept Psychology Bryn Mawr Coll Bryn Mawr PA 19010*

GONZALEZ, RICHARD JOSEPH, econ. cons.; b. San Antonio, Aug. 17, 1912; s. Rafael and Catarina (Trello) G.; A.B., U. Tex., 1931, M.A., 1932, Ph.D., 1934; m. Loraine O'Gorman, Dec. 19, 1936. Instr. econs. U. Tex., 1932-35, asst. prof., 1936-37; asst. prof. U. N.M., 1935-36; econ. adviser Humble Oil & Refining Co., 1937-51, dir., 1951-65, treas., 1953-59; now econ. cons.; dir. Master Computer Assos. Bd. dirs. Houston Symphony Soc., Houston Grand Opera Assn. Mem. Am. Econ. Assn., Am. Statis. Assn., Econometric Soc., Nat. Petroleum Council, Am. Petroleum Inst., Phi Beta Kappa. Home: 48 Tiel Way Houston, TX 77019. Office: PO Box 2180 Houston TX 77001

GONZALEZ, XAVIER, artist; b. Almeria, Spain, Feb. 15, 1898; s. Emilio and Gracia (Arpa) G.; grad. St. John B. de la Salle High Sch., Puebla, Mex.; night sch. student Art Inst. Chgo., 1921-23; m. Ethel Edwards, Aug. 24, 1935. Came to U.S. 1921, naturalized, 1931. Tchr., San Antonio, 1924; prof. art Newcomb Coll., Tulane U., 1930, Bklyn Mus., 1945; lectr. Nat. Coll. Assn., 1946, Met. Mus. N.Y., 1945. Exhibited N.Y.C., 1943, 46, 48.; retrospective Witte Mus., San Antonio, 1968. Represented in permanent colls. Whitney Mus., Met. Mus., Wellesley Coll., Delgado Mus., New Orleans, Witte Mus., San Antonio, Mus. Fine Arts, Seattle, IBM, N.Y. Artist in residence Western Res. U., Cleve. Guggenheim fellow. Recipient Nat. Arts Club gold medal, Audubon Artist gold medal, Am. Acad. Arts and Letters awards, Ellen P. Spever prize, 1958; Clara Obrig prize, Nat. Acad., 1962. Mem. Am. Water Color Soc., Am. Nat. Acad., Nat. Assn. Mural Painters (pres. 1968). Clubs: Artist Equity, Century (N.Y.C.). Home: 222 Central Park S New York City, NY 10019.

GONZALEZ-MUELA, JOAQUIN, educator; b. Madrid, Spain, Dec. 21, 1915; s. Joaquin and Constanza (Muela) Gonzalez; Ph.D., U. Madrid, 1946; m. Felicia Fogg, Mar. 27, 1957; children—Elena, John. Came to U.S., 1957. Lectr., Manchester (Eng.) U., 1952-57; prof. U. Ore., 1959-61, Western Res. U., 1961-64; prof. Spanish, Bryn Mawr Coll., 1965—. Guggenheim fellow, 1964; Am. Council Learned Socs. fellow, 1969. Mem. Modern Lang. Assn., Am. Assn. Tchrs. Spanish and Portuguese. Author: El infinitivo en el Corbacho, 1954; El lenguaje poético de la generación Guillen-Lorca, 1955; La realidad y Jorge Guillen, 1962; Editor: Pedro Salinas, 1969; Martinez de Toledo, 1970. Office: Bryn Mawr Coll Bryn Mawr PA 19010

GOOCH, GORDON, govt. ofcl.; b. Ft. Worth, Aug. 17, 1934; s. John Aubrey and Adrienne (Gordon) G.; A.B. with exceptional distinction in History, magna cum laude, Washington and Lee U., 1956; LL.B., J.D. with honors, U. Tex., 1961; m. Patricia Ellen Campbell, Aug. 23, 1958; children—Gordon C., Ellen A. Admitted to Tex. bar, 1961, also U.S. Supreme Ct., law clk. to chief justice of U.S., 1961-62; asso. firm Baker, Botts, Shephard & Coates, Houston, 1962-69; gen. counsel FPC, 1969—. Trustee Houston Legal Found., 1966-69, sec. 1966—68. Served to 1st lt. AUS, 1956-58. Named Outstanding Young Lawyer in Tex., Tex. Jr. Bar Assn., 1967, in Houston, Houston Bar Assn., 1967; recipient Outstanding Young Texan award Tex. Jr. C. of C., 1967. Mem. Am. Bar Assn., Phi Beta Kappa, Order of Coif. Editor in chief Tex. Law Rev., 1960-61. Home: 3549 Springland Lane NW Washington DC 20008 Office: 441 G St NW Washington DC 20426

GOOCH, HORACE, Jr., corp. exec.; b. Amarillo, Tex., 1908; grad. Washington and Lee U., 1931; m. Jane Bradford, Nov. 4, 1932; children—Sally, Bradford Cushing. A founder, chmn. bd., dir. Worcester Moulded Plastics Co.; dir. Essex Corp., Mechanics Nat. Bank, Peoples Savs. Bank. Bd. dirs. Hahnemann Hosp.; mem. Mass. Employees Group Ins. Commn.; pres. com. Leicester Jr. Coll.; adv. com. Div. Bus. Adminstrn., Clark U.; trustee Meadville (Ohio) Theol. Sch. Mem. Tex. Bar Assn., Worcester Art Mus., C. of C. (dir.; indsl. bur.), Worcester Legal Aid Soc., Soc. of Plastics Industry (past pres., past chmn. bd. dirs.), Newcomen Soc., Plastics Pioneers, Phi Kappa Psi, Phi Delta Phi. Moderator, mem. First Unitarian Ch. Clubs: Tatnuck Country, University (past pres.), Worcester. Home: 12 Massachusetts Av Worcester MA 01609 Office: 8 Drury Lane Worcester MA 01609

GOOCH, JAMES THOMAS, lawyer; b. Vanndale, Ark., Dec. 10, 1913; s. Samuel Amos and Augustus (Halk) G.; student Ark. State U., 1937, Ark. Law Sch., 1940; m. Edris Wyanna Yookadoo, Mar. 9, 1940; children—Edris Johanna (Mr. Wade Quinn, Jr.), Marilyn Kay.

(Mrs. Don Peterson). Admitted to Ark. bar, 1940; practiced in Wynne, 1940-46, Arkadelphia, 1954—; mem. firm Gooch & Gooch, 1940-46; U.S. atty. Eastern Dist. Ark., 1946-54; partner firm Lookadoo, Gooch & Lookadoo, 1954—. Vice pres., dir. Elk Horn Bank & Trust Co. Pres. U.S. Atty.'s Conf., 1948-50. Mem. War Meml. Stadium, Little Rock, 1946-67. Mem. Ark. Senate, 1940-44; chmn. Clark County Democratic Com., 1960—. Served to lt. USNR, 1942-45. Mem. Am. Judicature Soc., Am., Ark., S.W. Ark., Clark County bar assns. Home: 1215 Richardson St Arkadelphia AR 71923 Office: Lookadoo Bldg PO Box 357 Arkadelphia AR 71923

GOOCH, JOHN AUBREY, lawyer; b. nr. Ennis, Tex., Aug. 18, 1903; s. Robert E. and Della (Turner) G.; student U. Tex., 1921-22, 24-29; m. Adrienne G. Gordon, June 2, 1930; children—Robert Gordon, Adreienne Gay. Admitted to Tex. bar, 1929, since practiced in Ft. Worth; mem. firm Cantey, Hanger, Cravens & Munn. Dir. Tex. Electric Service Co., Balmorhea Ranches, Inc. Chmn. Mayor's Human Relations Com. Keynoter, chmn. Tex. Republican Conv., 1956. Dir. T. J. Brown and C. A. Lupton Found., Knet Found. Mem. Am., Tex., Ft. Worth-Tarrant County bar assns., Am. Coll Trial Lawyers, Am. Judicature Soc., Internat. Assn. Ins. Counsel (pres. 1953-54), Ft. Worth C. of C. (pres. 1959; dir.). Home: 4400 Ridgehaven Ct Ft Worth TX 76116 Office: First Nat Bank Bldg Fort Worth TX 76102

GOOD, BILL JEWEL, univ. adminstr.; b. Alma, Ark., May 1, 1924; B.S., Ark. State Tchrs. Coll., 1950; M.S., U. Ark., 1952; Ph.D. in Physics, La. State U., 1957; married; 2 children. Instr. physics U. Ark., 1952-54; asst. in physics La. State U., New Orleans, 1954-57, research asso., 1957-58, asso. prof., 1958-68, now prof., dean Coll. Sci. Served with USCGR, 1942-45. Mem. Am. Phys. Soc. Office: Coll Sci La State U New Orleans LA 70122*

GOOD, CLARENCE ALLEN, physician, radiologist; b. St. Joseph, Mo., Sept. 20, 1907; s. Clarence Allen and Sophie Love (Evans) G.; A.B., Williams Coll., 1929; M.D., Washington U., 1933; M.S. in Radiology, U. Minn., 1938; m. Virginia McClure, Sept. 6, 1930; children—Clarence Allen III, John McClure, Andrew Evans, Stephen Conrad. Asst. radiology Mallinkrodt Inst. Radiology, Washington U., 1933; intern medicine Barnes Hosp., St. Louis, 1934-35; fellow radiology Grad. Sch. Mayo Found., U. Minn., 1935-38, successively instr., asst. prof., asso. prof., prof. radiology, head sect. diagnostic roentgenology, Mayo Clinic, now sr. cons. diagnostic roentgenology, 1967- -. Diplomate Am. Bd. Radiology (sec., asst. treas., trustee). Fellow Am. Coll. Radiology; mem. A.M.A., Am. Roentgen Ray Soc. (pres.), Radiol. Soc. N.Am., Minn. Radiol. Soc. (past pres.), Phi Beta Kappa, Sigma Xi, Alpha Omega Alpha, Theta Delta Chi, Nu Sigma Nu. Home: 1211 7th St SW Rochester MN 55901 Office: Mayo Clinic Rochester MN 55901

GOOD, DALE EDWARD, fgn. service officer; b. Bluffton, O., May 24, 1920; s. Edward Earl and Leona Luella (Motter) G.; A.B., Bluffton Coll., 1942; M.A., Ohio State U., 1948; m. Lois Anne Whike, July 30, 1949; 1 dau. Elizabeth (Mrs. Edward B. Miller Jr.). Research asst. U. Ill., 1948-49; labor specialist N.P.A., 1951-52; internat. rep. trade union, 1949-51; labor attache Am. embassy, Athens, 1953-57; mem. staff Am. embassy, Tel Aviv, 1957-60; internat. relations officer Dept. of State, 1960-63; labor attache Am. embassy, Bonn, Germany, 1967—. Served to 1st lt. AUS, 1942-46. Contbr. profl. jours. Home: 1348 Woodland Av NW Canton OH 44703 Office: American Embassy 53 Bonn Bad Godesberg 1 Federal Republic of Germany

GOOD, DON LADOYT, educator; b. nr. Van Wert, O., Oct. 8, 1921; s. George Lewis and Dora Leota (Haines) G.; B.S. in Animal Husbandry, Ohio State U., 1947; M.S., Kan. State U., 1951; Ph.D. in Animal Sci. and Agrl. Econs., U. Minn., 1957; m. Jane Lenore Swick, Dec. 27, 1947; children—Linda, Craig, Gary. Instr., Kan. State U., 1947-49, asst. prof., 1949-53, asso. prof., 1953-61, prof., 1961—, head dept. animal sci. and industry, 1966—. Cons. AID, Nigeria, 1968, 69, Turkey, 1971. Pres., Fedn. Handicapped Children, Manhattan, Kan., 1965-68. Served with AUS, World War II; ETO, PTO. Mem. Am. Soc. Animal Sci., Intercollegiate Livestock Coaches Assn., Kan. Livestock Assn., Kan. Farm Bur., Am. Angus Assn., Farm House, Sigma Xi, Alpha Zeta, Gamma Sigma Delta. Republican. Methodist. Contbr. articles to profl. jours. Home: 2027 Sunnymeade Rd Manhattan KS 66502

GOOD, FREDERICK HOPKINS, physician; b. Holdrege, Neb., May 13, 1911; s. Winfred P. and Nora (McQueen) G.; A.B. (biochemistry fellow 1931-33), Colo. State Coll., 1933; B.S., U. Neb., 1936; M.D., U. Colo., 1938; m. Winifred Kinney, Sept. 1, 1935; children—Stephen F., Sherril Ann (Mrs. M. Timothy Bray). Intern Colo. Gen. Hosp., 1939-40, surg. resident, 1940-43; pvt. practice, Denver, 1945—; mem. active staff St. Joseph's, Mercy, Children's, St. Anthony's, Rose Meml. hosps., Craig Sanitarium; asso. clin. prof. surgery U. Colo. Med. Sch., 1955—; chmn. med. edn. com. Mercy Hosp., 1955—. Trustee Colo. Hosp. Service, 1946-47, pres., 1949- 60, commr. dist. IX, 1952-54; chmn. exec. com., dir. Med. Indemnity Am., 1958-61. Commr.-at-large Nat. Assn. Blue Shield Plans, 1956-60, chmn. exec. com., 1956-60, mem. joint exec. com., 1956-60, chmn. physicians relations com. Blue Shield Commn., also nat. v.p., 1964-65, nat. commr. at large, 1964-66, nat. pres., 1965-66; trustee Colo. div. Am. Cancer Soc., 1950-52. Dir. First Trust Corp., Denver. Trustee Sands House, Isaac Walton League, Goodwill Industries. Recipient Distinguished Service award U. Colo. Med. Sch., 1963, Med. Alumni award, 1964. Fellow A.C.S.; mem. Am. Assn. Med. Colls., Am. Assn. U. Profs., A.M.A., Internat. Coll. Surgeons, Southwestern Surg. Congress, Pan-Pacific Surg. Assn., Colo. (speaker ho. of dels. 1961-62, chmn. indoctrination com. 1957-59, chmn. med. services com. 1955; certificate of service 1959), Denver County (pres. 1949-50) med. socs. Presbyn. (deacon, elder). Author articles in field. Home: 9300 E Center Av Denver CO 80222 Office: 1245 E Colfax Av Denver CO 80231

GOOD, JOHN WILLIAM, former farm implement mfg. co. exec.; b. Moline, Ill., Dec. 11, 1915; s. Harry C. and Marguerite (Thompson) G.; grad. Hill Sch., 1935; B.A., Yale, 1939; m. Mildred McConnell, May 15, 1943; children—Pamela, Bettina, Victoria. Began with Deere & Co., and predecessors, Moline, 1939, mgr. export dept., 1956-58, became sec., 1958, now ret. Sec. dir. John Deare Found. Bd. trustees St. Katharine's Sch., Davenport, Ia. Served with USNR, 1941-46. Home: 2411 38th St Rock Island IL 61201

GOOD, LEONARD PHELPS, artist, educator; b. Chickasha, Okla., June 25, 1907; s. Jacob Calvin and Belle (Leonard) G.; B.F.A., U. Okla., 1927; student Art Students' League, N.Y.C., 1930, Clarence White Sch. Photography, N.Y.C., 1937, State U. Ia., 1940; m. Nancye Dooley, July 15, 1932 (dec. May 1969); 1 son, Leonard Jacob; m. 2d, Yoshie Tobe, Nov. 26, 1970. Tchr. pub. sch. art depts. Tex. and Okla., 1927-30; mem. faculty U. Okla. Sch. Art, 1930-50, U. Wis., 1950-52; prof. art Drake U., 1952—; vis. artist-in residence-Ia. State U., Ames, 1966, Shenandoah (Fl.) Community High Sch., 1970-71; curator paintings Mus. Art, U. Okla., 1935-50; exhibited paintings nat. exhbns. Am. Art, 1936, 37, traveling exhbns. Am. Fedn. Art, 1940-41; mem. acquisitions and exhbns. com. Des Moines Art Center, 1955-60; rep. permanent collections Oklahoma City Art Center, Okla. Hist. Mus., Philbook Art Center, Tulsa, Kan. Fedn. Arts, Milw. Art Center, Des Moines Art Center, Ia. Hist. Mus.; juror nat. exhbns. Mem. Art Dirs. Assn. Ia., Artists Equity, Omicron Delta Kappa (hon.), Delta Phi Delta (nat. pres. 1958-60). Home: 750 34th St Des Moines, IA 50312.

GOOD, ROBERT ALAN, educator, physician; b. Crosby, Minn., May 21, 1922; s. Roy Homer and Ethel Gay (Whitcomb) G.; B.A., U. Minn., 1944, M.B., 1946, Ph.D., 1947, M.D., 1947; M.D., U. Uppsala, Sweden, 1966; m. Joanne Finstad, May 21, 1967; children—Robert Michael, Mark Thomas, Alan Maclyn, Margaret Eugenia, Mary Elizabeth. Teaching asst. dept. anatomy U. Minn., Mpls., 1944-45, instr. pediatrics Med. Sch., 1950-51, asst. prof., 1951-53, asso. prof., 1953-54; Am. Legion Meml. research prof. pediatrics, 1954—, prof. microbiology, 1962—, Regents prof. pediatrics and microbiology, 1969—, prof., head dept. pathology, 1970—; intern U. Minn. Hosps., 1947, asst. resident pediatrics, 1948-49; vis. investigator Rockefeller Inst. for Med. Research, N.Y.C., 1949-50, asst. physician to Hosp., 1949-50; attending pediatrician Hennepin County Gen. Hosp., 1950—, cons., 1960—. Mem. Unitarian Service Commn. Med. Exchange Team to France, Germany, Switzerland and Czechoslovakia, 1958; cons. VA Hosp., Mpls., 1959-60; cons., sci. adviser Nat. Jewish Hosp., Denver and Childrens Asthma Research Inst. and Hosp., Denver, 1964-69; mem. study sects, USPHS, 1952-69; mem. expert adv. panel on immunology WHO, 1967—; cons. Merck & Co., N.J., 1968—; mem. President's Sci. Adv. Council on Biol. and Med. Sci., 1970; mem. adv. council Life Ins. Med. Research Fund. Bd. dirs., com. chmn. Minn. chpt. Arthritis Found., mem. adv. council Childrens Hosp. Research Found., Cin., 1954-58. Recipient Borden Undergrad. Research award U. Minn. Med. Sch., 1946, E. Mead Johnson First award, 1955, Theobald Smith award, 1955, Parke-Davis 6th Ann. award, 1962, Rectors medal U. Helsinki, 1963-64, Pemberton Lectureship award, 1966, R.E. Dyer Lectureship award, 1967, Clemons Von Pirquet Gold medal 9th Ann. Forum on Allergy, 1968, Presidents medal U. Padua, Italy, 1968, Tap Teen award March of Dimes, Mpls., 1969, John Stewart Meml. award Dalhousie U., 1969, Ricketts award U. Chgo., 1970, Gairdner Found. award, 1970, Albert Lasker Meml. Research award, 1970. Fellow Nat. Found. for Infantile Paralysis, 1947, Helen Hay Whitney Found. fellow, 1948-50, Markle Found. scholar, 1950-55. Fellow Acad. Multidisciplinary Research, A.A.A.S., N.Y. Acad. Sci.; mem. Am. Assn. History of Medicine, Am. Cancer Soc., Am. Fedn. Clin. Research, Am., Minn. (dir., past com. chmn.) heart assns., Am. Assn. Lab. Animal Sci., Am. Assn. Anatomists, Am., Western assns. immunologists, Am. Assn. U. Profs., Am., Mpls., Northwestern pediatric socs., Am. Rheumatism Assn., Am. Soc. Clin. Investigation (past pres.), Am. Soc. Exptl. Pathology, Am. Soc. Microbiology, Assn. Am. Physicians, Central Soc. Clin. Research (past pres.), Harvey Soc., Infectious Disease Soc. Am. (Squibb award 1968), Internat. Soc. Nephrology, Internat. Acad. Pathology, Internat. Soc. for Transplantation Biology, Leukemia Soc., Minn. Med. Assn., Am. Assn. Immunology (councilor 1970), Nat., Minn. acads. sci., Reticuloendothelial Soc., Soc. for Exptl. Biology and Medicine, Soc. for Pediatric Research, Am. Clin. and Climatol. Assn. (Gordon Wilson Gold medal 1967), Am. Acad. Allergy (Robert A. Cooke Gold medal 1968), Detroit Surg. Assn. (McGraw medal, 1969), Assn. Am. Med. Colls. (Borden award 1970), Phi Beta Kappa, Sigma Xi, Alpha Omega Alpha. Contbr. articles profl. jours. Office: Box 494 U Minn Hosps Minneapolis MN 55455

GOOD, ROBERT CROCKER, author; b. Mt. Vernon, N.Y., Apr. 7, 1924; s. Alfred Henry and Josephine (Crocker) G.; student Amherst Coll., 1942-43; B.A., Haverford Coll., 1945; B.D., Yale, 1951, Ph.D. in Internat. Relations, 1956; m. Nancy Louise Cunningham, Aug. 21, 1946; children—Stephen Lawrence, Karen Louise, Kathleen Jenifer. Dir. Am. Friends Service Com. Neighborhood Center, Frankfurt am/Main, Germany, 1947, adminstr. Internat. Student Seminars, Phila., 1948; instr., later asst. prof. internat. relations Social Sci. Found., U. Denver, 1953-58; research asso. Washington Center Fgn. Policy Research, Johns Hopkins, 1958-61, 1969— (Ford Found. grant); dir. Carnegie Endowment Seminars in Diplomacy, Washington, 1960-61; dir. Office Research and Analysis for Africa, State Dept., 1961-65; U.S. ambassador to Zambia, Lusaka, Central Africa, 1965- 69. Coordinator President elect Kennedy's Task Force on Africa, 1960. Pres. Neighbors, Inc., Wash., 1962-65. Rockefeller Found. fellow, 1960. Mem. Soc. Religion in Higher Edn., African Studies Assn. Co-author: Alliance Policy in the Cold War, 1959; Neutralism and Non-Alignment: The New States in World Politics, 1962. Co-editor: Reinhold Neibuhr on Politics, 1960; Foreign Policy in the Sixties: The Issues and the Instruments.

GOOD, ROLAND HAMILTON, Jr., educator, theoretical physicist; b. Toronto, Ont., Can., Oct. 22, 1923; s. Roland Hamilton and Marie (Smith) G.; came to U.S., 1948, naturalized, 1950; B.M.E., Lawrence Inst. Tech., 1944; M.A.E., Chrysler Inst. Engring., 1946; M.S., U. Mich., 1948, Ph.D., 1951; m. Ferol Hendrickson, May 7, 1944; children—Roland Hamilton III, Patricia Gail, Sue Marie. Engr., Chrysler Corp., Windsor, Ont. and Highland Park, Mich., 1942-47; instr. U. Cal. at Berkeley, 1951-53; mem. faculty Pa. State U., 1953-56; from asso. prof. to prof. physics Ia. State U., Ames, 1956—, distinguished prof. scis. and humanities, 1970—; physicist, sr. physicist Ames Lab. of U.S. AEC, 1956—; vis. asso. prof. U. Colo., summer 1958; NSF sr. postdoctoral fellow Inst. Advanced Study, Princeton, 1960-61; vis. prof. Inst. Math. Sci., Madras, India, 1968; guest Stanford Linear Accelerator Center, 1968-69. Fellow Am. Phys. Soc. Research, publs. theoretical physics, especially relativistic wave equations, polarization of elementary particles, metallic binding, electron emission from metals and spectroscopy of rare earths. Author: (with T.J. Nelson) Classical Theory of Electric and Magnetic Fields, 1971. Home: 1724 Meadowlane Ames IA 50010

GOODALE, MARCUS DOWD, banker; b. Newington, Conn., Nov. 2, 1908; s. Harry C. and Lila (Desell) G.; student Am. Inst. Banking, Rutgers U. Grad. Sch. Banking; m. Louise Pomeroy, May 23, 1936; children—Marcia (Mrs. Albert N. Graves III), Jeannette D. Began career with Conn. Bank & Trust Co., Hartford, v.p., 1950-63, sr. v.p., 1963-65, exec. v.p., 1965—; chmn. bd., dir. No. Data Services; v.p. CBT Data Services. Mem. Conn. regional adv. Council Small Bus. Adminstrn. Mem. exec. council Charter Oak council Boy Scouts Am. Treas. Conn. Republican Central Com., also mem. finance com. Bd. dirs., mem. exec. com. Children's Services of Conn.; v.p. bd. dirs. Greater Hartford Tb and Pub. Health Soc.; v.p., treas., chmn. budget and finance com. Windsor Library Assn.; bd. dirs. Combined Health Appeal for Bus. and Industry; corporator St. Francis Hosp. Mem. Hartford C. of C. Episcopalian. Clubs: Hartford; New Seabury (Mass.) Country. Conn.). Home: 10 Harvey Rd Windsor, CT 06095. Office: 1 Constitution Plaza Hartford CT 06115

GOODALE, ROBERT LINCOLN, educator; b. New Haven, Oct. 9, 1910; s. G. Frank and Isabel (McLean) G.; B.A. in English, Yale, 1932, B. Mus., 1937; m. Hope Kaufmann, Aug. 2, 1951. Instr. music Hollins Coll., 1937-42; mem. faculty Bryn Mawr Coll., 1946—, Alice Carter Dickerman prof. music, 1964—, chmn. dept., 1957—. Served to lt. comdr. USNR, 1942-45. Mem. Coll. Music Soc., Am. Musicol. Soc.; asso. mem. Am. Guild Organists. Pub. early Spanish choral music. Home: 2030 Old Gulph Rd Villanova PA 19085. Office: Bryn Mawr Coll Bryn Mawr PA 19010

GOODALL, DONALD BANNARD, educator; b. Los Angeles, Oct. 8, 1912; s. George Oliver and Margaret (Bannard) G.; A.B., U. Ore., 1935; grad. painting, Sch. Art Inst. Chgo., 1936; A.M., U. Chgo., 1938; Ph.D. (fellow) Harvard, 1969; m. Gladys Hobbs, May 5, 1940; children—Brooks, Anne, Hollis. Dir. Utah Art Center, Salt Lake City, 1938-42; with U. Tex., 1942-46, 1959—, chmn. art dept., 1945-46, prof., chmn. dept. art, dir., Univ. art mus., 1959—, acting dean Coll. of Fine Arts, 1965. Acting dean of sch. Todedo Art Mus., 1947-48; chmn. dept. fine arts U. So. Cal., 1948-59; Executive sec. Utah Inst. Fine Arts, 1940-42; sec. Utah Symphony Assn., 1941-42; exec. bd. Los Angeles Mus. Assn., 1950-56; trustee Pasadena Art Mus., 1956-60; bd. dirs., Tex. Fedn. Fine Arts, 1959—; bd. dirs., trustee Nat. Assn. Schs. of Art. Mem. Coll. Art Assn. (dir.), Am. Studies Assn., Sigma Nu. Club: Headliner's. Home: 836 E 37th St Austin TX 78705

GOODALL, ERNEST LORNE, paper co. exec.; b. Ottawa, Ont., Can., Apr. 10, 1901; s. Ernest Lionel and Violetta (Graham) G.; B.Sc., McGill U., 1924; m. Margaret Helen Little, Sept. 19, 1931; children—Marilyn Louise (Mrs. A. N. Chisholm), Margaret Noreen (Mrs. G. Cook), Robert Graham. With Dryden Paper Co. Ltd., Que., 1947—, chmn. bd., 1959—. Mem. bd. govs. Lakehead U., Port Arthur Gen. Hosp. Registered profl. engr., Ont. Mem. Canadian Pulp and Paper Assn., Profl. Engrs. Ont., Engring. Inst. Can. Address: 101 Summit Av Port Arthur Ontario Canada

GOODALL, ROBERT D., chem. co. exec.; b. Phila., May 4, 1912; s. Herbert W. and Ruth (Dorr) G.; ed. Yale, 1936; m. Mary Elizabeth Hopkins, Oct. 15, 1933; children— Pamela Dorr (Mrs. Howard M. Jelleme), Patricia Hancock (Mrs. Eugene Parker), Mary Elizabeth. With Detroit, Toledo & Ironton R. R., 1934-39; with Davison Chem. div. (formerly Davison Chem. Corp.) W.R. Grace & Co., 1939—, gen. sales mgr., 1947-50, asst. to v.p., 1950-55, asst. v.p., 1955-58, v.p., gen. mgr., 1958-63, exec. v.p., 1963-65, pres., Balt., 1965-67, became exec. N.Y.C., 1967, now dir.; pres. Davison Chem. Co., Ltd.; chmn. bd. dirs. Nuclear Fuel Services, Inc; dir. Md. Nat. Bank, G. Ober & Sons Co., H.M. Jelleme Constrn. Co. Chmn. steering com. Indsl. Relations Council, C. of C. of Met. Balt., 1964-; mem. Balt. City Econ. Devel. Commn., 1963-64. Mem. Mfg. Chemists Assn. (bd. dirs.). Home: 1019 Wagner Rd Ruxton MD 21204 Office: 7 Hanover Sq New York City NY 10005

GOODBARY, WILLIAM ALLAN, govt. ofcl.; b. Carney, Okla., July 18, 1915; s. James Russell and Martha Ann (Shoop) G.; B.S., Okla. State U., 1941; postgrad. S.D. State U., 1950-51; m. Dorris Sullivan, July 29, 1941; children—Robert Allan, Joan (Mrs. James M. Gass), Rhonda (Mrs. Larry A. Simpson), Marlyn (Mrs. Michael Curtis), Amelia, Alice. County agrl. agty. Kan. State U., Iola, 1941-49; state extension dairy specialist S.D. State U., Brookings, 1949-52; with AID, State Dept., 1952—, agriculturist Far E. br., Washington, 1961-62, food and agr. officer, Nicosia, Cyprus, 1962-64, Dacca, East Pakistan, 1964-68, dep. food and agr. officer, Lagos, Nigeria, 1968-69, regional food and agr. officer, Mbabane, Swaziland, 1969—. Mem. Am. Dairy Sci. Assn., Am. Jersey Cattle Club. Home: Box 8 Carney OK 74832 Office: Box 199 Mbabane Swaziland

GOODBODY, HAROLD P., business exec.; b. Toledo, 1905; grad Williams Coll., 1927. Sr. partner, former chmn. exec. com. Goodbody & Co., N.Y.C., now mng. partner. Trustee Pingry Sch., Elizabeth, N.J.; mgr. Morristown (N.J.) Hosp. Home: Brooklake Rd Florham Park Madison NJ 07932 Office: 2 Broadway New York City NY 10004

GOODBODY, JOHN COLLETT, publisher; b. Omaha, May 15, 1915; s. Maurice Fitzgerald and Nellie Jane (Collett) G.; grad. Kent Sch., 1933; A.B., Williams Coll., 1937; student Harvard Grad. Sch., 1939-41, 46; m. Harriet Tuthill Linen, Aug. 5, 1939; children—Margaretta (Mrs. Nicholas Niles), David Lister, Joan Tuthill. United Press corr., 1937; reporter Toledo News-Bee, 1938; asso. editor School Exec. mag., 1938; asst. sec. to pres. Williams Coll., 1939; teaching fellow Harvard, 1945-46; staff Colonial Williamsburg, 1946-61, spl. asst. to John D. Rockefeller III, 1949-50, v.p., 1957-61, cons., 1961—; pres. Seabury Press, N.Y.C., 1961—. Communications officer Served to lt. comdr. USNR, 1941-45. Mem. Gargoyle Assn., Chi Psi. Club: St. Andrews. Home: 49 Boulder Trail Bronxville NY 10708 Office: 815 2d Av New York City NY 10017

GOODCHILD, ANTHONY ALBERT, utilities exec.; b. London, Eng., May 11, 1928; s. Albert William and Florence (Greebe) G.; student Emanuel Sch., London, 1939-46; m. Anne Elizabeth Larson, Aug. 13, 1960; children—Christian Elizabeth, Peter Anthony Clay, Matthew Edward. Came to U.S., 1956, naturalized, 1967. Vice pres. operations Elliott Bus. Machines, Inc., Randolph, Mass., 1961-67; group v.p. Transitron Electronic Corp., Wakefield, Mass., 1967-69; pres. Smithcraft Lighting, Inc., Wilmington, Mass., 1969-70; group v.p. Internat. Utilities Corp., Phila., 1970—; chmn., pres., chief exec. officer Walworth Co. (Bala Cynwyd, Pa.); chmn., dir. Divcon, Inc. (Houston), Ireco, Inc. (Eugene, Ore.), Amvit, Inc. (Cleve.); dir. Walworth-Aloyco S.P.A. (Rome, Italy), Internat. Utilities Indsls. of U.S. Served with Brit. Army, 1946-48. Home: 135 Conshohocken State Rd Gladwyne PA 19083 Office: 1500 Walnut St Philadelphia PA 19102

GOODCHILD, CHAUNCEY GEORGE, educator; b. New Castle, Pa., June 18, 1912; s. James Dean and Jane Ellen (McKnight) G.; B.S., Westminster (Pa.) Coll., 1933, Doctor of Laws, 1961; Ph.D., N.Y. U., 1941; m. Hazel Gertrude Fisher, Dec. 6, 1934; children—David George, James Fisher, Susan Jane. Teaching asst. biology Westminster Coll., 1930-33, research asst. phys. chemistry, 1933-34, instr. biology, 1934-36, acting chmn. dept., 1935- 36; grad. teaching asst. N.Y.U., 1936-40, Sandham fellow biology, 1940- 41; instr. biology Coll. City N.Y., 1940-41; asso. prof. biology S.W. Mo. State Coll., Springfield, 1941-45, prof., 1945-52; instr. invertebrate biology Marine Biol. Lab., Woods Hole, Mass., 1943-52; asso. prof. biology Emory U., Atlanta, 1952-55, prof., 1955-60, Charles Howard Chandler prof., 1960—, chmn. dept., 1957-64, mem. NSF coop. fellowship com. at univ., 1958-61. Summer research Marine Biol. Lab., Woods Hole, 1943-52; mem. tng. grant com. NIH, 1957- 60, mem. com. internat. center med. research and tng., 1960-63. Chmn. publicity Easter Seal Drive, Springfield, Mo., 1949-52; bd. dirs. Greene County Soc. Crippled Children and Adults, 1949-52; pres. Springfield Civic Music Assn., 1951-52. Fellow A.A.A.S.; mem. Am. Soc. Zoologists, Am. Soc. Parasitologists, Am. Microscopical Soc., Assn. S.E. Biologists, Corp. Marine Biol. Lab., Am. Soc. Tropical Medicine and Hygiene, Soc. Systematic Zoology (exec. com. 1957-60), Am. Assn. U. Profs. (exec. com. Emory U. 1959-63), Sigma Xi. Kiwanian (dir. Springfield 1951-52). Author: Laboratory Manual of General Zoology, 1958; also research papers. Asst. editor Jour. Parasitology, 1956—, Emory U. Quar., 1959-69. Contbr. Ency. Britannica, Ency. Sci. and Tech. Home: 1000 Clifton Rd NE Atlanta GA 30307

GOODE, HERMAN AVITUS, retired savs. and loan assn. exec.; b. Clementsville, Ky., May 18, 1905; s. William Jerome and Mary (Mays) G.; ed. pub. schs.; m. Margaret Gallagher, Nov. 30, 1929; 1 son, James Bruce. Head teller Mut. Home Bldg. & Loan Assn., Dayton, O., 1927-36; chief teller Home Savs. & Loan Assn., Dayton, 1936-43; exec. v.p., sec. Western Fed. Savs. & Loan Assn., Los

Angeles, 1943-70, now dir. Republican. Club: Los Angeles Optimist. Home: 441 S Baldwin Av Arcadia CA 91006 Office: 600 S Hill St Los Angeles CA 90014

GOODE, JOHN MARTIN, mfg. co. exec.; b. Chgo., Sept. 24, 1934; s. Robert Charles and Alyce (Belz) G.; B.Sc., DePaul U. 1959; M.B.A., U. Chgo., 1966; m. Arlene A. Walendzuk, Oct. 29, 1955; children—John, Sue, Leslie, James. Owner J.M. Goode Maintenance Co., Chgo., 1953-57; accountant firm Shaw, Stout & Tobin, Chgo., 1957-58; asst. controller Gramer, Holdorson Transformer Co., Chgo., 1958-59; mgr. corp. accounting Motorola, Inc., Chgo., 1959-62; controller Erie div. Marathon Electric Co. (Pa.), 1962-63, Sola Electric div. Sola Basic Industries, Milw., 1963-66, Farm Equipment div. Allis-Chalmers Co., Milw., 1966-69; v.p., controller Maremont Corp., Chgo., 1969—; instr. Pa. State U., 1962-63. Bd. dirs. Holy Family Hosp., Des Plaines, Ill., C.P.A., Ill. Mem. Pa. Inst. C.P.A.'s, Ill. Soc. C.P.A.'s, Nat. Assn. Accountants, Financial Execs. Inst., Phi Sigma Phi. Home: 251 W 80th St Clarendon Hills IL 60514 Office: 168 N Michigan Av Chicago IL 60601

GOODE, MACKARNESS HUTCHINS, author; b. Atlanta, Mar. 15, 1913; s. Kenneth Mackarness and Cara (Hutchins) G.; grad. Culver Mil. Acad., 1931; B.A., Wesleyan U., Middletown, Conn., 1935, M.A., 1936; grad. student Harvard, 1939; m. Mary Ellen Mowbray, Sept. 1939 (div. 1955); children—Mackarness Mowbray, Martha Jerolaman; m. 2d, Marjorie B. Scott, June 1961. Tchr. Culver Mil. Acad., 1936-43; sr. exec. Am. Assn. Advt. Agys., 1947-52; mgr. pub. relations, advt. Irving Trust Co., 1952-55; exec. com. Farley Manning Assos., pub. relations agy., N.Y.C., 1955-60; v.p. devel. and pub. relations Wheaton Coll., Norton, Mass., 1960-62; v.p. devel. Cedar Crest Coll., Allentown, Pa., 1962-66; v.p. Acad. Natural Scis. of Phila., 1966-70; dir. devel. New Coll., Sarasota, Fla., 1970-71. Past trustee Wesleyan U. Served with USNR, 1943-45. Mem. Am. Pub. Relations Assn. (dir. N.Y. forge 1958-60), Psi Upsilon (trustee). Clubs: Forest Lakes Country (Sarasota). Author: First Aid for Writers, 1940; also articles on bus. and psychology. Home: 3520 Bayou Louise Lane Sarasota FL 33581

GOODE, RICHARD BENJAMIN, govt. ofcl.; b. Ft. Worth, July 31, 1916; s. Flavius M. and Laura Nell (Carson) G.; A.B., Baylor U., 1937; M.A., U. Ky., 1939; Ph.D., U. Wis., 1947; m. Liesel Gottscho, June 23, 1943. Economist, U.S. Bur. Budget, 1941-45, Treasury Dept., 1945-47; asst. prof. econs. U. Chgo., 1947-51; with IMF, Washington, 1951-59, 65—, dir. fiscal affairs dept., 1965—; mem. staff Brookings Instn., 1959-65; cons. Treasury Dept., 1947- 51, World Bank, 1964. Mem. Am. Econ. Assn., Royal Econ. Soc., Nat. Tax Assn., Am. Finance Assn. Author: The Corporation Income Tax, 1951; The Individual Income Tax, 1964. Editor Nat. Tax Jour., 1948-51. Home: 2939 Van Ness St. NW Washington, DC 20008. Office: Internat Monetary Fund Washington DC 20431

GOODE, WILLIAM JOSIAH, educator; b. Houston, Aug. 30, 1917; s. William J. and Lillian Rosalie (Bare) G.; B.A., U. Tex., 1938, M.A., 1939; Ph.D., Pa. State U., 1946; D.Sc. (hon.), Upsala U., 1970; m. Josephine Mary Cannizzo, Dec. 22, 1938 (div. 1946); children—Brian, Erich, Rachel (dec.), Barbara Nan; m. 2d, Ruth Siegel, Oct. 20, 1950; 1 son, Andrew Josiah. Instr. sociology Pa. State U., 1941-43; social sci. analyst Inter-Am. Statis. Inst., 1943-44; asst. prof. Wayne State U., 1946-50; asso. research dir. Columbia, 1950-52, asso. prof. sociology, 1952-56, prof., 1956—; vis. prof. Free U. Berlin, 1954. U.S. del. UN Conf. Aid to Tech. Undevel. Nations, 1963. Bd. dirs. sec. Social Sci. Research Council; gov., asso. dir. Bur. Applied Social Research; mem. behavioral scis. tng. com. Nat. Inst. Gen. Med. Scis., Nat. Inst. Mental Health, 1966-67. Served with USNR, 1944-45. Guggenheim fellow, 1965-66; recipient MacIver award Am. Sociol Soc., 1965, Burgess award Nat. Council Family Relations, 1969. Mem. Am. (exec. com., council 1959-62, pres. elect 1970-71), Eastern (pres. 1959-60, exec. com. 1959-61) sociol. socs., Am. Civil Liberties Union, Sociol. Research Assn. (exec. council; pres. 1967—). Author: Religion Among the Primitives, 1951; Methods in Social Research, 1952; After Divorce, 1956; Struktur Der Familie; World Revolution and Family Patterns, 1963; The Family, 1964; Family and Society, 1965; Dynamics of Modern Society, 1966. Editor sociol. series, 1953; asso. editor: Marrigae and Family Living, 1956. Contbr. articles profl. jours. Home: 435 W 119th St New York City NY 10027

GOODELL, CHARLES ELLSWORTH, lawyer, former U.S. Senator; b. Jamestown, N.Y., Mar. 16, 1926; s. Charles Ellsworth and Francesca (Bartlett) G.; A.B., Williams Coll., 1948; LL.B., Yale, 1951, M.A. (Ford Found. faculty fellow), 1952; hon. degree Houghton (N.Y.) Coll., Alfred U. (N.Y.), St. Bonaventure U. (N.Y.); m. Jean Rice, Aug. 28, 1954; children—William Rice, Timothy Bartlett, Roger Stokoe, Michael Charles Ellsworth, Jeffrey Harris. Instr., Quinnipiac Coll., New Haven, 1950-51; admitted to N.Y. bar, 1954, Conn. bar, 1951; congl. liaison asst. Dept. Justice, 1954-55; partner law firm Van Vlack, Goodell & McKee, Jamestown, N.Y., 1955-59, Roth, Carlson, Kwit, Spengler & Goodell, N.Y.C., 1971—; mem. 86th-87th Congresses, 43d Dist. N.Y.; mem. 88th-90th Congress, 38th Dist. N.Y., chmn. Planning and Research Com.; U.S. senator from N.Y., 1968-71. Chmn. Republican Com., Chautaugua County, 1958-59. Served as seaman USNR, World War II; 1st lt. USAAF, Korean War. Mem. Jamestown Jr., Jamestown (chmn. govtl. affairs com. 1956-58) chambers commerce, Am., Jamestown bar assns., Phi Beta Kappa, Gamma Sigma Chi. Episcopalian. Clubs: Capitol Hill, 86th Congress (Washington); Chautauqua County Young Republican. Home: 12 Elm Rock Rd Bronxville NY 10708

GOODELL, SOL, lawyer; b. St. Louis, Aug. 24, 1906; s. Abram and Jennie (Silverberg) G.; LL.B., U. Tex., 1929; m. Beatrice Cholden, Feb. 24, 1946; children—Thomas C., Susan Jean. Admitted to Tex. bar, 1929; asso. prof. law U. Tex. Law Sch., 1929-30; asso., then mem. firm Thompson, Knight, Simmons & Bullian, and predecessors, Dallas, 1930—. Dir. Carrier-Bock Co.; asst. sec. Tex. Instruments, Inc. Former chmn. bd. Greenhill Sch., Dallas. Served to capt. AUS, 1942-46. Mem. Am., Dallas bar assns., State Bar Tex., Jewish religion. Clubs: Dallas, Columbian (Dallas). Home: 5927 Joyce Way Dallas TX 75225 Office: Republic Nat Bank Bldg Dallas TX 75201

GOODEN, REGINALD HEBER, bishop; b. Long Beach, Cal., Mar. 22, 1910; s. Robert Burton and Alice Leonard (Moore) G.; A.B., Stanford U., 1931; S.T.B., Berkeley Div. Sch., New Haven, 1934, D.S.T., 1946; student U. Madrid, 1934- 35, Centro de Estudios Historicos, Madrid (Spain), 1934-35; m. Victoria Elena Fernandez de Mendia y Miranda; children—Reginald Heber, Hiram Richard. Ordained to ministry Protestant Episcopal Ch., 1934; hon. asst. chaplain Brit. Embassy Ch., Madrid, 1934-35; priest in charge St. Paul's Ch. and Sch., Camaguey, Cuba, 1935-39; dean Holy Trinity Cathedral, Havana, Cuba, 1939-45; bishop of missionary dist. P.E. Ch. in Panama C.Z., 1945—, also bishop in charge Ecuador, 1956-64. Pres. bd. Colegio Episcopal, Academia de Cristo, Instituto Episcopal. Chmn. bd. dirs., pres. bd. adminstrs. Bella Vista Children's Home, Panama City, C.Z.; mem. com. mgmt. Balboa-Armador Rd. U.S.O.; v.p. bd. trustees Panama Peace Corps, 1967-70. John Henry Watson fellow Berkeley Div. Sch. Mason. Club: The Breakers (Stanford U.). Home: 334 Gorgas Rd Ancon CZ Office: The Bishop's House Box R Balboa CZ

GOODEN, ROBERT BURTON, ret. clergyman, educator; b. Bolton, Eng., Sept. 18, 1874; s. James and Hannah (Burton) G.; came to U.S., 1888; B.A., Trinity Coll., Conn., 1902, M.A., 1904, D.D., 1922; B.D., Berkeley Div. Sch., 1904, D.D., 1931; Dr. Canon Law, Ch. Div. Sch. Pacific, 1966; m. Alice Leonard Moore, Nov. 7, 1904; children—Alice Mary, Carolyn Frances, Robert Burton, Reginald Heber, Muriel Margaret. Ordained deacon P.E. Ch., 1904, priest, 1905; rector St. Paul's Ch., Ventura, Cal., 1904-06, Trinity Ch., Escondido, 1906-07, St. Luke's Ch., Long Beach, 1907-12; headmaster Harvard Sch., 1912, v.p. bd. trustees, 1937-49; pres. Province of Pacific, 1946-50; v.p. bd. trustees Bishop's Sch., LaJolla, Cal.; suffragan bishop of Los Angeles, 1930-47, acting bishop, 1947-48. Sec. standing. com Diocese of Los Angeles, 1910-29, pres. standing com., 1929- 30, exam. chaplain, 1907-30, pres., 1929-30, mem. bd. Christian Edn., Diocese Los Angeles; mem. bd. Episcopal Home for Aged. Elected pres. bd. trustees, hon. life mem. Ch. Div. Sch. of Pacific, Berkeley, 1941; hon. life trustee Bishop's Sch., La Jolla, Cal.; trustee Bishop Gooden Home Alcoholic Men, Pasadena, Cal. Mem. Phi Beta Kappa, Alpha Chi Rho. Democrat. Contbr. P.E. Ch. Congress papers, 1927, P.E. Church press, 1928-. Home: 1629 Santa Maria Av Glendale, CA 91208.

GOODENOUGH, WARD HUNT, anthropologist; b. Cambridge, Mass., May 30, 1919; s. Erwin Ramsdell and Helen Miriam (Lewis) G.; grad. Groton (Mass.) Sch., 1937; A.B., Cornell U., 1940; Ph.D., Yale, 1949; m. Ruth Gallagher, Feb. 8, 1941; children—Hester G. (Mrs. Steven M. Gelber), Deborah L. (Mrs. Paul Gordon), Oliver R., Garrick G. Instr. anthropology U. Wis., 1948-49; mem. faculty U. Pa., 1949—, prof., 1962- -; vis. prof. Cornell U., 1961-62, vis. lectr., summer 1950; vis. lectr. Swarthmore Coll., spring 1955, Bryn Mawr Coll., fall 1955, U. Hawaii, summer 1959; vis. prof. Yale, spring 1969. Anthrop. studies in Truk, 1947, 64-65, Gilbert Islands, 1951, New Guinea, 1951, 54; Pacific Sci. bd. Nat. Acad. Scis.-NRC, 1962-66; standing com. anthropology and social scis. Pacific Sci. Assn., 1962-66; cons. Office Sci. and Tech., 1961-62. Mem. health com. Phila. Dist. Health and Welfare Council, 1963-64. Served with AUS, 1941-45. Mem. Telluride Assn., 1939-54; fellow Center Advanced Study Behavioral Scis., 1957-58. Mem. Royal, Am. (editor 1966-70) anthrop. assns. A.A.A.S. (v.p., chmn. sect. H 1971), Am. Ethnol. Soc. (pres. 1962), Soc. Applied Anthropology (pres. 1963), Linguistics Soc. Am., Am. Oriental Soc., Polynesian Soc., Phi Beta Kappa, Sigma Xi, Phi Kappa Phi. Author: Property, Kin and Community on Truk, 1951; Cooperation in Change, 1963; Explorations in Cultural Anthropology, 1964; Description and Comparison in Cultural Anthropology, 1970. Home: 204 Fox Lane Wallingford, PA 19086. Office: Univ Museum Philadelphia PA 19104

GOODENOW, DONALD IRVING, newspaper editor; b. Berkeley, Cal., Apr. 16, 1920; s. Harold and Mildred (Barcus) G.; student U. Cal. at Los Angeles, 1938-42; m. Grayce Stedman Van Tress, June 30, 1944; children—Guy Donald, Georgi Ann. Mem. editorial dept. Los Angeles Examiner, 1942-62; with Los Angeles Herald-Examiner, 1962—, mng. editor, 1964—. Mem. profl. journalism adv. com. U. Cal. at Los Angeles. Served with AUS, 1942-43. Mem. Am. Soc. Newspaper Editors. Club: Los Angeles Press. Office: 1111 S Broadway Los Angeles CA 90054

GOODFELLOW, ALEXANDER SCOTT, naval officer; b. Seattle, Feb. 15, 1917; s. Alexander Scott and Elizabeth (Shepardson) G.; student U. Wash., 1934-36; B.S., U.S. Naval Acad., 1940; M.S., Mass. Inst. Tech., 1947; m. Barbara Estelle Sorrick, Sept. 11, 1943; children—Alexander Scott, Jane Browning. Commd. ensign USN, 1940, advanced through grades to rear adm., 1966; comdg. officer U.S.S. Frank Knox, 1950-53; staff comdr. Cruisers Destroyers, Pacific Destroyer Div. 112, 1959-60; chief staff Cruiser Destroyer Flotilla 3, 1960-61; comdg. officer U.S.S. Paul Revere, 1961-62, U.S.S. Galveston, 1965-66; comdr. Cruiser Destroyer Flotillas 7 and 9, 1966-67; dep. chief navy material Navy Dept., Washington, 1967-69; comdr. operational test and evaluation force, Norfolk, Va., 1969—. Decorated Legion of Merit, Bronze Star. Mem. Marine Technol. Soc., Soc. Naval Engrs., Am. Ordnance Assn., Phi Delta Theta, Sigma Psi. Republican. Episcopalian. Club: Army-Navy Country (Washington). Home: 433 Dillingham Blvd Norfolk VA 23511 Office: Naval Sta Norfolk VA 23511

GOODFELLOW, JOSEPH WILLIAM, broadcasting co. exec. b. Bklyn., Sept. 24, 1909; s. Wallace W. and Alice (Strong) G.; B.A., St. Lawrence U., 1933; m. Mary Candace Tucker, Mar. 29, 1941; 1 son, Robin Tucker. With U.S. Rubber Co., 1933-43, asst. mgr. govt. sales dept., 1933-43; v.p. Jamestown Broadcasting Co. (N.D.), 1946-48; with NBC, 1949—, dir. sales WRC and WRC-TV, Washington, 1953-59, v.p. NBC, gen. mgr. WRC and WRC-TV, 1960—. Bd. dirs. Washington Better Bus. Bur. Mem. Radio and TV Exec. Soc., Md.-D.C. Broadcasters Assn. (pres.), Washington Broadcasters Club (pres.), Internat. Radio and TV Execs. Soc., Washington Bd. Trade, Washington Advt. Club (dir. 1953- 58), Alpha Tau Omega. Clubs: Broadcasters, Nat. Press., International, Congressional Country (gov.) (Washington). Home: 9129 Redwood Av Bethesda MD 20034 Office: 4001 Nebraska Av NW Washington DC 20016

GOODFELLOW, MILLARD PRESTON, publisher; b. Bklyn., May 22, 1892; s. George and Elizabeth (Dowling) G.; ed., N.Y. U. Sch. Journalism; m. Florence Haeussler, June 29, 1917; children—Alice, Millard Preston. Reporter, Bklyn. Eagle, 1907; successively dist. reporter, ct. reporter, sports writer, telegraph editor, copy reader, city editor and war corr., Bklyn. Times; asst. city editor N.Y. Evening Mail and spl. corr. on Mexican Border, N.Y. Times until 1919; successively circulation dir., advt. mgr. Bklyn. Eagle; asst. pub. N.Y. Am.; pres., pub., trustee Bklyn. Daily Eagle, 1932-38; pres., dir. Bklyn. Pub. Corp., B.D.E. Broadcasting Co., B.D.E. Properties Corp., Tri-County Pub. Corp., 1932-38, also M. P. Goodfellow & Co.; pres. Newspapers, Inc., Overseas Reconstrn. Inc., also pub. Pocatello (Fl.) Tribune. Bd. dirs. Boys Clubs Am. Served as 2d lt., S.C., World War I; col., Army of U.S., General Staff G-2, World War II; dep. dir. OSS, Washington, 1942-46; polit. adviser to comdg. gen., Korea, 1946. Decorated Mexican Border Service and World War I and II medals; hon. officer, mil. div. Most Excellent Order Brit. Empire; chevalier Order Polonia Restituta; officer's cross; comdr. Crown of Italy. Episcopalian. Mason. Clubs: Army and Navy (Washington); Society Old Brooklynites. Home: 2301 Connecticut Av NW Washington DC 20006 Office: 824 Connecticut Av NW Washington DC 20006

GOODFELLOW, THOMAS MACKEY, railroad exec.; b. Altoona, Pa., Oct. 1, 1907; s. Frank Addison and Edith (Mackey) G.; C.E., Cornell U., 1929; LL.D., L.I. U.; m. Dorothy Haak, May 26, 1934. With Pa. R.R. Co., 1924-54, successively apprentice, asst. on engring. corps., asst. supr. track, supr. track, asst. div. engr., Phila. Terminal div., 1944-45, div. engr., Columbus, O., 1945-47, Pitts., 1947-48, asst. supt. freight transp., Pitts., 1948, supt., Delmarva div., 1948-51, Fort Wayne div., 1951-53, Pitts. div., 1953-54; v.p., gen. mgr. L.I. R.R., 1954-56, pres., gen. mgr., 1956-67; pres. Assn. Am. Railroads, 1967-70, chmn., 1970—; dir. Riggs Nat. Bank. Chmn. U.S. Nat. commn. Pan Am. Ry. Congress. Chmn. Golden Spike Centennial Celebration Commn., 1967; chmn. Nat. R.R. Com. on Scouting. Bd. dirs. World Safety Inst., Nat. Capital Area council Boy Scouts Am., YMCA Met. Washington. Mem. Phi Delta Theta. Republican. Presbyn. Mason (Shriner). Home: 4917 Rockwood Pkwy Washington DC 20016 Office: 1920 L St NW Washington DC 20036

GOODFIELD, JUNE, author The Discovery of Time; (with Stephen Toulmin) Fabric of The Heavens: The Development of Astronomy and Dynamics. Address: care Harper & Row 49 E 33d St New York City NY 10016*

GOODFRIEND, ARTHUR, educator; b. N.Y.C., June 21, 1907; s. Samuel and Fannie Goodfriend; student Nat. Acad. Design, 1924; B.Sc., Coll. City N.Y., 1928; m. Edith Del Mar; children—Jill (Mrs. L. Craig Johnston), Arthur II, Bret Meredith. Merchandising dir. Amos Parrish & Co., N.Y.C., 1928- 35; around-the-world rep. Esquire mag., Herald Tribune, 1936-37; advt. dir. Goodall Corp., Sanford, Me., 1938-41; corr. N.Y. Times, Holiday, Life mags., other publs., Latin Am., 1948-49; mem. Joint Commn. on Rural Reconstrn., Canton, China, also Taipei, Formosa, 1949-50; fgn. service officer, New Delhi, India, 1958-60; Fed. Exec. fellow Brookings Instn., 1961-62; cons. for West Africa, USIA, 1963-65; spl. asst. to chancellor East-West Center, Honolulu, 1966-69; asst. to pres. People to People Health Found., (Project HOPE), 1969-70, prof. Am. Studies, New Coll. U. Hawaii, 1970—. Senior del. U.S. delegation to SEATO Conf., Manila, 1967. Served to lt. col., AUS, 1941-46; editor-in- chief Stars and Stripes, Europe, 1944-45, China, 1946. Decorated Legion of Merit, Bronze Star (U.S.); Croix de Guerre. Mem. N.H. Council World Affairs (dir.), Soc. Illustrators, Fgn. Service Assn. Clubs: Cannon, Press, Outrigger Canoe. Author: If You Were Born in Russia, 1952; The Only War We Seek, 1953; What Can a Man Believe?, 1954; What Can a Man Do?, 1955; Something is Missing, 1956; What is America?, 1957; Rice Roots, 1958; Stand Fast in Liberty, 1959; The Twisted Image, 1963; India: A Case Study in Intercultural Communication, 1962; Tomtoms and Transistors, 1966; The Cognoscenti Abroad, 1969; others. Contbr. articles govt. publs. Home: 3787-A Diamond Head Rd Honolulu HI 96816 Office: New College U Hawaii Honolulu HI 96816

GOODHART, ARTHUR LEHMAN, educator; b. N.Y.C., Mar. 1, 1891; s. Philip J. and Hattie (Lehman) G.; B.A., Yale, 1912, M.A., 1914, LL.D., 1948; B.A., LL.B., Cambridge (Eng.) U., 1914, M.A., 1918, LL.M., 1926, LL.D., 1931, D. Litt., 1969; D.C.L., Oxford (Eng.) U., 1931, N.Y.U., 1955; LL.D., Wesleyan U., 1940, U. Edinburgh, 1946, U. Cal., 1952, Queen's U., 1953, Columbia, 1954, London U., 1954, Princeton, 1956, Williams, 1956, Harvard, 1957, Dartmouth, 1957, Dalhousie U., Can., 1958, U. Pa., 1958, Melbourne U., 1959, Tulane, 1960; L.H.D., Cin. U., 1964; m. Cecily Carter, July 2, 1924; 3 sons. Admitted to bar, 1915; asst. corp. counsel, N.Y.C., 1915-17; counsel to Am. Mission to Poland, 1919; barrister at Law, Inner Temple, Eng., 1919; Hon. Bencher, Lincoln's Inn, 1938, King's Counsel, 1943; fellow and lectr. Corpus Christi Coll., Cambridge U., 1919, also sec. to vice chancellor of univ., 1921; vis. prof., Yale, 1929, Harvard Law Sch., 1964, U. Va. Law Sch., 1965, McGill U. Law Sch., 1966; prof. of jurisprudence and fellow Univ. Coll., Oxford U., 1931, master, 1951-63; asso. fellow Jonathan Edwards Coll., Yale, 1933; del. Oxford U. Press, 1942; fellow Nuffield Coll., Oxford, 1944, British Acad., 1952; curator Bodleian Library, 1947, hon. fellow Corpus Christi Coll. Cambridge, 1942, Trinity Coll., 1955, Trinity Hall, 1960; scholar-in-residence N.Y.C. Bar Assn., 1966- 67. Decorated knight comdr. Order Brit. Empire, 1948. Chmn. So. Region Price Regulation Com., 1940-48; mem. Monopolies Commn., 1954-57; mem. Royal Commn. to the Police, 1960—; chmn. Internat. Law Assn.; v.p. Société Internat. de Philosophie du Droit; pres. Internat. Assn. U. Profs., 1948; mem. Soc. Tchrs. Law (pres. 1950), Pedestrians Assn. (pres. since 1950), Am. Law Inst., Phi Beta Kappa, Alpha Delta Phi. Officer d'Academie of France, 1920. Mem. Lord Chancellor's Law Revision Comm., 1937; mem. Co. Law Revision Com., 1944; Alternative Remedies Com., 1945, Supreme Ct. Com., 1947; mem. Scottish Constn. Com., 1969. Clubs: Yale, City (New York); Athenaeum, Oxford and Cambridge (London); Queen's, Savile, University, Century (N.Y.C.). Author: Poland and the Minority Races, 1920; The General Strike, 1927; Essays in Jurisprudence and the Common Law, 1931; Precedent in English and Continental Law, 1934; What Acts of War are Justifiable, 1941; English Contributions to the Philosophy of Law, 1949; Five Jewish Lawyers of the Common Law, 1950; English Law and the Moral Law, 1954. Editor of Cambridge Law Jour., 1921, Law Quarterly Rev., 1926—. Address: University College Oxford, England.

GOODHART, GORDON E., physician, educator and psychiatrist; b. Riverside, Cal., July 12, 1913; s. Eugene Wesley and Sarah Elva (Gordon) G.; A.B., Occidental Coll., 1935; M.D., Stanford, 1943; m. Ruth M. Forrester, Aug. 10, 1941. Intern Los Angeles County Hosp., 1942-43, resident physician internal medicine, 1943-44, 46-48, chief outpatient services, 1948, chief physician tng., 1949-52; instr. medicine, sch. medicine U. So. Cal., 1949-50, asst. clin. prof., 1950-52, asso. prof. medicine, asso. dean sch. medicine, 1952-53, dir. med. extension edn., 1950-53, prof. medicine and dean sch. medicine, 1953-56; resident physician psychiatry, Brentwood N.P. Hospital, VA Center, Los Angeles, 1956-59; pvt. practice psychiatry, 1959—, asst. clin. prof. psychiatry U. Cal. at Los Angeles Sch. Medicine, 1959—; attending staff VA Center, 1959-69, cons., 1969—; psychiat. cons. Los Angeles County Dept. Mental health, Children's Bur. Los Angeles, So. Cal. Permanente Med. Group, T.R.W. Systems. Served as capt. M.C., U.S. Army, 1944-46. Fellow Am. Psychiat. Assn., Am. Acad. Psychoanalysis; mem. Am., Cal. med. assns., So. Cal. Psychiat. Soc. (council 1961-64), So. Cal. Psychoanalytic Inst. and Soc., Los Angeles Med. Soc., Nu Sigma Nu, Phi Gamma Delta. Office: 11665 W Olympic Blvd Los Angeles CA 90064

GOODHART, ROBERT STANLEY, educator; b. Altoona, Pa., July 19, 1909; s. Robert Stanley and Beatrice (Pape) G.; B.S., Lafayette Coll., 1930; M.D., N.Y.U., 1934, D.M.S. (Wyckoff fellow), 1940; Rockefeller Found. fellow, Oxford U., 1938-39; m. Sigrid Ericksen, Nov. 20, 1935; children—Eric Neil, William Haldor. Rotating intern Bklyn. Hosp., 1934-36; resident physician psychiatry Bellevue Hosp., N.Y.C., 1936-38, asst. clin. vis. physician, 1938-41, asst. vis. physician, 1941; asst. to dean N.Y.U. Coll. Medicine, 1939-40, asst. prof. medicine, 1942-47; research fellow Milbank Meml. Fund, 1941-42; sci. dir. Nat. Vitamin Found., 1946-67, pres. 1962-67; physician-in- charge Washington Heights Nutrition Clinic, N.Y.C. Dept. Health, 1948-67; lectr. pub. health, adminstrv. medicine Columbia, 1950—; adj. prof. community medicine Mt. Sinai Med. Sch., 1969—. Mem. com. nutrition in industry NRC, 1941-49, vice chmn., 1942-46, chmn., 1946-49, mem. food and nutrition bd., 1946-50; chmn. food com. welfare emergency div. N.Y.C. Dept. Welfare, 1950—; vice chmn. nutrition div. Health Council Greater N.Y., 1951-52; chmn. nutrition div. Welfare and Health Council, N.Y.C., 1953-55; pres. Food and Nutrition Council Greater N.Y., 1958-60; mem. subcom. on nutrition, adv. bd. com. on foods, Q.M. Research and Devel., Nat. Acad. Scis.-NRC, 1954-56, com. nutrition, 1960-63. Served from asst. surgeon to surgeon, USPHS, 1942- 46. Diplomate human nutrition Am. Bd. Nutrition. Fellow N.Y. Acad. Medicine (exec. sec. com. on med. education 1967—), N.Y. Acad. Scis., Gerontological Soc., Am. Pub. Health Assn.; mem. A.M.A., N.Y. County, N.Y. State med. socs., Am. Soc. Clin. Investigation, Am. Inst. Nutrition, Am. Soc. Clin. Nutrition, Harvey Soc., N.Y. Diabetes Assn. (dir. 1953—, chmn. com. on research 1953-55).

Author: Nutrition for You, 1958; The Teen-Ager's Guide to Diet and Health, 1964. Co-author: Manual of Clinical Nutrition, 1964. Editor: Modern Drugs and Modern Drug Ency., 1960-68. Co-editor: Modern Nutrition in Health and Disease 5 edits. Home: 67 Forest Rd Tenafly NJ 07670 Office: 2 E 103d St New York City NY 10029

GOODHARTZ, ABRAHAM SAMUEL, former coll. dean; b. Bklyn., Oct. 14, 1910; s. Jacob and Ida (Dudowitz) G.; A.B., Coll. City N.Y., 1932; M.A., Columbia, 1939; Ph.D., N.Y.U., 1951; m. Zena Frank, Dec. 29, 1934; children—Natalie Ruth, Dorothy Ann, Sima Beth. Tchr. English, Townsend Harris High Sch., N.Y.C., 1933-37; faculty Bklyn. Coll., 1938—, dean studies, 1960-71, emeritus, 1971, dir. div. grad. studies, 1960-63; vis. prof. higher edn. N.Y.U., 1953-61. Bd. dirs. Pride of Judea Children's Services, 1964—; exec. com. Nat. Hillel Commn., 1966—. Recipient Gold Service award Hillel Found., 1958. Mem. Modern Lang. Assn., Am. Assn. U. Profs., Kappa Delta Pi. Contbr. profl. jours. Editor: A Commitment to Youth, 1960. Home: 711 Montauk Ct Brooklyn NY 11235

GOODHEART, CLYDE RAYMOND, virologist; b. Erie, Pa., June 9, 1931; s. Edmund James and Helen (Husted) G.; B.S., Northwestern U., 1953, M.S., 1957, M.D., 1957; m. Barbara Jean Peterson, Dec. 26, 1953; children—Kenneth James, Karen Jean, Diane Louise. Research fellow Cal. Inst. Tech., 1958-61; asst. prof. pediatrics, then asso. prof. Childrens Hosp., Los Angeles, 1961-65; asso. mem., then mem. Inst. Biomed. Research, Edn. and Research Found., A.M.A., 1965-70; sr. microbiologist Rush-Presbyn.-St. Luke's Med. Center, Chgo., 1970—; tchr. microbiology U. Cal. at Los Angeles, 1961-64. Mem. Am., Ill. socs. microbiologists, A.A.A.S., N.Y. Acad. Scis., Biophysical Soc., Am. Soc. for Cell Biology, Phi Beta Kappa, Sigma Xi, Phi Rho Sigma. Author: An Introduction to Virology, 1969; papers in field. Home: 15 Sheffield Ct Lincolnshire Deerfield, IL 60015. Office: Growth Scis Center Hwy 45 at Winchester Rd Libertyville IL 60048

GOODIER, JOHN J., banker. Trust officer Bank of Del. Office: Bank of Del 300 Delaware Av Wilmington DE 19899*

GOODING, ROBERT CARPENTER, naval officer; b. New Orleans, June 27, 1918; s. Robert Fleming and Frances (Carruth) G.; B.S., U.S. Naval Acad., 1941; M.S., Mass. Inst. Tech., 1946; m. Joyce Waller, July 30, 1942; 1 son, Robert Fleming. Commd. ensign USN, 1941, advanced through grades to rear adm., 1969; mem. staff MINPAC maintenance and logistics, 1955-57; staff CTG 7.3, tech. dir., 1957-58; shipbuilding and repair supt. N.Y. Naval Shipyard, 1958-62; head navigation br. SPO, 1962-64, dep. tech. dir., 1964-65, tech. dir., 1965-68; comdr. Boston Naval Shipyard, 1968-69; vice comdr. NAVSHIPS, Dept. Navy, Washington, 1969—. Decorated Legion of Merit; recipient Parsons award Navy League, 1968. Mem. Soc. Naval Architects and Marine Engrs., Am. Soc. Naval Engrs., Sigma Xi. Contbr. articles profl. jours. Home: 1305 Trinity Dr Alexandria VA 22314 Office: Dept Navy Washington DC 20360

GOODKIND, LOUIS WILLIAM, lawyer; b. St. Paul, Aug. 29, 1914; s. Leo and Grace (Goldsmith) G.; B.A., Yale, 1936, LL.B., 1939; m. Jean Wald Morgenthau, Apr. 8, 1942; children—Barbara (Mrs. Jeffrey G. Pepper), Mary, Kathryn. Admitted to N.Y. bar, 1939, D.C. bar, 1951; pvt. practice, N.Y.C., 1939-40; asst. U.S. atty. So. Dist. N.Y., 1940-43; with CAB, Washington, 1943-52, sr. atty., 1943-46, asso. dir. Bur. Econ. Regulation, 1946-51, dep. dir. Bur. Air Operations, 1951-52; chief econ. def. div. Dept. State, Washington, 1952-56; partner Geenman, Zimet, Haines & Goodkind and predecessor firms, 1956—. Guest lectr. air transp. Am. U., 1946-51; apptd. acting village justice, Irvington, N.Y., 1971. Mem. U.S. delegations 3d Session Facilitation div. Internat. Civil Aviation Orgn., Buenos Aires, 1951, Consultative Group, Paris, 1953, Four Power Fgn. Ministers Meeting, Geneva, 1955. Mem. Alumni Bd. Yale. Mem. Village Democratic Com., Irvington, 1964-71; mem. Town Dem. Com., Greenburgh, N.Y.; County Dem. Com., Westchester, N.Y.; Past pres., trustee Green Acres Sch., Bethesda, Md.; sec., bd. dirs. Martha Graham Center Contemporary Dance; mem. corp. Neighborhood Playhouse Sch. of Theatre, N.Y.C. Mem. Assn. Bar City N.Y., Phi Beta Kappa, Phi Delta Phi. Clubs: Yale (N.Y.C.), National Aviation (Washington). Home: Harriman Rd Ivington NY 10533 Office: 1 New York Plaza New York City NY 10004

GOODKIND, RICHARD IRWIN, brokerage exec.; b. N.Y.C., Mar. 7, 1927; s. David A. and Ruth (Goldstone) G.; grad. Choate Sch., 1944; B.S., Northwestern U., 1949; m. Judith Kramer, Aug. 31, 1952; children—Richard Douglas, Jeffrey David, Lawrence Craig. With Ringwood Iron Mines, Inc., 1952-54; asst. to sr. exec. v.p. Merritt-Chapman & Scott Corp., 1955-57, 58-62; exec. v.p., dir. Tenn. Products & Chem. Corp., Nashville, 1962-63; dir. Tenn- Tex Alloy & Chem. Corp., Houston, 1963-65; partner Richard I. Goodkind Assos., mergers, acquisitions, N.Y.C., 1966—; pres. Goodkind & Co., Inc., mems. N.Y. and Am. stock exchanges. Conducted seminars Am. Mgmt. Assn. Mem. Mfg. Chemists Assn., Phi Epsilon Pi. Address: 711 Fifth Av New York City NY 10022

GOODLAD, JOHN INKSTER, educator; b. N. Vancouver, B.C., Can., Aug. 19, 1920; s. William James and Mary (Inkster) G.; teaching certificate Vancouver Normal Sch., 1939; B.A., U. B.C., 1945, M.A., 1946; Ph.D., U. Chgo., 1949; L.H.D., Nat. Coll. Edn., 1967, U. Louisville, 1968; m. Evalene M. Pearson, Aug. 23, 1945; children—Stephen John, Mary Paula. Tchr., Surrey Schs., B.C., 1939-41, prin., 1941-42; dir. edn. Provincial Sch. For Boys, B.C., 1942-46; cons. curriculum Atlanta Area Tchr. Edn. Service, 1947-49; asso. prof. Emory U., 1949-50, prof., dir. div. tchr. edn. Agnes Scott Coll. and Emory U., 1950-56; prof., dir. U. Chgo. Center Tchr. Edn., 1956-60; prof., dir. U. Elementary Sch. U. Cal., Los Angeles, 1960-, dean Grad. Sch. Edn., 1967- -. Chmn., Council on Coop. Tchr. Edn. Am. Council Edn., 1959-62; dir. research and devel. div. Inst. for Devel. of Ednl. Activities, 1966—. Fellow Internat. Inst. Arts and Letters; mem. Nat. Acad. Edn. (charter), Am. Ednl. Research Assn. (past pres.), A.A.A.S., Nat. Soc. Coll. Tchrs. Edn. (past pres.), Nat. Soc. For Study Edn. (dir.). Author: (with others) The Elementary School, 1956; Educational Leadership and the Elementary School Principal, 1956; Computers and Information Systems in Education, 1966; Behind the Classroom Door, 1970; (with Robert H. Anderson) The Nongraded Elementary School, 1959, rev., 1963; Planning and Organizing for Teaching, 1963; School Curriculum Reform, 1964; The Changing School Curriculum, 1966; School, Curriculum and the Individual, 1966. Author, editor: The Changing American School, 1966. Bd. editors Sch. Rev., 1956- 58, Jour. Tchr. Edn., 1958-60; contbg. editor Progressive Edn., 1955-58; mem. editorial adv. bd. Child's World, 1952-; chmn. editorial adv. bd. New Standard Ency., 1953-; chmn. ednl. adv. bd. Ency. Brit. Ednl. Corp., 1966-69. Contbr. chpts. to books, articles to profl. jours. Office: 1100 Glendon Av Los Angeles CA 90024 also U Cal Los Angeles CA 90024

GOODLING, GEORGE A., congressman; b. Loganville, Pa., Sept. 26, 1896; grad. Pa. State U.; 6 children. Fruit grower; dir. Peoples Bank of Glen Rock, White Rose Motor Club, Stewartstown Mut. Ins. Co.; mem. Pa. Ho. of Reps. 14 yrs.; mem. 87th-88th, 90-92d Congresses, 19th Dist. Pa. Exec. sec. Pa. Hort. Assn. Mem. Civil War Centennial Commn. Mem. Am. Legion, Pa. Farmers Assn., Grange, Gamma Sigma Delta. Republican. Mason (33), Elk. Address: Loganville PA 17342

GOODLOE, JOHN DUNCAN, III, lawyer, beverage co. exec.; b. Richmond, Ky., June 10, 1908; s. John Duncan and Anne (Ellison) G.; A.B., U. Ky., 1928; LL.B., Harvard, 1931; m. Helen Louise Hylton, Mar. 24, 1934 (div. 1952); children—John Duncan IV, Peter Hylton, Susan; m. 2d, Teresa G. Paulk, Oct. 4, 1954. News reporter Richmond (Ky.) Daily Register, 1924-26; asst. mgr. Lexington office of Louisville Courier Jour., 1926-27; city staff Lexington (Ky.) Herald, 1927-29; admitted to Ky. bar, 1931; atty. Fed. Farm Bd., Washington, 1931-32; atty. RFC, Washington, 1932-33; counsel Farm Credit Adminstrn., Washington, 1933-34; v.p., gen. counsel Commodity Credit Corp., Washington, 1934-40; v.p. Def. Supplies Corp., Washington, 1940-41; exec. asst. to chmn. RFC, 1941-43, gen. counsel, 1943-46, apptd. dir. RFC, 1946, chmn. bd. dirs., 1947; sec. Coca-Cola Co., Atlanta, 1948—, gen. counsel, 1955-69, v.p., corporate counsel, 1969—. Democrat. Mem. Brethren in Christ Ch. Home: 324 Pineland Rd NW Atlanta GA 30342 Office: 310 North Av Atlanta GA 30305

GOODLOE, ROBERT DOUGLAS, baritone; b. St. Petersburg, Fla., Oct. 5, 1936; s. Emerson Douglas and Mary (Gilmore) G.; B.S. in Journalism, Northwestern U., 1958, M.S., 1959; pupil of Harvey Brown, David Nott and Robert Larsen. Dir. publs. Simpson Coll., Indianola, Ia., 1961-64; appeared in operatic roles at Simpson Coll., Des Moines Civic Opera, also mus. comedy Kansas City (Mo.) Starlight Theatre; soloist Mpls. Symphony, 1964, Tulsa Philharmonic, 1966; winner Met. Opera Nat. Auditions, 1964, mem. co., 1964—; other appearances include Chatauqua Opera Assn., summer 1965, Chatauqua Music Festival, summer, 1966, Lake George Opera, summers 1966-69; appeared with San Francisco Opera, 1969. Mem. Sigma Alpha Epsilon. Home: 170 West End Av New York City, NY 10023. Office: Metropolitan Opera Lincoln Center New York City NY 10023

GOODMAN, ANDREW, business exec.; b. N.Y.C., Feb. 13, 1907; s. Edwin and Belle Dorothy (Lowenstein) G.; student U. Mich., 1924-26; m. Consuelo Manach, Sept. 29, 1935; children—Vivien, Mary Ann, Edwin Andrew, Pamela. With Bergdorf Goodman, 1926—, pres., 1951—, also dir.; pres. 754 Fifth Av. Inc., N.Y.C., 1953—, Fur Corp., Bergdorf Goodman Fur Corp.; dir. Guardian Life Ins. Co., H.M. Rayne, Ltd.; trustee Central Savs. Bank; mem. adv. bd. Mfrs. Hanover Trust Co. Dir. Fifth Av. Assn.; pres. Uptown Retail Guild; trustee Fashion Inst. Tech. Trustee-at-large Fedn. Jewish Philanthropies; chmn. retail stores exec. div. United Jewish Appeal; v.p. Am. Jewish Com.; bd. dirs. Better Bus. Bur., N.Y.C.; chmn. bd. Nat. Jewish Hosp., Denver. Served as lt., USN, 1944-46. Recipient Tobe award, 1960; Star of Solidarity (Italy). Club: Westchester Country (Rye). Home: Hilltop Pl Rye NY 10580 Office: 754 Fifth Av New York City NY 10019

GOODMAN, B. KENNETH, bus. exec.; b. Ohio, 1911; grad. U. Cal. at Los Angeles, 1932, U. Cal. Law Sch., 1935. Sec., gen. counsel Ryan Aero. Co., Continental Motors Corp., Continental Aviation & Engring. Corp., Wis. Motor Corp. Home: 13143 Ha Hana Rd Lakeside CA 92040 Office: Lindbergh Field San Diego CA 92135*

GOODMAN, BENJAMIN, lawyer; b. Memphis, Jan. 18, 1904; s. Ben and Leah A. (Hirsch) G.; A.B., Princeton, 1924; LL.B., Harvard, 1927. Admitted to Tenn. bar, 1926, since practiced in Memphis; mem. Armstrong, Allen, Braden, Goodman, McBride and Prewitt, 1932—. Gov. A.R.C., 1955-61, chmn. com. resolutions, 1954; pres. Memphis Acad. of Arts, 1955-59; mem. Tenn. Law Revision Commn., 1963-69 chmn. Memphis Arts and Sci. Commn., 1970—. Served from capt. to lt. col., USAAF, 1942-46. Mem. Am., Tenn., Memphis, Shelby County bar assns., Am. Judicature Soc. Home: 115 S. Rose Rd Memphis, TN 38117. Office: Commerce Title Bldg Memphis TN 38103

GOODMAN, BENNY, orchestra condr., clarinetist; b. Chgo., May 30, 1909; student Lewis Inst., Chgo.; studied clarinet with Franz Schoepp of Chgo. Symphony Orch.; m. Alice Hammond Duckworth, Mar. 1942; children—Rachel, Benjie. Began in orchestra Lake Mich. excursion boats; played in theatre orchestras in N.Y.C.; organized own orchestra, 1933; began popular Let's Dance radio program, 1934. Has conducted swing concerts at Carnegie Hall (N.Y.C.), Symphony Hall (Boston), Ravinia (Ill.) Park, Hollywood Bowl; clarinet soloist with Budapest String Quartet, N.Y. Philharmonic Symphony, Phila. Symphony, Rochester Symphony, and others; also concerts with various artists; radio programs including Camel Caravan, 1937-40, Old Gold, 1941; appeared in motion pictures, Big Broadcast of 1938, Hollywood Hotel; commentator on serious music WNEW; TV show Star Time; recorded for Columbia, Capitol and RCA Victor records; life story filmed, The Benny Goodman Story, 1956; reformed big band 1955 for engagements U.S. and abroad; organized new band 1958 Brussels World's Fair, toured Europe, 1959; appeared with London Philharmonic, 1961; State Dept. Cultural Exchange Program tour of Russia, 1962. Winner Internat. Jazz Critics Poll (clarinet); Apollo award, 1956. Mus. good-will ambassador on tour Far East, under auspices of Dept. of State and ANTA exchange program. Author: Kingdom of Swing (with Irving Kolodin). Known as the King of Swing. Address: 200 E 66th St New York City NY 10021

GOODMAN, BERNARD, educator; b. Phila., June 14, 1923; s. Louis and Fannie (Solomon) G.; A.B., U. Pa., 1943, Ph.D., 1955; m. Joyce Janet Willoughby, Mar. 3, 1950; children—David Nathan, Jonathan Bernard, Mark William. Stress analyst Internat. Harvester Co., Chgo., 1947-52; research asso. U. Mo., 1952, asst. prof., 1952-58, asso. prof., 1958-64, prof., 1964; prof. U. Cin., 1965—. Vis. scientist Argonne Nat. Lab., 1956-57, 61-62, 65-66, 70, Brookhaven Lab., 1960, Bell Telephone Lab., Murray Hill, N.J., 1967, Ohio U., 1969; vis. prof. Inst. Theoretical Physics, Uppsala, Sweden, 1962-63, Inst. Theoretical Physics, Gothenberg, Sweden, 1971-72. Guggenheim fellow, 1962-63. Fellow Am. Phys. Soc.; mem. A.A.A.S., Phi Beta Kappa, Sigma Xi. Home: 3411 Cornell Pl Cincinnati OH 45220

GOODMAN, BERNARD MAURICE, educator, musician; b. Cleve., June 12, 1914; s. Tobias and Ida (Josephs) G.; student Cleve. Inst. Music, 1932-35; B.S., Western Res. U., 1935; m. Margaret Ann Carfray, Sept. 1, 1937; children—Tobias William, Carl Jonathan. Tchr. instrumental music pub. schs., Cleve., 1935- 36; violinist Cleve. Orch., 1936-46; asst. prof. music, artist in residence Cornell U., 1946-47; prof. music, artist in residence U. Ill., 1947—; music dir., conductor U. Ill. Symphony Orch., 1950—, Champaign- Urbana Civic Symphony Orch., 1960—, Bloomington-Normal Symphony Orch., 1971—; mem. Walden String Quartet, 1934—. Mem. Internat. Cultural Exchange Program tour Western Europe with Walden String Quartet, summer 1949; mus. dir., conductor Internat. Cultural Exchange Program Tour Central and South Am. with U. Ill. Symphony Orch., 1964. Kulas Found. fellow advanced study, 1960. Mem. Phi Mu Alpha. Home: 412 W Nevada St Urbana IL 61801

GOODMAN, BERTRAM, painter; b. N.Y.C., Sept. 21, 1904; s. Saul and Rose (Cohen) G.; student Sch. Am. Sculpture, 1923-24, Art Students League, 1925; m. Marie Caputa, Aug. 18, 1928. Exhbns. include: Am. Watercolor Soc., Pa. Acad. Fine Arts, Bklyn. Mus., Art Inst. Chgo., Mus. Modern Art, Whitney Mus. Am. Art, Balt. Mus. Art, Okla. Art Center, Carnegie Art Inst., Fine Arts Gallery San Diego, Met. Mus. Art, Albany Inst. History and Art, Nat. Acad. Fine Arts, Phila. Art Alliance, Soc. Graphic Arts, Am. Soc. Etchers, N.A.D., Art Inst. and Sch. of Design, Kansas City, Mo., City Art Mus., St. Louis, Mus. New Mexico; one man exhbns. include: Butler Art Inst., Youngstown, O., Hudson Park Library, N.Y.C., The Research Studio, Maitland, Fla., Delgado Mus.; work in permanent collections of Bklyn. Mus., Library of Congress, Abbott Labs., Chgo., Butler (O.) Art Inst., Tenn. Wesleyan Coll., Norfolk (Va.) Mus., N.Y. Pub. Library Print Collection, Abraham Lincoln High Sch. Collection, N.Y.C., Mus. City N.Y.; work in lithography in Met. Museum, also pvt. collections. Dir. Village Art Center, N.Y.C.; has served on juries of Tiffany Awards, Bklyn. Soc. Artists (pres.), Nat. Assn. Women Artists. Recipient First Prize in watercolor Screen Publicists Guild, 1946; Purchase Prize, Abraham Lincoln Gallery, 1947; Jo and Emily Lowe prize (oil painting), 1956; awarded one man show, Emily Lowe Award Gallery, N.Y.C., 1956. Mem. Artists Equity Assn. (dir. 1955-56), Bklyn. Soc. Artists, Am. Soc. Graphic Artists (governing council). Club: Print (Phila.). Home and studio: 299 W 12th St New York City, NY 10014.

GOODMAN, CHARLES MORTON, architect; b. N.Y.C., Nov. 26, 1906; s. Harris and Jennie (Blomsten) G.; student U. Ill., 1925-28; B.S., Armour Inst. Tech., 1934; m. Charlotte K. Dodge, June 30, 1934; 1 dau., Lynn Lelah. Designing architect Treasury Dept., Washington, 1934-37; designer Washington Nat. Airport, Fed. Bldg., New Orleans, U.S. Govt. Group, N.Y. World's Fair; pvt. practice architecture, 1937—; head architect Air Transport Command, 1942-45; architect Am. U., Washington, 1946-50, Hollin Hills Community, Alexandria, Va., 1948-68, Officers' Club, Andrews AFB, Washington, Shopping Center, Lafayette, Ind.; cons. architect Nat. Homes Corp., Reynolds Metals Co., Tecfab Corp. Mem. tech. services adv. com., bldg. research adv. bd. Nat. Acad. Scis., 1958-60. Recipient biennial archtl. award Washington Bd. Trade, 1944, 48, 50, 55, 57, 64, 66, 69; Architect of the Year award Southwest Research Inst., 1951. Fellow A.I.A.; mem. Mus. Primitive Art N.Y., Assn. Engrs. and Architects in Israel, Am. Hort. Soc., Am. Craftsman's Council, Nat. Wildlife Fedn., Am. Forestry Assn., Nat. Council Archtl. Registration Bds., Washington Bd. Trade. Home: 514 N Quaker Lane Alexandria VA 22304 Office: 814 18th St NW Washington DC 20006

GOODMAN, CLARK DROUILLARD, nuclear physicist; b. Memphis, Sept. 9, 1909; s. J. Alma and Naomi (Clark) G.; B.S., Cal. Inst. Tech., 1932; Ph.D., Mass. Inst. Tech., 1940; m. Mary Ellen Hohiesel, Aug. 8, 1933 (dec. 1969); children—Gaye Ellen, Alan Clark; m. 2d, Deni O. Seinfeld, Jan. 12, 1970. Tech. aide div. 16 and 17, OSRD, 1942-45; sr. physicist Oak Ridge Nat. Lab., 1945-46; asso. prof. physics Mass. Inst. Tech., 1947-58; asst. dir. div. reactor devel. AEC, Washington, 1955-58; v.p. technique Schlumberger Ltd., Houston, 1958-62; v.p., tech. dir. Houston Research Inst., 1962-69; prof. physics U. Houston, 1963—, chmn. physics dept., 1966-68. Dir. Simmonds Precision Products, Inc. Sec. com. radio-activity NRC, 1939-47. Cons. Joint Congl. Com. Atomic Energy, 1961-62; mem. NASA Lunar and Planetary Missions Board; AEC Licensing and Regulations Panel. Fellow Am. Phys. Soc., Geol. Soc. Am.; mem. Nat. Acad. Sci. (chmn. com. radioactive waste disposal), Sigma Xi, Tau Beta Pi. Clubs: Warwick (Houston); Cosmos (Washington). Author: Science and Engineering of Nuclear Power, vols. I and II, 1947, 48; Introduction to Nuclear Power, 1955; Atomic Energy (in Japanese), 1957. Home: 8202 Broadway Houston TX 77017 Office: Univ Houston Houston TX 77004

GOODMAN, CONRAD EDWARD, greeting card co. exec., b. Kansas City, Mo., Nov. 14, 1912; s. Charles Edward and Marie (Hettenkemmer) G.; m. Marianna Blucher, Sept. 28, 1935; children—William Edward, Gail (Mrs. Thomas M. Johnston), Gary Conrad. With Hallmark Cards, Inc., 1929—, 1952-55, became exec. v.p., 1955, now chmn. exec. com., also dir. chmn. exec. com., pres. Hallmark Internat., 1966-; dir. Assns. Investment Fund, Inc. Bd. dirs. Hallmark Found.; mem. adv. bd. Kan. U. Sch. Bus.; trustee Childrens Mercy Hosp., Kansas City Gen. Hosp. and Med. Center, Kansas City Mental Health Found., Inst. Community Studies. Home: 6311 Norwood Rd Shawnee Mission, KS 66208. Office: Hallmark Cards Inc 25th and McGee St Kansas City MO 64141

GOODMAN, DAVID, author; b. N.Y.C., Sept. 14, 1894; s. Herman and Cecelia (Edelman) G.; A.B. (Pulitzer scholar), Columbia, 1917, A.M., 1918, Ed.D., 1951; m. Malvina Peterson, Dec. 8, 1924; children—Lawrence, Eric. Prin., Rhodes Prep. Sch., N.Y.C., 1929-55; columnist nat. syndicated column Marriage, Children and You with Bell Syndicate, N.Y.C., 1952—; profl. marriage counselor, 1970—. Mem. adv. council Parents Without Partners. Mem. Am. Assn. Marriage Counselors, Soc. for Sci. Study of Sex. Author: A Parent's Guide to the Emotional Needs of Children, 1959; Guidelines for a Healthy Marriage, 1967; What's Best For Your Child and You, 1966; Living From Within, 1968. Contbr. articles profl. jours. Address: 755 Pomander Walk Teaneck NJ 07666

GOODMAN, DONALD C., educator; b. Chgo. Nov. 24, 1927; s. Alexander Goodman and Freda (Mermelstein) G.; B.S., U. Ill., 1949, M.S., 1950, Ph.D., 1954; m. Martha Huggins, July 3, 1968; children—Brian and Eric (twins), Michael and Susan (twins), Elaine Alison; stepchildren—Bruce, Adam, Mitchell. Instr., U. Pa., 1954-56; mem. faculty U. Fla., 1956-68, prof., 1963-68, chmn. dept. anatomical scis., 1965-68, co-dir. Center Neurol. Sci., 1964-68; prof. anatomy, chmn. dept. State U. N.Y. Med. Center, Syracuse, 1968—. Mem. study sect. NIH. Served with AUS, 1946-48. Recipient Annual Research award Fla. chpt. Sigma Xi. Mem. Am. Assn. Anatomists, So. Soc. Anatomists, A.A.A.S., Am. Inst. Biol. Scientists, Sigma Xi. Author books and articles. Editor: Brain, Behavior and Evolution. Home: 5230 Wethersfield Rd Jamesville, NY 13078.

GOODMAN, EDWARD, dept. store exec.; b. N.Y.C., June 14, 1922; s. Abraham and Bertha (Kalchem) G.; student Polytechnic Prep. Country Day Sch., Bklyn., 1937-39; B.A., U.N.C., 1946; m. Barbara Penn, Oct. 6, 1946; children—John, William, Katherine. With Abraham & Straus, 1946—, pres., 1970—. Served with USMCR, 1942-45. Home: 1315 Club Dr Hewlett Harbor NY 11557 Office: 420 Fulton St Brooklyn NY 11201

GOODMAN, GEORGE JEROME WALDO, author, editor, communications exec.; b. St. Louis, Aug. 10, 1930; s. Alexander Mark and Viola (Cremer) G.; A.B. magna cum laude, Harvard, 1952; Rhodes scholar, Oxford (Eng.) U., 1954; m. Sallie Cullen Brophy, Oct. 6, 1961; children—Alexander Mark, Susannah Blake. Reporter, N.Y. Herald Tribune, 1952-54, Collier's mag., 1956, Barron's, 1957; contbg. editor, assc. editor Time and Fortune mags., 1958-60; portfolio mgr., v.p. Lincoln Fund, 1960-62; screenwriter, Los Angeles, 1962-65; co- founder New York mag., 1967, contbg. editor, v.p., 1967-; 1st editor Instl. Investor and Corporate Financing (formerly Investment Banking) mags., 1967—; exec. v.p., dir. Instl. Investor Systems 1969—; occasional lectr. Harvard Bus. Sch. Trustee Glassboro (N.J.) State Coll., 1967-, co-chmn. presdl. selection com., 1968; mem. adv. council econs. dept. Princeton, 1970—. Served with AUS, 1954-56. Recipient G.M. Loeb award for distinguished achievement in writing about bus. and finance U. Conn., 1969. Mem. Writers Guild Am. (West). Clubs: Harvard, Century (N.Y.C.) Author: (novel) The Bubble Makers, 1955; (novel) A Time for Paris, 1957; (novel) Bascombe, The Fastest Hound Alive, 1958; (novel) The

Wheeler Dealers, 1959; (pseudonym Adam Smith) The Money Game, 1968; (with Winthrop Knowlton) A Killing in the Market, 1958; also articles. Office: 140 Cedar St New York City NY 10006

GOODMAN, GEORGE JONES, educator, botanist; b. Evanston, Wyo., Nov. 5, 1904; s. Arthur Duane and Mary Elizabeth (Jones) G.; A.B., U. Wyo., 1926-29; M.S., Washington U., St. Louis, 1930, Ph.D., 1933; m. Marcia McCay, Dec. 19, 1948. Mem. faculty U. Okla., Norman, 1933-36, prof. botany, curator Herbarium, 1945—, curator botany Mus., 1945—, Regents prof. botany, head curator dept. botany and microbiology Stovall Mus., 1967—; mem. faculty Ia. State Coll., 1936-45, asso. prof., 1944-45; plant taxonomist Okla. Biol. Survey, 1950—. Mem. A.A.A.S., Am. Assn. U. Profs., Am. Fern Soc., Am. Soc. Plant Taxonomists, Bot. Soc. Am., Cal. Bot. Soc., New Eng. Bot. Club, Internat. Assn. Plant Taxonomists, Soc. Study Evolution, Torrey Bot. Club, Southwestern Assn. Naturalists (past pres.), Colo.-Wyo. Acad. Sci., Ia. Acad. Sci., Okla. Acad. Sci. (past pres.), Phi Beta Kappa, Sigma Xi, Phi Kappa Phi, Phi Sigma. Author: Spring Flora of Central Oklahoma, 1958; also numerous articles. Research on flora Okla.; taxonomic revisional work in flowering plants N.Am. Home: 1229 Avondale Dr Norman OK 73069

GOODMAN, HENRY ATLAS, orgn. exec.; b. Chattanooga, Sept. 3, 1924; s. Jay S. and Hazel L. (Atlas) G.; A.B., U. Chgo., 1944, A.M., 1950; m. Sigrid Urbich, Mar. 21, 1953; children—Davis Paul, Eleanore Blanche. Mem. staff Chattanooga Times, 1948-50; pub. relations Office U.S. High Commr. for Germany, 1951-53; research asso. Council State Govts., Chgo., 1953; staff Courier-Jour., Louisville, 1954-56; sci. and health editor Louisville Times, 1957-58; bd. editors Sci. Am., N.Y.C., 1959-64; exec. sec. Council Advancement Sci. Writing, 1964-. Advanced Sci. Writing fellow Columbia, 1958-59; cons.-editor in field; lectr. Bklyn. Coll., 1970. Mem. Nat. Assn. Sci. Writers. Address: 201 Christie St Leonia NJ 07605

GOODMAN, HENRY MAURICE, educator, physiologist; b. Glen Cove, N.Y., May 4, 1934; s. Ely Barney and Mary (London) G.; A.B., Brandeis U., 1956; A.M., Harvard, 1957, Ph.D., 1960; m. Sandra Jacobson, June 25, 1961; children—Michelle Zeva, Julie Myra, Carao Beverly. Jr. fellow Harvard, 1960-62; instr. physiology, Harvard Med. Sch., 1962, asso. physiology, 1962-65, asst. prof., 1965-69, asso. prof., 1969-70; prof. physiology, chmn. dept. U. Mass., Med. Sch., 1970—. Mem. Endocrine Soc., Am. Physiol. Soc., Am. Soc. Zoologist, N.Y. Acad. Scis. Research and pubs. on growth hormone and physiology of adipose tissue. Home: 58 High Rock Terrace Newton MA 02167 Office: 419 Belmont St Worcester MA 01604

GOODMAN, HENRY NELSON, educator, philosopher; b. Somerville, Mass., Aug. 7, 1906; s. Henry L. and Sarah (Woodbury) G.; B.S., Harvard, 1928, Ph.D., 1941; m. Katharine Sturgis, Aug. 13, 1944, Owner art gallery, Boston, 1929-41; instr. Tufts Coll., 1945-46; asso. prof., then prof. philosophy U. Pa., 1945-64; Wolfson prof. philosophy Brandeis U., 1964-67; research asso. edn. Harvard, 1967—, prof. philosophy, 1968—, dir. Project Zero, 1967—. Vis. lectr. Princeton, 1958; spl. lectr. U. London, Oxford U., Harvard, Cornell U., Mich. State U., Princeton. Served with AUS, 1942-45. Guggenheim fellow, 1946-47; felow Center Cognitive Studies, Harvard, 1962-63. Mem. Am. Philos. Assn. (pres. Eastern div. 1967); corr. fellow Brit. Acad. Author: The Structure of Appearance, 2d edit., 1966; Fact, Fiction and Forecast, 2d edit., 1965; Languages of Art, 1968; Problems and Projects, 1971. Office: Emerson Hall Harvard Univ Cambridge MA 02139

GOODMAN, JULIAN, broadcasting exec.; b. Glasgow, Ky., May 1, 1922; s. Charles Austin and Clara (Franklin) G.; student Western Ky. State Coll., 1939-42; A.B. in Econs., George Washington U., 1948; LL.D. (hon.), William Jewell Coll., 1967; m. Betty Davis, Oct. 13, 1946; children—Julie, John, Jeffrey, Gregory. News reporter in Ky.; news writer NBC, 1945-50, mgr. news, Washington, 1950-59, dir. news and pub. affairs NBC Network, 1959- 61, v.p. NBC News, 1961-65, exec. v.p., 1965, sr. exec. v.p. NBC, Inc., 1965, pres. 1966—, chief exec. officer, 1970—. Past chmn. radio and TV corrs. exec. com. U.S. Capitol. Recipient Robert E. Sherwood Meml. award, 1959. Mem. Radio-TV Corrs. Assn. (past pres.), Radio-TV News Directors' Assn., Broadcast Pioneers, The Players, Internat. Radio and TV Soc., Sigma Delta Chi. Clubs: Federal City (Washington); Winged Foot (Mamaroneck, N.Y.). Office: 30 Rockefeller Plaza New York City NY 10020

GOODMAN, LAWRENCE EUGENE, engring. educator; b. N.Y.C., Mar. 12, 1920; s. Joseph and Dorothy (Goldberger) G.; B.A., Columbia, 1939, B.S., 1940, Ph.D., 1949; M.S., U. Ill., 1942; m. Katherine Cecilia Lewis, Sept. 16, 1951; children—Jennifer Robin, Jeanne Harriet, Alice Abigail. Engr., sect. T, OSRD, 1943-46; NRC predoctoral fellow, 1947-48; tchr. Columbia, 1947-49, U. Ill., 1950-53, U. Minn., 1953—; sr. fellow NSF, 1962-63; prof. mechanics, head dept. civil and mineral engring. U. Minn., 1965-71; cons. in field, 1950—. Served with USNR, 1943-45. Recipient Distinguished Teaching award U. Minn., 1965. Fellow Am. Soc. C.E., Am. Soc. M.E. Contbr. profl. jours. Home: 1589 Vincent St St Paul MN 55108 Office: 107 Min Met Bldg Univ Minn Minneapolis MN 55455

GOODMAN, LEO A., educator, statistician; b. N.Y.C., Aug. 7, 1928; s. Abraham J. and Mollie (Sacks) G.; A.B. summa cum laude, Syracuse U., 1948; M.A., Princeton, 1950, Ph.D., 1950; m. Ann Haven Davidow, Aug. 28, 1960; children—Andrew Martin, Thomas Henry. Asst. prof. statistics, sociology U. Chgo., 1950-53, asso. prof., 1953-55, prof., 1955—, Charles L. Hutchinson Distinguished Service prof., 1970—; research tng. fellow Social Sci. Research Council, Princeton, 1950; Fulbright scholar, hon. research tng. fellow Social Sci. Research Council, Cambridge (Eng.) U., 1953-54; NSF sr. postdoctoral fellow, John Simon Guggenheim Meml. Found. fellow Cambridge U. and London Sch. Econs. and Polit. Sci., 1959- 60; vis. prof. math. statistics, sociology Columbia, 1960-61; com. statistics div. math. Nat. Acad. Scis.-NRC, 1961-64, chmn., 1963-64. Recipient MacLaren Advt. Research award Canadian Adv. Research Found., 1966; R.A. Fisher Meml. lecture Com. Pres. Statistical Societies, 1968. Fellow Inst. Math. Statistics (mem. council 1955-57), Am. Statis. Assn., A.A.A.S., Am. Sociol. Soc., Royal Statis. Soc.; mem. Internat. Statis. Inst., Internat. Union Sci. Study of Population, Econometric Soc., Biometric Soc., Am. Math. Soc., Am. Assn. U. Profs., Phi Beta Kappa, Sigma Xi. Clubs: Quadrangle, Princeton (Chgo.). Contbr. articles profl. jours., also to books. Home: 1126 E 59th St Chicago IL 60637

GOODMAN, LEO MAGILL, former fgn. service officer; b. Latvia, Dec. 7, 1909 (parents Am. citizens); s. Tobias and Emma (Magill) G.; B.S.S., Coll. City N.Y., 1931; student Columbia, 1931, LL.B., 1934, postgrad. Hunter Coll., 1942, Practicing Law Inst., N.Y.C., 1952, Indsl. Coll. Armed Forces, 1958-59, George Washington U., 1959. Admitted to N.Y. bar, 1934; practiced in N.Y.C. until 1944; atty., examiner Dept. Justice, 1941-42; chief trial div. U.S. War Crimes Group, Germany, 1946-47; chief adminstrn. German justice div. Office Mil. Govt. Bavaria, 1948-48; chief presiding judge for Bavaria. U.S. cts. of Allied High Commn. for Germany, 1948-54, justice Ct. of Appeals, 1954-55; legal adviser Am. Embassy, Vienna, Austria, 1955-57, 1st sec., consul, 1956-57; assigned Dept. of State, 1957-62; attended Nat. War Coll., 1962; consul gen. Am. Consulate Gen., Bremen, Germany, 1962-70. Mem. U.S. Adoption Rev. Bd. for Bavaria, 1948; U.S. mem. 4 power rations, deliveries and restitution directorate Allied Council for Austria, 1955-56, Joint Property Control and Restitution Commn. for Vienna, 1955-56, Fulbright Scholarship Selection Com. for Bavaria, 1953-54. Founder Leo Goodman Internat. Law Library, U. Munich (Germany), 1954; introduced Am. system of probation in Germany, 1950. Served with AUS, 1942-46; ETO; col. USAF Res. Decorated Bronze Star; recipient award City of Aachen, Germany, 1953. Mem. Am. Bar Assn., Am. Soc. Internat. Law, Am. Judicature Soc., Am. Assn. Comparative Study Law, Am. Fgn. Service Assn., Air Force Assn., Res. Officers Assn., Alumni Fedn. Columbia U., Diplomat and Consular Officers Ret., Nat. Def. Transp. Assn., Nat. Geog. Soc., United Seamen's Service Internat. Council, Am. C. of C. in Germany, Fed. Bar Assn., Kunstverein-Kunsthalle Bremen, Verein von Freuden des Fockemuseums Bremen, Buergerparkverein Bremen, Gesellschaft der Freunde der-Universitrieat Bremen e.V., Bremen Consular Corps, Carl Schurz Gesellschaft e.V., Ostasiatischer Verein Bremen. Clubs: zu Bremen; zur Vahr; Columbia University (N.Y.C.); Internat., Nat. Lawyers (Washington); Kiwanis. Author: Selected Opinions of Leo m. Goodman, 3 vols., 1954; Bavarian Digest of Current Legal Opinions, 1949. Address: care Dept of State Washington DC 20525

GOODMAN, LEON, chemist; b. Livingston, Mont., Dec. 16, 1920; s. Sam and Sadie Clara (Kopald) G.; student Fresno State Coll., 1937-40; B.S. in Chemistry, U. Cal. at Berkeley, 1941; Ph.D., U. Cal. at Los Angeles, 1950; m. Marilyn Gene Shear, Feb. 1, 1956; children—Laura Elizabeth, Andrew Bentley. Chemist, Los Alamos Sci. Lab., 1950-53; research asso., instr. U. So. Cal., 1953- 54; chemist Stanford Research Inst., 1955-70, chmn. dept. bio-organic chemistry, 1961-70; prof., chmn. dept. chemistry U. R.I. at Kingston, 1970—; spl. research chemotherapy cancer. Mem. Am. Chem. Soc., Chem. Soc. (London), N.Y. Acad. Scis., Sigma Xi. Home: 118 Woodruff Av Wakefield RI 02879 Office: Univ Rhode Island Kingston RI 02881

GOODMAN, LINDA, (Mrs. Sam O. Goodman), author; b. Parkersburg, W.Va.; d. Robert Stratton and Mazie (McBee) Kemery; grad. high sch.; m. William Herbert Snyder, Apr. 29, 1949 (dec. Oct. 1970); children—Melissa Anne, James, John Anthony, Sarah Elizabeth, William Dana; m. 2d, Sam O. Goodman, Sept. 28, 1955; children—Jill Kemery, Michael Aaron. Writer-broadcaster Letter From Linda radio shows WAMP (NBC), Pitts., 1958-61; writer Emphasis and Monitor for NBC network radio, 1962-64; continuity chief WHN Radio, N.Y.C., 1964-66. Mem. Universal Research Found., Sedona, Ariz., Assn. for Research and Enlightenment, Virginia Beach, Va. Speech writer for Whitney Young and Nat. Urban League, 1966-67. Named Dau. of Year, W.Va. Soc. Washington, 1971. Mem. A.F.T.R.A., Authors League Am., Writers Guild N.Y. Author: Sun Signs, 1968; Venus Trines at Midnight, 1970; Love Signs, 1971. Address: 490 West End Av New York City NY 10024 also 315 Carr Av Cripple Creek CO

GOODMAN, LOUIS S., prof. pharmacology; b. Portland, Ore., Aug. 27, 1906; s. Charles William and Dora (Hurwitz) G.; A.B., Reed Coll., 1928; M.D., M.A., U. Ore., 1932; postgrad. Johns Hopkins, 1932-33; Dr. Scis. (hon.), U. Man., 1965, U. Utah, 1969; m. Helen Ricen, Dec. 14, 1933; children—Carolyn, Debora. Teaching asst. psychology, Reed Coll., 1927-29; house officer in medicine Johns Hopkins Hosp., 1932-33; NRC fellow in pharmacology, Yale, 1934, instr. pharmacology and toxicology, 1935-37, asst. prof., 1937-43; prof. and chmn. dept. pharmacology and physiology, U. Vt., 1943-44; prof. and head dept. pharmacology, U. Utah, 1944- -. Mem. nat. bd. med. examiners Pharmacology Test Com., 1955-59; mem. nat. adv. Neurol. Diseases and Blindness Council, 1954-58; mem. adv. council Life Ins. Med. Research Fund, 1956-59; mem. adv. com. Pharmacology Service Center, Nat. Inst. Mental Health, 1957-63; chmn. pharmacol. tng. com. NIH, 1958-62; nat. adv. com. Mental Health Council, 1963-66, nat. adv. council health research facilities, 1966-70; mem. council on drugs A.M.A., 1958-61; mem. grad. council, research grants com. U. Utah, 1957-65; mem. med. bd. Myasthenia Gravis Found., 1953-59; mem. sci. bd. Nat. Neurol. Research Found., 1957-64; mem. sr. postdoctoral fellowship evaluation com. NSF, 1955-58. Fellow N.Y. Acad. Sci.; mem. Nat. Acad. Scis., Am. Acad. Neurology, Acad. Anesthesiology (hon.), Am. Soc. Pharmacolgy and Exptl. Therapeutics (past pres.), Soc. Exptl. Biology and Medicine, A.A.A.S., Am. Physiol. Soc., Phi Beta Kappa, Sigma Xi, Alpha Omega Alpha. Author: (with Gilman) Pharmacological Basis of Therapeutics, 1970. Editor: head dept. journalism Ala. Poly. Inst., Auburn, 1923-27; sec. to U.S. and Medicine, 1947-51; mem. editorial bd. Ann. Review of Pharmacology, 1959-65, Jour. of Exptl. Psychiatry, 1959—; contbr. to sci. publs. Home: 2926 Crestview Dr Salt Lake City UT 84108

GOODMAN, MARJORIE SMITH, educator, geographer; b. Caledonia, O., Dec. 19, 1916; d. Fred W. and Edith (Foos) Smith; B.S., Bowling Green State U., 1943; M.A., Syracuse U., 1947; Ph.D., Northwestern U., 1954; m. Robert J. Goodman, July 5, 1951. Tchr., Marion Co., O., 1937-41, Marion City schs., 1941-45, Chgo. Tchrs. Coll., 1949-50; with U.S. Govt., 1951-53; mem. expressway planning Detroit Met. Area Traffic Study, Mich. Hwy. Dept., 1954-55; became mem. faculty U. Detroit, 1955, former prof. geography, also chmn. dept., hon. prof. Karnatak U., Dharwar, India, 1961-62. Mem. Assn. Am. Geographers, Am. Assn. U. Profs., Nat. Council Geog. Edn., Soc. Women Geographers, Sigma Xi. Author: Exercises in Physical Geography, 1967. Spl. research aerial photo interpretation.

GOODMAN, MAURICE, holding co. exec.; b. N.Y.C., May 2, 1904; s. Benjamin F. and Sara (Hymans) G.; B.S., Columbia, 1923; m. Sara Strasbourger, Dec. 1, 1927; children—Jane M. (Mrs. Milton S. Pohl), Carol (Mrs. Richard Walter). Partner, Arnold & Co., 1927-36; with Ben Goodman & Son, 1936—, v.p., dir., 1948—; with Fuller Rodney & Co., 1939-41, Merrill & Lynch, 1941- 43; v.p. Liberty Fabrics, 1948-53, dir., 1951-53; v.p., treas. So. Coach Co., 1954-58; v.p., dir. Pueblo Transit Co., 1947-56; pres., dir. W. B. & S. Bus Lines, 1943-56; pres., treas., dir. Colorado Springs Transit Co., 1946—; pres., dir. BSF Corp., 1954-62; v.p., sec., dir. Savoy Industries, Inc., 1943-62, Standard Prudential Corp., 1967-71; chmn. bd., dir. Golden Cycle Corp., 1964—; dir. Inc., SOS Consol. Inc., Presidential Life Ins. Co., Internat. Food Service Systems, Inc., Hayes Internat. Corp., Willcox & Gibbs, Inc., The Thomas Holmes Corp. Clubs: Columbia University (N.Y.C.); Inwood (N.Y.) Country. Home: 125 Cedar Av Hewlett NY 11557 Office: 888 7th Av New York City NY 10019

GOODMAN, MICHAEL A., educator, architect; b. Lithuania, Jan. 7, 1903; s. Agran and Yacha (Barger) Gutman; came to U.S., 1920, naturalized, 1927; A.B., U. Cal. at Berkeley, 1925, M.A., 1927; m. Mildred Jacobs, Mar. 9, 1934; children—Michael A., Louise M. Faculty U. Cal. at Berkeley, 1927—, prof. architecture, 1945—, research architect for Inst. Transp. and Traffic Engring., U. Cal., 1971—; propr. firm Michael A. Goodman, architect, Berkeley, 1934—; prin. works include Lab. Chem. Bio-Dynamics, Life Scis. Bldg., Bio-Chemistry and Virus Lab. (all U. Cal. at Berkeley); County of San Mateo Hall of Justice and Records, Jail; East Bay Municipal Utility Dist. Adminstrn. Bldg.; Berkeley Pub. Health Adminstrn. Bldg.; First Savs. & Loan Office Bldg., Berkeley; one man exhbn. de Young Mus. and War Meml. Mus., San Francisco, 1934; participant annual shows throughout U.S., 1929—; rep. museums, pvt. collections. Sr. tech. def. planner Fed. Office Civilian Def. for 8 Western States, 1941-43; chmn. Berkeley City Planning Commn., 1954; pres. Bay Area Fedn. Planning Councils, 1964; chmn. Berkeley Housing Authority; mem. Redevel. Agy. City of Berkeley. Recipient Gold medal San Francisco Art Assn., 1925; award Fifty Prints of Year, Am. Graphic Artists Soc., 1930; 4 prizes state- wide exhbn. Cal. artists, 1929-34; Berkeley Citation for distinguished achievement and notable service to U. Cal., 1970. Fellow Coll. of A.I.A.; mem. Am. Inst. Planners. Am. Planning and Civic Assn., San Francisco Art Assn., San Francisco, Berkeley chambers commerce, San Francisco Mus. Art. Democrat. Club: Commonwealth (San Francisco). Contbr. archtl. publs. Home: 29 Northgate Av Berkeley CA 94708

GOODMAN, MURRAY, educator, chemist; b. N.Y.C., July 6, 1928; s. Louis and Frieda (Bercun) G.; B.S., Bklyn. Coll., 1949; Ph.D., U. Cal. at Berkeley, 1952; m. Zelda Silverman, Aug. 26, 1951; children—Andrew, Joshua, David. Postdoctoral fellow Mass. Inst. Tech., 1952-55; research fellow U. Cambridge (Eng.), 1955-56; mem. faculty Poly. Inst. Bklyn., 1956-71, prof. chemistry, 1964-71, dir. Polymer Research Inst., 1967-71; prof. chemistry U. Cal. at San Diego, 1971—. Recipient Distinguished Alumnus medal Bklyn. Coll., 1965. Mem. Am. Chem. Soc. Editor: Biopolymers Jour., 1963—. Research, publs. on structure of macromolecules; synthesized models of biopolymers and analyzed their structure and properties using spectroscopic methods. Home: 9760 Blackgold Rd La Jolla CA 92037

GOODMAN, NELSON, philosopher; b. Somerville, Mass., Aug. 7, 1906; s. Henry L. and Sarah E. (Woodbury) G.; B.S., Harvard Coll., 1928; Ph.D., 1941; m. Katharine Sturgis, Apr. 13, 1944. Operated art gallery, Boston, 1929-42; instr. philosophy Tufts Coll., 1945-46; asso. prof. U. Pa., 1946-51, prof., 1951-64; Harry A. Wolfson prof. philosophy Brandeis U., 1964-67; dept. psychology Harvard, dir. Project Zero, Grad. Sch. Edn., 1967—, prof. philosophy, 1968—; vis. lectr. Harvard, 1951, Princeton, 1958; spl. lectr. U. London, 1953; Alfred North Whitehead lectr. Harvard, 1962; John Locke lectr. Oxford U., 1962; vis. prof. edn. Harvard, 1967-68; Merriweather distinguished vis. prof. C.W. Post Coll., 1968; research fellow Center Cognitive Studies, 1962-65; dir. NSF Research Project, Brandeis U. Served as tech. sgt. AUS, 1942-45. Guggenheim fellow, 1946. Corr. fellow British Acad.; mem. Am. Philos. Assn. (pres. Eastern div. 1967), Assn. Symbolic Logic, Phi Beta Kappa. Author: The Structure of Appearance, 1951, 2d edit., 1966; Fact, Fiction and Forecast, 1955, 2d edit., 1965; Languages of Art, 1968; Problems and Projects, 1971. Contbr. articles to prof. jours. Address: Harvard U Emerson Hall Cambridge MA 02138

GOODMAN, OSCAR R., educator; b. Chgo., July 25, 1922; s. Benjamin and Anna (Faber) G.; B.S., Northwestern U., 1943; M.S., U. Wis., 1948, Ph.D., 1952, J.D., 1960. Mdse. control mgr. Alden's, Inc., Chgo., 1943-45; sr. market analyst Spiegel's, Inc., Chgo., 1945-46; instr. U. Wis., 1948-52; asso. prof. finance State U. Wash., 1953-56; asso. prof. finance U. Cal., Berkeley, 1956-58; vis. prof. U. Geneva, Switzerland, 1963, U. Mich., 1966; asso. prof. finance Northwestern U., 1958-65; prof. finance, chmn. finance dept. Roosevelt U., Chgo., 1966—; econ. cons. U.S. Dept. Justice Antitrust Div., U.S. House Banking and Currency Com.; expert witness U.S. Senate Com. on Antitrust and Monopoly; lectr. Nat. Trust Sch., Am. Bankers Assn. C.L.U. Mem. Am. Econ. Assn., Royal Econ. Soc., Am. Finance Assn., Am. Risk and Ins. Assn., Inst. Chartered Financial Analysts, Am., Ill. bar assns., Am. Assn. U. Profs. Jewish religion (v.p., dir. synagogue). Contbr. articles profl. jours. Home: 8100 S Loomis Blvd Chicago IL 60620

GOODMAN, PAUL, author, educator; b. N.Y.C., Sept. 9, 1911; B.A., Coll. City N.Y.; Ph.D., U. Chgo.; 1 dau. by 1st marriage, Susan; children by 2d marriage—Mathew R. (dec.), Daisy J. Tchr., U. Chgo., N.Y. U., Black Mountain Coll., also Inst. Gestalt Therapy, N.Y.C. and Cleve.; Knapp prof. U. Wis., 1964. Author: (criticism) Growing Up Absurd, Kafka's Prayer, 1947, The Structure of Literature, 1954, The Community of Scholars; (novels) The Facts of Life, 1946, The Break-up of Our Camp, 1950, Parents' Day, 1952, Stop-Light, 1942, The Empire City, 1959, Making Do, 1963; Compulsory Mis-Education, 1964; People or Personnel, 1965; Three Plays, 1965; Five Years, 1966; Like a Conquered Province, 1967; Adam and His Works, 1968; New Reformation: Notes of a Neolithic Conservative, 1970; (poems) Hawksweed, 1967, Homespun of Oatmeal Gray, 1970. Co-author: Communitas, 1947, Gestalt Therapy, 1951. Editor: Liberation, 1962—. Contbr. Commentary, Partisan Rev., Keyon Rev. Address: care Random House 457 Madison Av New York City NY 10022

GOODMAN, PERCIVAL, architect, planner; b. N.Y.C., Jan. 13, 1904; s. Barnet and Augusta (Goodman) G.; student Beaux Arts Inst. Design, Ecole Nat. des Beaux Arts, Am. Sch. Fine Arts (all France); m. Naomi Ascher, Sept. 28, 1944; children—Rachel, Joel. Vis. critic Sch. Architecture, N.Y.U., 1930-36; pvt. practice architecture, N.Y.C., 1936—; works include Balt. Hebrew Congregation, Temple Bethel, Springfield, Mass., Temple Bethel, Providence, Fairmount Temple, Cleve., Temple Emanuel, Denver, pub. schs., N.Y.C., Queensboro Coll., N.Y.C.; vis. critic city planning Columbia U., 1946, asso. prof. architecture, 1953- 66, prof., 1966—. Fellow A.I.A.; mem. Columbia U. Alumni Assn., Municipal Art Soc. Jewish religion. Author: (with Paul Goodman) Communitas, 1947, rev. edit., 1960. Illustrator Ltd. Editions Club. Contbr. articles encys. and mags. Home: 40 W 77th St New York City NY 10024 Office: 2114 Broadway New York City NY 10023

GOODMAN, RICHARD, business exec. Chmn., pres. GSC Enterprises, Inc. Office: 1950 N Mannheim Rd Melrose Park IL 60160*

GOODMAN, ROBERT NORMAN, plant pathologist, educator; b. Yonkers, N.Y., Dec. 15, 1921; s. Sidney William and Margaret (Fried) G.; B.S., U. N.H., 1948, M.S., 1950; Ph.D., U. Mo., 1952; m. Phoebe Newman, Sept. 4, 1949; children—Joyce Beth, Rachael Lea, Janet Faith. Grad. asst. U. N.H., 1948-50; grad. asst. U. Mo., 1950-52, asst. prof., 1952-55, asso. prof., 1955-61, prof., 1961—, chmn. dept. plant pathology, 1968—; postdoctoral fellow Swiss Fed. Inst. Tech., 1958-59, U. Leeds, Eng., 1965-66. Guggenheim Found. fellow, 1958-59; Lalor Found. fellow, 1958-59; NIH spl. fellow, 1965-66. Recipient U. Mo. Jr. Faculty Research award of merit, 1955. Mem. Am. Phytopathol. Soc., Am. Soc. Microbiology, Sigma Xi, Gamma Sigma Delta. Author: (with H.S. Goldberg) Antibiotics: Their Chemistry and Non- Medical Uses, 1959; Advances in Pest Control Research, 1961; Antibiotics in Agriculture, 1963; Biochemistry of Physiology of Infectious Plant Disease, 1967. Contbr. articles profl. jours. Home: 605 Crestland St Columbia MO 65201

GOODMAN, ROY MATZ, state senator, pharm. co. exec.; b. N.Y.C., Mar. 5, 1930; s. Bernard A. and Alice (Matz) G.; A.B. cum laude, Harvard, 1951, M.B.A. with distinction, 1953; m. Barbara Christine Furrer, June 28, 1955; children—Claire Barbara, Leslie Alice, Randolph Bernard. Dir. Ex-Lax, Inc., 1955—, pres., 1962- -; asso. buying and new bus. dept. Kuhn, Loeb & Co., investment, 1956-60; pres., dir. Roycemore, Inc., 1968-70; dir. Manhattan Industries, Ex-Lax, Ltd., Can., Ex- Lax Ltd., Eng.; mem. Bklyn. adv. bd. Chem. Bank N.Y. Trust Co., 1963- 65; dir. finance, finance admistr. City of N.Y., 1966-68; senator N.Y. State Assembly, 1968—, chmn. housing com., mem. finance, higher edn., social services, banking, civil service and pensions coms.; mem. joint legislative coms. on housing and community devel., environment mgmt. and natural resources. Mem. N.Y.C. Banking Commn., 1966-67; past trustee N.Y.C. Police Pension Fund, N.Y.C. Fire Dept. Pension Fund. Chmn. Parents Com., Dalton Schs. Devel. Program: trustee, chmn., exec. com Brotherhood-In-Action; mem. adv. council Inst. Philosophy and Politics of Edn. of Tchrs. Coll., Columbia. Exec. asst. to chmn. N.Y. State Assembly Jud. Com., 1963-64; asst. to atty. gen. State N.Y., 1960; pres. 9th A.D. Republican Club, 1963-64; del. N.Y. State Rep. Convs., 1966, 68, 70; treas. N.Y. County Rep. Com. Trustee Barnard Coll., Carnegie Hall Soc., Inc., Carnegie Hall Corp., Columbia Coll. Pharm. Scis., Dalton Schs., Freedom House, L.I. Coll. Hosp. Served to lt. USNR, 1953-56. Recipient Distinguished Service award (Young Man of Year), Jr. C. of C., 1966, Mt. Scopus citation Hebrew U., Jerusalem, 1968. Mem. Anti-Defamation League (bd. govs. N.Y.), Am. Arbitration Assn. (nat. panel arbitrators), Young Pres'. Orgn., N.Y. Soc. Security Analysts, Omicron Delta Epsilon (hon). Republican. Clubs: City, Wall Street, Harvard, Harvard Business School (N.Y.C.); Harvard (Boston); Century Country (Purchase, N.Y.). Home: 1035 Fifth Av New York City NY 10028 Office: 423 Atlantic Av Brooklyn NY 11217

GOODMAN, SAM RICHARD, food processing co. exec.; b. N.Y.C., May 23, 1930; s. Morris and Virginia (Gross) G.; B.B.A., Coll. City N.Y., 1951; M.B.A., N.Y.U., 1957, Ph.D., 1968; m. Beatrice Bettencourt, Sept. 15, 1957; children—Mark Stuart, Stephen Manuel, Christopher Bettencourt. Chief accountant John C. Valentine Co., N.Y.C., 1957-60; supr. budgets and analysis Gen. Foods. Corp., White Plains, N.Y., 1960-63; budget dir. Crowell Collier Pub. Co., N.Y.C., 1963-64; controller Nestle Co., Inc., White Plains, 1964—; lectr. N.Y.U. Inst. Mgmt., 1965-67; asst. prof. marketing Iona Coll. Grad. Sch. Bus. Adminstrn., 1967—; prof. finance and marketing Pace Coll. Grad. Sch. Bus. Adminstrn., 1969—. Served to lt. (j.g.) USNR, 1951-55. Mem. Financial Execs. Inst., Nat. Assn. Accountants, Am. Statis. Assn., Am. Econs. Assn., Planning Execs. Inst. Author: Techniques of Profitability Analysis; The Marketing Controller Concept; Prentice-Hall's Financial Management Series; also articles. Home: 12 Hidden Valley Dr Suffern NY 10901 Office: 100 Bloomingdale Rd White Plains NY 10605

GOODMAN, STANLEY JOSHUA, dept. store exec.; b. Montreal, Can., Mar. 23, 1910; s. Isaac and Jenny (Edinsweig) G.; B.A., McGill U., 1931, M.A., 1932; M.B.A., Harvard, 1934; m. Alice Therese Hahn, June 16, 1936; children—Ellen, John Edgar. Came to U.S., 1932, naturalized, 1940. With Arco Co., Cleve., 1934-36, C.I.T. Financial Corp., 1936-42, Interstate Dept. Stores, 1942-48; with May Dept. Stores Co., 1948—, v.p., 1958-67, pres. 1967—, chief exec. officer, 1969—, also dir., mem. exec. com.; pres. Famous-Barr Co., St. Louis, 1959-67; dir. Systems, Sci. & Software. Dir. Arts and Edn. Council, St. Louis; mem. Civic Progress, Inc.; bd. dirs. Am. Symphony Orch. League; mem. adv. com. Tobe-Coburn Sch. Fashion Careers, Fashion Inst. Tech; trustee Jefferson Nat. Expansion Meml. Assn.; vice chmn. St. Louis Symphony Soc.; dir. United Fund of St. Louis. Mem. Govtl. Research Inst. (dir.). Clubs: Harvard (St. Louis and N.Y.C.); Missouri Athletic (St. Louis); Stadium (St. Louis); Noonday, University; Creve CoeurRacquet; Rowfant (Cleve.). Contbr. articles Harper's mag., Harvard Bus. Rev. Home: 35 Briarcliff St Louis MO 63124 Office: May Dept Stores Co St Louis MO 63101

GOODMAN, STANLEY LEONARD, advt. exec.; b. N.Y.C., Jan. 21, 1920; s. Abraham and Leah (Fellman) G.; B.S. in Econs., Wharton Sch. U. Pa., 1941; certificate electronics U. Richmond, 1943; m. Anita Davis, Aug. 30, 1960; children—Patricia, Laurence: stepchildren—Marilyn Rice, Stuart Rice. Asst. to pres. Decca Records, Inc., N.Y.C., 1941-56; v.p., marketing dir. Grayson Robinson Stores, N.Y.C., 1956-61; club plan creative dir. Popular Mdse. Co., Inc., Passaic, N.J., 1961-62., dir. marketing, 1962-64; pres. Elliot, Goodman & Russell, Inc., advt., N.Y.C., 1964, EGR Travel Promotion, Inc., N.Y.C., 1969—, EGR Marketing, Inc., N.Y.C., 1968—, EGR Communications, Inc., Detroit, 1969—; pres., dir. EGR Communications, Inc., N.Y.C., 1968—; dir. Pub. Service Mut. Ins. Co., N.Y.C. Lectr., Am. Mgmt. Assn., 1964—; instr. marketing dept. Pace Coll. Mem. Sales Promotion Execs. Assn. (Sales Promotion Man of Year N.Y. 1959, internat. pres. 1960-62, honored Stanley Goodman grant, 1954—), Direct Mail Advt. Assn., Council Sales Promotion Agys. (pres. 1969-71), Am. Marketing Assn., Hundred Million Club, Westchester Alumni Assn. U. Pa. (v.p. 1966—). Contbr. articles to sales mags. Home: 46 Crosshill Rd Hartsdale NY 10530 Office: 292 Madison Av New York City NY 10017

GOODMAN, WALTER, author; b. N.Y.C., Aug. 22, 1927; s. Hyman and Sadie (Rybakof) G.; B.A. magna cum laude, 1949; M.A., Reading (Eng.) U., 1953; m. Elaine Egan, Feb. 10, 1951; children—Hal, Bennet. Lectr., Salzburg Seminar in Am. Studies, Breadloaf Writers Conf., U. Pa. Sch. Communications. Mem. Am. Civil Liberties Union, P.E.N. Author: The Committee, 1968; All Honorable Men, 1963; The Clowns of Commerce, 1957; Black Bondage, 1969; A Percentage of the Take, 1971; also numerous articles. Home: 4 Crest Dr White Plains, NY 10607.

GOODMAN, WILLIAM I., urban planner, educator; b. Detroit, June 24, 1919; s. Morris and Bella (Kecner) G.; A.B., Wayne State U., 1942, M.Pub. Adminstrn., 1950; M.City Planning, Mass. Inst. Tech., 1952; m. Pearl Joy Meisner, Dec. 28, 1946; children—Ann, Deborah. Planner, Detroit City Planning Commn., 1943-50; resident planner Adams, Howard & Greeley, Hartford, Conn., 1952-53; dir. rezoning study Boston City Planning Bd., 1953-54; asst. prof. city planning Harvard, 1953-56; asso. prof. urban planning U. Ill., Urbana, 1956-60, prof., 1960-65, chmn. dept. urban planning, 1965—. Planning cons., 1955—; cons. ICA, Govt. Costa Rica, U.S. Office Regional Econ. Devel. in Mass., Ill., Wis., S.D. Mem. Wabash Valley Interstate Commn., 1966—. Served with AUS, 1945. Recipient Merit award Am. Inst. Planners, 1969. Fulbright scholar to U.K., 1962-63. Mem. Urban Am., Internat. Fedn. for Housing and Planning, Am. Soc. Planning Ofcls. (edn. council), Am. Inst. Planners (v.p., past mem. bd. govs., adv. bd. Jour.), Assn. Collegiate Schs. of Planning (pres..). Author: Principles and Practice of Urban Planning, 1968. Contbr. articles to profl. jours. Home: 310 W Michigan St Urbana IL 61801

GOODMAN, WOLFE D., lawyer; b. Toronto, Ont., Can., Aug. 5, 1925; B.Commn., U. Toronto, 1946; LL.B., Osgoode Hall. Admitted to Ont. bar, 1949; now partner firm Goodman & Carr, Toronto; lectr. accounting in law, faculty of law U. Toronto, 1961-63, 65-69. Pres., Jewish Immigrant Aid Services of Can., 1967-69, sec., 1969—; chmn. budget and finance com. Canadian Jewish Congress, 1969—. Bd. dirs. Baycrest Centre for Geriatric Care. Mem. Canadian Bar Assn. (vice chmn. Ont. tax sect. 1966-67), Canadian Tax Found., Estate Planning Council Toronto. Office: 44 Victoria St Toronto 1 Ontario Canada*

GOODMAN, WOODROW I., coll. pres., b. Olive Hill, Ky., Aug. 21, 1918; s. William Preston and Myrtie Viola (Martt) G.; A.B., B.S. in Edn., Marion (Ind.) Coll., 1939; postgrad. Miami U., Oxford, O., summer 1939, Winona Lake (Ind.) Sch. Theology, summers 1942, 52; M.A. in Bibl. Lit., Wheaton (Ill.) Coll., 1947; D.D., Taylor U., 1952; D. Litt., Houghton Coll., 1956; m. Evelyn Marie Everest, Sept. 30, 1939; children—Annetta Marie, Dennis Ray, Sandra Kae. Tchr. pub. schs., O., Ind., Mich., 1939-45; ordained to ministry United Missionary Ch., 1942, Wesleyan Meth. Ch., 1959; pastor in Ind. and Mich., 1940-45; pres. Bethel Coll., Mishawaka, Ind., 1946-59; registrar Houghton (N.Y.) Coll., 1959-60; pres. Marion Coll., 1960—. Mem. United Missionary Gen. Conf., 1948, 52, 59, Wesleyan Meth. Gen. Conf., 1963, 66. Named Distinguished Citizen, Mishawaka, 1959. Mem. N.E.A., Nat. Holiness Assn., Nat. Assn. Evangelicals. Lion. Editor: Bethel Sunday School Series, 1952-56. Home: 501 E 43d St Marion IN 46952

GOODNIGHT, CLARENCE JAMES, educator; b. Gillespie, Ill., May 30, 1914; s. Charles A. and Phoebe (Personeus) G.; student Ill. Coll., 1932-33; A.A., Blackburn Coll., 1934; A.B., U. Ill., 1936, M.A., 1937, Ph.D., 1939; m. Marie Louise Ostendorf, Aug. 25, 1940; children—Ann Marie, Charles James. Instr. zoology U. Ill., 1936-39, 42-44, research asso., 1939-40; instr. biology Bklyn. Coll., 1940-42; instr. biology N.J. State Tchrs. Coll., 1944-46; asst. prof. biology Purdue U., 1946-49, asso. prof., 1949-55, prof., 1955-65; prof. biology, head dept. Western Mich. U., 1965—; cons. Sch. Sci. Curriculum Project U. Ill.; mem. com. Grad. Record Exam. Biology, Ednl. Testing Service, Princeton, N.J. Mem. A.A.A.S., Am. Assn. U. Profs., Ecol. Soc. Am., Am. Micros. Soc. (pres. 1971), Entomol. Soc. Am., Am. Soc. Limnologists and Oceanographers, Soc. Systemetic Zoology, Midwest Benthol. Soc. (sec.), Am. Inst. Biol. Scis., Am. Soc. Zoologists, Nat. Sci Tchrs. Assn., Nat. Assn. Biology Tchrs., Nature Conservancy, Phi Beta Kappa, Sigma Xi. Democrat. Unitarian. Author: (with M. L. Goodnight) Zoology, 1954; (with M.L. Goodnight and R.R. Armacost) Biology: An Introduction to the Science of Life, 1962; (with M. L. Goodnight and P. Gray) General Zoology, 1964; also articles. Home: 1633 Chevy Chase Blvd Kalamazoo, MI 49001.

GOODNOUGH, ROBERT ARTHUR, artist; b. Cortland, N.Y., Oct. 23, 1917; s. Leo J. and Hariett (Summers) G.; B.F.A., Syracuse U., 1940; M.A., N.Y.U., 1950; student New Sch. for Social Research, 1949, Ozenfant Sch. Art, 1950-51, Hoffman Sch. Art, 1951. Exhibited one-man shows at Tibor de Nagy Gallery, N.Y.C.; work exhibited in permanent collections Albright Art Gallery, Buffalo, Chgo. Art Inst., Mus. Modern Art, N.Y.C., Whitney Mus., N.Y.C., N.Y.U. Mus., R.I. Sch. Design Mus., N.C. Mus. Art; represented in pvt. collections; instr. painting N.Y.U., 1953, Fieldston Sch., Riverdale, N.Y., 1953-60, Cornell U., 1960. Served with AUS, 1941-45. Recipient award Chgo. Art Inst., 1962. Contbr. articles nat. mags. Home and studio: 122 Christopher St New York City, NY 10014.

GOODNOW, NATHAN BROOKS, lawyer; b. Detroit, Sept. 20, 1906; s. Edward Brooks and Dorothy (Atkinson) G.; LL.B., U. Detroit, 1930; J.D. (hon.), Detroit Coll. Law, 1965; m. Romalda Christine Wurm, Aug. 3, 1932; children—Judith Dorothy, Daniel Timothy. Admitted to Mich. bar, 1930, since practiced in Detroit; asso. firm Dykema, Gossett, Spencer, Goodnow & Trigg, and predecessor firm, 1933-42, partner, 1942—. Dir. City Nat. Bank Detroit, Abstract & Title Guaranty Co. subsidiary Lawyers Title Ins. Corp., Ernst Fuel & Supply Co., others. Mem. Mich. Commn. Traffic Safety, 1964; mem. Gov.'s Spl. Commn. Urban Problems, 1967-68. Bd. dirs. Pres.'s Lawyers Com. for Civil Rights Under Law, 1963—; trustee Marygrove Coll., Detroit, 1958—, Siena Heights Coll. Fellow Am. Bar Found.; mem. State Bar Mich. (commr. 1958-64, pres. 1964), Am., Detroit (dir. 1949- 56, pres. 1956) bar assns., Am. Coll. Trial Lawyers (regent 1968—), Am. Judicature Soc., Am. Inst. Mgmt., Delta Theta Phi, Alpha Sigma Nu. Clubs: Mackinaw Island yacht (dir.); Country of Detroit, Detroit, Detroit Athletic (pres. 1968-69, dir.), Economic of Detroit, Otsego Ski. Home: 75 Handy Rd Grosse Pointe Farms MI 48236 Office: Penobscot Bldg Detroit MI 48226

GOODPASTER, ANDREW JACKSON, army officer; b. Granite City, Ill., Feb. 12, 1915; s. Andrew Jackson and Teresa Mary (Mrovka) G.; student McLendree Coll., 1931-33; B.S., U.S. Mil. Acad., 1939; M.S.E., Princeton, 1949, M.A., 1949, Ph.D. in Internat Relations, 1950; m. Dorothy Dulahey Anderson, Aug. 28, 1939; children—Susan Delaney, Anne Morgan. Commd. 2d lt., C.E., A.U.S., 1939, advanced through grades to brig. gen., U.S. Army. 1956; comdg. officer 48th Engr. Combat Btn., World War II; strategic and policy staff duty, War Dept. Gen. Staff, 1944-47; spl. staff asst. SHAPE, 1940-54; dist. engr. C.E. San Francisco, 1954; def. liaison officer and staff sec. to President U.S., 1954-61; asst. div. comdr. 3d Inf. Div., 1961—; supreme allied comdr. Europe, 1969—. Decorated D.S.C., Silver Star, Legion of Merit with oak leaf cluster, Purple Heart with oak leaf cluster.†

GOODPASTURE, GRADY L., agrl. products co. exec.; b. Hillham, Tenn., May 5, 1909; s. R.M. and Katherine (Upton) G.; student N.M. Mil. Inst., 1930-32; m. Mollie Cleo Singletary, Jan. 20, 1934; children—Gradena, Rita (Mrs. H.K. Muldrow). Independent grain buyer, W. Tex., 1933-40; founder, 1940, since pres., chmn. bd. Goodpasture, Inc., Brownfield, Tex.; pres., chmn. bd. Western Ammonia Corp., Interstate Grain Corp., S. Plains Ready-Mix, Inc., Goodrow Corp., Service Marine, Inc., Shippers Stevedoring Co.; dir. Brownfield State Bank & Trust Co., Brownfield Savs. & Loan Assn., Brownfield State Co., G&B Computers, Inc. Trustee Baylor U., Wayland Coll., High Plains Research Found. Named Outstanding Man of Year, Wayland Coll., 1962, Outstanding Citizen, Brownfield C. of C., 1962, Outstanding Man, Tex. C. of C., 1963. Mem. Fertilizer Inst., Nat. Fertilizer Solutions Assn., Nat. Tex. grain and feed dealers assns., Am. Soc. Agronomy. Baptist (deacon 1955—). Patentee agrl. and related machinery. Home: 1011 E Tate St Brownfield TX 79316 Office: 902 W Broadway Brownfield TX 79316

GOODRICH, BAXTER DEE, utility exec.; b. Oklahoma City, July 9, 1913; s. Robert E. and Moye Aileen (Wilson) G.; student Ala. Poly. Inst., 1931-33; B.S. in Civil Engring., Rice U., 1935; m. Glennis McCrary Aug. 9, 1937. With W. M. Kellogg Co., 1935-36, United Gas Pipe Line Co., 1936-46; chief engr. Arctic Contractors, 1946-47; with Tex. Eastern Transmission Corp., 1947- -, pres., 1965—, also chief exec. officer; pres., chief exec. officer Transwestern Pipeline Co. Mem. gas industry group on tour USSR, 1961. Trustee Inst. Gas Tech. Served to lt. comdr. USNR, 1943- 46. Mem. Ind. Natural Gas Assn. (bd. dirs.), Am. Gas Assn. (bd. dirs., chmn. industry tech. adv. com.; award pipe line research com. 1964), Soc. Am. Mil. Engrs., Sigma Alpha Epsilon. Home: 615 Hunters Grove Houston, TX 77024. Office: PO Box 2521 Houston TX 77001

GOODRICH, BENN FLOYD, carbon co. exec.; b. Roulette, Pa., Sept. 13, 1910; s. Chauncey B. and Ruth C. (Jones) G.; grad. Elmire Bus. Coll., 1930; m. Helen Marbrie Hartwell, Sept. 17, 1932; 1 dau., Marbrie Ellen (Mrs. Neil William Beefelt). Asst. cashier State Bank of Paulette, 1930-33, 1st Nat. Bank of Coudersport (Pa.), 1933-42; asst. cashier Elk County Nat. Bank, Ridgway, Pa., 1942-46, now dir.; controller Stackpole Carbon Co., St. Marys, Pa., 1946-61, sec., 1961—, also dir.; sec., dir. Canadian Stackpole, Ltd.; dir. Kaul Hill Oil & Gas Co.; sec. Stackpole Fibers Co., Inc., Boston; sec., treas., dir. J.K.P. Hall Corp., St. Marys, 1958—; sec., dir. Phin, Inc., Bloomfield, N.J., Stackpole Components Co., Farmville, Va.; dir. Elk County Bank & Trust Co., Mc. Research Corp., mgmt. cons., 1935—. Pres., YMCA, Ridgway, 1955—, mem. state bd. dirs., 1957—. Bd. dirs. Bucktail council Boy Scouts Am.; chmn. bd. trustees Stackpole Hall Found. Mem. Nat. Assn. Cost Accountants. Episcopalian. Mason (32, Shriner), Kiwanian. Clubs: Elk County Country (past dir. Ridgway); St. Marys Country. Home: Bennsylvania Ridgway PA 15853 Office: Stackpole Carbon Co Stackpole St St Marys PA 15857

GOODRICH, DONALD WELLS, educator; b. Bklyn., N.Y., Jan. 20, 1898; s. Charles Howard and Matilda Antoinette (Brant) G.; grad. Phillips Exeter Acad., 1915; A.B., Williams Coll., 1919; A.M., Harvard, 1920; grad. student Columbia, 1923, 24; Litt.D. (honorary), Emerson Coll. 1958; D.Humanities, Suffolk U. 1969; m. Violet Elizabeth Walser, June 24, 1922; children—Donald Wells, Charles Howard, Alice Jacqueline. Master in English, Hoosac (N.Y.) Sch., 1921, Lawrenceville (N.J.) Sch. 1921-23; headmaster Great Neck (L.I.) Prep. Sch., 1923-28; sr. master lower sch. Tamalpais Sch., San Rafael, Cal. 1928-32; headmaster Calvert Primary Sch., Balt., 1932-40; ednl. research Harvard Grad. Sch. of Edn., 1940-42; registrar, dir. admissions, prof. humanities Suffolk U., Boston, 1947-56, dean, registrar, 1956-66, v.p. dean, 1966- 69, prof., 1969—. Served with S.A.T.C., Williams, 1918; capt. to lt. col. adj. gens. dept. AUS 1942-47. Mem. Pvt. Sch. Assn., Balt., 1932- 40, pres. 1937-38; mem. Ednl. Records Bur., N.Y., 1933-40, Country Day School Headmasters' Assn., 1939-42. Mem. Am. Conf. Acad. Deans, N.E.A., Phi Beta Kappa, Phi Delta Kappa. Conglist. Clubs: Rotary, State, Massachusetts Schoolmasters. Author Textbooks. Editor: G.I. Roundtable Discussion Pamphlets, U.S. Army, 1943-45. Home: 1 Boulder Brook Rd Wellesley MA 02181 Office: Suffolk U Boston MA 02114

GOODRICH, EDWARD THAYER, lawyer; b. Detroit, July 5, 1902; s. Clarence Edward and Virginia (Thayer) G.; student Assumption Coll., Windsor, Ont., Can., 1917-19, U. Detroit, 1919-24; LL.B., U. Detroit, 1924; m. Margaret Elizabeth Grix, Jan. 20, 1934. Admitted to Mich. bar, 1925, since practiced in Detroit; partner firm Hill, Lewis, Adams, Goodrich & Tait, and predecessors, 1952—. Dir. Palmer Shile Co., Detroit, 1960—, sec., 1964—. Mem. Delta Theta Phi. Republican. Roman Cath. Clubs: Detroit; Grosse Pointe (Mich.) Yacht; Lawyers (N.Y.C.). Home: 102 Handy Rd Grosse Pointe Farms, MI 48236 Office: Penobscot Bldg Detroit MI 48226

GOODRICH, FOSTER EDWARD, mfg. co. exec.; b. Cambridge, N.Y., Aug. 12, 1908; s. Edward and Bertha (Allen) G.; A.B., Colgate U., 1933; m. Dorothy Ada Morgan, Aug. 12, 1937 (dec.); children—Foster Allen, Ann Morgan, Donald William, Jon Edward, Pamela Jeanne, Trili. Dealer, Stanley Home Products, Inc., Utica, N.Y., 1932, successively coll. mgr. Hamilton, unit mgr. Schenectady, br. mgr. Watertown, dist. mgr. Syracuse, region mgr., asst. sales mgr., promotional sales mgr., gen. sales mgr., 1953-57, v.p. charge sales, 1957, 1st v.p., dir. sales, 1958, pres. Stanley Home Products, Inc., Westfield, Mass., 1960—, also dir.; dir. Third Nat. Bank Hampden Co. Dir. Frank Stanley Beveridge Found., Inc., Stanley Park of Westfield, Inc. Mem. alumni bd. Colgate U. Served with USNR, 1944-45. Mem. N.Y. Sales Exec. Club, Newcomen Soc., Explorers Club. Republican. Methodist. Home: 22 Tekoa Terrace Westfield MA 01085 Office: 333 Western Av Westfield MA 01085

GOODRICH, FRANCES, author; b. Belleville. N.J.; d. Henry Wickes and Madeleine Christy (Lloyd) Goodrich; B.A., Vassar Coll.; student Sch. Social Service, N.Y.C.; m. Robert Ames (div.); m. 2d, Hendrik Willem Van Loon (div.); m. 3d, Albert M. Hackett, Feb. 7, 1932. Actress Vassar Theatre; writer stage and cinema; collaborator (with Albert Hackett) stage plays, Up Pops the Devil, 1930, Bridal Wise, Great Big Doorstep, 1943, Diary of Anne Frank, 1955; motion pictures include Thin Man, Naughty Marietta, Ah Wilderness, Father of the Bride, Easter Parade, Seven Brides for Seven Brothers, others. Recipient Pulitzer prize (with Albert Hackett), for play Diary of Anne Frank. Mem. Dramatists Guild, Authors League. Clubs: Vassar, Cosmopolitan (N.Y.C.). Author: The Third Adam, 1967. Home: 88 Central Park W New York City NY 10023

GOODRICH, FRANK IVOR, former mfg. exec.; b. Dover, O., Dec. 13, 1905; s. Glenn I. and Minnie M. (Beans) G.; student Denison U.; m. Helen M. Lahm, Feb. 23, 1927. Various positions Eaton Corp., Detroit, former exec. v.p., dir., now ret. Bd. dirs. Hillsdale Coll. Mem. Soc. Automotive Engrs. Mason. Club: Union. Home: 65 Hunting Trail Moreland Hills OH 44022

GOODRICH, FREDERICK NORMAN, banker; b. Bklyn., Nov. 22, 1908; s. Charles Howard and Matilda Antoinette (Brant) G.; grad. Phillips Exeter Acad., 1926; A.B., Princeton, 1930; M.B.A., Harvard, 1932; m. Dorothy Raymond Frost, Aug. 4, 1934; children—David, Sally. With Central Hanover Bank & Trust Co., 1932-34; with U.S. Trust. Co. of N.Y., N.Y.C., 1934—, v.p., 1953-61, head investment div., 1958—, exec. v.p. 1961—; vice chmn. U.S. Trust Internat. Corp.; mng. dir. U.S. Trust London, Ltd.; dir. Southwestern Sugar and Molasses Co. N.Y.C. Treas. mem. bd. trustees Inst. Muscle Disease, N.Y.C.; trustee Anatolia Coll., Thessaloniki, Greece, Bangor (Me.) Theol. Sem. Mem. Nat. Council Chs. Conglist. (trustee). Clubs: India House, Princeton (N.Y.C.). Author pamphlets. Home: 56 Cadogan Lane London SW1 England Office: 45 Wall St New York City NY 10005

GOODRICH, HENRY CALVIN, packaging co. exec.; b. Fayetteville, Tenn., Apr. 24, 1920; s. Charles Landess and Maude (Baxter) G.; student Erskine Coll., 1938-39; B.S., U. Tenn., 1943; m. Billie Grace Walker, Sept. 10, 1943; children—Thomas Michael, William Walker, Sydney Lee. Engr., project engr., project mgr., mgr. sales, v.p., sr. v.p., dir. Rust Engring. Co., Birmingham, Ala. and Pitts., 1946-67; exec. v.p., dir. Inland Container Corp., Indpls., 1968-69, pres., chief exec. officer, 1970—; chmn., dir. Ga. Kraft Co., Rome, Ga.; dir. Protective Life Ins. Co., So. Natural Gas Co., Metalplate and Coatings, Ala. Gt. So. R.R. Pres., St. Vincents Hosp. Devel. Fund, Indpls., 1968-70. Served to lt., C.E., USNR, 1943-46. Fellow Am. Soc. C.E.; mem. Am. Iron and Steel Inst., T.A.P.P.I., Assn. Iron and Steel Engrs., Newcomen Soc., Kappa Alpha, Tau Beta Pi, Omicron Delta Kappa, Beta Gamma Sigma. Rotarian. Home: 7760 N College Av Indianapolis, IN 46240. Office: 120 E Market St Indianapolis IN 46206

GOODRICH, JAMES F., mfg. co. exec.; b. 1913; B.S., U. Mich., 1937; married. Naval architect, engr. Seattle-Tacoma Shipbldg. Corp., 1940-46; gen. supt., asst. gen. mgr. Todd Shipyards Corp., 1946-59, gen. mgr. Los Angeles div., 1959-64; exec. v.p. Bath Iron Works Corp., 1964-65, pres., dir., 1965-67; v.p., dir. Bath Industries, Inc., Milw., 1967—; dir. Congoleum-Nairn Inc., Pa. Crusher Corp. Served with U.S. Mcht. Marine, 1937-39. Office: 2100 N Mayfair Rd Milwaukee WI 53226*

GOODRICH, JOHN BERNARD, lawyer, ry. exec.; b. Spokane, Wash., Jan. 4, 1928; s. John Casey and Dorothy (Koll) G.; LL.B., Gonzaga U., 1954; m. Therese H. Vollmer, June 14, 1952; children—Joseph B., Bernadette M., Paula M., Andrew J., Philip M., Thomas A., Mary Elizabeth, Jennifer H., Rosanne M. Admitted to Ill. bar, 1955, Wash. bar, 1954; indsl. traffic mgr. Pacific N.W. Alloys, Spokane, 1950-54; asst. to gen. counsel Cromium Mining & Smelting Corp., Chgo., 1954-56; with Monon R.R., 1956-69, atty., gen. solicitor, 1956-66, sec., 1957-69, treas., 1959-66, v.p. law, 1966-69, also dir.; sec.-treas. I.C.R.R., Chgo., 1970—; pres., dir. subsidiaries

Chgo. & Indpls. Coal Co., Inc., Monon Coal Co., River Warehouse & Terminal Co.; sec., treas. Waterloo R.R., Miss. Valley Corp., Madison Coal Corp., Chgo. Produce Terminal. (all Chgo.). Mem. Traffic and Safety Commn., Park Forest, Ill., 1963-66; mem. Park Forest Recreation Bd., 1966—, chmn., 1969-70. Served with AUS, 1946-48. Mem. Am., Wash., Chgo. bar assns., Newcomen Soc. Republican. Roman Catholic. K.C. (4), Elk. Clubs: University, Economic (Chgo.). Home: 47 Apple Lane Park Forest IL 60466 Office: 135 E 11th Pl Chicago IL 60605

GOODRICH, JOHN QUINCY, banker; b. Glastonbury, Conn., July 1, 1906; s. Charles Edwards and Nellie B. (Griswold) G.; student U. Pa., 1926-28, Hartford chpt. Am. Inst. Banking, 1933-40, Stonier Grad. Sch. Banking, Rutgers U., 1946-48; m. Grace Angus Miller, May 12, 1934; children—Susan G. (Mrs. David L. Motycka), John Quincy. With State Savs. Bank Hartford, 1932-68, pres., 1964-68; pres., chief exec. officer, trustee State-Dime Savs. Bank, Hartford, 1968—; dir. Glastonbury Bank & Trust Co., Hartford Mut. Investment Fund, Savs. Bank Life Ins. Co., Church Homes, Inc. State rep. Nat. Assn. Bank Supervisors, 1968—; Incorporator, treas. Glastonbury Free Acad., 1944—; chmn. Glastonbury Bd. Finance 1958-68, Glastonbury Charter Revision Commn., 1968-69. Corporator Hartford Hosp., St. Francis Hosp. Inst. Living. Named Republican Man of Year, Glastonbury, 1968. Mem. Am. Inst. Banking, Greater Hartford C. of C., Greater Hartford Bd. Realtors, Home Builders Assn. Hartford County, Newcomen Soc. N. Am., Kappa Alpha. Home: 93 Farmcliff Dr Glastonbury CT 06033 Office: 39 Pearl St Hartford CT 06103

GOODRICH, KENNETH PAUL, coll. adminstr.; b. Elkhorn, Wis., 1933; s. Kenneth Potter and Helene (Keller) G.; A.B., Oberlin Coll., 1955; M.A., U. Ia., 1958, Ph.D., 1959; m. Elaine L. Ashby, June 12, 1954; children—Laurel Lynn, David Kenneth, Paul Ashby, Karen Elaine. Mem. faculty U. Pa. Phila., 1959-63; lectr., project asso. U. Wis., Madison, 1963-65; asso. prof. psychology Macalester Coll., St. Paul, 1965-68, chmn. dept. psychology, 1965-67, dean coll., 1967-69, prof. psychology, 1968—, dean and dir. ednl. resources, 1969-71, v.p. for acad. affairs and provost, 1971—. Mem. exec. com. Delaware County chpt. Am. Civil Liberties Union, Phila., 1960- 63; mem. Wis. Citizens for Fair Housing, Madison, 1963-65. Mem. Am. Assn. U. Profs., Am. Assn. Higher Edn. Home: 1944 Shryer Av W St Paul MN 55113 Office: Macalester College St Paul MN 55101

GOODRICH, LELAND MATTHEW, educator; b. Lewiston, Me., Sept. 1, 1899; s. Fred Bartlett and Alice Mae (Tibbetts) G.; A.B., Bowdoin Coll., 1920, Sc.D., 1952; A.M., Harvard, 1921, Ph.D., 1925; m. Eleanor Allen, June 30, 1928; children—Richard Allen, John Bradbury. Instr. polit. sci. Brown U., 1922-23, asst. prof. polit. sci. Brown U., 1926-31, asso. prof., 1931-46, prof. 1946-50; instr. govt. and law Lafayette Coll., 1925-26; prof. internat. orgn. and adminstrn. Columbia, 1950-67, acting chmn. dept. pub. law and govt., 1965-66, James T. Shotwell prof. internat. relations, 1967—; vis. lectr. in govt. Harvard, 1949-50; prof. internat. orgn. and adminstrn., Fletcher Sch. of Law and Diplomacy, 1944—; vis. prof. Sch. Internat. Affairs, Columbia, 1948-49; dir. World Peace Found., 1942-46, Belgian-Am. Ednl. Found. 1953—. Mem. Internat. Secretariat, UN Conf. on Internat. Orgn., 1945; chmn. bd. editors Internat. Orgn., 1946—. Trustee World Peace Found.; trustee overseer Bowdoin Coll. Mem. Fgn. Policy Assn. (chmn. R.I., 1928-35, sec. Providence com. Fgn. Relations, 1942-48), Am. Soc. Internat. Law (exec. council 1940-43), Am. Polit. Sci. Assn., Acad. Polit. Sci., Phi Beta Kappa, Psi Upsilon. Conglist. Author: (with Edvard Hambro) Charter of the United Nations: Commentary and Documents, rev. 1949; (with Anne Simons), The United Nations and the Maintenance of International Peace and Security, 1955; Korea: A Study of United States Policy in the United Nations, 1956; The United Nations, 1959. Editor: (with S. Shepard Jones and Denys Myers) Documents on Am. Foreign Relations, Vol. IV, 1942, Volumes V-VII (with Marie J. Carroll) (World Peace Found.) 1945, 46, 47; co-editor the United Nations in the Balance, 1965; mem. bd. editors Internat. Orgn. Author articles. Member Sec. Gen's, Com. to review orgn. and activities, UN Secretariat, 1961. Home: 460 Riverside Dr New York City NY 10027

GOODRICH, LLOYD, mus. officer and author; b. Nutley, N.J., July 10, 1897; s. Henry Wickes and Madeleine (Lloyd) G.; ed. Nutley High Sch., Art Students League and Nat. Acad. of Design (N.Y.C.); D.Fine Arts, Cornell Coll., Io., 1963, Colby Coll., 1964; m. Edith Havens, Jan. 12, 1924; children—David Lloyd, Madeleine Lloyd (Mrs. John J. Noble). With Macmillan Co., pubs., 1923-25; asso. editor The Arts, 1925-27, 1928- 29, European editor, 1927-28, contbg. editor, 1929-31; asst. art critic N.Y. Times, 1929; research curator Whitney Mus. Am. Art, 1935-47, asso. curator 1947-48, asso. dir., 1948-58, dir. 1958-68, advt. dir. 1968—; mem. N.Y. Regional Com., Pub. Works Art Project, 1933-34; founder, dir. Am. Art Research Council, 1942—; chmn. editorial bd. Mag. of Art, 1942-50; mem. editorial bd., Art Bull., Art in Am., 1946—; mem. adv. bd. Carnegie Study Am. Art; N.Y. Regional bd. Archives of Am. Art chmn., Com. on Govt. and Art, 1948—; mem. Nat. Council on Arts and Govt., 1954—, vice-chmn., 1962—; sec. Sara Roby Found., 1956—, also dir. Trustee, hon. v.p. Am. Fedn. Arts; mem. Smithsonian Art Commn.; co-chmn. Joint Artists- Mus. Com.; mem. council Coll. Architecture, Cornell U.; counseil Scientifique Internat., Enciclopedia dell'Arte; asso. seminar Am. Civilization, Columbia; mem. bd. trustees Whitney Mus. Am. Art, Am. Friends of Tate Gallery. Mem. Adv. Com. Art for the White House, 1960-63. Bd. dirs. Edward MacDowell Assn. Recipient Art in Am. award, 1959, art award Nat. Art Materials Trade Assn., 1964, award of merit Phila. Mus. Coll. Art, 1964. Fellow Am. Acad. Arts and Scis.; mem. Assn. of Art Mus. Dirs., Internat. Art Critics Assn., Drawing Soc., Am. Inst. of Interior Disigners (hon. mem.). Lectr. and writer on art, especially Am. art. Author books including: Thomas Eakins, 1933; Winslow Homer, 1944; Yasuo Kuniyoshi, 1948; Max Weber, 1949, Edward Hopper, 1950, John Sloan, 1952, Albert P. Ryder, 1959; Winslow Homer's America, 1969. Co-author: Am. Art of Our Century, 1961. Editor Research in American Art, 1945; Mus. and the Artist, 1958. Contbr. New Art in America, 1957. Office: Whitney Mus Am Art 945 Madison Av at 75th St New York City NY 10021

GOODRICH, MAX, univ. dean; b. Calboun, Mo., Dec. 11, 1905; s. Henry Charles and Elma Antoinette (Shafer) G.; B.A. cum laude, Westminster Coll., Fulton, Mo., 1927; Ph.D., U. Minn., 1936; m. Marian Jeannette Guyer, Aug. 24, 1929; children—Mary Lee Ann (Mrs. Roy T. Matthews), Marna Jean (Mrs. Clement J. Clarke III). Instr. math. Salt Lake City Collegiate Inst. 1927-29; asst. instr. physics U. Minn., 1929-36; faculty La. State U., Baton Rouge, 1936—, prof. physics, 1950—, dean Grad. Sch., on 1961—, leave, 1968-69; chief grad. acad. programs br. U.S. Office Edn., Washington, 1968-69. Mem. staff War Research Lab., U. Tex. 1945; sr. physicist Oak Ridge Nat. Lab., 1949, summers 1950, 52, 54. Mem. computer com. So. Regional Bd. 1968—. Fellow Am. Phys. Soc., A.A.A.S.; mem. Am. Assn. Physics Tchrs., Am. Assn. U. Profs., La. Acad. Sci., Sigma Xi (past pres. La. State U. chpt.), Sigma Pi Sigma, Omicron Delta Kappa, Phi Kappa Phi. Contbr. articles to profl. jours. Home: 5688 Forsythia Av Baton Rouge LA 70808

GOODRICH, NATHANIEL HERMAN, lawyer, govt. ofcl.; b. N.Y.C., June 30, 1914; s. Pincus and Frieda (Weinstein) G.; student Townsend Harris Hall, 1927-30; A.B., Cornell, 1934, LL.B., 1936; grad. Command and Gen. Staff Coll., 1945; sr. officers tng. course Air Force Sch. Applied Tactics, 1944; m. Marjorie A. Rosenthal, Oct. 4, 1954; children—Robert Dunbar, Thomas Neil. Admitted to N.Y. bar, 1936, U.S. Supreme Ct. bar, 1948, D.C. bar, 1954; staff atty. Am. Jewish Com., 1938-41; asst. to chief tax amortization div. Office Under Sec. War, 1941-42; legal adviser sec. div. Office War War Moblzn. and Reconversion, 1946; counsel President's Sci. Research Bd., 1947; exec. sec., counsel President's Spl. Bd. Inquiry Air Safety, 1947-48; counsel to comptroller Dept. Def., 1948, asst. gen. counsel, 1949, dep. gen. counsel, 1952-53, spl. asst. to sec. def., 1956; pvt. practice law, Washington, 1954-59; gen. counsel FAA, Washington, 1962-70; permanent mem. Atomic Safety and Licensing Bd. AEC, 1971—. Served to lt. col. USAAF, 1942-46; Office Asst. Chief of Air Staff Intelligence. Mem. Am. Bar Assn. Jewish religion. Clubs: Army and Navy (Washington), Federal City, Woodmont Country; Wings (N.Y.). Home: 4705 Drummond Av Chevy Chase MD 20015 Office: AEC Washington DC 20545

GOODRICH, PAUL W., business exec.; b. Oskaloosa, Ia., Sept. 2, 1906; s. Harry and Stella (Guthrie) G.; A.B., Drake U., 1928; LL.B., Chgo. Kent Coll. Law, 1931; M.B.A., U. Chgo., 1947; m. Virginia Davis, Feb. 6, 1932; children—William D., James W., Carolyn. Joined Chgo. Title & Trust Co., 1931, pres., 1953-69, chmn. bd., 1967—, chief exec. officer, 1953—; dir. Lincoln Nat. Corp., Swift & Co., Internat. Harvester, Peoples Gas Co., also Halsey Stuart & Co. Mem. Chgo. Police Bd. Trustee Drake U., Wesley Meml. Hosp., Field Museum of Natural History. Mem. Am., Ill., Chgo. bar assns., Chgo. Assn. Commerce and Industry (pres. 1959-60), Am., Ill. title assns., U.S. C. of C. (dir.). Republican. Methodist. Clubs: University, Economic, Chicago, Commercial, Mid-Am. (Chgo.). Home: 439 Sheridan Rd Kenilworth IL 60043 Office: 111 W Washington St Chicago IL 60602

GOODRICH, PIERRE FRIST, lawyer; b. Winchester, Ind., Sept. 10, 1894; s. James Putnam and Cora (Frist) G.; A.B., Wabash Coll., 1916, LL.D., 1949; LL.B., Harvard Law Sch., 1920; m. Dorothy Dugan, 1920; 1 dau., Nancy; m. 2d, Enid Smith, Feb. 1941. Admitted to Ind. bar, 1920, began practice at Winchester; mem. Macy & Goodrich, 1920-23, Mote & Goodrich, 1923-25, Goodrich, Emison & Campbell, 1928-39, Goodrich & Campbell, 1939-52, Goodrich, Campbell & Warren, 1952-61, Goodrich & Warren, Indpls., 1961—; pres., dir. Ind. Telephone Corp, 1935—, Peoples Loan & Trust Co.; chmn. Liberty Fund, Inc., Thirty- Five Twenty, Inc; dir. Pub. Telephone Corp. Served as 2d lt. U.S. Army, 1917-18. Trustee Found. for Econ. Edn., Inc. Mem. Mont Pelerin Soc., Am., Ind., Indpls. bar assns., Indpls., Ind. chambers commerce, Am. Legion, Athenaeum Turners, Phi Beta Kappa, Phi Beta Kappa Assos., Phi Gamma Delta. Republican. Presbyn. Clubs: University (N.Y.); Columbia; Woodstock. Office: 3520 Washington Blvd Indianapolis IN 46205

GOODRICH, RICHARD LANE, govt. ofcl.; b. Lynn, Mass., July 30, 1908; s. Philip and Bertha (Grouer) G.; B.S., Tufts U., 1931; postgrad. N.Y.U., 1931-32, Coll. City N.Y., 1936-37; m. Bernice Holz, Sept. 24, 1932; children—Brenton, Paul, Virginia. Instr. L.I.U., 1931-32; instr.-coach Westfield (N.J.) High Sch., 1932-41; exec. devel. technician Gen. Motors Inst., 1941-44; indsl. equipment specialist Ritterbush & Co., N.Y.C., 1944-47; personnel dir. Am. Cyanamid, 1947-49; mgmt. cons. Worden & Risberg, Phila., 1949-52; indsl. adviser USOM, Japan and Korea, 1952—; mgmt. cons-Republic China; adviser Corporacion de Fomento, Chile, 1953-54. Bd. dirs. Korea Inst. Sci. and Tech., Asian Productivity Orgn. Mem. Com. Internat. Orgn. Sci., Theta Delta Chi. Author: Top Management in Retrospect, 1967; Quo Vadis, Top Management, 1968; Top Management in Review, 1969. Home: Center Ossipee NH 03814 Office: APO San Francisco CA 96301

GOODRICH, ROBERT EDWARD, Jr., clergyman; b. Cleburne, Tex., June 9, 1909; s. Robert Edward and Moye (Wilson) G.; B.A., Birmingham-So. U., 1931; M.A., Perkins Theol. Sch., 1940; D.D., Centenary Coll., 1950; m. Thelma Quillian, June 5, 1939; children—Thelma Jean (Mrs. James Skinner), Lucy (Mrs. James Caswell), Robert Edward III, Paul Quillian. Ordained to ministry Methodist Ch., 1933; pastor in Port Arthur, Tex., 1935-37, Houston, 1937-44, El Paso, Tex. 1944-46, First Meth. Ch., Dallas, 1946—. Past chmn. jurisdictional council So. Central Jurisdiction Meth. Ch., also past chmn. jurisdictional TV, radio and film commn.; del. World Meth. Conf., 1966, Gen. Conf., 1952, 66, 60, 64, 68, 70. Trustee Southwestern U., So. Meth. U., Meth. Home for Children. Mem. Kappa Alpha. Author: What's It All About, 1955; Reach for the Sky, 1960; Lift Up Your Heart, 1961; On the Other Side of Sorrow, 1962, 70; Dear God Where Are You? 1969. Created 1st dramatic religious TV show, 1949; preacher on radio. Home: 3310 Fairmont St Dallas TX 75201 Office: 1928 Ross Av Dallas TX 75201

GOODRICH, WARREN M., lawyer; b. Lawton, Okla., Jan. 5, 1922; A.B. with honors, U. Fla., 1943, LL.B. with high honors, 1948. Admitted to Fla. bar, 1948; mem. firm Goodrich, Hampton, Thompson, Boylston, and Namack, P.A., Bradenton, Fla.; pros. atty., 1953-57. Mem. Fla. Constitution Revision Commn., Commn. on Aging. Chmn. Fla. Democratic Exec. Com., 1962—, chmn., 1962-66. Fellow Acad. Fla. Trial Lawyers (pres. 1962-63); mem. Am., Manatee County (pres. 1956-57) bar assns., Fla. Bar (past chmn. com. on econs. of bar, council of bar pres.'s), Law Sci. Acad., Am. Trial Lawyers Assn. (editor Jour. 1961—, Fla. committeeman 1962-63), Blue Key, Phi Beta Kappa, Phi Delta Phi, Phi Kappa Phi, Tau Kappa Alpha. Editor-in-chief U. Fla. Law Rev., 1949-50. Address: 406 13th St W Bradenton FL 33505

GOODSILL, MARSHALL M., lawyer; b. Galesburg, Ill., Oct. 19, 1916; s. Marshall Max and Margherita (Chase) G.; B.A. magna cum laude, U. Minn., 1935; LL.B., Harvard, 1937; m. Ruth Caley, Feb. 20, 1947; children—Kay, Curtis, Jane, John. Admitted to N.Y. bar, also Hawaii bar; asso. firm Cravath, Swaine & Moore, N.Y.C., 1940-41; partner firm Jenks, Kidwell, Goodsill & Anderson, and predecessors, Honolulu, 1950—. Sec. standing com. rules of practice and procedure Hawaii Supreme Ct., 1962—. Bd. dirs. Honolulu Community Theatre, 1960-62, Palama Settlement Study Com., 1967-68. Served to lt. comdr. USNR, 1941-45. Decorated Bronze Star; mem. Order Brit. Empire. Fellow Am. Bar Found.; mem. Hawaii Bar Assn., Phi Beta Kappa. Episcopalian. Club: Pacific (Honolulu). Home: 4258 PuuPanini Av Honolulu, HI 96816 Office: Financial Plaza of the Pacific Honolulu HI 96801

GOODSILL, STANLEY CHASE, accountant; b. Galesburg, Ill., Aug. 24, 1918; s. Marshall M. and Harriett M. (Chase) G.; B.B.A., U. Minn., 1940; M.B.A., Harvard, 1942; m. Marilyn Allenbaugh, June 14, 1951; children—Louise, Susan, Jeffrey. With Arthur Andersen & Co., C.P.A.'s, Chgo., 1941-42, Young, Lamberton & Pearson, C.P.A.'s, Honolulu, 1951-56; with Haskins & Sells, C.P.A.'s, 1956—, partner, New Haven, 1961. Served with AUS, 1943-45. Home: Peck Hill Rd Woodbridge CT 06525 Office: 900 Chapel Sq New Haven CT 06510

GOODSON, CARL EDWARD, educator; b. St. Louis, July 31, 1917; s. Harry Edward and Clara (Cummins) G.; A.B., William Jewell Coll., 1939; Th.M., So. Baptist Theol. Sem., 1944; Th.D., Central Baptist Theol. Sem., 1951; m. Rozelle Wordingham, May 31, 1944; children—Mary (Mrs. Lynn Clark), Nancy Lea, Margery (Mrs. Daniel Lumpkin), Charlotte Rose, Timothy Carl. Ordained to ministry Baptist Ch., 1940; pastor Baptist Ch. Smiths Grove, Ky., 1944-45, Columbia, Mo., 1945-46; mem. faculty Southwest Bapt. Coll., Bolivar, Mo., 1946-61; prof. Ouachita Bapt. U., Arkadelphia, Ark., 1961-68, v.p. for academic affairs, 1970—; dean Mo. Bapt. Coll., St. Louis, 1968-70. Mem. edn. commn. So. Baptist Conv., 1950-56; mem. hist. commn. Mo. Bapt. Conv., 1969-70. Mem. Nat. Collegiate Honors Council. Mem. Soc. Biblical Lit., Am. Acad. Religion, Kiwanian, Rotarian. Home: 144 Evonshire Dr Arkadelphia AR 71923

GOODSON, CHARLES L., lawyer; b. Franklin, Ga., Mar. 24, 1928; s. Tom W. and Ora Lee (Farr) G.; LL.B., U. Ga., 1950; m. Dorothy Enloe, June 30, 1954; children—Mary Jane, Paige Enloe, Ora Leigh, Charles L. Admitted to Ga. bar, 1950; practiced in Franklin and Newman, Ga., 1950-51, Newman, 1957-61, Atlanta, 1969—; adminstrv. asst. to U.S. Congressman Flynt, 1955-57; U.S. atty. No. Dist. Ga., 1961-69. Dir., atty. Bank of Heard County, Franklin. Mem. Ga. Ho. of Reps. from Heard County, 1953-55. Served to 1st lt. USAF, 1951-53. Decorated Bronze Star. Mem. Fed., Ga., Coweta County bar assns., Phi Alpha Delta. Democrat. Mason, Kiwanian, Elk. Club: Old War Horse Lawyers. Home: 4 Brookside Dr Newman GA 30263 Office: 15 1/2 Greenville St Newnan GA 30263

GOODSON, JAMES BUTLER, life ins. co. exec.; b. Waco, Tex., Aug. 15, 1923; s. William Lloyd and Susie (Butler) G.; B.B.A., U. Tex., 1948; m. Molly Barnes, Mar. 20, 1949; children—Laurie, Liza, James Butler, Thomas Barnes. Analyst, Rauscher, Pierce & Co., Dallas, 1948-52; with Southland Life Ins. Co., Dallas, 1952—, pres., 1969—, also dir., mem. exec. com.; chmn. finance com., dir., mem. exec. com. Nathan Hale Life Ins. Co. Treas., dir. Boys' Clubs Am., 1962-66; pres., dir. Children's Devel. Center, Dallas, 1967; mem. exec. com. Dallas Council Chs., 1967, bd. dirs., 1968; mem. Dallas Assembly, 1962—, Cotton Bowl Council 1962—; active United Fund, YMCA. Bd. dirs. Goodwill Industries Dallas, Hope Cottage, Dallas, Jr. Achievement Dallas. Served with AUS, World War II. Mem. Salesmanship Club Dallas (bd. dirs. 1965-66), Sigma Alpha Epsilon. Presbyn. (chmn. deacons 1961, elder 1962-65, deacon 1961—). Home: 3817 Gillon St Dallas TX 75205 Office: 1800 Southland Center Dallas TX 75201

GOODSON, LOUIE AUBREY, Jr., textile mfr., lawyer; b. Caswell County, N.C., Dec. 20, 1922; s. Louie Aubrey and Lenna Sue (Neal) G.; B.S., N.C. State Coll., 1943; LL.B., Georgetown U., 1951; m. Bernice Carroll, July 23, 1945; children—Louie Aubrey III, Gayle, Mark, Mary. Admitted to D.C. bar, 1951; patent searcher Fisher & Christen, 1948-51; partner Fisher, Christen & Goodson, Wash., 1953-62; chemist, patent liaison work Dan River, Inc., Danville, Va., 1946-48, house patent lawyer, asst. dir. research, 1951- 52, v.p., dir. research, 1959—; dir. Danville Industries, Inc., 1st Fed. Savs. and Loan, Danville. City planning commr., Danville. Trustee Averett Coll., Textile Research Inst. Served to capt., C.W.S., AUS, 1943- 46. Mem. Am. Patent Law Assn., Am., D.C. bar assns., Am. Chem. Soc., Am. Assn. Textile Chemists and Colorists. Republican. Baptist. Rotarian. Home: 174 Fairmont Circle Danville VA 24541 Office: Dan River Inc Danville VA 24541

GOODSON, MARK, TV producer; b. Sacramento, Jan. 24, 1915; s. Abraham Ellis and Fannie (Gross) G.; A.B., U. Cal., 1937; m. Bluma Neveleff, Feb. 16, 1941; children—Jill, Jonathan; m. 2d Virginia McDavid, Aug. 1956; 1 dau., Marjorie. Announcer, newscaster, dir. Radio Sta. KFRC, San Francisco, 1938-41; radio announcer, dir., N.Y.C., 1941-43; producer Appointment with Life, ABC, 1943; dir. Portia Faces Life, Young & Rubicam, advt. agy., 1944; radio dir. U.S. Treasury War Bond Drive, 1944-45; formed Goodson-Todman Prodns., with W. S. Todman, 1946, prod. radio show Winner Take All, 1946, Stop the Music, 1947, Hit the Jackpot, 1947-49; TV panel show What's My Line, 1949; developer, producer shows, 1950—, including It's News to Me, Name's the Same, I've Got a Secret, Fred Allen Show, Two for the Money, Beat the Clock, The Web; pres. Goodson-Todman Enterprises, producers TV shows To Tell the Truth, The Price is Right, The Rebel, Password, The Match Game, others; 1st v.p. Mid-Atlantic Newspapers, Inc.; chmn. bd. Central States Pub. Co.; 1st v.p. Capitol City Pub. Co.; v.p. New England Newspapers, Inc. Recipient nat. television award Great Britain, 1951; Emmy award Academy TV Arts and Scis., 1951, 52; Sylvania award. Mem. Acad. TV Arts and Sci. (pres. N.Y.C. 1957-58), Phi Beta Kappa. Home: 1 Beekman Pl New York City NY 10022 Office: 375 Park Av New York City NY 10022

GOODSON, MAX REED, educator; b. Garrett, Ill., Feb. 5, 1911; s. Otis Richard and Eva (Reed) G.; B.A., U. Ill., 1933, M.A., 1936, Ed.M., 1942, Ed.D., 1949; m. Margaret Catherine Schnapp, June 5, 1935; children—Nancy Kay, Charles Robert. Tchr. elementary sch., Tuscola, Ill., 1933-34; sci. tchr. Community High Sch., Mason City, Ill., 1934-35; prin. Dana Twp. High Sch., Ill., 1935-36; sci. tchr. Univ. High Sch., U. Ill., 1936-43, coordinator student teaching Coll. Edn., 1943-44; curriculum cons. Community High Sch., Blue Island, Ill., 1940-41; instr. edn., asst. prin. Univ. Sch., Ind. U., 1944-45; coordinator curriculum and instrn. Horace-Mann Lincoln Sch., N.Y.C., 1945-46, prin., 1946-47; asst. dean. coordinator research and service Ohio State U., 1947-57, prof. edn., 1949-57, asso. dean Coll. Edn., 1957; dean, prof. sch. edn. Boston U., 1957-62; editor-in-chief high sch. div. Ginn & Co., Boston, 1962-65; prof. ednl. policy studies U. Wis., Madison, 1965—, dir. Wis. Research and Devel. Center for Cognitive Learning, 1965-67, prin. investigator planned ednl. change, 1965-70; trustee Corp. Upper Midwest Regional. Ednl. Lab., Mpls., 1965—, pres., 1967-68; fellow Midwest Group for Human Resources, Kansas City, Mo.; prof. edn. U. Fla., summers 1948-50; prof. U. Va., summers 1951-53; policy com., staff Nat. Tng. Labs., Bethel, Me., 1949-60; dir. Midwest Center Human Relations Tng., 1954-57. Cons. Am. Cancer Soc., A.R.C., Lago Oil & Transport Co., Aruba, Dutch West Indies. Bd. govs. Human Relations Center, Boston U. Mem. N.E.A. (commn. on safety edn. 1955-59, Nat. Tng. Labs. Inst. for Applied Behavioral Scis. fellow), Mass. Council for Pub. Schs., Mass. Com. for Children and Youth, Am. Assn. Sch. Adminstrs., Phi Delta Kappa, Kappa Phi Kappa. Democrat. Unitarian. Author: (with Gale E. Jensen) Formal Organization in School Systems, 1956; 1960 Yearbooks of Nat. Soc. Study Edn.; also tech. reports, articles. Home: 506 Le Roy Rd Madison, WI 53704

GOODSON, RICHARD ALLEN, utility co. exec.; b. Jacksonville, Tex., Oct. 12, 1905; s. Richard Coke and Rena (Thompson) G.; B.S., Tex. A. and M. Coll., 1927; m. Nina Mae Brand, June 20, 1937; 1 dau., Rena Rozelle. Traffic asst. Southwestern Bell Telephone Co., Dallas, 1928-30, dist. traffic chief, Abilene, Tex., 1930-37, switchboard facilities engr., Dallas, 1937-43, various positions traffic dept., San Antonio, 1943-52, div. traffic supt., 1950-52, gen. traffic mgr., St. Louis, 1952-54, asst. v.p., 1954- 56, Tex. gen. mgr., Dallas, 1956-58, v.p., 1958-63; v.p. operations Am. Tel. & Tel. Co., N.Y.C., 1963-64, v.p. operations Southwestern Bell Tel. Co., St. Louis 1964-65, pres. 1965-70, chmn., chief exec. officer, 1970—; dir. Southwestern Bell, First Nat. Bank St. Louis, St. Louis Union Trust Co., Southwestern Life Ins. Co., Dallas Fed. Savs. & Loan Assn., Brown Shoe Co.,

Angelica Corp., Gen. Am. Life Ins. Co., Curlee Clothing Co. Mem. Civic Progress Inc. St. Louis. Bd. dirs. St. Louis Metropolitan YMCA, St. Louis Area council Boy Scouts Am.; mem. Mo. U. Adv. Council; campaign chmn. Greater St. Louis United Fund, Inc., 1968-69; chmn. State campaign com. Tex. United Fund, 1959-60., v.p. Dallas Council World Affairs 1962-63, Dallas Citizens Council; chmn. Tex. Research League, 1963; chmn. adv. bd. Salvation Army Tex. 1961-62, bd. dirs. Salvation Army, St. Louis; trustee Washington U., St. Louis. M.P.R.R. Research fellow Southwestern Legal Found. Mem. Dallas, St. Louis (bd. dirs.) chambers commerce, Municipal Opera Assn. Presbyn. (deacon) 1961-63. Clubs: Noonday, University, Racquet, Media, Bogey, Bellerive, St. Louis Round Table, Dallas Country (pres. 1963). Home: 14 McKnight Lane St Louis MO 63124 Office: 1010 Pine St Louis MO 63101

GOODSON, WALTER KENNETH, clergyman; b. Salisbury, N.C., Sept. 25, 1912; s. Daniel Washington and Sarah (Peeler) G.; A.B., Catawba Coll., 1934; also L.H.D.; student Duke Div. Sch., 1934-37, D.D., 1960; D.D., High Point (N.C.) Coll. 1951. Birmingham-So. Coll.; L.H.D., St. Bernard Coll.; LL.D., U., Ala; m. Martha Ann Ogburn, July 12, 1937; children—Sara Ann (Mrs. Larry M. Faust), Walter Kenneth Nancy Craven (Mrs. Thomas S. Johnson). Ordained to ministry Methodist Ch., 1939; pastor in Western N.C. Conf., 1935-64; bishop Birmingham area, 1964—. Del. World Conf. Meth. Ch., Oxford, Eng. 1951, Lake Junaluska, N.C., 1956, London, 1966, Denver, 1971; mem. Meth. World Council; bd. dirs. Meth. Com. Overseas Relief; mem. Mission Team to Gt. Britain, 1962, study team to France and Berlin, 1962; chmn. finance com. bd. missions, pres. commn. on religion and race, chmn. commn. on religion United Meth. Ch. Pres. J. B. Cornelius Found., 1946-64. Trustee Brevard Coll., Birmingham-So. Coll., Duke, Huntingdon Coll., Athens Coll., Miles Coll. Rotarian, Mason (32). Home: 2205 Vestavia Dr Birmingham AL 35216 Office: 1801 6th Av N Birmingham AL 35203

GOODSPEED, NORWICK R.G., banker. Vice pres., also treas. People's Savs. Bank of Bridgeport. Office: Main and State Sts Box 1580 Bridgeport CT 06602*

GOODSPEED, STEPHEN SPENCER, univ. adminstr.; b. Berkeley, Cal., Nov. 15, 1915; s. Thomas Harper and Florence (Beman) G.; A.B., U. Cal. at Berkeley, 1937, Ph.D., 1947; m. Grace Frances Halloran, May 12, 1938; 1 son, Roger Halloran. Instr. U. Cal. at Santa Barbara, 1946-49, asst. prof., 1949-55, asso. prof., 1955- 60, prof., 1960—, asst. to chancellor, 1958-60, vice-chancellor, 1960—; summer faculty U. Cal. at Berkeley, 1942, at Los Angeles, 1950, 59; cons. 4th Army and Western Def. Command, 1942; radio commentator, 1946- 49; mem. Standard Oil Co. Cal. Faculty Seminar, 1954, U.S. Army War Coll. Strategy Seminar, 1965. Vice pres., trustee Laguna Blanca Sch.; bd. dirs. UN Assn. Served from ensign to lt., USNR, 1942-46. Recipient Distinguished Service award Alpha Delta Phi, 1966. Mem. Am., Western polit. sci. assns., Pan-Am. Inst. History and Geography, West Coast Athletic Assn. (pres.), Pi Sigma Alpha. Club: Valley (v.p., dir.). Author: The Mexican President, 1955; Nature and Function of International Organization, 1967. Contbr. articles profl. jours. Home: 2221 Las Tunas Rd Santa Barbara, CA 93103.

GOODWILLIE, JOHN, advt. exec.; b. Wausau, Wis., May 26, 1910; s. Clarence James and Rhoda Ann (Day) G.; grad. Phillips Exeter Acad., 1929; B.A., Williams Coll., 1933; m. Mary Louise Rhodes, May 12, 1939 (div. Feb. 1961); 1 dau., Susan Rhodes; m. 2d, Lee Marko, Dec. 31, 1961; 1 dau., Kate. Asst. publicity dir. R. H. Macy Co., N.Y.C., 1935-41; copy writer, account exec. Benton & Bowles, 1945-47; dir. advt. and pub. relations Alexander Smith & Sons Carpet Co., 1948-51, v.p. charge advt. and pub. relations, 1951; account exec. Young & Rubicam, advt. agy., 1952-55; account exec. C. J. LaRoche & Co., Inc., N.Y.C., 1955-58, v.p., 1958-60, exec. v.p., vice chmn. plans bd., 1960-65; sr. v.p. Norman, Craig & Kummel, Inc., 1965-68; pres. John Goodwillie Inc. 1968—. Bd. dirs. United Fund, North Westchester, 1959-61, Irvington House, 1950—. Served to maj. USAAF, 1942-45. Mem. Mil. Order Fgn. Wars, Am. Iris Soc., Zeta Psi. Home: 106 E 17th St New York City NY 10003 Office: 415 E 52d St New York City NY 10022

GOODWIN, ALFRED THEODORE, judge; b. Bellingham, Wash., June 29, 1923; s. Alonzo Theodore and Miriam Hazel (Williams) G.; B.A., U. Ore., 1947. J.D., 1951; m. Marjorie Elizabeth Major, Dec. 23, 1943 (div. 1948); 1 son, Michael Theodore; m. 2d, Mary Ellin Handelin, Dec. 23, 1949; children—Karl Alfred, Margaret Ellen, Sara Jane, James Paul. Newspaper reporter Eugene (Ore.) Register-Guard, 1947-50; admitted to Ore. bar, 1951; practiced in Eugene until 1955; circuit judge Ore. 2d. Jud. Dist., 1955- 60; asso. justice Ore. Supreme Ct., 1960-69; U.S. dist. judge Dist. Ore., 1969—. Bd. dirs. Central Lane YMCA, Eugene, 1956-60, Salem (Ore.) Art Assn., 1960—; adv. bd. Eugene Salvation Army, 1956-60, chmn., 1959. Served to capt., inf., AUS. 1942- 46; ETO. Mem. Am. Judicature Soc., Am. Bar Assn., Inst. Jud. Adminstrn., World Peace Through Law Center, World Assn. Judges, Appellate Judges Conf., Order of Coif, Phi Delta Phi, Sigma Delta Chi, Alpha Tau Omega. Republican. Presbyn. (trustee Synod of Ore.). Contbr. articles Ore. Law Rev., 1949-51, student editor, 1950-51. Home: High 3430 SW Seymour St Portland OR 97201 Office: US Courthouse Portland OR 97205

GOODWIN, ANDREW JACKSON, investment banker; b. Anniston,, Ala., Oct. 18, 1911; s. Andrew Jackson and Viola (Farley) G.; grad. Hill Sch., Pottstown, Pa., 1930; A.B., Princeton, 1934; M.B.A., Harvard, 1936; grad. Command and Gen. Staff Sch., 1943; m. Charlotte Barton Head, Dec. 20, 1939 (div. Sept. 1963); children—Andrew Jackson, James Barton, Charlotte. With Dillon, Read & Co., investment bankers, N.Y.C., 1936-39; with First Nat. Bank, Anniston, Ala., 1939-40; v.p., dir. Anniston Nat. Bank, 1946-52; dir. Fed. Res. Bank of Atlanta, Birmingham br., 1952-53, Life Ins. Co. of Ala., Gadsden, 1952-53; commr. SEC, Washington, 1953-56; v.p., dir. Lee Higginson Corp., investment bankers, Chgo., 1956-64; mgr. Washington office Burton, Dana & Co., 1964-70; pres. Goodwin Investments, Inc., Anniston, 1970—. Commr. water bd., Anniston, 1952-53. Served at lt. col. F.A., AUS, 1940-46, asst., aide to undersec. war Robert Patterson, 1943-44; served PTO, ETO. Mem. Nat. Assn. Securities Dealers (bd. govs. 1961-64), Newcomen Soc., V.F.W., Am. Legion. Democrat. Episcopalian. Clubs: Anniston Country; Mountain Brook Country (Birmingham, Ala.); Capital City (Atlanta); Chevy Chase Country (Washington); Chicago, Attic (Chgo.); Shoreacres Country, Onewentsia Country (Lake Forest, Ill.). Home and office: 1230 Woodstock Av Anniston AL 36201

GOODWIN, BERNARD, lawyer, exec., educator; b. N.Y.C., Dec. 19, 1907; s. Mayer and Hannah (Wald) G.; Sc.B. cum laude, N.Y.U., 1928; J.D. cum laude, Harvard, 1931; children—Charles Stewart, Wendy Melinda, Alexandre Charles, Nadine Antonia. Lawyer, Seattle, 1931-34, N.Y.C., 1935—; lawyer, exec. Paramount Pictures Corp., 1934-57; sec., dir. Allen B. Dumont Labs., Inc., Clifton, N.J., 1938-55; pres., dir. Metro Media, Inc., N.Y.C., 1955-59; chmn. bd. Sunrise Broadcasting Corp., Ft. Lauderdale, Fla., 1965—; guest lectr. U. Mich. Law Sch., 1965-68, adj. prof. South Md. U. Law Sch., 1971—; prof. ospite U. Padua (Italy), 1970. Lay trustee U. Detroit, 1966—. Mem. Am., Wash., N.Y. State bar assns., Fed. Bar Council, Assn. Bar City N.Y., Am. Judicature Soc., A.S.C.A.P. (dir.), Acad. Motion Picture Arts and Scis., Am. Soc. Internat. Law, Broadcast Pioneers, Copyright Soc. U.S.A., Am. Arbitration Assn. (nat. labor panel), Phi Beta Kappa. Club: Harvard (N.Y.C.). Author books and articles on legal subjects. Address: 500 Fifth Av New York City NY 10036

GOODWIN, CLAUDE ELBERT, gas utility exec.; b. Ripley, W.Va., Aug. 9, 1910; s. Claud Earl and Marie (Vail) G.; A.B., W.Va. Wesleyan U., 1931, LL.B., W.Va. U., 1940; grad. student speech, Northwestern U., 1932; m. Ireta Joy Watson, Aug. 15, 1931; 1 dau., Judith (Mrs. Eugene L. Hayes). Admitted to W.Va. bar, 1941; mem. firm Goodwin & Goodwin Ripley, 1941-47; prof. W.Va. U. Coll. Law, 1947-48; sec., counsel United Fuel Gas Co., 1963-67; v.p., gen. counsel Charleston group companies Columbia Gas System, Inc., 1967—; dir. Atlantic Seaboard Corp., Ky. Gas Transmission Corp., Columbia Gas Ky., Inc., Columbia Gas W.Va., Inc., United Fuel Gas Co., Va. Gas Distbn. Corp., First Nat. Bank Ripley, Vail Furniture, Inc. Mem. bd. Sunrise, Charleston, museum and art gallery, 1969—; past pres., mem. alumni exec. council W.Va. U. Served with USNR, 1943-46. Decorated Commendation medal. Mem. Am., W.Va. bar assns., Fed. Power Bar Assn., Am. Judicature Soc., Order of Coif. Episcopalian (trustee). Editor-in-chief W.Va. Law Rev., 1939-40. Home: Evans Rd Ripley WV 25271 Office: 1700 MacCorkle Av Charleston WV 25325

GOODWIN, CRAUFURD DAVID, educator; b. Montreal, Que., Can., May 23, 1934; s. George R. and Roma (Stewart) G.; B.A., McGill U., 1955; Ph.D., Duke, 1958; m. Nancy Virginia Sanders, June 7, 1958. Came to U.S., 1962. Econ. research asst. Courtauld's Can., Ltd., 1955; lectr. econs. U. Windsor, Ont., 1958-59; exec. sec. Commonwealth Studies Center, Duke, also vis. asst. prof., 1959-60; hon. research fellow Australian Nat. U., 1960-61; asst. prof. econs. York U., Toronto, 1961-62; asst. prof. econs., asst. to provost Duke, Durham, N.C., 1962-63, asso. prof. econs., sec. to Univ., asst. to provost, 1963-64, asso. prof. econs., sec. Univ., asst. provost, 1964- 66, asso.. prof. econs., asst. provost, dir. internat. studies, 1966-68, prof. econs., vice proovost for internat. studies, 1968-69, prof. econs., vice provost, dir. internat. programs, 1969—; officer in charge European and internat. affairs Ford Found., 1971—. Smuts vis. fellow Cambridge U., 1967-68, Guggenheim fellow, 1967-68. Author: Canadian Economic Thought: The Political Economy of a Developing Nation 1814-1914, 1961; Economic Enquiry in Australia, 1966. Editor; (with W.B. Hamilton and Kenneth Robinson) A Decade of the Commonwealth 1955-64, 1966; (with I.B. Holley) The Transfer of Ideas, 1968; History of Political Economy, 1969—. Home: 2256 Cranford Rd Durham NC 27706

GOODWIN, DONALD LESLIE, govt. ofcl.; b. Brewer, Me., Feb. 22, 1923; s. Galen Leslie and Ethel Rose (Mayo) G.; A.B., U. Me.; student Am. U., 1949-50; m. Lillian Estes, Sept. 4, 1942; children—Larry, Judith, Alan. Tchr. pub. schs., Bucksport, Me., 1947-49; with Nat. Archives, 1949-50, Civil Service Intern Program, 1950; with records mgmt. Dept. State, 1950-53; with Diamond Ordnance Fuze Lab., Dept. Army, 1953-54; with Post Office Dept., 1954-56; cons. ICA, Iran, 1956-60; chief pub. adminstrn. div. Bur. Africa, AID, 1962-66; dep. dir. AID, Liberia, 1966-68, asst. dir. pub. adminstrn., Vietnam, 1968-70; with Bur. Vietnam, AID, Washington, 1970—. Recipient Congl. fellowship Am. Polit. Sci. Assn., 1965-66. Served to capt. AUS, World War II. Mem. Am. Polit. Sci. Assn., Am. Soc. Pub. Adminstrn., Soc. Internat. Devel. Club: Toastmasters. Address: AID Vietnam Bur Washington DC 20523

GOODWIN, EUGENE STERN, lawyer; b. Hartford, Conn., Oct. 24, 1915; s. I. M. and Sadie (Feingold) G.; A.B., U. Cal. at Los Angeles, 1936; LL.B., U. So. Cal., 1940; m. Madeline Rosenthal, Dec. 14, 1946; children—Theodore S., George M., Betty G. Admitted to Cal. bar, 1941, since practiced in Beverly Hills; partner firm Kaplan, Livingston, Goodwin, Berkowitz & Selvin, and predecessor firms, 1946—. Mem. Am., Beverly Hills, Los Angeles bar assns., Cal. State Bar, Am. Judicature Soc., Am. Arbitration Assn. (nat. panel arbitrators). Club: Brentwood Country. Home: 139 N Thurston Av Los Angeles CA 90049 Office: 450 N Roxbury Dr Beverly Hills CA 90210

GOODWIN, FRANCIS MARLON, Jr., steel co. exec.; b. Spokane, Wash., Nov. 2, 1910; s. Francis M. and Margaret (Carnan) G.; A.B., Harvard, 1931, M.B.A., 1933; student Emanuel Coll., Cambridge U. (Eng.), 1933-34; m. Ann Frances Sproule, July 13, 1946; 1 dau., Nancy Sproule. Nat. bank examiner Treasury Dept., 1935-41, 46-49; asst. dept. mgr. internat. div. Ford Motor Co., 1950-52, dept. mgr., 1952-56; asst. to treas. U.S. Steel Corp., N.Y.C., 1956-57, asst. treas., 1957-59, v.p., asst. treas., 1959—. Served from lt. (j.g.) to lt. comdr., USNR, 1942-46. Mem. Am. Mgmt. Assn., Am. Iron and Steel Inst., Bronxville Derby Assn., Nat. Fgn. Trade Council. Episcopalian. Clubs: St. Andrews Golf (pres. 1969-71), University (N.Y.C.); University (Washington). Home: 20 Homesdale Rd Bronxville NY 10708 Office: 71 Broadway New York City NY 10006

GOODWIN, FREDERICK MERRY, chem. co. exec.; b. Kansas City, Mo., June 13, 1908; s. Harry L. and Bertha L. (Merry) G.; student U. Mo., 1925-27; m. Maxine Maxwell, June 15, 1929; 1 son, Frederick Merry. With Thompson-Hayward Chem. Co., Kansas City, Mo., 1927—, exec. v.p., 1951-68, vice chmn. bd., 1968—, also dir. Mem. Drug. Chem. and Allied Trades Assn., Nat. Paint, Varnish and Lacquer Assn., Sigma Alpha Epsilon. Episcopalian. Home: 5411 Windsor Lane Shawnee Mission KS 66205 Office: 5200 Speaker Rd Kansas City KS 66106

GOODWIN, GEORGE Jr., educator; b. Hartford, Conn., June 29, 1921; s. George and Louise Whitney (Dodge) G.; grad. Deerfield Acad., 1939; A.B., Williams Coll., 1943; Ph.D., Harvard, 1955; m. Ellen Dean Safford, Dec. 15, 1951; children—Alice Safford, Emily Dodge, Maida Dean, George Putnam, William Tappen. Faculty, U. Mass., Amherst, 1947-62; prof. polit. sci., chmn. dept. U. R.I., 1962-65; prof. U. Mass., Boston, 1965—, also chmn. politics dept. Served with USAAF, 1943-45. Mem. Am., New Eng. polit. sci. assns., Am. Assn. U. Profs. Conglist. Author: (with E. Latham) Massachusetts Politics, 1960: The Little Legislatures, 1970; also articles. Editor: Congress: Anvil of American Democracy, 1967. Home: 38 Balcarres Rd West Newton MA 02165 Office: University of Mass Boston MA 02116

GOODWIN, GEORGE EVANS, pub. relations exec.; b. Atlanta, June 20, 1917; s. George and Carrie (Clark) G.; A.B. with cert. in journalism, Washington and Lee U., 1939; m. Lois Milstead, Nov. 2, 1940; children—Clark, Allen. Reporter, Atlanta Georgian, 1939, Charleston (S.C.) News and Courier, 1940, Washington (D.C.) Times-Herald, 1940-41, Miami Daily News, 1941-42; staff writer Atlanta Jour., 1945-52; exec. dir. Central Atlanta Improvement Assn., 1952-54; v.p. First Nat. Bank of Atlanta, 1954-64; exec. v.p. Bell & Stanton, Inc., 1965—, also dir.; exec. sec. Ga. Senatorial Transit Study Com., 1954; dir. Roy D. Warren Co. Trustee Oglethorpe U., Atlanta Arts Alliance. Served as lt., motor torpedo boat squadrons, Attu, New Guinea, the Philippines, 1942-45. Decorated Navy Unit Commendation; Purple Heart; Philippines Liberation ribbon with one star; Asiatic-Pacific theater ribbon with three stars. Recipient Pultizer Prize for local reporting, 1948; Sigma Delta Chi award for gen. reporting, 1948; Asso. Press of Georgia award for reporting, 1948 (all for story on Telfair Co., Ga., vote frauds); Pall Mall Big Story award, 1949. Mem. Public Relations Soc. Am., Delta Tau Delta, Sigma Delta Chi, Omicron Delta Kappa. Democrat. Presbyn. (elder). Home: 3302 Ivanhoe Dr NW Atlanta, GA 30327. Office: Peachtree Center Bldg Atlanta GA 30303

GOODWIN, HARRY EUGENE, journalist, educator; b. Council Bluffs, Ia., Dec. 19, 1922; s. Harry Lars and Mary Ellen (James) G.; B.A., U. Ia., 1946, M.A., 1947; m. Frances Jean Prudhon, July 3, 1943; children—Geri, Gibson Eugene, Susan, Michael Jay. Editor, The Daily Iowan, Iowa City, 1946-47; copy editor Balt. Sun, 1947-48; writer Asso. Press, Balt., 1948-50; columnist, reporter Washington Star, 1950-57; dir., prof. Sch. Journalism, Pa. State U., 1957-69, prof. Sch. Journalism, 1969—. Bd. dirs. Mellet Fund for a Free and Responsible Press, 1967—; mem. admissions com. Washington Journalism Center, 1968—. Served as 1st lt., 8th Air Force, USAAF, World War II. Mem. Pa. Soc. Newspaper Editors (hon.), Am. Assn. Schs. and Depts. Journalism (v.p. 1960-61), Assn. Edn. Journalism (chmn. div. mass communications and soc. 1966-67), Am. Council on Edn. for Journalism, Pa. Council for Mass Communications Studies (pres. 1969-71), Sigma Delta Chi, Omicron Delta Kappa. Home: 119 Bathgate Dr State College PA 16801 Office: School of Journalism Pennsylvania State University University Park PA 16802

GOODWIN, JOHN EDWIN, Sr., ret. corp. exec.; b. Topeka, May 13, 1902; s. John Edwin and May (Russell) G.; B.S., Lake Forest Coll., 1926; m. Thelma Peugh, May 1, 1926; children—Jacklyn, John Edwin. Machinist, Mo. Pacific Lines, 1926-27, enginehouse foreman, 1927-29, erecting foreman, 1929-32, schedule supr., 1932-33, prodn. engr., 1933-35, gen. foreman, 1935-39, shop supt., 1939-41, mech. supt., 1942-43; master mechanic Internat. Gt. No. Ry., 1941-42; asst. chief mech. officer C. & N.-W. Ry., 1943-45, chief mech. officer, 1945-48, v.p., exec. asst. to pres., 1948-52, v.p. charge operations, 1952-55, exec. v.p. 1955-57, ret., 1957; pres., dir. M & J Diesel Locomotive Filter Corp., pres. Trans-Am. Mfg. & Equipment Corp., 1958-59; v.p. U.S. Ry. Equipment Corp., 1959-60, pres. dir., 1960-63; v.p. U.S. Ry. Leasing Corp., 1959-60, pres., dir., 1960- 63; v.p. M.S. Kaplan Co., 1960-63; dir., mem. exec. com. First Fed. Savs. & Loan Assn. Chgo.; pres., dir. Am. Security Savs. & Loan Assn., Little Rock, 1964-70. Mem. Locomotive Maintenance Officers Assn. (past pres.), Assn. Am. R.R.'s (past vice chmn. gen. com. mech. div.), Coordinated Assns. (past chmn.), Lake Forest Alumni Assn. (past pres.), Northwestern U. Assos., Phi Pi Epilon (trustee). Episcopalian. Mason. Clubs: Tower (past pres., dir.); Western Railway (pres. 1948-49) (Chgo.); Country, Top of the Rock, Little Rock, Kiwanis (Little Rock). Home: 4 River Ridge Rd Little Rock AR 72207

GOODWIN, JOHN MITCHELL, lawyer; b. St. Louis, Mar. 5, 1921; s. John Mitchell and Theresa (Longinotti) G.; student St. Louis U., 1942; LL.B., Washington U., St. Louis, 1946; m. Mary Susan Farris, Feb. 15, 1947; children—Mary Ellen, John Mitchell III. Admitted to Mo. bar, 1946, since practiced in St. Louis; partner firm Hocker, Goodwin, Koenig, Gibbons & Fehlig, and predecessors, 1953—. Fellow Am. Coll. Trial Lawyers; mem. Bar Assn. St. Louis (pres. 1965- 66), Lawyers Assn. St. Louis (pres. 1952-53), Mo. Bar (bd. govs. 1966—, mem. exec. com. 1968—, v.p. 1970-71), Am. Bar Assn., Mo. Hist. Soc., Civil War Round Table (pres. 1962), Navy League U.S., Sigma Chi, Delta Theta Phi. Home: 460 Edgewood Dr Clayton, MO 63105 Office: 411 N 7th St St Louis MO 63101

GOODWIN, JOHN PAUL, advt. exec.; b. Shreveport, Mar. 3, 1908; s. James Edwin and Clara (Gilliland) G.; B.A., Centenary Coll., 1929; m. Marcia Edith Carl, Aug. 20, 1936. Various positions radio stas., La., Tex., 1929-38, advt. agys., Houston, 1939-42; free lance radio writer, producer, Hollywood, Cal. and Houston, 1942-46; pres. Steel Advt. Agy., 1946-49; established, operated Goodwin Advt. Agy., Houston, 1949-52; pres. Southwest Film Prodns., Inc., 1952-55; chmn. bd. Goodwin, Dannenbaum, Littman & Wingfield, and predecessors, Houston, 1955—; v.p., dir. sta. KTRK-TV, Houston, 1953-67; lectr. radio, TV, U. Houston, 1950-56. Trustee Variety Boy's Club; bd. dirs. Sam Houston Area council Boy Scouts Am.; past bd. dirs. Harris County chpt. Am. Cancer Soc. Mem. Radio and TV Execs. Assn. (pres. S. Tex. 1957), Houston Inst. Advanced Advt. Studies (pres. 1969), Am. (chmn. bd. S.W. council 1968), S.W. (pres. 1965) assns. advt. agys., Kappa Alpha. Episcopalian (lay reader). Rotarian. Clubs: Variety, Houston Press, Criterion, Knife & Fork, Pine Forest Country; Brae Burn Country, University. Home: 4723 Ivanhoe St Houston TX 77027 Office: 2400 W Loop S Houston TX 77027

GOODWIN, LOUIS PAYNE, cartoonist; b. Flintville, Tenn., Oct. 9, 1922; s. John B. and Lillie (Cate) G.; student Ark. Poly. Coll., 1941-42; B.A. in English lit., U. Chattanooga, 1948; m. Mary Elizabeth Adams, Feb. 23, 1946; children—Joyce Ann, Timothy Alan, Jonathan David. With VA, Columbus, O., 1948-52; advt. and editorial cartoonist Dispatch Printing Co., Columbus, 1952-62; editorial cartoonist Columbus Evening Dispatch, 1962—. Served with USNR, 1942-46. Recipient Cartoon award Freedoms Found., 1962, 63, 64, 65, 66, 67, 68; Cartoonists award Hwy. Safety Found., 1966. Mem. Assn. Am. Editorial Cartoonists. Republican. Baptist. Office: 34 S 3d St Columbus OH 43216

GOODWIN, MERRILL HARRY, assn. exec., ret. naval med. officer; b. Selma, Ind. May 19, 1911; s. William and India Moore (Dunkin) G.; student Ball State Coll., 1930-32; B.S., Ind. U., 1934, M.D., 1936; m. Josephine Deanne Voynic, Apr. 1, 1943; children—Michael Anne, Kimberley Dane. Intern U.S. Marine Hosp., Balt., 1936-37; commd. lt. (j.g.), M.C., U.S. Navy, 1937, advanced through grades to capt., 1953; grad. USAAF Sch. Aviation Medicine, 1938, USN Sch. Aviation Medicine, 1939; designated naval flight surgeon, 1939, naval aviator, 1944; exec. med. officer Naval Air Sta., Pensacola, Fla., 1948-51; head liaison sect. Bur. Medicine and Surgery, 1951-54; sr. med. officer Naval Air Sta., Barbers Point, Hawaii, 1954-56, Quonset Point, R.I., 1956-59; asst. chief for aviation medicine Bur. Medicine and Surgery, 1959-63; comdg. officer U.S. Naval Hosp., Pensacola, Fla., also dep. comdr. U.S. Naval Aviation Med. Center, 1963-67; retired, 1967; exec. v.p., sec.- treas. Aerospace Med. Assn., Washington, 1967—. Decorated 3 Presdl. unit citations, Philippine Def. medal. Diplomate Am. Bd. Preventive Medicine (mem., trustee; vice chmn. for aerospace medicine 1968-70) in aviation medicine. Fellow Aerospace Med. Assn. (exec. council 1962-65), Am. Coll. Preventive Medicine: mem. A.M.A., Am. Pub. Health Assn., Am. Inst. Aeros. and Astronautics, Am. Soc. Assn. Execs., Am. Assn. Med. Soc. Execs., Profl. Conv. Mgmt. Assn., Quiet Birdmen, Alpha Omega Alpha, Phi Beta Pi. Home: 1321 Macbeth St McLean VA 22101 Office: Aerospace Med Assn Washington DC 20001

GOODWIN, PAUL, clergyman; b. Lynn, Ark., Mar. 1, 1915; s. Joseph M. and Vera (Laferney) G.; student Ark. Tech. Inst., 1937-38, Ark. State U., 1939; D.B., Missionary Baptist Sem., Little Rock, 1945; m. Frieda Padgett, Dec. 24, 1941; children—Allen, David, Ann. Ordained to ministry Bapt. Ch., 1941; pastor in chs. in Ark., 1941-66, 71—; pres. Missionary Baptist Sem., 1966-71, prof., 1946-65, 71—; pres. Am. Bapt. Assn., 1964-65. Author: The Golden Age, 1944; In

His Hands, 1946; Seven Sermons, 1954; A Panoramic View of Bible Giving, 1964; Baptist Churches in All Ages, 1965. Address: Rt 1 Box 201 C Alexander AR 72002

GOODWIN, RICHARD HALE, botanist; b. Brookline, Mass., Dec. 14, 1910; s. Harry Manley and Mary Blanchard (Linder) G.; A.B., Harvard, 1933, A.M., 1934, Ph.D., 1937; m. Esther Bemis, Oct. 12, 1936; children—Mary (Mrs. Bruce K. Wetzel), Richard Hale. Asst. biology, Harvard, 1935-36; expedition Brit. E. Africa and Belgian Congo, 1937; Am.-Scandinavian fellow U. Copenhagen, 1937-38; instr. in botany U. Rochester, 1938-41, asst. prof., 1941-44; prof. botany and chmn. dept. Conn. Coll., New London, 1944—; dir. Conn. Arboretum, 1944-65, 67-68; commr. Conn. Geol. and Natural History Survey, 1945—; pres. Nature Conservancy, 1956- 58, 64-66, chmn. nat. council, 1966-68. Pres. Conservation and Research Found. Fellow Am. Acad. Arts and Scis., Rochester Acad. Sci.; mem. A.A.A.S., Am. Soc. Naturalists, Soc. for Developmental Biology, Soc. of Gen. Physiology, Bot. Society of Am., N.E. and Torrey bot. clubs, Am. Inst. Biol. Scis., Am. Soc. Plant Physiologists, Am. Soc. Plant Taxonomists, Conn. Acad. Arts and Scis., Am-Scandinavian Found., Gamma Alpha, Sigma Xi. Club: The Country. Connecticut College New London, CT 06320.

GOODWIN, RICHARD NARADOF, former govt. ofcl.; b. Boston, Dec. 7, 1931; s. Joseph C. and Belle (Fisher) G.; B.A. summa cum laude, Tufts U., 1953; LL.B. summa cum laude, Harvard, 1958; m. Sandra Leverant, June 15, 1958; 1 son, Richard Joseph. Admitted to Mass. bar, 1958; law clk. to Supreme Ct. Justice Frankfurter, 1958-59; spl. cons. subcom. legislative oversight U.S. Ho. of Reps., 1959; asst. to U.S. Senator Kennedy, 1959- 61; asst. spl. counsel to Pres. Kennedy, 1961; dep. asst. sec. state inter-Am. affairs, 1961-63; spl. asst. to Pres. of U.S., 1963-65; fellow Center Advanced Studies, Wesleyan U., 1965-67; vis. prof. Mass. Inst. Tech., 1967-68. Mem. Phi Beta Kappa. Author: The Sower's Seed, 1965; Triumph or Tragedy: Reflections on Vietnam, 1966. Address: 14 Chestnut St Boston MA 02108

GOODWIN, SIDNEY SILER, mining exec.; b. Corbin, Ky., May 3, 1906; s. Sidney Wallingford and Sarah (Casey) G.; B.S., U. Ky., 1928; grad. study U. Cin., 1928-30; m. Mattie Cromer, June 2, 1928; children—Sara, Judith (Mrs. F. B. Wolcott, III). Staff geologist Ky. Geol. Survey, 1928-30; successively geologist, mine foreman, chief geologist, supt. N.J. Zinc Co., Austinville, Va., 1930-47, v.p. mgr. mines, 1953—, dir., 1955—; v.p., dir. N.J. Zinc Exploration Co. of Can.; dir. Hedman Mines Ltd., Restigouche Mining Corp. Fellow Geol. Soc. of Am.; mem. Am. Inst. Mining and Metall. Engrs., Mining and Metall. Soc., Soc. Econ. Geologists, Newcomen Soc., Sigma Psi, Scabbard and Blade, Phi Sigma Kappa. Clubs: Engineers, Mining (N.Y.C.). Home: Ogdensburg NJ 07439 Office: 2045 City Line Rd Bethlehem PA 18017

GOODWIN, WILLARD E., urologist; b. Los Angeles, July 24, 1915; s. Willard and Olive (Belt) G.; A.B., U. Cal. at Berkeley, 1937; M.D., Johns Hopkins, 1941; m. Mary Pearson Josephs, Feb. 21, 1942; children—Mary Devereux, Peter Colt (dec.), Willard II. Mem. faculty Johns Hopkins Med. Sch., 1948-51; asst. prof. urology U. Cal. at Los Angeles, 1951—, prof., 1953—; chief urology Wadsworth VA Hosp., Los Angeles. Diplomate Am. Bd. Urology. Fellow A.C.S.; mem. A.M.A., Am. Urol. Assn., Pacific Coast Surg. Assn., Am. Surg. Assn., Am. Assn. Genitourinary Surgeons, Clin. Soc. Genitourinary Surgery, Assn. Univ. Surgeons. Research and numerous publs. on urol. surgery, kidney transplantation. Home: 254 Bronwood Av Los Angeles, CA 90049.

GOODWIN, WILLIAM RICHARD, bldg. products mfg. co. exec.; b. Pendleton, Ore., June 21, 1924; s. Carl W. and Pearl (Taylor) G.; B.A., Reed Coll., 1949, M.A., 1950; Ph.D., Stanford, 1955; m. Patricia Earnest, Mar. 3, 1956; children—Douglas, Richard, Barbara. With RAND Corp., Santa Monica, Cal., 1955; with System Devel. Corp., Paramus, N.J., 1957-65, asst. div. mgr., 1958, mgr. SAC system design div., 1959-65; owner W.R. Goodwin & Co., Fort Lee, N.J., 1965-69; v.p. corporate planning Johns-Manville Corp., N.Y.C., 1969-70, pres., chief exec. officer, 1970—, also dir.; pres., dir. several Johns-Manville subsidiaries. Trustee Elect Com. for Econ. Devel. Served with AUS, 1942-46. Home: 10 Soder Rd North Caldwell NJ 07006 Office: 22 E 40th St New York City NY 10016

GOODWYN, JOHN LANCASTER, judge; b. Montgomery, Ala., Oct. 13, 1903; s. Robert Tyler and Jessie (Lancaster) G.; A.B., U. Ala., 1925, LL.B., 1926; m. Elizabeth Hill, Apr. 16, 1931; children—Warren, Elizabeth Lancaster. Admitted to Ala. bar, 1926; practiced in Montgomery, 1926-40; mayor, Montgomery, 1946- 51; judge Ala. Supreme Ct. 1951—. Served with AUS 1940-46; PTO, disch. rank col. Home: 1567 Gilmer Av Montgomery AL 36104 Office: State Capital Montgomery AL 36104

GOODWYN, KENDALL WIRT, magazine editor; b. Springfield, Mass., June 28, 1911; s. William Wirt and Mabel Alice (Trask) G.; student N.Y.U., 1946-48; m. Helen Janet Zeman, Nov. 9, 1940; children—Pamela Kendall, Camilla Kendall. Engaged in advt. bus., 1933-38; free-lance mag. writer, 1938-40; asso. editor Popular Publs., pubs. Argosy, Adventure and Railroad mags., 1940-43, 46- 48, editor Adventure mag., 1948-51; copy dir. Popular Sci. mag., 1951- 56, asst. mng. editor, 1956-62, mng. editor, 1962—; editorial cons. audio-visual div. Popular Sci. Pub. Co., 1960-66, mem. mgmt. adv. bd., 1965-67. Served with AUS, 1943-46. Mem. A.A.A.S. Episcopalian. Clubs: Overseas Press (N.Y.C.); Philipse Manor (North Tarrytown). Home: 49 Merlin Av North Tarrytown, NY 10591. Office: 355 Lexington Av New York City NY 10017

GOODWYN, ULYSSES VINCENT, utility exec.; b. Cullman, Ala., Sept. 27, 1923; s. Andrew Sylvester and Thella (Quattlebaum) G.; B.S., U. Ala., 1947; LL.B., Birmingham (Ala.) Sch. Law, 1958; m. Mary Mozelle Anderson, July 15, 1944; children—Janet Leigh, William Vincent, Robert Andrew. With So. Natural Gas Co., Birmingham, 1947—, treas., 1964, v.p., treas., 1967-71, exec. v.p., 1971—, also dir.; dir. Offshore Co., 1966—; instr. U. Ala., 1946- 47. Admitted to Ala. bar, 1959. Served to capt., Q.M.C., AUS, 1943-46. Mem. Ala. Bar Assn., Beta Gamma Sigma, Pi Mu Epsilon, Delta Sigma Kappa. Club: Vestavia Country (Birmingham). Home: 2740 Altadena Rd Birmingham AL 35243 Office: Watts Bldg Birmingham AL 35203

GOODYEAR, AUSTIN, mfg. co. exec.; b. Buffalo, Nov. 18, 1919; s. Charles W. and Grace (Rumsey) G.; grad. St. Mark's Sch., 1939; student Yale, 1939-40; m. Louisa Robins, Mar. 30, 1940; children—Grace R. (Mrs. Franklin D. Roosevelt III), Thomas R., Cullen C. With Hewitt-Robins, Inc. div. Litton Industries, Stamford, Conn., 1941-70, successively apprentice machinist, prodn. mgr., asst. gen. mgr., gen. mgr., v.p., 1953-56, exec. v.p., 1956-58, pres., 1958-70; sr. v.p. Litton Industries, 1967-70; pres. Ellsworth Falls Lumber Co. Inc. (Me.), Ellsworth Builders Supply, Inc. Home: Brooklin ME 04616 Office: State St Ellsworth ME 04605

GOODYEAR, GEORGE FORMAN, lawyer; b. Buffalo, July 8, 1906; s. A. Conger and Mary (Forman) G.; Ph.B., Yale, 1927; LL.B., Harvard, 1931; m. Sarah Norton, June 22, 1932; children—Anne (Mrs. William H. Hudnut III), Mary (Mrs. Albert R. Gurney, Jr.), Sarah (Mrs. James M. Wadsworth). Admitted to N.Y. bar, 1936, since practiced in Buffalo; tech. rep. and patent atty. E. I. du Pont De Nemours, 1932-37; patent atty. Bean, Brooks, Buckley & Bean, patent attys., 1937-42; factory supr. Lake Ont. Ordance Works, 1942-43; patent atty. Curtiss-Wright Corp., 1942-45; sec., counsel Hewitt-Robins, Inc., 1945-52, Ky. Synthetic Rubber Corp., 1950-52; pres. WGR Corp., radio and TV broadcasting, 1953-57; pres. Chautauqua Broadcasting Corp, 1956-64; dir. Niagara Share Corp., Marine Midland Bank Western N.Y. Pres. Urban League, Buffalo, 1960, 64-66, Med. Found., Buffalo, 1957-65; 1st v.p., dir. Ellicott Community Redevel. Found.; mem. Buffalo Bd. Edn., 1965-70, pres. 1967-68; pres. Buffalo Philharmonic Orch. Soc., 1968-69; chmn. Hosp. Review and Planning Council Western N.Y., 1961-65; Mem. Buffalo Fine Arts Acad., Buffalo Hist. Soc., Am. Chem. Soc., Am., Erie County bar assns., Buffalo Soc. Natural Sci. (pres. 1948- 65). Clubs: Saturn, Tennis and Squash, Buffalo Country, Pack, Queen City Chess (Buffalo); Ocean Reef (Fla.); Coral Beach and Tennis (Bermuda); Cotton Bay (Bahamas). Home: 115 Meadow Rd Buffalo NY 14216 Office: Marine Trust Bldg Buffalo NY 14203

GOODYKOONTZ, CHARLES ALFRED, newspaper editor; b. Radford, Va., Dec. 29, 1928; s. Charles A. and Claudine (Noell) G.; student Emory and Henry Coll., 1946-48; m. Jean Shirley Beasley, Sept. 17, 1955; 1 son, Charles Alfred. Sports editor Radford News Jour., 1948-50; mem. staff Richmond (Va.) Times-Dispatch, 1952—, mng. editor, 1969—. Served with AUS, 1950-52. Mem. Sigma Delta Chi (pres. Richmond 1964-65). Co-editor: Virginia Travel Guide, 1968. Home: 8207 Shannon Hill Rd Richmond VA 23229 Office: 333 E Grace St Richmond VA 23219

GOODYKOONTZ, HARRY GORDON, clergyman, educator; b. Roanoke, Va., Dec. 13, 1906; s. John Tilden and Nellie (Williams) G.; A.B., Davidson Coll., 1927; B.D. (Moses D. Hoge fellow), Union Theol. Sem., Richmond, Va., 1931, Th.M., 1933, Th.D., 1937; m. Betty Warren Love, Dec. 30, 1933; children—Betty Love (Mrs. Mallory F. Miree), Nancy Williams (Mrs. James O. Chatham), Harry Gordon. Ordained to ministry Presbyn. Ch., 1931; asst. to pastor, Wilmington, N.C., 1927-28; asso. dir. youth work Presbyn. Ch. U.S. 1931-33, dir. student work, 1945-50; pastor in Fayetteville, Ark., 1933-39, Denton, Tex., 1939-45; prof. Christian edn. Louisville Presbyn. Theol. Sem., 1950—. Moderator Presbytery of Washburn, Ark., 1935, Presbytery of Dallas, 1943, Presbytery of Louisville, 1964; mem. com. chaplains Ky. Council Chs., 1953—; mem. profs. sect. div. Christian edn. Nat. Councils Chs., 1951—. Mem. Assn. for Profl. Edn. for Ministry, Acad. Religion and Mental Health, Omicron Delta Kappa, Phi Delta Theta. Democrat. Author: Christian Ways for College Days, 1949; Training to Teach (with Mrs. Goodykoontz), 1961; The Minister in the Reformed Tradition, 1963; The Persons We Teach, 1965. Home: 2406 Ashwood Dr Louisville KY 40205 Office: Theol Sem 1044 Alta Vista Rd Louisville KY 40205 NO. OF RECORDS 00490

GOOGIN, JOHN MELVIN, phys. chemist; b. Lewiston, Me., May 2, 1922; s. John Melvin and Helen (Hilton) G.; B.S. in Chemistry, Bates Coll., 1944, D.Sc. (hon.), 1968; Ph.D. in Phys. Chemistry, U. Tenn., 1953; m. Janet Harriet Horn, Mar. 19, 1949; children—Jacqueline Ann, Diane Joan, Laura Donna, Roxane Ivy. Chemist, Tenn. Eastman Corp., 1944-47; with Union Carbide Corp., 1947—, sr. staff cons., exec. offices nuclear div., 1968—. Recipient Ernest O. Lawrence Meml. award AEC, 1967. Mem. Am. Chem. Soc., A.A.A.S., Sci. Research Soc. Am., Am. Soc. Metals, Phi Beta Kappa, Sigma Xi. Unitarian (pres. 1962-64). Author, patentee in field. Home: 111 Orkney Rd Oak Ridge, TN 37830. Office: PO Box Y Oak Ridge TN 37830

GOOKIN, RALPH BURTON, food company exec.; b. Chariton, Ia., June 23, 1914; s. Albert Brisbine and Maude Mary (McFarland) G.; B.S., Northwestern, 1935; M.B.A., Harvard, 1940; m. Mary Louise Carroll, Dec. 11, 1948; children—Cristy Carroll, David Burton. With H. J. Heinz Co., Pitts., 1945—, comptroller, 1951-59, v.p. finance, 1959-64, exec. v.p. U.S. operations, 1964-66, pres., chief exec. officer, chmn. exec. com., 1966—, also dir.; dir. Westinghouse Electric, Bank of Am.; vice chmn. Grocery Mfrs. Am. Inc. Past pres., dir. Pa. Golf Assn.; past pres. Western Pa. Golf Assn.; exec. com. Pa. Economy League. Bd. dirs. Allegheny General Hosp. Shady Side Acad., United Fund Allegheny County; past pres. Financial Execs. Research Found. Mem. Financial Execs. Inst., Harvard Bus. Sch. Assn. Clubs: University, Duquesne (dir.), Oakmont, Fox Chapel (Pitts.); Laurel Valley Golf (Ligonier Pa.); Augusta (Ga.) Nat. Golf (gov.); Portmarnock Golf (Dublin, Ireland). Home: 101 Hickory Hill Rd Pittsburgh PA 15238 Office: 1062 Progress St Pittsburgh PA 15212

GOOLAGONG, EVONNE, tennis player; b. Griffith, New South Wales, Australia, July 31, 1951; d. Kenneth and Linda Goolagong. Internat. tennis competitor, 1970—; winner Wimbledon (Eng.) finals, 1971. Address: care Victor A Edwards 80 Duntroon Av Roseville New South Wales Australia

GOOSSEN, EUGENE COONS, educator, writer; b. Gloversville, N.Y., Aug. 6, 1920; s. Arthur B. and Carolyn E. (Coons) G.; student Corcoran Sch. Fine Arts, 1939-42; certificat Sorbonne, Paris, France, 1948; B.A., New Sch. Social Research, 1950; m. Jean A. Griffin, June 9, 1945; children—Theodore W., Mary Hayes. Free lance art critic, 1948—; critic corr. Monterey (Cal.) Peninsula Herald, 1948-58; prof. art, dir. exhbns. Bennington (Vt.) Coll., 1958-61; prof. art, chmn. dept. Hunter Coll., 1961—; cons. Grolier Soc., 1963-64; guest exhbn. dir. Mus. Modern Art, 1967-68, 71-72; Whitney Mus. Am. Art, 1968-69; mem. adv. com. Archives Am. Art; lectr. USIA and Sr. Fgn. Service Seminar, 1967. Mem. vis. arts com. Bennington Coll., 1966—; mem. N.Y. City Cultural Council, 1970—. Served to capt. USAAF, 1942-45; ETO. Decorated Air medal (6), D.F.C. (2), Silver Star, Presdl. citation (2); recipient Frank Jewett Mather citation excellence art criticism, 1958, citation Art News directing most significant art program, 1958. Guggenheim fellow, 1970. Mem. Internat. Art Critics Assn., Am. Assn. U. Profs., Am. Soc. Aesthetics, Coll. Art Assn. Author: Ellsworth Kelly, 1958; Three American Sculptors, 1959; Stuart Davis, 1959; The Art of the Real (also pub. in French), 1968; Helen Frankenthaler, 1969; also numerous articles. Contbg. editor Art Internat., 1957-61. Home: RFD 1 Buskirk NY 12028 Office: 695 Park Av New York City NY 10021

GOOSTREE, ROBERT EDWARD, educator; b. nr. Clarksville, Tenn., Sept. 23, 1923; s. William Lee and Lucy (Frech) G.; A.B., Southwestern at Memphis, 1943; M.A., State U. Ia., 1948, Ph.D., 1950; J.D., Am. U., 1962; m. Jane Rogers, July 16, 1955; children—Laura, Frederic, Samuel. Instr. polit. sci. U. Ia., 1946-50, U. Md., 1951-53; asst. prof. Am. U., 1953-56, asso. prof., 1956-60, prof., 1960-71, asst. dean Sch. Govt., 1958-62, acting dean, 1962-63, prof. law and govt., 1963-71, acting dean law sch., 1970-71; dean, prof. Capital U. Law Sch., Columbus, O., 1971—. Cons. John F. Kennedy Center for Performing Arts, Washington, 1964—. Served with AUS, 1943-46. Mem. D.C., Supreme Ct bars, Am., Fed. bar assns., Am. Polit. Sci. Assn., Am. Trial Lawyers Assn. Clubs: National Lawyers (Washington). Contbr. articles to legal jours. Home: 2274 Astor Av Columbus OH 43209

GOOTT, DANIEL, govt. ofcl.; b. N.Y.C., Apr. 23, 1919; s. Hyman and Min (Novak) G.; B.S.S., City Coll. N.Y., 1940; postgrad. Columbia, 1940-41; grad. Sch. Internat. Studies, Geneva, Switzerland, 1946; m. Sylvia Blousman, Aug. 29, 1940; children—Alan F., Eugene M. Asso. chief labor relations br. WPB, 1942-43; spl. asst. internat. labor affairs to under sec. state Dept. State, Washington, 1955-61, dep. coordinator internat. labor affairs Office Sec. State, 1961-62; 1st sec., labor attache Am. embassy, Paris, France, 1962-65; became chief spl. profl. affairs Office of Dep. Undersec. of State for Adminstrn., Washington, 1965, now labor and UN adviser Bur. European Affairs. Served with AUS, 1943-46. Mem. Am. Econ. Assn., Indsl. Relations Research Assn., Am. Fgn. Service Assn., Am. Acad. Polit. and Social Sci. Club: American (Paris). Home: 10904 Oakwood St Silver Spring MD 20850 Office: Bureau European Affairs Dept of State Washington DC 20520

GOPALLAWA, WILLIAM, gov.-gen. of Ceylon; b. Dullewre, Matale, Ceylon, Sept. 16, 1897; s. Tikiri Banda and Dullewa (Kumarihamy) G.; ed. Dharmaraja Coll., St. Anthony's Coll., both Kandy; grad. Law Coll., Colombo, 1924; LL.D., U. Ceylon, 1962, Vidyalankara U., 1962; D.Litt., Vidyodaya U., 1926; m. Seelawathie Rambukwella, 1928; children—Asoka, Moithra, Iranganie (Mrs. M. Ratwatte), Chintha (Mrs. Mediwaka). Tchr., 1918-20; proctor Supreme Ct. Ceylon, 1924; practiced in Matale, 1924-39; mem. Urban Council Matale, 1927-39, chmn., 1928-32; commnr. Kandy Municipal Council, 1939-52; municipal commnr., Colombo, 1952-57; ambassador of Ceylon to People's Repub. China, 1958-61, to U.S., concurrently to Cuba and Mexico, 1961-62; gov.-gen. Ceylon, 1962—. Chancellor U. Ceylon, Vidyodaya U., Vidyalankara U.; founder mem. Vidyartha Coll.; founder Dodandeniya Buddhist Sch., Matale; founder mem. Social Service League Matale; chmn. panel folk-songs and folk-dancing Arts Council Ceylon, 1954-56. Decorated mem. Order Brit. Empire. Mem. Young Men's Buddhist Assn. Buddhist. Rotarian (hon. mem., past pres. Kandy). Address Queen's House Colombo, Ceylon.

GORALSKI, ROBERT, radio-TV news corr.; b. Chgo., Jan. 2, 1928; s. Stanley and Caroline (Bielas) G.; B.S., U. Ill., 1949; student Sch. Advanced Internat. Studies, Johns Hopkins, 1960-61; Litt.D., William Jewell Coll., 1969; m. Margaret Anne Walton, Aug. 22, 1948; children—Douglas, Dorothy, Katherine. News Announcer WDWS, Champaign, Ill., 1948-51; combat corr. U.S. Navy, Korea, 1951-53; prodn. supr. Radio Free Asia, Tokyo, Japan, 1953-54; asst. rep. Asia Found., Karachi and Dacca, Pakistan, 1954-56; editor, desk supr. Voice of Am., Washington, 1956-61; White House and State Dept. and Pentagon corr. NBC News, 1961—. Served with USNR, 1945-46; PTO. Mass media fellow Ford Found. Fund Adult Edn., 1960-61. Recipient Du Pont-Columbia Journalism award 1970. Mem. Sigma Alpha Epsilon. Club: Nat. Press (Washington). Office: 4001 Nebraska Av NW Washington DC 20016

GORAN, MORRIS, educator; b. Chgo., Sept. 4, 1916; s. David and Sara (Klein) G.; B.S., U. Chgo., 1936, M.S., 1939, Ph.D., 1957; m. Cymia Walen, June 3, 1951; children—Marjorie, Ruth. Chemist Dearborn Chem. Co., 1941-42; asst. prof. physics Ind. U., 1942-43; scientist Manhattan Dist. Corps of Engrs., Oak Ridge, 1943-45; prof., chmn. dept. phys. sci. Roosevelt U., 1945—; cons. Plastofilm, Croft Ednl. Services; lectr. George Williams Coll., Elmhurst Coll. Pres. Lincolnwood Bd. Edn., 1959-68. Fellow Am. Inst. Chemists; mem. Am. Chem. Soc., Am. Phys. Soc., A.A.A.S., Am. Assn. Univ. Profs., History of Sci. Soc. Author: Story of Fritz Haber, 1967; The Future of Science, 1971. Contbr. articles profl. jours. Home: 7330 N Kilbourn St Lincolnwood IL 60646 Office: 430 S Michigan Av Chicago IL 60605

GORBATKO, LT. COL. VICTOR V., Russian cosmonaut; b. 1935; grad. Zhukovsky Air Force Engring. Acad. Mem. Russian Air Force, 1954—; research engr. on space ship Soyuz 7, 1969. Address: care Scientific Research Inst. Petrovsky Park Moscow, USSR.*

GORBMAN, AUBREY, biologist, educator; b. Detroit, Dec. 13, 1914; s. David and Esther (Korenblit) G.; A.B., Wayne U., 1935, M.S., 1936; Ph.D., U. Cal., 1940; m. Genevieve D. Tapperman, Dec. 25, 1938; children—Beryl Ann, Leila Harriet, Claudia Louise, Eric Jay. Research asso. U. Cal., 1940-41; instr. zoology Wayne U., 1941-44; Jane Coffin Childs fellow in anatomy Yale, 1944-46; asst. prof. zoology Barnard Coll., Columbia, 1946-49, asso. prof., 1949-53, prof., 1953-63, exec. officer dept. zoology, 1952- 55; prof. zoology U. Wash., Seattle, 1963—, chmn. zoology dept., 1963- 66; biologist Brookhaven Nat. Lab., 1952-58; Fulbright scholar College de France, Paris, 1951-52, Guggenheim fellow U. Hawaii, 1955-56; vis. prof. biochemistry Nagoya U. Japan, 1956, Tokyo U., 1960. Fellow A.A.A.S., N.Y. Zool. Soc., N.Y. Acad. Sci.; mem. Endocrine Soc., Am. Soc. Naturalists, Am. Soc. Zoologists, Soc. Exptl. Biology and Medicine, Phi Beta Kappa. Editor: Comparative Endocrinology; editorial bd. Endocrinology, 1957-61; editor-in-chief Gen. and Comparative Endocrinology. Home: 4218 55th Av NE Seattle WA 98105

GORCHELS, CLARENCE CLIFFORD, librarian; b. Oshkosh, Wis., Aug. 26, 1916; s. Arthur Frederick and Mary Elizabeth (Korsch) G.; B.S., Wis. State Coll., Oshkosh, 1940; B.L.S. (Wis. Library Assn. fellow 1944-45), U. Wis., 1945; M.S., Columbia, 1952, D.L.S., 1971; m. Eugenia Hayes, June 16, 1945; children—Catherine Marilee, Christopher Michael, Melissa Jean, Gregory Francis. With Wash. State U., 1945-58, chief tech. services div., 1947-50, chief readers service div., 1950-56, acting asst. dir. of libraries, 1956-58; vis. asst. prof. U. Wash. Sch. Librarianship, 1958-59; asso. library service Columbia Sch. Library Service, 1959-60; dir. libraries, chmn. dept. library sci. Central Wash. State Coll., Ellensburg, 1960-63; librarian Cal. State Coll. at Palos Verdes, 1963-66; dir. library Ore. Coll. Edn., 1966—; dir. World Affairs Inst., Wash. State U., 1958. Mem. adv. bd. Sch. Library Service, U. So. Cal., 1966—. Mem. Am. (council 1956-57, chmn. statistics com. 1952-54, 56-57, chmn. budgeting, costs and accounting com. 1965—), Pacific N.W. (vice chmn. 1956), Wash. State (mem. exec. bd.), Wash. State Sch. library assns., Assn. Coll. and Reference Librarians, Am. Assn. U. Profs., Cal. State Coll. Librarians (sec. 1963-65), Phi Alpha Theta, Kappa Delta Pi. Roman Catholic. Kiwanian. Editor Foreshadow, Bull. Regional Hist. Research, 1957—; asst. to editor Coll. and Research Libraries, 1959-62; books appraisal staff Library Jour., 1947—, abstractor Historical Abstracts, 1956—. Author articles. Home: 342 Stadium Dr S Monmouth OR 97361

GORDENKER, LEON, educator; b. Detroit, Oct. 7, 1923; s. Samuel and Anna (Posalsky) G.; A.B., U. Mich., 1943; student Inst. d'Etudes Politiques, Paris, France, 1951-52; M.A., Columbia, 1954, Ph.D., 1958; student Acad. Internat. Law, The Hague, Netherlands, 1958; m. Belia Emilie Strootman, Aug. 16, 1956; children—Robert Jan Mario, Hendrik Willem Paul, Emilie Elise Saskia. Journalist, A.P., 1943, Detroit Free Press, 1944-45; information officer NWLB, 1945; pub. information officer UN, 1945-53; instr. Dartmouth, 1956- 58; mem. faculty Princeton, 1958—, prof. politics, 1966—, faculty asso. Center Internat. Studies, 1963—; vis. prof. Columbia, 1967, Makerere U., 1969-70; cons. UN, 1961—. Mem. Am. Polit. Sci. Assn., Internat. Studies Assn. Author: The United Nations and the Peaceful

Unification of Korea, 1959; The UN Secretary-General and the Maintenance of Peace, 1967; The United Nations in the International System, 1971. Home: 492 Riverside Dr Princeton, NJ 08540.

GORDH, GEORGE RUDOLPH, educator; b. St. Paul, May 18, 1912; s. Gustaf Arvid and Agnes (Ostergren) G.; A.B., Macalester Coll., 1931; A.M., U. Minn., 1935; Th.M., So. Bapt. Theol. Sem., 1936; Ph.D., U. Chgo., 1941; m. Gwen Reed, June 2, 1943; children—George Rudolph, Robert Reed, William Hansford, Gwendolyn. Asst., then asso. prof. philosophy Mercer U., 1941-45; asst. prof. history theology U. Chgo., 1945-51; prof. religion Hollins (Va.) Coll., 1951—, chmn. div. humanities, 1963-68, 70—, chaplain, 1951-59; vis. lectr. ch. history Crozer Theol. Sem., 1959-60. Ordained to ministry Methodist Ch., 1964. Mem. Roanoke Council Human Relations, Roanoke Ministers Conf., Am. Acad. Religion. Democrat. Author: Christian Faith and Its Cultural Expression, 1962; also articles. Home: 815 Chester Av NW Roanoke, VA 24019. Office: Hollins Coll Hollins VA 24020

GORDIMER, NADINE, author; b. S. Africa, Nov. 20, 1923; d. Isidore and Nan (Myers) Gordimer; ed. Convent Sch., Springs, S. Africa; m. Reinhold Cassirer, Jan. 29, 1954; children—Oriane, Hugo. Recipient W. H. Smith award for Commonwealth Writers, 1961. Mem. Com. European Authors. Author: (story colls.) Soft Voice of the Serpent, 1953; Six Feet of the Country, 1956; Friday's Footprint, 1960; Not for Publication, 1965; (novels) The Lying Days, 1953; A World of Strangers, 1958; Occasion for Loving, 1963; The Late Bourgeois World, 1966. Address: 7 Frere Rd Parktown West Johannesburg, South Africa.

GORDIS, ROBERT, clergyman, author; b. Bklyn., Feb. 6, 1908; s. Hyman and Lizzie (Engel) G.; A.B. cum laude, Coll. City N.Y., 1926; Ph.D., Dropsie Coll., 1929; rabbi (with distinction), Jewish Theol. Sem. Am., 1932, D.D. 1950; m. Fannie Jacobson, Feb. 5, 1928; children—Enoch, Leon, David. Teacher, Hebrew Tchrs. Tng. Sch. for Girls, 1926-28, Yeshiva Coll., 1929-30, Sem. Coll. of Jewish Studies, 1931; lectr. Rabbinical Sch. Sem., 1937—, prof. bibl. exegesis 1940—; rabbi Rockaway Park (N.Y.) Hebrew Congregation, 1931-69, rabbi emeritus, 1969—. Adj. prof. religion Columbia, 1948-57; cons. Center Study Dem. Instn., Santa Barbara, Cal., 1960—; lectr. O.T., Union Theol. Sem., 1953-54; Sem. prof. Bible, Jewish Theol. Sem., 1961—; vis prof. religion Temple U., 1967-68, prof., 1968—; vis. prof. Bible, Hebrew U., Jerusalem. Chmn. soc. justice com. Rabbinical Assembly Am., 1935-37, mem. exec. council, 1935, del. Synagogue Council of Am. 1937-40, pres. Rabbinical Assembly, 1944-46; founder Beth-El (now Robert Gordis) Day Sch., Belle Harbor, L.I., N.Y., 1950; mem. council on religious freedom Nat. Conf. Christians and Jews; bd. dirs. Inst. Ch. and State, Villanova U. Overseas mission War-Navy depts., investigating religious condition armed forces Pacific, Asiatic theatres, 1946. Mem. Nat. Hillel Commn., nat. adminstrv. council United Synagogue Am.; bd. govs. Nat. Acad. Adult Jewish Studies; mem. Nat. Com. on Scouting; mem. Jewish Book Council of Am.; pres. Synagogue Council of Am., 1948-49; trustee Church Peace Union; cons. on religion Fund for the Republic. Asso. editor dept. of Bible, Universal Jewish Ency. Contbg. editor: Menorah Jour., Reconstructionist, Conservative Judaism; The Jewish Forum; Human Sexuality; bd. editors, Judaism (journal) 1942-68, editor, 1969—. Contbr. to jours. and mags. Author books including: Wisdom of Ecclesiastes, 1945; Conservative Judaism-An American Philosophy, 1945; Koheleth, The Man and His World, 1951; The Song of Songs, 1954; Judaism for the Modern Age, 1955; A Faith for Moderns, 1960; The Root and The Branch-Judaism and the Free Society, 1962; The Book of God and Man, A Study of Job, 1965; Judaism in A Christian World, 1966; Leave a Little to God, 1967; Sex and the Family in the Jewish Tradtion, 1967; Poets, Prophets and Sages, Essays in Biblical Interpretation, 1970. Editor: Judaism, 1970—. Lectr., radio and TV, pub. forums speaker. Home: 150 West End Av New York City NY 10023 Office: 3080 Broadway New York City NY 10027

GORDON, ANGUS NEAL, Jr., electric co. exec.; b. Henderson, Ky., Jan. 23, 1919; s. Angus Neal and Judith (Lyle) G.; grad. Phillips Acad., Andover, Mass., 1937; B.A., Yale, 1941, LL.B., 1948; m. Louise Patterson Stites, Nov. 21, 1942. Admitted to Conn. bar, 1948; with firm Wiggin & Dana, New Haven, 1948- 64, partner, 1953-64; pres., dir. United Illuminating Co., New Haven, 1964—; dir. Union Trust Co. Conn. Yankee Atomic Power Co., Electric Council New Eng. Vice pres., dir. New Haven Boys Club; Mem. Yale Devel. Bd. Served to lt. col. USAAF, 1941-46. Mem. Newcomen Soc. N. Am., Order of Coif, Phi Beta Kappa, Sigma Xi (asso.), Alpha Sigma Phi, Phi Delta Phi. Mem. United Ch. Club: Graduate Association, Lawn, Quinnipiack (New Haven); Branford Yacht. Home: 206 Armory St New Haven, CT 06511. Office: 80 Temple St New Haven CT 06506

GORDON, ARTHUR ERNEST, educator; b. Marlborough, Mass., Oct. 7, 1902; s. Arthur Ernest and Susan Esther (Porter) G.; A.B., Dartmouth, 1923; student Am. Acad. in Rome, 1923-25; Ph.D. (Johnston scholar), Johns Hopkins, 1929; m. Maddalena Belloni, Sept. 15, 1924; 1 dau., Paola (Mrs. Paola Zinnecker); m. 2d, Joyce A. Stiefbold, June 11, 1937. Instr. Latin, Dartmouth, 1925- 27; student asst. Johns Hopkins, 1927-28; instr. Latin, Western Res. U., 1928; asso. prof. Latin, ancient history, U. Vt., 1929-30; asst. prof. Latin, U. Cal. at Berkeley, 1930-32, asso. prof., 1932-51, prof., 1951- 70, emeritus, 1970—, chmn. dept. classics, 1953-59; prof. classical langs. Ashland (O.) Coll., 1970; sr. research fellow classical studies Am. Acad., Rome, 1948-49; Guggenheim fellow and Fulbright research scholar, 1955-56. Mem. 2d Internat. Congress Greek and Latin Epigraphy, Paris, 1952. Mem. adv. council, Sch. Classical Studies, Am. Acad. Rome, 1940-70, chmn., 1953. Mem. Philol. Assn. Pacific Coast (sec.-treas. 1935- 38, v.p. 1951, pres. 1952), Classical Assn. Pacific States (sec.-treas. 1944-47, 49-50), Classical Soc. Am. Acad. Rome (pres. 1951), Archaeol. Inst. Am. (lectr. 1953), Am. Philol. Assn., Classical Assn. (Eng.), Roman Soc. (Eng.), Société des Etudes Latines (Paris), Internat. Assn. for Latin Epigraphy. Clubs: Faculty (Berkeley); Sierra (San Francisco). Author: On the Origin of Diana, 1932; The Cults of Aricia, 1934; Epigraphica I-II, 1935-36; The Cults of Lanuvium, 1938; A Mysterious Latin Inscription in Cal., 1944; Supralineate Abbreviations in Latin Inscriptions, 1948; A New Fragment of the Laudatio Turiae, 1950; Q. Veranius, Consul A.D. 49, 1952; Potitus Valerius Messala, Consul Suffect 29 B.C., 1954; Notes on the Res Gestae of Augustus, 1969; On the Origins of the Latin Alphabet, Modern Views, 1970; (with Joyce S. Gordon) Contributions to the Palaeography of Latin Inscriptions, 1957, Album of Dated Latin Inscriptions, Parts I-IV, 1958-65, Three Latin Inscriptions of 52 B.C., 1965. Home: 125 Camino del Mar PO Box 97 Inverness CA 94937

GORDON, BASIL, educator; b. Balt., Dec. 23, 1932; s. Basil and Helen (Williams) G.; M.A., Johns Hopkins, 1953; Ph.D., Cal. Inst. Tech., 1956. Instr. Cal. Inst. Tech., 1956-57; asst. prof. math. U. Cal. at Los Angeles, 1959-63, asso. prof., 1963-67, prof., 1967—. Served with AUS, 1957-59. Alfred P. Sloan fellow, 1962-64. Mem. Math. Assn. Am., Pi Mu Epsilon. Editor of Pacific Jour. Mathematics, 1969-70, Jour. Combinatorial Theory, 1970—. Contbr. articles profl. jours. Research on number theory, combinatorics, group theory, and function theory. Home: 402 15th St Santa Monica CA 90402 Office: 405 N Hilgard St Los Angeles CA 90024

GORDON, BERNARD, food market exec.; b. Albany, N.Y., June 13, 1916; s. Frank and Sophie (Rabineau) G.; grad. high sch.; m. Ida Shapiro, Mar. 7, 1938; children—Paul N., Michael. Div. sales mgr. Fed. Tea Co., Springfield, Mass., 1937-46; pres. Save Way Food Markets, Schenectady, 1946—, Roida Realty Co., Schenectady, 1959—, Rosita Realty Co., Schenectady, 1966—, Arrowhead Assos. Realty Co., Schenectady, 1969—. Pres. N.Y. Capital dist. Retail Grocers, 1947; adviser Small Bus. Adminstrn., Schenectady, 1966-67. Bd. dirs. Jr. Achievement Schenectady, 1956—. Jewish religion (dir. temple 1957—). Mason (32, Shriner), Elk, mem. B'nai B'rith. Club: Shaker Ridge Country (Loudenville, N.Y.). Home: 44 Milner Av Albany, NY 12203. Office: 240 Broadway Schenectady NY 12305

GORDON, BRUCE RUTHVEN, educator; b. Schenectady, Mar. 13, 1916; s. Theodore W. and Mabel (Ashworth) G.; A.B., Brown U., 1937; M.A., N.Y. State Coll. at Albany, 1942; Ph.D., Syracuse U., 1950; m. Jean V. Ledden, May 17, 1943; children—Linda, Douglas. Instr. Oneonta State Tchrs. Coll., 1941- 42; instr., asst. prof. Colgate U., 1947-50; prof., chmn. dept. Romance langs. Emory U., 1950-63; prof. French and Spanish, head dept. linguistics and fgn. langs. U. Alaska, College, 1963—, presiding officer Univ. assembly, 1968-70; dir. Sweetbriar Jr. Year in France, 1959-60; asso. dir. Nat. Def. Edn. Act. Inst., Besancon, France, 1962—; dir. French Inst. U. Alaska, summers 1965-67, Alaska Conf. Modern Fgn. Langs., 1967; chmn. Fgn. Credentials Evaluation Com. for Alaska, 1966-71. Decorated Palmes Academiques French Govt. 1961-68. Mem. Am. Assn. Tchrs. French (past nat. v.p.), Am. Assn. Tchrs. Spanish and Portuguese, Alaska Fgn. Lang. Assn. (pres. 1967-69), Am. Assn. U. Profs., Instituto Internacional de Literatura Iberoamericana, Modern Lang. Assn., Am. Council Teaching Fgn. Langs. (dir. 1967-70). Contbr. profl. jours. Home: Box 5-046 College, AK 99701.

GORDON, BURGESS LEE, physician, editor; b. Spokane, Wash., Apr. 10, 1892; s. Burgess Lee and Raphaleta (Simpson) G.; A.B., Gonzaga U., 1912, LL.D., 1953; M.D., Jefferson Med. Coll., 1919; D.Sc., Woman's Med. Coll., 1957; m. Margaret Huston; 1 son, Burgess Lee. Intern Jefferson Hosp., Phila., 1919-21; resident physician Peter Bent Brigham Hosp., Boston, 1921-26; teaching fellow in medicine Harvard Med. Sch., 1923-26; pvt. practice specializing in internal medicine, Phila., 1926—; dir., physician-in-chief Barton Meml. and White Haven divs. of Jefferson Hosp., Pa. Hosp., 1946-51; clin. prof. medicine Jefferson Medical Coll. 1941-51, vis. prof. medicine, 1961—; dir. health and welfare fund for study of anthracosilicosis Jefferson Medical Coll. Hosp. 1941-51; pres. Woman's Med. Coll. Phila., 1951-57, Mullen prof. medicine, 1951-57; dir. edn., mem. med. bd. Lovelace Found. and Clin., Albuquerque, 1957-60, cons. med. edn., 1959—; asso. editor Jour. A.M.A., 1960-64, editor Current Medical Information and Terminology, 1966—, dir. office current medical terminology A.M.A., 1961—; cons. internal medicine and diseases of chest VA. Council Internat. Orgns. Med. Scis., Geneva; mem. Com. Internat. Med. Nomenclature, Geneva, 1968—. Served with M.C., AUS, 1942-46; ret. as col. Trustee Mercy-Douglass Hosp., 1947-57, Phila. Tb and Health Assn., 1938-57, Am. Coll. Sports Med. Fellowship Commn., Phila., 1952-54. Recipient Gold medal for contbns. in chest diseases Am. Coll. Chest Physicians, 1962. Fellow A.C.P., Am. Coll. Chest Physicians (past pres.); mem. N.M. State (hon.), Phila. County, Pa. med. socs., Am. Trudeau Soc., Am. Assn. Hist. Medicine, N.M. Soc. Biol. and Med. Research, Assn. Am. Physicians, Am. Soc. Clin. Investigation, Coll. of Physicians of Phila. (mem. council), Alpha Omega Alpha, Phi Chi. Clubs: Union League, University (Phila.). Author text books; also articles med. jours. Editor: Clinical Cardiopulmonary Physiology (textbook), Current Procedural Terminology, Thesaurus Med. Descriptors. Co-editor of Oxford Medicine, 1946-58, Advances in Cardiopulmonary Diseases, 1962—. Home: 1550 Lake Shore Dr Chicago, IL 60610. Office: 535 N Dearborn St Chicago IL 60610

GORDON, CAROLINE (Mrs. Gordon Tate), author; b. Todd County, Ky., Oct. 6, 1895; d. James Morris and Nancy Minor (Meriwether) Gordon; A.B., Bethany Coll., 1916; Litt.D., 1946; Litt.D., St. Mary's Coll., Notre Dame, Ind., 1964; m. Allen Tate, Nov. 2, 1924 (div.); 1 dau., Mrs. Percy H. Wood, Jr. Reporter, staff Chattanooga News, 1920-24; Guggenheim fellow, 1932; prof. English, Woman's Coll., U. N.C., 1938-39; lectr. creative writing Sch. Gen. Studies, Columbia, 1946—; vis. prof. English, U. Wash., 1953, U. Kan., 1956; writer in residence U. Cal. at Davis, 1962-63; lectr. creative writing New Sch. Social Research. Recipient 2d O. Henry Meml. award, 1934, $10,000 grant Nat. Council on Arts, 1966. Mem. Alpha Xi Delta. Roman Catholic. Author novels including: Aleck Maury, 1934; None Shall Look Back, 1937; The House of Fiction (with Allen Tate), 1950; The Strange Children, 1951; The Malefactors, 1956; How to Read a Novel (criticism), 1957; Old Red and Other Stories, 1963; The Glory of Hera, 1971. Contbr. to publs., rep. in anthologies. Address: The Red House Princeton NJ 08540

GORDON, CECIL FITZHUGH, investment banker; b. Anniston, Ala., Jan. 9, 1902; s. Frederick Elliott and Fanny Barclay (Hammond) G.; B.S., Dartmouth, 1923; m. Georgia Clinton Mackenzie, June 22, 1929; children—Barclay Fitzhugh, Graham Mackenzie. With First Nat. Bank, N.Y.C., 1924-25, N.Y.C. R.R., 1925-28; with Tucker, Anthony & R. L. Day, N.Y.C., 1928—, gen. partner, 1946-69, ltd. partner, 1970—; dir. Harvey Aluminum Inc. Trustee Huntington (L.I.) Hosp. Mem. Am. Hist. Assn. (trustee), Soc. Colonial Wars. Episcopalian. Clubs: Down Town Assn. (N.Y.C.); Gold Spring Harbor (L.I.) Beach (pres. 1955-56). Home: Laurel Hollow Rd Syosset NY 11791 Office: 120 Broadway New York City NY 10005

GORDON, CHARLES, govt. ofcl.; b. N.Y.C., Oct. 12, 1905; s. Louis and Sarah (Tannenbaum) G.; student Coll. City N.Y., 1923-26; LL.B., N.Y. U., 1927; m. Anne Chachanowsky, Mar. 17, 1940; children—Michael, Ellen. Admitted to N.Y. bar, 1929, also U.S. Supreme Ct.; atty., N.Y.C., 1929-39; with U.S. Immigration and Naturalization Service, 1939—, dep. gen. counsel, 1962- 66, gen. counsel, 1966—; adj. prof. law Georgetown U., 1963—. Active local civic orgns. and P.T.A. Recipient Annual Authorship award Fed. Bar Assn., 1965. Mem. Am. (vice chmn. com. immigration and nationality 1967—), Fed. bar assns. Author: (with Rosenfield) Immigration Law and Procedure, rev. edit., 1966. Home: 11810 Seven Locks Rd Rockville, MD 20854. Office: 119 D St NE Washington DC 20536

GORDON, COLIN D., educator; B.A., U. Alta., (Can.); M.A., Ph.D., U. Mich. Prof., chmn. dept. classics, vice dean Faculty of Arts and Sci., McGill U. Home: 144 Broadview Av Pointe Claire Quebec Canada*

GORDON, CYRUS HERZL, educator; b. Phila., June 29, 1908; s. Benjamin Lee and Dorothy (Cohen) G.; A.B., U. Pa., 1927, M.A., 1928, Ph.D., 1930; m. Joan Elizabeth Kendall, Sept. 22, 1946; children—Deborah J., Sarah Y., Rachel K., Noah D., Dan K. Instr. semitics U. Pa., 1930-31; field archaeologist, fellow Am. Schs. Oriental Research, Near East, 1931-35; teaching fellow Oriental Sem., Johns Hopkins, 1935-38; lectr. Bible, Smith Coll., 1938- 39, 40-41; mem. Inst. Advanced Study, Princeton, 1939-40, 41-42; prof. Assyriology and Egyptology, Dropsie U., Phila., 1946-56; prof. Near Eastern studies Brandeis U., Waltham, Mass., 1956—, chmn. dept. Mediterranean studies, 1958—, dir. Grad. Sch., asso. dean faculty, 1957-58. Vis. fellow humanities U. Colo., 1967; Gay lectr. Simmons Coll., 1970; vis. prof. N.Y.U., 1970-72; archaeol. explorations E. Mediterranean lands, 1957-58, 59, 61, 67, 68, 69, 70, 71. Trustee Boston Hebrew Coll.; corr. mem. Inst. Antiquity and Christianity Claremont Grad. Sch. and University Center; trustee Internat. Council for Etruscan Studies of Order of Holy Cross. Served as officer AUS, 1942-46; col. USAF Res.; flight comdr. Boston Air Res. Center, 1958-61; mobilization assignee Hdqrs. USAF, 1961-67. Harrison scholar U. Pa., 1928-29, Harrison fellow, 1929-30; fellow Am. Council Learned Socs., 1932-33, Am. Scandinavian Found., 1939; recipient Alumni award Gratz Coll., Phila., 1961. Fellow Am. Acad. Arts and Scis., Explorers Club; mem. Am. Hist. Assn., Am. Oriental Soc. (exec. com. 1964-67), Am. Philol. Assn., Archaeol. Inst. Am., Soc. Bib. Lit. and Exegesis. Author: Ugaritic Grammar, 1940; Ugaritic Handbook, 1947; Ugaritic Manual, 1955; The Living Past, 1941; Adventures in the Nearest East, 1957; Ugaritic Literature, 1949; Smith College Tablets, 1952; Introduction to Old Testament Times, 1953; The World of the Old Testament, 1958, rev. as the Ancient Near East, 1965; Before the Bible, 1963, rev. as The Common Background of Greek and Hebrew Civilization, 1965; Ugaritic Textbook, 1965, rev. with supplement, 1967; Ugarit and Minoan Crete, 1966; Evidence for the Minoan Language, 1966; Forgotten Scripts, 1968, rev. edit., 1971; Before Columbus, 1971. numerous articles. Contbg. editor Am. Jour. Archaeology, 1938-45; editorial council Encounter, 1956. Home: 130 Dean Rd Brookline MA 02146 Office: Brandeis U Waltham MA 02154

GORDON, DEXTER, tenor saxophonist, composer; b. Los Angeles, Feb. 27, 1923. Leading name band musician during 1940s, then combo leader during 1950s; composer, leader quartet, also actor in The Connection, 1960; lived and played in Europe, especially Denmark, 1962—; also produced Danish prodn. of The Connection; numerous appearances in nightclubs throughout Europe and U.S.; recording artist for Jazzland, Blue Note, Prestige, Epic records. Address: Andreas Bjørnsgd 22/5 Copenhagen K, Denmark.*

GORDON, DOUGLAS RODERICK, banker; b. Toronto, Can., Mar. 17, 1911; s. William E. and Olive (Kennedy) G.; student Walsh Inst. Accounting, 1946-49, NABAC Sch. Bank Auditors and Comptrollers, 1955-57; chartered bank auditor, 1968; m. Louise Kurz, Mar. 15, 1941; 1 son, Brian D. With Mfrs. Nat. Bank Detroit, 1935—, auditor 1958—. Instr. Bank Adminstrn. Inst., 1968. Served with AUS, 1943-46; ETO. Mem. Bank Adminstrn. Inst. (past pres. Detroit), Inst. Internal Auditors. Mason. Home: 1751 Highview Dearborn MI 48128

GORDON, EDGAR GEORGE, lawyer, bus. exec.; b. Detroit, Feb. 27, 1924; s. Edgar George and Verna (Hay), G.; A.B., Princeton, 1947; A.B., Harvard Bus. Sch., 1945; J.D., Harvard, 1950; m. Alice J. Irwin, Feb. 4, 1967; 1 son, David A. Admitted to Mich. bar, 1951, also to U.S. Supreme Ct. bar; asso. Poole, Warren & Littell, 1950-54; partner Poole, Warren, Littell & Gordon, Detroit, 1954-63; corporate counsel Hygrade Food Products Corp., 1963—, corporate sec., 1966—, v.p., 1968—; v.p., counsel City Nat. Bank, Detroit, 1969—; v.p., sec. Northern States Financial Corp., 1971—. Bd. dirs. Inter-City Community Clinic, 1961—. Served to lt. (j.g.) USNR, 1943-46. Mem. Am., Detroit (chmn. pub. relations com., 1963-65), Mich. bar assns, Am. Soc. Corporate Secs. Home: 210 Lothrop Rd Grosse Pointe Farms MI 48236 Office: Penobscot Bldg Detroit MI 48226

GORDON, EDGAR STILLWELL, educator, physician; b. Chgo., Nov. 6, 1907; s. Edgar Bernard and Edna (Stillwell) G.; B.S., U. Wis., 1927, M.A., 1929; M.D., Harvard, 1932; m. Lola A. Gray, June 27, 1936; children—Joan Elizabeth (Mrs. Arthur W. Owens), Stuart Gray, Robert Bruce. Intern, Billings Meml. Hosp., Chgo., 1932-34; resident medicine Mass. Gen. Hosp., Boston, 1935, U. Wis. Hosps., 1936; practice medicine specializing in endocrinology and metabolism, Madison, Wis., 1938—; faculty U. Wis. Med. Sch., 1938-, prof. medicine, 1952—, chief staff Univ. Hosp., 1970—. Cons. AEC, Oak Ridge Inst. Nuclear Studies, NASA; mem. program project com. Inst. Arthritis and Metabolic Diseases, NIH. Pres. bd. dirs. Wis. Idea Theater Found. Diplomate Am. Bd. Internal Medicine, Am. Bd. Nutrition. Mem. Assn. Am. Physicians, A.C.P., Am. Soc. Clin. Investigation, Central Soc. Clin. Research, Endocrine Soc., Am. Inst. Nutrition, Am. Diabetes Assn., Am. Clin. and Climatol. Assn., Am. Soc. Clin. Nutrition, Sigma Xi. Author: Nutritional and Vitamin Therapy, 1942. Editor: Steroid Hormones. Contbr. articles to profl. jours. Home: 1520 Wood Lane Madison WI 53705

GORDON, EDMUND WYATT, educator, psychologist; b. Goldsboro, N.C., June 13, 1921; s. Edmund Tayloe and Mabel (Ellison) G.; B.S., Howard U., 1942, B.D., 1945; M.A., Am. U., 1950; Ed.D., Columbia Tchrs. Coll., 1957; m. Susan Elizabeth Gitt, Nov. 6, 1948; children—Edmund T., Christopher W., Jessica G., Johanna S. Ordained to ministry Presbyn. Ch., 1945; field missionary, bd. nat. missions Presbyn. Ch. U.S.A., 1945-46; asst. dean men Howard U., 1946-50; asst. dir., counseling psychologist Morningside Community Center and Mental Health Service, N.Y.C., 1951-52; from part-time clin. asst. in psychiatry to part-time sr. psychologist N.Y. Med. Coll., 1952- 60; mem. staff Jewish Hosp. Bklyn., 1952-60, chief psychologist and supr., 1952-60; co-founder, co-dir. Harriet Tubman Clinic Children, N.Y.C., 1953-59; lectr. psychology L.I. U., 1958-59; lectr. spl. edn., asso. prof. edn., research asso. pediatrics, chmn. dept. spl. edn. Yeshiva U., 1959-61; mem. faculty Albert Einstein Coll. Medicine, Yeshiva U., 1961—, prof. Ferkauf Grad. Sch., 1965, past chmn. dept. ednl. psychology and guidance; research asst. prof. Albert Einstein Coll. Medicine, 1963—; chmn. dept. guidance, prof. edn. Tchrs. Coll. Columbia, 1968—. Research asso. Horace Mann Lincoln Inst.; vis. prof. div. behavioral scis. Harvard, summer 1966; cons. in field, 1964—. Mem. research grants rev. panel Bur. Ednl. Research, U.S. Office Edn., 1964- -; dir. div. research and evaluation, project Head Start, Office Econ. Opportunity, 1965-67. Pres. Rockland County (N.Y.) chpt. N.A.A.C.P., 1956-61. Fellow research conf. learning and ednl. process Stanford, 1964. Fellow Am. Psychol. Assn., Am. Orthopsychiat. Assn.; mem. N.Y. State Psychol. Assn. (pres. applied social div. 1965-66), Am. Ednl. Research Assn., Soc. Research Child Devel., A.A.A.S., Am. Personnel and Guidance Assn., Council Exceptional Children. Contbr. numerous articles to jours, Home: Cooper Morris Dr Pomona, NY 10970. Office: Tchrs Coll 523 W 120th St New York City NY 10027

GORDON, EDWARD, music assn. exec.; b. 1930. Former concert pianist; performed age 9 with Chgo. Symphony under Frederick Stock; asso. mgr. Grant Park summer concerts Chgo. Park Dist., 1958-65, mgr., 1965-68; gen. mgr. Ravinia Festival Assn., Chgo., 1968—. Home: 3470 Lake Shore Dr Chicago IL 60657 Office: Ravinia Festival Assn 22 W Monroe St Chicago IL 60603

GORDON, EDWARD S., educator; b. Chgo., May 2, 1919; s. Hyman and Hannah (Schulman) G.; M.B.A., U. Chgo., 1940; m. Frances Fogel, Aug. 31, 1941; children—Barbara, Kenneth, Joseph. Service specialist Spiegel, Inc., 1940-41; tchr. Austin Jr. Coll., 1941-42; chmn., prof. marketing Roosevelt U., Chgo., 1945—, asso. dean Walter E. Heller Coll. of Bus. Adminstrn., 1965-70, acting dean, 1970—; owner Am. Research Assos., 1947—; analyst Firestone Tire & Rubber Co., 1952; cons. research dir. Haywood Pub. Co., 1955-63; marketing cons. Arthur Retlaw & Assos., 1969—. Mem. sch. bd., Skokie, Ill., 1956-62; adv. com. Tri-County div. Ill. Sch. Bd. Assn., 1959-62. Trustee Roosevelt U., 1962-66. Served with USAF, 1942-

45. Ford Found. research fellow, 1962. Mem. Am. Marketing Assn. (v. p. Chgo. chpt. 1968-69), Nat. Retail Mchts. Assn. (careers com. 1963), Am. Assn. U. Profs., Assn. Indsl. Advertisers. Author: Home Improvement Course for Professional Plumbing and Heating Salesmen; Principles of Marketing; Your Efforts. Home: 8140 N Kildare Av Skokie IL 60076 Office: 430 S Michigan Av Chicago IL 60605

GORDON, EDWIN JAY, mfg. co. exec.; b. N.Y.C., Jan. 26, 1933; s. Charles and Pearl (Bland) G.; B.B.A., Coll. City N.Y., 1953; LL.B., Columbia, 1958; m. Roseann Abramson, June 19, 1955; children—Amy, Adam. Legal practice in Louisville, 1958-60; asso. firm Skaggs, Hays & Fahey, 1958-60; atty. Cities Service Oil Co., N.Y.C., 1960-63; asst. gen. counsel Gildden Co., Cleve., 1963-67; v.p., sec. Dayco Corp., Dayton, O., 1967—. Served with AUS, 1953-55. Office: 333 W 1st St Dayton, OH 45405.

GORDON, ELLIOTT MORTON, business exec.; b. Connersville, Ind., Apr. 14, 1909; s. Charles Taylor and Anna (Morton) G.; student U. Cal., 1928-29; B.S., Purdue U., 1932, hon. E.D., 1950; Sloan fellow Mass. Inst. Tech., 1938-39; m. Mary Hutchinson, Sept. 7, 1935; children—John Elliott, David William, Mary Gillette, James Peter. Chief engr., asst. supt. Moore Corp., Joliet, Ill., 1932-34; asst. personnel dir. Fleetwood Body Corp., Gen. Motors Corp., Detroit, 1934-35; indsl. engr. mgmt. div. Ernst & Ernst, Chgo., 1935-37; asst. to v.p. and prodn. engr. Griggs, Cooper & Co., St. Paul, 1937-40; dir., v.p., gen. mgr. Gorham Mfg. Co., Gorham Co., Alvin Corp.; v.p., dir. Mt. Vernon Silver Co.; dir. Black, Starr & Gorham, Inc., until 1956; pres., gen. mgr., dir. Towle Mfg. Co.; dir. Nat. Shawmut Bank of Boston, Millipore Filter Corp., New Eng. Tel. & Tel. Co. Former trustee Gov. Dummer Acad. Mem. Am. Soc. M.E., Am. Mgmt. Assn., Tau Beta Pi, Sigma Chi, Sigma Delta Chi. Clubs: Newcomen, University (N.Y.C.); Union (Boston). Home: Glenwood Rd Hampton Falls NH 03844 Office: Towle Mfg Co Newburyport MA 01950

GORDON, ERNEST, clergyman; b. Greenock, Scotland, May 31, 1916; s. James and Sarah Rae (Macmillan) G.; B.D., Hartford, 1948; S.T.M., Hartford Theol. Sem., 1949; student U. Glasgow, 1950-51; LL.D., Bloomfield Coll., 1957; D.C.L. (honorary), Bishop's U. of Can., 1966; became naturalized U.S. citizen, 1960; m. Helen McIntosh Robertson, Dec. 17, 1945; children—Gillian Margaret, Alastair James. Ordained to ministry Ch. of Scotland, 1950; dep. minister Paisley Abbey, 1950-52; supply minister Amagansett and Montauk chs., 1953-54; Presbyn. chaplain Princeton, 1954- 55, dean univ. chapel, 1955—. Danforth lectr. Davis and Elkins Coll., 1968; Turnbull preacher, Melbourne, Australia, 1969, Chmn., N.J. Mental Health Research and Devel. Fund. Served as capt. 93d Highlanders, 1939-46; PTO. Fellow Victoria Inst. London; mem. Royal Inst. Philosophy (London), Am. Soc. Ch. History, Renaissance Soc. Am., Ch. Service Soc. Am. (founder), Am. Acad. Polit. and Social Sci. Clubs: Century (N.Y.C.); Highland Brigade (London). Author: A Living Faith for Today, 1956; Through the Valley of the Kwai, 1962; Miracle on the River Kwai, 1963; Meet Me at the Door, 1969. Contbr. articles periodicals. Home: 17 Ivy Lane Princeton NJ 08540

GORDON, EUGENE ANDREW, fed. judge; b. Guilford Co., N.C., July 10, 1917; s. Charles Robert and Carrie (Scott) G.; A.B., Elon Coll., 1938; LL.B., Duke, 1941; m. Virginia Stoner, January 1, 1943; children—Eugene Andrew, Rosemary Anne. Admitted to N.C. bar, 1941; practiced law, 1946-64; mem. firm Young, Young & Gordon, Burlington, 1947-64; solicitor Alamance Gen. Co. Ct., 1947-54; county atty., Alamance Co. 1954-64; U.S. judge Middle Dist. N.C., 1964—. Former chmn. adv. bd. Salvation Army. Former nat. committeeman N.C. Young Democrats; former pres. Alamance Co. Young Democrats; chmn. Alamance Co. Dem. Exec. Com., 1954-64. Served to capt. AUS, 1942-46; comdg. officer N.G., Burlington, 1946-47. Mem. Alamance Co. Bar Assn. (past pres.), Burlington-Alamance County C. of C. (past pres.), Burlington Jr. C. of C., Phi Delta Phi. Clubs: Rotary (past pres.), American Business (Burlington). Home: 601 Currier Ct Winston-Salem NC 27104 Office: Winston-Salem NC 27102

GORDON, EZRA, architect; b. Detroit, Apr. 5, 1921; s. Abraham and Rebecca (Reimer) G.; student Roosevelt Coll., 1946-48; B.S., U. Ill., 1951; m. Jeanette Greenberg, Oct. 10, 1942; children—Cheryl P., Rana, Judith. Draftsman, Pace Assos. Architects, 1951-53; sr. planner Chgo. Plan Commn., 1953-54; project architect Harry Weese & Assos., 1954-61; partner Gordon-Levin & Assos., Chgo., 1961—; cons. Dept. Urban Renewal City Chgo. Bd. dirs. Hyde Park-Kenwood Community Conf. Served with AUS, 1942-45. Decorated Croix de Guerre with palm; recipient Honor award Dept. Housing and Urban Devel., 1967, A.I.A.-Chgo. C. of C., 1967, award A.I.A.-House & Home Mag., 1967, Distinguished Bldg. award A.I.A., 1969, 71, award City of Chgo. Beautification, 1969. Mem. A.I.A. Home: 5432 East View Park Chicago IL 60615 Office: 410 S Michigan Av Chicago IL 60605

GORDON, GEORGE LONGAN, Jr., lawyer; b. Kansas City, Mo., Feb. 10, 1901; s. George L. and Ernestine (Snead) G.; student U. Kan., 1936, Oxford U., 1937; J.D., Kan. City Sch. Law, 1924; m. Jane T. Hemingway, Sept. 2, 1930 (dec.); children—George Hemingway, Jean Arabell, Elizabeth Ernestine; m. 2d, Alice P. Scarritt, Sept. 14, 1966. Admitted to Mo. bar, 1924, U.S. Supreme Ct. bar, 1935; partner Gordon & Gilmore, 1934—, Lathrop, Righter, Gordon & Parker, 1956-70; gen. atty. Mo. & Ia., Atchison, Topeka & Santa Fe Ry., 1956-71; gen. counsel, dir. Bus. Men's Assurance Co., Am. Black, Sivalls & Bryson, Inc., 1946-69; sec.-treas., dir. Westport Television, Inc. Mem. exec. com. Mo. Pub. Expenditure Survey. Chmn. bd. trustees Children's Mercy Hosp.; trustee Linda Hall Library Sci. and Tech., U. Kansas City, 1953-65. Mem. Am., Mo. (chmn. trusts and real estate law com. 1947-51), Kansas City bar assns., C. of C., Assn. Life Ins. Counsel (exec. com. 1958-61), Am. Life Conv. (state v.p. 1953-54), Internat. Assn. Ins. Counsel, Lawyers Assn. Kansas City. Clubs: Kansas City Country, Kansas City. Home: 1025 W 55th St Kansas City MO 64113 Office: BMA Tower Kansas City MO 64108

GORDON, GEORGE SELBIE, research adminstr. govt. ofcl., b. Pittsfield, Mass., Apr. 28, 1919; s. George Selbie, Jr. and Celia Williams (Goodwin) G.; grad. Phillips Exeter Acad., 1937; A.B., Princeton, 1941; Ph.D. in Chemistry, Northwestern U., 1949; m. Anne Spencer Welch, Dec. 28, 1946; children—Peter Williams, Catherine Anne. Research engr. Gen. Electric Co., 1948-51; v.p. Titanium Zirconium Co., Inc., 1951-55; dir. research U.S. Potash Co., 1955-57; asso. dir. research U.S. Borax Research Corp., 1957-58; dir. chem. research Ill. Inst. Tech. Research Inst., Chgo., 1959-63, v.p., 1963-64; chief textile and apparel tech. center Inst. Applied Tech., Nat. Bur. Standards, Washington, 1964-66, chief office Engrng. Standards, Liaison and Analysis, 1966-67, chief Office Indsl. Services, 1967—. Served to lt. USNR, 1943-46. Mem. Am. Chem. soc., A.A.A.S., Phi Beta Kappa, Sigma Xi. Home: 4845 Broad Brook Dr Bethesda, MD 20014. Office: Nat Bur Standards Washington DC 20234

GORDON, H. STEPHAN, govt. ofcl.; b. Vienna, Austria, Dec. 4, 1922; s. Saul and Sabina (Spatz) G.; came to U.S., 1938, naturalized, 1944; A.B., Ind. U., 1947; LL.B., George Washington U., 1949; m. Irene Stewart Harris, May 17, 1946; children—Christopher David, Matthew Dallas. Atty. NLRB, 1949-54, trial atty. P.R. office, 1954-56, chief law officer Atlanta office, 1957- 59, asst. gen. counsel, 1959-61, asso. gen. counsel, 1961—. Served with AUS, 1944-46; ETO. Home: 2905 Covington Rd Silver Spring MD 20910 Office: 1717 Pennsylvania Av Washington DC 20006

GORDON, HAROLD, lawyer; b. Washington, Aug. 30, 1929; s. Frank and Mary (Portnick) G. A.A., George Washington U., 1959, J.D., Am. U. 1961; m. Ingrid Stern, Mar. 17, 1957; children—Marc Edmond, Gillian Leslie, David Keith. Admitted to D.C. bar, 1962, also U.S. Supreme Ct. bar, asst. corp. counsel D.C., 1962-64; partner firm Danzansky, Tydings, Dickey, Quint & Gordon, and predecessors, Washington, 1969—; lectr. municipal corps. Am. U., 1964. Dep. gen. counsel Democratic Nat. Com., 1968-69. Served with AUS, 1946- 49. Mem. Am., D.C. bar assns., Phi Alpha Delta. Mason. Home: 6121 Highboro Dr Bethesda MD 20034 Office: 1120 Connecticut Av NW Washington DC 20036

GORDON, HAROLD JOHN, bus. exec.; b. Chgo., Apr. 11, 1895; s. Daniel C. and Anna N. (Zeeveld) G.; Ph.B., U. Chgo., 1917; m. Ethel Rycroft Byford, Jan. 28, 1922; children—Ethel Ann (Mrs. A. J. Michael), Harold Rycroft, Frances Theresa (Mrs. J. R. Lee). Salesman Halsey, Stuart & Co., Inc., Chgo., 1917-26, dist. sales mgr., 1926-42, Chgo. sales mgr., 1942-67, v.p., 1947-67. Bd. govts. Internat. House (past pres.), U. Chgo. Alumni Found. (past pres.) Served as lt. USN, 1917-18. Mem. Delta Kappa Epsilon. Republican. Presbyn. Clubs: University, Chikaming Country (past pres). Home: 1150 N Lake Shore Dr Chicago IL 60611 Office: 123 S LaSalle St Chicago IL 60690

GORDON, HARRY BERNARD, jewelry co. exec.; b. Houston, Oct. 20, 1909; s. Morris Meyer and Ida (Sampson) G.; student U. Tex., 1926-28; B.S., Columbia, 1931; m. Aileen Becker, July 18, 1946; children—Frann, Harry Bernard, Douglas. With Gordon Jewelry Corp., Houston, 1931—, pres., dir., 1958—. Served to capt. Q.M. Corps, AUS, 1942-45. Mem. Beta Gamma Sigma, Phi Sigma Delta. Jewish religion (past pres. congregation). Club: Houston. Home: 3435 Westheimer Houston TX 77027 Office: 820 Fannin St Houston TX 77002

GORDON, HARRY HASKIN, physician, educator; b. Bklyn., Aug. 4, 1906; s. Samuel and Ida (Haskin) G.; B.A., Cornell U., 1926, M.D., 1929; D.Sc., Yeshiva U., 1969; m. Fayga Halpern, June 8, 1948; children—Charles, Deborah. Intern, Montefiore Hosp., N.Y.C., then New Haven Hosp., 1929-31; resident New Haven Hosp., then N.Y. Hosp., 1931-33; asso. attending pediatrician N.Y. Hosp., 1932-46; pediatrician-in-chief Colo. and Denver Gen. hosps., 1946- 52; pediatrician-in-chief Sinai Hosp., Balt., 1952-62; attending pediatrician Johns Hopkins Hosp., 1952-62; attending pediatrician Bronx Municipal Hosp. Center, 1962—; dir. Rose Fitzgerald Kennedy Center for Research in Mental Retardation and Human Devel., 1965—; asst. prof. Cornell U. Med. Coll., 1933-46; prof. pediatrics U. Colo., 1946-52; asso. prof. pediatrics Johns Hopkins U., 1952-62; prof. pediatrics Albert Einstein Coll. Medicine, 1962—, asso. dean, 1966-67, dean, 1967- 70; cons. in pediatrics Surgeon Gen. U.S. Army, 1947-62, U.S. Childrens Bur. for Maternal and Child Health and Crippled Childrens Services, 1948- 51; cons. Surgeon Gen. USPHS, 1949—; mem. food and nutrition bd. NRC, 1955-59; mem. Health Task Force, N.Y. Urban Coalition, 1970—. Career scientist Health Research Council City N.Y., 1962-67. Served from capt. to lt. col. M.C., AUS, 1942-46. ReRecipient Borden award for nutritional research Am. Acad. Pediatrics, 1944; Grover F. Powers Distinguished prof. Nat. Assn. for Retarded Children, 1963—. Fellow A.A.A.S.; mem. Am. Pediatric Soc. (past pres.), Soc. for Pediatric Research (past pres.), Nat. Assn. for Retarded Children (vice chmn. research adv. bd.), A.M.A., Am. Acad. Pediatrics, Am. Soc. for Clin. Investigation, Am. Assn. Mental Deficiency, Sigma Xi, Alpha Omega Alpha. Contbr. articles profl. jours. Home: 369 Orienta Av Mamaroneck NY 10543 Office: 1410 Pelham Pkwy S Bronx NY 10461

GORDON, HOWARD HENLEY, mgmt. cons.; b. Jamestown, N.C., May 10, 1899; s. James R. and Nancy Elizabeth (Henley) G.; B.S. in Agr., N.C. State Coll. Agr. and Engrng., 1919; grad. student Va. Poly. Inst.; m. Ethel M. Hindle, June 26, 1926; children—James D., Nancy H. Extension specialist N.C. and Va. extension services, 1925-34; dir. for Va., also regional dir. Farm Security Adminstrn., 1934-43; with So. States Coop., Richmond, Va., 1943-64, asst. gen. mgr., then gen. mgr., 1948-61; pres. Commodity Credit Corp., Dept. Agr., 1953-54; mgmt. cons., Richmond, 1961-64; pres., dir. Coop. Mills Va., Richmond, 1954-63, So. States Marketing Service, Richmond, 1954-63. Pres. Agrl. Conf. Bd. Va., 1956-58, exec. sec., 1963-69; cons. AID, 1966-67, Govt. India, 1966-67. chmn. Gov.'s Commn. Industry of Agr., 1966-69; pres. Nat. Council Farmer Coops., 1961-63; vice chmn. Am. Inst. Coop., 1961-62; U.S. del. Internat. Wheat Agreement Conf., Madrid, Spain, 1953; mem. labor mgmt. manpower com. region 2, Dept. Agr., 1960-63; adviser U.S. delegation FOA, 1961; del. Internat. Fedn. Agrl. Producers, Dubrounik, Yugoslavia, 1961, Dublin, Ireland, 1963. Recipient Certificate of Merit, Va. Poly. Inst., 1958, Agr. Bus. award Richmond Agrl. Grange, 1960; named Man of Year in Va. Agr., Progressive Farmer mag., 1959. Mem. Richmond (dir.), Va. chambers commerce, Central Richmond Assn. (dir.), Va. Farm Bur. Fedn., Va. Grange. Methodist (chmn. ofcl. bd., chmn. trustees). Home: 5909 Crestwood Av Richmond VA 23226

GORDON, IRA H., Jr., mfg. co. exec.; b. Cleve., 1922; ed. Miami U., 1944. Chmn., pres. Swift Industries Inc., United Dealers Corp., Gordon Swift Homes Co.; pres., dir. Rosmer Acres, Inc.; pres. Allgheny Mortgage Co., So. Swift Corp., Mercury Motor. Home: 126 Beechmont Rd Pittsburgh, PA 15206. Office: 241 Curry Hollow Rd Pittsburgh PA 15236

GORDON, IRVING, physician, educator; b. Cleveland, June 20, 1914; s. N. Beryl and Minna (Singer) G.; M.D., U. Mich., 1937; m. Toini Lefren, June 16, 1939 (dec. May 1967); children-James Norrby, Elizabeth Britt (Mrs. Michael Ascher), Thomas Rolf; m.2d. Francis Maxwell Hawkes, Oct. 18, 1968. Intern L.I. Coll. Med. Sch. Hosp., 1937-38, resident, 1938-39; fellow Rockefeller Found., 1941; profl. asso. commn. acute respiratory disease Army Epidemiological Bd., Ft. Brag; N.C. 1943-46 staff mem. div. labs. and research N.Y. State Health Dept., 1946-55, asst. dir. 1952-55; asso. prof. medicine and bacteriology Albany (N.Y.), Med. Coll., also asso. attending physician Albany Hosp., 1949-55; prof., chmn. dept. microbiology U. So. Cal. Med. Sch., 1955—, asso. dean., 1964-65; sr. attending physician U. So. Cal. Med. Center, 1956—. Diplomate Am. Bd. Pathology, Am. Bd. Microbiology, Nat. Bd. Med. Examiners. Mem. Nat. Insts. Health (mem. numerous coms.) Am. Cancer Soc. at Armed Forces Epidemiological Bd., Who, Nat. Tb Assn. Author research contributions to virology and infectious deseases. Contbr. to med., microbiol. textbooks. Editorial bd. sci. jours. Home: 375 S San Rafael Av Pasadena CA 90033 Office: U Southern Cal Med Sch Los Angeles CA 90033

GORDON, IRVING ARTHUR, educator; b. Minsk, Russia, Sept. 12, 1917; s. Elchonon P. and Rebecca (Lieberman) G.; came to U.S., 1924, now naturalized; B.A., U. Chgo., 1938; J.D., Northwestern U., 1947; m. Arline Leavitt, Feb. 15, 1942; children—David J., Jeffry I., Debra G., Susan R. Admitted to Ill. bar, 1947; practice in Chgo., 1947-66; clk. to Justice Sherman Minton, Ct. of Appeals 7th Circuit, 1947-48; prof. law Northwestern U., Chgo., 1966—. Mem. Gov.'s Research Group for Ill. Constl. Conv., 1970. C.P.A., Ill. Mem. Am., Chgo. bar assns., Order of Coif, Phi Beta Kappa. Contbr. articles profl. jours. Home: 5421 Cornell St Chicago IL 60615 Office: 357 E Chicago Av Chicago IL 60611

GORDON, JAMES BRAUND, mgmt. cons.; b. Battle Creek, Mich., July 30, 1911; s. James Howard and Emma (Braund) G.; B.A., Williams Coll., 1932; LL.B., Harvard, 1935; m. Evelyn H. Riley, Aug. 10, 1940; children—Constance, Douglas, Martha. Admitted to N.Y. bar, 1936, Mich. bar, 1944; practice in N.Y.C., 1936-44; gen. atty. Bendix Corp., 1944-67, sec., 1960-69, Washington counsel, 1969-71; mgmt. cons., 1971—. Mem. Unitarian- Universalist Laymens League (regional v.p. 1962-70), Greater Detroit Meml. Soc. (pres. 1964-69). Unitarian. Home: 1001 Wilson Blvd Arlington VA 22209 Office: Lawyers Search Div Exec Agy 1025 Vermont Av NW Washington DC 20005

GORDON, JAMES CAMERON, mfg. co. exec.; b. Chgo., Sept. 6, 1912; s. Andrew Cameron and Jean (Robertson) G.; student Beaux Arts Sch. Design, N.Y.C., 1931-33, Hillyer Coll., Hartford, Conn., 1934-35; m. Muriel Mercier, June 26, 1938; children—Robert C., Donna M., Janet M. With Seeburg Corp., Chgo., 1948- 66, exec. v.p., 1959-64, pres., dir., 1964-66; exec. v.p. Seeburg Internat., Inc., Chgo., 1961-64, pres., dir., 1964—; exec. v.p. Serose Corp., Zurich, Switzerland, 1961-66; pres., dir. Williams Electronics Corp., 1964-66; vice chmn. bd. Tel-A-Sign, Inc. Chgo., 1966-67; pres., NO. OF RECORDS 00057 chief exec. officer Theatre 16 Internat. Corp., Chgo., 1966—; pres. Cameron Internat. Ltd., 1967—, Cameron Mus. Industries Ltd., 1967— (both N.Y.). Music adviser Worlds Fair Music, N.Y.C., 1962. Mem. A.S.C.A.P. Clubs: Executives, Mid-America. Home: 73 Port Washington Blvd Flower Hill Roslyn NY 11576 Office: 82 S Bayles Av Port Washington NY 11050

GORDON, JAMES FLEMING, U.S. dist. judge; b. Madisonville, Ky., May 18, 1918; s. John F. and Ruby (James) G.; LL.B., U. Ky., 1941; m. Iola Young, Sept. 1, 1942; children-Maurice K. II, James Fleming, Marianna. Admitted to Ky. bar, 1941; practice in Madisonville, 1941-65; judge U.S. Dist. Ct., Western Dist. Ky.,Louisville, 1965—. Chmn. Ky. Pub. Service Commn., 1955-59. Speakers chmn. Ky. Democratic Party, 1955, campaign chmn., 1962. Bd. dirs. Clinic Found., Madisonville. Served to 1st lt., Judge Adv. Gen. Dept., AUS, 1941-46; PTO. Mem. Am. Coll. Trial Lawyers, Am. Legion, V.F.W., Phi Delta Phi. Home: 402 Mockingbird Hill Rd Louisville KY 40207 Office: Fed Bldg Louisville KY 40202

GORDON, JAMES ROYCROFT, mining exec.; b. Kingston, Ont., May 26, 1898; s. Byron and Edith Harriet (Leonard) G.; B.Sc. in chemistry, Queen's U., 1920, LL.D., 1955; m. Margaret Arthur, June 7, 1922 (dec.); children—James, David, Shirley (Mrs. Ralph Harrison), Ruth (Mrs. Fraser Parrott) m. 2d, Joan Ehretia Windus, 1955; 1 stepson, Brian. Research metallurgist M.J. O'Brien, Ltd., 1920-29; research Ont. Research Found., 1929-36; dir. research Internat. Nickel Co. of Can., Ltd., 1936-41, asst. to v.p., 1941-46, tech. asst. to v.p., 1946, asst. v.p., 1947-53, asst. gen. mgr., 1952, v.p., dir., gen. mgr. Canadian operations 1953, transferred N.Y. office as v.p., 1955, exec. v.p. Internat. Nickel Co. Can, Ltd., Internat. Nickel Co., Inc., 1957-60, pres., 1960-66, chmn. exec. com., dir., 1967-68, now dir., mem. exec. com.; hon. dir. Bank of N.Y.; dir. Gulf Oil Can. Ltd., Steel Co. of Can., Ltd., Borden Co., Can. Life Assurance Co., Babcock & Wilcox Co., N.Y. Trustee Queen's U. Bd. Gov.'s Ont. Research Found. Recipient. Platinum medal Canadian Inst. Mining and Metallurgy 1948, medal for advancement research Am. Soc. Metals, 1967, James Douglas gold medal Am. Inst. Mining, Metall, and Petroleum Engineers, 1957. Mem. Canadian Inst. Mining and Metallurgy, Am. Inst. Mining, Metall. and Petroleum Engrs., Am. Soc. Metals, Chem. Inst. Can., Mining Club, Engring. Inst. Can., Mining and Metall. Soc. Presbyn. (pres. bd. trustees; bd. mgrs. Am. Bible Soc.). Mason. Clubs: Toronto (Toronto); University, India House (N.Y.C.). Home: 57 Park Av New York City NY 10021 Office: 1 New York Plaza New York City NY 10004

GORDON, JOEL ETHAN, educator; b. Denver, May 9, 1930; s. Samuel Jerome and Margaret (Greinetz) G.; A.B., Harvard, 1952; student Magdalene Coll., Cambridge (Eng.) U., 1952-53; Ph.D., U. Cal. at Berkeley, 1958; M.A. (hon.), Amherst Coll., 1969; m. Pamela Ann Wonfor, Feb. 24, 1956; children—Peter Andrew, Stephen Eliot. Mem. faculty Amherst Coll., 1957—, prof. physics, 1968—; vis. and guest scientist Brookhaven Nat. Lab., 1962-67; mem. attached staff solid state physics div. Harwell (Eng.) Labs., 1964-65; Rockefellwr Found. spl. staff vis. prof. physics U. del Valle, Cali, Colombia, 1968-69. Mem. Am. Assn. Physics Tchrs. (chmn. resource letter com. 1967—), Am. Phys. Soc., A.A.A.S., Am. Assn. U. Profs., Phi Beta Kappa, Sigma Xi. Home: 43 Hitchcock Rd Amherst MA 01002

GORDON, JOHN, museum curator; b. Bklyn., Jan. 20, 1912; s. Charles A. and Margaret M. (Dunne) G.; A.B., Dartmouth, 1934. Adminstrv. asst. dept. circulating exhbns. Mus. Modern Art, 1944-45; sec. Bklyn. Mus., 1945-52, curator paintings and sculpture, 1952-59; curator Whitney Mus. Am. Art, 1959-69; dir. Soc. Four Arts, Palm Beach, Fla., 1969—. Corporate mem. McDowell Colony; mem. adv. bd. The Drawing Soc. Author: (exhibition catalogs) Face of America, Bklyn. Mus., 1959, Biennial Internat. Watercolor Exhbns., Bklyn. Mus., 1955, 57, 59, (with Una E. Johnson) 14 Painter-Printmakers exhbn., Bklyn. Mus., 1955; Karl Schrag, 1960; José de Rivera, 1961; Geometric Abstraction in America, 1962; Richard Pousette-Dart, 1963; A Selection of American Prints from the New York Hilton at Rockefeller Center, 1963; New York, New York, 1965; Louise Nevelson, 1967; Isamu Noguchi, 1967; Franz Kline, 1968; Jim Dine, 1970. Clubs: Everglades, Bath and Tennis (Palm Beach). Address: Soc Four Arts Four Arts Plaza Palm Beach FL 33480

GORDON, JOHN LUTZ, utility exec.; b. Lincoln, Ill., Oct. 10, 1899; s. Frank B. and Marian C. (Lutz) G.; B.S. in Elec. Engring., Milw. Sch. Engring., 1920, E.E., 1953; m. Ruth Coddington, Apr. 30, 1928; 1 dau., Marian (Mrs. Jack A. McCann). Cons. engr. Vaughan & Meyer, Milw., 1920-23; engr. C.A. Shaler Co., Waupun, Wis., 1923-26; with Central Ill. Electric & Gas Co. (now div. of Commonwealth Edison Co.), Rockford, 1926—, chmn. bd., 1963—; dir. Commonwealth Edison Co. Chgo., Alpine State Bank, Rockford, Ill., Elco Tool & Screw Corp., Rockford, Mt. Pulaski Telephone & Electric Co., Lincoln, Ill. Trustee Lincoln (Ill.) Coll., Rockford Coll.; bd. regents Milw. Sch. Engring.; bd. trustees Rockford Meml. Hosp. Served with AUS, World War I. Mem. Ill. (past v.p., chmn. econ. devel. com., dir.), Rockford (chmn. indsl. devel. com.) chambers commerce, Ill. S.A.R. Episcopalian. Rotarian, Mason (Shriner). Clubs: Rockford Country, Mid- Day, University (Rockford); Union League (Chgo.). Office: 303 N Main St Rockford IL 61101

GORDON, JOSEPH ELWELL, coll. dean; b. Deatsville, Ala., July 2, 1921; s. Joseph Elwell and Martha (Berry) G.; A.B., Birmingham-So. Coll., 1942; M.S., Auburn U., 1949; Ph.D., U. Chgo., 1951; m. Doris Elizabeth Smith, June 5, 1948; children—Cecile Lizabeth, Joseph Elwell, Melissa Innes. Tchr. math., Montgomery, Ala., 1946-48; instr. math. Auburn U., 1948-49; research asst. N. Central Assn. Colls. and Secondary Schs., Chgo., 1949-51; program analyst Air U., Maxwell AFB, 1951-54; mem. faculty Tulane U., 1954—, asst. prof. edn., 1958—, asso. dean admissions, 1957-63, dean Coll. Arts and Scis., 1964—. Served to lt. USNR, 1942-46. Mem. Omicron Delta Kappa, Phi Delta Kappa, Pi Kappa Alpha. Democrat. Presbyn. Home: 1108 Lowerline St New Orleans LA 70118

GORDON, JOSEPH HAROLD, lawyer; b. Tacoma, Mar. 31, 1909; s. Joseph H. and Mary (Obermiller) G.; B.A., Stanford, 1931; LL.B., U. Wash., 1935; m. Jane Wilson, Sept. 12, 1936 (dec.); children—Joseph H., Nancy Jane; m. 2d, Eileen Rylander, Jan. 7, 1967. Admitted to Wash. bar, 1935, since practiced in Tacoma; partner Gordon, Honeywell, Malonca, Peterson and Johnson. Personnel dir. Todd Pacific Shipyards, 1942-44. Mem. Am. (ho. dels., bd. govs. 1962—, treas. 1965—), Wash. State, Tacoma (past pres.) bar assns. Presbyn. (elder). Clubs: Rotary, Union, University, Tacoma Golf and Country. Home: 2819 N Junett St Tacoma WA 98407 Office: Puget Sound Bank Bldg Tacoma WA 98402

GORDON, KERMIT, instn. exec., economist; b. Phila., July 3, 1916; s. H. B. and Ida E. (Robinson) G.; B.A. with highest honors in Econs., Swarthmore Coll., 1938, LL.D., 1963; Rhodes scholar, U. Coll., Oxford, 1938-39; m. Mary King Grinnell, Dec. 26, 1941; children—Katherine, Emily, Andrew. Research asso. econs. Swarthmore Coll., 1939-40; Adminstrn. fellow Harvard, 1940-41, tchr. econs., 1950, 54; with OPA, 1941-43; spl. asst. Office Asst. Sec. Econ. Affairs, State Dept., 1945-46, cons., 1946-53; faculty Williams Coll. 1946-62, prof. econs., 1955-62, David A. Wells prof. polit. economy, 1961-62; mem. Council of Econ. Advisers, 1961-62; dir. Bur. of Budget, 1962-65; v. p. Brookings Instn., Washington, 1965-67, pres., 1967—. Asso. to adminstr. Merrill Found. for Advancement Financial Knowledge, 1947-56; cons. White House, 1950, OPS, 1951; exec. asso. Ford Found., 1956-57, dir. program econ. devel. and adminstrn., 1960-61, mem. bd. trustees, 1967—; mem. Council Fgn. Relations, 1967—; chmn. Health Ins. Benefits Adv. Council, 1965-67; mem. Social Security Adv. Council, 1969-71; mem. Gen. Adv. Com. on Arms Control and Disarmament, 1969—; trustee Com. Econ. Devel.; bd. mgrs. Swarthmore Coll., 1965—, vice chmn., 1970—. Served to 2d lt. AUS, 1943-45. Fellow Am. Acad. Arts and Scis.; mem. Am. Econ. Assn., Am. Assn. Rhodes Scholars, Phi Beta Kappa. Club: Cosmos (Washington). Bd. editors Am. Econ. Rev., 1958-60. Home: 2202 Wyoming Av NW Washington, DC 20008. Office: Brookings Instn 1775 Massachusetts Av N W Washington DC 20036

GORDON, LINCOLN, polit. economist; b. N.Y.C., Sept. 10, 1913; s. Bernard and Dorothy (Lerned) G.; A.B., Harvard, 1933; D. Phil. (Rhodes scholar), Oxford U. (Eng.), 1936; LL.D., Fairleigh Dickinson U., 1965, Columbia, 1967, Rutgers U., 1967, U. Md., 1968, Wash. Coll., 1968, U. Del., 1969; L.H.D., Loyola Coll., Balt., 1968; m. Allison Wright, June 25, 1937; children—Anne, Robert W., Hugh, Amy. Instr., faculty instr. govt. Harvard, 1936-41, William Ziegler prof. internat. econ. relations, 1955-61; research technician water, energy resources, U.S. Nat. Resources Planning Bd., Washington, 1939-1940; sr. econ. analyst adv. commn. Council Nat. Def., Washington, 1940; mem. staff requirements com. W.P.B., 1942, asst. and dep.-dir. program bur., 1943-44, dir. program bur., 1944, dep. vice chmn. program, 1944-45, program vice chmn., 1945; dir. bur. reconversion priorities Civilian Prodn. Adminstrn., 1945-46; asso. prof. bus. Harvard, 1946-47, prof. govt. and adminstrn., 1947-50; cons. U.S. Rep. UN AEC, 1946, Army and Navy Munitions Bd., Dept. of State, 1947, ECA, 1948; North Atlantic Council Com. of Three on non-mil. aspects of NATO, 1956; dir. program div. Office ECA spl. rep. in Europe, 1949-50; econ. adviser to spl. asst. to President, 1950-51; asst. dir. for Mut. Security Agy., 1951-52, chief mission to U.K., 1952-55, minister econ. affairs in Am. embassy, London, 1952-55; U.S. ambassador to Brazil, 1961-66; asst. sec. state for inter-Am. affairs, 1966-67; pres. Johns Hopkins U., Balt., 1967-71; prof. polit. economy Johns Hopkins Sch. Advanced Internat. Studies, Washington, 1971—. Dir. Equitable Life Assurance Soc. U.S. Bd. dirs. Center Inter-Am. Relations; trustee Com. for Econ. Devel. Decorated Grand Cross Order Quetzal (Guatemala); Grand Cross Order Cruzeiro do Sul (Brazil). Fellow Am. Acad. Arts and Scis.; mem. Am. Polit. Sci. Assn., A.A.A.S., Am. Econ. Assn. Council on Foreign Relations, Royal Econ. Soc., Am. Council Edn. (overseas devel. council), Phi Beta Kappa, etc. Club: Cosmos (Washington). Author: The Public Corporation in Great Britain, 1938; Government and the American Economy (with M. Fainsod), 1941, rev. edit. 1948; Fuel and Power in Industrial Location and National Policy, Nat. Resources Planning Bd., 1942; Representation of the U.S. Abroad (in part), 1956, rev. edit. 1964; (with Engelbert L. Grommers) United States Manufacturing Investment in Brazil, 1961; A New Deal for Latin America, 1963. Editor: Internat. Stability and Progress; U.S. Interests and Instruments, 1957; Fgn. Trade Policy, House Ways and Means Com., 1957. Contbr. articles and book revs. to periodicals. Home: 3069 University Terrace NW Washington DC 20016 Office: Johns Hopkins Sch Advanced Internat Studies 1740 Massachusetts Av NW Washington DC 20036

GORDON, MARGARET SHAUGHNESSY, economist; b. Wabasha, Minn., Sept. 4, 1910; d. Michael James and Mary (O'Brien) Shaughnessy; B.A., Bryn Mawr Coll., 1931; M.A., Radcliffe Coll., 1933, Ph.D., 1935; student London Sch. Econs., 1933-34; m. Robert Aaron Gordon, Aug. 15, 1936; children—Robert James, David Michael. Instr., Wellesley Coll., 1935-36; research fellow Harvard-Radcliffe Bur. Internat. Research, 1936-39; head research unit Export-Import office OPA, Washington, 1942-43; asst. research economist Inst. Indsl. Relations, U. Cal. at Berkeley, 1950-54, asso. dir., 1954—, lectr. social welfare, 1959—, lectr. econs., 1965—. Mem. Cal. Gov.'s Commn. on Employment and Retirement of Older Workers, 1959-60; mem. Personnel Bd., City of Berkeley, 1961-65, 70—; asso. dir. Carnegie Commn. on Higher Edn., 1969—; mem. Pres.'s Commn. on Income Maintenance Programs, 1968-69; cons. unemployment ins. U.S. Bur. Employment Security, 1962-66; adv. com. research devel. U.S. Social Security Adminstrn., 1965-68, chmn., 1966-67. Mem. council City of Berkeley, 1965-69. Fellow Gerontological Soc.; mem. Am. Econ. Assn., Indsl. Relations Research Assn., Western Gerontological Soc. (pres. 1961-62). Author: Employment Expansion and Population Growth, 1954; The Economics of Welfare Policies, 1963; Retraining and Labor Market Adjustment in Western Europe, 1965. Editor: Poverty in America, 1965; (with E. F. Cheit) Occupational Disability and Public Policy, 1963. Mng. editor Indsl. Relations, 1961-63, 65-66. Home: 984 Creston Rd Berkeley, CA 94708.

GORDON, MAX, theatrical producer; b. N.Y.C., 1892. Began career in vaudeville. Produced (with Albert Lewis) The Family Upstairs; The Jazz Singer; Easy Come, Easy Go; (alone) Three's a Crowd, 1930; The Band Wagon, 1931; The Cat and the Fiddle, 1931; Flying Colors, 1932; Design for Living, 1933; Roberta, 1933; The Shining Hour, Dodsworth, The Great Waltz, Spring Song, The Farmer Takes a Wife, 1934; Jubilee (with Sam H. Harris), Pride and Prejudice, 1935; Ethan Frome, The Women, St. Helena, 1936; Othello, 1937; Sing Out the News, 1938; Missouri Legend (with Guthrie McClintic), 1938; The American Way (with Sam H. Harris), 1939; My Sister Eileen, 1941; Junior Miss, 1942; The Doughgirls, 1942; Over Twenty-One, 1944; The Late George Apley, 1944; Born Yesterday, Park Avenue, Years Ago (all 1946); The Solid Gold Cadillac, 1953. Film producer; became dir. TV prodn., NBC, 1939. Author: (with Lewis Funke) Max Gordon Presents, 1963. Home: 30 W 54th St New York City NY 10019 Office: 1614 Broadway New York City NY 10019

GORDON, MELVIN JAY, mfg. co. exec.; b. Boston, Nov. 26, 1919; s. Jacob S. and Sadye Z. (Lewis) G.; B.A., Harvard, 1941, M.B.A., 1943; m. Ellen Rubin, June 25, 1950; children—Virginia Lynn, Karen Dale, Wendy Jean, Lisa Jo. Vice pres. Clear Weave Hosiery Stores, Inc., Boston, 1945-50; v.p. Tenn. Knitting Mills, Inc., Columbia, 1945-56; pres. P.R. Hosiery Mills, Inc., Arecibo, 1956-61; chmn. bd. Tootsie Roll Industries, Chgo., 1962—, pres., 1968—; partner Manchester Hosiery Mills (N.H.), 1946-69; pres. Hampshire Designers Inc., 1969—; adv. com. Mfrs. Hanover Bank, N.Y.C., 1967—. Mem. Pres.'s Citizens Adv. Com. Fitness Am. Youth, 1957-60, mem. exec. com., 1959-60; del. White House Conf. Econ. Issues, 1962, White House Conf. Youth Fitness, 1962; co-chmn. Com. Support Psychol. Offensive, 1961-63; dir., mem. exec. com. Council World Tensions, N.Y.C., 1960-65; chmn. Mass. Gov.'s Com. Youth Fitness, 1958-64; dir. New Eng. Econ. Edn. Council, 1960-63, N.H. Council on World Affairs, 1962-65; dir., chmn. exec. com. Citizen Exchange Corps, N.Y.C., 1964-66, hon. chmn. adv. council, 1966-67; del. Prime-Minister's Econ. Conf. Israel, 1968. Bd. overseers Harvard Coll. Vis. Com. Behavioral Scis., 1967—; dir. Inst. Man and Science. Mem. Young Presidents Orgn., Chief Execs. Forum, World Bus. Council, World Affairs Council Boston (treas., dir. 1966-67, v.p., dir. 1968—), New Eng. Soc. N.Y.C. Clubs: Harvard (Boston); Varsity (Harvard). Author: Better Than Communism, 1958. Home: 32 Monadnock Rd Wellesley Hills MA 02181 Office: PO Box 239 Manchester NH 03105

GORDON, MILTON A., investment banker; b. Chgo., Jan. 9, 1908; s. Julius H. and Diana (Edison) G.;Ph.B., U. Chgo., 1929, J.D., 1931; m. Elinor Loeff, Oct. 20, 1941; children—Stephen, Leslie Susan. Admitted to Ill. bar, 1931; practice in Chgo., 1931-43; pres. Morris, Mann & Reilly, Inc., Chgo., 1943-45; v.p., dir. Walter E. Heller & Co., Chgo., 1945-53; founder, 1953, TV Programs Am., Inc., N.Y.C., pres., 1953-58; founder, 1958, pres., now chmn. bd. M.A. Gordon and Co., Inc., N.Y.C.; pres. Halle & Stieglitz, Inc., N.Y.C. Mem. fiscal commn., N.Y.C., 1964-66; mem. Presdl. Delegation to Independence Celebration of Kenya, 1963. Home: 71 E 71st St New York City, NY 10021. Office: 52 Wall St New York City NY 10005

GORDON, MORTIMOR S., lawyer, mfg. exec.; b. N.Y.C., June 21, 1905; s Jacob and Rose (Stiefel) G.; A.B., Columbia Coll., 1925, LL.B., 1927; m. Helen Roth, June 11, 1931; children—Barbara Jane, Elaine. Admitted to N.Y. bar, 1927, since practiced in N.Y.C.; admitted to U.S. Supreme Ct., also other Fed. Cts.; dir., Continental Copper & Steel Industries, Inc., 1945—, pres., dir., 1956—, chmn. bd., chief exec. officer, 1970. Trustee Fedn. Jewish Philanthropies, N.Y.C., Police Athletic League; bd. visitors Columbia U. Sch. Law; adv. bd. Robert A. Taft Inst. Govt.; pres. Gordon Found., Inc. Mem. Am., N.Y. State bar assns., N.Y. Co. Lawyers Assn., Am. Iron and Steel Inst., Navy League U.S. (life mem.). Home: 150 Central Park S New York City NY 10019 Office: 100 E 42d St New York City NY 10017

GORDON, MYRON LEE, fed. judge; b. Kenosha, Wis., Feb. 11, 1918; s. Samuel and Janet (Ruppa) G.; B.A., U. Wis., 1939, M.A., 1939; LL.B., Harvard, 1942; m. Peggy Siesel, Aug. 16, 1942; children—Wendy, John, Polly. Admitted to Wis. bar, 1942; practiced in Milw., 1942-50; civil judge, Milw., 1950- 54, circuit judge, 1954-61; asso. justice Supreme Ct. Wis., 1962-67; U.S. dist. judge Eastern Wis., 1967—. Pres. Milw. Hearing Soc., 1951- 53. Served with USNR, World War II. Mem. D.A.V. (comdr. Wis. 1959), Phi Beta Kappa. Home: 7830 N Regent Rd Milwaukee, WI 53217. Office: Chambers US Dist Ct US Ct House Milwaukee WI 53233

GORDON, PAUL educator; b. Hartford, Conn., Jan. 1, 1918; s. Charles Dana and Anne Mabel (Hirshberg) G.; student Wesleyan U., Middletown, Conn., 1935-37; B.S. in Metallurgy, Mass. Inst. Tech., 1939, M.S., 1940, Sc.D., 1949; m. Evelyn Rubin, Oct. 16, 1941; children—Dana Charles, Jane Ellen. Research asso. metallurgy Mass. Inst. Tech., 1941-42, group leader Manhattan Project, 1942-47; mem. faculty Ill. Inst. Tech., 1949-50, 54—, prof. metall. engring., 1957—, chmn. dept., 1966—; asst. prof. Inst. Study Metals, U. Chgo., 1951-54. Mem. Am. Soc. Metals, Am. Inst. Mining and Metall. Engrs. (Mathewson gold medal 1957), Inst. Metals, A.A.A.S., Am. Soc. Engring. Edn., Engrs. Council Profl. Devel., N.Y. Acad. Sci., Sigma Xi. Author: Principles of Phase Diagrams in Materials Systems, 1968. Contbr. profl. jours., chpts. to books. Home: 1349 Chestnut Av Wilmette IL 60091

GORDON, PAUL JOHN, educator; b. N.Y.C., Oct. 14, 1921; s. Arthur L. and Georgiana (McDonough) G.; B.B.A., Coll. City N.Y., 1945; M.B.A., Cornell U., 1949; Ph.D., Syracuse U., 1958; m. Mary Brigid Keany, Jan. 28, 1950; children—Brian Joseph, Peter Christopher, Martha Ann, Hugh John, Paul John. With Brooks Bros., N.Y.C., 1941-43; with Lago Oil & Transp. Co., Ltd., Netherlands W. Indies, also Bayway Refinery, Linden, N.J. and Standard Oil Co. N.J., 1943-48; asst. prof. Cornell U., 1949-54; prof., chmn. dept. mgmt. Sch. Bus., Duquesne U., 1954-55; asso. prof., planning dir. grad. program hosp. adminstrn. Sch. Bus. Adminstrn., Emory U., 1956- 59; asso. prof. Grad. Sch. Bus., Ind. U., 1959-63, prof., chmn. dept. mgmt. adminstrv. studies, 1963-67, prof. mgmt., 1963—; chief U.S. Dept. State-Ford Found. party Ljubljana U., Yugoslavia, 1967; vis. prof. Trinity Coll., Dublin, 1967; vis. prof., Fulbright lectr. Instituto Post-Universitario Per Lo Studio Dell, Organizzazione Aziendale, Turin, Italy, 1963; Fulbright lectr., cons. Nat. U. Republic Uruguay, 1970; mem. U.S. AID Mgmt. Edn. Reconnaissance Survey, India, also Pakistan, 1971; cons. Internal Revenue Service, 1956—, Am. Coll. Hosp. Adminstrs., 1957—. Ford Found. grantee, 1963, 70; IBM fellow, 1965. Fellow Acad. Mgmt. (v.p. program 1967; pres. elect 1968, pres. 1969); mem. Am. Mgmt. Assn., Soc. Advancement Mgmt., Am. Soc. Pub. Adminstrn., Inst. Mgmt. Scis., Internat. Devel. Soc., Indsl. Relations Research Assn., Am. Assn. U. Profs. Contbr. profl. jours. Editor Acad. Mgmt. Jour., 1964-66, now editorial cons.; editorial cons. adv. bd. Bus. Horizons, Hosp. Adminstrn. Home: 1422 Winfield Rd Bloomington IN 47401

GORDON, PETER BENJAMIN, engr.; b. Montclair, N.J., Aug. 15, 1907; s. Louis and Fannie (Mattises) G.; B.C.E., Rutgers U., 1928; m. Alice I. Wylie, 1946. Engr. George E. Gibson Co., 1929-36; engr. Wolff & Munior, Inc., 1936—, treas., 1939-51, dir., 1940—, v.p., 1951-66, exec. v.p., 1966—. Lectr. air conditioning Bklyn. Eve. Tech. High Sch., 1934-38; instr. air conditioning evening div., coll. engring. N.Y. U., 1937-42, adj. assoc. prof. mech. engring. grad. div., 1946-52; assisted in design gaseous diffusion plant, Oak Ridge, 1943-46; vis. lectr. mech. engring. Princeton, 1946-49. Bd. dirs. Bldg. Research Inst., 1957—, v.p., 1957—, pres., 1966-67; v.p. C.H. Cronin of N.Y., Inc., 1962-66, Wolff & Munior-Cronin, Inc., 1970—; dir. Bldg. Research Adv. Bd., 1959- 63. Trustee, pres. John B. Pierce Found., 1959—. Recipient Distinguished Service award Mech. Contractors Assn. Am., 1956; F. Paul Anderson Medal award Am. Soc. Heating, Refrigerating and Air Conditioning Engrs., 1960. Fellow Am. Soc. Heating, Refrigerating and Air Conditioning Engrs. (mem. council 1952-58, pres. 1957); mem. Am. Soc. M.E., Phi Epsilon Pi. Home: 325 E 72d St New York City NY 10021 Office: 50 W 44th St New York City NY 10036

GORDON, RICHARD F., Jr., former astronaut, profl. football exec.; b. Seattle, Oct. 5, 1929; s. Richard F. Gordon; B.S. in Chemistry, U. Wash., 1951; postgrad. U.S Naval Post Grad. Sch., Monterey; m. Barbara Jean Field; children—Carleen Elizabeth, Richard F. III, Lawrence Joseph, Thomas Alan, James Edward, Diane Marie. Entered USN, 1951, advanced through grades to capt.; grad. All-Weather Flight Sch., Test Pilot Sch.; flight safety officer, asst. operations officer, ground tng. officer Fighter Squadron 96, Miramar, Cal.; now astronaut NASA Manned Spacecraft Center, Houston; pilot Gemini XI, 1966; command module pilot Apollo XII, 1969; exec. v.p. New Orleans Saints, 1972—. Winner Bendix Trophy Race from Los Angeles to N.Y., 1961. Office: New Orleans Saints New Orleans LA

GORDON, ROBERT AARON, economist; b. Wash., July 26, 1908; s. Harry Goldstein and Lena (Walpert) G.; A.B., Johns Hopkins, 1928; A.M., Harvard, 1931, Ph.D., 1934; m. Margaret Shaughnessy, Aug. 15, 1936; children—Robert James, David Michael. Instr., Harvard, 1931-38; asst. prof. U. Cal. at Berkeley, 1938-40, asso. prof., 1940-47, prof., 1947—, chmn. dept. econs., 1959-63; dir. Ford Found. Study Bus. Edn., 1956-58; Guggenheim Fellow, 1956-57; bd. dirs. Nat. Bur. Econ. Research, 1961—; chmn. Pres.'s Commn. on Employment and Unemployment Statistics, 1961-62. Officer, Combined, Raw Materials Bd., 1942-45; U.S. del. to Internat. Rubber Conf., 1944, 45. Mem. research adv. bd. Com. for Econ. Devel., 1954-58, 60-63; mem. Nat. Task Force Econ. Edn., 1960-61. Mem. Royal Econ. Society, Am. Econ. Assn. (exec. com. 1950-52, v.p. 1960), Phi Beta Kappa, Beta Gamma Sigma. Author: Business Leadership in the Large Corporation, 1945; Business Fluctuations, 1952, rev. edit., 1961; The Goal of Full Employment, 1967; also articles in econ. jours. Co-author: Higher Education for Business, 1959; Measuring Employment and Unemployment, 1962; Institutional Economics, 1963. Editor: Toward a Manpower Policy, 1967. Co-editor: Readings in Business Cycles, 1965; Prosperity and Unemployment, 1966. Home: 984 Creston Rd Berkeley CA 94708

GORDON, ROBERT BOYD, physicist, educator; b. East Orange, N.J., Dec. 25, 1929; s. Myron Boyd and Catherine (Rote) G.; B.S., Yale, 1952, D.Eng., 1955; m. Joan Parke Ruttiger, Sept. 13, 1952; children—Penelope, Margaret. Asst. prof. Sch. Mines, Columbia, 1955-57; mem. faculty Yale, 1957—, asso. prof. applied sci., 1960-68, prof. geophysics and applied sci., 1968—. Mem. Am. Phys. Soc., Am. Geophys. Union, Am. Inst. Mining and Metall. Engrs., Sigma Xi, Phi Beta Kappa. Author: (with R.M. Brick, A. Phillips) Structure and Properties of Alloys, 1965. Contbr. articles profl. jours. Home: 60 Dromara Rd Guilford CT 06437 Office: Box 2161 Yale Station New Haven CT 06520

GORDON, ROBERT CHARLES, ret. mag. exec.; b. Hingham, Mont., Oct. 23, 1915; s. Clarence Eugene and Delia Sophia (Lybeck) G.; m. Margaret Ruth Noble, Nov. 14, 1948; children—Dee Scott, Robert Charles. With E.M. Hale Pub. Co., 1945-46; sales mgr. Trans-Film, Inc., 1946-50; with Time Inc., 1950-70, asst. pub., 1960-61, advt. sales dir., 1961-68, corporate v.p., 1968-70; cons. Trade adviser Dept. Commerce, 1958. Mem. Sales Execs. Club. Clubs: Wee Burn Country; Hemisphere; New Canaan Field, Misquamicut, Watch Hill Yacht. Home: Brookside Rd New Canaan CT 06840 Office: Time & Life Bldg Rockefeller Center New York City NY 10020

GORDON, ROBERT EDWARD, coll. dean; b. N.Y.C., June 20, 1925; s. Lewis Francis and Claire (McEvoy) G.; A.B., Emory U., 1949; M.S., U. Ga., 1950; Ph.D., Tulane, U., 1956; m. Catherine Tigner, Sept. 16, 1948; children—Claire Catherine, Martha Lee. Curator, Highlands (N.C.) Museum Biol. Sta., 1949-50; mem. faculty N.E. La. State Coll., 1954-58, U. Notre Dame, South Bend, Ind., 1958—, prof. biology, 1966—, chmn. dept., 1964-67, asso. dean Coll. Sci., 1967-71, v.p. for advanced studies, 1971—. Mem. working party sci. publns. UNESCO, Phila., 1963, Paris, France, 1964; mem. panel primary publns. U.S.-Japan Coop. Sci. Program, Tokyo, 1965, 67; mem. sci. information council NSF, 1969—, chmn., 1971; biomed. communications study sect. NIH, 1967-71; mem. U.S. Nat. com. for F.I.D., 1969-71; mem. U.S. Nat. Com. for Internat. Union of Biol. Socs., 1969—; mem. standing com. communication sci. information Pacific Sci. Assn., 1967—, chmn., 1971—; chmn. bd. council biol. scis. information Nat. Acad. Scis.-NRC, 1967-68. Served with M.C., AUS, 1944-46. Fellow A.A.A.S. (council 1964-70), Herpetologists League; mem. Am. Inst. Biol. Sci. (nat. lectr. 1960-65, mem. at large bd. govs. 1968- 72), Am. Soc. Icthyologists and Herpetologists, Am. Soc. Zoology, Am. Soc. Naturalists, Council Biology Editors (sec. 1963-69), Ecol. Soc. Am., Herpetological Soc. Japan, Soc. Study Amphibians and Reptiles (chmn. 1971), Sigma Xi. Contbr. profl. jours. Editor, Am. Midland Naturalist, 1958-64; sect. editor Biol. Abstracts, 1963-69. Home: 19551 Oakdale Av South Bend IN 46637

GORDON, ROBERT EUGENE, lawyer; b. Los Angeles, Sept. 20, 1932; s. Harry M. and Minnie (Shafer) G.; A.B., U. Cal., at Los Angeles, 1954; LL.B., J.D., U. Cal., Berkeley, at 1959; postgrad. Middlebury Coll., Vt., 1958; Ford Found. fellow, U. Hamburg, Germany, 1959-60; m. Gail Yaras, Feb. 18, 1967; 1 son,Victor M. Lectr., Faculty Comparative Law, Luxembourg, 1960; admitted to Cal. bar, 1960; practice in Los Angeles, 1960-65. Beverly Hills, 1965—; asso. firm Lillick, Geary, McHose, Roethke & Myers, 1960-64, Schoichet & Rifkind, 1964-65, partner Baerwitz & Gordon, 1965-69; partner Ball, Hunt, Hart, Brown & Baerwitz, 1970—; lectr. Entertainment Law Center, U. So. Cal., 1964. Served with CIC, U.S. Army, 1954-56. Mem. Los Angeles Copyright Soc. (trustee). Office: 450 N Roxbury Dr Beverly Hills CA 90211

GORDON, ROBERT GEORGE, univ. dean; b. Pitts., Feb. 22, 1918; s. William and Josephine Emma (Mullen) G.; A.B., Denison U., 1939; B.D., Colgate-Rochester Div. Sch., 1942; M.A., Columbia, 1949, Ed.D., 1952; m. Betty Jane McClew, Sept. 12, 1945; children—Paul Richard, James Malcolm. Dean Freshmen Bucknell U., 1942; dean men, asso. prof. psychology Redlands U., 1946-48; asso. dean students Tex. U. 1948-54; dean men, dean students U. So. Cal., 1954-59; nat. dir. ednl. relations A.R.C., 1959-63; dean men Stanford, 1963-67; former vice-chancellor U. Tenn. Chmn. coll. adv. com. Los Angeles chpt. A.R.C., 1955—, bd. dirs. Palo Alto chpt., 1963—; mem. nat. student adv. con. YM-YWCA, 1960-62; cons. Hogg Found. Mental Hygiene; nat. ednl. adviser Nat. Indsl. Conference. Served to lt. comdr. USNR, 1943-46. Mem. Nat. Assn. Student Personnel Adminstrs. (exec. com.), Am. Coll. Personnel Assn. (commn. V), Tex. Personnel Assn., Cal. P.T.A. (hon. life), Blue Key, Omicron Delta Kappa, Tau Kappa Alpha, Lambda Chi Alpha, Phi Delta Kappa, Kappa Delta Pi, Alpha Phi Omega (v.p. 1959). Methodist. Editor: College Profile Series, 1960.

GORDON, ROBERT LATIMER, Jr., banker; b. Richmond, Va., Dec. 3, 1908, s. R. Latimer and Anne Moore (Talbott) G.; student U. Va., 1927-29; m. Charlotte Faulconer Epps, June 25, 1936 (dec. Aug. 1968); 1 dau., Charlotte Latimer; m. 2d, Lucylle Corey Farmer, Sept. 22, 1969. With First & Mchts. Nat. Bank of Richmond (Va.), 1929—, v.p., trust officer, 1951-62, exec. v.p., 1962-66, pres., 1966-69, chmn.,

1969—, also dir. Pres., Estate Planning Council of Richmond, 1962. Vice pres. Richmond area Community Chest, 1954, 58, campaign gen., 1956; chmn. Richmond-Henrico chpt. Nat. Found. Infantile Paralysis, 1954. Chmn. bd. St. Catherine's Sch., Richmond, 1960-63; bd. dirs. Sheltering Arms Hosp., Va. Diocesan Home for Aged; sec.-treas. Richmond Eye Hosp., 1952—; bd. govs., exec. com. United Givers Fund, 1963-. Served to lt. comdr. USNR, 1942-45. Mem. Assn. Res. City Bankers, Phi Kappa Psi, Episcopalian (vestry 1949-52, 59-62, treas. 1959-62, 67-71, sr. warden 1969-71). Clubs: Commonwealth, Country of Va. (dir., sec.-treas. 1957-59); Downtown (dir. 1962-63) (Richmond). Home: 706 Tiber Lane Richmond VA 23226 Office: 9th and Main Sts Richmond VA 23219

GORDON, ROBERT SIRKOSKY, Jr., physician; b. N.Y.C., Mar. 26, 1926; s. Robert Sirkosky and Dorothy (Dodson) G.; grad. Philips Exeter Acad., 1943; A.B., M.D., Harvard, 1949; m. Elizabeth Wilkins Brown, June 30, 1951; children—Hilary Ruth, Andrew Sirkosky, Peter Taylor, Dana Elizabeth. Intern, then resident Presbyn. Hosp., N.Y.C., 1949-53; investigator Nat. Heart Inst., 1953-61; chief clin. research Pakistan-SEATO Cholera Lab., 1961-64, tech. cons., 1964-69; clin. dir. Nat. Inst. Arthritis and Metabolic Diseases, Bethesda, Md., 1964—. Mem. Am. Physiol. Soc., Am. Soc. Clin. Investigation, Am. Fedn. Clin. Research, Assn. Am. Physicians. Republican. Episcopalian. Editorial bd. Jour. Lipid Research, 1965-68. Spl. research med. physiol. chemistry. Home: 3915 Prospect St Kensington MD 20014 Office: Nat Insts Health Bethesda MD 20014

GORDON, ROY GERALD, educator; b. Akron, O., Jan. 11, 1940; s. Nathan Gold and Frances (Teitel) G.; A.B. summa cum laude, Harvard, 1961, A.M. in Physics, 1962, Ph.D. in Chem. Physics, 1964; m. Myra Shela Miller, Dec. 24, 1961; children—Avra Karen, Emily Francine, Steven Eric. Jr. fellow Soc. of Fellows, Harvard, 1964-66, mem. faculty 1966—, prof., 1969—. Sloan Found. fellow, 1966-69. Mem. Am. Phys. Soc., Am. Chem. Soc. (award in pure chemistry 1972), Faraday Soc., Union of Concerned Scientists, Sigma Xi, Phi Beta Kappa. Theoretical research discovering forms of forces between molecules, way molecules collide with each other, motion of molecules in liquids and solids. Home: 22 Highland St Cambridge MA 02138

GORDON, RUTH, actress; b. Wollaston, Mass., Oct. 30, 1896; d. Clinton and Annie Tapley (Ziegler) Jones; ed. Wollaston Grammer sch., Quincy High Sch.; m. Garson Kanin, Dec. 4, 1942. Made first appearance Empire Theatre, N.Y.C., 1915, as Nibs in Peter Pan, with Maude Adams; other appearances include: Seventeen, 1917-19, Saturday's Children, 1928, The Church Mouse, 1930-31, Ethan Frome, 1935, The Country Wife, 1936-37, Nora in A Doll's House, 1938, Natasha in The Three Sisters, 1942-43, Over Twenty-One, 1943-45, The Leading Lady, 1948, The Smile of the World, 1949, The Matchmaker (London and Berlin), 1954, (N.Y.C.) 1955, The Good Soup, 1960, A Time to Laugh (in London), 1962, My Mother, My Father and Me, 1963, The Loves of Cass McGuire, 1966; (films) Mary Todd in Abe Lincoln in Illinois, 1939, Mrs. Ehrlich in Dr. Ehrlich's Magic Bullet, 1939, Inside Daisy Clover, 1965, Lord Love a Duck, 1966, Rosemary's Baby (Acad. award Best Supporting Actress), 1968, Whatever Happened to Aunt Alice?, 1969, Where's Poppa?, 1970; playwright, star A Very Rich Woman, 1965; (TV) Mommy in The American Dream, 1963. Mem. Screen Actors Guild, Actor's Equity, Writers Guild of Am., Acad. Motion Picture Arts and Scis. Author of plays: Over Twenty-One, Years Ago, The Leading Lady; screenplays (with Garson Kanin) A Double Life, Adam's Ribs, The Marrying Kind, Pat and Mike. Author: Myself Among Others, 1971. Contbr. to Readers Digest, Forum Mag., Atlantic Monthly, McCall's, Ladies Home jour., others. Office: 1041 N Formosa Hollywood CA 90046

GORDON, S. STEWART, univ. adminstr.; b. St. Louis, Sept. 14, 1912; s. Frank Newton and Louise (Isenman) G.; B.A., Westminster Coll., Fulton, Mo., 1933; M.A., U. Chgo., 1935, Ph.D., 1948; student U. Hawaii; m. Barbara Baker, Sept. 9, 1939; children—Jean Corbett, Donald Dunlop, Frank Huntly. Instr. English, U. Chgo., 1937-40, instr. English and edn., 1940-42, 46-47, asst. prof., 1947-53, asst. dean students humanities div., 1951-53; faculty fellow Fund for Advancement of Edn., 1952-53; asst. to exec. dean for four-year and profl. colls. State U. N.Y., 1953-55; asst. to editor Jour. Gen. Edn., 1953-55; dean, prof. Harpur Coll., State U. N.Y. at Binghamton, 1955-67, univ. v.p. for acad. affairs, 1965-71, exec. v.p., 1971—. Served as m-sgt. USAAF, 1942-45; weather forecaster. Mem. Modern Lang. Assn., Am. Assn. Higher Edn. Contbr. articles profl. jours. Home: 170 Leroy St Binghamton NY 13905

GORDON, SANFORD DANIEL, educator; b. Newark, N.J., June 23, 1924; s. Harry Louis and Beatrice (Safris) G.; student Tulane U., 1942; B.S. magna cum laude, N.Y. U., 1947, M.A., 1948, Ph.D., 1953; m. Alice Lillian Pressman, May 27, 1948; children—Ellen Ann, Eric Alan. Instr. econ. N.Y. U., 1948-50; mem. faculty State U. Coll., Oneonta, N.Y., 1950—, prof. econs., 1957—, chmn. dept., 1960—; econ. editor Kennikat Press., Inc., Port Washington, N.Y., 1970—; cons. govt., industry, pub. schs., 1954—. Mem. Parks Commn., also Charter Revision Com., Oneonta, 1957—; v.p. Oneonta Brotherhood, 1958. Served to sgt. USAAF, 1942-44. Recipient Kazajian Found. award, 1967. Mem. N.Y. Econ. Assn. (past pres.), Am. Assn. U. Profs. Author: (with J. Witchel), An Introduction to the American Economy, 1967; A Visual Analysis of the American Economy, 1968; (with G. Dawson) The American Economy, 1969. Lectr., writer pub. TV series The American Economy, Conversations on Economic Issues, 1970—. Home: 41 Union St Oneonta NY 13820

GORDON, SETH EDWIN, wildlife cons., writer; b. Richfield, Pa., Apr. 2, 1890; s. G.B.M. and Caroline (Wochley) G.; student New Bloomfield Acad., 1907, Pa. Bus. Coll., 1911; D.Sc., U. Mich., 1953; m. Dora Belle Silverthorn, Jan. 29, 1910; children—Seth Edwin, Phyllis Rowena (Mrs. John M. Stephenson). Pub. sch. tchr., Pa., 1907-11; stenographer-clk. Pa. Steel Co. (now Bethlehem Steel), 1911-13; game protector Pa. Game Commn., 1913-15, asst. sec., 1915-19, sec., chief game protector, 1919-26, exec. dir., 1936-48; conservation dir. Izaak Walton League Am., Chgo., 1926-31; pres. Am. Game Assn. N.Y.C., Washington, 1931-35; founder, sec. Am. Wildlife Inst., 1935; wildlife cons., writer, 1948-; cons. Cal. Wildlife Conservation Bd., 1948-51; dir. Cal. Dept. Fish and Game, 1951-59; mem., sec. Nat. Com. Wildlife Legislation, 1928-35; mem. forestry research adv. com. U.S. Dept. Agr., 1952-62; mem. Pres.' water pollution control adv. bd. to surgeon gen. U.S., 1958-61. Trustee, v.p. N. Am. Wildlife Found., 1947- -; pres. Keystone (Pa.) council Boy Scouts Am., 1946, mem. conservation com., 1956—. Recipient Founders award Izaak Walton League Am., 1959; named to Hall of Fame, 1969; Aldo Leopold award Wildlife Soc., 1967; Seth Gordon award Internat. Assn. Game, Fish and Conservation Commrs., 1970. Mem. Internat. Assn. Game, Fish and Conservation Commrs. (hon. life mem.; past pres.; gen. counsel 1964—), Western Assn. State Game and Fish Commrs. (hon. life), Am. Fisheries Soc. (hon. life mem., past pres.), Am. Forestry Assn. (past v.p.), Nat. Rifle Assn. (dir. 24 years, endowment mem., mem. hunting and conservation com. 1958-69), Wildlife Mgmt. Inst., Outdoor Writers Am., Wildlife Soc. (hon. life mem.), Izaak Walton League Am. (hon. nat. pres. 1961-62). Lutheran. Republican. Clubs: Cosmos (Washington); Wilderness (hon.) (Phila.). Home: 1390 7th Av Sacramento CA 95818

GORDON, THOMAS CHRISTIAN, Jr., judge; b. Richmond, Va., July 14, 1915; s. Thomas Christian and Ruth Nelson (Robins) G.; B.S., U. Va., 1936, LL.B., 1938. Admitted to Va. bar, 1937; asso. firm Parrish, Butcher & Parrish, Richmond, 1938- 40; asso., then partner firm McGuire, Woods, King, Gordon & Davis, and predecessor, Richmond, 1940-65; justice Supreme Ct. Appeals Va., 1965—; lectr. Law Sch., U. Va., 1970—. Trustee, past pres. Crippled Childrens Hosp., Richmond. Served to maj. AUS, 1941-45; Mem. Va. Bar Assn. (pres. 1963-64). Episcopalian (vestry, sr. warden). Bd. editors Va. Law Rev., 1937-38. Home: 300 W Franklin St Richmond, VA 23220. Office: PO Box 1315 Richmond VA 23210

GORDON, THURLOW MARSHALL, lawyer; b. Methuen, Mass., Nov. 20, 1884; s. Albert Brigham and Elizabeth Jane (Hamlet) G.; A.B. summa cum laude, Dartmouth, 1906; LL.B. cum laude, Harvard, 1911; m. Pauline Sawyer, Nov. 12, 1912; children—Thrulow M., Frances. Admitted to Mass. bar, 1911, U.S. Supreme Ct. bar, 1914, N.Y. Bar, 1918; spl. asst. Atty.-Gen. U.S., 1912-16; atty. FTC, 1916-17; asso. Spooner & Cotton, N.Y., 1917; partner McAdoo, Cotton & Franklin, now Cahill, Gordon, Sonnett, Reindel & Ohl. Trustee Mt. Desert Island Hosp. Mem. Am., N.Y. State, N.Y. City bar assns., Soc. Bus. Adv. Professions, Soc. Colonial Wars, English Speaking Union, Pilgrims, Acad. Polit. Sci. Republican. Episcopalian. Clubs: Century, University, Harvard, Down Town, Economic (N.Y.C.); Cosmos (Washington); Harbor (Seal Harbor, Me.); Bar Harbor, Pot and Kettle (Bar Harbor, Me.). Author various articles and speeches relating to fed. anti-trust laws. Home: 18 Stadium Rd Methuen MA 01844 Office: 80 Pine St New York City NY 10005

GORDON, ULYSSES SHORT, clergyman; b. Sardis, Miss., Dec. 3, 1893; s. Charles Law and Alice (Monroe) S.; A.B., Southwestern Coll., Memphis, 1915, D.D., 1930; B.D., Presbyn. Theol. Sem., Louisville, 1918; student Union Theol. Sem., N.Y., 1935-36, U. Fla., 1931-32; L.H.D., U. Fla., 1963. Ordained to ministry Presbyn. Ch., 1918; pastor, Charleston, Miss., 1919-22, First Ch., Starkville, Miss., 1922-26; asso. pastor Second Presbyn. Ch., Memphis, 1926-28, First Presbyn. Ch., 1928—. Served with U.S. Army, 1918-19. Dir. Columbia Theol. Sem., Atlanta; pres. Presbyn. Ednl. Assn. of South; moderator Synod of Fla., Presbyn. Ch.; mem. Gen. Assembly's Interchurch Relations Com. Trustee Montreat Coll. Recipient Centennial award and medal U. Fla., 1953. Mem. S.A.R., Interracial Council (chmn.), Pi Kappa Alpha (nat. chaplain), Fla. Blue Key. Mason (K.T.). Clubs: Rotary (Gainesville, Fla.), Alachua Sportsmans, (pres.), Univ. Athenium; Gainesville Golf and Country. Home: 1113 SW 2d Av Gainesville FL 32601

GORDON, WALLACE EMERSON, chem co. exec.; b. Detroit, Sept. 25, 1907; s. Donald Cassius and Alice Gordon (Hart) G.; A.B., Wayne U., 1927; M.S., U. Mich., 1931, Ph.D., 1933; m. Marion Searle, Sept. 10, 1930 (dec.); children—Roger B., Richard W.; m. 2d, Martha Fogg Ward, June 22, 1963. High sch. chemistry tchr., 1927-29; with DuPont Co., Wilmington, Del., 1933—, successively organic chemist exptl. sta., sales technologist Grasselli Chems. dept., mgr. agrl. chems. sales, asst. dir. sales, 1933-55, dir. advt. DuPont Co., Wilmington, 1955-57, asst. gen. mgr. Grasselli Chems. dept., 1957-59, asst. gen. mgr. indsl. and biochems. dept., 1959-61, gen. mgr., 1961-65, v.p., 1965—, also dir., mem. exec. com.; dir. Del. Trust Co. Bd. dirs. Found. Am. Agr., United Fund and Council Del. Member N.A.M. (dir.), Am. Chem. Soc., A.A.A.S., Soc. Chem. Industry, Mgmt. Execs. Soc., Phila. Soc. for Promoting Agr., Soc. Mayflower Descs., S.A.R., Sigma Xi, Phi Lambda Upsilon, Alpha Chi Sigma. Mason. Clubs: Union League (N.Y.C.); Wilmington Country (dir.), DuPont Country; Biderman Golf. Home: Greenville DE 19807 Office: Dupont Co Wilmington DE 19898

GORDON, WALTER, architect; b. Buffalo, Sept. 8, 1907; s. Walter William and Florence (Green) G.; B.S., Princeton, 1930, M.F.A. in Architecture, 1932; spl. student Yale, 1936-37, U. Paris (France), 1934; m. Margaret Murray, July 4, 1936. Curator, San Francisco Mus. Art, 1937-39; asst. dir. Portland (Ore.) Art Mus., 1939-41; practicing architect, Portland, 1946-58; prin. works include Southwest Hills Library, Portland, Alpha Phi sorority house, Corvallis, Ore., numerous residences Pacific N.W., coll. dormitories, faculty residence, library, Portland; dean Sch. Architecture, U. Ore., 1958-62; faculty mem. Reed Coll., 1962-65; sr. partner Gordon & Hinchliff, architects, 1962—. Design cons. Portland Devel. Commn., 1962—; mem. Ore. Bd. Architect Examiners, 1956-58, Portland Art Commn., 1955-57, Ore. Capitol Planning Commn., 1959-68. Trustee Portland Art Mus., 1947-51. Fellow A.I.A. (mem. nat. edn. com. 1960-62); mem. Phi Beta Kappa. Home: 2814 SW Labbe Av Portland OR 97202 Office: 10 Sw Ash St Portland OR 97202

GORDON, WALTER ARTHUR, judge; b. Atlanta, Oct. 10, 1894; s. Henry B. and Georgia (Bryant) G.; A.B., U. Cal. at Berkeley, 1918, J.D., 1922, LL.D., 1958; m. Elizabeth Fisher, July 22, 1920; children—Walter, Edwin, Betty. Policeman, Berkeley, Cal., 1919-30; asst. football coach U. Cal. at Berkeley, 1919-43; admitted to Cal. bar, 1923; practiced, 1923-44; atty. Golden State Ins. Co., Cal., 1935-44, adminstrv. adviser, 1944—; gov. V.I., 1955-58; judge Dist. Ct. of V.I., 1958—. Chmn. Adult Authority, State of Cal., 1945-55. Mem. bd., YMCA. Mem. Am. Prison Assn., Nat., Cal. parole and probation assns., Alpha Phi Alpha. Elk. Club: Commonwealth (San Francisco) Office: Dist Ct Charlotte Amalie St Thomas Virgin Islands

GORDON, WALTER LOCKHART, Canadian govt. ofcl; b. Toronto, Ont. Can., Jan. 27, 1906; s. Harry D.L. and Kathaleen H. (Cassels) G.; ed. Upper Can. Coll., also Royal Mil. Coll., Kingston; m. Elizabeth Marjorie Leith, 1932; children—Kyra (Mrs. Jean Montagu), Jane (Mrs. William Glassco), John Counsell Lockhart. Minister of finance, 1963-65, without portfolio, 1967; mem. Ho. of Commons for Toronto-Davenport, 1962-63; partner firm Clarkson, Gordon & Co., chartered accountants, 1935-63, Woods & Gordon, mgmt. cons., 1940-63; now pres. Privy Council, Govt. Can. Assisted with orgn. Fgn. Exchange Control Bd., 1939; spl. asst. to dep. minister finance, 1940-42; pres. Toronto Bd. Trade, 1947; chmn. nat. exec. com. Canadian Inst. Internat. Affairs, 1951-56; chmn. Royal Commn. Adminstrv. Classification in Pub. Service, 1946, Royal Commn. Can.'s Econ. Prospects, 1955, Com. Orgn. Govt. Ont., 1958, chmn. nat. campaign Liberal Party, 1962, 63. Bd. govs. U. Toronto, 1945-63. Home: 22 Chestnut Park Rd Toronto Ontario Canada Office: Parliament Bldgs Ottawa Ontario Canada*

GORDON, WILLIAM EDWIN, educator, physicist; b. Paterson, N.J., Jan. 8, 1918; s. William and and Mary (Scott) G.; B.A., Montclair (N.J.) State Coll., 1939, M.A., 1942; M.S., N.Y. U., 1946; Ph.D., Cornell U., Ithaca, N.Y., 1953; m. Elva Freile, June 22, 1941; children—Larry Scott, Nancy Lynn. Jr. high sch. tchr., 1939-41; asso. dir. elec. engring. research lab. U. Tex., 1946-48; research asso. Cornell U., Ithaca, N.Y., 1948-53, asso. prof., 1953-59, prof., 1959—; dir. Arecibo Ionospheric Obs., P.R., 1960-65, Walter R. Read prof. engring., 1965; spl. spl. research radio scattering; conceived, directed constrn. world's largest antenna reflector; v.p., dean engring. and sci., sci., prof. elec. engring. and space sci. Rice U., Houston, 1966—. Chmn. U.S. delegation Internat. Sci. Radio Union, 1960; chmn. com. sci. radio Nat. Acad. Scis., 1957-60; mem. adv. panel radio telescopes NSF, 1960-66; mem. devel. com. Inter Am. U.; trustee Corp. for Atmospheric Research. Served to capt. USAAF, 1942-46. Recipient Balth. Vander Pol award for distinguished research in radio sci., 1966; 50th Anniversary medal Am. Meteorol. Soc., 1970. Registered profl. engr., Tex. Fellow I.E.E.E. (chmn. profl. group on antennas and propagation 1964-65), Am. Geophys. Union; mem. Nat. Acad. Sci., Internat. Sci. Radio Union (internat. chmn. Commn. II), Am. Meterology Soc., A.A.A.S., Sigma Xi, Tau Beta Pi, Kappa Delta Pi, Sigma Kappa Nu, Phi Kappa Phi. Home: 12422 Mossycup Dr Houston, TX 77024.

GORDON, WILLIAM GLENN, mfg. co. exec.; b. Covington, 1922; s. William H. and Ora Nell (Barnes) G.; student Ohio U., 1941; B.B.A., U. Cin., 1948; student Solomon P. Chase Law Sch., Cin., 1948-49; m. Jean E. Kendall, Dec. 29, 1945; children—Carolyn, Richard, David, John. Asst. v.p. sales and corp. product planning Standard Oil Co. O., 1948-53; cons. McKinsey & Co., N.Y.C., 1953-57; dir. financial service IBM Corp., 1957-60; div. gen. mgr. Thompson Ramo Woolridge Corp., Michigan City, Ind., 1960-63; v.p., group exec. Studebaker Corp., 1963-65, v.p. operations, 1965- 67, pres., 1967—. Sect. chief local United Fund drive, 1964. Bd. dirs. Goodwill Industries, S. Bend, 1964. Presbyn. Home: 1229 Ridgedale Rd South Bend, IN 46614. Office: 1400 73d Av NE Minneapolis MN 55432

GORDON, WILLIAM JONES, Jr., bishop of Alaska; b. Spray, N.C., May 6, 1918; s. William Jones and Anna Barrow (Clark) G.; student Va. Episcopal Sch., 1932-36, U. N.C., 1936- 40; Va. Theol. Sem., 1940-43, D.D., 1953; m. Shirley Lewis, July 16, 1943; children—Paneen, William J. III, Rebecca, Anna. Deacon, St. Peter's Seward, Alaska, 1943; priest-in-charge St. Thomas' Mission, Pt. Hope, Alaska, 1943-48; consecrated bishop of Alaska, May, 1948. Chosen by Jr. C. of C. as one of 10 outstanding young men in U.S. for 1953. Democrat. Episcopalian. Home: 903 Kellum St Fairbanks AK 99701 Office: Box 441 Fairbanks AK 99701

GORDON, WILLIAM LIVINGSTON, educator; physicist; b. Tanta, Egypt, Jan. 17, 1927 (parents Am. citizens). B.S. Muskingum Coll., 1948; M.S., Ohio State U., 1950, Ph.D., 1954; m. Jean Crea, June 18, 1949; children—David W., Amy J., Timothy L. Instr. physics Ohio State U., 1954-55; mem. faculty Case Western Res. U., 1955—, prof. physics, 1968—. Mem. Am. Phys. Soc. ‡

GORDON, WILLIAM RICHARD, univ. ofcl.; b. Phila., Nov. 17, 1913; s. William Murray and Lucille Kerzie (Tribble) G.; B.S., U. Pa., 1936 m. Mary Alice Wagner, May 20, 1950; children—Anne Morrison, William Murray, Robert Duff, Douglas Andrew. Investment officer U. Pa., Phila., 1936-42, asst. treas., 1942- 55, treas., 1955—, asst. instr. accounting, corp. finance, investment banking Wharton Sch., 1937-57, treas. Hosp. and Grad. Hosp.; regional dir. The First Pa. Banking & Trust Co., Transp. Mut. Ins. Co., Finance Co. Pa. Curator arms Valley Forge Hist. Soc. Museum; commr. Valley Forge State Park. Bd. dirs. Revere Fund, Presbyn. Ministers' Fund, Harvest Fund; trustee Moore Sch. Elec. Engring.; v.p. U. Pa. Found., Inc. Served with 2d Regt., Arty., USCGR, 1942-46; capt., Gen. Staff Corps, Dept. Army, Washington, 1951-52. Mem. S.R., Soc. Colonial Wars Pa., Soc. War of 1912, St. Andrews Soc. of Phila., Mil. Order of Fgn. Wars U.S., Valley Forge Hist. Soc., Delta Psi. Presbyn. Clubs: Rittenhouse, St. Anthony (Phila.); Radnor Hunt. Home: 109 Arlington Rd Paoli, PA 19301. Office: 3451 Walnut St Philadelphia PA 19104

GORDON, WILLIAM TALBOTT, banker; b. Richmond, Va., Sept. 4, 1914; s. Robert Latimer and Anne (Talbott) G.; student U. Va., 1934-36; m. Eleanor Stuart Holladay, Aug. 23, 1943; children—Ellen S. (Mrs. Jesse Frank Williams), William Talbot, Anne M., James H. With Bank of Va., Richmond, 1936—, now pres., dir.; dir. Royal Sch. Labs., Inc., Ashland, Va., 1958-66, Apex Machine Mfg. Co., Inc., Richmond, 1959-64. Chmn. Va. Found. for Ind. Jr. Colls., 1969-71. Treas., bd. dirs. Va. Thanksgiving Festival, Inc.; bd. dirs. League Planned Parenthood. Served to lt. USNR, 1942-45. Mem. Am. Inst. Banking, Va., Richmond chambers commerce, Va. Soc. Creepers. Clubs: Commonwealth, Downtown (dir.) (Richmond). Home: 9912 Drouin Dr Richmond VA 23229 Office: 800 E Main St Richmond VA 23214

GORDANA, ALBERT GREGORIAN chemist, educator; b. Chicago, 1928; B.S. in Physics, Yale, 1950; Ph.D. in Chemistry, Harvard, 1956; m. Sally Ann Jones, July 5, 1957; children--Kenneth J., Nancy A. Chemist, Acme Chem. Co., Blue Island, Ill., 1950-51; director of Research Lab., Indsl. Chemicals Corp., Cambridge, Mass., 1956-60; project coordinator environmental sect. Steinmetz Assos., Chgo., 1960-61; v.p. for research Bauer Bros. Chem. Co., Inc., Memphis, 1961-64; asst. prof. chemistry Washington U., St. Louis, 1964-66, asso. prof., 1966-70, prof., 1970--, head of chemistry dept., 1970-71. Vis. prof. So. Ill. U., summer 1967, U. of Ore., 1969. Scoutmaster, Boy Scouts America, University City, Mo., 1968-70. Bd. dirs. Rest Haven Home for Elderly, 1960-61; trustee of the Lutheran Hosp., 1965-71. Served from lt. to capt., AUS, 1951-53. Mem. Am. Chem. Soc., Sci. Research Soc. Am. (chpt. treas. 1967), Am. Assn. Chemistry Tchrs., Am. Assn. U. Profs., Wildlife Soc., American Institute Chemists, Ecological Soc. Am. (chpt. sec.), Sigma Xi. Author: (with others) Basic Inorganic Chemistry, 1971. Contbr. articles to profl. jours., encys., also chpts. to books. Home: Fairfax Apts 7291 Windermere Dr University City MO 63105 Office: Dept Chemistry Washington University St Louis MO 63130

GORDONE, CHARLES, playwright; b. Cleve., 1926; grad. Cal. State Coll., 1952; m. Jeanne Warner; 1 dau. Actor off Broadway prodn. The Blacks; appeared in Of Mice and Men. Author: No Place to Be Somebody (Pulitzer prize for Drama). Office: Promenade Theatre Broadway and 7th St New York City NY 10014*

GORDY, BERRY, record co. exec.; children—T. James, Berry, Hazel Joy. Founder, pres. Motown Record Corp. Recipient Bus. Achievement award Interracial Council for Bus. Opportunity, 1967. Office: 6464 Sunset Blvd Hollywood CA 90028

GORDY, WALTER, educator; b. Miss., Apr. 20, 1909; s. Walter Kalin and Gertrude (Jones) G.; A.B., Miss. Coll., 1932, LL.D., 1959; M.A., U. N.C., 1933, Ph.D., 1935; Dr. honoris causa, U. Lille (France), 1955; m. Vida Brown Miller, June 19, 1935; children—Eileen, Walter Terrell. Asso. prof. math. and physics Mary Hardin-Baylor Coll., 1935-41; NRC fellow Cal. Inst. Tech., 1941-42; staff radiation lab. Mass. Inst. Tech., 1942-46; asso. prof. physics Duke, Durham, N.C., 1946-48, prof., 1948—, James B. Duke prof., 1958—. Vis. prof. U. Tex., 1958. Mem. NRC, 1954-57, 68—. Recipient Sci. research award Oak Ridge Inst. Nuclear Studies, 1949. Fellow Am. Phys. Soc. (chmn. S.E. sect. 1953-54, mem. council 1967—), A.A.A.S. (council 1955); mem. Radiation Research Soc. (mem. council 1961-64), Nat. Acad. Scis., Sigma Xi. Author: (with W.V. Smith, R.F. Trambarulo) Microwave Spectroscopy, 1953; (with Robert L. Cook) Microwave Molecular Spectra, 1970. Asso. editor Jour. Chem. Physics, 1954-58; Spectrochimia Acta, 1957-60; editorial bd. Radiation Research, 1969—. Home: 2521 Perkins Rd Durham NC 27706

GORE, ALBERT ARNOLD, former U.S. senator; b. Granville, Tenn., Dec. 26, 1907; s. Allen and Margie (Denny) G.; B.S., State Teachers Coll., Murfreesboro, Tenn., 1932; LL.B., Y.M.C.A. Night

Law Sch., Nashville, 1936; m. Pauline La Fon, Apr. 17, 1937; children—Nancy, Albert. Admitted to Tenn. bar, 1936, practiced in Carthage, Tenn.; commr. of labor, State of Tenn., 1936- 37; mem. from 4th Tenn. Dist.; 76th to 82d Congresses; U.S. senator, Tenn., 1953-70. Mem. U.S. delegation to UN Gen. Assembly. Mem. Tenn. Edn. Assn. Democrat. Baptist. Home: Carthage TN 37030

GORE, FRED CORDON, mfg. co. supr.; b. Washington, N.C., Oct. 3, 1915; s. Cicero Frederick and Margaret G. (Cordon) G.; B.S. in Chem. Engring., N.C. State Coll., 1937; m. Margaret Louise Jardot, Sept. 28, 1946; 1 dau., Diana Lynn. With E.I. duPont de Nemours & Co., Inc., Wilmington, Del., 1937—, area supr. exptl. sta., Wilmington, 1954—. Served to maj., Transp. Corps, AUS, 1942- 46: ETO. Mem. Am. Inst. Plant Engrs. (pres. Wilmington 1964, nat. asst. regional v.p. 1965-69), Faith Alive (nat. pres. 1970—), Brotherhood of St. Andrew (nat. pres. 1964—). Home: RD 2 Box 155 Hockessin, DE 19707. Office: DuPont Exptl Sta Wilmington DE 19803

GORE, GEORGE, mfg. co. exec.; b. Antofagasta, Chile, Apr. 30, 1912 (parents Am. citizens); s. James Bancroft and Georgia (Sarchet) G.; S.B., Harvard, 1934, LL.B., 1937; m. Virginia Laist, July 9, 1938; children—James Bancroft, Jeffrey Laist, Rosalba Laist. Admitted to Cal. bar, 1938; with firm O'Melveny & Myers, Los Angeles, 1939-41; with Northrop Corp., Beverly Hills, Cal., 1941—, gen. counsel, 1964—, sec., 1945—, v.p. 1964—. Mem. Am., Cal., Los Angeles Co. bar assns., Am. Soc. Corp. Sec. (nat. v.p., bd. dirs.). Home: 216 N Glenroy Av Los Angeles CA 90049 Office: 1800 Century Park East Los Angeles CA 90067

GORE, GEORGE WILLIAM, Jr., educator; b. Nashville, July 11, 1901; s. George William and Emma Joe (Hambrick) G.; A.B., DePauw U., 1923, LL.D., 1966; student U. Chgo., 1924; M.Ed., Harvard, 1928; Ph.D., Columbia, 1940; LL.D., U. Miami, 1969; Litt.D., U. Fla., 1969; m. Pearl M. Winrow, Sept. 4, 1927; 1 dau., Pearl Mayo. Sec. colored br. Y.M.C.A., Marion, Ind., 1923; head dept. English, Agrl. and Indsl. State Coll., Nashville, 1923-27, dean instrn., 1927-50; pres. Fla. A. and M. U., 1950-68, emeritus, 1968—; lectr. George Peabody Coll. Tchrs., Nashville, 1969—. Chmn. Conference on Coll. Projects, 1957-58; dir. Citizens Savings Bank, Nashville. Vice chmn. Fla. Civil Def. Council, 1966—. Trustee Nashville Kent Coll. Law, Fla. Meml. Coll.; rep. Nat. Bapt. Conv. Am., div. religious edn. Nat. Council Chs. Christ; mem. bd. control So. Regional Edn., 1950—; mem.-at-large nat. council Boy Scouts Am. Recipient DePauw U. Alumni citation, 1952; Distinguished Service award Nat. Newspaper Pubs. Assn., 1963; Medal of Honor, Alpha Phi Alpha, 1966. Mem. Assn. Coll. Honor Socs. (exec. com., v.p. 1957-61), Nat. Soc. Coll. Tchrs. Edn., Nat. Soc. Study Edn., Nat. Assn. Coll. Deans and Registrars (pres. 1937- 38), Am. Tchrs. Assn. (pres. 1949-51), N.E.A. (v.p. 1952-53, vice chmn. nat. commn. of def. of democracy through edn. 1954-58), Fla. Council Pres. (chmn. 1953-58), Agora Assembly, Assn. Colls. and Secondary Schs. (pres. 1950-51), Nat. Conf. Pres. Land Grant Colls. (exec. com. 1951-54), Alpha Kappa Mu (founder, pres. 1944-46, exec. sec., treas. 1946—), Fla. Assn. Colls. and Univs. (mem. exec. com. 1962- 63, recipient Distinguished Service certificate and medallion 1969), Delta Phi Delta, Sigma Pi Phi (grand sire archon 1954-56), Alpha Phi Alpha, Kappa Delta Pi (Service Key 1956), Beta Kappa Chi, Alpha Phi Omega, and Scabbard and Blade. Mason, Elk, K.P. Author: Negro Journalism, 1923; In-Service Improvement of Public School Teachers in Tennessee, 1940. Contbg. editor Quarterly Rev. Higher Edn. Among Negroes, 1935—. Home: 1211 Meharry Blvd Nashville TN 37208

GORE, JACK WORTER, editor, publisher; b. Evansville, Ind., Aug. 8, 1916; s. Robert Hayes and Lorena (Haury) G.; B.S., John B. Stetson U., 1939; m. Bettylou Stickrod, Nov. 19, 1941; children-John Christopher Richard Stewart, David Stephen, Laurence Douglas. Bus. mgr. Daytona Beach (Fla.) Sun- Record, 1939-40; with Ft. Lauderdale (Fla.) News, 1945—, columnist, cashier, sprots editor, 1945-47, editor, 1947-69, editor, publisher, 1969—; dir. Chgo. Tribune, N.Y. News Syndicate, N. Am. Co., Ft. Lauderdale. Served with USNR, 1941-45. Recipient First Place Editorial award Freedom Found., 1953, Distinguished Service award, 1969. Mem. C. of C., Sigma Delta Chi, Sigma Nu. Club: Coral Ridge Country (Fort Lauderdale). Home: 2800 NE 40th St Fort Lauderdale FL 33308 Office: 101 N New River Dr E Fort Lauderdale FL 33302

GORE, JEROME SIDNEY, clothing merchandising exec.; b. Chgo., Dec. 17, 1919; s. Alex Samuel and Rebecca (Spector) G.; B.S., U. Ill., 1941; m. Shirley Fay Zax, June 15, 1941; children—Stanley Norman, Lawrence Steven. With Hart Schaffner & Marx, Chgo., 1941—, asst. treas., 1955-60, v.p., 1960-66, group v.p., 1966-69, exec. v.p., 1969-70, pres., 1970—, also dir. Mem. adv. council U. Ill. Chgo. Circle Campus Coll. Bus. Adminstrn. Bd. dirs. Community Fund Chgo., Inc. Served with USNR, 1943-46. Mem. Beta Gamma Sigma (dirs. table). Clubs: Standard; Executives. Home: 856 Broadview Highland Park IL 60035 Office: 36 S Franklin St Chicago IL 60606

GORE, RICHARD TAYLOR, musician, educator; b. Takoma Park, Md., June 25, 1908; s. Herbert Charles and Pamela (Taylor) G.; A.B., Columbia, 1933, M.A., 1938; Victor Baier fellow ch. music, Hochschule fuer Musik, Berlin, Germany, 1936; Ph.D., U. Rochester, 1956; m. Adaline Heffelfinger, June 25, 1940; children—Peter Howell, Pamela Willard, Philip Andrew. Asst. prof. music Mt. Holyoke Coll., 1938-39; asso. prof., univ. organist Cornell U., Ithaca, N.Y., 1939- 45; prof. music, chmn. dept. Coll. Wooster (O.), 1945—, Olive Williams Kettering prof., 1955—, condr. Concert Choir, 1945—. Vis. prof. U. Cal. at Berkeley, 1956. Fellow Am. Guild Organists (dean Ithaca chpt. 1943-45); mem. Am. Musicol. Soc., Neue Bach-Gesellschaft. Composer works for chorus, solo voices, organ; editor, translator works by Bach, Buxtehude, Schuetz, others. Home: 1628 Cleveland Rd Wooster, OH 44691.

GORE, T.T., newspaper exec. Pres., Fort Lauderdale (Fla.) News. Office: Gore Newspapers Co 101 N New River Dr E Fort Lauderdale FL 33302*

GORE, WILLIAM L., missile and rocket co. exec.; b. 1917. With Aerojet-Gen. Corp., 1945—, v.p., 1958-64, sr. v.p. sales, 1964-69, corporate v.p., 1969—. Served with USMC, 1933-45; test pilot, also supr. testing both liquid and solid fuel jets. Fellow Am. Inst. Aero. and Astronautics; mem. Am. Rocket Soc. (past pres.). Address: care Aerojet-Gen Corp 9100 E Flair Dr El Monte CA 91734

GOREE, THOMAS MATT, newspaper editor; b. Athens, O., Apr. 16, 1928; s. Thomas Bryan and Imogene (Brown) G.; B.J., U. Mo., 1950; m. Margaret Anne Galliher, Aug. 16, 1950. Reporter, Springfield (Mo.) Leader and Press, 1950-56; copy editor Kansas City (Mo.) Star, 1956-61, former mem. staff, city editor; copy editor Chgo. Daily News, 1961-62. Served with AUS, 1946-47. Home: 6815 Main St Kansas City MO 64113

GOREN, CHARLES H., contract bridge expert, writer; b. Phila., Mar. 4, 1901; s. Jacob and Rebecca Goren; LL.B., McGill U., Montreal, Can., 1922, LL.M., 1923. Admitted to Pa. bar, 1923, since practiced in Phila.; Author various books including: Contract Bridge in a Nutshell, 1946; Point Count Bidding, 1950; Contract Bridge Complete, 1951; The Italian Bridge System, 1958; New Contract Bridge in a Nutshell, 1959; An Evening of Bridge with Charles Goren, 1959; Goren's Hoyle, 1961; Goren's Bridge Complete, 1963; Bridge is My Game, 1965; Go With the Odds, 1969. Goren on on Bridge, daily column syndicated by numerous newspapers including Chgo. Tribune, weekly column Sports Illustrated mag., 1944—. Home: 5767 Alton Rd Miami Beach FL 33140 ☆

GOREN, ZEYYAT, Turkish diplomat; b. Istanbul, Turkey, May 20, 1917; s. Ali and Fatma (Munevver) G.; M.A., Law Faculty Instanbul U., 1942; m. Hatice Saynur Edes, Mar. 10, 1961. City reporter, Daily Vatan, Istanbul, 1946-49; asst. mgn. editor Daily Cumhuriyet, Instanbul, 1949-52; fgn. corr. Daily Hurriyet, Istanbul, 1952-63; press attache, Stockholm, Sweden, 1963-66; dir. info., N.Y.C., 1966-68; asst. gen. mgr. Veb Ofset Publs., Inc., Instanbul, 1968-70; press counselor, Washington, 1970—; bur. mgr. for Turkey, UPI, 1947-63. Served as lt. Turkish Army, 1943-46. Mem. Internat. Press Inst. Zurich. Home: 5428 Nebraska Av NW Washington DC 20015 Office: 2523 Massachusetts Av NW Washington DC 20008

GORER, GEOFFREY EDGAR, author; b. London, Eng., 1905; ed. Charterhouse, Jesus Coll., Cambridge. Author: Exploring English Character, 1955; (with John Rickman) People of Great Russia, 1962; Africa Dances, 1962; Life and Ideas of the Marquis de Sade, 1963; American People, rev. edit., 1964; Death, Grief and Mourning, 1965; Bali and Angkor; Nobody Talks Politics; Himalayan Village; Modern Types; also articles in jours. Address: Sunte House Haywards Heath Sussex England

GORES, HAROLD BISMARK, educator, ednl. inst. exec.; b. Abington, Mass., Sept. 20, 1909; s. Louis and Carolyn (Stone) G.; B.S., State Coll., Bridgewater, Mass., 1931; Ed.M., Harvard, 1938, D.Ed., 1953; LL.D., Northeastern U., 1954; L.H.D., Williams Coll., 1963; D.Sc., Coll. Emporia (Kan.), 1960; m. Helen Edith Boothroyd, Apr. 17, 1937; children—Richard W., Judith E. Sweet, Prin. jr. high sch., Littleton, Mass., 1931-34; tchr. math., Lexington, Mass., 1934-35; tchr. math., guidance counsellor, Newton, Mass., 1935-39, adminstrv. asst., sec. sch. com., 1939-43, asst. supt. schs., sec. sch. com., 1943-49, supt. schs., 1949- 58; pres. Ednl. Facilities Labs., Inc., N.Y.C., 1958—; adj. prof. Grad. Sch., Union for Experimenting Colls. and Univs., Antioch Coll., Yellow Springs. Cons. Title III Elementary and Secondary Edn. Act and Title VI Higher Edn. Facilities Act; mem. Council Edn. Facilities Planners Cleve. Conf. New Eng. regional chmn. Fulbright Tchrs. Exchange Program, 1953- 57; nat. chmn. program of fellowships for high sch. tchrs. Fund for Advancement Edn., Ford Found., 1954-55; exec. com. Harvard Found. Advanced Study and Research, 1954-57; mem. President's Sci. Adv. Com., 1959; mem. Pres.'s Task Force adv. bd. Nat. Acad. of Scis.; adv. bd. on Edn., 1964, Pres.'s Task Force on Edn. of Gifted, 1968, Pres.'s Commn. on Instrnl. Tech., 1969; bldg. research adv. bd. Nat. Acad. of Scis.; adv. bd. Israel Edn. Fund. Trustee Independent Ednl. Services. Mem. A.I.A. (hon.), Harvard Grad. Sch. Edn. Alumni Assn. (pres.)., Kappa Delta Pi, Phi Delta Kappa. Clubs: University, Bonnie Briar Country (Larchmont, N.Y.). Home: 5 Dante St Larchmont NY 10538 Office: 477 Madison Av New York City NY 10022

GORES, JOSEPH NICHOLAS, author; b. Rochester, Minn., Dec. 25, 1931; s. Joseph Mathias and Mildred Dorothy (Duncanson) G.; B.A., U. Notre Dame, 1953; M.A., Stanford, 1961; m. Frances Susan Hall, Aug. 31, 1964. Investigator, L.A. Walker Co., San Francisco, 1955-57, 59; pvt. investigator David Kikkert & Assos., San Francisco, 1960-61, 65-66; tchr. Kakamega Boys Secondary Sch., Kenya, E. Africa, 1963-64; mgr./auctioneer Automobile Auction Co., San Francisco, 1968—. Served with AUS, 1958-59. Recipient Edgar Allan Poe award for A Time of Predators as best first novel Mystery Writers Am., 1969, also for Goodbye, Pops as best short story in Am. mags., 1969. Mem. Mystery Writers Am. (regional v.p. 1967, 69-70), Cal. Writers Club, Crime Writers Assn., Sci.-Fiction Writers Am. Republican. Roman Catholic. Author: A Time for Predators, 1969; Marine Salvage, 1971. Contbr. articles to profl. jours. Address: 540 Greenwich St San Francisco CA 94133

GORES, LANDIS, architect; b. Cin., Aug. 31, 1919; s. Guido and Paula Margaret (Landis) G.; A.B., Princeton, 1939; B. Arch., Harvard, 1942; m. Pamela Whitmarsh, Dec. 12, 1942; children—Catherine (Mrs. Dennis O. Lynch), Ainslie (Mrs. Davidson Gilligan), Valerie, Karl, Elizabeth Anne. Asso. with Philip C. Johnson, N.Y.C., 1945-51; individual archtl. practice, New Canaan, Conn., 1951—; lectr. Pratt Inst., 1947-48, 52-53. Served to maj. AUS, 1942-46. Decorated Legion of Merit, Order Brit. Empire. Recipient A.I.A. nat. honor award, 1955, Sao Paulo Bieniale, 1955, Award Merit, Boston Arts Festival, 1956, New Haven Festival Arts, 1959. Mem. A.I.A. (chmn. com. environmental awareness and visual edn. 1969—), Phi Beta Kappa. Republican. Episcopalian. Clubs: Field, Princeton (New Canaan). Contbg. bd. Jour. A.I.A., 1958-62. Address: 192 Cross Ridge Rd New Canaan CT 06840

GORGUZE, VINCENT THOMAS, elec. co. exec.; b. N.Y.C., May 3, 1918; s. Thomas and Edith (Pandell) G.; B.Sc. in Metall. Engring., U. Mich., 1941; postgrad. Columbia, U. Mich.; m. Gloria M. Hermann, July 18, 1955; 1 dau., Lynn Ellen. Engring. and prodn. mgr. Ford Motor Co., 1941-51; gen. mgr. metals processing div. Curtiss Wright Corp., 1951-60; pres. White-Rodgers Co., St. Louis, 1961-68; exec. v.p. Emerson Electric Co., 1968—; pres. U.S. Electric Motors Co., 1968—, also dir.; adv. dir. Emerson Electric Co.; dir. Emerson Electric Ltd., White-Rodgers Co. Served with USNR, 1944-46. Mem. Soc. Automotive Engrs., Am. Soc. Refrigeration and Air Conditioning Engrs., Nat. Elec. Mfrs. Assn., Am. Gas Assn., Gas Appliance Mfrs. Assn. Home: 3 Country Estate Frontenac MO 63131 Office: Old Gate Lane Milford CT 06460

GORHAM, DONALD R., clin. psychologist; b. Kalamazoo, May 23, 1903; s. Adelbert Leroy and Emma Louise (Rogers) G.; certificate Western State Tchrs. Coll., 1923; B.Th., Colgate U., 1926, M.A., 1927; scholar U. Pa., 1929-30, Ph.D., 1934; m. Elizabeth Ann Young, June 23, 1926; children—Ann Emily, Janet Susan. Prof., dir. Sch. Edn., Eastern Bapt. Theol. Sem., 1931-43; prof. edn. and psychology Keuka Coll., 1943- 50; clin. psychologist VA Neuro-psychiatric Hosp., Waco, Tex., 1950-59; prof. clin. psychology (part time) Baylor U., 1950- 59, cons. mem. staff, 1946-49, chief clin. psychology Canadaigua VA, 1946-47; cons. The Hogg Found., 1957-58; research psychologist VA Central Neuropshychiat. Research Lab., Perry Point, Md., 1959- coordinator research psychol. service VA Hosp., Perry Point, 1962-69; chief psychol. service VA Center, Bath, N.Y., 1969-70; cons. and ltd. pvt. practice, 1970—. Mem. Md. Bd. Examiners in Profl. Psychology. Fellow Internat. Council Psychology, Am. Psychol. Assn.; mem. Md. Psychol. Assn. Interam. Soc. Psychology. Author books including: Understanding Adults, 1948; Proverbs Test, 1954; (with J.E. Overall) Brief Psychiatric Rating Scale, 1961. Contbr. articles profl. jours. Home: Hill Acres Bluff Point NY 14417 ☆ Office: VA Center Bath NY ☆

GORHAM, EVILLE, educator; b. Halifax, N.S., Can., Oct. 15, 1925; s. Ralph Arthur and Shirley Agatha (Eville) G.; B.S. in Biology with distinction, Dalhousie U., 1945, M.Sc. in Zoology, 1947; Ph.D. in Botany, U. London (Eng.), 1951; m. Ada Verne MacLeod, Sept. 29, 1948; children—Kerstin, Vivien, Jocelyn, James. Lectr. botany U. Coll., London, Eng., 1951-54; sr. sci. officer Freshwater Biol. Assos., Ambleside, Eng., 1954-58; lectr., asst. prof. botany U. Toronto, 1958-62; asso. prof. botany U. Minn., Mpls., 1962-65, prof., 1966—, head dept., 1967-71; prof., head dept. biology U. Calgary (Alta., Can.), 1965-66. Mem. for Can., Internat. Commn. on Atmospheric Chemistry and Radioactivity, 1959-62; founding mem. Minn. Com. for Environmental Information, mem. exec. bd., 1968-70; mem. Scientists Inst. for Pub. Information, 1971—. Royal Soc. Can. fellow State Forest Research Inst., Stockholm, Sweden, 1950-51; NSF, AEC, NRC Can. grantee. Mem. Am. Soc. Limnology and Oceanography, Ecol. Soc. Am., Fedn. Am. Scientists, Internat. Assn. Pure and Applied Limnology, Nature Conservancy, Sigma Xi. Unitarian. Editorial bd. Ecology, 1965-67, Limnology and Oceanography, 1970-72. Contbr. articles to profl. jours. Home: 1933 E River Terrace Minneapolis MN 55414

GORHAM, FRANK DEVORE, Jr., petroleum co. exec.; b. St. Louis, June 4, 1921; s. Frank DeVore and Lillian (Hawley) G.; A.B., U. Mo., 1943; m. Marie Ellis Kelley, Sept. 1, 1947; children—Frank DeVore III, Daniel Kelly, Timothy Walker, Robert Hawley, Mark Linton. Petroleum geologist Creole Petroleum Co., Venezuela, 1946-49; dist. geologist Pure Oil Co., Denver, 1949-50; chief geologist Pubco Petroleum Corp., Albuquerque, 1950-60, exec. v.p., 1960- 65, pres., 1965—; dir. Bank of N.M. Served capt. AUS, 1943-46; MTO. Decorated Silver Star. Mem. Geol. Soc. Am., Am. Assn. Petroleum Geologists (pres. Rocky Mountain sect. 1959). Home: 218 16th St SW Albuquerque NM 87104 Office: PO Box 869 Albuquerque NM 87103

GORHAM, SAYLES, lawyer; b. Providence, Sept. 14, 1900; s. Frederick Poole and Emma Mary (Lapham) G.; Ph.B., Brown U., 1922; LL.B., Harvard, 1925; m. Ruth Mary Campbell, Apr. 25, 1931; children—John, Bradford, Nicholas Sayles, Desire Howland. Admitted to R.I. bar, 1925, since practiced in Providence; mem. firm Gorham & Gorham, 1959—. Mem. Am., R.I. (pres. 1960-61) bar assns. Mason. Home: 151 Meeting St Providence RI 02906 Office: 58 Weybosset St Providence RI 02903

GORHAM, WILLIAM, orgn. exec.; b. N.Y.C., Dec. 14, 1930; s. Jack and Fay (Blank) G.; student Mass. Inst. Tech., 1949-50; B.A., Stanford, 1952; m. Kathryn Aring, Dec. 15, 1951; children—Sarah, Nancy, Kim, Jennifer, Beckie. Pres. of Urban Inst., Washington, 1968—. Office: 2100 M St NW Washington DC 20037

GORIN, ERNEST BARTLEY, corp. exec.; b. Louisiana, Mo., Nov. 20, 1911; s. Ernest Bartley and Edith (Lynott) G.; student U. Chgo., 1928-30, Northwestern U., 1936-38; m. Mildred Sweeney, May 30, 1930; children—Walter Bartley, Thomas Bartley. Asst. mgr. Lapham-Hickey Steel Co., Chgo., 1928-32; budget dir. Montgomery Ward & Co., 1933-40; asst. controller Goldblatt Bros., Inc., 1940-43, Butler Bros., 1943-44; joined RCA Corp., N.Y.C., 1944, treas., 1949-51, v.p., treas. since 1951; dir. RCA Global Communications, Inc., 1950—, RCA Credit Corp., RCA de P.R., RCA Internat. Devel. Corp. Clubs: Rockefeller Center Luncheon, Economic, Treasurers (N.Y.C.); Innis Arden Golf (Old Greenwich, Conn.). Home: Wesskum Wood Rd Riverside CT 06878 Office: 30 Rockefeller Plaza New York City NY 10020

GORIN, IGOR, baritone; b. Grodak, Ukraine; grad. with high honors, Coll. and Conservatory Music, Vienna; Mus. D., Brigham Young U., 1956; m. Mary Smith, June 9, 1939. Came to U.S., 1934, naturalized, 1939. Concerts in Vienna, other cities, U.S., 1934—; singer radio programs Hollywood Hotel, Vicks Opera House, Magic Key, Ford Kraft, Texaco, Firestone, Bell Telephone hours; nation wide concert tours U.S., Can., Cuba, 1939—; appears with many opera companies; records for Allied Record Co.; appeared in motion pictures for M-G-M, motion picture Merry Wives of Nicolai; one of first singers to appear extensively for USO, Army camps and hosps.; appeared on NBC TV operas Germont La Traviata, 1957, Rigoletto, 1958. Recipient distinguished service award Nat. Soc. Utah Pioneers, awards A.S.C.A.P., Am. Fedn. Women's Clubs. Mem. A.S.C.A.P.

GORIN, JEAN, artist; b. St.-Emilien Blain, 1899; student Acad. de la Grande Chaumiere, Paris, also Ecole des Beaux Arts, Nantes. Strongly influenced by Matisse, Gleizes and Ozenfant's Purism; turned toward Neoplasticism, 1926; participant exhbn. Circle in the Square, 1930; exhbns. at Salon des Realites Nouvelles since found; retrospective shows at Mus. Fine Arts, Nantes, 1966, Stedelijk Mus., Amsterdam, 1967. Address: 18 Quatre Vents Paris 8e, France.*

GORIN, WILLIAM, retail co. exec.; b. Woburn, Mass., Feb. 8, 1908; s. Nehemias and Rebecca (Caban) G.; LL.B., Boston U., 1928; m. Helaine M. Falkson, May 14, 1945; children—Howard F., Ralph E. Pres. Gorin Stores Inc., Boston, 1928- -; dir. County Bank N.A., Cambridge, Mass. Trustee Nehemias Gorin Charitable Found. Home: 142 Hobart Rd Chestnut Hill MA 02167 Office: 1019 Commonwealth Av Boston MA 02215

GORINI, LUIGI, bacteriologist; b. Milan, Italy; grad. U. Pavia, 1925. Sci. researchist U. Milan, 1928; research fellow U. Paris, 1947; vis. investigator N.Y. U., 1955; mem. med. faculty Harvard, 1957—, now Am. Cancer Soc. prof. microbiology and molecular genetics. Recipient Ledlie prize for work on streptomycin Harvard, 1966. Mem. Nat. Acad. Scis., Am. Acad. Arts Scis. Home: 115 Longwood Av Brookline MA 02146

GORISEK, ALBIN ANTHONY, journalist; b. Warrensville Heights, O., June 8, 1932; s. Anton and Mary (Cimmerman) G.; student Miami U., Oxford, O., 1950-51; A.B., Western Res. U., 1955, postgrad. Law Sch., 1954-56; m. Suzanne J. Barto, June 17, 1961; children—A. Anthony, Kristin, Stephen Warn. Editor, Fairport Harbor (O.) Beacon, Geauga Times Leader, 1956-60; bur. chief Painesville (O.) Telegraph, 1960-62; news editor Chagrin Valley (O.) Herald, 1962-64; reporter Plain Dealer, Cleve., 1964-66, religion editor, 1966—; corr. Nat. Catholic Reporter, Religious News Service. Mem. Religion Newswriters Assn., Cleve. Newspaper Guild (mem. exec. bd., retirement bd.), Sigma Delta Chi. Club: Cleveland City, Home: 6400 Creekside Trail Solon OH 44139 Office: 1801 Superior Av NE Cleveland OH 44114

GORKIN, JESS, editor; b. Rochester, N.Y., Oct. 23, 1913; s. Barnett and Bessie (Berk) G.; B.A., U. Ia., 1936; m. Dorothy Kleinberg, June 23, 1940; children—Michael, Brett, Scott. Editor-in-chief Daily Iowan, Iowa City, 1936-37; asso. editor Look Mag., N.Y.C., 1937-41; originated and edited picture mag. for distbn. in friendly and occupied countries Photo Review, OWI, 1942-46; mng. editor Parade, N.Y.C., 1947-49, editor 1949—. Recipient Christopher Award, 1956, citation Overseas Press Club, 1955, editorial award Nat. Comdr. Am. Legion. Mem. So. Newspaper Pubs. Assn., Sigma Delta Chi. Club: Overseas Press. Home: 60 Bayne Pl White Plains NY 10605 Office: 733 3d Av New York City NY 10017

GORLIN, ROBERT JAMES, dentist, educator; b. Hudson, N.Y., Jan. 11, 1923; s. James Alter and Gladys Gretchen (Hallenbeck) G.; A.B., Columbia, 1943, postgrad. 1947-50; D.D.S., Washington U., 1947; M.S., Ia. State U., 1956; m. Marilyn Alpern, Aug. 24, 1952;

children—Cathy, Jed. Oral pathologist Bronx VA Hosp., N.Y.C., 1950-51; instr. dentistry Columbia, 1950-51; dental dir., pathologist Operation Blue Jay, Thule, Greenland, 1951-52; asso. prof. oral pathology U. Minn. Sch. Dentistry, 1956-58, chmn. div., 1956—, prof., 1958—; Fulbright exchange prof., also Guggenheim prof. Royal Dental Sch., Copenhagen, Denmark, 1961; chief dental service Glenwood Hills Hosp., 1962-63; staff Mt. Sinai Hosp.; cons. oral pathology VA Hosp., 1958—, Am. Jour. of Clin. Pathology; cons. dental and oral pathology div. Armed Forces Inst. Pathology, 1962—, WHO, 1968—. Bd. dirs. Minn. div. Am. Cancer Society. Group Health. Served as pfc. AUS, 1943-44, to lt. USNR, 1953-55. Diplomate Am. Bd. Oral Pathology. Fellow Am. Acad. Oral Pathology (pres. 1966-67); mem. Am. Acad. Dermatology, Am. Dental Assn., Internat. Assn. Dental Research (pres. Minn. div. 1959-60), Minn. Soc. Pathologists, Am. Soc. Human Genetics, Cancer Coordinators (pres. 1960- -), Internat. Acad. Pathology, Minn. Human Genetics League, Am. (pres. 1966-67) Internat. acads. oral pathology, Internat. Soc. Cranofacial Biology (pres. 1969-70), Sigma Xi. Omicron Kappa Upsilon. Cons. editor Stedman's Med. Dictionary, Geriatrics, Jour. Dental Research. Author: Syndromes of the Head and Neck, 1964; (with others) The Face-Genetic Disease, 1970; also articles profl. jours. Editor: Thoma's Oral Pathology, 1969; asso. editor: Am. Jour. Human Genetics. Home: 4600 Chatelain Terrace Golden Valley MN 55427

GORMAN, BURTON WILLIAM, educator; b. Mitchell, Ind., Mar. 29, 1907; s. William James and Minnie Rose (Burton) G.; A.B., Ind. U., 1930; M.S., 1936; Ph.D., George Peabody Coll. Tchrs. (Knudson F.), 1953; student U. Chgo., summers 1943, 45; m. Rebecca Evelyn Tolle, Dec. 29, 1931; children—Benjamin Lee, Joseph Tolle, John Burton. Tchr. history and music, Bardstown, Ky., 1930-36; supt. schs., Ohio County, Ind., 1936-37; prin. high sch., Lawrenceburg, Ind., 1937-39; counselor boys high schs., Connersville, Ind., 1939-42, high sch. prin., 1942-46, supt. schs., 1946-49; prin. Emmerich Manual Tng. High Sch., Indpls., 1949-51; prof., head edn. dept. De Pauw U., 1953-54; prof., head dept. secondary edn. Kent (O.) State U., 1954—. Vis. prof. Butler U., 1946. George Peabody Coll., 1948, 49, 51, 52, 53, 61, Ind. U., 1954, also U. N.C., U. Vt. Mem. N.E.A., Am. Assn. Sch. Adminstrs., Am. Assn. U. Profs., Phi Delta Kappa, Kappa Delta Pi, Acacia. Methodist. Mason, Kiwanian (pres. Connersville, 1946; lt. gov. 9th Ind. div., Internat., 1947). Author: Education for Learning To Live Together, 1969; The High School America Needs, 1971. Home: 1220 Lake Martin Dr Kent OH 44240

GORMAN, CLIFF, actor; b. N.Y.C., Oct. 13, 1936; s. Samuel and Ethel (Kaplan) G.; student U. N.M., 1954-55; B.S. in Edn., N.Y.U., 1959; m. Gayle Stevens, May 31, 1963. N.Y.C. appearances include Hogan's Goat, 1965, Ergo, 1968, The Boys in the Band, 1968, Lenny, 1971; mem. Jerome Robbins' Am. Theatre Lab., 1966-67; film appearance in Justine, 1969, The Boys in the Band, 1970; TV appearance The Trial of The Chicago Seven, 1970. Recipient Obie award, 1968. Office: care William Morris Agy 1350 6th Av New York City NY 10019

GORMAN, CORNELIUS EUGENE, physician; b. Lynchburg, Va., Dec. 8, 1906; s. James and Ellizabeth Jane (Magri) G.; student U. Va., 1924-26; B.A., Mt. St. Mary's Coll., 1928; M.D., Med. Coll. Va., 1932; M.A., Loyola U. of South, 1934; m. Mary Elizabeth Skender, Oct. 17, 1944; children—Cornelius, Joan, Thomas. Rotating internship St. Vincents Hosp., Norfolk, Va.; resident Hotel Dieu, New Orleans, Charity Hosp. of La., New Orleans; pvt. practice, New Orleans, 1934-40, 46—; established Gorman Med. Center, 1949; clin. instr. gynecology and obstetrics La. State U. Med. Center; prof. mico-anatomy, Loyola U. of South; mem. vis. staff Hotel Dieu Hosp., Charity Hosp. of La., Methodist Hosp., dir. Med. Center; vis. surgeon Metarie Hosp.; terminal surgeon 7515 ARTU, New Orleans. Served from maj. to col., M.C., AUS, 1940-45; developed and compiled physical standards for selection of inductees and phys. profiling of enlisted men. Invented Gorman solid blade low (outlet) obstet. forcep. Decorated Legion of Merit. Mem. A.M.A., La., So., La. State U. med. socs., Am. Bd. Abdominal Surgery, New Orleans, U.S. power squadrons, Nat. Rifle Assn., Phi Beta Pi, Pi, Sigma Zeta, Theta Beta. Roman Catholic. Democrat. Clubs: Rotary (pres. Carrollton; dist. gov. 1967- 68), Army-Navy. Home: 546 Lakeshore Pkwy New Orleans LA 70124 Office: 1626 S Carrollton Av New Orleans LA 70118

GORMAN, FRANK HERMON, former educator; b. Carrollton, Mo., Nov. 26, 1901; s. Claud David and May Ruth (Owells) G.; B.S. in Edn., Central Mo. State Tchrs. Coll., 1924; M.A., U. Mo., 1928. Ph.D., 1931; L.H.D., U. Omaha, 1967; m. Lena Elizabeth Coffman, June 28, 1922; 1 dau., Dorothy Ann (Mrs. John J. Watters). Prin. high sch., Mo., 1920-23; supt. schs., Golden City, Mo., 1924-27; instr., then asst. prof. edn., prin. Univ. Elementary Sch., U. Mo., 1927-41; prof., head dept. elementary edn. and reading clinic Butler U., 1941-48; prof. edn., head dept. Municipal U. Omaha, 1948-50, dean Coll. Edn., 1950-67, prof. ednl. adminstrn., 1967- 70, head dept., 1967-68; ret., 1970; dir. curriculum Omaha pub. schs., 1948-52. cons., 1952-56. Mem. bd. edn., Ralston, Neb., 1960-66; mem. adv. bd. Omaha Opportunity Sch., 1958-65. Trustee Neb. Heart Assn. Mem. N.E.A., Neb. Pub. Health Assn., Neb. Council Tchrs. of Edn., Council Exceptional Children, Am., Neb. assns. sch. adminstrs., Phi Delta Kappa, Kappa Delta Pi, Phi Sigma Phi, Sigma Tau Gamma. Mason, Lion. Author articles profl. jours. Co-author: Elementary School Organization and Management, 1950. Home: 8203 Oakwood St Ralston NB 68127

GORMAN, JOHN LEONARD, newspaper exec.; b. Palmyra. N.Y., May 8, 1906; s. Walter J. and Margaret E. (Hickey) G.; grad. Syracuse U., 1929; m. Mary Elizabeth Edwards, Aug. 23, 1934 (dec. Dec. 1955); children—Jane (dec.), John, Ann (Mrs. Timothy T. Schenck); m. 2d, Mary Lighthall Verbeck, Dec. 30, 1957; stepsons—K. Channing, Pieter L. Reporter Syracuse (N.Y.) Herald, 1929; pub. relations Syracuse U., 1930-32; copy reader Syracuse Post- Standard, 1933-41, editorial writer, 1941-47, city editor, 1947-53, mng. editor, 1953-59, exec. editor, 1959-60, 66—, editor, 1960-66. Mem. N.Y. State Fair Adv. Com. Bd. dirs. Syracuse Cerebral Palsy Clinic, N.Y. State div. Am. Cancer Soc., Onondaga chpt. A.R.C.; trustee Syracuse Pub. Library. Mem. Syracuse C. of C. (dir.), Asso. Press Mng. Editors Assn., N.Y. Asso. Press Assn. (pres. 1956), Am., N.Y. (pres. 1960-61) socs. newspaper editors, Syracuse U. Library Assn. (publs. com.), Pi Delta Epsilon, Sigma Delta Chi, Phi Kappa. Republican. Rotarian. Clubs: Syracuse Press, University (Syracuse). Home: 105 Kensington Rd Syracuse, NY 13210. Office: The Post-Standard Syracuse NY 13201

GORMAN, JOHN P., lawyer; b. Chgo., May 5, 1912; A.B., U. Notre Dame, 1934; J.D., Northwestern U., 1937. Admitted to Ill. bar, 1937; mem. firm Clausen, Hirsch, Miller and Gorman, Chgo. Fellow Am. Coll. Trial Lawyers, Internat. Acad. Trial Lawyers; mem. Am., Ill., Chgo. bar assns., Bar Assn. Seventh Fed. Circuit, Soc. Trial Lawyers, Fed. Ins. Counsel, Internat. Assn. Ins. Counsel, Phi Alpha Delta. Office: 135 S La Salle St Chicago IL 60603*

GORMAN, MIKE THOMAS FRANCIS. writer, assn. exec.; b. N.Y.C., Dec. 7, 1913; s. Frank and Mary (Naughton) G.; A.B., N.Y. U., 1934, postgrad., 1934-36; m. Ernestine Brown, June 3, 1946 (dec. June 1958); children—Michael, Patricia; m. 2d, Suzanne Mills, Feb. 6, 1960; 1 step-dau., Margaret. Advt., free-lance writer, 1936-41; reporter, cover gen. med. run Daily Oklahoman, 1945; writer numerous news stories and editorials in mental hosp. campaign; pioneered in establishment mental hygiene clinic in Okla., also mental hygiene orgn.; chief writer, dir. pub. hearings Pres.'s Commn. on Health Needs Nation, 1952-53; exec. dir. Nat. Com. vs. Mental Illness, Washington, 1953—. Mem. Menninger Found.; mem. Joint Commn. Mental Health of Children, 1966—; mem. nat. adv. mental health council USPHS, 1961—; mem. 1st U.S. Mental Health Delegation to USSR, 1967; mem. World Fedn. Mental Health; bd. dirs. Nat. Council Alcoholism. Served with USAAF, 1942-45. Recipient spl. Lasker award Nat. Com. Mental Hygiene, 1948; named one of 10 outstanding young men U.S. Jr. C. of C., 1949; Edward A. Strecker Meml. award, 1962. Fellow Am. Pub. Health Assn., Am. Psychiat. Assn. (hon.), Royal Soc. Health (Eng.), N.Y. Acad. Scis.; mem. Nature Conservancy, Phi Beta Kappa. Clubs: Nat. Press, Federal City, City Tavern (Washington). Author: Oklahoma Attacks Its Snake Pits, 1948; Every Other Bed, 1956; Psychiatry in the Soviet Union, 1969; Community Mental Health: The Search for Identity, 1970. Contbr. articles psychiat. and med. subjects to mags. Home: 2401 H St Washington DC 20037 Office: 1028 Connecticut Av Washington DC 20036

GORMAN, PATRICK EMMET, labor union exec.; b. Louisville, Nov. 27, 1892; s. Maurice and Ellen (Dwyer) G.; LL.B., U. Louisville, 1917; m. Harriet Lee Dove, June 1, 1914. Admitted to Ky. bar, 1917; joined Amalgamated Meat Cutters and Butcher Workmen of N.Am., 1911, bus. agt. Local 227, 1912-20, spl. organizer internat. union, 1917-20, gen. v.p., 1920-23, pres., 1923-42, sec.-treas., 1942—. Fraternal del. AFL to Brit. Trade Union Congress, 1948; exec. bd. Internat. Food and Drink Workers Assn., 1951—. Active numerous civic causes, 1920—. Mem. bd. Religion and Labor Council Am.; trustee Roosevelt U.; adv. com. trade union com. Harvard; pres. Eugene V. Debs. Found. Named St. Jude Man of Year, 1963; recipient Coronet award St. Edward's U., Austin, Tex., 1963, Clarance Darrow award, 1963, St. Joseph the Worker award, Buffalo, 1963, Good Am. award Chgo., 1963, Brotherhood award Chgo., 1963, Humanitarian award N.Y. Fur Industry 1964. Home: 2401 Newburg Rd Louisville, KY 40205. Office: 2800 N Sheridan Rd Chicago IL 60614

GORMAN, PAUL A., mfg. co. exec.; b. Carollton, Mo., Dec. 16, 1907; s. Frederick W. and Alice (Zellers) G.; B.S., U. Mo., 1929; m. Betty Edwards, July 12, 1930 (dec.); m. 2d, Betty Johnston, Nov. 14, 1964. With Western Electric Co., 1929-52, successively accountant, supt. accounting, indsl. relations, asst. engr. mfg., central zone mgr.; personnel dir. Am. Tel. & Tel. Co., 1952-53, asst. v.p. personnel, 1953-57, exec. v.p., 1959-64; v.p. def. projects Western Electric Co., 1954-56, v.p. finance, 1956, v.p. mfg., 1956-58, pres., 1964-69, also dir., mem. exec. com.; pres., chief adminstrv. officer Penn Central Co., 1969-70; chmn., pres. Internat. Paper Co., 1971—; dir. Bankers Trust Co., Campbell Soup Co., BT N.Y. Corp., Prudential Ins. Co. Am. Clubs: Canoe Brook Country (Summit, N.J.); Carlton 3 (Washington); University (N.Y.C.); Baltusrol Golf (Springfield, N.J.); Golf Stream Golf (Delray Beach, Fla.). Home: 255 Oak Ridge Av Summit NJ 07901

GORMAN, THOMAS KIELY, univ. ofcl., bishop; b. Pasadena, Cal., Aug. 30, 1892; s. John Joseph and Mary Elizabeth (Kiely) G.; student St. Patrick's Sem., Menlo Park, Cal., 1910-14, St. Mary's Sem., Balt., 1914-17; S.T.B., St. Mary's U., Balt.; J.C.L., Cath. U. Am., 1918; Docteur en Sciences Historiques, U. Louvain, 1925. Ordained priest Roman Cath. Ch., 1917; asst. pastor Oxnard, Cal., 1918-19, St. Vibiana's Cath., Los Angeles, 1919-22; mng. editor The Tidings, ofcl. organ Diocese of Los Angeles and San Diego, 1926-31; prof. medieval and modern history Mt. St. Mary's Coll., Los Angeles, also Immaculate Heart Coll., Hollywood, 1926-31; bishop of Reno (Nev.), 1931-52; titular bishop of Rhasus, coadjutor to bishop of Dallas, 1952-54; bishop of Dallas-Fort Worth, 1954-69, chancellor U. Dallas, 1956- -; asst. at Pontifical Throne, 1942. Episcopal chmn. press dept. Nat. Cath. Welfare Conf., 1952-57, asst. Episcopal chmn. Bur. Information, 1961-66. Grand Prior So. lieutenancy, Knight Grand Cross Equestrian Order Knights of the Holy Sepulchre. Democrat. Author: America and Belgium, 1925; Seventy-five Years of Catholic Life in Nevada, 1936. Pub.: The Nevada Register, 1932-52; The Texas Catholic, 1952-69. Home: 6435 Forest Lane Dallas TX 75230

GORMAN, WILLIAM JOSEPH, business exec.; b. Frankfort, Ky., Sept. 6, 1917; s. William J. and Genevieve (Weitzel) G.; B.C.S., U. Ky., 1939; m. Mary Jane Smith, Sept. 16, 1940; children—Mary Ann, Martha Lyn, Sarah, Susan, Elizabeth. Sales dept. B. F. Goodrich Rubber Co., Cin., 1939-40; asso. oil tax staff Leslie E. Martlew, Evansville, 1941-44, 46-48; gen. mgr. Ryan Oil Co., Evansville, 1949—; chmn. bd. So. Cal. Aircraft Corp., Ontario, Cal.; dir. Mahoe Developers, Ltd. Pres. bd. trustees Redevel. Commn., Evansville. Served as lt. 0478200USNR, 1944-46. Mem. Am. Petroleum Inst., Am. Assn. Oil Well Drilling U.S.N.R., 1944-46. Mem. Am. Petroleum Inst., Am. Assn. Oil Well Drilling Contractors, A.I.M. Home: 723 Lombard St Evansville IN 47715 Office: Court Bldg Evansville IN 47708

GORME, EYDIE, singer; b. N.Y.C., 1932; m. Steve Lawrence, Dec. 29, 1957; children—David and Michael. Export mgr. theatrical equipment co. to 1952; 1st profl. engagement as vocalist Tommy Tucker's band; various night club engagments; mem. Steve Allen's TV troupe Tonight Show, 1954; Broadway debut (with husband) in Golden Rainbow, 1967; appeared Copacobana, N.Y.C., Sands, Las Vegas, Nev., Latin Casino, Camden, N.J., Eden Roc, Miami, Fla.; recordings include Sound of Music, Amor. Chairwoman entertainment com. Cerebral Palsy. Recipient Grammy award as best female vocalist of year, 1967. Address: 40 W 55th St New York City NY 10017

GORMLEY, MARK MCGUIRE, librarian; b. Superior, Wis., Nov. 4, 1924; s. Mark Thaddaeus and Enid Beatrice Edith (Dolan) G.; B.S., Wis. State Coll., Superior, 1951; M.A. in Library Sci., Denver U., 1954; m. Margaret Joyce Dunn, June 8, 1948; children—Mary Patricia, Thomas John. Tchr., librarian Milltown (Wis.) High Sch., 1951-53; librarian Sr. High Sch., Janesville, Wis., 1953-56; spl. asst. to librarian Colo. State U. Library, 1956-57, asst. to dir. library, 1957-58, asst. dir. library, 1958-61, asso. prof. library sci., 1960-61; exec. sec. Assn. Coll. and Research Libraries, A.L.A., 1961-62; librarian, prof. library sci. U. Wis.-Milw. Library, 1962-70; prof. library sci., dir. univ. libraries Wayne State U., Detroit, 1970; dir. univ. libraries U. Mo., St. Louis, 1971—. Vis. prof. Grad. Sch. Librarianship, Denver U., summer 1962, 65. Served with U.S. Maritime Service, 1942- 43, with USNR, 1943-46. Mem. A.L.A. (life), Assn. Coll. and Research Libraries (life); mem. Nat. Microfilm Assn., Colo. (pres. 1959-60), Wis. library assns. Author articles. Home: 305 Ridge Trail Rd Chesterfield MO 63017

GORMLEY, ROBERT JAMES, lawyer; b. Oak Park, Ill., July 23, 1921; s. James R. and Mary (McGann) G.; B.S.C., Northwestern U., 1942, M.B.A., 1950, J.D., 1950; m. Mary A. Howard, Aug. 4, 1956; children—Philip V., Monica L. Accountant, Baumann, Finney & Co., Chgo., 1941-42, 46-47; lectr. finance Northwestern U., 1947-49; admitted to Ill. bar, 1950, siince practiced in Chgo.; mem. firm Bell, Boyd, Lloyd, Haddad & Burns, 1958—. Dir. Chgo. Title Ins. Co.; sec. Nat. Merit Scholarship Corp. Served with USNR, 1942-46. C.P.A., Ill. Mem. Am., Chgo. bar assns., Am. Inst. C.P.A.'s. Democrat. Roman Catholic. Clubs: University, Attic (Chgo.). Office: 135 S LaSalle St Chicago IL 60603

GORMLY, THOMAS WILSON, former banker; b. Pitts., Mar. 20, 1909; s. William Ross and Martha (Wilson) G.; B.S., U. Pitts., 1937; grad. Rutgers U. Grad. Sch. Banking, 1949; m. Lourene Blaine, July 7, 1932 (dec. 1967); children—Caryl (Mrs. Paul S. Gurski), William M., Christine (Mrs. Peter Whitten), Thomas; m. 2d, Aurelia Mannion, 1968. With Pitts. Nat. Bank and predecessor, 1925—, v.p., 1951-64, former sr. v.p.; instr. finance U. Pitts. evening Grad. Sch., 1948-52, Sch. Consumer Banking, U. Va., 1954-59. Chmn. North Allegheny Scholarship Orgn., 1953-57. Bd. dirs. North Hills Passavant Hosp. Served to lt. USNR, 1944-46. Mem. Am., Pa. (chmn. installment credit commn. 1956-59) bankers assns., Beta Gamma Sigma. Clubs: Pittsburgh Athletic, Duquesne, Shannopin Country (Pitts.). Contbr. profl. jours. Home: Gateway Towers Pittsburgh PA 15222

GORNICK, ALAN LEWIS, lawyer; b. Leadville, Colo., Sept. 23, 1908; s. Mark and Anne (Grayhack) G.; A.B., Columbia, 1935, LL.B., Columbia, 1937; m. Ruth L. Willcockson, Aug. 10, 1940 (dec. May 1959); children—Alan Lewis, Diana Willcockson (Mrs. Lawrence J. Richard, Jr.), Keith Hardin. Admitted to N.Y. bar, 1937, Mich. bar, 1948; practiced with Baldwin, Todd & Young, N.Y.C., 1937-41, Milbank, Tweed, Hope & Hadley, 1941-47; asso. counsel charge tax matters Ford Motor Co., Dearborn, Mich., 1947-49, dir. tax affairs, tax counsel, 1949-64; pres. Blvd. Center, Inc., Detroit, Meadow Brook Park Devel. Co.; dir. Bloomfield Center, Inc., Castleton Industries, Inc., N.Y.C., Brooks and Perkins, Inc., Detroit; v.p. Seagate Hotel, Inc., Delray Beach, Fla., Hidden Valley, Inc., Gaylord, Mich. Lectr. tax matters N.Y.U., Inst. Fed. Taxation, 1947—, Am. Bar Assn. and Practicing Law Inst. courses on fundamentals in federal taxation, 1946—, Am. Law Inst. courses in continuing legal edn., 1950—; spl. lectr. sch. bus. adminstrn. U. Mich., 1949, 53; adv. editor Nat. Tax Jour., 1952—. Chmn. finance com., exec. bd. Detroit area council Boy Scouts, Am., 1960—; pres. Mich. Assn. Emotionally Disturbed Children, 1962—. Mem. Columbia Coll. council Columbia U., N.Y.C. Trustee Council on World Affairs, Detroit. Recipient Gov.'s Spl. award State Colo., 1952. Mem. Am. Bar Assn. (council tax sect. 1957-58), Fed., Mich. bars, Detroit, N.Y. City (chmn. subcom. estate and gift taxes 1943-47) bar assns., Am. Law Inst., Tax Inst. Inc. (pres. 1954-55), U.S., Empire State chambers commerce, Council on Fgn. Relations, Nat. Tax Assn. (exec. com.), Internat. Fiscal Assn. (council, nat. reporter 6th Internat. Congress Fiscal Law, Brussels 1952), Internat. Law Assn., Assn., Ex-Mems. Squadron A, Nat. Fgn. Trade Council (mem. com. taxes 1950—). Automobile Mfrs. Assn. (chmn. com. on taxation 1960-62), Tax Execs. Inst. (pres. 1956-57), Fedn. Alumni Columbia (dir. 1946), Class 1935 Columbia Coll. (permanent pres.), N.Y. Adult Edn. Council (dir. 1939-45), Phi Delta Phi. Clubs: Bloomfield Hills (Mich.) Country; Bloomfield Open Hunt; Detroit, Detroit Athletic; University (Washington); Columbia University, Church (N.Y.C.); Lawyers of University of Michigan; Columbia University Alumni of Mich. (pres. 1950—). Author: Divorce, Separation and Estate Taxes, Estate Tax Handbook, 1952; Arrangements for Separation or Divorce, Handbook of Tax Techniques, 1952; Taxation of Partnerships, Estates and Trusts, rev. edit., 1952. Contbr. articles tax matters to profl. jours. Home: 150 Lowell Ct Bloomfield Hills MI 48013 Office: 1565 Woodward Av Bloomfield Hills MI 48013

GORNICK, JOSEPH LOUIS, advt. exec.; b. Pueblo, Colo., Aug. 16, 1925; s. Joseph Mark and Catherine (Deviney) G.; B.A., Yale, 1948; postgrad. Stanford, 1950; m. Margaret Gail Kennedy, Mar. 23, 1957; children—Juliana Joy, Lawrence Joseph. Account exec. Fuller, Smith & Ross, N.Y.C., then J.M. Mathes, N.Y.C.; marketing exec. McCann Erickson, N.Y.C.; account supr. Needham, Harper & Steers, N.Y.C.; v.p. Ellington, Inc., N.Y.C., until 1964; exec. v.p. West, Weir & Bartel, N.Y.C., 1965, sr. v.p. adminstrn. D'Arcy, MacManus, Intermarco, 1970—; dir. Merchandising Research, Inc. Served to 2d lt. USAAF, 1943-45. Mem. Am. Marketing Assn. Clubs: Yale (N.Y.C.); Yale of Fairfield County (Conn.). Home: 22 Crooked Mile Rd Westport CT 06880 Office: 347 Madison Av New York City NY 10017

GORNITZKA, ARNOLD REUBEN, clergyman; b. Seattle, Nov. 12, 1917; s. Odd and Anna Sophia (Munson) G.; B.A., St. Olaf Coll., 1939; B.Th., Luther Sem., 1943; D.D., Capitol U., 1959; m. Katherine Jorgenson, Aug. 1942 (dec.); m. 2d, Ruth Haanstad-Dahlquist, Oct. 2, 1945; children—Lynn (Mrs. James Kintzi), Katherine (Mrs. Wallace Brohough), Ann (Mrs. David Ziemer), Phoebe (Mrs. Nelson Demetrius). Ordained to ministry Lutheran Ch.; intern pastor, Watertown, S.D.; asso. pastor, Madison, Wis.; sr. pastor, Milw., 1944-56, Central Luth. Ch., Mpls., 1956-63; minister-on-extended-service; pres. Direction, Inc., Denver, 1963—; minister-at-large Am. Luth. Ch. Pres. Milw. Ministerium, Mpls. Ministerium; chmn. dept. urban ch. Am. Luth. Ch., 1957-69; radio broadcaster sta. WFOX, Milw., 1945- 56, stas. KSTP and WCAL, Mpls. and Northfield, 1956-63; series It's Your Life, 1958-59, Nat. Luth. Ch. TV series, 1959, series Direction, 1964, Art of Living on NBC, 1965; spl. cons. Hoover Worldwide Corp., William Kordsiemon & Assos. Mem. Mayor Milw. Com., Mayor Mpls. Adv. Com., Gov. Minn. Ethics Com., Mpls. Auditorium Com. Bd. dirs. Mpls. YMCA, Mpls., United Fund, Luther Coll., 1958-61, Interdenominational Urban Tng. Center, Chgo., 1962-66; bd. regents St. Olaf Coll., 1962—. Recipient Distinguished Service award mayor Mpls., certificate appreciation Mpls.; Town Tooper award Mpls. C. of C.; named hon. commodore Mpls. Aquatennial; hon. fire chief Mpls. Mem. Wis. Luth. Welfare Soc., Blue Key. Author: Sincerely Yours, 1956; Its Your Life, 1959; Who Cares, 1966. Home: 73 510 Pinyon St Palm Desert CA 92260 Office: 825 Petroleum Club Bldg Denver CO 80202

GORODETZKY, SERGE, physicist; b. Montpellier (Hérault), France, Apr. 16, 1907; s. Gregoire and Perel (Krementchoutsky) G.; Docteur ès-sciences, U. Paris, Sorbonne; m. Reine Guesnon, Mar. 26, 1936; children—Philippe, Francoise, Elisabeth. Career, Laboratoire de L'Institut du Radium, Laboratoire de Broglie; dir. de l'Institut de Recherches Nucléaires; prof. faculty sci. U. Strasbourg; examiner des Elèves à l'Ecole Polytechnique; research nuclear physics. Officer, Hon. Arty. Decorated officer Legion of Honor; commandeur de l'Instruction Publique; Commandeur de l'Ordre National du Merite. Fellow Am. Phys. Soc.; mem. de l'Institut de France, Académie des Sciences, de la Société Francaise de Physique. Home: 4 Rue Jacques Kablé 67 Strasbourg France Office: Institut de Recherches Nucléaires BP 16 Strasbourg-Cronenbourg (Bas-Rhin) France

GORODEZKY, ELI, lawyer; b. Kansas City, Kan., Mar. 15, 1909; s. Aaron Louis and Celia (Spector) G.; J.D., U. Ariz., 1933; m. Helen Gertrude Evans, Oct. 15, 1947. Admitted to Ariz. bar, 1933, since practiced in Phoenix; asst. city atty., 1938-40; partner firm Gorodezky, Marron & Diamond, 1955—. Chmn. Charter Rev. Com. Phoenix, 1967-70; sec. Neurol. Scis. Found.; pres. Barrow Neurol-Found., 1968-69, v.p., 1970; field dir. A.R.C., World War II; mem. Nat. Adv. Council Vocational Rehab., 1956-59; v.p. Nat. Soc. Crippled Children and Adults, 1954-56; pres. Ariz. Soc., 1950- 53. Bd. dirs. Maricopa County Better Bus. Bur. Named Citizen of Year, Phoenix Realty Bd., 1956, Man of Year, Phoenix Advt. Club, 1955. Mem. Am., Ariz., Maricopa County bar assns., Phoenix C. of C.,

Newcomen Soc., Phi Alpha Delta, Pi Delta Epsilon Clubs: Arizona, Cloud, ABC, Press (Phoenix). Home: 3701 E Pierson St Phoenix AZ 85018 Office: 3033 N Central Av Phoenix AZ 85012

GORODNITZKI, SASCHA, pianist, educator; b. Kiev, Russia, May 24, 1906; s. Ossip Borisovitch and Eugenia Samoilovna (Von Stein) G.; student Inst. Mus. Art, N.Y.C., 1919-24; grad. Juilliard Sch. Music, 1932; m. Virginia Waite Henderson, Oct. 2, 1942; 1 dau., Diane Sue. Soloist debut, N.Y. Philharmonic, 1930; annual recitals Carnegie Hall, 1931-53; annual concert tour N.Am., 1931- -; tchr. master classes Summer Sch. Juilliard Sch. Music, N.Y.C., 1932- 42, mem. maj. piano faculty, 1948—; mem. jury internat. piano competitions; tchr. master classes Temple U. Music Festival and Inst., 1968-70; recordings for Columbia, Capitol, Pickwick Records; appeared with U.S. symphony orchs., Phila., Chgo., Cleve., Cin., Pitts., Rochester, Nat. (Washington), Balt., St. Louis, Detroit. Denver, Dallas, Houston, many others. Mem. The Bohemians. Home: 285 Central Park W New York City, NY 10024. Office: Julliard School Lincoln Center Plaza New York City NY 10023

GORR, RITA, mezzo soprano. Debut as Frika in Die Walküre at Theatre Royal, Antwerp, 1949, later appeared in role at Bayreuth Festival, Covent Garden, London; debut at Met. Opera as Amneris in Aida, 1962; other appearances include Lyric Opera, Chgo. Recording artist for Angel, RCA Victor, Epic records. Address: care SA Gorlinsky Ltd 35 Dover St London W1 England

GORRELL, JUAN LEESE, pub. relations exec.; b. Florence, Italy, Jan. 22, 1910 (parents Am. citizens); s. Henry Horace and Mercedes Beatrice (Leese) G.; student Kansas City Jr. Coll.; m. Magdalena Jaén, Jan. 4, 1941; children—Magdalena N. (Mrs. Bruce Duncan Guimaraens), Cristina L. (Mrs. Harro von Zeppelin), Angela C.M. Feature writer Kansas City Jour.-Post, 1926-28; credit corr. mfg. cos., Kansas City and Chgo., 1928-32; with importing co., Guayaquil, Ecuador, 1933-36, mgr. br., Quito, Ecuador, 1936-42; vice consul Am. embassy, Quito, 1942-45, Windsor, Ont., 1946-50; asst. labor attaché, also 2d sec. Am. embassy, Paris, 1951-56; 1st sec., labor attaché Am. embassy, Guatemala City, 1957-59; officer charge Guatemalan affairs Dept. State, Washington, 1959-60, dep. pub. affairs adviser Bur. Inter Am. Affairs, 1960-62, acting pub. affairs adviser, 1962, exec. asst. to dep. asst. sec. state for Inter-Am. affairs, 1962-63; U.S. consul, Oporto, Portugal, 1963-68; exec. dir. N.Am. Assn. Venezuela, 1968—. Dir. Instituto Ecuatoriano-Americano, Quito, 1942-45; sec. Inter-Allied Com., Quito, 1941-42. Mem. Sociedad Juridico-Literaria (Quito), Club de la Union (Guayaquil). Address: North Am Assn of Venezuela Apartado 60835 Caracas Venezuela

GORRELL, LEONARD LEE, hotel exec.; b. Sutton, W. Va., July 16, 1911; s. Lee and Florrie (Arnold) G.; grad. Greenbrier Mil. Sch., 1931; m. Angela Corona, Sept. 12, 1937; 1 son, Leonard J. Exec. positions Park Central, Salisbury, Esplanade hotels, N.Y.C., 1933-43; gen. mgr. Sheraton Hotel, Phila., 1946-50, Springfield, Mass., 1950-52, Niagara Falls, Ont., Can., 1952- 54, Pasadena, Cal., 1954-56, Sheraton-Jefferson Hotel, St. Louis, 1956- 57, Princess Hotel, Bermuda, 1956-62, French Lick Sheraton Hotel (Ind.), 1962, Sheraton-Park Hotel, Washington, 1963-66; pres., gen. mgr. Sheraton Hawaii Corp., Honolulu, 1963—. Served as officer USNR, 1943- 46; lt. comdr. Res. Mem. Am., Hawaii hotel assns. Clubs: Rotary, Skal, Variety, Saints and Sinners. Home: Royal Hawaiian Hotel Honolulu HI 96815 96815 Office: Sheraton Hawaii Corp PO Box 8559 Honolulu HI 96815

GORSHIN, FRANK, actor; student acting Carnegie Inst. Tech.; m. Christina Gorshin; 1 son, Mitchell. Numerous TV, stage, film and nightclub appearances; Broadway debut in Jimmy. Served with AUS, 1953-55. Address: care Gregory Assos 736 N Doheny Dr Los Angeles CA 90069*

GORSKI, JACK, educator; b. Green Bay, Wis., Mar. 14, 1931; s. John R. and Martha (Kenney) G.; student Cal. Poly. Coll., 1949-50; B.S., U. Wis., 1953; postgrad. U. Utah, 1957; M.S., Wash. State U., 1956, Ph.D., 1958; m. Harriet M. Fischer, Sept. 9, 1955; children—Michael, Jo Anne. NIH postdoctoral fellow U. Wis., 1958-61; asst. prof., asso. prof. physiology U. Ill. at Urbana, 1961-66, prof. physiology 1967—, prof. biochemistry, 1969—. NSF research fellow Princeton, 1966-67; mem. NIH endocrinology study sect., 1966-70. Mem. Am. Soc. Biol. Chemists, Am. Physiol. Soc., Endocrine Soc., Am. Soc. Cell Biology. Democrat. Unitarian. Contbr. articles profl. jours.

GORSKI, PAUL, concert master; b. Chgo., Aug. 9, 1941; s. Henry and Eleanor (Wieczorek) G.; B.Mus., U. Ill., 1964, Mus.M., 1966; m. Letia Ferlen, Dec. 14, 1968. Asst. concertmaster Santa Fe Opera, 1964—; asso. concertmaster New Orleans Philharmonic, 1967—; staff U. Ill., 1965. Home: 1035 7th St Gretna LA 70053

GORSKI, ROGER ANTHONY, neuroendocrinologist, educator; b. Chgo., Dec. 30, 1935; s. Casimir Michael and Mary (Wajrowski) G.; B.S., U. Ill., 1957, M.S., 1959; Ph.D., U. Cal. at Los Angeles, 1962; m. Judith Ann Bentley, Sept. 6, 1959; children—Denise May, Kevin Bentley. Asst. prof. dept. anatomy Sch. Medicine, U. Cal. at Los Angeles, 1962-66, asso. prof., 1966-70, prof., 1970—, vice chmn. grad. affairs, 1967—. Vis. prof. dept. animal sci. Cornell U., 1968. Recipient Lederle Med. Faculty award, 1966. Mem. Am. Assn. Anatomists, A.A.A.S., Am. Physiol. Soc., Endocrine Soc., Internat. Brain Research Orgn., Soc. for Study Reproduction, Phi Beta Kappa. Editorial bd. Neuroendocrinology, 1967—, Anatomical Record, 1968—. Contbr. articles profl. jours. Home: 3832 Minerva Av Los Angeles CA 90066

GORSLINE, DOUGLAS W., artist; b. Rochester, N.Y., May 24, 1913; s. William Henry and Sarah (Warner) G.; student Yale, 1931-32, Art Students League, N.Y.C., 1932- 35; m. Elizabeth Evarts Perkins, Sept. 26, 1936; children—John Warner Jeremiah Evarts; m. 2d, Nel King, Apr. 17, 1959. Instr. Nat. Acad. Design; paintings exhibited Whitney Mus. Am. Art, N.Y.C., Carnegie Inst. Internat. Exhibit, Pitts., Pa. Acad., Phila.; exhibited Library of Congress, Chgo. Art Inst. Asso. Mem. N.A.D., Soc. Am. Etchers. His "Portrait of Thomas Wolfe" has achieved nat. prominence and reproduced often in newspapers and periodicals. Author: Farm Boy 1950: What People Wore (containing 2,000 Costume drawings) 1951. Office: Box 710 Grand Central Sta New York City NY 10017

GORSLINE, GEORGE WILLIAM, educator; b. Battle Creek, Mich., Dec. 19, 1923; s. James M. and Lora (Gates) G.; student Mich. Coll. Mining and Tech., 1942-43; B.S. in Agronomy, Va. Poly. Inst., 1948; M.S., Pa. State U., 1957, Ph.D., 1959; m. Anne Bonner, Aug. 9, 1947; children—George William, Gary B., Cynthia S. Asst. prof. agronomy Pa. State U., 1956-63, dir. consultation, applied programming, customer relations, Computer Center, Inst. for Sci. and Engring., 1963-65; dir. computer center Ohio U., 1965-67, also lectr. math.; prof., head computer sci. dept. Va. Poly. Inst. and State U., 1967—. Served with AUS, 1943-45. Fellow A.A.A.S.; mem. Am. Soc. Agronomy, Crop Sci. Soc. Am., Am. Assn. U. Profs., Assn. Computing Machinery, Sigma Xi, Phi Epsilon Phi, Gamma Sigma Delta. Contbr. profl. jours. Home: 624 Watson Lane NW Blacksburg VA 24060

GORSUCH, JOHN ELLIOTT, lawyer; b. Denver, Sept. 2, 1899; s. John C. and Nancy (Johnson) G.; A.B., U. Denver, 1921, LL.B., 1925; m. Freda H. Munz, Aug. 21, 1930; children—John Philip, Diane B. Long, David Ronald, Keith Edward. Admitted to Colo. bar, 1925, since practiced in Denver; partner Gorsuch, Kirgis, Campbell, Walker and Grover; dir. Security Nat. Bank of Denver, Warner Co., Inc. Lectr. U. Denver, U. Colo. Law Sch., Southwestern Legal Found. Chmn. Legal Aid Soc. Denver; vice chmn. Non-Ferrous Metals Commn., Nat. War Labor Bd. Mem. adv. bd. Denver YWCA. Bd. dirs. Denver Community Chest. Trustee U. Denver, Presbyn. Hosp., Florence Crittendom Home; mem. adv. bd. Mt. Airy Hosp. Mem. Assn. Life Ins. Counsel Am., Am. (mem. labor law com.), Denver (past pres.), Colo. (mem. bd. govs. 1947-48) bar assns., Denver Symphony Soc. (trustee), Denver Council Fgn. Relations, Colo. Conf. Social Workers, Am. Arbitration Assn. (adminstrv. law com.), Nat. Acad. Arbitrators (bd. govs.), Phi Beta Kappa, Beta Theta Pi. Mason (trustee Benevolent Fund Colo.). Clubs: Mile High, Denver, Denver Athletic, Press, Denver Country, Kiwanis (past internat. v.p.) (Denver), Wigwam. Home: 105 Albion St Denver CO 80220 Office: Security Life Bldg Denver CO 80220

GORSUCH, WILLARD BENSON, photographic processing co. exec.; b. Cin., Aug. 10, 1915; s. Harvey Lee and Lillie (Otte) G.; student Xavier U., Cin., 1932-33, J. Cin., 1933- 39; m. Joyce Robertson, May 21, 1943; 1 dau., Stephanie Ann. Controller Black-Clawson Co., 1946-57, v.p., 1964-65; controller Dole Corp., 1957- 61, v.p. corp. devel., 1961-64; treas. Technicolor, Inc., Hollywood, Cal., 1966—, also dir., exec. v.p.; dir. subsidiary company, Rome, also Asso. Employers Ins. Co., Ft. Worth. Served with AUS, 1942-46. C.P.A., Ohio. Mem. Am. Inst. C.P.A.'s Financial Execs. Inst. Home: 691 S Irolo St Los Angeles CA 90005 Office: Technicolor Inc 6311 Romaine St Hollywood CA 90038

GORTER, CORNELIS JACOBUS, physicist; b. Utrecht, Netherlands, Aug. 14, 1907; s. Harmanus Johan and Anne Christina (Van Eck) G.; grad. Nederlands Lyceum, The Hague, 1924; Ph.D., U. Leyden, 1932; D.Sc., U. Grenoble, 1955, U. Paris, 1963, U. Nancy, 1966, Canterbury U., 1969; hon. doctorate U. Cordoba (Argentina), 1968; LL.D., Dalhousie U., 1960; D.Sc., U. Colo., 1968; m. Lilla C.E.C. von Krogh, June 27, 1938; children—Fridtjof B., Herman J., Anne K., Lilla E.A.H. Scientist, Teylers' Found., Haarlem, Netherlands, 1931-36; reader U. Groningen, 1936-40; prof. U. Amsterdam, and dir. Zeeman Labor, 1940-46; prof. U. Leyden, dir. Kamerlingh Onnes Labor, 1946—. Recipient F. London award, 1968. Mem. Council Internat. Union Pure and Applied Physics (v.p. 1946-51, 60-66), Internat. Inst. Refrigeration (pres. tech. bd. 51-56, hon. pres. 1956—), Netherlands Found. for Research on Matter (pres. 1954-60), Royal Netherlands Acad. Scis. (pres. 1960-66), Royal Swedish Acad. Scis. (hon.), Am. Acad. Arts and Scis. (hon.), Am. Philos. Soc. (fgn.), Royal Flemish (hon.), Finnish (hon.) acads. sci., Royal Norwegian Sci. Soc., Sci. Soc. (hon. Liége, Belgium); fgn. research asso. Nat. Acad. Scis. Author: Paramagnetic Relaxation, 1947; Progress in Low Temperature Physics, Vol. I, 1955, Vol. II, 1957, Vol. III, 1961, Vol. IV, 1964, Vol. V, 1967, Vol. VI, 1970. Home: Burggravenlaan 3 Leyden, Netherlands. Office: Kamerlingh Onnes Lab Leyden Netherlands

GORTER, WYTZE, educator, economist; b. San Francisco, Apr. 27, 1914; s. Berend Wytze and Gerarda Maria (Jonker) G.; A.B., Stanford, 1936, Ph.D., 1948; m. Barbara Holmes, July 6, 1938; children—Ann, Christopher Berend. Instr., asst. prof. Central Wash. Coll. Edn., 1941-42; chief rev. and analysis OPA, Seattle, 1942-43, price exec., 1943; acting instr. Stanford, 1946- 47; lectr. econs. U. Cal. at Los Angeles, 1947-48, asst. prof., 1948-53, asso. prof., 1953-59, prof., 1959-64, chmn. dept., 1956-61; prof. econs., dean grad. div. U. Hawaii, Honolulu, 1964—, dir. research, 1965—. Served to 2d lt., Q.M.C., AUS, 1943-46. Carnegie research fellow Council Fgn. Relations, 1953-54; Fulbright lectr. internat. econs. U. Groningen, Netherlands, 1958-59; Guggenheim fellow, 1958-59. Mem. Am., Western (pres. 1962-63) econ. assns., Council Fgn. Relations, Western Assn. Grad. Schs. (pres. 1968-69). Author: (with G. H. Hildebrand) The Pacific Coast Maritime Shipping Industry, 1930-48, 2 vols., 1952, 54; United States Shipping Policy, 1956. Contbr. articles profl. jours. Home: 4351 Aukai Av Honolulu HI 96816

GORTIKOV, STANLEY MERRILL, record co. exec.; b. Los Angeles, May 14, 1919; s. Joseph and Goldie (Harris) G.; A.B., U. So. Cal., 1941; m. Judith Peyser, Mar. 31, 1957; children—Jeffrey, Julie, Jane, James, Scott. Prodn. mgr. L.K. Shapiro Co., 1949-60; dir. corp. devel. Capitol Records, Inc., 1960, sr. v.p. 1966-68, pres., 1968-69; v.p., then pres. Capitol Records Distbg. Corp., Hollywood, Cal., 1960-68; exec. v.p. Capitol Industries, Inc., 1969, pres., chief exec. officer, 1969-71; dir. KPFK Pacifica Corp. Founding mem. Center Study Democratic Instns. Trustee, Cal. Inst. Arts. Served to lt. col. AUS, 1941-45. Decorated Bronze Star medal. Home: 19812 Santa Rita St Woodland Hills CA 91364

GORTNER, ROSS AIKEN, Jr., biochemist, educator; b. Cold Spring Harbor, L.I., N.Y. June 2, 1912; s. Ross Aiken and Catherine (Willis) G.; student (Alumni scholar) Oberlin Coll., 1929-30; A.B. magna cum laude, U. Minn., 1933, M.A., 1934; Ph.D., U. Mich., 1937; M.A. (hon.), Wesleyan U., Middletown, Conn., 1948; m. Mary Priscilla Cahill, Dec. 20, 1938; children—Katherine Clarke (Mrs. David R. Singleton), Douglas Ross. Faculty fellow, grad. teaching asst. U. Mich., 1935-37; faculty Wesleyan U., Middletown, Conn., 1937—, prof. biochemistry, 1948—, dir. Sci. Center, 1967—. Fulbright lectr., Copenhagen, Denmark, 1954-55; vis. research prof. U. Giessen, Max Planck Inst. Biochemistry, Munich, Germany, 1961-62; asso. exec. sec. food and nutrition bd. NRC, 1943-44; dir. coll. sci. curriculum improvement program NSF, 1966-67; mem. bd. control Conn. Agrl. Expt. Sta., 1964—, sec., 1967—. Mem. council Middlesex Meml. Hosp. Sch. Nursing, 1948-54; corporator Middlesex Meml. Hosp., 1967—. Served to lt. USNR, 1944-46. Fellow A.S.S.S.; mem. Am. Chem. Soc., Am. Inst. Nutrition, Conn. Nutrition Council (chmn. 1952-54), Phi Beta Kappa, Sigma Xi, Phi Lambda Upsilon, Gamma Alpha, Alpha Chi Sigma. Club: Faculty (Middletown). Author: (with W. A. Gortner) Outlines of Biochemistry, 1949; (with P. E. Marsh) Federal Aid to Science Education: Two Programs, 1963; also articles. Home: 84 Bretton Rd Middletown, CT 06457.

GORTNER, WILLIS ALWAY, research adminstr., govt. ofcl.; b. Cold Spring Harbor, N.Y., Dec. 20, 1913; s. Ross Aiken and Catherine (Willis) G.; B.A. magna cum laude, U. Minn., 1934; Ph.D., U. Rochester, 1940; m. 2d, Susan Leet Reichert, Aug. 25, 1960; children—Willis Alway II, David Allen, Catherine Willis, Frederick Aiken. Research chemist Gen. Mills, Inc., Mpls., 1934-37, 40-42; teaching asst. biochemistry U. Rochester Med. Sch., 1937-40; asst. prof. biochemistry and chem. engring. Cornell U., 1943-45, asso. prof. biochemistry, 1945-48; head chemistry dept. Pineapple Research Inst. Hawaii, Honolulu, 1948-64; dir. human nutrition research div. Agrl. Research Service USDA, Beltsville, Md., 1964—. With Bikini Sci. Resurvey Team, 1947, Biorksten Research Found., Madison, Wis., 1953, NRC-Nat. Acad. Sci., 1957, Nat. Canners Assn. Research Lab., 1960-61, dept. nutritional scis. U. Cal. at Berkeley, 1963; affiliate grad. faculty U. Hawaii, 1956- 64. Recipient Thomas Andrews award for undergrad. research U. Minn., 1934. Fellow A.A.A.S.; mem. Am. Soc. Biol. Chemists, Am. Chem. Soc., Am. Inst. Nutrition, Inst. Food Technologists, Sigma Xi, Phi Lambda Upsilon, Alpha Chi Sigma. Clubs: Outrigger Canoe (Honolulu); Cosmos (Washington). Co-author; Principles of Food Freezing, 1948; co- editor, author: Outlines of Biochemistry, rev. edit., 1949. Contbr. articles to profl. jours. Patentee in field. Home: 12701 Lacy Dr Silver Spring, MD 20904. Office: Agrl Research Center Beltsville MD 20705

GORTON, JAMES ALLEN, musician; b. Corpus Christi, Tex., Feb. 13, 1947; s. Richard R. and Elizabeth (Sanders) G.; Mus.B. (Rochester Nat. scholar 1965-69), Eastman Sch. Music, 1969; m. Karen Barbara McDaniel, June 15, 1968; 1 dau., Elizabeth Helen. Studied oboe with Charles Morris, 1958-64, Louis Rosenblatt, 1964-65, John deLancie, 1965; 2d oboe Rochester Philharmonic Orch., 1966-69; 1st oboe Rochester Chamber Orch., 1967-69; oboist Mid-Am. Woodwind Quartet in residence Kan. State Tchrs. Coll., Emporia, 1969-71, lectr., 1969-71; asso. prin. oboe Pitts. Symphony Orch., 1971—; faculty Carlow Coll., Pitts., 1971—; mem. orch. Bach Festival, Bethlehem, Pa., 1967-69; 1st oboe N.H. Music Festival Orch., 1968-71; recording artist Decca and Deutsche Grammophon Gesellschaft labels, 1968-69. Bd. dirs. Kan. chpt. Young Audiences, Inc. Mem. Music Educators Nat. Conf. Home: 5256 Forbes Av Pittsburgh PA 15217 Office: 600 Pennsylvania Av Pittsburgh PA 15222

GORTON, JOHN GREY, govt. ofcl.; b. Sept. 9, 1911; M.A., Brasenose Coll., Oxford (Eng.) U.; m. Bettina Brown, 1935; 3 children. Senator for State of Victoria, Australian Parliament, 1949-68, govt. leader, 1967-68; minister for navy, 1958-63; minister assisting the minister for external affairs, 1960-63; minister-in-charge Commonwealth Sci. and Indsl. Research Orgn., 1962-68; minister for interior, 1963-64; minister for works and minister-in-charge commonwealth activities in edn. and research, 1963-66; minister for works, 1966-67; minister for edn. and sci., 1966-68; elected to Ho. of Reps., 1968—; prime minister, 1968-71, minister for def., 1971. Councillor, Kerang Shire, 1947-52, also pres.; mem. Lodden Valley Regional Com. Served to flight lt. Royal Australian Air Force, 1940-44. Mem. Liberal Party. Address: Parliament House Canberra A C T 2600 Australia

GORTON, SLADE, state ofcl.; b. Chgo., Jan. 8, 1928; s. Thomas Slade and Ruth (Israel) G.; A.B., Dartmouth Coll., 1950; student Northwestern U. Law Sch., 1950-51; LL.B., Columbia, 1953; m. Sally Jean Clark, June 28, 1958; children—Tod, Sarah Jane, Rebecca. Admitted to Wash. bar, 1953; practiced in Seattle, 1953-69; partner firm Little, Gandy, Palmer, Slemmons & Holcomb, 1965-69; atty. gen. Wash., Olympia, 1969—. Mem. Wash. Ho. of Reps., 1959-69, majority leader, 1967-69, mem. legislative council, 1961-69. Trustee Pacific Sci. Center, Seattle, Forward Thrust, Seattle. Served with AUS, 1946-47, to 1st lt. USAF, 1953-56. Mem. Am., Wash., Seattle bar assns., Phi Beta Kappa. Clubs: Seattle Tennis, Washington Athletic (Seattle). Home: 2622 S Capitol Way Olympia WA 98501 Office: Temple of Justice Olympia WA 98501

GORTON, THOMAS ARTHUR, composer, pianist, educator; b. Oneida, N.Y., Mar. 12, 1910; s. Thomas Joel and May Lovica (Kelley) G.; Mus.B., Eastman Sch. Music, Rochester, N.Y., 1932, Mus.M., 1935, Ph.D., 1948; m. Catherine Geib Urlass, Nov. 11, 1933; 1 dau., Judith Louise (Mrs. Leonard F. Parkinson). Teaching fellow Eastman Sch. Music, Rochester, N.Y., 1933-35; instr. David Hochstein Music Sch., Rochester, 1933-35; instr. music Riverside (Cal.) Jr. Coll., 1935-37; condr. Riverside Community Opera Assn., 1935-37; head piano dept. Memphis Coll. Music, 1937-38, U. Tex., 1938- 44; dir. Sch. Music, Ohio U., 1947-50; dean Sch. Fine Arts, U. Kan., Laurence, 1950—, condr. Univ. Little Symphony, 1950—; pianist St. Louis Symphony, 1943, Houston Symphony, 1939, Rochester Civic Orch., 1932-35. Mem. acad. music com. Cultural Presentations Program, Dept. State. Served to lt. USNR, 1944-46. Mem. Nat. Assn. Schs. Music (pres. 1958-62, chmn. devel. council 1962-65, chmn. commn. on curricula 1965-70, cons. commn. on undergrad. studies 1970—), Kan. Music Tchrs. Assn., Nat. Assn. Music Execs. State Univs., Nat. Council Fine Arts Deans, Phi Mu Alpha, Kappa Kappa Psi, Pi Kappa Lambda. Composer music including: Symphony No. 1, 1947; Variations on a Welsh Folk-Tune for symphonic band, 1949; also piano pieces and songs. Home: 831 Illinois St Lawrence KS 66044 ☆

GORWITZ, BERTRAM KALL, army officer; b. Duluth, Minn., May 10, 1920; s. Victor and Ann (Kall) G.; B.S., U. Md., 1962; M.B.A., George Washington U., 1965; postgrad. Indsl. Coll. Armed Forces, 1965, Harvard, 1967; m. Margie Marie Daugherty, Jan. 5, 1952; children—Cynthia Ann, David Kall, Patricia Nora, Joanna Marie. Commd. 2d lt. U.S. Army, 1943, advanced through grades to brig. gen., 1968; comdg. gen. 18th Airborne Corps Arty., Ft. Bragg, N.C., 1967-69; comdg. gen. I Corps Arty., Korea, 1969; dep. chief of information Dept. Army, 1970; comdg. gen. and asst. div. comdr. 23d Inf. Div., Vietnam, 1971—. Troop chmn. Nat. Capitol Area council Boy Scouts Am., 1966-67; ofcl. Little League Baseball, 1966. Decorated Legion of Merit with 2 oak leaf clusters, Air medal; D.S.M. (Vietnam). Mem. Nat. Sojourners, Heroes of 76 (camp comdr.), Harvard, George Washington U., U. Md. alumni assns., Hall of Fame Field Arty. Sch., Phi Kappa Phi. Clubs: Toastmasters International (pres.) (Washington); Century Parachute (Ft. Bragg, N.C.). Home: 8312 Orange Ct Alexandria VA 22309

GOSE, GEORGE BLOCKER, former life ins. co. exec.; b. Shelbina, Mo., Apr. 4, 1910; s. John Thomas and Eugene Burrus (Blocker) G.; A.B., U. Cal. at Los Angeles, 1931, LL.B., 1934; m. Helen West Ralston, Mar. 27, 1937; children—Jean Ralston, Margaret, John Edward. Admitted to Cal. bar, 1934, practiced in Los Angeles, 1934-42; with Pacific Mut. Life Ins. Co., 1942-70, gen. counsel, 1949-70, v.p., 1950-55, exec. v.p., dir., 1955-70, now ret., dir. Music Center Lease Co., Theater & Forum Lease Co., Coca-Cola Bottling Co. of Los Angeles, City Market of Los Angeles. Chmn. bd. Los Angeles Civic Light Opera Assn. Served as lt. USNR, 1943-46. Mem. Los Angeles C. of C. (dir. 1952-61, v.p. 1955-57, pres. 1958), Cal., Los Angeles bar assns., Delta Tau Delta, Phi Delta Phi. Clubs: California, Sunset (Los Angeles), Parma Valley Country. Home: 2021 Paseo del Sol Palos Verdes Estates CA 90274

GOSHKO, JOHN MYRON, journalist; b. Swampscott, Mass., July 29, 1933; s. Edward Earl and Gertrude (Gordon) G.; A.B., U. Pa., 1955; M.S. in Journalism, Columbia, 1959; m. Linda Levitt, Apr. 17, 1962; children—Anthony, Matthew, Gertrude, Jean. Reporter, rewriteman Mpls. Tribune, 1959-61; mem. staff Washington Post, 1961—, Latin Am. corr., 1965-69, Germany corr., 1970—. Served to 1st lt. AUS, 1955-58. Recipient Citation for Excellence in Internat. Reporting Oversees Press Club, 1969, Edwin Stout Meml. award, 1970, Washington-Balt. Newspaper Guild award, 1969, Maria Moors Cabot prize, 1970. Columbia-Ford Found. fellow internat. reporting, 1963-64. Jewish religion. Author articles, book revs. Home: Schleich Strasse 8 Bonn Venusberg West Germany Office: Adenauer Allee 270 Bonn West Germany

GOSHORN, JOHN ARTHUR, former army officer; b. Chambersburg, Pa., Dec. 9, 1911; s. John H. and Nettie (Kennedy) G.; B.S. in Civil Engring., Va. Mil. Inst., 1934; student Command and Gen. Staff Sch., 1942, Command and Gen. Staff Coll., 1947, Nat. War Coll., 1956; M.B.A., Harvard, 1951, student Advanced Mgmt.

Program, 1960; m. Louise Needy, June 15, 1935; children—Margaret E. (Mrs. Louis J. Casarett), Barbara (Mrs. William A. Bruchey), John Arthur, Linda (Mrs. Barry T. Hirsch). Engr., York Corp., 1934-40; commd. 2d lt. U.S. Army Res., 1934, 1st lt. U.S. Army, 1946, advanced through grades to maj. gen., 1965; various assignments in U.S., 1940-44; exec. officer 476th QM Group, ETO, 1944-45, comdg. officer, 1945; insp. gen. 12th Armored Div., ETO, 1945-46; instr. Command and Gen. Staff Coll., 1947-49; chief gen. supplies sect., supply br. QM div. Hdqrs. U.S. Army Europe, 1951-52; asst. for supply operations Hdqrs. and Hdqrs. Co. 53d QM Base Depot, U.S. Army Europe, 1952-54; chief clothing and equipage br. Office QM Gen., 1954-55; spl. staff officer Mil. Clothing and Textile Supply Agy., Phila., 1956, exec. officer, 1956-57; dep. QM Hdqrs. U.S. Army Japan/8th U.S. Army (rear), Japan, 1957-58; dep. QM Hdqrs. U.S. Army Pacific, Hawaii, 1958-60; chief procurement, planning and prodn. div. Office Dep. Chief Staff Logistics, Dept. Army, 1960-61, asst. dir. procurement, 1961- 62; dep. dir. procurement and prodn. Hdqrs. U.S. Army Materiel Command, 1962-63; dir. procurement Office Asst. Sec. Army (Installations and Logistics), 1963-66; dir. contract adminstrn. services Def. Supply Agy., 1966-68; comdg. gen. U.S. Army, Japan, 1968-70, retired, 1970. Commr. Nat. Capital area council Boy Scouts Am., 1964-68, v.p. Far East Council, 1968-70. Decorated D.S.M. with 2 oak leaf clusters, Legion of Merit, Bronze Star. Home: 420 St George Ct Satellite Beach FL 32935

GOSLINE, ROBERT BRADLEY, lawyer; b. Toledo, Jan. 9, 1913; s. Robert Gates and Ella Irene (Bradley) G.; A.B. cum laude, U. Toledo, 1933; J.D., Ohio State U., 1936; m. D. Martha Long, Nov. 29, 1941; children-Robert Bradley, William H., Mary G. (Mrs. Raymond P. Conrad). Admitted to Ohio bar, 1936, since practiced in Toledo; asso., partner Shumaker, Loop & Kendrick and predecessor firms, 1936—, head litigation dept., 1964—. Chmn. Bd. Bar Examiners for Ohio Supreme Ct., 1960-61. Chmn. March of Dimes Lucas County, 1951; mem. City Charter Commn., Maumee, O., 1951. Mem. City Council, Maumee, 1952-54. Sec., trustee Boys Club Toledo. Served to maj. AUS, 1942-46. Fellow Am. Coll. Trial Lawyers; mem. Am., Ohio, Toledo (past pres.) bar assns., Nat. Assn. R.R. Trial Counsel, Phi Delta Phi. Presbyn. (trustee, elder). Home: 232 E Wayne St Maumee OH 43537 Office: 811 Madison Av Toledo OH 43624

GOSLING, GLENN DONALD, publisher; b. Overisel, Mich., Sept. 29, 1909; s. Edward and Berendiena (Fynewever) G.; student Grand Rapids Jr. Coll., 1925-27; A.B., U. Mich., 1931, M.A., 1931; B.A. (Rhodes scholar), Oxford (Eng.) U., 1933, M.A., 1938; m. Laura Marshall, Mar. 24, 1942 (dec.); 1 dau., Anne Laura. Tchr. writing, English lit. Olivet (Mich.) Coll., 1934-41, mem. staff Olivet Writers Conf., summers 1936-41; editor trade dept. Henry Holt & Co., N.Y.C., 1941-50; editor-in-charge U. Cal. Press, Los Angeles, 1950-56, sr. editor, Berkeley, 1956-62; dir. U. Mich. Press, 1962—. Served with CIC, AUS, 1942-46. Mem. Am. Assn. Rhodes Scholars, Phi Kappa Phi, Kappa Tau Alpha. Home: 2229 Needham Rd Ann Arbor MI 48104 Office: U Mich Press Ann Arbor MI 48104

GOSLING, JOHN ALFRED, symphony condr.; b. Trenton, N.J., May 18, 1928; s. John Coates and Clara (Neuman) G.; student Juilliard Sch. Music, 1946-48, Cath. U. Am., 1956-59; m. Margaret Ellen Register, June 10, 1950; 1 dau., Susan Jeanne. Trumpet player Dallas Symphony Orch., 1947-48, St. Louis Symphonietta, 1949-50; condr. Cath. U. Am. Orch., Washington, 1956-59, Dept. Agr. Symphony Orch., 1959-60, Monterey County Symphony Orch., Carmel, Cal., 1961-67, Erie (Pa.) Philharmonic, 1967—. Founder Monterey Peninsula Choral Soc., 1962; founder, dir. Music from Bear Valley Festival, Cal., 1969. Served with USMCR, 1950-60. ANTA grantee, 1962. Mem. Phi Mu Alpha. Address: G Daniel Baldwin Bldg Erie PA 16501

GOSLING, ROBERT A., chem. co. exec.; b. 1913; student Oberlin Coll.; B.S., Yale, 1936; postgrad. Chgo. Kent Coll. Law, Northwestern U.; married. Second v.p., asst. cashier No. Trust Co., 1951-57; sec., treas. Manitowoc Co., Inc., 1957-62; controller Koehring Co., 1962-64; v.p., sec., treas. Am. Shipbldg. Co., 1964-67; controller Thiokol Chem. Corp., Bristol, Pa., 1968-69, controller, asst. sec., 1969—. Served with USNR, 1942-45. C.P.A., Pa. Office: Newportville Rd Bristol PA 19007*

GOSMAN, ALBERT LOUIS, educator; b. Detroit, May 27, 1923; s. Saul and Eva (Cohen) G.; B.S., U. Mich., 1950; M.S., U. Colo., 1955; Ph.D., U. Ia., 1965; m. Marguerite Emilie Lemieux, Mar. 9, 1946; children—Erica Jan, Stephanie Frances. Asst. prof. Colo. Sch. Mines, 1950-55, 58-62; research engr. Northrop Aircraft, Inc., Los Angeles, 1956-58; asso. prof. Wayne State U., Detroit, 1965-67; prof., chmn. mech. engring. dept., asso. dean engring. Wichita (Kan.) State U., 1967—. Research engring. cons. cryogenics Nat. Bur. Standards. Served with C.E., AUS, 1943-45. Recipient Outstanding Tchr. awards Colo. Sch. Mines, 1952, 53, Best Tchr. award Wayne State U., 1967. Ford Found. fellow, 1964-65. Mem. Am. Soc. M.E. (dir. Midwest sect.), Am. Soc. Engring. Edn., Blue Key, Sigma Xi, Phi Kappa Phi, Pi Tau Sigma, Alpha Tau Omega. Author monograph; contbr. chpt. to Tech. Navair Manual of Oxygen/Nitrogen Cryogenic Systems, 1971. Home: 244 Bonnie Brae Wichita KS 67207

GOSNELL, CHARLES FRANCIS, NO. OF RECORDS 00033 librarian; b. Rochester, N.Y., July 7, 1909; s. James Francis and Alameda (Whipple) G.; A.B., U. Rochester, 1930; B.S., Columbia, 1932, M.S., 1937; Ph.D., N.Y.U., 1943; certificate Centro de Estudios Históricos, Madrid, Spain, 1934; m. Patria Aran-Soler, Mar. 31, 1934; children—Alice, Rita; m. 2d, Helen Louise Kuhlman, Dec. 29, 1951; children—Marsh Kuhlman, Deborah, Susan, Catherine. Student asst. U. Rochester Library, 1927, asst., 1928-31; corr. Rochester Democrat and Chronicle, 1928-30; reference asst. N.Y. Pub. Library, 1931-37; librarian, asso. prof. Queens Coll., 1937-45; asso. Sch. Library Service, Columbia, 1943-47; asst. commr. edn., N.Y., 1949-62; state librarian, N.Y. State, 1945-62; dir. libraries, prof. library adminstrn. N.Y. U., 1962—; spl. cons., library orgns., and assns., library mus. and historic bldgs. for fire protection, library lighting. U.S. del. to UNESCO Conf. on Libraries, Sao Paulo, Brazil, 1951; head UNESCO survey pub. library services in Colombia, S.Am., 1959; cons. to Ford Found. and U. Brasilia, Brazil, 1963—; cons. Inter-am. Devel. Bank, 1966-67. Sec. N.Y. State Freedom Train Commn., N.Y. Cultural Heritage Found.; trustee Pub. Affairs Information Service, Mohawk-Caughnawaga Mus., Fonda, N.Y., Skidmore Coll., Saratoga Springs, N.Y.; chmn. Council Nat. Library Assns., 1956-57; past pres. Nat. Assn. State Libraries. Recipient Grand Cross Eloy Alfaro Internat. Found., 1968; comdr. Order Jacques Ignace Fresnel (Haiti); Good Citizenship gold medal S.A.R.; Benjamin Franklin fellow Royal Soc. Arts, London. Mem. A.L.A. (mem. exec. bd. 1953-57, pres. library adminstrn. div. 1966-67), N.Y. Library Assn. (pres. 1968-69), Middle Atlantic Regional Library Council (bd. dirs.), various spl. library assns., nat., state and local bibliog. and library assns., and also assns. in related fields, such as statis., archivist and hist. socs. Mason (33, grand historian, grand master N.Y., chmn. conf. grand masters N.Am. 1968-69, hon. grand master Guanabara, Rio de Janeiro, hon. mem. supreme council Brazil, Henry Price medalist grand lodge Mass.). Clubs: Grolier, Masonic, N.Y. University (N.Y.C.); Rotary, University (Albany). Author several books latest being: New York State's Freedom Train, 1948: Copyright Grab-bag, 1968; also articles to profl. publs. Home: 11 Orchard Circle Suffern NY 10901 Office: NY U Libraries Washington Sq New York City NY 10003 ☆ NO. OF RECORDS 00067

GOSNELL, HAROLD CORNELIUS, clergyman; b. Syracuse, N.Y., July 17, 1908; s. Cornelius Parsons and Carrie (Fawcett) G.; B.A., Syracuse U., 1930; B.D., Episcopal Theol. Sch., Cambridge, Mass., 1930-33; D.D., U. of South, 1956; m. Marjorie O. Adams, Aug. 29, 1932; children—Judith (Mrs. James M. Cavender III), Harold, Cornelius. Ordained to ministry Episcopal Ch., 1933; rector St. John's Ch., Marcellus, N.Y., 1933-36, All Saints Ch., Fulton, N.Y., 1936- 38, Holy Trinity Ch., Lincoln, Neb., 1938-48, St. Mark's Ch., San Antonio, 1948-68; bishop Diocese W. Tex., San Antonio, 1968—. Mem. exec. bd., trustee Diocese W. Tex.; mem. Nat. Commn. Ch. in Human Affairs; mem. Armed Forces Commn. Episcopal Ch.; mem. exec. council, program and budget com., com. on pastoral devel. Episcopal Ch.; mem. bd. Gen. Commn. on Chaplains and Armed Forces Personnel; dep. Episcopal Gen. Convs., 1940, 43, 46, 49, 52, 55, 58, 61, 64, 67. Pres. Allied Childrens Services, 1958-64, San Antonio Council of Chs., 1963-64. Bd. dirs. United Fund (pres. 1962-63), Community Chest, Good Govt. League, 1952— (all San Antonio); chmn. bd. St. Mary's Hall, San Antonio, Tex. Mil. Inst.; regent U. of South, Sewanee, Tenn. Served with USNR, 1942-46; ret. capt. Res. Mem. Psi Upsilon. Mason (33 Shriner). Rotarian (past pres. San Antonio). Club: Oak Hills Country (San Antonio). Home: 342 E Terra Alta San Antonio TX 78209

GOSNELL, JOHN RAINSFORD, ins. co. exec.; b. Sherman Mills, Me., Feb. 26, 1915; s. George Thomas and Pearl (Allen) G.; B.A., Brown U., 1941, LL.D., 1968; m. Evelyn Coulson, Oct. 24, 1942; children—Susanne, John R. With Paul Revere Corp., Worcester, Mass., 1946—, pres., 1969—, also dir.; with Paul Revere Life Ins. Co., Worcester, 1946—, vice chmn. finance com., 1968—, also dir.; chmn. finance com., dir. Paul Revere Variable Annuity Ins. Co., Worcester, 1965—; chmn. exec. com., dir. Avco Corp., Greenwich, Conn., 1970—; dir. Worcester Bancorp., Midland Glass Co. Trustee, chmn. investment com. Brown U., Worcester Hahnemann Hosp. Served to lt. USNR, 1942-46. Clubs: Worcester Country,, Worcester, Sagemace Country. Home: Parsonage Lane Greenwich CT 06831 Office: 1275 King St Greenwich CT 06830

GOSS, CHARLES MAYO, educator; b. Peoria, Ill., Feb. 16, 1899; s. Charles Edward and Frances Wade (Mayo) G.; A.B., Yale, 1921, M.D. cum laude (Goodrich scholar), 1926; m. Josephine Cowell, Aug. 14, 1928; children—Elizabeth C. (Mrs. Henry Chodkowski), Frances M. (Mrs. L. J. Vergne), Marianna (Mrs. B. Lewis Slaten). Instr. anatomy Yale, 1926-29, Columbia, 1929-31; asst. prof. anatomy Columbia, 1931-38; prof. anatomy U. Ala., 1938-47, La. State U., 1947-66; vis. prof. anatomy George Washington U., Washington, 1966—. Research work in exptl. embryology, cytology, histology; mng. editor Anat. Record, 1948- 68; prof. extraordinary anatomy U. Costa Rica, San Jose, 1961; mem. com. for Handbook of Biol. Data, NRC; hon. U.S. mem. Internat. Anat. Nomenclature Com. Recipient Distinguished Alumnus award Bradley U. 1956. Guggenheim fellow, 1956. Mem. Inst. Am. Affairs Med. Mission to survey med. schs. in Colombia. Mem. Am. Assn. Anatomists (exec. com. 1947-51, pres. 1964-65), Am. Assn. Phys. Anthropologists, Soc. Exptl. Biol. and Medicine, Am. Assn. History Medicine, History of Sci. Soc., Sigma Xi, Alpha Omega Alpha, Beta Theta Pi, Nu Sigma Nu. Republican. Episcopalian. Author: A Brief Regional Anatomy of the Human Body, 1970. Editor med. texts; editor Grays Anatomy 25th edit., 1948, 26th edit., 1954, 27th edit., 1959, 28th edit., 1966. Contbr. articles to med. jours. Home: 7809 Moorland Lane Bethesda MD 20014 Office: Dept Anatomy 1335 H St Washington DC 20005

GOSS, CHESTER C., finance and leasing co. exec.; b. Ft. Scott, Kan., May 10, 1921; s. Chester Curtis and Verla (Buckmaster) G.; A.B., Kan. State Tchrs. Coll., Pittsburg; LL.B., Fordham U., 1951; grad. Advanced Mgmt. Program, Harvard; m. Adrienne Helen Lucey, Feb. 10, 1946; children—Graydon, Robert, Virginia, Donna, Adrienne. With CIT Corp., 1946—, v.p. sales CIT Corp. and CIT Leasing Corp., 1965-67, exec. v.p., 1967-68, pres., 1968—, also dir. Served to lt. (j.g.) USNR, World War II. Home: 11 Homestead Pky E New Shrewsbury NJ 07724 Office: 650 Madison Av New York City NY 10022

GOSS, DONALD ARTHUR, educator, physician; b. Morristown, N.J., May 1, 1934; s. Frank A. and Claire (Burnett) G.; A.B., Hamilton Coll., 1955; M.D., Harvard, 1959; m. Marilyn G. Noel, Oct. 18, 1958; children—Donald Sturgis, Karen Noel. Intern surgery Vanderbilt U. Hosp., 1959-60, resident obstetrics and gynecology, 1960-61; resident surgery Peter Bent Brigham Hosp., Boston, 1961-62; resident obstetrics and gynecology Boston Lying-In Hosp., Free Hosp. for Women, 1962-65; faculty Vanderbilt U. Sch. Medicine, Nashville, 1966—, prof. obstetrics and gynecology, chmn. dept., 1966—. Med. dir. Planned Parenthood Nashville. Served with USAF, 1965-66. Fellow Am. Coll. Obstetricians and Gynecologists; mem. Endocrine Soc., Am. Fertility Soc., Internat. Fertility Soc., A.A.A.S., Central Assn. Obstetricians and Gynecologists, N.Y. Acad. Scis. Home: 627 Westview Av Nashville TN 37205

GOSS, GEORGE AUGUSTUS, Jr., former mfg. co. exec.; b. N.Y.C., Nov. 15, 1920; s. George Augustus and Estelle (Farrel) G.; B.A., Yale, 1942; m. Claire Leader, Sept. 11, 1948; children—George Augustus III, Edwin Leader, Dirck Waterhouse, Helene Farrel. With Scovill Mfg. Co., 1946—, gen. mgr. Waterville (Conn.) div., 1958-59, v.p., 1959-65, v.p., 1965-71, also dir., now ret.; dir. U.S.M. Corp., Boston, Eastern Co., Naugatuck, Conn., Colonial Bank & Trust Co., Waterbury; incorporator Waterbury Savs. Bank, 1960-66. Bd. dirs. Greater Waterbury Indsl. Devel. Corp., 1960—; sec. Middlebury (Conn.) Zoning Commn., 1952-57. Mem. council Mattatuck Mus.; trustee McTernan Sch., Waterbury, pres., 1966; trustee Waterbury Hosp., pres., 1966-67; corporator Waterbury Found. Served to capt. AUS, 1942-46. Decorated Bronze Star medal. Mem. Am. Ordnance Assn., Aubudon Soc. Coastal Conn. (dir.). Newcomen Soc. Clubs: Links (N.Y.C.); Laurentian (Canada); Lake Placid (N.Y.); Hillsboro (Fla.). Home: Topsy Lane Middlebury CT 06762

GOSS, JAMES HASSELL, former exec.; b. Paris, Ark., Sept. 22, 1907; s. Samuel and Mary Angeline (Berry) G.; B.S. in Mech. Engring., U. Ark., 1930; grad. advanced mgmt. program Harvard; m. Doris Almira Bunce, June 18, 1930; children—James Herbert, Cynthia Bunce. Design engr. Gen. Electric Co., West Lynn, Mass., 1931-47, asst. mgr., mgr. engring. indsl. control, Schenectady, 1947-51, asst. to div. gen. mgr. small apparatus div., Lynn, 1951, mgr. mfg. maj. appliance dept., Louisville, 1951-53, dept. gen. mgr. home laundry dept., 1953-55; pres. Canadian Gen. Electric Co., Ltd., Toronto, 1955-57; v.p., group exec., Gen. Electric Co., N.Y.C., 1957-68; pres. Automatic Sprinkler Corp. of Am., 1968-71, now ret.; also dir.; dir. Pantasote, Internat. Nickel Co. of Can., Ltd. Mem. Assn. Profl. Engrs. Ont., I.E.E.E. Home: Pilots Point Captains Dr Westbrook CT 06498

GOSS, JAMES WALTER, oil co. exec.; b. Farmerville, La., Mar. 18, 1924; s. Walter Frank and Lovie (Hollis) G.; B.S., La. State U., 1949; m. Mertie Henry, Jan. 1, 1953; children—James Walter, Kimberly. With Gen. Am. Oil Co. Tex., Dallas, 1949—, v.p. charge land dept., 1960—, exec. v.p., dir., mem. exec. com., 1970—. Served with USNR, 1943- 45. Mem. Ind. Petroleum Assn. Am. (dir.), Am., Dallas (past pres., dir.) assns. petroleum landmen, Midcontinent Oil and Gas Assn., Tex. Ind. Producers and Royalty Owners Assn., Am. Petroleum Inst., Lambda Chi Alpha. Clubs: Dallas Athletic, Petroleum, Texas (Dallas). Home: 3509 Centenary Dr Dallas TX 75225 Office: Meadows Bldg Dallas TX 75206

GOSS, JOSEPH WILLIAM, judge; b. Terre Haute, Ind., Nov. 10, 1925; s. Joseph William and Dorothy (Posey) G.; student Washburn U., 1943-44; B.S., U. Cal. at Los Angeles, 1946; J.D., Stanford, 1949; m. Patricia N. Mann, Aug. 11, 1958; children—Walter Woodbridge, Sarah Hope. Confirmation asst. E. F. Hutton & Co., Los Angeles, 1945-46; admitted to Cal. bar, 1950, also So. dist. U.S. Dist. Ct. Cal., U.S. Supreme Ct.; practiced in Los Angeles, 1950, Santa Barbara, 1953, Oxnard, 1953-59, Sacramento, 1959-61; civilian atty. Logistics div. Hdqrs. European Command Communications Zone, Fontainebleau (Seine-et-Marne) and Orleans (Loiret), France, 1950-51; civilian atty., chief distbn. sect. G-4 div. Hdqrs. U.S. Army Europe Communications Zone, Orleans, 1952, procurement officer, legal asst. to chief Gen. Purchasing div., 1952-53; city atty., Oxnard, 1953-59; adminstrv. adviser to state controller, Sacramento, 1959-61; judge Municipal Ct., Oxnard-Port Hueneme Jud. Dist. Cal., 1961-65, persiding judge, 1963-65; asso. justice High Ct. Trust Ty. Pacific Islands, Saipan, Mariana Islands, 1965-66, Majuro, Marshall Islands, 1966-68, also temporary judge dist. ct. Guam, 1965-67; asso. justice High Ct., Am. Samca, 1967—, acting chief justice, 1970. Commr., Oxnard Planning Commn., 1953-59; mem. So. Cal. Planning Congress, 1954-59; mem. Ventura County Planning Conf., 1957-59. Bd. dirs. Boys Club Oxnard, 1961-65, Ventura County council Boy Scouts Am., 1963-65; vice chmn., bd. dirs. Ventura County Council on Alcoholism, 1963-65. Served to lt. (j.g.) USNR, World War II. Mem. World Assn. Judges (del. from Trust Ty.), Am., Fed. bar assns. Home: Box 577 Pago Pago American Samoa 96920

GOSS, RICHARD JOHNSON, educator, biologist; b. Marblehead, Mass., July 19, 1925; s. Donald Chapin and Ruth (Johnson) G.; A.B., Harvard, 1948, Ph.D., 1952; m. Marcella Hyde, June 2, 1951; children—Stephen Harley, Elizabeth Alden. Instr. biol. and med. scis. Brown U., 1952-54, asst. prof., 1954-58, asso. prof., 1958-64, prof., 1964—. Corp. mem. Opportunities, Inc. Trustee Mt. Desert Island Bio. Lab., 1960-64. Served with inf., AUS, 1943-45. Fellow Carnegie Instn. of Washington Dept. Embryology, 1960-61. Mem. R.I. Zool. Soc. (pres., dir.), Am. Soc. Zoologists (chmn. div. developmental biology 1969), A.A.A.S. (sec. sect. biol. scis.). Author: Adaptive Growth, 1964; Principles of Regeneration, 1969. Editor: (with W.N. Nowinski) Compensatory Renal Hypertrophy, 1969. Research on regeneration of animal appendages and on regulation of organ and tissue growth. Home: 24 Winsor Dr Barrington RI 02806 Office: Brown Univ Providence RI 02912

GOSS, WESLEY PERRY, mining co. exec.; b. Garland, Kan., Nov. 4, 1899; s. Frank Bailey and Lola May (Perry) G.; B.S., U. Cal., 1922; m. Nellie F. McIntosh, Apr. 5, 1923; children—John Wesley, Patricia Caroline. Asst. supt. United Verde Copper Co., Jerome, Ariz., 1933-34; gen. supt. Park City (Utah) Consol. Mines Co., 1934-37; mine supt. O'Kiep Copper Co., Namaqualand, South Africa, 1937-41; asst. gen. mgr. Gray Eagle Copper Co., Happay Camp, Cal., 1942-44; v.p., gen. mgr., dir. Magma Copper Co., 1944- 53, pres., gen. mgr., dir., 1954—; v.p., gen. mgr., dir. Magma Ariz. R.R., 1944—. Mem. Ariz. Copper Tariff Bd. Mem. Ariz. Bd. Regents, 1963-70. Mem. Am. Inst. Mining and Metall. Engrs., Am. Mining Congress, Mining and Metall. Soc. Am., Am. Legion. Home: Box 676 San Manuel AZ 85631 Office: Box M San Manuel AZ 85631

GOSSAGE, STEVENSON MILNE, R.R. ofcl.; b. London, Eng., Dec. 6, 1905; s. Alfred Milne and Bertha (Pillans) S.; B.Sc. in Engring., Univ. Coll., U. London, 1926; M.Sc. in Transp., Yale, 1934; m. Edith Chatfield, May 6, 1935; children—Jonathan Frederick Milne, Edith Abigail; m. 2d, Eva Marie Huldschinsky, Apr. 19, 1958. With Canadian Pacific Ry. Co., 1926—, v.p. Eastern region, Toronto, 1958-59, v.p., gen. mgr., Toronto, 1959-62, v.p., gen. mgr. Prairie region, Winnipeg, 1962-64, v.p., co. services, Montreal, 1964-66, v.p. co., 1966-71, also dir., mem. exec. com.; chmn. preparatory commn. for metric conversion Dept. Industry, Trade & Commerce, 1971—. Trustee Bishops U. Mem. Am. Assn. R.R. Supts. (dir.), Canadian C. of C., Canadian Inst. Internat. Affairs (dir.). Clubs: University (Montreal), Montreal Badminton and Squash; Manitoba; National (Toronto). Home: Clubs: Manitoba; Winnipeg Squash Racquet; National (Toronto). Home: 590 Cote St Antoine Rd Westmount Montreal 6 Quebec Canada Office: Dept Industry Trade Commerce Tower B Place de Ville Ottawa Ontario Canada

GOSSELIN, JOHN WILLIAM, lawyer; b. Aurora, Ill., Feb. 20, 1934; s. John Stephen and Betty (Willoughby) G.; student Wabash Coll., 1952-53; B.A., Beloit Coll., 1953- 56; LL.D., U. Chgo., 1959; m. Judith Ann Wheeler, Sept. 14, 1956; children—Kathleen, Gabrielle, John Wheeler, Thomas Willoughby. Admitted to Ill. bar, 1959; practice in Aurora, 1959-66, Batavia, 1966—; asso. Thomas P. O'Malley, 1959-61; pvt. practice, 1961-66; partner Benson, Mair & Gosselin, 1966—. City atty. Batavia, 1964—; chmn. Tri-Cities Legal Aid. Mem. Am., Ill., Kane County bar assns. Home: Lockwood Hall Batavia IL 60510 Office: 18 E Wilson St Batavia IL 60510

GOSSELIN, ROBERT EDMOND, educator; b. Springfield, Mass., Sept. 2, 1919; s. A. Edmond and Grace (Pettengill) G.; A.B., Brown U., 1941; Ph.D., U. Rochester, 1945, M.D., 1947; m. Ruth L. Smith, June 26, 1948; children—Peter Gordon, Andrea Lee. Med. intern Yale service Grace-New Haven Hosp., 1947-48; instr. pharmacology U. Rochester, 1948-52, asst. prof. pharmacology, scientist atomic energy project, 1954-56; prof., chmn. dept. pharmacology and toxicology Dartmouth Med. Sch., 1956—; dir. poison information center Hitchcock Hosp., 1957—. Cons. USPHS, 1959-63, U.S. Army Chem. Corps, 1954-59; mem. toxicology study sect. USPHS, 1964-68; mem. toxicology study sect. FDA, 1966-69. Pres., Norwich Devel. Assn., 1965. Served with AUS, 1944-46; to capt., M.C., U.S. Army, 1952-54. Mem. Am. Physiol. Soc., Am. Soc. Exptl. Pharmacology and Therapeutics, A.A.A.S., Toxicology Soc., N.Y. Acad. Scis., Phi Beta Kappa, Sigma Xi. Contbr. articles to profl. jours. Home: Elm St Norwich VT 05055 Office: Dartmouth Med Sch Hanover NH 03755

GOSSETT, ED, judge; b. Sabine Parrish, La., Jan. 27, 1902; s. Edward L. and Sarah Anne (McKinley) G.; A.B., U. Tex., 1924, L.L.B., 1927; m. Mary Helen Moseley, May 20, 1939; children—Glenn, Judy, Jane, Melissa, Stephen, Murray. Admitted to Tex. bar, 1927; practiced in Vernon and Wichita Falls, 1927-32; dist. atty. 46th Jud. Dist. Tex., 1933-37; mem. 76th-81st congresses from 13th Dist. Tex.; gen. atty. for Tex. S.W. Bell Telephone Co., 1951-67; judge Criminal Dist. Ct. 5, Dallas County, Tex., 1967—. Chmn. U.S. Savs. Bonds Program for Tex., 15 years. Mem. Am., Dallas (pres. 1960) bar assns., East Tex. C. of C. Democrat. Presbyn. Mason. Club: Dallas City (v.p.). Home: 3916 Gillon Av Dallas TX 75205 Office: County Courthouse Dallas TX 75205

GOSSETT, OSCAR MILTON, advt. exec.; b. N.Y.C., May 27, 1925; s. Oscar Percival and Helen (Deutsch) G.; student Stevens Inst. Tech., 1943-44, 46-47, Columbia, 1947-48; m. Anna C. Scheid, May 29, 1949; children—Susanne, Michael, Thomas, Lorraine, James M. With

Compton Advt., Inc., 1949—, pres., 1968- -. Chmn. bus. and advt. sect. Am. Cancer Soc., N.Y.C.; chmn. council ministries United Methodist Ch., Ridgefield, Conn. Served with USNR, World War II. Mem. Am. Assn. Advt. Agencies. Inventor mobile of solar system. Home: RD 1 South Salem NY 10590 Office: 625 Madison Av New York City NY 10022

GOSSETT, WILLIAM THOMAS, lawyer; b. Gainesville, Tex., Sept. 9, 1904; s. James Tillman and Orrie B. (Laverty) G.; A.B., U. Utah, 1925, LL.D., 1961; LL.B., Columbia, 1928; LL.D., Kalamazoo Coll., 1965, Coe Coll., 1947, Bethany Coll., 1962, Tuskegee Inst., 1966, Detroit Coll. Law, 1967, Oakland U., 1967, Duke, 1968, U. Mich., 1968, Drury Coll., 1969, Brown U., 1969, U. Dallas, 1969; H.H.D., Wayne U., 1957; m. Elizabeth Evans Hughes, Dec. 19, 1930; children—Antoinette Carter, William T., Elizabeth Evans. Admitted to N.Y. bar, 1929; practiced in N.Y., 1929-47; assisted in reorgn. of Fox West Coast Theaters Corp., 1932-35, Wesco Corp., 1934, Fox Film Corp., 1935; assisted in defense Aluminum Co. of Am. in govt. anti-trust dissolution suit, 1937-41; gen. counsel Bendix Aviation Corp., 1943-47, dir. 1946-47; mem. firm Hughes, Schurman & Dwight, 1935- 37, Hughes, Hubbard & Ewing (and predecessor firm), 1937-47; v.p., gen. counsel, dir., mem. exec. and adminstrn. coms. Ford Motor Co., 1947- 1962; served as dep. spl. rep. for trade negotiations, Washington, 1962-63; counsel Dykema, Wheat, Spencer, Goodnow & Trigg, Detroit, Michigan, 1964-70; partner Dykema, Gossett, Spencer, Goodnow & Trigg, 1970—. Dir. One William St. Fund, Inc., Dart Industries, Inc., Twentieth Century Fox Film Corp. Chmn. board United Negro Coll. Fund., 1961-67; life trustee Columbia U. Mem. bd. trustees Riverside Ch., N.Y.C., 1935-47, pres. 1947; trustee Cranbrook Found., Bloomfield Hills, Mich., Atlanta U., Morehouse Coll., Harper Hosp., Detroit. Bd. dirs. Detroit Symphony Orch. Recipient Amity award Women's div. Am. Jewish Congress, 1955, ann. Brotherhood award Detroit Round Table, National Conf. Christians and Jews, 1958, Layman of Year award Detroit Council Chs., 1960. Fellow Am. Bar Found. (pres. 1964-66, dir.); mem. Am. (pres. 1968-69), N.Y., Detroit bar assns., Nat. Legal Aid Assn. (dir.), Assn. Bar City of N.Y., State Bar Mich., Order of Coif, Beta Theta Pi, Delta Theta Phi. Republican. Baptist. Clubs: Detroit, Detroit Athletic, Bloomfield Hills Country (Detroit); The Links (N.Y.C.); Metropolitan (Washington). Home: 420 Goodhue Rd Bloomfield Hills MI 48013 Office: Penobscot Bldg Detroit MI 48226

GOSSICK, LEE VAN, air force officer; b. Meadville, Mo., Jan. 23, 1920; s. Clark and Myrtle (Staats) G.; B.S. in Aero. Engring., Ohio State U., 1951, M.S., 1951; grad. Air War Coll., 1959; grad. Advanced Mgmt. Program, Harvard, 1961; m. Ruth Matter, Apr. 29, 1942; children—Roger V., Cynthia L. Aviation cadet, 1941-42; commd. 2d lt. USAAF, 1942, advanced through grades to maj. gen. USAF, 1968; fighter pilot 87th Fighter Squadron, North Africa, 1942- 43; various research and devel. posts, 1951-64; comdr. Arnold Engring. Devel. Center, 1964-67; dep. for F-111 aero. systems div. Wright- Patterson AFB, O., 1967-68, vice comdr. div., 1968-69, comdr., 1969-70; dep. chief staff systems Hdqrs. Air Force Systems Command, Andrews AFB, Md., 1970-71, chief of staff, 1971—. Decorated D.S.M., Legion of Merit with oak leaf cluster, D.F.C., Air medal with 9 oak leaf clusters; named Distinguished Alumnus, Ohio State U., 1960, Centennial Achievement award, 1970; recipient Vandenberg trophy Arnold Air Soc., 1967. Fellow Am. Inst. Aeros. and Astronautics. Home: 1306 Vandenberg Dr Andrews AFB Washington DC 20331 Office: DCS/Systems Hdqrs Air Force Systems Command Andrews AFB Washington DC 20331

GOSSMAN, FRANCIS JOSEPH, bishop; b. Balt., Apr. 1, 1930; s. Frank M. and Mary Genevieve (Steadman) G.; B.A., St. Mary Sem., Balt., 1952; S.T.L., N. Am. Coll. in Rome, 1955; J.C.D., Cath. U. of Am., 1959. Ordained priest Roman Cath. Ch., 1955; asst. pastor Basilica of the Assumption, Balt., 1959-68; asst. chancellor Archdiocese of Balt., 1959-65; pro-synodal judge Balt. Tribunal, 1961, vice officialis Tribunal of Archdiocese of Balt., 1962-65, officialis, 1965; made papal chamberlain with title Very Rev. Monsignor, 1965; elected to Senate of Priests of Archdiocese, 1967-68; adminstr. Cathedral of Mary Our Queen, 1968; named aux. bishop of Balt. and titular bishop of Agunto, 1968; apptd. vicar gen., 1968; now urban vicar for Archdiocese of Balt. Mem. Balt. Community Relations Commn., 1969-70; mem. exec. com. Md. Food Com., Inc., 1969-70. Trustee, Good Samaritan Hosp. Mem. Canon Law Soc. Am., Nat. Conf. Cath. Bishops, U.S. Cath. Conf. Home: 848 Hollins St Baltimore MD 21201 Office: 320 Cathedral St Baltimore MD 21201

GOSSMAN, JEFFREY L., educator; b. Glasgow, Scotland, May 31, 1929; s. Norman and Sarah (Gold) G.; M.A., U. Glasgow, 1951; D.E.S., U. Paris (France), 1952; D.Phil., St. Anthony's Coll., Oxford (Eng.) U., 1958; m. Eva Reinitz, Mar. 13, 1963; 1 dau., Janice Naomi. Came to U.S., 1958. Asst. lectr. U. Glasgow, 1957-58; faculty Johns Hopkins, Balt., 1958—, prof. French lit., 1966—. Home: 34 Over Ridge Ct Baltimore MD 21210

GOTAAS, HAROLD BENEDICT engr., educator; b. Mellette, S.D., Sept. 3, 1906; s. Halfdan C. and Emma E. (Cady) G.; B.S., U. S.D., 1928, Sc.D. (hon.), 1955; M.S., Ia. State Coll., 1930; S.M., Harvard, 1937, Sc.D., 1942; D.Eng., Rose Poly. Inst., 1969; m. Alice McLaughlin, Apr. 10, 1931; 1 son, Richard McLaughlin. With Am. Bridge Co., Ambridge, Pa., 1930-31, Ia. Hwy Commn., Ames, 1931, Clinton (Ia.) Bridge Works, 1931-32; asst. prof. civil engring. U. S.D., 1932-36; asst. prof., later prof. san. engring. U. N.C., 1937-42; also cons. engr., 1937-42; entered U.S. Army, 1942; assigned as chief engr. and asst. dir., div. of health and sanitation, Inst. Inter-Am. Affairs, 1942-44, dir. div. health and sanitation and exec. v.p., 1944-45, pres. inst., 1945-46; prof. san. engring. U. Cal., 1946-57, dir. San. Engring. Labs., 1949-57, chmn. div. civil engring., 1948-54; dean The Tech. Inst., Northwestern U., Evanston, Ill., 1957-70, prof. civil engring., 1957-67, Walter P. Murphy prof., 1967—. spl. cons., environmental health study sect. USPHS, 1948- 54; cons. WHO, 1954—; mem. nat. health adv. council U.S. Dept. Health, Edn. and Welfare, 1956-60; mem. com. on bio-astronautics NRC, 1959-60; mem. engring. panel NSF, 1960-63; mem. Gt. Lakes Commn., chmn. pollution control com., 1961-65; chmn. water resources com. N.E. Ill. Planning Commn.; mem. Ill. Water Pollution and Water Resources Commn., 1966-69; mem. Rockefeller Mission to Latin Am., 1969. Served from capt. to col. San. Corps, U.S. Army, 1942-46. Decorated Legion of Merit, Cross of Boyaca (Colombia), Order of Honor and Merit (Haiti), Order of Merit (Chile), Order of Condor of Andes (Bolivia); recipient awards including James Croes and Rudolph Hering medals, Harrison P. Eddy medal, Kenneth Allen award, Wisdom award Honpr; Engr. of Year award Ill. Soc. Profl. Engrs., 1962. Mem. Nat. Acad. Engring. (hon.), Am. Soc. C.E. (chmn. research com. 1959-60), Am. Soc. Engring. Edn., Am. Pub. Health Assn., Inter-Am. Assn. San. Engrs. (pres. U.S. sect. 1959), Am. Water Works Assn., Water Pollution Control Assn. (pres. Cal. sect. 1951-52), Engring. Coll. Research Council (dir. 1959-62), Engrs. Joint Council, Am. Environmental Engring. Inter-soc. Bd. (dir., v.p.), Planetarium Soc. Chgo. (dir. 1958-62), Phi Kappa Phi, Tau Beta Pi, Sigma Xi, Delta Omega, Chi Epsilon, Kappa Sigma, Sigma Phi Delta. Clubs: University (Evanston); Economic (Chgo.). Author books, articles in field. Home: 618 Colfax Evanston IL 60210 ☆

GOTESKY, RUBIN, philosopher, educator; b. Ploscк, Poland, July 4, 1906; s. Philip and Katherine (Habuse) G.; naturalized Am. citizen, 1927; B.A., N.Y.U., 1928, M.A., 1930, Ph.D., 1939; m. Frances Elizabeth Pickens, Aug. 5, 1947; children-James Kenneth, Stephen Francis. Instr., L.I. U., 1930-38; instr. N.Y.U., 1945-47; asso. prof. Tulane U., 1947-48; asso. prof. U. Ga., 1948-60; prof. No. Ill. U., Dekalb, 1960—; vis. prof. U. Chgo., summer 1949, Emory U., summer 1962, Rutgers U., summer 1963, N.Y.U., summer 1948, Ripon Coll., 1970; cons. HumRRO, 1958-60. Nat. vice chmn. Unitarian Service Com., 1958; pres. Carolinas Unitarian Conf., 1958-60, Ill. Philosophy Conf., 1963-65. Served with AUS, 1942-45. Fellow Philosophy of Edn. Soc.; mem. Mind Assn., Am. Philos. Assn., Assn. Symbolic Logic, John Dewey Soc., So. Soc. Philosophy and Psychology (past pres.), Phi Kappa Phi, Pi Mu Epsilon, Phi Delta Kappa. Author: Liberalism In Crisis, 1948; (with others) Struggle for Tomorrow, 1954; Excellence, 1965; Personality, 1967. Editor: Philosophy Forum, Quarterly, 1967—; Current Topics in Contemporary Thought, 1968—. Cons. editor: Humanist, 1955-58. Contbr. to Ency. of Morals, Collier Ency., Ency. of Philosophy Contbr. articles profl. jours. Home: 604 W Lincoln Hwy DeKalb IL 60115

GOTHELF, SY PAUL, dept. store exec.; b. Bklyn., Oct. 21, 1927; s. Adolph and Tillie (Altman) G.; student Bklyn. Coll., 1944-45, Mass. Inst. Tech., 1947, Coll. City N.Y., 1948-49; m. Betty Kahn, Dec. 25, 1947; children-Amy Beth, Carrie Lyn. From Stockboy to dept. mgr. Lerner Shops, 1948-50; asst. to pres. Grayson Robinson, 1956-62; mdse. coordinator Spartans, 1962-65; asst. to exec. v.p. operations adminstrn. Arlan's Discount Dept. Stores, Inc., N.Y.C., 1965—, also v.p. charge operations. Served with Signal Corps, AUS, 1945-46. Home: 32 Buckingham Circle Pinebrook NJ 67058 Office: 393 7th Av New York NY 10001

GOTO, YASUO BARON, educator; b. Japan, Nov. 20, 1901; s. Asakichi and Nami (Inaba) G.; came to U.S., 1902, naturalized, 1945; B.S., U. Hawaii, 1924; Sc.D. (hon.), Ore. State U., 1959; m. Pear Kimiko Kawasaki, Sept. 9, 1933; children—Leora Nami (Mrs. Melvin Hirose), Ray Ai-ji. Mem. faculty U. Hawaii, 1928—, dir. extension service Coll. Tropical Agr., 1955-62, sr. prof. agr., 1958-64, vice chancellor Inst. Tech. Interchange of East-West Center, 1962-69; established Internat. Coop. Center, Office Territorial Gov. Hawaii, 1954-55; cons. to govts. and industry, 1950—. Dir. Ewa Sugar Plantation, 1957-61, Grand Pacific Life Ins. Co., 1957- 63, Aloha Airlines, 1946-69, Shirokiya Inc., 1959—, Capital Investment Co., 1962—, Honolulu Star-Bull., 1963—, Internat. Savs. & Loan Assn., 1963—, Bishop Trust Co., 1963—. Chmn. Hawaii UN Week, 1955, Hawaii World Brotherhood Week, 1957, Hawaii Farm City Week, 1957, 58, Hawaii Cancer Crusade, 1963, Honolulu Tb campaign, 1964; del. Pacific Sci. Congress, 1961, 66; mem. U.S. Commn. S. Pacific Commn., 1964—, Pacific Sci. Bd. of Nat. Acad. Scis., 1966-69. Trustee Charles R. Hemenway Scholarship Trust Fund, 1962, Hawaii Vets. Meml. Fund, 1947—, Met. Hawaiian YMCA, 1945-55, Mid-Pacific Inst., 1937—, Hawaii 4-H Found., 1961—; mem. adv. com. Kamehameha Schs., 1964-68. Served with AUS, World War II. Recipient World Brotherhood citation, 1956, Paul S. Bachman award Pacific and Asian Affairs Council, 1957; named citizen of year Civitan Club, 1961. Mem. Hawaii Acad. Sci., Friends of Bishop Mus., Friends of Foster Garden, Friends of East-West Center, Honolulu (bd. dirs. 1960-62), Honolulu Japanese (bd. dirs. 1964- 69) chambers commerce. Rotarian. Home: 2243 Hoonanea St Honolulu HI 96822

GOTSCHLICH, GEORG-DIETER, German diplomat; b. Berlin, Germany, Mar. 22, 1931; s. Franz and Margarete (Fickler) G.; student U. Muenster (Germany), 1951, 53-55, Georgetown U. Law Sch., 1952; m. Christa Leuffen, Aug. 29, 1959; children—Michael, Wolfdieter, Tilman. Passed law state exam, 1955, great exam, 1959; state atty., Northrhine-Westphalia, Germany, 1959; with German Finance Adminstrn., 1960—, personal asst. to state sec. German Finance Ministry, 1968-69, financial counselor, Germany embassy, Washington, 1970—. Home: 7921 Falstaff Rd McLean VA 22101 Office: 4645 Reservoir Rd NW Washington DC 20007

GOTSHALK, DILMAN WATER, educator; b. Trenton, N.J., Sept. 11, 1901; s. William Calvin and Josephine (Walters) G.; A.B., Princeton, 1922; Ph.D., Cornell, 1927; m. Naomi Irene Smith, Oct. 17, 1930; children—Richard Allan, Mary Laine. Instr. English lit. Mohegan Lake Sch., N.Y., 1922-24; acting prof. philosophy Colgate U., 1927; instr. philosophy U. Ill., Urbana, 1927-30, asst. prof., 1930-36, asso. prof., 1936-43, prof. philosophy, 1943- 65, prof. philosophy emeritus, 1965—, chmn. dept., 1951-61. Fellow A.A.A.S.; mem. Am. Philos. Assn. (v.p. Western div. 1947-48, 49-50, pres. 1950-51, chmn. nat. bd. officers 1951, Carus lecture com. 1952, chmn. 1953-65), Am. Soc. Aesthetics (trustee 1952-55, pres. 1957-59, del. soc. to Am. Council Learned Socs. 1959-61), Am. Assn. U. Profs. Author: Structure and Reality, 1937, 68; Metaphysics in Modern Times, 1940; Art and the Social Order, 1947, 51, 62; The Promise of Modern Life, 1958; Patterns of Good and Evil, 1963; Human Aims in Modern Perspective, 1966; The Structure of Awareness, 1969; Twentieth Century Theme, 1971. Contbr. to Heritage of Kant, 1939, Ency. of the Arts, 1946, P.F. Collier's Gen. Ency., 1951, A Modern Book of Esthetics, 1952, 60, Problems of Aesthetics, 1953; also other books and various philos. periodicals. Home: 413 E Butler St Olney IL 62450 Office: Gregory Hall U Ill Urbana IL 61801

GOTSHALL, ROY JORDAN, corp. exec.; b. 1920; B.A., Dartmouth, 1942; married. With Arthur Andersen & Co., C.P.A.'s Phila., until 1949; with Air Products and Chems. Inc., 1949—, now treas. Address: PO Box 538 Allentown PA 18105

GOTT, EDWIN HAYS, steel exec.; b. Pitts., Feb. 22, 1908; s. Leonard Hays and Isabel (Dalzell) G.; B.S. in Indsl. Engring., Lehigh U., 1929; m. Mary Louise Carr, Oct. 6, 1934; children—Elizabeth C. (Mrs. John A. Byerly, Jr.), Edwin H., Barbara D. (Mrs. J. Paul Martha). With U.S. Steel Corp., 1937- -, successively indsl. engr. Ohio Works, indsl. engr., Clairton Works, Gary Steel Works, asst. div. supt. maintenance Gary Steel Works, asst. div. supt. Central Mills, asst. gen. supt. service depts., asst. gen. supt. South Works, Chgo., gen. supt. Youngstown Dist. Works, gen. mgr. operations-steel, 1937-56, v.p. operations-steel, 1956-58, v.p. prodn., steel producing divs., 1958-59, adminstrv. v.p. central operations, 1959, exec. v.p. prodn., 1959-67, pres., chief adminstrv. officer, 1967-68, chmn., chief exec. officer, 1969—, also dir., chmn. operations policy com.; dir. Reactive Metals, Inc., Mellon Nat. Bank & Trust Co. Trustee Children's Hosp. Pitts., Lehigh U.; chmn. bd. trustees U.S. Steel Found.; v.p., mem. exec. bd. Nat. Boy Scouts Am., mem. exec. bd. Allegheny Trails Council; mem. exec. com. Allegheny Conf. Community Devel.; bd. dirs. United Fund Allegheny County, Internat. Iron and Steel Inst., Am. Iron and Steel Inst., Pitts. Regional Planning Assn., Pitts. Urban Transit Council; trustee Carnegie-Mellon U., Nat. Safety Council, Automotive Safety Found. Mem. Newcomen Soc. N.Am., U.S. Naval Inst., Navy League U.S., Assn. Iron and Steel Engrs., Pa. Soc., Eastern States Blast Furnace and Coke Oven Assn., Western Pa. Engrs. Soc., Business Council, The Presidents. Clubs: Fox Chapel Golf, Pittsburgh Athletic Assn., Duquesne (Pitts.); Longue Vue Country (Verona, Pa.); Links (N.Y.); Laurel Valley Golf: Rolling Rock; Pine Valley Golf; Augusta (Ga.) Nat. Golf. Home: 213 Hampton Rd Fox Chapel Pittsburgh PA 15215 Office: 525 William Penn Pl Pittsburgh PA 15230

GOTT, RODNEY CLEVELAND, mfg. exec.; b. Bklyn., Sept. 11, 1911; s. Charles Cleveland Dodge and Florence Brush (Hutchinson) G.; B.S., U.S. Mil. Acad., 1933; m. Lydia Gilpin McAdam, Dec. 22, 1933; children—Peter Hartley, Rodney Cleveland, Alan Vaughn. Asst. to sales mgr. Am. Radiator & Standard San. Corp., N.Y.C., 1935-41; v.p. Am. Machine & Foundry Co., N.Y.C., 1946-54, exec. v.p., 1954-62, pres., 1962-70, chmn., 1968—; dir., chmn. exec. com., chmn. bd. dirs. and mgmt. all subsidiaries and divs. AMF Inc.; dir. Bulova Watch Co., Inc., Black & Decker Mfg. Co., Towson, Md., Asso. Diry Goods Corp.; trustee Franklin Savs. Bank. Trustee, Am. Mus. Natural History. Served as 2d lt., C.E., U.S. Army, 1933-35; col. with brig. gen. command F.A., 1941-46. Decorated Silver Star, Legion of Merit, Bronze Star with oak leaf cluster, Purple Heart; Croix de Guerre avec palme (France). Mem. Mil. Order Loyal Legion U.S., Army Ordnance Assn. Episcopalian. Clubs: Bedford (N.Y.) Golf and Tennis; Shenorock (Rye, N.Y.); Union League, The Links (N.Y.C.). Home: Sarles St Mt Kisco NY 10549

GOTT, VINCENT LYNN, physician; b. Wichita, Kan., Apr. 14, 1927; s. Henry Vivian and Helen (Lynn) G.; B.A., Wichita U., 1951; M.D., Yale, 1953; m. Iveagh Foreman, Sept. 4, 1954; children—Deborah Lynn, Kevin Douglas, Cameron Bradley, Intern U. Minn. Hosp., 1953-54; resident surgery U. Minn. Hosps., 1954-60; asst. prof. surgery U. Wis., 1960-65; asso. prof. surgery Johns Hopkins, 1965-68, prof., 1968—; cardiac surgeon in charge Johns Hopkins, Hosp., 1965—. Served with USNR, 1945-46. Recipient Hektoen gold medal, A.M.A., 1957; John and Mary R. Markle scholar, 1962. Fellow A.C.S.; mem. Am. Surg. Assn., Soc. Univ. Surgeons, Am. Assn. Thoracic Surgery, Soc. Thoracic Surgeons, Soc. Vascular Surgeons, Am. Heart Assn. Contbr. articles profl. jours. Co-developer Gott-Daggett artificial heart valve, 1963; developer graphite-benzalkonium-heparin coating for plastic surfaces. Home: 203 Kemble Rd Baltimore MD 21218

GOTTEHRER, BARRY, city ofcl., journalist; b. Bronx, N.Y., Jan. 25, 1935; s. Arthur and Hilda (Klein) G.; B.A., Brown U., 1956; M.S. in Journalism, Columbia, 1957; m. Judith Loeffler, Jan. 19, 1958 (div. Aug. 1967); children—Andrea Brett, Gregg. Copy and state legislative editor New Bedford (Mass.) Standard Times, 1958-59; asso. editor Sport Mag., 1959-60; press editor, also sports editor Newsweek mag., 1960-63; editor, also writer investigative series, New York City in Crisis, N.Y. Herald Tribune, 1964-65, columnist Inside New York, 1965; asst. to Mayor John Lindsay of N.Y.C., 1966-69, exec. asst. to mayor, 1970—, also chmn. Mayor's Urban Action Task Force, Mayor's Commn. on Youth; lectr. in journalism Columbia U., 1970—. Youth coordinator Pres.'s Council on Youth Opportunity. Served with AUS, 1957. Recipient Gold Typewriter award Newspaper Reporters Assn. N.Y., 1965; James Wright Brown award Deadline Club N.Y.C., 1965; Ralph Jonas award Urban Center, L.I. U., 1965; award Hundred Year Assn. N.Y.C., 1965; award City Club N.Y.C., 1965; Bronze medal Citizens Budget Commn., N.Y.C., 1966; George Polk Meml. award L.I.U., 1966. Mem. Mag. Sports Writers Assn. (pres. 1962), Am. Acad. Polit. and Social Sci. Jewish religion. Author: Football Stars of 1962, 1962; Basketball Stars of 1964, 1964; Football Stars of 1964, 1964; Giants of New York, 1964; New York City in Crisis, 1965. Contbr. nat. mags., annals. Home: 256 W 21st St New York City NY 10011 Office: City Hall New York City NY 10007

GOTTESMAN, ARTHUR EDWARD, lawyer; b. Hillside, N.J., July 29, 1937; s. Joseph J. and Sadonia (Herskowitz) G.; A.B., U. Chgo., 1954; LL.B., Yale, 1957; m. Allison Pierce Coudert, Apr. 22, 1963; children—Polly Moore, Catherine C. Admitted to N.Y. bar, 1959; with firm Coudert Bros., N.Y.C., 1959-62, partner, London (Eng.) office, 1962-70; partner Gottesman & Partners, 1970—. Asst. dir. Arden House Conf. Continuing Legal Edn., 1959. dir. Mattel, Ltd. Fellow Assn. Bar City N.Y. (staff sec. spl. com. fed. conflict-of-interest laws, 1958-59, sec. spl. com. study commitment procedures, 1960-62); mem. Am. Bar Assn., Am. Fgn. Law Assn. (sec.), Am. Soc. Internat. Law, Am. C. of C. U.K. (dir., chmn. legislative com.), Soc. Italic Handwriting; hon. mem. Law Soc. (London). Co-author: The Association of the Bar of the City of New York, 1958; also articles. Club: Reform (London). Home: 25A Bryanston Sq London W 1 England Office: Aldwych House Aldwych London W C 2 England

GOTTFRIED, KURT, physicist, educator; b. Vienna, Austria, May 17, 1929; s. Salomon and Augusta (Werner) G.; B.Eng., McGill U., 1951, M.S., 1952; Ph.D., Mass. Inst. Tech., 1955; m. Sorel B. Dickstein, June 26, 1955; children-David M., Laura S. Came to U.S., 1952, naturalized, 1965. Jr. fellow Soc. Fellows, Harvard, 1955-58; research fellow Inst. Theoretical Physics, Copenhagen, 1958-59; research fellow Harvard, 1959-60, asst. prof. physics, 1960-64; asso. prof. physics Cornell U., Ithaca, N.Y., 1964-68, prof. physics, 1968—. Mem. Am. Phys. Soc. author: Quantum Mechanics, 1966. Address: Lab Nuclear Studies Cornell U Ithaca NY 14850

GOTTLIEB, ABRAHAM MITCHELL, hosp. dir., physician; b. Chgo., Feb. 22, 1909; s. Michael and Frieda (Mantus) G.; B.S., U. Ill., 1930, M.D., 1934; m. Florence Handelman, May 23, 1934; children—Joel David, Judith Ann (Mrs. Harry Givelber). Mem. house staff Cook County Hosp., Chgo., 1933-35; staff physician Hines (Ill.) VA Hosp., 1937-38; internist VA Hosp., Tuscaloosa, Ala., 1938-39; chief cardiologist VA Hosp., Wood, Wis., 1939-42; chief cardiology, dir. profl. services, cons. internal medicine VA Hosp., Dearborn, Mich., 1946- 59; hosp. dir. VA Hosp., Madison, Wis., 1959-68, VA Hosp., Palo Alto, Cal., 1968—; from instr. to asso. prof. medicine Wayne State U. Med. Sch., 1946-59; from asso. prof. to prof. medicine U. Wis. Med. Sch., 1959-68; prof. medicine Stanford Med. Sch., 1968—. Served as med. officer U.S. Army, 1935-37; served to col. USAAF, 1942-46. Decorated Bronze Star. Diplomate Am. Bd. Internal Medicine. Fellow A.C.P.; mem. A.M.A., Assn. Mil. Surgeons U.S., Am. Physicians Art Assn. (pres. 1971—), Omicron Alpha Tau (nat. v.p. 1935), Phi Delta Epsilon. Contbr. articles to profl. jours. Home: 611 Willow Rd Menlo Park CA 94025 Office: 3801 Miranda Av Palo Alto CA 94304

GOTTLIEB, ADOLPH, artist; b. N.Y.C., Mar. 14, 1903; s. Emil and Elsie (Berger) G.; studied in Europe, 1921-22, m. Esther Dick, June 12, 1932. One-man shows various pvt. galleries, 1930—; executed mural Post Office, Yerrington, Nev., 1939; ten- year retrospective exhbn. Bennington Coll., Williams Coll., 1954; retrospective exhbn. Jewish Mus., 1957; exhbns. Paris, 1947, 52, 59, Tokyo, 1952, London, 1959; designer Ark curtains Congregation B'nai Israel, Millburn, N.J., 1952, Congregation Beth El, Springfield, Mass., 1953; designer stained glass facade Park Av. Synagogue, N.Y.C., 1954; one-man shows at Guggenheim Mus., Whitney Mus. Am. Art; represented permanent collections Met. Mus. Art, Mus. Modern Art, Whitney Mus. Am. Art, Tel Aviv Mus., Bklyn. Mus., U. Neb., Soc. Four Arts, Isaac Dalgado Mus., Smith Coll., Guggenheim Found., U. Miami, Detroit Inst., others. Winner mural award for Nev., U.S. Treasury competition, 1939, first prize Bklyn. Soc. Artists, 1944; purchase award U. Ill., 1951; Carnegie Internat. 3d prize, 1961; Grand Prix, Sao Paulo Bienal, 1963. Home: 27 W 96th St New York City NY 10025 Studio: 380 W Broadway New York City NY 10013

GOTTLIEB, JACQUES S., physician; b. Trinidad, Colo., Feb. 2, 1907; s. David Hart and Sara (Sanders) G.; student State U. Colo., 1923-25; B.S., Harvard, 1928, M.D., 1932; m. Helen Mae White, Dec. 19, 1934; children—Marilyn Lee, Jacquelyn, David. Clin. asst. psychiatry, 1932-33; asst. internist Worcester (Mass.) State Hosp., 1933-34, asst. internist Meml. Found. Neuro-Endocrine Research, 1935; intern Worcester Hahnemann Hosp., 1935-36; resident psychiatry Psychopathic Hosp., Iowa City, 1936-37, asst. physician, chief outpatient dept., 1937- 40, sr. physician, 1940-41, asst. dir., 1941-53; asso. psychiatry U. Ia., 1937-40, asst. prof. psychiatry, 1940-43, asso. prof. psychiatry, 1943-47, prof. psychiatry, 1947-53; chmn. dept. psychiatry and neurology U. Miami (Fla.), 1953-55, prof. psychiatry, 1953-55; dir. inst. Jackson Meml. Hosp., Miami, 1953-55; dir. Lafayette Clinic, Mich. Dept. Mental Health, Detroit, 1955—; prof. psychiatry Coll. Medicine, Wayne State U., 1955- -, also chmn. dept.; med. adv. council VA, 1962-66. Mem. tng. com. Nat. Inst. Mental Health, 1956-59, mem. program-project com., 1961-64. Recipient Gold medal Soc. Biol. Psychiatry, 1969. Diplomate Nat. Bd. Med. Examiners, Am. Bd. Psychiatry and Neurology (dir. 1959-66, v.p. 1965, pres. 1966). Mem. A.M.A., Am. Psychiat. Assn. (council 1957-60, exec. com. 1959-60), Am. Acad. Psychoanalysis, Am. Psychosomatic Soc., A.A.A.S. (council 1954). Mich. Soc. Neurology and Psychiatry (pres. 1962-63), Mich., Wayne County med. socs., Alpha Omega Alpha. Author numerous articles. Home: 1712 Lafayette Towers W Detroit MI Office: 951 E Lafayette St Detroit MI 48207

GOTTLIEB, JAMES E., dept. stores co. exec.; b. Mpls., 1924; B.S., U. Minn., LL.B., 1949; married. Admitted to Minn. bar; exec. v.p. Equity Capital Co., 1950-66; with Gamble-Skogmo Inc., Mpls., 1968—, sr. v.p. real estate, 1969—; dir. Red Owl Stores, Inc., Gamble Alden Life Ins. Co. Home: 1654 Pinehurst St St Paul MN 55116 Office: 5100 Gamble Dr Minneapolis MN 55416*

GOTTLIEB, LEO, lawyer, b. N.Y.C., June 21, 1896; Ph.B., Yale, 1915; LL.B., Harvard, 1920; m. Tekla Picard Landauer, Nov. 23, 1922; children —Elinor Carol, Leo (dec.). Admitted to N.Y. Bar, 1921; asso. Root, Clark, Buckner & Howland, N.Y.C., 1920-25, partner of firm and successor firms, 1925-46, Cleary, Gottlieb, Friendly & Cox, N.Y.C. and sucessor firm Cleary, Gottlieb, Steen & Hamilton, 1946—; dir. Sci. Am., Inc., Midland Capital Corp., Newsday, Inc.; mem. N.Y. adv. com. Anglo-Lautaro Nitrate Corp. Mem. N.Y. Co. Lawyers Assn. (past pres., dir.). Home: 120 E 81st St New York City NY 10028 Office: 52 Wall St New York City NY 10005

GOTTLIEB, LEWIS, banker; b. Baton Rouge, Aug. 11, 1894; s. Joe and Rebecca (Hahn) G.; A.B., La. State U., 1913, LL.B. with honors, 1916. Admitted to La. bar, 1916; v.p. City Nat. Bank of Baton Rouge, 1934-46, pres., 1946-57, chmn. bd., 1957—; sec., dir. Lottie Land & Devel. Co., Inc.; pres., dir. Baton Rouge Realty Co., Ltd., Standard Motors, Inc.; dir. Pan-Am. Life Ins. Co., New Orleans br. Fed. Res. Bank, Atlanta. Past pres. United Givers Fund of Greater Baton Rouge; mem. nat. budget com. United Community Funds and Councils Am., Nat. Social Welfare Assembly, 1954—. Mem. bd. suprs. La. State U. A. and M. Coll., Baton Rouge, 1939-40, 50-58, chmn., 1954-56; trustee Delgado Mus. Art, New Orleans. Recipient Brandeis award, 1960, Golden Deeds award, 1960, Brotherhood award Nat. Conf. Christians and Jews, 1963. Mem. La. Bankers Assn. (pres. 1955-56), Baton Rouge C. of C. (pres. 1932-34), La. State U. Alumni Fedn. (pres. 1931-35), Tau Kappa Alpha, Phi Kappa Phi, Omicron Delta Kappa, Zeta Beta Tau (Man of Year award 1963). Home: 714 Drehr Av Baton Rouge LA 70806 Office: 124 N 3d St Baton Rouge LA 70801

GOTTLIEB, MANUEL, educator; b. Grass Valley, Cal., Aug. 29, 1913; s. Samuel and Ethel (Spiegel) G.; B.A., U. Minn., 1937; M.A. in Econs., U. Cal. at Berkeley, 1941; Ph.D., Harvard, 1953; m. Margaret Rush, Oct. 2, 1944; children—Elizabeth (Mrs. David Kohlenberg), Deborah (Mrs. Larry Kent), Judith, Samuel. Wholesale rug and carpet salesman, 1938-41; with U.S. Govt., 1942-48; mem. faculty U. Wis.-Milw., 1959—, prof. econs., 1962- -, on leave as research prof. Econ. Research Bur., U. Dar Es Salaam, Tanzania, Africa, 1971—. Candicate for mayor in Milw. primary, 1967; chmn. platform com. Milwaukee County Democratic Party, 1962-65. Littauer fellow Harvard, 1950-52. Mem. Internat. Union Sci. Study Population. Author: The German Peace Settlement and the Berlin Crisis, 1960; also articles. Home: 3051 N Prospect St Milwaukee WI 53211

GOTTLIEB, MELVIN BURT, physicist; b. Chgo., May 25, 1917; s. Ezra Benjamin and Sara (Hotz) G.; B.S. in Math., U. Chgo., 1940, Ph.D., 1951; m. Golda Gehrman, June 26, 1948; children—Martha Ellen, Paula Gay. Mem. research staff radio research lab. Harvard, 1943-46; instr., then research asst. U. Chgo., 1946-50; asst. prof. physics Ia. State U., 1951-54; head exptl. physics project Matterhorn, Princeton, 1954-56, asso. dir. project, 1956-61, prof., dir. plasma physics lab., 1961—; spl. research cosmic rays, plasma physics. Mem. standing com. on controlled thermonuclear reactions AEC; mem. phys. sci. research evaluation group Air Force Office Sci. Research. Pres., Princeton Community Democratic Orgn. Bd. dirs. Council Community Services, Princeton, 1956-59. Fellow Am. Phys. Soc. (chmn. plasma physics div. 1959-60, mem. council, exec. com.); mem. Phi Beta Kappa, Sigma Xi. Home: 24 Lake Lane Princeton NJ 08540

GOTTLIEB, PHILIP MORRIS, allergist; b. Phila., Apr. 12, 1912; s. Paul and Bertha (Brav) G.; B.A. (Simon Muhr scholar 1928), U. Pa., 1932, M.D., 1935; m. Betty A. Fried, May 1, 1938 (div. Aug. 1964); children—Susan Lynne, Roberta Jo, James Joseph; m. 2d, Adele W. Bruner, Oct. 10, 1965. Intern, Phila. Gen. Hosp., 1935-37, asst. clinic physician, 1939-58; resident Childrens Seashore House, Atlantic City, 1937; med. resident Mt. Sinai Hosp., N.Y.C., 1938-39; practice medicine specializing in allergy, Phila., 1939—; asso. allergist Albert Einstein Med. Center, 1939-60, attending physician allergy sect., 1960—; allergist Kensington Hosp., 1949—; chief allergy Oxford Hosp., 1957-63; allergist Sidney Hillman Med. Center, 1951—, research coordinator, 1958-63 (all Phila.); regional cons. Jewish Nat. Home Asthmatic Children, Denver, 1956—; nat. physicians adv. bd. Nat. Jewish Hosp., Denver, 1960—; cons. allergist Deborah Sanitorium and Hosp., Browns Mills, N.J., 1951—, Moss Rehab. Hosp., Phila., 1961—; faculty U. Pa. Sch. Medicine, 1940-61, asso. medicine, 1950-61. Co-chmn. physicians div. Allied Jewish Appeal, Phila., 1960-63. Served to capt., M.C., AUS, 1943-46. Diplomate Am. Bd. Internal Medicine (allergy). Fellow Am. Coll. Allergists (pres. 1961-62), Am. Acad. Allergy, A.C.P. (life), Internat. Assn. Allergology (a founder); hon. mem. Asociacion Argentina de Alergia e Inmunologia; mem. Allergy Found. Am. (dir., exec. com.), Pa. Allergy Assn. (regent 1958-62, pres. 1963-64), Phila. Allergy Soc. (past pres.), A.M.A. (chmn. sect. on allergy 1964-66), Phi Beta Kappa, Alpha Omega Alpha. Mason; mem. B'nai B'rith (past trustee). Author: (with Dr. Erich Urbach) Allergy, 2d edit., 1946. Mem. editorial bds. jours. in field. Contbr. numerous articles. Home: 1242 Oliver Rd Huntingdon Valley PA 19006 Office: Medical Arts Bldg Philadelphia PA 19102

GOTTLIEB, ROBERT ADAMS, publisher; b. N.Y.C., Apr. 29, 1931; s. Charles and Martha (Keen) G.; B.A., Columbia, 1952; postgrad. Cambridge (Eng.) U., 1952-54; m. Maria Tucci, Apr. 26, 1969; children—Roger, Elizabeth. Editor-in-chief, v.p. Simon & Schuster, 1955-68; editor-in-chief, exec. v.p. Alfred A Knopf, Inc., N.Y.C., 1968—. Mem. Phi Beta Kappa. Home: 228 E 48th St New York City NY 10017 Office: 201 E 50th St New York City NY 10022

GOTTMANN, JEAN, geographer, educator; b. Kharkov, Russia, Oct. 10, 1915; s. Elie and Sonia (Ettinger) G.; Bacc. Lettres, U. Paris, 1932, D. Et. Sup. in History and Geography, 1934, Docteur es Lettres, 1970; LL.D., U. Wis., 1968; M.A, Oxford, 1968; D.Sc., So. Ill. U., 1969; m. Bernice Adelson, Aug. 11, 1957. Asst. dept. geography Sorbonne, Paris, 1937-40; several times mem. Inst. Advanced Study, Princeton, N.J., 1942-65; cons. Bd. Econ. Warfare, FEA, 1942-44; instr. Princeton, 1943; lectr., asso., then asso. prof. Johns Hopkins, 1943-48; adviser French Ministry of Nat. Economy, Paris, 1945-46; dir. studies and research, dept. social affairs UN, N.Y.C., 1946-47; research asso. Conseil National de la Recherche Scientifique, Paris, 1948-51; prof. Institut d'Etudes Politiques, U. Paris, 1948-60; prof. Ecole des Hautes Etudes, Paris, 1960—; prof. geogrpahy Oxford (Eng.) U., 1968—. Research dir. study of megalopolis Twentieth Century Fund, N.Y.C., 1956-61; vis. prof. Columbia, 1949, 56, U. Geneva (Switzerland), 1950, U. Durham (Eng.), 1951, Hebrew U., Jerusalem, 1956, U. Pitts., 1962, So. Ill. U., 1964, Laval U., 1964, U. Cal. at Berkeley, 1966, U. Wis.-Milw., 1968; fellow Hertford Coll., Oxford, Chmn. commn. on regional planning Internat. Geog. Union, 1949-52. Trustee Research Group European Migration Problems, The Hague, Netherlands. Recipient Charles P. Daly medal Am. Geog. Soc., 1964; Bonaparte-Wyse award Paris Geog. Soc., 1962. Fellow Royal Geog. Soc. (London); mem. Am. Geog. Soc., Assn. Am. Geographers, Regional Plan Assn. N.Y., Assn. de Geographes Francais, Assn. Francaise de Science Politique, Royal Netherlands Geog. Soc. (hon.). Author: A Geography of Europe, 1950; Virginia at Midcentury, 1955; Megalopolis, 1961, others. Office: Sch Geography Mansfield Rd Oxford England

GOTTSCHALK, ALFRED, coll. pres.; b. Oberwesel, Germany, Mar. 7, 1930; s. Max and Erna (Trum-Gerson) G.; A.B., Bklyn. Coll., 1952; B.H.Lit., Hebrew Union Coll.-Jewish Inst. Religion, 1957, M.A. with honors, 1957; Ph.D., U. So. Cal., 1965, S.T.D. (hon.), 1968, D.H.L. (hon.), 1971; m. Jeannie Schrag, June 28, 1953; children—Marc Hillel, Rachel Lisa. Came to US., 1939, naturalized, 1945. Rabbi, 1957; mem. faculty, adminstr. Hebrew Union Coll.-Jewish Inst. Religion, Los Angeles, 1957—, prof. Bible and Jewish religious thought, 1965—, pres. coll., 1971—. Mem. interreligious inst. Loyola U., Los Angeles, 1965—; mem. Mayor's Community Devel. Adv. Com., Los Angeles, 1965—, Pres.'s Com. on Equal Employment Opportunity, 1964—, Gov.'s Poverty Support Corps Program, 1964-66, Community Redevel. Agy. Adv. Bd., 1965—. State Dept. research grantee, 1963, Guggenheim fellow, 1967, 69. Mem. Am. Civil Liberties Union, Union Am. Hebrew Congregations and Central Conf. Am-Rabbis (trustee), Am. Assn. U. Profs., N.E.A., Soc. Sco. Study Religion, Am. Acad. Religion Soc-Bibl. Lit and Exgens.s, Internat. Conf. Jewish Communal Service, Western Israel Exploration Soc., So. Cal. Assn. Liberal Rabbis (past pres.), So. Cal. Jewish Hist. Soc. (v.p.), World Union Jewish Studies, Am. Jewish Com., (exec. com.), Jewish Fedn. Council Greater Los Angeles, World Union Progressive Judiasm (v.p.). Author: Your Future As A Rabbi-A Calling that Counts, 1967; Hesed in the Bible, 1967; The Future of Human Community, 1967; The Man Must be the Message, 1968. Home: 10563 Holman Av Los Angeles CA 90046

GOTTSCHALK, CARL WILLIAM, physician, educator; b. Salem, Va., Apr. 28, 1922; s. Carl and Lula (Helbig) G.; B.S., Roanoke Coll., 1942, Sc.D., 1966; M.D., U. Va., 1945; m. Helen Marie Scott, Nov. 22, 1947; children—Carl S., Walter P., Karen E. Intern, asst. resident, resident in medicine Mass. Gen. Hosp., Boston, 1945-52; research fellow physiology Harvard, 1948-50; fellow U. N.C. Med. Sch., Chapel Hill, 1952-53, faculty, 1953—, Kenan prof. medicine and physiology, 1969—; established investigator Am. Heart Assn., 1957-61, career investigator, 1961; Bowditch lectr., 1960; Harvey lectr., 1962. Mem. physiology study sect. NIH, 1961-65; mem. research career award com. Nat. Inst. Gen. Med. Scis., 1965-69, mem. physiology tng. com., 1970—; chmn. com. chronic kidney disease Bur. Budget, 1966-67; adv. com. biol. and med. scis. NSF, 1967-69, vice chmn. 1968, chmn., 1969. Pres. Children's Theatre N.C., 1967-68. Served to capt., M.C., AUS, 1946-48. Recipient N.C. award, 1967, Modern Medicine Distinguished Achievement award, 1966, Horsley Meml. prize U. Va., 1956, Homer W. Smith award N.Y. Heart Assn., 1970. Mem. Assn. Am. Physicians, Am. Physiol. Soc., Am. Soc. Clin. Investigation, Am. Clin. and Climatol. Assn., Soc. Exptl. Biology and Medicine, A.C.P., Am. Assn. U. Profs., Am. Acad. Arts and Scis., Phi Beta Kappa, Sigma Xi. Author papers on physiology of kidney. Home: 1300 Mason Farm Rd Chapel Hill NC 27514

GOTTSCHALK, CHARLES MAX, librarian, govt. ofcl.; b. Bochum, Germany, Feb. 2, 1928; s. Josef and Elsbeth (Ermeler) G.; came to U.S., 1941, naturalized, 1949; B.E.S. in Physics, Cleve. State U., 1950; M.A., Pa. State U., 1951; M.S. in L.S., Catholic U., 1966; m. Marianne Ida Besser, Dec. 24, 1948; children—Diane Linda, Leslie Anne, Research analyst Library of Congress, 1951-54, phys. sci. adminstr., head reference sect., sci. and tech. div., 1956-62, chief stack and reader div., 1962, head systems identification and analysis sect., 1962-63; instrumentation physicist Nat. Bur. Standards 1954-56; information systems specialist AEC, 1963-66, dir. libraries, 1966-69; sr. officer Internat. Atomic Energy Agency, Vienna, Austria, 1969—. Lectr. Dept. Agr. Grad. Sch., 1964—; cons. Arctic Inst. N.Am., 1954-59; research asst. Ohio State U., 1958-59; exec. sec. operating com. Fed. Council Sci. and Tech. Com. on Sci. and Tech. Information, 1965, exec. sec. panel edn. and tng., 1965-66, mem. panel information scis. and tech., 1966—, mem. nuclear cross sect. adv. group, 1965—. Served with AUS, 1946-47, USMCR, 1947-49. NSF grantee, 1961-62. Mem. Am. Nuclear Soc., Am. Phys. Soc., A.A.A.S., Am. Soc. Information Sci., N.Y. Acad. Scis., Am. Soc. Metals, Beta Phi Mu. Author articles, monographs. Office: Internat Atomic Energy Agy 1011 Vienna Austria

GOTTSCHALK, HANS W., educator; b. Berlin, Germany, Dec. 31, 1914; s. Richard and Margaret (Dittmann) G.; came to U.S., 1923, naturalized, 1936; B.A., N.Y.U., 1941, M.A., 1943; Ph.D., U. Ia., 1949; m. Anna Elizabeth Schmelzle, Nov. 20, 1941. Asst. head sales order dept. Am. Bemberg Corp. and N.Am. Raye Corp., N.Y.C., 1936-43; Eastern office mgr. Ill. Zinc Co., N.Y.C., 1943- 45; instr. English dept. Ohio State U., 1947-50; asst. prof. Wis. State Coll., Eau Claire, 1950-53; sr. tchr. New Lincoln Sch., N.Y.C., 1954; asst. prof. Duquesne U., 1954-55; asso. prof., prof. English, chmn. dept. State U. N.Y., Geneseo, 1955—. Cons. English linguistics project U.S. Office Edn., State U. N.Y., Buffalo, 1963-65; dir. Nat. Def. Edn. Act Insts. in English, 1966, 68, evaluator proposals Instns. in English, 1966-67. Fellow N.Y. State English Council; mem. Am. Assn. U. Profs., Nat. Council Tchrs. English (dir.), Nat. Soc. Study Communication, Linguistic Soc. Am., Modern Lang. Assn., Kappa Delta Pi, Phi Delta Kappa. Democrat. Roman Catholic. Contbr. articles to profl. jours. Home: 16 Main St Geneseo NY 14454

GOTTSCHALK, JOHN SIMISON, govt. ofcl.; b. Berne, Ind., Sept. 27, 1912; s. Thurman Arthur and Nellie Louise (Simison) G.; A.B. in Biology, Earlham Coll., 1934, LL.D., 1966; M.A. in Zoology, Ind. U., 1943; m. Edith E. Liechty, Apr. 17, 1937; children—Sara Nell (Mrs. George W. Davis VI), Thomas Andrew. With Ind. Dept. Conservation, 1930-41, supt. fisheries, 1937-41; with U.S. Fish and Wildlife Service, 1945—, chief div. fisheries Bur. Sport Fisheries and Wildlife, 1957-59, dir. N.E. region, Boston, 1959-64, dir., Washington, 1964-69, asst. to dir. Nat. Marine Fisheries Service, Dept. Commerce, 1969—. Recipient Nash Conservation award Am. Motor Co., 1955. Mem. Am. Fisheries Soc. (v.p. 1941, 62-63, pres. 1963-64), Wildlife Soc. (past v.p.), Am. Inst. Biol. Scis., Sigma Xi. Home: 4664 34th St N Arlington VA 22207 Office: Dept Commerce Washington DC 20235

GOTTSCHALK, LOUIS, educator; b. Bklyn., Feb. 21, 1899; s. Morris Frank and Anna (Krystall) G.; A.B., Cornell U., 1919; A.M., 1920, Ph.D., 1921; D.Litt. (hon.), Augustana Coll., 1954; Doctor honoris causa, U. Toulouse (France), 1957; D.H.L., Hebrew Union Coll., 1963; LL.D., U. Louisville, 1960; m. 2d, Fruma Kasdan, Dec. 16, 1930; children—Alexander, Paul Abo. Asst. in history Cornell U., 1919; instr. history U. Ill., 1921-23; asst. prof. history U. Louisville, 1923-25, asso. prof., 1925-27; asso. prof. modern history U. Chgo., 1927-35, prof., 1935-59, Gustavus F. and Ann M. Swift Distinguished Service professor, 1959-64, prof. emeritus, 1964—, chmn. dept. history, 1937-42; vis. prof. U. Ill., Chgo. Circle, 1966—, asso. dir. honors program, 1968—; summer apptmts. univs.; Fulbright Distinguished lectr., Japan, 1968. Pres. Chgo. Bd. Jewish Edn., 1942-45; chmn. B'nai B'rith Hillel Commn. 1963-69, hon. chmn., 1969- -. Col. a.d.c. to gov. of N.M., 1966—. Apprentice seaman, USNRF, 1918. AAF Com. Historians, 1943-44. Mem. Social Sci. Research Council, 1955-63. Fellow Center for Advanced Study Behavioral Scis., 1957-58. Mem. Am. Hist. Assn. (pres. 1953), Am. Assn. Univ. Profs., Am. Friends of Lafayette (exec. com.), Am. Acad. of Arts and Scis., Am. Philos. Soc., Société des Etudes Robespierristes, Société d'Histoire Moderne, Conf. on Jewish Relations (mem. council), Am. Council Learned Socs. (vice chmn. 1965-67), Phi Beta Kappa, Zeta Beta Tau (hon.). Recipient Guggenheim fellowship, 1928-29, 54-55; medal of merit Union Fédérale des Anciens Combattants de France, 1938; Princeton Bicentennial Medal, 1946; Newberry Library fellowship, 1946; U. Louisville Sesquicentennial, 1948; James H. Hyde Prize, 1948; Chevalier Legion of Honor, 1953; Fulbright research award, 1954-55, 68; award by Am. Council Learned Societies, 1959. Club: Quadrangle. Author books including: The Letters of Lafayette to Washington, 1945; Lafayette between the American and the French Revolution (1783-1789), 1950; Understanding History, 1950, 2d edit., 1969. Editor: Generalization in the Writing of History, 1963. Author, editor: Vol. IV UNESCO Scientific and Cultural History of Mankind. Co-author publs. including: Europe and the Modern World, 2 vols. 1951-54; Lafayette in the French Revolution, 1969; contbr. articles to mags. Asst. editor Jour. Modern History, 1929-43, acting editor, 1943-45; asso. editor several hist. periodicals. Participant in radio and public forums. Home: 5551 University Av Chicago IL 60637 ☆

GOTTSCHALK, WALTER HELBIG, mathematician, educator; b. Lynchburg, Va., Nov. 3, 1918; s. Carl and Lula (Helbig) G.; B.S., U. Va., 1939, M.A., 1942, Ph.D. in Math., 1944; M.A. (hon.), Wesleyan U., Middletown, Conn., 1964; m. Margaret Hemsworth, Aug. 27, 1952; children—Heather, Steven. From instr. to prof. math. U. Pa., 1944-63, chmn. dept., 1955-58; prof. math. Wesleyan U., 1963—, chmn. dept., 1964-69, 70-71. Mem. Inst. Advanced Study, Princeton, 1947- 48; research asso. Yale, 1960-61. Mem. Am. Math. Soc. (asso. editor proc. 1954-56, asso. sec. for East 1971—), Math. Assn. Am., Soc. Indsl. and Applied Math., Am. Assn. U. Profs., Phi Beta Kappa, Sigma Xi. Democrat. Unitarian. Author: (with G.A. Hedlund) Topological Dynamics, 1955. Mem. editorial bd. Math. Systems Theory, 1967—. Contbr. articles to profl. jours. Home: 41 Bretton Rd Middletown CT 06457

GOTTSCHALL, EDWARD MAURICE, assn. exec.; b. N.Y.C., Dec. 28, 1915; s. Myer and Stephanie (Kraus) G.; B.S., Coll. City N.Y., 1937; M.S., Columbia, 1938; m. Lee Beatrice Natale, Feb. 6, 1943; 1 son, Robert J. Mng. editor Graphic Arts Prodn. Yearbook, Colton Press, 1937-51; editor, Art Direction, 1952-69; sr. editor Popular Merchandising Co., Passaic, N.J., 1964-67; co-pub., editorial dir. Advt. Trade Publs., Inc., 1967-69; exec. dir. Am. Inst. Graphic Arts, N.Y.C., 1969—; lectr. Pratt Inst. Evening Art Sch., 1947-64, N.Y. U., 1955-64. Served with USAAF, 1942-45; ETO. Mem. Type Dirs. Club (past pres.; Spl. award, 1963), Phi Delta Pi. Mason. Author: (with F.C. Rodewald) Commercial Art As A Business, 3d edit., 1972. Co-editor: Advertising Directions, vols. 1-4, 1960-64. Editor Typographic i, 1969—. Home: 2504 Pine Grove Ct Yorktown Heights NY 10598 Office: 1059 3d Av New York City NY 10021

GOTTSCHALL, MORTON univ. dean; b. N.Y.C., Oct. 16, 1894; s. Edward and Miriam (Spillenger) G.; A.B., Coll. City N.Y., 1913; J.D., N.Y.U., 1917; m. Frances Greenfield, Oct. 16, 1947. With City U. N.Y., 1913—, successively asst. tutor and tutor, instr. in history 1918-23, asst. prof., 1923-29, asso. prof., 1928-33, prof., 1933—, dean Coll. of Liberal Arts and Sci., 1934—, served as recorder, 1919-34, also taught classes in business law and legal philos.; pres. Student Houses at City Coll., Inc., 1936-55; v.p. City Coll. Press. 1949—; sec. of City Coll. Fund, 1953—. Mem. Acad. Polit. Sci., Am. Acad. Polit. and Social Sci., Am. Assn. Univ. Profs., City Coll. Alumni Assn. (pres. 1955-57), Phi Beta Kappa. Club: City College. Home: 430 W 24th St New York City NY

GOTTSDANKER, ROBERT M., educator, psychologist; b. Los Angeles, Mar. 25, 1917; s. Theodore and Elizabeth (Levitan) G.; A.B., U. Cal. at Berkeley, 1938, Ph.D., 1941; m. Josephine Schlatter, May 22, 1945; children—Gerald Lee, Anne Elizabeth. Personnel research technician Social Security Bd., 1941-42; instr. psychology George Washington U., 1942-43; job analyst Kaiser Corp., 1943- 44; research asso. Nat. Def. Research Com., 1944-45 from instr. to asst. prof. psychology Tufts Coll., 1946-49; now prof. psychology U. Cal. at Santa Barbara, chmn. dept., 1955-60, 64-65. Grant cons. NSF. Fellow Am. Psychol. Assn.; mem. Psychonomic Soc., Phi Beta Kappa. Cons. editor Jour. Engring. Psychology, Jour. Motor Behavior; editorial cons. Psychonomic Sci., Perception and Psychophysics. Home: 282 Loma Media Rd Santa Barbara CA 93103

GOTTSHALL, RALPH KERR, chem. mfg. co. exec.; b. Landsale, Pa., Dec. 31, 1905; s. Harvey S. and Alice (Kerr) G.; B.S. magna cum laude, Lafayette Coll., 1927, D.Sc., 1959; m. Lorraine Lively, Sept. 4, 1929. With Atlas Chem. Industries, Inc., 1927—, dir. sales, 1943-48, asst. gen. mgr. explosives dept., 1948-50, v.p. and dir., 1951-52, exec. v.p., dir., 1952, pres., 1953-58, chmn. bd., pres., 1958-66, chmn. bd., 1966-71; dir. I.C.I. Am., Allegheny Corp., Alan Wood Steel Co., Diamond State Telephone Co., News-Jour. Co. Mem. Nat. Indsl. Conf. Bd. Vice chmn. bd. dirs. Wilmington (Del.) Med. Center; life trustee, chmn. bd. trustees Lafayette Coll. Mem. Mfg. Chemists Assn. (past dir.), Am. Mining Congress, Phi Beta Kappa Alpha Chi Sigma, Kappa Phi Kappa, Kappa Delta Rho. Clubs: University (N.Y.C.); Wilmington, Wilmington Country; Lusby (Md.); Chesapeake Country. Home: 1004 Barley Mill Rd Westover Hills Wilmington DE 19806 Office: Atlas Chem Industries Inc Wilmington DE 19899

GOTTWALD, BRUCE COBB, chem. co. exec.; b. Richmond, Ind., Sept. 28, 1933; s. Floyd Dewey and Anne Ruth (Cobb) G.; B.S., Va. Mil. Inst., 1954; postgrad. U. Va., Inst. Paper Chemistry, Appleton, Wis.; m. Nancy Hays, Dec. 22, 1956; children—Bruce Cobb, Mark Hays, Thomas Edward. With Albemarle Paper Mfg. Co., 1956—, v.p., sec. parent co. Ethyl Corp., 1962-64, exec. v.p., sec., 1964-70, pres., dir., 1970—, dir. First Mchts. Corp. Trustee Randolph Macon Woman's Coll.; bd. govs. St. Christophers Sch. Clubs: Chemists (N.Y.C.); Commonwealth (Richmond). Home: 4502 Coventry Rd Richmond VA 23221 Office: 330 S 4th St Richmond VA 23219

GOTTWALD, FLOYD DEWEY, corp. exec.; b. Richmond, Va., May 22, 1898; s. William H. and Mary A. Gottwald; student William and Mary Coll.; m. Anna Cobb, Nov. 17, 1920; children—Floyd Dewey, Bruce Cobb. Asst. paymaster Richmond Fredericksburg & Potomac R.R. Co., 1917-18; with Albemarle Paper Co., Richmond, 1918—, successivley export mgr., asst. sec., sec., prodn. mgr., v.p., exec. v.p., chmn. bd., now chmn. com.; dir. Ethyl Corp. Trustee U. Richmond. Mem. Richmond C. of C. Baptist. Mason. Clubs: Commonwealth, Country of Virginia. Home: 3907 Sulgrave Rd Richmond VA 23221 Office: 330 S 4th St Richmond VA 23217

GOTTWALD, FLOYD DEWEY, Jr., chem. co. exec.; b. Richmond, Va., July 29, 1922; s. Floyd Dewey and Ann (Cobb) G.; B.S., Va. Mil. Inst., 1943; M.S., U. Richmond, 1951; m. Elizabeth Morris Shelton, Mar. 22, 1947; children—William M., James T., John D. With Albemarle Paper Co., Richmond, 1943—, sec., 1956- 57, v.p., sec., 1957-62, pres., 1962—, also dir.; exec. v.p. Ethyl Corp., 1962-64, vice chmn., now chmn.; dir. Va. Commonwealth Bankshares, Inc., Seaboard Coast Line R.R. Co. Mem. Port Adv. Commn., Richmond, 1963—. Served to 1st lt. AUS, 1943-46. Decorated Bronze Star medal, Purple Heart. Mem. Va. Inst. Sci. Research (trustee), T.A.P.P.I., Paper Industry Mgmt. Assn., Am. Petroleum Inst. Home: Herndon Herndon Rd Richmond VA 23229 Office: 330 S 4th St Richmond VA 23217

GOTWALS, CHARLES PLACE, Jr., lawyer; b. Muskogee, Okla., May 19, 1917; s. Charles Place and Anna M. (Koehler) G.; A.B. U. Okla., 1938, LL.B. 1940; m. Mary Frances Brownlee, Jan. 31, 1948; children—Charles William, James Robert, Frances Ann, Virginia Hunt. Admitted to Okla. bar, 1940, since practiced in Tulsa; partner firm Gable, Gotwals, Hays, Rubin & Fox, 1960—; gen. counsel, dir. 4th Nat. Bank Tulsa, 1958—; counsel, dir. sec. Conard Investment Co.; gen. counsel, dir. Mid Continent Casualty Co., Quaker Life Ins. Co., Okla. Surety Co. Served to maj. AUS, 1942-46; ETO. Decorated Bronze Star medal. Mem. Am., Tulsa County (sec. 1949), Okla. bar assns., Am. Judicature Soc., Order of Coif, Phi Beta Kappa, Phi Delta Phi, Beta Theta Pi. Episcopalian (vestryman, jr. warden 1956-60). Kiwanian (pres. 1961). Clubs: Tulsa, Summit. Home: 1108 Woodward Blvd Tulsa OK 74114 Office: 4th Nat Bldg Tulsa OK 74119

GOTWALS, VERNON DETWILER, Jr., musician, educator; b. Conshohocken, Pa., Nov. 12, 1924; s. Vernon Detwiler and Helen (Jones) G.; student Drew U., 1941-43; A.B., Amherst Coll., 1947; M.F.A., Princeton, 1951; m. Carol Joyce, June 13, 1953; children—Frank, Thomas, Philip. Instr. music Princeton, 1951-52; faculty Smith Coll., Northampton, Mass., 1952—, prof. music, 1966—, chmn. dept., 1962-68, 71—. Served with AUS, 1943-45. Mem. Am. Assn. U. Profs., Music Library Assn., Am. Musicol. Soc., Am. Guild Organists, Phi Beta Kappa. Author: (with Philip Keppler) La Sfera armoniosa of Paolo Quagliati, 1957, Brahms's Folk Songs for Women's Voices, 1968; Joseph Haydn, 18th Century Gentleman and Genius, 1963. Home: 45 Washington Av Northampton MA 01060

GOTZES, HUBERT RICHARD, publishing co. exec.; b. Chgo., May 29, 1926; s. Hubert and Werra (von Puttkamer) G.; B.S.C., Loyola U., Chgo., 1951; m. Jane M. Lawson, Nov. 16, 1957. With R.R. Donnelley & Sons Co., Chgo., 1947—, exec. sales dept., 1958-59, v.p. sales, 1959-67, v.p., div. dir. Warsaw (Ind.) mfg. div., 1967-68, v.p., staff asst. to pres., 1968-69, sr. v.p., 1969—. Served with USNR, 1944-46. Clubs: Chicago Yacht, Caxton (Chgo.). Home: 3035 Indian Wood Wilmette IL 60091 Office: 2223 South Pkwy Chicago IL 60616

GOUDGE, ELIZABETH DE BEAUCHAMP, Brit. author; b. Somerset, Eng., Apr. 24, 1900; d. Henry Leighton and Ida de Beauchamp (Collenette) Goudge; student Art Sch. of Reading U. Eng., 1920-22; unmarried. Handicraft tchr., 1922; profl. writer 1932—. Fellow Royal Soc. Lit.; mem. P.E.N. Club. Mem. Ch. of Eng. Author: Island Magic, 1932; Middle Window, 1933; City of Bells, 1934; Pedlar's Pack, 1935; Towers in the Mist, 1936; Three Plays, 1937; Sister of the Angels, 1938; The Bird in the Tree, 1940; Smoky-House, 1940; The Golden Skylark, 1941; The Castle-on-the-Hill, 1941; The Blue Hills, 1942; Green Dolphin Street, 1944 (chosen by the Lit. Guild, U.S.A., winner Metro-Goldwyn-Mayer prize); The Little White Horse (juvenile); winner Carnegie medal (Eng.); Pilgrims Inn (Lit. Guild selection); God So Loved the World; Gentian Hill; The Valley of Song (juvenile); The Heart of the Family; The Rosemary Tree, 1956; The White Witch, 1957; My God and My All, 1959; The Dean's Watch, 1960; The Scent of Water, 1963; A Book of Comfort, 1964; A Diary of Prayer, 1966; Book of Peace, 1967; Christmas Book 1967; Child From the Sea, 1970. Address: Rose Cottage Peppard Common Henley-on-Thames England

GOUDGE, MONSON FRASER, mining engr.; b. Windsor, N.S., Can., Apr. 15, 1895; s. Michael Grant and Grace Stewart (Dakin) G.; B.A., King's Coll., 1916, D.C.L., 1959; B.S., N.S. Tech. Coll., 1921, D.Eng., 1962; m. Alice Muriel Piggott, Oct. 23, 1930; children—Margaret (Mrs. Robert Malcolm Black), Michael Grant. Research on petroleum Imperial Oil, Ltd., Halifax, N.S., 1921-23; with Dept. Mines, Ottawa, Ont., 1923-58, chief indsl. minerals div., 1946-58; pvt. cons. practice indsl. minerals, 1958—. Served with arty. Canadian Army, 1916-19. Recipient Gold medal Profl. Inst. Pub. Service Can., 1942; McCharles prize and medal U. Toronto, 1957. Mem. Canadian Inst. Mining and Metallurgy (life, Selwyn A. Blaylock Gold medal 1953, chmn. indsl. minerals div.), Am. Inst. Mining, Metall. and Petroleum Engrs. (Hal Williams Hardinge award 1967, dir. Soc. Mining Engrs., chmn. indsl. minerals div.), Profl. Engrs. Ont. Mem. United Ch. of Can. Clubs: Rideau Curling, Royal Ottawa Golf. Contbr. articles to profl. jours. Patentee in field. Address: 208 4th Av Ottawa Ontario Canada K1S 2L8

GOUDSMIT, SAMUEL ABRAHAM, physicist, editor; b. The Hague, Netherlands, July 11, 1902; s. Isaac and Marianne (Gompers) G.; student U. Amsterdam; Ph.D., U. Leiden (Netherlands), 1927; D.Sc., Case Inst. Tech., 1958; m. Jaantje Logher, Jan. 19, 1927 (div. 1960); 1 dau., Esther Marianne; m. 2d, Irene Bejach Rothschild, 1960. Came to U.S., 1927. Faculty U. Mich., 1927, prof. physics, 1932-46; Rockefeller fellow, 1926, Guggenheim fellow, 1938; vis. prof. Harvard U., 1941; prof. physics Northwestern U., 1946- 48; vis. prof. Rockefeller U., 1955—; on leave to Radiation (Radar) Lab. Mass. Inst. Tech. and Eng., 1942-46; sr. scientist Brookhaven Nat. Lab., 1948-70; editor-in-chief Am. Phys. Soc., 1951—. Detailed to War Dept. as chief sci. intelligence mission in Europe, 1944-45. Decorated Medal of Freedom, officer Order of Brit. Empire; recipient Research Corp. Sci. award, 1954; Max Planck medal German Phys. Soc., 1965. Fellow Am. Phy. Soc., Netherlands Phys. Soc., Nat. Acad. Scis., Am. Nuclear Soc.; mem. Am. Philos. Soc.; corr. Netherlands Royal Acad. Scis. Jewish religion. Author books including: Alsos, 1947. Founder Phys. Rev. Letters. Contbr. sci. articles to profl. jours. Discoverer (with G.E. Uhlenbeck) of so-called spin of Electron, 1925. Office: Brookhaven National Lab Upton NY 11973

GOUGER, MATTHEW M., corp. exec.; b. Tilden, Tex., Mar. 2, 1905; s. Robert O. and Cornelia May (Porter) G.; B.B.A., U. Texas, 1928; m. Mary Louise Goehring; 1 dau., Ann Virginia. Comml. mgr. Community Pub. Service Co., Ft. Worth, Tex., 1930-35; gen. mgr. eastern div. Western Light & Telephone Co.; v.p. and dir. East Bethlehem Water Co., 1935-41; asst. gen. supt. Nat. Tube Co., Div. U.S. Steel Corp., 1941-45; mgr. personnel, Pitts. Plate Glass Co., 1945-46; v.p. and dir. Glenn L. Martin Co., Balt., 1947-48) v.p., mem. mgmt. com. Gen. Aniline & Film Corp., N.Y.C.; pres. Data-Graphic Systems, Inc.; exec. v.p., dir. Frick Co., Waynesboro, Pa., 1960-62; chmn. bd., pres. Temmsco, Inc., Matthew M. Gouger Assos., Waynesboro, Pa.; chmn. bd. Testone Electrostatics Corp. Mem. Am. Mgmt. Assn. (v.p., exec. com., mem. personnel planning council), N.A.M. (indsl. relations com.), Quiet Birdmen, Sigma Iota Epsilon. Conglist. Clubs: University (Pitts.); Waynesboro (Pa.) Country; Manhasset Bay Yacht, Rotary; New York Yacht, Economic (N.Y.C.). Home: RD 5 Waynesboro PA 17268 Office: Waynesboro PA 17268

GOUGH, BETTY CATHERINE, fgn. service officer; b. Wis., July 18, 1920; B.S., Oshkosh State Tchrs. Coll., 1942; postgrad. George Washington U., 1944, Georgetown U., 1950. Tchr. pub. sch., 1942-43; clk.-typist Dept. State, 1943-46, research asst., 1946-48, fgn. affairs analyst, 1948-49, asst. internat. orgn. affairs, 1949-50, fgn. affairs officer, 1950-57; French lang. trainee Fgn. Service Inst., 1957; 2d sec., consul, Paris, 1957-59; 1st sec. U.S. mission to Internat. Atomic Energy Agy., Vienna, 1959-65, U.S. mission to UN and other internat. orgns., Geneva, 1965—. Home: 2 av de Bude Geneva Switzerland

GOUGH, HARRISON GOULD, psychologist, educator; b. Buffalo, Minn., Feb. 25, 1921; s. Harry B. and Aelfreda (Gould) G.; A.B. summa cum laude, U. Minn., 1942, A.M. (Social Sci. Research Council fellow 1946-47), 1947, Ph.D., 1949; m. Kathryn H. Whittier, Jan. 23, 1943; 1 dau., Jane Kathryn. Asst. prof. psychology U. Minn., 1948-49; asst. prof. U. Cal. at Berkeley, 1949-54, asso. prof., 1954-60, prof., 1960—, asso. dir. Inst. Personality Assessment and Research, 1964-67, chmn. dept. psychology, 1967—. Cons. VA, 1951—. Dir. Cons. Psychologists Press, Inc., 1956—. Mem. research adv. com. Cal. Dept. Corrections, 1958-64, Cal. Dept. Mental Hygiene, 1964- 69, Gov.'s Cal. Adv. Com. Mental Health, 1968—, citizens adv. council Cal. Dept. Mental Hygiene, 1968-71; clin. projects research revision com. Nat. Inst. Mental Health, 1968-72. Served to 1st lt. AUS, 1942-46. Fulbright research scholar, Italy, 1958-59, 65-66; Guggenheim fellow, 1965-66. Mem. Am., Western, Cal. (pres. 1961-62) psychol. assns., Internat. Assn. Applied Psychology, Internat. Inst. Arts and Letters, Phi Beta Kappa, Sigma Xi. Club: Commonwealth (San Francisco). Author: California Psychological Inventory. Chmn. bd. editors U. Cal. Publs. in Psychology, 1956-58; adv. editor Jour. Cons. and Clin. Psychology, 1956- -, Jours. Abnormal Psychology, 1964—; asso. editor Jour. Cross-Cultural Psychology, 1969—; editorial bd. Jossey-Bass, Inc., 1966—. Home: 10 Florida Av Berkeley CA 94707

GOUGH, HARRY PATTERSON, elec. mfg. co. exec.; b. Greencastle, Ind., Dec. 31, 1909; s. Harry B. and Mary Margaret (Patterson) G.; A.B., DePauw U., 1929; m. Janice Earl, Oct. 13, 1939; children—Judith Ann, Larry Patterson, Margaret Jane, David Earl. With Gen. Electric Co., 1929—, mgr. sales and distbn. maj. appliance div., San Francisco, 1956-61, became regional v.p., San Francisco, 1961, now v.p., gen. mgr. Mem. bd. govs. San Francisco Bay Area Council. Served to lt. USNR, 1943-46. Mem. Cal., San Francisco, Oakland chambers of commerce, Pacific Coast Elec. Assn. (dir.), Northwest Electric Light and Power Assn., Nat. Indsl. Conf. Bd., Cal. Mfrs. Assn. (sec.), Cal. Mfrs. Freight Assn. (dir.), Cal. Taxpayers Assn., San Francisco Conv. and Visitors Bur., Mchts. and Mfrs. Assn. Los Angeles (dir.). Presbyn. Clubs: Electric Stock Exchange, Rotary (San Francisco); California (Los Angeles); Alta (Salt Lake City) Peninsula Golf and Country (San Mateo, Cal.); Rainier (Seattle). Home: 71 Heather Dr Atherton CA 94025 Office: 235 Montgomery St San Francisco CA 94106

GOUGH, JOSEPH EDWARD, edn. ofcl.; b. Amarillo, Tex., Nov. 10, 1910; s. Edward C. and Jane Teresa (Cavanaugh) G.; student Creighton U., 1929-30; B.A., St. Louis U., 1934, M.A., 1937, Ph.L., 1939, S.T.L., 1944. Tchr. St. Louis U. High Sch., 1937-40; ordained priest, Roman Catholic Ch., 1943; asst. prin. Creighton Prep. Sch., Omaha, 1945-48; asst. dean Rockhurst Coll., 1948-49, dean, 1949-66; dir. financial aids St. Louis U., 1966-67; dir. studies Mo. Province Ednl. Inst., Soc. of Jesus, 1967-71; asst. for edn. Mo. Province Ednl. Inst., 1971—. Mem. N. Central Assn. Acad. Deans, Jesuit Ednl. Assn., Nat. Cath. Edn. Assn., Am. Assn. Higher Edn. Home: 221 N Grand Blvd St Louis MO 63103

GOUGH, ROBERT E., newspaper exec; Gen. mgr. New Orleans Times-Picayune and States Item, Times-Picayune Pub. Corp. Office: 3800 Howard Av New Orleans LA 70140*

GOUGLER, LAWRENCE W., banker; b. 1919; B.S., U. Ill.; married. With No. Trust Co., Chgo., 1946- -, adminstrv. v.p., sec., 1963-70, sr. v.p., sec., 1970—. Served with AUS, 1942-46, 50-52. Address: 50 S LaSalle St Chicago IL 60690

GOULARD, EVERETT MAURICE, lawyer; b. Bayonne, N.J., Aug. 23, 1913; s. Thomas and Eva Adele (Fitzgerald) G.; A.B., Cornell U., 1934; LL.B., Harvard, 1937; m. Marion Reed Ganzenmuller, June 12, 1935; children—James Everett, Sarah Reed. Vice pres. Pan Am. World Airways, Inc., N.Y.C., 1954-71; partner firm Poletti, Freidin, Prashker, Feldman & Gartner, 1971—. Served to lt. col. AUS. Mem. Delta Tau Delta. Clubs: Wee Burn Country (Darien); Union League. Home: 18 Overbrook Lane Darien CT 06820 Office: 777 3d Av New York City NY 10018

GOULD, ALVIN R., food co. exec.; b. Seattle, May 16, 1922; s. Charlie I. and Laura (Klos) G.; grad. pub. schs.; m. Ruth Nelson, May 25, 1946; children—Stephen Charles, Jon Patrick. Mem. engring. dept. Pacific Car & Foundry Co., Renton, Wash., 1943-45, asst. mgr. indsl. sales, 1945-48, mgr. indsl. sales, 1948-55, gen. sales mgr., 1956-60; gen. sales mgr. Peterbilt Motors Co., Newark, Cal., 1961-64; v.p., dir., gen. sales mgr. Honolulu Iron Works Co., 1964-66, exec. v.p., dir., chief operating officer, 1966, pres., dir., chief exec. officer, 1966—; group pres. Food Equipment Group Ward Foods Inc., N.Y.C., 1970—; pres., dir. Honiron Philippines, Inc., Manila, P.I., J & L Engring. Co., Inc.; chmn., dir. Tweedy Holdings Ltd., Burnley, Eng.; dir. Holsum Hawaii Baking Inc., Honolulu. Haleakala Storage & Transfer Inc., Kahului, Maui, Hawaii. Mem. nat. export expansion Council Dept. Commerce, 1969-73, chmn. regional export expansion council, 1969-73. Trustee Hawaii Pacific Coll. Mem. Hawaii C. of C. (chmn. trade com. 1968-69), Hawaii World Trade Assn. (mem. exec. com. 1968-69). Rotarian. Clubs: Waialae Country; Outrigger Canoe. Home: 987 Waiholo St Honolulu HI 96821 Office: 570 Auahi St Honolulu HI 96822

GOULD, ARTHUR FREEMAN, engr., educator; b. Lynn, Mass., Mar. 24, 1916; s. Frank Neil and Alice Louise (Crowley) G.; S.B., Mass. Inst. Tech., 1938; M.S., Lehigh U., 1949; m. Anne Stinson Pallister, June 14, 1941; children—Carol Anne, Robert Arthur, David Richard. Indsl. engr. Congoleum-Nairn, Inc., Kearny, N.J., 1938-39; supt. woodworking dept. Milton Bradley Co., Springfield, Mass., 1945-46; prodn. control mgr. Menswear div. Textron, Inc., Northampton, Mass., 1946-47; instr. mech. engring. Lehigh U., Bethlehem, Pa., 1947- 48, asst. prof., 1948-51, asso. prof. indsl. engring., 1951-52, head dept. indsl. engring., dir. curriculum indsl. engring., 1952—, Alcoa prof. indsl. engring., 1967-68. Dir. Gen. Electric Co. Mfg. Engring. Workshop Seminars, 1955-60. Served from 2d lt. to col., Ordnance Corps, U.S. Army, 1939-45. Registered profl. engr., Pa. Mem. Am. Soc. Engring. Edn. (chmn. indsl. engring. div. 1957-58, mem. gen. council 1958-60), Am. Inst. Indsl. Engrs. (editor operations research div.), Nat. Council Indsl. Engring. Dept. Heads (sec. 1966, chmn. 1968-69), Am. Soc. M.E., Am. Soc. Tool and Mfg. Engrs. (chmn. engr. conf. com. 1961-63), Inst. Mgmt. Scis., Operations Research Soc. Am., Am. Prodn. and Inventory Control Soc. (nat. edn. com. 1970—), Sigma Xi, Theta Delta Chi, Pi Gamma Mu, Alpha Pi Mu. Author: (with Charles W. Lytle) Manufacturing Equipment and Processes, 1951. Home: 835 Pine Top Dr Bethlehem PA 18017

GOULD, AUSTIN JUDSON, photog. supplies mfg. exec.; b. Stillwater, Okla., Dec. 12, 1910; s. Parley A. and Zora (Langford) G.; B.S., Okla. State U., 1931; Ph.D., Princeton, 1934; m. Catherine Allen, Dec. 25, 1934; children—Michael, Allen. With Eastman Kodak Co., Rochester, N.Y., 1934-, beginning as chemist, successively asst. supt. film base dept., supt., asst. mgr. film mfg., asst. to gen. mgr., 1954-56, mgr. film mfg., 1956-59, v.p., 1959—, dir., 1969—. Mem. Am. Chem. Soc., Photog. Soc. Am. Soc. Photog. Scientists and Engrs., Nat. Export Expansion Council, Internat. C. of C. (trustee U.S. council), Nat. Fgn. Trade Council (dir.). Home: Huntington Hills Rochester NY 14622 Office: 343 State St Rochester NY 14608

GOULD, BENJAMIN Z., lawyer; b. Chgo., July 27, 1913; s. Samuel and Fanny (Tendrich) G.; A.B., U. Chgo., 1935, J.D. cum laude, 1937; m. Shirley Handleman, Nov. 22, 1942; children—Frederick G., Edward S., Barbara F. Admitted to Ill. bar, 1937, since practiced in Chgo.; asso. firm Schradzke, Gould & Ratner, and predecessors, 1937-49, sr. partner, 1949—. Sec., gen. counsel, dir., Henry Crown (Ill.) & Co.; sec., gen. counsel Material Service Corp. subsidiary Gen. Dynamics Corp., Marblehead Lime Co., Freeman Coal Mining Corp.; v.p., gen. counsel, dir. Century-America Corp.; sec., gen. counsel, dir. Thomas B. Bishop Co., San Francisco; sec., v.p., gen. counsel, dir. Standard Forgings Corp.; dir., sec., gen. counsel Exchange Bldg. Corp., Burton-Dixie Co., LaSalle Corp., Mascar Corp., Santa Barbara Research Park, Inc., University Exchange Corp.; sec., gen. counsel Sioux City and New Orleans Terminal Corp., Sioux City and New Orleans Barge Lines; gen. counsel, dir. Central Cold Storage Co. Bd. dirs. Hebrew Theol. Coll. Served with USCGR, World War II. Mem. Am. Arbitration Assn. (mem. nat. panel), Chgo. Council Fgn. Relations, Am. Soc. Corporate Secs., Internat., Am., Ill., Chgo. bar assns., Navy League U.S., Am. Judicature Soc., Phi Beta Kappa. Jewish religion (dir. Chgo. congregations). Clubs: Executive, Standard, One Hundred (Chgo.). Home: 1170 Michigan Av Wilmette IL 60091 Office: 300 W Washington St Chicago IL 60606

GOULD, BERNARD ALBERT, govt. ofcl.; b. Chelsea, Mass., Jan. 30, 1912; s. Harry and Rebecca (LeVine) G.; B.C.S., N.Y.U., 1936, J.D., 1941; postgrad. George Washington U., 1937-38; m. Edith Solomon, June 16, 1936; children—Susan Deborah (Mrs. Gary O. Goldsmith), John Richard. Admitted to N.Y. State bar, 1942, also U.S. Supreme Ct.; with r.r. industry, N.Y.C., 1929-36; various positions in govt. service, 1936—; dir. Bur. Enforcement, ICC, Washington, 1967—; instr. interstate commerce law and procedure N.Y.U.; lectr. transp. law to industry and legal groups and seminars. Bd. dirs. J.F.K. Bldg. Fund for Retarded, Prince Georges Assn. for Retarded Children. Recipient Distinguished Service citation for war transp. activities, 1945. Mem. Alpha Epsilon Pi. Home: 9205 Sligo Creek Pkwy Silver Spring MD 20901 Office: ICC 12th and Constitution Av Washington DC 20423

GOULD, BERNARD SIDNEY, educator, biochemist; b. Boston, Oct. 15, 1911; s. Charles and Dina (Ulin) G.; S.B., Mass. Inst. Tech., 1932; Ph.D., U. London, (Eng.), 1932; postdoctoral U. Louvain, (Belgium), 1935; m. Sophie Ginzberg, Sept. 8, 1938; children—Michael, Jonathan, David. Asst. prof. biology Mass. Inst. Tech., 1937-43, asso. prof., 1943-69, prof., 1969—; vis. prof. Weizmann Inst. (Israel), 1960, Boston U., 1968; cons. to industry. Vice pres. Am. Assn. Jewish Edn., 1970—; vice chmn. Com. Jewish Edn.; mem. Council Jewish Fedns. and Welfare Funds, 1969—. Trustee Combined Jewish Philanthropies, Boston, 1960—; v.p. Hebrew Coll., Boston, 1960-71, chmn. bd., 1971—. Mem. Soc. Am. Biochemists, Sigma Xi. Jewish religion (life trustee congregation). Club: New Century of Boston (pres. 1952-53). Editor: Treatise on Collagen, 1970. Contbr. articles profl. jours. Home: 25 Cotswold Rd Brookline MA 02146 Office: 77 Massachusetts Av Cambridge MA 02138

GOULD, CARL MAURICE, lawyer; b. Toronto, Can., Oct. 14, 1913; s. S. and Bess (Green) G.; student U. Toronto, 1930-33; LL.B., Loyola U., Los Angeles, 1942, J.D., 1968; m. Joyce Capilouto Dec. 16, 1924; children—Beth, Tony. Came to U.S., 1940, naturalized, 1942. Admitted to Cal. bar, 1942; with Hill, Farrer & Burrill, Los Angeles, 1943—, partner, 1945—; specializing labor law; atty. constrn. industry, trade assns. in mfg. and service industries. Served with AUS, World War II. Mem. Am., Fed., Cal., Los Angeles bar assns. Home: 4240 Navajo St Toluca Lake North Hollywood CA 91602 Office: 445 S Figueroa Los Angeles CA 90017

GOULD, CHARLES LESSINGTON, newspaper exec.; b. Youngstown, O., Aug. 17, 1909; s. Fred Jay and Kathleen Helen (Murphy) G.; spl. student Northwestern U.; LL.D., Golden Gate Coll., 1963; m. Peggy Ann Shannon, Mar. 30, 1951; children—Charles Lessington, Michael Edward. Machinist, Steel & Tubes, Inc., Cleve., 1927-28; engr. Am. Tel. & Tel., Cleve., 1928-29; reporter, writer, promotion mgr. Cleve. News, 1930-34; sales promotion mgr. Universal Match Corp., Chgo., 1934-35; writer, radio announcer, promotion dir. Chicago American, 1935-42; plans dir. N.Y. Jour-American, 1946-50, asst. pub., 1951-61; pub. San Francisco Examiner, 1961—, San Francisco News Call Bull., 1962-65; v.p. San Francisco Newspapers div. Hearst Corp. Mem. Cal. Gov.'s Communication Com.; mem. hon. com. San Francisco council Girl Scouts U.S.A. Bd. govs. San Francisco Bay Area council United Bay Area Crusade. Served from lt. (j.g.) to capt. USNR, 1942-46; dir. combat photography U.S. Navy, Korea, 1950-51. Recipient gold medal award Freedoms Found., 1964, 65. Mem. San Francisco C. of C. (dir.), San Francisco Conv. and Visitors Bur. (dir.), Advt. Assn. of West (trustee), San Francisco Advt. Club, No. Cal. World Affairs Council (trustee), Naval Order U.S. (San Francisco commandry), Naval Res. Assn., Navy League (nat. dir.). Clubs: Westchester (N.Y.) Country; San Francisco Press and Union League; Bohemian. Home: 336 Poett Rd Hillsborough CA 94010 Office: 110 Fifth St San Francisco CA 94119

GOULD, CHARLES PERRY, lawyer; b. Los Angeles, Mar. 11, 1909; s. Thomas Charles and Viola Frank (Keeney) G.; student Pomona Coll., 1926-28; Ph.B., U. Chgo. 1930; LL.B., U. So. Cal., 1932; m. Mary Dalrymple, Sept. 1, 1932; children—Thomas Charles, Mary (Mrs. Robert Lancefield), Anne (Mrs. Thomason). Admitted to Cal. bar, 1932; asso. firm Frankley & Spray, Los Angeles, 1932- 35; mem. firm Spray, Gould & Bowers, 1935—. Dir. Golden State Bank, Gould Music Co., Cal. Bankers Trust Co. Served to lt. comdr. USNR, 1942-45. Mem. Am. Bar Assn., Internat. Assn. Ins. Counsel, Nat. Club Assn. (pres. 1962, dir.), World Affairs Council, Navy League U.S., Legion Lex, Delta Theta Phi. Republican. Episcopalian. Elk. Clubs: Jonathan, Los Angeles, (Los Angeles); Balboa Bay (Balboa, Cal.); California Book (San Francisco); Town Hall (Los Angeles). Home: 1200 Old Mill Rd San Marino CA 91108 Office: 3075 Wilshire Blvd Los Angeles CA 90017

GOULD, CHESTER, cartoonist; b. Pawnee, Okla., Nov. 20, 1900; s. Gilbert R. and Alice M. (Miller) G.; student Okla. A. & M. U., 1919-21; grad. Northwestern U., 1923; m. Edna Gauger, Nov. 6, 1926; 1 dau., Jean. Cartoonist Hearst Publs., 1924-29, Chgo. Tribune, 1931—; creator cartoon Dick Tracy, 1931, appearing in Chgo. Tribune-N.Y. News Syndicate, Inc., and syndicated newspapers. Mem. Nat. Cartoonists Soc., Lambda Chi Alpha. Clubs: Tavern, Lake Zurich Golf, Woodstock Country. Home: Woodstock IL 60098 Office: Tribune Tower Chicago IL 60611

GOULD, EDWIN SHELDON, educator, chemist; b. Los Angeles, Aug. 19, 1926; s. Ben and Margaret (Mandel) G.; B.S., Cal. Inst. Tech., 1946; Ph.D., U. Cal. at Los Angeles, 1950; m. Marjorie McFarlin, Jan. 25, 1952; children—Richard Forrest, Kirk Benson. Instr. Polytech. Inst. Bklyn., 1950-52, asst. prof., 1952-56, asso. prof. chemistry, 1956-59; sr. inorganic chemist Stanford Research Inst., 1959-66; prof. San Francisco State Coll., 1966-67, Kent State U., 1967—. Mem. London, Am. chem. socs., U.S. Volleyball Assn., Amateur Chamber Music Players Assn. Author: Inorganic Reactions and Structure, 1962; Mechanism and Structure in Organic Chemistry, 1959. Research inorganic chemistry. Home: 1583 Morris Rd Kent OH 44240

GOULD, ELLIOTT, actor; b. Bklyn., Aug. 29, 1938; s. Bernard and Lucille (Raver) Goldstein; student Profl. Children's Sch., N.Y.C., 1955, Columbia, 1955- 56; pupil of Vladmir Protevitch, Jerome Swinford, Sonya Box, Bill Quinn, Colin Romoff; m. Barbra Streisand, Mar. 21, 1963; 1 son. Theatrical appearances include Rumple, 1957; Say, Darling, 1958; Irma La Douce, 1960; I Can Get It For You Wholesale, 1962; On The Town, 1963; TV appearances in Once Upon A Mattress, 1964; appeared in film Bob & Carol & Ted & Alice, 1969. Mem. Artists Equity Assn., A.F.T.R.A. Address: care Bregman 630 3d Av New York City NY*

GOULD, GEORGE HALE, banker, lawyer; b. Mpls., Aug. 29, 1923; s. Edward Spalding and Florence (Ainsworth) G.; B.S., U. Minn., 1947, J.D., 1949; grad. Sch. Savs. Banking, Brown U., 1962; m. Kathleen A. Holte, Nov. 11, 1949; children—Scott Ainsworth, Reed Douglas, Kathleen Ann. Admitted to Minn. bar, 1949; atty. Minn. Dept. Taxation, 1949-52; spl. asst. atty. gen. Minn., 1952-56; sec., gen. counsel Farmers and Mechanics Savs. Bank, Mpls., 1956—, also v.p., lectr., extension div. U. Minn., 1954-55. Active local Boy Scouts Am. Served with AUS, 1943-46. Mem. Minn., Hennepin Co. bar assns. Episcopalian. Clubs: Minneapolis Athletic, Six O'Clock (Mpls.). Home: 6515 Waterman Av Edina MN 55343 Office: 90 S 6th St Minneapolis MN 55402

GOULD, GEORGE JEAN, lawyer; b. Toledo, Dec. 25, 1901; s. Abraham and Anna (Faber) G.; student U. Toledo, 1920-21, Detroit City Coll., 1921-22; LL.B., U. Mich., 1925; m. Elizabeth Davies, Sept. 1, 1928; children—Nancy G. (Mrs. Harland M. Britz), Elizabeth G. (Mrs. Guillermo Herrera). Admitted to Ohio bar, 1925; mem. firm Doyle, Lewis & Warner, Toledo, 1932—. Mem. Toledo Bd. Community Relations, 1950-56. Chmn. Citizens for Kennedy Com. Lucas County, O., 1960. Pres. Toledo UN Assn.; trustee Indiana Av. YMCA. Served with U.S. Army, 1917-18. Recipient Am. Bar Assn. award, 1950. Mem. Ohio, Toledo (pres. 1949-50), Lucas County bar assns., Nat. Assn. R.R. Counsel, Am. Trial Lawyers Assn. Home: 3137 Kenwood Blvd Toledo OH 43606 Office: Nat Bank Bldg Toledo OH 43604

GOULD, GLENN HERBERT, pianist, composer; b. Toronto, Can., Sept. 25, 1932; s. Russell Herbert and Florence (Greig) G.; student Royal Conservatory of Music, Toronto, 1943-52; sr. matriculation, Malvern Collegiate, Toronto, 1951. Profl. debut as soloist Toronto Symphony Orch., 1947; U.S. debut in recital, Washington, 1955; concert tours U.S., 1956-59, Europe, 1958; European debut as soloist Moscow Philharmonic Orch., 1957; recorded Bach's Goldberg Variations, Columbia Records, 1956, Beethoven Sonatas, Opus 109, 110, 111, Bach Concerto in D and F minors, Beethoven Concerto in B flat and C majors, Bach Partitas Nos. 5, 6, Haydn Sonata in E flat major, Mozart Sonata C major; composer: A String Quartet (world premiere Canadian Broadcasting Corp., 1956; first pub. performance Stratford (Ont.) Mus. Festival 1956). Home: 32 Southwood Dr Toronto 8 Ontario Canada Office: care Harold Holt Ltd Wigmorest London W1 England

GOULD, GORDON THOMAS, Jr., air force officer; b. Mobile, Ala., Jan. 7, 1916; s. Gordon Thomas and Minnie (Gaston) G.; B.S., U.S. Mil. Acad., 1941; M.S., Mass. Inst. Tech., 1950; grad. Air War Coll., 1954; m. Lois Sameth, June 12, 1941; children—Gordon Thomas III, Beverly L., Darcy A. Commd. 2d lt. USAAF, 1941, advanced through grades to lt. gen., 1971; served as signal and communications officer, China, 1944-46; chief communications- electronics div. Hdqrs. SAC, Offutt AFB, Neb., 1960-64; dep. comdr. Hdqrs. Air Force communications service Scott AFB, Ill., 1964-65; dir. command control and communications Hdqrs. USAF, Washington, 1965-71; dir. Def. Communications Agy., 1971—. Decorated Legion of Merit with 2 oak leaf clusters; Spl. Vest Order Yun Hui (China). Fellow I.E.E.E., A.A.A.S.; mem. Armed Forces Communications and Electronics Assn. (v.p.), Sigma Xi. Home: 9144 Leghorn Pl Fairfax VA 22030 Office: Defense Communications Agy Washington DC 20305

GOULD, IRA A., Jr., educator; b. Atchison, Kan., Sept. 28, 1905; s. Ira Alfred and Waunettia H. (Adams) G.; B.S.A., W.Va. U., 1931; M.S., Mich. State Coll., 1933; Ph.D., U. Wis., 1938; m. Genevieve M. Wilson, May 4, 1929; 1 son, Kaye Harter; m. 2d, Dorothy C. Drake, Dec. 24, 1970. Staff dairy mfrs. Mich. State Coll., 1933, instr., 1934-38, asst. prof., 1938-42, asso. prof., 1942-44; prof. dairy mfrs. U. Md., 1944-49; chmn. dept., prof. dairy tech. Ohio State U., 1949-70; chief of party USAID, Udaipur, India, 1970—. Dir. R & D Assos. Cons. to dairy and sci. orgns. U.S. del. XIV Internat. Dairy Congress, Rome, 1956; adviser U.S. delegation XV Congress, London, Eng., 1959; lectr. XVI Congress, Copenhagen, 1962; UNICEF cons. dairy edn., Near and Middle East, 1960; cons. dairy programs UNICEF-FAO, 1966. Recipient Borden award for research Am. Chem. Soc., 1946, award of honor Am. Dairy Sci. Assn., 1966. Fellow A.A.A.S.; mem. Am. Dairy Sci. Assn. (dir. 1951-53, v.p., pres. 1955-56), Inst. Food Tech., Wash. Acad. of Sci., Internat. Assn. Milk, Food Sanitarians, Phi Lambda Upsilon, Alpha Zeta, Gamma Sigma Delta. Methodist. Author sci. articles. Asso. editor of Jour. Dairy Sci., 1941-51. Home: 3007 Shady Hill Ct Columbus OH 43221

GOULD, JACK, (John Ludlow), journalist; b. N.Y.C., Feb. 5, 1914; s. John Warren DuBois and Evelyn Louisa (Fisk) G.; grad. Brown Sch., N.Y.C., 1932; m. Carmen L. Lewis, Nov. 25, 1938; children—Lewis Ludlow, Richard John, Robert DuBois. Reporter N.Y. Herald Tribune, 1932-37; drama dept. N.Y. Times, 1937-42, radio and TV dept., 1942-44, critic radio and television, 1944—. Recipient Variety award, 1951, George Polk award, 1953, Page-One award, 1953; Peabody award, 1957; Columbia U. Sch. Journalism award, 1970. Author: All About Radio and Television. Contbr. to mags. Home: Lighthouse Lane Old Greenwich CT 06870 Office: 229 W 43d St New York City NY 10036

GOULD, JAMES FREDERICK, entertainment co. exec.; b. Plymouth, Eng., Sept. 30, 1908; s. John and Lillian (Edwards) G.; student London (Eng.) Coll., 1923; m. Ethel Louise MacLean, Apr. 29, 1933; children—Donald Bruce, Robert Louis. Came to U.S., 1929, naturalized, 1938. Asst. cashier, bookkeeper Dakin Bros. Ltd., London, 1925-29; mem. accounting dept. Radio Keith Orpheum Corp., 1930-32; with Radio City Music Hall, N.Y.C., 1932—, exec. v.p., 1964- 66, pres., 1966—. C.P.A., N.Y. Mem. N.Y. State Soc. C.P.A.'s. Home: Middle Rd Harbor Acres Sands Point NY 11050 Office: 1260 Av Americas New York City NY 10020

GOULD, JAY REID, educator; b. N.S., Can., Mar. 15, 1906; s. Lealon B. and Eleanor W. (West) G.; came to U.S., 1929, naturalized, 1939; B.A., Acadia (N.S.) U., 1926; M.A., Harvard, 1929; postgrad. Columbia, 1933-34; m. Rebecca P. Ritter, Dec. 11, 1941; children—Lee P., Emilie W. Reporter, Halifax (N.S.) Herald, 1928-29; tchr. East Greenwich (R.I.) Acad., 1927-28; faculty Rensselaer Poly. Inst., Troy, N.Y., 1929—, Louis E. Laflin prof. English, 1954—, chmn. dept. language and lit., 1968—, dir. Tech. Writers Inst., 1953—. Cons. indsl. firms, 1954—. Recipient medal Pi Delta Epsilon, 1961. Fellow Soc. Tech. Writers and Pubs., Am. Bus. Communication Assn.; mem. Nat. Council Tchrs. English, Am. Med. Writers Assn., Am. Bus. Writers Assn., Edn. Coll. Theatre Assn. Author: Career Opportunities in Technical Writing, 1964; (one act plays) The Running Tide, 1952, The Long Silence, 1960, Steps from Beyond, 1954, The Death of the Hired Man, 1956, The Necklace (adaptation), 1969; co-author: Exposition: Technical and Popular, 1947; Technical Reporting, 1959. Editor Rensselaer Rev. Grad. Studies, 1960-66; exec. editor Jour. Tech. Writing and Communication, 1970—; also numerous articles. Home: 372 Pinewoods Rd Troy NY 12180

GOULD, JEAN ROSALIND, writer; b. Greenville, O., May 25, 1919; d. Aaron J. and Elsie E. (Elgutter) Gould; A.B., U. Toledo, 1939. Free-lance writer, 1941—; works include short stories, biographies; editorial re-writer, radio-script writer. Committeewoman dist. Democratic party, N.Y.C., 1961-62. Fellow, MacDowell Colony, Huntington Hartford Found., Wurlitzer Found. Mem. Nat. Journalism and Communications Soc., PEN Club, Theta Sigma Phi, Phi Kappa Phi. Author: Miss Emily, 1946; Robert Frost, The Aim Was Song, 1964; The Poet and Her Book: A Biography of Edna St. Vincent Millay, 1969; others. Address: c/o Dodd Mead & Co 79 Madison Av New York City NY 10016

GOULD, JOHN PHILIP, Jr., economist, educator; b. Chgo., Jan. 19, 1939; s. John Philip and Lillian (Jicka) G.; B.S. with highest distinction, Northwestern U., 1960; Ph.D. (Earhart Found. fellow), U. Chgo., 1966; m. Kathleen J. Hayes, Sept. 14, 1963; children—John Philip III, Jeffrey Hayes. Faculty, U. Chgo., 1965—, asso. prof. econs., 1969—. Spl. asst. econ. affairs to sec. labor, 1969-70; spl. asst. to dir. Office Mgmt. and Budget, 1970; past chmn. econ. policy adv. com. Dept. Labor. Recipient Wall St. Jour. award, 1960; Am. Marketing Assn. award, 1960. Mem. Econometric Soc. (chmn. local arrangements 1968). Contbr. Microeconomic Foundations of Employment and Inflation Theory, 1970; articles to profl. jours. Home: 5524 S Kimbark Av Chicago IL 60637

GOULD, JOHN THOMAS, farmer, author; b. Brighton, Mass., Oct. 22, 1908; s. Franklin Farrar and Hilda Dobson (Jenkins) G.; A.B., Bowdoin Coll., 1931, Litt.D., 1968; m. Dorothy Florence Wells, Oct. 22, 1932; childrenJohn Thomas, Kathryn MacLeod. Began newspaper work as country corr. in 1923; after 1931 joined weekly Brunswick (Me.) Record, covered area for many urban dailies; operates orchard and row-crop farm; at present devotes time to farming, writing weekly Dispatch from Farm in Christian Sci. Monitor; co-owner, editor Lisbon Enterprise, Lisbon Falls, Me., 1945-51; dir. Publicity Goddard Coll., Plainfield, Vt., 1940-42. Mem. Me. Devel. Commn., Sea and Shore Fisheries, 1942-43; pres. Assn. N.E. Fence Viewers; chief quint of N.E. Intermediary Tract of Guild of Former Pipe Organ Pumpers. Mem. N.E. Vet. Journalists Assn. (pres. 1961-62), Grange. Mason. Author: New England Town Meeting, 1940; Pre-Natal Care for Fathers, 1941; Farmer Takes a Wife, 1945; The House That Jacob Built, 1947; And One to Grow On, 1949; Neither Hay nor Grass, 1951; The Fastest Hound Dog in the State of Maine, 1953; Monstrous Depravity, 1963; Parables of Peter Partout, 1964; You Should Start Sooner, 1965; Last One In, 1966; Europe on Saturday Night, 1968; The Jonesport Raffle, 1969; Twelve Grindstones, 1970; The Shag Bag, 1972. Editor and pub. Box 199 RFD No 1 Lisbon Falls ME 04252

GOULD, KENNETH LAWRENCE, newspaper exec.; b. Miami, Fla., Jan. 31, 1925; s. Kenneth Leroy and Mary (Wilson) G.; B.A., Coll. William and Mary, 1947; m. Helen Marilynn Brand, Aug. 12, 1950; children—Alison DeLong, Lawrence Brand, Meredith Wanner. Reporter, Richmond (Va.) News Leader, 1946-50, 52-54, asst. city editor, 1954-58; city editor Roanoke (Va.) Times, 1958-59; asst. city editor Richmond News Leader, 1959-63, city editor, 1963-69, mng. editor, 1969—. Served with USNR, 1943-46, 50-52. Mem. Va. Press Assn., A.P. Mng. Editors Assn., Sigma Delta Chi. Episcopalian. Club: Salisbury Country (Chesterfield County, Va.). Home: 10409 Medina Rd Richmond VA 23235 Office: 333 E Grace St Richmond VA 23219

GOULD, KINGDON, Jr., U.S. ambassador; b. Laurel, Md., 1924. Chmn. bd. Murray Corp.; ambassador to Luxembourg, 1969—. Address: care American Embassy Luxembourg*

GOULD, LAURENCE MCKINLEY, educator; b. Lacota, Mich., Aug. 22, 1896; s. Herbert and Anna (Updike) G.; B.S. magna cum laude, U. Mich., 1921, M.A., 1923, Sc.D., 1925, LL.D., 1954; Sc.D. (hon.). Poly. Inst. Bklyn., 1931, Union Coll., 1958, Columbia, 1959, U. Notre Dame, 1960; LL.D., Coe Coll., 1945, Macalester Coll., 1946, Dartmouth, 1959, N.Y. U., 1959, Brandeis U., 1961, Wooster Coll., 1962, U. Minn., 1962, St. Olaf Coll., 1962, Harvard, 1962, Occidental Coll., 1961, Kalamazoo Coll., 1963; L.H.D., Ripon Coll., 1951, Southwestern at Memphis, 1953, Wayne State U., 1958, Carlton Coll., 1962; D. Litt. (hon.), Chgo. Med. Sch., 1955; m. Margaret Rice, Aug. 2, 1930. Instr. geology U. Mich., 1921-26, asst. prof., 1926-30, asso. prof., 1930-31; prof. geology Carleton Coll., 1932-45, pres., 1945-63, pres. emeritus, 1963—; prof. geology U. Ariz., Tucson, 1963—. Asst. dir., geologist U. Mich. Greenland Expdn., 1926; asst. dir. and geographer Putnam Baffin Island Expdn., 1927; 2d in command and geologist-geographer Byrd Antarctic Expdn., 1928-30. Dir. Antarctica program, U.S. Nat. Com., IGY, 1957-58; chmn. polar research com. Nat. Acad. Scis.; U.S. rep. spl. com. on Antarctic research Internat. Council Sci. Unions, 1963-66. Trustee, Ford Found., Carnegie Found. for Advancement Teaching, 1958-62; mem. nat. sci. bd. NSF, 1952-62. In ambulance service, U.S. Army, 1917-19; with Italian Army, summer, 1918; participated in St. Mihiel and Meuse Argonne offensives, France; with Army of Occupation, Germany. Chief, Arctic section Arctic, Desert and Tropic Information Center, USAAF, 1942-44. Awarded Congl. gold medal, 1931; Cross of St. Olaf, 1st Class, Royal Norwegion Order. Del. Internat. Congress of Geodesy and Geophysics, Edinburgh, 1936, 17th Internat. Geol. Congress, Moscow, 1937. Mem.-at- large nat. council Boy Scouts Am. Recipient Navy Distinguished Pub. Service award, 1959, Explorers Club medal, 1957. Fellow Geol. Soc. Am., A.A.A.S. (past pres.), Am. Geog. Soc. (David Livingston medal 1930); mem. Assn. Am. Geographers, Minn. Acad. Sci. (pres. 1938-39), Arctic Inst. N. Am. (chmn. bd. govs. 1946), Am. Meteorol. Soc., Council on Fgn. Relations, Phi Beta Kappa (pres., senator-at-large, United chpts.), Sigma Xi, Pi Kappa Alpha, Sigma Gamma Epsilon; life mem. Nat. Geog. Soc., Geog. Soc. Chgo. (Gold medalist 1931), Am. Legion; hon. life mem. Rotary Internat.; corr. mem. Phila. Geog. Soc. Clubs: Explorers: Minneapolis, Skylight (Mpls.); Old Pueblo Club (Tucson); Cosmos (Washington); Century, University (N.Y.C.). Author: Cold—the Record of an Antarctic Sledge Journey, 1931; also papers on geology Baffin Island and Antarctica, and pleistocene geology of upper Mississippi Valley. Home: Route 8 Box 131 Tucson AZ 85710

GOULD, LESLIE, financial cons.; b. Phila., Feb. 8, 1902; s. Alexander and Rosa Montgomery (Jenks) G.; student Bellefonte (Pa.) Acad. 1920-21; grad. Elmira Free Acad. 1921; m. Althea Mundorff O'Hanlon, June 14, 1957. Reporter, Advertiser, Telegram and Herald, Elmira, 1918-20; police reporter Rochester Democrat-Chronicle, N.Y., 1921-22; copyreader Syracuse Herald, 1922-23; telegraph editor Atlantic City Press 1923-25; rewrite, Los Angeles Times, 1925; copyreader and editor st. sale edits. Oakland (Cal.) Tribune 1925-28; financial reporter Asso. Press, N.Y.C., 1928-29; financial reporter N.Y. Post, 1929-30; financial editor N.Y. Jour. American, 1930-66, N.Y., World Jour. Tribune, 1966-68; condr. daily column Behind the News in Business, syndicated by King Features Service, 1948-68. Trustee Beekman-Downtown Hosp., N.Y.C. Clubs: Dutch Treat (gov.), Coffee House, Metropolitan, Amateur Comedy, Recess. Home: 200 E 66th St New York City NY 10021

GOULD, LYMAN JAY, educator; b. N.Y.C., May 5, 1925; s. David and Yvette (Pearlman) G.; A.B. cum laude, Colby Coll., 1948; M.A., U. Mich., 1949, Ph.D., 1958; m. Ann Rodney, Aug. 30, 1950; children-Ellen Yvette, Michael Rodney. Teaching fellow U. Mich., 1952; instr. U. Vt., 1953-57, asst. prof., 1957-61, asso. prof., 1961-66, dir. program of Latin Am. studies, 1962- 65, prof., 1966—, chmn. dept. polit. sci., 1966—, chmn. Center for Area Studies, 1965-69. Mem. Burlington City Charter commn., 1958-60, Burlington Com. on community relations, 1957-62, Jud. Council of Vt., 1967-69. Served with AUS, 1943-46, U. Vt. summer faculty research grantee, 1960, 65, U.Vt. Ford Found. travel grantee, 1963. Mem. Am. Polit. Sci. Assn., Latin Am. Studies Assn., Phi Beta Kappa, Pi Gamma Mu. Author: People, Power and Politics, 1961; La Ley Foraker, 1969. Contbr. essays to periodicals. Home: 25 University Terrace Burlington VT 05401

GOULD, MICHAEL, lawyer; b. Mozir, Russia, Nov. 25, 1905; s. David and Sophie (Chaitman) G.; came to U.S., 1909, naturalized, 1928; J.D., U. Mich., 1928; m. Gladys Maibaum, Oct. 14, 1941; children—Ellen Claire, Janet Elizabeth. Admitted to Mich. bar, 1928, D.C. bar, 1946; practiced in Detroit, 1928-34; spl. atty. penal div. Gen. Counsel Office, Internal Revenue Service, 1934-36; spl. atty. tax div. Dept. Justice, 1936-42, spl. asst. to atty. gen., 1946; partner firm Surrey, Karasik, Gould & Greene, Washington, 1952-69; counsel firm Jacobs and Speiller, Washington, 1969- -; lectr. ann. Inst. Fed. Taxation, N.Y. U., 1957, 60. Served to lt. USNR, 1942-46. Mem. Am., Fed., Mich. bar assns., Am. Judicature Soc. Contbr. profl. jours. Home: 3322 McKinley St NW Washington DC 20015 Office: Woodward Bldg Washington DC 20005

GOULD, MILTON SAMUEL, lawyer; b. N.Y.C., Oct. 8, 1909; s. David H. and Ida (Berman) G.; B.A., Cornell U., 1930. L.B., 1933; m. Eleanor Greenburg, 1936; children—Patricia, Judson, Jonathan. Admitted to N.Y. bar, 1933; asso. with fed. judge Samuel H. Kaufman, 1933-48; spl. atty. investigation and prosecutions violations immigration and naturalization laws Dept. Justice, 1935-37; partner firm Kaufman & Cronan, and successors, N.Y.C., 1938-48, Gallop, Climenko & Gould, N.Y.C., 1948-64; sr. partner firm Shea, Gallop, Climenko & Gould. Dir., chmn. exec. com. Elgin Nat. Watch Co.; dir., gen. Counsel Citizens Utilities Co., 1945-70; dir. Friendly Frost, Inc., Tex. Oil & Gas Corp., Coastal States Gas Producing Co., Corpus Christi, Tex. Lectr. Am. Mgmt. Assn., Practicing Law Inst.; lectr. in law Cornell Law Sch., 1970—. Chmn. lawyers div. United Jewish Appeal, N.Y.C. Mem. N.Y. County Lawyers Assn., Assn. Bar City N.Y., Newcomen Soc. N.Am. Clubs: Tower (Ithaca); Lake Waramug Golf (New Preston, Conn.); Cornell, Lawyers, Manhattan (N.Y.C.). Home: 35 E 75th St New York City NY 10021 also Warren CT 06754 Office: 330 Madison Av New York City NY 10017

GOULD, MORTON, composer, conductor; b. Richmond Hill, L.I., N.Y., Dec. 10, 1913; s. James and Frances (Arkin) G.; student pub. schs., Richmond Hill; married; four children. Played piano and composed at age of four; concertized extensively as composer pianist during early years; vaudeville and stage work, radio; on staff of Music Hall at age 17, later NBC staff; at age 21 conducted and arranged series of programs over WOR Mutual, Columbia networks; guest condr. major symphony orchs.; concert and radio appearances, Europe, 1966; major compositions played by Toscanini, Mitropolous, Monteux, Stokowski, Rodzinski, Reiner, Golschmann, etc. Works include: 3 symphonies, Foster Gallery, Concerto for Orchestra, Latin Am. Symphonette, Spirituals, Cowboy Rhapsody, Lincoln Legend, Venice, etc. Wrote music and appeared film Delightfully Dangerous; wrote music for stage show Billion Dollar Baby; commd. by Ballet Theatre to write music for ballet Fall River Legend; wrote mus. score Arms and the Girl, Windjammer; wrote and conducted symphony for Band for West Point sesquicentennial celebration, 1952; wrote Tap Dance Concerto; CBS-TV documentary series entitled World War I; musical host Nat. Ednl. TV series, The World of Music Morton Gould. Composer: Inventions, 1953; Dance Variations, 1953; Showpiece for Orchestra, 1954; Cinerama Holiday, 1954; Declaration, symphonic narrative for orchestra, 1957; Jekyll and Hyde Variations, for orchestra, 1957; St. Lawrence Suite, 1958; Dialogues for Piano and Orchestra; Venice for Double Orchestra; Vivaldi Gallery; Columbia; Troubador Music; Soundings; also shorter works; RCA Victor and recording artist. Mem. A.S.C.A.P., Nat. Assn. Composers and Conductors, Am. Soc. Composers, Am. Symphony Orch. League (dir.), Authors and Pubs. (dir., chmn. symphony and concert com.). Address: 609 Fifth Av New York City NY 10017

GOULD, ROY WALTER, physicist; b. Los Angeles, Apr. 25, 1927; s. Roy Walter and Rosamonde (Stokes) G.; B.S., Cal. Inst. Tech., 1949, Ph.D., 1956; M.S., Stanford, 1950; m. Ethel Savage Stratton, Aug. 23, 1952; children—Diana Stratton, Robert Clarke. Mem.

faculty Cal. Inst. Tech., 1955-70, prof. elec. engring. and physics, 1962-70; asst. dir. research controlled thermonullear research AEC, 1970—. Served with USNR, 1945-46. Fellow Am. Phys. Soc., I.E.E.E.; mem. Nat. Acad. Engring. Home: 6609 Selkirk Dr Bethesda MD 20034 Office: AEC Washington DC 20545

GOULD, SAMUEL BROOKNER, ret. univ. chancellor; b. N.Y.C., Aug. 11, 1910; s. Nathaniel and Lina (Brookner) G.; A.B., Bates Coll., 1930, LL.D., 1957; A.M., N.Y.U., 1936, LL.D., 1965; postgrad. Oxford (Eng.) U., 1931, Cambridge (Eng.) U., 1934, Harvard, 1941; LL.D., Wilberforce U., 1960, Union Coll., 1965, U. Cal., 1968, U. Akron, 1968, U. Pitts., 1970; L.H.D., Alfred U., 1966, Hamilton Coll., 1970; Litt.D., Colgate U., 1969; D.Sc., Albany Med. Coll., 1970; m. Laura J. Ohman, Dec. 24, 1936; 1 son, Richard Allan. Staff work sta. WEAN, Providence, 1931, sta. WTHT, Hartford, Conn., 1938; tchr. William Hall High Sch., West Hartford, Conn., 1932-38; head dept. speech Brookline (Mass.) Schs., 1938-47; prof. radio and speech, dir. div. radio, speech, theatre Boston U., 1947-50, asst. to pres., 1950-53; sr. asso. Cresap, McCormick & Paget, mgmt. engrs., 1953; cons. to sta. WARA, Attleboro, Mass., 1949-51; pres. Antioch Coll., Yellow Springs, O., 1954-59; chancellor U. Cal. at Santa Barbara, 1959-62; pres. Ednl. Broadcasting Corp., 1962-64; chancellor State U. N.Y., Albany, 1964-70, chancellor emeritus, 1970—. Dir. Nat. Comml. Bank & Trust Co. Albany, McKinsey & Co., Blue Cross of Northeastern N.Y., Inc. Chmn. bd. Research Found. State U. N.Y.; gen. chmn. Inst. Man and Sci., Rensselaerville, N.Y.; trustee Ednl. Testing Service; mem. Bd. Dormitory Authority, State N.Y.; bd. dirs. N.Y. State Higher Edn. Assistance Corp., Albany Orch. Assn.; bd. govs. Inst. Am. Studies, Paris; hon. bd. Max Reinhardt Research Inst., Salzburg-Vienna, Austria; trustee JDR 3d Fund, Ednl. Change Inc., Charles F. Kettering Found., Salk Inst.; mem. N.Y. State Adv. Council on Higher Edn.; mem. Ill. Gov.'s Commn. to Study Role and Needs Non-Pub. Higher Edn.; chmn. Gov.'s Com. Minority Employment Opportunities in News Media; Gov.'s Past Vietnam Planning Com.; mem. N.Y. State Council Advancement Indsl. Research and Devel., N.Y. State Health Planning Commn., N.Y. State Social Devel. Planning Commn., N.Y. State Joint Legislative Com. Higher Edn.; adv. com. Coll. Student Personnel Inst., vice-chmn. Internat. standing com. Univs. and Quest for Peace; mem. nat. com. U.S. Peoples Fund for Support of UN; mem. adv. council on grad. edn. U.S. Office Edn. Served as lt. comdr. USNR, World War II, PTO. Mem. Assn. Colls. and Univs. State N.Y. (v.p.), Nat. Assn. State Univs. and Land-Grant Colls. (dir.), Am. Council Edn. (dir.), Assn. Advt. Councils (dir.), Pilgrims U.S., N.Y. State Hist. Assn. (trustee), Phi Beta Kappa, Alpha Epsilon Rho, Delta Sigma Rho. Clubs: Bates College, University, Century (N.Y.C.); Fort Orange, Albany Country (Albany, N.Y.). Author: Knowledge Is Not Enough, 1959; (with S.A. Dimond) Training the Local Announcer, 1950; Today's Academic Condition, 1970. Home: 1 Benjamin Franklin Dr Sarasota FL 33577

GOULD, SYLVESTER EMANUEL, physician, educator; b. Detroit, July 31, 1900; s. Jude and Sarah (Stolarsky) G.; A.B., U. Mich., 1920, M.D., 1924, M.S., 1939, D.Sc., 1942; grad. study pathology under Dr. Ludwig Pick, Berlin, Germany, 1927- 28; m. Minna Blumenthal, July 22, 1926; children—Joyce (Mrs. Ronald M. Rothstein), Carol (Mrs. Berton A. Leon), Mark. Intern N.Y. City Hosp., 1924-26; asst. resident physician Montefiore Hosp., N.Y.C., 1926-27; pathologist-in-chief, dir. clin., pathology labs. Wayne County Gen. Hosp., Mich., 1932-63, hon. mem. med. staff, 1963—; instr. pathology, Coll. Medicine, Wayne U., 1935-37, asst. prof., 1938-48, asso. prof., 1949-50, clin. prof. pathology, 1951-53, prof. pathology, 1953- 64, prof. pathology emeritus, 1964—; prof., chmn. dept. pathology, U. Detroit Sch. Dentistry, 1956-62; research asso. pathology U. Mich., 1951-59, lectr. in pathology, 1959-63, research asso. pathology AEC Lab., 1951-56; Mich. Meml. Phoenix Project, 1951-61; Claude Bernard prof. U. Montreal, 1960; vis. prof. pathology U. Miami, 1963-66, adj. prof., 1966—; chief of research in pathology Atomic Bomb Casualty Commn., Hiroshima, Japan, 1966-67. U.S. rep. 1st Internat. Conf. Trichinosis, Warsaw, 1960; exec. com. Internat. Commn. Trichinosis, 1960—; chmn. Nat. Conf. on Trichinosis, 1952, 54, Continuing Com. on Trichinosis, 1952—; cons. pathology Sumby Meml. Hosp., River Rouge, Mich., 1939—, Sinai Hosp., Detroit, 1953—; hon. mem. med. staff Boulevard Gen. Hosp., Detroit, 1963—. Pres. Hampton Sch. P.T.A., 1951-52. Trustee Detroit Inst. Cancer Research, 1946-64, treas., 1956-61; trustee O.A. Brines Scholarship Fund, 1960-67. Chmn. Mich. SSS Adv. Bd., 1941-45. Diplomate clin. pathology and pathologic anatomy Am. Bd. Pathology. Mem. Internat. Acad. Pathology, Mich. Med. Soc. (del. 1934-58), Am. Soc. Parasitologists, A.A.A.S., Am. Assn. Pathologists and Bacteriologists, Am. Soc. Clin. Pathologists, Coll. Am. Pathologists (gov. 1957-62), Mich. (pres. 1946-47), Japanese (hon. mem.) path. socs., Sigma Xi. Author: Trichinosis, 1945. Spanish transl., 1952; (with others) Microscopic Pathology, 1964. Editor: Pathology of the Heart, 1953, 60, 68, Spanish translation 1956; Trichinosis in Man and Animals, 1969. Co- editor: The Acute Abdomen, 1966. Editor Am. Jour. Clin. Pathology, 1946- -, editor-in-chief, 1946-56; editor Bull. of Coll. Am. Pathologists, 1957-60, Bull. of Pathology, Am. Soc. Clin. Pathologists, 1965-70. Editorial bd. Internat. Pathology. Home: 801 Venetian Way Miami FL 33139

GOULD, WILLIAM RICHARD, utility exec., engr.; b. Provo, Utah, Oct. 31, 1919; s. William Gilbert and Pauline Eva (Faser) G.; B.S. in Mech. Engring., U. Utah, 1942; postgrad. Mass. Inst. Tech., U. Cal. at Los Angeles, U. Ida.; m. Erlyn Arvilla Johnson, Mar. 20, 1942; children—Erlyn Sharon, William Richard, Gilbert John, Wayne Raymond. With So. Cal. Edison Co., 1948—, mgr. engring. dept., 1962-63, v.p. engring., constrn., planning power supply and nuclear energy, 1963-67, sr. v.p., 1967—; dir. Energy Services, Inc., Mono Power Co., Electric Systems Co. Chmn. project mgmt. bd. Bolsa Island Nuclear Project, bd. of Control Mohave Project, Cal. Tech. Services Adv. Council. Active local Boy Scouts Am.; mem. water resources commn. So. Cal.; mem. sci. and engring. com. U. Redlands; bd. councilors Sch. Engring., U. So. Cal.; chmn. mgmt. com. WEST Assos., mem. bd. control Four Corners Project. Served to lt. USN, 1942-47. Recipient plaque Cal. Soc. Profl. Engrs., 1968. Registered profl. engr., Utah, Cal. Fellow Am. Soc. M.E. (Engr. of Month 1968), Inst. Advanced Engring. (Engr. of Year 1970); mem. Newcomen Soc. N.Am., Assn. Edison Illuminating Cos., Edison Electric Inst., Pacific Coast Elec. Assn., Internat. Conf. Large Electric Systems, Los Angeles C. of C. Mem. Ch. of Jesus Christ of Latter Day-Saints. Club: Electric. Home: 6441 Shire Way Long Beach CA 90815 Office: 601 W 5th St Los Angeles CA 90017

GOULDING, PHIL G., mgmt. cons.; b. San Francisco, Mar. 28, 1921; s. Alfred Thomas and Miriam M. (Fleck) G.; B.S., Hamilton Coll., 1943; m. Anne Catherine Wright, Apr. 30, 1949; children—Barry, Kent, Laura, Nancy, Philip. Reporter, Cleve. Plain Dealer, 1947-65, mem. Washington bur., 1950-65; dep. asst. sec. of def. for pub. affairs, Washington, 1965-67, asst. sec. of def. for public affairs, 1967-69; scholar in residence Aspen Inst. Humanistic Stuides, 1969; v.p., dir. Earl Newsom & Co., N.Y.C., 1969-70, pres., 1970—. Served from ensign to lt. (j.g.), USNR, 1943-46; ETO, PTO. Mem. Delta Upsilon. Episcopalian. Club: National Press (Washington). Author: Confirm or Deny: Informing the People on National Security, 1970. Home: 7210 Glenbrook Rd Bethesda MD 20014

GOULDNER, ALVIN WARD, educator, sociologist; b. N.Y.C., July 29, 1920; s. Louis and Estelle (Fetbrandt) G.; B.B.A., Bernard Baruch Coll., 1941; M.A., Columbia, 1945, Ph.D., 1953; m. Janet Lee Walker, Feb. 5, 1966; children—Richard Lee, Alan Jeremy, Andrew Ward, Alessandra Walker. Asso. prof. sociology U. Buffalo, 1947-51, Antioch Coll., Yellow Springs, O., 1952-54; asso. prof. U. Ill. at Urbana, 1954-57, prof., 1957-59; prof., chmn. dept. sociology Washington U., St. Louis, 1959-64, Max Weber Research prof., 1967—; lectr. Free U. Berlin (Germany), 1965, Stockholm (Sweden) Sch. Econ., 1965, Hebrew U., Jerusalem, Israel, 1966, Warsaw (Poland) U., 1966; founder, editor-in-chief Trans-Action mag., 1963-66; editor-in-chief New Critics Press, St. Louis, 1969—; editor Bobbs-Merrill Reprint Series, 1960—; cons. editor Penguin Books, London, Eng., 1969—; fellow Center Advanced Study Behavioral Scis., 1961-62. Mem. Am. Sociol. Assn., Soc. Study Social Problems Soc., Sic, Psychol. Study Social Issues, Soc. Study Social Problems, (pres. 1962). Author: Patterns of Industrial Bureaucracy, 1954; Wildcat Strike, 1954; (with R.A. Peterson) Notes on Technology and the Moral Order, 1962; Enter Plato, 1965; Coming Crisis of Western Sociology, 1970. Editor: Studies in Leadership: Leadership and Democratic Action, 1950; Emile Durkheim's Socialism and Saint-Simon, 1958; (with H.P. Gouldner) Modern Sociology, 1963; (with S.M. Miller) Applied Sociology, 1965. Home: 9 Washington Terrace St Louis MO 63112

GOULET, CHARLES RYAN, mgmt. cons.; b. Fond du Lac, Wis., Oct. 13, 1927; s. Charles N. and Irene (Ryan) G.; B.A., Beloit Coll., 1951; M.B.A., U. Chgo., 1953; m. Jeanne Comfort, Aug. 18, 1951; 1 son, Christopher Robert. Adminstrv. resident Jefferson-Hillman Hosp., Birmingham, Ala., 1952-53; adminstrv. asst., asst. supt. Cleve. City Hosp., 1953-55; asst. prof. U. Pitts., 1955-58; asso. dir. Johns Hopkins Hosp., 1958-62; dir. U. Chgo. Hosps. and Clinics, Chgo., 1962-69; prof. hosp. adminstrn. U. Chgo., 1962-69, asso. dir. program in hosp. adminstrn., 1962-69; prin. Cresap, McCormick and Paget, Inc., mgmt. cons., Chgo., 1969—. Exec. sec. Assn. U. Programs in Hosp. Adminstrn., 1962-65; pres. Chgo. Hosp. Council, 1968; treas. Ill. Hosp. Assn., 1969; mem. exec. com. Council Teaching Hosps., Assn. Am. Med. Colls., 1966-69. Mem. adv. council Kellogg Found., 1965-67. Bd. dirs. Hyde Park Dept. YMCA, 1966-68, Coop. Blood Replacement Plan, Home for Destitute Crippled Children, 1965-69, Chgo. Home for Incurables, 1966-69, Harvard-St. George Sch. Chgo., Hosp. Planning Council Met. Chgo., 1968-69, Comprehensive Health Planning, Chgo.; mem. gov. commn. Cook County Hosp., 1969-70. Served to 2d lt., Med. Adminstrn. Corps, AUS, 1946-47. Recipient Bachmeyer award U. Chgo., 1953. Fellow Am. Coll. Hosp. Adminstrs.; mem. Am., Ill. hosp. assns., Assn. Tchrs. Preventive Medicine, Phi Kappa Psi. Clubs: Kiwanis, Quadrangle (Chgo.); Chikaming Country (Lakeside, Mich.). Home: 1001 S Batavia Av Geneva IL 60134 Office: 100 W Monroe St Chicago IL 60603

GOULET, ROBERT G., singer; b. Lawrence, Mass., Nov. 26, 1933; s. Joseph and Jeanette (Gauthier) G.; student Royal Conservatory Music, Toronto, Ont., Can.; m. Carol Lawrence, Aug. 1963; children—Christopher, Michael; one dau. (by previous marriage), Nicolette. Formerly appeared as star of Canadian TV also radio; Broadway debut in Camelot, 1960; star, leading Am. TV programs; own CBS-TV spl. An Hour With Robert Goulet, own ABC-TV spl. The Bob Goulet Show, 1969; also BBC-TV spl., London, Eng.; appearing various supper clubs, including N.Y.C., Las Vegas; Columbia rec. artist; star of films Honeymoon Hotel, I'd Rather Be Rich; Underground; starred on Broadway in The Happy Time (Tony award for best mus. actor). Recs. include: My Love Forgive Me (album) (Gold rec.); Robert Goulet's Wonderful World of Christmas (album). Recipient Emmy award for TV version of Brigadoon. Home: Los Angeles CA 90052 Office: care Rogo Prodns The Plaza Hotel New York City NY 10019

GOULIAN, MEHRAN, physician, biochemist, hematologist, educator; b. Weehawken, N.J., Dec. 31, 1929; s. Dicran and Shamiram (Mzrakjian) G.; A.B., Columbia, 1950, M.D., 1954; m. Susan Hook, Aug. 5, 1961; children—Eric, Mark, Jonathan. Intern Barnes Hosp., St. Louis, 1954-55; resident Mass. Gen. Hosp., Boston, 1958-59, 61; fellow hematology Harvard, 1960, 62-63; fellow hematology Yale-New Haven Hosp., 1959-60; fellow biochemistry Stanford, 1965-67; instr. medicine Harvard Med. Sch., 1963-65; asso. prof. medicine, research asso. biochemistry U. Chgo.-Argonne Cancer Research Hosp., 1967-69, asso. prof. and biochemistry, 1969-70; prof. medicine U. Cal. at San Diego, 1970—. Served with USPHS, 1955-57. Home: 8433 Prestwick Dr La Jolla CA 92037

GOURLEY, DESMOND ROBERT HUGH, pharmacologist, educator; b. Thunder Bay, Can., Nov. 2, 1922; s. Hugh and Ida (Wilson) G.; B.A., U. Toronto, 1945, Ph.D., 1949; postgrad. U. Freiburg, 1968-69; m. Marjorie Edith Curl, Sept. 6, 1946; children—Robin C., David W., Alan W.H., Bruce D., Donald R. Demonstrator in zoology U. Toronto, 1945-49; research asst. U. Va., Charlottesville, 1949-51, asst. prof., 1951-53, asso. prof., 1953-62, prof. pharmacology, 1962—, acting chmn. dept. pharmacology, 1965, chmn. 1967-68, mem. Senate, 1966; mem. U.S. Pharmacopeial Conv., 1960. Fellow A. Von Humboldt Found., Germany, 1968. Mem. Am. Physiol. Soc., Am. Soc. Pharmacology and Exptl. Therapeutics, Pharmacology Soc. Can., Soc. for Exptl. Biology and Medicine, Va. Acad. Sci. Author: Interactions of Drugs with Cells, 1971. Contbr. articles profl. jours. Home: 225 Carrsbrook Dr Charlottesville VA 22901

GOURLEY, JAMES EDWIN, librarian; b. Birmingham, Ala., June 13, 1908; s. Ed. and Addie (Ozena) G.; A.B., Howard Coll., Birmingham, 1930; B.S., Columbia, 1931; postgrad. U. Tulsa; m. Virginia B. Ewing, Nov. 10, 1934; children—Dorothy Ewing, James Edwin. Page, jr. library asst. Birmingham Pub. Library, 1922-30; reference asst. N.Y. Pub. Library, 1930-37; dir. Pub. Library, Charlotte, N.C., 1937-39; asst. to librarian Racquet and Tennis Club, N.Y., 1933-37; librarian Tulsa Pub. Library, 1939-62; chief of Aero Center Libraries FAA, 1962—. Served as lt. USNR, 1942-45. Mem. A.L.A., Oklahoma Library Assn. (past pres.), Sigma Nu, Kappa Phi Kappa. Democrat. Methodist. Compiler: (with Robert M. Lester) The Diffusion of Knowledge, 1935; Regional American Cookery, 1936; Eating Round the World, 1937. Contbr. articles profl. jours. Home: 5708 NW 31 Oklahoma City OK 73127 Office: Will Rogers Field PO Box 1082 Oklahoma City OK 73105

GOURLEY, RONALD ROBERT, architect; b. St. Paul, Oct. 5, 1919; s. Robert Thomas and Eva Irene (Cardle) G.; B.Arch., U. Minn., 1943; M.Arch., Harvard, 1948; m. Phyllis Mary McDonald, Apr. 10, 1950; children—Robert McDonald, Karen Ellen, Geoffrey James. Instr. architecture Mass. Inst. Tech., 1948- 53; vis. prof. Royal Acad., Copenhagen, Denmark, 1952; prof. architecture Harvard, 1953-70; partner firm Sert, Jackson & Gourley, Cambridge, Mass., 1958-64; co-founder, partner Integrated Design Services Group, Cambridge, 1966—; pvt. practice, Cambridge, 1954-58, 64-66; prin. works include U. N.H. Meml. Union Bldg., Harvard Married Student Housing, Cunningham Found. Bldg. Served with AUS, 1944-46. Mem. A.I.A., Boston Soc. Architects, Boston Archtl. Center. Club: St. Botolph. Home: 1 Frost Terrace Cambridge MA 02140 also Middle Rd Chilmark MA 02535

GOURLEY, WALLACE S., judge; b. Wellsville, O., Aug. 4, 1904; s. Harry A. and Mary Margaret (Barclay) G.; LL.B., Ohio State U., 1929, LL.D.; m. Mildred R. Plunkett, Mar. 30, 1934. Admitted to Ohio bar, 1929, Pa. bar, 1931; 1st asst. dist. atty. Washington County, Pa., 1936-44; mem. Pa. Senate, 1941-45; judge U.S. Dist. Ct. for Western Dist. Pa., 1945-51, chief judge Western Dist. Pa., 1951—. Rep. to 3d Jud. circuit Jud. Conf. U.S. Mem. Nat. adv. Com. on Intercircuit Assignments, Nat. Com. on Trial Practice and Technique. Mem. Am., Pa., Washington County, Allegheny County bar assns., Am. Judicature Soc., Delta Theta Phi, Alpha Sigma Phi. Author: Gourley Instant Research Index Service, 6 vols. Home: Bigelow Apts Pittsburgh PA 15219 Office: US Courthouse Pittsburgh PA 15219

GOUSE, S. WILLIAM, Jr., univ. dean; b. Utica, N.Y., Dec. 15, 1931; s. S. William and Charlotte Virginia (Parzych) G.; S.B., S.M., Mass. Inst. Tech., 1954, Sc.D., 1958; m. Jacqueline Ann McLaughlin, Aug. 6, 1955; children—Linda Ellen, S. William III. Instr. mech. engring. Mass. Inst. Tech., 1956-57, asst. prof., 1957-61, 62-65, asso. prof., 1965-67, lectr., 1967-68; prof. mech. engring., prin. research engr. Transportation Research Inst. of Carnegie-Mellon U., 1967-69; staff mem. Office Sci. and Tech. of Exec. Office of the Pres., Washington, 1969-70; asso. dean Carnegie Inst. Tech. and Sch. Urban and Pub. Affairs of Carnegie-Mellon U., 1971—; cons. to industry. Served with ordnance, AUS, 1961-62. Visking Corp. fellow, 1954-55; Gen. Elec. Co. W.Rice Jr. fellow, 1955-56; recipient Ralph Teetor award Soc. Automotive Engrs., 1966. Contbr. articles profl. jours. Home: 3037 Sturbridge Ct Allison Park PA 15101 Office: Carnegie-Mellon Univ Pittsburgh PA 15213

GOUSHA, RICHARD PAUL, supt. of schs.; b. Balt., Sept. 3, 1923; s. Paul T. and Emma (Cartwright) G.; A.B., Heidelberg (O.) Coll., 1947; M.A., Western Res. U., 1949; Ed.D., Ind. U., 1960; m. Catherine Morris, Aug. 20, 1949; children—Catherine Anne, Michael Richard. Tchr., Bettsville, O., 1947- 48; local sch. exec., Putnam County, O., 1949, McCutchenville, O., 1950- 53, Woodville, O., 1954-56; supt. schs., Amherst, O., 1956-59; asst. to dir. research and field service Ind. U. Sch. Edn., 1959; supt. pub. schs., Cuyahoga Falls, O., 1960-64; supt. pub. instrn. Del., 1964-67; supt. pub. schs., Milw., 1967—. Mem. interim steering com. Edn. Commn. of States, 1965-67; ex officio mem., sec. Higher Edn. Adv. Com. Del., 1964-67; chmn. Nat. Schs. Com. Econ. Edn.; vis. prof. U. Wis.-Milw. Sch. Edn., summer 1970. Mem. Mental Health Planning Com. Milwaukee County; mem. adv. com. Milw. Children's Ct.; mem. Wis. regional bd. Nat. Conf. Christians and Jews; chmn. Wis. council Econ. Edn.; mem. exec. com., Council Great City Schs. Bd. dirs. Milwaukee County chpt. A.R.C., Milw. Symphony Orch., Milw. Tech. Coll.; trustee Jt. Council on Econ. Edn.; bd. govs. Jr. Achievement Southeastern Wis. Served with inf. AUS, World War II; ETO. Decorated Bronze Star. Mem. Am. Assn. Sch. Adminstrs., Ohio P.T.A. (hon. life), Phi Delta Kappa. Presbyn. Rotarian, Mason. Club: Schoolmasters of Wis. Home: 2840 N Menomonee River Pkwy Milwaukee WI 53222 Office: 5225 W Vliet St Milwaukee WI 53208

GOVAN, JAMES FAUNTLEROY, librarian; b. Chattanooga, May 9, 1926; s. Gilbert Eaton and Christine (Noble) G.; B.A., U. of South, 1948; postgrad. Inst. Hist. Research, U. London (Eng.), 1951-52; M.A., Emory U., 1955; Ph.D., Johns Hopkins, 1960; m. Ann Henegar Bright, June 6, 1952; children—James Gardner, Andrew Eaton, Christine Noble, David Bright. Asst. prof. history U. of South, 1949; readers services librarian U. Ala., 1955-60; head librarian Trinity U., 1961-65, Swarthmore (Pa.) Coll., 1965—, lectr., 1969—; prof. history Trinity U., 1961-65. Chmn. coll. and univ. div. Tex. Library Assn., 1963-64, chmn. com. coll. library standards, 1964, mem. library devel. com., 1964-65; cons. Hampshire Coll. Library Conf., 1967. Bd. dirs. Pa. Union Catalogue, 1966—, treas., 1968—. Served with USNR, 1944-46, AUS, 1953-55. Council Library Resources fellow, 1970. Mem. A.L.A., Phi Beta Kappa, Beta Phi Mu. Author: The Pat Ireland Nixon Collection, 1965. Home: 730 Yale Av Swarthmore PA 19081

GOVAN, MARY CHRISTINE NOBLE, author; b. N.Y.C., Dec. 12, 1898; d. Stephen Edward and Mary Helen (Quintard) Noble; student U. Chattanooga, 1916-17; m. Gilbert Eaton Govan, June 10, 1918; children—Emily Payne, Mary Quintard, James Fauntleroy. Writer, 1928—. Mem. Julia Ellsworth Ford Found. Com., 1939-40. Mem. League Women Voters, Authors League. Democrat. Episcopalian. Author books including: Jennifer's House, 1945; The Pink Maple House, 1950; The Surprising Summer, 1951; Tilly's Strange Secret, 1953; The Superduper Car, 1953; Rachel Jackson (juvenile), 1955; Mystery at Shingle Rock, 1955; The Year The River Froze, 1960; Mystery at the Mountain Face, 1956, Mystery at Moccasin Bend, 1957, Mystery at the Indian Hide-out, 1957, Mystery at the Deserted Mill, 1958, Mystery of the Vanishing Stamp (juvenile), 1958, Mystery at The Haunted House, 1959, Mystery at Plum Nelly, 1959, Mystery at Fearsome Lake, 1960, Mystery at Rock City, 1960, Mystery at the Weird Ruins, 1964 (all in collaboration with Emmy Govan West); Mystery of the Dancing Skeleton, 1960; Mystery at the Snowed-in Cabin, 1961; Willow Landing, 1961; The Delectable Mountain, 1962; Number 5 Hackberry Street, 1964; Mystery at the Echoing Cave, 1965; Return to Hackberry Street, 1967; Curious Clubhouse, 1967; short story, "Miss Winter and the Wind" in O. Henry Prize Collection, 1947, in Stories Not For the Nervous (Hitchcock), 1965; Phinny's Fine Summer-World, 1968; Mr. Alexander and the Witch, 1969; The Trash-Pile Treasure, 1970. Book reviewer Chattanooga Times; contbr. to newspapers and mags. Lectr. Address: 400 Laurel Lane Lookout Mountain TN 37350 ☆

GOVE, HARRY EDMUND, educator, nuclear physicist; b. Niagara Falls, Can., May 22, 1922; s. Harry Golden and Lucia (Olmsted) G.; B.Sc., Queen's U., Kingston, Ont., 1944; Ph.D., Mass. Inst. Tech., 1950; m. Elizabeth Alice dePencier, Aug. 20, 1945; children—Pauline Lucia, Diana Elizabeth. Came to U.S., 1963, naturalized, 1969. Research asst. Nat. Research Council, Chalk River, Can., 1945-46, Mass. Inst. Tech., 1946-50, research asso., 1950-52; asso. research officer Atomic Energy of Can., Ltd., Chalk River, 1952-59, br. head nuclear physics, 1956-63, sr. research officer, 1959-63, on leave with Niels Bohr Inst., Copenhagen, 1961-62; prof. physics, dir. nuclear structure research lab. U. Rochester, 1963—. Mem. vis. com. Mass. Inst. Tech. Lab. Nuclear Research, 1966-68, Argonne Nat. Lab. physics div., 1966-69, Queen's U. Coll. Engring., 1968-70; mem. adv. com. physics div. NSF, 1969—; mem. ad hoc panel on meson factories Office Sci. and Tech., 1963; mem. selection panel NSF Postdoctoral Fellows, 1967, 69, 70. Pres. Metro Act of Rochester, Inc., 1970-71. Served from sublt. to lt., Royal Canadian Navy, 1944-45. Fellow Am. Phys. Soc.; mem. Canadian Assn. Physicists. Democrat. Episcopalian. Club: Cosmos (Washington). Contbr. articles profl. jours. Home: 52 Poplar Dr Rochester NY 14625

GOVE, PHILIP BABCOCK, editor; b. Concord, N.H., June 27, 1902; s. John McClure and Florence Amy (Babcock) G.; A.B., Dartmouth, 1922, Litt.D., 1963; A.M., Harvard, 1925; Ph.D., Columbia, 1941; m. Grace Edna Potter, Aug. 17, 1929; children—Norwood B., Susan (Mrs. Rosser A. Rudolph, Jr.), Doris. Instr. English, Rice Inst., 1924-27, N.Y.U., 1927-42; William Bayard Cutting traveling fellow Columbia, 1939-40; asst. editor Merriam-Webster dictionaries, Springfield, Mass., 1946-51, mng. editor, 1951-52, gen. editor, 1952-61, editor in chief, 1961—. Mem. editorial bd. Ency. Brit.; mem. adv. bd. Center for Documentation,

Communication Research, Western Res. U. Served as lt. comdr. USNR, 1942-46. Mem. Linguistic Soc. Am., Am. Dialect Soc., Nat. Council Tchrs. English, Modern Lang. Assn., Internat. Soc. Gen. Semantics, Coll. English Assn., English Grad. Union (Columbia), Johnson Soc. of London, Nat. Soc. for Study Communications, Phi Gamma Delta. Author: The Imaginary Voyage in Prose Fiction, 1941. Editor: The Role of the Dictionary, 1967. Contbr. articles to learned jours. Home: Old Patrick Rd Warren MA 01083 Office: G & C Merriam Co Springfield MA 01101

GOVE, ROGER MADDEN, physician; b. Mechanicsburg, O., Nov. 30, 1914; s. Thurman Harrison and Leah Marie (Madden) G.; B.A., Ohio State U., 1937, M.D., 1941; m. Eleaner Jane Rooney, June 15, 1938; children—Jon Duane, Janet Marie (Mrs. David Dye), Joann Leah (Mrs. Jerry Webb) and Judith Lynn (twins). Intern White Cross Hosp., Columbus, O., 1941-42; resident psychiatry Columbus State Hosp., 1942, 45-46; Commonwealth Fund fellow child psychiatry Children's Service Center Wyoming Valley, Wilkes Barre, Pa., 1946-47; dir. Upper Miami Valley Guidance Center, Piqua, O., 1947-50; supt. Columbus State Sch., 1950-54, 58-66; asst. commr. Ohio Div. Mental Hygiene, 1966—, chief Bur. Mental Retardation, 1954, 66—; supt. Juvenile Diagnostic Center, Columbus, 1954-58; clin. asst. prof. psychiatry and pediatrics Ohio State U. Coll. Medicine, 1951- -. Chmn. Task Force Mental Retardation Planning Ohio, 1963-65; mem. com. long term care United Cerebral Palsy Assn., 1963—. Trustee Urbana (O.) Coll., 1964—. Served to capt., M.C., USAAF, 1942-45. Fellow Am. Assn. Mental Retardation (chmn. exam. bd. 1963-67); mem. Am., Ohio (pres. 1961) psychiat. assns. Home: 4230 Ongaro Dr Columbus OH 43204 Office: 65 S Front St Columbus OH 43215

GOVE, SAMUEL KIMBALL, educator; b. Walpole, Mass., Dec. 27, 1923; student Mass. State Coll., 1941-43; B.S. in Econs., U. Mass., 1947; M.A. in Polit. Sci., Syracuse U., 1949. Research asst. govt. and pub affairs U. Ill., 1950-51, research asso., 1951-54, mem. faculty, 1954—, prof. polit. sci., 1966—, dir. Inst. Govt. and Pub. Affairs, 1967—. Staff asst. Nat. Assn. Assessing Officers, 1949; mem. research staff Ill. Commn. Study State, Govt., 1950-51; cons. Ill. Dept. Finance, 1951-53; research staff Nat. Municipal League, 1955-56; exec. asst. Ill. Auditor Pub. Accounts, 1957; cons. Ill. Legislative Council, 1959, Ill. atty. gen., 1961; program coordinator Ill. Legislative Staff Intern Program, 1962—; mem. com. financing higher edn. Ill. Master Plan Higher Edn., 1963; mem. Ill. Commn. Orgn. Gen. Assembly, 1965-69, 70—, Ill. Commn. State Govt., 1965-67; cons. elections ABC, 1964, 66, 68; chmn. Champiagn (Ill.) County Economic Opportunity Council, 1966-67; staff legislative research fellow Am. Polit. Sci. Assn., 1966—; cons. Am. Council Edn., 1966-67; sec. Local Govts. Commn., 1967-69; staff dir. Ill. Constn. Study Commn., 1968-69; exec. sec. Gov. Ill. Constn. Research Group, 1969-70; mem. Ill. Constn. Study Commn., 1969-70; mem. Nat. Com. R, 1969—; mem. adv. council Ill. Dept. Local Govt. Affairs. Served to lt. (j.g.) USNR, 1943-46. Mem. Am. Assn. U. Profs. (past chpt. pres..), Am. Polit Sci. Assn., Am. Soc. Pub. Adminstrn. (past chpt. chmn.; chmn. univs. govtl. research conf. 1969—), Govtl. Research Assn. (bd. dirs. 1969—), Ill. Hist. Soc., Midwest Cong. Polit. Scientist, Nat. Municipal League. Author numerous articles. Home: 2006 Bruce Dr Urbana IL 61801 Office: Inst Govt and Pub Affairs Urban-Champaign Campus Urbana IL

GOVER, ROBERT, author; b. Phila., Nov. 2, 1929; s. Bryant Addison and Anna (Wall) G.; B.A., U. Pitts., 1953; m. Mildred Vitkovich, Mar. 15, 1955 (div. 1966); m. 2d, Jeanne-Nell Gement, Dec. 1968; 1 son, Bryant. Author: One Hundred Dollar Misunderstanding, 1962; The Maniac Responsible, 1963; Here Goes Kitten, 1964; Poorboy At The Party, 1966; J.C. Saves, 1968. Home: 540 Picacho Lane Montecito CA 93103

GOVIER, GEORGE WHEELER, engr., adminstr.; b. Nanton, Alta., Can., June 15, 1917; s. George Arthur and Gertrude (Wheeler) G.; B.A.Sc. in Chem. Engring., U. B.C., 1939; M.Sc. in Phys. Chem., U. Alta., 1945; Sc.D. in Chem. Engring., U. Mich., 1949; m. Doris Eda Kemp, Feb. 23, 1940; children—Gertrude Rose, Katherine Mary, Susan Elizabeth. Faculty U. Alta., 1940—, prof. chem. engring., 1948—, head dept. chem. and petroleum engring., 1948-49, dean faculty engring., 1959-63; part-time prof. engring., U. Calgary, 1963—. Mem. Oil and Gas Conservation Bd. Alta., 1948—, dep. chmn. bd., 1959-62, chmn. bd., 1962—; mem. Canadian nat. com. World Petroleum Congress, 1961—; mem. of Alta. Univs. Commn., 1968—. Registered prof. engr. Province Alta. Fellow Chem. Inst. Can. (chmn. chem. engring. div. 1948-49, vice chmn. 1959-60, councillor 1951-52), Engring. Inst. Can. (chmn. chem. engring. div. com. tech. operations 1961-63); mem. Can. Inst. Mining and Metallurgy (chmn. petroleum and natural gas div. 1950-51; pres. 1966-67), Am. Inst. Chem. Engrs., Assn. Profl. Engrs. Alta. (pres. 1957-58, mem. council 1959-60), Lambda Chi Alpha. Club: Calgary Petroleum. Contbr. numerous tech. papers to tech. lit. Mem. editorial bd. Chemistry in Can., 1950-52, Can. Jour. Chem. Engring., 1957—. Home: 1507 Cavanaugh Pl Calgary Alberta Canada Office: 603 6th Av SW Calgary Alberta Canada

GOVINDJEE, educator; b. Allahabad, India, Oct. 24, 1933; s. Visheshwar Prasad and Savitri (Asthana) Asthana: B.Sc., U. Allahabad, 1952, M.Sc., 1954; Ph.D., U. Ill., 1960; m. Rajni Varma, Oct. 24, 1957; children—Anita Govindjee, Sanjay Govindjee. Came to U.S., 1956. Lectr. in botany U. Allahabad, 1952-54; grad. fellow U. Ill., Urbana, 1956-58, USPHS postdoctoral trainee biophysics, 1960-61, mem. faculty, 1961—, asso. prof. botany and biophysics, 1965-69, prof., 1969—. Mem. Am. Assn. U. Profs., A.A.A.S., Am. Soc. Plant Physiologists, Biophys. Soc. Am., Am. Inst. Biol. Sci., Sigma Xi. Author: Photosynthesis, 1969. Contbr. profl. jours. Home: 1101 McHenry St Urbana IL 61801

GOVONI, ALBERT PETER, editor, writer; b. Hudson, Mass., Jan. 10, 1914; s. Rodolph and Caterina (Guidotti) G.; B.A., U. Wash., 1935; m. Joanne Ellyn Cron, May 29, 1948; children—Stephen, Catherine. Newspaper reporter, 1931-36; fgn. corr., Europe, S.Am., Central Am., 1936-41; free-lance mag. writer, 1945-48; editor True Detective, Master Detective, Ofcl. Detective mags., 1948—, pres. True Detective Pub. Corp.; records editor, critic Saga mag. Mem. citizens adv. council Nat. Police Officers Assn. Am. Served with USAAF, 1941-45. Named to Police Hall of Fame, 1964. Mem. Honor Legion N.Y.C. Police Dept., Internat., N.Y. State assns. chiefs police. Author: The Lawrence Welk Story, 1967; A Boy Named Cash—The Johnny Cash Story, 1970. Home: 39 Horton St Rye NY 10580 Office: 206 E 43d St New York City NY 10017

GOW, JAMES STEELE, ret. found. exec.; b. Pitts., Jan. 3, 1895; s. Harry Campbell and Elizabeth Gray (Steele) G.; ed. Pitts. Acad., 1909-12; A.B. cum laude, U. Pitts., 1916, LL.D., 1938; Ed.M., Harvard, 1927; m. Hazel Evelyn Steele, May 10, 1917; children—James Steele, Don Wallace, Robert Campbell. With U. Pitts., 1916-30, head dept. pub. relations until 1918, financial sec., 1918-20, asst. to pres., 1920-24, exec. sec. of Univ., 1924-29, dean adminstrn., 1929; exec. dir. Falk Found., Pitts., 1930-65. Austin fellow in edn., Harvard, 1924-25; lectr. ednl. sociology U. Pitts., 1925-35. Instr. O.T.S., U.S. Army, 1918; sec. Bd. Hospitalization for War Vets (U.S. Treasury Dept.), 1920. Trustee Children's Hosp.; mem. bd. Leon Falk Family Trust. Recipient Alan M. Scaife award for leadership in edn., 1964. Mem. Phi Beta Kappa, Omicron Delta Kappa, Pi Tau Alpha, Delta Mu Delta, Sigma Alpha Epsilon. Republican. Baptist. Clubs: Duquesne (Pitts.); Williams Country (Weirton, W.Va.). Home: 3955 Bigelow Blvd Pittsburgh PA 15213

GOW, ROBERT HAIGH, farming exec.; b. Paris, France, Apr. 26, 1933 (parents Am. citizens); s. Ralph F. and Eleanore (Haigh) G.; B.S., Yale, 1955; m. Patricia Alice Lawson, July 20, 1957; children—Laura Lawson, David Frederick, Heather Haigh. Indsl. engr. Electro-Chem. div. Norton Co., Chippawa, Ont., Can., 1955-56, supr. indsl. engring., sec. growth com., Worcester, Mass., 1958-61; pres. Champlain-Zapata Plastics Machinery, Inc., Caldwell, N.J., 1961-63; v.p., treas. Zapata Off-Shore Co., Houston, 1963-67, exec. v.p., 1967-69; pres., dir. Zapata Norness, Inc., 1969-70; chmn. bd., chief exec. officer Stratford of Tex., Inc., Houston, 1969—, also dir.; dir. Southdown, Inc., Australian Land & Cattle Co., Ltd., Digicon, Inc. Served to 1st lt. USAF, 1956-58. Mem. Houston Soc. Financial Analysts, Young Presidents Orgn., Tau Beta Pi. Club: Yale (past pres.) (Houston). Home: 3656 Ella Lee Lane Houston TX 77027 Office: Tenneco Bldg Houston TX 77002

GOWAN, ARTHUR MITCHELL, univ. adminstr.; b. Cleghorn, Ia., Dec. 1, 1910; s. William and Annie (Mitchell) G.; B.A., U. No. Ia., 1932; M.A., U. Ia., 1939; Ph.D., Ia. State U., 1947; m. Marjorie Mace, June 19, 1940; children—Barbara (Mrs. Donald K. Watkins), Sandra (Mrs. Gary R. Kirk). Adminstr. secondary sch., Nevada, Ia., 1932-42; supr. math. U.S. Naval Tng. Sch., Ia. State U., 1942-44; asst. to dean of engring. Ia. State U. at Ames, 1944-46, asst. registrar, 1946-51, registrar, 1951-65, dean admissions and records, 1965—. Ford Found. cons. Nat. Engring. U., Lima, Peru, 1965. Mem. Ames City Planning Commn., 1970—. Mem. Am. Assn. Collegiate Registrars and Admissions Officers, Am. Assn. Higher Edn., Phi Kappa Phi, Phi, Mu Epsilon. Kiwanian (lt. gov. Neb.-Ia. dist. 1965). Home: 610 9th St Ames IA 50010

GOWANS, ALAN, author, educator; b. Toronto, Can., Nov. 30, 1923; s. C. Allan and Ruth (Meek) G.; came to U.S., 1948, naturalized, 1957; M.A., U. Toronto, 1946; M.F.A., Princeton, 1948, Ph.D., 1950; m. Ruth Louisa Perry, June 18, 1948; children—Peter Alan, Jane Madeline, John Edward, Abigail Ruth. Instr. art history Rutgers U., 1948-53; asst. prof. art history Middlebury (Vt.) Coll., 1953-54; dir. Felming Mus., U. Vt., 1954-56; chmn. dept. art and art history U. Del., 1956—, prof. art history, 1960—; chmn. div. art and art history U. Victoria (B.C., Can.), 1966—; vis. prof. U Edinburgh (Scotland), fall 1964, U. Stockholm (Sweden), spring 1965. Grantee Am. Council Learned Socs., 1949. Mem. Soc. Archtl. Historians (bd. dirs. 1959-66, sec. 1961-64, 1st v.p. 1970—), Inst. for Study Universal History (pres. 1970—). Episcopalian. Author: Church Architecture in New France, 1955; Looking at Architecture in Canada, 2d edit., 1966; The Face of Toronto, 1960; Images of American Living, Four Centuries of Architecture and Furniture (Alice Davis Hitchcock award 1965), 1964; The Restless Art, A Study of Painting and Painters, 1750-1950, 1966; King Carter's Church, 1969; The Unchanging Art, A Study of Illustration, Comics, Cartoons, Advertising, TV, etc., 1970. Address: 3980 Locarno Lane Victoria British Columbia Canada

GOWDY, CURTIS, sportscaster; b. Green River, Wyo., 1919; grad. U. Wyo., 1942; m. Jerre Dawkins, June 1949; children—Cheryl Ann, Curtis, Trevor. Formerly broadcaster for radio stas. in Cheyenne, Wyo. and Oklahoma City; with Mel Allen broadcast N.Y. Yankees Baseball Team games, 1949-51; announcer for Boston Red Sox Baseball Team games, 1951-66; broadcaster Am. Football League games, 1961—; also host sports documentaries. Served with USAAF, 1942-43. Named Sportcaster of Year, Nat. Assn. Sportwriters and Sport Broadcasters, 1967. Address: care NBC 30 Rockefeller Plaza New York City NY 10022*

GOWEN, JAMES EMMET, ry. co. exec.; b. Phila., Apr. 22, 1895; s. Francis Innes and Alice (Robinson) G.; grad. St. Paul's Sch., 1913; A.B., Princeton, 1917; LL.B., U. Pa., 1921; m. Sally Drexel Henry, June 25, 1925; children—Francis I., Howard H. Admitted to Pa. bar, 1921; with legal dept. Pa. R.R. Co., 1921-30, dir., 1942—; v.p. Phila. Sav. Fund Soc., 1930-33; pres., dir. Western Sav. Fund Soc., 1933-39; pres., chmn. bd. Girard Trust Bank, Phila., 1939-60; dir. Camden Fire Ins. Assn., Pa. Gen. Ins. Co., Potomac Ins. Co., Phila., Balt. and Washington R.R. Co., Pitts., Youngstown and Ashtabula Ry. Co., Manor Real Estate Co., Mut. Assurances Co., Pa. Gen. Fire Ins. Co. Served with U.S. Navy, 1917-21. Democrat. Clubs: Philadelphia, Rabbit (Phila.); Schuylkill (Pa.). Home: Chestnut Hill Philadelphia PA 19118 Office: Girard Trust Bldg Philadelphia PA 19102

GOWEN, SAMUEL EMMETT author; b. LaVergne, Tenn., Sept. 10, 1902; s. George Washington and Nona Elizabeth (Duffel) G.; ed. pub. sch., LaVergne; m. Claire Loeb, May 31, 1941. Reporter Memphis News Scimitar, Memphis Comml. Appeal, 1922-25; field sec. Fla. Lumber & Millwork Assn., winter 1925; reporter Bronx Home News, 1926; editor The Fourth Estate, 1927; publicity dir. Better Bus. Bur. N.Y., 1927-29; mng. dir. Emmett Gowen Ltd., Belize, Brit. Honduras. Served as pvt. USMC, 1919-23; expdns. in Mexico and Central Am. Mem. Authors League Am., Outdoor Writers Assn. Am. Author: Racketeers, an Expose, 1930; Mountain Born, 1932; Dark Moon of March, 1933; Old Hell, 1937; The Rebel Drum, 1945; The Joys of Fishing, 1961; Expedition Holy Book, 1967; The Adventure Coast (translation La Costa de Adventura); short stories in Yale Review, Atlantic, Esquire and others; articles in Americas, True the Man's Mag., Field and Stream, Outdoor Life, Sports Afield, Sports Illustrated, others. Mem. adv. council Who's Who in Am. Home: La Vergne TN 37086

GOWETZ, IRENE, lawyer; b. Worcester, Mass., Aug. 28, 1907; d. Arthur E. and Alice (Hemenway) Gowetz; LL.B. cum laude, Northeastern U., 1929; m. Carl A. Remington, June 18, 1959. Admitted to Mass. bar, 1929; partner firm Bowditch, Gowetz and Lane, Worcester, 1950—. Chmn. Mass. Ballot Law Commn., 1955-58. Bd. dirs. Girls Clubs Am., 1955—. Republican. Home: Troon Way New Seabury MA 02536 Office: 340 Main St Worcester MA 01608

GOWLING, ERNEST GORDON, lawyer; b. Ottawa, Ont., Can., June 4, 1903; LL.D., Osgoode Hall; m. Aileen Isabell Harston, Oct. 12, 1929; 1 son, William Gordon. Called to Ont. bar, 1926; created Queen's Counsel; sr. mem. firm Gowling & Henderson, Ottawa. Mem. Canadian (past pres.), Am. (hon.) bar assns. Mason. Clubs: Rideau, Country. Home: 305 Clemow Av Ottawa Ontario K1S 2B7 Canada Office: 116 Albert St Ottawa Ontario Canada also Box 466 Terminal A Ottawa Ontario KIN853 Canada*

GOWON, YAKUBU, Nigerian govt. ofcl.; b. Lur Pankshin Div., Nigeria, Oct. 19, 1934; s. Yohanna and Saratu Gowon; ed. Govt. Coll., Zaria, Royal Mil. Acad., Sandhurst, Staff Coll., Camberley and Joint Services Coll., Latimer, Eng.; m. Victoria Hansatu, 1969; 1 son, 1 dau. Advanced through grades to maj. gen. Nigerian Army, 1967; adj. Nigerian Army, 1960; mem. peacekeeping force, UN, Cong., 1960-61; adj.-gen. Nigerian Army, 1966, chief of staff, 1966; head Fed. Mil. Govt., comdr. in chief Armed Forces of Nigeria, 1966—. Office: Supreme Hdqrs State House Dodan Varracks Lagos Nigeria*

GOYAN, JERE EDWIN, educator; b. Oakland, Cal., Aug. 3, 1930; s. Gerald H. and Lucille (Johnson) G.; B.S., U. Cal. Sch. Pharm., 1952, Ph.D., 1957; m. Patricia B. Mesirow, Aug. 24, 1952; children—Rebecca, Terrence H., Andrea. Asst. prof. pharmacy U. Mich., 1956-61, asso. prof., 1961-63; asso. prof. pharmacy and pharm. chemistry U. Cal. at San Francisco, 1963-65, prof., 1965—, asso. dean Sch. Pharmacy, 1966-67, dean, 1967—. Fellow A.A.A.S.; mem. N.Y. Acad. Scis., Am. Assn. U. Profs., Am. Pharm. Assn., Acad. Pharm. Scis., Cal. Pharm. Assn., Am. Pub. Health Assn., Rho Chi, Kappa Psi, Sigma Xi, Phi Lambda Upsilon. Home: 318 Rydal St Mill Valley CA 94941 Office: 3d and Parnassus Avs San Francisco CA 94122

GOYEN, CHARLES WILLIAM, author; b. Trinity, Tex., Apr. 24, 1915; s. Charles Provine and Mary Inez (Trow) G.; B.A., Rice U., 1937, M.A., 1939; m. Doris Roberts, Nov. 10, 1963. Asso. in English, Columbia, 1964-66; sr. editor trade dept. McGraw Hill, 1966-71. Recipient mus. awards (words and music) A.S.C.A.P., 1964, 65, 68, 70, 71. Guggenheim fellow, 1950, 52; Ford Found. grantee, 1963-64. Author: (novels) The House of Breath, 1950, In a Farther Country, 1955, The Fair Sister, 1963; (short stories) Ghost and Flesh, 1952, The Faces of Blood Kindred, 1960; (plays) The House of Breath, 1956, The Diamond Rattler, 1960, Christy, 1964; also critical pieces in N.Y. Times, 1950—. ‡

GOYNE, JAMES BEVAN, physician, med. adminstr.; b. Ashland, Pa., Apr. 25, 1911; s. John G. and Cora A. (Bevan) G.; B.S., Pa. State U., 1933; M.D., Jefferson Med. Coll., 1937; m. Jean Zemaitis, Aug. 2, 1950. Intern Cooper Hosp., Camden, N.J., 1937-38; gen. practice medicine, Gettysburg, Pa., 1938-42, Lawrenceville, N.J., 1946-50; resident in psychiatry Trenton (N.J.) State Hosp., 1950-51, Univ. Clincs, Phila., 1952-53; mem. staff N.J. State Hosp., Trenton, 1953-58, asst. med. dir., 1958-63, med. dir., 1963- 66; med. dir. Morris County Guidance Clinic, Morristown, N.J., 1967- -; pvt. practice psychiatry, 1953—; instr. U. Pa. Sch. Medicine, 1953- 66; cons. Lehigh U., Bethlehem, Pa. Served with M.C., AUS, 1942- 46. Mem. A.M.A., Morris County Med. Soc., Am. Psychiat. Assn., N.J. Neuro-Psychiat. Soc. Address: Morris County Guidance Clinic Court House Morristown NJ 07960

GOYTISOLO, JUAN, author; b. Barcelona, Spain, 1931; ed. univs. Barcelona, Madrid. Went to Paris, France, 1957, making frequent trips back to Spain; reporter for French jours. in Cuba, 1965. Author: The Young Assassins, Fiestas, Island of Women, Mejor la Destruccion, El Fuego, The Party's Over. Address: care Grove Press Inc 80 University Pl New York City NY 10003*

GOZONSKY, MOSES JAMES, former govt. ofcl.; b. Laconia, N.H., Sept. 10, 1923; s. Archie and Ida (Halperin) G.; B.S., U. N.H., 1947, M.A., 1950; M.S., Columbia, 1950; m. Eileen Ruth Charney, Oct. 14, 1951. Instr. dept. econs. and bus. adminstrn. U. N.H., 1948-49; bus. economist Bur. Labor Statistics, Dept. Labor, Washington, 1950-51, labor economist wage and hour div., 1951-53; cons. United Steelworkers Am. Com. on Ret. and Older Workers, 1957- 61, with Murray W. Latimer, indsl. relations cons., Washington, 1954-61; dep. asst. for problems of elderly and handicapped Dept. Housing and Urban Devel., Washington, 1961-69; cons. U.S. Senate Com. on Aging, 1961. Mem. exec. bd. govt. div. United Jewish Appeal, Washington. Research dir. Sr. Citizens for Kennedy and Johnson, Washington, 1960. Served with USAAF, 1943-45. Mem. Alumni Assn. Sch. Bus. Columbia, N.H. State Soc. Washington (pres. 1970-71, past v.p., dir.), Am. Pub. Welfare Assn., Phi Sigma Delta. Club: U. N.H. Alumni (past pres. Washington). Home: 700 7th St SW Washington, DC 20024. Office: Dept Housing and Urban Devel 7th and D Sts SW Washington DC 20410

GOZZANO, FRANCESCO, journalist; b. Rome, Italy, Jan. 14, 1930; s. Matteo Umberto and Natalia (Labroca) G.; law degree, Turin (Italy) U., 1953; m. Mariapiera Casolaro, Oct. 15, 1958; children—Simone, Natalia, Stefano. With daily newspaper Avanti, 1949—, fgn. editor, editoralist, 1957—; editoralist several Italian and European magazines. Mem. directory bd. Turin Socialist Party, 1949-53; mem. fgn. policy com. Italian Socialist Party, 1961—. Recipient Fgn. Journalism award U. Cal. at Los Angeles, 1967; St. Vincent Internat. Journalism award Italy, 1967. Mem. European Journalist Assn. (v.p. Italian sect. 1965—, mem. directory bd. Brussels 1965—). Home: 21 via San Calepodio Rome Italy 00152 Office: 22 via della Guardiola Rome Italy 00186

GRABACH, JOHN ROBERT, artist; b. Greenfield, Mass.; s. John Robert and Genevefa (Asam) G.; student Art Students League, N.Y.C.; m. Anna Thompson. Instr. Newark Sch. Fine and Indsl. Art, 1930—; one man shows include Art Inst. Chgo., 1930, Grand Central Galleries, N.Y.C., 1952, Montclair (N.J.) Art Mus., 1950, Meml. Art Gallery, Rochester, N.Y., 1935; group exhbns. include Springfield (Mass.) Art Mus., Audubon Artists, Pa. Acad. Fine Arts, Nat. Acad. Design, Detroit Inst. Arts, Corcoran Gallery Art, Art Inst. Chgo., Carnegie Inst., Los Angeles Mus., Buffalo Fine Arts Acad., Pan Am. Exhbn. (Los Angeles), Panama Pacific Internat. Exposition (San Francisco), Old White Art Colony, White Sulphur Springs, W. Va., Richmond (Ind.) Pub. Art Gallery, Art Club Phila., Montclair Art Mus., Gallery Sci. and Art (N.Y. Worlds Fair 1940), Meml. Art. Gallery (Rochester), J.B. Speed Meml. Mus., Louisville, Cin. Mus., Art Assn. Indpls., City Art Mus., St. Louis, Toledo Mus. Art, Columbus (O.) Gallery Fine Arts; rep. permanent collections Phila. Art Alliance, Art Inst. Chgo., Vanderpoel Art Assn., Chgo., John Herron Art Inst., Indpls., Corcoran Gallery Art, IBM Gallery, Norton Mus. (Fla.), Sea Isle (Fla.), Newark Mus., also pvt. colls. Recipient Peabody prize Art Inst. Chgo., 1930, Sesnam gold medal Pa. Acad. Fine Arts, 1927, Preston Harrison prize Los Angeles Mus., 1928, 2d William A. Clark prize and silver medal Corcoran Gallery Art, 1932, IBM medal N.Y. World Fair, 1940, R. Stern prize Audubon Artists, 1953, hon. mention Salmagundi Club, 1961, Herman Wick prize, 1961, gold medal of honor Am. Artists Profl. League, 1965, Knickerbocker Artists, N.Y., 1965. Mem. Phila. Water Color Club, Irvington Art Mus. Assn. (dir.), Audubon Artists, Salmagundi Club. Author: Drawing and Painting the Human Figure, 1956. Address: 915 Sanford Av Irvington NJ 07111

GRABAR, OLEG, educator; b. Strasbourg, France, Nov. 3, 1929; s. Andre and Julie (Ivanova) G.; B.A. magna cum laude, Harvard, 1950; licence d'Histoire, U. Paris, 1950; Ph.D., Princeton, 1955; m. Terry Ann Harris, June 9, 1951; children—Nicolas Howard, Anne Louise. Came to U.S., 1948, naturalized, 1960. Instr., U. Mich., 1954-55, asst. prof., 1955-59, asso. prof., 1959-64, prof., 1964-69; dir. Am. Sch. of Oriental Research, Jerusalem, Jordan, 1960-61, v.p., 1968—; prof. fine arts Harvard, 1969—. Mem. Coll. Art Assn. (bd. dirs. 1968-72), Archeol. Inst. Am., Mediaeval Acad. Am., German Archeol. Inst., Middle Eastern Studies Assn. Author: Coinage of Tulunids, 1957; Islamic Architecture and its Decoration, 1967; Sasanian Silver, 1967. Editor Ars Orientalis, 1957-71. Contbr. articles profl. jours. Dir. Mich.-Harvard excavations in Syria, 1964-71. Home: 18 Suzanne Rd Lexington MA 02173 Office: Fogg Museum Cambridge MA 02138

GRABBER, JOHN LEROY, mfg. co. exec.; b. Colon, Mich., June 6, 1916; s. Rex Leroy and Grace (Hughey) G.; A.B., Kalamazoo Coll., 1939; J.D., George Washington U., 1943; children—Helen V., John E., Jeffrey N. Admitted to D.C. bar, 1943; with legal office Q.M.C.,

AUS, Chgo., 1952-53, Martin Co., Balt., 1953-60; sec., gen. counsel Fairchild Hiller Corp., 1960-70; with Fecor Industries, York, Pa., 1970—. Pres. Jr. Bar Assn. D.C., 1948. Mem. Am. Bar Assn. Barristers. Home: 337 Brentwood Dr Apt 18E York PA 17403 Office: Fecor Industries Ltd York PA 17405

GRABER, PAUL JAMES, educator; b. Tulsa, Nov. 7, 1908; s. John E. and Dora M. (Kiser) G.; B.S., U. Mo., 1931, A.M., 1933; postgrad. Ohio State U., 1933-34, U. Tex., 1941-42; m. Lucy I. Raxter, Aug. 5, 1937; children—Roberta, John, James. Instr. accounting Ohio State U., 1934- 36; mem. staff Arthur Andersen & Co., N.Y.C., 1936-37; asst. and asso. prof. accounting Okla. A. and M. Coll., 1937-44, (on leave) U. Tex., 1941-42; resarch asst. Am. Inst. Accountants, N.Y.C., 1944-46; prof. accounting, head dept. U. Tulsa, 1946—. Asst. prof. accounting U. Mo., summers 1935, 40; Fulbright lectr. Nederlandsch Economisch Hogesch., Rotterdam, 1966-67. C.P.A., Okla., 1939. Mem. Am. Inst. C.P.A.'s, Am. Accounting Assn. (dir. research 1947-49), Okla. Soc. C.P.A.'s, Southwestern Social Sci. Assn. Editor: Common Carrier Pipe Line Operations and Accounting, Okla. C.P.A., 1947-54. Contbr. C.P.A. Rev. Manual, also articles to accounting jours. Home: 1312 S Jamestown Tulsa OK 74112

GRABNER, GEORGE JOHN, mfg. co. exec.; b. Muskogee, Okla., Aug. 25, 1918; s. George and Helen (Leitch) G.; B.A., Western Res. U., 1939; postgrad. Harvard Grad. Sch. Bus. Adminstrn., 1940; m. Monica Meyer, June 24, 1950; children—George John, Jan, Heidi, John, Thomas. Asst. mgr. Ernst & Ernst, C.P.A.'s, Cleve., 1946-57; v.p., dir. Cyrus Eaton Interests, 1957-58; financial v.p., treas. Weatherhead Co., Cleve., 1958-63, exec. v.p., 1963-65, pres., dir., 1965-70; pres., dir. Weatherhead Co. Can., Ltd., 1966-70, LPG Leasing Corp., Cleve., 1958-70; pres., chief exec. officer, dir. Lamson & Sessions Co., 1970—; dir. Narragansett Capital Corp., Fisher Food Co., Nat. City Bank Cleve.; trustee 1st Union Realty. Vice pres. Cleve. area council Boy Scouts Am., 1966—. Trustee Western Res. U., Univ. Sch.; bd. chmn. Greater Cleve. Growth Assn., 1966-69; chmn. Cleve. Devel. Found., 1966-69; dir. Ednl. Research Council. Served to 1st lt. USAAF, 1942-45. C.P.A., Ohio. Mem. Ohio Soc. C.P.A.'s, Am. Ordnance Assn. (past pres., dir.). Clubs: Union, Mayfield Country (Cleve.); Pepper Pike (O.) Country. Home: Oxgate Lane Daisy Hill Hunting Valley OH 44022 Office: 5000 Tiedman Rd Cleveland OH 44144

GRACE, GEORGE R., life ins. co. exec.; b. Cin., June 16, 1910; B.S. in Bus. Adminstrn., U. Cin., 1933; LL.B., Chase Coll. Law, 1943. Admitted to Ohio bar, 1943; with Ohio Nat. Life Ins. Co., 1924—, sec.-treas., 1963-67, v.p., sec., 1967—. Active local United Appeal. Mem. Clifton Town Meeting. Fellow Life Office Mgmt. Assn. Inst.; mem. Life Ins. Agy. Mgmt. Assn., Am. Life Conv., Internat., Cin. claim assns., Order Curia, Delta Sigma Pi, Kappa Psi Delta. Mason (Shriner). Home: 8000 Ludlow Av Cincinnati OH Office: Ohio Nat Life Ins Co William Howard Taft Rd at Highland Av Cincinnati OH*

GRACE, HAROLD LEO, Jr., hosiery mfg. co. exec.; b. Decatur, Ill., Dec. 27, 1924; s. Harold Leo and Helen M. (Bradshaw) G.; B.A. cum laude, DePauw U., Greencastle, Inc., 1948; m. Carolyn Faye Wilson, June 26, 1948; children—Robert Wilson, Janet Lynn. Vice pres. Nat. Asso: Mills, Indpls., 1955-59; exec. v.p. Nat. Mills, N.Y.C., 1959-66, pres., chief exec. officer, 1966-68; vice chmn. apparel and accessories group, corporate v.p. U.S. Industries, Inc., N.Y.C., 1968-69, exec. group chmn. apparel and accessories group, corporate exec. v.p., 1969—, also dir. Bd. govs. Empire State Club. Served with USNR, 1943-46. Mem. Nat. Assn. Hosiery Mfrs. (dir.), Am. Apparel Mfrs. Assn. (dir.), Phi Gamma Delta. Club: Huntington (L.I.) Crescent. Home: 33 Renwick Av Huntington NY 11743 Office: 350 Fifth Av New York City NY 10001

GRACE, J. PETER, bus. exec.; b. Manhasset, L.I., N.Y., May 25, 1913; s. Joseph Peter and Janet (Macdonald) G.; student St. Paul's Sch., Concord, 1927-32; B.A., Yale, 1936; LL.D., Mt. St. Mary's Coll., Manhattan Coll., Fordham U., Boston Coll., U. Notre Dame, Belmont Abbey, Stonehill Coll.; Dr. Latin Am. Relations, St. Joseph's Coll.; m. Margaret Fennelly, May 24, 1941; children—Joseph Peter III, William, Michael, Margaret, Mary, Nora, Patrick, Teresa, Christopher. With W.R. Grace & Co., 1936—, asst. sec., 1940, mgr., 1942, sec., 1942, dir., 1943—, v.p., 1945, pres., 1945—; dir. Kennecott Copper Corp., Brascan Ltd., First Nat. City Corp., First Nat. City Bank, Ingersoll-Rand Co., Magnovox Co., Stone & Webster, Inc., Deering Milliken, Inc.; trustee Atlantic Mutual Ins. Co. Chmn. gen. com., dir., mem. finance com. Greater N.Y. Co-ordinating Com. on Released Time; chmn. bd. trustees Am. Inst. for Free Labor Devel.; mem. Greater N.Y. Councils, Nassau County adv. bd. Boy Scouts Am.; bd. dirs., pres. Cath. Youth Orgn. of Archdiocese of N.Y.; mem. inter-Am. hon. sponsoring com. Mus. of Modern Art; bd. dirs. Boys Clubs Am., Grace Found.; pres., trustee Grace Inst., St. Vincent's Hosp. and Med. Center, N.Y.C. bd. mgrs. Roman Cath. Orphan Asylum; treas. Nat. Cath. Community Service; mem. Cardinal's Com. of the Laity; trustee, mem. finance com., exec. com., pres.'s com. greater N.Y. Notre Dame U.; council Yale Inst. Internat. Studies; adv. bd. N.Y. Foundling Hosp.; sponsor trustee, treas. Nat. Jewish Hosp., Denver; nat. adv. council Peace Corps. Decorated knight of Grand Cross, Equestrian Order Holy Sepulchre of Jerusalem; decorated by govts. of Colombia, Chile, Ecuador, Panama, Peru. Mem. Internat. C. of C. (trustee U.S. council), Newcomen Soc., Peruvian Am. Assn., Colombian- Am. C. of C., Downtown-Lower Manhattan Assn. (dir.), Council on Fgn. Relations, Inc., Pan Am. Soc. of U.S. Roman Catholic. Knight of Malta (Am. chpt., bd. founders). Clubs: Racquet and Tennis, Madison Square Garden (gov.), Links, India House (gov.), Links Golf (N.Y.C.); Meadow Brook, Pacific Union (San Francisco); Everglades. Home: 41 Shelter Rock Rd Manhasset NY 11030 Office: 5 Hanover Sq New York City NY 10004

GRACE, JOHN JOSEPH, social welfare adminstr.; b. Jersey City, May 26, 1902; s. Joseph J. and Elizabeth (Mitchell) G.; grad. Salvation Army Sch. Officers Tng., N.Y.C., 1922; m. Alice Owen, Apr. 18, 1930. Commd. officer Salvation Army, 1922, various field adminstrn. appointments, 1922-45; territorial pub. relations dir., N.Y.C., 1945-47; divisional comdr., Buffalo, 1947- 50, Phila., 1950-61; former nat. chief sec., adminstrv. asst. to nat. comdr., N.Y.C. Home: 530 Overlook Rd Philadelphia PA 19128

GRACE, OLIVER RUSSELL, bus. exec.; b. Great Neck, N.Y., Dec. 2, 1909; s. Morgan H. and Ruth (Eden). G.; student Phillips Andover Acad.; Ph.B., Yale, 1930; m. Anne Chilton McDonnell, Nov. 29, 1934 (div. 1944); children—Helen Miller (Mrs. Ralph McDermid, Jr.), Ann Chilton (Mrs. Ratus Lee Kelly), Ruth Elizabeth (Mrs. Wayne Jervis); m. Lorraine Graves, Oct. 23, 1949; children—Lorraine, Gwendolyn, Oliver Russell, John Sheffield. Statistician Grace Nat. Bank, N.Y.C., 1930-36; partner Sterling, Grace & Co., 1936—; chmn. Andersen Labs., West Hartford, Conn., 1959—; dir. Alpha Portland Cement Co., Gondas Corp., Republic Gear Co. Pres. N.Y. Cancer Research Inst., Inc., 1953-58, 66—. Mem. Nat. Inst. Social Scis., Newcomen Soc., N.Y. C. of C. Episcopalian. Clubs: Regency Whist, Down Town Assn., River (N.Y.); Edgartown (Mass.) Yacht. Home: 14 E 90th St New York City, NY 10028. Office: 39 Broadway New York City NY 10006

GRACE, RICHARD EDWARD, engring. educator; b. Chgo., June 26, 1930; s. Richard Edward and Louise (Koko) G.; B.S. in Metall. Engring., Purdue U., 1951; Ph.D., Carnegie Inst. Tech., 1954; m. Consuela Cummings Fotos, Jan. 29, 1955; children—Virginia Louise, Richard Cummings. Asst. prof. Purdue U., Lafayette, Ind., 1954-58, asso. prof., 1958-62, prof., 1962—, head sch. of materials sci. and metall. engring., 1965—, head div. interdiciplinary engring. studies, 1970; cons. to midwest industries. Mem. engring. edn. and accreditation com. Engrs., Council for Profl. Devel. Mem. Am. Soc. for Metals (tchr. award 1962), Am. Inst. of Mining, Metall. and Petroleum Engrs., Am. Soc. for Engring. Edn., Am. Assn. U. Profs., Sigma Xi, Phi Gamma Delta. Rotarian, Elk. Contbr. articles to profl. jours. Home: 2204 Huron Rd West Lafayette IN 47906 Office: Purdue Univ Lafayette IN 47907

GRACE, THOMAS L., airlines exec.; b. Neb., June 28, 1911; married; 1 dau. Supt. flight and space control Slick Airways, 1946, supt. operation, 1946-49, v.p. operation, 1949-50, v.p. operation, gen. mgr., 1950, pres., 1950-54, following consolidation with Flying Tiger Line, Inc., 1954, became exec. v.p. of new corp., then v.p. operations Northeast Airlines; now pres. Ozark Air Lines, Inc. Served as pilot USAAF, 1942-46. Office: Lambert Field St Louis MO 63145

GRACE, WALTER LAW, ins. co. exec.; b. Albany, N.Y., July 4, 1924; s. Charles J. and Lucile C. (Walter) G.; student Johns Hopkins, 1942-43; B.S., U. Mich., 1948, M.A., 1949; m. Janet C. Fletcher, Mar. 3, 1945; children—John F., Susan W., Ellen L. With Mass. Mut. Life Ins. Co., Springfield, 1949—, successively asst. group actuary, asst. actuary, asso. group actuary, asso. actuary, 1951-62, head pension dept., 1960-66, 2d v.p., 1962-66, 2d v.p. and actuary, 1966—; v.p. MML Investment Co. Corporator Wesson Meml. Hosp., Springfield. Served to 1st lt. USAAF, 1942-47. Fellow Soc. Actuaries (treas. 1960-62, sec. 1962-65, gov. 1965-68, 70—). Home: 8 Wilbraview Dr Wibraham MA 01095 Office: 1295 State St Springfield MA 01101

GRACE, WILLIAM EDWIN, trailer mfr.; b. Ft. Worth, Apr. 27, 1908; s. James and Anna (Christelles) G.; student pub. schs.; m. Mary Corinne Funderburk, Feb. 19, 1929; children—William Edwin, John P. Bookkeeper Hobbs Mfg. Co., Ft. Worth, 1930, office mgr., 1931-33, credit mgr., 1933-35, sales mgr., 1935-37, v.p., gen. mgr., 1937-41, exec. v.p. charge overall operations, 1941-55; v.p. Freuhauf Corp., charge Hobbs Trailer div. and Southwestern div., 1955-58, pres., 1958—, chief exec. officer, 1959—, dir.; pres. W. E. Grace Finance Co., 1934—, Ft. Worth Leasing Co.; pres., dir. Freuhauf Trailer Co. Can., Ltd., Dixie, Ont., Fruehauf Distbg. Co., Detroit; v.p., gen. mgr. Trailer Finance Co., 1935—, Truckers Loan Co., 1937—, Distbrs. Finance Co., 1938—, Eastwood Apts., Inc., 1940—; partner Grace Oil Co.; dir. Trailer Acceptance Co., Ltd., Dixie, Ont., Fruehauf Finance Co., Detroit, Freuhauf France, S.A., Paris, Freuhauf Internat., Ltd., Vaduz, Liechtenstein, Crane Fruehauf Trailers, Ltd., London, Tex. Motor Transport Co. Bd. dirs. Boy Scouts Am. Mem. Truck Trailer Mfrs. Assn. Am. (past pres.), Livestock Haulers Assn. (sec.- treas. 1945—). Clubs: Rotary (past pres.), Boat, Admiral's, Ridglea Country, Shady Oaks Country (Ft. Worth); Ostego Ski (Gaylord, Mich.); Grosse Pointe Yacht (Grosse Pointe Shores, Mich.); Detroit Athletic, Country of Detroit. Home: 21 Webber Pl Grosse Point Shores MI 48236 Office: 10900 Harper Av Detroit MI 48213

GRACE, WILLIAM PORTER, real estate co. exec.; b. Dardanelle, Ark., Oct. 14, 1908; s. William Porter and Bertha (Cox) G.; B.S., B.A., U. Ark., 1931; LL.B., So. Law U., 1963; m. Eleanor Curry, Nov. 16, 1936; children—William Porter III, Perry Rutledge. With HOLC, 1936-38, Memphis C. of C., 1938-50; with Union Planters Nat. Bank, Memphis, 1950-70, exec. v.p., 1963-68, pres., 1968-69, vice chmn., 1970; pres., dir., vice chmn., dir. John A. Cooper Co., Inc., Bella Vista, Ark., 1971—; dir. Grace Devel. Co. Bd. dirs. Am. Indsl. Devel. Council, 1956; pres. So. Indsl. Devel. Council, 1952, bd. dirs., 1948; chmn. Memphis Community Chest, 1955, Nat. Alliance Businessmen, Memphis & Shelby County Port Com.; bd. dirs. Memphis chpt. A.R.C., 1960—; exec. com. Shelby United Neighbors, 1964-70, Meth. Hosp., Memphis, 1960—. Served with U.S. Army, 1933-36, 41-45. Decorated Legion of Merit; Order Brit. Empire; Croix de Guerre (France). Mem. Am., Tenn. bankers assns. Mason. Clubs: Memphis Country, University (Memphis). Home: 9 Longdon Lane Bella Vista AR 72712 Office: John A Cooper Co Inc Bella Vista AR 72712

GRACIA, ALBERT JOSEPH, ret. rubber co. exec.; b. Cambridge, Mass., Oct. 11, 1905; s. Joseph Morris and Anna (Laubinger) G.; B.S. in Chem. Engring., Mass. Inst. Tech., 1928; grad. Advanced Mgmt. Program, Harvard, 1950; m. Josephine Buswell, June 21, 1929; children—Janet (Mrs. Roger H. Michael), Judith (Mrs. Frank Haims). With Goodyear Tire & Rubber Co., 1928-69, dir. research and devel., 1956-61, v.p. research, 1961-69, ret., 1969. Pres. United Community Council Summit Co., O., 1960-62; v.p. Ohio Citizens Council, 1965-68; mem. nat. budget com. United Funds and Councils Am., 1960—; mem. nat. council Christian social action United Ch. Christ, 1965—. Trustee Defiance Coll. Fellow A.A.A.S., Am. Inst. Chemists; mem. Am. Chem. Soc., Am. Nuclear Soc., Am. Inst. Chem. Engrs. Conglist. Mason. Home: 2414 Kensington Rd Akron OH 44313

GRACIDA, RENE HENRY, clergyman; b. New Orleans, June 9, 1923; s. Henry J. and Mathilde (Derbes) G.; student Rice U., 1942-43; B.S. in Architecture, U. Houston, 1950; postgrad. U. Fribourg, Switzerland, 1950, St. Vincent Coll., Latrobe, Pa., 1951-53, St. Vincent Maj. Sem., 1953-60. Faculty, U. Houston Sch. Architecture, 1948-51; practice architecture with Donald Bartheline & Assos., Houston, 1949-51; ordained deacon Roman Catholic Ch., 1958, priest, 1959; asst. pastor Holy Family Parish, North Miami, Fla., 1961-62, St. Coleman Parish, Pompano Beach, Fla., 1962-63, St. Matthew Parish, Hallandale, Fla., 1963-64; adminstr. St. Ambrose Parish, Deerfield Beach, Fla., 1964; asst. pastor Visitation Parish, North Dade, Fla., 1964-65; adminstr. St. Ann Parish, Naples, Fla., 1966-67; pastor Nativity Parish, Hollywood, Fla., 1967-69; mem. Archdiocesan Bldg. Commn., Archdiocese of Miami, 1961—, sec., 1962-65, chmn., 1967—, chmn. West Coast Deanery, Human Relations Bd., 1966-67, senator Priests Senate, 1967-69, archdiocesan consultor, 1967—, chmn. Broward Deanery, Human Relations Bd., 1967-69, chancellor, 1968—, treas., 1969—, vicar gen., 1969—. Pres. Community Action Fund. Served with USAAF, 1943-45. Decorated Air medal. Mem. Liturgical Arts Soc., Tex., Fla. socs. architects, A.I.A., Liturgical Conf., Nat. Assn. for Community Devel., Guild for Religious Architecture. Important archtl. works include remodelling St. Vincent Archabbey Basilica, Latrobe, Ch. of the Nativity, Hollywood, St. Ambrose Ch., Deerfield Beach. Home: 7525 NW 2d Av Miami FL 33138 Office: 6301 Biscayne Blvd Miami FL 33138

GRACY, JOHN SHIRLEY, ret. utility exec.; b. Smyrna, Tenn., Oct. 17, 1902; s. Brainard Bradshaw and Mittie Gresham (Moore) G.; student Davidson Coll., 1920-22; A.B., U. Fla., 1924; m. Margaret Breckenridge Owens, Feb. 15, 1929. Owner J. Shirley Gracy & Co., ins. and real estate, St. Petersburg, Fla., 1925- 27; with Fla. Power Corp., St. Petersburg, 1927-67, ins. dir., 1929-37, personnel dir., 1937-47, v.p., 1947-59, sr. v.p., 1959-67, also dir.; dir. ERC Corp., Employers Reins. Corp., Kansas City, Mo.; chmn. bd. Abilities, Inc. of Fla., Clearwater, 1959-62, 69—; now bus. cons. Nat. vice chmn. for Fla. fund and membership drive A.R.C., 1960, chmn. S.E. area adv. council, 1962, bd. govs., 1964-70; chmn. Fla. Merit System Council, 1958-60; dir. So. Indsl. Relations Conf., 1945—, chmn., 1963-65. Bd. dirs. Nat. Assn. for Mental Health, United Community Funds and Councils Am.; trustee Mus. Fine Arts, St. Petersburg, v.p., 1964-66, 71—. Mem. Newcomen Soc. N.Am., Sales Execs. Conf., Fla. Blue Key, Beta Theta Pi. Democrat. Presbyn. Home: 230 Bandera Way St Petersburg FL 33704 Office: 22 Fifth St N St Petersburg FL 33701

GRAD, ARTHUR, ednl. adminstr.; b. Austria, Jan. 31, 1918; s. Herman and Helen (Selinger) G.; B.S. cum laude, Coll. City N.Y., 1938; A.M., Columbia, 1939; Ph.D., Stanford, 1948; m. Irene Smiley, June 21, 1946; children—Susan, Laura. Phys. sci. aide Nat. Bur. Standards, 1941; mathematician U.S. Coast and Geodetic Survey, 1941-46; research asso., acting instr. Stanford, 1946-48; mathematician Office Naval Research, 1948-53; lectr. U. Md., 1949-53; mathematician Inst. Math. Scis., N.Y. U., 1953-54; head math. br. Office Naval Research, 1954-59; program dir. math. scis., head math. scis. sect. NSF, 1959-63; asso. dean grad. div. Stanford, 1963-64; dean Grad. Sch., prof. math. Ill. Inst. Tech., Chgo., 1964-71; pres. Poly. Inst. Bklyn., 1971—. Mem. council Asso. Midwest Univs., 1964-68; examiner Commn. Instns. Higher Edn., North Central Assn. Colls. and Secondary Schs., 1967-71; rep. Engring. Coll. Research Council, 1964-71, Argonne Univs. Assn., 1967-71; cons. deptl. sci. devel. sect. NSF, 1967-68; mem. com. on sources and forms of support div. math. Nat. Acad. Scis.-NRC, 1969—, chmn., 1970—; mem. exec. com. Bklyn. Instl. Council, 1971—. Mem. A.A.A.S., Am. Math. Soc., Math Assn. Am. Contbr. articles to profl. jours. Home: 37 Washington Sq W New York City NY 10011

GRAD, BERNARD JOHN, architect; b. Newark, Dec. 28, 1908; s. Frank and Kitty (Furst) G.; B.Arch., U. Pa., 1932; certificate Ecole des Beaux Arts, Fontainebleau, France, 1931; m. Marian Newfield, Mar. 12, 1937; children—Peter, Susan. With Frank Grad & Sons, architects and engrs., Newark, 1932—, gen. partner, 1936—; v.p., dir. 570 Broad St. Co., 494 Broad St. Corp. (both Newark); prin. works include master plan N.J. Capitol Devel. Program, 1958, N.J. Labor and Industry Bldg., 1963, N.J. Cultural Center, 1963, Rutgers Coll. Engring., 1963, Newark Underground Parking Garage, 1961, N.J. regional office bldgs. for Prudential Ins. Co. in Linwood, 1958, in Millville, 1960, six NATO air bases in France, 1954, Naval Air Turbine Test Sta., W. Trenton, N.J., 1954, 2 office bldgs. for Mut. Benefit Life Ins. Co., Newark, 1957, accounting and data processing center for Atlantic City Electric Co., 1960, research and computer center for Am.- Standard Co., Piscataway Twp., N.J., 1963, nat. adminstrv. center and freight terminal for Sea-Land Service, Inc., Elizabeth, N.J., 1963. Chmn. constrn. industry div. N.J. campaign for Radio Free Europe; mem. Newark Bd. Standards. Trustee Newark Boys Clubs. Fellow A.I.A. (bd. govs. N.J.); mem. Am. Soc. Mil. Engrs., Army Ordnance Assn., Nat. Council Archtl. Registration Bds., Tau Sigma Delta, Zeta Beta Tau. Home: Sycamore Av Elberon NJ 07740 Office: 11 Commerce St Newark NJ 07102

GRADISON, WILLIS DAVID, Jr., investment broker; b. Cin., Dec. 28, 1928; s. Willis David and Dorothy (Benas) G.; A.B., Yale, 1948; M.B.A., Harvard, 1951, D.C.S., 1954; m. Helen Ann Martin, June 25, 1950; children—Ellen, Anne, Margaret, Robin, Beth. With W. D. Gradison & Co., Cin., 1949; research asst., also research associate of Harvard Bus. Sch., 1951-53; asst. to under sec. of treasury, 1953-55; asst. to sec. of health, edn. and welfare, 1955-57; gen. partner W. D. Gradison & Co., 1958—. Mem. Cin. City Council, 1961-71; mayor, Cin., 1971—. Home: 6 Elmhurst Pl Cincinnati OH 45208 Office: Dixie Terminal Bldg Cincinnati OH 45202

GRADWOHL, BERNARD SAM, lawyer; b. St. Joseph, Mo., Apr. 5, 1905; s. Ben W. and Hattie (Hilpp) G.; A.B., U. Neb., 1923, J.D. cum laude, 1924; LL.M., Columbia, 1925; m. Elaine Mayer, June 21, 1928; children—John Mayer, David Mayer. Admitted to Neb. bar, 1926, since practiced in Lincoln; nat. exec. sec. Am. Interprofl. Inst., editor Quar., 1942-66, pres., 1966-67, pres. Lincoln chpt., 1948-49. Nat. adv. bd. Am. Council Judaism, 1944-68, co-chmn. nat. com. religious programs, 1949-58, mem. exec. com., 1954-58; mem. bd. Lincoln Social Welfare So., 1944-45, exec. council Neb. Welfare assn., 1947-49; past pres. Open Forum Club; past chmn. Lincoln bd. Nat. Conf. Christians and Jews, chmn. Nebraskans Say America is Beautiful Com., 1970—. Mem. Am., Neb., Lincoln (past treas.) bar assns., Lincoln, Omaha assns. fire fighters, Lincoln C. of C., Izaak Walton League, Phi Beta Kappa, Order Coif, Delta Sigma Rho. Jewish religion. Mason (Shriner). Clubs: Open Forum (Lincoln); Hillcrest Country (past pres.). Home: 1633 Crestline Dr Lincoln NB 68506 Office: Lincoln Benefit Life Bldg Lincoln NB 68508

GRADY, JOHN HENRY, computer co. exec.; b. San Mateo, Cal., Jan. 10, 1928; s. John H. and Monica (Klatt) G.; A.A., Coll. San Mateo, 1949; B.S., U. Cal. at Berkeley, 1951; m. Alexandra Diepenbrock, Dec. 29, 1956; children—Kathleen, John Henry, Carolyn, James. With Am. President Lines, 1951-52; with IBM, 1952—, dir. stockholder relations, Armonk, N.Y., 1963-65, asst. sec., 1965-70, sec., 1970—. Served with AUS, 1945-47. Mem. Am. Soc. Corporate Secs., Stockholder Relations Soc. N.Y. Club: Innis Arden Golf (Old Greenwich, Conn.). Home: Grove Lane Greenwich CT 06830 Office: Old Orchard Rd Armonk NY 10504

GRADY, JOSEPH HAROLD, judge, ex-mayor; b. Williamsport, Pa., Feb. 27, 1917; s. Thomas Leo and Edythe (Grange) G.; B.A. magna cum laude, Loyola Coll., Balt., 1938; LL.B., U. Md., 1942; m. Patricia Grogan, May 26, 1942; children—Maureen Ann, Joseph Harold, Katheen Ann, Thomas Leo. Admitted to Md. bar, 1942; spl. agt. FBI, 1942-47; asst. states atty., Balt., 1947-55, dep. states atty., 1955-56, states atty., 1956-59; mayor of Balt., 1959-62; asso. judge Supreme Court of Baltimore, 1962—; instr. U. Md. Sch. Law, Mt. Vernon Law Sch., Balt., 1949-58. Mem. Md., Balt. bar assns., States Attys. Assn. Md. (pres. 1957-59), Nat. Assn. Pros. Attys. (dir. 1957-59), Soc. Friendly Sons St. Patrick of Balt. (pres. 1959), Order of Coif. Democrat. Roman Catholic. K.C. (4). Home: 209 Goodale Rd Baltimore MD 21212 Office: Court House Baltimore MD 21202

GRADY, MARION BEHETHLAN, librarian, educator; b. La Crosse, Fla., Oct. 9, 1910; d. Seymour and Behethlan (Tucker) G.; B.S., Fla. State U., 1933; B.L.S., George Peabody Coll. Tchrs., 1938; M.A., U. Chgo., 1943, Ph.D., 1951. Pub. sch. librarian, 1933-39; instr. library sci. George Peabody Coll. Tchrs., librarian Peabody Demonstration Sch. Libraries, 1939-42; librarian Minot (N.D.) State Tchrs. Coll., 1944-45; librarian, head dept. library sci., prof. library sci. Ball State U., Muncie, Ind., 1945-69; librarian, prof. library sci. Ambassador Coll., Pasadena, Cal., 1969—. Mem. Assn. Coll. and Research Libraries, A.L.A., N.E.A., Am. Assn. Higher Edn., Am. Assn. U. Profs., Beta Phi Mu, Delta Zeta, Pi Gamma Mu, Kappa Delta Pi. Contbr. articles to profl. jours. Home: PO Box 2730 Sta D Pasadena CA 91105

GRADY, STAFFORD R., banker; b. Grand Rapids, Mich., Apr. 9, 1921; s. Stafford R. and Josephine (Cusick) G.; A.B., George Washington U., 1943, LL.B., 1945; m. Roberta Patterson, Aug. 26, 1950; children—Stafford R., Maureen H., Shaun. Admitted to Mich. bar, 1945, D.C. bar, 1945, Cal. bar, 1952; law clk. to U.S. Ct. Appeals Justice Stephens, 1945-47; asst. U.S. atty., Washington, 1947-51; spl. atty. Internal Revenue Service, 1951-52; partner firm Mackay,

McGregor and Bennion, Los Angeles, 1952-63; ins. commr., Cal., 1963-66; pres. First Western Bank, Los Angeles, 1966—, chmn. bd., 1968—; dir. Econ. Resources Corp., Pacific Employers Ins. Co., Educators Life Ins. Co., Surety Life Ins. Co., Cal.-Western States Life Ins. Co. Mem. Cal. Gov.'s Traffic Safety Com., Cal. Traffic Safety Found., Nat. Hwy. Safety Adv. Com., Los Angeles chpt. Nat. Safety Council. Trustee Occidental Coll.; regent Loyola U. at Los Angeles. Mem. Assn. Res. City Bankers, Cal. Bankers Assn. (dir.). Office: 548 S Spring St Los Angeles CA 90013

GRADY, THEODORE FREED lawyer, corp. exec.; b. Kent, O., 1922; B.A., Yale, 1943, LL.B., 1944; m. Mae Reed, May 2, 1949; 1 son. Admitted to Massachusetts bar, 1944; practiced in Boston, 1947--; gen. counsel Acme Mfg. Co., Boston, 1966--; dir. 1st Nat. Bank. Home: 23 Beacon St Boston MA 02107

GRADY, THOMAS J., bishop; b. Chgo., Oct. 9, 1914; s. Michael and Rose (Buckley) G.; S.T.L., St. Mary of Lake Sem., Mundelein, Ill., 1938; student Gregorian U., Rome, 1938-39; M.A. in English, Loyola U., Chgo., 1944. Ordained priest Roman Catholic Ch., 1938; prof. Quigley Prep. Sem., Chgo., 1939-45; procurator St. Mary of Lake Sem., 1945-56; dir. Nat. Shrine Immaculate Conception, Washington, 1956-67; titular bishop Vamalla, aux. bishop Chgo., 1967—; Chgo. Archdiocesan dir. seminaries and post-ordination priestly tng., 1967—; pastor St. Hilary Ch., Chgo., 1968—; chmn. Chgo. Archdiocesan Liturgical Commn., 1968—. Chmn. bishops' com. on priestly formation Nat. Conf. Catholic Bishops, 1969—. Home: St. Hilary Rectory 5600 N Fairfield Av Chicago, IL 60645. Office: PO Box 1979 Chicago IL 60690

GRAEBNER, HERBERT CONRAD, educator; b. Bay City, Mich., Jan. 3, 1908; s. M.G. and Emma (Umbach) C.; B.S., Valparaiso (Ind.) U., 1930; postgrad. Northwestern U., 1930- 31; M.B.A., U. Pa., 1948; m. Mildred Fessel, Aug. 24, 1933; children—James, Jane. Supt. A.J. Rehmus Constrn. Co., Bay City, Mich., 1931-32; instr. econs. Valparaiso U., 1932-35, asst. bus. mgr., 1935-39; prof. econs. Westminster Coll., 1939-46; v.p. Econ. Found Pa., 1942-46; prof. econs., dean coll. bus. adminstrn. Butler U., 1948-55; dean, trustee Am. Coll. Life Underwriters, 1955-64, v.p. and dean, 1964-67, exec. v.p., treas., 1967-70; pres., dir. Bldg. Owners and Mgrs. Inst. Internat., 1970—; chmn. bd. Certified Med. Reps. Inst., 1967—; dir. MPEP, Inc. Mem. Am. Acad. Polit. and Social Sci., Adult Edn. Assn., Am. Risk and Ins. Assn., Am. Assn. U. Profs., Phi Kappa Phi, Sigma Iota Epsilon. Lutheran. Author articles profl. jours. Contbg. and/or cons. editor several bus. handbooks. Home: 149 Clemson Rd Bryn Mawr PA 19010

GRAEBNER, NORMAN ARTHUR, educator; b. Kingman, Kan., Oct. 19, 1915; s. Rudolph William and Helen (Brauer) G.; B.S., Milw. State Tchrs. Coll., 1939; M.A., U. Okla., 1940; Ph.D., U. Chgo., 1949; m. Laura Edna Baum, Aug. 30, 1941; children—Harriet, Norman Brooks, Emily. Asst. prof. Okla. Coll. for Women, 1942-43, 46-47; from asst. prof. to prof. Ia. State Coll., 1948- 56; vis. prof. Stanford, 1952-53, summer 1959; prof. history U. Ill., Urbana, 1956-67, chmn. dept. history, 1961-63; Edward R. Stettinius prof. modern Am. history U. Va., 1967—; Commonwealth Fund lectr. U. Coll., London, Eng., 1958; Fulbright lectr. U. Queensland, Brisbane, Australia, 1963. Served to 1st lt. AUS, 1943-46. Mem. Am., So. hist. assns., Orgn. Am. Historians, Am. Assn. U. Profs. Lutheran. Author: Empire on the Pacific, 1955; The New Isolationism, 1956; Cold War Diplomacy, 1962; co-author: A History of the United States, 2 vols., 1970; A Hstory of the American People, 1970. Editor: The Enduring Lincoln, 1959; Politics and the Crisis of 1860, 1961; An Uncertain Tradition: American Secretaries of State in the Twentieth Century, 1961; The Cold War: Ideological Conflict or Power Struggle, 1963; Ideas and Diplomacy, 1964; Manifest Destiny, 1968. Contbr. articles to hist. jours. Home: 109 Kerry Lane Charlottesville VA 22901

GRAEBNER, WALTER, advt. cons.; b. Prairie Twp., O. Dec. 16, 1909; s. Rev. John R. and Hedwig (Sievers) G.; student U. of Wis., 1928-31; m. Jean Fairchild Bellis, Nov. 10, 1933 (div.); children—Gretchen, John; m. 2d, Constance Grange Lailey, Oct. 2, 1948. Employed by Time, Inc., 1931-53, as correspondent in Chgo., London and Moscow, chmn., mgr. dir. Erwin Wasey, Ruthrauff & Ryan, Ltd., 1953-63; advt. pub. relations cons. Interpublic, Ltd., London, Eng., 1963—. Mem. Alpha Delta Phi. Lutheran. Author: Round Trip to Russia, 1943; Conversation in London (with Stephen Laird), 1942. Editor; (with Allan. A. Michie), Their Finest Hour, 1941; Lights of Freedom, 1942; My Dear Mr. Churchill, 1965; Home: 34 Albion St London W2 England Office: 25 Upper Brook St London W1 England

GRAEFFE, EDWIN OTTO, coll. dean; b. Brussels, Belgium, May 1, 1900; s. Otto Robert and Constance Marianne (Ellis) G.; LL.M., U. Goettingen, 1920; LL.D., U. Tuebingen, 1923; m. Catherine Lawrence, May 4, 1930; 1 dau., Catherine Constance. Came to U.S., 1926, naturalized, 1935. China import, export bus., 1923-26; export dept. Kelvinator Corp., 1926-28; prof. social sci. U. Detroit, 1928-32; prof. social sci. Lawrence Inst. Tech., 1932-40, head dept. bus. adminstrn., 1940-51, dean, 1951—, dir. Sch. Indsl. Mgmt., 1964—. Home: 4 E Court Pleasant Ridge MI 48069 Office: 2100 W Ten Mile Rd Southfield MI 48075

GRAETTINGER, JOHN SELLS, educator, physician; b. Ontario, Cal., June 24, 1921; s. Rupert Frederick and Alice (Sells) G.; candidate A.B., Harvard, 1943, M.D., 1945; m. Elizabeth Dun Shorey, June 29, 1946; children—John Sells, William Frederick, Alan Mitchell, Robert Shorey, George Douglass. Intern Harvard med. service Boston City Hosp., 1945-46, asst. resident, 1946, 48-49; research asst. cardiology and internal medicine U.S. Naval Sch. Aviation Medicine, Pensacola, Fla., 1949-53; dir. sect. cardio-respiratory diseases, dept. medicine Presbyn. Hosp., also Presbyn.-St. Luke's Hosp., Chgo., 1953-68; chmn. div. medicine Presbyn.-St. Luke's Hosp., Chgo., 1966-70; asst. prof. U. Ill. Coll. Medicine, 1953-58, asso. prof., 1958-64, prof. medicine, 1964-70; prof. medicine Rush Presbyn.- St. Luke's Med. Center, Rush Med. Coll., also dean student and faculty affairs at coll., 1970—. cons. to surgeon-gen. USPHS, 1965—, VA Hosp., Hines, Ill., 1954—. Pres. Bishop Anderson Found., 1960-62, bd. dirs., 1954—; bd. dirs. Chgo. Heart Assn. Served to lt. U.S. Navy, 1946-53. Diplomate Am. Bd. Internal Medicine. Fellow A.C.P.; mem. Am. Soc. Clin. Investigation, Central Soc. Clin. Research, Assn. U. Cardiologists (councillor 1964-69, pres. 1969-70), Chgo. Soc. Internal Medicine (v.p. 1970-71), Inst. Medicine Chgo., N.Y. Acad. Sci. Clubs: Harvard (chmn. scholarship com. 1962-64, dir. 1968—), University, Yacht (Chgo.). Publs., monographs on the heart and circulation. Home: 720 S County Line Rd Hinsdale, IL 60521. Office: 1753 W Congress Pkwy Chicago IL 60612

GRAETZER, JOHN STEPHEN, Jr., advt. exec.; b. N.Y.C., June 20, 1908; s. John Stephen and Katharine (Lamlein) G.; grad. Phillips Acad., Andover, Mass., 1925; Ph.B., Yale, 1930; m. Marian Jane Menard, Mar. 6, 1942; children—Peter Menard, Kurt Stephen, Eric Delore, Anthony Menard. Program mgr. OWI, 1942-45; advt. exec. Lennen & Mitchell, N.Y.C., 1945-58; sales promotion mgr. Nat. Distillers Corp., 1948-52; with LaRoche McCaffrey & McCall, 1952—, exec. v.p., 1960-71, account mgr., 1971—. Chmn. zoning appeals bd., Tuxedo Park, N.Y., 1958—; treas. Tuxedo Park Sch., 1958—. Mem. Scroll and Key, Alpha Delta Phi. Home: Tuxedo Park NY 10987 Office: 575 Lexington Av New York City NY 10022

GRAF, DONALD LEE, geochemist, educator; b. Elma, Ia., Jan. 24, 1925; s. John and Anna Marie (Nelson) G.; Geol. Engr., Colo. Sch. Mines, 1945; M.A., Columbia, 1947, Ph.D., 1950. Geologist, Ill. Geol. Survey, 1949-61, geochemist, 1963-65; prof., dir. grad. studies hydrogeology, dept. geology and geophysics U. Minn., 1965-69; prof. dept. geology U. Ill., Urbana, 1969—. Research fellow Harvard, 1961-63. Fellow Geol. Soc. Am., Mineral. Soc. Am. (award 1960), Am. Geophys. Union; mem. Tau Beta Pi. Author articles on geochemistry carbonate rocks and sediments, origin subsurface brines. Address: Dept Geology University of Ill Urbana IL 61801

GRAF, EDWIN CHARLES, physician; b. Chgo., Sept. 3, 1914; s. Clarence Z. and Lillian J. (Andrews) G.; B.S., Northwestern U., 1935, B.M., 1939, M.D., 1940; m. Miriam O. Mayfield, Apr. 19, 1943; children—James and Thomas (twins), Paul. Intern St. Luke's Hosp., Chgo., 1939-41; practice of medicine, Chgo., specializing in urology, 1946—; dept. urology Presbyn.-St. Luke's Hosp.; attending staff Cook Co. Hosp., Inst. of Medicine, Chgo.; teaching staff U. Ill. Med. Sch. Served to maj., USAAF, 1943-46. Diplomate Am. Bd. Urology. Fellow A.C.S.; mem. A.M.A. Home: 331 Abbotsford Rd Kenilworth IL 60043 Office: 310 S Michigan Av Chicago IL 60604

GRAF, FRANKLIN H., research co. exec.; b. Somonauk, Ill., 1911; grad. U. Ill., 1933; married. With A.C. Nielsen Co., Chgo., 1937—, now exec. v.p.; dir. A.C. Nielsen Co. Ltd. of Can. Home: 148 Eddy Lane Northfield IL 60093 Office: 2101 W Howard St Chicago IL 60645*

GRAF, HERBERT, stage dir.; b. Vienna, Austria, Apr. 10, 1903; s. Max and Olga (Hoenig) G.; grad. State Acad. Music; Doctor Phil. et Mus., U. Vienna, 1925; m. Liselotte Austerlitz, Feb. 28, 1927; 1 son, Werner. Came to U.S., 1934, naturalized, 1943. Formerly stage dir. Municipal Theatre Muenster; former chief stage dir. opera houses of Breslau and Frankfurt/Main, Germany; stage dir. Met. Opera Co., 1936-49; head opera dept. Curtis Inst., Phila., 1949-60; gen. mgr. Municipal Opera House, Zurich, Switzerland, 1960-63. Author: The Opera and Its Future in America, 1941; Opera for the People, 1951; Producing Opera for America, 1961. Home: Indian Hill Rd Bedford NY 10506 ‡

GRAF, LEROY PHILIP, educator; b. Fremont, O., Mar. 17, 1915; s. John Charles and Rose (Hammel) G.; A.B., Oberlin Coll., 1936; M.A., Harvard, 1937, Ph.D., 1942; m. Ruth Adena Peal, June 12, 1942; children—Christina, Melissa, Jeremy Peal. Tutor-instr. Harvard-Radcliffe Coll., 1942-43; instr. Tufts Coll., 1943-44; instr. Ohio State U., 1944-45; asso. prof. U. Tenn., Knoxville, 1945-50, prof., 1950—, head history dept., 1965—; co-editor Andrew Johnson Papers editorial project; vis. prof. Houston U., summer 1956; vis. prof. Vanderbilt U., summer 1960. Mem. State Adv. Com. on Nat. Historic Preservation Act, 1969—, Knoxville Round Table, 1957—, Nat. Conf. Christians and Jews, 1957—. Bd. dirs. Tenn. Council on Human Relations. Mem. Am., So. (mem. council 1956-58) hist. assns., Orgn. Am. Historians, Am. Assn. U. Profs. (mem. council 1964-66), Am. Studies Assn., Hakluyt Soc., Phi Beta Kappa, Phi Kappa Phi. Unitarian. Co-editor: The Papers of Andrew Johnson: Vol. 1 1823-51, 1967, Vol. 2 1852-57, 1970. Home: 5717 Westover Dr Knoxville TN 37919

GRAF, PAUL LUTHER, clergyman; b. North Lima, O., Oct. 22, 1914; s. John Henry and Henrietta Augusta Louisa (Tiemann) G.; A.B., Thiel Coll., 1936, D.D., 1954; B.D., Northwestern Luth. Theol. Sem., Mpls., 1940, M. Div., 1971; m. Ruth Esther Baer, Oct. 30, 1933; children—Paul, James, Karen, Kristin, Ruth Anne, Jon. Ordained to ministry Lutheran Ch., 1940; pastor Faith Luth. Ch., Walters, Minn., 1940-42, Trinity Luth. Ch., Kenosha, Wis., 1942-48; stewardship dir. Evang. Luth. Synod of N.W., 1948-50; pastor Holy Trinity Luth. Ch., Mpls., 1950-69; dir. Luth. Social Service Minn. Found., 1969-. Pres. bd. world missions Luth. Ch. Am., 1958-64, mem. bd. Am. missions; pres. bd. social ministry Minn. Synod, 1963-69; chmn. directing com. Luth. Evangelism Mission U.S. and Can., 1956-57; del. Constituting Conv., Luth. Ch. Am.; v.p. Luth. Social Services of Minn., 1960-69; mem. Alcoholic Task Force Hennepin County. Pres., Day Activity and Tng. Center Council Hennepin County, Minn. Synod Housing Corp.; chmn. Twin City Met. Strategy Com. Pres. bd. dirs. Minn. Vols. Am.; bd. dirs. Martin Luther Manor, Mpls., Bethesda Hosp., St. Paul, 1967-69. Home: 5145 17th Av S Minneapolis MN 55417 Office: 2414 Park Av S Minneapolis MN 55404

GRAF, UTA, soprano, educator; b. Karlsruhe/Baden, Germany, Jan. 5, 1915; s. Lukas and Martha (Weiss) Graf; Abiturienten reife, Humanistisches Gymnasium Bruchsal/Baden, 1933; teaching diploma in voice Dr. Hoch's Konservatorium, Frankfurt/Main, 1937; 1 dau., Angèle Aimée Georgette Breyer. Came to U.S., 1948, naturalized, 1954. Made debut under composer Wolfgang Fortner, 1938; debut Düsseldorf Opera House, 1940-41; leading soprano Stadttheater Aachen, 1941-43, Koeln Opera, 1943-44, San Francisco Opera Co., 1949-51, Royal Opera, Covent Garden, London, 1950- 51, Nederlandsche Opera, Amsterdam, 1955-58; operatic, recital, concert appearances under numerous noted condrs. in U.S., Can., Europe, S.Am.; tchr. voice Vassar Coll., 1949, Pa. Coll. Women, 1953, New Eng. Conservatory Music, Boston 1958-66, Manhattan Coll. of Music, N.Y.C., 1964—, Phila. Mus. Acad., 1968—; pvt. tchr. vocal technique and interpretation, N.Y.C., 1960-; artist in residence, Aspen, Colo., 1950.‡

GRAFE, PAUL, constrn. engr., contractor; b. Clay City, Ind., Apr. 19, 1895; s. John Henry and Margaret (Edmonds) G.; grad. Rose Poly. Inst., 1920, D.Eng. (hon.), 1950; spl. study U. Glasgow (Scotland); m. Helen Louise Thickstun, Dec. 11, 1917; children—Helen, Louise, Paula. Engr. Pa. R.R., 1919; timekeeper, supt. C.R. Cummins Co., constructing belt line for Pa. R.R. in Detroit, also substructure for Marysville Power Plant for Detroit Edison Co.; with Grafe-Callahan Constrn. Co., Los Angeles and Dallas, 1922—, in charge constrn. work, v.p., pres., now chmn. bd.; supervised Ill. River levee work, River De Pere's sewer project in St. Louis, Marseilles (Ill.) Canal, Mississippi River levees in Ark. and Mo., Bagnell Dam found. on Osage River, Mo., Madden Dam, C.Z., All-Am. Canal, Cal., dam and tunnels on Casper Alcova project, Wyo., shafts, tunnels on Delaware Aqueduct for Bd. of Water Supply, City of N.Y.; work on Shasta Dam, Central Valley Project, Redding, Cal., Prado Dam, Orange County Flood Control, Cal., Caddoa (Colo.) Dam, pipe and tunnel sects. of San Diego Aqueduct, Granby Dam and pumping plant, Horsetooth Dam, Soldiers Canyon Dam on Colo. Big Thompson project, Hungry Horse Dam, Mont., Davis Dam, Ariz., Duchesne Tunnel, Utah, tunnels for City of Chgo., constrn. NASA Hdqrs., Colorado Springs, Colo., Titan Missile Base, Mountain Home, Idaho; exec. dir. on secret war work in Pacific, N.W. Can. and Brit. Isles; constructing water tunnels Bd. Water Supply, N.Y. Served in engring. dept. Motor Transport Corps in France and Scotland, 1917-19. Breeder thoroughbred and quarter horses, Aberdeen Angus cattle. Regent Loyola U., Los Angeles; bd. dirs. Carrie Estell Doheny Found.; bd. mgrs. Rose Poly. Inst., Terre Haute, Ind. Mem. Acad. Polit. Sci., Los Angeles World Affairs Council. Republican. Roman Catholic. Clubs: California, Los Angeles Country, Greater Los Angeles Press (Los Angeles); Union (Panama); City, Petroleum (Dallas); Tyee (B.C.); Rancheros Visitadores (Santa Barbara). Home: Ferndale Ranch Santa Paula CA 93060 Office: 714 W Olympic Blvd Los Angeles CA 90015

GRAFF, ALFRED CARL, banker; b. Phila., Dec. 26, 1907; s. E. Richard and Caroline (Grauer) G.; student Wharton Sch. U. Pa., Grad. Sch. Banking Rutgers U.; advanced mgmt. program Harvard; m. Louise C. Roth, Jan. 6, 1934; children—Richard P., William M.; m. 2d, Georgette M. Voetsch, Oct. 1968. With Ninth Bank & Trust Co., Phila., 1923-29; with First Pa. Banking and Trust Co., Phila., 1929—, beginning in comptroller's dept., successively asst. treas., asst. v.p., treas., v.p. and treas., 1929-56, sr. v.p., 1956-63, exec. v.p. 1963—; dir. Stock Clearing Corp., Am. Dredging Co., Conemaugh & Black Lick R.R. Co., Patopsco & Back Rivers R.R. Co., Phila., Bethlehem, New Eng. R.R. Co., S. Buffalo Ry. Co., Steelton & Highspire R.R. Co., Skytop Lodges, Inc., Pocono Hotels Corp., V.I. Nat. Bank, Cambria and Ind. R.R. Co. Asso. trustee U. Pa.; vice chmn. bd. mgrs. Grad. Hosp. Mem. bd. publs., chmn. finance com., mem. exec. com. Lutheran Ch. Am. Mem. Am. Bankers Assn., Res. City Bankers Assn. Clubs: Harvard Business School, Racquet, Cricket (Phila.). Home: 3908 Henry Av Philadelphia PA 19129 Office: First Pa Banking and Trust Co 15th and Chestnut Sts Philadelphia PA 19101

GRAFF, EMIL GEORGE, ret. ins. co. exec., lawyer; b. Beatrice, Neb., Sept. 15, 1902; s. Frederick and Mary (Moschel) G.; A.B., Creighton U., 1922; LL.B., U. Detroit, 1925; m. Amelia Bunbury, Nov. 25, 1943. Admitted to Mich. bar, 1925; practiced in Detroit, 1925-26; with investment dept. Mich. Mut. Life Ins. Co., Detroit, 1926-27, Nat. Life Ins. Co. of U.S.A., Chgo., 1927-34, Hercules Life Ins. Co., Chgo., 1934-38; with Wash. Nat. Ins. Co., Evanston, Ill., 1938-67, 3d v.p., 1950-60, treas., 1960-67, v.p., dir., 1963-67. Pres., MacDowell Soc. Evanston. Served with AUS, 1942-43. Mem. English Speaking Union, Chgo. Council Fgn. Relations, Evanston Hist. Soc., Lyric Opera Guild. Roman Catholic. Home: 472 Sheridan Rd Evanston IL 60202. Office: 10 S LaSalle St Chicago IL 60603

GRAFF, GEORGE STEPHEN, aerospace co. exec.; b. N.Y.C., Mar. 16, 1917; s. George Russell and Marjory Eleanor (Dolan) G.; A.B. cum laude, DeSales Coll., Toledo, 1939; B.Aero. Engring., U. Detroit, 1942; m. Mary Rita Shaughnessy, Oct. 3, 1942; children—Mary Ann, George Stephen, James Russell, Thomas Gerald, Maureen Rita. Draftsman, Continental Aviation & Engring. Corp., Detroit, 1940-42; with McDonnell Aircraft Co., 1942—, dir. system tech., 1961- 64, v.p. engring. tech., 1964-68, v.p. engring., 1968-70, exec. v.p., 1970-71, pres., 1971—, also dir.; v.p. McDonnell Douglas Corp., 1971. Mem. subcom. stability and control NACA, 1951-56; mem. subcom. aerodynamic stability and control NASA, 1956-58, com. missile and spacecraft aerodynamics, 1959-61, com. aircraft aerodynamics, 1964-65, chmn. aircraft aerodynamics com., 1965-67, mem. research and tech. adv. com. on aeros., 1967-71. Mem. industry com. Parks Coll., St. Louis, 1950-58. Recipient trophy for design excellence, 1942. Asso. fellow Am. Inst. Aeros. and Astronautics (regional dir., chmn. com. aircraft design 1964-67); mem. Tau Beta Pi. Home: 9 Ridgemoor Dr Clayton MO 63105 Office: PO Box 516 St Louis MO 63166

GRAFF, HENRY FRANKLIN, educator; b. N.Y.C., Aug. 11, 1921; s. Samuel F. and Florence Babette (Morris) G.; B.S., Coll. City N.Y., 1941; M.A., Columbia, 1942, Ph.D., 1949; m. Edith Krantz, June 16, 1946; children—Iris Joan, Ellen Toby. Fellow history Coll. City N.Y., 1941-42, tutor history, 1946; lectr. history Columbia, 1946-47, instr. to asso. prof., 1946-61, prof. history, 1961—, chmn. dept. history, 1961-64; lectr. Vassar Coll., 1953. Chmn. advanced placement com. Am. history, Coll. Entrance Exam. Bd., 1959-63; mem. Nat. Hist. Publs. Commn., 1965—; acad. cons. Gen. Learning Corp., Time-Life Books; cons. editor Alfred A. Knopf, Inc. Served to 1st lt. AUS, 1942-46. Recipient citation War Dept.; Am. Council Learned Socs. fellow, 1942; Townsend Harris medal City Coll. N.Y., 1966. Mem. Orgn. Am. Historians, Middle States Council Social Studies, Am. Hist. Assn., Author's Guild, P.E.N., Nat. Council Social Studies, Phi Beta Kappa. Author: Bluejackets with Perry in Japan, 1952; (with Jacques Barzun) The Modern Researcher, 1962, rev. edit., 1970; (with Clifford Lord) American Themes, 1963; (with John A. Krout) The Adventure of the American People, 2d edit., 1968; The Free and the Brave, 1968; Thomas Jefferson, 1968; American Imperialism and the Philippine Insurrection, 1969; The Tuesday Cabinet, 1970. Cons. editor Life's History of the United States, 1963-64. Contbr. articles to profl. jours. Home: 47 Andrea Lane Scarsdale NY 10583 Office: Fayerweather Hall Columbia U New York City NY 10027

GRAFF, MAURICE OTTO, univ. ofcl.; b. Minier, Ill., Oct. 7, 1907; s. Otto and Mary E. (Munder) G.; B.Ed., Ill. State Normal U., 1929; M.A., State U. Ia., 1937, Ph.D., 1941; m. Elizabeth R. Wilson, June 17, 1934; children—Barbara Jean (Mrs. David Smith), Janice Rae (Mrs. James Gerlach). Tchr. high schs., Ill., 1929-40; faculty Wis. State Univ., La Crosse, 1941—, dean Coll., 1952-63, v.p. acad. affairs, 1963—. Asst. wage stblzn. dir., asst. disputes dir., then disputes dir., 8th Regional WLB, Dallas, 1942-46; mem. labor arbitration staff Fed. Mediation and Conciliation Service, 1946—. Mem. Am. Arbitration Assn. Home: 2303 Johnson St La Crosse WI 54601

GRAFF, WILLIAM, architect; b. Budapest, Hungary, June 19, 1925; s. William and Clara (Pejtsik) G.; M.A. in Arch., Royal Jozsef Nador Tech. U., Budapest, 1949; m. Clara Lenke Marot, Dec. 19, 1959; children—Marcella, Carlo, Guido, Mattias. Came to U.S., 1954, naturalized, 1959. With Marani & Morris, Toronto, Ont., Can., 1951-53, John B. Parkin, Toronto, 1953-54, Maguolo & Quick, Balt., 1954-56, Hugh Stubbins, Cambridge, Mass., 1956- 59, the Architects Collaborative, Cambridge and Rome, Italy, 1959-62, Soc. General Immobilare, Rome and Washington, 1962-67; partner Holle & Grabb, Washington, 1967—; prin. works include 330 Beacon St., Boston, 1958, U. Baghdad (Iraq), 1960, Pl. Victoria, Montreal, Que., Can., 1962, Watergate Apts., Washington, 1963-66, Port Royal Apts., Montreal, 1963, 1801 K St. N.W., Wash., Jefferson Plaza, Alexanderia; Internat. Club Bldg., Washington, 1971. Home: 3735 T St NW Washington DC 20007 Office: 5272 River Rd Washington DC 20016

GRAFFIS, HERB, writer; b. Logansport, Ind., May 31, 1893; s. William Herbert and Elizabeth (Markley) G.; student Northwestern U., 1912-16; m. Dorothy Vaughan, Jan. 7, 1917; 1 son, William H. Telephony mag., 1912-16, Gas Age, 1917-27; sports writer, columnist Chgo. Times, 1935; sports columnist Esquire, 1934; editor Golfdom and Golfing mags., 1927; columnist Chgo. Sun-Times, 1950-65. Pres., Nat. Golf Fund. Mem. Nat. Golf Found. (dir.), Sigma Delta Chi. Clubs: Knollwood, Headline (past pres.), Press (past pres.), Ind. Society of Chicago (past pres.). Home: 3 Little Carlos Lane Fort Myers Beach, FL 33931.

GRAFFLIN, ALLAN LYLE, physician; b. Balt., May 10, 1906; s. Charles F. and Margaret (Cassell) G.; student Balt. City Coll.; A.B., Johns Hopkins, 1925, M.D., 1930; m. Catherine Dennis, Jan. 30, 1937; children—Mary Douglas, Dennis, David Marshall. Instr. and tutor biochem. scis. Harvard, 1930-32, instr., 1932-34, asso., 1934-37; asst. prof. anatomy Harvard Med. Sch., 1937-46; fellow John Simon Guggenheim Meml. Found., 1934, 37; sr. fellow in cancer research, dept. medicine Coll. Phys. and Surgs., N.Y.C., 1946-47, dept. pharmacology N.Y.U. Coll. Medicine, 1947-48; prof. anatomy and dir. dept. anatomy Johns Hopkins U. Sch. Medicine, 1948-57; resident ophthalmology Henry Ford Hosp., 1957- 59, asso. surgeon dept. ophthalmology, 1959-64. Served as maj., lt. col. and col. M.C., U.S. Army, 1942-46. Diplomate Am. Bd. Ophthalmology. Fellow Am. Acad. Ophthalmology and Otolaryngology, A.A.A.S.; mem. Am. Chem. Soc., Am. Assn. Anatomists, A.M.A., Mass. Med. Soc., Am. Physiol. Soc., Sigma Xi, Phi Beta Kappa, Alpha Omega Alpha. Contbr. to sci. jours. Home: 6 Walker Rd Manchester MA 01944 Office: 2 Orchard Lane Danvers MA 01923

GRAFFMAN, GARY, pianist; b. N.Y.C., Oct. 14, 1928; s. Vladimir and Nadia (Margolin) G.; student Curtis Inst. Music, 1936-46, Columbia, 1947-48; m. Naomi Helfman, Dec. 5, 1952. Soloist debut Phila. Orch., 1947; first U.S. tour, 1951, S.Am. tour, 1955, European tour, 1956, Asian-Australian tour, 1958, South African tour, 1961; solo appearances with N.Y. Philharmonic, Boston, Chgo., Cleve., San Francisco, Los Angeles symphony orchs., Philharmonia London, London Symphony, Halle Orch. of Manchester, Royal Liverpool Philharmonic, Berlin, Lisbon, Oslo, Warsaw philharmonics, Johannesburg, Sydney, Melbourne orchs., Cape Town Symphony, others; rec. artist with N.Y., Phila., Boston, Cleve., Chgo., San Francisco orchs., also solo recs. Recipient Rachmaninoff Fund spl. award, 1948, Leventritt award, 1949. Fulbright scholar, 1950; Ford Found. fellow, 1962. Address: care Judson Management 119 W 57th St New York City NY 10019

GRAFLUND, JOHN HENRY, corp. exec.; b. Moline, Ill., June 6, 1918; s. Frederick and Mildred (Claus) G.; grad. with high honors, U. Ill., 1941; m. Marjorie Thorngren, Oct. 3, 1941; children—Linda, Jack, Connie, James. With Deere & Co., 1941—, beginning as internal auditor, successively factory works auditor, asst. comptroller, 1941-56, comptroller, 1956-60, gen. mgr. John Deere Harvester Works, 1960-63; v.p. for overseas mfg. Deere & Co., S.A., 1963-66, v.p. overseas adminstrn., 1966-70, v.p., 1970—, also dir.; pres. John Deere Ltd., Hamilton, Ont., Can., 1970—; dir. Lutheran Mut. Life Ins. Co. Mem. Agribus. Industry Adv. Com., 1968. Pres., dir. Moline Luth. Hosp.; bd. regents Wartburg Coll.; bd. dirs. Agribus. Council. Mem. Am. Inst. C.P.A.'s. Elk. Home: 432 Townsend E Burlington Ontario Canada Office: John Deere Rd Moline IL 61265 also John Deere Ltd Hamilton Ontario Canada

GRAFLY, DOROTHY, writer; b. Paris, France, July 29, 1896 (parents Am. citizens); d. Charles and Frances (Sekeles) Grafly; brought to U.S. in infancy; B.A., Wellesley, 1918; grad. work under Prof. George P. Baker of Harvard, 1918-19; m. Charles Hawkins Drummond, Aug. 9, 1946. Art critic, Phila. North American, 1920-25, art editor and editorial and feature writer, 1925; art editor Public Ledger, Phila., 1925-34; art critic Evening Publ. Ledger, 1934; art editor Phila. Record, 1934-42; spl. corr. Christian Sci. Monitor, 1920-63; Phila. corr. Am. Mag. of Art to 1928; curator of collections Drexel Inst., 1934-45; dir. mag. publicity Phila. Art Alliance, 1944-48; dir. research and art Philip Rangan Assos., 1942-48, contbg. editor American Artists, 1946-56; contbg. critic Art Digest (under name Dorothy Drummond), to 1953; art editor Tempos Mag., Philadelphia, 1955-59, The Evening and Sunday Bull., 1956-70; lectr. art Temple U., 1938-39, Drexel Inst., 1940- 42. Fellow in perpetuity Pa. Acad. Fine Arts, 1957. Elected Distinguished Dau. Pa., 1960. Mem. Art Alliance, Alumnae Assn. Wellesley Coll., Pi Gamma Mu. Clubs: Contemporary, Art Alliance, New Century Guild (Phila.), Phila. Altrusa (charter mem.; pres. 1930-32), hon. mem. Phila. Water Color Club; Nat. Travel, Nat. Geog., Am. Assn. Museums, Phila. Mus. Art, Am. Fedn. Arts, P.A.F.A. Wrote and produced Masque of Night; Masque of Life; The Phoenix; Metamorphosis; Imagesall produced Gloucester, Mass., 1914-20; winner prize for one-act play, Plays and Players' Club, Phila., 1921. Author: History of the Philadelphia Print Club, 1929; series of American art biographies under title Parade of American Art, 1936-37; series of articles dealing with living European sculptors, nat. "What Sells" series, Am. Artist, 1948- 49. Contbr. Dictionary Am. Biography, Ency. Brit. and to mags. Editor-pub. of Art in Focus. Lectr. on art. One of six American critics invited by Chicago Art Inst. to broadcast over nat. hook-up at opening of 1934 Century of Progress Expn. Art Exhbn. Address: 131 N 20th St Philadelphia PA 19103 (summer) 1233 Washington St Gloucester MA 01930

GRAFTON, ARTHUR WALLACE, lawyer; b. Hsuchoufu, China, Jan. 4, 1907 (parents Am. citizens); s. Thomas B. and Letitia Hart (Taylor) B.; B.A., Presbyn. Coll. of S.C., 1928; LL.B., U. Louisville, 1930; m. Betty Lou Mikell, Feb. 21, 1946; children—Arthur Wallace, Mikell Taylor. Admitted to Ky. bar, 1930, since practiced in Louisville; asso. firm Woodward, Dawson & Hobson and predecessor firm, 1933-36, Wyatt, Grafton & Sloss, and predecessors, 1937- -. Mem. Ky. Senate, 1953-57. Served to lt. col. USAAF, 1943-45. Mem. Am., Ky., Louisville bar assns., Am. Judicature Soc. Home: Prospect KY 40059 Office: M E Taylor Bldg Louisville KY 40202

GRAFTON, CONNIE ERNESTINE, librarian; b. Hubbard, Tex., Jan. 17, 1913; d. Louis Dormer and Connie Imogene (Newton) Grafton; A.B., Trinity U., 1933; A.B. in L.S., U. Okla., 1934; M.A., U. Chgo., 1940; postgrad. Sch. Edn., City U. N.Y., 1971—. Student asst. Trinity U. library, 1930-33; reference asst. circulation dept. Cin. Pub. Library, 1936-41; tri-county librarian, Person, Caswell and Orange County libraries, N.C., 1941-45; head extension div. Va. State Library, Richmond, 1945-56; dir. Ia. State Traveling Library, 1956-71. Pres. Ia. Council Community Improvement, 1965-67; chmn. adult edn. com. Ia. Commn. Sr. Citizens; mem. Ia. Inter-govtl. Relations Commn., 1966—. Named woman of yr., Va., 1951. Mem. Assn. State Libraries (sec. 1960-61), Assn. Library Trustees (2d v.p. 1957-58), Southeastern (exec. bd. 1949-50), Am. (counselor at large 1964), Va. (pres. 1948-49), Ia. (exec. bd. 1956-66) library assns., Ia. Assn. Sch. Libraries, C. of C., Va. Council Human Relations, Southeastern (exec. bd. 1955-56), Mo. Valley (Ia. State rep. 1960-62), Ia. (pres. 1959-60, exec. bd. 1960-66) assns. adult edn., Adult Edn. Assn. U.S.A. (Ia. membership coordinator 1958-66, sec. 1966-67, exec. com. 1968—) Pi Gamma Mu. Jewish religion. Editor N.C. Libraries, 1942-44, Va. Library Bull., 1945-56, Ia. Library Quar., 1956-71.

GRAFTON, SAMUEL, publishing co. exec.; b. N.Y.C., Sept. 4, 1907; A.B., U. Pa., 1929; m. Edith Kingstone, June 28, 1931; children—Abigail Alice, John William, Anthony Thomas. Editorial writer Phila. Record, 1929-34; asso. editor N.Y. Post, 1934-49; writer daily column I'd Rather Be Right (N.Y. Post, Chgo. Sun-Times, St. Louis Star-Times, Los Angeles Daily News, Phila. Inquirer, other newspapers), 1939-49; editor Lithopinion, 1966-69; pres. Grafton Publs., Inc., N.Y.C., 1969—; editor Youth Report and Addiction and Drug Abuse Report. Decorated chevalier Legion of Honor (France). Author: All Out, 1940; An American Diary, 1943; A Most Contagious Game, 1955. Contbr. to McCall's and other mags. Address: 667 Madison Av New York City NY 10021

GRAGAN, PHILIP A., dept. store exec.; b. 1931; B.A., George Washington U., 1953, J.D., 1959. With firm Covington & Burling, 1959-65; with Woodward & Lothrop Inc., 1965—, sec., counsel, 1968—. Served with AUS, 1953-55. Address: Woodward and Lothrop Inc 11th F and G Sts NW Washington DC 20013*

GRAGG, LOGAN, psychiatrist; b. Lexington, Ky., Aug. 30, 1916; s. Logan and Louise (Creighton) G.; A.B., Transylvania Coll., 1937; M.D., U. Louisville, 1941; m. Mary Park Avery, June 12, 1940; children—Ann (Mrs. Russell Lay), Wyatt Logan, Susan Park. Intern Good Samaritan Hosp., Lexington, 1941-42; resident Louisville Gen. Hosp., 1945-47; practice medicine, specializing in psychiatry, Lexington, 1947-49; mem. psychiat. staff, chief phys. medicine rehab. VA Hosp., Lexington, 1949-53, psychiatrist, 1970—; clin. dir. Eastern State Hosp., Lexington, 1953-56, supt., 1956-70; dir. Franklin County Child Guidance Clinic, Frankfort, Ky., 1956-64; cons. dept. psychology U. Ky., 1956-60. Bd. dirs. Central Ky. Mental Health Assn., Central Ky. Mental Health Center. Served to capt., M.C., AUS, 1942-45; PTO, ETO. Fellow Am. Psychiat. Assn.; mem. A.M.A., Ky. Med. Assn., Ky. Psychiat. Assn. (past pres.), Alpha Kappa Kappa, Kappa Alpha. Democrat. Mem. Christian Ch. Kiwanian. Home: No 7 Tanglewood Lexington, KY 40505. Office: 427 W 4th St Lexington KY 40508

GRAGG, WILLIFORD, ins. co. exec.; b. Memphis, June 11, 1914; s. Ovie H. and Ruth Graves (Williford) G.; student Southwestern U., 1931-32; LL.B., U. Tenn., 1936; m. Grace Clement Bailey, Oct. 19, 1940; 1 dau., Frances Ann. Admitted to Tenn. bar, 1936; practiced in Memphis, 1936-37; agt. FBI, 1942-43; with U.S. Fidelity & Guaranty Co., Balt., 1937-42, 46—, v.p., 1956-59, exec. v.p., 1959-63, sr. exec. v.p., 1963-70, pres., 1970—, also dir.; dir. Fidelity & Guaranty Life Ins. Co., Fidelity Ins. Co. Can., First Nat. Bank Md., Provident Savs. Bank, Del Mar, Co., Fidelity & Guaranty Ins. Underwriters, Inc. Trustee Greater Balt. Med. Center; bd. govs. Presbyn. Eye, Ear and Throat Hosp., Balt.; bd. dirs. Balt. chpt. A.R.C.; bd. overseers Goucher Coll. Mem. Balt. C. of C. (dir.), Alpha Tau Omega. Presbyn. (elder). Clubs: Center, Maryland, Merchants, Baltimore Country. Home: 109 Churchwarden's Rd Baltimore MD Office: US Fidelity and Guaranty Co Baltimore MD 21203

GRAHAM, ALBERT BRUCE, audiologist, speech pathologist; b. Oil City, Pa., Aug. 8, 1919; s. Albert Vanderlin and Octavia (Kellogg) G.; A.B., Colo. State Coll. Edn., 1940; A.M., U. Denver, 1949; Ph.D., Northwestern U., 1953; m. Mary Margaret Zeller, June 4, 1943; children—Janice, Michael. Tchr. high sch. drama, Coolidge, Kan., 1940-42; prin. Schofield High Sch., Schofield Barracks, Hawaii, 1946-48; dir. Speech and Hearing Clinic, also Cerebral Palsy Center, Bowling Green State U., 1951-52; chief div. audiology and speech pathology Henry Ford Hosp., Detroit, 1952—. Bd. dirs. Detroit Hearing and Speech Center, 1956—, pres., 1961-62, 66-67; bd. dirs. Mich. Assn. Better Hearing and Speech, 1967—; mem. profl. adv. council United Cerebral Palsy Assn. Mich., 1960—, chmn., 1968-69; bd. dirs. Nat. Assn. Hearing and Speech Agys., 1960—, 1st v.p., 1968-69; mem. speakers bur. United Found., Detroit; survey cons. Commn. on Accreditation Rehab. Facilities, 1970—. Served with USAAF, 1942-46. Fellow Am. Speech and Hearing Assn.; asso. fellow Am. Acad. Ophthalmology and Otolaryngology; mem. Acad. Aural Rehab., Mich. Speech and Hearing Assn. (pres. 1957), Council Exceptional Children; asso. mem. Detroit Otol. Soc. Editor Sensorineural Hearing Processes and Disorders, 1967. Home: 3236 Lincoln St Dearborn MI 48124 Office: Henry Ford Hospital 2799 W Grand Blvd Detroit MI 48202

GRAHAM, ALICE MILLETT, home economist, ret. coll. dean; b. Hebron, Me.; d. Ralph Linwood and Alice (Campbell) Millett; student U. Ia., 1925-27, U. N.M., 1936-37; B.S., N.M. Western Coll., 1930; M.S., Ia. State Coll., 1939; m. Hoyt Conlin Graham, Aug. 22, 1927 (dec. 1936). Instr. home econs. Ia. State Coll., 1939-41, U. Tenn., 1941-44; dean home econs. La. Poly. Inst., Ruston, 1944-70. Recipient Cardinal Key. Mem. Am. Home Econs. Assn., Am. Vocational Assn., Am. Assn. U. Women, Delta Sigma Epsilon, Phi Kappa Phi. Home: 408 Pinecrest Dr Ruston LA 71270

GRAHAM, ANGUS FREDERICK, educator, microbiologist, b. Toronto, Ont., Can., Mar. 28, 1916; s. Frederick J. and Mary (Ball) G.; came to U.S., 1958, naturalized, 1963; B.A.Sc., U. Toronto, 1938, M.A.Sc., 1939; Ph.D., U. Edinburgh (Scotland), 1942, D.Sc., 1952; m. Jacqueline Francoise Poirier, July 3, 1955; children—Robert J., Andrew D., Paul F. Lectr. biochemistry Carnegie Teaching fellow U. Edinburgh, 1942-47; research asso. Connaught Med. Research Labs., U. Toronto, 1947-58, asso. prof. microbiology, 1953-58; mem. Wistar Inst. Anatomy and Biology, Wistar prof. microbiology U. Pa., Phila., 1958-70; prof., chmn. dept. biochemistry McGill U., Montreal, Que., 1970—. Eleanor Roosevelt Internat. Cancer fellow Institut du Radium, Paris, France, 1964-65. Mem. Canadian Soc. Microbiology, Am. Soc. Microbiologists, N.Y. Acad. Scis., A.A.A.S. Editor-in-chief Jour. Cellular Physiology, 1965-70; editorial bd. Jour. Virology, 1964—. Research and publs. on chemistry of enzymes and viruses, especially mechanism of multiplication of viruses in living cells. Home: 447 Strathcona St Westmount Quebec Canada Office: Dept Biochemistry McGill U Montreal 2 Quebec Canada

GRAHAM, BILL, theatre mgr.; degree in bus. administrn. Coll. City N.Y. Came to U.S., 1942. Former producer San Francisco Mime Troupe; producer Fillmore West, San Francisco, Fillmore East, N.Y.C. Address: Fillmore West 1545 Market St San Francisco CA 94103

GRAHAM, BILLY, evangelist; see Graham, William Franklin.

GRAHAM, BRUCE, research scientist; b. Crete, Neb., Dec. 26, 1916; s. Charles C. and Mabel (Douglas) G.; student Ore. Coll. Edn., 1933-35, U. Ore., 1936, 37, 39; B.S., Ph.D., Ore. State Coll., 1945; m. Hermine Meta Zwanck, June 1, 1937; children—Bruce D., Kim L., Paul A., Robert A., Janice H. Prin., Ore. pub. schs., 1935-41; research antimalarial chemotherapy, 1942-45, chemistry color photography, 1945-52, organic chemistry and biol. scis., 1952—; now prof. U. Southwestern La., Lafayette; pres. Gulf South Research Inst., Baton Rouge, 1965-69. Mem. Am. Chem. Soc. (chmn. Santa Clara Valley 1955-56), Western Pharm. Soc., A.A.A.S., Sigma Xi, Phi Kappa Phi. Contbr. articles in field. Home: 4900 Claycut Rd Baton Rouge LA 70806

GRAHAM, BRUCE DOUGLAS, pediatrician; b. Roberts, Wis., Dec. 15, 1915; s. Francis J. and Mary (Turner) G.; A.B., U. Ala., 1939; M.D., Vanderbilt U., 1942; m. Louise Alice Rowekamp, Jan. 21, 1946; children—John Gardiner, Mary Augusta, Anne Louise. Intern U. Mich. Hosp., 1942-43, resident dept. pediatrics, 1946-48, dir. pediatric labs., 1949-59; faculty pediatric dept. U. Mich., 1948-59, asso. prof., 1954-59, prof., 1959; prof., head dept. pediatrics U. B.C., 1959-63; pediatrician-in-chief Vancouver (B.C., Can.) Gen. Hosp., 1959-63; chief pediatrics Children's Hosp., Vancouver, 1961-63; prof., chmn. dept. pediatrics Ohio State U. Coll. Medicine, 1964—; chief staff Children's Hosp., Columbus, O., 1964-70, med. dir., 1970—; chief pediatric div. U. Hosp., Ohio State U., 1964—; med. dir. Children's Hosp. Research Found., Columbus, 1966—. Mem. med. adv. com. state Crippled Children's Bur.; mem. Med. Adv. Bd. on Ednl. Film Prodn.; mem. Greater Dublin Community Council. Served to maj., M.C., AUS, 1943-46. Diplomate Am. Bd. Pediatrics. Mem. Soc. Pediatric Research, Am. Pediatric Soc., A.M.A., Am. Acad. Pediatrics, A.A.A.S., Assn. Am. Med. Colls., Midwest Soc. Pediatric Research, Ohio Med. Assn., Central Ohio Pediatric Soc., Acad. Medicine Columbus and Franklin County, Assn. Med. Sch. Pediatric Dept. Chairmen, Am. Pub. Health Assn., Am. Assn. Maternal and Child Health, Med. Center Alumni Soc. U. Mich., Central Ohio Biomed. Engring. Community Council (charter), Sigma Xi, Alpha Omega Alpha. Home: 4915 Brand Rd Dublin OH 43017 Office: 561 S 17th St Columbus OH 43205

GRAHAM, BRUCE JOHN, architect; b. La Cumbre, Bogota, Colombia, Dec. 1, 1925 (parents Am. citizens); s. Charles Stewart and Angelica (Gomez de la Torre) G.; student U. Dayton, 1942-43, Case Sch. Applied Scis., 1944-46; B.Arch., U. Pa., 1948; m. Jane Johnson, Sept. 1, 1960; children—George, Lisa, Mara. With firm Holabird, Root & Burgee, Chgo., 1949-51; chief design Chgo. office Skidmore, Owings & Merrill, 1951-60, gen. partner, Chgo., 1960—; prin. works include Inland Steel Bldg., Brunswick Bldg., Conn. Mut. Life Ins. Co., Gateway I, II, Equitable Bldg., John Hancock Bldg., Sears Tower (all Chgo.), Upjohn Bldg., Kalamazoo, Bus. Men's Assurance Co., Kansas City, Mo., Shell Bldg., Houston, Boots Hdqrs. Bldg., Nottingham, Eng. Adviser Washington U. Sch. Architecture, St. Louis. Trustee Chgo. Ednl. TV Assn. Served with USNR, 1943-46. Fellow A.I.A. (1st honor award for Bus. Men's Assurance Co. Bldg., 1963); mem. Soc. Contemporary Am. Art (pres. 1968-69), Art Inst. Chgo. Home: 2215 N Cleveland Chicago IL 60614 Office: 30 W Monroe St Chicago IL 60603

GRAHAM, CHARLES JOHN, coll. pres.; b. Peru, Ill., May 29, 1929; s. John William and Pauline (Powell) G.; A.B., U. Ill., 1950, M.A., 1951, Ph.D., 1955; m. Florence Yvonne Ure, Sept. 2, 1951; children—John Charles, James Spencer, David Powell. Mgmt. intern Navy Dept., 1953-54, contract negotiator Bur. Ships, 1954; from instr. to prof. polit. sci. Wis. State U., River Falls, 1954-63, chmn. dept. social scis., 1962-63; vis. lectr. U. Wis., summer 1957, U. Ill., summer 1959; legislative asst. to Senator Proxmire, 1960-61; dean Coll. Art and Scis., Wis. State U., Whitewater, 1963-70, asst. to pres. for fed. programs, 1965-68, acting chmn. dept. polit. sci., 1970-71; pres. Saint Cloud State Coll., St. Cloud, Minn., 1971—. James W. Garner fellow polit. sci., 1951-52, 52-53. Mem. Am., Midwestern polit. sci. assns., Am. Assn. Higher Edn., Am. Assn. U. Profs., Phi Beta Kappa, Phi Kappa Phi. Methodist. Rotarian (pres. Whitewater 1969-70). Home: 9 Highbanks Pl St Cloud MN 56301

GRAHAM, CLARENCE R., librarian; b. Louisville, Feb. 28, 1907; s. Samuel J. and Lillian Ellen (Paris) G.; student U. N.C., 1924-27; A.B., U. Louisville, 1934; B.S. in L.S., Western Res. U., 1935; postgrad. Northwestern U., 1937-38; m. Esther Charlotte Lothman, Feb. 28, 1930; 1 dau., Carolyn. Student asst. U. N.C. Library, 1925-27; field rep. N.C. State Dept. Health, Raleigh, 1924-25; dept. statistics Brown & Williamson Tobacco Co., Louisville, 1929-30; librarian Parkland Jr. High Sch., Louisville, 1930-34; asst. to librarian Louisville Free Pub. Library, 1935-36; dir. Nat. Coll. of Edn. Library, Evanston, Ill., 1936-42; librarian Louisville Free Pub. Library, 1942—; instr. library scis. U. Louisville, 1946-51. Vis. asso. prof. library sci. U. Ky., spring 1963. Mem. Louisville Labor Mgmt. Com. Treas. Jr. Art Gallery. Bd. dirs. Children's Theatre, Nat. Conf. Christians and Jews. Mem. A.L.A. (chmn. com. libraries and television 1949-50, pres. 1950-51), Ky. Library Assn. (pres. 1947), Southeastern Library Assn. (pres. 1948-50), Newcomen Soc. N.Am., English Speaking Union, Louisville Urban League. Clubs: Louisville Library (pres. 1948-49), Filson, Arts, Rotary (Louisville). Co-founder, 1947, and cons. to free "Neighborhood Colleges" in br. libraries sponsored by U. Louisville, Free Pub. Library. Author: First Book of Public Libraries, 1959. Contbr. articles to profl. jours. Home: 1028 Cherokee Rd Louisville KY 40204 Office: 301-333 Library Pl Louisville KY 40203

GRAHAM, DAVID, corp. ofcl.; b. No. Ireland, Mar. 11, 1905; s. William J. and Agnes J. (Clark) G.; came to U.S. as Commonwealth Fellow, 1927, naturalized, 1942; grad. Queens U., 1926; grad. Mass. Inst. Tech., 1929, Harvard Sch. Bus., 1931; m. Clover E. Henry, Sept. 1933; children—Rae H. (dec.), David (dec.), Philip; m. 2d, Florence Ruth Comer, Oct. 1948. Asso. with J. P. Morgan & Co., N.Y.C., 1931-32; dir. J. Walter Thompson Co., London, 1932-37, L. Rose & Co., Ltd., London, 1934-43; treas. W. Va. Pulp and Paper Co., N.Y.C., 1945-48; financial v.p. Weyerhaeuser Timber Co., Tacoma, Wash., 1948-52; financial v.p., dir. Standard Oil Co. (Ind.), 1952-62; chmn. corporate finance dept., gen. partner Hornblower & Weeks-Hemphill, Noyes, N.Y.C., 1962-69; dir. Gen. Fireproofing Co., Del. Labs., Inc., Olinkraft, Inc., Tecumseh Products Co. Pres. Weyerhaeuser Timber Found., 1948-51. Chief pulp sect. Pulp and Paper Br. WPB, 1942; dir. Office of Pulp Allocation, Forest Products Bur., 1943. Mem. bd. govs., bd. dirs. Chgo. chpt. A.R.C.; dir., past pres. Community Fund, Chgo. Trustee Northwestern U., Woodrow Wilson Nat. Fellowship Found. Mem. Harvard Bus. Sch. Alumni Assn., Am. Inst. E.E., N.A.M. (dir. 1949-51, 57-62), Chgo. Planetarium Soc. (trustee). Presbyn. Clubs: The Links, India House, Wall Street, Harvard, Union League (N.Y.C.); Chicago, Commercial (Chgo.); Ocean, Country of Fla. (Delray Beach); Willow Point Country (Alexander City, Ala.). Home: RFD 755 Delray Beach FL 33444 Office: 8 Hanover St New York City NY 10004

GRAHAM, DAVID TREDWAY, educator, physician; b. Mason City, Ia., June 20, 1917; s. Evarts Ambrose and Helen (Tredway) G.; B.A., Princeton, 1938; M.A., Yale, 1941; M.D., Washington U., St. Louis, 1943; m. Frances Jeanette Keesler, June 14, 1941; children-Norma VanSurdam, Andre Tredway, Polly Brewster. Intern Barnes Hosp., St. Louis, 1944, asst. resident medicine, 1944-45, 47-48; research fellow medicine Cornell U. Med. Coll., 1948-51; asst. prof. medicine Washington U. Med. Sch., 1951-57, asst. prof. psychiatry, 1956-57; mem. faculty U. Wis. Med. Sch., 1957—, prof. medicine, 1963—, asso. chmn. dept., 1969—, asst. dean and/or chmn. med. sch. admissions, 1964-69; vis. prof. psychiatry U. Va. Sch. Medicine, 1960. Alternate delegate Democratic Nat. Conv., 1968. Served to capt., M.C., AUS, 1945- 47. Mem. A.M.A., Am. Fedn. Clin. Research, Am. Psychosomatic Soc. (council 1952-55, 64-67), Soc. Psychophysiologic Research (bd. dirs. 1964-67, pres. 1969-70), Central Soc. Clin. Research, Soc. Biol. Psychiatry. Editor Clin. Research Proc., 1954-59. Home: 2927 Harvardd Dr Madison WI 53705

GRAHAM, DEE MCDONALD, educator; b. Dixon, Miss., Oct. 11, 1927; s. Homer Yancy and Pearl (Nicholson) G.; B.Sc., Miss. State U., 1950; M.S., Ia. State U., 1951, Ph.D., 1954; m. Marjory May Cox, Jan. 4, 1948; children—Dee McDonald, Kenneth L., Thomas R., Timothy A., Robert D., Marjory F., Michael A. Asso. prof. Clemson U., 1953-58; asso. dir. research Pet Inc., 1958-66, tech. dir., 1967-69; prof. food sci. and nutrition, chmn. dept. U. Mo., Columbia, 1969—. Cons.; speaker in field. Mem. subcom. food additives Nat. Acad. Sci., 1970. Served with AUS, 1946-48. Mem. Evaporated Milk Assn. (chmn. research and devel. council 1956-66), Am. Dairy Sci. Assn., Am. Acad. Pediatrics, A.A.A.S., Sigma Xi. Presbyn. (elder 1964-67). Mason (32), Kiwanian. Patentee in field. Home: 1105 S Glenwood Columbia MO 65201

GRAHAM, DONALD, univ. dean; b. Lansing, Kan., Dec. 13, 1917; s. Frank L. and Bertha (Carrington) G.; B.S., Kan. State Coll., Pittsburg, 1939, M.S. 1940; Ph.D. in History, State U. Ia., 1953; m. Allene Louise Boyer, Oct. 21, 1943. Mem. faculty Buena Vista Coll., Storm Lake, Ia., 194655; mem. faculty Wis. State U.-Whitewater, 1955—, dean Sch. Grad. Studies, 1965—; cons. U.S. Office Edn. Served with USAAF, 1941-45. Home: 1246 W Melrose St Whitewater WI 53190

GRAHAM, DONALD GOODNOW, lawyer; b. Ft. Worth, Tex., Dec. 9, 1894; s. Theodore F. and Carrie (Knight) G.; B.S., Coe Coll., 1916; LL.B., Harvard, 1921; m. Juanita Fisher, Sept. 2, 1919; children—Richard Fisher, Donald Goodnow. Admitted to Wash. bar, 1921; also U.S. Supreme Ct., U.S. Fed. Cts., Wash. State Cts., U.S. Tax Ct.; practice in Seattle, 1921-; asst. U.S. atty., 1924-25; pvt. practice, 1925—; sr. mem. Graham, Dunn, Johnston & Rosenquist, 1930—. Dir. Fisher Flouring Mills Co., Fisher's Blend Sta., Inc., San Juan Fishing & Packing Co., West Coast Airlines, Inc., Columbia River Packers. Chmn. advance gift sect. United Good Neighbor Fund, 1936. Treas. Republican Primary campaign U.S. Senate, Janet Tourtellotte, 1950. Pres., bd. dirs. U. Wash. Arboretum Found.; bd. dirs. O.D. Fisher Charitable Found.; former gov. for Wash. Nat. Aero. Assn. Served to 1st lt. USAAF, 1917-19, to col., 1942-45. Mem. Am., Wash., Seattle bar assns., Seattle C. of C. (past sect. chmn.), Order Daedalians, Am. Judicature Soc. Episcopalian. Clubs: Rainier, Sea Tennis, Sea Golf, Quiet Birdmen. Home: 1900 Shenandoah Dr E Seattle, WA 98102. Office: Seattle First National Bank Bldg Seattle WA 98104

GRAHAM, DONALD MARTIN, banker; b. Pitts., Sept. 10, 1913; s. Robert T. and Jane C. (Martin) G.; A.B., Northwestern U., 1933, J.D., 1936; m. Josephine D. Hall, Sept. 10, 1936; children—Robert, Alan, Mary J., Boyd. Admitted to Ill. bar; asso. firm Mayer, Brown & Platt, and predecessor firms, Chgo., 1936-44, partner, 1945-52; v.p. Continental Ill. Nat. Bank and Trust Co., Chgo., 1953-60, vice chmn. bd., 1960-69, chmn. bd., chief exec. officer, 1969—, also dir.; dir. Abbott Labs., U.S. Gypsum Co., Texaco, Inc., N.Y.C., Ill. Power Co., Decatur, Marcor, Inc. (formerly Montgomery Ward), Clow Corp., Chgo. Chmn. of bd. of commrs. Chgo. R.R. Terminal Authority. Mem. citizens bd. U. Chgo., Loyola U.; bd. dirs. Met. Housing and Planning Council; trustee Chgo. Wesley Meml. Hosp., treas. 1968—; mem. bd. advisers Mercy Hosp.; trustee Notre Dame (Ind.) U., Ill. Inst. Tech. Mem. Am., Ill., Chgo. bar assns., Am. Bankers Assn., Am. Inst. Banking, Assn. Res. City Bankers, Chgo. Assn. Commerce and Industry (dir.), Transp. Assn. Am. (chmn.), Sigma Alpha Epsilon, Phi Alpha Delta. Methodist. Clubs: Bankers, Law, The Chgo., Commercial, Economic, Executives, Union League (Chgo.); Dairymen's Country (Boulder Junction, Wis.); Glen View; John Evans of Northwestern University (chmn.); the Brook (N.Y.C.). Home: 2247 Orrington Av Evanston IL 60201 Office: Continental Ill Nat Bank and Trust Co 231 S LaSalle St Chicago IL 60690

GRAHAM, DONALD S., sugar co. exec. Gen. counsel Am. Crystal Sugar Co. Office: Am Sugar Crystal Sugar Co PO Box 419 Denver CO 80201*

GRAHAM, DONALD WILLIAM, air force officer; b. San Francisco, Aug. 5, 1917; s. John Bremner and Nellie May (Hoey) G.; B.S., U. Cal. at Berkeley, 1939; M.B.A., Harvard, 1952; m. Dorothy Wray Reesman, Aug. 3, 1946; children—Catherine Ellen, Ralph Bremner and Bruce William (twins). Commd. 2d lt., U.S. Army, 1938, advanced through grades to maj. gen. USAF, 1965; operations officer, exec. officer 357th Fighter Group, Cal. and Eng., 1943-44, group comdr., 1944; with Air Material Command, Wright Field, Dayton, O., 1946-50; with office asst. for materiel program control, hdqrs. USAF, 1952-53; dep. exec. and exec. officer to under sec. Air Force, 1953, exec. officer to asst. sec., 1953-55; dep. comdr. 10 Air Div., Alaska, 1955- 58; dir. tactical and supports systems Aero. Systems Center, Air Force Logistics Command, Wright-Patterson AFB, O., 1959-60; comdr. central contract mgmt. region Air Force Logistics Command/Air Force System Command, 1960-62; dep. chief staff materiel, hdqrs. Mil. Air Transport Service, 1962-65, comdr. Eastern Transport Air Force (now named 21 Air Force, Mil. Airlift Command), 1965-67; dir. maintenance engring. Air Force Logistics Command, Wright-Patterson AFB, O., 1967-68, dep. chief staff maintenance engring., 1968-69; asst. dep. chief staff systems and logistics U.S. Air Force Hdqrs., 1969—. Decorated D.S.M., Legion of Merit, Silver Star, Air Medal with 3 oak leaf clusters, D.F.C. with 1 oak leaf cluster, French Croix de Guerre with palm. Office: Asst Dep Chief Staff Systems and Logistics Hdqrs USAF Washington DC 20330

GRAHAM, DUNSTAN, educator; b. Princeton, N.J., Aug. 17, 1922; s. Frank Dunstone and Mary Louise (Power) G.; B.S. in Engring., Princeton, 1943, M.S. in Engring., 1947; student Cornell U., 1949, U. Buffalo, 1950; m. Arline Marie Roech, Dec. 23, 1944; children—Bruce, Geoffry. Draftsman, Fleetwings, Inc., Bristol, Pa., 1943; aerodynamicist Boeing Airplane Co., 1947-48; flight research engr. Cornell Aero. Lab., 1948-50; gen. engr. USAF All Weather Flying Div., Wright-Patterson AFB, 1950-55; chief engr. flight controls Lear, Inc., 1955-59; tech. dir. Systems Tech., Inc., Princeton, N.J., 1959—; prof. aero. engring. Princeton, 1959-; guest lectr. U. Cal. at Los Angeles, 1965-68. Served to 2d lt. USAAF, 1943-46, to 1st lt. USAF, 1951- 53. Fellow I.E.E.E.; asso. fellow Am. Inst. Aero and Astronautics; mem. Am. Assn. U. Profs., Sigma Xi. Asso. editor Jour. Franklin Inst., 1960- -. Home: 54 McClean Circle Princeton, NJ 08540.

GRAHAM, ELIZABETH M., lawyer; b. Bklyn., Nov. 8, 1907; d. Joseph W. and Margaret (Harding) Graham; student Hunter Coll.; LL.B., Fordham U., 1929; m. John H. Michels, Sept. 29, 1933. Admitted to N.Y. bar, 1930; law clk. Emmet, Marvin & Martin, 1927-30, asso. lawyer, 1930-44, partner, 1944-71; dir. Louise Smith Corp. Trustee, Traphagen Sch. Fashion. Mem. Bar Assn. City of N.Y., N.Y. State Bar Assn., Phi Delta Delta. Republican. Roman Catholic. Home: Box 202 Waverly Pl Shelter Island Heights NY 11965 Office: 48 Wall St New York City NY 10005

GRAHAM, ELMER ALBERT, petroleum co. exec.; b. Evansville, Ind., Oct. 6, 1926; s. William J. and Mary (Grimwood) G.; B.S., Evansville Coll., 1949; grad. Advanced Mgmt. Program, Harvard, 1966; m. Sally Ann Shoupe, Sept. 29, 1956; children—Rick William, William Earl, Terri Ellen. With Marathon Oil Co., Findlay, O., 1955—, asst. treas., 1961-62; treas., 1967-68, v.p., treas., 1969—; treas. Marathon Internat. Oil Co., 1962-66; dir. First Nat. Bank Findlay. Past pres. Blanchard Valley Hosp. Assn.; mem. Findlay Bd. Edn.; mem. bd. Hancock County Joint Vocational Sch. Served with USNR, 1943-46. Mem. Am. Petroleum Inst., Nat. Assn. Credit, Financial Execs. Inst. Presbyn. Elk, Rotarian. Clubs: Catawba Island Yacht; Detroit Yacht; Marco Polo. Home: 931 Oakdale Dr Findlay, OH 45840. Office: 539 S Main St Findlay OH 45840

GRAHAM, ERWIN HERMAN, automobile co. exec.; b. Detroit, Jan. 28, 1921; s. Jacob and Marie Pauline (Schulz) G.; certificate accounting, Bus. Inst., Walton Sch. Commerce, 1943; m. Ellen Marie Eliasen, Sept. 12, 1944; children—Leigh Ellen, Michael Randall. Cost accountant Parke, Davis & Co., 1939-43; pub. accountant Ernest & Ernst, 1945-51; comptroller's staff Chrysler Corp., 1951-54, comptroller DeSoto div., Detroit, 1954-58, comptroller corp., 1958-67, v.p., 1964—. Bd. dirs. YMCA Met. Detroit. Served to 1st lt. USAAF, 1943-45. C.P.A., Mich. Mem. Am. Inst. C.P.A.'s, Mich. Assn. C.P.A.'s, Financial Execs. Inst. Clubs: Detroit Athletic, Detroit Golf. Home: 529 Lake Shore Rd Grosse Pointe Shores MI 48236 Office: 341 Massachusetts Av Detroit MI 48231

GRAHAM, ERWIN MONTGOMERY, Jr., army officer; b. Pensacola, Fla., Nov. 18, 1917; s. Erwin M. and Ruth (Granberry) G.; B.S., Miss. State Coll., 1938; M.S., Ph.D., Mass. Inst. Tech., 1950; grad. Ordnance Center and Sch., 1953, Command and Gen. Staff Coll., 1957, Armed Forces Staff Coll., 1961, Naval War Coll., 1965; m. Mary Douglass Biederman, Jan. 20, 1955; children—Diana S. (Mrs. Howard Edels) Elizabeth A., Janet L., David E., Mary Douglass. Commd. 2d lt. U.S. Army, 1938, advanced through grades to maj. gen., 1970; staff officer G-4, France, 1944-45; chief instrument lab APG, 1947; 1st comdt. Ordnance GM Sch., 1952; comdg. officer Ordnance Procurement Center, Norway, 1953-54, France, 1955-56; comdg. officer 74th Ordnance Bn., Korea, 1961-62; asst. chief of staff logistics 7th Logistics Commd., Korea, 1962; comdt. U.S. Army Missile and Munitions Center and Sch., 1965-67; comdg. gen. U.S. Army Ordnance Sch., 1967-68, U.S. Army Ammunition Procurement and Supply Agy., 1968-69, U.S. Army Munitions Command, 1970—. Mem. exec. council Boy Scouts Am., 1965-67, 70-71; mem. exec. com. United Fund, 1970-71. Decorated Legion of Merit, Bronze Star, Army Commendation medal with oak leaf cluster (U.S.), Croix de Guerre (France), Order of Nichan Tftikhar (Tunisia). Mem. Am. Ordnance Assn., Assn. U.S. Army, Dover C. of C. (dir.), Kappa Sigma. Episcopalian. Home: Quarters 112 Picatinny Arsenal Dover NJ 07801 Office: US Army Munitions Command Dover NJ 07801

GRAHAM, EVARTS AMBROSE, Jr., newspaper editor; b. St. Louis, Feb. 4, 1921; s. Evarts A. and Helen (Tredway) G.; B.S., Harvard, 1941; m. Perugina Adler, June 30, 1951; children—Helen, Sarah. With St. Louis Post-Dispatch, 1941—, mng. editor, 1968—. Bd. dirs. Community Sch., St. Louis, Asso. Harvard Alumni. Served with AUS, 1942-46. Home: 5136 Westiminster Pl St Louis MO 63108 Office: 1133 Franklin Av St Louis MO 63101

GRAHAM, FLORENCE R., (Mrs. David Graham), lawyer; b. Princeton, Mo., July 9, 1918; d. George Paul and Hettie (Johnson) Comer; B.A., U. Md., 1939; J.D., Northwestern U., 1955; m. David Graham, Oct. 23, 1948. Asso. economist U.S. govt., Washington, 1941-44; research dir. Far East-Am. Council Commerce and Industry, N.Y.C., 1945-48; admitted to Ill. bar, 1955, N.Y. bar, 1963; mem. firm Graham and Stevenson, Chgo., 1955-70. Mem. nat. com. White House Conf. Children and Youth, 1960; mem. Ill. Commn. on Children, 1961, Commn. on Pub. Aid and Assistance Ill., 1957-61. Bd. dirs., trustee Ill. Children's Home and Aid Soc.; bd. dirs. Family Service Assn. Am., also sec. Mem. Ill., Chgo. bar assns. Clubs: Woman's Athletic, Fortnightly, Arts (Chgo.). Home: PO Box 631 Ridgefield CT 06877

GRAHAM, FORD MULFORD, oil co. exec.; b. Sumner, Mich., May 29, 1911; s. Frederick Joseph and Anna (Mulford) G.; A.B., Alma Coll., 1932; LL.B., U. Mich., 1938; m. Maxine Ingold, July 22, 1933; children—Shirley (Mrs. Louis Wiginton), John J. Div. landman Humble Oil & Refining Co., 1938-46; La. mgr. mineral div. Gaylord Container Corp., 1946-54; independent oil operator, 1954-58; pres. Citizens Nat. Bank in Hammond, La., 1954-57, chmn. bd., 1957-61; v.p. Monterey Oil Co., 1958-60, v.p., dir. Monterey Pipe Line Co., 1960; v.p. La. Land & Exploration Co., New Orleans, 1960, pres., 1961- 67, chief exec., 1962-67, chmn. bd. and chief exec. officer, 1967—, also dir.; dir. Halliburton Co., Hibernia Nat. Bank & Trust Co. New Orleans. Mem. Nat. Petroleum Council, 1963-70; bd. dirs. Am. Petroleum Inst. State crusade chmn. Am. Cancer Soc., 1964-65. Trustee Gulf Research Inst. Clubs: Houston; Boston, New Orleans Country (New Orleans); Racquet and Tennis (N.Y.C.). Home: Woodland Park Hammond LA 70401 Office: Baronne Bldgs New Orleans LA 70112

GRAHAM, FRANCES KEESLER 0(Mrs. David Tredway Graham), psychologist, educator; b. Canastota, N.Y., Aug. 1, 1918; d. Clyde C. and Norma (Van Surdam) Keesler; B.A., Pa. State U., 1938; Ph.D., Yale, 1942; m. David Tredway Graham, June 14, 1941; children—Norma, Andrew, Polly. Acting dir. St. Louis Psychiat. Clinic, 1942-44; instr. Barnard Coll., 1948-51; instr. Sch. Medicine, Washington U., St. Louis, 1942-48, 53-55, research asso., 1953-57; research asso. U. Wis., Madison, 1957-64, asso. prof., 1964-68, prof. pediatrics and psychology, 1968—. Cons. Nat. Inst. Neurol. Diseases and Blindness perinatal research br.; mem. exptl. psychology research review com. Nat. Inst. Mental Health, 1970-74. Recipient Research Scientist award Nat. Inst. Mental Health, 1964-74. Mem. Am. Psychol. Assn., Soc. Research Child Devel., Soc. Psychophysiol. Research, A.A.A.S., Phi Beta Kappa, Sigma Xi. Mem. editorial bd. Jour. Exptl. Child Psychology, 1964-67, Child Devel., 1966-68, Jour. Exptl. Psychology, 1968—, Psychophysiology, 1968—. Contbr. articles profl. jours. Home: 2927 Harvard Dr Madison WI 53705

GRAHAM, GEORGE ADAMS, polit. scientist; b. Cambridge, N.Y., Dec. 23, 1904; s. Andrew Allen and Anna Katherine (Adams) G.; A.B., Monmouth Coll., 1926, LL.D., 1959; A.M., U. Ill., 1927, Ph.D., 1930; m. Rosanna Grace Webster, Aug. 20, 1930; children—Andrew Allen, Lora Katherine (Mrs. C. R. K. Lunt), Mary Margaret (Mrs. Kurt J. Jenne). Instr., Monmouth Coll., 1927-28; asst. U. Ill., 1929-30; faculty Princeton, 1930-58, instr., 1930-31, asst. prof., 1931-39, asso. prof., 1939-45, prof., 1945-58, chmn. dept. politics, 1946-49, 52- 55; dir. govtl. studies Brookings Inst., 1958-67; exec. dir. Nat. Acad. Pub. Adminstrn., 1967—. Mem. staff Detroit Bur. Govt. Research, 1929-30; with U.S. Bur. Budget, 1942-46, as adminstrn. cons., 1942-43, Chief War Supply sect., 1943-45, sec. Com. on Records War Adminstrn., 1944-45, chief Govt. Orgn. Br. and asst. chief Div. Adminstrv. mgmt., 1945; cons., 1945-46; chmn. com. on Indian Affairs, Hoover Commn. on Orgn. Exec. Br. Govt., 1948, staff dir., task force on personnel and civil service, 1953- 54; cons. Senate subcom. Ethics in Govt., 1951; dir. pub. affairs program Ford Found., 1956-57. Mem. Am. Polit. Sci. Assn., Am. Soc. Pub. Adminstrn., Theta Chi. Presbyn. Clubs: Kenwood, Cosmos. Author books including: Education for Public Administration, 1941; (with Henry Retning) Regulatory Administration, 1943; Morality in American Politics, 1952; America's Capacity to Govern, 1960. Home: 6901 Granby St Bethesda MD 20034 Office: 1225 Connecticut Av Washington DC 20036

GRAHAM, GEORGE GORDON, physician; b. Hackensack, N.J., Oct. 4, 1923; s. Charles Stewart and Angelica (Gomez de la Torre) G.; A.B., U. Pa., 1941, M.D., 1945; m. Simone H. Custer, Mar. 3, 1949; children—Marianne, Alexander, Monica, Carol. Intern, resident Brit. Am. Hosp., Lima, Peru, 1946-48, staff pediatrics, 1948-50, 52-55, dir. research, 1960—; research resident U. Pa. Hosp., 1951; resident pediatrics Balt. City Hosp., 1955-56, asso. chief pediatrician, 1965—; asso. prof. pediatrics Johns Hopkins U., 1965—, prof. human nutrition, 1968—; staff pediatrician Cleve. Clinic, 1957-59; lectr. nutrition Mass. Inst. Tech., 1962-65; vis. prof. nutrition Agrarian U. Peru, 1962-65. Mem. com. amino acids Food and Nutrition Bd. of NRC, 1966—; cons. nutrition A.I.D., NIH. Recipient Orden al Merito Agricola (Peru), 1964. Diplomate Am. Bd. Pediatrics, Am. Bd. Nutrition, Mem. Am. Inst. Nutrition, Am. Soc. Clin. Nutrition, Soc. Pediatric Research, Am. Pediatric Soc. Mem. editorial bd. Jour. Nutrition, 1968—, Jour. Clin. Nutrition, 1969—. Research infantile malnutrition, its long-term effects, its prevention by new protein sources. Home: Golf Course Rd W Owings Mills MD 21117 Office: 615 N Wolfe St Baltimore MD 21205

GRAHAM, GEORGE WILLIAM, hosp. adminstr., educator; b. Quebec, Que., Can., Oct. 9, 1916; s. Charles Ruthefoord and Margaret (Fraser) G.; B.S., McGill U., 1937, M.D., C.M., 1941; diploma hosp. adminstrn., U. Toronto, 1950; m. Dorothy Elizabeth Phinney, June 1, 1944; children—David, Susan, Lynda. Came to U.S., 1949, naturalized, 1954. Admitting officer Royal Victoria Hosp., Montreal, Que., Can., 1942-49; pvt. practice medicine, Montreal, 1942-49; asst. dir. Strong Meml. Hosp., Rochester, N.Y., 1950-54; asst. prof. hosp. adminstrn. U. Rochester, 1950-54; exec. dir. Ellis Hosp., Schenectady, 1954—; lectr. pub. health and adminstrv. medicine Columbia U., N.Y.C., 1960. Fellow Am. Coll. Hosp., Adminstrs.; mem. Med. Soc. County Schenectady, Sight Conservation Soc. Northeastern N.Y. (past pres.). Schenectady C. of C., Am. (chmn. council profl. practice 1962-64, trustee 1965-67, pres. 1968-69), Northeastern (past pres.) hosp. assns., Hosp. Assn. N.Y. State (trustee 1965—), Med. Soc. State N.Y., Doctors and Lawyers Group Rochester (hon. life), Am., N.Y. State pub. health assns., Nat. League Nursing, Soc. Med. Adminstrs. (pres.) Clubs: Mohwak, Mohawk Golf (bd. govs. 1971-73), Curling (Schenectady). Home: 1056 Nott St Schenectady NY 12309 Office: 1101 Nott St Schenectady NY 12308

GRAHAM, GERALD JAMES, mfg. co. exec.; b. Chgo., Feb. 20, 1897; s. James W. and Mary (McNulty) G.; student Northwestern Sch. Commerce. With Armour & Co., 1916-19; salesman Charles Boldt Glass Co., 1919-22; v.p. Graham Bottle Co., 1922- 24; v.p. Carroll-Graham Glass Co., 1924-37; dist. mgr. Anchor Hocking Glass Corp., Chgo., 1937-42; pres. Lummis-Graham Glass Co., 1942-48, Graham Glass Co., 1949—; v.p. Thatcher Glass Mfg. Co., Inc., 1958—; pres. Graynat Packaging Co., Chgo.; dir. Am. Window Glass Co., Linco Products Co. Served with USN, 1918-19. Mem. Am. Legion. Clubs: South Shore Country, Ill. Athletic, International, Chicago Figure Skating, Tavern (Chgo.); Minocqua (Wis.) Country. Home: 1000 Lake Shore Dr Chicago IL 60611 Office: 307 N Michigan Av Chicago IL 60601

GRAHAM, GORDON MARION, air force officer; b. Ouray, Colo., Feb. 16, 1918; s. Alexander and Margaret (Wilson) G.; B.S., U. Cal. at Berkeley, 1940; M.S., U. Pitts., 1948; children—Eloise L., Helen H., G. Alexander E.; m. 2d, Vivian Fox, Dec. 4, 1968. Grad. Flying School, 1941, commd. 2d lt. USAAF, 1941, advanced through grades to lt. gen. USAF, 1968; comdr. 354th Fighter Squadron, 1944-45, 361st Fighter Group, 1945; asst. chief staff operations 8th Fighter Command, 1945-46; dep. asst. chief staff operations 10th Air Force, Brooks AFB. Tex., 1946; comdr. 182d Base Unit Res. Tng. Detachment, Carswell AFB, Tex., 1946-47; comdr., 178th Base Unit Res. Tng., Brooks AFB, 1947; chief target analysis div. Office Dir. Intelligence, Hdqrs. USAF, 1949-53; dir. targets, directorate intelligence Hdqrs. Far East Air Force, 1953-55; dep. comdr. 31st Strategic Fighter Wing, Turner AFB, Ga., 1955, comdr., 1955-59; chief tactical div., directorate operations Hdqrs. USAF, 1959-60, dep. dir. operational forces, 1961-62; comdr. 4th Tactical Fighter Wing, Seymour Johnson AFB, N.C., 1962-63; vice comdr. Hdgrs. 19th Air Force, 1963-64; dep. operations Hdqrs. Tactical Air Command, Langley AFB, Va., 1964-66, vice comdr. 7th Air Force, Pacific Air Forces, 1966-67; comdr. 9th Air Force, Shaw AFB, S.C., 1967-68; vice comdr. Tactical Air Command, Langley AFB, Va., 1968-70; comdr. U.S. Forces Japan, 5th Air Force, 1970—. Decorated D.S.M., Silver Star, Legion of Merit, D.F.C. with oak leaf cluster, Air medal with 28 oak leaf clusters, Joint Service Commendation medal, Air Force Commendation ribbon. Mem. Am. Inst. Mining, Metall. and Petroleum Engrs., Am. Fighter Aces Assn., Air Force Assn., Order Daedalians, Nat. Rifle Assn. (life), Tau Beta Pi. Home: Hdqrs 5th Air Force Box 151 APO San Francisco CA 96525

GRAHAM, HARRY THOMPSON, corp. exec.; b. Bogalusa, La., Aug. 10, 1913; s. Harry Edmund and Anna (Thompson) B.; student U. Fla., 1930-33, George Washington U., 1934; m. Mary Elizabeth Walsh, June 29, 1940; children—James Scott, Katherine Elizabeth, John Thompson. With Gen. Refractories Co., 1937-69, v.p., 1953-64, pres., vice chmn., 1968-69; pres. Sciencope, Inc., 1970—; Served to lt. USNR, 1942-46. Mem. Am. Iron and Steel Inst., Am. Inst. Mining, Metall. and Petroleum Engrs., Am. Iron and Steel Engrs. Republican. Episcopalian. Clubs: Merion Golf (Ardmore); Pine Valley Golf (Clementon, N.J.); Rolling Rock, Laurel Valley Golf (Ligonier, Pa.). Home: 200 Cedarbrook Rd Ardmore PA 19003 Office: 2 Oriole Av Media PA 19063

GRAHAM, HENRY MAITLAND, ins. co. exec.; b. Sawyerville, Que., Can., Apr. 10, 1903; s. Henry M. and Henrietta Maria (Cromwell) G.; came to U.S., 1905, naturalized, 1920; student Northeastern Coll., 1943; m. Rhona Ford, Oct. 28, 1959; children—Joanne G. (Mrs. George E. Martinez), Sandra G. (Mrs. Robert P. Bahre). With Monarch Life Ins. Co., 1925—, treas., 1948-64, exec. v.p., 1964- 66, pres., 1966-68, now dir.; v.p., treas. Springfield-Monarch Ins. Cos., 1959-68; exec. v.p. Springfield Life Ins. Co., 1964-66, pres., 1966- 68, now dir.; dir. Monarch Capital Corp., Security Nat. Bank, Springfield. Home: Hall Hill Rd Somers CT 06071 Office: 1250 State St Springfield MA 01109

GRAHAM, HERBERT WILLIAM, ret. biologist; b. New Brighton, Pa., Dec. 18, 1905; s. William H. and Christina (Jahns) G.; B.S., U. Pitts., 1929; Am.M., Stanford, 1934, Ph.D., 1938; m. Ruth Thompson, June 14, 1930; children—Anne H., David H. Chemist and biologist, Carnegie Expdn., Carnegie Instn. of Washington, 1929-38; prof. of biology and convenor Sch. of Sci., Mills Coll., Oakland, Cal., 1938-48; oceanographer Philippine Fishery Program, U.S. Fish and Wildlife Service, Manila, 1949-50, dir. Red Tide Lab., Sarasota, Fla., 1950-51, dir. Woods Hole Lab., 1951-70, ret. 1970. Mem. A.A.A.S. (mem. council, 1943-49), Western Soc. Naturalists (v.p., 1940, sec.-treas. 1943- 49). Author books and articles on marine biology and oceanography. Home: 36 Wilson Rd Woods Hole MA

GRAHAM, HOWARD BARRET, publishing co. exec.; b. Boston, Dec. 7, 1929; s. Robert M. and Belle (Brown) G.; B.A., Syracuse U., 1951; m. Janet L. Greenstone, July 8, 1951; children—Ronni M., Erica. Gen. mgr. sch. supply div., sales mgr. ednl. div. Milton Bradley Co., Springfield, Mass., 1954-63; gen. mgr. jr. book div. McGraw-Hill Co., 1964-69; pres., dir. Franklin Watts Inc., N.Y.C., 1970—; dir. Franklin Watts Ltd., Mulberry Press, Inc. Served with USAF, 1951-53. Mem. Mensa, Zeta Beta Tau. Home: 25 E 83d St New York City NY 10028 Office: 575 Lexington Av New York City NY 10022

GRAHAM, HUGH DAVIS, educator; b. Little Rock, Sept. 2, 1936; s. Otis L. and Lois (Patterson) G.; B.A. magna cum laude, Yale, 1958; M.A. (Woodrow Wilson fellow 1960-61, 63-64), Stanford, 1961, Ph.D., 1964; m. Ann Clary, June 11, 1966; 1 son, Hugh Patterson. History instr. Foothill Coll., Los Altos, Cal., 1962-64; asst. prof. San Jose (Cal.) State Coll., 1964-65; tng. officer, regional dir. Peace Corps,

Washington, 1965-66; vis. asst. prof. history Stanford, 1966-67; asso. prof. history Johns Hopkins, Balt., 1967-71, acting dir. Inst. So. History, 1969-70; chmn. dir. social scis. U. Md. Balt. County, 1971—. Co-dir. history task force Nat. Com. on Causes and Prevention of Violence, 1968-69. Served to 1st lt., arty. USMCR, 1958-60. Recipient Merit award Am. Assn. State and Local History, 1968. Guggenheim fellow, 1970-71. Mem. Am., So. hist. assns., Orgn. Am. Historians, Am. Assn. U. Profs. Author: Crisis in Print, 1967. Co-editor: Violence in America, 1969; editor Huey Long, 1970; Violence, 1971. Home: 213 Southway Baltimore MD 21218 Office: 5401 Wilkens Av Baltimore MD 21228

GRAHAM, JACK A., b. San Rafael, Cal., 1910; sec. San Diego Gas and Electric Co. Home: 5688 Marne Av San Diego, CA 92120. Office: 101 Ash St San Diego CA 92112*

GRAHAM, JACKSON, transp. exec.; b. Mosier, Ore., June 27, 1915; s. A. E. and Nada (Clark) G.; B.S. in Civil Engring., Ore. State U., 1936; postgrad. Mass. Inst. Tech., 1939-40; Nat. War Coll., 1958-59; m. Mabel Lee Dowlin, July 4, 1943; children—Ona Lee, Jackson Reade. Commd. 2d lt., C.E., U.S. Army, 1936, advanced through grades to maj. gen., 1963; comdr. combat engr. regt., ETO, World War II; comdr. all aviation engrs., Korea, 1954; dir. civil works Army Engrs., 1963-66, ret., 1967; gen. mgr. Washington Met. Area Transit Authority, 1967—. Decorated D.S.M., Legion of Merit; Medal of Merit (Brazil). Mem. Sigma Phi Epsilon. Mason. Home: 2836 Fort Scott Dr Arlington, VA 22202. Office: 950 S L'Enfant Plaza SW Washington DC 20024

GRAHAM, JAMES R., banker; b. Pitts., 1911; grad. Haverford Coll., 1933; LL.B., U. Pitts., 1937. Vice pres., trust officer Liberty Nat. Bank, Buffalo. Home: 18 Heathwood Dr Williamsville NY 14221 Office: PO Box 889 Buffalo NY 14240*

GRAHAM, JARLATH JOHN, magazine editor; b. Chgo., Dec. 18, 1919; s. Jarlath John and Isabelle Marie (Corboy) G.; B.A., U. Chgo., 1949; m. Elizabeth Grace Carlson, Aug. 23, 1958; children by previous marriage—Carol (Mrs. Glen Gilchrist), Karen. With Advt. Age, weekly bus. publ., Chgo., 1950—, editor, 1969—; v.p. Crain Communications Inc., Chgo., 1963—. Mem. cabinet U. Chgo.; bd. dirs. Bateman Sch., Chgo. Served to capt. AUS, World War II. Mem. Sigma Delta Chi. Contbr. Ency. Brit., 1966—. Home: 322 Belden Av Chicago IL 60614 Office: Advertising Age Magazine 740 N Rush St Chicago IL 60611

GRAHAM, JEAN CHARTERS, polit. worker; b. Columbia, Mo., Dec. 31, 1914; d. Werrett Wallace and Jessie (Allen) Charters; A.B. in Labor Econs., U. Wis., 1935; A.M. in Pub. Law, Columbia, 1936; Ph.D. in Polit. Sci., U. Chgo., 1942; m. Charles Andrew Graham, Dec. 27, 1941; children—Judi, Charles A., Margaret. Research, Pub. Adminstrn. Clearing House and Civil Service Assembly, Chgo., 1936-41; personnel staff Office Emergency Mgmt., 1942- 43; adminstrv. staff Social Sci. Found., U. Denver, 1943-44, adj. asst. prof. dept. polit. sci., 1967-70. Active precinct, county, state activities Democratic Party, 1944—; mem. Dem. Nat. Com. from Colo., 1960-68; mem. Nat. Women's Adv. Council on Poverty OEO, 1967-69. Home: 2345 Routt St Denver, CO 80215.

GRAHAM, JOHN, architect; b. Seattle, May 8, 1908; s. John and Hallie Corrine (Jackson) G.; B.F.A., Yale, 1931; m. Marjorie Belle Clark, Feb. 20, 1943; children—Jane Jackson, Barbara Ann, John Thomas. With Allied Store Corp., also The Bon Marche, Seattle, 1931-37; with John Graham, architect, Seattle, 1931-37; partner firm Graham & Painter, N.Y.C., 1937- 41; head Graham Constrn. Co., constrn. housing devel., Washington, 1941- 46, John Graham & Co., architects, Seattle, 1946—, N.Y.C. 1955—; prin. works include shopping centers, office bldgs. Mem. A.I.A. Office: 444 Fifth Av New York City NY 10018 also 1426 Fifth Av Seattle WA 98101

GRAHAM, JOHN BORDEN, medical educator; b. Goldsboro, N.C., Jan. 2, 1918; s. Ernest Heap and Mary (Borden) G.; B.S., Davidson Coll., 1938; M.D., Cornell U., 1942; m. Ruby Barrett, Mar. 23, 1943; children—Charles Barrett, Virginia Borden, Thomas Wentworth. Asst. Cornell U., 1943-44; mem. faculty U. N.C., Chapel Hill, 1946—, Alumni Distinguished prof. pathology, 1966—, asso. dean medicine for basic scis., 1968-70, dir. genetics tng., 1961—. Mem. genetics tng. com. USPHS, 1962-66, chmn., 1967-71; mem. pathology test com. Nat. Bd. Med. Examiners, 1963-67; mem. Internat. Com. Hamostasis and Thrombosis, 1963-67; cons. Environmental Health Center, USPHS. Markle scholar in med. sci., 1949-54. Recipient Gardner award U. N.C., 1968. Mem. A.M.A., A.A.A.S., Elisha Mitchell Sci. Soc. (pres. 1963), Am. Assn. U. Profs., Soc. Exptl. Biology and Medicine, Am. Soc. Exptl. Pathology, Assn. U. Pathologists, Am. Assn. Pathologists and Bacteriologists, Am. Soc. Human Genetics (pres. 1971), Internat. Soc. Hematology, Am. Soc. Biol. Sci., Mayflower Soc., Sigma Xi. Democrat. Presbyn. Clubs: Cosmos (Washington). Publs. on co-discovery of Stuart Factor in blood clotting; among first to map genes on human X-chromosome; descriptions of inherited diseases in humans. Home: 108 Glendale Dr Chapel Hill NC 27514

GRAHAM, JOHN FISHER, banker; b. Swampscott, Mass., May 7, 1916; s. John L. and Alberta (Fisher) G.; A.B., Dartmouth, 1938; grad. Bentley Sch. Accounting and Finance, 1942; m. Barbara Thomas, Jan. 21, 1939; children—Kent, Gail, Cheryl (Mrs. Gary Schwandt), John Fisher. With Charles F. Rittenhouse & Co., C.P.A.'s, Boston, 1941-47; with Norfolk County Trust Co., Brookline, Mass., 1947—, exec. v.p., 1968—, also dir.; dir. Metal Bellows Corp., Yankee Capital Corp. Home: 2 Bryden Rd Weston MA 02193 Office: 1319 Beacon St Brookline MA 02147

GRAHAM, JOHN J., bishop. Ordained priest Roman Cath. Ch., 1938; aux. bishop Phila. and titular bishop of Sabrata, 1963—. Address: 6161 N 5th St Philadelphia PA 19120*

GRAHAM, JOHN JOSEPH, mfg. and financial co. exec.; b. Phila., July 18, 1915; s. Walter Thomas and Laura Cecilia (McGowan) G.; grad. Wharton Sch., U. Pa., grad. Advanced Mgmt. Program, Harvard, 1955; m. Kathryn Mary Brady, Nov. 28, 1942; 1 dau., Elaine Marie. With RCA, 1947- 61, div. v.p., gen. mgr. RCA, 1959-61; v.p., area gen. mgr. N.Am., also dir. Internat. Tel. & Tel. Co., 1961-64; v.p. Curtiss-Wright Corp., also pres., gen. mgr. Wright Aeor. div., 1964-66; group v.p. Gen. Dynamics Corp., N.Y.C., 1966-69; pres., chief exec. officer, dir. DCL, Inc., Saddle Brook, N.J., 1969—. Recipient Distinguished Alumni award Wharton Sch., U. Pa. Mem. I.E.E.E. (sr.), Navy League, Newcomen Soc., Pa. Soc., Sigma Kappa Phi. Club: Union League (N.Y.C.). Home: 110 Chestnut Ridge Rd Saddle River NJ 07458 Office: DCL Inc Park/80 Plaza East Saddle Brook NJ 07662

GRAHAM, JOHN MACDOUGALL, lawyer, educator; b. N.Y.C., Nov. 29, 1915; s. Kelley and Valerie (Atherton) G.; grad. Groton Sch., 1934; A.B., Harvard, 1938; LL.B., Columbia, 1941; m. Barbara Putnam, June 19, 1939; 1 dau., Katherine; m. 2d, Janet Weldon, July 4, 1947; children—Gerrit, Samuel W. Admitted to N.Y. bar, 1942; with firm Spence, Windels, Walser, Hotchkiss & Angell, N.Y.C., 1941-42; with Office Gen. Counsel, Navy Dept., 1945-46, Office Naval Research, 1946-48; mem. law dept. Port of N.Y. Authority, 1948-51; tchr. history Mary Inst., Ladue, Mo., 1951-55, Thomas Jefferson Sch., Kirkwood, Mo., 1955-56, Grosse Pointe Univ. Sch., Grosse Pointe Woods, Mich., 1956-60; headmaster Latin Sch., Chgo., 1960-70, exec. dir. Guild of Independent Schools, Cleveland, Ohio. Address: 2204 Demington Dr Cleveland Heights OH 44118

GRAHAM, JOHN MEREDITH, II, ret. mus. dir.; b. Floyd Co., Ga., Dec. 23, 1905; s. Samuel Lowry and Lila (Berry) G.; student Lehigh U., 1927-28, in Paris, 1929-31, in Rome, 1935-36; grad. N.Y. Sch. Fine and Applied Arts, 1931. Curator decorative arts Bklyn. Mus., 1939-50; dir., curator collections Colonial Williamsburg, 1950-70, v.p., 1961-70; circulated Wedgwood Exhbn. throughout museums in U.S. and Can., 1948; completed restoration and furnishings of interior Van Cortlandt Manor House for Sleepy Hollow Restoration, 1958; adviser White House Fine Arts Com.; lectr. fine arts; frequent radio and TV speaker. Hon. bd. govs. Wedgwood Internat. Seminar; trustee, cons. Campbell Mus. Mem. Soc. Archtl. Historians, English Ceramic Circle, Pewter Collectors Club of N.Y. (past v.p.), Delta Tau Delta. Club: Church (N.Y.C.) Author: Popular Art in America, 1939; American Pewter, 1949. Co-author: Wedgwood, A Living Tradition, 1948. Editor: Old Pottery and Porcelain Marks (C. J. Thorne), 1947. Home: Libby House Mentone AL 35984

GRAHAM, JOHN WEBB, lawyer; b. Toronto, Ont., Can., Sept. 10, 1912; s. George Wilbur and Rosaline (Webb) G.; student Upper Can. Coll., 1920-30; B.A., Trinity Coll. U. Toronto, 1933; Barrister-at-law, Osgoode Hall Law Sch. (Can.), 1936; m. Velma Melissa Taylor, June 19, 1941; children—Edward Samuel Rogers (stepson), Ann Taylor Faulds. Corporate trust officer Toronto Gen. Trusts Corp., 1936-39; solicitor Daly, Thistle, Judson & McTaggart, Toronto, 1946-48; gen. counsel Imperial Life Assurance Co. Can., Toronto, 1949-58; partner firm Payton, Biggs & Graham, Toronto, 1958—; chmn. bd. Bramalea Telecable Ltd., Coaxial Colourview Ltd., Reliance Ins. Co. Canada, Travelers Life Ins. Co. Can., Rogers Broadcasting Ltd., Rogers Cabel TV Ltd.; dir. numerous cos., including Bulk Fertilizer Ltd., Charter Oak Fire Ins. Co., Distination Transport Ltd., Kentnor Holdings Ltd., Travelers Ins. Co. Mem. exec. com. Trinity Coll., Toronto, 1960—, also chmn., 1966-69. Pres. St. Paul's Progressive Conservative Assn., 1957-61. Served with Royal Canadian Armoured Corps, 1939-46; ETO. Decorated Efficiency Decoration, 1944; named lt. col. Gov. Gen's Horse Guards, 1970, Queen's Counsel, 1956. Mem. Canadian Bar Assn., York County Law Assn., Lawyers' Club Toronto, Assn. Life Ins. Counsel, Canadian Tax Found., Bd. Trade Met. Toronto, Estate Planning Council Toronto, Progressive Business Men's Club Met Toronto (v.p. 1968-70). Sigma Chi (internat. pres. 1971—). Mem. Conservative party. Mem. Anglican Ch. Can. Clubs: Albany, Granite, Royal Canadian Mil. Inst. (Toronto); Muskoka Lakes Golf and Country (Port Carling, Ont.); Hartford (Conn.). Home: 405 Glenayr Rd Toronto 349 Ontario Canada Office: 400 University Av Toronto 100 Ontario Canada

GRAHAM, JOHN WILLIAM, Jr., coll. pres.; b. Dayton, O., May 25, 1915; s. John William and Louise (Whipps) G.; B.C.E., Ohio State U., 1939; C.E., Princeton, 1940; D.Sc., Carnegie Inst. Tech., 1950; L.H.D., St. Lawrence U., 1968; m. Ruth E. Orr, Feb. 7, 1942; children—Judith Ann, Kathleen, John William III, Margaret Louise. Engr. fabricated steel constrn. div. Bethlehem Steel Corp., Rankin, Pa., 1940-42, 45-46; instr. to asso. prof. civil engring., asst. dean Coll. Engring. and Sci., dean students Carnegie Inst. Tech., P.Hs., 1946-56; v.p. Cooper Union, 1956-59; dean engring. U. Rochester, 1959-66; pres. Clarkson Coll. Tech., Potsdam, N.Y., 1966- -. Dir., Marine Midland Trust Co. No. N.Y. Served from 2d lt. to maj. C.E., AUS, 1942-46. Registered profl. engr., Pa., N.Y. Mem. Rochester Engring. Soc., Am. Soc. C.E., Am. Soc. Engring. Edn., Nat. Soc. Profl. Engrs., Sigma Xi, Tau Beta Pi, Chi Epsilon, Phi Kappa Phi. Home: 71 Pierrepont Av Potsdam NY 13676

GRAHAM, JOSEPH COOPER, Jr., pub.; b. Phila., 1902; s. Joseph Cooper and Margaret Williamson (Kennedy) G.; student pub., pvt. schs.; 1 son, Cooper Carrington. With Grolier, Inc., N.Y.C., 1936—, exec. v.p., 1936-47, vice chmn. 1947-60, now v.p., dir., mem. finance com. of Profit Sharing Trust; pres., dir. Ins. Mgmt. Corp., Balt.; v.p. Balt. Co. Mortgage Co., Towson; sec.-treas., dir. Hill Farm, Inc., Meadowood Inc., Brooklandville Flynn and Emrich, Federated Credit Corp., Americana Corp., N.Y.C., Grolier Devel. Corp., Welles Ins. Co.; dir., chmn. exec. com. Loyola Fed. Savs. & Loan Assn.; mem. Towson adv. bd. First Nat. Bank. Home: 100 W Cold Spring Lane Baltimore MD 21210 Office: 575 Lexington Av New York City NY 10022

GRAHAM, KATHARINE, newspaper co. exec.; b. N.Y.C., June 16, 1917; d. Eugene and Agnes (Ernst) Meyer; student Vassar Coll., 1935-36; A.B., U. Chgo., 1938; m. Philip L. Graham, June 5, 1940 (dec. 1963); children—Elizabeth Morris (Mrs. Yann R. Weymouth), Donald Edward, William Welsh, Stephen Meyer. Reporter, San Francisco News, 1938-39; mem. editorial staff Washington Post, 1939-45, also Sunday, circulation and editorial depts.; pres. Washington Post Co., 1963—; dir. Bowaters Mersey Paper Co., Ltd. Mem. adv. com. to John F. Kennedy Sch. Govt. Inst. Politics, Harvard; mem. pub. policy com. Advt. Council. Trustee George Washington U., Com. for Econ. Devel., Am. Assembly, U. Chgo., The Urban Inst.; governing bd. Bus. Com. for Arts; bd. dirs. Nat. Center for Resource Recovery; mem. steering com. Nat. Urban Coalition. Recipient Gold medal for distinguished services to humanity Nat. Inst. Social Scis., 1970. Mem. the Conf. Bd., Inter-Am. Press Assn. (bd. dirs., mem. exec. com.), Sigma Delta Chi, Theta Sigma Phi. Clubs: Women's Nat. Press, 1925 F Street (Washington); Cosmopolitan (N.Y.C.). Home: 2920 R St NW Washington DC 20007 Office: 1515 L St NW Washington DC 20005

GRAHAM, KENNETH L., educator; b. Coffeyville, Kan., Apr. 25, 1915; s. Ethan L. and Maud (Huff) G.; B.A., State U. Ia., 1936; M.A., Northwestern U., 1939; Ph.D., U. Utah, 1947; m. Barbara Louise Fowler, Dec. 15, 1945 (dec. July 1969); children—Greg Fowler, Sherry Lynn. Speech, drama tchr. Watertown (S.D.) High Sch., also North Kansas City (Mo.) High Sch.; dir. Sch. of Theatre, Cain Park Theatre, Cleveland Heights, O., summers 1941, 42, 46, 47; faculty speech, communication, theatre arts dept. U. Minn., asst. prof., 1948-51, asso. prof., 1952-56, prof., 1957—, chmn. dept., 1963-71, vice chmn. dept. theatre arts, 1971—, dir. Univ. theatre, 1971—. Vice pres., trustee Am. Playwrights Theatre. Served with USNR, 1942- 45. Fellow Am. Ednl. Theatre Assn. (exec. sec.-treas. 1946-58, 2d v.p. 1962, 1st v.p. 1963, pres. 1964); mem. Citizens League Mpls., ANTA (dir. 1959-61), Beta Theta Pi. Methodist. Office: 4 Folwell Hall U Minn Minneapolis MN 55455

GRAHAM, KENNETH N., banker; m. Lucene Glock; 1 dau., Ann G. Wilsmann. Sr. v.p. Winters Nat. Bank and Trust Co. Mem. Ohio Bankers Assn. (chmn. trust div., v.p.). Home: 3215 Southdale Dr Dayton OH 45409 Office: 40 N Main St Dayton OH 45402

GRAHAM, LEWIS TEXADA, univ. dean, biologist; b. Alexandria, La., Oct. 2, 1914; s. George Mason and Aimee (Texada) G.; B.S., U. Southwestern La., 1936; M.S. (Research fellow 1936-38), La. State U., 1938; Ph.D., Ia. State U., 1947; m. Justine Bruner, Aug. 12, 1939; childrenLewis Texada, Elizabeth Marie. Instrn., then research asso. and asso. extension entomologist Ia. State U., 1938-42; asso. prof. entomology U. Neb., 1942-43; mem. faculty U. Southwestern La., 1946-, prof. biology, 1952-, head dept., 1954-, dir. Vermilion Bay Marine La., 1958-64, dean of Coll. of Liberal Arts, 1965-. Served to commander USNR, 1943-45, 51-52. Mem. Entomol. Soc. Am., Assn. Southeastern Biologists. La. Entomologists Soc. (chmn. exec. com. 1954, 58, 62), La. Acad. Sci., La. Tchrs. Assn., La Mosquito Control Assn. (dir. 1961-). Am. Soc. Oceanography, Sigma Xi, Phi Kappa Phi, Gamma Sigma Delta, Omicron Delta Epsilon, Sigma Pi. Kiwanian. Home 701 Harding St Lafayette LA 70501

GRAHAM, LLOYD KENNETH, mem. Democratic Nat. Com.; b. Cashmere, Wash., July 1, 1906; s. Fred C. and Clara (Bollman) G.; ed. pub. schs., Ore., also Internat. Corr. Schs.; m. Blanche J. Padgett, Mar. 14, 1931; childrenJames E., Carol Ann (Mrs. John S. Edgar), Fred C. With Astoria (Ore.) Budget, 1920-24, Columbian Daily, Vancouver, Wash., 1924-25; pressman San Francisco Examiner, 1924-25, Vancouver Columbian, 1925-37, Ore. Jour., Portland, 1937-41, Seattle Post Intelligencer, 1941-42, 51-55, Columbian Daily, 1955-57; with Internat. Corr. Schs., 1942-51, supt. Ore. div. 1945-51; with Security Savesco, Inc., Seattle, 1961-, sec., 1963-, also dir.; pres., dir. Savesco Mortgage, Inc., Seattle, 1964-: mem. exec. bd. Bank of Tacoma, 1965-. Chmn. Clark County (Wash.) Dem. Com., 1947-56; treas. Nine County Dem. League, 1948-53, chmn., 1953-54; chmn. statewide Jefferson-Jackson Day dinner, 1951; co-chmn. Jefferson-Jackson dinner com., 1963; mem. Senator Magnuson dinner com., 1961, Senator Jackson's dinner com., 1963, Gov. Rosellini's dinner com., 1963; mem. Wash. Dem. Finance Com., 1953-54, chmn., 1957-61; co-dir. Senator Magnuson's campaign, 1962; mem. King County Dem. Finance Com., 1963-64; co-chmn. Wash. Com. Election Dem. House, 1964; chmn. President Johnson's Wash. Finance Com., 1964; mem. Dem. Nat. Com. for Wash., 1964-; del. Dem. Nat. Conv., 1948, 52, 56, chmn. Wash. delegation, 1960. First chmn. polit. action com. Clark, Skamanoa and West Klickitat Central Labor Council, 1934, chmn. scale com., 1941, v.p. Seattle Webb local, 1941, pres. Portland Webb's Pressmans Union, 1955-56. Mason, Elk. Club: Variety-Tent 46. Home: 2323 W Newton Seattle WA 98199 Office: 1312 2d Av Seattle WA 98101

GRAHAM, MAE, librarian; b. Florence, S.C., Sept. 29, 1904; d. John Wesley and Augusta (Currie) Graham; A.B., Women's Coll., U N.C., 1925; B.L.S., U. Ill., 1934; M.L.A., Johns Hopkins, 1967. Tchr. N.C. high schs., 1925-28; librarian sr. high sch., High Point, N.C., 1928-33, 1935- 36, Kingsport, Tenn., 1934-35; asst. prof. library sci. dept. Coll. William and Mary, 1936-42, asso. prof., acting head dept., 1942-46; dir. summer sch. for tchr.-librarians Fisk U., summers 1936-41; editor sch. libraries sect. Wilson Library Bull., 1937-38; vis. instr. library sch. U. Ill., summer 1942; chief placement office A.L.A., 1946-47; supr. sch. libraries Md. Dept. Edn., 1947-68, asst. dir. div. library extension, 1968—. Sch. library adviser information and edn. sect. SCAP, 1947. Mem. Va. (v.p. 1938), Am. (council 1944-46, 61-65, pres. div. libraries children and young people 1950-51, exec. bd. 1952-56), Md. (1st v.p., pres. 1953) library assn., Md. Tchrs. Assn., N.E.A. Contbr. articles to library, edn. publs. Home: 4105 Bedford Rd Baltimore MD 21207 Office: State Office Bldg 301 W Preston Baltimore MD 21201

GRAHAM, MARTHA, dancer, choreographer; b. Pitts., May 11, 1894; studied with Ruth St. Denis; LL.D., Mills Coll., Brandeis U., Smith Coll., Harvard, 1966, also numerous others. Soloist, Denishawn Co., 1920, Greenwich Village Follies, 1923; faculty Eastman Sch., 1925; debut as choreographer-dancer 48th St. Theatre, N.Y.C., 1926; founder, artistic dir. Martha Graham Dance Co., Martha Graham Sch. Contemporary Dance; Guggenheim fellow, 1932; choreographer 144 works including Appalachian Spring, Letter to the World, Clytemnestra, with music composed by Aaron Copland, Paul Hindemith, Carlos Chavez, Samuel Barber, Gian-Carlo Menotti, William Schuman; guest soloist leading U.S. orchs. in solos Judith, Triumph of St. Joan; Guggenheim fellow, fgn. tours with Martha Graham Dance Co., 1950, 54, 55-56, 60, 62-63, 67, 68, some under auspices U.S. Dept State; U.S. tours, 1966, 70, sponsored by Nat. Endowment for Arts. Recipient Aspen award, 1965; Creative Arts award Brandeis U., 1968; Distinguished Service to Arts award Nat. Inst. Arts and Letters, 1970; Handel medallion City of N.Y., 1970; others. Address: 316 E 63d St New York City NY 10021

GRAHAM, MARTIN HAROLD, educator: b. N.Y.C., July 12, 1926; B.Elec. Engring., Poly. Inst. Bklyn., 1947, D.Elec. Engring., 1952; M.Sc., Harvard, 1948; m. Selma Weitzman, Jan. 22, 1949; children—Andrew, Lisa. Engr., Brookhaven Nat. Lab., 1948-57; asso. prof. elec. engring. Rice U., 1957-60, prof. elec. engring., 1960-66, dir. computer project, 1957-66; prof. elec. engring. U. Cal. at Berkeley, 1966-68, prof. computer sci., 1968—, chmn. dept. computer sci., 1971—, asso. dir. computer center, 1966-69; cons. in field, 1957—. Served with USNR, 1944-46. Fellow I.E.E.E.; mem. Assn. Computing Machinery, Am. Assn. U. Profs., Sigma Xi, Eta Kappa Nu, Tau Beta Pi. Home: 3060 Buena Vista Way Berkeley CA 94708

GRAHAM, MORTIMER ELLIOTT, lawyer; b. Oil City, Pa., Oct. 18, 1901; s. Lyman Lincoln and Luella (Barnes) G.; A.B. cum laude, Allegheny Coll., 1922; LL.B. cum laude, U. Pa., 1925; m. Grace E. Budd, July 7, 1925; children—Nancy Lee (Mrs. Charles W. Brown), Douglas Hume. Admitted to Pa. bar, 1925; dist. atty., Erie County, 1932-40; sec., v.p., gen., counsel Hammermill Paper Co., 1948-66; partner firm Knox, Graham, Pearson, McLaughlin & Sennett, Pitts., 1967—. Dir. Erie Indemnity Co., 1952—, chmn. bd., 1970—; dir. Hammermill Paper Co., 1962-66, Nat. Fuel Gas Co., 1965—, Erie Family Life Ins. Co., 1967—, Lyons Transp. Lines, 1970—. Mem. Gov. Pa. Commn. Constl. Revision, 1964-66; pres. United Fund Erie County, 1956-57; trustee, mem. ecclesiastical ct. Episcopal Diocese Erie, 1966—. Chmn. Erie County Republican Com., 1932-34, 66-70; del. Rep. Nat. Conv., 1964, 68. Served to lt. comdr. USNR, 1942-45. Mem. Phi Beta Kappa, Order of Coif. Home: 322 Mohawk Dr Erie PA 16505 Office: 23 W 10th St Erie PA 16501

GRAHAM, OTTO EVERETT, Jr., athletic dir.; b. Waukegan, Ill., Dec. 6, 1921; s. Otto Everett and Cordonna (Hayes) G.; B.A., Northwestern U., 1944; m. Beverly Jean Collinge, Oct. 7, 1945; childrenDuey, Sandy, David. Quarterback with Cleve. Browns, 1946-55; coach Coll. All-Stars vs. Nat. Football League champions, 1958-65; athletic dir., head football coach USCG Acad., New London, Conn., 1959-66, athletic dir., 1970—; gen. mgr., head coach Washington Redskins, 1966-68. Pres. Fellowship Christian Athletes, 1956-57. Bd. dirs. Washington YMCA, 1967- -. Served with USNR, 1944-45; now capt. USCG. Named All Am. in Football and Bakeball, 1943; All Pro Quarterback, 1951, 52, 54, 55. Home: Heritage Rd East Lyme CT Office: Athletic Dept USCG Academy New London CT 06320

GRAHAM, RICHARD ALTON, govt. ofcl.; b. Chgo., Nov. 6, 1920; s. Louis Alton and Estelle (Stone) G.; B.Mech. Engring., Cornell U., 1942; m. Nancy Aring, Dec. 21, 1949; children—Peggy Sue, Charles Louis, Richard Alton, Nancy Aring, John Pietre. Sales mgr. Graham Transmissions Inc., Menomonee Falls, Wis., 1946-61; co-founder, v.p. Jordan Controls Inc., Milw., 1955-61; dir. recruitment Peace Corps, 1961-62, acting dir. pub. affairs, 1962-63, dir. in Tunisia, 1963-65; mem. Equal Employment Opportunities Commn., Washington, 1965-66; dir. Nat. Tchrs. Corps., 1966-71; spl. asst. dir. ACTION for

Ednl. Programs, 1971—. Chmn. E. Mequon (Wis.) Sch. Bd., 1955. Pres. Thiensville-Mequon Republican Club, 1959- 61. Served with USAAF, 1943-46. Registered profl. engr., Wis. Mem. Tau Beta Pi Psi Upsilon. Patentee variable speed transmissions, elec. and electric control devices. Home: 1511 33d St NW Washington DC 20007 Office: ACTION 806 Connecticut Av NW Washington DC 20525

GRAHAM, RICHARD HARPER, lawyer, broadcasting co. exec.; b. San Diego, May 8, 1911; s. John A. and Edith (Harper) G.; student N.Y. U., 1929-30; J.D., Loyola U., Los Angeles, 1936; m. Ethel Stevens, June 3, 1937; children—Hollis Ann (Mrs. John N. Hosfield, Jr.), Alan S. Admitted to Cal. bar, 1937; atty. RCA, Hollywood, Cal., 1937-41, Pacific coast counsel, 1941-43, 46-57; v.p. law Pacific div. NBC, Burbank, 1957—. Served from lt. (j.g.) to lt. USNR, 1943-46; lt. comdr. Res., 1946-53. Recipient citation Navy Dept., 1945. Mem. Am. Bar Assn., So. Cal. Symphony Assn. Club: Flintridge Riding. Home: 1036 San Marino Av San Marino CA 91108 also Lake View Dr Palmdale CA 93550 Office: 3000 W Alameda Blvd Burbank CA 91505

GRAHAM, ROBERT BRUCE, financial exec.; b. Winnipeg, Man., Can., Feb. 25, 1917; s. George MacGillivray and Mary Lockhart (Smith) G.; Chartered Accountant, Queen's U., 1951; m. Joy Willemar Cooke, Dec. 28, 1950; children—Alan Bruce, Jock David. Came to U.S., 1962, naturalized, 1969. Supr., chief auditor Can. Safeway Ltd., Vancouver, B.C., Can., 1952-60; controller internat. div. Hooker Chem. Corp., Vancouver, N.Y.C., 1960-67; controller Austin, Nichols & Co., N.Y.C., 1967-69, treas., 1969—, also dir.; dir. Austin, Nichols N.Y. Corp., Austin Nichols Distilling Co., Inc. Served with Canadian Army, 1941-45. Mem. Canadian, B.C. insts. chartered accountants, Financial Execs. Inst. Presbyn. (elder, clk. session). Home: 74 Kent Av Hastings-on-Hudson NY 10706 Office: 58th St and 55th Dr Maspeth NY 11378

GRAHAM, ROBERT EDWARD, glass co. exec.; b. Clarion, Pa., Aug. 15, 1910; s. Walter A. and Katherine L. (Ormston) G.; B.S., Georgetown U., 1931; m. Elizabeth L. Goodwin, Sept. 1, 1934; 1 dau., Judith Ann. With Owens-Ill. Glass Co., 1934-, successively with mfg. plants, 1934-41, then salesman, mgr. processed foods, N.Y.C., mgr. processed foods sales div., Toledo, mgr. N.Y. sales br., 1941-57, v.p. corp., also gen. mgr. glass container div., 1957-, exec. v.p., 1962, dir., 1963, charge internat. operations, 1964, also pres., dir. many overseas operations. Bd. dirs. Mercy Hosp. Clubs: Seaview Country (Absecon, N.J.); Toledo Yacht, Toledo, Inverness (Toledo); Catawba Cliffs Beach. Home: 2148 Emkay Dr Toledo OH 43606 Office: PO Box 1035 Toledo OH 43601

GRAHAM, RUSSELL A., mfg. co. exec.; b. Chgo., Feb. 27, 1914; s. Harry M. and Lucile (Crains) G.; B.S. in Mech. Engring., Ill. Inst. Tech., 1937; M.B.A., U. Chgo., 1948; m. Shirley S. Solborg, Sept. 8, 1940; children—Robert Crain, Gary Lee, Janice Sue. With Maremont Automotive Products Co., Chgo., 1936-51, works mgr., Cicero, Ill., 1941-51; with Maremont Corp., Chgo., 1951—, exec. v.p. div. Saco-Lowell Shops, 1961-62, pres, 1962—, also corp. dir. and div. dir.; dir. South Carolina Nat. Bank, Greenville. Mem. bd. edn. dist. 200, Oak Park and River Forest (Ill.) High Sch., 1956-61, pres., 1961; mem. Greenville County Art Mus. Commn., 1969—. Bd. mgrs. St. Francis Municipal Hosp., Greenville, 1968—. Registered profl. engr., Ill. Mem. Am. Textile Machinery Assn. (dir., pres. 1967, 68), Am. Mgmt. Assn., Soc. Automotive Engrs., Soc. Advancement Mgmt. Kiwanian. Clubs: Greenville Country, Poinsett (Greenville); Corinthian Yacht (Chgo.). Home: 925 Cleveland Av Greenville SC 29601 Office: Saco-Lowell Shops Saco-Lowell Sq Easley SC 29640

GRAHAM, SAM F., hotel co. exec.; b. Buckholts, Tex., 1917; ed. U. Tex., 1939. Treas. Hilton Internat. Co. Home: Rocky Ridge Rd Westport CT 60880 Office: 301 Park Av New York City NY 10022*

GRAHAM, SHEILAH, columnist. Came to U.S., 1933, and since engaged in newspaper work; now condr. movie column in Hollywood Citizen News; writer of syndicated column relating to movies, also TV program and mags. Author: Beloved Infidel (with Gerald Frank), 1958, film 1959; College of One, 1967. Appeared in film College Confidential, 1960. Address: care Hollywood Citizen News Hollywood CA 90028

GRAHAM, SHIRLEY LOLA, (Mrs. W. E. B. DuBois), author, composer; b. Indpls., Nov. 11, 1906; d. David Andrew and Etta (Bell) Graham; B.A., Oberlin Coll., 1934, M.A., 1935; postgrad. (Julius Rosenwald fellow 1938-40), Yale U. Drama Sch., 1939-41, N.Y. U., 1944- 46, Guggenheim fellow, Sorbonne U., Paris, France, 1946-47; m. Shadrach T. McCants (div. 1928); 1 son, David Graham; m. W.E. Burghardt DuBois, Feb. 14, 1951. Composer words and music; music drama Tom-Tom, prod. 1932; opera for children Little Black Sambo (dir. 1st prodn.), 1938. Author: (with George Lipscombe) Dr. George Washington Carver, Scientist, 1944; Paul Robeson, Citizen of the World, 1946; The Story of Phillis Wheatley, 1949; There was Once a Slave, 1947; Your Most Humble Servant, 1949, Jean Baptiste Pointe de Sable, Founder of Chicago, 1953; The Story of Pocahantas, 1954; Booker T. Washington, Educator, 1955. Trustee Library of Intercultural Studies, 1955—. Recipient Julian Messner award, 1947, Anisfield-Wolf award, 1950, Nat. Acad. Arts and Letters award, 1950. Mem. Kappa Delta Pi, Sigma Delta Theta. Club: P.E.N. Home: PO Box 2797 Accra Ghana Office: care Dir Pub Relations 1 W 39th St New York City NY 10018

GRAHAM, STERLING EDWARD, newspaper pub.; b. Cleve., May 16, 1892; s. Thomas C. and Jennie (Wright) G.; A.B., Columbia, 1915; m. Jane Peterson, Feb. 26, 1921; (dec. 1965); children—Thomas R., Sterling Edward, Jane E. (Mrs. Joseph H. Champ); m. 2d, Dorothy Pratt, July 14, 1966. Display advt. salesman Cleve. Plain Dealer, 1924-28, local advt. mgr., 1928-31, advt. dir., 1931-43, gen. mgr., 1943-53; pres., dir. Forest City Pub. Co., pub. Cleve. Plain Dealer, 1953-63, ret. Served as capt. inf. U.S. Army, 1917-19. Mem. Ohio (dir.), Cleve. (pres. 1950-51, dir.) chambers commerce, Am. Legion. Rotarian. Clubs: Union, Madison Country, Automobile (dir.), Advertising, City, Cleveland Skating (Cleve.). Home: 13710 Shaker Blvd Shaker Heights OH 44120 Died May 24, 1971

GRAHAM, THOMAS, investment banker; b. West Union, Ia., Jan. 12, 1901; s. Thomas J. and Elizabeth Malcolm (Connor) G.; student Fargo Coll. Acad., Phillips Andover Acad., Princeton, U. Louisville, U. Ky.; m. Charlotte Henriques, June 20, 1931; 1 son, Thomas. Pres., dir. Thomas Graham Co.; chmn., dir. Mchts. Ice & Cold Storage Co., Arctic Ice Co.; v.p., dir. Seymour Water Co. Ind.; treas., dir. 133 S. 4th St. Bldg. Corp.; dir. Churchill Downs, Inc., Ky. Fire & Casualty Underwriters Inc., Louproco Realties Inc., Kentucky Stone Co., Ky. State Armory Corp.; dir., mem. exec. com. Ky. Water Service Co. Mem. Nat. Democratic Club. Trustee Hanover (Ind.) Coll. Mem. Def. Orientation Conf. Assn. (1st pres. 1951), Municipal Finance Officers Assn. (asso.), Nat. Municipal League N.Y. (mem. council), Nat. Security Traders Assn. (past pres.), Nat. Assn. Small Bus. Assn. (dir.), Investment Bankers Assn. (past gov.). Mason, Elk. Clubs: Filson, Pendennis, Louisville Country (Louisville); Rotary, Advertising, Frankfort Country Bankers, Princeton (N.Y.C.); Lake Shore Internat. (Chgo.); Thoroughbred (Lexington, Ky.). Home: 531 Fairfield Dr Louisville KY 40206 Office: 310 W Liberty Louisville KY 40202

GRAHAM, THOMAS WESLEY, clergyman, educator; b. Carlsbad, Ont., Can., Oct. 12, 1882; s. John and Margaret Marion (Snyder) G.; grad. Ottawa Collegiate Inst., 1899; A.B., U. of Toronto, 1903; student McCormick Theol. Sem., 1904-07; Free Ch. Coll., Glasgow, Scotland, 1907-08; D.D., Macalester Coll., 1920; m. Kate Fullerton, June 16, 1910 (dec. Jan. 1958); m. 2d, Beatrice B. Smith, Oct. 1, 1959. Came to U.S., 1904, naturalized citizen, 1920. Sec. Univ. Y.M.C.A., Toronto, 1903-04, Univ. Y.M.C.A., U. of Minn., 1909-12; ordained Prebyn. ministry, 1908; pastor Andrew Ch., Minneapolis, 1912- 20; prof. homiletics, Oberlin Grad. Sch., 1920-48, dean Grad. Sch. of Theology, 1923-48; counsellor on religious work YMCA, N.Y.C., 1948-59; asst. minister First Presbyn. Ch., Greenwich, Conn., 1959-68, minister emeritus 1st Presbyn. Ch., 1968—. Represented The Bd. for Chrisitan Colleges in China, Taipei, Formosa, 1953-54. College preacher at many colleges and univs.; lectr. at many student confs, in U.S. and Can., also for World's Student Christian Fed. Awarded Alumni Medal for distinguished service to Oberlin Coll., 1949. Mem. Nat. Bd. YMCA chmn. Centennial Com. Nat. Council YMCA; counsellor on religion, Y.M.C.A. of N.Y.C. mem. Nat. Com. Student Y.M.C.A.; mem. Internat. Com. Y.M.C.A. Army Y.M.C.A. sec., Ft. Snelling, Minn., and Paris, France, 1917-19; bd. dirs. Greenwich (Conn.) Community Chest, Mem. Fgn. Policy Assn. Clubs: Quill, Shanghai Tiffin, Canadian Soc. (N.Y.C.); The Belle Haven (Greenwich, Conn.). Editor: The Story of Jesus, 1925. Author religious articles. Home: 133 North St Greenwich CT 06830 Office: First Presbyn Ch Greenwich CT 06830 Died June 4, 1971.

GRAHAM, VINCENT JOSEPH, retail co. exec.; b. Chgo., Nov. 11, 1918; s. Charles J. and Grace (Walter) G.; B.A., Loyola U., 1941; m. Dorothy Zeller, June 6, 1942; childrenVincent Joseph, Susanne, Diane. With Sears, Roebuck & Co., Chgo., 1946-, now divisional v.p.; dir. Sears Bank & Trust Co. Served with AUS, 1943-46; ETO. Mem. Chgo. Assn. Commerce and Industry, Am. Legion. Roman Catholic. Home: 6243 N Knox Av Chicago IL 60646 Office: 925 S Homan Av Chicago IL 60607

GRAHAM, WALKER RYAN ALLEN, corp. exec.; b. Muncie Ind., July 13, 1917; s. George Montgomery and Nola Edna (Ryan) G.; A.B., U. Mich., 1938; m. Ruthe Caroline Willey, June 24, 1939. Copywriter, account exec. McCann-Erickson, Inc., Detroit, 1939-42, v.p., group head, 1953-56; copy chief, account supr. Grant Advt., Inc., 1946-49; v.p. charge Detroit office Geyer Advt., Inc., 1949- 53; v.p., creative dir., chmn. plans bd. D. P. Brother & Co., Detroit, 1956-61; became exec. v.p. Willey Sign Co., Mt. Clemens, Mich., 1961; dir. merchandising Chrysler-Plymouth div. Chrysler Corp. until 1964; with W. B. Doner & Co., advt., 1964; v.p. Fugazy Travel and Incentive, Inc.; v.p. Marketing Diners Fugazy, Inc.; pres. WRAG. & Assos., 1970—. Advt. dir. Romney for Gov. Com. Chmn. educator com. Mich. council Am. Assn. Advt. Agys., mem. nat. bd. govs.; advt. chmn. United Found. of Detroit. Served as lt., naval aviation, USNR, 1943-46. Mem. Sales Promotion Execs. Assn., Theta Chi, Kappa Delta Phi. Clubs: Players (pres.), Detroit Boat, Adcraft (Detroit); Druids. Author one-act plays. Editor: Service Engring. (quar.), 1942. Home: 2501 Iroquois Detroit MI 48214 Office: 2600 Detroit Bank and Trust Bldg Detroit MI 48226

GRAHAM, WALLACE HARRY, surgeon; b. Highland, Kan., Oct. 9, 1910; s. James Walter and Elizabeth Marie (Veneman) G.; student Central Mo. State, Warrensburg, Mo., 1928- 32; B.S., Creighton U., 1934, M.D., 1936; student U. Vienna, 1937, U. Budapest, 1938, Royal Coll. of Surgeons, Edinburgh Scotland, 1939; m. Velma Ruth Hill, Sept. 15, 1935; children—Wallace Scott, Heather Ellen, Bruce Douglas. Served externship Mass. Gen. Hosp., Boston, 1935; internship and pres. house staff Kansas City Gen. Hosp., Kansas City, Mo., 1936; personal physician to Pres. of the U.S., Sept. 12, 1945; profl. lectr. in surgery George Washington U. Sch. Medicine and asso. surgeon George Washington U., Washington; surg. staff Bapt. Meml., Research, Menorah, St. Margarets hosps. (Kansas City, Mo.); sect. chief surgery Walter Reed Gen. Hosp., Washington; founder Fountain Plaza Corp., Kansas City, Mo.; hon. mem. faculty U. of Santo Domingo, Dominican Republic; research worker in cancer; special asst. to the surgeon general USAF, sr. flight surgeon. Mem. Presdl. Spl. Mission to Guatemala City and the Middle East; USAF delegate to Internat. Coll. Medicine and Pharmacy, Mexico City, Internat. Symposium of High Altitude Biology, Lima, Peru. Entered active service with U.S. Army as 1st lt., advanced through the grades to maj. gen., 1951; chief of 24th Evacuation Hosp. Surgical Service in combat, 1942- 45. Decorated Bronze Star, Purple Heart (U.S.); chevalier Legion of Honor, Croix de Guerre with palm (France); Distinguished Service Order, Hon. Companion (Great Britain); officer Order of Orange-Nassau with crossed sabres and rosette (Netherlands); officer Order of Leopold with palm and attrition; comdr. Order of Finlay, (Cuba); Order Italian Star of Solidarity, 2d Class; Croix de Guerre with palm (Belgium); comdr. Order of Mil. Merit (Brazil); Cross of Comdr. of the Royal Order of the Phoenix (Greece). Elected to Hall of Fame, Creighton U., 1945. Certified fellow Internat. Coll. Surgeons. Fellow A.C.S.; mem. Aero Med. Assn., Royal Soc. Medicine, A.M.A., Mo., Jackson County (Mo.), D.C. med. socs., Mo., D.C., George Washington U. surg. socs., Pan Am. Surg. Assn. (v.p.), Assn. Mil. Surgeons U.S., Res. Officers Assn., Am. Legion, Phi Rho Sigma. Democrat. Baptist. Clubs: Cosmopolitan, Kansas City and District of Columbia. Contbr. numerous articles to med. and surgical pubs. Home: 5157 Ward Parkway Kansas City MO 64112 Office: 1815 E 63d St Kansas City MO 64130

GRAHAM, WALTER WAVERLY, Jr., educator; b. College Grove, Tenn., Dec. 1, 1906; s. Walter Waverly and Bettie (Hatcher) G.; B.A., Vanderbilt U., 1929, M.A., 1930; Ph.D., George Peabody Coll., 1943; m. Irene Turner, Aug. 6, 1931; childrenWalter Waverly III, Jane Turner. With Vanderbilt U., 1930-, instr. math., 1930-41, asst. prof., 1941-43, asso. prof. applied math., 1946-50, prof., 1950-51, prof., head dept., 1951-69, prof., 1969—. Served from lt. (j.g.) to lt. USNR, 1943-46; tchr. math. U.S. Naval Acad., 1943-46. Mem. Am. Math. Assn., Am. Soc. Engring. Edn., Tenn. Acad. Sci., Sigma Xi, Omicron Delta Kappa. Methodist. Mason. Home: 128 Alton Rd Nashville TN 37205

GRAHAM, WILLIAM B., pharm. exec.; b. Chgo., July 14, 1911; s. William and Elizabeth (Burden) G.; S.B. cum laude, U. Chgo., 1932, J.D. cum laude, 1936; m. Edna Kanaley, June 15, 1940; children—Elizabeth (Mrs. Dennis Muckerman), Margaret (Mrs. Benson Caswell), Robert B., William J. Admitted to Ill. bar, 1936; patent lawyer Dyrenforth, Lee, Chritton & Wiles, 1936-40; mem. Dawson & Ooms, 1940-45; v.p., mgr. Baxter Labs., Inc., Morton Grove, Ill., 1945-53, pres., chief exec. officer, 1953-71, chmn. bd., chief exec. officer, 1971—, also dir.; dir. First Nat. Bank, Chgo., Culligan Inc., UARCO, Borg Warner Co., Bell & Howell, Inc. Bd. dirs., past pres. Community Fund Chgo.; bd. dirs. Lyric Opera Chgo.; trustee Crusade of Mercy Nat. Fund Grad. Nursing Edn., U. Chgo., Ravinia Festival Assn., Orchestral Assn., Evanston Hosp. Recipient V.I.P. award, 1963. Mem. Am. Pharm. Mfrs. Assn. (past pres.), Ill. Mfrs. Assn. (dir., past pres.), Pharm. Mfrs. Assn. (dir., past chmn.), Phi Beta Kappa, Sigma Xi, Phi Delta Phi. Clubs: Chicago, Commonwealth, Mid-Am., Commercial, Westmoreland (Chgo.); University, Links (N.Y.C.). Home: 40 Devonshire Lane Kenilworth IL 60043 Office: 6301 Lincoln Av Morton Grove IL 60053

GRAHAM, WILLIAM BUTTERWORTH, corp. exec.; b. Providence, Nov. 6, 1916; s. William John and Florence (Butterworth) G.; B.S., U. Mass., 1938; M.B.A., Harvard, 1941; m. Ruth A. Hall, Aug. 30, 1941; 1 dau., Jane Elizabeth (Mrs. Richard J. Murphy, Jr.). Accounting supr. Talon, Inc., Meadville, Pa., 1941-50; tax adminstr. Weatherhead Co., Cleve., 1950-61, treas., 1961—; treas. Hyco, Inc., Ashland, O., 1969—; treas. LPG Leasing Corp., Cleve., 1961-70, sec., treas., 1970—, also dir. Asst. sec. Weatherhead Found., 1963-66, sec.-treas., 1966-70. Mem. Greater Cleve. Growth Assn., Treasurers Club Cleve. (bd. dirs. 1968-71, pres. 1970-71). Presbyn. (elder, trustee). Mason (32). Club: Canterbury (Cleve.). Home: 2436 Newbury Dr Cleveland Heights OH 44118 Office: 300 E 131st St Cleveland OH 44108

GRAHAM, WILLIAM DONALD, physician, ret. army officer; b. Birmingham, Eng., Oct 5, 1905; s John and Lilian (Abels) G.; came to U.S., 1915, naturalzied, 1922; B.Sc., U. Minn., 1930, M.D., 1931; M.P.H., U. Cal. at Berkeley, 1949; m. Dorothy Margaret Quinlen, Apr. 7, 1934; 1 dau., Ann (Mrs. Gerald E. Bouchoux). Pvt. practice medicine and surgery, Hanska, Minn., 1931-34; commd. in M.C., U.S. Army, 1934, advanced through grades to maj. gen.; exec. dir. Dependents Medicare Program, 1960-62; comdg. gen. Tripler Army Med. Center, Honolulu, also chief surgeon U.S. Army, Pacific, 1962-65; dep. dir. Hawaii Regional Med. Program, U. Hawaii, 1966-68. Decorated D.S.M., Legion of Merit. Fellow A.C.P., Am. Coll. Hosp. Adminstrs., Assn. U.S. Army, Assn. Mil. Surgeons, Phi Rho Sigma. Episcopalian. Rotarian, Mason (Shriner). Home: 420 Poipu Dr Honolulu HI 96821

GRAHAM, WILLIAM FRANKLIN, educator, evangelist; b. Charlotte, N.C., Nov. 7, 1918; s. William Franklin and Morrow (Coffey) G.; A.B. Wheaton (Ill.) College, 1943; Th.B., Fla. Bible Sem., Tampa, 1940; D.D., LL.D., Houghton (N.Y.) Coll., 1950, Baylor U., William Jewell Coll., LL.D., The Citadel., numerous other hon. degrees; m. Ruth McCue Bell, Aug. 13, 1943; childrenVirginia Leftwich, Anne Morrow, Ruth Bell, William Franklin, Nelson Edman. Ordained to ministry Baptist Ch.; minister First Church, Western Springs, Ill.; founder program Songs in the Night, WCFL, Chgo., 1943-45; 1st v.p. Youth for Christ, Internat. 1945-48; pres. Northwestern Coll., Mpls., 1947-52; chmn. bd. World Wide Pictures, Inc.; nationwide evangelistic campaigns, 1949-; speaker weekly Hour of Decision radio program (occasional telecast) ABC, Mut., Yankee, Inter-Mountain, Canadian and Australian networks and world-wide shortwave, 1950-; founder, pres. Billy Graham Evangelistic Assn.; editor-in-chief Decision Mag.; United Bible Socs., 1963—. Recipient numerous awards, including Bernard Baruch award, 1955; Humane Order of African Redemption, 1960; gold award George Washington Carver Meml. Inst., 1963; Horatio Alger award, 1965. Author: Calling Youth to Christ, 1947; Revival in Our Times, 1950; America's Hour of Decision, 1951; Korean Diary, 1953; Peace with God, 1953; The Secret to Happiness, 1955; My Answer, 1960; World Aflame, 1965; The Challenge; also writer of daily newspaper column. Made numerous preaching trips to Europe; has preached in nearly every country of world. Home: Montreat NC 28757 Office: 1300 Harmon Pl Minneapolis MN 55403

GRAHAM, WILLIAM HUGH, advt. co. exec.; b. Winnipeg, Man., Can., May 18, 1912; s. Robert Blackwood Whidden and Louisa (Ramwell) G.; B.A., U. Man., 1935; m. Catherine Eleanor Godfrey, Mar. 25, 1940; 1 son, William Hugh Godfrey. Copywriter MacLaren Advt. Co. Ltd., Toronto, Ont., Can., 1938-47, account exec., 1947-56, v.p., 1956-64, exec. v.p., 1964-. Pres. trustee Galion Community Center. Served wtih Canadian Army, 1940-45. Mem. Newcomen Soc. Clubs: Univ. (Toronto); Manitoba (Winnipeg). Author: The Tiger of Canada West, 1962. Home: PH 6 131 Bloor St W Toronto 5 Ontario Canada and Belleview Farm Greenbank Ontario Canada Office: 111 Richmond St W Toronto Ontario Canada

GRAHAM, WILLIAM HUGH, electronics co. exec.; b. Dayton, O., Jan. 11, 1919; s. Charles Walter and Katherine (Ernst) G.; student mech. engring., U. Dayton, 1942; m. Mary Emerson Glotfelter, Oct. 26, 1940; childrenJohn W., Barbara A. (Mrs. Richard Corman). Spl. asst. to works mgr. Nat. Cash Register Co., Dayton, 1937-47; gen. mgr. Crosley div. Avco Mfg. Corp., Cin., 1947-55; exec. v.p. Magnavox Co. of Tenn., Greeneville, 1955-59; pres. Metals Engring. Co., Greenville, 1959; pres., dir. North Electric Co., Galion, O., 1959—. Mem. exec. bd. Johnny Appleseed Area council Boy Scouts Am., also mem. nat. council, vice chmn. Region IV; trustee, pres. Galion Community Center. Mem. Newcomen Soc. Home: Rural Route 4 Box 636 Galion OH 44833 Office: 553 S Market St Galion OH 44833

GRAHAM, WILLIS SPRAGINS, entertainment exec.; b. Florence, Ala., Oct. 29, 1919; s. Willis Ramey and Edna Bibb (Spragins) G.; m. Katherine Rowena Dinkins, May 2, 1942. Mem. advt. dept. Memphis Comml. Appeal-Press Scimitar, 1940-42; free-lance writer, 1946; promotion dir. radio sta. WSM, Nashville, 1946- 48; v.p. Noble-Dury & Assos., Inc., Nashville, 1948-55, pres., 1956-63, chmn. bd., 1963-66; chmn. bd. Show Biz, Inc., Nashville; pres. Show Biz Music, Inc., Willis Graham Prodns., Inc. Served with AUS, 1942-46; CBI. Mem. Broadcast Music. Clubs: Belle Meade, Richland Country, Cumberland (Nashville). Composer (popular songs); Christmas Morn, 1959; Johnny Reb, 1960; Mickey's Tune, 1964; Too Tired to Run Anymore, 1965; Hoss, He's The Boss, 1965; Christmas at the Opry, 1966; Opry Theme, 1967; I Can't Remember to Forget, 1968; Moning, 1970. Contbr. fiction and non-fiction to various nat. mags. Home: 4410 Chickering Lane Nashville TN 37215 Office: Show Biz Inc and Show Biz Music Inc Baker Bldg Nashville TN 37202

GRAHAME, ORVILLE FRANCIS, lawyer, bus. exec.; b. Palo, Ia., Apr. 2, 1904; s. Samuel G. and Dawn (Booth) G.; B.A., U. Ia., 1925, J.D., 1929; m. Paula Patton, Nov. 3, 1923; 1 dau., Sarah Jane (Cairns). Admitted to Ia. bar, 1929, N.Y. bar, 1932, Mass. bar, 1940, U.S. Supreme Ct. bar, 1954; asso. Guardian Life Ins. Co., 1929-39, asst. sec., 1936-39; chmn. law com., dir. Paul Revere Life Ins. Co., Worcester, Mass., Paul Revere Variable Annuity Ins. Co., Paul Revere Corp. and several affiliated cos.; dir. Avco Corp., Worcester Devel. Corp. Mem. nat. adv. com. White House Conf. Aging, 1959-61, tech. com. on income, 1971-72. Exec. com. Health and Accident Underwriters Conf., 1954-55; author, sponsor concept of guaranteed renewable adjustable premium accident and sickness ins., 1948; mem. Mass. Pension Commn., 1953-55; mem. Mass. Variable Annuity Commn., 1956- 60; mem. Zoning Appeals Bd., Worcester, 1958-63; mem. com. on employment and retirement Nat. Council Aging; mem. Bus. Com. for Tax Reduction, 1963-64. Bd. dirs. Worcester Red Cross, 1957-63, 66—, U. Ia. Found., Ia. Law Sch. Found., 1970—. Mem. N.Y. County Republican Com., 1934-36. Recipient Distinguished Service award U. Ia., 1964. Fellow Ins. Inst. Am.; mem. Am. Judicature Soc., Am., Mass., Worcester County bar assns., Assn. Bar City N.Y., N.Y. County Lawyers Assn., Acad. Polit. Sci., English-Speaking Union, Assn. Life Counsel, Am. Life Conv., Ins. Econs. Soc. Am. (pres. 1954-55), Worcester Hist. Soc., Worcester Music Festival Assn., Newcomen Soc., Phi Alpha Delta, Order of Coif. Republican. Unitarian. Mason (Shriner). Clubs: Rotary, University, Worcester, Westboro Country. Author: (with others) The

Life Insurance Contract, 1953; also legal articles. Mem. editorial bd. Insurance Decision, 1933-37. Home: 6 Bancroft Tower Rd Worcester MA 01609 Office: 27 Elm St Worcester MA 01608

GRAINGE, FLOYD MARVIN, educator; b. Toledo, Ia., Oct. 8, 1920: s. John Mossen and Lucille Evaline (Shugart) G.; B.S. in Indsl. Edn., Ia. State U., 1949, M.S. in Vocational Edn., 1953; Ed.D., U. Cal. at Los Angeles, 1967; m. Theresa Arlene Sarazine, June 2, 1941; childrenCatharine Anne, Barbara Eileen. Tchr. indsl. arts and math. Ames (Ia.) High Sch., 1949-53; mem. faculty Long Beach State Coll., 1953-, prof. indsl. arts, 1962-, chmn. indsl. arts dept., 1962-69, asso. dean Sch. Applied Arts and Scis., 1969—, co-dir. Aero-Space Work Shop, 1958—. Mem. planning com. Long Beach Sabin on Sunday Program; mem. radio communications com. for local cancer and polio drives. Served with USNR, World War II. Mem. Cal. Edn. Assn., Am., Cal. indsl. edn. assns., Amateur Radio Relay League, Radio Amateur Civil Emergency Service, Asso. Radio Amateurs Long Beach (pres. 1962, dir. 1963), Holy Name Soc., Long Beach Civic Light Opera Assn., Civil Def. Communications, Am. Vocational Assn., Phi Delta Kappa, Phi Kappa Phi, Epsilon Pi Tau, Elk. Home: 4414 Whitewood Av Long Beach CA 90808

GRAINGER, DELBERT WILLIAM, lawyer; b. Salt Lake City, Aug. 24, 1925; s Delbert J. and Margaret (Brown) G.; B.S., U. Utah, 1950, LL.B., 1951, J.D., 1967; m. Gayle Hodge, June 28, 1949; children—William Douglas, Karen Diane. Admitted to Utah bar, 1951. Ariz. bar, 1960, also Utah Supreme Ct. Ariz. Supreme Ct., U.S. Supreme Ct.; practice in Salt Lake City, 1951-53, Phoenix, 1953—; pvt. practice, 1951-53; with claims dept. State Farm Ins. Co., 1953-60; mem. firm Lewis & Roca, 1960—, partner, 1965—. Served with USNR, 1943-46. Mem. Fedn. Ins. Counsel, Internat. Assn. Ins. Counsel, Am. Bd. Trial Advs., Phoenix Assn. Def. Counsel (past pres.). Home: 7013 E Belleview St Scottsdale AZ 85257 Office: 114 W Adams St Phoenix AZ 85003

GRAINGER, JAMES EDMUND, motion picture exec.; b. N.Y.C.; s. James R. and Veronica Grainger; student Fordham U. Salesman, Fox Studios; producer for Fox, Universal, Warner Bros., Republic; pres., gen. mgr. Edmund Grainger Prodns., 1950; exec. producer RKO Prodns.; pres. RKO Pictures Corp., RKO Radio Pictures, Inc.; producer Riders of the Purple Sage, Diamond Jim Brady, Love before Breakfast, Sutter's Gold, Magnificant Brute, International Squadron, Flying Tigers, The Fabulous Texan, Wake of the Red Witch, Sands of Iwo Jima, Flying Leathernecks, The Racket, One Minute to Zero, Blackbeard the Pirate, Split Second, Devil's Canyon, Second Chance, The French Line, Treasure of Pancho Vila, Great Day in the Morning, Bundle of Joy, The Sheepman, Torpedo Run, Green Mansions, Home from the Hill, Never So Few. Served as maj. AUS, World War II. Address: 708 N Foothill Rd Beverly Hills CA 90210

GRALLA, ARTHUR ROBERT, naval officer; b. Bklyn., Apr. 21, 1913; s. Abraham and Ella (Alpert) G.; student Bklyn Coll., 1928-30; B.S., U.S. Naval Acad., 1934; student U.S. Navy Postgrad. Sch., 1940-41; M.S. in Elec. Engring., Mass. Inst. Tech., 1942; grad. Armed Forces Staff Coll., 1950, Naval War Coll., 1953; m. Mildred Charlotte Lesser, May 31, 1936; childrenArthur Robert Jr., Richard Jeremy. Commd. ensign U.S. Navy, 1934, advanced through grades to vice adm., 1969; assigned duty ashore and afloat, 1934-43; gunnery officer U.S.S. Reno, 1943-45, U.S.S. Macon, 1945-46; comdg. officer U.S.S. Buckley, 1946-47; assigned Office Chief Naval Operations, also mem. Air Def. Bd., 1947-50; current operations officer staff comdr. in chief Naval Forces Eastern Atlantic and Mediterranean, 1950-52; comdr. Destroyer Div. 202, 1953-54, Destroyer Squadron 20, 1954; adminstrv. aide to dep. chief naval operations, 1954-56; comdg. officer Naval Ordnance Test Unit, Patrick AFB, Fla., 1956-57, naval missile test ship U.S.S. Norton Sound, 1957-58; system dir. surface weapons systems Navy Bur. Ordnance, 1958-59; dir. missiles research and devel. Bur. Naval Weapons, 1959; comdr. Destroyer Flotilla 2, 1960-61; dep. comdr. Mil. Sea Transp. Service, 1961-63; dep. chmn., chmn. Joint Chiefs of Staff, spl. studies group, 1963-64; comdr. South Atlantic force U.S. Atlantic Fleet, 1964-66; comdr. Naval Ordnance Systems Command, 1966-69; naval insp. gen., 1969-70; comdr. Mil. Sealift Command, 1970—. Decorated D.S.M., Legion of Merit with gold star, Navy-Marine Corps medal, Bronze Star with gold star and combat V, Joint Service Commendation medal. Mem. Sigma Xi. Home: Quarters L-1 Washington Navy Yard Washington DC 20390 Office: Comdr Mil Sealift Command Navy Dept Washington DC 20390

GRAM, HARVEY B., Jr., investment banker; b. Washington, Aug. 31, 1903; s. Harvey B. and Virginia Lee (Jones) G.; Ph.B., Wesleyan U., Middletown, Conn., 1927; m. Mary Worthington Dunbar, June 18, 1936; children—Harvey B. III, W. Dunbar, John Worthington (dec.). With Spencer Trask & Co., N.Y.C., 1927- 30, J.G. White & Co., 1930-32; with Johnston, Lemon & Co. Washington, 1932—, gen. partner, 1936—; v.p., sec., dir. Washington Mut. Investors Fund, Washington Mut. Investors Plan; dir., mem. exec. com. Govt. Employees Corp., Govt. Employees Financial Corp., Govt. Employees Ins. Co., Govt. Employees Life Ins. Co., Criterion Ins. Co. (all Washington); dir. Internat. Gen. Industries, Inc., Washington, D.C. Paper Mills, Inc., Washington, Financial Internat. Corp., Washington, Nat. Press Bldg. Corp., Washington, Telcom., Inc., McLean, Va. Trustee Davis Meml. Goodwill Industries, Washington. Served to lt. col. USAAF, 1942-45. Mem. Investment Bankers Assn. (bd. govs.), S.A.R. (trustee), Alpha Delta Phi. Clubs; University (pres. 1960-62) (Washington); Columbia Country (bd. govs. 1961-64) (Chevy Chase, Md.); Burning Tree (Bethesda, Md.). Home: 3514 Overlook Lane NW Washington DC 20016 Office: Southern Bldg Washington DC 20005

GRAMATKY, HARDIE, artist, author; b. Dallas, Apr. 12, 1907; s. Bernhard and Blanche (Gunner) G.; student Stanford U., 1926-28, Chouinard Art Sch., 1928-30; m. Dorothea Cooke, Aug. 20, 1932; 1 dau., Linda Anne (Mrs. Kendall Borden Smith). Engaged as artist-reporter Fortune mag., 1937-39; illustrator True, Today's Woman, Collier's, Cosmopolitan, etc., 1940—; supr. prodn. tng. films for Army Air Force, 1942-45. Commd. artist-of-war in Vietnam, Air Force, 1966. Represented permanent collections Bklyn. Mus., Chgo. Art Inst., Toledo Art Mus., Mus. Fine Arts, Springfield, Mass.; children's book illustrations in Kerlan collection U. Minn. Numerous watercolor prizes including Chgo. Internat. 1939, Am. Watercolor Soc., 1941, 52, Audubon Artists, 1945, 52, Salmagundi award, 1952, Conn. Watercolor Soc., 1969, Soc. of Illustrators, 1970. Mem. Am. Watercolor Soc. (bd. control 1953—), Soc. Illustrators (dir. 1940-41), Cal. Watercolor Soc. (dir. 1935-36), N.A.D. Conglist. Author, illustrator: (children's books) Little Toot, 1939 (Lewis Carroll Shelf award U. Wis. 1969); Hercules, 1940; Loopy, 1941; Creepers Jeep, 1948; Sparky, 1952; Homer and The Circus Train, 1957; Bolivar, 1961; Nikos and the Sea God, 1963; Little Toot on the Thames, 1964; Little Toot on the Grand Canal, 1968; Happy's Christmas, 1970. Address: 60 Roseville Rd Westport CT 06880

GRAMBLING, ALLEN ROWELL, lawyer; b. Tyler, Tex., Oct. 26, 1891; s. Allen M. and Ella (Rowell) G.; LL.B., U. Tex., 1912; m. Marion Hogan, June 24, 1919; childrenJohn Allen, Patricia (Mrs.E. R. Harvey). Admitted to Tex. bar, 1913; now mem. firm Hardie, Grambling, Sims & Galatzan; dir., gen. atty. El Paso (Tex.) Natural Gas Co. 1946—; dir., v.p. Lea Co. Gas Co. 1941—; dir. First State Bank El Paso. Pres. Sch. Bd., C. of C., Community Chest, El Paso. Bd. dir., v.p. Providence Meml. Hosp. Fellow Am. Bar Found. Mem. Am., Tex. State, Fed. Power Commn., El Paso bar assns. Kiwanian (pres.). Home: 615 Hague St El Paso TX 79902 Office: Natural Gas Co Bldg El Paso TX 79901

GRAMBSCH, PAUL VICTOR, educator; b. Dayton, O., Mar. 14, 1919; s. Rinold Herman and Victoria Catherine (Danecker) G.; B.A., North Central Coll., 1941; M.A., U. Miss., 1947; D.B.A., Ind. U., 1955; m. Ada Elizabeth Branch, June 20, 1945; childrenE. Donald, Paul Victor, Kathryn, Nancy, Richard, William, Anne, Mary. Instr. Equality (Ill.) Twp. High Sch., 1940-42; asst. prof., acting chmn. dept. economics U. Miss., 1948-50; asso. prof. mgmt. Tulane U. Sch. Bus. Adminstrn., 1952-60; dean Sch. Bus. Adminstrn., U. Minn., 1960-70, prof. mgmt., 1970—; mgmt. cons. Educator cons. U.S. Gen. Accounting Office; dir. research project on univ. goals Ford Found., 1970-71. Pub. interest dir. Fed. Home Loan Bank, Des Moines, 1971—; dir. Northwest Growth Fund, Inc. Mem. Gov.'s Adv. Commn. to Dept. Bus. Devel., 1961- 63, Upper Midwest Regional Export Expansion Council; chmn. Gov's Tax Study Com., 1962. Served as lt. USNR, 1942-46. Mem. Am. Econ. Assn., Acad. Mgmt. (bd. govs.), Inst. Mgmt. Scis., Financial Execs. Inst., Indsl. Relations Research Assn., Mpls. C. of C., So. Econ. Assn., Beta Gamma Sigma, Delta Sigma Pi. Episcopalian. Clubs: Rotary, Campus (Mpls.). Author: (with E. Gross) University Goals and Academic Power. Home: 4800 Emerson Av S Minneapolis MN 55409

GRAMLEY, DALE HARTZLER, found. exec.; b. Loganville, Pa., Sept. 23, 1905; s. Andrew D. and Ada Laura (Meals) G.; A.B., Albright Coll., 1926, Litt.D., 1949; S.M., Columbia, 1929; LL.D., Moravian Coll. and Theol. Sem., 1950; Litt.D. (hon.), Wake Forest Coll., 1955; LL.D. (hon.), Davidson Coll., 1960; m. Caroline Lois Illick, Dec. 27, 1929; children—Hugh Andrew, William Eugene, Dale Illick, Stephan Edward. Reporter, asst. editor York (Pa.) Dispatch, 1926-28; copy-reader N.Y. Jour. Commerce, 1929; instr. journalism Lehigh U., 1929-33, asst. prof., 1933-35, asso. prof., 1935-42, dir. journalism courses, 1931-42, editor Univ. News, 1936-42; asst. to pres. Moravian Coll. and Theol. Sem., 1942-44; editor Bethlehem (Pa.) Globe-Times, 1944-49; v.p., dir. Bethlehem WGPA Charities, Inc., 1947-49; v.p. Old Salem, Inc. 1950-71; pres. Salem Acad. and Coll., Winston-Salem, 1949-71; exec. dir. Z. Smith Reynolds Found., 1971—; dir. Triangle Broadcasting Co. Alumnus trustee Albright Coll., 1931-40; trustee Moravian Coll. and Theol. Sem., 1947- 50; v.p. Moravian Music Found.; bd. dirs. N.C. Gov.'s Sch., 1965-71, Reynolda House, Inc., 1966-71; pres. Piedmont U. Center N.C., 1964-69. Mem. Winston-Salem C. of C. (pres. 1968, chmn. bd. 1969), Pi Delta Epsilon. Democrat. Moravian. Rotarian. Clubs: Forsyth Country; Winston-Salem Automobile (dir.). Home: 331 S Main St Winston-Salem NC 27101

GRAMLEY, EUGENE TITUS, banker; b. Spring Mills, Pa., Dec. 10, 1899; s. Titus M. and Agnes (Loose) G.; B.S. in Elec. Engring., Pa. State U., 1920; student Am. Inst. Banking; m. Polly R. Powell, June 28, 1923; 1 dau., Ann K. (Mrs. John I. Freed). Security salesman Redmond & Co., 1922-23; with Citizens Nat. Bank, Lewiston, Pa., 1923-46, cashier, trust officer, dir., 1936- 46; pres. Milton Bank & Safe Deposit Co. (Pa.), 1946-; dir. Fed. Res. Bank Phila., 1961-. Regional chmn. group 5, Pa. banking and investment div., war finance com. Treasury Dept., 1941-45; mem. Pa. Banking Bd., 1952-58; mem. faculty Pa. Bankers Assn. summer sch., Bucknell U., 1958- 61. Pres. Lewistown Community Chest, 1938-39, Milton Community Chest, 1948-49. Mem. exec. bd. Pa. State U., 1952-60, athletic adv. bd., 1940- 48; bd. dirs. Milton Council Boy Scouts Am., 1950-56, Milton Salvation Army, 1948-51. Served to 2d lt., inf., U.S. Army, World War I. Mem. Pa. Bankers Assn. (chmn. group 5, 1941), Pa. State U. Alumni Assn. (past pres.), Am. Legion. Lutheran (council). Mason, Elk. Home: RD 1 Milton PA 17847 Office: Milton Bank and Safe Deposit Co Milton PA 17847

GRAMLING, LEA GENE, educator; b. High Springs, Fla., Nov. 3, 1908; s. George Eugene and Anne (Edwards) G.; Ph.G., U. Fla., 1931, B.S. in Pharmacy, 1935, M.S. in Pharmacy, 1936, Ph.D., 1938; m. Margaret Mixson, Sept. 18, 1933; 1 son, Lea Gene. Retail pharmacist, 1931-34; asst. prof. Coll. Pharmacy, George Washington U., 1938-43, acting adminstr. coll., 1942-43; tchr. Sci. and math. Dunnellon (Fla.) High Sch., 1945-46; faculty Coll. Pharmacy, U. Fla., 1946-, prof., 1956-59, chmn., prof. pharm. chemistry, 1959-. Served to 2d lt. AUS, 1943-45. Fellow A.A.A.S.; mem. Am. (co-recipient Ebert award 1938), Fla. pharm. assns., Fla. Acad. Sci., Am. Chem. Soc., S.A.R., Sigma Xi, Gamma Sigma Epsilon (nat. sec. 1946-50, 54-56, nat. pres. 1950-54), Phi Kappa Phi, Rho Chi, Phi Sigma, Phi Eta Sigma, Delta Chi, Scabbard and Blade. Presbyn. (deacon). Home: 640 NW 36th Terrace Gainesville FL 32601

GRAMLING, OLIVER S., former press assn. exec., author; b. Tallahassee, Fla., Aug. 30, 1904; s. David F. and Edna (Oliver) G.; student Oglethorpe U.; Litt. B., Columbia; m. Vera Johnson, 1950. Began newspaper work at age fifteen with So. papers; spl. assignments on N.Y. Times, 1926-27; with A. P., N.Y.C., 1927-69, reporter, 1927-30, news supr., cable and polit. reporting, 1932-33, chief of service in Pa. and W.Va., Pitts., 1933-36, exec. asst. charge membership dept. in N.Y. office, 1937-40, assisted devel. A. P. news report for radio, 1941, asst. gen. mgr., 1946-62; v.p. Press Assn., Inc. (broadcast subsidiary), 1941-62. Wrote stories on Italian mass flight, dirigible Akron disaster, Ohio River floods, etc. Mem. Soc. Am. Hstorians, Boar's Head (Oglethorpe), Broadcast Pioneers. Clubs: Dutch Treat, Silurians, Overseas Press. Author: APThe Story of News, 1940; Free Men Are Fighting, 1942; Back from Africa (play produced in Atlantia Theater), 1924. Contbr. to mags. Home: PO Box 4424 Fort Lauderdale FL 33304

GRAMM, DONALD, opera singer; b. Milw., Feb. 26, 1927; s. Rinold H. and Victoria (Danneker) Grambsch; student piano and organ Wis. Coll. Music, Wis. Conservatory, 1935-44; student Chgo. Mus. Coll., 1944-49. Radio singer Chgo. Theater of the Air, Hymns of All Churches, Club Time, Best of All, 1947-55; soloist recitals U.S., Alaska, Can., 1945-47; soloist Hollywood Bowl, Tanglewood, Ravinia (Chgo.), May festivals, Ann Arbor, Mich., Cin, Alaska Festival, Anchorage, 1959, 60, 61, Santa Fe Opera Assn., 1960—, Stratford (Ont.) Festival, 1963, Miami Opera, 1965, also Met. Opera Co. 1964—; singer with symphony orchs., N.Y.C., Boston, Phila., Pitts., Chgo., San Francisco, Los Angeles, others; leading bass baritone, N.Y.C. Opera, 1952—, Chgo. Lyric Theatre, 1960, New Orleans Opera Assn., 1957-58; roles include Marriage of Figaro, La Cenerentola, Carmen, Boheme, others; appeared as Moses in Am. premiere of Moses and Aron, 1966; singer NBC-TV Opera Theatre, Tulsa opera, 1963, Berlin Festwochen, 1961, Opera Nacional, Mexico City, Mexico, 1965, The Festival of Two Worlds, Spoleto, Italy, 1967, Aix-en- Province Festival, France, 1969, Chgo. Lyric Opera, 1968; appeared Am. Die Jacobsleiter, Santa Fe, 1968. Recipient award Chicagoland Music Festival, 1943, Oliver Ditson scholarship, 1945-46, Paul LaValle award, 1947, Ford Found. program for solo artists, 1962. Mem. Am. Guild Mus. Artists, Am. Fedn. TV and Radio Artists, Santa Fe (N.M.) Opera Assn. Club: Forty (Chgo.). Address: care Columbia Artists Mgmt Inc 165 W 57th St New York NY 10019

GRAMMATER, RUDOLF DIMITRI, constrn. co. exec.; b. Detroit, Nov. 29 1910; s. D. M. and Amelia (Busse) G.; student accountancy and bus. adminstrn., Pace Inst., 1928- 32; LL.B., Lincoln U., 1937; m. Fredricka W. Cook, Aug. 18, 1943; 1 son, Douglas. Admitted to Cal. bar, 1938; with Bechtel Corp., San Francisco, 1941—, treas., v.p., 1955-62, v.p., 1962—, dir., 1960—; v.p., dir. subsidaires. Mem. San Francisco Com. Fgn. Relations. Trustee Golden Gate Coll. C.P.A., Cal. Mem. Am., San Francisco bar assns., State Bar Cal., Am. Inst. C.P.A.'s, Cal.. Soc. C.P.A.'s, C. of C. Clubs: Stock Exchange, Commonwealth, Bankers (San Francisco); Menlo Country (Redwood City). Home: 270 Eleanor Dr Woodside CA 94062 Office 50 Beale St San Francisco CA 94119

GRAMPP, WILLIAM DYER, educator; b. Columbus, O., Aug. 22, 1914; A.B. U. Akron, 1936; A.M., U. Chgo., 1942, Ph.D., 1944; student Columbia, 1941; children—Wendy P., Heather M., Christopher W. Mem. editorial staff Akron Times-Press, 1937- 38, Press Wireless, Paris, France, 1938, Chgo. Tribune, London, Eng., 1939; instr. Adelphi Coll., 1942; vice consul econ. sect. Am. embassy, Rome, Italy, 1944-45; asst. prof. econs. Elmhurst Coll., 1942-44; asst. prof., then prof. econs. Coll. Commerce, DePaul U., 1945-46; mem. faculty Coll. Bus. Adminstrn., U. Ill., 1947—, prof. econs., 1957—; vis. prof. Lake Forest (Ill.) Coll., U. Cal. at Los Angeles, Ind. U., Coll. City N.Y., U. Wis. Mem. Am. Econ. Assn. Author: The Manchester School of Economics, 1960; Economic Liberalism, 1965. Editor: (with E.T. Weiler) Economic Policy, 3d edit., 1961. Home: 5426 Ridgewood Ct Chicago IL 60615

GRAMS, BOB, cartoonist; Cartoonist Balt. News. Office: Lombard and South Sts Baltimore MD 21203*

GRANATELLI, ANTHONY, corp. exec.; b. Dallas, 1923. Pres. STP Corp., Paxton Products Co. Home: 25 Bridlewood Rd Northbrook IL 60062 Office: 125 Oakton St Des Plaines IL 60018*

GRANBERRY, EDWIN PHILLIPS, educator, author; b. Meridian, Miss., Apr. 18, 1897 s. James Asaph and Elizabeth Jane (Phillips) G.; student U. Fla., 1916-18; A.B., Columbia, 1920; postgrad. Harvard, 1922-24; D.Litt., Rollins Coll., 1943; m. Mabel Leflar, Mar. 22, 1924; childrenEdwin Phillips, Julian Maddux, Hal Maurice. Asst. prof. Romance langs. Miami U., Oxford, O., 1920-22; master Latin and French, Stevens Sch., Hoboken, N.Y., 1925-32; Irving Bacheller prof. creative writing Rollins Coll., Winter Park, Fla., -, writer-in-residence, 1970. Served with USMCR, World War I. Recipient O. Henry Meml. prize for best short-short story in Am. mags., 1932. Mem. Authors League Am., Kappa Alpha. Club: Harvard Central Florida. Author: The Ancient Hunger, 1927; Strangers and Lovers, 1928; The Erl King, 1930; A Trip to Czardis, 1967; (plays) Hitch Your Wagon to a Star, 1924; The Falcon, 1950. Translator: L'Amour Nuptial (A Man's Life), 1931; La Belle Journee (A Lover's Return), 1933. Home: 201 Phelps Av Winter Park FL 32789

GRANBERY, EDWIN CARLETON, Jr., architect; b. Bklyn., Apr. 21, 1913; s. Edwin Carleton and Julia Kinport (Barr) G.; B.A., Yale, 1935, B.F.A., 1938; s. Diana Allyn, Feb. 8, 1942; children—Joya Weld, Pamela, Carleton Allyn. Architect, James Gamble Rogers, N.Y.C., 1937, Norman Bel Geddes, N.Y.C., 1938, John Russell Pope, N.Y.C., 1939, Philip L. Goodwin, N.Y.C., 1940, Coolidge-Granbery, New Haven, 1946-47, Carleton Granbery, 1948-63, Granbery Cash & Assos., New Haven, 1964-69, Carleton Granbery Assos., New Haven, 1970—. Pres., chmn. bd. Norwich Water Power Co., Norwich, Conn., 1955-63; instr. design Yale, 1946-47; cons. in field. Head div. United Fund, New Haven, 1958-59; mem. Guilford Charter Commn., 1960, Citizens Action Com., New Haven, 1956-70; chmn. Urban Beautification Com., New Haven, 1967-70, Conn. Beautification Com., 1968. Mem. Republican Town Com., Guilford, Conn., 1952-70. Bd. dirs. Day Prospect Hill Sch., New Haven. Served to lt. comdr. USNR, 1941-45. Recipient awards excellence archtl. design Boston Arts Festival, 1958, New Haven Festival Arts, 1960, Am. Fedn. Arts, 1960, Conn. Bldg. Congress, 1966, 68, 71, Am. Assn. Sch. Adminstrs., 1960-64. Mem. A.I.A. (chmn. com. 1967), Conn., N.Y. (award 1968) assns. architects, Zeta Psi. Episcopalian. Clubs: New Haven Lawn; Sachem's Head Yacht (commodore Guilford 1971—); Yale (N.Y.C.). Contbr. articles to profl. jours. Works include Yale University Press, Foote Sch., New Haven, Crown St. Parking Garage, Quinnpiac Sch., Christ Ch. Parish House and Rectory, others. Home: Old Quarry Leetes Island Guilford CT 06437 Office: 112 Whitney Av New Haven CT 06510

GRAND, GORDON, Jr., chem. ofcl.; b. Orange, N.J., Mar. 14, 1917; s. Gordon and Emma (Dill) G.; grad. The Hill Sch., 1934; B.A., Yale, 1938; LL.D., Harvard, 1941; m. Ruth Young, Feb. 27, 1943; children—Minette, Gordon III, Lorna, Diana, Timothy Grand. Tchr. Millbrook (N.Y.) Sch., 1938-39; admitted to N.Y. bar, 1943, to practice before U.S. Supreme Ct.; lawyer Spence, Hotchkiss, Parker & Duryee, N.Y.C., 1946-48; counsel Rep. mems. Ways and Means Com., U.S. Congress, 1948-52; clk. Ways and Means Com., 83d Congress, 1953; asst. to pres. Olin Industries, Inc., 1954-55, corporate v.p., 1955-63, vice chmn. bd., exec. v.p., 1964-65, pres., chief exec. officer, 1965—, chmn., 1966-67; dir. Nat. Starch & Chem. Co., 1st Nat. City Bank, Prudential Ins. Co. America, Squibb Beechnut. Gov. Young Rep. Club N.Y.C., 1947-48. Trustee, vice chmn. Tax Found., Inc. Served to maj. U.S. Army Res., ret. Decorated Bronze Star medal; 2 croix de Guerre (France). Clubs: Metropolitan (Washington); Links, Yale (N.Y.C.). Author: Federal Legislative Process, 1951; Proposals for Revising the Tax System, 1954. Home: Knollwood Dr Greenwich CT 06830 Office: 120 Long Ridge Rd Stamford CT 06904

GRAND, JOHN LOUIS ROCHON, architect, educator; b. Washington, Nov. 12, 1909; s. Jean Louis and Reine Agnes (Rochon) G.; student George Washington U., 1926-28; B.S., Catholic U. Am., 1931. A.M., 1932; Certificate in architecture Beaux Arts Inst. Design, 1933; postgrad. U.S. Dept. Agr. Grad. Sch., 1936, Columbia, summer 1938, Art Students League, 1938; studied under Seward Hume Rathbun, 1924-26, Frederick V. Murphy, 1928-32, Frederick Kiesler, 1938; m. Winifred Mary Metcalfe, June 14, 1939; childrenJeanne Metcalfe, Kathleen Rochon. Draftsman Murphy and Omsted, Washington, 1929-32; asst. architect Allied Architects, Office Q.M. Gen., War Dept., Upman and Adams, Waddy B. Wood, 1932-35; head exhbns. Housing div., PWA, 1935-36; pvt. practice, Washington, 1936-37; faculty, U. Fla., Gaineille, 1937—, prof. architecre, 1947—, head dep., 1948-56. Served to capt., Corps Engrs., U.S. Army, 1942-46. Registered architect, D.C., Fla. Mem. Soc. Beaux Arts Architects (asso.), Beaux Arts Inst. Design (hon.), A.I.A. (Fla. No. chpt. v.p. 1950, 56; dir. 1951, 53-55, pres. 1952, sec. 1961-69, treas. South Atlantic regional council 1957-59, treas. Fla. dist. 1959-61), Fla. Assn. Architects (dir. 1949, 53). Home: 1908 NW 10th Av Gainesville FL 32601

GRAND, JOSEPH H., lawyer; b. Luck, Poland, Aug. 24, 1896 s. Mitchell and Ida (Cotlar) G.; student Brown U.; LL.B., Washington U., 1919; m. Evalyne Schnepf, Aug. 15, 1920; children—Judith (Mrs. Jerome Rubenstein), Ruth (Mrs. Charles Decker), Paul Robert. Admitted to Mo. bar, 1918; practice in St. Louis; sr. partner Jones, Hocker, Gladney & Grand and successor firms, 1937-56, Grand Peper, Martin & Roudebush and successor firms, 1957-65; counsel Bryan, Cave, McPheeters & McRoberts, 1966-; city atty. University

City, 1924- 31; instr. Mo. statutory law City Coll. Law and Finance, 1927-31; pres., gen. counsel, dir. Mo. Natural Gas Co.; v.p., gen. counsel, dir. Commerce Bank of University City; dir., treas., asst. sec. counsel Mt. Olive & Staunton Coal Co.; dir. Mo. Utilities Co. Mem. Am. Bar Assn., Mo. Bar, Bar Assn. St. Louis, Phi Delta Phi. Home: 220 N Kingshighway St Louis MO 63108 Office: Boatmen's Bank Bldg St Louis MO 63101

GRAND, STANLEY IRWIN, govt. ofcl.; b. N.Y.C., Aug. 7, 1920; s. Morris and Dora (Smerling) G.; Ph.B., U. Wis., 1941; div.; childrenStanley Irwin, Jon Thomas, Robert James. Field asst. Social Security Bd., Madison, Wis., 1941-43; economist OPA, 1943-44; newswriter Office Coordinator Interam. Affairs, 1944; regional specialist Am. Republics affairs Dept. State, 1945-48; press officer Am. embassy, Lima, Peru, 1948-50; asst. to asst. sec. state for Interam. Affairs, Dept. State, 1950- 55; 1st sec. Am. embassy, Rio de Janeiro, Brazil, 1955-56; dept. head Fgn. Service Inst., 1956-58; polit. officer, disarmament and outer space in UN, Dept. State, 1958-59; fgn. affairs cons. to Senator Lyndon B. Johnson, 1960; dep. asst. adminstr. capital devel. AID, 1965-66; asst. dir. AID Mission to Argentina, 1966-70; asst. dir. Office Devel. Resources, Bur. Inter-Am. Affairs-Bur. for Latin Am., Washington, 1970—. Mem. U.S. del. U.S.-Brazil meeting to renegotiate Bilateral Civil Air Agreement, 1957; adviser U.S. del. 13th Gen. Assembly UN, 1958, U.S. del. UN ad hoc com. outer space, 1959, 14th Gen. Assembly UN, 1959, Inter-Am. Nuclear Energy Commn., 1959, UN Disarmament Commn., 1959, NATO Parliamentarians Meeting, Paris, 1960, 3d meeting bd. govs. Interam. Devel. Bank, Buenos Aires, Argentina, 1962; U.S. observer 2d meeting bd. govs. Central Am. Bank Econ. Integration; Managua, Nicaragua, 1962; mem. U.S.-Puerto Rican Status Commn., Washington; U.S. del. 1st Inter-Am. Coop. Conf., Buenos Aires, 1968. Served with AUS, 1944-45; Italy. Life mem. Wis. Union, U. Wis. Clubs: Nat. Press, Internat. (Washington); Yacht of Argentina; University of Buenos Aires. Office: LA/DR AID Washington DC 20523

GRANDIN, THOMAS B., writer, bus. analyst, radio sales exec., photographer; b. Cleve., July 19, 1907; s. George Wilbert and Mabel Gordon (Burnham) G.; grad. Kent (Conn.) Sch., 1926; B.A., Yale, 1930; postgrad. Ecole des Sciences Politiques, Paris (France), 1931, U. Berlin (Germany), 1932; m. Natalia Parligras, Feb. 8, 1940 (dec.); children—Thomas, George, Natalia; m. 2d, Beulah Thompson Paul, Mar. 21, 1970. Research analysis and writing, 1933-38, on railroad and truck transp. for Internat. C. of C., on internat. finance for Council on Fgn. Relations, on polit. use of radio and techniques of persuasion for Rockefeller Found.'s Geneva Research Centre; spl. corr. in France for C.B.S., 1938, covering Munich crisis; bus. rep. and chief corr. C.B.S., France, 1939-40; chief editor Fgn. Broadcast Intelligence Service, Fed. Communications Commn., 1942-43, dir. operations in U.S. and abroad, confidential govt. mission to Algeria, Tunisia, Italy, Egypt, Turkey, India and England; war corr. Am. Broadcasting Co., 1944, officially qualified U.S. Army parachutist, broadcast all U.S. networks first eyewitness radio report Normandy landings, Omaha beachhead; apptd. spl. asst. to dir. of news ABC, 1945; account exec. D'Arcy Advt. Co., 1946; bus. analyst Soc. Savs., Cleve., 1947-48; nat. fleet sales mgr. Hull-Dobbs, Inc., 1949-50; now engaged in writing and freelance photography. Club: Nat. Press (Washington). Author: The Political Use of Radio, 1939, also mag. articles and lectrs. Address: 290 S Alu Rd Wailuku HI 96793

GRANDJANY, MARCEL, harpist, composer; b. Paris, France, Sept. 3, 1891; s. Eugene and Marie Jeanne (Hugo) G.; mus. edn. Nat. Conservatory Music, Paris, 1900-12; studied composition with Taudou and Vidal, harp with Renié and Hasselmans; m. Georgette H. Boulanger, May 20, 1919; 1 son, Bernard. Came to U.S., 1936, naturalized, 1945. Debut as concert artist on harp, Paris, Jan. 24, 1909; played in recitals and with orchs. throughout France; London debut, 1922; N. Y. debut at Aeolian Hall, 1924, later soloist with N.Y. Symphony Orch.; annual tours, Europe, U.S. and Can.; head harp dept. Fontainebleau (France) Summer Sch., 1921-35; head harp dept. Juilliard Sch. Music, N.Y.C., 1938—; gave Master Classes Conservatoire de Musique, Province Que., Montreal, 1943-63; mem. faculty Manhattan Sch. Music, 1956-66. Founder Am. Harp Soc., 1962. Mem. A.S.C.A.P. Club: Bohemians. Prin. compositions include: Aria in classic style for harp and string orch.; Poem for harp, horn and orch.; Rhapsodie for harp; The Colorado Trail, Fantaisie for harp; Children's Hour, suite for harp; Fughetta and Divertissement for harp; Cadenza for the Handel harp Concerto in B flat; Cadenza for the Mozart Concerto for Flute and Harp; Realization of the Sonata for Harp by C. Ph.E. Bach, 1964. Address: 235 W 71st St New York City NY 10023

GRANDY, CYRUS WILEY, banker; b. Norfolk, Va., Mar. 22, 1920 s. Cyrus Wiley and Mary Carter (Randolph) G.; grad. Episcopal High Sch., Alexandria, Va., 1939; student U. Va., 1939-41; m. Ann Sterrett, Nov. 13, 1943; childrenCarter Randolph, Cyrus Wiley V., Hatch Dent Sterrett. With Nat. Bank Commerce, Norfolk, 1941-42; with Office Coordinator Information and successor, OSS, 1942-45; with Investment Corp. Norfolk (co. name changed to United Va. Mortgage Corp.), 1945-, v.p., 1956-64, pres., 1964-; v.p. Investment Corp. Va., 1960- 64, pres., 1964-68; dir. Mut. Assurance Soc. Va. (Richmond), Norfolk- Justice Ins. Corp., Charters Devel. Corp., United Va. Bank, Seaboard Nat., Property Mgmt. Corp., Forbes Candy Co., Williamsburg Va. Trustee, treas. Norfolk Mus. Arts and Scis., Norfolk Acad.; trustee Norfolk Gen. Hosp. (pres. 1968- 70); chmn. bd. Renewal, Inc.; v.p. Norfolk Historic Found.; v.p., trustee Mary F. Ballentine Home Aged, Norfolk, Howard Assn., Norfolk; bd. dirs. Tidewater Cancer Soc., Norfolk, United Communities Fund , Navy YMCA, Norfolk, Order Cape Henry 1607, Hampton Roads chpt. Navy League U.S. Mem. Newcomen Soc. N. Am. Episcopalian (past sr. warden). Clubs: Norfolk Yacht and Country (pres. 1962-64), Harbor (Norfolk); Princess Anne Country (Virginia Beach). Home: 1421 W Princess Ann Rd Norfolk VA 23507 Office: 215 E Plume St Norfolk VA 23510

GRANELLI, GERALD JOHN JERRY, musician; b. San Francisco, Dec. 30, 1940; s. Jack and Ida (Icardi) G.; student San Francisco State Coll., 1958-60; m. Jacqueline Giorgi, Nov. 27, 1960; 1 son, J. Anthony. With Vince Guaraldi Trio, 1962-, John Handy, 1965, Denny Zeitlin Trio, 1964-67, Earl Hines, 1965, John Hendricks 1965-66, Mose Allison, 1965-67, Ornette Colman, 1968; original partner in devel. and orgn. Light Sound Dimension, 1968; cons., tchr. San Francisco rock groups. Home: 802 Camelia St Berkeley CA 94710 Office: 448 Shotwell St San Francisco CA 94110

GRANEY, MAURICE RICHARD, univ. dean; b. Indpls., Apr. 1, 1907; s. John Richard and Mary Ann (Sullivan) G.; B.S. in Indsl. Edn., Purdue, 1935, M.S., 1937, Ph.D., 1942; m. Catherine Connor, Sept. 28, 1935; children-Catherine Loretta (Mrs. Allen Drexier), Maurice Richard, David John (dec.). From instr. to asst. prof. gen. engring. Purdue U., 1935-43, head div. tech. insts., 1943-50, head dept. indsl. mgmt., also dir. indsl. mgmt. ednl. services, 1952-56; supt. edn. and tng. Inland Steel Co., Chgo., 1950-51; dean Sch. Engring., U. Dayton, 1956—. Sch. and curricular examiner North Central Assn. Colls. and Secondary Schs., 1956—, Engrs. Council Profl. Devel., 1947—; chmn. sub- com. tech. insts. of council, 1956-60. Trustee Engrs. Found. Ohio, 1964—; pres. Engring. and Sci. Inst. Dayton, 1970—; trustee Sinclair Community Coll., 1965—. Registered profl. engr., Ohio. Mem. Am. Soc. Engring. Edn. (gen. council 1960-61), A.A.A.S., Nat. Soc. Profl. Engrs. (chmn. bd. trustees for inst. for certification of engring. technicians 1963-64), Newcomen Soc., Sigma Xi, Tau Beta Pi. Roman Catholic. Clubs: Engineers (pres. 1966-67), Rotary (pres. 1969- 70) (Dayton, Ohio). Author: The Technical Institute, 1964. Contbr. articles profl. jours. Home: 3164 Ridgeway Rd Dayton OH 54419

GRANGAARD, BERNHARD CLARENCE, banker; b. Rogers, N.D., Apr. 5, 1911; s. Melvin O. and Agnes (Brusegaard) G.; J.D., U. Minn., 1933; m. Mary Pettit, June 13, 1936; children—Robert P., Richard C., Carol Ruth. Credit investigator Fed. Res. Bank Mpls., 1933-40; cashier First Nat. Bank, Windom, Minn., 1941- 42; asst. cashier Nat. Bank S.D., Sioux Falls, 1943-44; cashier First Nat. Bank Grand Forks, N.D., 1944-45; asst. v.p. Seattle-First Nat. Bank, 1946-51, v.p., 1951-62; chmn., pres., dir. Central Nat. Bank and Trust Co., Des Moines, 1962—; pres. Central Nat. Bancshares, Inc., Ia. Bus. Devel. Credit Corp.; dir. Hawkeye Security Ins. Co., Northeastern Ins. Co., United Security Ins. Co. Mem. Greater Des Moines Com.; mem. bd. Des Moines Indsl. Bur. Trustee Drake U. Mem. Ia. Bankers Assn., Assn. Res. City Bankers, Des Moines C. of C. (dir.), Phi Delta Theta, Phi Alpha Delta. Lutheran. Clubs: Des Moines, Wakonda (Des Moines). Home: 20 37th St Des Moines IA 50312 Office: Central Nat Bank and Trust Co Des Moines IA 50304

GRANGER, CARL VICTOR, med. educator; b. Bklyn., Nov. 26, 1928; s. Carl V. and Marie (Henson) G.; A.B., Dartmouth, 1948; M.D., N.Y.U., 1952; m. Helen Bolden, Feb. 9, 1951; children—Glenn, Marilyn. Intern Meadowbrook Hosp., Hempstead, N.Y., 1952-53, resident pathology, 1953; gen. practice medicine, Huntington, N.Y., 1954; resident phys. medicine and rehab. Walter Reed Gen. Hosp., 1955-58; asst. chief phys. medicine Letterman Gen. Hosp., 1958-61; instr. to asst. prof. phys. medicine Yale, 1961-67, asso. clin. prof. phys. medicine and rehab., 1967-68; prof., chmn. dept. physl. and rehab. medicine Tufts U., 1968—; physiatrist in chief Rehab. Inst. of New Eng. Med. Center Hosps.; lectr., cons. Mem. med. adv. bd. Nat. Multiple Sclerosis Soc.; survey cons. Commn. Accreditation of Rehab. Facilities. Served to maj. AUS, 1954-61. Diplomate Am. Bd. Phys. Medicine and Rehab. Fellow Am. Acad. Phys. Medicine and Rehab. (gov. 1970); mem. Conn. Soc. Phys. Medicine (pres. 1966-68), Am., Mass. heart assns., Am. Congress Rehab. Medicine, Am. Assn. Electromyography and Electrodiagnosis (pres. 1968-69), A.M.A., Am. Rehab. Found., Internat. Rehab. Med. Assn. Contbr. articles profl. jours. Home: 16 Beechwood St Cohasset MA 02025 Office: 185 Harrison Av Boston MA 02111

GRANGER, DAVID, investment banker; b. N.Y.C., June 26, 1903; s. David and Felicia (Newton) G.; student Phillips Exeter Acad., 1917-19; Ph.B., Yale, 1924; student Christ's Coll., Cambridge (Eng.) U., 1924-25, U. Caen, 1926; m. M. Lee Mason, May 5, 1950; 1 son, Mason. Partner, Granger & Co., N.Y.C., 1926-, sr. partner, 1946-; dir. 642 Park Corp. Mem. N.Y. Stock Exchange, 1926—. Bd., dir. Southampton Hosp.; alumni council Phillips Exeter Acad.; adv. council Grosvenor Neighborhood House, N.Y.C.; trustee St. Luke's Hosp., N.Y.C.: v.p. Museum City N.Y.; mem. exec. comm. Repertory Theater of Lincoln Center Guild; adv. council Victoria Home for Aged, Ossining, N.Y. Served from 1st lt. to maj., USAAF, 1942- 45. Decorated Order Brit. Empire. Mem. English-Speaking Union (nat. v.p.), St. George's Soc. (v.p.), Pilgrims U.S. Episcopalian (vestry). Clubs: Church (past trustee, v.p.), Yale, University, Brit. Luncheon, City Midday, Metropolitan Opera (N.Y.C.); Bath (London); Nat. Golf Links Am.; Shinnecock Hills Golf (Southampton, N.Y.); Travellers (Paris); Lyford Cay (Nassau, Bahamas). Home: 640 Park Av New York City NY 10021 Office: 111 Broadway New York City NY 10006

GRANGER, JEFFREY SOLON, stockbroker; b. N.Y.C., June 21, 1891; s. David and Mimmie (Neuburn) G; student N.Y. Mil. Acad., Corwall-on-the-Hudson, 1903-05, Phillips-Exeter Acad., 1905-09; Ph.B., Brown U., 1913; LL.B., Columbia, 1916; m. Carolyn Sears, Apr. 5, 1921; children-Ann (Mrs. Andrew Laszlo), Jeffrey Sears. Mng. and sr. partner Granger & Co., 1919—; pres., chmn. bd. Fed. Match Corp. 1928-29; chmn. bd. Harvill Corp., Los Angeles, 1944-56; dir. Dempster Investment Co., Evanston, Ill.; mgr. and partner Granger Ranches, Ennis, Mont., pres. Indian Creek Ditch Co., Cameron Ditch Co., Mont. Served as 2d lt. U.S. Army, 1917-19. Mem. Am. Stock Exchange, Chgo. Bd. Trade, N.Y. Produce Exchange, Commodity Exchange, Am. Arbitration Assn. (arbitrator), Mil. Order World Wars, N.E. Soc., St. George's Soc. N.Y., Phillips-Exeter Alumni Assn. Clubs: Brown U. (pres.), Touchdown, Church, Bankers Am. (N.Y.C.); Riverside Country (Bozeman, Mont.); Turf and Field. Home: 1155 Park Av New York City NY 10028 Office: 111 Broadway New York City NY 10006

GRANGER, LESTER B., social service administr.; b. Newport News, Va., Sept. 16, 1896; s. William Randolph and Mary (Turpin) G.; grad. Dartmouth, 1918; postgrad. N.Y. U., 1921; profl. studies, N.Y. Sch. Social Work, 1925; D.H.L. (hon.), Dartmouth, 1946, Wilberforce U., 1947; LL.D., Oberlin Coll., 1952, Morris Brown Coll., 1952, Va. State Coll., 1953; D.H.L., Columbia, 1954; m. Harriet Forrester Lane, Aug. 11, 1923. Extension worker N.J. State Manual Sch., Bordentown, 1922-34; workers' ednl. sec. Nat. Urban League, 1934-38; sec. on Negro welfare Welfare Council of N.Y.C., 1938-40; asst. exec. sec. Nat. Urban League, 1940-41, exec. dir., 1941-61; Edgar B. Stern distinguished vis. prof. Dillard U., New Orleans, 1962-66; vis. prof. urban sociology, 1966—. Mem. President's com. on Equal Opportunity in Armed Services; chmn. Fed. Adv. Council on Employment Security. Decorated comdr. Royal Order of Phoenix (Greece); recipient Navy Medal for Distinguished Civilian Service, Pres.'s Medal for Merit. Vice pres. Am. Assn. Social Workers, 1942; pres. Nat. Conf. Social Work, 1952, Internat. Conf. Social Work, 1961; hon. pres. Internat. Council Social Welfare, 1964; bd. dirs. Council Social Work Edn. Home: Congress Dr New Orleans LA 70126

GRANGER, SHELTON B., educator; b. Harrisburg, Pa., Feb. 21, 1921; s. Augustus T. and Katherine (Harris) G.; A.B., Howard U., 1942; M.S., Columbia, 1947; m. Dorothy Steele, June 18, 1943; children—Carol (Mrs. B.C.M. Nesmith), Katherine B. (Mrs. P.H. Cosby), Diane L., Shelton H., Richelle G. Field worker with N.Y. Urban League, 1946-47; dir. indsl. activities Cleve. Urban League, 1947-51; exec. dir. Mpls. Urban League, 1951-58; field instr., guest lectr. U. Minn., also Western Res. U., 1951-62; cons. charitable founds., social agys., govt. agys., 1951-62; exec. dir. Cleve. Urban League, 1958-62; dir. youth devel. unit Dept. Health, Edn. and Welfare, Washington, 1962-63, dep. asst. sec. dept., 1965-66, dep. asst. sec. for internat. affairs, 1966-69; asso. prof. polit. sci., cons. on urban affairs Macalester Coll., St. Paul, 1969—; chief of human resources devel. div. Bur. Latin Am., AID, 1963-64. Mem. U.S. Del. 12th Pan. Am. Congress on Children OAS, Argentina, 1963; UN Commn. on Social Devel., 1966, 67, 68, UN Econ. and Social Council, Geneva, 1966. Bd. dirs. Guthrie Theatre Found., St. Paul Health and Welfare Council. Guest lectr. U. Md., 1968. Served to 1st lt. AUS, 1942-46. Recipient citations for civic and pub. service Mpls. Urban League, 1958, City Council Cleve., 1959, Health and Welfare Council Nat. Capital Area, 1967, Washington Urban League, 1967, Urban League Cleve., 1968. Mem. Nat. Assn. Social Workers, Nat., Internat. confs. social welfare, Council Social Work Edn. Club: Internat. (Washington). Home: 1832 Kenwood Pkwy Minneapolis MN 55405 Office: Macalester College St Paul MN 55105

GRANGER, STEWART, (James Lablache Stewart), actor; b. London, Eng., May 6, 1913; s. James and Frederica (Lablache) Stewart; student Epsom Coll., 1926-30, Webber-Douglas Sch. of Dramatic Art, London, 1932-34; m. Elspeth March, Sept. 10, 1938 (div.); children—Jamie, Lindsay; m. 2d, Jean Simmons, Dec. 20, 1950 (div.); m. 3d, Caroline Lecerf, Aug., 1964. Stage actor Hull Repertory Theater, Birmingham Repertory Theater, Malvern Festivals, Old Vic Co., London, 1934-38; in moving pictures in Eng., 1939-49, including Caesar and Cleopatra, Adam and Evalyn; under contract to M-G-M since 1949, pictures include King Solomon's Mines, Scaramouche, Prisoner of Zenda, Salome, Young Bess, All the Brothers Were Valiant, Beau Brummell, Green Fire, Moonfleet, Bhowani Junction, The Last Hunt, The Little Hut, Gun Glory, Sodom and Gomorrah, North to Alaska, Swordsman of Siena, Rampage at Apache Wells, Frontier Hellcat, the Secret Invasion, Flaming Frontier, the Trygon Factor, others.

GRANGER, WILLIAM WOODARD, Jr., food co. exec.; b. Norfolk Va., Mar. 10, 1919; s. William Woodard and Grace (Williams) G.; student Coll. William and Mary, 1938-40; m. Norma White, Sept. 7, 1946; children—Shirley W., Gail P., William Woodard III. With Norfolk Shipbldg. & Dry Dock Corp., 1940; with Beatrice Foods Co., and subsidiaries, 1946—, mgr. Meadow Gold Dairies, Inc., Pitts., 1963-66, regional v.p. Northeastern region, 1966—. Served with AUS, 1942-45. Home; 5 White Fawn Lane Pittsburgh PA 15238 Office: 1050 Freeport Rd Pittsburgh PA 15238

GRANICK, DAVID, economist, educator; b. N.Y.C., Jan. 13, 1926; s. Harry and Ray (Weiss) G.; B.S.S., Coll. City N.Y., 1944; M.A., Columbia, 1948, Ph.D., 1951, certificate Russian Inst., 1949; m. Kaete Loette Boenheim, Sept. 12, 1950; children—Steve, Barbara Liza, Jim Timothy. Asso. prof. econs. Fisk U., 1951-57; asst. prof. econs. Carnegie Inst. Tech., 1957-59; asso. prof. U. Wis., Madison, 1959-62, prof. econs., 1962—. Econ. affairs officer UN Secretariat, summers 1951, 52; research asso. U. N.C., 1953- 54, Russian Research Center, Harvard, 1956-57; sr. research scholar U. Glasgow (Scotland) 1959-60; dir. d'etudes Associe, Ecole Pratique des Hautes Etudes, U. Paris, 1963-64; vis. prof. U. Manchester (Eng.), 1964; exec. sec. U. Wis. Russian Area Program, 1965-66; sr. research fellow European Inst., Columbia, 1966-67. Served with AUS, 1944-46. Social Sci. Research Council fellow, 1949-50; Guggenheim fellow, 1956-57; Fulbright fellow, 1959-60; Internat. Research and Exchanges Bd. fellow, Rumania, Hungary, Poland, 1970-71. Mem. Am. Econ. Assn., Assn. for Study Soviet-Type Econs. (exec. com. 1967-68), Phi Beta Kappa. Rotarian. Author: Management of Industrial Firm in the USSR, 1954; The Red Executive, 1960; The European Executive, 1962; Soviet Metalfabricating and Economic Development, 1967. Contbr. articles to profl. jours. Home: 4249 Manitou Way Madison WI 53711

GRANICK, SAM, biochemist; b. N.Y.C., Feb. 16, 1909; s. Aaron and Dora (Ustin) G.; B.S., U. Mich., 1929, M.S., 1933, Ph.D., 1938; m. Elsa Bachman, 1938; children—Donna, Joel Leonor. Mem. staff Rockefeller Univ., 1938—, mem., prof. biochemistry, 1964—, Harvery lectr., 1949. Mem. Nat. Acad. Scis., Am. Soc. Naturalists (v.p. 1963), Am. Soc. Biol. Chemists, Am. Chem. Soc., Society for Developmental Biology (pres. 1967), Am. Soc. Plant Physiologists, Bot. Soc. Am. Home: 43-17 48th St Long Island City NY 11104 Office: Rockefeller Univ York Av and 67th St New York City NY 10021

GRANIK, HANNAH BELLE, TV and radio producer; b. N.Y.C., Nov. 19, 1909; d. Samuel and Regina (Fallick) Hayne; grad. Brown's Bus. Coll., Bklyn., 1927; m. Theodore Granik, June 7, 1931; children—William Robert, Marian Ruby (Mrs. Stephen Good). Supr., coordinator Youth Wants to Know, 1951—, Am. Forum of the Air, 1928—, All Am. Wants to Know, 1960—, Women Want to Know, 1955—; primitive painter, 1963—. Vice pres. CATV Enterprises, Inc., Riverdale Sect., Bronx, N.Y. Mem. Nat. Council Jewish Women, Friends Brandeis U. Mem. U.S. Reps. Radio and TV Gallery. Mem. B'nai B'rith. Home: 2601 Woodley Pl NW Washington DC 20008 Office: 2660 Woodley Rd NW Washington DC 20008

GRANING, HARALD MARTIN, govt. ofcl., physician; b. Mpls., Feb. 14, 1912; s. Martin Kristian and Laura Elise (Kaaberg) G.; B.S., U. Minn., 1934, B.M., 1937, M.D., 1938; M.P.H., Johns Hopkins, 1940; m. Thelma Dagmar Forus, July 5, 1938; children—Harald Martin, Karen Ann (Mrs. Robert Gardner), George Edward. Commd. USPHS, 1938, asst. surgeon gen., 1963; assigned hosp. service and quarantine, 1940, Pedro, Cal., 1938-39, plague lab., San Francisco, 1940, field epidemiology and exec. officer, 1942-43; dir. Kitsap County Health Dept., Bremerton, Wash., 1941; med. officer civil affairs U.S. Navy, 1944-45; dir. div. local health services Ga. Dept. Health, 1945-47; cancer control cons., New Orleans, 1947-48; chief state and local health services, Washington, 1948-50, regional med. dir. region V, 1951-58, region II, 1958-63, asst. surgeon gen., chief div. hosp. and med. facilities, Washington, 1963-68, dir. health facility planning and constrn. service, 1968—. Recipient Meritorious Service medal USPHS, 1963. Diplomate Am. Bd. Preventive Medicine. Fellow Am. Pub. Health Assn. (sec. joint com. study edn. pub. health 1959—, chmn. health officers sect. 1962-63), Am. Coll. Hosp. Adminstrs. (hon.); mem. A.M.A., Am. Assn. Hosp. Cons. (hon.), Am. Hosp. Assn. (ho. of dels.), Am. Dietetic Assn. (hon.). Home: Route 1 Box 187 Severna Park MD 21146 Office: 5600 Fishers Lane Rockville MD 20852

GRANIT, RAGNAR ARTHUR, neurophysiologist; b. Finland, Oct. 30, 1900; grad. Swedish Normallyceum, Helsinki, Finland, 1919; M.D., Helsinki U., 1927; hon. degrees from Oslo, Oxford, Hong Kong, Loyola U., Chgo., Pisa, others; m. Baroness Daisy Bruun; 1 son, Michael. Docent, Helsinki U., 1932-37, prof. physiology, 1937-40; fellow med. physics Eldridge Reeves Johnson Research Found., U. Pa., 1929-31; mem. staff Royal Caroline Inst., Stockholm, Sweden, 1940-67, emeritus mem., 1967—, prof. neurophysiology, 1946- 67; Thomas Young orator Phys. Soc. London (Eng.), 1945; Silliman lectr. Yale, 1954; Sherrington lectr., London, 1967, Liverpool, 1970; vis. prof. Rockefeller U., N.Y.C., 1956-66, St. Catherine's Coll., Oxford, 1967, Smith-Kettlewell Inst. Med. Sci., San Francisco, 1969, Fogarty Internat. Center, NIH, Bethesda, Md., 1971-72. Co-recipient Nobel prize in medicine, 1967; recipient Donders, Retzius, Sherrington, Purkinje medals; 3d Internat. St. Vincent prize, 1961; Jahre prize Oslo U., 1961. Mem. Royal Swedish Acad. Sci. (pres. 1963-65, v.p. 1965-69), Royal Soc. London (fgn. mem.), Nat. Acad. Sci. (U.S.), Am. Philos. Soc., Indian Acad. Sci. (hon.), Acad. di Med. (hon.) (Turin), Physiol. Soc. Eng., Physiol. Soc. U.S., Am. Acad. Arts and Scis. (hon.), Royal Danish Acad. Sci. Author: Ung Mans Väg till Minerva, 1941; Sensory Mechanism of the Retina, 1947; Receptors and Sensory Perception, 1955; Charles Scott Sherrington, An Appraisal, 1966; Basis of Motor Control, 1970; Regulation of the Discharge of Motoneurons, 1971. Address: 14 Eriksbergsgatan 11430 Stockholm Ö Sweden

GRANNIS, CHANDLER BRINKERHOFF, editor; b. Union Vale, N.Y., May 17, 1912; s. Percy and Maude (Brinkerhoff) G.; A.B., Columbia, 1934; m. Martha Elisabeth Winckler, Oct. 25, 1947; children—John Chandler, Peter Brinkerhoff. Asst., then asso. editor Publishers Weekly, 1936-62, sr. editor, 1962-67, editor-in- chief, 1968-71, editor-at-large, 1971—; dir. R.R. Bowker Co., N.Y.C., 1957-68. Bd. dirs. Mental Health Materials Center, 1965—, pres., 1971—. Served with AUS, 1942-45. Mem. Am. Inst. Graphic Arts, Bibliog. Soc. Am., Book Club Cal., Am. Vets. Com. Democrat. Conglist. Editor, co-author: What Happens in Book Publishing, rev. edit., 1967; editor: Heritage of the Graphic Arts, 1972. Office: 1180 Av Americas New York City NY 10036

GRANRUD, CARL FRITHIOF, lawyer; b. Decorah, Ia., Sept. 13, 1896; s. John E. and Amalie (Olsen) G.; B.A., St. Olaf Coll. 1918; LL.B., Minn. Coll. Law, Mpls., 1921; LL.D., Carthage Coll., 1956, Concordia Theol. Seminary; L.H.D., Wagner Coll.; m. Agnes Bjorneby, Oct. 20, 1920; childrenRobert, Marian, Carolyn. Admitted to Minn. bar, 1921, since practiced in Mpls. Mem. adv. bd. Concordia College, Moorhead. Minn. Chmn. bd. Lutheran Brotherhood. Pres. Ins. Fedn. Minn., 1963-66. Mem. Mpls. C. of C. (v.p., dir), Minn. Bar Assn., Nat. Fraternal Congress Am. (v.p., mem. exec. com.). Clubs: Minneapolis Athletic, Minneapolis, Midland Hills Country. Home: 607 Delaware St SE Minneapolis MN 55414 Office: 527 2d Av S Minneapolis MN 55401

GRANSTROM, MARVIN LEROY, educator; b. Anaconda, Mont., Sept. 25, 1920; s. Carl August and Alida Sophia (Eckstrom) G.; B.S., Morningside Coll., 1942; B.S. in Civil Engring., Ia. State Coll., 1943; M.S. in San. Engring., Harvard, 1947, Ph.D., 1955; m. Ruth Maybelle Olsen, Jan. 1, 1944; childrenDavid Marvin, Kay Ruth, Chris Carl. Engring. aide Soil Conservation Service, Whiting, Ia., 1939; cons. engr., Sioux Falls, S.D., 1946; instr. civil and san. engring. Case Inst. Tech., 1947-49; asso. prof. san. engring. U. N.C., 1949-58; prof. civil engring. Rutgers U., New Brunswick, N.J., 1958—. Research participant Oak Ridge Nat. Labs., 1954; cons. Nat. Engring. Sch., Lima, Peru, 1955-57. Served with USMCR, 1943-46. Research grantee N.C., 1953, NIH, 1954-58, NSF, 1954-63, Army Chem. Center, 1961- 64, surgeon gen. U.S. Army, 1962, Office Water Resources Research, Dept. Interior, 1965; fellow Nat. Found., 1946-47, USPHS, 1952-53. Mem. Am. Chem. Soc., Am. Soc. C.E., Am. Water Works Assn., Am. Water Resources Assn., Tau Beta Pi, Sigma Xi, Delta Omega, Chi Epsilon. Author articles in field. Home: 1796 Watchung Av Plainfield NJ 07060 Office: Rutgers Univ New Brunswick NJ 08903

GRANT, ALAN JULIUS, electronics co. exec.; b. Chgo., Dec. 18, 1925; s. Hugo Bernard and May (Gardner) G.; B.S., Ill. Inst. Tech., 1946, M.S., 1948; grad. Inst. for Mgmt., Northwestern U., 1961; m. Margaret Stewart, Dec. 21, 1946; children—Pamela Rose, Deborah May, Bruce David. Instr. elec. engring. Ill. Inst. Tech., Chgo., 1946-49; with N.Am. Aviation, Inc. (Autonetics), Anaheim, Cal., 1949-64, v.p., gen. mgr. data systems div., 1962-64; pres. guidance and control systems div. Litton Industries, Inc., Woodland Hills, 1964-65; exec. v.p. Lockheed Electronics Co. div. Lockheed Aircraft Corp., Plainfield, N.J., 1965-68, pres., 1968-69, also v.p. parent co.; group v.p., dir. Fairchild Camera and Instrument Corp., Mountain View, Cal., 1969-70; exec. v.p. Aerojet-Gen. Corp., El Monte, Cal., 1970—. Served with USNR, 1944-46. Sigma Xi, Tau Beta Pi, Eta Kappa Nu, Pi Delta Epsilon. Home: 1632 Galaxy Dr Newport Beach CA 92660 Office: 9100 E Flair Dr El Monte CA 91734

GRANT, ARNOLD MONROE, lawyer; b. N.Y.C., Jan. 7, 1908; s. Samuel and Hana (Weinberg) G.; grad. Ethical Culture Grammar Sch., 1920, Dwight Prep. Sch., 1923; B.A., Syracuse U., 1927, LL.B. cum laude, 1929; m. 2d, Bess Myerson, May 1, 1962 (div.); 1 dau., Barbara; children (by previous marriage)—Nancy (Mrs. Mayer), Sally (Mrs. Morse). Admitted to N.Y. bar, 1929, Cal. bar, 1945, D.C. bar, 1962, ICC bar, 1945; in pvt. practice law, specializing in corporate, financial and tax matters, N.Y. and Cal. Dir., Continental Airlines, Inc., Kayser-Roth Corp., Wells, Rich & Greene, Inc., and others. Trustee Syracuse U., St. John's Coll., Annapolis and Santa Fe, Eleanor Roosevelt Meml. Found., Center for Study Dem. Instns.; bd. visitors Law Coll., Syracuse U. Recipient Distinguished Service award Law Coll., Syracuse U., 1963; Human Relations award Am. Jewish Com., 1964; Cum Laude award Syracuse U. Alumni Assn., 1964. Mem. Assn. Bar City N.Y., Justinian Soc., Phi Kappa Phi. Clubs: Harmonie (N.Y.C.); Hollywood Country (N.J.); Tamarisk, Hillcrest (Cal.). Home: 1 Sutton Sq New York City NY 10022 Office: 660 Madison Av New York City NY 10021

GRANT, BEN JOSEPH, editor; b. Dothan, Ala., July 20, 1909; s. Ben Joseph and Ethel (Dowman) G.; B.S., U. Fla., 1931; m. Elizabeth Brubaker, Aug. 9, 1938; children—William Dowman, Richard Martin, Martha Watts (Mrs. Mark Bedner). Staff writer Jacksonville (Fla.) Jour., 1932-35; staff writer A.P., Fla. Bur., 1935- 36, Washington Bur., 1936-42; asso. editor U.S. News and World Report, Washington, 1946-52, asst. exec. editor, 1952-65, asso. exec. editor, 1965-67, mng. editor, 1968-70, exec. v.p., 1970—; dir. U.S. News & World Report, Inc., Nat. Press Bldg. Corp. Served from 1st lt. to maj. USAAF, 1942-46. Decorated Legion of Merit; recipient citation of merit as distinguished alumnus U. Fla., 1953. Clubs: National Press (past pres.), Internat., Kenwood Golf and Country (Washington); Plantation (Hilton Head Island, S.C.). Home: 7000 Orkney Pkwy Bethesda MD 20034 also N Sea Pines Dr Hilton Head Island SC 29928 Office: 2300 N St NW Washington DC 20037

GRANT, CARY, actor; b. Bristol, Eng., Jan. 18, 1904; s. Elias and Elsie (Kingdom) Leach; student Fairfield Acad. Somerset, Eng., 1914-19; m. Virginia Cherill, Feb. 1934 (div. Sept. 1934); m. 2d, Barbara Hutton July 8, 1942 (div. Aug. 1945); m. 3d, Betsy Drake; m. 4th, Dyan Cannon, July 22, 1965 (div.); 1 dau., Jennifer. Came to U.S., 1921, naturalized, 1942. Began as actor in New York, 1921, playing successively in Golden Dawn, Polly, Boom Boom, Wonderful Night, Street Singer, and Nikki; starred in motion pictures Mr. Lucky, Arsenic and Old Lace, Destination Tokyo, None But the Lonely Heart, The Bishop's Wife, I Was a Male War Bride, The Bachelor and the Bobby Soxer, Every Girl Should be Married, Mr. Blandings Builds His Dream House, Crisis, People Will Talk, Room for One More, Monkey Business, Dream Wife, To Catch a Thief, Pride and the Passion, An Affair to Remember, Indiscreet, Houseboat, Kiss Them for Me, North by Northwest, Operation Petticoat, Grass Is Greener, That Touch of Mink, Charade, Father Goose, Walk, Don't Run. Mem. Ch. of Eng. Address: Universal Internat Pictures Universal City CA 91608 ☆

GRANT, CHARLES LEON, govt. ofcl.; b. Chester, S.C., June 14, 1915; s. Leon Mills and Ethel Janie (Lee) G.; student George Washington U., 1936-37, Grad. Sch. U.S. Dept. Agr., 1939-40; m. Nellie Flora Oliver, Sept. 18, 1940; childrenPhyllis Anne, Elizabeth Jane, Charles Wayne. Accountant U.S. Weather Bur., 1935-41; fiscal accountant, budget analyst, asst. to dir. finance and chief div., Office Budget and Finance, Dept Agr., 1941- 53, dep. dir. finance, 1953-57, dir. finance, 1957—. Baptist. Home: 4922 N 27th St Arlington VA 22207 Office: Dept of Agriculture Washington DC 20250

GRANT, CLAUDE WILSON, educator; b. Holbrook, Ida., Aug. 16, 1918; s. Carter Eldrige and Pamela (Smith) G.; student U. Utah, 1936-38, M.S., 1947; student U. So. Cal., 1941-42, Utah State U., 1943; B.S., U. Houston, 1946; Ph.D., U. Minn., 1950; m. Minerva Unice, June 11, 1944; children—Claude Wilson, Renae Lynn. Instr. U. Minn., 1947-49; asst. prof. edn. psychology U. Utah at Salt Lake City, 1949-51, prof., 1955-57, chmn. dept., 1970—, prof., dir. instl. studies, 1965-70; asso. prof. psychology, edn. Syracuse (N.Y.) U., 1951-55; prof. edn. N.Y.U., 1957-65; cons. VA, sch. systems, bus., colls., pvt. social service founds. Served to 1st lt. USAAF, 1943-46. Fellow Am. Psychol. Assn.; mem. Am. Personnel and Guidance Assn., Am. Ednl. Research Assn., Am. Assn. U. Profs. Contbr. articles profl. jours. Home: 5576 Dunbarton Dr Salt Lake City UT 84117

GRANT, DANIEL ROSS, univ. pres.; b. Little Rock, Ark., Aug. 18, 1923; s. James Richard and Gracie (Sowers) G.; B.A., Ouachita Bapt. U., 1945; M.A., U. Ala., 1946; Ph.D., Northwestern U., 1948; m. Betty Jo Oliver, June 17, 1947; children—Carolyn, Shirley, Ross. Asst. prof. polit. sci. Vanderbilt U., 1948-54; asso. prof., 1954-63, prof., 1963-70; pres. Ouachita Bapt. U., 1970—; vis. prof. municipal govt. and planning Thammasat U. (Bangkok), 1958-59; cons. U.S. Adv. Commn. Introgovtl. Relations, 1962-67; asso. dir. Harris County Home Rule Commn., Houston, 1957. Mem. adv. com. federalism and met. govt. Nat. Com. Econ. Devel., 1969—; dir. Urban and Regional Devel. Center of Vanderbilt U., 1969-70. Mem. So. Bapt. Found., 1959-60. Mem. Am., So. polit. sci. assns., Am. Soc. Pub. Adminstrn., Am. Assn. Univ. Profs. Rotarian. Author: The Christian and Politics, 1968; (H.C. Nixon) State and Local Government in America, rev. ed., 1968; (with others) The States and the Metropolis, 1968; Metropolitan Surveys: a Digest, 1958; (with others) Government and Politics: an Introduction to Political Science, rev. edit., 1971; Plan of Metropolitan Government for Nashville and Davidson County, 1956. Home: 1049 N Phelps Circle Arkadelphia AR 71923

GRANT, DANIEL TIMOTHY, coll. pres.; b. Attapulgus, Ga., Sept. 14, 1914; s. Henry Wilgo and Lula (Burney) G.; B.A., Morris Brown Coll., 1939, D.D. (hon.), 1964; M.Ed., Atlanta U., 1949; student Ohio State U., 1951-53; certificate U. Ga., 1968; LL.D. (hon.), Union Bapt. Sem., 1970; m. Emma Slack, May 21, 1941; children—Lula Carolyn, Floyd Goodman, Barbara Ann (Mrs. Jim Adams), Frances Danette. Tchr. Savannah State Coll., 1939-40, Albany State Coll., 1956-57; pres. Daniel Payne Coll., Birmingham, Ala., 1969—. Founder Family Coop. Union, Bainbridge, Ga., 1953. Trustee Morris Brown Coll., 1963-70. Recipient plaque for meritorious service, Ga. Tchrs. and Educators Assn., 1965. Mem. N.E.A., Phi Beta Sigma. Mason. Author: When the Melon is Ripe, 1956. Address: 6415 Washington Blvd Birmingham AL 35212

GRANT, DAVID ALEXANDER, psychologist; b. Des Moines, May 17, 1916; s. Alexander Haswell and Charlotte Elizabeth (David) G.; student Kan. City Jr. Coll., 1934-36; B.A., State U. Ia., 1938; M.A., U. Wis., 1939; Ph.D., Stanford, 1941; m. Mary Lucille Brodie, July 22, 1938; children—Marjorie E. Skuldt, Douglas Henry, Edward Alexander. Prof. psychology U. Wis., 1948-, Clark L. Hull research prof. psychology, 1967—, chmn. dept., 1950-54, 70—; vis. prof. psychology U. Cal. at Berkeley, 1959-60; lectr. Northwestern U., 1948, Stanford, 1949, Columbia, 1953; U. Cal. at Los Angeles, U. So. Cal., 1955. Mem. sect. psychology-anthropology, NRC, 1957-59; study sect. exptl. psychology NIH, 1960—. Social psychologist War Dept., 1944. Fellow Am. Psychol. Assn. (pres. exptl. psychology div. 1961); mem. Am. Statis. Assn., Psychometric Soc., Inst. Math. Statistics, Soc. Exptl. Psychologists, Midwestern (sec.- treas. 1949-52, pres. 1953), Wis. (exec. com.) psychol. assns., Psychonomic Soc. (governing bd. 1960-66, chmn. governing bd. 1965). Clubs: Sierra; Am. Alpine. Author articles psychol. jours. Asso. editor Jour. Exptl. Psychology, 1957-62, editor, 1962-. Cons. editor Psychol. Rev. and Jour. Gen. Psychology. Home: 113 Ely Pl Madison WI 53705

GRANT, DAVID MCMURRAY, educator; b. Oelwein, Ia., Aug. 17, 1913; s. Frederick B. and Ruth (McMurray) G.; B.A., Ia. State Tchrs. Coll., 1935; M.A., U. Ia., 1940; Ph.D., Stanford, 1953, post-doctoral student, 1959; m. Elinor Brokaw, Apr. 3, 1937; childrenGrace Elinor, Virginia Ruth. Tchr. pub. schs., Ia., 1935-40; prof., chmn. dept. speech Hastings (Neb.) Coll., 1940-44; prof., dept. English and speech Cal. State Polytech. Coll., San Luis Obispo, 1950-. Chmn. trustees San Luis Obispo Library, 1960-; mem. San Luis Obispo County chpt. Am. Cancer Soc., 1962-. Served to lt. (j.g.) USNR, 1944-47. Mem. Council Tchrs. English, Am. Speech Assn., Am. Legion Disabled Am. Vets., Pi Kappa Delta, Delta Sigma Rho, Phi Delta Kappa. Presbyn. Mason. Kiwanian. Contbr. articles profl. jours. Home: 290 Chaplin Lane San Luis Obispo CA 93401

GRANT, DAVID MORRIS, educator; b. Salt Lake City, Mar. 24, 1931; s. David L. and Lucille (Greenwood) G.; B.S., U. Utah, 1954, Ph.D., 1957; m. Reva L. Carlow, Sept. 11, 1953; children—David J., Linda, Heidi, Karen, John C. Instr. chemistry U. Ill., 1957-58; asst. prof. chemistry U. Utah, 1958-62, asso. prof., 1962-66, prof., 1966—, chmn. dept., 1962—. Recipient scholastic award, Am. Inst. Chemists, 1954, gold medal, Cal. sect. Am. Chem. Soc., 1969. Research in nuclear magnetic resonance, especially in devel. of expt. and theory of carbon-13 magnetic resonance. Contbr. articles profl. jours. Home: 370 A St Salt Lake City UT 84103 Office: University of Utah Salt Lake City UT 84112

GRANT, DONALD K., constrn. co. exec.; b. Portland, Ore., Oct. 27, 1907; s. Brotherton Wentworth and Janet (McKay) G.; A.B., LL.B., Willamette U., 1929; LL.B., Harvard, 1935; m. Evelyn High Grant, June 15, 1931; children—Judith Allen (Mrs. Arnold V. Allen), Virginia (Mrs. Ted A. Cook), Donald McKay. Admitted to bar; with firm Davis & Harris, Portland, 1929-32, Maguire, Shields & Morrison, Portland, 1935-41; with Guy F. Atkinson Co., 1941—, now v.p.; Mgmt. mem. Nev. Test Site Constrn. Labor Bd., Pres. San Mateo County (Cal.) Community Chest, San Mateo County United Fund, San Mateo County YMCA, Treas., dir. Atkinson Found.; trustee, bd. govs. Willamette U., 1950—; bd. dirs. San Francisco YMCA, 1950—; trustee San Mateo Union High Sch. Dist., 1948-56. Mem. Asso. Gen. Contractors Am. (bd. dirs.). Office: Guy M Atkinson Co 10 W Orange St San Francisco CA

GRANT, EDWARD DONALD, chem. mfg. exec.; b. Glascow, Scotland, June 18, 1897; s. Charles and Jemina (McDonald) G.; came to U.S., 1909, naturalized, 1922; A.B., Austin Coll., Sherman, Tex., 1920, Litt. D., 1933; postgrad. Y.M.C.A. Grad Sch., 1924- 25; M.A., George Peabody Coll. for Tchrs., 1929; L.H.D., Southwestern U. at Memphis, 1954; m. Georgia Voyles, July 14, 1921; 1 son, Edward Donald. Profl. fund raiser, 1920-21; sec. edn. and promotion Fgn. Mission Bd., Presbyn. Ch. in U.S., 1921- 34, also acting sec. Com. on Stewardship and Finance, 1931-35, exec. sec. Bd. Edn., Richmond, Va., 1934-52; mem. personnel bd. City of Richmond, 1950-52; dir. instns. State of La., 1952-58; pres. Grant Chem. Co., 1958-69; chmn. bd. Grant-Lehr Corp., 1962-65; sec.-treas. Gramor Chems., Inc., 1965-68; chmn. bd., pres. Roadways Internat. Corp.; treas. Plasticos Y Estabalizadones, S.A., Mexico. Pres., Baton Rouge YMCA, 1969,70; past pres. Am. Leprosy Missions, Inc.; moderator Presbyn. Ch. in U.S., 1962-63, dir. bd. ch. extension, 1959-67. Recipient Pub. Service award La. Coll., 1954; La. Mental Health award, 1955. Served as 2d lt. U.S. Army, 1918. Mem. Phi Delta Kappa. Democrat. Presbyn. Mason. Author: The Ambassador Supreme, 1933. Del. to Internat. Missionary Council. Madras. India, 1938, to World Council of Christian Edn., Birmingham, Eng., 1947. Home: 638 Carol Marie Dr Baton Rouge LA 70806 Office: 1911 N 4th St Baton Rouge LA 70802

GRANT, EVVA H., editor; b. Rock Island, Ill., Feb. 22, 1913; d. Morris and Ida (Learner) Handelman; A.B., Augustana Coll., 1934; A.M., State U. Ia., 1937; m. Herman Grant, June 5, 1934; 1 son, David. Tchr. pre-sch. and parent edn. St. Louis, 1936-37; asst. editor Nat. Parent-Teacher mag., 1938-40, editor, 1940—, editor-in-chief Nat. Congress Parents-Tchrs.; interpreter on Baxters radio program sponsored by P.T.A. and NBC. Vis. Lectr. Northwestern U., summers 1945, 46, cons. pub. adv. bd. FOA, 1954; gen. council U.S., nat. com. Internat. Union Family Orgns.; mem. bd. cons. Mental Health Materials Center. Mem. Ednl. Assn. Am. (pres. 1941-43, exec. com. 1943-45), Nat. Assn. Nursery Edn. (adv. bd. 1945-47), Am. Child Guidance Found. (adv. bd.), N.E.A., Delta Kappa Gamma, Sigma Xi. (asso.). Author: Parents and Teachers as Partners, 1971. Cons. editor; Community Life in a Democracy (Nat. Congress Parents and Teachers), 1942; editor: Guiding Children as They Grow, 1959; PTA Guide to What's Happening in Education, 1965. Contbr. to ednl. jours. Home: 2600 N Lakeview Chicago IL 60614 Office: 700 N Rush St Chicago IL 60611

GRANT, FRANCES RUTH, editor, lecturer; b. Abiquiu, N.M.; d. Henry and Sarah (Spiro) Grant; ed. Hunter Coll. High Sch., Barnard Coll. and Sch. Journalism, Columbia U., 1918; unmarried. Studied music with Albert Von Doenhoff, Ernest Bloch, and others, 1910-21. Dir. Roerich Museum, 1921-27, 1927-37 (with its Central Asiatic Expdn., 1928). Sent by Roerich Museum to all Latin-American nations to study plan for Inter-Am. cultural interchange; brought back pioneer contemporary Latin-Am. Art Exhibit, 1929, and arranged subsequent expositions of Latin-Am. Art. Lectured Inst. for Advanced Edn. (Brazil), Nat. Museum (Buenos Aires), U. of Santiago (Chile), Nat. Acad. Peru, Nat. Museum Bolivia, Ministry Edn. Mexico, 1930, Nat. Acad. Bogota, repeated tour, 1941 (also corr. for N. Am. Newspaper Alliance); instrumental in negotiation of Treaty for Protection of Cultural Sites (signed by 21 Republics of Am.) in 1935; sec. Internat. League for Rights of Man (U.N. consultative orgn.); sec.-gen. Inter-Am. Assn. for Democracy and Freedom. Recipient Gold Medal award, Republic, Costa Rica, 1955; decorated Dame. Order of Liberation, Spanish Rep. Govt., Order Condor of Andes (Bolivia), Order Francisco Morazan, the Liberator (Honduras), Grand Officer Order Merit of Duarte, Sanchez & Mella (Dominican Republic). Pres. Pan- Am. Women's Assn. since its founding, 1930; shortwave news commentator to Latin Am. over C.B.S., 1938-40; spl. programs, shortwave WRUL, 1940-41 (in Spanish); awarded hon. membership by the Ateneo of Caracas, Comite Cultural Argentina, Federacion de Madres de Peru, Decorated Commander Order of the Liberator (Venezuela). Asso. editor, Musical American, 1918-22; managing editor Super Market Merchandising, 1938-57. Author and editor of books. Editor Hemispherica (monthly rev. directed to Latin Am). Contbr. of articles. Home: 310 West End Av New York City NY 10023 Office: 20 W 40th St New York City NY 10018 ☆

GRANT, FRANCIS COMMISKEY, shipping co. exec.; b. Ft. Sam Houston, Tex., May 1, 1913; s. Walter S. and Marjorie (Commiskey) G.; A.B., Yale, 1936; m. Penelope G. Hunter, Mar. 21, 1947; 1 son, Matthew S. With U.S. Lines, 1947-69, v.p., dir., 1964-69; chmn. bd. pres. Rice Trailer Agy., Inc., Monkton, Md., 1969—; ind. marine and labor cons. Gen. chmn. marine sect. Nat. Safety Council, 1966-67. Home: Cold Comfort Farm Monkton MD 21111 Office: PO Box 23 Monkton MD 21111

GRANT, FRED RUSSELL, mfg. co. exec.; b. San Francisco, Oct. 17, 1920; s. Fred E. and Antoinette (Meyers) G.; A.B. summa cum laude, U. San Francisco, 1942; m. Celeste J. Healy, May 11, 1946. Jr. accountant Rheem Mfg. Co., San Francisco, 1945-57, asst. comptroller, 1957-63, comptroller, 1963-68, v.p., 1969—. Served with AUS, 1942-45. Mem. Nat. Assn. Accountants (past pres. San Francisco chpt.), Am. Accounting Assn., Financial Execs. Inst. Republican. Roman Catholic. Home: 69 Morningside Dr San Francisco CA 94132 Office: 801 Chesley Av Richmond CA 94804

GRANT, HAROLD WINFIELD, aviation and telecommunications cons., ret. air force officer; b. Louisville, Oct. 16, 1906; s. William Edward and Daisy Dean (Nolen) G.; B.S., Northwestern U., 1928; m. Dorothy Louise Silvis, Mar. 21, 1934; childrenMichael Winfield, Lina, Bruce Dundon. Commd. 2d lt. AC, U.S. Army, 1929, advanced through grades to lt. gen., 1962; vice comdr. Japan Air Def. Force, 1952-54; dep. comdr. Fifth Air Force, 1954-55, U.S. Taiwan Def. Command, 1955-57; dep. for operations Air Def. Command, 1957-58; dir. communications-electronics Hdqrs. USAF, 1958-60, dir. telecommunications, 1960-61; comdr. Air Force Communications Service, 1961-62; dep. adminstr. FAA, Washington, 1962-65; ret., 1965; dir. telecommunications policy Dept. Def., 1965-70; aviation and telecommunications cons., 1970—. Decorated D.S.M., Legion Merit with 2 oak leaf clusters, FAA decoration for exceptional service (U.S.); Order British Empire; Ulchi Distinguished Mil. Service medal with gold star (Korea); Medal Cloud and Banner (China); Comdr. Cross with star Icelandic Order of Falcon. Mem. Quiet Birdmen, Beta Theta Pi. Home: 2420 44th St NW Washington DC 20007

GRANT, HERBERT B., trust co. exec.; b. Norwalk, Conn., 1917; grad. Union Coll., 1939. Sr. v.p. County Trust Co., White Plains, N.Y. Trustee Council for the Arts in Westchester, Inc., Hackley Sch. Home: Indian Hill Rd Bedford NY 10506 Office: 235 Main St White Plains NY 10602*

GRANT, HOMER HAMILTON, Jr., pres. tech. inst.; b. Wenatchee, Wash., Feb. 12, 1908; s. Homer Hamilton and Georgia (Sanders) G.; B.S. in Elec. Engring., U. Wash., 1932, M.S. in Elec. Engring., 1933, E.E., 1946; Sc.D., Northrop Inst. Tech., 1965; m. Beth Huntley, Jan. 7, 1933; 1 dau., Sydney Gail (Mrs. George K. McCauley). Mgr., Western Union Telegraph Co., 1926-33; chief div. research and statistics, research engr. Wash. State Dept. Pub. Service, 1934-39; statistician Bonneville Power Adminstrn., U.S. Dept. Interior, 1939-40; on leave to Nat. Resources Com. and Wash. State Planning Council, 1937; research engr. charge transp. research div. and transp. economist Cal. Pub. Utilities Commn., 1940-43; asst. to v.p. and gen. mgr. transp. engr. Key System, Oakland, Cal., 1943- 46; cons. engr. in mgmt., 1946—; prof. indsl. engring. U. So. Cal., 1948-67, head dept., 1954-67, mem. exec. com. sch. engring., 1953-62, acting dean sch. engring., 1959-60, asso. dean, 1960-62, acting head dept. elec. engring., 1960-62; pres. Northrop Inst. Tech., Inglewood, 1967—. Pres. Aquatic Research, Inc., and Climax Mfg. Co., 1959-62. Cons. on indsl. engring., gen. mgmt., feasibility, transp., electric rates, and/or value engring.; tech. research evaluator U.S. Dept. Transp., 1967- -; cons. Hanford Atomic Products operation Gen. Electric Co., 1957; dir. Tri-County Sanitation Study, Ore., 1958; cons. U.S. Army Mgmt. Engring. Tng. Agy., 1962-66; mem. bd. transp. rate experts Los Angeles Bd. Transp., 1952-61; mem. statewide adv. com. for pvt. schs. and colls. adv. to State Supt. Pub. Instrn., 1964-67. Mem. nat. research adv. com. Am. Transit Assn., 1946; mem. Rapid Transit Action Group, 1948; mem. U. Pres. Transp. Com., 1950. Registered profl. engr., Wash., Cal.; pub. accountant, Cal. Fellow Am. Inst. Indsl.

Engrs. (chmn. small plants session nat. conf. 1958); sr. mem. I.E.E.E. (chmn. mgmt. sessions nat. conf. 1956, mem. Nat. Mgmt. Com., 1956-57); mem. Los Angeles, Inglewood (v.p. 1970), Long Beach (chmn. transp. com. 1952) chambers commerce, Nat. Soc. Profl. Engrs., Am. Soc. Engring. Edn. (chmn. Pacific S.W. sect. 1959-60), Am. Assn. U. Profs., Sigma Xi, Tau Beta. Pi, Alpha Tau Omega, Phi Kappa Phi, Alpha Pi Mu (hon.). Mason (32). Author reports on mgmt., indsl. engring., utilities and transp. Home: 228 N Hillcrest Blvd Inglewood CA 90301 Office: 1155 W Arbor Vitae St Inglewood CA 90301

GRANT, HUGH GLADNEY, commentator, journalist, lectr., former diplomat; b. Birmingham, Ala., Sept. 2, 1888; s. William Curtis and Minnie Becket (Gladney) G.; A.B., Howard Coll., Birmingham, 1910, A.M., 1916, LL.D., 1935; A.B., Harvard, 1912; A.M., George Washington U., 1931; m. Cora Dean Hibbs, Aug. 9, 1916; 1 dau., Louise Esther (Mrs. Robert C. Kennedy). Corr., Birmingham News and other So. newspapers, 1910-13; with Birmingham Bd. Edn., 1913-17; with Fed. Bd. for Vocational Edn., 1919-21; mem. staff Ala. State Dept. Edn., 1921-23; asso. prof. polit. sci., head dept. journalism Ala. Poly. Inst., Auburn, 1923-27, sec. to U.S. Senator H.L. Black of Ala., 1927-33; in div. of Western European affairs Dept. of State, 1933-35; E.E. and M.P. of U.S. to Albania, 1935 until closing of Legation, Sept. 1939, to Thailand (Siam), 1940-41; with Dept. State, 1939-40; lectr. writer, also radio commentator on nat. and internat. questions. An organizer and mem. Com. for Free and Ind. Albania; speaker Dem. Nat. Conv., 1936; guest speaker Albanian-Am. Nat. Orgn. Conv., Phila., 1952; mem. exec. com. Fedn. for Constl. Govt.; mem. nat. policy com. for Am.; organizer, States' Rights Council Ga., pres. 1954; mem. Ind. candidates nat. com. 1956 campaign. Served with U.S. Army, 1918. Decorated Order of Skanderbeg (Albania); recipient Liberty award Congress of Freedom, 1959. Mem. Ala. Soc. of Washington (pres., 1934-35), Sons Confederate Vets. (camp comdr. 1966-67), Pi Gamma Mu, Pi Kappa Alpha. Mason, Elk. Clubs: Kiwanis (chmn. internat. relations com. Augusta 1968); Speakers (Harvard). Author govtl. publs. Contbr. to newspapers. Made tour of Balkan countries, 1937 studying political and economic trends. In charge Am. Legation, Tirana, Albania, at time of Italian invasion, 1939; had last audience granted to any fgn. rep. by King Zog, the day before Italian invasion; guest of H.M. Leka, heir to throne of Albania, Washington, 1970. Following return from Thailand late in 1941, made nation-wide lecture tour, speaking on the "Far Eastern Situation." Also speaker for War Dept. in orientation lecture program for soldiers and aviators in U.S. Army camps and aviation fields, organized ednl. program for disabled veterans of World War II in State of Ore., 1943-44, also Oliver Gen. Hosp., Augusta, Ga. Address: Room 638 Bon Air Retirement Club and Hotel Augusta GA 30904

GRANT, JAMES ALAN CLIFFORD, educator; b. Grand Forks, N.D., June 19, 1902; s. William Lewis and Margaret (Spotswood) G.; student U. Cal. at Los Angeles, 1920-22, LL.D., 1969; A.B. Stanford, 1924, M.A., 1925, Ph.D., 1927; m. Helen Marjorie Allison, July 14, 1928; children—William Allison, Beverly Gale (Mrs. Neil A. Holmberg). Fellow and asst. polit. sci., Stanford, 1925-27, vis. asst. prof., 1936; clk. judiciary com., Cal. Assembly, 1927; instr. polit. sci., U. Wis., 1927-29, asst. prof., 1929-30; asst. prof. polit. sci., U. Cal. at Los Angeles, 1930-36, asso. prof., 1936-40, prof. 1940—, chmn. dept., 1939-42, dean div. social scis., 1950-59; acad. asst. to pres. U. Cal. (statewide), 1966—. Spl. adviser to pres. and minister justice of Republic of Vietnam, in 1956. Vice chmn. 10th Regional War Labor Bd., 1943-45; Loyalty Bd. 12 U.S. Civil Service Dist., 1949-53; permanent com. Oliver Wendell Holmes Devise, 1970—. Active in labor arbitration 1943—; vice chmn. Los Angeles City Employee Relations Bd., 1971—. Social Sci. Research Council fellow, 1931-32, recipient sr. research award, 1959-60; Guggenheim fellow in Latin Am., 1942-43; Fulbright prof. Johns Hopkins, Bologna, Italy, 1963-64; cons. editor, Social Science Abstracts, 1931-33. Mem. Am. Polit. Sci. Assn. (bd. editors 1938-41; exec council 1944-46; exec. com. 1950-51; v.p., 1953-54), Internat. Bar Assn. (justice Brit. sect.), Selden Soc., Nat. Acad. Arbitrators, Scabbard and Blade, Phi Beta Kappa, Pi Sigma Alpha, Pi Gamma Mu, Sigma Delta Pi. Contbr. Selected Essays on Constitutional Law, 1938; Our Common Law Constitution, 1960; El Control Jurisdiccional de la Constitucionalidad de las Leyes: Una Contribución de las Américas a la Ciencia Politica, 1963; also papers on constl. and comparative law. Home: 13160 Riviera Ranch Rd Los Angeles CA 90049

GRANT, JAMES INGE, former steel steel fabricating co. exec.; b. Denton, Tex., Aug. 21, 1909; s. Hugh Robert and Laila (Inge) G.; student Engring. Sch., So. Meth. U., 1928-31; m. Alice Sutton, Mar. 17, 1934; children—Alice Ann (Mrs. Stanley L. Smith), James Inge, William Sutton. With Wyatt Industries, Inc., and predecessor, 1928-68, v.p. charge operations, 1955-62, pres., 1962-67, chmn. bd., 1968-68, co. merged into U.S. Industries, Inc., 1968, vice chmn. energy equipment group, 1969-71; pres. Steel Tank Constrn. Co., 1955—; dir. Austin Steel Co., Dallas, Gt. So. Ins. Co., North Side State Bank, Houston, Bank Southwest, Houston. With WPB, 1943; industry mem. Regional Wage Stablzn. Bd., 1951-52. Mem. Tex. N.G., 1926-37. Registered profl. engr., Tex. Mem. Steel Plate Fabricators Assn. (dir. 1964, 68), N.A.M. (dir. 1968), Salesmanship Club Dallas (dir. 1950), Tex. Soc. Profl. Engrs., Kappa Alpha. Presbyn. (elder). Clubs: Dallas Country (pres. 1952), Dallas (Dallas); Houston Country, Houston. Home: 6235 Valley Forge Houston TX 77027

GRANT, JAMES PINEO, found. exec.; b. Peiping, China, May 12, 1922; s. John Black and Charlotte (Hill) G.; A.B., U. Cal., 1943; LL.B., Harvard, 1951; m. Ethel Henck, Dec. 30, 1943; children—John Putnam, James Dickinson, William Joseph. Rep. UNRRA in North China, 1946-47; cons., spl. asst. to dir. U.S. Econ. Aid Mission to China, 1948-49, 50; asso. Covington & Burling, Washington, 1951-54; regional legal counsel for U.S. Econ. Aid Missions in South Asia, 1954-56; dir. U.S. Econ. Aid Mission to Ceylon, 1956-58; spl. asst. to dir. ICA, 1958, dep. dir. ICA, Washington, 1958-61; dep. asst. sec. state for Near Eastern and South Asian affairs, 1962-64; dir. U.S. Econ. Aid Mission to Turkey, 1964-67; asst. adminstr. AID, Washington, 1967- 69; pres. Overseas Devel. Council, 1969—. Commr., Commn. on Churches Participation in Devel., World Council of Chs., 1970—. Served as capt. AUS, 1943-45; CBI. Decorated Bronze Star with cluster; Breast Order of Yun Hui (China); recipient Distinguished Pub. Service award AID, 1961. Mem. Council Fgn. Relations, Bar Assn. D.C. Club: Metropolitan (Washington). Home: 2871 Tilden St NW Washington DC 20008 Office: 1717 Massachusetts Av NW Washington DC 20036

GRANT, JOHN BENJAMIN, lawyer; b. Willimantic, Conn., May 1, 1908; s. Frederick Benjamin and Ida (Lincoln) G.; B.A., Yale, 1930, LL.B., 1932; m. Eleanor Quin, July 14, 1934; children—John Benjamin, Frances (Mrs. Gary C. Moore), Judith (Mrs. William D. McMeekin), Eleanor II (Mrs. Theodore R. Grave). Admitted to Conn. bar, 1933, since practiced in New Haven; mem. firm Tyler, Cooper, Grant, Bowerman & Keefe, 1944—; instr. law New Haven Coll., 1942-46. Dir., counsel 2d Fed. Savs. & Loan Assn.; dir. F.D. Grave & Son Inc.; sec., dir. Conn. Radio Found. Inc., 1944-67. U.S. concillation commr. in farm bankruptcies, 1942-46; judge Orange Town Ct., 1939-43. Mem. bd., sec. Orange Zoning Commn., 1941-51. Mem. adv. bd. New Haven Area Rehab. Center. Mem. Am., Conn., New Haven bar assns., Newcomen Soc. N.Am., Phi Alpha Delta. Episcopalian (vestry). Clubs: Point Judith Country (Narragansett, R.I.); New Haven Country. Quinnipiack (New Haven). Home: Arnolda Charlestown RI 02813 Office: 205 Church St New Haven CT 06509

GRANT, JOHN FRANCIS, banker; b. East Machias, Me., July 25, 1918; s. Arthur J. and Sarah (McDonald) G.; A.B., U. Me., 1948; m. Margaret Wells Libby, June 8, 1947; childrenJohn E., Robert A., Richard A. With Merrill Trust Co., Bangor, Me., 1937-, asst. treas., 1948-54, v.p., 1954, exec. v.p., 1955- 58, dir., 1958, pres., 1959—, chmn., 1969—; dir. Cole's Express (Bangor), Me. Bonding & Casualty Co., Me. Recreation Authority. Mem. bd. U. Me. Found.; trustee Bangor Pub. Library; dir., v.p. Bangor Humane Soc.; trustee, pres. Eastern Me. Med. Center. Served to lt. col. USAF, World War II, Korea. Mem. Phi Beta Kappa, Phi Kappa Phi. Home: 311 W Broadway Bangor ME 04401 Office: 2 Hammond St Bangor ME 04401

GRANT, JOHN L., business exec.; b. Los Angeles, Oct. 26, 1922; B.A., Union Coll., 1945; M.B.A., Harvard, 1949; m. Carolyn Jane Hubbell, Dec. 9, 1960. With First Pa. Banking & Trust Co., Phila., 1949-60; asst. treas. Sinclair Oil Corp., 1960-66, treas., 1966-68; treas. Sinclair Internat. Oil Co., 1960-68; v.p. treas. Sinclair Refining Co., 1960-68, Sinclair Venezuelan Oil Co., 1960-68; v.p. Atlantic Richfield Co. 1968-70; exec. v.p. finance Am. Standard, Inc., N.Y.C., 1970—. Home: 160 E 48th St New York City NY 10017 Office: 40 W 40th St New York City NY 10020

GRANT, LEE, (Lyova Haskell Rosenthal), actress; b. N.Y.C.; d. A.W. and Witia (Haskell) Rosenthal; student Juiliard Sch. Music, Neighborhood Playhouse Sch. of Theatre, Met. Opera Ballet Sch. Stage debut at age 3, N.Y.C.; appeared at Green Mansions Theatre, Warrensburg, N.Y.; Broadway debut in Joy to the World, 1948; roles include plays Joy to the World, Detective Story, Arms and the Man, I Am a Camera, They Knew What They Wanted, Gigi, Wedding Breakfast, A Hole in the Head, Two for the Seesaw, The Tender Trap, Silk Stockings, The Maids; also in films, TV. Nominated Acad. award, 1952; recipient Cannes Film Festival award, 1952, Village Voice Off-Broadway award, 1964, Emmy award for outstanding single performance, 1971. Address: 3000 W Alameda Burbank CA 91503*

GRANT, LINDSEY, fgn. service officer; b. Chapel Hill, N.C., Sept. 8, 1926; s. Daniel Lindsey and Anne Morgan (Majette) G.; student Deep Springs (Cal.) Coll., 1943-44, Hobart Coll., 1944; B.A. in History, Cornell U., 1948; postgrad. Yale, 1954-55; m. Burwell Marshall, June 20, 1952; childrenAnne Paige, Gordon Lindsey. Joined U.S. Fgn. Service, 1949; assigned Washington, 1949-50, Hong Kong, 1950-52, Singapore, 1952-54; econ. assignments, Hong Kong, 1955-58, Taipei, 1958-61; officer charge mainland China affairs State Dept., 1961-63, dir. Office Asian Communist Affairs, 1963-65, chief Asian Communist areas div. Bur. Intelligence and Research, 1968-69; 1st Sec. Am. embassy, New Delhi, 1965-68; mem. staff Nat. Security Council, Washington, 1969-70, detailed to Nat. War Coll., 1970-71, mem. planning and coordination staff Office of Sec. State, 1971—. Served to ensign USNR, 1944- 46. Mem. Telluride Assn., Phi Beta Kappa, Phi Kappa Phi. Home: 650 Beach View Dr St Simons Island GA 31522 Office: Dept of State Washington DC 20520

GRANT, LOU, cartoonist; Editorial cartoonist Oakland Tribune. Office: 401 13th St Oakland CA 94612*

GRANT, M. DONALD, chmn. bd. N.Y. Mets Profl. Baseball Team. Address: Shea Stadium Roosevelt Av and 126th Av Flushing NY 11368

GRANT, MURRAY, physician, govt. ofcl.; b. London, Eng., June 24, 1926; s. Abrahm and Jenny (Harbour) G.; student U. London, 1944-46; M.D., St. George's Hosp. Med. Sch., U. London, 1949; D.P.H., U. Toronto, 1950; m. Trudy Shein, Nov. 25, 1951; childrenBradley, Schuyler, Stephanie, Darryl, Valerie. Intern Toronto East Gen. Hosp., 1949; asst. health officer Balt. Co. Health Dept., Towson, Md., 1950-51; commr. health Cattaraugus Co. Health Dept., Olean, N.Y., 1951-55; dir. health Clay Co. Health Dept., Liberty, Mo., 1955-57; asst. health officer Prince George Co. Health Dept., Cheverly, Md., 1957-59, health officer, 1959-62; dir. pub. health D.C. Dept. Pub. Health, 1962-; clin. prof. George Washington U., Georgetown U., Howard U. Fellow Am. Pub. Health Assn.; mem. D.C. Med. Soc., Assn. State and Territorial Health Officers, U.S. Conf. City Health Officers, Am. Assn. Pub. Health Physicians, Met. Health Officers Assn. (pres. 1964- 66). Author: Handbook on Preventive Medicine and Public Health Contbr. articles profl. jours. Home, 7105 Loch Lomond Dr Bethesda, MD 20034. Office: 1875 Connecticut Av NW Washington DC 20009

GRANT, NICHOLAS JOHN, educator; b. South River, N.J., Oct. 21, 1915; s. John and Mary (Sudnik) G.; S.B., Carnegie Inst. Tech., 1938; Sc.D., Mass. Inst. Tech., 1944; m. Anne T. Phillips, Sept. 12, 1942 (dec. Apr. 1957); children—Anne P., William D., Nicholas P.; m. 2d, Susan Mary Cooper, Aug. 1963; children—Johnathan, Katharine. Metallurgist Bethlehem Steel Co., 1938- 40; mem. faculty Mass. Inst. Tech., 1942-, prof. metallurgy, 1955-, dir. Center Materials Sci. and Engring., 1968—; pres., dir. N.E. Materials Lab., Inc., 1954-66, tech. dir. Investment Castings Inst., 1954-; cons. industry, 1947—. Vice pres. Nitralloy Corp. U.S.A.; dir. Gen. Diode Corp., Loomis-Sayles Mut. Fund, Alfa Inorganics. Inc., Indsl. Materials Tech., Inc., Electronic Instrument & Splty. Corp. Mem. materials com. NASA, 1958-67. Recipient distinguished service award Investment Castings Inst., 1956; Merit award, Carnegie Mellon U. Mem. Am. Soc. Metals, Am. Inst. Mining, Metall. and Petroleum Engrs., Inst. Metals (London), Am. Soc. Testing and Materials, Sigma Xi, Tau Beta Pi, Theta Tau, Alpha Xi Epsilon. Contbr. articles profl. jours., chpts. in books. Home: 10 Leslie Rd Winchester, MA 01890. Office: Massachusetts Inst Technology Cambridge MA 02139

GRANT, PHILIP RUSSELL, tobacco co. exec.; b. Carney's Point N.J., Apr. 11, 1923; s. George W. and Helen (Cussons) G.; B.A., Middlebury (Vt.) Coll., 1944; LL.B., U. Pa., 1950; m. Ann Clark Ransom, Mar. 9, 1945; childrenBrian Ransom, Julie Clark, Jane Cussons. Admitted to N.Y. bar, 1951; asso. atty. firm Cravath, Swaine & Moore, N.Y.C., 1950-53, Perkins, Daniels & Perkins, N.Y.C., 1953-57; partner firm Perkins, Daniels & McCormack, and predecessors, 1957-66; v.p., gen. counsel P. Lorillard Co., 1966-. Served to lt. (j.g.) USNR, 1943-47. Mem. Assn. Bar City N.Y., Alpha Sigma Phi. Unitarian-Universalist. Club: Bonnie Briar Country (Larchmont, N.Y.). Home: 211 Griffen Av Scarsdale, NY 10853. Office: 200 E 42d St New York City NY 10017

GRANT, RICHARD ANGUS, cement mfg. exec.; b. Los Angeles, Apr. 16, 1909; s. Daniel Garfield and Nannie (Dillon) G.; B.A., Stanford U., 1931, LL.B., 1935; m. Dorothy Louise Duque, Jan. 21, 1939; childrenRichard, Louise, Melinda, Susan, Andrew, Joseph. Admitted to Cal. bar, 1936; staff law office Richard J. Dillon, Los Angeles, 1936-43; v.p., gen. counsel Fullerton Oil Co., Los Angeles, 1943-54; pres. dir. Cal. Portland Cement Co., officer, exec., 1955- ; officer, exec., dir. Arizona Portland Cement Co., Los Angeles, 1955- ; dir. Dan Murphy Co., Los Angeles Investment Co., Fed. Ice & Cold Storage Co., Robinson Bldg. Co., Community TV of So. Cal. Trustee Valentine Found., Santa Catalina Found., Dan Murphy Found., Harvey Mudd Coll., Cath. Welfare Bur., Los Angeles Archdiocese, The Tidings, newspaper Los Angeles Archdiocese; dir. Los Angeles Civic Light Opera. Decorated knight comdr. Order St. Gregory the Great, Pope Pius XII. Mem. Oil Producers Agy. Cal. (dir. 1943-55, pres. 1954, 55), Mchts. and Mfrs. Assn. (dir. 1960-63), Portland Cement Assn. (chmn. bd. 1963-), Los Angeles C. of C. (dir. 1959-61), Am., Los Angeles bar assns., State Bar Cal. Home: 655 Hillside Terrace Pasadena CA 91105 Office: 612 S Flower St Los Angeles CA 90017

GRANT, ROBERT ALLEN, judge; b. Marshall County, Ind., July 31, 1905; s. Everett F. and Margaret E. (Hatfield) G.; A.B., U. Notre Dame, 1928, LL.B., 1930; m. Margaret Anna McLaren, Sept. 17, 1933; children—Robert A., Margaret Ann. Admitted to Ind. bar, 1930, U.S. Supreme Ct. bar, 1940; practiced in South Bend, Ind.; dep. pros. atty., St. Joseph County, 1935-36; mem. 76th-80th congresses from 3d Ind. Dist.; U.S. dist. judge No. Dist. Ind., 1957—, chief judge, 1961—. Mem. Am., Ind., bar assns., S.A.R. Republican. Methodist. Mason (33, K.T., Shriner), Rotarian, Elk, Eagle; Order DeMolay (internat. supreme council, Ind. exec. officer). Clubs: Columbia (Indpls.); Indiana (South Bend); Union League (Chgo.). Home: 1607 East Wayne St South Bend IN 46615 Office: Federal Bldg South Bend IN 46624

GRANT, ROBERT ENGLAND, investment co. exec.; b. Albany, N.Y., Nov. 10, 1924; s. Benjamin William and Violet England (Rowell) G.; A.B., Brown U., 1948; M.B.A., Harvard, 1950; m. Cynthia Ann Kirk, Aug. 25, 1951; childrenRobert England, David Kirk, James Wickersham. With Kidder, Peabody & Co., 1950- 57; financial v.p. Plough, Inc., 1957-60; v.p., group exec. Textron, Inc., 1960-67, group v.p., 1967-69; pres. Grant Capital Mgmt. Corp., Providence, 1969—; chmn. exec. com., dir. Am. Bakeries Co., Chgo.; dir. The Outlet Co., Providence. Trustee Providence (R.I.) Country Day Sch. Served as aviator USNR, World War II. Home: 139 Nayatt Rd West Barrington, RI 02890. Office: 76 Westminster St Providence RI 02903

GRANT, ROBERT MCQUEEN, educator; b. Evanston, Ill., Nov 25, 1917; s. Frederick Clifton and Helen McQueen (Hardie) G.; A.B., Northwestern U., 1938; student Episcopal Theol. Sch., 1938-39, Columbia, 1939-40; B.D., Union Theol. Sem., 1941; S.T.M., Harvard, 1942, Th.D., 1944; D.D., Seabury- Western Theol. Sem., 1969; m. Margaret Huntington Horton, Dec. 21, 1940; children-Douglas McQueen, Peter Williams, Susan Hardie, James Frederick. Ordained to ministry P.E. Ch., 1942; minister St. James Ch., South Groveland, Mass., 1942-44; instr. to prof. N.T., U. of South, 1944- 53, acting dean, 1947; vis. lectr. U. Chgo., 1945, research asso., 1952-53, asso. prof., 1953-58, prof., 1958—. Vis. lectr. Vanderbilt U., 1945-47; Fulbright research prof. U. Leiden, 1950-51; Guggenheim fellow, 1950, 54, 59; vis. lectr. Seabury-Western Theol. Sem., 1954-55; lectr. Am. Council Learned Soc., 1957-58; vis. prof. Yale, 1964-65; dir. Anglican Theol. Review; asso. editor Vigiliae Christianae, Jour. of Religion. Mem. Soc. Bibl. Lit. and Exegesis (pres. 1959), Am. Soc. Ch. History (pres. 1970, co-editor), Chgo. Soc. Bibl. Research (pres. 1963-64), Phi Beta Kappa, Alpha Delta Phi. Clubs: Quadrangle (Chgo.); Authors (London). Author: Second-Century Christianity, 1946; The Bible in the Church, 1948; Miracle and Natural Law, 1952; The Sword and the Cross, 1955; The Letter and the Spirit, 1957; Gnosticism and Early Christianity, 1959; (with D.N. Freedman) the Secret Says of Jesus, 1960; Gnosticism: an Anthology: The Earliest Lives of Jesus, 1961; Historical Introduction to the New Testament, 1963; The Apostolic Fathers, Vol. I, 1964, Vol. II (with H.H. Graham), 1965, Vol. IV, 1966; U-Boats Destroyed 1914-1918, 1964; The Formation of the New Testament, 1965; History of Early Christian Literature (revision from E.J. Goodspeed); The Early Christian Doctrine of God, 1966; After the New Testament, 1967; U-Boat Intelligence 1914-1918, 1969; Augustus to Constantine; Theophilus of Antioch Ad Autolycum, 1970. Home: 5728 Harper Av Chicago IL 60637

GRANT, ROBERT YEARINGTON, govt. ofcl.; b. Seattle, 1913; s. Charles Ernst and Amy Jane (Mahon) G.; B.S., U. Wash., 1938, postgrad., 1939-40; m. Eleanor May Lewis, May 24, 1941. Chief geologist Cornucopia Gold Mines, Ore., 1940-41; chief mining and geology div. Gen. Hdqrs. Supreme Comdr. Allied Powers, Japan, 1946-51; asst. dir. for industry Mut. Security Agy., Dept. State, Taiwan, 1952-58, industry-transp. officer Fgn. Operations Adminstrn., Indonesia, 1958-62, industry officer AID, Ceylon-Guatemala, 1962-63, dep. provisional dir. AID, Dacca, East Pakistan, 1964-68, spl. asst. to dir. AID, Islamabad, Pakistan, 1968-70, asst. dir. population and health AID, Islamabad, 1970—. Served from lt. to lt. col., AUS, 1941-45. Recipient Dept. Army commendation for meritorious civilian service, 1951, Dept. State Meritorious Honor award, 1971. Fellow Geol. Soc. Am., A.A.A.S.; mem. Am. Geophys. Union, Am. Geol. Inst., Am. Inst. Mining Engrs. Club: Washington Athletic (Seattle). Contbr. articles profl. jours. Home: 14044 36th Av Seattle WA 98125 Office: Islamabad Dept State Washington DC 20521

GRANT, STEPHEN WALKLEY, publisher; b. Elyria, O., Jan. 9, 1909; s. John Hiram and Margaret Knowlton (Hall) G.; grad. Deerfield (Mass.) Acad., 1926; A.B., Amherst Coll., 1930, Litt. D., 1970; m. Cornelia Blodget Hawley, May 22, 1936; children-Cornelia Ann (Mrs. Andrew L. Nichols), Stephen Hall. Instr., Deerfield Acad., 1930-31; with Houghton Mifflin Co., Boston, 1931-, mgr. coll. dept., 1952-63, v.p., 1962-63, pres., 1963—. Mem. Psi Upsilon. Home: 78 Leighton Rd Wellesley, MA 02181. Office: 2 Park St Boston MA 02107

GRANT, THOMPSON DOANE, headmaster; b. Bangor, Me., Apr. 18, 1909; s. Frederick Howard and Fannie (Chandler) G.; A.B., Colby Coll., 1932, M.A., 1934; m. Frances Taylor Parke, June 5, 1936; childrenCharles F., Susan F., Thompson Doane. Asst. headmaster Pebble Hill Country Day Sch., DeWitt, N.Y., 1942- 52; headmaster Carteret Sch., West Orange, N.J., 1953-56, Morristown Sch., 1956-. Leader Great Books Found., Syracuse, N.Y., 1948-52. Bd. dirs. Family Service of Morris County; past pres. Boarding Sch. Headmasters' Assn. Middle States. Mem. N.J. Assn Ind. Schs. (v.p. 1961-63; trustee), Phi Delta Theta. Methodist (trustee). Rotarian (past pres. Morristown). Home: Morristown School Wippany Rd Morristown NJ 07960

GRANT, VIRGIL VESCO, mfg. exec.; b. Grantsburg, Ill., Feb. 25, 1913; s. Robert F. and Dorothy (Simmons) G.; B.S., U. Ill., 1935; m. Esther Lundberg, June 6, 1936; childrenLois Margaret, Linda Kay. With accounting dept. Caterpillar Tractor Co., Peoria, Ill, 1936-41, domestic credit mgr., 1941-42, supr. auditing div., 1942-44, asst. treas., 1944-46, treas., 1946-56, v.p., 1962—, v.p. fgn. trade group, 1956-60; pres. Caterpillar Overseas S.A., Geneva, Switzerland, 1960-62; dir. First Fed. Savs. & Loan Assn., Peoria. Mem. Nat. Assn. Accountants. Clubs: Peoria Country, Creve Coeur. Home: 7422 Edgewild Dr Peoria IL 61614 Office: Caterpillar Tractor Co Peoria IL 61602

GRANT, WALTER KING, financial exec.; b. Jefferson, Ala., July 27, 1906; s. William Sandowski and Mabel (Kirven) G.; student U. Ga., 1923-24; m. Helen Burney, Apr. 4, 1936; children—Walter King, Helen (Mrs. W. Henry Maddox III), Constance (Mrs. Charles K. Browning). Broker, mem. New Orleans Cotton Exchange and Chicago Bd. Trade, 1936-38; broker, pres. So. Discount Co., Atlanta, 1936—, chmn. bd., 1970—; dir. SCI Systems, Inc., Huntsville, Ala. Trustee Atlanta chpt. Big Bros. Am., Boys Estate; bd. dirs. Met. YMCA. Mem. Delta Tau Delta. Presbyn. (chmn. bd. trustees, elder). Rotarian. Clubs: Commerce, Capital City (Atlanta). Home: 1720 W Wesley Rd NW Atlanta GA 30327 Office: 919 W Peachtree St NE Atlanta GA 30309

GRANT, WALTER KING, Jr., discount co. exec.; b. Atlanta, Sept. 24, 1939; s. Walter King and Helen (Burney) G.; B.A., Vanderbilt U., 1961; M.B.A., Ga. State U., 1967; m. Eleanor McPhail, Dec. 1, 1961; children—Walter King III, Hugh McPhail, Eleanor Suttles. With So. Discount Co., Atlanta, 1961—, pres., 1970—; pres. Consumer Life Ins. Co.; chmn. bd. Henson Furniture Co. Mem. adv. bd. Salvation Army, Atlanta, Goodwill Industries, Atlanta. Trustee Trinity Sch., Atlanta. Mem. Ga. Consumer Finance Assn. (chmn. bd. 1970-71), Sigma Alpha Epsilon. Clubs: Capital City, Piedmont Driving (Atlanta). Home: 353 Argonne Dr N W Atlanta GA 30305 Office: 919 W Peachtree St NE Atlanta GA 30309

GRANT, WALTER RANDOLPH, elec. co. exec.; b. Trenton, N.J., June 18, 1910; s. Harris P. and Elma M. (Waite) G.; B.S., U. Pa., 1934; m. Joyce A. Gafford, Feb. 12, 1949; children—Kathleen S., Sally E., Nancy M., Laurie Jean. Traveling auditor Gen. Electric Co., 1934-45; sec.-treas. Locke Insulator Co., Balt., 1945-47, Hotpoint, Inc., Chgo., 1947-52, v.p., 1950-52; v.p., treas. Packard Motor Car Co., Detroit, 1952-54; v.p. finance Studebaker-Packard Corp., Detroit, 1954-55, N.Y.C., R.R., 1955-68; exec. v.p. Penn Central, 1968; exec. v.p. Consol. Edison Co. N.Y., Inc., 1968—: Clubs: Indian Harbor Yacht, Milbrook (Greenwich, Conn.). Home: Orchard Dr Milbrook Greenwich CT 06830 Office: 4 Irving Pl New York City NY 10003

GRANT, WILLIAM, lawyer; b. Estes Park, Colo., Aug. 29, 1910; s. William West and Gertrude (Hendrie) G.; A.B. magna cum laude, Dartmouth, 1931; LL.B. cum laude, Harvard, 1938; m. Helen Prindle, June 6, 1938; childrenWilliam West, Melanie, Mary, Gertrude, Charles Hendrie. Partner, Boettcher- Newton & Co., stockbrokers, N.Y.C., 1933-34, mem. N.Y. Stock Exchange, 1934-35; admitted to Colo. bar; mem. firm Grant, Shafroth, Toll & McHendrie, Denver, 1940-. Pres. Met. TV Co. (KOA radio-TV), 1952-63, chmn. bd., 1963-68; pres. Sangre de Cristo Broadcasting Co. (KOAA-TV and KCSJ radio), Pueblo, 1968—; dir. Colo. Nat. Bank, Hendrie Investment Co., Denver. Chmn. Colo. Heart Fund drive. Chmn. Democratic State Central Com., 1965-69. Trustee Colo. Found. Research Tb. Served from lt. (j.g.) to lt. comdr., USNR, 1942-46. Decorated Bronze Star medal. Mem. Casque and Gauntlet, Phi Beta Kappa, Psi Upsilon. Rotarian. Clubs: Arapahoe Hunt, Denver, Denver Country. Home: 101 S Humboldt St Denver CO 80209 Office: 1700 Western Fed Bldg Denver CO 80202

GRANT, WILLIAM CALLOWAY, advt. exec.; b. Dallas, Aug. 9, 1906; s. William Calloway and Birdie (Henderson) G.; student So. Meth. U., 1924-28, LL.D., 1955; student Tex. U. Law Sch., 1928-29; m. Mary Waller, Nov. 29, 1930; children—Constance (Mrs. Philip Gardner Meyers), Roberta (Mrs. Donald C. Flynn), Carole (Mrs. Andrew Clarkson), William. Conducted system of advt., Dallas, 1929-31; with R.R. Donnelley & Sons Co., 1932-34, W.F. Hall Printing Co., 1934-35; established Grant Advt., Inc. hdqrs. Dallas, 1935, opened office in Chgo., 1937, N.Y.C., 1940, Mexico City and Monterrey, Mexico, 1941, Rio de Janeiro, São Paulo and Buenos Aires, 1943, Miami, Caracas, 1944, London, Toronto, 1945, Hollywood, 1946, Bombay, Calcutta, 1947, Karachi, Hongkong, Manila, Cape Town, Johannesburg, Durban, Panama City, 1948, Santiago, 1949, New Delhi, 1950, Madras, India, San Francisco, Montreal, 1952, Bangkok, 1956, Salisbury, 1957, Ceylon, Singapore, 1958, Kuala Lumpur, 1961, Dacca, 1962, and others, now chmn. bd., chief exec. officer Grant Advt., Inc.; chmn. bd. Grant Advt. Internat., Inc., subsidiaries; dep. pres. Bahamas Nat. Trust, 1960, pres., 1961. Dir. Nat. Outdoor Advt. Bur., 1960—. Exec. dir. U.S. Commn., Inter-Am. Devel. Commn., 1943; mem. adv. com. to improve Inf. morale, 1951; dir. Chgo. Maternity Center, 1951-55; pres., dir. Chgo. Commn. UNICEF, 1967-68, dir. U.S. Commn., 1968. Mem. exec. com. Don Belding Internat. Grant-in-Aid Fund at Tex. Tech. Coll., 1968; overseer Redmond Coll., 1968-69. Decorated Order of Cruzeiro do Sul, Brazilian govt. Mem. Phi Delta Theta. Conglist. (trustee). Clubs: Indian Hill Golf, University, Executives, Tower (Chgo.); Detroit Athletic; Internat. Trade (dir. 1968-69). Home: 33 Indian Hill Rd Winnetka IL 60093 Office: 10 S Riverside Plaza Chicago IL 60606

GRANT, WILLIAM DOWNING, ins. co. exec.; b. Kansas City, Mo., Feb. 10, 1917; s. William Thomas and Frances (Downing) G.; A.B., U. Kan., 1939; grad. Wharton Sch. Finance, 1940; m. Mary Noel, June 24, 1941; childrenLaura Noel, William Thomas II. With Bus. Men's Assurance Co., Kansas City, Mo., 1941—, v.p. charge reins., 1951-56, exec. v.p., 1956-60, pres., 1960-69, chmn. bd., pres., 1969—; dir. City Nat. Bank & Trust Co., U.P.R.R., Kansas City Power & Light Co. Chmn. elect Am. Life Conv. Mem. Pres.'s Commn. on Financial Structure and Regulation. Nat. trustee Am. Field Service. Trustee Conservatory Music of U. Mo. at Kansas City, S.S. Huebner Found. for Ins. Edn., Union Pacific R.R. Found. Served as comdr. USNR, World War II. Mem. Am. Coll. Life Underwriters (trustee). Home: 5821 Brookbank lane Shawnee Mission KS 66208 Office: BMA Tower Kansas City MO 64141

GRANT, WILLIAM RUSSELL, journalist; b. Winchester, Ky., July 5, 1943; s. R. Russell and Mary (Rees) G.; B.A., U. Ky., 1965, M.A., 1967; m. Linda Alice Mills, June 4, 1966; 1 dau., Elizabeth Mitchell. Reporter, Louisville Courier-Jour., 1965; Washington corr. Collegiate Press Service, 1965-66; instr. journalism U. Ky., 1966-67; reporter Lexington (Ky.) Leader 1967-68; edn. editor Detroit Free Press, 1968—. Mem. Sigma Delta Chi, Omicron Delta Kappa. Home: 4385 Lakeview St Detroit MI 48215 Office: 321 W Lafayette St Detroit MI 48231

GRANT, WILLIAM THOMAS, merchant; b. Stevensville, Pa., June 27, 1876; s. William T. and Amanda Louise (Bird) G.; educated high sch., Malden, Mass.; LL.D., Bates Coll., 1947; L.H.D., U. Miami, 1960; m. Lena Blanche Brownell, Oct. 5, 1907 (dec.); children—Helen (Mrs. Francis Allchin), Marian (Mrs. John R. Henry); m. 2d, Beth Bradshaw, Sept. 3, 1930 (dec.); 1 dau., Shirley (Mrs. Harrington E. Drake Jr.). Founder, 1906, hon. chmn. bd. W.T. Grant Co., chain of dept. stores. Founder, 1936, now hon. chmn. bd. The Grant Found., Inc. Mem. N.E. Historic Genealogical Soc. Home: Greenwich CT 06830 Office: 1441 Broadway New York City NY 10018

GRANTHAM, DON L., food co. exec.; b. Toledo, Ill., May 7, 1911; s. Courtland and Clara (Elrod) G.; student Eastern Ill. Coll., 1933; C.P.A., U. Ill., 1943; m. Mary Elizabeth Burke, May 15, 1937; children—Mark Burke, Maralee, Barbara Ann, Gregory Elrod. With Beatrice Foods Co., 1934—, Eastern regional v.p., 1961-65, v.p. charge dairy div., 1965-66, exec. v.p. of co., 1966—, also dir.; pres. subsidiary Meadow Gold Products Co. Bd. dirs. Milk Industry Found., Nat. Dairy Council. Mem. Internat. Assn. Ice Cream Mfrs. (dir.), Ill. C. of C. (bd. dirs.). Presbyn. Kiwanian (life). Clubs: Exmoor Country (Highland Park, Ill.); Mid-Day (Chgo.); Eldorado Country (Palm Desert, Cal.); Pinehurst (N.C.) Country. Home: 201 N Greenbay Rd Lake Forest IL 60045 Office: Beatrice Foods Co 120 S La Salle St Chicago IL 60603

GRANTHAM, EMERY ARDEN, naval officer; b. nr. Weatherford, Tex., Dec. 4, 1914; s. Emery Lycurgus and Minnie (Grable) G.; B.S., U.S. Naval Acad., 1937; M.S., Mass. Inst. Tech., 1941; certificate Harvard Bus. Sch., 1948; m. Mary Louise Graham, Mar. 25, 1950. Commd. ensign USN, 1937, advanced through grades to rear adm., 1965; Pacific Fleet maintenance officer, Pearl Harbor, Hawaii, 1962-65; dep. comdr. Naval Ship Systems Command, Washington, 1965-67; dir. ships material readiness div. Office Chief Naval Operations, Washington, 1967-. Decorated Legion of Merit, Bronze Star medal. Mem. Soc. Naval Architects and Marine Engrs., Am. Soc. Naval Engrs. Club: Army-Navy Country (Arlington, Va.).

GRANTHAM, ROBERT GORDON, lawyer; b. Terry, Miss., July 29, 1912; s. Joseph Wyatt and Margaret (Bracey) G.; B.A., Millsans Coll., Jackson, Miss., 1934; LL.B., U. Miss., 1937; m. Jessie G. Smith, Nov. 5, 1937; childrenShelby Smith, Ann Lucinda, Margaret Bracey. Admitted to Miss. bar, 1937; adjuster Md. Casualty Co., Jackson, Miss., 1937; spl. agt. FBI, 1937-45; practice in Jackson, 1945-; mem. firm Brunini, Everett, Grantham & Quin, 1950-. Appeal agt. for Miss., SSS, 1957-62. Adv. bd. St. Dominic-Jackson Meml. Hosp., 1954-; mem. bd. United Givers Fund Jackson, 1958. Mem. Am., Miss., Hinds County (pres. 1964-65) bar assns., Kappa Alpha, Phi Delta Phi, Alpha Psi Omega, Blue Key. Home: 2135 Eastover Dr Jackson MS 39211 Office; First Nat Bank Bldg Jackson MS 39205

GRANTHAM, ROY EMERY, lawyer; b. nr. Fairfax, Okla., Jan. 26, 1907; s. Amos Dean and Flora Lillian (McCarty) G.; A.B., LL.B., U. Okla., 1934, Ed.M., 1940; m. Martha Elizabeth Young, Dec. 24, 1933; children-Marcia Lea (Mrs. Vernon L. Moore), Linda Roy (Mrs. Thomas A. McNew). Instr. pub. schs., Kay County, Okla., 1927-30; job order accountant Empire Oil Co., Ponca City, Okla., 1930-31; instr. Panama (Okla.) pub. schs., 1934-35, Ponca City pub. schs., 1934-41; admitted to Okla. bar, 1934; county atty. Kay County, 1941-42; practice in Ponca City, 1947—; counsel, dir. Pioneer Nat. Bank, Ponca City. Mem. Gov. Okla. Crime Commn.; mem. President's Com. for Hiring Handicapped. Mem. Okla. Senate from Dist. 20, 1950—. Bd. dirs. Kay County Assn. Retarded Children. Served with AUS, 1942-47. Decorated Commendation ribbon. Mem. Am., Okla., Kay County bar assns. Democrat. Home: 325 S 12th St Ponca City OK 74601 Office: 313 N 4th St Ponca City OK 74601

GRANVILLE, MAURICE FREDERICK, Jr., petroleum co. exec.; b. La Grange, Tex., Oct. 26, 1915; s. Maurice Frederick and Dorathea (von Rosenburg) G.; B.S. in Chem. Engring., U. Tex., 1937; Sc.M. in Chem. Engring., Mass. Inst. Tech., 1939; m. Janet Knotts, Jan. 13, 1945; children—Carol McCoy (Mrs. Peter Blyberg), Frederick Lloyd. With Texaco Inc. 1939—, organizer chem. div.. Port Arthur, Tex., 1955-58, gen. mgr. petrochem. dept., 1958-60, v.p. petrochem. dept., 1960-67, v.p. strategic planning and asst. chmn., 1967-70, pres., dir., 1970-71, chmn. bd., 1971—. Bd. dirs. Am. Petroleum Inst. Mem. Am. Inst. Chem. Engrs., Tau Beta Pi, Delta Kappa Epsilon, Phi Lambda Upsilon. Conglist. Clubs: Country (Darien); Cloud (N.Y.C.). Home: Morley Lane Darien CT 06820 Office: 135 E 42d St New York City NY 10017

GRANVILLE-SMITH, WALTER, Jr., advt. cons.; b. Bellport, N.Y., June 20, 1905; s. Walter and Jessie May (Stout) Granville-S.; B.S. summa cum laude (Rufus Choate scholar), Dartmouth, 1926; m. Jean Masson, Apr. 5, 1930; childrenWalter, III, Beverly (Mrs. George A. Bullwinkel). With Young & Rubicam, Inc., 1928-33; v.p., media dir. Ruthrauff & Ryan, Inc., 1934-47; v.p., dir. media planning Biow Co., Inc., 1947-55; v.p. William Esty Co., Inc., 1955-65; advt. cons., 1965-. Mem. Phi Beta Kappa, Zeta Psi. Republican. Episcopalian. Clubs; Larchmont Yacht, Dartmouth; Coral Beach (Bermuda). Home: 17 Winfield Av Harrison NY 10528

GRAPP, WESLEY GLEASON, govt. ofcl.; b. Aberdeen, S.D., Oct. 19, 1918; s. Walter C. and Mame (Gleason) G.; student No. State Tchrs. Coll., Aberdeen, 1936-38; Ph.B., U. N.D., 1942; J.D., Creighton U., 1944; m. Carolyn Kunik, Aug. 23, 1943; childrenMary, Elizabeth, William, James. Admitted to Neb. bar, 1944, also U.S. Supreme Ct.; with FBI, 1946—, spl. agt. charge various field divs., 1956—, Los Angeles div., 1964—. Served to lt. (j.g.) USNR, 1944-46; PTO. Mem. Cal. (exec. com.), Los Angeles County (exec. com.) peace officers assns., Am. Legion, V.F.W., U. N.D., Creighton U. alumni assns., Chief Spl. Agts. Assn. So. Cal., Internat. Assn. Chiefs Police, Internat. Footprinters Assn., C. of C. Los Angeles (adv. mem. law and order com.), Soc. Friendly Sons St. Patrick, Beta Theta Pi, Phi Beta Phi. Roman Catholic. K.C. Clubs: Los Angeles, Los Angeles Athletic, One Hundred, Anchor, Kiwanis, Newman, Roorag, Rotary, Silver Dollar, YMCA Boosters (Los Angeles). Office: FBI Federal Bldg 11000 Wilshire Blvd Los Angeles CA 90024

GRAPSKI, LADISLAUS F., hosp. adminstr.; b. Larksville, Pa., May 17, 1917; s. Edward and Hedwig (Surowinski) G.; R.N., Mills Sch. Nursing for Men, N.Y.C., 1938; student U. Neb., 1938-39; B.S., U. Denver, 1942; M.B.A., U. Chgo., 1943; m. Dorothy Kuhn, May 17, 1941; childrenLadd, Edward, Robert, Mary Ann, Richard, Barbara. Doctors asst. St. Elizabeth's Hosp., Lincoln, Neb., 1938-39; asst. supr., instr. med. techniques U. Colo. Sch. Medicine and Hosps., 1939-41; asst. to resident physician St. Joseph's Hosp., Denver, 1941-42; asst. personnel officer Billings Gen. Hosp., Indpls., 1943-44; adminstr. Halifax Dist. Hosps., Daytona Beach, Fla., 1946-47; spl. lectr., exec.-dir. Univ. Hosp., Loyola U., 1947-51; asso. dir., asst. sec. bd. trustees Johns Hopkins Hosp., 1951-58; dir. Univ. Hosp., asso. dean Sch. Medicine, U. Md., Balt., 1958-64; dir. Loyola Univ. Hosp., asso. dean Stritch Sch. Medicine, Chgo., 1964-68; pres. Allegheny Gen. Hosp., Pitts., 1968—. Spl. lectr., preceptor Grad. Sch. Hosp. Adminstrn., U. Chgo.; lectr. hosp. adminstrn. George Washington U.; hosp. cons., 1946-. Served with AUS, 1944-46. Fellow Am. Coll. Hosp. Adminstrs. (bd. examiners, chmn. bd. publs.); mem. Hosp. Council Md. (chmn. adminstrs. sect., mem. exec. com., trustee), Md., D.C., Del. hosp. assns., Am. Hosp. Assn. (chmn. mgmt. systems com., mem. ho. dels.), Am. Assn. Med. Colls. (ho. of dels.), Council Teaching Hosps. (chmn. exec. com.), Am. Mgmt. Assn., Am. Pub. Health Assn. Home: Fairway Rd Route 3 Sewickley, PA 15143. Office: 320 E North Av Pittsburgh PA 15212

GRASER, CLARENCE FRANCIS, indsl. designer; b. Toledo, Oct. 14, 1923; s. Ottomar and Irene (Frommer) G.; B.S. in Indsl. and Mech. Engring., U. Mich., 1948; m. Gladys Augusta Haefele, May 26, 1951; children—Nancy Jane, Gary Michael, Jay Francis, Thomas Jeffrey. With Gen. Electric Co., 1948-59, mgr. product planning portable appliances, 1955-57, 58-59; cons. product planning and indsl. design European Productivity Agy., Paris, France, 1957-58; mgr. indsl. design data systems div. IBM Corp., 1959-64; dir. indsl. design Westinghouse Electric Corp., 1964—. Mem. Conn. Study of Role Pub. Edn., 1958-59; adviser Jr. Achievement Co., Bridgeport, Conn., 1958-59. Adv. bd. Bridgeport Sheltered Workshop, 1956-57. Recipient Master Design award Product Engring. Mag., 1962; internat. design award Am. Inst. Interior Designers, 1966; Design in Housewares award Nat. Housewares Mfrs. Assn., 1966, 68. Mem. Indsl. Designers Soc. Am., Alpha Sigma Phi. Home: 2654 Charing Rd Columbus OH 43221 Office: 300 Phillippi Rd Columbus OH 43228

GRASS, ALEXANDER, retail co. exec.; b. Scranton, Pa., Aug. 3, 1927; s. Louis and Rose (Breman) G.; LL.B., U. Fla., 1949; m. Lois Lehrman, July 30, 1950; children—Linda Jane, Martin L., Roger L., Elizabeth Ann. Admitted to Fla. bar, 1949, Pa. bar, 1953; individual practice law, Miami Beach, Fla., 1949-51; v.p. Rite Aid Corp., Shiremanstown, Pa., 1952-66, pres., 1966-69, chmn., chief exec. officer, 1969—; dir. Penn Pacific Corp., Phoenix. Nat. chmn. United Jewish Appeal, 1970—, mem. nat. exec. com., 1968-70; pres. Harrisburg (Pa.) Jewish Fedn., 1970—. Served with USNR, 1945-46. Mem. Nat. Am. Wholesale Grocers Assn. (dir.). Jewish religion (dir. temple). Rotarian. Home: 1611 Baldwin Lane Harrisburg PA 17110 Office: Trindle Rd and Railroad Av Shiremanstown PA 17013

GRASS, GUNTER WILHELM, writer; b. Danzig, Oct. 16, 1927; studied sculpture with Sepp Magesh, painting with Otto Pankok, Kunstakademie (Düsseldorf), 1949; Acad. Fine Arts (Berlin), 1953; m. Anna Margareta Grass, 1954; children—Franz, Raoul, Laura, Bruno. Began as a writer of poems, dramatic scenes, also worked as a drummer and washboard accompanist with jazz band; lectr., reader Harvard, Yale, Smith Coll., also Goethe House, Poetry Center YM-YWCA, 1964. Mem. German Mil. Service, 1943-45. Recipient lit. prize, Gruppe 47; French award for best fgn. lang. book The Tin Drum, 1962. Mem. Berlin Acad. Fine Arts. Roman Catholic. Author: The Tin Drum (pub. German, other langs.), 1959; (plays) Die Bösen Koche, Noch zehn Minuten bis Buffalo, Hochwasser, 1957, Onkel, Onkel, 1965; (poetry) Gleisdreeck, 1960, Die Vorzüge der Windhühner, 1965; Cat and Mouse, 1961; The Dog Years, 1963; Selected Poems, 1966; Ausgefragt, 1967; Four Plays, 1967; New Poems, 1968; Plebeians Rehearse the Uprising, 1966; Davor, 1968; Ortlich Betäubt, 1969. Home: Niedstrasse 13 Berlin 41 Germany

GRASSELLI, CAESAR AUGUSTIN, II, ret. chem. co. exec.; b. Cleve., Feb. 17, 1901; s. Thomas S. and Emilie (Schmidt) G.; A.B., Cornell U., 1924; m. Elizabeth Hunkin, Oct. 12, 1929; 1 dau., Josephine Eugenia (Mrs. Thomas G. Winter). With Grasselli Chem. Co. (became subsidiary duPont 1928), 1925-29; with E. I. duPont de Nemours & Co., Wilmington, London, Eng., 1930-55, ret., 1955. Trustee, chmn. pres.'s council PMC Colls.; mem. Cornell U. Council. Trustee Wilmington Med. Center. Chmn. local bd. SSS. Served from maj. to col., AUS, 1942-46; ETO, MTO. Decorated Legion of Merit, Order Brit. Empire. Home: 1100 Blackshire Rd Wilmington DE 19805 Office: Hotel Dupont Wilmington DE 19899

GRASSHOF, ALEX, writer, producer, dir.; b. Boston, Dec. 10, 1930; student psychology and English, Tufts Coll., 1949-50; B.A. in Cinema, U. So. Cal., 1953. Film editor, 1954; writer, producer, dir. mental health documentary Emotion Stress. 1955, The Jailbreakers, 1956, Roy on the Run, 1960; formed Grassco Prodns., 1959; producer, dir. series The Story of for TV. Recipient Oscar award for best documentary Young Americans, 1968. Address: care Columbia Pictures Corp 711 Fifth Av New York City NY 10022*

GRASSI, JOSEPH GERALD, educator; b. Rochester, N.Y., July 16, 1919; s. Andrew and Phyllis (DeFelice) G.; A.B., St. Bernard's Coll., Rochester, 1942; M.A., Cath. U. Am., 1949; postgrad. (Italian Govt. fellow), U. Florence (Italy), 1953-55; Ph.D., U. Buffalo, 1960. Lectr., Howard U., 1947; instr. La Salle Coll., Phila., 1948-53; asst. prof. Rochester Inst. Tech., 1955-61; prof. Fairfield (Conn.) U., 1961—, also chmn. philosophy dept., dir. Humanities Summer Inst. Served with USNR, 1941-43. Mem. Am. Philos. Assn., Metaphys. Soc. Am., Phenomenological and Existential Soc., Soc. for Philos. and Pub. Affairs. Author: The Political Philosophy of B. Croce, 1960; The Need for Dissent, 1969; Toward A Philosophy of Credit, 1970. Home: 2178 Kings Hwy E Fairfield CT 06430

GRASSO, ELLA T., (Mrs. Thomas A. Grasso), congresswoman; b. Windsor Locks, Conn., May 10, 1919; d. James and Maria (Oliva) Tambussi; student pvt. schs.; B.A. magna cum laude, Mt. Holyoke Coll., 1940, M.A., 1942; m. Thomas A. Grasso, Aug. 31, 1942; children—Susane, James. Asst. in dept. econs. and sociology Mt. Holyoke Coll., 1942; apptd. asst. state dir. research War Manpower Commn., 1943-46. Mem. Conn. Legislature, 1953, 55, asst. house leader, 1955; state sec. State of Conn., 1958-70; mem. 92d Congress from 6th Dist. Conn. Nat. committeewoman from Conn. Democratic Party, 1956-58, chmn. state platform com., 1958, 60, 62, 64, 66, 68, nat. platform com., 1960, co-chmn. resolutions com. Dem. Nat. Conv., 1964, 68; del., Dem. floor leader Constl. Conv., 1965. Mem. Com. 100 for Hartford U.; mem. Bd. Fgn. Scholarships, 1960-66. Assn. Mental Health, Conn. Inst. Blind, Bd. dirs. Windsor Locks Pub. Library; hon. dir. Urban League Greater Hartford; mem. adv. bd. Hartford, Am. Com. Italian Migration. Recipient Amita award as outstanding women of Italian parentage, 1959, Am. Heritage award, 1961, Americanism award Conn. Valley council B'nai B'rith, 1963, Italian-Am. Gold medal Conn. lodge Order Sons of Italy in Am., 1963; named Woman of Year, Hartford Bus. and Profl. Womens Club, 1964; recipient Silver Apple award Conn. Edn. Assn., Most Distinguished Service citation Am. Legion, Knight in Order Merit Republic Italy, 1968. Mem. Am. Assn. U. Women, Conn. Council Catholic Women (dir.), Order of Sons of Italy, League Women Voters, Kappa Delta Pi (citation Central Conn. State Coll. chpt. 1960). Clubs: Mt. Holyoke (Hartford); Pilot. Office: Cannon Office Bldg Washington DC 20515

GRATTAN, CLINTON HARTLEY, author; b. Wakefield, Mass., Oct. 19, 1902; s. Leonard and Laura (Campbell) G.; A.B., Clark Coll., Worcester, Mass., 1923; D. Litt., Clark U., 1953; m. Beatrice Kay, Oct. 22, 1926 (div. 1934); m. 2d, Marjorie Sinclair Campbell, June 3, 1939; childrenRosalind Campbell (Mrs. Arthur von Au), Jennifer Hartley (Mrs. Alan Corner), Jacqueline Allison (Mrs. Conrad Smeeth), John Hartley. Head dept, English, Urbana (O.) Jr. Coll., 1923-25; writer, 1925-; vis. fellow Australian Nat. U., 1960; curator Grattan Collection of Southwest Pacificana, univ. prof. history U. Tex., 1964—. Author books including: Way We Fought, 1929, 66; Bitter Bierce: A Mystery of American Letters, 1929, 66; The Three Jameses: A Family of Minds, 1932 62; (with Paxton Hibben) The Peerless Leader: William Jennings Bryan, 1929, 67; Introducing Australia, 1942, rev. edit., 1947; Australia (U.N. Series), 1947: (with Sylvan Hoffman) News of the World, 1953; In Quest of Knowledge, 1955; The United States and The Southwest Pacific, 1961; The Southwest Pacific: A Modern History, 2 vols., 1963. Editor publs. including: Such is Life, by Tom Collins, 1948; American Ideas about Adult Education 1710-1951, 1959, Collaborator News of the Nation, 1944, and others. Contbr. articles on Australia 1945 edit. Ency. Americana. Contbr. to Harpers, Am. Mercury, Scribners and other nat. mags., 1924-; writer on Australian affairs, 1927—. Awarded grant by Carnegie Corp., N.Y.C., to study social devel. of Australia, 1937-38. Home: 702 Spofford St Austin TX 78704

GRATZ, HOMER TUCKER, govt. ofcl.; b. Louisville, Dec. 11, 1906; s. Hugh Turney and Ora (Tucker) G.; grad. Sheldon Bus. Sch., Chgo., 1926, Greenville (Ill.) Coll., 1927; m. Julie Boyd Gratz. U.S. collector customs, Hawaii, 1950-52; pres., chmn. bd. Better Brands, Ltd., Honolulu, 1952-64; pres. Pepsi-Cola of Hawaii, 1964; v.p. Windward Properties, 1948—; Hawaii dir. U.S. Dept. Commerce, 1964—. Chmn. Pacific War Meml. Commn.; pres. Aloha council Boy Scouts of Am., 1963-66; chmn. Pacific National Cemetery in Puowaina. Served from lt. to comdr. USNR, 1938-45; capt. Res. ret. Recipient commendations for meritorious and outstanding service PTO; recipient Silver Beaver award Boy Scouts Am., 1957. Mem. Res. Officers Assn. (nat. v.p. 1951-52), Naval Res. Officers Assn. Hawaii (pres. 1947), Am. Legion, V.F.W., Navy League (pres. Hawaii 1967), U.S. C. of C. Presbyn. Mason (Shriner). Clubs: Outrigger Canoe, Rotary (pres. 1966-67) (Honolulu). Address: Alexander Young Bldg 1015 Bishop St Honolulu HI 96813

GRAU, ALBERT A., educator; b. Switzerland, 1918; s. Albert G. and Martha (Koehler) G.; came to U.S., 1926, naturalized, 1938; B.S. with distinction and honors in Math., U. Mich., 1940, M.S., 1941, Ph.D. in Math., 1944; m. Doris Teague, June 15, 1965; 1 dau., Doris Anne. Univ. fellow U. Mich., 1941-44, instr., 1944-45, Horce H. Rackham postdoctoral fellow, 1944-45; mem. Inst. Advanced Study, 1944-45; instr.. Drake U., 1945-46; asst. prof. U. Ky., 1946-47; asso. prof. U. Ala., 1947-48; U. Okla., 1948-56; sr. mathematician Oak Ridge Nat. Lab., 1956-63; prof. Northwestern U., 1963—; cons. Argonne Nat. Lab., 1966—; lectr. George Washington U., 1947, U. Tenn., 1957-60. Bd. dirs. Grace Inst. Bible, Oklahoma City, 1951-52. Mem. Am. Math. Soc., Math. Assn. Am., Assn. Computing Machinery, Soc. Indsl. and Applied Math., Phi Beta Kappa, Sigma Xi, Phi Kappa Phi, Mem. Gospel Ch. Author: (with others) Translation of Algol 60, 1967; also articles. Home: 826 Milburn St Evanton IL 60201

GRAU, SHIRLEY ANN, (Mrs. James Kern Feibleman), writer; b. New Orleans, July 8, 1929; d. Adolph and Katherine (Onions) Grau; B.A., Tulane U., 1950; m. James Kern Feibleman, Aug. 4, 1955; children—Ian, James, Nora Miranda, William, Katherine. Writer for Holiday, New Yorker, New World Writing, Mademoiselle, Sat. Eve. Post, Atlantic, The Reporter, 1954—. Author: The Black Prince and Other Stories, 1955; The Hard Blue Sky, 1958; The House on Coliseum Street, 1961; The Keepers of the House (Pulitzer prize for fiction 1965), 1964. Mem. Phi Beta Kappa. Office: care Brandt and Brandt 101 Park Av New York City NY 10017

GRAUBARD, SEYMOUR, lawyer; b. N.Y.C., Mar. 8, 1911; s. John and Edna (Kiesler) G.; A.B., Columbia, 1931, LL.B., 1933; m. Blanche Kazon, Aug. 24, 1941; 1 dau., Katherine (Mrs. William Calvin). Admitted to N.Y. bar, 1933; legislative asst. to bd. aldermen, N.Y.C., 1934-35; partner Joseph D. McGoldrick, N.Y.C., 1936-37; law sec. to comptroller N.Y.C., 1937-41; sec. to justice supreme ct. N.Y. County, 1942, 45-46; practice in N.Y.C., 1949- -; mem. firm Graubard, Moskovitz, McGoldrick, Dannett & Horowitz, 1969- -; lectr. municipal govt. N.Y.U., New Sch. Social Research, 1938-40. Mem. N.Y.C. Commn. Govtl. Operations, 1959-61, N.Y.C. Transition Com., 1965, Coordinating Council Criminal Justice, 1967—. Nat. chmn. Anti- Defamation League, B'nai B'rith, 1970—. Trustee Fund for N.Y.C., N.Y.C. Pub. Events Com., City Univ. Constrn. Fund. Served to maj. AUS, 1942-45. Mem. Assn. Bar City N.Y. (past chmn. com. city cts.), N.Y. State Bar Assn., N.Y. County Lawyers Assn. Clubs: City (trustee past pres.), Harmonie (N.Y.C.). Author: (with Joseph D. McGoldrick) Building Regulation in New York City, 1944; also articles. Home: 993 Park Av New York NY 10028 Office: 345 Park Av New York NY 10022

GRAUBART, ELLA, lawyer; b. Boston, Sept. 30, 1896; d. Samuel and Dora (Trattner) Graubart; B.A., Hunter Coll., 1917; postgrad. N.Y.U., 1922-24; LL.B., U. Pitts., 1927; m. Charles Frederick Covert Arensberg, Aug. 18, 1949; 1 dau., Nancy Bay. Admitted to Pa. bar, 1927, since practiced in Pitts.; prvt. practice, 1927-34; asso. Patterson, Crawford, Arensberg & Dunn, 1934-40, partner, 1940-45, sr. partner, 1945-. Dir. Imperial Glass Co. Trustee Point Park Coll. Mem. Am., Pa., Allegheny County bar assns., Am. Judicature Soc., Internat. Law Assn. Unitarian. Club: Figure Skating (pres.), Harbor, Rolling Rock, Golf (Pitts.). Author: Yesterdays Laws and To-days Accidents; also articles. Home: 834 Amberson Av Pittsburgh PA 15232 Office: First Nat Bank Bldg Pittsburgh PA 15222

GRAUE, LOUIS C., educator; b. Louisana, Mo., Dec. 23, 1923; s. Louis J. and Ruth (Foreman) G.; B.S., U. Chgo., 1947, M.S., 1948; Ph.D., Ind. U., 1950; m. Patricia J. Hock, June 24, 1949; childrenGeoffrey, Nancy, David. Instr., then asst. prof. Sacramento State Coll., 1950-56; asso. prof. Coe Coll., Cedar Rapids, Ia., 1956-59; faculty Bowling State (O.) U., 1959-, now prof. math., chmn. dept. Served to lt. (j.g.) USNR, 1944-46. Home: 624 Campbell Hill Rd Bowling Green OH 43402

GRAUER, BENJAMIN FRANKLIN, radio, TV reporter: b. N.Y. C., June 2, 1908; s. Adolph and Ida Kunstler (Goldberg) G.; B.S.S., Coll. City N.Y., 193O; m. Melanie Kahane, Sept. 25, 1954. Played in motion pictures and theatre, 1915-25; employed with NBC 193O—, covering every type of spl. event and news broadcast including Olympic games, 1932, presdl. inaugurations, 1937—, Dem. and Rep. convs. since 1944; United Nations Conf., 1945; Paris, Conf., 1946; Israel-Arab War, 1948; Gen. Assembly, Paris, 1948; Berkshire Music Festival, 1949; Brit. Coronation, 1953; UN Security Council, 1960. NBC Symphony under Toscanini, 1940-54; Spanish commentator on Telstar, 1962; master ceremonies NBC's Atlantic Spotlight (with BBC.). Moderator TV panel show, It's a Problem. Producer- narrator, Senor Ben and His PanAm. Hwy. of Melody; narrator of the TV documentary, March of Medicine; editor-host of TV program Big Story; host-commentator radio program ToscaniniThe Man Behind the Legend; reporter Daily Bus. Trends; moderator TV panel program Newslight; communicator Monitor program; co-producer of Shaw's Mrs. Warren's Profession. Recipient George Sandham prize Coll. City N.Y., 1930; Nat. winner, H.P. Davis announcers award, 1944; Alumnae Service medal, 1949; Civilian Service citation, U.S. Army, 1951; Crusade for Freedom citation, 1953; recipient Man of Year Award Nat. Fedn. Temple Brotherhood, 1955; decorated Chevalier, Legion of Honor. Mem. Bibliog. Soc. Am., Nat. Music League (pres.), Acad. TV Arts and Scis. (nat. sec.), OPC Corr. Fund (pres.), Tau Delta Phi, Sigma Delta Chi. Clubs: Overseas Press (trustee), Grolier. Author: March on Pharoah, 1932; Bernal Diaz Reborn, 1956. Editor: NBC News Picture Book of the Year, 1967, 68, 69. Home: 29 E 63d St New York City NY 10021 Office: NBC Radio City New York City NY 10020

GRAULTY, WILLIAM WILLARD, banker; b. Troy, N.Y., Dec. 30, 1923; s. William and Grace (Colton) G.; B.A., Dartmouth, 1946; LL.B., Harvard, 1951; m. Dorothy Burke Yeomans, Oct. 4, 1968; children by previous marriageWilliam Willard, Colton D., Susan, Martha, Henry H., Roger D. Admitted to Conn. bar, 1951; with firm Robinson, Robinson & Cole, Hartford, 1951-56; with Conn. Bank & Trust Co., Hartford, 1956-, exec. v.p., 1967-; dir. Nat. Fire Ins. Co. Trustee, chmn. bd. Renbrook Sch., West Hartford, Conn., 1962-68. Served with USNR, 1943-45. Mem. Conn. Bankers Assn. (chmn. trust div. 1966-68). Episcopalian (vestryman 1955-58, 60-63, 66-69). Homme: 27 Talcott Notch Rd Avon CT 06001 Office: 1 Constitution Plaza Hartford CT 06115

GRAUMANN, HUGO OSWALT, plant scientist, agrl. adminstr.; b. Granite, Okla., May 31, 1913; s. G. and Amelia (Neumann) G.; B.Sc., Okla. State U., 1938, M.Sc., 1940; Ph.D., U. Neb., 1950; m. Modelle S. Pattillo, Aug. 7, 1935; 1 dau., DeEstye (Mrs. Merle Richman). Asst. agronomist Okla. State U., 1938-40, asst. prof. agronomy, then asso. prof., 1941-47; res. agronomist U.S. Dept. Agr., Lincoln, Neb., 1947-53, Beltsville, Md., 1953-58, agrl. adminstr. forage and range research br. Agrl. Research Service, Beltsville, 1958-65, agrl. adminstr. crops research div., 1965-66, 68-70, dep. dir. sci. and edn., 1967, dir. plant sci. research div., 1971—; spl. research plant breeding in alfalfa. Fellow Am. Soc. Agronomy, A.A.A.S.; mem. Am. Genetic Assn., Crop Sci. So. Am. (pres. 1964), Sigma Xi, Alpha Zeta, Phi Kappa Phi, Phi Sigma, Gamma Sigma Delta. Home: 1714 Edgewater Pkwy Silver Spring MD 20903 Office: Plant Industry Station Beltsville MD 20705

GRAVAGNO, EMILIO ANTHONY, musician; b. Chgo., Jan. 13, 1934; s. David and Domenica (Lo Galbo) G.; diploma Curtis Inst. Music, 1958; student music edn. Southeastern La. Coll., DePaul U., 1951-54; m. Ann Clara Chastain, Oct. 18, 1953; children—Daniel, John, Cary. With New Orleans Symphony, 1958-60, Balt. Symphony, 1962-67; with Phila. Orch., 1967—. Tchr. doublebass Glassboro State Coll. Mem. Phi Mu Alpha. Home: 15 E Albemarle Av Lansdowne PA 19050 Office: 230 S 15th St Philadelphia PA 19102

GRAVEL, CAMILLE FRANCIS, Jr., lawyer; b. Alexandria, La., Aug 10, 1915; s. Camille F. and Aline (Delvaille) G.; student Notre Dame U., 1931-35, La. State U., 1935-37, Cath. U. Am., 1937-39; m. Katherine David, Nov. 26, 1939; children—Katherine Ann, Mary Eileen (Mrs. Richard B. Cappell), Martha Louise (Mrs. Thomas A. Antoon), Camille III, Grady, Eunice (Mrs. Joseph Mitchell), Virginia (Mrs. Larry Carbo), Lynn, Mark, Gregory. Admitted to La. bar, 1940, practiced in Alexandria; asst. dist. atty., Rapides Parish, 1942; atty. La. tax collector, 1943-45; asst. city atty., 1945-48; atty. La. tax commn., 1949-52; sr. partner Gravel, Roy & Burnes; dir. Payne Gravel Corp., So. Ventures Corp., Couvel Corp., Myci Corp., Holiday Builders, Inc. Mem. Nat. Citizen's Com. for Community Relations, 1964; mem. Gov.'s Adv. Commns. on Workmen's Compensation Laws and Tax Laws La., 1964-65; spl. counsel on medicare to gov. La., 1966-67; Gov's spl. counsel on health, 1967. Mem. Democratic Nat. Com., 1954-60, La. Dem. State Central Com., 1948-64; presdl. elector, 1952; del. Dem. Nat. Conv., 1956, 60, 64, chmn. La. delegation, 1956, rep. 12 so. states on nat. exec. com., 1955-60. Bd. dirs. Cath. Charities, Diocese of Alexandria; bd. advisers N. Central Cath. Register. Decorated knight of St. Gregory (Pope Pius XII). Fellow Internat. Acad. Trial Lawyers (bd. dirs. 1960), Law Sci. Acad.; mem. Am., La. (bd. govs. 1969-71), Alexandria (pres. 1949-50) bar assns., Am. Trial Lawyers Assn. (asso. editor law jour. Cath. U. Am. Alumni Assn. (nat. bd. govs. 1960-68 pres. alumni chpt. 1962-68), Notre Dame Law Assn. (dir. 1960-66, 1962-63), Am. Legion, Law Sci. Acad., Internat. Soc. Barristers, Kappa Sigma, Phi Delta Phi. K.C. (4), Elk. Clubs: City (Baton Rouge). Home: 3214 Carol St Alexandria LA 71301 Office: 611 Murray St Alexandria LA 71301

GRAVEL, MIKE, U.S. senator; b. Springfield, Mass., May 13, 1930; s. Alphonse and Maria Gravel; student Assumption Coll., Worcester, Mass., 1949-50, Am. Internat. Coll., Springfield, 1950-51; B.S. in Econs., Columbia, 1956; m. Rita Jeannette Martin, Aug. 25, 1959; childrenMartin, Lynn. Engaged in real estate, 1958; mem. Alaska Ho. of Reps. from Anchorage, 1962-68, speaker of house, 1964-66; U.S. senator from Alaska, 1969-. Past pres. Anchorage Tb Assn. Served with AUS, 1951-54. Author: Jobs and More Jobs, 1968. Home: PO Box 2283 Anchorage AK 99501 Office: US Senate Washington DC 20510

GRAVEL, RAIMEAU EMILE, Canadian diplomat; b. Gravelbourg, Sask., Can., Sept. 3, 1912; s. Maurice and Rosie (Lemelin) G.; B.A., U. Ottawa, 1934; M.Commerce, U. Montreal, 1938; B.Econ. Sci., U. San Marcos, Lima, Peru, 1951; m. Anita Larrain del Campo, Oct. 11, 1947; children—Richard James, Maurice, Raineau. Sec. Retail Merchants Assn. Can., 1938-39; asst. gen. agt. for Que., 1939-41; assigned Canadian embassies in Chile, Argentine, Peru, Santo Domingo and Venezuela, 1945-60; consul gen., Hamburg, Germany, 1960-64; comml. counsellor, charge d'affairs, Santiago, Chile, 1964-69; consul, head of post, Detroit, 1970—. Served to lt. comdr. Royal Canadian Navy, 1941-45. Decorated Coronation medal (Queen Elizabeth): comdr. Order Merit (Santo Domingo and Chile). Mem. Econ. Club Detroit. Clubs: Detroit; Union (Santiago). Home: 8162 E Jefferson St Detroit MI 48214 Office: First Fed Bldg 1001 Woodward Av Detroit MI 48214

GRAVENSTEIN, JOACHIM STEFAN, educator, anesthesiologist; b. Berlin, Germany, Jan. 25, 1925; Dr. med., U. Bonn (Germany), 1951; M.D., Harvard, 1958; m. Alix Trutschler, Aug. 27, 1949; childrenNikolaus, Alix, Frederike, Stefan, Ruprecht, Dietrich, Constanze, Katharina. Came to U.S., 1952, naturalized, 1959. Resident and staff appointments anesthesia Mass. Gen. Hosp., 1952-58; fellow, tchr. Harvard Med. Sch., 1952-58; chief anesthesiology Coll. Medicine, U. Fla., 1958-69; prof. anesthesiology, chmn. dept. Case Western Res. Med. Sch., 1969-. Mem. Am. Soc. Anesthesiology, Am. Soc. Pharmacology and Exptl. Therapeutics. Home: 15000 Shaker Blvd Shaker Heights OH 44120 Office: University Hospitals 2065 Adelbert Rd Cleveland OH 44106

GRAVER, HAROLD ANDERSON, business exec.; b. Colton, S.D., Jan. 28, 1905; s. Ole Peter and Annie (Austin) Anderson; B.A., Northwestern U., 1928, M.A., 1935, Ph.D., 1941; m. Gertrude Askew, Feb. 14, 1946; children—Anne Askew, Kingsbury Gene. Guidance counselor secondary schs., Chgo., 1928-38; admissions dir. Northwestern U. Dental Sch., Chgo., 1938-42; psychol. cons. Rohrer, Hibler & Replogle, Chgo., 1944-46; personnel dir., v.p., sec., dir. Hardware Mut. Casualty Co., Stevens Point, Wis., 1946—; v.p., sec. Hardware Dealers Mut. Fire Ins. Co., 1946-70; v.p., sec., dir. Sentry Life Ins. Co., 1958—, Sentry Life Ins. Co. N.Y., 1966—; sec.; dir. Sentry Plan Inc., 1960- 69, The Sentry Corp., Wilmington, Del., 1967—; sec. Sentry Ins. Mgmt., Ltd., London, 1969-70; pvt. practice as cons. psychologist, Stevens Point, 1970—; coop. edn. coordinator Wis. State U., Stevens Point, 1970—. Sec. bd. edn. Stevens Point Sch. Vocational and Adult Edn., 1959-70. Pres., dir. Sentry Found., 1964-70. Served to lt. USNR, 1942-44. Diplomate Am. Bd. Examiners in Profl. Psychology. Fellow Am. Psychol. Assn.; mem. Midwestern, Wis. psychol. assns. Rotarian. Home: 402 Greenbriar Av Stevens Point WI 54481

GRAVER, WILLIAM JEFFERIS, fgn. service officer; b. Balt., Mar. 25, 1922; s. William Harold and Frances (Williams) G.; B.A., Washington and Jefferson Coll., 1943; m. Rosemary Smith, Mar. 29, 1952; childrenJefferis William, Christopher Tobin. Civilian employee USAAF and USAF, 1942-51; with Dept. of Army, Germany, 1952-58, Washington, 1958-61; joined U.S. Fgn. Service, 1961; assigned Am. embassy, Berlin, Germany, 1961-66; with Bur. European Affairs Dept. State, Washington, 1966-69; polit. officer Am. embassy, Vienna, Austria, 1969—. Served with USAAF, World War II. Mem. Phi Beta Kappa. Home: 3228 Highland Lane Fairfax VA 22030

GRAVES, ALBERT AUGUSTUS, banker; b. Newark, O., Apr. 20, 1906; s. Winslow Warren and Lola (Vanatta) G.; ed. Denison U.; grad. Stonier Grad. Sch. Banking, 1949; m. Edda Eileen Foster, May 22, 1928; children—Patricia, Ann (Mrs. William Austin), With Central Nat. Bank, Cleve., 1928-35, First Nat. Bank, Utica, O., 1935-43; with Central Trust Co., Cin., 1943—, sr. v.p., 1969—. Sr. thesis examiner Stonier Grad. Sch. Banking; tchr., chmn. adv. bd. Am. Inst. Banking. Bd. dirs., treas. Vol. Bur. of Cin. United Appeal. Mem. Cin. Clearing House Assn. (pres.), Am. Bankers Assn. (chmn. program instrn. com.), Cin. Bankers Club. Home: 1033 Sea Sage Dr Delray Beach FL 33444 Office: 308 Race St Cincinnati OH 45202

GRAVES, ALLEN WILLIS, religious educator; b. Rector, Ark., Jan. 20, 1915; s. James Henry and Anna Joyce (Keaster) G.; B.Ed., So. Ill. U., 1935; Th.M., So. Bapt. Theol. Sem., 1939, Th.D., 1942; m. Helen Elizabeth Cannan, June 1, 1937; children—Joyce (Mrs. Carl Olney), John Raymond, Dorothy (Mrs. William Dinwiddie), David, Virginia (Mrs. John Weisz), Thomas. Pub. sch. tchr., Herrin, Ill., 1935-36; ordained to ministry Bapt. Ch., 1935; pastor in Ill. and Ky., 1935-41; dir. young peoples work Bapt. Tng. Union Dept., Bapt. Sunday Sch. Bd., Nashville, 1941-43; pastor in Fla., 1943-45, Va., 1945-50, Okla., 1950-55; dean Sch. Religious Edn., So. Bapt. Theol. Sem., 1955-69, adminstrv. dean, 1969—. Mem. So. Bapt. Religious Edn. Assn. (pres. 1962-63). Author: Christ in my Career, 1958; Church Committee Manual, 1958; (with B.B. McKinney) Let us Sing, 1943; Using and Maintaining Church Property, 1965; The Church at Work: A Handbook of Church Polity, 1971. Home: 328 S Birchwood Av Louisville KY 40206

GRAVES, AUSTIN TAYLOR, business exec.; b. Louisville, Sept. 19, 1908; s. W J. and Eva S. (Raplee) G.; B.S., U. Ky., 1929; m. Mary Hill Goodall, Oct. 27, 1935; children—Linda, Austin Taylor. Asso. with Marshall Field & Co., Chgo., 1930, v.p., gen. operating mgr., 1946-53; pres. John Wanamaker, N.Y., 1953-55; pres., dir. Products of Asia, Inc., 1955-64; pres., dir. Products of India, Inc., 1959-64; exec. v.p. Gruen Industries, Inc., N.Y.C., 1966-67, pres., 1967—, also dir. Former dir. Child Welfare League of Am., Inc.; former trustee, sec. Ill. Children's Home and Aid Soc.; former v.p. Chgo. Crime Commn.; mem. bus. adv. com. U. Wis., Green Bay. Mem. Phi Mu Alpha, Delta Sigma Pi, Beta Gamma Sigma. Mem. Christian Ch. Clubs: University, Tokeneke. Home: 9 Sunswyck Rd Darien CT 06820 Office: Gruen Industries Inc 20 W 47th St New York City NY

GRAVES, BENJAMIN BARNES, univ. pres.; b. Jones County, Miss., Nov. 5, 1920; s. Thomas Cannon and Velma (Barnes) G.; B.A., U. Miss., 1942; M.B.A., Harvard, 1947; Ph.D., La. State U., 1961; LL.D., U. Ala., 1970; m. Hazeline Wood, May 25, 1946; children—Benjamin Barnes, Janis Elizabeth, Cynthia Wood. Staff and supervisory positions Humble Oil Co., 1947-60; spl. lectr. Coll. Bus. Adminstrn., La. State U., 1959-60, asst. prof., 1960-62; asso. prof. U. Va., 1962-64; Milner prof. indsl. econs. U. Miss., 1964-65; pres. Millsaps Coll., Jackson, Miss., 1965-70, U. Ala. in Huntsville, 1970—. Guest lectr. Mid-South Exec. Devel. Program, La. State U., 1962-68, also asso. dir. program, 1961-62; guest lectr. mgmt. program Natural Resources Mgrs., Pa. State U., 1962-, Va.-Md. Sch. Banking, U. Va., 1962-. Pres. Miss. Found. Ind. Colls., 1967-68; mem. com. human investigation U. Miss. Sch. Medicine, 1964-; v.p. Miss. Jr.-Sr. Coll. Conf., 1968-69; pres. Miss. Assn. Colls., 1969-70; mem. exec. com. Ind. Coll. Funds Am.; mem. adv. com. Am. Council on Edn.'s Inst. for Coll. and U. Adminstrs. Mem. exec. bd. Andrew Jackson council Boy Scouts Am., 1966—. Bd. dirs. Jackson Symphony Assn., 1965—. Served to lt. (s.g.) USNR, 1942-46. Mem. Acad. Mgmt., Am. Marketing Assn., Southwestern Social Sci. Assn., So. Econ. Assn., A.I.M. (president's council), Jackson C. of C., Pi Kappa Alpha (mem. centennial com. 100), Omicron Delta Kappa. Methodist. Rotarian. Author articles in field. Home: 703 Adams St SE Huntsville AL 35801

GRAVES, BERT I., former oil co. exec.; b. St. Paul; s. Charles and Ellen (Ufford) G.; student pub. schs.; m. Grace Guthrie, Dec. 3, 1918. With Tide Water Asso. Oil Co. and predecessor co., 1909-53, in various capacities in San Francisco, Shanghai, and N.Y.C., v.p., dir., chmn. operating com. Eastern div., hdqrs., N.Y.C.; pres. B. I. Graves Assos., petroleum cons., N.Y.C. and San Francisco, 1953-69; dir. Dodge Land Co., San Francisco, United Life & Accident Co., Concord, N.H. Club: Bohemian (San Francisco). Home: 150 W Edith Av Los Altos CA 94022

GRAVES, CHARLES L., bus. exec.; b. 1916; B.C.E., U. Louisville, 1938. With various constrn. cos., 1938-46; with J. Ray McDermott & Co., Inc., 1946-, v.p., 1955-64, exec. v.p., 1964-, also dir. Address: Box 60035 New Orleans LA 70160

GRAVES, DONALD CHARLES, Jr., advt. exec.; b. Detroit, Nov. 2, 1931; s. Donald Charles and Virginia (Zimmer) G.; student City Coll. N.Y., 1949-50, U. Cal. at Los Angeles, 1950-51; m. Josephine Marie Cacciapalle, Feb. 4, 1953; childrenWalter, Donald Charles III, Jess. With ABC, 1948-49, Hearst Newspapers, 1949-50, CBS-TV and Radio and affiliates, 1950-56; with Zimmer, Keller & Calvert, Inc., Detroit, 1956-71, pres., 1965-71; sr. v.p., asst. to pres. Ross Roy, Inc., 1971—; chmn. bd. Vernor-Wagner Corp., Cin., 1966—. Chmn. advt. United Found. Detroit, 1967; mem. Nat. council Boy Scouts Am., 1966-68. Served with USMCR, 1947-48. Mem. Adcraft Club Detroit (bd. dirs. 1968—), Am. Assn. Advt. Agys. (chmn. Mich. council 1967). Home: Bloomfield Hills MI 48013 Office: 28 W Adams Av Detroit MI 48226

GRAVES, DOUGLAS FOCH, banker; b. Appleton, Minn., Nov. 11, 1918; s. James and Pearl (Perrin) G.; B.S., Ia. State U., 1942, M.S., 1949; m. Barbara Ruth Giese, Feb. 1, 1942; children-Heidi (Mrs. Gary Downing), Douglas K., Thomas C., Deborah (Mrs. Thomas Reitinger), James H., Jeffrey D. Extension specialist Ia. State Coll. Found., 1946-49; asst. sec. No. Trust Co., Chgo., 1949-57; 2d v.p. Harris Trust Co., Chgo., 1957-61; v.p. 1st Nat. Bank, Freeport, Ill., 1961-68; pres. Nat. Mfrs. Bank, Neenah, Wis., 1968-69, Nat. Bank of Commerce, Jackson, Tenn., 1970—; dir. Carlson-Knowlton, Inc.; lectr. Grad. Schs. Banking, Rutgers U., U. Wis. Mem. Sch. Bd., Freeport, Ill., 1966-68; adviser Jr. Coll., Freeport, 1967-70. Pres. Ill. Brain Research Found.; past bd. dirs. YMCA, Freeport, Community Chest, Neenah, Wis.; trustee Nat. Brain Research Found., Ill. Sch. Banking. Served to capt. AUS, 1942-46. Recipient Ia. State servicekey, 1965. Mem. Am., Ill. (pres.) socs. farm mgrs., Robert Morris Assos., Ia. State U. Nat. Alumni Assn. (past pres.), Phi Delta Theta. Republican. Episcopalian. Author: (with others) Agricultural Credit, 1969. Writer syndicated column for bank publ. Contbr. articles popular mags. Home: 231 Elmwood Dr E Jackson TN 38301 Office: PO Box 189 Jackson TN 38301

GRAVES, EBEN MONTGOMERY, lawyer; b. Saginaw, Mich., Apr. 1, 1903; s. James C. and Nellie (Montgomery) G.; grad. Worcester Acad., 1921; B.S. in Chem. Engring., U. Mich., 1926; LL.B., Fordham U., 1930; m. H. Marion Ward, Dec. 4, 1930; children—Deborah Ward (Mrs. Hugh T. Nolin), James Montgomery, Eben Montgomery. Admitted to N.Y. bar, 1930, also U.S. Supreme Ct.; practice in N.Y.C., 1927—; partner firm Brumbaugh, Graves, Donohue & Raymond, and predecessors, 1935—. Mem. exec. com., del. Nat. Patent Council; mem. internat. indsl. property panel State Dept. Organizing mem. Citizen's Sch. Study Council, Fairfield, Conn.,

1946-50; exec. com. Yale- Fairfield Study Elementary Teaching, 1954-60. Trustee Fairfield Country Day Sch., Wakeman Meml.; bd. dirs. Southport Area Assn. Mem. Bar Assn. City N.Y., N.Y. Patent Law Assn., Am. Bar Assn., Am. Judicature Soc., Am. Patent Law Assn. (pres. 1967-68), Sigma Phi (exec. com. 1935-64). Clubs: Pequot Yacht (bd. govs. 1960-65) (Southport, Conn.); Country of Fairfield (pres. 1950-51); Downtown Assn. (N.Y.C.); Appalachian Mountain. Home: Sasco Point Southport CT 06490 Office: 90 Broad St New York City NY 10004

GRAVES, EDGAR BALDWIN, educator; b. Phila., Sept. 30, 1898; s. Frederic and Mary (Baldwin) G.; A.B., Haverford Coll., 1919, A.M., 1922; LL.D., 1969; Ph.D., Harvard, 1929; postgrad. Inst. Hist. Research, London, 1926-27; m. Beatrice Palmer, June 30, 1927; childrenStephen Palmer (dec.), Barbara (Mrs. William Starnes). Instr. physics Haverford Coll., 1920-22; mem. faculty Hamilton Coll., Clinton, N.Y., 1927-, prof. history, 1936-, McEwen prof., 1968-69, dean civilian program, 1943-44. Mem. Fulbright Com. Cultural History, 1950-54. Harvard Traveling fellow, 1926-27; Am. Council Learned Socs. fellow, 1929, 35, 61; fellow Mediaeval Acad., 1932, 35, Am. Philos. Soc., 1954; Humanities sr. fellow Nat. Found., 1967-68. Mem. Am. Hist. Assn., Mediaeval Acad. Am. (councillor 1950-53), Phi Beta Kappa. Editor: (W.E. Lunt) Accounts Rendered by Papal Collectors in England, 1317-78, 1968. Contbr. profl. jours. Home: 318 College Hill Rd Clinton NY 13323

GRAVES, EDWARD S., lawyer; b. Lynchburg, Va., Dec. 30, 1909; A.B., Washington and Lee U., 1930, M.A., 1931; LL.B., Harvard, 1935. Admitted to Va. bar, 1938; partner firm Edmunds, Williams, Robertson, Sackett, Baldwin & Graves, Lynchburg. Served to lt. comdr. USNR, 1942-45. Mem. Internat., Am., Va., Lynchburg (pres. 1948) bar assns., Assn. Bar City N.Y., Phi Beta Kappa, Omicron Delta Kappa. Office: 916 Main St Lynchburg VA 24504*

GRAVES, FRED HILL, librarian; b. Rockdale, Tex., Feb. 11, 1914; s. Fred Hill and Etta Sherman (Loper) G.; B.A., S.W. Tex. State Coll., San Marcos, 1935; postgrad. U. Tex., 1938, 41, U. Chgo., 1943-46; M.S., Columbia, 1954. Successively tchr. English, librarian, prin. Rockdale (Tex.) High Sch., 1935-43; asst. librarian Bemidji (Minn.) State Coll., 1943-44; acting librarian Hardin-Simmons U., 1944-45; librarian Tex. A. and I. U., Kingsville, 1945-51; asst. to dean Sch. Library Service, Columbia, 1952-54, vis. lectr., spring terms 1968, 70, 71; asst. prof. Grad. Sch. Library Service, Rutgers U., 1954-60; vis. instr. So. Conn. State Coll., New Haven, fall 1960; head librarian Cooper Union, N.Y.C., 1960—. Mem. Am., N.Y. library assns., N.Y. Tech. Services Librarians (exec. bd. 1960-66, pres. 1965-66). Editor Tex. Library Jour., 1948-49. Home: 360 E 55th St New York City, NY 10022.

GRAVES, GERALD WILLIAM, municipal ofcl.; b. Alpena, Mich., July 28, 1923; s. Joseph and Mary J. (Panowic) G.; B.S., U.S. Mcht. Marine Acad., 1943; M.A., Mich. State U., m. Donna I. Rouleau, Feb. 16, 1952; children—Jeri, Donna, Amy, Billy. Exec. dir. Mich. Good Rds. Fedn., also sec. Mich. Joint Legislative Com. Hwy. Needs, 1954-61; city treas. City of Lansing (Mich.), 1961-69, mayor, 1969—. Exec. sec. Lansing Old Newsboys Assn. Rep. Mich. Legislature, 1950-54; sec. Mayor's Com. Human Relations, Lansing, 1961-62. Served to lt. comdr., U.S. Mcht. Marine, World War II. Eagle. Contbr. articles periodicals. Home: 1704 W Shiawassee Lansing MI 48915 Office: City Hall Lansing MI 48933

GRAVES, GRANT OSTRANDER, educator, physician; b. Columbus, O., Jan. 21, 1905; s. Henry and Kathleen (Ostrander) G.; B.A., Ohio State U., 1926, M.A. in Anatomy, 1929, M.D., 1932; m. Helen Louise Pierson, July 18, 1940; childrenScott, Heather, Holly. Intern Duke U. Hosp., 1932-33; resident Univ. Hosp., Columbus, 1933-34; mem. faculty Ohio State U., 1935-, prof. anatomy, 1959-, chmn. dept., 1962-, asst. clin. prof. medicine, 1947-, asst. prof. radiology, 1947-. Mem. exec. bd. Central Ohio Blue Cross, 1960-65. Diplomate Am. Bd. Internal Medicine. Life fellow A.C.P.; mem. Am., Ohio med. assns., Columbus Acad. Medicine (pres. 1951), Alpha Omega Alpha. Home: 3821 Maize Rd Columbus OH 43224

GRAVES, HAROLD KEASTER, sem. pres.; b. Sale Creek, Tenn., Mar. 25, 1912; s. James Henry and Joyce (Keaster) G.; B.Ed., So. Ill. U., 1933; Th.M., So. Bapt. Theol. Sem., 1937, Th.D., 1940; LL.D., Okla. Bapt. U., 1952; m. Frieda Mae Kommer, Sept. 29, 1933; children—Nancy Jo (Mrs. McLaughlin), Harold Keaster. Ordained to ministry Bapt. Ch., 1935; pastor First Bapt. Ch., Jeffersonville, Ind., 1936-41, Chickasha, Okla., 1941-45, Bartlesville, 1945-52; pres. Golden Gate Bapt. Theol. Sem., Mill Valley, Cal., 1952—. Pres. Okla. Bapt. Gen. Conv., 1947-48, dir., 1943-48. Trustee Okla. Bapt. U., 1947-51, chmn., 1951; trustee So. Bapt. Theol. Sem., 1946-52. Mem. Kappa Phi Kappa. Democrat. Mason, Rotarian (dist. gov. R.I. 1969-70). Club: Commonwealth (San Francisco). Author: The Nature and Functions of a Church. Home: 10 Chapel Dr Mill Valley CA 94941

GRAVES, HAROLD NATHAN, Jr., internat. ofcl., author; b. Manila, Philippines, Jan. 20, 1915 (parents Am. citizens); s. Harold Nathan and Florida (Tolbert) G.; A.B., Princeton, 1935; M.S., Columbia, 1936; m. Alta Frances Judy, July 9, 1937; childrenStephen Tolbert, Thomas Perry, Michael Allen. Research asst. Literary Digest, 1936; asso. editor Pathfinder mag., 1936-39; dir. Princeton Listening Center, 1939-41; asst. to dir. fed. broadcast intelligence service FCC, 1941-43; Washington corr. Providence Jour. and Evening Bull., 1946-50; dir. information Internat. Bank Reconstrn. and Devel., 1950-67, Internat. Devel. Assn., 1960-67, Internat. Finance Corp., 1956-57, 61-67; asso. dir. devel. services dept. Internat. Bank for Reconstrn. and Develop., Internat. Devel. Assn., 1967-. Served to lt. (j.g.) USNR, 1943-45. Decorated Order Crown 3d class (Thailand). Club: Cosmos (Washington). Home: 4816 Grantham Av Chevy Chase MD 20015 Office: 1818 H St NW Washington DC 20433

GRAVES, HAROLD P., utility exec.; b. Groton, N.Y., 1917; A.B., Calvin Coll., 1938; J.D., U. Mich., 1941; married. Atty., Consumers Power Co., Jackson, Mich., 1953-55, gen. atty., 1955-58, gen. counsel, 1958-70, v.p., gen. counsel, 1970—. Dir., gen. counsel No. Mich. Exploration Co.; dir. Mich. Gas Storage Co. Home: 605 S Durand St Jackson MI 49203 Office: 212 W Michigan Av Jackson MI 49201*

GRAVES, HAROLD THEODORE, Jr., banker; b. Jamestown, N.D., Nov. 26, 1904; s. Harold Theodore and Lenna (Ford) G.; B.S., U. Pa., 1926; m. Mary Gertrude Burke, Oct. 24, 1932; 1 son, Harold Theodore III. With Guaranty Trust Co. N.Y., 1927-28; with First of Boston, 1928-36; partner N.Y. Stock Exchange firm, 1936-37; v.p., dir. Summit Trust Co. (now Summit and Elizabeth Trust Co.) (N.J.), 1937-57, exec. v.p., dir., 1957-58, now chmn. bd., dir.; dir. C.R. Bard, Inc., Murray Hill, N.J. Treas., trustee Overlook Hosp.; bd. dirs. Shaw U., Raleigh, N.C. Home: 29 Whittredge Rd Summit NJ 07901 Office: 367 Springfield Av Summit NJ 07901

GRAVES, HARRY PARKER, ret. publisher; b. Providence, Nov. 14, 1905; s. John Caunt and Anne (Parker) G.; B.S., Middlebury Coll., 1927; m. Mary Witherbee Owen, Sept. 28, 1938; 1 dau., Nancy Anne (Mrs. L. G. Rieger). Asst. to v.p. Brown & Sharpe Mfg. Co., Providence, 1927-31; coll. rep. Macmillan Co., N.Y.C., 1931-37; v.p. Cordon Co., N.Y.C., 1937-39; West Coast mgr. McGraw-Hill Book Co., San Francisco, 1939-44, mgr. coll. dept., N.Y.C., 1944-46, v.p., 1946-54, v.p., Western dist., 1954-69; ret., 1969. Bd. govs. San Francisco Bay Area Council; bd. dirs. San Francisco Employers Council. Mem. Marin County C. of C. (dir.), Delta Kappa Epsilon. Clubs: Press (San Francisco); Meadow (Fairfax). Home: 50 Rancheria Rd Kentfield CA 94904

GRAVES, JAMES MADISON, lawyer, farmer, rancher; b. Washington County, Ky., July 25, 1912; s. Richard C. and Selena (Drury) G.; A.B., U. Louisville, 1936, LL.B., 1938; m. Beverly McDonald, May 20, 1939; 1 dau., Beverly Jean. Admitted to Ky. bar, 1938, since practiced in Louisville; mem. firm Boehl, Stopher, Graves & Deindoerfer, 1938—. Mem. Am., Ky. State, Louisville bar assns. Home: 10 A Commodore Apts 2140 Bonnycastle Av Louisville KY 40205 also Perryville KY 40468 Office: Kentucky Home Life Bldg Louisville KY 40202

GRAVES, LAWRENCE MURRAY, mathematician; b. Topeka, Aug. 7, 1896; s. William James and Sarah Prescott (Cowgill) G.; A.B., Washburn Coll., 1918, Sc.D., 1941; A.M., U. Chgo., 1920, Ph.D., 1924; m. Josephine Mary Wells, Aug. 27, 1924 (dec. Oct. 1970), children—Robert Lawrence, John Lowell, Anne Lowell (Mrs. Gahn). Instr. math. Washington U., St. Louis, 1920-22; Nat. Research fellow, Harvard, 1924-26; asst. prof. math. U. Chgo., 1926-30, asso. prof., 1930-39, became prof., 1939, now retired; vis. asso. prof. U. Mich., 1930, Stanford, summer 1937; vis. prof. Ind. U., 1947-48; vis. prof. Ill. Inst. Tech., 1961-66. Served with AEF, 1918-20. Mem. applied math. panel Nat. Def. Research Com., 1944-46. Fellow A.A.A.S. (v.p., chmn. sect. A 1952); mem. Am. Math. Soc. (v.p. 1943-44; editorial com. Bull. 1938-43), Math. Assn. Am. (v.p. 1950-51), Sigma Xi. Episcopalian. Clubs: Literary (v.p. 1950- 51), The Quadrangle (Chgo.). Author: The Theory of Functions of Real Variables, 1946. Mem. editorial com. Am. Jour. Math. 1946-50; chmn. editorial com. Internat. Congress Mathematicians, Cambridge, Mass., 1950. Contbr. articles on calculus of variations and functional analysis to math. jours. Home: 315 N La Grange Rd La Grange Park IL 60525

GRAVES, MADISON BAYLES, lawyer; b. N.Y.C., Nov. 5, 1910; s. Horace Cutler and Elsa (Lehmaier) G.; A.B., Harvard, 1931, LL.B., 1934; m. Jane Douglass Willcox, May 21, 1950; children—Madison Bayles II, Horace Cutler II, Lyndon Busbey, Jane Douglass II. Newspaper reporter, 1923- 27; admitted to Mass. bar, 1934, Nev., 1941; practice of law, Boston, 1934-40; mem. firm Morse, Graves, Parraquirre & Rose, Ltd., and predecessor, 1941—; asst. to district atty. Clark County Nev., 1941; deputy city atty., Las Vegas, 1942; U.S. district attorney, 1954-55. Pres. Las Vegas Community Chest, 1948. Chmn. bd. Las Vegas Little Theater, 1951. Served as lt. USNR, 1942-46; now lt. comdr. Mem. State Bar of Nev. (pres. 1960-61), Am., Clark County (pres. 1947) bar assns., Internat. Assn. Ins. Counsel, C. of C., Vets. Fgn. Wars (vice comdr. 1947, judge adv. 1948), Am. Legion (nat. pub. relations commn. 1953—, post comdr. 1946, judge adv. Nev. 1947, vice comdr. 2d dist. 1948, dept. comdr. 1952; dir. 1962 Conv. Corp. Nev.), 40 and 8 (advocate), Amateur Athletic Union, Airplane Owners and Pilots Assn., Clark County Sheriff's Aero Squadron. Eagle, Footprinter, Elk, Mason (32, Shriner). Republican. Clubs: Press (Las Vegas); Hualapai (Las Vegas). Home: 2323 Palomino Lane Las Vegas NV 89107 Office: 200 Las Vegas Blvd Las Vegas NV 89101

GRAVES, MILFORD, musician, percussionist; b. Jamaica, N.Y., Aug. 20, 1941; s. Marvin and Gonive (Williams) G.; student City Coll. N.Y., 1959-60; m. Lois Harris, Jan. 4, 1958; children—Kevin, Lenne, Renita, Kim. Appearances include Newport Jazz Festival, 1965, New Music Concert, Judson Hall, N.Y.C., 1964-65, Town Hall, N.Y.C., 1965, Downbeat mag. summer concert, N.Y.C., 1965, also Improvisations, film short, 1965; recording artist Esp Records.‡

GRAVES, MORRIS COLE, artist; b. Fox Valley, Ore., Aug. 28, 1910; s. Edwin Lyman and Helen (Malson) G. Works exhibited Seattle Art Mus., 1936-56, Mus. Modern Art, 1942, Arts Club Chgo., 1943, Cal. Palace Legion of Honor, 1948, Whitney Mus. Am. Art, 1956; retrospective exhbns. in 1956 in Mus. Fine Arts, Boston, De Young Meml. Mus., San Francisco, others; one man shows Univ. Gallery, Mpls., 1943, Detroit Inst. Art, 1943, Phillips Gallery, Washington, 1943, 54, Santa Barbara Mus. Art, 1948, Los Angeles County Mus., 1948, Art Inst Chgo., 1948, Beaumont (Tex.) Art Mus., 1952, Oslo (Norway) Kuntsforening, 1955, Bridgestone Gallery, Tokyo, 1957; annual exhibitions Philadelphia Art Alliance, 1946, N.Y. World's Fair, 1939, Art Inst. Chgo., 1947, Tate Gallery, London, 1946, 56, Solomon R. Guggenheim Mus., N.Y.C., 1956, others; works rep. permanent collections Art Inst. Chgo., Balt., Cleve., San Francisco museums of art, Detroit, Milw. art insts., Mus. Modern Art, Phillips Gallery, Museum of Contemporary Art, Dublin, Ireland, also the Whitney Mus. Am. Art, Tate Gallery London, and others; retrospective show at Pavilion Gallery, Balboa, Cal., 1963; U.S. State Dept. travelling show Europe, Asia, 1957. Brussells Fair, 1958. Recipient 1st purchase prize Seattle Art Mus., 1933, Harris medal Art Inst. Chgo., 1947, Blair prize, 1948, purchase prize U. Ill., 1955; Guggenheim fellow, 1946; Windsor award, 1957; grant Nat. Inst. Arts and Letters, 1956. Mem. Nat. Inst. Arts and Letters. Home: Loleta CA 95551 Office: care Willard Gallery 23 W 56th St New York City NY 10019

GRAVES, NELSON MONTGOMERY, indsl. cons.; b. Buffalo, May 14, 1895; s. Luther P. and Nellie (White) G.; Ph.B., Yale, 1916; m. Mary Beaty Herod, May 22, 1920; 1 son, Nelson Montgomery. Asso. McDougall-Butler Co., Inc., Buffalo, 1920-37; pres. Barcalo Mfg. Co. div. Mohasco Industries, Inc., 1939-66; now indsl. cons.; trustee Buffalo Savs. Bank; ltd. partner Common, Dann & Co., mems. N.Y. stock exchange, Buffalo, 1967—. Republican. Presbyn. Club: Buffalo. Home: 130 Oakland Buffalo NY 14222

GRAVES, OSCAR ALBERT, Jr., lawyer; b. Hope, Ark., Oct. 16, 1936; s. Oscar Albert and Alice (Pritchard) G.; B.A., Hendrix Coll., Conway, Ark., 1958; LL.B., Harvard, 1961; m. Judith Myers Brannan, July 18, 1958; children—Julie Anne, Allison. Admitted to Ark. bar, 1961, since practiced in Hope; partner Graves & Graves, 1961—. Pres., dir. So. Mills; dir. Citizens Nat. Bank of Hope, So. Grain & Elevator Corp., Hope Leasing Co., Inc., Storage, Inc. Dep. pros. atty., Hempstead County, 1962-66. Mem. Hope City Council, 1963-66. Trustee Pioneer Washington Restoration Found., Hope Sch. Bd. Mem. Ark., S.W. Ark., Hempstead County bar assns. Methodist (trustee). Home: 404 E 14th St Hope AR 71801 Office: Box 458 Hope AR 71801

GRAVES, PETER, actor; b. Mpls., Mar. 18, 1926; s. Rolf C. and Ruth E. (Duesler) Aurness; ed. U. Minn., 1949; m. Joan E. Endress, Dec. 16, 1950; children—Kelly Jean, Claudia King, Amanda Lee. Engaged in motion pictures and TV, 1951—; star TV series Mission Impossible, 1967—. Hon. Cal. chmn. Am. Cancer Soc., 1968. Served with USAAF, 1944- 45. Recipient Outstanding Achievement award U. Minn., 1968. Mem. Phi Kappa Psi. Address: care Fred Barman Assos 9255 Sunset Blvd Los Angeles CA 90069

GRAVES, RALPH, mag. editor; b. Washington, Oct. 17, 1924; s. Ralph and Elizabeth (Evans) G.; B.A., Harvard, 1948; m. Patricia Monser, Oct. 14, 1950 (div.); childrenWilliam, Katherine; m. 2d, Eleanor Mackenzie, Oct. 27, 1958; childrenSara, Andrew. Staff, Life mag., 1948-, successively reporter, writer, 1948-58, articles editor, 1958-61, asst. mng. editor, from 1961, now managing editor of Life sr. staff editor Time, Inc., 1968. Author: Thanks for the Ride, 1949; The Lost Eagles, 1955. Home: 1158 Fifth Av New York City NY 10029 Office: 1271 6th Av New York City NY 10009

GRAVES, RAY, lawyer; b. Seattle, Feb. 23, 1924; s. Ralph Raymond and Naomi (Capron) G.; B.A., Wash. State Coll. 1950; LL.B., Duke, 1952; m. Joan Catherine Kikkert, May 19, 1946; children-Valerie Ann, Jon Carlton. Admitted to Wash. bar, 1952, since practiced in Tacoma; pvt. practice, 1952-60; partner Murray, Scott, McGavick & Graves and predecessor firm, 1960—; mem. Wash. Bd. Bar Examiners, 1968—. Pres., dir. Western Land Mgmt., Inc. Served with USMCR, 1943-46. Mem. Inter-Am., Am., Wash. bar assns., Am. Judicature Soc., Order of Coif. Republican. Presbyn. Mason (32). Clubs: Tacoma Country and Golf, Roesburg (Ore.) Country. Contbr. articles profl. jours. Home: 12101 Clover Creek Dr Tacoma WA 98499 Office: Washington Bldg Tacoma WA 98402

GRAVES, ROBERT, (von Ranke), author; b. London, Eng., 1895; s. Alfred Perceval and Amy G.; ed. Charterhouse Sch. and John's Coll., Oxford. Captain Royal Welch Fusiliers, 1915. Became prof. English litt., Egyptian U., 1926. Author numerous book since 1928, latest publications being: Collected Poems, 1939; Sergeant Lamb's Am., 1940; Proceed, Sergeant Lamb, 1941; Long Week- End (with Alan Hodge), 1941; Story of Marie Powell, wife to Mr. Milton, 1942; Reader Over Your Shoulder (with Alan Hodge), 1943; Golden Fleece, 1944 (U.S., Hercules My Shipmate); King Jesus, 1946, The White Goddess, 1947; Watch the North Wind Rise, 1948; The Isles of Unwisdom, 1949; The Golden Ass, 1951; Greek Myths, 1954; The Nazarene Gospel Restored (with Joshua Podro), 1953; Homer's Daughter, 1955; Collected Poems, 1955; Crowning Privilege, 1956; They Hanged My Saintly Billy, 1957; Five Pens in Hand, 1958; The Anger of Achilles, 1959; Collected Poems, 1961; The Penny Fiddle, 1961; (with Raphael Patai) Hebrew Myths, 1963; New Poems, 1963; Collected Short Stories; Man Does, Woman Is, 1964; Love Respelt, 1965; Poetic Craft and Principles, 1967; Poems 1965-68, 1969; On Poetry: Collected Talks and Essays, 1969; Poems about Love, pub. 1969; 90 others; works, manuscripts permanent exhbn. Lockwood Meml. Library Buffalo U.; prof. of poetry Oxford U., 1961-66; A.B. Little lecturer Mass. Inst. of Tech., 1963. Recipient Russell Loines award for poetry Am. Acad. and Nat. Inst. Arts and Letters, 1958; gold medal award Nat. Poetry Soc. Am., 1960; Gold medal for poetry, Mexican Cultural Olympics, 1968. Home: Deya, Mallorca, Spain. Address: care Watt and Sons 10 Norfolk St London WC2 England

GRAVES, ROBERT LAWRENCE, educator, mathematician; b. Chgo., Sept. 1, 1926; s. Lawrence Murray and Josephine (Wells) G.; B.A., Oberlin Coll., 1947; M.A., Harvard, 1948, Ph.D., 1952; m. Barbara Junette Sward, Oct. 20, 1951; childrenSusan Johanna, Julia Lowell, Christine Craig, Virginia Anne. Teaching fellow Harvard, 1949-51; supervisory and research positions Standard Oil Co. (Ind.), 1951-58; mem. faculty Grad. Sch. Bus., U. Chgo., 1958-, prof. applied math., 1965-. Served to ensign USNR, 1944-46. Mem. Am. Math. Soc., Math. Assn. Am., Operations Research Soc., Inst. Mgmt. Sci., Assn. Computing Machinery (co-chmn. spl. interest group for math. programming 1961-63). Episcopalian. Club: Quadrangle (U. Chgo.). Author: (with H.B. Thorelli) INTOP, The International Operations Simulation, 1964. Editor: (with Philip Wolfe) Recent Advances in Mathematical Programming, 1963. Home: 830 Park Dr Flossmoor IL 60422 Office: Grad Sch Business Univ Chicago Chicago IL 60637

GRAVES, THOMAS ASHLEY, Jr., coll. pres.; b. Buffalo, July 3, 1924; s. Thomas Ashley and Esther (Brittain) G.; grad. Phillips Exeter Acad., 1942; B.A., Yale, 1947; M.B.A., Harvard, 1949, D.B.A. (Ford Found. fellow), 1958; m. Zoe Ann Wasson, June 12, 1962; children—Thomas, Stephe, Mary, Andrew, Elizabeth. Research asst., adminstrv. asst. to dean, asst. dean, asso. dir. doctoral program Harvard. Grad. Sch. Bus. Adminstrn., 1950-60; dir. IMEDE, Internat. Mgmt. Devel. Inst., Lausanne, Switzerland, 1960-64; asso. dean, dir. Internat. Center for Advancement of Mgmt. Edn., Stanford Grad. Sch. Bus., 1964-67; asso. dean. Harvard Grad. Sch., 1967-71; pres. Coll. William and Mary, Williamsburg, Va., 1971—. Mem. adv. bd. CEI Mgmt. Devel. Inst., Geneva, Switzerland, IDEA Mgmt. Devel. Inst., Buenos Aires, Argentina. Trustee Clark U.; bd. curators Transylvania U. Served with USNR, 1943-46. Club: Commonwealth (Richmond, Va.). Home: President's House Coll William and Mary Richmond VA 23185

GRAVES, WALLACE BILLINGSLEY, univ. pres.; b. Ft. Worth, Feb. 10, 1922; s. Ellery George and Edith (Billingsley) G.; B.A., U. Okla., 1943; M.S., Tex. Christian U., 1947; Ph.D., U. Tex., 1953; m. Barbara Jeanne Abey, Nov. 20, 1943; childrenDavid W., Emily B., John R., Julia A. Teaching fellow Tex. Christian U., 1946-47, U. Tex., 1947-50; prof. polit. sci. DePauw U., 1950-58; vis. prof. Butler U., summer 1956; Armstrong prof. govt., dean men Tex. Wesleyan Coll., 1958-63, asst. to pres., 1963-65; acad. v.p. U. Pacific, 1965-67; pres. U. Evansville (Ind.), 1967-. Mem. exec. bd., chmn. home service com. Tarrant County chpt. A.R.C., 1960-65; exec. bd. Buffalo Trace council Boy Scouts Am., 1968-. Trustee Evansville Day Sch., 1967-; dirs. Ft. Worth Assn. Retarded Children, 1963-65, World Affairs Council, Stockton, Cal., 1965-67; adv.-bd. Carl Duisberg Soc., 1960-. Served with AUS, 1943-45. Ford fellow, summer 1951, 55. Mem. Am. Assn. Ind. Coll. and Univ. Presidents (bd. dirs.), Am. Assn. U. Profs., Gold Key, Blue Key, Sigma Nu, Pi Sigma Alpha. Rotarian. Club: Commonwealth (San Francisco); Columbia (Indpls.). Contbr. profl. jours. Home: 1700 Lincoln Av Evansville IN 47714

GRAWEMEYER, HENRY CHARLES, mfg. co. exec.; b. Louisville, Sept. 3, 1912; s. John Adolph and Elise (Scheirich) G.; B.S. in Chem. Engring., U. Louisville, 1934; m. Lucy Martin, July 9, 1937; childrenNancy (Mrs. Donald Robbins), Martha (Mrs. Russell Colton), Marian (Mrs. Richard Hall). With Reliance Universal Inc., Louisville, 1934-70, mgr. Chgo. plant, 1942-57, chmn. bd., 1958-70; chmn. bd. Plastic Parts, Inc., Shelbyville, Ky., 1970—; dir. Gamble Bros. Co., Louisville, Commonwealth Life Ins. Co., Louisville Martin Sweets Co., H.J. Scheirich Mfg. Co., Louisville. Trustee U. Louisville. Mem. Sigma Tau. Presbyn. (elder). Club: Pendennis (Louisville). Home: 2571 Cherosen Rd Louisville KY 40205 Office: Box 63 Shelbyville KY 40065

GRAY, ALLEN DANIEL, Jr., corp. exec.; b. Wilkinsburg, Pa., July 16, 1924; s. Allen Daniel and Ina (Thistlethwaite) G.; B.S., Pa. State U., 1949; M.S., Colo. Sch. Mines, 1952; m. Mary McFall, Sept. 18, 1948; childrenDouglas Allen, Cynthia Lee, Leslie Anne. Pres., dir. Susquehanna Corp., Denver, 1959-62; pres., dir. Edgemont Corp., Golden Glass Corp.; exec. v.p., dir. Terra chems. Internat., Inc., 1964-68; v.p., dir. Energy Devel. Co., Energy Reserves, Inc., Cimmred, Inc. Pres., bd. dirs. Sioux City Hist. Assn.; bd. dirs. Sioux City Art Center, Sioux City Concert Course. Mem. Am. Inst. Mining and Metall. Engrs., Am. Mining Congress, Theta Xi. Clubs: Hawkeye, Sioux City Country. Home: 3935 Orchard Sioux City IA 51104 Office: Orpheum Electric Bldg Sioux City IA 51102

GRAY, ARTHUR, banker; b. Canton, O., Sept. 11, 1891; s. Simon and Sarah (Stone) G.; student pub. schs., Can.; m. Beatriz Lerner, Jan. 13, 1920; children-Joan (Mrs. Samuel Untermyer), Arthur. Sr. partner Arthur Gray & Co., N.Y.C., 1937—; pres. Arthur Gray Corp., 1939—. Chmn. bd. Lerner Marine Lab., Am. Mus. Natural History; gov. Internat. Game Fish Assn.; bd. dirs. Nat. Hosp. for Speech Disorders. Mem. Am. Arbitration Assn. (founder 1922, dir.). Home: 2 E 61st St New York City NY 10021 Office: 730 Fifth Av New York City NY 10019

GRAY, ARTHUR, Jr., investment broker; b. N.Y.C., Dec. 21, 1922; s. Arthur and Beatriz (Lerner) G.; student Lawrenceville (N.J.) School, 1937-40; student Mass. Inst. Tech., 1941-42; m. Adele Hall, Dec. 1944 (div. 1954); children—Michael H., Kathleen W., John M., Wendy L.; m. 2d, Betty Johnson; children—Lydia, Elisabeth. Asso. with Kuhn, Loeb & Co., 1945-53; pres. Michael Myerberg Prodns., 1953-57; exec. v.p., dir. A.M. Kidder & Co., Inc., 1957-59; sr. partner Rossmann, Gray & Co., mems. N.Y. Stock Exchange. Pres. bd. Boys Athletic League, 1960-64, Speech Rehab. Inst., 1970—. Chmn. spl. events Citizens for Eisenhower-Nixon, 1952. Trustee Am. Mus. Natural History; v.p., dir. Lerner-Gray Found.; bd. dirs., mem. exec. com. Presbyn. Progress Found. Served to 1st lt. USAAF, 1942-45. Decorated D.F.C., Air medal with 4 oak leaf clusters. Mem. Am. Arbitration Assn. (dir.), Sigma Alpha Epsilon. Clubs: Wall Street, Lambs (N.Y.C.); Silvermine Golf (Norwalk, Conn.). Home: Maple Hill Farm Barnegat Rd Pound Ridge NY 10576 Office: 40 Wall St New York City NY 10005

GRAY, CARL ALBERT, mfr. co. exec.; b. Worcester, Mass., Dec. 12, 1900; s. Charles Albert and Lillian (Hanson) G.; B.S., Dartmouth Coll., 1923; m. Barbara L. Brown, Apr. 10, 1928; childrenLinda Lathrop, Vernon Carlton, Harvey Lathrop. Began with Am. Steel & Wire Co., Worcester, Mass.; apprentice Osgood Bradley Car Co., Worcester, 1923-24, Colgate Co., Jersey City, 1924-27; with Bankers Trust Co., N.Y.C., 1927-33; v.p. Capewell Mfg. Co., Hartford, Conn., 1933-37; v.p., dir. Whitney Mfg. Co., Hartford, 1937-40; pres., dir. Grenby Mfg. Co., Plainville, Conn., 1940-54; pres. Graham Mfg. Co., Needham, Mass., 1954-69; dir. Omark Industries, United Elastic Corp., Easthampton, Mass. Chmn. Conn. Reemployment Commn.; mem. Conn. Commn. for Reconversion, 1944-47. Mem. Conn. Def. Council; mgmt. adviser tng.-within- industry WPB, Conn. state dir. WPB, 1941-42, chmn. state adv. com., 1942-43, mem. New Eng. regional adv. com., 1942-45; mem. Conn. State War Council, 1943-45; mem. Gov.'s Commn. to Study Edn. in Conn., 1948-50. Chmn. exec. com. Hartford Indsl. Foremen's Club, 1936-39; bd. dirs. Hartford Y.M.C.A., 1936-43, former bd. dirs. internat. assn.; mem. budget com. Hartford Community Chest, 1937-39. Trustee Willston Acad., Mt. Desert Hosp.; mem. adv. council Sch. Engring., U. Conn.; trustee Springfield (Mass.) Coll., mem. exec. com. Recipient Distinguished Service citation for originating job-tng. schs. in Conn. to aid employment, Am. Legion. Mem. U.S.C. of C. (com. on mfr. 1945-47), Am. Soc. Tool Engrs., Conn. Vocational Assn. (pres. 1940—), Internat. Assn. Pub. Services (hon.), Phi Gamma Delta, Delta Sigma Rho, Kappa Phi Kappa. Clubs: Racquet and Tennis, Union, River (N.Y.C.); Hartford (ex-gov.), Hartford Tennis (ex-gov.); Farmington Golf. Author: Connecticut Plan for Postwar Employment. Contbr. articles and editorials to jours. Home: Seal Harbor ME 04675

GRAY, CHARLES T., lumberman; b. Oaksdale, Wash., Feb. 19, 1907; s. George J. and Ethel M. (Thomas) G.; A.B., U. Cal. at Los Angeles, 1929; m. Lenore J. Gillick, Dec. 27, 1932; childrenCharles L., Lenore M. Office clk. Yosemite Lumber Co., Merced Falls, Cal., 1929-33; office mgr. Feather River Lumber Co., Delleker, Cal., 1933-35, asst. mgr., 1935-37, gen. mgr., 1937; spl. asst. to W. S. Johnson, Am. Box Corp., San Francisco, 1937-40; gen. mgr. Stockton Box Co. (Cal.), 1940- 47, v.p., 1947, pres., dir., 1948-65; v.p., dir. Trinity Alps Lumber Co., 1948-66; pres., dir. Ore. Creek Lumber Co., 1945-52; v.p. Am. Forest Products Corp. (formerly Am. Box Corp.), 1948-53, dir., 1948-, exec. v.p., 1954-55, pres., 1956-; pres., dir. Am. Forest Properties, Inc., White Plains, Cal., 1962—; dir. Bendix Corp. Mem. Cal. (dir. 1968- -), San Francisco chambers commerce, Western Wood Products Assn. (v. p. 1959), Cal. Forest Protective Assn. (pres. 1959), Nat. Forest Products Assn., Western Wooden Box Assn., Delta Sigma Phi, Alpha Kappa Psi. Presbyn. Mason (32, Shriner). Clubs: Commonwealth, Olympic (San Francisco). Home: 516 Arballo Dr San Francisco CA 94132 Office: 2740 Hyde St San Francisco CA 94119

GRAY, CLARKE THOMAS, educator; b. Norwood, O., May 7, 1919; s. Charles W. and Adelaide (Clarke) G.; B.S., Eastern Ky. State Coll., 1941; Ph.D., Ohio State U., 1949; postgrad. (Guggenheim fellow) U. Oxford (Eng.), 1959-60; M.A. (hon.), Dartmouth, 1964; m. Mary Agnes Finneran, July 18, 1942; childrenEileen Ann, Charles William II. Dir. biol. control William S. Merrell Co., Cin., 1943-45; research fellow Nat. Tb Assn., 1946-48; instr. bacteriology Ohio State U., Columbus, 1948-49; biochemist Leonard Wood Meml. Found., also research asso. bacteriology and immunology Harvard Med. Sch., 1949-59; faculty Dartmouth Med. Sch., Hanover, N.H., 1960—, prof. microbiology, 1962-, chmn. dept., 1965-. Mem. A.A.A.S., Am. Soc. Microbiology, Am. Soc. Biol. Chemists, N.Y. Acad. Scis., Sigma Xi. Contbr. articles to profl. jours. Home: 3 Read Rd Hanover, NH 03755.

GRAY, CLEVE, artist; b. N.Y.C., Sept. 22, 1918; s. Jacob and Sylvia (Fields) G.; grad. Phillips Acad., Andover, Mass., 1936; B.A. summa cum laude, Princeton, 1940; m. Francine du Plessix, Apr. 23, 1957; childrenThaddeus Ives, Luke Alexander. One-man shows J. Seligmann Gallery, 1947-50, 52, 54, 57, 59, Staempfli Gallery, 1960, 62, 64, Saidenberg Gallery, 1965, 67, Betty Parson Gallery, Addison Gallery Am Art, 1969, Honolulu Acad. Fine Arts, 1970, also shows in Can., France, Italy; exhibited in group shows, 1946-, including Whitney Mus. annuals, U. Ill. annuals, Guggenheim Mus., 1961, 65, Chgo. Art Inst., 1946, 61, U. Neb. annuals, Corcoran Mus. annuals; permanent collections Whitney Mus., Met. Mus., Guggenheim Mus., R.I. Sch. Design Mus., Wadsworth Atheneum, Columbus Mus., Krannert Art Mus., Honolulu Acad. Fine Arts, N.Y.U. Mus., U. Cal. at Berkeley, U. Ill. Mus., Vanderbilt U. Mus., Columbia, Nat. Collection, Sheldon Meml. Gallery, also others. Trustee R.I. Sch. Design. Served with AUS, 1943-46. Mem. Phi Beta Kappa. Club: Century Assn. (N.Y.C.). Author, editor: David Smith by David Smith, 1968; John Marin by John Marin, 1970. Contbr. editor Art in America. Address: Graystones Cornwall Bridge CT 06754

GRAY, DONALD JAMES, educator; b. Spokane, Jan. 16, 1908; s. William James and Nellie (Simpson) G.; B.S., U. Wash., 1931, M.S., 1933, Ph.D., 1937; m. Rose Marie Vettraino, Nov. 25, 1966; children by previous marriageRobert Keith, Donald Garry. From teaching fellow in anatomy to instr. anatomy, U. Wash., 1931-39; mem. faculty Stanford Sch. Medicine, 1939-, prof. anatomy, 1949-, acting exec. head dept. anatomy, 1953-54, 61-; USPHS sr. research fellow, acting asso. prof. anatomy Wayne State U. Coll. Medicine, 1947-48, USPHS spl. fellow, guest prof. anatomy, 1959-60. Fellow A.A.A.S.; mem. Am. Assn. Anatomists, Am. Assn. Phys. Anthropologists, Am. Assn. U. Profs., Sigma Xi. Author: (with others) Anatomy, a Regional Study of Human Structure, 1963; also articles. Home: 611 Salvatierra Stanford CA 94305

GRAY, DONALD JOSEPH, educator; b. Waukegan, Ill., Sept. 21, 1927; s. Harold Joseph and Katherine (Kennedy) G.; Ph.B., Loyola U., Chgo., 1950; M.A., U. Minn., 1951; Ph.D., Ohio State U., 1956; m. Mary-Alice Olentine, June 26, 1954; children-Julie, Susannah. Instr. English, Ind. U., Bloomington, 1956-59, asst. prof., 1959-63, asso. prof., 1963-68, prof., chmn. dept. English, 1968—; book rev. editor Victorian Studies, 1956-64; cons. U.S. Office Edn., 1965-69. Served with USAAF, 1946-47. Mem. Moder Lang. Assn., Nat. Council Tchrs. English, Am. Assn. U. Profs. Home: 1913 Sussex Dr Bloomington IN 47401

GRAY, EARL QUINCY, lawyer; b. Higgins, Tex., Jan. 24, 1891; s. Eli Clark and Nancy Adelaide (Patton) G.; A.B., U. Okla., 1910; S.B., U. Chgo., 1911, J.D. cum laude, 1913; m. Lucile D. Roberts, July 2, 1921; childrenRoger K., Nancy L. (Mrs. Nancy Cheek). Admitted to Okla. bar, 1913, practiced in Pauls Valley, 1913-14, Ardmore, 1914-; mem. Gray & Poindexter and predecessor firms, 1914-50; pvt. practice, 1950-. Cattle ranching Johnston and Murray counties; oil operations Carter, Stephens, Gravin & Marshall Co.; oil royalty, other investment interests; dir. First Nat. Bank, Ardmore. Mem. Okla. Securities Commn., 1958-59. Pres. Chickasaw council Boy Scouts Am., 1935-36; chmn. Community Chest campaign, Ardmore, 1965; chmn. com. bldg. campaign Okla. Bar Center, 1960-61. Bd. dirs. Okla. Soc. for Crippled Children, 1950—, pres., 1970—. Fellow Am. Bar Found.; mem. Am. (Okla. del. 1963—), Okla. (pres. 1957, chmn. com. adminstrn. justice which submitted constl. amendment creating spl. ct. for removal judges for cause, mem. 3-man com. to investigate corruption in Okla. Supreme Ct., 1964-65, resulting in removal and disbarment of 2 mems. of the ct.) Carter County (past pres.) bar assns., Nat. Conf. Bar Presidents (mem. council 1961—, treas. 1963-70, vice chmn. 1970-71), Ind. Producers Assn., Am. Judicature Soc. (dir. 1959-63), Okla. Bar Found. (trustee 1957—, pres. 1963-65), Okla. Cattlemen's Assn., Order of Coif, Phi Beta Kappa. Rotarian (pres. 1933-34; dist. gov. 1953-54, mem. constn. and by-laws com. 1955-57, chmn. 1957-58). Home: 401 O Street SW Ardmore OK 73401 Office: 9 / W Main St Ardmore OK 73401

GRAY, EDWARD C., cons.; b. Bklyn.; s. Edward and Mary (Kuhn) Gray; B.C.S., N.Y.U.; m. Dorothea Baier, Mar. 25, 1944; 1 dau., Dorothy Joan (by 1st marriage). Held various positions with the N.Y. Stock Exchange 1918—, including, sec. bus. conduct com., dir. dept. of mem. firms, exec. v.p., ret.; now cons. Oppenheim, Appel, Dixon & Co., C.P.A.'s. Home: 6 Hawthorn Dr Westfield NJ 07090 Office: 140 Broadway New York NY 10005

GRAY, EDWARD ZIGMUND, aircraft co. exec.; b. Portland, Ore., Oct. 8, 1915; s. John H. and Anna S. (White) G.; B.S. in Civil Engring, Ore. State U., 1938; postgrad. engring. aerodynamics, U. Wash.; m. R. Faith Brown, Sept. 2, 1939; childrenEdward Z., Theresa. Hydraulic engr. U.S. Geol. Survey, 1938-40; with Boeing Co., 1943-63, dir. systems engring. directorate, 1958-59, program devel. mgr. advanced space systems, aerospace div., 1959-63; dir. advanced manned missions program, manned space flight NASA, 1963-67; asst. to pres. Grumman Aircraft Engr. Corp., Bethpage, N.Y., 1967-. Asso. fellow Am. Inst. Aeros. and Astronautics. Home: RFD 3 Fiddlers Green Huntington NY 11743 Office: Grumman Aircraft Engr Corp Bethpage NY 11714

GRAY, ELISHA, II, corp. exec.; b. N.Y.C., Sept. 7, 1906; s. David Edgerton and Olive (Rawlins) G.; B.S., Mass. Inst. Tech., 1928; LL.D., Mich. State U., 1965, Evansville Coll., 1966; m. Helen Carolyn Battin, Feb. 8, 1930; children-Michael, Linda, Elisha. With Sears, Roebuck & Co., Chgo. and Newark, 1928-33; v.p., gen. operating mgr. Cutler Shoe Co., Chgo., 1933-38; joined Whirlpool Corp., St. Joseph, Mich., 1938, v.p., 1940, dir., 1943, exec. v.p., 1947, pres. 1949-62, chmn. bd. 1958-; chmn., dir. Warwick Electronics, Inc., 1967—; dir. A.O. Smith, Milw., Gen. Foods Corp. Mem. Bus. Council; mem. Corp. Mass. Inst. Tech., 1963-68; chmn. bd. Council Better Bus. Bureaus, Inc., 1970—. Bd. govs. Am. Nat. Red Cross, 1962-68. Clubs: Augusta National Golf; University, Chicago, Point o' Woods (Benton Harbor, Mich.); Fifth Avenue (N.Y.C.). Home: Nickerson Av Benton Harbor MI 49022 Office: Whirlpool Corp Benton Harbor MI 49022

GRAY, ERNEST WESTON, educator; b. Scituate, Mass., Dec. 19, 1902; s. Ernest Weston and Dora Frances (Harwood) G.; student Northeastern U., 1919-22; Ph.B., Brown U., 1924, A.M., 1926; Ph.D., Harvard, 1931; m. Gladys Margaret Bauer, June 24, 1926; 1 dau., Anne Harwood. Instr. English, Brown U., 1925-28; asst. prof. English, asso. prof., prof. Coll. William and Mary, Norfolk (Va.) div., 1931-47; prof. English, U. Toledo, 1947—, chmn. dept. English, 1949-60, dir. honors program, 1965. Mem. Coll. English Assn., Nat. Council Tchrs. English, Am. Assn. U. Profs., Phi Beta Kappa, Phi Kappa Phi. Home: 402 E Dudley St Maumee OH 43537 Office: U of Toledo Toledo OH 43606

GRAY, FRANCES M., educator; b. Little Rock, Jan. 6, 1910; d. Daniel L. and Nancy (Miller) Gray; B.A., Southwestern at Memphis, 1930; M.A., U. Chgo., 1939; M.S., Columbia. 1954; LL.D., Whitworth Coll., 1959. Field dir. A.R.C., 1944-46; exec. sec. Presbyn. Ch. U.S.A., 1946-50, rep. for overseas mission in Africa and Middle East, 1950-56; prof. religion and social studies Beirut (Lebanon) Coll. for Women, 1956-59. pres., 1959- 65; pres. Damavand Coll., Teheran, Iran, 1965—. Recipient gold medal in edn., Lebanon, 1965. Home: Box 1326 Teheran Iran

GRAY, FRANCIS CALLEY, banker; b. Chestnut Hill, Mass., Jan. 22, 1890; s. Morris and Flora (Grant) G.; A.B., Harvard, 1912, LL.B., 1915, D.C.S., Suffolk U., 1952; L.H.D., Tufts Coll., 1954; m. Helen Rotch Bullard, Sept. 16, 1916; children-Morris, Francis Calley, John Bullard. Practiced law with Ropes, Gray, Boyden & Perkins, 1915-22; partner Shattuck & Gray, 1922-28; v.p., later pres., Lee, Higginson Trust Co., 1928-32; v.p. Fiduciary Trust Co., 1932-44, dir., 1932-66, pres., 1944-57, chmn. bd., 1957-61; dir. Colonial Fund, Inc., State St. Investment Corp.; trustee Chase Fund of Boston, Shareholders Trust of Boston, Income and Capital Shares of Boston; trustee, mem. investment bd. Provident Inst. Savs., 1925-65. Sec., Mass. Gen. Hosp., 1920-30, trustee, 1935-, chmn. bd. trustees, 1946-64, pres., 1964—; treas., trustee Radcliffe Coll., 1930-70, Rotch Traveling Scholarship; bd. mgrs. Greater Boston Charitable Trust; trustee Boston U., 1940-65, hon. trustee, 1965—; trustee King's Chapel, Humane Soc. Commonwealth Mass.; bd. dirs. Hosp. Planning for Greater Boston, Inc. Mem. Boston Sch. Com., 1926-32, chmn. 1928-30; mem. Council Boston Bar Assn., 1928-30; gen. chmn. Greater Boston 1940 Community Fund campaign; mem. Mass. Emergency Pub. Works Commn., 1933-34, Boston Sch. Ho. Commn., 1943-45; mem. exec. com. Greater Boston Community Survey, 1947-49; dir. N.E. Conf. Christians and Jews, Del., Mass. Republican Pre-Primary Conv., 1936; alternate del Rep. Nat. Conv., 1944; mem. Mass. Eisenhower Sponsoring Com. Served as 1st lt. 303d F.A., 1917-19, World War I; maj. to col. Mass. State Guard, World War II. Fellow Am. Acad. Arts and Scis. Clubs: Somerset (Boston); Tavern. Home: 62 Beacon St Boston MA 02108 Office: 10 Post Office Sq Boston MA 02109

GRAY, FRANK, Jr., U.S. judge; b. Franklin, Tenn., Feb. 25, 1908; s. Frank and Mary Hall (Philips) G.; LL.B., Cumberland U., 1928; m. Faye Anders, Feb. 14, 1941. Admitted to Tenn. bar, 1928; practice in Franklin, 1928-61; U.S. judge Middle Dist. Tenn., 1961-. Mayor of Franklin, 1947-61. Mem. bd. trustee Battle Ground Acad., Franklin. Mem. Am., Tenn. (bd. govs. 1956-58) bar assn., Am. Judicature Soc. Democrat. Presbyn. Home: 1003 Adams St Franklin TN 37064 Office: US Courthouse Nashville TN 37203

GRAY, FRANKLIN DINGWALL, lawyer; b. Mpls., July 19, 1904; s. William Irving and Isabelle Wenonah (Welles) G.; B.A. magna cum laude, U. Minn., 1925; B.A. in Jurisprudence (Rhodes scholar), Oxford (Eng.) U., 1927, B.C.L., 1928, M.A., 1953; m. Laura Erf, June 18, 1932; 1 dau., Ellen (Mrs. John I. Horton, Jr.). Admitted to Minn. bar, 1929; partner firm Haverstock, Gray, Plant, Mooty and Anderson, and predecessors, Mpls., 1942—; lectr. bus. law Sch. Bus. Adminstrn., U. Minn., 1937-45. Dir. Midland Nat. Bank of Mpls. Fellow Am. Coll. Trial Lawyers; mem. Am., Minn. bar assns., Am. Arbitration Assn. (Twin Cities council), U. Minn. Alumni Assn. (pres. 1963-64), Phi Beta Kappa, Theta Delta Chi. Rotarian (pres. Mpls. 1965-66). Home: 5253 Richwood Dr Minneapolis, MN 55436. Office: Roanoke Bldg Minneapolis MN 55402

GRAY, FREDERIC COLBERT, former air force officer; b. nr. Palestine, Tex., Oct. 6, 1911; s. Frederic Chesterfield and Winifred (Ward) G.; B.A., Abilene Christian Coll., 1931; grad. AC Advanced Flying Sch., 1934, Army Command and Gen. Staff Sch., 1943, Air War Coll., 1950, Army Air Forces Staff Officers Course, 1944, RAF Sch. Army Coop., 1944; m. Dorothy Gretchen Robins, Apr. 6, 1940 (div. 1946); children—Frederic C. III, Robin Gray; m. 2d, Elizabeth Kittredge Collisson, Sept. 27, 1948; 1 step dau., Nancy Elizabeth (Mrs. Loren E. Warner). Commd. 2d lt. USAAF, 1935, advanced through grades to brig. gen. USAF, 1959; fighter pilot, 1934-44; flew Spitfires with RAF in Eng., 1941; comdr. 78th Fighter Group, Eng., 1944- 45; dir. fighter operations Hdqrs. VIII Air Force, Eng., 1945; comdr. Majors Field, Greenville, Tex., 1945, La Junta AFB, Colo., 1945-46; instr. Air N.G., 1946-49; comdr. 35th Fighter Wing, Korea, 1950-51; insp. gen. Hdqrs. Far East Air Forces, Tokyo, 1951-53; dir. flying tng. Hdqrs. Air Tng. Command, Scott AFB, Ill., 1953-54; comdr. Tyndall AFB (Fla.) Fighter Interceptor Tng. Wing, 1954-56; dep. comdr. Crew Tng. Air Force, Randolph AFB, Tex., 1956-57; dep. chief staff, operations, dep. comdr. 12th Air Force, Waco, Tex., 1957-60; asst. dep. operations, asst. dep. plans Hdqrs. Tactical Air Command, Langley AFB, Va., 1960-63; comdr. U.S. Logistics Group, Ankara, Turkey, 1963-65; vice comdr. Hdqrs. First Air Force, Stewart AFB, N.Y., 1965-68, ret. Decorated Silver Star, Legion Merit with 3 oak leaf clusters, D.F.C., Air medal with 5 oak leaf clusters; Croix de Guerre with palm (France); comdr. Order British Empire. Mem. Air Force Assn., Order of Daedalians, Air Force Acad. Athletic Assn. (charter). Rotarian (hon.). Home: 7 E 63d St New York City NY 10021

GRAY, GEORGE, mural painter; b. Harrisburg, Pa., Dec. 23, 1907; s. George Zacharias and Anna Margaret (Barger) G.; ed. Harrisburg Tech. High Sch., Sch. Indsl. Art, Phila., 1927-30, Acad. Fine Arts, Wilmington, Del., 1931-33, Art Students League, N.Y.C., Howard Pyle Sch. Illustration, Wilmington. Designer stage scenery, N.Y.C., 1926; invited to sketch scenes of army life in various forts and camps; tchr. anatomy and figure constrn. while attending art classes, Phila., Wilmington; later staff artist U.S. Inf. Jour., U.S. Cav. Jour., Washington, N.Y. Nat. Guardsmen, Pa. Nat. Guard Mag.; mural painter patron Gen. J. Leslie Kincaid, pres. Am. Hotels Corp., N.Y.C., 1934—; murals exhibited in hotels throughout U.S., including MacArthur of Battan, Hotel Jefferson-Clinton, Syracuse, N.Y.; Gen. George Rogers Clark, Louisville, Ky.; 3 murals Hist. L.I., Suffolk County Savs. and Loan Bank, Babylon, L.I.; mural painting Brooklyn Bridge, Seamen's Ch. Inst., N.Y.C.; hist. picture map Hotel Huntington (L.I.); mil. artist Engring. Bd., Ft. Belvoir, Va.; combat artist U.S. Coast Guard Hdqrs., Washington. Life fellow Royal Soc. Arts (London); mem. Am. Mil. Inst., Co. Mil. Collectors and Historians, Nat. Soc. Mural Painters, Am. Vets. Soc. Artists, Am. Artists Profl. League, Nat. Hist. Soc. (founding mem.), Assn. Mil. Surgeons U.S., U.S. Naval Inst., Armed Forces Mgmt. Inst., Navy Art Cooperation and Liaison Com. (chmn.). Clubs: Arts (Washington); Salmagundi (N.Y.C.). Address: Salmagundi Club 47 Fifth Av New York City NY 10003 ☆

GRAY, GORDON, broadcasting co. exec.; b. Balt., May 30, 1909; s. Bowman and Nathalie Fontaine (Lyons) G.; A.B., U. N.C., 1930; LL.B., Yale, 1933; m. Jane Boyden Craige, June 11, 1938 (dec. July, 1953); children—Gordon, Burton Craige, Boyden, Bernard; m. 2d, Nancy Maguire Beebe; step-childrenCameron, Alexandra, Schuyler Beebe. Admitted to N.Y. bar, 1934, N.C. bar, 1936; asso. Carter, Ledyard & Milburn, 1933-35, Manly, Hendren & Womble, 1935-37; pres. and pub. Piedmont Pub. Co., Winston-Salem Jour., Twin City Sentinel, also operator radio sta. WSJS, 1935-47; asst. sec. Army, Dept Def., 1947-49, sec. of Army, 1949-195O; spl. asst. to President of U.S., Apr.-Nov. 1950; pres. U. N.C., Feb. 1950; asst. sec. def. for internat. security affairs 1955-57; dir. office def. mblzn., 1957-58; spl. asst. to Pres. for nat. security affairs, 1958-61; chmn. bd. Piedmont Pub. Co., 1961-69, Triangle Broadcasting Co., 1969—; dir. R.J. Reynolds Tobacco Co., Am. Security & Trust Co. Trustee Fed. City Council; mem. Pres.' Fgn. Intelligence Adv. Bd., 1961-. Chmn. Nat. Trust for Historic Preservation; trustee Corcoran Art Gallery, Brookings Instn. Dir. Psychol. Strategy Bd., July- Dec. 1951; mem. N.C. State Senate, 1938-42, 1946-47. Served as pvt. U.S. Army, commd. 2d lt., Inf., discharged as capt., Inf., 1942-45. Mem. Phi Beta Kappa, Delta Kappa Epsilon, Phi Delta Phi. Democrat. Episcopalian. Clubs: Alibi, Chevy Chase, Burning Tree, Metropolitan (Washington). Home: 1224 30th St NW Washington DC 20007

GRAY, GORDON L., educator; b. Hampton, Ia., May 18, 1924; s. Leroy Ernest and Arianna (Oldham) G.; B.A., Cornell Coll., 1948; M.A., Northwestern U., 1951, Ph.D., 1957; m. Barbara Ann Smith, Feb. 5, 1949; children—David Gordon, Jonathan William. Radio announcer and newsman, 1948-50; broadcast coordinator NBC-TV, Chgo, 1951; instr. to asso. prof. television and radio Mich. State U., 1953-67; prof. communications, chmn. dept. radio, TV and film Temple U., 1967—. Program asso. Ednl. TV and Radio Center, Ann Arbor, Mich., 1956-57; Fulbright scholar Inst. Edn. U. Leeds, U.K., 1965-66. Served to staff sgt., AUS, 1943-46. Mem. Assn. Profl. Brodcasting Edn. (dir.), Speech Communication Assn., Assn. Edn. in Journalism, Univ. Film Assn. Methodist. Office: School of Communications and Theater Temple University Philadelphia PA 19122

GRAY, HAMILTON, educator, civil engr.; b. Gardiner, Me., July 26, 1910; s. Charles Henry and Grace Duncan (Hamilton) G.; B.A., Harvard, 1933, M.S. in Engring., 1934, Sc.D., 1938; m. Prudence M. Jones, Sept. 5, 1936 (dec. Oct. 1965); children—Faith Harriet, Priscilla Hamilton (Mrs. David D. Platt); m. 2d, Barbara J. Bidwell, Oct. 21, 1966; 1 son, Charles Hamilton. Asst. civil engring. Harvard Grad. Sch. Engring., 1934-36; soil technician Moran & Proctor, N.Y.C., 1936-40; asst. prof. civil engring. N.Y. U., 1940-45; prof. U. Me., soils engr. Me. Hwy. Commn., 1945-55; prof. Ohio State U., Columbus, 1955—, chmn. civil engring., 1955-71. Cons. civil engr., 1942—. Fellow Am. Soc. C.E. (A.M. Wellington award 1958), mem. Asso. Hwy. Research Bd., Sigma Xi, Phi Kappa Phi, Tau Beta Pi. Home: 2675 Haverford Rd Columbus OH 43220

GRAY, HAROLD EDWIN, former airline exec.; b. Guttenberg, Ia., Apr. 15, 1906; s. Otis Elmer and Bertha (Hagensick) G.; student State U. Ia., 1922-25, U. Detroit, 1926- 28, M. Engring. (hon.), 1939; m. ExaBell Sublett, Sept. 12, 1929; children—Harold (dec.), Frank. Pilot, Ford Motor Co., 1928; with Pan Am. World Airways, 1929-70, div. mgr. Pacific-Alaska div., 1947-49, v.p., 1949-52, v.p. Atlantic div., 1952-53, exec. v.p. Atlantic div., 1953-60, exec. v.p. overseas div., 1960-64, pres., 1964-68, chmn., chief exec. officer, 1968-70, also dir. Mem. steering com. N.Y. Gov.'s Commn. on Social Problems. Fellow Am. Inst. Aeros. and Astronautics. Clubs: Sky, Stanwich, Cotton Bay, Blind Brook, Economic of N.Y. Home: 535 Park Av New York City NY 10021

GRAY, HARRY BARKUS, educator, chemist; b. Woodburn, Ky., Nov. 14, 1935; s. Barkus and Ruby (Hopper) G.; B.S., Western Ky. U., 1957; Ph.D., Northwestern U., 1960; m. Shirley Barnes, June 2, 1957; children—Victoria Lynn, Andrew Thomas. Postdoctoral fellow U. Copenhagen, 1960-61; faculty Columbia, 1961- 66, prof., 1965-66; prof. chemistry Cal. Inst. Tech., Pasadena, 1966—. Vis. prof. Rockefeller U., Harvard, U. Ia., Pa. State U., Yeshiva U.; cons. govt., industry. Recipient Fresenius award, 1970; Shoemaker award, 1970; Franklin Meml. award, 1967. Mem. Am. Chem. Soc. (award pure chemistry 1970), Alpha Chi Sigma, Phi Lambda Upsilon. Author: Electrons and Chemical Bonding, 1965; Molecular Orbital Theory, 1965; Ligand Substitution Processes, 1966; Basic Principles of Chemistry, 1967; Chemical Dynamics, 1968; Chemical Principles, 1970; Models in Chemical Science, 1971. Home: 2015 Glen Springs Rd Pasadena CA 91107

GRAY, HARRY JACK, business exec.; b. Augusta, Ga., Nov. 18, 1919; B.S. with honors, U. Ill., 1941, M.S., 1947; m. Barbara Helen Sander; childrenPam, Vicky Lynn. Instr., U. Ill., 1946-47; sales mgr. truck div. Esserman Motor Sales, Chgo., 1947-50; exec. salesman Platt, Inc., Chgo., 1950-51; exec. v.p., gen. mgr. Greyvan Lines, div. Greyhound Corp., Chgo., 1951-54; pres. U.S. Engring. div. Litton Industries, Van Nuys, Cal., 1956-; v.p. Litton Industries, Beverly Hills, Cal., 1958-; group v.p., 1961-64, sr. v.p. for finance and adminstrn., 1964-67, exec. v.p., 1967-69, sr. exec. v.p., 1969-71, also dir.; pres. United Aircraft, Hartford, Conn., 1971—. Served to capt. AUS, 1941-46. Decorated Silver Star medal, Bronze Star medal. Mem. Inst. Electronic and Elec. Engrs., Nat. Sales Exec. Club, N.A.M. (dir), Alpha Delta Sigma, Kappa Tau Alpha. Clubs: Bel Air Bay Beach (Los Angeles); N.Y. Athletic (N.Y.C.); Bel Air Country. Office: 400 Main St Hartford CT 06108

GRAY, JAMES ALEXANDER, coll. ofcl.; b. Winston-Salem, N.C., Dec. 12, 1920; s. James Alexander and Pauline Lizette (Bahnson) G.; A.B., U. N.C., 1941; M.B.A., Harvard, 1943; m. Yvonne Winifred Jackson, Aug. 12, 1944; children—Susan Winifred, James Alexander, David Bahnson; m. 2d, Evelyn Mashburn Cuddy, Nov. 28, 1970. Mfrs. rep., 1946-49; with Jour. and Sentinel newspapers, Winston-Salem, 1949-61, gen. mgr., 1957- 59, pub. 1959-61; exec. dir. Winston-Salem Found., 1961-62; exec. dir. Mobile (Ala.) Historic Devel. Commn., 1970-71; dir. devel. Salem Coll., Winston-Salem, 1971—. Mem. N.C. Hwy. Commn., 1953-57; chmn. Winston-Salem United Fund campaign, 1958. Bd. visitors Bowman Gray Sch. Medicine, 1959-70; pres. Old Salem, Inc., 1950-53, 63-70. Served to lt. USNR, 1943-46. Named Young Man of Year, Winston-Salem Jr. C. of C., 1949. Mem. Home Moravian Ch. Rotarian. Home: Salem Sq Winston-Salem NC 27108

GRAY, JAMES C., former steel co. exec.; b. Elco, Pa., 1904; grad. Pa. State U., 1925. Former adminstrv. v.p. U.S. Steel Corp. Past pres. Soc. Mining Engrs. Home: 4049 Crayton Rd Naples FL 33940

GRAY, JAMES CLARKE, educator; b. Schenectady, Dec. 1, 1902; s. James and Violet (Yorkston) G.; B.A., Syracuse U., 1925, M.A., 1927; Ph.D., U. Chgo., 1929; m. Arlisle Miller, Oct. 1, 1933; 1 son, James Roy. Mem. faculty Western Res. U., 1929-60; prof. biology State U. N.Y. at New Paltz, 1960—, chmn. div. sci. and math., 1960-70. Fellow A.A.A.S., Ohio Acad. Sci.; mem. N.Y. Acad. Scis., Cal. Acad. Sci., Am. Inst. Biol. Sci., Sigma Xi, Phi Kappa Phi, Beta Beta Beta. Home: 5 Parker Lane New Paltz NY 12561

GRAY, JAMES LORNE, atomic energy co. exec.; b. Brandon, Man., Mar. 2, 1913; s. James Bruce and Sarah Edna (Elder) G.; B.Eng., U. Sask., 1935, M.Sc. in Mech. Engring., 1938; LL.D., 1961; D.Sc., U. B.C., 1961; m. Anne Evelyn Lawrence, June 1, 1940; 1 son, James Michael. Canadian Gen. Electric Co. Test Course, 1938-39; lectr. U. Sask., 1939; asst. dir. gen. Dept. Reconstrn. & Supply, Ottawa, 1945-46; asst. to pres. Montreal Armature Works Ltd., Montreal, 1946-47; sci. asst. to pres. Nat. Research Council, Ottawa, 1947-49; chief adminstrn. NRC, Chalk River, 1949-52; gen. mgr. Atomic Energy of Can., Ltd., Chalk River, 1952-53, v.p. adminstrn., operation, 1954-58, pres., 1958—. Served to wing comdr. RCAF, 1939-45. Decorated Companion Order of Can. Clubs: Royal Ottawa Golf, Rideau Club (Ottawa); Deep River Curling, Royal Automobile St. George's Hill Golf (London, Eng.), Travellers (Paris, France). Home: 25 Beech Av Deep River Ontario Canada Office: 275 Slater St Ottawa Ontario K1P 5H9 Canada

GRAY, JEROME BETHEL, advt. exec.; b. Harrisburg, Pa., July 18, 1899; s. Norman D. and Alice (Hoopes) G.; student Hill Sch., 1916-19; m. Miriam Fertig, Nov. 13, 1920; childrenAlice, Jane; m. 2d, Thelma Packman, July, 1961. Staff mem. Barta Press, Cambridge, Mass., 1921-23; service mgr. Franklin Printing Co., Phila., 1923-27; partner Gray & Rogers, advt. agy., Phila., 1927-64; pres. Gray & Rogers, Inc., advt. agy., Phila., 1964-67, chmn. bd., chief exec. officer, 1967-. Republican. Episcopalian. Clubs: Poor Richard, Art Directors; Racquet, Midday, Merion Golf. Home: The Dower House West Chester PA 19380 Office: 12 S 12th St Philadelphia PA 19107

GRAY, JOANNE HASTINGS, mem. Republican Nat. Com.; b. Birmingham, Ala., Dec. 1, 1921; d. Littleberry Byrd and Virginia I. (Jenkins) Haley; student Lindenwood Coll., 1939-40; B.A., U. Colo., 1943, postgrad. sociology, 1943; m Daniel Gray, Apr. 29, 1946; childrenDaniel Allan, Robert Byrd. With Continental Airlines, 1943-46, dir. stewardess tng., 1945-46; instr. stewardess tng. U. Denver, 1947; clk. Colo. Sentate, 1963-65. Republican precinct committeewoman, 1960-68, dist. capt., 1967-68; Colo. co-chmn. Goldwater campaign, 1964, Schauer campaign, 1966; mem. Rep. Nat. Com. for Colo., 1968—, sec. Regional Western States, 1969—. Mem. bd. U. Colo. Devel. Found,, 1961-63; bd. dirs. Planned Parenthood Found., 1964-66. Recipient Certificate of Merit award U. Colo., 1956, Asso. Alumni Recognition award, 1961. Mem. U. Colo. Alumni Assn. (bd. dirs. 1958-60), Delta Gamma. Home: 2850 E Flora Pl Denver CO 80210 Office: 1711 Pennsylvania Av Denver CO 80203

GRAY, JOHN DAVIS, lawyer; b. Blairstown, N.J., Mar. 1, 1914; s. Jesse Martin and Anna Blair (Vail) G.; grad. Hill Sch., 1932; A.B., Princeton, 1936; LL.B., Harvard, 1939; m. Mary D. Washburn, Aug. 26, 1939; children—Stephen Vail, Pauline, Samuel O., David A.C. Admitted to N.Y. bar, 1940; with Consol. Edison Co., N.Y.C., 1939-69, asst. sec. dir. finance, 1960-62, treas., 1962-68, sec., 1968-69; partner law firm Washburn & Gray, N.Y.C., 1969—. Treas., Elec. Light & Power Exhibit, N.Y. World's Fair, 1964. Served with USNR, 1944-46. Mem. Edison Elec. Inst. (treas.), Am. Soc. Corp. Secs. Am., N.Y. State bar assns., Assn. Bar City N.Y., Am. Judicature Soc. Clubs: University, Edison Engineering, Down Town Assn., Princeton (N.Y.C.); Edgewood. Home: 153 E 82d St New York City NY 10028 Office: 36 W 44th St New York City NY 10036

GRAY, JOHN DELBERT, apparel co. exec.; b. Petersburg, Ind.; s. John Daniel and Emma Louise (Rudolph) G.; m. Ruth Josephine Campbell, Dec. 31, 1936 (dec. 1966); children—John Douglas, Thomas Campbell, Andrew Michael, Stephen Joseph; m. 2d, Ann Milligan, May 1, 1971. Divisional mdse. mgr. Mandel Bros., Chgo., 1931-42; pres. Baskin Stores, Chgo., 1945-48; pres. Wallachs, Inc., N.Y.C., 1948-61; chmn., chief exec. officer Hart Schaffner & Marx; dir. W.T. Grant Co., First Nat. Bank of Chgo.; trustee Mut. Life Ins. Co. N.Y. Bd. dirs. Better Bus. Bur. Met. Chgo., Jr. Achievement, Chgo., Mid-Am. chpt. A.R.C., Evanston Hosp.; trustee Better Govt. Assn., Chgo. Orchestral Assn., Chgo. Ednl. TV Assn.; asso. Northwestern U. Served as maj., spl. asst. to dep. dir. spl. services div. AUS, World War II. Named Man of Year, Asso. Men's Wear Retailers, 1950; Golden Fleece award Nat. Assn. Wool Mfrs., 1958. Mem. Clothing Mfrs. Assn. (dir.), Ill. Mfrs. Assn. (dir.), Brit.-Am. (dir.), U.S. (dir.) chambers commerce, Chgo. Assn. Commerce and Industry (pres., dir.). Presbyn. Clubs: Pere Marquette Rod and Gun; Mid-America; Glen View, Chicago Athletic, Chicago Curling, Mid-Day, Commercial, Economic, Tavern, Old Elm, Eldorado, Chicago; Links (N.Y.C.). Home: 480 Voltz Rd Northbrook IL 60062 Office: 36 S Franklin St Chicago IL 60606

GRAY, JOHN ELLIS, banker; b. Bay City, Tex., Mar. 3, 1907; s. John W. and Millie M. (Nicholson) G.; B.A., U. Tex., 1934, M.A., 1936; LL.D., Centenary Coll., Shreveport, 1949; m. Mary M. Hahn, June 4, 1930; children—Jean Carolyn (Mrs. James T. Richardson), Mary Ann (Mrs. Paul W. Pigue, Jr.). Tchr., athletic dir., dean mem. Lamar State Coll. Tech. (formerly Lamar Coll.), 1932-40, pres., 1941-51; with First Security Nat. Bank (formerly First Nat. Bank), Beaumont, Tex., 1952—, pres., dir., 1959-71, chmn. bd., 1971—; dir. Enterprise Co., Gateway Nat. Bank. Vice chmn. Tex. Chmn. Higher Edn., 1961-66; chmn. coordinating bd. Tex. Coll. and Univ. System, 1966—; pres. Beaumont United Appeals, 1965, Beaumont Young Men's Bus. League. Served to lt. USNR, 1944- 45. Recipient Golden Deeds award Beaumont Exchange Club, 1963; Distinguished Citizen award Home Builders Assn. Sabine Area, 1966. Mem. Am., Tex. bankers assns., Beaumont C. of C. (past pres.), Phi Delta Kappa, Delta Sigma Pi, Sigma Nu (Legion of Honor award 1956). Methodist. Rotarian. Clubs: Beaumont, Beaumont Country. Home: 4460 University Dr Beaumont TX 77705 Office: PO Box 3391 Beaumont TX 77704

GRAY, JOHN HUBERT, clergyman, coll. dean; b. Cupertino, Cal., Jan. 27, 1924; s. Clyde Peter and Margaret (Oddie) G.; B.A. in Philosophy, Gonzaga U., 1948; M.A. in English, Loyola U. at Los Angeles, 1952; Ph.D., U. London, (Eng.), 1961. Ordained priest Roman Catholic Ch., 1955; mem. faculty U. Santa Clara, (Cal.), 1949—, instr. English, 1949-51, asst. prof., 1961-67, asso. prof., 1967—, chmn. English dept., 1963-68, dean Coll. Humanities, 1968—. Trustee Mexican-Am. Cultural Found., v.p., 1968-70; bd. dirs. Family Service Orgn. Mem. Modern Lang. Assn. Am., Am. Assn. for Higher Edn. Home: 820 Alviso St Santa Clara CA 95053

GRAY, JOHN JUSTIN, coll. dean; b. New Concord, O., Nov. 21, 1919; s. Charles Irving and Faith (McCall) G.; Mus.B., U. Mich., 1942; Mus.M., Eastman Sch. Music, U. Rochester, 1945; D.Mus. Arts, U. So. Cal., 1960; m. Patricia May Brunton, Dec. 28, 1947; children—Stephen, Christine, Cynthia. Supr. music Charlevoix (Mich.) pub. schs., 1944-45; asst. prof. Ohio State U., 1945-46; asso. prof. U. Mont., 1946-58; prof. music Cal. State Coll., Fullerton, 1961—, asso. dean Sch. Letters, Arts and Sci., 1965-68, dean Sch. Arts, 1968—. Mem. Am. Musicol. Soc., Music Educators Nat. Conf. (life), Coll. Bank Dirs. Nat. Assn., Am. Assn. U. Profs., Phi Mu Alpha Sinfonia, Kappa Kappa Psi, Pi Kappa Lambda. Contbr. articles to profl. jours. Home: 1201 Lindendale Av Fullerton CA 92631

GRAY, JOHN STEPHENS, physiologist; b. Chgo., Aug. 11, 1910; s. Joseph William and Carrie (Weston) G.; B.S., Knox Coll., Galesburg, Ill., 1932; M.S., Northwestern U., 1934, Ph.D., 1936, M.D., 1946; m. Elma Nash, June 15, 1935; childrenAnn R., Virginia B. Instr. in physiology Northwestern U., 1936-40, asst. prof. 1940-45, asso. prof., 1946, prof., 1946—, Nathan Smtih Davis prof., 1946-70; research physiologist A.A.F. Sch. of Aviation Medicine, Randolph Field, Tex., 1942-45. Mem. A.A.A.S., Am. Physiol. Soc., Soc. Exptl. Biology and Medicine, Chgo. Westerners, Sigma Xi, Phi Gamma Delta. Author: Pulmonary Ventilation and Its Physiological Regulation. Contbr. research articles in physiology and in Am. frontier history to various publs. Home: 422 15th St Wilmette IL 60091 Office: 303 E Chicago Av Chicago IL 60611

GRAY, JOSEPH ROOT, lawyer, brewing co. exec.; b. Lansing, Mich., Sept. 26, 1907; s. William F. and Edna P. (Root) G.; B.S. Northwestern U., 1930, J.D., 1933; married to Willo C. Austin, Sept. 13, 1958. Admitted to Ill. bar, 1933; asso. firm (and succeeding firms) Cooke, Sullivan & Ricks, Chicago, 1933- 48; partner Daily, Dines, White & Fiedler Chgo., 1949-51; asst. sec., asso. gen. counsel Pabst Brewing Co., Chgo., 1951-57, v.p., asst. sec., asso. gen. counsel, 1957-59, v.p., sec., gen. counsel, Milwaukee, Wis., 1959—. Served from pvt. to 1st lt., Signal Corps and judge adv. gen. dept., AUS, 1943-46. Mem. Am., Wis., Ill., Chgo. and Milw. bar assns., Delta Sigma Pi. Home: 2244 W Club View Dr Glendale WI 53209 Office: 917 W Juneau Av Milwaukee WI 53201

GRAY, KENNETH JAMES, congressman; b. West Frankfort, Ill., Nov. 14, 1924; s. Thomas J. and Anna (Reed) G.; grad. high sch.; m. Gwendolyn June Croslin, Nov. 27, 1943; 1 dau., Diann. Owner Gray Motors, West Frankfort, 1942-54; mem. 84th to 87th U.S. Congresses, 25th District of Ill., mem. 88th- 92d Congresses, 21st Ill. District. Served as sergeant AUS, 1943-45. Mem. Am. Legion, Vets. Fgn. Wars, 40 and 8, Jr. C. of C. of Ill. (v.p.), Walking Dog Found. Elk. Eagle. Kiwanian. Address: 411 East Main St West Frankfort IL 62896

GRAY, LESLIE R., ret. dairy co. exec.; b. London, Can., 1904; ed. U. Western Ont., 1925. Vice pres. finance, sec., treas., dir. Silverwood Dairies, Ltd.; sec., treas., dir. Kwik Shops Ltd., Uplands Dairy Shops (1967) Ltd.; dir. Silverwood Investors. Ltd., Silverwood Employee Holdings Ltd., Silverwood Lawrence Holdings Ltd. Sec., treas. A.E. Silverwood Found. Home: 717 Hillcrest Dr London Ontario Canada

GRAY, MILTON HEFTER, lawyer; b. Chgo., Dec. 2, 1910; s. Jacob S. and Fannie (Hefter) G.; A.B., Northwestern U., 1931, J.D., 1934; m. Florence Adele Subin, Apr. 12, 1937; children—Roberta (Mrs. Paul L. Katz), James. Admitted to Ill. bar, 1934; asso. and partner Gardner, Carton & Douglas, 1934-43; pvt. practice, Chgo., 1943-60; mem. firm Altheimer, Gray, Naiburg & Strasburger, Chgo., 1960—; commr. Supreme Ct. Ill., 1957-62, 66-68, 70—. Vice pres., sec., dir., Blackstone Mfg. Co., Inc., Noma-World Wide, Inc.; dir. Alloy Mfg. Co. Lectr., Am. Inst. Banking, 1943-45, U. Ill. Law Sch., 1953, Northwestern U. Law Sch., 1956, Harvard Law Sch., 1967. Pres., N. Shore council Boy Scouts Am., 1957-59, exec. bd. region VII, 1959—, vice chmn., 1966-68, chmn. 1968-70, mem. nat. exec. bd., 1968—. Recipient Silver Beaver, Silver Antelope, Distinguished Eagle Scout Citizens awards Boy Scouts Am. Mem. Am. (com. state regulation securities 1961—, com. fed. regulation securities 1963—), Ill. (past chmn. corp. and securities laws sect.), Chgo. (past chmn. corp. law com., past chmn. securities law com., bd. mgrs. 1966-68, 1st v.p. 1970-71, pres. 1971—) bar assns. Co-drafter: Ill. Not for Profit Corporation Act, 1945; Ill. Securities Law, 1953. Editorial bd. Ill. Bus. Corp. Act Annotated, 1947. Contbr. articles to legal publs. Home: 420 Lakeside Pl Highland Park IL 60035 Office: 1 N LaSalle St Chicago IL 60602

GRAY, MYLES MCCLURE, ins. co. exec.; b. Lansing, Mich., Aug. 28, 1932; s. Carlyle Avery and Lucile (Meitz) G.; B.B.A. with distinction, U. Mich., 1954; m. Marilyn Ida Osberg, Feb. 14, 1953; children—Kathleen, David, Patricia. Div. mgr. Nat. Life & Accident Ins. Co., Nashville, 1954-58; from asst. actuary to exec. v.p., actuary United Benefit Life Ins. Co., Omaha, 1958- 67; v.p., actuary Gen. Reins. Life Corp., N.Y.C., 1967-69, Cal. Western States Life Ins. Co., Sacramento, 1969—. Bd. dirs. Sacramento Area chpt. A.R.C. Fellow Soc. Actuaries; mem. Am. Acad. Actuaries, Pacific States Actuaries Club, Alpha Kappa Psi, Phi Kappa Phi, Beta Gamma Sigma. Republican. Presbyn. (finance com., elder). Clubs: Sutter; Arden Hills Swim and Tennis. Home: 4041 Crondall Dr Sacramento CA 95825 Office: 2020 L St Sacramento CA 95814

GRAY, NORMAN BRIGGS, judge; b. Bloomfield, Neb., Oct. 24, 1902; s. George and Caroline Alice (Leigh) G.; LL.B., U. Neb., 1928; m. Alma May Sanders, Nov. 26, 1938; childrenNorma Lee, Susan Ann. Sec. Pub. Service Commn., Wyo., 1932-38; trial examiner, FPC, 1938-42; pvt. practice, Cheyenne, 1942-47, 51-60; atty. gen. Wyo., 1947-50, 60-63; supreme ct. justice, 1963—, chief justice Wyo. Supreme Ct., 1969-70. Mem. Sigma Alpha Epsilon, Phi Delta Phi. Democrat. Home: 100 W First Av Cheyenne WY 82001 Office: Supreme Ct Bldg Cheyenne WY 82001

GRAY, NORMAN HAMBLIN, govt. ofcl.; b. Birmingham, Ala., Jan. 31, 1915; s. David Elmer and Bertha (Hamblin) G.; student Newberry Coll., 1934, N.C. State U., 1935-36; A.B., George Washington U., 1953, M.A., 1954; student Harvard Grad. Sch. Edn., 1954-55; Ed.D., Am. U., 1961; m. Ann Elaine Lamond, Oct. 19, 1940; children—N. Bruce, Kirk Lamond. Mem. Inspection Bd., U.K., Can. and N.Z., 1940-43, engring. aide, 1943-45; pres., gen. mgr. Monanock Industries, Keene, N.H., 1946-52; teacher, prin. Fairfax, Va., and Prince Georges County, Md., 1952-60; research group dir. Bur. Naval Personnel, 1960-62; human factors support dir. USN, 1962-64; tng. dir. Peace Corps, 1969-70; asst. exec. dir. Pres.'s Council Youth Opportunity, Washington, 1970—. Dir. No. Va. Heart Assn., 1960-62. Served with USNR, World War II; PTO. Republican. Mason. Developer Navy's 1st man machine and human requirements center, 1966-68, concept. of Peace Corps' lang. culture and Environmental Inst., 1970. Home: 2209 Dunhaven St San Diego CA 92110 Office: 801 19th St NW Washington DC 20006

GRAY, PAUL EDWARD, tech. inst. chancellor; b. Newark, Feb. 7, 1932; s. Kenneth Frank and Florence (Gilleo) G.; S.B., Mass. Inst. Tech., 1954, S.M, 1955, Sc.D., 1960; m. Priscilla Wilson King, June 18, 1955; children—Virginia Wilson, Amy Brewer, Andrew King, Louise Meyer. Mem. faculty Mass. Inst. Tech., 1960-71, Class of 1922 prof. elec. engring., 1968-71, dean Sch. Engring., 1970-71, chancellor, mem. corp., 1971—. Dir. Shawmat Nat. Bank, Boston, 1971—. Trustee Wheaton Coll., Mass. Served to 1st lt. AUS, 1955-57. Recipient C.E. Tucker award teaching Mass. Inst. Tech. Fellow Am. Acad. Arts and Scis.; mem. I.E.E.E. (publs. bd. 1969-70), A.A.A.S., Sigma Xi, Eta Kappa Nu, Tau Beta Pi, Phi Sigma Kappa. Mem. United Ch. Christ (deacon 1969—). Home: 5 Sheffield Rd Winchester MA 01890 Office: 77 Massachusetts Av Cambridge MA 02139

GRAY, PETER, biologist; b. London, Eng., June 4, 1908; s. Oscar and Dorothy (Selby) G.; student, Imperial Coll. Sci. U. London, 1925-31, A.R.C.S., 1929, D.I.C., 1933; B.Sc., London Hons. Zool., 1929, Ph.D., 1931; m. Freda Dolman, July 29, 1933; 1 son, Peter John (dec.). Came to U.S. 1937, naturalized, 1944. Asst., Royal Coll. Sci., 1927-29; zoologist Norwich Castle Museum, 1929-31; lectr. embryology U. Edinburgh (Scotland), 1931-37; Rockefeller traveling fellow U. Rochester, 1937-38; asso. prof. U. Pitts., 1939-43, prof., 1943-64, acting head dept. biol. scis., 1945, head dept. biol. scis., 1947-64, Andrey Avinoff prof. biology, 1964—. Section editor biol. abstracts, World War II, dir. research projects OSRD and AAF. Term mem. bd. dirs. Carnegie Mus., 1968—. Fellow A.A.A.S., Royal Micros. Soc.; mem. Am. Soc. Zool., Am. Assn. Anatomists, Am. Micros. Soc. (pres. 1963-64), Soc. Indsl. Microbiology (dir. 1962-65), Am. Assn. U. Profs., Phi Beta Kappa, Sigma Xi, Phi Sigma, Alpha Epsilon Delta (hon. life). Clubs: Rolling Rock (Ligonier, Pa.); Pittsburgh Golf. Author books including: The Microtomist's Formulary and Guide, 1954; The Mistress Cook, 1956; Handbook of Basic Microtechnique, 1964; General Zoology, 1964; Dictionary of the Biological Sciences, 1967; articles scientific jours.; two patents. Editor-in-chief: Encyclopedia of Biological Sciences, 1961. Home: 5131 Ellsworth Av Pittsburgh PA 15232 Office: U Pitts Pittsburgh PA 15213

GRAY, RICHARD GEORGE, journalist, educator; b. Tacoma, Wash., Feb. 24, 1932; s. Leo James and Olive (Masterman) G.; A.B., Whitworth Coll., 1954; M.A., U. Minn., 1956, Ph.D., 1964; m. Ida Ruth Higgins, Aug. 5, 1956; childrenChristopher Devin, Grant Allen. News editor Tacoma Star, 1955; teaching asst. U. Minn., 1957-58; reporter, rewrite man, feature writer St. Louis Post- Dispatch, 1958-61; corr. Life mag., 1959-61; asst. prof. Northwestern U., 1961-66, asso. prof. journalism, 1966-68; nat. dir. Project Pub. Information, U.S. Office Edn., Madison, Wis., 1966-68; prof., chmn. dept. journalism Ind. U., Bloomington, 1968-; cons. U.S. Office Edn. State Depts. Edn., 1966-. Cons. Danforth Found., 1959-61, 68-. Danforth fellow, 1954-59, Lincoln scholar, 1950-51. Mem. Whitworth Coll. Alumni Assn. Bd. (dir.), Chgo. Presbyn. Bd. Research, Northwestern U. Bd. Religion, Nat. Scholastic Press. Assn. (judge 1954-), Am. Soc. Newspaper Editors (edn. com.,), Assn. Collegiate Presses (judge 1955- 65), Assn. for Edn. in Journalism (accrediting com.), Am. Assn. U. Profs., A.P. Mng. Editors Assn. (freedom information com.), Soc. for Religion in Higher Edn., Sigma Delta Chi. Democrat. Presbyn. Author: Freedom of Access to Government Information, 1965; Education and Communication in a Dynamic Society, 1969; From Personal Relations to Public Relations, 1969. Contbr. articles profl. jours. Home: RR 1 Marlin Hills Bloomington IN 47401

GRAY, ROBERT DAVIS, economist, educator; b. Warren, Pa., Oct. 14, 1909; s. Robert Elmer and Clara Florence (Davis) G.; B.S. in Econ., U. Pa., 1930, postgrad. Grad. Sch., 1930-36; m. Mary V. Adams, Dec. 23, 1942; 1 dau., Mary Belinda. Research asst. and asso. indsl. research dept. U. Pa., Phila., 1927-39, instr. in industry, 1934-37; asst. prof. econs. U. Conn., 1937-40; spl. research asst. Life Office Mgmt. Assn., 1939-40; asso. prof. econs. and indsl. relations Cal. Inst. Tech., 1940-42, dir. Indsl. Relations Center, 1941—, prof. econs. and indsl. relations, 1942—. Mem. Cal. Personnel Bd., 1944-63, v.p., 1946- 47, pres., 1947-49, 1958-60; bd. adminstrs. Cal. State Employees Retirement System, 1956-63; dir. Family Service Pasadena (Cal.), 1946-49, pres., 1947-48; mem. adv. council Cal. Dept. Employment, 1967-69. Trustee Assn. Ind. Cal. Colls. and Univs. Fellow Acad. Mgmt.; mem. Personnel and Indsl. Relations

Assn. (life), Tournament of Roses Assn., Pasadena C. of C., Civic Assn. of Pasadena (dir. 1950-56, pres. 1953- 54), Am. Soc. Personnel Adminstrs., Am. Soc. Tng. Dirs., Am. Assn. U. Profs. Roman Catholic. Clubs: Athenaeum, Twilight. Author books, 1929—, latest pubs. include: A Guide to Systematic Wage and Salary Administration, 1959; The Roles of Benefit Plans in Protection, Compensation, and Cost, 1960; Supervision of Engineers, 1964; Evaluating the Personnel Department, 1965; Conducting an Employee Opinion Poll, 1966; Supervisor of the 70s, 1970. Editor: Frontiers of Industrial Relations, 1959. Home: 2486 Morslay Rd Altadena, CA 91001.

GRAY, ROBERT HANES, educator, lawyer; b. Mt. Hope, W.Va., Dec. 3, 1909; s. William Robert and Mary (Hanes) G.; B.S., Washington and Lee U., 1931, LL.B., 1936; M.B.A., Harvard, 1933; student Yale Law Sch., 1933; LL.M., Columbia, 1941, J.S.D., 1942; m. Lois Dinger, Dec. 6, 1933 (div. 1962); childrenCelie Jane Gray (Mrs. David Rosenau), Robert Hanes. Admitted to Va. bar, 1935, W.Va. bar, 1936; instr., then asst. prof. econs. and law Washington and Lee U., 1936-40; asst. prof. law U. Louisville, 1941-42; with firm Cravath, Swaine & Moore, N.Y.C., 1942-45; tax atty. Bethlehem Steel Corp., 1946-52, asst. comptroller, 1952-55, dir., treas. fgn. subsidary cos., 1956-59; chancellor Diocese of Nassau and Bahamas, 1960-61; vis. scholar Columbia, 1961-62; lectr., prof. law Washington and Lee U., 1963—; subsitute judge Appomattox County (Va.), 1967—. Dir. Bank of Mt. Hope, 1935-50. Mem. Appomattox County Sch. Bd., 1967—. Served with AUS, 1945-46: PTO. Mem. Am., Va., W.Va. bar assns., Order of Coif, Phi Beta Kappa, Beta Gamma Sigma, Kappa Sigma Phi Alpha Delta. Democrat. Episcopalian. Lion. Club: Falling River (Appomattox). Author: (with Lott) Law in Medical and Dental Practice, 1942; Some Constitutional and Legal Aspects of Deductions from Gross Income, 1942. Home: Appomattox VA 24522. Office: Tucker Hall Washington and Lee U Lexington VA 24450

GRAY, ROCKWELL, tool mfg. exec.; b. Muskegon, Mich., Jan. 26, 1912; s. Curtis Rockwell and Dorothy (Spalding) W.; Ph.B., Brown U., 1934; m. Margaret E. Horton, Oct. 31, 1936 (dec. July 1967); children-Rockwell, Spalding, Channing; m. 2d. Alice H. Mays, June 14, 1969. Credit man Gen. Motors Acceptance Corp., Providence, R.I., 1934-42; with Brown & Sharpe Mfg. Co., N. Kingtown, R.I., 1942—, asst. treas. and asst. sec., 1952-68, treas. 1968—; Dir. Tools Capital Corp. 1958—, Brown & Sharpe Internat. Capital Corp., 1968—, Pleasant Valley Land Co., 1968—. Club: Providence Art. Home: 225 Shady Hill Dr East Greenwich RI 02818 Office: Precision Park North Kingstown RI 02852

GRAY, RUSSELL, heating and ventilating exec.; b. Schenectady, Aug. 16, 1907; s. William J. and Mabel (Smith) G.; B.S., U. Ky., 1933; m. Dorothy Carlan, May 9, 1936; childrenSheila, Dennis, Barbara, William, Robert. With Carrier Corp., Syracuse, N.Y., 1933, successively constrn. asst. dealer sales engr., staff asst. to pres., dealer dist. mgr. Dallas office, asst. mgr. direct sales, Syracuse, dist. sales mgr., Atlanta, dir. marketing services, Syracuse, asst. gen. mgr. Unitary Equipment div., 1933-55, v.p. and gen. mgr. Unitary Equipment div., 1955-60, pres. Carrier Air Conditioning Co., div. Carrier Corp., 1960-66, exec. v.p., dir. Carrier Corp., 1967-. Mem. Air Conditioning and Refrigerating Inst. (past pres.), Am. Soc. Heating and Air Conditioning Engrs., Tau Beta Pi, Pi Tau Sigma. Club: Century (Syracuse). Home: Highbridge St Fayetteville NY 13066 Office: Carrier Pkwy Syracuse NY 13201

GRAY, TRUMAN STRETCHER, educator; b. Spencer, Ind., May 3, 1906; s. Clarence Truman and Bessie Lee (Stretcher) G.; B.S. in Elec. Engring., U. Tex., 1926, B.A., 1927; S.M., Mass. Inst. Tech., 1929, Sc.D., 1930; m. Isabel Gilliam Crockford, June 20, 1931. Asst. physics U. Tex., 1924-27; research asst. Mass. Inst. Tech., 1927-28, Coffin fellow, 1928-29, Saltonstall fellow, 1929- 30, instr., 1930-35, mem. faculty, 1935-, prof. elec. engring., 1960-; engr. Leeds and Northrup Co., summer 1929, Gen. Electric Co., summer 1935, Naval Ordnance Lab., summer 1941; cons. indsl. firms, govt. labs., 1942-. Fellow I.E.E.E. (chmn. instruments and measurements com. 1945- 47); mem. Am. Soc. Engring. Edn., Phi Beta Kappa, Sigma Xi, Tau Beta Pi, Eta Kappa Nu, Phi Mu Alpha, Pi Kappa Alpha. Author: Applied Electronics, 2d edit., 1954. Contbr. sci. periodicals, books, handbooks, reports. Home: 22 Hayes Av Lexington MA 02173 Office: Mass Inst Tech Cambridge MA 02139

GRAY, WADE HAMPTON, former coal co. exec.; b. Dunlap, Tenn., June 17, 1906; s. Lawrence and Savannah (Hixson) G.; grad. Knoxville (Tenn.) Bus. Sch., 1927; m. Dorothy Eleanor Yoakley, Jan. 15, 1938. Fuel clk. So. Ry. System, Knoxville, 1927-31; sales Va. Iron Coal & Coke Co., Roanoke, 1931-41; salesman Walter Bledsoe & Co., Knoxville, 1941-43, asst. mgr. So. div., 1943-48, div. mgr., St. Louis, 1948-61, v.p. sales, 1961-63; v.p. sales Peabody Coal Co., St. Louis, 1963-71. Presbyn. Home: 1954 Iowa Av NE St Petersburg FL 33703

GRAY, WALTER FRANKLIN, banker; b. Denver, 1929; s. Walter F. and Alice (Fassig) G.; B.S., Northwestern U., 1951; J.D., Loyola U., Chgo., 1957; m. Susan Mair, Mar. 26, 1955; children—Constance M., Stuart F. Admitted to Ill. bar, 1957; v.p. The First Nat. Bank of Chgo., 1953-69; exec. v.p., dir. Merc.-Safe Deposit and Trust Co., Balt., 1969—; dir. Merc. Bankshares Corp., Ellicott Machine Corp.. Monumental Corp., Monumental Life Ins. Co. Chmn. bd. Community Relations Com. Balt.; active Balt. Urban Coalition. Trustee, St. Paul Sch. for Boys, Balt. Served with USAF, 1951-53. Mem. Am., Chgo., Ill. bar assns., Econ. Club of Chgo., Alpha Tau Omega. Clubs: Center of Baltimore, Maryland; Elkridge. Home: 915 Poplar Hill Rd Baltimore MD 21210 Office: 2 Hopkins Plaza Baltimore MD 21203

GRAY, WALTER H., former bishop; b. Richmond, Va., Aug. 20, 1898; s. William Cole and Irena Hanswood (Talley) G.; student Coll. William and Mary, U. Richmond Law Sch.; B.D., Va. Episcopal Theol. Sem., 1928, D.D. (hon.), 1941; S.T.D., Berkeley Div. Sch., 1940, D.C.L., 1969; S.T.D., Trinity Coll., Hartford, Conn., 1941; D.D., U. Richmond, 1954, Wycliffe Coll., Toronto, Can., 1962; D.C.L., U. of South, 1960; L.H.D., U. Hartford, 1962; m. Virginia Stuart Hutchinson, Feb. 4, 1933; children—Agatha Ashton (Mrs. J.T. Cabaniss, Jr.), Parke Hanswood. Admitted Va. bar, 1925; ordained deacon P.E. Church, 1928, priest, 1929; asst. rector St. John's Ch., West Hartford, Conn., 1928-32; dean Nativity Pro-Cathedral, Bethlehem, Pa., 1932-36; dean Christ Church Cathedral, Hartford, 1937-40; suffragan bishop Diocese of Conn., 1940-45, bishop coadjutor, 1945-51, bishop, 1951-69. Pres. Province of New Eng., Protestant Episcopal Ch.; chmn. 3d Lambeth Conf. Com., 1958, Nat. Council, P.E. Ch.; chmn. com. arrangements Anglican Congress 1954; pres. Ch. Missions Pub. Co.; trustee Trinity Coll., Hartford, St. Stephen's Sch., Rome, Italy; pres. trustees Colt Bequest, corporator Inst. of Living, Mt. Sinai Hosp., Hartford. Served with 29th Div., U.S. Army, 1917-19. AEF; 2d lt. inf., later 1st lt., Cav., O.R.C. to 1933. Mem. S.R. Va., Soc. Colonial Wars (Conn. chaplain and chaplain gen.), Soc. Cincinnati (Conn. chaplain), Kappa Alpha, Delta Theta Phi. Clubs: Farmington (Conn.) Country; University Hartford; Graduates (New Haven); Commonwealth (Richmond). Editor: Pan Anglican. Author: Our Belief, 1945; Faith in the Right (anthem), 1945; Fut. Course of the Anglican Communion, 1946; A Bishop's Carol (anthem), 1966. Home and office: 100 Westerly Terrace Hartford CT 06105

GRAY, WARREN PHILIPS, banker; b. Franklin, Tenn., Oct. 6, 1911; s. William Francis and Mary (Philips) G.; grad. Rutgers U. Grad. Sch. Banking, 1948; m. Nancy Lee Thompson, Dec. 26, 1936; childrenMary Ann (Mrs. William M. Tate, Jr.), Frances Phyllis. Clk., First Bank & Trust Co., Franklin, 1929-31, Harpeth Nat. Bank, Franklin, 1931-34; with Third Nat. Bank, Nashville, 1934—, cashier, 1963—, sr. v.p., 1965-70, exec. v.p., 1970—; treas. Presbyn. Apts. Active local A.R.C., United Givers Fund; treas. Tenn. Children's Home Soc. Trustee Battle Ground Acad., Franklin, Ind. Mem. Bank Adminstrn. Inst. (nat. treas. 1967-69), Financial Execs. Inst. (pres. Nashville 1964-65), Am. Inst. Banking (pres. Nashville 1940-41). Presbyn. (elder). Clubs: Richland Country, City (Nashville). Home: 4103 Estes Rd Nashville TN 37215 Office: Third Nat Bank Bldg Nashville TN 37202

GRAY, WELLINGTON BURBANK, educator; b. Albany, N.Y., Apr. 25, 1919; s. Wellington and Lilla Maude (Burbank) G.; B.S., Kutztown (Pa.) State Coll., 1947; M.A., N.Y.U., 1948, Ed.D., 1954; student Pa. State U., U. Phillippines; m. Norma Laree Wallace, Dec. 26, 1942; childrenBruce Wellington, Brian Erwin. Art supr. pub. schs., Connellsville, Pa., 1947-49; art dir. Highland Park (Ill.) High Sch., 1949-54; dean Art Sch., Edinboro (Pa.) State Coll., 1954-56; dean Sch. Art, East Carolina U., Greenville, N.C., 1956—; lectr. fine arts Alliance Coll., 1955-56; instr. N.Y.U., summers 1950, 51; hon. faculty Q.M. Sch., Ft. Lee, Va. Partner Gray Assos., design cons., Greenville, 1960—; paintings in permanent collections Atlanta, Akron, O., Albany, N.Y., Highland Park, Mobile, Greenville; exhibited Carnegie Inst. Tech., Art Inst. Chgo., Albany Inst. History and Art; one man shows Highland Park, Greenville, Erie, Pa. Sec. Pitt County Republican Com. Served to lt. col., AUS, World War II; PTO. Mem. Internat. Assn. Deans of Fine Arts, Am. Assn. U. Profs., Nat. Art Edn. Assn., Am. Inst. Interior Designers, mem. Southeastern Arts Assn. (co-chmn. coll. tchrs. art com.), Nat. Soc. Interior Designers (v.p. S.E. chpt.), Phi Delta Kappa, Kappa Delta Pi, Delta Phi Delta. Episcopalian. Author: Student Teaching in Art, 1960; also articles. Adv. bd. Colorcast and Design Quar. Home: 2001 Brook Rd Greenville NC 27834

GRAY, WILLARD FRANKLIN, univ. adminstr.; b. Flint, Tex., Dec. 25, 1913; s. John Franklin and Leona (Booth) G.; B.S. in Elec. Engring., Tex. Tech. U., 1934; M.S. in Elec. Engring., Tex. A. and M. U., 1940; m. Clotyde Roberts, Jan. 2, 1937; children—Jay Willard, Paula Kay (Mrs. Clyde Samuel Precise). Jr engr. Tex. Power & Light Co., Dallas, 1934-37; faculty Tex. Tech. U., 1937-46, asso. prof. elec. engring., 1943-46; asst. prof. elec. engring. Mass. Inst. Tech. 1946-47; faculty U. Ala., University, 1947-66, prof. elec. engring., head dept., 1959-66, asst. v.p. acad. affairs, 1966-68, asst. v.p. adminstrn., 1968-71, asso. acad. v.p., dean adminstrn., 1971—. Cons. to bus., industry, 1950—. Mem. panels evaluation applications for undergrad. instnl. equipment NSF, 1965-66; mem. Charles LeGeyt Fortescue fellowship panel I.E.E.E. 1966—; mem. Ala. Bd. Registration for Profl. Engrs. and Land Surveyors, 1969—, Nat. Council Engring. Examiners, 1969—. Registered profl. engr., Ala. Mem. Am. Soc. Engring. Edn. (chmn. elec. engring. div. 1964-65, chmn. prizes and award com. div. elec. engring. 1967-70, chmn. scholarship com. 1971—, mem. awards bd. 1971—), I.E.E.E. (chmn. scholarship com. 1971—, mem. awards com. 1971—), Nat. Soc. Profl. Engrs., Am. Assn. U. Profs., Tau Beta Pi, Eta Kappa Nu, Theta Tau, Pi Tau Chi. Methodist. Home: 21 Windsor Dr Tuscaloosa AL 35401 Office: PO Box 3625 University AL 35486

GRAY, WILLIAM ASHLEY, Jr., mfg. co. exec.; b. St. Louis, Dec. 3, 1915; s. William Ashley and Mary (Stephens) G.; grad. St. Louis Country Day Sch., 1935; m. Anne Sullivan, Mar. 31, 1942; children—William Ashley III, John Sullivan. Field rep. Am. Automobile Ins. Co., 1935-41; sales rep. Scullin Steel Co., 1945-54; v.p. Pioneer Silica Products Co., 1954-57; with Gen. Steel Industries, Inc., St. Louis, 1957—, v.p., asst. to pres., 1961-62. exec. v.p., 1962-64, pres., chief exec. officer, 1964—, also dir.; dir. First Nat. Bank St. Louis. Past campaign chmn., exec. com. United Fund Greater St. Louis; v.p., dir. Civic Progress, St. Louis; exec. bd. St. Louis Area council Boy Scouts Am.; 1st v.p. St. Louis Children's Hosp. Trustee St. Louis Country Day Sch., Ladue Chapel. Served to maj. AUS, 1941-45. Decorated Bronze Star. Mem. Ry. Progress Inst. (past chmn.), St. Louis C. of C. (dir.). Clubs: St. Louis Country, Racquet, Noonday, St. Louis; Chicago; Links (N.Y.C.). Home: 710 S Hanley St Louis MO 63105 Office: One Memorial Dr St Louis MO 63102

GRAY, WILLIAM LAFAYETTE, Jr., lawyer; b. Laurens, S.C., Nov 10, 1902; s. William L. and Mary (Dunklin) G.; A.B., Wofford Coll., 1923; postgrad. U. S.C., 1923-24; law student Harvard, 1925-26; J.D. U. Fla., 1927; LL.D. (hon.), Wofford Coll., 1965; m. Jean Hancock, June 10, 1931; 1 son, William Lafayette III. Admitted to Fla. bar, 1927: partner Huber, Clements & Blackwell, Miami, 1927-30; asst. county solicitor Dade County, Fla., 1931-32; 1st asst. gen. counsel Fla. Power & Light Co., Miami, 1933-41; partner Blackwell, Walker & Gray, Miami, 1941—; mem. Wofford Assos., 1966—; mem. spl. com. on drafting rules of civil procedure Fla. Indsl. Commn., 1947. Chmn. large donations Coral Gables chpt. A.R.C., 1945; pres. Dade County unit Am. Cancer Soc., 1963; dir. Coral Gables Youth Center; troop com. Boy Scouts Am. Chmn. inst. on continuing legal edn. U. Miami, 1960-; bd. dirs., treas. World Center for Liturgical Studies, 1965-68; mem. Fla. Bd. Bar Examiners, 1960- 65; bd. dirs. Crime Commn. Greater Miami, 1966-. Fellow Am. Coll. Probate Counsel; mem. Am. Soc. Internat. Law, Am., Dade County (dir. 1960-62, 63-66. pres. 1941) bar assns., Fla. Bar (bd govs. 1966-67), C. of C., Junior C. of C., S.A.R., Kappa Sigma, Phi Alpha Delta. Methodist (steward, trustee). Clubs: Century (bd. govs. 1965—), Kiwanis (Coral Gables); Miami (founder mem.); Beale Law (Harvard); Riviera Country (bd. govs., sec.); Committee of 100 (Miami Beach, Fla.). Home: 600 Alhambra Circle Coral Gables FL 33134 Office: First Federal Bldg Miami FL 33132

GRAY, WILLIAM LATIMER, cons.; b. Lincoln, Neb., Apr. 26, 1894; s. William Leonard and Mary (Latimer) G.; B.S., Harvard, 1917; m. Margaret Morton Platt, Feb. 14, 1931; children—William Latimer, Samuel Packwood Morton. Clk., First Nat. Bank Boston, 1917, v.p., 1928-47, sr. v.p., 1947-59; dir. Platt & Co., Inc., Stone Indsl. Corp., Helmerich & Payne, Inc., Bamden Corp. Danbury. Clubs: Country (Brookline); Somerset, Harvard (Boston); Beverly Yacht (Marion); Knickerbocker (N.Y.C.). Home: Saffron Walden Wareham MA 02571

GRAY, WILLIAM PAUL, assn. exec.; b. Marston, Mo., Aug. 26, 1911; s. James W. and Lela L. (Mainord) G.; B.S., Colo. State A. and M. U., 1936; M.S., Colo. State U., 1953; postgrad. Mich. State U., 1957; m. Edna May Glover, Mar. 21, 1941. Tchr. vocational agr., 1936-41, 46-52; flight instr. Inland and United airlines, 1941-44; asst. state supr. vocational agr. edn., exec. sec. Future Farmers Am., Colo., 1952-53, nat. exec. sec., 1957-, also sec. nat. bd. trustees, sec., and trustee Future Farmers Am. Found., Inc., 1957—; asst. prof. agr. edn. Colo. State U., 1953-57. Specialist Agrl. Youth Orgns., 1957-66; vocational tech. edn. programs specialist U.S. Office Edn., 1966—. Mem. Pres.'s Commn. on Handicapped. Bd. govs. Agr. Hall of Fame, 1958—; bd. dirs. Nat. Safety Council, nat. chmn. youth safety conf., 1966-68, exec. com. Nat. Youth Conf., 1961—. Served to lt. Transp. Corps, AUS, 1944-45. Named Hon. Am. Farmer, 1950, Hon. State Farmer, Colo., Miss. Mem. Nat. Grange, Alpha Zeta, Alpha Tau Alpha, Kappa Kappa Tau. Mason (32, Shriner). Author: Preflight for Commercial Pilots, 1950; Colo. Manual Supervised Farming Programs, 1954; Adv's Guide Teach. FFA, 1968; Nat. FFA Manual, 1970-71. Home: 520 S Court House Rd Arlington VA 22204 Office: Dept Health Edn and Welfare US Office Edn Washington DC 20203 also National FFA Center Alexandria VA 22313

GRAY, WILLIAM PERCIVAL, judge; b. Los Angeles, Mar. 26, 1912; s. Jacob L. and Catherine (Percival) G.; A.B., U. Cal. at Los Angeles, 1934; LL.B. cum laude, Harvard, 1939; m. Elizabeth Polin, Nov. 8, 1941; childrenRobin Marie, James Polin. Admitted to Cal. bar, 1941; legal sec. to Harold M. Stephens, U.S. Ct. Appeals, Washington, 1939-40; with firm O'Melveny & Myers, lawyers, Los Angeles, 1940-41; pvt. practice, Los Angeles, 1945- 49; partner Gray, Pfaelzer & Robertson, Los Angeles, 1950-66; U.S. dist. judge Central Dist. of Cal., 1966-. Spl. asst. to atty. gen. U.S., 1958- 64; chmn. Cal. Conf. State Bar Dels., 1952. Trustee Ch. of Lighted Window, La Canada. Served fron 1st lt. to lt. col., AUS, 1941-45. Fellow Am. Bar Found.; mem. Am. Judicature Soc. (dir. 1961-64), Am., Los Angeles County (pres. 1956) bar assns., State Bar Cal. (bd. govs. 1960-63, pres. 1962-63). Home: 5495 Burning Tree La Canada CA 91011 Office: U S Court House Los Angeles CA 90012

GRAY, J. S., editor, writer, pub.; b. Clio, Mich., Feb. 20, 1890; s. John Wesley and Ida Caroline (Smith) G.; A.B., Adrian Coll., 1910, LL.D. (hon.), 1938; m. Harriett Taylor, Sept. 10, 1912; childrenThorne (Mrs. David C. Hawley), Grattan, Whitmore. Reporter, editorial writer Adrian (Mich.) Telegram, 1911-17, mng. editor, 1919-27, v.p., 1927—; pres. and editor Monroe (Mich.) Evening News, 1927—. Trustee Adrian Coll. Served as arty. officer, A.E.F., U.S. Army, 1917-19. Recipient Bronze medal journalism U. Minn., 1949; Inland Press citation for pub. service, 1946. Mem. adv. com. WPB and Civilian Prodn. Adminstrn., 1942-45; mem. nat. adv. council Journalism Sch. Adminstrs. Mem. Am. Newspaper Pubs. Assn. (dir. chmn. freedom of press com. 1950-57), Mich. Hist. Soc. (dir.), Am. Soc. Newspaper Editors, Inland Daily (past pres.), Mich. (past pres.), Inter Am. press assns., Mich. Asso. Press Editorial Assn. (past pres.), Internat. Press Inst., Am. Legion (life). Mason (life). Clubs: Detroit Press, U. Mich. Press (past pres.), Washington Press. Collector, annotator hist. maps of southeast Mich. A sponsor of Mich. law under which penal fines are devoted to establishment and maintenance of township libraries. Home: 448 N Macomb St Monroe MI 48161 Office: 20 W First St Monroe MI 48161

GRAYBEAL, SIDNEY NORMAN, govt. ofcl.; b. Butler, Tenn., May 20, 1924; s. Lyman B. and Mary Dove (Hazelwood) G.; student Cortland (N.Y.) State Tchrs. Coll., 1940-42; B.S. in Transp., U. Md., 1949, M.B.A. in Air Transp., 1950; m. Josephine Graybeal, May 7, 1948; children-Douglas Lee, Joan Louise. Div. chief fgn. missile and space activities CIA, 1950-64; dep. asst. dir. bur. sci. and tech. U.S. Arms Control and Disarmament Agy., 1964—. Mem. strategic weapons panel Dept. Def., 1961-64; mem. U.S. delegation to Strategic Arms Limitations Talks, Helsinki, 1969, 70, Vienna, 70. Served as pilot USAAF, World War II; PTO. Decorated D.F.C., Air medal with 3 oak leaf clusters. Mem. Am. Inst. Aeros. and Astronautics, Air Force Assn., Sigma Chi, Phi Kappa Phi, Beta Gamma Sigma. Presbyn. Home: 11501 Parkedge Dr Rockville MD 20852 Office: Dept of State Washington DC 20520

GRAYBIEL, ASHTON, physician; b. Port Huron, Mich., July 24, 1902; s. William and Lucy Ann (Young) G.; A.B., U. So. Cal., 1924, A.M., 1925; M.D., Harvard, 1930; m. Moira Barkley Martin, Mar. 23, 1934; children—Ashton L., Ann M. Moseley Traveling fellow, 1932-33; Dalton fellow, 1933-34; Intern Mass. Gen. Hosp., Boston, 1930-32; cardiac clinic, 1934-42; asso. Harvard Fatigue Lab., 1936-42; instr. medicine and grad. courses Harvard, 1940-42, research staff, 1942-45; dir. research Naval Aerospace Med. Inst., Pensacola, Fla., 1945-70, spl. asst. sci. programs, research labs., head psychophysiology labs, 1970—. Recipient Theodore C. Lyster award for researches in aviation medicine, 1950; Legion of Merit, 1952, with gold star, 1967; Adm. William S. Parsons award for sci. and technical progress Navy League, 1960; The Eric J. Liljencrantz award for contbns. aviation and space medicine, 1961; John J. Jeffries Award, 1962, Melbourne W. Boynton award for space medicine, 1962; Groedel Meml. award Am. Coll. Cardiology, 1962; Hubertus Strughold award for space medicine, 1963; Arnold J. Tuttle award aviation medicine, 1965; Capt. Robert Dexter Conrad award for tech. and sci. achievement in research and devel. for Navy, 1965. Diplomate Am. Bd. Preventive Medicine (aviation med.). Fellow Aerospace Med. Assn. (pres.), A.A.A.S.; mem. Am. Coll. Cardiology (past pres.), Assn. Mil. Surgeons, Am. Coll. Sports Medicine, Internat. Acad. Aviation Medicine, Space Medicine Assn., Am. Physiol. Soc., Am. Heart Assn., Am. Inst. Aeros. and Astronautics, Fla. Acad. Scis., Internat. Acad. Astronautics (trustee). Club: Cosmos (Washington). Author: Clinical Electrocardiography, 1950; Electrocardiography in Practice (with P.D. White, L.Wheeler, C. Williams), 3d edit., 1952. Home: PO Box 4063 Warrington FL 32507 Office: Naval Aerospace Med Research Lab Naval Aerospace Med Inst Pensacola FL 32512

GRAYDON, ALLAN, lawyer; b. Toronto, Ont., Can., Jan. 21, 1898; s. Richard Albert and Sarah Jane (Hughes) G.; student Royal Mil. Coll. of Can., Kingston, 1915-17; A.B., U. Toronto, 1921; student Osgoode Hall Law Sch., 1921-24; m. Elizabeth Palmer, Sept. 20, 1934; childrenJane, Barbara. Called to the bar, Ont., 1924, counsel to firm Blake, Cassels & Graydon; chmn. Barcelona Traction, Light and Power Co., Ltd.; dir. Abitibi Power & Paper Co., Ltd., Transcontinental Timber Co., Ltd., Steel Co. Can., Ltd., others. Officer Royal Arty., British Army, 1917-19. Mem. Canadian Bar Assn. Home: 408 Russell Hill Rd Forest Hill Village Toronto Ontario Canada Office: 25 King St W Toronto Ontario Canada

GRAYHACK, JOHN THOMAS, educator, urologist; b. Kankakee, Ill., Aug. 21, 1923; s. John and Marie (Keckich) G.; B.S., U. Chgo., 1945, M.D., 1947; m. Elizabeth Houlihan, June 3, 1950; childrenElizabeth, Anne Marie, Linda Jean, John, William. Intern medicine Billings Hosp., Chgo., 1947; intern gen. surgery Johns Hopkins Hosp., 1947-48, asst. resident, 1948-49, fellow urology, 1949- 50, asst. resident, 1950-52; resident urology, 1952-53; dir. Kretchmer Lab., Northwestern U. Med. Sch., 1956—, prof. urology, 1963—, chmn. dept. Cons. VA Research Hosp., Gt. Lakes Naval Sta. Served to capt. USAF, 1954-56. Recipient Outstanding Achievement award USAF. Fellow Am. Cancer Soc., 1949-50, Damon Runyon Fund, 1953-54. Diplomate Am. Bd. Urology. Mem. A.M.A., Ill., Chgo. med. socs., Am. Urology Assn., Chgo. Urology Soc., Endocrine Soc., Soc. Genito- urology Surgeons, Nephrology Soc., Phi Beta Kappa, Alpha Omega Alpha, Editor Year Book of Urology, 1963—; mem. editorial bd. Urology Digest, Jour. Investigative Urology, Surgery, Gynecology and Obstetrics. Home: 95 N Park Rd LaGrange IL 60525 Office: 303 E Chicago Av Chicago IL 60611

GRAYSON, CHARLES JACKSON, Jr., ednl. adminstr. b. Ft. Necessity, La., Oct. 8, 1923; s. Charles Jackson and Daphne (DeGraffenreid) G.; B.B.A., Tulane U., 1944; M.B.A., U. Pa., 1947; D.B.A., Harvard, 1959; m. Barbara Schmidt, Aug. 7; children-Christopher Jackson, Michael Wiley, Randall Charles. Instr.,

then asst. prof. Sch. Bus. Adminstrn., Tulane U., 1947-55, asso. prof., 1959- 63, asso. dean Sch. Bus. Adminstrn., 1961-63, dean, prof. Sch. Bus. Adminstrn., 1963-68; dean, prof. Sch. Bus. Adminstrn., So. Meth. U., 1968—; chmn. Price Commn., Washington, 1971—; vis. prof. Grad. Sch. Bus., Stanford, spring 1967; prof. IMEDE, Mgmt. Devel. Program, Switzerland, 1963-64. Reporter, New Orleans Item, 1949-50; spl. agt. FBI, Washington, 1950-52; partner James E. O'Neill & Assos., New Orleans, 1952-53 Served with USNR, 1943-46. C.P.A., La. Mem. Operations Research Soc. Am., Inst. Mgmt. Scis., Am. Finance Assn., Beta Gamma Sigma, Delta Tau Delta. Author: Decisions Under Uncertainty: Drilling Decisions by Oil and Gas Operators, 1960. Contbr. articles to profl. publs. Home: 4228 Hallmark Dr Dallas TX 75229

GRAYSON, JAMES MCDONALD, educator; b. Bland, Va., Aug. 6, 1913; s James McNutt and Ida Saunders (Newberry) G.; B.S., Va. Poly. Inst., 1935, M.S., 1937; Ph.D., Ia. State U., 1941; m. Margaret Lee Lawrence, Aug. 4, 1945; childrenNancy Louise, Elizabeth Ann, Janet Margaret, Mary Ellen. Faculty Va. Poly. Inst., Blacksburg, 1935—, prof., head research entomology, 1954-59, prof., chmn. dept. entomology, 1959-; asst entomologist Va. Agrl. Expt. Sta., 1943- 46. Presented invitational talks sci. research Internat. Congress Plant Protection, Hamburg, Germany, 1957, Vienna, Austria, 1967, PASB/WHO Seminar, Panama City, 1958; del. 11th Internat. Congress Entomology, Vienna, 1960, London, 1964. Fellow Gen. Edn. Bd., 1939-40. Mem. Entomol. Soc. Am. (chmn. sect. B 1958-59, Eastern br. 1960-61), Va. Acad. Sci., Sigma Xi, Phi Kappa Phi, Alpha Zeta. Home: 1300 Oak Dr Blacksburg VA 24060

GRAYSON, KATHRYN, singer; b. Winston-Salem, N.C.; student M.-G.-M. Studio Schoolhouse. Stage appearances in musicals include The Merry Widow, 1961, Naughty Marietta, 1961, Rosalina, 1963, Camelot, 1963-64, also S. Am. tour in Show Boat; motion picture appearances include Rio Rita, As Thousands Cheer, Anchors Aweigh, Till the Clouds Roll By, Show Boat, The Desert Song, So This Is Love, Kiss Me Kate, The Vagabond King; numerous appearances on concert stage, TV and radio, also recording artist.*

GRAYSON, RICHARD CARL, r.r. exec.; b. Cuba, Mo., Dec. 16, 1920; s. William James and Lenna (James) G.; student Columbia, 1955; m. Evelyn Honey, Sept. 24, 1939; children—Susanne, Shari, Richard Carl. With St. Louis-San Francisco Ry. Co., 1941—, v.p. operations, Springfield, Mo., 1964-68, pres., 1969—; chmn. bd., pres., dir. Quanah, Acme & Pacific Ry. Co.; pres., dir. Clarkland, Inc., Clarkland Royalty, Inc., Data Tabulating Corp., Frisco Transp. Co., 906 Olive Corp.; chmn. bd., dir. N.M. & Ariz. Land Co.; dir. Ill. Terminal R.R. Mem., dir. Assn. Am. R.R.'s, Western R.R. Assn., Assn. Southeastern R.R.'s, Terminal R.R. Assn. St. Louis, Transp. Assn. Am. Home: 13642 Peacockfarm Rd St Louis MO 63131 Office: 906 Olive St St Louis MO 63101

GRAYSON, ROBERT ALLEN, advt. exec., educator; b. N.Y.C., Oct. 8, 1927; s. Julius and Lillian (Davidson) G.; B.S., U. Ill., 1948; M.B.A., N.Y. U., 1962, Ph.D., 1968; m. Suzanne B. Bomse, June 18, 1960; children—Peter, Jocelyn, Andrea. Vice pres. Henry S. Harris Assos., mgmt. cons., 1952-58; v.p. marketing I. Rokeach & Sons, 1958-62; new products mgr. Lever Bros., 1962-68; sr. v.p., mem. exec. com. Daniel & Charles, Inc., N.Y.C., 1968-71; chmn. Grayson Assos., Inc., Englewood, N.J., 1971—. dir. Am. Commonwealth Ins. Co.; asso. prof. gen. bus. adminstrn. N.Y. U., Grad. Sch., 1966—. Mem. Am. Marketing Assn. (pres. 1969-70), Inst. Mgmt. Sci., Am. Assn. U. Profs., Acad. Mgmt. Author: Introduction to Marketing, 1971. Editor: Marketing and the Computer, 1967. Home and office: 269 Fountain Rd Englewood NJ 07631

GRAYSON, WALTON GEORGE, III, lawyer; b. Shreveport, Aug. 18, 1928; s. Walton George, Jr. and Mary Alice (Lowrey) G.; A.B., Princeton, 1949; LL.B., Harvard, 1952, m. Bennetta McEwen Purse, May 20, 1955; children-Walton IV, Mark Christopher, Bennett Purse, Dwight Philip. Admitted to Tex. bar, 1952, since practiced in Dallas; partner firm Atwell, Grayson & Atwell, 1961- 69; sr. partner Grayson & Simon, 1969—; gen. counsel, v.p., dir. Southland Corp., 1961—; asst. counsel Gt. Nat. Life Ins. Co., 1955-69. Mem. grievance com. 5th dist. Tex., 1957-66. Regional v.p. class of 1949, Princeton, 1961—, gen. solicitation chmn. capital funds drive Dallas area, 1960. Served with USNR, 1952-54. Mem. Am., Tex., Dallas bar assns. Mem. Disciples of Christ. Mason (32). Clubs: Dallas Petroleum; Princeton (N.Y.C.). Home: 10525 Strait Lane Dallas TX 75229 Office: 4 Lemmon Park E Dallas TX 75204

GRAYSTON, J. THOMAS, educator; b. Wichita, Kan., Sept. 6, 1924; s. Jesse T. and Luzia B. (Thomas) G.; student Carleton Coll., 1942-43; B.S., U. Chgo., 1947, M.D., 1948, M.S., 1952; m. Joan R. Byers, Dec. 27, 1947; children—Susan, Jesse, David. Intern, Albany (N.Y.) Med. Sch., 1948-49; Seymour Coman fellow preventive medicine U. Chgo., 1949-50, asst. resident medicine, 1950-51; epidemiologist epidemic intelligence service USPHS, U. Kan. Med. Center, 1951-53; chief resident medicine U. Chgo., 1953-54, instr. medicine, 1953-55; fellow Nat. Found. Infantile Paralysis, 1954-56; asst. prof. medicine U. Chgo., 1955-60, asso. prof., 1960; chief div. microbiology and epidemiology U.S. Naval Med. Research Unit 2, Taipei, Taiwan, 1957-60, cons., 1960—; prof. preventive medicine, chmn. dept. Sch. Medicine, U. Wash., 1960-70, dean Sch. Pub. Health and Community Medicine, 1970-71, prof. dept. epidemiology and internat. health, 1971—, mem. exec. com. Regional Primate Research Center, 1964-70, research affiliate 1967-70, v.p. for health affairs Health Scis. Center, 1971—, attending physician medicine Univ. Hosp., Seattle, 1960—. Asso. mem. commn. acute respiratory diseases Armed Forces Epidemiological Bd., 1962-65, mem., 1965—; mem. research and engring. adv. panel biology and medicine Dept. Def., 1963-67, sci. group trachoma research WHO, 1963, virology and rickettsiology study sect. NIH, 1963-67; mem. internat. centers com. Office Internat. Research, NIH, 1967-68; geog. medicine br. Nat. Inst. Allergy and Infectious Diseases, 1968-71. Diplomate Am. Bd Internal Medicine, Am. Bd. Preventive Medicine. Fellow Am. Coll. Preventive Medicine (v.p. gen. preventive medicine 1970—), Am. Pub. Health Assn.; mem. Am. Assn. Immunologists, Am. Assn. Physicians, Am. Epidemiological Soc., Am. Fedn. Clin. Research, Am. Soc. Clin. Investigation, Am. Soc. Tropical Medicine and Hygiene, Assn. Tchrs. Preventive Medicine, Infectious Diseases Soc., Internat. Epidemiological Assn., Soc. Exptl. Biology and Medicine, Western Assn. Physicians, Western Soc. Clin. Research, Sigma Xi. Contbr. numerous articles to profl. jours. Office: Health Scis Center U Wash Seattle WA 98195

GRAZIANI, SANTE, artist; b. Cleve., Mar. 11, 1920; s. Giovanni and Cleonice (Riccardi) G.; student Cleve. Sch. Art, 1938-41; B.F.A., Yale, 1943, M.F.A., 1948; m. Jacquelee McMurry, Apr. 22, 1944; children-Michael, Alexandra, Gregory Philip. Instr. drawing and painting Sch. Fine Arts, Yale, 1946-51; dean Whitney Sch. Art, 1950-51; head Sch. Worcester (Mass.) Art Mus., 1951—. Executed murals for Bluffton (O.) PO, 1941, Columbus PO, 1942, Springfield (Mass.) Mus. Fine Arts, 1947, Holyoke (Mass.) Pub. Library, 1949-51, Burncoat Sch., Worcester, 1954, Am. Battle Monument, Henri-Chapelle, Belgium, 1957, Creativity, Mayo Clinic, 1969; prep. drawings, color sketches Springfield murals; exhibited various museums, schs., galleries throughout U.S., 1947-50; one-man exhbns. at Babcock Galleries, N.Y.C., 1962, 63, 65, 67, 69, 71. Kanegis Gallery, Boston, 1964, 65, 66, 67, 68, 69, 70, U. Conn., Storrs, 1970, Fairweather-Hardin Gallery, Chgo., 1970, Allentown (Pa.) Art Mus., 1970. Served with AUS, 1943-46; conducted army arts contest PTO, with culminating exhbn. Imperial Household Mus., Tokyo, Japan, 1946; Recipient Pulitzer prize, 1942; won internat. competition for mural Springfield Mus. Fine Arts, 1943; Edwin Austin Abbey prize, 1948; Gold medal award Archtl. League N.Y., 1951, Boston Art Dirs. Club, 1954; spl. drawing award Norfolk (Va.) Mus., 1961. Mem. Nat. Soc. Mural Painters. Home: 2 Eastwood Rd Shrewsbury MA 01545 Office: Worcester Arts Mus Worcester MA 01545

GRAZIANO, FRANK JOSEPH, corp. exec.; b. Jersey City, Feb. 25, 1918; s. Samuel and Catherine (Lacava) G.; B.E.E., U.S. Naval Acad., 1940; M.S. in Mech. Engring., Mass. Inst. Tech., 1945; student advanced mgmt., N.Y.U., 1947; m. Jo- Anne Divisek, Apr. 22, 1946; childrenGayle, James, Joseph, David. Commd. ensign USN, 1940, advanced through grades to comdr.; assigned PTO and Atlantic, World War II; engring. duty officer, serving various engring. and mfg. mgmt. positions, 1945-55; resigned, 1955; v.p. mfg., dir., sec. Monarch Machine Tool Co., 1955-61; dir. operations Continental Copper & Steel Industries, Inc., 1961-63; with Am. Can Co., 1963-69, group v.p., gen. mgr. Canco, Glass and Plastic Products Group, 1964-67, v.p., gen. mgr. mfg., 1967-68, sr. v.p. adminstrn., 1968-69; pres., chief exec. officer Crompton & Knowles Corp.; mem. bd. dirs. Chemplex Corp. Mem. Community Citizens Advisory Bd., 1960—. b. County Com. on Edn. Chmn. bd. trustees United Fund, Shelby County, O., 1959. Clubs: Kiwanis (pres. Shelby County, 1961; Sky (N.Y.C.). Home: 3O Westview Rd Short Hills NJ 07078 Office: 100 Park Av New York City NY 10017

GRAZIANO, JOSEPH THOMAS, shipping co. exec.; b. Hoboken, N.J., Nov. 30, 1910; s. Alexander and Marianna (Pescatore) G.; student Pace Inst., 1930; m. Helen O'Keefe, Dec. 1, 1934; childrenMarian, Margaret, Joseph Thomas. With Am. Smelting & Refining Co., 1930-52; asst. controller Am. Export Lines, Inc., N.Y.C., 1952-55, controller, 1955-58, v.p., controller, 1958-63, v.p. govt. contracts adminstrn., 1963—. Mem. council Borough of Wood-Ridge, N.J., 1954-56. Mem. Assn. Water Transp. Accounting Officers (pres. 1960), Nat. Assn. Accountants. K.C. Home: 435 North Av Wood Ridge NJ 07075 Office: 26 Broadway New York City NY 10004

GRAZIER, JOSEPH ALBERT, mfg. exec.; b. Tyrone, Pa., Sept. 10, 1903; s. John Howard and Olive Maude (Grammer) G.; A.B., Lafayette Coll., Easton, Pa., 1925, L.H.D., 1956; LL.B., U. Pa., 1928; m. Marian Messner, Nov. 1, 1930. With Sullivan & Cromwell, N.Y.C., 1928-37, Berlin rep., 1933-35; with Am. Standard Corp. 1937—, asst. sec., 1939-47, sec., 1947-51, v.p., 1951-52, exec. v.p. 1952-53, pres., 1953-66, dir., mem. exec. com., 1952-, chmn., 1965-68; dir. Atlantic Richfield Co., Bristol-Myers Co., Nat. Cash Register Co., First Nat. City Bank, First Nat. City Corp., Johns- Manville Corp. Chmn., Nat. Indsl. Conf. Bd., 1966-68, trustee, 1959—, life councillor, 1968—; cons. Econ. Devel. Council, N.Y.C., Vice pres. bd. trustees Lafayette Coll.; bd. dirs. Internat. Center N.Y.; bd. Advt. Council, 1960-63, mem. pub. policy com., 1963—. Served as lt. col. Transp. Corps, AUS, 1942-45. Decorated grand officer Order of Merit (Italy). Mem. Order of Coif, Phi Beta Kappa, Phi Delta Phi. Republican. Presbyn. Clubs: University, Blind Brook, River, Pinnacle, The Links (N.Y.C.); Duquesne (Pitts.). Home: 435 E 52nd St New York City NY 10022 Office: 6 E 43d St New York City NY 10017

GRAZIOTTI, U. ADRIANO, artist, geometrician, historiographer; b. Carpenedolo, nr. Brescia, Italy, May 7, 1912; s. Filippo Antonio and Onorina G. (Pandolfi) G.; B.A., Inst. Superiore d'Arte, Monza, Italy, 1935, M.A., 1936; diploma di Maturita Artistica, Liceo Artistico, Florence, Italy, 1937; licenza del Corso di Scultura, L.C.S., Facolta di Architettura, Royal Acad. Fine Arts, Florence, 1940; student Slovenska Vysoka Skola Technicka' v Bratislava, Czechoslovakia, 1942-44; postgrad. Royal Acad. Fine Arts, Rome, 1940-41; jr. coll. teaching certificate, Cal., 1964; M.A., Western Res. U., 1952. Came to U.S., 1948, naturalized, 1955. Asst. prof. fine arts Royal Acad. Fine Arts, 1945-47; co-dir. Sch. Life Drawing, Circolo Artistico Internazionale Roma, 1946-47; prof. human anatomy Inst. d'Arte Beato Angelico for study ecclesiastic art, Rome, 1947-48; lectr. art Notre Dame Coll., Cooper Art Sch., Cleve. Inst. Art, Art Colony, 1949-52; asst. prof. human anatomy Cal. Coll. Arts and Crafts, Art League Cal., 1954-55; dir., lectr. Graziotti Studio Fine Arts, San Francisco, 1955-66; rep. permanent collections Civic Mus., Bratislava, City Hall, Carpenedolo, Cleve. Mus. Art; projects include monument St. Benedict, Cleve., murals life of Thomas Edison, Milan, O., 1952, Capriccio Italino, mural Italian Consulate, Cleve., 1951, monument Spirit of Christopher Columbus, San Francisco, 1957, New Generation Conquers space, 1958, Our Time, 1964, bust Pres. Kennedy, 1964, Catarinella, 1966; discoverer, classifier 22 contact twinned polyhedral forms; discoverer geometric method to determine 19 prin. duals of semi-regular archimedean polyedra, 125 origins of Platonic bodies auto-produced and inscribed within each other; drew, composed Hist. Chart of Polyhedra, 1966; lectr. Math. Inst.; prof. perspective and anatomy Stanislaus State Coll., Turlock, Cal., 1967—. Vis. writer Pacific Sci. Center, Seattle, 1967. Recipient Thiel award for portrait, Cal., 1955; John F. and Anna Lee Stacey fellow Cal. Fellow Internat. Inst. Arts and Letters. Mem. Dante Alighieri Soc. (pres. Midwest chpt. 1952). Author: Graziotti on Polyhedra, 1962; manuscripts: Optical Sensations in Geometry, 1967-70, Geometry of Repeating Design, 1965, Treatise on Normal Perspective, 1960-67, Forme Assolute e Immaginaire della Materia nello Spazio, 1955-67, History of Polyhedra. Reconstructed 14 semi-regular, stellated and interlinked lost polyhedra invented by Leonardo da Vinci, 1966-67. Contbg. author L'Arte, other publs. Discovered lost painting by Michelangelo di Caravaggio, Pasadena, 1963. Disproved authenticity of a sculpture declared erroneously an original Cellini in De Young Mus. of San Francisco. Address: Carpenedolo Via Santa Croce Brescia Italy 25013

GREACEN, NAN, artist; b. Giverny, France, Mar. 6, 1908; d. Edmund and Ethol (Booth) Greacen; student Friends Sem., N.Y.C., 1914-21, Brearley Sch., 1921-26, Grand Central Sch. Art, 1926-39; m. Rene Bard Faure, Dec. 9, 1935; childrenNancy Greacen, René Booth. Instr. painting Grand Central Art Sch., 1931—; one-man exhibits Montross Gallery, N.Y.C., Guild Hall, East Hampton; exhibited Corcoran Gallery, World's Fair, N.A.D. dir. Westchester Gallery For The Arts. Recipient Hallgarten prize Nat. Acad., 1936; Nat. Arts Club medal, 1937; Montclair Art Mus. medal, 1938; Flower Painting award, 1939; mem. annual award Nat. Arts Club, 1940; Grand Central award, 1941; Cooper prize Nat. Assn. Women Artists, 1942; 1st prize Hudson Valley Art Assn., 1947; Julian Detmer award, 1950; 1st prize Yonkers Art Exhibit, Jane Peterson prize for flower painting Allied Artists Ann., 1st prize Scarsdale Art Assn., 1951; Silver medal Katherine Lorillard Wolfe Womans Exhibit, 1953; portrait prize Scarsdale Art Exhibit, 1955; Chester Eldredge Award, Hudson Valley Art Assn., 1956; 1st prize oil painting Manhattan Savs. Bank Exhibit Westchester Artists, 1963; 1st award Nat. Arts Club ann. exhibit, 1964, Best in Show award Katherine Lorillard Wolf Exhbn., 1965; 1st prize for landscape N.A.C., 1967. Mem. N.A.D., Allied Artists Am. Nat. Arts Club, Painters and Sculptors Gallery Assn., Nat. Assn. Women Artists, Audubon Artists, Hudson Valley Art Assn. (gold medal and citation 1966, Grumbacher award 1968). Clubs: Coral Beach (Bermuda); Ponte Vedra. Author: Still-Life is Exciting, 1969; The Magic of Flower Painting, 1971. Home: 184 San Juan Dr Ponte Vedra Beach FL 32082

GREAN, ALEXANDER MICHAEL, Jr., lawyer, business exec.; b. N.Y. City, Jan. 19, 1906; s. Alexander M., Sr., and Anna A. (Kurtz) G.; student Wesleyan U., Middletown, Conn., 1924-25; A.B., Columbia, 1927; LL.B., 1930; m. Muriel E. Goodliffe, Jan. 18, 1936; childrenMichael A., Linda A., Luara J. Admitted N.Y. State bar, 1931, practiced as asso. Sullivan & Cromwell, N.Y. City, 1930-38; treas. Ward Baking Co., 1938-41, v.p., atty., 1941-, dir., 1957-; dir. Brit. Arkady Co., Ltd., 1953-; Served as industry mem. Nat. War Labor Bd., Region II, 1942-45; member Wage Stabilization Bd., Region II, 1952- 53. Mem. Nat. Council Pvt. Motor Truck Owners (dir. 1942—, pres. 1942-45). Mem. Assn. Bar of City of N.Y., Chi Psi, Phi Delta Phi. Lutheran. Clubs: University (New York City); Apawamis, (Rye, N.Y.). Editor: Columbia Law Rev., 1928-30. Home: 125 Central Av Rye NY 10580 Office: 475 Fifth Av New York City NY 10017

GREASER, MAYLIN H., dredging co. exec.; b. North Wales, Pa., Jan. 15, 1909; s. John B. and (Band) G.; B.S. in Civil Engring., Pa. State U., 1930; m. Ruth N. Philipp, Mar. 13, 1943. Engaged in constrn. and dredging bus., 1930-; with Am. Dredging Co., Phila., 1949—, successively gen. supt., dir., 1951—, v.p., 1953, pres., 1954—; dir. Phila. Maritime Exchange; bd. mgrs. Ivy Hill Cemetery Co., Phila. Served as lt. col. C.E., AUS, 1942-45. Mem. Soc. Am. Mil. Engrs. (past pres., dir. Phila. post), Franklin Inst., Post of Phila. Maritime Soc. (past pres.), Vessel Owners & Pilots Assn., Am. Soc. C.E., Delaware Valley Council (past pres.), Newcomen Soc. N.Am., Am. Legion, Phila. Bourse, Seamens Church Inst. (bd. mgrs.), Pa. Soc., Permanent Internat. Assn., Nav. Congress. Presbyn. (trustee). Clubs: Cricket, Engineers, Racquet, Downtown, Union League (Phila.); Seaview Country (Absecon, N.J.); Skytop (Pa.). Home: Cricket Rd Flourtown, PA 19031. Office: 12 S 12th St Philadelphia PA 19107

GREASON, ARTHUR LEROY, Jr., coll. dean; b. Newport, R.I., Sept. 13, 1922; s. Arthur LeRoy and Pauline (Brown) G.; B.A., Wesleyan U., Middletown, Conn., 1945; M.A., Harvard, 1947, Ph.D., 1954; m. Pauline Schaaf, Dec. 29, 1945; childrenRandall Mark, Katherine, Douglas Bradford. Asst. to dean Wesleyan U., 1945-46; teaching fellow English, Harvard, 1948-52; mem. faculty Bowdoin Coll., 1952-, asso. prof. English, 1961-66, prof., 1966- -, dean students, 1962-66, dean of Coll., 1966—. Sec.-treas. New Eng. Assn. Colls. and Secondary Schs. Trustee Hyde Sch., Bath, Me. Kent fellow Soc. Religion Higher Edn., 1946. Mem. Phi Beta Kappa. Conglist. Home: 256 Maine St Brunswick ME 04011

GREATHOUSE, GLENN ARTHUR, nuclear cons.; b. West Salem, Ill., Aug. 16, 1903; s. Chester A. and Alta (Brown) G.; B. Ed., Ill. State Normal U., 1927; M.S., U. Ill., 1929; Ph.D., Duke U. (fellow 1930-31), 1931; m. Edith Mary Bennett, Aug. 22, 1925; children—Rosemary, Glenna Lu. Tchr., Arenzville (Ill.) High Sch., 1925- 26; asst. in research U. Ill., 1927-3O; asst. prof. biophysics, U. Md., 1931-36; physiologist USDA, Washington, 1936-44, lectr. Grad. Sch., 1935-44; dir. Army-Navy Nat. Def. Research Com. Information Center, 1944-45; dir. Prevention of Deterioration Center NRC, Nat. Acad. Scis., 1945-55, sci. adviser, 1955—. interim prof. chem. engring. U. Fla., 1951-56, prof. nuclear engring., 1956-60, head dept., 1957-60; pres., treas. Nuclear Research Chem., Inc., 1955- 67; spl. cons. Mallincrodt Chem. Works, St. Louis, 1967-. Mem. sci. com. Office Sci. Research and Devel., 1944-45; spl. cons. office chief ordnance Army Dept., Washington 1944-45; head nuclear cons. Commonwealth Mass., 1959-63; mem. U.S.-Brit. Sci. Mission to Eng., Europe, Africa and Panama, 1945; U.S. del. second World Conf. on Peaceful Use of the Atom, Geneva, 1958. Recipient Nat. Def. Research Com. award; Bur. Ordnance Devel. award U.S. Navy; His Majesty's medal for services in the cause of freedom Brit. Govt. Mem. Am. Nuclear Soc., Am. Chem. Soc., A.A.A.S., Wash. Acad. Sci., Sigma Xi, Phi Sigma, Sigma Phi Sigma. Author: (with Wessel) Deterioration of Materials-Causes and Preventive Techniques, 1954. Contbr. articles to profl. publs. Home: The Towers Apt Dayton Beach, FL 32020. Office: Spl Cons Mallincrodt Chem Works Ormond Beach FL 32074 also Greathouse Consulting Services PO Box 332 Ormond Beach FL 32074

GREATHOUSE, JOE STEPHEN, Jr., hosp. dir.; b. Lewisport, Ky., June 18, 1929; s. Joe Stephen and Lydia (Edwards) G.; B.S., U. Ky., 1951; M.H.A. with distinction, Northwestern U., 1957; divorced; children—Amy, Joan. Asst. registrar U.S. Air Force Hosp., Maxwell AFB, Ala., 1951-53; asst. bus. mgr. Central State Hosp., Lakeland, Ky., 1953-54, bus. mgr., 1954-55; adminstrv. resident U. Louisville Med. Center, 1956-57; asst. dir. Vanderbilt U. Hosp., 1957-59, asso. dir., 1959-65, adminstrv. dir., 1965-67, dir., 1967—; preceptor hosp. adminstrn. George Washington U., U. Ala., Wash. U., Xavier U.; cons. Nat. Insts. Health. Mem. Tenn. Pub. Health Council, 1970—; mem., sec. State Medicaid Med. Adv. Com., 1968—; pres. Nashville Regional Eye Bank. Bd. dirs. Travelers Aid. Fellow Am. Coll. Hosp. Adminstrs.; mem. Tenn. Hosp. Assn. (pres. 1967-68), Middle Tenn. Hosp. Council, Met. Nashville Hosp. Adminstrs. Assn., Nat. League Nursing, Tenn. Hosp. Assn. (chmn. budget com. 1968-71, chmn. council on finance 1969-71, chm legislative com. 1968—), chmn. council govt. and pub. affairs 1970—), Mid-Cumberland Health Planning Council, Assn. Am. Med. Colls. Methodist. Kiwanian. Home: 214 Old Hickory Blvd Nashville TN 37221 Office: Vanderbilt U Hosp Nashville TN 37203

GREAVES, DONALD CRITCHFIELD, educator, physician; b. Minot, N.D., June 26, 1924; s. John Perce and Adelaide (Hamilton) G.; student Mont. State U., 1942-43, 44-45, Yale, 1943-44; M.D., Washington U., St. Louis, 1949; B.S., U. Mont., 1959; m. Jean McGregor, Oct. 2, 1954; children—Mary McGregor, Donald Critchfield. Intern, Salt Lake City Gen. Hosp., 1949-50; form jr. asst. resident psychiatrist to resident psychiatrist Payne Whitney Psychiat. Clinic, N.Y.C., 1950-54, asst. attending psychiatrist, 1954-55; asst. in psychiatry, then instr. psychiatry Cornell U. Med. Coll., 1951-55; asso. prof. psychiatry, neurology, behavioral scis. U. Okla. Sch. Medicine, 1955-58; prof. psychiatry, head dept. U. Kan. Sch. Medicine, 1958—; chief in-patient psychiatry service U. Okla. Hosps., 1955-58; attending psychiatrist VA Hosp., Oklahoma City, 1955- 58; cons. psychiatrist student health service Okla. State U., 1955-58, VA hosps., Kansas City, Mo., Wadsworth, Kan., 1958—, Winter VA Hosp., Topeka, 1958-63. Spl. asst. to dir. Nat. Inst. Mental Health, 1968-69. Mem. Gov. Kan. Adv. Commn. State Instl. Mgmt., 1958-63, 66—. Diplomate Am. Bd. Psychiatry and Neurology (examiner 1957—). Mem. A.A.A.S., A.M.A., Am. Psychiat. Assn., Assn. Am. Med. Colls., Am. Psychosomatic Soc., N.Y. Acad. Sci., Acad. Psychoanalysis. Contbr. articles to profl. jours. Home: 7259 Eby Dr Shawnee Mission KS 66204 Office: Kan U Med Center 39th and Rainbow Blvd Kansas City KS 66103

GREAVES, HALBERT SPENCER, educator; b. Ephraim, Utah, Oct. 19, 1907; s. Peter and Catherine (Mortensen) G.; B.A., U. Utah, 1929, postgrad., 1950, 54; M.S., Northwestern U., 1932, U. Berlin, 1936; Ph.D., U. Wis., 1941; m. Afton Martha Christensen, June 9, 1938; childrenPeter Morris, Jerald Richard. Tchr., Ephraim High

Sch., 1929-31, 33-34, Carbon County High Sch., Price, Utah, 1932-33; faculty Utah State Agrl. Coll., Logan, 1936-40; 41- 42, 45-46, acting head speech dept., 1939-40; mem. faculty U. Utah, 1946- , prof., 1951-, head speech dept., 1961-69; faculty Purdue U., 1936, U. Wis., 1940-41, Western State Tchrs. Coll., Gunnison, Colo., summer 1946, USAF, Tuscaloosa, Ala., summer 1948, U.S. Naval Postgrad. Sch., Monterey, Cal., summers 1962-64. Opera dir. Utah Centennial Commn., 1947; chmn. Utah Am. Legion High Sch. Oratorical Contest, 1951-63. Fellow Mountain States Telephone Co., summer 1961. Served to lt. (j.g.) USNR, 1942-45. Mem. Speech Communication Assn., Western Speech Assn. (pres. 1965), So. Speech Assn., Speech Arts Assn. Utah (past pres.), Am. Legion, Pi Kappa Alpha, Theta Alpha Phi, Phi Eta Sigma. Mem. Ch. of Jesus Christ of Latter-day Saints. Author articles in profl. jours and chpts. in books. Home: 1904 Herbert Av Salt Lake City UT 84108

GREAVES, THOMAS GUY, Jr., lawyer; b. Lynchburg, Va., Apr. 19, 1918; s. Thomas Guy and Ellen duVal (Radford) B.; B.S. in Econs., Wharton Sch. U. Pa., 1939; LL.B., U. Ala., 1947; m. Annie Jean Bell, Feb. 28, 1942; childrenThomas Guy III, Mac Bell. Admitted to Ala. bar, 1948, since practiced in Mobile; partner firm Hand, Arendall, Bedsole, Greaves & Johnston, 1952—. Pres. Mobile County chpt. A.R.C., 1966-68; pres. Episcopal Churchmens Assn. Ala., 196O-61; mem. Ala. Bar Found., U. Ala. Law Sch. Found. Served to capt., inf. AUS, 1941-45. Fellow Am. Bar Found.; mem. Am. (ho. dels. 1959-, chmn. standing com. Am. Citizenship 1960-63, com. documents of title 1959-62; chmn. rules and calendar com. 1970—, vice chmn. com. draft of ho. of dels. 1960-63; chmn. bar activities sect. 1965-66; mem. exec. council young lawyers sect. 1953-55; mem. adv. bd. jour. 1961-63; bd. govs. 1966-69), Ala. (pres. young lawyers 1948-49), Mobile County (pres. 1968) bar. assns., Am. Judicature Soc. (dir. 1959-63), Fedn. Ins. Counsel (dir. 1963-65), Am. Counsel Assn. (exec. com. 1960-63), Conf. Personal Finance, Mobile C. of C. (chmn. govt. affairs com. 1962-63), U. Ala Law Sch. Alumni Assn. (pres. 1963-64), Am., Ala. law insts., English Speaking Union (pres. 1970), Delta Kappa Epsilon, Phi Delta Phi, Phi Eta Sigma. Home: 77 Clarise Circle Mobile AL 36608 Office: First Nat Bank Bldg Mobile AL 36602

GREAVES, WILLIAM, film maker; b. N.Y.C., Oct. 8, 1926; s. Garfield G. and Phillis (Muir) G.; student Film Inst., Coll. City N.Y., 1949-51, New Inst. Film and TV, N.Y.C., 1950-51. Featured actor on Broadway, screen, radio and TV, 1946-52; mem. prodn. staff Nat. Film Bd. Can., 1952-60; founder, dir. Canadian Drama Studio, Montreal, Toronto and Ottawa, 1953-63; pub. information officer Internat. Civil Aviation Orgn., 1962-63; mem. prodn. staff UN TV, 1963-64; ind. documentary film maker, 1964—; exec. producer Black Jour., 1968-70. Initiator Nat. Assn. Black Media Producers, 1970. Recipient Emmy award Nat. Acad. TV Arts and Scis., 1970; Russwurm award Nat. Newspaper Pubs. Assn. Am., 1970. Mem. N.Y. Actors Studio. ‡

GREBANIER, BERNARD, author; b. N.Y.C., Mar. 8, 1903; s. Benjamin and Ottillie (von Storenberg) G.; A.B., Coll. City N.Y., 1926; M.A., N.Y. U., 1930, Ph.D., 1935; m. Frances Winwar, Sept. 22, 1925 (div. Dec. 1942). Instr., Coll. City N.Y., 1926-30; faculty Bklyn. Coll., 1930—, prof. English, 1957-63, prof. emeritus, 1963—; Lectr., Pace Coll., 1958-63; lectr. adult edn. Hofstra Coll., 1971; lectr. poetry workshop Delbrook Coll., Riverton, Va., 1971; dir. plays Off-Broadway including Phaedra, Othello, Merchant of Venice, King Lear, Oedipus the King, The Importance of Being Ernest, Recipient Samuel French award for best teaching in playwriting, 1957, 58. Mem. Poetry Soc. Am., P.E.N., Author's Guild. Author: (with S. Thompson) English Literature and its Backgrounds, 2 vols., 1939-40; (with H. Hintz) Modern American Vistas, 1941; Fauns, Satyrs and a Few Sages, 1945; Mirrors of the Fire, 1946; Essentials of English Literature, 2 vols., 1948-49; (with V. Hopper) Essentials of European Literature, 2 vols., 1950-51; Bibliography of European Literature in English Translation (with V. Hopper), 1953; The Other Love, 1957; Racine's Phaedra, an English Acting Version in Verse, 1958; (with S. Reiter) College Writing and Reading, 1958; Moliere's The Misanthrope, an English Acting Version, 1959; (with S. Reiter) An Introduction to Imaginative Literature, 1960; The Heart of Hamlet, 1960; Playwriting, 1961; Chaucer, 1962; Milton, 1962; The Truth about Shylock, 1962; Moliere, 1963; Rousseau, 1963; Thornton Wilder, 1963; Shakespeare's Henry IV, Part I, 1964; The Great Shakespeare Forgery, 1965; Armenian Miniatures, 1967; The Uninhibited Byron, 1970; Edwin Arlington Robinson, 1971; The Angel in the Rock, 1971; also contbr. to encys., mags. Home: 215 W 88th St New York City NY 10024 Office: Cyrilly Abels 119 W 57th St New York City NY 10019

GREBANIER, MICHAEL PETER, musician, educator; b. Bklyn., Apr. 27, 1937; s. Joseph Phillip and Lillian (Greenberg) G.; diploma Curtis Inst. Music, 1958; m. Patricia Parr, Mar. 7, 1959; children—Loren, Steven. With Pitts. Symphony Orch., 1958-59, solo violincellist, 1963—; with Cleve. Orch., 1959-63; tchr. Duquesne U., 1963-70, Temple U., 1970—; ann. solo appearances with Pitts. Symphony Orch., Pitts. Chamber Orch., solo recitals. Recipient Naumberg award, 1957. Home: 120 N Lang Av Pittsburgh PA 15208 Office: Heinz Hall Pittsburgh PA

GREBE, MARGUERITE LUCKETT, co. exec.; b. Washinton; d. Joseph E. and Florence (Balderston) Luckett; ed. high sch.; m. H.C. Grebe, July 11, 1921 (dec. June 1, 1952). With H.C. Grebe & Co., Inc., Chgo., 1952—, now pres. Clubs: Yacht, Lake Shore (Chgo.). Home: 2052 Lincoln Park W Chicago IL 60614 Office: 3250 N Washtenaw Chicago IL 60618

GREBER, ARTHUR CASPER, drug mfg. co. exec.; b. Cin., Apr. 9, 1915; s. Henry H. and Minnie (Kruse) G.; Chem. Engr., U. Cin., 1938; m. Irma S. Hoeweler, June 10, 1939; 1 son, Alan H. Engring., prodn. supr. Procter & Gamble Co., 1934- 43; chief engr. Schenley Industries, Cin., 1943-55; asst. to v.p. mfg. Smith, Kline & French Labs., 1955-56; v.p. mfg., dir. Clopay Corp., Cin., 1956-60; v.p. Richardson-Merrell, Inc. (formerly Vick Chem. Co.), N.Y.C., 1960—, exec. v.p. Tulox-Lumelite-Bradley div. Registered profl. engr., Ohio, Md., Pa., Ky., Ind. Mem. Nat. Soc. Profl. Engrs., Am. Inst. Chem. Engrs., Engring. Soc. Cin., Tau Beta Phi. Home: Milton Harbor House Milton Rd Rye NY 10580 Office: 122 E 42d St New York City NY 10017

GREBER, EDWARD GEORGE, telephone co. exec.; b. Dallas, Oct. 7, 1916; s. Edward George and Hettie (Woodcock) G.; B.S. in Elec. Engring., Purdue U., 1937; m. Eula Lee James, Apr. 6, 1940; childrenMartha (Mrs. James Michael Crawford), James, and Nancy. Employed with Southwestern Bell Telephone Co., 1935- 50, 1955-60, v.p., gen. mgr., 1957-59; plant service engr., then plant operations engr. Am. Tel. & Tel. Co., 1950-55; v.p. operations dir., exec. com. N.J. Bell Telephone Co., 1960-62; v.p. operations N.Y. Telephone Co., 1963-65; v.p. operations Southwestern Bell Telephone, 1965-, also dir., mem. exec. com.; dir. Boatmen's Nat. Bank, St. Louis. Trustee St. Louis Children's Hosp., St. Louis Ednl. TV Council. Mem. I.E.E.E., C. of C. Met. St. Louis, Newcomen Soc. North Am., Delta Tau Delta, Tau Beta Pi, Eta Kappa Nu. Clubs: Racquet, Noonday, Clayton, Media, Bellerive Country (St. Louis); Seaview Country (Absecon, N.J.). Home: 33 Bellerive Country Club Grounds St Louis MO 63141 Office: 1010 Pine St St Louis MO 63101

GRECO, CHARLES P., clergyman; b. Rodney, Miss., Oct. 29, 1894; s. Frank P. and Carmela (Testa) G.; student Jesuit Coll., New Orleans, 1904-07, Jefferson Coll., Convent, La., 1908; St. Joseph Sem., St. Benedict, La., 1907-13; American Coll., Louvain, Belgium, 1913-14, U. Fribourg, Switzerland, 1914-18. Ordained priest Roman Catholic Ch., July, 1918; asst. pastor, Houma, La., 1918-23, vice chancellor and chancellor of New Orleans, 1923-26, adminstr. and pastor of St. Maurice Ch., 1926-45, Sec., Defender of Marriage Bond, presiding judge of Matrimonial Court, 1923-46; vicar gen. New Orleans, 1944-46; bishop Alexandria 1946—. K.C. (supreme chaplain 196O—). Editor-in-chief, Cath. Action of South, 1944-46. Address: PO Drawer 191 Alexandria LA 71301

GRECO, DICK A., Jr., mayor; b. Tampa, Fla., Sept. 14, 1933; s. Dick A. and Evelyn (Cotarella) G.; student U. Fla.; B.S., U. Tampa, 1956; m. Dana Hepinstall, Apr. 3, 1953; childrenRichard L., Dana L., Darcy L. Councilman, City of Tampa, 1963-67, major, 1967—. V.p., King-Greco Hardware Co., Inc. Pres. Travelers Aid Soc.; v.p. Davis Islands Civic Center. Bd. dirs. MacDonald's Tng. Center, Fla. League Municipalities. Named Outstanding Young Man of Year, Jr. C. of C., 1965; mem. Nat. Skeet Champion-All Am. Skeet Team, 1950-51. Mem. Ybor City C. of C. (dir.). Home: 112 Lodoga St Tampa FL 33606 Office: City Hall Florida Ave and JF Kennedy Blvd Tampa FL 33602

GRECO, GEORGE JOSEPH, fgn. service officer; b. Nesquehoning, Pa., Aug. 26, 1912; s. George Joseph and Salvatrice (Moretta) G.; A.B., Mt. St. Mary's Coll., Md., 1935; M.A., Columbia, 1941; m. Ligia J. Villafane, June 12, 1937; 1 dau., Juliana. Dir. orch. Cunard-White Star Line, 1933; tchr., later supr. Pub. Sch. System P.R., 1936-42; news broadcaster, Eng., P.R., 1941; edn. project dir., local com. Inter-Am. Affairs, Dominican Republic, 1942-45, spl. rep. Inter-Am. Edn. Found., 1945-48, chief field party edn. Inst. Inter-Am. Affairs, Dominican Republic, 1948, 51-52, Bolivia, 1948-50, Ecuador, 1950-51; U.S. dir. TCA, Dominican Republic, 1952-54; U.S. chief edn. adviser ICA, Peru, 1954-61; chief West Coast div. S.A., ICA, 1961, supervisory internat. relations officer, 1961-62; chief human resources div. AID, Peru, 1962-64, asst. dir. agy., 1964-71, Dominican Republic, 1971—. Coach trainer nat. track and field, Dominican Republic, 1947; observer Indian Conf., Cuzco, Peru, 1949; U.S. del. UNESCO Regional Conf. Free and Compulsory Edn. in Latin Am., Peru, 1956; adv. U.S. del. 2d Inter-Am. Meeting Ministers of Edn., Peru, 1956; adv. 1st nat. edn. survey Nat. Peruvian Govt., 1956-57; U.S. del. Internat. Conf., Santiago, Chile, 1962, Interam. Edn. Conf., Chile, 1962. 59. Address: care Am embassy Dominican Republic

GRECO, JOHN D., banker. Sr. v.p. operations First New Haven Nat. Bank. Office: 1 Church St Box 502 New Haven CT 06502*

GRECO, JOSE choreographer; b. Montorio nei Frentani, Italy, Dec. 23, 1918; s. Paolo Emilio and Carmela (Bucci) G.; brought to U.S., 1928, naturalized, 1928; student Leonardo da Vinci Art Sch., N.Y.C.; studied dancing with Helene Veola; m. Nila Amparo, Aug. 16, 1946. First profl. appearance as dancer in Carmen, N.Y. Hippodrome Opera Co., 1937; joined Gloria Belmonte in engagement at La Conga, N.Y.C. (profl. name Ramon Serrano), 1938; tchr. dancing, hotels and resorts, 1936-45; appeared with Argentinita, 1943, toured U.S., 1943-45, guest appearances Ballet Theater at Met. Opera House; dancer ballets including Ravel's Bolero, de Falla's El Amor Brujo, Capriccio Espagnol, Carmen; Spanish debut with Ballet Español, Madrid, 1946; choreographer cana y Farruca, Sentimento, Polo, others; choreographer, dancer for motion picture Manolete, 1948; organized company Ballets y Bailes de Espana, 1948, appeared Barcelona, Paris, also Norway, Sweden, Denmark, other European countries, toured Argentina, Uruguay, Chile, Peru, 1950, appeared Sadler's Wells Theater, London, 1951; North Am. debut with Spanish Ballet, Shubert Theater, N.Y.C., 1951; tours of U.S. 1951—. Home: 224 W 49th St New York City NY 10019 Office: 1740 Broadway New York City NY 10019

GRECO, SALVATORE J., univ. dean; b. Richmond, Cal., Jan. 25, 1921; s. Joseph and Bessie (Bonocorso) G.; B.S. in Pharmacy (Lehn and Fink medal), Duquesne U., 1942; Ph.D., U. Md., 1948; m. Betty J. Hicks, May 21, 1946; childrenTom, Janet, Amy, Sheryl, Robert, Marianne. Asst. prof. chemistry Temple U. Sch. Pharmacy, Phila., 1948-49; asst. prof. pharmacy George Washington U., 1949-52, asso. prof., 1952-56; asso. prof. pharmacy, asst. to dean Creighton U., Omaha, 1956-58, prof. pharmacy, dean Sch. Pharmacy, 1958—. Served with AUS, 1943-46. Mem. Am. (past pres. Washington), Neb., Omaha pharm. assns., Am. Inst. History Pharmacy, Am. Assn. Coll. Pharmacy (chmn. com. relationships bds. and colls.), Sigma Xi, Rho Chi (1st pres. Duquesne U.), Kappa Psi, Alpha Sigma Nu. Roman Catholic. Contbr. articles to profl. jours. Home: 4004 Maple St Omaha NB 68111

GREDE, WILLIAM, J., business exec.; b. Milw., Feb. 24, 1897; s. Henry L. and Fanny (Runkel) G.; student U. Wis.; LL.D., George Williams Coll., Carroll Coll.; Dr. Bus. Adminstrn., Northland Coll.; m. Margaret Weiss, Sept. 17, 1919; children—Janet, Betty. With foundry, Decatur, Ill., 1917-20; with Liberty Foundry, Milw., 1920—, pres., 1923-40, pres. successor co., Grede Foundries, Inc., 1940-60, chmn. bd., 1960—; chmn. exec. com. J.I. Case Co., 1956-61, dir., 1953-61, pres., chmn. bd., 1960-61; class B dir. 7th Fed. Res. Bank, 1947-61; pres., dir. Coatings, Inc.; dir. Kingsford Co., Thomas Industries, Inc. Mem. nat. council YMCA (pres. 1952-54). Recipient William H. McFadden Gold Medal, Foundrymen's Soc., 1953; gold medal for good citizenship S.A.R., 1953. Mem. Gray Iron Research Inst., Am. Foundrymen's Soc., Wis. Mfrs. Assn., N.A.M. (pres. 1952, dir.), Gray Iron Founders Assn., Steel Founders Soc. of Am., John Birch Soc. (mem. council), Delta Upsilon. Home: Elm Grove WI 53122 Office: 1320 S 1st St Milwaukee WI 53201

GREEHY, WILLIAM E., petroleum co. exec.; b. 1936; B.B.A., St. Mary's U., 1960; married. Auditor, Price Waterhouse & Co., 1960-61; sr. auditor Humble Oil & Refining Co., 1961-63; controller Coastal States Gas Producing Co., Corpus Christi, Tex., 1968—, v.p., 1969—. Served with USAF, 1954-58. Office: Petroleum Tower Corpus Christi TX 78401*

GREEK, DAROLD I., lawyer; b. Kunkle, O., Mar. 30, 1909; s. Albert F. and Iva (Shaffer) G.; student Bowling Green State U., 1926-28; LL.B., Ohio State U., 1932; m. Catherine Johnson, Oct. l2, 1935 (dec. 1962); 1 son, Darold I; m. Elizabeth Tracy Ridgley, Sept. 18, 1970. Admitted to Ohio bar, 1932; treas. Williams County, O., 1932-33; atty. Ohio Dept. Taxation, 1934-36; practice in Columbus 1937-; partner firm George, Greek, King, McMahon & McConnaughey, and predecessors, 1937—. Mem. Am., Ohio, Columbus (pres. 1966-67) bar assns. Presbyn. Rotarian. Clubs: University; Columbus Country (Columbus); Golf. Home: 8 Lake of the Woods Point Galena OH 43021 Office: 100 E Broad St Columbus OH 43215

GREELEY, ANDREW MORAN, sociologist, educator; b. Oak Park, Ill., Feb. 5, 1928; s. Andrew T. and Grace (McNichols) G.; A.B., St. Mary of Lake Sem., 1950, S.T.L., 1954; M.A., U. Chgo., 1961, Ph.D., 1961. Ordained priest Roman Catholic Ch., 1954; asst. pastor Ch. of Christ the King, Chgo., 1954-64; program dir. Nat. Opinion Research Center, Chgo., 1961—; lectr. sociology U. Chgo.; prof. sociology of edn. U. Ill. at Chgo. Circle; cons. Hazen Found. Commn. Recipient Cath. Press Assn. award for best book for young people, 1965, Thomas Alva Edison award for radio broadcast, 1963. Mem. Am. Sociol. Assn., Am. Cath. Sociol. Soc. (pres.), Soc. for Sci. Study Religion, Religious Research Assn. Author: The Church and the Suburbs, 1959; Strangers in the House, 1961; Religion and Career, 1963; (with Peter H. Rossi) Education of Catholic Americans, 1966. Contbr. articles profl. jours. Home: 1012 E 49th St Chicago IL 60653 Office: 6030 S Ellis Av Chicago IL 60637

GREELEY, ARTHUR WHITE, govt. ofcl.; b. Washington, Aug. 1, 1912; s. William Buckhout and Gertrude Maxwell (Jewett) G.; M.F., Yale, 1935; B.S.F., U. Wash., 1934; m. Anne Elizabeth Sturmer, June 18, 1938; childrenJanet (Mrs. Brace N. Rodenhiser), Lynne. With U.S. Forest Service, 1935-, asst. chief nat. forest protection and devel., 1959-62, asst. chief, then dep. chief nat. forest resource mgmt., 1962-66; asso. chief U.S. Forest Service, 1966—. Mem. Pres. Quetico-Superior Com., 1956—. Mem. Soc. Am. Foresters, Am. Soc. Range Mgmt., Soil Conservation Soc. Am., Am. Forestry Assn., Alpha Delta Phi. Methodist. Home: 8312 Thoreau Dr Bethesda MD 20034 Office: Dept Agr South Bldg Washington DC 20025

GREELEY, DANA MCLEAN, clergyman; b. Lexington, Mass., July 5, 1908; s. William Roger and Morjory Ellen (Houghton) G.; B.S., Harvard, 1931, S.T.B., 1933; D.D., Meadville Theol. Sch., 1951, Tufts U., St. Lawrence U., Emerson Coll., Calvin Coolidge Coll.; m. Deborah Webster, Dec. 27, 1931; children—Faith Scovel, Rosamond Hamlin, Cynthia Mc-Elwain, Penelope Elwell. Ordained to ministry Unitarian Ch., 1932; minister, Lincoln, Mass., 1932- 34, Concord, N.H., 1934-35, Arlington St. Ch., Boston, 1935-58; sec. Am. Unitarian Assn., 1945-53, pres. 1958-61; pres. Unitarian Universalist Assn. N.Am., 1961-69; pres. Internat. Assn. for Liberal Christianity and Religious Freedom, 1969—; minister First Parish, Concord, 1970—. Vis. prof. Meadville Theol. Sch. U. Chgo.; co-chmn. World Conf. on Religion and Peace, Nat. Inter- Religious Peace Com. Hon. pres. Citizens Crime Com. New Eng.; past pres. Unitarian Service com.; past pres. Mass. Council Chs.; dir. Benevolent Fraternity, Isles of Shoals Assn., Home for Aged Women, Boston Urban League. Trustee St. Laurence Theol. Sch., Emerson Coll.; past mem. vis. coms., bd. overseas Harvard. Mem. Unitarian Universalist Ministerial Union, Mass. Bible Soc. (v.p.), Delta Upsilon. Rotarian. Clubs: Harvard Musical Assn., Appalachian Mountain; Harvard (Boston, N.Y.C.). Author: Toward Larger Living, 1945; A Message to Atheists, 1948; 25 Beacon St. and Other Recollections, 1971. Home: 276 Main St Concord MA Office: First Parish Concord MA

GREELEY, JOSEPH MAY, advt. cons.: b. Winnetka, Ill., Sept. 13, 1902; s. Morris Larned and Anne (Foote) G.; student Phillips Exeter Acad.; B.S. Harvard, 1925, M.B.A., 1927; m. Margery Gerould, Dec. 18, 1928 (div. June 1958): children—Margery (Mrs. Forrest I. Watson), Samuel Joseph May; m. 2d, Elizabeth Knode Conrad, Apr. 8, 1961. Advt. mgr. Quaker Oats, Ltd., London, Eng., 1930-39; asst. gen. mgr. Hecker Products Corp., N.Y.C., 1939-41; account exec. Pedlar & Ryan, N.Y.C. 1941-42; v.p. Dancer, Fitzgerald, Sample, Chgo., 1942-48; v.p. Leo Burnett, Chgo., 1948-55, v.p. charge marketing, 1955-58, exec. v.p. marketing services, 1958-70, also former dir., mem. exec. com., now cons., 1971—. Clubs: Minneapolis; Harvard (N.Y.C.); University Curling (Chgo.); Harvard of Chicago (pres., dir.), Mid-America, Indian Hill. Home: 955 Green Bay Rd Hubbard Woods IL 60093 Office: Prudential Bldg Chicago IL 60601

GREELEY, PAUL WEBB, surgeon; b. Waterman, Ill., July lO, 1902; s. Paul Eber Norman, and Maud Nancy (Webb) G.; A.B., U. Ill., 1923; M.D., Northwestern U., 1928; m. Eunice Cooksey Goebel, June 12, 1927; 1 son, Paul Julius Goebel. Rotating intern Evanston (Ill.) Hosp., 1927-28, gen. surgery tng. under Dr. Frederick Christopher, 1928-31; pvt. practice medicine specializing in gen. surgery, Chgo., 1931-34, plastic surgery, 1936—; clin. asst. gen. surgery Northwestern U. Med. Sch. Chgo., 1930-34; vol. asst. plastic surgery to Sir Harold Gillies and Sir Archibald McIndoe, London, additional tng. in plastic surgery in Freiburg, Munich, Vienna, 1934-35; clin. prof. surgery, head dept. plastic surgery U. Ill. Coll. Medicine, Chgo., 1937-70; prof. plastic surgery Rush Presbyn.-St. Lukes Med. Center, Chgo., 1971—; attending plastic surgeon, chief plastic surgery service U. Ill. Hosp., Presbyn.-St. Lukes Hosp.; cons. plastic surgeon West Side VA Hosp., Municipal Tb Sanitarium, Chgo., U.S. Naval hosps., Great Lakes, Ill. and San Diego. Served with M.C., USNR, 1943-46; now rear adm. Res., res. cons. plastic surgery Bur. Medicine and Surgery, Dept. Navy, 1947—. Diplomate Am. Bd. Plastic Surgery (bd. govs. 1951-58). Mem. Am. Soc. Plastic and Reconstructive Surgery (pres. 1950-51), Am. Assn. Surgery Trauma, Am. Assn. Plastic Surgeons, A.C.S., A.M.A., Am., Western, Central surg. assns., Internat. Fedn. Plastic Surgeons, Am. Assn. Ry. Surgeons, Ill. Med. Soc., Inst. Medicine Chgo., Chgo. Surg. Soc. (v.p. 1960), Argentine Soc. Plastic Surgeons (hon.), Internat. Soc. Surgeons, Warren H. Cole Surg. Soc., Kappa Delta Rho, Omega Beta Pi, Nu Sigma Nu. Clubs: University (Chgo.); Indian Hill (Winnetka, Ill.). Contbr. numerous monographs to profl. lit., chpts. to textbooks. Home: 1410 Sheridan Rd Wilmette IL 60091 (summer) Castle Park MI 49422 (winter) LaJolla CA 92037 Office: 310 S Michigan Av Chicago IL 60604 ☆

GREELEY, ROLAND BRADFORD, educator; b. Lexington, Mass., Oct. 22, 1910; s. William Roger and Marjory (Houghton) G.; A.B., Harvard, 1931, M. City Planning, 1961; m. Marian Mills Kimball, July 27, 1935; childrenWilliam Bradford, Warren Kimball, Edward Houghton, David McLean, Sally Anne. Chief planning technician New Eng. Regional Planning Commn., Boston, 1935-43; planning engr. Fed. Works Agy., Boston, 1943-44; research asso. Am. Pub. Health Assn., 1944-45; mem. faculty Mass. Inst. Tech., 1945-, prof. city planning 1961-, dir. admissions, 1961-. Mem. Lexington (Mass.) Planning Bd., 1933-35, 63-68, chmn., 1967-68; chmn. Lexington Sch. Sites Com., 1957-62; mem. Greater Boston Census Tract Commn., 1947-. Pres. Star Island Corp., 1960-. Pres. Lexington Vis. Nurse Assn., 1950-51; mem. standing com. Mass. Trustees of Reservations, 1961-67; mem. Mass. Com. Children and Youth, 1959-62, Gov. Mass. Com. Historic Site Preservation, 1963-65; Pres. Unitarian Service Pension Soc., 1947-58; clk. United Unitarian Appeal, 1953-55; pres., treas. Unitarian Young Peoples Religious Union, 1934-39; mem. Unitarian-Universalist Goals Com., 1965-67. Mem. Am. Inst. Planners (bd. govs. 1950-53, mng. editor jour. 1945-52, sec.-treas. New Eng. chpt. 1947-48), Am. Soc. Planning Ofcls., Unitarian-Universalist Laymen's League, Delta Upsilon. Rotarian. Co-author: Integration of the New England Regional Plan 1942; Regional Planning Study, Farmington Valley, Conn., 1957; Master Plan, Town of Gandhidham, India, 1952; Greater Bangkok Plan, Bangkok, Thailand, 1960. Home: 1359 Massachusetts Av Lexington MA 02173 Office: Mass Inst Tech Cambridge MA 02139

GREELEY, SAMUEL SEWALL, lawyer; b. Winnetka, Ill., Sept. 14, 1914; s. Samuel Arnold and Dorothy (Goffin) G.; A.B., Harvard, 1936, LL.B., 1939; m. Irene E. Mares, Oct. 28, 1945; children—Sara S., Samuel Sewall. Admitted to Ill. bar, 1939; practice in Chgo., 1939-42, 46-51; gen. counsel Masonite Corp., Chgo., 1951-69, sec., 1958-69, treas., 1961-64, financial v.p. 1964-66, exec. v.p., 1966-69, pres., 1969—, also dir.; dir. Masonite Co. Can., Ltd. Served to lt. comdr. USNR, 1942-46. Mem. Am., Fed., Ill., Chgo. bar assns., Legal

Club. Clubs: Tower, Economic (Chgo.): Indian Hill (Winnetka). Home: 800 Tower Rd Winnetka IL 60093 Office: 29 N Wacker Dr Chicago IL 60606

GREELEY, WALTER FRANKLIN, corp. exec.; b. Framingham, Mass., July 14, 1931; s. Sidney Foote and Annette (Stiles) G.; A.B. cum laude, Harvard, 1953, LL.B., 1960; student U. Amsterdam (Netherlands), 1956-57; m. Alida Daale, Feb. 23, 1957; childrenWalter Franklin, Robin, Jennifer, John David. Admitted to Mass. bar, 1960; with Cabot Corp., Boston, 1960—, gen. counsel, sec., 1967-69, v.p., 1969—. Sec. Internat. Center New Eng. Served with USNR, 1953-56. Mem. Am., Boston (chmn. com. internat. legal practice 1967) bar assns., Am. Soc. Corp. Secs. Home: 17 Maugus Av Wellesley MA 02181 Office: 125 High St Boston MA 02110

GREEN, ABEL, editor of Variety; b. N.Y.C., June 3, 1900; s. Seymour A. and Berta (Raines) G.; student N. Y. U.; m. Gracelyn Adele Fenn, June 3, 1921. Organizer theatrical news coverage European, N. African, S. Am. capitals for Variety mag., 1929-30; as theatrical trade reporter, writer, editor recognized as an authority on contemporary film, TV, radio, stage, music, nightclub, concert, Tin Pan Alley, vaudeville 1921—; editor of Variety 1933—. Co-author, producer Philco-Variety Radio Hall Fame, coast-to-coast, Blue Network radio hour. Author: Mr. Broadway, Warner Bros. film saga of Variety's founder- editor-publisher, the late Sime Silverman, 1947; Tin Pan Alley; Outward Bound and Gagged; Show Biz (From Vaude to Video) (with Joe Laurie, Jr.), 1952. Editor: Variety Music Cavalcade, 1952, latest rev. edit., 1971; The Spice of Variety, 1953; ann. anthologist, Show Biz, Am. Peoples Ency.; contbr. articles on theatrical world to nat. mags. Mem. Motion Picture Pioneers, Skeeters, A.S.C.A.P. Club: Variety (N.Y.C.). Address: 55 Central Park W New York City NY 10023

GREEN, ABNER LEON, educator; b. Oakland, La., Mar. 31, 1888; s. William Morris and Emily Frances (McCormick) G.; A.B., Ouachita Coll., 1908; LL.B., U. Tex., 1915; postgrad. U. Mich., 1921; M.A. (hon.), Yale, 1928; LL.D., La. State U., 1938; m. Notra Anderson, Dec. 22, 1909; children—Notra Nevin, Leon. Indsl. and land devel., Jones County, Tex., 1908-11; admitted to Tex. bar, 1912, began practice in Austin; mem. Rector & Green, 1912-15; adj. prof. law U. Tex., 1915-18; with Locke & Locke, Dallas, 1918; mem. Wynne, Johnson, Green & Morgan, Fort Worth, 1919-20; prof. law U. Tex., 1921-26, prof. law, 1947-58, prof. law, 1960—; prof. law, dean Sch. Law, U. N.C., 1926-27; vis. prof. law Yale, 1927, asso. prof. law, 1927-28, prof., 1928-29; prof. law, dean Sch. Law, Northwestern U., 1929-47; prof. law U. Cal. Hastings Coll. Law, 1958-59. Adv. editorial council Jour. Criminal Law and Criminology. Mem. Tex., Conn., Ill., Chgo. bars, Philos. Soc. Tex., Order of Coif (nat. sec.-treas. 1963-70), Phi Delta Phi. Democrat. Unitarian. Author: Rationale of Proximate Cause, 1927; Judge and Jury, 1930; The Judical Process in Tort Cases, 1931, 2d edit., 1939; Injuries to Relations, 1940; My Philosophy of Law, 1941; Traffic Victims: Tort Law and Insurance, 1958; The Litigation Process in Tort Law, 1966. Co- author: Cases on The Law of Torts, 1968; Injuries to Relations, 1968. Contbr. to legal periodicals. Home: 207 Yaupon Valley Rd Austin TX 78746

GREEN, ADOLPH, actor, playwright, lyricist; b. N.Y.C., Dec. 2, 1915; s. Daniel and Helen (Weiss) G.; student pub. schs., N.Y.C.; m. Phyllis Newman, Jan. 31, 1960; children—Adam, Amanda. Writer, author (with Betty Comden) On the Town, 1944-45; Billion Dollar Baby, Two on the Aisle, Wonderful Town, Take Me Out to the Ball Game, Good News, Barkleys of Broadway, Band Wagon, Singing in the Rain, Bells are Ringing, 1960; Do Re Mi, 1960; Subways are for Sleeping, 1962; Fade Out-Fade In, 1964; (with Betty Comden and Jules Styne) Say Darling, 1959; screenplays (with Betty Comden) Auntie Mame, What a Way to Go; Co-author Applause. Co-recipient Donaldson award for Wonderful Town, 1953; Tony award for co-writer music and lyrics for Hallelujah Baby and co- writer best score, 1967-68, for Applause as best mus., 1970. Address: care John Springer Assos Inc 667 Madison Av New York City NY 10021

GREEN, ALICE, librarian; b. nr. Burlington, Kan., Sept. 20, 1916; d. Roy J. and Eliza (Carleton) Green; student Amarillo Coll., 1933-35, W. Tex. State Coll., 1935-37; B.S. in L.S., U. Okla., 1938. Librarian, Tex. Mil. Coll., Terrell, 1938-39; gen. asst. Tex. State Library, Austin, 1939-41; asst. librarian Mary E. Bivins Meml. Library (formerly Amarillo Pub. Library), 1941-47, librarian, 1947-. Mem. Am., Southwestern, Tex. library assns., Am. Assn. U. Women, Delta Kappa Gamma. Club: Altrusa. Home: 3704 Clearwell St Amarillo TX 79109 Office: 1000 Polk St Box 2171 Amarillo TX 79105

GREEN, BEN CHARLES, judge; b. Cleve., Jan. 4, 1905; s. Isadore and Rose (Mailman) G.; A.B. cum laude, Western Res. U., 1928; LL.B., 1930, J.D., 1968; m. Sylvia E. Chappy, Nov. 20, 1940; 1 dau., Rosemary A. Admitted to Ohio bar, 1930; practiced in Cleve., 1930-61; atty. Fed. Land Bank, Louisville, 1933-35; spl. counsel to atty. gen. Ohio, 1937-38; mem. law dept., real estate cons. City of Cleve., 1944-50; mem. bd. elections, 1950-61; U.S. dist. judge No. dist. Ohio, 1961—. Chmn. Bd. Elections Cuyahoga County, Ohio, 1952-55, 59-61; trustee Ohio Assn. Elections Ofcls., 1955-61; Treas. Cuyahoga County Democratic Com., 1948-61; del. Dem. Nat. convs., 1948, 52. Trustee, Nat. Conf. Christians and Jews, 1963—. Mem Ohio, Cleve., Fed., Cuyahoga County bar assns., Nat. Lawyers Club, Order of Coif. Club: Beechmont Country (Cleve.) Home: 3280 Belvoir Blvd Beachwood OH 44122 Office: US Courthouse Cleveland OH 44114

GREEN, BERT FRANKLIN, Jr., psychologist; b. Honesdale, Pa., Nov. 5, 1927; s. Bert Franklin and Emily May (Brown) G.; A.B., Yale, 1949; M.A., Princeton, 1950, Ph.D., 1951; m. Hasseltine Beck Robinson, Apr. 29, 1961; children—Malcolm Edward. Mem. psychology group Lincoln Lab., Mass. Inst. Tech., 1951-62, leader, 1958-62; cons. RAND Corp., 1961; prof. psychology Carnegie Inst. Tech., Pitts., 1962-69, head psychology dept., 1962-67; prof. psychology Johns Hopkins U., Balt., 1969-. Mem. Am. Psychol. Assn., Am. Statis. Assn., Psychometric Soc., Psychonomic Soc., A.A.A.S. Author: Digital Computers in Research, 1963. Home: 1010 Malvern Av Baltimore MD 21204

GREEN, CARL A., lawyer; b. Buffalo, Aug. 27, 1927; s. Harry and Nettie (Greener) G.; LL.B., U. Buffalo, 1950; m. Ruby Saltzman, May 25, 1952; childrenWilliam N., Betsy S., Frances E., Amy B. Admitted to N.Y. bar, 1950, since practiced in Buffalo; mem. firm Lipsitz, Green, Fahringer, Roll, Schuller & James, 1964—; instr. N.Y. Sch. Indsl. and Labor Relations, Cornell U., 1956—. Bd. dirs. Neighborhood House, 1967-70, Citizens Council Human Rights, 1965-69, East Side Community Orgn., 1967- 70, Legal Aide Bur. Buffalo, 1969-72, Goals for Met. Buffalo. Served with USNR, 1945-46. Fellow Internat. Acad. Law and Sci.; mem. N.Y., Erie County bar assns., Bar Assn. Erie County (dir. 1967- 70), Erie County Trial Lawyers Assn. (dir. 1969-72), Am. Arbitration Assn. (nat. panel arbitrators). Home: 170 Fairlawn Dr Eggertsville, NY 14226. Office: 1 Niagara Sq Buffalo NY 14262

GREEN, CASPAR DUNHAM, govt. ofcl.; b. Hiram, O., Feb. 13, 1915; s. Perry Luther and Mabel (Alden) G.; A.B., Hiram Coll., 1936; M.A., Ohio State U., 1939; m. Mary Pauline Peet, Jan. 17, 1959; children by previous marriageLemuel Ransom, Alden James, Emily Jane, Edward Velazquez Peet. Instr. German, Hiram (O.) Coll., 1937; supr. P.R. Dept. Edn., 1937-38, 39-40; with Fgn. Service, Dept. State, 1941—, vice consul, Havana, Cuba, 1941, Concepcion, Chile, 1942, Guayaguil, Ecuador, 1944; sec. Am. embassy, Helsinki, Finland, 1945; with No. European Affairs div., 1947-50; consul, Maraciabo, Venezuela, 1950-52; 1st sec. Am. embassy, Rio de Janeiro, Brazil, 1952-54; teaching, studying, 1954-58; program officer USOM, Port au Prince, Haiti, 1958-60, econ. adviser, Port-of-Spain, Trinidad, 1960-61; desk officer AID, Colombia, 1961- 63; dep. dir. AID Mission to Chile, 1963-66, Office Caribbean Affairs, Dept. State, 1966-70; dep. asso. dir. AID Mission to Brazil, Recife, 1970-71; consul gen., asso. dir., 1971—. Contbr. to nat. mags., Writers Source Book, 1956. Home: RD 2 Mantau OH 44255 Office: Am Consulate Gen Recife Brazil

GREEN, CECIL HOWARD, geophys. engr.; b. Manchester, Eng., 1900; s. Charles Henry and Maggie (Howard) G.; student U. B.C.; S.B. in Elec. Engring., Mass. Inst. Tech., 1923, S.M., 1924; D.Eng., Colo. Sch. Mines, 1953; D.Sc., U. Tulsa, 1961; U. Sydney (Australia), 1961, U. B.C., 1964, So. Meth. U., 1967; LL.D., Austin Coll., 1966; m. Ida M. Flansburgh, Feb. 6, 1926. Research engr. A.C. engring. dept. Gen. Electric Co., Schenectady, 1924-26; research engring. Raytheon Mfg. Co., Cambridge, Mass., 1926-28, Fed. Telegraph Co., Palo Alto, Cal., also Newark, 1928-30; chief Geophys. Service, Inc., Dallas, 1930-36, supr., 1936-41, v.p., 1941-50, pres., 1950-56, chmn. bd., 1956-59, hon. chmn., 1959—; dir. Tex. Instruments, Inc. Mem. study com. on oceanography Tex. Ho. of Reps.; mem. Nat Commn. Coop. Edn. Trustee Scripps Clinic and Research Found., Woods Hole Oceanographic Inst., Tex. Research Found., S.W. Med. Found., So. Meth. U. Found. for Sci. and Engring., St. Mark's Sch. Tex., Tex. Christian U.; trustee, mem. exec. com. Austin Coll.; life mem. corp., mem. vis. com. dept. physics, chmn. vis. com. earth and planetary scis. Mass. Inst. Tech.; mem. com. earth scis. Stanford. Mem. Mass. Inst. Tech. Alumni Assn. (pres. 1968-69), Soc. Exploration Geophyisists (past pres., hon. life mem.), Am. Assn. Petroleum Geologists, European Assn. Exploration Geophysicists, Mexican Assn. Petroleum Geologists, Assn. Grad. Edn. on Research (N. Tex. chmn.), Dallas Geol. Soc. (hon. life), Dallas Geophys. Soc. (hon. life). Clubs: Dallas Country, Dallas Petroleum. Home: 3908 Lexington Av Dallas, TX 75205. Office: PO Box 5474 MS 230 Dallas TX 75222

GREEN, CHARLES EDWARD, lawyer; b. Woodstock, Ill., Jan. 4, 1894; s. Thomas Patrick and Mary (Dacy) G.; LL.B., Chgo.-Kent Coll. Law, 1915; postgrad. Sorbonne U., 1919; m. Lucile C. Black, Sept. 5, 1920; children-Donna (Mrs. Robert V. Nystrom), Elaine (Mrs. John R. Coath). Admitted to Ill. bar, 1915, since practiced in Chgo.; gen. counsel Motorola, Inc. Served with inf. U.S. Army, AEF, 1918. Mem. Ill., Chgo. bar assns., Soc. Trial Lawyers. Clubs: Mid-Day, Butterfield Country (Hinsdale, Ill.). Home: 1223 Park Av River Forest IL 60305 Office: 77 W Washington St Chicago IL 60602

GREEN, CONSTANCE MCLAUGHLIN, author; b. Ann Arbor, Mich., Aug. 21, 1898; d. Andrew Cunningham and Lois Thompson (Angell) McLaughlin; student U. Chgo., 1914-16; A.B., Smith Coll., 1919, Litt.D., 1963; M.A., Mt. Holyoke Coll., 1925; Ph.D., Yale, 1937; m. Donald Ross Green, Feb. 14, 1921 (dec. 1946); children—Lois Angell (Mrs. Jack Ladd Carr), Donald Ross, Elizabeth L. Faculty, U. Chgo., 1919-20, Mt. Holyoke Coll., 1925-32, Smith Coll., 1939-47; historian Army Ordnance Dept., Springfield, Mass., 1942-45, A.R.C., Washington, 1947-48; chief historian ordnance Army Hist. Div., Dept. Def., 1948-51; historian research and devel. bd. Office Sec. Def., 1951-54; dir. Washington History Project, Am. U., 1954-60. Commonwealth Fund lectr. Univ. Coll., U. London, 1951. Grantee Rockefeller Found., Capelbrook Found. Recipient Pulitzer prize for History, 1963. Mem. Am. Hist. Assn., Econ. History Assn., U.S. Capitol Hist. Soc., Washington Lit. Soc. Author: Washington, Village and Capital, 1800- 1878, Vol. 1, 1963; Washington: Capitol City, 1963; American Cities in the Growth of the Nation, 1965; Eli Whitney and the Birth of American Technology, 1965; The Rise of Urban America, 1965; The Secret City: A History of Race Relations in the Nations Capital, 1967; others. Contbr. to various jours., books, Ency. Brit., Ency. Am., book revs. Address: 19 2d St NE Washington DC 20002

GREEN, CURTIS HARLAN, architect; b. Mpls., Mar. 29, 1925; s. Richard T. and Hazel (Ohman) G.; B.Arch., U. Minn., 1946; M.Arch., Mass. Inst. Tech., 1948; m. Marjorie E. Lee, Sept. 9, 1947; children—Hollyce, Jill, Shelley, Leslie. With architects' offices in Mpls., St. Paul and Milw., 1945-53; propr. Hammel. Green & Abrahamson, Inc., and predecessors. St. Paul, 1953—; lectr. U. Minn. Sch. Architecture, 1950-54; partner Graphic Properties. Prin. works include St. Bede Priory, Eau Claire, Wis. (A.I.A. nat. citation), Benedicta Arts Center, Coll. St. Benedict, St. Joseph. Minn., Fine Arts Center, Gistavus Adolphus Coll., St. Peter, Minn. Mem. Mpls. Inst. Arts, Walker Art Center A.I.A. Lutheran. Clubs: Minneapolis Golf; Midland Hills Country. Home: 608 Turnpike Rd Minneapolis MN 55416 Office: 2675 University Av St Paul MN 55114

GREEN, DALE MONTE, judge; b. Outlook, Wash., Apr. 27, 1922; s. Carey W. and Minnie M. (Gunness) G.; B.A. in Econs. and Bus., U. Wash., 1948, B.S. in Law, 1949, LL.B., 1950; m. Maxine Spencer, June 30, 1946; children—Judith Louise, Frederick William. Admitted to Wash. bar, 1950; practiced in Spokane, 1954; asst. U.S. dist. atty. Eastern Dist. Wash., 1954-56; trial atty. civil div. Dept. Justice, Washington, 1956-58; U.S. dist. atty. Eastern Dist. Wash., 1958-60; mem. Sherwood, Tugman & Green, Walla Walla, Wash., 1960-69; judge Wash. Ct. Appeals Div. III, Spokane, 1969—. Served with AUS, 1943-46. Mem. Am., Fed., Wash., Walla Walla bar assns., Am. Judicature Soc. Methodist, Rotarian, Mason. Editorial bd. Wash. Law Rev., 1949-50. Home: S 3914 Cook Spokane WA 99202 Office: Broadway Centre Bldg Broadway and Jefferson Spokane WA 99201

GREEN, DAVID, ins. co. exec.; b. N.Y.C., Mar. 31, 1899; s. Joseph and Sarah (Rosenstein) G.; Naval Engr., Lehigh U., 1922; LL.B., Rutgers U., 1926; m. Jeannette Katchen, Mar. 25, 1926; childrenJoan (Mrs. Michael Miron) (dec), Alice (Mrs. Robert Fried). Engr., Fed. Shipbldg. Co., 1923; admitted to N.J. bar, 1926, practiced in Newark, 1926-46; incorporator Motor Club of Am. Ins. Co., Newark, 1928, dir., 1928-, pres., 1954-; pres., dir. Motor Club Fire & Casualty Co., Motor Club Am., Garden State Life Ins. Co., MCA Ins. Co. Active state, county, city safety councils. Served with U.S. Army, 1918; from lt. to lt. comdr., USNR, 1942-45. Recipient Service award Def. Research Inst., 1968. Mem. Fedn. Ins. Counsel (pres. 1964-65, chmn. bd. 1965-66), Internat., Inter-Am., Am. (publs. vice chmn., asso. editor Forum 1966-67), N.J., Essex County bar assns., Am. Soc. Naval Engrs., N.J. Soc. Profl. Engrs., Nat. Assn. Ind. Insurers (v.p. gov. 1963—, past pres.), Nat. Conf. Lawyers, Ins. Cos. and Adjusters, Pi Lambda Phi. Republican. Jewish religion. Mason, Kiwanian (past pres.). Home: 15 Lowell Pl West Orange, NJ 07052. Office: 484 Central Av Newark NJ 07107

GREEN, DAVID, Jr., educator; b. Chgo., Feb. 14, 1923; s. David and Gertrude (Strauss) G.; B.S., DePaul, U.; 1947; M.B.A., U. Chgo., 1948, Ph.D., 1956; C.P.A., Ill., 1951; m. Nova Muir, Sept. 12, 1948; childrenKatherine, Nova. Mem. faculty U. Chgo., 1949-, prof. accounting, 1963-; vis. prof. accounting Fla. State U., 1963-64, Middle East Tech U., 1967-68, U. Birmingham, 1968; fiscal and accounting cons. City Chgo., 1957-63. Served with AUS, 1943-45. Editor Jour. Accounting Research, 1963-67. Home: 5519 Cornell Chicago IL 60637

GREEN, DAVID EZRA, educator; b. N.Y.C., Aug. 5, 1910; s. Herman and Jennie (Marrow) G.; B.A., N.Y.U., 1930, M.A., 1932; Ph.D., Cambridge (Eng.) U., 1934; m. Doris Cribb, Apr. 15, 1935; childrenRowena (Mrs. Larry Matthews), Pamela (Mrs. Joseph Baldwin, Jr.). Beit Meml. Research fellow Cambridge, Eng., 1934-40; fellow Harvard, 1940-41; with enzyme lab. Coll. Phys. and Surg., Columbia, 1941-48; asso. prof. biochemistry Columbia, 1947; co- dir. Inst. Enzyme Research, U. Wis., 1948-, prof. enzyme chemistry, 1948-. Recipient Paul-Lewis Labs. award enzyme chemistry, 1946. Fellow Am. Acad. Arts and Scis.; fgn. fellow Royal Flemish Acad. Arts and Scis.; mem. Am. Soc. Biol. Chemists, Nat. Acad. Scis., Am. Chem. Soc., Harvey Soc., Biochem. Soc., Am. Soc. Cell Biology, Phi Beta Kappa, Sigma Xi. Author: Mechanisms of Biological Oxidations, 1939; Molecular Insights into the Living Process, 1967. Home: 1525 Sumac Dr Madison WI 53705

GREEN, DAVID HENRY, banker; b. Worcester, Mass., Feb. 8, 1921; s. Herbert H. and Florence (Knapp) G.; B.A., Wesleyan U., Middletown Conn., 1942; M.B.A., Harvard, 1943; m. Betty Jeppson, June 23, 1951; children—Anne L., Susan E., David Henry, Charles J., Sarah C. Asst. treas. Valley Bank & Trust Co., Springfield, Mass., 1946-51; sr. v.p. Worcester County Nat. Bank,, 1952- 65; sr. v.p. New Eng. Mchts. Nat. Bank, Boston, 1965—; dir. Mass. Higher Edn. Assistance Corp., Fed. St. Capital Corp., L.G. Balfour Co. Gen. chmn. 1965 Greater Worcester Golden Rule Red Cross Fund; sect. chmn. Mass. Bay United Fund Corporate Gifts div. 1969-70 campaign. Trustee Worcester Found. Exptl. Biology, Worcester Acad., Fenn Sch.; trustee, treas. Pine Manor Jr. Coll. Served to capt. AUS, 1943-46. Home: 675 Sudbury Rd Concord MA 01742 Office: Prudential Center Boston MA 02199

GREEN, DAVID KENNETH, mfg. co. exec.; b. Phila., Nov. 5, 1932; s. Frank and Edith (Bossler) G.; B.S. in Accounting, Pa. State U., 1958; C.P.A., N.J., 1962; m. Veronica T. Picarro, July 11, 1956; children—Kenneth D., Susan L. Pub. accountant Price Waterhouse & Co., C.P.A.'s, N.Y.C., 1958-64; internal auditing Am. Cyanamid Co., 1964-66; with Singer Co., 1966-69, controller U.S. consumer products div., 1968-69; v.p. Morgan Guaranty Trust Co., N.Y.C., 1969; comptroller Union Camp Corp., Wayne, N.J., 1969—. Served with AUS, 1953-54. Mem. Am. Inst. C.P.A.'s Financial Execs. Inst. Home: 129 Westview Rd Upper Montclair NJ 07043 Office: 1600 Valley Rd Wayne NJ 07040

GREEN, EARL LEROY, geneticist; b. Meadville, Pa. Aug. 7, 1913; s. George Graytric and Iva Pearl (Lewis) G.; B.S., Allegheny Coll., 1935, Sc.D. (honoris causa), 1960; Ph.D., Brown U., 1940; m. Margaret Creighton, July 4, 1940. From instr. to prof. genetics dept. zoology Ohio State U., 1941-56; geneticist div. biology and medicine AEC, 1953-55; dir. The Jackson Lab. Bar Harbor, Me., 1956—. Adv. com. biology and medicine AEC, 1963-69; sci. adv. com. New Eng. Regional Primate Research Center, 1966-68. Served as capt. USAAF, 1943-46; chief dept. statistics Sch. Aviation Medicine. Mem. Biometrics Soc., Genetics Soc. Am., Am. Genetics Assn., Am. Soc. Naturalists (sec. 1959-61), Phi Beta Kappa, Sigma Xi. Rotarian. Editor: Biology of the Laboratory Mouse 2d edit., 1966. Home: Seeley Rd Bar Harbor ME 04609 Office: Jackson Lab Bar Harbor ME 04609

GREEN, EDITH, congresswoman; b. Trent, S.D. Jan. 17, 1910; d. James Vaughn and Julia (Hunt) Starrett; student Willamette U., 1927-29; B.S., U. Ore., 1939; postgrad. Stanford, 1944; LL.D., U. Alaska; H.H.D., Culver-Stockton Coll.; L.H.D., Eureka Coll.; LL.D., Goucher Coll., Linfield Coll., Gonzaga U., Seattle U., Hood Coll., Boston Coll., Regis Coll., St Xavier Coll., Keuka Coll.; D.P.H., Bethany Coll.; hon. degrees Reed Coll., Oberlin Coll., Georgetown U., Miami U., Yale, Williamette U., U. Portland, Tex. Christian U.; children—James S., Richard A. Tchr. sch., Salem. Ore., 1930- 41; comml. radio work KALE, Portland, 1944-45, free lance, 1943-47; dir. pub. relations Ore. State Edn. Assn.; mem. of 84th-92d Congresses, 3d Ore. Dist., mem. edn. and labor com. Congl. del. NATO Conf., London, 1959; mem. U.S. Commn. UNESCO.; mem. Pres.' Commn. on Status of Women. Del. Democratic Nat. Conv., 1956, 60, 64, 68, chmn. state delegation, 1960-68. Recipient Brotherhood award, B'nai B'rith, 1956, Women of Year award Amvets, 1958; Community service award Nat. Assn. Colored Womens Clubs, 1962; Edn. Service award Am. Coll. Pub. Relations Assn., 1964; Top Hat award Bus. and Profl. Women's Clubs Am., 1965; Distinguished Service award U. Ore., 1967, others. Democrat. Mem. Christian Ch. Office: U S Court House Portland OR 97205 also Rayburn House Office Bldg Washington DC 20515

GREEN, EDWARD AVERILL, actuary, ins. exec.; b. Morgantown, W.Va., May 14, 1907; s. Robert Rodman and Mary Lyon (Purinton) G.; student Rutgers U., 1925-28; A.B., Yale, 1930; m. Doris Harriette Hinman, Aug. 12, 1933; childrenDeborah (Mrs. William D. Morrison), Martha (Mrs. David K. Cuthbert). With actuarial dept. State Mut. Life Assurance Co., Worcester, Mass., 1930-41, asst. actuary, 1941-46, asso. actuary, 1946-48; 2d v.p. John Hancock Mut. Life Ins. Co., Boston, 1948-54, v.p., 1954-56, v.p., group actuary, 1956-69, sr. v.p., group actuary, 1969—; instr. bus., statistics and forecasting Worcester br. Northeastern U., 1939-42. Mem. joint group com. Life Ins. Assn. Am. and Am. Life Conv., 1946-57. Mem. budget com. Newton (Mass.) Community Chest, 1956-57, chmn., 1958; gov's com. studying pension laws of Mass., 1954-55. Fellow Soc. Actuaries; mem. Boston Actuaries Club. Club: Brae Burn Country (West Newton, Mass.). Home: 35 Pickwick Rd West Newton MA 02165 Office: 200 Berkeley St Boston MA 02116

GREEN, EDWARD JAMES, mgmt. cons.; b. Rochester, N.Y., Oct. 19 1908; s. James Franklin and Bessie (Cox) G.; A.B., Bethany (W.Va.) Coll., 1930; C.L.U., 1933; student Grad. Sch. Pub. Adminstrn., Am. U., 1948-49; M.P.A., Grad. Sch. Pub. and Internat. Affairs, U. Pitts., 1961; m. Eleanor Greco, June 30, 1947; childrenEdward James, Robert Alan, Gayle, Meredith. Vice pres., dir. McCready Pension Engrs., Inc., Indpls., 1933-40; various positions with U.S. Govt., 1941-52; exec. asst. to pres. Westinghouse Air Brake Co., Pitts., 1953-59, v.p. planning and marketing, 1959-65; v.p., dir. Westinghouse Air Brake Internat. Corp., 1957-65; pres. Edward J. Green Assos., 1965-67; pres., dir. Planning Dynamics, Inc. 1967—; dir. Ryan Homes, Inc., Dickerson Constrn. Co. Mem. Ind. Senate, 1941; personal asst. to Pres. Eisenhower, 1952. Mem. nat. export council U.S. Dept. Commerce; indsl. adv. council long range planning service Stanford Research Inst., 1961-66. Served to comdr. USNR, 1941-47. Decorated Legion of Merit. Mem. U.S., Pa., Pitts. (v.p., dir. 1958-62) chambers commerce, Nat. Municipal League (council 1958), N.A.M., Nat. Conf. Bd., Am. Mgmt. Assn. (planning council), Machinery and Allied Products Inst., Am. Marketing Assn. (v.p.) Ry. Progress Inst. (co- chmn. pub. affairs council), Phi Kappa Tau, Tau Kappa Alpha. Clubs: Duquesne, Civic of Allegheny County (dir. 1958-62). Author: Planning for Profit and Growth, 1963; Workbook for Corporate Planning, 197O. Lectr. in field. Home: 5619 Kentucky Av Pittsburgh PA 15232 Office: 3 Gateway Center Pittsburgh PA 15222

GREEN, EDWARD MELVIN, banker; b. Milledgeville, Ga., Nov. 22, 1904; s. Edward Melvin and Ann (Craig) G.; student Center Coll. of Ky., 1920-21; B.S., Princeton, 1925. Mem. North China dept. Standard Oil Co. of N.Y., N.Y.C., 1925-28; with Bell Tel. Co. of Pa., 1929; with Dauphin Deposit Trust Co., Harrisburg, Pa., 1929—, pres., 1966-70, chmn. bd., 1969—. Pres. Pa. Council Chs., 1962-64; commnr. Pa. Human Relations Commn., 1964-68. Bd. mgrs. Harrisburg Hosp.; adv. bd. Harrisburg State Hosp.; trustee Wilson Coll. Served with USNR, 1942-46. Mem. Sigma Chi. Democrat. Presbyterian. Clubs: Princeton (N.Y.C.); Nassau (Princeton, N.J.), Harrisburg Country Club. Home: 1519 N Front St Harrisburg PA 17102 Office: 213 Market St Harrisburg PA 17105

GREEN, ERNEST, coll. adminstr.; b. Columbus, Ga., Oct. 15, 1938; s. Albert and Susie (Marshall) G.; B.S., U. Louisville, 1962; m. Wylene Jackson, June 14, 1956; children—Zachary, Derek, Ernest II. Football player Cleve. Browns, 1962-68; asst. vice-provost for student affairs Case Western Res. U., 1969—. Pres., trustee C.R.E.S.T., Inc.; trustee Vocational Guidance and Rehab. Service, Cleve. Scholarship Program, Big Bros. Cleve., Shaker Heights Recreation Bd. Active Gov. Nelson Rockefeller's presdl. campaign. Named one of 10 outstanding young men in Cleve., Cleve. Jr. C. of C., 1970; mem. East All Star Football Squad, 1966-67. Home: 3633 Riedham Rd Shaker Heights OH 44120 Office: 10900 Euclid Av Cleveland OH 44106

GREEN, FITZHUGH, govt. ofcl.; b. Jenkintown, Pa., Sept. 12, 1917; s. Fitzhugh and Natalie W. (Elliot) G.; grad. St. Paul's Sch., 1936; student Princeton, 1940; M.A., Boston U., 1963; 1 dau., Penelope. Fgn. sales and advt. exec. Vick Chem. Co., 1946-49; div. mgr., advt. sales promotion Life mag., 1949-52; asst. to chmn. FTC, 1953-54; with USIA, 1954-66; dir. USIS Laos, 1955-56, Israel, 1956-58, chief pvt. enterprise div., 1958-60, dir. USIS, Belgian Congo, 1960, Republic of Congo, Leopoldville, 1960-62, student Naval War Coll., 1962-63, USIA rep. U.S. Mission to UN, dir. Fgn. Corrs. Center, N.Y.C., 1964-65; dep. dir. personnel and tng. USIA, 1965-66; spl. asst. oceanography, fgn. affairs to U.S. Senator Claibourne Pell, 1966-68; dep. dir. Far East operations, 1968-70; asso. adminstr. Environmental Protection Agy., 1971—. Psychol. warfare cons. Am. U. 1959. Dep. vice chmn. Nat. Citizens for Eisenhower, 1954; Republican candidate for Congress, 1970. Trustee, mem. exec. com. Washington chpt. Nat. Multiple Sclerosis Soc. Served from ensign to lt. USNR, 1942-46; PTO. Clubs: University, Federal City (Washington); Explorers, Racquet and Tennis (N.Y.C.). Home: Bellevue Av Newport RI 02840 Office: Environmental Protection Agy Washington DC 20460

GREEN, FLETCHER MELVIN, educator; b. Gainesville, Ga., July 12, 1895; s. Robert Chambers and Mary Mahalia (Haynes) G.; Ph.B., Emory U., 1920, Litt.D., 1957; A.M., U.N.C., 1922, Ph.D., 1927; U. Chgo., 1925; Litt.D., Washington and Lee U., 1960; m. Mary Frances Black, Aug. 16, 1930; children—Fletcher Melvin II, Mary Carolyn, Robert Ramsey, Elizabeth Haynes. Teacher history, Lindsey-Wilson Prep. Sch., 1920-21; fellow in history, Univ. of N.C., 1921-22, instr. 1922-23; prof. history, Sparks Coll., 1923-24; asst. prof. history Vanderbilt U., 1924-25; fellow Inst. for Research in Social Sci., U. of N.C., 1925-27; asst. prof. history U. of N.C., 1927-30, asso., 1930-33, prof., 1936-46, Kenan prof. 1946—, chmn. dept. history, 1953-60; prof. history, Emory U., 1933-36; lectr. summer schs., Coll. of William and Mary, U. of Tenn., Duke, U. of Mo., Columbia, 49, 50, Vis. prof. history, Harvard, 1944-45, vis. prof. Stanford U., summer, 1956, Northwestern U., summer, 1957; Lamar lectures Mercer U., 1968; Harmsworth prof. Am. history Oxford Univ., 1968-69. Member exec. bd. N.C. Dept. Archives and History, 1955-; research fellow Huntington Library, 1967. Served in M.C., U.S. Army, with A.E.F., 1918-19. Mem. Am., Miss. Valley (Exec. council 1946-49, bd. editors rev. 1955-56, pres. 1960-61), So. (pres. 1945), Ga. hist. assns., Agrl., N.C. (pres. 1953) hist. socs., N.C. Lit. and Hist. Assn. (pres. 1955), Alpha Tau Omega, Phi Beta Kappa. Democrat. Methodist. Club: Chapel Hill Country. Author: Essays in Southern History, 1949; The Lides Go South and West, 1952; The Ferry Hill Plantation Journal Jan. 4, 1938-Jan. 15, 1939, 1961. Co- author: Travels in the New South, Vol. I., The Postwar South, 1865-1900. Editor: The Civil War and Reconstruction in Florida (William Watson Davis), 1964; Memorials of a Southern Planter (Susan Dabney Smedes), 1965; Southern Wealth and Northern Profits (Thomas Prentice Kettell), 1965. Editor, contbr. hist. jours.; bd. editors Jour. So. History, 1935-36, 41-46. Home: Laurel Hill Rd Chapel Hill NC 27514 ☆

GREEN, FRANCIS JOSEPH, bishop; b. Corning, N.Y., July 7, 1906; student St. Joseph's Coll., St. Patrick's Sem., Cal. Ordained priest Roman Catholic Ch., 1932; domestic prelate, 1950, vicar-gen. Diocese of Tucson; apptd. aux. bishop, 1953, coadjutor bishop, 1960, bishop of Tucson, 1960. Address: 192 Stone Av Tucson AZ 85701

GREEN, FRANK LESTER, librarian; b. Seattle, Jan. 15, 1931; s. Lester Charles and Lois Janet (Covington) G.; B.A., Seattle Pacific Coll., 1953; S.T.B., Harvard, 1958; M.L.S., U. Wash., 1959. Reference asst. U. Wash. Library, 1959-60; reference librarian Pacific Luth. U., Tacoma, 1960-62; librarian Ch. Div. Sch. Pacific, Berkeley, Cal., 1962-66, Wash. Hist. Soc., Tacoma, 1966—. Cons. Grad. Theol. Union, Berkeley, 1965. Served with AUS, 1953-55. Mem. Spl. Libraries Assn., Western History Assn., Am. Assn. State and Local History. Episcopalian. Author guides to library collections. Editor: Wash. Hist. Soc. News Notes, 1972—. Home: 319 N Tacoma Av Tacoma WA 98403 Office: 315 N Stadium Way Tacoma WA 98403

GREEN, FRANK WILLIAM, cosmetic co. exec.; b. N.Y.C., Aug. 17, 1925; s. Frank W. and Margeurite (Murphy) G.; B.A., Brown U., 1949; m. Norma Truxell, Feb. 3, 1948; children—F. William, Felicity, Nathaniel. With Fieldcrest Mills, Inc., Eden, N.C., 1952-71, pres., dir., 1971—; pres., dir. Lanuin-Charles of the Ritz, 1971—. Served with AUS, 1942-45. Mem. Am. Textile Mfrs. Inst. (mem. market com. 1969—). Clubs: Union League, Metropolitan (N.Y.C.). Home: 8 Butlers Island CT 06820 Office: 730 Fifth Av New York City NY 10019

GREEN, GEORGE LARNED, corp. exec.; b. Providence, Oct. 27, 1908; s. J. Larned and Grace (Naylor) G.; B.S., Yale 1931; m. Jessie Sparrow, Jan. 25, 1936; children—Mary L. (Mrs. Richard L. Urevig), Wendy K. (Mrs. Craig A. Ross), Cecily K. (Mrs. Dennis Dunlop). Trainee, Continental Ill. Nat. Bank, 1931-34; service engr., sales engr., salesman, asst. v.p. sales Union Asbestos & Rubber Co., 1934-44; v.p. H.K. Porter Co., Chgo., 1944-47; Western sales mgr. Am. Locomotive Co., Chgo., 1947-48; mgr. miscellaneous sales Pullman-Standard, Chgo., 1948-49, v.p. sales, 1953-61, v.p. charge marketing, 1961-64, v.p., gen. mgr., 1965-67, pres., 1968-70; pres. Trailmobile, 1968-70; exec. v.p. Pullman Inc. Transp. Group, 1971—; dir. Pullman, Inc., Pullman Bank & Trust Co., Pullman Transport Leasing Co., Trailor, S.A. (France), Trailmobile de Mexico, S.A., Canadian Trailmobile Ltd. Mem. adv. com. Transp. Center Northwestern U. Mem. Chgo. Assn. Commerce and Industry (dir.). Clubs: Chicago; Glenview (Ill.); Biltmore Forest (Asheville, N.C.); Mountain Brook (Birmingham); Home: 999 Woodland Dr Glenview IL 60025 Office: 200 S Michigan Av Chicago IL 60604

GREEN, GERALD, author; b. Bklyn., 1922; grad. Columbia, also Columbia Sch. Journalism; m.; 3 children. Formerly with Internat. News Service; with NBC, intermittently 1950-, producer Today show with Dave Garroway, also Wide Wide World, Chet Huntley Reporting; producer, writer various TV documentaries. Mem. Writers Guild Am., Phi Beta Kappa. Author: Sword and the Sun, 1954; The Last Angry Man, 1957; The Lotus Eaters, 1959; The Heartless Light, 1961; The Portofino PTA, 1962; The Legion of Noble Christians, 1965; (with Lawrence Klingman) His Majesty O'Keefe, 1948; (with Philip Rubin) Solitary Metastases. Address: care NBC 30 Rockefeller Plaza New York City NY 10020

GREEN, GUY, film dir.; b. Somerset, Eng. 1913. Prejectionist, camera asst. Film Advt. Co., 1933-35; camera asst. Elstree Studios, 1935; camera operator films including One of Our Aircraft Is Missing, In Which We Serve, This Happy Breed; dir. Allied Film Makers Ltd. Photographed: The Way Ahead, Great Expectations, Oliver Twist, Captain Horatio Hornblower, I Am a Camera; dir. River Beat, Tears for Simon, House of Secrets, Sea of Sand, The Angry Silence, The Mark, Light in the Piazza, Diamond Head; writer, dir. A Patch of Blue, 1965; dir. The Magus, 1967, John Brown's Body, 1968-69. Address: care Noel Singer 315 S Beverly Dr Beverly Hills CA 90212

GREEN, HARRY, newspaper publisher; b. Phoenix, Jan. 14, 1904; s. Samuel Steele and Alice (Kay) G.; A.B. in econs., U. Redlands, 1922-26; m. Mercedes Reussenzehn, Jan. 6, 1934; 1 dau., Floradel. Editor trade papers, Western Canner and Packer and West Coast Builder, 1926-32; bus. mgr. Ventura County Star-Free Press, 1934-45; gen. bus. mgr. John P. Scripps newspapers 1945—; pres. Watsonville Newspapers, Inc., Tulare Newspapers, Inc. Chmn. Draft Bd. SSS. 145. 1940-45. Mem. Audit Bur. Circulation (bd. dirs. 1965-), Cal. Newspaper Pubs. Assn. (pres. 1963), Cal. Newspaperboy Found., Inc. (pres. 1949-50), Ventura C. of C. (pres. 1939), Sigma Delta Chi. Kiwanian (pres. 1939). Home: 9801 Sierra Vista Av La Mesa CA 92041 Office: 306 Scripps Bldg San Diego CA 92101

GREEN, HARRY EDWARD, lawyer; b. Coshocton, O., Sept. 19, 1911; s. William and Jenny (Nobley) B.; B.S. summa cum laude, Princeton, 1933; LL.B. cum laude, Harvard, 1936; m. Molly Morse Leachman, June 1, 1946; children—William Strother, Sara McLaurin, Nancy M. Admitted to Ohio bar, 1936, N.Y. bar, 1947, Ill. bar. 1958; practice law with Squire, Sanders & Dempsey, Cleve., 1936-42; asso. firm Armstrong & Keith, N.Y.C., 1946-47; gen. counsel, dir. W.I. Sugar Corp., 1947-52, v.p. sec. gen. counsel, dir., 1952-58; gen. practice law, N.Y.C., 1946-58; dir., gen. counsel Melchior, Armstrong, Dessau Co., Ridgefield, N.J., 1948-59; gen. counsel Container Corp. Am., Chgo., 1958-59, v.p., gen. counsel, 1960-63, sr. v.p., 1963—; v.p. Marcor Inc., 1968—; dir. Faith Investment Co., Albany, N.Y. Chmn. exec. com. Chgo. chpt., bd. dirs. Nat. Found.; bd. dirs., pres. Windham Children's Service, 1955-58. Served from 2d lt. to lt. col. USAAF, 1942-46; now col. Res. Decorated Legion of Merit. Mem. Am., Ill. bar assns., Bar Assn. City N.Y., Am. Arbitration Assn. (chmn. Chgo. adv. council). Clubs: Chicago, University (Chgo.); International Trade (dir. Chgo.). Home: 181 Birch St Winnetka IL 60093 Office: 38 S Dearborn St Chicago IL 60603

GREEN, JACK PETER, med. scientist; b. N.Y.C., Oct. 4, 1925; s. Maurice and Tillie (Herman) G.; B.S., Pa. State U., 1947, M.S., 1949; Ph.D., Yale, 1951, M.D., 1957; postgrad. Poly. Inst., Copenhagen, 1953-55, Inst. de Biologie Physico-Chimique, Paris, 1964-65; m. Arlyne Genevieve Frank, Oct. 25, 1958. Vis. scientist Poly. Inst., Copenhagen, 1953-55, Inst. de Biologie Physico-Chimique, Paris, 1964-65; asst. prof. Yale, 1957-61, asso. prof., 1961-66; asso. prof Cornell U. Med. Coll., 1966-68; prof., chmn. dept. pharmacology Mt. Sinai Sch. Medicine, 1968—. Mem. research grant rev. com. USPHS. Recipient Claude Bernard Vis. Professorship, U. Montreal, 1966. Mem. N.Y. Acad. Sci., Am. Chem. Soc., Am. Soc. Biol. Chemists, Soc. Drug Research, N.Y. Acad. Medicine, Harvey Soc., A.A.A.S., Am. Soc. Pharmacology and Exptl. Therapeutics, Internat. Soc. Quantum Biology, Sigma Xi, Alpha Omega Alpha, Phi Lambda Upsilon, Gamma Sigma Delta. Contbr. articles profl. jours. Mem. editorial bds. profl. jours. Home: 1212 Fifth Av New York City NY 10029 Office: Mt Sinai Sch Medicine Dept Pharmacology Fifth Av at 100th St New York City NY 10029

GREEN, JAMES WESTON, educator, physiologist; b. Elkins, W.Va., May 16, 1913; s. James Weston and Adah (Harshbarger) G.; B.S., Davis-Elkins Coll., 1935; postgrad. U. Pa., 1940-41; Ph.D., Princeton, 1948; m. Erika Roth, July 8, 1961; children—James Philip, Stephen Henry. Faculty, Rutgers U., New Brunswick, 1948—, prof. physiology, 1961—, chmn. dept. physiology and biochemistry, 1962-67, chmn. dept. physiology, 1967—, dir. grad. physiology program, 1968-. Bd. dirs. Wesley Found., Rutgers U. Served to capt. AUS, 1942-46. Ford Found. fellow, 1953-54. Mem. Am. Physiol. Soc., Soc. Gen. Physiologists. Methodist (bd. stewards). Editor: New Developments in Tissue Culture, 1961. Home: 409 Grant Av Highland Park NJ 08904 Office: Rutgers U New Brunswick NJ 08903

GREEN, JAMES WYCHE, sociologist, govt. ofcl.; b. Alton, Va., Aug. 5, 1915; s. William Ivey and Mary (Crowder) G.; B.S. with honors, Va. Poly. Inst., 1938, M.S., 1939; postgrad. Duke, 1947-48; Ph.D., U. N.C., 1953; student Sch. Advanced Internat. Studies, Johns Hopkins, 1959; m. Pearl O'Neal Cornett, Mar. 2, 1940; 1 dau., Margaret Lydia. Research fellow Va. Poly. Inst., 1938-39; research field supr. Va. Expt. Sta., 1939; asst. specialist program planning N.C. State Coll. Extension Service, 1939-42; v.p. Greever's, Inc., 1946; tchr. high sch., farm operator, 1946-47; asst. prof. rural sociology N.C. State Coll., 1949-54; from asso. chief to chief community devel. adv. to Govt. of Pakistan, Karachi, 1954-59; prof. rural sociology dept. Cornell U., Ithaca, N.Y., 1960; community devel. adviser Govt. of So. Rhodesia, AID, 1960-64, chief community devel., local govt. adviser Govt. of Peru, 1964-67, with AID, Washington, 1967—. Served from 1st lt. to capt. AUS, 1942-46. Decorated Croix de Guerre with silver star (France); Croix de Guerre with palm (Belgium); Bronze Star with cluster. Fellow Am. Sociol. Assn., Soc. for Applied Anthropology; mem. So. Sociol. Soc., Rural Sociol. Soc., Res. Officers Assn., Alpha Kappa Delta, Omicron Delta Kappa, Alpha Zeta, Phi Kappa Phi. Conglist. Contbr. articles to profl. jours. Home: 5304 N 1st Pl Arlington VA 22203 Office: US AID State Dept Washington DC 20523

GREEN, JEROME KEITH, mfg. co. exec.; b. Highland, Ill., July 5, 1936; s. I. Frank and Florence (Kircher) G.; m. Kathy Jane Haefelin, June 26, 1965. Sr. accountant Price Waterhouse & Co., C.P.A.'s, Chgo., 1960-64; with J.I. Case Co., Racine, Wis., 1964-, corp. controller, 1967-69, v.p. finance, 1969-. Served as 2d lt. AUS, 1967. C.P.A., Ill. Mem. Am. Inst. C.P.A.'s. Home: 3040 N Main St Racine WI 53402 Office: 700 State St Racine WI 53402

GREEN, JOHN, (Johnny), composer, condr.; b. N.Y.C., Oct. 10, 1908; s. Vivian and Irma (Jellenik) G.; student, N.Y. Mil. Acad., Cornwall-on-Hudson; A.B., Harvard, 1928; m. Bunny (Bonnie) Waters, Nov. 20, 1943; children—Barbara, Kathe, Kim. Arranger for Guy Lombardo, 1927; accompanist for Gertrude Lawrence, Ethel Merman, James Melton, 1931-33; commd. by Paul Whiteman to write The Night Club Suite, 1932, performed Symphony Hall, Boston, 1932, Lewisohn Stadium, 1933, B.B.C. Orch., London; arranger, composer, condr. Paramount's Eastern studios, 1930-32; composer Coquette, 1928, I'm Yours, 1930, Out of Nowhere, 1932, Body and Soul, 1931, I Cover the Waterfront, 1933, You're Mine You, 1933, Fantasia for piano, Music for Elizabeth, 1939, The Trembling of A Leaf, 1952, motion picture score Raintree County, 1957; organized dance band and toured U.S., 1933-40; appeared on radio programs with Ruth Etting, Jack Benny, Fred Astaire, Christopher Morley, 1933-37; starred on Philip Morris program, 1938-39; featured condr. N.Y. Paramount Theatre, Bklyn. Paramount Theatre, State Theatre, Mpls.; rec. artist, 1932—; composer, mus. dir. motion pictures, Hollywood, 1942—; composer music, condr. weekly radio program The Man Called X, 1947-48; gen. mus. dir. M-G-M Pictures, 1949-58; 1st original dramatic score for film TV, Bernadette, 1958; producer TV films for Desilu; dir. music motion pictures Rhapsody, Brigadoon, High Society, The Great Caruso, Summer Stock, 1950-58; condr. Hollywood Bowl, 1949—; guest condr. various symphony orchs., 1953—; condr. motion pictures West Side Story, Pepe, 1960-61; music dir., adaptor, condr. motion picture Bye Bye Birdie, 1962-63; composer- condr. TV films The Proud Earth, 1960, Miami Undercover, 1961; composer score TV series Empire, 1962-63; music dir., permanent condr. Promenade Concerts, Los Angeles Philharmonic Orch., 1959-61; condr., music dir. Cinderella, CBS-TV, 1965; composer UN film Who Has Seen The Wind, 1965; mus. dir., arranger film Lionel Bart's Oliver, 1967-68. Mem. Cal. Com. on Pub. Edn.; gov.-at-large Performing Arts Council Los Angeles Music Center. Chmn bd. Young Musicians Found. Recipient Downbeat Spl. award radio dramatic music, 1948; Academy awards for Easter Parade, 1948, American in Paris, 1952, Merry Wives of Windsor, 1953, West Side Story, 1962, Oliver, 1968; Golden Globe award for Inspector General, 1949; Nat. citation Am. Fedn. Music Clubs, 1955. Mem. Acad. Motion Picture Arts and Scis. (life), A.S.C.A.P., Dramatist's Guild, Am. Fedn. Musicians, P.T.A. (life), Screen Composers Assn. U.S.A. (pres.). Club: Harvard (N.Y.C., So. Cal.) Address: 903 N Bedford Dr Beverly Hills CA 90210

GREEN, JOHN ALDEN, educator; b. Cardston, Alta., Can., Nov. 4, 1925; s. John H.F. and Olivia (Thornhill) G.; came to U.S., 1952, naturalized, 1961; B.A., Brigham Young U., 1954 M.A., 1955; Ph.D., U. Wash., 1960; m. Michele Therese Jugant, Aug. 27, 1954; children—John Scott, Jeffrey Paul, Evan Curtis, Alan Merrill, Kerry Anne, Cammie Suzanne. Spl. instr. French, Boeing Aircraft Co., Renton, Wash., 1958-59; asst. prof. U. N.D., 1960- 63, dir. Summer NDEA Inst., 1962; asso. prof., chmn. dept. U. Wichita, 1963-64; asso. prof. Brigham Young U., Provo, Utah, 1964-68, prof., 1968- -, chmn. dept., 1969—. Served with RCAF, 1944-46. Contbr. to Research on Lang. Teaching: An Annotated International Bibliography for 1945-61, 1962. Contbr. articles profl. jours. Home: 623 S 590 E Orem UT 84057 Office: Brigham Young U Provo UT 84601

GREEN, JOHN CAWLEY, lawyer; b. Washington, Mar. 2, 1910; s. Kirt and Linda (Cawley) G.; B.S., U.S. Naval Acad., 1934; J.D., Georgetown Univ., 1940; m. June Lazenby, Sept. 5, 1936. Admitted to D.C. bar, 1939; examiner U.S. Patent Office, 1936-40; chief engr. Nat. Inventors Council, examining and analyzing civilian inventions directed to def. effort in cooperation with Armed Services, 1940-56, exec. dir., 1956-63; exec. sec., Publ. Bd., 1945-63, also in charge of release of fed. research data; adviser to Dept. of State and Internat. Cooperation Adminstrn.; dir. Office Tech. Services U.S. Dept. of Commerce, Washington, 1945-63, charge release fgn. sci. reports; dir. research Research and Devel. div. Office Emergency Planning, 1963-66; dir. Office Analysis and Research, 1966-67; practice law, Washington, 1967—; pres. John C. Green Assos., Inc., 1968- -; cons. Tech. adviser Internat. Conf. on Alien Patents, London, 1946. Recipient His Majesty's medal for services in cause of freedom (U.K.), 1948; award for sci. efforts U.S. Sec. of Army and Navy, exceptional service medal sec. of Commerce; medal Royal Swedish Acad. Engrng. Scis., 1963. Fellow A.A.A.S; mem. Fed. Bar Assn., Nat. Fedn. Sci. Abstracting and Indexing Services (pres. 1963-64). Clubs: Cosmos, Army Navy Country (Washington). Home: Joyce Lane Arnold MD 21012 Office: Washington Bldg 15th and New York Av NW Washington DC 20005

GREEN, JOHN GISBURNE, former newspaperman; b. Washington, Sept. 23, 1904; s. William Ezra and Nellie Blanche (Gisburne) G.; student Ohio State U., 1921-25; m. Evelyn Campbell, Sept. 19, 1926; childrenEdward Gisburne, James Robert. Reporter Sandusky (O.) Register, 1924; telegraph editor Portsmouth Sun, 1925, Canton (O.) Daily News, 1925-26; rewrite desk Cleve. Press, 1926; news editor Canton Daily News, 1926-30; copyreader Canton Repository, 1930-31, editor, 1957-69; mng. editor Mansfield (O.) News, 1931-33; mng. editor Portsmouth Times, 1934-46, editor, 1946-57. Mem. adv. council Ohio State U. Sch. Journalism. Mem. Am. Soc. Newspaper Editors, Sigma Delta Chi, Pi Delta Epsilon. Unitarian. Clubs: Ohio State University. Home: 11130 Nocturne Ct Sun City AZ 85351

GREEN, JOHN JOSEPH, indsl. scientist; b. Portsmouth, Eng., Nov. 9, 1905; s. George Edward and Elizabeth (Jarmey) G.; B.S., Portsmouth Municipal Coll., London U., 1925; B.S., A.R. C.S., Royal Coll. Sci., London U., 1928, D.I.C. (Busk studentship in aeros.), 1929, Ph.D. (Beit Sci. Research fellow), 1930; m. Winifred Maud Pascoe, May 31, 1930; children—Lorna, Janet. Apptd. to staff NRC Can., 1930, head aerodynamic sect., 1935-43; commd. squadron leader RCAF, chief research engr. RCAF Test and Devel. Establishment, 1943- 45; chief research aero. engr. Air Transport Bd., 1945-49; chief, div. "B", Def. Research Bd., spl. adv. to chief air staff RCAF, 1949-55; def. research mem. Canadian Joint Staff, Washington, 1955-59, chief supt. Canadian Armament Research and Devel. Establishment, Quebec, 1959-63; dir. research Litton Systems (Can.) Ltd., 1963—. Commonwealth lectr. Royal Aero. Soc., London, Eng., 1955. Can. nat. del. council of adv. group on aero. research and devel. NATO, 1952-59; chmn. Sci. Council Study Aero. Research and Devel., 1968. Chmn. Daniel Guggenheim Medal Bd. of Award, 1966, Mem., 1967; vice chmn. Laura Taber Barbour Flight Safety Award Bd., 1966. Decorated mem. Order Brit. Empire, 1943; recipient King's Commendation for valuable service in the air, 1945; Imperial Coll. of Sci. and Tech. Gov's. prize in physics, 1928. Fellow Royal Aero. Soc., Am. Inst. Aeros. and Astronautics, Canadian Aero. Space Inst. (pres. 1954-55, 62-63); mem. Canadian Research Mgmt. Assn. (vice chmn. mgmt. bd. 1967-69, chmn. 1969- -), Internat. Council Aero Scis. (chmn. exec. bd. 1968—), Am. Astronautical Soc. (sr.), Inst. Nav., Soc. Automotive Engrs., Am. Assn. Airport Execs. (hon. life). Clubs: Rideau (Ottawa): Cosmos (Washington) Contbr. tech. papers to profl. lit. Editor-in-chief Canadian Aero. and Space Inst. Jour. Home: 22 Princess Ann Crescent Islington Ontario Canada Office: 1790 Woodward Dr Ottawa Ontario Canada

GREEN, JOHN ORNE, Jr., lawyer, drug co. exec.; b. Erie, Pa., Jan. 1, 1922; s. John Orne and Harriot Cox (O'Brien) G.; grad. Lawrenceville Sch., 1940; A.B., Yale, 1943; LL.B., Harvard, 1948; m. Phyllis Booth, Jan. 13, 1945; children John Orne 3d, Edward Townsend, George Thomas. Admitted to N.Y. bar, 1950, N.J. bar, 1960; asso. Mudge, Rose, Guthrie & Alexander, N.Y.C., 1948-51; gen. atty., asst. sec. Johnson & Johnson, New Brunswick, N.J., 1951-62; v.p. Permacel div., 1956-58; asst. sec., asst. gen. counsel Richardson-Merrell Inc., N.Y.C., 1962-65, sec., asst. gen. counsel, 1965-66, gen. counsel, sec., 1966—; dir. Ortho Pharm. Corp., 1961-62, v.p., 1970—. Mem. Bd. Improvement Assessors, Princeton Twp., 1961-62; mem. Township Com., Princeton, 1963-65. Dir., chmn. class agts. Yale Alumni Fund, 1948-63. Served to lt. USNR,

1943-46. Mem. Am., N.J., N.Y. State, Mercer County bar assns., Assn. Bar City N.Y., Am. Soc. Corporate Secs., Pharm. Mfrs. Assn., Proprietary Assn. Clubs: Yale (N.Y.C.); Capitol Hill (Washington); Bedens Brook (Princeton, N.J.); Vineyard Haven Yacht (gov. 1965—). Home: 299 Edgerstoune Rd Princeton NJ 08540 Office: 122 E 42d St New York City NY 10017

GREEN, JOHN PLATH, lawyer; b. Dallas, Dec. 11, 1910; s. George Athel and Nora (Rape) G.; LL.B., U. Tex., 1938; m. Margueritte Francine Tatom, Sept. 6, 1941; children—John Randall, Nancy Robin. Admitted to Tex. bar, 1938; asso., partner firm Storey, Sanders, Sherrill & Armstrong, Dallas, 1938-48; partner firm Sanders, Lefkowitz & Green, Dallas, 1950-65, Green, Gilmore, Chrisman & Rothpletz, Dallas, 1967—. Chmn., Dallas County Hist. Survey Com., 1942-46. Trustee Dallas Ind. Sch. Dist., Dallas Pub. Library; mem. Dallas Bd. Edn. Bd. dirs. Little Bethel Cemetery Found. Served with AUS, 1942-46. Decorated Legion of Merit, Bronze Star medal. Mem. Am., Dallas bar assns., State Bar Tex. Presbyn. (elder 1953—). Author: Henry Cabaniss and His Descendants, 1955. Home: 7517 Mason Dell Dr Dallas TX 75230 Office: First Nat Bank Bldg Dallas TX 75202

GREEN, JOHN RAEBURN, lawyer; b. St. Louis, Mar. 30, 1894; s. John Findley and Eleanor Essie (Ibbotson) G.; A.B., Westminster Coll., St. Louis, 1914, LL.D., 1954; LL.B., Harvard, 1917; LL.D., Washington U., 1959; m. Elisabeth Haskell Cox, Dec. 24, 1917; children—Richard Cox (dec.), Elisabeth Cox (Mrs. Samuel C. Hair), John Raeburn, Lewis Cox, Henry Ibbotson (dec.). Admitted to Mo. bar, 1915, U.S. Supreme Ct., 1919; legal drafting officer Dept. State, 1918-19; mem. legal sec. secretariat League of Nations, 1920-21; mem. firm Judson, Green & Henry (name now Green, Hennings & Henry), St. Louis, 1919—. Apptd. by U.S. Supreme Ct. to represent habeas corpus petitioners, 1944-45, spl. master in Tex. vs. N.M. (Rio Grande litigation), 1952-57. Dir. various corps. Mem. council Washington U., 1957—; adv. council St. Louis U. Sch. Law, 1958—; v.p. Jefferson Nat. Expansion Meml. Assn. (exec. com.). Trustee Westminster Coll., chmn. bd. 1953-55; bd. dirs., sec. St. Luke's Episcopal Presbyn. Hosp., 1947-53. Served as 2d lt., 35th inf. U.S. Army, 1917-18. Recipient Newspaper Guild Civic award, 1955. Mem. Am. Law Inst., Am., Mo., St. Louis bar assns., Lawyers Assn. St. Louis, Assn. Bar City N.Y., Am. Soc. Internat. Law, Internat. Law Assn. (Am. br.), Am. Judicature Soc., Harvard Law Sch. Assn. (council 1948-61), Am. Soc. Legal History, S.R., Mo. Hist. Soc., Am. Legion, Order of Coif (hon.), Phi Delta Theta, Zeta Tau Delta, Phi Delta Phi (hon.). Democrat (nominee for Congress 1928). Presbyn. Clubs: Noonday, University (St. Louis); Army and Navy (Washington); Harvard (N.Y.C.); Automobile of Missouri (bd. govs.). Author: Liberty Under the Fourteenth Amendment, 1942. Contbr. to law revs. Home: 901 Glenridge Clayton MO 63105 Office: Boatman's Bank Bldg St Louis MO 63102

GREEN, JOHN ROOT, educator; b. Alameda, Cal., Sept. 19, 1920; s. John Doughty and Helen Mary (Root) G.; B.S. in Chemistry, U. Cal. at Berkeley, 1941, M.A., 1950, Ph.D. in Physics (Westinghouse, Whiting fellow), 1950; m. Anna Vallevik, Sept. 13, 1951; children—John Vallevik, Mary Alice, Jane Katherine. Research chemist Cal. Ink Co., Berkeley, 1941-42; teaching asst. U. Cal. at Berkeley, 1946-48; asst. prof. physics U. N.M. at Albuquerque, 1950-55, asso. prof., 1955-62, prof. physics, 1962—; mem. staff Los Alamos Sci. Lab., 1951; NSF sci. faculty fellow U. Oslo (Norway), 1957-58; Fulbright prof. physics U. Aleppo (Syria), 1966-67. Mem. Albuquerque Legal Aid Soc., 1969—. Mem. Sandoval County Democratic Grass Roots Com., 1963-69. Served with USAAF, 1942-46 (capt. Res., 1946-52). Mem. Am. Assn. U. Profs., Am. Phys. Soc., Sigma Xi, Phi Beta Kappa, Pi Mu Epsilon. Research in cosmic radiation, dielectric properties and phase transformations in the organic solid state. Home: S S Box 115 Corrales NM 87048

GREEN, JOHN WILLARD, oil co. exec.; b. Albuquerque, July 22, 1912; s. John W. and Flossie (Floyd) G.; student Baylor U., 1932-35; m. Peggy Byrn, Dec. 21, 1936; childrenJoan B. (Mrs. Barry Jeffrey), Mike B. Vice pres. Texaco Inc., 1960-61, exec. v.p., 1961—; dir. Caltex Petroleum Corp., Texaco Can. Ltd. Mem. Am. Petroleum Inst. Home: 16 Dewart Rd Greenwich CT 06832 Office: 135 E 42d St New York City NY 10017

GREEN, JOHN Y., banker. Sr. v.p. First and Merchants Nat. Bank, Richmond, Va. Office: 9th and Main Sts Richmond VA 23217*

GREEN, JOSEPH, coll. dean; b. N.Y.C., Oct. 1, 1916; s. Abraham and Fannie (Blacksberg) G.; B.S., N.Y.U., 1939, M.A., 1947, Ed.D., 1960; m. Sylvia Cohen, Oct. 9, 1947; childrenLaura Ann, Cynthia. Asst. purchasing agt. Boy Scouts Am., 1939-40; tchr. Warwick (N.Y.) High Sch., 1941-43; instr. Bergen Jr. Coll., Teaneck, N.J., 1946-47, Packard Jr. Coll., N.Y.C., 1948-54; mem. faculty Fairleigh Dickinson U., 1954-, prof. accounting and mgmt., 1960- , dean Coll. Bus. Adminstrn., 1966-, asst. provost, 1963-66; vis. prof. U. P.R. summers, 1964-66. Cons. A.I.M., 1956, Bergen County (N.J.) Planning Bd., 1965-; del. White House Conf. Youth, 1941, White House Conf. Internat. Coop., 1965; mem. Bergen Co. Commn. Resources and Econ. Devel. Served with USAAF, 1943-46. Mem. Am. Assn. U. Profs., Am. Mgmt. Assn., Ednl. Press Assn. Am. (regional dir.), Beta Gamma Sigma, Delta Pi Epsilon, Alpha Phi Omega. Mng. editor The Clearing House, 1955-61, editor, 1961-. Home: 15 Brown Pl Bergenfield NJ 07621 Office: Fairleigh Dickinson U Teaneck NJ 07666

GREEN, JOSHUA, Jr., banker; b. Seattle, Dec. 9, 1908; s. Joshua and Laura (Turner) G.; student Thacher Sch. (Cal.), 1921-25, Lawrenceville (N.J.) Sch., 1925- 26, Harvard, 1927-29; m. Elaine Brygger, Dec. 29, 1931; childrenJoshua, Frances Scandrett. Messenger, Peoples Nat. Bank of Wash., Seattle, 1929-32, asst. cashier, 1932-37, v.p., 1937-42, exec. v.p. 1946-, pres., 1949-62, chmn. bd., 1962-; v.p. Joshua Green Corp., 1936-60, pres., 1960—; dir. Rainier Cos., Inc., Safeco Corp., Pay'n Save drugs, Inc. Served from lt. (j.g.) to comdr., USNR, 1941-45. Mem. Wash. Soc. S.R., Seattle C. of C. Clubs: Rainier, Seattle Golf, Wash. Athletic, University (Seattle). Home: The Highlands Seattle WA 98177 Office: 1414 4th Av Seattle WA 98101

GREEN, JULIAN, author; b. Paris, France, Sept. 6, 1900; s. Edward and Mary (Hartridge) G.; ed. in France, U. Va. Recipient Grand Prix, Nat. des Lettres, Paris, 1966; Grand Prix de Littérature, Acadéemie Française, 1970. Mem. French Acad., Phi Beta Kappa. Author: Mont-Cinere (Avarice House), 1925; Adrienne Mesurat (The Closed Garden), 1927; Leviathan (The Dark Journey), 1929; Le Voyageur sur la Terre (Christine), 1930; Epaves (The Strange River), 1931; Le Visionnaire (The Dreamer), 1934; Minuit (Midnight), 1936; Personal Record (1928-1939), 1939; Varouna, 1940; Then Shall the Dust Return, 1941; Memories of Happy Days, 1942; Journal (1940-1943), 1946; Si j'etais vous. . ., 1947; Journal (1943-1945), 1949; Moira, 1950; Sud, 1953; L'Ennemi, 1954; Journal (1949-1954), 1955; Le Malfaiteur, 1956; L'Ombre, 1956; Le Bel Aujourd'hui, 1958; Chaque Homme dans sa Nuit, 1960; Partir avant le jour, 1963; Mille chemins ouverts, 1964; Terre lointaine, 1966; Vers l'Invisible, 1968; L'Autre, 1971. Address: care Plon 8 rue Garancière Paris 6 France

GREEN, JUNE LAZENBY, (Mrs. John Cawley Green), U.S. judge; b. Arnold, Md., Jan. 23, 1914; d. Eugene H. and Jessie T. (Briggs) Lazenby; J.D., Am. U., 1941; m. John Cawley Green, Sept. 5, 1936. Admitted to Md. bar, 1943, D.C. bar, 1945; pvt. practice law, Washington, 1947-68, Annapolis, Md., 1950-68; claims adjuster Lumbermans Mut. Casualty Co., Washington, 1942-43, claims atty., 1943-47; judge U.S. Dist. Ct. for D.C., 1968-. Bar examiner, Washington, 1963-68. Named Woman Lawyer of Year, 1965. Fellow Am. Acad. Matrimonial Lawyers; mem. Inter-Am., Am., Md. bar assns., Bar Assn. D.C. (dir.), Women's Bar Assn. D.C. (pres. 1955-57), Kappa Beta Pi. Clubs: Nat. Lawyers, Zonta. Home: 246 Joyce Lane Arnold MD 21012 Office: U S Courthouse Washington DC 20001

GREEN, KENNETH W., lawyer; b. St. Paul, 1923; B.S., U. Minn., 1947, LL.B., 1949. Admitted to Minn. bar, 1949, D.C. bar, 1964; mem. firm O'Connor, Green, Thomas, Walters & Kelly, Mpls. Mem. Hennepin County, Ramsey County, Minn. bar assns. Office: 845 Northwestern Bank Bldg Minneapolis MN 55402*

GREEN, LEON, Jr., mech. engr.; b. Austin, Tex., Aug. 13, 1922; s. Leon and Notra (Anderson) G.; B.S. in Physics, Cal. Inst. Tech., 1944, M.S. in Mech. Engring., 1947, Ph.D., 1950; m. Eleanor Broome Samuels, Apr. 14, 1951; children—John Anderson, Emily Broome, Charles Leon. With N.Am. Aviation, Inc., 1949-51, Aerojet-Gen. Corp., 1951-59, Aeronutronic div. Ford Motor Co., 1959-62; chief scientist Lockheed Propulsion Co., 1962-64; sci. dir. research and tech. div. Air Force Systems Command, Washington, 1964-67; dir. planning Lockheed Aircraft Corp., 1967-70; exec. sec. Def. Sci. Bd., Dept. Def., 1970—. Asso. fellow Am. Inst. Aeros. and Astronautics; mem. Am. Soc. M.E., Am. Ordnance Assn., Solar Energy Soc., Combustion Inst., Research Soc. Am., World Future Soc., A.A.A.S., Am. Acad. Polit. and Social Sci., Sigma Xi. Club: Cosmos (Washington). Contbr. articles to profl. jours. Home: 5140 Westpath Way Washington DC 20016 Office: The Pentagon Washington DC 20301

GREEN, LESLLE H., automotive materials co. exec.; b. Detroit, June 18, 1886; s. Edmund Henry and Caroline M. (Betz) G.; ed. pub. schs. of Detroit; m. Edith M. Cornyn, Sept. 28, 1907; 1 son, Robert Newton. Pres Automotive Materials Corp., 1921-48, chmn. bd., 1948—; chmn. bd. Standard Cotton Products Co., Flint, Mich.; dir. Detroit Bank & Trust Co. Trustee Brighton (Mich.) Hosp., Detroit Mus. Art Founders Soc., St. Peter's Home for Boys, Detroit. Mem. Detroit Zool. Soc. Episcopalian. Clubs: Detroit, Detroit Athletic, Recess; Bloomfield Hills Country, Forest Lake Country (Bloomfield Hills, Mich.). Home: Turtle Lake Farms Bloomfield Hills MI 48013 Office: Fisher Bldg Detroit MI 48202

GREEN, LOUIS CRAIG, educator, astrophysicist; b. Macon, Ga., Feb. 2, 1911; s. Edward Melvin and Ann Field (Craig) G.; A.B., Princeton, 1932, M.A., 1933, Ph.D., 1937; m. Elizabeth Hazard Ufford, July 27, 1940. Tchr. math. and astronomy Allegheny Coll., 1937-41, Haverford Coll., 1941-, prof. astronomy, 1953-, chmn. physics dept., 1963-65, provost, 1965-68, acting pres., summer 1967; tchr. math Swarthmore Coll., 1944, physics Bryn Mawr Coll., 1944-46; dir. Strawbridge Meml. Obs.; vis. prof. Max Planck Inst. Physics and Astrophysics, Munich, Germany, summer 1959; mem. Inst. for Advanced Study, Princeton, 1962-63, 68-69. Guggenheim fellow, 1955- 56. Fellow Am. Phys. Soc.; mem. Am. Astron. Soc., Phi Beta Kappa, Sigma Xi. Contbr. articles to profl. jours. Home: 791 College Av Haverford PA 19041

GREEN, M. EDWIN, architect; b. Kerhonkson, N.Y., July 1, 1896; s. Moses E. and Viola J. (Haskin) G.; A.B., Carnegie Inst. Tech., 1920; grad. student Fountainbleu Sch. Fine Arts, France, 1932; m. Gladys W. Wilson, Sept. 1, 1922; childrenAndrew Wilson, Moses Edwin, Elizabeth DeWitt. Asst. dir., bur. sch. bldgs. Dept. Pub. Instrn. Commonwealth of Pa., 1920-22; partner Lawrie & Green, Harrisburg, 1922—. Past pres. bd. of architectural registration Commonwealth Pa.; mem. bd. trustees Kiskiminetas Springs Boys Prep. Sch.; treas. Historical Found. Pa., Served as 1st lt. 94th Aero Squadron, 1st Pursuit Group. Decorated Croix de Guerre (France). Recipient Alumni Merit award Carnegie Inst. Tech. Fellow A.I.A. (past chmn. joint com. modular coordination, past pres. Central Pa. chpt.); mem. Pa. (past dir.), Harrisburg (past dir.) C.'s of C., Pa. Soc. Architects (past pres.), Harrisburg Art Assn., Pa. Dept. Labor and Industry (mem. bldg. adv. bd.), Modular Bldg. Standards Assn., Order of Daedalians, Beta Theta Pi. Methodist (past pres. ch. bd. trustees). Mason. Clubs: Kiwanis, Torch, Country (Harrisburg); Wing. Prin. archtl. works include: Dauphin County Ct. House, Harrisburg, Cumberland County Ct. House, Carlisle, Hunt Meml. Library at Carnegie Inst. Tech., Commonwealth of Pa. William Penn Meml. Mus. and Archives Bldg., numerous hosps., schs., indsl. bldgs., hotel, coll. bldgs. Home: RFD 1 Dauphin PA 17018 Office: 321 N Front St Harrisburg PA 17101

GREEN, MARCUS HERBERT, educator, biologist; b. Harrisburg, Pa., July 31, 1905; s. Herbert Ritchie and Katherine (Grosz) G.; B.S. in Biology, Albright Coll., 1929; M.S., U. Pitts., 1935; Sc.D., Lebanon Valley Coll., 1964; m. Leona Gladys Christopher, Apr. 26, 1930; childrenThomas Francis, John Foster. High sch. instr., 1929-30; mem. faculty Albright Coll., Reading, Pa., 1930—, prof. biology, 1962-66, Henry Pfeiffer prof. biology, 1966-; dir. devel. program scis. for non-sci. majors; cons. in field. Mem. steering com. Friends of Reading Pub. Mus., 1966. Recipient award for service to mankind Del. dist. Sertoma Club, 1956; Christian R. and Mary F. Lindbeck Found. award for distinguished teaching, 1963. Mem. A.A.A.S., Am. Assn. Profl. Biologists, Fedn. Am. Soc. Exptl. Biology, Mengel Natural History Soc. (past pres.), Pa. Acad. Sci. (past v.p.), Sigma Xi, Pi Gamma Mu. Mem. United Ch. Christ (past elder). Mason. Research and publn. the vascular system, interactions of brain and skull, dental hypertrophy in rodent. Home: 1138 Spring St Reading PA 19604

GREEN, MARGUERITE, educator; b. Chgo., Sept. 2, 1922; d. Edward A. and Mary (Prindeville) Green; B.A., Barat Coll., 1943; M.A., Cath. U. Am. 1953, Ph.D., 1956; postgrad. U. Mich., Sophia U., Tokyo, Japan. Joined Religious of Sacred Heart, 1944; tchr. high sch. Acad. Sacred Heart, Chgo., 1946-49; prof. history and polit. sci. Barat Coll., Lake Forest, Ill., 1949—, chmn. dept. history, 1958-. Mem. Am., Cath. hist. assns., Am. Polit. Sci. Assn. Author: The National Civic Federation and the American Labor Movement, 1900 to 1925, 1956. Address: Barat Coll Lake Forest IL 60045

GREEN, MARSHALL, fgn. service officer; b. Holyoke, Mass., Jan. 27, 1916; s. Addison Loomis and Gertrude (Metcalf) G.; grad. Groton Sch., 1935; A.B., Yale, 1939; m. Lispenard Seabury Crocker, Feb. 14, 1942; children—Marshall Winthrop, Edward Crocker, Brampton Seabury. Pvt. sec. to Am. ambassador to Japan, 1939-41; vice consul career, sec. Diplomatic Service, 1945; assigned Wellington, New Zealand, 1946-47; acting officer in charge Japanese affairs Dept. State, 1947-50; 1st sec. embassy, consul, Stockholm, Sweden, 1950-55; assigned Nat. War Coll., 1955-56; regional planning adviser for Far East, Dept. State, 1956-59, acting dep. asst. sec. of state, 1959-60, minister counselor Am. embassy, Korea, 1960-61; Am. consul gen. Hong Kong, personal rank of minister, 1961-63; dep. asst. sec. for Far Eastern affairs Dept. State, 1963-65; ambassador extraordinary and envoy plenipotentiary to Indonesia, 1965- 69, asst. sec. state for East Asian-Pacific affairs, 1969—; personal rank of career minister, 1966—. Mem. U.S. team in Paris for Vietnam negotiations, 1969. Served to lt. USNR, 1942-45. Episcopalian. Clubs: Metropolitan, Chevy Chase (Washington). Home: 5063 Millwood Lane NW Washington DC 20016 Office: Dept State Washington DC 20520

GREEN, MAYER ALBERT, physician: b. Pitts., May 29, 1909; s Oscar and Elizabeth (Rosenbloom) G.; B.S., U. Pitts., 1929, M.D., 1932; m. Phyllis Blumenfeld, Feb. 6, 1938; children—Patricia Sue (Mrs. Sanford Berman), Richard Lee, Nancy Carole (Mrs. Allen Satenberg). Intern Montefiore Hosp., Pitts., 1932-33, resident roentgenology, 1933-34; asst. med. dir. Mt. Sinai Hosp., N.Y.C., 1937-38, clin. asst. adult and pediatric allergies, 1938- 39; instr. allergy U. Pitts., 1933-37; pvt. med. practice, Pitts., 1933- ; lectr., sr. physician, head allergy dept. Columbia Hosp.; cons. Braddock Gen. Hosp., St. John's Hosp., Jewish Home for Aged, Ohio Valley Gen. Hosp., The Children's Asthma Research Inst. and Hosp., Homestead Hosp., Dever; lectr. allergy to nurses Homestead, Columbia hosps.; sr. physician dept. allergy Montefiore Hosp.; clin. asst. prof. dept. dermatology, allergy sect. U. Pitts. Sch. Medicine; med. dir. Allergy Found. Am. Regional cons. nat. adv. com. Asthmatic Children's Found.; mem. sponsoring com. Am. Bd. Allergy and Immunology, 1970—; mem. profl. adv. com. Group Against Smog and Air Pollution, 1970. Bd. dirs. Assn. Convalescent Homes and Hosps. Asthmatic Children; founder, advisor Mayer A. Green Allergy Found. Served to capt., M.C., AUS, World War II. Diplomate allergy Am. Bd. Internal Medicine. Fellow Internat. Assn. Allergists. (hon.), A.C.P., Am. Coll. Chest Physicians (chmn. allergy com. 1964-69), Am. Coll. Allergists (pres. 1962-63; mem. scientific and ednl. council 1965-70, chmn. 1968-70), Acad. (alternate del. allergy sect., allergy sect. del. 1970—), Am. Acad. Allergy; mem. A.A.A.S., N.Y. Acad. Sci., Assn. Am. Med. Colls., Western Pa. Soc. Clin. Hypnosis (bd. govs. 1969), Am. Soc. Certified Allergists, Pa. Allergy Assn. (pres. 1964- 65), Pitts. Allergy Soc. (past pres.), West Coast Allergy Soc. Pa., Allegheny County medical socs., Pitts. Med. Forum (past pres.), Am. Med. Writers Assn., Assn. Argentina de Alergiae Inmunologia (hon.), Internat. Soc. Internal Medicine, Grad. Club (past pres.), Phi Delta Epsilon. Mason (past master). Editorial bd. Annals of Allergy, Indsl. Medicine and Surgery. Contbr. articles profl. jours. Home: 5535 Darlington Rd Pittsburgh, PA 15217. Office: 6113 Jenkins Arcade Pittsburgh PA 15222

GREEN, MELVILLE SAUL, educator, physicist; b. Jamaica, N.Y., June 9, 1922; s. Maurice S. and Ella (Prichep) G.; B.A., Columbia, 1944; M.A., Princeton, 1947, Ph.D., 1952; m. Vivian Grossman, Feb. 12, 1950; children—Aliza, Joel. Mem. faculty, U. Chgo., 1947-51; research asso. Inst. Fluid Dynamics and Applied Math., U. Md., 1951-54; chief statis. physics sect. Nat. Bur. Standards, Washington, 1954-68; prof. physics Temple U., Phila., 1968—. Vis. lectr. Weitzmann Inst. Sci., Rehovoth, Israel, 1958; with Office of Asst. Sec. Commerce for Sci. and Tech., Washington, 1963; OAS lectr. in statis. mechanics Inst. Polytechnico Nacional de Mexico, 1964, dir. course critical phenomena Enrico Ferm; Summer Sch. Physics, Varenna, Italy, 1970. Recipient Gold medal for Distinguished Achievement in Fed. Service, U.S. Dept. Commerce, 1965. Fulbright grantee, 1957, Guggenheim fellow, 1957. Fellow Am. Phys. Soc.; mem. Washington Philos. Soc., Washington Acad. Scis. Editor: (with J.V. Sengers) Critical Phenomena: The Report of a Conference, 1965. Bd. editors Phys. Rev., 1944—, Jour. Math. Physics, 1953-65, 71—, Jour. Physics of Fluids, 1966—. Research in statis. mechanics, especially theory of irreversible processes, theory of dense systems, kinetic theory of gases, critical phenomena. Home: 2345 N 52d St Philadelphia PA 19131

GREEN, MICHAEL JOSEPH, bishop; b. St. Joseph, Mich., Oct. 13, 1917; s. Michael Joseph and Margaret Mary (Kennedy) G.; student St. Joseph Sem., Grand Rapids, Mich., 1938-41; B.A., St. Gregory Sem., Cin., 1943; postgrad. St. Mary Sem. of West, Norwood, O., 1943-46; D.Cannon Law, Lateran U., Rome, Italy, 1954. Ordained priest Roman Catholic Ch. 1946; made domestic prelate, 1959; aux. bishop of Lansing, Mich., 1962-67; bishop Diocese of Reno, 1967—. Home: 843 Marsh Av Reno NV 89502 Office: PO Box 1211 Reno NV 89504

GREEN, MILTON DOUGLAS, educator; b. Central City, Colo., May 16, 1903; s. William Samuel and Josephine (Anderson) G.; A.B., U. Mich., 1926, J.D., 1928; LL.M., Columbia, 1938, J.S.D., 1944; m. Geraldine Isabelle Knight, Dec. 21, 1928; childrenAnn, Daniel Edward. Admitted to Colo. bar, 1929, Wash. bar, 1947, Mo. Bar., 1954; with law firms Hodges, Wilson & Rogers, Denver, 1929, McComb & Strong, 1929-30; mem. firm McComb & Green, 1930-37; instr. law U. Colo., 1937-38 asso. prof., 1940-41, prof., 1941-45, acting dean, 1943-45; asso. prof. law U. Utah, 1938-40; prof. law U. Wash., 1945-53; dean, prof. law Washington U., St. Louis, 1953-59; vis. prof. sch. law N.Y.U., 1959-60, prof. law, 1960-67, acting dir. Inst. Jud. Adminstrn., 1959-60, asso. dir., 1960-63, resident Master Hayden Hall, 1964-66; prof. Hastings Coll. of the Law, U. of Cal., 1967—; vis. prof., summers, U. Mich., 1941, Standford, 1948, U. So. Cal., 1953, 1958. Chmn. Clayton, Mo. charter commn., 1956-57. Compliance commr. WPB, also Civilian Prodn. Adminstrn., 1943-47; pub. panel mem. War Labor Bd., 1943-45; hearing commr. NPA, 1951-53. Mem. Am., Mo., Wash., San Francisco bar assns., Am. Law Inst., Bar Assn. St. Louis, Am. Arbitration Assn., Phi Beta Kappa, Phi Delta Phi (nat. pres. 1959-61), Theta Chi, Order of Coif. Author: Mental Incompetency to Make a Contract or a Will, 1944; Trial by Jury (motion picture), 1948; Alternatives and Preliminaries to the Trial of a Civil Action, 1961. Contbr. Collier's Ency., 1959, Grolier's Ency., 1962, also profl. jours. Home: 2030 Vallejo San Francisco CA 94123

GREEN, MORRIS, educator, physician; b. Indpls., May 27, 1922; s. Coleman and Rebecca (Oleinick) G.; A.B., Ind. U., 1942, M.D., 1944; m. Janice Barber Gorton, Mar. 11, 1955; children—David Schuster, Alan Coleman, Carolyn Ann, Susan Elaine, Marcia Ruth, Sylvia Rebecca. Intern, Ind. U. Med. Center, 1945; resident pediatrics U. Ill. Research and Ednl. Hosps., 1947-49; instr. pediatrics U. Ill. Coll. Medicine, 1949-52; asst. prof. Yale Sch. Medicine, 1952- 57; faculty Ind. U. Sch. Medicine, Indpls., 1957—, prof. pediatrics, 1963— ; chmn. dept. pediatrics, physician-in-chief James Whitcomb Riley Hosp. for Children, Indpls., 1967—. Served to capt. M.C., AUS, 1945-47. Mem. Am. Pediatric Soc., Soc. Pediatric Research, Am. Fedn. Clin. Research, Am. Acad. Pediatrics, A.M.A., Soc. Research Child Devel., Phi Beta Kappa, Sigma Xi, Alpha Omega Alpha. Author: (with others) Pediatric Diagnosis; 2d edit., 1962. Co-editor: Ambulatory Pediatrics, 1968; editorial bd. Pediatrics, Current Problems in Pediatrics. Home: 5716 Washington Blvd Indianapolis IN 46220

GREEN, MORTON, educator; A.B., M.A., U. Kan.; Ph.D., U. Cal. Mem. faculty S.D. Sch. Mines and Tech., 1950—, now prof. biology, head dept., also curator vertebrate paleontology. Address: care Dept Biology SD Sch Mines and Tech Rapid City SD*

GREEN, OSCAR U., business exec.; b. 1912; married. With Greif Bros. Corp., Delaware, O., 1937—, v.p., 1961-70, pres., dir., 1970—. Served with AUS, 1942-45. Office: Greif Bros Corp Delaware OH 43015*

GREEN, OTIS HOWARD, educator; b. Monroe, Mich., Dec. 11, 1898; s. John Howard and Cora Letitia (Dike) G.; A.B., Colgate U., 1920; A.M., Pa. State Coll., 1923; Ph.D., U. Pa., 1927, Litt.D., 1969; postgrad. Centro de Estudios Historicos, Madrid, Spain, summer 1922; m. Mabel Warburton Barnett, June 11, 1924; childrenEleanor Irving, Paul Barnett. Tchr. French and Spanish, Peddie Sch., Hightstown, N.J., 1920-21; instr. Romance langs. Pa. State Coll., 1921-23; instr. Spanish, U. Pa. 1923-28, asst. prof., 1928-36, asso. prof. Romance langs., 1936-39, prof., 1939-69, prof. emeritus, 1969—, chmn. dept., 1938-45. Vis. prof., U. Colo., summers 1934, 36, 48, 49, 50, 57, Duke, summer 1968; mem. adv. council dept modern langs. Princeton, 1942- 59. Decorated Comendador de la Order de Isabel La Catolica. Guggenheim fellow, 1964-65. Mem. Am. Council Learned Socs. (com. of Renaissance studies 1942-50), Hispanic Soc. Am. (trustee), Modern Lang. Assn. Am. (1st v.p. 1961, 67, pres. 1968), Medieval Acad. Am., Modern Humanities Research Assn., Am. Assn. Tchrs. Spanish, Renaissance Soc. Am. (adv. council, 1954-64, 68-70), Phi Beta Kappa, Kappa Delta Rho. Republican. Baptist. Author books including; The Life and Works of Lupercio Leonardo de Argensola, 1927; Courtly Love in Quevedo, 1952. Editor: Lucio V. Mansilla, Una Excursion a los Indios Ranqueles, 1944; Torres Naharro and the Drama of the Renaissance, 1961; Spain and the Western Tradition: The Castilian Mind in Literature from El Cid to Calerón, 4 vols., 1963-66; co-editor Hispanic Rev. Contbr. articles to profl. jours. Home: 60 E Levering Mill Rd Bala-Cynwyd PA 19004

GREEN, PAUL ELIOT, author, tchr.; b. Lillington, N.C., Mar. 17, 1894; s. William Archibald and Betty Lorine (Byrd) G.; grad. Buies Creek (N.C.) Acad., 1914; A.B., U. N.C., 1921, postgrad., 1921-22; postgrad. Cornell U., 1922-23; Litt.D. (hon.) Davidson Coll., Western Res. U., U. N.C., U. Louisville, Berea Coll., Campbell Coll.; m. Elizabeth Atkinson Lay, July 6, 1922; childrenPaul Eliot, Nancy Byrd, Betsy McAllister, Janet McNeill. Prof. dramatic art U. N.C., 1939-44. Editor, The Reviewer, 1925. Mem. exec. com. U.S. Nat. Commn. for UNESCO; del. UNESCO conf. at Paris. Guggenheim fellow, 1928-29. Mem. Nat. Inst. Arts and Letters, 1941. Author plays and various works, 1925— including Faith of Our Fathers (play), 1950; Peer Gynt (modern adaptation Ibsen's play), 1951; Dramatic Heritage (Essays), 1953; Wilderness Road (play), 1955; The Founders (play), 1956; The Confederacy (play), 1958; Drama and the Weather (Essays), 1959; Wings for to Fly (play), 1959; The Stephen Foster Story (play), 1959; Plough and Furrow (essays), 1963; Five Plays, 1963; Cross and Sword (play), 1964; The Sheltering Plaid (play), 1965; Texas (play), 1966; Texas Songbook, 1967; Words and Ways (stories), 1968; Sing All a Green Willow (play), 1969; The Honeycomb (play); Home to My Valley (stories), 1969; Trumpet in the Land (play), 1970. In Abraham's Bosom awarded Pulitzer prize for best American play, 1927. Address: Old Lystra Rd Chapel Hill NC 27514

GREEN, PAUL MARTIN, coll. dean.; b. East Liverpool, O., Apr. 26, 1902; s. Edward Lawrence and Annie J. (Martin) G.; A.B., Miami U., 1926, LL.D., 1952; M.S., U. Ill., 1927, Ph.D., 1933, postgrad. law, 1933-34; m. Hilda Jane McCoy, Sept. 9, 1930; 1 dau., Jane Ellsworth. Prof. accounting U. Fla., 1934, 41; head research accountant FHA, 1934-37; dep. adminstr. charge accounting OPA, 1941-47; controller AEC, 1947-50; professorial lectr. George Washington U., 1949; controller ECA, 1950-52; asst. dir. charge accounting OPS, 1951-52; instr. accounting, finance U. Ill., 1926-34, asst. prof. econs. in charge corp. finance, 1937-41, prof. head div. mgmt., 1949-51, dean Coll. Commerce and Bus. Adminstrn., 1952- 67, emeritus, 1967—, prof. mgmt., 1952-57, prof. bus. adminstrn., 1957- 67, emeritus, 1967—, dir. Grad. Sch. Bus. Adminstrn., 1952-54, 59- 67, emeritus, 1967—; dean Coll. Bus. Adminstrn., prof. Fla. Tech. U., 1967-68; exec. dean for bus. schs., prof. bus. and econs. Stetson U., Deland, Fla., 1968-69. Cons. accounting and mgmt. govt. agys.; dep. asst. sec. def., 1961-62. Pres., Council for Profl. Edn. for Bus., 1959-60. Mem. Am. Econ. Assn., Am. Accounting Assn., Royal Econ. Soc., Fed. Govt. Accountants Assn., Am. Statis. Assn., Am. Assn. Collegiate Schs. Bus. (pres. 1957-58), Am. Finance Assn., Phi Beta Kappa, Phi Kappa Phi, Delta Sigma Pi (scholarship key 1926), Beta Alpha Psi, Phi Delta Phi, Beta Gamma Sigma, Artus, Beta Nu Kappa, Sigma Iota Epsilon, Pi Gamma Mu, Sigma Alpha Epsilon. Presbyn. Club: Union League (Chgo.). Contbr. articles to tech. publs. Home: 601 W Delaware Av Urbana IL 61801 Office: David Kinley Hall Urbana IL 61801

GREEN, RICHARD CALVIN, utility exec.; b. Kansas City, Mo., Dec. 12, 1925; s. Ralph J. and Nell (Schrorer) G.; B.S. in Bus. Adminstrn., U. Mo., 1950; m. Ann G. Gabelman, May 10, 1952; childrenSuzanne, Cassandra, Richard, Pamela, Robert. With Mo. Pub. Service Co., Kansas City, 1941-, exec. v.p., 1953- 58, pres., 1958-, chmn. bd., 1963-; pres. dir. Green Securities, Inc., 1962-. Sunrise Seed and Implement Co., 1947-; dir. City Nat. Bank & Trust Co., Kansas City. dir., mem. bd. finance com. Business Men's Assurance Co., Pres. Kansas City Crime Commn. Bd. dirs. Kansas City area council Boy Scouts Am., Kansas City Indsl. Found.; bd. trustees U. Mo. Kansas City, Southwest Atomic Energy Assn.; trustee, mem. exec. com. Kansas City Conservatory Music; sec., dir. Starlight Theatre Assn ; bd. govs. Am. Royal; hon. dir. Rockhurst Coll. Recipient Outstanding Boss award Mo. Jr. C. of C., 1954, Distinguished Service award Kansas City Jr. C. of C. 1958. Citation of Merit award U. Mo., 1963. Mem. Phi Gamma Delta, Elk. Clubs: Eldorado (Palm Desert, Cal.); Marco Polo (N.Y.C.); Kansas City Country; Saddle and Sirloin. Home: 1235 W 65th St Kansas City MO 64113 Office: 10700 E Hwy 50 Kansas City MO 64138

GREEN, ROBERT CLAY, Jr., retail co. exec.; b. Columbia, Tenn., Oct. 20, 1932; s. Robert Clay and Inez (Stephens) G.; B.S., Bowling Green Coll. Commerce, 1959; m. Carol Kasparian, May 23, 1964. Auditor, Ernst & Ernst, Shelbyville, Tenn., 1959; auditor Genesco, Inc., Nashville, 1959-62, adminstrv. v.p. retail apparel for men, N.Y.C., 1962-66, now dir.; controller S.H. Kress & Co., N.Y.C., 1966-67, treas., 1967, adminstrv. v.p., 1967—, also dir. Served with USAF, 1952-56. Recipient Superior Achievement Recognition award Genesco, Inc., 1966. Mem. Menswear Retailers Am. (group vice-chmn.), Pi Tau Nu (past pres.). Democrat. Methodist. Club: Downtown Athletic. Author: (with others) Menswear Merchandising and Accounting Manual, 1966. Home: 102-10 66th Rd Forest Hills NY 11375 Office: 114 Fifth Av New York City NY 10011

GREEN, ROBERT HOLT, educator, physician; b. Charleston, S.C., Oct. 31, 1911; s. Walter Guerry and Daisie (Holt) G.; B.A., U. of South, 1933; postgrad. U. N.C., 1933-34; M.D., Johns Hopkins, 1938; M.A. (hon.), Yale, 1967; m. Audrey Greet Johnston, Apr. 29, 1943; children—Robert Holt, Barbara Johnston, William Guerry. Intern medicine Strong Meml. Hosp., Rochester, N.Y. 1938-39; fellow medicine, asst. resident medicine Lakeside Hosp., Cleve., 1939- 41; NRC fellow med. scis., asst. resident physician Rockefeller Inst. Hosp., N.Y.C., 1941-42, NRC fellow med. scis., 1946-47; faculty Yale Sch. Medicine, 1947-60, 67—, prof. medicine, 1967-69, prof. pathology and medicine, 1970—; pvt. practice internal medicine, Madison, Conn., 1953-57; asso. sci. dir. Health Research Council N.Y.C., 1960-64; asso. prof. medicine, then prof. medicine N.Y. U. Sch. Medicine, 1960-67; chief med. service VA Hosp., N.Y.C., 1964-67; vis. physician 3d and 4th med. divs. Bellevue Hosp. Center, N.Y.C., 1965-67; attending medicine Univ. Hosp., N.Y.C., 1965-67; cons. physician internal medicine Willowbrook State Sch., Staten Island, N.Y., 1961-67; asso. chief staff research VA Hosp., West Haven, Conn., 1967—; prof. medicine, also dean Coll. Medicine, Med. U. S.C., 1969-70. Served to lt. comdr. USNR, 1942-46. Commonwealth Fund fellow, summer 1961. Diplomate Am. Bd. Internal Medicine. Mem. Am. Assn. Immunologists, Am. Fedn. Clin. Research, A.M.A., Am. Soc. Clin. Investigation, Harvey Soc., Infectious Diseases Soc. Am., Conn., New Haven County med. socs., Soc. Exptl. Biology and Medicine, Phi Beta Kappa, Sigma Xi. Contbr. numerous articles to profl. jours. Editor Yale Jours. Biology and Medicine, 1952-53. Home: 26 Lovers Lane Madison CT 06443 Office: VA Hosp W Spring St West Haven CT 06516

GREEN, ROBERT HORTON, lawyer; b. Menan, Ida., Nov. 16, 1927; s. Charles Wesley and Lola (Leavitt) G.; B.S., Brigham Young U., 1951; LL.B., U. Utah, 1956, J.D., 1963; m. Irene Rowan, Aug. 11, 1950; children—Shauri, Shelli, Staci, Robert Horton. Admitted to Ariz. bar, 1957, since practiced in Phoenix; asso. firm Romley, Kaplan, Robbins & Green, 1957-63, partner, 1963—. Sustaining mem. Boy Scouts Am. Bd. dirs. Legal Aid Soc. Ariz., Phoenix Assn. Def. Counsel. Served with USNR, 1945-46. Mem. Am., Maricopa County bar assns., state bars Ariz., Utah, Am. Bd. Trial Advs., Def. Research Inst., Lawyers Club Phoenix, Phi Delta Phi. Republican. Clubs: Arizona, Mountain Shawdows Country (Phoenix). Home: 4828 E Calle Tuberia Phoenix AZ 85018 Office: Arizona Title Bldg Phoenix AZ 85003

GREEN, ROBERT LAMAR, agrl. engr.; b. Moultrie, Ga., Nov. 15, 1914; s. Louis Pinkney and Bessie (Tillman) G.; B.S., U. Ga., 1934; M.S., Ia. State Coll., 1939; grad. Command and Gen. Staff Coll., 1944; Ph.D. (fellow Gen. Edn. Bd.), Mich. State U., 1953; m. Frances Cowan, June 7, 1940; 1 son, Robert Lamar. Terracing foreman Soil Erosion Service, Athens, Ga., 1934; camp engr. Civilian Conservation Corps., Bartow County, Ga., 1935; jr. agrl. engr. Soil Conservation Service, Lawrenceville, also Americus, Ga., 1936- 38, work unit conservationist, Lawrenceville, 1939-47; asst. prof. agrl. engring. La. State U., 1947-50, 53-54; agrl. engr. U.S. Spl. Tech. and Econ. Mission to Indonesia (ECA, MSA, TCA, FOA), Djakarta, Indonesia, 1951-53; supt., agrl. engr. S.E. Tidewater Expt. Sta., Dept. Agr., 1954-58; state drainage engr., Md., 1958—; head dept. agrl. engring. U. Md., 1958—, coordinator Water Resources Research Center, 1965-. Chmn. Spl. Gov.'s Com. to study shore erosion Md., 1960-66; chmn. Spl. Gov.'s Com. for Conservation and Devel. Natural Resources, 1960-66; mem. Md. Water Resources Commn., 1964—; chmn. Md. Water Scis. Adv. Bd., 1968- -. Served from 1st lt., cav., to maj., armor, AUS, 1941-46; col. Res., ret. Registered profl. engr., Ga., Md. Fellow Am. Soc. Agrl. Engrs. (chmn. Washington D.C.-Md. sect. 1961-62, rep. to NRC 1959-66, bd. dirs. 1969-71); mem. Am. Soc. Engring. Edn. (chmn. Mid- Atlantic sect. 1965-66), Sigma Xi, Tau Beta Pi, Phi Kappa Phi, Epsilon Sigma Phi. Episcopalian. Rotarian. Contbr. articles profl., trade jours. Home: 4201 Van Buren St Hyattsville MD 20782 Office: U Md College Park MD 20740

GREEN, ROBERT SMITH, engr., educator; b. Lafayette, Ind., Dec. 17, 1914; s. Arthur D. and Nellie Floss (Smith) G.; B.S. in Civil Engring., Purdue U. 1936, M.S.E., 1942; m. Katheryn Jane Harshman, Dec. 25, 1938; 1 dau., Katheryn Anne. Engr., Am. Bridge Co., 1936, Sinclair Refining Co., 1937, Carnegie-Ill. Steel Corp., 1937-38, Purdue U., 1938-40, Panama Canal, 1940-41, Blaw Knox Corp., 1941-42, Weirton Steel Co., 1942-47; exec. dir. engring. expt. sta., prof. welding engring. Ohio State U., Columbus, 1947-58, asso. dean Coll. Engring., exec. dir. engring. expt. sta., 1958—. Program dir. consortium of 9 Am. univs. assisting in devel. of Indian Inst. Tech., Kanpur, India, 1964-66. Served from ensign to lt. (j.g.) USNR, 1943-46. Mem. Am. Soc. M.E., Am. Soc. C.E., Am. Welding Soc., Am. Soc. for Metals, Nat. Soc. Profl. Engrs., Am. Soc. for Engring. Edn. Home: 211 Medick Way Worthington OH 43085 Office: Ohio State U Columbus OH 43210

GREEN, ROBERT THOMAS, lawyer; b. Shelby, O.; s. Thomas Jefferson and Blanche (Skiles) G.; B.A., Amherst Coll., 1927; LL.B., Harvard, 1931; m. Ruth Judd, June 22, 1935 (dec. 1958); childrenRobert Thomas, James J., Jeffrey S., Judith E.; m. 2d, Ann Kirkby, Feb. 14, 1964. Admitted to Ohio bar, 1931; practice in Shelby, 1936-; partner firm Long, Green & Long, 1936-. Chmn. bd. Autocall Co., Shelby, 1950-68. Chmn. Ohio Bd. Bar Examiners, 1962-63, Nat. Conf. Bar Examiners, 1965- 66. Mem. Phi Beta Kappa. Home: 13 E Gaylord Av Shelby OH 44875 Office: Insurance Bldg Shelby OH 44875

GREEN, ROY ORVAL, educator; b. Longford, Kan., Oct. 8, 1905; s. Matthew Eric and Ella (Baringer) G.; B.S., Kan. State Coll., 1930; M.S., U. Wis., 1932, Ph.D., 1934; M.A. (hon.), Harvard, 1946; D.Sc., U. Buffalo, 1960, Kan. State U., 1968; m. Eunice Estella Hauserman. Sept. 5, 1931; children—Ann Louise, Marjorie, Nancy. Research asst. in zoology Harvard, 1935-38; research asso. Squibb Inst. for Med. Research, New Brunswick, N.J., 1938-44; asst. prof. dental sci., Harvard Sch. Dental Medicine, 1944-46. asso. prof., 1946-49, prof. dental sci., 1949, dean, 1952-67; prof. anatomy, 1956-61; acting head dept. anatomy Harvard Med. Sch., 1956-59, dir. lab. Human Reprodn, and Reproductive biology, 1967—; John Rock prof. population studies Harvard Sch. Pub. Health, 1967—; mem. bd. visitors Pitts. U., 1958-62. Chmn. com. on dentistry NRC, 1956-61; mem. endocrinology study sect. USPHS, NIH; med. adv. bd. Nat. Pituitary Agy., 1963-67. Mem. exec. com. Worcester Found. for Exptl. Biology, 1969—. Recipient Schering award Endocrine Soc., 1957; Henry Dale medal Soc. for Endocrinology, Gt. Britain, 1967. Fellow A.A.A.S., N.Y. Acad, Sci., Am. Acad. Arts and Scis., Am. Coll. Dentists, Obstet. Soc. Boston (hon.); mem. Am. Cancer Soc. (chmn. adv. com. on personnel for research), New Eng. Bd. Higher Edn. (commn. on dental edn.), Soc. for Study Reprodn., Internat. Soc. Endocrinology (pres. 1968—), Soc. Exptl. Biology and Medicine (v.p. 1967, pres, 1969), Am. Assn. Anatomists, Am. Soc. Zoologists, Am. Physiol. Soc., Endocrine Soc. (chmn. publs. com. 1963-70, pres. 1966), Soc. Endocrinology (Gt. Britain), A.A.A.S., Internat. Assn. Dental Research, Boston Soc. Biologists; mem. Am. Acad. Dental Sci., Laurentian Hormone Conf. (com. on arrangements), Harvard Odontological Soc., Mass. Dental Soc. (hon.), Am. Dental Assn. Contbr. chpts. on hormones. Editor in chief Endocrinology, 1952, 63. Editor: Textbook of Histology, 1953, 2d edit., 1966; The Parathyroids, 1961; Human Fertility and Population Problems, 1963. Co-editor Handbook of Physiology, Sect. on Endocrinology, Am. Physiol. Soc., 1968. Home: 56 Upland Rd Brookline MA 02146 Office: Harvard Medical School 25 Shattuck St Boston MA 02115

GREEN, SAMUEL MAGEE, II, educator, artist; b. Oconomowoc, Wis., May 22, 1909; s. Raymond W. and Gwenthleen (Kaine) G.; grad. Haverford Sch., 1928; student Pa. Acad. Fine Arts, 1928-29; B.A., Harvard, 1933, Ph.D., 1945; m. Helen Bagenstose, June 23, 1934; childrenJonathan Standish, Samuel Adams, Gwynthlyn Hoague. Instr. art Wellesley Coll., 1938-40; teaching asst. Harvard, 1940-41; asst. prof. fine arts Colby Coll., 1943-47, curator art collection, 1945-47, asso. prof. fine arts, first semester, 1947-48; prof. art Wesleyan U., Middletown, Conn., 1948-; vis. prof. art Harvard, summer 1949, U. Colo., summer 1952, Yale, 1960-61; mem. Salzburg Seminar Am. Studies, summers 1953, 54, winter, 1958; rep. permanent collections Library of Congress, Fogg Mus. at Harvard, Smith Coll. Mus. Art, others. Mem. Coll. Art Assn., Soc. Archtl. Historians. Author; American Art, A Historical Survey, 1966; also articles. Home: Meriden Rd Middletown CT 06457

GREEN, THOMAS FITZGERALD, univ. prof.; born Athens, Ga., Aug. 6, 1903; s. Thomas Fitzgerald and Hope (Linton) G.; A.B., U. of Ga., 1925, LL.B., 1927; J.S.D., U. Chgo., 1931; m. Jane Oliver, Dec. 8, 1955. Admitted to Ga. bar, 1927; practiced law with Green & Michael, Athens, Ga., 1927-29; asso. prof. U. Ga., 1929-32, prof. law, 1932-67 (on leave 1941-46); state atty. OPA, 1942- 43; prin. atty. U.S. Dept. of Agr. and War Food Adminstrn., 1943-46; chmn. efficiency rating com. Office of Solicitor, U.S. Dept. of Agr., 1946; vis. prof. Vanderbilt U. 1956-57; Alumni Found. Distinguished prof. U. Ga., 1967-69, prof. emeritus, 1969—. Mem. Ga. Prison Study Commn.; former mem. bd. of dirs. Athens YMCA. Mem. adv. com. on rules evidence Jud. Conf. U.S. Recipient Ross award. Am. Bar Assn., 1940. Mem. Am. Assn. U. Profs. (nat. sec., 1941-42; mem. council, 1943-45), Phi Beta Kappa, Phi Kappa Phi, Sphinx, Chi Phi, Phi Delta Phi. Democrat. Methodist. Rotarian (past pres., Athens, Ga.). Author: Practical Summary of Negotiable Instruments, 1938; Georgia Law of Evidence, 1957. Contbr. articles to law jours. Home: Lullwater Dr Athens GA 30601

GREEN, THOMAS GEORGE, architect; b. Ackley, Ia., July 12, 1931; s. Thomas Chalmers and Marie Angeline (Dentel) G.; B.A., U. Chgo., 1951, B.D., 1955; B.Arch., Yale, 1959. With Architects Collaborative, 1959-65, asso., 1964-65; asso. Benjamin Thompson & Assos., architects, Cambridge, Mass., 1966—; ordained to ministry United Ch. of Christ, 1955. Commd. minister Bd. Homeland Ministries, 1962-69. Eliel Saarinen Traveling fellow Yale, 1959. Mem. A.I.A., Delta Upsilon. Democrat. Club: Yale (Boston). Important works include Greylock Residential Houses, williams Coll., High Sch., Bennington, Vt., Design Research Bldg., Harvard Sch. Edn. Library, Cambridge. Home: Boston MA 02116 Office: Cambridge MA 02138

GREEN, WILLIAM CLINTON, lawyer; b. Tyler, Fla., Jan. 14, 1907; s. William Henry and Nettie Loraine (Brooks) G.; student U. Fla., 1926-27, U. Miami (Fla.), 1927; m. Phoebe Diehl, Jan. 28, 1955; childrenClinton Marvin Tyler, Janice (Mrs. Fred Grothe), Marjorie Jeanette, Melinda Jane, Melissa Anne, Melanie Roberta, Marcia Loreen. Admitted to Fla. bar, 1930, since practiced in Miami; mem. firm Green & Hastings, 1961-; dir. U. Miami Law Center, 1960-. Dir. for Fla. compensation dept. Fed. Civil Works Adminstrn., 1934. Served to 1st lt., judge adv. gen. dept. AUS, World War II; 1st lt. Res. Fellow Am. Coll. Trial Lawyers; mem. Am., Fla., Dade County (bd. dirs. 1960) bar assns., Law Sci. Acad. Am., Judge Adv. Gen. Assn., Am. Judicature Assn., Soc. Am. Mil. Engrs. Nat. Assn. Claimants Counsel Am., Acad. Fla. Trial Lawyers, Mil. Order World Wars, Res. Officer Assn., Sigma Phi Epsilon. Club: Miami Beach Rod and Reel. Home: 2616 Country Club Prado Coral Gables FL 33134 Office: Biscayne Bldg 19 W Flagler St Miami FL 33132

GREEN, WILLIAM E., Jr., banker. Vice pres., also omptroller Citizens and So. Nat. Bank. Office: 300 Bull St Box 9586 Savannah GA 31402*

GREEN, WILLIAM FREDERICK, adminstrv. psychiatrist; b. New Milford, Conn., Feb. 5, 1906; s. Frederick Rockwell and Catharine Ann (Turrill) G.; S.B., Harvard, 1928, M.D., 1932; m. Adrienne LaBauve, Jan. 29, 1945; 1 son, William Frederick. Intern L.I. Coll. Hosp., Bklyn., 1932-33; house officer Boston Psychopathic Hosp., 1933-35, Bellevue Hosp., N.Y.C., 1935-36, Hartford (Conn.) Retreat, 1936-38, sr. psychiatrist Bellevue Hosp., 1938-40; clin. dir. Fairfield Hills Hosp., Newtown, Conn., 1940-41, supt., 1946—; lecturer in psychiatry Yale Sch. Medicine, 1946-. Served as lt. comdr. M.C., U.S.N.R., 1941-46. Mem. A.M.A., Am. Psychiat. Assn. Conn. Med. Soc., Conn. Soc. Psychiatry and Neurology. Fairfield Co. Med. Assn., N.E. Soc. Psychiatry. Author articles med. jours. Home: Fairfield Hills Hospital Newtown CT 06470

GREEN, WILLIAM JOHN, educator, painter; b. Shawano, Wis., Jan. 4, 1942; s. Thomas Raymond and Mary Grace (Wandrey) G.; B.F.A., U. Notre Dame, 1964; M.F.A., U. Wis., 1967; m. Alynne Pfeiffer, Aug. 24, 1963; children—Anna Katherine, Phillip William. Tchr. painting, design Murray (Ky.) State U.; tchr. drawing, design Western Ky. U., Bowling Green. Recipient Jacques Silver medal fine arts U. Notre Dame, 1954; Louis Ritman prize Chgo. Art Inst., 1964, William Bartels prize, 1965. Home: 1340 State St Bowling Green KY

GREEN, WILLIAM JOHN, paper co. exec.; b. Muncie, Ind., July 25, 1915; s. George Wyatt and Blanche (Young) G.; student Ball State U., 1933-34, Ind. U., 1938-39; m. Judith Heiman, May 24, 1964; children—Stephen John, Philip Wyatt, Douglas Hanson, Christina Fields, Nicholas William. Sales mgr. Ball Bros. Co., Muncie, 1939-44; pres. Stone & Co., Louisville, 1944-52; pres. Thatcher Glass Mfg. Co., N.Y.C., 1952-62; chmn. bd. Clevepak Corp., N.Y.C., 1962—; dir. Distillers Corp.-Seagram's Ltd. Home: Oregon Rd Mt Kisco NY 10549 Office: 375 Park Av New York City NY 10020

GREEN, WILLIAM JOSEPH, congressman; b. Phila., June 24, 1938; s. William Joseph and Mary E. (Kelly) G.; grad. St. Joseph's Coll., 1960, Villanova Law Sch.; m. Patricia Anne Kirk; children—William Joseph, Katherine Kirk. Mem. 88th-92d Congress 5th Dist. Pa. Democrat. Address: House Office Bldg Washington DC 20515

GREEN, WILLIAM THOMAS, orthopedic surgeon; b. Waucoma, Ia., Aug. 29, 1901; s. William L. and Jessie Aiken (Scott) G.; A.B., Ind. U., 1921, A.M., 1922, M.D., 1925, D.Sc. (hon.). 1960; M.A. (hon.) Harvard, 1962; m. Gladys Griffith, Dec. 18, 1930; childrenWilliam T., Janet (Mrs. Henry W. Vaillant), Elisabeth Ann (Mrs. John T. Fogerty). Intern. Ind. U. Hosp., 1925-26; asst. resident gen. surgery, Henry Ford Hosp., Detroit, 1926-27, resident orthopedic surgery, 1928-29; asst. resident gen. surgery Peter Bent Brigham Hosp., 1929-30, asso. orthopedic surgery, 1933-46, chief orthopedic surgeon 1946-68, surgeon emeritus, 1968-; resident orthopedic surgery Children's Hosp., Boston, 1930-31, vis. orthopedic surgeon, 1932-46, orthopedic surgeon-in-chief, 1946—; asst. orthopedic surgery Harvard Med. Sch., 1934-40, asst. prof., 1940-46, clin. prof. orthopedic surgery, co-head dept., 1947-62, Harriet M. Peabody prof. orthopedic surgery, 1962-68, emeritus, 1968-, co-head dept., 1962-; dir. Mass. Infantile Paralysis Clinics, 1946-68, Mary MacArthur Meml. Respiratory and Rehab. Unit, 1950-68, program in phys. therapy Simmons Coll., 1948-68. Diplomate Am. Bd. Orthopaedic Surgery (past pres.). Mem. Am. Acad. Orthopaedic Surgeons (past pres.), Am. Acad. Cerebral Palsy (past pres.), Am. Acad. Pediatrics, Société Internationale de Chirurgie Orthopédique de Traumatologie, Brit. Orthopaedic Assn (hon.), Am. Orthopedic Assn., Assn. Bone and Joint Surgeons, Soc. Pediatric Research, Orthopedic Research Soc., N.E. Surg. Soc., Societa Italiana Di Ortopedia and Traumatologia (hon.). Phi Beta Kappa, Sigma Xi, Alpha Omega Alpha. Contbr. articles in field. Research orthopedic surgery, rehab. of children, human growth. Home: 126 Prospect St Belmont MA 02178 Office: 300 Longwood Av Boston MA 02115

GREENACRE, PHYLLIS, physician; b. Chgo., May 3, 1894; d. Isaiah Thomas and Emma (Russell) Greenacre; S.B., U. Chgo., 1913; M.D., Rush Med. Coll., 1916; m. Curt Paul Richter, Sept. 30, 1919 (div.); children—Ann (Mrs. William A. Roy), Peter. Faculty Johns Hopkins U. Med. Sch., 1917- 27; prof. clin. psychiatry Cornell U. Med. Coll., N.Y.C., 1935—; faculty N.Y. Psychoanalytic Inst., 1942—, pres., 1948-50, Freud Lectr., 1953; Brill Meml. lectr., 1956, Sloan lectr., 1969. Recipient Blackwell award, 1955, 62. Diplomate Am. Bd. Psychiatry and Neurology. Fellow N.Y. Acad. Medicine, Am. Psychiat. Assn; mem. Am. Psychoanalytic Assn., N.Y. Psychoanalytic Soc. (pres., 1956-57), Internat. Psychoanalyt. Assn. (treas. 1955-61), Phi Beta Kappa, Alpha Omega Alpha. Author: Trauma Growth and Personality, 1952; Swift and CarrollA Psychoanalytic Study, 1955; The Quest For the Father: A Study of the Darwin-Butler Controversy, 1963. Editorial bd. Psychoananlytic Study of the Child, 1945—. Contbr. articles to profl. jours. Address: 501 E 87th St New York City NY 10028

GREENAWALT, KENNETH WILLIAM, lawyer; b. Town of Wall Street, Colo., Oct. 9, 1903; s. William Eckert and Cora May (Cornell) G.; LL.B., Cornell U., 1927; m. Martha Frances Sloan, Sept. 3, 1929; children—William Sloan, Robert Kent, Ann Cornell, Kim Chandler. Admitted to N.Y. bar, 1929; since practiced in N.Y.C.; asso. Sackett, Chapman, Brown & Cross, 1927-30, Davies, Auerbach & Cornell, 1930-39, Davies, Auerbach, Cornell & Hardy, 1939-44, mem. firm, 1944-49, and successor firm, Davies, Hardy Ives & Lawther, 1949—. Mem. Edgmont Sch. Dist. Bd. Edn., Scarsdale, N.Y., 1957-62, Met. Opera Guild; mem. bd. regents L.I. Coll. Hosp. Recipient Woodford prize, Cornell, 1927, Am. Bar Assn. Gavel award, 1962, George Washington Honor medal Freedoms Found., 1962. Mem. U.S. Supreme Ct. bar, various fed. cts. Fellow Am. Coll. Trial Lawyers; mem. Soc. for Religion in Higher Edn. (bd. dirs.), Am. Acad. Polit. Sci., Am. (coms.), N.Y. (coms.), Westchester County bar assns., Am. Judicature Soc., Bar Assn. City of N.Y. (coms.), Am. Acad. Polit and Social Sci. Cornell Law Assn., N.Y. State Vet. Med. Soc. (hon.), Vet. Med. Assn. N.Y.C. (hon.), Sigma Delta Chi, Phi Sigma Kappa, Phi Delta Phi, Sphinx Head. Democrat. Conglist. (trustee). Clubs: Cornell of N.Y. City and Westchester Country; Westchester County Tennis (past pres.); Fox Meadow Tennis (Scarsdale); Harbor View (N.Y.C.). Contbr. to legal publs.; guest participant radio, tv programs. Home: 65 Highridge Rd Hartsdale NY 10530 Office: 2 Broadway New York City NY 10004

GREENAWAY, DONALD, univ. ofcl.; b. Frankfort, Mich., Apr. 14, 1911; s. George Henry and Mary Elizabeth (Orr) G.; B.A., Mich. State U., 1934; LL.D., Northwood Inst., 1970; m. Louise Constance Wadsworth, June 27, 1936; 1 dau., Jeanne Elizabeth (Mrs. Robert Mattice); m.2d, Lorraine Katherine Muellenbach, July 6, 1958; dau., Karen. Hotel adminstrn. and mgmt., 1934-41; food service exec. Trans World Airlines, 1946-47; prof. hotel adminstrn. Coll. Bus., Wash. State U., 1947-51; prof. adminstr.-dir. Sch. Hotel, Restaurant and Instl. Mgmt., Coll. Bus., Mich. State U., 1951-58; exec. v.p. Nat. Restaurant Assn., Chgo., 1958-70; asso. dean Sch. Hotel and Restaurant Mgmt., U. Houston, 1970—. Dir., Wilkensburg Hotel Co. (Pa.), Hotel Elkhart (Ind.). Mem. Gov. of Wash.'s Com. for Devel. State Wash., 1950-51; pres., founder Nat. Council Hotel and Restaurant Edn., 1946; adviser USPHS, USAF World-Wide Food Service; mgmt. cons. Soc. Advancement Food Service Research; mem. 5th Internat. World Food Congress; mem. U.S. Travel Service also trade assn. adv. com. U.S. C. of C.; trade missions to Europe auspices Dept. Commerce. Bd. dirs. Govs. Confs. Tourism Pacific N.W. 1947-49, Pacific N.W. Trade Assn., 1947-48. Served to capt. USAAF, 1942-46. Mem. Am. Assn. U. Profs., Am. Soc. Assn. Execs., Execs. Forum, Mich., Resort Assn., Mich. Pa. hotel assns., Food Execs. Assn., Internat. Ho-Re-Ca, Confrerie de la Chaine des Rotisseurs, Theta Chi, Alpha Kappa Psi. Rotarian. Author: Manual for Resort Operations, 1950; also monographs, papers, articles. Home: 5580 Longmont St Houston TX 77027

GREENAWAY, EMERSON, former librarian; b. Springfield, Mass., May 25, 1906; s. James and Sara Elizabeth (Lilley) G.; A.B. in L.S., U. N.C., 1935; B.S., U. Mass., 1927, L.H.D., 1952; Litt.D., Western Md. Coll., 1950, Drexel Inst. Tech., 1959; LL.D., Temple U., 1958; m. Helen Kidder, June 18, 1938; children—Ann, Jane (Mrs. John G. Sampson). Reference asst. City Library Assn., Springfield, Mass., 1928-30; supr. brs. and asst. librarian, Pub. Library, Hartford, Conn., 1930-34, 36; spl. asst. Enoch Pratt Free Library, Balt. 1935, librarian, 1945-51; librarian Pub. Library, Fitchburg, Mass., 1937-40, Free Pub. Library, Worcester, Mass., 1940-45; lectr. library adminstrn., Simmons Coll. Sch. Library Sci. Boston, 1942-45, Columbia U. Grad. Sch. Library Sci., 1963-64; dir. The Free Library of Phila., 1951-69. Dir. Forest Press, Inc. Cons. in pub. libraries for UNESCO, 1947-49. Mem. Adult Ednl. Council, Mus. Council, Spl. Library Council, all Phila.; Nat. Adv. Commn. Libraries, 1967; adv. com. Internat. Book and Library Programs; Pa. Adv. Council Library Devel., 1957-68; books across the sea com. English Speaking Union. Trustee Schuylkill Valley Nature Center, pres., 1970—; trustee Harcum Jr. Coll., Union Library Catalog, Phila., 1952-69, Phila. Art Alliance. Recipient 1954 Good Govt. award, 1955; Citation, Phila. Jr. C. of C. and U.S. C. of C.; Lippincott award A.L.A., 1955, Distinguished Achievement award Drexel Inst., 1965, Merit award Phila. Art Alliance, 1969. Mem. A.L.A. (council 1954—, exec. bd. 1954-60, pres., 1958- 59), Mass. (life), Pa., Md. (life) library assns., Franklin Inst. (library com.), Am. Philos. Soc. (councilor, library com.), Internat. Fedn. Library Assns. (exec. com. pub. libraries sect.). Clubs: Franklin Inn, Philobiblon; Science and Arts (Germantown); Boy's (New London, N.H.); Baltimore Bibliophiles; Appalachian Mountain. Home: 97 E Bells Mill Rd Philadelphia PA 19118 als New London NH 03257

GREENBAUM, DAVID, musician; b. Glasgow, Scotland, Mar. 29, 1908; s. Barnet and Annie (Wasserstrum) G.; ed. Scottish Nat. Acad., Royal Coll. Music London; m. Hilda Feinblatt, Apr. 29, 1938; children—Joan (Mrs. William Goldsmith), Marvin. Studied with W.E. Whitehouse, London; cellist Scottish Nat. Symphony, London Philharmonic Orch. at Covent Garden, 1937, BBC recitals, N.Y. Philharmonic Orch., 1941-46; mem. Cleve. Orch., 1940-44, Metropolitan Opera Co., 1944-48, Chgo. Symphony Orch., 1948—; solo cellist Russian Ballet, N.Y.C., 1939, Tommy Dorsey Orch., 1944; faculty Settlement Sch. Music, Cleve., 1940, Roosevelt U., Chgo., 1957. Named Chicagoan of Year for Outstanding Achievement, 1971; recipient Certificate of Merit for Outstanding Cultural Achievement from Mayor Daley, 1971; recipient Dir.'s scholarship Royal Coll. London, 1928-30. Home: 6818 N Ashland Blvd Chicago IL 60626 Office: 220 S Michigan Av Chicago IL 60604

GREENBAUM, DOROTHEA SCHWARCZ, sculptor; b. Bklyn., June 17, 1893; d. Max and Emma (Indig) Schwarcz; m. Edward S. Greenbaum, Oct. 21, 1920; children—David S., Daniel W. One man shows, N.Y.C., Washington, San Francisco, others; sculpture rep. permanent collections, Whitney, Moscow, Newark, Balt., Ogunquit (Me.), Toledo, N.J. state museums, Pa. Acad. of Arts, also many univ. museums, pvt. collections. U.S. del. 1st Internat. Conf. Arts, Venice, 1952; mem. advisory com. to combat artists U.S. War Dept., 1943-45. Recipient Widener Meml. medal Pa. Acad., 1941; grant Acad. Arts and Letters, 1947; medal of honor Nat. Assn. Women Artists, 1953; Cybis Purchase prize, Blumenthal Purchase prize (both N.J. State Mus.). Mem. Sculptors Guild (founding mem.). Audubon Artists, Nat. Inst. Arts and Letters, N.J. Council Arts. Home and studio: 104 Mercer St Princeton NJ 08540

GREENBAUM, JAMES RICHARD, food distbg. co. exec.; b. Cleve., July 3, 1933; s. Harold and Miriam (Lion) G.; B.A., Tulane U., 1955; m. Peggy Strauss, Jan. 29, 1955; children—Robert Strauss, James R., Clifford Harold. Vice pres., dir. Malone & Hyde, Inc., Memphis, 1967; pres., dir. F. Strauss & Son, Inc., Monroe, La., 1970—; chmn. bd. Strauss Distbrs. Ark., 1961—, Northgate Devel. Corp., Monroe, 1964—; exec. v.p., Strauss Liquor Corp., Monroe, 1957—, Falstaff Distbrs. Monroe Inc. 1957—, Gulf Inland Corp., Houston, 1959—; v.p. F. Strauss & Son Inc., Tallulah, La., 1957—; dir. S & D Realty, Little Rock; asst. sec. F. Strauss & Son, Inc., New Orleans, 1961—. Bd. dirs. Carolyn Rose Strauss Rehab. Center, Twin Cities YMCA, United Givers Fund, La. chpt. Nat. Soc. Crippled Children and Adults, United Jewish Fund N.E. La. Served as lt. AUS, 1955-57. Mem. Nat. Am. Wholesale Grocers Assn. (dir.), Zeta Beta Tau. Jewish religion (past pres., dir. temple). Clubs: Bayou DeSiard, Lotus (Monroe). Home: 3400 Deborah Dr Monroe LA 71201 Office: 2930 Commerce Av Monroe LA 71201

GREENBAUM, ROBERT SIMON, banker; b. N.Y.C., Sept. 29, 1922; s. Simon and Lottie (Rown) G.; grad. Am. Inst. Banking, 1949, Exec. Mgmt. Sch. N.Y. State Bankers Assn., 1961; student Bank Mgmt. Inst. N.Y.U., 1959; m. Adele Boltax, July 17, 1955; childrenRandy, Robert Charles, Laurie Jean. With Trade Bank & Trust Co., N.Y.C., 1939—, auditor, 1957-62, comptroller, 1962-70, v.p., 1970—. Active Am. Jewish Com., 1967. Served with F.A., AUS, 1943-46. Mem. Bank Adminstrn. Inst. (mem. exec. com. N.Y. chpt). Mason. Home: Valley Stream, NY 11580. Office: 592 Fifth Av New York City NY 10036

GREENBERG, BEN NORTON, surgeon; b. Omaha, May 30, 1903; s. Samuel and Rose (Coren) G.; A.B., U. Neb., 1925, B.Sc. in Medicine, 1926, M.D., 1928. Intern U. Neb. Hosp., 1928-30; Postgrad. Manhattan Eye and Ear Hosp., N.Y.C., 1930-32; resident Babies Hosp.-Columbia U. Med. Center, 1933; ship surgeon Am. Export and Grace Steamship Lines, 1934; practice medicine, specializing in eye, ear, nose and throat, York, Neb., 1934—; staff York Gen. Hosp. Chmn. Coordinating Council for Pub. Higher Edn. in Neb.; mem. nat. adv. council Center Disease Control, Atlanta. Bd. dirs. Neb. div. Am. Cancer Soc.; trustee Neb. Med. Found.; regent U. Neb., 1953-, pres. bd., 1957, 63, 68, v.p., 1967-70. Recipient Distinguished Service award Nat. Assn. Governing Bds. State Univs., 1962; Service to Mankind award Sertoma Internat., 1964. Diplomate Nat. Bd. Med. Examiners. Fellow A.M.A.; mem. A.C.S., Neb. Med. Assn. (councilor 1955-61), Nat. Assn. Governing Bds. State Univs. and Allied Insts. (pres. 1961-62, pres. found. 1961—), York County Med. Soc. (past pres.). Mason, Rotarian (Cadwallader award 1969). Home: McCloud Hotel York NB 68467 Office: First Nat Bank Bldg York NB 68467

GREENBERG, BERNARD GEORGE, educator; b. N.Y.C., Oct. 4, 1919; s. Samuel nd Lillie (Kidansky) G.; B.S., Coll. City N.Y., 1939; Ph.D., N.C. State U., 1949; m. Ruth Esther Marck, Apr. 7, 1946; children—Stanley Marc, Frances Kay, Raymond Seth. Chmn. dept. biostatistics Sch. Pub. Health, U. N.C., 1949—; Kenan prof., U. N.C., 1969—; cons. WHO, NIH. Served to capt., inf., AUS, 1941-46; ETO. Recipient Bronfman prize, Am. Pub. Health Assn., 1966. Fellow Internat. Statis. Inst.; mem. Biometric Soc. (pres. 1971), Am. Statis. Assn., Am. Pub. Health Assn. Jewish religion. Editor: (with A.E. Sarhan) Contributions to Order Statistics; asso. editor of Review Internat. Statis. Inst. Contbr. articles profl. jours. Home: 425 Brookside Dr Chapel Hill NC 27514

GREENBERG, BYRON STANLEY, newspaper exec.; b. Bklyn., June 17, 1919; s. Albert and Bertha (Getleson) G.; student Bklyn. Coll., 1936-41; m. Helena Marks, Feb. 10, 1946; children—David, Eric, Randy. Circulation mgr. N.Y. Post, 1956-62, circulation dir., 1962-63, bus. mgr., 1963—; sec., dir. N.Y.. Post Corp., 1966—. Served with AUS, 1942-45. Home: 2920 Harbor Rd Merrick NY 11566 Office: 210 South St New York City NY 10002

GREENBERG, CARL, journalist; b. Boston, Aug. 19, 1908; s. Harry and Fannie (Herman) G.; student extension div. U. Cal. at Los Angeles, 1927; m. Gladys Bilansky, July 12, 1930; 1 son, Howard Allan. Reporter Los Angeles Evening Express, 1926-28, City News Service of Los Angeles, 1928-33, Los Angeles Examiner, 1933-43, polit. editor, 1943-62; polit. writer, mem. editorial bd. Los Angeles Times, 1962-68, 68-, polit. editor, mem. editorial bd., 1966-68. Disaster acting gov. Cal., 1959-67. Served as coxswain USCGR, World War II. Recipient 1st prize for best news story So. Cal. Newspaper Writers, Los Angeles chpt. Theta Sigma Phi, 1944; Silver award Cal.-Nev. Asso. Press, 1957. Mem. Order of Hound's Tooth (charter), Coast Guard League, Sigma Delta Chi, Kappa Tau Alpha. Mem. B'nai B'rith. Club: Greater Los Angeles Press. Home: 6001 Canterbury Dr Culver City CA 90230 Office: Times-Mirror Sq Los Angeles CA 90053

GREENBERG, CHARLES, psychiatrist; b. N.Y.C., Mar. 18, 1906; s. Enoch and Rachel (Greenberg) G.; student Fordham U., 1923-25; B.S., N.Y.U., 1927; postgrad. Dartmouth, 1927-29; M.D., U. Chgo., 1931; m. Ruth Ostroff, Apr. 21, 1940; childrenEllen Ann (Mrs. Allwyn Levine), Nina Jean. Intern City Hosp., N.Y.C., 1931-33; resident psychiatry Grasslands Hosp., Valhalla, N.Y., 1933-34, Syracuse Psychiat. Hosp., 1934-35; practice medicine, specializing in psychiatry, Wingdale, N.Y., 1935-52, Sonyea, N.Y., 1952- 57, Rome, N.Y., 1957-; asst. dir. Harlem Valley State Hosp., 1935-52; dir. Craig Colony Sch. and Hosp., 1952-57, Rome State Sch., 1957—. Guest lectr. Upstate Med. Center, Syracuse, N.Y. Bd. dirs. United Fund, Rome. Served to lt. comdr. USNR, 1943-46. Recipient Stuckart Meml. award for service to mentally retarded, 1963. Diplomate Am. Bd. Psychiatry and Neurology. Fellow Am. Psychiat. Assn. (past br. pres.), Am. Assn. on Mental Deficiency; mem. Livingston County (past sec.-treas.), Oneida County med. socs. Mason, Rotarian. Address: Rome State Sch Box 550 Rome NY 13440

GREENBERG, EDWARD, economist, educator; b. Jersey City, June 22, 1936; s. Abraham and Sylvia (Dechowitz) G.; B.S., N.Y.U., 1957; M.S., U. Wis., 1959, Ph.D., 1961; m. Joan B. Siegel, June 14, 1959; children—Arthur M., Lisa J. Instr., U. Wis., 1961-62, asst. prof., 1962-63; asst. prof. Washington U., St. Louis, 1963-65, asso. prof., 1965-69, Ford Found. faculty fellow, 1965-66, prof., chmn. dept. econs., 1969—. Cons. Midwest Program Airborne Television, 1963-64, Fed. Res. Bank of St. Louis, 1963-65, Social Security Adminstrn., 1965, Rand Corp., 1967-69, President's Task Force on Communications Policy, 1968. Bd. dirs. B'Nai Amoona Synagogue. Mem. Am. Econ. Assn., Econometric Soc. Democrat. Home: 7307 Princeton Av University City MO 63130 Office: Box 1208 Washington U St Louis MO 63130

GREENBERG, FRANK, lawyer; b. Chgo., July 21, 1910; s. Samuel and Sophie (Nowosenitz) G.; Ph.B., U. Chgo., 1930, J.D. cum laude, 1932; m. Bernice Jenks, Nov. 12, 1938. Admitted to Ill. bar, 1932, since practiced in Chgo.; partner firm Greenberg, Keele, Lunn & Aronberg, and predecessors, 1938—. Dir. Tee-Pak, Inc., Oppenheimer Casing Co. Chmn. spl. inquiry Commn. Ill. Supreme Ct., 1969. Gen. counsel Nat. P.T.A., 1949- -. Served to lt. comdr. USNR, 1942-45. Mem. Am., Ill., Chgo. (chmn. grievance com. 1963, inquiry com. 1959-60, bd. mgrs. 1964-66, 1967—, pres. 1969-70) bar assns. Clubs: Standard (Chgo.); Army, Navy (Washington). Home: 320 W Oakdale Av Chicago, IL 60657. Office: N LaSalle St Chicago IL 60602

GREENBERG, HANK, baseball club exec.; b. N.Y.C., Jan. 11, 1911; student N.Y.U., 1930; m. Caral Gimbel, 1946 (div. 1959); 3 children. With Detroit Tigers farm team, 1930-33, major league team, 1933-4O, 46-47; sold to Pittsburgh Pirates, 1947; farm dir. Cleveland Indians, 1948-49, gen. mgr., 1949-57, dir. reorgn. of club, 1956; v.p., treas., gen. mgr. Chgo. White Sox, 1959-61, past dir. Served with AUS, 1940-46. Elected to baseball's Hall Fame, 1956; recipient most valuable player award Am. League, 1935, 40; former major league home run champion. Home: 16470 S Park Blvd Shaker Heights OH 44120 Office: White Sox Baseball Club 324 W 35th St Chicago IL 60616*

GREENBERG, HOWARD, govt. ofcl.; b. N.Y.C.., Feb. 8, 1911; s. Jacob Mayer and Rose (Stein) G.; B.C.S. with highest honors, Benjamin Franklin U., 1937, M.C.S., 1938; m. Rose Kaufman, Aug. 24, 1931; 1 dau., Cynthia Irene. Chief budget and finace Civilian Conservation Corps, Dept. Interior, 1935-41; financial and adminstrv. mgmt. OPA, 1942-46; owner retail food market, 1946; dep. dir. budget War Assets Adminstrn., 1946-48; pres. wholesale-retail liquor corp., 1949; with budget office HHFA, 1950; with Gen. Services Adminstrn., 1951-53, 54-62, 63-66, commnr. utilization and disposal service, 1963-66; dep. comptroller Small Bus. Adminstrn., 1953, dep. adminstr. for investment, 1966-67, dep. adminstr., 1967-69; dir. found. study, select com. on small bus. U.S. Ho. of Reps., 1969-70, staff dir., 1970—; asso. dir. charge mgmt. Peace Corps, 1962-63; asst. prof. accounting Benjamin Franklin U., 1937-44; lectr. Civil Service Commn. insts., 1959-69; cons. chief staff U.S. Army, 1949. Recipient Outstanding Achievement award Fed. Govt. Accountants Assn., 1963; Meritorious Service award Gen. Services Adminstrn., 1961; Distinguished Service award, 1967, Adminstrs. Spl. Service award, 1968 (both Small Bus. Adminstrn.). Mem. Fedn. Govt. Accountants Assn. Democrat. Jewish religion. Home: 7426 Arrowwood Rd Bethesda MD 20034 Office: House Select Committee on Small Business Rayburn House Office Bldg Washington DC 20515

GREENBERG, IRWIN MORTON, psychiatrist; b. Bklyn., Sept. 21, 1930; s. Max and Clara (Passweg) G.; B.A. summa cum laude, N.Y.U., 1951, M.D., 1955; D.M.S. (USPHS fellow), State U. N.Y., Downstate Med. Center, 1968; Intern, L.I. Coll. Hosp., 1955-56; resident Bronx Municipal Hosp. Center-Albert Einstein Coll. Medicine, 1956-58, Nat. Inst. Mental Health, 1959-60; clin. asso. Nat. Inst. Mental Health, 1958-60; staff psychiatrist Hillside Hosp., Glen Oaks, N.Y., 1960-67; chief of service Bronx State Hosp., 1967-68, dep. dir., 1968-69; dir. Creedmoor State Hosp., Queens Village, N.Y., 1969-71; chief, div. psychiatry Waterbury Hosp., Waterbury, Conn., 1972—; asst. clin. prof. psychiatry Albert Einstein Coll. Medicine, 1967; adj. prof. psychology York Coll., Queens, N.Y., 1970-71; mem. faculty Yale U. School Med., 1972—. Chmn. comprehensive care com. Queens Fedn. Mental Health and Mental Retardation Agys., 1970—. Bd. dirs. Queenborough Council for Social Welfare; mem. adv. com. Queens County Mental Health Soc. Fellow Am. Psychiat. Assn.; mem. A.M.A., A.A.A.S., Am. Psychol. Assn. Address: Waterbury Hospital Robin St Waterbury CT 06720

GREENBERG, J. MAYO, astrophysicist, educator; b. Balt., Jan. 14, 1922; s. Henry and Ree (Goldenberg) G.; Ph.D., Johns Hopkins, 1948; m. Naomi Slovin, June 21, 1947; children—Toby, Joshua, Shelly, Jonathan. Physicist NACA, Langley Field, Va., 1944-46; asst. prof. U. Del., Newark, 1948-51; research asso. Inst. for Fluid Dynamics and Applied Math., U. Md., 1951-52; asst. prof. physics Rensselaer Poly. Inst., Troy, N.Y., 1952-56, asso. prof., 1956-57, prof., 1957-70, dir. astronomy 1967-70; leading prof. dept. astronomy and space sci. State U. N.Y., Albany, 1970—; mem. faculty Enrico Ferni Internat. Summer Sch., Varenna, Italy, 1961; mem. Inst. Advanced Study Princeton, N.J., 1965-66. OEEC sr. vis. fellow U. Leiden (Holland), 1961, initiated new chair Lab. Astrophysics, 1968-69. Mem. Internat. Scientific Radio Union Commn. VI; mem. organizing com. Commn. 34 Internat. Astron. Union or Nebulae and Interstellar Matter; mem. organizing com. various internat. meetings. Fellow Am. Phys. Soc.; mem. Internat. Astron. Union, Am. Astron. Soc., Sigma Xi. Developed and applied theories of scattering of light by small particles, theories of potential scattering, studies on interstellar matter. Home: 2126 Union St Schenectady NY 12309 Office: Dept Astronomy and Space Sci State U NY at Albany Albany NY

GREENBERG, JACK, lawyer; b. N.Y.C., Dec. 22, 1924; s. Max and Bertha (Rosenberg) G.; A.B., Columbia, 1945, LL.B., 1948; LL.D., Morgan State Coll., Central State Coll., 1965; m. Sema Ann Tanzer, Feb. 19, 1950 (div. 1970); children—Josiah, David, Sarah, Ezra; m. 2d, Deborah M. Cole, 1970. Admitted to N.Y. bar, 1949; research asst. N.Y. State Law Revision Commn., 1949; asst. counsel N.A.A.C.P. Legal Def. and Ednl. Fund, 1949-61, dir.-counsel, 1961—; argued in sch. segregation, sit-in, other cases before U.S. Supreme Ct. Bd. dirs. Mexican Am. Legal Def. Fund. Served to lt. (j.g.) USNR, 1943-46. Fellow Am. Coll. Trial Lawyers; mem. Am. (commn. to study FTC, adv. com. to spl. com. on crime prevention, sect. on individual rights and responsibilities), N.Y. State (exec. dir. spl. com. study state antitrust laws 1956—) bar assns., Bar Assn. City N.Y. Author: (with H. Hill) Citizens Guide to Desegregation, 1955; Race Relations and American Law, 1959. Contbr. articles legal jours. Home: 22 Knightsbridge Rd Great Neck NY 11021 Office: 1172 Park Av New York City NY 10028

GREENBERG, JOANNE, author; b. Bklyn., Sept. 24, 1932; d. Julius Lester and Rosalie (Bernstein) Goldenberg; B.A., Am. U., 1955; m. Albert Greenberg, Sept. 4, 1955; children—David, Alan. Tchr. exptl. class etymology Jefferson County (Colo.) Sch. System, 1963—. Recipient H. & E. Daroff Meml. award fiction, 1963; Fromm-Reichmann award Am. Acad. Psychoanalysis, 1967. Author: The King's Persons, 1963; I Never Promised You A Rose Garden, 1964; The Monday Voices, 1965; Summering, 1966; In This Sign, 1970 (Kenner award 1971). Address: Route 3 Box 321 Golden CO 80401

GREENBERG, JOSEPH H., educator; b. Bklyn. May 28, 1915; s. Jacob and Florence (Pilzer) G.; A.B., Columbia, 1936; Ph.D. in Anthropology (Social Sci. Research Council fellow), Northwestern U., 1940; m. Selma Berkowitz, Nov. 23, 1940. Faculty U. Minn., 1946-48; asst. prof. Columbia, 1948-53, asso. prof., 1953-57, prof. anthropology, 1957-62; prof. Stanford, 1962-, also chmn. com. on African studies; dir. Nat. Def. Edn. Act. African Lang. and Area Center, 1967—. Vis. prof. Summer Linguistic Inst., Mich. U., 1957, U. Minn., 1960; mem. panel anthropology and philosophy and history of sci. NSF, 1959-61; vis. prof. summer inst. U. Colo., 1961; dir. West African Langs. Survey, 1959-. Served with Signal Intelligence Corp., AUS, 1940-45. Stanford fellow, 1958-59; Ford Found. grantee, 1952, 57-62; recipient Demobilization award Social Sci. Research Council, 1945-46; Guggenheim award, 1954-55; Haile Selassie award for

African research, 1967. Mem. Am. Anthropol. Assn. (rep. to gov. bd. Internat. Inst. 1955—, 1st distinguished lectr. 1970), Linguistic Soc. Am. (exec. com. 1953-55), West African Linguistics Soc. (chmn. 1965-66), African Studies Assn. (exec. com. also com. on langs. and linguistics, 1959—, pres. 1964-65), Nat. Acad. Scis., Phi Beta Kappa. Author: Languages of Africa, 1963; Essays in Linguistics, 1957; Universals of Language, 1963; Influence of Islam on a Sudanese Religion, 1946; Anthropological Linguistics: An Introduction, 1968. Co-editor, Word, 1950-54; asso. editor Jour. of African Langs., 1962-. Home: 860 Mayfield St Stanford, CA 94305.

GREENBERG, LEON ARNOLD, educator; b. New Britain, Conn., Apr. 27, 1907; s. Max and Sarah (Wallof) G.; Ph.B., Yale, 1930, Ph.D., 1933; m. Lillian Freeman, July 24, 1934; children—Richard, Martha, Robert. Mem. faculty Yale, 1933-62, successively instr., asst. prof., asso. prof., asso. dir. lab. applied physiology, 1933-55, dir. lab. applied physiology, 1955-62; prof. physiology, dir. research lab. Rutgers U. and Center Alcohol Studies, New Brunswick, N.J., 1962—. Author, lectr. Mem. A.A.A.S., Am. Physiol. Soc., Nat. Safety Council, N.Y. Acad. Scis., Sigma Xi. Inventor of Alcometer. Pres., asso. editor Quar. Jour. Studies on Alcohol. Home: 91 Philips Dr Princeton NJ 08540 Office: Rutgers U New Brunswick NJ 08903

GREENBERG, MAURICE RAYMOND, ins. co. exec.; b. N.Y.C., May 4, 1925; s. Jacob and Ada (Rheingold) G.; pre-law certificate U. Miami (Fla.), 1948; LL.B., N.Y. Law Sch., 1950; J.D. (hon.), New Eng. Sch. Law, 1970; m. Corinne Phyllis Zuckerman, Nov. 12, 1950; childrenJeffrey W., Evan G., Lawrence S., Cathleen J. Admitted to N.Y. bar, 1953; with Continental Casualty Co., 1952-60, v.p. charge marketing and advt., accident and health dept., 1959-60; pres., dir. Am. Home Assurance Co., 1962-69, chmn., dir., 1969—; pres. Ins. Co. State Pa., 1962—, Am. Internat. Life Assurance Co. N.Y., 1962-68, chmn., dir., 1968—; v.p. C.V. Starr & Co., Inc., 1961-66, exec. v.p., 1966-68, pres., dir. 1968-; vice chmn. dir. Am. Internat. Reins. Co.; pres., dir. Transatlantic Ins. Co., 1967-; pres. Am. Internat. Group 1967—; chmn., dir. Nat. Union Fire Ins. Co., 1968—, Commerce and Industry Ins. Co., 1968—; pres., dir. C.V. Starr and Co., 1968—. Trustee N.Y. Law Sch., Coll. Ins. Served to capt. with AUS, World War II, also Korea. Decorated Bronze Star medal. Mem. Young Pres. Orgn., N.Y. Bar Assn., Fgn. Policy Assn., Sigma Alpha Mu. Clubs: Bankers, Casualty and Surety (N.Y.C.); India House. Home: 1001 Park Av New York City NY 10028 Office: 102 Maiden Lane New York City NY 10005

GREENBERG, MAX, labor union ofcl.; b. N.Y.C., Aug. 6, 1907; s. Isaac and Mollie (Beigel) G.; m. Billie Garfinkle, Sept. 21, 1929; childrenMartin Lewis, Marsha Lee. Joined retail men's furnishing union, 1929; organized Retail Union of N.J., local 108, 1936, pres., 1936-54; v.p. Retail, Wholesale and Dept. Store Union, 1946-54. pres., 1954-; exec. bd. CIO, 1954-55; mem. gen. bd. AFL-CIO, 1955—, v.p., 1967—; mem. exec. bd. AFL-CIO indsl. union dept., mem. adminstrv. com. AFL- CIO com. polit. edn. Mem. regional bd. War Labor Bd., World War II; mem. N.J. Bd. Mediation, 1949-54; mem. labor adv. council Pres.'s. Com. on Equal Employment Opportunity, also U.S. Office Econ. Opportunity. Bd. dirs. Inst. Collective Bargaining and Group Relations, also A. Philip Randolph Inst. Home: 47 Stanford Av West Orange NJ 07052 Office: 101 W 31st St New York City NY 10001

GREENBERG, MILTON, corp. exec.; b. Carteret, N.J., Apr. 21, 1918; s. David and Eva (Salzer) G.; student Coll. City N.Y., 1934-40; B.A., N.Y.U., 1943; M.P.A., Harvard, 1954; Sc.D., Canaan Coll., 1962; m. Maxine Carol Baer, June 30, 1948; childrenEve Diane, David Max, Alan Baer. Research and devel. planner Air Force Cambridge Research Center, 1947-49, dep. dir. operations and planning Geophysics Research div., 1947-54, dir. Geophysics Research Directorate, 1954-58; pres. Geophysics Corp. of Am. (name changed to GCA Corp.), 1958—. First chmn. tech. mgmt. council, Air Research and Devel. Command, U.S. del. to XIth Gen. Assembly, Internat. Union Geodesy & Geophysics, 1957; mem. Upper-Air Rocket & Satellite Research Panel; mem. central radio propagation lab. adv. panel of Nat. Acad. Scis., 1963-1966. Served from cadet to maj. USAAF, 1942-47; geophysicist. Recipient exceptional civilian service citation USAF, 1957. Trustee Coll. Advanced Sci., Canaan, N.H. Mem. A.A.A.S., Am. Geophys. Union, Am. Meteorol. Soc., Internat. Assn. Geomagnetism and Aeronomy, Internat. Assn. Meteorology and Atmospheric Physics, Internat. Union Geodesy and Geophysics, U.S. Rocket and Satellite Research Panel, Am. Inst. Aeros. and Astronautics, Sci. Research Soc. of Am., Mu Chi Sigma, Beta Lambda Sigma. Editor-in-chief Planetary and Space Science, 1957-62, editorial adv. bd., 1962-. Home: 46 Sagamore Dr Andover MA 01810 Office: GCA Corp Burlington Rd Bedford MA 01730

GREENBERG, MOSHE, educator; b. Phila., July 10, 1928; s. Simon and Betty (Davis) G.; B.A. with honors, U. Pa., 1949, Ph.D., 1954; M.H.L., Jewish Theol. Sem Am., 1954; m. Evelyn Doris Gelber, June 21, 1949; children—Joel, Raphael, Ethan. Asst. prof. Hebrew, U. Pa., Phila., 1954-57, asso. prof., 1957- 61, prof. Biblical studies, 1961-65, A.M. Ellis prof. Hebrew and Semitic langs., 1965-70; vis. prof. Bible, Jewish Theol. Sem. Am., N.Y.C., 1966- 70; vis. lectr. Hebrew U. Jerusalem (Israel), 1961, prof. Bible, 1970- -. Mem. Bible translation com. Jewish Publ. Soc. Am., 1966—. Recipient Harbison award Danforth Found., 1967. Guggenheim fellow, 1961. Fellow Am. Acad. Jewish Research; mem. Biblical Colloquium, Am. Oriental Soc., Soc. Biblical Lit., Phi Beta Kappa. Author: The Hab/piru, 1955; The Religon of Israel, 1960; Introduction to Hebrew, 1965; Understanding Exodus, 1969. Monograph editor Jour. Biblical Lit., 1959-66; div. editor Ency. Judaica, 1968—. Home: 29 Benjamin of Tudela St Jerusalem Israel Office: Department of Bible Hebrew U Jerusalem Israel

GREENBERG, NATHAN, accountant; b. Worcester, Mass., May 17, 1919; s. Samuel and Ida (Katz) G.; B.S. in Bus. Adminstrn., Boston U., 1942; m. Mimi Aaron, Mar. 12, 1950; children—Henry Aaron, Ruthanne. With Internal Revenue Service, 1945-47; v.p. finance Gt. Am. Plactics Co., Worcester, Mass., 1948—, also dir.; mng. partner Nathan Greenberg & Assos., C.P.A.'s, Worcester, 1958—; treas., sec. King's Dept. Stores, Inc., now financial v.p., sec., dir.; dir. Berkshire Frocks, Inc. Trustee Nathan and Mimi Greenberg Charitable Trust, Jewish Home for Aged, Jewish Community Center, Jewish Fedn. Served with AUS, 1942-45; ETO. Decorated Bronze Star. C.P.A., Mass. Fellow Am. Inst. C.P.A.'s., Mass. Soc. C.P.A.'s., Controllers Inst. Am.; mem. Mu Sigma. Club: Mt. Pleasant Country (v.p. 1962—Boylston, Mass.). Home: 5 Santult Lane Worcester MA 01609 Office: 390 Main St Worcester MA 01608

GREENBERG, OSCAR WALLACE, educator, physicist; b. N.Y.C., Feb. 18, 1932; s. Joseph Jacob and Betty (Sklower) G.; B.S., Rutgers U., 1952; A.M., Princeton, 1954, Ph.D., 1957; m. Yael Shapiro, May 27, 1969. Instr., Brandeis U., 1956-57; NSF postdoctoral fellow Mass. Inst. Tech., 1959-61; faculty U. Md., College Park, 1961—, prof. physics, 1967—. Mem. Inst. Advanced Study, fall 1964-65; vis. asso. prof. Rockefeller U., 1965-66; vis. prof. Tel-Aviv U., 1968- 69. Served to 1st lt. USAF, 1957-59. Sloan research fellow, 1964-66; Guggenheim fellow, 1968-69. Fellow Am. Phys. Soc.; mem. Am. Math. Soc., Phi Beta Kappa. Home: 902 Kenbrook Dr Silver Spring MD 20902 Office: Dept Physics Astronomy Univ Md College Park MD 20742

GREENBERG, PAUL, newspaperman; b. Shreveport, La., Jan. 21, 1937; s. Ben and Sara (Ackerman) G.; B. Journalism, U. Mo., 1958, M.A. in History, 1959; student Columbia Grad. Sch., 1960-62; m. Carolyn Levy, Dec. 6, 1964; children—Daniel, Ruth Elizabeth. Lectr. Am. history Hunter Coll., 1962; editorial page editor Pine Bluff (Ark.) Comml., 1962-66, 67—; Syndicated columnist, 1970—; editorial writer Chgo. Daily News, 1966- 67. Served to capt. AUS, 1969. Recipient Grenville Clark award for best editorial, 1964; Pulitzer prize editorial writing, 1969; award Nat. Newspaper Assn., 1968. Republican. Jewish religion. Home: 2406 W 39th St Pine Bluff AR 71601 Office: 300 Beech St Pine Bluff AR 71601

GREENBERG, SAM U., chem. mfg. co. exec.; b. Stamford, Conn., Sept. 20, 1907; s. Isaac and Mary (Wittenberg) G.; B.S., U. Cal., 1929; m. Edith Wilson, Mar. 18, 1932; children—Sydne (Mrs. K. Howard), Robert David. Tech. dir. Cal. Ink Co., 1940-42; tech. mgr. Dorward & Sons Co., 1943-46; mgr. resin dept. Pacific Paint & Varnish Co. subsidiary Sears, Roebuck & Co., 1947-50, gen. mgr., 1951-53, Sears, Roebuck Paint & Wallpaper Factories, 1953-56; pres., dir. DeSoto Chem. Coatings, Inc. (name changed to DeSoto, Inc.), 1956-67, chmn, bd., chief exec. officer, 1967-68, chmn. exec. com., 1969-71, also dir. Mem. Am. Chem. Soc., Sigma Xi, Sigma Alpha Mu. Office: 1700 Mt Prospect Rd Des Plaines IL 60018

GREENBERG, SANFORD DAVID, computer corp. exec.; b. Buffalo, Dec. 13, 1940; s. Carl and Sarah (Fox) G.; A.B., Columbia, 1962, M.B.A., 1966; M.A., Ph.D. (Woodrow Wilson fellow Woodrow Wilson Dissertation fellow), Harvard, 1965, postgrad. Law Sch., 1965-66, (Marshall scholar) Oxford (Eng.) U., 1964-65; m. Susan Beth Roseno, Aug. 12, 1962; children—Paul Eric, James Albert. Asst. prof. govt. Columbia, N.Y.C., 1965; faculty Center for Internat. Affairs, Harvard, Cambridge, Mass., 1966; asst. to Pres.'s sci. adviser, Washington, 1966-67; dir. corporate devel. System Devel. Corp., Washington, 1967-68; chmn. bd. EDP Tech., Inc., Washington, 1968-71; vice chmn. KMS Industries, 1971—. Pres., Columbia Coll. Class of 1962. Trustee Nat. Braille Press, Charles River Acad., Cambridge Ford's Theatre Soc., Opera Soc. Washington; bd. dirs. Nat. Com. on U.S.-China Relations. Named One of 10 Outstanding Young Men of Boston, One of 4 Outstanding Young Men of Mass., One of 10 Outstanding Young Men Am., 1966; White House fellow. Mem. Young Presidents Orgn., Am. Polit. Sci. Assn., Am. Hist. Assn., Oxford Union Soc., Assn. Computing Machinery, Phi Beta Kappa, Zeta Beta Tau. Clubs: Federal City; Harvard of N.Y., International, Harmonic. Patentee device for compression and expansion of speech. Home: 700 New Hampshire Av NW Washington DC 20037 Office: 2600 Virginia Av NW Washington DC 20037

GREENBERG, SIMON, educator, rabbi; b. Horoshen, Russia, Jan. 8, 1901; s. Morris and Bessie (Chaidenko) G.; brought to U.S., 1905; naturalized, 1924; student U. Minn., 1920-21; A.B., Coll. City N.Y., 1922; Rabbi, Jewish Theol. Sem., N.Y.C., 1925; Ph.D., Dropsie Coll., Phila., 1932; D.D., Jewish Theol. Sem. Am., 1950; postgrad. Hebrew U. in Jerusalem, Am. Sch. for Oriental Research, Jerusalem, 1924-25; m. Betty Davis, Dec. 13, 1925; childrenMoshe, Daniel Asher. Rabbi, Har Zion Temple, Phila., 1925-46; lectr. Jewish edn. Jewish Theol. Sem., 1932-41, asso. prof. edn., 1941-48, provost, 1946, prof. edn. and homiletics, 1947—, acting pres., 1948-49, vice chancellor, v.p. faculties, 1951; dir. U. Judaism Los Angeles, 1948-58, pres., 1958-66, chancellor, 1966—. Bd. dirs. Phila. Psychiat. Hosp. Pres. Rabbinical Assembly Am., 1937-39; past pres. Avukah- Intercoll. Zionist Orgn., Phila. br. United Synagogue, Phila. Bd. Jewish Ministers; mem. nat. exec. com. Zionist Orgn. Am. pres. Phila. br., 1941-44, chmn. nat. edn. com., 1943-45; exec. dir. United Synagogue Am., 1950-53; mem. exec. com. World Zionist Orgn.; chmn. United Synagogue Commn. on Jewish Edn., 1962-67; mem. praesidium World Council on Jewish Edn., 1964-68; past mem. chaplains religious council U. Pa. Fellow Con. on Sci., Philosophy and Religion. Author: Living as a Jew Today; 1939; The Harishon Series, 1942; Ideas and Ideals in the Jewish Prayer Book, 1940; The First Year in the Hebrew School; A Teacher's Guide, 1945; The Conservative Movement in Judaism, 1954, Israel and Zionism, Conservative Approach, 1955; God, Man, Torah and Israel, 1957; The SeminaryAn Evaluation, 1960; Foundations of a Faith, 1968; Words of Poetry 1970. Home: 420 Riverside Dr New York City NY 10025 Office: 3080 Broadway New York City NY 10027

GREENBLATT, LOUIS, lawyer; b. Austria, Sept. 24, 1905; LL.B., N.Y. U., 1926. Admitted to N.Y. State bar, 1928, U.S. Supreme Ct. bar, 1964; mem. firm Tenzer, Greenblatt, Fallon and Kaplan; lectr. Practising Law Inst., 1956—. Mem. Assn. Bar City N.Y. (mem. real property com. 1957-60), N.Y. County Lawyers Assn. Contbr. articles to profl. jours. Office: Pfizer Bldg 235 E 42d St New York City NY 10017*

GREENBLATT, MILTON, psychiatrist; b. Boston, June 29, 1914; s. Julius and Sophia (Bolonsky) G.; A.B. summa cum laude, Tufts U., 1935, M.D. cum laude, 1939; m. Gertrude Anna Rogers, June 10, 1941; children—David John, Daniel Lawrence. Charleston research fellow, instr. physiology Tufts U. Sch. Medicine 1939-40, prof. psychiatry, 1963—, Alpha Omega Alpha lectr., Bergendahl Meml. lectr., 1963; intern gen. medicine Beth Israel Hosp., Boston, 1940-41; intern psychiatry Mass. Mental Health Center, Boston, 1941-42, dir. Electroencephalography Lab., 1942-63, sr. physician, 1943- 45, dir. labs., research, 1946-63, dir. clin. psychiatry, 1953-57, asst. supt., 1957-63; practice medicine specializing in psychiatry, Boston, 1941—; supt. Boston State Hosp., 1963-67; asso. clin. prof. psychiatry Med. Sch. Harvard, 1958-63, lectr. psychiatry, 1963—, lectr. dept. social relations, 1957-63; Eugene Barrera Meml. lectr. Albany Med. Sch., 1955; Israel Strauss Meml. lectr. Hillside Hosp., N.Y.C., 1962; lectr. div. psychiatry Sch. Medicine Boston U., 1963—. Cons. on research WHO; cons. Nat. Inst. Mental Health; commnr. Mass. Dept. Mental Health, 1967—. Chmn., Task Force on Research Mass. Mental Health Planning Project, 1963-64; mem. profl. adv. council Nat. Assn. Mental Health; mem. Vol. Program Pres.'s Task Force on War Against Poverty, 1964. Trustee U. Mass.; bd. dirs. Am. Bd. Psychiatry and Neurology. Fellow Am. Psychiat. Assn. (Hofheimer prize 1951, Gold Medal award as supt. Boston State Hosp. 1964, past pres. No. New Eng. Dist. br., chmn. com. community aspects psychiatry, councilor 1966-69, chmn. commn. on drug safety 1966-68), Boston Med. Library; mem. Mass. Soc. Research Psychiatry (past pres.), Mass. Med. Soc. (past chmn. sect. psychiatry, neurology), Am. Coll. Neuropsychopharmacology (past pres.), Group for Advancement Psychiatry Am. Psychopath. Assn., A.A.A.S., Am. Acad. Neurology. Club: Harvard (Boston). Author: (with others) From Custodial to Therapeutic Patient Care in Mental Hospitals, 1955; Author, editor: Studies in Lobotomy, 1950; (with Harry C. Solomon) Frontal Lobes and Schizophrenia, 1953; (with others) the Patient and the Mental Hospital, 1957; (with Benjamin Simon) Rehabilitation of the Mentally Ill; Social and Economic Aspects, 1959; (with others) The Prevention of Hospitalization, 1963, Drug and Social Therapy in Chronic Schizophrenia, 1965. Editor: (with others) Mental Patients in transition, 1961, College Students in a Mental Hospital, 1962, Halfway House: A Sociocultural and Clinical Study of Rutland Corner HouseA Transitional Aftercare Residence For Female Psychiatric Patients, 1965; Threat of Impending Disaster, 1965; Seminars in Psychiatry; (with others) Poverty and Mental Health, 1967; (with others) Adolescents in a Mental Hospital, 1968; (with others) Dynamics of Institutional Change, 1971. Asso. editor: Am. Jour. Psychiatry, 1965—; editorial bd. Quar. Jour. Studies on Alcohol, 1958—, Jour. Health and Human Behavior, 1959—, Psychiatric Opinion, 1962—; Psychophysiology, 1963-68, Comprehensive Psychiatry, 1965—, New Eng. Jour. Medicine, Existential Psychiatry. Home: 11 Burnside Rd Newton MA 02161 Office: Dept Mental Health 190 Portland St Boston MA 02114

GREENBURG, DAN, author; b. Chgo., June 20, 1936; s. Samuel and Leah (Rozalsky) G.; B.F.A., U. Ill., 1958; M.A., U. Cal. at Los Angeles, 1960; m. Nora Ephron, Apr. 9, 1967. Copywriter, Lansdale Co., Los Angeles, 1960- 61, Carson Roberts Advt., Los Angeles, 1961-62; mng. editor Eros mag., N.Y.C., 1962-63; copywriter Papert, Koenig, Lois, advt., N.Y.C., 1963- 65; free-lance writer, N.Y.C., 1965—. Recipient Silver Key award Advt. Writers Assn. N.Y.C., 1964. Mem. Dramatists Guild, Authors Guild Am., A.F.T.R.A. Author: How To Be a Jewish Mother, 1964; Kiss My Firm But Pliant Lips, 1965; How to Make Yourself Miserable, 1966; Chewsday, 1968; Jumbo the Boy and Arnold the Elephant, 1969; Philly, 1969; Porno-Graphics, 1969; (plays) Arf, 1969; The Great Airplane Snatch, 1969; also articles. Contbr. to Off- Broadway rev. Oh, Calcutta!, 1969. Home: 323 E 50th St New York City NY 10022

GREENE, ALVIN CARL, Tv producer, author; b. Abilene, Tex., Nov. 4, 1923; s. Alvin Carl and Marie (Cole) G.; B.A., Abilene Christain Coll., 1948; m. Betty Dozier, May 1, 1950; children—Geoffrey, Mark, Eliot, Meredith Elizabeth. Mem. staff Abilene Reporter-News, 1948-52, amusements editor, 1957-60; book store owner, Abilene, 1952-57; spl. instr. Hardin-Simmons U., 1957; book editor, editorial columnist Dallas Times Herald, 1960-68, editor editorial page, 1963-65; staff U. Tex., Austin, 1968-69; exec. editor Southwestern Hist. Quar., 1968-69; exec. producer KERA-TV, Dallas, 1970-71; free-lance writer, 1950—. Served with USNR, 1943-46; PTO, CBI. Recipient award Nat. Conf. Christians and Jews, 1964. Dobie-Paisano fellow, 1968. Mem. Tex. Inst. Letters (pres. 1969-71, award 1964), Tex. Electric Railroaders Assn. Presbyn. Club: Dallas Press. Author: A Personal Country, 1969; Living Texas, 1969; The Last Captive, 1971. Home: 10640 Lennox Lane Dallas TX 75229

GREENE, ANTHONY STORM, constrn. equipment co. exec.; b. Aurora, Ill., Apr. 28, 1925; s. William B. and Jane (Smith) G.; B.S., U. Cal. at Los Angeles, 1948; m. Barbara Anderson, Aug. 31, 1946; children—Christopher Storm, Mary Kimberly. With Barber-Greene Co. and subsidiaries, Aurora, 1948—, pres. B/G Can. (Toronto), 1956-63, v.p. internat., Aurora, 1963-69, dir., 1966—, exec. v.p., 1969-71, pres., 1971—; dir. B/G Americas, B/G Australia, B/G do Brazil, B/G Europa (Netherlands), B/G Eng., Growth Industry Shares, Inc., Chgo. Mem. exec. bd. Boy Scouts Am. Served with USMCR, 1943-46. Mem. Constrn. Industry Mfrs. Assn., Conveyor Equipment Mfrs. Assn., Ill., Aurora (v.p. 1966-67) chambers commerce. Home: 123 S Evanslawn Av Aurora IL 60507 Office: 400 N Highland Av Aurora IL 60507

GREENE, ARTHUR ALBERT, Jr., lawyer; b. Washburne, Me., Sept. 6, 1914; s. Arthur A. and Bertha (Hamlin) G.; B.A., Dartmouth, 1936; J.D. with distinction, U. Mich., 1939; m. Geraldine Giles, July 5, 1938; childrenArthur Giles, Richard Erwin. Admitted to N.H. bar, 1939; mem. firm Greene & Greene, North Conway, 1939-41, Sheehan & Phinney, Manchester, 1941-43; rent atty. OPA, N.H., 1944; partner firm McLane, Carleton, Graf, Greene & Brown, Manchester, 1944—. Mem. N.H., Manchester (pres. 1967) bar assns. Conglist. (trustee 1968—). Mason. Contbr., bd. govs. N.H. Bar Jour., 1962—. Home: 2367 Elm St Manchester NH 03104 Office: 40 Stark St Manchester NH 03101

GREENE, BALCOMB, artist; b. Niagara Faols, N.Y., May 22, 1904; s. Bert Stillman and Florence (Stover) G.; A.B., Syracuse U., 1926; A.M., N.Y.U., 1940; postgrad. U. Vienna, 1926-28; m. Gertrude Glass, 1926 (dec. 1956); m. 2d, Terry Trimpen, 1961. Tchr. Dartmouth, 1928-31; asso. prof. Carnegie Inst. Tech., Pitts., 1942-59; one man show J.B. Neumann's New Art Circle, N.Y.C., 1947, Arts and Crafts Center, Pitts., 1953, Bertha Schaefer Gallery annually, 1950-61, Am. U., 1957, Brookhaven Nat. Lab., 1959, Centre Culturel American, Am. embassy, Paris, 1960, Retrospective Exhbn. at Whitney Mus. Am. Art, N.Y.C., 1961, Saidenberg Gallery, N.Y.C., 1962- 68, Feingarten Galleries, Los Angeles, 1963, 64, Feingarten Galleries, Chgo., 1963, Art Center, Los Angeles, 1964, Tampa (Fla.) Art Inst. 1966, Santa Barbara (Cal.) Mus. Art, 1966, Phoenix Art Mus., 1966, Berenson Gallery, Bay Harbor Islands, Fla., 1968, 70, Fairweather-Hardin Gallery, Chgo., 1969, Adele Bednasz Galleries, Los Angeles, 1970, 71, Forum Gallery, N.Y.C., 1970, others; represented in permanent collections Mus. Modern Art, Whitney Mus. Am. Art, Solomon Guggenheim Mus., Met. Mus. (all N.Y.C.), Carnegie Inst., Pitts., Walker Art Center, Mpls., U. Neb., Joselyn Mus., Omaha, numerous others; also pvt. collections. Mem. Am. Fedn. Arts, Theta Beta Phi. Club: Cosmopolitan. Editor Art Front, 1935-36. Contbr. profl. pubs. Home: Montauk Point Long Island NY 11954 also 2 Sutton Pl S New York City NY 10022 Studio: 345 E 52d St New York City NY 10022

GREENE, BRUNO H., legal educator; b. Lwow, Austria-Hungary, Mar. 18, 1905; s. Joseph N. and Claire (Lieber) G.; J.U.D., U. Vienna (Austria), 1927; B.S., Columbia, 1949; LL.B., Rutgers U., 1952; m. Blanche Aberbach, Dec. 22, 1935; 1 dau., Josephine (Mrs. Carl J. Bachmann, Jr.). Admitted to Vienna bar, 1934, Minn. bar, 1966; individual practice law, Vienna, 1934-38; asst. law librarian Rutgers U., 1949-52; asst. prof. law Syracuse U., 1952-59, law librarian, 1952-59; prof. law, dir. law library U. Minn., 1960—; legal cons. Ford Found. grantee, 1959-60. Mem. Am. Bar Assn., Fgn. Law Assn., Order Coif. Contbr. articles legal jours. Home: 48 Groveland Terrace Minneapolis MN 55403

GREENE, BRYDON S., advt. exec.; b. N.Y., Mar. 8, 1911; s. Henry Ward and May (Hall) G.; student Chauncy Hall, 1930, Mass. Inst. Tech., 1931-33; B.F.A., Yale, 1935; m. Virginia Hitchcock, Jan. 2, 1938 (dec. Sept. 1955); 1 dau., Judith Lenox; m. 2d, Mary Will Kilgore, July 19, 1959. Design dept. Gen. Motors Corp., 1935-36; with Chrysler Corp., 1936-37; asst. advt. mgr. Lever Bros., 1938-45; with N.W. Ayer & Son, Inc., Phila., 1945-, v.p., mgr. Phila. office, 1952-56, dir., 1955-, v.p. in charge exec. service, 1956-68, exec. v.p., 1968—. Clubs: Merion Golf (Haverford, Pa.); Racquet (Phila.); San Francisco Golf. Home: 1100 Union St San Francisco CA 94119 Office: N W Ayer & Son Inc 2470 Crocker Plaza San Francisco CA 94104

GREENE, BURTON, composer, pianist; b. Chgo., June 14, 1937; s. Henry M. and Yvette (Bolner), G.; student U. Ill., 1955-56. Town Hall and Judson Hall concerts, 1964, Jazz Composers concerts, 1965, Music in Our Times series, 1966, 67, N.Y. State Council Arts coll. tour, 1966, Eastern colls. tours, 1967, 68, Jazz Interactions concerts, 1967, Jazz clubs concerts, 1967, Village Theatre concerts, 1967; tchr. Henry St. Music Sch.; lectr. New music, Compser for solo piano and small orch. Recording artist ESP Disk Recording, (with quartet) Columbia Records. Address: 193 Eldrige St New York City NY 10002

GREENE, CHARLES CASSIUS, advt. exec.; b. Sullivan, Ill., June 6, 1897; s. Cassius Wilbur and Katherine (Mouser) G.; Ph.B., U. Chgo., 1919, J.D., 1921; postgrad. Sch. Commerce Northwestern U., 1932-33; m. Ursula Lally. Account exec. Albert Frank, advt., Chgo., 1926-31, Carroll Dean Murphy advt., Chgo., 1931-36; v.p. Critchfield & Co., advt., Chgo., 1936-40, Buchanan & Co., advt., Chgo., 1940-44; v.p., resident mgr., dir. Doremus & Co., advt. and pub. relations, Chgo., 1944-70, cons., 1970—. Served as 2d lt., inf., U.S. Army, World War I. Admitted to Ill. bar. Mem. Pub. Relations Soc. Am. (past pres. Chgo., nat. v.p.), Chgo. Athletic Assn., Phi Beta Kappa, Ill. C. of C., Phi Kappa Psi, Phi Delta Phi. Republican. Rotarian. Clubs: Chicago Press, Executives, South Shore County. Home: 1642 E 56th St Chicago IL 60637 Office: 208 S La Salle St Chicago IL 60604

GREENE, CHARLES HERBERT, educator; b. Troy, Pa., Sept. 26, 1904; s. Charles Nelson and Minna (Silliman) G.; A.B., Haverford Coll., 1926; A.M., Harvard, 1927, Ph.D., 1930; m. Winifred Moores, July 16, 1930; childrenCharles Moores, David Graham, Megan Elizabeth. Research chemist Corning Glass Works, 1930-31, 37-53; faculty instr. Harvard, 1931-37; prof. glass sci. State U.N.Y. Ceramic Coll. Alfred U., 1953-70; prof. Nat. U. Cordoba, Argentina, 1971—. Fellow Am. Ceramic Soc., A.A.A.S., mem. Am. Chem. Soc., Soc. Glass Tech., Internat. Glass Commn., Phi Beta Kappa, Sigma Xi, Phi Kappa Phi, Alpha Chi Sigma, Lambda Chi Alpha. Rotarian. Home: Jerico Hill P O Box 804 Alfred NY 14802

GREENE, DAVID HERBERT, educator; b. Boston, Nov. 4, 1913, s. Herbert Alva and Anne (Roche) G.; B.A., Harvard, 1936, M.A., 1938, Ph.D., 1943; m. Catherine J. Healy, June 24, 1939; childrenJudith (Mrs. Bruce Fields), Catherine J., Gail E., David G., Helen C. Instr. English Coll., New Rochelle, 1939-41; asst. prof. U.S. Naval Acad., 1941-46; mem. faculty N.Y.U., 1946-, prof. English, 1959-, head all univ. dept. English, 1964-. Served to lt. (j.g.) USNR, 1943-45; ETO. Rockefeller fellow, 1955-56; Fulbright Research fellow, Ireland, 1962-63. Mem. Modern Lang. Assn., Royal Soc. Antiquarians Ireland, Am. Com. Irish Studies. Author: (with Vivian' Merchier) 1000 Years of Irish Prose, 1952; An Anthology of Irish Literature, 1954; Short Stories of Chekhov, 1959; (with Dan H. Laurence) Bernard Shaw, The Matter with Ireland, 1962; (with E.M. Stephens) J.M. Synge, 1871-1909, 1959. Home: 29 Washington Sq W New York City NY 10011

GREENE, E. MILO, investment banker; b. Czernowitz, Austria, Feb. 2, 1898; s. Leopold and Cecelia (Zwickel) G.; student U. Vienna (Austria), 1919, U. Hamburg (Germany), 1922; m. Helen Margaret Stiefel, Jan. 15, 1932 (div. 1950); 1 son, John Peter; m. 2d, Lucette Olivar, June 27, 1951. Came to U.S., 1925, naturalized, 1938. Exec. officer grain import-export firm, Hamburg and Berlin, Germany, 1920-25; with H. Hentz & Co., N.Y.C., 1925—, mgr. fgn. dept., 1934-36, gen. partner charge fgn. dept., 1937—, mem. exec. com., 1960—, sr. partner, 1964—, also hon. chmn. bd.; dir. Lee Nat. Corp., Hookah Filter Corp., N.Y.C. Served to lt., inf. Austrian Army, World War I. Mem. N.Y. C. of C. Clubs: Harmonie, Marco Polo (N.Y.C.). Home: 993 Park Av New York City NY 10028 Office: H Hentz & Co 72 Wall St New York City NY 10005

GREENE, FRANCIS THORNTON, lawyer; b. N.Y.C., May 29, 1908; s. Frederick Stuart and Grace Emily (Clapp) G.; student St. Paul's Prep. Sch.; grad. Albany Acad., 1926; A.B., Va. Mil. Inst., 1930; LL.B., Harvard, 1933; m. Byrd Harrison Tucker, Oct. 28, 1933; children—Frances Bland, Stuart Thornton. Admitted to N.Y. bar, 1934; asso. Haight, Smith, Griffin & Deming, N.Y.C., 1933-34; staff gen. counsel's office SEC, Washington, 1934- 37, asst. dir. trading and exchange div., 1937-41; partner Tucker, Mays, Cabell & Moore, Richmond, Va., 1946-49; spl. counsel Sec. Def., Washington, 1949-50; dep. gen. counsel Fed. Maritime Bd., 1950-52, gen. counsel, 1952; exec. v.p. Washington office Am. Mcht. Marine Inst., 1953-55, pres., 1955-56; mem. Surrey, Karasik & Greene, 1956—. Served as comdr. USNR, 1941-45. Mem. Am., Va., D.C., Fed. bar assns. Episcopalian. Clubs: Metropolitan (Washington); Whitehall, Harvard (N.Y.C.). Contbr. numerous articles to profl. jours. Home: Hunting Ridge Warrenton VA 22186 Office: 1156 15th St NW Washington DC 20005

GREENE, FRED, educator; b. N.Y.C., Jan. 12, 1923; s. Max and Clara (Passweg) G.; B.A. magna cum laude, Coll. City N.Y., 1943; M.A., Yale, 1948, Ph.D., 1950; m. Ruth Light, Mar. 21, 1959; childrenAlicia Janet, Evelyn Paula, Joseph Steven, Carolyn Joan. Mem. faculty Williams Coll., Williamstown, Mass., 1949—, prof. polit. scis., 1961—, chmn. dept., 1968—; faculty Nat. War Coll., 1957-58; research analyst State Dept., 1962-63, dir. Office Research E. Asian and Pacific Affairs, 1966-68, cons., 1963-66, 68—. Served with AUS, 1942-46. Recipient Superior Honor award State Dept., 1968. Mem. Am. Polit. Sci. Assn., Phi Beta Kappa. Author: The Far East, 1957; Dynamics of International Relations, 1964; American Policy and the Security of Asia, 1968. Home: 54 South St Williamstown MA 01267

GREENE, FREDERICK DAVIS, II, educator; b. Glen Ridge, N.J., July 9, 1927; s. Phillips Foster and Ruth (Altman) G.; grad. Phillips Andover Acad., 1944; B.A., Amherst Coll., 1949; Ph.D., Harvard, 1952; m. Theodora Elizabeth Whatmough, June 5, 1953; children—Alan, Carol, Elizabeth, Phillips. Research asso. U. Cal., Los Angeles, 1952-53; instr. dept. chemistry Mass. Inst. Tech., Cambridge, 1953-55, asst. prof., 1955-58, asso. prof., 1958-62, prof., 1962—. Served with USNR, 1945-46. Alfred P. Sloan fellow, 1958-62, NSF Sr. Postdoctoral fellow, 1965-66. Mem. Am. Chem. Soc., Chem. Soc. (London), Am. Acad. Arts and Scis., Phi Beta Kappa. Editor-in-chief Jour. Organic Chemistry, 1962-. Contbr. articles sci. jours. Home: Winchester MA 01890 Office: Dept Chemistry Mass Inst Tech Cambridge MA 02139

GREENE, GEORGE BENJAMIN, Jr., air force officer; b. Laurens, S.C., Apr. 20, 1914; s. George Benjamin and Helen Louise (Crisp) G.; B.S., Clemson U., 1935; grad. flying tng., Kelly Field, Tex., 1938, Air War Coll., 1953; m. Jane Drake, Jan. 20, 1940; children-Susan, Charles Drake, Jacquelin. Commd. 2d lt. USAAF, 1935, advanced through grades to maj. gen. USAF, 1962; pilot and group engring. officer 8th Pursuit Group, Va. and N.Y., 1938-41; comdr. 35th Pursuit Squadron, New Guinea, 1941-43; group exec. officer 8th Pursuit Group, New Guinea, 1942-43; group Comdg. officer 423 Reconnaissance Fighter Group, La., 1943, 54th Fighter Group, Fla., 1943; asst. A-3, Hdqrs. III Fighter Command, Fla., 1943-44, Hdqrs. 3d Air Force, Fla. and Va., 1944-46; A-3 Tactical Air Command, Langley Field, Va., 1946-47; asst. chief staff, later chief staff Hdqrs. 6th Fighter Wing, C.Z., 1947- 48; asst. dep. chief, then dep. chief staff operations, Hdgrs. Cairo, C.Z., 1948-50; chief combat operations, operations and tng. Hdqrs. EADF, 1950-51; wing comdr. Hdqrs. 4710th Air Def. Wing, Del., 1951-52, Hdqrs. 4708th Air Def. Wing., Mich., 1953-56; dep. chief staff personnel Hdqrs. Air Def. Command, Ent AFB, Colo., 1956-59, chief staff, 1959-60; dep. comdr. Hdqrs. 17th Air Force, Ramstein AFB, Germany, 1960-61; dep. chief staff operations Hdqrs. USAFE, Wiesbaden, Germany, 1961-63; dir. mil. personnel Hdqrs. USAF, 1963-67; comdr. Lackland Mil. Tng. Center, Tex., 1967-. Decorated D.S.C., Silver Star, Legion of Merit, D.S.M., Air medal, numerous area and service ribbons. Mem. Air Force Assn., Night Fighters Assn., Order Daedalians. Home: 3260 Walnut St NE St Petersburg FL 33704

GREENE, GRAHAM, author; b. Berkhamsted, Hertfordshire, Eng., Oct. 2, 1904; s. Charles Henry and Marion (Raymond) G.; ed. Berkhamsted Sch., Balliol Coll., Oxford; hon. Litt.D., Cambridge U., 1962; hon. D.Litt., Edinburgh U., 1967; m. Vivien Dayrell-Browning, 1927; 1 son, 1 dau. Sub-editor London Times, 1926-30; lit. editor Spectator, 1940-41; with Fgn. Office, 1941-44; dir. Eyre & Spottiswoode, Ltd., 1944-48; dir. Bodley Head, 1958-68. Decorated Companion of Honour; Hon. fellow Balliol Coll. Author: Babbling April, 1925; The Man within, 1929; The Name of Action, 1930; Rumour at Nightfall, 1932; Stamboul Train, 1932; It's a Battlefield, 1934; England Made Me, 1935; The Basement Room (short stories), 1935; Journey Without Maps, 1936; A Gun for Sale, 1936; Brighton Rock, 1938; The Lawless Roads, 1939; The Confidential Agent, 1939; The Power and the Glory (Hawthornden prize 1940), 1940; British Dramatists, 1942; The Ministry of Fear, 1943; Nineteen Stories, 1947; The Heart of the Matter, 1948; The Third Man, 1950; The Lost Childhood & Other Essays, 1951; The End of the Affair, 1951; Essais Catholiques, 1953; Twenty-One Stories, 1954; Loser Takes All, 1955; The Quiet American, 1955; Our Man in Havana, 1958; A Burnt-Out Case, 1961; In Search of a Character, 1961; A Sense of Reality, 1963; The Comedians, 1966; May We Borrow Your Husband? and Other Comedies of the Sexual Life (short stories), 1967; Collected Essays, 1969; Travels with My Aunt, 1969; (plays) The Living Room, 1953, The Potting Shed, 1957, The Complaisant Lover, 1959; Carving a Statue, 1964; (for children, with Dorothy Graigie) The Little Train, 1947, The Little Fire Engine, 1950, The Little Horse Bus, 1952, The Little Steamroller, 1953; (screenplays) Brighton Rock, 1948; The Fallen Idol, 1948; The Third Man, 1949; Our Man in Havana, 1960; The Comedians, 1967. Address: Care Bodley Head 9 Bow St London WC 2 England

GREENE, HOKE SMITH, chemist, univ. adminstr.; b. Gray, Ga., Aug. 20, 1906; s. Samuel Alexander and Susan (Zellner) G.; A.B., Mercer U., 1927, D.Sc., 1963; M.S., U. Cin., 1928, Ph.D., 1930; fellow Inst. Internat. Edn. to Technische Hochschule, Karlsruhe, Germany, 1931-32; m. Stella Catherine Potter, Dec. 19, 1936. Chem. Supr. E.I. DuPont de Nemours & Co., 1930-31, 32-34; asst. prof. chem. engring. U. Cin., 1934-39, asso. prof., 1939-45, prof., head chemistry dept., 1945-56, fellow Grad. Sch. of Arts and Scis., 1947—, dean of grad, sch., 1947-59, dean acad. adminstrn., 1956-59, v.p., dean faculties, 1959-66, v.p. acad. affairs, 1966-67, v.p. research, 1967—. Cons. chemistry and bacteriologist; rep. from U. Cin. to Argonne Nat. Labs., U. Chgo., lectr. Registered chem. engr., Ohio. Fellow Ohio Acad. Sci.; mem. Fgn. Policy Assn. (dir. Cin. 1947-51), Am. Chem. Soc. (nat. councilor 1945-46, chmn. Cin. sect. 1948), A.A.A.S., Midwest Conf. Grad. Deans (v.p. 1947-48), Sigma Xi, Alpha Chi Sigma, Phi Lambda Upsilon, Omicron Delta Kappa. Clubs: Rotary, Torch (dir. 1947-50). Home: 2347 Vista Pl Cincinnati OH 45208

GREENE, SIR HUGH CARLETON, pub. co. exec., brewer; b. Berkhamsted, Eng., Nov. 15, 1910; s. Charles H. and Marion (Raymond) G.; B.A., Merton Coll., Oxford U., 1935, M.A., 1958; m. Helga Guinness, 1934; children—Graham, James; m. 2d, Elaine Shaplen, Sept. 24, 1951; children—Christopher, Timothy; m. 3d, Tatjana Sais, May 11, 1971. Mem. Berlin staff Daily Telegraph, 1934-38; chief corr., Berlin, 1938-39, Warsaw corr., 1939; head German service BBC, 1940-46; controller broadcasting Brit. zone Germany, 1946-48; head Eastern European services BBC, 1949-50; head Emergency Information Services, Malaya, 1950-51; asst. controller overseas services BBC, 1952-55, controller overseas services, 1955-56, dir. adminstrn., 1956-58, dir. news and current affairs, 1958-59, dir. gen., 1960-69, bd. govs., 1969-71; chmn. Bodley Head Pub. Co., Greene, King & Sons Ltd. Served with RAFVR, 1940. Decorated Order Brit. Empire; knight comdr. St. Michael and St. George. Author: (with Graham Greene) Spy's Bedside Book, 1957; The 3rd Floor Front, 1969; The Rivals of Sherlock Holmes, 1970; Cosmopolitan Crimes, 1971. Office: 9 Bow St London WC 2E 7AL England

GREENE, IRVING LEWIS, publisher; b. N.Y.C., Feb. 20, 1908; s. Andrew and Goldie (Schlesinger) G.; student Columbia, 1926-27, Am. Inst. Banking, 1928-29; m. Harriet Altschul, Apr. 2, 1933; 1 son, Andrew Frank. Asst. br. mgr. Bank of U.S., N.Y.C., 1924-30; asst. gen. sales mgr. Todd Co., Rochester, N.Y., 1932-50; pres., dir. Gerlach Barklow Co., Joliet, Ill., Artographic Corp., Joliet, 1951; v.p., gen. sales mgr. Products Corp., Newark, 1956-58; exec. v.p. United Printers & Pub., Inc., 1959-63, gen. mgr. all domestic operations, 1961-63; pres. Barker Greeting Card Co., Cin., 1963-64; with Allen Kander Assos., N.Y.C., 1964—; owner I.L. Greene Co., N.Y.C., 1967—. Payroll Savs. cons. U.S. Treasury, 1947-50. Past pres. Joliet Jewish Welfare Chest. Mem. Nat. Assn. Cost Accountants, Nat. Sales Execs. Club, Ill. C. of C. Clubs: Friars; Lake Isle Country. Home: 200 E 78th St New York City NY 10022 Office: 3 E 54th St New York City NY 10022

GREENE, GEORGE FREDERICK educator, biologist; b. Ames, Ia.; B.A., Ia. State U., 1936, M.A., 1937, Ph.D. with honors, 1940. Instr., Ia. State U., 1946-47; asst. prof. biology Johns Hopkins, 1947-50, asso. prof., 1950-62, prof., 1962--, chmn. dept., 1963-69; vis. lectr. Stanford, 1970-71. Active Boy Scouts Am., 4-H Club. Served with AUS, 1940-46. Mem. Am. Soc. Biologists, Md. Biologists, A.A.A.S., Am. Acad. Arts and Scis., Phi Beta Kappa. Home: 48936 W Hancock Blvd Baltimore MD 20206

GREENE, JAMES ETHERIDGE, univ. dean; b. Columbus, Ga., Feb. 22, 1911; s. Robert C. and Eleanor (Jenkins) G.; D.V.M., Auburn U., 1933, M.S., 1939; m. Mary Lynton McGehee, Oct. 22, 1934; children—James Etheridge II, Bruce McGehee, Edward Chesley, Mary Katherine. Jr. vet. U.S. Bur. Animal Industry, 1935; grad. asst. anatomy Ala. Poly. Inst., Auburn, 1937-38, asso. prof. small animal surgery and medicine, 1938-42, head depts. large and small animal surgery, 1946-58, dean Sch. Vet. Medicine, 1958—. Nat. cons. USAF, 1965-66; cons. div. physician manpower, gen. research support sci. adv. and rev. com. USPHS; mem. commn. on edn. for health professions Nat. Assn. State Univs. and Land Grant Colls. Councilman, Auburn City, Ala., 1955-56. Served to maj. USAAF, 1942-46. Mem. Am. Vet. Med. Assn. (chmn. exec. bd. 1965-66), Ala. Vet. Medicine Assn. (pres. 1957), Sigma Xi, Omicron Delta Kappa, Phi Eta Sigma, Phi Zeta. Clubs: Auburn Country, Rotary, Auburn Faculty. Author: (with J.V. LaCroix) Questions and Answers, 1951; (with W.S. Bailey) Metazoan Infections, Canine Medicine, 1953. Contbr. chpt. on Infectious Diseases, Yearbook of Agriculture, 1956. Contbr. articles profl. jours. Home: 517 Sanders St Auburn AL 36830

GREENE, JAMES NICHOLAS, mfg. and retailing co. exec.; b. Danbury, Conn., Dec. 29, 1909; s. Michael W. and Catherine (Brennan) G.; student Yale, 1926, Columbia, 1927; m. Jane Allen, Apr. 18, 1938; children—James N., Catherine (Mrs. William Hellauer), Michael, Peter. Vice pres., F.H. Lee Co., Danbury, 1929-54; treas., asst. to pres. Montecatini Soc., Milan, Italy and N.Y.C., 1955-63; v.p., sec. Botany Industries, Inc., N.Y.C., 1963—; dir. Fashion Park, Botany Products, Broadstreets Inc., Weber Heilbroner Inc., Harris Frank, Levensohn Bros. & Co. Mem. Conn. Bd. Edn., 1954-66; chmn. speakers bur. A.R.C., 1941—; mem. Pres.'s Com. Edn., 1960. Mem. Conn. Democratic Central Com., 1950—; candidate for Conn. Gen. Assembly, 1956. Mem. Conn. N.G., 1936-41. Recipient citation A.R.C., 1950. Mem. Am. Mgmt. Assn. Elk, Rotarian (past pres. Newtown, Conn.), K.C. (4, dist. dep. 1946-51). Home: Tauntnon Hill Newtown CT 06470 Office: 1290 Av Americas New York City NY 10019

GREENE, JEROME ALLAN, advt. exec.; b. N.Y.C., Mar. 25, 1934; s. Morris and Tessie L. (Abrams) G.; B.A. in Marketing, Coll. City N.Y., 1960; m. Ruth Doris Bronnenmayer, Apr. 28, 1956; 1 son, Richard Harris. Marketing research account supr. Ted Bates & Co., N.Y.C., 1965-66; mgr. consumer research J.B. Williams Co., N.Y.C., 1966-68; research account supr. Rumrill-Hoyt Inc., N.Y.C., 1968-70; dir. marketing research Marsteller, Inc., N.Y.C., 1970—. Served with USAF, 1953-57. Mem. Am. Marketing Assn. Club: Metropolitan New Jersey-New York Belgian Sheepdog (chmn. bd. dirs.). Home: 111 Warren Dr Matawan NJ 07747 Office: 866 3d Av New York City NY 10022

GREENE, JOHN JAMES, Canadian govt. ofcl.; b. Toronto, Ont., Can., June 24, 1920; s. Pete and Andree (Champagnol) G.; B.A., U. Toronto, 1948; grad. Osgoode Hall, 1950; m. Corinne Bedore, Sept. 2, 1948; children—Glenn, Peter, Jocelyn, Stephanie, Virginia. Called to Canadian bar, 1950; practice in Arnprior, Ont., 1950-65; mem. Ho. of Commons, 1963—; co-chmn. spl. joint com. Senate and Ho. of Commons on Consumer Credit; minister of agr. of Can., 1965-68; minister energy, mines and resources, 1968—. Canadian del. 54th Inter-Parliamentary Union Conf., Dublin, Ireland, 1965; chmn. UN/FAO World Food Program Pledging Conf., 1966; vice chmn. meeting ministers agr. to OECD, Paris, France, 1966. Served to flight lt. Canadian Air Corps, 1941-45. Decorated Distinguished Flying Cross. Mem. Canadian Legion, Mem. Liberal Party. Mem. Anglican Ch. Clubs: Rideau, Royal Ottawa Golf, Ottawa Hunt and Golf; University (Toronto); Niagara Falls (Canada). Home: 323 John St Arnprior Ontario Canada Office: House of Commons Parliament Bldgs Ottawa Ontario Canada

GREENE, JOHN WILLIAM, Jr., physician; b. East Orange, N.J., July 25, 1926; s. John William and Illinois (Dowler) G.; B.S., U. Pitts., 1948; M.D., U. Pa., 1952; m. Eugenie W. Wuichet, Sept. 4, 1954; children—Eugenie, Susan, Isobel. Intern U. Pa. Hosp., 1952-53, resident obstetrics and gynecology, 1953- 56; research fellow, then research asso. obstetrics and gynecology U. Pa. Sch. Medicine, 1956-59, asst. prof., 1959-63; prof. obstetrics and gynecology, chmn. dept. U. Ky. Coll. Medicine, Lexington, 1963—. Trustee Frontier Nursing Service, 1966—. Served with AUS, 1944-46. Recipient Great Tchr. award U. Ky., 1970. Diplomate Am. Bd. Obstetrics and Gynecology (asso. examiner). Fellow A.C.S., Am. Coll. Obstetricians and Gynecologists; mem. A.M.A., Am., Central assns. obstetricians and gynecologists, Soc. Gyneclogic Investigation. Author: (with others) Induction of Labor, 1965; also numerous papers. Home: 420 Bristol Rd Lexington KY 40502

GREENE, JOSEPH NATHANIEL, Jr., fgn. service officer; b. N.Y.C., Apr. 9, 1920; s. Joseph N. and Nanine (Pond) G.; grad. Hotchkiss Sch., 1937; B.A., Yale 1941; m. Edith Cowles, Mar. 21, 1942 (div. Aug 1960); children—Alice W., Nancy W., Edith E.; m. 2d, Christine O'Hara, Apr. 22, 1961; children—Joanna, John, stepdau. Susan O'Hara. Asst. instr. Phillips Acad., 1941, vice consul, Montreal, Que., Can., 1942, 3d sec., vice consul, Ottawa, Ont., Can., 1943; staff mem. U.S. Adv. Council, Allied Control Commn. for Italy, 1944; fgn. service officer, Trieste, 1946; 2d sec. vice consul., Rome, 1947-49; desk officer Dept. State Washington, 1949-52; consul, Singapore, 1952-54; 1st sec., Bonn, Germany, 1954-56; dep. dir. exec. secretariat Dept. State, Washington, 1956, spl. asst. to Sec. State, 1957-59; assigned Imperial Def. Coll., London, 1960; counselor embassy, dep. chief mission, Lagos, Nigeria, 1961-63; minister- counselor, dept. chief mission Am. embassy, New Delhi, India, 1963-68; dep. adminstr. Bur. Security and Consular Affairs, 1968-69, dep. asst. sec. state internat. orgn. affairs, 1969-70; minister-counselor, dep. chief mission Am. embassy, London, 1970-71; diplomat-in-residence Brandeis U., Waltham, Mass., 1971-72. Served with USNR 1944-46. Mem. Am. Fgn. Service Assn. Clubs: Metropolitan (Washington); Yale (N.Y.C.). Office: care Dept State Washington DC 20525

GREENE, JULE BLOUNTE, govt. ofcl.; b. Dublin, Ga., Aug. 15, 1922; s. Jule B. and Bette (O'Neal) G.; A.B., Mercer U., 1949, LL.B., 1950; m. George Williams, Aug. 22, 1952; childrenJames Herschel, Bradley O'Neal. Admitted to Ga. bar, 1950, Supreme Ct. bar, 1960; atty, SEC, Atlanta, 1950-53, Washington, 1956-58, atty.-in-charge, Miami, Fla., 1958-69, regional adminstr., Atlanta, 1969-; pvt. practice law, Macon and Waycross, Ga., 1953-56. Mem. Atlanta Fed. Exec. Bd., 1969-, Interagy. Bd. U.S. Civil Service Examiners, 1969-. Served with A.C., AUS, 1942-46. Recipient award for exemplary achievement in pub. adminstrn. William A. Jump Meml. Found., 1958. Mem. Fed. Bar Assn. (pres. S. Fla. chpt. 1961), Ga. Bar Assn., Kappa Alpha, Baptist. Rotarian. Home: 186 River Valley Rd NW Atlanta GA 30328 Office: 1371 Peachtree St NE Atlanta GA 30309

GREENE, LAURENCE FRANCIS, educator; b. Chgo., Jan. 11, 1912; s. Morris and Rose (Fledler) G.; B.S., U. Chgo., 1932; M.D., Harvard, 1936; Ph.D. in Urology, U. Minn., 1942; m. Rosalyn R. Ravits, June 24, 1951; childrenEdith, Richard, Nancy, James. Intern St. Luke's Hosp., Chgo., 1936-38; fellow Mayo Found., 1938-42; cons. urology Mayo Clinic, Rochester, Minn., 1942—; mem. Mayo Grad. Sch. Medicine, U. Minn., 1943—, prof. urology, 1963—. Mem. adv. bd. Am. Family Physician GP. Bd. dirs. Minn. Orch. Assn., 1966-, chmn. Rochester com., 1965-; bd. dirs. Rochester Festival Music, 1965-66; pianist, mgr. Notochords Orch., Rochester, 1958—. Am. Bd. Urology. Fellow A.M.A.; mem. Am. Urol. Assn., Am. Fertility Soc., Minn. Surg. Soc., Am. Soc. Nephrology, Soc. U. Urologists, Internat. Soc. Urologists, Sigma Xi; corr. mem. La Soc. Mexicana de Urologia, Soc. Medico-Quirurgica del Guayas. Contbr. profl. jours. Home: 1033 Plummer Circle Rochester, MN 55901. Office: 200 1st St SW Rochester MN 55901

GREENE, LAWRENCE VIVANS, retired army officer; b. Washington, Aug. 23, 1917; s. Douglass Taft and Eleanora (Lenihan) G.; B.S., U.S. Mil. Acad., 1941; m. Margaret Page Lindsay, May 9, 1942; children—Lawrence Douglass (dec. 1968), Anne Page (Mrs. Victor A. Skinner). Commd. 2d lt. U.S. Army, 1941, advanced through grades to brig. gen., 1967; staff asst. to Nat. Security Council planning bd., 1958-61; sr. adviser to minister of def. Korea, 1961-63; asst. dep. chief of staff for personnel Continental Army Command, Fort Monroe, Va., 1963-65; comdr. Combat Devels. Command armor agy., Fort Knox, Ky., 1965-67; comdg. gen. 3d inf. Div., also chief staff V Corps, Europe, 1967-69; comdg. gen. U.S. Army Tng. Center, Ft. Knox, 1969-70; asst. chief of staff for personnel Hdqrs. Mil. Assistance Command, Vietnam, 1970-71; retired, 1971. Decorated Silver Star, D.S.M., Legion of Merit, Bronze Star, Army Commendation medal, Joint Service Commendation medal. Mem. Assn. U.S. Army, U.S. Armor Assn., Mil. Order World Wars. Home: Box 104E Star Route 1 Beaufort SC 29902

GREENE, LEE SEIFERT, polit. scientist; b. Esbon, Kan., May 31, 1905; s. Eugene C. and Margaret E. (Cline) G.; B.M., U. Kan., 1927, A.B., 1930; postgrad. (German-Am. exchange fellow) U. Leipzig, 1930-31; A.M., U. Wis., 1932, Ph.D., 1934; student Brooking Instn., 1933-34, U. Mich., summer 1935; Social Sci. Research Council post-doctoral fellow, 1937-38; m. Dorothy H. Kuersteiner, Dec. 24, 1932; childrenHarriet Lee, Robert Everist. Instr. music U. Kan., 1926-30; instr. U. Wis., 1934-36; research asso. and supr. pub. adminstrn. TVA, 1936-37, 1938-41; lectr. U. Tenn., Knoxville, 1937, asst. prof. polit. sci., 1938-39, asso. prof., 1939-45, prof., 1945—, Distinguished prof., 1965—, acting head dept. polit. sci., 1942-46, head, 1946-71, dir. Bur. Pub. Adminstrn., 1945—; exec. dir. Harris County (Houston) Home Rule Commn., 1956-57; exec. sec. Knoxville, Knox County Met. Charter Commn., 1957-59; cons. Knoxville Met. Planning Commn., 1960; vis. prof. U. Ala., summer 1948, U. Cal., Los Angeles, summer 1949, Duke U., summer 1950, Syracuse U., 1950-51, U. Ga., 1961, 65. Mem. civil service bd., Knoxville, 1941-47, chmn., 1945-47. Cons. TVA, 1941-42, So. Regional Edn. Bd., 1952-53, FOA, 1954. Chmn. research com. Constl. Conv., Tenn., 1953; cons. ICA, 1955, Memphis Charter Com. mem., 1967, Shelby County Structure Com., 1969. Public panel mem. and labor arbitrator, Nat. War Labor Bd., Nat. Wage Stblzn. Bd., U.S. Conciliation Service, Fed. Mediation and Conciliation Service; arbitrator TVA; mem. nat. panel arbitrators Am. Arbitration Assn. Mem. Am., So. (pres. 1957-58) polit. sci. assns., Nat. Municipal League, Am. Soc. Pub. Adminstrn., Nat. Inst. Pub. Affairs (trustee 1961-71), Phi Beta Kappa, Phi Kappa Phi, Pi Kappa Lambda, Beta Theta Pi, Phi Mu Alpha. Mason. Author: (with V.H. Brown and Evan A. Iverson) Rescued Earth, The Public Administration of Natural Resources in Tennessee, 1948; (with D.R. Grant) A Future for Nashville, 1952, Metropolitan Harris County, 1957; (with R.S. Avery) Government in Tennessee, 1962, 2d edit., 1966; (with George Parthemos) American Government: Policies and Functions, 1967; (with M.E. Jewell, D.R. Grant) The States and the Metropolis; (with Dye and Parthemos) American Government: Theory, Structure and Process, 1969. Editor: (with R. deV. Williamson) Five Years of British Labour, 1945-50, 1950, Resources and Policy, 1951. Editor The Jour. of Politics, 1953-57, asso. editor, 1949-52. Spl. editor Conservatism, Liberalism, and Natl. Issues (Annals Am. Acad.), 1962, City Bosses and Political Machines, 1964 Contbr. articles. Home: 1410 Tugaloo Dr Knoxville TN 37919

GREENE, LORNE, actor; b. Ottawa, Ont., Can., Feb. 12, 1915; s. Daniel and Dora Greene; ed. Queen's U. (Can.), Neighborhood Playhouse Sch. of Theatre, N.Y.C.; m. Nancy Anne Deale, Dec. 1961. Am. debut in The Prescott Proposals, N.Y.C., 1953; starred in Stratford (Ont.) Shakespeare Festival, 1955; Broadway appearances include Speaking of Murder, 1956, Edwin Booth, 1958; appeared with New Play Soc., Earl Grey Players, Toronto, Ont.; founder, dir., actor Jupiter Theater, Toronto; commentator documentary film Churchill's Island; acted in motion pictures including The Silver Chalice, 1954, Tight Spot, 1955, Autumn Leaves, 1956, Peyton Place, 1957, The Hard Man, 1957, Gift of Love, 1958, The Buccaneer, 1958, The Trap, 1959; regular on TV series Bonanza. Served with RCAF. Mem. Actors Equity Assn., Screen Actors Guild, A.F.T.R.A. Address: Care NBC 30 Rockefeller Plaza New York City NY 10020

GREENE, MARK RICHARD, educator; b. Imbler, Ore., Oct. 28, 1923; s. Homer Cooper and Adah (Hicks) G.; A.B., Stanford, 1947, M.B.A., 1949; Ph.D., Ohio State U., 1955; m. Fanney Runolfs, Dec. 31, 1946; children—Irving Edward, Robert, Erik. Asst. prof. bus. adminstrn. U. Ore., 1949-51; lectr. Stanford, 1952; asst. Ohio State U., 1952-53; asst. prof. marketing Washington U., 1953-55; asso. prof. bus. adminstrn. U. Ore., Eugene, 1955-58, asso. prof. ins., 1958-61, prof., head dept. marketing, ins. and transp., 1961-67, dir. Center For Internat. Bus. Studies, 1967-70, acting dean Sch. Bus. Adminstrn., 1964-65; Distinguished prof. ins. U. Ga., Athens, 1970—. Inst. Basic Math. for Application to Bus. fellow Harvard, 1959-60; vis. prof. marketing Denver U., summer 1955; vis. prof. ins. U. of Cal., Los Angeles, summer 1965. Exec. sec. Am. Assn. Collegiate Schs. Bus., 1953-55. Served with USAAF, 1943-46. Mem. Am. Marketing Assn., Am. Finance Assn., Am. Risk and Ins. Assn. (pres. 1968-69), Phi Theta Kappa, Beta Gamma Sigma, Alpha Kappa Psi. Conglist. Author: Risk and Insurance, 1962, 2d edit., 1968; The Role of Employee Benefit Structures in Manufacturing Industry, 1964; Risk Aversion, Insurance and the Future, 1971; co-author: Mathematical Methods and Models in Marketing, 1962. Contbr. articles profl. to jours. Home: 335 St George Dr Athens GA 30601

GREENE, MICHAEL JOSEPH LENIHAN, ret. army officer; b. West Point, N.Y., July 4, 1919; s. Douglass Taft and Eleanora (Lenihan) G.; student Drexel Inst. Tech., 1936-37; B.S., U.S. Mil. Acad., 1941; M.A., U. Va., 1951; grad. Army Command and Gen. Staff Coll., 1943, U.S. Naval War Coll., 1959, U.S. Army War Coll., 1969; m. Ruth Eileen Conner, Jan. 1, 1946; children—Mary (Mrs. Richard Wesley Monk), Rebecca (Mrs. Michael Henrik Fellows), Michael J.L., Katharine. Commd. 2d lt. U.S. Army, 1941, advanced through grades to brig. gen., 1968; sec. Gen. Staff, U.S. 7th Army, Germany, 1956-58, Army Gen., Staff, Office Asst. Sec. Def., 1959-63; asst. African affairs Mil. Assistance Command, Vietnam, 1963-65; comdr. 2d Brigade, 1st Armored Div., Ft. Hood, Tex., 1965-66; fellow Council Fgn. Relations, 1966-67; asst. to chmn. Joint Chiefs Staff, 1967-68; dep. comdt. Army War Coll., 1968-70; asst. comdr. 25th Div., Vietnam, 1970-71; comdg. gen. Army Hdqrs. Area Command for Vietnam, 1971; ret., 1971. Decorated Silver Star, Legion Merit with 2 oak leaf clusters, D.F.C., D.S.M. Bronze Star, Air medal with 17 oak leaf clusters, Army Commendation medal, Purple Heart. Mem. Assn. Grad. U.S. Mil. Acad., Alumni Assn. U. Va., Assn. U.S. Army, Council on Fgn. Relations, Inst. for Strategic Studies, Middle East Inst., Middle East Studies Assn. Home: 8501 Cyrus Pl Alexandria VA 22308

GREENE, NATHAN IRA, former banker; b. Rochester, N.Y., Mar. 6, 1906; s. Myron W. and Laura (Lancaster) G.; A.B., Bowdoin Coll., 1928; m. Esther Newlin Smith, July 3, 1931; children—Timothy Gilpin, Nathanael N., Jane Priscilla (Mrs. Peter Dean Stephens). Trainee, N.Y. Trust Co., N.Y.C., 1928-31; v.p. Canal Nat. Bank, Portland, Me., 1931-55; v.p. Newton-Waltham Bank & Trust Co., Waltham, Mass., 1955-63, pres., chmn., 1963-70, chmn. bd., 1970-71; trustee Newton Savs. Bank (Mass.). Trustee Waltham Hosp.; overseer Bowdoin Coll. Home: 48 Cloyster Rd South Portland ME 04106

GREENE, NICHOLAS MISPLEE, educator, physician; b. Milford, Conn., July 11, 1922; s. Joseph N. and Nanine W. (Pond) G.; B.S., Yale, 1944, M.A., 1955; M.D., Columbia, 1946; m. Elizabeth R. Miller, May 21, 1946; childrenNicholas P., Cynthia R., Joseph Nathaniel II. Intern Presbyn. Hosp., N.Y.C., 1946-47; resident anesthesiology Mass. Gen. Hosp., Boston, 1949-51; vis. fellow U. Edinburgh (Scotland) and Royal Infirmary, 1951; asst. anesthetist Mass. Gen. Hosp., also instr. anesthesia Harvard Med. Sch., 1951-53; asso. prof. anesthesiology, asst. prof. pharmacology U. Rochester Sch. Medicine, also dir. anesthesia Strong Meml. Hosp., 1953-55; prof. anesthesiology, lectr. pharmacology Yale Sch. Medicine, also dir. anesthesia Yale-New Haven Hosp., 1955—. Served to lt. (j.g.), M.C., USNR, 1947-49. Diplomate Am. Bd. Anesthesiology. Mem. Assn. Univ. Anesthetists, Am. Soc. Anesthesiologists, Internat. Anesthesia Research Soc., N.E. Soc. Anesthesiologists, A.M.A., N.E. Med. Soc., Sigma Xi. Author Articles in field. Home: 1220 Ridge Rd Hamden, CT 06517. Office: 789 Howard Av New Haven CT 06504

GREENE, RALEIGH WILLIAMS, Jr., banker, lawyer; b. St. Petersburg, Fla., May 26, 1927; s. Raleigh Williams and Anne (Kenny) G.; B.S., B.A., U. Fla., 1950, LL.B., 1951; m. Nancy Hardison, Oct. 25, 1947; children—Raleigh Williams III, Michael Edward, Patricia Anne, Mark Christopher, Mary Evelyn. Admitted to Fla. bar, 1951; mem. firm Grazier, Feilding, Greene & Coit, 1951-54, Grazier, Greene & Coit, 1954-60, Greene & Davenport, 1960-67, Harrison, Greene, Mann, Davenport, Rowe & Stanton, 1967—; dir. First Fed. Savs. & Loan Assn., St. Petersburg, 1952—, v.p., 1963-64, gen. counsel, 1960-68, exec. v.p., 1964-68, pres., chief exec. officer, 1970—; dir. Founders Financial Corp. Fla., St. Louis Cardinals, 1940—. Chmn. bd. trustees St. Leo (Fla.) Coll. Served with AUS, 1946-48. Mem. Am., Fla., St. Petersburg bar assns., Kappa Alpha, Phi Delta Phi. Democrat. Roman Catholic. K.C. Home: 1239 43d Av N St Petersburg FL 33703 Office: First Fed Bldg PO Box 1509 St Petersburg FL 33731

GREENE, RICHARD LEIGHTON, educator; b. Rochester, N.Y., Jan. 18, 1904; s. James Gereau and Ruth (Leighton) G.; A.B., U. Rochester, 1926; A.M., Princeton, 1927; Ph.D., 1929; A.M. (hon.), Wesleyan U., 1956; m. Eleanor Foulkes Curtiss, June 5, 1944 (dec. 1950); stepsons—Stephen Alan Curtiss, Peter Andrew Curtiss. Instr. English, U. Rochester, 1929- 30, asst. prof., 1930-34, prof., 1934-42, Joseph H. Gilmore prof., chmn. dept. English, 1942-46; pres. Wells Coll., Aurora, N.Y., 1946- 50; vis. prof. English, Purdue U., 1951-52, U. Cal. (Berkeley), 1952-53, Cal. Inst. Tech., 1953-54; Frank B. Weeks vis. prof. English, Wesleyan U., Middletown, Conn., 1954-56, prof., 1956-60, Wilbur Fisk Osborne prof. English, 1960—. Research fellow Am. Council Learned Socs., 1931-32; vis. fellow Princeton, 1963-64, 68. Mem. Am. Musicological Soc., Modern Humanities Research Assn., Renaissance Soc. Am., Modern Lang. Assn., Mediaeval Acad. Am., Am. Assn. U. Profs., Johnsonians, Phi Beta Kappa, Alpha Delta Phi (Samuel Eells award 1963, pres. 1946-47). Republican. Presbyn. Clubs: University (hon., Rochester); Princeton (N.Y.C.); Graduates (New Haven); Nassau (Princeton). Editor; The Early English Carols, 1935; A Selection of English Carols, 1962. Contbr. articles, revs. to philol. jours. Office: Dept English Wesleyan U Middletown CT 06547

GREENE, RICHARD THADDEUS, savs. and loan exec.; b. Charleston, S.C., July 18, 1913; s. Richard Thaddeus and Martha (Black) G.; B.S., Hampton Inst., 1938; postgrad. N.Y.U., 1949, Wharton Sch. Banking and Finance U. Pa., 1938-39, Am. Savs. and Loan Inst., 1960-61; m. Virginia Lea, June 6, 1942; children—Cheryll, Richard Thaddeus. Asst. treas. Citizens & So. Bank & Trust Co., Phila., 1938-41; bus. mgr. Asso. Pubs., Inc., N.Y.C., 1945-58; sec., bus. mgr. Interstate United Newspapers, N.Y.C., 1958-60; with Carver Fed. Savs. & Loan Assn., N.Y.C., 1960—, v.p., 1966-68, exec. v.p., 1968-69, pres., 1969—; dir. Thrift Assns. Service Corp., Urban Devel. Corp. Treas. Bedford Stuyvesant Youth in Action, 1963-66; treas. N.Y.. Urban League, 1968—; bd. dirs. Citizens Budget Commn., 1969. Bd. mgrs. Bedford YMCA. Served with AUS, 1941-45; maj. Res. Named Omega Man of Year, 1967, Citizen of Year, 1969. Mem. U.S. Savs. and Loan League, N.Y. Hampton Alumni, Omega Psi Phi. Presbyn. (elder). Home: 117-41 193d St St Albans NY 11412 Office: 75 W 125th St New York City NY 10027

GREENE, ROBERT HARGRAVE, Jr., banker; b. Newark, July 7, 1929; s. Robert Hargrave and Lillie Mae (Snead) G.; student Va. Poly. Inst., 1948-50; LL.B., diploma in accounting LaSalle Extension U., 1955; certificate in savs. mgmt. Am. Inst. Banking, 1956; postgrad. U. Wis. Sch. Bank Adminstrn., 1967; m. June Mary Litterer, Sept. 27, 1952; children—Susan Ann, Robert Hargrave III, Pamela Mae. Asst. auditor Howard Savs. Instn., Newark, 1950-68; asst. auditor Bank of Commonwealth, Detroit, 1968-69, auditor, 1969-70, v.p., auditor, 1970. Mem. Bank Adminstrn. Inst. (sec. Detroit chpt. 1971—), Inst. Internal Auditors, Mich. High Sch. Athletic Assn. (ofcl. football 1959—). Home: 536 Fox River Dr Bloomfield Hills MI 48013 Office: 719 Griswold St Detroit MI 48231

GREENE, ROBERT ZEMON, vending co. exec.; b. Calumet, Mich., Dec. 28, 1898; s. Benjamin and Yetta (Yedor) G.; student pub. schs.; m. Nancy Jane Mickle, May 27, 1950. Sr. salesman IBM, 1914-20; intro. cigarette vending machine nationwide, 1927; founder with William H. Rowe, Rowe Cigarette Service Co., Inc., 1928, pres., 1928—, successor firm Rowe Corp. subsidiary I.T.T. Canteen Corp.; chmn. bd. P O P Assos., Inc., Plastetics, Inc.; dir. ITT Cante. Pres. Robert Z. Greene Found. Mem. Hall of Fame of Boston Conf. on Distbn.; life mem. ANTA. Trustee U. Miami, Mt. Sinai Hosp. Greater Miami, Cedars Lebanon Hosp. Mem. Am. Order Assn. Nationale Des Crois de Guerre of France (hon.), Nat. Automatic Merchandising Assn. (founder, dir., past pres.), U.S.C. of C., Soc. Advancement Mgmt. Clubs: Kiwanis (past dir.); National Sales Executives; Westview Country (Miami, Fla.); Harmonie. Author articles on automatic merchandising. Home: 112 Central Park W New York City NY 10023 Office: 31 E 17th St New York City NY 10003

GREENE, RONALD ROWE, educator, physician; b. Roslyn, Wash., Jan. 28, 1908; s. Ronald A. and Louise (Rowe) G.; B.S., Gonzaga U., 1929; M.D., Northwestern U., 1934, M.S., 1937; m. Elizabeth Paul, Sept. 21, 1935; children—Judith L., Eric P. Intern, St. Luke's Hosp., Chgo., 1934-35, resident 1935-36; pvt. practice medicine specializing in obstetrics and gynecology, Chgo., 1936—; faculty obstetrics and gynecology Northwestern Med. Sch., 1937-71, Anna Lapham prof., 1954-71; prof. obstetrics, gynecology U. Ill. Med. Sch., 1971—; mem. staff Ill. Masonic Hosp. and Med. Center, 1971—. Served with M.C., USNR, 1942-45. Mem. Am. Gynecol. Soc., Am. Assn. Obstetrics and Gynecology, Soc. Gynecol. Investigation, Am. Cytological Soc., Am. Coll. Obstetrics and Gynecology, A.M.A. Home: 904 Monroe St Evanston IL 60202 Office: 720 N Michigan Av Chicago IL 60611

GREENE, STEPHEN, painter; b. N.Y.C., Sept. 19, 1918; s. William and Augusta (Lasky) G.; art student Nat. Acad. Design, 1936-37, Art Student's League, 1937-38; B.F.A., U. Ia., 1942, A.M., 1945; m. Sigrid de Lima, 1953; 1 dau., Alison de Lima. Instr. art Ind. U., 1945-46, Washington U., St. Louis, 1946-47, Parsons Sch. Design, N.Y.C., 1947-56, Pratt Inst., N.Y.U., Art Students League; artist in residence Princeton, 1956-59; guest critic Columbia, 1961-64, asst. prof., 1964-67; asso. prof. Tyler Sch. Art, Temple Univ., 1968-; one-man show Durlacher Bros., N.Y.C., 1947, 49, 52, Grace Borgenicht Gallery, 1955, 58, 59, Staempfli Gallery, 1961, 64, 66, 69; retrospectives Dana and De Cordova Mus., 1953, Princeton, 1956, The Corcoran Gallery of Am. Art, 1963; exhbns. Whitney Mus., Art Inst. Chgo., Nat. Acad. Design, Milw. Art Inst., Va. Mus. Fine Arts, Met. Mus., Bklyn. Mus., Mus. Modern Art, Carnegie Internat., Musee d'Art Moderne of Paris, Found. Maeght, France; represented permanent collections Wadsworth Athenaeum, Hartford, Conn., St. Louis City Art Mus., Pasadena (Cal.) Art Mus., Va. Mus. Fine Arts, Rockhill Nelson Gallery, Detroit Inst. Art, Whitney Mus., Met. Mus., Corcoran Gallery, Washington, San Francisco Art Mus., Art. Inst. Chgo., Fogg Art Inst., Addison Gallery, Mus. Modern Art, Tate Gallery, London, Guggenheim Mus., High Art Mus., Atlanta, Chase Manhattan Bank, Tenn. Fine Arts Center, Rose Art Mus. Brandeis U., others; also in pvt. collections; represented Sao Paolo (Brazil) Biennal, 1961. Recipient purchase prize Va. Mus. Fine Arts, 5th biennial contemporary Am. painting, 1946; 2d prize Kearney Meml., Milw. Art Inst., 1946; bd. dirs. award John Herron Art Mus., 1946; 1st prize ann. contemporary Am. painting Cal. Palace Legion of Honor, 1947; Prix de Rome, 1949; purchase prize Contemporary Am. Painting Exhibit, Isaac Delgado Mus., New Orleans, 1958; Corcoran Fourth prize, 1965; $2,500 award Nat. Inst. Arts and Letters, 1967; $5,000 grant Council of the Arts, 1967. Home: Box 408 A Storms Rd Valley Cottage NY 10989

GREENE, STEWART, advt. agy. exec.; b. N.Y.C., June 24, 1928; s. Harry and Yetta (Katz) Greenbaum; B.S., N.Y. U., 1949; postgrad. Parsons Sch. Design; m. Iris Katz, Feb. 6, 1950; children—Lisa, Eric. Co-founder Wells, Rich, Greene, Inc., N.Y.C., 1966, sr. v.p., chief operating officer for creative services, 1966—. Recipient Art Dirs. Gold medal Internat. Broadcasting Finest Comml. in World Award, Andy award for Alka-Seltzer stomach comml., Am. Film Festival's Best Campaign award for Alka-Seltzer, 1965- 66, Art Dirs. Gold medal, Andy award for Benson & Hedges disadvantages comml., Am. Film Festival's Best Campaign award for Benson & Hedges, 1966- 67. Clubs: Corinthians (L.I.); Knickerbocker Yacht (Port Washington, L.I.). Pioneer Braniff colored airplanes. Home: 1815 Heritage Way Manhasset LI NY 11030 Office: Wells Rich Greene Inc 767 Fifth Av New York City NY 10022

GREENE, THOMAS MCLERNON, educator; b. Phila., May 17, 1926; s. George Durgin and Elizabeth (McLernon) G.; B.A., Yale, 1949, Ph.D., 1955; student U. Paris (France), 1949-51; m. Liliane Massarano, May 20, 1950; childrenPhilip James, Christopher George, Francis Richard. Mem. faculty Yale, 1954-, prof. English and comparative lit., 1966-, chmn. directed studies program, 1965-68. Served with AUS, 1945-47. Recipient Harbison prize for distinguished teaching Yale, 1968; grantee Am. Council Learned Socs., 1963-64; Guggenheim fellow, 1968-69. Mem. Modern Lang. Assn., Dante Soc. Am., Renaissance Soc. Am. Author: The Descent From Heaven: A Study in Epic Continuity, 1963; Rabelais: A Study in Comic Courage, 1970. also articles. Co- editor: The Disciplines of Criticism: Studies in Literary Theory, Interpretation and History, 1968. Home: 125 Livingston St New Haven CT 06511

GREENE, TOM E., Jr., banker; b. Macon, Ga., 1919. Pres., 1st Nat. Bank & Trust Co. in Macon. Home: 169 Country Club Rd Macon GA 31204 Office: 606 Cherry St Macon GA 31201

GREENE, WESLEY HAMMOND, educator; b. Romney, W.Va., June 14, 1907; s. Stuart Hardy and Virginia (Hammond) G.; student Randolph-Macon Acad. (Front Royal), 1918-23; A.B., Randolph-Macon Coll., 1927; A.M., U. of Va., 1929; m. Marie Zoé Mercier, June 21, 1937; childrenSteven Hardy, Richard Stuart, Roger Hammond. History teacher, Handley High Sch., Winchester, Va., 1927-28; pres. Internat. Film Bur., Inc., 1936-41, pres. and dir. 1945—; co- ordinator of distribution, Nat. Film Bd. of Dominion Govt. of Can., 1941- 45; dir. Coll. Film Center; ednl. and documentary film cons.; distbr. of films for Mental Health Film Bd., 1951—.; Okla. State Dept. of Health, 1952—. Mem. bd. dirs. Trans-World Film, Inc. Producer of the films Tierra Mexicana, 1947; Jefferson the Architect, 1949; Facts about Projection, 1950; Tom Sawyer and Mark Twain, 1950; distributor: Producing a Play (7 film series), 1951, Living Science Film Series, French Film Reader Series, Nat. Film Bd. of Can. Films, John Nash Ott, Jr., Prodns., and other films. Nat. Council for Social Studies, Scientific Film Assn. (London), Chicago Film Council World Film Festival (chmn. Chgo., 1947), Chgo. Sci. Film Soc. (co-founder, dir.), Chgo. French Film Soc. (founder), Am. Polit. Sci. Assn., Am. Soc. Pub. Adminstrn., Phi Beta Kappa. Democrat. Methodist. Clubs: Ill. Athletic: Executives, City, Quadrangle, Rotary (Chgo.). Home: 1232 E 57th St Chicago, IL 60637 Office: 332 S Michigan Av Chicago IL 60604 ☆

GREENEBAUM, SAMUEL LEWIS, lawyer; b. Louisville, Nov. 20, 1902; s. Samuel Lewis and Cora (Popper) G.; A.B. cum laude, U. Mich., 1924; LL.B., Harvard, 1927; m. Rita Levine, Jan. 29, 1956; children—John S., Jane (Mrs. Richard Eskind). Admitted to Ky. bar, 1927, D.C. bar; since practiced in Louisville; now sr. mem. firm Greenebaum, Grissom, Doll Matthews & Boone; asst. county atty. Jefferson County, Ky., 1930-33. Pres., Community Chest of Louisville and Jefferson County, 1948-49. Mem. Am., Ky., Louisville bar assns., Assn. Bar City N.Y., Zeta Beta Tau. Home: 2567 Cherosen Rd Louisville KY 40205 Office: Ky Home Life Bldg Louisville KY 40202

GREENER, EVAN HERBERT, educator; b. Bklyn., Sept. 8, 1934; s. Max W. and Rebecca (Fishgold) G.; B. Metall. Engring., Bklyn. Poly. Inst., 1955; M.S., Northwestern U., 1957; Ph.D., 1960; m. Sybil Brown, Dec. 22, 1957; children—Catherine, Irene. Asst. prof. materials sci. Marquette U., Milw., 1960-63, asso. prof. materials sci., 1963-64; asso. prof., chmn. dept. biol. materials Northwestern U. Dental Sch. and Med. Sch., Chgo., 1964-69 prof., chmn., 1969—. Internat. Assn. Dental Research, Am. Soc. Testing and Materials, Mem. Am. Ceramic Soc., Am. Phys. Soc., Am. Soc. for Metals, Am. Assn. Dental Schs., A.A.A.S., Am. Inst. Mining, Metall. and Petroleum Engrs., Am. Assn. U. Profs., Sigma Xi, Phi Lambda Upsilon. Home: 9418 Ironwood Lane Des Plaines IL 60016 Office: 311 E Chicago Av Chicago IL 60611

GREENEWALT, CRAWFORD HALLOCK, business exec.; b. Cummington, Mass., Aug. 16, 1902; s. Frank Lindsay and Mary Elizabeth (Hallock) G.; ed. William Penn Charter Sch., 1914-18, B.S. in Chem. Engring., Mass. Inst. Tech., 1922; D.Sc., U. Del., 1940, Northeastern U., 1950; E.D. (hon.), Rensselaer Poly. Inst., 1952; LL.D., Columbia, 1953, Williams Coll., 1953; Sc.D., Boston U., 1953; D.C.S., N.Y.U., 1954; D.Eng., Poly. Inst. Bklyn., 1954; D.Sc., Phila. Coll. Pharmacy and Sci., 1955, Drexel Inst. Tech., 1961, Hamilton Coll., 1970; LL.D., Kenyon Coll., 1958, Kan. State U., Temple U., 1960, U. Pa., 1961, Swarthmore Coll., 1961, U. Notre Dame, 1965, Bowdoin Coll., 1965, Yale, 1969; L.H.D., Jefferson Med. Coll., 1960; m. Margaretta Lammot du Pont, June 4, 1926; childrenNancy Crawford Frederick, David, Crawford Hallock. With E. I. du Pont de Nemours & Co., 1922—, asst. dir. exptl. sta., chem. dept., 1939, chem. dir. Grasselli chem. dept., 1942, tech. dir. explosives dept., 1943, asst. dir. devel. dept., 1945; asst. gen. mgr. pigments dept., 1945, v.p., 1946-48, pres., 1948-62, chmn. bd., 1962-67, chmn. finance com., 1967—; dir. Equitable Trust Co., 1935-43, E.I. du Pont de Nemours & Co., Christiana Securites Co., Morgan Guaranty Trust Co., The Boeing Co. Mem. Bus. Council. Bd. Dirs. Winterthur Corp., Mass. Inst. Tech., Phila. Orch. Assn. New Sch. Music. Trustee Longwood Found., Carnegie Instn.; regent Smithsonian Instn. Recipient John Fritz medal Am. Inst. Chem. Engrs., 1962. Mem. Am. Inst. Chem. Engrs., Am. Inst. Chemists, Soc. Chem. Industry, Am. Acad. Arts and Scis., Nat. Acad. Scis., Am. Chem. Soc., A.A.A.S., Am. Philos. Soc., Nat. Geog. Soc. (trustee), Theta Chi, Tau Beta Pi. Clubs: Wilmington, Wilmington Country, du Pont Country; Royal Bermuda Yacht. Author: The Uncommon Man, 1959; Hummingbirds, 1960; Bird Song: Acoustics and Physiology, 1968. Home: Greenville DE 19807 Office: Du Pont Bldg Wilmington DE 19898

GREENFIELD, ALEXANDER, lawyer; b. Wilmington, Del., Jan. 19, 1929; s. Abraham and Annie (Colton) G.; A.B., U. Del., 1949; LL.B., U. Pa., 1953; m. Lucille Ogden, June 1, 1965 (div.). Admitted to Del. bar, 1953; pvt. practice, Wilmington, 1956, 59-60; dep. atty. gen. Del., 1957-58; atty. FCC, 1960- 61; U.S. atty. Dist. Del., 1961-69; spl. asst. to pres. Off-Track Betting Corp., N.Y.C., 1971—; dir. legislative affairs N.Y. State Consumer Protection Bd., 1970-71. Pres., Del. Ednl. TV Assn., 1959-60; mem. Non-Partisan Com. for Good Govt. Co-chmn. govt. unit United Community Fund No. Del.; adv. bd. Del. Valley Regional Med. Program, 1967-68. Mem. Del., D.C. bar assns., Am. Assn. UN (pres. Del. 1959-60, v.p. Delaware br. 1968), Del. Mental Health Assn., Prisoners Aid Soc. Home: 11 E 87th St New York City NY 10028 Office: 1501 Broadway New York City NY

GREENFIELD, ALFRED M., condr., educator; b. St. Paul, Mar. 14, 1902; s. Jospeh William and Edith Mary (Stripe) G.; student Inst. Musical Art, N.Y.C., 1922-25, David Mannes Sch., N.Y., 1925-26, N.Y. U, 1924-27; m. Elsie Holbrook Learned, June 15, 1925 (dec. Feb. 1967); 1 son, William Edward; m. 2d, Nancy Ann Harris, May 19, 1970. Organist, Virginia Avenue Ch. (Swedenborgen), St. Paul, 1920, First Ch. Christ Scientist, St. Paul, 1921-22, Calvary P.E. Ch., N.Y.C.; 1923-24, Fifth Ch. Christ Scientist, N.Y.C., 1924-41; condr. Oratorio Soc. of N.Y.C., 1943-55, hon. condr., 1955—. Instr., N.Y.U., 1925-29, asst. prof. 1929-34, asso. prof., 1934-46, prof. music, 1946-68; adminstr. chmn. dept. music U. Coll., 1930-59; tchr. oratorio interpretation and conducting Union Theol. Sem., Sch. of Sacred Music, 1945-55; vis. prof. various ednl. instns., summers; prof. choral music U.S. Dept. State specialist program, Colombia, S. Am., 1962-63; U.S. specialist Dominican Republic, 1969. Condr. of Bach Festival Choir, Rollins Coll., 1946, Handel's Messiah Salt Lake Oratorio Soc., Mormon Tabernacle, 1947, 1948, also with Shreveport Civic Chorus, Dallas Symphony Orch., Shreveport, La., Twin City Chorus and Mpls. Symphony Orch. for Nat. Conv. Am. Guild Organists, 1954, Mozart Club Chorus and Orch., Winston-Salem, N.C., 1958, 65, 66, 67, in Carnegie Hall with Oratorio Soc. N.Y. and Orch., 1958; condr. Messiah with chorus and orch., Ridgecrest, N.C. and Glorietta, N.M., 1965; Fulbright lectr. Nat. U., Bogotá, Colombia, 1961, 64. Prof. honorario Universidad de Cartagena, 1962. Dir. Army Specialist Tng. Unit Glee Club, Air Cadet Singers, N.Y.U., World War II. Decorated Camilo Torres (Colombia). Hon. asso. N.Y. Hist. Soc.; mem. Am. Guild Organists, Juilliard Alumni Assn., Music Library Assn., Phi Kappa Tau. Club: Andiron, Saint Wilfrid, New York Univ. Faculty (Heights), Bohemians (N.Y.). Composer: (anthems) Blessed Be Thou, Lord God of Israel; Inner Light; Here, O My Lord; (solos) The Shepherd's Way; Blessed Be Thou; Watchful Shepherds; Wild Bird; Je Me Demande; The Hem of His Garment; (organ) Prelude in Olden Style; (solo) Here, O My Lord, 1948; The Earth Is the Lord's (Anthem), 1950; Quodlibet (for organ), 1959. Editor: University Glee Club series, 1931-. Home: 1931 Buena Vista Rd Winston-Salem NC 27104

GREENFIELD, BRUCE HAROLD, lawyer, banker; b. Phila., Mar. 12, 1917; s. William I. and Bertha (Kauffman) G.; B.A., Duke, 1938; LL.B., Yale, 1941; m. Adele Gersh, Sept. 18, 1955; children—Gregory Richard, Elizabeth Susan, Margaret Alison. Admitted to Pa. bar, 1941; atty. Office Tax Legislative Counsel, Treasury Dept., 1941-48; partner firm Folz, Bard, Kamsler, Goodis & Greenfield, Phila., 1949-53; v.p. Bankers Securities Corp., Phila., 1953- 59, exec. v.p., 1959-70, pres., 1970—; treas., dir. radio sta. WSMB, Inc., New Orleans, 1957—; pres., dir. Land Title Bldg. Corp., Phila., 1956—; treas. Bellevue-Stratford Hotel Corp., Phila., 1957—; dir. Bankers Bond & Mortgage Guaranty Co. Am., Briarcliff Candy Corp., City Stores Co., Continental Bank, Phila., Northeast Corner Walnut & Juniper Sts., Inc., Gold Trading Stamp Co., Phila. Lectr., N.Y. U., Tulane U., Am. U. tax insts. Treas., trustee Albert M. Greenfield Found.; trustee, exec. com. Fedn. Jewish Agys. Greater Phila.; bd. dirs. Phila., Am. Jewish Com.; bd. dirs., v.p. finance Girl Scouts U.S.A. Phila. Served to maj. USAAF, 1942-46. Mem. Am., Fed., Pa., Phila. bar assns., Tax Execs. Inst. (pres. Phila. 1964-65), Judge Adv. Assn., Res. Officers Assn., Lawyers Club Phila., Phi Beta Kappa. Democrat. Clubs: Yale, Locust, Variety (Phila.). Contbg. author Practicing Law Inst., Prentice-Hall Tax Ideas Service, Taxes mag. Home: 210 Barker Rd Wyncote PA 19095 Office: 1401 Walnut St Philadelphia PA

GREENFIELD, DONALD, banker. Sr. v.p. People's Nat. Bank Wash., Seattle. Office: 1414 4th Av Seattle WA 98111*

GREENFIELD, ELIZABETH MURPHY, (Mrs. Albert Greenfield), civic worker; b. Camden, N.J., Dec. 1, 1912; d. Walter Eugene and Janet (Harbage) Murphy; LL.D., Drexel Inst. Tech., 1964; L.H.D., Ursinus Coll., 1965; m. Albert Greenfield, Jan. 14, 1952; childrenTheodore Hallstrom II, Janet Hallstrom. Exec. dir. Phila. br. Fgn. Policy Assn., 1947-49, World Affairs Council of Phila., 1949-52; chmn. bd. Albert M. Greenfield Found.; former chmn. bd. trade and convs., mem. recreation coordination bd., Phila.; former v.p. Fgn. Policy Assn.; former exec. sec. Phila. group Nat. Policy Committee. Mem. Bd. Pub. Edn., Phila.; mem. Pa. Bd. Edn.; chmn. Pa. Council for Basic Edn. Mem. nat. bd. Woman's Med. Coll. Pa.; bd. govs. Mus. Coll. Art; bd. dirs. Inst. Contemporary Art at U. Pa., Phila. Mus. Art, Blue Cross of Phila.; asso. trustee U. Pa.; trustee Phila. Coll. Art; bd. govs. Phila. br. English Speaking Union; bd. mgrs. U. Pa. Mus. Mem. League Women Voters (past pres. Phila.), Am-Italy Soc. Phila. (v.p., mem. exec. com.). Unitarian. Club: Cosmopolitian (Phila.). Address: Rittenhouse Square Philadelphia PA 19103

GREENFIELD, GEORGE B., physician; b. N.Y.C., May 4, 1928; s. Jacob and Rose (Wolf) G.; B.A., N.Y.U., 1949; M.D., State U. Utrecht, Netherlands, 1956; m. Barbara Anne O'Driscoll, Mar. 3, 1956; children—Edward James, Sheelagh Anne. Intern, Bridgeport (Conn.) Hosp., 1956-57; resident radiology Presbyn.-St. Lukes Hosp. Chgo., 1957-60; practice medicine, specializing in radiology, Chgo., 1960—; radiologist Cook County Hosp., 1961-66, asst. dir. diagnostic radiology, 1966-69; asso. prof. radiology U. Ill., 1966-69; prof., chmn. dept. radiology Chgo. Med. Sch. and Mt. Sinai Hosp. Med. Center, 1969—; prof. radiology Cook County Grad. Sch. Medicine. Served with U.S. Army, 1951. Diplomate Am. Bd. Radiology. Mem. A.M.A., Chgo. Med. Soc., Chgo. Roetgen Soc., Am. Coll. Radiology, Radiol. Soc. N.Am., Inst. Medicine Chgo., Assn. U. Radiologists, Soc. of Chmn. Acad. Radiology Depts., A.A.A.S. Author: Radiology of Bone Diseases, 1969. Contbr. articles profl. jours. Home: 4855 Greenleaf Av Lincolnwood IL 60646 Office: Mt Sinai Med Center 15th St and California Av Chicago IL 60608

GREENFIELD, GORDON KRAUS, business exec., b. Phila., June 16, 1915; s. Albert Monroe and Edna Kraus (Paine) G.; grad. Lawrenceville (N.J.) Sch., 1933; A.B., Princeton, 1937; m. Harriet F. Copelin, Feb. 6, 1945; children—Juliet (Mrs. Jallabert), Gordon Kraus, Faith, Hope, James Donald. Pres., dir. City Specialty Stores, N.Y.C., 1953-60, America Copr., N.Y.C., 1960-64, Franchard Corp., N.Y.C., 1965-68; v.p., dir. Penson Freight Corp., 1968-69; chmn. bd. Q-Tr, Inc., N.Y.C., 1968—; dir. Bankers Securities Corp., Loft Candy Corp., Market Place Products Inc. Pres., dir. Arthritis Found. N.Y. chpt.; vice chmn. bd. Manhattan Sch. Music; trustee Theodore Roosevelt Assn., Nat. Conf. Christians and Jews. Served to lt. (s.g.) USNR, 1940-45. Mem. Confrerie des Chevaliers du Tastevin. Clubs: Princeton (N.Y.C.); Stage Harbor Yacht (Chatham, Mass.). Home: 1 W 72d St New York City, NY 10023 also Quasson Rd Chaathan MA 02633 Office: 342 W 40th St New York City NY 10018

GREENFIELD, IRVING H., lawyer; b. Nov. 15, 1902; s. Hyman and Fannie (Javitz) G.; LL.B., St. Lawrence U., 1924; m. Ethel Rudaw, Mar. 19, 1944 (dec. July 1968); children—Collin Wild, Lois Barbara; m. 2d, Molly Spirn, July 6, 1971. Admitted to N.Y. bar, 1924, since practiced N.Y.C.; mem. firm. Greenfield, Lipsky & Bress; with Metro-Goldwyn-Mayer (formerly Loew's, Inc.), 1922-69, asst. sec., 1944-54, sec., 1954-58. Home: 275 Central Park W New York City NY 10024 Office: 310 Madison Av New York City NY 10017

GREENFIELD, JAMES LLOYD, newspaper exec.; b. Cleve., July 16, 1924; s. Emil and Belle (Speiser) G.; B.A., Harvard, 1949; m. Margaret Ann Schwertley, July 16, 1954. With Cleve. Press, 1939-41, Voice of Am., 1949-50; corr. for Time mag. in Korea and Japan, 1951-55, bur. chief, New Delhi, India, 1956-57, dep. bur. chief, London, Eng., 1958-61; chief diplomatic corr. Time-Life, Washington, 1961-62; dep. asst. sec. state pub. affairs, 1962-64; asst. sec. state for pub. affairs, 1964-66; asst. v.p. internat. affairs Continental Airlines, Los Angeles, 1966-68; v.p. Westinghouse Broadcasting Co., N.Y.C., 1968-69; fgn. editor N.Y. Times, 1969—. Club: Reform (London, Eng.); Harvard (N.Y.). Home: 850 Park Av New York City NY 10021 Office: New York Times New York City NY 10036

GREENFIELD, JONAS C., educator. Prof. semitic langs. U. Cal. at Berkeley. Office: 1229 Dwinelle Hall U Cal Berkeley CA 94720*

GREENFIELD, MEG, journalist; b. Seattle, Dec. 27, 1930; d. Lewis James and Lorraine (Nathan) Greenfield; B.A. summa cum laude, Smith Coll., 1952; Fulbright scholar Newnham Coll., Cambridge (Eng.) U., 1952-53. With Reporter mag., 1957-68, Washington editor, 1965-68; editorial writer Washington Post, 1968-70, dep. editorial page editor, 1970—. Mem. Phi Beta Kappa. Home: 2909 Olive St NW Washington DC 20007 Office: 1515 L St NW Washington DC 20005

GREENFIELD, NORMAN SAMUEL, educator, psychologist; b. N.Y.C., June 2, 1923; s. Max and Dorothy (Hertz) G.; B.A., N.Y. U., 1948; M.A., U. Cal. at Berkeley, 1951, Ph.D., 1953; m. Marjorie Hanson Klein, May 17, 1969; children—Ellen Beth, Jennifer Ann, Susan Emery. Fellow med. psychology Langley Porter Clinic, U. Cal. Med. Center, 1949-50; VA Mental Health Clinic trainee, San Francisco, 1950-53; instr. clin. psychology U. Ore. Med. Sch., 1953-54; from asst. prof. to prof. psychiatry U. Wis. Med. Sch. at Madison, 1954—; asso. dir. Wis. Psychiat. Inst., U. Wis. Center for Health Scis., 1964—. Served with USAAF, 1943-46. Mem. Am. Psychol. Assn., Soc. Psychophysiol. Research, Am. Psychosomatic Soc., Am. Assn. U. Profs. Co-editor Handbook of Psychophysiology; Psychoanalysis and Current Biological Thought; Psychophysiological Correlates of Psychological Disorder; The New Hospital Psychiatry. Office: Dept Psychiatry University Hosps Madison WI 53706

GREENFIELD, ROBERT KAUFFMAN, lawyer; b. Phila, Mar. 30, 1915; s. William I. and Bertha (Kauffman) G.; A.B., Swarthmore Coll., 1936; LL.B., Harvard, 1939; m. Louise Rose Stern, June 20, 1937; childrenLinda (Mrs. Sheldon P. Davis), Mary (Mrs. David R. Beck), William Stern, James Robert. Admitted to Pa. bar, 1939, since practiced in Phila.; asso. firm Goodis, Greenfield & Mann, and predecessor, 1939-46, partner, 1947-. Trustee Greenfield Real Estate Investment Trust; dir. First Investment Securities Co., Gateway Ins. Co., Barco, Inc., McCullough-Howard & Co., Inc. Vice pres. Nat. Community Relations Adv. Council, 1965-68; sec., mem exec. com. Conv. and Tourist Bur. Phila., 1942—; commr., v.p. Phila. Fellowship Commn., 1965—; pres. Jewish Community Relations Council Phila., 1962-65. Pres. Moss Rehab. Hosp., 1969—; exec. com. Council Performing Arts Phila., 1964- 70; trustee Fedn. Jewish Agys. Phila., 1964—; mem. Phila. regional bd. Nat. Conf. Christians and Jews, 1966-; pres. Phila. chpt. Am. Jewish Com., 1966-68; bd. dirs. Phila. Grand Opera Co., 1950-61, Pa. Coll. Podiatric Medicine, 1967—; pres. Housing Adv. Service Corp., 1968—, Symphony Club Phila., 1968—. Served with USNR, 1945. Mem. Am., Phila. bar assns., Phi Beta Kappa. Clubs: Socialegal, Peale, Midday (Phila.). Home: 8221 Fairview Rd., Elkins Park PA 19117 Office: 1315 Walnut St Philadelphia PA 19107

GREENFIELD, SANFORD RAYMOND, architect; b. N.Y.C., Feb. 3, 1926; s. Harry Leon and Dorothy (Shaefer) G.; student Mich. State Coll. Liberal Arts, 1946-48; B.Arch., Mass. Inst. Tech., 1952, M.Arch., 1954; postgrad. New Sch. for Social Research N.Y.C., 1953, L'Inst. d'Urbanisme, Paris, 1954-55; m. Stella Berger, Oct. 12, 1952; children—Lise, Daniel, Stefanie. Faculty, Sch. Architecture and Planning, Mass. Inst. Tech., 1955-57; with Samuel Glazer, Boston, 1958-60; partner Carroll & Greenfield, architects, Boston,, 1960—; dir. edn. Boston Archtl. Center; cons. ednl. planning; lectr. Mass. Coll. Art. Served with USNR, 1944-46. Fulbright scholar, 1954-55. Fellow A.I.A.; mem. Boston Soc. Architects, Assn. Collegiate Schs. Architecture (dir.). Jewish religion. Editor: Architecture and the Computer, 1964; Forces Shaping The Role of The Architect, 1966; Systems, 1968. Contbr. articles profl. jours. Important works include Library St. John's Sem. Office: 729 Boylston St Boston MA 02116

GREENFIELD, TAYLOR HATTON, govt. ofcl.; b. Balt., Dec. 17, 1905; s. Amos Hatton and Lillian Estelle (Taylor) G.; LL.B., U. Balt., 1940; m. Mildred Sophia Albert, Sept. 15, 1928; children—Lillian (Mrs. Jerome Tilles), Millette. Admitted to Md. bar, 1949; exec. Glenn L. Martin Co., 1929-43, Gen. Motors, 1944-45; field dir. A.R.C., Germany, 1945-46; property and supply supr. War Assets Adminstrn., 1946-48; practice law, Balt., 1949-51; with Hayes Aircraft Co., Birmingham, Ala., 1951-55; adviser to Govt. Vietnam, 1955-62; mem. tech. adv. staff AID, Far East Bur., 1962-67, dir. Far East Logistics Office, 1965-67 chief logistics USOM, Bangkok, Thailand, 1967—. Recipient meritorious honor award AID, 1966. Mem. Md. Bar, Md. Natural History Soc., Hawaii Malocological Soc. Civitan. Home: 350 Scientists Cliffs Calvert County MD 20676 also: Thailand 508 Bangkok Apt 588/3 Petchburii Bangkok Thailand Office: USOM APO San Francisco CA 96346

GREENFIELD, WILBERT, coll. dean; b. Seven Springs, N.C., July 18, 1933; s. William Street and Mattie (Flannagan) G.; B.S., A. and T. State U. N.C., 1956; M.S., U. Ia., 1958; Ph.D., 1960; m. Felicia Black, Aug. 22, 1959; children-Rifka La Zonya, Tanya Winifret. Research asst. U. Ia., 1957-60; prof. biology, head biology dept. Jackson (Miss.) State Coll., 1960-67, dir. Summer Insts. in Biology, 1963-67, asso. dean Sch. Liberal Studies, 1967, dean of instrn., 1967-70, dean academic affairs, 1970—; cons. sci. dept. Magnolia High Sch., Moss Point, Miss. sponsored by grants from Paper Co. Found., 1963-67; mentor Am. Council of Edn. Academic Adminstrv. Internship Program, 1968-69; dir. Summer Insts. in Biology for high sch. tchrs., sponsored by grants from NSF, 1962-66. Scoutmaster Andrew Jackson council Boy Scouts Am., 1962; mem. bd. Jackson Urban League, 1968; mem.. Miss. Ednl. TV Bd., 1968; mem. bd. Farish St. br. YMCA, 1969; com. mem. Miss. Interagency Commn. on Mental Illness and Retardation, 1970. Recipient Outstanding Young Man of Year award Beta chpt. Omega Psi Phi, 1968. Mem. Miss. Acad. Sci., Sigma Xi, Alpha Kappa Mu, Beta Kappa Chi, Tri Beta, Omega Psi Phi. Home: 1341 Rockdale Dr Jackson MS 39213

GREENFIELD, WILLIAM DUMONT, former air force officer; b. Dayton, O., Sept. 15, 1914; s. Earl S. and Lillian (Rager) G.; B.S. in Bus. Adminstrn., Miami U., Oxford, O., 1936; grad. USAAF flying schs., 1939, 40, Army Air Force Tactical Sch., 1942, Army Lang. Sch., 1949, Air War Coll., 1953, Air Force Manpower Mgmt. Tng. Program, 1954, Command and Staff Sch., 1955; m. Nancy Pribe, Oct. 21, 1942; children—William Dumont, Linda, Ann. Commd. 2d lt. USAAF. 1940, advanced through grades to maj. gen. USAF, 1965; various assignments, U.S., Eng., Australia, New Guinea, France, 1941-44; chief combat analysis br. USAAF Bd., Orlando, Fla., 1944-45; chief allocation br., operations div. Hdqrs. USAAF, 1946-49; chief USAF mission to Venezuela, Maracay, 1949-52; comdr. 4706th Def. Wing, O'Hare Internat. Airport, Park Ridge. Ill., 1953-54, dep. comdr., 1954-55; comdr. 4711th Air Def. Wing, Presque Isle AFB, Me., 1955-56; asst. dep. operations Eastern Air Def. Force, Stewart AFB, N.Y., 1956-58; comdr. 316th Air Div., USAF in Europe, 1958-60, Syracuse Air Def. Sector, Hancock Field, N.Y. 1960-61; vice comdr. 26th Air Div., Hancock AFB, 1961-62; comdr. Boston Air Def. Sector, Stewart AFB, 1962-63, Chgo. Air Def. Sector, Truax Field, Wis., 1963-64; asst. dep. chief staff operations Hdqrs. Air Def. Command, Ent AFB, Colo., 1964-65, dep. chief staff operations, 1965-67, ret., 1967. Decorated D.F.C., Bronze Star, Air medal with 7 oak leaf clusters; Croix de Guerre with palm (France, Belgium); Air Force cross (Venezuela). Life mem. Delta Tau Delta. Home: 1110 Vega Dr Colorado Springs CO 80906

GREENHILL, J. P., gynecologist, obstetrician; b. N.Y.C., Feb. 28, 1895; s. Charles and Fanny (Pearl) G.; B.S., Coll. City N.Y., 1915; M.D., Johns Hopkins, 1919; m. Olga B. Hess, Mar. 16, 1929. Resident house officer Johns Hopkins Hosp., 1919-20; asst. resident Sinai Hosp., Balt., 1920-21; first resident Chgo. Lying-in Hosp., 1921-23, later sr. attending obstetrician; sr. attending obstetrician, gynecologist Michael Reese Hosp., Chgo., 1931—; attending gynecologist Cook County Hosp., Chgo., 1925—, chmn. dept., 1941-47; prof. gynecology Cook County Grad. Sch. Medicine, 1936—; asso. obstetrician Northwestern U., 1922-32; prof. obstetrics, gynecology, vice chmn. dept. Loyola U., Chgo., 1933-47; hon. prof. Nat. U., Peru. Mem. White House Conf. Com., 1930. Decorated chevalier Legion of Honor. 1957, conseiller d'Honneur, Inst. Endocrinologie, Haiti, 1960; recipient Fulbright Travel award, 1962. Diplomate Am. Bd. Obstetrics and Gynecology (charter). Fellow A.C.S. (life), Am. Coll. Obstetrics and Gynecology (charter), Am. Acad. Psychomatic Medicine, Chgo. Inst. Medicine; hon. fellow Internat. Coll. Surgeons (treas., trustee), Internat. Fertility Soc. (charter, v.p.); mem. Am. Med. Writers Assn., A.M.A. (chmn. com. female genital system for standard nomenclature diseases and operations), Ill., Chgo. med. socs., Am. Pub. Health Assn., Central Assn. Obstetrics and Gynecology (charter), Am. Geriatric Soc., Chgo. Gynecol. Soc. (pres. 1954- 55), A.A.A.S., Am. Assn. Anatomists, Venereal Disease Assn., Johns Hopkins Med. and Surg. Assn., Ill., N.Y. acads. scis., Am. Assn. Study Internal Secretions, Am. Soc. Cancer Control, Soc. Sci. Study Sex (charter), Am. Soc. Abdominal Surgeons, Pan-Pacific Surg. Assn.; hon. mem. obstet. and gynecol. socs. S. Africa, Dominican Republic, Chile, Argentine, Panama, Brazil, Uruguay, Venzuela, Portugal, Algeria, Turkey, Guatemala, Hawaii, Philippines, Cuba, W.Va.; gynecol. socs. France, Germany, Brazil, S.W., Med. Assn. Maternity Hosp. Lima, Peruvian Acad. Surgeons, Hollywood Acad. Medicine, fertility socs. Brazil, Argentina, Portugal. Author: Obstetrics for the General Practitioner, 1935; Office Gynecology, 8th edit., 1965; Obstetrics in General Practice, 4th edit., 1948; Obstetrics, 13th edit., 1965; Surgical Gynecology, 4th edit., 1969; Analgesia and Anesthesia in Obstetrics, 2d edit., 1962 (trans. Japanese, Spanish, Portuguese, Italian, Serbian); The Miracle of Life, 1971. Editor: (with J.B. DeLee) Year Books of Obstetrics, 1923-31; Year Book of Gynecology, 1931-42; Year Book of Obstetrics and Gynecology, 1942—; book rev. editor Fertility and Sterility, 1949-67. Book reviewer, mem. editorial bd. numerous med. jours. U.S., Europe, S.Am. Editor: Hosp. Publs., Inc., 1964. Home: 175 E Delaware Chicago IL 60611 Office: 55 E Washington St Chicago IL 60602

GREENHILL, J. RAYMOND, retail store exec.; b. Cross Plains, Tex., Mar. 20, 1913; s. Jesse Monroe and Alice (Steen) G.; B.A., U. Cal. at Los Angeles, 1935; m. Mary Foster, Sept. 15, 1935; childrenRobert F., Raymond M. Buyer, Golden Rule Dept. Store, St. Paul, 1935-36, Powers Dry Goods Dept. Store, Mpls., 1937-47, v.p., merchandise mgr., 1947-50; v.p., dir. Stewart & Co., Balt., 1950-57, pres., 1958-66; v.p. J.W. Robinson Co., Los Angeles, 1966—; v.p. Asso. Dry Goods Corp., N.Y.C., 1958; pres. Delivery of Balt.; dir. Cavendish Trading Corp. (N.Y.C.), Gibson Island Corp. Bd. dirs. Greater Balt. Com., Com. for Downtown, Better Bus. Bur., Mayor's Coordinating Council, Howard St. Assn., chmn. United Fund Appeal; bd. dirs Eye Bank of Md. Commr., Balt. Econ. Devel. Commn. Mem. Retail Mchts. Balt. (pres., dir.), Nat. Retail Mchts. Assn., Lambda Phi Alpha. Clubs: Maryland, University (Balt.); Gibson Island (bd. govs.) (Md.); Riviera Tennis; Los Angeles Athletic. Home: 1825 Via Visalia, Palos Verdes CA 90274 Office: care J W Robinson Co 7th and Grand, Los Angeles CA

GREENHILL, JOE judge; b. Houston, July 14, 1914; s. Joe Robert Jr. and Violet (Stanuell) G.; B.A., U. Tex., 1936, B.B.A., 1936, LL.B., 1939; m. Martha Shuford, June 15, 1940; childrenJoe Robert IV, William Duke. Admitted to Tex. bar, 1938; partner firm Bryan, Suhr, Bering and Bell, Houston, 1939-41, Dougherty & Greenhill, Austin, 1950-57; briefing atty. Supreme Ct. Tex., 1941-42, 46, now justice; asst. atty. gen. State of Tex., 1947-48, 1st asst. atty. gen., 1948-50. Served from ensign to lt., USNR, 1942-46. Mem. Am. Bar Assn., State Bar Tex. (chmn. mineral sect. 1957-58, jud. sect. 1969-70), Philos. Soc. Tex., Ex-students Assn. U. Tex. (exec. council), Order of Coif, Phi Beta Kappa, Phi Delta Theta. Mason, (33) Lion (past pres.). Home: 3204 Bridle Path Austin TX 78703 Office: Supreme Ct of Tex Austin TX 78711

GREENHILL MAURICE HERZBERGER psychiatrist; b. Terre Haute, Ind., Aug. 16, 1909; s. Louis Lester and Estelle (Herzberger) G.; A.B., U. Rochester, 1931; M.D., U. Chgo., 1936; m. Estelle Markin, Sept. 6, 1936; childrenLaurence, William, Andrew, Barry. Postgrad. study psychiatry Worcester (Mass.) State Hosp., 1937- 39, Mass. Gen. Hosp., Boston, 1939-40, Boston City Hosp., 1940-41; faculty Harvard Med. Sch., 1939-41; asso. prof. Duke U. Sch. Medicine, 1943-52; prof. psychiatry U. Md., 1952-55; prof. psychiatry, chmn. dept., dir. Psychiat. Inst., U. Miami (Fla.), 1955-57; dir. Community Mental Health Bd., N.Y.C., 1957-58; clin. prof. psychiatry Albert Einstein Coll. Medicine, N.Y.C., 1957-65, prof. clin. psychiatry, 1966-67, prof. psychiatry, 1968—, dir. psychiatry hosp., 1966—. Coordinator tng. and research High Point Psychiat. Hosp., Port Chester, N.Y., 1958-; pvt. practice psychiatry, 1958-; research and ednl. cons. to numerous med., govt., social agys.; cons. Nat. Inst. Mental Health; spl. cons. surgeon-gen. U.S. Army, UPSHS. Bd. dirs. Highland Hosp., Ashville, N.C.; trustee Gralnick Found., N.Y.C. Rockefeller Found. fellow, 1940-41; Diplomate Am. Bd. Psychiatry and Neurology. Fellow Am. Psychiat. Assn. mem. A.A.A.S., Group Advancement Psychiarty (chmn. com. on med. edn.), Am. Psychosomatic Soc., Assn. Research Nervous and Mental

Diseases, Phi Beta Kappa, Sigma Xi, Alpha Delta Phi. Author: Evaluation in Mental Health, 1955. Contbr. profl. jours. Home: 70 Hampton Rd Scarsdale NY 10583 Office: Eastchester NY 10709

GREENHUT, MELVIN LEONARD, economist, educator; b. N.Y.C., Mar. 10, 1921; s. Ab and Lillian (Frudman) G.; Ph.D., Washington U., 1951; m. Elmara Margaret Griffith, Mar. 24, 1944; children—Margaret Lee, Pamela Jo, John Giffith, Patricia Lynn. Asst. prof. econs. Auburn (Ala.) U., 1948-52; asso. prof. econs. Miss. State Coll., 1952-53; prof. bus. and econs., chmn. social relations div. Rollins Coll., 1953-57; prof. econs. Fla. State U., 1957-59, 62-66; asso. dean Sch. Bus., U. Richmond, 1959-62; prof., head dept. econs. Tex A. and M. U., College Station, 1966-69, distinguished prof. econs., 1969—. Vis. prof. Mich. State U., 1963; cons. Rountree Assos., Richmond, Va., 1959, A.T. & T. risk and uncertainty com., 1961-62, Atlantic Research Corp., 1962; cons. to pres. Amerad Corp., 1962-64; cons. So. Conf. Council State Govts., 1964- 66, Bur. Bus. Research, Memphis State U., 1965-66; mem. nat. econ. policy com. and econ. adv. council U.S. C. of C. 1960-63. Served to maj. AUS, World War II. Mem. Am., So. (past v.p.) econ. assns., Regional Sci. Assn. (councillor), Econometric Soc., Delta Chi, Omicron Delta Gamma. Lutheran (trustee). Author: Plant Location in Theory and in Practices, 1956; (with Frank Jackson) Intermediate Income and Growth Theory, 1961; Full Employment, Inflation and Common Stocks, 1961; (with Marshall R. Colberg) Factors in the Location of Florida Industry, 1962; Microeconomics and the Space Economy, 1963; (with Tate Whitman) Essays on Southern Economic Development, 1964; A Theory of the Firm in Economic Space, 1970. Editor: So. Econ. Jour., 1966- 68; cons. editor Indsl. Devel., 1959-62. Contbr. articles profl. jours. Home: 3107 Camelot Bryan TX 77801 Office: Dept Econs Tex A and M U College Station TX 77843

GREENKORN, ROBERT ALBERT, educator; b. Oshkosh, Wis., Oct. 12, 1928; s. Frederick John and Sophie (Phillips) G.; student Oshkosh State Coll., 1951-52; B.S., U. Wis., 1954, M.S., 1955, Ph.D., 1957; m. Rosemary Drexler, Aug. 16, 1952; children—David Michael, Eileen Anne, Susan Marie, Nancy Joanne. Postdoctoral fellow Norwegian Tech. Inst., 1957-58; research engr. Jersey Prodn. Research Co., Tulsa, 1958-63; lectr. U. Tulsa, 1958-63; asso. prof. theoretical and applied mechanics Marquette U., Milw., 1963- 65; asso. prof. Sch. Chem. Engring., Purdue U., Lafayette, Ind., 1965-67, prof., head Sch. Chem. Engring., 1967—. Served with USN, 1946- 51. Decorated D.F.C., Air medal with two oak leaf clusters. Mem. Am. Inst. Chem. Engrs., Soc. Petroleum Engrs., Am. Inst. Mining, Metall. and Petroleum Engrs., Am. Chem. Soc., Sigma Xi, Phi Eta Sigma, Tau Beta Pi, Phi Gamma Delta. Roman Catholic. Author: (with D.P. Kessler) Transfer Operations, 1971. Contbr. articles profl. jours. Patentee in field. Home: 151 Knox Dr West Lafayette IN 47906

GREENLAW, RALPH WELLER, educator; b. N.Y.C., July 21, 1917; s. Ralph Weller and Georgianna (Hallock) G.; grad. Phillips Exter Acad., 1933-34; B.A., Amherst Coll., 1938; M.A., Princeton, 1947, Ph.D., 1952; m. Alice Palmr Handforth, June 15, 1940; children—David Henry (dec.), Claire Hallock. With Dodwell & Co. Ltd., N.Y.C., 1939-42; asst. prof. history State U. Ia., 1949-53; asst. prof. Wellesley Coll., 1953-59; dir. program dept. CARE, Inc., 1959-62; vis. asso. prof. Brown U., 1962-63; asso. prof. N.C. State U., 1963-65; prof., head dept. history, 1965—; dir. tng. 1st Peace Corps Unit for Colombia, 1961, Unit for Chile, 1964. Served to 1st lt. AUS, 1942-45; ETO. Decorated Bronze Star. Mem. Am., So. hist. assns., Am. Assn. U. Profs., Soc. for French Hist. Studies. Gen. editor: (series) Problems in European Civilization, 1956-71; spl. editor: The Economic Origins of the French Revolution—Poverty or Prosperity?, 1958. Home: 1307 Duplin Rd Raleigh NC 27607

GREENLAW, ROBERT PIPER, mfg. co. exec.; b. Boston, Jan. 14, 1917; s. Clarence A. and Emma E. (Piper) G.; m. Marion Weir Wallace, Aug. 31, 1940; childrenJanice Elizabeth, Lorraine Clare (Mrs. James Stampone, Jr.), M. Wynne (Mrs. Keller). Admitted to practice U.S. Tax Ct., 1946. With Bank of N.Y., 1934-36, Royal Indemnity Co., 1936-38, Standard Statistics Copr., 1938-41; with Am. Home Products Corp., N.Y.C., 1941—, head tax dept., 1950-61, treas., dir., 1963—, v.p., 1967—, exec. com., 1970. Bd. supts. New Brunswick Theol. Sem., 1961-63. Council financial execs. Nat. Indsl. Conf. Bd. Patron Internat. Oceanographic Found. Mem. Newcomen Soc. Mem. Reformed Ch. (elder). Clubs: Treasurers; Seaview Country (Absecon, N.J.); Morehead City Country (N.C.). Home: 60 Sutton Place S New York City NY 10022 Office: 685 3d Av New York City NY 10017

GREENLEAF, LELAND BURLIEGH musical instrument mfg. co. exec.; b. Wauseon, O., Aug. 12, 1904; s. Carl Dimond and Deacon (Jennings) G.; student U. Chgo., 1923-24, also Internat. Corr. Schs., spl. night classes, Notre Dame U. and Purdue U.; m. Pauline Isbell, Oct. 1, 1932; childrenHarriet (Mrs. Robert A. Schoeller), Carroll (Mrs. Peter Perez), Charlotte A. (Mrs. Thomas Mittle). With Foster Machine Co., Elkhart Ind., 1924-28; with C. G. Conn Limited, Elkhart, 1928—, v.p., 1953-58, pres., 1958—, also chmn., bd. dirs.; dir. St. Joseph Valley Bank, Elkhart. Bd. dirs. Elkhart United Fund. Mem. Am. Soc. M.E., Nat. Assn. Band Instrument Mfrs. (dir.), Am. Music Conf. Rotarian (bd. dirs. Elkhart). Patentee in field. Home: 1449 Greenleaf Blvd., Elkhart IN 46514 Office: 1101 E Beardsley Av Elkhart IN 46514

GREENLEAF, ROBERT KIEFNER cons.; b. Terre Haute, Ind., July 14, 1904; s. George W. and Burchie M. (Kiefner) G.; B.A., Carleton Coll., 1926, D.H.L., 1969; m. Esther E. Hargrave, Sept. 26, 1931; children—Newcomb, Elizabeth, Madeline. With Ohio Bell Telephone Co., 1926-29; with Am. Tel.&Tel. Co., 1929-64, dir. mgmt. research, 1957-64; faculty Dartmouth Grad. Sch. Financial Mgmt., 1950-58, Salzburg Seminar in Am. Studies, 1968; exec. in residence Fresno State Coll., 1968. Cons. Ford Found., R.K. Mellon Found., 1962—, Giovanni Agnelli Found., 1968—; vis. lectr. Harvard Bus. Sch., Sloan Sch. Mgmt., Mass. Inst. Tech., 1962-63; pres. Center for Applied Studies. Trustee Russell Sage Found., 1957-65; vis. com. Harvard Div. Sch. Mem. Soc. Friends. Club: Harvard (N.Y.C.). Home: Old Street Rd Peterborough NH 03458

GREENLEAF, THOMAS R., business exec.; b. 1927; married. With Chem. Leaman Tank Lines Inc., Downington, Pa., 1951—, now exec. v.p., dir. Office: 520 E Lancaster Av Downington PA 19335*

GREENLEE, HOWARD SCOTT, coll. dean; b. Chgo., Feb. 13, 1919; s. James T. and Edith (Scott) G.; A.B., U. Chgo., 1939, A.M., 1941, Ph.D., 1950; postgrad Columbia, 1953- 54; m. Helen L. Schwarz, Oct. 4, 1941; childrenSarah, David Scott. Tchr. pub. schs., Woodstock, Ill., 1941-42; asst. Salzburg Seminar in Am. Studies, 1948; vis. asst. history U. Chgo., 1950; asso. prof. history, asso. dean Simpson Coll., 1950-55; asso. dean, prof. history Southwestern U., 1955-56; dean coll., prof. history Park Coll., 1956-58; dean Coe Coll., 1958-65; prof. history Tuskegee Inst. (Ala.), 1965- 68, acting dean Coll. Arts and Scis., 1967-68; dean faculty Antioch Coll., Yellow Springs, O., 1968-71; acad. dean, prof. history Windham Coll., Putney, Vt., 1971—. Cons.-examiner N. Central Assn. Colls. and Secondary Schs. Served to lt. USNR, 1942-46. Faculty fellow Fund for Advancement Edn., 1953-54; travel grantee Carnegie Corp. Ednl. Adminstrn., 1960. Mem. Am. Assn. U. Profs., Orgn. Am. Historians. Presbyn. Office: Windham Coll Putney VT 05346

GREENLEE, JOHN ALDEN, coll. pres.; b. Richland, Ia., Sept. 7, 1911; s. John Amzi and Martha (Logsdon) G.; B.A., U. Ia., 1930, M.A., 1931, Ph.D., 1934; m. Lillian Ruth Witte, Dec. 13, 1955. Prof., asst. to dean scis. Ia. State U., 1949- 59; dir. engring. personnel and edn. Collins Radio Co., Cedar Rapids, Ia., 1959-65; v.p. acad. affairs Cal-State Coll., Los Angeles, 1965-66, pres., 1966—. Served with USNR, World War II. Decorated Bronze Star medal. Mem I.E.E.E., Am. Soc. Engring. Edn., South Pasadena, Los Angeles chambers commerce, Phi Delta Kappa, Phi Kappa Phi, Alpha Kappa Psi, Pi Gamma Mu, Beta Sigma Pi. Home: 5O Oak Hill Lane South Pasadena CA 91030 Office: 5151 State College Dr Los Angeles CA 90032

GREENLEIGH, ARTHUR DASHEW, business exec., mgmt. cons.; b. N.Y.C., May 8, 1903; s. Abraham Morris and Sadie (Dashew) G.; A.B., U. Cal. at Los Angeles, 1929; M.A., U. So. Cal., 1930; postgrad. N.Y. Sch. Social Work, Columbia, 1931-32; m. Frances Nasatir, July 3, 1928; children—Stephen Henry, Esther Ellen. Social worker Big Bros. Assn., Los Angeles, 1928-31; dir. div. adminstrv. surveys N.Y. State Temporary Emergency Relief Adminstrn., 1932-34; dir. field service Cal. Relief Adminstrn., 1934-36; exec. dir. Los Angeles County Bur. Pub. Assistance, 1936-39; lectr. grad. sch. U. So. Cal., 1936-39; asst. exec. dir. Nat Refugee Service, N.Y.C., 1939-42; asst. to exec. dir. War Manpower Commn., Washington, 1942-44; dir. for Italy Am. Joint Distbn. Com., Rome, 1944, dir. for France, Paris, 1945, dep. European dir., Paris, 1946-47; mem. exec. com. Am. Council Vol. Agys. Fgn. Service, 1948—; mem. exec. com. U.S. Com. for Care European Children, 1948-53; mem. nat. adv. com. U.S. Displaced Persons Commn., Washington, 1948-50, chmn. com., 1950-52; asso. exec. dir. United Service New Ams., N.Y.C., 1948-50, exec. dir. 1950-54; exec. dir. United Hias Service (merger Hebrew Immigrant Aid Soc. and United Service for New Ams., 1954-56; pres. Greenleigh Assos. Inc., 1956—; pres. Fed. Warehouse & Storage Co., Los Angeles; v.p. Fed. Crating Co., Los Angeles; sec.-treas. Fed. Transfer Co., Los Angeles, 1964—. Mem. exec. com. Am. Immigration Conf., 1954; vice chmn. Internat. Conf. Non-Govtl. Orgns. Interested in Migration, 1951-52, chmn. 1952-53; cons. to U.S. del. Internat. Migration Conf., Naples, 1951, Intergovtl. Migration Conf., Brussels, 1951. Fellow Am. Sociol. Assn.; mem. Am. Assn. Social Workers, A.A.A.S., Am. Mgmt. Assn., Am. Pub. Welfare Assn., Am. Acad. Polit. and Social Sci., Am. Soc. for Pub. Adminstrn., Innternat., Nat. confs. social welfare, Nat. Conf. Jewish Social Welfare, Nat. Council Family Relations, Fgn. Policy Assn., Zeta Beta Tau, Psi Chi. Jewish religion. Author articles on immigration, pub. welfare, pub. adminstrn., human relations. Home: 920 Park Av New York City NY 10028 Office: 355 Lexington Av New York City NY 10017 also 127 N Dearborn Av Chicago IL 60602

GREENLEY, WILLIAM FAIRCHILD, Jr., banker; b. Newark, Mar. 5, 1913; s. William Fairchild and Mary (Moore) G.; B.A. cum laude, Princeton, 1935; postgrad. Columbia, 1936-37, Fordham U., 1937-38; m. Ann T. Donnelly, Oct. 11, 1965. Sr. v.p. Fidelity Union Trust Co., Newark, 1955—; pres., dir. Essex Investment Co., Akron Investment Co.; sec., dir. Commerce Investment Co., Broad Agy., Inc. Mem. exec. com. Investment Council N.J., 1960—; mem. Financial Adv. Commn. County Essex, 1962—; Trustee Benedictine Found., Elizabeth, N.J. Mem. N.J., Greater Newark chambers commerce, N.J. Bankers Assn. Nat. Indsl. Conf. Bd., Nat. Council Cath. Men, Friendly Sons St. Patrick. Democrat. Clubs: Downtown, Essex (Newark); Princeton (N.Y.C.); Spring Lake Bath and Tennis, Spring Lake Golf and Country. Home: 220 Lorraine Av Spring Lake NJ 07762 Office: 765 Broad St Newark NJ 07102

GREENLIEF, FRANCIS STEVENS, army officer; b. Hastings, Neb. July 27, 1921; s. Walter and Florence (Hayden) G.; student U. Neb., 1939-40; grad. Officers Candidate Sch., 1942, U.S. Army Aviation Sch., 1969, Command and Gen. Staff Coll., 1951; m. Mavis Burt, Nov. 4, 1941; children—Barbara, Carol, Robert, Michelle, Kevin and Constance (twins). Mem. Neb. N.G., 1940—; enlisted as pvt. U.S. Army, 1940, advanced through grades to maj. gen., 1965; served in ETO, 1944-53; with N.G. Bur., 1960—, dep. chief, 1965—. Decorated Silver Star, Bronze Star, Purple Heart with 3 oak leaf clusters, Combat Ing. wings, Army Aviator wings; Croix de Guerre with Etoile de Vermeil (France). K.C., Elk. Home: 5101 N 10th St Arlington VA 22205 Office: Nat Guard Bureau Washington DC 20310

GREENOUGH, ALLEN JACKSON, former railroad exec.; b. San Francisco, Sept. 20, 1905; s. Earnest Allen and Nellie (Jackson) G.; B.S. in Civil Engring., Union Coll., Schenectady, 1928, Dr. Engring. (hon.), 196O; m. Jean Lytel, Apr. 8, 1933; children—Allen Lytel, Norman Jackson; m. 2d, Julie McCormack Waterman, Oct. 29, 1966. With Pa. R.R., 1928-68, engring. dept., 1928-45, operating dept., 1945-53, v.p. 1953-59, pres., 1959-68, ret., 1968; dir. Lehigh Valley R.R. Co., Mchts. Warehouse Co., Detroit, Toledo & Ironton R.R., Raymond Internat., Inc., Girard Trust Bank, United N.J. R.R. & Canal Co.; trustee Penn Mut. Life Ins. Co., Union Coll. Mem. Soc. Colonial Wars, Chi Psi, Sigma Xi. Clubs: Round Hill (Greenwich); Pine Valley Golf; Metropolitan; The Presidents. Episcopalian. Home: Round Island Greenwich CT 06830

GREENOUGH, WILLIAM CROAN, ins. co. exec.; b. Indpls., July 27, 1914; s. Walter Sidney and Katharine (Croan) G.; A.B., Ind. U. 1935, LL.D., 1966; M.A., Harvard, 1938, Ph.D., 1949; m. Doris Decker, Jan. 4, 1941; childrenDavid William, Walter Croan, Martha Alice. Asst. to dean, instr. Ind. U. Sch. Bus., 1937-38, asst. to pres., 1938-4O, personnel dir, 194O-41; asst. to pres. Tchrs. Ins. and Annuity Assn. Am., 1941-43, 46-48, v.p., 1948-55, exec. v.p., 1955-57, pres., 1957-62, chmn., pres., 1963-67, chmn., chief exec. officer, 1967—, also trustee; v.p. Coll. Retirement Equities Fund, 1952-55, exec. v.p., 1955-57, pres., 1957-62, chmn., pres., 1963-67, chmn., chief exec. officer, 1967—, also trustee; trustee Dry Dock Savs. Bank, First Nat. City Bank Trust Bd. Dir. Turner Constrn. Co. Mem. commn. on faculty and staff benefits Assn. Am. Colls., 1958-64, mem. commn. on students and faculty, 1964-66, mem. commn. on coll. adminstrn., 1966-; adv. council N.Y. U. Pres.'s Council for Grad. Sch. Arts and Sci., 1965-67; mem. Harvard Grad. Soc. Council, 1965—; adv. council edn. and world affairs, com. internat. activities U.S. Office of Edn., 1963-64; mem. com. on 2d regional plan Regional Plan Assn., N.Y.C., 1966-, bd. dirs. 1967-. Trustee Found. Library Center, 1961-67, Russell Sage Found., Devereux Found.; bd. dirs. Ind. U. Found., The Aspen Inst. Recipient Distinguished Alumni Service award Ind. U., 1960, Elizur Wright award variable annuity writing, 1961. Served from ensign to lt., USNR, 1943-45. Decorated Bronze Star medal. Mem. Life Office Mgmt. Assn., Am. Pension Conf., Am. Econs. Assn., Am. Finance Assn., Am. Assn. U. Profs., Am. Risk and Ins. Assn., Phi Beta Kappa. Clubs: Harvard, Century Assn. (N.Y.C.). Author: College Retirement and Insurance Plans, 1948; A New Approach to Retirement Income, 1951; (with Dr. F. P. King) Retirement and Insurance Plans in American Colleges, 1959, Benefit Plans in American College. Editor: Pension Planning in the U.S., 1952; also numerous articles in field. Home: 870 UN Plaza Office: 730 3d Av New York City NY 10017

GREENSON, RALPH ROMEO, educator, psychoanalyst; b. Bklyn., Sept. 20, 1911; s. Joel O. and Katherine (Goldberg) G.; student Columbia, 1928-30; M.D., U. Berne (Switzerland), 1934; m. Hildegard Troesch, July 14, 1935; children—Daniel, Joan (Mrs. Andreas Aebi). Intern, Cedars of Lebanon Hosp., Los Angeles, 1934-35; resident U. Vienna, Austria, 1935-36; pvt. practice medicine, Beverly Hills, Cal., 1936-42, 46—; tng. analyst Los Angeles Psychoanalytic Inst., Beverly Hills, 1947—; clin. prof. psychiatry U. Cal. at Los Angeles Med. Sch., 1951—. Chmn. sci. adv. bd. Found. for Research in Psychoanalysis, 1964—. Served to maj. M.C., AUS, 1942-46. Mem. Am. Psychoanalytic Assn., Los Angeles Psychoanalytic Soc. (pres. 1951-53). Author: The Technique and Practice of Psychoanalysis, vol. I, 1967. Contbr. articles to profl. jours. Home: 902 Franklin St Santa Monica CA 90403 Office: 465 N Roxbury Dr Beverly Hills CA 90210

GREENSPAN, BERNARD, educator; b. N.Y.C., Dec. 17, 1914; s. Harry and Yetta (Siegel) G.; B.S., Bklyn. Coll., 1935, M.A., 1936; postgrad. Columbia, 1936-38; Ph.D., Rutgers U., 1958; NSF faculty fellow, U. Cal., Berkeley, 1958-59; postgrad. Rensselaer Poly. Inst., 1960; m. Beatrice Meltzer, Aug. 26, 1939; children—Valerie Helen (Mrs. Robert M. Davidson), Ellen Freda (Mrs. Daniel J. Delaney). Instr., Bklyn. Coll., 1935-44; instr. Poly. Inst. Bklyn. 1943-44; instr. Drew U., Madison, N.J., 1944-47, asst. prof., 1947-58, asso. prof., 1958-59, prof., chmn. math. dept., 1959—, dir. NSF Summer Math. Inst., 1962—, dir. Math. Inservice Inst., 1961—; assistantship Rutgers U., 1952; cons., lectr. math. Out of Hours Program, N.J. Bell Telephone Lab., Whippany, 1953-58; vis. prof. U. Santa Clara, summer 1961, Rutgers U., summer 1971; table leader reader advanced placement exams. Ednl. Testing Service, 1966—. Mem. Am. Math. Soc., Math. Assn. Am. (past chmn. exec. com. N.J. sect.), Assn. Math. Tchrs. N.J., Am. Assn. U. Profs., Sigma Xi, Pi Mu Epsilon, Sigma Phi. Contbr. articles profl. jours. Home: 44 Cathedral Av Florham Park NJ 07932 Office: Drew U Madison NJ 07940

GREENSPAN, DONALD, mathematician, educator; b. N.Y.C., Jan. 24, 1928; s. Louis and Jessie (Scholnick) G.; B.S., N.Y. U., 1948; M.S., U. Wis., 1949; Ph.D., U. Md., 1956; m. Ruth Lucas, July 3, 1957; childrenJames, Marc, Rona. Instr., U. Md., 1948-56; research engr. Hughes Aircraft Co., 1956-57; asst. prof. Purdue U., 1957-61, asso. prof. 1961-62; permanent mem. U. Wis. Math. Research Center, Madison, 1962-68, prof. computer scis., cons. to U. Wis. Computing Center, 1965—. Lectr., Am. Math. Assn., 1963-64, U. Mich. Summer Conf., 1964-; referee NRC, NSF. Served with USAF, 1953. Mem. Am. Math. Soc., Am. Phys. Soc., Assn. Computing Machinery, Am. Civil Liberties Union, N.A.A.C.P., Americans Dem. Action. Author: Theory and Solution of Ordinary Differential Equations, 1960; Introduction to Partial Differential Equations, 1961; Introductory Numerical Analysis of Elliptic Boundary Value Problems, 1965; Introduction to Calculus, 1968; Lectures on the Numerical Solutions of Linear, Singular, and Nonlinear Differential Equations, 1968. Editor: Numerical Solutions of Nonlinear Differential Equations, 1966. Contbr. numerous articles to profl. jours. Home: 817 Hiawatha Dr., Madison, WI 53711.

GREENSPAN, HARVEY PHILIP, educator, applied mathematician; b. N.Y.C., Feb. 22, 1933; s. Louis and Jessie (Scholnick) G.; B.S., Coll. City N.Y., 1953; M.S., Harvard, 1954, Ph.D., 1956; m. Mirian Gordon, Sept. 6, 1953; children—Elizabeth, Judith. Asst. prof. applied math. Harvard, 1957-60; faculty Mass. Inst. Tech., Cambridge, 1960—, prof. applied math., 1964—. Bd. govs. Israel Inst. Tech. Author: Theory of Rotating Fluids, 1968. Editor: Studies in Applied Mathematics, 1969. Home 15 Chatham Circle Brookline MA 02146 Office: Mass Inst Tech Cambridge MA 02139

GREENSPAN, MARTIN physicist; b. N.Y.C., May 8, 1912; s. Barnett and Jennie (Myerson) G.; B.S., Cooper Union Inst. Tech., 1934; m. Lillian Rosalie Gunsberg, Dec. 26, 1937; children—Robert, Miriam, Ruth. Physicist, Nat. Bur. Standards , Washington, 1935—, chief sound sect., 1967—. Vis. lectr. Univ. Cal. at Los Angeles, 1958-59; adj. prof. Catho. U. of Am., 1968—; mem. U.S. nat. com. Internat. Union Pure and Applied Physics, 1966—; mem. NRC, 1969—. Recipient Meritorious Service award Commerce, 1949, 61. Fellow Acoustical Soc. Am. (pres. 1966-67), Am. Phys. Soc., Washington Acad. Scis., A.A.A.S. (mem. council 1966-67). Contbr. profl. jours., encys. Asso. editor Jour. Acoustical Soc. Am., 1961-66; editor sect. C., Jour. Research Nat. Bur. Standards, 1962-. Spl. research elasticity and acoustics. Home: 12 Granville Dr., Silver Spring MD 20901 Office: Nat Bur Standards Washington DC 20234

GREENSPAN, RICHARD HENRY, educator, radiologist; b. N.Y.C., Apr. 25, 1925; s. Benjamin and Sara (Lipschitz) G.; A.B., Columbia, 1945; M.D., Syracuse U., 1948; m. Lydia C. Selmanoff, June 20, 1952; children—Daniel Edward, Benjamin, Helen, Martha. Intern Michael Reese Hosp., Chgo., 1948-50; resident U. Minn. Hosps., 1950-52, fellow, 1955-57; instr., then asst. prof. U. Minn. Med. Sch., 1957-59; from asst. prof. to prof. Yale Sch. Medicine, 1960-68; prof. radiology U. Cal. Med. Sch. San Francisco, 1968—, cons. Cardiovascular Research Inst., 1968—; cons. VA Hosp., San Francisco, 1968—. Mem. tng. com. NIH, 1965-67, 69—, chmn. angiography com., 1968—. with USAF, 1952-54. Am. Cancer Soc. fellow, 1956-57; NSF sr. postdoctoral fellow, 1966-67. Diplomate Am. Bd. Radiology. Mem. Assn. U. Radiologists (exec. com.), Radiol Soc. N. Am., Am. Coll. Chest Physicians, Am. Coll. Radiology, Am. Heart Assn., Am. Roentgen Ray Soc., A.A.A.A.S., Am. Thoracic Soc., Conn. Med. Soc., Conn. Thoracic Soc., New Eng. Roentgen Ray So., N.Y. Acad. Sci., Minn. Med. Found., Royal Soc. Medicine, Syracuse U. Med. Sch. Alumni Assn., Alpha Omega Alpha hon. med. Canadian, Toronto radiol. socs. Contbr. profl. jours. Asso. editor Investigative Radiology, 1965—. Home: 606 The Alameda Berkeley CA 94707 Office: Dept Radiology San Francisco Med Center San Francisco CA 94121

GREENSPUN, HERMAN MILTON, newspaper pub.; b. Bklyn., Aug. 27, 1909; s. Samuel J. and Anna (Fleischman) G.; student St. John's Coll., 1930-32; LL.B., St. John's Sch. Law, 1934; m. Barbara Joan Ritchie, May 21, 1944; childrenSusan Gail, Brian Lee, Jane Toni, Daniel Alan. Admitted to N.Y. bar, 1936; pvt. law practice, N.Y.C., 1936-46; pub. mag. Las Vegas Life, 1946-47; owner, pub. Las Vegas Sun, N. Las Vegas News, 1950—; owner Colorado Springs (Colo.) Sun, 1970—; editorial writer, columnist Las Vegas Sun, 1950-; pres. Las Vegas Sun, Inc., 1950- -, KLAS-TV, Las Vegas TV, Inc., 1954-68; owner Sun Outdoor Advt. Co. Bd. dirs. Sun Youth Found. Served from pvt. to maj., AUS, 1941-46; ETO. Decorated Croix de Guerre with silver star; Conspicuous Service cross State N.Y.; recipient Outstanding Journalist award Jewish War Vets, 1957. Mem. Nev. Press Assn. (pres. 1957), Am. Legion, V.F.W., D.A.V. Clubs: Nat. Press; Overseas Press; Variety; Friars; Paradise Valley Golf and Country (pres., dir.). Author Where I Stand (autobiography). Home: 545 Griffith Av Las Vegas NV 89104 Office: 900 S Commerce St Las Vegas NV 89106

GREENSTEIN, FRED IRWIN, educator, polit. scientist; b. N.Y.C., Sept. 1, 1930; s. Arthur Aaron and Rose (Goldstein) G.; B.A., Antioch Coll., 1953; M.A., Yale, 1956, Ph.D., 1960; m. Barbara Elferink, July 14, 1957; childrenMichael, Amy, Jessica. Instr., Yale, 1959-62, vis. prof., 1965-68; mem. faculty Wesleyan U., Middletown,

Conn., 1963-, prof. polit. sci., 1966-; vis. prof. U. Essex (Eng.), 1968-69. Served with AUS, 1953-55. Fellow Center Advanced Study Behavioral Scis., 1964-65; NSF sr. postdoctoral fellow, 1968-69. Mem. Am. Polit. Sci. Assn. (editorial bd. 1968-), Am. Assn. U. Profs., Soc. Psychol. Study Social Issues. Author: (with R. E. Lane and J.D. Barber) Introduction to Political Analysis, 2d edit., 1965; The American Party System and the American People, 1970; Children and Politics, 2d edit., 1969; Personality and Politics, 1969; (with M. Lerner) A Source Book for the Study of Personality and Politics, 1971. Home: 32 Summit Pl Middletown CT 06457

GREENSTEIN, JESSE LEONARD, astronomer; b. N.Y.C., Oct. 15, 1909; s. Maurice and Leah (Feingold) G.; student Horace Mann Sch. for Boys, 1921-25; A.B., Harvard, 1929, A.M., 1930, Ph.D., 1937; m. Naomi Kitay, Jan. 7, 1934; childrenGeorge Samuel, Peter Daniel. Engaged in real estate and investments, 1930-34; Nat. Research fellow, 1937-39; asso. prof. Yerkes Obs., U. of Chgo., 1939-48; research asso. McDonald Obs., U. Tex., 1939-48; mil. research under OSRD (optical design), Yerkes Obs., 1942-45; Lee A. DuBridge prof. astrophysics, also exec. officer for astronomy Cal. Inst. Tech., also staff mem. Hale Obs., 1949—, chmn. of faculty of inst. 1965-67; mem. obs. com., Hale Observatories; mem. staff Owens Valley Radio Obs.; cons., also com. mem. NASA and NSF on astronomy and radio astronomy, chmn. astronomy survey Nat. Acad. Scis., 1969-71; vis. prof. Princeton, 1955, Inst. for Advanced Studies, 1964, 68-69, lectr. in field Mem. bd. overseers Harvard, 1965-71. Named Cal. Scientist of Year, 1964. Asso. Royal Astron. Soc. Mem. Astron. Soc. Pacific (dir., Bruce medalist), Am. Astron. Soc. (councillor 1947- 50, v.p. 1955-57), Internat. Astron. Union (pres. commn. on spectroscopy 1952-58), Nat. Acad. Scis. (councillor, com. on sci. and pub. policy 1965—), Am. Acad. Arts and Scis., Am. Philos. Soc., Phi Beta Kappa. Club: Athenaeum (Pasadena). Author sections of treatises, Astrophysics, 1951; Modern Physics for the Engineer, 1953; Vistas in Astronomy. 1956. Corresponding editor Annales d'Astrophysique, Paris, Astrophysical Letters. Editor: Stellar Atmospheres, 1960. Contbr. sci. articles; author govt. reports. Home: 2057 San Pasqual St Pasadena CA 91107

GREENSTEIN, JULIUS SIDNEY, educator, biologist; b. Boston, July 13, 1927; s. Samuel and Helen (Shriber) G.; B.A., Clark U., 1948; M.S., U. Ill., 1951, Ph.D., 1955; postdoctoral study Harvard Med. Sch., 1966; m. Joette Mason, Aug. 23, 1954; children—Gail Susan, Jodi Beth, Jay Mason, Blake Jeffrey, Joette Elise. Mem. faculty U. Mass., 1954-59; faculty Duquesne U., Pitts., 1959-70, chmn. dept. biol. scis., 1961-70, prof., 1964-70; prof., chmn. dept. biology State U. N.Y., Fredonia, 1970—; vis. lectr. Am. Inst. Biol. Scis., 1966—. Mem. Carnegie Civic Symphony Orch. Mem. sci. adv. bd. Human Life Found. Served in armored div. AUS, World War II. Recipient Wisdom award Honor, 197O. Mem. Am. Assn. Anatomists, Am. Inst. Biol. Scis., Internat. Fertility Assn., A.A.A.S., Am. Soc. Zoologists, Am. Fertility Soc., Soc. Study Fertility (Eng.), Council Biol. Editors, Pa. (editorial bd. 1963—) N.Y. State acads. sci., Soc. Study Reprodn., Am. Assn. U. Profs. (pres. Duquesne chpt.), Soc. Developmental Biology, Sigma Xi, Phi Sigma. Editor: Internat. Jour. Fertility, 1958—; contbr. to understanding of causes and prevention of reproductive failure in mammals by studying early developmental stages of embryo, nature of male and female reproductive organs and endocrine glands; developed new techniques for staining specimens and smears; investigated relationship of specific diseases to normal reproductive performance; publs. profl. jours. Home: 12 Birchwood Dr Fredonia NY 14063

GREENSTEIN, PHILIP, educator; b. N.Y.C., Oct. 26, 1905; s. Samuel and Sarah (Brody) G.; B.S., N.Y.U., 1927. M.S., 1939; m. Dorothy Fischer. June 25, 1944; 1 son, Elliot. Faculty N.Y.U., 1927—, successively asst. instr. elec. engring., instr., asst. prof., asso. prof., 1927-48, prof., 1948—, project dir., 1941—, research coordinator sponsored projects, 1951—; cons. N.Y. Telephone Co., 1961-66. Cons. City N.Y., 1941-42. I.E.E.E., Sigma Xi, Tau Beta Pi, Eta Kappa Nu. Contbg. editor Van Nostrand's Sci. Ency. Home: 164 Church St New Rochelle NY 10805

GREENWALD, JOSEPH ADOLPH, U.S. ambassador; b. Chgo., Sept. 18, 1918; s. Jacob and Lena (Corman) G.; student U. Pa., 1936-38; B.A. in Econs., U. Chgo., 1941; LL.B., Georgetown U., 1951; m. Mary Virginia Doyle, Dec. 12, 1942; children—John, Bruce, Jane. Admitted D.C. bar 1951; internat. economist U.S. Dept. State, 1947, U.S. resident representative Internat. economist orgns., Geneva, Switzerland, 1952-55, chief comml. policy br. Office Internat. Trade, Dept. of State, 1955-58, 1st sec., asst. comml. attache Am. embassy, London, Eng., 1958-63; dir. Office of Internat. Trade, Dept. State, 1963-65, dep. asst. sec. state for internat. trade policy, 1965-69; U.S. ambassador to Orgn. for Econ. Cooperation and Devel., 1969—. Chmn. U.S. delegation UN Conf. on Trade and Devel., 1968. Mem. D.C. Bar, Phi Beta Kappa. Home: 12 rue Weber Paris 16 France Office: 19 rue Franqueville Paris 16 France

GREENWALL, FRANK KOEHLER, mfg. exec.; b. N. Y.C., May 6, 1896; s. Henry and Hattie (Koehler) G.; student pub. schs., N.Y.C.; m. Anna Alexander, Jan. 4, 1921; childrenSusan (dec.), Nancy (Mrs. C. Richard MacGrath). With Nat. Starch & Chem. Corp. and predecessor firms, 1920-, beginning as salesman, successively treas., v.p. sales, 1920-38, pres., dir. 1938-58, chmn. bd., chief exec. officer, 1958-64, chmn. bd., 1964-69, chmn. exec. com., 1969—; dir., treas. Hotel Pierre, N.Y.C. Hon. trustee Corn Refiners Assn., Inc.; trustee Susan Greenwall Found.; dir. Keep Am. Beautiful, Monmouth Med. Center. Served USNRF, World War I. Mem. Adhesive Mfrs. Assn. Clubs: Pinnacle, Madison Sq. Garden (N.Y.C.); Ocean Beach (Elberon, N.J.). Home: 2 E 61st St New York City NY 10021 Office: 750 3rd Av New York City NY 10017

GREENWALT, HOWARD, ch. ofcl.; b. Roodhouse, Ill., Apr. 30, 1912; s. Bida and Rebecca (Baker) G.; A.B., Ill. Coll., 1935, D.D., 1968; B.D., Garrett Bible Inst., 1940; D.D., Ill. Wesleyan U., 1964; m. Helen Henard, June 21, 1936; children—Sylvia Anne (Mrs. Peter Bushell), Robert Irl. Ordained as deacon Meth. Ch., 1941, elder, 1942; pastor, Lovelock, Nev., 1940-43, South San Francisco, 1943-48, San Leandro, Cal., 1948-53; supt. central dist. Cal.-Nev. Conf., Modesto, Cal., 1953-56; asso. sec Commn. on Promotion and Cultivation, Evanston, I11., 1956-66, gen. sec., 1966-68; asso. gen. sec. div. interpretation program council United Methodist Church, 1968—. Bd. dirs. Kendall Coll., Evanston. Author: Look-A-Graf, 1954; Ideas and Helps for District Superintendents, 1957. Home: 42O Pinecrest Lane Wilmette IL 60091 Office: 1200 Davis St Evanston IL60201

GREENWALT, ROBERT ROGENE, mfg. co. exec.; b. Mt. Vernon, Ill., Oct. 24, 1923; s. G. Gale and Lena (Blackburn) G.; m. Jeanne Stranderfer, Dec. 14, 1946; children—Gayle, Roben, Todd, Nicholas. Vice pres. Mpls. Moline Co., 1956-58; sr. v.p. White Consol. Industries, Cleve., 1958-68; exec. v.p. Bath Industries, Inc., Milw., 1968—. Served to lt. USNR. Decorated Air medal with six stars. Home: 4914 W Parkview Dr Mequon WI 53092 Office: 2100 N Mayfair Rd Milwaukee WI 53226

GREENWALT, TIBOR JACK, physician; b. Budapest, Hungary, Jan. 23, 1914; s. Bela and Irene (Foldes) G.; came to U.S., 1920, naturalized, 1943; B.A. summa cum laude, N.Y. U., 1937, M.D., 1937; m. Shirley Johnson, Aug. 6, 1960 (dec. Sept. 1970); 1 son, Peter H.; m. 2d, Pia Glas, Feb. 27, 1971. Intern pathology and bacteriology Mt. Sinai Hosp., N.Y.C., 1937-38; rotating intern Kings County Hosp., Bklyn., 1938-40; resident medicine Montefiore Hosp., N.Y.C., 1940-41; research asso. New Eng. Med. Center, Boston, 1941-42; med. dir. Milw. Blood Center, 1947-66; faculty medicine Marquette U. Sch. Medicine, 1948-66, prof. medicine, 1963-66; cons. hematology VA Hosp., Wood, Wis., 1946-66, Milw. County Gen. Hosp., 1948-66; cons. Clin. Center NIH, 1967—; med. dir. blood program A.R.C., 1967—; clin. prof. medicine George Washington U. Sch. Medicine, 1967—. Chmn. com. blood and transfusion problems Nat. Acad. Scis.-NRC, 1963-66; mem. hematology study sect. NIH, 1960-63, chmn., 1970-72; mem. Internat. Panel Blood Donors of Rare Types, 1965—, Interdepartmental Com. Nat. Blood Program Research, 1967—; vis. prof., speaker throughout U.S., 1960—. Served to maj. M.C., AUS, 1942-46. Recipient Gold medal Caduceus Soc., N.Y. U., 1933; Jr. Achievement award for outstanding contbn. sci., 1958; Distinguished Citizen's award Allied Vets. Council, 1963. Diplomate Am. Bd. Internal Medicine. Mem. A.M.A., Am. Assn. Blood Banks (v.p. 1959-60, med. dir. central file rare donors 1960-66, John Elliot award 1966), Internat. Soc. Hematology, A.C.P., A.A.A.S., Internat. Soc. Blood Transfusion (pres. 1966-72), Am. Soc. Clin. Pathologists, Central Soc. Clin. Research, Am. Soc. Hematology (treas. 1963-67), Am. Assn. Immunologists, D.C. Acad. Medicine, Soc. Exptl. Biology and Medicine, Am. Soc. Human Genetics, Sigma Xi, Alpha Omega Alpha. Author: (with others) Hemolytic Syndromes, 1942; (with Shirley Greenwalt) Coagulation and Transfusion in Clinical Medicine, 1965. Editor: (with Graham A. Jamieson) The Red Cell Membrane, 1969, Formation and Destruction of Blood Cells, 1970, Glycoproteins of Plasma and Membranes, 1971; editor, contbr. Immunogenetics, 1967; editor-in-chief Transfusion, 1960-66, asso. editor, 1966—; editorial bd. Gen. Principles of Blood Transfusions, 1962—, Vox Sanguinis, 1956—, Haematologia, 1968—. Contbr. numerous papers to profl. lit. Home: 4617 Kenmore Dr NW Washington DC 20007 Office: ARC 17th and D Sts NW Washington DC 20006

GREENWAY, JAMES COWAN, Jr., zoologist, museum trustee; b. N.Y.C., Apr. 7, 1903; s. James Cowan and Harriet Miller (Lauder) G.; A.B., Yale, 1926; m. Mary Frances Oakes, June 29, 1961. Asso. curator birds Mus. Comparative Zoology, Harvard, 1933-51, curator birds. 1952-60; trustee Am. Mus. Natural History, N.Y.C., 1960—. Served with USNR, 1942-45. Decorated Bronze Star; Dragon d'Annam; Million d'Elephants et Parasol Blanc (Laos). Clubs: The Brook (N.Y.C.); Somerset (Boston). Author: Extinct and Vanishing Birds of the World, 1958. Editor: (with E. Mayr) Birds of the World, vol. 9, 1959. Address: Mead's Point Greenwich CT 06830

GREENWAY, JOHN SELMES rancher, hotel exec.; b. Santa Barbara, Cal., Oct. 11, 1924; s. John Campbell and Isabella Dinsmore (Selmes) G.; B.A., Yale, 1949; LL.B., U. Ariz., 1954. Owner, Ariz. Inn, Tucson, 1958—, pres. Quarter Circle Double X Ranch, Inc., Williams, Ariz., 1963—; dir. So. Ariz. Bank, Tucson. Pres. bd. trustees Ariz.-Sonora Desert Mus., Tucson; trustee St. John's Coll., Santa Fe; bd. dirs. Ariz. Hist. Soc., U. Ariz. Found., Tucson. Address: 1634 N Olsen Av Tucson AZ 85719

GREENWELL, RICHARD DEARING, state ofcl.; b. Glasgow, Ky., Oct. 1, 1940; s. Henry Russell and Rachel (Dearing) G.; student Bethel Jr. Coll., 1958-60; B.S., Murray State U., 1964; m. Cynthia Dale Thompson, June 8, 1963; children—Rachel Elizabeth, Margaret Elaine. Announcer radio sta. WKOA, Hopkinsville, Ky., 1960-61; recreation dir. Western State Hosp., Hopkinsville, Ky., 1965-66, purchasing dir., 1966, personnel officer, 1966-67, asst. hosp. adminstr., 1967-68; adminstr. Frankfort (Ky.) State Hosp. & Sch., 1968-70; adminstr. div. Mental Retardation, Dept. Mental Health, Commonwealth of Ky., Frankfort, 1970—. Mem. Sigma Chi. Home: 318 Senate Dr Frankfort KY 40601 Office: PO Box 678 Frankfort KY 40601

GREENWOOD, ERMA GRIFFITH, lawyer; b. Honaker, Va., Feb. 10, 1917; d. Arthur Tazewell and Maude (Catron) Griffith; A.B., Duke, 1937, LL.B., 1939; m. Porter Greenwood, Dec. 21, 1939 (div. June 1951). Admitted to Va. bar, 1938, Tenn. bar, 1943; partner Griffith & Greenwood, Lebanon, Va., 1939-43; asso. Poore, Kramer & Overton, Knoxville, Tenn., 1943-48; partner Kramer, Dye, McNabb & Greenwood 1948-63; sr. partner Kramer, Dye, Greenwood, Johnson & Rayson, 1963—. Sec. central com. E. Tenn. Community Improvement Program, 1959, pres., 1963; mem. budget com. Community Services Council, Knoxville, 1961-63, admissions com., planning council, 1964. Bd. dirs. Tenn. River and Tributaries Assn. Mem. Am., Tenn. (past pres. Woman's conf.; chmn. negligence and ins. sect. 1968-69), Knox County bar assns., Bus. and Profl. Women's Club, Tau Kappa Alpha. Methodist. Clubs: Quota, Deane Hill Country. Home: 3305 Montlake Dr Knoxville TN 37920 Office: Valley Fidelity Bank Bldg Knoxville TN 37901

GREENWOOD, GEORGE JOSEPH, Jr., former banker; b. Green Bay, Wis., Apr. 14, 1906; s. George J. and Matilda C. (Pellegrin) G.; pre-standard, standard, grad. certificate Am. Inst. Banking; grad. Grad. Sch. Banking at Rutgers, 1952; m. Kathleen M. Carr, June 18, 1929; children—George J., K. Colleen (Mrs. Peter B. Dannenfelser), Daniel D., Elizabeth, Nannette (Mrs. Terrence Giomi). Messenger, Hibernia Comml. & Savs. Bank, Portland, Ore., 1922, comml. teller, 1927; utility clk. Bank of Cal. Nat. Assn., Portland, 1931, departmental mgr., 1935-42, asst. mgr. 1942-47, v.p. head office, San Francisco, 1947-68; exec. mgr. Western Ind. Bankers, San Jose, Cal., 1968-70. Recipient certificate of merit award Sec. Navy for work as state chmn. citizens com. for raising funds Navy Relief Soc. Mem. Am. Inst. Banking (nat. exec. council 1942, nat. v.p. 1945, nat. pres. 1946, life mem. Portland chpt.), Am. (regional v.p.), Ore. (state chmn. coms. 6 yrs.) bankers assns. Republican. Roman Catholic. Kiwanian. Clubs: Stock Exchange, Commercial (San Francisco); Peninsula Golf and Country (San Mateo). Home: 5051 Cribari Vale San Jose CA 95135

GREENWOOD, JAMES, Jr., physician; b. Seguin, Tex., July 19, 1907; s. James and Ella L. (Harris) G.; A.B., Rice Inst., 1927; M.D., U. Tex., 1931; m. Mary Pedan Cox, June 22, 1935; children—James, Alexander William, Mary Grace (Mrs. Jon Knolle), Marvin Harris, Nancy Lee (Mrs. James I. Riddle), Andrew Pedan. Postgrad. work Phila. Gen. Hosp., 1931-35; pvt. practice neurosurgery, Houston, 1935—; clin. prof. of neurosurgery Baylor U. Coll. Medicine, 1943—, acting chmn. div. neurosurgery 1943-55, chmn. 1956-57; chmn. div. neurosurgery Meth. Hosp.; chmn. Jefferson Davis Hosp., 1940- 46, St. Joseph's Infirmary, 1940-49; pres. staff Meth. Hosp., 1957-59; cons. neurosurgery VA Hosp., M.D. Anderson Hosp. Cancer Research. Diplomate Am. Bd. Neurol. Surgery. Fellow A.C.S.; mem. Harvey Cushing Soc., S.W. Surg. Congress, Am. Acad. Neurol. Surgery, Tex. Surg. Soc. (past pres.), So. Neurosurg. Soc. (past. pres.), Tex. Neuropsychol. Soc. (past pres.), Soc. of Brit. Neurol. Surgeons (hon.), Alpha Omega Alpha, Phi Rho Sigma. Democrat. Episcopalian. Contbr. articles neurosurg. publs. Amateur radio (W5PB) operator since 1920. Home: 1839 Kirby Dr Houston TX 77019 Office: Hermann Professional Bldg Houston TX 77025

GREENWOOD, JAMES WARD, Canadian diplomat, physicist; b. Winnipeg, Can., May 13, 1925; s. James Arthur and Marion (Evans) G.; B.Sc., U. Man., 1946; M.A., U. Minn., 1953; m. Dorothy F. Swancar, June 4, 1949; children—Nancy Jean, Douglas James. Lectr., U. Man., 1946-49; with Atomic Energy of Can. Ltd., Chalk River Ont., 1954-59, head internat. relations, Ottawa, Ont., Can., 1959-67; alternate gov. for Can., IAEA, Vienna, Austria, 1964-65; sci. counsellor Canadian embassy, Washington, 1967—. Home: 5315 Albemarle St Washington DC 20016 Office: 1746 Massachusetts Av Washington DC 20036

GREENWOOD, JAMES WILLIAM, Jr., mgmt. cons.; b. Phila., Sept. 3, 1912; s. James and Emily (Tither) G.; student Temple U., 1929-31, 45-46, U. Pa., 1943-45; B.S., Am. U., 1949, M.A. in Pub. Adminstrn. 1960; m. Mary Agnes Sweeney, June 5, 1930; childrenJames William, Albert Francis, Kenneth Robert, Mary Kathryn, Kay. Fiscal accountant Soil Conservation, Service U.S. Dept. Agr., 1936-41; fiscal accountant Central Adminstrv. Services, Office Emergency Mgmt., 1941-42; adminstrv. officer Nat. War Labor Bd., 1942-46; dir. adminstrv. mgmt. WSB, 1946-47, acting exec. dir., 1947, liquidation officer, 1947; dir. adminstrv. mgmt. Fed. Mediation and Conciliation Service, 1947-50, asso. dir., 1950- 53; asst. dir. labor relations Glass Container Mfrs. Inst., 1954-56; cons., 1956—; mem. planning staff Internal Revenue Service, Washington, 1957; dir. Bur. Mgmt. Methods, Pa. Gov's. Office, 1957-59; chief mgmt. analysis staff Office Sec. Health, Edn. and Welfare, 1959-61, dir. Office Mgmt. Policy, 1961-67, dir. Office Mgmt. Planning, 1967-68, asst. to asst. sec. for adminstrn., 1968-69; mem. faculty U.S. Dept. Agr. Grad. Sch., 1963—. Finance officer 2d ann. conf. FAO, Copenhagen, 1946. Exec. fellow Brookings Instn., Washington, 1968-69. Mem. Am. Acad. Polit. and Social Sci., Am. Soc. Pub. Adminstrn., Am. Polit. Sci. Assn. Soc. Gen. Systems Research. Home: 7314 Lois Lane Lanham MD 20801

GREENWOOD, ROBERT EWING, educator, mathematician; b. Navasota, Tex., June 21, 1911; s. Robert E. and Lula (Lewis) G.; B.A., U. Tex., 1933; postgrad. Brown U., 1935-36; M.A., Princeton, 1938, Ph.D., 1939; m. Mary Maud Brown, Dec. 15, 1951; 1 dau., Barbara Frances. Faculty, U. Tex., Austin, 1938—, now prof. math. Contbr. reports for various research agys., articles to math. jours., Collier's Ency. Study of probability, numerical methods, combinatory analysis. Home: 3203 Breeze Terrace Austin TX 78722

GREENWOOD, WILLIAM FRANK, banker; b. Nashville, Aug. 9, 1924; s. Vayne K. and Eleanor (Steele) G.; grad. Rutgers U. Grad. Sch. Banking, 1961; m. Reba Capps, June 14, 1946; children—William Frank, Lisa Claire. Asst. prodn. mgr. Baird Ward Printing Co.; Nashville, 1946-47; prodn. supr. Genesco, Inc., 1947-49; account exec. Gen. Outdoor Advt. Co., 1949-51; with First Am. Nat. Bank, Nashville, 1951—, exec. v.p., 1965-69, vice chmn. bd., 1969-, also dir. Pres. Nashville Mental Health Assn., 1966-69, Vis. Nurse Service, Nashville, 1962-64;vice chmn. bd. United Givers Fund Nashville, 1960-61; mem. bus. adv. bd. Middle Tenn. State U.; chmn. pres.'s adv. bd. Trevecca Coll. Bd. dirs. Council of Community Services, Tenn. Mental Health Assn., 1967—, local council Boy Scouts Am., 1964-67, Nashville Salvation Army, 1967-; trustee, treas. Disciples of Christ Hist. Soc., 1961-, Disciples of Christ. Hist. Found., Nashville, 1961-. Served with USNR, 1943-46. Mem. Nashville C. of C., Am. Inst. Banking, Assn. Res. City Bankers. Mason. Club: Belle Meade Country (Nashville). Home: 225 Clarendon Ave Nashville TN 37205 Office: 326 Union St Nashville TN 37202

GREENWOOD, WILLIAM HENRY, Jr., ins. co. exec.; b. Whitinsville, Mass., May 3, 1915; s. William Henry and Mary (Carpenter) G.; A.B. magna cum laude, Dartmouth, 1937, M.C.S. with distinction, Amos Tuck Sch. Bus. Adminstrn., Dartmouth, 1938; m. Eleanor Marie Apple, Sept. 17, 1943; childrenWilliam Henry III, Gail E. With Provident Mut. Life Ins. Co., Phila., 1938-, asst. ins. supr., 1950-56, asso. ins. supr., 1956-61, v.p. underwriting 1961-67, sr. v.p. ins., 1967-. Active United Fund Phila.; sec. Life Ins. Med. Research Fund, Rosemont, Pa., 1962—. Served to lt. USNR, 1942-45; PTO. Fellow Life Office Mgmt. Assn. Inst.; mem. Home Office Life Underwriters Assn. (past pres.), Health Ins. Assn. Am., Phi Beta Kappa, Sigma Alpha Epsilon. Clubs: Racquet, Dartmouth (Phila.). Home: 671 Berry Lane Upper Providence Media PA 19063 Office: 4601 Market St Philadelphia PA 19101

GREEP, HARRY PETERSON, savs. and loan assn. exec.; b. Chgo., Mar. 7, 1914; s. Carl F. and Hulda (Peterson) G.; student U. Ill., 1932, Northwestern U., 1934; grad. Am. Savs. & Loan Inst., Chgo., 1936; m. Catherine E. Portscheller, Apr. 23, 1939; childrenPatrice Lea, Stephen Michael, Shari-Lea. Credit man Bell Savs. & Loan Assn., Chgo., 1935-37; teller, credit man First Fed. Savs. & Loan Assn., Miami, Fla., 1938-44, mortgage officer, 1946; organizer, pres. Greep & Merrill, Inc., Ft. Lauderdale, Fla., 1946-52; founder, pres., dir. Atlantic Fed. Savs. & Loan Assn., Ft. Lauderdale, 1952—; organizer Investment Corp. Fla., 1955, chmn. bd., 1955-62, cons., 1963- 66; organizer, dir. Home Owners Life Ins. Co., 1960. Cons. AID, 1961-; mem. Ft. Lauderdale, Bd. Adjustment, 1953-66; mem. adv. com. naval affairs 6th Naval Dist., 1958-. Nat. asso. Boys Clubs Am., 1961-67; pres. Broward County club, 1966-69, founding dir., 1965; pres. Broward County chpt. Am. Cancer Soc., 1957-60, bd. dirs., 1955-, Fla. Crusade chmn., 1964; v.p., bd. dirs. Opera Guild Ft. Lauderdale, 1953-70, Broward Citizens bd. U. Miami, 1970—; mem. seminar and inst. adv. com. Nova U. Advanced Tech., Ft. Lauderdale, 1964-; mem. bd. South Fla. Edn. Center, Ft. Lauderdale, 1964—; hon. dir. Ft. Lauderdale Symphony Soc., 1960-; hon. trustee Pine Crest Sch., Ft. Lauderdale, 1966-68; mem. adv. board Holy Cross Hosp., 1968—. Served with USNR, 1944-46. Decorated Francisco de Miranda medal (Venezuela). Mem. Ft. Lauderdale C. of C. (dir. 1964-68), Navy League (founder 1958; past pres. Ft. Lauderdale council), Nat. League Insured Savs. Assns. (pres. 1965-66), Econ. Soc. South Fla. Elk. Clubs: Le Club International, Lauderdale Yacht (Fort Lauderdale); Hundred (Broward Country). Home: 524 Isle of Capri Fort Lauderdale FL 33301 Office: 1750 E Sunrise Blvd Fort Lauderdale FL 33304

GREER, CARL CRAWFORD, petroleum co. exec.; b. Pitts., June 12, 1940; s. Joseph Moss and Gene (Crawford) G.; B.S., Lehigh U., 1962; Ph.D., Columbia U., 1966; m. Jerrine Ehlers, June 16, 1962; children—Caryn, Michael. Asso. in bus. Columbia U., 1964-66, asst. prof. banking and finance, 1966-67; retail marketing mgr. Martin Oil Service Inc., Alsip, Ill., 1967-68, exec. v.p., 1968, pres., dir., 1968—; dir. First Nat. Bank Blue Island. Mem. Beta Theta Pi, Tau Beta Pi, Beta Gamma Sigma, Omicron Delta Kappa. Presbyn. Home: 1 Strauss Lane Olympia Fields IL 60461 Office: 4501 W 127th St Alsip IL 60658

GREER, DON SWINT, banker; b. Mt. Pleasant, Tex., Mar. 16, 1908; s. Jesse Wade and Dee (Swint) G.; B.S. in Mech. Engring., Harvard, 1929, B.B.A., 1930; m. Charlotte Mason, Apr. 12, 1930 (dec., 1968); children-Diane Wedgwood (Mrs. Edward P. Williams), Charlotte Mason (Mrs. Stuart P. Carlisle); m. 2d, Paulina Moxley, Dec. 30, 1969. Pres., J.W. Greer Co., Wilmington, Mass., 1930-68, also subsidiaries in Can., Eng., Australia; pres. Wire Belt Co. of Am., 1930-66; pres. Wire Belt Co., Ltd., 1960—; pres., dir. Harvard Trust Co., Cambridge, Mass., 1969—; dir. Baystate Corp., Boston. Chmn.

bd. Selectman, Winchester, Mass.; pres. Asso. Industries Mass., Boston; trustee Longyear Found., Brookline, Mass., Lesley Coll., Cambridge; mem. corp. Northeastern U. Recipient citiation for excellent performance in World War II war material prodn. USN, 19—. Registered profl. engr., Mass. Mem. Tau Beta Pi, Alpha Sigma Phi. Christian Scientist. Clubs: Harvard (Boston), Yacht (St. Thomas, V.I.). Home: 1010 Memorial Dr Cambridge MA 02138

GREER, GERMAINE, author; b. nr. Melbourne, Australia, Jan. 29, 1939; d. Eric Reginald and Margaret May Mary (Lanfrancam) Greer; B.A. with honors in English and French Lit., U. Melbourne, 1959; M.A. with honors in English, U. Sydney (Australia), 1961; Ph.D. (Commonwealth scholar), Newnham Coll. of Cambridge U. (Eng.), 1964; m. May 1968 (separated). Lectr. English, U. Warwick (Eng.), 1967—. Author: The Female Eunuch, 1970. A leader women's liberation movement. Address: care U Warwick Coventry Warwickshire England

GREER, JOHN JAMES, interior designer; b. Washington, July 18, 1913; s. John J. and Mildred (Steuart) G.; student U. Pa., 1932-34, George Washington U., 1935-37, Pa. Acad. Fine Arts, 1933-34. Co-ordinator home furnishings and design Woodward & Lothrop dept. store, Washington, 1942- 47; pres., chmn. bd. John J. Greer-Maurice D. Blum Assos., Inc., Washington, 1948—; designer, decorator numerous clubs, offices, pvt. homes, apts., embassies. Mem. bd. Internat. Sch. Interior Design. Mem. Friends Corcoran Gallery, Washington; chmn. environmental design com. Filene Center-Wolf Trap Farm Park for Performing Arts, Vienna, Va.; mem. bicentennial fashion com. Washington's Bicentennial, 1776-1976. Recipient design certificate of merit Upholstery Leather Group, 1955; Interior of Year award Materna Assos., N.Y.C., 1954. Mem. Am. Inst. Designers (pres. D.C. chpt. 1966-68). Clubs: Washington Arts (pres., chmn. bd. 1970-71); City Tavern. Address: 1212 Potomac St NW Washington DC 20007 (summer) 416 Pilot Town Rd Lewes DE 19958

GREER, JOSEPH EPPS, architect; b. Seattle, Feb. 13, 1923; s. Joseph and Gertrude (Greene) G.; B.A., U. Wash., 1948, B.Arch., 1950; m. Francoise Aubert, Sept. 15, 1957; children—Christine, Eric, Alan. Pvt. practice architect and engr., 1951—; sr. partner, gen. mgr. White-Greer Assos., Washington, Paris, France, Geneva, Switzerland, 1960—. Served with USMCR, 1942-46. Fellow Am. Soc. C.E., Inst. Dirs. (London), Societe des Ingenieurs Civils de France; mem. A.I.A. (Scholastic award 1950), Archtl. Assn. (London), Societe des Amis des Chateaux de la Loire (France) (life), Delta Kappa Epsilon, Tau Sigma Delta. Episcopalian. Clubs: Seattle Tennis; Directors (London); Cercle Haussmann (Paris). Home: 6 rue Boutard Neuilly-sur-Seine 92 France Office: 26 rue du Renard Paris (4) 75 France

GREER, JOSEPH MOSS, steel co. exec.; b. Paris, Mo., Feb. 27, 1915; s. James Kirkland and Katherine (Moss) G.; B.S., Northwestern U., 1936; m. Gene Crawford, Aug. 1, 1936 (dec. Aug. 1948); children—Carl Crawford, James Kirkland II; m. 2d, Mary Anne Thompson, Jan. 14, 1950 (dec. Feb. 1971). Trainee, Gen. Electric Co., 1936-37; with U.S. Steel Corp., 1937—, gen. mgr. prodn. planning, 1956-65, v.p. prodn. planning, 1965—. Mem. Mt. Lebanon (Pa.) Twp. Zoning Bd. Adjustment, 1956-60. Mem. Am. Iron and Steel Inst., Assn. Iron and Steel Engrs. Clubs: University, Duquesne (Pitts.); St. Clair Country (Bridgeville, Pa.). Home: 4 Parkridge Lane Pittsburgh PA 15228 Office: 600 Grant St Pittsburgh PA 15230

GREER, JOSEPH PHILIP, hospital dir.; b. Boone, N.C., Apr. 3, 1922; s. Isaac Garfield and Willie Celia (Spainhour) G.; grad. Mars Hill Acad., 1939; B.S., Wake Forest Coll., 1943; student hosps. adminstrn., U. Chgo., 1949-50; m. Sarah Amelia Reich, July 1, 1950. Dist. supr. Broyhill Furniture Factories, 1946-49; asst. dir. U. N.C. Hosp., Chapel Hill, 1950-55; dir. St. Lukes Hosp., Chgo., 1955-59; dir. Children's Hosp. Medical Center, Boston, 1959-62; dir. Children's Memorial Hosp., Chgo., Ill., 1962-66, exec. v.p., 1966—; dir. Asso. Hosps. Laundry, Inc., Hosp. Purchasing Corp. Chmn. pub. relations and pub. information com. Chgo. Hosp. Council. Mem. citizens com. U. Ill.; trustee Bishop Anderson Found. Served with U.S. Maritime and Merchant Marine, 1943-46. Mem. Am. Hosp. Assn., Chgo. Welfare Council, Council Frgn. Relations, Greater Boston Hosp. Assn. (trustee), Hosp. Adminstrs. Study Soc., Phi Kappa Psi. Home: 1448 Lake Shore Dr Chicago IL 60610 Office: 2300 Children's Plaza Chicago IL 60614

GREER, MICHAEL, actor; b. Galesburg, Ill. Theatrical appearance in Fortune and Men's Eyes, 1969; films include The Gay Deceivers; Fortune; The Magic Garden of Stanley Sweetheart; author comedy material for Phyllis Diller, Debbie Reynolds, Rip Taylor, Larry Storch. Address: 46 E 65th St New York City NY*

GREER, ROGER CLEMENT, librarian; b. Chatfield, Minn., Apr. 29, 1928; s. Richard and Henrietta (Sorenson) G.; A.B., St. John's U., Collegeville, Minn., 1950; postgrad. Columbia, 1954-55; M.L.S., Rutgers U., 1956, Ph.D., 1964; m. Natalia Markulis, Jan. 9, 1954; children—Wanda, Marc, Felicia. Asst., Bklyn. Pub. Library, 1954-55; bus. and tech. librarian Linden (N.J.) Pub. Library, 1956-57; head processing unit Purdue U. Library, 1957-60; instr. Rutgers U. Grad. Sch. Library Service, 1960-64; dir. libraries State Univ. Coll., Potsdam, N.Y., 1964-67; asst. dean Sch. Library Sci., Syracuse U., 1967-68, dean, 1968-, asso. prof., 1967-; lectr. library studies U. Hawaii, summer 1965-66; spl. research on U.S. Nat. Bibliographies, 1961-64. Mem. adv. bd. Mater Dei Coll., Ogdensburg, N.Y., 1966—. Pres. North Country Reference, Research and Resources Council, 1964-66, trustee, 1964-67, hon. trustee, 1967-. Served with USNR, 1945-46, U.S. Army, 1951-54. Mem. N.Y. Library Assn. (pres. coll. and univ. libraries sect. 1968-69), Assn. Coll. and Research Libraries, Am. Assn. Information Sci., Aircraft Owners and Pilots Assn., Onondaga Hill Vol. Fire Dept. Democrat. Roman Catholic. Contbr. articles to jours. Home: 5011 Skyline Terrace Syracuse NY 13215

GREER, S. MARCUS, former bus. exec.; b. Pittsburg, Tex., 1899; grad. U. Tex., 1921; m. Margaret Griffith; children—John Marcus, Robert Griffith, Margaret McLean (Mrs. Camp). Dir. Terrell State Bank, (Tex.); dir., mem. exec. Jefferson Standard Life Ins. Co., Greensboro, N.C.; vice chmn. bd. dirs. First City Nat. Bank of Houston, pres., 1963-69, now dir.; dir. Am. Nat. Ins. Co., Galveston, Heights State Bank, Houston. Trustee Moody Found., Galveston, Meth. Hosp., Houston, Baylor Coll. Medicine, Houston. Home: 5607 Bordley St Houston TX 77027 Office: First City Nat Bank Houston TX 77002

GREER, SCOTT A., sociologist; b. Sweetwater, Tex., Oct. 25, 1922; s. Azzie Allen and Mary (Scott) G.; A.B., Baylor U., 1946; M.A., U. Cal. at Los Angeles, 1951, Ph.D., 1952; m. Ann Louise Lennarson, Dec. 1969; 1 dau., Eve Shannon; m. 2d, Ann Lennarson, Dec. 1969. Faculty, U. Cal. at Santa Barbara, 1951-52, Occidental Coll., 1952-56; chief sociologist Met. St. Louis Survey, 1956-57; faculty Northwestern U., Evanston, Ill., 1957—. Cons., lectr., writer in field. Recipient Ariz. Quar. Poetry award, 1961. Fellow Am. Sociol. Assn.; mem. Sociol. Research Assn. Author: Social Organization, 1955; The Last Man In, 1959; Exploring the Metropolitan Community (with others), 1960; The Emerging City, 1962; Governing the Metropolis, 1962; Metropolitics, 1963; Urban Renewal and American Cities, 1965; The New Urbanization, 1968; The Logic of Social Inquiry; The Concept of Community, 1969; (poetry) The Landscape Has Voices, 1946, Via Urbana, 1964. Former asso. editor Urban Affairs Quar., Am. Sociol. Rev. Office: Dept of Sociology Northwestern U Evanston IL 60201

GREER, T.D., chem. co. exec.; b. Greenville, S.C., 1931. Vice pres., asst. to pres. Texize Chems. Inc., Greenville, 1955-62, v.p. consumer products div., 1962-67, sr. v.p. marketing and sales, 1967-69, pres., dir., 1969—; pres. Simoniz Co. subsidiary Morton Internat. Inc.; v.p., dir. Norwich Pharmacal Co. Served with USNR, 1951-56. Home: Route 6 Knollwood Dr Greenville SC 29607 Office: PO Box 368 Greenville SC 29602*

GREER, THOMAS HOAG, educator, historian; b. Bklyn., Apr. 18, 1914; s. Thomas H. and Lillian E. (Marmion) G.; A.B., U. Cal. at Berkeley, 1935, M.A., 1936, Ph.D., 1938; m. Margarette M. Cheney, Dec. 17, 1939; children—Thomas M., Margarette E. Instr., San Diego State Coll., 1938-42; supt. USAAF Pre-Flight Sch., Santa Ana, Cal., 1942-44; chief hist. studies Air Hist. Office, 1946-47; faculty Mich. State U., Lansing, 1947—, prof. humanities 1956—, chmn. dept., 1963-68. Served to capt. USAAF, 1943-46. Faculty fellow Am. Council Learned Socs., 1952. Recipient Distinguished Faculty award Mich. State U., 1960. Mem. Am. Hist. Assn., Orgn. Am. Historians, Am. Assn. U. Profs., Am. Studies Assn., Phi Beta Kappa, Pi Gamma Mu. Author: American Social Reform Movements, 1949; USAAF in World War II, vol. VI, 1955; Development of Air Doctrine in Army Air Arm, 1955; What Roosevelt Thought, 1958; Curriculum Building in General Education, 1960; Brief History of Western Man, 1972. Gen. editor: Classics of Western Thought, 1964. Home: 427 Collingwood Dr East Lansing MI 48823

GREER, WALTER EUGENE, Jr., textile exec.; b. Belton, S.C., Sept. 24, 1902; s. Walter Eugene and Inez (Campbell) G.; A.B., Furman U., 1923; m. Sue Vaughn, July 15, 1924; 1 dau., Margaret (Mrs. Walter H. Kroening). Sec. and asst. treas. Judson Mills, Greenville, S.C., 1928-45; with Burlington Mills Corp., Greensboro, N.C., 1945-68, v.p., dir., 1947-52, exec. v.p., 1952-55; exec. v.p., dir. Burlington Industries, Inc., 1955- 68. Chief synthetic fabric sect. Textile, Clothing and Leather Bur., WPB, 1943-45. Baptist. Club: Greensboro (N.C.) Country. Home: 305 Kimberly Dr Greensboro NC 27408

GREET, WILLIAM CABELL, educator; b. El Paso, Tex., Jan. 28, 1901; s. William Dement and Eleanor Love (Martin) G.; A.B., U. of South, 1920, D. Litt., 1959; postgrad. Harvard Law, 1920- 21; A.M., Columbia, 1924, Ph.D., 1926; m. Katherine Hyde, Sept. 11, 1926; 1 dau., Anne Hyde (Mrs. John E. Cushing). Tutor in English, U. Tex., 1921-22; instr. U. of South, 1922, U. Colo., 1924, U. Cal., 1925; lectr. Barnard Coll., Columbia, 1926-27, instr. 1927-29, asst. prof., 1929-38, asso. prof., 1938-46, prof., English, 1946-53, McIntosh prof., 1953-66, emeritus, spl. lectr., 1966-69; lectr. Bryn Mawr Coll., 1937-41, 45; vis. prof. U. Montpellier and U. Aix-en-Provence, France, 1950-51, U. Ariz., 1969, U. Zagreb and U. Ljubljana (both Yugoslavia), 1969-70. Guggenheim fellow, 1952; dir. recordings Am. speech and modern poets; editor Am. Speech mag., 1933-52; speech cons. CBS, 1937-39, 40—; chmn. editorial adv. com. Funk and Wagnalls Coll. Standard Dictionary, 1942-48; adv. editor Am. Coll. Dictionary, 1942-68; chmn. adv. com. Century Cyclopedia of Names, 1948—; chmn. adv. com. Thorndike-Barnhart dictionaries, 1949—; adviser Walt Disney Prodns., 1947; linguistic adviser Scott, Foresman Basic Reading Program, 1956—. Mem. Modern Lang. Assn. Am., Am. Dialect Soc., Nat. Council Tchrs. English, Linguistic Soc. Am., Internat. Assn. U. Profs. English, Phi Gamma Delta. Democrat. Episcopalian. Clubs: Century, Columbia Faculty. Editor. Author: World Words, 1944, 1948; (with others) Listen, Speak, and Write (a series), 1960—; My Little Pictionary (child's dictionary), 1962; My Second Pictionary, 1964; In Other Words, a Beginning Thesaurus, 1968; In Other Words, a Jr. Thesaurus, 1969. Contbr. to mags. Home: 1201 Alta Vista Rd Santa Barbara CA 93103

GREEVER, LEDDY L., aircraft mfg. co. exec.; b. 1913. In retail drug bus., 1928-41; with Beech Aircraft Corp., Wichita, Kan., 1941—, v.p., 1950-56, v.p. sales, 1956-60, v.p., dir., 1960—. Office: 9709 E Central Av Wichita KS 67206*

GREEVER WILLIAM ST. CLAIR, educator, historian; b. Lexington, Va., July 22, 1916; s. Gustavus Garland and May St. Clair (Stocking) G.; B.A., Pomona Coll., 1938; M.A., Harvard, 1940, Ph.D., 1949; m. Janet Elizabeth Groff, Aug. 24, 1951; 1 dau., Barbara Clair. Instr. bus. history Northwestern U., 1947-49; mem. faculty U. Ida., 1949-, chmn. dept. history, 1956-, prof. history, 1958—. Served with AUS, 1942-46. Guggenheim fellow, 1958-59. Mem. Am. Hist. Assn. (council Pacific Coast br. 1957-59), Orgn. Am. Historians, Am. Assn. U. Profs. (pres. local chpt. 1955-56), Phi Beta Kappa. Author: Arid Domain: The Santa Fe Railway and Its Western Land Grant (prize Pacific history Pacific Coast br. Am. Hist. Assn. 1954), 1954; The Bonanza West: The Story of the Western Mining Rushes (Spur award best nonfiction Western, Western Writers Am. 1963), 1963. Bd. editors Pacific Hist. Rev., 1956-58. Contbr. profl. jours. Home: 315 S Hayes St Moscow ID 83843

GREGG, CHARLES STONE, pub. co. exec.; b. N.Y.C., May 27, 1928; s. William Burr and Dorothy (Kilbourne) G.; grad. Lawrenceville Sch., 1945; student U. Nanking, 1948-49, Lingnan U., 1949, Columbia, 1949-50; m. Patricia Hagerty, Nov. 15, 1951; children—Peter Paul, John, Dorothy, Catherine, James, Thaddeus. Reporter, N.Y. Daily News, 1952-57; pub. relations dir. N.Y. Central System, 1957-59; editor NBC, 1959-63; pres. Gregg Press, Upper Saddle River, N.J., 1963—, Gregg, D'Alessandre Assos., Washington, 1970—. Sec., Ridgewood Pub. Library, 1968—. Vice chmn., finance chmn. N.J. Democratic party, 1966-69, candidate for Congress, 1968. Trustee Montclair State Coll. Served with AUS, 1945-48. Fellow Peabody Mus., Salem, Mass.; Pintard fellow N.Y. Hist. Soc. Mem. Fgn. Policy Assn., Nat. Wildlife Fedn., Alliance Francaise, N.A.A.C.P. Editor: Am. Imperialism Series, The Am. Journalists, Am. Environmental Studies, N.Y. Times, 1970-71. Home: 33 Maynard Ct Ridgewood NJ 07450 Office: 121 Pleasant Av Upper Saddle River NJ 07458

GREGG, DAVIS WEINERT educator; b. Austin, Tex., Mar. 12, 1918; s. Davis Alexander and Lorene (Murff) G.; B.B.A., U. Tex., 1939; M.B.A., U. Pa., 1940, Ph.D., 1948; m. Mildred Grace McDaniel, May 15, 1942; childrenMary Cynthia Davis William. Underwriter Aetna Casualty & Surety Co., Hartford, Conn., 1940- 41; asst. prof. naval sci. U. Minn., 1945-46; prof. ins. Ohio State U., 1948-49, Grad. Sch. Bus. Stanford, 1949; asst. dean Am. Coll. Life Underwriters, Phila., 1949-51, dean, 1952-53, trustee, 1951-, pres., 1954—. Dir. 1st Internat. Ins. Conf., Internat. Ins. Seminars; past chmn. Commn. on Ins. Terminology. Mem. adv. council on continuing edn. Princeton Theol. Sem.; v.p. bd. pensions United Presbyn. Ch. Trustee Charles W. Griffith Meml. Found. for Ins. Edn.; chmn. governing com. McCahan Found. Basic Research in Security, Risk and Insurance, 1965-. Mem. Am. Risk and Ins. Assn. (pres. 1961), A.A.A.S., Am. Econ. Assn., Am. Sociol. Assn., Acad. Polit. and Social Sci., Am. Soc. Chartered Life Underwriters (dir.), Beta Gamma Sigma. Presbyn. (ruling elder). Clubs: Overbrook Golf Club; Union League (Phila.). Author: An Analysis of Group Life Insurance, 1950; Group Life Insurance, 1964; Insurance Courses Outside the United States, 1960. Editor: Irwin Series in Insurance and Economic Security; Life and Health Insurance Handbook 1964; World Insurance Trends, 1960; Property and Liability Insurance Handbook, 1965. Home: 820 Castlefinn Lane Bryn Mawr PA 19010 Office: 270 Bryn Mawr Av Bryn Mawr PA 19010

GREGG, DONALD CROWTHER, educator; b. Marlboro, N.H., June 25, 1913; s. Arthur E. and Ida May (Crowther) G.; B.S., U. Vt., 1935; M.S., U. N.H., 1937; Ph.D., Columbia, 1941; m. Florence Bentley Green, May 29, 1943; children—Bentley Crowther, Fulton Mills. Asst. chemistry U. N.H., 1935-37, Columbia, 1937-39; research chemist Wallace & Tiernan Products, Belleville, N.J., 1940-41; faculty Harvard, 1940; vis. lectr., summer 1946; instr., asst. prof. Amherst (Mass.) Coll., 1941-46; prof. U. Vt., 1952—, Pomeroy prof. chemistry, 1963—; vis. prof. U. Fla., 1962-63; sci. faculty fellow NSF, 1962-63. Trustee Fletcher Free Library, 1964—. Fellow Am. Inst. Chemists, Vt. Acad. Arts and Scis.; mem. Am. Chem. Soc. (chmn. Western Vt. sect. 1953), Am. Assn. U. Profs. (pres. Vt. chpt. 1953-55), New Eng. Assn. Chemistry Tchrs. (hon.), New Eng. Acad. Sci. (pres. 1965-66), Vt. Library Trustees Assn. (pres. 1968-69), Sigma Xi (pres. Vt. chpt. 1952-53), Alpha Chi Sigma, Phi Lambda Upsilon, Sigma Delta Xi. Clubs: Sagamore Beach Colony, Burlington Tennis (v.p.; dir. 1959-62). Author Principles of Chemistry, 3d edit., 1968; College Chemistry, 2d edit., 1965; Chemistry in the Laboratory, 1966. Home: 60 University Terrace Burlington VT 05401

GREGG, DONALD EATON, research physiologist; b. Bridgeport, Conn., Mar. 24, 1902; s. Hugh Gilmore and Julia (Ober) G.; B.S. in Chemistry, Colgate U., 1924; M.S. (Porter fellow 1928-30), U. Rochester, 1929, Ph.D., 1930, M.D., 1946; m. Maria Grana, Jan. 1927; children—James Alan, William Gilmore, John Bruce. Instr. physiology Western Res. U. Med. Sch., 1930-34, asst. prof., 1934-39, asso. prof., 1939-44; chief research physician Med. Research Lab., Dept. Army, Ft. Knox, Ky., 1946-50; chief dept. cardiorespiratory diseases Walter Reed Army Inst. Research, Washington, 1950—. Recipient Exceptional Civilian Service award Sec. Army, 1959, Distinguished Civilian Service award Dept. Def., 1961, Presdl. award for distinguished fed. civilian service, 1962. Fellow Am. Coll. Cardiology, Am. Coll. Chest Physicians; mem. Am. Physiol. Soc., Am. Heart Assn. (exec. com. basic sci. sect.; Research Achievement award 1963), A.A.A.S., Am. Soc. Study Arteriosclerosis, Inter-Am. Cardiol. Soc., Soc. Exptl. Biology and Medicine, Peruvian Nat. Cardiol. Soc., Italian Soc. Exptl. Biology, Phi Beta Kappa, Sigma Xi, Alpha Omega Alpha. Author: The Coronary Circulation in Health and Disease, 1950. Contbg. author: Ency. of the Cardiovascular System, 1959; The Physiological Basis of Medical Practice, 1961; Man's Dependence on the Earthly Atmosphere, 1962; Blood Vessels and Lymphatics, 1962; Handbook of Physiology, 1963; Shock-Pathogenesis and Therapy, 1962; Coronary Heart Disease, 1963; The Etiology of Myocardial Infarction, 1963; Oxygen in the Animal Organism, 1964; The Coronary Circulation and Energetics of the Myocardium, 1967; Heart Failure: Pathophysiological and Clinical Aspects, 1968; Microcirculation as Related to Shock, 1968. Cons. editor: Circulation Research, Am. Jour. Physiology, Am. Heart Jour., Am. Jour. Cardiology. Author numerous articles to profl. jours. Home: 3535 Chevy Chase Lake Dr Chevy Chase MD 20015 Office: Walter Reed Army Inst Research Washington DC 20012

GREGG, DOUGLAS CLARK, oil co. exec.; b. San Luis Obispo, Cal., 1908; A.B., Stanford, 1930, LL.B., 1933; married. Admitted to Cal. bar; with firm Andrews, Blanche & Kline, 1933-39; asst. counsel Union Oil Co., Los Angeles, 1939-63, gen. counsel, 1963-69, v.p., gen. counsel, 1969—; v.p., dir. Minerals Exploration Co.; asst. sec., dir. Unoco Ltd.; dir. Collier Carbon & Chem. Corp., Pure Oil Middle East, Inc., Ras Al Khaimah Oil Co., Sully-Miller Contracting Co., Union Oil Devel. Co., Union Oil Exploration & Prodn. Co. Home: 690 Bradford St Pasadena CA 91105 Office: Union Oil Co Cal Union Oil Center Los Angeles CA 90017

GREGG, EARLE COVINGTON, educator; b. Cleve., Aug. 22, 1918; s. Earle C. and Elsie (Emms) G.; B.S., Case Inst. Tech., 1940, M.S., 1941, Ph.D., 1949; student Cornell U., 1941-42, Mass. Inst. Tech., 1942-43, Columbia, 1943-45; m. Dorothy C. Davies, June 27, 1942; childrenLynn Dianne, Suzanne C. Research asso. Cleve. Clinic Found., 1937-41, Mass. Inst. Tech., 1942-43, Columbia, 1943-45; asso. prof. Case Inst. Tech., 1949-58; asso. prof. radiology Western Res. U., Cleve., 1958-65, prof., 1965—; cons. physicist St. Lukes, Highland View, Crile VA, Luth. hosps.; partner Biophys. Specialties Co., 1947-64; dir. Hamlet Devel. Corp., Hamlet Health Center. Bd. dirs. Cleve. Hearing and Speech Center; trustee Hamlet Found. Fellow Am. Phys. Soc.; mem. Radiation Research Soc., Biophys. Soc., Cleve. Physics Soc. (past pres.), Radiol. Soc., Am. Cancer Soc. Contbr. articles to profl. jours. Patentee in field. Asso. editor Jour. Applied Physics, 1953-56. Home: 328 N Main St Chagrin Falls OH 44022 Office: Wearn Labs Western Res U Cleveland OH 44106

GREGG, HAROLD LARUE, banker; b. Harmony, Pa., Mar. 26, 1910; s. Fred H. and Idella (Reichenbach) G.; grad. Rutgers U. Grad. Sch. Banking, 1947; m. Katherine Hemerly, Oct. 27, 1932. With Union Nat. Bank, Pitts., 1929—, sr. v.p., 1967—, sec., 1964—. Home: 125 Crestview Dr Pittsburgh PA 15236 Office: PO Box 837 Pittsburgh PA 15230

GREGG, HUGH, cabinet mfg. co. exec., former gov. N.H., b. Nashua, N H., Nov. 22, 1917; s. Harry A. and Margaret R. (Richardson) G.; grad. Phillips Exeter Acad., 1935; A.B., Yale, 1939; LL.B., Harvard, 1942; LL.D. U. N.H. 1953; M.A., Dartmouth, 1953; D.C.L., New Eng. Coll., 1954; m. Catherine M. Warner, July 24, 1940; children—Cyrus Warner, Judd Alan. Admitted to N.H. bar, 1942, Mass., 1948; practice of law, Nashua, since 1942, mem. Sullivan, Gregg & Horton; former pres., treas. Gregg & Son, Inc., Nashua, N.H.; gov. of N.H. 1953- 55; chmn. bd. Indian Head Nat. Bank Nashua; pres. treas. Gregg Cabinets Ltd., Chambly, Que.; dir. Wildcat Mountain Corp., N.H. Indian Head Nat. Bank, Manchester, N.H. Bankshares, Inc.; clk., former co-pub. N.H. Profiles; former mem. adv. bd. Am. Mut. Liability Ins. Co. Mem. Nat. Exec. Res. Pres. Nashua Fresh Air Camp; aiderman-at-large, Nashua, 1948-50, mayor, 1950. Dir. New Eng. Council, 1952-55, pres. 1955- 57. Spl. agt. Army CIC, 1942-46, 50-52. Mem. Nat. Inst. Wood Kitchen Cabinets (first v.p.), Canadian Kitchen Cabinet Assn. (dir.), Am. Legion, V.F.W. Home: RFD 3 Gregg Rd Nashua NH 03060 Office: 148 Main St Nashua NH 03060

GREGG, JAMES CALVIN, lawyer; b. Ebensburg, Pa., Dec. 26, 1924; s. Oliver E. and Sophie Gregg; student Ind. State Tchrs. Coll., 1946-47; LL.B., George Washington U., 1950; m. Dora Osterstock, June 9, 1951; children—Gregory Michael, Watson W. Admitted to D.C. bar, 1950, Va. bar, 1953; partner firm Gregg & Tait, Washington, 1950-57; partner firm MacLeay, Lynch, Bernhard and Gregg, Washington, 1957—. Vice pres., dir. Asso. Realty Mortgage Co. Served with USAAF, 1943-46. Mem. Va. State Bar, Defense Research Inst., Phi Delta Phi. Home: 3156 N 21st St Arlington VA 22001 Office: 1625 K St NW Washington DC 20006 also: 3132 10th St N Arlington VA 22201

GREGG, LUCIUS PERRY, Jr., univ. adminstr.; b. Henderson, N.C., Jan. 16, 1933; s. Lucius Perry and Rachel (Jackson) G.; B.S. with distinction, U.S. Naval Acad., 1955; S.M., Mass. Inst. Tech., 1961; student Cath. U. Am., 1961-62; m. Doris Marie Jefferson, May 30, 1959; 1 son, Lucius Perry III. Research scientist, instrumentation lab. Mass. Inst. Tech., 1960-61; research adminstr. Hdqrs. Office Aerospace Research, USAF, 1961-62; project scientist Air Force Office Sci. Research, 1962-63; dir. Office Research Coordination, Northwestern U., 1965-, instr. mech. engring. and astron. sci., also asso. dean scis., 1966-. Mem. adv. council State Tech. Services Ill., 1966-; mem. Nat. Acad. Sci. Com. on NASA U. Relations, 1967-; mem. Ill. Urban Area Study Commn., 1968-; chmn. edn. com. Evanston Anti-Poverty Council Office Econ. Opportunity, 1967; mem. citizens adv. com. on human relations Evanston High Sch., 1968. Bd. dirs. United Community Services, Evanston, 1967-, Community Hosp., Evanston, 1967—; trustee Universities Research Assn. Served to capt. USAF, 1955-65; capt. Res. Recipient Bausch & Lomb Math. and Sci. award, 1950; certificate of recognition Washington Acad. Scis., 1964; named one of 10 outstanding young men Chgo. Jr. Assn. Commerce and Industry, 1966; named Man of Year, Service Guild, Evanston, 1966. Home: 2000 Sheridan Rd Evanston IL 60201

GREGG, R. FRANK, conservation exec.; b. Denver, Dec. 15, 1925; s. John D. and Viola L. (Gerald) G.; student Kan. State U., 1943; B.A. in Journalism, U. Colorado, 1949; m. Virginia A. Shea, August 30, 1952; children—Scott F., Sara A. Bldg. editor Institutions mag., Chgo., 1949-51; dir. publs. Colo. Dept. Game and Fish, also editor Colo. Outdoor mag., 1951-57; exec. dir. Izaak Walton League Am., also editor Outdoor Am. mag., 1957-61; central states forest adv. bd. U.S. Forest Service, 1957-61, staff asst. Office Sec. Interior, 1962-63; exec. dir. Citizens Com. For Outdoor Recreation Resources Review Commn. Report, 1963-65; vice pres. Conservation Found., Wash., 1965—. Mem Pres.' Com. on Quetico-Superior, 1961-63. Served as pvt., inf., AUS 1943-46. Mem. Outdoor Writers Assn. Am., Izaak Walton League Am., Am. Fisheries Soc. Rotarian. Home: 6428 Hollins Dr Bethesda MD 20034 Office: 1250 Connecticut Av NW Washington DC 20036

GREGG, RICHARD ALEXANDER, educator; b. Paris, France, Aug. 22, 1927; s. Alan and Eleanor (Barrows) G.; grad. Deerfield (Mass.) Acad., 1945; A.B., Harvard, 1951, M.A., 1952; Ph.D., Columbia, 1962; m. Francoise Bouriez, June 6, 1953; 1 son, Jonathan Alan. Instr. Russian lang. Amherst (Mass.) Coll., 1957-58; instr. Russian lang. and lit. Brown U., 1959-60; from instr. to asso. prof. Russian lang. and lit. Columbia, 1960-69; prof. Russian, chmn. dept. Vassar Coll., 1970—. Served with USAAF, 1946-47. Ford Found. fellow, 1955-56; U.S. Govt. fellow, Leningrad, 1958-59; Guggenheim fellow, 1965-66. Mem. Modern Lang. Assn., Am. Assn. Advancement Slavic Studies. Author: F.I. Tiutchev: The Evolution of a Poet, 1965; also articles. Home: 64 Boardman Rd Poughkeepsie NY 12603

GREGG, RICHARD NELSON, museum dir.; b. Kalamazoo, Sept. 4, 1926; s. Sherman U. and Elizabeth (Dye) G.; student Western Mich. U., 1945-47; B.F.A., Cranbrook Acad. Art, 1949, M.F.A., 1950; m. Patricia Dunbar, June 17, 1952; children—William S., Joel D. Instr., Cranbrook Sch. Boys, 1950-51; instr. Worcester (Mass.) Art Mus., 1951-54; dir. Kalamazoo Art Inst., 1954-56; curator Toledo Art Mus., 1956-59; head edn. Art Inst. Chgo., 1959-61; dir. Paine Art Center, Oshkosh, Wis., 1961-69; dir. Joslyn Art Mus., Omaha, 1969—. Served with USAAF, 1945-46. Mem. Am. Assn. Museums, Art Mus. Dirs. Assn. Unitarian-Universalist. Rotarian. Address: Joslyn Art Museum 24th and Dodge Sta Omaha NB 68102

GREGG, RUSSELL TAAFFE, educator; b. Fairfield, Ill., July 24, 1903; s. John Lewis and Bertha Lee (Taaffe) G.; B.S., U. Ill., 1928, M.A., 1929, Ph.D., 1934; m. Genevieve Catherine Owen, June 7, 1930; children—Jane Gregg Steinhauer, Richard Owen. Rural sch. tchr., Wayne County, Ill., 1923-24; elementary sch. tchr., Fairfield, 1924-25; asst. in edn. U. Ill., 1928-33; instr. edn., asst. prin. U. Ill. High Sch., 1933-36, supr. visual aids library, 1933-36; asst. prof. edn. Syracuse U., 1936-39, asso. prof. edn., 1939-42, dir. curriculum workshops, 1939-42, supr. ednl. film library, 1938-42; asso. prof. edn. U. Wis.-Madison, 1945-48, prof. ednl. adminstrn., 1948—, chmn. dept. ednl. adminstrn., 1967-70, dir. Fellowship Program in Urban Sch. Adminstrn., 1968-70, dir. Research Tng. Program for State Dept. Edn. Personnel, 1967; vis. prof. U. So. Cal., 1950, U. Cal., Berkeley, 1955, U. Cal., Los Angeles, 1960. Cons. Pa. Gov.'s Com. on Edn., 1960; participant Wilton Park (Eng.) Internat. Conf., 1971; cons., coordinator Nat. Project Staff Devel. in State Ednl. Agencies, 1971-72. Pres. Shorewood Hills (Wis.) Bd. Edn., 1952-58. Trustee Univ. Council for Ednl. Adminstrn., 1958-61. Served to lt. comdr. USNR, 1942-45. Decorated Navy Commendation medal. Mem. Am. Assn. Sch. Adminstrs., Internat. Com. on Ednl. Adminstrn., Am. Ednl. Research Assn., Am. Friends of Wilton Park, Nat. Conf. Profs. Ednl. Adminstrn. (dir. 1946-49, pres. 1948-49), Am. Assn. U. Profs., N.E.A., Nat. Soc. for Study Edn., Wis. Edn. Assn., Acacia, Phi Kappa Phi, Phi Eta Sigma, Phi Delta Kappa, Kappa Delta Pi. Conglist. Rotarian. Clubs: University (Madison), Blackhawk Country (Shorewood Hills, Wis.). Co-editor, author: Administrative Behavior in Education, 1957. Author: (with others) A Functional Program of Teacher Education, 1941, Schools in Our Democratic Society, 1951, Personal Expenditures for High School Education, 1951, The County Superintendency in Wisconsin, 1957, Instructional Change and Its Relationship to Decision Making in School Systems, 1966, The School Board as an Agency for Resolving Conflicts, 1967, Wisconsin Educational Assessment Study, 1969. Mem. editorial adv. bd. Sch. Exec. mag., 1955-60. Home: 1202 Edgehill Dr Madison WI 53705

GREGG, WALTER EMMOR, steel co. exec.; b. Louisville, Jan. 12, 1914; s. Walter E. and Ethel (Barrett) G.; B.A., U. Del., 1936; m. Anne Roberson, Oct. 8, 1938; children—Walter Emmor, Mary Ann (Mrs. Nathaniel F. Tarbox II). With Remington Arms Co., 1936-50; v.p., asst. gen. mgr. Rem-Cru Titanium, Inc., Midland, Pa. 1950-58; asst. dir. operations, 1953-55, v.p., asst. gen. mgr., 1955-58; with Crucible Steel Co. Am., 1958-68, v.p. operations, 1960-63, sr. v.p., 1963-67, exec. v.p., 1967, also dir.; sr. exec. v.p. NVF Co., now pres., dir.; pres. Sharon Steel Corp.; dir., vice chmn. bd. Crucible Steel Internat., Crucible Steel Can. Trustee Geneva Coll., Beaver Falls, Pa. Mem. Am. Iron and Steel Inst., Am. Mgmt. Assn., Assn. Iron and Steel Engrs., Soc. for Advancement Mgmt. Clubs: Duquesne (Pitts.); Beaver Valley Country. Home: 675 Woodlawn Dr Sharon PA 16146 Office: Sharon Steel Corp PO Box 291 Sharon PA 16146

GREGOIRE, PAUL, archbishop; b. Verdun, France, Oct. 24, 1911; s. Albert and Marie (Lavoie) G.; Grand Sem., Montreal, 1937; Ph.D., S.T.L., License in Letters, M.A. in History, diploma pedagogy. Ordained priest Roman Cath. Ch., 1937; dir. Sem. de Ste-Thérèse; prod. philosophy edn. l'Ecole Normale Secondaire, l'Inst. Pedagogique; chaplain of students U. Montreal, 1950-61; bishop, 1961; aux. to archbishop of Montreal, also vicar gen. and dir. Office for the Clergy; apostolic adminstr. Archdiocese Montreal, 1967-68, archbishop, 1968—. Pres., French sect. Episcopal commn. ecumenism Canadian Cath. Conf., 1965; presided over numerous diocesan commns., 1965—. Office: Archbishop's Palace 1071 Rue de la Cathedrale Montreal 3 Quebec Canada

GREGOR ARTHUR, poet; b. Vienna, Austria, Nov. 18, 1923; s. Benjamin and Regine (Reiss) Goldenberg; came to U.S., 1939, naturalized, 1945; B.S. in Elec. Engring., Newark Coll. Engring., 1945. Engaged in engring., 1954, journalism, 1956-61; sr. editor Macmillan Co., 1962-70. Recipient 1st Appearance prize Poetry mag., 1948. Mem. P.E.N. Author: Octavian Shooting Targets, 1954; Declensions of a Refrain, 1957; Basic Movements, 1966; Figure in the Door, 1968; A Bed by the Sea, 1970; The Selected Poems of Arthur Gregor, 1971; also books for children. Contbr. maj. lit. revs. and magazines. Home: 49 Greenwich Av New York City NY 10014

GREGOR, HOWARD FRANK, educator, geographer; b. Two Rivers, Wis., Apr. 7, 1920; s. Stephen Phillip and Emily (Drissen) G.; B.S., U. Wis., 1946, M.S., 1947; Ph.D., U. Cal. at Los Angeles, 1950; m. Marjorie Evelyn Onley, Dec. 26, 1950; 1 dau., Marsha Evelyn. Instr. geography Ind. U., 1950-51; analyst CIA, Washington, 1951-53; vis. asst. prof. geography U. Ore., 1953-54; asst. planner Los Angeles County Regional Planning Commn., 1954-55; asst. prof. geography San Jose (Cal.) State Coll., 1955-60; asst. prof. geography U. Cal. at Davis, 1960-64, asso. prof., 1964-69, prof., chmn. dept., 1969—. Served with USAAF, 1942-45. Decorated D.F.C., Air Medal with 1 silver and 3 bronze oak leaf clusters. Mem. Assn. Pacific Coast Geographers (pres. 1960), Assn. Am. Geographers (pres. Pacific coast div. 1960), Am. Geog. Soc., Sigma Xi, Pi Gamma Mu, Phi Delta Kappa. Author: Environment and Economic Life, 1963; Geography of Agriculture: Themes in Research, 1970. Contbr. articles profl. jours. Home: 1309 Beech Lane Davis CA 95616

GREGORIADES, JOHN GREGORY, Greek diplomat; b. Istambul, Sept. 6, 1922; s. Gregory and Maria (Caloutas) G.; degree polit. sci., Athens U., 1945; M.A., Columbia, 1947; m. Ioanna Simeonoglou, June 9, 1951; 1 son, Gregory. With Ministry of Fgn. Affairs of Greece, 1952—; mem. Permanent Mission to UN, 1955-61; dir. Desk Turkish Affairs, 1961-62; asst. to Dir. Gen., 1962-63; mem. Permanent Delegation to NATO, 1963-67; consul gen. in Istambul, 1967-69; counselor, dep. chief mission Greek embassy, Washington, 1969—. Served with Hellenic Army, 1950-52. Decorated Order of George I and the Phoenix (Greece), Legion of Honor (France), Order of Nassau (Netherlands), Order of Leopold (Belgium), Order of Danebrog (Denmark), Order of Merit (Spain, Italy and Germany), Order of Holy Sepulcre. Home: 1001 Wilson Blvd Roslyn Arlington VA 22209 Office: 2221 Massachusetts Av Washington DC 20008

GREGORY, CHARLES A., lawyer; b. Lovington, Ill., Oct. 2, 1902; A.B. magna cum laude, Harvard, 1923, LL.B., 1927. Admitted to Ark. bar, 1926, Hawaii bar, 1927; mem. firm Cades, Schutte, Fleming & Wright, Honolulu. Mem. Bar Assn. Hawaii, Phi Beta Kappa. Office: 1st Hawaiian Bank Bldg Honolulu HI 96808*

GREGORY, CHARLES FRANCIS, medical educator; b. Battle Creek, Mich., Aug. 21, 1919; s. Charles Bernard and Ione (Cooper) G.; B.S., Ind. U., 1942, M.D., 1944; m. Dorothy Jane Pyle, Aug. 21, 1944; children—Charles Bernard, Michael Manion. Intern Wayne County Gen. Hosp., Eloise, Mich., 1944-45; resident Leila Hosp., Battle Creek, 1946-48, Methodist Hosp., Indpls., 1948-50, Ind. U. Med. Center, 1951-52; instr. orthopedic surgery Ind. U. Med. Sch., 1954-56; asso. prof., chmn. orthopedic surgery U. Tex. Southwestern Med. Sch., Dallas, 1956-61, prof. orthosurgery, 1961—. Nat. cons. orthopedics surgeon gen. USAF; mem. surgery adv. bd. Shrine Hosps. Crippled Children. Served with M.C., USNR, 1945-46, 52-54. Recipient award research Kappa Delta, 1952. Diplomate Am. Bd. Orthopedic Surgery. Mem. A.M.A., Am. Orthopedic Assn., Am. Acad. Orthopedic Surgery. Home: 5700 Stonegate Dr Dallas TX 75209

GREGORY, CHARLES OSCAR, educator, labor arbitrator; b. Derby, Conn., Apr. 22, 1902; s. Louis L. and Grace (Spencer) G.; A.B., Yale, 1924, LL.B., 1926; m. Mary Palache, Dec. 26, 1928; children—David Palache, Judith. Admitted to Conn. bar, 1926, N.Y. bar, 1927; practiced in N.Y.C. with Root, Clark, Buckner, Howland & Ballantine; asst. prof. law U. Wis., 1928-30; asso. prof. U. Chgo., 1930-41, prof., 1941-49; prof. law U. Va., 1949-67, John B. Minor prof. law, 1958-67; permanent umpire and arbitrator, collective agreements, 1943—, part time lectr. U. Conn. Law Sch. Solicitor U.S. Dept. Labor (on leave from U. Chgo.), 1936- 37. Chmn. Nat. Enforcement Commn., 1953. Mem. atty. gen.'s Nat. Com. Studt Anti-Trust Laws, 1953-55; mem. labor relations panel AEC, 1959—. Mem. Phi Beta Kappa, Alpha Delta Phi, Phi Delta Phi, Order of the Coif. Democrat. Conglist. Author: Labor and the Law, rev. edit., 1958; (with Harry Kalven) Cases and Materials on Torts, 1959, rev. edit., 1969. Contbr. Ency. Brit. Address: Route 1 Box 241-A Jaffrey NH 03452

GREGORY, CHRISTOF ROBERTS mfg. exec.; b. Lima, O., Apr. 1, 1932; B.S., U. San Francisco, 1954; M.S., Stanford University, 1956; m. Rosemarie Lois Brown, May 15, 1955; 1 son, Anthony Robinson. Sales rep. Ames-Brockton Fabricated Products, Akron, O., 1956-58, sales mgr. Coshocton, Ohio, 1959-61, gen. manager plant, 1961-68, v.p. sales, 1968--. Instr. bus. Coshocton Jr. College, 1968-69. Mem. Coshocton C. of C. (vice president 1967-68, pres. 1969-70), English Speaking Union, Coshocton Sertoma Club, Nat. Assn. Mfrs., Sales Executives Institute, Phi Beta Kappa, Sigma Chi, Phi Mu. Democrat. Mem. Christian Ch. (lay reader). Mason (32, Shriner). Clubs: Coshocton Country, Coshocton City, Running Deer Country. Home: 2d Av Coshocton OH Office: 3d Av Coshocton OH

GREGORY, DICK, comedian; b. St. Louis, 1932; student So. Ill. U., 1951-53, 55-56; m. Lillian Smith, 1959; children—Michele, Lynne, Paula, Pamela, Stephanie, Gregory, Christian. Miss. entertainer Esquire Club, Chgo.; opened night club Apex, Robbins, Ill.; master ceremonies Roberts Show Club, Chgo., 1959-60; night club appearances, Akron, Milw., Chgo., 1960, San Francisco, Hollywood, numerous other cities, 1961—; comedy act Playboy Club, Chgo., 1961; TV guest appearances Jack Parr show, others; record albums Dick Gregory in Living Black and White, Dick Gregory: The Light Side-Dark Side, others; lectr. univs. throughout U.S. Peace and Freedom Party candidate, 1968. Served with AUS, 1953-55. Winner Mo. mile championship, 1951, 52; named Outstanding Athlete, So. Ill. U., 1953. Author: From the Back of the Bus; Nigger, 1964; What's Happening, 1965; The Shadow That Scares Me; Write Me In; No More Lies, 1971. Home: 1451 E 55th St Chicago IL 60637 Office 79 W Monroe Chicago IL 60603

GREGORY DONALD MUNSON, lawyer; b. San Francisco, Jan. 21, 1897; s. Warren and Sarah (Hardy) G.; A.B., U. Cal. at Berkeley, 1920; LL.B., Harvard, 1923; m. Josephine Wallace, May 21, 1924; childrenJoan (Mrs. Thomas C. Benet), Donald Munson. Admitted to Cal. bar, 1924, since practiced in San Francisco, mem. firm Chickering & Gregory, 1926—. Del. Commn. for Relief in Belgium, 1916-17, Served as 2d lt. F.A., U.S. Army, 1917-19; lt. col. Adj. Gen. Dept., AUS, 1942-45. Mem. Astron. Soc. Pacific (dir.), Am., San Francisco bar assns., State Bar of Cal., Am. Judicature Soc. Clubs: Pacific Union, Sierra, Commonwealth (San Francisco); Burlingame (Cal.) Country. Home: 940 Green St San Francisco CA 94138 Office: 111 Sutter St San Francisco CA 94104

GREGORY, EDWARD WADSWORTH, Jr., univ. prof.; b. Chase City, Va., Sept. 29, 1903; s. Edward Wadsworth and Kate Winn (Cleveland) G.; A.B., U. Va., 1925, M.A., 1926, Ph.D., 1931; m. Margaret Louise Jeffreys, Aug. 28, 1934; 1 son, Allen Wadsworth. Instr. sociology, U. Va., 1925-28; asst, prof. sociology, U. Ala., 1928-29, asso. prof., 1929-35, prof., 1935-45; prof. sociol. U. Md., 1946; prof. sociol. U. Richmond (Va.) 1946—. Chmn. Tuscaloosa Co. (Ala.) Bd. Pub. Welfare, 1940-43; pres. Ala. Conf. Social Work, 1941-42; pres. Va. Council Social Welfare, 1950-51; mem. Commn. on Aging, Virginia, 1962-68; chmn. Welfare and Instns. Va., 1964-71. Chmn. adv. bd. Pub. Welfare, Richmond, 1953-55; pres. Richmond Area Community Council, 1951-53. Mem. War Price and Rationing Bd. of Tuscaloosa Co., 1942-43; mem. commn. on Reorgn. State Govt., Va., 1947. Commd. lt., U.S.N.R., Jan. 1943, lt. comdr., Oct. 1945 (on active duty, Feb. 1943-Jan. 1946). Mem. Am. Sociol. Soc., So. Sociol. Soc. (pres. 1939), Nat. Council on Family Relations (nat. adv. council, 1939-42), Am. Assn. U. Profs., Va. Social Sci. Assn. (pres. 1951-52), Family and Children's Service Richmond (bd. dirs.), Delta Sigma Phi, Delta Sigma Rho, Phi Beta Kappa, Phi Delta Kappa, Alpha Kappa Delta. Raven. Methodist. Club: Country of Va.; Torch. Author: Introductory Sociology (with Lee Bidgood), 1939. Co-author: Social Control, 1947, rev. ed., 1956. Contbr. articles to jours. Address: U Richmond Richmond VA 23220

GREGORY, GEORGE, surgeon; b. Burlington, Mass., 1921; M.D., Tufts U., 1948. Intern Los Angeles County Gen. Hosp., 1948-50, resident gen. surgery, 1951-55, sr. surg. resident, 1954-55, mem. active staff, 1956—; resident thoracic surgery Olive View Sanitarium, Los Angeles, 1955-56; mem. active staff Hollywood Presbyn. Hosp., Holy Cross Hosp.; asst. prof. surgery Loma Linda Coll., 1956—; now also personal physician to President Johnson. Diplomate Am. Bd. Surgery. Mem. A.M.A. Address: 13320 Riverside St Sherman Oaks CA 91413*

GREGORY, GEORGE MITCHELL, investment banker; b. Bklyn., Feb. 10, 1905; s. William H. and Elizabeth (Mitchell) G.; student St. Paul's Sch., 1918-23, Trinity Coll., 1924-28; m. Marjorie Waddell, Jan. 25, 1933 (dec.); 1 son, Robert H.; m. 2d, Mary Louise Feitner, Sept. 17, 1957; childrenGay H., Richard Hyde. With Theodore Prince & Co., 1928-29. Kountze Bros., 1929-31, Foster & Co., Inc., 1932-35; pres., dir. Gregory & Son, Inc., N.Y.C., 1935-; sr. partner Gregory & Son, N.Y. c. Mem. St Andrews Soc., S.A.R. Clubs: Bankers of America, Canadian, Union League (N.Y.C.); Brooklyn; South Bay Golf. Bay Shore Yacht (L.I.); Everglades, Bath and Tennis (Palm Beach, Fla.). Home: 40 Lawrence Lane Bay Shore NY 11706 also 140 Brizilian Av Palm Beach FL 33480

GREGORY, GUSTAV ROBINSON, economist, forester; b. Cass City, Mich., Sept. 1, 1915; s. William Alfred and Erna May (Roeser) G.; B.S., Central Mich. U., 1938; B.S. in Forestry, U. Mich., 1940, M.F., 1940; Ph.D., U. Cal. at Berkeley, 1953; m. Edna Ann Hano, Mar. 26, 1943; children-Bonnie Ann, Robin Scott, Sharolyn Kay. Timber cruiser U.S. Forest Service, West Coast, 1940, jr. research forester Allegheny Forest Expt. Sta., Beltsville, Md., 1941-42, forest economist E. Tex. br. So. Forest Expt. Sta., Nacogdoches, 1945-49; George Willis Pack asst. prof. resource econs. Sch. Natural Resources, U. Mich., Ann Arbor, 1952-55, asso. prof., 1955-60, prof., 1960-; chief analysis, survey sect., forestry div. FAO, Rome, Italy, 1960-61, forestry coordinator world indicative plan, Rome, 1966-67; cons. Treasury Dept., 1962, spl. fund UN, Mexico, 1963, Mexican Govt., summer 1964, Harvard Center Internat. Affairs, Liberia, 1965, Ford Found., India, 1970; co-dir. Seminar Tropical Hardwood Marketing, West Berlin, 1961, sr. economist timber study Pub. Land Law Rev. Commn. Served to lt. USNR, 1942-45. Mem. Soc. Am. Foresters (past chmn. div. econs.), Am. Econ. Assn., Phi Beta Kappa, Sigma Xi, Phi Kappa Phi, Phi Sigma, Xi Sigma Pi, Gamma Alpha. Contbr. articles profl. jours. Home: 2704 Brockman Blvd Ann Arbor MI 48014

GREGORY, HARRY K., mfg. co. exec.; b. 1914; ed. Coll. City N.Y., 1936; M.B.A., Harvard, 1939. Treas., Beaunit Corp., 1966—, also dir. Home: 46 Old Estate Rd Manhasset NY 11030 Office: 261 Madison Av New York City NY 10016*

GREGORY, HORACE VICTOR, poet, critic; b. Milw., Apr. 10, 1898; s. Henry Bolton and Anna Catherine (Henkel) G.; student German-English Acad., Milw., 1914-19, Milw. Sch. Fine Arts, 1913-16; B.A., U. Wis., 1923; m. Marya Zaturenska, Aug. 21, 1925; children—Joanna Elizabeth, Patrick Bolton. Free-lance writer, 1923-34, contbg. to New Republic, The Nation, Atlantic Monthly, Hound and Horn, Poetry mag. (Chgo.), New Verse (London), etc.; lectr. poetry and critical theory Sarah Lawrence Coll., Bronxville, N.Y., 1934—; editor New Letters in Am., 1937; Guggenheim fellow, 1951. Recipient Lyric prize Poetry mag., 1928, Helen Haire Levinson prize, 1934; Russell Loines award for poetry Am. Inst. Arts and Letters, 1942; fellowship award Acad. Am. Poets, 1961; Bollingen prize in poetry, 1965. Mem. Nat. Inst. Arts and Letters. Translator. Author: Chelsea Rooming House (verse), 1930; several books, 1930—, latest being A History of American Poetry, 1900-1940 (in collaboration with Marya Zaturenska), 1946; Selected Poems, 1951; Amy Lowell; Portrait of the Poet in Her Times, 1958; The World of James McNeil Whistler, 1959; Medusa in Gramercy Park (new poems), 1961; The Dying Gladiators and Other Essays, 1961; (with Marya Zaturenska) The Crystal Cabinet, 1962; Collected Poems, 1964; Love Poems of Ovid, new English version, 1964; Dorothy Richardson: An Adventure in Self-Discovery, 1967; The House on Jefferson Street: A Cycle of Memories (autobiography), 1971. Editor: The Triumph of Life, 1943; Selected Poetry of Robert Browning, 1956; (with Marya Zaturenska) The Mentor Book of Religious Verse, 1957, The Crystal Cabinet: An Invitation to Poetry, 1962, The Silver Swan, 1966; Henry Wadsworth Longfellow: Evangeline and Other Tales and Poems, 1964; Selected Poems of E.E. Cummings, 1965; asso. editor The Tigers Eye; editor The Portable Sherwood Anderson, 1949-71, The Selected Poems of George Gordon Lord Byron, 1969. Address: Palisades Rockland County NY 10964

GREGORY, IAN WALTER, educator, psychiatrist; b. London, Eng., July 14, 1926; s. Ernest Walter and Anna (Buckner) G.; B.A., U. Cambridge (Eng.), 1946, M.B., 1948, M.A., 1951, M.D., 1956; D. Psychiatry, U. Toronto (Can.), 1954; M.P.H., U. Mich., 1959; m. Eleanor Jean Dingwall, June 10, 1950; children—Robert Dalziel, Mary Elizabeth, Heather Jean, Roderick Ian. Came to U.S., 1959, naturalized, 1964. Instr. psychiatry U. Western Ont., 1955-58; Commonwealth Fund fellow U. Mich., 1958-59; asst. prof., then asso. prof. psychiatry U. Minn., 1959-65; prof. psychiatry, chmn. dept. Ohio State U., Coll. Medicine, 1965—. Cons. div. research grants NIH, 1963-65. Gold medal in psychiatry U. Toronto, 1954. Fellow Am. Psychiat. Assn. mem. of Delta Omega, Phi Kappa Phi. Author: Psychiatry: Biological and Social, 1961; (with E. Rosen) Abnormal Psychology, 1965; Fundamentals of Psychiatry, 2d edit., 1968; also articles. Home: 2019 Upper Chelsea Rd Columbus OH 43221

GREGORY, JAMES, librarian; b. Hendersonville, N.C., Dec. 24, 1923; s. James Parker and Hattie (Cochran) G.; A.B., Eastern Ky. State U., 1944; M.A., U. N.C., 1945; M.S. in L.S., Columbia, 1955. Head catalogue N.Y. Hist. Soc., 1956- 64, librarian, 1965-. Mem. N.Y. Tech. Services Libraries (pres. 1965- 66), Am., N.Y. State

Library assns., Grolier Club, Bibliog. Soc. Am. Episcopalian (trustee). Home: 224 Riverside Dr New York City NY 10025 Office: 170 Central Park W New York City NY 10024

GREGORY, JOHN MASON MOODY, Jr., tobacco co. exec.; b. Durham, N.C., Feb. 5, 1907; s. John Mason Moody and Mary (Barksdale) G.; A.B., Duke, 1929; m. Katherine Jamieson, Apr. 18, 1936; children—John Mason Moody III, Andrew Jamieson. With Am. Leaf Orgn. Imperial Tobacco Co. Gt. Britain and Ireland, Ltd., and predecessor, 1929—, pres., 1963—; pres. Brit. Leaf Tobacco Co. Can., Ltd., 1964—. Mem. Durham City Council, 1945-57; bd. dirs. N.C. Citizens Assn. Trustee Atlantic Christian Coll., Greenfield Acad. Served with USNR, World War II. Mem. Wilson C. of C. (div.), Alpha Tau Omega. Democrat. Episcopalian. Clubs: Hope Valley Country, TOBAC (Durham); Country N.C. (Pinehurst); Dunes Golf and Beach (Myrtle Beach, S.C.); Commonwealth (Richmond, Va.); Wilson Country. Home: 400 Wilshire Circle Wilson NC 27893 Office: PO Box 1848 Wilson NC 27893

GREGORY, JOSEPH TRACY, educator, paleontologist; b. Eureka, Cal., July 28, 1914; s. Frank C. and Edith (Tracy) G.; A.B., U. Cal. at Berkeley, 1935, Ph.D., 1938; postgrad. Inst. Meteorology, U. Chgo., 1943-44; m. Jane Everest, Feb. 21, 1949; children—Carl Douglas, Sarah Jane. Lectr. zoology Columbia, 1939; WPA paleontology lab. supr. Tex. Bur. Econ. Geology, 1939-41; instr. geology U. Mich., 1941-46; asst. prof., then asso. prof. geology Yale, 1946-60, curator vertebrate paleontology Peabody Mus., 1946-60; prof. paleontology, also curator lower vertebrates Mus. Paleontology, U. Cal. at Berkeley, 1960—, chmn. dept. paleontology, 1960-65, 71—, dir. mus., 1971—. Served with AUS, 1942-46. Fellow Geol. Soc. Am.; mem. Am. Soc. Mammalogists, Am. Soc. Zoologists, Soc. Study Evolution, Soc. Vertebrate Paleontology (sec.-treas. 1954-57, pres. 1958), Paleontol. Soc., Phi Beta Kappa, Sigma Xi. Co-editor Am. Jour. Sci., 1955-60. Office: Dept Paleontology U Cal Berkeley CA 94720

GREGORY, L.H., journalist; Sports editor Portland Oregonian. Office: 1320 SW Broadway Portland OR 97201*

GREGORY, LLOYD JEFFERSON, advt. exec.; b. Beeville, Tex., Apr. 19, 1899; s. Charles Hardy and Mollie Beulah (Keller) G.; B.J., U. Tex., 1922; m. Myrtle Marie Hayden, July 15, 1922 (dec.); children—Lloyd Jefferson, Martha Jane, Myrtle Marie; m. 2d, Lura Riley Seale, Nov. 27, 1961. Reporter, sports editor Austin (Tex.) Statesman, 1921-22; tchr. journalism U. Tex., 1922-25; corr. A.P., Austin, 1925-27; polit. writer Houston Post, 1927, sports editor, 1927-36, mng. editor, 1936-47, v.p., gen. mgr., 1947-51; owner Lloyd Gregory & Assos., advt. Vice pres. Tex. Air and Water Resources Found. Served with USMC, World War. Mem. Sigma Delta Chi. Presbyn. Clubs: Houston Press, Houston University. Writer sports articles. Home: 5424 Holly Springs Houston TX 77027 Office: 3901 Westheimer Houston TX 77027

GREGORY, SISTER MARY, med. librarian; b. County Clare, Ireland, Jan. 7, 1912; d. Joseph and Norah (O'Grady) Linnane; came to U.S., 1930, naturalized, 1943; grad. St. Joseph Sch. Nursing, Houston, 1940; student Houston U., 1941-48. Joined Congregation Sisters of Charity of Incarnate Word, Houston, 1930; nurse supr. St. Joseph's Hosp., Houston, 1940-48; nurse supr., organizer central supply dept. St. Michael's Hosp., Texarkana, Ark., 1948-56, librarian, 1956-57; librarian St. Elizabeth Hosp., Beaumont, Tex., 1957—. Mem. Nat. Nurses Assn., Med. Library Assn. Roman Catholic. Pioneer med. libraries in Texarkana and S.E. Tex.; research in med. library progress. Home: 2830 Calder Av Beaumont TX 77706 Office: St Elizabeth Memorial Library Box 5405 Beaumont TX 77706

GREGORY, MERRILL V., banker; b. Colfax, Wis., Oct. 1916; s. G.I. and Mabel (Morrison) G.; B.A., U. Wis., 1938; m. Lillian Hutton, 1941; 1 dau., Betty Jane. Spl. agt. FBI, 1940-52; practice as C.P.A., Houston, 1953; comptroller Tex Nat. Bank Commerce, Houston, 1954-60, v.p., comptroller, 1960-63, sr. v.p., 1964—, asst. to chmn., 1970—; dir. 1st Nat. Bank, Stafford, Tex. Pres., bd. dirs. Day Care Assn. Mem. United Fund Agy.; mem. adv. com. Community Council Research Bur. Served with AUS, 1945; USNR, 1945-46. Mem. Am. Inst. C.P.A.'s. Tex. Soc. C.P.A.'s, Financial Exec. Inst. Presbyn. (deacon). Mason. Clubs: Houston, Lakeside Country (Houston). Home: 5327 Bordley Dr Houston TX 77027 Office: PO Box 2558 Houston TX 77001

GREGORY, PAUL, producer; b. Waukee, Ia., Aug. 27, 1920; s. James Clifford and Esther May (Taylor) Lenhart; student Drake U., m. Janet Gaynor, 1965. Head concert div. Music Corp. Am., 1947-48; started Charles Laughton reading tours, 1948; prod. Don Juan in Hell, 1951, John Brown's Body, 1952, Caine Mutiny Court Martial, 1953, Elsa Lancaster's Pvt. Music Hall, 1953, Agnes Moorehead in That Fabulous Redhead, 1954, Three for Tonight, 1955, (motion picture) The Night of the Hunter, 1954, The Rivalry, 1957, (motion picture) The Naked and the Dead, 1958, The Marriage-Go-Round, 1958, 59, 60, The Pink Jungle, 1959, Captains and the Kings, 1961, Prescription Murder, 1962, Lord Pengo, 1963, Seven Ways of Love, 1963, Dame Judith Anderson as Hamlet, 1970. Recipient N.Y. Critics award for prodn. of Don Juan in Hell, 1952, Outer Circle Critics award for Caine Mutiny Court Martial, Alumni Distinguished Service award Drake U., 1959. Hon. mem. Theta Alpha Phi. Address: PO Box 847 Beverly Hills CA 90213

GREGORY, ROBERT HAMILTON, investment banker; b. Bklyn., Dec. 19, 1934; s. George M. and Marjorie (Waddell) G.; grad. Kent Sch., 1953; student U. Pa., 1957; m. Evelyn C. Lawrence, Sept. 24, 1965; children by previous marriage—Robert Hamilton, William Prescott. With Gregory & Sons, N.Y.C., 1956—, partner, 1961—. Mem. Investment Assn. N.Y., St. Andrews Soc. N.Y., S.A.R., Delta Psi. Clubs: N.Y. Yacht, Union League (N.Y.C.); Bayberry Beach and Tennis (Islip, N.Y.). Home: Office: 40 Wall St New York City NY 10005

GREGORY, ROBERT TODD, educator; b. Owensboro, Ky., Mar. 19, 1920; s. Richeson Todd and Jennie (Howard) G.; student Georgetown Coll., Ky., 1937-38; B.S., U.S. Naval Acad., 1942; M.S., Ia. State U., 1948; Ph.D., U. Ill., 1955; m. Margaret Kathryn Bentzinger, Dec. 29, 1944; children—Rosalie Jane, Carl Richeson. Instr. math. Fla. State U., 1949-50; research asst. U. Ill., 1950-55; asst. prof. math. U. Cal., Santa Barbara, 1955-59; asso. prof., prof. math. U. Tex., Austin, 1959—, sr. research mathematician Computation Center, 1959-70, prof. math., 1963—, prof. math. and computer scis., 1966—, acting chmn. dept. computer scis., 1966-68, dir. Center Numerical Analysis, 1970—. Served with USN, 1942-46. Mem. Am. Math. Soc., Math. Assn. Am., Soc. for Indsl. and Applied Math., Assn. for Computing Machinery, Sigma Xi. Author: Numeral Systems, 1963, co-author: A Collection of Matrices for Testing Computational Algorithms, 1969; A Survey of Numerical Mathematics, 2 vols., 1972. Contbr. articles profl. jours. Home: 2703 Mountain Laurel Dr Austin TX 78703

GREGORY, ROSS, educator; b. Washington, Ind., Feb. 11, 1933; s. Norrell and Bertha Beatrice (Jones) G.; A.B., Ind. U., 1959, M.A., 1961, Ph.D. (U. fellow), 1964; m. Shirley Ann Heines, Dec. 15, 1961; children—Theresa M., Graham T., Darren M. Asst. prof. history W.Va. Inst. Tech., Montgomery, 1963-66; asst. prof. history Western Mich. U., Kalamazoo, 1966-69, asso. prof., 1969—. Served with AUS, 1954-56. Am. Philos. Soc. grantee, 1967; Western Mich. U. fellow, 1969. Mem. Orgn. Am. Historians, Am. Hist. Assn. Author: Walter Hines Page: Ambassador to St. James's, 1970 (Frederick Jackson Turner award). Contbr. articles to profl. jours. Home: 2812 Romence Rd Kalamazoo MI 49002

GREGORY, RUTH WILHELMENE, librarian; b. West Point, Neb., Feb. 20, 1910; d. Edward George and Wilhelmene (Plieth) Gregory; A.B., U. Neb., 1933; L.S., U. Wis., 1938. Gen. library asst. Lincoln (Neb.) City Library, 1934-36; librarian editorial dept. Rotarian mag., Chgo., 1937; acting librarian Stevens Point (Wis.) Pub. Library, 1938-39; asso. librarian Waukegan (Ill.) Pub. Library, 1939, head librarian, 1939-; exec. sec. div. pub. libraries, A.L.A., 1946-48. Sec. Waukegan City Planning Commn., 1950-57. Sec. bd. dirs. Lake County Mus. of History. Mem. Round Table (v.p., editor 1948-49), A.L.A. (council 1951-54, chmn. jury on citation of trustees 1952-53, pres. pub. libraries div. 1954-55, exec. bd. 1956-60 Ill. Library Assn. (pres. 1947-48, mem. planning bd. 1951-54), Am. Assn. U. Women (pres. Waukegan br. 1949-51), YWCA, P.E.O., League of Women Voters, Kappa Delta. Clubs: Chicago Library; Woman's (Waukegan). Editor: Public Libraries, 1947-48. Home: 2035 Walnut St Waukegan IL 60085 Office: Waukegan Pub Library Waukegan IL 60085

GREGORY, WALTON CARLYLE, educator; b. Amherst, Va., Aug. 12, 1910; A.B., Lynchburg Coll., 1934; A.M., U. Va., 1935, Ph.D., 1940; Asst. prof. biology Tenn. Poly., 1940- 42; asst. prof. agronomy N.C. State U., 1942-47, asso. prof., 1947- 50, prof., 1950—, now also William Neal Reynolds prof. crop sci. Recipient Fleming prize U. Va., 1940; research award Va. Acad. Sci., 1940. Mem. Am. Bot. Soc., Am. Genetics Soc. Home: 3808 Blue Ridge Rd Raleigh NC 27609*

GREGORY WILLIAM HAMILTON, III investment banker; b. N.Y.C., Dec. 31, 1929; s. William Hamilton and Edith (Crowley) G.; grad. St. Paul's Sch., Concord, N.H., 1948; student Hobart Coll., 1948-51; divorced; childrenCarol, William Hamilton IV, Jennifer, Stuart; m. 2d, Elizabeth Finlayson. Began career with Gregory & Sons, N.Y.C., 1951-, partner, 1955-; dir. Seeman Bros. Mem. Investment Assn. N.Y., Bond Club N.Y., St. Andrews Soc. N.Y. Clubs: Racquet and Tennis, Union League, City Midday, Harbor View (N.Y.C.); Nat. Golf Links (Southampton, N.Y.); Everglades (Palm Beach, Fla.). Home: 334 E 69th St New York City NY 10021 Office: 40 Wall St New York City NY 10005

GREGSTON, GENE, newspaper editor; b. Marlow, Okla., May 19, 1925; s. Roy Lee and Elsie (Lamb) G.; student U. Mo., 1943, U. Okla., 1946-47; m. Donna Patricia Bettis, June 3, 1945; children—Donna Gene, Richard Patrick. Sports editor Odessa (Tex.) Am., 1947-48; sports writer Ft. Worth Star- Telegram, 1949-58; sports editor Evening Tribune, San Diego, 1958-64, exec. news editor, 1964-65, mng. editor, 1965-70, editor, 1970-71; editor San Diego Union, 1971—; dir. San Diego Plating Co. Bd. dirs. San Diego Conv. and Visitors Bur. Served with USAAF, 1943-45. Mem. San Diego Soc. Natural History (dir.), Greater San Diego Sports Assn. (dir.), Sigma Delta Chi. Home: 4899 Atlanta Dr San Diego CA 92115 Office: 940 3d Av San Diego CA 92112

GREHL, MICHAEL TREE, newspaper editor; b. Evanston, Ill., Dec. 6, 1928; s. Paul Michael and Jean (Tree) G.; A.A., North Park Jr. Coll., 1949; B.A., U. Ill., 1952; m. Audrey Ann Ewert, Sept. 13, 1957. Mng. editor Morris (Ill.) Daily Herald, 1952, Carbondale (Ill.) So. Illinoisan, 1952-56, Comml. Appeal, Memphis, 1957-69; editor Evansville (Ind.) Press, 1969—, police reporter Anchorage Daily Times, 1956-57. Bd. dirs. Salvation Army, Evansville's Future, Inc. Served with AUS, 1946-47. Mem. Evansville C. of C. (dir.), Am. Soc. Newspaper Editors. Rotarian. Clubs: Evansville Country, Petroleum. Home: 100 Logwood Dr Evansville IN 47710 Office: 2d and Vine Evansville IN 47701

GREIBER, CLARENCE LEONARD, Vocational cons.; b. Sauk City, Wis., June 11, 1905; s. Herman J. and Katherine (Little) G.; A.B., U. Wis., 1929, A.M., 1943; m. Mary A. Diebold, Sept. 5, 1931; 1 son, Robert John. Asst. sec. Wis. State Bd. Vocational and Adult Edn., 1929-31, sec. 1931-43, state dir. and exec. officer, 1944-70; cons. in Vocational and tech. edn., 1971—; supr. adult edn. program WPA, 1936-42, supervised devel. Wis. Edn. for aliens citizenship program under Nat. Citizenship Edn. Program, 1941-42; bd. trustees Stout Inst., 1944-55, State Radio Council, Govs. Ednl. Adv. Com.; pres. Am. Vocational Assn., 1946. State dir. Vocational Tng. for War Prodn. Workers Program, 1944-46; state dir. Food Prodn. War Tng. Program, 1944-46; mem. adv. comm. on vocational edn. U.S. Office of Edn., 1951-53; mem. Gov.'s Com. on Law Enforcement and Crime. Mem. bd. visitors Stout State U. Served as lt., USNR, 1943-44. Mem. Nat. Assn. State Dirs. Vocational Edn. (pres. 1955), Am. Legion, Phi Delta Kappa. Roman Catholic. K.C., Elk. Club: Nakoma Country. Home: 2707 Kendall Av Madison WI 53705

GREIDINGER, B. BERNARD, educator, accountant; b. N.Y.C., Mar. 30, 1906; s. Max and Fannie (Oster) G.; B.B.A., Coll. City N.Y., 1928; M.S., Columbia, 1932, Ph.D., 1939; C.P.A., N.Y., 1930. Partner Beame & Greidinger C.P.A., 1929- 42; prof. accounting grad. sch. bus., N.Y.U., 1948—; sr. partner Greidinger and Co., C.P.A., 1946—; prof. accounting U. Cal. at Los Angeles, summer 1947; lectr. accounting Coll. City N.Y., 1930-39, Rutgers U., 1940-46; past dir., mem. exec. com. U.S. Hoffman Machinery Corp. Rep. dir. gen. UNRRA at inception Internat. Refugee Orgn., 1946; financial adv., chief financial operations UNRRA, 1946-47; cons. budget adv. com. Army-Air Force Post Exchange Serv., 1948; cons. to chief ordnance Dept. of Army, N.Y. dist., 1952—; nominated by Pres. Truman as mem. Renegotiation Bd., 1952; spl. cons. to comptroller N.Y., 1955; cons. to internat. co-operation adminstrn. of U.S. State Dept., 1956; coordinator, N.Y.U., U.S. Operation Mission (internat. cooperation adminstrn.), Israel, 1956; mem. Temp. Commn. City Finances, N.Y.C., 1965-66, mem. citizens' commn. on future of City U. N.Y., 1970—. Served with finance dept. AUS, 1942-44, as maj. to lt. col., USAAF, 1944-46, chief budget fiscal div., 2d Air Force, chief tech. service div., Office of Chief Finance, AUS, World War II; col., USAF Res., 1950—. Mem. Am. Inst. C.P.A.'s, N.Y. State Soc. C.P.A.'s, Am. Accountants Assn., Nat. Assn. Accountants, Acad. Polit. Scis. Mason. Clubs: Columbia, New York University Faculty Author: Accounting Requirements of the Securities and Exchange Commission, 1941; Preparation and Certification of Financial Statements, 1950; Filings with the Securities and Exchange Commission, 1966; also articles profl. jours. Contbr.: Financial Handbook, 3d rev. edit., 1948; co-author, contbr. to Big Business Methods for Small Business, 1952. Home: 8100 Bay Pkwy Brooklyn NY 11214 Office: 1441 Broadway New York City NY 10018

GREIF, HERBERT, shoe mfg. co. exec.; b. Bklyn., June 9, 1918; s. Samuel and Rose (Scalettar) G.; B.A., Bklyn. Coll., 1939; LL.B., St. Lawrence U., 1947; M.E. in Aero. Engring., U.S. Naval Acad. Postgrad. Sch., 1945; D.Juris, Bklyn. Law Sch., 1969; m. Helen Brand, Jan. 3, 1943; children—Jon Meredith, Barbara Dean (Mrs. Charles Wolfe), Ellen Beth, Debra Susan. Buying, mdse. mgmt. positions with Abraham & Straus, Inc., Bklyn., 1938-47, Cohen Bros., Jacksonville, Fla., 1947-49, Davison-Paxton Co., Atlanta, 1949-51; gen. mdse. mgr. R.H. White, Inc., Boston, 1952-57, Grand-Way div. Grand Union Co., East Paterson, N.J., 1958-61; pres., dir., mem. exec. com. Geo. E. Keith Co., Brockton, Mass., 1961—, also pres., treas., dir. 11 subsidiaries; dir., mem. exec. com. Educator Biscuit Co., Lowell, Mass.; dir. Ofcl. Films, Inc., N.Y.C. Lectr., Am. Marketing Assn., 1956. Mem. adv. com. Nat. Alliance Businessmen; mem. nat. UN Day com. UN Assn.; mem. Nat. Planning Council. Served to lt. USNR, 1942-46. Mem. Nat. Retail Mchts. Assn., Brockton C. of C. (dir.), Nat. Footwear Mfrs. Assn. (dir.), New Eng. Footwear Assn. (dir.). Home: 5 Moose Hill Pky Sharon MA 02067 Office: 100 Perkins Av Brockton MA 02403

GREIF, ROGER LOUIS, educator, physiologist; b. Balt., Aug. 23, 1916; s. Leonard L. and Amy (Frederleicht) G.; B.S., Haverford Coll., 1937; M.D., Johns Hopkins, 1941; m. Carol Clement Prince, July 24, 1950; children—Peter Clement, Nicholas Peabody, Matthew Payson. Fellow in Medicine Johns Hopkins Hosp., 1946-47; asst. physician Rockefeller Inst. Hosp., N.Y.C., 1947-53; faculty Cornell U. Med. Coll., N.Y.C., 1953—, prof. physiology and biophysics, 1965—; cons. Health Research Council N.Y.C., chmn. metabolic disease panel, 1962-64. Mem. Harvey Soc. (mem. council 1962-65), Soc. Exptl. Biology and Medicine (sec. N.Y.C. chpt. 1962), Am. Physiol. Soc., Am. Fedn. Clin. Research, Soc. Gen. Physiologists, Endocrine Soc., Phi Beta Kappa, Alpha Omega Alpha. Research, numerous publs. on albuminuria in nephrosis, in treatment of malaria, in hormone-enzyme relationships, comparative physiology of kidney; mechanism of action of thyroid hormones and of hormone synthesis by thyroid gland. Home: 534 E 87th St New York City NY 10028

GREIG, THOMAS CURRIE, wholesale distbr.; b. Edinburgh, Scotland, Dec. 16, 1931; s. Thomas Currie and Elsie E. (Bell) G.; M.A., U. Edinburgh, 1953. With Peat, Marwick, Mitchell & Co., Toronto, Can., 1956-62, acting mgr., 1961-62; with M. Loeb Ltd., Ottawa, 1962—, v.p., treas., 1965-67, sr. v.p., treas., 1967-71, exec. v.p. finance, 1971—. Served to lt. Royal Navy, 1953-56. Club: Laurentian (Ottawa). Home: 195 Clearview Av Ottawa Ontario Canada Office: 400 Industrial Av Ottawa Ontario Canada

GREIG, WALTER, coll. pres.; b. Austin, Tex., Nov. 16, 1906; s. Walter and Elizabeth (Kopperl) G.; student U. Tex., 1924-30; B.S., Cleary Coll., 1949, B.B.A., 1960, M.B.A., 1961, Sc.D., 1962; D.C.Sc., Drake Coll., 1964; m. Shirley Jean Coker, Dec. 7, 1946; children—Carol Ann, Walter Coker. Admitted to Tex. bar, 1931, Mich. bar, 1946; pvt. practice law, Austin, Tex., 1931-41, Detroit, 1946-47; exec. sec. Mich. Liquor Control Commn., 1947-49; asst. to pres. Cleary Coll., 1949, trustee, sec. bd., 1950-51, exec. v.p., 1951-70, pres., treas. bd. trustees, 1970—. Mich. indsl. ambassador, 1962-64; mem. Ypsilanti Civil Service Commn., 1963—. Bd. dirs. Ypsilanti Area Indsl. Devel. Corp., 1970-71. Served to capt., AUS, 1941-46. Mem. Ypsilanti Bd. Commerce (v.p. 1956-57, dir. 1955-58), Washtenaw Av. Bus. and Profl. Assn. (chmn. 1970—), Mil. Order Fgn. Wars (Mich. comdr. 1958-59), Tex., Mich. bar assns. Mason (Shriner, Jester). Home: 1223 Washtenaw Av Ypsilanti MI 48197

GREINDL, JOSEF, chamber singer; b. Munich, German, Dec. 23, 1912; studied voice with Paul Bender, 1932-36. Appeared Municipal Theatre, Krefeld, 1936, Municipal Opera, Dusseldorf, 1938, German State Opera, Berlin, 1942, Municipal Opera, Berlin-Charlottenburg, 1948; participant music festivals, Bayreuth, 1943, 44, 52-69, Salzburg, 1949-52, Zurich and Luzerne, 1951, 52; guest engagements operatic assembles, Met. Opera, N.Y.C., La Scala, Milan, Teatro San Carlo, Naples, Buenos Aires, Rome Venice, Paris, Lisbon, Vienna, Chgo., Mexico City, Tokyo; concerts. London, Paris, Stockholm, Amsterdam, The Hague. others. Bass voice. Recipient Kunstpreis der Stadt Berlin Bundesverdienstkreuz 1, Klasse; Kritikerpreis der Stadt Berlin; Max Reinhardt medal Salzburg Festival. Address: Kuechelstr Ia 8 Munich 55 Federal Republic of Germany

GREINER, EDWARD DAVID, indsl. mfg. exec.; b. Peoria, Ill., Mar. 11, 1920; s. Fritz O. and Ethel K. (Mohn) G.; student U. Ill., 1937-38; B.S., Bradley U., 1941; m. Dorothy M. Janssen, July 31, 1943; children—David (dec.), Joel, Dan, Mark A., John R. Accountant R. G. LeTourneau, Inc., Peoria, 1941- 42, asst. treas., 1946-53, sec.-treas. LeTourneau-Westinghouse Co., Peoria, 1953-59; v.p. finance Westinghouse Air Brake Co., Pitts., 1959- 63; v.p. Cherry-Burrell Corp., Chgo., 1963-64; asst. to pres. Masonite Corp., Chgo., 1965-70, v.p. adminstrn., 1970—. Served to lt. USNR, 1942-46. Home: 557 N Washington St Hinsdale IL 60521 Office: 29 N Wacker Dr Chicago IL 60606

GREINER, FRANCIS LASHA, former banker; b. Syracuse, N.Y., Apr. 11, 1906; s. William Edward and Ida (Thomas) G.; B.A. in Econs., Stanford, 1925; m. Frances Ila Pelton, Sept. 8, 1929; children—William LaSha, Susan (Mrs. Roy A. Carley). With Wells Fargo Bank, San Francisco, 1926-71, sr. v.p., chmn. comml. loan com., 1967-71. Home: 235 Somerset Rd Oakland CA 94611

GREINER, MORRIS ESTY, Jr., TV exec.; b. Mpls., Nov. 7, 1920; s. Morris Esty and Irene Marie (O'Connell) G.; A.B., Duke, 1942; m. Dorothy J. Carter, May 23, 1946; 1 son, Derek Carter. Promotion mgr. radio sta. WHB, Kansas City, Mo., 1946-50; editor Swing mag., 1946-50; copy dir. Rogers & Smith, advt. agts., Kansas City, Mo., 1950-51, radio and tv dir., 1951-53; mgr. tv sta. WHB, Kansas City, Mo., 1953-54, tv sta. KMBC, Kansas City, Mo., 1954-64; mgr. tv sta. WMC, Scripps-Howard Broadcasting Co., Memphis, 1964-66, v.p. Scripps Howard, 1966—; gen. mgr. stas. WMC-TV, WMC, WMC-FM, Memphis, 1966—. Dir. NBC TV Affiliates Bd. Dels., 1969—; faculty Memphis State U., 1968-70. Pres., Red Ballon Players, 1969-70, bd. dirs., 1968—; pres. Greater Memphis State, 1970-71, bd. dirs., 1966—; steering chmn. United Memphis, 1970-71. Trustee Memphis State U. Found.; bd. dirs. Memphis Speech and Hearing Center, Shelby United Neighbors, Mid-South Fair Assn., Memphis Area Better Bus. Bur., Memphis Vol. Placement Program, United Memphis. Served to lt. USNR, 1942-46. Named Boxer Breeder of Year, 1955. Regional Emmy winner Nat. Acad. TV Arts and Scis., 1971. Mem. Nat., Tenn. assns. broadcasters, Maximum Service Telecasters. Home: 280 Waring Rd Memphis TN 38117 Office: 1960 Union Av Memphis TN 38104

GREISEN, KENNETH INGVARD, educator, physicist; b. Perth Amboy, N.J., Jan. 24, 1918; s. Ingvard C. and Signa (Nielsen) G.; student Wagner Coll., 1934-35; B.S., Franklin and Marshall Coll., 1938; Ph.D., Cornell U., 1942; m. Elizabeth C. Chase, Apr. 12, 1941; children—Eric Winslow, Kathryn Elise. Instr. Cornell U., 1942-43, asst. prof., 1946-48, asso. prof., 1948-50, prof., 1950—; scientist Manhattan Project, Los Alamos, 1943-46. Fellow Am Phys. Soc.; mem. Am. Astron. Soc., Internat. Astron. Union, Am. Assn. Physics Tchrs., A.A.A.S. Research cosmic rays. Home: 201 Wyckoff Av Ithaca NY 14850

GREISER, MELVIN RUDOLPH, business exec.; b. Cin., Nov. 29, 1900; s. Rudolph A. and Mary E. (Meyer) G.; B.S., Tri-State Coll., 1921, Dr. Eng. (hon.), 1959; m. Ada C. Brickner, Jan. 27, 1926; children—M. Neil, Rhea, Lyra, Alan, Ronald. With Carthage Mills, Inc., Cin., 1921—, beginning as laborer, various capacities becoming successively v.p. prodn., 1st v.p., 1921-41, pres., 1941—, also gen. mgr.; dir. Central Trust Co. Former mem. Cin. Planning Commn. Bd.

dirs. Jr. Achievement, Inc. Mem. Soc. Advancement Mgmt. (past nat. v.p.), A.I.M. (asso.), Cin. C. of C. (past pres., dir.), Am. Chem. Soc., Hist. and Philos. Soc. Am., Newcomen Soc. Episcoplian. Clubs: La Coquille (Palm Beach, Fla.); Queen City (Cin.); Whitehall (Chgo.). Home: 1330 Hillcrest Rd Cincinnati OH 45224 Office: 124 W 66th St Cincinnati OH 45216

GREISINGER, JOSEPH HENRY, former banker; b. Toledo, Sept. 11, 1904; s. Namon S. and Josephine (Sherwood) G.; student Ohio State U.; m. Grace Marie Baker, June 17, 1928; 1 dau., Diane Lee (Mrs. Ronald E. Felty). Asst. mgr. Ernst & Ernst C.P.A.'s, Toledo, 1934-58; comptroller Toledo Trust Co., 1958-70. C.P.A., Ohio. Home: 310 Fernwood St Delta OH 43515

GRELLINGER, JOHN BENJAMIN, bishop; b. Milw., Nov. 5, 1899; s. Christopher J. and Anna L. (Schwister) G.; student Marquette U., 1918-19, St. Francis Sem., 1922-24; S.T.D., North Am. Coll., 1930; Ph.D., Gregorian U., 1932. Ordained priest Roman Catholic Ch., 1929; curate St. Paul's U. Chapel, Madison, Wis., 1932-36; prof. philosophy St. Francis Sem., Milw., 1936-49; apptd. Titular Bishop of Syene, aux. to Bishop of Green Bay, Wis., June 1949, consecrated, July 1949. Address: Bear Creek WI 54922

GREMILLION, CURTIS LIONEL, Jr., hosp. adminstr.; b. Slaughter, La., Feb. 26, 1924; s. Curtis Lionel and Beatrice (Watson) G.; B.A. in Psychology and Music, U. Southwestern La., 1948; postgrad. in psychology La. State U., 1948-49, 53; m. Rosemary Duhon, Dec. 8, 1951; children—Suzanne Lynelle (Mrs. Walden), Curtis Lionel III, Monique Angele. Profl. musician, 1940-43, 46-51; staff psychologist E. La. State Hosp., Jackson, 1949—, dir. psychology and social service depts., 1953- 57, asst. supt., 1957-62, adminstr., 1961, 62-64, acting supt., 1964-66, asso. adminstr., 1966—. Chmn., East Feliciana Parish United Givers Fund, 1960; regional chmn. Am. Heart Assn., 1968—. Bd. dirs. United Givers East La. State Hosp., 1957-62, regional chmn. A.R.C., 1954-55, 62, Boy Scouts Am., 1964-69, Am. Heart Assn., 1963, Am. Cancer Soc., 1963-64, bd. dirs. So. Behavioral Research Found. Served with USNR, 1943-46. Recipient Outstanding Leadership and Service award La. Dept. Hosps., 1966. Mem. La. Psychol. Assn. (charter), So. Sociol. Assn., La. Music Therapy Assn. (mem. bd. 1966—), Am. Legion, Internat. Platform Assn., Psi Chi, Sinfonia, Pi Gamma Mu, Kappa Delta Pi. Democrat. Baptist. Lion. Club: New Orleans Jazz. Address: Residence 121 E La State Hosp Jackson LA 70748

GREMILLION, JACK PAUL FAUSTIN, La. atty. gen.; b. Donaldsonville, La., June 15, 1914; s. William Kossuth and Genca (Henderson) G.; student La. State U., 1931-37; m. Doris McDonald, Jan. 12, 1942; children—Jack Paul Faustin, William McDonald, Wayne Francis, Doris H. Admitted to La. bar, also Fed. Cts., U.S. Supreme Ct., 1941; practice of law, 1937—; atty. Dept. Revenue, 1940- 42; 2d asst. dist. atty. Parish of East Baton Rouge, 1952-53, 1st asst., 1953-56, atty. gen. State of La., 1956—. Served as 1st lt. 106th and 3d inf. divs., AUS, 1942-45. Mem. Am., La., East Baton Rouge bar assns., Nat. Assn. Attys. Gen., Am. Legion (past post pres.), Mil. Order World Wars, Baton Rouge C. of C., Nat. Assn. County and Pros. Attys. K.C., Elk. Clubs: Lions, Young Men's Business (pres. 1940) (Baton Rouge). Address: 5475 Capital Heights Av Baton Rouge LA 70806

GREMSE, ALBERT RUDOLPH, constrn. co. exec.; b. Bklyn., Sept. 14, 1907; s. Ferdinand R. and Elise (Detrich) G.; student N.J. Law Sch., 1926-27; B.C.S., N.Y.U., 1933; m. Jean Elizabeth Faust, Mar. 26, 1941; children—Joan, Kathleen, Helen, Martha (Mrs. James Norris, Jr.), David. Chief accountant Fidelity Union Title & Mortgage Guarantee Co., Newark, 1925-37; sr. accountant Haskins & Sells, Newark, 1937-39; chief accountant Sperry Products, Inc., Hoboken, N.J., 1939-43; tax supr., controller Va. Bridge Co., Roanoke, 1943-52; asst. controller Am. Bridge div. U.S. Steel Corp., Pitts., 1952-55; sec., controller, dir. Blount Bros. Corp., Montgomery, Ala., 1955-71, v.p., treas., 1965-71, now dir.; v.p., sec., treas. Blount, Inc., 1971—; dir. B.F. Shaw Co., Pipeco Steel Co. Inc., Mid-Am. Housing, Inc., Global Erectors Inc., Indiana Bridge Co., Inc., Paramount Equipment Rental & Sales, Blount Bros. Enterprises, Interstate Inns. Mem. Montgomery County Pensions and Security Bd., 1969—, vice chmn., 1970—. Mem. council com. Boy Scouts Am., 1955—; mem. del. assembly Montgomery Area United Appeal, 1970—. Treas., exec. com. Montgomery County Republican Party, 1955—. Bd. dirs. St. James Sch.; v.p., trustee Am. Youth Found. N.H. Recipient Silver Beaver award Boy Scouts Am., 1964. Mem. Financial Execs. Inst. (dir., past pres. Birmingham chpt.), Am. Mgmt. Assn., Newcomen Soc. N.Am., Sigma Sigma Sigma. Methodist. Club: Optimist (past lt. gov., pres.) Montgomery). Home: 9 S Haardt Dr Montgomery AL 36105 Office: 79 Commerce St Montgomery AL 36104

GRENE, MARJORIE GLICKSMAN, educator; b. Milw., Dec. 13, 1910; d. Harry and Edna (Kerngood) Glicksman; B.A., Wellesley Coll., 1931; M.A., Radcliffe Coll., Harvard, 1934, Ph.D., 1935; m. David Grene, Dec. 17, 1938 (div. 1961); children—Ruth (Mrs. Ruth Alscher), Nicholas. Mem. faculty Monticello (Ill.) Coll., 1936-37, U. Chgo., 1937-44; vis. prof. Northwestern U., summer 1951; mem. faculty U. Manchester, Eng., 1957-58, U. Leeds, Eng., 1958-60, Queen's U., Belfast, No. Ireland, 1960-65; prof. philosophy U. Cal. at Davis, 1965—, chmn. dept., 1966—; vis. prof. U. Tex., Austin, 1967-68; Philip Merlan lectr. Scripps Coll., 1971. German-Am. Exchange fellow, 1931-32, Alice Freeman Palmer fellow, 1935-36, Lucy Martin Donnelley fellow, 1960-61; Faculty research lectr. U. Cal. at Davis, 1971. Mem. Soc. Phenomenology and Existential Philosophy, Metaphysical Soc. Am., Am. Philos. Assn. (pres. Pacific div. 1971—), Sigma Xi. Author: (with T.V. Smith) From Descartes to Kant, 1940; Dreadful Freedom: A Critique of Existentialism, 1948; Heidegger, 1957; A Portrait of Aristotle, 1963; The Knower and the Known, 1966; Approaches to a Philosophical Biology, 1969. Editor: The Anatomy of Knowledge, 1969; Toward A Unity of Knowledge, 1969; Knowing and Being, 1969; Interpretations of Life and Mind, 1971; also articles. Home: 40 Walnut Lane Davis CA 95616

GRENFELL, JOYCE, entertainer, writer; b. London, Eng., Feb. 10, 1910; d. Paul Phipps and Nora Langhorne; m. R. P. Grenfell, Dec. 12, 1929. Free lance journalist, also writer light verse for Punch, later radio critic The Observer. 1936- 39; actress on stage, Farjeons Little Revu, 1939; writer radio plays, including series A Note With Music; (with Stephen Potter) The How Series; appeared on stage in Noel Coward's Sigh No More, others; appeared own show J. G. Requests the Pleasure, on Broadway, toured U.S., Can., 1956-57, 58, 60. Gt. Britain, 1960; concert tours Gt. Britain, 1961, 62, Australia, New Zealand, Hong Kong, Singapore, 1963, Can., 1964 Switzerland, 1964, England, Australia, New Zealand 1966, England, 1967, U. S., 1967, colls. and univs. in U.S.A., 1967, U.K., 1967, 68, also Australia and Hong Kong, 1969; appeared on the Ed Sullivan Television Show, also David Susskind's Festival Performing Arts TV Hour; 2 TV solo hour programmes BBC, 1964; wrote and played in How Now to Listen, 1962; filmed Old Dark House, 1962; The Americanization of Emily, 1963; The Yellow Rolls Royce, 1964. Served Pilkington Com. TV and Radio in United Kingdom, 1960; adv. council BBC, 1964. Decorated Order of the British Empire. Mem. Soc. Women Writers and Journalists (pres.). Address: care Christopher Mann Ltd 140 Park Lane London W 1 England

GRENIER, GEORGE HAMPTON, inst. dean; b. N.Y.C., Jan. 12, 1920; s. George Garfield and Mary (Bair) G.; B.E.E.E., Cooper Union Inst., 1950; M.E.E., N.Y. U., 1956; Ph.D., Mont. State U., 1967; m. Helen Biadaszkiewicz, Jan. 17, 1941; children—Christine (Mrs. David Rusch), Myra (Mrs. Vincent Stanley), James Hampton, Theodore Robert. Broadcast technician WBNX Broadcasting Co., N.Y.C., 1937-51; chief electronics engr. Langevian Mfg. Corp., 1951-53; advanced products engr. Gen. Electric Co., Syracuse, N.Y., 1954-60; asso. prof. elec. engring. U. Toledo, 1960-67; project leader directed research Mitre Corp., Bedford, Mass., 1967-68; chmn. elec. engring. Detroit Inst. Tech., 1968-69, dean Coll. Engring., 1969—; cons. Gen. Electric Co., 1960-63, Ill. Inst. Gas Tech., 1964, Argonne Labs., 1964, Y.S. Army Tank Arsenal Command, 1967. Served with AUS, 1943-46; ETO. Nat. Sci. fellow, 1964-66. Mem. I.E.E.E., Am. Soc. Engring. Edn., Am. Assn. U. Profs., Engring. Soc. Detroit. Club: Economic of Detroit, Patentee electronic control system. Home: 1019 Michigan Av Ann Arbor MI 48104 Office: 2300 Park Av Detroit MI 48201

GRENIER, GERARD J., bldg. materials co. exec.; b. 1931; married. With Peat, Marwick, Mitchell & Co., C.P.A.'s, 1953-59; controller Champion Home Builders Co., Dryden, Mich., 1960-70, sec.-treas., 1970—. C.P.A., Mich. Office: 5573 E North St Dryden MI 48428*

GRENIER, JOHN EDWARD, lawyer; b. New Orleans, Aug. 24, 1930; s. Charles Desire and Beatrice (Schaumburg) G.; LL.B., Tulane U., 1953; LL.M., N.Y. U., 1957; m. Lynne Dea Youmans, June 12, 1953; 1 son, John Beaulieu. Admitted to La. bar, 1953, N.Y. bar, 1957, Ala. bar, 1959; practice in N.Y.C., 1956-57, Birmingham, 1957—; asso. Burke & Burke, 1956-57; atty. So. Natural Gas Co., 1957-58; partner Bradley, Arant, Rose & White, 1959-66, Lange, Simpson, Robinson & Somerville, 1967—. Lectr. continuing legal edn. Ala. Bar Assn. Pres., Birmingham Civic Ballet; chmn. Beaux Arts Krewe. Chmn., Jefferson County Young Republicans, 1960-61, Ala. Young Rep. Fedn., 1961-62, Ala. Rep. Exec. Com., 1962-65; So. regional dir. Goldwater for Pres. Com., 1963-64; exec. dir. Rep. Nat. Com., 1964, mem., 1964-65; Rep. candidate U.S. Senator for Ala., 1966. Bd. dirs. Jefferson County Com. for Econ. Opportunity. Served to capt. USMCR, 1953-56. Mem. Ala., La., N.Y. bar assns., Fitzpatrick Hounds, Midland Hounds. Club: Mountain Brook (Ala.) Country. Home: 90 Country Club Blvd Birmingham AL 35213 Office: City Fed Bldg Birmingham AL 35203

GRENNEN, JOSEPH E., educator; b. N.Y.C., Sept. 3, 1926; s. James J. and Dorothy (Gallagher) G.; B.S., Holy Cross Coll., 1947; M.A., Fordham U., 1954, Ph.D., 1960; m. Mary Margaret Nesbitt, June 17, 1950; children—James, Jean, Patricia, Christopher, Peter, Mary. Instr. Regis (N.Y.) High Sch., 1947-50; edn. adv. U.S. Army, Munich, Germany, 1950-55; instr. Fordham U., 1956-59, asst. prof. English, 1959-64, asso. prof., 1964-70, prof., 1970—, chmn., 1965—; mem. editorial com. Chaucer Variorum Edition. Mem. Modern Language Assn. (vice-chmn. nat. conv. 1965), Mediaeval Acad. Am., Am. Assn. U. Profs. Roman Catholic. Home: 45 Ontario Rd Bellerose Village NY 11426 Office: Dept English Fordham U Bronx NY 10458

GRESHAM, LUNIA PAUL, educator; b. Portales, N.M., Jan. 3, 1911; s. Lunia Houston and Caroline (Anderson) G.; A.B., Bethany-Peniel Coll., 1933; M.A., U. Okla., 1934; Ph.D., Vanderbilt U., 1943; m. Martha Elizabeth De Witt, June 10, 1936; childrenLoren Paul, Daniel Kay, Instr. history Bresee Coll., Hutchinson, Kan., 1935-36, instr. Trevecca Nazarence Coll., 1936-54, dean, 1946-54; dean Honolulu Christian Coll., 1954-55; prof. history Pasadena Coll., 1955-66, dean instrn., 1966— chmn. div. social sci., 1958-66. Mem. Tenn. Hist. Soc., So. Hist. Assn., Phi Delta Lambda (nat. pres. 1948-52). Author articles in field. Home: 1419 Bresee Av Pasadena CA 91104

GRESHAM, NEWTON, lawyer; b. Jewett, Tex., July 21, 1905; s. Edward Alexander and Beulah Benton (Selman) G.; A.B., Sam Houston State Tchrs. Coll., 1924; LL.B., U. Tex., 1930; m. Mary Frances Stone, July 3, 1933; 1 dau., Susan Frances. Admitted to Tex. bar, 1930, since practiced in Houston; partner firm Fulbright, Crooker, Freeman, Bates & Jaworski, and predecessor, 1937—. Dir. Great Nat. Life Ins. Co., Houston Bank and Trust Co. Mem. bd. regents State Tchrs. Colls. Tex., 1959-65 (pres. bd. regents 1963-65); mem., vice chmn. coordinating bd. Tex. Coll. and Univ. System; trustee St. Luke's Episcopal Hosp., Houston. Fellow Am. Bar Found., Am. Coll. Trial Lawyers; mem. Internat. Assn. Ins. Counsel, Fedn. Ins. Counsel, State Bar of Tex. (pres. 1956-57), Order of the Coif, Phi Delta Phi, Alpha Chi, Alpha Tau Omega. Clubs: Coronado, River Oaks Country (pres. 1950) (Houston). Home: 1935 Olympia Dr Houston TX 77019 Office: Bank of Southwest Bldg Houston TX

GRESHAM, OLLIE WILSON, lawyer; b. Tulsa, May 5, 1933; s. Ollie M. and Carrimae (Wood) G.; LL.B., U. Tulsa, 1958; m. Patricia Z. Blakey, May 1, 1959; children—David Wayne, Michael Blake. Admitted to Okla. bar, 1958, since practiced in Tulsa; mem. firm Van Cleave, Thomas & Liebler, 1958-68; partner Van Cleave, Gresham, Liebler, Dalton & Bevins, 1968—; pub. defender Tulsa County, 1960-61. Served to 1st lt. USAF, 1961; to maj. Okla. Air N.G., 1968—. Named Outstanding Lawyer in Tulsa,, Tulsa County Bar Assn., 1963. Mem. U. Tulsa Alumni Assn. (past pres.). Democrat. Club: University (past pres.) (Tulsa). Home: 6848 E 59th St Tulsa OK 74145 Office: 905 Mayo Blvd Tulsa OK 74103

GRESHAM, PERRY EPLER, coll. pres.; b. Covina, Cal., Dec. 19, 1907; s. George Edward and Mary Elizabeth (Epler) G.; A.B summa cum laude, Tex. Christian U., 1930, B.D., 1933, LL.D., 1949; postgrad. U. Chgo., 1932-33, Columbia, 1931-41; Litt.D., Culver-Stockton Coll., 1954, U. Cin., 1966; L.H.D., Chapman Coll., 1964; Ed.D., Transylvania, 1965; Pd.D., Youngstown U., 1966; m. Elsie Stanbrough, Dec. 9, 1926 (dec. Mar. 1947); 1 son, Glen Edward; m. 2d, Mrs. Alice Fickling Cowan, May 6, 1953; 1 dau., Nancy. Prof. philosophy Tex. Christian U., 1936-42; minster U. Christian Ch., Ft. Worth, 1933-42, Seattle, 1942-45, Central Woodward Christian Ch., Detroit, 1945-53; feature writer Detroit Free Press, 1950-52; pres. Bethany (W.Va.) Coll. 1953—. Mem. study com. Commn. on Faith and Order, World Council Chs., 1948-60; pres. W.Va. Found. Colls., 1954-58; clergy industry commn. N.A.M., 1957-65; commn. on liberal edn. Assn. Am. Colls., 1963—; chmn. North Central Assn. Colls. and Univs., 1964-66; pres. Internat. Conv. Christian Chs., 1960-61. Dir. Found. for Econ. Edn., 1960—, chmn. bd., 1966-68; bd. dirs. Fedn. Regional Accrediting Commns. Higher Edn. Dir. Chesapeake & Potomac Telephone Cos. Bd. dirs. Lawrence Inst. Tech., Detroit. Mem. Am. Philos. Soc. Internat. Robert Burns Soc., Internat. Platform Assn., Alpha Chi. Mason (Shriner). Clubs: University (N.Y.C.); Duquesne (Pitts.); Williams Country (Weirton), Rotary, Fort Henry (Wheeling); Skytop (Pa.); Royal Scottish (Glasgow); Authors' (London). Author: Incipient Gnosticism in the New Testament, 1933; Disciplines of the High Calling, 1954; The Sage of Bethany, 1960; Answer to Conformity, 1961. Home: Highland Hearth Bethany WV 26032

GRESHAM, ROBERT COLEMAN, govt. ofcl.; b. Booneville, Miss., Nov. 12, 1917; s. J.F. and Pearl (Bellamy) G.; A.A., Sunflower Coll., Miss., 1938; B.C.S., Southeastern U., Washington, 1942; m. Katherine Wootten, Oct. 8, 1955; children—Robin (Mrs. Keith T. Groseclose), D. Jackson. Spl. agt., exec. FBI, 1938-53; asst. dir. research Council State Chambers Commerce, Washington, 1953-65; Republican staff dir. Ho. Appropriations Com., U.S. Congress, 1965-69; commr. ICC, Washington, 1969—. Republican. Episcopalian. Home: 14712 Claude Lane Silver Spring MD 20904 Office: 12th and Constitution Av NW Washington DC 20423

GRESHAM, RUPERT N., lawyer; b. Luling, Tex., Apr. 7, 1892; s. Robert Hall and Jennie Lee (Robinson) G.; legal student U. Tex.; m. Gertrude Negley, June 8, 1921; children—Rupert N., Susan (Mrs. James W. Crudgington). Admitted to Tex. bar, 1916, U.S. Circuit Ct., 1918, U.S. Supreme Ct., 1945; now mem. Gresham, Davis, Gregory, Worthy & Moore. Fellow Am. Bar Assn. (Ho. dels. 1956—, mem. council tax sect. 1959-62); mem. San Antonio Bar Assn., State Bar Tex. (pres. 1954-55, chmn. com. real estate, trust and probate law, chmn. tax sect.), Am. Law Inst., S.W. Legal Found., Order of Coif (hon.). Contbr. articles to profl. jours. Home: 421 Howard St San Antonio TX 78212 Office: Nat Bank of Commerce Bldg San Antonio TX 78205

GRESOV, BORIS VLADIMIR, economist; b. Russia, Aug. 7, 1914; s. Paul Vladimir and Maria de (Suzor) G.; B.A. with honors, Cambridge (Eng.) U., 1938, M.A. with honors, 1952; m. Letitia Coxen Graham, June 21, 1945; childrenWinston Graham, Christopher Leo. Came to U.S., 1938, naturalized, 1944. Prodn. mgr. Compania Nacional Minera de Taxco S.A., to 1945; v.p. Industrias Y Minas S.A., Mexico, 1945-49; cons. economist Shields & Co., 1949-52, Walston & Co., 1952-54; mem. adv. bd. Axe Sci. & Electronic Corp., N.Y.C., 1957-61; cons. economist E.W. Axe & Co., N.Y.C.; chmn. bd., chief exec. officer, dir Shattuck Denn Mining Corp., 1958-60, chmn. exec. com., dir., 1962; mem. exec. com., dir. Western Devel. Co., Del., 1958-61; chmn. bd., dir. Standard Metals Corp., 1963—, chmn., pres., 1965—; founder, pres. Excelsior Fund, Inc., 1963—. Mem. A.I.M. (pres.'s council), Union Soc. (Cambridge), N.Y. Soc. Security Analysts, Confrerie de la Chaine des Rotisseurs (chevalier). Roman Catholic. Clubs: University, Broad Street, Economic, Metropolitan (N.Y.C.); Long Island; Westhampton Country (L.I.); Surf (Quoque, L.I.). Home: 900 Fifth Av New York City NY 10021 Office: 1345 Av of Americas New York City NY 10019

GRESSITT, JUDSON LINSLEY, entomologist; b. Tokyo, Japan, June 16, 1914; s. James Fullerton and Edna (Linsley) G.; student Am. Sch. in Japan, 1931, Stanford U.; B.S., U. Cal. at Berkeley, 1938, M.S., 1939, Ph.D., 1945; m. Margaret Kriete, Mar. 20, 1941; childrenSylvia Anne, Rebecca Louise, Edna Carolyn, Ellyn Elizabeth. Asst. zoology U. Cal., 1938-39, research fellow, 1944-45; instr. Lingnan U., Canton, China, 1939-43, interned by Japanese Army; asst. prof., 1946-48, asso. prof., 1948-51; mem. Pacific Sci. Bd., 1951- 52; staff Bishop Mus., 1953—, chmn. entomology dept., 1955—, L.A. Bishop Distinguished Chair zoology, 1964-; research trips to Taiwan, 1932-66, West China, 1940, 48, S.E. Asia, 1954-66, Ryukyu Islands, 1932 34, 45, 63, 64, Laos, 1965, Vietnam, 1940, 60, Micronesia, New Guinea, 1955-70 Solomon Islands, New Hebrides, New Caledonia, Samoa, Fiji, Tahiti, Hawaii, Philippines, Antarctica, 1945-68, Arctic, 1969. Chmn., Gov.'s Com. on Preservation Sci. Areas, 1969-; cons. NIH, 1961-65, polar research Nat. Acad. Scis., 1965-68; affiliate grad. faculty U. Hawaii, 1955-. Mem. Hawaiian Entomol. Soc. (pres. 1955), Entomol. Soc. Am., Entomol. Soc. Japan, Pacific Coast Entomol. Soc., Soc. Systematic Zoology, A.A.A.S. Author: Chrysomelidae of China and Korea (with S. Kimoto); Insects of Campbell Island. Editor: Pacific Basin Biogeography; Entomology of Antarctica, 1967. Editor of Pacific Insects, Jour. Med. Entomology. Contbr. sci. articles profl. publs. Home: 1053-A Ilima Honolulu HI 96817 Office: Bishop Museum PO Box 6037 Honolulu HI 96818

GRETEMAN, FRANK HENRY, bishop; b. Willey, Ia., Dec. 25, 1907; s. Bernard and Mary (Meissner) G.; A.B., Loras Coll., 1929; S.T.L., N.Am. Coll., Rome, Italy, 1932; J.C.L., Cath. U., 1937. Asst. pastor St. Augustine Ch., Spokane, Wash., 1933-35; pastor Assumption Ch., Merrill, Ia., 1937-41, St. Michael's Ch., Sioux City, 1941-50, Holy Spirit Ch., Carroll, 1950-65; aux. bishop, vicar gen. Sioux City Diocese, 1965-70, bishop 1970—. Mem. Canon Law Soc. Am. Home: 2221 Nebraska St Sioux City IA Office: 1821 Jackson St Sioux City IA 51104

GRETHER, HENRY MORONI, Jr., univ. dean; b. Salt Lake City, Jan. 29, 1920; s. Henry Moroni and Grace (Howell) G.; B.A., U. Utah, 1943, J.D., 1947; LL.M., U. Minn., 1948; m. Jane Child, June 16, 1944; children—Deborah, Henry Moroni III, Sharon Elise. Admitted to Neb. bar, 1949, U.S. Supreme Ct. bar; practiced in Lincoln, 1949—; instr. law U. Neb., 1948-51, asst. prof., 1951-54, asso. prof., 1954-57, prof., 1957—, dean, 1966—; asst. atty. gen. Neb., 1950; spl. atty. Neb. Rds. and Irrigation, 1954-57; spl. asst. atty. gen. Neb., 1957-60; minority counsel U.S. Senate Judiciary Com., 1960. Pres., Cornhusker Dairy Queen, Inc., 1970—; dir. Lincoln Agr. Credit Corp.; trust cons. Union Bank & Trust Co. Mem. Lincoln City Zoning Commn., 1950-60. Served with USAAF, 1943-46. Recipient Outstanding Mem. award Neb. Bar Assn., 1968. Mem. Nat. Conf. Commrs. Uniform State Laws (Neb. commr.), Am. Law Inst., Am. Bar Assn., Am. Judicature Soc., Am. Legion, Delta Phi, Phi Alpha Delta. Mem. Ch. of Jesus Christ of Latter-day Saints. Elk. Author: Cases and Materials on Water Rights, 1949; Restatement of the Law of Security. Nebraska Annotation, 1950. Contbr. articles to profl. jours. Home: 6721 Rexford Dr Lincoln NB 68506

GRETSCH, FRED, Jr., musical instrument, mfg. co. exec.; b. Bklyn., Mar. 10, 1905; s. Frederick and Charlotte (Sommer) G.; B.A., Cornell U., 1926; m. Helen A. Mooney, May 24, 1952; 1 dau., Helen Marie. With The Fred Gretsch Co. Inc., Bklyn., 1926—, treas., 1930—, pres., 1948—, dir., 1930—; chmn. bd. trustees The Lincoln Savs. Banks, chief exec. officer, 1971—. dir. D.H. Baldwin Co., Taylor & Co. Trustee Indsl. Home for Blind; mem. council Cornell U. Served with USNR, 1942-46. Mem. Bklyn. C. of C. (dir. 1952—), Nat. Assn. Band Instrument Mfrs. (dir. 1971—). Clubs: North Hempstead Country; Manhasset Bay Yacht; Cornell (N.Y. C.). Home: 71 Bellows Lane Manhasset NY 11030 Office: 60 Broadway Brooklyn NY 11211

GREULACH, VICTOR A. botanist; b. Convoy, O., Dec. 6, 1906; s. John Adam and Margaret (Giessler) G.; A.B. (Rector scholar), DePauw U., 1929; M.S., Ohio State U., 1933, Ph.D. (U. scholar), 1940; m. Elizabeth Dunnells, Oct. 6, 1934; childrenDorothy Gould, Mary Susan, Vicki Elizabeth. Instr. botany Ohio Wesleyan U., Lakeside, summer 1929; instr. biology Muskingum Coll., 1933-35; asst. prof. biology U. Houston, 1935-41, asso. prof., 1941-44, chmn. div. biol. scis., 1944-46; supr. natural sci. sect. City of Houston Parks and Recreation Dept., 1944-46; asso. prof. botany A. & M. Coll. Tex., 1940-49; asso. prof. botany U. N.C., 1949-51, prof., 1951—, chmn. dept. botany, 1960-72, dir. botany conf., 1959-61, 63. Co-dir. NSF Inst. Sci. Tchrs., 1957-61; vis. prof. U. N.H., summers 1962, 63; profl. asst. NSF, summer 1958, cons., 1958- 62. Mem. biology exam. com. Coll. Entrance Exam. Bd., 1963-68; mem. subcom. on coll. edn., biology div. Nat. Acad. Scis., 1955-58; exec. dir. Commn. on Undergrad. Edn. in Biol. Scis., 1964-65. Fellow A.A.A.S., Tex. Acad. Sci. (pres. eastern sect. 1944-45); mem. Bot. Soc. Am., Assn. Southeastern Biologists (editor bull. 1954-59, pres. 1960-61), N.C. Acad. Scis. (pres. 1963-64), Elisha Mitchell Sci. Soc. (editor Jour. 1966—), Sigma Xi (pres. N.C. 1959-60), Phi Sigma, Phi Epsilon Phi.

Methodist. Author: (with others) Plants An Introduction to Modern Botany, 1962, 2d edit., 1967; Botany Made Simple, 1968; Plant Structure and Function, 1972. Contbr. articles to profl. jours. Address: Univ of North Carolina Chapel Hill NC 27514

GREULICH, WILLIAM WALTER, anatomist; b. Columbus, O., July 24, 1899; s. Richard B., and Louise M. (Greily.) G.; Ph.B., Kenyon Coll., 1926; A.M., U. Denver, 1927; Ph.D., Stanford, 1934; Sc.D. (hon.), Kenyon Coll., 1967; m. Mildred A. Libby, Oct. 11, 1924; children—James Libby, Richard Curtice. Instr. biology, Regis Coll., 1927-28, U. Colo., 1928-31; teaching fellow anatomy Stanford, 1931-34; Gen. Edn. Bd. fellow anatomy Yale Sch. Medicine, 1934-36, asst. prof. anatomy, 1936-39, asso. prof. anatomy, phys. anthropology, 1939- 40; prof. phys. anthropology, anatomy, dir. Brush Found., Western Reserve U. Sch. Medicine, 1940-44; prof. anatomy Stanford Sch. Med., 1944-64, prof. emeritus, 1964—, exec. head dept., 1949-62, vis. prof. dept. pediatrics, 1969—. Dir. Brush Found., 1940-49; sr. Fulbright lectr. Makerere Med. Sch. Kampala, Uganda, 1958-59; travel fellow. Carnegie Corp. N.Y.; lectr. under auspices Brit. Med. Assn., Australia and New Zealand, 1946; cons. NRC; Com. on Atomic Casualties; Anthropology Survey, Children of Guam, M.I., 1947; study growth and devel. Japanese children who survived atomic bombing of Hiroshima and Nagasaki, 1947-52; sci. adviser U.S. High Commr. for Germany, Bonn, 1952-54; chmn. U.S. Ednl. Commn. in Fed. Republic of Germany (Fulbright Com.) 1953-54; sci. attache Am. embassy, London. 1961-66; asst. to dir. growth and devel. sect Nat. Inst. Child Health and Human Devel., Bethesda, 1966-68, research biologist, 1968-71. Recipient Viking Fund medal and award in phys. anthropology, 1959. Sci. fellow Zool. Soc. London; mem. A.A.A.S., Am. Assn. Anatomists (chmn. com. on anat. nomenclature, U.S.A. rep. internat. com. on anat. nomenclature exec. com. 1945-50, 1st v.p. 1956-58), Am. Assn. Phys. Anthropologists (pres. 1959-61, mem. exec. com.), Soc. for Research Child Devel. (pres. 1955-57), Anat. Soc. Gt. Britain and Ireland, Deutsche Anatomische Gesellschaft, Soc. for Adolescent Medicine (hon.), Sigma Xi, Alpha Omega Alpha. Club: Athenaeum (London). Asso. editor Am. Jour. Phys. Anthropology, 1940-44, Anat. Record, 1948-62, Growth, 1950-62, Am. Jour. Phys. Medicine, 1959-63; Zeitschrift für Mikroskopischanatomische Forschung, Acta Geneticae Medicae et Gemellologiae. Home: 1736 Oak Creek Dr Palo Alto CA 94304 Office: Dept Anatomy Stanford U Stanford CA 94305

GREVE, DONALD JOE, carpet co. exec.; b. Oklahoma City, Dec. 18, 1933; s. Joe and Wilma Jean (Cook) G.; student Oklahoma City U., 1952; m. Janna Sue McGee, June 6, 1954; children—Jeanna Kim, John Robert. With Barnett Home Furnishings, Oklahoma City, 1953-62, owner, 1955-62; founder, 1962, since chmn. bd. Sequoyah Industries, Inc., mfr. and seller tufted carpets, Oklahoma; dir. First Okla. Bank & Trust Co., Sulphur, Okla., First Wagoner Bank & Trust Co. (Okla.), Plaza Nat. Bank, Bartlesville, Okla., Plaza Mgmt. Co., Oklahoma City; adv. dir. Furst Nat. Bank, Bethany, Okla. Bd. dirs. N.A.M., Nat. Council Small Bus. Devel. Mem. Putnam City (Okla.) Bd. Edn., 1961—, pres., 1968—; mem. Warr Acres (Okla.) City Council, 1956—; chmn. finance Okla. Democratic Party. Bd. visitors U. Okla.; trustee Water Devel. Found. Okla., Oklahoma City U. Named Okla. Outstanding Small Businessman, 1965, 66, 67, Nation's Outstanding Small Businessman, 1966, One of America's Ten Outstanding Young Men, 1967. Methodist (lay leader). Mason. Home: 3125 Lakeview Manor Dr Bethany OK 73008 Office: 4545 N Lincoln Blvd Oklahoma City OK 73105

GREVE, JOHN PAUL, oil co. exec., lawyer; b. Urbana, Kan., Aug. 16, 1906; s. Benno and Anna Gertrude (Sellman) G.; student St. Mary's Coll., 1927; J.D., St. Louis U., 1930; m. Florence Louise Hohl, Aug. 14, 1936; children—Margaret Ann (Mrs. Bruce T. Brown), John Paul. Admitted to Okla. bar, 1930, Mo. bar, 1931; atty. Mid-Continent Petroleum Corp., 1930-57; with DX Sunray Oil Co., 1955-59, gen. counsel, 1955-59, dir., 1957-60; gen. atty. Sunray DX Oil Co., 1959-67; v.p., gen. counsel DX div. Sun Oil Co., Tulsa, 1967—. Mem. Am., Okla., Tulsa County bar assns., Am. Judicature Soc. Home: 1704 S Delaware Pl Tulsa OK 74104 Office: PO Box 2039 Tulsa OK 74101

GREY, HARVEY J., lawyer; b. Winnipeg, Man., Can., Sept. 2, 1924; B.A., U. B.C. (Can.), 1948, LL.B., 1949. Admitted to B.C. bar, 1949; partner firm Harper, Gilmour, Grey & Co., Vancouver, B.C. Mem. Canadian (chmn. ins. law sect. 1966-68), Vancouver (pres. 1970—) bar assns., Law Soc. B.C. Office: 409 Granville St Vancouver 2 British Columbia Canada*

GREY, JAMES DAVID, clergyman; b. Princeton, Ky., Dec. 18, 1906; s. George Lindsay and Lucy Ann (Kenny) G.; A.B., Union U., Jackson, Tenn., 1929, D.D., 1938; Th.M., Southwestern Bapt. Theol. Sem., Ft. Worth, 1932; LL.D., La. Coll., Pineville, 1952; D.D., Baylor U., 1953; m. Lillian Gaines Tooke, Sept. 16, 1927; children-Martha Ann, Mary Beth. Ordained to ministry Bapt. Ch., 1925; pastor Tabernacle Ch., Ennis, Tex., 1931-34, First Ch., Denton, Tex., 1934-37, First Ch., New Orleans, 1937—; minister radio program The Gospel Hour, New Orleans, 1940—, Bapt. Hour, 1940, 52. Mem. bd. Met. Area Com. (New Orleans), 1966—. Organizer, mem. bd. dirs. La. Moral and Civic Found., 1943-56, pres., 1953-56; pres. bd. trustees La. Coll., 1960-61; bd. dirs. United Fund Greater New Orleans, Council for a Better La., Salvation Army (gulf states area); mem. bd. Information Council of Americas; pres. New Orleans Fedn. Chs., 1957; dir. Met. New Orleans Crime Commn. Pres. La. Bapt. Conv., 1948-50, So. Bapt. Conv., 1951-53; mem. exec. com. Bapt. World Alliance 1950-70. Pres. Met. Crime Commn., New Orleans, 1968-69; mem. La. Commn. on Law Enforcement and Adminstrn. Justice, 1968-70; mem. New Orleans Council on Naval Affairs. Bd. dirs. Heddlen Stanton Manor, Inc., So. Bapt. Hosps. Named Ky. col., 1950. Mem. Alpha Tau Omega. Kiwanian (bd. dirs. 1946-47). Author religious booklets and contbr. to Bapt. periodicals. Home: 4524 S Galvez St New Orleans LA 70125 Office: 4301 St Charles Av New Orleans LA 70115

GREY, JERRY, aerospace scientist; b. N.Y.C., Oct. 25, 1926; s. Abraham and Lillian (Danowitz) G.; B.S., Cornell U., 1947, M.S., 1949; Ph.D., Cal. Inst. Tech., 1952; m. Vivian Hoffman, June 27, 1948; children—Leslie Ann, Jacquelyn Eve. Instr. thermodynamics Cornell U., 1947-49; engine devel. engr. Fairchild Co. 1949-50; hypersonic aerodynamicist Guggenheim Aerospace Lab., Pasadena, Cal., 1950-51; sr. engr. Marquardt Co., 1951- 52; prof., dir. Nuclear Propulsion Research Lab., Princeton Sch. Engring. and Applied Sci., 1952-67; pres. Greyrad Corp., N.Y.C., 1959—. Served with USNR, 1944-46. Mem. Am. Inst. Aeros. and Astronautics (v.p.), Am. Astronautical Soc., Am. Soc. M.E., Am. Soc. Testing Materials, Am. Rocket Soc. (past chpt. pres.), N.Y. Acad. Sci., Sigma Xi, Tau Beta Pi, Phi Kappa Phi. Editor: (with Vivian Grey) Space Flight Report to the Nation, 1962. Address: 359 W 21st St New York City NY 10011

GREY, JOEL, actor; b. Cleve., 1932; s. Mickey Katz; m. Jo Wilder, June 1958; childrenJennifer, Jimmy. Began stage career in childhood, traveling with father as standup comic, song and dance man; played Chez Paris, Chgo., at age 18; appeared in with nat. touring co. of Stop the World, on Broadway in Stop the World, Come Blow Your Horn, and Half a Sixpence; role in Broadway musical Cabaret, 1966-67; TV appearances on Password, Snap Judgment, Our Place, Dean Martin Show, Jackie Gleason show, others. Recipient Tony award for performance in Cabaret, 1967. Address: care Ashley Famous Agy Inc 9255 Sunset Blvd Hollywood CA 90069

GREY, REX BURTON, mfg. co. exec.; B. el Paso, Tex., Oct. 27, 1920; s. Rex and Georgie Mary (Ferris) G.; B.S. in Mech. and Elec. Engring., Tex. A. and M. Coll., 1941; m. Natalie C. Tandy, May 2, 1942; 1 son, Rex Oliver. With Gen. Elec. Co., 1945-55, mgr. mfg. Trumbull div., 1952-55; chmn. ITT (U.K.) Industries, 1964-, Standard Telephones & Cables Ltd., Creed Co., Supersonics (Zambia), STC (S. Africa), Supersonics (Rhodesia, Zambia), ITT (Zambia), ITT (Maroc), ITT (Iran), ITT (Algeria), ITT (Nigeria); pres. ITT Africa and Middle East; v.p. dir. Internat. Standard Electric Co., ITT (Europe); v.p. Internat. Tel & Tel. Corp. Mem. Am. Mgmt. Assn. Mason (Shriner). Home: 10 Park Crescent London W 1 England Office: STC House 190 Strand London W C 2 England

GREY, WHEELER, lawyer; b. Des Moines, Dec. 3, 1908; s. John Chester and Maude (Wheeler) G.; student Mich. State U., 1925-27; B.A., J.D., George Washington U., 1931; m. Allene Carew May, July 1, 1933 (dec. 1967); children—Wheeler, Stephen Carew, Allene Carew; m. Peggy Burton Green, Feb. 27, 1969. Admitted to D.C. bar, 1931, N.J. bar, 1933, Wash. bar, 1938; practiced in N.J., 1933-37; partner firm Jones, Grey, Bayley & Olsen, Seattle; dir. John Fluke Mfg. Co., Inc., Seattle Hardware Co., MWK Internat. Co. Ltd., Fluke Internat. Corp., Rupert Fish Co., Western Aluminum Co., Standard Veneer & Timber Co., Coast Oyster Co. Active Black Found., Jerry Lorentson Found., Goodwill Industries, Seattle, United Good Neighbors. Served to lt. col. Judge Adv. Gen.'s Dept., AUS, 1943, Civil Affairs Dept., War Dept. Gen. Staff, 1943-46. Decorated Legion of Merit; Officer, Order Brit. Empire. Mem. Am., Internat., Wash., N.J., D.C. bar assns., Seattle C. of C. (pres. 1960-61), Japan-Am. Soc. Seattle (pres. 1961-62), Psi Upsilon. Republican. Rotarian (pres. Seattle 1965-66). Home: 6648 NE 60th St Seattle WA 98115 Office: Norton Bldg 801 2d Av Seattle WA 98104

GREY, WILLIAM LEON, wire and cable co. exec.; b. Bklyn., Mar. 24, 1916; s. Joseph Charles and Theresa Charlotte (Olsen) G.; B.S. in Mech. Engring., N.Y.U., 1937; LL.B., Bklyn. Law Sch., 1950; grad. Advanced Mgmt. Program, Harvard, 1957; m. Marguerite Felicia Kefer, Aug. 31, 1940; childrenRichard William, Carol Lynne. Admitted to N.Y. bar, 1950; with Anaconda Wire and Cable Co., 1939—, gen. counsel, v.p., 1958-65, adminstrv. v.p., 1965-66, exec. v.p., 1966, pres., 1967—, also dir.; dir. Anaconda Electronics Co., Anaheim, Cal., Condumex, Mexico City. Mem. Am. Bar Assn., N.Y. County Lawyers Assn. Clubs: Union League (N.Y.C.); Scarsdale Golf. Home: 25 Cross Hill Rd Hartsdale NY 10530 Office: Anaconda Wire & Cable Co 605 3d Av New York City NY 10016

GRIBBEL, JOHN, II, securities co. exec.; b. Chestnut Hill, Pa., June 10, 1916; s. Wakeman Griffin and Margaret Douglas (Latta) G.; B.S., Yale, 1938; m. Natalie Fox Elkins, June 28, 1938; children—John III, Natalie G. (Mrs. Wayne S. Thomas). Cadet engr. Phila. Electric Co., 1938-41; sales engr. Budd Co., Phila., 1945-47; dist. sales mgr. Am. Meter Co., Phila., 1947-51; v.p. Riverside Metal Co. (N.J.), 1951-54; chmn. exec. com. Elkins Morris Stroud & Co., Phila., 1965—. Trustee Germantown (Pa.) Acad., Abington Meml. Hosp. Pres., Pa. Acad. Fine Arts, 1970—. Served to lt. comdr. USNR, 1941-45. Episcopalian (vestryman). Clubs: Union League (Phila.) Huntingdon Valley (Pa.) Country; Bald Peak (N.H.) Country. Home: 2141 Paper Mill Rd Huntingdon Valley PA 19006 Office: Stock Exchange Bldg Philadelphia PA 19103

GRIBBIN, JOHN HAWKINS, librarian; b. Charleston, S.C., Sept. 22, 1920; s. Robert Emmet and Emma (Jenkins) G.; A.B., U. N.C., 1942; B.L.S., U. Cal. at Berkeley, 1947, M.L.S., 1950; Ph.D., U. Chgo., 1958; m. Lenore Evelyn Sipes, Mar. 3, 1951. Documents librarian U. Mo., 1947-49; geology librarian, instr. Library Sch., U. Tex., Austin, 1950-51; asso. librarian Rice U., 1953- 54; librarian Nat. Acad. Scis., Washington, 1955-61; asso. librarian U. N.C., 1961-66; library dir. Tulane U., New Orleans, 1966—. Chmn. sectional com. U.S. Standards Inst., 1965-68. Served as officer AUS, 1942-46. Mem. Am., Southeastern, La. library assns., Assn. Southeastern Research Libraries (chmn. 1971-73), Kappa Alpha. Episcopalian. Editor: Industrial Research Laboratories of the U.S., 1960; Scientific and Technical Societies of the U.S. and Canada, 1961; The Southeastern Librarian, 1965-66. Home: 1430 Jackson Av New Orleans LA 70130

GRIBBLE, LLOYD RAYMOND, coll. dean; b. Fairchance, Pa., Sept. 7, 1906; s. Russell Thornton and Lou Ella (Martin) G.; B.S., Waynesburg Coll., 1929; M.S., W. Va. U., 1931, Ph.D., 1935; m. Myrtle Elizabeth Ekhardt, June 10, 1927; 1 dau., Joanne Marie (Mrs. Daniel Edward Lebo, Jr.). Instr. zoology Waynesburg Coll., summer 1929; mem. faculty W. Va. U., 1929-, prof. zoology, 1947- , asso. dean Coll. Arts and Scis., 1961-. Mem. adv. council Monongalia Gen. Hosp. Sch. Nursing, 1949-62, chmn., 1953-62. Fellow A.A.A.S. (council 1953-60); mem. W. Va. Acad. Sci. W. Va. Assn. Acad. Deans, Am. Soc. Zoologists, Sigma Xi, Alpha Epsilon Delta (nat. pres. 1953-60; nat. councilor 1960-68). Author: Comparative Anatomy Laboratory Manual, 1950. Home: 819 Riverview Dr Morgantown WV 26505

GRIBBLE, WILLIAM CHARLES, Jr., army officer; b. Ironwood, Mich., May 24, 1917; s. William Charles and Maud (Slade) G.; student Mich. Technol. U., 1934-37, D. Engring. (hon.), 1969; B.S., U.S. Mil. Acad., 1941; M.S., U. Chgo., 1948; postgrad. Nat. War Coll., 1960-61; m. Martha Jane Watson, June 21, 1941; childrenWilliam Charles III, Nancy Jane, Donald James, Judith Ann. Commd. 2d Lt. U.S. Army, 1941, advanced through grades to lt. gen., 1971; staff mem. Los Alamos Sci. Lab., 1948- 52; staff AEC, 1953-56; with Alaska Engr. Dist., 1956-60; with Office Chief Army Engrs., 1961-63; div. engr. North Central Engrs. Div., 1963; dir. research and devel. Army Material Command, 1963-66; dep. asst. chief of staff Dept. Army Gen. Staff, 1966-69; comdg. gen. U.S. Army Engr. Center, 1969-70; chief research and devel. Dept. Army, 1971—. Decorated D.S.M., Legion of Merit medal with oak leaf cluster. Registered profl. engr., D.C. Mem. Am. Ordnance Assn., Soc. Am. Mil. Engrs., Assn. U.S. Army, Tau Beta Pi, Theta Tau. Home: 9045 Patton Blvd Alexandria VA 22309 Office: Dept Army The Pentagon Washington DC 20310

GRIBBS, ROMAN S., mayor of Detroit; b. Detroit, Dec. 29, 1925; s. Roman and Magdeline (Widziszewski) Grzyb; B.S., magna cum laude, U. Detroit, 1952, LL.B., 1954; m. Katherine Stratis, June 12, 1954; children—Paula, Carla, Christopher, Rebecca, Elizabeth. Admitted to Mich. bar, 1954; tchr. law and accounting U. Detroit, 1952; asst. pros. atty. Wayne County, Mich., 1956-64; pvt. practice law Shaheen, Gribbs & Shaheen, 1964-66; presiding referee Traffic Ct., 1966-68; sheriff Wayne County, 1968-69; mayor of Detroit, 1970—. Mem. Presdl. Commn. Civil Def. Adv. Commn., 1970-74. Served as sgt. AUS, World War II. Mem. Nat. League of Cities (exec. com.), U.S. (trustee), Mich. (pres.) confs. mayors, Delta Sigma Phi, Blue Key. Democrat. Roman Catholic. Office: City-County Bldg Detroit MI 48226

GRICE, BENNING MOORE, state justice; b. Hawkinsville, Ga., Sept. 16, 1909; s. Warren and Clara (Rumph) G.; A.B., Mercer U., 1931, LL.B., 1932; m. Mary Flavia Calhoun, Oct. 18, 1941; childrenBenning Moore, Ann Victoria, Warren C. Admitted to Ga. bar, 1932, practiced in Macon, 1933-60; asso. justice Supreme Ct. of Ga., 1961-. Mem. Ga. Bd. Bar Examiners, 1957-60. Pres. Central Ga. council Boy Scouts Am., 1955-58. Mem. Ga. Ho. of Reps., 1939- 42. Trustee Ga. Indsl. Home, 1937-42, 47-49, YMCA, 1948-66. Served from lt. (j.g.) to lt. comdr., USNR, 1942-45. Voted Macon's Outstanding Young Man by civic clubs, 1940. Mem. Am., Ga., Macon Circuit (pres.1953-54), Macon, Atlanta bar assns., Mercer U. Alumni Assn. (pres. law chpt. 1950-51), Kappa Alpha. Baptist (deacon). Mason (32). Clubs: Kiwanis (pres. 1951), Idle Hour Golf and Country (Macon); Atlanta Athletic, Capitol City (Atlanta). Home: 3065 High Point Dr Macon GA 31204 Office: State Judicial Bldg Atlanta GA 30334

GRICE, H. PAUL, educator. Prof. philosophy U. Cal. at Berkeley. Office: 314 Moses Hall U Cal Berkeley CA 94720*

GRICE, HARWOOD VINSON, banker; b. Dallas, Aug. 15, 1915; s. Harwood Newman and Ada May (Vinson) G.; B.S. with honors, So. Meth. U., 1935; m. Kathryn Gentry, Dec. 14, 1953; children by previous marriage—Harwood Vinson, Edward Cowan. Asst. v.p. Republic Nat. Bank, Dallas, 1934-48; with United Cal. Bank, Los Angeles, 1948—, sr. v.p., 1959-63, exec. v.p., 1963—. Bd. dirs. Better Bus. Bur., Los Angeles. Served to lt. (s.g.) USNR, 1942-45. Mem. Robert Morris Assos., Mchts. and Mfrs. Assn., Lambda Chi Alpha, Beta Gamma Sigma, Phi Eta Sigma, Alpha Theta Phi. Methodist. Clubs: Wilshire Country, Stock Exchange, Beavers (Los Angeles); Shadow Mountain Golf (Palm Desert, Cal.). Home: 1014 Highland St South Pasadena CA 91030 Office: 600 S Spring St Los Angeles CA 90014

GRIDER, HAL LOUOWN, lawyer; b. Altus, Okla., Dec. 2, 1929; s. Hugh B. and Hallie (Young) G.; B.B.A., W.Tex. State U., 1959; LL.B., U. Okla., 1962; 1 son, Victor Roderick. Admitted to Okla. bar, 1962, since practiced in Altus; legal adviser county officers Jackson County, 1967—; asst. dist. atty. 3d Judicial Dist. Okla., 1967—. Bd. dirs. Altus chpt. A.R.C., Black Beaver council Boy Scouts Am. Served with AUS, 1946-47, USN, 1948-56. Mem. Altus C. of C. (past dir.). Baptist. Mason (32), Kiwanian, Elk. Club: Altus Golf and Country. Home: 409 N Main St Altus OK 73521 Office: N B C Bldg Altus OK 73521

GRIEBEL, RICHARD HERMAN, corp. exec.; b. Liberty, N.Y., Apr. 4, 1924; s. Joseph F. and Libbie R. (Henry) G.; A.B., Dartmouth, 1946; postgrad. Columbia, 1946, Grad. Exec. Devel. Program, Ind. U., 1956; m. Elaine A. Gretzkowski, Jan. 26, 1946; children—R. Nelson, Douglas M., Barbara E. With RCA, 1946- 53, Farnsworth Electric Co., 1953-58, Raytheon Co., 1958-59; v.p. Internat. Tel.&Tel. Corp., 1960-62, also pres. Kellogg Telecommunications div., group exec. Comml. Telecommunications group and pres., gen. mgr. Kellogg Switchboard & Supply Co.; pres., chmn. bd., dir. Fairbanks, Morse and Co., N.Y.C., 1963-67; v.p., dir. Fairbanks Whitney Corp., N.Y.C., 1963-64; v.p., group exec., dir. Colt Industries, Inc., 1964-67; chmn. bd. Canadian Locomotive Co., Ltd., Kingston, Ont., Can., 1963-67, Pratt & Whitney Machine Tool Co., Hartford, Conn., 1963- 64, Colt Firearms Co., Hartford, 1963-64, pres., chief exec. officer, dir. P. Ballantine & Sons, 1967-69; pres., chief exec. officer, dir. Lehigh Valley Industries, Inc., 1969—. Overseer, Hanover Inn, Hanover, N.H., 1968—. Served to capt. USMCR, 1942-45. Mem. Am. Inst. Indsl. Engrs., Am. Soc. Tool Mfg. Cos., Am. Soc. Naval Engrs., Assn. U.S. Army, Armed Forces Communications and Electronics Assn., Nat., Def. Transp. Assn. (dir.), Am. Ordnance Assn. Clubs: Rockaway River Country (Denville, N.J.); Union League, Economics (N.Y.C.). Home: 609 Mountain Rd Smoke Rise NJ Office: 200 E 42d St New York City NY 10017

GRIEM, PAUL D., corp. exec.; m. May Griem; children—Paul D., Robert F., Susan. V.p., Hunt Foods & Industries, Inc., also pres. W.P. Fuller & Co. div.; v.p., gen. mgr. West Coast operations Anchor Hocking Glass Corp. Treas., dir. Cal. Assn. Mental Health; dir. Orange County Assn. Mental Health, Laguna Beach Festival of Arts, Laguna Beach Civic League; dir., mem. exec. com. Nat. Assn. Mental Health. Home: 2017 Ocean Way Laguna Beach CA 92651 Office: 4855 E 52d Pl Los Angeles CA 90022

GRIER, EDWARD J., meat co. exec.; b. Ottumwa, Ia., 1906; ed. Creighton Coll., 1931. Vice pres., sec., dir. John Morrell & Co. K.C., Elk. Office: 208 S La Salle St Chicago IL 60604*

GRIER, HARRY DOBSON MILLER, art museum exec.; b. Phila., Jan. 23, 1914; s. Edwin Stanley and Ethel Milnor (Miller) G.; B.S. in Architecture, Pa. State U., 1935; postgrad. art, archaeology Princeton, 1935-38; postgrad. Inst. d'Art et d'Archeologie, U. Paris (France), summer 1936, N.Y. U. Inst. Fine Arts, 1939-41. Architect, archaeol. field asst. Princeton Expdn. for Excavation Antioch and Vicinity, 1937; lectr., later asst. to dean, dept. edn. Met. Mus. Art, 1938-46; asst. dir. Mpls. Inst. Arts, 1946-51; asst. dir. Frick Collection, 1951-64, dir., 1964—. Adv. council Princeton Art Mus. Trustee Internat. Exhbns. Found., Amon Carter Mus. Western Art, Ft. Worth; bd. dirs. Am. Friends Attingham, sponsors Nat. Trust Summer Sch. for study historic Houses Eng. Served to maj. AUS, 1941-46; ETO. Decorated Bronze Star with oak leaf cluster; officer Order of Leopold II. Mem. Museums Council N.Y.C. (chmn. 1962-64), Nat. Com. Drawing Soc., Am. Inst. Interior Designers, Coll. Art Assn., Am. Italy Soc. (dir.), Internat. Council Museums, Am. Assn. Museums, Assn. Art Mus. Dirs. (pres. 1968-69, trustee, treas. 1970—). Home: 16 E 84th St New York City NY 10028 also Brookside Farm Cottage Oxford PA 19363 Office: 1 E 70th St New York City NY 10021

GRIER, HERBERT EARL, scientist; b. Chgo., July 3, 1911; s. Herbert Earl and Martha (Sleeter) G.; B.S., Mass. Inst. Tech., 1933, M.S., 1934; D.Sc. (hon.), U. Nev., 1967; m. Dorothy Jean Whitcomb, Sept. 5, 1954; children—Herbert Earl, III, Joan, David Louis. Cons. engr. Mass. Inst. Tech., 1934-47; sr. v.p. EG&G, Boston and Las Vegas, 1947—; pres., dir. CER Geonuclear Corp., Las Vegas, 1965—; dir. Reynolds Elec. & Engring. Co., Inc., Las Vegas, 1969—; dir. Aerovox Corp., 1st Nat. Bank Nev. Pres. So. Nev. Indsl. Found., 1965-66; mem. nat. adv. bd. Desert Research Inst. of U. Nev., 1965—. Trustee Nev. So. U. Land Found. Recipient Certificate of Appreciation, Sec. Army, 1954. Registered profl. engr., Mass., Nev. Colo. Mem. Mass., Nev. socs. registered profl. engrs., Mass. Inst. Tech. Alumni Assn., Health Physics Soc. Research in ultra high-speed photography and devel. of stroboscopic and flash lighting techniques, atomic weapons. Home: 200 Rancho Circle Las Vegas NV 89107 Office: 120 E Flamingo Rd Las Vegas NV 89114

GRIER, PAUL LIVINGSTON, librarian; b. Clover, S.C., May 26, 1914; s. William Pressly and Nellie Brownlee (Bigham) G.; A.B., Erskine Coll., 1936; A.B. in L.S., U. N.C., 1938; A.M., U. Mich., 1947; m. Eleanor Jane Meacham, Aug. 16, 1947. Library asst. Washington Pub. Library, 1936-40; librarian Hampden-Sydney Coll., 1940-42, 46—. Served from ensign to lt. USNR, 1942-46. Mem. evaluating coms. for So. Assn. Colls. and Schs. Mem. A.L.A.

Southeastern, Va. library assns., Assn. Am. Museums, English Speaking Union, Assn. for Preservation Va. Antiquities, Sigma Upsilon. Presbyn. (elder). Home: Hampden-Sydney VA 23943

GRIER, WILLIAM HARRIS, textile mfr.; b. Ft. Mill, S.C., Nov. 21, 1901; s. Robert F. and Bessie (Caldwell) G.; B.S., Clemson Coll., 1923; LL.D., 1963; m. Lila Atkinson, Sept. 20, 1930; children:William Harris, John Buford. With Pacific Mills, Lawrence, Mass., 1924-25, Lyman, S.C., 1925-27, Thomaston (Ga.) Mills, 1927-29, Commander Mills, Sand Springs, Okla., 1929-33; with Rock Hill Printing & Finishing Co., 1933—, exec. v.p., 1947-58, pres., 1958-; pres. Lyman Printing & Finishing Co., 1958-; dir. Bus. Development Corp. S.C.; bd. dirs. M. Lowenstein & Sons, Inc., N.Y.C., since 1950; dir. Fed. Res. Bank of Richmond, Piedmont & Northern Ry., Charlotte. Bd. dirs. Carolinas United Community Services, Charlotte. Trustee of Winthrop College, Rock Hill, N.C. Member Rock Hill C. of C., S.C. Mfrs. Assn. (dir.), Soc. Advancement Management. Presbyn. (elder). Club: Executives. Home: 604 Charlotte Av Rock Hill SC 29730 Office: Rock Hill Printing & Finishing Co Rock Hill SC 2973O

GRIES, GEORGE ALEXANDER, univ. dean; b. Cambridge, Mass., May 2, 1917; s. John Mathew and Ethel (Goff) G.; A.B., Miami U., Oxford, O.; M.S., Kan. State U., 1940; Ph.D., U. Wis., 1942; m. Mary Lou Carpenter, May 26, 1939; childrenJames C., Judy L. Asst. plant pathologist Conn. Agr. Expt. Sta., 1942-45; asso. prof., then prof. plant physiology Purdue U., 1945-60; research demonstrator U. Wales, Swansea, Eng., 1957-58; prof. plant pathology, head dept. U. Ariz., 1960-66, prof. head biol. scis., 1966-68; dean arts and scis. Okla. State U., 1968-. Mem. Commn. Edn. in Agr. and Natural Resources, 1961-69; mem. Commn. Undergrad. Edn. in Biol. Scis. 1969-71; governing bd. Am. Inst. Biol. Sci., 1970—. Recipient Silver Beaver award Boy Scouts Am. Mem. Am. Phytopathol. Soc. (councillor-at-large 1966-68), Bot. Soc. Am., Nat. Assn. Biology Tchrs., Nat. Assn. Coll. Tchrs. Agr., Phi Beta Kappa, Sigma Xi, Phi Kappa Phi, Phi Sigma. Contbr. profl. jours. Home: 23 Brentwood Dr Stillwater OK 74074

GRIES, JOHN PAUL, coll. dean; b. Washington, June 7, 1911; s. John Matthew and Ethel Martha (Goff) G.; A.B., Miami U. (Ohio), 1932; M.S., U. Chgo., 1933, Ph.D., 1935; m. Virginia Overbeck, July 5, 1933; children—John Charles, Donald Alan. Geologist, Ill. Geol. Survey, 1935-36; from instr. to asst. prof. geology S.D. Sch. Mines and Tech., Rapid City, 1936-44; from asso. prof. to prof., 1946—, dir. grad. studies, 1951-66, dean grad. div., 1966—; geologist Magnolia Petroleum Co., Midland, Tex., 1944-46; geol. cons. in groundwater, engring. geology non-metallics, mineral fuels. Participant Am. Geol. Inst., Internat. Field Inst., Paris Basin, summer 1965. Mem. Geol. Soc. Am., Am. Inst. Mining, Metall. and Petroleum Engrs., Am. Assn. Petroleum Geologists, Paleontol. Soc., Rapid City Astron. Soc. (treas.). Rotarian. Contbr. articles profl. jours. Home: 238 St Charles St Rapid City SD 57701

GRIES, KONRAD, educator; b. N.Y.C., Feb. 17, 1911; s. Charles A. and Ella (Dempwolff) G.; student Sorbonne, 1929, U. Munich, 1930; B.A., Coll. City N.Y., 1931; M.A., Columbia, 1933, Ph.D., 1948; m. Anne Zeeb, Apr. 16, 1933; children—Christian, David, Peter, Daniel. Tchr. Latin, Townsend Harris Hall High Sch., 1931-37; tchr. German, Grover Cleveland High Sch., N.Y.C., 1937; from tutor to prof. classical langs., chmn. dept. classical, oriental langs. Queens Coll., Flushing, N.Y., 1937—, supr. English Lang. Inst., 1950-69. Chmn. cub pack 272 Boy Scouts Am., Queens, 1945-57. Mem. Am. Assn. U. Profs. (past pres. Flushing chpt.), Am. Philol. Assn., Am. Classical League, Classical Assn. Atlantic States, N.Y. Classical Club (past pres.), Phi Beta Kappa. Author: The Constancy of Livy's Latinity, 1949. Bus. mgr., asso. editor, editor The Classical Outlook, 1945—. Contbr. articles to philology jours. Home: 45-31 171st Pl Flushing NY 11358

GRIESBACH, GEORGE ALBERT, overseas trader; b. N.Y.C., June 9, 1890; s. Albert and Rose (Seligmann) G.; ed. in Hamburg, Germany; m. Elsie Hirsch, Nov. 5, 1922; 1 dau., Dorothy (Mrs. William A. Salant). Co-owner, J. Gerber & Co., Inc., N.Y.C., 1920-. Decorated Chevalier of Leopold Order of Belgium. Home: The Willows Pomona NY 10970 also 140 E 56th St New York City NY 10025 Office: J Gerber & Co Inc 855 Av of Americas New York City NY 10001

GRIESEDIECK, JOSEPH E., brewery exec.; b. St. Louis, Mar. 1, 1919; s. Alvin and Mary (O'Donnell). G.; B.S., Cornell U., 1940; m. Judith Powers, Feb 27, 1943; children—Joseph, Ellen, Ann, Judith, Carroll. Chief engr. Falstaff Brewing Corp., 1945-48, asst. to pres., 1948-51, v.p., asst. gen. mgr., 1952-53, pres., 1953—, chmn. bd., mem. exec. com., 1970—. Served with USNR, 1941-45. Mem. Acad. Sci. (St. Louis), Master Brewers Assn. Am., Tau Beta Pi. Roman Catholic. Clubs: Old Warson Country, University Noonday, Cornell, St. Louis Country (St. Louis, N.Y.C.), Racquet; California. Home: 800 Barnes Rd Ladue MO 64724 Office: 5050 Oakland Av St Louis MO 63110

GRIESEMER, RICHARD ALLEN, educator, veterinarian; b. Andreas, Pa., May 8, 1929; s. Harold H. and Edna Amanda (Wehr) G.; D.V.M., Ohio State U., 1953, Ph.D., 1959; m. Marilyn Joann Stauf, Jan. 20, 1951; children—James, Thomas, William. Instr. vet. pathology Ohio State U., 1953-55, 57-59, asst. prof., 1959-61, asso. prof., 1961-64, prof., 1964-71, chmn. dept., 1967-71; prof. vet. pathology U. Cal., Davis, 1971—; asso. dir. Nat. Center Primate Biology, 1971—. Mem. animal resources adv. com. NIH, 1969-73, biohazards adv. com. Nat. Cancer Inst., 1969—; mem. subcom. standards for dogs and cats Nat. Acad. Sci., Inst. Lab. Animal Resources, 1967—. Served to capt. USAF, 1955-57. Mem. Am. Vet. Med. Assn. (Gaines award and medal 1968), Am. Coll. Vet. Pathologists, Am. Soc. Exptl. Pathology, Internat. Acad. Pathology, Am. Soc. Microbiology, A.A.A.S., Am. Soc. Vet. Clin. Pathologists, Assn. Gnotobiotics. Home: 704 Radcliffe Dr Davis CA 95616

GRIEST, THEODORE REED, architect; b. Cheyenne Wells, Colo., Aug. 14, 1898; s. John E. and Annie (Campbell) G.; B.S. in Architecture, Kan. State U., 1923; postgrad. Harvard, 1929-30; m. Frances H. Crarey, Jan. 24, 1931. Archtl. draftsman and designer, Chgo., Boston, Topeka, 1923-33; practicing architect, Topeka, 1933-56; cons. architect, Topeka, 1956—. Mem. Topeka City Planning Com., 1957-59; planning cons. Topeka Urban Renewal, 1962-70; mem. Kan. Registration and Examining Bd. for Architects, 1949-58; engring. adv. council Kan. State U. 1959-62. Bd. dirs. Topeka YMCA. Served with U.S. Army, 1918. Recipient Distinguished Service award Sch. Engring. and Architecture, Kan. State U., 1960. Fellow A.I.A. (regional jud. com.; pres. Kan. 1946-47), Sigma Tau. Address: 208 Country Club Dr Topeka KS 66611

GRIEVE, HAROLD WALTER, interior designer; b. Los Angeles, 1901; s. Alexander and Maria (Chapman) G.; m. Jetta Goudal, Oct. 11, 1930. Motion picture art dir., 1921-27, designing prodns. for Rex Ingram, Mary Pickford, Ernst Lubitsch, Marshal Neilan, Sam Goldwyn; also Costumes for Ben Hur, Rome, 1925; interior designer, Los Angeles, 1927-; interiors include homes for Howard Greer, Blanche Sweet, John Gilbert, Colleen Moore, Jack Benny, Norma Scherer, Lily Pons, numerous others. Served from lt. to comdr. 1942-46; designed CIC plot-radar and nite fighter unit; capt. USNR. Recipient Spl. Fabric Design award Am. Inst. Decorators, 1948. Fellow Am. Inst. Decorator (nat. pres. 1957-59).‡

GRIEVE, PIERSON MACDONALD, diversified co. exec.; b. Flint, Mich., Dec. 5, 1927; s. P.M. and Margaret (Leamy) G.; B.S. in Bus. Adminstrn., Northwestern U., 1950; postgrad. U. Minn., 1955-56; m. Florence R. Brogan, July 29, 1950; children—Margaret, Scott, Bruce. With Caterpillar Tractor Co., Peoria, Ill., 1950-52; staff engr. A.T. Kearney & Co., mgmt. consultants, Chgo., 1952-55; pres. Rapin-Wax, Mpls., 1955-62; exec. Questor Corp. (formerly Dunhill Internat. Inc.), Todedo, 1962—, chief exec. officer, 1967—; dir. Ward Foods, Inc., N.Y.C., A.G. Spalding & Bros., Inc., Chicopee, Mass. Served with USNR, 1945-46. Mem. Kappa Sigma. Episcopalian. Clubs: Toledo (Toledo); Metropolitan (N.Y.C.). Home: 2105 Orchard Rd Toledo OH 43606 Office: 1801 Spielbusch Av Toledo OH 43601

GRIEVES, ROBERT BELANGER, educator; b. Evanston, Ill., Oct. 15, 1935; s. Roy and Marie (Belanger) G.; B.A. in Russian, Northwestern U., 1956, M.S. in Chem. Engring., 1959, Ph.D. in Chem. Engring., 1961; m. Sandra Lee Artman, Dec. 10, 1966; children—Christopher Robert, Jaime Robert. Asst. prof. civil engring. Northwestern U., Evanston, 1961-63; from asst. prof. to asso. prof. civil and environmental engring. Ill. Inst. Tech., Chgo., 1963-67; prof., chmn. chem. engring. dept. U. Ky., Lexington, 1967—, dir. grad. tng. program in air pollution control, 1968—. Cons. to industry in air and water pollution control. Mem. Am. Inst. Chem. Engrs., Am. Water Works Assn., Water Pollution Control Fedn., Phi Beta Kappa, Sigma Xi, Tau Beta Pi. Contbr. articles to profl. jours. Home: 3195 Burnham Ct Lexington KY 40503

GRIFFEN, RICHARD DANIEL, food co. exec.; b. Tarrytown, N.Y., Apr. 11, 1916; s. Charles Daniel and Isabel B. (Bushell) G., B.A., Coll. City N.Y., 1938; LL.B., N.Y.U., 1942; m. Sara C. Cannady, Dec. 24, 1939; childrenSusan T., Richard Daniel, Sara Elizabeth. Admitted to N.Y. bar, 1942; with firm Sullivan & Cromwell, N.Y.C., 1942-50; corp. sec. Best Foods, Inc., N.Y.C., 1950-58, Corn Products Co., N.Y.C., 1958-. Served with USNR, 1943-45. Mem. Assn. Bar City N.Y., Am. Soc. Corp. Secretaries, Delta Kappa Epsilon. Home: 124 Woodside Dr Greenwich CT 06830 Office: 717 Fifth Av New York City NY 10022

GRIFFENHAGEN, EDWIN O., cons. mgmt. engr.; b. Chgo., Ill., Jan. 14, 1886; s. Oscar Fred and Anna Maria (Kleinhans) G.; B.S. in C.E., Ill. Inst. Tech., 1906, C.E., 1909; m. Christine A. Gloeckler, Jan. 7, 1909; childrenRuth Christine (Mrs. Newton Du Puy), Elinor Jane (Mrs. David B. Truman). Mining engring., Alaska, 1906; bldg. engr., C.M. & St. P. Ry., 1907-09; archtl. engr. Chgo., 1909, orgn. tech. work, Civil Service Commn., 1910; head indsl. engring. dept., Arthur Young & Co., Chgo., N.Y.C., 1911-19, with colleagues took over business of indsl., engring, dept. 1920, and since practiced as Griffenhagen & Assos. cons. mgmt. engrs.; cons. Griffenhagen-Kroeger, Inc., 1959—. Reorganized Canadian Gov't. depts., 1918- ret. naval officer; b. Phila., Jan. 12, 1906; s. Joseph Richard and Maude (Spicknall) G.; B.S., U.S. Naval Acad., 1927; M.S. in Aero. Engring., U. Mich., 1937; grad. Nat. War Coll., 1951; m. Camilla Yvonne Ganteaume, Sept. 14, 1935 (dec.); children-Linda (Mrs. Harry Collins II), Charles Donald; m. 2d., Marion Hopkins Schaefer, Nov. 21, 1964. Commd. ensign USN, 1927, advanced through grades to adm., 1963; designated naval aviator; duty in battleships, destroyers, 1927-30; attached U.S.S. Enterprise, 1937-40; flight test officer Naval Air Sta., Anacostia, 1940-42; comdr. Carrier Air Group 9, U.S.S. Essex, 1942- 43; operations officer T.F. 58 Pacific, 1943; mem. Joint War Plans Com. Joint Chiefs Staff, 1944; comdg. officer U.S.S. Croatan, 1945-46; plans officer U.S. Atlantic Fleet, 1946-47; strategic plans div. Operations Navy, 1948-50; plans officer U.S. Pacific Fleet, 1951-53; comdg. officer U.S.S. Oriskany, 1953-54; spl. asst. to chmn. Joint Chiefs of Staff, 1955-56; comdr. Carrier Div. 4, 1947-48; dir. strategic plans Navy Dept., 1959-60; comdr. Seventh Fleet, 1960-61; dep. chief naval operations, 1962-63; comdr. in chief USN Forces Europe, 1963-65; comdr. in chief allied forces So. Europe, 1965-68. Decorated D.S.M. with gold star, Bronze Star medal, Presdl. citations; supreme comdr. Order of George the First (Greece); knight Grand Cross Order of Republic (Italy); comdr. Philippine Legion Honor; Order Mil. Merit with silver star (Korea); Order of Double-Rays of Rising Sun (Japan); Medal of Pao-Ting (China). Episcopalian. Clubs: Chevy Chase (Md.); Army and Navy, Metropolitan, Tavern Association (Washington); Army and Navy Country (Arlington, Va.); American (London, Eng.); Circolo dell'Unione (Naples, Italy); Royal and ancient Golf of St. Andrews (Scotland); New York Yacht (N.Y.C.). Home: 4610 Dexter St SW Washington DC 20007

GRIFFETH, PAUL LYMAN, educator; b. Sturgis, Mich., Aug. 3, 1919; s. Shirley C. and Edna M. (Kaechele) G.; B.A., Mich. State U., 1941; M.A., U. Ia., 1955; Ph.D., 1958; m. Phyllis Mae Dean, Jan. 17, 1942; children—Gary Dean, Lindsey Jo. Officer, Walstrom-Griffeth Co., Harbor Springs, Mich., 1946-52; asst. dean men U. Ia., 1953-56, dean men, 1956-58; dean students Western Mich. U., Kalamazoo, 1958-66, v.p. student services, 1966-70, prof. counseling and personnel, 1970—. Dir. First Fed. Savs. & Loan Assn. Kalamazoo. Past pres. Constance Brown Speech and Hearing Center. Served with USNR, 1941-46. Mem. Mich. Coll. Personnel Assn. (past pres.), Council Mich. Guidance and Personnel Assns. (past pres.), Am. Personnel and Guidance Assn., Sigma Nu, Omicron Delta Kappa, Phi Delta Kappa. Presbyn. (elder). Kiwanian. Home: 5231 Colony Farm Rd Kalamazoo MI 49001

GRIFFIN, AMOS CLARK, biochemist, educator; b. Newton, Utah, May 16, 1917; s. Amos R. and Della (Petersen) G.; B.S., Utah State U., 1939; M.S., Mich. State U., 1941; postgrad. U. Cal. at Berkeley, 1941-42; Ph.D., U. Wis., 1947; m. Cleo L. Lundstrom, Aug. 16, 1939; children—Douglas C., Paul A., Brent L., Robert A., Janis. Postdoctoral fellow chemistry Stanford, 1947- 48, prof. chemistry, 1948-54; prof., head dept. biochemistry U. Tex. M.D. Anderson Hosp. and Tumor Inst., Houston, 1954-63, Am. Cancer Soc. prof. biochemistry, 1963—; head dept. biochemistry Baylor U. Coll. Medicine, Houston, 1955-62; cons. Meth. Hosp., Houston, 1959-70. Served with AUS, 1942-46. Mem. Am. Soc. Biol. Chemists, Am. Assn. for Cancer Research, Biochem. Soc. (London), Soc. for Exptl. Biology and Medicine, Am. Chem. Soc. Contbr. over 200 articles, chpts. to profl. publs. Home: 1800 Holcombe Blvd Houston TX 77025

GRIFFIN, ARVAL WESLEY, former banker; b. Fair Play, Mo., Sept. 2, 1905; s. John L. and Lucy Jane (Eddy) G.; student pub. schs.; m. Margaret Kelley May 22, 1937; children —John W., Kathryn J. With Nehawka (Neb.) Bank, 1924-26, Continental State Bank, Lincoln, Neb., 1926-28, Elmwood State Bank (Neb.), 1928-29; with Continental Nat. Bank, 1929-60, successively asst. trust officer, trust officer, v.p. and trust officer, exec. v.p., 1957-60; exec. v.p. 1st Nat. Bank & Trust Co., Lincoln, starting 1960, also dir. Republican. Conglist. Mason. Home: 4627 A St Lincoln NB 68510

GRIFFIN, CHARLES CARROLL, historian; b. Tokyo, Japan, May 24, 1902; s. Charles Sumner and Mary Avery (Greene) G.; student U. Ill., 1920-21; A.B., Harvard, 1922; A.M., (fellow) Columbia, 1933, Ph.D., 1937; m. Jessica Frances Jones, Aug. 27, 1934; children—Thomas Carroll, Samuel (dec.), Nancy Evarts. With fgn. dept. First Nat. Bank of Boston, 1922-23; Cia. Argentina de Cemento Portland, 1923-25, Cia. Uruguaya de Cemento Portland, 1925-30; rep. in Spain of European Mission, Library of Congress, 1931-32; faculty Vassar Coll., Poughkeepsie, N.Y., 1934-67, prof. history, 1944-67, chmn. dept. history, 1944-46, 50-52, 60-64, dean faculty, 1965-67; dir. Asso. Colls. Mid-Hudson area, 1968-69. Exchange prof., Venezuela, 1940-41; div. Am. reps. State Dept., 1943-44; vis. prof. U. Wis., 1949-50, U. de Chile, Santiago, 1954, Harvard, 1959-60, Columbia, 1966, Princeton, 1968; Fulbright lectr., Chile, 1966. Author: United States and the Disruption of the Spanish Empire 1810-1822, 1937; Latin America, 1944; The National Period in the History of the New World, 1961; Los temas sociales y economicos en la epoca de la independencia, 1962; Ensayos Soliel historia de America, 1970. Contbr., editor Concerning Latin American Culture, 1940; Latin America-A Guide to the Historical Literature, 1971; contbg. editor Handbook of Latin American Studies, 1940-43, 55-58. adv. bd., 1958-65, chmn., 1960-65; editorial bd. Hispanic Am. Hist. Rev. 1944-53, mng. editor, 1950-53, adv. bd., 1954—. Home: 14 Main St Hyde Park NY 12538

GRIFFIN, CHARLES DONALD, ret. naval officer; b. Phila., Jan. 12, 1906; s. Joseph Richard and Maude (Spicknall) G.; B.S., U.S. Naval Acad., 1927; M.S. in Aero. Engring., U. Mich., 1937; grad. Nat. War Coll., 1951; m. Camilla Yvonne Ganteaume, Sept. 14, 1935 (dec.); children-Linda (Mrs. Harry Collins II), Charles Donald; m. 2d., Marion Hopkins Schaefer, Nov. 21, 1964. Commd. ensign USN, 1927, advanced through grades to adm., 1963; designated naval aviator; duty in battleships, destroyers, 1927-30; attached U.S.S. Enterprise, 1937-40; flight test officer Naval Air Sta., Anacostia, 1940-42; comdr. Carrier Air Group 9, U.S.S. Essex, 1942- 43; operations officer T.F. 58 Pacific, 1943; mem. Joint War Plans Com. Joint Chiefs Staff, 1944; comdg. officer U.S.S. Croatan, 1945-46; plans officer U.S. Atlantic Fleet, 1946-47; strategic plans div. Operations Navy, 1948-50; plans officer U.S. Pacific Fleet, 1951-53; comdg. officer U.S.S. Oriskany, 1953-54; spl. asst. to chmn. Joint Chiefs of Staff, 1955-56; comdr. Carrier Div. 4, 1947-48; dir. strategic plans Navy Dept., 1959-60; comdr. Seventh Fleet, 1960-61; dep. chief naval operations, 1962-63; comdr. in chief USN Forces Europe, 1963-65; comdr. in chief allied forces So. Europe, 1965-68. Decorated D.S.M. with gold star, Bronze Star medal, Presdl. citations; supreme comdr. Order of George the First (Greece); knight Grand Cross Order of Republic (Italy); comdr. Philippine Legion Honor; Order Mil. Merit with silver star (Korea); Order of Double-Rays of Rising Sun (Japan); Medal of Pao-Ting (China). Episcopalian. Clubs: Chevy Chase (Md.); Army and Navy, Metropolitan, Tavern Association (Washington); Army and Navy Country (Arlington, Va.); American (London, Eng.); Circolo dell'Unione (Naples, Italy); Royal and Ancient Golf of St. Andrews (Scotland); New York Yacht (N.Y.C.). Home: 4610 Dexter St NW Washington DC 20007

GRIFFIN, CHARLES HUDSON, congressman; b. nr. Utica, Miss., May 9, 1926; s. Charles Farris and Nora (Shelton) G.; B.S. in Pub. Adminstrn., Miss State U., 1949; m. Angelina Pedrotti, Nov. 8, 1953. Aide to U.S. Rep. John B. Williams, 1949-68; mem. 90th-92d congresses 3d Dist. Miss. Served with USNR, 1944-46. Mem. V.F.W. (life). Am. Legion. Democrat. Mem. Disciples of Christ Ch. Moose, Mason (Shriner). Home: W Main St Utica MS 39175 Office: Longworth House Office Bldg Washington DC 20515

GRIFFIN, CLAIBOURNE EUGENE, educator; b. Rocky Mount, N.C., Oct. 15, 1929; s. Claibourne Eugene and Virginia (Perry) G.; student Phillips Andover Acad., 1946-47; B.A., Princeton, 1951; M.S., U. Va., 1953, Ph.D., 1955; m. Barbara Anne Reif, Dec. 13, 1959; children—Clay William, Eric Allan, Amy Elizabeth. USPHS fellow, Cambridge U., 1955-57; instr. U. Pitts., 1957-58, asst. prof., 1958-62, asso. prof., 1962-66, prof. dept. chemistry, 1966-69; adj. sr. fellow Mellon Inst., 1966-69; prof., chmn. dept. chemistry, U. Toledo, 1969—; cons. Stauffer Chem. Co., 1962—, Strem Chem. Co., 1970—. Mem. Am. Chem. Soc., Chem. Soc. (London), Sigma Xi, Phi Lambda Upsilon. Contbr. articles profl. jours. Home: 2249 University Hills Blvd Toledo OH 43606

GRIFFIN, CLARE ELMER, educator; b. Allegan, Mich., Mar. 22, 1892; s. Frank and Ethel May (Lewis) G.; B.A., Albion (Mich.) Coll., 1914; M.A., U. Ill., 1915, Ph.D., 1918; m. Florence Lovina Parsons, Dec. 27, 1917; childrenFrances Ethel (Mrs. Edward S. Bres., Jr.), Nancy Letitia (Mrs. Miron W. Neal). Instr. econs. Dartmouth, 1916-17; instr. transp. Johns Hopkins, 1917-18; expert U.S. Shipping Bd. and Central Bur. of Planning and Statistics, Washington, 1919; asso. prof. marketing, U. Mich. 1919-27, prof. marketing, 1925-43, dean Sch. Bus. Adminstrn. and dir. Bur. Bus. Research, 1927-43, Fred. M. Taylor prof. of bus. econs. since 1943. Ednl. dir. Detroit chpt. Am. Inst. Banking, 1923-25. Mem Nat. Adv. Com. on War Tng. U.S. Office of Edn., 1941-44. Econ. cons. to Cement Inst., Am. Meat Inst. and other orgns.; research staff Com. for Econ. Devel., 1943-46. Pres. Am. Assn. Collegiate Schs. of Bus., 1942-43. Served as 1st lt., U.S. Army, 1918- 19. Mem. Am. Econ. Assn., Am. Marketing Assn, Research Club (U. Mich.), Phi Beta Kappa, Delta Sigma Rho, Phi Kappa Phi. Club: University. Author: Principles of Foreign Trade, 1924; Life History of Automobiles, 1926; Enterprise in a Free Society, 1949; Britain, a Case Study for Americans, 1950; An Economic Approach to Antitrust Problems, 1951; The Free Society, 1965. Contbr. articles in various profl. jours. Home: 21 Ridgeway Ann Arbor MI 48104 Office: U Mich Sch Bus Adminstrn Ann Arbor MI 48104

GRIFFIN, CORNELIUS JOSEPH, Jr., oil co. exec.; b. Somerset, Mass., May 25, 1911; s. Cornelius Joseph and Mary E. (Donahue) G.; grad. Bradford Durfee Tech. Inst., 1932; student advanced mgmt. program Harvard, 1957; m. Mary S. Harrison, June 17, 1939; childrenBonny, Louise. Div. mgr. Lago Oil & Transp. Co., Aruba, 1940-50; mgr. Belot Refinery, Havana, Cuba, 1951-54; dir. Esso Standard Oil, S.A., Havana, 1954-58; pres. Esso Brasileira de Petroleo, Rio de Janeiro, Brazil, 1958-62, exec. v.p., dir. Creole Petroleum Corp., Caracas, Venezuela, 1962-. Mem. N.Am. Assn. Caracas (dir. 1965-66), Am. C. of C. Caracas. Home: Calle Otama Qta La Machera Valle Arriba Caracas Venezuela Office: Apartada 889 Caracas Venezuela

GRIFFIN, DONALD REDFIELD, biologist; b. Southampton, N.Y., Aug. 3, 1915; s. Henry Farrand and Mary (Redfield) G.; B.S., Harvard, 1938, A.M., 1940, Ph.D., 1942; m. Ruth Marion Castle, Sept. 6, 1941; childrenNancy Jean, Janet Redfield, Margaret Louise, John Hadley. Asst. biology and jr. fellow Harvard, 1938- 41, research asso. 1942-45. prof. zoology, 1953-66, chmn. dept. biology, 1962-65; successively asst. prof., asso. prof., prof. zoology Cornell, 1946-53; prof. animal behavior and comparative physiology Rockefeller U., 1966-; researcher comparative physiology (animals, birds and bats). Mem. Nat. Acad. Sci., Am. Acad. Arts and Scis.; Am. Soc. Physiology, Soc. General Physiologists, Am. Soc. Zoologists, Ecol. Soc. Am., Phi Beta Kappa, Sigma Xi, Author: Listening in the Dark, 1958; Echoes of Bats and Men, 1959; Animal Structure and Function, 1962; Bird Migration, 1964 (Science award 1965). Contbr. tech. papers sci. jours., semi- popular mags. Home: 52 Willow St Belmont MA 02178 Office: Rockefeller U New York City NY 10020

GRIFFIN, EDWARD JOHN, educator; b. Homestead Pa., Apr. 6, 1909; s. Edward J. and Mary C. (Havican) G.; A.B., Duquesne U., 1930, M.A., 1933; Ph.D., U. Pitts., 1947; m. Margaret Koessler, July 3, 1935; childrenEdward M., Mary Elizabeth. Tchr., Homestead pub. schs., 1930-41; asst. jr. high sch. prin., then jr. high sch. prin. West Mifflin (Pa.) pub. schs., 1941-48; lectr. sch. adminstrn. Duquesne U., 1945-48; lectr. edn. Cath. U. Am., summers 1942-48; mem. faculty U. San Francisco, 1948-, prof. edn., 1953- , chmn. dept., 1956-. Grad. cons. St. Mary's Coll., Notre Dame, Ind., 1964; field researcher Nat. Study Cath. Edn., Notre Dame, 1963; Cal. liasion rep. Am. Assn. Colls. Tchr. Edn., 1963-65; vice chmn. edn. commn. Jesuit Edn. Assn., 1967, chmn., 1970-71. mem. acrediting commn. Western Cath. Edn. assn., 1957-; chmn. adult tng. San Francisco exec. council Boy Scouts Am., 1960-64; chmn. adv. council, community cultural arts program San Francisco Unified Sch. Dist., 1967. Recipient Silver Beaver award Boy Scouts Am., 1948; state rep. award Am. Assn. Colls. Tchr. Edn., 1963- 65. Mem. Nat., Nat. Cath. edn. assns., Nat. Assn. Secondary Sch. Prins., Cal. Assn. Secondary Sch. Adminstrs., Nat. Cath. Guidance Assn., Am.. Assn. U. Profs., Internat. Reading Assn., Phi Delta Kappa. K.C. Club: Commonwealth (San Francisco). Author articles in field, also contbg. editor several books. Home: 470 Colon Av San Francisco CA 94127

GRIFFIN, GEORGE ELLISON, diversified co. exec.; b. St. Louis, Feb. 15, 1921; s. Thomas Joseph and Ursula (Tockstein) G.; B.S. magna cum laude, St. Louis U. Sch. Commerce and Finance, 1948, LL.B., 1956; m. Beverly Joy Benson, Sept. 9, 1944; children—Dennis Michael, Terence James, Rory Ellison, Maureen Joy, Douglas Paul, Laurie Ann. Admitted to Mo. bar, 1957; staff asst. to controller Stix, Baer & Fuller, St. Louis, 1948-51; sr. tax accountant Touche, Ross, Bailey & Smart, Detroit, 1951-54; adminstrv. asst. McDonnell Aircraft Corp., St. Louis, 1954; asst. treas., sec. Orbit Corp., St. Louis, 1955-57; exec. asst. McDonnell Aircraft Corp., St. Louis, 1957-59, mgr. corp. budgets, 1959-61; mgr. profit analysis Ling-Temco-Vought, Inc., Dallas, 1961, mgr. tax, financial planning, 1962, asst. treas., 1963-65, dir. corporate financial planning, 1966, v.p. corp. financial plans, 1967-70, sr. v.p., chief financial officer, 1970—, also dir.; dir. Jones & Laughlin Steel Corp., LTV Aerospace Corp., LTV Electrosystems, Inc., LTV Ling Altec, Inc., Wilson & Co., Inc. Lectr. corp. finance, budgeting, St. Louis U. Sch. Commerce and Finance, 1960-61. Served with USNR, 1942-43, USAAF, 1943-45. Decorated Air medal with oak leaf cluster, Purple Heart. C.P.A., Mich. Mem. Financial Execs. Inst. Roman Catholic. Home: 4252 Shady Hill Dr Dallas TX 75229 Office: PO Box 5003 Dallas TX 75222

GRIFFIN, GEORGE RICHARD, banker; b. Tampa, Fla., Sept. 4, 1903; s. James A. and Nannie M. (Johnson) G.; B.S. in Econs., Wharton sch., U. Pa., 1925; m. Mildred D. Macdonald, July 14, 1952; childrenDonald W., Gordon G. With Exchange Nat. Bank of Tampa, Fla., 1925—, dir., 1935—, v.p. 1940-52, pres., 1952-67, chmn. bd., 1967-69, chmn. emeritus, 1969—; vice chmn., dir. Exchange Nat. Bank of Winter Haven, Fla., 1951—; chmn., dir. Exchange Bank of Temple Terrace, Fla.; pres. Tampa Investment Securities Co., Tampa; dir. Gen. Telephone Co. Fla., Gen. Portland Cement Co., Dallas, Fla. Steel Corp., Tampa, Founders Life Assurance Corp., Tampa, Indsl. Devel. Corp. Fla. Trustee U. Tampa. Served from lt. to lt. comdr. USNR, 1942-46. Mem. Fla. Bankers Assn. (pres. 1956). Episcopalian. Home: 3106 Sunset Dr Tampa FL 33609 Office: 610 Franklin St Tampa FL 33602

GRIFFIN, GEORGE ROBERT, educator; b. Indpls., Sept. 2, 1914; s. Will C. and Elizabeth (Morgan) G.; B.S. in Chemistry, Ind. U., 1936; M.A., Boston U., 1938; Ph.D., Mass. Inst. Tech., 1941; m. Dorothy Wilkinson, July 31, 1938; children Russell M., Elizabeth Anne (Mrs. Vallerand), Constance Jeanne, George W. Research chemist Am. Cyanamid Co., 1941-44; group leader Dewey and Almy Chem. Co., 1944-48; asst. prof. chemistry U. R.I., 1948-51; research mgr. New Polymers Cry-O-Vac, Cambridge, Mass., 1951-54; head dept. chemistry Lowell Tech. Inst., 1954-. Mem. Am. Chem. Soc., Sigma Xi. Home: Middlesex Rd Box 105 Tyngsboro MA 01879 Office: 1 Textile Ave Lowell MA 01854

GRIFFIN, GEORGE WORTHAM, Jr., bus. exec.; b. St. Paul, Apr. 14, 1914; s. George W. and Mary (Davis) G.; B.B.A., U. Minn., 1936; m. Evelyn Savage, Mar. 8th, 1941; children-Patricia (Mrs. Stewart), Gail, Suzanne. Pub. relations dept. Gen. Electric Co., Schenectady, 1937-38; producer pub. service programs radio sta. WGY, Schenectady, 1939-40; advt., bus. mgr. G-E Review, 1940-41; mgr. G-E News Bur., Schenectady, 1946-52; dir. pub. relations Sylvania Electric Products Inc., 1952-58, v.p., 1958—; v.p. parent co. Gen. Telephone & Electronics Corp., 1959-. Lt. col. AUS, 1941-45. Mem. Pub. Relations Soc. Am., I.E.E.E., Am. Mgmt. Assn. Conglist. Club: New Canaan Field. Home: Carter St New Canaan CT 06840 Office: 730 3d Av New York City NY 10017

GRIFFIN, GERALD EDWARD, newspaperman; b. Lincoln, Neb., Dec. 16, 1907; s. Edward William and Mary Agnes (Bergers) G.; A.B., U. Neb., 1929; m. Amy G. Olsen, June 15, 1929; children Mary (Mrs. Robert Simms), Ellen (Mrs. John Burgoyne), Sally (Mrs. George Hickey). Editor, U. Neb. alumni mag., 1928-30; mem. Sunday staff Balt. Sun, 1930-34, mem. Washington bur., 1934-47, chief London bur., 1947-49, Washington bur. staff, 1949-64, chief bur., 1955-64, editor, 1964-. Served at lt. (j.g.) USNR, 1944-45. Clubs: National Press, Gridiron, Overseas Writers (Washington). Home: 4414 Underwood Rd Baltimore MD 21218 Office: The Sun Baltimore MD 21203

GRIFFIN, GWYN, author: A Last Lamp Burning; Operational Necessity; Scorpion on a Stone. Address: care GP Putnam's Sons 200 Madison Av New York City NY 10016*

GRIFFIN, HENRY LUDWIG, press photographer; b. Balt., May 19, 1916; s. Harry and Teresa (Grill) G.; student high sch., Balt.; m. Barbara Hupp, July 14, 1937; childrenRonald Edward, Carole Roberta. With Asso. Press, 1932-, news photographer, 1934-; war corr., 1942-45; chmn. Senate Press Photographers Gallery, 1956-62, chmn. legislative com., 1962—. Recipient of citation War Dept., commendation Navy Dept. Mem. White House News Photographers Assn. (life). Moose. Home: 3214 Gumwood Dr University Hills MD 20742 Office: 1300 Connecticut Av Washington DC 20036

GRIFFIN, ISABEL KINNEAR, newspaper corr.; b. nr. Lexington, Va.; d. John Joseph Lyle and Rachael (Lackey) Kinnear; student Longwood Coll., Farmville, Va.; m. Bulkley Southworth Griffin, July 8, 1926 (dec. 1967); d. Charmian (Mrs. John Clark Jr.). Washington corr., feature writer Bulkley S. Griffin News Bur., 1924-; Washington corr. Worcester Gazette, Springfield Union, New Bedford Standard Times, 1942-; pres. Griffin-Larrabee News Bureau, 1967- . Chmn. Mrs. Roosevelt's White House Press Conf. Assn., 1943-44. Mem. White House Corr. assn., Senate and House Press Galleries. Clubs: Women's Nat. Press, Am. Newspaperwomen's, Nat. Democratic Women's Internat., City Tavern (Washington). Home: 4817 Woodway Lane Washington DC 20016 also Middlesex Beach DE Office: Nat Press Bldg Washington DC 20004

GRIFFIN, JAMES BENNETT, anthropologist, educator; b. Atchison, Kan., Jan. 12, 1905; s. Charles Bennett and Maude (Bostwick) G.; Ph.B., U. Chgo., 1927, A.M., 1930; Ph.D. (fellow in aboriginal N. Am. ceramics 1933-36), U. Mich., 1936; m. Ruby Fletcher, Feb. 14, 1936; childrenJohn Bennett, David Moss, James Chapman. Research asso. Mus. Anthropology, U. Mich., 1936-41, asst. curator, archaeology, 1937-42, asso. curator, 1942-45, curator, 1945—, dir. Mus. Anthropology, 1946—, lectr. econ. and polit. geography, war tng. program, 1943-44; asso. prof. anthropology, 1945-49, prof., 1949—, chmn. anthropology sect. Mich. Acad. Sci., Arts and Letters, 1936-37, 1943-44; field research in Ill., 1928, 29, 48, in Pa., 1930, in Ind., 1933, in Miss. and Ark., 1940, 41, in Mexico, 1946, in Mich., 1948, Ill. and Mo., 1950; mem. faculty field sch. univs. Cal., Mich., Tex. in 26th Summer Sch. of Nat. U., Mexico City, 1946. U.S. sec. for New World Archaeology of the Permanent Council of Internat. Union of Prehistoric and Protohistoric Scis., 1948—, mem. exec. com. and permanent council, 1962—; pres. com. on anthropology Pan-Am. Inst. Geography and History, 1954-59. Recipient Viking Fund medal and award in archeology, 1957. Fellow A.A.A.S. (sect. H., 1945, past sect. com. and v.p.). Am. Anthropol. Assn. (pres. Central States br., 1948-49), Soc. for Am. Archaeology (asst. editor, 1936-46, asso. editor 1946-50; 1st v.p., 1945-46, exec. com. 1945-46, 195O-53, pres. 1951-52); mem. Wash. Acad. Sci. Nat. Acad. Sci., Am. Quaternary Assn. (sec. 1970—), Sociedad Mexicana de Antropologia, Sigma Xi, Phi Sigma. Club: Faculty (Ann Arbor). Author: Archaeological Survey in the Lower Mississippi Alluvial Valley, 1940-47, Vol. 25 (with others), 1950. Author, editor: Archeology of Eastern United States, 1952. Contbr. articles to profl. jours. Office: University Museums Bldg Ann Arbor MI 48104

GRIFFIN, JAMES EDWARD, educator; b. Columbus, O., Dec. 17, 1922; s. Don Wallace and Belle (Eason) G.; B.A., Western Md. Coll., 1944; certificate phys. therapy, Duke, 1946, M.A., 1948; Ph.D., U. Pa., 1959; m. Frances Lenora Roberts, Sept. 22, 1948; children—Karl Edward, Bruce William, Karen Lorraine. Staff phys. therapist Duke Med. Center, 1946-48; sr. phys. therapist Hosp. Chronic Illness, Rocky Hill, Conn., 1948-53; mem. faculty U. Pa., 1953-70, prof. phys. therapy, 1969-70; prof. phys. therapy, chmn. dept. State U. N.Y. at Buffalo, 1970—. Fellow Internat. Soc. Med. Hydrology and Climatology; mem. Am. Phys. Therapy Assn. (chmn. sect. research 1968-70), Phila. Physiol. Soc., Am. Congress Rehab. Medicine, N.Y. Acad. Scis., Assn. Schs. Health Related Professions (chmn. com. equivalency 1969-71). Home: 1640 Dodge Rd East Amherst NY 14051 Office: 264 Winspear Av Buffalo NY 14215

GRIFFIN, JERALD LEE, silicone mfg. co. exec.; b. Detroit, Feb. 21, 1926; s. J. A. and Beulah (Childers) G.; student Central Mich. U., 1943, Lawrence Coll., 1944; B.B.A., U. Mich., 1952, M.B.A., 1952; P.M.D., Harvard, 1964; m. Valetta May Batchelor, Dec. 25, 1944; children—Steve, Kathleen (Mrs. Gary Allen Fenwick), Christine, Janet. Ind. contractor Mich. Bell Telephone Co., 1950-52; asst. credit mgr., div. controller, internat. controller, treas. Dow Corning Corp., Midland, Mich., 1952—; dir. Chem. Bank & Trust Co., Midland Bahamas Co., Ltd., Franchise Foods Internat. Chmn. Sen. Griffin Finance Com. Republican Party, 1966. Mem. exec. com. Mich. United Fund. Served to lt. USNR, 1943-49. Mem. Midland C. of C., Alpha Kappa Psi. Kiwanian. Home: 1421 Airfield Lane Midland MI 48640 Office: 3901 S Saginaw St Midland MI 48640

GRIFFIN, JOHN ARNOLD, III, (Johnny), saxophonist b. Chgo., Apr. 24, 1928. With Art Blakey, Thelonious Monk, others, late 1950's; formed quintet with Eddie (Lockjaw) Davis, 1960-62, performances Paris, France, Stockholm, Sweden, London, Eng., 1962-63, N.Y.C., 1963; concerts France, Italy, Germany, Switzerland, Belgium, also club dates, 1963-66. Record albums include: Change of Pace; (with Eddie Davis) Tough Tenor Favorites: Night Lady; (with Wes Montgomery) Full House; (with Raymond Fol) Four Seasons. Address: 432 E 46th St Chicago IL 60653*

GRIFFIN, JOHN COY, steel co. exec.; b. Holley, N.Y., Jan. 22, 1916; s. John Lawrence and Edna (Coy) G.; A.B., U. Mich., 1937, J.D. with distinction, 1939; m. Marjorie Carney, Jan. 4, 1941; childrenRobert C., Christine. Admitted to Pa. bar, 1939, Ohio bar, 1960; atty. Nat. Supply Co., Pitts., 1946- 59; with Armco Steel Corp., Middletown, O., 1959-, sec., gen. atty., 1968-. Bd. dirs. Middletown-Butler unit Am. Cancer Soc., 1966-, trustee Humane Assn. Miami Valley, 1962-; mem. Butler County Welfare Adv. Bd., 1965-. Served to capt. AUS, 1942-46. Decorated Purple Heart. Mem. Am., Ohio bar assns., Delta Theta Phi. Presbyn. Club: Brown's Run Country (Middletown). Home: 1600 Schirm Dr Middletown OH 45042 Office: 703 Curtis St Middletown OH 45042

GRIFFIN, JOHN DOUGLAS, assn. exec.; b. Hamilton, Ont., Can., June 3, 1906; s. Herbert Spohn and Edith Moore (Robinson) G.; student Hamilton Collegiate Inst.; B.A., U. Toronto, 1929, M.D., 1932, M.A., 1933, postgrad. psychology, 1932-33; postgrad. Hosp. for Sick Children in Toronto, 1933; Rockefeller fellow postgrad. psychiatry, 1934-36; m. Erica Maude Withrow, Sept. 22, 1934; childrenCharles Peter Morecroft, John David Anthony. Staff Nat. Com. Mental Hygiene (now Canadian Mental Health Assn.), 1936-39, med. dir., 1939-41, gen. dir., 1953-; asst. psychiatrist Clinic Psychol. Medicine, Hosp. Sick Children, 1937-41; cons. personnel devel. Moore Corp., Inc., 1945-51; cons. mental health program Canadian Broadcasting Corp., 1945-56; spl. lectr. Sch. Social Work, U. Toronto, 1946-56; mem. psychiat. panel Def. Research Bd., 1949-57; mem. Canadian adv. com. mental health to Fed. Govt., 1950—; mem. Inter-Am. Council Psychiat. Assn., 1967-69. Served to col. M.C., Royal Canadian Army, 1941-45. Mem. Can., Ont. med. assns., Toronto Acad. Medicine, Am. (council), Canadian (pres. 1967-68), Ont. psychiat. assns., Canadian Pub. Health Assn., Canadian Edn. Assn. Clubs: Faculty (U. Toronto); National Yacht. Author: (with W. Line and S.R. Laycock) Mental Hygiene-A Manual for Teachers, 1938; (with Tyhurst, Chalke, et al.) More for the Mind, 1963; The Law and Mental Disability, 1968. Author popular, sci. articles. Home: 18 Bracondale Hill Rd Toronto Ontario Canada Office: 52 St Clair Av E Toronto 7 Ontario Canada

GRIFFIN, JOHN EDWARD, druggist; b. Zion, Ill., Nov. 2, 1908; s. Roy Bennett and May (Putnam) G.; B.A., Morningside Coll., 1934; student Northwestern U., summer 1936, Harvard Grad. Sch. Bus. Adminstrn., 1936-38; m. Sara Elizabeth Bozarth, Mar. 17, 1950; childrenJon Taylor, Mark Edward, Susan Mary. Personnel dir. Morningside Coll., 1932-34; tchr., prin. Primghar (Ia.) High Sch., 1934-37; gen. accountant Beech Aircraft, 1942-43; pres. Lewis Drug Stores, 1946—, Griffson Realty, 1960—, G.E.F. Realty, 1963—; v.p. Eckland Drugs, Mankato, Minn., 1956-69, Fredin Realty, 1957—; dir. Northwestern Nat. Bank, Raven Industries, Dakota House Motel Properties. Mem. Sioux Falls Bd. Edn., 1955-60, pres., 1958-60; mem. exec. com. Gov.'s Lay Conf. of Edn., 1961-62; mem. exec. com. State Master Plan for Higher Edn., 1969—; mem. adv. council S.D. State U., 1956-65. Mem. adv. council State Republican Party, 1954—. Bd. dirs. Great Plains Zoo, 1957—, Crippled Children's Hosp. and Sch., 1967—, Morningside Coll., 1968—. Served with AUS, 1943-45. Recipient Distinguished Alumni award Morningside Coll., 1960. Mem. Greater S.D. Assn. (dir. 1956-68; pres. 1960-61), U.S. (dir. 1958-68, v.p., 1962-65), Sioux Falls (pres. 1952-53) chambers commerce, Beta Gamma Sigma (hon.). Presbyn. Mason (Shriner). Clubs: Minnehaha Country, Rotary (pres. Sioux Falls 1955-56). Home: 1712 Edgewood Pl Sioux Falls SD 57103 Office: 309 S Phillips Av Sioux Falls SD 57102

GRIFFIN, JOHN HENRY, fraternal ofcl., physician; b. Peabody, Mass., May 19, 1914; s. John Henry and Mary Theresa (Kiley) G.; A.B., Boston Coll., 1935; M.D., Tufts U., 1939; m. Mary Louise McDonagh, Feb. 21, 1942; children—Clare Theresa (Mrs. James K. Ittner , Jr.), Mary Louise (Mrs. George M. Sullivan, Jr.), John Henry III, Thomas Paul, Gerald McDonagh, Kathryn Kiley, James Wills, Peter Charles, Christopher Patrick. Intern Malden (Mass.) Hosp., 1939-40, St. Elizabeth's Hosp., Washington, 1940-41; pvt. practice in medicine and surgery, Hughesville, Md., 1947-64; chief staff Physician's Meml. Hosp., La Plata, Md., 1952-57; mem. K.C., 1947-, faithful navigator 4, 1957-60, dep. of Md., 1960, supreme dir., 1960-, dep. supreme knight, 1964-66, supreme physician, 1966-. Mem. Charles County (Md.) Devel. Commn., 1958-65. Treas. Charles County Democratic Com., 1958-62. Served to comdr. U.S. Navy, 1941-47; PTO. Decorated Knight of St. Gregory. Mem. Am., So. med. assns., Medico-Chirurgical Faculty Md., Charles County Med. Soc. (past pres.), Am. Legion. Roman Cath. Club: Hawthorne Country (past pres.), (La Plata). Home: 239 Kings Hwy North Haven CT 06473 Office: PO Drawer 1670 New Haven CT 06507

GRIFFIN, JOHN HOWARD, author, photographer; b. Dallas, June 16, 1920; s. Jack W. and Lena Mae (Young) G.; certificate of studies, Conservatoire de Fontainebleau, 1946; certificates from Benedictines and Dominicans in France; LL.D., Bellarmine U., m. Elizabeth Ann Holland, June 2, 1953; childrenSusan Michele, John Howard, Gregory Parker, Amanda Claire Dominique. Author syndicated columns for the Internat. News Service and also King features, 1957-60; student primitive cultures, intergroup and intercultural relations ships; lectr., 1950-. Recipient award Nat. Assn. Negro Women; Christian Culture award, 1966; co-recipient Pope John XXIII Pacem in Terris, Peace and Freedom Award, 1964. Mem. Am. Soc. of Mag. Photographers. Author: (novels) Devil Rides Outside, 1952, Nuni, 1956; (history) Land of the High Sky, 1959; (non-fiction) Black Like Me (Anisfield Wolf award Sat. Rev. 1961), 1961; (non-fiction) The Church And The Black Man, 1968; A Hidden Wholeness: The Visual World of Thomas Merton, 1970; also articles, short stories, photo- journalistic studies. Address: 3816 W Biddison Ft Worth TX 76109

GRIFFIN, JOHN TOOLE, broadcasting co. exec.; b. McAlester, Okla., May 3, 1923; s. John T. and Ada (Toole) G.; B.S. in Bus., Okla. U., 1947; m. Martha L. Watson, Apr. 25, 1959; children—John W., David F. Pres., Griffin Grocery Co., Muskogee, Okla., 1943—, Griffin TV, Inc., and predecessors, Muskogee, 1943—; dir. Citizens Nat. Bank, Muskogee, Okla. Gas & Electric Co. Chmn. bd. Muskogee Gen. Hosp.; pres. Five Civilized Tribes Mus., Muskogee. Trustee Okla. Health Sci. Found. Served with AUS, 1943-45. Mem. Young Pres. Orgn., Phi Gamma Delta, Beta Gamma Sigma. Methodist. Home: 600 Robb St Muskogee OK 74401 Office: 111 S Cherokee St Muskogee OK 74401

GRIFFIN, JOSEPH ALOYSIUS, clergyman, soc. exec.; b. Dickson City, Pa., Feb. 26, 1901; s. Charles D. and Julia E. (O'Connor) G.; A.B., Holy Cross Coll., Worcester, Mass., 1923; student St. Bernard's Sem., Rochester, N.Y., 1923-27, U. Louvain, Belgium, 1930-31, Inst. Francaise, Cologne, Germany, summer 1931; A.M., Catholic U. Am., 1930, Ph.D., 1932. Ordained priest Roman Cath. Ch.; asst. pastor East Stroudsburg, Pa., 1927, Blossburg, PA., 1927-28, Williamsport, 1928; prof. history and chaplain Marywood Coll., Scranton, Pa., 1932-38; head history dept. U. Scranton, 1938; chaplain St. Joseph's Hosp., Scranton, 1938; examiner jr. clergy and candidates for Diocese of Scranton, 1932; pastor St. Catherine's, Moscow, Pa., 1944-52, Ss. Peter and Paul's, Towanda, Pa., also dean Bradford and Sullivan counties, 1952-67; domestic prelate, 1958—. Mem. Am. Cath. Hist. Assn. Democrat. Author: The Contribution of Belgium to the Catholic Church in America, 1932; contbr. to Records of Am. Cath. Hist. Soc. Emmanuel, History of Diocese of Scranton. Address: 715 Hawthorne St Avoca PA 18641

GRIFFIN, KYLE, journalist. Sports editor Memphis Comml. Appeal. Office: 495 Union Av Memphis TN 38101*

GRIFFIN, LELAND MILBURN, educator; b. Kansas City, Kan., Apr. 9, 1920; s. Herbert Lester and Cliffe (Connell) G.; A.B., U. Mo., 1941, M.A., 1942; Ph.D., Cornell U., 1950; m. Dorothy M. Schlotzhauer, July 4, 1943; childrenDorothy Lee, Charles James Grant, Andrew Dion Crispin. Asst. prof. speech Washington U., St. Louis, 1950-54; asso. prof., chmn. dept. speech Boston U., 1954-56; asso. prof. speech Northwestern U., Evanston, Ill., 1956-64, prof. speech, 1964-; prof. speech Garrett Theol. Sem., 1958-68. Served to lt (j.g.) USNR, 1943-46. Recipient Citation of Merit award U. Mo., 1971. Mem. Am., Central States speech assns., Am. Assn. U. Profs., Phi Kappa Phi. Republican. Baptist. Asso. editor: Quar. Jour. Speech, 1954-59, 69-71, Central States Speech Jour., 1950- 52, 64- 66. Contbr. articles to profl. jours. Home: 1940 Orrington Ave Evanston IL 60201

GRIFFIN, MALVERN ULYSSES, lawyer; b. Huntsville, Ala., May 27, 1924; s. Malvern Ulysses and Harriett (Beasley) G.; student Vanderbilt, 1942-43; B.S., U. Ala., 1950, LL.B., 1951; m. Linda Anne Condra, Dec. 5, 1963; children—Griff, Tracy Anne. Admitted to Ala. bar, 1951, since practiced in Huntsville; asso. Griffin, Ford, Caldwell & Ford, 1951-60; mem. firm Griffin & Griffin, 1960—. Pres., Huntsville Lit. Assn. Bd. dirs. Regional Boys Club. Served with USNR, 1943-46. Recipient Boys Club Pub. Service award, 1969. Mem. Fed., Ala., Huntsville-Madison County bar assns., Delta Kappa Epsilon. Democrat. Presbyn. (deacon). Kiwanian. Club: Acme (Huntsville). Contbr. articles to profl. jours. Home: 308 Shadybrook St Huntsville AL 35801 Office: 206 Eustis Av Huntsville AL 35001

GRIFFIN, MARVIN ANTHONY, educator; b. Butler Springs, Ala., Mar. 28, 1923; s. Randolph Simpson and Linnie (Barrett) G.; B.S., Auburn U., 1949; M.S. Engring., U. Ala., 1952; D.Eng., Johns Hopkins, 1960; m. Jane Pearle A. L'Herisson, Sept. 4, 1949; children—Margaret Lynn, John Marvin, Barbara Lee, Elizabeth Ann. Chief operations analysis Anniston Ordnance Depot (Ala.), 1949-51; sr. mfg. engr. Western Electric Co., Winston-Salem, N.C., 1952-55; chief engring. Cumberland Mfg. Co., Chattanooga, 1955-57; instr. Johns Hopkins, 1957-60; chief indsl. engr. Matson Navigation Co., San Francisco, 1960-61; prof. indsl. engring. U. Ala., 1961—, chmn. dept., 1966—, dir. computer sci., 1969—; mgmt. cons. to industry, govt. Served to comdr. USNR, 1943-47; PTO. Sr. postdoctoral fellow, Johns Hopkins, 1969. Registered profl. engr., Ala. Mem. Operations Research Soc. Am., Am. Statis. Assn., Am. Inst. Indsl. Engrs. (bd. dirs. 1954-55, chpt. pres. 1959-60), Am. Soc. Engring. Edn., Inst. Mgmt. Sci., Assn. Computing Machinery. Contbr. articles profl. jours. Home: 93 Claymont Dr Tuscaloosa AL 35401 Office: PO Box 6316 University AL 35486

GRIFFIN, SISTER MARY, educator; b. Chgo., Dec. 25, 1916; d. Michael Anthony and Margaret (O'Connor) Griffin; B. Music Edn., Mundelein Coll., Chgo., 1939, A.B., 1947; A.M., Catholic U. Am., 1950; Ph.D. (scholarship 1958-59, fellowship 1961), Fordham U., 1961. Joined Congregation of Sisters of Charity, 1939; instr. piano and

English, Clarke Coll., Dubuque, Ia., 1944-53; asst. prof. English, Mundelein Coll., 1953-60, acad. dean, 1960- 67; research fellow English, Yale, 1968-69; prof. English, Alcorn A. and M. Coll., Lorman, Miss., 1969—. Mem. upperclass awards com. Ill. Scholarship Commn., 1963-65; mem. Deans' Workshop, Harvard, 1964; mem. planning com. Johnston Coll., U. Redlands (Cal.), 1968-69. Summer scholar U. London (Eng.), 1961. Mem. Am. Assn. U. Women, Modern Lang. Assn., Am. Conf. Acad. Deans (exec. com. 1964-68), Assn. Higher Edn. (exec. com. 1966- 68), Am. Council on Edn. (com. on acad. affairs 1965-68), Kappa Gamma Pi. Editor: (Charles Burney) The Trial of Midas II, 1961. Address: Alcorn A and M College Lorman MS

GRIFFIN, MERV EDWARD, entertainer, TV producer; b. San Mateo, Cal., July 6, 1925 s. Mervyn Edward and Rita (Robinson) G.; student San Mateo Coll., 1942-44; m. Julann Elizabeth Wright, May 18, 1958; 1 son, Anthony Patrick. Performer Merv Griffin Show radio sta. KFRC, San Francisco, 1945-48; vocalist Freddy Martin's Orch., 1948-52; contract player, star So This is Love, Warner Bros., 1953-55; TV master ceremonies, 1958—, Merv Griffin Show, NBC-TV, 1962-63, Westinghouse Broadcasting Co., 1965-69, CBS-TV, 1969—; pres. Griffin Prodns., producers TV show Jeopardy, 1964; owner several radio stas., 1965—; owner Racing Patrol Inc. Miami, Fla. Mem. Cath. Actors Guild Am. (sr. v.p. 1963—). Address: 162 W 48th St New York City NY 10017

GRIFFIN, OSCAR O'NEAL, Jr., govt. ofcl.; b. Daisetta, Tex., Apr. 28, 1933; s. Oscar O'Neal and Myrtle Ellen (Edgar) G.; B. Journalism, U. Tex., 1958; m. Patricia Lamb, July 28, 1955; children—Gwendolyn Ann, Amanda Karen. Editor, Canyon (Tex.) News, 1959-60, Pecos (Tex.) Ind., 1960-62; reporter Houston Chronicle, 1962-66, White House corr., 1966-69; asst. dir. pub. affairs U.S. Dept. Transp., Washington, 1969—. Served with AUS, 1953-55. Recipient award for investigative reporting Southwest Journalism Forum, 1963; Pulitzer prize for local reporting not under pressure of edit. time, 1963. Mem. White House Corrs. Assn., Sigma Delta Chi. (Distinguished Service in Journalism award Ft. Worth chpt. 1962, Courage in Journalism award Des Moines chpt. 1963, award for gen. reporting nat. orgn. 1963). Clubs: National Press, Houston Press. Home: 6424 Woodridge Rd Alexandria VA 22312 Office: 400 7th St NW Washington DC 20591

GRIFFIN, RICHARD GEORGE, librarian; b. Tampa, Fla., June 24, 1927; s. Richard George and Esther Lee (Hubert) G.; A.B., Morehouse Coll., 1949; M.L.S., Atlanta U., 1951; postgrad. Sch. of Law, U. Tenn., summer 1958; m. Dolores Griffin, July 2, 1965; children—Felicia Rene, Eric Hubert. Circulation librarian, Tex. So. U., 1950-54, univ. librarian, 1954-57, instr. govt., 1953-57; asst. librarian, Knoxville Coll., 1957-58; dir. libraries, N.Y. Inst. Tech., Old Westbury, 1959—; library cons., Wilmington Coll., New Castle, Del., 1968-71. Served with AUS, 1946-47. Mem. A.L.A., Assn. for Higher Edn., N.Y. Library Assn. Home: 733 Franklin St Westbury NY 11590

GRIFFIN, RICHARD THOMAS, newspaper editor; b. Chgo., Dec. 22, 1932; s. George D. J. and Edna Mary (Healy) G.; B.S., Loyola U., Chgo., 1954; m. Catherine Nord, Jan. 23, 1954; children—Karen E., Gregory T., Lizabeth, Diana, Jennifer Rebecca. With City News Bur. Chgo., 1951-54; mem. staff Chgo. Daily News, 1958-, financial editor, 1965-. Served as officer USNR, 1955-58. Mem. Soc. Am. Bus. Writers (bd. govs. 1966-). Home: 3959 Garden Av Western Springs IL 60558 Office: 401 N Wabash Av Chicago IL 60611

GRIFFIN, ROBERT ALLEN, ret. newspaper exec.; b. Kansas City, Mo., Sept. 27, 1893; s. William and Francesca (Black) G.; B.A., Stanford, 1917; LL.D., Occidental Coll., m. 2d, Hester Hyde Hately, June 27, 1935; children (by former marriage)—Jeanne Andree, Nancy Allen. Reporter Portland Oregonian, 1919, later with Portland Jour., sec. to Prince C. Lubomirski, first Polish minister to U.S., 1919-20; dir. Polish Bur. Information, 1920-21; mgr. Am. Polish C. of C., 1921; founder, editor, pub. Monterey Peninsula Herald, 1922-63, pres., 1963-70; opened radio sta. KDON, Del Monte California, 1935. Dep. chief China Aid Mission, ECA, 1948-49; headed Dept. State Econ. Mission to S.E. Asia, 1950; dir. Far East program div. of ECA, 1950, spl. rep. ECA and Mut. Security Agy. to Far East, 1951-52, resigned 1952; dir. Monterey Found; mem. exec. com. Asian Found. Served in World War I. 1917-19; to col. AUS, 1941-45; ETO. Decorated D.S.C., Silver Star, Bronze Star, Legion of Merit with oak leaf cluster, Purple Heart with oak leaf cluster: chevalier Legion of Honor, Croix de Guerre with palm (French). Mem. Internat. Press Inst., Monterey Inst. Fgn. Studies (dir.), Am. Legion, Legion of Valor, Phi Delta Theta, Sigma Delta Chi. Clubs: Metropolitan (Washington); University (N.Y.C.); Press (San Francisco); Cypress Point (Pebble Beach, Cal.); Old Capital (Monterey, Cal.); Union Interalliee (Paris, France); St. James (London, Eng.). Editor and co-author: The Sch. of the Citizen Soldier, 1942. Home: Pebble Beach CA

GRIFFIN, ROBERT P., U.S. senator; b. Mich., Nov. 6, 1923; s. J.A. and Beulah M. Griffin; A. B., B.S., LL.D., Central Mich. Coll.; J.D., U. Mich.; LL.D., Eastern Mich. U., 1969, Albion Coll., Western Mich. U., Grand Valley State Coll.; D.H.L., Hillsdale (Mich.) Coll. 1969; J.C.D., Rollins Coll.; Ed.D., No. Mich. U.; D.Pub. Service, Detroit Inst. Tech.; m. Marjorie J. Anderson; four children. Admitted to Mich. bar; practiced in Traverse City, 1950-56; mem. 85th-89th Congresses 9th Dist. Mich.; mem. U.S. senate, 1966—, mem. coms. on commerce, finance, rules and adminstrn., minority whip, 1969—. Served inf. AUS, World War II: ETO. Named Outstanding Young Man of Nation, U.S. Jr. C. of C., 1959. Mem. Am., Mich. bar assns., Am. Legion. Republican. Elk, Kiwanian. Co-author Landrum- Griffin Act. Office: Senate Office Bldg Washington DC 20510

GRIFFIN, ROBERT STUART, univ. adminstr.; b. Brinson, Ga., Dec. 8, 1903; s. Henderson Virgil and Mary Elizabeth (Hearn) G.; B.S., Ore. State U., 1928; A.M., U. So. Cal., 1935, Ph.D., 1941; m. Marquerite Eunice Welch, Dec. 24, 1934; 1 son, Robert Leven. Instr., Ore. State U., 1927; mem. faculty U. Nev., 1928—, prof. English and speech, 1944—, coordinator army tng. programs, 1943-44, adminstrv. asst. to univ. pres., acting dean men, 1944-46, dean men, coordinator for vet. affairs, 1946-52, chmn. dept. English, 1953-55, chmn. dept. speech and drama, 1955—, dir. intercollegiate forensics, 1928—. Commnr., Reno Housing Authority, 1944-50; officer Nev. Wing, Civil Air Patrol, 1960—; mem. Sheriff's possee, 1960—. Founder, pres., bd. dirs. Cedar Flat Community Assn., Lake Take, Cal., 1950—. Recipient Distinguished Alumni award Delta Sigma Rho-Tau Kappa Alpha, 1968; Spl. Forensics Honor, Stanford, 1969. Mem. Pacific Forensic League (pres. 1932—), Western Interfrat. Conf. (co-founder), Am. Assn. U. Profs., Nat. Assn. Deans and Advisers of Men, Speech Assn. Am., Western Speech Assn., Blue Key, Delta Sigma Rho (nat. v.p. 1956-64; Pacific regional gov. combined Delta Sigma Rho-Tau Kappa Alpha 1965—), Phi Kappa Phi, Sigma Alpha Epsilon. Democrat. Methodist. Contbr. numerous articles and book revs. to profl. jours. Home: 1390 Mallory Lane Reno NV 89502

GRIFFIN, ROBERT THOMAS, govt. ofcl.; b. Somerville, Mass., July 3, 1917; s. Michael and Cecilia (Rourke) G.; B.S., Boston Coll., 1939; M.A. in Pub. Adminstrn., Boston U., 1954; postgrad. Harvard Grad. Sch. Pub. Adminstrn., 1954-55; m. Mary Ellen Mulcahy, Sept. 10, 1960; childrenMary Catherine, Christiane Marie, Justine Dufresne. Regional mgr. War Assets Adminstrn., 1946-49; with Gen. Services Adminstrn., 1950-56, 58-, spl. asst. to adminstr., 1961-62. asst. adminstr., 1962-70, asst. commr. property mgmt., 1970—. Conferee White House Conf. Natural Beauty, 1964, Pres.'s Fed. Agy. Task Force on Cost Reduction, 1965; adminstrv. cons. Govt. of Iran, 1956-58. Served with USCGR, 1943-46. Mem. Am. Soc. Pub. Adminstrn., D.A.V. Club: Washington Athletic. Home: 8003 Kerry Lane Chevy Chase MD 20015 Office: 6105 18th and F Sts NW Washington DC 20405

GRIFFIN, RUSSELL ALFRED, univ. dean; b. Lorain, O., July 11, 1905; s. Fred Myron and Olwen (Reese) G.; A.B., Hillsdale Coll., 1929; M.A., Western Res. U., 1932, Ph.D., 1940; m. Jane Carol Geddes, Aug. 9, 1958; one dau., Pamela Jane. Asst. instr. in speech Hillsdale Coll., 1928-29; in bus., 1929-35; instr. English, Case Western Res. U., 1935-42, asst. prof., 1942-47, asso. prof., 1947-, asst. dean Adelbert Coll., 1941-45, dir. admission, 1942-45, dean of men, 1945-58, dean students, 1951-, asso. dean, 1958—, dean of summer session, 1968. Served as lt. in USNR, 1943-45. Recipient distinguished alumni award Hillsdale Coll., 1957. Mem. Nat. Assn. Student Personnel Adminstrs., Am. Assn. U. Profs., Ohio Deans of Men, Delta Tau Delta, Theta Alpha Phi, Sigma Tau Delta, Omicron Delta Kappa, Pi Delta Epsilon. Home: 2827 Van Aken Blvd Cleveland OH 44120

GRIFFIN, THOMAS MCLEAN, banker; b. Lake Placid, N.Y., Sept. 12, 1922; s. Nathaniel Edward and Anne Waters (McLean) G.; grad. Phillips Acad., Andover, Mass., 1940; A.B., Harvard, 1943, LL.B., 1949; m. Hope Wiswall, July 16, 1949; children—Richard Wiswall, Anne McLean, Thomas McLean, David Coggin. Admitted to Mass. bar, 1950; mem. legal staff State Mut. Life Assurance Co. Am., 1949-58; asst. v.p., asso. counsel Old Colony Trust Co., Boston, 1958-67; v.p., cashier, sec. bd. dirs. First Nat. Bank Boston, 1967—; clk., dir. Bank Boston Internat., First Bank Financial Corp.; clk., treas. First Nat. Boston Corp.; sec. First Capitol Corp. Boston; corporator Salem Five Cents Savs. Bank (Mass.). Trustee Salem Athenaeum. Served to lt. (j.g.) USNR, 1943-46; comdr. Res. Mem. Boston Bar Assn., Boston Council Fgn. Relations. Club: Eastern Yacht (Marblehead, Mass.). Home: 14 Beckford St Salem MA 01970 Office: 67 Milk St Boston MA 02106

GRIFFIN, WILLIAM HANCOCK, lawyer; b. Huntsville, Ala., June 10, 1930; s. Malvern U. and Harriett (Beasley) G.; LL.B., U. Ala., 1958; m. Elisabeth Lamar Jones, Apr. 25, 1959; children—Elisabeth Lamar, William Hancock. Admitted to Ala. bar, 1958, since practiced in Huntsville; partner Griffin & Griffin, 1958—; city prosecutor Huntsville 1958-62, city recorder, 1962—; city atty. Madison, 1969—. Served with USAF, 1950-53. Mem. Ala., Huntsville bar assns., Ala. Municipal Judges Assn., Phi Delta Theta. Presbyn. Kiwanian. Club: Acme Internat. (Huntsville). Home: 1703 Fagan Circle SE Hunstville AL 35801 Office: 206 Eustis Av Huntsville AL 35801

GRIFFIN, WILLIAM LESTER HADLEY, shoe co. exec.; b. Edwardsville, Ill., May 17, 1918; s. Ralph D. and Julia (Hadley) G.; A.B., Williams Coll., 1940; LL.B., Washington U., 1947; m. Phoebe M. Perry, Apr. 1, 1942; children—Dustin H. II, Lockwood Perry, Peter Burley. Admitted to Mo. bar, 1947; counsel Wohl Shoe Co., St. Louis, 1947-51, asst. sec. treas., 1950-51; sec. Brown Shoe Co., St. Louis, 1954-64, v.p., 1964-66, exec. v.p., 1966-68, pres., 1968—, chief exec. officer, 1969—, chmn. exec. com., 1971—; also dir.; dir. Boatmen's Nat. Bank, St. Louis, Boatmen's Bancshares, Beecham Inc. Trustee Washington U.; bd. dirs. St. Louis Symphony Soc., Neighborhood Assn., Govtl. Research Inst., Mo. Pub. Expenditure Survey, Arts and Edn. Council St. Louis, St. Luke's Hosp., St. Louis. Served from ensign to lt. USNR, 1941-45; as lt. comdr., Korea, 1951-52. Mem. Am. Footwear Mfrs. Assn. (past chmn.), Met. C. of C., Phi Gamma Delta, Phi Delta Phi. Republican. Home: Mason Rd St Louis MO 63131 Office: 8400 Maryland Av St Louis MO 63105

GRIFFIN, WILLIAM MARVIN, ins. co. exec.; b. Hartford, Conn., June 20, 1926; s. Samuel M. and Florence E. (Smith) G.; A.A., U. Hartford, 1949; B.S., U. Pa., 1952; m. Shirley Klotzbaugh, May 1, 1954; 1 dau., Martha. Sec. investments Conn. Gen. Life Ins. Co., Hartford, 1952-64; sr. v.p. Hartford Fire Ins. Co., 1964—, also dir., dir. subsidiaries; dir. Tex. Utilities Co.; asso. bd. dirs. Conn. Bank & Trust Co. Bd. dirs. Conn. Inst. for Blind. Served with AUS, 1945-46. Clubs: Hartford Golf, Hartford Gun; Downtown Athletic (N.Y.C.). Home: 149 Stoner Dr West Hartford CT 06107 Office: 690 Asylum Av Hartford CT 06115

GRIFFIN, WILLIAM THOMAS, lawyer; b. N.Y.C., Sept. 27, 1905; s. John and Alice (Doonan) G.; A.B. summa cum laude, Holy Cross Coll., 1927; LL.B. cum laude, Fordham, 1930; m. Joan Mannix, Jan. 10, 1934; children—Christine, William, Gabrielle, Peter. Admitted to N.Y. bar, 1931, since practiced in N.Y.C.; former v.p. law, N.Y., New Haven and Hartford Ry. Co. Corp.; dir. New Eng. Transp. Co., Am. Trust Co.; dir., v.p. gen. counsel, Roper Realization Co., Inc., John L. Roper Lumber Co., Norfolk So. Land Co.; dir. v.p. lawyer, Providence Produce Warehouse Co. Member Am., Fed. bar assns., Am. Judicature Soc., Nat. Lawyers Club, N.Y. Law Inst., N.Y. County Lawyers Assn., Assn. ICC Practitioners, Internat. Assn. Barristers. Clubs: New York Athletic (N.Y.C.), Quinipiack (New Haven); Richmond County Country (S.I., N.Y.); Princess Anne Country (Virginia Beach, Va.). Home: 37 Howard Av Grymes Hill NY 10301 Office: 161 William St New York City NY 10038

GRIFFING, JOSEPH BRUCE, educator; b. Tempe, Ariz., Feb. 24, 1919; s. John B. and Anna M. (Kelly) G.; B.S., Ia. State U., 1941, M.S., 1947, Ph.D., 1948; Roosevelt fellow, U. San Marcos, Lima, Peru, 1941-42; NRC fellow, U. Cambridge (Eng.), 1953-55; m. Penelope M. Scott, Sept. 1, 1950; children—Cynthia, Steven, Joan, Deborah. Instr. genetics Ia. State U., 1947-48, asst. prof., 1948-53; prin. research officer plant industry Commonwealth Sci. and Indsl. Research Orgn., Australia, 1955-57, sr. research fellow, 1957-59, sr. prin. research scientist, 1959-65, chmn. genetic sect., 1960-62; Mershon prof. genetics Ohio State U., 1965—, chmn. dept., 1967—. Bd. dirs. Ohio State U. Research Found. Served with AUS, 1943-46. Chilean-Pan.-Am. fellow, 1942. Mem. Genetics Soc. Am., Am. Soc. Naturalist, A.A.A.S., Ohio Acad. Sci., Sigma Xi, Gamma Sigma Delta. Home: 4235 Clairmont Rd Columbus OH 43220

GRIFFIS, ELLIOT, composer, pianist, educator; b. Boston, Jan. 28, 1893; s. William Elliot and Katharine Lyra (Stanton) G.; student Ithaca (N.Y.) High Sch., Ithaca Coll. (music), 1909-13, Yale Sch. Music, (studied under Horatio Parker), 1913-15, Yale Sch. Fine Arts, 1915-16, N.E. Conservatory Music, 1917-18 (studied under G.W. Chadwick, Stuart Mason, Lee Pattison); also studied in London, Paris, Vienna; hon. Mus.D., N.Y. Coll. Music, 1937. Instr. piano playing Grinnell (Ia.) Coll., 1920-22, Bklyn. Settlement Sch., 1923-24; head theory dept. St. Louis Inst. Music, 1935-36; dir. Westchester Conservatory, White Plains, 1942-43; tchr. piano and theory; lectr., lecture recitalist; radio appearances as pianist and accompanist. Composer: (for orchestra) First Symphony; A Persian Fable (ballade); Montevallo Suite; Paul Bunyan, Colossus (symphonic poem); Variations for Strings; symphony for strings, Fantastic Pursuit (performed under Sevitzky, Phila., 1941); (chamber music) 3 String Quartets; Quintet; Suite for Trio; Sonata for Violin and Piano; Wood Wind Quartet; (for piano) Sonata; Letters from a Maine Farm; A Set of Eight; Rousseau Variations; Transmutations; (for voice) Song Cycle: Sunlight and Shadow; A Caravan from China Comes; Men Are the Devil; El Dorado, others; Port of Pleasure (one act opera), 1960; 3 long playing records of original compositions. Served as judge for the Guild of Piano Teachers. Awarded Julliard scholarship, 1922, Pulitzer traveling fellowship, 1931. Served with Chem. Warfare Service, U.S. Army, 1918-19. Mem. A.S.C.A.P., Am. Soc. Composers and Condrs., Phi Mu Alpha Sinfonia. Episcopalian. Author: Rain in May, 1918. Contbr. to jours. Address: 141 N Swall Dr Los Angeles CA 90048

GRIFFIS, NIXON, business exec.; b. N.Y.C., Oct. 23, 1917; s. Stanton and Dorothea (Nixon) G.; Hotchkiss Sch., 1936, Cornell, 1940; children—Hughes, Elizabeth Hethea, Nixon Stanton. With Brentano's, Inc., from 1948, chmn. bd., dir. 1949—; pres., chmn. bd., dir. Brentano's, Inc., of Cal., 1949—; now with N.Y. Acquarium-Osborne Labs.; dir. Colonial Co., New Canaan, Conn. Bd. dirs. Griffis Found. Served with Signal Corps, AUS, 1940-45. Clubs: Racquet and Tennis; Cornell; Explorers; N.Y. Athletic; New Canaan Field. Home: 455 E 57th St New York City NY 10022 Office: NY Acquarium-Osborne Labs Brooklyn NY 11202

GRIFFIS, STANTON, investment banker; b. Boston, Mass., May 2, 1887; s. William Elliot and Katharine Lyra (Stanton) G.; A.B., Cornell U., 1910; LL.D., Union College, 1944; m. Dorothy Nixon, June 19, 1912; children—Theodora, Nixon. Fruit grower, Medford, Oregon, 1910-14; partner Hornblower & Weeks-Hemphill, Noyes, investment bankers, N.Y.C., 1914—. On govt. bus. Eng., Sweden, Finland, Spain and Portugal, 1942-43; chief Motion Picture Bur. (domestic br.) O.W.I., 1943-44; special rep. U.S. Govt. to Sweden, Apr. 1944; apptd. ambassador to Poland, 1947, Egypt, 1948, Argentine, 1949, Spain, 1951-52, Commr. Am. Red Cross, Pacific Ocean Areas, 1944- 45. Awards: Medal for Merit, Medal of Freedom, Treasury Medal for War Bond work; Motion Picture Assn. Medal. Served as capt. on Gen. Staff, during World War I. Trustee Cornell U., Am. Hist. Soc.; dir. Meml. Hosp., Nat. Hosp. for Speech Disorders. Clubs: Cornell, Links Golf, Recess, Racquet and Tennis, Links (New York); Everglades, Seminole (Palm Beach). Author: Lying in State, 1952. Home: Palm Beach FL 33480 Office: 8 Hanover St New York City NY 10004

GRIFFIS, WINFORD ELDON, utility co. exec.; b. Little Rock, Feb. 13, 1916; s. Charles Henry and Dora (McKnight) G.; m. Annette M'Liss Frellsen, Feb. 20, 1937. With Ark. Power & Light Co., 1928-42; treas. Capital Transp. Co., Little Rock, 1942-51; v.p. finance Birmingham Transit Co. (Ala.), 1951-64; sec., treas. Dallas Power & Light Co., 1964—. Home: 5521 Meletio Lane Dallas TX 75230 Office: 1506 Commerce St Dallas TX 75201

GRIFFITH, ANDY, actor; b. Mt. Airy, N.C., June 1, 1926; student U. N.C.; m. Barbara Edwards; children—Andy Sam, Dixie Nan. With wife, performed for civic clubs, night clubs; TV debut as monologuist Ed Sullivan show; Broadway debut as illiterate hillbilly draftee in No Time for Sergeants, 1955, (also in motion picture); motion pictures include Angel in my Pocket, A Face in the Crowd, Onionhead, 1958, Second Time Around role Broadway musical comedy Destry, 1959; recording What It Was Was Football; TV star Andy Griffith Show, 1960-69, Headmaster, 1970, The New Andy Griffith Show, 1970—; recording star Capitol Records. Home: North Hollywood CA 91603 Office: care Richard O Linke Assos Inc 4000 Warner Blvd Burbank CA 91505

GRIFFITH, BRODIE SHEPPARD, newspaper editor; b. Saluda, S.C., Mar. 14, 1899; s. John Franklin and Elizabeth (Keziah) S.; student Erskine Coll., 1916-17, LL.D., 1967; LL.D., Davidson Coll., 1966; m. Thelma Cobb Wilkinson, Dec. 18, 1920; children—Gail Elizabeth (Mrs. W.C. Dowd, II), Myra Elise (Mrs. Norman L. Moore). Reporter, Greensboro (N.C.) Record, 1919-21, Greensboro Daily News, 1921-23; state editor Charlotte (N.C.) News, 1923- 25, mng. editor, 1925-48, exec. editor, 1948-55, gen. mgr., 1955-59, editor, gen. mgr., 1959-65, asso. pub., 1965-66; became v.p., sec., gen. mgr. Charlotte News Pub. Co., Inc., 1955; v.p., treas., dir. Knight Pub. Co., v.p., asso. pub., 1968—, gen. mgr. Charlotte Observer and Charlotte News, 1966-68; treas., dir. Observer Transp. Co.; editor N.C. Legion News, 1937-69; dir. Knight Newspapers, Inc., Bank of Charlotte. Chmn., N.C. Urban Affairs Com.; mem. Charlotte Zoning Bd. Adjustment, 1949-50, mem. and chmn. Planning Bd, 1950-51. Served with U.S. Army, 1917-19; AEF. Mem. Am. Newspaper Pubs. Assn., N.C. Press Assn. (pres. 1969-70), Am. Legion 40 and 8, Newcomen Soc., Sigma Delta Chi. Baptist. Mason (K.T., Shriner). Club: Charlotte City. Home: 330 Ridgewood Av Charlotte NC 28209 Office: Knight Pub Co PO Box 2138 Charlotte NC 28201

GRIFFITH, CALVIN ROBERTSON, baseball club exec.; b. Montreal, Que., Can., Dec. 1, 1911; s. James and Jane (Davies) Robertson; adopted by Clark C. Griffith, 1923; brought to U.S., 1921; ed. Staunton Mil. Acad., 1928-32, George Washington U., 1932-35; m. Natalie N. Niven, Feb. 1, 1940; childrenClark C., N. Corinne, Clare. Sec. Chattanooga Baseball Club, 1935-37, pres., 1937, mgr., 1937; pres., mgr., treas. Charlotte Club, 1938-41; v.p. Washington Am. League Baseball Club, 1943-55, pres., 1955-61; pres. Minn. Twins, Am. League, 1961—. Dir. First Southdale Nat. Bank, Mpls. Mem. planning com. Profl. Baseball, also rules com., also alternate mem. exec. com. Bd. dirs., state chmn. Christmas Seal campaign Minn. Tb and Health Assn.; bd. dirs. St. Paul Winter Carnival Assn. Named Baseball exec. of Yr., 1965. Presbyn. Home: 552 W Ferndale Rd Wayzata MN 55391

GRIFFITH, DAVID WILLIAM, library dir.; b. Johnstown, Pa., Mar. 10, 1922; s. William and Pearl (Swank) G.; B.A. in Edn., U. Pitts., 1948; M.L.S., Carnegie Inst. Tech., 1950; m. Doris Marie Wilson, May 1, 1948; childrenDebra Ann, Bruce Michael. Reference librarian Cambria Free Library, Johnstown, Pa., 1948- 49; library dir. Pub. Library Steubenville, O., 1950-64, Youngstown (O.) Pub. Library, 1965-. Trustee Butler Art Inst., Youngstown, 1967-. Served with USAAF, 1943-45. Mem. A.L.A. (life), Ohio Library Assn. (pres. 1961, chmn. legislative com. 1966-68). Rotarian (chmn. mag. com. 1966-67, editor The Clatter 1967-68). Home: 20 Timothy Knoll Dr Poland OH 44514 Office: 305 Wick Av Youngstown OH 44503

GRIFFITH, EDWIN CLAYBROOK, educator; b. Hague, Va., May 24, 1915; s. Richard Lee and Sarah Lee (Brown) G.; A.B., Hampden-Sydney Coll., 1936; M.A., U. Va., 1939, Ph.D., 1940; m. Mary Owen Hill, Dec. 28, 1940; children—Martha Anne, Richard Lee III. Instr. govt. Marshall (Va.) High Sch., 1936-37; instr. econs. Berea Coll., summer 1940; prof. econs. U. Ga., 1940-46; faculty Washington and Lee U., Lexington, Va., 1946—, prof., 1950—, head dept., 1959—. Labor arbitrator Fed. Mediation and Conciliation Service, 1950—; pres. Community Chest, Lexington, 1956-57; mem. planning commn., Lexington 1957-62., chmn., 1956-60; mem. Lexington Sch. Bd., 1960-71, chmn., 1968-71; hon. chmn. Lexington United Fund, 1968; pres. Stonewall Jackson Hosp., Lexington, 1964-68. Mem. Am., So. econs. assns., Va. Social Sci. Assn., Am. Arbitration Assn., Phi Beta Kappa, Omicron Delta Kappa, Beta Gamma Sigma. Episcopalian (vestryman). Lion (past pres. Lexington). Home: 29 Sellers Av Lexington VA 24450

GRIFFITH, ERNEST STACEY, editor, writer; b. Utica, N.Y., Nov. 28, 1896; s. George and Elizabeth (Stacey) G.; A.B., Hamilton Coll., 1917, L.H.D., 1959; D.Phil., Oxford U., 1925; Litt.D., W. Va. Wesleyan, 1957; m. Margaret Dyckman Davenport, June 8, 1929; childrenMargaret Dyckman, Elizabeth Alison, Lawrence S. Cameron, Julia Bourne, Stephen Loyal. Preceptor in econs. Princeton, 1920-21; warden Univ. Settlement, Liverpool, Eng., 1923-28; lectr. dept. govt. Harvard, 1929-30; dean lower div., prof. comparative govt., Syracuse U., 1930-35; dean. Grad. Sch., prof. polit. sci. Am. U., 1935-40; dir. legislative reference service, Library Congress, 1940-58; dean Sch. Internat. Service, Am. U., 1958-65; cons. editor Praeger series U.S. Govt. Depts. and Agys., 1966- -. Rhodes Scholar, N.Y.; lectr. Swarthmore Coll., 1941; Stokes lectr. N.Y.U., 1951; Fulbright lectr. Oxford, 1951-52, Internat. Christian U., Tokyo, 1966-67; lectr. Birmingham U., Manchester U., U. Oslo, U. Swansea. Served in Naval Air Force, 1918. Pres. Washington Council Social Agys., 1943-47; Washington chmn. Nat. Conf. Christians and Jews, 1940-41. Mem.-at-large. Bd. Missions and Ch. Extension, Methodist Ch., 1947-51; del. World Council of Chs., New Delhi, 1961; mem. Am. Nat. Commn. for UNESCO, 1963-66; cons. in fgn. policy, platform com., 1968; Nat. Republican Com., mem. D.C. Planning Commn., 1946-47. Mem. Am. Polit. Sci. Assn. (exec. council, 1939-42, chmn. research com. 1942-47, program com. 1949, v.p. 1958-59), Nat. Municipal League, Am. Soc. Pub. Adminstrn., Wilderness Soc. (council 1937-55, treas., 1940-50, 58-), Nat. Acad. Econs. and Polit. Sci. (pres. 1958-63), Nat. Acad. Pub. Adminstrn. (hon.), Phi Beta Kappa, Phi Kappa Phi, Delta Upsilon. Republican. Methodist. Clubs: Potomac Appalachian Trail, Cosmos. Author: The Modern Government in Action, 1942; Congress: Its Contemporary Role, rev. edit. 1967; The American System of Government, 1953, 4th rev. edit., 1966, Italian, German and Korean edits., 1957-58, edits. numerous fgn. langs. Editor and co-author Research in Political Sience, 1948. Editor, Congressional Anthology, rev. edit. 1958. Holder misc. speed and endurance records in mountain climbing. Home: 1941 Parkside Drive NW Washington DC 20012

GRIFFITH, FRANK WELLS, utility co. exec.; b. Ft. Dodge, Ia., July 1, 1921; s. Frank Whitcombe and Gladys (Wells) G.; B.S. in Gen. Engring., Ia. State U., 1947; utility mgmt. course U. Mich., 1960; m. Betty Marie Harrelson, Sept. 12, 1945; children—Clark Wells, Steven Harrelson, Jon Lance. Gen. engr. U.S. Gypsum Co., Sweetwater, Tex., 1947-48; with Ia. Pub. Service Co., Sioux City, Ia., 1948—, asst. to pres., 1961-63, v.p. operations, 1963-65, exec. v.p., 1965-66, pres., chmn. bd., also dir.; dir. Security Nat. Bank. Dir. Edison Electric Inst. Chmn., Wagon Wheel Dist. Boy Scouts Am., 1959; dir. Ia. Coordinating Com. for Higher Edn.; gen. chmn. United Fund; commr. Ia. Devel. Commn., 1970-73. Bd. dirs. Woodbury County Crippled Children Soc., Sioux City Symphony Assn., Sioux City Art Center, Planned Parenthood, St. Lukes Med. Center, Siouxland Blood Bank; trustee Westmar Coll. Served to maj. USAAF, 1941-45; CBI. Mem. Am. Soc. M.E., Am., Midwest (pres.) gas assns., Am. Pub. Works Assn., N. Central Electric Assn. (pres.), Sioux City C. of C., Nat. Rifle Assn. (life). Episcopalian (vestryman). Mason (Shriner), Rotarian. Clubs: Sioux City Country, Sioux City Engineers, Toastmasters (past pres.), Knife and Fork (Sioux City). Home: 4455 Perry Way Sioux City IA 51104 Office: PO Box 778 Sioux City IA 51102

GRIFFITH, HAROLD MELVIN, steel co. exec.; b. Clinton, Ill., July 4, 1904; s. Melvin M. and Anna (McGaw) G.; B.S. in E.E., Chgo. Tech. Coll., 1926; student Advanced Mgmt. Program, Harvard, 1949; m. Fredrica Schneider, Sept. 14, 1927; children—Gretchen (Mrs. Harold R. Skeels), Shirley (Mrs. George Russell). Steel works metallurgist Bethlehem Steel Co., 1926-30, Jones and Laughlin Steel Co., 1930-36; with The Steel Co., of Can., Ltd., Hamilton, 1936—, beginning as metallurgist, successively asst. open hearth supt., open hearth supt., asst. works mgr., works mgr., asst. to the pres., 1936-53, v.p., 1953-64, exec. v.p., 1964-66, pres., 1966-68, pres., chief exec. officer, 1968—, also dir.; dir. Toronto, Hamilton & Buffalo Ry. Co., Canadian Gen. Electric Co. Ltd., Ontario Steel Products Co. Ltd., Steetley of Can. Ltd., Steetley Industries Ltd., Toronto-Dominion Bank. Mem. Am. Iron and Steel Inst. (dir.), Internat. Iron and Steel Institute (dir.), Am. Inst. Mining, Metall. and Petroleum Engrs. (past chmn. open hearth steel com.). Home: 1404 Old Mill Towers 39 Old Mill Rd Toronto 590 Ontario Canada Office: Steel Co of Canada Ltd PO Box 205 Toronto-Dominion Centre Toronto 111 Ontario Canada

GRIFFITH, HUGH, actor; b. Anglesey, Wales, May 30, 1912 s. William and Mary (Williams) G.; ed. (Gold medal), Royal Acad. Dramatic Art, London; D.Litt. (hon.), U. of Wales; m. Adelqunde M.B. von Dechend, Oct. 27, 1947. Appeared on Broadway in Look Homeward Angel, Andora; motion pictures include, Ben Hur (recipient of the Academy award for role of Sheik), 1960, Exodus, 1961, The Counterfeit Traitor, Mutiny on the Bounty, Tom Jones, How to Steal a Million, 1965, The Chastity Belt, Oh Dad, Poor Dad . . ., The Fixer, Oliver, also appeared in Two Times Two; TV appearances include The Waltz of the Toreadors, Treasure Island, The Citadel, The Inn of the Flying Dragon, Dare I Weep, Dare I Mourn. Served as officer Royal Welch Fusiliers, British Army, 1940-46. Hon. Druid of Welsh Gorsedd of Bards. Club: Garrick (Ldn). Office: London Internat 11-12 Hanover St Park St London W 1 England

GRIFFITH, JOHN STEVENSON, exec.; b. Los Angeles, Feb. 16, 1901; s. John Tomlinson and Adele (Wedemeyer) G.; grad. high sch.; m. Helen Hostetter, July 25, 1928; childrenJohn Stevenson, Miriam G. Jones. Investment securities, 1920- 37, real estate devel. and mgmt., gen. ins., 1935—; pres. John S. Griffith & Co., developers comml. property, 1950-; propr. John S. Griffith, Ins., 1935-; pres. City Securities Co., Pomona Valley Center; chmn. bd. Far West Financial Corp.; managing partner Buena Park Co.; dir. Norris Thermador, Am. Pipe & Constrn. Co., State Mutual Savs. and Loan Assn. Trustee Cal. Inst. Tech. Clubs: California, Yacht (Los Angeles); Newport (Cal.) Harbor Yacht; Santa Ana (Cal.) Country; San Gabriel (Cal.) Country. Home: 1435 Orlando Rd Pasadena CA 91106 Office: Far West Financial Corp 626 Wilshire Blvd Los Angeles CA 90017

GRIFFITH, LYNN B., judge; b. West Farmington, O., Oct. 30; 1886; s. Herbert F. and Lovira (Snyder) G.; A.B., Oberlin Coll., 1910; LL.B., Western Res. U., 1914; m. Stata Norton Miller, Sept. 9, 1916; childrenDavid Miller, Patricia Ann, Lynn B. City solicitor, Warren, O., 1925-26; county pros. atty., 1927- 28; common pleas judge, Trumbull County, O., 1931-50; judge Ct. of Appeals, 7th Dist. Ohio, 1950-62; judge Supreme Ct. of Ohio, 1962-; mem. Letson, Letson & Griffith, Warren, O., 1965-. Dir. First Nat. Bank, Girard, O., Girard Fed. Savs. & Loan Assn. Pres. Warren Pub. Library, Oakwood Cemetery Assn,; chmn. adv. bd. YWCA. Home: 4205 E Market St Warren OH 44484 Office: Judiciary Bldg Columbus OH 43215 also Union Savs and Trust Bldg Warren OH 44482

GRIFFITH, PAUL HOWARD, corp. exec., bus. cons.; b. Uniontown, Pa., Apr. 8, 1897; s. David Ambrose and Annie May (Fleegle) G.; student Salem Coll.; m. Pearl Jennewine, June 30, 1920; children—Nancy Lee (Mrs. Robert R. Sweeney), Paul Howard. Partner, D.A. Griffith & Son, wholesale dairy products, Uniontown, 1919-32, Hutchinson-Griffith Motor Co., Brownsville, Pa., 1928-30; owner Paul H. Griffith Industries, Washington, 1940—; chmn. bd. Militronics, Inc., Alexandria, Va.; pres. Creative Chems., Inc., C.D. Distbrs., Inc., Potomac, Md.; exec. v.p. Buchart, Inc., architects and engrs., York, Pa., 1956—; now with Buchart-Horn, cons. engrs.; asst. sec. def., 1949-50. Pres., U.S. Small Bus. Council, 1954- 55; exec. mem. Nat. Selective Service (Presdl.) Appeal Bd., 1949- 59; mem. Am. tech. mission to India, also asst. to Louis Johnson, personal rep. of Pres. in Middle and Near East, 1942; served as mem. bd. to establish essential activities and critical occupations War Manpower Commn. and SSS; chief Vets. Personnel div. SSS; adminstr. Retng. and Reëmployment Adminstrn., Office Manpower Moblzn.; asst. exec. Office Undersec. of War; chmn. Pa. Vets. Commn. Pres., Religious Heritage Am. Bd. dirs. Arms of Friendship. Served with U.S. Army, World War I; to col. AUS. Decorated U.S., France, Belgium (World War I), U.S., France, Greece, Italy (World War II). Mem. Soc. Am. Mil. Engrs., Engrs. Soc. Pa., Am. Rd. Builders Assn., Am. Legion (nat. comdr. 1946-47). Republican. Mem. Christian Ch. (elder, trustee, mem. bd.). Club: Army and Navy (Washington). Home: 11121 River Rd Potomac MD 20854 Office: Metromedia Bldg 5151 Washington Av NW Washington DC 20016

GRIFFITH, ROBERT KENASTON, fabricated metal products co. exec.; b. Canton, O., Mar. 5, 1917; s. Louis Eugene and Mary Wygant (Kenaston) G.; B.S., Lafayette Coll., 1940; night student Wharton Sch., U. Pa. 1953-55; m. Edna Adele Roth, Nov. 1, 1942; cildren—Robert Kenaston, Adele Harley, Louis Eugene II, Mary Anne, Martha Wygant. With Riley Stoker Corp., Worcester, Mass., 1940-41, 46-, v.p., treas., 1956- 60, pres., treas., 1960-69, chief exec. officer, 1966-69, v.p., treas., dir. Badenhausen Co., Cornwells Heights, Pa. 1956—; asst. sec., dir. A.W. Cash Co., Decatur, Ill., 1956—; pres., treas. Robert K. Griffith & Assos., Inc., East Woodstock, Conn., 1971—; v.p., dir. Union Iron Works, Erie, Pa.; dir. Mechanics Nat. Bank, Worcester. Incorporator Hahnemann Hosp., Worcester. Mem. Am. Soc. M.E., Am. Soc. Ins. Mgmt., Zeta Psi. Republican. Home: Box 48 East Woodstock CT 06244

GRIFFITH, ROBERT LYN, airlines executive; b. Rochester, N.Y., Sept. 11, 1907; s. Harri and Inez Jane (Harris) G.; A.B., Cornell U., 1929, LL.B. with spl. honors, 1935; m. Thelma Alberta Parks, July 5, 1935 (div. June 1950); 1 dau., Martha Lyn; m. 2d, Carrie Woods Capps, Nov. 28, 1950. Instr. accounting Cornell U., 1929; admitted to N.Y. bar, 1935, practiced in Rochester, 1935-42; asso. firm Root, Clark, Buckner and Ballantine, N.Y.C., 1942, 43, Pruitt, Hale and Coursen, 1943-46; asst. gen. counsel Am. Airlines Inc., 1943-46, asst. sec., 1946-48; asst. to pres. Delta Air Lines, Inc., 1948-50, 55-59, v.p., 1959-; attorney OPS, 1951-53; chief office compliance Civil Aero. Board, Washington, 1953-55. District commr. Rochester area Boy Scouts, 1940-42. Mem. Alpha Sigma Phi, Phi Delta Phi, Phi Kappa Phi. Order of Coif. Clubs: Wings (N.Y.C.); Nat. Aviation; Aero, Cornell (Washington). Mng. editor, Cornell Law Quar., 1934, 35. Home:

GRIFFITH, ROBERT WILSON, ins. co. exec.; b. Custer, Mont., Apr. 30, 1915; s. William T. and Helena (Shoemaker) G.; B.S., Ohio State U., 1937; m. Jane Needham, Aug. 6, 1942; children—Ann (Mrs. Darrel Dreher), Lynn. Underwriter, Nationwide Mut. Ins. Co., Columbus, O., 1937-40, statistician, 1940-49, actuary, 1949—, v.p., actuary, 1966—; v.p., actuary Nationwide Mut. Fire Ins. Co., Nationwide Gen. Ins. Co. Served with Ordnance Corps, AUS, 1942-46. Mem. Am. Acad. Actuaries, Sigma Nu. Presbyn. (trustee). Mason. Home: 40 Wilson Dr Worthington OH 43085 Office: 246 N High St Columbus OH 43216

GRIFFITH, SAMUEL BLAIR II, author, lectr., cons.; b. Lewistown, Pa., May 31, 1906; s. Henry Foster and Marguerite (Fitzgerald) G.; B.S., U.S. Naval Acad., 1929; D.Phil., Oxford U., Eng., 1961; m. Beele Gordon Nelson, Dec. 21, 1929; children—Belle Gordon (Mrs. Harry Bailey Heneberger), Jane Serrill (Mrs. Robert Kyger Rushing (div.). Commd. 2d lt. USMC, 1929, advanced through grades to brig. gen., 1956; staff, corps commdr., Tientsin, China, staff 7th Fleet, 1945-46; comdg. officer U.S. Marine Forces, Tsingtao, China, 1946-47; staff U.S. Naval War Coll., Newport, R.I., 1947-50; chief of staff Fleet Marine Force Atlantic, 1951-52; mem. staff U.S. Comdr.-in-Chief, Europe, 1953-56; ret., 1956; research fellow Council on Fgn. Relations, N.Y., 1964-67; research asso. Hoover Instn., Stanford, 1967-68; cons. aerospace systems div. Bendix Corp., Ann Arbor, Mich., 1965-67, Stanford Research Inst., Menlo Park, Cal. and Washington, 1968-70, Hoover Instn., Stanford, 1967-68, Inst. for Def. Analysis, Washington, 1968-69; lectr. Nat. War Coll., Washington, 1966-68, Air War Coll., Maxwell AFB, Ala., 1967-70, Naval War Coll., Newport, R.I., 1965, 68, Army War Coll., Carlisle, Pa., 1970. U.S. Mil. Acad., 1966, U.S. Naval Acad., 1968, U. Cal. at Berkeley, 1969, Stanford, 1968, Commonwealth Club, San Francisco, 1967, League Women Voters, Washington, 1968, Washington and Lee U., 1969, U. Va., 1969. Mem. Nat. Com. on U.S.-China Relations, N.Y.C., 1966-71; mem. vis. com. East Asian Studies, Harvard, 1967-70. Decorated D.S.C., Navy Cross, Purple Heart, Order Cloud and Banner, Republic of China. Mem. Inst. for Strategic Studies, London, Eng., Council on Fgn. Relations, N.Y.C., Assn. for Asian Studies, New Coll. Soc., 1st Marine Div. Assn., 1st Marine Raider Assn., U.S. Naval Acad. Alumni Assn., Marine Corps Assn. Author: Mao Tse-tung: On Guerrilla War, 1962; Sun Tzu: The Art of War, 1963; The Battle for Guadalcanal, 1963; Peking and People's Wars, 1966; The Chinese People's Liberation Army, 1968; also articles. Address: Norcross Lodge RFD 1 Mt Vernon ME 04352

GRIFFITH, THOMAS, editor; b. Tacoma, Dec. 30 , 1915; s. Thomas and Anne (O'Reilly) G.; A.B., U. Wash., 1936; postgrad. (Nieman fellow) Harvard, 1942-43; m. Caroline Coffman, Sept. 26, 1937. Reporter, asst. city editor Seattle Times, 1936- 42; contbg. editor Time Mag., 1943-49, nat. affairs editor, 1949-51, fgn. news editor, 1951-60, asst. mng. editor, 1960-63; sr. staff editor Time, Inc. publs., 1964-67; editor Life mag., 1968-. Mem. Council Fgn. Relations, Hammer and Coffin, Fir Tree, Sigma Delta Chi. Clubs: Harvard, Century Assn., Coffee House (N.Y.C.). Author: The Waist High Culture, 1959. Home: 25 East End Av New York City NY 10028 Office: Time and Life Bldg Rockefeller Center New York City NY 10020

GRIFFITH, THOMAS LEE, Jr., superior ct. judge; b. Albia, Ia., Mar. 5, 1902; s. Thomas Lee and Carrie Liza (Thomas) G.; ed. U. So. Cal., 1922-26, Law Sch., 1925-26; LL.B., Southwestern U., 1928; m. Portia Louise Broyles, Apr. 9, 1933; children—Thomas Lee III, Greta Louise, Liza Jane. Admitted to Cal. bar, 1931, since practiced in Los Angeles; judge municipal ct., Los Angeles, 1953-69, superior ct., Los Angeles, 1969—. Mem. Am., Los Angeles bar assns., Omega Psi Phi. Republican. Baptist. Home: 4219 Don Ortega Pl Los Angeles CA 90008 Office: 111 N Hill St Los Angeles CA 90012

GRIFFITH, WILLIAM EDGAR, educator; b. Remsen, N.Y., Feb. 19, 1920; s. William G. and Sarah G. (Mitchell) G.; A.B., Hamilton Coll., Clinton, N.Y., 1940; M.A., Harvard, 1941, Ph.D., 1950; m. Ingeborg Maria Ehrhardt, Apr. 10, 1948; childrenEvelyn Elizabeth, Dorothy Isabelle, Oliver William. Teaching fellow Harvard, 1948-50; asst. to pres. Free Europe Com., 1950-51, polit. adviser, Munich, Germany, 1951-58; research asso. Center Internat. Studies, Mass. Inst. Tech., 1958-65, prof. polit. sci., 1965- ; prof. Soviet diplomacy Fletcher Sch. Law and Diplomacy, 1962-; cons. to govt., 1959-. Served to 1st lt. AUS, 1942-46. Mem. Council Fgn. Relations. Author: Albania and the Sino-Soviet Rift, 1963; The Sino- Soviet Rift, 1964; Sino-Soviet Relations, 1964-1965, 1967. Editor: Communism in Europe, 2 vols., 1964, 66. Home: 19 Peacock Farm Rd Lexington MA 02173 Office: 30 Wadsworth St Cambridge MA 02139

GRIFFITHS, DANIEL EDWARD, univ. dean; b. Bridgeport, Conn., May 8, 1917; s. Frederick George and Helen (Quist) G.; B.Ed., Central Conn. State Coll., 1940; M.Ed., U. N.H., 1949; Ph.D., Yale, 1952; m. Priscilla Tomlinson, June 22, 1946; children—Priscilla Ann, Michael Edward. Asst. prof. edn. Colgate U., 1949-52; prof. edn. State Coll. Tchrs., Albany, N.Y., 1952-55; dir. coop. devel. pub. sch. adminstrn., asso. coordinator ednl. research N.Y. State Dept. Edn., 1955-56; asso. prof., then prof. edn. Columbia Tchrs. Coll., 1956-61; asso. dean N.Y. U. Sch. Edn., 1961-65, dean, 1965—. Dir. devel. criteria of success in sch. adminstrn. project, coop. research br. U.S. Office Edn., 1957-61, dir. devel. taxonomies of orgnl. behavior in edn. project, 1964—, mem. ednl. processes panel, 1964-67; dir. N.Y.C. Study Tchr. Mobility, 1963. Pres., Sch. Bd. Greenburgh, N.Y., 1961-64. Served with USAAF, 1943-46. Mem. Am. Ednl. Research Assn., Am. Assn. Sch. Adminstrs., Nat. Conf. Profs. Ednl. Adminstrn., Pub. Edn. Assn. (trustee). Author: Human Relations in School Administration, 1956; Administrative Theory, 1959; Organizing Schools for Effective Education, 1962; Administrative Performance and Personality, 1962; The School Superintendent, 1967. Editor: Behavioral Science and Educational Administration, 1964; Taxonomies of Organizational Behavior in Education, 1969. Editorial bd. Library of Edn., 1961-67, chmn., 1964-67. Home: 54 Clarendon Rd Scarsdale NY 10583 Office: NY U Washington Sq NY 10003

GRIFFITHS, GEORGE FINDLEY, business exec.; b. Chgo., Feb. 18, 1906; s. George Harold and Mabel May (Green) G.; student U.S. Mil. Acad., 1925- 27; B.A., Amherst Coll., 1929; m. Marion E. Winterrowd, Feb. 15, 1941; children—Jean Winterrowd, William Harold, Judith Holland, Robert Pennell. Salesman, United Screw & Bolt Corp., 1929-31, U.S. Steel Corp., 1931-38; salesman Sharon (Pa.) Steel Corp., 1938-40, dist. mgr. sales, 1940-46, gen. mgr. sales, 1946-47, v.p., gen. mgr. sales, 1947-49; asst. to exec. v.p. Acme Steel Co., Chgo., 1950-51, asst. to pres., 1952, v.p. 1953-58, exec. v.p. sales, 1958-60, pres., chief exec. officer, chmn. exec. com., 1961-64, dir., 1954- 64; chmn. bd., chief exec. officer Interlake Steel Corp. (merger Acme Steel Co. and Interlake Iron Corp. 1964), 1964-69, chmn. bd., 1969-71, also dir., mem. exec. com.; dir. Midland Ross Corp., Pullman Trust & Savs. Bank, Bliss & Laughlin Industries, Inc. Bd. dirs. Jr. Achievement of Chgo.; trustee Ill. Inst. Tech., Igalls Meml. Hosp., Village of Hinsdale, 1959-63. Mem. exec. com. IIT Research Inst. Mem. Am. Iron and Steel Inst., Ill. C. of C., Psi Upsilon. Republican. Christian Scientist. Clubs: Executives (dir.), Mid-Am., University (dir.), Chicago (Chgo.); Hinsdale (Ill.) Golf; Commercial. Home: 439 E 6th St Hinsdale IL 60521 Office: 310 S Michigan Av Chicago IL 60603

GRIFFITHS, GEORGE HAROLD, found. ofcl.; b. Cleve., June 11, 1910; s. George Harry and Elizabeth (Morgan) G.; B.A., Ohio Wesleyan U., 1932; postgrad. Columbia, 1935- 38, New Sch. Social Research, 1938-39; m. Laura Olive Jenkins, Sept. 22, 1947. Instr. English, Lingnan U., Canton, China, 1932-34; visitor Fed. Emergency Relief Adminstrn., Cleve., 1934-35; project dir. WPA, Cleve., 1936; staff Nat. Adv. Com. on Use Motion Pictures in Edn., 1937-38; cons. motion picture project Progressive Edn. Assn., 1938; writer ERPI Classroom Films, 1937-39, research asso., 1939-42; contract employee tng. film br. Bur. Aero., Navy Dept., 1942-43; N.Y. regional dir. div. visual aids for war tng. U.S. Office Edn., 1943-46; producer Ency. Brit. Films, 1946, dir. prodn., 1949-51; West Coast regional rep. and dir. mass media Fund for Adult Edn., 1951-54, exec. asst. to pres., 1954-56, v.p., treas., 1956- , bd. dirs., 1962-; asso. program dir. edn. div. Ford Found., 1961-67, program officer div. edn. and research, 1967-, also asso. program dir. Fund Advancement Edn., 1961-67, sec.-treas., mem. bd dirs., 1967-. Mem. Phi Beta Kappa, Omicron Delta Kappa, Delta Sigma Rho, Delta Tau Delta. Club: City Island (N.Y.) Yacht. Home: 300 Pelham Rd New Rochelle NY 10805 Office: Ford Foundation 320 E 43d St New York City NY 10017

GRIFFITHS, HENRY JOSEPH, educator; b. Cambridge, Eng., July 4, 1910; s. Joseph and Ethel Mary (Payne) G.; B.S.A., McGill U., 1932, M.S., 1935, Ph.D., 1939; D.V.M., Ia. State U., 1943; m. Anne Martha Franklin, Apr. 8, 1943. Came to U.S., 1939, naturalized, 1952. Grad. asst. McGill U., 1932-39, Ia. State U., 1939-43; instr. Ont. Vet. Coll., 1946-47; asso. prof. Wash. State U., 1947-48; asso. prof. U. Minn., St. Paul, 1948-53, prof., 1953, asst. dean Coll. Vet. Medicine, 1955-58, prof., head vet. pathology, 1965-71, prof. vet. parasitology, 1971—. Served to capt. M.C., Royal Canadian Army, 1943-46. Recipient Distinguished Tchr. award U. Minn., 1963, All Univ. recognition award, 1967. Mem. Am., Minn. vet. med. assns., Conf. Research Workers Animal Diseases, Am. Soc. Parasitologists, Am. Assn. Vet. Parasitologists, World Assn. Advancement Vet. Parasitology, Sigma Xi, Phi Zeta, Gamma Sigma Delta. Contbr. articles to profl. jours. Home: 1845 W Larpenteur Av St Paul MN 55113

GRIFFITHS, MARTHA WRIGHT, congresswoman; b. Pierce City, Mo.; d. Charles Elbridge and Nelle (Sullinger) Wright; A.B., U. Mo., 1934; J.D., U. Mich., 1940; m. Hicks G. Griffiths. Admitted to Mich. bar, 1941; contract negotiator Detroit Ordnance Dist., 1942-46; practice law Griffiths & Griffiths, Detroit, 1946—; mem. Mich. Ho. Reps., 1948-52; judge, recorder Detroit Recorder's Ct., 1953; mem. 84th- 92d Congresses, 17th Mich. Dist., mem. joint econ. com., house com. ways and means, chmn. subcom. fiscal policy. Mem. Detroit City Election Commn. Democrat. Office: Longworth House Office Bldg Washington DC 20515 also 14615 Grand River Detroit MI 48227

GRIFFITHS, PHILLIP A., educator. Prof. math. Princeton. Office: Princeton U 702 New Fine Princeton NJ 08540*

GRIFFO, JAMES VINCENT, Jr., educator; b. Bklyn., Sept. 17, 1928; s. James Vincent and Delsie (Ceruti) G.; B.S., U. Ky., 1952, M.S., 1953; Ph.D., U. Fla., 1960; m. Sally Jean Stieren, Nov. 20, 1954; children—James Vincent III, Lauren Carol, Kenneth Charles. Tchg., research asst., U. Fla., 1956-60; instr. biology, Fairleigh Dickinson U., 1960-61; project leader Wildlife Diseases, U.S. Dept. Interior Fish and Wildlife Service, Laurel, Md., 1961-62; asst. prof. biology, Fairleigh Dickinson U., 1962-63, chmn. biology, 1963-66, acting campus dean, 1966, asso. prof., 1967-69, campus dean, 1967, prof., 1969—, campus dean, 1967—, campus provost, 1971—. Trustee All Souls Hosp., Morristown, N.J. Served with AUS, 1953-55. Mem. Am. Soc. Mammalogists, Wildlife Fedn. Republican. Roman Catholic. Rotarian. Home: 33 Sherbrooke Dr Florham Park NJ 07932 Office: Fairleigh Dickinson U 285 Madison Av Madison NJ 07940

GRIGG, AUSTIN EARNEST, univ. dean; b. Richmond, Va., July 24, 1919; s. Crawford Field and Etta (Earnest) G.; B.A., Richmond Coll., 1940; M.A., U. Richmond, 1947; Ph.D., U. Ia., 1957; m. Helen Webb, Sept. 2, 1952; 1 son, Kenneth Carver. Asst. prof. psychology, U. Richmond, psychologist, Tucker Hosp., Richmond, 1948-55; USPHS research fellow, U. Ia., 1955-57; dir. grad. studies, clin. psychology, U. Tex., Austin, 1957-60; prof. psychology, U. Richmond, 1960-64, chmn. dept. psychology, 1964-67, dean Richmond Coll., 1967—; cons. Va. State Police Tng. Sch., 1964—, Human Devel. Project,

Richmond Pub. Schs., 1964-66. Mem. Gov.'s Commn. on Mental Health, 1963-64. Bd. dirs. Meml. Guidance Clinic, Richmond; trustee Collegiate Schs., Richmond. Served to 2d lt. USAAF, 1943-46. Fellow Am. Psychol. Assn.; mem. Am. Assn. Higher Edn., So. Assn. Deans, Va. Acad. Sci. (treas.), A.A.A.S., Va. Psychol. Assn. (pres. 1962-63), Sigma Xi, Omicron Delta Kappa, Pi Kappa Alpha. Kiwanian. Club: Willow Oaks Country (dir. 1967-70, v.p. 1970) (Richmond). Contbr. articles profl. jours. Home: 3112 Fellsway Circle Richmond VA 23225

GRIGG, CHARLES MEADE, sociologist, educator; b. Richmond, Va., Nov. 1, 1918; s. Joseph W. and Nellie A. (Chockley) G.; B.S., Coll. William and Mary, 1948; M.A. U. N.C., 1950, Ph.D., 1952; m. Virginia E. Caffee, Aug. 23, 1947; childrenCharles M., John W., Joseph G., Ruth E. Asst. prof. Brown U., 1952-55; mem. faculty Fla. State U., Tallahassee, 1955-, prof. sociology, dir. Inst. Social Research, 1950—, asso. dean arts and scis., 1966—. Chmn. Gov. Fla. Com. Employment Handicapped, 1963- -, Gov.'s Commn. Law Enforcement and Justice. Served to capt. USAAF, 1941-46. Fellow Am. Sociol. Assn.; mem. So. Sociol. Soc. (exec. com.), Population Assn. Author: (with L.M. Killian) Leadership and Conflict of Racial Crisis in America, 1963; Graduate Education, 1965. Editor: (with C.N. Millican) Setting for Higher Education in Florida, 1963; (with K.S. Miller) Mental Health and the Lower Social Classes. Home: 2500 Harriman Circle Tallahassee FL 32302

GRIGG, ELMER LEE, lawyer; b. Springfield, Mo., Feb. 14, 1919; s. Elmer Lonzo and Margaret (Sims) G.; student U. Tulsa, 1946-51; m. Betty Joan Loesel, Mar. 1, 1946; children—Alan R., James L., Thomas J. Admitted to Okla. bar, 1951, since practiced in Tulsa; mem. firm Houston, Klein & Davidson, 1951—; gen. counsel Tulsa County Med. Soc. Served with AUS, 1943-45. Mem. Am., Okla., Tulsa bar assns., Okla. Assn. Def. Counsel, Def. Research Inst., Phi Beta Gamma. Democrat. Presbyn. Home: 3704 S Sandusky St Tulsa OK 74135 Office: 404 S Boston St Tulsa OK 74103

GRIGG, FRANCIS NEPHI, food co. exec.; b. Nampa, Ida., May 6, 1913; s. Parley M. and Thankful Halsey (Gardener) G.; m. Addie Christine Crummett, Dec. 24, 1936; children—Delma (Mrs. Wayne E. Saunders), Janet (Mrs. Dale B. McLane), Billie Louise, Laurel Francis, Karen Marie, David Nephi, Steven Richard, Jeri Christine. Engaged in corn and vegetable raising, 1920-48; engaged in freezing corn on the cob, 1948-51; formed Ore. Frozen Foods, Inc., 1951; formed Ore-Ida Potato Products, Inc. (now Ore-Ida Foods, Inc.), 1951, pres., 1951-, also chmn. bd.; pres. Latter Day Saints Mission, Edinburgh, Scotland, 1969—; dir. H. J. Heinz Co., Pittsburgh, Pa. Mem. Ore. Indsl. Devel. Com., 1961-; marketing adv. council Sch. Bus. Adminstrn., U. Ore., 1962-. Pres. Ore-Ida council Boy Scouts Am., mem. exec. bd. N.W. regions XI, 1962—, council rep. to nat. bd., 1958—. Trustee Treasure Valley Community Coll., Ontario, Ore. Mem. Frozen Potato Products Inst. (dir., past pres.), Nat. Frozen Food Assn. (dir.). Mem. Ch. of Jesus Christ of Latter Saints (bishop 1942-52, high councilman Nyssa Stake 1955-69). Address: Scottish Mission Boroughfield 32 Colinton Rd Edinburgh 10 Scotland also PO Box 60 Ontario OR 97914

GRIGG, HAMBLETT CHARLES, beverage exec.; b. St. Louis, Apr. 20, 1905; s. Charles Leiper and Lucy E. (Alexander) G.; grad. Cleveland High Sch., St. Louis; m. Margaret E. Blanke, Feb. 11, 1939; childrenCharles Robert, Douglas Wells. Commercial artist, 1924-26; in advt. sign business, 1927-28; salesman Seven-Up Co., St. Louis, 1929-35, advt. mgr., 1935-39, gen. mgr., 1939- 40, pres., 1940-65, chmn. bd., 1965-, also dir.‡

GRIGG, JOSEPH WILLIAMS, fgn. corr.; b. Bangor, Me., Aug. 23, 1910; s. Joseph Williams and Anna Prentiss (Stearns) G.; grad. Westminster Sch., London, England, 1929; student of Trinity Coll., Cambridge, England, 1929-32; B.A., Cambridge U., 1932, M.A., 1966; m. Jerry Abbott, Apr. 4, 1944 (dec. 1959); childrenMargaret, Richard Abbott; m. 2d, Margaret Meikle, November 19, 1960. Corr. London office N.Y. Sun, 1932-34; corr. United Press, London, 1934-39, 1957, Berlin, 1939-42, Washington, 1942-43, war corr., 1943-45, chief corr. and mgr. for France, Paris, 1945-51, chief corr. and mgr. for Germany, Frankfurt and Bonn, 1951-57, chief European corr. United Press Internat., 1957-60, news mgr. Western Continental Europe and N. Africa, 1960-66, chief European corr. United Press Internat., 1966-. Mem. Anglo-Am. Press Assn. Paris (pres. 1965), Fgn. Press Assn. in Germany, Assn. Am. Corres. in London, Fgn. Press Assn. in London. Clubs: Wig and Pen (London). Overseas Press of Am. Co-author: This is the Enemy, 1942. Home: 80A Oakwood Ct London W 14 England Office: United Press Internat 8 Bouverie St London EC 4 England

GRIGG, MILTON LATOUR, architect; b. Alexandria, Va., Apr. 18, 1905; s. James Fossett and Mary Emily (Glasgow) G.; student U. Va., 1924-29; m. Grace Vestal Thomas, Sept. 1, 1930; m. 2d, Ella Albian Repass, May 18, 1940. Draftsman, designer Perry, Shaw & Hepburn, Boston, architects for restoration Colonial Williamsburg, Va., 1929-33; pvt. practice architecture, Alexandria and Charlottesville, Va., 1933—, specializing restoration, chs., restoration, including Monticello, Edgemont, other historic sites; sr. partner Grigg, Wood Browne & Williams; architect Am. embassy, Canberra, Australia. Cons. Nat. Council Chs., commn. architecture Luth. Ch. Am., U.S. Park Service. Mem. Planning Commn. Charlottesville, chmn. Bldg. Code Rev. Bd.; pres. Interfaith Research Center, N.Y.; comptroller Internat. Congress on Religious Architecture. Bd. dirs. Va. Archtl. Found. Civilian service with C.E., 1942-45, chief design hosps., mil. structures. Fellow A.I.A. (religious bldg. com., regional dir. Middle Atlantic region); mem. Ch. Archtl. Guild Am. (pres.), Guild for Religious Architecture (pres.), Delta Sigma Phi, Theta Tau, Omicron Delta Kappa (hon. mem.), Scarab. Episcopalian. Clubs: Cosmos (Washington); Farmington, Colonade (Charlottesville). Contbr. numerous papers to tech. lit. Home: 2033 Hessian Rd Meadowbrook Hills Charlottesville VA 22903 Office: 404 8th St NE Charlottesville VA 22901

GRIGGS, DAVID TRESSEL, geophysicist; b. Columbus, O., Oct. 6, 1911; s. Robert F. and Laura (Tressel) G.; A.B., Ohio State U., 1932, A.M., 1933; jr. fellow Harvard, 1934-41; m. Helen Avery, May 4, 1946; children—Nicola F., Stephen F. Research asso. radiation lab. Mass. Inst. Tech., 1941-42; chief nuclear energy sect. Project RAND, 1946-48, cons., 1948—; prof. geophysics Inst. Geophysics and Planetary Physics, U. Cal. at Los Angeles, 1948—; chief scientist USAF, 1951-52, sci. adv. bd., 1952—; chmn. ballistic systems div. adv. group USAF, 1963-65; cons. Armed Forces Spl. Weapons Proj., 1951-56; cons. various govtl. agys., also AEC; mem. Nat. Geog. Soc. Expdn. to Valley 10,000 Smokes, 1930; lectr. Lowell Inst., 1938; dir. FMA, Inc., Inglewood, 1960-67. Expert cons. Office Sec. of War, 1942-46; chief sci. adv. group Far East Air Forces, 1945; sci. adv. group U.S. Strategic Air Force, 1944-45; mem. Def. Sci. Bd., 1964- -, Army Sci. Adv. Panel, 1965—, OST Panel for Earthquake Prediction, 1965-66; asso. sci. adviser COMUSMAC, Vietnam, 1968. Decorated Purple Heart, 1944, President's Medal for Merit, 1946; USAF award for exceptional civilian service, 1953; Bucher medal Am. Geophys. Union, 1970; Centennial Achievement award Ohio State U., 1970. Fellow Geol. Soc. Am., Am. Phys. Soc.; mem. Nat. Acad. Sci., Am. Geophys. Union (pres. sect. tectonophysics 1964-68), Am. Acad. Arts and Scis., Phi Beta Kappa, Sigma Xi. Clubs: Cosmos (Washington); Riviera Country (Los Angeles). Author: Rock Deformation, 1960. Home: 190 Granville Av Los Angeles CA 90049

GRIGGS, EARL LESLIE, educator; b. N.Y.C., Apr. 15, 1899; s. Edward Howard and Mary P. (Little) G.; student, Princeton U., 1917-19; A.B., U. of Colo., 1922; A.M., Columbia, 1923; Ph.D., U. of London, England, 1927, D.Lit., 1956; m. Grace Evelyn Riley, July 30, 1923. Instructor of English, U. of Minnesota, 1923-25; asst. prof. English, U. of Ore., 1927-28; U. of Mich., 1928-34; asso. prof. English, U. of Mich., 1934-39; prof. English, U. of Pa., 1939-47; prof. English U. Cal. at Los Angeles, 1947-62, faculty research lectr., 1961; dean grad. div. U. Cal., Santa Barbara, 1962-67; dir. edn. abroad program in U.K. and Ireland, 1967-69; hon. research asso. Univ. Coll., London, 1968-69; vis. prof. U. Cal., 1945-46, and summers U. of Colorado, 1934, 36, 38, Duke U., 1937-41, Ohio State U., 1942, N.Y.U., 1950. Served as pvt., U.S. Army, 1918. Received Lloyd traveling fellowship, 1930-31. Henry Russell award, 1931, Huntington Library fellowship, 1945-46. F. Royal Soc. of Lit. Mem. Modern Language Assn. Am., Charles Lamb Soc. (v.p.), Phi Beta Kappa, Phi Kappa Phi, Phi Delta Kappa, Kappa Delta Pi. Club: Cosmos. Author: Hartley Coleridge-His Life and Work, 1929; Thomas Clarkson, The Friend of Slaves, 1935. American, edit., 1938; Coleridge Fille, A Biography of Sara Coleridge, 1940. Editor: Unpublished Letters of Samuel Taylor Coleridge (2 vols.), 1932; The Best of Coleridge, 1934; Coleridge-Studies by Several Hands on the Hundredth Anniversary of His Death (with Edmund Blunden), 1934; Letters of Hartley Coleridge (with G.E. Griggs), 1937; Wordsworth and Coleridge, 1939; New Poems of Hartley Coleridge, 1942; Henry Christophe & Thomas Clarkson, 1952; Collected Letters of Samuel Taylor Coleridge, Vols I-VI, 1956-69. Contbr. to English and Am. jours. Home: 3323 Cliff Dr Santa Barbara CA 93105

GRIGGS, JAMES HENRY, univ. dean; b. New Monmouth, N.J., Oct. 21, 1912; s. James Edward and Deborah Ann (Roberts) G.; A.B., Harvard, 1932; M.A., Columbia Tchrs. Coll., 1933, Ed.D., 1940; m. Anne Elizabeth Cameron, Sept. 1, 1936; children—Carol Ann, Nancy Jane. High sch. tchr. Middletown (N.J.) Township High Sch., 1933-34; elementary sch. tchr., Des Moines, Ia., 1934-36; successively demonstration sch. tchr., asst. dir. demonstration sch., dean instrs., Nat. Coll. Edn., Evanston, Ill., 1936-48; dir. tchr. edn. Western Mich. U., Kalamazoo, 1948-56, dean Sch. Edn., 1956—. Pres. Coop. Ednl. Research Lab., Inc., 1967—. Mem. Mich. Adv. Commn. Tchr. Edn. and Certification, 1956—. Served to 2d lt. AUS, 1944-46. Mem. Nat., Mich. edn. assns., Phi Delta Kappa, Kappa Delta Pi. Baptist. Rotarian. Contbg. author: Curriculum Readers, 1937-38. Home: 2609 Bruce Dr Kalamazoo

GRIGGS, MARC MICHAEL, advt. exec.; b. Washington, Conn., Aug. 15, 1921; s. Robert Wadsworth and Anna Margaret (Michael) G.; grad. Hotchkiss Sch., 1940; B.A., Williams Coll., 1943; m. Kathleen Bulley, Oct. 9, 1948; children—Marc Michael, Amanda H., Kathleen W., Timothy W. With Batten, Barton, Durstine & Osborn, N.Y.C., 1946—, account exec., 1947-61, v.p., 1961—. Chmn. fund drive Greenwich chpt. of the A.R.C., 1957. Trustee Hotchkiss Sch.; chmn. Williams Coll. Alumni Fund, 1968—. Served as 1st lt. USMCR, 1943-46. Mem. Hotchkiss Sch. Alumni Assn. (pres. 1958-60). Clubs: Williams (gov. 1950—, pres. 1969—) (N.Y.C.); Field (Greenwich). Home: 159 Park Av Greenwich CT Office: 383 Madison Av New York City NY 10017

GRIGGS, ROBERT STEPHENSON, lawyer; b. Hartford, Conn., July 31, 1925; s. Edward Fry and Margaret (Stephenson) G.; grad. Loomis Inst., Windsor, Conn., 1940-43; B.S. in Bldg. Engring. and Constrn., Mass. Inst. Tech., 1949, B.S. in Civil Engring., 1949; J.D., U. Wash., 1952; m. Jessiemay Wilson, July 10, 1946; children—Linda Lucille, Susan Karen, Gayle Wilson, Charles Stephenson, Jean Anne. Admitted to N.Y. bar, also P.R. bar; asso. firm Cravath, Swaine & Moore, N.Y.C., 1952-54; partner firm McConnell, Valdes, Kelley & Sifre, and predecessor, San Juan, P.R., 1958—. Trustee Episcopal Theol. Sem. Caribbean, Carolina, P.R., 1959—; chancellor Episcopal Diocese P.R., 1963—. Served to 1st lt. AUS and USAAF, 1943-46. Mem. Colegio de Abogados de P.R., Am. Bar Assn., Assn. Bar City N.Y., Order of Coif, Tau Beta Pi. Episcopalian. Rotarian. Club: P.R. Bankers. Home: Carr Acueductor Km 15 1 Guaynabo PR Office: GPO Box 4225 San Juan PR 00936

GRIGGS, THOMAS NEWELL, lawyer; b. Bellevue, Pa., May 20, 1903; s. Thomas Campbell and Christine (Newell) G.; B.S., Carnegie Inst. Tech., 1924; J.D., U. Pitts., 1928; m. Anne Hathaway Kiskaddon, July 13, 1928; 1 dau., Eleanor Christine (Mrs. Francis B. Nimick, Jr.). Admitted to Pa. bar, 1928; partner Griggs, Moreland, Blair & Douglass, Pitts., since orgn. Pres., dir. Island Properties, Inc.; dir., mem. exec. com. G.C. Murphy Co.; dir. Washington Oil Co., Morgan & Lindsey, Inc., Terry Farris Stores, Inc., M & L Equipment Co., M & L Realty Co., Morris Stores Corp. Chmn. adv. com. U.S. Dist. Ct., Western Dist. of Pa. Recipient Alumni Award of Merit, Carnegie Inst. Tech. Mem. bd. govs. Amen Corner; mem. bd. dir. D. T. Watson Home for Crippled Children. Mem. Am. (mem. first bd. Jr. Bar Conf.), Allegheny Co. (pres., chmn. exec. com.), Pa. (gov.) bar assns., Am. Judiciary Soc., Am. Law Institute, Engineers Soc. of Western Penn., U. of Pitts. Sch. Law Alumni Assn. (past pres.), Phi Kappa Psi, Theta Tau, Delta Theta Phi. Clubs: Allegheny Country, Duquesne, Harvard-Yale-Princeton, Law, Tax (Pitts.), Edgeworth. Home: Spanish Tract Rd Edgeworth Borough Sewickley RD PA Office: Henry W Oliver Bldg Pitts 15222

GRIGNON, HENRI GEORGES, govt. ofcl.; b. Providence, Feb. 11, 1919; s. George O. and Pamela (Sauvageau) G.; B.Accounts, Hill Coll., Woonsocket, R.I., 1938; M.Comml. Sci., Columbus U., 1940; grad. Command and Gen. Staff Coll., Ft. Leavenworth; m. Elizabeth G. Barksdale, May 25, 1940; children—Robert G., Thomas A. With U.S. Govt., 1939—; asst. dir. Office Security, Dept. State, 1964—. Served with inf., AUS, World War II; ETO; lt. col. Res. Decorated Bronze Star with oak leaf cluster, Combat Inf. badge. Roman Cath. Home: 8814 Lewinsville Rd McLean VA 22101 Office: Dept of State Washington DC 20520

GRIGSBY, JOHN LAMBERT, educator; b. Kansas City, Mo., July 19, 1928; s. John Lambert and Dessie (Thornburgh) G.; A.A., Kansas City Jr. Coll., 1949; B.S. in Edn., U. Kan., 1951, M.A., 1955; diploma (French govt. fellow), U. Paris (France), 1955; Ph.D. (Harrison fellow, Fels fellow), U. Pa., 1960; m. Carol Marie Schatzel, June 30, 1956. Asst. prof. modern langs. U. Okla., 1960-62; asst. prof. French, U. Cal. at Berkeley, 1962-67; asso. prof. Romance langs., Washington U., St. Louis, 1967-69, chmn. dept., 1968-71, prof., 1969—. Served with USMC, 1946-48. Grantee Am. Philos. Soc., 1966. Mem. Internat. Arthurian Soc. (sec.-treas. Am. br. 1967—), Modern Lang. Assn. Am., Mediaeval Acad. Am., Societe de linguistique romane. Author: The Middle French Liber Fortunae, 1967; co-author: Joufroi de Poitiers, 1971. Asst. editor Romance Philology Quarterly. Contbr. articles, revs. medieval French lit. to profl. jours. Home: 531 E Dr St Louis MO 63130

GRIGSBY, JOHN LYNN, machinery and equipment co. exec.; b. Tulsa, Apr. 28, 1924; s. James Arnette and Lynette (Kimmons) G.; B.S. in Elec. Engring., U. Colo., 1949; M.S., Stanford, 1956, Ph.D., 1959; m. Virginia Ruth Eck, July 15, 1950; children—David A., Sharon L., Susan E., Gloria J. Radio operator FCC, Tex., Neb., 1942,43; engr. Gen. Elec. Co., Pittsfield, Mass., Syracuse, N.Y., 1949-52; research asso. Stanford, 1953-59; chief engr., v.p. applied tech. div. Itek Corp., Palo Alto, Cal., 1960-70, exec. v.p., 1970—. Served with USAAF, 1943-46. Mem. I.E.E.E. (sr.), Sigma Xi, Tau Beta Pi, Eta Kappa Nu, Sigma Tau. Research and devel. in active and passive electronic countermeasures systems. Home: 729 Viola Pl Los Altos CA 94022 Office: 3410 Hillview Av Palo Alto CA 94304

GRIKA, LARRY ARNOLD, musician; b. Chgo., Oct. 14, 1932; s. Samuel and Celia (Goldberg) G.; Mus.B., Chgo. Mus. Coll., 1954; Mus.M., Roosevelt U., 1955; postgrad. Cath. U., DePaul U.; m. Pearl Millman, Aug. 8, 1966; children—Marc Uriel, Lauren J., Deborah. Instr. music Lewis Coll., North Shore Acad. Arts, Rizzo Sch. Music, 1951-55; with Lyric Opera, Chgo., 1954, 55; instr. music history and violin Antioch (O.) Coll., 1959-62; 1st violinist Cin. Symphony Orch., 1962-64, Phila. Orch., 1964—; mem. Phila. Orch. com., 1967-68, 68-69. Served with AUS, 1956-59. Recipient Oliver Ditson award, 1953, 54. Home: 215 Philellena Rd Cherry Hill NJ 08034 Office: 230 S 15th St Philadelphia PA 19103

GRILE, LESTER LEROY, supt. schs.; b. Jay County, Ind., Oct. 8, 1917; s. Daniel F. and Luella (Rockwell) G.; A.B., Ind. U., 1939, M.A., 1948; LL.D., Taylor, Upland, Ind., 1964; m. Ella Glendening, Aug. 10, 1940; 1 dau., Lane I. Tchr., 1939-43, 47-48; elementary sch. prin., 1948-50, 52-53; jr. high sch. prin., 1953-55; adminstrv. asst. to supt. schs., Ft. Wayne, Ind., 1955-61, supt. schs., 1961—. Chmn. edn. div. Ft. Wayne United Fund; mem. bldg. com. for Ft. Wayne Fine Arts Center. Served to 1st lt. AUS, 1943-46, 50-52. Mem. N.E.A., Nat. Assn. Sch. Adminstrators, Ft. Wayne C. of C., Phi Delta Kappa. Methodist. Home: 6914 Hiltonia Dr Fort Wayne 46809 Office: 1230 S Clinton St Fort Wayne IN 46802

GRILICHES, ZVI, educator, economist; b. Kaunas, Lithuania, Sept. 12, 1930; came to U.S., 1951, naturalized, 1960; student Hebrew U., Jerusalem, 1950-51; B.S., U. Cal. at Berkeley, 1953, M.S., 1954; M.A., U. Chgo., 1955, Ph.D., 1957; m. Diane Asseo, Apr. 26, 1953; children—Eve, Marc. Asst. prof. econs. U. Chgo., 1956-59, asso. prof., 1960-64, prof., 1964-69; prof. Harvard U., 1969—; research asso. Nat. Bur. Econ. Research, 1959-60; vis. prof. Econometric Inst., Netherlands Sch. Econs., Rotterdam, 1963-64; vis. prof. Hebrew U., 1964; cons. Rand Corp., Brookings Instn., bd. govs. Fed. Res. System, Ford Found., NSF. Served with Israeli Army, 1948-49. Fellow Am. Acad. Arts and Scis., Econometric Soc., Am. Statis., A.A.A.S.; mem. Am. Econ. Assn. (J.B. Clark medal 1965), Am. Farm Econ. Assn. (award of merit 1958, 59, 60, 65), Royal Econ. Soc. Author articles in field. Am. editor: Rev. Econ. Studies. Co-editor: Econometrica. Home: 89 Dorset Waban MA 02168

GRILL, LAWRENCE J., housing co. exec.; b. Chgo., Nov. 5, 1936; s. Samuel S. and Evelyn (Wollack) G.; B.S. with honors, C.P.A., U. Ill., 1958; postgrad. U. Chgo., 1959-60; LL.B., Northwestern, 1963; m. Joan V. Krimston, Dec. 16, 1961; 1 son, Steven Eric. Audit and tax mgr. Arthur Anderson & Co., Chgo., 1959-60; admitted to Ill. bar, 1963; with firm Aaron, Aaron, Schimberg & Hess, Chgo., 1963-64, Gendel, Raskoff, Shapiro & Quittner, Los Angeles, 1964-66; sec., gen. counsel Traid Corp., Los Angeles, 1966-69; v.p., sec., corp. counsel Kaufman & Broad, Inc., Los Angeles, 1969—; dir. subsidiaries. Served with AUS, 1958-59. C.P.A., Ill. Home: 4622 Via Aquesta Tarzana CA 91356 Office: 10801 National Blvd Los Angeles CA 90064

GRILLO, JOANN, mezzo soprano; b. Bklyn., May 14, 1939; d. John D. and Lucile (DePierre) Grillo; student Hunter Coll., 1957-59, N.Y. Coll. Music, Am. Acad. Dramatic Arts; studied voice with Marinka Gurewich, Kathryn Long courses Met. Opera; m. Richard Kness, 1967; 1 son, John Richard. Appeared in Aida, Madame Butterfly, N.Y. City Opera, 1962; European debut in Werther at Gran Teatro Liceo, Barcelona, 1963; appeared with Paris Opera, Teatro San Carlo, Naples, Zurich Stadttheatre, Bellas Artes of Mexico City, 1963, Isreal Nat. Opera, Opera of Marseille, 1964, Frankfort Opera-Carmen, Amneris, Jocasta, 1967-68; debut with Met. Opera, N.Y.C., 1963, resident artist, 1963—; toured U.S. for Civic Concert Orgn., 1959, 1961; presented concerts in Europe, Latin Am. Roman Catholic. Home: 1550 75th St Brooklyn 10028 Office: Metropolitan Opera Assn New York City NY 10018

GRIMALDI, JOHN VINCENT, safety engr., educator; b. N.Y.C., Sept. 6, 1916; s. Ottavio V. and Ernestine H. (Lima) G.; B.S., N.Y.U., 1939, M.A., 1941, Ph.D., 1955; B. Chem. Engring., Poly. Inst. Bklyn., 1951; m. Joan Formichella, Jan. 28, 1942; childrenJacqueline Anne, John Gardner. Safety dir. Grumman Aircraft Engring. Corp., Bethpage, N.Y., 1941-44; research engr. Assn. Casualty and Surety Co.'s N.Y.C., 1945-46, dir. research and engring. div., 1946-56; cons. safety and plant protection Gen. Electric Co., 1956-61, health safety and plant protection, 1961-67; lectr. safety edn. N.Y.U., 1951-61, adj. asst. prof., 1961-64, adj. asso. prof., 1964- 67, prof., 1967—, dir. Center for Safety, 1967—. Chmn. govt. agys. steering com. President's Conf. Occupational Safety, 1948-5O; mem. Pres.' Com. Employment Handicapped, 1950—; bd. dirs. Nat. Safety Council, Greater N.Y. Safety Council; bus. research adv. com., also com. work industry statistics, Dept. Labor, 1951—. Commr. parks, Village of Bellerose, N.Y., 1959-60, trustee, 1970—. Mem. Bd. Standards Rev. Am. Nat. Standards Inst., U.S. Sec. Labor's Occupational Safety and Health Adv. Com. Health, Edn. and Welfare Occupational Safety and Health Study Sect. Recipient Arthur Williams Meml. Research fellow award Am. Mus. Safety, 1944-45, 54-55; certificate patriotic civilian service U.S. Army, 1958; Founders Day award N.Y.U., 1956. Fellow Am. Soc. Safety Engrs. (pres. 1961-62), Am. Inst. Chemists, Am. Soc. M.E. (chmn. exec. com. safety div. 1949-51); mem. Am. Chem. Soc., Am. Standards Assn., Nat. Fire Protection Assn. Episcopalian (mem. vestry). Author: The Physically Impaired-A Guide to Their Employment, 1945; Applying Systems Analysis Techniques in Safety Situations, 1968. Co- author: Ground Safety in Aviation Operations, 1951; Safety ManagementAccident Cost and Control, 1956, rev. edit., 1963. Contbg. editor: Production Handbook, 1969. Editorial bd. Jour. Safety Research Contbr. profl. jours. Home: 23 Commonwealth Blvd Bellerose NY 11426 Office: 15 Washington Mews Washington Sq New York City NY 10003

GRIMALDI, PRINCESS GRACE OF MONACO, (Grace Patricia Kelly); b. Phila., Nov. 12, 1929; d. John and Margaret (Majer) Kelly; student Raven Hall Acad., Phila., Stevens Sch., Phila., Am. Acad. Dramatic Arts, N.Y.C.; m. Rainier III, Prince of Monaco, Apr. 19, 1956; children—Caroline Louise Marguerite, Albert Alexander Louis Pierre, Stephanie Marie Elizabeth. Actress in plays, Old Acad. Players Theatre, Phila., 1939, Broadway play The Father, 1949; screen debut Fourteen Hours, 1951; films include: High Noon, Mogambo, Dial M for Murder, Rear Window, The Country Girl, Bridges at Toko-Ri, To Catch a Thief, The Swan, High Society. Recipient Acad. Award for role in Country Girl, 1954. Pres. Monegasque Red Cross; hon. pres. Girl Guides of Monaco, A.M.A.D.E.; chmn. organizing com. Centennial of Monte Carlo; hon. pres. Monaco-U.S.A. Assn.; pres. Princess Grace Monaco Found., Garden Club Monaco. Address: The Palace Principality of Monaco

GRIMES, BARTLETT TORREY, ins. co. exec.; b. Detroit, Jan. 19, 1930; s. Edwin Loomis and Bernice (Torrey) G.; B.B.A., U. Mich., 1951, M.B.A., 1952; m. Geraldine Smith Burke, June 6, 1953; children—Bartlett Torrey, Kelly Burke, Nancy Geraldine. Supr. statement analysis sect. credit dept. Nat. Bank Detroit, 1952-55; asst. to v.p. charge bank's investment portfolio Bank Cal., N.A., San Francisco, 1955-59; mgr. bond investment portfolio Fireman's Fund Am. Ins. Cos., 1959-60, asst. treas., mgr. bond investment portfolio, 1960- 63, treas., mgr. bond investment cash flow banking, 1963-67; v.p., treas. bond investments, cash flow Fund Am. Cos. and affiliates, 1967—. Dir. Intercontinental Reins. Co., Bermuda, Am. Express Investment Mgmt. Co., Am. Ins. Co., Fireman's Fund Ins. Co. of Tex. Finance com. Nat. Council Alcoholism, San Francisco. Mem. bd. adminstrn. Pub. Employees Retirement System of Cal. Served with AUS, 1952-54. Mem. Municipal Forum N.Y., San Francisco Bond Club, Security Analysts San Francisco, Financial Officers No. Cal. (chmn.), Beta Gamma Sigma, Zeta Psi. Republican. Club: Commonwealth of California. Home: 70 Woodbine Dr Mill Valley CA 94941 Office: 3333 California St San Francisco CA 94118

GRIMES, BURTON PIPER, psychiatrist, med. director; b. Lake Crystal, Minn., Nov. 13, 1909; s. Henry Burton and Mary Elizabeth (Piper) G.; student Macalester Coll., 1927-28; B.A., U. Minn., 1930, M.B., M.D., 1932; m. C. Ruth Bones, Nov. 14, 1936; 1 dau., Sarah Elizabeth. Intern, Mpls. Gen. Hosp., 1933-34, resident, 1934-35; gen. practice medicine, 1935-37; staff physician St. Peter (Minn.) State Hosp., 1937-40, asst. supt., 1946-48, supt., 1948- 63, med. dir., 1963-. Served with M.C., AUS, 1940-46; mem. Res. Fellow Am. Psychiat. Assn.; mem. A.M.A., Minn. Med. Assn., Nicollet LeSueur County Med. Soc., Assn. Med. Supts. Mental Hosps., Minn. Soc. Neurol. Scis., Res. Officers Assn. Mason (Shriner), Rotarian. Address: St Peter State Hospital St Peter MN 56082

GRIMES, DAVID CHARLES, savs. and loan assn. exec. b. Omaha, Apr. 15, 1925; s. George and Eva (Miller) G.; B.A., Yale, 1945, fellow Trumbull Coll., 1963; M.A., Cambridge (Eng.) U., 1950; m. Suzanne Olander, Dec. 30, 1949; childrenDavid E., Susan H., George F. With Wall St. Jour., 1950-51; with Republic Nat. Bank, Dallas, 1951-64, v.p., 1958-64; pres., dir. Brentwood Financial Corp., Los Angeles, 1964-66; pres., dir. Brentwood Savs. and Loan Assn., Los Angeles, 1964-, chmn. bd., 1966-; chmn. bd. Family Security Life Ins. Co., Los Angeles, 1966-; v.p., dir. First Brentwood Corp., Los Angeles, 1966-. Mem. Town Hall, Los Angeles, Founding friend Harvey Mudd Coll.; chmn. alumni bd. Yale. Served as aviator USNR, 1943-46. Club: Yale of So. Cal. (bd. dirs.). Home: 202 S Rockingham Av Los Angeles CA 90049 Office: 12001 San Vicente Blvd Los Angeles CA 90049

GRIMES, HENRY ALONZO, bassist; b. Phila., Nov. 3, 1935. Played with groups of Gerry Mulligan, Tony Scott, Sonny Rollins, Grimes, 1957-; appeared with Cecil Taylor, Perry Robinson, also others, worked with Mose Allison; made record Into the Hot. Address: 272 E 7th St New York City NY 10009*

GRIMES, J. FRANK, former assn. exec.; b. Chgo., Dec. 17, 1881; s. Joseph Lawrence and Mary Ann (Mapes) G.; ed. pub. schs.; m. Barbara C. Adam, Jan. 28, 1903 (dec. Mar. 1951); children—John Franklin, Donald Robert, Douglas Adam, Helen Margaret; m. 2d, Alice Curry Burton, June 1954. Began Marshall Field & Co., Chgo., in charge group of cash boys, 1896; became accountant Corbin & Sons Co., Chgo.; paymaster Armour & Co., Chgo.; accountant, dept. mgr. Tolerton & Warfield Co., wholesale grocers, Sioux City, Ia., 1906-13; sales mgr. Baker-Vawter Co., Benton Harbor, Mich., Chgo., 1913- 17; partner William W. Thompson & Co., C.P.A.'s, Chgo., 1917-33; founder, 1926, pres. Ind. Grocers Alliance (IGA) Am., 1926-52; pres. subsidiary distbg. cos. Wash., Cal., N.Y., Can.; pres. Marketing Specialists, Inc.; in 1952 ret. pres. Market Splty. Co. Food Products Co. Am., Neighbor Products Co., Chgo. Offset Printing Co.; dir. Progressive Wholesale Grocery Co., No. N.Y. Grocery Co., Western N.Y. Grocery Co. Bd. dirs. Nat. Vol. Group Inst. Former chmn. Ind. Food Distbrs. Council; pres. Gt. Lakes Found.; mem. Ill. State Food Marketing Com.; adv. com. surplus foods War Food Adminstrn.; food adv. com. OPA Mem. Chgo. Art Inst. (life), Chgo. Farmers. Clubs: Union League, Illinois Athletic, Westmoreland Country; Beach and Tennis (La Jolla, Cal.). Home: 1001 Center La Jolla CA 92037

GRIMES, JOHN R., banker; b. Chgo., Sept. 13, 1931; A.B., U. Chgo., 1952, J.D., 1955, M.B.A., 1961. With First Nat. Bank Chgo., 1958-, trust officer, 1963- 65, sec., 1965-69, v.p., sec., 1969—; admitted to Ill. bar. Mem. Am., Ill., Chgo. bar assns., Chgo. Estate Planning Council, Am. Soc. Corporate Secs. Home: 2112 B N Hudson Chicago IL 60614 Office: First National Bank Chicago IL 60670

GRIMES, STEPHEN HENRY, lawyer; b. Peoria, Ill., Nov. 17, 1927; s. Henry Holbrook and June (Kellar) G.; student Fla. So. Coll., 1946-47; B.S. in Bus. Adminstrn., U. Fla., 1951, LL.B., 1954; m. Mary Fay Fulghum, Dec. 29, 1951; childrenGay Diane, Mary June, Sue Anne, Sheri Lynn. Admitted to Fla. bar, 1954, since practiced in Bartow; partner firm Holland and Knight, 1956-. Dir. Fla. Nat. Bank, Bartow. Mem. adv. bd. Polk County Juvenile Ct., 1966-. Bd. dirs. Bartow Meml. Hosp., 1958-61, Bartow Library, 1968- -; trustee Polk Jr. Coll., Winter Haven, Fla., 1967-70, chmn., 1969-70. Served with USNR, 1951-53. Mem. Am., 10th Circuit (pres. 1965) bar assns., Fla. Bar, Bartow C. of C. (pres. 1964), Fedn. Ins. Counsel. Episcopalian (sr. warden 1964-65). Rotarian (pres. Bartow 1957-58, dist. gov. 1960-61). Club: Peace River Country (pres. 1966-67) (Bartow). Home: 1950 El Paso St E Bartow FL 33830 Office: 245 S Central Av Bartow FL 33830

GRIMES, TAMMY, actress, singer, comedienne; b. Lynn, Mass., Jan. 3O, 1936; d. Luther Nichols and Eola Willard (Niles) Grimes; grad. Beaver Country Day Sch., 1951: grad. with honors Stephens Jr. Coll., 1953; m. Christopher Plummer, Aug. 16, 1956 (div. 1960); 1 dau., Amanda Michael. Mem. staff Westport Playhouse, Conn., 1954; N.Y. debut in Neighborhood Playhouse, 1955; singer, actress Littlest Review, Off Broadway Phoenix Theatre, 1956; appeared Stratford (Ont.) Shakespeare Festival, 1958; performed Cambridge (Mass.) Drama Festival, in Shakespeare's Twelfth Night, summer 1959; role of Moll in Marc Blitzstein's opera, The Cradle Will Rock, N.Y.C. Center, 1960; role in Unsinkable Molly Brown, on Broadway, 1961-62, later on tour; TV performer NBC-TV on Omnibus, 1959, Hollywood Sings, 1960, series Hour of Great Mysteries, 1960; in Four Poster, CBS-TV, 1962; appeared in Broadway prodn. Rattle of A Simple Man, 1964, High Spirits, 1965-66; appeared in film Three Bites of the Apple, 1966. Recipient Comoedia Matinee Club award, 1961; Antoinette Perry award, 1960; Variety Drama Critics award, 1961, Tony award for Private Lives, 1970. Republican. Office: care Actors Equity Assn 226 W 47th St New York City NY 10036

GRIMES, WILLIAM ALEXANDER, lawyer; b. St. Louis, June 7, 1904; s. William Hearne and Isabelle (Seguenot) G.; A.B. magna cum laude, Harvard,1925, LL.B., 1928; m. Adela Lawrance Ax, Feb. 13, 1934. Admitted to Md. bar, 1929, since practiced in Balt.; mem. firm Ober, Grimes and Shriver, and predecessors, 1931-; asst. gen. counsel Fed. Alcohol Adminstrn., 1934; mem. adv. com. admiralty rules U.S. Supreme Ct., 1960—. Dir. Fingles Co., 1955—; asst. sec. F. and M. Schaefer Brewing Co., 1963-. Served to maj. AUS, 1942- 45. Recipient 1st prize for thesis Chgo. Trust Co., 1925. Mem. Am., Md. (chmn. com. fed. jud. appointments 1964-65, 67-68, bd. govs. 1968-69), Balt. bar assns., Maritime Law Assn. (exec. com. 1960-63), Phi Beta Kappa. Clubs: Rule Day, Round Table, Harvard, Baltimore Country, Elkridge, Center (Balt.). Author: Financing Automobile Sales on the Time Payment Plan, 1926; also sects. in books. Home: 8 St Martin's Rd Baltimore MD 21218 Office: Md Nat Bank Bldg Baltimore MD 21202

GRIMLEY, JAMES HENDERSON, Jr., baking co. exec.; b. Boston, Feb. 7, 1921; s. James Henderson and Emma (Dolan) G.; B.S., Fordham Coll., 1941; m. Lucille Mokros, Aug. 3, 1957; childrenEllen, Paul, Barbara, Joan. With Continental Baking Co., Rye, N.Y., 1941-, now comptroller. Home: 23 Blue Ridge Dr Stamford CT 06903 Office: PO Box 731 Halstead Av Rye NY 10580

GRIMM, CARL HUGO, composer, conductor, organist; b. Zanesville, O., Oct. 31, 1890; s. Carl William and Ida (Goetzinger) G.; ed. pub. schs. Cin.; studied piano, organ and theory with his father, composition with Edgar Stillmon-Kelley, and orchestration with Frank van der Stucken; largely self taught in composition and orchestration; hon. Mus.D., Cin. Cons. Music, 1930; m. Alberta Kumler, June 17, 1922; children—Carl Albert, Mary Carolyn. Organist and choir dir. Immanuel Reformed Ch., 1907-12, Mt. Auburn Bapt. Ch., 1912-24, Mt. Auburn Presbyn. Ch., 1924-27, Knox Presbyn. Ch., 1938-52, Reading Rd. Temple, 1910-22, Isaac M. Wise Temple (all, Cin.) 1922—; pvt. tchr. piano, organ, music theory, 1907-31; head composition dept., Cin. Cons. Music, 1931-52; condr., Cin. Cons. Music Symphony Orch., 1944-52. Awarded, $1,000 prize for orchestral work by Nat. Fedn. Music Clubs, 1927; $1,000 prize for choral and orchestral work by MacDowell Club N.Y., 1930. Mem. Phi Mu Alpha, Pi Kappa Lambda. Mason. Presbyn. Club: Torch. Served as sgt. U.S. Army, 1918. Compositions: (for orchestra) Erotic Poem (tone poem); Thanatopsis (tone poem); Abraham Lincoln (tone poem); 116th Psalm (tone poem); Five Pictures for Peter and Wendy (suite); overture, Pennsylvania, for State U.; Cantata for Whittier, 150th anniversary year; Scherzo Fantaisie for Piano and Orchestra; Montana (two impressions); Victory Overture; Symphony in F minor; Byzantine Suite (for small orchestra); (chamber music) String Quartet; Serenade for Wind Instruments; Four Stencils for Flute, Cello, Piano; Fantaisie for Two Clarinets, Cello, Piano; Sonata for Cello and Piano; Song of Songs (chorus and orchestra); Feast of Kol Folk (chorus and orchestra); Concertino for Trumpet and Orchestra; Christmas Concerto; Five Designs for Brass Ensemble; Variations on Mooz Zur for Chorus and Organ; also cantatas, anthems, services for synogogue, piano and organ pieces, etc. Orch. compositions have been played by Cin., Chgo., Rochester, Los Angeles, Indpls., Huntington, Dayton and Fed. symphony orchs., Cin. Cons. Orch., Jordon Conservatory Orch. (Indpls.), Cin. Civic and Cin. chamber orchs., Columbus, O., Sacramento and Schenectady orchs., Detroit Little Symphony, Ohio Sinfonietta; Communion Services for choir, organ and string orch.; Gothic mass for choir, organ, string and brass instruments. Home: 6746 Shawnee Run Rd Cincinnati OH 45243

GRIMM, DONALD E., corp. exec.; b. Charleston, W.Va., Feb. 23, 1930; s. George B. and Rhea (Byerly) G.; student Johns Hopkins, 1946-51; m. Ruth A. Hassink, Dec. 29, 1949; childrenBeverly, Patricia, Carol, Rebecca. Financial analyst Bur. of Budget, Office Sec. Def., 1951-62; budget dir. Grace Lines, Inc., N.Y.C., 1962-66, v.p., treas., 1966-68; v.p. W.R. Grace and Co., N.Y.C., 1968-. Office: 7 Hanover Sq New York City NY 10004

GRIMM, EDITH RAMBAR, dept. store exec.; b. Seneca Falls, N.Y., Jan. 17, 1908; d. Mitchel J. and Florence (Kutner) Rambar; Ph.B., U. Chgo., 1927; postgrad. U. Mich., 1927-28; m. Emery G. Grimm, Aug. 31, 1929 (dec. Mar. 19, 1959). Tchr. math. Detroit pub. schs., 1927-29; supr. personal shopping service Marshall Field and Co., Chgo., 1935; with Carson Pirie Scott and Co., Chgo., 1935—, asso. gen. mdsg. mgr., 1958-63, v.p., 1963—. Chmn. retail adv. bd. Bride's mag., 1946-48. Regional dir. Chgo. Fashion Group, 1949-50; mem. adv. council Tobé-Coburn Sch., 1965—. Chmn. gen. mdse. div. Chgo. Heart Fund, 1964. Recipient Victory award and citation for war bond sales, 1945; named one of ten outstanding women bus. and community leaders in Chgo., 1959. Mem. Home Fashions League, Am. Inst. Decorators (nat. jury mem. for design competition 1953, design awards jury 1964), U. Chgo. Alumni Assn. (exec. bd. and senate 1952-53, chmn. improved activities com. 1954), Fashion Group, Nat. Council Women U.S., Internat. Platform Assn. Club: Arts (Chgo.). Home: 900 N Michigan Av Chicago IL 60611

GRIMM, EDWARD ELIAS, banker, ret. naval officer; b. York, Pa., Dec. 1, 1910; s. Walter Elwood and Mary (Craumer) G.; B.S., U.S. Naval Acad., 1933; M.B.A., George Washington U., 1952; m. Ernestine Bernardin, June 1, 1936; children—Edward Anthony, Diana Michelle (Mrs. Robert Dean Brotherton). Commd. ensign U.S. Navy, 1934. advanced through grades to rear adm., 1964; comdg. officer in U.S.S. 1934, Repertus, 1949-51; assigned Office Chief Naval Operations, 1952-55, 60- 63; comdg. officer in U.S.S. Sierra, 1955-56; asst. dir. budget and reports Office Navy Comptroller, 1956-59; comdr. Destroyer Squadron 30, 1959-60, Destroyer Squadron 6, 1960; comdg. officer in U.S.S. Des Moines, 1960; comdr. Cruiser Destroyer Flotilla 6, 1963-64; dep. dir. operations Nat. Mil. Command Center, Joint Chiefs of Staff, 1964-65; dir. budget and reports Dept. Navy, 1965-68; comdr. Tng. Command, Pacific Fleet, San Diego, 1968-69; ret., 1969; asst. v.p. Wells Fargo Bank, San Diego, 1969-71, v.p., 1971—. Decorated Legion of Merit (2), Purple Heart; Korean Presdl. citation; Order Prince Henry the Navigator (Portugal). Mem. U.S. Naval Acad. Alumni Assn., Navy League, San Diego C. of C., World Affairs Council San Diego, S.-W. Naval Commandry, Rest and Aspiration Soc. Kiwanian. Clubs: Army-Navy Country (Arlington, Va.); Cuyamaca (San Diego); Uplifters. Home: 3440 Bangor Pl San Diego CA 92106 Office: Wells Fargo Bank San Diego Hdqrs 500 Broadway San Diego CA 92101

GRIMM, GOETZ, automobile importing co. exec.; b. Gotha, Germany, May 16, 1928; s. Otto R. and Elfriede (Schmidt) G.; grad. Gymnasium Ernestinum, Gotha, 1948; m. Ursula A. M. Schneider, Sept. 25, 1959; childrenAndrea, Kathrin. Apprentice, Voigtlaender and Sohn, Braunschweig, Germany, 1948-50; exec. position in financial field Volkswagenwerk AG, Wolfsburg, Germany, 1950- 59; sec. Volkswagen Am., Inc., Englewood Cliffs, N.J., 1959-70, v.p. finance and adminstrn., also sec., 1970—. Home: 15 Addison Terrace Old Tappan NJ 07675 Office: 818 Sylvan Av Englewood Cliffs NJ 07632

GRIMM, HAROLD JOHN, educator; b. Saginaw, Mich., Aug. 16, 1901; s. Henry Frederick and Ella Emelie (Lepien) G.; A.B., Capital U., 1924; grad. Evang. Luth. Theol. Sem., Columbus, O., 1927; M.A., Ohio State U., 1928, Ph.D., 1932; student U. Leipzig, 1929-30, U. Hamburg, summer 1930; Litt.D., Carthage Coll., 1965; m. Thelma Jayne Rickey, Aug. 31, 1931; 1 dau., Jane (Mrs. H.S. Minton). Instr. Capital U., 1925-29, asst. prof., 1930-33, asso. prof., 1933-36, prof., chmn. dept., 1936-37; asst. prof. history Ohio State U., 1937-42, asso. prof., 1942-47, prof., 1947- 54; prof. history 1958—, chmn. dept., 1958-66, regents' prof., 1968—. prof. history, chmn. dept. Ind. U., 1954-58; Fulbright teaching fellow U. Freiburg i. Br., 1954. Mem. bd. dirs., v.p. Found. for Reformation Research. Mem. bd. edn. Bexley pub. schs. Fellow Royal Soc. Arts (Gt. Britain), Royal Hist. Soc. (Gt. Britain); mem. Am. Hist. Assn., Am. Soc. Ch. History (past pres.), Am. Soc. Reformation Research (past pres.), Hansischer Geschichtsverein, Am. Assn. U. Profs., Phi Beta Kappa, Phi Alpha Theta (hon. life 1965). Lutheran. Rotarian. Club: Ohio State University Faculty. Author: Martin Luther as a Preacher, 1929; Western Civilization (with Tschan and Squires), 2 vols., 1942; The Reformation Era, 1954; Luther and Culture (with G.W. Forell and T. Hoelty Nickel), 1960. Editor: Luther's Works, Vol. 31, 1957. Am. editor Archiv fuer Reformationsqeschichte, 1949-62, editorial bd., 1962—. Contbr. articles profl. publs. Home: 76 N Stanwood Rd Columbus OH 43209

GRIMM, PETER, real estate exec.; b. N.Y.C., Jan. 12, 1886; s. Adam and Josephine (Henry) G.; B.S., Columbia, 1911; m. Harriet Lawrence, Feb. 11, 1922; children—Peter, Laurie. Real estate broker Stephen H. Tyng and Co., N.Y.C., 1911-20; owner real estate bus., 1920-29; pres., dir. William A. White and Sons, 1929-44, dir., chmn. bd., 1944; dir. various cos.; spl. asst. to sec. Treasury Dept., 1935-36; minister USOM to Italy. Pres., dir. Grand Central Art Galleries; pres. Sailors Snug Harbor, 1951, 52. Vice pres., trustee Citizen's Budget Com.; chmn. Mayor's Com. on Taxation, 1932-54; mem. N.Y.C. Plan Commn., 1934; mem. real estate adv. bd. War Dept., 1941; mem. race and housing commn. Fund for Republic, 1963-64; mem. Mayor's Fiscal Commn., 1963-64; chmn. Mayor's Com. for Gracie Mansion, 1963, pres. com., 1964-65. Exec. com. Nat. Inst. Social Scis., 1960-65; pres. N.Y.C. Baseball Fedn., 1963-65; chmn. Columbia Coll. Council, Netherland Am. Found.; dir., mem. exec. com. United Cerebral Palsy Assn.; trustee, chmn. real estate com. Presbyn. Hosp.; trustee N.Y. Zool. Soc.; bd. dirs. Nat. Book Com. Served from capt. to maj., A.S., U.S. Army, 1917-18. Decorated grand officer Order Cristobal Colon (Dominican Republic); comdr. Order Orange- Nassau (Netherlands); grand officer Order Merit Republic of Italy; Order of St. John of Jerusalem (Great Britain); recipient Columbia U. medal for social service, 1934, Alumni medal, 1954, Alexander Hamilton medal, 1965; Plaque for Distinguished Service, Municipal Art Soc. N.Y.C., 1965; citation for distinguished service Explorer's Club, 1965; Man of Year award Realty Found., 1965; Bi-annual award Fifth Av. Assn. N.Y., 1967. Fellow Royal Soc. Fine Arts London; mem. N.Y. State C. of C. (pres. 1946- 48), Am.-Italy Soc. (pres. 1958-65). Clubs: Rockefeller Center, University, Columbia University, Century, Pinnacle, Grolier, Explorers' (N.Y.C.); Long Island Country; Piping Rock (L.I.); Bohemian (San Francisco). Home: 104 E 68th St New York City NY 10021 Office: 51 E 42d St New York City NY 10017

GRIMM, REINHOLD, educator; b. Nuremberg, Germany, May 21, 1931; s. Eugen and Anna (Käser) G.; student U. Erlangen (Germany), 1951-52, Ph.D., 1956; student U. Colo., 1952-53; m. Anneliese Schmidt, Sept. 25, 1954; 1 dau., Ruth Sabine. Faculty German lit. U. Erlangen, 1957-61, U. Frankfurt (Germany), 1961-67; vis. prof. Columbia, also N.Y. U., spring 1967; Alexander Hohlfeld prof. German, U. Wis., 1967—. Recipient Förderungspreis der Stadt Nürnberg, 1964; Guggenheim fellow, 1969-70. Mem. Modern Lang. Assn., Am. Assn. Tchrs. German, Am. Assn. U. Profs. Author numerous books including: Strukfuren, 1963; Bertolt Brecht, 3d edit., 1971; Gottfried Beun, 2d edit., 1962. Editor books including: Deutsche Romantheorien, 2d edit., 1971; Deutsche Dramentheorien, 1971; co-editor, Basis, 1970—, Monatshefte, 1967—, German Studies, 1968—. Contbr. articles to profl. jours. Home: 3983 Plymouth Circle Madison WI 53705

GRIMM, WILBUR WINFIELD, educaor; b. Cleve., Dec. 3, 1906; s. William H. and Caroline (Buescher) G.; B.S., Coll. of Wooster, 1930; A.M., Miami U., Oxford, O., 1932; Ph.D., Ohio State U., 1937; m. Dorothy Martin, June 6, 1936; children—Judith Ann (Mrs. William W. Southwick), Thomas Martin, Richard Alan, Nancy Jean (Mrs. William N. Erickson). Prof. natural scis. Lincoln Meml. U., Harrogate, Tenn., 1935-41; prof. biology Bradley U., Peoria, Ill., 1941—, chmn. dept. biology, 1941-64, dean Peoria Coll., 1946-64, asso. dean Grad. Sch., 1964-65, dean, 1965—. Pres. Bradley U. Town and Gown Club, 1967-68; v.p. Vis. Nurses Assn., 1970. Mem. Ill. (past pres.), Peoria (past pres.) acads. sci., Ill. Assn. Jr. Colls. (past pres.), Sigma Xi, Phi Kappa Phi, Phi Eta Sigma, Phi Sigma, Sigma Alpha Epsilon. Republican. Presbyn. (elder). Rotarian. Home: 1021 N Glenwood St Peoria IL 61606

GRIMOND, JOSEPH, Brit. M.P.; b. St. Andrew, Scotland, July 29, 1913; s. Joseph Bowman and Helen Lydia (Richardson) G.; B.A. in Politics, Philosophy and Econs. with 1st class honours (Brackenbury scholar), Balliol Coll., Oxford U.; hon. D.C.L., LL.D.; m. Laura Miranda Bonham Carter, June 1938; children—John, Grizelda, Magnus. Dir. personnel European officer UNRRA, 1945-47; sec. Nat. Trust for Scotland, 1947-49; M.P. for Orkney and Shetland, 1950—; leader Liberal Party, 1956-67. Rector, Edinburgh (Scotland) U., 1960-63, Aberdeen U., 1969—; chancellor U. Kent, 1970—. Served to maj. Brit. Army, 1939-45. Author: the Liberal Future, 1959; The Liberal Challenge, 1963. Home: Old Manse of Firth Kirkwall Orkney Scotland Office: House of Commons London SW 1 England

GRIMSLEY, JAMES ALEXANDER, Jr., army officer; b. Florence, S.C., Nov. 14, 1921; s. James Alexander and Anne (Darby) G.; B.S., The Citadel, 1942; M.A., George Washington U., 1964; m. Jessie Lawson, Dec. 8, 1945; children—James Alexander III, Anne, William. Mgr., Peoples Gas Co., Florence, 1946-48; commd. 2d lt. U.S. Army, 1942, advanced through grades to brig. gen., 1970. Decorated Silver Star medal, Legion of Merit, Bronze Star medal, Purple Heart, Combat Inf. badge. Mem. Assn. U.S. Army, U.S. Armor Assn. Episcopalian. Home: 6758 Marshall St Fort Hood TX 76544 Office: Hdqrs 2d Armored Div Fort Hood TX 76544

GRIMSON, KEITH SANFORD, physician, educator; b. Munich, N.D., Apr. 21, 1910; s. Judge Gudmundur and Ina (Sanford) G.; B.A., U. N.D., 1930, B.S., 1931; M.D., U. Chgo., 1934; m. Ardyce Mozelle Johnson, Oct. 16, 1934; childrenRoger Connell, Baird Sanford, Keith Sanford. Intern, Presbyn. Hosp., Chgo., 1934; fellow, resident surgery U. Chgo., 1935-39, instr. dept. surgery, 1940- 42; Belgian Am. Ednl. Found. Research fellow with Prof. C. Heymans, Ghent, Belgium, 1939-40; asst. prof. surgery Duke U. Sch. Medicine, Durham, N.C., 1943- 48, prof., 1948-; prof. surgery Duke Hosp.; cons. A.M.A., U.S. Dept. Health, Edn. and Welfare, Am. Heart Assn., surg. and med. socs. Fellow A.C.S.; mem. Am., So. surg. assns., Am. Physiol. Soc., Am., So. socs. clin. research, Am. Heart Assn., Am. Soc. Pharmacology and Exptl. Therapeutics, Soc. U. Surgeons, Sigma Xi, Phi Delta Theta, Alpha Kappa Kappa. Presbyn. Asso. editor Ann. Revs. of Internal Medicine, 1952-, The Am. Surg. Jour., 1953-, Modern Medicine, 1955-. Contbr. profl. jours. Home: 3313 Devon Rd Hope Valley Durham NC 27707

GRINDEL, CARL WILLIAM, clergyman, educator; b. Staten Island, N.Y., Mar. 21, 1905; s. Gustav William and Catherine Elizabeth (Larkin) G.; grad. St. John's Prep. Sch., Bklyn., 1921; B.A., St. Joseph's Coll., Princeton, 1925; student St. Vincent's Sem., Phila., 1925-30; Ph.D., Collegio Angelico, Rome, Italy, 1932. Ordained priest Roman Cath. Ch., 1930; prof. philosophy St. Joseph's Coll., Princeton, N.J., 1932-35; prof. philosophy St. John's U., Jamacia, N.Y., 1935-48, grad. prof., 1948-, chmn. dept. philosophy, 1957-65. Del. Internat. Congress Medieval Philosophy, Louvain, Belgium,

1958, Internat. Congress Philosophy, 1958, 63, 68, Internat. Thomistic Congress, Rome, 1960, 65. Recipient award Freedom's Found., 1955. Mem. Am. Cath. Philos. Assn. (pres. 1961-62), Am. Acad. Polit. and Social Sci., Am. Philos. Assn., Metaphysics Soc. Am., Société Internationale pour l'Etude de la Philosophie Médievale. Editor, contbr. Concept of Freedom, 1955. Address: St John's U Jamacia NY 11432

GRINER, JOHN F., labor union ofcl.; b. Camilla, Ga., Aug. 7, 1907; s. Will and Dollier (Shiver) G.; LL.B., Columbus U., Washington; m. Claranell Nicholson, Nov. 27, 1936; childrenJohn F., Remer Will. With various railroads, 1925-36; adjudicator, liaison officer, labor relations officer U.S. Railroad Retirement Bd., 1936-62; nat. pres. Am. Fedn. Govt. Employees, 1962-. Mem. Order R.R. Telegraphers, Am. Train Dispatchers Assn.; hon. mem. Brotherhood R.R. Trainmen, R.R. Yardmasters Am., Brotherhood R.R. Signalmen. Democrat. Baptist. Mason (Shriner). Home: 10225 Kensington Pky Kensington MD 20795 Office: 400 1st St NW Washington DC 20001

GRINGS, WILLIAM (Washburn), educator; b. Superior, Wis., Mar. 19, 1918; s. William Wilker and Jessie (Washburn) G.; A.B., U. Dubuque, 1940; M.A., U. Ia., 1941, Ph.D., 1946; m. Hilda Balster, Aug. 27, 1942; children—Carol Ann, Janet Marie, Steven Frederick, Elaine Ethel. Asst. prof. psychology U. Denver, 1946-47; faculty U. So. Cal., Los Angeles, 1947—, prof. psychology, 1960—, chmn. dept., 1960-68. Cons. govt. mil. depts., also mem. assns. Served to 1st lt. USAAF, 1942-45. Fellow Am. Psychol. Assn., A.A.A.S.; mem. Psychometric Soc., Cal., Los Angeles County (pres. 1960-61 psychol. assns., Soc. Psychophysiol. Research (pres. 1967-68), Sigma Xi, Author: Laboratory Instrumentation in Psychology 1954. Contbr. research papers to profl. lit. Home: 7806 Cowan Av Los Angeles CA 90045

GRINKER, ROY RICHARD, Sr., psychiatrist, psychoanalyst; b. Chgo., Aug. 2, 1900; s. Julius and Minnie (Friend) G.; S.B., U. Chgo., 1919; M.D., Rush Med. Coll., 1921; m. Mildred Barman, July 24, 1924; 1 son, Roy Richard. Instr. neurology Northwestern U., 1925; instr. neurology U. Chgo., 1927-29, asst. prof., 1929-31, asso. prof., 1931-35, asso. prof. psychiatry, 1935-36, also chief psychiat. div., 1935-36; chmn. dept. neuropsychiatry, also dir. Inst. for Psychosomatic and Psychiat. Research and Tng., Michael Reese Hosp., Chgo., 1946—; clin. prof. psychiatry U. Ill., 1951-66; prof. psychiatry Pritzker Med. Sch., U. Chgo., 1969—. Served as student Army Tng. Corps, 1917; col. M.C., 1942- 45. Decorated Legion of Merit. Recipient Maj. Raymonds Longacre award for sci. contbn. to aviation medicine, 1955; Profl. Achievement award U. Chgo. Alumni Assn., 1969; Gold Medal award Soc. Biol. Psychiatry, 1970; Salmon medal N.Y. Acad. Medicine, 1970. Fellow A.A.A.S., N.Y. Acad. Scis., Am. Coll. Neuropharmacology; mem. Am. Psychopathology Assn., Acad. Psychoanalysis (pres. 1961), Am. Assn. Research in Nervous and Mental Diseases, Am. Assn. Neuropathologists, Am. Neurol. Assn., Am. Psychiat. Assn., Am. Psychoanalytic Soc., A.M.A. (editor-in-chief archives neurology, psychiatry 1956-59, archives of gen. psychiatry 1959- 69), Sigma Xi. Clubs: Standard, Ravisloe Country. Author: Neurology; Psychosomatic Research; The Borderline Syndrome, also numerous other sci. publs.; co-author: Men Under Stress; War Neuroses, Anxiety and Stress; The Phenomena of Depressions; Psychiatric Social Work. Editor: Mid-Century Psychiatry, Toward a Unified Theory of Human Behavior. Home: 910 N Lake Shore Dr Chicago IL 60611 Office: Michael Reese Hosp 29th and Ellis Av Chicago IL 60616

GRINKER, ROY RICHARD, Jr., psychiatrist; b. Chgo., Apr. 25, 1927; s. Roy Richard and Mildred (Barman) G.; Ph.B., U. Chgo., 1947; M.D., Harvard, 1952; postgrad. Chgo. Inst. Psychoanalysis, 1956-62; m. Florence Schwartz, Oct. 19, 1958; children—Jennifer, Roy Richard III. Intern, Mary Hitchcock Meml. Hosp., Hanover, N.H., 1952-53; resident Michael Reese Hosp. and Med. Center, Chgo., 1953-54, 55-56; resident U. Ill. Hosp., 1954-55; instr. neurology and psychiatry Northwestern U. Med. Sch., 1962-63; mem. faculty Inst. Psychoanalysis, 1966-. Served with USNR, 1945-46. Fellow Am. Psychiat. Assn.; mem. Am. Psychoanalytic Assn., A.M.A., Nu Sigma Nu. Contbr. profl. jours. Home: 237 E Delaware Pl Chicago IL 60611 Office: 664 N Michigan Av Chicago IL 60611

GRINNELL, ERNEST DOANE, Jr., r.r. ofcl.; b. Flint, Mich., Sept. 30, 1920; s. Ernest Doane and Ruth (Drum) G.; A.B., Dartmouth, 1942; LL.B., Washington U., St. Louis, 1948; m. Jean McMillan, May 19, 1945 (dec. Feb. 1971); children—Ernest Doane III, Margaret, Jeffrey; m. 2d, Christine E. Drew, Aug. 14, 1971. Admitted to Mo. bar, 1948; pvt. practice, St. Louis, 1948-51; mem. legal dept. St. L.-S.F. Ry., 1951-69, gen. counsel, v.p., 1961-69, v.p. traffic and indsl. devel., 1969—; v.p. traffic and indsl. devel. Frisco Transp. Co., Quanah Acme & Pacific R.R. Co., 1969—; gen. counsel Frisco Employees Hosp. Assn., 1961-67; dir. Clarkland, Inc., Clarkland Royalty, Inc., Frisco Transp. Co., 906 Olive Corp.; v.p., gen. counsel N.M. & Ariz. Land Co., 1961-69; counsel Tulsa Union Depot Co., 1961-69. Vice pres. Dartmouth Alumni Council, 1967-68. Served to capt. F.A., AUS, 1942-46. Decorated Purple Heart, Bronze Star medal. Mem. Am. Bar Assn., Bar Assn. St. Louis, Assn. ICC Practitioners, Nat. Freight Traffic Assn., Sigma Chi, Phi Delta Phi. Clubs: Traffic (N.Y.); St. Louis Traffic. Home: 722 Dominion Dr Frontenac MO 63131 Office: 906 Olive St St Louis MO 63101

GRINTER, LINTON E., engr., educator; b. Kansas City, Mo., Aug. 28, 1902; s. Linton Earl and Mary Mandeville (Masterson) G.; B.S., U. Kan., 1923, C.E., 1930; M.S., U. Ill., 1924, Ph.D. (Univ. fellow), 1926; LL.D., Ariz. State U., 1962; Sc. D. (hon.), U. Akron, 1969; m. Constance Louise Hall, Oct. 19, 1926; children—Mary Constance, Lawrence Edward. Part-time draftsman and engr., 1923-26; engr., designer Standard Oil Co. of Ind., Whiting, 1926-28; asso. prof. civil enging. Tex. A. and M. Coll., 1928-29, prof. structural enging., 1929-37; dean grad. div., dir. civil enging. Armour Inst. Tech., Chgo., 1937-39, v.p. and dean grad. div., 1939-40; v.p. and dean Grad. Sch., Ill. Inst. Tech., 1940-46, research prof., 1946-52; dean grad. sch. and dir. research U. Fla., Gainesville, 1952-69, exec. v.p., 1969—. Cons. War Manpower Commn., 1943; coordinator 6th Service Command of Army Specialized Tng. Program, 1943-44; cons. Ency. Brit. on tech. articles, 1944—; cons. to bd. control So. Regional Edn., 1950—, also mem. commn. on grad. studies; del. Internat. Tech. Congress, also Internat. Congress for Applied Mechanics, Paris, France, 1946, Internat. Congress Enging. Edn., Zurich, 1954; cons., chmn. Panel on Heavy Equipment, Research and Devel. Bd., Office Sec. of Def., 1949—; mem. bd. univ. reps. Argonne Nat. Lab. Recipient Lamme medal for enging. edn., 1958. Mem. Am. Soc. C.E. (chmn. exec. com. mechanics, 1950-51), Am. Soc. M.E., Western Soc. Engrs. (chmn. civic com. 1948-50, bd. dirs. 1950-52), Am. Concrete Inst., Internat. Assn. Bridge and Structural Engrs., Am. Soc. for Enging. Edn. (chmn. Ill.-Ind. sect. 1947-48, pres. 1953-54, chmn. com. evaluation of enging. edn., 1952-56), Engrs. Council for Profl. Devel. (pres. 1965-67), Sigma Xi (mem. exec. com. 1969—, chmn. nat. study tech. edn. 1970-71), Tau Beta Pi, Chi Epsilon, Gamma Alpha. Clubs: University, Armour Faculty, Beach and Tennis (pres. 1948) (Chgo). Author numerous books since 1936; co-author Engineering Preview, 1945; Numerical Methods of Analysis in Engineering, 1949; Engineering Mechanics, 1952; numerous papers and monographs. Home: 2256 NW 4th Pl Gainesville FL 32601 ☆

GRIP, CARL MANFRED, Jr., univ. dean; b. Rockford, Ill., May 21, 1921; s. Carl Manfred and Nora Elizabeth (Bostrum) G.; A.B., Beloit Coll., 1946; Ph.D., U. Chgo., 1956; children—Jeffrey Carl, Jeremy Alan, Timothy Harris. Research asst. U. Chgo., 1946, dir. univ. house system, 1950-54, asso. dir. community orgn. research project, 1953-54, lectr., 1954-56; asst. dean men U. Ill., 1947-50; dean men, asso. dept. psychiatry Temple U., 1956-66, clin. asst. prof. psychology, 1966-68; dean Coll. Liberal Arts, chmn. Met. Studies Center, prof. psychology Ill. Inst. Tech., Chgo., 1968—. Faculty Phila. Psychoanalytic Inst., 1956-66; lectr. weekly TV program The Adolescent, 1957-58. Dir. Fellowship House, 1958-68; commr. Phila. Fellowship Commn., 1963-68. Chmn. nat. adv. bd. Nat. Student's Assn. 1960-61. Mem. Am. Personnel and Guidance Assn., Nat. Assn. Student Personnel Adminstrs. (v.p. 1960-61), Am. Psychol. Assn., A.A.A.S., Am. Assn. for Higher Edn., Sigma Xi, Beta Theta Pi. Office: Ill Institute Technology Chicago IL 60616

GRIPPE, PETER, sculptor, printmaker, painter; b. Buffalo, Aug. 8, 1912; s. Leonardo and Josephine (Orlando) G.; student Albright Art Sch., Buffalo, 1923-25, Art Inst. Buffalo, 1929-35, Atelier 17, N.Y.C., 1944-47; m. Florence Berg, Apr. 21, 1940; 1 stepson, Ronald Roseman. Student tchr. sculpture Art Inst. Buffalo, 1934-35; instr. sculpture, drawing Fed. Arts Project, N.Y.C., 1939-42; instr. sculpture Black Mountain Coll., 1948; instr. drawing design Pratt Inst., 1949-50; instr. sculpture Smith Coll., 1951- 52; dir., instr. etching and engravings Atelier 17, 1951-53; now prof. fine arts Brandeis U. One-man show Orrefors Gallery, N.Y.C., 1942, Willard Gallery, N.Y.C., 1944, 45, 46, 48, Brandeis U., 1957, Paridot Gallery, 1957, 59, Nordness Gallery, N.Y.C., 1960, 63; group exhibitions Whitney Mus. Am. Art, Wildenstein Gallery, Library of Congress, Art Inst. Chgo., Bklyn. Mus., Worcester Art Mus., U. Chgo., Met. Mus. Art, Mus. Modern Art, Carnegie Inst. Borgenight Gallery, Pa. Acad. Fine Art, Stable Gallery, Addison Gallery Am. Art, numerous others; prints exhibited Achenbach Found. of Graphic Arts, San Francisco, Nat. Gallery Art, Washington, Boston Mus. Fine Arts, Balt. Mus. Art, Met. Mus. Art, Mus. Modern Art, others; rep. permanent collections Albright Art Gallery, Addison Gallery Am. Art, Library of Congress, N.Y. Pub. Library Print Collection, Tel Aviv Mus., Met. Mus. Art, Whitney Mus. Art, Mus. Modern Art, N.Y.C., Nat. Gallery, Washington, others. Recipient purchase prize Bklyn. Mus., 1947; prize for print Met. Mus. Art; Charles M. Lea award Print Club. Phila., 1953; 1st prize for sculpture Boston Arts Festival, 1955; sculpture award Nat. Council U.S. art, 1955, R.I. Arts Festival, 1961; Guggenheim fellow for sculpture, 1964-65; commn. to design medallion for ann. creative arts award Brandeis U., 1957, 7 1/2 ft. bronze figure for Theodore Shapiro Forum, 1963. Two sculpture murals Puerto Rican Information Center, N.Y.C., 1959. Club: Artists (N.Y.C.). Author: 21 Etchings and Poems. Address: 1190 Boyslton St Newton MA 02164

GRISANTI, EUGENE PHILIP, flavors and fragrances co. exec.; b. Buffalo, Oct. 24, 1929; s. Nicholas D. and Victoria (Pantera) G.; A.B. magna cum laude, Holy Cross Coll., 1951; LL.B., Boston U., 1953; LL.M., Harvard, 1954; m. Anne Couming, June 29, 1953; children—Marylee, Christopher, Eugene Paul. Admitted to Mass. bar, 1953, N.Y. bar, 1954; mem. firm Fulton, Walter & Halley, N.Y.C., 1954-60; gen. atty. Internat. Flavors & Fragrances Inc., N.Y.C., 1960-64, sec., gen. atty., 1964-70, v.p., sec., gen. atty., 1970—. Mem. Essential Oil Assn. U.S. (bd. dirs.), N.Y.C. Bar, Am. bar assns., Am. Soc. Corp. Secs., Flavor and Extract Mfrs. Assn. U.S. (bd. dirs.), Research Inst. for Fragrance Materials (sec.). Club: Larchmont Yacht. Home: 8 Oxford Rd Larchmont NY 10538 Office: 521 W 57th St New York City NY 10019

GRISCOM, W.E., savs. and loan assn. exec. Exec. v.p. Golden West Savs. and Loan Assn., Oakland Cal. Office: 1632 Franklin St Oakland CA 94612*

GRISDALE, JOHN THOMAS, architect; b. Mpls., Sept. 30, 1904; s. Charles and Frances (Orvis) G.; student U. Minn., 1924-26, U. Pa., 1928; m. Catherine J. Hanford, Jan. 31, 1931; 1 son, Hanford Gillespie. Partner Carroll, Grisdale & Van Alen, Phila., 1946—; works include bldgs. for U. Pa., Lincoln U., LaSalle Coll., Pa. Mil. Coll., Haverford Coll., office bldgs., govt. bldgs., NASA Bldg. (Washington), additions and parking facility Nat. Insts. Health (Bethesda, Md.), Fed. Aviation Agy. (Washington). Mem. com. Phila. Housing Assn., Citizens Council City Planning. Pres. Phila. Child Study Center, 1965-66. Fellow A.I.A.; mem. Phila. Art Alliance, Pa. Soc. Architects (past sec.). Club: Rittenhouse (Phila.). Home: 2 Browns Lane Radnor PA 19087 Office: 6 Penn Center Plaza Philadelphia PA 19103

GRISMER, RAYMOND LEONARD, educator, author; b. Schenectady, N.Y., Mar. 30, 1895; s. Charles Valentine and Luna M. (Leonard) G.; A.B., U. Vt., 1916; Rhodes Scholar, Oxford U., Eng., 1916-17; M.A., Ohio State U., 1922; Ph.D., U. Cal., 1930; m. Mildred Best, Aug. 20, 1919; children—Jean, Raymond, William. Tchr., Mercersburg Acad., Pa., 1917-18, The Hill Sch., Pottstown, Pa., 1919-20; instr. romance langs. Ohio State U., 1920-24; head modern lang. dept. Oklahoma City U., 1924-27 asso. Spanish, U. Cal., 1927-31; asst. prof. U. Minn., 1931-34, asso. prof. 1934-49, prof. romance langs, 1949- 66, prof. emeritus of Romance langs., 1966—. Mem. Am. Assn. Tchrs. Spanish, Modern Lang. Assn. Am., Phi Beta Kappa. Tau Kappa Epsilon. Author: Pageant of Spain (with D.K. Arjona), 1939; Reference Index to Twelve Thousand Spanish-American Authors, 1939; Sailing the Spanish Main, 1940; New Bibliography of the Literatures of Spain and Spanish America (with M.B. Grismer, J. Magraw; 7 vols.), 1941-46; A Brief Spanish Grammar for Beginners, 1942; Spanish Short Stories (with R.H. Olmsted), 1943; Buenos Vecinos, Buenos Amigos (with C.I. Arroyo), 1943; Short Spanish Review Grammar (with D.K. Arjona), 1943; Tales of Spanish America (with N.B. Adams), 1944; Influence of Plautus in Spain Before Lope de Vega, 1944; Easy Spanish-American Reader (with M.W. Molinos. E.D. Corbett), 1945; Elementary Spanish Conversations (with L.C. Keating) 1946; Cervantes: A Bibliography, Vol. I, 1946, Vol. II, 1963; Liberatadores y Defensores (with Roy and Margarita Mills), 1953; Bibliography of Lope de Vega, Vols. I and II, 1964-65; Bibliography of the Drama of Spain and Spanish America, Vols. I and II, 1967; and others. Contbr. articles jours. Home: South Pasadena FL 33707

GRISSINGER, JAMES ADAMS, educator; b. Bklyn., Oct. 5; s. James Leroy and Ethel (Adams) G.; B.S., Ohio State U., 1946, M.A., 1947, Ph.D., 1957; m. Jo Ann Smith, July 8, 1950; children-Lynnan, Beth. Grad. asst. Ohio State U., 1946-47; instr. Coll. Wooster (O.), 1949-50; asst. prof. Otterbein Coll., 1950-55, asso. prof., 1955-58, prof., 1958—, chmn. dept. speech and theatre, 1951—; cons. bus. and profl. speech. Mem. Westerville (O.) City Council, 1958- 70, chmn., 1968-70; presiding judge Westerville Election Precinct, 1960- 70. Served to 2d lt. USAF, 1943-46; PTO. Mem. Ohio Assn. Coll. Tchrs. Speech (pres. 1966), Pi Kappa Delta (recipient province distinguished service award 1968; nat. v.p. 1969), Sigma Alpha Epsilon. Clubs: Antique Auto Am. (regional v.p. 1970). Contbr. articles profl. jours. Home: 111 Central Av Westerville OH 43081

GRISSOM, DONALD BAUER, life ins. co. exec.; b. Judsonia, Ark., Mar. 12, 1919; s. Walter J. and Mayme (Bauer) G.; student U. Ark., 1946-47; m. Medora E. Beal, Dec. 27, 1945; children—Jane Elizabeth, Robin Bauer. Cashier, So. Nat. Ins. Co., Little Rock, Ark., 1936-46, dir., v.p., 1946-48; asst. to pres. Midwestern United Life Ins. Co., Fort Wayne, Ind., 1949-50, sec., 1950—, dir., 1952—, v.p., 1955-64, 1st v.p., 1964-70, exec. v.p., 1970—; dir., v.p. Am. Travelers Life Ins. Co., Indpls., 1960-61; dir., pres. Ill. Mid-Continent Life Ins. Co., Chgo., 1964-65; dir., v.p., treas. Transcontinental Motor Inns, Inc.; dir., sec., treas. Varied Industry Plan, Inc.; dir., pres. Exec. Mgmt. Corp.; dir., chmn. bd. Transcontinental Motor Hotels, Inc.; dir. Fund Distbrs. Inc. (Fort Wayne); dir. chmn. bd. Metro Linen, Inc., Dallas. Mem. com. investments and valuation of assets Assn. Ind. Legal Reserve Life Ins. Cos., 1970—. Mem. world services com. YMCA, 1962-70. Bd. dirs. Am. Cancer Soc. Served with AUS, 1942-45. Decorated Bronze Star. Conglist. (moderator, deacon, trustee). Clubs: Fort Wayne Country; Summit. Home: 3003 Kingsley Dr Fort Wayne IN 46805 Office: 7551 US Hwy 24 W Fort Wayne IN 46804

GRISSOM, PINKNEY, lawyer; b. Tippah County, Miss., July 7, 1897; s. James Henry and Charlotte Anna (Mathis) G.; student North Tex. State Coll., 1916-17; LL.B., Washington and Lee U., 1920; m. Karl Ruth Simmons, Jan. 1, 1921; children—Pinkney, John, David. Tchr. rural sch., 1917-18; admitted to Tex. bar, 1920; asso. Thompson, Knight, Wright & Simmons, Dallas, 1921- 34, a sr. partner, 1934-68, of counsel, 1968—; atty. specializing trial practice, 1921—; lectr. on malpractice, other medico-legal problems of physicians Research fellow, mem. medico-legal com., chmn. ins. div. (1957) Southwestern Legal Found. Fellow Am. Coll. Trial Lawyers, Internat. Acad. of Trial Lawyers, Am. Bar Found.; mem. Am. and Dallas (chmn. 1955) bar assns., Tex. State Bar, Internat. Assn Ins. Counsel. Fedn. Ins. Counsel, Order of Blue Goose Internat., Engr Club of Dallas, Phi Delta Phi, Phi Sigma Kappa. Mason (Shriner). Clubs: Dallas Exchange (pres. 1940), Dallas Athletic, Insurance (Dallas); DAC Country, The Carriage. Home: 4204 Stanhope St Dallas TX 75205 Office: Republic Nat Bank Bldg Dallas TX 75201

GRISSOM, ROBERT LESLIE, educator, physician; b. Decatur, Ill., Mar. 5, 1917; s. Leo L. and Ruth (English) G.; student Millikin U., 1934-37; B.S., M.S., M.D., U. Ill., 1937-41; m. Virginia B. Beal, Oct. 28, 1944; children—Nancy, Carol, Leslie, Timothy. Mem. faculty U. Ill. Coll. Medicine, Chgo., 1946-53, asst. prof., 1950-53; faculty U. Neb., Omaha, 1953—, prof. internal medicine, chmn. dept., 1956-70, prof., head div. cardiology, dept. internal medicine, 1970—. Markle scholar, 1950-56. Mem. Sigma Xi. Contbr. articles to tech. jours. Cardiovascular research. Home: 5521 Harney St Omaha NB 68132

GRIST, RERI, coloratura soprano; b. N.Y.C.; student High Sch. Music and Art, N.Y.C.; grad. Queens Coll. Appeared on Broadway in West Side Story, 1957; with Santa Fe Opera Co., 1959; debut, N.Y.C. Opera, 1959; appeared with Cologne (Germany) Opera as queen of the night in Magie Flute and starring role in The Nightingale; mem. Zurich (Switzerland) Opera Co.; other appearances in Europe include Corent Garden, La Scala, Vienna (Austria) State Opera also as Zerbinetta in Adriadne auf Naxos at Salzburg (Austria) Festival, Recipient Blanch Thebom award for voice, 1958. Address: care Met Opera Assn 147 W 39th St New York City NY 10018 *

GRISWOLD, ALEXANDER BROWN, investment banker; b. Balt., Apr. 19, 1907; s. Benjamin Howell, Jr., and Bessie M. (Brown) G.; A.B., Princeton, 1928; postgrad. Trinity Coll., Cambridge, Eng., 1929. Entered employ Alex Brown & Sons, Balt., 1930, mem. firm since 1931. Pres. Breezewood Found. Republican. Author: Dated Buddha Images of Northern Siam; other works on Oriental art epigraphy and history. Home: Breezewood Found Monkton MD 21111 also Krishnavana House 777 Bang Plat Tonburi Thailand Office: Breezewood Found Monkton MD 21111

GRISWOLD, ARTHUR STEWART, former utilities exec.; b. Rocky Hill, Conn., Sept. 22, 1898; s. William Francis and Margaret Adah (Williams) G.; M.E., Cornell U., 1922; m. Bessie Grace Moody, June 18, 1927. Instr. mech. enging. labs. Cornell U., 1920-22; with Detroit Edison Co., 1922-64, asst. to pres., 1952-57, v.p., 1957-64; v.p., gen. mgr. Power Reactor Devel. Co., 1964-68. Cons. ECA, 1948-52; staff officer war utilities WPB, 1941-45. Registered profl. engr., Mich. Mem. Edison Electric Inst. (chmn. elec. power survey com. 1954- 68), N.A.M (atomic energy com.), Atomic Indsl. Forum, Am. Soc. M.E., Nat. Dist. Heating Assn., Enging. Soc. Detroit. Clubs: Engineers (N.Y.C.); Detroit; Orchard Lake (Mich.) Country. Home: 5015 Pon Valley Bloomfield Hills MI 48013 Office: 1911 First St Detroit MI 48226

GRISWOLD, BENJAMIN HOWELL, III, banker; b. Balt., Oct. 29, 1911; s. B. Howell and Bessie M. (Brown) G.; student Gilman Country Sch., Balt., 1919-29; A.B., Princeton, 1933; m. Arabella Leith Symington, Oct. 8, 1936; children—Benjamin Howell IV, Jack S., Lelia Leith, Nancy Montague. With Alex, Brown & Sons, investment bankers. Baltimore, 1933—, partner, 1935—; dir. Black & Decker Mfg. Co., Olin Corp., Fidelity & Deposit Co. Md., Rouse Co. Trustee Good Samaritan Hosp., Johns Hopkins. Clubs: Maryland, Elkridge, Green Spring Valley Hunt, Elkridge-Harford Hunt (Balt.); Metropolitan (Washington); Links (N.Y.C.); Buck's (London). Home: Fancy Hill Monkton MD 21111 Office: 135 E Baltimore St MD 21202

GRISWOLD, BRUCE, lawyer; b. Cleveland Heights, O., 1916; A.B., Harvard, 1938; LL.B., Case Western Res. U., 1947. Admitted to Ohio bar, 1947; now mem. firm Calfee, Halter, Calfee, Griswold & Sommer, Cleve. Mem. Am., Ohio State, Cleve. bar assns., Phi Delta Phi, Phi Beta Kappa, Order of Coif. Office: Central Nat Bank Bldg Superior Av and E 9th St Cleveland OH 44114*

GRISWOLD, CLAYTON TRACY, clergyman, exec.; b. Elmira, N.Y., May 12, 1901; s. Tracy Beadle and Mary Lovina (Carrier) G.; A.B., Amherst Coll., 1923; student U. Paris, 1925-26; S.T.B., Biblical Sem. in N.Y. 1927; D.D. (hon.), Huron Coll., 1949; m. Miriam Rittenhouse Mayne, June 1, 1925; childrenDavid, Lincoln, Maud Mary, Katharine. Ordained to ministry Presbyn. Ch., 1927; asst. pastor, First Ch., Cortland, N.Y., 1927-30; pastor, Hobart, N.Y., 1930- 34, Watkins Glen, N.Y., 1934-39; sec. youth work Presbyn. Gen. Council, N.Y.C., 1939-48; exec. dir. radio and television Presbyn. Ch., U.S.A., 1948-58; exec. sec. Mayne Ednl. Fund, 1958-. Served as sergt., N.Y. N.G., 1918-19. Trustee Bibl. Sem. in N.Y., 1941-50, Mayne Ednl. Fund (Newark). Mem. gen. bd. Nat. Council Chs.; chmn. Broadcasting and Film Committee 1953-55; North Am. representative World Com. for Christian Broadcasting. Hon. life mem. Westminster Fellowship, 1948. Mem. Phi Delta Theta. Clubs: Lake Mohawk Golf, Sparta Chess. Author: The Youth Budget Plan, 1942; Youth Budget Program Guide, 1948; Religious Radio Expediters, 1949. Co-author: Broadcasting Religion, 1954. Home: 550 West Shore Trail Sparta NJ 07871

GRISWOLD, DONALD J., diversified industries exec.; b. 1919; student Miami U., Oxford, O., 1938-39, U. Cin., 1939-41; B.S., LL.B., U. Ore.; married. Admitted to Ore. bar; asst. atty. gen. State of Ore., 1951-57; partner firm Pattullo, Gleason, Griswold & Hinson,

Portland, 1958-67; sec., gen. counsel Omark Industries Inc., Portland, 1967—. Served with USMCR, 1941-45. Office: 2100 SE Milport Rd Portland OR 97222*

GRISWOLD, EDWARD MANSFIELD, educator; b. New Haven, Mar. 28, 1905; s. Edward Parmelee and Jennie (Mansfield) G.; B.S. in Engring., Carnegie Mellon U., 1927; M.S. in Edn., U. Pa., 1939; m. Catharine Andres Wescoe, Oct. 28, 1939; children—Mary Catharine (Mrs. William T. Cunningham, Jr.) (dec.), Edward Robert. Engr., Am. Foundry Equipment Co., Mishawaka, Ind., 1927-28, Metals Coating Co. Am., Phila., 1928-29, Weston Electric Instrument Co., Newark, 1929-30; tchr. Stonington (Conn.) High Sch., 1932-42; instr. Cooper Union Advancement Sci. and Art., N.Y.C., 1942-47, asst. prof., 1947-52, asso. prof., 1952-62, prof. mech. engring., 1962-71, prof. emeritus, 1971—, dir. NSF program 1959-62; cons. engr. Shades Inc., 1944-49, Byrne Assos., 1948-53, Kidde Mfg. Co., 1945, The Singer Co., 1963-69; vis. engr. Bell Telephone Labs., 1954-58. Dir. summer camp for disadvantaged children of N.Y., Cooper Union, N.Y. College Bound Corp., 1969. Registered profl. engr., N.J. Mem. Am. Soc. Engring. Edn. (Distinguished Service award engring. design graphics div. 1969, nat. chmn. 1961-62), Nat. Soc. Profl. Engrs., Am. Assn. U. Profs., Pi Tau Sigma. Presbyn. (elder). Home: 141 Washington Av Chatham NJ 07928 Office: Cooper Sq New York City NY 10003

GRISWOLD, ERNEST, educator; b. Milan, Kan., Aug. 13, 1905; s. Chester Ward and Mary (Fairbrother) G.; A.B., U. Kan., 1927, Ph.D., 1934; m. Marvel Silva Legg, June 6, 1931; children—Norman Ernest, Mary (Mrs. James Howard McMechan), Virginia (Mrs. Harold Wayland Fearing), William Chester, Catherine (Mrs. Henry Burt Person), Stephen Lawrence. Mem. faculty U. S.D., Vermillion, 1931-47, asso. prof. chemistry, 1939-45, prof., 1945-47; asso. prof. U. Kan., Lawrence, 1947-55, prof., 1955—. Mem. Am. Chem. Soc., Sigma Xi, Phi Beta Kappa, Alpha Chi Sigma. Methodist. Author: Chemical Bonding and Structure, 1968; (with others) Inorganic Chemistry, 1960; also articles. Home: 2217 Massachusetts St Lawrence KS 66044

GRISWOLD, ERWIN NATHANIEL, lawyer, govt. ofcl.; b. East Cleveland, O., July 14, 1904; s. James Harlen and Hope (Erwin) G.; A.B., A.M., Oberlin Coll., 1925; LL.B., Harvard, 1928, S.J.D., 1929; L.H.D., Tufts Coll., 1949, Case Inst. Tech., 1950; LL.D., U. B.C., 1949, Brown U., 1950, U. Sidney, U. Melbourne, 1951, Dalhousie U., 1952, Harvard, Amherst Coll., 1953, Columbia, U. Richmond, 1954, Brandeis U., 1956, U. Mich., 1959, Northwestern U., 1960, Notre Dame U., Allegheny Coll., 1961, U. Toronto, 1962, Williams Coll., 1966, Tulane U., Boston Coll., Princeton 1968; D.C.L., U. Western Ont., 1961, U. Toronto, 1962, U. Edinburgh, Georgetown U., 1963, Oxford U. 1964; D.Litt., Western Res. U., 1967; m. Harriet Allena Ford, Dec. 30, 1931; children—Hope Eleanor (Mrs. Daniel Murrow), William Erwin. Admitted to Ohio bar, 1929, Mass. bar, 1935; practiced with Griswold, Green, Palmer & Hadden, Cleve., 1929; atty. office solicitor gen., spl. asst. to atty. gen., Washington, 1929-34; asst. prof. law Harvard, 1934-35, prof., 1935-46, dean, Charles Stebbins Fairchild prof. law, 1946-50, dean, Langdell prof. law, 1950-67; solicitor gen. U.S., 1967—. Mem. Alien Enemy Hearing Bd. for Mass. 1941-45; cons. expert U.S. Treasury Dept., 1942; mem. U.S. Civil Rights Commn., 1961-67. Trustee Oberlin Coll., Bradford Jr. Coll., 1942-49, Tchrs. Ins. and Annuity Assn., 1942-46, Harvard Law Rev. Assn., 1938-67; bd. dirs. Am. Bar Found. Pres., Assn. Am. Law Schs., 1957-58. Fellow Am. Acad. Arts and Sci. (v.p. 1946-48); mem. Am. (ho. of dels. 1957—), Mass. bar assns., Am. Law Inst., Am. Philos. Soc., Phi Beta Kappa. Clubs: Harvard (N.Y.C.); Burning Tree, Cosmos (Washington); Century Assn. (N.Y.); Athenaeum (London); Charles River Country. Author: Spendthrift Trusts, 1936; 2d edit., 1947; Cases on Federal Taxation, 1940; 6th edit., 1966; Cases on Conflict of Laws (with others), 1941, rev. edit., 1964; The Fifth Amendment Today; Law and Lawyers in The United States. Home: 36 Kenmore Rd Belmont MA 02178 Office: Dept Justice Washington DC 20530

GRISWOLD, GORDON COX, pub. utility co. exec.; b. Denver, May 24, 1911; s. Robert Gray and Mary (Cox) G.; B.S. in Econs., Wharton Sch. of U. Pa., 1933; m. Emily Ryer, Mar. 2, 1931; childrenGordon C., John R., Alan R. With Bklyn. Union Gas Co., 1933-, v.p., treas., 1957-61, exec. v.p., 1961-68, pres., 1968-, also dir.; chmn. adv. bd. Chem. Bank N.Y. Trust Co.; trustee, mem. exec. comm. South Bklyn. Savs. Bank; dir. Utilities Mut. Ins. Co., pres., 1968-69. Cons. gas planning div. Petroleum Adminstrn. Def., 1951-52; Bklyn. utility chmn. United Hosp. Fund, 1957-61, gen. chmn. 1964, chmn. Bklyn. adv. bd., 1965—; mem. Scotch Plains (N.J.) Bd. Edn., 1941-47; chmn. budget com. United Fund, Westfield, N.J., 1961-62, 2d vp., 1962, pres. bd. trustees 1962, 63. Bd. dirs., pres. Downtown Bklyn. Assn.; bd. dirs. United Hosp. Fund N.Y. Mem. Soc. Gas Lighting, Am. Gas Assn. (dir; past chmn. com. econs, 1954-55; chmn. mng. com. gen. mgmt. sect. 1960-61; adv. council assn. 1962; conv. chmn. 1964; finance com. of bd, 1965-66, chmn. finance com. 1970-71), N.Y. Soc. of Security Analysts, Bklyn. C. of C., Inst. Gas Tech. (trustee), Newcomen Soc., S.R., Sigma Chi. Conglist. Clubs: Brooklyn; Broad Street (N.Y.C.); Echo Lake Country (Westfield). Home: 847 Shadowlawn Dr Westfield NJ 07090 Office: 195 Montague St Brooklyn NY 11201

GRISWOLD, JOHN ALFRED, educator; b. Cerro Gordo, Ill., Jan. 17, 1907; s. Earl A. and Harriet (Balch) G.; A.B., James Millikin U., 1929; A.M., Columbia, 1930, Ph.D., 1934; m. Ellen Melrose, June 9, 1936. Instr. econs. Butler U., 1930-32; asst. prof. econs. St. Louis U., 1934-37; asso. prof., prof. finance U. Okla., 1937-46; prof. finance Amos Tuck Sch., Dartmouth, 1946-; analyst Security Analysis Bur., St. Louis, 1936; econ. cons. New Eng. Tel. & Tel. Co., 1950-51. Served as maj. USA AF, 1942-46. Mem. Am. Econ. Assn., Am. Finance Assn. Conglist. Author: A History of the Federal Reserve Bank of Chicago, 1936; The Banking Situation (with H Parker Willis and others), 1937; Cash Flow Through a Business, 1955, The Capital Budget, 1956; (with Frank C. Pierson and others) The Education of American Business Men, 1959; Use of Funds in American Manufacturing, 1965. Home: Hopson Rd Norwich VT 05055 Office: Amos Tuck School Hanover NH 03755

GRISWOLD, JOHN CARROLL, bus. exec.; b. Decatur, Ill., Oct. 3, 1901; s. Harry Ross and Edna Cantrell (Graves) G.; student Millikin U., 1919-21, LL.D., 1964; spl. courses Chgo. Kent Coll. Law, 1921-23; m. Marguerite Bessire, July 22, 1922; children—Jacqueline Louise (Mrs. John V. Earls), David Ross. Clk., Continental Casualty Co., Chgo., 1922-25, resident v.p. in charge Chgo. office, 1931-36; with Rollins Burdick Hunter Co., 1925-31; dir., v.p. Fred S. James & Co., Chgo., 1936, mgr. N.Y.C. office, 1939- 45; founder, pres., dir. Griswold & Co., Inc., N.Y.C., 1945-62; exec. com., dir. Marsh & McLennan, Inc., 1962-69; v.p. W.R. Grace & Co., 1949- 55, dir., 1950—, exec. v.p., 1955-64; gen. partner Eastman Dillon, Union Securities & Co., 1964—; sr. v.p., dir., 1971—; dir. Metromedia, Inc., Marlennan Corp., Boothe Computer Corp., Safety First Shoes, Inc., Am. Standard, Inc., Alexander S. Onassis Corp., Mich. Gas Utilities Co., Victory Carriers. Turstee Athens (Greece) Coll., Millikin U. (Decatur). Postgrad. Inst. Osteo. Medicine and Surgery. Mem. U.S. Srs. Golf Assn., Sigma Alpha Epsilon, Phi Delta Phi. Presbyn. Clubs: Links, Wall Street, Brook (N.Y.C.); Chicago; Blind Brook (Portchester, N.Y.); Bohemian, Pacific-Union (San Francisco). Home: 655 Park Av New York City NY 10021 Office: 1 Chase Manhattan Pl New York City NY 10005

GRISWOLD, JOHN SLOANE, indsl. designer; b. Lenox, Mass., July 26, 1914; s. William E.S. and Evelyn (Sloane) G.; grad. Hotchkiss Sch., 1933; B.A., Yale, 1937; student bus. sch., Harvard, 1937-38; m. Anna L. Greenway, June 25, 1938; childrenSusan, Ursula, John S., Evan, Edward Charles. Furniture buyer W. & J. Sloane, 1938 41, v.p., treas., 1949-51, dir. until 1954; with U.S. Maritime Commn. under Sloane contract, 1941-45; v.p. Co. of Master Craftsmen, 1945-51; owner John S. Griswold Assos., N.Y.C., 1950-55; mem. firm Griswold, Heckel & Keiser Assos., Inc., N.Y.C., 1955-65; pres. Exhbn. Services Internat., 1965-69; pres. Plant-Griswold Assos., 1969—. Dir., mem. exec. com. Boys Clubs Am., Inc.; trustee, pres. Children's Aid Soc. Trustee Pomfret Sch., Internat. Coll., Beirut. Home: Meads Point Greenwich CT 06830 Office: 355 Lexington Av New York City NY 10017

GRISWOLD, RALPH ESTY, landscape architect; b. Warren, O., Aug. 22, 1894; s. William Tudor and Mabel (Hull) G.; B.S., Cornell U., 1916, M. Landscape, Design, 1917; student Am. Art Tng. Center, Paris, 1919, Am. Acad., Rome, 1920-23; m. Dorothy Elizabeth Griffith, July 14, 1920; 1 dau., Romola (Mrs. Gordon Brady). Landscape architect A.D. Taylor, Cleve., 1923-27, Nicolet & Griswold, Pitts., 1927-30; pvt. practice, Pitts., 1930—; now partner Griswold, Winters and Swain; commissions include Longue Vue, Fox Chapel, Rolling Rock Country Club, Buhl Found., Chatham Village Housing, Aluminum Co. Am. Lab., Cyrus McCormick, Lessing Rosenwald, Mrs. Max Ascoli, Edgar Kaufman; cons. Pitts. Housing Authority; supt. Bur. Parks, Pitts., 1934-45; cons. Fed. Housing Authority, U. Pitts., Westminster Coll., Ga. Warm Springs Found., Pa. Coll. for Women, R.B. Mellon Estate, Jones Laughlin Steel Corp., also several municipalities and schs. on landscape, recreation improvements; resident landscape architect Am. Acad., Rome, 1949-50; landscape architect Am. Mil. Cemetery, Anzio, Italy; architect landscape restoration Athenian Agora, Am. Sch. Classical Studies, Athens, Greece; research fellow in landscape architecture of Dumbarton Oaks Research Library and Collection; hist. research for Williamsburg on 18th Century gardens. Dir. Pa. Parks Assn., Western Pa. Conservancy; mem. sponsoring com. Allegheny Conf. on Community Devel. Served as 1st lt., engrs., camouflage, A.E.F., 1917-19. Recipient Sarah Gildersleeve Fife award Garden Club Am., also Gold medal of Honor; Gold Cross of Royal Order of George I, Paul King of Hellenes. Fellow Am. Soc. Landscape Architects; mem. A.I.A. (hon.), Nat. Acad. Design (asso.). Clubs: Pittsburgh Architectural (pres. 1930-31), Longue Vue; Century Assn. (N.Y.C.); Cosmos (Washington). Contbr. Garden Dictionary, Historic Architecture of Western Pa., also to tech. and popular mags. Home: Indian Aprings Apt Indian Springs Rd Williamsburg VA 23185 Office: Williamsburg Nat Bank Bldg Williamsburg VA 23185

GRISWOLD, RETTIG ARNOLD, surgeon; b. Peru, Ind., Apr. 17, 1898; s. Edward Harvey and Georgine (Rettig) G.; A.B., Harvard Coll., 1921; M.D., U. Louisville, 1925; m. Bonita Bligh, Aug. 8, 1923; children—Rettig Arnold, Bonita, Georgine, Annalee. Grad. tng. in pathology Louisville City Hosp. and U. Louisville, 1925-27; grad. tng. in surgery Western Res. U. and Lakeside Hosp., Cleve., 1927-32; asso. prof. surgery U. Louisville Med. Sch., 1932-37, prof. and head dept. surgery, 1938-52, prof. surgery, 1952—. Cons. surgeon St. Joseph Infirmary, Ky. Bapt., Meth. and Evang., St. Anthony hosps., Kosair Crippled Children Hosp., John W. Norton Meml. Infirmary. Served as lt. j.g., Flying Corps USN, 1917-21; naval aviator, overseas service, 10 mos.; served to col., M.C., AUS, 1942-44; cons. in surgery 4th Service Command; chief Surg. Service Walter Reed Gen. Hosp., Washington, 1943. Decorated Legion of Merit (U.S.); Mil. Order of Ayacucha (Peru); recipient Citation Navy Dept.; Surgeon's award for distinguished service to safety Nat. Safety Council, 1963. Fellow A.C.S. (2d v.p. 1957-58), Am., Central surg. assns., mem. Societe Internationale de Chirurgie, Am. Assn. for Surgery of Trauma (founder; pres. 1951-52), Am. Bd. Surgery (founders' group), Soc. Surgery Alimentary Tract (a founder), Southeastern Surg. Congress (1st v.p. 1963-64), Western, So. surg. assns., A.M.A., So. Med. Assn. Alpha Kappa Kappa, Alpha Omega Alpha. Republican. Episcopalian. Club: Pendennis. Home: 27 Stone Bridge Rd Louisville KY 40207 Office: Med Towers South Louisville KY 40202

GRIZZARD, GEORGE, actor; b Roanoke Rapids, N.C., Apr. 1, 1928; s. George Cooper and Mary Winifred (Albritton) G.; B.A., U. N.C., 1949. Appeared at Arena Stage, Washington, 1950, 52-54; Broadway appearances include The Desperate Hours, 1955, The Happiest Millionaire, 1956-57, The Disenchanted, 1958- 59, Face of a Hero, 1960, Big Fish, Little Fish, 1961, Mary, Mary, 1962, Who's Afraid of Virginia Woolf?, 1962, The Glass Menagerie, 1965, You Know I Can't Hear You When the Water's Running, 1967; The Gingham Dog, 1969, Inquest, 1970; also appeared with Assn. Producing Artists, N.Y.C., 1961-62, Tyrone Guthrie Theatre, Mpls., 1963-65; film appearances include From The Terrace, 1960, Advise and Consent, 1961, Warning Shot 1967, Happy Birthday, Wanda June, 1971. Mem. Kappa Alpha. Club: Players. Home: New Preston CT 06777 Office: care Becker & London 15 Columbus Circle New York City NY 10023

GROBEN, ROBERT, lawyer; b. Buffalo, N.Y., Oct. 8, 1909; s. Arthur and Thekla (Rodenbach) G.; A.B., Cornell U., 1931, LL.B., 1934; m. Jane Beattie, May 1, 1936; children—Robert B., William B. Admitted to N.Y. bar, 1934; asso. firm Ferris, Hughes, Dorrance & Goben, Utica, N.Y., 1937-45, mem. firm, 1945—. Dir. Homestead Savs. & Loan Assn. of Utica, Hurd Shoe Co., Oreco of Utica, Inc., Central N.Y. Abstract Co., First Utica Corp., Mohawk Data Sciences Corp., Divine Bros. Co., Munson Mill Machinery Co. Mem. N.Y. State Senate, 1947-48. Bd. dirs. Children's Hosp. and Rehabilitation Center of Utica; bd. dirs. Utica Boys Club Inc. Served with USNR, 1942-45. Mem. Am., N.Y. State, Oneida County bar assns. Mason. Clubs: Fort Schuyler, Sadaquada Golf, Longboat Key Golf. Home: 6 Prospect St Utica NY 13501 Office: First Nat Bank Bldg Utica NY 13503

GROBMAN, ARNOLD BRAMS, coll. dean; b. Newark, Apr. 28, 1918; s. Samuel H. and Sophia (Brams) G.; B.S., U. Mich., 1939; M.S., U. Rochester, 1941, Ph.D., 1943; m. Hulda Gross, Feb. 20, 1944; childrenMarc Ross, Beth Allison. Instr. zoology U. Rochester, 1943-44; research asso. Manhattan project, 1944- 46; mem. faculty U. Fla., 1946-59, dir. Fla. State Mus., 1952-59; dir. biol. scis. curriculum study U. Colo., 1959-65; dean Coll. Arts and Scis., prof. zoology Rutgers U., New Brunswick, N.J., 1965-67, dean Rutgers Coll., prof. zoology, 1967-; cons. to govt., industry, founds. and ednl. instns., 1954-. Mem. Acad. Zoology in India (council 1961-64, exec. com. 1967- 69), A.A.A.S. (council 1961-65), Am. Assn. Museums (chmn. coll. and univ. mus. sect. 1958, mus. tng. com. 1960-63), Am. Ednl. Research Assn., Am. Inst. Biol. Scis. (gov. bd. 1950-61, chmn. Gainesville meeting 1954, exec. com. 1958-61), Am. Soc. Ichthyologists and Herpetologists (bd. govs. 1964—, sec. 1952-57, pres. 1964), Am. Soc. Naturalists, Am. Soc. Zoologists, Assn. Am. Med. Colls., Assn. Higher Edn., Assn. Southeastern Biologists, Assn. Supervision and Curriculum Devel., Asian Assn. Biol. Edn., Biol. Scis. Curriculum Study (chmn. steering com. 1965—), Biol. Soc. China, Biol. Soc. Washington, Colo., Nat. edn. assns., Colo.-Wyo. Acad. Sci., Am. Assn. U. Profs., Fla. Acad. Sci., Fla. Found. Future Scientists (chmn. 1957-59), Genetics Soc. Am., Herpetologists League, Philippine Assn. Sci. Tchrs., Nat. Assn. Biology Tchrs. (pres. 1966), Nat. Assn. Research Sci. Teaching, Nat. Sci. Tchrs. Assn., Nature Conservancy, Newcomen Soc., N.J. Acad. Scis., Sci. Soc. Thailand, Soc. Study Evolution, Soc. Systematic Zoology, Soc. Vertebrate Paleontology, Southeastern Museums Conf. (pres. 1955-57), Assn. Tropical Biology, Sigma Xi, Phi Sigma, Alpha Epsilon Delta. Mem. div. biology and agr. NRC-Nat. Acad. Scis., 1954-58, com. adult edn., 1956-58; sec. U.S. nat. com. Internat. Union Biol. Scis., 1966-69. Recipient Fred H. Stoye prize Am. Soc. Ichthyologists and Herpetologists, 1941; A Cressy Morrison prize N.Y. Acad. Scis., 1943; Macalaster award Nat. Assn. Biology Tchrs., 1966. Author: (with others) Island Life: A Study of the Land Vertebrates of Eastern Lake Michigan, 1948; Our Atomic Heritage, 1951; (with others) Genetics Effects of Chronic X-irratiation Exposure in Mice 1960; (with others), BSCS Biology Implementation in the Schools, 1964; The Changing Classroom, 1969. Editor: Social Implications of Biological Education, 1970. Office: Rutgers U New Brunswick NJ 08902

GROBSTEIN, CLIFFORD, educator; b. N.Y.C., July 20, 1916; s. Aaron Joshua and Birdie (Yurdin) G.; B.S., Coll. City N.Y., 1936; M.A., U. Cal. at Los Angeles, 1938, Ph.D., 1940; m. Rose Gruver, Aug. 6, 1938; childrenPaul, Joan; m. Ruth Hirsch Beloff, June 12, 1966. Instr. zoology Ore. State Coll., 1940- 43; sr. research fellow USPHS, 1946-47; biologist Nat. Cancer Inst., 1947-57; prof. biology Stanford, 1957-65, exec. head dept. biol. scis., 1963-65; chmn. dept. biology U. Cal. at San Diego, 1965—. now dean Sch. Medicine, vice chancellor health scis. Cons. NSF, NIH, Am. Cancer Soc. Served to capt. USAAF, 1943-46. Recipient Brachet award Royal Acad. Scis. Belgium, 1959. Fellow Am. Acad. Arts and Scis.; mem. Am. Soc. Zoologists (past pres.), Am. Soc. Cell Biologists, Internat. Inst. Embryology, Soc. Study Devel. and Growth (past pres.), Nat. Acad. Scis. Home: 2651 Greentree Lane La Jolla CA 92037

GRODEN, JOHN FRANCIS, lawyer; b. Watertown, Mass., Mar. 16, 1908; s. Michael F. and Flavia D. (Grady) G.; A.B., Boston Coll., 1930; LL.B., Harvard, 1933; m. Helen Mead Wires, Aug. 12, 1940; childrenSarah, Helen, Frances, Edith, John Frances. Admitted to Mass. bar, 1933, since practiced in Boston; partner firm Withington, Cross, Park & Groden, 1947-. Sec.-treas. U.S. Figure Skating Assn., 1961-67. Served to comdr. USNR, World War II. Decorated Sec. Navy Spl. Commendation. Fellow Am. Coll. Trial Lawyers; mem. Am., Boston, Cambridge bar assns., Boston Coll. Alumni Assn. (treas. 1958- 59), Mass. Arms Collectors, Company Mil. Collectors. Clubs: Wardroom, Varsity, Skating, Harvard (Boston); Cohasset (Mass.) Yacht. Home: 12 Summit Rd Lexington MA 02173 Office: 73 Tremont St Boston MA 02108

GRODINS, FRED SHERMAN, educator, physiologist; b. Chgo., Nov. 18, 1915; s. Abe E. and Minnie (Levine) G.; B.S., Northwestern U., 1937, M.S., 1940, M.D., 1942, Ph.D., 1944; m. Sylvia Johnson, Mar. 28, 1942. Instr., Northwestern U., 1942- 44, asso. prof., 1947-50, prof. physiology, 1950-67; asst. prof. U. Ill., 1946, asso. prof., 1947; prof. elec. engring. and physiology U. So. Cal., 1967—. Mem. physiology tng. com. NIH, 1964-68, biomed. engring. tng. com., 1968—; cons. Rand Corp., 1964—. Served to capt. USAAF, 1944-46. Mem. Am. Physiol. Soc., Biomed. Engring. Soc., Soc. Exptl. Biology and Medicine, A.A.A.S., Sigma Xi, Phi Beta Kappa, Alpha Omega Alpha, Phi Lambda Upsilon. Author: Control Theory and Biological Systems, 1963. Research in physiology, biomed. engring. Home: 26 Chuckwagon Rd Rolling Hills CA 90274 Office: Univ So California Los Angeles CA 90007

GRODZINS, LEE, educator, physicist; b. Lowell, Mass., July 10, 1921; s. David Melvin and Taube (Bialoblotsky) G.; B.S., U. N.H., 1946; M.S., Union Coll., 1948; Ph.D., Purdue U., 1954; m. Lulu F. Anderson, Dec. 16, 1956; children—Dean David, Henry Jacob. Research asst. Gen. Electric Research Lab., 1946-48; instr. Purdue U., 1954-55; with Brookhaven Nat. Lab., 1955-59; faculty Mass. Inst. Tech., Cambridge, 1959—, prof. physics, 1966—; cons. USN, industry. Guggenheim fellow, 1964-65, 71-72. Fellow Am. Phys. Soc. Research, publs. on symmetry properties, particularly parity non-conservation and nuclear spectroscopy, particularly electromagnetic moments of excited nuclear states. Home: 14 Stratham Rd Lexington MA 02173 Office: Dept Physics Mass Inst Tech Cambridge MA 02139

GROEL, FREDERICK HENRY, lawyer, ins. exec.; b. Newark, Jan. 15, 1899; s. Charles and Augusta N. (Schiener) G.; A.B., Princeton, 1921; LL. B., Harvard, 1924; m. Audrey Berdine, June 21, 1929; childrenMarjory Eve (Mrs. James S. Ward), Berdine. Admitted to N.J. bar, 1924, practiced in Newark, 1924-40; asst. corp. counsel City Newark, 1927-33; with Prudential Ins. Co. of Am., 1940-65, v.p., sec., 1948-61, exec. v.p., 1961-65; asso. prof. Rutgers U., 1926-38; dir., chmn. trust com. 1st Nat. State Bank of N.J.; dir. Triangle Industries Inc. Mem. N.J. Legislature, 1926-27. Mem. bd. United Hosps. (Newark), Newark Mus., N.J. State Safety Council, N.J. Econ. Devel. Council; mem. N.J. Tercentenary Commn.; pres., mem. Newark Indsl. Devel. Corp.; pres. Newark 300 Anniversary Com. Served as seaman USN, World War I. Mem. Am., N.J., Essex County bar assns., N.J. C. of C. (pres.), N.J. Hist. Soc. (mem. bd.). Republican. Clubs: Princeton, Essex (Newark); Advertising (mem. bd.), Harvard (N.Y.); Short Hills, Baltusrol Golf; Bay Head Yacht. Home: 10 Joanna Way Short Hills NJ 07078 Office: 550 Broad St Newark NJ 07102

GROESCHEL, AUGUST HERMAN, hosp. adminstr., physician; b. Jersey City, May 31, 1908; s. August Herman and Margaret (Murphy) G.; A.B., Holy Cross Coll., 1927; M.D., Columbia, 1931, M.S., 1947; m. Mary T. Molloy, Feb. 21, 1933 (dec. 1945); children—Peter, Moya, Noel; m. 2d, Eileen D. Bosquett, Jan. 3, 1946; children—Margaret, Catherine. Intern French Hosp., N.Y.C., 1931-33, N.Y. Nursery and Child's Hosp., 1933-34; pvt. practice, Sussex, N.J., 1934-40; asst. med. dir. Health Ins. Plan Greater N.Y., 1947-48; asst. dir. N.Y. Hosp., 1948-52, asso. dir., 1954-66, adminstr., 1967-69; exec. dir. Phila. Gen. Hosp., 1952-54; v.p. N.Y. Hosp.-Cornell Med. Cnter, 1970—; asst. prof. pub. health and preventive medicine Cornell U. Med. Coll., 1954—; spl. cons. surgeon gen. USPHS, 1959—, surgeon gen. U.S. Army, 1954—. Pres. Community Blood Council Greater N.Y., 1959—; bd. dirs. Group Health Ins., Inc., N.Y., 1961—; med. control bd. Health Ins. Plan Greater N.Y., Inc., 1957—, bd. dirs., 1963—; treas. Career Center Social Services, 1966-70; mem. nat. health resources adv. com. Office Emergency Planning, Exec. Offices President, 1963-68, also chmn. com. blood, health adviser to dir., 1969—, chmn. nat. health resources adv. com., 1969—; chmn. nat. adv. com. on selection physicians, dentists and allied specialists SSS, 1969—; bd. dirs. Am. Bur. Med. Aid to China, 1968—, 1st v.p., 1969, pres., 1970, hon. pres., 1971; mem. Nat. Bd. Med. Examiners, 1970—. Trustee Marymount-Manhattan Coll., N.Y.C., La Guardia Hosp., N.Y.C. Served to lt. col. AUS, 1941-45. Decorated Legion of Merit. Fellow A.M.A., N.Y. Acad. Medicine, Am. Pub. Health Assn., Am. Coll. Hosp. Adminstrs.; mem. Am. Hosp. Assn. Author: (with Emanuel Hayt and Lillian R.

Hayt) Law of Hospital, Physician and Patient, 1952; (with Emanuel Hayt and Dorothy McMullan) Law of Hospital and Nurse, 1958. Home: NY Hosp 68th St New York City NY 10021

GROEZINGER, LELAND BECKER, lawyer; b. San Francisco, June 17, 1907; s. Emile August and Emma (Becker) G.; A.B., U. Cal. at Berkeley, 1927; J.D., Harvard, 1930; m. Clara-Catherine Hudson, Sept. 30, 1939; children—Leland Becker, Marlene Margaret (Mrs. James S. Doak). Admitted to Cal. bar, 1930; dep. legislative counsel State of Cal., 1930-31; practice in San Francisco, 1931—; asso. Pillsbury, Madison & Sutro, 1931-46; mem. firm Allan, Miller & Groezinger, 1946-55, Allan, Miller, Groezinger, Keesling & Martin, 1955- 66, Miller, Groezinger, Pettit, Evers & Martin, 1966-69, Miller, Groezinger, Pettit & Evers, 1970—. Mem. Am. Bar Assn. (past chmn. sect. ins. and negligence law, past state del.). Home: 2164 Hyde St San Francisco CA 94109 Office: 650 California St San Francisco CA 94108

GROFE, FERDE, (Ferdinand Rudolph von Grofé), composer, conductor; b. at N.Y. City, Mar. 27, 1892; s. Emil and Elsa Johanna (Bierlich) von G.; ed. primary school, Los Angeles; private school in Germany; St. Vincents, Los Angeles; early musical training by his mother, his grandfather, Bernhardt Bierlich (1st cellist Los Angeles Symphony Orchestra), and by his uncle, Julius Bierlich (concertmaster of same orchestra); studied harmony and counterpoint with C.E. Pemberton at U. of Southern Calif.; studied piano with Homer Grunn, Los Angeles and Herman Wasserman, N.Y. City; orchestra scores with Maestro Pietro Floridia of N.Y.C., Mus.D., Ill. Wesleyan U., 1946; m. Ruth Harriet MacGloan, May 11, 1929; children—Ferdinand Rudolf, Jr., Anne Carlin; m. 2d, Anna May Lempton, Jan. 12, 1952. Orchestra conductor on radio programs; has made personal appearances as conductor at Hollywood Bowl, Lewisohn Stadium, Gershwin Memorial Program, Robin Hood Dell (Phila.), Carnegie Hall Concerts (1937-38), New York World's Fair (Ford Exhibit, Novachord Ensemble, 1939-40). Mem. Am. Soc. of Composers. Authors and Publishers Phi Mu Alpha. Clubs: Nat. Travel, N.Y. Athletic; Bohemian, (San Francisco). Mason (K.T., 32, Shriner). Compositions: Tabloid Suite, Mississippi Suite, March for Americans, Grand Canyon Suite, Kentucky Derby, Knute Rockne, Three Shades of Blue Suite, Christmas Eve, An American Biography (based on the life of Henry Ford), Ode to the Star Spangled Banner, Café Society Ballet, Ode to Freedom, Trylon and Perisphere, Symphony in Steel, Wheels Suite, Hollywood Suite, Blue Flame, "Ruby" from Jewel Tones, Miss Mischief, Free Air, Templed Hills, 1941; Daybreak, 1942; Uncle Sam Stands Up, Skylines, 1943; Broadway at Night, 1945; Aviation Suite, 1946; Deep Nocturne, 1947; and some twenty others, 1948—. Address: 8268 Sunset Blvd Los Angeles CA 90046

GROFF, JOHN ROBERT, hydraulic turbine mfr.; b. New Holland, Pa., Mar. 9, 1898; s. Benjamin Franklin and Anna Catherine (Lintner) G.; student Franklin and Marshall Coll., Pa. State Coll.; m. Emily Caroline Moores, June 1, 1922; 1 dau., Virginia Ann (Mrs. Gilbert Graves). Hydraulic engr. James Leffel & Co. Springfield, O., 1920-26, dir., 1926—, sales mgr., exec. sec., 1929-38, v.p., 1938-40, pres., gen. mgr., 1940—; dir. Ohio Edison Co.; dir., chmn. bd. Springfield Bank (merger State Bank of South Charleston, O. and Savs. Soc. of Springfield). Adv. com. heavy machinery NPA, 1945; trustee Ohio Pub. Expenditure Council; mem. U.S. nat. com., council Internat. Electrotech. Commn. Pres. Springfield Community Fund and War Chest, 1942-45; pres. United Appeals Fund, Springfield and Clark County, 1954-69; Bd. dirs. Wittenberg U.; pres., trustee Springfield Found. Recipient Community Leadership award Wittenberg U. 1959; Community Service award V.F.W. of U.S.A., 1966. Mem. Nat. Elec. Mfrs. Assn. (chmn. hydraulic turbine industry), Am. Soc. M.E., Springfield C. of C. (pres. 1937-39), Greater Springfield and Clark County Assn. (pres. 1945), Clark County Hist. Soc. Rotarian (past pres.). Clubs: Springfield Country, Literary, Van Dyke (Springfield); Engineers (N.Y.C.). Home: 4465 National Rd E Springfield OH 45505 Office: 426 East St Springfield OH 45505

GROFF, ROBERT ARMAND, physician; b. Phila., May 11, 1903 s. Henry Clemens and Estella (Rosenberger) G.; B.A., U. Pa., 1925, M.D., 1928; m. Georgiana Ketchum Hallenbeck, July 29, 1933. Faculty neurosurgery U. Pa. Med. Sch., 1930—, prof., 1957—; vol. asst. Dr. Harvey Cushing, Peter Bent Brigham Hosp., Boston, 1931-32; clin. clk. Nat. Hosp., Queen's Sq., London, Eng., 1933-34; research neurosurgery Hosp. U. Pa., 1934; faculty U. Pa. Grad. Sch. Medicine, 1937—, prof., 1953—; asst. prof. surgery Jefferson Med. Coll., 1941-45; chief neurosurgery U. Pa. Grad. Hosp., Phila. Served to col. AUS, 1942-46. Diplomate Am. Bd. Neurology and Psychiatry, Am. Bd. Neurosurgery. Mem. A.M.A., Pa., Philadelphia County med. socs., Phila. Neurol. Soc., Soc. Research Nervous and Mental Diseases, Phila. Acad. Surgery, Soc. Neurol. Surgeons, A.C.S., Harvey Cushing Soc., Am. Neurol. Assn., Congress Neurol. Surgeons, Coll. Physicians Phila. Club: Philadelphia Country. Home: Presidential Apts Philadelphia PA 19131 Office: Med Tower 255 S 17th St Philadelphia PA 19103

GROGAN, J. EDMUND, lawyer; b. Santa Rosa, Cal., Oct. 3, 1903; s. James E. and Cecelia (Wirtz) G.; B.S., U. Cal. at Berkeley, 1926; postgrad. Bolt Sch. Law, 1926-27; J.D., Southwestern U., Los Angeles, 1930; m. Rose Marie McInerny, June 10, 1933 (dec.); children—James C., Patricia (Mrs. R.R. Hines), Mary, Catherine. With Ceco Corp., Chgo., 1928-69, sr. v.p. legal and financial, 1964-69, now dir.; dir. Moews Seed Co., Granville, Ill.; admitted to Cal., Neb., Ill. bars, 1931; with firm Jenner & Block, Chgo., 1969—. Trustee Meyer-Ceco Found. Home: 165 N Kenilworth Av Oak Park IL 60301 Office: 135 S LaSalle St Chicago IL 60603

GROGAN, JOHN J., mayor; b. Hoboken, N.J., Mar. 26, 1914; s. John and Catherine (May) G.; student St. Peters Parochial Sch., 1925; Columbia, 1945; m. Eileen McNulty, June 5, 1937; childrenJames Peter, Patricia Ann. Mem. A.F. of L. Steamfitters Union, 1930; exec. sec., treas. Local 15 Shipbuilder's Union, 1937-42; v.p., gen. exec. bd. Internat. Union Marine, Shipbuildings Workers Am. C.I.O., 1941; pres. Hudson Co. C.I.O. Council, 1943-44; v.p. Labor Com. Palestine, 1944; mem. Nat. Italian-Am. Commn., Dallas TX 75205 Office: 5323 Hines Blvd Dallas TX 75235 ☆

GROH, CLIFFORD JOHN, lawyer, state legislator; b. Ramapo, N.Y., Apr. 1, 1926; s. Marcel and Helen (Jaworski) G.; B.S., St. Lawrence U., 1948; J.D., U. N.M., 1951; m. Lucy Bright Woodruff, Aug. 22, 1949; children—Clifford John II, Paul Woodruff, Lucy Elizabeth. Admitted to N.M. bar 1952, to Alaska bar, 1953; gen. counsel First Fed. Savs. & Loan Assn., Anchorage, Nat. Bank Alaska; chmn., dir. Security Title and Trust Co.; partner firm Groh, Benkert and Greene, 1966—; mem. Alaska Senate, 1970—. First pres. Operation Statehood, 1953; chmn. Alaska Constl. Research Com., 1955; mem. Anchorage Ind. Sch. Bd., 1955-59, 62-63, pres., 1958-59; assemblyman Greater Anchorage Area Borough, 1964-66; mem. Anchorage City Council, 1963-67, acting mayor of Anchorage, 1966-67. Served to lt. USNR 1943-46, 50-52. Mem. Am., Alaska (bd. govs., 1958-61, pres. 1960- 61), Anchorage bar assns., Am. Judicature Soc. Republican. Episcopalian. Home: 1576 Coffey Lane Anchorage AK 99501 Office: 430 C St Anchorage AK 99501

GROHMANN, HANS VICTOR, advt. exec.; b. Jersey City, Jan 7, 1903; s. William Martin and Marie Johanna (Tamm) G.; B.S., Cornell U., 1928; m. Margaret E. Haver, June 24, 1944; children—Gwendolyn Anne (Mrs. Archer B. des Cognets), Victor Nelson, William Haver. Cornell U. rep. Gen. Foods Corp., 1926-28; asst. mgr. Hotel Walt Whitman, Camden, N.J., 1928-29; asst. mgr. charge advt. Hotel Lexington, N.Y.C., 1929-30; account exec. Harry Latz Co., advt., 1930-31; co-founder Needham & Grohmann, advt., N.Y.C., 1931, pres., 1939- 70, chmn., treas., 1970—. Instr., lectr. advt. and pub. relations Cornell U., 1939—; propr., operator Havendale Farm, Sussex, N.J., 1941—. Pres., Tenafly (N.J.) Community Chest, 1953-54, Tenafly All-Sports Assn., 1962-63, Citizens Ednl. Council, Tenafly, 1958-59; chmn. communications com. Christian Sci. Pavilion, N.Y. World's Fair, 1964-65. Trustee Cornell U. Recipient award of commendation for ednl. activities Hotel Sales Mgrs. Assn., 1960. Mem. Am. Assn. Advt. Agys. (past treas. N.Y., chmn. bd. ins. trust 1962-65), Discover Am. Travel Orgns. (sec. bd. dirs.), Am. Hotels and Motels Assn. (mem. People-to-People com.), Resort Representation Service (pres. 1952—), Cornell Soc. Hotelmen (past pres.), Phi Gamma Delta (pres. Cornell chpt. 1961-69). Clubs: Cornell (pres. 1962-64), Farm (dir.), Touchdown, University (N.Y.); Rockefeller Center Luncheon (gov., pres. 1963-67). Author: Advertising Terminology, 1952; 30 Year Calendar, 1961. Home: 232 Hudson Av Tenafly NJ 07670 Office: 30 Rockefeller Plaza New York City NY 10020

GROLLMAN, ARTHUR, research physician; b. Balt., Oct. 20, 1901; s. Simon and Bessie Flora (Karu) G.; A.B., Johns Hopkins, 1920, Ph.D., 1923, M.D., 1930; student U. Chgo., 1924-25, U. Mich., 1926; m. Anna Louise Costello, Mar. 1926; children—Arthur Patrick, Catherine Anne, Evelyn Frances. Instr. chemistry Grad. Sch. Johns Hopkins, 1923-24, asso. prof. physiology Med. Sch., 1930-32, asso. prof. pharmacology and therapeutics, 1932-41; Guggenheim Meml. fellow U. London, Med. Acad. Dusseldorf, U. Berlin, U. Heidelberg, 1930- 31; research prof. medicine Bowman Gray Sch. Medicine, Winston-Salem, N.C., 1941-44; prof. medicine and chmn. dept. exptl. medicine Southwestern Med. Coll., Dallas, 1944—, acting prof. pharmacology and chmn. dept. physiology and pharmacology, 1946-50; cons. internal medicine Baylor U.; cons. VA Hosp., USAAF Hosp., Wilford Hall, Lackland AFB; nat. civilian cons. to Surg. Gen. USAF, Surgeon (R) USPHS, 1945-50; hon. prof. medicine Guadalajara, Mexico; Gorgas lectr., 1946; Long lectr., 1952, Boynton lectr., 1958, Duluth lectr., 1956. Mem. adv. bd. U. Dallas. Recipient Guggenheim Meml. award, 1930, Marchman awrd, 1950; Oscar B. Hunter award Am. Therapeutic Soc., 1968. Fellow A.C.P., N.Y. Acad. Scis.; mem. Am. Physiol. Soc., A.M.A., Am. Soc. Pharmacology and Therapeutics, Fed. Soc. Biology, Phi Beta Kappa, Sigma Xi. Author: Cardiac Output of Man, 1932; The Adrenals, 1936; Pharmacologand Experimental Therapeutics, 1965, 7th edit., 1970; Acute Renal Failure: Pathogenesis and Treatment, 1954; Clinical Endocrinology, 1964. Editor: The Functional Pathology of Disease, 1963; Research on peritoneal lavage, adrenals, endocrinology, circulationand hypertension. Contbr. chpts., articles to profl. publs. Mem. revision com. US Pharmacopoea 1960-70. Home: 3501 Princeton Av Dallas TX 75205 Office: 5323 Hines Blvd Dallas TX 75235

GROLLMES, EUGENE E., educator, clergyman; b. Seneca, Kan., Nov. 9, 1931; s. Edward Anthony and Josephine (Roeder) G.; A.B., St. Louis U., 1957, M.A., 1961; Ph.D., Boston Coll., 1969. Joined Soc. of Jesus, 1951, ordained priest Roman Cath. Ch., 1964; chmn. religious life workshop St. Louis U., 1966; chmn. Jesuit Edn. Workshop, Denver, 1969; acad. dean Regis Coll., 1970—. Mem. Nat. Cath. Edn. Assn., Common Cause. Editor: Vows But No Walls: Analysis Religious Life, 1967; Catholic Colleges in Secular Mystique, 1970. Home: 3539 W 50th Parkway Denver CO 80221

GROMAN, ARTHUR, lawyer; b. Los Angeles, Sept. 13, 1914; s. Lou and Tinnie (Lurie) G.; A.B. magna cum ladue, U. So. Cal., 1936; LL.B., Yale, 1939; children—Richard, Steven; m. Miriam Shanedling, Aug. 14, 1969; children—Alan, David, Deborah. Admitted to Cal. bar, 1939; atty. Gen. Counsel's Office, Treasury Dept., 1939-41, Bur. Internal Revenue, 1941-44; sr. partner Mitchell, Silberberg & Knupp, Los Angeles. Dir. Occidental Petroleum Corp., Telautograh Corp. Co-founder, lectr. Tax Inst., U. So. Cal., 1948. Trustee Cal. Inst. Cancer Research. Fellow Am. Coll. Trial Lawyers; mem. Yale Law Sch. Alumni Assn. So. Cal. (pres.), Phi Beta Kappa, Order of Coif. Club: Hillcrest Country (dir.). Bd. editors Yale Law Jour., 1938-39. Home: 520 Stonewood Dr Beverly Hills CA 90210 Office: 1800 Century Park E Los Angeles CA 90067

GROMBACH, JOHN V., gen. bus. cons.; b. New Orleans, La., Jan. 2, 1902; s. André and Marcelle (Valentin) G., ed. Va. Mil. Inst.; B.S., U.S. Mil. Acad., 1923; U.S. Service Schs., 1923-27; C.E., N.Y. State Univ., 1929; licensed profl. engr., New York, 1929; m. 2d, Olga Alice Lohinecz, July 17, 1959. Commd. 2d lt. U.S. Army, 1923; police and prison officer, Govenor's Island, N.Y., 1923-25; head coach 2d Corps (all service) football team, 1923-26; acting jr. mil. attaché, Paris, 1924; asst. provost marshal, Panama Canal Zone, 1926-28; liaison officer between War Dept. and motion picture producers and tech. adviser to N.Y. theatre producers during army service; resigned as lt., U.S. Army, 1928; writer and producer, radio and motion picture studios; Judson Radio Program Corp. (subsidiary of Columbia Broadcasting and Paramount Publix, latter firm became Grombach Prodns.; Inc., of which is pres.); pres. Jean V. Grombach, Inc., 1929-41, Adv. Recording Service, 1930-41; recalled to army service, 1941. Col. War Dept. Gen. Staff, MIS, chief, liaison br. between War Dept. and State dept. F.B.I., F.C.C., etc., 1942- 46; Brigadier Gen. N.Y.N.G. Reserve, 1956. Pres. Indsl. Reports, Inc., 1942—; pres. Universal Service Corp., 1947—; bus. cons., N.Y.C. Awarded Legion of Merit, 1946, Army Commendation Medal, N.Y. State Conspicuous Service Cross. Intercollegiate heavy-weight boxing champion, 1922, army champion, 1924, mem. U.S. Olympic boxing team, Paris, 1924; sec. Internat. Amateur Boxing Fedn., 1924-28; Nat. and Internat. fencing championships, 1924- 40; mem. U.S. Internat. fencing teams, London, 1926, Paris, 1937, Nat. Open (Masters) Epée Champion, 1950; mem. U.S. Olympic Games Com., 1956, 60, 64, 68; sec. gen. Internat. Fencing Fedn., 1960-64. Clubs: New York Athletic, N.Y. Fencers, Union (Panama), Army, Navy (Washington). Author: How to Box; Radio Prodn. Touch Football, Saga of Sock, Olympic Cavalcade of Sports; also major radio programs, 1930-40; latest book, The 1968 Olympic Guide. Contbr. to mags. Radio sports commentator. Home: 220 Central Park S New York City NY 10019 also Little Farm Richmond MA 01254 Office: 111 W 57th St New York City NY 10019

GROMYKO, ANDREI A., U.S.S.R. diplomat, b. Gomel Region, U.S.S.R., July 6, 1909; grad. high school, 1928, teachers coll., 1931; student Economic Inst., Moscow, 1931-36 M.A., 1936; m. Lydia D. Grinevich; childrenAnatoli, Emila. Senior scientific worker, Economic Inst., Acad. of Scis. of USSR, 1936-39, also lectured at Moscow univs.; chief Div. Am. Countries, People's Commissariat of Foreign Affairs, May-Oct. 1939; counselor, USSR, Embassy, Washington, Oct. 1939-Aug. 1943, also minister to Cuba; ambassador to U.S. Aug. 1943-Apr. 1946, to Britain, 1952-53. Apptd. USSR rep. on Security Council of UN Orgn., Mar. 1946; deputy minister for Foreign Affairs of USSR, 1946-49; apptd. 1st dep. fgn. minister USSR, Mar. 1949-57, fgn. minister, 1957-. Address: The Kremlin Moscow USSR

GRONDAHL, HILMAR, music editor Portland Oregonian. Address: 5233 SW Hewett Blvd Portland OR 97221 •

GRONDAHL, TEG CONRAD, assn. exec.; b. Red Wing, Minn., Sept. 23, 1908; s. Gilbert Lars and Lavina (Peterson) G.; A.B. cum laude, U. Minn., 1930, grad. study, 1931- 32; m. Kathryn Fenstermaker; one dau., Kristina Conrad (Mrs. Peter M. Bear). Engaged as reported and editor United Press Assn., 1935- 42; editor overseas br. O.W.I., 1942-44; chief psychol. warfare team, Calcutta, India, 1944-45; rep. psychol. warfare matters India-Burma Theatre Command, Calcutta, 1945; dir. U.S. Information Service, Bangkok, Thailand, 1945, pub. affairs officer, 2d sec. U.S. Embassy, 1946-49; dep. dir. Office Internat. Information, Dept. of State, 1949-52; counselor of embassy and chief public affairs officer New Delhi, India, 1952-53; exec. asso. Am. Univs. Field Staff, 1953-56, asso. dir., 1956-61, acting exec. dir., 1961, exec. dir., 1961-; cons. Ford Found, 1957-60. Vis. prof. S.E. Asian studies Cornell, 1951-52. Awarded Emblem for meritorious civilian service (India-Burma Theater command). Mem. Iron Wedge, Council Fgn. Relations, Assn. Asian Studies, Asia Soc., Sigma Delta Chi, Sigma Phi Epsilon. Home: 45 Sutton Pl S New York City NY 10022 Office: 535 Fifth Av New York City NY 10017

GRONER, FRANK SHELBY, hosp. administr.; b. Stamford, Tex., Sept. 25, 1911; s. Frank S. and Laura (Wyatt) G.; B.A., Baylor U., 1934; LL.D., Tex. Bapt. Coll., 1946, Union U., 1952, Baylor U., 1969; m. Daisy Amanda McFearin, Dec. 12, 1936; Dean sch. bus. Coll. of Marshall (Tex.), 1934-36; asst. adminstr. So. Bapt. Hosp., New Orleans, 1936-43, adminstr., 1943-46; adminstr. Bapt. Meml. Hosp., Memphis. 1946-. Cons. USPHS; cons. Div. Hosp. and Med. Facilities, also Bur. Family Services on Med. Matters, U.S. Dept. Health, Edn. and Welfare; exec. dir. Health, Edn. and Research Found. Mem. Surgeon General's adv. com. on Nat. Health Survey. Bd. govs. exec. com. Blue Cross; bd. dirs. A.R.C., Am. Cancer Soc., Memphis Community Chest. Dollar-a- Year Man, Washington, 1942-45. Recipient of Justin Ford Kimball award, 1964, Distinguished Service award Am. Hosp. Assn., 1966; Distinguished Service award Memphis and Shelby County Med. Soc., 1967; Gold medal award Am. Coll. of Hosp. Adminstrs., 1968. Mem. Am. (pres., chmn. council hosp. planning and plant operation, chmn. hosp. architects qualifications, trustee; past president), La. (past pres.), Tenn. (past pres.) hosp. assns., Southeastern Hosp. Conf. (past pres.), Southwide Bapt. Hosp. Assn. (past pres.), So. Inst. Hosp. Adminstrs. (pres., dir.), Internat. Hosp. Fedn. (del.). Baptist. Home: 649 Sweetbriar Rd Memphis TN 38117 Office: 899 Madison Av Memphis TN 38103

GRONER, JOHN VAUGHAN, lawyer; b. Norfolk, Va., Sept. 21, 1901: s. Duncan Lawrence and Anne (Vaughan) G.; student U. Va., 1922; m. Dorothy Teter, Dec. 29, 1954; childrenBarbara (Mrs. E. Sheldon Spicer, Jr.), Sally Anne (Mrs. William B. Terry, Jr.), Anne Vaughan (Mrs. Walter G. Spilsbury), Beverly Jane. Admitted to Va. bar, 1921, D.C. bar, 1926, N.Y. bar, 1931; practiced in Norfolk, 1922-26; spl. asst. atty. gen., Washington, 1926-29; mem. firm Fish & Neave, N.Y.C., 1929—. Home: 9 Mansion Pl Greenwich CT 86830 Office: 277 Park Av New York City NY 10017

GRONER, POWELL CAMPBELL, lawyer, corp. exec.; b. Norfolk, Va., Feb. 13, 1892; s. John Archibald Campbell and Elizabeth Stith (Powell) G.; ed. U. Va.; m. Marjorie Hayes Wolcott, July 18, 1917; childrenPowell Campbell, William Wolcott. Admitted to bar Va., 1913, N.Y., 1915, Ill., 1918, Mo., 1925, Kan., 1928, U.S. Supreme Ct., 1928; asso. with William H. Page, Chgo. and N.Y.C., 1913-22; rep. Newman, Saunders & Co., investment bankers N.Y.C. and New Orleans, 1922-27; counsel, reorgn. com. Kansas City Rys. Co., 1924-27; pres. and dir. Kansas City Pub. Service Co. and Wyandotte Rys. Co., 1927-57; pres., dir. Kansas City Pub. Service Motor Transport Co. 1935-57; dir. Pierce Industries and subs., 1958-61; mem. law firm Watson, Ess, Groner, Barnett & Whittaker, Kansas City, Mo., 1926-50, Rice, Groner, Nugent and Baska, Kansas City, Kan., 1958-66; pvt. practice, 1966—; dir. Westgate State Bank, Kansas City, Kan.; sec., dir. Sherold Crystals, Inc. and subsidiaries, 1964-70. Gen. chmn. Kansas City Allied Charities Campaign, 1938; gen. chmn. Red Cross War Fund Campaign, Jackson County, 1943, dir., 1943-50. Dir. C. of C. Kansas City, Mo., 1932-34, 38-40; mem. exec. com. Am. Transit Assn., 1932-34, v.p., 1941-42, pres., 1942-43. Nat. councillor of U.S. C. of C., 1932-40, dir., 1943-54, v.p., 1947-49, 51-54, mem. exec. com., 1944-45, 47-49, 51-53. Chmn. Transp. and Communications Com., 1943-47, Labor Relations Com., 1952-53, Nat. Def. Com., 1953-54; mem. Pres.'s labor-mgmt. conf., Washington, 1945; mem. Kansas City Charities Com., 1939- 49. Trustee Kansas City Art Inst.; chmn. Trustee Kansas City Philharmonic Orch., 1933-1941; chmn. exec. com. Conservatory of Music, Kansas City, 1934-53, pres. 1944-46, chmn., 1954; mem. Jud. Council Mo., 1934-35; bd. dirs. Boys Clubs of Am., 1951-62. Mem. Am., Mo. bar assns., Lawyers Assn. (Kansas City, Mo.), Wyandotte County Bar (Kansas City, Kan), Phi Sigma Kappa, Delta Sigma Chi. Episcopalian. Clubs: University, Kansas City, Kansas City Country. Press (Kansas City); River. Home: 420 E Armour Blvd Kansas City MO 46109 Office: Huron Bldg Kansas City KS 66101

GRONNEBERG, ROLF BREDA, banker; b. Drammen, Norway, Jan. 31, 1917; s. Nils Breda and Anna H. (Haug) G.; ed. in Norway; certificate Am. Inst. Banking, 1959; grad. Nat. Assn. Bank Auditors and Controllers Grad. Sch., U. Wis., 1962; m. Helen Gudrun, Apr. 30, 1947; childrenRolf Breda, Richard Nils. Came to U.S., 1949, naturalized, 1952. Accountant, Standard Baatbyggeri, Drammen, 1943-46, Norges Kooperative Landsforening, Oslo, Norway, 1946-49; with Indsl. Nat. Bank R.I., Providence, 1949-, controller, 1965-; sec. Providence, Clearing House Assn.; sec.-treas. Exchange Real Estate Co., Providence. Mem. Nat. Assn. Bank Auditors and Controllers (adv. bd. Boston 1967-, chmn. finance com. regional conf. Boston 1967). Lutheran (trustee). Home: 70 Hyland Av East Greenwich RI 02818 Office: Indsl Nat Bank Rhode Island Providence RI 02903

GRONOUSKI, JOHN AUSTIN, univ. dean; b. Dunbar, Wis., Oct. 26, 1919; s. John Austin and Mary (Riley) G.; student Oshkosh (Wis.) State Tchrs. Coll., 1938-41; Ph.B., U. Wis., 1942, Ph.M., 1947, Ph.D., 1955; m. Mary Louise Metz, Jan. 24, 1948; children—Stacy, Julie. Instr. econs. U. Me., 1948-50; research asso. Fedn. Tax Adminstrs., instr. Roosevelt U. Evening Sch., Chgo., 1952-56; mem. staffs studying Wis. and Mich. income tax adminstrn., instr. Wayne State U., 1956-59; research dir. Wis. Dept. Taxation and U. Wis. Tax Impact Study, exec. dir Wis. Revenue Survey Commn., 1959; commr. taxation Wis., 1960-63; postmaster gen. U.S., 1963-65; U.S. ambassador to Poland, 1965-68; dean Lyndon B. Johnson Sch. Pub. Affairs, U. Tex., Austin, 1969—. Lectr., writer. Mem. adv. council to pres. Alliance Coll. Trustee Nat. Urban League, St. Edwards U. Served to 1st lt. USAAF, 1942-45; ETO. Mem. Am. Econ. Assn., Nat. Tax Assn., Polish Inst. Arts and Scis. Democrat. Roman Catholic. Contbr. articles to profl. jours. Home: 610 E 43d St Austin TX 78751

GRONOWICZ, ANTONI, author; b. Rudnia, Poland, July 31, 1913; s. Antoni and Paulina (Dorocinska) G.; Ph.D., U. Lwow (Poland), 1937; m. Sophia Shymanska, June 8, 1940; childrenAnthony Boleslaw, Gloria Andrea. Came to U.S., 1938, naturalized, 1962. Decorated Polonia Restituta Order (Poland); recipient Polish Nat. Lit. prize, 1938; Ford Found. grantee, 1959. Mem. Authors League Am., P.E.N., Cath. Poetry Soc. Am., Cath. Press Assn. Author: (poetry) Prosto w Oczy, 1936, Bunt Walki, 1937, Melodia Switow, 1939; (essays) Byki Czystej Poezji 1936, Pattern For Peace, 1951; (novels) I Chlopi Ida od Wschodu, 1937, Bolek, 1942, Hitler's Woman, 1942, Four From The Old Town, 1944, The Piasts, 1945, Gallant General, 1946, Virtue in Four Positions, 1965; (art theory) Harmonizm, 1938; (plays) Niedroga Recepta, 1938, A Comedy of Angels, 1957, Chiseler's Paradise, 1958, Modjeska, 1962; (biog. novels) Paderewski, 1942, Chopin, 1943, Tchaikovsky, 1944, Rachmaninoff, 1946, Modjeska-Her Life and Lovers, 1956; (biography) Béla Schick and the World of Children, 1954; Greta (play), 1967; The United Animals (play), 1967, The Great Soc. (play), 1968; The Quiet Vengeance of Words (poetry), 1968; Forward Together (play) 1969. Address: 132 E 82d St New York City NY 10028

GROOME, HARRY CONNELLY, Jr., advt. exec.; b. Phila., Dec. 23, 1908; s. Harry Connelly and Mary (Upton) G.; grad. St. Paul's Sch., 1926; B.A., Princeton, 1931; LL.B., U. Pa., 1934; m. Sarah C. Zantzinger, June 25, 1932; children—Margaret S. (Mrs. M. Todd Cooke Jr.), Harry Connelly III, Clark. With N.W. Ayer & Son, 1935—, sr. v.p. finance and adminstrn., 1967—. Chmn. Fife Hamil Meml. Health Center, 1955-60; mem. bd. Delaware County Council Econ. Edn., 1966-. Bd. dirs. Babies Hosp., 1946-55; bd. dirs. St. Christopher's Hosp., 1960—, chmn., 1967-70; bd. dirs. Delaware Valley Hosp. Council. Served to maj. AUS and USAAF, 1942-46. Republican. Episcopalian. Contbr. profl. jours. Home: 514 E Evergreen Av Philadelphia PA 19118 Office: NW Ayer & Son W Washington Sq Philadelphia PA 19106

GROOMS, HARLAN HOBART, judge; b. Jeffersonville, Ky., Nov. 7 1900; LL.B., U. Ky.; m. Angeline M.; childrenHarlan Hobart, Ellen Elizabeth, John Franklin, Angeline. Admitted to Ky. bar and Ala. bar; practiced in Birmingham, Ala., 1926-53; former mem. Spain, Gillon, Grooms & Young; U.S. Dist. judge, No. Dist. of Ala., 1953—. Trustee Samford U., Birmingham Bapt. Hosps. Mem. Am., Ala. bar assns., Phi Alpha Delta, Omicron Delta Kappa, Pi Kappa Alpha. Baptist. Club: Civitan. Home: 2625 Crest Rd Birmingham AL 35223 Office: Box 34 Birmingham AL 35202

GROOMS, RED, artist; b. Nashville, June 2, 1937; student Peabody Coll., Chgo. Art Inst., Hofmann Sch., Provincetown, Mass. One-man exhbns. include Sun Gallery, Provincetown, 1958, Reuben Gallery, N.Y.C., 1960, Tibor de Nagy Gallery, 1963, 65-67, 69-70, Artists Guild, Nashville, 1962, Allan Frumkin Gallery, Chgo., 1967, John Bernard Myers Gallery Discount Store, 1971, Happenings: A Play Called Fire, Sun Gallery, 1958, Burning Bldgs., N.Y.C., 1958; group exhbns. include Chgo. Art Inst., 1964, Delancey St. Mus., N.Y.C., 1959, 60, also Provincetown/Chrysler Mus.; movie with Rudi Burckhardt, Shoot the Moon, 1962; commd. (with Mimi Gross) for mural Centre Modern Culture, Florence, Italy; rep. permanent collections Cheekwood Fine Arts Mus., Nashville, Raleigh (N.C.) Mus. Art. Address: 186 Grand St New York City NY 10012*

GROOMS, REGINALD LESLIE, educator, painter; b. Cin., Nov. 16, 1900; s. Harry Murray and Regina Caroline (Diehl) G.; student Art Acad. Cin., Academie Julian, Paris; pvt. art studies; m. Jessie Macy Roberts, Aug. 11, 1941 (dec.). Instr. drawing and painting Coll. Applied Arts, U. Cin., 1925-46, asst. prof., 1946-51, asso. prof., 1951-55, Alfred P. Streitman prof. art, 1955- 71, emeritus, 1971—; landscape instr. Cin. Art Acad., summers 1925-53. Works exhibited Cin. Art Mus., Butler Art Inst., Pa. Acad., Art Inst. Chgo., Kearney Gallery, Milw., Ball State Tchrs. Coll.; one-man shows U. Kan., Art Inst. Cin; works represented permanent collections Ball State Coll. Mus., U. Cin., Cin. Pub. Schs.; lectr., demonstrator painting technique and styles and art theory. Recipient award Ohio Water Color Soc., 1946. Mem. Cin. Art Club (dir., past pres.), Cin. Profl. Artists (dir.), Cin. MacDowell Soc. (dir., past pres.), Am. Soc. Aesthetics. Club: Torch (Cin.). Home: 3436 Lyleburn Pl Cincinnati OH 45220

GROOT, JOHAN JACOB, geologist; b. Amsterdam, Netherlands, Nov. 25, 1918; s. Wiebe and Aagje (Mars) G.; M.A., U. Amsterdam, 1945, Doctorandus, 1947; m. Catharina Repko, June 21, 1945; childrenOlga, Eric, Research asso. U. Amsterdam, 1945-47; research asso., studying environmental factors of desert and semi-desert of West Africa for Q.M. Gen. Office, Dept. Def., U. Md., 1947-49; lectr. geography, geology U. Del., 1949-51, prof. geology, 1956- 69; state geologist Del., 1951-69; project dir. UN in Bolivia, 1969-; sr. research asso. Columbia U. Fellow Geol. Soc. Am.; mem. A.A.A.S., Am. Geophys. Union, Assn. Am. State Geologists, Royal Dutch Geog. Soc. Author papers on palynology. Home: Av Bustamente Calcoto La Paz Bolivia Office: Naciones Unidas Casilla 686 La Paz Bolivia

GROOVER, MARY AGNES, see Brown, Mary-Agnes.

GROPP, ARMIN HENRY, univ. adminstr.; b. Antigo, Wis., Sept. 21, 1915; s. William E. and Emilie (Kater) G.; B.A., U. Ore., 1943, M.A., 1945, Ph.D. with honors, 1947; m. Clare Elizabeth Morgan, Aug. 31, 1944; childrenWilliam, Kathryn. Chemist, Standard Oil Co. Cal., 1945; research asso. U. Ore., 1947; mem. faculty U. Fla., 1947-64, prof. chemistry, 1955-64; dean Grad. Sch., U. Miami, 1964-65, v.p., dean faculties, 1965-; cons. to industry. Treas. Young Republican Fedn. Ore., 1941-42. Mem. Am. Chem. Soc., Am. Inst. Chemists, Phi Beta Kappa, Sigma Xi (Research award Ore. chpt. 1947), Phi Kappa Phi, Alpha Chi Sigma, Delta Upsilon. Democrat. Lutheran. Home: 6090 SW 116th St Miami FL 33156 Office: Univ Miami Ashe Bldg Coral Gables FL 33124

GROPPER, WILLIAM, artist; b. N.Y.C., Dec. 3, 1897; s. Harry and Jennie (Nidel) G.; student N.A.D., 1913-14, N.Y. Sch. Fine and Applied Art, 1915-18; m. Sophie Frankle, Oct. 10, 1924; children—Gene, Lee. Began as artist N.Y. Tribune, 1919; illustrator many books; Ford Found. award artist in residence under Am. Fedn. Art, 1965; artist in residence Tamarind Lithographic Workshop, Los Angeles, 1967. Murals: U.S. Post Office, Freeport, L.I.; New Interior Bldg., Washington; Wayne State U., Detroit; Schenley Corp., N.Y.; stain glass windows Temple Har Zion, River Forest, Ill.; represented Met. Mus. Art, Mus. Modern Art, Whitney Mus. Am. Art (all N.Y.C.), Mus. Western Art, Moscow, USSR, Hartford (Conn.) Mus., Art Inst. Chgo., Phillips Meml. Mus., Washington, Dr. Paul Sachs Coll., Fogg Art Mus., Mus. of City N.Y., Bklyn. Mus., Cambridge, Mass., St. Louis Art Mus., Newark Mus., Walker Art Center, Minn., U. Ariz., Pa. Acad. Art, Phila. Mus. Art, Library of Congress, Ency. Brit. collection, Abbott collection, U. Me., Los Angeles County Mus., John Herron Art Inst. Recipient Collier prize for illustration, 1920; Harmon prize, 1930; Young Israel prize, 1931, 3d prize Carnegie Inst., for Don Quixote, 1946, Gimbel collection, 1946; Artists for Victory lithograph prize, 1944; John Herron Art Inst. prize for lithography, 1944; Los Angeles County Mus. purchase award, 1945. John Simon Guggenheim fellow, 1937. Mem. Inst. Arts and Letters, Soc. Am. Graphic Artists, Artists Equity Assn. Author books including: Portfolio of Caucasian Studies, 1950; American Folklore Lithographs, 1953; The Little Tailor, 1954; The Lost Conscience, 1955; (lithographs) Capricios, 1957; Portfolio of Twelve Etchings. Illustrator numerous books, most recent being: The Crime of Imprisonment (George Bernard Shaw), 1945; Here Comes Daddy (Gale T. Parks), 1951; Hound Dog Moses and the Promised Land (W.D. Edwards), 1954. Contbr. to mags. Home: 33 Hickory Dr Great Neck Estates NY 11021

GROS, ANDRE, internat. justice; b. 1908; ed. univs. Lyons and Paris. Asst. law faculty, Paris, 1931; asst. prof. U. Nancy, 1935, U. Toulouse, 1937; univ. prof. pub. law, 1938-; mem. Ministry Fgn. Affairs, 1939; prof. polit. sci. Rio de Janerio U., 1939, 41-42; legal counsellor French embassy in London; French rep. War Crimes Commn., London, 1945; legal adviser French delegation Council Fgn. Ministers and Peace Conf., Paris, 1946; legal adviser Ministry Fgn. Affairs, 1947; prof. Ecole Nationale d'Administration, Paris, 1947; mem. Permanent Ct. of Arbitration, The Hague, 1950; del. Commn. for Rhine, 1950; agt. Internat. Ct. of Justice, 1950-60, judge, 1964—; counselor d'Etat, 1954; mem. Inst. Internat. Law, 1965; mem. UN Internat. Law Commn., 1961. Decorated comdr. Legion of Honor, Croix de Guerre. Address: Judge of France Internat Court of Justice Peace Palace The Hague Netherlands

GROS, ROBERT RICHART, utilities co. exec., commentator; b. Salt Lake City, July 11, 1914; s. S. V. R. and Gladys (McConaughy) G.; B.A. with great distinction, Stanford, 1935, postgrad., 1935-36; m. Evelyn Weyher, July 23, 1937 (div. Sept. 1952); children—Elizabeth Ann, Barbara Jane; m. Mellanie Brillant, Dec. 26, 1968. Teaching asst., debating coach Stanford, 1936-37; with Pacific Gas & Electric Co., San Francisco, 1937—, advt. mgr., 1944-55, v.p., 1955-65, v.p. pub. relations, 1965—. Cons., lectr. USN; cons., nat. dir. Am. Council on NATO, 1956-61. Exec. chmn. 10th commemoration UN, 1955, exec. vice chmn. 20th Commemoration, 1965. Recipient Distinguished Pub. Service medal Navy Dept., 1958; Silver Advt. medal Am. Fedn. Advt., 1966; George Washington medal Freedoms Found., 1957, 59, 61, 63-66; UN 20th Anniversary medal U Thant, 1965. Mem. Advt. Assn. of West (pres. 1953-54). Advt. Council (dir.), Navy League U.S. (nat. dir.), Californians (pres. 1959-62), San Francisco Civic Light Opera Assn. (dir.), Cal. Newspaper Pubs. Assn., Cal. Press Assn., Pub. Relations Soc. Am., Phi Beta Kappa. Republican. Episcopalian. Clubs: San Francisco Press, Circumnavigators (chmn. No. Cal.), Commonwealth of Cal., San Francisco Advertising (pres. 1953-54), Stock Exchange (San Francisco). Lectr., commentator on world affairs. Home: 163 Britton Av Atherton CA 94025 also 1750 Taylor St San Francisco CA 94133 Office: 245 Market St San Francisco CA 94105

GROSBARD, ULU, theatrical dir.; b. Antwerp, Belgium, Jan. 9, 1929; s. Morris and Rose (Tennenbaum) G.; B.A. with honours, U. Chgo., 1950, M.A. with honours, 1952; student Yale Drama Sch., 1952-53; m. Rose Gregorio, Feb. 24, 1965. Came to U.S., 1948, naturalized, 1954. Theatrical prodns. include The Days and Nights of Beebee Fenstermaker, 1962; The Subject Was Roses (Pulitzer prize), 1964; A View From the Bridge, 1965, The Investigation, 1966; That SummerThat Fall, 1967; TV prodns. include Far Rockaway, 1966, The Investigation, 1967; co-producer Days and Nights of Beebee Fenstermaker, 1962, A View From the Bridge, 1965, TV spl. The Investigation, 1966; dir. The Price, 1968; (film) The Subject was Roses, 1968; co-producer, dir. "Who is Harry Kellerman and Why is He Saying Those Terrible Things About Me?" (film), 1971. Served with AUS, 1953-55. Recipient Vernon Rice award Drama Desk, 1965; Obie award Village Voice, 1965. Mem. Soc. Stage Dirs. and Choreographers, Dirs. Guild Am., Dramatist Guild. Office: 29 W 10th St New York City NY 10011

GROSE, CLARENCE HERMAN, educator; b. Gilboa, W.Va., Aug. 30, 1896; s. Walter Richmond and Maria (Scintilla Rader) G.; B.S., W.Va. Wesleyan Coll., 1916, Ped.D. (hon.), 1940; M.A., U. Pitts., 1927, Ph.D., 1940; LL.D., Allegheny Coll., 1950; m. Esther Mae Troeger, Aug. 29, 1931; 1 dau., Karen Jean (Mrs. William J. Rice, Jr.). Tchr. high sch., Buckhannon, W.Va., 1914-15, Salem, W.Va., 1916-17, Huntington, W.Va., 1917-22; prin. Cammack Jr. High Sch., Huntington, 1922-24; prin. jr. high sch., Ambridge, Pa., 1924-30, supt. schs., 1930-31; supt. schs., Mt. Lebanon, Pa., 1931-35, Erie, Pa., 1935-49; dep. supt. Pa. Dept. Pub. Instrn., Harrisburg, 1949-52; pres. State Tchrs. Coll., California, Pa., 1952-56; dep. supt. pub. instrn., Pa., 1956-58; asso. sec. Pa. Council Edn., 1956-58, also sec., bd. pres. Pa. State Tchrs. Colls., 1956-58, prof. ednl. adminstrn., dir. ednl. placement office Sch. Edn., U. Pitts., 1958-68, emeritus prof. edn., dir. ednl. placement, 1968—. Recipient Gov.'s citation for service to edn. handicapped, 1958; award for distinguished services to edn. Pa. Dept. Pub. Instrn., 1964; Distinguished Ednl. Leadership award Tri- State Area Sch. Study Council, 1967; Alumni Achievement award Sch. Edn. U. Pitts., 1968. Mem. Am. Assn. Sch. Adminstrs. (adv. council 1945-51), Pa. Assn. Dist. Supts. (pres. 1940), Pa. Edn. Assn. (pres. 1945), N.E.A. (chmn. tax edn. and sch. finance com. 1947-48), Pa. Assn. Health, Phys. Edn. and Recreation (Layman's Trophy 1947), Pa. Instnl. Tchr. Placement Assn. (pres. 1961), Phi Delta Kappa (nat. Commn. on support pub. edn. in U.S. 1948-49). Home: 841 California Av Pittsburgh PA 15202

GROSE, HERSCHEL GENE, educator; b. Clinton County, Ind., Feb. 1, 1921; s. Herschel K. and Anna M. (Heaton) G.; B.S., Ind. Central Coll., 1942; Ph.D., Ind. U., 1951; m. Charlotte Mable Wilson, Apr. 14, 1944; children—Ruth Suzanne (Mrs. Warren G. Williamson), Steven Lee, David Lee, Sandra Jeanne, Gregory Gene, Bonnie Louise. Tech. supr. U.S. Rubber Co., Indpls., 1941-43; research chemist E.I. duPont de Nemours & Co., Waynesboro, Va., 1951-53 prof., head dept. chemistry Marietta (O.) Coll., 1953—. Served with USNR, 1943-46. Mem. Am. Chem. Soc., A.A.A.S., Ohio Acad. Sci. Conglist. Home: 215 Ingleside Av Marietta OH 45750

GROSE, PETER BOLTON, fgn. corr.; b. Evanston, Ill., Oct. 27, 1934; s. Clyde Leclare and Carolyn (Trowbridge) G.; B.A., Yale, 1957; M.A.; Oxford (Eng.) U., 1959; m. Claudia Kerr, Sept. 11, 1965; childrenCarolyn Bronia, Stephanie Kim. Corr. with A.P. in London, 1959-60, Congo and W. Africa, 1961-62; corr. N.Y. Times, 1963—, assigned Paris, 1963, chief corr. Vietnam, 1964, chief Moscow bur., 1965-67, diplomatic corr., Washington, 1967-70, chief corr. Israel, 1970—. Clubs: Yale (N.Y.C.); Federal City (Washington); Oxford, Cambridge (London). Office: Lishkat Haitonuth Jerusalem Israel

GROSECLOSE, ELGIN economist, author; b. Waukomis, Okla., Nov. 25, 1899; s. M. Clarence and Della (Wishard) G.; A.B., U. Okla., 1920; M.A., Am. Univ., 1924, Ph.D., 1928; m. Louise Elizabeth Williams, June 25, 1927; children—Sarah Jane (Mrs. Peter Theodoropoulos), Nancy Margaret (Mrs. Herold Witherspoon), Hildegarde Elsa (Mrs. Earl Bender), Suzy French (Mrs. Kenneth Labaugh). Tchr., Presbyn. Mission Sch., Tabriz, Persia (now Iran), sec. Persia Relief Com., 1920-23; spl. agt. U.S. Dept. Commerce, 1923-26; asst. U.S. Trade Commr., 1926; with Guaranty Trust Co., N.Y.C., 1927-30; asso. editor Fortune, also lectr. Coll. City N.Y., 1930-32; asst. prof. bus. adminstrn. U. Okla., 1932-38; economist telephone investigation FCC, 1935-38; economist U.S. Treasury Dept., 1938-43; treas.-gen. Iran, 1943; head firm Elgin Groseclose, Econ. Counsel, 1944-59; Groseclose, Williams and Assos., financial analysts and cons., 1959-; exec. dir. Inst. for Monetary Research, 1961—. Founder Welfare of Blind, Inc.; bd. dirs. Internat. Council for Christian Leadership, 1953-65. Recipient Near East Relief medal; Am. Booksellers award, 1939; Found. for Lit. award, 1940. Mem. Okla. Soc. Washington (pres. 1945- 46), Washington City Bible Soc. (pres., bd. dirs.), Phi Beta Kappa, Phi Delta Phi, Alpha Kappa Psi, Delta Sigma Rho, Delta Tau Delta. Episcopalian. Clubs: Nat. Economists, Cosmos (Washington). Author: MoneyThe Human Conflict, 1934; The Persian Journey of the Rev. Ashley Wishard and His Servant Fathi, 1937; Ararat, 1939; The Firedrake, 1942; Introduction to Iran, 1947; The Carmelite, 1955; The Scimitar of Saladin, 1956; Money and Man, 1961; Fifty Years of Managed Money, The Story of the Federal Reserve, 1966; also monographs. Home: 4813 Woodway Lane NW Washington DC 20016 Office: 1010 Vermont Av NW Washington DC 20005

GROSETH, HAAKON BJARNE, advt. exec.; b. Mpls., Dec. 20, 1905; s. Johannes T. and Sanna (Stigum) G.; A.B., U. Minn., 1929; M.B.A., Graduate Sch. U. Chgo., 1963; m. Mary Ann Reardon, Feb. 8, 1937; childrenJohn Michael, Mary Ann (Mrs. John H. Nichols, Jr.), and Robert Theodore, Rolf Stigum, Sanna Jane. Sales promotion rep. Dollenmayer Advt. Agy., 1929; jr. salesman Pillsbury Flour Mills Co., 1929-30; advt. dept. Armstrong Linoleum Co., 1930; market research, account exec. Paul Teas Advt. Agy., Cleve., 1930-31; advt. mgr. George A. Hormel & Co., Austin, Minn., 1931- 36; merchandising dir. Knox Reeves Advt. Co., 1937-39; account and merchandising exec. Ruthrauff & Ryan, Inc., Chgo., 1939-44, v.p. 1944—, dir. 1953-57; exec. v.p., in charge Chgo. operations, mem., exec. com., 1957-58; exec. v.p., Erwin Wasey, Ruthrauff & Ryan, Inc., 1958-64, dir.; sr. v.p. Clyne Maxon Advt., Inc., N.Y.C., 1964-66; sr. v.p. Fuller, Smith & Ross Advt., Inc., 1966-68; marketing cons., 1968-. Mem. Phi Gamma Delta. Clubs: Chgo. Press; Hinsdale (Ill.) Golf; Milbrook (Greenwich, Conn.); Duquesne (Pitts.). Address: 705 Treasure Boat Way Sarasota FL 33581

GROSH, RICHARD JOSEPH, mech. engr., univ. dean; b. Ft. Wayne, Ind., Oct. 29, 1927; s. Joseph A. and Vera (Vogeding) G.; B.S., Purdue U., 1950, M.S., 1952, Ph.D., 1953; m. Susan Marie Ankenbruck, June 24, 1950; children—Katherine, Anton, Richard, John, Jane, Suzanne. Research, devel. Capehart Farnsworth Corp., Ft. Wayne, 1950-51; asst. prof. mech. engring. Purdue U., Lafayette, Ind., 1953-56, asso. prof., 1956-58, prof., 1958-71, head Sch. Mech. Engring., 1961-65, asso. dean engring., 1965-67, dean, 1967-71; pres. Rensselaer Poly. Inst., Troy, N.Y., 1971—. Dir. indsl. devel. Purdue Research Found.; v.p. McClure Park, Inc., 1964-66; dir. AMF Inc., Ecol. Sci. Corp., 1st Fed. Savs. & Loan Assn.; cons. Allison div. Gen. Motors Co. Bd. dirs., lay adv. bd. St. Elizabeth Hosp., Ind. Ednl. Services Found. Served with CIC, USAAF, 1946-47. Mem. Nat. Acad. Engring., Am. Inst. Aeros. And Astronautics, Am. Soc. for Engring. Edn. Pi Tau Sigma, Sigma Pi Sigma, Tau Beta Pi. Cons. editor Charles E. Merrill Book Co. Contbr. articles to profl. jours. Home: 2005 Tibbits Av Troy NY 12181

GROSHANS, WERNER, artist; b. Eutingen, Germany, July 6, 1913; s. Emil and Anna (Jung) G.; came to U.S., 1927; grad. Newark Sch. Fine and Indsl. Arts, 1932; m. Yetta Abramowitz, June 3, 1944. Exhibited group shows Whitney Mus. Carnegie Inst., Met. Mus., Butler Inst., N.A.D., Montclair Mus. Art, Parrish Art Mus., Newark Mus., Audubon Artists, Silvermine Guild, AFA Traveling Exhbn., Hirschl-Adler Gallery, Springfield (Mass.) Mus. Fine Arts, Kennedy Gallery, Wadsworth Atheneum, U. Md., 1966-67, Quinata Gallery, Nantucket, Mass., 1969, Centenary Coll. (2-man exhbn.) Hackettstown, N.J., 1969, Okla. Mus. Art, 1969, others; represented permanent collections Davenport (Ia.) Municipal Art Gallery, Ct. Gen. Sessions, Washington, Newark Mus., Newark Pub. Library, N.A.D. Collection, Ency. Brit. collection, New Britain (Conn.) Mus. Am. Art; also pvt. collections. Chmn. fine arts dept. Jersey City Mus., 1966-69. Recipient Thomas B. Clarke award N.A.D., 1960; Henry Ward Ranger Fund purchase prize, 1961; 1st prize Montclair Art Mus., 1961; Pauline Wick award, 1961; Painters and Sculptors award, 1964; Silver medallion N.J. Tercentenary Exhbn., 1964; Famous Artists Sch. award, 1965; Margaret C. Cooper award, 1966; Gold medal, Ligonier, Pa., 1966; N.J. Artist of Year award, 1966; Edward C. Roberts Meml. award New Britain Mus. Am. Art, 1969. Nat. academician N.A.D. (Council 1970—) Mem. Audubon Artists, Conn. Acad. Fine Arts, Allied Artists, Assn. Artists N.J., Painters and Sculptors Soc. N.J. (v.p. 1967—). Address: 941 Blvd E Weehawken NJ 07087 Office: Robert Schoelkopf Gallery 825 Madison Av New York City NY

GROSPIRON, A. F., labor union exec.; b. Burton, Tex., Apr. 17, 1916; s. Emil Carl and Ella (Werner) G.; ed. pub. schs., Tex.; m. Etta Mae Taylor, Mar. 17, 1937; childrenLynn Rhea (Mrs. Conrad Keniston), Alvin Gene. Refinery operator Am. Oil Co., 1935-51; with Oil, Chem. and Atomic Workers Internat. Union, 1951-, sec.-treas., 1962-65, internat. pres., 1965-; dir. Mainland Bank & Trust Co., Texas City, Tex., 1961-62. Democrat. Methodist. Home: 2771 S Eaton Way Denver CO 80227 Office: 1840 California St Denver CO 80201

GROSS, ABRAHAM, rabbi, educator; b. Bklyn., June 29, 1928; s. Joseph and Tillie (Lauer) G.; rabbi Ch'san Sofer Rabbinical Sem., 1952; B.B.A., Coll. City N.Y., 1951; M.S. Edn., Yeshiva U., 1959; 6th yr. profl. certificate Hunter Coll., 1968; m. Hannah Leah Stern, Dec. 18, 1952; children—Israel Meyer, Elijah Moses, Vitel, Adel Binah, Hilda Mindy, Solomon Abel. Rabbi, Young Israel of Coll. Av., Bronx, N.Y., 1953-63, Congregation Adath Jeshurum, Bronx, 1963-68, Young Israel of Vanderveer Park, Bklyn., 1968—; asst. prin. pub. schs., N.Y.C., 1966—. Mem. Community Planning Bd. 4, Bronx, 1966-69; active Bonds for Israel, Yeshiva, Beth Jacob movements. Treas., Charles and Ana Elenberg Found. Mem. Rabbinical Alliance Am. (pres. 1969-71), Met. Bd. Orthodox Rabbis (treas. 1965-69). Home: 2720 Av J Brooklyn NY 11210 Office: 2815 Farragut Rd Brooklyn NY 11210

GROSS, AVRUM MICHAEL, lawyer; b. N.Y.C., Feb. 25, 1936; s. Joel and Theresa (Stavisky) G.; B.A., Amherst Coll., 1957; J.D., Mich. Law Sch., 1960; m. Sharon Ruth Robinson, Dec. 21, 1958; children-Jody Ann, Alan Stuart. Admitted to Alaska bar, 1961, since practiced in Juneau; legal counsel Alaska Legislative Council, 1960-61; asst. atty. gen. Alaska, 1961-63, chief Appellate div., 1962-63; asso. Faulkner, Benfield, Boochener & Doogan, 1963-64, partner, 1964—. Alternate del. Nat. Democratic Conv., 1968. Pres. Juneau-Douglas Concert Assn., S.E. Alaska chpt. Am. Civil Liberties Union; pres., bd. dirs. Juneau Receiving Home; v.p. Juneau Centennial Commn. Mem. Alaska, Juneau bar assns., Alaska, Intergrated Bar (v.p., bd. govs.). Home: 328 Coleman St Juneau AK 99801 Office: 311 N Franklin St Juneau AK 99801

GROSS, BENJAMIN SAMUEL, former radio-TV editor, critic, author; b. Birmingham, Ala., Nov. 24, 1891; s. Aldolph and Sarah (Kaufman) G.; student Tulane U., 1911-12; LL.B., U. Ala., 1914; m. Kathleen Cotter, Dec. 31, 1921. Reporter, feature writer Birmingham News, 1911-14; admitted to Ala. bar, 1915; with law office Banks, Deedmeyer & Birch, Birmingham, 1915- 17; reporter Bronx (N.Y.) Home News, 1919; editor World Traveler mag., N.Y.C., 1919-20; reporter, columnist N.Y. Morning Telegraph, 1922-23; reporter, feature writer N.Y. Morning Telegraph, 1922-23, N.Y. Am., 1923;

reporter-rewriteman A.P., N.Y.C., 1924; reporter, labor editor, radio-TV editor and critic, N.Y. Daily News, 1925-71; news, polit. commentator radio stas. WMCA, N.Y.C., 1940-41; spl. commentator polit. convs., NBC, 1944; commentator sts. WPIX-TV, N.Y.C., 1948. Served with 348th Inf., 87th Div., U.S. Army, 1918-19; AEF in France. Mem. Radio Pioneer U. Ala. Alumni Assn. Clubs: National Press (Washington); Overseas Press (N.Y.C.). Author: (book) I Looked and I Listened, 1955, 70; (with M.H. Aylesworth) Men, Mikes and Money; (comedy) Husbands, 1927; (comedy) (with Charles Zerner) What This Town Needs, 1937. Author numerous articles popular mags., newspapers, lectr. Home: 360 E 55th St New York City NY 10022 Office: NY Daily News 220 E 42d St New York City NY 10017

GROSS, BERNARD JOEL, corp. exec.; b. Chgo., Feb. 28, 1918; s. Jerry and Anna (Burrows) G.; grad. Exec. Program U. Chgo., 1953, M.B.A., 1953; m. Judith Bazelon, Nov. 14, 1942; children—Michael, Susan, John. Writer, exec. Meyer-Both Co., Chgo., 1936-41; copywriter Leo Burnett Co., Chgo., 1945-46; with Edward H. Weiss & Co., Chgo., 1947—, exec. v.p., 1959-62, also dir., sr. v.p. McCann-Erickson, Inc., 1962-65; exec. v.p. Johnstone, Inc., N.Y.C., 1965; sr. v.p. McCann-Erickson, Inc., gen. corp. exec. Interpub. Inc., 1966; v.p., gen. mgr. products div. Helene Curtis Industries, Inc., Chgo., 1966-70; group v.p., gen. mgr. Amtico div. Am. Biltrite Rubber Co., Inc., Trenton, N.J., 1971—. Former mem. Ill. Council Econ. Advisers, Ill. Com. Trade Expansion. Mem. Council U. Chgo. Clubs: Press (Chgo.); Standard. Office: PO Box 2151 Trenton NJ 08607

GROSS, BERNARD JOSEPH, mfg. co. exec.; b. St. Louis, Nov. 6, 1908; s. Bernard and Johanna (Reiss) G.; B.S. in Metallurgy, U. Mo., 1933; grad. Advanced Mgmt. Program Harvard, 1960; m. Adelaine M. Murphy, Sept. 17, 1937; children—Robert B., Raymond F. Engr., Key Co., East St. Louis, Ill., 1933-39, sales mgr., 1939-45, v.p. sales, 1945-47, pres., 1947-55; v.p. marketing W.K.M. Valve div. ACF Industries, Inc., Houston, 1955-67, v.p. marketing, N.Y.C., 1967—. Registered profl. engr., Mo. Mem. Alloy Castings Inst., Valve Mfrs. Assn. (pres.), Am. Petroleum Inst., Sales Exec. Club N.Y., Phi Kappa Theta, Theta Tau. Club: Pinnacle (N.Y.C.). Home: 303 E 57th St New York City NY 10022 Office: ACF Industries Inc 750 3d Av New York City NY 10017

GROSS, BERTRAM MYRON, educator, govt. ofcl.; b. Phila., Dec. 25, 1912; s. Samuel and Regina (Glass) G.; B.A., U. Pa., 1933, M.A., 1935; m. Nora Faine, Sept. 4, 1938; children—David, Larry, Samuel, Theodore. With information div. U.S. Housing Authority, 1938-41; external lectr. Grad. Sch., Dept. Agr., 1939-40; chief reports unit OPA, 1941; research and hearings dir., com. small bus. U.S. Senate, 1942-43, staff dir. subcom. war contracts, 1943-44, econ. adviser to chmn. banking and currency com., 1945-46; comd. seminar adminstrn. for govt. ofcls., also external lectr. Sch. Govt., George Washington U., 1946-47; external lectr. Hebrew U., Jerusalem, 1955-56, vis. prof. adminstrn., 1956-60; prof. adminstrn. Maxwell Sch. Citizenship and Pub. Affairs, Syracuse U., 1960-61, 1963-68; dir. Center for Urban Studies Wayne State U., 1969-70; Distinguished prof. urban affairs and planning Hunter Coll. City U. N.Y.; vis. prof. U. Cal. at Berkeley, spring 1962, Harvard Grad. Sch. Bus. Adminstrn., fall 1962-63. Spl. asst. to adminstr. FSA, 1946; exec. sec. Council Econ. Adviser to Pres., 1946-51; mem. then vice chmn. Arlington County (Va.) Planning Commn., 1950-52; research dir. Democratic Nat. Com., 1952; chmn. Nat. Capital Regional Planning Council, 1952-53; cons. UN Korean Reconstrn. Adminstrn., 1952-53; mem. econ. adv. staff Office Prime Minister Israel, 1953-55, econ. adviser Office Minister Finance, 1955-56; mgmt. cons. El Al, Israel Nat. Airlines, 1956-57, 59; cons. Ford Found. in India, also Indian Inst. Pub. Adminstrn., New Delhi, 1961; mem. summer study group, com. space efforts and soc. Am. Acad. Arts and Scis., 1962; chmn. Internat. Group Studies Nat. Planning, 1965-69; chmn. com. nat. planning research Am. Soc. Pub. Adminstrn., 1965—; cons. social indicators to sec. Dept. Health, Edn. and Welfare, 1966-67. Fellow Center Advanced Research Behavioral Scis., 1961-62; Faculty research fellow Social Sci. Research Council, 1961-62. Mem. Am. Polit. Sci. Assn. (chmn. com. polit. parties 1951-52; Woodrow Wilson award 1953). Author: The State of The Nation; Social Systems Accounting, 1966; Legislative Struggle: A Study in Social Combat, 1953; (with Will Lumer) The Hard Money Crusade, 1954; The Managing of Organizations, 2 vols., 1964; Organizations and Their Managing, 1968. Editor: A Great Society?, 1968; Social Goals and Indicator for American Society: I, 1967, 2, 1967; Action Under Planning, 1967; National Planning Series, 1965-67; Social Intelligence for America's Future, 1969; New Styles of Planning in Post-Industrial America, 1971. Address: 444 E 82d St New York City NY 10028

GROSS, CALVIN EDWARD, educator; b. Los Angeles, Apr. 8, 1919; s. Harry Edward and Telah May (Calvin) G.; A.B., U. Cal. at Los Angeles, 1940; M.S., U. So. Cal., 1947; Ed. D., Harvard, 1955; L.H.D. (hon.), Carnegie-Mellon U., 1963; Pd.D. (hon.), Manhattan Coll., 1963; LL.D., Ripon Coll., 1963, U. Akron, 1963; m. Bernice Marjorie Hayman, Mar. 29, 1946; children—Georgette Louise, Gary, Glenn. Grad. asst. math. Ore. State U., 1940-41; tchr. math. dept., chmn., registrar, vice prin. Los Angeles city schs., 1946-50; supt. schs., Weston, Mass., 1951-56, Niskayuna Central Sch. Dist., Schenectady, 1956-58, Pitts., 1958-63; supt. schs., N.Y.C., 1963-65; dean Sch. Edn., U. Mo., Kansas City, 1965- -. Adv. com. on new ednl. media U.S. Dept. Health, Edn. and Welfare; chmn. study com. Gov.'s Conf. on Edn., 1968; mem. commn. on edn. for teaching profession Nat. Assn. State Univs. and Land-Grant Colls., mem. com. on govt. relations Am. Assn. Colls. for Tchr. Edn.; chmn. com. on budget and finance Nat. Council for Accreditation Tchr. Edn. Chmn. exec. com., pres. bd. trustees Mid-Continent Regional Ednl. Lab. Trustee Carnegie-Mellon U., Ednl. Testing Service, Nat. Conf. Christians and Jews; mem. vis. com. Harvard U. Summer Sch.; adv. com. Kamehameha Schs. Served in AUS, 1941-46. Mem. Am. Assn. Sch. Adminstrs., Joint Council Econ. Edn. (trustee), Cleve. Conf., Mo. Tchrs. Assn., Internat. Platform Assn., Phi Beta Kappa. Club: Harvard (N.Y.C.). Co-author: Research for Tomorrow's Schools: Disciplined Inquiry for Education, 1969. Address: Sch Edn U Mo Kansas City MO 64110

GROSS, CHAIM, sculptor, teacher; b. Austria, Mar. 17, 1904; s. Moses and Lea (Sperber) G.; student Beaux Arts Inst., N.Y.C., 4 yrs., Ednl. Alliance Art Sch., N.Y. City, 4 yrs.; D.F.A., Franklin and Marshall Coll., 1970; m. Renee Nechin, Dec. 13, 1932; children—Yudie, Mimi L. Came to U.S., 1921, naturalized, 1934. Tchr. sculpture, Ednl. Alliance Art Sch., N.Y.C., 1927—, Mus. Mod. Art, 1952-57; New Sch. for Social Research, N.Y., 1948—. One-man shows at Gallery 144, N.Y.C., 1932, Boyer Gallery, Phila. and N.Y.C., 1935, 37, Newark, 1939; Assn. Am. Artists, N.Y.C., 1942, 45, 47, 52, 53, Duveen-Graham Gallery, N.Y.C., 1957, Forum Gallery, N.Y.C., 1962, Whitney Mus. Am. Art, N.Y.C., 1959, Medici II Gallery, Miami Beach, Fla., 1971, numerous others; Artists for Victory Exhbn., Met. Mus., N.Y.C. 1942; carved in stone, over-door panel FTC Bldg., Washington; carved in wood a panel for post office, Irwin, Pa., 1942; executed 2 groups shown at N.Y. World's Fair, 1939, for France overseas and Switzerland bldgs.; exhibited in numerous group shows including Whitney Mus. Modern Art, Newark Mus. Art, Bklyn. Mus. Art; represented in permanent collections Met. Mus., Mus. Modern Art, Whitney Mus. Am. Art, N.Y.C.; Bklyn., Newark museums, Worcester Art Mus., Andover Mus. of Art, Brandeis U., Smith Coll., Jewish Mus. of Art, Abraham Lincoln Sch. and numerous other pub. bldgs. and museums. Made 3- reel ednl. motion picture "Tree Trunk to Head," demonstrating technique of wood carving. Awarded nat. competition prize for "Alaskan Snowshoe Mail Carrier," Washington, D.C., sect. of Fine Arts, 1936; silver medal for "Offspring," Paris Expn., 1937; 2d prize "Lillian Leitzell," Artist Victory Exhibition, N.Y.C., 1942; first mention Nat. Acad. Philadelphia, 1954; anonymous prize Audubon Soc., 1955; 1st prize (water color), Cape Cod Art Assn., 1951; 3d prize (sculpture), Boston Art Festival, 1954; Arts, Letters Grant, Nat. Acad. Arts, Letters, N.Y.C., 1956; Hon. Mention prize Audubon Soc., N.Y.C., 1957, numerous others. Mem. bd. Sculptors Guild. Mem. Ednl. Alliance Alumni Assn., Nat. Inst. Arts and Letters (Award of Merit medal and prize for sculpture 1963). Author: A Sculptor's Progress, an Autobiography, 1938; Fantasy Drawings, 1956; Technique of Wood Carving, 1957. Has illustrated children's books by Naftoli Gross. Carves in wide variety woods. Works also illustrated several books and collections. Address: 526 W Broadway New York City NY 10012

GROSS, COURTLANDT SHERRINGTON, aircraft corp. exec.; b. Boston, Nov. 21, 1904; s. Robert H. and Mabel (Bell) G.; student St. George's Sch., 1919-23; A.B., Harvard, 1927; m. Alexandra van R. Devereux, July 18, 1939; childrenAlexandra Devereux (dec.), Courtlandt Devereux, Mary L. Wanamaker Fenwick (step-dau.). Clk., salesman Lee Higginson & Co., Boston, 1927-29; buyer, dir. Viking Flying Boat Co., New Haven, 1929-32; Eastern rep. Lockheed Aircraft Corp., N.Y.C., 1932-40, v.p., gen. mgr., dir., Burbank, 1943-52, exec. v. p., dir., 1952- 56, pres., dir., 1956-61, chmn. bd., chmn. exec. com., 1961-67, now chmn. finance com., dir.; pres., dir. Vega Aircraft, Burbank, 1940-43; dir. Lockheed Aircraft Corp., Burbank, Cal., Phila. Contributionship for Ins. Houses from Loss by Fire, Atlantic Richfield Corp., Electric Storage Battery Corp., Girard Trust Bank, Smith Kline & French Labs.; trustee Penn Mut. Life Ins. Co. Episcopalian. Home: 1230 Arrowmink Rd Villanova PA 19085 Office: 2 Girard Plaza Philadelphia PA 19102

GROSS, ERIC TARAS BENJAMIN, educator, elec. engr.; b. Vienna, Austria, May 24, 1901; s. Berthold and Sophie (Gerstman) G.; E.E., Tech. U., Vienna, 1923, D.Sc., 1932; m. Catharine B. Rohrer, Aug. 14, 1942; children—Patrick Walter, Elizabeth Sophia, Margaret Joan. Came to U.S., 1939, naturalized, 1943. Elec. engr. in industry with emphasis on heavy electric power engring., 1923-40; asst. prof. elec. engring. Cornell U., 1940-45; prof. elec. engring. Ill. Inst. Tech., 1945-62; chmn. electric power engring., Philip Sporn prof. engring. Rensselaer Poly. Inst., Troy, N.Y., 1962—; cons. War Dept., 1942-45. Registered profl. engr., Ill., N.Y., Vt. Chartered engr., U.K. Fellow N.Y. Acad. Scis., I.E.E.E., A.A.A.S., Inst. Elec. Engrs. (London); mem. Am. Arbitration Assn. (mem. nat. panel), Am. Soc. Engring. Edn. (Best Paper prize Chgo. sect. A.I.E.E. 1953), Panamerican Congress on Engring. (v.p. for U.S. 1970—), Eta Kappa Nu (nat. pres. 1953-54). Contbr. articles profl. jours. Home: 2525 McGovern Dr Schenectady NY 12309 Office: Rensselaer Poly Inst Troy NY 12181

GROSS, ERNEST ARNOLD, lawyer; b. N.Y.C., Sept. 23, 1906; s. Arnold and Caroline (Fleisher) G.; B.S., Harvard Coll., 1927; student Oxford U., 1927-28; LL.B., Harvard, 1931; Geneva Sch. of Internat. Studies, summers 1929, 1930; m. Kathryn Watson, Sept. 1, 1933; childrenSuzanne, Peter, Catherine. Admitted to bar, 1933; asst. legal adviser, Dept. of State, 1931-33; div. counsel, N.R.A., 1933-34; gen. counsel graphic arts coordinating com., Printing and Publishing Industries, 1934-36; asso. gen. counsel, Nat. Assn. Mfrs., 1936-38; asso. gen. counsel for enforcement, Nat. Labor Relations Bd., 1938-43; dep. asst. sec. of state for Occupied Areas, 1946-47, legal adviser, Dept. of State, Washington, 1947; asst. sec. state, 1948; partner Curtis, Mallet-Prevost, Colt & Mosle, 1954-; chmn. bd. Internat. Mgmt. & Engring. Group Ltd.; dir. United Printers & Publishers. Mem. U.S. delegation to Far Eastern Commn.; U.S. rep. on U.N. peace comm. to 1953; del. to 3d, 5th and 6th U.N. Gen. Assembly Sessions; pres. Freedom House, 1953; trustee Carnegie Endowment for Internat. Peace; dir., v.p. Asia Soc.; chmn. dept. internat. relations Nat. Council Chs. of Christ Am. Trustee Barnard Coll.; pres. Woodrow Wilson Found. Commd. capt., U.S. Army, 1943, advanced lt. col., 1944; became chief econs. sect. Civil Affairs Div., War Dept. Gen. Staff; adviser to U.S. delegation ILO, 1944; chmn. exec. comm. Free Europe Com., 1964—; trustee African- Am. Inst. Decorated Legion of Merit, Order of Brit. Empire, European Theatre Ribbon. Mem. Am. Bar Assn., Am. Soc. Internat. Law, UN Assn. (vice chmn.). Author: The United Nations-Structure for Peace, 1964; articles in Dept. of State Bulletins, N.Y. Times Mag., other periodicals. Home: 146 Central Park W New York City NY 10023 Office: 100 Wall St New York City NY 10005

GROSS, FRITZ A., electronics co. exec.; b. Germany, Oct. 8, 1910; s. Fritz and Anna (Hörmann) G.; came to U.S., 1912, naturalized, 1920, grad. Lowell (Mass.) Inst., 1930, grad. course electronics, 1931; m. Olive Nelson, Aug. 14, 1937; children-Jane, Martha, Susan. Design engr. S.H. Couch Co., Quincy, Mass. 1932-34; with Raytheon Co., Lexington, Mass., 1934—, mgr. heavy electronic equipment operations, 1958-60, vice pres., gen. mgr. equipment div., 1960-68, v.p. engring., 1968—. Tech. adv. radio aids to navigation USN, 1946. Recipient Certificate of Merit commendation USN, 1946. Registered profl. engr., Mass. Fellow I.E.E.E.; mem. Am. Soc. Naval Engrs., Armed Forces Communications and Electronics Assn. Home: 71 Westland Rd Weston MA 02193 Office: Raytheon Co Lexington MA 02173

GROSS, GERALD J., book pub.; b. Jersey City, Oct. 10, 1921; s. David and Faye (Weberman) G.; B.S.S., Coll. City N.Y., 1946; m. Flora Finn, Jan. 24, 1943; childrenSarah Kerstin, Adam Anthony. Formerly with Reynal & Hitchcock, N.Y.C., then prodn. mgr., editor Harcourt, Brace & Co., also v.p., mng. editor Pantheon Books, N.Y.C., now sr. v.p. Macmillan Co., N.Y.C.; lectr. Columbia Sch. Gen. Studies, N.Y.U. Grad. Sch. Book Pub. Trustee library bd., Weston, Conn. Served to 2d lt., navigator, USAAF, World War II; ETO. Mem. Am. Inst. Graphic Arts (past bd. dirs.). Home: Godfrey Rd Weston CT 06880 Office: 60 Fifth Av New York City NY 10011

GROSS, HAL RAYMOND, bishop; b. Walla Walla, Wash., Jan. 15, 1914; s. John J. and Millie (Hale) G.; student Ore. State U., 1931-36; J.D., Willamette U., 1939; student Ch. Div. Sch. of Pacific, 1946, D.D., 1965; m. Evelyn Blyth Kerr, July 22, 1933; 1 dau., Patricia Ann (Mrs. Charles E. Ernst). Admitted to Ore. bar, 1939; pvt. practice in Corvallis, 1939-42; atty. Ore. Unemployment Compensation Commn., 1942-44; ordained to ministry Episcopal Ch., 1946; pastor U. Ore., 1946-47; rector St. Paul's Ch., Oregon City, 1947-61; Archdean Episcopal Diocese Ore., 1961-65; suffragan bishop Ore., 1965-. Trustee Ch. Div. Sch. of Pacific, 1950- 55. Mem. Ore. Bar Assn., Phi Delta Theta. Democrat. Elk, Rotarian (hon.). Home: 200 Burnham Rd Lake Oswego OR 97034 Office: 11800 SW Military Lane Portland OR 97219

GROSS, HAROLD BANCROFT, lawyer, corp. exec.; b. Providence, Mar. 28, 1908; s. George Lord and Ethel Maude (Chace) G.; grad. cum laude, Phillips Exeter Acad. (N.H.), 1926; A.B. magna cum laude, Williams Coll. (Mass.), 1940; LL.B. cum laude Harvard 1933; m. Virginia Bleh North, Oct. 3, 1957. Admitted to Rhode Island bar, 1933, New Hampshire bar 1938, N.Y. bar, 1954; with Hinckley, Allen, Tillinghast and Wheeler, Providence, R.I., 1933-36; prin. atty., Social Security Bd., Washington 1936-37; instr. English, Phillips Exeter Acad., 1937-42; counsel, Bur. of Aeronautics, U.S. Navy Dept., 1946-47; asst. gen. counsel, Navy Dept., 1947-49, gen. counsel, 1949-53; with Am. Cyanamid Co., 1953-57, head legal dept., 1957-63, gen. mgr. law div., 1963-68, sec., gen. counsel, 1968-. Served with USN, 1942-46. Mem. Am. Law Inst., Am. Bar Assn., Phi Beta Kappa, Alpha Delta Phi, Harvard Law Assn. Episcopalian. Home: 47 Pines Lake Dr E Wayne NJ 07470 Office: Am Cyanamid Co Berdan Av Wayne NJ 07470

GROSS, JOHN ARTHUR, patent lawyer; b. Chgo., July 14, 1906; s. Arthur and Ann (Carroll) G.; B.S. in Chem. Engring., U. Ill., 1927; student Georgetown U., 1928-30; LL.B., DePaul U., 1932; m. Lila Ann Millarkey, Aug. 25, 1934; children—J. Michael, Dennis A., Terrence R. Plant control engr. Van Schaack Bros. Chem. Works, Chgo., 1927-28; patent examiner U.S. Patent Office, 1928-30; admitted to Ill. bar, 1932, U.S. Supreme Ct. bar, 1947; practiced in Chgo., 1932—; patent atty. firm Charles W. Hills, 1930—; mem. firm Hill, Sherman, Meroni, Gross & Simpson, 1943—. Registered profl. engr., Ill. Mem. Am. Patent Law Assn., Fed., 7th Fed. Circuit, Chgo. (chmn. patent, trademark and copyright com. 1959-62), Am., Ill. bar assns., Patent Law Assn. Chgo. (chmn. various coms. 1947-59, pres. 1968), Am. Chem. Soc., Soc. Automotive Engrs., Chgo. Assn. Commerce and Industry, Delta Theta Phi. Roman Catholic. Clubs: Union League (Chgo.); North Shore Country (Glenview, Ill.). Home: 15 Winfield Dr Winnetka IL 60093 Office: 53 W Jackson Blvd Chicago IL 60604

GROSS, JOHN BIRNEY, coll. dean; b. Barbourville, Ky., Aug. 24, 1924; s. John Owen and Harriet (Bletzer) G.; A.B., DePauw U., 1948; B.D., S.T.M., Drew U., 1953; Ph.D., George Peabody Coll., 1958; m. Lois Feldkircher, July 8, 1948; childrenJohn Birney II, Steven Louis. Ordained to ministry Meth. Ch., 1950; minister, in Mendham, N.J., 1950-53; dean chapel Centenary Coll. Women, Hackettstown, N.J., 1953-56; asst. to pres. Fla. So. Coll., Lakeland, 1958-59, dean acad. affairs, 1959-65; dean coll. Mt. Union Coll., Alliance, O., 1965-67, v.p., 1967-68; dean coll. Tex. Wesleyan Coll., Ft. Worth, 1968-. Co-chmn. membership drive Community Concerts, Alliance, 1968; mem. Crandel alumni scholarship com. DePauw U., 1967. Bd. dirs. Lakeland chpt. A.R.C., 1963-65, Community Concerts, Lakeland, 1963-65, Casa Manana Playhouse, Ft. Worth, 1968—. Served with AUS, 1943-46. Kellog fellow George Peabody Coll., 1956-58. Mem. Am. Assn. Acad. Deans, Assn. Acad. Deans, So. Assn. Schs. and Colls., Phi Delta Kappa, Kappa Delta Pi, Phi Mu Alpha. Democrat. Kiwanian. Home: 4912 Boulder Lake Rd Fort Worth TX 76103

GROSS, LAMBERT JOHN, corp. exec.; b. Bklyn., May 1, 1915; s. John Lambert and Charlotte Marie (Reiber) G.; B.A., Princeton, 1937; M.B.A., N.Y.U., 1941; m. Shirley Allison Wolfe, May 2, 1936. Pub. accountant R. G. Rankin and Co., C.P.A.'s, 1937-43; treas. Autoflight Corp., 1943-44; sec. Adel Precision Products Corp., 1944-47; v.p., controller Electric Boat Co., 1949-52; v.p. finance, dir. Gen. Dynamics Corp., 1952-60; v.p. finance Combustion Engring., Inc., 1960—, dir., 1964—; asst. to chmn. Canadair, Ltd., 1949-60. C.P.A., N.Y., Cal. Mem. Am. Mgmt. Assn., Financial Execs. Inst. Clubs: University, Princeton (N.Y.C.); Elm (Princeton, N.J.); Ridgewood Country. Office: 277 Park Av New York City NY 10017

GROSS, LEONARD, mfg. co. exec.; b. Phila., June 9, 1921; s. Philip P. and Rose (Cohen) G.; student Temple U., 1938-40, U.S. Naval Acad., 1944-45; m. Miriam Zimmerman, July 2, 1944; childrenLeslie Faye, Elise Ricki, Andrew Peter. With Philco Corp., 1945-60, mdse. mgr., 1958-60; v.p. vending div. Seeburg Corp., Chgo., 1960-62, exec. v.p. operations, 1962-; pres. Shelen Corp., Chgo., 1961-; pres., chmn. Golf Ball, Inc., Chgo., 1963- -; dir. Evergreen Gardens Inc., Chgo. Div. chmn. Crusade of Mercy, Chgo., 1962. Served to lt. comdr. USNR, 1940-45. Decorated Bronze Star, Purple Heart. Mem. Ill. C. of C. Home: 3200 Lake Shore Dr Chicago IL 60657 Office: 5816 S Lowe Av Chicago IL 60621

GROSS, LEROY, sugar co. exec.; b. N.Y.C., Aug. 11, 1926; s. Morris and Sarah (Leichter) G.; B.S., in Accounting, N.Y. U., 1948; postgrad. Fordham U. Sch. Law, 1951-53; M.B.A. in Accounting, N.Y. U., 1955; m. Betty Koch, Aug. 28, 1949; children—Michael Stephen, Kenneth Richard, Emily Jayne. With SuCrest Corp., N.Y.C., 1948—, internal audit mgr., 1962-65, corp. accounting mgr., 1965-69, controller, 1969—; lectr. N.Y. U., 1968—. Served with USAAF, 1946-47. Mem. Inst. Internal Auditors, Am. Accounting Assn., Nat. Assn. Accountants. Home: 23 Moccasin Pl Monsey NY 10952 Office: 120 Wall St New York City NY 10005

GROSS, LIONEL GRANT, lawyer; b. Sheridan, Wyo., May 1, 1925; s. Bert and Eva (MacIntyre) G.; Ph.B., U. Chgo., 1947, J.D., 1950; m. Lois C. Gordon, June 19, 1949; children—Susan Rae, David Brian. Admitted to Ill. bar, 1950; since practiced in Chgo.; asso., partner Altheimer, Gray, Naiburg, Strasburger & Lawton, 1950. Served to 1st lt. AUS, 1943-46. Mem. Am., Ill., Chgo. bar assns. Home: 1361 Lincoln Av S Highland Park IL 60035 Office: 1 N LaSalle St Chicago IL 60601

GROSS, LLEWELLYN ZWICKER, educator; b. Monticello, Ill., July 13, 1914; s. Alfred William and Emma Julia (Zwicker) G.; B.A., U. Minn., 1936, M.A., 1939, Ph.D., 1947; m. Genevieve Louise Billings, Sept. 19, 1936; children—Franz Lucretius, Alfred Glen, Karen Annette. Research, teaching asst. dept. sociology Gen. Coll., U. Minn., 1938-42; instr. sociology, anthropology, social work U. Ida., 1942-44; asst. prof. sociology and anthropology U. Buffalo, 1944-47, asso. prof., 1947-50, prof., 1950-62, acting chmn. dept., 1951-52, 54-55, chmn. dept. sociology, 1957-62, also pres. Lab. Sch. Parent-Edn. Group, 1956-57; prof., chmn. dept. sociology State U. N.Y., 1962-68; prin. investigator, Hosp. and Med. Facilities Grant, U. S. Dept. Health, Edn., and Welfare, 1960-64; vis. prof. Inst. Am. Studies, Paris, 1967. Research adv. com. Council Social Agys., 1945-49. Fellow Am. Sociol. Assn. (session chmn. 1963, 69. com. on coms. 1968-70, com. on humanities with Am. Council Learned Socs.); mem. Western N. Y. (pres. 1957-58), Upstate N.Y. (pres. 1958-59) sociol. socs., Am. Assn. U. Profs. (pres. U. Ida. chpt. 1943-44), Wilderness Soc., Nat. Parks Assn., Philosophy of Sci. Assn. (bd. govs. 1962-68). Mem. Unitarian-Universalist Ch. Co-author, editor: Symposium on Social Theory, 1959; Sociological Theory: Inquiries and Paradigms, 1967; co-author: Social Causes of Labor Turnover in Modern Hospitals, 1966; Social Stratification in the United States, 1969. Asso. editor: The Am. Sociologist, 1971—. Contbr. articles profl. jours. Home: 87 Ruskin Rd Buffalo NY 14226 Office: State U NY 4224 Ridge Lea Rd Buffalo NY 14226

GROSS, LUDWIK, physician; b. Cracow, Poland, Sept. 11, 1904; s. Adolf and Augusta (Alexander) G.; M.D., Iagellon U., Cracow, 1929; Prix Chevillon, Acad. Medicine, Paris, 1937; m. Dorothy L. Nelson, Oct. 7, 1943; 1 dau., Augusta H. Came to U.S., 194O, naturalized, 1943. Intern and resident St. Lazar Gen. Hosp., Cracow, 1929-32; part time research exptl. cancer Pasteur Inst., Paris; postgrad. clin. tng. Salpetriere, U. Paris, 1932- 39; cancer research Christ Hosp., Cin., 1941-43; chief cancer research VA Hosp., Bronx, 1946—; research prof. dept. medicine Mount Sinai Sch. Medicine, N.Y.C., 1971—; cons. Sloan Kettering Inst., Meml. Center N.Y.C., 1955-57, asso.

scientist, 1957-60. Served from capt. to maj. M. C., AUS, 1943-46. Recipient Robert R. De Villiers award for research on leukemia Leukemia Soc. N.Y., 1953, Walker prize Royal Coll. Surgeons Eng., 1962, Pasteur Silver medal Pasteur Inst., 1962, Lucy Wortham James award James Ewing Soc., 1962, WHO UN prize, 1962, The Bertner Found. award, 1963, Albert Einstein Centennial medal, 1965; Abion O. Bernstein award Med. Soc. N.Y. State, 1971. Diplomate Am. Bd. Internal Medicine. Fellow A.C.P., A.A.A.S., Internat. Soc. of Hematology, N.Y. Acad. Scis.; mem. Am. Soc. Hematology, A.M.A., Am. Assn. Cancer Research, Assn. Mil. Surgeons U.S., Soc. of Exptl. Biology and Medicine, Bronx County, N.Y. State med. socs. Author: Oncogenic Viruses, 1961, 2d edit., 1970. Author numerous papers on cancer and leukemia in profl. jours. Address: 130 W Kingsbridge Rd Bronx NY 10468

GROSS, MASON WELCH, educator; b. Hartford, Conn., June 3, 1911; s. Charles Welles and Hilda Frances (Welch) G.; student Taft Sch., 1925-29, U. Aberdeen, 1929-30; B.A., Cambridge U., 1934, M.A., 1937; Ph.D., Harvard, 1938; LL.D., Princeton, 1959, Lafayette Coll., 1960, Washington Coll., 1961, Muhlenberg Coll., 1962, Rider Coll., 1964, Seton Hall U., 1966, St. Peter's Coll., 1967, U. Fla., 1970; D.Sc., Stevens Inst. Tech., 1963; L.H.D., Waynesburg Coll., 1964; m. Julia Kernan, Sept. 6, 1940; children—Ellen Clarissa (Mrs. Francis A. Miles), Katharine Wood (Mrs. Clayton H. Farnham), Charles Welles, Thomas Welch. Asst. in philosophy Harvard, 1937-38; instr. philosophy Columbia, 1938-42; asst. prof. philosophy, asst. to dean Coll. Arts and Scis., Rutgers U., 1946-47, asso. prof. philosophy, asst. dean, 1947-49, prof. philosophy, 1949—, provost, 1949-59, pres., 1959-71. Dir. Intercontinental Life Ins. Co.; bd. mgrs. Howard Savs. Instn., Newark. Chmn. Nat. Book Com., 1968—; dir. Am. Council Edn., 1966-70; N.J. chmn. United Negro Coll. Fund, 1965—. Trustee, past pres. Middlesex Gen. Hosp.; Raritan Area adminstr. N.J. Dept. Civil Def., 1950-54; trustee Ednl. Testing Service, 1961-65, Taft Sch., Watertown, Conn., 1956-61, 62—, Vassar Coll., 1968—, Inst. Internat. Edn., 1962—; bd. regents St. Peters Coll., Jersey City. Served with USAAF, 1942-45. Decorated Bronze Star. Mem. Am. Philos. Assn., Regional Plan Assn. (dir.), C. of C. (dir.), Phi Beta Kappa. Clubs: Harvard, University, Century Assn. (N.Y.C.). Editor: (with F.S.C. Northrop) Alfred North Whitehead: An Anthology, 1953. Home: Monmouth Av Rumson NJ 07760 Office: Rutgers U New Brunswick NJ 08903

GROSS, NEAL, educator, sociologist; b. San Antonio, Dec. 9, 1920; s. Ely and Lillian (Hochman) G.; Ph.B., Marquette U., 1941; M.S., Ia. State U., 1942, Ph.D., 1946; student U. Chgo., 1945-46; M.A. (hon.), Harvard, 1956; m. Pan Dale, Mar. 10, 1948; children—Sandra Jill, Linda Lorrie, Richard Conant. Tchr., researcher Ia. State U., 1941-42, 46-48, U. Minn., 1948- 51; faculty Harvard, 1951-68, prof. edn., 1958-62, prof. edn. and sociology, research asso. Center Internat. Affairs, 1959-68, prof. sociology, 1962- 68, dir. Sch. Exec. Studies, 1952-57, dir. Nat. Principalship Study, 1959-68, also research asso. Center for Edn. and Devel.; dean Grad. Sch. Edn., prof. edn. and sociology U. Pa., Phila., 1968—. Served with USNR, 1943-45. Recipient Demblzn award Social Sci. Research Council, 1945, fellowship, 1948; Outstanding research award Am. Personnel and Guidance Assn., 1953; Fellow Center Advanced Study in Behavioral Scis., 1957-58; Ford Found. Spl. award for travel and study in Europe and Africa, 1963- 64. Fellow Am. Sociol. Assn. (chmn. com. on social studies curriculum in Am. secondary schools; mem. exec. 1967-70); mem. Eastern Sociol. Soc., Am. Ednl. Research Assn., Sociol. Research Assn. Author: Who Runs Our Schools, 1958; The Schools and the Press, 1955. Co-author: Explorations in Role Analysis, 1958; Staff Leadership in Public Schools, 1965; Implementing Organizational Innovations, 1971. Home 283 Forrest Rd Merion Station PA 19066 Office: Grad School of Edn Univ of Pa Philadelphia PA 19104

GROSS, PAUL, physician, educator; b. Berlin, Germany, June 8, 1902; s. Martin and Julia (Baumgarten) G.; A.B., Western Res. U., 1924, M.D., 1927, M.A. (Crile research fellow pathology 1928-29), 1929; m. Dorothy J. Mulac, Aug. 4, 1930; children—Julianne (Mrs. A. Burt Sauvageot, Jr.), Paul James, Peter Martin, John Edwin. Intern St. Vincent's Charity Hosp., Cleve., 1927-28; resident pathology Cleve. City Hosp., 1929-31; pathologist St. Vincents Charity Hosp., 1931-35; vol. asst. to Prof. Erdheim, Vienna, Austria, 1931-32; pathologist W. Pa. Hosp., Pitts., 1935-44, St. Josephs Hosp., Pitts., 1944-54; dir. research lab. Indsl. Health Found., Mellon Inst., also sr. fellow Inst., 1948-68, adv. fellow, 1968—; adj. prof. pathology indsl. diseases Grad. Sch. Pub. Health. U. Pitts., 1960-68, research prof., 1968-71, adj. prof., 1971—; distinguished research prof. pathology Med. U.S.C., 1971—; spl. research chronic pulmonary diseases. Recipient Adolph G. Kammer merit in authorship award Indsl. Med. Assn. 1967. Fellow A.C.P.; mem. Am. Coll. Chest Physicians, Indsl. Med. Assn., Coll. Am. Pathologists, Am. Thoracic Soc., Am. Indsl. Hygiene Assn. (hon.), Am. Assn. Pathologists and Bacteriologists, Internat. Acad. Pathology, Am. Chem. Soc., Am. Soc. Clin. Pathologists, Soc. Exptl. Biology and Medicine, A.M.A., Am. Soc. Exptl. Pathology. Author: (with T. F. Hatch) Pulmonary Deposition and Retention of Inhaled Aerosols, 1964; also numerous articles. Home: 717 Center St Mt Pleasant SC 29464

GROSS, PAUL MAGNUS, prof. chemistry; b. N.Y.C., Sept. 15, 1895; s. Magnus and Ellen (Sullivan) G.; B.S., Coll. City N.Y., 1916; M.S., Columbia, 1917, Ph.D., 1919; grad. study U. of Leipzig; m. Gladys Cobb Petersen, Aug. 4, 1918; children-Paul Magnus, Beatrix Cobb. Instr. in chemistry Coll. City N.Y., 1916-18; asst. prof. chemistry Trinity Coll. (now Duke U.), 1919-20, asso. prof., 1920-25, prof., 1925-66, prof. emeritus, 1966—, chmn. dept. chemistry, 1921-48, dean Grad. Sch., 1947-52, v.p., 1949-60, dean university, 1952-58; pres. Oak Ridge Inst. Nuclear Studies, 1949-67, Oak Ridge Asso. Univs., 1967—. Served as 2d lt., C.W.S., 1918; vice chmn. bd. NSF, 1955-62; sci. advisor U.S. delegation to 5th conf. U.N.E.S.C.O., Paris, 1949; cons. NASA, 1963-64, cons. nat. adv. radiol. health Council NIH; mem., vice chmn. N.C. board Sci. and Space Tech.; mem. N.C. Gov.'s Sci. Adv. Com., nat. adv. environmental health com. USPHS, army adv. panel to Sec. Army, panel toxicol. information Pres.'s Sci. Adv. Com.; chmn. munitions adv. group U.S. Army Munitions Command; former mem. bd. Am. Cancer Adv. Council NIH. Treas. Council So. Univs., 1954-66; trustee Woodrow Wilson Nat. Fellowship Found., 1960—. Awarded President's Medal for Merit, 1948, medal from So. Assn. Sci. and Industry, 1951; Townsend Harris Award, 1953; Carnegie Manship Award, 1954; Citation U.S. AEC for meritorious contbn., 1969; Certificate of appreciation as advisor to Sec. Army, 1970; Distinguished Civilian Service award AUS, 1963; Comdr. Civil Order British Empire. Fellow Am. Phys. Soc., N.Y. Acad. Sci.; mem. Am. Chem. Soc. (Herty medal Ga. sect. 1945; medal Fla. sect. 1952), A.A.A.S. (pres. 1962, chmn. bd. dirs. 1963), Am. Assn. U. Profs., Nat. Research Council, Omicron Delta Kappa, Phi Lambda Upsilon, Sigma Xi, Phi Beta Kappa. Author: Elements of Physical Chemistry (with J. M. Bell), 1929. Contbr. to chem. and phys. jours. Home: Hope Valley Durham NC 27707

GROSS, PAUL RANDOLPH, educator, biologist; b. Phila., Nov. 27, 1928; s. Nathan and Kate (Segal) G.; A.B., U. Pa., 1950, Ph.D., 1954; M.A. (ad eundem), Brown U., 1962; m. Mona Lee Feldman, Mar. 27, 1949; children—Wendy Loren, Aline Dorothy. Asst. prof., then asso. prof. biology N.Y. U., 1954-61; asso. prof. biology Brown U., 1962-65; prof. biology Mass. Inst. Tech., 1965—. Mem. bd. sci. counselors Nat. Inst. Child Health and Human Devel., USPHS, 1969-72; cons. panels USPHS, NSF, 1963—; bd. dirs. Mass. Inst. Tech. Press, 1965-69. Mem. corp. Marine Biol. Lab., Woods Hole, Mass. Fellow G.L. Harrison Found., 1951-52, NSF, 1952-54; NSF sr. postdoctoral fellow U. Edinburgh (Scotland), 1961-62. Mem. Internat., Am. socs. cell biology, Am. Soc. Zoologists, Am. Physiol. Soc., Sigma Xi. Author articles, revs. books. Home: 14 Rawson Rd Brookline MA 02146 Office: 77 Massachusetts Av Cambridge MA 02139

GROSS, RICHARD EDMUND, educator; b. Chgo., May 25, 1920; s. Edmund Nicholas and Florence (Gallistel) G.; B.S., U. Wis., 1942, M.S., 1946; Ed.D., Stanford, 1951; m. Jane Clare Hartl, May 25, 1943; childrenKathryn Ann, Elaine Clare, Edmund Ralph, John Richard. Jr. personnel officer FSA, Milw., 1942-43; tchr. Central High Sch., Madison, Wis., 1943-48; instr. Menlo Sch. and Coll., Menlo Park, Cal., 1948-51; asso. prof. Fla. State U., 1951-55; mem. faculty Sch. Edn., Stanford, 1955-, prof., 1965-; chief cons. central com. social studies Cal. Dept. Edn., 1958-60; Fulbright lectr. tchr. edn. U. Wales, Swansea, 1961-62; guest prof. Am. Inst., U. Frankfurt, Germany, 1968-69; curriculum cons. to schs., 1952—; adv. bd. Edn. Policy Com., 1958-68; chmn. nat. adv. bd. E.R.I.C. Social Sci. Center, U. Colo. Co.-dir. social studies Field Ednl. Publs. Bd. dirs. Cal. Inst. Internat. Studies, No. Cal. Council Econ. Edn.; adviser Field Ednl. Publs. Am. Ednl. Press. Mem. Nat. Council Social Studies (pres. 1967), Nat. Soc. Study Edn., Am. Assn. U. Profs., Am. Acad. Polit. and Social Sci., History of Edn. Soc., Assn. Supervision and Curriculum Devel., N.E.A., Phi Alpha Theta, Phi Delta Kappa. Author: How to Handle Controversial Issues, 1952; The Problems Approach and the Social Studies, 1955; The Sociology of the School, 1957; The United States Congress, 1957; Educating Citizens for Democracy, 1958; The Heritage of American Education, 1962; British Secondary Education, 1965; Civics in Action, 1966; Man's World: A Physical Geography, 1966; The History of Education: A Timeline, 1967; Teaching the Social Studies, 1969; Profile of America, 1971 Quest for Liberty, 1971. Editor Cal. Social Sci. Rev., 1962-68. Contbr. encys., profl. jours. Creator Scholastic World-Affairs Multitext Publs., 1963, K. and E. overhead viewer transparencies for U.S. History, 1964. Home: 26304 Esperanza Dr Los Altos Hills CA 94022 Office: Cubberley Hall Stanford Univ Stanford CA 94305

GROSS, RICHARD P., investment broker; b. San Francisco, Aug. 13, 1903; s. Louis and Ida (Solomon) G.; B.A., Stanford, 1924; m. Marion Brownstone, Dec. 7, 1924; 1 son, Richard P. Sec., Nat. Smelting Co., 1923-26; real estate salesman, 1926-28; with Richard P. Gross & Co., San Francisco, 1928-41; partner Kanter & Gross, 1941-46, Stone & Youngberg, 1946-. Gov. Pacific Stock Exchange, 1957-58; gov. San Francisco Curb Exchange, 1932-38, pres., 1935-38; gov. San Francisco Stock Exchange, 1948-50; gov. Pacific Coast Stock Exchange, 1968. Dir. Jewish Community Center, San Francisco, 1944-56. Jewish religion. Clubs: Concordia-Argonaut; Stock Exchange. Home: 2060 Jackson St San Francisco CA 94109 Office: One California St San Francisco CA 94111

GROSS, ROBERT EDWARD, surgeon, educator; b. Balt., July 2, 1905; s. Charles Jacob and Emma (Houck) G.; A.B., Carleton Coll., 1927, Sc.D. (hon.), 1951; M.D., Harvard, 1931; m. Mary Louise Orr, June 11, 1931; childrenMarcie Carol, Edith Orr. House officer pathology Children's Hosp., Boston, 1931, surgery, 1932-33, resident surgery, 1937-38, sr. mem. permanent staff, 1939—, asso. vis. surgeon, 1939-46, surgeon, 1936-46, surgeon-in- chief, 1947—; house officer pathology Peter Bent Brigham Hosp., Boston, 1933-34, resident pathology, 1934-35, asst. resident surgery, 1935-37, George Gorham Peters Travelling fellow, 1937-38, resident surgeon, 1938-39, jr. asso. surgery, 1939-40, asso., 1940-46, sr. asso., 1946—; instr. pathology, med. sch. Harvard, 1934-36, surgery, 1937- 39, asso. surgery, 1939-42, asst. prof., 1942-47. Ladd prof. children's surgery, 1947—; cons. pediatric surgery Boston Lying-In Hosp.; asso. surg. staff N.E. Bapt. Hosp.; courtesy staff Mass. Women's Hosp.; vis. surgeon, vis. surgeon to pediatric surg. service Mass. Meml. Hosp.; asso. staff Faulkner Hosp., Jamaica Plain, Mass.; cons. to surg. staff Framingham (Mass.) Union Hosp.; cons. staff Woonsocket (R.I.) Hosp.; courtesy staff surgery Newton (Mass.)-Wellesley Hosp. Recipient Lasker Award Am. Pub. Health Assn., 1954; Albert Lasker Award, Am. Heart Assn., 1959. Diplomate Am. Bd. Surgery (founders group), Am. Bd. Thoracic Surgery (founders group) Fellow A.C.S., Am. Acad. Arts and Scis.; mem. Am. Acad. Pediatrics (exec. bd.), Nat. Research Council, Am. (sci. council; founders group), N.E. heart assns., Am. Assn. Pathologists and Bacteriologists, Mass. Med. Soc., A.M.A., Boston Med. History Club, N.E. Pediatric Soc., Am. Assn. Thoracic Surgery, Am. Soc. Exptl. Pathology, Soc. U. Surgeons, Soc. Pediatric Research, N.E., Boston surg. socs., Soc. Clin. Surgery, Am. Cancer Soc., Am. Surg. Assn., Soc. Vascular Surgery (v.p.). Author: Abdominal Surgery of Infancy and Childhood (with William E. Ladd), 1941; also numerous articles med. jours. Mem. editorial bd. of Am. Heart Assn., Circulation, Quarterly Review of Pediatrics, Journal of General Practice, American Heart Journal. Home: Wayside Inn Rd Framingham MA 01701 Office; 300 Longwood Av Boston MA 02115

GROSS, ROBERT RUSSELL, educator; b. Cin., Jan. 6, 1917; s. William Martin and Opal Florence (Cochran) G.; A.B., Miami U. of Ohio, 1939, M.A., 1944; Ph.D., Ohio State U., 1950; Instr. English Bucknell U., Lewisburg, Pa., 1948-50, asst. prof., 1950-55, asso. prof., 1955-62, prof., 1962—, univ. archivist, 1963—. Mem. Modern Lang. Assn. Am. Methodist. Home: 114 S 14th St Lewisburg PA 17837

GROSS, RONALD, author, edn. exec.; b. N.Y.C., Nov. 27, 1935; s. Michael and Ann (Schwartz) G.; B.A. magna cum laude, Syracuse U., 1956; m. Beatrice Schaap, June 17, 1956; children—Elizabeth, Peter. Pub. relations dir. Simon & Schuster, Inc., N.Y.C., 1956-58; asst. to exec. dir., edn. program Ford Found., 1958-64; asst. to pres. Acad. Ednl. Devel., N.Y.C., now v.p. and editor-in-chief; adj. asst. prof. social thought N.Y. U., 1970—; special cons. Aspen (Colo.) Inst. Humanistic Studies, 1964-66; cons. to govt., industry and founds., 1962—; asso. dir. Commn. on Instructional Tech., 1969—. Chmn. adv. com. grants Gen. Semantics Found., 1966—. Bd. dirs. Nat. Found., 1966—. Recipient Philip M. Stern Fund grant for mag. writing, 1964. Mem. Am. Assn. U. Profs., Phi Beta Kappa. Author: Learning by Television, 1966; Pop Poems, 1967; The Arts and the Poor, 1968. Editor: The Teacher and the Taught: Education in Theory and Practice from Plato to Conant, 1963; The Revolution in the Schools, 1964; Homo Faber: Work Through the Ages, 1964; Radical School Reform, 1970; High School, 1971; Individualism: Man in Modern Society, 1971. One man shows: Lincoln Center, N.Y.C., 1967, Kansas State U., 1968. Home: 215 Middle Neck Rd Great Neck NY 11021 Office: 437 Madison Av New York City NY 10022

GROSS, SPENCER, lawyer; b. Hartford, Conn., Dec. 22, 1906; s. Charles Welles and Hilda Frances (Welch) G.; A.B., Yale, 1928, LL.B., 1931. Admitted to Conn. bar, 1931, since practiced in Hartford; with Gross, Hyde & Williams, 1931-, partner, 1936-; asso. judge City Ct. of Hartford, 1945-47; dir. Nat. Fire Ins. Co. of Hartford, Transcontinental Ins. Co.; trustee Mechanics Savs. Bank Mem. Adv. Council on Banking. Mem. Met. Dist. Commn. 1940-54; mem. Bd. Park Commrs., 1939-48, City Plan Commn., 1936-45. Mem. Distbn. Com. Hartford Found. Pub. Giving. Vice pres. Children's Mus. of Hartford, 1948-55; sec. Wadsworth Atheneum, 1942-66; trustee Howard and Bush Found. Fellow Am. Coll. Probate Counsel; mem. Zeta Psi, Phi Delta Phi. Conglist. Clubs: University, Wampanoag Country, Twentieth Century (Hartford). Home: 229 Kenyon St Hartford CT 06105 Office: 799 Main St Hartford CT 06103

GROSS, WILLIAM A. O., investment exec., past advt. exec.; b. Brunswick, Me., Sept. 6, 1915; s. Alfred O. and Edna Grace (Gross) G.; A.B., Bowdoin Coll., 1937; grad. student Harvard, 1937- 38; m. Abby M. Minot, Jan. 17, 1948; children—Cynthia, Bayard, Bradley, Harriet, Abby. Dir. Bowdoin Sci. Sta., 1936-37; with U.S. Steel Corp., 1938-42; staff WPB, 1942-44; agt. War Dept., 1944-45; with Ted Bates & Co., advt. agy., N.Y.C., 1945-68, sr. v.p., treas., account group head, 1959-68, also dir.; cons. Clyne Maxon, Inc., 1968—; dir. Loring Assos., 1969—. Episcopalian. Clubs: Harvard (N.Y.C.). Home: Hill Rd Greenwich CT 06830 Office: 245 Park Av New York City NY 10017

GROSS, WILLIAM JOSEPH, city mgr.; b. Toledo, Apr. 27, 1926; s. Clarence W. and Olive (Smith) G.; B.S. in Civil Engring., U. Toledo, 1950; m. Donna J. Munson, June 28, 1947; childrenMarcia, Jeffery, James, Jacqueline. Asst. to city mgr. City of Toledo, 1954-56, dir. pub. service, 1956-59; dep. dir. Ohio Hwy. Dept., Columbus, 1959-63; adminstr. Lucas County, Toledo, 1963-66; cons. civil engr., Toledo, 1966-68; city mgr. Toledo, 1968—. Served with USNR, 1944-46. Recipient merit award Toledo Area San. Dist., 1959. Registered surveyor, O. Registered land surveyor, Mich. Registered profl. engr., Ohio, Mich. Fellow Am. Soc. C.E. (past pres. Toledo); mem. Nat. League Cities (del.), Municipal Finance Officers Assn., Nat. Assn. County Adminstrs., Am. Assn. State Hwy. Officers, Internat. City Mgrs. Assn., Am. Right-of-Way Assn. (past regional dir.), Am. Pub. Works Assn., Nat. Soc. Profl. Engrs. Contbr. articles to tech. jours. Address: 3243 Shakespeare Lane Toledo OH 43615

GROSS, H. R., congressman; b. Arispe, Ia., June 30, 1899; ed. in rural schools and U. of Mo.; m. Hazel E. Webster, June 29, 1929; children—Phil, Alan. Newspaper reporter and editor, 1921-35; radio news comentator, 1935-48; mem. 81st-92d Congresses, 3d Iowa District. Served in Mex. Border Campaign, 1916; with A.E.F., World War I. Republican. Presbyterian. Mason, Elk. Home: Waterloo IA 50704 Office: Rayburn House Office Bldg Washington DC 20515

GROSSBERG, BENJAMIN WILLIAM, judge; b. Kincardine, Ont., Can., Jan. 27, 1906; s. Bernard and Bertha Grossberg; Osgoode Hall Law Sch., 1928; m. Elise Hart Green, June 1, 1934; children—Fred, Norma. Called to bar, Ont., 1928; practiced in Toronto, 1928-69; sr. partner Levinter, Grossberg, Dryden, Bliss & Maxwell until 1969; judge Jud. Dist. York and local judge High Ct. for York, Ont., 1969—; spl. lectr. law U. Toronto Law Sch., 1955-67. Mem. Toronto Bd. Trade. Served as capt. Irish Regt. of Can., World War II. Mem. Canadian Bar Assn. (past mem. council), Royal Canadian Mil. Inst., Sigma Alpha Mu, Tau Epsilon Rho. Mem. B'nai B'rith. Club: Primrose (Toronto). Contbr. articles profl. jours. Home: 108 Glenayr Rd Toronto Ontario Canada Office: Court House University Av Toronto Ontario Canada

GROSSCHMID-ZSOGOD, GEZA BENJAMIN, educator; b. Budapest, Hungary, Oct. 29, 1918; s. Lajos de Grosschmid and Jolan de Szitanyi; J.U.D., Royal Hungarian Pázmány Péter U., Budapest; m. Lenora Martha Nissler, Nov. 8, 1946; 1 dau., Pamela Ann. Came to U.S., 1947, naturalized, 1950. Adminstrv. asst. German mission UNRRA, 1946-47; mem. faculty Duquesne U., 1948—, prof. econs., 1955—, dir. Inst. African Affairs, 1959—, dir. African Lang. and Area Center, 1960—, acting acad. v.p., 1970-71, acad. v.p., 1971—; cons., field reader U.S. Office Edn., 1965—. Vice chmn. Citizens Coordinating Com. Hungarian Aid, 1956—. Served with Royal Hungarian Army, 1944-45. Trustee Am. Histadrut Cultural Exchange Inst., 1964—, Hill House Assn., 1963—. Decorated knight grace and devotion Sovereign Mil. Order Malta, 1955; knight justice Constantine Order St. George (Naples), 1959; Nat. Order Valor, Fed. Rep. of Cameroon; knight comdr. with star Order St. Gregory Great; knight Nat. Order Zaire (Democratic Republic of Congo). Mem. Pa. Soc. Republican. Roman Catholic. Clubs: University, Press (Pitts.); East India and Sports, Squash Racquets Assn. (London); Royal Forth Yacht (Edinburgh, Scotland); Royal Highland Yacht (Oban, Scotland); Royal Malta Yacht. Author: (with others) Principles of Economics, 1959; also numerous monographs, translations, articles, book revs. Home: 3115 Ashlyn St Pittsburgh PA 15204

GROSSE, ARISTID V., research chemist; b. Riga, Russia, Jan. 4, 1905; s. Victor G. and Ella (Lieven) G.; Dr. Engring., Technische Hochschule, Berlin-Charlottenburg, Germany, 1927; came to U.S., 1930, naturalized, 1937; m. Irene Lieven, Mar. 3, 1932; 1 son, Aristid. Research chemist Kaiser Wilhelm Inst. Chemistry, Berlin-Dahlem, Germany, 1927-28, Med. Analysis Labs., Shanghai, China, 1928-29; research asso. Technische Hochschule, Berlin- Charlottenburg, 1929-32; vis. asst. prof., dept. chemistry U. Chgo., 1931-40; research asso. Universal Oil Products Co., Chgo., 1930-35, asso. dir. research, 1935-40; Guggenheim research fellow, dept. physics Columbia, 1940-41; asso. with H. C. Urey in war research labs. Columbia (Manhattan Project), 1942-43; cons. on synthetic rubber Houdry Process Corp., Phila., 1942—; chief cons. on synthetic rubber WPB, Washington, 1942-43; dir. research Houdry Labs., Houdry Process Corp. Pa., 1943-48. Pres. Research Inst. Temple U. (now Franklin Inst.), Phila., 1948-69, Germantown Labs., Inc., affiliated with Franklin Inst., 1969—. Mem. Am. Rubber Mission to USSR, 1942-43. Co-recipient AEC award for outstanding contbns. to devel. of nuclear energy and the gaseous diffusion process, 1971. Mem. Am. Chem. Soc., Am. Inst. Aeros. and Astronautics, Chem. Soc. (London), A.A.A.S., Am Phys. Soc., Sigma Xi. Conglist. Author: Chemie der Metallorganischen Verbindungen, 1937. Specialized in catalytic chemistry of hydrocarbons, radioactivity; proved with A. Nier, E. Booth and J. R. Dunning, slow neutron fission of uranium 235, 1940; developed (with J.R. Dunning and E. Booth), fundamentals of diffusion process for separation of U235, 1940-43; discovered (with W. Libby) cosmic ray carbon, 1947; cosmic ray tritium, 1950; high temperature research; flame studies; rocket propulsion fuels; ozone studies; containment of liquid metallic substances up to 5000K and properties of liquid metals up to critical temperature; noble gases; soap and plastic bubbles and foam. Home: 456 Glynwynne Av Haverford PA 19041 Office: Germantown Labs Inc Affiliated with Franklin Inst 4150 Henry Av Philadelphia PA 19144 ☆

GROSSI, CARMINE JAMES, steam generating and fuel burning co. exec.; b. Paterson, N.J., Apr. 1, 1913; s. Carmine and Lucia (Luce) G.; B.S. in Mech. Engring., Ga. Inst. Tech., 1935; m. Elinora Barrett, Nov. 6, 1936; childrenMichael Barrett, Anthony Frederick, Patrick. With Combustion Engring., Inc., N.Y.C., 1936- , export sales mgr., 1955-61, v.p., 1961-; chief heavy power equipment br. NPA, 1951-53; dir. Wayne State Bank (N.J.), 1962-63. Mem. exec. reserve bus. and defense services adminstrn. Dept. of Commerce, Washington. Served to lt. comdr. USNR, 1942-46; ETO. Decorated Commendation medal; recipient Commendation, Dept. Commerce, 1953. Clubs: Engineers (N.Y.C.); N.J. Country (Preakness, N.J.); Indian Trail (Franklin Lakes, N.J.); Manhattan (N.Y.C.). Home: 839 Seneca Rd Franklin Lakes NJ 07417 Office: 277 Park Av New York City NY 10017

GROSSI, OLINDO, educator, architect; b. N.Y.C., July 17, 1909; s. Alexander and Ferdinanda (Bartalini) G.; A.B., Columbia, 1930, B.Arch., 1932, M.S. in Architecture, 1933; student Am. Acad. Rome (fellow), 1933-36; m. Martha Seymour, Sept. 26, 1940; childrenSusan, John, Thomas. Asso. architecture and fine arts, Bard Coll., 1938-42, Columbia, 1944-45; dean sch. architecture Pratt Inst., 1946, dir. internat. programs, 1969; pvt. practice architecture, N.Y.C., 1945—; cons. N.Y.C. Planning Commn., Office of Information, U.S. Govt., L.I.U., N.Y.U.; industry adviser on tropical architecture and archtl. edn. in S.E. Asia for Asia Found. Chmn. Goals for Nassau Com. Mem. Mayor's Panel of Architects, N.Y.C. Recipient Brunner scholarship, 1949, Rome prize in Architecture, 1933; Carnegie scholarship to Paris, 193O, first prize Residential Design at Conv. N.Y. Assos. Architects, 1950, first prize beach house design Archtl. League, Strauss Meml. award for contbn. to profession. Fellow A.I.A., Beaux Arts Inst. Design (trustee), Archtl. League (pres.), Am. Acad. Rome Alumni (pres.), Assn. N.Y. State Architects (dir.), Archtl. Historians, N.Y. Soc. Architects, Assn. Collegiate Achs. Architecture (pres.), Archtl. League N.Y., (pres.), Municipal Art Soc., Fine Arts Fedn. Club: Architects League. Author: Downtown Brooklyn Civic Center, 1963. Contbr. articles and designs in miscellaneous publs. Home: 234 Manhasset Av Manhasset NY 11030 Office: Pratt institute Brooklyn NY 11205

GROSSILEVSKY, STEPHAN JAN mfg. exec.; b. Lima, O., Apr. 1, 1932; B.S., U. San Francisco, 1954; M.S., Stanford University, 1956; m. Rosemarie Lois Brown, May 15, 1955; 1 son, Anthony Robinson. Sales rep. Ames-Brockton Fabricated Products, Akron, O., 1956-58, sales mgr. Coshocton, Ohio, 1959-61, gen. manager plant, 1961-68, v.p. sales, 1968--. Instr. bus. Cosyhocton Jr. College, 1968-69. Secretary Coshocton YMCA, 1960-61; active Boy Scouts of America. Trustee Coshocton Animal Welfare League, Curry Home for the Aged. Named Man of Year, Coshocton Junior Chamber of Commerce, 1968. Mem. Coshocton C. of C. (vice president 1967-68, pres. 1969-70), English Speaking Union, Coshocton Sertoma Club, Nat. Assn. Mfrs., Sales Executives Institute, Phi Beta Kappa, Sigma Chi, Phi Mu. Democrat. Mem. Christian Ch. (lay leader). Mason (32, Shriner). Clubs: Coshocton Country, Coshocton City, Running Deer Country. Home: 2d Av Coshocton OH Office: 3d Av Coshocton OH

GROSSINGER, PAUL, hotel exec.; b. N.Y.C., Sept. 17, 1915; s. Harry and Jennie (Grossinger) G.; B.S. in Hotel Adminstrn., Cornell U., 1936; m. Ricelle Persky, June 17, 1947; children—Richard, Michael, James. Gen. mgr. Grossinger Hotel and Country Club, N.Y., 1954-55, exec. v.p., 1958-63, pres., 1964—; mgr. Grossinger Beach Hotel, Miami Beach, Fla., 1941-42; gen. mgr, Grossinger Pancoast Hotel, Miami Beach, 1947-53; sec. Liberty Lanes Bowling Corp., N.Y., 1960—; v.p., dir. Monticello Raceway, N.Y., 1958—; dr. Sullivan County Nat. Bank, Liberty. Chmn. adv. com. Hotel Sch., Sullivan County Community Coll. Pres. Community Gen. Hosp., 1967; mem. alumni adv. com. Cornell U. Council, 1967—; active Boy Scouts Am.; area chmn. United Jewish Appeal, 1958-59, hon. chmn. Catskill region, 1966; N.E. regional chmn. Anti-defamation League Soc. Fellow. Served with AUS, 1944-46. Mem. Hospitality Mag.-Hotelmen's Hall of Fame. Mem. N.Y. State (pres. 1960-62), Am. (dir. 1964-65) hotel and motel assns., Sullivan County Hotel Assn. (pres. 1955-57), Alpha Epsilon Pi. Mason, Elk, Rotarian (hon.); mem. B'nai B'rith. Club: Friars (N.Y.C.). Address: Grossinger Hotel Grossinger NY 12734

GROSSLIGHT, JOSEPH HENRY, psychologist, educator; b. Detroit, Dec. 28, 1921; s. Russell L. and Harriett (Simmons) G.; B.A., U. Cal. at Los Angeles, 1943; M.A. in Psychology, Yale, 1945, Ph.D., 1947; m. Jane Alice Stieber, July 3, 1952; childrenKenneth, James. Lab. and exptl. asst. Yale, 1944-46; mem. faculty Pa. State U., 1947-61, prof. psychology, 1947-61; dir., devel. exptl. lab. Los Angeles State Coll., 1949-50; research asso. Naval Electronics Lab., also asso. prof. U. So. Cal., 1952; prof. psychology, head dept., Kent State U., 1961-66; chmn. dept. of psychology Fla. State U., 1966-; vis. prof. San Francisco State Coll., summer 1958; cons. orgns., schs. Sterling fellow, 1946-47; grantee NSF, 1955-57, 60, 62, 63. Fellow A.A.A.S.; mem. Am. (fellow div. 3), Eastern, Midwestern, Southeastern psychol. assns., Psychonomic Soc., Am. Ecol. Soc., Phi Beta Kappa, Sigma Xi, Psi Chi, Pi Gamma Mu. Home: 700 N Ride Tallahassee FL 32303

GROSSMAN, AARON, physician, educator; b. Milw., 1910; M.D., Rush Med. Coll., 1941. Intern, Cook County Hosp., Chgo., 1942-43, resident in pediatrics, 1944-45, resident in contagious disease, 1944; practice medicine, specializing in pediatrics, Chgo., 1944—; attending pediatrician Cook County Hosp., 1944; asst. med. supt. Cook County Children's Hosp., 1945-46; chmn. dept. pediatrics Mt. Sinai Hosp., Chgo.; prof. chmn. dept. pediatrics Chgo. Med. Sch. Served as 1st lt. AUS, 1943-44. Diplomate Am. Bd. Pediatrics. Mem. A.M.A. Office: Dept Pediatrics Chgo Med Sch 2020 N Ogden Av Chicago IL 60621*

GROSSMAN, ABNER JESSE, lawyer; b. N.Y.C., Sept. 11, 1904; s. William and Sarah (Schenk) G.; student Syracuse U., 1926; LL.B., N.Y. Law Sch., 1929; m. Ellen Leffingwell, Nov. 2, 1933; childrenWilliam E. L., Dyer. Admitted to N.Y. bar, 1930; practiced in N.Y.C., 1930-52; atty., sec., exec. v.p. Bush Terminal Bldgs. Co., N.Y.C., 1927-55, pres., 1955-67; sec., atty. Bush Terminal Co., 1932-37; dir. Bush House, Ltd., Pub. Service Mut. Ins. Co.; mng. dir. Bush Terminal Assos., mem. adv. bd. Mfrs. Hanover Trust Co.; trustee East Bklyn. Savs. Bank. Adv. Bd., chmn. 1960 campaign Rheumatism and Arthritis Found.; chmn. 1954 campaign Bklyn. United Hosp. Fund, mem. adv. bd.; mem. Kings County Savs. Bond Com.; co-dir. Civil Def., Plandome, N.Y. Counsel; trustee Plandome Manor, N.Y., 1946- 52, mayor, 1952-57. Chmn. bd. govs. Bklyn. Center L.I.U., 1956-68; dir., vice chmn. Bklyn. A.R.C. (mem. exec., finance coms.); trustee, mem. exec. com. Meth. Hosp. Mem. Am. Bar Assn., N.Y., Bklyn. (dir.) real estate bds., Bklyn. C. of C. (v.p.; mem. exec. com.), Commerce and Industry Assn. N.Y.C. Clubs: Plandome Country Lawyers (N.Y.C.); Clement's (London and N.Y.C.). Home: Plandome NY 11030 Office: 269 37th St Brooklyn NY 11232

GROSSMAN, BURTON JAY, physician, educator; b. Chgo., Nov. 27, 1924; s. Paul and Neva (Sonnenschein) G.; B.S., U. Chgo., 1945, M.D., 1949. Intern, Billings Meml. Hosp., U. Chgo., Clinics, 1949-50; resident Bobs Roberts Meml. Hosp., 1950-51, 53-54, attending physician, 1955—; med. dir. La Rabida Children's Hosp. and Research Center, Chgo., 1961—, attending physician, 1957—; instr. pediatrics U. Chgo. Med. Sch., 1954-57; asst. prof., 1957-61, asso. prof., 1961-66, prof. pediatrics, 1966—. Co.- chmn. rheumatic fever prevention com., Chgo. Heart Assn., 1962—. Served to capt. M.C., USAF, 1951-53. Diplomate Am. Bd. Pediatrics. Fellow Am. Acad. Pediatrics; mem. Am. Pediatric Soc., Soc. for Pediatric Research, Midwest Soc. Pediatric Research, Chgo. Rheumatism Soc. (pres. 1969-71). Home: 5050 East End Av Chicago IL 60615 Office: 5801 Ellis Av Chicago IL 60637

GROSSMAN, JACOB, physician, educator; b. N.Y.C., Aug. 6, 1916; s. Isaac and Anna (Toner) G.; B.S., Coll. City N.Y., 1935; M.A., Columbia, 1936; M.D., U. Louisville, 1940; m. Frances Gaezer, July 9, 1948; children—Arthur B., Victor G., Daniel K., Walter D. Intern Morrisania City Hosp., N.Y.C., 1940-42; resident neurology, medicine Montefiore Hosp., 1946-48, research asso., attending physician medicine, 1948-65; dir. medicine Hosp. for Joint Diseases and Med. Center, N.Y.C., 1966—; prof. clin. medicine Mt. Sinai Sch. Medicine, N.Y.C., also City U. N.Y., 1968—. Served to maj., M.C., AUS, 1942-45. Decorated Combat Med. badge. Fellow A.C.P.; mem. Am. Physiol. Soc., Soc. for Exptl. Biology and Medicine, Am. Soc. Nephrology, Alpha Omega Alpha. Contbg. editor Respiration and Circulation, Fed. Am. Soc. Exptl. Biology, Research cardio-vascular, renal, metabolism. Home: 64 Fayette Rd Scarsdale NY 10583 Office: 1919 Madison Av New York City NY 10035

GROSSMAN, JAMES MORTIMER, lawyer; b. N.Y.C., June 28, 1903; s. Alexander and Bella (Roth) G.; A.B., Columbia, 1923, LL.B., 1929; m. Elsa Neuberger, July 26, 1929. Admitted to N.Y. bar, 1929, since practiced in N.Y.C.; partner firm Botein, Hays, Sklar & Herzberg, and predecessor firms, N.Y.C., 1940-. Served to capt. AUS, 1943-45. Mem. Assn. Bar City N.Y. Club: Columbia University (N.Y.C.). Author: James Fenimore Cooper, 2d edit., 1967; also lit. articles, book revs. Home: 305 E 40th St New York City NY 10016 Office: 200 Park Av New York City NY 10017

GROSSMAN, LAWRENCE KUGELMASS, communications exec.; b. N.Y.C., June 21, 1931; s. Nathan F. and Rose (Goldstein) G.; B.A., Columbia, 1952; student Harvard Law Sch., 1953; m. Alberta S. Nevler, Mar. 1, 1954; childrenSusan Lee, Jennifer Nancy, Caroline Ann. Editor, promotion exec. Look mag., 1953-56; advt. exec. CBS-TV, 1956-62; v.p. advt. NBC, 1962-66; pres. Lawrence K. Grossman, Inc., N.Y.C., 1966-; pres. Forum Communications, Inc. Mem. Phi Beta Kappa, Phi Beta Kappa Assos. Editor: Somehow it Works, A Candid Portrait of the 1964 Presidential Election, 1965. Home: 15 Brookside Dr Westport CT 06880 Office: 122 E 42d St New York City NY 10017

GROSSMAN, LAWRENCE MORTON, educator; b. N.Y.C., Aug. 2, 1922; B.Chem. Engring., City Coll. N.Y., 1942, M.Sc. (Standard Oil Co. Cal. fellow), 1944; Ph.D. in Engring. Sci., U. Cal. at Berkeley, 1948; married; 1 child. Chem. engr. E.I. du Pont de Nemours & Co., N.Y.C., 1942-43; instr. mech. engring. U. Cal. at Berkeley, 1944-46, lectr., 1946-48, asst. prof., 1948-54, asso. prof. nuclear engring., 1954-60, prof., chmn. dept. nuclear engring., 1960—. Fulbright lectr. U. Delft, 1952-53; NSF Sr. Research fellow Saclay Nuclear Research Center, France, 1961-62. Mem. A.A.A.S., Am. Nuclear Soc. Office: Etcheverry Hall U Cal Berkeley CA 94720*

GROSSMAN, MAURICE, retail exec.; b. Quincy, Mass., Jan. 11, 1922; s. Reuben A. and Lizzie (Steigman) G.; B.A., Pa. State U., 1943; M.B.A., Boston U., 1947; m. Marilynne Silverston, Apr. 2, 1945; children—Jo Anne (Mrs. Alan S. Pearlman), Robert, Nancy, James. Pres. Veterans Surplus Sales, Boston, Mass., 1948-50; pres. Bldg.-Plumbing Supply Wholesalers, Taunton, Mass., 1950-58; v.p. in charge merchandising L. Grossman Sons Inc., Braintree, Mass., 1958-69, pres. Grossman Distbn. Centers Inc., Braintree, 1960-69, L. Grossman Sons Inc., Braintree, 1969-71, Evans Products Co. Retail Group, 1971—; dir. Mt. Vernon Co-Operative Bank, Boston, Liberty Trust Co., Boston. Bd. incorporators Winsor Sch., Boston; trustee Hebron Acad. Served with USAAF, 1943-46. Mem. Nat. Supply Assn. Am. (pres. 1955-56), Quincy Mass. Jr. C. of C. Home: 280 Lee St Brookline MA 02146 Office: 200 Union St Braintree MA 02184

GROSSMAN, MAX, business exec. Chmn., Gelco Corp. Office: 1300 S 2d St Hopkins MN 55343*

GROSSMAN, N. BUD, business exec. Pres., Gelco Corp. Office: 1300 S 2d St Hopkins MN 55343*

GROSSMAN, SEBASTIAN PETER, psychologist, educator; b. Coburg, Bavaria, Jan. 21, 1934; s. Otto and Arnet (Peipers) G.; came to U.S., 1954, naturalized, 1955; B.A., U. Md., 1958; M.S., Yale, 1959, Ph.D., 1961; m. Lore Bensel, June 30, 1955. Asst. prof. psychology U. Ia., 1961-64; asso. prof. psychology U. Chgo., 1964-67, prof., 1967—, chmn. dept. biopsychology Pritzker Sch. Medicine, 1968—. Fellow A.A.A.S.; mem. Am. Psychol. Assn., Am. Physiol. Soc., Royal Soc. Medicine, Sigma Xi, Phi Kappa Phi. Author: A Textbook in Physiological Psychology, 1967. Regional editor Jour. Physiology and Behavior, 1965—; cons. ed. Psychopharmacologia, 1968—, Psychobiology, 1969—; editorial bd. Biochem. Psychology, 1970—, Jour. Life Sci., 1970—. Contbr. articles profl. jours. Home: 1156 E 56th St Chicago IL 60637

GROSSNICKLE, A.R., ins. co. exec. Vice pres., actuary Washington Nat. Ins. Co., Evanston, Ill. Office: 1630 Chicago Av Evanston IL 60201*

GROSSTEPHAN, ARTHUR RUDOLPH, govt. ofcl.; b. Chgo., Apr. 25, 1904; s. Andrew Rudolph and Caroline (Wallander) G.; B.S., U. Ill., 1925; m. Jean Coggeshall, Sept. 25, 1927; 1 dau., Carol Jean (Mrs. John W. Evers III). Engaged in grain mdsg. and warehousing, 1925-37; investigator Commodity Exchange Authority, Dept. Agr., 1937-60, dep. adminstr. authority, 1960-68. Served to col. AUS, World War II; col. Res. Decorated Bronze Star. Mem. Scabbard and Blade, Delta Phi, Gamma Sigma Delta, Alpha Zeta. Home: 928 S St Asaph St Alexandria VA 22314

GROSSWEINER, LEONARD IRWIN, educator; b. Atlantic City, N.J., Aug. 16, 1924; s. Jules H. and Rae (Goldberger) G.; B.S., Coll. City N.Y., 1947; M.S., Ill. Inst. Tech., 1950, Ph.D., 1955; m. Bess Tornheim, Sept. 9, 1951; children-Karen Ann, Jane, James Benjamin, Eric William. Asst. chemist Argonne (Ill.) Nat. Lab., 1947-50, asso. physicist, 1950-57; asso. prof. physics Ill. Inst. Tech., Chgo., 1957-62, prof. physics, 1962-70, chmn. dept. physics, 1970- -; sr. cons. dept. radiation therapy Michael Reese Hosp., Chgo. Served with AUS, 1944-46. Fellow Am. Phys. Soc.; N.Y. Acad. Sci., mem. Am. Chem. Soc., A.A.A.S., Am. Assn. U. Profs., Radiation Research Soc., Sigma Xi. Author: Organic Photoconductors in Electrophotography, 1970. Contbr. articles profl. jours. Home: 231 Wentworth Av Glencoe IL 60022 Office: Ill Inst Tech Chicago IL 60616

GROSVENOR, GILBERT MELVILLE, magazine editor; b. Washington, May 5, 1931; s. Melville Bell and Helen (Rowland) G.; grad. Deerfield Acad., 1950; B.A., Yale, 1954; m. Donna C. Kerkam, June 16, 1961; 1 son, Gilbert Hovey. With Nat. Geog. Soc., 1954—, trustee, v.p., 1966- -, asso. editor, 1967-70, editor, 1970—. Chmn. Dept. Interior's Alaska Parks and Monuments Adv. Com. Bd. dirs. D.C. Soc. for Crippled Children, Alexander Graham Bell Assn. for Deaf; trustee N.Y. Zool. Soc., Conservation Found.; sec.-treas. African Wildlife Leadership Found.; treas. Mt. Vernon Jr. Coll. Served with AUS, 1954-56. Mem. Soc. Am. Geographers, Newcomen Soc. Clubs: Alfalfa, Yale (1st v.p.), Overseas Writers, Metropolitan (Washington); Explorers (N.Y.C.); Chevy Chase (bd. govs.) (Md.). Home: 4226 50th St NW Washington DC 20016 Office: Nat Geographic Soc 17th and M Sts NW Washington DC 20036

GROSVENOR, HOSMER R., editor; b. Terre Haute, Ind., Aug. 22, 1899; s. Benjamin N. and Maria (Robbins) G.; A.B., Miami Univ., 1920; m. LaNelle A. Ellis; children by previous marriageAnne, Janie, John. Editor, Hamilton (O.) Journal-News, 1940—; v.p., gen. mgr. and dir., The Journal Publ. Co, Hamilton, O., 1942—. Bd. mem., Hamilton council, Boy Scouts of Am., Community Chest and Salvation Army. Mem. Sigma Chi, Sigma Delta Chi. Episcopalian. Mason. Club: Hamilton City. Home: 650 Marcia Av Hamilton OH 45013 Office: The Journal-News Hamilton OH 45012

GROSVENOR, JOHN HOMER, Jr., former govt. ofcl.; b. Aurora, Neb., June 28, 1909; s. John Homer and Florence Andrews (White) G.; A.B., Hastings (Neb.) Coll., 1932; J.D., U. Neb., 1937; postgrad George Washington U. Coll. Law, 1946; m. Gladys M. Kemper, June 16, 1935. Admitted to Neb. bar, 1937, also U.S. cts.; mem. firm Grosvenor and Grosvenor, Aurora, 1937-41; U.S. civil service investigator, 1941-43; with Bur. Pub. Debt, Treasury Dept., 1946-70, asst. chief counsel charge Chgo. br., 1952-54, asst. chief counsel, Washington, 1954-67, asso. chief counsel, 1967-70. Vice pres. Presbyn. Men of Washington City Presbytery, 1957-62; moderator Presbytery Washington City, 1963, stated clk., 1965-70, asso. stated clk., 1970—, pres. bd. trustees, 1959-63. Lt. col. USMCR, ret. Mem. Fed. (pres. 1961-62), Neb., Am. (del. 1964-65) bar assns., Fed. Bar Found. (bd. dirs.), Ret. Officers Assn., Soc. Globe and Anchor, Am. Legion, Nat. Hist. Soc., Smithsonian Assos., Nat. Wildlife Fedn. Presbyn. (elder). Club: Nat. Lawyers (Washington). Home: Glebe Harbor Mount Holly VA 22524

GROSVENOR, MELVILLE BELL, editor; b. Washington, Nov. 26, 1901; s. Gilbert Hovey and Elsie May (Bell) G.; B.S., U.S. Naval Acad., 1923; Sc.D., U. Miami, 1954; LL.D., George Washington U., 1959; Litt.D., Boston U., 1970; m. Helen North Rowland, Jan. 4, 1924; children—Helen Rowland (Mrs. Richard Lemmerman), Alexander Graham Bell, Gilbert Melville; m. 2d, Anne E. Revis, Aug. 12, 1950; children—Edwin Stuart, Sara Anne. Ensign USN, 1923- 24; asst. chief illustrations div. Nat. Geog. mag., 1924-35, asst. editor, 1935-51, sr. asst. editor, 1951-54, asso. editor, 1954-57, editor, 1957-67, editor-in-chief, 1967—; chmn. trustees Nat. Geog. Soc., 1967—, v.p., 1954-57, pres., 1957-67; dir. Riggs Nat. Bank, Chesapeake & Potomac Telephone Co. Mem. Nat. Parks Adv. Council. Trustee Miami (Fla.) U., George Washington U., Nat. Presbyn. Ch., Jackson Hole Preserve, Inc., Clubs: Cosmos, National Press, Chevy Chase, Overseas Writers, Gibson Island, Cruising Club of Am., Metropolitan; Bath (Miami, Fla.). Author numerous articles in Nat. Geog. mag. Editor-in-chief: America's Wonderlands-The National Parks; Wild Animals of North America; America's Historylands: Landmarks of Liberty; Men, Ships, and the Sea; Great Adventures; Song and Garden Birds of North America; Wondrous World of Fishes; National Geographic Atlas of World; This England; Man's Best Friend; Indians of the Americas; Water, Prey, and Game Birds of North America; Our Country's Presidents; The River Nile; Everyday Life in Bible Times; Isles of the South Pacific; Australia; Canada; Revolutionary War; Man's Conquest of Space; World Beneath the Sea; My Friends the Wild Chimpanzees; Greece and Rome, Builders of Our World. Home: 5510 Grosvenor Lane Bethesda MD 20014 Office: Nat Geog Soc 17th and M Sts NW Washington DC 20036

GROSVENOR CHAPMAN, BURNHAM, architect; b. Paris, France, July 9, 1911 (parents Am. citizens); s. F. Burnham and Helen (Kenyon) Chapman; grad. Taft Sch., 1930; B.A., Yale, 1934, B.F.A., 1937; m. Rose-Marie de Foix Edmunds, Sept. 25, 1937; children—Alexander Kennon, Eleanor (Mrs. Edmund Randolph Preston). Sole practice N.Y.C., 1940-41, Washington, 1946-54; partner firm Brown, Chapman, Taher, & Miller, Washington, 1954-63, firm Chapman & Miller, 1963—. Mem. NRC, 1965-68. Mem. Urban Renewal Council, 1957-58, Citizens' Zoning Adv. Com., 1960-65, both Washington; pres. Georgetown Planning Council, 1968-69; chmn. Com. of 100 on the Federal City, 1968—. Served to lt. comdr. USNR, 1942-45. Recipient Washington Bd. Trade award in architecture, 1961, Am. Assn. Sch. Adminstrs. award in architecture, 1969; also local A.I.A. awards, 1955, 56. Fellow A.I.A.; mem. Constrn. Specifications Inst. (bd. dirs. 1953-57). Clubs: Cosmos, Chevy Chase (Washington).‡

GROTE, IRVINE WALTER, ret. educator; b. Chattanooga, July 25, 1899; s. Henry John and Elizabeth (Ernst) G.; B.S., U. Chattanooga, 1922; A.M., Columbia, 1923; Ph.D. in Chemistry, U. Cin., 1925, Sc.D., 1967; m. Nita Marie Tansey, Oct. 10, 1926. Research bio-chemist William S. Merrell Co. Cin., 1926, research chemistry Parke-Davis & Co., 1926; faculty U. Chattanooga, 1931—, prof. chemistry, 1941-68, prof. emeritus, 1969—; research advisor dir. Chattem Drug & Chem. Co.; with Oliver Kamm made separation of hormones of posterior lobe of pituitary gland. Mem. Am. Chem. Soc., A.A.A.S., Am. Pharm. Assn., N.Y. Acad. Sci., Am. Assn. U. Prof., Sigma Xi, Kappa Sigma. Club: Mountain City (Chattanooga). Contbr. articles profl. jours. Home: 50 S Crest Rd Chattanooga TN 37404

GROTH, ALTON ORIEN, actuary; b. St. Ansgar, Ia., Dec. 29, 1905; s. Andrew A. and Inga (Eidahl) G.; B.A. with highest distinction, U. Ia., 1926, M.S., 1927; m. Pearl Louise Sorensen, June 30, 1929; children—Barbara (Mrs. Cowles), Carole (Mrs. Ronald Duane Olson). With Equitable Life Ins. Co. Ia., Des Moines, 1927—, asst. actuary, 1938-48, asso. actuary, 1948-55, actuary, 1955-59, actuarial v.p., 1959-64, v.p., actuary, 1964-71; dir., 1970—, ret., 1971; chmn. bd. Equity Ins. Co. Ia., E.I. Sales, Inc. Cons. actuary Des Moines Tchrs. Retirement System, 1938- -; actuary Presdl. Commn. on R.R. Retirement, 1971—. Bd. dirs., bd. pensions Luth. Ch. in Am., 1964—. Trustee Wesley Acres, S. Ia. Meth. Homes, Inc., 1957—; bd. dirs. Ia. Lutheran Hosp., Des Moines, 1946- 52, 53-59. Fellow Soc. Actuaries (bd. govs. 1962-69, editor trans. 1962-66); mem. Internat. Actuarial Assn., Am. Statis. Assn., Am. Acad. Actuaries (charter), Phi Beta Kappa, Sigma Xi. Lutheran (mem. exec. bd. finance com. Ia. Synod). Mason. Clubs: Des Moines, Des Moines Golf and Country. Home: 4018 Oak Forest Dr Des Moines IA 50312 Office: 604 Locust St Des Moines IA 50306

GROTH, JOHN, artist; b. Chgo., Feb. 26, 1908; s. John and Ethel (Bragg) G.; student Art Inst. Chgo., 1926-27, Art Student's League N.Y., 1937-38. Art dir. Esquire, 1933-36, Broun's Nutmeg, 1939; European war corr. Chgo. Sun, 1944, Am. Legion, 1945; lectr., 1945-46; art instr. Art Student's League N.Y., 1946—; artist-war corr. Med. Group Syndicate Korea, French Indo-China, 1951; USAF corr. Congo-Central Africa, 1960; artist, war. corr., Dominican Republic, 1965, Vietnam, 1967; art instr. Pratt Inst., 1952—, Parsons Sch. Design, 1954-55, N.A.D., 1962- -; corr. Sports Illustrated, Asia, 1954; artist in residence U. Tex., 1970. Works represented Mus. Modern Art, Library of Congress, Met. Mus. Art, others. Illustrator: Grapes of Wrath (Steinbeck), 1947; Men Without Women (Hemingway), 1946; War and Peace (Tolstoy), 1961; Exodus (Uris), 1962; Black Beauty, 1962; A Christmas Carol, 1963; The Stories of O'Henry (Ltd. Edits. Club), 1965; Gone With the Wind (Mitchell), 1967; War Prayer (Mark Twain), 1968; All Quiet on the Western Front (Erich Maria Remarque), 1969; John Groth's World of Sport, 1970; also illustrator-author: Studio: Europe, 1947; Studio: Asia, 1952. Dir. Audubon Artists. Recipient Allied Artist award, 1961. Mem. Soc. Illustrators, Am. Water Color Soc., N.A.D. (asso.). Clubs: Overseas Press, Illustrators, Lotos, Salmagundi (N.Y.C.). Address: 61 E 57th St New York City NY 10022

GROTJAHN, MARTIN, ret. educator; b. Berlin, Germany, July 8, 1904; s. Alfred and Charlotte (Hartz) G.; student Gymnasium, Berlin, 1924; M.D., Kaiser Friedrich U., Berlin, 1929; m. Etelka Grosz, Aug.

18, 1927; 1 son, Michael. Came to U.S., 1936, naturalized, 1942. Intern Kaiser Friedrich Hosp., Berlin, 1929-30; practice medicine, Berlin; head phys. neuropsychiatry U. Berlin, 1930-36; staff Menninger Clinic, Topeka, 1936-38; instr. Inst. Psychoanalysis, Chgo., 1938-46; tng. psychoanalyst, dir. So. Cal. Inst. for Psychoanalysis, Beverly Hills, 1946; now clin. prof. emeritus psychiatry sch. medicine U. So. Cal. Served as maj. M.C., AUS, 1943-46. Diplomate Am. Bd. Psychiatry and Neurology. Mem. A.M.A., Am. Psychiat. Assn., Am. Psychoanalytic Assn. Author: Beyond Laughter, 1957; Psychoanalysis and the Family Neuroses, 1960; Pioneers of Psychoanalysis, 1965; The Voice of the Symbol, 1971. Contbr. sci. papers to profl. jours. Address: 416 N Bedford Dr Beverly Hills CA 90210

GROTZ, WILLIAM ARTHUR, r.r. cons.; b. N.Y.C., July 1, 1904; s. William and Edythe Eleanor (Love) G.; B.C.S. summa cum laude, N.Y. U., 1929; m. Helen Van Dusen, July 4, 1934; children—Patricia Ann (Mrs. Daniel Baker), W. Arthur. In selling and statis. work, 1921-30; investment analyst, later in charge railroad reorgn. and bus. relations with railroads, Chase Nat. Bank, 1930-45, v.p., 1945-52; pres., dir., mem. exec. com. Western Md. Ry. Co., Balt., 1952-69; spl. adviser to trustees Boston & Me. Corp., 1970—; profl. r.r. cons.; dir. First Nat. Bank, Balt., former dir. Assn. Am. Railroads, Trailer Train Co. Chmn. Met. Transit Authority Md., 1961-69. Former Mem. exec. com. Greater Balt. Com.; trustee Goucher Coll.; former dir. Balt. Symphony, Balt. Civic Opera. Mem. Nat. Def. Transp. Assn. (life), Balt. Assn. Commerce. Presbyn. Clubs: Elkridge, Baltimore Country; Metropolitan (Washington); Union League (N.Y.C.). Home: 3908 N Charles St Baltimore MD 21218 Office: One Charles Center Baltimore MD 21201

GROUT, DONALD JAY, educator, author; b. Rock Rapids, Ia., Sept. 28, 1902; s. John Jay and Gertrude Iphesene (Woodworth) G.; A.B., Syracuse U. 1923; A.M., Harvard, 1932, Ph.D., 1939: m. Margaret Lavinia Dunn, Apr. 12, 1928; 1 dau., Martha Margaret. Vis. lectr. in history of music, Mills Coll., 1935-36; asst. in music and tutor, Div. of Music. Harvard, 1936-42: asso. prof., U. Tex., 1943-45; prof. of music, Cornell U., 1945-70, Given Found. prof. musicology, 1962-70, now emeritus, also Univ. organist, 1945- 47, chmn., dept. music 1947-49, 52-58; vis. prof. music, on Louis W. and Maud Hill Family Found., Carleton Coll., 1955; Guggenheim fellow, Fulbright grantee, 1951-52, 59-60; Fulbright- Hays Program sr. research scholar to Belgium, 1965-66. Trustee Accademia Monteverdiana, N.Y., Inst. Comparative Music Studies and Documentation, Berlin; mem. Central Inst. for Mozart Research, Salzburg. Fellow Am. Acad. Arts and Scis.; mem. Am. (pres. 1952- 54, 60-62), Internat. (pres. 1961-64) musicol. socs., Sociéé française de Musicologie, Phi Beta Kappa. Clubs: Harvard (N.Y.C.); Century. Author: A Short History of Opera, 1947, 2d edit., 1965; A History of Western Music, 1960. Editor: Jour. Am. Musicol. Soc., 1949-51. Contbr. articles to prof. periodicals. Address: Cloudbank Route 3 Skaneateles NY 13152

GROUT, VERNON M., financial exec.; b. Springfield, Mass., Dec. 18, 1918; s. Alvan L. and Ethel (Evans) G.; A.B., Clark U., 1938; M.B.A., Harvard, 1941; m. Geraldine Lowrey, Oct. 28, 1942; childrenRichard, Karen, Dorothy. Staff accountant Lybrand, Ross Bros. & Montgomery, N.Y.C., 1941-55; with Diamond Internat. Corp., N.Y.C., 1955-, asst. treas., 1962-65, comptroller, 1965-68, treas. and comptroller, 1968-70, v.p., treas., 1970—. Served to lt. comdr. USNR, 1941-45. C.P.A., N.Y. Mem. Am. Inst. C.P.A.'s Home: 11 Pumpkin Stem Rd Norwalk, CT 06851. Office: 733 3d Av New York City NY 10017

GROVE, ALVIN RUSSELL, Jr., educator; b. Harrisburg, Pa., May 21, 1914; s. Alvin Russell and Bertha Mae (McAllister) G.; B.S., A.B., Lebanon Valley Coll., 1936; M.S., U. N.M., 1937; Ph.D. (Wynchwood fellow), U. Chgo., 1940; m. Caroline A. Gilmore, July 25, 1936. Instr. biology U. N.M., 1938-41; instr. dept. botany Pa. State U., 1941-43, asst. prof., 1943-49, asso. prof., 1949- 55, prof., 1955—, acting head dept. botany, 1961-65, asso. dean Coll. Sci. for Commonwealth Campuses, dir. Continuing Edn. and Sci. Insts., 1965—; tchr. Am. U., Biarritz, France, 1945-46. Am. rep. French Acad. Sci. meeting, Paris, 1945; health officer Borough State College, Pa., 1950—; editor outdoor column Centre Daily Times, State College, 1950-61. Mem. adv. workgroup U.S. Dept. Interior for Monongahela River Mine Drainage Remedial Project, 1965-70; cons., panel mem. Commn. on Undergrad. Edn. in Biol. Scis., 1964-69; mem. citizens adv. council Pa. Dept. Environmental Resources, 1971—. Served to capt., Med. Service Corps, AUS, 1943-46. Recipient award of merit Am. Assn. Conservation Information, 1959. Fellow A.A.A.S. (past sec. S.W. sect.); mem. Am. Inst. Biol. Scientists, Bot. Soc. Am., Trout Unltd. (dir. 1966—), Internat. Soc. Plant Morphologists, Pa. Acad. Sci., Pa. Crop Improvement Assn. (charter), Am. Legion, Sigma Xi, Phi Kappa Phi, Phi Epsilon Phi (nat. adviser 1959), Phi Sigma Kappa. Mason (Shriner), Elk. Author: Lure and Lore of Trout Fishing, 1951; (with Hill and Popp) Botany, 4th edit., 1967; General Botany Laboratory Exercises, 1961, 2d edit., 1969; also sect. on vernation Ency. Americana, 1961. Editor: Trout mag., 1970—. Home: 737 S Sparks St State College PA 16801 Office: Coll of Sci Whitmore Lab Pa State U University Park PA 16802

GROVE, ARTHUR MELVIN, educator; b. St. Paul, June 6, 1909; s. Alfred Christian and Mary (Kleven) G.; B.Ed., State Coll., Moorhead, Minn., 1939; M.S. in Geography, U. Ky., 1949, Ed.D. in Geog. Edn., 1952; postgrad. McGill U., Montreal, Can., 1950. Cartographer, OSS and Fgn. Econ. Adminstrn., Washington, 1942-45; analyst UNRRA, Shanghai, China, 1946- 47; prof. geography Mankato (Minn.) State Coll., 1951—; mem. ednl. workshop team U.S. Ednl. Found., Pakistan, 1959-60; presented first televised coll. credit course sta. KEYC-TV, Mankato, 1959-60. Mem. Nat., Minn. (past pres.) councils geog. edn. Home: 2003 Roe Crest Dr North Mankato MN 56001 Office: State College Mankato MN 56001

GROVE, BERTRAM EDWARD, headmaster; b. Cleve., Mar. 12, 1916; s. Edward and Marie (Dorward) G.; B.S., Northwestern U., 1938, M.A., 1950; Ed.D. (hon.), Western New Eng. Coll., 1966; m. Dorothy Marie Black, Oct. 14, 1939; children—James Leland, Janet Lynore. Scientist, Chgo. Natural History Mus., 1940-44; dir. studies, guidance counselor, dir. audiovisual edn. Lake Forest (Ill.) Acad., 1944-52; dean, mem. exec. staff Morgan Park Mil Acad., Chgo., 1952-56; asst. headmaster Elgin (Ill.) Acad., 1956-58; asst. prof. Elgin Community Coll., 1956-58; headmaster Carteret Sch., West Orange, N.J., 1958-60; headmaster, pres. Webster (Mass.) Acad., 1960-68; headmaster Golden Hills, Acad., Ocala Fla., 1968-69, Graham-Eckes Sch., Palm Beach, 1969—. Spl. officer Ill. Dept. Conservation, 1946; chmn. fund raising campaign Lake Forest March of Dimes, 1946; mem. Mayor's Com. on Juvenile Delinquency, Chgo., 1955; mem. Gov.'s Adv. Com. Youth Service Bd. Mass., 1962-69; mem. Tchr. Edn. Adv. Council, Fla., 1969; lt. col., aide de camp to gov. Ga., 1967. Chief judge Lake Forest Election Bd., 1950-52; adminstrv. asst. Republican Nat. Conv. Chgo., 1952; Rep. candidate congressman, 1956. Adv. bd. L'Ecole En Famille, Liege, Belgium. Mem. N.E.A., Air Force Assn., Mil. Order World Wars, A.A.A.S., Inland Bird Banding Assn., Nat. Assn. Biology Tchrs., Assn. Edn. by Radio, New Eng. Assn. Colls. and Secondary Schs., Nat., Mass. assns. ind. schs., Nat. Assn. Sch. Adminstrs., Mass. Secondary Sch. Prins. Assn., Council Basic Edn., Fraternal Order Police, Fla. Sheriffs Assn., Ret. Officers' Assn., Marine Tech. Soc., English Speaking Union, Res. Officers Assn. (regional v.p. 1955), C. of C. (dir.), New Eng. Assn. Coll. Admissions Counselors, Mass. Police Assn., Ancient Order of Deep, Am. Legion, Internat. Platform Assn., Exec. and Profl. Hall of Fame (chmn.), S.A.R., Order of Lafayette, Sigma Xi, Sigma Alpha Epsilon, Beta Beta Beta, Sigma Gamma Epsilon. Presbyn. Clubs: Army and Navy (Chgo.); Gezira Sporting (Cairo, Egypt); Officers (Ft. Sheridan, Ill.); Golden Hills Turf and Golf (Ocala); Beach, Kiwanis, Republican (Palm Beach, Fla.). 233 W Indies Dr Palm Beach FL 33480

GROVE, BRANDON HAMBRIGHT, Jr., fgn. service officer; b. Chgo., Apr. 8, 1929; s. Brandon Hambright and Helen Julia Grove; A.B., Bard Coll., 1950; M.P.A., Princeton, 1952; m. Marie Cheremeteff, Nov. 1, 1959; children—John C., Catherine, Paul C., Mark C. Joined U.S. Fgn. Service, 1959; vice consul, Abidjan, Ivory Coast, also Conseil de l'Entente States, 1959-61; staff asst. to undersec. state, 1961-62; spl. asst. to dep. undersec. state for adminstrn., 1962-63; spl. asst. to Am. ambassador, New Delhi, India, 1963-65; U.S. liaison officer to city govt., Berlin, Germany, 1965-69; dir. Office Panamanian Affairs, State Dept., 1969-71; mem. Sr. Seminar in Fgn. Policy, 1971-72; asst. instr. Princeton, 1953. Served to lt. USNR, 1954-57. Recipient Meritorious Honor award State Dept., 1970. Mem. Am. Fgn. Service Assn. Home: 4938 Quebec St NW Washington DC 20016 Office: Dept of State Washington DC 20520

GROVE, DAVID LAWRENCE, economist; b. Boston, Apr. 25, 1918; s. Lawrence Roger and Emily (Becker) G.; grad. Boston Latin Sch., 1935; A.B. magna cum laude, Harvard, 1940, M.A., 1941, M.P.A., 1941, Ph.D., 1952; m. Lois Pawlowski, May 13, 1942; 1 dau., Carolyn Anne. Economist, Fed. Res. Bd., 1944-52; adviser monetary and banking problems, Paraguay, 1944, 51, Ecuador, 1947, 57, 58, Guatemala 1945, 46, 56, 62, 65, Philippines, 1948, 49, Colombia, Chile, 1950, Israel, 1964; chief economist Bank Am., San Francisco, 1952-58, v.p., head internat. relations, 1961-62, v. p., head bond investment dept., 1962-63, v.p., 1959-63; v.p., econ. adviser Fed. Res. Bank San Francisco, 1963-64; v.p., economist Blyth & Co., N.Y., 1965-66; chief economist IBM, 1966-69, v.p.; chief economist, 1969—; lectr. Am. U., 1952, Center of Latin Am. Monetary Studies, Mexico, 1954-56, 58, 64, 66. Mem. Time mag. panel economists, Several U.S. Govt. adv. coms.; bd. dirs., Nat. Bur. Econ. Research. Served with OSS, 1942-44. Decorated officer Order of Merit (Ecuador). Mem. Am. Econ. Assn., Am. Finance Assn., Phi Beta Kappa. Episcopalian. Author articles in field Mem. editorial bd. Financial Analysts Jour. Home: The Knoll Armonk NY 10504 Office: Old Orchard Rd Armonk NY 10504

GROVE, EUGENE FOREST, educator; b. Sheldon, Ill., July 28, 1915; s. Perle Forest and Janie Hathaway (Kissack) G.; B.M., Ill. Wesleyan U., 1937, M.M., 1939; Mus. Ed. D., Ind., U., 1951; spl. student Ill. State Normal U., 1935, 37, Columbia Tchrs. Coll., 1946; m. Margaret Rogers, May 30, 1942; childrenMichael, Margaret Jane, Thomas. Music tchr. Leaf River (Ill.) schs., 1937-38; dir. music Lanark (Ill.) pub. schs., 1938-41; head music dept. Atlantic Christian Coll., Wilson, N.C., 1941-43, Alma (Mich.) Coll., 1943-53; teaching fellow Ind. U., 1949-51; dir. choral groups Central Mich. U., Mt. Pleasant, 1953-59, prof. music, 1956—, head dept., 1959-. Mem. Mich. Music Tchrs. Assn. (pres. 1960-62), Mich. Edn. Assn., Am. Assn. U. Profs., Music Tchrs. Nat. Assn., Music Educators Nat. Conf., Mich. Music Educators Assn., Mich. Sch. Vocal Assn., Phi Mu Alpha (life). Presbyn. Home: 400 Crescent Dr Mount Pleasant MI 48858

GROVE, PHILIP HARVEY, constrn. engr.; b. Atlantic City, N.J., Oct. 4, 1904; s. Philip Bruner and Mignon (Lee) G.; C.E., Rensselaer Poly. Inst., 1925; m. Harriet Flaherty, July 17, 1926; childrenBarbara (Mrs. Guy P. Simoni), Jane (Mrs. George F. Pritchard), Winthrop Denison, Elizabeth (Mrs. Frederick W. Schweizer). Founder, 1929, pres. Grove, Shepherd, Wilson & Kruge, Inc., N.Y.C., now also chmn. bd.; founder 1951, now pres. MacLean-Grove & Co., Inc., rock and sub-aqueous tunnel construction, New York City, also dir. Trustee Rensselaer Poly. Inst. Mem. Am. Soc. C.E., Soc. Am. Mil. Engrs., Delta Kappa Epsilon. Clubs: Metropolitan, Canadian (N.Y.C.). Home: 781 Fifth Av New York City NY 10022 Office: 400 Madison Av New York City NY 10017

GROVE, ROBERT ECCLES, advt. exec.; b. Pitts., Apr. 23, 1891; s. John Williamson and Eliza (Eccles) G.; B.S. in Econs., U. Pitts., 1914; m. Louise Wolfe, Dec. 17, 1925. Began as salesman, 1914; asst. to pres. Tenn. Iron & Chem. Co., Pitts., 1919-23; in advt. 1923—, now chmn. bd., dir. Ketchum, MacLeod & Grove, Inc. Trustee Presbyn.-U. Hosp., Pitts. Served as 2d lt. AS, U.S. Army, 1917-18. Mem. Am. Assn. Advt. Ags. (sec., treas. 1954-55), Pitts. Advt. Club (past pres.), Sigma Alpha Epsilon, Omicron Delta Kappa. Republican. Presbyn. (elder). Clubs: Duquesne, Fox Chapel Golf (Pitts.); Rolling Rock (Ligonier, Pa.). Home: 415 Parr Plaza Apts 128 N Craig St Pittsburgh PA 15222 Office: 4 Gateway Center Pittsburgh PA 15222

GROVE, WILLIAM JOHNSON, physician; b. Ottawa, Ill., Mar. 23, 1920; s. Joseph Roy and Florence (Johnson) G.; B.S., U. Ill., 1941, M.D., 1943, M.S. in Surgery, 1949; m. Betty Pedigo, Mar. 23, 1944; children—William Johnson, Pamela J. Holly Lynn. Intern U. Ill. Research and Ednl. Hosps., 1944, asst. resident surgery, 1949-50, chief resident surgery, 1951-52; asst. resident surgery, Hines VA Hosp., 1950-51; mem. faculty U. Ill. Coll. Medicine, 1951—, prof. surgery, 1964—, dean, 1968-70, exec. dean, 1970—; attending surgeon Cook County Hosp., Chgo., 1952-54, U. Ill. Research and Ednl. Hosps.; cons. Hines VA Hosp., Presbyterian-St. Luke's Hosp., Chgo. Served to capt. AUS, 1944-47. Fellow A.C.S.; mem. A.M.A., Assn. Am. Med. Colls., Central, Chgo. surg. socs., Western Surg. Assn., Soc. Univ. Surgeons, Am. Heart Assn., Internat. Cardiovascular Soc., Warren H. Cole Soc., Soc. Clin. Surgery, Am. Surg. Assn., Inst. Medicine Chgo., Sigma Xi, Alpha Omega Alpha; Phi Delta Epsilon. Author numerous articles in field. Home: 664 58th St Hinsdale IL 60521 Office: 1853 W Polk St Chicago IL 60612

GROVEN, LOUIS JEAN, Belgian diplomat; b. Kerniel, Belgium, Feb. 18, 1910; s. Henri Jean and Antoinette Josephine (Notelaers) G.; M.S., U. Brussels, 1934, Ph.D., 1947; m Simone Gabrielle Radart, Dec. 13, 1937; children—Annie (Mrs. Douglas Long), Claude-Michel, Jean-Pierre. Mem. faculty U. Brussels, 1934-55, asso. prof. physics, 1954-55; sci. counselor, Washington, 1955—. Decorated Order Crown, laureate Concours Bourses de Voyage, Belgium, 1946; UNESCO fellow, 1952. Mem. Societe Francaise de Physique, Am. Phys. Inst., Am. Nuclear Soc. Author: Emission de Rayons Pares Gaz Rarefies, 1939. Home: 6401 Shadow Rd Chevy Chase MD 20015 Office: 3330 Garfield St Washington DC 20008

GROVENSTEIN, ERLING, Jr., educator, chemist; b. Miami, Fla., Nov. 12, 1924; s. Erling and Lois (Nesbitt) G.; B.S. in Chemistry, Ga. Sch. Tech., 1944; Ph.D. in Organic Chemistry, Mass. Inst. Tech., 1948; m. Catherine Gangwer, Sept. 4, 1954 (dec. 1961); childrenJohn Nesbitt, Alfred Enloe; m. 2d, Lillian Anne Enloe, June 23, 1962. Research asso. Mass. Inst. Tech., summer 1948; mem. faculty Ga. Inst. Tech., 1948-, Julius Brown prof. chemistry, 1965- ; research participant Oak Ridge Nat. Lab., summers 1949, 54. Mem. Am. Chem. Soc. (vis. asso. com. profl. tng.), Chem. Soc. (London), Ga. Acad. Sci., Am. Assn. U. Profs., Sigma Xi (Monie Ferst research award Ga. Inst. Tech. chpt. 1956), Phi Kappa Phi, Alpha Chi Sigma. Presbyn. (elder). Home: 2424 Briarmoor Rd NE Atlanta GA 30345

GROVER, ANTHONY CHARLES, underwriter; b. Oct. 13, 1907; student Westminster Sch.; m. Marguerite Beatrice Davies, June 27, 1931; 1 son, 1 dau. Underwriting mem. Lloyd's, London, Eng., 1936—, dep. chmn., 1958, chmn., 1959-60, dep. chmn., treas. Lloyd's Register of Shipping, 1956-58, 61, chmn., 1963- -; chmn. Lifeguard Assurance Ltd.; dir. F. Bolton & Co. (Holdings) Ltd., Bolton, Ingham (Agy.) Ltd., Grover, Bolton & Co., Ltd., Shellbridge Property Investment Co., Ltd. Chmn. N. European sect. London C. of C. Served as maj. Coldstream Guards, 1940-44. Clubs: Guards, Whites, Pratts, Woking Golf, Honourable Co. of Edinburgh Golfers, Rye Golf; Royal St. George's Golf (Sandwich); Royal Worlington, Newmarket Golf. Home: Marella Hook Heath Woking Surrey England Office: Lloyd's Register of Shipping 71 Fenchurch St London EC 3 England

GROVER, CHARLES STRAUDER, patent lawyer; b. Frankfort, Ind., Mar. 25, 1888; s. James H. and Carrie (DeVault) G.; B.S., Purdue U., 1910; LL.B., George Washington U., 1916; m. Mary Hedgcock, July 2, 1911; children—James, Stuart. Engr., Gen. Electric Co., 1910-11; examiner U.S. Patent Office, 1911-16; admitted to D.C. bar, 1915, Mass. bar, 1916; with Boston patent firm 1916—, formerly Roberts, Roberts & Cushman, now Roberts, Cushman & Grover; dir. Technicolor Motion Picture Corp. Mem. bd. appeals City of Newton. Trustee Garland Sch. Mem. Am., Mass., Boston bar assns., Am. Patent Law Assn., Tau Beta Pi. Clubs: St. Botolph (Boston); Brae Burn Country (Newton, Mass.). Home: 38 Vista Av Auburndale MA 02166 Office: 31 Milk St Boston MA 02109

GROVER, FREDERIC JOHN, educator; b. Paris, France, June 25, 1920; s. Frederick James and Marie- Hermance (Dagan) G.; Licence-es-Lettres, Sorbonne, Paris, 1940; Ph.D. in Romance lit., U. Cal. at Berkeley, 1954; m. Gloria Clare Waldron, Aug. 19, 1949; childrenClaire Anne, Eve Marie. Came to U.S., 1949, naturalized, 1952. Exec. asst. Mil. Permit Office, N.Y.C., 1949- 51; teaching asst. U. Cal. at Berkeley, 1951-54; from asst. prof. to prof. Swarthmore Coll., 1954-67; prof. French lit. U. B.C., Vancouver, Can., 1967-. Mem. French Underground, 1941-44; served to capt. French Army, 1944-49. Guggenheim fellow, 1959-60; fellow Am. Council Learned Socs., 1965; research grantee Am. Philos. Soc., 1961. Author: Drieu La Rochelle and the Fiction of Testimony, 1958; Drieu La Rochelle, 1963; Sur Les Ecrivains, 1964. Home: 4553 Langara St Vancouver 8 British Columbia Canada

GROVER, JAMES RUSSELL, Jr., congressman; b. Babylon, N.Y., Mar. 5, 1919; s. James Russell and Christine (English) G.; A.B., Hofstra Coll., 1941; LL.B., Columbia, 1949; m. Mary F. Fullerton, Apr. 23, 1943; childrenNancy, Jean, James Roberts, Jill. Admitted to N.Y. bar, 1950; pvt. practice, Babylon, 1951- -; mem. N.Y. State Assembly from Suffolk Dist., 1957-62; mem. 88th to 92d Congresses from 2d Congl. Dist. N.Y. Served with AUS, 1942-43, with USAAF, 1943-46. Mem. VFW, Am. Legion. Republican. Roman Catholic. Lion. Home: 185 Woodsome Rd Babylon NY 11702 Office: 1801 Argyle Sq Babylon NY 11702 and Longworth Office Bldg Washington DC 20525

GROVER, MYRON ROBERTS, Jr., univ. dean, physician; b. Boston, Dec. 5, 1927; s. Myron Robert and Treasa (Riley) G.; B.A., Bowdoin Coll., 1950; M.D., Cornell U., 1954; M.S., U. Ore., Med. Sch., 1956; m. Geraldine Ann Walker, June 30, 1956; children—Susan, Rob, Penny. Intern U. Ore. Med. Sch. Hosps. and Clinics, then resident internal medicine; asst. med. dir. U. Ore. Med. Sch., 1958-67, asst. prof. medicine, 1958-68, dir. continuing med. edn., 1965—, program coordinator Ore. Regional Med. Program, 1967-68, prof. medicine, 1968—, asso. dean, 1968—. Mem. N.W. Regional Med. Library Adv. Bd., 1968—. Mem. Gov.'s Council on Health Manpower, 1969—; mem. local sch. com. Garden Home Sch., 1970—. Served with AUS, 1946-47. Mem. Assn. Am. Med. Colls. (mem. com. on research on student affairs 1968—). Editorial bd. Northwest Medicine, 1964—. Home: 7720 SW 91st St Portland OR 97223

GROVER, NORMAN LAMOTTE, theologian, philosopher; b. Topeka, Feb. 9, 1928; s. LaMotte and Virginia Grace (Alspach) G.; B. Mech. Engring., Rensselaer Poly. Inst., 1948; B.D., Yale, 1951, S.T.M., 1952, Ph.D., 1957; m. Anne Stottler, June 24, 1950; childrenJennifer Jean, Peter Neal, Rebecca, Sandra. Mem. faculty Hollins (Va.) Coll., 1954-57, asst. prof. religion, 1956-57; ordained to ministry Presbyn. Ch., 1952; head dept. philosophy and religion Va. Poly. Inst. and State U., 1957—, prof. philosophy and religion, 1961—. Mem. supervising com. So. leadership tng. project Fund for Republic, 1955-56; asso. Danforth Found., 1958—, sr. asso., 1962—, chmn. Va., N.C. and S.C. conf., 1962—; psychotherapeutic counsellor Blacksburg Community Counselling Center, 1962-65. Mem. Am. Assn. U. Profs. (pres. Va. Poly. Inst. 1961-62), N.A.A.C.P., Am., Va. (pres. 1969) philos. assns., So. Soc. Philosophy and Psychology, Am. Acad. Religion, Blacksburg Ministerial Assn., Va., Montgomery County councils human relations, Am. Civil Liberties Union, Am. Acad. Arts and Scis., Delta Phi. Clubs: University (Blacksburg, Va.); Cosmopolitan (Va. Poly Inst.); Yale (Va.). Home: 705 Burruss Dr NW Blacksburg VA 24060

GROVER, ROBERT LAWRENCE, tool co. exec.; b. Chgo., Sept. 28, 1910; s. Donald and Martha (Bates) G.; B.S., Northwestern U., 1931, J.D., 1934; m. Ruth W. Dean, May 12, 1934; childrenKathleen C., Patricia R., Barbara E., Robert Lawrence, Donald D., Margaret E. Admitted to Ill. bar, 1934, Wis. bar, 1943; practice in Chgo., 1934-42; with Snap-on Tools Corp., Kenosha, Wis., 1942—, exec. v.p., 1964-66, pres. 1966—, also dir.; dir. Weidenhoff Corp., Twin Disc, Inc. Pres. Kenosha County council Boy Scouts Am., 1960-65. Bd. dirs. Kenosha Pub. Library and Museum; bd. govs. Dominican Coll.; chmn. bd. govs. Boston Coll. Franchise Study Center; bd. assos. Carthage Coll. Recipient Silver Beaver award Boy Scouts Am. Mem. Am. Bar Assn., Am. Mgmt. Assn., Order of Coif, Phi Beta Kappa. Conglist. Home: 5420 83d Pl Kenosha WI 53140 Office: 8028 28th Av Kenosha WI 53140

GROVER, VINOD KUMAR, Indian diplomat; b. Lahore, India, Dec. 11, 1938; s. Amar Nath and Kanta (Bhagat) G.; B.A., St. Stephen's Coll., New Delhi, 1958; M.A., Cambridge (Eng.) U., 1961; m. Reva Chopra, Apr. 26, 1962. With Indian Fgn. Service, 1961—, under sec. Ministry Fgn. Affairs, New Delhi, 1965-68; comml. counselor Indian embassy, Washington, 1968—. Vice chmn. Internat. Cotton Adv. Com., 1970—. Home: 4701 Willard Av Chevy Chase MD 20015 Office: 2107 Massachusetts Av Washington DC 20008

GROVER, WILLIAM LUTHER, hosp. adminstr.; b. Columbus, O., July 16, 1919; s. William E. and Leona (George) G.; B.A., Ohio State U., 1940, postgrad., 1940-41, M.D., 1944; m. Geraldine A. Morris, Sept. 15, 1943; children—Gregory William, James Elliott, Cynthia Sue, Carol Anne. Intern U.S. Naval Hosp., Bainbridge, Md., 1944; resident Ohio State U. Hosp., 1946-49; psychiatrist Columbus State Hosp., 1949-54; supt. Cleve. State Hosp., 1954—. Mem. Cuyahoga County Mental Health and Retardation Bd. Dist. commr. Boy Scouts

Am., 1959-60. Served as lt. M.C., USNR, World War II and Korea. Certified mental hosp. adminstr., Am. Psychiatric Assn. Mem. Ohio Med. Assn., Cleve. Acad. Medicine, Am., Ohio psychiat. assns., Cleve. Soc. Neurology and Psychiatry, Assn. Med. Supts. Mental Hosps., Am. Acad. Religion and Mental Health, Royal Soc. Health. Home: 5671 Cumberland Dr Cleveland OH 44125 Office: 4455 Turney Rd Cleveland OH 44105

GROVERMAN, WILLIAM HEALD, Jr., naval officer; b. Covington, Ky., Nov. 4, 1909; s. William Heald and Belle Virginia (Marr) G.; grad. Peddie Sch., 1928; B.S., U.S. Naval Acad., 1932; grad. Naval War Coll., 1951; m. Lady Helen Parnell (dec.); m. 2d, Paola Castanedo Copeland, May 15, 1953; 1 foster son, A. Wallace Grafton. Commd. ensign U.S. Navy, 1932, advanced through grades to rear adm., 1961; assigned various ships, 1932-41; instr. chemistry, ordnance and marine engring. Naval Acad., 1941; exec. officer destroyer U.S.S. Radford, 1941-43; comdr. U.S.S. Philip, Guadalcanal, 1943, then mem. staff Comdr. Destroyers U.S. Atlantic Fleet, to 1945; comdg. officer U.S.S. DeHaven, 1945; head undersea warfare br. Office Naval Research, 1946-50; comdr. Destroyer Div. 122, 1951-52; chief staff officer Comdr. Fleet Tng. Group, Guantanamo Bay, Cuba, then mem. staff Comdr. in Chief Atlantic Fleet, 1952-57; comdr. Cruiser U.S.S. Des Moines, 1957-58; attached Office Dep. Chief Naval Operations for Devel., Washington, 1958-62; comdr. Cruiser Destroyer Flotilla 3, Long Beach, Cal., 1963-65; dir. Anti-Submarine Warfare div. Office Chief Naval Operations, Washington, 1965-67; comdr. Western Sea Frontier, Treasure Island, San Francisco, 1967-. Decorated Silver Star medal with cluster; Bronze Star medal with 2 clusters, Presdl. Unit citation (U.S.); Korean Presdl. Unit citation. Clubs: Boston (New Orleans); Bohemian, Pacific Union, St. Francis Yacht (San Francisco); Cypress Point (Pebble Beach); Propeller. Office: Comdr Western Sea Frontier Treasure Island San Francisco CA 94130

GROVES, EARL WILSON, pianist, educator; b. Balt., Apr. 16, 1917; s. Norman John and Sarah Jane (Morgan) G.; tchr.'s certificate in piano, Peabody Conservatory Music, 1937, in theory, 1938, ch. organist's certificate cum laude, 1938, B.Mus., 1939, M.Mus., 1941; B.S., Johns Hopkins, 1948; postgrad. musicology Columbia, 1951-53; pupil piano P. Tallarico, R. Casadesus, E. Steuermann. Organist, choir master Balt. chs., 1935-41; mem. faculty Vassar Coll., 1945-, prof. music, 1962-, chmn. dept., 1967-70; piano soloist Peabody, Vassar, Clarion and Boston Pops orchs.; ensemble and recital appearances. Served with AUS, 1941-44. Recipient Thomas prize Peabody Conservatory, 1940, Harold Randolph prize, 1941; Faculty fellow Fund Advancement Edn., 1951-52; Vassar Coll., 1960-61, 70-71. Mem. Am. Assn. U. Profs., Coll. Music Soc., Dutchess County Music Assn. (bd. dirs., v.p. 1955-60, 66-). Democrat. Episcopalian. Home: 10 Vassar Lake Dr Poughkeepsie NY 12601

GROVES, FRANK MALVON, contractor; b. Butler, Jo., Jan. 22 1887; s. Stephen Jasper and Mary Ann (Frederickson) G.; student pub. schs. and pvt. studies; m. Hazel Olive Nelson, Sept. 25, 1915; childrenFrances Mary, Franklin Nelson. With S.J. Groves & Sons Co., Mpls., 1905-, pres., 1918-, chmn. bd., 1950-; pres. and/or dir. subsidiary and affiliated cos. Recipient co. Army citations. Mem. U.S. C. of C., N.A.M., Asso. Gen. Contractors Am., Moles. Club: Athletic (Mpls.). Home: 4885 E Lake Harriet Blvd Minneapolis MN 55401

GROVES, GERALD ALEXANDER, govt. ofcl.; b. Mt. Mansfield, Jamaica, Apr. 10, 1916; s. George Reginald and Agnes (Prestwidge) G.; L.S.E., London (Eng.) U., 1957; postgrad. Internat. Coll., Elsinore, Denmark, 1957; m. Bernice O'Connor, Aug. 6, 1957; children-Gerald Alexander, Marguerite. Asst. clk. courts, Kingston, Jamaica, 1937-44, assst. clk. legislature, 1948-53; adminstrv. officer, asst. sec. Colonial Secretariat, Kingston, 1953-57; prin. asst. sec., asst. undersec. Ministry Home Affairs, 1956-68; consul gen. of Jamaica in N.Y.C., 1968—. Home: 215 E 68th St New York NY 10021 Office: 200 Park Av New York S1NY 10017

GROVES, HARRY EDWARD, lawyer; b. Manitou Springs, Colo., Sept. 4, 1921; s. Harry A. and Dorothy A. (Cave) G.; B.A., U. Colo., 1943; J.D., U. Chgo., 1949; LL.M., Harvard, 1959; m. Dolores Ruth Hale (div. 1947); 1 son, Sheridon Hale; m. 2d, Evelyn Frances Apperson, Dec. 23, 1949. Admitted to N.C., Tex. and Ohio bars, also U.S. Supreme Ct.; staff asst. Am. Council Race Relations, Chgo., 1949; asst. prof. law N.C. Coll. Law, 1949-51; pvt. practice law, Fayetteville, N.C., 1952-56; prof., dean Sch. Law, Tex. So. U., 1956-61; head dept. law U. Singapore, 1962-64, dean Faculty of Law, 1963-64; dir. minority groups project Assn. Am. Law Schs., 1964-67; vis. prof. constl. law, U. Malaya, Singapore, 1960- 62; vis. prof. law U. Wash., 1965-66; pres. Central State U., Wilberforce, O., 1965-68; pvt. practice law, Dayton, O., 1970—; prof. Law Sch., U. Cin., 1968-70; vis. prof. U. Utah, 1968, U.N.C., 1970. City councilman, Fayetteville, 1955-56. Chmn. bd. dirs. Dayton-Miami Valley Consortium, 1968. Served with AUS, 1943-46, 50-51. Author: Comparative Constitutional Law: Cases and Materials; The Constitution of Malaysia. Contbr. articles to profl. jours. Home: Route 5 Xenia OH 45385 Office: 1526 W 3d St Dayton OH 45407

GROVES, JOHN HURST, lawyer; b. E. Chicago, Ind., Oct. 4, 1908; s. Hurst Kohler and Edith S. (Johnson) G.; A.B., U. Mich., 1930, LL.B., 1933; student accounting Northwestern U. Sch. Commerce, 1934-36; m. Mary E. Sisco, Feb. 2, 1935; 1 son, Hurst Kohler II. Admitted to Ind. bar, 1932, Ill. bar, 1933; with firm Cooke, Sullivan & Ricks, Chgo., 1933-34; partner firm Lawyer & Garrett, Chgo., 1934-38, Evans & Hebel, Indpls., 1938-42, Barnes, Hickam, Pantzer & Boyd, Indpls., 1942—. Gen. counsel Ind. Gas Co., Inc.; counsel Indpls. Power & Light Co. Bd. dirs. Central Newspapers Found., Inc. Served with USNR, 1944-46. Mem. Am., Ind. (chmn. corp. law com. 1946-48), Indpls., 7th Circuit bar assns., Indpls. Com. Fgn. Relations, Ind. Soc. Chgo., Art Assn. Indpls., Sigma Phi Epsilon. Republican. Presbyn. Clubs: Columbia, Lawyers (past pres.), Woodstock Country, Traders Point Hunt (Indpls.); Lawyers (Ann Arbor, Mich.). Home: 4240 Roland Rd Indianapolis IN 46208 Office: Merchants Bank Bldg Indianapolis IN 46204

GROVES, MARION HERBERT, educator; b. Medicine Lodge, Kan., Feb. 18, 1910; s. Herbert St. Clair and Martha (Pepoon) G.; B.S., Phillips U., 1933; Ph.D., U. Chgo., 1950; m. Arleen Elizabeth Daffer, Nov. 21, 1943 (div. May 1959); 1 son, Marshall Ray; m. to Mildred Ann Blakesley, June 1, 1963; childrenMariann, Montgomery. Minister Disciples Church, 1933, minister, Stafford, Kansas, 1934-37, Larned, Kansas, 1937-41; clinical intern at the Elgin State Hosp., 1942-43; chief psychologist Cook County Criminal Ct., 1943-45; psychologist VA counselling service U. Chgo., 1945; instr. U. Chgo., 1945-47; lectr., dir. psychol. lab. U. Cal. at Santa Barbara, 1947-49; asst. prof. psychology Ill. Inst. Tech. 1950-54, asso. prof., 1954—, asst. dean Grad. School, 1951-58, asso. dean, 1958-69, acting dean Grad. Sch., 1962-64; lectr. neurology, psychiatry Northwestern Med. Sch., 1954—. Cons. Ventura County (Cal.) Juvenile Ct., 1948-49; Nat. Assn. Fgn. Student Affairs grantee as participant 1st World Conf. on Internat. Houses and Centers, Paris, 1961; mem. Inter- Univ. Com. on Travel Grants for exchange scholars with Russia and Eastern Europe, 1963-68; cons. dept. neurology and psychiatry Chgo. Med. Sch., 1964—. Bd. govs. Internat. House, Chgo., 1961—. Charter clin. fellow Behavior Therapy and Research Soc.; mem. Am. Psychol. Assn., A.A.A.S., Am. Assn. U. Profs., Am. Soc. Engring. Edn., N.E.A., Ill. Soc. Personality Study (pres. 1957-58), Nat. Assn. Fgn. Student Affairs (regional chmn. 1962-64, mem. resolutions com. 1969), Assn. for Higher Edn., Sigma Xi. Club: University. Contbr. articles to psychol. and psychiat. publs. Home: 72 Shore Dr Ogden Dunes Portage IN Office: 3300 S Federal St Chicago IL 60616

GROVES, RICHARD HULBERT, army officer; b. Honolulu, July 10, 1923; s. Leslie Richard and Grace (Wilson) G.; student Princeton, 1940-42; B.S., U.S. Mil. Acad., 1945; M.S., Harvard, 1950; M.A., George Washington U., 1964; postgrad. U.S. Army Engr. Sch., 1951-52, U.S. Army Command and Gen. Staff Coll., 1956-57, Air War Coll., 1963-64; m. Patricia Hook, Oct. 14, 1945; children—Carolyn, Patricia, Richard W., Ann L. Comd. 2d lt. U.S. Army, 1945, advanced through grades to brig. gen., 1969; company comdr., battalion adjutant 1st Div., Germany, 1945-49; asst. dist. engr., Mobile, 1950-51; aide to chief of engrs., 1952-55; company comdr. aviation engr. units, B.W.I., 1955-56; mem. staff and faculty U.S. Army Engr. Sch., Ft. Belvoir, Va., 1957-60; chief of maintenace Am. Battle Monuments Commn., Paris, France, 1960-62; battalion comdr. 8th Div., Germany, 1962-63; div. chief Office Chief of Staff, U.S. Army, Washington, 1964-66; mil. asst. to Sec. Army, Washington, 1966-67; comdg. officer 159th Engr. Group, Vietnam, 1967-68; dep. dir. civil works Office Chief Engrs., Washington, 1968—; tchr. Cath. U., 1957-58, George Washington U., 1958-60. Decorated Legion of Merit with oak leaf cluster, Bronze Star for valor with oak leaf cluster, Air medal with 2 oak leaf clusters, Army Commendation medal, Chuong My medal; Fellow Am. Soc. C.E.; mem. Nat. Soc. Profl. Engrs., Am. Soc. Mil. Engrs. Author: (with Leslie R. Groves) Now It Can Be Told, 1962. Home: 1203 Westgrove Blvd Alexandria VA 22307 Office: Office Chief of Engineers Washington DC 20314

GROVES, ROBERT ALVIN, hotel exec.; b. Jacksonville, Ill., Aug. 11, 1910; s. James A. and Maria (Ellis) G.; student Ill. Coll., 1928-31; m. Joan O'Neal, Oct. 17, 1946; childrenRichard O'Neal, Jo Ann. Gen. mgr. The Town House, Los Angeles, 1937-42, Sherry-Netherland, N.Y.C., 1948-49, La Quinta Hotel, Palm Springs, Cal., 1950-53, Hilton Arrowhead Springs, San Bernardino, Cal., 1953-54, Beverly Hilton, Beverly Hills, Cal., 1954-; mgr. Palmer House, Chgo., 1946-47, Mayflower Hotel, Washington, 1947-48; v.p. Hilton Hotel Corp., 1961-. Lectr. hotel adminstrn. Cornell U. Vice pres. Crescent Bay council Boy Scouts Am., 1959-; gen. chmn. Beverly Hills Community Chest, 1959-60. Served to lt. col. USAAF, 1942-46. Recipient Community Chest award United Charities, 1959. Mem. Cal. (v.p. 1961-), So. Cal. (pres. 1942) hotel assns., Cal. Hotel and Motel Assn. (pres. 1964, chmn. bd. 1965), Beverly Hills C. of C. (v.p. 1956-61, dir. 1956-, pres. 1961- 62); Sigma Xi. Mason. Clubs: Los Angeles Country, Bel Air Bay (dir. 1966-70) (Los Angeles); Rotary, Cherry Hills Country (Denver); Pauma Valley (Cal.) Country. Address: Denver Hilton Hotel 1550 Court Pl Denver CO 80201

GROVES, ROBERT W., banker. Chmn. bd. emeritus Savannah Bank and Trust Co. Office: 2 E Bryan St Box 9947 Savannah GA 31402*

GROVES, WALLACE, financier; b. Norfolk, Va., Mar. 20, 1901; s. James S. and Lillie (Edwards) G.; M.A., B.Sc., LL.B., LL.M., Georgetown U., Washington, 1924; LL.D. (hon.), Ursinus Coll., Collegeville, Pa.; m. Georgette Cusson; children—Gordon, Gene, Graham, Gary, Gayle. Admitted Md. bar, 1925; practiced law until 1931, then went to N.Y. to engage in reorgn. and mgmt. industrial and financial concerns; formerly pres. and chmn. bd. Phoenix Securities Corp.; founder of Freeport, Bahamas; pres. Grand Bahama Port Authority, Freeport Med. Authority, Freeport Ednl. Authority, Freeport Trust Co.; chmn. bd. Grand Bahama Port Authority Ltd. Founder, Wallace Groves Found., Inc., a charitable orgn. Address: PO Box 5 Freeport Grand Bahama Island Bahama Islands

GROW, JOHN, lawyer; b. Tuscaloosa, Ala., Sept. 21, 1934; s. James Augustus and Altona (Way) G.; B.S., U. Ala., 1961, LL.B., 1962; m. Hercilia Herrera, Jan. 16, 1957; children-Angela Gail, Carla Marie, John, Christopher Winston, Barbara Carol. Admitted to Ala. bar, 1962; practice in Montgomery, 1962-63, Mobile, 1963—; law clk. Frank M. Johnson, U.S. dist. judge, 1962-63; partner Armbrecht, Jackson & De Mouy, 1963—. Pres. Friends of Mobile Pub. Library. Served to 1st lt. U.S. Army, 1954- 58. Mem. Am., Ala., Mobile bar assns., Maritime Law Assn. U.S., Mobile Area C. of C., Ala. Alumni Assn. (pres. Mobile chpt.), Bench and Bar, Phi Alpha Delta, Omicron Delta Kappa. Editor-in-chief Ala. Law Review, 1961-62. Home: 2733 S Belvedere Circle Mobile AL 36606 Office: Mchts Nat Bank Mobile AL 36602

GROW, RICHARD WILLIAM, educator; b. Lynndyl, Utah, Oct. 31, 1925; s. Joseph Henry and Helen Mary (Horne) G.; B.S., U. Utah, 1948, M.S., 1949; Ph.D. (Sylvania Electric Products fellow, Nat. RCA fellow), Stanford, 1954; m. Peggy Anne Staub, Sept. 3, 1947; childrenRichard Feramorz, Robert Joseph, David William, Margaret Anne. Electronic scientist Naval Research Lab., Washington, 1949-51; research asso. Stanford Electronics Lab., 1953-58; asso. research prof. elec. engring. dept. U. Utah, Salt Lake City, 1958-64, asst. dir. high velocity lab., 1958-59, dir., 1959-62, dir. microwave device and phys. electronics lab., 196O-, research prof. elec. engring. dept., 1964-66, chmn. dept., 1965-, prof., 1966-; cons. Gen. Electric Microwave Lab., 1954-59, Litton Industries, 1959, 68-, Eitel-McCullough, Inc., 1959, Microwave Electronics Corp., 1959-68, Northrop Corp., 1969—, Bur. Radiol. Health, Pub. Health Service, 1970—; with Hughes Research Lab., Malibu, Cal., summer 1969. Served with USNR, 1944-46. Mem. I.E.E.E. (sr. mem.), Sigma Xi, Phi Eta Sigma, Tau Beta Pi, Phi Kappa Phi. Contbr. articles to profl. jours. Home: 4311 Spruce Circle Salt Lake City UT 84117

GRUBB, CHARLES B., banker; b. Poughkeepsie, N.Y., 1912; ed. Colgate U., 1936. Pres. trust officer; Poughkeepsie Savs. Bank, partner Campbell Parking Sta.; dir. Empire Nat. Bank. Home: 6 St Johns Pkwy Poughkeepsie NY 12601 Office: 21 Market St Box 31 Poughkeepsie NY 12602

GRUBB, H. DALE, govt. ofcl.; b. Henryetta, Okla., Apr. 23, 1925; s. Hiram D. and Buena Vista (Troth) G.; B.A. in Journalism, U. Okla., 1951; m. Martha Ann Ports, July 8, 1967. With U.S. Secret Service, 1951, NASA, 1959-60, Avco Corp., 1960-68; spl. asst. to Pres. Nixon, 1969-70; asst. adminstr. legislative affairs NASA Hdqrs., Washington, 1970—. Served as pilot USAAF, World War II. Mem. U. Okla. Alumni Assn. (pres. Washington chpt. 1962), Delta Tau Delta. Clubs: Nat. Press, Nat. Aviation, Fed. City, Nat. Space (pres. 1965-66) (Washington); Burning Tree (Bethesda, Md.). Home: Watergate West Washington DC 20037 Office: NASA Hdqrs Washington DC 20546

GRUBB, HOMER VERNON, educator; b. Rockville, Ind., July 12, 1916; s. Marion Henry and Olus (Harmless) G.; B.S. in Chem. Engring., Purdue U., 1938, M.S. in Chem. Engring., 1941; Ph.D., Ga. Inst. Tech., 1951; m. Sara Jane Cole, June 12, 1943; 1 dau., Sara Ann. Research asst. engring. expt. sta. U. Mo., 1939-; mem. faculty Sch. Chem. Engring., Ga. Inst. Tech., 1939-, prof. chem. engring., 1958-, dir. Sch. Chem. Engring., 1960-; spl. instr. Purdue U., summer 1941, Bell Aircraft Corp., 1943-45, Oglethorpe U., 1944; cons., 1943-. Dir. Plastic Films Corp., Atlanta. Registered profl. engr., Ga. Mem. Am. Int. Chem. Engrs., Sigma Xi, Alpha Chi Sigma, Tau Beta Pi, Phi Lambda Upsilon. Home: 3146 Downwood Circle NW Atlanta GA 30327 Office: 225 North Av NW Atlanta GA 30332

GRUBB, KENNETH MACLEOD, publishing exec.; b. Chgo., Feb. 15, 1908; s. Joseph E. and Amanda (MacLeod) G.; A.B., Miami U., 1931, A.M., 1934, Litt.D., 1964; postgrad. U. Túbingen (Germany), 1932-33; m. Elenore H. Scheel, Feb. 20, 1937; children—Frederick K., Amanda M. Instr. German, U. Chgo., 1934-37; sales mgr. Gen. Motors Acceptance Corp., 1937-41; v.p. Prentice-Hall, Inc., 1941-51; with Allyn & Bacon, Inc., Boston, 1951—, pres., 1953-70, chmn. bd., 1971—, also dir. Served to maj. USAAF, 1942-46. Conglist. Clubs: Downtown, Algonquin (Boston); Concord Country; Union League (Chgo.). Home: Camino Acoma Santa Fe NM 87501 Office: 470 Atlantic Av Boston MA 02210

GRUBB, KENNETH PHILIP, U.S. dist. judge; b. Mauston, Wis., Sept. 14, 1895; s. George S. and Lucy (Nuzum) G.; student Northwestern U., 1914-17; LL.B., U. Wis., 1921; m. Marguerite Nuzum, Dec. 27, 1921; children—Dr. Kenneth P., Barbara (Mrs. William E. Weiner). Admitted to Wis. bar, 1921; asso. Quarles, Spence & Quarles, 1921-30, partner, 1940-55; U.S. dist. judge, Milwaukee, 1955-; dist. judge rep. from 7th Circuit on Judicial Conf. of U.S., 1964. Served as 2d lt. U.S. Army, World War I. Fellow Am. Coll. Trial Lawyers; mem. State Bar Wis., Am., Milw. bar assns., Bar Assn. 7th Fed. Circuit, Internat. Assn. Ins. Counsel (pres. 1948-49), Order of Coif, Sigma Chi, Phi Delta Phi. Mason. Clubs: Milwaukee, Athletic. Contbr. to Successful Jury Trials (Appleman), 1952. Home: 2138 E Lafayette Pl Milwaukee WI 53202 Office: Federal Bldg Milwaukee WI 53202

GRUBB, WILSON LYON, physician, educator; b. Balt., Nov. 26, 1910; s. Harry and Eleanor (Chaney) G.; grad. St. Albans Sch., Washington, 1929; A.B., Johns Hopkins, 1932, M.D., 1937; m. Margot J. Carter, 1967; 1 son, James Carter. Intern bacteriology and pathology Boston Children's Hosp. Med. Center, 1937-38, intern pediatrics, 1938-40; asst. resident pediatrics Johns Hopkins Hosp., 1940-41; pvt. practice pediatrics, Balt., 1941—; pediatrician-in-chief Union Meml. Hosp., Balt., 1961—; attending pediatrician Greater Balt. Med. Center, 1943—; attending pediatrician Ch. Home and Hosp., Balt., 1942—, chief pediatrics, 1956-61; pediatric cons. Childrens Hosp., Happy Hills Convalescent Hosp., Childrens Rehab. Inst.; asst. prof. pediatrics Johns Hopkins Med. Sch., 1957—; clin. asst. prof. pediatrics Sch. Medicine, U. Md. spl. research juvenile diabetes, adoptions, infant feeding. Diplomate Am. Bd. Pediatrics. Fellow Am. Acad. Pediatrics (chmn. for Md. 1966-70, alternate dist. chmn. 1970—); A.M.A., Md. Diabetes Assn. (pres. 1966—), Med. and Chirurgical Faculty Edn., Nat. Kidney Found., Md. Hist. Soc., Phi Beta Kappa, Phi Kappa Psi. Episcopalian. Clubs: Pithotomy (Johns Hopkins Med. Sch.); Johns Hopkins, Churchmens, Tudor and Stuart, Baltimore Country (Balt.); St. Petersburg (Fla.) Yacht. Home: 3607 Greenway Baltimore MD 21218 Office: 5820 York Rd Baltimore MD 21212

GRUBBS, EDWARD JOSEPH, educator; b. Los Angeles, July 22, 1934; s. Thomas Whitfield and Mary (Pfund) G.; A.B., Occidental Coll., 1956; Ph.D., Mass. Inst. Tech., 1959; m. Mary Jo Schmith, Dec. 15, 1963; children—June Marie, Alan Whitfield. Postdoctoral research asso. U. Ill., 1960-61; mem. faculty San Diego State Coll., 1961—, prof. chemistry, 1968—. Grantee Research Corp., NSF, NIH; Humboldt Found. fellow, Germany, 1968-69. Mem. Am. Chem. Soc. Contbr. articles profl. jours. Home: 3955 El Canto Dr Spring Valley CA 92077 Office: Dept Chemistry San Diego State Coll San Diego CA 92115

GRUBBS, FRANCIS OLMSTED, educator; b. Harrisburg, Pa., Feb. 23, 1908; s. Henry Alexander and Edith Clarke (Holmes) G.; student The Hill Sch., Pottstown, Pa.; A.B., Princeton, 1930; student Sorbonne U., Paris, 1930, Middlebury French Sch., 1931-33, Harvard U., 1937; L.H.D., Trinity Coll., Hartford, Conn., 1961; m. Frances Eleanor Jones, Aug. 1, 1936; children—Eleanor Olmsted (Mrs. Charles A. Rice III), Dennis Holmes. French tchr. Loomis Sch., Windsor, Conn., 1930-46, chmn. modern lang. dept., dir. studies, 1946-52, acting headmaster, 1952, headmaster, 1952-67; pres. Loomis Inst., 1967—. Pres. New Eng. Assn. Colls. and Secondary Schs., 1965-66. Bd. dirs. Newington Children's Hosp., 1965-70. Served as lt. USNR, 1943-46, officer in charge ednl. services Phila. Naval Hosp. Recipient citation for rehab. amputees, blind and deaf, Surgeon Gen. Navy, 1946. Pres. Walks Found., Inc., 1968-70. Mem. Headmasters Assn., Windsor Hist. Soc., Newcomen Soc., Conn. Assn. Ind. Schs. (mem. exec. com.). Conglist. Clubs: Princeton (N.Y.C.); Windsor. Address: Loomis Sch Windsor CT 06095

GRUBBS, HENRY ALEXANDER, educator; b. Bala, Pa., Mar. 1, 1904; s. Henry Alexander and Edith Clarke (Holmes) G.; A.B., Princeton, 1923, Ph.D., 1927; student Johns Hopkins U., 1919-20, Université de Bordeaux, 1924-25; m. Mireille Olga Masson, Feb. 17, 1931; 1 dau., Diane (Mrs. W. Savage). Instr. French, Princeton, 1923-24, 27-30, asst. prof., 1931-42; bookman Am. Book Co., 1942-43; asso. editor Ziff-Davis Pub. Co., 1943-44; prof. French, Oberlin Coll., 1944-70, head dept. Romance langs., 1944-56, chmn. French and Italian, 1956-59; asst. prof. French, Columbia, summer, 1936. Research fellow Am. Council of Learned Socs., 1930-31; research grantee, Am. Philos. Soc., 1939; Fulbright Postdoctoral Research fellow, France, 1952. Decorated Chevalier des Palmes Academiques. Mem. Modern Lang. Assn. Am., Central States Modern Lang. Tchrs. Assn., Phi Beta Kappa. Democrat. Author: Damien Mitton: bourgeois honnête homme, 1932; Jean-Baptiste Rousseau; his life and works, 1941; Paul Valery, 1968; co-author, editor, textbooks in French. Contbr. to learned jours, in France and U.S. Home: Constellations de Fabron Bloc "Lyre" Blvd de l'Ouest 06 Nice France

GRUBE, KARL P., mfg. co. exec.; b. Aurora, Ill., 1911; grad. Stanford, 1935; married. Engr., Douglas Aircraft Co., 1928-48; in charge All Steel Equipment Inc., Aurora, 1948-55, pres., treas., chief exec. officer, 1955-71, chmn. bd., chief exec. officer, 1971—; pres., treas. Roach Appleton Mfg. Co.; dir. Union Spl. Machine Co., Sears Bank & Trust Co., CIT Financial Corp. Elk. Office: PO Box 871 Aurora IL 60507*

GRUBER, JACOB WILLIAM, educator; b. Pitts., Feb. 26, 1921; s. Frank and Rebecca (Rosenberg) G.; B.A., Oberlin Coll., 1942, M.A., 1947; Ph.D., U. Pa., 1952; m. Shirley Moskowitz, Feb. 3, 1946; children—Ruth Ellen, Frank Judah, Samuel David. Instr. N.Y. U., 1947-48; from instr. to prof. anthropology Temple U., 1948- -, chmn. dept. anthropology, 1963-70, dir. Coll. program in Rome, 1970- -. Democratic committeeman, 1949-55. Served with AUS, 1942-45. Fellow Am. Anthrop. Assn., Royal Anthrop. Inst., A.A.A.S.; mem. Soc. Am. Archeology, Am. Assn. Phys. Anthropologists, History of Sci. Soc., Phila. Anthrop. Soc. (editor 1967). Author: A Conscience in Conflict: Life of St. George Mivart, 1960. Contbr. articles profl. jours. Home: Via Antonio Nibby 3 00161 Rome Italy Office: Anthropology Dept Temple U Philadelphia PA

GRUBER, KARL, Austrian diplomat; b. May 3, 1909; grad. Inst. Tech.; J.D., LL.D., U. Vienna; m. Helga Ahlgrimm, 1939. Began with Austrian Postal Adminstrn., 1934; mem. resistance movement to Nazis, 1938-45; gov. of Tyrol, 1945; minister of fgn. affairs, Austria, 1945-53; Austrian ambassador to U.S., 1954—; asso. prof. econs. U. Vienna. Mem. People's Party. Author: Politik der Mitte; Full Employment; From Liberation to Liberty. Address: Austrian Embassy 2343 Massachusetts Av NW Washington DC

GRUBER, WILLIAM EDWARD, lawyer; b. Alva, Okla., Apr. 6, 1914; s. Merl M. and Ruth (Herod) G.; B.A., Northwestern State Coll., Alva, 1934; LL.B., U. Okla., 1937, J.D., 1970; m. Cleo Bailey, Oct. 16, 1937; children—Patricia (Mrs. Nelson Myers), John S., Thomas W. Admitted to Okla. bar, 1937; practice in Alva, 1939-42, 65- -; county atty. Woods County, 1939-42; spl. agt. FBI, Washington 1942- 64; mem. firm Morford, Benson & Gruber, 1965—; city atty. Alva, 1965—. Prof. law enforcement Northwestern State Coll., 1969-70. Mem. Okla. Crime Commn. Mem. council Gt. Salt Plains council Boy Scouts Am., Enid, Okla., 1968—. Mem. Am., Okla., Woods County bar assns., Alva C. of C., U. Okla. Assn., Northwestern State Coll. Alumni Assn. Baptist. Home: 820 Locust St PO Box 512 Alva OK 73717 Office: 615 Barnes St PO Box 488 Alva OK 73717

GRUBER, WILLIAM PAUL, journalist; b. Chgo., May 2, 1932; s. Frank and Gisella (Rudelitch) G.; B.S. in Journalism, U. Ill., 1954. Asst. editor Community News, Woodstock, Ill., 1954-55; reporter, markets editor U.P.I., 1958-63; mem. staff Chicago's Am., 1963—, financial editor Chgo. Today, 1968—. Served with AUS, 1955-57. Mem. Am. Soc. Bus. Writers, Sigma Delta Chi. Club: Chgo. Press. Home: 6030 N Sheridan Rd Chicago IL 60626 Office: 441 N Michigan Av Chicago IL 60611

GRUBERG, MARTIN, educator; b. N.Y.C., Jan. 28, 1935; s. Benjamin and Mollie (Stolnitz) G.; B.A., Coll. City N.Y., 1955; Ph.D., Columbia, 1963; m. Rosaline Kurfirst, Mar. 25, 1967. Agt.-adjudicator Passport Agy., Dept. State, N.Y.C. 1960-61; tchr. social studies Pelham (N.Y.) High Sch., 1961-62; instr. polit. sci. Hunter Coll., 1961-62; tchr. social studies James Monroe and Seward Park High Schs., N.Y.C., 1962-63; asst. prof. polit. sci. Wis. State U. at Oshkosh, 1963-66, asso. prof., 1966-69, prof., chmn. dept., 1969—, dir. pre-law program, 1966-69. Pres. Oshkosh Human Rights Council, 1966-68; v.p. Winnebago chpt. Nat. Orgn. Women, 1970-71. Recipient Am. Legion Aux. Americanism award, 1949, N.Y. State Scholarship, 1952, Buckwar award, 1955, Steigman award, 1955, Columbia grantee, 1961, 62, Wis. Regents' Research grantee, 1964-70. Mem. Am., Midwest, Wis. polit. sci. assns., Law and Soc. Assn., Aurelian Soc. Optimist. Author: Women in American Politics, 1968; newspaper column Women: Our Largest Minority, The Paper for Central Wisconsin, 1970-71, Spotlight on Women for Oshkosh Northwestern, 1971. Broadcast 16 weeks Civil Rights Revolution Wis. State FM Network, 1969. Contbr. articles encys., prof. jours. Home: 2020 Wisconsin St Oshkosh WI 54901

GRUBERT, CARL, cartoonist; b. Chgo., Sept. 10, 1911; s. Karl and Christine (Schwartz) G.; B.S., U. Wis., 1934; student Chgo. Acad. Fine Arts, 1929-30; m. Gloria Alexander, Feb. 27, 1937; children—Carleen, Carl; m. 2d, Lorraine Whitney, July 13, 1946; children—Jon, Jan, James, Jean. Creator, cartoonist The Berrys, internationally syndicated cartoon, 1942; exhibitions at the Nat. Cartoonists Soc. Exhibit, 1950, 51, Met. Mus. Art, 1951, Library of Congress, 1941. Staff artist Great Lakes Bull., Pub. Information 9th Naval Dist., 1944-45. Recipient U.S. Treasury award of Merit, 1950, Freedom's Found. Medal, 1950. Mem. Nat. Cartoonists Soc. Lion, Elk. Home: 918 Woodland St Des Plaines IL 60017

GRUCHACZ, ROBERT S., food co. exec.; b. Bloomfield, N.J., May 15, 1929; s. Stanley A. and Mae (Zalenski) G.; B.S., Seton Hall U., 1950; M.B.A., N.Y. U., 1971; m. LaVerne T. Stein, Mar. 2, 1957; children—Robert S., Thomas A., Christopher J. With Arthur Young & Co., C.P.A.'s, 1955-58, Sterling Drug Inc., N.Y.C., 1958-65; controller Nat. Biscuit Co., 1965—. Served as 1st lt. USAF, 1952-54. C.P.A., N.J. Mem. Am. Inst. C.P.A.'s, Financial Execs. Inst. Home: 61 Rockledge Dr Livingston NJ 07039 Office: 425 Park Av New York City NY 10022

GRUEHN, HERMAN LAWRENCE, pub. utilities exec.; b. Baltimore, Sept. 7, 1900; s. John and Margaret (Schlaffer) G.; B.S. in econs., U. Pa., 1924, grad. study, 1929-30; C.P.A., Md., 1927; m. Lillian Siebert, June 4, 1926; children—Robert L., Janet E., Wayne H. Vice chmn. Equitable Trust Co.; dir. Savs. Bank of Balt. Clubs: Annapolis Yacht, Maryland. Home: 117-C Cross Keys Rd Baltimore MD

GRUEN, DAVID HENRY, corp. exec.; b. Buffalo, Aug. 12, 1929; s. Edward Charles and Florence (Knoche) G.; B.A., Cornell U., 1951, M.B.A., 1954; m. Reba Jean Stoffer, Aug. 12, 1953 (div. 1970); children—David E., Stephen P., Cathryn E., Edward Charles II, William A. Sr. accountant Arthur Andersen & Co., N.Y.C., 1954-59; asst. treas. Marine Midland Banks, Inc., 1959-60, asst. v.p., 1960-63, v.p., treas., 1963-69; sr. v.p. Marine Midland Bank-Western, 1969—. Served from 2d lt. to 1st lt., USAF, 1951-53. C.P.A., N.Y. Mem. Am. Inst. C.P.A.'s, Tax Execs. Inst., N.Y. Soc. C.P.A.'s, Bank Adminstrn. Inst., Nat. Assn. Bus. Economists, Financial Execs. Inst. Home: 105 Elmwood Park Tonawanda NY 14150 Office: 241 Main St Buffalo NY 14203

GRUEN, VICTOR, architect; b. Vienna, Austria, July 18, 1903; s. Adolph and Elizabeth Lea (Levy) Gruenbaum; student Tech. Inst. and Acad. Fine Arts, Vienna; m. Lazette Van Houten, Sept. 28, 1951 (dec.); children(by former marriage) Michael Stephen, Margaret; m. Kemija Salihefendic, February 28, 1963. Came to U.S., 1938, naturalized 1943. Bldg. supervisor Edmund Melcher, and engr. Steiner, Vienna, 1923-32; own practice architecture, designed important residential and commercial projects, Austria, Germany, Czechoslovakia, with office at Vienna, 1932-38; archtl. practice, N.Y.C., later additional offices at Los Angeles, and Chgo., Europe; pres. Victor Gruen Planning and Architecture, Inc., Switzerland; planning and archtl. cons. to state and city govts. and pvt. orgns. in France, Belgium, Vienna, Austria, Scandinavian countries; projects for J.L. Hudson Co., (Northland, Eastland regional shopping centers; shown Nat. Gallery, Washington, as a part of A.I.A. centennial exhibit), Westland Regional Shopping Center, Dayton Company, Minneapolis (Southdale regional shopping center); city planning projects Ft. Worth, Kalamazoo, Mich., Boston; planning redevel. city Core Fresno, Cal., Paterson, N.J., Rockville Center, N.Y. Lectr. before profl. orgns., also in European countries. Formed Victor Gruen Found. for Environmental Planning, Los Angeles. Awarded So. Cal. A.I.A. award for Archtl. Merit, 1949, honor award, 1951; Av. of the Americas Assn. plaque, 1952; award of merit (Northland Shopping Center), A.I.A., 1954, planning citation, Downtown Redevel. for Greater Fort Worth, Tex.; Progressive Architecture's 4th ann. design award program, 1957. Exhibited, 1952, 53 Gold Medal exhibits, Archtl. League of N.Y., VIII Pan Am. Congress of Architects, Mexico City, 1952, Sokolniki Park, Moscow, 1959, Internat. Congress Food Distribution, Lausanne, Switzerland, 1959. Dir. Citizens' Housing and Planning Council N.Y., Inc. Registered architect in Cal., D.C., Va., Tex., N.Y., N.J., Nev., Md. Fellow A.I.A.; mem. Am. Arbitration Assn., Am. Inst. Planners, Nat. Assn. Housing and Redevel. Ofcls., Yale Arts Assn. (charter mem., exec. com.), Mich. Soc. Architects, Urban Land Inst. Clubs: Economic (Detroit); Archtl. League of N.Y. Author: How to Live with Your Architect, 1950; (with Larry Smith) Shopping Towns, U.S.A.; The Heart of Our Cities, 1964. Home: 315 N Beverly Glen Blvd Los Angeles CA 90024 Office: Goldeggasse 7 1040 Wien Vienna Austria

GRUENBERG, FREDERICK PAUL, civic worker; b. Minneapolis, Minn., Nov. 19, 1884; s. John and Charlotte (Mayberg) G.; bro. Benj. C. Gruenberg; student Coll. City of N.Y., 1898-99, DeWitt Clinton High Sch., 1899-1902; B.C.S., New York U., 1911; post-grad. study U. Pa., 1916-18; m. Bertha Sanford, Dec. 29, 1909; childrenEdith (Mrs. Stephen M. Harris), John, 2d. Began as bookkeeper, 1902; engaged in financial and accounting work, Wall Street, 8 yrs.; dept. head Brown Bros. & Co., Philadelphia, 3 yrs.; with Philadelphia Bur. of Municipal Research, 10 yrs. (dir. 8 yrs.); mem. Phila. Charter Revision Com., 1917-19 (sec. 1917); treas. Bankers Bond & Mortgage Co. and Bankers Securities Corp. (both Phila.), 7 yrs.; apptd. pub. service commr. of Pa. by Gov. Pinchot, 1931, for term expiring 1940 (commn. abolished by Legislature, Mar. 31, 1937); directed nation-wide study of governmental research for Social Sci. Research Council, June 1937-38; exec. sec. City Charter Com. of Phila., 1938-40; area rent dir. Phila. Defense Rental Area, Office of Price Adminstrn., 1942-44; exec. dir., treas. Samuel S. Fels Fund, 1944-59, cons.; volunteer settlement resident, Southwark House and Coll. Settlement, 1911-14; spl. lectr., Hobart Coll., Geneva, N.Y., 1917-18; mem. faculty Pa. Sch. for Social Work, 1917-24. Asst. in office of chmn. U.S. Shipping Bd., Washington, latter part of World War I. Former trustee Nat. Farm School, Doylestown, Pa. Dir. Phila. Housing Assn., Crime Prevention Assn. of Phila.; past dir. Pa. Public Edn. Assn.; past mem. adv. bd. Inst. Local and State Govt., U. Pa. Recipient Samuel S. Fels award for civic and social service, 1966. Mem. Am. Polit. Sci. Assn. (mem. council 1921-24), Am. Acad. Polit. and Social Sci., Nat. Municipal League, Governmental Research Assn. (chmn. 2 terms). Mem. Am. Soc. for Pub. Adminstrn.; mem. Pa. Polit. Sci. and Pub. Adminstrn. Assn., Phila. Com. on Pub. Affairs, Lambda Sigma Phi, Phi Alpha Sigma. Ind. Republican. Mem. Ethical Soc. Clubs: Constitutional (Phila.), The Franklin Inn. Address: 1530 Locust St Philadelphia PA 19102

GRUENBERG, ROBERT, newspaperman; b. Chgo., Sept. 13, 1922; s. Samuel and Fannie (Cohen) G.; B.Ph., Northwestern U., 1953; m. Ruth Schwartz, Sept. 18, 1943; children—Mark Jonathan, Jeremy Ethan. Reporter, Chgo. Daily News, 1941- 61; Evening Star, Washington, 1961-62; Washington corr. Chicago's Am., 1962-66; reporter Chgo. Daily News, 1966—, now Washington corr. Chmn. Chgo. Daily News unit of the Chgo. Newspaper Guild, AFL-CIO, 1956, mem. exec. bd. guild, 1957. Served with inf. AUS, 1943-46. Recipient Page One award Chgo. Newspaper Guild, 1955, 6O, 69, 70; 1st Ann. James P. McGuire Meml. award Ill. div. Am. Civil Liberties Union, 1968; Marshall Field award, 1969. Contbr. articles Nation mag., Progressive mag. Home: 4018 Ingersol Dr Silver Spring MD 20902 Office: Nat Press Bldg Washington DC 20004

GRUENBERG, ROBERT PERSHING, trade assn. exec.; b. Bklyn., July 29, 1918; s. James and Mary (Debrowsky) G.; B.S., U. Ill., 1940, M.S. in Commerce, 1941; m. Imogene Chandler, June 10, 1941; childrenJames Chandler, Imogene Mary, Peter Colby. With Nat. Home Furnishings Assn., Chgo., 1941—, v.p. charge service, 1960-65, exec. v.p., sec., 1965—; vice chmn. Central council Nat. Retail Assn., 1970; mem. bd. Am. Retail Fedn., dir. services for affiliates So. Retail Furniture Assn.; dir. Home Furnishings Council, 1966—. Served to lt. USNR, World War II; PTO. Club: Merchants and Manufacturers (dir.). Home: 263 Merton Av Glen Ellyn, IL 60137. Office: Nat Home Furnishings Assn Merchandise Mart Chicago IL 60654

GRUENBERG, SIDONIE MATSNER, (Mrs. Benjamin C. Gruenberg), writer, lecturer; b. in Austria, June 10, 1881; d. Idore and Augusta Olivia (Bassechés) Matzner; ed. Höhere Töchterschule, Hamburg, Germany, 1894; Ethical Culture Sch., N.Y., 1897, spl. student, normal tng. dept., same, 1905-06; grad. student Tchrs. Coll., Columbia 1906-10; m. Benjamin C. Gruenberg, Ph.D., June 30, 1903; childrenHerbert M., Richard M., Hilda (Mrs. David Krech), Ernest M. With Child Study Assn. Am. (formerly Fedn. for Child Study) 1906-, dir. 1923-50, spl. cons., 1950—; chmn. Nat. Council for Parent Edn., 1947-51; lectr. in parent edn., Tchrs. Coll. (Columbia), 1928-36, 47, N.Y. U. 1936-37, 40, U. Colo., 1940, 42. Chmn. sub-com. of White House Conf. on Child Health and Protection, 1930; mem. White House Conf., 1940, Pres.' Conf. on Home Building and Home Ownership, 1931, adv. commn. on children in wartime, U.S. Children's Bur., 1942; mem. com. communications, Mid-Century White House Conf., 1950. Mem. editorial bd. Jr. Lit. Guild 1929—, Parents Mag., 1926-43; "Child Study"; editorial cons. to Fawcett Publs., 1943-45; cons. on family relationships, Woman's Day, 1947-49; spl. cons. Doubleday & Co., 1950-. Fellow A.A.A.S.; mem. Am. Social Hygiene Assn. (hon. life), Assn. Childhood Edn., Nat. Assn. for Nursery Edn., Campfire Girls, Pub. Edn. Assn., Nat. Pub. Housing Conf., N.Y. State Conf. on Marriage and the Family, Nat. Orgn. for Pub. Health Nursing. Dir. Pub. Affairs Com., 1947-; dir. Social Legislation Information Service, 1947-61. Author many books for children and parents, 1914-, later ones: The Wonderful Story of How You Were Born, 1952, rev., 1959, new rev. edit., 1970, trans. into Japanese, Norwegian, Swedish; Parents' Guide to Everyday Problems of Boys and Girls: Guiding Your Child from Five to Twelve, 1958. Co-author: Parents, Children and Money, 1933; (with Hilda Sidney Krech) The Many Lives of Modern Woman, 1952; (with Benjamin C. Gruenberg) Children for the Childless, 1954; (with Benjamin C. Gruenberg) The Wonderful Story of You, 1960. Editor: Our Children: A Handbook for Parents, 1932; Parents Questions, 1936, rev. edit. 1948; The Family in a World at War, 1942; Favorite Stories Old and New, 1942, rev. edit. 1955; More Favorite Stories Old and New, 1948, rev. 1960; Let's Read a Story, 1957; Let's Read More Stories, 1960; Let's Hear a Story, 1961; Kinds of Courage, 1962; The Encyclopedia of Child Care and Guidance, 1953, rev. edit., 1967. Home: 100 Central Park S New York City NY 10019. Office: 277 Park Av New York City NY 10017

GRUENE, HANS FRIEDRICH, research engr.; b. Braunschweig, Germany, May 24, 1910; s. Eduard Hugo Hans and Anna Alwine (Bertram) G.: Dipl. Ing., Tech. Hochschule Braunschweig, 1935; Dr.-Ing., 1941; m. Edith Geier, Dec. 23, 1937; childrenKarin, Peter. Came to U.S., 1945, naturalized, 1954. Research engr. AEG and Siemens Schuckertwerke A.G., 1935-43, Rocket Research Center, Peenemünde, 1943-45; rocket research engr. for U.S. Army, Ft. Bliss, Tex., Huntsville, Ala., 1945, 61—; engaged in launch vehicle devel. NASA 1961; dir. launch vehicle operations Marshall Space Flight Center, Launch Operations Center, Cape Kennedy, Fla., 1963-64; dir. launch operations John F. Kennedy Space Center, Cocoa Beach, Fla., 1964—. Mem. Am. Inst. Aeros. and Astronautics. Contbr. to Handbook of Astronautical Engineering. Home: 129 La Riviere Rd Cocoa Beach FL 32931 Office: John F Kennedy Space Center Cocoa Beach FL 32899

GRUENING, ERNEST, U.S. senator, editor, author; b. N.Y. City, Feb. 6, 1887; s. Emil and Phebe (Fridenberg) G.; grad. Hotchkiss Sch., Lakeville, Conn., 1903; A.B., Harvard, 1907, M.D., 1912; LL.D., U. Alberta, 1950, U. Alaska, 1955, Brandeis U., 1958; L.H.D., Wilmington Coll.; m. Dorothy E. Smith, Nov. 19, 1914; childrenErnest (dec.), Huntington Sanders, Peter B. (dec.). Reporter, spl. article writer, editor various newspapers, 1911-20; mng. editor The Nation, 1920-23, and editor, 1933-34; nat. dir. of publicity, LaFollette Progressive Presidential Campaign, 1924; founder Portland (Me.) Evening News, 1927, editor until 1932, contbg. editor, 1932-37; editor N.Y. Evening Post, Feb.-Apr. 1934, mem. Cuba Commn. Fgn. Policy Assn., 1934; dir. Div. Territories and Island Possessions, U.S. Dept. Interior, 1934-39, adminstr. P.R. Reconstrn. Adminstrn, 1935-37; fed. emergency relief adminstr. for P.R., 1935-36; mem. Alaska Internat. Hwy. Commn. 1938-42. Gov. of Alaska, 1939-53; keynoter, Alaska Constnl. Conv., 1955; elected provisional U.S. Senator from Alaska, 1956-58, Senator 58-69. Gen. adviser to the U.S. delegation to 7th Pan Am. Conf., Montevideo, 1933. Cons. Population Crisis Com., 1968—. Recipient Hadassah award, Geo. W. Norris award, Herbert H. Lehman award, Margaret Sawyer award; decorated Order of Aztec Eagle, Mexico. Mem. Phi Beta Kappa. Clubs: Harvard (N.Y.); Cosmos (Washington). Rotarian. Editor: These United States. Author: Mexico and Its Heritage, 1928; The Public Pays, 1931; The State of Alaska, 1954; An Alaska Reader, 1967; The Battle for Alaska Statehood, 1967. Contbr. various books and mags. Home and office: 7926 W Beach Dr Washington DC 20012

GRUENTHER, ALFRED M., retired army officer, corp. exec.; b. Platte Center, Neb., Mar. 3, 1899; s. Christian M. and Mary (Shea) G.; B.S., U.S. Mil. Acad., 1919; grad. F.A. Sch., 1920, Command and Gen. Staff Sch., 1937, Army War Coll., 1939; hon. degrees from 38 univs. and colls., including Harvard, Yale, Columbia, Dartmouth, Holy Cross; m. Grace E. Crum, Aug. 22, 1922; children—Donald Alfred, Richard Louis. Commd. 2d lt. F.A., 1918, and advanced through grades to gen., 1951; chief of staff, Third Army, 1941-42; dep. chief of staff, Allied Force Hdqrs., 1942-43; chief of staff, Fifth Army, 1943-44; chief of staff, 15th Army Group, 1944-45; dep. comdr. U.S. Forces in Austria, 1945; dep. comdt. Nat. War Coll., Washington, 1945-47; dir. Joint Staff, Joint Chiefs Staff, 1947-49; dep. chief of staff for plans and operations Army Gen. Staff, 1949-51; chief of staff SHAPE, 1951-53, Supreme Allied Comdr. in Europe, 1953-56, ret. 1956. Pres. A.R.C., 1957-64; dir. Pan Am. World Airways, N.Y. Life Ins. Co., Federated Dept. Stores, Dart Industries, Inc. Mem. Bus. Council; mem. Pres.' Com. for Traffic Safety, 1961-67; gen. adv. com. Arms Control and Disarmament, 1966-69; gen. adv. com. Fgn. Assistance Programs, 1965-69; mem. Pres.' Commn. on Heart Disease, Cancer and Stroke, 1964-66; mem. Pres.' Commn. for an All-Volunteer Army, 1969-70. Bd. dirs. Inst. for Def. Analyses. Decorated D.S.M. with 2 oak leaf clusters (U.S.); Companion of the Bath (British); Grand Cross Legion d'Honneur, Medaille Militaire (France); Comdr. Order Mil. Merit (Brazil); Mil. Order of Italy; Grand Cordon, Order of Leopold (Belgium); Knight, Order of Malta; Grand Cross, Royal Order of Saviour (Greece); Grand Cross, Order of Orange-Nassau (Netherlands); Grand Cross, Order of Couronne de Chene (Luxembourg); Grand Cross of Aviz (Portugal); Grand Cross of Merit Fed. Republic of Germany. Mem. World Bridge Fedn. (hon. pres. 1965—), English-Speaking Union (chmn. 1966-68). Clubs: Metropolitan, Army-Navy (Washington). Address: 4101 Cathedral Av NW Washington DC 20016

GRUENTHER, HOMER H., travel agy. exec., former govt. ofcl.; b. Platte Center, Neb., May 23, 1900; s. Christian M. and Mamie (Shea) G.; student Christian Bros. Sch., St. Joseph, Mo., St. Thomas Coll., St. Paul, Creighton U., Omaha, 1919-21; m. Elizabeth Mahoney, Aug. 14, 1926. Entered newspaper work as sports editor Omaha Daily News; sec. Neb. State Senate, 1933; became sec. to Congressman (later Senator) Edward R. Burke, Washington, 1933; became adminstrv. asst. to Sec. Commerce Jasse Jones. 1941; sec. to Senator Kenneth Wherry, 1946-51, then to successor Senator Fred Seaton, 1951-52; spl. aide to Gen. Eisenhower, 1952; spl. asst. to Presidents Eisenhower, Kennedy and Johnson, 1953- 1953- -65; pres. Travel Agy., Washington, 1966—. Co-author Burke-Wadsworth Bill for creation SSS 1940; writer Wherry Bill for creation SSS 1940; writer Wherry Mil. Housing Bill, authorizing pvt. constrn. multiple housing projects on Army bases, St. Lawrence Seaway and Colorado River projects. Home: 4000 Cathedral Av NW Washington DC 20016

GRUHL, ALFRED, utility co. exec.; b. Milw., Nov. 19, 1902; s. Frederick and Emma (Schroeder) G.; B.A., U. Wis., 1925; m. Helen Vanderveer, Dec. 1940; children—Frederick, James, Edward. With Wis. Electric Power Co., 1932-69, pres., 1962-67, chmn., 1967-69, also dir.; dir. affiliated Wis. Michigan Power Co., Wis. Natural Gas Co., others. Mem. Wis. Utilities Assn. (pres. 1951). Home: 7610 N Christie Dr Tucson AZ 85718

GRULEE, CLIFFORD GROSSELLE, Jr., physician, educator; b. Chgo., June 9, 1912; s. Clifford Grosselle and Margaret (Freer) G.; B.A., Williams Coll., 1933; M.D., Northwestern U., 1937; m. Mary Evelyn Lewis, Feb. 14, 1943; 1 son, Clifford Grosselle III. Rotating intern St. Luke's Hosp., Chgo., 1937-38; house officer bacteriology, pathology and clin. pediatrics Boston Childrens Hosp., 1938-42, chief resident pediatrics, 1942; Rockefeller fellow pediatrics U. Minn., 1946-47; asst., then asso. prof. pediatrics U. Tex. Med. Sch., 1947-49; faculty Tulane U. Sch. Medicine, 1949-63, prof. pediatrics, 1956-63, dir. grad. medicine, 1956-63, asso. dean Sch. Medicine, 1958- 63, acting dean, 1960, mng. editor bull. med. faculty, 1952-63; prof. pediatrics, dean Coll. Medicine, U. Cin., 1963-; cons. to surgeon gen. Brooke Gen. Hosp., San Antonio, 1948-49; cons. pediatrics Keesler Field, Miss., 1952-59; chmn., directing med. staff Cin. Gen. Hosp., Christian R. Holmes Hosp.; chmn. deans com. Cin. VA Hosp.; physician cons. VA, 1970-71. Served to capt., M.C., AUS, 1942- 45. Diplomate Am. Bd. Pediatrics. Mem. Am. Acad. Pediatrics (chmn. com. juvenile delinquency 1962-65), Soc. Pediatric Research, Am. Pediatric Soc., Am. Assn. Med. Colls. (chmn. Midwest-Great Plains region 1969-70, exec. com. 1970—), Alpha Omega Alpha (chpt. councillor), A.M.A., Phi Delta Theta, Phi Rho Sigma. Office: Coll of Medicine U Cin Cincinnati OH 45219

GRULICH, NORMAN HENRY, advt. exec.; b. Woodcliff, N.J., June 20, 1926; s. Dezeo Richard and Edith (Latinovits) G.; A.B., Columbia, 1950; m. Celeste Reed Seymour, July 24, 1957; children—Victoria Mary, Valerie Edith. Vice pres. Benton & Bowles, Inc., 1955-60; treas., exec. v.p. Papert, Koenig, Lois, Inc., N.Y.C., 1960-67, pres., dir., 1967-69; pres., chmn. Viva Assos., N.Y.C., 1969—; chmn. Davis Mfg. Co., Knoxville, Tenn., 1969—. Mem. com. broadcast and publicity div. Greater N.Y. Fund. Mem. Columbia Coll. Alumni Assn., Psi Upsilon. Club: Coral Reef Yacht Home: 180 E 79th St New York City NY 10021 Office: 101 Park Av New York City NY 10017

GRUMAN, ROBERT CLAYTON, prosthetist; b. Mpls., Mar. 1, 1922; s. Adelbert Paul and Charlotte (Blanchard) G.; student Carleton Coll., 1940-43, U. Mich., 1943; B.B.A., U. Minn., 1947; m. Beverly Jane Taylor, Dec. 21, 1947; children—Gregory, William, Nancy. With Winkley Artificial Limb Co., Mpls., 1947—, pres., 1957—, pres. Protheses Orthipedique, Inc., Quebec, Can., 1957-64, Marks Artificial Limb Co., N.Y.C., 1957—, Winkley Co., Des Moines, Davenport, Ia., Ft. Lauderdale, Fla. and Buffalo, 1957—; sec.-treas. Am. Prosthetics, Inc., Mpls., 1963—. Served with USAAF, 1943-46. Area vice chmn. Mpls. United Fund, 1962. Mem. Am. Orthotics and

Prosthetics Assn. (regional dir. 1960-61; v.p. 1962; pres. 1964), Minn., (pres. 1960), Nat. rehab. assns., Am. Legion, Am. Bd. Certification Orthotists and Prosthetists. Kiwanian. Home: 4511 Westwood Lane Minneapolis MN 55416 Office: 4130 Hwy 55 Minneapolis MN 55422

GRUMBACH, MELVIN MALCOLM, physician, educator; b. N.Y.C., Dec. 21, 1925; s. Emanuel and Adele (Weil) G.; student Columbia Coll., M.D., Columbia, 1948; m. Madeleine F. Butt, Dec. 1, 1951; children—Ethan Malcolm, Kevin Lawrence, Anthony Havemayer. Resident pediatrics Babies Hosp., Presbyn. Hosp., N.Y.C., 1949-51; vis. fellow Oak Ridge Inst. Nuclear Studies, 1952; postdoctoral fellow, asst. pediatrics Johns Hopkins Sch. Medicine, 1953-55; mem. faculty Columbia Coll. Physicians and Surgeons, 1955-66, asso. prof. pediatrics, 1961-66; from asst. attending pediatrician to asso. attending pediatrician, head pediatric endocrine div. and postdoctoral tng. program pediatric endocrinology Babies Hosp. and Vanderbilt Clin., Columbia-Presbyn. Med. Center, 1955-66; prof. pediatrics, chmn. dept. U. Cal. Sch. Medicine, San Francisco, 1966—; dir. pediatric service U. Cal. Hosps., 1966- -; vis. prof. Vanderbilt U., 1961, Emory U., 1962, U. Western Ont., 1962, U. N.C., 1963; domestic lectr. Jour. Pediatrics Edn. Found., 1962; Alpha Omega Alpha lectr. State U. N.Y. Downstate Med. Center, 1961, U. Cal. at San Francisco, 1966; Univ. lectr. U. Zurich, 1971; cons. Letterman Gen. Hosp., Children's Hosp., San Francisco, U.S. Naval Hosp., Oakland, Cal., Dept. Health , Edn. and Welfare, NIH, Nat. Bd. Med. Examiners, 1964-68. Mem. human embryology and devel. study sect. NIH, 1962-66, endocinology study sect., 1967-71, bd. sci. counselors Nat. Inst. Child Health and Human Devel., 1971—; mem. com. on research Nat. Found.; mem. adv. com. Inst. Human Devel., U. Cal. at Berkeley; adv. bd. Nat. Pituitary Agy., 1965-69; trustee, mem. exec. com. San Francisco chpt. Nat. Found. Served to capt., M.C., USAF, 1951-53. Postdoctoral fellow Nat. Found. Infantile Paralysis, 1953- 55; recipient Joseph M. Smith prize Columbia, 1962, Career Scientist award Health Research Council City N.Y., 1961-66; Silver medal Bicentennial Columbia Coll. of Physicians and Surgeons, 1967; Borden award Am. Acad. Pediatrics, 1971. Diplomate Am. Bd. Pediatrics, Nat. Bd. Med. Examiners. Fellow Am. Acad. Pediatrics, N.Y. Acad. Sci.; mem. A.A.A.S., Am. Pediatrics Soc., Am. Soc. Clin. Investigation, Am. Soc. Human Genetics, Harvey Soc., Western Soc. Pediatric Research, Soc. Pediatric Research, Teratology Soc., Endocrine Soc. (councillor 1968—), Soc.Study Reprodn., European Soc. Pediatric Endocrinology (corr. mem.), Western Assn. Physicians, Cal. Acad. Medicine, Western Soc. Clin. Research, Sigma Xi, Alpha Omega Alpha. Club: University (N.Y.C.). Author articles in field, contbr. med. and sci. books. Asso. editor, mem. editorial bd. Jour. Clin. Endocrinology, 1957-70; adv. editor Jour. Pediatrics, 1966—; asso. editor: Pediatric Research, 1970—, Barnett Pediatrics, 14th and 15th edits., Current Topics in Experimental Endocrinology, 1968—; editorial bd. Biology of Reproduction, 1968-70. Home: 230 Santa Clara Av San Francisco CA 94127 Office: Dept Pediatrics U Cal Sch Medicine at San Francisco San Francisco CA 94122

GRUMBLES, LEIAND CREED, educator, veterinarian; b. Star City, Ark., Sept. 21, 1921; s. James Rufus and Martha (Baker) G.; student Lamar State Coll., Beaumont, Tex., 1940; D.V.M., Tex. A. and M. U., 1945, M.S., 1957; postgrad. R.I. State U., 1947; m. Helen Beatrice Battle, Sept. 18, 1943; childrenPaula Ruth, Jane Sallie. Pvt. practice vet. medicine, 1945-46; asst. prof. R.I. State U., 1946-48, La. State U., 1948-49; mem. faculty Tex. A. and M. U., 1949-53, 55-, prof., 1957-, head dept. vet. microbiology, 1967-. Cons., pres. Animal Disease Research Workers So. States, 1965. Served with USAF, 1953-55. Recipient Faculty award service and achievement Southwestern Veterinarian, 1957. Mem. Am. Coll. Vet. Microbiologists (v.p. 1967), Am. Assn. Avian Pathologists (chmn. 1967), Am., Tex. (award 1967) vet. med. assns. Baptist. Lion. Research infectious diseases animals. Editor Avian Diseases, 1967-. Home: Route 4 Box 616 Bryan TX 77801 Office: Tex A and M U Coll Station TX 77843

GRUMHAUS, HAROLD FRANCIS, newspaper exec.; b. Naperville, Ill., Apr. 19, 1903; s. Henry R. and Adeline (Heitzler) G.; ed. U. Ill., 1925; m. Helen Royoll Dean, Apr. 14, 1928; children—Peter D., David D. With Celotex Corp. until 1934; with Chgo. Tribune, 1934—, bus. mgr., 1960- 64, gen. mgr., 1964-68, pub., 1969—; pres. Tribune Co., 1966-70, vice chmn., 1970-71, chmn., 1970—, chief exec. officer, 1968—, also dir.; pres. Chgo. Tribune Co., 1967-71, chmn., chief exec. officer, 1971—; chmn. Ill. Atlantic Corp., Ont. Paper Co., Ltd. Que., North Shore Paper Co.; dir. WGN Continental Broadcasting Co. Mem. Northwestern U. Assos. Trustee McCormick-Patterson Trust, Robert R. McCormick Charitable Trust. Former trustee Village of Hinsdale. Treas., v.p., dir., mem. exec. com. Research Inst., Am. Newspaper Pubs. Assn., 1957-63, pres., 1963-65, now mem. labor relations com. Trustee Beloit Coll., Northwestern U., Godair Home for Aged, Hinsdale; chmn. Mid-Am. chpt. A.R.C., 1969-71; mem. citizens bd. U. Chgo.; mem. U. Ill. Found.; mem. lay bd. trustees Loyola U., Chgo. Mem. Chgo. Newspaper Pubs. Assn. (pres. 1962, 63, 66, 67). Clubs: Chicago, Economic, Commercial, Tavern (Chgo.); Onwentsia, Old Elm (Lake Forest, Ill.); Royal Poinciana Golf (Naples, Fla.). Home: 675 Woodland Rd Lake Forest IL 60045 Office: Chicago Tribune 435 N Michigan Av Chicago IL 60611

GRUMMAN, LEROY RANDLE, aircraft engring. exec.; b. Huntington, N.Y., Jan. 4, 1895; s. George T. and Grace E. (Conklin) G.; M.E., Cornell U., 1916; grad. student Mass. Inst. Tech., 1918-19; D.Eng., Poly. Inst. Bklyn. 1949; LL.D., Adelphi Coll., 1961; m. Rose Marion Werther, Mar. 19, 1921; childrenMarion Elinor (Mrs. Ellis L. Phillips, Jr.), Florence Werther (Mrs. Fred Hold), Grace Caroline (Mrs. A.C. Nelson), David Leroy. Engring. dept. N.Y. Telephone Co., 1916-17; aero. engr. Loening Aero. Engring. Corp., N.Y.C., 1920-29; pres. Grumman Aircraft 66, hon. chmn., 1966-. Trustee emeritus Cornell U. Served as lt., U.S. Navy, 1917-20. Recipient Presdl. medal for Merit, 1945, Daniel Guggenheim medal, for notable achievements in aeros.; 1948, Frank M. Hawks Meml. award, 1958. Hon. fellow Inst. Aero. Scis., mem. Soc. Automotive Engrs. Presbyn. Clubs: Country (North Hempstead, L.I.); Yacht (Manhasset Bay, L.I.); The Creek (Locust Valley, L.I.); N.Y. Yacht, Cornell (N.Y.); Riomar Country (Vero Beach, Fla.). Home: 77 Bayview Rd Plandome NY 11030 Office: Bethpage NY

GRUMMITT, OLIVER JOSEPH, educator; b. Cleve., Jan. 16, 1910; s. Joseph James and Hannah (Gleine) G.; A.B., Oberlin Coll., 1932; M.A., Western Res. U., 1934, Ph.D., 1936; DuPont postdoctoral fellow chemistry, Cornell U., 1936-38. From instr. to asso. prof. chemistry Case Western Res. U., 1938-54, prof., 1954—, chmn. dept. chemistry, 1958-62; research cons. Sherwin-Williams Co., 1939-. Chem. investigator in Germany, U.S. Army, Dept. Commerce, 1946. Fellow A.A.A.S.; mem. Am. Chem. Soc., Am. Assn. U. Profs., Am. Assn. Oil Chemists, Phi Beta Kappa, Sigma Xi, Alpha Chi Sigma. Home: 15949 Cleviden Rd East Cleveland, OH 44112.

GRUNAUER, MORTIMER, real estate exec.; b. N.Y.C., June 3, 1889; s. Reuben and Delia (Abrahams) G.; B.S. in Civil Engring., N.Y.U., 1910. With Bing & Bing, Inc., N.Y.C., 1912—, dir., 1931—, exec. v.p., 1955-56, pres., 1956-67, vice chmn. bd., 1967-70, chmn., 1970—; dir. Bijur Lubricating Co., Dorset Hotel Corp. Served with U.S. Army. 1918-19. Fellow Am. Soc. C.E. K.P. Home: 30 W 54th St New York City NY 10019 Office: 119 W 40th St New York City NY 10018

GRUNBAUM, ADOLF, educator, author; b. Cologne, Germany, May 15, 1923; s. Benjamin and Hannah (Freiwillig) G.; came to U.S., 1938, naturalized, 1944; B.A., Wesleyan U., Middletown, Conn., 1943; M.S. in Physics, Yale, 1948, Ph.D, in Philosophy, 1951; m. Thelma Braverman, June 26, 1949; 1 dau., Barbara Susan. Mem. faculty Lehigh U., 1950-60, prof. philosophy, 1955-56, Selfridge prof. philosophy, 1956-60; vis. research prof. Minn. Center Philosophy of Sci., 1956, 59; Andrew Mellon prof. philosophy, dir. Center Philosophy of Sci., U. Pitts., 1960—. Chmn. sect. philosophy of phys. scis. Internat. Congress for Logic and Philosophy of Sci., Jerusalem, Israel, 1964, Bucharest, Rumania, 1971. Mem. governing bd. Inst. Unity Sci. Physicist div. war research Columbia, World War II. Recipient J. Walker Tomb prize Princeton, 1958; honor citation Wesleyan U., 1959. Fellow A.A.A.S. (v.p. sect. L 1963), Philosophy Sci. Assn. (rep. to Internat. Union for History and Philosophy of Sci.), Am. Philos. Assn. (mem. exec. com.), Philosophy of Sci. Assn. (pres. 1965-70), Inst. for Fundamental Studies Assn., Phi Beta Kappa, Sigma Xi. Author: Philosophical Problems of Space and Time, 1963; Modern Science and Zeno's Paradoxes, 1967; Geometry and Chronometry in Philosophical Perspective, 1968; also numerous articles. Editorial bd. Ency. Philosophy, 1961—; bd. editors Philosophy Sci., 1959—, Am. Philos. Quar., Philosopher's Index, Studies in History and Philosophy of Science. Home: 2270 McCrea Rd Pittsburgh PA 15235

GRUNDMANN, ALBERT WENDELL, educator; b. Salt Lake City, Sept. 1, 1912; s. Bastian and Alberdiena (Legger) G.; B.A., U. Utah, 1937, M.A., 1939; Ph.D., Kan. State U., 1942; m. Janice Faith Isenberg, Dec. 20, 1947; 1 son, Kenneth. Research asst. Kan. State Coll., 1939-42; faculty dept. environmental biology U. Utah, Salt Lake City, 1946—, prof., 1963—, dept. chmn., 1963-70. Served from 1st lt. to maj., San. Corps, AUS, 1942-45. Mem. Am. Soc. Parasitologists, Am. Soc. Tropical Medicine and Hygiene, Helminthological Soc. Washington, A.A.A.S., Am. Microscopic Soc., Kan. Entomol. Soc., Phi Beta Kappa, Sigma Xi, Phi Kappa Phi, Gamma Sigma Delta. Mem. Ch. of Jesus Christ of Latter-day Saints. Contbr. articles to profl. jours. Home: 2374 Sheridan Rd Salt Lake City UT 84108

GRUNDMANN, CHRISTOPH JOHANN, educator; b. Berlin, Germany, Dec. 29, 1908; s. Bruno Johann and Mathilde (Bolomey) G.; Dipl. Chem., U. Berlin (Germany), 1931, Ph.D., 1933; Dr.Phil. Habil, U. Heidelberg (Germany), 1937; m. Lieselotte M. Mieth, Mar. 1, 1963; 1 son by previous marriage, Henning J. Chem. researcher acad. instns. and pvt. cos., Germany, 1933-51; staff Research Found., Ohio State U., 1958-60; dir. research and devel. Gen. Cigar Co., Lancaster, Pa., 1958-60; sr. fellow Mellon Inst., Pitts., 1961—; prof. chemistry Carnegie-Mellon U., Pitts., 1967—; patent cons., 1961—; research cons. Olin Mathieson Chem. Corp., 1952-58. Mem. patent adv. com. Interior Dept., 1960-62. Mem. N.Y. Acad. Scis., Am. Chem. Soc., Gesellschaft Deutschen Chemiker, Sigma Xi. Club: R.K. Duncan (Pitts.). Research and numerous publs. and patents in organic, medicinal, polymer chemistry. Mailing Address: Home: 1519 Williamsburg St Pittsburgh PA 15235

GRUNDSTEIN, NATHAN DAVID, educator; b. Ashland, O., Sept. 19, 1913; s. Samuel Lewis and Rose J. (Kolinsky) G.; B.A., Ohio State U., 1935, M.Sc., 1936; Ph.D., Syracuse U., 1943; LL.B., George Washington U., 1951; m. Dorothy Deborah Davis, Nov. 12, 1938; children-Miriam R. (Mrs. Bruce R. Levin), Margaret J. (Mrs. Rachmat Kartadjoemena), Leon D., Robert H. Legal research asst. Office Head Atty., Dept. Agr., 1939-40; adminstrv. asst. to asst. commr. FDA, 1940-41; adminstrv. officer, exec. asst. to vice chmn. for labor prodn. WPB, 1941-47; prof. pub. law and adminstrn. Wayne State U., 1947- 58; admitted to Mich. bar, 1954; prof. adminstrn. Grad. Sch. Pub. and Internat. Affairs, U. Pitts., 1958-64; prof., dir. grad. program pub. mgmt. sci. Case Western Res. U., 1964—; cons. to govt. and industry. Mem. Inst. Mgmt. Sci., Urban and Regional Information Systems Assn., Soc. Gen. Systems Research, Am. Soc. Legal Philosophy, Mich. Bar Assns., Am. Assn. U. Profs., Phi Beta Kappa, Order of Coif. Jewish religion. Author: Adminstrative Practice and procedure Under the Federal Plant Quarantine Act, 1940; Administrative Practice and Procedure Under the Federal Food, Drug and Cosmetic Act, 1941; Industrial Mobilization for War, Vol. I, Part III, 1947; Cases and Readings on Adnministrative Law (with F. Davison), 1952; Presidential Delegation of Authority in Wartime, 1961; Administrative Law and the Regulatory System, rev. edit., 1968. Home: 2872 Washington Blvd Cleveland Heights OH 44118 Office: Baker Hall Sch Mgmt Case Western Res Univ Cleveland OH 44106

GRUNEBAUM, ERICH O., investment banker; b. Essen, Germany, Mar. 26, 1902; s. Ernst and Agathe (Hirschland) G.; student pub. schs.; m. Gabriele Hildegard Newman, Oct. 21, 1933; children—Ernest Michael, Eva Irene, David Francis. Came to U.S., 1941, naturalized, 1947. With N.Y. Hanseatic Corp. 1942-, pres., 1948-59, chmn. bd. 1959—; chmn. bd., dir. Nyhaco Credit Corp., Ltd.; dir. Aberdeen Mfg. Corp., Peruinvest Internat. N.V., Curacao, N.Am., COFIEC-Compania Financiera Privada, Quito, Ecuador, Peruinvest Compania de Fomento e Inversiones S.A., Lima, Peru. Home: 11 Cotswold Way, Scarsdale, NY 10583. Office: 60 Broad St New York City NY 10004

GRUNEBAUM, KURT H., corp. exec.; b. Essen, Germany, Aug. 11, 1905; s. Ernst and Agathe (Hirschland) G.; m. Anneliese Eichwald, Dec. 27, 1929; 1 son, Peter K. Came to U.S., 1941, naturalized, 1947. Joined N.Y. Hanseatic Corp., N.Y. City, 1941, exec. v.p., 1947-59, pres., 1959—, also dir.; pres., dir. Nyhaco Credit Corp., Ltd.; vice chmn. bd., dir. Canal-Randolph Corp.; dir. United Stockyards Corp., Security Title & Guaranty Co., Standard Internat. Corp., Greater N.Y. Mut. Ins. Co., Ins. Co. Greater N.Y. Home: 100 Muchmore Rd Harrison NY 10528 Office: 60 Broad St New York City NY 10004

GRUNEWALD, DONALD educator; b. N.Y.C., Feb. 9, 1934; s. Harry A. and Tina (Gegner) G.; A.B., Union Coll., 1954; M.A., Harvard, 1955, M.B.A., 1959, D.B.A., 1962. Instr., U. Kan. Sch. Bus., 1959-60; lectr. Boston U. Coll. Bus. Adminstrn., 1961-62; research agt. Harvard U. Grad. Sch. Bus., 1962; asst. prof. Rutgers U. Grad. Sch. Bus., 1962-65, asso. prof., 1965-67; dean, prof. Suffolk U. Coll. Bus. Adminstrn., Grad. Sch. Adminstrn., 1967-69, v.p., dean Coll. Liberal Arts and Scis. and Coll. Journalism, 1969—; v.p., dir. Southern House, Inc.; propr. Boston Athenaeum; ednl. cons. Served as lt. USAF, 1955-57. Mem. Am. Econ. Assn., Acad. Mgmt., Am. Hist. Assn., Am. Polit. Sci. Assn. Roman Catholic. Rotarian (bd. dirs. Boston 1971-72). Club: Harvard (N.Y.C.). Author: Cases in Business Policy, 1962; (with Moranian, Reidenbach) Business Policy and Its Environment, 1964; (with H. Bass) Public Policy and the Modern Corporation, 1966; Small Business Management, 1966; (with Fenn, Katz) Business Decision Making and Government Policy, 1966; (with Funk) Managerial Finance,1969. Home: 151 Tremont St Boston MA 02111

GRUNEWALD, THEODORE JOSEPH, advt. exec.; b. Bklyn., Oct. 31, 1924; s. Theodore J. and Ellen C. (Jackman) G.; B.S., N.Y.U., 1948; m. Dorothy M. Nedwick, Oct. 9, 1949; children—Carol Lynn, Theodore Joseph, Steven Paul. TV-radio producer William Esty Co., 1948-49, mgr. TV dept., 1950-52; dir. TV and radio Doyle Dane Bernbach, 1952-53; with Hicks & Griest, 1953-65, dir. TV and radio, v.p., 1953-57, dir., prin., 1957-65, sr. v.p., 1959-65; pres., dir., prin. Bliss/Grunewald, Inc., N.Y.C.; chmn. Synoptic Systems Corp.; dir. Churchill Marketing Corp., Council for Marketing. Active in Stamford Good Govt. Assn., Greater New York Fund. Served with USAAF, 1943-46; ETO. Mem. Alpha Delta Sigma, Alpha Kappa Psi. Home: Bartina Lane Stamford CT 06902 Office: 360 Lexington Av New York City NY 10017

GRUNOW, JOHN E. D., mining co. exec.; b. N.Y.C., Oct. 6, 1919; s. William R. and Edwina (Dearden) G.; B.S., Columbia, 1942; LL.B., Harvard, 1948; m. Betty Letsch, June 19, 1942; children—John E. D., Steven P., Andrew L. Thomas A., Patricia A., Peter T. Sec., counsel Newmont Mining Corp., N.Y.C., 1948-62, now dir., also officer, dir. various affiliated cos.; pres., dir. Atlantic Cement Co., Inc., N.Y.C., 1962-66; v.p. Martin Marietta Co., N.Y.C., 1967—, pres. Rock Products div., 1969—; pres. Marietta Resources Internat., N.Y.C., 1969—. dir. Potter Instrument Co.; spl. asst. to pres. Columbia N.Y.C., 1967. Trustee William J. Matheson Found., Inc., Boyce Thompson Inst. for Plant Research, Rollins Coll. Mem. Am. Inst. M.E. Clubs: Racquet and Tennis, Mining (N.Y.C.); Innis Arden Golf Club, Inc. (Old Greenwich). Home: 22 Ballwood Rd Old Greenwich CT 06870 Office: 277 Park Av New York City NY 10022

GRUNWALD, ERNEST MAX, educator; b. Wuppertal, Germany, Nov. 2, 1923; s. Fred and Gertrude (Lowenstein) G.; came to U.S., 1939, naturalized, 1945; B.A., U. Cal. at Los Angeles, 1944, B.S., 1944, Ph.D., 1947; m. Esther Richter, Mar. 17, 1952; 1 dau., Judith. Research chemist Portland Cement Assn., 1947; research fellow Columbia, 1948; asso. prof., then prof. Fla. State U., 1949-60; research chemist Bell Telephone Labs., 1960; prof. Brandeis U., 1964—. Mem. Friends Grunwald Graphic Arts Found., U. Cal. at Los Angeles, 1966—. F. B. Jewett fellow, 1948; Chaim Weizmann fellow, 1955; Sloan fellow, 1958-60. Fellow Am. Acad. Arts and Scis.; mem. Am. Chem. Soc. (award pure chemistry 1959), Am. Phys. Soc. Author: (with R. H. Johnson), Atoms, Molecules and Chemical Change, 1960; (with J. E. Leffler) Rates and Equilibria of Organic Reactions, 1963; also numerous research papers. Office: Chemistry Dept Brandeis Univ Waltham MA 02154

GRUNWALD, HENRY ANATOLE, editor-writer; b. Vienna, Austria, Dec. 3, 1922; s. Alfred and Mila (Loewenstein) G.; came to U.S., 1940, naturalized, 1948; A.B., N.Y.U., 1944; m. Beverly Suser, Jan. 7, 1953; children—Peter, Madeleine, Lisa. Editorial staff Time mag., 1945-, sr. editor, 1951-, fgn. editor, 1961- -, asst. mng. editor, 1966-68, mng. editor, 1968- . Mem. A.S.C.A.P., Phi Beta Kappa. Contbr. to Life and Horizon mags.; Salinger, a Critical and Personal Portrait, 1962; Churchill, The Life Triumphant, 1965; The Age of Elegance, 1966. Home: 50 E 72d St New York City NY 10021 Office: Time and Life Bldg Rockefeller Center New York City NY 10020

GRUNWALD, JOSEPH, economist; b. Vienna, Austria, June 25, 1920; s. Arthur and Marie (Laub) G.; came to U.S., 1938, naturalized, 1943; B.S., John Hopkins, 1943; Ph.D., Columbia, 1950; m, Sheila Katz, June 2, 1949; children-Peter, Kenneth, Timothy. Personnel mgr. Textile Mfg. Co., Balt., 1940-43; lectr. Rutgers U., 1946-47, Columbia, 1947; asst. prof. Adelphi Coll., 1947-50; econ. adviser to gov. P.R., 1950-52; acting dir., econ. div. P.R. Planning Bd., 1950-52; lectr. Coll. City N.Y., 1952-54; prof. econs. U. Chile, 1954-61, dir. Inst. Econs., 1954-61, acad. mem., 1964—; cons. Ford Found., 1960-68; prof. econs. Yale, 1961- 63; lectr. Johns Hopkins, 1963—; sr. fellow charge Latin Am. econ. studies Brookings Instn., 1963—. Chmn. joint com. Latin Am. Studies Social Sci. Research Council-Am. Council Learned Socs., 1962-; mem. adv. bd. Hispanic Found., Library of Congress, 1964—; mem. com. experts, alliance mem. Com. Internat. Exchange of Persons, 1971; mem. econ. screening com. Fulbright Awards, 1965-68; mem. com. indsl. and transp. research Joint U.S.-Brazil Sci. Program, Nat. Acad. Scis., 1966-68, 70—. Decorated Order Bernando O'Higgins (Govt. of Chile). Mem. Am. Econ. Assn., Internat. Devel. Soc., Internat. Assn. Research in Income and Wealth, Inter-Am. Planning Soc. Author: National Budgeting in Norway, 1950; (with others) Economic Development of Puerto Rico, 1951; The Economic Development of Chile, 1956; (with others) Latin American Trade Patterns, 1965; (with P. Musgrove) Natural Resources in Latin American Development, 1970; (with others) Latin American Economic Integration and the United States, 1971. Regional editor Columbia Jour. World Bus., 1965 -66; mem. adv. bd. Jour. Common Market Studies, 1965—. Home: 8206 Kenfield Ct Bethesda MD 20034 Office: 1775 Massachusetts Av NW Washington DC 20036

GRUPP, WILLIAM JOHN, educator; b. Rochester, N.Y., June 3, 1922; s. William J. and Hilda S. (Becker) G.; B.A., U. Toronto, 1945; M.A., Cornell U., 1947, Ph.D., 1949; m. Helen B. Foley, July 28, 1945; children—Mary Colleen (Mrs. John H. Clark, Jr.), Marie Teresa, Catherine Anne, Judith Elizabeth, William J. Instr. to asso. prof., head dept. modern langs. U. Notre Dame, 1949-61; cultural attache Am. Embassy, Buenos Aires, Argentina, 1961-64; sect. chief U.S. Office of Edn., 1965-67; prof., chmn. dept. Spanish and Portuguese, U. Colo., 1967—. Served as pilot USAAF, 1942-45; ETO. Decorated Air medal. Mem. Am. Council Teaching Fgn. Langs., Rocky Mountain Modern Lang. Assn., Rocky Mountain Council Latin Am. Studies. Democrat. Roman Catholic. Home: 6731 Lakeview Dr Boulder CO 80303

GRUPPE, KARL HEINRICK, sculptor; b. Rochester, N.Y., Mar. 18, 1893; s. Charles Paul and Helen Elizabeth (Mitchell) G.; student art, Royal Acad., Antwerp, Belgium, and Art Student League, N.Y.C.; pupil of Karl Bitter, N.Y.C., 1912-15; m. Betty A. Clarke, Oct. 9, 1948; 1 dau., Elizabeth Mitchell Gruppe. Chief sculptor, monument restoration project, Dept. Parks, N.Y.C. 1934-37. Served with USMC, 1918-19. Academician, N.A.D., first v. p., 1956-59. Bd. dirs. Art Commn. Assos., Nat. Sculture Soc. (pres. 1950). Recipient St. Gaudens prize Art Students League, 1912, Avery prize Archtl. League, 1920, Helen Foster Barnett prize, 1926; Saltus gold medal N.A.D., 1952: Dessie Greer prize, 131st Ann. Exhbn. N.A.D., 1956; Lindsey Morris Meml. prize Nat. Sculpture Soc., 1968; Elizabeth Watrous Gold medal for sculpture, N.A.D., 1969; medal of honor, Nat. Arts Club, 1970. Club: Century Assn. (N.Y.C.). Home: 138 Manhattan Av New York City NY 10025

GRUSKIN, MARY J., (Mrs. Alan D. Gruskin), art dealer; b. Italy; d. Mauro Bovio and Tina Simone; student Cooper Union, Traphagen Sch. Design, Grand Central Art Sch., N.Y. Sch. Design, Art Students League; m. Alan D. Gruskin, July 16, 1940; children—Richard B., Robert A. Designer for china; dress buyer Martin's, Bklyn., 1937-40; assembled paintings for Art-in-Industry collections; assisted arrangement contemporary Am. artists group for design of print fabrics; illustrated book jacket and story for book House That Runs Itself; art dir. Midtown Galleries, 1944—, dir., 1970. Trustee Assn. for Arts N.J. Mus., Trenton. Mem. Nat. Council Women U.S. Home: Stockton NJ 14784 Office: 11 E 57th St New York City NY 10022

GRUSON, SYDNEY, newspaper editor; b. Dublin, Ireland, Dec. 16, 1916; s. Harry and Edith (Black) G.; m. Flora Lewis, Aug. 17, 1945; children—Kerry Lewis, Sheila Clare, Lindsey David. Naturalized U.S. citizen, 1962. With Canadian Press, 1931-43; mem. staff N.Y. Times, 1944—, chief Bonn (Germany) Bur., 1958-63, chief London (Eng.) Bur., 1963-65, fgn. news editor, 1965- 66, editor, chief exec. officer Internat. Edit., 1966-67; asso. pub. Newsday, Garden City, L.I., 1968; asst. to pub. N.Y. Times, 1969-71, v.p., 1971—. Served as war corr. U.S. 9th Army, 1944-45, Jewish religion. Home: 211 Central Park W New York City NY 10024 Office: 229 W 43d St New York City NY 10036

GRUSSING, BON DIRCK, advt. exec.; b. Chippewa Co., Minn., Jan. 27, 1904; s. Dirck and Jennie (Bontjes) G.; A.B., Carleton Coll., Northfield, Minn., 1927; student Mpls. Coll. Law, 1930-32; postgrad. U. Minn., 1963-66; m. Evelyn Florence Pearson, July 18, 1936; children—Bon Dirck, Theodore, Bruce Douglas. Sales mgr. Northfield (Minn.) Iron Co., 1928; real estate loan appraiser, 1928-29; publicity mgr. Redpath Chautauqua, 1929; salesman Proctor & Gamble, Mpls., 1929- 30, Shaw-Walker, Chgo., also Mpls., 1931-35; copywriter, dir. pub. relations, advt. and sales promotion mgr. Minneapolis-Moline Co., Mpls., 1935-56, dir. merchandising, 1956; v.p., dir. merchandising Brown & Bigelow, 1956-57; v.p., dir. sales Louis F. Dow Co., 1957-67; nat. account exec. Osborne-Kemper-Thomas, 1967-68; dist. mgr. Shaw-Banton, 1968-69; dir. Grussing & Assos., Inc., 1968—. Rep. candidate 7th Congl. Dist. Minn., 1928. Chmn. adv. council Farm Equipment Inst., 1947-54; bd. dirs. 10,000 Lakes Assn. Recipient George Washington Medal of Honor, Freedoms Found; Izak Walton League award. Mem. Soil Conservation Soc. Am., Advt. Fedn. Am., Army Ordnance Assn. Republican. Conglist. Mason (32, Shriner). Clubs: Athletic, Golden Valley Golf, Automobile, Advertising (Mpls.). Author: How to Tune Your Sales Appeal to the Farmer's Wave Length in Sales Management, 1945; From Adam to Atom, 1947; co-author: Land of Plenty. Contbr. articles trade papers. Writer, producer, dir. many travelogs, conservation and ecology movies. Home: 21386 Via Straits Lane Villa Pacific Huntington Beach CA 92646 Office: 1784 Monrovia Av Costa Mesa CA 92627

GRUT, FLEMMING, architect; b. Copenhagen, Denmark, Sept. 28, 1911; s. Harold and Harriet (Bottern) G.; grad. The Royal Acad. Fine Arts, 1938; m. Erni Skovgaard-Petersen, Nov. 1, 1941; children—Harald, Nicolai, Rikke. Partner firm Tyge Holm & F. Grut, Copenhagen, Denmark, 1941—. Mem. Copenhagen City Council, 1950-70, 1st vice-chmn., 1962-70. Hon. fellow A.I.A.; mem. Internat. Soc. for Rehabilitation of Disabled (pres. 9th World Congress, 1963), Fedn. Danish Architects (chmn. 1954-60). Home: 55 Stockholmsgade DK 2100 Copenhagen O Denmark Office: 77 St Kongensgade DK 1264 Copenhagen K Denmark

GRUZEN, BARNETT SUMNER, architect; b. Riga, Latvia, July 25, 1903; s. Max and Ida (Friedman) G.; came to U.S., 1905, naturalized, 1925; B.Arch., Mass. Inst. Tech. 1926, M.Arch., 1928; grad. work, Ecole des Beaux Arts, Paris, France, 1930; m. Ethel Brof, Aug. 7, 1930; children—Jordan Lee, Maxson Stewart. Rotch travelling scholar in Europe. 1930-32; now prin. Gruzen and Partners, Architects-Engrs., N.Y.C. and Newark, 1932—; prin. works include U.S. mission to UN bldg., 1959, Albert Einstein Coll. Medicine, 1954, Rutgers U. dormitories and related facilities, 1954, VA Hosp., Wilkes-Barre, Pa. (Nat. Honor award A.I.A. 1951), 1952, Canton (O.) City Hall, 1960, N.Y. Sch. Printing, N.Y.C., 1955, Passaic (N.J.) High Sch. (one of five 1st prizes for sch. design Sch. Exec. mag. 1955), 1949, monument and park for Theodore Herzl (3d prize World Zionist Orgn. 1951). 1951, also other high schs., shopping centers, mil. installations; new campus for State U. N.Y., Rutgers U.; new police headquarters for N.Y.C. Bd. dirs. Israel Inst. Tech., Haifa, 1935—; chmn. archtl. div. United Jewish Appeal, N.Y.C., 1951, Fed. Jewish Philanthropies, N.Y.C. 1952-53. Recipient 1st prize archtl. competition for development new state capitol, N.J., from A.I.A., 1945. Registered profl. engr., N.J. Fellow A.I.A.; mem. Nat. Council Archtl. Registration Bds., Nat. Soc. Profl. Engrs., N.J. Soc. Architects, N.Y. State Assn. Architects, Soc. Am. Mil. Engrs., Am. Hosp. Assn., Archtl. League of N.Y., Am. Technion Soc., Am. Arbitration Assn. Club: Mass. Inst. Tech. (N.Y.C.). Author articles, papers, also chpt. in book. Home: 1 W 72d St New York City NY 10023 Office: 1700 Broadway New York City NY 10019

GRYDER, JOHN WILLIAM, educator; b. Los Angeles, Nov. 6, 1926; s. William Thomas and Myrtle (Bogart) G.; B.S., Cal. Inst. Tech., 1946; Ph.D., Columbia, 1950; m. Rosa Meyersburg, Sept. 1, 1949; childrenDavid Jonas, Katherine Ann, Thomas William. Jr. scientist Brookhaven Nat. Lab., 1948-49; mem. faculty Johns Hopkins, 1949-, prof. chemistry, exec. officer dept., 1966-; bd. govs. Center Research Instrn. and Curricuium in Sci. and Math., 1965-68. Mem. steering com. Baltimore County-City Sci. Seminars, 1958-. Chmn. bd. mgrs. Levering Hall YMCA, 1966-. Mem. Am. Chem. Soc., Am. Assn. U. Profs., Am. Phys. Soc., Sigma Xi, Tau Beta Pi. Democrat. Contbr. jours. Home: 2006 W Rogers Av Baltimore MA 21209

GRYMES, DOUGLAS, mfg. exec.; b. St. Louis, Feb. 6, 1914; s. Douglas and Mary E. (Croghan) G.; student Southwestern U., Memphis. 1932-33, Spring Hill Coll., Mobile, Ala., 1933-36, Advanced Mgmt. Program, Harvard, 1953; m. Lillian Wood, July 20, 1940; childrenGlen, Virginia. With Ayer & Lord Tie Co., 1935-36, Nat. Lumber & Creosoting Co., 1936-40; with Koppers Co., Inc., Pitts., 1940-, successively Pitts. dist. sales mgr. forest products div., asst. mgr. r.r. sales, mgr. r.r. sales, div. sales mgr., exec. asst. to v.p. and gen. mgr., 1940-55, v.p., 1955-58, v.p., gen. mgr., 1958-66, exec. v.p., 1966-70, pres., 1970—, also dir.; dir. Gen. Steel Industries. Dir. United Fund Allegheny County, Pitts., Pitts.-Allegheny County chpt. A.R.C., Health Research Services Found.; v.p., mem. exec. com. East Boroughs Council, Boy Scouts Am.; trustee Mercy Hosp. Pitts.; bd. regents Spring Hill Coll., Mobile, Ala. Mem. Am. Iron and Steel Inst., Am. Wood Preservers Inst. (dir.), Am. Ordnance Assn., Brit. Wood Preserving Assn., Ry. Tie Assn. (past pres., mem. exec. com.), Am. Wood Preservers Assn. Republican. Roman Catholic. Clubs: University, Duquesne; Laurel Valley Golf, Rolling Rock (Ligonier, Pa.). Home: 18 Churchill Rd Pittsburgh PA 15235 Office: Koppers Bldg Pittsburgh PA 15219

GRYP, F.A., savs. and loan assn. exec. Pres., mgr. Palo Alto Salinas Savs. and Loan Assn. Office: 300 Hamilton Av Palo Alto CA 94301*

GUARD, DAVE, musician; b. Honolulu, Oct. 19, 1934; s. Carl Jackson and Marjorie Elizabeth (Kent) G.; B.A. in Econs., Stanford, 1956; m. Gretchen Ballard, Nov. 4, 1957; childrenCatherine Kent, Thomas Jonathan, Sarah Shannon. Leader, Kingston Trio, 1957-61, Whiskeyhill Singers, 1962; moved to Australia, 1962; folk music adviser Jazz Meets Folks, TV series for Australian Broadcasting Commn., 1964; host TV music series Dave's Place, 1965-66; pres. Britannia Enterprises, Ltd., 1960-; dir. Granada Music BMI, 1961-66; recording artist for Capitol Records; Kingston Trio recorded 11 albums, Whiskeyhill Singers recorded 2; 5 albums recorded in Australia as accompanist; Whiskeyhill Singers recorded sound track for film How The West Was Won, 1962 (Acad. award 1962); Kalimba soloist, 1967. Recipient 7 Gold Record award, 2 Grammy awards. Author: Colour Guitar, 1967. Home: 27 Morella Rd Wale Beach NSW Australia Office: Care Brobeck Phleger & Harrison 111 Sutter St San Francisco CA 94104

GUARD, RAY WESLEY, educator, metallurgist; b. Lafayette, Ind., Nov. 28, 1927; s. Arthur Thomas and Cleo (Gross) G.; B.S. in Metall. Engrng., Purdue U., 1947, Ph.D., 1952; M.S., Carnegie Inst. Tech., 1948; m. Edwina Louise Nichols, Oct. 16, 1948; children—Daniel Thomas, Neil Russell, Randall Brian, Alan Edward, Celia Louise. Instr., Purdue U., 1948-50; research asso. Gen. Electric Co., 1952-60, mgr. diamond process devel., 1960-62; mgr. metallurgy br. Gen. Precision Ind., 1962-63; group leader metall. service North Am. Aviation Sci. Center, 1963-66; prof. metall. engrng., head dept. Mich. Tech. U., 1966-70; dean Sch. Engring., U. Tex., El Paso, 1970—; adj. asso. prof. metall. engrng. Rensselaer Poly. Inst., 1956-60. Dir. Copper Industries Devel. Corp., 1967-70. Bd. dirs. Portage Lake United Fund, 1968-70. Federated Metals Co. scholar, 1947; recipient Best Paper award Am. Inst. Chem. Engrng., 1960. Mem. Am. Inst. Mining, Metall. and Petroleum Engrs. (chmn. high temperature materials com. 1959-60), Am. Soc. Metals (chmn. trans. com. 1959-60), Am. Ceramic Soc., Iron and Steel Inst. (Great Britain), Inst. Metals (Great Britain), A.A.A.S., Tau Beta Pi Phi Lambda Upsilon. Patentee in field. Home: 5840 Pebble Beach Dr El Paso TX 79912

GUARINI, FRANK J., Jr., state senator; b. Jersey City, N.J., Aug. 20, 1924; s. Frank J. and Caroline (Critelli) G.; B.A., Dartmouth Coll., 1946; J.D., N.Y.U., 1950, LL.M., 1955; student The Hague Acad. Internat. Law (Netherlands). Admitted to N.J. bar, 1951, also U.S. Supreme Ct.; partner firm Guarini & Guarini, Jersey City, 1951—; mem. N.J. Senate, 1966—, chmn. air and water pollution and pub. health com., 1967-68. Mem. nat. bd. dirs. A.R.C.; bd. dirs. Hudson County Bar Assn.; trustee St. Peter's Coll., Jersey City; trustee Christ Hosp., Jersey City. Served to lt. USNR, 1942-46; PTO. Recipient Man of Year award Jersey City, 1966. Mem. Hudson County (trustee), N.J. State (gen. council) bar assns., Jersey City C. of C. (bd. dirs.), Internat. Law Assn., Hague Acad. Internat. Law (trustee), Phi Delta Phi, Alpha Delta Phi. Clubs: Bergen Carteret University Hudson County (Jersey City). Home: 608 Newark Av Jersey City NJ 07306 Office: 610 Newark Av Jersey City NJ 07306

GUARNACCIA, SAMUEL, educator; b. Wakefield, Mass., Oct. 1, 1908; s. Giuseppe and Pietra (Caruso) G.; A.B., Middlebury (Vt.) Coll., 1930, M.A., 1936; postgrad. Boston U., 1939-40; m. Jean Stafford Hayden, Dec. 27, 1940; childrenGina (Mrs. Kenneth W. Burton), Samuel. Instr., Roxbury Sch., Cheshire, Conn., 1930-36, N.Y. Mil. Acad., Cornwall-on-Hudson, 1936-39; mem. faculty Middlebury Coll., 1940-68, prof., dean Spanish sch., 1947- 68, dir. Grad Sch. Spanish in Spain, 1952-53, 57-58, 62-63, 67-68; dir. Peace Corps, Peru, 1964-65; dir. admissions and scholarships Verde Valley Sch., Sedona, Ariz., 1968—. Mem. Vt. com. of patrons Alliance for Progress with Honduras, 1966-68. Active local A.R.C. drives. Served to lt. USNR, 1944-46. Mem. Am. Assn. U. Profs., Am. Assn. Tchrs. Italian, Dante Soc. Am. Address: Verde Valley School Sedona AZ 86336

GUARRERA, FRANK, concert baritone; b. Phila., Dec. 3, 1924; s. Anthony and Rosaria (Cavallaro) G.; grad. Curtis Inst. Music, 1948; m. Adelina Di Cintio, Oct. 14, 1944. Made debut in U.S. at Phila. Pop Concert, 1946; sang with Norfolk (Va.) Symphony, 1947; operatic debut as Silvio in Il Pagliacci, N.Y.C. Center, 1947; awarded $1000 in Met. Opera Auditions of the Air, sponsored by Farnsworth Radio and Television Corp., also contract with Met. Opera for 1948-49; invited by Arturo Toscanini to La Scala, Italy, for anniversary program dedicated to Boito, and there made debut in role of Fanuel in Nerone, also sang leading role in The Pearl Fishers and role in The Love of Three Kings, 1948; has sung over 35 leading roles at Met. Opera House and in every Opera Co. in U.S. Served with USNR, 1943-46. Address: care Metropolitan Opera House New York City NY 10018

GUBA, EGON GOTTHOLD, educator; b. Chgo., Mar. 1, 1924; s. Oswald and Rosina (Schell) G.; A.B., Valparaiso U., 1947; M.A., U. Kan., 1950; Ph.D., U. Chgo., 1952; m. Elaine Vivian Thompson, June 21, 1947; children-Christianne Joan, Susan Carol, Philip Paul. Instr. math. physics Valparaiso U., 1947-48; research asso. U. Chgo., 1951-53, instr., 1952-56, asst. prof. edn., 1956- 57; asso. prof. edn. U. Kansas City, 1957-58; research asso. Community Studies, Inc., Kansas City, Mo., 1957-58; successively research asso., asso. prof., prof. bur. ednl. research and service Ohio State U., 1958- 66, dir. bur. ednl. research and service, 1961-65, asst. dir. Sch. Edn., 1965-66; prof. edn. Ind. U., 1966—, asso. dean acad. affairs Sch. Edn., 1968-. Dir. Nat. Inst. for Study Ednl. Change, 1966-. Served with C.E. AUS, 1943-46. Mem. A.A.A.S., Am. Psychol. Assn., Am. Sociol. Soc., Am. Statis. Assn., Am. Ednl. Research Assn., Phi Delta Kappa. Editor: Theory into Practice, until 1966. Home: 2305 Sussex Dr Bloomington IN 47401 Office: Sch Edn Ind U Bloomington IN 47401

GUBELMANN, WALTER STANLEY, indsl. realty corp. exec.; b. Buffalo, N.Y., June 16, 1908; s. William S. and Juliette E. (Metz) G.; student Philips Andover Academy.; A.B., Yale, 1931; Postgraduate in bus. administrn., at Columbia U., 1931-33; m. Barton Green, Nov. 1, 1941; children—William Samuel, II, James Barton. Pres. Realty & Indsl. Corp., 1935—, patents, investments and real estate; dir. Potter Instrument Co., Plainview, L.I., N.Y. Trustee, pres. Soc. Four Arts, Palm Beach, Fla. Mem. Palm Beach Civic Assn., Yale Coll. Alumni Bd. Served as capt. AUS, World War II. Clubs: Racquet and Tennis, N.Y. Yacht (organizer and mgr. Constellation syndicate, winner Am.'s cup 1964), Cruising of America, Leash (all N.Y.C.); Seawanhaka Yacht (Oyster Bay, N.Y.); Piping Rock, Beaver Dam Winter Sports (Locust Valley, N.Y.); Corinthian Yacht (Phila.); Royal Swedish Yacht Club (Stockholm, Sweden); Clambake, Bailey's Beach (Newport, R. I.); Bar Harbor (Me.) Yacht; Northeast Harbor (Me.) Yacht; Everglades (gov.), Seminole, Bath and Tennis (Palm Beach, Fla.); Metropolitan (Washington); Newport Reading Room; Wyandanch Shooting (Smithtown, L.I.). Home: Southerly Centre Island Oyster Bay NY 11771 160 Via del Lago Palm Beach FL also 1 E 66th St New York City NY 10021 Office: 375 Park Av New York City NY 10022

GUBLER, V. GRAY, lawyer; b. Santa Clara, Utah, Jan. 11, 1910; s. John G. and Alyce (Gray) G.; A.B., U. Utah, 1932, LL.B., 1935; m. Loreta Newton, Nov. 23, 1937; childrenRichard Newton, John Gray, David Michael, James Leslie. Admitted to Nev. bar, 1936, since practiced in Las Vegas; dep. dist. atty. Clark County, 1940-43, dist. atty., 1943-47. Mem. Nev. Bd. Bar Examiners, 1937-50. Mem. Am., Clark County bar assns., State Bar Nev. (bd. govs. 1950-59, pres. 1958-59), Am. Coll. Trial Lawyers, Am. Coll. Probate Counsel, Order of Coif, Phi Kappa Phi, Tau Kappa Alpha. Elk (past dist. dep. grand exalted ruler Nev.), Kiwanian (past pres. Las Vegas). Home: 1139 S 5th Pl Las Vegas NV 89104 Office: 1st Nat Bank Bldg 3d and Carson Sts Las Vegas NV 89101

GUBOW, LAWRENCE, U.S. dist. judge; b. Detroit, Jan. 10, 1919; s. Jacob and Dora (Rubin) G.; A.B., U. Mich., 1940, LL.B., 1950, hon. certificate real estate, 1958, hon. certificate in building; m. Estelle Schmalberg, June 27, 1948; children—David Mark, Mona Joy, Janey Ann. Admitted to Mich. bar, 1951; practicing atty., 1951-53; dir. investigations Mich. Corp. and Securities Commn., 1953, dep. commr., 1953-56, commr., 1956-61; U.S. atty. Eastern Dist. Mich., 1961-68; U.S. dist. judge Eastern Dist. Mich., 1968—. Chmn. investment companies com. N. Am. Securities Adminstrn., 1958-61; mem. Gov. Mich. Com. Study Housing Law for State, 1959-60, Gov. Mich. Com. Study Tax Procedures for State, 1959-60, Gov. Mich. Task Force Studying Govt. Reorgn. Field Vets. Affairs, 1959-60, Gov. Mich. Task Force Studying Govt. Reorgn. Field Tax Procedures and Collections, 1959-60. Pres. Jewish War Vets. Meml. Home Assn., 1960-62; gen. chmn. Jewish War Vets. Nat. Conv., 1962; judge advocate Allied Vets. Council Wayne County, 1956- 58, legal adviser, 1962—, chmn. legislative council, 1956-59; treas. Jewish Community Council Met. Detroit, 1959-62, v.p., 1962-68, pres., 1968-71; bd. govs., mem. exec. com. Jewish Welfare Fedn., 1968—; mem. exec. com. Nat. Community Relations Adv. Council, 1969—. Chmn. 17th Dist. Young Democratic Club, 1953-55, Dem. Housing Com. Mich., 1958- 61. Bd. dirs. Jewish Nat. Fund, Detroit Service Group. Served to capt., inf., AUS, 1941-48. Named Wayne County Vet. of Year, 1958, Mich. Vet. of Year, 1959; recipient Civic award Eastern Mich. Realty Assn., 1959, Distinguished Service award Detroit Real Estate Brokers Assn., 1961; Outstanding Federal Administrator award, 1967; Man of the Year award Jewish War Veterans, 1967; Distinguished Service award Yeshiva Univ., 1969. Mem. Am., Fed., Mich., Detroit bar assns., Am. Judicature Soc., Nat. Assn. License Law Ofcls., Jewish War Vets. (Bronze Medal award 1960, 69; comdr. Mich. 1956-57, nat. exec. com. 1957- 64), Am. Legion (judge advocate Mich. 1960-61), 106th Inf. Div. Assn. (pres. 1956-57), AMVETS, V.F.W., Disabled Am. Vets., Disabled Officers Assn., Ret. Officers Assn., Real Estate Alumni Mich. (hon.), Fed. Bus. Assn. (treas.), Fed. Exec. Assn. (v.p. 1966-67), U. Mich. Alumni Assn. Detroit (bd. govs. 1969-). Home: 4397 Sunningdale Dr Bloomfield Hills MI 48013 Office: Federal Bldg Detroit MI 48226

GUBSER, CHARLES S., congressman; b. Gilroy, Cal., Feb. 1916; s. Charles Henry and Ella Oma (Matlack) G.; student San Jose (Cal.) State Jr. Coll., 1932-34; A.B., U. Cal., 1937, grad. student, 1937-39; m. Joan Fay Brimberry, Jan. 8, 1939; 1 dau., Marcia Jeanne. Secondary sch. tchr. Gilroy Union High Sch., 1939- 43; operator truck farm, Cal., 1940-50; assemblyman 29th Dist., Cal. Legislature, 1950-52; mem. 83d-92d Congresses, 10th Dist. Cal. Mem. Kappa Alpha. Mason, Elk, Rotarian. Office: Rayburn Bldg Washington DC 20515

GUCKER, FRANK THOMSON, chemist; b. Phila., Apr. 8, 1900; s. Frank Thomson and Louise Oliphant (Fulton) G.; B.A., Haverford Coll., 1920, A.M., 1921, LL.D., 1966; Ph.D., Harvard U., 1925; m. Eleonore Dubois Harris, 1925; childrenFrank Fulton, Katharine Harris (Mrs. Herbert H. Hand). Research asst. Harvard U., 1924-25; nat. research fellow. Cal. Inst. Tech., 1925-27; research fellow, Harvard U., 1927-28; research chemist, duPont Co., 1928-29; asst. prof. Northwestern U., 1929- 36, asso. prof., 1936-42, prof. 1942-47; prof. and chmn. dept. of chemistry Ind. U., 1947-51, dean Coll. Arts and Scis., 1951-65, research prof. chemistry, 1965-70, research prof. emeritus chemistry, 1970—, dir. research on phys. chemistry aerosols, 1970—. Chief tech. aide Nat. Def. Research Com., 1941-42; mem. com. phys. Chemistry NRC, 1951-54; regional councilor Office Ordnance Research, 1951-54, mem. com. on awards in Chemistry under the Fulbright Act, 1954, chmn., 1955-59. Cons. Nat. Sci. Found. (mem. adv. panel chemistry div. math., phys., engrig. scis., 1957-60, chmn. 1958-59); cons. Ford Found. Latin Am. Program, 1965; exec. com. Inter-Univ. Com. Travel Grants, 1966-69. Mem. Oak Ridge Nat. Lab. Adv. Com., Reactor Chemistry, 1961- 63. Mem. exec. com. Am. Council Academic Deans, 1961-65; mem. commn. on liberal learning Assn. Am. Colls., 1966-68, chmn. 1968, exec. com. spl. com. liberal studies, 1968. Mem. alumni council Haverford Coll., 1957-60. Fellow Carnegie Instn., 1940-50. Fellow A.A.A.S., Ind. Acad. Sci.; Am. Soc. Testing Materials (instrumentation subcom. com. methods atmospheric sampling and analysis), Am. Assn. U. Profs., Am. Chem. Soc. (asso. editor Chem. Revs. 1950-53; sec.-treas. 1952-53, chmn. elect 1953-54, chmn. div. phys. and inorganic chemistry 1954-55; councilor, chmn. council policy com. 1959-61, mem. com. nominations and elections 1963-68, sec. 1964-66, chmn. 1967-68), Phi Beta Kappa (chpt. pres. 1965-66), Alpha Chi Sigma, Sigma Xi, Phi Lambda Upsilon. Presbyn. Club: Faculty Men's (Ind. U.). Author: (with Ralph L. Seifert) Physical Chemistry, 1966; textbooks; also articles assn. jours. Home: 1125 E Hunter Av Bloomington IN 47401 summer Melvin Village NH 03850 Office: Indiana U Bloomington IN 47401 ☆

GUDE, GILBERT, congressman; b. Washington, Mar. 9, 1923; s. Adolph E. and Inez (Gilbert) G.; student U. Md., 1941-43; B.S., Cornell U., 1948; M.A., George Washington U., 1958; m. Jane Wheeler Callaghan, June 19, 1948; children—Sharon, Gilbert, Gregory, Daniel, Adrienne Ann. Co-owner landscape nursery A. Gude Sons Co., Rockville, Md., 1948—; mem. Md. Ho. of Dels. from Montgomery County, 1953-58, Senate, 1962-66; mem. 90th-92d Congresses, 8th Dist. Md., mem. house dist. com., govt. operations com. Chmn. Montgomery County Republican State Central Com., 1960. Chmn. Montgomery County Heart Fund, 1958; bd. dirs. Montgomery County Tb and Heart Assn.; trustee Md. Assn. Retarded Children, Md. Tb Assn. Served with AUS, 1943-46; PTO. Recipient Distinguished Service award Bethesda Jr. C. of C., 1955; Golden Rule award Md. Congress PTA, 1966. Mem. Pi Kappa Phi, Phi Sigma Kappa. Catholic. Rotarian. Home: 5411 Duvall Dr Bethesda MD 20016 Office: Cannon House Office Bldg Washington DC 20515

GUDEMAN, EDWARD, investment banker; b. Chicago, Oct. 9, 1906; s. Edward and Clara (Asher) G.; B.A., Harvard, 1927; m. Frances Alschuler, Oct. 12. 1932; children—Jon Edward. Stephen Edward. Formerly v.p. and dir. Sears, Roebuck & Co.; formerly dir. One William Street Fund, Inc., Brunswick Corp., Globe Union Corp., Whirlpool Corp., Warwick Corp., Schnadig Corp.; under-sec. Commerce, 1961-63; partner Lehman Bros., investment bankers, 1963-69, ltd. partner, 1969—; bd. dirs. Marcor, Inc., Esquire Corp. Montgomery Ward & Co. Former exec. dir. President's Adv. Com. on Labor Mgmt Policy. Trustee Nat. Council on Crime and Delinquency; mem. adv. council U. Chgo. Grad. School Bus. Clubs: Lake Shore Country (Glencoe, Ill.); Century Country (Purchase, N.Y.); Montego Bay Tennis (Jamaica), Mid America, Harvard (Chgo.). Home: 142 E 65th St New York City NY 10021 Office: 1 William St New York City NY 10004

GUE, RONALD LEE, medical computing co. exec.; b. Washington, Sept. 12, 1938; s. George Irving and Doris Lavinia (Hawkins) G.; B.Engring. Sci., Johns Hopkins, 1960; Ph.D., 1964; Patricia A. McDaniel, July 11, 1959 (div. Oct. 1966); m. 2d, Peggy C. Nutt, Dec. 1966; children—Kevin Randolph, Kathleen Anne, Lisa Karen. Faculty, U. Fla., Gainesville, 1964-67, asso. prof., 1965-67; prof., dir. Computer Scis. Center, So. Methodist U., Dallas, 1967-70; pres. MEDICUS Corp., Dallas, 1970—; cons. VA, 1964—. Gilman fellow Johns Hopkins, 1962-64; USPHS grantee, 1968-70. Mem. Am. Assn. U. Profs., Assn. for Computing Machinery (pres. Dallas chpt. 1969-70), Am. Inst. Indsl. Engrs. (dir. operations research div. 1966-68, editorial bd. transactions 1964-71), Am. Soc. Engring. Edn. (long-range planning com. 1966-68), Operations Research Soc. Am. (chmn. 39th nat. meeting 1971). Author: (with M.E. Thomas)

Mathematical Methods in Operations Research, 1968; also articles. Home: 3883 Turtle Creek Blvd Dallas TX 75214 Office: Expressway Tower Dallas TX 75206

GUEDEL, JOHN, radio and TV writer, producer; b. Portland, Ind., Oct. 9, 1913; s. Walter Morris and Hazel McKee (Bimel) G.; student U. Cal. at Los Angeles, 1931-32; m. Beth Pingree, August 15, 1936; children—John Kenneth, Heidi Beth; m. 2d, Helen Parrish, August 3, 1956; m. 3d, Valerie McDonald, June 27, 1968. Motion picture writer Our Gang series, Bohemian Girl (Laurel and Hardy) Hal Roach Studio, Culver City, Cal., 1933-37; v.p. in charge radio Dan B. Miner Advt. Co., Los Angeles, 1937- 41; Russel M. Seeds Advt. Co., Chgo., 1942-44; pres. John Guedel Radio Prodns., Hollywood, 1942—; writer, producer People Are Funny 1938—, House Party 1945—, Tommy Dorsey show, 1943-44, Charlotte Greenwood show, 1944, Life With Linkletter TV show 1950—, Earn Your Vacation show, 1949-50; producer Groucho Marx radio and TV shows 1947—, Red Skelton show, 1943-46; former producer TV show Anybody Can Play, On The Go, For Better or Worse. Partner Peterson-Guedel Family Center, 1959—. Cons. U.S. Dept. State, 1952. Mem. Radio Writers Guild, Radio and TV Dirs. Guild (pres. 1949-50), Nat. Acad. TV Arts and Scis. (pres. Hollywood chpt.). Author: Tornado, 1942. Home: 27070 Malibu Cove Colony Dr Malibu CA 90265 Office: 8321 Beverly Blvd Los Angeles CA 90048

GUEDEN, HILDE, concert singer; b. Vienna, Austria; d. Italo F. and Frieda (Brammer) Geiringer; student Acad. Music, Vienna, also dramatics with Max Reinhardt Sch.; m. Robert Josef; m. 2d. Lacy L. Herrmann, Feb. 28, 1952. Operatic debut Zurich State Opera, 1939; lyric, coloratura soprano; debut Staatsoper, Munich, Germany, 1941, Royal Opera, Rome, 1942; appeared Salzburg Festivals, 1946—; debut LaScala, 1946, Met. Opera, 1951; appeared Vienna State Opera, 1955, also participated concert tours European cities, orchestra concerts with Phila., Chgo. orchs., TV programs Eng., U.S. Recipient title Kammersängerin, Pres. of Austria, 1950, golden record Decca London, 1958, grand cross for sci. and art Pres. Austria, 1950, silver rose Vienna Philharmonic Orch., 1959, Le Discobole, Académie du Disque Francais, 1961; decorated Cross of Danebrog Order (Denmark). Mem. Royal Naval Assn., Sigma Alpha Iota. Home: 26 Washington Sq N New York City NY 10011 Office: Metropolitan Opera New York City NY 10023

GUENTHER, CARL FREDERIC, architect; b. Cleve., Apr. 8, 1909; s. Herman Richard and Marie Sophia (Brandt) G.; B.Arch., Western Res. U., 1930; diploma architecture Fontainebleau (France) Sch. Fine Arts, 1930; certificate Beaux Arts Inst. Design, N.Y.C., 1931; spl. student (24th Paris prize in architecture), Ecole des Beaux Arts, Paris, 1931-34; m. Marie Anne Davis, June 29, 1936 (div. Feb. 1952); children—Ann Christine (Mrs. Michael R. Stadler), Florence Anne (Mrs. Thomas J. Connole); m. 2d Laverne Jane Bell, Oct. 10, 1952. Designer, Walter R. MacCornack, Architect, Cleve., 1934-35; chief design, asso. architect, Great Lakes Exposition, 1935-37; pvt. practice, Cleve., 1937-39; partner Miller & Guenther, Cleve. 1939-42; sr. project planner region V, Fed. Pub. Housing Authority, 1942-44; asso. and chief designer Maier-Outcalt- Dickerson & Assos., Cleve., 1944-45; partner Outcalt, Guenther and Assos., Cleve., 1945-60, Outcalt, Guenther and Van Buren, architects, Cleve. 1960-62, Outcalt-Guenther Partners, Cleve., 1962-68, ret.; critic, lectr. archtl. design Western Res. U., 1934- 41. Author programs, mem. juries Beaux Arts Inst. Design, 1934—; mem. Architects Educators Conf., 1953, 54. Adv. com. to reorganize Sch. Architecture, Western Res. U., 1950-51, trustee univ., 1951- 56, gov., 1957-68. Recipient two individual awards U.S. Post Office competition, 1938; first award for suburban location of office bldg., 1956; Flat Glass award Pitts. Plate Glass Co., 1957. Fellow A.I.A. (com. nat. honor awards 1956-57; past pres. Cleve.); mem. Fla. Assn. A.I.A., Nat. Inst. Archtl. Edn., Fontainebleau Alumni Assn. Clubs: Pontiac Game (Sheenboro, Que., Can.); Royal Poinciana Golf, Naples Sailing (Naples, Fla.). Author articles. Home: 322 Harbour Dr Naples FL 33940

GUENTHER, GEORGE CARPENTER, govt. ofcl.; b. Reading, Pa., Aug. 27, 1931; s. John H. and Eleanor (Carpenter) G.; A.B. in Psychology, Amherst Coll., 1952; m. Kathleen Lance Coyle, Oct. 20, 1962; children—George Carpenter, Todd C., John E. Pres., John H. Guenther Hosiery Co., Reading, 1955-67; dep. sec. Pa. Dept. Labor and Industry, 1967-69; dir. Bur. Labor Standards, Dept. Labor, 1969-71, sec. labor for occupational safety and health, 1971—. Bd. dirs. Nat. Safety Council. Chmn., Fed. Safety Council. Served with USNR, 1952-55. Mem. Am. Soc. Safety Engrs. Home: 5508 Wilson Lane Bethesda MD 20014 Office: Dept of Labor Washington DC 20210

GUENTHER, JACK EGON, lawyer; b. San Antonio, Dec. 14, 1934; s. Egon E. and Camilla (Mallepell) G.; B.B.A., U. Tex., Austin, 1956; LL.B. magna cum laude, St. Mary's U., 1959; LL.M. in Taxation, N.Y. U., 1960; m. Valerie Urschel, Feb. 1, 1964; children—Charles Urschel, Abigail Camilla, Jack Egon. Practice pub. accounting, San Antonio, 1957-59; admitted to Tex. bar, 1959; practice in San Antonio, 1960—; atty. Cox, Smith, Smith, Hale & Guenther and predecessor firm, 1961—, partner, 1965—; pres. North Loop Volkswagen, Inc., 1965—; dir. Pearl Brewing Co., Southdown, Inc.; adj. prof. law St. Mary's U.; lectr. various tax insts. Trustee St. Luke's Episcopal Sch. Served to capt., Judge Adv. Gen. Corps, AUS, 1957. C.P.A., Tex. Mem. Am., Tex. bar assns., Tex. Soc. C.P.A.'s, Sigma Chi, Phi Delta Phi. Episcopalian. Office: Nat Bank of Commerce Bldg San Antonio TX 78205

GUENTHER, ROBERT WALLACE, mag. editor; b. Van Nuys, Cal., Aug. 30, 1929; s. Earl L. and Marie A. (Angel) G.; B.A., Los Angeles State Coll., 1955; m. Helen J. Fitz, Apr. 14, 1954; children—Jane L., Anne K. Reporter, copy editor Los Angeles Daily News, 1948-53; travel editor, asst. Sunday editor, then editor Home mag. Los Angeles Times, 1954-69; editor House Beautiful mag., N.Y.C., 1969—. Served with AUS, 1951-53. Home: 136 Locust Rd Briarcliff Manor NY 10510 Office: 717 Fifth Av New York City NY 10022

GUENZEL, PAUL WALTER, corp. exec.; b. Chgo., Jan. 8, 1910; s. Louis and Alice (Paepcke) G.; A.B., Williams Coll., 1931; m. Elizabeth Skinner, Sept. 10, 1938; children—Elizabeth Alice, William Skinner. With Container Corp. Am., Chgo., 1931—, asst. sec., 1947-48, asst. sec. and asst. treas., 1948- 49, now v.p., treas., dir.; dir. Pioneer Trust & Savs. Bank. Bd. dirs. Children's Meml. Hosp.; trustee N. Shore Country Day Sch. Found.; bd. dirs. Peninsula Arts Assn., Taxpayers Fedn. Ill.; pres., dir. Chestnut St. Corp. Mem. Phi Delta Theta. Clubs: University, Chicago (Chgo.); Indian Hill (Winnetka, Ill.). Home: 1630 Sheridan Rd Wilmette IL 60091 Office: One First Nat Plaza Chicago IL 60670

GUERARD, ALBERT JOSEPH, writer, educator; b. Houston, Nov. 2, 1914; s. Albert Leon and Wilhelmina (Macartney) G.; A.B., Stanford, 1934, Ph.D., 1938; A.M., Harvard, 1936; m. Mary Maclin Bocock, July 11, 1941; children—Catherine Collot, Mary Maclin, Lucy Lundie. Faculty Harvard, 1938-61, beginning as instr. English, successively faculty instr., asst. prof., asso. prof., 1941-54, prof. English, 1954-61; prof. English, Stanford, 1961—. Served as tech. sgt. psychol. warfare br. AUS, World War II. Rockefeller fellow, 1946-47, Fulbright fellow, 1950-51, Guggenheim fellow, 1956-57, Ford fellow, 1959-60. Recipient Paris Review Fiction prize, 1963; Nat. Found. Arts fellowship, 1967-68. Mem. Am. Acad. Arts and Scis., Phi Beta Kappa. Author: The Past Must Alter, 1937; Robert Bridges, 1942; The Hunted, 1944; Maquisard, 1945; Joseph Conrad, 1947; Thomas Hardy, 1949; Night Journey, 1950; Andre Gide, 1951; Conrad the Novelist, 1958; The Bystander, 1958; The Exiles, 1963, English edit., 1962. Co-editor: The Personal Voice, 1964. Home: 635 Gerona Rd Stanford CA 94305

GUERASSIMOV, LUBEN NIKOLOV, Bulgarian diplomat; b. Targovishte, Bulgaria, Sept. 9, 1906; s. Nikola Nikolov and Stephka (Titkova) G.; student Sofia U., 1927-31; m. Vera Todorova, Dec. 17, 1946; children—Andrey, Nikolai, Stephen. Ambassador to Hungary, 1949-51; dep. fgn. minister, 1951-56; ambassador to USSR, 1956-63; ambassador at large at Fgn. Ministry of P.R. of Bulgaria, Sofia, 1963-65; ambassador to U.S.A., Washington, 1965-. Decorated Order of Georgy Dimitrov. Home: 1629 Van Buren St NW Washington DC 20012 Office: 2100 16th St NW Washington DC 20009

GUERIN, DEAN PATRICK, investment banker; b. St. Paul, Feb. 21, 1922; s. Joseph H. and Della (Booth) G.; B.S. in Bus. Adminstrn., Boston U., 1949; m. Jo Alice Maryman, Sept. 3, 1959; children—Dean William, Susan Jane, Stephen Patrick, Mark Joseph. With Sperry Gyroscope Co., N.Y.C., 1940-42; registered rep. Chas. A. Day & Son, Boston, 1946-49, Dallas Rupe & Son, 1949-51; pres. Eppler, Guerin & Turner, Inc., Dallas, 1951—; dir. Aaronson Bros. Stores Corp., First Worth Corp., Kreisler Mfg. Corp., ProChemco, Inc., John Roberts, Inc., The Circle K Corp., Redman Industries, Inc., Houston Oil & Minerals Corp., Trinity Industries, Howard B. Wolf, Inc., Zale Corp. Asso. mem. Am., Midwest, N.Y. stock exchanges. Mem. Municipal Adv. Council Tex., 1955—. Served with USMCR, 1942-46; PTO. Mem. Investment Bankers Am. Home: 4747 Miron Dr Dallas TX 75220 Office: First Nat Bank Bldg Dallas TX 75221

GUERIN, JOHN WILLIAM, artist; b. Houghton, Mich., Aug. 29, 1920; s. Omer Francis and Mildred Montague (Miller) G.; student Am. Acad. Art, Chgo., Art Students League, N.Y.C., Escuela de Bellas Artes, San Miguel, Mexico; m. Anne Walden Dewey, Dec. 28, 1948. Prof. art U. Tex., 1953—; artist in residence Skowhegan (Me.) Sch. Painting and Sculpture, 1960; one man exhbns. include Kraushaar Galleries, N.Y.C., 1960, 63, 68, Ft. Worth Art Center, 1956, 64, 65, Marion Kooglar McNay Art Inst., San Antonio, 1961, 65, Centennial Mus., Corpus Christi, Tex., 1963, Carlin Galleries, Ft. Worth, 1962, 64, 67; group exhbns. include Met. Mus. Art, Whitney Mus. Art, Art Inst. Chgo., Corcoran Mus. Art, Carnegie Inst.; rep. permanent collections Chrysler Mus., Provincetown, Mass., Joslyn Mus., Omaha, New Britain (Conn.) Mus., Houston Mus., Dallas Mus., U. Notre Dame Art Gallery, Colorado Springs (Colo.) Fine Art Center. Served with USAAF, 1942-45. Grantee Am. Acad Arts, 1959, U. Tex., 1960; recipient Henry Ward Ranger Fund Purchase prize N.A.D., 1958; Research Inst. grant U. Tex., 1960, 66. A.N.A. Life member Art Students League, N.Y.C. Episcopalian. Home: 3400 Stoneridge Rd Austin TX 78746

GUERLAC, HENRY EDWARD, educator; b. Ithaca, N.Y., June 14, 1910; s. Othon Goepp and Helen Elizabeth (Finch) G.; A.B., Cornell, 1932, M.S., 1933; Ph.D., Harvard, 1941; m. Lucy Rita Carey, Aug. 27, 1941; childrenLucy Anne, Anne Christine, Suzanne Goepp. Asst., Harvard Fatigue Lab., 1934-35, jr. fellow, Harvard Soc. Fellows, 1935-38; instr., tutor history, Harvard, 1938-41; asst. prof., chmn. dept. history of sci., U. Wis., 1941-43; historian Radiation Lab., Mass. Inst. Tech. under Office Sci. Research and Devel., 1943-46; prof. history of sci., Cornell, 1946-64, Goldwin Smith prof. history of sci., 1964—, dir. Soc. for Humanities, 1970—. Mem. Inst. Advanced Study, Princeton 1953- 55. Mem. Académie Internationale d'Histoire des Sciences (pres. 1959-65). Fellow Am. Acad. Arts and Scis., Royal Soc. Arts (London); mem. Internat. Soc. for History of Ideas, Am. Hist. Assn., A.A.A.S. (mem. council 1947-50), History of Sci. Soc. (pres. 1957-60), Am. Assn. U. Profs., Sigma Xi. Author: Official History of Radar Development Joint Auspices of the Armed Services and OSRD, 1946; Report on present state of field of history of science to Ninth Internat. Congress of Historical Scis., 1950; Lavoisier-the Crucial Year, 1961. Contbr. articles gen. hist. of sci., hist. of chemistry, history of French sci. Home: 3 Fountain Pl Ithaca NY 14850

GUERNSEY, JANET BROWN, (Mrs. William Guernsey), educator; b. Germantown, Pa., May 2, 1913; d. Clarence M. and Luella (Conwell) Brown; A.B., Wellesley Coll., 1935; A.M., Harvard, 1948; Ph.D., Mass. Inst. Tech., 1955; m. William G. Guernsey, June 20, 1936; children—Richard M., David W., Michael W., Robert G., Madeleine. Instr. dept. physics Wellesley Coll., 1942-48, asst. prof., 1948-55, asso. prof., 1955-61, prof., 1961-69, Louise S. McDowell prof., 1969—, chmn. dept. physics, 1967—. Mem. A.A.A.S., Am. Phys. Soc., Am. Assn. Physics Tchrs., Am. Assn. U. Profs., Phi Beta Kappa, Sigma Xi. Home: Sabrina Farm Wellesley MA 02181

GUERNSEY, JOHN, journalist. Edn. editor Portland Oregonian. Office: 1320 SW Broadway Portland OR 97201*

GUERNSEY, JOSEPH SHEDD, savs. and loan exec.; b. Orlando, Fla., Oct. 14, 1918; s. Joseph Welburn and Emelyn Evans (Shedd) G.; student Citadel Mil. Coll., 1936-37; B.A., U. Fla., 1940; postgrad., Harvard, U. Fla.; m. Virginia Shepperd Leps, June 12, 1954; children—Joseph Welburn, Virginia Elizabeth, Mary Emelyn, Priscilla Jean. Salesman, S.Kendrick Guernsey & Assos., Orlando, 1940-41; pilot Pan Am. Airways, 1945-46; salesman McNut-Heasley Real Estate, Orlando, 1946-47; founder Guernsey-Green-Slemons Real Estate and Ins., Orlando, 1947-67; founder Orlando Fed. Savs. and Loan Assn., 1949—; dir. Founders Life Assurance Co. Fla., Tampa. Pres. Young Democrats, Orlando, 1947-48. Chmn. bd. Coll. of Orlando (formerly Orlando Jr. Coll.), 1969-71, Lake Highland Prep. Sch., 1970-71. Bd. trustees Rollins Coll., Winter Park, Fla. Served with USAAF, 1940-45. Mem. Fla. Savs. and Loan League (pres. 1956), Fla. Mental Health Assn. (pres. 1962-63), V.F.W., S.A.R. Presbyn. (ruling elder). Rotarian (pres. Orlando 1970-71). Clubs: Orlando Country, University. Home: 1611 Spring Lake Dr Orlando FL 32804 Office: 77 E Livingston St Orlando FL 32801

GUERNSEY, OTIS LOVE, Jr., critic, editor; b. N.Y.C., Aug. 9, 1918; s. Otis L. and Margaret (Henderson) G.; student Taft Sch., Watertown, Conn.; B.A., Yale, 1940; m. Dorianne Downe, Dec. 11, 1943. With N.Y. Herald Tribune, 1941-60, successively copy boy, reporter, asso. film and drama critic, film critic and drama critic, arts editor, 1955-60; story cons. CBS, 1957-59; free lance writer, 1960—; editorial cons. New Eng. Guide, 1960—; drama critic and sr. editor Show mag., 1963-64; arts editor Diplomat mag., 1965-67; lectr. on modern theater. Mem. N.Y. Newspaper Guild, N.Y. Film Critics (past chmn.), N.Y. Drama Critics Circle, Dramatists Guild, Phi Beta Kappa. Clubs: Coffee House, Century Assn. (N.Y.C.). Author original film stories, also articles on stage and screen. Editor: The Dramatists Guild Quar., 1964—; Best Plays series of theater yearbooks, 1965—. Address: North Pomfret VT 05053

GUERRA, EMILIO LOUIS, educator; b. Hoboken, N.J., Aug. 27, 1909; s. Francesco and Maria (Parano) G.; A.B., Coll. City N.Y., 1931, M.S. in Edn., 1933; Ph.D., N.Y. U., 1942; m. Alice Hendler, Dec. 12, 1931; 1 son, Robert. Tchr. Spanish, Italian and French, N.Y.C. high schs., 1932-39, community coordinator Benjamin Franklin High Sch., N.Y.C., 1939-43; chmn. dept. fgn. langs., 1943-57; supr. teaching English as a 2d lang. high sch. div. N.Y.C. pub. schs., 1957-63, acting dir. for lang., 1963-65; prof., head div. fgn. langs. and internat. edn. N.Y. U., 1965—; instr. gen. lang. Adelphi U., 1955-59; adj. asso. prof. Romance langs. N.Y. U., 1957-65; Smith-Mundt lectr. U. Central del Ecuador, 1956, 57, U. de Guayaquil (Ecuador), 1957; Fulbright lectr. U. Nat. de Buenos Aires, 1958; lectr. applied linguistics Nat. Def. Edn. Act Inst., Ohio State U., 1962; lectr. Inst. Guatemalteco Americano, 1956, 57. Named cavaliere dell' ordine Al Merito Della Repubblica Italiana, 1967. Mem. Am. Assn. Tchrs. Spanish and Portuguese (pres. N.Y. chpt. 1938), Am. Assn. U. Profs., Am. Assn. Tchrs. French, Am. Assn. Tchrs. Italian, N.E.A., Internat. Linguistic Assn., Am. Assn. Sch. Adminstrs., Modern Lang. Assn., N.Y. State Fedn. Fgn. Lang. Tchrs., Am-Council Tchrs. Fgn. Lang., Assn. Supervision and Curriculum Devel., Am. Soc. Italian Legion of Merit, Phi Delta Kappa. Author: Getting to Know Spain and Latin America, 1957; A First Course in Spanish, 1961; A Second Course in Spanish, 1965. Home: 116 40 Park Lane S Kew Gardens NY 11418 Office: New York Univ Washington Sq New York City NY 10003

GUERRANT, DAVID EDWARD, food co. exec.; b. Elizaville, Ky., Sept. 27, 1919; s. William Upton and Claire (Jordan) G.; B.S., Kan. State U., 1941; m. Charlotte L. Lander, Feb. 6, 1942; children—Stephen, Jeffrey. With Potts-Turnbull Agy., Kansas City, Mo., 1941-48; creative dir. Campbell-Ewald Co., Chgo., 1948-51; with John W. Shaw Advt., Inc., Chgo., 1951-61, pres., 1959-61; pres. MacFarland, Aveyard & Co., Chgo., 1961-64; v.p. marketing Libby, McNeill & Libby, Chgo., 1964-68, pres., chief exec. officer, 1968—, chmn. bd., 1971—, dir., 1967—. Presbyn. Clubs: Chicago Athletic Assn., Mid Am. (Chgo.); Westmoreland Country (Wilmette, Ill.). Home: 38 Park Lane Golf IL 60029 Office: 200 S Michigan Av Chicago IL 60604

GUERRANT, EDWARD OWINGS, educator; b. Danville, Va., Feb. 2, 1911; s. Peter Dutois and Grace (Owings) G.; A.B., Davidson Coll., 1933; M.A., U. So. Cal., 1939, Ph.D., 1942; m. Helen Louise Daggett, Feb. 14, 1936 (dec.); 1 dau., Helen Louise (Mrs. Stewart A. Toy); m. 2d, Charlotte Edwina Tompkins, Aug. 12, 1944; childrenLucy Allison, Edward Owings. Instr. history Cal. Inst. Tech., 1942-44; polit. analyst Office Coordinator Inter-Am. Affairs, 1944-45, State Dept., 1945-46; asso. prof., then prof history Davidson Coll., 1946-54; mem. faculty Cal. State Coll. at Los Angeles, 1954-, head dept., 1957-64, prof. history, 1960, chmn. dept. history, 1966-69; vis. summer prof. U. So. Cal., 1947-54; vis. prof. history U. Hawaii, 1963. Ford fellow, 1952-53. Mem. Phi Beta Kappa, Phi Delta Theta. Presbyn. (ruling elder). Author: Roosevelt's Good Neighbor Policy, 1950; Modern American Diplomacy, 1954: Herbert Hoover and Franklin D. Roosevelt: Comparisons and Contrasts, 1960; (with K.A. Martyn) Toward A More Perfect Union, 1967. Home: 1431 N Coolidge Av Pasadena CA 91104 Office: 5151 State College Dr Los Angeles CA 90032

GUERRERO, E.T., petroleum engr., educator; b. Richmond, Tex., Nov. 2, 1924; s. Agustin and Herminia (Trevino) G.; B.S. in Petroleum and Mech. Engring., Tex. A. and M. Coll., 1949, M.S., 1950, Ph.D., 1953; m. Isabelle Arredondo. May 28, 1949; childrenPhillip, Gregory, Elizabeth, and David. Roustabout, Magnolia Petroleum Co., 1952; instr. petroleum engring. Tex. A. and M. Coll., 1952-53; petroleum reservoir engr. Seeligson Engr. Com., San Antonio, 1953-56; trustee's prof., head dept. petroleum engring., dir. information services dept. U. Tulsa, 1956-65, dean, 1966—. Registered profl. engr. Mem. Nat. Okla. socs. profl. engrs., Soc. Petroleum Engrs., Am. Petroleum Inst., Am. Soc. Engring. Edn., Am. Inst. Mining, Metall. and Petroleum Engrs., Am. Documentation Inst., Sigma Xi, Tau Beta Pi, Pi Epsilon Tau. Episcopalian. Mason. Home: 1741 S Darlington Av Tulsa OK 74112

GUERRERO, JOSE, artist; b. Granada, Spain, Oct. 29, 1914; s. Emilio Garcia Lopez and Gracia Guerrero Padial; student Escuela de Artes y Oficios, Granada, 1931-35, Escuela de Bellas Artes de San Fernando, Madrid, 1940-44, Ecole de Beaux Arts, Paris, 1946-47; m. Roxane Whittier Pollock, Apr. 25, 1949; children—Lisa Gracia, Antonio. Exhbt. one man shows at Secolo Gallery, Rome, 1948, Lou Cosyn Gallery, Brussels, 1950, Buchholz Gallery, Madrid, 1950, Betty Parsons Gallery, N.Y.C., 1954, 57, 58, 60, 63, Rose Fried Gallery, N.Y.C., 1964, Juana Mordo Gallery, Madrid, 1964, 67, Buchholz Gallery, Munich, 1965, Buchholz Gallery, Lisbon, 1967, French and Co., N.Y.C., 1970, Graham Gallery, N.Y.C., 1970, Ostermalm Gallery, Stockholm, Sweden, 1970; rep. in permanent collections at Albright-Knox Gallery (Buffalo), Art Inst. Chgo., Carnegie Inst. (Pitts.), Chase Manhattan Bank, Guggenheim Mus., New Sch., Whitney Mus., N.Y.U. Gallery (all N.Y.C.), Cuenca Mus. (Spain), Houston Mus. Fine Arts, Museo de Arte Contemporaneo (Madrid), Pa. Acad. Fine Arts, Toronto Art Gallery, Yale U. Gallery, Hopkins Art Center at Dartmouth Coll., Gotteborg Mus., Gothenburg, Sweden, La. Mus., Humlebaek, Denmark; mem. faculty New Sch., N.Y.C., 1962-65. Decorated Chevalier de l'ordre des arts et des lettres (French); recipient grant Graham Found. for Advanced Studies in Fine Arts. Home: 406 W 20th St New York City NY 10011 also Plaza del Trabuco No 1 Cuenca Spain also Nerja (Malaga) Spain

GUERRERO, LUIS M., banker; b. Santo Domingo, Dominican Republic, July 23, 1924; s. Luis M. and Maria (Gomez) G.; diploma comml. studies, Inst. Comml. Rivas, 1944, accountant diploma, 1952; D.Pharmacy, U. Autonoma de Santo Domingo, 1950. With govt. offices, Dominican Republic, 1944-53; asst. dir. econ. research dept. Central Bank Dominican Republic, 1963-68, econ. adviser, 1958-60; prof. accounting U. Autonoma de Santo Domingo, 1958-65; dir. econ. research dept. Central Bank Dominican Republic, 1960-63, sec. monetary bd., 1960-61, mgr., 1963-65, vice gov., 1965—; undersec. state for finance, 1963. Mem. Pharm. Assn. Roman Cath. Clubs: Executives, Santo Domingo Country, Naco Sports, Yacht (Santo Domingo). Home: 15 Calle 6 Ensanche Naco Santo Domingo Dominican Republic Office: Banco Central Pedro Henriques Urena Santo Domingo Dominican Republic

GUERRERO, MANUEL FLORES LEON, governor of Guam; b. Agana, Guam, Oct. 25, 1914; s. Jose L.G. Leon and Maria Luian (Flores) G.; ed in Guam; LL.D., West Virginia Inst. Tech., 1968; m. Delfina T. Tuncap, Oct. 18, 1934; childrenAlfredo, Lolita (Mrs. Charles J. Huxel, Jr.), Rudolpho, Evelyna (Mrs. Floyd Bonner), Teresita (Mrs. Paul DeDominico), Manuel Flores Leon Guerrero, Patricia. With Guam Govt., 1930-48, 50-, asst. sec. Guam, 1956-60, adminstrv. staff officer 6th Guam Legislature, 1960-61, sec. of Guam, 1961-63, gov. of Guam, 1963-. Bd. dirs., v.p. Guam Comml. Corp., 1946- 48, fiscal adviser, controller, 1948-49. Mem. Guam Congress Ho. of Assembly, 1948-50, chmn. finance com., 1948-50; mem. 1st Guam Legislature, 1950-52, chmn. rules and land transfer bd. coms., 1950-52. Mem. U.S. delegation 4th S. Pacific Conf., New Caledonia, 1963; U.S. observer S. Pacific Conf., 1962; alternate U.S. commnr. to S. Pacific Commn., 1961, permanent U.S. commissioner, 1964-. Capt., Guam Militia. Mason (Shriner). Home: PO Box 223 Agana Guam Office: Governor's Office Agana Guam

GUERRERO GOMEZ, PABLO E., consul gen. of Dominican Republic in Los Angeles. Address: 747 Lillian Way Los Angeles CA.*

GUERRI, WILLIAM G., lawyer; b. Higbee, Mo., Mar. 30, 1921; A.B., Central Meth. Coll., 1943; LL.B., Columbia, 1946. Admitted to N.Y. bar, 1946, Mo. bar, 1947; mem. firm Thompson, Mitchell, Douglas, Neill & Guerri, St. Louis. Mem. Am. Bar Assn., Am. Law Inst., Am. Judicature Soc., Mo. Bar, Bar Assn. Met. St. Louis, Phi Delta Phi. Mem. bd. editors Columbia Law Rev., 1945-46. Office: 705 Olive St St Louis MO 63101*

GUERTIN, ALFRED N., actuary; b. Hartford, Conn., Mar. 11, 1900; s. N. P. and Mary L. (Belanger) G.; B.S., Trinity Coll., 1922, M.S. (hon.). 1951; m. Rhoda R. Thomas, Jan. 28, 1933; childrenA. Thomas, Robert P. Mem. actuarial dept. Conn. Mut. Life Ins. Co., Hartford, 1922-29; chief asst. actuary N.J. Dept. Banking and Ins., Trenton, 1929-32, actuary, 1932-45; actuary Am. Life Conv., Chgo., 1945-65; actuarial cons., 1965-; pres. Scholarships for Ill. Residents, Inc., Chgo., 1951-65, hon. chmn., 1965- -; spl. adviser taxation life ins. cos., U.S. Treasury Dept., 1955. Chmn. spl. com. Nat. Assn. Ins. Commrs., recommendations resulted in widespread enactment of standard non-forfeiture and valuation laws, 1937-42. Bd. dirs. Sigma Nu, Inc. Ednl. Found. Recipient Elizur Wright Ins. Lit. award, 1945; named to Ins. Hall Fame at Ohio State U., 1967. Fellow Soc. Actuaries (bd. govs. 1960-63); asso. Inst. Actuaries of Gt. Britain, Casualty Actuarial Soc.; mem. Am. Risk and Ins. Assn., Am. Acad. Actuaries, Sigma Nu. Clubs: Metropolitan (N.Y.C.); Union League (Chgo.). Contbr. articles in actuarial and ins. publs. Home: 503 Lake Dr Princeton NJ 08540 Office: 2 Pennsylvania Plaza New York City NY 10001

GUESS, WALTER EUGENE, lawyer, state legislator; b. Tutwiler, Miss., Dec. 30, 1932; s. Thomas L. and Ralda (Bailey) G.; B.A. in Econs., Coll. William and Mary 1955; LL.B., U. Va., 1959; m. Carolyn Bailey Suber, July 14, 1956; children—Carl Thomas, John Bailey, Philip Mosby, Gretchan Jean. Asst. field solicitor, 1959-61; admitted to Alaska bar, 1961, since practiced in Anchorage; partner Ely, Guess, Rudd & Havelock, 1961—; mem. Alaska Ho. of Reps., 1965—, chmn. judiciary com., 1965-66, vice chmn. commerce com., 1965-66, mem. spl. house com. on Pub. Service Commn. legislation, 1965, House minority whip, 1967-68, chmn. Minority Caucus, 1967-68, chmn. Alaska State Legislative Council, 1969-71, vice chmn., 1971—, majority floor leader, 1969-70, chmn. local govt. com., 1969-70, spl. com. on monetary policy, 1969-70, speaker house, 1971—. Vice chmn. Gov.'s Adv. Com. on Econ. Devel., 1962-64; spl. asst. to Gov. Post Alaska Earthquake of 1964 as liaison to Anchorage Banking Community; mem. Alaska Export Expansion Council, Dept. Commerce, 1966—. Mem. Alaska devel. council Alaska Meth. U.; participant Eagleton Inst. Polit. Sci. Served to capt., arty. AUS, Army, 1963. Mem. Fed. (past pres.), Va., Alaska, Anchorage bar assns., Alaska (mem. Alaska Nippon Kai), Anchorage chambers commerce. Home: 3226 Upland Dr Anchorage AK 99501 Office: 1016 W 16th Av Anchorage AK 99501

GUEST, BARBARA, author, poet; b. Wilmington, N.C., Sept. 6, 1920; d. James Harvey and Ann (Hetzel) Pinson; A.B., U. Cal. at Berkeley, 1941; m. Lord Stephen Haden-Guest, Aug. 1948 (div. 1954); 1 dau., Hon. Hadley; m. 2d, Trumbull Higgins, Aug., 1954; 1 son, Jonathan van Lennep. Editorial asso. Art News, 1951-53. Yaddo fellow, 1958; recipient Longview award Longview Found., 1960. Author: (plays) The Ladies Choice, 1953, The Office, 1961, Port, 1965; (poems) The Location of Things, 1960, Poems, 1963, The Blue Stairs, 1968; (with B. H. Friedman) Robert Goodnough, Artist, 1962; (with Sheila Isham) I Ching: Poems and Lithographs, 1969. Address: 1148 Fifth Av New York City NY 10028

GUEST, LEON CECIL, Jr., financial exec.; b. Camden, N.J., June 20, 1914; s. Leon Cecil and May Ivens (Hall) G.; student U. Pa., evenings 1933-38; m. Martha Carolyn Downing, June 18, 1938; children-Barbara G. Adams, Susan G. Yancey, Stephen D. Adminstr. mortgages and real estate investments Provident Trust Co., Phila., 1935-42; auditor E.I. du Pont de Nemours & Co., 1942-43; with Sylvania Electric Products, Inc., 1943-69, successively auditor, mgr. internal auditing, divisional controller, controller, 1953-62, sr. v.p. adminstrn., 1962-69, also dir.; v.p. finance, sec. Huyck Corp., Stamford, Conn., 1969—, also dir.; v.p., controller Gen. Telephone & Electronics Corp., until 1962; dir. Arkwright Boston Mut. Ins. Co., MONY Fund. Mem. Financial Execs. Inst. (past pres.), Am. Mgmt. Assn. Clubs: Union League, Wee Burn Country. Home: Stony Brook Rd Darien CT 06820 Office: 733 Summer St Stamford CT 06901

GUEST, MAURICE MASON, educator, scientist; b. Fredonia, N.Y., July 30, 1906; s. Maurice S. and Daisy (Mason) G.; A.B., U. Mich., 1930; Ph.D., Columbia, 1941; m. Alice Rhoda Avery, Aug. 16, 1936; children—Avery Mason, John Andrew. Field asst. U.S. Dept. Agr. Bur. of Entomology, 1930-31; sci. tchr. Sherman (N.Y.) High Sch., 1931-36; instr. physiology Columbia, 1936-40, research asso., 1940-42; asso. prof. physiology Wayne U. Coll. Medicine, 1946-51; prof., chmn. dept. physiology U. Tex. Med. Br., Galveston, 1951—. Mem. Med. Adv. Bd. Film Prodn. Served to maj. USAAF, 1942-46. Mem. Am. Physiol. Soc., A.A.A.S., Am. Assn. U. Profs., Soc. for Exptl. Biology and Medicine, Internat. Hematol. Soc. Contbr. articles profl. jours. Asso. editor Microvascular Research. Home: 1409 Harbor View Dr Galveston TX 77550

GUEST, RAYMOND RICHARD, former U.S. ambassador; b. N.Y.C., Nov. 25, 1907; s. Frederic Edward and Amy (Phipps) G.; student McGill U., 1927-28, Yale, 1928-31; m. Elizabeth Polk, June 1935; childrenRaymond Richard, Elizabeth Stevens, Virginia; m. 2d, Caroline Murat, June 1960; childrenArchille Murat, Laetitia Amelia. Horse breeder, cattle farmer, King George, Va., 1931-; spl. asst. to sec. def., 1945-47; dir. Bessemer Securities, Inc., 1947; commr. Va. Game and Inland Fisheries, 1960-65; U.S. ambassador to Ireland, 1965-68. Chmn. fund raising drive Front Royal Hosp., 1950. Del. Nat. Democratic convs., 1940, 48, 60; mem. Va. Senate, 1947-53. Trustee Va. Mus. Fine Arts. Served to comdr. USNR, 1941-46. Decorated Legion of Merit, Bronze Star medal; Croix de Guerre; Order British Empire; Danish Def. medal; Norwegian Cross. Mason (32). Clubs: Racquet and Tennis, Jockey (N.Y.C.); Commonwealth (Richmond, Va.). Home: Powhatan Plantation King George VA 22485 Office: 245 Park Av New York City NY 10017

GUEST, ROBERT HENRY, educator; b. East Orange, N.J., May 3, 1916; s. James Henry and Charlotte (Newbould) G.; A.B. cum laude, Amherst Coll., 1939; M.A., Columbia, 1941, Ph.D., 1960; M.A. (hon.), Dartmouth Coll., 1963; m. Kate Hay, Dec. 18, 1942; childrenDavid Hartley, Gregory Alan, John Hay, Peter Staples. Dir. indsl. relations Lamerick Yarn Mills (Me.), 1941-42; sr. field examiner NLRB, 1946-47; mem. field research staff Labor and Mgmt. Center, Yale, 1948-52, asso. dir. research tech. project, 1952-60; partner Charles R. Walker Assos., mgmt. cons., New Haven, 1952-61; staff cons. Douglas Williams Assos., mgmt. cons., N.Y.C., 1959-61; prof. bus. adminstrn. Amos Tuck Sch., Dartmouth, 1960-63, prof. orgn. and adminstrn., 1963-66, prof. orgnl. behavior, 1966—. Mediator Conn. Labor-Mgmt. Com. Econ. Devel., 1960; mem. N.H. Gov.'s Mental Health Com., 1964; mem. N. H. Aeros. Commn., 1968; mem. mgmt. adv. panel NASA, 1969. Am. del. World Student Christian Conf., Amsterdam, 1939. Mem. exec. com. N.H. State Democratic Party. Served USNR, 1942-45. Recipient Book of Yr. award Nat. Orgn. Devel. Council, 1963. Fellow Am. Sociol. Soc.; mem. Soc. Applied Anthropology, Soc. History Tech., Alpha Delta Phi. Author: (with C. R. Walker) The Man on the Assembly Line, 1952; (with C. R. Walker and A. N. Turner) The Foreman on the Assembly Line, 1957; Organizational Change: The Effect of Successful Leadership 1962; (with others) Hospital Policy: Process and Action. Contbg. editor: Changing Forces in American Society. Home: 8 Barrett Rd Hanover NH 03755

GUEST, WILLIAM SELMAN, naval officer; b. Rome, Ga., July 3, 1913; s. William Sanford and Ann (Selman) G.; B.S., U.S. Naval Acad., 1935; m. Tina Louise Innes, Dec. 20, 1962; children—Robert Scott, Douglas Everette. Commd. ensign U.S. Navy, 1935, advanced through grades to rear adm., 1962; first carrier based aviator to sink Japanese ship, 1942; chief staff Pacific Carrier Task Force, 1944-45; chief staff Pacific Naval Air Force, 1961-62; comdr. Carrier Task Force (flagship Constellation) in Gulf Tonkin attacks, S. China Sea, 1964; dep. comdr. Naval Striking Forces So. Europe (NATO), Naples, Italy, 1965-67; comdr. Task Force 65 in recovery H bomb off Palomaros, Spain, 1966; comdr. Naval Air Res. Force, 1967-69; dep. mgr. manned spacecraft recovery Dept. Def., 1969-70; comdr. Task Force 140 Atlantic Indian Ocean Area Recovery Forces for Apollo 13; comdr. Mil. Sealift, Pacific, 1970—. Vice pres. San Francisco chpt. Nat. Def. Transp. Assn. Decorated Navy Cross, D.S.M., Legion of Merit, Air medal, Bronze Star. Clubs: N.Y. Yacht; Cuyamaca (San Diego); U.S. Propeller; California Golf (San Francisco); Athenian-Nile (Oakland). Contbr. articles profl. jours., travel mags. Home: Corpus Christi TX Office: Com MSC PAC Oakland CA 94625

GUETTEL, HENRY ARTHUR, producer; b. Kansas City, Mo., Jan. 8, 1928; s. Arthur Abraham and Sylva (Hershfield) G.; student Wharton Sch. of U. Pa., 1944-47, U. Kansas City, 1947-48; 1 dau. by previous marriage, Laurie C.; m. 2d, Mary Rodgers, Oct. 14, 1961; childrenMatthew Rodgers (dec.), Adam Arthur, Alexander Burton. Stage mgr. on Broadway and TV, also stock companies, 1949-60; gen. mgr. Royal Ballet Canada, 1953-54; producer nat. touring companies The Best Man, Sound of Music, Camelot, Oliver, then also gen. mgr. Music Theatre of Lincoln Center, touring companies The Merry Widow, Kismet, Carousel, Annie Get Your Gun, Show Boat, 1964-67; mng. dir., then v.p. Am. Nat. Opera Co., 1967-68; prodn. supr. theatre concerts Music Theatre, Lincoln Center, 1966-69; lectr. in field. Mem. theatrical adv. panel N.Y. State Council of Arts, 1965-70; cons. theatre to State U. N.Y., 1969-70; bd. dirs. Chelsea Theatre Center, N.Y.C., 1966—; bd. dirs. Performing Arts Repertory Theatre, N.Y.C., 1971—. Served with AUS, 1954-56. Mem. League N.Y. Theatres, Internat. Assn. Concert Mgrs. Address: 115 Central Park W New York City NY 10023

GUETZKOW, HAROLD, educator; b. Milw., Aug. 16, 1915; A.B. in Social Scis., U. Chgo., 1936; Ph.D. in Psychology, U. Mich., 1948; m. Lauris L. Steere, 1944; children—James, Gay, Daniel. Instr., then asst. prof. psychology, also coordinator ONR Conf. research project U. Mich., 1945-50; asso. prof., then prof. Grad. Sch. Indsl. Adminstrn., also dir. Social Sci. Lab., Carnegie Inst. Tech., 1950-57; prof. polit. sci., psychology and sociology Northwestern U., 1957-, Gordon Scott Fulcher prof. in decision-making, 1966—, co-dir. internat. relations program, 1957—, dir. Northwestern U./ARPA simulated internat. processes project, 1964—; distinguished vis. scholar Ednl. Testing Service, 1965; cons. to govt. and industry, 1948—. Fellow Center Advanced Study Behavioral Scis., 1956-57; master fellow econ. devel. and adminstrn. program Ford Found., 1958-63; vis. research scholar Carnegie Endowment for Internat. Peace, 1970-71. Author: (with others) Organizations, 1958; (with others) Simulation in International Relations: Developments for Research and Teaching, 1963; (with B.E. Collins) A Social Psychology of Group Processes for Decision-Making, 1964; (with Cleo H. Cherryholmes) Inter- Nation Simulation Kit, 1966; also articles, monographs. Editor: Simulation in Social Science, 1962; Groups, Leadership and Men, 2d edit., 1963. Address: 1834 Sheridan Rd Evanston IL 60201

GUFFEY, DONAL DEXTER, gas co. exec.; b. Kingston, Mo., Apr. 11, 1926; s. John William and Elsie M. (Palmer) G.; student Park Coll., 1944-46; B.S., Northwestern U., 1947; LL.B., U. Mo., 1951. Admitted to Mo. bar, 1951; asst. atty. gen. Mo., 1951-60; practice law, Kansas City, Mo., 1960-63; commr. Mo. Pub. Service Commn., 1963-68; atty., gen. counsel The Gas Service Co., Kansas City, Mo., 1968—, also v.p., dir. Served with USNR, 1944-46. Mem. Am., Mo. bar assns., Kansas City Lawyer's Assn., Am. Gas Assn., C. of C. Methodist. Club: Kansas City. Home: 4545 Wornall St Kansas City MO 64111 Office: Gas Service Co Scarritt Bldg Kansas City MO 64142

GUFFEY, JAMES ROGER, banker; b. Kingston, Mo., Sept. 11, 1929; s. John William and Elsie M. (Palmer) G.; B.S. in Bus. Adminstrn., U. Mo. at Columbia, 1952, LL.B., J.D., 1958; m. Sara C. Carmack, Feb. 7, 1959; children—James Michael, Sara Elizabeth. Admitted to Mo. bar, 1958; practice in Kansas City, 1958-68; partner firm Fallon, Guffey & Jenkins, 1965-68; v.p., gen. counsel, sec. Fed. Res. Bank Kansas City, 1968—; instr. bus. law U. Mo. at Columbia, 1956-57; instr. uniform comml. code Am. Inst. Banking, 1968-69. Served with AUS 1952-54. Mem. Am., Mo., Kansas City bar assns., Kansas City Lawyers Assn., Am. Judicature Soc., Phi Gamma Delta, Phi Delta Phi. Home: 5207 Sunset Dr Kansas City MO 64112 Office: 925 Grand Av Kansas City MO 64198

GUFFIN, GILBERT L., clergyman; b. nr. Marietta, Ga., Aug. 5, 1906; s. William Thomas and Nora (Eubanks) G.; A.B., Mercer U., 1930, D.D., 1955; B.D., Eastern Bapt. Theol. Sem., 1935; Th.M., 1938, Th.D., 1941; LL.D., Atlanta Law Sch., 1951; m. Lorene Parrish, Aug. 23, 1930; children—Gilbert Truett, Orville Thomas. Ordained to ministry Bapt. Ch., 1927; prin. Jr. High Sch., Mabelton, Ga., 1927-28, Elizabeth Jr. High Sch., Marietta, 1930-33; pastor field chs. nr. Marietta, 1927-33, First Ch., Merchantville, N.J., 1935-42, Jasper, Ala., 1942-47; dean Bapt. Seminar, Walker Coll., 1942-47; dir. extension div. Christian tng. Howard Coll. (now Samford U.), Birmingham, 1947-49, dean of religion, chmn. extension div., 1961-71; pres. Eastern Bapt. Theol. Sem., Phila., 1950-61, trustee, 1961—; pres. Eastern Bapt. Coll., 1952-61, trustee, 1961—; Layne lectr. New Orleans Bapt. Theol. Sem., 1958; mem. bd. lectrs. Freedom's Found. Bd. dirs. Ala. Bapt. Conv., 1942- 47, mem. exec. com. 1945-47; exec. bd. N.J. Bapt. Conv.; bd. dirs. Bham Council of Christian Edn., 1970—; bd. advisers Bible Land Tours Assn., 1956-57; dir. Pa. Theol. Sem. Found., Inc., 1955-61; dir., trustee Watchman-Examiner Found., N.Y.; trustee Ala. Temperance League (now Ala. Council Alcohol Problems), 1943-49, 61—; bd. mgrs. Council Missionary Coop., Am. Bapt. Conv., 1953-61, pres. sem. presidents and deans, 1958-59; mem. Guatemala-Ala. Partners of Alliance, 1969—. Recipient Freedoms Found. awards, 1960, 61. Mem. Greater Birmingham Pastors' Assn. (exec. com. 1962-63, 67—), Ala. Writer's Conclave, Omicron Delta Kappa. Mason, Rotarian (past pres.). Author: How To Run A Church, 1948; Called of God, 1951; Pastor and Church, 1955; El Pastor La Iglesia, 1955; The Gospel in Isaiah, 1968. Editor: What God Hath Wrought, 1960. Editor Walker Bapt. Herald 1944-47. Writer Monthly Bible Studies for Royal Service, 1964-68; co-author Helps for Study of Missionary Message of Bible; The Pentatouch, Joshus and Malichi. Contbr. to religious publs., Life and Work Ann. 1966-67, 67-68 (for Bapt. Sun. Sch. bd. So. Bapt. Conv.). Originator Howard Plan extensive edn.; condr. European tour, messenger Bapt. World Alliance, Atlanta, 1939, Copenhagen, 1947, Cleve., 1950, London, 1955, Rio de Jenario, 1960, Miami, 1965, Tokyo, 1970; tours in 45 countries; condr. Holy Land tour, 1955, 63, Around-the-World tour, 1970. Home: 2832 Vestavia Forest Pl Vestavia Hills Birmingham AL 35216

GUGELOT, PIET CORNELIS, educator; b. Bussum, The Netherlands, Feb. 24, 1918; s. Pieter Cornelis and Anna (Arnold) G.; Physics degree, Fed. Sch. Tech., Zurich, Switzerland, 1940, Ph.D., 1945; m. Ursula Federspiel, June 27, 1944; 1 son, Oliver C. Came to U.S., 1947, naturalized, 1954. Research asso. Phys. Inst., Fed. Sch. Tech., Zurich, 1940-47; research asso. Princeton, 1947-49, asst. prof., 1949-56; dir. Inst. for Nuclear Research, Amsterdam, The Netherlands, prof. nuclear physics U. Amsterdam, 1956-66; prof. physics U. Va., Charlottesville, 1966—; vis. prof. U. Wash., 1954; vis. scientist Oak Ridge Nat. Lab., 1959, U. Cal., Livermore, 1960; vis. prof. Stanford, 1963-64, Fermi Inst., U. Chgo., 1970. Dir. NASA Space-Radiation Lab., 1966; cons. NASA Langley Research Center, Los Alamos Sci. Lab. Fellow Am. Phys. Soc.; mem. Swiss, Netherlands, European phys. socs., A.A.A.S., Gesellschaft Ehemaliger Polytechn., Sigma Xi. Contbr. articles profl. jours. Office: Dept Physics U Va Charlottesville VA 22901

GUGGENHEIM, PEGGY, art collector and patron; b. N.Y.C., Aug. 26, 1898; d. Benjamin and Florette (Seligman) Guggenheim; m. Lawrence Vail, Mar. 15, 1923; children—Sindbad, Pegeen (Mrs. Rumney); m. 2d, Max Ernst, Dec. 30, 1941. Directed, financed gallery Guggenheim Jeune, London, Eng., 1938-39, Art of This Century, N.Y.C., 1943-47, Mus. Palazzo Venier dei Leoni, Venice, Italy, 1951-; exhbns. of pvt. collection through Europe, 1951-. Named hon. citizen of Venice, 1962. Author: Out of This Century, 1946; Una Collezionista Ricorda, 1956; Confessions of An Art Addict, 1960; also articles, introductions. Address: Palazzo Venier dei Leoni 701 San Gregorio Venice Italy

GUGGENHEIM, RICHARD E., state govt. ofcl.; b. Cin., Jan. 5, 1913; s. Eli F. and Eva (Stransky) G.; A.B., U. Mich., 1934; LL.B., Harvard, 1937; m. Carol J. Rice, Sept. 21, 1942 (dec. 1958); children—Jane, Polly, Richard R.; m. 2d, Alice W. Joseph, Feb. 27, 1967. Admitted to Ohio bar, 1937, admitted to Supreme Court of U.S., 1942; with Dept. Justice, 1940-42, 46-50, atty. civil and anti trust div., 1946-50; dep. gen. counsel ESA, 1950-51; with U.S. Shoe Corp., 1951-71, v.p., 1960-71, sec., 1964-71; dir. FHLB, Cin., 1965-70; dir. Dept. Liquor Control, State of Ohio, 1971—. Mem. Mayor Cin. Friendly Relations Com., 1958-59; chmn. Ohio Civil Rights Commn., 1959-62; mem. Ohio Constl. Rev. Commn., 1970—. Chmn. platform com. Ohio Democratic Party, 1966, 68-70. Served maj. AUS, 1942-46. Mem. Am., Ohio, Cin. bar assns., Miami Soc., Pub. Health Fedn. Jewish religion. Home: 2470 Grandin Rd Cincinnati OH 45208 Office: 33 N 3d St Columbus OH 43215

GUGGENHEIMER, RANDOLPH, lawyer; b. N.Y.C., Nov. 14, 1907; s. Charles S. and Minna (Schafer) G.; B.A., Yale, 1928; LL.B., Harvard, 1931; m. Elinor S. Coleman, June 2, 1932; childrenCharles S. II, Randolph C. Admitted to N.Y. bar, 1932; partner Guggenheimer & Untermyer, N.Y.C., 1936-; dir. Ideax Corp., Tenn. Corp., Chester Cable Corp., Cinema V, Ltd., Cinema V Distbg., Ltd. Chmn. bd. Mills Coll. of Edn.; dir. Hosp. for Joint Diseases, and Andrew Freedman Home, 1938—. Served from 1st lt. to maj. USAAF, 1942-45; ETO. Mem. Am., N.Y. State bar assns., N.Y. County Lawyers Assn., Assn. Bar City New York. Clubs: Bankers of America, Manhattan Chess (dir.), Yale (N.Y.C.); Century Country (Purchase, New York). Home: 1095 Park Av New York City NY 10028 Office: 80 Pine St New York City NY 10005

GUGGENHIME, RICHARD ELLAS, lawyer; b. San Francisco, Sept. 19, 1908; s. David J. and Elsa (Triest) G.; A.B., Stanford, 1929; LL.B., Harvard, 1932; m. Charlotte M. Johnson, Mar. 2, 1939; children—Richard J., David J. Admitted to Cal. bar, 1932; asso. Heller, Ehrman, White & McAuliffe, San Francisco, 1932-33, 34-39, partner, 1939-41, 46—; pres. Union Sugar Co., F-K Land Co.; dir. Wells Fargo Bank, N.A., Fireman's Fund Ins. Corp., Consol. Foods Corp. Pres. San Francisco Community Chest, 1952; bd. dirs. San Francisco Symphony Assn.; pres. Rosenberg Found., 1954-57; trustee Stanford U., 1958—, pres. bd. trustees, 1964-67. Served from lt. (j.g.) to comdr., USNR, 1941-45. Decorated Bronze Star medal with gold star. Mem. Am., San Francisco bar assns., Phi Beta Kappa. Bd. editors Harvard Law Rev., 1932. Home: 65 Raycliff Terrace San Francisco CA 94115 Office: 44 Montgomery St San Francisco CA 94104

GUGLER, ERIC, architect; student Armour Inst. Tech. and Art. Inst. Chgo.; A.B., Columbia, 1911; McKim fellow, Am. Acad. in Rome, 1911-14. Architectural works include Exec. Office Bldg. of The White House Washington, Oval Room. Office of the Pres. of U.S., cabinet room, The White House Piano for the East Room, and Adams inscription for dining room; Forman Schools, Litchfield, Conn.; meml. to Harvey Firestone, Akron, O., to Drs. William and Charles Mayo, Rochester, Minn.; Anzio- Nettuno Meml., Italy, Am. Battle Monuments Commn.; bldgs. Wabash Coll., Crawfordsville, Ind.; mural decoration, chronological tables, historical geography (in assn. with historians and other mural painters), The Ednl. Bldg., Capitol Park, Harrisburg, Pa.; houses for Katharine Cornell, others; memls. to Waldo Hutchins, Theodore Roosevelt, Franklin D. Roosevelt, Anna Eleanor Roosevelt. Recipient 1st prize Chgo. War Meml., 1929. Fellow A.I.A.; mem. N.A.D., Nat. Inst. Arts and Letters, Archtl. League N.Y. Club: Century Assn. (N.Y.C.). Home: Box 156 Palisades NY 10964 Office: 101 Park Av New York City NY 10017

GUIDO, BEATRIZ, author; b. Rosaria, Argentina. Dec. 13, 1924; d. Angel and Berta (Eirin) Guido; student Faculty Philosophy and Lit., U. Buenos Aires; pupil of B. Croce and Guido di Ruggiero, Rome, Italy, of Gabriel Marcel, The Sorbonne, Paris, France; m. Leopoldo Torre Nilsson, June 29, 1959. Author: The Angel's House (1st prize EMECE editors Buenos Aires), 1954; La Caida (trans. to film); Fin de Fiesta (trans. to film); La Mano en la Trampa (trans. to film; 1st prize Festival Cinematographique, Cannes, France), 1961; End of the Day; Escandalos y Soledades, 1971. Address: Av Quintana 245 PBA Buenos Aires Argentina

GUIDOTTI, GUIDO, educator, biochemist; b. Florence, Italy, Nov. 3, 1933; s. Mario and Jiun (Casao) G.; came to U.S., 1951, naturalized, 1959; M.D., Washington U., St. Louis, 1957; Ph.D., Rockefeller U., 1963; M.S. (hon.), Harvard. 1968; m. Judith Ann Sanders, May 28, 1967; 1 son, Guido. Intern, then asst. resident Barnes Hosp., St. Louis, 1957-59; mem. faculty Harvard, 1963—, prof. biochemistry, 1969—. Mem. Am. Soc. Biol. Chemists, A.A.A.S., Harvey Soc., Sigma Xi. Home: 67 Sparks St Cambridge MA 02138

GUILBERT, CHARLES MORTIMER, clergyman; b. Parral, Mexico, Nov. 6, 1908; s. Henry Mortimer and Kitty Belle (Brown) G.; Ph.B., U. Chgo., 1934; S.T.B. magna cum laude, Seabury- Western Theol. Sem., 1936, S.T.D. honoris causa, 1959; m. Elizabeth Houston Lay, June 6, 1936; childrenElizabeth (Mrs. Edward Jennings), Thomas G. P. Ordained to ministry Protestant Episcopal Ch., 1936;

vicar, Ashland, Ore., 1937-40, Coquille with Bandon, Ore., 1940-43; dean St. Stephen's Cathedral, Portland, Ore., 1943-49; dir. promotion and Christian edn. Diocese Cal., San Francisco, 1949-56; rector St. Clement's Ch., Berkeley, Cal., 1957-61; sec. Nat. Council P.E. Church, New York, 1961-62; sec. Exec. Council, P. E. Church, N.Y.C., 1962-7O; sec. Gen. Conv., 1964—, registrar historiographer, 1967—, sec.-treas., exec. officer, 1971—. Mem. standing com. P.E. Diocese Oregon, 1943- 49, Cal., 1957-61, diocesan counsel, Ore., 1943-49, Cal., 1957-59; examining chaplain to bishops of Ore. and Cal. 1942-49, 50-53, sec. provincial synod and council Province Pacific, 1953-61; dep. to gen. conv. Episcopal Ch., 1946, 49, 52, 55, 58, 61, mem. nat. council, 1958- 61. Trustee St. Helen's Hall, Portland, 1943-49, St. Margaret's House, Berkeley, 1958-61. Named hon. canon Grace Cathedral, San Francisco. Mem. Ch. Hist. Soc. Custodian, Standard Book of Common Prayer; mem., sec. Standing Liturgical Commn., 1963-. Home: 455 E 57th St New York City NY 10022 Office: 815 2d Av New York City NY 10017

GUILD, DOUGLAS SCOTT, telephone co. exec.; b. Honolulu, July 28, 1907; s. John and Mary (Knox) G.; student Armour Inst. Tech., 1928-29; m. Janet Carter, Aug. 15, 1936; 1 son, Robert C. With Hawaiian Telephone Co., 1922-, v.p. operations, 1950-62, pres., 1962—, also dir.; dir. Bank Hawaii, Sheraton Hawaii Corp., First Ins. Co. Hawaii, Ltd., Dillingham Corp., Hawaiian Western Steel Ltd. Mem. Gov.'s Adv. Com. on Sci. and Tech. Bd. dirs. Queen's Med. Center; mem. bus. adv. council Coll. Bus. Adminstrn., U. Hawaii. bd. govs. Hawaii Employers Council. Mem. Armed Forces Communications and Electronics Assn., Assn. U.S. Army, Air Force Assn. (Oahu chpt.), Navy League U.S. Home: 140 Wailupe Circle Honolulu HI 96821 Office: PO Box 2200 Honolulu HI 96805

GUILD, HENRY RICE, lawyer; b. Boston, Feb. 14, 1896; s. Samuel Eliot and Jessie (Motley) G.; student Noble and Greenough Sch., Delham, Mass., 1902-13; A.B., Harvard, 1917, LL.B., 1922; m. Martha Pintard Bayard, Oct. 1, 1927 (dec. Dec. 1970); children—Henry R., Sheila, Bayard. Partner law firm Herrick, Smith, Donald, Farley & Ketchum, Boston; mem. exec. com., dir. Boston Edison Co.; trustee Public Reservations, Boston Personal Property Trust, Century Shares trust; dir. Tampa Elec. Co.; dir., mem. exec. com. Fiduciary Trust Co. Served as ensign and lt. (j.g.), chief g.m., USN, World War I. Vice pres., trustee Mass. Gen. Hosp. 1939—; gen. chmn. Greater Boston Community Fund Campaign, 1941, chmn. exec. com., 1944-46; pres. Greater Boston Community Council Social Agys., 1942-44; chmn. adv. council Mass. Dept. Pub. Welfare, 1945-46. Mem. Boston Bar Assn. (council), Mass. Bar Assn., Audubon Soc. (dir.). Republican. Unitarian. Clubs: Boston Harvard; Longwood Cricket (pres. 1932-35); New England Lawn Tennis Assn. (pres. 1936- 37); Commercial of Boston; Tavern; Dedham Country and Polo; Country (Brookline, Mass.). Home: 1150 South St Needham MA 02192 Office: 294 Washington St Boston MA 02108 ☆

GUILD, LURELLE VAN ARSDAL, indsl. designer; b. N.Y.C., Aug. 19, 1898; s. Thomas Lurelle and Alice Taylor (Gumble) G.; student King Sch., Stamford, Conn., 1916; Bachelor of Painting, Syracuse Sch. Fine Arts, 1920; m. A. Louise Eden, Nov. 31, 1929; 1 dau., Cynthia Eden. Actor, 1914-17; magazine and advt. illustrator, indsl. designer, N.Y.C., 1927—; pres., owner Lurelle Guild Assos., N.Y.C., Dale Decorators, Milestone Village Museum, Noroton, Conn. (restoration complete town circa 1780). Adviser Nat. Housing Authority; dir. Regional Planning Commn., N.Y.C. of Fairfield Co., chmn. Darien Town and Planning Commn. Works exhibited in Metropolitan Mus., Mus. Modern Art, Los Angeles Mus., etc. Recipient Art Dirs. Club medal for paintings and drawings in color done through J. Walter Thompson Advt. Agency, 1924; Arents medal Syracuse U., 1941, Jordan Marsh award, Modern Plastics award, Fashion Acad. award for Household products (Westinghouse), 1951. Fellow Am. Soc. Indsl. Designers; mem. Am. Inst. Decorators, Art Dirs. Club, Soc. Indsl. Designers, Delta Kappa Epsilon. Republican. Presbyn. Club: Am. Dutch Treat. Author: Geography of American Antiques, 1929; New Geography of American Antiques, 1947; Bluebook of Interior Decoration, 1938; A Course in Period Furniture, 1934. Editor: Pictorial Review, Delineator. Works published in Ladies Home Journal, House and Garden, House Beautiful, Better Homes and Gardens. Designer: Interior of Alcoa Steamships; N.Y., N.H. & H. R.R. cars, locomotives, Alcoa Museum, Westinghouse small appliances. Home: Long Neck Point Rd Darien CT 06820 also Tanglewood Farm Smith's Parish Bermuda Office: 1844 Boston Post Rd Darien CT

GUILD, NELSON PRESCOTT, coll. pres.; b. Keene, N.H., Nov. 20, 1928; s. Louis F. and Hope (Mason) G.; B.A., U. N.H., 1953; M.A., Pa. State U., 1955, Ph.D., 1958; m. Margaret Adele Graf, June 24, 1950; children—Douglas, Matthew. Asst. prof. govt. Hamilton Coll., Clinton, N.Y., 1958-64, asso. prof., 1964-66; dean Frostburg (Md.) State Coll., 1966-69, pres., 1969—. Served with USAF, 1946-49. Mem. Am. Polit. Sci. Assn., Am. Assn. U. Profs. Author: Introduction to Politics, Essays and Readings (with Kenneth T. Palmer), 1968. Home: 28 Teaberry Lane Frostburg MD 21532

GUILD, WALTER RUFUS, educator; b. Ann Arbor, Mich., Oct. 25, 1923; s. Stacy Rufus and Florence Ruth (White) G.; student Swarthmore Coll., 1941-43, N.Y. U., 1943-44; B.S., U. Tex., 1948, M.A., 1949; Ph.D., Yale, 1951; m. Ellen Christine Sangster, Feb. 22, 1946; 1 son, Thomas D. Instr. physics Yale, 1951-54, asst. prof. biophysics, 1954-60, radiation safety officer 1955-60; asso. prof. biochemistry Duke, 1960-65, prof., 1965—. Mem. internat. fellowship rev. com. NIH Fogarty Internat. Center, 1968-72. Served from pvt. to 1st lt. USAAF, 1943-46. A.E.C. predoctoral fellow, 1950-51; NIH sr. postdoctoral fellow, 1970-71. Mem. Am. Soc. Biol. Chemists, Biophys. Soc., Radiation Research Soc., Genetics Soc. Am., A.A.A.S., Am. Soc. Microbiology, Fedn. Am. Scientists, Sigma Xi. Editorial bd. Radiation Research, 1964-67. Contbr. articles to sci. jours. Home: 2625 McDowell St Durham NC 27705

GUILDS, JOHN CALDWELL, Jr., educator; b. Columbia, S.C., Feb. 27, 1924; s. John Caldwell and Lucille (Folk) G.; A.B., Wofford Coll., 1947; A.M., Duke, 1949, Ph.D., 1954; m. Carolee Green Heriot, July 3, 1947; children—Carolee Heriot, Reba Lucille, John Caldwell III. Instr., Duke, 1949-52; asst. prof Clemson U., 1952-54; asso. prof., E. Central State Coll. 1954-56; mem. faculty Tex. Tech. U., Lubbock, 1956-64, prof. English, chmn. dept., 1962-64; prof. English, head dept. U. S.C., Columbia, 1964-70, vice provost, 1970—; Smith-Mundt prof. Am. lit. U. Damascus, 1959-60. Pres. S. Atlantic Assn. Depts. English, 1971. Served with AUS, 1943-46; ETO. Decorated Purple Heart, Bronze Star. Mem. Modern Lang. Assn. Am., Modern Humanities Research Assn., Internat. Assn. U. Profs. English. Gen. editor: The Centennial Edition of the Writings of William Gilmore Simms. Contbr. profl. jours. Home: 1321 Milford Rd Columbia SC 29206

GUILER, LEONARD KENT, merchandising exec.; b. Pitts., Mar. 23, 1913; s. Leonard Kent and Lucy (Hechelman) G.; grad. Shady Side Acad., 1931; B.A., Amherst Coll., 1935; student Cornell U., 1933, 35; m. Ruth Dauchy, June 2, 1944; childrenJeffery Kent, Peter Scott. Sr. staff accountant Price Waterhouse & Co., C.P.A.'s, N.Y.C., 1935-43; auditor S. H. Kress & Co., N.Y.C., 1943-52, asst. treas., 1953-57, treas., 1958-61, v.p., finance, treas., 1961-65; v.p., mem. bd. govs. Genesco, Inc., 1965-. Clubs: Manhattan, Amherst (chmn.), University Glee (dir.) (N.Y.C.). Home: 52 E 91st St New York City NY 10028 Office: 730 Fifth Av New York City NY 10019

GUILES, ROGER EARL, coll. pres.; b. LaValle, Wis., Dec. 24, 1907; s. Earl and Wilhelmina (Roloff) G.; B.E., Wis. State Coll., 1930; Ph.M., U. Wis., 1935, Ph.D., 1949; m. M. Margaret Washburn, June 12, 1934; childrenJanet Lou (Mrs. John Hubbell), Jon Roger. Tchr. math., physics, Cazenovia, Wis., 1930-31, prin. high sch., 1931-34; prin. Richland County Normal Sch., 1934-37; dir. curriculum pub. schs., Superior, Wis., 1937-42; dean Wis. State Coll., Platteville, 1942-59; pres. Wis. State U., Oshkosh, 1959—. Mem. White House Commn. Children and Youth, 1954-55. Mem. N.E.A., Nat. Soc. Study Edn., Wis. Research Assn. (pres.), Wis. Congress Parents and Tchrs. (past v.p.), N. Central Assn. Colls. and Secondary Schs., Phi Kappa Delta. Conglist. Mason, Kiwanian. Contbr. articles ednl. jours. Home: 842 Algoma Blvd Oshkosh WI 54901

GUILFORD, JOY PAUL, psychologist; b. Marquette, Neb., Mar. 7, 1897; s. Edwin Augustus and Arvilla (Monroe) G.; A.B., U. Neb., 1922, A.M., 1924; Ph.D., Cornell, 1927; LL.D. (hon.), U. Neb., 1952; Sc.D., U. So. Cal., 1962; m. Ruth S. Burke, Sept. 8, 1927; 1 dau., Joan S. Instr. psychology U. Ill., 1926-27; asst. prof. psychology U. Kan., 1927-28; asso. prof., prof. psychology U. Neb., 1928-4O, dir. Bur. Instructional Research, 1938-4O; prof. psychology U. So. Cal., 1940-67, now prof. emeritus. Served to col. USAAF 1942-45. Decorated Legion of Merit. Fellow A.A.A.S., Am. Psychol. Assn. (pres., 1949-50); mem. Psychometric Soc. (pres. 1937-38), Nat. Acad. Scis., Soc. Exptl. Psychologists, Midwestern (pres., 1939-40), Western (pres., 1946-47), So. Cal., Cal. State psychol. assns., Soc. Multivariate Exptl. Psychologists, Cal. Color Soc. (pres. 1948-49), Blue Key, Phi Beta Kappa, Sigma Xi, Phi Sigma, Psi Chi, Phi Delta Kappa, Pi Kappa Alpha, Phi Kappa Phi. Democrat. Author: Psychometric Methods, 1936, 1954; others. Home: PO Box 1288 Beverly Hills CA 90213 Office: U So Cal Los Angeles CA 90007 ☆

GUILFORD, RICHARD GRISWOLD, educator; b. Mpls., Oct. 18, 1909; s. Paul Willis and Ella (Griswold) G.; B.A., Carleton Coll., 1932, M.A. in Social Work, U. Chgo., 1939, Ph.D., 1960; m. Dorothy Cramer, Aug. 23, 1941; children—Mary Ellen, Dale, William, Barbara. Social worker Ill. Children's Home and Aid Soc., Chgo., 1938-40; field rep. Minn. Div. Social Welfare, 1940-42; prof. Sch. Social Work U. Minn., 1946-55, 71—; dir. Grad. Sch. Social Work, U. Neb., 1955-71. Served to lt. comdr. USNR, 1942-46; lt. comdr. Res. ret. Mem. Nat. Assn. Social Workers, Council Social Work Edn., Am. Assn. U. Profs., Am. Pub. Welfare Assn. Author book and document revs., articles. Home: 4024 Queen Av S Minneapolis MN 55410

GUILFOYLE, GEORGE H., bishop; b. N.Y.C., Nov. 13, 1913; s. James J. and Johanna (McGrath) G.; A.B., Georgetown U., 1935; student St. Joseph's Sem., 1939-44; J.D., Fordham U., 1939; student N.Y. Univ. School Banking, 1945; LL.M., Columbia, 1946; LL.D., St. Francis College, 1958, Manhattan Coll., 1962, Iona Coll., 1966; Lit.D., St. Joseph's Coll., Phila., 1968; Ordained priest Roman Cath. Ch., 1944, named papal chamberlain, 1955, domestic prelate, 1958; admitted to N.Y. bar, 1940, asst. St. Patrick's Cathedral, 1944-45, St. Andrew's Ch., 1944-46; asst. chancellor, also asst. St. Elizabeth's Ch., N.Y.C., 1946-47; with Catholic Charities, N.Y.C., 1947-66, exec. dir., 1956-66; episcopal vicar Richmond County (S.I.), also pastor St. Peter's Ch., 1966-68; bishop of Camden, N.J., 1968-. Asso. moderator coordinating com. Cath. Lay Orgns. Archdiocese N.Y., 1954-57; archdiocesan consultor, 1960-68; nat. spiritual dir. Soc. St. Vincent de Paul, 1966-. Pres. Nat. Conf. Cath. Charities, 1959-61, bd. dirs., 1959-67; mem. N.Y.C. Adv. Bd. Pub. Welfare, 1960-66; mem. Archdiocesan Commn. for Community Planning, 1964- 68. Bd. dirs. Nat. Shrine Immaculate Conception; trustee Seton Hall U. Recipient John Carroll award Georgetown U., 1963; Knight grand cross Equestrian Order Holy Sepulchre Jerusalem. Home: 455 Madison Av New York City NY 10022 Office: 122 E 22d St New York City NY 10010

GUILFOYLE, JOHN W., bus. exec.; b. 1921; student Wilson Jr. Coll., Northwestern U.; m. With Internat. Tel. & Tel. Corp., 1951-, v.p. operations subsidiary Fed. Elec. Corp., then pres., 1959-64, pres. subsidiary Am. Cable & Radio Corp., 1964, v.p. parent co., 1964-, v.p., group exec. Far East and Pacific, 1966-. Served with USAAF, World War II. Address: 621 Industrial Av Paramus NJ 07653 *

GUILFOYLE, MERLIN JOSEPH, bishop; b. San Francisco, July 15, 1908; s. John Joseph and Teresa (Bassity) G.; student St. Joseph's Coll., Mountain View, Cal., 1925-27, St. Patrick's Sem., Menlo Park, Cal., 1927-33; Dr. Canon Law, Cath. U., 1937. Ordained Priest Roman Cath. Ch., 1933, designated monsignor, Domestic Prelate, by Pope Pius XI, 1949, consecrated aux. bishop, San Francisco, 1950; pastor Mission Dolores Basilica, 1950-70; mil. vicar Armed Forces, 1948; bishop of Stockton, Cal., 1970—. Home: 205 E Harding St Stockton CA 95204 Office: 1105 N Lincoln St Stockton CA 95204

GUILLARD, GEORGE WILLIAM, former bank exec.; b. Paterson, N.J., Aug. 21, 1903; s. Louis and Marie (deRichaud) G.; student Trinity Coll., 1921-23; m. Gertrude Mortensen, Nov. 10, 1934. Asst. cashier Hartford Nat. Bank & Trust Co. (Conn.), 1923-37, cashier. 1937-42, v.p., cashier, 1942-45, v.p. charge operations, 1945-56, sr. v.p., 1956-60, exec. v.p., dir., then vice chmn., now ret. Treas., director Conn. Higher Edn. Assistance Corp. Corporator Hartford Hosp., Hartford YMCA, Mt. Sinai Hosp., St. Francis Hosp. Mem. Hartford C. of C., Wetherfield Bus. and Civic Assn., Newcomen Soc. N. Am., Trinity Coll. Alumni Assn. (past nat. treas.). Conglist. Mason (32 Shriner). Home: 854 Ridge Rd Wethersfield CT 06109 Office: 777 Main St Hartford CT 06103

GUILLE, FRANCES VERNOR, educator; b. Atlanta, Mar. 1, 1908; d. B. Frank and Margaret Davis (Baker) Guille; student Muskingum Coll., 1926-27; B.A., Coll. of Wooster, 1930; M.A., Western Res. U., 1936; postgrad. Middlebury Lang. Sch., summers 1934, 38, Ohio State U., summer 1940; Docteur de l'Université, U. Paris, 1949. Tchr., Fairview High Sch., Cleve., 1930-37; tchr. French, Coll. of Wooster, O., 1937—, prof., 1955—, chmn. dept. French, 1969—, acting dean women, 1944-46; instr. math. and geopolitics Naval Flight Prep. Sch., 1943-44; tchr. Central Mich. Coll., summer 1950, Western Res. U., summer 1955; dir. Wooster-in-Paris Summer Program, 1951-59, Crossroads-Africa group to Sénégal, summer 1960, Corr. Bur. for Students of French, 1953—. Recipient Research grants Gt. Lakes Coll. Assn., 1967, 68; decorated chevalier des Palmes Académiques; French Govt. scholar, 1947-49, Vis. scholar Radcliffe Coll., 1961-62. Mem. Am. Assn. Tchrs. French (past pres. Ohio chpt.), Modern Lang. Assn., Am. Assn. U. Women (past pres. local chpt.), Midwest, Ohio modern lang. assns., Am. Council on Teaching Fgn. Langs., Assn. Depts. Fgn. Lang., Phi Beta Kappa, Phi Sigma Iota, Delta Sigma Rho. Presbyn. Author: François-Victor Hugo et son Oeuvre, 1950; (with Bonthius, Davis, Drushal and Spencer) Independent Study Programs in the U.S., 1957. Editor: Le Journal d'Adèle Hugo, Vol. I, 1968, Vol. II, 1971. Asso. editor Wooster Alumni Mag., 1941-44. Home: 1508 Overlook Dr Wooster OH 44691

GUILLEMIN, ERNEST ADOLPH, prof. engring; b. Milwaukee, Wis., May 8, 1898; s. Victor and Erna (Jacobsen) G.; B.S., U. of Wis., 1922; S.M., Mass. Inst. Tech., 1924; Ph.D., U. of Munich, 1926; m. Mary Lanier Moran, May 29, 1929 1 dau., Mary Grace. Asst. in elec. engring., Mass. Inst. Tech., 1922-24, instr., 1926-28, asst. prof., 1928-36, asso. prof., 1936-44, prof., 1944-60; Webster prof. of electrical engring., 1960-; Saltonstall traveling fellow 1924-26; cons. Radiation Lab., 1940-44, Raytheon Mfg. Co., 1946—. Edgerton, Germeshausen & Greer, Inc., 1965—; mem. adv. bd. Hycon Eastern, Cambridge. Awarded President's Certificate of Merit 1948; medal of honor Inst. Radio Engrs., 1961. Fellow Inst. Radio Engrs., Am. Inst. Elec. Engrs., Am. Acad. Arts, Scis., Royal Society Arts (London); mem. Eta Kappa Nu, Tau Beta Pi, Sigma Xi. Mason. Author: Communication Networks, Vols. I and II, 1931 and 1935; Mathematics of Circuit Analysis, 1949; Introductory Circuit Theory, 1953; Synthesis of Passive Networks, 1957; Linear Physical Systems, 1963; collaborator; Electric Circuits, 1940. Applied Electronics, 1943. Home: 41 Woodlawn Av Wellesley Hills MA 02182 Office: Mass Inst Tech Cambridge MA 02138

GUILLEMIN, ROGER, educator, physiologist; b. Dijon, France, Jan. 11, 1924; s. Raymond and Blanche (Rigollot) G.; B.A., U. Dijon, 1941, B.Sc., 1942; M.D., Faculty of Medicine, Lyons, France, 1949; Ph.D., U. Montreal, 1953; m. Lucienne Jeanne Billard, Mar. 22, 1952; children-Chantal Claude Marie, Francois Jean Marie, Claire Marguerite Marie, Helene Marie, Elizabeth Marie, Cecile Marie. Came to U.S., 1953, naturalized, 1965. Intern, resident univs. hosps., Dijon, 1949-51; asso. dir., asst. prof. Inst. Exptl. Medicine and Surgery, U. Montreal, 1951-53; asso. dir. dept. exptl. endocrinology Coll. de France, Paris, 1960-63; mem. faculty Baylor U. Coll. Medicine, 1953—, adj. prof. physiology, 1970—; resident fellow Salk Inst., 1970—. Mem. Am. Physiol. Soc., Endocrine Soc. (council), Soc. Exptl. Biology and Medicine, A.A.A.S., Internat. Brain Research Orgn., Internat. Soc. Research Biology Reprodn., Soc. Neuro scis. Home: 7316 Encelia Dr La Jolla CA 92037 Office: Salk Inst Box 1809 San Diego CA 92112

GUILLERMIN, JOHN, dir. The Blue Max, Rapture, The Waltz of the Toreadors, Guns at Batasi, P.J., House of Cards, The Bridge at Remagen. Address: care GAC 9025 Wilshire Blvd Beverly Hills CA 90211*

GUILLERY, RAINER WALTER, educator; b. Greifswald, Germany, Aug. 28, 1929; s. Hermann and Eva (Hackel) G.; B.Sc. in Anatomy, U. Coll., London, Eng., 1951; Ph.D., 1954; m. Margot Cunningham Pepper, Dec. 21, 1954; children—Peter, Edward, Philip, Jane. Came to U.S., 1964. Asst. lectr. Univ. Coll., London, Eng., 1954-57, lectr., 1957-63, reader, 1963-64; asso. prof. U. Wis. at Madison, 1964-68, prof. anatomy, 1968—. Mem. Asm. Assn. Anatomists, Soc. for Neurosci., Am. Soc. Cell Biology, Anatom. Soc. Gt. Britain. Research central nervous system, synapses, degeneration, visual pathways. Home: 225 Princeton Av Madison WI 63705

GUILMARTIN, JAMES L., lawyer; b. Boston, Nov. 3, 1917; A.B., Harvard 1941; J.D., St. Johns U., 1945; children—Kenneth Kells, Susan Liane (dec. 1956), Nancy Leydon, Laurie, James. Admitted to N. Y. bar, 1945, to Fla. bar, 1951; practiced in Miami; former U.S. atty. So. Dist. Fla.; mem. Guilmartin, Gaine & Gaine. Mem. Fla. Bar, Dade County, Fed., Am. bar assns., Assn. Bar City N.Y., Am. Judicature Soc., Phi Delta Phi. Home: 5615 Orduna Dr Coral Gables FL 33146 Office: Dade Fed Bldg Miami FL 33131

GUIN, JUNIUS FOY, Jr., lawyer; b. Russellville, Ala., Feb. 2, 1924; s. Junius Foy and Ruby (Pace) G.; student Ga. Inst. Tech., 1940-41; J.D., U. Ala., 1947; LL.D., Magic Valley Christian Coll., 1963; m. Dorace Jean Caldwell, July 18, 1945; children—Janet Elizabeth, Judith Ann, Junius Foy III, David Jonathan. Admitted to Ala. bar, 1948, since practiced in Russellville; sr. partner Guin, Guin, Bouldin & Porch, 1948—; commr. Ala. Bar, 1965—, 2d v.p., 1969-70. Pres. Abstract Trust Co., Inc.; sec. Iuka TV Cable Co., Inc. Haleyville TV Cable Co., Inc.; dir., gen. counsel First Nat. Bank of Russellville, Franklin Fed. Savs. & Loan Assn. of Russellville. Chmn. Russellville City Planning Com., 1954-57. Republican county chmn., 1954-58; candidate for U.S. Senator from Ala., 1954. Served to 1st lt., inf., AUS, 1943-46. Mem. Am. Radio Relay League, Assn. Ins. Attys., Am. Counsel Assn., Am. (mem. com. on regional meetings), Ala. (com. chmn.), Franklin County bar assns., Ala. Law Inst. (bd. dirs. 1969—), Am. Trial Lawyers Assn., World Peace Through Law Center, Ala. Def. Lawyers Assn., Ala. Plaintiffs Lawyers Assn., Farrah Law Soc., Phi Beta Kappa, Delta Chi. Mem. Ch. of Christ (elder). Rotarian. Home: 2005 Wilson Av NW Russellville AL 35653 Office: 500 N Jackson St PO Box 940 Russellville AL 35653

GUINIER, EWART, educator; b. Panama, C.Z., May 17, 1910; s. Howard Manoah and Marie Louise (Beresford) G.; student Harvard Coll., 1929-31; B.S. cum laude, City Coll. N.Y., 1935; M.A., Columbia, 1939; J.D., N.Y.U., 1959; M.A. (hon.), Harvard, 1969; m. Eugenia Paprin, Oct. 16, 1945; children—Clothilde Yvonne Stenson, Lani Carol, Sary Elisabeth, Marie Louise. Asst. v.p. Haarlem Research Lab., N.Y.C., 1933-35; dir. Intake Welfare Dept., N.Y.C., 1935-37; examiner, dir. Service Rating Bur., N.Y.C., 1937-41; internat. sec.-treas. CIO Pub. Workers, 1946-53; realtor Queens Home Sales Co., 1955; account exec. Arthur Milton Agy., ins., N.Y.C., 1956; cons. Pensions, Newark, 1953-54, N.Y.C., 1954—, Govt. of Sierra Leone, 1961-62; co-producer Ballad for Bimshire and other plays, N.Y.C., 1963; exec. dir. Brownsville Community Council, Inc., 1965-66; asso. dir. Agys. Intramerica Life Ins. Co., N.Y.C., 1966; asso. dir. Urban Center, Columbia, 1968-69; dir. Douglass Urban Corp., 1969—; prof., chmn. Afro Am. studies Harvard, 1969—, dir. W.E.B. DuBois Inst. for Afro-Am. Research, 1969—; founder, chmn. Jamaica coordinating council Harlem Affairs Com., also adv. bd. Black Heritage: A History of Afro-Americans. Chmn. Queens Urban League, 1962-68. Am. Labor Party candidate for Boro Pres. of Manhattan, 1949. Bd. dirs. Pub. Edn. Assn., N.Y. Urban League, Queens Coll. Speech and Hearing Center, Center for Urban Edn. Served with AUS, 1942-46. Urban fellow Columbia, 1969. Mem. African-Am. C. of C., N.A.A.C.P. (life mem.), Acad. Polit. Sci. Contbr. articles profl. jours. Home: 29 Robinson St Cambridge MA 02138

GUINN, DICK HENRY, naval officer; b. Palestine, Tex., Mar. 27, 1918; s. Jack Simpson and Ruby Aurelia (Johnson) G.; student U. Tex., El Paso, 1934-36; B.S., U.S. Naval Acad., 1941; postgrad. Nat. War Coll., 1959-60; m. Muriel Parker, July 25, 1942; children—Daryl Hale (Mrs. Wayne Bruce Wilson), Charlsa Jaqueline Claire. Commd. ensign USN, 1941, advanced through grades to vice adm., 1970; comdg. officer Fighter Squadron Two Able, 1947-48; staff operations officer, exec. officer Field Command, Armed Forces spl. weapons project, 1949-52; exec., comdg. officer Night Fighter Squadron 3, 1952-54; operational requirements officer Office Chief Naval Operations, 1954-56; comdg. officer Carrier Air Group Six, 1956-57; weapons readiness officer staff comdr. Naval Air Force, Atlantic Fleet, 1957-58; officer, detailer Bur. Naval Personnel, 1958-59; operations officer 7th Fleet Staff, 1960-61; comdg. officer U.S.S. Rigel, 1962-63, U.S.S. Forrestal, 1963-64; aviation capts. detailer Bur. Naval Personnel, 1964; program appraiser Office Sec. Navy, 1964-65; comdr. Carrier Div. Four, 1965-67; chief Naval Air Basic Tng., Naval

Air Sta., Pensacola, Fla., 1967-69; dep. chief Naval Personnel, Washington, 1969-70, chief, 1970—. Trustee Naval Hist. Found., Naval Aviation Mus.; bd. mgrs. Navy Relief Soc. Decorated Navy Cross, Legion of Merit, Air medal with gold star. Mem. Order of Daedalians. Rotarian. Home: Quarters A 3701 Nebraska Av NW Washington DC 20016 Office: Chief Naval Personnel Navy Dept Washington DC 20370

GUINN, GEORGE EARL, coll. pres.; b. Mossville, Miss., Aug. 21, 1912; s. David Howard and Martha Inez (Easterling) G.; A.B., La. Coll., 1937; student Southwestern Bapt. Theol. Sem., 1938-39; Th.M., New Orleans Bapt. Theol. Sem., 1942, Th.D., 1944; D.D., Mercer U. (Ga.), 1961; LL.D., William Jewell Coll., 1970; m. Gail Holmes, July 13, 1937 (dec. 1969); 1 dau., Peggy Elaine (Mrs. Herschel Wood Crump); m. 2d, Neva Norsworthy DeMoss, June 12, 1970. Ordained to ministry Bapt. Church, 1933; pastor First Ch., Sterlington, La., 1937-41, Jennings, La., 1941-45, Bossier City, La., 1945-48; head dept. homiletics Southwestern Bapt. Theol. Sem., Fort Worth, 1948-51; pres. La. Coll., Pineville, 1951—. Trustee Acadia Bapt. Acad., Eunice, La., 1941-48, Baton Rouge Gen. Hosp., 1944-45. Chmn. La. Bd. Instns., 1956-58; v.p. La. Found. Pvt. Colls., 1953- 54, pres. 1954-55, 60-61, 64-65, 67-68; v.p. La. Coll. Conf., 1953-54; mem. edn. commn. So. Bapt. Conv., 1952-58, 68—; mem. commn. on colls. and univs. So. Assn. Colls. and Schs. 1961-67, 68—, pres. 1970-71. Mem. Pi Kappa Delta. Mason, Rotarian. Co-author So. Bapt. Preaching, 1959. Home: 1127 College Dr Pineville LA 71360

GUINN, JOHN ALONZO, univ. pres.; b. New Braunfels, Tex., Mar. 10, 1905; s. Marvin E. and Irma K(lappenbach) (Hatton) G.; A.B., U. Tex., 1929, A.M., 1929, Ph.D. (advanced univ. fellow in English 1938), 1939; student U. Chgo., summer 1936, U. Heidelberg, 1931; m. Bessie Alice Mitchell, Sept. 18, 1943; childrenJohn A., Cecily Denise and Diana Evelyn (twins). Rural sch. prin., McQueeney, Tex., 1925-27; instr., later head English dept. Schreiner Inst., Kerrville, Tex., 1929-37, dean students, head English dept., 1939-42; supt. schs., Alice, Tex., 1946-49; pres. San Angelo Coll., 1949-1950, Tex. Woman's U., Denton, 1950—. Summer tchr. S.W. Tex. State Tchrs. Coll., 1938, 48, U. Tex., 1947; dir. Univ. State Bank. Pres. Denton County United Fund, 1962-63. Mem. Bd. Control for So. Regional Edn., 1963—. Served with USNR, 1942-45, instr. Advanced Naval Intelligence Sch., N.Y.C., PTO, 1944-45, comdr. to capt. USNR, 1953-60. Decorated two combat citations, Commendation and Commendation medal, 8th Naval Dist. Intelligence award, 1963. Presbyn. Clubs: Rotary (pres. Kerrville 1936, dist. gov. 1941); City (Dallas). Address: Box 23925 TWU Sta Denton, TX 76204.

GUINNESS, ALEC, actor; b. London, Eng., Apr. 2, 1914; s. Andrew and Agnes (Cuffe) Geddes; student Pembroke Lodge, Southbourne, Hantshire, 1922-27, Roborough, Eastbourne, Sussex, 1927-32; scholarship Fay Compton Dramatic Studio, 1934; D.F.A. (hon.), Boston Coll., 1962; m. Merula Salaman, June 20, 1938; 1 son, Matthew. Copywriter advt. agy., 1933; first profl. appearance in Libel, 1934; first part Osric in Hamlet, 1934; played Old Vic Theater, 1936-37, 38-39, John Gielgud's Theater, 1937-38; toured Europe, 1939; film actor, Great Expectations, 1946, Oliver Twist, 1947-48, also Man in the White Suit, The Mudlark, Lavender Hill Mob, Malta Story, Kind Hearts and Coronets, The Captain's Pleasure; The Bridge on the River Kwai, Horse's Mouth, All at Sea, Our Man in Havana, Tunes of Glory, A Majority of One, H.M.S. Defiant, The Comedians, Lawrence of Arabia, Fall of the Roman Empire, Dylan (recipient 1963 Tony award for performance), Dr. Zhivago, 1965, Situation Hopeless, 1965, But Not Serious, 1965, Hotel Paradise, 1966, The Quiller Memorandum, 1966; N.Y. state appearances, Flare Path, Cocktail Party. Recipient Acad. award, best actor, 1957. Knight Bachelor, 1959. Clubs: Athenaeum, Garrick (London). Address: Kettlebrook Meadows Steep Marsh Petersfield Hantshire England

GUINZBURG, THOMAS, publisher; b. N.Y.C., Mar. 30, 1926; s. Harold K. and Alice M. (Reizenstein) G.; student Hotchkiss Sch., 1940-44, Yale, 1946-50; m. Rita Gam, 1956 (div. 1963); children—Kate Thornton, Michael Thomas; m. 2d, Rustine Unger, June 21, 1967. Editor, Paris Review, 1952-53; with The Viking Press, Inc., N.Y.C., 1953- -, pres., 1962—; dir. Franklin Publs., 1966-69, exec. com., 1969; bd. govs. Yale U. Press, 1968—. Bd. dirs. Am. Book Pubs. Council, 1967-70, exec. com., 1969-70; dir. Assn. Am. Pubs., 1970—. Served with USMCR, World War II. Address: 625 Madison Av New York City NY 10022

GUION, ROBERT MORGAN, educator, psychologist; b. Indpls., Sept. 14, 1924; s. Leroy Herbert and Carolyn (Morgan) G.; B.A., State U. Ia., 1948; M.S., Purdue U., 1950, Ph.D., 1952; m. Mary Emily Firestone, June 8, 1947; children—David Michael, Diana Lynn, Keith Douglas, Pamela Sue, Judith Elaine. Vocational counselor Purdue U., 1948-51, research fellow, 1951-52; mem. faculty Bowling Green (O.) State U., 1952—, prof. psychology, 1964—, chmn. dept., 1966-71. Vis. prof. U. Cal. at Berkeley, 1963-64, U. N.M., summer 1965; tech. adviser Dept. Personnel Services, State Hawaii, summer 1970; cons. in field, 1954—. Served with AUS, 1943-46. Recipient James McKeen Cattell award Am. Psychol. Assn. 1965. Mem. Am., Midwestern, Ohio psychol. assns., Internat. Assn. Applied Psychology, Sigma Xi, Pi Chi. Methodist. Author: Personnel Testing, 1965. Home: 632 Haskins Rd Bowling Green OH 43402

GUIREY, FRED MELVILLE, architect; b. Oakland, Cal., Dec. 6, 1908; s. Fred William and Emily Caroline (Sorby) G.; student U. Ariz., 1927-28, U. Cal. at Berkeley, 1928-30, B.A., 1933; m. Catherine Louise Bolen, Dec. 28, 1939; children—Caroline Rogue, Sherry Lynn. Landscape engr. Ariz. Hwy. Dept., 1933-42; site planner, office engr. Leeds, Hill, Barnard & Jewett, 1942-46; prin. Guirey & Quist, 1946-47; prin. Guirey & Jones, Architects, 1947-50; architect Fred M. Guirey, Phoenix, 1950-59; prin. Guirey, Srnka, Arnold & Sprinkle, Phoenix, 1959—. Chmn. Maricopa County Parks Commn., 1956—; mem. Tonto Nat. Forest Multiple Use Adv. Council, 1963—. Bd. dirs. Goodwill Industries, 1957-64, pres., 1963; bd. dirs. Phoenix Mus. Theatre, 1956-63. Fellow A.I.A. (sec. Ariz. chpt. 1946); mem. Am. Arbitration Assn., Ariz. Acad., Delta Chi. Mason (Shriner), Kiwanian. Club: Dons (pres. 1940) (Phoenix). Home: 300 E Missouri St Phoenix AZ 85012 Office: 3800 N Central Av Phoenix AZ 85012

GUIS, C.H., savs. and loan assn. exec. Pres., Prudential Savs. and Loan Assn., San Gabriel, Cal. Office: PO Box 67 526 W Las Tunas Dr San Gabriel CA 91776*

GUIZADO, EDUARDO CAMACHO, educator, author; Licenciado en Filosofia y Letras. U. de los Andres, Bogota, Colombia, Doctor en Filosofia y Letras, U. Madrid, 1962. Prof. U. de los Andes, also dean students 196364, dean Sch. Arts and Scis., 1964—; vis. prof. Spanish Sch., Middlebury Coll., 1967, 68. Recipient Nobel prize in lit., 1967. Author: Estudios de literatire colombrand, Siglos XVI y XVII, 1965; La poesia de Jose Asuncion Silva, 1967; also articles of Spanish Am. poetry and novel. Address: care Spanish Sch Middlebury Coll. Middlebury, VT 05753.*

GULICK, CLARENCE SWIFT, govt. ofcl.; b. N.Y.C., Apr. 26, 1920; s. Luther H. and Helen (Swift) G.; A.B., Swarthmore Coll., 1941; M. Pub. Adminstrn., Harvard, 1947, Ph.D., 1948; m. Frances D. Anderson, Dec. 19, 1942; childrenSidney Luther, Michael Anderson. With War Dept., 1941-42, WPB, 1942-43; program officer Agy. Internat. Devel and predecessor agencies, 1948-; assigned Dublin. Ireland, 1948-50, Karachi, Pakistan, 1959-61, Nat. War Coll., 1963; chief policy planning div., program coordination staff Agency Internat. Devel., 1964-65, asst. dir. (program) U.S. AID Nigeria, 1965, U.S. AID, New Delhi, India, 1965-. Served with USNR, 1943-46. Mem. Am. Econ. Assn., Irish Statis, and Social Inquiry Soc., Nigerian Econ. Soc., Indian Econ. Assn. Club: Kenwood (Washington). Home: 4702 De Russey Pky Chevy Chase MD 20015 Office: US AID New Delhi Dept State Washington DC 20521

GULICK, EDWARD VOSE, educator, historian; b. Tacoma, May 30, 1915; s. Walter Vose and Eleanor (Brooks) G.; grad. Phillips Andover Acad., Andover, Mass., 1933; B.A., Yale, 1937, M.A., 1942, Ph.D. in History, 1947; m. Elizabeth Whitney Merrill, Dec. 20, 1941; children—Susan Patricia, David Brooks. Tchr. English, Yale-in-China, Changsha, Hunan, China, 1937-39; mem. faculty Wellesley (Mass.) Coll., 1947—, prof. European, Far Eastern history, 1961—. Served in camps and unit Civilian Pub. Service, 1943-46. Mem. Am. Hist. Assn., Assn. Asian Studies, Am. Fern Soc., W. Wales Naturalists Trust, Phi Beta Kappa. Author: Europe's Classical Balance of Power, 1955. Home: 741 Washington St Wellesley MA 02181

GULICK, JAMES WHARTON maritime transp. cons.; b. Newport News, Va., Dec. 9, 1910; s. James Wharton and Maude (Coleman) G.; student Hampden-Sydney Coll., 1928-30, Nat. U., 1941- 43; m. Elsie Cummins, Oct. 2, 1937 (dec. 1967); children—Diana Jo, James Wharton. Sec. to U.S. Congressman Bland, 1930-33; clk. merchant marine and fisheries com. U.S. Ho. of Reps., 1933-41; legislative rep. bur. marine insp. and navigation Dept. Commerce, 1941-42; with Bur. Customs, 1942-62, dep. commr., 1952-62; dep. maritime adminstrn. Dept. Commerce, also mem. Maritime Subsidy Bd., 1962-66, acting maritime adminstrn., chmn. Maritime Subsidy Bd., 1966-69, ret., 1969; cons. maritime transp. Muller, Fox and Pennington, 1969—. Served with AUS, 1943-45. Mem. Fed., D.C. bar assns., Nat. Defense Transp. Assn. (v.p.), Pi Kappa Alpha. Delta Theta Phi. Presbyn. (elder). Club: Propeller of U.S. (v.p., bd. govs. Washington). Home: 10300 Wood Rd Fairfax VA 22030 Office: 1145 19th St NW Washington DC 20036

GULICK, JOHN, educator; b. Newton, Mass., Apr. 18, 1924; s. Millard Burr and Alida (Carey) G.; A.B. magna cum laude, Harvard, 1949, A.M., 1951, Ph.D., 1953; m. Margaret G. Eaton, Apr. 10, 1946; children—Stehen M., James C., Anne S. Teaching fellow Harvard, 1951, 53; lectr. Am. U. of Beirut, 1952; instr. Adelphi Coll., 1953-55; asst. prof., asso. prof., prof. anthropology U. N.C., Chapel Hill, 1955—, chmn. dept. anthropology, 1965-70; dir. Cross-Cultural Lab., Inst. Research Social Sci., U. N.C., 1955-59, bd. dirs. Human Relations Area Files, 1959-66. Served with Am. Field Service, 1943-44; with AUS, 1944-46. Fellow Am. Anthrop. Assn., N.Y. Acad. Scis.; mem. So. Anthrop. Soc. (pres. 1968-69), Phi Beta Kappa. Author: Social Structure and Culture Change in a Lebanese Village 1955; Cherokees at the Crossroads, 1960; (with Charles E. Bowerman) Adaptation of Newcomers in the Piedmont Industrial Crescent, 1961; Tripoli: A Modern Arab City, 1967. Editor: Dimensions of Cultural Change in the Middle East, 1965; co-editor: Symposium on Cherokee and Iroquois Culture, 1961. Home: 1029 Highland Woods Chapel Hill NC 27514

GULICK, LUTHER HALSEY, government administrator; b. Osaka, Japan, Jan. 17, 1892; s. Sidney Lewis and Cara M. (Fisher) G.; A.B., Oberlin, 1914, A.M., 1915, Litt. D., 1939; student Training Sch. for Pub. Service, N.Y. Bur. Municipal Research, 1915-17; research staff, 1917; Ph.D., Columbia, 1920, LL.D., 1954; LL.D., Whitman Coll., 1952; m. Helen McKelvey Swift, 1917 (dec. 1969); children—Clarence Swift, Luther Halsey; m. 2, Carol Willis Moffett, 1970. Served as sec. Joint Spl. Com. on Budget, Mass. Gen. Court; asst. chief of sect. Council Nat. Def., World War I; capt. statistics branch of Gen. Staff; formerly staff mem. in pub. finance and taxation, N.Y. Bur. Municipal Research, dir., 1920-60 city dminstr., N.Y.C., 1954-56; pres. Inst. Pub. Adminstrn., 1920-62. Counsel of research staff legislative coms. and tax depts. various states. Eaton prof. municipal sci. and adminstrn., Columbia, 1931-42; lectr. various univs. and profl. orgns. Cons. numerous govtl. agencies, adminstr. various govtl. orgns. for research and investigation, during and following World War 2 yrs. Mem. staff U.S. Reparations Mission, Moscow, Potsdam, Tokyo, Manila, 1945, Paris, Brussels, Nuremberg, Vienna, 1946; cons. fgn. govts. and UN, 1953-68, Com. Econ. Devel. Trustee Oberlin Coll., 1940-48, Nat. Recreation Assn., Nat. Audubon Soc., Nat. Planning Assn. Recipient Butler medal Columbia, 1939; citations Am. Soc. Pub. Adminstrn., 1964, Nat. Municipal League, 1964, Internat. City Mgrs. Assn., 1966. Mem. Am. Polit. Sci. Assn. (past pres.), Am. Soc. Pub. Adminstrn. (past pres.). Phi Kappa Pi, Phi Beta Kappa. Republican. Conglist. Clubs: University, Greensboro Yacht. Author: numerous books, latest: Administrative Reflections, World War II, 1947; American Forest Policy, 1952; Modern Management for the City of N.Y., 1953; METRO: Changing Problems and Lines of Attack, 1957; Metropolitan Problems and American Ideas, 1962; also reports, brochures, articles. Editor several publs. Home: 404 Riverside Dr New York City NY 10025 also Greensboro VT 05841 Office: 55 W 44th St New York City NY 10036 ☆

GULICK, LUTHER HALSEY, Jr., educator; b. Bklyn., Sept. 23, 1922; s. Luther Halsey and Helen (Swift) G.; B.A., Oberlin Coll., 1943; M.A. in Geography, U. Chgo., 1948, Ph.D., 1952; postgrad. U. Pa., 1966-67; m. Melba Christensen, June 18, 1948; childrenLeslie Carmen, Alan Christensen, Lisa Louise. Asst. prof. geography Fla. State U., 1948-49; asso. prof. Winona (Minn.) State Coll., 1952-62; prof. geography, chmn. dept. State U. N.Y. Coll. at Potsdam, 1962-; field research P.R., 1950-51. Mem. Potsdam Planning Bd., 1965—, chmn., 1968—. Salisbury and Walgreen fellow, 1947-48; Fulbright grantee, Pakistan, 1959-60. Served with AUS, 1943-46. Mem. Assn. Am. Geographers, Nat. Council Geog. Edn., Assn. Asian Studies, Phi Beta Kappa. Author articles, chpts. in books. Home: 3 Broad St Potsdam, NY 13676.

GULICK, MERLE AMERSON, life ins. exec.; b. Jackson, Mich., 1906; s. Frank M. and Maud Mae (Dickes) G.; grad. Hobart Coll., 1930; LL.D., Hobart and William Smith Colls., 1966; m. Edna Zeller, Apr. 28, 1934 (dec. April 1960); 1 son, Peter L.; m. 2d, Helen Manzo Hindmarsh, Nov. 1, 1962. Asso. with Equitable Life Assurance Soc., N.Y.C., 1930—, successively service supr. group dept., mgr. Phila. group office, mgr. N.Y. Group dept., exec. asst. to pres., gen. mgr. group dept., 2d v.p., 1930-52, v.p., 1952-60, v.p. pub. relations-personnel, 1960- 68, v.p. corporate affairs, 1968—. Exec. vice chmn. Greater N.Y. Fund, 1939; chmn. greater N.Y. men's com. United Negro Coll. Fund, Inc., 1953, mem. steering com., 1953-55; chmn. greater N.Y.C. com. Nat. Fund Med. Edn.; mem. exec. com. Com. on Alcoholism, Community Council Greater N.Y., mem Manhattan Council on Alcoholism; co-chmn. labor mgmt. com. on alcoholism, 1967-70. Trustee Hobart and William Smith Coll. 1950-68, chmn. bd., 1957-68, now hon. trustee bd. dirs. N.Y.C. Cancer Com.; chmn. exec. com. N.Y.C. div. Am. Cancer Soc.; bd. dirs. Nat. Football Found. and Hall of Fame Inc., Nat. Assn. Prevention Blindness, West Side Assn. Commerce; trustee Morehouse Coll.; bd. advisers Internat. U. Communications mem. Council execs. on co. contbns. Nat. Indsl. conf. Bd. Served with USCGR, 1942-46; chief port security div.; capt. res. Decorated Legion of Merit; recipient Marts and Lundy medal, 1965; named to Football Hall of Fame, 1965. Mem. Ins. Soc. N.Y., N.Y. C. of C. (chmn. ins. com., mem. exec. com., 1966-68), Nat. Council Alcoholism (pres. 1963-65), Pub. Relations Soc. Am., Newcomen Soc. N.A., Coast Guard League (founder), Holland Soc. N.Y., S.A.R., Kappa Alpha (nat. pres. 1951). Clubs: Overseas Press; Hobart (N.Y.C.): River, Touchdown; Madison Square Garden. Home: 40 Central Park S New York City NY 10019 Office: 1285 Av of the Americas New York City NY 10019

GULICK, SIDNEY LEWIS, coll. dean; b. Kobe, Japan, Aug. 17, 1902; s. Sidney L. and Cara May (Fisher) G.; A.B., Oberlin Coll., 1923; M.A., 1925; Ph.D., Yale, 1931; m. Evelyn Mary Bade, July 31, 1931; children—Marian Harris (Mrs. Kirk Wilson), Sidney Lewis III. Tchr. English, piano Doshisha U., Kyoto, Japan, 1923-24; asso. pub. speaking U. Cal. at Berkeley, 1927-30; instr. English, U. Rochester, 1931-35; asst. prof. English, Mills Coll., 1935- 45; asso. prof. English, San Diego State Coll., 1945-49, prof. English, 1949-69, prof. emeritus, 1969—, dean arts and scis., 1959-69, emertius, 1969- -, adminstrv. adviser, 1969—. Served as chief procurement and placement dist. postal censor San Francisco Office of Censorship, 1942-45. Mem. Modern Lang. Assn., Am. Assn. U. Profs., Philol. Assn. Pacific Coast, Shakespeare Assn. Am. Conglist. Club: Cal. Writers. Author: A Chesterfield Bibliography to 1800, 1935; Some Unpublished Letters of Lord Chesterfield, 1937; Gulick Vocabulary Survey, 1957, 61. Contbr. essays, articles to learned publs. Home: 10301 Sierra Vista La Mesa CA 92041 Office: San Diego State Coll San Diego CA 92115

GULICK, WALTER LAWRENCE, educator, psychologist; b. Summit, N.J., July 4, 1927; s. Walter Lawrence and Carol (Dewey) G.; A.B., Hamilton Coll., Clinton, N.Y., 1952; M.A. (Theta Delta Chi Fellow), U. Del., 1955, (hon.), Dartmouth, 1968; Ph.D., (psychology scholar 1955-57), Princeton, 1957; m. Winifred Bourn Frazee, Oct. 18, 1952; children—Hans, Tod, Kristina. Mem. faculty U. Del., 1957-64, prof. psychology, 1963-64, chmn. dept., 1964-65; prof. psychology Dartmouth, Hanover, N.H., 1965—; chmn. dept., 1970—. Vis. prof. U. Vt., summer 1966; cons. Princeton on grant to E.G. Wever, 1957-61, Presbyn. Hosp., Phila., 1961-63; editorial cons. Oxford U. Press, 1963, McGraw-Hill Pub. Co., 1966-67; panel cons. NSF, 1966. Served with AUS, 1946-48. Recipient Nat. Service award, 1955; Dale prize music Hamilton Coll., 1952. Mem. N.Y. Acad. Scis., Eastern, N.H. psychol. assns., Psychonomic Soc., Phi Beta Kappa, Sigma Xi (pres. Dartmouth chpt. 1967-68), Psi Chi (pres. U. Del. chpt. 1954-55). Author: Hearing: Physiology and Psychophysics, 1971. Contbr. profl. jours. Research vision and hearing. Home: Meadow Lane Hanover NH 03755

GULL, CLOYD DAKE, librarian, educator; b. Lorain, Ohio, June 17, 1915; s. Cloyd DeLaney and Margaret Louise (Dake) G.; A.B., Allegheny Coll., 1936; A.B. in Library Sci., U. Mich., 1937, A.M., 1939; m. Dorothy Turner Phelps, Aug. 31, 1943; children—Marilyn Virginia, Evan Howd, Janet Phelps, Thomas Alexander. Asst. Gen. Library, U. Mich., 1937-39; periodicals librarian N.C. State Coll., Raleigh, 1939-42; various adminstrv. positions, processing dept. office, navy research sect., catalog maintenance div.,. union catalog div. Library of Congress, Washington, 1945-52; tech. analyst Documentation, Inc., Washington, 1952-54; adminstrv. officer, div. engring. and indsl. research Nat. Acad. Scis.- NRC, Washington, 1954-58; information systems analyst computer dept. Gen. Elec. Co., 1958-60, cons. analyst information processing def. systems dept., 1960-63; prof. library sci. Ind. U., 1964-67, MEDLARS liaison officer Nat. Library Medicine, 1967-68; rep. cons. Document Systems, Inc., 1968-69; pres. Gull & Assos., 1969—. Chmn. com. on dissemination technolinformation about materials and materials research NRC, 1958-59; chmn. U.S. nat. com. Internat. Fedn. Documentation, 1960-63, mem., 1963-66. Chmn. recreation adv. planning com., Rockville, Md., 1954-57. Served to lt. USNR, 1942-45. Mem. Am. Soc. for Information Sci. (pres. 1959-60), Spl. Libraries Assn. (pres. Ind. chpt. 1966-67), A.L.A. (councillor 1962-65), Md., D.C., Rockville (trustee, pres. 1954-59) library assns., Phi Beta Kappa, Phi Kappa Phi, Alpha Chi Rho. Episcopalian. Contbg. author: Studies in Coordinate Indexing, Vol. 1, 1953, Punched Cards: Their Application to Science and Industry, rev. edit., 1958. Contbr. articles library and documentation periodicals. Home: 4200 Dresden St Kensington, MD 20795.

GULLAGE, JAMES TRUETT, lawyer; b. Camp Hill, Ala., Sept. 13, 1937; s. James and Lula (Middlebrooks) G.; B.S., Ala. Poly. Inst., 1960; J.D., U. Ala., 1960; m. Julia Claire Smith, May 29, 1960; children-Lisa Claire, Lauri Jill. Admitted to Ala. bar, 1960, U.S. Supreme Ct. bar, 1966; practice in Opelika, 1968—; tchr. bus. law U. Md., European div., 1965; partner Walker, Hill & Gullage, 1969—. Bd. dirs. E. Ala. Comprehensive Mental Health Clinic Lee County Council for Dependent and Neglected Children. Served to maj. U.S. Army, 1960-68. Decorated Army Commendation medal with oak leaf cluster. Mem. Am., Ala., Lee County bar Assns., Bench and Bar. Home: 1302 Claire St Opelika AL 36801 Office: 205 S 9th St Opelika AL 36801

GULLANDER, WERNER PAUL, assn. exec.; b. Big Rapids, Mich., July 19, 1908; s. Paul and Elvira Esther (Werner) G.; B.S., U. Minn., 1930; LL.D. (hon.), U. Puget Sound, 1966; m. Dorothy Mae Becker, July 12, 1930; children—Barbara Louise (Mrs. Donald Nelson Weinberger), Judith Maria. Accounting trainee Gen. Electric Co., 1930-33, traveling auditor, 1933-38, supervising auditor, 1938-44; sec., treas. Gen. Electric Supply Corp. 1945-48, dist. mgr., 1948-51; financial v.p. Weyerhaeuser Co., Tacoma, 1952-60; exec. v.p., dir. Gen. Dynamics Corp., 1960-62; pres. N.A.M., N.Y.C., 1962—; dir. Zurn Industries, Inc. Mem. Pres.'s Com. Employment of Handicapped. Mem. Conf. Bd., Nat. Export Expansion Council, Newcomen Soc. N. Am., Internat. C. of C. (U.S. council trustee), Financial Execs. Inst., Tau Kappa Epsilon. Mason (Shriner). Clubs: Washington Athletic, 101 (Seattle); Siwanoy Country (Bronxville, N.Y.); University, Economic (N.Y.C.). Home: 72 W Pondfield Rd Bronxville NY 10708 Office: 277 Park Av New York City NY 10017

GULLEDGE, CHARLES GLENN, mfg. co. exec.; b. Marion, Ill., Oct. 4, 1919; s. Basyle Glenn and Ethel Minnie (Binkley) G.; B.S. in Mech. Engring., Washington U., St. Louis, 1941, grad. student, 1949; grad. student, Harvard-Mass. Inst. Tech., 1944; m. Patricia M. Moore, Jan. 19, 1944; children—Ann Dee, Patrick Forrest, Christopher Moore; m. 2d, Elizabeth Ann Wright, Dec. 29, 1960; children—George H. Price, Allen Wright Price, Suz-Ann Price Stephenson. From engr. to mgr. armament sales Emerson Electric Mfg. Co., St. Louis, 1946-56, asst. v.p., 1956-58, v.p., gen. mgr. electronics and avionics div., 1958- 60; pres., dir. Dynalectron Corp., and predecessor, Washington, 1960—; pres., dir. Hydrocarbon Research, Inc., N.Y.C., 1964—, Metrodyn Corp., Pan Am. Hydrocarbon Research, Inc., Hydrocarbon Realty Inc., Dytel, Ltd.; dir. Air Carrier Service Corp., Internat. Fuel Corp., Liberia Refining Co., Hydrocarbon Engring., S.A., Airtech Service, Inc., Dynair, Inc., Vegas Valley Electric Inc., Seeger Electric Co., Griffin Constrn. Co., Griffin Electric Co., Frazier Elec. Constrn., Inc. Trustee Dynalectron Corp. Pension Trust. Served to capt. USMCR, 1943-46. Mem. Nat. Aerospace Services Assn. (pres., dir. 1963-64), Nat. Aero. Assn., Air

Force Assn., Army Aviation Assn. Am., Am. Petroleum Inst., Theta Xi. Clubs: Engineers (St. Louis); Nat. Aviation (Washington); Le Club Internat; Metropolitan. Home: Normandy House 1701 N Kent St Arlington VA 22209 Office: 2233 Wisconsin Av NW Washington DC 20007

GULLEDGE, EUGENE A., govt. ofcl.; b. Greensboro, N.C., 1920. Past pres. Nat. Assn. Home Builders; asst. sec. mortgage credit Dept. Housing and Urban Devel., also fed. housing commnr., 1969—. Address: 811 Vermont Av NW Washington DC 20410*

GULLEN, GEORGE EDGAR, Jr., ednl. adminstr.; b. Detroit, Mar. 6, 1914; s. George Edgar and Alice Maud (Seruton) G.; J.D., Wayne State U., 1936; m. Mary Ruth Gullen, Jan. 9, 1937; children—Nancy (Mrs. George Scheffler), George Edgar III, Gail (Mrs. Paul Fitzsimmons), Kathryn (Mrs. Luis Jauregui), Carolyn (Mrs. Neil Spink), Christopher, Frederick, John. Admitted to the Mich. bar, 1936; asst. sec. Detroit Motors Corp., 1940-55, dir., 1945-55; dir. labor relations Am. Motors Corp., Detroit, 1955-66, v.p. indsl. relations, 1963-66; v.p. univ. relations Wayne State U., 1966—. Mem. panel arbitrators Am. Arbitration Assn. Moderator S.E. Mich. Assn. Cong. Chs. Bd. dirs., v.p. Mich. United Fund; dir. nat. bd. YMCA's North Am. and Can.; past pres. Detroit YMCA, 1955-57; pres. Nat. Council YMCA's, 1966—; dir. Nat. Assn. of Mental Health. Recipient Alumni award Wayne State U., 1962. Mem. Indsl. Relations Research Assn. Mason. Home: 5245 N Adams Rd Route 1 Pontiac MI 48057 Office: McKenzie Hall Detroit MI 48226

GULLEY, HALBERT EDISON, educator; b. Sesser, Ill., Nov. 21, 1919; s. Roy Arbi and Mary Alice (Martel) G.; B.Ed., So. Ill. U., 1940; M.A., State U. Ia., 1941, Ph.D., 1948; m. Nadine Ellen Dauderman, June 28, 1941; children—Gerald Baird, Ellen Elizabeth, William Bruce. Tchr., Hannibal (Mo.) High Sch., 1941- 42; head speech br. Shrivenham (Eng.) Am. U., 1945; instr. communications skills State U. Ia., 1946-48; mem. faculty U. Ill., 1948- 67, prof. speech, 1960-67, dir. Exptl. Research Lab. Pub. Address, 1959- 63, head div. gen. studies, 1963-67; prof. speech Colo. U., 1967-68; prof., chmn. dept. speech U. Ky., Lexington, 1968-70; chmn. dept. speech No. Ill. U., DeKalb, 1970—. Chmn. bd. U. Ill. YMCA, 1963-64; bd. dirs. United Fund Campaign County, 1963- 64. Served to capt., inf., AUS, 1942-46. ETO. Decorated Purple Heart. Mem. Central States (exec. sec. 1956-57), Ill. (pres. 1954-55) speech assns., Speech Assn. Am., Am. Assn. U. Profs., Delta Sigma Rho. Mem. Christian Ch. (chmn. bd. 1960-61). Author: Essentials of Discussion and Debate, 1955; Discussion, Conference and Group Process, 1960, 2d edit., 1968; (with Phillips R. Biddle) Essentials of Group Discussion, 1969; also articles. Home: 122 Ilehamwood Dr DeKalb IL 60115

GULLEY, LYLE FOXWELL, mfr.; b. Balt., June 28, 1908; s. Thomas W. and Clara (Foxwell) G.; B.S., Johns Hopkins, 1930; m. Mary Ruth Jameson, Sept. 6, 1948; childrenLyle F., Thomas III. With Granite City Steel Co. (Ill.), 1951- , dir. purchases, 1951-52. works mgr., 1952-56, v.p. charge operations, 1956-65, exec. v.p., gen. mgr., dir., 1965—, now pres. and dir.; v.p., dir. City Machine & Mfg. Co., Cleve., 1956-; dir. Clepit Co., Cleve. Clubs: Mo. Athletic, Glen Echo Country Racquet, Bellerive Country (St. Louis). Home: 1 Coach 'N Four St Louis MO 63131 Office: 20th and Madison Av Granite City MO 63650

GULLEY, WILBUR PAUL, Jr., banker; b. Little Rock, Aug. 8, 1923; s. Wilbur Paul and JaJa Douglas (Ashburn) G.; A.B. in Bus. Adminstrn., Duke, 1947; m. Mary Elizabeth Bragg Hunt, Mar. 13, 1971; children by previous marriage—Wilbur Paul III and William H. (twins), James Ransom, Michael. With Gulley Ins. Agy., Little Rock, 1947, partner, mng. officer, 1947-58; with Pulaski Fed. Savs. & Loan Assn., Little Rock, 1947—, sec., 1948-58, v.p., 1958, pres., 1959—, also dir.; dir. Security Mortgage Ins. Co., Baton Rouge, Pres. Better Bus. Bur. Ark., 1962; gen. chmn. United Fund campaign, Pulaski County, Ark., 1963-64; v.p. Little Rock Boys Club, 1970-71. Trustee, pres. George W. Donaghey Found.; trustee; chmn. bd. Ark. State U., 1969, sec., treas. trustees, 1971. Served with USNR, 1943-46. Mem. Southwestern Savs. and Loan Conf. (pres. 1960-61), Savs. Assn. Retirement Fund (trustee 1960-65), U.S. (mem. exec. com. 1963-66), Pulaski County (pres. 1964), Ark. (pres. 1965-66) savs. and loan leagues, Little Rock C. of C. (pres. 1968), Phi Beta Kappa, Sigma Alpha Epsilon, Beta Omega Sigma. Methodist (bd. stewards). Rotarian. Clubs: Country, Little Rock, Capital (Little Rock). Home: 5525 Grandview St Little Rock AR 72207 Office: 400 W 3d St Little Rock AR 72201

GULLICKSEN, WILLARD A., assn. exec. Pres., Forest Products Research Soc. Office: 2119 Churchill St Chicago IL 60647*

GULLICKSON, GLENN, Jr., educator, physician; b. Mpls., July 9, 1919; s. Glenn and Grace (Stellwagen) G.; B.A., U. Minn., 1942, M.D., 1945, Ph.D., 1961; m. Glenna A. Swore, May 18, 1937; children—Mary, Glenn III. Intern, Gallinger Municipal Hosp., Washington, 1944-45; faculty U. Minn. Med. Sch., Mpls., 1946—, asso. prof. phys. medicine and rehab., 1961-66, prof. phys. medicine and rehab., 1966—, asst. dir. Rehab. Center, 1954-61, dir., 1961—. Exec. dir. Am. Congress Phys. Medicine and Rehab., 1960-66; mem. exam. com. phys. therapists Minn. Bd. Med. Examiners, 1961-71, pres., 1968-71; mem. med. adv. com. Minn. Soc. for Crippled Children and Adults, 1967—; fellow council on cerebrovascular disease Am. Heart Assn.; mem. neurol. scis. research tng. com. Nat. Inst. Neurol. Diseases and Blindness, 1965-69; exec. com. Joint Com. Stroke Facilities, 1969—. Served to lt. (s.g.), M.C., USNR, 1945-46, 53-54. Diplomate Am. Bd. Phys. Medicine and Rehab. Mem. A.M.A. (prin. rep. interspecialty com. 1968—), Minn., Hennepin County med. socs., A.A.A.S., Am. Assn. U. Profs., Nat., Minn. rehab. assns., Minn. Med. Found., Am. Acad. Phys. Medicine and Rehab. (gov., v.p. 1968-69, pres. 1970-71), Am. Bd. Phys. Medicine and Rehab., Assn. Am. Med. Colls., N.Y. Acad. Scis., Sigma Xi. Home: 217 Holly Rd Hopkins MN 55343 Office: Medical Center Univ Minn Minneapolis MN 55455

GULLIKSEN, HAROLD OLIVER, educator; b. Washington, July 18, 1903; s. Charles and Signe Matilda (Engebretsen) G.; A.B., U. Wash., 1926, A.M., 1927; Ph.D., U. Chgo., 1931; m. Dorothy Eleanor Palmer, Sept. 6, 1930; children—Eleanor Louise (Mrs. John Willliam McLauchlin), Katherine Jean (Mrs. Leon Goodrich). Research asso. Mooseheart (Ill.) Lab. for Child Research, 1931-33; research asst. U. Chgo., 1933-34, mem. bd. examiners, 1934-40, asst. prof. psychology, 1938-42, asso. prof., 1942- 45, dir. research project Nat. Def. Research Com. (on leave from U. Chgo.), 1942-45; research sec. Coll. Entrance Examination Bd., Princeton, N.J., 1945-48; prof. psychology Princeton U., 1945—; research adviser Ednl. Testing Service, Princeton, 1948—. Fellow Am. Statis. Assn., Am. Psychol. Assn.; mem. Psychometric Soc. (mng. editor Psychometrika 1942-49, pres. 1945), A.A.A.S., Am. Assn. U. Profs., Inst. Math. Statistics, Sigma Xi, Phi Beta Kappa. Author: Theory of Mental Tests. Editor: (with Samuel Messick) Psychological Scaling; (with Norman Frederikson) Theory and Applications, 1960. Contbr. to Mathematical Psychology, 1964. Home: 12 Aiken Av Princeton NJ 04540

GULLIN, LARS, baritone saxophonist, composer; b. Sweden, May 4, 1928. Formerly clarinetist in mil. band, also classical composer, pianist; baritone saxophonist, 1949; joined Arne Dommerus, 1951; recorded with numerous artists visiting Sweden; active in Italy, 1958-59; recording artist for Roost, Verve records. Recipient award as new star Down Beat Critic Poll, 1954. Address: care Atlantic Records 1841 Broadway New York City NY 10023

GULLING, RICHARD ALBERT, mfg. co. exec.; b. Akron, O., 1921; ed. U. Notre Dame, 1943. Treas. Timken Roller Bearing Co., Canton, O. Home: 1304 Washington Blvd Louisville, OH 44641. Office: 1835 Dueber Av SW Canton OH 44706

GULLION, EDMUND ASBURY, univ. ofcl.; b. Lexington, Ky., Mar. 2, 1913; s. Allen Wyant and Ruth (Matthews) G.; A.B., Princeton, 1935; grad. Nat. War Coll., 1949; LL.D., U. Louisville, 1969; m. Patricia Palmer, Sept. 2, 1961. Became vice consul, Marseilles, France, 1937; U.S. fgn. service officer, 1937-64, Dept. State, 1938, vice consul Salonika, Greece, 1939; third sec., London, 1942; 3d sec., London, 1943; chargé d'affaires, Helsinki, 1943; 2d sec., Stockholm, 1944; with Dept. State, Washington, 1945-60; counselor of legation, Saigon 1950; fgn. service insp., 1957; acting dept. dir. U.S. Disarmament Adminstrn., 1960, dep. dir., 1961; Am. ambassador Republic Congo, 1961; career minister, 1962; now dean Fletcher Sch. Law and Diplomacy, Tufts U., Medford, Mass., 1965—. Bd. dirs. World Peace Found., Boston, World Affairs Council, Boston. Mem. Council Fgn. Relations N.Y., Am. Acad. Arts and Scis., Am. Polit. Assn., Am. Fgn. Service Assn., Inst. Strategie Studies. Clubs: Metropolitan (Washington); Lansdowne, London. Address: Tufts U Fletcher Sch Law and Diplomacy Medford MA 02155

GULLIVER, ASHBEL GREEN, ret. educator, lawyer; b. N.Y.C., Nov. 23, 1897; s. William Curtis and Louisa (Green) G.; student Groton (Mass.) Sch., 1910-15; B.A., Yale, 1919, LL.B., cum laude, 1922, M.A. (hon.), 1935; m. Eugenia B. Porter, Dec. 18, 1926; childrenWilliam Curtis, Anne Porter, Ashbel Green. Admitted to N.Y. bar, 1923, engaged in gen. practice law, N.Y.C.; asso. with Alexander & Green, 1922-27; mem. faculty Yale U. Sch. Law, 1927—, asst. prof. law, 1927-31, asso. prof. law, 1931-35, prof. law, 1935-65, Garver prof. law emeritus 1965—, asst. dean, 1934-39, acting dean, 1939, dean, 1940-46. Fellow Timothy Dwight Coll., Yale, 1935-48. Served to 2d lt. F.A., U.S. Army, 1918, Mem. Conn. State Bd. Pardons, 1936-59, Alien Enemy Hearing Bd. of Dist. Conn., 1942-45, Conn. Post-War Planning Bd., 1943-45; chmn. Conn. State Bd. Labor Relations 1945-55, 64; arbitrator labor, motion picture and contract cases. Mem. Wolfs Head of Yale, Beta Theta Pi. Author: Future Interests, 1959; (with Clark, Lusky and Murphy) Gratuitous Transfers, 1967. Contbr. to legal periodicals. Home: Norwich VT 05055

GULLIVER, HAROLD STRONG, journalist; b. Valdosta, Ga., Sept. 25, 1935; s. Harold Strong and Augusta (Rentz) G.; B.A., Yale, 1957; postgrad. Free U. West Berln, 1957-58; m. Marian Godwin, Jan. 13, 1962; 1 son, Harold Strong III. Reporter, Macon (Ga.) Telegraph, 1960; pub. relations dir. Valdosta State Coll., 1960-62; reporter Atlanta Constitution, 1962-65, asso. editor, 1970—; employee State of Ga., 1965-67; reporter A.P., 1967-69. Pres. Fulton County Young Democrats, 1966-67. Served with USMCR, 1959-60. Rotary Internat. Found. fellow, 1957-58. Mem. Atlanta Press Club (pres.). Author: (with Reg Murphy) The Southern Strategy, 1971. Home: 85 E Park Lane NE Atlanta GA 30309 Office: 10 Forsyth St Atlanta GA 30302

GULLIVER, WILLIAM HENRY, lawyer; b. Portland, Me., Feb. 9, 1904; s. William Henry and Agnes Margaret (Gilroy) G.; A.B., Bowdoin Coll., 1925; LL.B., Harvard, 1928; m. Catherine P. McGahan, Sept. 3, 1939 (dec. Jan. 1964); childrenWilliam, Ann Derby (Mrs. David G. Hanes), Catherine James; m. 2d, Elin A. Tulloch, Dec. 29, 1965. Admitted to Mass. bar, 1928, since practiced in Boston; partner firm Powers, Hall, Montgomery & Weston, 1950-. Dir. Reece Corp., Torrington Mfg. Co., Workingsmens Coop. Bank, Raymond Engring., Inc., Marriner & Co., Inc., Dolan Steel Co., Inc. Chmn. Wellesley (Mass.) Adv. Com., 1947-50; chmn. Port of Boston Commn., 1953-57. Treas., dir. Frances E. Willard Homes, Boston, 1945-, pres., 1965-; bd. overseers Bowdoin Coll., 1965-. Mem. Am., Mass., Boston bar assns., Clubs: Harvard, Algonquin (Boston); Longwood Covered Courts (Brookline, Mass.). Home: 81 Beacon St Boston MA 02108 Office: 30 Federal St Boston MA 02110

GULLY, ARNOLD JARVIS, educator; b. Preston, Miss., July 8, 1921; s. John William and Martha (Jarvis) G.; B.S. in Chem. Engring., Auburn U., 1947; M.S., La. State U., 1950, Ph.D., 1951; m. Katharine Jordan, Dec. 18, 1945 (dec. 1968); children—Katharine, Jane, John, Martha; m. 2d, Lois Schallenberger Marmion, May 23, 1969. Quality control chemist Hercules Powder Co., 1947-48; prof. chem. engring. Miss. State U., 1951-59; research supt. Texaco Inc., 1959-63; prof. chem. engring., head dept. Tex. Tech. U., Lubbock, 1963-68, asso. dean engring., 1968—. Process engr. AEC, summers 1952, 53, Columbian Carbon Co., summer 1956, Mobil Oil Co., summer 1958. Served to lt. (j.g.) USNR, 1943-46. Mem. Am. Chem. Soc., Am. Inst. Chem. Engrs., Am. Soc. Engring. Edn., Sigma Xi, Tau Beta Pi, Omicron Delta Kappa, Phi Lambda Upsilon. Contbr. profl. jours. Home: 2406 Slide Rd Lubbock TX 79407

GULTON, LESLIE KAY, corp. exec.; b. Budapest, Hungary, June 5, 1901; s. Martin Rudolph and Ilka (Tandlich) G.; Ph.D., U. Graz, Austria, 1922; m. Edith Monath, Dec. 19, 1923; 1 dau., Marian (Mrs. Daniel Malcolm). Came to U.S., 1939, naturalized, 1945. First asst. Inst. Colloid Research, Frankfurt/Main, Germany, 1922-25; various exec. positions in Germany and France, 1925- 39; chmn. bd., pres. Gulton Industries, Inc., Metuchen, N.J., 1940-69; chmn. bd. Vernitron Corp., Carlstadt, N.M., 1969—. Mem. Chemists Club N.Y.C., Am. Chmn. Soc. Home: 425 Highview Rd Englewood NJ 07631 Office: Vernitron Corp Empire Blvd and Terminal Lane Carlstadt NJ 07072

GUM, MOY FOOK, educator; b. Honolulu, Oct. 29, 1924; s. William Wah Fong and Daisy (Mau) G.; A.B., U. Chgo., 1951, M.A., 1953, Ph.D., 1961; m. Dorothy Mew Ung Lee, Jan. 18, 1951; children—Gregory Shih-Ping, Elinor Mei-Hua, Aileen Mei-Mei, Joellyn Mei-Ying. Translator-interpretor State Dept., CBI, 1947-48; research asst. U. Hawaii, 1951-52; instr. George Williams Coll., 1955; instr., head Counseling Office, U. Minn., Duluth, 1956-61, asst. prof., head Counseling Office, 1961-62, asso. prof. psychology, dir. grad. studies, 1962-67, prof. psychology, dir. grad. studies, 1967- 70, prof. psychology, head dept. psychology, dir. grad. studies, 1970—; cons. pupil personnel sect. Minn. Dept. Edn., 1967—; dir. NDEA Elementary Guidance and Counseling Inst., 1968-69, EPDA Elementary Guidance and Counseling Fellowship Program, 1969-70. Del., Democratic Farm and Labor State Conv., 1970. Served with AUS, 1943-47; CBI, PTO. Recipient Faculty-Staff Leadership award U. Minn., 1960; USPHS grantee, 1955. Mem. Am., Minn. personnel and guidance assns., Am., No. Minn. psychol. assns., Am. Assn. U. profs., Phi Delta Kappa. Home: 1617 Cliff Av Duluth MN 55811

GUMBART, WILLIAM BARNUM, lawyer; b. Norwalk, Conn., Feb. 14, 1892; s. Edward H. and Mary Frances (Barnum) G.; A.B., Dartmouth Coll., 1913; law student Columbia; LL.B., Yale, 1915; m. Lucy Adele Finch, Oct. 18, 1919; childrenMary, William B. Admitted to Conn. bar, 1916, to Mass. bar, 1916, since practiced in New Haven; now of counsel Tyler, Cooper, Grant, Bowerman and Keefe; lectr. Conn. law Yale U. Sch. Law, New Haven, 1924-44; fellow Davenport Coll. of Yale; trustee Conn. Savs. Bank; dir. Berger Bros. Co., So. Conn. Gas Co., Alling Paper Co. Served as 1st lt. Q.M.C., U.S. Army, 1917-19; with A.E.F., France, 1918- 19. Former trustee Hopkins Grammar Sch.; past pres. New Haven Community Chest; former chmn. New Haven chpt. A.R.C. Fellow Am. Bar Found.; mem. Am., Conn. (past pres.) bar assns., Phi Beta Kappa. Republican. Conglist. Clubs: Graduate, Quinnipiack (former pres.), Rotary, Country. Home: 55 Laurel Rd Hamden CT 06511 Office: 205 Church St New Haven CT 06509

GUMBINER, JULIAN LEE, investment banker; b. Centralia, Ill., Apr. 9, 1909; s. Charles and Augusta (Woolner) G.; student U. Chgo., 1927-29; m. Gladys MacDowell, June 6, 1932; children—Donald, Judith. Various positions securities firms, Chgo., Mpls., St. Paul, Kansas City, 1929—; exec. v.p., dir. Stern Brothers & Co., Kansas City, 1957—: v.p., dir. Central Coal & Coke Corp.; dir. Gateway Sporting Goods Co., Berkley Industries, Inc., Volume Shoe Corp., Robo-Wash, Inc., Nat. Beef Packing Co., Frank Paxton Co., Nat. Bellas Hess, Inc., Cook Chem. Co., Rival Mfg. Co.; mem. finance com. Old Am. Ins. Co. Home: 455 E 55th St Kansas City MO 64110 Office: 9 W 1Oth St Kansas City MO 64105

GUMBLETON, THOMAS J., bishop; b. Detroit, Jan. 26, 1930; s. Vincent E. and Helen (Streintrager) G.; B.A., Sacred Heart Sem. Col.; J.C.D., Pontifical U. of the Lateran, Rome. Ordained priest Roman Cath. Ch., 1956; asso. pastor St. Alphonsus Parish, Dearborn, Mich., 1956-60; asst. chancellor Archdiocese Detroit, 1960-61; vice chancellor, 1965-68, aux. bishop, 1968—, vicar gen., 1968—. Address: 1234 Washington Blvd Detroit MI 48226

GUMMERE, JOHN, ins. co. exec.; b. Mt. Holly, N.J., Feb. 12, 1928; s. John Westcott and Ruth (Clark) G.; B.A., Yale, 1949; m. Eleanor Frances Greene, Oct. 9, 1954; childrenCynthia Clark, John Greene. With Phoenix Mut. Life Ins. Co., Hartford, Conn., 1949-, sec. charge underwriting dept., 1961-64, 2d v.p., 1964-65, v.p., 1965-. Bd. dirs. Children's Services Conn.; pres. Capitol Regional Mental Health Assn. Fellow Soc. Actuaries; mem. Home Office Life Underwriters Assn., Inst. Home Office Underwriters, Sigma Xi. Office: 1 American Row Hartford CT 06115

GUMMERE, WALTER COOPER, mfg. co. exec.; b. Columbus, O., Apr. 24, 1917; s. Walter Cooper and Glenn (Becker) G.; A.B., Brown U., 1940; M.B.A., U. Louisville, 1953; m. Virginia Lee Jeffries, Jan. 10, 1942; childrenVirginia (Mrs. Peter O. Haggerty), Deborah (Mrs. Charles W. Lilgendahl), Rebecca Jane. Chief indsl. engr. Colgate Palmolive Co., 1947-53; gen. supt., dir. Rich's Inc., Atlanta, 1953-57; personnel adminstr. Montgomery Ward & Co., Chgo., 1957-60; v.p., gen. mgr. Plasti-Line Inc., Knoxville, Tenn., 1960- 62; mgm. cons., 1962-63; with Tappan Co., 1963-, exec. v.p., 1966-, also dir.; dir. Farmers Savs. & Trust Co., Mansfield Brass and Aluminum Co. Mem. bd. Johnny Appleseed council Boy Scouts Am. Served to capt. AUS, 1942-46. Mem. Mansfield C. of C. (exec. com.), Delta Upsilon, Phi Beta Kappa. Presbyn. Home: Rebel Run Farm RD 6 Mansfield OH 44903 Office: 180 Park Av W Mansfield OH 44902

GUMMO, BLANCHARD STANLEY, artist, educator; b. Lock Haven, Pa., Feb. 3, 1906; s. Clarence Kent and Marilla (Stouck) G.; B.A., Yale, 1926, B.F.A., 1931; pvt. studies Hobson Pittman and Alexander Brook. Chmn. dept. art Bucknell U., 1931-68, prof. art, 1931—; painter, works exhibited Pa. Acad. Fine Arts, Allied Artists Am., Springfield (Mass.) Art League, Conn. Acad. Fine Arts, Butler Art Inst. (Youngstown, O.), Ind. Tchrs. Coll. Coop. Art Exhbns., Pepsi-Cola Shows, Cin. Mus., Chgo. Art Inst.; works rep. permanent collections Pa. Acad. Fine Arts, Bucknell U., Trinity Luth. Ch., Milton, Pa., pvt. collectors; one-man shows Lock Haven State Coll., Bucknell U., Susquehanna U., Wilkes Coll., Everhart Mus. (Scranton), Annie Halenbake Ross Library (Lock Haven), Lake Worth, Delray Beach pub. Libraries, Norton Gallery (West Palm Beach). Mem., adviser Lewisburg (Pa.) Council on Arts. Recipient medal for figure composition and portrait, Soc. Washington Artists, 1935, 1st prize for oils, Art Assn. Harrisburg, 1941, 52, 1st mention for oils, Springfield Art League, 1938, 1st prize for oils, Coop. Art Exhbns., 1949, M. Grumbacher hon. mention award, Fla. Internat. Art Exhbn., 1952. Mem. Midstate Artists, Artists Equity Assn., Delta Upsilon, Pi Alpha, Theta Alpha Phi. Republican. Methodist. Home: 402 W Church St Lock Haven PA 17745 Office: 219 Market St Lewisburg PA 17837

GUMP, RICHARD BENJAMIN, merchant; b. San Francisco, Jan. 22, 1906; s. Abraham Livingston and Mabel (Lichtenstein) G.; student Stanford, 1924-25, Cal. Sch. Fine Arts, 1931; m. Agnes Marie Fraser, Aug. 31, 1945 (div. Dec. 1960); 1 son by prev. marriage—Peter. Stock boy with S. & G. Gump Co., San Francisco, 1925-26, draftsman, 1926-27, European buyer, 1929-30, head designer Gump's Honolulu, 1939-41, v.p., gen. mgr. S. & G. Gump Co., San Francisco, 1944-47, pres., 1947—; pres. Gump's, Inc. since orgn., 1950. Served as mem. import adv. com. U.S. Dept. Commerce, 1946-48. Organizer, condr. Guckenheimer Sour Kraut Band. Recipient Star of the Solidarity of Italy, 1954. Mem. Redwood Empire Assn. (dir. 1947-48, 1949-52), San Francisco Art Assn. (sec.), Am. Acad. of Asian Studies (treas. 1957), San Francisco C. of C. (world trade com. 1948, 49, 50), A.S.C.A.P., Am. Inst. Decorators (asso. mem.). Clubs: Marin Golf and Sports, Rotary, Press, Lake Merced Golf and Country. Composer all types of music from popular band arrangements to symphonic and religious choral works; recording artist; lectr. Author: Jade, Stone of Heaven, 1962; Good Taste Costs No More, Watercolorist.

GUMPEL, HUGH artist; b. N.Y.C., Feb. 3, 1926; s. Morris and Helen (Stapleton) G.; student Columbia, Art Students League; m. Dorothy Werner, June 2, 1952; childrenDavid, Carolyn. Painter in water color and oil, 1950-; instr. Nat. Acad. Design, summer 1962; instr. painting pvt. classes Mamaroneck Studio; exhibited Butler Art Inst., Audubon Artists, Nat. Acad. Design. Am. Water Color Soc.; rep. permanent collections Norfolk Mus., Art Inst. of Zanesville, O., Somner Found., N.Y. Hosp. Recipient two grants Louis Comfort Tiffany Found.; purchase award Henry Ward Ranger Fund, N.A.D.; Am. Artist citation. A.N.A. Mem. Am. Water Color Soc. (mem. bd. 1960, corr. sec. 1961-62, Grand award with Gold medal of Honor 1968). Address: 335 Rushmore Av Mamaroneck NY 10543

GUMPERT, EMIL, judge; b. Stockton, Cal., Jan. 14, 1895; s. William and Sarah (Gellert) G.; student Columbia, 1919-20, Washington and Lee U., 1919; LL.D., U. of Pacific; m. Ruth Kenner, July 18, 1925; 1 son, William Kenner. Admitted to Cal. bar, 1916, trial and corp. lawyer, Stockton, 1916-47; judge Superior Ct. Cal., Los Angeles, 1956—. Mem. adv. panel Cal. Youth Authority, 1953. Fellow Am. Coll. Trial Lawyers (founder, pres. 1950-51, chmn. bd. regents 1952-53, chancellor 1953—), Am. Bar Found. (life); mem. Los Angeles World Affairs Council, State Bar Cal. (gov. 1950-53, pres. 1951-52), Am. Bar Assn., Am. Judicature Soc., Am. Legion. Mason (Shriner). Mem. B'nai B'rith. Chmn. bd. editors Cal. Jury Instructions. Home: 149 S. Woodburn Dr Los Angeles CA 90049 Office: Superior Ct Bldg Los Angeles CA 90012

GUNADIRDJA, ABDURRAHMAN, Indonesian diplomat; b. Tanggerang, Indonesia, Apr. 26, 1926; s. Chassan and Nursari (Djohan) G.; B.A., U. Indonesia, 1955; M.A., Far Eastern U., Manila, 1960; m. Mastura binti Hadji Noordin, Sept. 22, 1968; 1 son, Eddy Masman. Vice consul, Indonesian Consulate Gen., Hongkong, 1956-57, Singapore, 1957-58; 3d sec. Indonesian embassy, Manila, Philippine Islands, 1958-60; dir., editor English newspaper Indonesian Herald, Djakarta, 1961-63; 1st sec. Indonesian embassy, Peking, People's Republic China, 1963-64, Tokyo, Japan, 1965-67; chief pub. relations Dept. Fgn. Affairs, Djakarta, 1967-71; minister counsellor Indonesian embassy, Washington, 1971—. Home: 4701 Willard St Chevy Chase MD 20016 Office: 2020 Massachusetts Av Washington DC 20036

GUNCKEL, JAMES EUGENE, educator; b. Indpls., June 8, 1914; s. Don A. and G. Beatrice (Stanley) G.; student U. Cin., 1934-36; B.S. in Edn., Miami U. (O.), 1938; M.A., Harvard, 1941, Ph.D., 1945; m. Roberta Jean Longworth, Aug. 30, 1941; childrenFred James, Nancy Katherine. Librarian, Dayton (O.) Pub. Library, 1928-34; folder operator McCall Pub. Co., 1934-36; grad. asst. botany Miami U., 1938-39; teaching fellow Harvard, 1939-43; spl. coordinator Army-Navy tng. program in biology 1943-45, instr. biology, 1945-46; mem. faculty Rutgers U., 1946-, prof. botany, 1957-, chmn. dept., 1954-; research collaborator biology dept. Brookhaven Nat. Lab., 1951-57, cons., 1950-; research contract AEC, 1951-. Del. 8th Internat. Congress of Botany, Paris, 1954. Recipient Waksman Found. in France award, 1959-60. Mem. Torrey Bot. Club (editor bull. 1960-62, pres. 1965). Bot. Soc. Am. Gen. Sect. (sec. 1953-56, editorial bd. 1957, chmn. 1958-60), Internat. Soc. Plant Morphologists, Am. Soc. Plant Physiologists, Radiation Research Soc., Soc., Study Growth and Development, Sigma Xi. Mem. Reformed Ch. Contbr. articles profl. jours., encys. Home: 29 Crestwood Dr Somerville NJ 08876 Office: Botany Dept Rutgers U New Brunswick NJ 08903

GUNDER, ROGER W., chem. co. exec.; b. Ft. Wayne, Ind., Feb. 8, 1909; ed. high sch. and business school, San Diego; m. Mary Runyon. With McKesson & Robbins, 1927-34; with Stauffer Chem. Co., 1934—, exec. v.p., 1965-67, pres., chief exec. officer 1967—, also dir., chmn. exec. com.; vice chmn., dir. Stauffer Wacker Silicone Corp.; dir. toyo-Stauffer Chem. Co., Am. Chem. Corp., Calhio Chems., Inc., Montrose Chem. Corp. of Cal. Mem. Mfg. Chemists Assn. (chmn. exec. com., dir.). Clubs: French (San Francisco); Greenwich Country; Bohemian (San Francisco); Sky, Board Room, Economic (N.Y.C.); Menlo Country (Menlo Park, Cal.). Office: 299 Park Av New York City NY 10017

GUNDERSEN, JAMES NOVOTNY, educator; B.S., U. Wis., 1949; M.A., U. Cal., 1955; Ph.D., U. Minn., 1958. Prof., head dept. geology U. Ariz., Tucson. Office: Dept Geology U Ariz Tucson AZ 85721*

GUNDERSEN, SVEN MARTIN, physician; b. LaCrosse, Wis., Sept. 12, 1904; s. Adolf and Helga (Isaksaetre) G.; student U. Wis., 1922-25; M.D., Harvard, 1929; m. Harriet Elizabeth Adams, June 23, 1934; childrenKaren (Mrs. Alan Jay Lerner), Pamela (Mrs. Ralph English Miller). Intern, East med. service Mass. Gen. Hosp., Boston, 1929-31; asst. resident, then resident New Haven Hosp., 1931-33; practice in Boston, 1933-37; physician Hitchcock Clinic, Hanover, N.H., 1937-69, chmn. bd. dirs., 1960-64; instr. medicine Yale Med. Sch., 1932-33; asst. medicine Harvard Med. Sch., 1933-37; clin. prof. medicine Dartmouth Med. Sch., 1961-69; cons. N.H. Dept. Health; sr. cons. VA; mem. Doctors' Com. Med. Care of Elderly Through Social Security, 1963, White House Conf. Health, 1965. Mem. N.H., Grafton County med. socs., Am. Heart Assn., Am. Rheumatism Assn., A.C.P. (gov. for N.H.), Am. Clin. and Climatological Assn., Am. Trudeau Soc., Phi Beta Kappa, Beta Theta Pi, Nu Sigma Nu. Democrat. Author articles serum treatment pneumonia, diabetes, atypical pneumonia. Home: Balch Hill Hanover, NH 03755. Office: 2 Maynard St Hanover NH 03755

GUNDERSON, HARVEY JONES, lawyer; b. San Francisco, Aug. 29, 1906; s. Andrew Bennett and Clara (Jones) G.; A.B., U. Mich., 1928, LL.B., 1930; grad. in economics, U. S. D., 1930; m. Alwayne Burkhart, Dec. 2, 1933. Admitted to bar. S.D., 1929, since in practice of law, Vermillion, S.D., Washington partner law firm Gunderson & Gunderson; engaged in business individually as agent and farmer, Vermillion, 1930—; counsel Mpls. agy. Reconstrn. Finance Corp., 1932-35, Washington, 1935-41, asst. gen. counsel, 1941—; gen. counsel Disaster Loan Corp., 1937-45; asst. gen. counsel Metals Reserve Co., Washington, 1940-42, gen. counsel, 1942-44, exec. v. p., gen. counsel, 1944-45; exec. dir. Office of Metals Reserve, R.F.C., 1945. Dir. R.F.C., Fed. Nat. Mortgage Assn., 1945-5O, Weylin Corp.; eastern rep. Transam. Corp., 1950-53; partner Gunderson & Fuller, Washington, 1950—; pres. H. J. Gunderson & Assos.; dir. Gt. Western Malting Co., Alkali, Inc. Pres. Williams Found. U.S.A. Served as lt. col. Cav., AUS. Prodn. Divisions, Hdqrs. A.S.F., 1942-45. Mem. Am. (life), Fed. bar assns., State Bar S.D., Nat. Lawyers Club, U.S. Cav. Assn., Phi Delta Theta, Phi Alpha Delta, Sigma Delta Chi, Scabbard and Blade. Republican. Mason. Clubs: Denver; Capitol Hill, Burning Tree, Congressional, Metropolitan, Aviation (Washington). Home: 205 Lewis St Vermillion SD also 3335 Stuyvesant Place NW Washington DC 20015 Office: Nat Bank of South Dakota Bldg Vermillion SD 57069 also Wyatt Bldg 777 14th NW Washington DC 20006

GUNDERSON, NORMAN OLE, educator; b. Laramie, Wyo., Sept. 10, 1918; s. Ole and Esther Amelia (Peterson) G.; B.S., U. Wyo., 1939, M.S., 1947; C.E., Stanford, 1955; m. Bonne Jeane Davis, July 18, 1942; children—John Davis, Cherie Lynn. Engr., Wyo. Hwy. Dept., U.S. Soil Conservation Service, U.S. Bur. Reclamation, 1939-41; faculty U. Hawaii, 1947-48; faculty San Jose State Coll., 1948—, dean engring., 1956-70, dir. Cybernetic Systems Program, 1970—; cons. planning City of San Jose. Served from 2d lt. to maj. AUS, 1941-46. Registered profl. engr., Cal. Mem. Am. Soc. C.E., Nat. Soc. Profl. Engrs., Am. Soc. Engring. Edn., Res. Officers Assn. Am., A.A.A.S., World Futures Soc., Am. Acad. Arts and Scis., Soc. for Gen. Systems Research Assn. for Systems Mgmt., Phi Kappa Phi, Sigma Chi. Republican. Clubs: Engineers (San Jose); Commonwealth of California. Home: 1465 Weaver Dr San Jose CA 95125

GUNDERSON, ROY MELVIN, educator; b. Ecorse, Mich., May 1, 1930; B.S., Ill. Inst. Tech., 1951; M.S., U. Wis., 1952; Ph.D. (fellow), Brown U., 1956. Asst. in math. U. Wis., Madison, 1951-52; asst. in applied math. Brown U., 1953-55; mathematician U. Chgo., 1955; dir. research U. Paris (France), 1955-56; research engr. Boeing Aircraft Co., 1956-57; asst. prof. math. Ill. Inst. Tech., Chgo., 1957-60, asso. prof., 1960-63; prof. math. U. Wis.-Milw., 1963—. Cons. Armour Research Found., 1957, 59-60, Bendix Systems div. Bendix Corp., 1960-61. NSF research grantee, 1958-60. Mem. Am. Math. Soc., Soc. Natural Philosophy. Office: Dept Math U Wis-Milw Milwaukee WI 53201*

GUNDERSON, SHERMAN EDWARD, educator; b. Waupaca, Wis., Sept. 3, 1906; s. Gunder and Bessie (Salverson) G.; Ph.B., Ripon Coll., 1927; A.M., Columbia, 1931; Ph.D., State U. Ia., 1951; m. Alma E. Walter, June 20, 1928; childrenThomas, Sheridah, John. High sch. tchr., debate coach, Two Rivers, Wis., 1927- 43; high sch. tchr., Madison, Wis., 1943-46; with faculty Wis. State U. at Oshkosh, 1946-, prof. econs., 1954-, chmn. dept., 1956-63, dean Sch. Letters and Arts, 1963-66, v.p. program devel. and staffing, 1966- 70; cons. First Nat. Bank Oshkosh, 1963. Bd. dirs. Wis. Tchrs. Retirement System, 1956—. Mem. Am. Econ. Assn., Assn. Higher Edn., Assn. Gen. and Liberal Studies, Artus Soc. Mason, Rotarian. Home: 1720 Chestnut St Oshkosh WI 45901

GUNDY, CHARLES LAKE, investment exec.; b. Toronto, Ont., Can., Feb. 6, 1905; s. James Henry and Serena Lake (Clarke) G.; student Appleby Coll., Oakville, Ont., 1913-23, U. Toronto, 1923-26; LL.D., U. Toronto, 1969; m. Virginia Diana Antoinette Ritchie, June 2, 1939. With Wood, Gundy Ltd., Toronto, Ont., Can., 1926—, sales mgr., 1939-41, v.p., 1945-48, pres., 1948-67, chmn., 1967—, also dir.; partner Wood, Gundy & Co.; dir. Abitibi Paper Co., Ltd., Can. Cement Lafarge Ltd., Canron Ltd., Canadian Niagara Power Co., Dominion Life Assurance Co., Domtar Ltd., Massey-Ferguson Ltd., Simpsons, Ltd., Simpsons-Sears, Ltd., United Corps., Ltd. Chmn. bd. trustees Hosp. for Sick Children. Served to maj. with Canadian Army, 1941-45. Mem. Canadian Soc. Clin. Investigation (hon.), Canadian Assn. for Advancement of Health Scis. (founding), Investment Dealers' Assn. Can. (hon. pres. 1961, chmn. sr. adv. com. 1969—), Bd. Trade, Zeta Psi. Mem. United Ch. Can. Clubs: Toronto, Golf, York (Toronto); Canadian (London, Eng.); Echo Beach Fishing, Mount Royal, St. James (Montreal); Vancouver (B.C.); Beaver Winter, Hunt, Glenmajor Angling. Home: 43 Russell Hill Rd Toronto Ontario Canada Office: Royal Trust Tower PO Box 274 Toronto Dominion Centre Toronto 111 Ontario Canada

GUNDY, HOWARD B., ednl. adminstr. Dean Sch. Social Work U. Ala. Office: Sch Social Work U Ala University AL 35486*

GUNKLER, CARL ANDREW, Jr., banker; b. Ft. Wayne, Ind., Jan. 23, 1920; s. Carl A. and Bertha C. (Niebergall) G.; student Grad. Sch. Banking Rutgers U., 1951; m. June B. Denton, May 23, 1946; 1 son, Andrew C. With Lincoln Nat. Bank & Trust Co., Ft. Wayne, 1939—, sr. v.p., dir., 1968—; asso. dir. Shipshewana State Bank (Ind.). Pres., Ft. Wayne Conv. Bur., 1963-64; treas., dir. Jr. Achievement Ft. Wayne; mem. exec. bd. Anthony Wayne council Boy Scouts Am., 1962—; mem. Purdue Econ. Edn. Adv. Bd., 1960—. Served with USAAF, 1942-46. Mem. Financial Execs. Inst., Ind. Bankers Assn. Episcopalian. Clubs: Press, Orchard Ridge Country (pres. Ft. Wayne 1966-67). Home: 5615 Indiana Av Fort Wayne IN 46807 Office: 116 E Berry St Fort Wayne IN 46802

GUNN, BILL, (William Harrison Gunn), actor, writer; b. Phila., July 15, 1934; s. William Harrison and Louise (Alexander) G.; student pub. schs. Phila. Actor stage, TV, films, 1955- ; appeared in Antony and Cleopatra, 1962, Take a Giant Step. Served with USNR. Democrat. Author: (play) Marcus in the High Grass, 1960; All the Rest Have Died, 1964. Address: care Bertha Case 42 W 53d St New York City NY 10019

GUNN, FRANK LEROY, retired army officer; b. Crawfordville, Ga., Mar. 21, 1920; s. Fortson L. and Eva (Herndon) G.; B.S., U. Ga., 1941; postgrad. Yale, 1946; grad. Army Command and Gen. Staff Coll., 1952, Armed Forces Staff Coll., 1955, Army War Coll., 1959, U. Pitts. Grad. Sch. Bus., 1963; m. Doris Yates, June 2, 1941; children—Lacy Kathryn, Frank Leroy. Commd. 2d lt. U.S. Army, 1941, advanced through grades to brig. gen., 1964; asst. chief, then chief Tng. Div., Office Dep. Chief of Staff for Mil. Operations, Dept. Army, Washington, 1959-61; chief of staff 1st Cav. Div., Korea, 1961-62; chief strategic studies group Army Inst. Advanced Studies, Carlisle Barracks, Pa., 1962-64; dep. comdg. gen. Army Tng. Center, Inf., Ft. Ord, Cal., 1964-66; asst. dep. chief of staff for unit tng. and readiness Hdqrs. U.S. Continental Army Command, Ft. Monroe, Va., 1966; comdg. gen. U.S. Army Recruiting Command, Hampton, Va., 1966-68; asst. div. comdr. 9th Inf. Div., Vietnam, 1968-69; asst. chief of staff for mil. assistance U.S. Mil. Assistance Command, Vietnam, 1969-70; dep. chief of staff for intelligence Hdqrs. CONARC, Ft. Monroe, 1970, dep. chief of staff for force devel., 1970-71; retired, 1971; dir. manpower planning Coop. Area Manpower Planning System, 1971—. Decorated D.S.M. with oak leaf cluster, Silver Star with 2 oak leaf clusters, Legion of Merit, D.F.C., Bronze Star with oak leaf cluster, Air medal with 19 oak leaf clusters, Joint Service Commendation medal, Army Commendation medal, Purple Heart with oak leaf cluster, Combat Inf. badge; French Croix de Guerre avec palme; Belgian Fourragere; Vietnam Cross of Gallantry with palm, Vietnam Army Distinguished Service Order 1st class, Vietnam Navy Service medal honor class, Vietnam Civil Actions Honor medal 1st class. Home: 320 Beauregard Heights Hampton VA 23369 Office: 2019 Cunningham Dr Hampton VA 23366

GUNN, GEORGE PURNELL, ret. bishop; b. Winona, Miss., Oct. 11, 1903; s. Elijah Steirling and Susan Ellwood (Carter) G.; grad. Protestant Episcopal Theol. Sem., Alexandria, Va., 1930, D.D., 1948; student Va. Episcopal Sch., Lynchburg, 1921-23; U. Va., 1924-27; m. Frances Hawkins Purnell, Sept. 3, 1930; children—George Purnell Jr., James Steirling. Carter Tredway. Ordained deacon Protestant Episcopal Ch., 1929, priest, 1930; consecrated bishop, 1948; rector Moore Parish, Altavista. Va., 1930-32, Ch. of the Good Shepherd, Norfolk, Va., 1932-48; bishop coadjutor Diocese So. Va., 1948-50, diocesan (sr. bishop), Apr. 1950-71. Dean Tidewater Convocation. Pres. bd. trustees St. Paul's Poly. Inst. Lawrenceville, Va.; trustee P.E. Theol. Seminary, Chathan Hall, Episcopal H.S., Stuart Hall, Boy's Home, Jackson-Feild Home. Bd. dirs. Travelers Aid; bd. dirs., mem. exec. com. Tidewater council Boy Scouts Am., Norfolk chpt. A.R.C. Mem. Order First Families of Va., Phi Delta Theta. Mason, Rotarian (bd. dirs.). Home: 1326 Cloncurry Rd Lochaven Norfolk VA 23505

GUNN, LEWIS BURWELL, banker; b. Richmond, Va., Aug. 20, 1905; s. Randolph Wellford and Alla (Jones) G.; student bus. adminstrn. U. Richmond, 1929-30; grad. Am. Inst. Banking, 1929; m. Dorothy Ryce, Apr. 14, 1934; children—Margaret V. (Mrs. James B. Farinholt, Jr.) (dec.), Lewis Burwell. With State-Planters Bank of Commerce & Trusts, Richmond, Va., 1922-71, clk., asst. trust officer, trust officer, 1922-42, v.p. and trust officer charge trust dept., 1942-61, dir., 1945-71, exec. v.p., 1961-63, vice chmn. bd., 1963-70; vice chmn. bd. United Va. Bankshares, Inc., 1963-70, dir., 1963—; dir. Publishers Envelope Co., Chesapeake Corp. Va., Mut. Assurance Soc. Va. Mem. investment com. Richmond Instructive Vis. Nurses Assn. to 1971. Bd. dirs. Collegiate Schs., Richmond, Richmond Eye Hosp., Richmond Meml. Hosp., Ellis-Olsson-Chesapeake Found., West Point, Va. Mem. Phi Kappa Sigma. Home: 1808 Monument Av Richmond, VA 23220. Office: 900 E Main St Richmond VA 23219

GUNN, MOSES, actor; b. St. Louis, Oct. 2, 1929; s. George and Mary (Briggs) G.; foster mother, Jewel C. Richie; A.B., Tenn. State U., 1959; m. Gwen Landes, July 25, 1966; 1 dau., Kirsten Sarah. Theatrical appearances include The Blacks, 1962-63, In White America, 1963-64, Day of Absence, 1965, Measure for Measure, 1965, A Hand is on The Gate, 1966, Aavron in Titus Andronicus, 1957, Negro Ensemble Co., 1967-68; TV Appearances include N.Y. Police Dept., Of Mice and Men, The FBI; film Nothing But a Man, 1962. Served with AUS, 1954-57. Recipient Obie award, 1967-68; Jersey Jour. award for best actor, 1967-68. Mem. Theta Alpha Phi. Address: 463 W 2d St New York City NY 10009

GUNN, PAUL JAMES, educator, artist; b. Guys Mills, Pa., June 21, 1922; s. Theodore Jacob and Sarah (Beck) G.; B.S. in Art Edn., Edenboro (Pa.) State Tchrs. Coll., 1947; M.F.A., Cal. Coll. Arts and Crafts, 1948; m. Elaine Marie Almgren, June 8, 1946; childrenThomas Jay, Steven Ray. Mem. faculty Ore. State U., Corvallis, 1948—, prof. art, 1964—, also chmn. dept.; exhbns. include Oakland (Cal.) Art Mus., 1951, Denver Art Mus., 1951, Internat. Bordighera (Italy) Biennial 1957, Portland Art Mus., 1953, Seattle Art Mus., 1954, Cheney-Cowles Mus., Spokane, 1956; represented in permanent collections Portland Art Mus., Cheney-Cowles Mus., Seattle Art Mus., Am. Information Service Collection, Athens, Greece, Bibliotheque Nationale, Paris, France, Victoria and Albert Mus., London, Eng. Served with USNR, 1943-46: PTO. Home: 1440 Kings Rd Corvallis, OR 97330.

GUNN, STANLEY VEERIN, rocket propulsion engr.; b. Portland, Ore., May 21, 1923; s. Reuben Veerin and Christina (Rouwenhorst) G.; B.S. in Mech. Engring., Mich. State U., 1947; M.S., Purdue U., 1949, Ph.D., 1953; m. Doris Elaine Clonts, Sept. 9, 1945; childrenTibby Marie, Nancy Carol, Karen Christine, Susan Katherin. Instr., research asst. Purdue U., 1948-52; propulsion engr. guided missile dept. Gen. Electric Co., 1952-53; sr. research engr., supr., project engr., program engr. and program mgr. Rover program, Rocketdyne div. North Am. Aviation, 1953-; research ignition lags hypergolic rocket propellants. Served at 1st lt., combat engrs., AUS, 1943-46. Mem. Am. Rocket Soc. (chmn. nuclear propulsion com.), Sigma Xi. Home: 22454 Gilmore St Canoga Park CA 91304 Office: 6633 Canoga Av Canoga Park CA 91303

GUNN, THOMSON WILLIAM, poet; b. Gravesend, Eng., Aug. 29, 1929; s. Herbert Smith and Ann Charlotte (Thomson) G.; B.A., Trinity Coll., Cambridge (Eng.) U., 1953. Came to U.S., 1954. Tchr. English, U. Cal. at Berkeley, 1958-66; ordained minister Universal Life Ch., 1969. Author: Fighting Terms, 1954; The Sense of Movement, 1957; My Sad Captains, 1961; Touch, 1967; Moly, 1971. Address: 1216 Cole St San Francisco CA 94117

GUNN, WILLIAM GEORGE, firearms co. exec.; b. Springfield, Mass. Sept. 29, 1909; s. James and Annie C. (Knowles) G.; m. Doris P. Halsted, Aug, 3, 1931; 1 son, Donald W. Draftsman small motor engring. dept. Westinghouse Electric Co., 1927- 29; with Smith & Wesson, Inc., Springfield, 1929-, exec. v.p., 1962-63, pres., 1963-, group v.p. Bangor Punta operations, 1968-, also dir.; dir. 3d Nat. Bank. Mem. Am. Ordnance Assn. Mason. Club: Suffield Country. Home: 31 Wendover Rd Suffield CT 06078 Office: 2100 Roosevelt Av Springfield MA 01109

GUNNEMANN, LOUIS HERMAN, educator: b. Indpls., Dec. 12, 1910; s. Louis and Lydia Amelia (Amt) G.; B.A., Lakeland Coll., Plymouth, Wis., 1932; B.D., Mission House Theol. Sem., Plymouth, 1935, D.D., 1952; Th.M., Princeton Theol. Sem., 1953; m. Johanna Diedericke Menke, June 4, 1935; children—Judith Ann (Mrs. Bruce R. Pullen), Jon Peter, Joanne Ruth (Mrs. Allan J. Dempsey). Ordained to ministry United Ch. Christ, 1935; pastor in Tipton, Ia., 1935-41, Immanuel United Ch. Christ, Lafayette, Ind. 1941-52; tchr., dean Mission House Theol. Sem., Plymouth, Wis., 1953-62, United Theol. Sem. Twin Cities, New Brighton, Minn., 1962—; scholar-in-residence Harvard, 1968. Chmn. commn. worship United Ch. Christ, 1961-, corp. mem. bd. homeland ministries, 1961-; sec. Am. Assn. Theol. Schs., 1964-; mem. adminstrv. com. N.Am. area council Alliance Ref. Chs., 1960—. Editorial com. Theology and Life, 1959—. Home: 600 Driftwood Rd New Brighton, MN 55112. Office: 3000 5th St NW New Brighton MN 55112

GUNNENG, ARNE, Norwegian diplomat; b. Oslo, Norway, Dec. 1, 1914; s. Andreas Christian and Jenny (Gronholdt) G.; LL.B., Oslo U., 1937; m. Ingrid Fleischer, Feb. 11, 1939; childrenThale, Hedda, Nora. Joined Norwegian Fgn. Service, 1945; 1st sec. embassy, Washington, 1945-48; assigned Ministry Fgn. Affairs, 1948-50; charge d'affaires, Warsaw, Poland, 1950-51; counsellor, Stockholm, Sweden, 1951-52; dep. permanent rep. N. Atlantic Council, Paris, France, 1952-55; ambassador to Can., 1955-59; dir. gen. polit. affairs Ministry Fgn. Affairs, 1959-62; ambassador to Sweden, 1962-66, to U.S., 1966-. Home: 3401 Massachusetts Av NW Washington, DC 20007.

GUNNERSON, JAMES HOWARD, educator; b. Aurora, Neb., Nov. 28, 1922; s. Joe. E. and Mabel Murl (Brickner) G.; B.S., U. Neb., 1949, M.A., 1950; postgrad., Harvard, 1950-54, Ph.D., 1963; m. Dolores Alice Bellamy, Jan. 3, 1944; 1 son, James Lawrence. Curator, Mus. Anthropology, U. Utah, 1954-60; asst. prof. anthropology No. Ill. U., DeKalb, 1963-64, asso. prof., 1964-69, prof., 1969—. Served with USAAF, 1943-46. Thaw fellow Peabody Mus., Harvard, 1962-63. Fellow Am. Anthrop. Assn., Current Anthropology (asso.); mem. Soc. Am. Archaeology, A.A.A.S., Sigma Xi. Contbr. articles profl. jours. Home: 545 Garden Rd DeKalb IL 60115

GUNNESS, ROBERT CHARLES, chem. engr., b. Fargo, N.D., July 28, 1911; s. Christian I. and Elizabeth (Rice) G.; B.S., Mass. State Coll., Amherst, 1932; M.S., Mass. Inst. Tech., 1934, D.Sc., 1936; m. Beverly Osterberger, June 18, 1936; childrenRobert Charles, Donald Austin, Beverly Anne. Asst. prof. chem. engring. Mass. Inst. Tech., 1936-38; research dept. Standard Oil Co. Ind., 1938-47, mgr. research, 1947-51, asst. gen. mgr. mfg. 1952-54, gen. mgr. supply and transp., 1954-56, exec. v.p., 1956-65, pres., 1965—; dir., 1953; dir. Inland Steel Co., Harris Trust & Savs. Bank. Vice chmn. research and devel. bd. Dept. Def., 1951. Trustee U. Chgo.; life mem. Mass. Inst. Tech. Corp.; past pres. John Crerar Library. Mem. Am. Inst. Chem. Engrs. (council 1951), Am. Chem. Soc., Am. Petroleum Inst., Sigma Xi, Phi Kappa Phi, Kappa Sigma. Clubs: Commercial, Chicago (Chgo.); Flossmoor (Illinois) Country; Chemists (N.Y.C.); Cosmos (Washington); Glen View. Home: 1110 Lake Shore Dr Chicago IL 60611 Office: 910 S Michigan Av Chicago IL 60680

GUNNING, ROBERT CLIFFORD, mathematician, educator; b. Longmont, Colo., Nov. 27, 1931; s. Clifford Henry and Inez (Wilhelm) G.; A.B., U. Colo., 1952; M.A., Princeton, 1953, Ph.D., 1955; m. Wanda S. Holtzinger, July 9, 1966. NSF fellow U. Chgo., 1955-56; faculty Princeton, 1956—, prof. math., 1966—; vis. prof. U. Sao Paulo, Brazil, 1957; Sloan fellow, 1958-61; asst. dir. studies, prof. math. St. Catharines Coll., Cambridge U., 1959-60; vis. prof. U. Munich, 1967; mem. editorial bd. Princeton U. Press, 1969-73. Mem. Am. Math. Soc., Societe Mathematique de France, Phi Beta Kappa, Sigma Xi. Clubs: Princeton (N.Y.C.); Nassau (Princeton). Author: (with H. Rossi) Analytic Functions of Several Complex Variables, 1965; Lectures on Riemann Surfaces, 1967; Lectures on Complex Analytic Varieties, 1970. Office: Fine Hall Box 37 Princeton NJ 08540

GUNSALUS, IRWIN CLYDE, educator; b. Sully County, S.D., June 29, 1912; s. I. Clyde and Anna (Shea) G.; B.S., Cornell U., 1935, M.S., 1937, Ph.D., 1940; m. Merle La Mont, Aug. 17, 1935; children-Gene, Glen, Ann, Robert, Richard; m. 2d, Carolyn Faust, June 16, 1951 (dec. Jan. 1970); children—Carolyn Kristina, Kristin Carla; m. 3d, Dorothy Clark, Nov. 21, 1970. From instr. to asso. prof. Cornell U., Ithaca, N.Y., 1937- 46, prof. bacteriology, 1946-47, Ind. U., 1947-50; prof. bacteriology U. Ill., Urbana, 1950-55, prof. biochemistry, 1955—, head biochemistry div. chem. dept., 1955-66, Center for

Advanced Study, 1966-67. Vis. prof. microbiology U. Cal. at Berkeley, summer 1949; discovered coenzyme from vitamin B6; isolated, syntheses and function lipoic acid; occurrance anaerobic hexose monophosphate fermentation mechanisms; biol. control of growth and energy supply. Guggenheim fellow, 1949, 59, 68; Nat. Acad. Scis., 1966. Co- recipient Mead Johnson award biochemistry, 1946. Fellow A.A.A.S.; mem. N.Y. Acad. Sci., Am., Brit. biochem. and microbiol. socs., Am. Chem. Soc., Am. Physiol. Soc., Genetic Soc. Am., Sigma Xi, Phi Kappa Phi, Alpha Chi Sigma. Home: 2002 S Race St Urbana IL 61801

GUNSETT, HELEN TOSSEY, mem. Democratic nat. com.; b. Van Wert, O., Oct. 5, 1909; d. Ira and Lucy (Stuckey) Tossey; student Ohio State U., 1927-29; m. Luther Gunsett, Feb. 2, 1936. Mem. Ohio Dem. Exec. Com., 1950-; charter mem. Ohio Young Dem. Exec. Com.; mem. Ohio Dem. Central Com. from 5th Dist., 1950-; trustee Federated Dem. Women Ohio, 1955-57; vice chmn. Van Wert County Dem. Exec. Com., 1956-58; mem. Dem. Nat. Com. from Ohio, 1956-; alternate at large Dem. Nat. Conv., 1956, del. at large, 1960, 64, co-chmn. credentials com., 1964. Mem. Van Wert Bd. Health, 1956-; mem. Presdl. bd. advisers Fed. Reformatory for Women; vice chmn. Van Wert Civic Planning Com. Incorporator Van Wert County Hist. Soc.; mem. twig group Van Wert Hosp.; dir. women's aux. Ohio br. Starr Commonwealth Sch. Boys, local A.R.C., YWCA and Am. Heart Assn. Mem. League Women Voters, D.A.R., Columbus Urban League, UN Assn., Kappa Delta. Clubs: Van Wert Country Democratic Women's (pres.), Van Wert Woman's (pres. 1954-56). Address: 2636 Nottingham Rd Columbus, OH 43221.

GUNSON, LEO JOSEPH, business exec.; b. Phila., July 5, 1896; s. John D. and Mary F. (Cahill) G.; student Notre Dame Acad., Phila., 1902-08, St. Joseph's Coll., 1908- 12, U. Pa., 1914-17; m. Florence G. Cullen, June 29, 1922; children—Mary Elizabeth, Leo Joseph, Jr. With Publicker Industries, Inc. 1924—, now vice chmn., treas., dir.; pres., dir. Continental Distilling Corp., Oak Hickory Distilling Corp. Served to 1st lt. 312th Machine Gun Bn., World War I. Decorated knight grand cross Order Holy Sepulchre. Mem. Am. Legion. Clubs: Philadelphia Country, Midday (Phila.); Chemists (N.Y.C.). Home: 1810 Rittenhouse Sq Philadelphia PA 19103 Office: 1429 Walnut St Philadelphia PA 19102

GUNTER, ELDER, city manager; b. Douglass, Kan., Jan. 9, 1916; s. D.F. and Mary (Elder) G.; B.A., U. Wichita, 1938; m. Martha Ann Daniels, June 2, 1938; children-Rebecca, Catherine, Daniel, Mark. Asst. to city mgr., Wichita, Kan., 1938-45; city mgr., Newton, Kan., 1945-47, Junction City, Kan., 1947-50, University City, Mo., 1950-58, Des Moines, 1958-63, Pasadena, Cal., 1963-66; program adminstr. Ford Found. Overseas Devel. Program Mideast and Africa, 1966-67; dep. asst. sec. Dept. Housing and Urban Devel., 1967-68; city mgr. Yonkers, N.Y., 1968-69, Stockton, Cal., 1969—. Mem. Internat. City Mgrs. Assn. (pres. 1962), Cal. League Cities. Rotarian (pres. 1958). Author articles in field. Home: 6237 Shenandoah Pl Stockton CA 95207

GUNTER, GORDON, zoologist; b. Goldonna, La., Aug. 18, 1909; s. John O. and Joanna (Pennington) G.; B.A., La. State Normal Coll., 1929; M.A., U. Tex., 1931, Ph.D., 1945; m. Frances M. Hudgins, Sept. 7, 1957; childrenEdmund Osbon, Harry Allen; children by previous marriageCharlotte A. (Mrs. Bobby G. Wood), Miles G., Forrest P. Biologist, U.S. Bur. Fisheries, intermittently, 1931-38; marine biologist Tex. Game, Fish and Oyster Commn., 1939-45; research scientist Inst. Marine Sci., U. Tex., 1945-49, dir., 1949-55; prof. zoology Marine Lab., U. Miami (Fla.), 1946-47; sr. marine biologist Scripps Instn. Oceanography, 1948-49; dir. Gulf Coast Research Lab., Ocean Springs, Miss., 1955—, also prof. biology U. Miss. and U. So. Miss., prof. zoology Miss. State U. Tex. area cons. Office Coordinator Fisheries, 1942-45; adv. panel comml. seafoods div. La. Commn. Wild Life and Fisheries, 1953-54; vice chmn. biology, com. treatise on marine ecology NRC, 1942-57; sci. adv. panel Gulf State Marine Fisheries Commn., 1956—; mem. bd. advisors Fla. Bd. Conservation. Fellow Internat. Oceanographic Found.; mem. Am. Fisheries Soc., Am. Ornithologists Union, Am. Soc. Ichthyologists and Herpetologists, Am. Soc. Limnology and Oceanography, Am. Soc. Mammalogists, Am. Soc. Naturalists, Am. Soc. Zoologists, Ecol. Soc. Am., La., Miss., New Orleans acads. scis., Nat. Shellfisheries Assn., Internat. Acad. Fishery Scientists, Wildlife Soc., Am. Inst. Fishery Research Biologists, Miss. Acad. Scis. (pres. 1964-65), Sigma Xi, Phi Kappa Phi. Author articles in field. Address: Gulf Coast Research Lab Ocean Springs MS 39564

GUNTER, JOHN BROWN, Jr., dept. store exec.; b. Johnstown, Pa., May 22, 1919; s. John Brown and Mary (Barr) G.; student Valley Forge Mil. Acad. Jr. Coll., 1937-39; B.S., U. Md., 1941; m. Dorothy Mulhollen, July 5, 1942; 1 dau., Jerrol Louise (Mrs. Benjamin Hinchman IV). Exec. dir. Johnstown Community Chest, 1946-48; trainee, mgr. Sears, Roebuck & Co., 1948-52; adminstrv. asst. Penn Traffic Co., Johnstown, 1952-58, controller, 1958-62, asst. treas., 1962-65, sec., 1965—. Served to lt. col. AUS, 1941-46; ETO. Decorated Order Brit. Empire, Bronze Arrowhead. Mem. Phi Delta Theta. Republican. Presbyn. Mason. Home: 2215 Crabtree Lane Johnstown PA 15905 Office: 319 Washington St Johnstown PA 15905

GUNTER, JOHN WADSWORTH, economist; b. Sanford, N.C., Feb. 17, 1914; s. Herbert Brown and Lucy Hadassah Hosp.; asst. pathology Mt. Sinai Hosp., N.Y.C., 1935-36, asst. hematology, 1937-39; mem. faculty Columbia Coll. Phys. and Surg., 1939- -, clin. prof. rehab. medicine, 1964-68, prof. emeritus and spl. lectr., 1968—; attending physician Columbia Presbyn. Med. Center, 1962-; 1st med. officer UN Secretariat, 1949-51; physician Mrs. Eleanor Roosevelt, 1945-62; med. dir. Blythdale Children's Hosp., Valhalla, N.Y., 1951-68, med. dir. emeritus, 1968—; charge phys. medicine and rehab. service S.S. Hope, 1962-63. Mem. adv. council edn. and vocational rehab. Dept. Health, Edn. and Welfare, 1963- 66; mem. med. adv. bd. Medico, 1963-; U.S. del. Am. Assn. UN to World Fedn. UN Assns. at Bangkok, 1954, Geneva, 1955, Brussels, 1958, Warsaw, 1961, N.Y.C., 1963, New Delhi, 1965. Fellow Am. Acad. Phys. Medicine and Rehab.; mem. A.M.A., Am. Congress Rehab. Medicine. Contbr. med. jours. Home: 55 E 74th St New York City, NY 10021. Office: 121 E 60th St New York City NY 10022

GUNTHER, FRANK ALEXANDER, corp. exec.; b. N.Y.C., Feb. 3, 1908; s. Alexander K. and Barbara (Hertel) G.; student Columbia, 1925-26, Wagner Coll., 1939-40; m. Lillian Marie Madden, Sept. 17, 1930; children—Frank M., Robert C. With Radio Engring. Labs. div. Dynamics Corp. Am., L.I. City, N.Y., 1927—, asst. radio engr., radio engr., chief engr., v.p., 1927-59, exec. v.p., 1959-60, pres., 1960—; exec. v.p. Dynamics Corp. of Am., 1962—. Mem. nat. industry adv. com. FCC, 1962-69. Mem. Richmond County Grand Jurors Assn., 1946—. Bd. dirs. Armstrong Meml. Research Found. (pres. 1968—). Served to maj. USAAFR, 1941-46. Recipient Distinguished Service award Armed Forces Communications and Electronics Assn., 1969; DeForest Audion award Vet Wireless Operations Assn., 1969. Fellow I.E.E.E., Radio Club Am. (pres. 1956-58); mem. Armed Forces Communications and Electronics Assn. (pres. 1961-63, bd. dirs.), U.S. Air Force Assn., Am. Radio Relay League. Episcopalian. Clubs: Richmond County Country, Richmond County Yacht (N.Y.); N.Y. Yacht. Contbr. articles profl. jours. Home: 10 Highpoint Rd Dongan Hills NY 10304 Office: 501 Fifth Av New York City NY 10017

GUNTHER, GERALD, educator; b. Usingen, Germany, May 26, 1927; s. Otto and Minna (Floersheim) G.; brought to U.S., 1938, naturalized, 1944; B.A., Bklyn. Coll., 1949; M.A., Columbia, 1950; LL.B., Harvard, 1953; m. Barbara Kelsky, June 22, 1949; children—Daniel Jay, Andrew James. Admitted to N.Y. bar, 1955; law clk. Judge Learned Hand, 1953-54, Chief Justice Earl Warren, 1954-55; asso. firm Cleary, Gottlieb, Friendly & Hamilton. N.Y.C., 1955-56; asso. prof. law Columbia, 1956-59, prof., 1959-62; prof. law Stanford, 1962—; lectr. polit. sci. Bklyn. Coll., 1949-50; research dir. com. constl. simplification N.Y. Inter-law Sch., 1957-58; dir. Columbia Fed. Cts. and History Project, 1957-59. Served with USNR, 1945-46. Recipient distinguished alumnus award Bklyn. Coll., 1961; Guggenheim fellow, 1962- 63; fellow Center Advanced Study in Behavioral Scis., 1969-70; Fulbright- Hays lectr., Ghana, 1970. Mem. Am. Hist. Assn. (mem. com. Littleton- Griswold Fund 1968—). Author: Cases and Materials on Constitutional Law, 8th edit., 1970; Cases and Materials on Individual Rights in Constitutional Law, 1970; John Marshall's Defense of McCulloch versus Maryland, 1969. Bd. overseers Harvard Law Rev., 1967—. Contbr. articles profl. jours. Home: 858 Lathrop Dr Stanford CA 94305

GUNTHER, GOTTHARD, educator; b. Arnsdorf, Germany, June 15, 1900; s. Richard and Klara (Karwat) G.; student Heidelberg U., 1921-22; Ph.D., Berlin U., 1932; m. Marie Hendel, Oct. 1, 1929. Came to U.S., 1940, naturalized, 1948. Asst., Leipzig U., 1935-38; Carnegie lectr. U. Stellenbosch, S.Africa, 1938-40; asst. prof. Colby Coll., Me., 1943-45; research asso. Bollingen Found., 1955-56; regular vis. prof. Hamburg U., Germany, 1956—; asso. prof. U. Ill. at Urbana, 1961-66, prof., 1966—. Mem. Internationale Hegel Vereinigung and Int. Hegel gesellschaft. Co-editor Grundlagenstudien aus Kybernetik und Geisteswissenschaft, 1960-71. Home: 504 W White St Champaign IL 61820 Office: E E Res Lab U Ill Urbana IL 61801

GUPTA, OM PRAKASH, dental educator; b. Rupar, India, Feb. 8, 1926; s. Harish Chandra and Purnima (Devi) G.; B.S., Agra (India), Coll. 1945; B.D.S. Bombay (India), U. 1950; M.S., Harvard, 1954, Dr.P.H., 1959; M.S.D., N.Y.U., 1958; D.M.D., U. Pitts., 1967; m. Yamuna Gaitonde, Dec. 17, 1957; children—Pradeep, Praveen, Sareeta. Came to U.S., 1952, naturalized, 1963. Research asso. Coll. Dentistry, N.Y.U., 1956-58; asst. prof. dept. applied materia medica and therapeutics U. Ill. Coll. Dentistry, 1958-60; dir. Dental Coll., prof. dental surgery Trivandrum, India, 1960-63; prof., head dept., pub. health and preventive dentistry, grad. periodontics Sch. Dental Medicine, U. Pitts., 1963—, prof. pub. health practice Grad. Sch. Pub. Health, U. Pitts., 1965—; cons. VA hosps., Leech Farm, Pa., 1964—, Pitts., 1966—. Mem. P.T.A. of Greentree, Pitts., 1964—. Fellow A.A.A.S., Internat. Coll. Dentists; mem. Am. Dental Assn. (asso.), Am. Acad. Periodontics, Am. Pub. Health Assn., Internat. Assn. Dental Research, Fedn. Dentaire Intanat., Sigma Xi. Home: 1026 Dale Dr Pittsburgh PA 15220

GUPTA, SURAJ NARAYAN, physicist, educator; b. Haryana, India, Dec. 1, 1924; s. Lakshmi N. and Devi (Goyal) G.; M.S., U. Delhi (India), 1946; Ph.D., U. Cambridge (Eng.), 1951; m. Letty Gupta, July 14, 1948; children—Paul, Ranee. Came to U.S., 1953, naturalized, 1963. Imperial Chem. Industries fellow U. Manchester (Eng.), 1951-53; vis. prof. physics Purdue U., 1953-56; prof. physics Wayne State U., 1956-61, Distinguished prof. physics, 1961—; vis. physicist Argonne Nat. Lab., Brookhaven Nat. Lab., Nat. Research Council Can. Fellow Am. Phys. Soc., Nat. Acad. Scis. India. Author articles on relativity, gravitation, quantum electrodynamics, nuclear physics, high-energy physics. Home: 1300 E Lafayette Blvd Detroit MI 48207

GUPTILL, LEIGHTON, publisher; b. Bklyn., May 27, 1920; s. Arthur Leighton and Ethel M. (Weir) G.; B.A., Colgate U., 1942; m. Louise Post Hubert, July 14, 1945; children—Ann Louise, William Leighton. Publisher, Am. Artist mag., 1956-63; pres. Watson-Guptill Publs., Inc., pubs. art and music books, N.Y.C., 1956-62, v.p., 1963—, dir. publs. music book div., 1963—. Mem. Publs. Advt. Club. N.Y.C., Conn. Playmakers, Vets. Hosp. Radio and TV Guild, Am. Legion, Am. Theatre Organ Enthusiasts, Am. Fedn. Musicians, Phi Gamma Delta. Mason (32, Shriner). Clubs: Innis Arden Golf (Old Greenwich, Conn.); University (Darien, Conn.). Home: 116 Camp Av Darien CT 06820 Office: 165 W 46th St New York City NY 10036

GURASH, JOHN THOMAS, ins. holding co. exec.; b. Oakland, Cal., Nov. 25, 1910; s. Nicholas and Katherine (Restovic) G.; student Loyola U. Sch. Law, Los Angeles, 1936, 38-39; m. Katherine Mills, Feb. 4, 1934; 1 son, John N. With Am. Surety Co. N.Y., 1930-44; with Pacific Employers Ins., Co., 1944—, chmn. bd., 1968—; v.p. Ins. Co. N.Am., 1966-70; exec. v.p., dir. INA Corp., 1968-69, chmn., pres., chief exec. officer, dir., 1969—; dir. Ins. Co. N.Am., Life Ins. Co. N.Am., Adela Investment Co. S.A., Girard Trust Bank, Girard Co., Phila. Savs. Fund Soc. Active local YMCA, Pasadena Art Mus., Los Angeles Civic Light Opera Assn., Founders of Music Center Los Angeles, Crime Commn. Phila., So. Cal. Bldg. Funds, Greater Phila. C. of C., Phila. Orch. Assn., Greater Phila. Movement, World Affairs Council Phila., Internat. House Center. Trustee San Gabriel Valley Scout Found., Thomas Jefferson Univ. Hosp.; mem. council Orthopaedic Hosp., Los Angeles; bd. dirs. Hosp. Survey Com. Clubs: California, 100 (Los Angeles); Oakmont Country (Glendale, Cal.); Thunderbird Country (Palm Springs, Cal.); Merion Golf (Ardmore, Pa.); Pine Valley (N.J.) Golf; Brook (N.Y.C.). Home: 191 Presidential Blvd Bala Cynwyd PA 19004 also 1141 S Orange Grove Blvd Pasadena CA 91105 Office: 1600 Arch St Philadelphia PA 19101

GURD, FRANK ROSS NEWMAN, educator, biochemist; b. Montreal, Que., Can., Jan. 20, 1924; s. Fraser Baillie and Jessie (Newman) G.; grad. cum laude Phillips Exeter Acad., 1941; B.S., McGill U., 1945, M.S., 1946; Ph.D., Harvard, 1949; m. Ruth Sights, June 12, 1956; children—Fraser, Kathleen, Martha, Charles. Came to U.S., 1946, naturalized, 1954. Asst. dir. Bur. Med. Research, Equitable Life Assurance Soc., N.Y.C., 1955-59; asst. prof. clin. biochemistry Med. Coll. Cornell U., 1955-60; prof. biochemistry Sch. Medicine, Ind. U., 1960-66, prof. chemistry, 1965—. Chmn. biophysics and biophys. chemistry B study sect. NIH, 1968-70. John Simon Guggenheim and Helen Hay Whitney fellow dept. biochemistry Sch. Medicine, Washington U., 1954-55. Mem. Am. Soc. Biol. Chemists, Am. Chem. Soc., Biophys. Soc., N.Y. Acad. Scis., A.A.A.S., Sigma Xi. Author: Chemical Specificity in Biological Interactions, 1954; (with D.J. Hanahan) Chemistry of the Lipides, 1960. Editorial bd. Jour. Biol. Chemistry, 1966—. Research, publs. on lipoprotein isolated from blood; combination of proteins with certain metal salts; identification of sites of binding and effects on conformation; modes of combination of metal ions with peptides; chem. modification of proteins to correlate structure in solution with that in crystalline state. Home: 2600 Fairoaks Lane Bloomington IN 47401

GURD, FRASER NEWMAN, medical educator; b. Montreal, Can., Mar. 19, 1914; s. Fraser Baillie and Jessie Gibson (Newman) G.; B.A., McGill U., 1934, M.D., 1939; M.Sc., U. Pa., 1947; m. Mary Louise Moore, Dec. 19, 1938; children—Patricia (Mrs. Douglas S. Pryde), Katharine (Mrs. H. Garry Chaplin), Mary (Mrs. Edgar G. Goss), Susan (Mrs. Brian G. Bexton), Deborah. Asst. surgeon to surgeon in chief Montreal Gen. Hosp., 1948—; prof. surgery McGill U., 1963—. Served to capt., M.C., Royal Canadian Army, 1941-46; ETO. Fellow A.C.S. (nat. regent 1964); mem. Royal Coll. Physicians and Surgeons of Can., Central Surg. Assn. (pres. 1967-68), Am. Assn. Surgery of Trauma (pres. 1967-68), Canadian Assn. Clin. Surgeons (pres. 1967-69), Am. Surg. Assn., Soc. Univ. Surgeons, James IV Surg. Soc., Internat. Surg. Group. Research on surg. care, shock, fluids and nutrition, med. edn. Home: 3180 The Boulevard Montreal 217 Quebec Canada

GURDJIAN, ELISHA STEPHENS, neurological surgeon; b. Smyrna, Turkey, Apr. 18, 1900; s. Stepan and Beruke (Hagopian) G.; M.S., U. Mich., 1924, M.D., 1926, Ph.D., 1927; m. Dorothy Eileen Kratz, May 29, 1933; children—Edwin, Joan, Ronald, Richard. Came to U.S., 1920, naturalized, 1930. Intern U. Mich. Hosp., 1925-27, 28-30, Rochester Gen. Hosp., N.Y., 1927-28; practice of medicine, Detroit, 1930—, specializing neurological surgery; head neurosurg. service Grace Hosp., Detroit. 1938-70; prof. neurological surgery Wayne U., 1949-56, chmn. dept. neurosurgery, 1956-70, dir. Bioengineering Research Center, 1966-70, prof. emeritus, 1970—. Recipient Bronze medal 1948, Gold medal, 1960, Roentgen Ray Soc.; Silver Hektoen medal Am. Med. Assn., 1967. Diplomate Am. Bd. of Neurol. Surgery (mem. bd., v.p. 1966-68). Fellow A.C.S. (chmn. adv. council neurology 1952); mem. A.M.A. (chmn. sect. on nervous and mental diseases 1960), Am. Assn. Neurol. Surgeons, Cushing Soc., Congress Neurological Surgeons, Am. Neurol. Assn. (v.p. 1969), Am. Assn. Anatomists, Am. Assn. Surgery Trauma, Central Surg. Assn., Central Neuropsychiat. Assn., Soc. Neurol. Surgeons, also Sigma Xi, Phi Sigma, Alpha Omega. Author: (with Dr. J.E. Webster) Operative Neurosurgery, 1952; (with Dr. Webster) Mechanism, Diagnosis and Management of Head Injury, 1958; Operative Neurosurgery, 1964; Cranial and Intracranial Supperation, 1969. Editor: (with L. M. Thomas) Operative Neurosurgery, 1970; Impact Injury and Crash Protection, 1970, Neckache and Backache, 1970. Contbr. articles med. publs. Home: 19385 Renfrew Rd Detroit MI 48221

GUREWITSCH, ARNO DAVID, physician, educator; b. Zurich, Switzerland, Oct. 31, 1902; s. Aron David and Maria (Markovitch) G.; student Berlin (Germany) U., 1921-23, 27-29; M.D., U. Basel (Switzerland), 1933; postgrad. tng., Basel, Vienna, London nd N.Y.C.; m. Nemone Balfour, Aug. 13, 1937; 1 dau., Grania Marion; m. 2d, Edna Perkel, Feb. 23, 1958; 1 dau., Maria Anna. Came to U.S., 1935, naturalized, 1943. Intern, Jeusalem; resident Hadassah Hosp.; asst. pathology Mt. Sinai Hosp., N.Y.C., 1935-36, asst. hematology, 1937-39; mem. faculty Columbia Coll. Physicians and Surgeons, 1939—, clin. prof. rehab. medicine, 1964-68, prof. emeritus, spl. lectr., 1968—; attending physician Columbia Presbyn. Med. Center, 1962—; 1st med. officer UN Secretariat, 1949-51; physician Mrs. Eleanor Roosevelt, 1945-62; med. dir. Blythdale Children's Hosp., Valhalla, N.Y., 1951-68, med. dir. emeritus, 1968—; charge phys. medicine and rehab. service S.S. Hope, 1962-63. Mem. adv. council edn. and vocational rehab. Dept. Health, Edn. and Welfare, 1963- 66; mem. med. adv. bd. Medico, 1963—; U.S. del. Am. Assn. UN to World Fedn. UN Assns. at Bangkok, 1954, Geneva, 1955, Brussels, 1958, Warsaw, 1961, N.Y.C., 1963, New Delhi, 1965. Fellow Am. Acad. Phys. Medicine and Rehab.; mem. A.M.A., Am. Congress Rehab. Medicine. Contbr. med. jours. Home: 55 E 74th St New York City NY 10021 Office: 121 E 60th St New York City NY 10022

GURFEIN, MURRAY IRWIN, judge; b. N.Y.C., Nov. 17, 1907; s. Louis and Rose (Feld) G.; A.B., Columbia, 1926; LL.B., magna cum laude, Harvard, 1930; m. Eva Hadas, Aug. 6, 1931; children—Abigail (Mrs. Robert Hellwarth), Susan Hadas (Mrs. Arthur Rosett). Admitted N.Y. bar; law sec. U.S. Circuit Judge Julian W. Mack, 1930-31; asst. U.S. atty. So. Dist. N.Y., 1931-33; pvt. law practice, N.Y.C., 1933-35; chief asst. investigation organized crime to Hon. Thomas E. Dewey, 1935-38; asst. dist. atty., N.Y. County, 1938-42; partner Judd and Gurfein, N.Y.C., 1946-54 Goldstein, Judd and Gurfein, 1955-68, Goldstein, Gurfein, Shames & Hyde, 1968-71; judge U.S. Dist. Ct., So. Dist. N.Y., 1971—. Mem. N.Y. State Temporary Commn. Courts, 1953-58. Former pres. United Hias Service, Internat. Council Jewish Social and Service Orgns. Served as lt. col., chief intelligence Psychol. Warfare Div., Supreme Hdqrs. Allied Expeditionary Force, OSS and U.S. Army; asst. to Hon. Robert H. Jackson, U.S. Chief Counsel in Nuremberg Trials, 1942-45. Decorated Legion of Merit; Hon. Officer of British Empire; Croix de Guerre (France). Fellow Am. Coll. Trial Lawyers, Am. Bar Found.; mem. N.Y. County Lawyers Assn., Am., N.Y. State bar assns., Assn. Bar City N.Y., Council Fgn. Relations, Phi Beta Kappa. Clubs: Columbia U., Harmonie, Lawyers (N.Y.C.). Home: 530 Park Av New York City NY 10021 Office: US Courthouse Foley Sq New York City NY 10007

GURIN, H.M., assn. exec. Exec. officer Am. Astron. Soc., Princeton, N.J. Office: 211 Fitz Randolph Rd Princeton NJ 08540*

GURIN, SAMUEL, biochemist; b. N.Y.C., July 1, 1905; s. Morris and Rose (Zwinig) G.; B.A., Columbia, 1928, M.S., 1930, Ph.D., 1934; NRC fellow, U. Ill., 1935- 37; D.Sc., LaSalle Coll., 1965, Phila. Coll. Pharmacy, 1961; m. Celia Zall, June 14, 1930; children—Robert N., Richard S. Mem. faculty U., prof. biochem. U. Pa., 1951-70, chmn. dept., 1954-70, dean Med. Sch., 1961-70; prof. biochemistry U. Fla. Med. Sch. and Dept. Biol. Scis., Gainesville, 1970—. Mem. metabolism panel NRC. Mem. Am. Soc. Biol. Chemists, Am. Chem. Soc. Mem. editorial bd. Jour. Biol. Chemistry. Home: 706 SW 21st Av Gainesville FL 32601

GURKO, LEO, educator; b. Warsaw, Poland, Jan. 4, 1914; s. Adolph and Renia (Kaye) G.; came to U.S., 1917, naturalized, 1926; B.A., Coll. City Detroit, 1931; M.A., U. Wis., 1932, Ph.D., 1934; m. Miriam Berwitz, Feb. 3, 1934; childrenStephen, Jane. Faculty Hunter Coll., 1939-, prof. English, 1957-, chmn. dept., 1954-60. Fellow Fund for Advancement Edn., 1953-54. Mem. Modern Lang. Assn. Author: The Angry Decade, 1947; Heroes, Highbrows and the Popular Mind, 1953; Tom Paine, Freedom's Apostle, 1957; Joseph Conrad; Giant in Exile, 1962; The Two Lives of Joseph Conrad, 1965; Ernest Hemingway and the Pursuit of Heroism, 1968. Home: 258 Riverside Dr New York City, NY 10025.

GURLAND, JOHN, educator; b. Ottawa, Can., Jan. 6, 1917; s. Max and Bella (Spivak) G.; B.A., U. Toronto, Ont., Can., 1939, M.A., 1942; Ph.D., U. Cal. at Berkeley, 1948; m. Vera Frances Green, June 26, 1946; childrenMarsha, Iva. Came to U.S., 1945, naturalized, 1955. Benjamin Pierce instr. math Harvard, 1948-49; asst. prof. statistics U. Chgo., 1949-52; asso. prof., then prof. statistics Ia. State U., 1952-60; prof. Math. Research Center, U. Wis., Madison, 1960-63, prof. statistics, 1963—. Fellow Am. Statis. Assn., Inst. Math. Statistics, Royal Statis. Soc., Am. Pub. Health Assn., A.A.A.S.; mem. Biometric Soc., Math. Assn. Am., Internat. Statis. Inst. (phys. sci. sect.). Contbr. articles profl. jours. Editor: Stochastic Models in Medicine and Biology, 1964. Home: 3521 Sunset Dr Madison, WI 53705.

GURLEY, SAM, Jr., steel co. exec.; b. Metropolis, Ill., Aug. 19, 1917; s. Sam and Susan (Snyder) G.; B.S. in Chem. Engring., U. Mo., 1939; m. Norma Thomasine Williams, July 12, 1941; children—Phillip S.,

Susan E. (Mrs. Mechling). Vice pres. sales Peichold Chems., Inc., 1948-52, H.M., Porter, Inc., 1952-55, Olin Mathieson Chem. Corp., 1955-57; pres., chief exec. officer Tubesales, 1957—. Served to lt. comdr. USNR, 1939-44. Mason. Home: 1362 Galaxy Dr Newport Beach CA 92660 Office: 2211 Tubeway Los Angeles CA 90022

GURNEY, CLIFFORD WILLIAM, educator; b. Chgo., Apr. 11, 1924; s. Clifford John and Margaret (Kuehner) G.; B.S., U. Chgo., 1948, M.D., 1951; m. Doris Blanche Arnett, June 18, 1949; childrenEllen Ruth, Beth Margaret, Melissa Ann, Paul, Gwendolyn. Intern U. Mich., 1951-52, resident internal medicine, 1952- 55; vis. scientist Churchill Hosp., Oxford, Eng., 1960-61; asso. prof. medicine U. Chgo., 1960-65, prof. medicine and physiology, 1965; prof. medicine, chmn. dept. Rutgers U. Med. Sch., 1966-69; prof. medicine, chmn. dept. U. Kan. Med. Sch., Kansas City, 1969—, research erythropoietin and stem cell kinetics. Mem. CARE medico emergency med. team to Algeria, 1962. Served to 1st lt. USAAF, 1943-46: ETO. John and Mary Markle scholar med. scis., 1959-64. Diplomate Am. Bd. Internal Medicine. Mem. Am. Soc. Clin. Investigation, Assn. Am. Physicians, Central Soc. Clin. Research, A.M.A., Brit. Radiation Research Soc., Phi Beta Kappa, Sigma Xi, Alpha Omega Alpha. Contbr. med. jours. Home: 6508 Belinder Av Shawnee Mission, KS 66208. Office: Dept Medicine Univ of Kansas Medical School Kansas City KS 66208

GURNEY, EDWARD JOHN, U.S. senator; b. Portland, Me., Jan. 12, 1914; s. Edward J. and Nellie (Kennedy) G.; B.S., Colby Coll., 1935; LL.B., Harvard, 1938; LL.M., Duke, 1948; m. Natalie Ahlborn, Aug. 1, 1941; children—Jill, Sarah. Admitted to N.Y. bar, 1939, Fla. bar, 1949; practice law in N.Y.C., 1938-41, Winter Park, Fla., 1948—; mem. 88th-90th congresses, 11th Dist. Fla.; mem. U.S. Senate from Fla., 1968—. Dir. Comml. Bank. Winter Park. City commr., Winter Park, 1952-58, mayor, 1961-62. Served to lt. col. AUS, 1941-46: ETO. Decorated Silver Star medal, Purple Heart. Mem. Am., Fla., N.Y. bar assns., Am. Legion, V.F.W., Res. Officers Assn., Alpha Tau Omega. Republican. Conglist. Rotarian. Home: 800 Greentree Dr Winter Park FL 32789 Office: New Senate Office Bldg Washington DC 20510

GURNEY, JAMES PAUL, rose cons.; b. Lansdowne, Pa., Mar. 22, 1915; s. Henry Brandon and Lillie (Crossland) G.; student N.Y. Tech. and Agrl. Inst., 1941; B.S., U. Md., 1950; m. Elizabeth Gessford Ebaugh, Dec. 21, 1945; children—Helen Jessie, Katharine Elizabeth. Exec. sec. Am. Rose Soc., Columbus, O., 1953-61; sec. Am. Rose Found.; rose cons. O.M. Scott & Sons Co., Marysville, O., 1961-62; lectr. on roses to radio, TV, other groups. Mem. Christian Sci. Com. on Publs. for Ohio; sec. City of Columbus Park of Roses Commn. Mem. Clintonville Bus. Men's Assn., Harrisburg Rose Soc. (pres. 1952), Pi Alpha Xi. Home: 1777 Guilford Rd Columbus, OH 43221. Office: East Broad Bldg Columbus OH 43215

GURNEY, JAMES THOMAS, lawyer; b. Ripley, Miss., Jan. 24, 1901; s. James Andrew and Mary Jane (Shepherd) G.; A.B., Miss. Coll., 1919; student U. Chgo., 1919-20, Columbia, 1919; LL.B., Cumberland Univ., Lebanon, Tenn., 1922, J.D., 1928; LL.D., Stetson U., 1970; m. Blanche Johnson, Mar. 5, 1925; 1 son, J. Thomas. Mem. faculty Miss. Woman's Coll., Hattiesburg, 1919-21; admitted to Fla. bar, 1922, and since practiced in Orlando. Asso. gen. counsel, dir. Bankers Nat. Life Ins. Co., dir., gen. counsel Fla. Telephone Corp.; counsel Minute Maid Co. dir. Coca- Cola Co.; dir. Beneficial Finance Co., Citizens Nat. Bank Orlando. Gen. counsel Orlando Utilities Commn.; mem. Fla. Supreme Court com. for redrafting common law rules of procedure 1945; mem. examining bd. Fla. Parole Commn., 1945; chmn. bd. control Fla. Insts. of Higher Learning, 1945-1949. Trustee New Orleans Bapt. Theol. Sem., 1960-67; bd. dirs. Children's Home Soc. of Fla. Recipient Certiticate Merit, 1953, Distinguished Service award Stetson U., 1958, Distinguished Service citation New Orleans Bapt. Theol. Sem. and So. Bapt. Found., 1967; award Pres. Ind. Colls. Fla., 1970. Fellow Am. Bar Found., Am. Coll. Trial Lawyers; mem. Am. (com. on life ins. law, vice chmn. 1944-47, admissions, 1944-48; assn. and adv. spl. com. on pub. relations 1944-46, adminstrv. law 1945, chmn. Fla. membership com. on ins. sect., 1946-48), Fla. State (pres. 1942-43), Orange County bar assns., Am. Life Conv. (legal sect.), Assn. of Life Ins. Counsel (exec. com. 1946-48), Orange County Budget Commn. (chmn. 1935-42), Orlando Community Chest (gen. chmn.), C. of C. (pres. 1930, nat. council 1940-41), Fla. Blue Key (hon.), Newcomen Soc., Alumni Assn. U. Fla. (hon.). Democrat. Baptist. Clubs: Lions Internat. (dist. gov. 35th dist. 1928), Univ., Orlando Country. Author: Life Insurance Law of Florida, 1934; Disability Claims Resort to Equity, 1940; World War II Construction of War Clauses, 1946. Contbr. articles to Fla. Bar Jour. Home: 1701 N Spring Lake Dr Orlando FL 32804 Office: 203 N Magnolia Av The Gurney Bldg Orlando FL 32801

GURNHAM, CHARLES FREDERICK, chem., san. engineer; b. Ludlow, Mass., Oct. 19, 1911; s. George Frederick and Ella Bertha (Hendrick) G.; B.S., Yale, 1932; M.Ch.E., N.Y.U., 1940, D.Eng.Sc., 1942; m. Vivian Wikander, Aug. 25, 1934; childrenSandra J. (Mrs. Richard J. Barman), Diane W. (Mrs. Peter L. LaPorte), Robert H., Roy F. Chemist, Smith Paper Co., Lee. Mass., 1932-34; chem. engr. Ludlow Mfg. Assos. (Mass.), 1934- 36, Naugatuck Chem. Co. (Conn.), 1936-38; asst. prof. chem. engring. Pratt Inst., 1938-41; chem. engr. Air Reduction Co., Stamford, Conn., 1942-44, Whitney Blake Co., Hamden, Conn., 1944-48; prof., head dept. chem. engring. Tufts U., 1949-52, Mich. State U., 1952-61; prof. environmental engring. and chem. engring. Ill. Inst. Tech., Chgo. 1962- 68, chmn. dept. environmental engring., 1966-68; v.p., mgr. midwest operations Cyrus William Rice & Co., Water Mgmt. Cons., Chgo., 1967-69; now pres. Gurnham and Assos., Inc., Chgo.; ind. cons. chem. and san. engr., 1961-. Del. from electroplating industry to Nat. Tech. Task Com. on Indsl. Wastes USPHS, 1950-57, del. from mining industry, 1957-61, vice chmn., 1955, chmn. 1956. Recipient Distinguished Alumnus citation N.Y. U., 1955; spl. recognition Am. Inst. Plant Engrs., 1970. profl. engr., Registered N.Y., Ind., Ill., Mich. Diplomate Am. Acad. Environmental Engrs. Mem. Am. Water Works Assn., Am. Soc. C.E., Am. Inst. Chemists, Am. Inst. Plant Engrs., Am. Chem. Soc. Am. Inst. Chem. Engrs., Water Pollution Control Fedn., Sigma Xi, Tau Beta Pi, Phi Lambda Upsilon, Alpha Chi Sigma, Sigma Pi Sigma. Author: Principles of Industrial Waste Treatment, 1955; Industrial Wastewater Control, 1965. Home: 505 N Lake Shore Dr Chicago IL 60611 Office: 223 W Jackson Blvd Chicago IL 60606

GURR, LENA, artist; b. Bklyn., Oct. 27, 1897; d. Hyman and Ida (Gorodnick) Gurr; ed. Bklyn. Tng. Sch. for Tchrs.; student Art Students League, N.Y.C. and France; m. Joseph Biel, Nov. 24, 1931 (dec.). Artist in oil, water color, lithography, serigraphy, wood cuts; art tchr. jr. high sch. system, N.Y.C., 1918- 44; represented in permanent collection of Biro-Bidjan Museum, U.S.S.R., oil painting landscape-Nice, France, lithograph Snowy Vistas bought by Pennell Fund for Library of Congress, oil painting in Tel Aviv, Israel; represented as Am. contemporary art N.Y. World's Fair, 1939-40; oil paintings Ain Harod Mus. Israel, Heywood Broun Collection, Contemporary Art Collection, Atlanta, Brandeis U., Marvin Small Collection; serigraphs N.Y. Pub. Library, State Library of Cal., Kan. State Coll., U. Wis., Va. Mus. of Fine Arts, Reading (Pa.) Mus., Howard U., Coll. Nat. Assn. U. Women, Met. Mus., U, Syracuse, Safed Mus., Israel, Brasenose Coll., Oxford, Eng., Norfolk (Va.) Museum, Jersey City State Coll., Smithsonian Instn., Washington, Boston Pub. Library, Marx Collection, Provincetown Art Assn., Butler Inst. Am. Art, Youngstown, O., Chrysler Mus., Provincetown, Mass., Slater Meml. Mus., Norwich, Conn., Otero Jr. Coll., LaJunta, Colo, Phila. Museum, Kalamazoo Art Inst., Bklyn. Mus., Fairleigh Dickinson U., St. Peter's Coll.; oil painting Sunday Funnies being exhibited in larger museums U.S. in Portraits of America exhbn. sponsored by Artists for Victory and Pepsi-Cola Co.; exhibited numerous one-man shows in oil painting, prints, 1949; exhibited important shows, 1932—, including Carnegie Inst., Corcoran Museum, Phila. Acad., Va. Mus., Met. Mus. Recipient numerous awards latest being prize Nat. Soc. of Painters in Casein, 1961, 2d prize for oil Cape Cod Art Assn., 1962-63; Samuel Mann Meml. prize for casein Nat. Assn. Women Artists, 1963, Marion K. Haldenstein prize for oil, 1964; Grumbacher prize, 1964, Grumbacher award for oil Painters and Sculptors Soc. N.J., 1966, Benedictine award for oil, 1966; Abbot Treadwell prize for graphics Nat. Assn. Women Artists, 1967; 1st hon. mention for oil Cape Cod Art Assn., 1968; Jersey City Mus. medal Painters and Sculptors Soc. N.J.; W. Alden Brown prize Nat. Soc. Painters in Casein, 1971; Molly Morpeth Canaday prize Nat. Soc. Women Artists, 1971. Mem. Nat. Soc. Painters in Casein, Provincetown Art Assn., Nat. Assn. Women Artists, N.Y. Soc. Women Artists, Bklyn. Soc. Artists, Audubon Artists, Artists Equity (v.p.), Am. Color Print Soc., Soc. Am. Graphic Artists, Painters and Sculptors Soc. N.J., Casein Soc., Print Club of Albany. Home: 71 Remsen Av Brooklyn NY 11212 Studio: 10 E 23d St New York City NY 10010

GURR, TED ROBERT, educator; b. Spokane, Wash., Feb. 21, 1936; s. Robert Lucas and Anne (Cook) G.; B.A. (Wilson Nat. fellow 1957), Reed Coll., 1957; postgrad. Woodrow Wilson Sch. Pub. and Internat. Affairs, Princeton, 1957-58; Ph.D., N.Y. U., 1965; m. Erika Brigitte Klie, Feb. 20, 1960; children—Lisa Anne, Andrea Mariel. Asst. editor, then asso. editor Am. Behavioral Scientist, 1961-64; asst. to dir. N.Y.U. office research services, N.Y.C., 1962-64; mem. faculty Princeton U., 1965-69, research asso., 1965-67, asst. prof. politics, 1967-69, asso. dir. workshop in comparative politics, 1966-69; asso. prof. polit. sci. Northwestern U., 1969—. Co-dir. hist. and comparative task force Nat. Commn. on Causes and Prevention of Violence, 1968-69. Recipient Woodrow Wilson Fedn. award for best book in polit. sci. Why Men Rebel, 1970. Ford Found. faculty fellow, 1970. Mem. Am. Polit. Sci. Assn., Peace Research Soc., Internat. Studies Assn., Phi Beta Kappa. Author: (with A. de Grazia) American Welfare, 1961; Why Men Rebel, 1970; (with C. Ruttenberg) Cross National Studies of Civil Violence, 1969; (with H.D. Graham) Violence in America; Historical and Comparative Perspectives, 1969. Editorial bd. World Politics, 1970—, Comparative Political Studies, 1968—; co-editor: Sage Professional Papers in Comparative Politics, 1969—. Office: 1818 Sheridan Rd Northwestern U Evanston IL 60201

GURSEY, FEZA, Turkish physicist, educator; b. Instanbul, Turkey, Apr. 7, 1921; s. Reshid A. and Remzive (Hisar) G.; B.S., Istanbul, 1944; Ph.D., Imperial Coll., U. London, 1950; postgrad. Cambridge U., 1950-51; m. Suha Pamir, Oct. 9, 1952; 1 son, Yusuf. Asst. physics dept. Istanbul U., 1952-54, docent, 1954-57; vis. physicist Brookhaven Nat. Lab., 1957-58; mem. Inst. for Advanced Study, Princeton, N.J., 1958-60, 63-64; vis. asso. prof. Columbia, 1960-61; prof. physics Middle East Tech. U., Ankara, 1961—; vis. prof. Yale, New Haven, 1965-67, prof. physics, 1969—; mem. Turkish Atomic Energy Agy., 1962-63; mem. Turkish Nat. Sci. and Tech. Research Council, 1965-67. Recipient Sci. prize Turkish Nat. Sci. and Tech. Research Council, 1968. Mem. Turkish, Am. phys. socs. Editor: Group Theoretical Methods and Concepts in Elementary Particle Physics, 1964. Contbr. articles Profl. jours. Home: 1066 Whitney Av Hamden CT 06517 Office: Yale U Physics Dept New Haven CT 06520

GURTIN, MORTON EDWARD, educator; b. Jersey City, Mar. 7, 1934; s. Saul and Irene (Hoffman) G.; B.M.E., Rensselaer Poly. Inst., 1955; Ph.D., Brown U., 1961; m. Leatrice Thelma Kagan, June 12, 1955; children—Amy Lynn, William Robert. Structures engr. Douglas Aircraft Co., 1955-56, Gen. Elec. Co., 1956-59; research asso. Brown U., 1961-62, asst. prof., 1962-64, asso. prof., 1964-66; prof. mathematics Carnegie Mellon U., 1966—; cons. to industry. Mem. Soc. Natural Philosophy, Am. Math. Soc., Sigma Xi. Author: (with B.D. Coleman, I Herrera, and C. Truesdell) Wave Propagation in Dissipative Media, 1965. Co-editor: Springer Tracts in Natural Philosophy. Contbr. articles profl. jours., chpt. in handbook. Home: 732 College Av Pittsburgh PA 15232

GURTNER, WENDELL JONES, rubber co. exec.; b. Wabash, Ind., Mar. 19, 1913; s. Frank F. and Maude (Jones) G.; student Manchester Coll., 1933-35, Ind. U., 1936; m. Edna Lucille Horton, Dec. 16, 1954. Controller indsl. products div. Gen. Tire & Rubber Co., Wabash, Ind., 1937-57; controller, treas. A.M. Byers Co., Pitts., 1957-61, V.P. finance, dir., 1961—; asst. treas, Gen. Tire & Rubber Co., Akron, O., 1962-65, treas., 1965-. Mem. Nat. Assn. Accountants, Am. Mgmt. Assn., Financial Execs. Inst. Mem. Soc. Friends. Mason (Shriner), Elk. Club: Congress Lake Country. Home: 3386 W Bath Rd Akron, OH 44313. Office: Gen Tire & Rubber Co One General St Akron OH 44309

GURWITSCH, ARON, educator; b. Wilna, Russia, Jan. 17, 1901; s. Meyer and Eva (Bloch) G.; student U. Berlin, 1918-21, U. Frankfurt, 1921-28; Ph.D., U. Goettingen, 1928; m. Alice Stern, Apr. 1929. Came to U.S., 1940, naturalized, 1946. Research fellow Prussian Ministry Scis., Arts and Pub. Instrn., Berlin, Germany. 1929-33; lectr. Institut d'Histoire des Scis. Sorbonne, Paris, 1933-40; research fellow Caisse Nationale de la Recherche Scientifique, Paris, 1939-40; vis. lectr. philosophy Johns Hopkins, 1940-42; instr. physics Harvard, 1943-46; vis. lectr. math. Wheaton Coll., Norton, Mass., 1947-48; asst. prof. math. Brandeis U., 1948-51, asso. prof. philosophy, 1951-59; prof. philosophy Grad. Faculty Polit. and Social Sci. New Sch. for social research. N.Y.C., 1959—. Fulbright Exchange prof. philosophy U. Cologne (Germany), 1958-59; vis. prof. philosophy Columbia, 1962, U. P.R., 1963, U. Mainz (Germany), 1968. Mem. Am. Assn. U. Profs., Am. Philos. Assn., Internat. Phenomenological Soc. (mem. council), Soc. Phenomenology and Existential Philosophy, History of Sci. Soc., Société Francaise de Philosphie. Author: Théorie du Champ de la Conscience, 1957; The Field of Consciousness, 1964; Studies in Phenomenology and Psychology, 1966. Mem. editorial bd. Philosophy and Phenomenological Research, 1940; Social Research, 1964. Cons. editor: Studies in Phenomenology and Existential Philosophy, 1963; Phenomenologica, 1966; Conscientia, 1966; mem. editorial bd. Man and World, 1968. Contbr. articles profl. jours. Home: 820 West End Av New York City, NY 10025.

GURY, JEREMY, writer, advt. exec.; b. N.Y.C., Mar. 2, 1913; s. Abraham and Rebecca (Silverman) G.; M.A., Columbia, 1935; m. Louise Hutchison, Feb. 24, 1950; children—Michael Collister, Melissa Jeremie. Contbg. editor The Spur, N.Y.C.; mng. editor Stage Mag., N.Y.C., 1936; sr. script writer We the People, 1937; copy chief Ferry Hanley Advt. Agy., N.Y.C., 1938-41; copy dir. Donahue & Coe, N.Y.C., 1941-47; sr. writer Ted Bates & Co., N.Y.C., 1948-53, creative supr., v.p., 1956-59, v.p., 1959—, creative dir., 1959-68, mem. exec. com., 1962—, dep. chmn. bd. dirs., creative services, 1968—; creative dir. Benton & Bowles, N.Y.C., 1953-56; pres. Quadrant Communications, 1971—. Chmn. pub. relation com. Inst. Internat. Edn., 1960—, trustee, 1964—; Sch. Design; bd. advisers Univ. Film Study Center, 1971. Served with AUS, 1941-44. Mem. Am. Assn. Advt. Agys. Sch. Design. Served with AUS, 1941-44. Mem. Am. Assn. Advt. Agys. Author: The Round and Round Horse, 1943; (play) The Hither and Thither of Danny Dither, 1956; The Wonderful World of Aunt Tuddy, 1958. Librettist: The Mighty Casey, 1953. Home: Orchard Hill Rd Katonah NY 10536 Office: 666 Fifth Av New York City NY 10019

GUSBERG, SAUL BERNARD, educator; b. Newark, Aug. 3, 1913; student U. Mich., 1934; M.D., Harvard, 1937; Sc.D, Columbia, 1948; m. Dorothy Cushner, June 17, 1938; 1 son, Richard. Research fellow Collis P. Huntington Hosp., Harvard U.; resident obstetrics, gynecology Sloane Hosp. for Women, Columbia-Presbyn. Med. Center, 1946, asst. attending obstetrician and gynecologist Sloane Hosp. for Women, Francis Delafield Hosp., Vanderbilt Clinic, 1946-53, asso. attending, 1954-62; asst. prof. clin. obstetrics and gynecology Coll. Phys. and Surg., Columbia, 1953, asso. prof., 1953-62, clin. prof., 1962-66; obstetrician and gynecologist-in-chief Mt. Sinai Hosp., N.Y.C., prof., chmn. obstetrics and gynecology Mount Sinai Sch. Medicine City U. N.Y., 1965—. Bd. dirs. N.Y. div. Am. Cancer Soc., chmn. adv. com. on research and therapy, 1962, pres.-elect N.Y. div., 1966, pres., 1967-70. Fellow Royal Belgian Soc. Obstetrics and Gynecology (hon.), N.Y. Acad. Sci., A.C.S., Am. Gynecol. Soc., Am. Radium Soc. (v.p. 1968), Am. Coll. Obstetricians and Gynecologists (chmn. com. on malignant disease 1965-70), Am. Assn. Obstetricians and Gynecologists, Soc. Gynecologic Oncologists; mem. Am. Profs. Obstetrics and Gynecology, Soc. Gynecol. Investigation, N.Y. Obstet. Soc. (pres. 1962-63), Am. Soc. Cytology (v.p 1962), Soc. Pelvic Surgeons, Phi Beta Kappa, Sigma Xi. Club: Harvard (N.Y.C.). Contbr. articles on pelvic surgery to profl. jours. Asso. editor Obstetrics and Gynecology. Research, papers on gynec. cancer. Home: 257 Palisade Av Dobbs Ferry NY 10522 Office: 1176 Fifth Av New York City NY 10029

GUSEWELLE, CHARLES WESLEY, journalist; b. Kansas City, Kan., July 22, 1933; s. Hugh L. and Dorothy (Middleton) G.; B.A. in English, Westminster Coll., 1955; m. Katie Jane Ingels, Apr. 17, 1966; children—Anne Elizabeth, Jennifer Sue. Reporter, Kansas City (Mo.) Star, 1955-66, editorial writer of fgn. affairs, 1966—. Served to lt. AUS, 1956-58. Contbr. short stories to Brit., Am. lit. quars. Home: 1212 W 73d St Kansas City MO 64114 Office: 1729 Grand Av Kansas City MO 64108

GUSHMAN, JOHN LOUIS, corp. exec.; b. Lima, O., May 29 1912; s. Louis Alexis and Belle (Whitney) G.; B.A., Ohio State U., 1934, J.D., 1936; certificate of completion Inst. Mgmt., Northwestern U., 1953; m. Helen Louise Little, Sept. 11, 1937; children—Sally Louise, Susan Little, John Louis. Admitted to Ohio bar, 1936; practiced law with Williams, Eversman & Morgan, Toledo, 1936-47; counsel glass container div., mem. legal dept. Owens Ill. Glass Co., 1947-53; v.p., gen. mgr. internat. div., dir. Owens-Ill. Inter-Am. Corp., 1953-61, also fgn. subsidiaries; pres., chief operating officer, dir. Anchor Hocking Glass Corp., 1961-67, pres., dir. chief exec. officer, 1967-71, chmn. bd., chief exec. officer, 1971—; chmn. bd., dir. Anchor Cap & Closure Corp. Can., Ltd., Anchor Hocking Inter-Am., Ltd., Gas Transport, Inc.; pres., dir. Standard Glass Mfg. Co., Lancaster, Glass Crafters, Inc.; former pres. Owens-Ill. Internat.; dir. Federal Reserve Bank of Cleve., Western Elec., F.W. Woolworth Co., Moldcraft, Inc., Phoenix Glass Co., Plastics, Inc., Ravenscroft Ltd. Trustee, Ohio State U. Served as maj. USAAF, World War II. Mem. Am. Bar Assn., Phi Beta Kappa, Phi Delta Theta, Order of Coif. Presbyn. Home: 6 Timberlane Heights Lancaster OH 43130 Office: Anchor Hocking Glass Corp Lancaster OH 43130

GUSSMAN, HERBERT, oil producer; b. N.Y.C., Aug. 25, 1911; s. Samuel and Lottie (Simon) G.; A.B., Cornell U., 1933; m. Roseline Nadel, Apr. 14, 1935; childrenEllen J. (Mrs. Stephen Adelson), Barbara (Mrs. Stephan J. Heyman). With Res. Drilling Co., Tulsa, 1940—, chmn. bd., 1950—; dir. M.P. R.R. Co., 1956—, Tulsa Fed. Savs. & Loan Assn., Mississippi River Corp. Exec. v.p. Tulsa Philharmonic Soc. Mem. Tulsa C. of C. (dir.), Phi Mu Alpha. Home: 4644 S Zunis Av Tulsa OK 74105 Office: 1st Nat Bank Bldg Tulsa OK 74103

GUSSMAN, LAWRENCE, chem. specialty co. exec.; b. Irvington, N.J., Dec. 23, 1915; s. Samuel and Lottie (Simon) G,; B.A., Columbia, 1937, B.S., 1938, Chem. Engr., 1939; m. Catharine Raymond Moore, Dec. 31, 1939; children—William Raymond, Margaret Elaine, John Albert. Chem. engr. Research Found., 1939- 40; with Stein, Hall & Co., Inc. and subsidiaries, N.Y.C., 1940—, pres., dir., 1953—; pres., dir. Eastern Me. Starch Co., Inc., 1955—, Stein-Davies Co., 1952—; chmn. bd. Stein, Hall So., Inc., 1958—; dir. Guardian Mut. Fund, Meyhall Chem. A.G., Meypro Ltd., Switzerland, Meypro. N.V., Holland, Hall Trading Corp., Zaandam, Holland, Stein, Hall Ltd., Stein, Hall S.A. (Pty.), Ltd., Hindustan Gum & Chem. Co., India, Pakistan Gum & Chem. Co., Karachi. Mem. Columbia Engring. Sch. Council, U. Me. Pulp and Paper Found.; pres. bd. Albert Schweitzer Fellowship; bd. dirs. Chief Execs. Forum. Decorated Knight of Malta. Mem. T.A.P.P.I., Am. Inst. Chem. Engrs., Am. Chem. Soc., Am. Assn. Chemists and Colorists, Envelope Mfrs. Assn. Clubs: Pinnacle, Chemists (N.Y.C.). Home: 14 Cooper Rd Scarsdale NY 10583 Office: 605 3d Av New York City NY 10016

GUSSOW, ROY, sculptor; b. Bklyn., Nov. 12, 1918; s. Abraham and Mildred (Jaffe) G.; diploma ornamental horticulture N.Y. State U., Farmingdale, 1938; B.A. in Product Design, Inst. Design, Chgo., 1948; m. Mary Maynard, Oct. 10, 1946; children—Olga, Mimi, Jill. Exhbns. include Art Inst. Chgo., 1947- 49, Joslyn Mus., Omaha, 1949-50, Pa. Acad., 1951-59, Detroit Inst. Art, 1959, Met. Mus., 1951, Whitney Mus., 1956, 62, 64, 66, 68, Kansas City Art Mus., 1950, Arts Club, Chgo., 1966, Colorado Springs Art Center, 1951; rep. permanent collections High Mus., Atlanta, N.C. State Art Mus., Ackland Mus., Chapel Hill, N.C., Bklyn. Mus., Whitney Mus., Mus. Modern Art, N.Y.C., also pvt. collections; commissions include Dept. Commerce, 1956, Lenoir Rhyne Coll., 1957, Coop. Savs. & Loan Assn., Wilmington, N.C., 1959, N.C. State Coll., 1961, Cal. Mus. Sci. and Industry, 1962, Phoenix Mut. Life Ins. Co., Hartford, Conn., 1963, Equitable Life Assurance Soc. U.S., N.Y.C., 1964, Tulsa Civic Center, 1968, Xerox Corp., 1969; tchr. sculpture, design Bradley U., Peoria, Ill., 1948, Colorado Springs Fine Arts Center, 1949-51, Sch. Design, N.C. State Coll., 1951-62; adj. prof. sculpture Sch. Architecture, Pratt Inst., 1962-68. Served with AUS, 1942-45: ETO. Recipient hon. mention Pa. Acad., 1958, N.C. Mus. Art, 1957, 61; purchase award N.C. Mus. Art, 1952, 61, Ford Found., 1960, 62; Nat. Gold medal for exhbn. bldg. arts Archtl. League N.Y., 1962, 65. Address: 40-40 24th St Long Island City NY 11101 also care Borgenicht Gallery 1018 Madison Av New York City NY 10021

GUST, DEVENS, lawyer; b. Phoenix, Aug. 31, 1918; s. John Lewis and Ada (Rebstock) G.; A.B., Stanford, 1940, LL.B., 1942; m. Mary Elizabeth Montgomery, Sept. 1, 1942; childrenJohn Devens, Morgan Montgomery. Admitted to Ariz. bar, 1943; practice law in Phoenix, 1946—; mem. firm Gust Rosenfeld and Divilbess, 1946—; dir. Valley Nat. Bank Ariz. Served as lt (j.g.) USNR, 1941-46. Mem. Am., Ariz.,

Maricopa County (past pres.) bar assns., State Bar Ariz. (past pres.). Home: 4707 E Porter Dr Phoenix AZ 85018 Office: Security Bldg Phoenix AZ 85004

GUSTAD, JOHN WILBERT, coll. pres.; b. St. Paul, Oct. 28, 1922; s. John and Mary Elizabeth (Stringer) G.; A.B. cum laude, Macalester Coll., 1943; M.A., U. Minn., 1948, Ph.D., 1949; 1 dau., Ann Kathryn; m. Dorris Adams Burdick. Teaching asst. dept. psychology U. Minn., 1946, instr., 1947-49; asst. prof. psychology, dir. counseling service Vanderbilt U., 1949-52; vis. asst. prof. George Peabody Coll., summer 1950; mem. seminar improvement undergrad. instrn. psychology Cornell U., summer 1951; operations analyst research Dept. Army, Korea, 1952; asso. prof. psychology, dir. counseling service U. Md., 1952- 56; cons. USN Sch. Hosp. Adminstrn., Bethesda, Md., 1952; cons. VA Vocational Counseling Service, Washington, 1953-59; mem. seminar on occupational choice theory Ohio State U., summer 1954; prof. psychology, dir. counseling center U. Md., 1956-60; cons. sci. teaching improvement program A.A.A.S., 1957-58; project dir. Coll. Teaching Career Research Project, 1957-58; cons. Yale U. Sch. Math. Study Group, 1958-60; vis. prof. Harvard, summer 1959; dir. coll. tchr. program New Eng. Bd. Higher Edn., 1959-60; dean Coll. Liberal Arts, Alfred U., 1960-63, acting dean Grad. Sch., 1962-63; provost and dean coll. New Coll., 1963-66; vis. prof. higher edn. and psychology Ohio State U., 1965-66, asso. dean Coll. Arts and Scis., 1966-68; coordinator Neb. State Colls., 1968-69; pres. Ft. Hays Kansas State Coll., 1969—. Dir. 1st Nat. Bank of Hays. Bd. dirs. Hadley Regional Med. Center. Served to lt. (s.g.), USNR, 1943-46. Fellow Am. Psychol. Assn. (council reps. 1954-57, bd. profl. affairs 1957-60), A.A.A.S.; mem. Am. Assn. U. Profs., Am. Council Edn. (commn. on acad. affairs), Am. Assn. Higher Edn. (chmn. com. on teaching), Kan C. of C., Sigma Xi, Phi Delta Kappa, Pi Phi Epsilon. Presbyn. Rotarian. Club: Smoky Hill Country. Author: Improving Undergraduate Instruction in Psychology; Graduate Education in Psychology; How to Interview; The Choice of a Career in College Teaching; numerous articles in psychol. jours. Home: President's Residence Fort Hays Kansas State Coll Hays KS 67601

GUSTAFSON, ALTON HERMAN, educator; b. Brockton, Mass., Sept. 16, 1904; s. Claus Adolph and Gerda Wilhemina (Anderson) G.; B.S., Mass. Agrl. Coll., 1926; M.A., Harvard, 1928, Ph.D., 1930; m. Maude Elinor Bosworth, June 24, 1929; children—William Eric, Peter Bosworth, Thomas Alton. Austin teaching fellow Harvard, 1928-30; instr. biology Williams Coll., 1930-35, asst. prof., 1935-41, asso, prof., 1941-44, prof., 1944-46, acting dean, 1944- 46; prof. biology Bowdoin Coll., Brunswick, Me., 1946—, chmn. dept. biology, 1946-70. NSF teaching fellow, 1959-60, Mem. Bot. Soc. Am., A.A.A.S., Am. Assn. U. Profs., Phycological Soc. Am., N.E. Bot. Club, Am. Soc. Limnology and Oceanography, Nat. Shellfish Assn., Am. Inst. Biol. Scis., Sigma Xi, Phi Kappa Phi, Phi Sigma Kappa. Home: 261 Maine St Brunswick ME 04011

GUSTAFSON, ELMER T., corp. exec.; b. Omaha, Nov. 9, 1902; s. Charles Edward and Hilda (Sandstrom) G.; B.S. in Mech. Engring., U. Neb., 1925; m. Mabel H. Erickson, Sept. 30, 1928; 1 son, John A. Chmn. bd., dir., chief exec. officer Ceco Corp. Chgo. Ill. Mem., Ill. C. of C., Concrete Reinforcing Steel Inst. (past dir.), Profl. Engrs. Soc. D.C., Aluminum Archtl. Mfrs. Assn. (past dir.). Lutheran. Clubs: Mid America, Executives, Union League (Chgo.); La Grange (Ill.) Country. Home: 626 S Kensington Ave LaGrange IL 60525 Office: 5601 W 26th St Chicago IL 60625

GUSTAFSON, JAMES M., educator; b. Norway, Mich., Dec. 2, 1925; s. John O. and Edith (Moody) G.; B.S., Northwestern U., 1948; B.D., Chgo. Theol. Sem. and U. Chgo., 1951; Ph.D., Yale, 1955; m. Louise Roos, Sept. 3, 1947; childrenKarl, Greta, John, Birgitta. Ordained to ministry United Ch. of Christ, 1951; pastor, Northford, Conn., 1951-54; asst. dir. Study Theol. Edn. in Am., 1954-55; mem. faculty Yale Div. Sch., 1955-71, prof. Christian ethics, 1963-71, chmn. dept. religious studies, 1964-67, prof. religious studies, 1971—, acting chmn., 1970-71. Bd. dirs. United Theol. Sem., New Brighton, Minn., 1961—. Served with AUS, 1944-46. Kent fellow, 1953; Guggenheim fellow, 1959-60, 67-68. Mem. Soc. Sci. Study Religion, Am. Acad. Religion, Am. Soc. Christian Ethics (pres. 1969), Inst. Society, Ethics and the Life Scis. (bd. dirs.). Author: (with H.R. Niebuhr and D.D. Williams) The Advancement of Theological Education, 1957; Treasure in Earthen Vessels; The Church as a Human Community, 1961; Christ and the Moral Life, 1968; The Church as Moral Decision Maker, 1970. Home: 57 Northside Rd North Haven, CT 06473. Office: 409 Prospect St New Haven CT 06510

GUSTAFSON, JOHN EMIL, physician; b. Akeley, Minn., Apr. 6, 1924; s. Emil John and Lily (Lystad) G.; student Hamilton Coll., 1944; M.D., Columbia, 1949; m. Betty Mae Chapman, June 23, 1945; children—Nancy Fae, John Leroy. Intern Ia. Meth. Hosp., 1949-50, resident, 1951-53; dir. United Heart Sta. Ia. Methodist Hosp., 1959-69, dir. Emergency Room Service, 1969—. Served with AUS, 1943-46, 1951-52. Life master Am. Contract Bridge League. Mem. A.M.A., Ia., Polk County med. socs., Am., Ia., Polk County pediatric socs., Am., Ia. (past state and div. pres.) heart assns. Contbr. articles to profl. jours. Home: 1 56th St Des Moines IA 50312 Office: 1200 Pleasant St Des Moines IA 50309

GUSTAFSON, JOHN KYLE, mining co. exec.; b. Chgo., Mar. 13, 1906; s. Lewis and Irene Stoddard (Baker) G.; A.B., Washington U., St. Louis, 1927; A.M., Harvard, 1928, Ph.D., 1930; D.Sc., Mich. Coll. Mining and Tech., 1963; m. Elizabeth Brigham, June 11, 1930; children—Lewis Brigham, Judith (Mrs. Walter Lyall Milde), Andrew Baker. Geologist with various cos. Can., Australia, 1930-39; in charge Toronto office, Hollinger Exploration Ltd., 1939-42, 1st expdn. to Labrador and Ungava, 1942; adviser Metals Res. Co., Washington, 1942- 44; chief geol. Newmont Mining Corp., Magma Copper Co. and affiliated cos., 1944-49; cons. Zinc Corp. Ltd., New Broken Hill Consol. Ltd., Australia, 1947; cons. geologist M.A. Hanna Co., 1950-56, dir. explorations, 1956-60; v.p. Hanna Mining Co., and predecessor corp., 1953-60; pres. Homestake Mining Co., 1961-70, chief exec. officer, 1962-70, chmn., 1970—, also dir.; dir. United Cal. Bank, Pacific Indemnity Group. Dir. raw materials AEC, 1947-48, mgr. raw materials operations, 1948- 49, mem. adv. com. raw materials, 1950-59; mem. NSF advisory panel mineral exploration research, 1952-59; mem. adv. council Inst. Geophysics and Planetary Physics, U. Cal., 1961-68; mem. pres. council Cal. Inst. Tech., 1968-69. Mem. overseers com. to visit dept. geol. scis. Harvard, 1961-67; trustee Washington U., St. Louis, 1962-70. Fellow Geol. Soc. Am. (mem. council 1957-60), Soc. Econ. Geologists (councilor 1949-51, v.p. 1961-62, pres. 1966-67); mem. Am. Inst. Mining, Metall. and Petroleum Engrs., Canadian Inst. Mining and Metall., Mining. Metall. Soc. Am. (Daniel C. Jackling award 1971), Am. Mining Congress (bd. govs. 1962-67), Phi Beta Kappa, Sigma Xi, Sigma Chi. Clubs: Cosmos (Washington); Engineers, Stock Exchange, World Trade Golden Gate Angling and Casting, Pacific Union (San Francisco); Claremont Country (Oakland, Cal.). Home: 206 The Uplands Berkeley CA 94705 Office: 650 California St San Francisco CA 94108 ☆

GUSTAFSON, WESLEY A., former neurosurgeon; b. Waukegan, Ill., Mar. 5, 1909; s. Axel and Victoria (Johnson) G.; M.D., U. Ill., 1934; m. Jennie Robinson; 2 sons, 1 dau. Intern, Ill. Research and Edn. Hosp., Chgo., 1933-34, resident neurosurgery, 1934-35, resident gen. surgeon, 1935-37, asso. neuro-surg.; fellow neuro-pathology Albert Merritt Billings Hosp., Chgo., 1937-38; clk. Nat. Hosp., London, Eng., 1938; fellow neuro-surgery, Lahey Clinic, Boston, 1938-39; attending neurosurgeon Henrotin, Augustana, Garfield Park, Ravenswood hosps., Chgo.; attending neurosurgeon McAllen Municipal Hosp.; cons. neuro-surgeon Gt. Lakes Naval, U.S. Marine, Bethany Meth. hosps.; clin. prof. neurosurgery U. Ill; now ret. Del. surgery Internat. Congress Neurosurgeons. Served as lt. M.C., AUS, 1946. Specialist nerve surgery of heart disease. Diplomate Pan Am. Med. Assn. Mem. A.M.A., Warren Cole Soc., Am. Acad. Neurol. Surgery, Chgo. Surg. Soc., Harvey Cushing Soc., Inst. Medicine Chgo., Miss. Valley Med. Soc., Interurban, So., Chgo. neurol. socs., So. Neurosurg. Soc., Nu Sigma Nu, Sigma Xi. Club: University. Contbr. articles in field to profl. jours. Home: Route 1 Box 269A McAllen TX 78501 Office: First Nat Bank Bldg McAllen TX 78501

GUSTAFSON, WINTHROP ADOLPH, educator; b. Moline, Ill., Oct. 14, 1928; s. Gustav A. and Katherine (Wenger) G.; B.S., U. Ill., 1950, M.S., 1954, Ph.D., 1956; m. Sarah Elizabeth Garner, Aug. 3, 1957; children—Charles Lee, Stanley Scott, John Winthrop. Research scientist Lockheed Missiles & Space Co., Palo Atto, Cal., 1956-60; asso. prof. Sch. Aeros., Astronautics and Engring. Scis., Purdue U., Lafayette, Ind., 1960-66, prof., 1966—; vis. prof. U. Cal. at San Diego, 1968; research engr. Allison div. Gen. Motors Co., Indpls., summer 1962; mem. tech. staff Bell Telephone Labs., Whippany, N.J., summer 1966; cons. Goodyear Aerospace Corp., Akron, O., 1964. Served to 1st lt. USAF, 1951-53. Mem. Am. Inst. Aeros. and Astronautics, Am. Soc. Engring. Edn., Sigma Xi. Contbr. articles profl. jours. Home: 209 Lindberg Av West Lafayette IN 47906 Office: Purdue U Lafayette IN 47907

GUSTAV, ADOLF, VI, King of Sweden; b. Stockholm, Sweden, Nov. 11, 1882; s. King Gustaf V and Victoria, Princess of Baden; ed. pvt. tutors; student U. Uppsala, 1902-03, U. Oslo, 1903-04; hon. degrees, U. Lund, 1918, Princeton, Yale, and Clark univs., 1926, Cambridge U., 1929, Dorpat U., 1932, Harvard, 1938, Stockholm U., 1944, Helsingfors U., 1952; Oxford, 1955; m. Margaret, Princess of Great Britain and Ireland, June 15, 1905 (dec. 1920); children—Gustaf Adolf, Duke of Vasterbotten (dec., 1947); Sigvard; Ingrid, Queen of Denmark; Bertil, Duke of Halland, Carl Johan; m. 2d, Lady Louise Mountbatten, former Princess of Battenberg, Nov. 3, 1923 (dec. 1965). Crown Prince, 1907-50, King of Sweden, 1950—. Commd. to Army, 1902, advanced through grades to gen., 1932. Promoter humanistic research in general in Sweden; an organizer Swedish humanistic scholarship; a founder and pres. Swedish Archaeol. Inst. in Rome, 1925, in Athens, 1948; pres. Humanistic Research Fund, 1928-50. Royal Acad. Hist. and Antiquities, 1945-50, Swedish-Chinese Research Com. from its foundation 1922; of Swedish Cyprus Com., 1926—. Active part in archaeol. excavations in Sweden, Greece, Cyprus and China. Pres. Swedish Olympics Com., 1912. Mem. Swedish Sports Fedn. (pres. 1903-33), Central Assn. Promotion Athletics (pres. 1907-33), Nat. League Against Tuberculosis (hon. pres.). Swedish Export Assn. (hon. pres.); fgn. mem. Académie des Inscriptions et Belles Lettres; mem. numerous other Swedish, fgn. socs., Archeol. Inst. d.deutschen Reiches, British Acad. clubs. Interested in archaeology and art, particularly ancient Chinese art. Address: Royal Palace Stockholm Sweden

GUSTAVSON, CARL GUSTAV, educator; b. Vinton, Ia., Aug. 3, 1915; s. Carl Linus and Edla (Gustafson) G.; A.B., Augustana Coll., 1937; M.A., U. Ill., 1938; Ph.D. (Pres. White fellow 1938-40), Cornell U., 1942; m. Caryl Jennings, June 30, 1943; children—Carl, Eric, Martha. Instr., Lake Forest Coll., 1942- 43; asst. prof. Miami (O.) U., 1943-45; asst. to asso. prof. Ohio U., 1945-56, acting chmn. dept., 1955-56, prof. history 1956-, chmn. dept., 1961-65; research, Munich, Germany, 1960, Spain and Vienna, 1966; vis. prof. summer Emory U., 1949, Cornell U., 1950, Wayne State U., 1955, U. Ill., 1961, U. Cin., 1964, Western Res. U., 1965, U. Ga., 1968, U., Pacific, 1969; Fulbright fellow U. Uppsala (Sweden), 1969. Del. XI Internat. Congress Hist. Socs., Stockholm, 1960. Ford Found. Fellow, 1953-54; grantee Am. Philos. Soc., 1956, 64; recipient Baker Research award, 1965. Mem. Am. History Assn., Am. Assn. U. Profs., Ohio Acad. History (pres. 1964-65; ann. award 1956), French Hist.-Soc., Am.-Scandinavian Found., Societe d'Histoire Moderne (Paris), Phi Beta Kappa, Phi Alpha Theta, Pi Gamma Mu, Lambda Chi Alpha. Episcopalian. Club: Swedish (Chgo.). Author: A Preface to History, 1955; The Institutional Drive, 1966; Europe in the World Community Since 1939, 1970. Home: 14 Utah Pl Athens OH 45701

GUSTAVSON, DEAN LEONARD, architect; b. Salt Lake City, June 27, 1924; s. Ernest L. and Leona (Hansen) G.; B.Arch., U. Cal. Berkeley, 1951; student U. Utah, 1946-47; m. Barbara Knight, Apr. 28, 1944; children—Mark Steven, Lisa Ann, Clint Knight. Pvt. practice architecture, Salt Lake City, 1953—; pres. Dean L. Gustavson Assos., architects and planners, Salt Lake City, 1957—; pres. Nat. Council Archtl. Registration Bds., 1969-70; co-chmn. Internat. Com. Archtl. Registration, 1970—. Chmn. planning Salt Lake City's Second Century Plan, 1960-62. Served with USAAF, 1942-46. Fellow Am. Inst. Architects, A.I.A. (pres. Utah 1959-60); mem. Salt Lake C. of C. Home: 5775 Highland Dr Salt Lake City UT 84121 Office: 15 N West Temple Salt Lake City UT 84103

GUSTIN, ARNO ANTHONY, ednl. adminstr.; b. Flasher, N.D., June 18, 1906; s. John and Gertrude (Schmidt) G.; B.A. with honors, St. John's U., Collegeville, Minn., 1929; M.A., Cath. U. Am., 1934; Ph.D., U. Minn., 1945. Joined Order St. Benedict, 1927, ordained priest Roman Cath. Ch., 1933; prin. St. John's Prep. Sch., 1936-40; registrar St. John's U., Collegeville, Minn., 1944-52, acad. dean, 1952-58, pres., 1958-64, prof. edn., 1944-58, chmn. dept., 1954-58, prof. edn., asso. in devel., 1964-65, dir. asso. and fellow programs, 1970—; pres. Mary Coll., Bismarck, N.D., 1965-70. Mem. Minn. Adv. Com. Tchr. Edn., 1947-52; pres. Minn. Pvt. Coll. Council, 1958-59, Minn. Pvt. Coll. Fund, 1960-61; participant Minn. Assembly on Fed. Govt. and Higher Edn., 1961; an organizer Tri- Coll. program of St. Cloud State Coll., Coll. St. Benedict, St. John's U., 1958; mem. exec. com. Dakota-Asso. Colls. Consortium of Research Devel. Mem. Nat. Cath. Edn. Assn. (chmn. deans meeting 1954), Assn. Am. Colls., Assn. Minn. Colls., N.E.A., Am. Ednl. Research Assn., N.D. Edn. Assn., Collegeville C. of C., Phi Delta Kappa. Contbr. articles, revs. to periodicals. Home: St John's Abbey Collegeville MN 56321

GUSTIN, HARLEY WEMPLE, lawyer; b. Salt Lake City, Apr. 22, 1902; s. Frank Jasper and Dora (Harley) Gustin; LL.B., U. Utah, 1924; m. Margaret Strunk, Dec. 7, 1945; children—(by previous marriage) Violet Eugenia (Mrs. John C. McKay), Beverly Jane (Mrs. K.F. Campbell), Frank Johannesen. Admitted to Utah bar, 1924, and since practiced in Salt Lake City; mem. firm Gustin & Gustin. Asst. dist. atty. Third Jud. Dist. of Utah, 1933-34. Fellow Am. Coll. Trial Lawyers; mem. Salt Lake City Bd. Edn., 1933-39. Mem. Utah State (commr. 1948), Am., Salt Lake County (pres. 1951) bar assns., S.A.R., Sigma Chi, Delta Theta Phi. Episcopalian. Mason (Shriner), Elk. Club: University. Home: 2545 Verona Circle Salt Lake City UT 84117 Office: Walker Bank Bldg Salt Lake City UT 84111

GUSTIN, RALPH LIVINGSTON, Jr., lawyer, ins. co. exec.; b. West Somerville, Mass., Mar. 7, 1918; s. Ralph Livingston and Ruth Elizabeth (Haskell) G.; grad. Phillips Exeter Acad., 1936; A.B., Harvard, 1940, LL.B., 1943, grad. Advanced Mgmt. Program, 1960; m. Margaret McAfee, Oct. 15, 1949 (div. Sept. 16, 1966); children—Ralph Livingston III, Nancy Gail (dec.), Lisa Joan, Roger McAfee; m. 2d, Marie-Louise de Coriolis Wheeler, May 3, 1968; step children—Allison Gates Wheeler, Cynthia Howe Wheeler. Admitted to Cal. bar, 1947, Mass. bar, 1953, U.S. Supreme Ct. bar; asso. McCutchen, Thomas, Matthew, Griffiths & Greene, San Francisco, 1947-53; asso. counsel John Hancock Mut. Life Ins. Co., Boston, 1953-57, 2d v.p., counsel, 1957-62, v.p., gen. solicitor, 1962-65, v.p., gen. counsel, 1965-66, sr. v.p., gen. counsel, 1967—. Sec., bd. dirs. United Fund of Greater Boston, Mass. Bay United Fund. Served from pvt. to maj., USAAF, 1941-46. Mem. Am., Boston bar assns., Cal. State Bar Assn., Life Ins. Counsel, Nat. Assn. Securities Dealers (bd. govs.). Am. Life Conv. Conglist. Home: 27 Colgate Rd Wellesley MA 02181 Office: 200 Berkeley St Boston MA 02117

GUSTINE, GERALD RICHARD, mfg co. exec.; b. Keeler, Mich., July 20, 1910; s. Arthur and Ada (MacMillan) G.; A.B., U. Mich., 1932; m, Phyllis Lee Dye, Aug. 21, 1937; childrenRobert Dye, Beverly Jane, Patricia Ann. With King-Seeley Thermos Corp., Ann Arbor, Mich., 1935-, v.p. charge sales, 1955-58, gen. mgr. King-Seeley div., 1958-63, exec. v.p. corp., 1963-65, pres., 1965—, also dir. Active Ann Arbor United Fund. Mem. Ann Arbor C. of C. (dir.), Lambda Chi Alpha. Home; 2540 Londonderry St Ann Arbor MI 48104 Office: 315 S 1st St Ann Arbor MI 48108

GUSTLIN, PHILIP RAYMOND, lawyer; b. Santa Ana, Cal., Sept. 25, 1934; s. Paul Raymond and Evelyn (Jumper) G.; B.S., U. Cal. at Los Angeles, 1957; J.D., U. So. Cal., 1963; m. Hansel C. Huss, 1958 (div.); children—Holly, Gretchen P., Caroline. Jr. auditor, sr. auditor Peat, Marwick, Mitchell & Co., C.P.A.'s, 1957-59; with Electronic Specialty Co., 1959-68, asst. controller, controller, gen. counsel, gen. mgr., 1963-64, gen. mgr., 1964-66, asst. to pres., 1966-67; gen. mgr. Los Angeles Electronics, 1967-69; exec. v.p. Tasker Industries, 1969-71; pvt. practice law, Los Angeles, 1971—; admitted to Cal. bar, 1964. Served with AUS, 1957. C.P.A., Cal. Mem. Cal. Soc. C.P.A.'s, Los Angeles Bar Assn., Cal. Bar, Am. Inst. C.P.A.'s, Nat. Assn. Atty.-C.P.A.'s, Sigma Nu. Clubs: Jonathan; Verdugo; Multnomah Athletic. Home: 8715 Sunset Plaza Los Angeles CA 90069 Office: 1800 Century Park E Century City Los Angeles CA 90067

GUSTON, PHILIP, painter; b. Montreal, Can., June 27, 1912; student Otis Art Inst. Exhibited Whitney Mus. Modern Art, 1941-55, Pa. Acad. Fine Arts, 1944, Boston Mus. Fine Arts, 1946, also Guggenheim Mus., 1954, galleries Paris, Rome, Barcelona, London; one-man show Midtown Gallery, 1945. Peridot Gallery, 1952, Egan Gallery, 1953; represented in collections City Art Mus., St. Louis, Washington U., Va. Mus. Fine Arts, Ill. Wesleyan U., U. Ia., U. Ill., Met. Mus. Art, others. Instr. art U. Ia., 1941-45, Washington U., 1945-47, N.Y.U., 1947-. Recipient prize N.Y. World's Fair, 1939, Carnegie Inst., 1945; med. prize Va. Mus. Fine Arts, 1946; Guggenheim fellow, 1948; Prix de Rome, 1949; grant Am. Acad. Arts and Letters, 1948. Contbr. articles, illustrations art mags. Address: Woodstock NY 12498

GUTCHE, GENE, composer; b. Berlin, Germany, July 3, 1907; s. Maxmillian and Flora (von Zerbst) G.; came to U.S., 1925; M.A., U. Minn., 1950; Ph.D., State U. Ia., 1953; m. Marion Frances Buchan, Dec. 1, 1935. Guggenheim fellow, 1963-65. World premieres include Piano Concerto Opus 24, Mpls. Summer Session, 1956, Third String Quartet Opus 12 No. 3, Arts Quartet, 1958, Holofernes Overture Opus 27 No. 1, Mpls. Symphony, 1959, Rondo Capriccioso Opus 21, N.Y. Chamber Orch., 1960, Concertino for Orch. Opus 28, Mpls. Summer Session, 1961, Fourth String Quartet Opus 29 No. 1, Fine Arts Quartet, 1962, Symphony IV Opus 30, Albuquerque Symphony, 1962, Timpani Concertante Opus 31, Oakland Symphony, 1962, Symphony V for Strings Opus 34, Chautauqua Festival, 1962, Bongo Divertimento Opus 35, St. Paul Chamber Orch., 1962, Raquel Opus 38, Tulsa Philharmonic, 1963, Genghis Khan Opus 37, Mpls. Symphony, 1963, Rites in Tenochtitlan Opus 39, St. Paul Chamber Orch., 1965, Gemini Opus 41, Mpls. Summer Session, 1966, Hsiang Fei Opus 40, Cin. Symphony, 1966, Rites in Tenochtitlan Opus 39 No. 1, New Orleans Symphony, 1967, Classic Concerto for Chamber Orch. Opus 44, St. Paul Chamber Orch., 1967, Aesop Fabler Suite Opus 43, Fargo-Moorhead Symphony, 1968, Epimetheus USA Opus 46, Detroit Symphony, 1969. Recipient Minn. State Centennial prize, 1958, Luria award, 1959, prize Albuquerque Nat. Composition, 1962, prize Oscar Espla Internat. Composition, 1962, XVI Premio Citta di Trieste, 1969, Louis Moreau Gottschalk Gold medal, 1970; commns. include St. Paul Philharmonic, 1962, St. Paul Arts and Scis., 1965, regents U. Minn., 1966, Fargo-Moorhead Symphony, 1967, Detroit Symphony, 1969. Mem. Am. Fedn. Musicians, Am. Composers Alliance, Am. Music Center. Contbr. articles profl. jours. Address: Galaxy Music Corp 2121 Broadway New York City NY 10023

GUTE, HERBERT JACOB, artist, educator; b. Jeffersonville, N.Y., Aug. 10, 1907; s. Rudolph Herman and Martha (Mueller) G.; B.F.A., Yale, 1933; m. Catherine M. Schaefer, Oct. 18, 1936; childrenHerbert Schaefer, David Mueller. Staff artist Dure-Europos Expdn., 1933-35; tchr. U. Va., 1937; mem. faculty Yale, 1938—, asst. prof. drawing and painting, 1936—; fellow Calhoun Coll., 1955-; exhbns. include Am. Water Color Soc., 1949-, Silvermine Guild, 1956-, Boston Art Festival, 1938, Watercolor U.S.A., 1961, 200 Years of Am. Watercolor, Met. Museum of Art, 1965; represented permanent collections O'Hara Coll., Sweetbriar Coll., Yale Art Gallery, Dept. Interior, Louvre, Dura, Paris, France, Jewish Mus., Dura, IBM collection, Antheneum, Hartford, Conn., Walker Art Mus., others; chmn. from Am. Battle Monuments Commn. for mural U.S. Mil. Cemetery, Cambridge, Eng., 1953-54. Adviser on art therapy for mentally ill Conn. Mental Hosp., 1949-53. Recipient Muriel Alvord prize Yale, 1935, 1st prize Conn. Contemporary Painting, Springfield, Mass., 1951, 2d Internat. Hallmark award, 1954. A.N.A.; mem. Audubon Soc., Phila. Water Color Club, Silvermine Guild, Am. Water Color Soc. Club: Yale (New Haven). Illustrator; (M. Rostovtzeff) Dura Europos, 1936; (J. Geise) Man in the Western World, 1940. Rep. Ten Best Books of the Year, 1941-48. Home: Box 1605 Art Yale Sta New Haven CT 06520

GUTERBOCK, HANS GUSTAV, educator; b. Berlin, Germany, May 27, 1908; s. Bruno Gustav and Margarethe (Auer) G.; student U. Berlin, 1926-27, U. Marburg, 1928-29; Ph.D., U. Leipzig, 1934; m. Frances Hellmann, Sept. 2, 1940; children—Walter Michael, Thomas Martin. Came to U.S., 1949, naturalized, 1955. Asst., Berlin (Germany) Museum, 1933-35; asso. prof. Hittitology, U. Ankara (Turkey), 1936-48; guest lectr. U. Uppsala (Sweden), 1948-49; with Oriental Inst., U. Chgo., 1949—, prof. Hittitology, 1956—, Tiffany and Margaret Blake Distinguished Service prof., 1969—. Mem. German expdn. Boghazkoy, Turkey, 1933-35, U. Chgo. expdn., 1958, 59, 61, 64, 66, 68; pres. Am. Research Inst. in Turkey, 1968—. Mem. Am. Oriental Soc., Am. Schs. Oriental Research, Internat. Soc. Oriental Research, Deutsche Orient-Gesellschaft, German Archaeol. Inst. Author: (Hittite text) Kumarbi, 1946; (Hittite seals) Siegel aus Bogazkoy, 2 vols., 1942; also articles. Home: 5617 S Drexel Av Chicago IL 60637

GUTERMUTH, CLINTON RAYMOND, conservationist, naturalist; b. Fort Wayne, Ind., Aug. 16, 1900; s. Henry Christian and Alice Virtue (Zion) G.; student U. Notre Dame, 1918-19; grad. Am. Inst. Banking, 1927, postgrad., 1927-28; m. Ila Bessie Horm, Mar. 4, 1922. Asst. cashier St. Joseph Valley Bank, Elkhart, Ind., 1922-34; dir. div. edn. Ind. Dept. Conservation, Indpls., 1934-40, dir. div. fish and game, 1940-42; Ind. rent dir. OPA, Indpls., 1942-45; exec. sec. Am. Wildlife Inst., Washington, 1945-46; v.p. Wildlife Mgmt. Inst., 1946—. Chmn. Natural Resources Council Am., 1959-61; exec. com. Am. com. adv. council Pub. Land Law Rev. Commn., 1964-70. Trustee, sec. N.Am. Wildlife Found., Inc., 1945—; trustee, v.p. Stronghold (Sugarloaf Mountain) Inc., 1947—; bd.dirs., treas. World Wildlife Fund, 1961—. Recipient Leopold medal Wildlife Soc., 1957; Fishing Hall of Fame, Sportsman's Club Am. Distinguished Service award Nat. Assn. Soil Conservation Dists., 1958; Meritorious service award Nat. Watershed Congress, 1963; Nat. Service award Keep Am. Beautiful, 1965; Nat. Conservation award Mich. United Conservation Clubs, 1968; Distinguished Service award Nat. Wildlife Fedn., 1969; Horace M. Albright medal Am. Scenic and Historic Preservation Soc., 1971. Mem. Nat. Rifle Assn. (life mem., dir.), Izaak Walton League Am. (life), Outdoor Writers Assn. Am., The Wildlife Soc. (hon. mem., trustee), Nat. Audubon Soc., Wilderness Soc., Am. Fisheries Soc., Internat. Assn. Game, Fish and Conservation Commrs., Am. Forestry Assn., Am. Soc. Range Mgmt., Conservation Edn. Assn., Nat. Parks Assn., Polar Inst. N.Am., Soil Conservation Soc. Am. (hon.), Artic Inst. N.Am., Zool. Soc. (N.Y.), Mason (32, K.T.). Clubs: Cosmos, Nat. Press (Washington); Explorers; Boone and Crockett; Camp Fire N.Y.C. (hon.); Booneville (Ind.) Press; Elkhart (Ind.) Conservation; Miami (Fla.) Sailfish; Tanana Valley (Alaska) Sportsmen's; Outdoor Boating Am. (hon.). Author: Where to Go in Indiana, Official Lake Guide, 1938; Quips and Queries page on natural history, Outdoor Indiana, 1934-42; W.M.I. bi-weekly Outdoor New Bulletin, 1947-50. Co-author; The Fisherman's Encyclopedia, 1950; The Standard Book of Fishing, 1950. Program chmn. ann. N.Am. Wildlife Conf. 1946—. Numerous articles and lectures on various phases of natural resource restoration. Home: 4801 Connecticut Av NW Washington DC 20008 Office: Wire Bldg Washington DC 20005

GUTH, DONALD JOHN, corp. exec.; b. Manning, Ia., Mar. 24, 1916; s. T. R. and Laura (Guth) McCann; student Capital City Comml. Coll., 1934, Am. Inst. Bus., 1935, Harvard, 1952; m. Josephine C. Lindsey, Mar. 16, 1934; 1 son, Donald D. Clk., Mut. Benefit Life Ins. Co., Des Moines, 1934-35; accountant Ford Motor Co., Des Moines, 1935-42; comptroller, treas., chief financial officer Solar Aircraft Co., Des Moines, N.Y.C., San Diego, 1942-61; controller, chief accounting officer Collins Radio Co., Dallas, 1961-68; v.p. GF Industries, Inc., Dallas, 1969—; v.p., dir. Gen. Earth Minerals Corp., Dallas, 1969—; v.p., treas. Varo, Inc., Garland, Tex., 1971—; dir. Swift Ohio Corp., Kenton, 1970—, Constrn. Products Corp., Miami, Fla., 1971—, Varo-Semiconductor, Inc., Garland, 1971—. Pres. Taxpayers Assn., Des Moines and San Diego. Served with Ia. State Guard, 1942-45. Recipient Remington Rand trophy as pres. Nat. Assn. Accountants, 1948. Mem. Financial Execs. Inst. (nat. dir., past pres. Dallas and Ia. chpts., past nat. v.p.), Nat Assn. Accountants (past nat. v.p., mem. nat. exec. com., past pres. Des Moines chpt., council continuing ednl. policies 1965-68), Am. Accounting Assn. Home: 212 1832 Royal Lane Dallas TX 75230 Office: Garland Bank & Trust Bldg Garland TX 75040

GUTH, RAYMOND CHARLES, food co. exec.; b. Bklyn., Nov. 3, 1921; s. Eugene and Grete (Kuhn) G.; A.B., Harvard, 1943, LL.B., 1948; m. Dorothy J. Lobrano, Aug. 31, 1963; children—Raymond Charles, Dorothy Jean. Admitted to N.Y. bar, 1949; firm Klein, Alexander & Cooper, N.Y.C., 1948-49, McCanliss & Early, N.Y.C., 1949-51; with Amstar Corp., 1953—, asst. sec., counsel, 1961-65, sec., 1965—. Served to lt. (j.g.) USNR, 1943-46, to lt., 1951-53. Mem. N.Y. State Bar Assn., Am. Soc. Corporate Secs. Presbyn. Club: Harvard (N.Y.C.). Home: 1172 Park Av New York City NY 10028 Office: 1251 Av of Americas New York City NY 10020

GUTHE, ALFRED KIDDER, anthropologist, educator; b. Detroit, Apr. 30, 1920; s. Carl Eugen and Grace Ethel (McDonald) G.; student U. N.C., 1937-39; A.B., U. Mich., 1941, Ph.D., 1956, M.A., U. Chgo., 1948; m. Lois Frances Kuhlman, Sept. 2, 1944; childrenCarol Jean, Nancy Lee, Janet Tate, Philip Bruce, Martin Eugene, Donald Edward. Jr. anthropologist, then curator anthropology Rochester (N.Y.) Mus. Arts and Scis., 1949-61; lectr. anthropology U. Rochester, 1949-61; head dept. anthropology U. Tenn., Knoxville, 1961-71, dir. Frank H. McClung Mus., 1961—, archaeol. research Notheastern U.S. Treas. N.Y. State Archaeol. Assn., 195O-58, v.p., 1958-62; mem. archaeol. adv. council Tenn. Dept. Conservation, 197O—. Served with USNR, 1942-45. Fellow Am. Anthrop. Assn.; mem. Soc. Am. Archaeology, Tenn. Assn. Mus. (pres. 1963-65), Sigma Xi. Unitarian. Kiwanian. Author articles. Editor Tenn. Archaeologist, 1961-; asst. editor (N.E.) Am. Antiquity, 1952-61, (N.E.) Abstracts of New World Archaeology, 1959-62. Home: 8008 Chesterfield Dr Knoxville, TN 37919.

GUTHEIM, FREDERICK, writer, cons,; b. Cambridge, Mass., Mar. 3, 1908; s. August G. and Augusta (Meiser) G.; A.B., U. Wis., 1931; postgrad. in pub. adminstrn. U. Chgo., 1933-35; m. Mary Purdon, June 8, 1935; 1 son, Nicholas. Staff mem. Inst. for Govt. Research, Brookings Instn., 1931-33; with fed. housing and planning agys., 1935-47; spl. staff writer for New York Herald-Tribune, 1947-50; asst. exec. dir. Am. Inst. Architects, 1950-53; pvt. practice as planning cons., 1953-; staff dir. Joint Com. on Washington Met. Problems, U.S. Congress, 1958-60: pres. Washington Center for Met. Studies, 196O-65. Vis. prof Williams Coll., 1969; distinguished vis. prof. environmental studies Central Wash. State Coll., 1970. Commr., Upper Montgomery County (Md.) Planning Com., 1950-57; mem. Nat. Capital Regional Planning Council, 1952-57; mem. President's Council on Pa. Av., 1962-64, President's Task Force on Natural Beauty, 1964; mem. Potomac Planning Task Force, 1965-67. Served with AUS, 1943-45. Decorated Order of Lion (Finland). Mem. Italian Town Planning Inst. (hon.), A.I.A. (hon.), Am. Inst. Planners. Author: Houses for Family Living, 1948; Rethinking Urban Redevelopment (with Coleman Woodbury), 1949; The Potomac, 1949; Housing as Environment, 1953; 100 Years of Architecture in America, 1957; Alvar Aalto, 1960. Editor: Frank Lloyd Wright on Architecture, 1941; adv. editor for architecture and planning Mag. of Art, 1935-40; corr. editor Urbanistica, 1950-58, Progressive Architecture, 1954-59. Archtl. critic Washinton Post, 1960- 62. Home: Mt Ephraim Dickerson MD 20753 Office: 1750 Pennsylvania Av Washington DC 20006

GUTHEIM, ROBERT JULIUS, govt. ofcl.; b. Washington, Dec. 30, 1911; s. August G. and Augusta (Meiser) G.; B.S. in C.E., Harvard, 1933, M.B.A., 1935; m. Bernice A. Howard, June 19, 1937; childrenGeorge C., August W. Travel in Europe, studying elec. cable mfg., 1935; mem. staff Gen. Cable Corp., 1935-39; asst. engr. system planning bur. Potomac Electric Power Co., Washington, 1939-43; civilian asst. to head guided missile and electronics program, Bur. Ordnance, Dept. of Navy, electronics program, Bur. Ordnance, Dept. of Navy, 1946-55; mem. staff asst. sec. navy for material, 1956, staff spl. asst. to sec. def. for guided missiles, 1956- 57; staff dir. plans and coordination Office Dir. Guided Missiles, Office Sec. Def., 1957-59; chmn. spl. com. adequacy of range facilities Dept. Def., 1957-59; staff missiles Office Dir. Def. Research and Engring., 1959-60; mgmt. officer space scis. NASA, 1961-63, program planning officer space scis. and applications, 1963—; lectr. in mgmt. problems, 1957—. Served from lt. (j.g.) to lt. comdr., USNR, 1943-46; captain Reserve; comdg. officer Naval Reserve Weapons Unit 664, 1963-64. Registered mech. and electrical engr., D.C. Mem. Nat. Space Club. Lutheran. Clubs: Kenwood Country (Bethesda, Md.); Harvard (Washington and N.Y.C.). Contbr. to Ency. Brit. Home: 5210 Goddard Rd Bethesda MD 20014 Office: Fed Office Bldg 6 Washington DC 20546

GUTHKE, KARL SIEGFRIED, educator; b. Lingen, Germany, Feb. 17, 1933; s. Karl Hermann and Helene (Beekman) G.; came to U.S., 1956; M.A., U. Tex., 1953; Dr.phil., U. Göttingen (Germany), 1956; M.A. (hon.), Harvard, 1968; m. Dagmar von Nostitz, Apr. 24, 1965. Mem. faculty U. Cal. at Berkeley, 1956-65, prof. German lit., 1962-65; prof. German lit. U. Toronto, 1965-68, Harvard, 1968—; vis. prof. U. Colo., 1963, U. Mass., 1967. Guggenheim fellow, 1965. Mem. Schiller Gesellschaft, Hebbel Gesellschaft, Am. Lessing Soc. (pres.). Author: Englische Vorromantik und deutscher Sturm und Drang, 1958; (with Hans M. Wolff) Das Leid im Werke Gerhart Hauptmanns, 1958; Geschichte und Poetik der deutschen Tragikomödie, 1961; Gerhart Hauptmann: Weltbild im Werk, 1961; Haller und die Literatur, 1962; Der Stand der Lessing-Forschung: Ein Bericht über die Literatur, 1932-1962, 1965; Modern Tragicomedy: An Investigation into the Nature of the Genre, 1966; Die Moderne Tragikomödie: Theorie und Gestalt, 1968; Wege zur Literatur: Studien zur deutschen Dichtungs und Geistesgeschichte, 1967; Gotthold Ephraim Lessing (with Heinrich Schneider), 1967; Hallers Literaturkritik, 1970; Die Mythologie der entgötterten Welt: Ein literarisches Thema von der Aufklärung bis zur Gegenwart, 1971. Co-editor: Lessings Werke, 1971-72. Home: Hillside Rd Lincoln MA 01773 Office: Boylston Hall Harvard Univ Cambridge MA 02138

GUTHMAN, EDWIN O., editor; b. Seattle, Aug. 11, 1919; s. Otto and Hilda (Leiser) G.; A.B., U. Wash., 1941; m. Jo Ann Cheim, July 6, 1947; children—Lester, Edwin, Gary, Diane. Entered U.S. Army, 1941, commd. 2d lt., 1942, advanced to capt., 1945; served as reconnaissance officer, 339th inf. Regt., 85th Div., ETO; disch., 1946; reporter Seattle Star, 1946-47, Seattle Times, 1947-61; dir. pub. information Dept. Justice, 1961-64; press asst. Senator Robert Kennedy, 1965; nat. news editor Los Angeles Times, 1965—. Recipient Purple Heart, Silver Star medal Recipient Pulitzer prize for nat. reporting, 1949; Nieman fellow Harvard, 1950-51. Author: We Band of Brothers, 1971. Home: 1436 N Capri Dr Pacific Palisades CA 90272 Office: Los Angeles Times Los Angeles CA 90053

GUTHMANN, WALTER S., educator, chemist; b. Chgo., Apr. 3, 1907; s. William B. and Ida (Seligmann) G.; B.S., Yale, 1928, Ph.D., U. Chgo., 1932; m. Edith Greenbaum, Oct. 16, 1940; children—Babette (Mrs. David Steinbrecher), William Alan. Co-founder Edwal Labs., Chgo., 1933, v.p., 1933-41, pres., 1947-53; pres. Ringwood Chem. Co., 1953-58, Morton Chem. Co., 1958-61; mem. faculty Roosevelt U., Chgo., 1961—, prof. chemistry, 1965—, chmn. dept., 1966—. Cons. in field, 1935—; dir. Ventron Corp., 1958—. Mem. Bd. Edn. dist. 111, Highland Park, Ill., 1953-59; chmn. jr. coll. com. Highland Park-Deerfield, 1962-67. Served to maj., C.W.S., AUS, 1941-45. Mem. Am. Chem. Soc. (dir. Chgo. sect. 1963—, nat. councilor 1965- -), Mfg. Chemists Assn. (chmn. edn. activities com. 1963-65), Soc. Chem. Industry, Sigma Xi. Clubs: Chemists (Chgo.); Yale (N.Y.C.). Contbr. articles to jours. Research in organo-metallic reactions. Home: 695 Euclid Av Highland Park, IL 60035. Office: 430 S Michigan Av Chicago IL 60605

GUTHRIE, ALBERT NELSON, educator; b. Carlsbad, N.M., Sept. 10, 1903; s. Daniel Burleson and Lillie May (Hill) G.; B.S., U. Ariz., 1926, Ph.D., U. Ill., 1930; m. Edna Mary Howe, June 5, 1929 (dec. June 1962); 1 son, Daniel Albert, Instr. physics Columbia, 1930-36; mem. faculty U. R.I., 1936-43, head dept. physics, 1936-43, prof., 1942-43; mem. faculty Bklyn. Coll., 1943- , prof. physics, 1956-, chmn. dept., 1956-; research physicist Hudson Labs., Columbia, 1952-, dir., 1954-56. Liaison scientist London (Eng.) br. office Office Naval Research, 1961. Fellow Am. Phys. Soc.; mem. Am. Assn. Physics Tchrs., Acoustical Soc. Am., A.A.A.S., Am. Assn. U. Profs., Sigma Xi, Delta Chi. Episcopalian (vestry). Home: 3215 Av H Brooklyn NY 11210

GUTHRIE, ALFRED BERTRAM, Jr., author; b. Bedford, Ind., Jan. 13, 1901; s. Alfred Bertram and June (Thomas) G.; student U. Wash., 1919-20; A.B., U. Mont., 1923, Litt. D., 1949; m. Harriet Larson, June 25, 1931 (dec.); children—Alfred Bertram III, Helen Larson; m. 2d, Carol B. Luthin, Apr. 3, 1969. Reporter Lexington, (Ky.) Leader, 1926- 29, city editor, editorial writer, 1929-45, exec. editor, 1945-47; teacher creative writing, U. Ky., 1947-52. Recipient Pulitzer prize for distinguished fiction, 1950. Nieman fellow Harvard, 1944-45. Author: The Big Sky, 1947; The Way West, 1949; These Thousand Hills, 1956; The Big It, 1960; The Blue Hen's Chick, 1965; Arfive, 1971. Contbr. stories, articles to mags.; also author of screen plays. Home: 2600 Queen St Missoula MT 59801

GUTHRIE, ARLO, folk singer, composer; b. 1947; s. Woody and Marjorie Guthrie. Performed at Newport Festival, 1967. Composer; Alice's Restaurant; Chilling of the Evening; Ring-around the-Rosy Rag; Now and Then; I'm Going Home; The Motorcycle Song; Highway in the Wind, others; record albums include Alice's Restaurant, Arlo. Address: Reprise Records 4000 Warner Blvd Burbank CA 91503

GUTHRIE, DWIGHT RAYMOND, educator; b. Apollo, Pa., Sept. 6, 1902; s. Alexander S. and Sarah (McCullough) G.; A.B., Grove City (Pa.) Coll., 1925; S.T.B. (fellow 1929), Western Theol. Sem., 1929; S.T.M., Hamma Div. Sch., 1935; D.D. (hon.). Cedarville (O.) Coll., 1938; Ph.D., U. Pitts., 1949; student U. Edinburgh (Scotland), 1930-32; m. Julia I. Clevenger, July 15, 1931. Tchr., Apollo (Pa.) High Sch., 1925-26; ordained to ministry Presbyn. Ch., 1929; pastor, Indpls., 1929-30, Cedarville, O., 1932-37, Springfield, O., 1937-42, Oil City, Pa., 1942-46, Johnstown, Pa., 1946-50; prof. religion and philosophy Grove City (Pa.) Coll., 1950—. Moderator Dayton (O.) Presbytery, 1937; archon Pitts. Cleric Club, 1969. Republican. Mason, Kiwanian (pres. Grove City 1967). Author: John McMillan, The Apostle of Presbyterianism in the West, 1952; co-author: The Presbyterian Valley, 1958; The Imcomparable Snowden, 1961. Contbr. articles jours. Home: 440 E Washington Blvd Grove City, PA 16127.

GUTHRIE, EUGENE HARDING, physician; b. Washington, Apr. 9, 1924; s. Marshall Crapon and Harriet Ellen (Harding) G.; student Haverford Coll., 1942, Duke, 1943, U. N.C., 1945-47; M.D., George Washington U., 1951; M.P.H., U. Mich., 1955; m. Elizabeth Schultz, June 5, 1948; childrenStephen Harding, Linda Elizabeth, Michael Dustin, Matthew Chapin and Leslie Ann (twins), Melissa Ellen. Intern USPHS Hosp., Balt., 1951-52, house officer, 1952- 53; commd. USPHS, 1951, med. dir., 1959; assigned Cal., 1955-56; chief sch. health and rural health activities, then chief program officer Bur. State Services, USPHS, 1959-62; chief neurol. and sensory disease service br., div. chronic diseases USPHS, 1962, chief div., 1962-65; asst. surgeon gen. for operations USPHS, 1966, asso. surgeon gen. USPHS, 1966-68; exec. dir. Md. Comprehensive Health Planning Agy., 1968- ; clin. asso. prof. community medicine and internat. health Georgetown U. Sch. Medicine, 1968—; asso. in pub. health adminstrn. Johns Hopkins U. Sch. Hygiene, 1970—; chmn. bd. dirs. Am. Acad. Comprehensive Health Planning, 1969—; staff dir. surgeon gen's adv. com. smoking and health, 1963. Mem. interdeptl. com. health sch. aged child Dept. Health, Edn. and Welfare, 1957-59, com. agrl. migrants, 1957- 59; alt. mem. interagy. adv. group Pres.' Council Youth Fitness, 1957-59; mem. working group Pres.' Com. Migratory Labor, 1957-59; cons. health and fitness Boy Scouts Am., 1958-59; mem. commd. officers awards bd. USPHS, 1963-64; mem. med. com. Pres.' Commn. Employment Handicapped, 1963-68; sec. Nat. Interagy. Council on Smoking and Health, 1964-66. Mem. exec. bd. Chevy Chase Recreation Assn., 1963- 69. Served with M.C., USCGR, 1942-45. Recipient Meritorious Service medal USPHS, 1964; named Asso. Press Man of Year in Science, 1964. Mem. A.M.A., Am. Pub. Health Assn., USPHS Commd. Officers Assn. (exec. com.), U.S.-Mexico Border Pub. Health Assn., Am. Sch. Health Assn., Smith-Reed- Russel Med. Soc., Armed Forces Relief and Benefit Assn. (dir. 1966-68), Assn. Mil. Surgeons, Am. Hosp. Assn. (mem. council on planning 1971—), Delta Omega, Phi Delta Theta, Nu Sigma Nu. Asso. editor Jour. Sch. Health, 1960-63. Home: 3908 Aspen St Chevy Chase MD 20015 Office: Medical Arts Bldg 101 W Read St Baltimore MD 21201

GUTHRIE, GEORGE RALPH, Jr., real estate devel. corp. exec.; b. Phila., Mar. 12, 1928; s. George Ralph and Myrtle (Robertson) G.; B.S. in Econs., U. Pa., 1948; m. Roberta Elizabeth Stanton, Jan. 30, 1958; children—Mary Elizabeth, Brenda Ann. With I-T-E Imperial Corp., Phila., 1948-70, controller, financial planner, 1960-68, treas., 1968-69, v.p. finance, 1969-70; v.p. finance N. U. Winston Corp., N.Y.C., 1970—; dir. Oxford First Corp. Lectr. budgetary control Grad. Coll. Bus. Adminstrn., Drexel Inst. Tech., Phila., 1957-63. Active United Fund Phila. Area, 1959-70; vice chmn. services div. com. Health and Welfare Council Phila., 1965-67, chmn. 1967-68, also bd. dirs., v.p., mem. exec. com.; mem. young married com. Phila. Charity Ball, 1958—; adviser Delaware Valley (Pa.) Jr. Achievement, 1959-60. Bd. dirs. Family Service Phila.; bd. dirs., treas., mem. exec. com. Nationalities Service Center Phila., 1963-70, 1st v.p., 1966-69, pres., 1969-70. Mem. Internat. Council Shopping Centers, Phila. Jr. C. of C. (dir. 1958-59; named Outstanding Freshman 1956). Club: Cricket (Phila.). Home: 295 Claremont Av Montclair NJ 07042 Office: 711 Fifth Av New York City NY 10022

GUTHRIE, SIR GILES CONNOP MCEACHARN, bus. exec.; b. 1916; ed. Eton and Magdalene Coll., Cambridge U. m. Rhona Stileman, 1939; 3 children (1 dec.). Former mng. dir. Brown Shipley & Co., Ltd.; former dep. chmn. N. Central Finance, Ltd., past dir. Prudential Assurance Co., Ltd., Radio Rentals, Ltd., others; chmn., chief exec. British Overseas Airways Corp., 1964-68; mem. bd. Brit. European Airways, 1959-68; now chmn. Air Transport Ins. S.A., Lausanne, Switzerland; mcht. banker. Served with Fleet Air Arm, World War II. Baronet, 1945; decorated Order Brit. Empire, D.S.C.; recipient (with C.W.A. Scott). Portsmouth-Joannesburg Air Race prize, 1936. Home: Rozel Jersey C 1 England

GUTHRIE, HARVEY HENRY, Jr., educator; b. Santa Paula, Cal., Oct. 31, 1924; s. Harvey Henry and Emma (Aubrey) G.; B.A., Mo. Valley Coll., 1944; student Union Theol. Sem., N.Y.C., 1944-45; S.T.B., Gen. Theol. Sem., N.Y.C., 1948, S.T.M., 1953, Th.D., 1958; m. Doris Mignonette Peyton, Dec. 29, 1945; childrenLawrence Harvey, Lynn Frances, Stephen Temple, Andrew Simpson. Ordained to ministry Episcopal Ch., 1947; vicar St. Martha's Ch., White Plains, N.Y., 1947-50; fellow, instr. Gen. Theol. Sem., N.Y.C., 1950-58; mem. faculty Episcopal Theol. Sch., Cambridge, Mass., 1958-, prof. O.T., 1964-, asso. dean, 1967-69, dean, 1969—, Vis. lectr. Columbia University, 1955-56; vis. prof. Andover Newton Theol. Sch., 1966-67. Democrat. Author: God and History in the Old Testament, 1960; Israel's Sacred Songs, 1966. Home: 4 Berkeley St Cambridge, MA 02138.

GUTHRIE, HENRY BLANDY, lawyer; b. N.Y.C., June 6, 1902; s. Henry Blandy and Ada (McMahan) G.; grad. Hill Sch., 1920; A.B., Princeton, 1924; J.D., Harvard, 1927; m. Elizabeth A. Guthrie, June 22, 1932. Admitted to N.Y. bar, 1928; asso. Shearman & Sterling, N.Y.C., 1927-41, mem. firm, 1941—; v.p., dir. Goelet Estate Co., 1950—, Rhode Island Corp., 1950—; dir. Doubleday & Co. Chmn. bd. trustees Big Bros., 1948-55, sponsor, 1955—, v.p. Big Bros. Am., 1951-55; trustee St. Luke's Hosp. Center, 1952-, v.p., 1959-63, chmn. exec. com., 1963-66, pres., 1966-70, co-chmn., 1970—; trustee Mt. Desert Island Hosp., 1962-71; trustee Green-Wood Cemetery, 1962—, v.p., 1963- 65, pres., 1965—; bd. dirs. United Hosp. Fund N.Y. Mem. Am., N.Y. bar assns., Assn. Bar City N.Y., Phi Beta Kappa. Clubs: Racquet and Tennis, Brook, Downtown Association (N.Y.C.); Cap and Gown (Princeton, N.J.). Home: 169 E 70th St New York City NY 10021 Office: 53 Wall St New York City NY 10005

GUTHRIE, HUNTER, educator; b. N.Y.C., Jan. 8, 1901; s. Jacob Francis and Mary (Ross) G.; A.B., Woodstock (Md.) Coll., 1923, A.M., 1924; S.T.D., Gregorian U., Rome, Italy, 1931; student Tronchiennes, Belgium, 1931-32, univs., Berlin, Munich, Freiburg, 1932-37; Dr. de. l'U., Univ. Paris, 1937. Entered Soc. of Jesus, 1917; ordained priest Roman Cath. Ch., 1930; last vows, Paris, 1934; instr. rhetoric English, Latin, Virgan Sem., P.I., 1924-25, English, Latin, econ., Ateneo de Manila, P.I., 1925-27; prof. history philosophy Woodstock (Md.) Coll., 1937-40 prof., head grad. philosophy Fordham, 1940-43; dean grad. sch. Georgetown U., 1943-49, pres., rector, 1949-52; prof., head dept. philosophy St. Joseph's Coll., Phila., 1952—. Latin American specialist Dept. State, 1954, 58. Decorated Grand Cross of Alfonso X el Sabio (Spain); officer Legion Honor and Merit (Haiti); recipient Freedom award Valley Forge, 1950; Air U. award, 1958. Mem. Internat. Mark Twain Soc., Cath. Commn. for Intellectual and Cultural Affairs (co-founder), Am. Cath. Philos. Assn., Am. Acad. Polit. and Social Sci., Nat. Cath. Edn. Assn., U.S. Commn. on Reconstrn. Edn., Inst. of Religious Studies (mem. com., guest prof.), Assn. Am. Colls. (vis. prof.), Medieval Acad. Am., Am. Philos. Assn., Nat. Fund Med. Edn. Author: Modern Trends in Am. Culture, 1923; Introduction au probleme de l'histoire de la Philosophie, 1937; Symposium on American Catholic Education, 1941; History of Theology, 1968. Asst. editor Dictionary of Philosophy. Home: St Joseph's Coll Philadelphia PA 19131

GUTHRIE, JOHN ALEXANDER, educator; b. Fraserburgh, Scotland, July 20, 1907; s. John P. and Margaret (Rutherford) G.; A.B., U. Man. (Can.), 1929; A.M., U. Wis., 1932; Ph.D., Harvard, 1939; m. Ida Waldon, Sept. 13, 1938; childrenFrances, Gordon. Came to U.S., 1931, naturalized, 1943. Instr., Harvard, 1938-40; asst. prof. econ. Wash. State U., Pullman, 1940-43, asso. prof., 1943-47, prof. econ., dir. bur. econ. and bus. research, 1947—. Mem. Am., Western (pres., 1950) econ. assns. Author: The Newsprint Paper Industry: An Economic Analysis, 1941; The Economics of Pulp and Paper, 1950; Economics, 1957, rev. 1969; Western Forest Industry; The Economic Outlook, 1961. Home: 1403 Upper Dr Pullman WA 99163

GUTHRIE, JOHN CONAUGHTY, fgn. service officer; b. N.Y.C., Mar. 21, 1916; B.A., Williams Coll., 1937; M.A., Columbia, 1939; postgrad. George Washington U., 1947; m. Audrea L. Barthol, Dec. 19, 1945; 1 son, William John. Instr. langs. Lingnan U. (China),

1939-45; research analyst Dept. State, Washington, 1946-49, intelligence research specialist, 1950-52, chief polit. br., div. research for USSR and Eastern Europe, 1952, chief Soviet fgn. br., 1952-54, dep. dir. Office Soviet Union Affairs, 1960-61, dir., 1961-64; assigned Am. embassy, Moscow, 1949-50, 1st sec., consul, 1955-57, minister-counselor, 1965-67; selection bd. 1967; bd. examiners for fgn. service, 1968, acting exec. dir., 1969; council polit. affairs, Bangkok, 1957-60; diplomat-in-residence Grinnell Coll., 1969-70; counselor Am. embassy, Stockholm, Sweden, 1970—. Home: 4109 Mason Ridge Dr Annandale VA 22003 also Strandvägen 63 Stockholm Sweden

GUTHRIE, JOHN HIRAM, cattle rancher; b. Porterville, Cal., Nov. 27, 1913; s. Charles Lester and Florence (Manter) G.; student pub. sch.; m. Marian Elizabeth Kleinhans, Dec. 26, 1935; childrenJohn Lester, Lou Ann. Rancher, Porterville, Cal., 1932—. Mem. Bd. Edn., Tulare County, 1956-57; mem. Cal. Livestock San. Com., 1948-60; adv. com. to regional forester U.S. Forest Service, 1950-61; mem. Cal. bd. dirs. Nat. Cowboy Hall of Fame, 1957-59. Named Cal. Livestock Man of Year, San Francisco C. of C., 1956. Mem. Visalia Prodn. Credit Assn. (past dir.), Am. Nat. Cattlemen's Assn. (pres. 1966-67), Cal. Cattle Feeders Assn. (past pres., dir.), Cal. Farm Bur. Marketing Assn., Terra Bella Meml. Dist. (past dir.), Cal. (past pres.), Tulare County (past pres.) cattlemens assns. Mason; mem. Order Eastern Star. Address: 237 N Sierra Vista Porterville, CA 93257.

GUTHRIE, JOHN REILEY, army officer; b. Phillipsburg, N.J., Dec. 20, 1921; s. John Milton, Jr., and Claire (Reiley) G.; grad. Blair Acad., 1938; A.B. with honors, Princeton, 1942; grad. Command and Gen. Staff Coll., 1944, Nat. War Coll., 1961; m. Rebecca Jane Jeffers, June 18, 1947; children—Rebecca Claire, Michael Reiley, John Jeffers, Peter Blair, Margaret, Kevin McCammon. Commd. 2d lt. U.S. Army, 1942, advanced through grades to maj. gen., 1969; served in Hawaii and Japan, World War II; asst. to mil. attache, London, Eng., 1946-49; with 39th Field Arty. Bn. and 3d Inf. Div. Arty., U.S., Japan and Korea, 1949-51; comdr. 602d F.A. Bdn., 1952-53; mem. staff and faculty F.A. Sch., 1953-56; mil. asst. exec. officer to Sec. of Army, 1958-60; staff CINCPAC, 1961-64; comdr. 25th Inf. Div. Arty., chief of staff 25th Inf. Div., 1964-65; mem. Orgn. Joint Chiefs of Staff, 1965-66; dir. developments Dept. of Army, 1966-67; asst. div. comdr. 2d Inf. Div., 1967-68; dir. research, devel. and engring. U.S. Army Materiel Command, Washington, 1969—. Decorated Legion of Merit with 2 oak leaf clusters, B.S.M. with 2 oak leaf clusters, Joint Service Commendation Medal, Army Commendation Medal. Mem. Assn. U.S. Army. Republican. Presbyn. Clubs: Princeton (Washington); Nassau (Princeton). Army staff action officer for devel. and launching of 1st U.S. artificial earth satellite, Explorer I (Jupiter C29), 1958. Home: 7420 Walton Lane Annandale VA 22003 Office: Hdqrs US Army Materiel Command Washington DC 20315

GUTHRIE, LOUIS CHARLES, banker; b. Gilchrist, Ill., Oct. 25, 1918; s. Leroy and Ruby (Gasaway) G.; B.S., Stonier Grad. Sch. Banking Rutgers U., 1962; m. Juanita J. Hilton, Oct. 20, 1941; children—Sheila (Mrs. Joseph France), Terry W. With Gary Nat. Bank, Gary, Ind., 1936—, sr. vice-pres., 1967—. Served to capt. AUS, 1941-46. Decorated Bronze Star. Mem. Gary C. of C., Am. Legion. Mem. Christian Ch. Office: 504 Broadway Gary IN 46402

GUTHRIE, MEARL RAYMOND, Jr., educator; b. Eldorado, Kan., Oct. 4, 1922; s. Mearl Raymond and Pauline Marie (Benz) G.; student U. Tulsa, 1941-43; B.S., Ball State U., 1948, M.A., 1949; Ph.D., U. Minn., 1953; m. Lolita Ann Thayer, July 21, 1946; childrenScott Raymond, Carla Ann. Property accountant for constrn. firm, customer service rep. Pub. Service Co. of Okla., 1940-43; grad. asst. Ball State U., 1948-49; teaching asst. U. Minn., 1949-50; mem. faculty U. Cin., 1950-54; mem. faculty Bowling Green State U., 1954-, chmn. dept. bus. edn., 1957-; chmn. div. bus. adminstrn. Coll. of V.I., 1965-66. Prod. film strips on gen. and bus. math. Ednl. Devel. Labs., 1961. Chmn. fund drive Boy Scouts, Bowling Green. Served with AUS, 1943-46. Mem. Ohio Archaeol. Soc., Black Swamp Archaeol. Assn. (pres.), Nat. Assn. for Bus. Tchr. Edn. (mem. exec. bd.), Nat. Bus. Edn. Assn. (treas., nat. council, state membership chmn., dir. nat. student membership), Ohio Bus. Tchrs. Assn. (pres.), Delta Pi Epsilon (chpt. pres.), Pi Omega Pi (nat. organizer, nat. v.p., nat. pres.), Beta Gamma Sigma, Sigma Zeta, Kappa Delta Pi. Presbyn. (elder; chmn. Christian edn. com.). Author: Workbook for Briefhand, 1958; Alphabetical Indexing, 1965. Co-author: Today's Business Mathematics, 1967. Contbr. profl. articles ednl. periodicals. Home: 128 N Grove St Bowling Green OH 43402

GUTHRIE, PAUL NEWMAN, economist, labor historian, arbitrator; b. Greene County, Tenn., Dec. 3, 1903; s. William Lawson and Sally L. (Berry) G.; A.B., U. of Tenn., 1926; B.D., Union Theol. Sem., N.Y.C. 1932; M.A., Columbia, 1932, Ph.D., 1946; m. N. Mary Sheaffer, Aug. 27, 1932; children—Paul Newman, Jr., Robert Sheaffer. Asso prof. econs. and sociology Randolph-Macon Woman's Coll., Lynchburg, Va., 1935-40, prof., 1940-42; dir. Disputes Div., Region IV, Nat. War Labor Bd., 1943-44, vice chmn. and pub. mem., 1944-46; chmn. So. Textile Commn., 1945; dir. Wage Stabilization Div., Nat. Wage Stabilization Bd., 1946; prof. econs. U. of N.C., 1946—; arbitrator labor disputes, 1946—; pub. mem. W.S.B., Region IV, 1951-52, Washington, 1952. Referee for the Nat. R. R. Adjustment Bd.; mem. numerous presdl. emergency bds. in r.r. and air line labor disputes. Mem. Am., Southern econ. assns., Nat. Acad. of Arbitrators (pres. 1957), Phi Beta Kappa, Democrat. Author: (with others), The Path I Trod, 1940. Home: Chapel Hill NC 27514

GUTHRIE, RAMON, poet; b. N.Y.C., Jan. 14, 1896; s. Harry and May (Hollister) G.; doctorat en droit, U. Toulouse (France), 1922; Litt.D. (hon.), Dartmouth, 1971; m. Marguerite Maurey, Apr. 8, 1922. Asst. prof. U. Ariz., Tucson, 1924-27; prof. Romance langs. Dartmouth, 1930-63. Served with U.S. Army, 1916-19, OSS, 1943-45. Decorated Silver Star. Author: Trobar Clus, 1923, A World Too Old, 1927, Graffiti, 1959, Asbestos Phoenix, 1968, Maximum Security Ward, 1970. Address: Norwich VT 05055

GUTHRIE, RANDOLPH HOBSON, lawyer; b. Richmond, Va., Nov. 5, 1905; s. Joseph Hobson and Thomasia Harris (Parkinson) G.; B.S., The Citadel, 1925; LL.B. magna cum laude, Harvard, 1931; m. Mabel Edith Welton, Mar. 24, 1934; children—Randolph Hobson, Jo Carol, George Gordon. Admitted to N.Y. bar, 1932, since practiced in N.Y.C.; sr. partner Mudge, Rose, Guthrie & Alexander; chmn. bd. Studebaker Corp., Studebaker-Worthington, Inc., 1963-71, chmn. exec. com., 1971—; chmn. bd. UMC Industries, Inc., 1969—. Bd. dirs. Boys Clubs Am. Mem. Am., N.Y. bar assns., N.Y. County Lawyers Assn., Assn. Bar City N.Y., Kappa Alpha. Clubs: Down Town Assn., Harvard (N.Y.C.); Baltusrol Golf (Springfield, N.J.). Episcopalian. Home: 157 Lake Dr Mountain Lakes NJ 07046 Office: 20 Broad St New York City NY 10005

GUTHRIE, ROBERT LEE, lawyer; b. Salado, Tex., Feb. 13, 1900; s. Dr. James Edwin and Eugenia (Shofner) G.; B.A., Baylor U., 1921; M.A., Brown Univ., 1922; student Princeton, 1923-24; B.A. (Rhodes scholar), Oxford U., 1926, B.C.L., 1927; m. Martha Dee Schwartz, June 4, 1954. Admitted to Tex. bar, 1927, U.S. Supreme Ct., 1954; practice of law, Dallas, 1927-42, 53- -; partner Johnson, Guthrie, Woodburn & Hunter. Mem. Dallas Civil Service Bd., 1935-41. Served from capt. to lt. col., USAAF, 1942-46; U.S. judge Allied High Commn. for Germany, 1946-53. Decorated Bronze Star. Mem. Tex. Bar Assn., Oxford Union, Oxford Soc., Phi Delta Theta. Club: Dallas Athletic. Home: 6623 Park Lane Dallas TX 75225 Office: Republic Bank Bldg Dallas TX 75201

GUTHRIE, WILLIAM STONE, savs. and loan assn. exec.; b. Columbus, O., Apr. 4, 1912; s. Curtis C. and Florence (Stone) G.; A.B., Ohio State U., 1932, A.M., 1939; postgrad. Columbia, 1940-41; m. Mary G. Titus, May 22, 1936; children—David W., Stephen T., Philip C., Susan J. Dir. student aid programs N.Y.A. in Ohio, 1934-36; dir. student employment, asst. dean of men Ohio State U., Columbus, 1936-42, acting jr. dean, coll. arts and scis., 1943-46, jr. dean, dir. univ. orientation programs, 1947-55, asso. dean coll. arts and scis., 1956, exec. dean student relations, 1957-61; pres. Buckeye Fed. Savs. and Loan Assn., Columbus 1961-70, chmn. bd., 1967—; trustee Galbreath First Mortgage Investments. Chmn. Devel. Com. Greater Columbus; Former chmn. bd. Blue Cross, Columbus Symphony Orch., United Community Council; chmn. Ohio State U. Devel. Fund. Mem. Columbus Area C. of C. (past chmn. bd.), Kappa Sigma. Clubs: Rotary, Faculty. Author: Annual Studies of Applications to the Professional Schools and Colleges in U.S., 1948-52. Home: 2214 Johnston Rd Columbus OH 43220 Office: 36 E Gay St Columbus OH 43215

GUTIERREZ, JULIO CESAR, Paraguay diplomat; b. Bogado, Paraguay, Feb. 11, 1920; s. Emilio and Amalia (Arrechea) G.; degree pub. accountant, Nat. Comml. Sch., 1943; D. in Econ. Scis., U. Asuncion, 1953; postgrad Inst. Latin Am. Monetary Studies, Mexico, 1954; m. Beatriz Ferrari, Aug. 26, 1963; children—Leticia, Norah Lia, Hugo Cesar, Rodrigo. Comptroller banks in Paraguay, 1949-56; adviser to Minister Finance, 1956-58; financial controller Paraguay, 1958-62; econ. counselor, Washington, 1962—; exec. dir. Inter-Am. Devel. Bank, Washington, 1962-71; prof. Sch. Economy, U. Asuncion, Paraguay, 1959-62; mem. faculty Economy Coll. Paraguay, 1955—. Mem. Inter-Am. Soc. Econ. Devel. Home: 5504 Surrey St Chevy Chase MD 20015 Office: 808 17th St NW Washington DC 20577

GUTIERREZ-CANO, JOAQUIN, Spanish business exec.; b. Madrid, Spain, Nov. 29, 1920; s. Jose F. Gutierrez- Segura and Pilar Cano de Benito; law degree, Central U., Madrid, 1943; m. Maria Isabel Vallejo Zaldo, June 1, 1950; children—Maria del Pilar, Maria Isabel, Maria Patricia, Maria Lourdes. Joined Spanish diplomatic service, 1946; consul in Hamburg, Germany, 1948; econ. counselor, Bonn, Germany, 1951-58; chmn. Nat. Fruit Growers and Exporters Assn., also mem. Spanish Parliament of Cortes, 1958-61; vice sec. nat. for econs., mem. Parliament (Cortes), permanent mem. Nat. Econ. Council Spain, exec. dir. Bank of Spain, exec. dir. Indsl. Devel. Bank, 1961-63; exec. dir. Internat. Bank Reconstrn. and Devel., Internat. Devel. Assn., also Internat. Finance Corp., representing Spain, Italy, Greece and Portugal, 1963-68; exec. dir. Empresa Nacional Calvo Sotelo of Spain, 1961—, Banco de Valladolid, Banco Espanol in Germany; chmn. Asso. Engring. Companies Spain, Montoro Petrochem. Co. Decorated grand cross Civil Merit, grand cross Cisneros, grand officer Merit in Agr., Mil. Merit cross, War medal, 1936-39 (Spain); grand officer Ordine del Merito alla Republica Italiana; comdr. Bunderverdienstkreuz (Germany); grand officer Order Don Henrique (Portugal). Roman Catholic. Clubs: Country, Club XXI (Madrid); Lasarte (Fuenterrabia, Spain). Home: Felipe IV No 5 Madrid Spain Office: Velasqula 74 Madrid Spain

GUTKIN, SYDNEY A., lawyer; b. N.Y. City, May 7, 1907; s. Charles and Rose (Shapiro) G.; student Townsend Harris Hall Prep. Sch., 1923; B.S., Coll. City of N.Y., 1927; LL.B., Columbia, 1929; m. Beatrice Marx, Apr. 9, 1931; children—Martin John, Linda Carol. Admitted to N.Y. bar, 1929, N.J. bar, 1931, D.C. bar, 1937; practice of law, Trenton, N.J., 1932-36, Newark, since 1939 specializing in federal taxation and tax practice; now mem. firm of Gutkin and Miller; revisor N.J. Law Revision Commn., 1929-32; asso. Office Chief Counsel, U.S. Bur. Internal Revenue, 1936-38; asso. prof. law Rutgers U., 1951—; lectr. on taxation Tax Inst. of N.Y.U., U. W.Va., Pa. State Coll., U. Miami, U. Pitts., R.I. State Coll., Marquette U., N.J. and N.U. insts. for Practicing Lawyers. Mem. planning com. N.Y.U. Tax Inst.; chmn. Rutgers U. Fed. Tax Inst.; mem. bd. trustees Newark Beth Israel Hosp. Trustee Kessler Inst. Mem. Am., N.J. State and Essex County bar assns. Jewish religion. Mason. Clubs: Down Town (Newark, N.J.); Old Red Bank Yacht; Mountain Ridge Country (West Caldwell, N.J.). Author Security Transactions, Co-author: Estate Tax Handbook; Handbook of Tax Techniques: Tax Avoidance vs. Tax Evasion, 1958. Contbr. articles to law and tax jours. Home: 377 S Harrison St East Orange NJ 07018 Office: 744 Broad St Newark NJ 07102

GUTKNECHT, JOHN WILLIAM, lawyer, banker; b. Toledo, June 17, 1909; s. Otto William and Ida C. (Gohlke) G.; J.D., Ohio No. U., 1932; m. Mary Oletha Buck, July 12, 1934; 1 dau., Kristine A. (Mrs. Jerry Courtney). Admitted to Ohio bar, 1932, since practiced in Fostoria; city solicitor, Fostoria, 1935-40; judge Fostoria Municipal Ct., 1945-48; pvt. practice, 1948—; pres., dir. Comml. Bank & Savs. Co., 1952—; dir. John B. Rogers Producing Co., Seneca Lumber & Millwork, Inc., Ohm, Inc. Gen. chmn. Fostoria chpt. A.R.C., 1946; pres. Fostoria Hosp. Assn., 1960-67. Served to maj., C.E., AUS, 1942-45; PTO. Decorated Bronze Star medal with oak leaf cluster. Mem. Ohio Bar Assn., Sigma Phi Epsilon. Republican. Mason (Shriner). Home: 901 Van Buren St Fostoria OH 44830 Office: 118 W Tiffin St Fostoria OH 44830

GUTMAN, JONATHON AUSTIN lawyer, corp. exec.; b. Kent, O., 1922; B.A., Yale, 1943, LL.B., 1944; m. Mae Reed, May 2, 1949; 1 son. Admitted to Massachusetts bar, 1944; practiced in Boston, 1947--; gen. counsel Acme Mfg. Co., Boston, 1966--; dir. 1st Nat. Bank. Home: 23 Beacon St Boston MA 02107

GUTMAN, MONROE C., banker; b. N.Y.C. Oct. 15, 1885; s. Sanders and Pauline (Bernstein) G.; A.B. magna cum laude, Harvard, 1905, M.A., 1906; m. Pauline Ehrich, Oct. 8, 1917 (div.); m. 2d, Edna Cullman, Nov. 24, 1932 (dec.). Began in brokerage bus., 1905; with firm Bernhard, Scholle & Co., 1910; joined Lehman Bros., N.Y.C., 1922, partner 1927—; dir., mem. exec. com. Lehman Corp. Trade distbr. U.S. War Trade Bd., World War I. Hon. chmn. bd. trustees Montefiore Hosp. and Med. Center. Jewish religion. Clubs: Harvard, Harmonie (N.Y.C.). Home: 480 Park Av New York City NY 10022 Office: 1 William St New York City NY 10004

GUTMAN, ROBERT, educator; b. N.Y.C., Aug. 3, 1926; s. Bert and Beatrice (Thailhein) G.; A.B., Columbia, 1946, Ph.D. (social psychiatry fellow, also Social Sci. Research Council fellow), 1955; postgrad. Princeton, 1952, London (England) Sch. Economics, 1952-53; m. Sonya Rudikoff, Sept. 17, 1950; children—John A.D., Elizabeth C.R. Instr., then asst. prof. sociology Dartmouth, 1949-57; mem. faculty Rutgers U., 1957—, dir. grad. studies sociology, 1966-68; vis. prof. Stanford, 1964, Bartlett Sch. Architecture, London U., 1966, Sch. Architecture and Urban Planning, Princeton, 1969-71; vis. fellow Inst. Architecture and Urban Studies, N.Y.C., 1967-68, Graham Found. fellow, 1968-69; Class of 1913 lectr. in architecture Princeton, 1971-72. Fellow social psychiatry Columbia, 1948-49; fellow Social Sci. Research Council, 1952-53; Research fellow Population Council, 1952-53; Faculty Research fellow Rutgers U., 1965-66, 70-71. Mem. Population Assn. Am. (bd. dirs. 1963-66), Am. Sociol. Assn. (liaison rep. interprofl. com. on environmental design), Am. Statis. Assn. Author: (with others) The Mark of Oppression, 1951; The Accuracy of Vital Statistics in Massachusetts, 1842-1901, 1956; Birth and Death Registration in Massachusetts, 1960; Site Planning and Social Organization, 1964; (with others) Neighborhood, City and Metropolis, 1970; also articles, revs. Asso. editor Am. Sociol. Rev., 1961-63; adv. editor Am. Jour. Sociology, 1962-65. Home: 200 Hun Rd Princeton NJ 08540 Office: Rutgers Univ New Brunswick NJ 08903 also Princeton Univ Princeton NJ 08540

GUTMAN, ROBERT WILLIAM, educator, author; b. N.Y.C, Sept. 11, 1925; s. Theodore and Elsie Gutman; B.A., N.Y.U., 1945, M.A., 1948. Mem. faculty New Sch. Social Research, N.Y.C. 1956- 57, Coll. City N.Y., 1955-57, U. State N.Y. Fashion Inst. Tech., 1957—, Bayreuth (Germany) Festival Master Classes (a founder), 1959-61. Author: Volsunda Saga, 1962; Richard Wagner: The Man, His Mind and His Music, 1968. Address: 370 Riverside Dr New York City NY 10025

GUTMANN, JAMES, educator; b. N.Y.C., Apr. 11, 1897; s. Carl nd Lilly (Liebmann) G.; A.B., Columbia, 1918, A.M., 1919, Ph.D., 1936; m. Jeanette Mack, Feb. 3, 1920; children—Barbara Rosenkrantz, Carl Mack, Alice Brandfonbrener. Tchr. ethics Ethical Culture Sch., N.Y.C., 1918-28; asso. leader Soc. Ethical Culture, 1927-30; with Columbia U., 1920—, successively lectr. philosophy, instr., asst. prof., asso. prof., 1923-48, prof. philosophy, 1948-62, prof. emeritus, 1962—, chmn. dept., 1952-61, dir. univ. seminars, 1970—. Mem. exec. com. Com. To Abolish Capital Punishment; mem. East- West Philosophers Conf., U. Hawaii, 1969. Bd. dirs. Encampment for Citizenship, Riverside Health Com., N.Y.C. Mem. Am. Assn. U. Profs., Am. Philos. Assn., Phi Beta Kappa. Club: Columbia Faculty. Author: Schelling: Of Human Freedom, 1936; Personal Integrity, 1961. Co-author: Naturalism and Historical Understanding, 1967; Horizons of a Philosopher, 1963; Ethics and Social Justice, 1970. Editor: Marcus Aurelius' Meditations, 1963; Spinoza's Ethics, 1968. Editorial bd. Studies in Romanticism (Boston U.). Home: 39 Claremont Av New York City NY 10027

GUTMANN, MAX, retail stores co. exec.; b. Germany, 1922; married. With Bee-Gee Shoe Corp., 1953-61, co. acquired by Elder-Beerman Stores Corp., Dayton, O., 1961; exec. v.p. Elder-Beerman Stores Corp., 1961-70, pres., chief operating officer, dir., 1970—; v.p., dir. Elbee Charge It Corp., McCook Wholesale. Home: 3100 Marlay Rd Dayton OH 45406 Office: 153 E Helena St Dayton OH 45405*

GUTOWSKY, HERBERT SANDER, educator; b. Bridgman, Mich., Nov. 8, 1919; s. Otto and Hattie (Meyers) G.; A.B., Ind. U., 1940; M.S., U. Cal. at Berkeley, 1946; Ph.D., Harvard, 1949; m. Barbara Stuart, June 22, 1949; childrenDaniel Kurt, Robb Edward, Christopher Carl. Faculty U. Ill. at Urbana, 1948—. prof. chemistry, 1956—, head div. phys. chemistry, 1956-63, head dept. chemistry and chem. engring., 1967-70, dir. Sch. Chem. Scis., head dept. chemistry, 1970—. Mem. adv. bd. Petroleum Research Fund, 1959-61; mem. selection and scheduling com. Gordon Research Conf., 1959-64, 68—, trustee, 1969—; mem. chemistry panel NSF, 1963-66. Served to capt., chem. warfare service, AUS, 1941-45. Recipient 1966 $5000 Irving Langmuir award Gen. Electric Found. Guggenheim fellow, 1954-55. Fellow Am. Phys. Soc., A.A.A.S., Am. Acad. Arts and Scis.; mem. Nat. Acad. Scis., Am. Chem. Soc. (chmn. div. phys. chemistry 1966-67), Faraday Soc., Am. Assn. U. Prof., Phi Beta Kappa, Sigma Xi. Home: 508 S Ridgeway St Champaign IL 61820 Office: Noyes Lab Urban IL 61801

GUTSCHE, CARL DAVID, educator; b. LaGrange, Ill., Mar. 21, 1921; s. Frank Carl and Vera (Mutchler) G.; B.A., Oberlin Coll., 1943; Ph.D., U. Wis., 1947; m. Alice Eugenia Carr, June 4, 1944; children—Clara Jean, Betha Lynn, Christopher Glenn. With U.S. Dept. Agr. Office Sci. Devel., 1943-44; instr. chemistry Washington U., St. Louis, 1947-48, asst. prof., 1948-51, asso. prof., 1951-59, prof., 1959—, chmn. dept., 1970—; cons. to industry. Mem. Am. Chem. Soc. (chmn. St. Louis sect. 1959, dir.), Chem. Soc. (London), Am. Assn. U. Profs., Phi Beta Kappa, Sigma Xi. Author: The Chemistry of Carbonyl Compounds, 1967; Carbocyclic Ring Expansion Reactions, 1968. Contbr. articles profl. jours. Home: 6933 Kingsbury Blvd University City MO 63130 Office: Washington Univ St Louis MO 63130

GUTSCHICK, RAYMOND CHARLES, educator; b. Chgo., Oct. 3, 1913; s. Anthony William and Bessie (Kostaka) G.; student J. Sterling Morton Jr. Coll., Cicero, Ill., 1932-34; B.S. in Engring. Physics, U. Ill., 1938, M.S. in Geology, 1939, Ph.D., 1942; m. Alice Edna Augusta Lude, July 2, 1939; children—Alice Antoinette, Raal Emily. With Aluminum Ore Co., Rosiclaire, Ill., summer 1942, 46-47; instr. U. Ill., 1942-43; staff Magnolia Petroleum Co. (Socony), Oklahoma City, 1943-45, Gulf Coil Co., Oklahoma City, 1947; asst. to asso. prof. U. Notre Dame (Ind.), 1947-54, prof., 1954—, chmn. dept. geology, 1956-70. Vis. prof. Ind. U., summers 1951-52, 56-62, 69. Fellow Geol. Soc. Am., A.A.A.S.; mem. Am. Assn. Petroleum Geologists, Paleontol. Soc., Internat. Assn. Sedimentologists, Soc. Econ. Paleontology and Mineralogy, Assn. Geol. Tchrs. Research Assn., Am. Inst. Profl. Geol., Sigma Xi. Contbr. articles to profl. jours. Home: 53176 W Oakmont Dr South Bend IN 46637 Office: University of Notre Dame Notre Dame IN 46556

GUTTENBERG, WILLIAM STUART, elec. mfg. co. exec.; b. Paterson, N.J., Oct. 9, 1922; s. Charles and Celia (Goteiner) G.; B.S. in Elec. Engring., Newark Coll. Engring., 1944; M.S., N.Y.U., 1947; m. Adele Rita Basch, Feb. 15, 1948; childrenFrances, Charles. Chief engr. Bogue Electric Mfg. Co., Paterson, 1952-59, v.p., 1959-61, exec. v.p., 1963-64, pres., 1965-, also mem. bd. dirs.; dir. of Thiel, Inc. Served with AUS, 1944- 45, Mem. I.E.E.E., Am. Ordnance Assn., Am. Arbitration Assn., Engine Generator Mfrs. Assn. (dir.), Paterson C. of C. (dir.). Mason. Home: 143 Mackay Dr Tenafly NJ 07670 Office: 100 Pennsylvania Av Paterson NJ 07509

GUTTENPLAN, HAROLD ESAU, food co. exec.; b. Flushing, N.Y., Oct. 12, 1924; s. Adolph and Mollie (Penner) G.; B.A., Queens Coll., 1948; M.B.A., N.Y. U., 1951; m. Jeanette Harris, Apr. 17, 1948; children—Bruce David, Mark Stuart. Statistician printing ink div. Sun Chem. Corp., 1948-49; cost accountant, chief accountant, asst. treas. DCA Food Industries, Inc., N.Y.C., 1949-66, treas., 1966—. Cub Scout leader Nassau County Thunderbird council Boy Scouts Am., 1955-63. Served with USAAF, 1943-45; PTO. Recipient Anti-Defamation League citation award, 1968. Mem. Alpha Phi Omega (pres. 1947-48). Mem. B'nai B'rith (pres. Sagamore lodge 1963-64). Home: 26 Roberta Lane Syosset NY 11791 Office: 919 3d Av New York City NY 10022

GUTTENTAG, JACK MARK, educator, economist; b. Bklyn., Dec. 9, 1923; s. Sidney W. and Fannie (Coon) G.; B.S., Purdue U., 1948; Ph.D., Columbia, 1958; m. Doris Wallach, June 5, 1955; childrenWilliam, Adam. Market analyst FHA, 1952- 54; economist

Fed. Res. Bank N.Y., 1954-62; prof. finance Wharton Sch., U. Pa., 1962-; mem. sr. research staff Nat. Bur. Econ. Research, 1968- ; cons. in field, 1962-. Served with inf., AUS, 1943-46; ETO. Mem. Am. Econ. Assn., Am. Finance Assn. (bd. dirs. 1968-70), Lambda Alpha. Author: Banking Structure and Performance, 1967; also monographs, articles. Home: 300 W Sedgwick St Philadelphia PA 19119

GUTTER, ROBERT HAROLD, orch. conductor; b. N.Y.C., June 16, 1938; s. Jerome Sidney and Mathilda (Bressler) G.; B.Music, Yale, 1959, M.Music, 1960; m. Bernadette Janet Boyle, Sept. 14, 1959; children—Deborah Carole, and Cheryl Lynn. Conductor Des Moines Symphony, 1967-69, Springfield (O.) Symphony, 1969-71, Springfield (Mass.) Symphony, 1970; guest conductor Albuquerque Symphony, 1970, Colorado Springs, Colo., 1970, New Orleans Opera, 1969, Siena, Italy, 1970, Palazzo Pitti, 1970; asst. prof. U. Wis. at Madison, 1964-67; asso. prof. Drake U., also lectr. Wittenberg U., 1969-70. U.S. State Dept. grantee, 1962, as conductor for Nat. Orch. of Uruguay. Mem. Am. Fedn. Musicians, Am. Symphony Orch. League, Am. Assn. U. Profs. Home: 36 Falmouth Rd Longmeadow MA 01106 Office: Springfield Symphony Orch 49 Chestnut St Springfield MA 01103

GUTTING, FERD J., brewery exec.; b. St. Louis, 1910; ed. La Salle Extension U.; married. Sec., treas., dir. Griesedieck Bros. Brewery Co., until 1958; with Falstaff Brewing Corp., St. Louis, 1958—, asst. treas., 1964-67, v.p. planning, 1967-68, v.p., controller, 1968—. Home: 4 Meadow Acres Ladue MO 63124 Office: 5050 Oakland Av St Louis MO 63166*

GUTTMACHER, ALAN FRANK, physician; b. Balt., May 19, 1898; s. Adolf and Laura (Oppenheimer) G.; A.B., Johns Hopkins, 1919, M.D., 1923; D.Sc. (hon.), Brandeis U., Dartmouth Coll., 1970; m. Leonore Gidding, July 22, 1925; children—Ann (Mrs. Robert Loeb), Sally (Mrs. Eric Holtzman), Susan (Mrs. Ben Green). Intern Johns Hopkins Hosp., 1925-26; asst. in anatomy Johns Hopkins, 1923-24, U. Rochester, 1924-25; various positions from resident to asso. prof. obseterics Johns Hopkins. 1926-52; practice medicine, specializing in obstetrics and gynecology, Balt., 1929-52, N.Y.C., 1952—; former chief obstetrics and gynecology Mt. Sinai Hosp.; emeritus prof. obstetrics-gynecology Mt. Sinai Med. Sch.; vis. prof. Einstein Med. Sch. Pres. Planned Parenthood Fedn., 1962; bd. dirs. Margaret Sanger Research Bur. Recipient Lasker award, 1947; Bronfman award, 1970. Diplomate Am. Bd. Obstetrics and Gynecology. Fellow Assn. Obstetrics and Gynecology, N.Y. Acad. Medicine, N.Y. Obstet. Soc. (past pres.). Author: Life in the Making, 1933; Into This Universe, 1937; Pregnancy and Birth, 1957; Babies by Choice or Chance, 1959; (with J. Rovinsky, Williams, Wilkins) Complications of Pregnancy, rev., 1965; Complete Book of Birth Control, 1961; Planning Your Family, 1964; Birth Control and Love, 1969; Understanding Sex, 1970. Home: 1185 Park Av New York City NY 10028 Office: 810 7th Av New York City NY 10019

GUTTMAN, HELENE NATHAN, (Mrs. Newman Guttman), microbiologist, educator; b. N.Y.C., July 21, 1930; d. Arthur and Mollie (Bergovoy) Nathan; B.A., Bklyn. Coll., 1951; A.M. (Andelot fellow), Harvard, 1956; M.A., Columbia, 1958; Ph.D. (Rutgers scholar), Rutgers U., 1960; m. Newman Guttman, Apr. 4, 1962. Research technician Pub. Health Research Inst., N.Y.C., 1951-52; control bacteriologist Burroughs- Wellcome, Inc., Tuckahoe, N.Y., 1952-53; vol. researcher Haskins Labs., N.Y.C., 1952-53, research asst., 1953-56, research asso., 1956-60, staff microbiologist, 1960-64; lectr. dept. biology Queens Coll., N.Y.C., 1956- 57; research collaborator Brookhaven Nat. Labs., Upton, L.I., N.Y., 1958; guest investigator Botanisches Institut der Technisches Hochschule, Darmstadt, Germany, 1960; research asso. dept. biol. scis. Goucher Coll., Towson, Md., 1960-62; vis. asst. research prof. dept. medicine Med. Coll. Va., Richmond, 1960-62; asst. prof., then asso. prof. dept. biology N.Y. U., 1962-67; asso. prof. dept. biol. scis. U. Ill. at Chgo. Circle, 1967-69, prof., 1969—, mem. grad. faculty dept. microbiology Med. Sch., 1969—. Recipient Thomas Jefferson Murray prize Theobald Smith Soc., 1959; spl. award for work in Germany, Deutscher Forschungs Gemeinschaft, 1960. Fellow Dazian Found., 1956. Fellow A.A.A.S., Am. Inst. Chemists; mem. Soc. Am. Bacteriologists (pres.'s fellow 1957), Tissue Culture Soc., Am. Soc. Neurochemistry, Neuroscis. Soc., Am. Soc. Microbiologists, Am. Soc. Cell Biology (past com. chmn.), Am. Soc. Clin. Nutrition, Am. Soc. Plant Physiology, Am. Soc. Tropical Medicine and Hygiene, Soc. Indsl. Microbiologists, Soc. Gen. Microbiologists (Eng.), Soc. Protozoology (mem. exec. com.), Soc. Exptl. Biology and Medicine, Biophysics Soc., N.Y. Acad. Scis., Sigma Xi, Sigma Delta Epsilon. Contbr. articles to profl. jours. Home: 916 60th Pl Downers Grove IL 60515 Office: Dept Biol Scis U Ill at Chgo Circle Box 4348 Chicago IL 60680

GUTTMAN, IRWIN, educator; b. Montreal, Que., Can., Apr. 23, 1930; s. Samuel Saul and Anna (Kahn) G.; B.S., McGill U., Montreal, 1951; M.A., U. Toronto, 1953, Ph.D., 1955. Asst. prof. dept. math. U. Alta. (Can.), 1955-57; research asso. dept. math. Princeton, 1957-59; asso. prof. dept. math. McGill U., Montreal, Que., Can., 1959-62; vis. asso. prof. dept. statistics U. Wis., Madison, 1962-63, prof., 1963- -. Author: (with S.S. Wilks) Introductory Engineering Statistics, 1965, 2d edition (also with J.S. Hunter), 1971; Statistical Tolerance Regions: Classical and Bayesian, 1970. Contbr. articles profl. jours. Home: 139 W Wilson St Madison WI 53703

GUTWIRTH, MARCEL MARC, educator; b. Antwerp, Belgium, Apr. 11, 1923 (parents Am. citizens); s. Jacob Nahum and Frieda (Willner) G.; student N.Y.U., 1941-42; A.B., Columbia, 1947, M.A., 1948, Ph.D., 1950; m. Madelyn Katz, June 20, 1948; children—Eve, Sarah, Nathanael. Mem. faculty Haverford (Pa.) Coll., 1948—, Johns Hopkins, 1967, Queens Coll., 1968, Bryn Mawr Coll., 1969. Bd. dirs. Childbirth Edn. Assn. Greater Phila., 1961-64. Served with AUS, 1943-46; ETO. Fulbright postdoctoral fellow, Paris, France, 1953-54; Am. Council Learned Socs. fellow, 1964-65, Guggenheim fellow, 1971-72. Mem. Am. Civil Liberties Union, Modern Lang. Assn., Am. Assn. Tchrs. French, Am. Assn. U. Profs. Jewish religion. Author: Molière ou l'invention comique, 1966; Jean Racine: un itinéraire poétique, 1970; Stendhal, 1971. Home: 753 College Av Haverford PA 19041

GUTZMAN, WAYNE WALLACE, univ. dean; b. Kensington, Kan., Mar. 22, 1916; s. William Carl and Hulda (Wachs) G.; A.B., Ft. Hays (Kan.) State Coll., 1936; M.S., U. Ia., 1937, Ph.D., 1941; m. 2d, Patricia Jane Doll, Nov. 5, 1964; children by previous marriage—Susan, Kathleen, Howard, Ellengrav, Carl. Instr. math. Hunter Coll., N.Y.C., 1941-42; asst. prof. math. U.S. Naval Postgrad. Sch., 1946- 47; prof. math. U. S. D., Vermillion, 1947-63, dean Grad. Sch., 1963—. Served to capt. USNR, 1942-46, 51-53, 62-63. Mem. Am. Math. Soc., Inst. Math. Statistics, Math. Assn. Am., Sigma Xi. Home: 215 N Pine St Vermillion, SD 57069.

GUVENDIREN, EKREM ESAT, Turkish diplomat; b. Cyprus, Mar. 1, 1931; s. Ahmet Esat and Fatma (Esat) G.; m. Gunes Guvendiren, Jan. 25, 1962; children—Ahmet Esat, Cevdat Esat. Called to English bar, 1953; with Turkish Govt. Ser., 1957—, diplomatic ser., 1959—; 2d sec. Turkish embassy, Prague, Czechoslovakia, 1963-64; Turkish consul, Aleppo, Syria, 1966-68; dir. CENTO and tech. assistance sects. Ministry Fgn. Affairs; 1st sec. Turkish embassy Washington, 1970—. Home: 7/7 Mesnevi Sokak Ankara Turkey Office: 1606 23d St NW Washington DC 20008

GUY, BASIL, educator; b. Lynn, Mass., Apr. 12, 1926; s. Basil J.T. and Emma M. (Houchin) G.; B.A., Bowdoin Coll., 1949; M.A., Yale, 1951, Ph.D., 1955. Mem. faculty U. Cal. at Berkeley, 1954—, prof. French, 1968—, acting chmn. dept., 1963-64, 68-69. Served with AUS, 1944-46. Decorated Bronze Star medal; Jr. Sterling fellow Yale, 1950- 53; Fulbright scholar, 1953-54; Commn. Relief Belgium fellow, 1960-61; Guggenheim fellow, 1964-65; Humanities Research fellow U. Cal., 1971-72. Mem. Modern Lang. Assn., Philol. Assn. Pacific Coast, Phi Beta Kappa. Author: The French Image of China, 1963. Home: 2816 Claremont Av Berkeley CA 94705

GUY, CHARLES ARMOR, editor, pub.; b. Balt., Mar. 30, 1902; s. Charles Adams and Jennie (Armor) G.; B.A., U. Okla., 1923; LL.D., Tex. Tech. U., 1968; m. Grace Moore, Sept. 21, 1930; childrenCharles Armor, Dorrance Herbert, George Moore. Reporter Tulsa World, 1917-18, El Reno (Okla.) American, 1922-23, Bristow (Okla.) Record, 1923; editor Lubbock (Tex.) Plains Jour., 1924-25, Lubbock Evening Jour., 1925-26; editor, pub. Lubbock Avalanche-Jour., 1926-; v.p., dir. El Paso Times; dir. Globe- News Publ. Co., Amarillo, Tex., Fort Worth and Denver Railway Co., Fort Worth. Pres., Panhandle-South Plains Fair; mem. Tex. Commn. on Alcoholism; dir. Tex. Election Bd. Mem. Tex., West Tex. (past pres.) press assns., Tex. Asso. Press Editors Assn. (past pres.), Am. Soc. Newspaper Editors (past dir.), Sigma Delta Chi, Phi Gamma Delta. Presbyn. Mason (Shriner, 33). Clubs: Rotary, Lubbock (Tex.) Country, Lubbock. Home: 3509 43d St Lubbock TX 79413 Office: Avalanche-Jour 720 Av J Lubbock TX 79401

GUY, GEORGE FREDRIK, lawyer; b. Cheyenne, Wyo., May 4, 1904; s. Benjamin Field and Eva Madeline (Goldsmith) G.; J.D., Wyo. U., 1927; m. Lucille C. Schopf, Aug. 27, 1936; 1 dau., Georgina Carol. Admitted to Wyo. bar, 1927, since practiced in Cheyenne; asst. pros. atty. Laramie County, 1928; city police judge, 1930-31, city atty., Cheyenne, 1948-52; atty. gen. Wyo., 1955-57; now sr. partner firm Guy, Williams, White & Mulvaney, Cheyenne. Def. counsel trial Japanese Gen. Tomayuki Yamashita, Manila, P.I., 1945; judge advocate gen. Wyo. N.G., 1948-62. Mem. Wyoming Legislature, 1949-51. Mem. Wyo. State Bar (pres. 1966-67), Am. Legion, V.F.W., Alpha Tau Omega. Elk, Mason. Home: 4019 Carey Av Cheyenne WY 82001 Office: 1600 Van Lennen Av Cheyenne WY 82001

GUY, ROBERT JEFFERSON, hosp. adminstr.; b. Summitville, Ind., Aug. 22, 1912; s. Daniel Jefferson and Bertha (Dobson) G.; student La. State U., 1936-37; B.A., Emory U., 1940; m. Martha Elizabeth Jackson, Aug. 30, 1940; childrenRobert Leland, Carol Lynn, Elizabeth Elaine. Asst. to adminstr. Ga. Bapt. Hosp., Altanta, 1940-43; gen. mgr. Ridgecrest Bapt. Assembly, 1946-50; adminstr. Baton Rouge Gen. Hosp., 1950-62, Mo. Bapt. Hosp., St. Louis, 1962-. Trustee YMCA, Baton Rouge, 1955-61, pres., 1957-58. Served from 2d lt. to capt., AUS, 1943-46. Fellow Am. Coll. Hosp. Adminstrs. (regent 1967-71); mem. Am. (del. 1970-71), Am. Protestant, Bapt., Mo. (pres. 1969, trustee) hosp. assns., Hosp. Assn. Met. St. Louis (treas. 1967-69, pres. 1970), Sigma Chi. Democrat. So. Baptist. Rotarian. Home: 3031 N Ballas Rd St Louis MO 63131 Office: 3015 N Ballas Rd St Louis MO 63131

GUY, WILLIAM LEWIS, gov. N.D.; b. Devils Lake, N.D., Sept. 30, 1919; s. William Lewis and Mable (Leet) G.; B.S., N.D. Agrl. Coll., 1941; M.A., U. Minn., 1946; m. Elizabeth Jean Mason, Jan. 30, 1943; children—William Lewis III, James Mason, Deborah Jean, Holly Elice, Nancy Jo. Salesman, Balthouser-Moyer Livestock Agts., West Fargo, N.D., 1946; asst. county agt., Cass County, N.D., 1947; propr. Guy-Bean Farm Store, West Fargo, 1947-50; instr. agrl. econs. N.D. Agrl. Coll., 1952-58; mem. N.D. Ho. of Reps., 1959-61, asst. minority leader, 1959; gov. N.D., 1961—. Mem. Pres.'s Commn. on Health Facilities, 1968; Pres.'s election observer in South Vietnam, 1967; organizer, chmn. Midwest Govs. Conf., 1962, 63; chmn. Nat. Gov.'s Conf., 1967, 68; chmn. Council State Govts., 1967. Mem. N.D. Dem. Central Com., 1950—. Served from ensign to lt. (s.g.), USNR, 1942-45. Mem. N.D. Agrl. Coll. Alumni Assn. (pres. 1948). Presbyn. (trustee). Office: State Capital Bismarck ND 58501

GUY, WILLIAM THOMAS, Jr., educator; b. Abilene, Tex., Dec. 11, 1919; s. William Thomas and Viola (Broughton) G.; B.S. in Mech. Engring., Tex. A. and M. Coll., 1940; M.A., U. Tex., 1948; Ph.D., Cal. Inst. Tech., 1951; m. Valeree Commander, Dec. 30, 1941; childrenPaul William, Gary Boyd, Greg Alan. Design engr. land turbine div. Westinghouse Electric Corp., 1940-42; instr. applied math. U. Tex., 1946-48; inst. scholar, grad. asst. Cal. Inst. Tech., 1948-51; faculty U. Tex., 1951-, prof. math., chmn. dept., 1959-, research scientist, cons. Def. Research Lab., 1953-; math. cons. Tex. Research Assos., Austin, 1960-. Vis. lectr. for secondary schs., 1959, 60, for colls., 1961, for Math. Assn. Am.; dir. summer inst. elementary sch. personnel Nat. Sci. Found., 1960; mem. commn. math Tex. Edn. Agy. Bd. dirs. U. Tex. YMCA. Served to maj., C.E., AUS, 1942- 46. Recipient Lemuel Scarbrough Found. award for excellence in teaching, 1956. Fellow A.A.A.S., Tex. Acad. Sci. (v.p. math. div.; dir. vis. lectr. program 1959-60); mem. Math. Assn. Am. (past chmn. Tex.), Am. Soc. Engring. Edn. (chmn. math. div.), Am. Math. Soc., Indian Math. Soc., Sigma Xi, Tau Beta Pi, Sigma Pi Sigma. Methodist (ofcl. bd.). Mason. Home: 4602 Madrona Dr Austin TX 78731

GUYER, BYRON, educator; b. Brownwood, Tex., Oct. 16, 1915; s. Byron Clyde, Sr., and Helen (Tidd) G.; B.A., San Diego State Coll., 1938; M.A., U. Cal. at Berkeley, 1941; Ph.D., Stanford, 1947; m. Marjorie Houk, Nov. 23, 1938; childrenRobert, Susan. Instr. Stanford, 1945; asst. prof. English, Humboldt State Coll., 1946, U. Cal. at Davis, 1947-50; head dept. English Diablo Valley Coll., 1950-55, Los Angeles State Coll., 1955—. Mem. Cal. Assn. English Councils, Internat. Inst. Arts and Letters (life), Modern Lang. Assn. Author: (with Donald A Bird) Patterns of Thinking and Writing, 1959; (with John Bushman and Marvin Laser) Language In Your Life, Vol. 3, 1967. Home: Pasadena CA Office: 5151 State College Dr Los Angeles CA 90032

GUYER, DAVID LEIGH, found. exec.; b. Pasadena, Cal., Sept. 24, 1925; s. Leigh Davis and Emily (Shuford) G.; B.A., Stanford, 1948; m. Carol Penney, June 21, 1952; children—Cynthia Lorraine, Grant Penney, Alissa Carolyn, Shelly Diane, Marion Leslie, Leigh Jonathan. With UN, 1950-60, dep. resident rep. Tech. Assistance Bd., India, 1955-58, chief Tech. Assistance Bd., India, 1955-58, chief Tech. Assistance Recruitment Office for N.Am., 1959-60; with U.S. Mission to UN, 1960-65, adviser polit. and security council affairs, 1962-65; v.p. devel. and pub. affairs Inst. Internat. Edn., 1965-71; exec. dir. Community Devel. Found.-Save the Children Fedn., N.Y.C., 1971—. Bd. dirs. YMCA Internat. Com., Town Sch., N.Y.C., Collegiate Sch., N.Y.C., Freedom House, World Edn., Johnson Coll., Redlands, Cal. Mem. Fgn. Policy Assn. (bd. dirs.), Alpha Tau Omega. Episcopalian. Clubs: River (N.Y.C.); Maidstone (Easthampton). Author: Ghana and the Ivory Coast-The Impact of Colonialism in an African Setting. Home: 112 E 78th St New York City NY 10021 Office: 345 E 46th St New York City NY 10017

GUYER, GORDON EARL, educator; b. Kalamazoo, May 30, 1926; s. Clifford and Hazel (Boughton) G.; B.S., Mich. State U., 1950, M.S., 1952, Ph.D., 1954; m. Norma Lake, Dec. 16, 1950; childrenDawn, Daniel. Mem. faculty Mich. State U., Lansing, 1953—, prof. entomology, 1961—, chmn. dept., 1962—. On leave to U. Cal. at Riverside, also Ore. State U., 1961. Mem. Entomol. Soc. Am. (chmn. N. Central br. 1963-64), Canadian Entomol. Soc., Mich. Acad. Sci., Arts and Letters, Sigma Xi. Spl. research applied entomlgy, aquatic ecology. Home: 862 Whitman Dr East Lansing MI 48823

GUYTON, ARTHUR CLIFTON, educator; b. Oxford, Miss., Sept. 8, 1919; s. Billy Sylvester and Mary Katherine (Smallwood) G.; A.B., U. Miss., 1939; M.D., Harvard, 1943; m. Ruth Alice Weigle, June 12, 1943; childrenDavid Lee, Robert Allan, John Richard, Steven William, Catherine A., Jean M., Douglas, James, Thomas, Gregory Paul. Intern Mass. Gen. Hosp., 1943, asst. resident, 1946; acting asso. prof. physiology, U. Tenn. Med. Sch., 1947, asso. prof. pharmacology, 1947-48; prof. and chmn. dept. physiology and biophysics, U. Miss., 1948—; cons. editor Clin. Medicine, 1950-51; mem. internat. bd. editors, sec. Cardiovascular diseases, Excerpta Medica; cons. editor Jour. Applied Physiology, Am. Jour. Cardiology, Am. Jour. Physiology. Mem. exec. com., teletherapy evaluation bd. Oak Ridge Inst. Nuclear Studies, 1952-53. Served in med. research USN, 1944-46. Awarded Commendation Citation by Army for wartime research; chosen one of Ten Outstanding Young Men of Am. by U.S. Jr. C. of C., 1951; recipient Ida Gould award, A.A.A.S., 1959. Fellow Am. Coll. Cardiology (v.p. 1965-66), A.A.A.S.; mem. Am. Heart Assn., Am. Fedn. Clin. Research, A.M.A., Am. Physiol. Soc., Miss. Acad. Sci. (pres. 1963-64), So. Soc. for Clin. Research (pres. 1956-57), Circulation Soc., Miss. Heart Assn. (pres. 1955-56), Alpha Omega Alpha, Pi Kappa Pi, Sigma Alpha Epsilon, Tau Kappa Alpha, Alpha Kappa Kappa, Phi Eta Sigma, Alpha Epsilon Delta, Omicron Delta Kappa. Author textbooks, also Function of the Human Body, 1959, 3d edit., 1969; Textbook of Medical Physiology, 1961, 4th edit., 1971; Circulatory Physiology: Cardiac Output and Its Regulation, 1963. Contbr. articles in profl. jours. Home: 234 Meadow Rd Jackson MS 39206 Office: Miss Medical Center Jackson MS 39216

GUYTON, JACK SMALLWOOD, educator; b. Ingomar, Miss., Oct. 12, 1914; s. Billy Sylvester and Mary Katherine (Smallwood) G.; student U. Miss., 1930-31; A.B., U. N.C., 1933; M.D. cum laude, Harvard, 1937; m. 2d, Barbara Bayne, May 22, 1964; 1 dau. by previous marriage, Susan Elizabeth (Mrs. James H. Rock). Successively intern, asst. resident, fellow, resident ophthalmology Johns Hopkins U. Hosp., 1937-42, asst. prof. ophthalmology Med. Sch., 1942-44, asso. prof., asst. dir. Wilmer Ophthalmol. Inst., 1944-54; chmn. dept. ophthalmology Henry Ford Hosp., Detroit, 1954—; chmn. dept. biomath. and computer scis. Edsel B. Ford Inst. 1967—. Mem. Am. Ophthalmol. Socs., Am. Acad. Ophthalmology and Otolaryngology, Assn. Research Ophthalmology, Pan Am. Congress Ophthalmology, A.M.A., Mich. Med. Soc., Phi Beta Kappa, Sigma Xi, Alpha Omega Alpha. Home: 402 University Pl Grosse Pointe, MI 48230. Office: 2799 W Grand Blvd Detroit MI 48202

GUYTON, ROBERT POOL, banker; b. Blue Mountain, Miss., Mar. 31, 1937; s. Albert J. and Birma Elizabeth (Pool) G.; B.B.A., U. Miss., 1958; M.B.A., Harvard, 1966; m. Katherine Cole Taylor, June 15, 1960; children—Robert Pool, Randall Taylor. Joined Deposit Guaranty Nat. Bank, Jackson, Miss., 1960, asst. cashier, 1963-66, asst. to pres., 1966-69, sr. v.p., 1969, exec. v.p., 1969-71; pres., dir. Nat. Bank of Ga., Atlanta, 1971—; dir. Miss. Chem. Co., Yazoo City, First Miss. Corp. Jackson, First Nat. Bank of New Albany (Miss.). Bd. dirs. Miss. Indsl. and Spl. Service, Miss. Econ. Council (treas. 1970), Miss. Art Assn., Miss. Opera Assn., Miss. Council Econ. Edn.; trustee Blue Mountain Coll., 1970-71. Served to 1st lt. AUS, 1958-60. Named Outstanding Young Man of Year, Miss. Jr. C. of C., 1968. Mem. Am. Bankers Assn. (urban affairs com. 1970—), U. Miss. Alumni Assn. (exec. com. 1970-71), Jackson C. of C. (dir.), Omicron Delta Kappa, Sigma Chi. Baptist (chmn. bd. 1969). Clubs: Country of Jackson (bd. govs. 1970-71); Capital City Petroleum, Patio (Jackson); Atlanta City. Home: 700 Montana Rd NW Atlanta GA 30327 Office: Nat Bank Ga Box 1234 Atlanta GA 30301

GUZMAN, GERMAN DE LA MELENA, banker. Mgr., Banco Central de Reserva Del Peru, Lima. Office: Esquina Lampa Y Ucayali Lima Peru*

GUZMAN WEST, GUILLERMO, journalist; m. Rosa Maria Covarrubias; children—Elisa, Consuelo. Photographer, reporter, mgr. Tiempo S.A. de CV, Mexico City. Coordinator gen. Pub. Library Commn. Home: Angel Urraza 1104 Dept 3 Mexico City 12 Mexico Office: Barcelona 32 Mexico City 6 Mexico

GUZZETTA, DOMINIC JAMES, univ. pres.; b. Fredonia, N.Y., July 21, 1919; s. James and Josephine (Giordano) G.; student U. Alfred, 1937-38, U. Rochester, 1950-51, Syracuse U. 1951-52; B.A. cum laude, U. Buffalo, 1948, M.Ed., 1951, Ed.D., 1953; LL.D., Akron U. 1968, Kent State U.; D.S.Sc., Marian Coll.; m. Nola Miller, Aug. 8, 1942; children—JoAnne Nola, Elaine Marie. Tchr. pub. schs., 1948- 51; asst. dean Millard Filmore Coll., 1951-53; supr. productivity program FOA, Washington, 1953-54; asst. dean evening and adult edn. div. U. Akron (O.), 1954-56, dean, 1956-59, prof. edn., 1960-68, dir. summer session, 1956-59, acting dean Coll. Edn., 1958-59, dean gen. coll., 1959- 62, v.p., dean adminstrn., 1962-66, sr. v.p., provost, 1966-68, coordinator research, 1959-62, pres., prof. higher edn., 1971—; pres., prof. history Marian Coll., Indpls., 1968-71. Cons., evaluator higher edn. N. Central Assn. Pres., Cuyahoga Falls City Bd. Edn. Served from pvt. to capt., AUS, 1940-46; lt. col. Ohio N.G. Mem. Ohio Coll. Assn. (pres. adult edn. sect.), Am. Soc. Tng. Dirs. (pres. N.E. Ohio chpt.), Assn. Univs. Evening Colls., Adult Edn. Assn., Internat. Inst. Akron (pres.), Am. Assn. Sch. Adminstrs., Ind. Conf. on Higher Edn., Nat. Conf. Christians and Jews, Kappa Delta Pi, Alpha Sigma Lambda, Phi Delta Kappa, Chi Sigma Nu, Omicron Delta Kappa. Rotarian. Club: Indianapolis Literary. Home: 856 Mayfair Rd Akron OH 44303

GUZZO, LOUIS R., exec. editor Seattle Post-Intelligencer. Address: Hearst Pub Co 6th and Wall Sts Seattle WA 98121 *

GWALTER, L. IVIMY, church ofcl.; b. E. Orange, N.J.; d. Henry L. and Lucy Lydia (Ivimy) Gwalter; student langs., Geneva, Switzerland, 1907-08; grad. Mus. Art Inst., N.Y.C., 1913. Second reader Third Ch. Christ, Scientist, N.Y.C., 1922-25; authorized tchr. C.S., 1940—; asso. editor C.S. Jour., C.S. Sentinel, Heralds of C.S., 1947-48; mem. C.S. bd. dirs. First Ch. Christ, Scientist, Boston, 1948-68. Trustee Under the Will of Mary Baker Eddy, 1948-68; trustee Christian Sci. charitable instns., 1948-68. Home: 250 Beacon St Boston MA 02116 Office: 1028 Statler Office Bldg Boston MA 02117

GWATHMEY, ROBERT, artist; b. Richmond, Va., Jan. 24, 1903; s. Robert and Eva Mortimer (Harrison) G.; student N.C. State Coll., 1924-25, Maryland Inst., 1925- 26, Pa. Acad. Fine Arts, 1926-30; m. Rosalie Dean Hook, Nov. 2, 1935; 1 son, Charles. Work purchased for permanent collections Carnegie Mus., Pitts., Telfair Mus., Savannah, Ga., 1944, Boston Mus., Va. Mus., Richmond, Va., Pa. Acad., Phila., San Diego Mus., Los Angeles Mus., Springfield (Mass.) Mus., IBM Corp., U. Tex., U. Okla., Ala. Poly. Inst. Butler Art Inst., Youngstown,

O., Rochester Meml. Gallery, U. Ga., U. Ill., Whitney Mus., Mus. Modern Art, Sao Paulo, Brazil, others. Recipient of First prize Contemporary Water Color Annual, San Diego Mus., 1941, second prize Carnegie Inst. Annual, 1943, second prize Pepsi-Cola Annual, 1946, Grant, Nat. Acad. of Arts. Letters, 1946, second prize Birmingham Mus., 1956, fourth prize Corcoran Gallery, 1957; Fellowship prize Pa. Acad. Fine Arts, 1958. Instr. Cooper Union. Address: Amagansett NY 11930

GWIAZDA, HENRY JOHN, lawyer, judge; b. New Britain, Conn., June 24, 1910; s. Ignacy and Julia (Smigel) G.; student Williston Acad., 1929-31, Mass. Inst. Tech., 1931- 32; B.A., Wesleyan U., Middletown, Conn., 1936; LL.B., U. Conn., 1939; m. Emily B. Cieszynski, July 13, 1938; childrenHenry John II, Ronald E. Admitted to Conn. bar, 1939, since practiced in New Britain; judge City and Police Ct., New Britain, 1941-43; dir. Peoples Savs. Bank New Britain, 1948-, counsel, 1950-60; judge Probate Ct., 1954-; chmn. Nat. Selective Service Appeal Bd., 1965-70; dir. Conn. Probate Assembly Seminar. Mayor, New Britain, 1946-50; candidate treas. Conn., 1948. Served with AUS 1944-46. Mem. Conn., Hartford County New Britain bar assns., Polish Nat. Alliance, Polish Falcons Am., V.F.W., Catholic War Vets., Am. Legion, Disabled Am. Vets., Beta Theta Pi. Clubs: National Capitol Democratic, Shuttle Meadow Country. Home: 580 Shuttle Meadow Av New Britain CT 06051 Office: 177 Columbus Blvd New Britain CT 06051

GWIAZDA, STANLEY JOHN, coll. dean; b. Phila., Feb. 14, 1922; s. Nicholas and Pauline (Stanczak) G.; B.S. in Mech. Engring., Drexel Inst. Tech., 1944, M.S., 1952; m. Regina R. Grzeskowiak, Nov. 26, 1944; 1 dau., Marianne C. Mem. faculty Drexel U., 1946—, asso. prof. mech. engring., 1952—, dean Eve. Coll., 1963—. Bd. dirs. Phila. Govt. Tng. Inst., 1963—. Served to lt. (j.g.) USNR, 1944-46; PTO; lt. comdr. Res. Mem. Assn. U. Eve. Colls., Am. Soc. Engring. Edn., Assn. Higher Edn., Adult Edn. Assn., Engrs. Club Phila., Res. Officers Assn. (1st v.p. Navy N.J. dept. 1971-72), Pi Tau Sigma, Alpha Sigma Lambda, Cross Keys. Roman Catholic. Author: (with J. H. Billings) Advanced Machine Design, 1958. Home: 2001 Wayne Av Haddon Heights NJ 08035 Office: Drexel Evening Coll Philadelphia PA 19104

GWIN, JOHN DURDEN, govt. ofcl.; b. Tchula, Miss., Apr. 15, 1906; s. Walter Keirn and Mary (Wolfe) G.; B.A., Davidson Coll., 1928. With Nat. City Co., N.Y.C., 1928- 30, Harris, Forbes & Co., N.Y.C., 1930-31, R.H. Macy & Co., N.Y.C., 1931- 32, various banks, 1932-36; with U.S. Treas. Dept., 1936—, spl. asst. to comptroller of currency, Washington, 1965-66, acting dep. comptroller, 1966-67, dep. comptroller currency, 1967—. Mem. Fed. Exec. Bd., Atlanta, 1963-65; instr. Interagy. Sch. for Examiners, Washington, 1958-62. Recipient Meritorious Service award Treasury Dept., 1969. Mem. Phi Gamma Delta. Presbyn. Lion (past sec.). Clubs: Capital City (Atlanta); University (Washington), Army Navy Country (Arlington, Va.). Home: 2301 E St NW Washington DC 20037 Office: Main Treas Bldg Pennsylvania Av and 15th St Washington DC 20220

GWINN, DAVID, dairy industry exec.; b. S.I., N.Y., July 25, 1911; s. Ralph W. and Essie (O'Daniel) G.; grad. Deerfield Acad., 1930; student Williams Coll., 1931-32; m. Ethel Elizabeth Bechtold, Sept. 23, 1933; children—John C., Richard H., Nancy V., Martha E. Dairyman, mgr. dairy plants, Atlanta, also Daytona Beach, Fla., 1932-40; mgr. Pennbrook Milk Co., Phila., 1940-41, pres., 1941—. Owner Dairy Museum, Phila.; del. Internat. Dairy Congress, Hague, 1954, Rome, 1957. Trustee Phila. Mus. Art; bd. dirs. Pa. Acad. Fine Arts. Mem. Phila. Orchestra Mens Com. Republican. Clubs: Orpheus, Racquet, Radnor Hunt, Merion Cricket, Franklin Inn, Corinthian Yacht (Phila.). Penn, Rittenhouse. Contbr. articles on dairy industry. Home: Monk Rd Gladwyne PA 19035 Office: Lombard and 27th Sts Philadelphia PA 19146

GWINN, HERBERT CATHER, elec. appliance mfg. co. exec.; b. Anderson, Ind., Mar. 21, 1905; s. Marshall and Margaret (Cather) G.; student Walton Sch. Commerce, 1927; m. Ethel Elmer, Mar. 8, 1941; 1 dau., Diane Gwen. With Sunbeam Corp., Chgo., 1928—, treas., 1944-70, v.p., 1955-63, exec. v.p., 1963-70, now dir., mem. exec. com., chmn. finance com.; chmn. bd. Sunbeam Equipment Corp., 1958-70, chmn. bd. Sunbeam Internat., 1961-70; chmn. bd. dir. H.W. Crane Co.; dir. Protection Mut. Ins. Co. Clubs: South Shore Country, Chicago Yacht. Home: 1425 Franklin Av River Forest IL 60305 Office: 15 N 9th Av Maywood IL 60153

GWINN, ROBERT P., elec. appliance mfg. exec.; b. Anderson, Ind., June 30, 1907; s. Marshall and Margaret (Cather) G.; Ph.B., U. Chgo., 1929; m. Nancy Flanders, Jan. 20, 1942; children—John Marshall, Richard Herbert. With Sunbeam Corp., 1936—, gen. sales mgr. elec. appliance div., 1951-52, v.p., dir., 1952, pres., 1955-71, chmn. bd., chief exec. officer, 1971—; pres. Sunbeam Appliance Service Co., 1952—; dir. Ency. Brit., First Nat. Bank of Chgo., Riverside Nat. Bank, Continental Casualty Co., Continental Assurance Co., Borg Warner Corp., CNA Financial Corp., Ball Corp. Trustee Hanover Coll., U. Chgo., U. Chgo. Cancer Research Found. Mem. Elec. Assn. Chgo. (dir.), Ill. C. of C. (dir., v.p.), Brit.-Am. C. of C. in Midwest (dir.), Alpha Sigma Phi. Clubs: Chicago, University (Chgo.); Riverside (Ill.) Country; Commercial, Economic. Home: 144 Fairbanks Rd Riverside IL 60546 Office: 5400 Roosevelt Rd Chicago IL 60650

GWINN, WILLIAM DULANEY, educator, phys. chemist; b. Bloomington, Ill., Sept. 28, 1916; s. Walter E. and Allyne (Dulaney) G.; A.B., U. Mo. 1937, M.A., 1939; Ph.D., U. Cal. at Berkeley, 1942; m. Margaret Boothby, July 11, 1953; children—Robert B., Ellen, Kathleen. Teaching asst. U. Cal. at Berkeley, 1939-42, mem. faculty, 1942—, prof. phys. chemistry, 1955—, research prof. Miller Research Inst., 1961-62. Vis. prof. chemistry U. Minn., Mpls., 1969-70; spl. research molecular structure, microwave spectroscopy, quantum mechanics, direct digital control. Guggenheim fellow, 1954; Sloan fellow, 1955-59; recipient citation merit U. Mo., 1964. Fellow Am. Phys. Soc.; mem. Phi Beta Kappa, Sigma Xi, Pi Mu Epsilon. Asso. editor Jour. Chem. Physics, 1962-64. Home: 8506 Terrace Dr El Cerrito CA 94530 Office: Dept Chemistry Univ California Berkeley CA 94720

GWINN, WILLIAM PERSONS, aircraft exec.; b. N.Y.C., Sept. 22, 1907; s. Frederick W. and Clare (Persons) G.; student Gunnery Prep. Sch., Washington, Conn., 1923-25; Dr. Engring. (hon.), Rensselaer Poly. Inst., 1956; D.Sc. (hon.), Trinity Coll., 1961; m. Joyce Clark, Nov. 29, 1934 (dec. 1957); children—William Clark, Linda Clare, Michael; m. 2d, Mary Berry Devoe, 1958 (dec. 1969); m. 3d, Rachel Coleman Witman, 1970. Joined Pratt & Whitney Aircraft div. United Aircraft Corp., East Hartford, Conn., 1927, engr., 1929-34, West Coast rep., Los Angeles, 1934-39, asst. sales mgr., 1939-42, asst. gen. mgr., 1942, acting gen. mgr., 1943, gen. mgr. 1944- 56, v.p. United Aircraft Corp., 1946-56, pres., dir., chief adminstrv. officer, 1956-67, chmn., chief exec. officer, dir., 1968—; dir. First Nat. City Bank N.Y., The F & M Schaefer Corp., United Aircraft of Can., Ltd., United Aircraft Internat., Shell Oil Co., Hartford Nat. Bank & Trust Co., Hartford Nat. Corp., Conn. Mut. Life Ins. Co., Orenda, Ltd. Nat. chmn. U.S. Indsl. Paroll Savs. Com., 1968. Mem. def. industry adv. council Dept. Def.; nat. def. com. N.A.M.; vice chmn. airlines and aircraft sub-council Pres.'s Nat. Indsl. Pollution Control Council. Bd. dirs. Hartford Hosp. Trustee Trinity Coll. (life), Naval Aviation Mus. Assn., Rensselaer Poly. Inst. Conn., Marine Hist. Assn., Mystic Seaport. Mem. Aerospace Industries Assn. (gov.), Transp. Assn. Am. (dir.). Clubs: Hartford, Hartford Golf; Conquistadores del Cielo, N.Y. Yacht, Essex Yacht, Burning Tree, Sky, Fishers Island Country; Country Florida; Delray Beach Yacht. Home: 60 Ledyard Rd West Hartford CT 06117 Office: 400 Main St East Hartford CT 06108

GWYNN, JOHN MINOR, educator; b. Glade Spring, Va., Aug. 13, 1897; s. Price Henderson and Mary Waters (Minor) G.; A.B., U. N.C., 1918, A.M., 1927; postgrad. U. Chgo., 1927; Ph.D., Yale, 1935; m. Janie Sue Stacy, June 6, 1925; 1 son, John Minor. Elementary sch. teacher, Leaksville, N.C., 1919; high sch. tchr. and prin., Leaksville, 1919-20, Reidsville, 1920- 24; instr. in Latin, U. N.C., 1924-26, asst. prof. edn., 1927-36, also supt. schs., Chapel Hill (part of univ. work), 1932-37, asso. prof. edn. and dir. curiculum lab., 1936-45, prof. edn., dir. curriculum lab., 1945-54, prof. edn., mem. administrv. bd. sch. edn., 1954-68; instr. Yale, 1933-35. Mem. Del. State Sch. Survey, 1946. Served as 2d lt., inf., U.S. Army, 1918. Mem. Nat. Soc. Study Edn., Am. Assn. Sch. Adminstrs., Assn. for Supervision and Curriculum Devel., Nat. Assn. Secondary Sch. Prins., Nat. Vocational Guidance Assn., Am. Acad. Polit. and Social Sci., Nat. Soc. Advancement Edn., Am. Edn. Fellowship (v.p.), N.E.A., Classical Assn. Middle West and South, Phi Beta Kappa, Phi Delta Kappa. Presbyn. Mason (Shriner). Author: Curriculum Principles and Social Trends, 1943, rev. edits., 1950, 60, 69. Editor: (with W. Carson Ryan and A. K. King) Secondary Education in the South, 1946; (with A. J. Atkins) Teaching Alcohol Education in the Schools, 1959; Theory and Practice of Supervision, 1961; asso. editor The High Sch. Jour. (U. N.C.), 1929-49, mng. editor, 1930-31; chmn., editor U. (Chapel Hill) instn.-wide Tchr. Edn. Self-Study, 1963-64. Home: 514 North St Chapel Hill NC 27514 Died Jan. 16, 1971.

GYGI, HANS A., cement co. exec.; b. Switzerland, 1906; grad. Fed. Inst. Tech. (Switzerland), 1929. Chmn. bd., pres. Dundee Cement Co. (Mich.). Home: Hellgasse Wildegg Switzerland Office: Dundee Cement Co PO Box 317 Dundee MI 48131*

GYLES, MARY FRANCIS, educator; b. Blackville, S.C., Dec. 24, 1918; d. Ronald Corbin and Valeria (Still) Gyles; A.B., U. N.C., 1939, A.M., 1945, Ph.D. (fellow), 1949; postgrad. (fellow), U. Chgo., 1945-46, Cambridge (Eng.) U., 1948. Belgian-Am. research fellow, Brussels, Belgium, 1947-49; asst. prof. Memphis State U., 1949-57; asst. prof. Bklyn. Coll., 1957-63, asso. prof. ancient history, 1963-, acting chmn. dept. history, 1962-63, chmn., 1964-. Mem. Am. Hist. Assn., Am. Assn. U. Women (exec. bd. 1961- 64, fellowship chmn. 1963-64), Am. Assn. U. Profs. (chpt. v.p., 1955- 56), Cercle des Alumni de la Fondation Universitaire de la Belgique, Phi Beta Kappa, Phi Alpha Theta. Author: Pharaonic Policies and Adminstration, 663-323 B.C., 1959; (with W.E. Caldwell) The Ancient World, 1966. Co-editor: Laudatores Temporis Acti, 1964. Contbr. articles on early Roman Empire period to profl. jours. Home: 129 Cockonoe Av Babylon NY 11702 Office: Dept History Bklyn Coll City U NY Bedford and H Avs Brooklyn NY 11210

GYORGY, PAUL, physician; b. Nagy Varad, Hungary, Apr. 7, 1893; M.D., U. Budapest, 1915, (hon.), Heidelberg U., 1958; m. Margaret A. John, Oct. 23, 1920. Came U.S., 1935, naturalized, 1941. Prof. pediatrics Heidelberg U., 1920-33; research fellow U. Cambridge (Eng.), 1933-35; vis. research prof. Western Res. U., 1935-44; prof. pediatrics U. Pa., Phila., 1944-58, emeritus, 1958—. Chmn. organizing com. 5th Internat. Congress on Nutrition, Washington, 1960; chmn. protein adv. group WHO, FAO, UNICEF. Recipient Borden award Am. Inst. Nutrition and Acad. Pediatrics; Mendel award Am. Inst. Nutrition; Goldberger award A.M.A.; Markle fellow U. Toronto; Howland award Am. Pediatric Soc., 1968. Pioneer in discovery riboflavin, vitamin B6, biotin, growth factors in human milk, exptl. dietary liver injury. Home: 201 Curwen Rd Rosemont PA 19010 Office: Phila Gen Hosp Philadelphia PA 19104

HAACK, ROBERT W., stock exchange exec.; b. 1917. Partner, Robert W. Baird & Co., Milw.; pres. Nat. Assn. Securities Dealers, Inc., 1964-67; pres. N.Y. Stock Exchange, 1967—. Address: NY Stock Exchange Office of the Pres 11 Wall St New York City NY 10005*

HAAG, GEORGE HAROLD WALDO, architect; b. Phila., July 14, 1910; s. John Samuel and Anna (McCambridge) H.; B.Arch., U. Pa., 1934; m. Janina Garstka, Aug. 9, 1936; children—Mark, Evan and Eric (twins), Gary. Architect firm Berninger & Bower, Jenkintown, Pa., 1936-39, firm Berninger, Haag & d'Entremont, 1946-50, firm Haag & d'Entremont, 1950—. Mem. Council City Ivyland, Pa., 1960—, chmn. Planning Commn., 1964—; mem. exec. com. Bucks County Council Boy Scouts Am., 1963—; mem. adv. com. Pa. Bd. Edn., 1964—; mem. tech. adv. com. Pa. Dept. Edn., 1964—. Served to lt. comdr. USNR, 1942-45. Recipient numerous awards for excellence in design, 1951—. Fellow A.I.A. (mem. nat. judiciary com.); mem. Pa. Soc. Architects (past pres.), Soc. Archtl. History, Phila. Art Alliance. Projects have included several schools, including Unami, Klinger & Log Coll., Chalfont and Southampton, Pa., Central Bucks Jr. and Sr. High Sch., Centennial Sr. High Sch., Doylestown, Pa., Upper Dublin Municipal Bldg., Ft. Washington, Pa. Home: Green Meadows Ivyland PA 18974 Office: 445 Cedar St Jenkintown PA 19046

HAAG, WILLIAM GEORGE, educator, anthropologist; b. Henderson, Ky., Aug. 15, 1910; s. William George and Lillian (Kreipke) H.; B.S., U. Ky., 1932, M.S., 1933; Ph.D., U. Mich., 1948; m. Hope Sullivan, Dec. 25, 1937; children—William George 3d, John Martin, Forrest Kreipke, Alaric Sullivan. Field archeologist TVA, 1934, 36-37; curator Mus. Anthropology, U. Ky., 1937-49, asst. prof. anthropology, 1938; asso. prof. U. Miss., 1949-52; mem. faculty La. State U., 1952—, prof., 1955-66, curator Museum Anthropology, Alumni prof. anthropology, 1966—, chmn. dept. geography and anthropology, 1961-63; field expdns. in Tenn., 1934, Ala., 1936-37, Ky., 1937-41, Miss., 1950-51, Cape Hatteras, 1954-55, Carolina coast, 1956-57, Mexico, 1959, St. Lucia and Martinique, 1960-61, Nicaragua, 1970. Served to 1st lt. USAAF and AUS, 1942-45. Fellow Am. Anthrop. Assn., A.A.A.S.; mem. Soc. Am. Archaeology, archeol. socs. La., Ark., Tenn., N.C., Sigma Xi, Gamma Alpha, Beta Beta Beta, Phi Sigma, Sigma Gamma Epsilon, Delta Tau Delta, Omicron Delta Kappa, Phi Kappa Phi. Author: Aborginal Dogs, 1948; Archeology of Coastal North Carolina, 1958. Editor Southeastern Archaeol. Conf., 1939-59; asst. editor Am. Antiquity, 1947-50. Home: 330 Magnolia Wood Av Baton Rouge LA 70808

HAAGENSEN, C.S., metals co. exec.; b. Milw., May 18, 1916; s. William and Inger (Jackson) H.; B.A., Beloit Coll., 1939; student U. Wis., 1939-40; m. Gail Morse, Apr. 4, 1941; children—Stuart M., Scott R., Rick S. With Allis Chalmers Mfg. Co., 1939-51; dir. indsl. and pub. relations Ampco Metal, Inc. (now Ampco-Pitts. Corp.), Milw., 1951-63, corp. sec., 1963—, v.p., since 1966—, now asst. corp. sec. Mem. bus. adv. bd. Wis. gov.'s council for econ. devel. of the state. Bd. dirs. Milw. YMCA, chmn. drive, 1958; bd. dirs. Family Service Milw. Mem. Pub. Relations Soc. Am., Indsl. Relations Assn. Wis. (pres. 1951-52), Mgmt. Club Milw. (pres. 1954-55), Wis. C. of C., N.A.M., Employers Assn. Milw., Milw. Press Club, Milw. Assn. Commerce. Conglist. (council). Clubs: Westmoor Country (past pres.); Wauwatosa Curling (past pres.). Home: 14575 Woodridge Circle Brookfield WI 53005 Office: 1745 S 38th St Milwaukee WI 53201

HAAGENSEN, KENNETH WILLIAM, c. of c. exec.; b. Milw., Feb. 7, 1911; s. William and Inger (Jackson) H.; B.A., Beloit Coll., 1934; M.A., U. Wis., 1936; m. Dorothy Philips, Nov. 30, 1940; children—Kenneth D., Mark P., Karen A. Dir. pub. relations Allis Chalmers Mfg. Co., West Allis, Wis., 1946-63, asst. to v.p. marketing, pub. relations, 1963-66; exec. v.p. Wis. State C. of C., 1966—; author, lectr.; cons. U.S. Com. Econs. and Statistics. Dir. Green Bay Packers. Bd. dirs. Henry Vilas Park Zool. Soc., Circus World Mus. Mem. Pub. Relations Soc. Am. (pres. 1958), Canadian Pub. Relations Soc. (internat. v.p. 1963—), Sigma Delta Chi, Alpha Kappa Delta, Delta Sigma Rho. Home: 37428 Indian Mound Rd Oconomowoc WI 53066 Office: 411 W Main St Madison WI 53701

HAAGEN-SMIT, ARIE JAN, educator, bio-organic chemist; b. Utrecht, Holland, Dec. 22, 1900; B.A., M.A., Ph.D., Rijks U., Utrecht. Head asst. dept. organic chemistry U. Utrecht, 1929-34; lectr. organic chemistry Harvard, 1936-37; mem. faculty Cal. Inst. Tech., 1937—, prof. bio-organic chemistry, 1940-71, prof. emeritus, 1971—, also dir. Plant Environmental Labs. Mem. Air Sanitation Com. Cal.; mem. Sci. Com. Los Angeles County; biochem. adv. com. AEC; cons. Los Angeles County Air Pollution Control Dist., abatement br. Dept. Health, Edn. and Welfare, Nat. Center Air Pollution; chmn. Air Resources Bd. Cal., President's Task Force on Air Pollution. Trustee Arboretum Found. Los Angeles County. Decorated knight Order Orange Nassau, 1947; recipient Chambers award Air Pollution Assn. Am.; Community Service award D.A.R.; Hodgkins medal Smithsonian Instn., Washington; B.Y. Morrison Lecture award Dept. Agr., 1970. Fellow N.Y. Acad. Scis.; mem. Am. (Fritzsche award 1950, Tolman award Cal. sect. 1962), Swiss, Dutch chem. socs., Nat. Acad. Scis.; corr. mem. Royal Acad. Sci. (Netherlands). Author articles in field. Spl. research isolation and synthesis plant hormones. Home: 416 S Berkeley Av Pasadena CA 91107

HAAK, HAROLD HOWARD, ednl. adminstr.; b. Madison, Wis., June 1, 1935; s. Harold J. and Laura (Kittleson) H.; B.A., U. Wis., 1957, M.A., 1958; Ph.D., Princeton, 1963; m. Betty L. Steiner, June 25, 1955; children—Alison Marie, Janet Christine. Asst. prof., asso. prof. polit. sci., pub. adminstrn. and urban studies San Dieto State Coll., 1962-69, dean Coll. Profl. Studies, prof. pub. adminstrn. and urban studies, 1969-71; acad. v.p. Fresno State Coll., 1971—. Mem. County of San Diego Employee Relations Panel, 1969-71. Mem. Phi Beta Kappa, Phi Kappa Phi. Home: 6331 N 11th St Fresno CA 93710

HAAK, ROBERT ARNOLD, paper mfr.; b. Bayside, L.I., N.Y., Mar. 29, 1913; s. Robert and Bertha (Arnold) H.; B.S., Hamilton Coll., 1933; m. Julia D. Cookingam, Sept. 5, 1936; chiildren—Jill Louise (Mrs. Barry Adels), Barbara Jane (Mrs. Mark A. Cane). With Gt. No. Paper Co. (now div. Great No. Nekoosa Corp.), 1934—, mem. sales dept., asst. mgr. sales, mgr. sales, v.p. product devel., 1934-58, v.p., mgr. sales, 1958- 61, v.p. sales, 1961-66, pres., 1966—, mem. exec. and finance coms., dir.; pres. Gt. No. Bd. Sales Corp. Mason. Club: Red Hook (N.Y.) Golf. Home: The Willows Clinton Corners NY 14850 also 137D Heritage Hill Rd New Canaan CT Office: 522 Fifth Av New York City NY 10036

HAAKENSTAD, OTTO, life ins. co. exec., lawyer; b. Havnik, Norway, Dec. 7, 1901; s. Ole and Marie (Olson) H.; brought to U.S., 1907, naturalized, 1934; student N.D. Agrl. Coll.; m. Lillian Peterson, June 30, 1925; children—Dale L., Ardith L. (Mrs. Harlan Holly), Alan Otto. Admitted to N.D. bar, 1926, also Fed. Ct. bars, U.S. Supreme Ct. bar; mem. firm Burnett, Bergesen & Haakenstad, Fargo, to 1953; spl. atty. U.S. Dept. Justice, Fargo, 1935- 44; co-founder Western States Life Ins. Co., Fargo, 1930, sec., 1930-44, pres., 1944-68, chmn., 1968—; dir. Fargo Nat. Bank, N.D. Vice pres. Am. Life Conv., 1948-57, mem. exec. com., 1957—, pres., 1960—. Mem. bd. admissions and budget, past chmn. Fargo United Fund. Mem. Fargo (past dir.), N.D. (dir. 1965-69) chambers commerce Inst. Life Ins. (dir. 1965-69), Am. N.D. bar assns. Lutheran (trustee). Mason (grand master N.D. 1969-70); mem. Red Cross of Constantine. Clubs: Fargo Country, Lions (past dep. dist. gov.) (Fargo): Minneapolis Athletic. Home: 1718 S 7th St Fargo ND 58102 Office: Western States Life Bldg Fargo ND 58102

HAAN, AUBREY EDWIN, ednl. cons.; b. Sherwood, N.D., July 24, 1908; s. Klaas Mello and Foskea (Zuidema) H.; student So. Ore. State Coll., 1926-28; B.S., U. Ore., 1931; M.A., Stanford, 1938, Ed.D., 1940; m. Norma Stangle, Apr. 29, 1944; children—Peter, Mary, Linda. Sch. prin., Tillamook, Ore., 1928-30; supt. sch., Riverton, Ore., 1931-36; research asst. Regional Planning Project, Stanford, 1937-39; instr. ednl. psychology Wash. Coll., 1942- 44; exec. sec. Council Civic Unity, San Francisco, 1944-45; dir. Stewart Demonstration Sch., U. Utah, 1945-48; prof., U. Hawaii, 1948-51: chmn. ednl. adminstrn. San Francisco State Coll., 1955-60, dean Sch. Edn., 1962-68; cons. in field, 1948—. Chmn. bd. Ednl. Cons. and Community Planners, 1966—; bd. dirs. Architects and Asso. Professions, Inc., 1965- -. Recipient Eugene F. Saxton award Harper Bros., 1948. Mem. Phi Delta Kappa. Author: Elementary Curriculum, Theory and Research, 1961; Education for Open Society, 1962; Readings in Professional Education, 1963. Home: 1143 Hillview Rd Alamo CA 94507 Office: 1600 Holloway St San Francisco CA 94132

HAAR, CHARLES MONROE, lawyer, educator; b. Antwerp, Belgium, Dec. 3, 1920; s. Benjamin and Dora (Eisner) H.; brought to U.S., 1921, naturalized, 1926; A.B., N.Y.U., 1940; LL.B., Harvard, 1948; M.A., U. Wis., 1941; LL.D. (honorary) Lake Erie U., 1968; m. Natalie Zinn, 1946; children—Jeremy, Susan Eve, Jonathan. Admitted to N.Y. bar, 1949, U.S. Supreme Ct., 1968; practice of law, N.Y.C., 1949-52; asst. prof. law Harvard, 1952-54, prof., 1954-66, 69—; chmn. Joint Center for Urban Studies, Mass. Inst. Tech. and Harvard, 1969—; dir. Charles River Assos.; asst. sec. met. devel. Dept. Housing and Urban Devel., Washington, 1966-69. Chief reporter Am. Land Inst. project model code land devel., 1964-66; mem. Cambridge Redevel. Authority, Met. Area Planning Council: chmn. Pres.'s Task Force Preservation Natural Beauty, Task Force on Model Cities, on Suburban Problems. Cons. AID, HHFA, U.S. Senate Subcom. Govtl. Operations, state and city agys. Pres. Regional and Urban Planning Implementation, Inc.; bd. dirs. Zelda Zinn Found. Served from ensign to lt. (j.g.), USN, 1942-46. Mem. Am. Acad. Arts and Scis., Am. Inst. Planners, Brit. Town Planning Inst., Phi Beta Kappa. Author: Land Planning Law in a Free Society; Land-Use Planning, 1959; Federal Credit and Private Housing, 1960; Law and Land, 1964; Golden Age of American Law, 1966. Editor: Beacon Classics of the Law. Contbr. articles law, planning jours. Home: 1 Kennedy Rd Cambridge MA 02138 Office: Harvard Law Sch Cambridge MA 02138

HAAR, EMILE ALPHONSE, life ins. co. exec.; b. Corning, N.Y., Jan. 16, 1902; s. Jean George and Marie (Burgan) H.; grad. Corning Free Acad., 1918; m. Agnes Angela Conklin, Oct. 18, 1924; childrenJean George, Ella Cecilia (Mrs. William E. Burden), Mary Monica (Mrs. Robert B. Wall). With Maccabees Mut. Life Ins. Co.,

Detroit, 1921-, pres., 1964-68, chmn. bd., 1968-. Clubs: Detroit, Economic (Detroit). Home 70 Troy-del Way Williamsville NY 14221 Office: 25800 Northwestern Hwy Southfield MI 48076

HAAS, F. OTTO, mfg. co. exec.; b. Phila., 1915; student Amherst Coll., also Princeton. Chmn. bd., mem. exec. com. Rohm & Haas Co.; dir. Phila. Nat. Bank, INA Corp., Standard Pressed Steel. Bd. dirs. Pa. Mfrs. Assn. Office: Independence Mall West Philadelphia PA 19105

HAAS, FELIX, univ. dean; b. Vienna, Austria, Apr. 20, 1921; s. Adolf and Marianne (Schick) H.; came to U.S., 1939, naturalized, 1943; B.S., Mass. Inst. Tech., 1948, M.S., 1949, Ph.D., 1952; m. Violet Bushwick, Apr. 17, 1948; childrenRichard Allen, Elizabeth Ann, David Robert. Instr., Lehigh U., 1952-53; Fine research lectr. Princeton, 1953-55; asst. prof. U. Conn., 1955-56; mem. faculty Wayne State U., 1956-61, asso. prof. math., 1957- 60, chmn. dept., 1860-61; head div. math. sci. Purdue U., 1961-62, dean Sch. Sci., 1962-, prof. math., 1961-; math. cons. to industry, 1952-. Served with AUS, 1943-46. Mem. Am. Math. Soc., Am. Math. Assn., Am. Soc. Engring. Edn., Am. Assn. U. Profs., A.A.A.S. Contbr. articles profl. jours. Office: Purdue Univ Lafayette IN 47907

HAAS, FREDERICK PETER, corp. exec.; b. Yonkers, N.Y., Oct. 16, 1911; s. John George and Margaret Mary (McDevitt) H.; grad. Phillips Acad., Andover, Mass., 1931; B.A., Yale, 1935, LL.B., 1938; m. Mary Helen Parke, Feb. 8, 1941; children—Susanne Phyfe (Mrs. Bruce W. Harned), Margaret McDevitt, Harriet Parke. Admitted to N.Y. bar, 1939; asso. firm Webster & Garside, N.Y.C., 1938-46; partner firm Webster, Sheffied, Fleischmann, Hitchcock & Chrystie, and predecessors, N.Y.C., 1946-65; gen. counsel, dir. Liggett & Myers Inc., N.Y.C., 1965—, v.p., 1967—; dir. Paddington Corp., N.Y.C., Austin-Nichols, N.Y.C., Nat. Oats Co., Inc., Brite Industries, Inc., Earl Grissmer Co., Inc. Served to lt. USNR, 1943-46. Fellow Am. Coll. Trial Lawyers; mem. Am., N.Y. State bar assns., Assn. Bar City N.Y. (sec. 1959-61). Clubs: University (N.Y.C.); Tokeneke (Darien). Home: 137 Raymond St Darien CT 06820 Office: 630 Fifth Av New York City NY 10020

HAAS, GEORGE AARON, lawyer; b. N.Y.C., July 6, 1919; s. Herman Joseph and Violt (Cowen) H.; A.B., Princeton, 1940; LL.B., Yale, 1947; m. Miriam Durkin, Aug. 1942; children—Thomas Leonard, Karen Ann (Mrs. Michael Davenport), James G.D. Admitted to Ga. bar, 1947, since practiced in Atlanta; partner Dunaway, Shelfer, Haas & Newberry and predecessor firms, 1947—. Sec., dir. Suburban Investments, Inc., Lucerne Corp., East Freeway Corp., Crescent View Corp., Mountain View Corp., Lake Placid Corp., Parker Products, Inc. Mem. hosp. and health div. Atlanta Community Council, 1962-68; mem. tech. assistance com., del. White House Conf. on Children and Youth, 1970; state trustee from Ga., Nat. Easter Seal Soc. for Crippled Children and Adults, 1959-65, mem. exec. com., 1961-65, v.p., 1963-65, 1st v.p., 1965-66, mem. ho. of dels., 1965—, bd. dirs., 1965- -, chmn. formula rev. bd., mem. relations and standards rev. com., 1967- 69, pres., 1969—; trustee Ga. Easter Seal Soc. for Crippled Children and Adults, 1955—, sec., 1957-58, pres., 1959-61, chmn. ho. of dels., 1967—. Bd. dirs. Fulton-DeKalb chpt. Nat. Found.; mem. med. adv. bd. Ga. chpt. Am. Phys. Therapy Assn. Served to capt., F.A., AUS, World War II. Mem. Am., Ga., Atlanta bar assns., Lawyers Club Atlanta, Atlanta C. of C. (past chmn. health com.). Kiwanian. Club: Standard (past sec., dir.) (Atlanta). Home: 2860 Ridgewood Circle NW Atlanta GA 30327 Office: 90 Fairlie St NW Atlanta GA 30303

HAAS, HAROLD, ch. ofcl.; b. Union City, N.J., Nov. 9, 1917; s. Joseph August and Magdalena (Bonin) H.; student U. Jena (Germany), 1938, U. Oslo (Norway), 1947; A.B., Wagner Coll., Staten Island, N.Y., 1939, D.D., 1958; M.A., U. Pa., 1942; Ph.D., Drew U., 1952; m. Evelyn Johnsen, May 23, 1942; childrenMarilyn Susan, Carolyn Sandra (Mrs. Paul E. Henry, Jr.). Ordained to ministry Lutheran Ch., 1942; pastor in Rochester, N.Y., Linden, N.J. and Jersey City, 1942-57; exec. sec. bd. social missions United Luth. Ch. Am., 1957-62, bd. social ministry, 1963-66; dean of coll. Wagner Coll., 1966-70; exec. sec. divs. of mission and welfare services Luth. Council in U.S.A., 1971—, Mem. gen. bd. Nat. Council Chs., 1956-65; rep. to Luth. Council U.S.A., 1967—; mem. bd. world missions Luth. Ch. Am., 1968-70; del. and visitor Luth. World Fedn. assemblies, Sweden, 1947, Germany, 1952, U.S., 1957, Finland, 1963; del. numerous confs. Nat. Council Chs. Mem. nat. bd. Nat. Conf. Social Welfare, 1963-66. Author: Marriage, 1960; also articles, chpts. in books. Home: 21 Lakeland Rd Staten Island, NY 10314.

HAAS, HOWARD GREEN, bedding mfr.; b. Chgo., Apr. 14, 1924; s. Adolph and Marie (Green) H.; student U. Chgo., 1942; B.B.A., U. Mich., 1948; m. Carolyn Werbner, June 4, 1949; children—Jody, Jonathan. Promotion dir. Esquire, Inc., Chgo., 1949-50; advt. mgr. Mitchell Mfg. Co., Chgo., 1950-52, v.p. advt., 1952-56, v.p. sales, 1956-58; sales mgr. Sealy, Inc., Chgo., 1959-60, v.p. marketing, 1960-65, exec. v.p., 1965-67, pres., 1967—; exec. v.p. Ind. Spring Corp., 1967; pres. Sealy Sleep Products, Ltd. (Toronto), 1967; pres. Sealy Spring Corp., 1970; dir., exec. com. Old Equity Life Ins. Co. Gov. Am. Furniture Mart. Mem. nominating com. Glencoe Sch. Bd. Trustee Haas Family Charitable Trust; mem. parents adv. com. U. Rochester. Served to 1st lt., USAAF, 1943-45; ETO. Decorated Air Medal with 3 oak leaf clusters. Mem. Nat. Assn. Bedding Mfrs. (trustee, exec. com.), Art Inst. Chgo., Soc. Contemporary Art. Democrat. Jewish religion. Mason (Shriner). Club: Birchwood Tennis (Highland Park, Ill.). Office: 666 N Lake Shore Dr Chicago IL 60611

HAAS, JOHN CHARLES, company exec.; b. Haverford, Pa., May 22, 1918; s. Otto and Phoebe (Waterman) H.; student Episcopal Acad., 1928-36; A.B., Amherst Coll., 1940; M.S., Mass. Inst. Tech., 1942. Various positions with Rohm & Haas Co., Phila., 1942—, dir., 1948—, vice chmn. bd., 1959—, exec. v.p. and head adminstrn. div., 1962—. Lt. USNR, 1942-46. Mem. Am. Chem. Soc., Am. Inst. Chem. Engrs. Home: 330 Spring Mill Rd Villanova PA 19085 Office: care Rohm & Haas Co Philadelphia PA 19106

HAAS, JOSEPH MARSHALL, oil co. exec.; b. Alexandria, La., June 21, 1927; s. Samuel and Lulu Susan (Haupt) H.; B.Mech. Engring., Ga. Inst. Tech., 1949; m. Mary Louise Nance, June 4, 1949 (dec. Jan. 1950); 1 son, Samuel Douglas; m. 2d, Marion Barker, Apr. 9, 1954; children—Joseph Marshall, Suzanne M., Thomas B., Katherine L. With Gen. Am. Oil Co., Dallas, 1949—, asst. v.p. prodn. and engring., 1957-60, v.p. engring., 1960—; v.p., dir. Haas Investment Co., Haas Land Co., La. Central Land and Improvement Co.; pres., dir. Avoyelles Wholesale Grocery Co., Ltd. Mem. nat. adv. bd. Ga. Inst. Tech., 1968—. Served with USNR, 1945-46. Mem. Am. Petroleum Inst., Am. Inst. Mining and Metall. Engrs., Ind. Petroleum Assn. Am. (chmn. productive capacity com.), Tau Beta Pi, Sigma Chi, Pi Tau Sigma. Methodist. Mason (32, Shriner). Clubs: Northwood; Texas; Engineers; North Texas Georgia Tech Club (past president, sec.). Home: 6830 Orchid Lane Dallas TX 75230 Office: Meadows Bldg Dallas TX 75206

HAAS, LEONARD CLARENCE, univ. pres.; b. Eau Claire, Wis., Feb. 17, 1915; s. Lee Leon and Laura (Brown) H.; B.E., Wis. State Coll., Eau Claire, 1935; M.A. in Philosophy, U. Wis., 1938: student Columbia, 1939, U. So. Cal., 1940; Ph.D., U. Minn., 1954; LL.D., St. Olaf Coll., Northfield, Minn., 1968; m. Dorellen Marie Lambert, Mar. 31, 1941; childrenKaren Marie, Kristine Kay. Tchr. elementary sch., Watertown, S.D., 1935-37; grad. asst. history U. Wis., 1937-38; dir. guidance, faculty Wausau (Wis.) Sr. High Sch., 1938-41; faculty Inst. Hist. and Polit. Sci., Wis. State U., Eau Claire, 1941-44, 46-48, dir. tchr. tng. and placement, 1944-46, dean of instrn., registrar, 1948-59, pres., 1959—. Dir. Am. Nat. Bank. Vice pres. Eau Claire City Council, 1949-55, pres., 1955-57. Bd. dirs. Eau Claire Community Chest, United Cerebral Palsy; trustee Eau Claire Pub. Library; adv. council Luther Hosp.; bd. dirs. Bd. of College Edn. of Am. Lutheran Ch.; com. div. coll. and univ. work Nat. Lutheran Council; chmn. Council Presidents Wis. State Univs. Recipient Luth. layman's award, 1957; Kiwanis Achievement award for civic service, 1957. Mem. Wis. League Municipalities (dist. v.p. 1954), N.E.A., Wis. Com. Gen. Edn. (chmn. 1956), Wis. Assn. Higher Edn. (pres. 1968), Am. Assn. Coll. Registrars, Hesperia Lit. Soc., Phi Kappa Phi, Phi Delta Kappa, Kappa Delta Pi, Pi Kappa Delta. Lutheran (bd. edn.). Club: Kiwanis (pres. Eau Claire 1952; lt. gov. 1952). Home: 5985 North Shore Dr Eau Claire WI 54701

HAAS, LESTER CARL, architect; b. Shreveport, La., Apr. 9, 1913; s. Jacob and Hanna (Kahn) H.; B.A., Johns Hopkins, 1933; B.Arch., U. Pa., 1936; postgrad. Ecole Des Beaux-Arts, N.Y.C., 1936-37; diplome Fontainebleau, France, 1939; student Am. Acad., Rome, Italy, 1940; m. Niki Kal, Nov. 1, 1942; children—Dale Frances, Catherine Kal (Mrs. Fred Donald Youngswick). Archtl. apprentice W. Pope Barney, Phila., 1936-39; architect Robert & Co., 1940-41; practice arch. in Shreveport, 1946-65; partner Haas & Massey & Assos., architects, Shreveport, 1966—. Pres. Travelers Aid, 1951, Childrens Service Bur., 1952, Courtyard Players Civic Theatre, 1954, A.R.C., 1963-65, Nat. Conf. Christians and Jews, 1965-69 (nat. bd. 1970-73), St. Vincent Acad. Parents Club, 1966-67, Lyric Ball, 1967; v.p. Caddo-Bossier Assn. Retarded Children, 1957, United Fund, 1963-67, Caddo Found. Exceptional Children, 1967—; adv. bd. Congregation Daughters of the Cross, 1965-69 (all Shreveport). Served from ensign to lt., USNR, 1942-45; Recipient Merit award 2d Internat. Lighting Exposition, 1947; John Stewardson Travelling scholar architecture, 1939. Fellow A.I.A. (pres. N.La. chpt. 1955, exec. com. Gulf States regional council 1956); mem. Constrn. Specifications Inst. (pres. Shreveport chpt. 1970-71), La. Architects Assn., Shreveport Jr. (past v.p.), Shreveport (past officer) chambers commerce, Am. Legion, D.A.V., Tau Sigma Delta. Jewish religion (pres. congregation 1967, 68). Clubs: Petroleum, Downtown (founder, past v.p.), Centime (past pres.) (Shreveport). Co-author weekly column Ark-La-Tecture, 1967—. Principal works include Pioneer Bank and Trust Co., Shreveport main office and 7 br. banks, 1948-70; KTBS offices, radio and TV studios, Shreveport, 1948-66; Caddo Sch. Exceptional Children, Shreveport, 1956; La Sands Western Hills Motel, Bossier City, La., 1957; St. Pius X Sch., convent and sanctuary alterations, N. Shreveport 1962; Barksdale Officer Club, Barksdale AFB, La., 1965; Northwestern State U. at Shreveport, 1966; Middle Creek Elementary Sch., Many, La., 1969; C-Bare Adult Workshop, Shreveport, 1970; Adminstrv. Center, Caddo Parish Sch. Bd., Shreveport, 1971. Home: 1031 Dudley Dr Shreveport LA 71104 Office: Haas & Massey 1400 Line Av Shreveport LA 71101

HAAS, MARY ROSAMOND, linguist, educator; b. Richmond, Ind., Jan. 23, 1910; d. Robert J. and Leona (Crowe) Haas; A.B., Earlham Coll., 1930; student U. Chgo., 1930- 31; Ph.D., Yale, 1935; divorced. Fellow Am. Council Learned Socs., 1941- 43, 44-46; lectr. U. Cal. at Berkeley, 1942-44, 46-47, asst. prof., 1947- 53, asso. prof., 1953-57, prof., 1957-, acting chmn. dept. linguistics, 1956-57, chmn., 1958-64, faculty research lecturer, 1964-65; also program coordinator Survey California Indian Langs., 1964—; vis. prof Summer Inst. Linguistics, U. Alberta, 1967; Linguistic Soc. Am. prof. Linguistic Inst., Ohio State U., summer 1970. Fellow, Center for Advanced Study Behavioral Scis., Stanford, 1967-68. Guggenheim fellow, 1964-65; senior fellow National Endowment for the Humanities, 1967-68. Mem. Linguistic Soc. Am. (v.p. 1956, pres. 1963), Linguistic Circle of N.Y. Ethnohistory Conf., Am. Anthrop. Assn., Am. Folklore Soc., Am. Oriental Society. Author: Tunica, 1941; (with Heng R. Subhanka) Spoken Thai, 2 vols., 1946-48: Tunica Texts, 1949; Tunica Dictionary, 1953; Thai Reader, 1954; Thai Vocabulary, 1955; Thai System of Writing, 1956; Thai- English Student's Dictionary, 1964; The Prehistory of Languages, 1969. Home: 1065 Keith Av Berkeley, CA 94708.

HAAS, MERRILL WILBER, geologist, oil co. exec.; b. Albert, Kan., July 9, 1910; s. Frederick William and Ella (Keller) H.; student Kan. U., 1928-31; B.A. in Geology, U. Mich., 1932; postgrad. Harvard, 1932-33; m. Maria Lara, June 10, 1944; childrenMariella, Merrill Wilber, Maria Cecilia, Frederick Harold. Paleontologist, Humble Oil & Refining Co., Houston, 1933-34. Lago Petroleum Corp., 1934-38; div. geologist Standard Oil Co., Venezuela, 1938-49, area geologist, N.J., 1949-59; with Carter Oil Co., Tulsa, 1950-, successively chief geologist exploration mgr., dir., v.p., 1957-; v.p. Humble Oil & Refining Co., Houston, 1960-. Recipient Erasmus Haworth Distinguished Alumni award U. Kan., 1961, Distinguished Service citation, 1966. Fellow Geol. Society America; member of Am. Assn. Petroleum Geologists, Tulsa Geol. Soc., Am. Petroleum Inst., Paleontol. Research Inst., Mid-Continent Oil and Gas Assn., Houston Geological Soc., Texas Gulf Coast Historical Society, Sigma Gamma Epsilon, Acacia. Methodist. Mason. Club: Petroleum. Home: 10910 Wickwild St Houston, TX 77024. Office: Humble Oil & Refining Co Humble Bldg Houston TX 77001

HAAS, PAUL RAYMOND, co. exec.; b. Kingston, N.Y., Mar. 10, 1915; s. Frederick J. and Amanda (Lange) H.; A.B., Rider Coll., Trenton, 1934; postgrad. U. Tex., 1939; m. Mary F. Diedrick Aug. 30, 1936; children—Rheta Marie, Raymond Paul, Rene Marie. Accountant, Arthur Andersen & Co., C.P.A.'s, N.Y.C. and Houston, 1934-41; with La Gloria Oil & Gas Co. (now subsidiary Tex. Eastern Transmission Corp.), Corpus Christi, Tex., 1941- 59, v.p., treas., dir., 1947-59; adminstrv. v.p. Tex. Eastern Transmission Corp., Houston, 1958-59; pres., chmn. bd. Prado Oil & Gas Co., 1959-66, Wiltex Corp., 1950-65, Garland Co., 1956-65, Citronelle Oil & Gas Co., 1967-69, Corpus Christi Leaseholds, Inc., 1968—, Corpus Christi Oil and Gas Co., 1968—, Metalsales Corp., 1970—; 1961—; dir. Corpus Christi Savs. & Loan Assn., Guaranty Nat. Bank and Trust Co.; exec. com., dir. Kaneb Pipe Line Co., Am. Nat. Ins. Co.; ind. oil and gas operator, 1959—. Trustee Corpus Christi Ind. Sch. Dist., 1951-58, pres., 1956-58; mem. Tex. Bd. Edn., 1962—, Gov.'s Com. Edn., 1966-69. Trustee Paul and Mary Haas Found., 1954—, Robert T. Wilson Found., 1954—, Rider Coll., 1959-67, Moody Found., 1966—, Found. Center, 1970—, Council on Founds., 1970—, C.P.A., Tex. Presbyn. (elder). Home 36 Hewit Dr Corpus Christi TX 78404 Office: Driscoll Bldg Corpus Christi TX 77701

HAAS, PETER EDGAR, mfr.; b. San Francisco, Dec. 20, 1918; s. Walter A. and Elise (Stern) H.; student Deerfield Acad., 1935-36; A.B., U. Cal., 1940; postgrad. Harvard, 1943; m. Josephine Baum, Feb. 1, 1945; children—Peter E., Michael Stern, Margaret Elizabeth. Asst. prodn. mgr. Levi Strauss & Co., San Francisco, 1946-51, v.p., dir., 1951-58, exec. v.p., 1958-71, pres., 1971—; chmn. bd. dirs. Great Western Garment Co. (Edmonton, Alta.); dir. Crocker-Citizens Nat. Bank, Fibreboard Corp. Vice pres. Jewish Welfare Fedn.; mem. civilian adv. com. Presidio of San Francisco. Named a leader of tomorrow Time mag., 1953. Mem. Cal. Acad. Scis. (treas.), Cal. Alumni Fedn. (trustee). Republican. Jewish religion. Home: 313 Maple St San Francisco CA 94115 Office: 98 Battery St San Francisco CA 94106

HAAS, ROBERT GREEN, advt. exec.; b. Chgo., Sept. 14, 1921; s. Adolph R. and Marie (Green) H.; student U. Ill., 1940-41, Western Mich. U., 1944-45; m. Carolyn Buhai, June 29, 1947; children—Andrew Robert, Mari Beth, Betsy Ann, Thomas Michael, Karen Sue. Pres. Robert Haas Advt., 1960-63, Bronner & Haas Advt., 1963-67; exec. v.p. Gray-North Advt. Agy., Chgo. 1967- -; dir. Barnaby's Inc. Served with USNR, 1942-46. Mason. Home: 280 Sylvan Rd Glencoe IL 60022 Office: Merchandise Mart Chicago IL 60654

HAAS, RUTH ALICE, coll. pres.; b. Syracuse, N.Y., Mar. 30, 1903; d. Frederick W. and Mary E. (Marra) Haas; A.B., Syracuse U., 1924, B.S., 1925, M.A., 1928, LL.D., 1946; grad. student Yale, 1933-35; Ed.D., R.I. Coll. Edn. Tchr. history and civics Watertown (N.Y.) High Sch., 1924-27; instr. polit. sci. Maxwell Sch. Citizenship, Syracuse U., 1927-31; asst. personnel dept., 1928-31; dean Western Conn. State Coll., 1931-46, pres., 1946-. Mem. Com. on Cooperation with Fed. Authorities in Matters Pertaining to higher edn. Bd. dirs. Danbury (Conn.) Library; trustee Danbury Hosp. Mem. Eastern States Assn. Profl. Schs. for Tchrs. (pres. 1947), New Eng. Assn. Tchrs. Colls. (pres. 1949), Conn. Council Higher Edn. (pres. 1959-), Am. Assn. Univ. Women, N.E.A., Conn. Edn. Assn., Kappa Delta Pi, Alpha Kappa Delta, Delta Kappa Gamma. Address: Western Conn State Coll Danbury CT 06810

HAAS, VINTON BENJAMIN, Jr., educator; b. Terre Haute, Ind., Aug. 30, 1923; s. Vinton Benjamin and Mayme Catherine (Hartzler) H.; B.S., Rose Poly. Inst., 1943: M.S., Mass. Inst. Tech., 1949, Sc.D., 1956; m. Jeanne Reak, Mar. 25, 1944; children—Catherine Elizabeth (Mrs. David Francis Bean), Vinton Benjamin III, Douglas Francis, Marjorie Ellen. Test engr. Gen. Electric Co., 1946-47; instr. Mass. Inst. Tech., 1947-49, 53-56; asst. prof. N.D. State Coll., 1949-50; asst. prof. U. Conn., 1950-53, asso. prof., 1956, prof., 1957—, head elec. engring. dept., 1968—; dir. research project IBM Corp., 1961-63. Served with C.E. AUS, 1943-46. Mem. I.E.E.E., Am. Soc. Engring. Edn., Sigma Xi, Tau Beta Pi, Eta Kappa Nu. Home: 1 Storrs Heights Rd Storrs CT 06268

HAAS, WALTER A., business exec; b. San Francisco, 1889; s. Abraham and Fannie (Koshland) H.; B.L., U. Cal., 1910; m. Elise Stern, Oct. 18, 1914; childrenWalter A., Peter, Rhoda (Mrs. R. N. Goldman). Pres., dir. Levi Strauss & Co., San Francisco, 1928-56, chmn., dir., 1956-70, hon. chmn. bd., dir., 1970—; pres. Iris Securities Co., 1927—; pres. Levi Strauss Realty Co.; dir. Pacific Intermountain Express Co., Pacific Gas & Electric Co. Mem. adv. council U. Cal. Sch. Bus. Adminstrn. Former pres. San Francisco C. of C., San Francisco War Chest; former dir., mem. exec. com. World Affairs Council, San Francisco Federated Fund; former v.p. Mt. Zion Hosp.; trustee Mills Coll.; past pres. Jewish Welfare Federation; past pres. Recreation and Park Commn., City and County of San Francisco; member Blyth-Zellerbach Com. Served as 2d lt. F.A., World War I. Republican. Jewish religion. Clubs: Family, Concordia-Argonaut, Stock Exchange (San Francisco); St. Francis Yacht; Bankers (San Francisco). Home: 2100 Pacific Av San Francisco CA 94115 Office: 98 Battery St San Francisco CA 94111

HAAS, WALTER A., Jr., business exec.; b. San Francisco, Jan. 24, 1916; s. Walter A. and Elise (Stern) H.; A.B., U. Cal., 1937; M.B.A., Harvard; m. Evelyn Danzig, Mar. 16, 1940; children—Robert Douglas, Elizabeth Jane, Walter Jerome. Personnel dir. Levi Strauss & Co., 1946-52, v.p., dir., 1952-58, pres., dir., 1958-71, chmn. bd., chief exec. officer, 1971—; dir. Bank of Am., Pacific Tel. & Tel. Co. Bd. dirs. Mt. Zion Hosp. Named outstanding young man of the year San Francisco Jr. C. of C., 1951; Distinguished Achievement award Mfrs. and Wholesalers Assn. San Francisco, 1951; named leader of tomorrow Time mag., 1953. Mem. Nat. Alliance Businessmen (dir., region chmn.). Home: 2666 Broadway San Francisco CA 94115 Office: 98 Battery St San Francisco CA 94111

HAAS, WARREN JAMES, librarian; b. Racine, Wis., Mar. 22, 1924; s. Samson Henry and Laura (Jacobson) H.; A.B., Wabash (Ind.) Coll., 1948; B.L.S., U. Wis., 1950; m. Peggy Anne Tinker, June 14, 1947; childrenAnne Bruington, Warren James, William Henry. Asst. librarian Racine Pub. Library, 1950-52, Johns Hopkins, 1952-59; cons. Council Higher Ednl. Instns. in N.Y.C., 1959-60; asso. librarian Columbia, 1961-66, dir. libraries, 1970—; dir. libraries U. Pa., 1966-69; cons. on library bldgs. Bd. dirs. Assn. Research Libraries, 1967—, pres., 1970. Served with USAAF, 1943-46. Mem. A.L.A. Club: Grolier (N.Y.C.).

HAAS, WILLIAM PAUL, coll. pres.; b. Newark, May 31, 1927; s. Joseph J. and Elizabeth (Ryan) H.; A.B., Providence Coll., 1948; S.T.L., Pontifical Inst., Washington, 1954; Ph.D., U. Fribourg (Switzerland), 1962; D.B.A. (hon.), Bryant Coll., Providence, 1966; LL.D., U. R.I., 1967, Brown U., 1969; D.D., Conn. Wesleyan U., 1969; D.H.L., R.I. Coll., 1970. Ordained as priest Roman Cath. Ch., 1953; prof. theology and philosophy Emmanuel Coll., Boston, 1954-60; prof. philosophy Providence Coll., 1962-63, pres., 1965-71; asso. prof. U. Notre Dame, 1963- 65; inaugurated spl. program religious studies Purdue U., 1963-65; prof. contemporary theology Wabash Coll., Crawfordsville, Ind., 1964-65; Corporator Providence Instn. Savs.; dir. R.I. Hosp. Nat. Bank, Providence, 1968—, Narragansett Electric Co., 1970—. Mem. R.I. Council Arts, 1967—, R.I. Adv. Council State Tech. Services Act 1965, 1967-; mem. commn. learning Assn. Am. Colls., 1966-69; adv. council extension and continuing edn. Dept. Health, Edn. and Welfare, 1966-; mem. commn. humanities in schs. Nat. Found. on Arts and the Humanities, 1967—. Bd. dirs. R.I. Philharmonic Orch., R.I. Found. Repertory Theatre, R.I. Urban Coalition, Packard Manse (center ecumenical studies), 1965-67; trustee John R. Kennedy Meml. Fund R.I., 1966—, New Eng. Colls. Fund, 1970—; mem. corp. Butler Hosp., Providence, 1966—; bd. dirs. United Fund R.I., 1968— chmn. R.I. com. Rhodes Scholarship Trust, 1969, mem., 1970. Mem. Am. Soc. Aesthetics, Nat. Cath. Edn. Assn. (exec. com. coll. and univ. dept. 1970—). Clubs: British Empire, University, Art (Providence). Author: The Conception of Law and the Unity of Peirce's Philosophy, 1964. The Contemporary Arts, 1965; also articles. Address: Providence Coll Providence, RI 02918.

HAASE, CARL ALVIN, ins. co. exec.; b. Mpls., June 19, 1915; s. Alvin and Helen (Peterson) H.; B.B.A., U. Minn., 1938; postgrad. U. Man., 1948-50; m. Patricia Mary Graff, Nov. 15, 1944; 1 dau., Mary (Mrs. Mokhtar Abdoli Namvar). Asst. actuary N. Am. Life & Casualty Co., Mpls., 1937-48; v.p. Nelson & Warren, Consulting Actuaries, Kansas City, (Mo.), 1950-58; chief actuary Investors Syndicate Life Ins. & Annuity Co., Mpls., 1958-70, pres., 1970—; v.p. ins. operations Investors Diversified Services, Inc., Mpls., 1970—. Served with USAAF, 1942-46. Fellow Soc. Actuaries; mem. Am. Acad. Actuaries (charter), Phi Sigma Kappa. Home: 5950 Wolfberry Lane Minneapolis MN 55422 Office: 8th St and Marquette Av Minneapolis MN 55402

HAASE, MILTON C., banker; b. Waupun, Wis., Nov. 28, 1916; s. August J. and Lena Wilhelmina (Hacker) H.; B.A., Lawrence U., 1937; postgrad. Stonier Grad. Sch. Banking, Rutgers U., 1960; grad. Am. Inst. Banking; m. Mary Elizabeth Mills Minter Thomson, June 18, 1938; children—Ashley Thomson, Milton Craig. With 1st Nat. Bank Chgo., 1937—, v.p., head comml. loan div. K, 1962—. Mem. president's council Bus. Assos., Elmhurst Coll. Mem. I.E.E.E., Am. Inst. Banking, Chgo. Assn. Commerce and Industry, Chgo. Research and Devel. Council, Robert Morris Assos., Nat. Planning Assn., Newcomen Soc. N.Am., Phi Gamma Delta. Clubs: Barrington Hills; University, Bankers, Mid- America (Chgo.). Home: 505 N Lake Shore Dr Chicago IL 60611 Office: One First Nat Plaza Chicago IL 60670

HAASE, PAUL, association exec.; b. N.Y.C., July 11, 1907; s. Paul F. and Betty (Fleisher) H.; B.S., N.Y. U., 1930; m. Corinne Trost, June 27, 1934; childrenLinda Corinne, Norman Lewis. Reporter N.Y. World, 1929-31; mng. editor Credit and Finance Mgmt., 1931-33; with Nat. Assn. Credit Men, 1931-43, dir. pub. relations, 1933-43; mng. editor The Controller, asst. mng. dir. Controllers Inst. Am., 1943-53, mng. dir., 1953-62; mng. dir. Financial Exec. Inst., 1962-67, exec v.p., 1967-69, cons. to pres. 1969—. Pres. Conf. on Assn. Publicity, 1942. Mem. Nat. Assn. Pub. Relations Counsel (dir. 1943-46, treas. 1944-47), Pub. Relations Soc. Am. (treas. 1953). Contbr. articles mags. Home 58 E River Rd Rumson NJ 07760 Office: 50 W 44th St New York City NY 10036

HAASE, RICHARD HENRY, educator; b. Cleve., Feb. 27, 1924; s. Harold M. and Fern (Dyer) H.; B.S. in Aero.Engring., Purdue U., 1945; M.B.A., Tulane U., 1949; Ph.D., U. Cal. at Los Angeles; m. Kathleen I. Deane, June 9, 1951; children-Deane D., David R., Diane M. With CONVAIR Corp., 1946-47, Gen. Electric Co., 1947-51, 65-67; lectr. engring., asst. head engring. extension U. Cal. at Los Angeles, 1951-61; mem. tech. staff RAND Corp., 1961-65; prof. statistics, head finance and statistics dept. Drexel U., 1967—; cons. in field. Served with USNR, 1943-46. Faculty fellow NSF, 1959-60. Mem. Sigma Xi, Pi Tau Sigma, Tau Beta Pi, Alpha Kappa Psi. Home: 326 Lenape Dr Berwyn PA 19312 Office: Drexel Univ Philadelphia PA 19104

HAASE, WALTER, assn. exec.; b. Appleton, Wis., Jan. 27, 1920; s. Walter Godfrey and Elisabeth (Sauer) H.; student Northwestern Coll., Watertown, Wis., 1937- 38; B.B.A., U. Minn., 1941; m. Evelyn Hope Stoll, Aug. 31, 1946; childrenGretchen Elizabeth, David, Amy. Auditor Touche, Niven & Co., Mpls., 1941-42; financial analyst Equity Corp. and affiliates, N.Y.C., 1946-49; with Am. Assn. Advt. Agencies, Inc., N.Y.C., 1949—, exec. sec.- treas., 1955—. Served with Ordnance Corps, AUS, 1942-46. Mem. Beta Gamma Sigma. Lutheran. Home: 62 Tunstall Rd Scarsdale NY 10583 Office: 200 Park Av New York City NY 10017

HAASS, ERWIN HERMAN, lawyer; b. Detroit, Feb. 18 1904; s Otto C. and Minnie (Peters) H.; A.B., U. Mich., 1925, J.D., 1927; m. Virginia Allmand, Oct. 5, 1937; childrenFrederick, Robert, Stephen, Susan, Sandra. Admitted to Mich. bar, 1927; asso. Race, Haass & Allen, Detroit, 1927-30; partner Hitt, Brewer & Haass, Detroit, 1930-41, McGraw, Haass, Selander, Farmes & Lawrence, and predecessor firms, Detroit, 1941-, also dir.; sec. Ross Roy, Inc., Detroit; dir. First Nat. Bank North Broward County, Lighthouse Point, Fla., City Nat. Bank, Detroit, Pettibone Mulliken Corp., Chgo. Served to lt. col. AUS, 1942-46. Clubs: Country, Detroit, Boat, Detroit Athletic, Grosse Pointe (Detroit); Royal Palm Yacht and Country (Boca Raton, Fla.). Home: 84 Stephens Rd Grosse Pointe Farms MI 48236; also 991 Hillsboro Beach Pompano Beach FL 33062 Office: Guardian Bldg Detroit MI 48226

HAASS, IRVING B., investment adviser; b. N.Y.C., Aug. 16, 1917; s. Nathan and Beatrice (Mauss) H.; B.A., Bklyn. Coll., 1938; m. Marcella Rosenthal, July 15, 1943; childrenBarbara, Richard. Instr. Bklyn. Coll., 1947-49; partner David J. Greene & Co., mems. N.Y. Stock Exchange; dir. Am. Color-type, 1957-58, Rapid American Corp., 1958-59, Brown Co., Berlin, N.H., 1960—. Served to sgt. AUS, 1942-46. Mem. N.Y. Soc. Security Analysts, Bklyn. Coll. Alumni Finance Assn. (v.p.). Club: Mill River (N.Y.). Home: 77 Cardinal Dr East Hills NY 11576 Office: 30 Wall St New York City NY 10005

HABA, ALOIS, composer; b. Vizovice, June 21, 1893; ed. Kromeritz Sch., also conservatories Prague, Vienna, Berlin. Prof., Acad. Music Prague, 1945—. Mem. Czechoslovak Acad. Scis. and Arts in Prague, Société Internationale pour la Musique Contemporaine. Composer numerous works including Cesta Zivota, Fantaisie Symphonique; (operas) Matka, Novázeme, Prijd Království tvé. Author books on music. Address: care U druzstva Práce 59 Prague 4 Podolí Czechoslovakia *

HABACH, GEORGE FREDERIC, mech. engr.; b. N.Y.C., Aug. 2, 1907; s. George Frederic and Marie (Veith) H.; M.E., Stevens Inst. Tech., 1929; M.M.E., Bklyn. Poly. Inst., 1936; m. Helen Selma Wislicenus, Oct. 8, 1939; 1 dau., Elizabeth Mary (Mrs. E. M. McCollum). With Worthington Corp. Harrison, N.J., 1929-70, successively engr. design and application centrifugal pumps, product engr. chem. and end suction pumps, chief engr. centrifugal pump dept., mgr. engring. Harrison div., 1929-55, v.p. charge engring., 1955-59, v.p. charge adminstrn., 1959-67, adminstrv. v.p., 1967-68, pres., 1968-70, also dir.; v.p. adminstrn. Studebaker-Worthington, Inc., 1968-70; v.p. mgmt. div. Creative Logic Corp., Paramus, N.J., 1971—; instr. mech. engring. dept. Bklyn. Poly. Inst. 1937-41, adj. prof., 1941- 52. Treas. Glen Ridge Taxpayer Assn., 1953-56, dir., 1956-61; chmn. alumni fund council Bklyn. Poly. Inst., 1958-61, alumni rep. corporate bd. dirs., pres. alumni assn., 1965-66; mem. adv. com. mech. engring. Newark Coll. Engring. Registered profl. engr., N.J. Fellow Standards Engrs. Soc.; mem. Nat. Soc. Profl. Engrs., Am. Soc. M.E. (standardization com., chmn. exec. com. gen. engring. dept., dir. 1965—; v.p. gen. engring. policy bd., exec. com., chmn. tech. activities com.; pres. 1968-69), N.J. C. of C. (citizen com.), Am. Standards Assn. (chmn. sect. com. 1954-61, mem. standard review com. 1969-70), Am. Mgmt. Assn., Alumni Assn. Stevens Inst. Tech. (dir., pres. 1969-70, chmn. long range policy and planning com. 1971—), Pi Tau Sigma, Tau Beta Pi. Home: 20 Cambridge Rd Glen Ridge NJ 07028 Office: Creative Logic Corp Paramus NJ

HABAS, EUGENE J., investment cons.; b. N.Y.C., Oct. 14, 1908; s. Joseph and Celia (Rodstein) H.; student Columbia and N.Y.U., 1927-33; m. Sylvia Seltzer, Feb. 15, 1933; children—Linda B., Wendy A. Engaged in investment business, 1926-65; mgr. research dept. Fenner & Beane, brokers, 1936-41; N.E. regional economist OPA, 1941; with Lehman Corp., 1942-44; sr. v.p. Hugh W. Long & Co., Inc.; v.p. Fundamental Investors, Inc. Diversified Investment Fund, Inc., Diversified Growth Stock Fund, Inc., Westminster Fund, Inc., 1944-62; pres., treas., dir. Mut. Investment Fund, Inc., 1962-64; pres., dir. Mut. Mgmt. Co., Inc., 1962- 64; exec. v.p. Sel-Rex Corp., 1965-69, dir., 1960-70; pres., dir. Meaker Co. 1966-68; mng. dir. Hooker Metal Finishing Internat., 1969; investment/business cons., 1971—. Trustee Maplewood, S. Orange Adult Sch., 1960-68, pres. bd. trustees, 1964-66. Mem. N.Y. Soc. Security Analysts (pres. 1939-40). Club: Harbor View (N.Y.C.). Editor Analysts Jour., 1945-46. Home: 4390 Exeter Dr Sarasota FL 33577

HABBE, DONALD EDWIN, coll. dean; b. Milw., Jan. 20, 1931; s. John Edwin and Anna May (Lewis) H.; B.A., Denison U., 1952; M.S., U. Wis., 1954, Ph.D., 1957; m. Lois Ann Preucil, Dec. 27, 1953; children—Donald, Peter, Susan, Thomas. Fgn. service officer Dept. State, Washington, and Mexico, 1956-59; from asst. prof. to prof. polit. sci. U. S.D., Vermillion, 1959-67, asso. dean Coll. Arts and Scis., 1967-69, dean, 1970—; Rockefeller fellow Fgn. Policy Assn. UN, 1961-62; vis. prof. Grad. Sch. Internat. Studies, U. Denver, 1964-65. Mem. Am. Polit. Sci. Assn., Internat. Studies Assn. Home: 230 S Yale St Vermillion SD 57069

HABBERTON, BENJAMIN GEORGE, lawyer; b. Mt. Carmel, Ill., Sept. 22, 1902; s. William Peck and Helen (Redman) H.; A.B., DePauw U., 1924; LL.B., Harvard, 1931; m. Sarah Turpin, June 15, 1946: children—Alice, Anne. Admitted to Tex. bar, 1933; mem. Dallas law firms, 1933-49; resident atty. Texas Centennial Central Expn., 1935-37; spl. asst. to atty. gen. U.S., 1949-51; dep. commr. Immigration and Naturalization, 1951-54; partner firm Fistere & Habberton, Washington, 1959—; chief legal adv. br. U.S. Mil. Govt. for Germany, 1946-47. Chmn. Com. Am. Ch. of Berlin, Germany, 1947-62; exec. council Episcopal Diocese Washington, 1958-60. Dir. Episcopal Home for Children, Washington, 1954-60. Served as intelligence officer USAAF, 1942-46. Mem. D.C., Tex. bars, Am. Bar Assn. Episcopalian. Clubs: Army and Navy (Washington); Harvard (N.Y.C.). Home: 3103 Hawthorne St Washington DC 20008 Office: 910 17th St Washington DC 20005

HABE, HANS, author; b. Budapest, Hungary, Feb. 12, 1911; s. Imre and Blanca (Marton) H.; student univs. Vienna (Austria) and Heidelberg (Germany), 1929-30; m. Licci Balla, Apr. 5, 1958; children—Anthony Miklos, Marina Elizabeth. Editor-in-chief Der Morgen, Vienna, 1934-36; League of Nations corr. Prager Tagblatt, 1936-39; editor-in-chief various newspapers, including all publs. mil. gov.'s press sect., Germany, 1945-46. Bd. govs. Halfa U. Served to maj. AUS, 1942-46. Decorated Bronze Star with oak leaf cluster; Croix de Guerre (Luxembourg); Fellow Boston U., 1966. Mem. P.E.N. Author of books including: A Thousand Shall Fall, 1941; (novels) Walk in Darkness, 1948; Off Limits, 1957; Ilona, 1960; The Countess, 1962; The Mission, 1966; Christopher and His Father, 1967; The Poisoned Stream, 1969. Address: Casa Acacia Ascona Ticino Switzerland

HABECK, IRWIN JOHN, educator; b. Winona, Minn., May 7, 1904; s. Albert Ernst and Anna (Wenk) H.; A.B., Northwestern Coll., 1924; Luth. Sem., Wauwatosa, Wis., 1927; m. Dorothy Bertha Seefeldt, Aug. 1, 1929; childrenJohn Albert (dec.), Daniel. Ordained ministry Lutheran Ch., 1927; pastor, Minocqua, Wis., 1927-33, Immanuel Ch., Medford, Wis., 1933-40, St. Peter's Ch., Wevauwega, Wisconsin, 1940-50, Bethesda Ch., Milw., 1950-63, Gloria Dei-Bethesda Ch., 1963-66; v.p. Wis. Evang-Luth. Synod, 1947-66; prof. Wis. Luth. Sem., 1966-. Dir. Northwestern Pub. House, Milw. Editorial bd. Wis. Luth. Quar. Contbr. religious publs. Home: 11805 N Seminary Dr Mequon WI 53092

HABER, BERNARD D., mfg. co. exec.; b. N.Y.C., Jan. 29, 1919; s. Julius and Bertha (Silver) H.; B.S. in Aero. Engring., U. Mich., 1940: grad. student Ohio State U., 1946-48; m. Miriam Miller, Mar. 30, 1941; children—Jonathan D., Ruth Phyllis. With N.Am. Rockwell Corp., 1954—, asst. to pres., 1961-63, charge research and engring., 1963-64, v.p. research and engring., 1964—. Mem. adv. council Cal. Assembly Sci. and Tech. 1961—. Served as aero. engr. USAAF, 1940-48, USAF, 1950-54. Fellow Am. Inst. Aero. and Astronautics; mem. Aerospace Industries Assn. Am. (aerospace tech. council), Soc. Automotive Engrs. (exec. com.). Office: 1700 E Imperial Hwy El Segundo CA 90246

HABER, FRANCIS COLIN, educator; b. Flint, Mich., Apr. 21, 1920; s. Arthur and Amelia (Glenfield) H.; student U. Ia., 1940-41; B.A., U. Conn., 1948; M.A., Johns Hopkins, 1951, Ph.D., 1957; m. Ruth M. Owens, 1943 (div.); 1 son, Robert O. Asso. editor Md. Hist. Mag., 1952-53; reference librarian Peabody Inst. Library, 1953-55; editor Md. Hist. mag., librarian, Md. Hist. Soc., Balt., 1955-58; asst. prof. U. Fla., 1958-63, asso. prof., 1963-66; prof. U. Md., College Park, 1966—, chmn. dept. history, 1968—. Served with U.S. Mcht. Marine, 1941-45. Recipient Am. Philos. Soc. grants, 1958-64, Folger fellow, 1962. Mem. History of Sci. Soc., Am. Hist. Assn., Internat. Soc. for Study of Time, Johns Hopkins History of Ideas Club. Club: Cosmos (Washington). Author: Age of the World: Moses to Darwin, 1959; (with others) Forerunners of Darwin, 1959. Contbr. articles profl. jours. Home: 2450 Virginia Av NW Washington DC 20037 Office: Dept History U Md College Park MD 20742

HABER, PHILMORE JOSEPH, lawyer; b. Cleve., May 24, 1895; s. Marcus and Rickie (Lorber) H.; A.B., Western Res. U., 1915; LL.B., Cleve. Law Sch., 1917; m. Constance Mayer, Mar. 14, 1918; children—Richard, James. Admitted to Ohio bar; formerly sr. partner, now of counsel Burke, Haber & Berick. Past vice chmn. Cuyahoga County Mental Health Commn. Past Trustee Mt. Sinai Hosp. Cleve. Mem. Cleve. C. of C., Citizens League, Nat. Conf. Christians and Jews (past co-chmn.). Clubs: Oakwood Country (past trustee), City. Home: 13900 Shaker Blvd Cleveland OH 44120 Office: Central Nat Bank Bldg Cleveland OH 44114

HABER, RALPH NORMAN, educator; b. Lansing, Mich., May 15, 1932; s. William and Fannie (Gallas) H.; B.A., U. Mich., 1953; M.A., Wesleyan U., Middletown, Conn., 1954; Ph.D., Stanford, 1957; Postdoctoral fellow Med. Research Council, Applied Psychology Unit, Cambridge, Eng., 1970-71; m. Ruth Lea Boss, July 24, 1961; children—Sabrina Beth, Rebecca Ann. Research asso. Inst. for Communication Research, Stanford, 1957-58; instr. psychology San Francisco State Coll., 1957-58; asst. prof. psychology Yale, 1958-64; asso. prof. psychology U. Rochester, N.Y., 1964-67, prof. psychology, 1967-70, prof. psychology and visual sci., 1970—, chmn. dept. psychology, 1967-70, mem. Faculty Senate, 1968-70; sec., mem. steering com., 1969-70; vis. scientist Med. Research Council Applied Psychology Unit, Cambridge Eng., 1970-71; chmn., divisional maj. III, Yale, 1959-64; vis. asst. prof. New Sch. for Social Research, 1963; research cons. VA, 1967—; adv. editor for exptl. psychology Holt, Rinehart & Winston Book Pubs., 1969—. Mem. Nat. Acad. Sci.-NRC Com. on Vision, 1970—. Committeeman, 18th Ward, Brighton (N.Y.) Democratic Party, 1967—. Founding mem., trustee Coll. Admission Prep. Program, Rochester. Behavioral Sci. fellow Ford Found., 1953-54. Fellow Am. Psychol. Assn.; mem. Eastern Psychol. Assn., Psychonomics Soc., A.A.A.S., Optical Soc. Am., Sigma Xi, Pi Lambda Phi. Editor: Current Research on Motivation, 1966; Contemporary Theory and Research on Visual Perception, 1968; Information Processing Approaches to Visual Perception, 1969. Contbr. articles profl. jours. Home: 55 Avon Rd Rochester NY 14625

HABER, WILFRED, educator. Chmn. dept. rehab. edn. N.Y. U. Office: Sch Edn NY U Washington Sq New York City NY 10003*

HABER, WILLIAM, educator, economist; b. Rumania, Mar. 6, 1899; s. Leon and Anna (Stern) B.; brought to U.S., 1909; B.A., U. Wis., 1923, M.A., 1926, Ph.D., 1927; grad. work U. Wis. and Harvard, 1924-25; L.H.D. honoris causa, Hebrew Union Coll., 1961, Mich. State U., 1970; Ph.D. (hon.), Hebrew U., Jerusalem, 1971; m. Fannie Gallas, Aug. 31, 1924; children—Ralph, Alan. Labor mgr. Hart, Schaffner & Marx, 1923; instr. econs. U. Wis., 1926-27; asso. prof. econs. Mich. State Coll., 1927-36; prof. econs. U. Mich., 1936—, chmn. dept., 1962-63, dean Coll. Lit., Sci. and Arts, 1963-68, spl. adviser to exec. officers, 1968—. Cons. Social Security Bd., 1939- 45, cons. Nat. Resources Planning Bd., 1940-44, chmn. com. long-range work and relief policy, 1941-44; spl. asst. to dir. Bur. Budget, 1942, mem. conf. post war relief readjustment of civilian and mil. personnel, 1943, chief planning div., 1942; dir. Bur. Program Requirement, War Manpower Commn. 1943, asst. exec. dir. 1944; adviser on manpower to dir. Office War Moblzn. and Reconversion, 1945, cons. 1945- 46; mem. Am. Assn. Social Security (com. post-def. planning), 1941, U.S. Employment Service (tech. bd. on occupational research program), 1940, chmn. Fed. Adv. Council on Employment Security, 1948—, mem. Manpower Cons. Com., Nat. Resources Security Bd., Nat. Def. Agy., 1947- 48; mem. pub. adv. com. Area Redevel. Adminstrn., Dept. Commerce, 1962, mem. regional export expansion council, 1962; panel Am. Arbitrators Assn.; mem. Nat. Academy Arbitrators; mem. Social Science Research Council (com. on econ. security), 1941—; mem. indsl. com. (for paper products, rubber and textiles) Wage and Hour Adminstrn., 1941; mem. Adv. Council on Social Security, 1938-39; cons. on manpower to sec. of labor, and Def. Manpower Adminstrn., Adviser on Jewish affairs to comdr.-in-chief U.S. Forces in Germany and Austria. 1948- 49; mem. Presidents Task Force on Depressed Areas, 1961. Exec. com. Am.-Jewish Com., 1945—; chmn. nat. Hillel commn. B'nai B'rith, 1949-64, hon. chmn., 1964—; pres. Am. ORT Fedn. (rehab. through training), 1951; pres. central bd. World ORT Union, 1955—. Bd. dirs. United Service for New Americans, 1947—. bd. govs. Hebrew U., Jerusalem, 1968—; trustee Brandeis U., 1969—. Recipient John Dewey award League Indsl. Democracy, 1960, John Lendrum Mitchell award indsl. relations U. Wis., 1924; Wertheim fellow for research indsl. relations, Harvard, 1925. Mem. Am. Econ. Assn., Am. Pub. Welfare Assn., Soc. Pub. Adminstrn., Indsl. Relations Research Assn. (pres. 1960). Author: Industrial Relations in the Building Industry, 1930; Unemployment Relief and Economic Security, 1936; The Cost of Financing Unemployment Insurance in Michigan, 1952; Labor Relations and Productivity in the Building Trades (with H. L. Levinson), 1955; co- author: Post War Economic Reconstruction, 1945; The Michigan Economy: Its Potentials and Its Problems, 1960; (with Wilbur J. Cohen) Social Security Program Problems and Policies, 1961; (with others) Michigan in the 1970s, 1965; (with Merrill G. Murray) Unemployment Insurance in the American Economy, 1966. Editor: Readings in Social Security, 1948, Labor in a Changing America, 1966; co-editor: Manpower in the United States. 1954, Contbr. to Survey Graphic, Social Service Rev. Pub. Adminstrn. Rev., Am. Sociol. Rev., others. Home: 530 Hillspur Rd Barton Hills Ann Arbor MI 48105 ☆

HABERL, HERBERT WILLIAM, Jr., accountant; b. E. Orange, N.J., Oct. 25, 1928; s. Herbert William and Mary Elizabeth (Behen) H.; became Canadian citizen, 1942; B. Commerce, Loyola Coll., Montreal, Can., 1953; m. Margaret Ann O'Brien, Dec. 28, 1954; children—Susan Eileen, Herbert William, James Edward, Kevin John, Patrick Joseph, Michael David. With Ernst & Ernst, chartered accountants, 1953—, resident mgr., Vancouver, B.C., Can., 1963—; lectr. extension dept. Loyola Coll., 1958-61. Pres. Shaughnessy Little League, 1970-71. Mem. St. Peter and Paul Sch. Bd., Vancouver, 1965—. Chartered accountant, Que., Man. Mem. Inst. Chartered Accountants B.C. Clubs: Gyro, Point Grey Golf and Country (Vancouver). Home: 1578 W 26th Av Vancouver British Columbia Canada Office: 424-602 W Hastings St Vancouver British Columbia Canada

HABERLER, GOTTFRIED, educator; b. Purkersdorf, Austria, July 20, 1900; s. Franz and Francisca (Mosing) H.; came to U.S., 1936: Dr. rer. pol. U. Vienna, 1923, J.D., 1925; postgrad. U. London, Harvard Univ. and other Am. univs., 1927-29; m. Friedericke Kaan, 1931. Lectr., later prof. econs. and statistics U. Vienna (with interruptions), 1928-36; vis. lectr. econs. and statistics, Harvard U., 1931-32, mem. faculty, 1936—, now prof. internat. trade; expert attached to financial sect. League of Nations, Geneva, 1934-36. With bd. govs. Fed. Res. System, Washington, 1943; chmn. bd. Nat. Bur. Econ. Research, 1956-. Fellow Royal Econ. Soc.; mem. Am. (pres. 1963), Internat. (pres. 1950-53, now hon. pres. econ. assns., Econometric Soc. Author books including Prosperity and Depression, 3d edit., 1942; Quantitative Trade Controls, Their Causes and Nature, 1943. Contbr. to econ. jours. and mags. Home: 2 Mercer Circle Cambridge MA 02138*

HABERLY, LOYD, writer, educator; b. Ellsworth, Ia., Dec. 9, 1896; s. Lewis Benote and Nora (Galligan) H.; student Reed Coll., 1915-18; A.B., Harvard, 1921; M.A. (Rhodes Scholar), Oxford U., 1924; LL.D., Fairleigh Dickinson Univ., 1954; m. Virginia Dean, 1942; 1 son, David Tristram. Organizer, operator Seven Acres Press, Eng., 1925-34; dir. Gregynog Pres., Wales, 1934-36; excavator Notley Abbey, Buckshire, 1933; lectr. Harvard, 1938; staff U. N.H. Writer's Conf., 1940-; asst. prof. Washington U., 1942- 45; asso. prof. vets. coll. U. Mass., 1945-48; prof., chmn. dept. English, Fairleigh Dickinson University, 1948-59, dean of arts and sciences, 1959-66, academic head Wroxton Coll., Banbury, Eng., 1965-68, Distinguished professor of humanities, 1968-. Served with 13th Inf., U.S. Army, World War I; member Mo. Nat. Guard, World War II. Mem. Poetry Society Am. (pres. 1963-68). Author: Collected Poems, 1931; Medieval English Pavingtiles, 1937; Silent Fame, 1945; Pursuit of the Horizon, a Biography of George Catlin, 1948; Highlights, a Book of Verse, 1960. Writer, illustrator, printer, binder of numerous hand-press books, 1926- . Editor: Pliny's Natural History, compacted edit. 1956. Home: 171 Montross Av Rutherford NJ 07070 Office: Grad Center of Fairleigh Dickinson U Wroxton Abbey Banbury England

HABERMAN, ALAN L., food chain store exec.; b. 1929; A.B., Harvard, 1951, M.B.A., 1953; married. Exec. v.p. Hills Supermarkets, Inc., 1960-65; pres. Hills Korvette Supermarkets, div. E.J. Korvette Inc., 1965-66; with First Nat. Stores, Inc., 1966—, exec. v.p., 1967—, also dir. Address: 5 Middlesex Av Somerville MA 02143

HABERMAN, FREDERICK WILLIAM, educator; b. Duquesne, Pa., May 11, 1908; s. Louis Henry and Maude (McLaughlin) H.; A.B., Allegheny Coll., 1930; A.M., U. Wis., 1936; Ph.D., Cornell U., 1947; m. Helen Louise Power, June 16, 1934; childrenFrederick William IV, Ann Marwood (Mrs. Gene L. Armstrong). Tchr., Harborcreek (Pa.) High Sch., 1930-32; instr. Allegheny Coll., 1932-36, asst. prof., 1942-43; instr. Princeton. 1938- 42; faculty U. Wis., 1947-, successively asst. prof., asso. prof., 1949- 52, prof., 1952—, chmn. dept. speech, 1954-70. Mem. bd. edn. Joint dist. 1, towns of Middleton and Madison, Wis., 1951-54. Served to lt. (s.g.) USNR, 1943-46. Mem. Am. Assn. U. Profs., Speech Assn. Am., Central States, Wis. speech assns., Phi Kappa Phi, Delta Sigma Rho, Phi Delta Theta. Author: (with James W. Cleary) Rhetoric and Public Address: A Bibliography, 1947-61, 1964. Contbr. essays profl. jours., books. Home: 5760 Bittersweet Pl Madison, WI 53705.

HABERMAN, PHILIP SANFORD, lawyer, assn. exec.; b. Lodi, Wis., Aug. 11, 1913; s. Reno John and Tressa Mabel (Axon) H.; Ph.B., U. Wis., 1941, LL.B., 1947; m. Ernestine O. Anderson, Aug. 17, 1939; 1 dau., Gail Marie. Admitted to Wis. bar, 1947, since practiced in

Madison; asst. sec. League Wis. Municipalities, 1935-42; exec. sec. Me. Municipal Assn., 1942-43, Wis. Legislative Council, 1947-48; legislative counsel Wis. State Bar Assn., 1949-55, exec. sec., 1948-56, exec. dir., 1957—. Served as lt. (j.g.) Supply Corps, USN, 1943-46. Recipient Reginald Heber Smith award, 1964. Mem. exec. com. Am. Municipal Assn., 1942-43. Mem. Am. Bar Assn. (commn. organized crime 1950-52, mem. council sect. bar activities 1949-54, adv. com. pub. relations 1956, spl. com. on econs. of law practice 1957-64, spl. com. profl. corps. 1964-68), Scribes, Conf. Bar Assn. Secs. (chmn. 1951), Phi Alpha Delta, Artus. Author articles on law enforcement and law office mgmt. Home: 705 Huron Hill Madison WI 53711 Office: 402 W Wilson St Madison WI 53703

HABERMAN, PHILLIP WILLIAM, Jr., lawyer; b. St. Louis, Mar. 30, 1905; s. Phillip William and Blanche (Altheimer) H.; A.B., Princeton, 1926; LL.B., Columbia, 1929; m. Helen Liebman, July 30, 1933; children-Charles, Norma. Admitted to N.Y. bar, 1929; asst. counsel Seabury Investigations, N.Y.C., 1930-32; asst., acting corp. counsel City of N.Y., 1934-37; practice in N.Y.C., 1929—; mem. firm Proskauer, Rose, Goetz & Mendelsohn, 1945—. Chief asst. counsel Rapp ¸ Coudert Legislative Com. to Investigate Communism in N.Y. pub. schs., 1940-42; mem. Temporary State Commn. on Govtl. Activities, N.Y.C., 1960-61; mem. N.Y.C. Charter Revision Commn., 1961; mem., vice chmn. Commn. on State-Local Fiscal Relations, 1962-65. Pres. Mt. Sinai Hosp. Sch. Nursing, 1951-60, now mem. bd. dirs.; v.p., bd. dirs. Legal Aid Soc. N.Y.; treas., trustee, exec. com. Practising Law Inst.; trustee Mt. Sinai Hosp., N.Y.C., Simon's Rock, Great Barrington, Mass. Served with USAAF, 1942-45. Fellow Am. Bar Found., Am. Coll. Trial Lawyers; mem. Assn. Bar City of N.Y. (chmn. exec. com. 1958-59, v.p. 1959-60), Am., N.Y. State bar assns., N.Y. County Lawyers Assn., Am. Arbitration Assn. (dir., mem. exec. com. 1963-69). Clubs: Princeton, Harmonic (N.Y.C.), Campus (Princeton, N.J.); Century Country (Purchase, N.Y.). Home: 1133 Park Av New York NY 10028 Office: 300 Park Av New York NY 10022

HABERMEYER, HOWARD WILLIAM govt. ofcl.; b. Aurora, Ill., Mar. 26, 1915; s. William G. and Marie (Schneider) H.; student pub. schs., Aurora; m. Helen Lorraine Braithwaite, July 2, 1938; childrenHoward William, Kent Leigh. Electrician's helper C.B. & Q. R.R., 1934-35; successively messenger, clk., supr. U.S. R.R. Retirement Bd., 1936-47, asst. bur. dir., 1947-52, dir., 1952-56, chmn., 1956—. Served with AUS, 1944-46. Recipient Arthur S. Flemming award U.S. Jr. C. of C., 1955, scholarship to mgmt. sch. Am. Mgmt. Assn., 1955. Mem. Am. Legion. Lutheran. Moose. Home: 175 Westlawn Av Aurora IL 60506 Office: 844 Rush St Chicago IL 60611

HABETLER, GEORGE JOSEPH, educator, mathematician; b. McKees Rocks, Pa., Oct. 31, 1928; s. Stephen and Mary (Tisenay) H.; B.A. summa cum laude, Duquesne U., 1949; D.Sc., Carnegie Inst. Tech., 1952; m. Clementine S. Williams, July 13, 1953; childrenChristy Susan, Linda Rae, Mark Gregory. Research scientist Knolls Atomic Power Lab., Gen. Electric Co., Schenectady, 1952-64; prof. math. Rensselaer Poly. Inst., Troy, N.Y., 1964—. Mem. Am. Math. Soc., Am. Phys. Soc. Indsl. and Applied Math. Author papers, reports founds. and numerical analysis involved in neutron diffusion problems in reactor theory. Home: Lee Av Rexford NY 12148. Office: Math Dept Rensselaer Poly Inst Troy NY 12180*

HABIB, PHILIP CHARLES, fgn. service officer; b. Bklyn., Feb. 25, 1920; s. Alex and Mary (Spiridon) H.; B.S., U. Ida., 1942; Ph.D., U. Cal. at Berkeley, 1952; m. Marjorie W. Slightam, Aug. 27, 1942; childrenPhyllis A., Susan W. Fgn. service officer, 1949-; 3d sec. Am. embassy, Ottawa, Can., 1949-51; 2d sec. Am. embassy, Wellington, New Zealand, 1952-54; research specialist Dept of State, Washington, 1955-57; consul Am. consulate gen., Port of Spain, Trinidad, 1958-60; fgn. affairs officer Dept. State, 1960-61; counselor for polit. affairs Am. embassy, Seoul, Korea, 1962-65, Saigon, Vietnam, 1965-67; personal rank of minister, 1966-67, personal rank of ambassador, 1969—; dep. asst. sec. State for East Asian and Pacific affairs, 1967-69; mem. U.S. delegation to meetings on Vietnam, Paris, 1968—. Served from pvt. to capt. AUS, 1942-46. Recipient Rockefeller Pub. Service award, 1969. Roman Catholic. Office: Dept State Washington DC 20520

HABIF, DAVID V., surgeon, educator; b. Cin; M.D., Columbia, 1939. Successively intern, asst. resident surgery, resident surgery, attending surgery Presbyn. Hosp., N.Y.C., 1939-47; now prof. surgery Columbia Coll. Phys. and Surg. Served with AUS, 1942-45. Decorated Bronze Star, Presdl. Citation with 2 oak leaf clusters. Diplomate Am. Bd. Surgery. Fellow A.C.S.; mem. A.M.A., Soc. Exptl. Biology and Medicine, Am. Surg. Assn., Soc. Univ. Surgeons, Halsted Soc., Soc. Surgery Alimentary Tract. Address: 622 W 168th St New York City NY 10032

HACAULT, ANTOINE JOSEPH LEON, bishop; b. Bruxelles, Man., Can., Jan. 17, 1926; s. Francois and Irma (Mangin) H.; B.A., U. Man., 1947; theol. student, St. Boniface Maj. Sem., 1947-51; S.T.D., Angelicum U., Rome, 1954. Ordained priest Roman Cath. Ch., 1951; chaplain St. Boniface Sanatorium, 1954; prof. theology St Boniface Maj. Sem., 1954-64; dir. diocesan rev. Les Cloches de Sain Boniface, 1961; personal theologian to archbishop of St. Boniface, also council expert 2d Vatican Ecumenical Council, 1962-64; bishop titular of Media, aux. bishop of St. Boniface, 1964—; rector Coll. St. Boniface 1967-69. Address: 151 Av de la Cathedrale Saint Boniface Manitoba Canada

HACHE, HARRY, sports editor San Diego Union-Tribune. Address: 940 3d Av San Diego CA 92112*

HACK, HOWARD E., painter; b. Cheyenne, Wyo., July 6, 1932; student Cal. Coll. Arts and Crafts, Mills Coll.; B.S., U. San Francisco. Exhbns. include San Francisco Drawing and Print Annual, 1961, Oakland (Cal.) Mus. Art, 1953, 55, 57, 60, Jack London S Festival, 1956, 61, Carnegie Inst., Pitts., 1964; rep. permanent collection Oakland Mus. Art. Recipient prize San Francisco Chronicle, 1949; purchase prize Oakland Mus. Art, 1960; prize Jack London Sq. Festival, 1961; Rosenthal award painting, 1966. Address: 9 Mission St San Francisco CA 94105*

HACKAMACK, LAWRENCE CARROLL, educator; b. New Truxton, Mo., Sept. 17, 1921; s. Lawrence Henry and Martha Louise (Denser) H.; B.A., Culver Stockton Coll., 1944; M.S., Western Ill. State U., 1948; Ph.D., U. Ia., 1956; m. Beatrice Irene Littlefield, June 15, 1946; children—Susan Ann, David Lee. Sales corr. A.P. Green Co., Mexico, Mo., 1944-46; tchr. Vista (Cal.) Sch. System, 1948-50; instr. Neb. State Tchrs. Coll., Wayne, 1950-53; grad. asst. U. Ia., 1953-54; asso. prof. U. Mass., 1955-61; prof., head mgmt. dept. No. Ill. U., DeKalb, 1961—; cons. to metal working machine cos.; cons. VA, 1957. Sec.-treas. Haish Meml. Hosp. Fund, DeKalb; adviser Marketron, Inc., Wheaton, Ill. Served with USAAF, 1942-43. Ford Found. fellow Cornell U., 1958. Mem. Am. Prodn. and Inventory Control Soc. (editorial bd.), Acad. Mgmt., Soc. for Advancement Mgmt., Lambda Chi Alpha, Sigma Iota Epsilon, Beta Gamma Sigma. Methodist (chmn. ofcl. bd.). Home: 205 Joanne St DeKalb IL 60115

HACKBERT, HARLAN LUND, lawyer; b. Appleton, Wis., Aug. 16, 1906; s. Paul Lewis and Lou (Lund) H.; A.B., Lawrence Coll., 1927; J.D., U. Mich., 1930; m. Joanne Williams, Dec. 7, 1940 (div. 1962); children—Susan Bright (Mrs. Peter Shire), Paul Lewis II, Peter Harlan, Richard Lund, Nancy Lou. Admitted to Wis. bar, 1930, Ill. bar, 1931; asso. firm Knapp, Cushing, Hershberger & Stevenson, and predecessors, Chgo., 1930-44, mem., 1945-54; mem. firm Stevenson, Conaghan, Hackbert, Rooks & Pitts, and predecessors, Chgo., 1954-66, Hackbert, Rooks, Pitts, Fullagar & Poust, Chgo., 1966-. Mem. Evanston (Ill.) Welfare Council, 1959-60; mem. exec. com. Evanston Sch. Dist. 65 Caucus, 1954-57; mem. lay adv. council Evanston Twp. High Sch., 1956-59. Bd. dirs. Christopher House, Chgo., 1952-65. Fellow Am. Coll. Trial Lawyers; mem. Am., Ill., Chgo. bar assns., State Bar Wis., Soc. Trial Lawyers (pres. 1953), Nat. Assn. R.R. Trial Counsel (pres. 1959-61, exec. com. 1956-), Am. Judicature Soc., Phi Beta Kappa, Order of Coif. Republican. Presbyn. Clubs: University, Legal, Law (Chgo.). Home: 1550 N Lake Shore Dr Chicago IL 60610 Office: 208 S LaSalle St Chicago IL 60604

HACKEL, EMANUEL, educator; b. Bklyn., June 17, 1925; s. Henry N. and Esther (Herbstman) H.; student N.Y.U., 1941-42; B.S., U. Mich., 1948, M.S., 1949; Ph.D., Mich. State U., 1953; m. Elisabeth Mackie, June 24, 1950; childrenLisa M., Meredith Anne, Janet M. Fisheries biologist Mich. Dept. Conservation, 1949; mem. faculty Mich. State U., East Lansing, 1949-, prof. natural sci., 1962-, chmn. dept. natural sci., 1963-, asst. dean coll., 1958-63; research fellow the Galton Laboratory, Univ. Coll., London, Eng., 1970-71. Vis. investigator blood group research unit The Lister Inst., London, Eng., 1956-57. Served to lt. (j.g.) USNR, 1943-47; lt. comdr. Res. Recipient Cooley Meml. award Am. Assn. Blood Banks, 1969. Mem. Assn. Gen. and Liberal Studies (sec.-treas. 1962-65), Am. Assn. U. Profs., A.A.A.S., Genetics Soc. Am., Am. Soc. Human Genetics, Am., Mich. (v.p. 1970—) assns. blood banks, Am. Inst. Biol. Sci., Biometric Soc., N.Y. Acad. Scis., Sigma Xi, Phi Kappa Phi. Author: Guide to Laboratory Studies in Biological Science, 1951; Studies in Natural Science, 1953; Natural Science, 1955, Vols. 1, 2, 3, 1952-63; also articles on genetics, human blood group immunology and chem. nature of blood group antigens to sci. jours. Editor: Natural Science, 1963; The Search for Explanation-Studies in Natural Science, Vols. 1, 2, 3, 1967-68; Laboratory Manual for Natural Science, Vol. 1, 2, 3, 1967-68. Home: 244 Oakland Dr East Lansing MI 48823

HACKENBERG, ISAAC JAMES, lawyer; b. Cleve., Dec. 13, 1938; s. Henry Wilson and Violet (Havel) H.; B.A., Baldwin-Wallace Coll., 1961; J.D., Western-Res. U., 1964; m. Betty Lou Blewett, June 22, 1963; children—Susan Lynn, James Scott. Admitted to Ohio bar, 1964, since practiced in Painesville; partner Baker, Byron & Hackenberg, 1964—. Chmn. exec. com. Lake County Civil Def., 1969—. Councilman, Mentor, O., 1968-70, mayor, pres. council, 1970—. Mem. Ohio, Lake Coty bar assns., Am. Arbitration Assn. Republican. Methodist. Rotarian. Home: 9722 Old Johnnycake Ridge Rd Mentor OH 44060 Office: Cleveland Trust Bldg Painesville OH 44077

HACKER, ANDREW, educator; b. N.Y.C., Aug. 30, 1929; s. Louis Morton and Lilian (Lewis) H.; A.B., Amherst Coll., 1951; M.A., Oxford U., 1953; Ph.D., Princeton, 1955; m. Lois Sheffield Wetherell, June 17, 1955; 1 dau., Ann. Instr. govt. Cornell U., Ithaca, N.Y., 1955-56, asst. prof., 1956-60, asso. prof., 1960-66, prof., 1966-71; prof. polit. sci. Queens Coll., City U. N.Y., 1971—; cons. Nat. Indsl. Conf. Bd., Brookings Instn., Rockefeller Bros. Fund, Nat. Council Chs. of Christ in Am., Am. Jewish Com. Mem. Am. Polit. Sci. Assn., Am. Assn. U. Profs., Phi Beta Kappa. Republican. Author: Political Theory: Philosophy, Ideology, Science, 1960; Congressional Districting, 1963; The Study of Politics, 1963; The Corporation Take-Over, 1964; The End of the American Era, 1970. Home: 20 W 64th St New York City NY 10023 Office: Dept Polit Sci Queens Coll City U NY Flushing NY 11367

HACKER, HAROLD SCHWORM, librarian; b. Buffalo, July 9, 1916; s. Joseph Frederick and Henrietta Catherine (Schworm) H.; A.B., Canisius Coll., 1937; B.L.S., U. Buffalo, 1941. Dir. pub. relations Grosvenor Library, Buffalo, 1941-44, Buffalo Pub. Library and Grosvenor Library, 1945-46; adminstrv. asst. Grosvenor Library, 1946-47, dir., 1952-53; 1st dep. dir. Erie County Pub. Library 1948-52; dir. Rochester (N.Y.) Pub. Library and Monroe County Library System, 1954—. Mem. Gov. Dewey's Com. on Library Aid, 1949; vice chmn. Commr. of Edn.'s com. on pub. library service, 1956-58, mem. com. on research and reference resources, 1960-62; mem. Gov.'s Com. Libraries, 1965-66; chmn. Commr. Edn.'s com. library devel., 1967-70; Trustee St. John Fisher Coll.; trustee, treas. John F. Wegman Found.; trustee Rochester Area Ednl. TV Assn., pres., 1960-67. Recipient Velmak. Moore Meml. award, 1963; Education award Civic Devel. Council, 1968; Helen Stone Jones award, 1969. Fellow Rochester Mus. Arts and Scis.; mem. Am., N.Y. (pres. 1947 library assns., Rochester C. of C., Vol. Edn. Council (pres. 1960-61), Inter-Museum Council Rochester (pres. 1954-56). Home: 1077 East Av Rochester NY 14607 Office: Rochester Pub Library Rochester NY 14604

HACKER, HILARY BAUMANN, clergyman; b. New Ulm, Minn., Jan. 10, 1913; s. Emil and Sophia (Baumann) H.; student Nazareth Hall, St. Paul, Minn., 1928-32, St. Paul Sem., 1932-38, J.C.B., Gregorian Univ., Rome, Italy, 1939. Ordained priest Roman Cath. Ch., 1938; asst. pastor Ch. of Nativity, St. Paul, June-Oct. 1938; asst. pastor Ch. of Most Holy Trinity, Winsted, Minn., 1939-41; vice chancellor Archdiocese of St. Paul, June-Sept. 1941, chancellor 1941-45, vicar gen., 1945-56; bishop of Bismarck, N.D., 1956- -. Home: 420 Raymond St Bismarck ND 58501 Office: Box 1575 Bismarck ND 58501

HACKER, JOSEPH BLAKEMAN, fraternal orgn. exec., lawyer; b. Manchester, Ky., Mar. 10, 1911; s. David Lyttle and Josephine Gardner (Burchell) H.; A.B., Maryville (Tenn.) Coll., 1932; LL.B., Chattanooga Coll. Law, 1937; student Louisville Presbyn. Theol. Sem., 1932-33, U. Chattanooga, 1946; m. Alline Koons, Sept. 23, 1933; childrenIberus Joseph, Robert Gordon. Admitted to Tenn. bar, 1939; engaged in real estate and tax law, 1933-. Mem. K.P., 1939-, grand chancellor Tenn., 1947-48, a rep. Tenn. to Supreme Lodge, 1954-60, supreme vice chancellor, 1960-62, supreme chancellor, 1962-64, supreme sec., 1964-68, supreme tribune K.P. Supreme Lodge, 1968-. Served with USNR, World War II. Mem. Sigma Delta Kappa. Presbyn. (elder). Address: 2716 Bennett Av Chattanooga TN 37404

HACKER, LOUIS MORTON, educator, author, editor; b. N.Y.C., Mar. 17, 1899; s. Morris and Celia (Waxelbaum) H.; A.B., Columbia, 1922 (Class of 1920), A.M., 1923; M.A., Oxford U., Eng., 1948; LL.D., U. Hawaii, 1953; m. Lillian Lewis, June 26, 1921 (died 1952); children—Andrew, Betsy (Mrs. Roy Dexheimer); m. second, Beatrice Larson Brennan, June 17, 1953. Asst. editor New Internat. Ency., 1923-25, 28-29; assistant editor Ency. of Social Scis., 1932-34; lectr. history and econs., summer sessions Univ. Wis., 1937, Ohio State U., 1939, Utah State Agrl. Coll., 1945, U. Hawaii, 1953; lectr. econs. dept. Columbia, 1935-42, asst. prof., 1942-44, asso. prof., 1944-48, prof., 1948-67, professor emeritus, since 1967-, director of the School of Gen. Studies, 1949-52, dean, 1952-58; mem. faculty New Sch., 1940, 43-48, Am. Inst. Banking, 1940-43; Harmsworth prof. Am. history (Fellow Queens Coll.), Oxford U., 1948-49; faculty Yeshiva U., 1958-59; lectr. Cambridge U., 1952, Army War Coll., 1952-, National War Coll., 1953-54, 57; visiting distinguished professor Pennsylvania State University, 1959-60; Bode Memorial lecturer Ohio State U., 1960; vis. distinguished prof. Fairleigh Dickinson U., 1967- 68; Relm Found. research fellow, 1967-68. Served S.A.T.C., 1918. Guggenheim fellow, 1948, 1958-59; Benjamin Franklin fellow Royal Soc. Arts, Eng., 1963. Member Am. Assn. for Middle East Studies (director), American History Association, American Economic Association. Econ. History Assn., P.E.N., Authors League, Mt. Pelerin Society, Phi Beta Kappa. Republican. Clubs: Athenaeum Club (London); Pilgrims (New York City). Author: United States Since 1865 (with B. B. Kendrick), 1932; Farmer is Doomed, 1933; Short History of the New Deal, 1934; The United States: A Graphic History, 1937; American Problems of Today, 1938; Triumph of American Capitalism, 1940; Shaping of the American Tradition, 1947; New Industrial Relations (with others), 1948; England and America: The Ties That Bind, 1948; Government Assistance to Universities in Great Britain (with H. W. Dodds and L. Rogers), 1952; United States in the 20th Century (with H. S. Zahler), 1952; Alexander Hamilton in the American Tradition, 1957; American Capitalism, 1957; Larger View by the University, 1961; The World of Andrew Carnegie, 1865- 1901, 1968; The Course of American Economic Growth and Development, 1970. Editor: (and co-author with Allan Nevins) The United States and its Place in World Affairs, 1918-43; Capitalism and the Historians (with others), 1954. Editor: American Century Series; Major Documents in American Economic History, 2 Vols., 1961. Home: 430 W 116th St New York City, NY 10027

HACKERMAN, NORMAN, univ. pres., chemist; b. Balt., Mar. 2, 1912; s. Jacob and Anna (Raffel) H.; A.B., Johns Hopkins, 1932, Ph.D., 1935; m. Gene Allison Coulbourn, Aug. 25, 1940; children—Patricia Gale, Stephen, Sally, Katherine. Asst. prof. Loyola Coll., Balt., 1935-39; research chemist Colloid Corp., 1936-40; chemist USCG, S.I., 1939-41; asst. prof. Va. Poly. Inst., Blacksburg, 1941-43; research chemist Kellex Corp., 1944; asst. prof. chemistry U. Tex., 1945-46, asso. prof., 1946-50, prof., 1950-70, chmn. dept., 1952-61, dir. corrosion research lab., 1948-61, dean research and sponsored programs, 1960-61, v.p., provost, 1961-63, vice chancellor acad. affairs, 1963-67, pres., 1967-70; prof. chemistry Rice U., Houston, 1970—, pres., 1970—; cons. in corrosion, 1946—, in surface chem., 1948—. Chmn. Gordon Corrosion Research Conf., 1950; chmn. Inter Soc. Corrosion Com., 1956-58; chmn. Gordon Research Conf. Chemistry, 1959. Mem. Nat. Sci. Bd., NSF; chmn. bd. trustees Argonne Univs. Assn., 1969—; bd. dirs. Gordon Research Confs., 1970—. Recipient Whitney award Nat. Assn. Corrosion Engrs., 1956; Joseph J. Mattiello Meml. lectr. Fedn. Socs. Paint Tech., 1964; Southwest Regional award Am. Chem. Soc., 1965; Palladium medalist Electrochem. Soc., 1965. Fellow N. Y. Acad. Scis., A.A.A.S.; mem. Nat. Acad. Scis., Am. Chem. Soc. (bd. editors, 1956-62, exec. com., colloid div. 1955-58), Electrochem. Soc. (pres. 1957-58), Faraday Soc., A.A.A.S., Nat. Assn. Corrosion Engrs. (dir. 1952-55, chmn. com. on edn. Corrosion Research Council 1957—), Sigma Xi, Phi Lambda Upsilon, Alpha Chi Sigma, Phi Kappa Phi. Tech. editor Jour. Electrochem. Soc., 1950-68, editor, 1969—; interim editor Electrochem. Tech., 1965-68; adv. editorial bd. Corrosion Sci.; editorial bd. Catalysis Reviews. Home: President's House Rice Univ Houston TX 77001

HACKES, PETER SIDNEY, radio-TV news corr.; b. N.Y.C., June 2, 1924; s. John R. and Ruth (Misch) H.; B.A., Grinnell Coll., 1948; M.A., U. Ia., 1949; Litt.D., Newberry Coll.; L.H.D., Grinnell Coll.; m. Mary Ellen Propper, Mar. 30, 1954; children—Pamela Townsend, Carole Austin, Peter Quinn. With radio sta. WELM, Elmira, N.Y., 1946-47, WSUI and KXIC, Iowa City, 1948-49, WAKR, Akron, O., 1949-50, WHAS, Louisville, 1950-52; Washington corr. CBS, 1952-55; Washington corr. NBC, 1955—, Def. Dept. corr., 1956-67, anchorman NBC World News Roundup, 1957-61, also reporter spl. activities NASA, State Dept., White House, U.S. Congress, polit. convs., elections, Chilean earthquake, Hungarian revolt airlift, every manned space flight, others. Mem. Nat. Commn. on Fire Prevention and Control. Served to lt. (j.g.) USNR, World War II. Recipient TV Emmy award for Apollo coverage. Mem. Radio-TV Corrs. Assn., Chatham (Mass.) Conservation Assn., Sigma Delta Chi. Club: Stage Harbor Yacht (Chatham). Office: 4001 Nebraska Av NW Washington DC 20016

HACKETT, ALBERT, author, actor; b. N.Y.C., Feb. 16, 1900; s. Maurice and Florence (Spreen) H.; studied with pvt. tutors; student Profl. Children's Sch., N.Y.C.; m. Frances Goodrich, Feb. 7, 1931. Began as child actor; appeared in theatre, in motion pictures for Lubin Moving Picture Co., Phila., 1911-14; appeared N.Y. state in Up the Ladder, Nervous Wreck, Whoopee, others; writer (with Frances Goodrich) Up Pops the Devil, 1931, Bridal Wise, 1932, The Great Big Doorstep, 1942, Diary of Anne Frank, 1955; motion pictures include Thin Man, Naughty Marietta, Ah, Wilderness; Father of the Bride, Easter Parade, Seven Brides for Seven Brothers, others. Recipient Pulitzer prize (with Frances Goodrich) for play Diary of Anne Frank. Mem. Players, Dramatists Guild, Screen Writers Guild. Home: 88 Central Park W New York City NY 10023*

HACKETT, BOBBY, trumpeter; b. Providence, Jan. 31, 1915; s. William F. and Rose (Mulvaney) H.; ed. pub. schs., Providence; m. Edna L. Lee, July 26, 1937; children—Barbara, Ernie. Trumpeter with Horace Heidt Band, 1939, Glenn Miller Band, 1941-42, NBC staff orch., 1943, Glen Gray Band, 1944- 45, Paul Whiteman Band and ABC staff orch., 1947—; recording artist for Capitol, Columbia, Epic Records, also Benny Goodman Concert Group; frequent TV concerts. Mason. Home: Indian Hill Rd Chatham MA

HACKETT, BUDDY, actor; b. Bklyn., Aug. 31, 1924; s. Philip and Anna (Geller) Hacker; ed. pub. schs., Bklyn.; m. Sherry Cohen, June 12, 1955; children—Sandy Zade, Ivy Julie, Lisa Jean. Theatrical appearances include Call Me Mister, 1946, Lunatics and Lover, 1954, I had A Ball, 1964; motion picture appearances include Walking My Baby Back Home, 1953, Gods Little Acre, 1958, Music Man, 1960, Brother Grimm, 1961, It's a Mad, Mad, Mad, Mad World, 1962, Golden Head, 1963; cafe and nightclub appearances throughout U.S. Recipient Donaldson award, 1955, Venice Film Festival award, 1961. Home: 75 Bluff Av Palisade NJ 07024 Office: 33 W 42d St New York City NY 10036*

HACKETT, CHARLES E., Jr., physician, educator; b. Portsmouth, N.H., 1920; M.D., Columbia, 1944. Intern, Bellevue Hosp., N.Y.C., 1944-45; asst. resident in neurosurgery Neurol. Inst. N.Y., 1945-46, 49-50, resident in neurosurgery, 1951; research asso. N.Y. Med. Sch., 1948, Columbia, 1950; instr. surgery U. Kan., Kansas City, 1952-58, asso. prof. neurosurgery, 1958-64, prof., 1964—, also head sect. neurosurgery. Served to lt. (j.g.) M.C., USNR, 1946-47. Diplomate Am. Bd. Neurol. Surgery. Mem. Coll. Neurol. Surgeons, A.M.A. Office: U Kan Sch Medicine Kansas City KS 66101*

HACKETT, CHARLES MEGGINSON, newspaper editor; b. Wilmington, Del., Apr. 3, 1909; s. Harry Clifford and Elizabeth (Megginson) H.; student U. Del., 1927-29, U. Pa., 1929-31; m. Dorothy Hartmann, Oct. 10, 1930; children—Charles Michael, Henry

Clay; m. 2d, Marjorie Regestein, Apr. 5, 1954; 1 dau., Cynthia. With Wilmington Eve. Jour., 1927-28; reporter Wilmington Every Eve., 1929-30, Phila. Record, 1930-34; reporter, city editor Wilmington Star, 1934-37; press Officer E.I. du Pont de Nemours & Co., Inc., 1937-64; v.p., exec. editor News-Jour. Papers, Wilmington, 1964-68; pres. News-Jour. Pub. Co., 1968—; lectr. Boston U., 1950-54, U. Pa., 1952-56. Mem. Del. Planning Commn. Mem. Am. Soc. Newspaper Editors, Am. Newspaper Pubs. Assn., Sigma Delta Chi. Home: Plaza Apts Wilmington DE 19806 Office: 831 Orange St Wilmington DE 19898

HACKETT, JAMES J., retail co. exec.; b. 1907. With Scheuer & Co., textile brokers, 1936-47; with J. P. Stevens & Co. Inc., 1947—, exec. v.p., 1968—, pres. Woolens and Women's Wear div., 1970—, also dir. Address: 1460 Broadway New York City NY 10036*

HACKETT, JOHN FRANCIS, bishop; b. New Haven, Dec. 7, 1911; s. Thomas J. and Anna (Whalen) H.; student St. Thomas Sem., Bloomfield, Conn., 1929-31, Seminaire St. Sulpice, Issy and Paris, France, 1931-36; LL.D. (honorary), Fairfield University, 1953; LL.D., Providence College, 1960. Ordained priest, Roman Cath. Ch., 1936; asst. pastor St. Aloysius Ch., New Canaan, Conn., 1936-45; sec. Bishop of Hartford, 1945-52; asst. chancellor Diocese of Hartford, 1945-51, vice chancellor, 1951-52, chancellor, 1953-59, vicar- gen., 1954-; apptd. Titular Bishop of Helenopolis in Palaestina, Auxiliary Bishop of Hartford, 1952. Home: 1109 Prospect Av West Hartford, CT 06105. Office: 134 Farmington Av Hartford CT 06105

HACKETT, JOHN THOMAS, economist; b. Fort Wayne, Ind., Oct. 10, 1932; s. Harry H. and Ruth (Greer) H.; B.S., Ind. U., 1954, M.B.A., 1958; Ph.D., Ohio State U., 1961; m. Ann E. Thompson, July 24, 1954; children—Jane, David, Sarah, Peter. Instr. Ohio State U., 1958-61; asst. v.p., economist Fed. Res. Bank, Cleve., 1961-64; dir. planning Cummins Engine Co., Columbus, Ind., 1964—, v.p. finance, 1966—. Served to 1st lt. AUS, 1954-56. Mem. Am. Econ. Assn., Financial Execs. Inst., Am. Finance Assn., Bus. Economists Assn., Internat. C. of C. (com. internat. monetary relations of U.S. council). Home: 1005 Hawthorne Dr Columbus IN 47201 Office: 1000 5th St Columbus IN 47201

HACKETT, WARREN THEODORE, orgn. exec.; b. Chgo., Mar. 16, 1906; s. Philip John and Lillian (Lawson) H.; student U. Ill.; m. Kathryn Volz, Mar. 23, 1956; 1 dau., Dorothy Joanne (Mrs. Samuel T. Johnston). Salesman, Hokinson & Jenks, realtors, Evanston, Ill., 1927-28; salesman, security analyst T. L. Chapman & Co., security dealers, 1928-32; sales mgr. Larson Co., Green Bay, Wis., 1932-34; propr. Heath & Co., Cin., 1934-40; partner Haydock & Co., investment counsellors, Cin., 1940-47; with Huntington Nat. Bank, Columbus, O., 1947-71, sr. v.p., trust officer, 1947-71; vice chmn. Am. Econ. Found., 1971—; dir. Columbus Auto Parts Co., Lupher Drilling Co. Pres. Big Brothers Assn. Columbus, 1965; pres., mem. bd. House of Hope for Alcoholics, 1960—; bd. dirs. Davis Found., Berkstone Fund, O'Bleness Found., Am. Econ. Found., Citizens Evaluation Inst.; trustee Ohioana Library, Ohio Information Com., Columbus Area Devel. and Tng. Sch. Mem. Columbus Area C. of C. Chi Phi, Symposiarchs Frat. (nat. bd.). Mason (32), Rotarian. Author: How to Prosper Under Freedom (Distinguished Leadership award Ohio Information Com., Sertoma's Service to Mankind award, George Washington honor certificate award Freedom Found.). Home: 9592 Lake of the Woods Dr Galena OH 43021 Office: 222 E Town St Columbus OH 43215

HACKETT, WILLIAM THOMAS, Jr., state ofcl.; b. Port Gibson, Miss., Dec. 17, 1924; s. William Thomas and Lois (Hightower) H.; student Ga. Sch. Tech., 1943; A.B., Mercer U., 1949; m. Mary Frances Aultman, Dec. 3, 1944; childrenWilliam Thomas III, Michael A., Neil M. With Waterways Expt. Sta., Vicksburg, Miss., 1948-49, Forest (Miss.) C. of C., 1949-51, Canton (Miss.) C. of C., 1953- 56, Madison Woodworking Co., Canton, 1956-59, Jones & Yandell Mfg. Co., Canton, 1959-60, Meridian (Miss.) C. of C., 1960-61; exec. v.p. Miss. Agrl. and Indsl. Bd., Jackson, 1961-64; exec. dir. La. Dept. Commerce and Industry, Baton Rouge, 1964-. Served with USNR, 1943-46, 51-53. Mem. Am., So. indsl. devel. councils, Nat., So. assns. state devel. agys. Home: 6350 Peggy St Baton Rouge, LA 70808. Office: PO Box 44185 Capitol Sta Baton Rouge LA 70804

HACKETT, JAMES WALLACE, glass co. exec.; b. Cumberland, Md., May 8, 1912; s. Edward S. and Margaret (White) H.; B.Sc. in Engring. Physics, Ohio State U., 1939; D.Sc. (honorary), U. Toledo, 1966; Ehrensenator, Tech. U. Vienna (Austria), 1968; m. Eloise Munger, Dec. 19, 1942; children—Jeanne E., Margaret M., Karen I. Phys. metallurgist research labs. div. Gen. Motors Corp., 1939-43; process engr. Owens-Corning Fiberglas Co., 1943-44; asst. dir. research Victor Adding Machine Co., 1944-45; with Owens-Ill., Inc. (formerly Owens-Ill. Glass Co.), Toledo, 1945—, dir. research, 1953-56, 58-61, v.p. adminstrv. div., v.p. research and engring., 1963-66, v.p. and tech. dir., 1966—. Spl. cons. to dir. armament U.S. Strategic Air Force Europe, 1945; co. rep. to Indsl. Research Inst., 1954-, chmn. membership com., 1961-62. Pres. Toledo Hearing League, 1958-59, bd. dirs., 1951-60; com. chmn. Toledo United Appeal, 1959-61; mng. mem. Easter Seal Soc. Lucas County, 1960-; sci. adv. com. Ohio Bd. Regents; Former trustee Packaging Found., Inc.; bd. dirs. Ohio State U. Research Found. Registered profl. engr., Ohio. Fellow Am. Ceramic Soc.; mem. A.A.A.S., Soc. Hist. Tech., Soc. Chem. Industry, Ohio Soc. Profl. Engrs. (mem. adv. council), Tau Beta Pi, Phi Eta Sigma, Sigma Pi Sigma. Kiwanian (past pres. Toledo). Home: 3014 Plumbrook Rd Toledo Maumee OH 43537 Office: 1700 N Westwood Av Toledo OH 43607

HACKLER, JOHN BYRON, III, architect; b. Pekin, Ill., Mar. 31, 1925; s. John Byron and Josephine (Walters) H.; B.Arch., Carnegie-Mellon U., 1949; m. Patricia Ann Baum, June 29, 1948; children—Catherine Frances, John Byron IV, Ann Frost. Pvt. practice architecture, 1950-53; with Foley, Hackler, Thompson, Lee, 1953-65; partner John Hackler & Co., Peoria, Ill., 1965—; pres. Domey, Ltd.; vis. critic archtl. design U. Ill., 1969-70; dir. Ill. Valley Pub. Telecommunications Corp. Dir. Upgrade, Inc. Dir. Mid-Am. Hearing Research Fedn. Served with USAAF, 1943-45. Research housing for migrant workers, systems for low and moderate income housing, integrated bldg. systems, health care delivery systems, implementation of ednl. information. Office: Commercial National Bank Bldg Peoria IL 61602

HACKLER, VICTOR, newspaper man; b. Gregory, S.D., Feb. 2, 1906; s. Joy M. and Nellie (Tisue) Hackler; B.A., U. Neb., 1927; m. Harriet Corey (div.); children—Robert, Kent (dec.); m. 2d, Mrs. Grethel Crawford Lloyd. Received early training as reporter and corr. on Omaha (Neb.) Bee; with Associated Press, 1927-71, staff mem. Omaha, Milw., Duluth, Chgo., N.Y., chief of bur., Milw., 1934-36, Chgo., 1937-42, exec. asst. to gen. mgr., N.Y.C., 1942, gen. financial editor, 1943, chief N.Y. Bur., 1944-45, news editor, London, 1945-48, assigned to exec. news staff, N.Y., 1948-50, gen. exec., 1951-71, cons., 1971—; editor Asso. Press Mng. Editors Assn. Redbook, 1953-71; nat. coordinator A.P. Election Coverage, 1950-71. Bd. mgrs. Network Election Service, 1964, News Election Service, 1966-71. Mem. Phi Kappa Psi, Sigma Delta Chi. Home: 4704 Rue Bayou Sanibel Island FL 33957 Office: 50 Rockefeller Plaza New York City NY 10020

HACKLEY, HOWARD HAYWARD, govt. ofcl.; b. Washington, Mar. 13, 1909; s. David Kibler and Frances (Settle) H.; B.A., U. Va., 1929. LL.B., 1931; LL.M., Columbia, 1932; m. Rose O'Connor, July 26, 1941; childrenJohn David, Steven Walsh. With Fed. Res. Bd., 1933-, asst. counsel, 1939-51, asst. gen. counsel, 1951- 57, gen. counsel, 1957-67, assistant to the board, 1968-, also gen. counsel of federal open market committee, 1957-. Mem. Phi Beta Kappa, Order of Coif. Methodist. Home: 5116 Marlyn Dr Washington DC 20016 Office: Federal Reserve Board Washington DC 20551

HACKLEY, SHERLOCK DRESSER, aeronautical co. exec.; b. Berkeley, Mar. 6, 1910; s. Roy C. and Alice (Dresser) H.; B.S., U. Cal. at Berkeley, 1934; m. Helena Johnson, Mar. 12, 1953. Gen. supt. L. E. Dixon, Bent Bros. & Johnson, Met. Aqueduct, Los Angeles, 1934-37, R. G. Clifford, San Francisco, also Redding, Cal., 1937-38, Shea Kaiser, N.Y.C., 1938-40; gen. supt. Kaiser Co., Mare Island, Cal., 1940-42, asst. to exec. v.p. Kaiser Steel Co., 1942-43; v.p., gen. mgr. Kaiser Metals Products, Bristol, Pa., 1946, Kaiser Fleetwings, Inc., 1946; v.p. Henry J. Kaiser Co., 1950-67, Kaiser Industries Corp., 1956- 67; mng. dir., chmn. Island Flying Service Ltd., Out Island Airways, Ltd., Nassau, The Bahamas, 1968—. Mem. Am. Inst. Aero. Scis., Am. Mil. Engrs., Clubs: Lyford Cay (Nassau, Bahamas); Racquet and Tennis (N.Y.C.); Rolling Rock (Ligonier, Pa.); Conquistadores del Cielo (N.M.); Deepdale Golf (Manhasset, N.Y.); Clove Valley (N.Y.) Rod and Gun; Home: Long Point Farm Oxford MD 21654

HACKMAN, GENE, actor. Appeared in stage prodns. Any Wednesday, Poor Richard, Children from Their Games, A Rainy Day in Newark, The Natural Look; tv roles include My Father, My Mother, The F.B.I., The Invaders, The Iron Horse, others; film roles include Lilith, Bonnie and Clyde (Acad. award nomination for best supporting actor), First to Fight, Out by the Country Club, Hawaii, Riot, The Split, The Gypsy Moths, Downhill Racer, Marooned, I Never Sang for My Father, Doctor's Wives. Address: George Morris Agy 355 N Canon Dr Beverly Hills CA 90210*

HACKNEY, ROGER, corp. exec.; b. Wellington, Feb. 9, 1902; s. Edward T. and Mabel C. (Rogers) H.; B.S., U. Kan., 1924; m. Margaret Flaherty, Aug. 27, 1928; children—Ann (Mrs. Jack Webb), Cynthia (Mrs. Donald Matthews). Constrn. engineer Thompson Starrett, N.Y.C., 1924-26, Hegeman Harris, N.Y.C., 1926-28; investment banker Eastman Dillon, 1928-34, Foster Marvin, 1934-41; treas. Johns Manville Corp., 1942-59, dir., v.p. for finance, 1959-67, sr. operating v.p., 1961-67; pres., treas., dir. Halcyon Fund, Inc., N.Y.C., 1967-70; dir. Polymer Corp. Bush Universal, Inc., Universal Airlines Co. (both N.Y.C.), Johns Manville Iceland and Kisilidjan H. F. Mem. Sigma Nu, Tau Beta Pi, Theta Tau. Clubs: Union League; Larchmont Yacht. Home: 20 Maple Av Larchmont NY 10538

HACKNEY, VICTOR CHARLES, physician; b. Kansas City, Mo., Feb. 25, 1917; s. Charles Vivan and Floye (Allard) H.; student U. Louisville, 1936-37; B.A., Colgate U., 1940; M.D., Yale, 1943; m. Stella Louise Fischer, Oct. 25, 1945. Asst. resident surgery New Haven Hosp., 1947-48; asst. resident pathology U. Okla. Hosp., 1949-52; resident dermatology Indpls. Gen. Hosp., 1949-52; pvt. practice, Cal., 1952-62; with Lilly Research Labs., Indpls., 1956- 57; prof., chmn. dept. dermatology Ind. U. Med. Center, 1963-; dir. dermatology Marion County Gen. Hosp., Indpls., 1963-. Served with M.C., USNR, World War II. Fellow dermal pathology Armed Forces Inst. Pathology, Washington. Diplomate Am. Bd. Dermatology. Mem. Am. Acad. Dermatology, Am. Soc. Dermatopathology (charter), Pacific Dermat. Soc., Assn. Am. Med. Colls., A.C.P. Home: 5262 Olympia Dr Indianapolis IN 46208*

HADDAD, BARBARA, journalist; b. Canton, O., Dec. 18, 1937; d. George Michael and Laverne (Smith) Haddad; B.A. with honors, Swarthmore Coll., 1959; M.S. in Journalism with honors, Columbia, 1960; student U. Vienna (Austria), summer 1960; m. Vincent F. Ryan, November 25, 1967; 1 dau., Jennifer Maria. With pub. information dept. Lincoln Centre, N.Y.C., 1960; reporter Adirondack Daily Enterprise, also Lake Placid News, Saranac Lake, N.Y., 1960; asst. pub. relations dir. N.Y. Med. Coll., also Flower-Fifth Av. Hosp., N.Y.C., 1961-62; music and art editor Denver Post, 1962-69, editorial writer, 1969-70, TV editor, 1970—. Recipient Sacket prize in law of libel Columbia, 1960. Mem. Mortar Bd. Home: 640 Race St Denver CO 80206 Office: 650 15th St Denver CO 80201

HADDAD, JERRIER ABDO, elec. mfg. co. exec.; b. N.Y.C., July 17, 1922; s. Abdulmassih Abdo and Rashida (Shaker) H.; B.S. in Elec. Engring., Cornell U., Ithaca, N.Y., 1945; D.Sc. (hon.), Union Coll.; m. Margaret Van Hamlin, June 25, 1944; children—Mary (Mrs. Jerry DeGarmo), Helen (Mrs. Elias Abu Shaheen), Suzanne, Albert John, Alexander Lansdowne. Teaching asst. Cornell U., 1944- 45; with IBM Corp., 1945—, began as lab. tech., successively various engring. positions, lab. mgr., dir. advanced machine devel., gen. mgr. spl. engring. products div., 1945-59, gen. mgr. advanced systems devel. div., 1959-61, v.p. data systems div., 1961-62, v.p. system design and engring., 1962-63, dir. tech. and engring., 1963-67, v.p. engring., programming and tech., 1967-70, v.p., lab. dir., 1970—; dir. Am. Dist. Telegraph Co. Mem. adv. council Coll. Engring., Cornell U.; trustee Clarkson Coll. Tech. Recipient order of Cedars medal Lebanese Republic. Fellow I.E.E.E.; mem. Assn. Computing Machinery, Nat. Acad. Engring., Nat. Acad. Sci. (mem. computer sci. and engring. bd.), A.A.A.S., Sigma Xi, Tau Beta Pi, Eta Kappa Nu. Patentee in field, plus fgn. filing. Home: 162 Macy Rd Chilmark Park Briarcliff Manor NY 10510 Office: Box 390 Poughkeepsie NY*

HADDAD, KHALIL, diplomat of Lebanon; b. Lebanon, Aug. 4, 1930; s. Michel K. and Manneh (Dagher) H.; LL.B., Sacred Heart Coll., Beirut, Lebanon, 1947; student, U. St. Joseph, Beirut, 1951; internat. studies, Paris, 1963; m. Jacqueline Samaha, Nov. 21, 1962; childrenMichele, Philip. Attache embassy, Bagdad, 1953; charge d'affaires, Teheran, 1955-56; vice consul, Cairo, 1956-57, consul, 1957-59; charge d'affaires, Sudan, 1959-60; alternate del. to UN Gen. Assembly, 1960-62; 1st sec., Paris. 1962- 64: consul gen., Detroit, 1964-66, N.Y.C., 1966—. Founder many Am.- Lebanese clubs in U.S. Hon. mem. Am. Assn. Commerce and Industry, N.Y.C. C. of C. Home: 9 E 76th St New York City NY 10021*

HADDAD, WILLIAM FREDERICK, journalist, corp. exec.; b. Charlotte, N.C., July 25, 1928; s. Charles Frederick and Esther (Nowack) H.; A.A., St. Petersburg (Fla.) Jr. Coll., 1951; B.A., Columbia, 1954. spl. student Sch. Journalism, 1953-54. Sch. Pub. Law and Govt., 1958; grad. student Russian and Chinese, Georgetown U. and Linguistics Inst., 1954-56; m. Kate Roosevelt, Oct. 17, 1959; children—Laura, Andrea, Camilla. Cons. to U.S. Senate Judiciary Com., 1955; pub. relations, later staff dir. subcom. to investigate juvenile delinquency, 1955; asst. to U.S. Senator Kefauver on world tour, 1955, spl. asst. presdl. primaries, 1955-56, exec. mgr. in v.p. campaign, 1956; systems engr. mil. applications RCA, 1957; gen. assignment reporter N.Y. Post, 1957-60, on leave as asso. dir. planning, coordination and evaluation Peace Corps, Washington, 1961-63; with N.Y. Herald Tribune, 1963-64; insp. gen. and asst. dir. Office Econ. Opportunity, 1965-66; pres. U.S. Research & Devel. Corp., 1966-68, pres., chief exec. officer, 1968—; co-pub. Manhattan Tribune. Sec.-gen. Internat. Conf. Middle Level Manpower, 1962; mem. N.Y.C. Bd. Edn., 1968- 69; chmn. N.Y. State Council on Continuing Edn., 1970—; bd. dirs. N.Y. Bd. Trade; bd. dirs. N.Y. Urban Coalition, Boys Brotherhood Republic, Crossroads Africa, Encampment for Citizenship; bd. govs. Am. Jewish Congress. Organizer Council New York Democrats, N.Y.C., 1957; exec. com. N.Y. Com. for Democratic Voters, N.Y.C., 1959-60; asst Robert Kennedy presdl. campaign, 1960, Robert Kennedy presdl. primaries, 1968. Served with U.S. Merchant Marine, 1945-50. Co-recipient (with Joe Kahn) awards for crusading reporting or for exposés of municipal corruption from George Polk Meml. Found., 1958, 59, from N.Y. Newspaper Guild, 1958, 59, Am. Newspaper Guild, 1959, Newspaper Reporters Assn., 1959; recipient Byline award Newspaper Reporters Assn., 1960; Page One award, 1965; Littauer fellow, 1957, 64. Author: (with Richard Goodwin) The Hidden Force, 1962; (with Douglas Pugh) Black Economic Development, 1968. Office: Chrysler Bldg New York City NY

HADDEN, GERALD ROBINSON, utilities exec.; b. Beacon, N.Y., Nov. 12, 1910; s. James H. and Pauline J. (Wright) H.; E.E., Rensselaer Poly. Inst., 1931; m. Marjorie Ann Nichols, Nov. 28, 1935 (dec. Aug. 1958); childrenValerie (Mrs. Theodor P. Krauss), Judith (Mrs. Eugene R. Buck); m. 2d, Mariana Sarrica, Nov. 23, 1960. Employed, Consol. Edison Co. of N.Y., Inc., 1931-68, asst. v.p., 1956-58, v.p., 1958-68; v.p. T. Frederick Jackson, Inc., Long Island City, 1968-. Vice chmn. exec. bd. A.R.C. Served lt. comdr. USNR, 1942-46. Mem. N.Y. Soc. Profl. Engrs., I.E.E.E., N.Y. Bldg. Congress (bd. govs.), Alpha Tau Omega. Clubs: Engineers, Manhattan, Union League (N.Y.C.); Seaview Country (Absecon, N.J.); Winged Foot Country. Home: 135 E 83d St New York City, NY 10028. Office: 42-12 28th St Long Island City NY 11101

HADDEN, JOHN ALEXANDER, lawyer; b. Cleve., July 11, 1886 s. Alexander and Frances (Hawthorne) H.; A.B., Harvard, 1908, LL.B., 1910; m. Marianne Elisabeth Millikin, Jan. 7, 1922; childrenJohn Alexander, Alexander Hawthorne, Elisabeth Severance Alexander. Admitted Ohio bar, 1910; now mem. firm Arter, Hadden, Wykoff & Van Duzer; asst. dist. atty. No. dist. Ohio, 1912-13; dir., mem. exec. com. Youngstown Steel Door Co., Erie R.R. Co.; dir. Union Bank of Commerce, Enos Coal Mining Co., Enoco Collieries, Inc. Dep. regional dir. WPB, 1942-43. Trustee Elizabeth Severance Prentiss Found.; trustee, mem. exec. com. U. Hosp.; Ohio chmn. Harvard Law Sch. Fund, 1944. Mem. Ohio Legislature, 1925-31. Served as sgt. Troop A, 1st Squadron, Ohio N.G. on Mexican border, 1916-17; capt. 135th F.A., U.S. Army, 1917-19; with A.E.F., 1918-19. Mem. Am. Bar Assn., Ohio, Cleve., bar assns., Sigma Alpha Epsilon. Republican. Clubs: Union, Tavern, Kirtland, 50 (Cleveland); Ottawa, Shooting (Fremont. O.). Home: 2787 Fairmont Blvd Cleveland OH 44118 Office: Union Commerce Bldg Cleveland 14 OH 44114*

HADDEN, MAYO ADDISON, naval officer; b. Holland, Mich., Aug. 14, 1916; s. Mayo Addison and Marguerite Elizabeth (Leenhouts) H.; B.A., Hope Coll., 1938; student Naval War Coll., 1953-54, Nat. War Coll., 1960-61; fellow Center Internat. Affairs Harvard, 1965-66; m. Lorain Erma Grant, Feb. 27, 1942; children—Mayo Addison III, Michael Grant, Jon Marta (Mrs. Donald D. Winter), Merry Lorain. Asst. advt. mgr. Spring-Air Co., Holland, 1938-41; joined USN, 1941, commd. ensign, 1941, advanced through grades to rear adm., 1969; naval aviator, 1942, service African and Pacific theaters; comdg. officer Fighter Squadron 73, 1949; comdr. U.S.S. Graffias, 1963-64, U.S.S. Hornet, 1964-65; dep. dir. operations Office Politico-Mil. Affairs Dept. State, 1966-68; comdr. Iceland Def. Force, 1968-70; comdr. Fleet Air Wings Atlantic Fleet, 1970—: Decorated Silver Star, Legion of Merit, D.F.C. with 2 stars, Air medal with 2 stars, Navy Commendation medal, Purple Heart with 2 stars; comdr. Icelandic Order Falcon. Mem. Fighter Aces Assn., Fleet Res. Assn., Nat. War Coll. Alumni Assn. Club: Army-Navy Country (Washington). Home: 276 Pine Av Holland MI 49423 Office: NAS Brunswick ME 04011

HADDOCK, AUBURA GLEN, educator; b. Jasper, Ark., May 29, 1935; s. Walter Lee and Zada (Owens) H.; B.S. in Math., State Coll. Ark., 1954; M.S. in Math., Okla. State U., 1958, Ph.D., 1961; m. Bobbie Sue Fugett, Oct. 1, 1954; children—Debbie Sue, Glen David, Vicky Denise, DeeAnn. Tchr. Carlisle (Ark.) High Sch., 1955-57; asso. prof. Ark. Coll., 1961-64, prof., dean, 1964-66; asso. prof. U. Mo. at Rolla, 1966-68, prof., chmn. math. dept., 1968—. Dir. Batesville Devel. Corp., 1964-65. Recipient Outstanding Service award Ark. Coll., 1966. Mem. Am. Math. Soc., Math. Assn. Am. (gov. 1970-73), Am. Soc. Engring. Edn., Sigma Xi. Baptist. Rotarian. Contbr. articles profl. jours. Home: Route 4 Box 27 Rolla MO 65401

HADDOCK, IRA FREDERICK, rear adm. U.S. Navy. Address: Bureau of Naval Personnel Dept of Navy Washington DC 20390*

HADDON, MATHEW CARL, aircraft exec.; b. Holly, Mich., June 21, 1908; s. Mathew J. and Margaret E. (Ryan) H.; B.S., U. Mich., 1931; m. Lillian Josephine Penzotti, May 31, 1931; childrenRichard Paul, Dean Kildare (dec.). Chief engr. Stearman-Hammond Aircraft, 1936-38; project engr. Svenska Aeroplan A.B., Linkoping, Sweden, 1938-39; project engr. Lockheed Aircraft Corp., 1940-52. chief project engr. Cal. div., 1952-56, chief engr., 1956-58, marketing dir., 1958-59, v.p., gen. mgr. for Los Angeles, Avionics & Indsl. Products div. Lockheed Electronic Co., 1959- 60; v.p. Lockheed Aircraft Corp., gen. mgr. Cal. div., 1960-61, corporate group vice president, 1965-67, exec. v.p., 1967-70, sr. adviser, dir., 1970—; pres. Lockheed-Cal. Co., 1961-63, corporate v.p. sci. and engring., 1963- 65; Trustee, So. Cal. Sch. Theology, Claremont, Pomona Coll. Fellow Inst. Aeros. and Astronautics; mem. Am. Helicopter Soc., Tau Beta Pi. Methodist. Clubs: Verdugo (Glendale, Cal.); Commonwealth (San Francisco). Home: 1680 Larco Way Glendale CA 91202 Office: 2555 N Hollywood Way Burbank CA 91503

HADDON, WILLIAM, Jr., profl. inst. exec.; b. Orange, N.J., May 24, 1926; s. William and Anna (Herrstrom) H.; S.B., Mass. Inst. Tech., 1949; M.D., Harvard, 1953, M.P.H. magna cum laude, 1957; m. Gene Billo, June 16, 1956; children—Jonathan, Charles, Robert. Research fellow microbiology, postdoctoral fellow Nat. Found. Infantile Paralysis, Harvard Sch. Pub. Health, 1954-55, research asso., 1955-56; dir. driver research center N.Y. Dept. Health, 1957-61, dir. epidemiology residency program, 1961-65, acting asst. commnr. pub. health research devel. and evaluation, 1963-64; asst. prof., then asso. prof. epidemiology Albany (N.Y.) Med. Coll., Union U., 1960-66, asso. dir. div. chronic disease services, 1964-66; spl. asst. for traffic safety planning to undersec. transp. Dept. Commerce, 1966; adminstr. Nat. Hwy. Safety Agy., also Nat. Traffic Safety Agy., Dept. Commerce, 1966-67; dir. Nat. Hwy. Safety Bur., Dept. Transp., 1967-69; pres. Ins. Inst. Hwy. Safety, Washington, 1969—. Mem. com. mil. accidents Armed Forces Epidemiological Bd., 1965- 69; mem. Council Med. Adminstrs., 1966-70; mem. com. alcohol and drugs Nat. Safety Council, 1960—; mem. U.S. delegation com. on challenges modern society N. Atlantic council NATO, 1969; mem. com. emergency med. services Nat. Acad. Sci./NRC, 1970—. Served with USAAF, 1944-45. Recipient Nat. Safety Council-Met. Life Ins. Co. award merit research accident prevention, 1963; Arthur Williams Meml. award World Safety Research Inst., 1966; Modern Medicine award for distinguished achievement, 1969; Bronfman prize Am. Pub. Health Assn., 1969. Fellow Am. Pub. Health Assn. (mem. council environment 1970—); mem. Am. Epidemiological Soc., Sigma Xi, Delta Omega. Unitarian. Author: (with E. A. Suchman and D. Klein) Accident Research, Methods and Approaches, 1964; also articles. Home: 7506 Hamilton Spring Rd Bethesda MD 20034 Office: Ins Inst Hwy Safety Watergate 600 NW Washington DC 20037*

HADDOX, BENJAMIN EDWARD, educator, sociologist; b. Orlando, Fla., Dec. 11, 1923; s. James Henry and Lily (Caldwell) H.; A.B. magna cum laude, Stetson U., 1945; B.D., So. Bapt. Theol. Sem., 1950; M.A., U. Fla., 1960. Ph.D., 1962; m. Geraldine Hayes, Sept. 14, 1942; children—Benjamin Edward, Cheryl Ann, John Stephen. Ordained to ministry Bapt. Ch., 1945; minister in Fla., 1950-62; asst. prof. sociology Miss. State U., 1962-64; asst. prof., acting chmn. dept. sociology Stetson U., 1964-66; prof., head dept. sociology Butler U., Indpls., 1966—; research in Bogota, Colombia, 1961. Miss. rep. regional research project low income families, 1962-64. U.S. Steel Found. fellow, 1960-62. Mem. Am. Assn. U. Profs. (pres. Butler U. chpt. 1968-69), A.A.A.S., Am. Sociol. Assn., Ohio Valley, Midwest. So. sociol. socs., Latin Am. Studies Assn., Phi Beta Kappa, Phi Kappa Phi. (pres. Butler chpt. 1971-72). Democrat. Mem. Christian Ch. Author: Sociedad y Religion en Colombia, 1965; Joint Decision Making Patterns and Related Factors Among Low Income Families, 1965; also articles. Home: 327 Buckingham Dr Indianapolis IN 46208*

HADDY, FRANCIS JOHN, educator physician; b. Walter, Minn., Sept. 6, 1922; s. Thomas J. and Frances (Shaheen) H.; student Luther Coll., Decorah, Ia., 1940-42; B.S., U. Minn., 1943, B.M., 1946, M.D., 1947, M.S. in Physiology, 1949, Ph.D. in Physiology (Am. Heart Assn. fellow), 1953; m. Theresa Eileen Brey, Sept. 21, 1946; children—Richard, Carol, Alice. Intern, Mpls. Gen. Hosp., 1946-47; fellow internal medicine Mayo Found., 1949-51; asst. prof. physiology and medicine Northwestern U. Med. Sch., 1953-61; clin. investigator VA Research Hosp., Chgo., 1957-59; prof. physiology, chmn. dept., asso. prof. medicine U. Okla. Med. Center, 1961-66; prof. physiology, chmn. dept. Mich. State U. Sch. Medicine, East Lansing, 1966—. Recipient Carl J. Wiggers award, 1966. Diplomate Am. Bd. Internal Medicine. Mem. Am. Physiol. Soc., Am. Soc. Clin. Investigation. Mem. editorial bd. Am. Jour. Physiology, 1963—, Jour. Applied Physiology, 1963-69, procs. Soc. Exptl. Biology and Medicine, 1969—, cardiovascular study sect. NIH, 1963-69, tng. com. A, Nat. Heart and Lung Inst., NIH, 1970. Home: 900 Audubon Rd East Lansing MI 48823

HADEN, CLARENCE RUPERT, Jr., bishop; b. Ft. Worth, May 30, 1910; s. Clarence Rupert and Marguerite W. (Collins) H.; B.A., Baylor U., 1931; student Union Theol. Sem., N.Y.C., 1932-34; S.T.B., Seabury-Western Theol. Sem., 1936, D.D., 1952; m. Essie Lucille Jones, Feb. 1, 1935; 1 dau., Nedah Louise (Mrs. David E. L. Egan). Mem. staff purchasing and accounting depts. Armour & Co., Ft. Worth; sales, advt. Pangburn Candy Co., Ft. Worth; ordained deacon P.E. Ch., 1936, priest, 1936; minister in charge St. Barnabas Ch., Denton Tex., St. Paul's Ch., Gainesville, Tex., 1936-37; rector St. John's Ch., Corsicana, Tex., 1937-41, St. Matthew's Ch., Houma, La., 1941-43, St. Paul's Ch., New Orleans, 1943-45, St. Philip's Ch., Durham, N.C., 1945-51; exec. dir., presiding bishop's com. on layman's work U.S., 1951-53; dean Grace and Holy Trinity Cathedral, Kansas City, Mo., 1953-57; mem. nat. council Episcopal Ch., 1954-57; bishop coadjutor Diocese of Sacramento, 1957, diocesan bishop, 1958—; Nat. Council Chs. interchange preacher to Eng., 1956. Chmn. dept. missions, exec. council Diocese of Dallas, 1938-41, examining chaplain, 1940-41; chmn. dept. Christian edn., mem. exec. council Diocese of La., 1942-45; exec. council Diocese of W. Mo., 1953-57, pres. standing com., 1955-57. Dir. Durham Community Chest, 1950-51, pres., 1951; dir. United Charities, 1937-41, chmn. ann. campaign, 1940; dir. Family Service, Inc.; bd. mgrs. Gaudet Normal and Indsl. Sch., New Orleans; trustee St. Augustine's Coll., Raleigh, N.C. Fellow Coll. Preachers of Washington; mem. United Church Men (bd. mgrs.), Brotherhood of St. Andrew (nat. chaplain), Denton Ministerial Union (v.p.), Corsicana Ministerial Alliance (pres. 1940-41), Lambeth Conf. Anglican Bishops (London), Kappa Epsilon Alpha. Clubs: Rotary, Kiwanis. Author religious articles, booklets. Home: 1800 Rolling Hills Rd Sacramento CA 95825

HADER, BERTA HOERNER (Mrs. Elmer Stanley Hader), writer, illustrator; b. San Pedro, Coahuila, Mexico; d. Albert and Adelaide (Jennings) Hoerner; student, U. of Wash., 1909-12; Calif. Sch. of Design, San Francisco, 1915-18; m. Elmer Stanley Hader, July 14, 1919. Began as fashion designer, 1914; newspaper artist, San Francisco Bulletin, 1916-18; miniature portrait painter, 1916-37; illustrator and writer of children's books since 1919. Author and co-author numerous books, later ones: Little Stone House, 1944; Rainbow's End, 1945; The Skyrocket, 1946; Little Chip, 1958; Reindeer Trail, 1959; Mr. Billy's Gun, 1960; Quack-Quack, 1961; Little Antelope, 1962. Illustrator with Elmer Stanley Hader: Adventures of Theodore Roosevelt, Humpy, Stripey; The Big Snow, 1948 (awarded Caldecott Medal). Author illustrator (with husband): Little Appaloosa, 1949; Squirrely of Willow Hill, 1950; Lost in the Zoo, 1951; Little Whitefoot, 1952; The Friendly Phoebe, 1953; Wish on the Moon, 1954; Home on the Range, 1955; The Runaways, 1956; Ding Dong Bell, 1957; Snow in the City, 1963; Two is Company, Three's a Crowd, 1965. Contbr. stories and drawings to mags. Home: River Rd Grand View-on-Hudson NY 11227 ☆

HADER, ELMER STANLEY, illustrator, writer; b. Pajaro, Calif., Sept. 7, 1889; s. Henry and Lena (Nyberg) H.; student Calif. Sch. of Design, San Francisco, 1907-10; Julian Acad., Paris, France, 1912-14; m. Berta Hoerner, July 14, 1919. Began as landscape artist and portrait painter, 1914; illustrator and writer of children's books since 1919. Zoning adminstr. Village of Grand View-on-Hudson, N.Y., 1925-; mem. adv. bd. dirs. Hudson River Conservation Soc. Served camoufluer, engrs., U.S. Army in World War, 1918-19. Author and co-author numerous books, later ones The Little Stone House, 1944; Rainbow's End, 1945; The Skyrocket, 1946; Little Chip, 1958; Reindeer Trail, 1959; Mr. Billy's Gun, 1960; Quack-Quack, 1961; Little Antelope, 1962. Illustrator (with Berta Hoerner Hader): Bingo Is My Name, Here, Bingo, Humpy, Stripey, The Big Snow, 1948 (awarded Caldecott Medal). Author, illustrator (with wife): Little Appaloosa, 1949; Squirrely of Willow Hill, 1950; Lost in the Zoo, 1951; Little White Foot, 1952; The Friendly Phoebe, 1953; Wish on the Moon, 1954; Home on the Range, 1955; The Runaways, 1956; Ding Dong Bell, 1957; Snow in the City, 1963; Two is Company, Three's a Crowd, 1965. Contbr. stories and drawings to mags. Home: River Rd Grand View-on-Hudson NY 11227 ☆

HADIDIAN, DIKRAN YENOVK, librarian; b. Aintab, Turkey, June 9, 1920; s. Yenovk Haroutune and Helen (Koundakjian) H.; came to U.S., 1946, naturalized, 1956; B.A., Am. U. Beirut, 1944; B.D., Hartford Theol. Sem., 1948; M.A., Hartford Sch. Religious Edn., 1949; S.T.M., Hartford Sem. Found., 1950; M.S. in L.S., Columbia, 1960; m. Jean Root Wackerbarth, June 9, 1948; children—Eric Dikran, Andrew Dikran. Instr. Oak Grove Sch., Vassalboro, Me., 1950-52, Sweet Briar Coll., 1952-57; librarian Hartford Sem. Found., 1957-66, Pitts. Theol. Sem., 1966—, also vis. faculty U. Pitts., 1969—. Mem. corp. bd. United Ch. World Ministries, 1971—. Dir. Pitts. Chamber Music Soc. Mem. Studiorum Novi Testamenti, Soc. Bibl. Literature, Am. Assn. Univ. Profs., Am. Theol. Library Assn. Chmn. editorial bd. of Perpsective, 1967-72; editor series Bibliographia Tripotamopolitana, 1969—. Contbr. articles profl. jours. Home: 4137 Timberlane Dr Allison Park PA 15101 Office: 616 N Highland Av Pittsburgh PA 15206

HADJIMARKOS, DEMETRIOS MARKOS, educator; b. Athens, Greece, Mar. 30, 1912; s. Markos G. and Euterpi (Stamatakes) H.; D.D.S., U. Athens, 1931; M.S.D., Northwestern U., 1943; M.P.H., Harvard, 1946; m. Clara Budlong, Sept. 22, 1954; 1 dau., Marcia-Charlotte. Came to U.S., 1940, naturalized, 1948. Asso. prof. Ore. State U., 1946-52; asst. prof. U. Ore. Dental Sch., Portland, 1953-55, asso. prof., 1955-57, prof., chmn. dept. preventive dentistry, 1957—. Fellow A.A.A.S., Am. Pub. Health Assn. Greek Orthodox. Author: chpts. in books. Contbr. articles profl. jours. Home: 4400 SW Idaho Dr Portland OR 97221

HADLEY, DONALD BOYD, financial writer; b. Grinnell, Ia., Dec. 24, 1903; s. Elam Jessup and Minnie Mae (Boyd) H.; A.B., Grinnell Coll., 1925; postgrad. U. Wis., 1927-28; m. Avo Oma Rice, June 7, 1930; childrenDonald Henry. Asst. state editor Des Moines Register-Tribune, 1925-26; night editor Des Moines bur. A.P., 1926-27; U. Wis. campus corr. Milw. Jour. and copy desk of Wis. State Jour., 1927-28; mng. editor Capitol Hill Beacon, Oklahoma City, 1928-31; bus. editor, editor Washington facts and figures Washington Star, 1936-56, financial editor, daily columnist, 1950-69; free lance writer, 1969-. Mem. Newcomen Soc. Am., Am. Inst. Banking (life, outstanding service award Washington chpt.), Financial Analysts, Sigma Delta Chi. Republican. Conglist. Mason. Club: Exchequer. Home: 9409 Woodland Dr Silver Spring MD 20910

HADLEY, ELBERT HAMILTON, univ. adminstr.; b. Springville, N.Y., July 10, 1913; s. Bert Nelson and Ruth (Oyer) H.; student Wheaton Coll., 1932-34; B.S., U. Mich., 1936, M.S., 1938; Ph.D., Duke 1940; m. Edna Ruth Baker, Dec. 26, 1941; children—Marilyn Ruth, Phyllis Elaine (Mrs. Bryce Ashley Babcock). Teaching asst. Duke 1938-40; sr. research chemist E.I. duPont de Nemours & Co., Niagara Falls, N.Y., 1940-47; asso. prof. So. Ill. U., Carbondale, 1947-56, prof., 1956—, asst. chmn. chemistry dept., 1961-65, asst. dean Coll. Liberal Arts and Scis., 1965-70, asso. dean basic scis., 1970—; vis. prof. Kabul U., Afghanistan, 1960. Recipient Smith-Mundt grant State Dept. for Afghanistan, 1960. Mem. Am. Chem. Soc., Electrochem. Socs., A.A.A.S., Am. Assn. U. Profs., Am. Inst. Chemists, Sigma Xi, Alpha Chi Sigma. Baptist. Contbr. articles profl. jours. Patentee in field. Home: 1002 Briarwood Dr Carbondale IL 62901

HADLEY, FREDERIC MURRAY, coll. pres.; b. Telluride, Colo., July 13, 1907; s. Murray N. and Florence (Henley) H.; A.B., Amherst Coll., 1928; m. Mary Jane Schillinger, Nov. 26, 1936; childrenFrederic Murray, Patricia. With Eli Lilly & Co., Indpls., 1928-60, successively asst. cashier, asst. treas treas., 1928-53, dir., exec. v.p., 1953-60; dir. Host Internat., Mchts. Nat. Bank, H-C Industries, Indpls., Buehler Corp., Indpls. Vice pres. Wabash Coll., Crawfordsville, Ind., 1961-66; pres. Ind. Vocational Tech. Coll., Indpls., 1966—. Mem. adv. com. Nat. Tchr. Corps. Bd. dirs. Earlham Found., 1960-; trustee Amherst Coll., 1960-66. Mem. Ind. C. of C. (dir.). Club: Sixty (pres. 1969-). Home: 6484 N Chester St Indianapolis IN 46220 Office: 99 E 106th St Indianapolis IN 46280

HADLEY, HAMILTON, ret. lawyer; b. New Haven, Jan. 13, 1896; s. Arthur Twining and Helen Harrison (Morris) H.; ed. Groton Sch., 1908-14; B.A., Yale, 1919, LL.B. cum laude, 1923; m. Emily Hammond Morris, July 13, 1929; 1 dau., Anne (Mrs. John Keith Howat). Partner, law firm Winthrop, Stimson, Putnam and Roberts, N.Y.C., 1929-40; trustee U.S. Trust Co., N.Y.C., 1936-68, hon. trustee, 1968—; v.p., dir. Am. Superpower Corp., 1929-40; in period of orgn. and original financing v.p. Niagara Hudson Power Corp., Commonwealth and So. Corp.; dir. Research Corp., 1930-57. Dir. and trustee The Brearley Sch., 1930-54; asso. fellow Branford Coll., Yale, 1939—; former councillor Am. Geog. Soc.; gov. N.Y. Hosp., 1947-65, hon. gov., 1966-, pres., 1953-57. Served as capt. A.E.F., U.S. Air Service, World War I. Life mem. Am. Mus. Natural History, Acad. Polit. Sci., Am. Geog. Soc.; mem. Assn. Bar City N.Y., Am., N.Y. State bar assns. Clubs: Century Assn., Down Town Assn., Yale (N.Y.); New Haven Lawn, Graduates, Elizabethan (New Haven). Author: A Free Order, 1963. Address: Armonk NY 10504

HADLEY, HERBERT MOTTER, religious orgn. exec.; b. Manchester, Okla., Nov. 26, 1915; s. James Perry and Gertrude Edith (Motter) H.; A.B., Friends U., Wichita, Kan., 1939; M.A., U. Pa., 1947; m. Ruthanna Davis, July 6, 1946; childrenCarol A., Helen H., Stephen J. Sec., Friends Meetings, Washington, 1947-55; gen. sec. Friends World Com. Consultation, Birmingham, Eng., 1956-62; editor Friends World News, 1959-62; exec. sec. Friends World Com., Am. sect., Phila., 1962-. Mem. Friends Hist. Assn., Nat. Geog. Soc. Home: 7018 Clearview St Philadelphia PA 19119. Office: 152-A N 15th St Philadelphia PA 19102

HADLEY, JOHN MICHAEL, pub. co. exec.; b. St. Louis, Sept. 23, 1927; s. Leo George and Marsulite Stewart (Nolker) H.; B.A., Washington U., St. Louis, 1950; m. Polly Rolwing, Oct. 16, 1954; childrenPolly Rolwing, Nancy Stewart, Sally Catherine, Laura Nolker. With U.S. Fgn. Service, 1951-53, assigned embassy, Bonn, Germany, 1951, Moscow, USSR, 1952-53; with Hadley Dean Glass Co., St. Louis, 1954-55; with Curtis Pub. Co., 1955-67, pub. Ladies Home Jour., 1963-67, also v.p. co.; exec. v.p. Popular Sci. Pub. Co., 1967—. Served with USNR, 1945-46. Mem. Mag. Pubs. Assn. (dir. 1964-66), Phi Delta Theta. Club: University (N.Y.C.). Home: 20 Park Av Greenwich CT 06830 Office: 355 Lexington Av New York City NY 10017

HADLEY, KATHERINE BLODGETT, former coll. trustee; b. Grand Rapids, Mich., Jan. 13, 1898; d. John W. and Minnie (Cumnock) Blodgett; ed. The Spence Sch., N.Y., 1914-16; A.B., Vassar, 1920; m. Morris Hadley, July 12, 1919; childrenArthur Twining II, Katherine Morris (Mrs. Charles Michel), John W.B., Helen Barbara (Mrs. Dixon L. Stanton). Trustee Vassar Coll., 1942-62, chmn. bd., 1945- 53; mem. Planned Parenthood Fedn. Am. (dir. 1935-45, chmn. exec. com. 1943-45); dir. Internat. Social Service, Inc (pres. Am. br. 1958-65, v.p 1965—), Vis. Nurse Service N.Y., Inst. Internat. Edn. Republican. Presbyn. Club: Colony (N.Y.), Cosmopolitan. Home: Lloyd Neck Huntington NY 11743

HADLEY, MORRIS, lawyer; b. New Haven, Mar 21, 1894; s. Arthur Twining and Helen Harrison (Morris) H.; grad. Groton Sch., 1912; B.A., Yale, 1916, LL.D., 1963; LL.B., Harvard, 1921; m. Katherine Cumnock Blodgett, July 12, 1919; children—Arthur Twining II, Katherine Morris Michel, John W.B., Barbara (Mrs. Dixon L. Stanton). Admitted to N.Y. bar, 1922, began practice, N.Y.C.; partner firm Milbank, Tweed, Hadley and McCloy and predecessor firms, N.Y.C., 1924—. Served in Conn. N.G., 1915-16; commd. maj. 302d Field Arty., U.S. Army, 1917; served with A.E.F. in Meuse-Argonne campaign, 1918; mem. staff, Army of Occupation, 1919. Fellow corp. Yale U., 1940-62; trustee Carnegie Corp., 1947-67, chmn., 1955-66; trustee N.Y. Pub. Library, pres., 1943-58; trustee Pierpont Morgan Library. Mem. Am., N.Y. State, N.Y. County bar assns., Assn. Bar City of N.Y. Republican. Conglist. Clubs: Century, Down Town (N.Y.C.). Author: The Citizen and the Law, 1941; Arthur Twining Hadley, 1948. Home: 71 E 71st St New York City NY 10021 also Lloyd Harbor NY 11978 Office: 1 Chase Manhattan Plaza New York City NY 10005

HADLEY, PAUL ERVIN, educator; b. South Ovid, Mich., July 17, 1914; s. Ervin C. and Viola M. (Barnes) H.; A.B., Occidental Coll., Los Angeles, 1934; A.M., U. So. Cal., 1946, Ph.D. in Comparative Lit., 1955; m. Virginia Faye Last, May 15, 1945; 1 dau., Deborah Faye. Tchr., El Monte (Cal.) Union High Sch., 1935-42; exec. sec. Centro Cultural Paraguayo Americano, Asunción, Paraguay, 1943-44; head Cultural Insts. unit U.S. Dept. State, Washington, 1945; instr. internat. relations U. So. Cal., Los Angeles, 1945-47, asst. prof., 1947-55, asso. prof., 1955-64, prof., 1964—, dean summer session, 1966—, dean U. Coll. and summer session, 1966—; exec. sec. Inst. World Affairs, 1948—; chmn. Pacific Coast Council Latin Am. Studies, 1956-57; mem. Woodrow Wilson Fellowship selection com. Region XV, 1960-67; fgn. leader and specialist program Am. Council on Edn., 1960-62; mem. State Com. on Continuing Edn., 1966—. Chmn. edn. sect. Town Hall of Cal., 1965-68, chmn. internat. relations sect., 1969—. Mem. Assn. U. Summer Sessions (pres. 1970-71), Inst. Internat. Edn. (mem. adv. bd. So. Cal. region), Nat. U. Extension Assn. (chmn. region VI 1970), Adult Educators Greater Los Angeles (chmn. 1970), Phi Beta Kappa, Pi Sigma Alpha. Presbyn. (elder). Home: 3098 Menlo Dr Glendale CA 91208 Office: U So Cal Los Angeles CA 90007

HADLOCK, WENDELL STANWOOD, museum dir.; b. Islesford, Me., May 12, 1911; s. George R. and Edna (Campbell) H.; A.B., U. Me., 1936; M.A., U. Pa., 1946; m. Susan Sadler, July 3, 1936; 1 dau., Jean Campbell. Curator hist. collection, Islesford, Me., summers 1929-35; curator Robert Abbe Mus. of Stone Age Antiquities, Bar Harbor, Me., 1936-50; mus. asst. Peabody Mus., Salem, Mass., 1948-49, adminstrv. asst., 1949-50; dir. William A. Farnsworth Library and Art Mus., Rockland, Me., 1951-; archeol. explorations, Me., New Brunswick, Conn.; cons. Maine Hwy. Commn.; historian, archeologist Acadia Nat. Park. Fellow Am. Anthrop. Soc.; mem. Am. Acad. Arts and Sciences, Am. Archeol. Soc., Am. Folklore Soc., Newcomen Soc. N.Am., Sigma Xi. Contbr. articles archeol., hist. jours. Home: 133 Lake View Dr Rockland ME 04841 Office: William A Farnsworth Library and Art Museum Rockland ME 04841

HADLOW, EARL BRYCE, lawyer; b. Jacksonville, Fla., July 29, 1924; s. Earl Crichton Bryce and Emily Hadlow Bryce; student Clemson Coll., 1941-43; A.B., Duke, 1947, LL.B., 1950; m. Nancy Ann Petway, Apr. 5. 1969; children by previous marriage Richard B., Janet V. Admitted to Fla. bar, 1950, since practiced in Jacksonville; partner firm Mahoney, Hadlow, Chambers & Adams, and predecessors, 1956-; asst. solicitor Duval County, 1952-53. Dir. Barnett First Nat. Bank, Jacksonville. Trustee, gen. counsel Jacksonville U., 1965-; sec., counsel Children's Home Soc. Fla., 1964- . Served with AUS, 1943-46. Fellow Am. Coll. Probate Counsel; mem. Am., Jacksonville (pres. 1966) bar assns., Fla. Bar (bd. govs. 1967-), Order of Coif, Phi Delta Phi, Alpha Tau Omega. Republican. Episcopalian. Author articles. Home: 3412 University Blvd N Jacksonville FL 32211 Office: PO Box 4099 Jacksonville FL 32201

HADSEL, FRED LATIMER, U.S. ambassador; b. Oxford, O., Mar. 11, 1916; s. Fred Latimer and Mary (Perine) H.; A.B., Miami U., Oxford, O., 1937; M.A., Clark U., 1938; Ph.D., U. Chgo., 1942; grad. student U. Grenoble (France), 1933, Freiburg U. (Germany), 1938; m. Winifred Nelson, Oct. 21, 1942; children—Mary C., Winifred R., Jane L. Instr. Rutgers U., 1946; with Dept. of State, 1946; assigned hist. research German Affairs Office, exec. secretariat Bur. Near Eastern, S. Asian and African Affairs, 1946-56; dir. Office So. Africa Affairs, 1956-57; 1st sec. Am. embassy, London, Eng., 1957-61; dep. chief mission Am. embassy, Addis Ababa, Ethiopia, 1961- 62; adviser Bur. African Affairs, Dept. State, 1963-64, dir. Office Inter-African Affairs, 1964; U.S. ambassador to Somalia, 1969-71 to Ghana, 1971—. Professorial lectr. polit. sci. George Washington U., 1947-57, 63—, master Grad. Council, 1947-57. Served from pvt. to maj., AUS, 1942-46. Mem. Phi Beta Kappa, Beta Theta Pi, Omicron Delta Kappa, Phi Eta Sigma. Contbr. articles profl. jours. Address: care Dept of State Washington DC 20520

HAEBERLI, WILLY, educator, scientist; b. Zurich, Switzerland, June 17, 1925; s. Paul and Clara (Christen) H.; Ph.D., U. Basel (Switzerland), 1952; m. Heidi Speiser, Jan 6, 1954; children—Martin Peter, Paul Eric, Frances Barbara. Came to U.S., 1952. Research asso. U. Wis., Madison, 1952-54, asst. prof. physics, 1956-59, asso. prof., 1959-61, prof., 1961-; research asso. Duke, 1954-56; vis. prof. U. Basel, 1961-62. Fellow Am. Phys. Soc.; mem. Sigma Xi. Editor proceedings 3d Internat. Conf. on Polarization Phenomena. Contbr. research papers to tech. publs. Research in polarization of neutrons, protons and deutrons; designer of polarized-ion sources. Office: U Wis Dept Physics Madison WI 53706

HAEBERLIN, JOHN BENJAMIN, Jr., physician; b. Chgo., Sept. 25, 1909; s. John Benjamin and Carolyn (Parrott) H.; B.Sc., U. Chgo., 1930; M.D., C.M., McGill U., 1935; m. Clare Rogerson, Mar. 21, 1936; children—Susan, John. Intern Ill. Research and Edn. Hosp., Chgo., 1936-37; practice of medicine, 1937—, specializing dermatology, 1943—; fellow dermatology U. Ill., 1946-49, clin. asst. prof. dermatology, 1948—; chmn. dept. dermatology Presbyn. Hosp., 1953-59, Presbyn.-St. Lukes Hosp., Chgo., 1959-68. Served from lt. to maj., AUS, 1942-46. Diplomate Am. Bd. Dermatology and Syphilology. Mem. Ill., Chgo. med. socs., A.M.A., Chgo. Dermatological Soc. (pres. 1967), American Acad. Dermatology, Soc. Investigative Dermatology, Am. Dermatological Assn., Wine and Food Soc., Psi Upsilon. Home: Ranchos de Placitas Box 84 Placitas NM 87043

HAECKEL, GERALD BURSETH, oil co. exec.; b. Lewistown, Mont., Oct. 20, 1929; s. Christopher A. and Anne (Burseth) H.; student Mont. State Coll., 1947-48; B.S., U. Pa., 1952; m. Joanne L. Dings, Mar. 17, 1956; childrenJohn, Peter, Stephen. With N.Y. Life Ins. Co., N.Y.C., 1952-66, v.p., 1965-66; v.p. finance Fla. Gas Co., Winter Park, 1966-68; v.p. Hamilton Bros. Oil Co., Denver, 1968—. Served with USNR, 1948-49. Home: 525 Circle Dr Denver CO 80206 Office: 1600 Broadway Denver CO 80202

HAEFF, ANDREW V., scientist; b. at Moscow, Russia, Dec. 30, 1904; s. Vasily A. and Klavdia A. (Makaroff) H.; E.E., M.E., Poly. Inst., 1928; M.S., Cal. Inst. Tech., 1929, Ph.D., 1932; m. Sonya I. Bibikoff. Oct. 22, 1936; 1 son, Andre. Spl. research fellow Cal. Inst. Tech., 1932-33; research engr. RCA, 1934- 41; cons. electronics, head electron tube research br. Naval Research Lab., 1941-50; head electron tube lab. Hughes Aircraft Co., Culver City, Cal., 1950-53, v.p., dir. research, 1954-64, cons. gen. mgr., 1961-64; sr. scientist TRW Space Technology Labs., Redondo Beach, Cal., 1965-66; dir. phys. electronics lab. TRW Systems, Redondo Beach, 1966—. Panel electronics, research and devel. bd. U.S. Dept. Def., also adv. group on electron tubes. President of Santa Monica Symphony Assn., 1968. Recipient Harry Diamond Meml. award Inst. Radio Engrs., 1950. Fellow Am. Phys. Soc., Inst. Radio Engrs.; mem. A.A.A.S. Contbr. articles profl. jours. Patentee in field. Home: 11134 Bellagio Rd Los Angeles, CA 90049. Office: TRW Systems Redondo Beach CA 90277

HAEFLIGER, ERNST, tenor; b. Davos, Switzerland, July 6, 1921; s. Johann and Flaad (Paula) H.; degree music tchr. Music Acad., Zurich, Switzerland, 1943; m. Anna Hadorn, July 16, 1954; childrenChristine, Michael, Andreas. Concert debut, 1943; opera debut, 1949; concert tours throughout Europe, 1945—; leading lyrical tenor Deutsche Oper, Berlin, 1952-; participant festivals Aixen-Provence, Glyndebourne, Salzburg, Lucerne, Munich; N. Am. debut at Vancouver Festival, 1959; rec. artist Columbia Records, Deutsche Grammophone. Recipient German Critics prize, 1955: Chappel Gold medal, 1956. Home: Konzertgesellschaft Zurich Steinwiesstrasse 2 Zurich 7 Switzerland*

HAEGER, LEONARD GEORGE, architect; b. St. Louis, Dec. 2, 1906; s. Leonhard and Ida (Wolf) H.; B.Arch., Washington U., 1928, M.Arch., 1933; m. Nancy Leigh, Feb. 16, 1935; 1 son, John Winthrop. Practice of architecture, St. Louis, 1928- 38; chief architect Nat. Youth Adminstrn., Mo., 1939-41; dir. engring., then asst. dir. research Housing & Home Finance Agy., 1946-50; dir. research Nat. Assn. Homebuilders, Washington. 1950-54; tech. dir. Levitt & Sons, Inc., 1954-58; research cons. and mem. editorial staff House and Garden Mag., 1958-70; prof. architecture Cal. State Polytech. Coll., San Luis Obispo, 1970—. Bd. dirs. Nat. Safety Council, 1953-55. Served as lt. comdr. C.E., USNR, 1942-46, war plans div. Bur. Yards and Docks, Washington. Recipient award for bldg. standardization Am. Standards Assn., 1956. Mem. NRC (dir., bd. govs. Bldg. Research Inst.), A.I.A., Am. Concrete Inst., Am. Soc. Testing and Materials. Club: Army and Navy (Washington). Author: Comprehensive Design Manual for Roofing Systems; also tech. papers on housing. Home: 1153 High Rd Santa Barbara CA 93108 Office: Cal State Polytech Coll San Luis Obispo CA 93401

HAEGER, PHYLLIS MARIANNA, assn. exec.; b. Chgo., May 20, 1928; d. Milton O. and Ethel (Mohr) Haeger; B.A., Lawrence U., 1950; M.A., Northwestern U., 1952. Midwest editor Tide mag., Chgo., 1953-55; account exec. Allied Pub. Relations, Inc., Chgo., 1955-56; with Smith, Bucklin & Assos., Inc., Chgo., 1956—, dir. pub. relations, 1961-63, v.p. for pub. relations, 1963—, also dir. Home: 535 N Michigan Av Chicago IL 60611 Office: 111 E Wacker Dr Chicago IL 60601

HAEHL, JOHN GEORGE, Jr., utility exec.; b. Bklyn., Aug. 16, 1922; s. John George and Madeline (Hamilton) H.; B.S. cum laude, U. So. Cal., 1949; m. Helene Richardson, Oct. 17, 1945; childrenConstance, Victoria. Mgr., Price Waterhouse & Co., C.P.A.'s, N.Y.C., Rochester and Syracuse, N.Y., 1949-61; with Niagara Mohawk Power Corp., Syracuse, 1961-, controller, 1965—, v.p., 1968—. Mem. N.Y. State Bus. Adv. Com., 1966—. Bd. dirs. Syracuse Community Chest, 1965—. Trustee Cazenovia (N.Y.) Coll., 1968—. Served with USNR, 1942-46. C.P.A., N.Y. Mem. Am. Inst. C.P.A.'s, N.Y. State Soc. C.P.A.'s, Financial Execs. Inst., Edison Electric Inst., Gyro Internat. Episcopalian. Club: Onondaga Golf and Country (Fayetteville, N.Y.). Home: 22 Lynacres Blvd Fayetteville, NY 13066. Office: 300 Erie Blvd W Syracuse NY 13202*

HAEKKERUP, PER, former diplomat from Denmark, parliamentarian; b. Ringsted, Denmark, Hans Kristen and Petra Johanna Jensen (Sanddahl) H.; student polit. economy U. Copenhagen; m. Karen Margrethe Hurup, Apr. 5, 1939. Mem. City Council of Copenhagen, 1946-50; mem. Folketing (Parliament) from Copenhagen County, 1950—, floor-leader Social-Democratic party; fgn. minister Denmark, 1962-66. Mem. Consultative Assembly of Council Europe, 1953-62; head Danish delegation to Gen. Assembly UN, 1961, 62. Pres. Social-Democratic Youth Movement, 1946-52; gen. sec. Internat. Union Socialist Youth, 1946-54; editor econ. policy Aktuelt, Social-Democratic daily, 1956-61; pres. N. Atlantic Council. Home: Niels Juelsgade 13 Copenhagen K Denmark. Office: Folketinget Christiansborg Copenhagen Denmark*

HAENIGSEN, HARRY WILLIAM, cartoonist; b. N.Y.C., July 14, 1900; s. Harry W. and Patricha (Crimmins) H.; student Art Students League, 1919; m. Jeannette E. Kerr, June 13, 1925; 1 dau., Jeanne Kerr (Mrs. Jorn Prokop). Illustrator columns, spl. sects. art dept. N.Y. Evening World, 1919-21; mag. illustrator Photoplay, Motion Picture, 1922; comic illustrator, editorial cartoonist nat. mags.; daily cartoon series N.Y. World, 1924- 31, King Features Syndicate, 1931-37; animated cartoons, 1938-39; creator comic Our Bill, N.Y. Herlad Tribune Syndicate, 1939, Penny, 1943, now pub. U.S., Can., S.A., P.I., Europe. Bd. dirs. Bucks County Playhouse, New Hope, Pa., Playhouse Inn; faculty Famous Artists Schs. cartoon course. Mem. Nat. Cartoonists Soc. (exec. bd.), Soc. Illustrators, Phila. Acad. Fine Arts, Modern Mus. N.Y.C. Club: Coffee House (N.Y.C.). Author: Our Bill, His Life and Times, 1947; Penny, 1953; Penny Party Book, 1954; (TV play) Penny, 1954. Home: New Hope, PA 18938 Office: Herald Tribune Syndicate 230 W 41st St New York City NY 10036*

HAENSZEL, WILLIAM MANNING, educator, bio-statistician; b. Rochester, N.Y., June 19, 1910; s. William Edward and Myrtle (Manning) H.; B.A., U. Buffalo, 1931, M.A., 1932; m. Helen Margery Clark, July 26, 1946; childrenCharles Edward, Priscilla Clark, James Irving. Statistician, N.Y. State Dept. Health, 1934-47; dir. bur. vital statistics Conn. Dept. Health, Health, 1947-52; head biometrics sect. Nat. Cancer Inst., 1952-57, asst. chief biometry br., 1957-62, chief, 1962-; lectr. pub. health Yale Sch. Medicine, 1949- 52; adj. prof. biostatistics U. Pitts. Grad. Sch. Pub. Health, 1966-. Mem. U.S. Nat. Com. Vital and Health Statistics, 1964-68; mem. com. human adaptability Nat. Acad. Sci., 1965; commn. epidemiology and cancer prevention Internat. Union Against Cencer, 1966-70; mem. working party methodology of cancer epidemiology WHO, 1965-; chmn. com. studies migrant populations Internat. Union Against Cancer; 1966-70; cons. U.S. Joint Com. Cancer Staging and End-Results, 1961-; cons. WHO, 1961-, Colombia Nat. Com. Against Cancer, 1963-; chmn. orgn. com. Internat. Assn. Cancer Registries, 1967; mem. com. epidemiology and statistics Am. Cancer Soc., 1960-70. Recipient Superior Service award Dept. Health, Edn., Welfare, 1967-. Fellow A.A.A.S., Am. Statis. Assn. (chmn. biometrics sect. 1965-66); mem. Am. Pub. Health Assn. (chmn. statis. sect. 1955-56); mem. Am. Epidemiological Soc., Biometrics Soc.; Regional adv. bd. 1955-57). Author papers in field. Editor: Epidemiological Study of Cancer and Other Chronic Diseases, 1966. Home: 103 Floral Dr Gaithersburg, MD 20760. Office: Nat Cancer Inst Bethesda MD 20014

HAERUM, GUNNAR, Norwegian diplomat; b. Fredrikstad, Norway, May 20, 1923; s. Aksel and Astrid (Arnesen) H.; LL.B., U. Oslo, 1948; m. Ilma-Rita Niiranen, Oct. 30, 1954; 1 son, Jan Erik. Sec., Ministry Fgn. Affairs, Oslo, 1949; attache Norwegian embassy, Washington, 1952-54, sec., Madrid, Spain, 1954-57; sec. Ministry Fgn. Affairs, Oslo, 1957-60; sec. Norwegian embassy Buenos Aires, 1960-64; head div. Office Bilateral Econ. Relations, Ministry Fgn. Affairs, Oslo, 1964-69; minister counselor Norwegian embassy, Washington, 1969—. Home: 4905 Sangamore Rd Washington DC 20016 Office: 3401 Massachusetts Av NW Washington DC 20007

HAESE, GUNTER, sculptor; b. Kiel, Germany, Feb. 18, 1924; s. Max and Emma (Kruger) H.; student Art Sch. Plon, Germany, 1947-49, Art Akademie Dusseldorf, 1950- 58; m. Ursula Schwinge, Apr. 27, 1950; 1 son, Gunter-Georg. Exhibited one man shows at Mus. Ulm, Germany, 1964, Mus. Modern Art N.Y.C., 1964, London, 1965, 33d Biennale, Venice, 1966, Kunsthalle Dusseldorf, 1967, Kunstnernes Hus, Oslo, 1968, 1Oth Biennale, Sao Paulo, 1969; attended 5 Guggenheim Internat. Exhbn., N.Y.C., 1967. Served with AUS, 1942-45. Recipient D.E. Bright prize, Venice, 1966, Cornelius Preis Dusseldorf, 1967, Guggenheim award, N.Y., 1968. Home: 23 Kaiserstrasse Dusseldorf Germany

HAEUSSERMANN, WALTER, aero. devel. engr.; b. Kuenzelsau, Germany, Mar. 2, 1914; s. Otto and Margarete (Henn) H.; B.S., Inst. Tech., Stuttgart, Germany, 1935; M.S., Inst. Tech., Darmstadt, Germany, 1938, Dr. Ing., 1944; m. Ruth Knos, Mar. 24, 1940. Came to U.S., 1948, naturalized, 1954. Research and devel. engr. German Rocket Research Center, Peenemuende, also Inst. Applied Physics, Darmstadt, 1939-45; scientist Inst. Tech., lectr. Coll. Engring., Darmstadt, 1946-47; supr., aero. devel. engr. Guided Missile Research and Devel., Ft. Bliss, Tex., 1948- 50; supr. aero. devel. engring. Ordnance Missile Lab., Redstone Arsenal, Ala., 1950-56; supervising phys. scientist, devel. operations div. Army Ballistic Missile Agy., Guidance and Control Lab., 1956-58, aero. research adminstr., dir. lab., 1958-60; dir. astrionics lab. George C. Marshall Space Flight Center, NASA, Huntsville, Ala., 1960-69, dir. Central System Engring., 1969—; mem. grad. faculty elec. engring. Auburn (Ala.) U. Fellow American Astronautical Soc. Am. Inst. Aeros. and Astronautics; mem. Rocket City Astro. Assn., Inst. Navigation, Sigma Xi. Home: 1067 Sandlin Av SE Huntsville AL 35801 Office: Central System Engring Geo C Marshall Space Flight Center NASA Huntsville AL 35812

HAFEN, LEROY R., historian; b. Bunkerville, Nev., Dec. 8, 1893; s. John George and Mary Ann (Stucki) H.; A.B., Brigham Young U., 1916; M.A., U. Utah, 1919; Ph.D., U. Cal., 1924; Litt.D., U. Colo., 1935; m. Ann Woodbury, Sept. 3, 1915; children—Norma (dec.), Karl LeRoy. Tchr. high sch., Bunkerville, Nev., 1916-18, prin., 1918-20; teaching fellow U. Cal., 1920-23; tchr. A. to Zed Sch., Berkeley, Cal., 1923-24; exec. dir. and state historian State Hist. Soc. Colo., 1924-54; now prof. history Brigham Young U.; prof. history U. Denver; vis. prof. Am. history U. Glasgow, Scotland, 1947-48. Fellow Huntington Library, 1950-51. Editor Colorado Mag., 1925-54. Mem. Am., Western hist. assns., Orgn. Am. Historians, Utah Writers League, Colo. Authors League, Denver Westerners, Utah Westerners. Club: Riverside Country. Author: The Overland Mail, 1926; Broken HandLife of Thomas Fitzpatrick (with W.J. Ghent), 1931; ColoradoThe Story of a Western Commonwealth, 1933; Fort Laramie and the Pageant of the West, 1834-1890 (with F.M. Young), 1938; Western America (with C.C. Rister), 1941, 50, (with W.E. Hollen and C.C. Rister), 1970; Colorado, a Story of the State and Its People (with Ann Woodbury Hafen). 1943; Colorado and Its People (2 vols.), 1948; The Colorado Story (with Ann W. Hafen), 1953, 67. Editor: (with J.H. Baker) History of Colorado, 3 vols., 1927; The Past and the Present of the Pike's Peak Gold Region (by Henry Villard), 1932; Pike's Peak Gold Rush Guide Books of 1859 (1941); The Colorado Gold Rush of 1859 (1941); Diaries of the Gold Rush, 1859 (1942); Ruxton of the Rockies (1950); Life in the Far West (1951); (with Ann W. Hafen) The Far West and the Rockies Series, 15 vols., 1954-62; The Hafens of Utah, 1962; Mountain Men series, 1964—. Contbr. Jour. of Am. History, Pacific Hist. Rev., Am. Hist. Rev., Dictionary Am. Biography, Dictionary Am. History, World Book Ency., Atlas of Am. History, Ency. Brit., Ency. Americana. Home: 1102 Fir Av Provo UT 84601

HAFER, GEORGE HORACE, lawyer; b. Abbottstown, Pa., Mar. 18, 1905; B.S., Gettysburg Coll., 1925; LL.B., Dickinson Sch. Law, 1932. Admitted to Pa. bar, 1932; partner firm Metzger, Hafer, Keefer, Thomas and Wood, Harrisburg; gen. counsel SSS, 1944-46. Mem. Nat. Conf. Commrs. Uniform State Laws, 1951-56, Procedural Rules Com. Supreme Ct. Pa., 1957—. Mem. Am., Fed., Pa., Dauphin County bar assns., Judge Advocate's Assn. (pres. 1949-50), Phi Beta Kappa. Office: 208-210 Walnut St Harrisburg PA 17108*

HAFERBECKER, GORDON MILTON, univ. adminstr.; b. Antigo, Wis., July 19, 1912; s. August A. and Elizabeth (Becker) H.; B.Ed., Wis. State U.-Stevens Point, 1939; M.A., Northwestern U., 1942; Ph.D., U. Wis., 1952; m. Erma R. Groth, May 29, 1937; children-Judith (Mrs. John A. Miller), John. Rural tchr. nr. Antigo, 1931-37; high sch. tchr., Antigo, 1939-42, Beloit, Wis., 1942- 45; instr. Wis. State U.-La Crosse, 1945-46; prof. econs. U. Wis.-Milw., 1946-56; dean instr. Wis. State U.-Stevens Point, 1956-62, v.p. acad. affairs, 1962—, acting pres., 1967; fact-finder, labor arbitrator, 1964--. Dir. First Fed. Savs. & Loan Assn., Stevens Point. Mem. Gov. Wis. Tax Adv. Com., 1959-60; chmn. Portage County chpt. A.R.C., 1963-64. Mem. Am. Econ. Assn., Indsl. Relations Research Assn. Rotarian (pres. Stevens Point 1962-63). Author: Wisconsin Labor Laws, 1958. Home: 1600 Brawley St Stevens Point WI 54481

HAFFNER, CHARLES CHRISTIAN, III, printing co. exec.; b. Chgo., May 27, 1928; s. Charles Christian and Clarissa (Donnelley) H.; grad. Philips Exeter Acad., 1946; B.A., Yale, 1950. m. Anne P. Clark, June 19, 1970. With R.R. Donnelley & Sons Co., Chgo., 1951—, treas., 1962-68, v.p. and treas., 1968—, also dir.; chmn. bd. dirs. Lakeside Bank, 1970. Bd. dirs. Chgo. Nursery and Half Orphan Asylum; trustee Morton Arboretum, Art Inst. of Chgo. Served to 1st lt. USAF, 1952-54. Mem. Nature Conservancy (dir. Ill. chpt.). Clubs: Chicago, Racquet, Caxton (Chgo.). Home: 1524 N Astor St Chicago IL 60610 Office: 2223 South Park Way Chicago IL 60616

HAFFNER, CHARLES CHRISTIAN, Jr., manufacturer; b. Bloomville, O., March 15, 1895; s. Charles Christian and Minnie (Zahner) H.; ed. St George's Sch., Newport, R.I., 1911-14; A.B., Yale, 1919; m. Clarissa Donneley, Oct. 10, 1925; children— Clarissa Gaylord, Charles Christian, Frances Ann, Phoebe Louise. Served as capt. Field Arty. A.E.F., 1918; exec. v.p. City Nat. Bank & Trust Co., 1933-34; treas., v.p., pres. R. R. Donnelley and Sons, 1934-52, chief exec. officer, chmn. bd., 1952-64, chmn. finance com., 1964—. Chmn. bd. directors Lakeside Bank, 1965-70, Col., F.A., Ill. N.G., 1931, brig. gen., 1940; served as maj. gen. AUS, 1942, comdg. 103 div. Mem. N.A.M. (nat. v.p. 1953-55), Ill. Mfrs. Assn. (pres. 1954), U.S. C. of C. (past dir.), Chicago Assn. Commerce and Industry (past dir.). Clubs: Chicago, University, Commercial (Chgo.); Ontwentsia (Lake Forest). Home: 902 N Green Bay Rd Lake Forest IL 60045 Office: 2223 South Park Way Chicago IL 60616

HAFREY, DANIEL JACQUES, fgn. service officer; b. Dniepropetrovsk, USSR, Feb. 5, 1920; s. Anany Yagda-Ogly and Lea (Freidberg) Hanukajev; came to U.S., 1940, naturalized, 1942; B.A. magna cum laude, U. Minn., 1946, postgrad., 1954-56; postgrad. London Sch. Econs. and Polit. Sci., 1949-50; m. Monique Louise Justine Tourneur, Mar. 28, 1947; children—Leigh G., Anne C., Joye L. Copy reader Mpls. Tribune, 1947-52, editor, 1952-55, reporter 1955-61; acting cultural affairs officer Am. Embassy, Leopoldville, Congo, 1961-62; information officer, Am. Embassy, Bangui, 1962-63; asst. information officer, Vienna, Austria, 1963-64, information officer, 1965-68; 1st sec. press and culture, Bucharest, Rumania, 1968—; part-time tchr., research asst. U. Minn., 1950-56. Active P.T.A., Mpls., also Am. and French schs. in Leopoldville, Vienna and Bucharest. Served with AUS, 1942-46; PTO, ETO. Recipient meritorious honor award Regional Projects Office, Am. Embassy, Vienna, 1967. Mem. Am. Newspaper Guild, Phi Beta Kappa, Sigma Delta Chi. Club: Minnesota Press. Home: 42 Strada Snagov Bucharest Rumania Office: Am Embassy Bucharest Rumania

HAFSTAD, LAWRENCE RANDOLPH, physicist; b. Mpls., June 18, 1904; s. Bernt Andrew and Ellen (Bruem) H.; B.S., U. Minn., 1926; Ph.D., Johns Hopkins, 1933; m. Mary Cowen; 1 son, William A. Engr., Northwestern Bell Telephone Co., Mpls., 1920-28; physicist, Carnegie Instn. of Washington, (D.C.), 1928-42; staff Applied Physics Lab., Johns Hopkins, Silver Spring, Md., 1942-45, dir. research, 1945-47; dir. Inst. Coop. Research, 1947-49; exec. sec. Research and Devel. Bd., Office of Sec. of Def., 1947-49; named first director Reactor Devel. Div., AEC, 1949-55; dir. Atomic Energy Div. Chase Manhatten Bank, 1955; v.p. Gen. Motors Corp., director research labs., 1955-69; director Atomic Power Devel. Assos.; trustee Power Reactor Devel. Corp. Cons. exec. office of Pres., dir. research and engring. Dept. Def.; mem. gen. adv. com. AEC; chmn. com. on undersea warfare Nat. Acad. Scis., Washington, 1967—. Trustee Cranbrook Inst. Sci., Johns Hopkins Carnegie Endowment for Internat. Peace; mem. adv. council Fund for Peaceful Atomic Devel. Recipient (with M. A. Tuve) A.A.A.S. award for research and devel. 1,000,000-volt vacuum tube, 1931; medal for merit from Sec. Navy for maj. contbn. in devel. of significant improvements in ordnance for Army and Navy, 1946; King's medal in def. of Freedom, Brit. Govt., 1946; Proctor prize Sci. Research Soc. Am., 1956; Kettering award George Washington University. Fellow American Phys. Soc., Am. Inst. Radio Engrs.; mem. Am. Geophys. Union, Washington Philos. Soc., Washington Acad. Scis., Am. Inst. E.E., Indsl. Research Inst., Soc. Automotive Engrs., Sigma Xi, Tau Beta Pi. Clubs: Orchard Lake Country (Mich.); Cosmos (Washington); Century Assn. (N.Y.C.). Contbr. articles to tech. jours. Home: Willow Point Chester MD 21619 Office: Nat Acad Scis 2100 Pennsylvania Av NW Washington DC 20013

HAFT, HERBERT H., drug stores exec. Pres., Dart Drug Corp. Office: 3301 Pennsy Dr Landover MD 20785*

HAGAN, CHARLES BANNER, educator; b. Irwin, Va., Jan. 27, 1905; s. Patrick C. and Nannie (Dingus) H.; A.B., Emory and Henry Coll., 1926; A.M., U. Va., 1928; Ph.D., Duke, 1933; m. Dorothy Veinus, Apr. 18, 1938; children—Patricia Gray, John Lee. Asst. polit. sci. U Ill., 1934-35, asso. polit. sci., 1937-52, prof. polit. sci., 1952-67, chmn. dept., 1961-65; prof. polit. sci. U. Houston, 1967—, chmn. dept., 1968-71; instr. Smith Coll., 1935-37; vis. lectr. Harvard, 1942-44; vis. prof. Duke, 1971-72; staff Office Intelligence Research, Dept. State, 1952-53; Fulbright lectr. U. Sydney, 1957-58; lectr. U. New South Wales (by the U.S. Australian Ednl. Found.), 1966. Mem. Am., So. polit. sci. assns., Am. Assn. U. Profs., Midwest Conf. Polit. Scientists, Pi Sigma Alpha (pres. 1968). Author: (with Neil F. Garvey) Blueprint for Democracy, 1954; (with Emmette S. Redford) American Government and the Economy, 1965; also articles. Home: 2330 Hilton 16 Durham NC 27707

HAGAN, G. ELLIOTT, congressman; b. Sylvania, Ga., May 24, 1916; student U. Ga., Emory U., John Marshall Law Sch.; m. Frances Bryant; children—G. Elliott, Charles Franklin, Frances Bryant. Engaged in life ins., estate planning; sec.-treas., dep. dir. Ga. Bd. Workmen's Compensation, 1946; Ga. mem. Nat. Council State Govts.; Past mem. Ga. Ho. of Reps., Ga. Senate; mem. 87th-92d congresses 1st Ga. Dist. Dist. dir. OPS, 1951- 52, dep. regional dir. Atlanta office, 1953. Bd. dirs. Grace Home; trustee Tift Coll. Served with Signal Corps, AUS, World War II. Mem. Am. Legion, Farm Bur., Ga. Press Assn. (bd. mgrs. 1941-42), Million Dollar Round Table (life), Marine Tech. Soc. (dir. sect.). Democrat. Baptist. Mason (Shriner), Elk, Rotarian. Home: Sylvania GA 30467 Office: Rayburn House Office Bldg Washington DC 20515

HAGAN, JOHN LOGAN, fgn. service officer; b. Dungannon, Va., Aug. 31, 1913; s. James Bernard and Agnes (Richmond) H.; B.S. in Fgn. Service, Georgetown U., 1942; m. Maria Teresa Surroca, May 28, 1948; children—Patricia, Monica, Jacqueline, John Logan, M. Tara, M. Teresa. Joined U.S. Fgn. Service, 1943; vice consul, prin. officer Puntarenas, Costa Rica, 1944, San Jose, Costa Rica, 1944-48, Lisbon, Portugal, 1948-50; asst. attache, vice consul, Rio de Janeiro, Brazil, 1951-53; consul, prin. officer, Antofagasta, Chile, 1953-55; consul, attache, Dublin, Ireland, 1955-56; 2d sec., consul, 1956-60; fgn. affairs officer Office Internat. Confs., State Dept., 1960-64; consul. gen., Calgary, Alta., Can., 1965-67, Bangkok, Thai. 1967-70, Johannesburg, South Africa, 1970-71; fgn. affairs officer Bur. Internat. Orgns., Dept. State, Washington, 1971—. Adviser numerous U.S. delegations to internat. meetings; pres. Ireland-Am. Soc. Dublin, 1960. Home: Dungannon VA Office: Dept State 10/HDC Washington DC 20520

HAGAN, ROBERT LYLE, univ. dean; b. Kewanee, Ill., Mar. 17, 1913; s. James Jackson and Carrie (Lyle) H.; certificate, Goodman Theatre, Art Inst. Chgo., 1935, B.F.A., 1946, M.F.A., 1947; Ph.D., Western Res. U., 1949; postgrad. U. Mexico, 1959; m. Joyce Tallyn Hagan, Dec. 24, 1946; children—Colette, Adrienne, Denise, James, Robert. Actor, Circuit Theatre Players, Chgo., 1935; actor-dir. Beverly Shores Summer Theatre, Michigan City, Ind., 1935; actor Fed. Theatre Project, Chgo., 1936, 38-39; actor-stage mgr. Old Globe Shakespeare Co., San Diego, 1936; sports announcer, 1937; dir. Ft. Wayne (Ind.) Civic Theatre, 1940-41, Country Playhouse, Lake Wawasse, Ind., summer 1941; radio actor, announcer, Chgo., 1936-49; actor Cleve. Playhouse, 1947; dir. Shaker Heights (O.) Players, 1947-49, also Ind. U. Theatre and Brown County Playhouse; asst. prof. speech and theatre Ind. U., 1949-54; dean Sch. Speech and Theatre, prof. speech and theatre, dir. univ. theater Eastern N.M. U., Portales, 1954—. Chmn. mil. affairs com. Roosevelt County C. of C., 1968; mem. nat. council USO; co-chmn. N.M. USO. Served with USNR, 1942-45. Mem. Am. Ednl. Theatre Assn., ANTA, Am. Assn. U. Profs., N.M. Edn. Assn., Speech Assn. Am., S.W. Theatre Conf., Nat. Theatre Conf., N.M. Speech Assn., N.M. Hereford Assn., Am. Legion. Rotarian, Elk. Author articles in field. Editor S.W. Theatre Topics. Home: 1503 S Avenue A Portales NM 88130

HAGAN, THOMAS WILLIAM, govt. ofcl.; b. Dallas, Aug. 18, 1913; s. Michael Edward and Margaret (Mahoney) H.; student So. Meth. U., 1929-31; B.J. cum laude, U. Tex., 1933; m. Virginia Margaret Moody, Aug. 24, 1942; children Thomas William, Michael Garland, Virginia Margaret, Elizabeth Ann. Engaged as night editor Daily Texan, 1932; reporter Dallas Morning News, 1933; Broward Co. corr., real estate editor, asst. city editor, Sunday editor Miami Daily News, 1933-41, Washington corr., 1941-46, chief editorial writer, 1946-51, editor, 1951-57; chief Washington Bur., Cox Nespapers, 1957-61; dep. asst. dir. pub. affairs OCDM, 1961; director information division Office Emergency Planning, 1961-62, emergency information officer, 1962-69, chief war information services, 1969—; Washington corr. Dayton (O.) Daily News, 1941-46. Mem. citizens bd. U. Miami. Awarded Pulitzer prize (with others) for editorial campaign Miami Daily News, 1938; scholarship Am. Press Inst., Columbia, 1947; prize for editorial writing Fla. Asso. Dailies, 1949, 1951. Mem. Am. Soc. Newspaper Editors (mem. membership com. 1953-54), Nat. Conf. Editorial Writers, Internat. Press Inst., Hist. Assn. South Fla. (mem. bd. dirs., pres.), Florida Society of Editors (treasurer 1957-). White House Corr. Assn.

Montgomery County Historical Soc., Sigma Delta Chi, Sigma Phi Epsilon. Roman Catholic. Club: Nat. Press. Home: 5611 Cromwell Dr Washington, DC 20016. Office: Executive Office Bldg Annex Washington DC 20504

HAGAN, WALLACE WOODROW, geologist; b. Griggsville, Ill., Feb. 3, 1913; s. Warren L. and Mabel Rea (Bruner) H.; B.S., U. Ill., 1935, M.S. (Grad. scholar 1935-36), 1936, Ph.D. (Grad. fellow 1936-37, 40-41), 1942; summer sudent U. Mo., 1937; m. Mary Elizabeth LeVan, Nov. 30, 1940; children—Elizabeth Annette, Karen Rea (Mrs. Annette, Karen Rea (Mrs. James A. Wade). Began career as park geologist Mesa Verde Nat. Park, summer 1935; field asst. Geol. Soc. Am. studies, summers 1935, 36; asst. petroleum Geologist J.V. Wicklund Devel. Co., Detroit, 1937-39; cons. geologist, Greenville, Ky. and Urbana, Ill., 1939-40; geologist charge ground water sect., div. geology Ind. Dept. Conservation, 1942-44; geologist Sohio Petroleum Co., 1945-48, Felmont Oil Corp., 1948-52; cons. geologist, Owensboro, Ky., 1952-58; dir., state geologist Ky. Geol. Survey, 1958—. Mem. topographic mapping com. Ky. C. of C., 1947-51; adv. bd. Ky. Geol. Survey, 1952-58, ex officio mem., 1958—; Am. Assn. State Geologists rep. to Dept. of Interior Geol. Survey div. com. water data for public use, Washington, 1968-71; rep. governor Kentucky research com. Interstate Oil Compact Commn., 1958-70, chmn. com., 1965-66; bd. dirs. Ky. Conservation Congress, also mem. natural resources devel. com. and mineral resources subcom., 1961-64; chmn. quality water com. Ky. Water Resources Study Commn., 1959; rep. gov. Ky. Nat. Water Research Symposium, 1961. Fellow Geol. Soc. Am. (vice chmn. S.E. sect. 1957); mem. Am. Assn. Petroleum Geologists (dist. rep. Great Lakes 1954), Ind.-Ky. (exec. officer 1955-56), Lexington geol. socs., Palentological Soc., Assn. Am. State Geologists (statistician 1963-66, v.p. 1966-67, pres. 1968-69, 69-70, chmn. liaison com. 1966-68), Geol. Soc. Ky. (pres. 1966-67), Ky. Acad. Sci., Ky., Ill. mining insts., Phi Beta Kappa, Sigma Xi, Phi Kappa Phi, Sigma Gamma Epsilon. Methodist (ofcl. bd.). Rotarian. Contbr. articles profl. jours. Home: 317 Jesselin Dr Lexington KY 40503 Office: Ky Geol Survey Univ Ky Lexington KY 40506

HAGARTY, PAUL LEONARD, bishop; b. Greene, Ia., Mar. 20, 1909; s. James Herbert and Lucy Belle (O'Connell) H.; B.A., Loras Coll., Dubuque, Ia., 1930, LL.D., 1950; L.H.D., St. Bernards (Ala.) Coll., 1966, Belmont Abbey Coll., 1964. Jr. meteorologist, Modena, Utah, 1931; ordained priest Roman Catholic Ch., 1936; tchr. biology St. John's Prep. Sch., Collegeville, Minn., 1936-37; missionary, Nassau, Bahamas, 1937-50; titular bishop Arba, vicar apostolic Bahamas, 1950; bishop of Nassau, 1960—. Address: PO Box N-8 187 Nassau Bahamas

HAGEDORN, ROBERT HARRY, banker; b. St. Bernard, O., June 30, 1920; s. Harry G. and Frieda (Flatt) H.; student U. Cin., 1938-40, 44-46; grad. NABAC Sch. Banking, U. Wis., 1959; m. Susan Koncz, Jan. 9, 1954; 1 dau., Margot. From jr. accountant to sr. accountant Ernst & Ernst, C.P.A.'s, Cin., 1944-51; with Central Trust Co., Cin., 1951—, auditor, 1963-69, asst. v.p., 1969—. Served to 2d lt. AUS, 1942-44. Mem. Bank Adminstrn. Inst. Home: 3730 Yellowstone Dr Cincinnati, OH 45239.

HAGEL, RAYMOND CHARLES, publishing co. exec.; b. Jersey City, Sept. 5, 1916; s. Morris and Theresa (Feigenbaum) H.; B.S. cum laude, N.Y.U., 1937; m. Ruth Block, May 30, 1941; children—Keith W., Wendy A. Promotion mgr. McGraw-Hill Pub. Co., 1938-42, 45-48; pres. Smith, Hagel & Knudsen, Inc., N.Y.C., 1948-59; pres. P.F. Collier & Son Corp., N.Y.C., 1959-60, chmn. bd., 1961-65; exec. v.p. Crowell-Collier Pub. Co. (name changed to Crowell Collier and MacMillan, Inc. 1965), 1959-60, pres., chief exec. officer, 1960—, chmn. bd., 1964—, also dir. Trustee Coll. of New Rochelle, 1970—. Served with USNR, 1942-45. Mem. Fgn. Policy Assn., Alpha Delta Sigma, Beta Gamma Sigma. Clubs: Economic (dir.), Lotos, Publisher's Lunch (N.Y.C.). Home: 2 Broadview Rd Westport CT 06880 Office 866 3d Av New York City NY 10022

HAGEL, ROGER S., chain food store exec.; b. 1918; married. Propr. supermarket, 1944-59; regional v.p. Arden-Mayfair, Inc., 1959-67; dir. store operations A.J. Bayless Markets, Inc., Phoenix, 1967-68, sr. v.p., dir. retail operations, 1968-69, pres., chief exec. officer, 1969—, also dir. Office: 111 E Buckeye Rd Phoenix AZ 85004*

HAGELMAN, CHARLES WILLIAM, Jr., educator; b. Houston, Nov. 9, 1920; s. Charles William and Anna Marie (Griffin) H.; B.A., U. Tex., 1942, Ph.D. (fellow 1952-53), 1956; M.A., Columbia, 1947; student Washington U., St. Louis, 1942, Va. Mil. Inst., 1943-44; m. Elizabeth Drisler Sloan, Sept. 7, 1946; childrenLucy Ann, Charles William III, John Francis. Part-time instr. English, Columbia, 1946-47; instr. Muhlenberg Coll., 1947-51, U. Tex., 1953-55; instr., then asst. prof. and asso. prof. U. Houston, 1955-59; prof. English, head dept. Lamar State Coll., Beaumont, Tex., 1959-66; prof. English, asso. dean humanities Coll. Arts and Scis. U. Toledo (Ohio), 1966-68; prof. English, chmn. dept. No. Ill. U., Dekalb, 1968—; tech. writing cons., 1956—; editorial cons. Survival Planning Project Houston-Harris County Area, 1956-57, Business Rev. mag., 1957-59. Rep. Lamar State Coll. to So. Humanities Conf., 1961- . Served with AUS, 1942-46. Mem. Modern, South Central lang. assns., Keats-Shelley Assn., Am. Studies Assn., Am. Assn. U. Profs., Nat. Council Tchrs. English, Conf. Coll. Composition and Communication, Conf. Coll. Tchrs. English (pres.), Phi Kappa Phi. Episcopalian. Recipient of United States Steel Co. award for outstanding achievement teaching U. Houston, 1958. Editor, author introduction A Vindication of the Rights of Woman, 1966; (with Robert J. Barnes) A Concordance to Byron's Don Juan, 1967. Contbr. articles profl. jours. Office: Dept English No Ill U Dekalb IL 60115

HAGEMAN, CARL HENRY, mfg. exec.; b. Lorain, O., Feb. 26, 1912; s. Carl Henry and Flo May (Kissling) H.; B.S., Harvard, 1933; m. Isabelle W. Close, Apr. 24, 1938; childrenKathleen A., Robert H. With Union Carbide Corporation. New York City 1933—, beginning in works lab. Carbon Products div. Fostoria, O., successively at Carbon Products Plants in Clarksburg, W.Va., Columbia, Tenn., Niagara Falls, N.Y., Chgo., Morgantown, N.C., transferred to N.Y.C. office, 1944, asst. mgr., then mgr. indsl. relations metals div., 1947-53, asst. mgr., then mgr. indsl. relations for corp. 1953-56, vice pres. indsl. relations, 1956-61, vice president of corporation, 1961—, Mem. American Mgmt. Assn., Mfg. Chemists Assn., Commerce and Industry Assn., N.Y., Nat. Urban League. Mason. Clubs: Harvard (N.Y.C.); Apawamis (Rye, N.Y.). Home: Adams Place Harrison, NY 10528. Office: 270 Park Av New York City NY 10017

HAGEMAN, ELMER LAVERNE, union ofcl.; b. Ford, Kan., May 13, 1905; s. Oscar Y. and Rella (Imel) H.; m. Evelyn T. Kelly, Apr. 5, 1941; 1 dau., Helen. Morse operator, printer operator, telegraph technician Western Union, 1921-46; regional pres. Western Union div. Comml. Telegraphers Union, Eastern region, 1947- 53, nat. pres. Western Union div., 1953—, internat. pres. United Telegraph Workers, AFL-CIO, 1963—. Home: 4205 4th St S Arlington VA 22204 Office: Dupont Circle Bldg Washington DC 20036

HAGEMAN, HOWARD GARBERICH, clergyman; b. Lynn, Mass., Apr. 19, 1921; s. Howard G. and Cora E. (Derfler) H.; grad. Albany Acad., 1938; A.B., Harvard, 1942; B.D., New Brunswick Sem., 1945; D.D. (hon.), Central Coll., 1957; m. Carol Christine Wenneis, Sept. 15, 1945. Ordained to ministry Reformed Ch., 1945; minister North Reformed Dutch Ch., Newark, 1945—; exchange lectr. S. Africa, 1956; lectr. New Brunswick, Bloomfield, Princeton sems. Pres. gen. synod Reformed Ch. Am., 1959-60. Mem. Societas Liturgica (internat. treas. 1967—), Holland Soc. N.Y. (asso. domine), Phi Beta Kappa. Author: Lily Among the Thorns, 1952; We Call This Friday Good, 1961; Pulpit and Table, 1962; The Book that Reads You, 1962; Predestination, 1963; That the World May Know, 1965; Advice to Mature Christians, 1965. Home: 595 Parker St Newark NJ 07104 Office: 510 Broad St Newark NJ 07102

HAGEMANN, HENRY FREDERICK, Jr., banker; b. St. Louis, May 24, 1906; s. Henry Frederick and Helen Ann (Oonk) H.; B.S., Washington U., St. Louis, 1926; m. Leita Perkins Amory, Mar. 15, 1940; children—Louise Amory, Helen Ann, Leita, Henry Frederick III. With municipal bond dept. Kauffman, Smith & Co., St. Louis, 1926-29; mgr. bond dept. Boatmen's Nat. Co., St. Louis, 1929-33; asst. v.p., mgr. bond dept. Boatmen's Nat. Bank, St. Louis, 1933-38, v.p., 1938-43, v.p. banking div., 1943-46; pres., chief exec. officer Nat. Rockland Bank of Boston, 1946 (Nat. Rockland Bank consol. with Webster & Atlas Nat. Bank 1948), Rockland-Atlas Nat. Bank, 1948-61; pres., chief exec. officer State Street Bank & Trust Co., Boston, 1961-65, chmn., pres., chief exec. officer, 1965-70, chmn., chief exec. officer, 1970-71, dir., mem. exec. and trust couns., 1971—; pres. 18th St. Bldg. Co., St. Louis; dir., mem. exec. com. Southwestern Pub. Service Co., Dallas, Petrolite, St. Louis; mem. finance com., dir. N.E. Mut. Life Ins. Co., Boston: trustee, mem. investment com. Provident Instn. for Savs. Trustee Infants' Hosp., Lying- in-Hosp., Museum of Sci. Mem. Sigma Chi, Beta Gamma Sigma. Clubs: The Country (Brookline); Somerset, Union, Algonquin (Boston); Kittansett (Marion). Home: 37 Woodman Rd Chestnut Hill MA 02167 Office: 225 Franklin St Boston MA 02110

HAGEMEYER, EDWARD W., banker; B. N.Y.C., 1914. Pres., Farmers Bank of Del., Dover. Treas., mem. exec. com., bd. dirs. United Community Fund No. Del.; mem. Nat. Budget and Consultation Com. Bd. dirs. West End Neighborhood House Inc., Assn. Greater Wilmington Neighborhood Centers, Inc.; trustee, chmn. finance commn. Del. State Coll. Home: 43 Paschall Rd Wilmington DE 19803 Office: 8 Loockerman St Dover DE 19901*

HAGEN, EVERETT E., educator, economist; b. Holloway, Minn., July 5, 1906; s. John J. and Marthea (Moe) H.; A.B., St. Olaf Coll., 1927; M.A., U. Wis., 1932, Ph.D., 1941; m. Ruth Alexander, June 4, 1937. Tchr. high schs., Minn. and Wis., 1927- 36; instr. econs. Mich. State Coll., 1937-42; economist Nat. Resources Planning Bd., 1942-43, OSS, 1943, to bd. govs. Fed. Res. System, 1943- 45; econ. adviser, chief div. fiscal policy and program planning Office War Moblzn. and Reconversion, Washington, 1945-46; chief fiscal analyst Bur. of Budget, 1946-48; prof. econs. U. Ill., 1948-51, chmn. dept., 1950-51; econ. adviser Govt. of Burma, 1951-53; vis. prof. econs. Center internat. Studies, Mass. Inst. Tech., 1953-58, prof. econs., 1958—, prof. polit. sci., 1964—, dir. center, 1970—; econ. adviser Govt. of Japan, 1956. Mem. Am. Econ. Assn., Royal Econ. Soc., Am. Acad. Arts and Scis., Phi Beta Kappa. Author: Handbook for Industry Studies, 1956; Economic Development of Burma, 1956; On the Theory of Social Change, 1962; Economics of Development, 1968; co-author: The Sioux on the Reservation, 1960; Economics and The Emerging Nations, 1961. Editor: Planning Economic Development, 1963. Contbr. profl. jours. Home: 100 Memorial Dr Cambridge MA 02142

HAGEN, GEORGE LEON, chem. co. exec.; b. Bancroft, Ida., Sept. 8, 1924; s. George William and Mabel (Waddell) H.; student Mont. Sch. Mines; B.Sc. in Chem. Engring., U. Wash., 1948, B.Sc. in Indsl. Engring., 1951; m. Anita Louise Rowe, Aug. 31, 1946; children—Richard Lee, Judy Ann, Paul Evan, Phillip Bradley. Indsl. engr. methods Boeing Airplane Co., 1948-51; with Reichhold Chems. Inc., Seattle, 1951-61, plant engr., sales rep., 1956- 61; with Reichhold Chems. (Can.) Ltd., Weston, Ont., 1961—, v.p., 1963—, exec. v.p., 1964-66, pres., 1966—, chief exec. officer, 1971—, also dir.; chmn. bd. Can. Printing Ink Co., Ltd., Toronto, Ont., 1968—. Mem. Toronto Bd. Trade. Served with USNR, 1943-45. Registered profl. engr., Wash., B.C. Mem. Am. Inst. Chem. Engrs., Forest Products Research Soc., Soc. Plastic Engrs., T.A.P.P.I., Am. Mgmt. Assn., Phi Kappa Psi. Clubs: Mississauqua Golf and Country; Port Credit Yacht. Patentee formaldehyde mfg. Home: 1485 Mildmay Ct Clarkson Ontario Canada Office: Reichhold Chems (Can) Ltd 1919 Wilson Av Weston Ontario Canada

HAGEN, JOHN P., astronomer; b. Amherst, N.S., Can., July 31, 1908; s. John T. and Ella Bertha (Fisher) H.; B.S., Boston U., 1929, Sc.D., 1959; M.A., Wesleyan U., Middletown, Conn., 1931; postgrad. Yale, 1931-33; Ph.D., Georgetown U., 1949; Sc.D., Fairfield U., 1958, Loyola U., 1959, Adelphi Coll., 1959; Sc.D., Mount Allison (Canada), 1960; m. Edith W. Soderling, Oct. 12, 1935; children—J. Peter, E. Christopher. Research asso. Wesleyan U., 1931-35; supt. atmosphere and astrophysics div., devel. microwave radar, radio astronomer, mem. various eclipse expdns. Naval Research Lab., Washington, 1935-58; asst. dir. space flight devel. NASA, 1958-60, dir. OUNC, 1960-62; prof. astronomy Pa. State U., 1962—, head dept. astronomy, 1966—. Project dir. Earth Satellite Project; lectr. Georgetown U. Recipient Presdl. Certificate of Merit; Distinguished Service medal U.S. Navy, 1958. Fellow Inst. Radio Engrs., Am. Acad. Arts and Scis., Royal Astron. Soc (Eng.); mem. Am. Astron. Soc., Internat. Astron. Union, Washington Acad. Scis., U.R.S.I. (past chmn. nat. com.), Phi Beta Kappa, Sigma Xi. Home: 613 W Park Av State College PA 16801 Office: Whitmore Pa State U University Park PA 16802

HAGEN, UTA, actress; b. Gottingen, Germany, June 12, 1919; d. Oskar F. L. and Thyra A. (Leisner) H.; m. Herbert Berghof, Jan. 24, 1951; 1 dau., Leticia. Played Ophelia, Dennis, Mass., 1937, Nina in Sea Gull, N.Y.C., 1938, Key Largo, 1939, Vicki, 1942, Othello, 1943-45, Whole World Over, Faust, Masterbuilder, 1947, Angel Street, 1948, Street Car Named Desire, 1948, Country Girl, 1950; G. B. Shaw's Saint Joan, 1951-52, Tovarich, City Center, 1952, In Any Language, 1952; The Deep Blue Sea, 1953; The Magic and the Loss, 1954; The Island of Goats, 1955; A Month in the Country, 1956; Good Woman of Setzvan, 1957; Who's Afraid of Virginia Wolff, 1962-64; The Cherry Orchard, 1968; tchr. acting Herbert Berghof Studio, N.Y.C., 1947—. Recipient Perry award, Critics award, Donaldson award best actress, 1951; Tony award, 1963; Critics award for best actress 1963-64 season. Address: Herbert Berghof Studio 120 Bank St New York City NY 10014

HAGENAH, WILLIAM JOHN, lawyer, corp. exec., b. Reedsburg, Wis., Jan. 25, 1881; s. John Henry and Catherine (Meyer) H.; B.L., U. Wis., 1903, LL.B., 1905, LL.D., 1956; LL.D. Northland Coll., 1952; m. Florence Doyon, July 26, 1913; children- -Florence Catherine, William John. Statistician, Wis. Bur. Labor, 1905; dep. commr. labor, 1906; chief financial and legal depts. Wis. R.R. Commn., 1907-10, cons. expert, 1911; engr. and analyst, specializing in pub. service commn. practice, cons. City of Chgo., 1910-11; made appraisals and rate studies of gas, telephone, traction, electric and water utilities for states, municipalities or corps., covering one or more of such utilities in Akron, Butte, Chgo., Cleve., Dayton, Detroit, Des Moines, Duluth, Indpls., Louisville, N.Y.C., Omaha, Portland (Ore.), St. Louis, Springfield (Mass.), Toronto, Wichita, Birmingham, Columbus, Montreal, Washington, Milw., Houston, Seattle, St. Paul, Los Angeles, Mobile, Jacksonville, Tulsa, Balt., Pitts., Erie, Charleston, Grand Rapids, Cin., San Francisco, Nashville, Chattanooga, also Rio Janeiro, Sao Paulo and other cities in Brazil, cities in Mexico and W.I., 1911-28, as mem. Hagenah & Erickson, 1916-28; v.p., spl. counsel Byllesby Engring. and Mgmt. Corp., 1928-31; mem. Hagenah & Flynn, counsel for Standard Gas & Electric Co. and subsidiaries, 1931- 38; pres. Pub. Utility Engring. and Service Corp., 1938-42; dir. and chmn. bd. Schering Corp., Bloomfield, N.J., 1942-52; dir. Mather Stock Car Co., 1947-56, chmn. bd., 1953-56; dir. Adams and Westlake Co., 1948-65, Aladdin Industries, Ltd. (London, Eng.), Alladin Industries, Inc. (Nashville), N.Am. Car Corp. (Chgo.), 1955-70. Vice pres. Nat. Electric Light Assn., 1932; v.p. Edison Elec. Inst., 1933-35, trustee, 1935-43; chmn. Utilities Publ. Com., Washington. past pres. Glencoe Bd. Trustees; trustee Rush Med. Coll., Chgo., 1937-69, Northland Coll., Ashland, Wis. Seabury-Western Theol. Sem., Evanston, Ill.; Alonzo Mather Home for Ladies, Evanston, Ill. (pres.); v.p., chmn. U. Wis. Found.; chmn. Alonzo Mather Found., Chgo. hon. trustee Rush, Presbyn. and St. Lukes Med. Center, Chgo., 1969. Mem. Am., Ill., Chgo., Wis. bar assns., Wis. Acad. Sci. and Letters, Wis. Soc. (pres.), Phi Alpha Delta, Delta Sigma Rho. Republican. Episcopalian. Mason. Clubs: Chicago, Mid-Day, Union League (Chgo.); Skokie Country (Glencoe, Ill.). Home: Glencoe IL 60022

HAGENAH, WILLIAM JOHN, Jr., chewing gum mfg. exec.; b. Chgo., Aug. 3, 1920; s. William John and Florence (Doyon) H.; A.B., Princeton, 1942; children—William, Philip, Blanny, John; m. 2d, Marjorie Clark. With Wm. Wrigley Jr. Co., Chgo., 1945—, asst. to treas., 1953-59, v.p., asst. treas., 1959—; dir. Wm. Wrigley Jr. Co., Ltd., Amurol Products Co., Wrigley Import Co., L.A. Dreyfus Co., Four-Ten Corp., Chgo. Nat. League Ball Club, Inc. Served to lt. USNR, 1942-45. Home: 92 Woodley Rd Winnetka IL 60093 Office: 410 N Michigan Av Chicago IL 60611

HAGENDORN, WILLIAM, credit card exec., lawyer; b. Bklyn., Sept. 1, 1925; s. William V. and Florence (Hull) H.; A.B., Princeton U., 1944; J.D., Harvard, 1949; LL.M., N.Y.U., 1952. Admitted to N.Y. bar, 1949, since practiced in N.Y.C.; asso. firm Carter, Ledyard & Milburn, N.Y.C., 1961-65; gen. counsel Am. Express Co., 1965—, Wells Fargo & Co., 1965-68, Equitable Securities, Morton & Co., N.Y.C., 1966—. Adviser to com. uniform consumer credit code Nat. Conf. Uniform State Laws, 1966-68. Served with inf. AUS, 1944-46. Mem. Assn. Bar City N.Y., Bklyn. Bar Assn. Clubs: University, Princeton (N.Y.C.). Home: 120 E 81st St New York City NY 10028 Office: 65 Broadway New York City NY 10006

HAGENSTEIN, WILLIAM DAVID, forester, assn. exec.; b. Seattle, Mar. 8, 1915; s. Charles William and Janet (Finigan) H.; B.S. in Forestry, U. Wash., 1938; M. Forestry, Duke, 1941; m. Ruth Helen Johnson, Sept. 2, 1940. With Dept. Agr., Hat Creek, Cal., 1938, Eagle Logging Co., Sedro-Woolley, Wash., 1939, U.S. Forest Service, N. Bend, Wash., 1940; forester W. Coast Lumbermen's Assn., Seattle and Portland, Ore., 1941-43, 45-49; sr. forester FEA, S. and Central Pacific Theaters of war and Costa Rica, 1943-45; mgr. Indsl. Forestry Assn., Portland, 1949—, exec. v.p., 1956—; H.R. MacMillan lectr. forestry U. B.C., 1952; Benson Meml. lectr. U. Mo., 1966; cons. forest engr. U.S.N., P.I., 1952. Trustee Wash. Forestry Conf., 1948—; trustee Keep Ore. Green Assn., 1957—, v.p., 1970-71; adv. trustee Keep Wash. Green Assn., 1957—; v.p., dir. Western Forestry Center, 1965—; mem. forestry com. Portland C. of C., 1948—, chmn., 1960-62; trustee Ore. Mus. Sci. and Industry, 1968—; forestry adv. com. Nat. Forest Products Assn., 1949—; mem. U.S. Forest Products Trade Mission, Japan, 1968. Recipient Charles Lathrop Pack Found. prize in forestry U. Wash., 1938; Forest Mgmt. award Nat. Forest Products Assn., 1968. Registered profl. engr., Wash., Ore. Fellow Soc. Am. Foresters (council 1958-63, pres. 1966-69); life mem. Am. Forestry Assn. (hon. v.p. 1966-69), mem. Commonwealth Forestry Assn., Xi Sigma Pi. Repbulican. Author: (with Wackerman and Michell) Harvesting Timber Crops, 1966; also numerous articles. Asso. editor Jour. Forestry, 1946- 53. Home: 3062 SW Fairmount Blvd Portland OR 97201 Office: 1410 SW Morrison St Portland OR 97205

HAGENY, WILLIAM JOSEPH, educator; b. Oswego, N.Y., June 30, 1907; s. William and Katherine (Cronin) H.; B.S., Hobart Coll., 1930; M.S., Syracuse U., 1932; Ed.D., Columbia, 1946; m. Mildred Boyce, Jan. 29, 1934 (dec. Oct. 1962); children—Jean (Mrs. James Lahey), Hannah (Mrs. A. Anderson); m. 2d, Frances Long, Dec. 27, 1965. Tchr. history high schs., N.Y., N.J., 1930-37; prin. high sch., Cold Spring, N.Y., 1937-38, supervising prin., 1938-58; prof. edn. State U. N.Y. Coll. at New Paltz, 1958-69, prof. edn., chmn. dept. adminstrn. and supervision, 1969—. Exec. sec. Mid-Hudson Sch. Study Council, 1958-71; pres. N.Y. State Council Adminstrv. Leadership, 1957; mem. joint legislative com. N.Y. State revision edn. law, 1965-68; mem. Council E.R.I.E., 1966-71. Mem. bd. edn., New Paltz Central Sch., 1961-69. Trustee Regional Ednl. Supplementary Center, Ulster County Community Coll. Mem. N.Y. State Assn. Secondary Sch. Prins. (pres. 1956), N.E.A., N.Y. State Sch. Bds. Assn., Collegiate Assn. for Devel. of Ednl. Adminstrn. (pres. 1971), Nat. Orgn. Legal Problems Edn. Republican. Club: Paltz (New Paltz). Author: Handbook on New York State Education Law, rev. biennially, 1945—; The Teacher and the Law in New York State, 1968; Legal Status of Principals, 1970; Landmark Cases and Commissioner's Decisions—N.Y. State, 1971. Contbr. articles profl. jours. Home: 46 Plattekill Av New Paltz NY 12561

HAGER, CARL, educator; b. Plymouth, Ind., Oct. 15, 1911; s. Frank and Catherine (Rafferty) H.; A.B., U. Notre Dame, 1935, A.M., 1941; Mus.B., DePaul U., 1950, Mus.M., 1951. Ordained priest Roman Catholic Ch., 1939; instr., asst. prof. U. Notre Dame, 1941-56, asso. prof. music, 1956-68, prof., 1968—, chmn. dept. music, 1956-. Mem. Ind. Music Tchrs. Assn., South Bend Recorder Soc., South Bend Chamber Music Soc. Composer: And Time Shall Be No Longer, a cantata, 1963; Parish Mass in English, 1965. Home: U Notre Dame Music Dept Notre Dame, IN 46556.

HAGER, CYRIL FRANCIS, educator; b. Marshfield, Wis., Mar. 7, 1914; s. Anton James and Josephine (McNamee) H.; B.A., U. Wis., 1936, M.A., 1937, Ph.D., 1942; postgrad. Cornell U., 1938-39; m. Margaret Ruth Wood, Sept. 11, 1937; 1 son, Anthony Wood. Instr., Cornell U., Ithaca, N.Y., 1938-39; asst. prof. Eastern Ky. State Coll., Richmond,, 1940-42; with A.R.C., China, India, 1943-44; asst. prof. Mich. State U., 1944-45; asso. prof., dept. chmn. Syracuse U., 1945-49; ednl. dir., adviser Air War Coll., Maxwell AFB, 1949-56; dean Sch. Fgn. Affairs, Fgn. Service Inst., U.S. Dept. State, 1956-58; dir., asso. dean Coll. Liberal Arts, Pa. State U., University Park, 1958, dir. Center Continuing Liberal Edn., prof. social sci. and internat. policy studies, 1958—; cons. Dept. State, Ford Found., U.S. Senate Com. on Govt. Operations, Pa. Dept. Pub. Instrn., Pa. Dept. Community Affairs. Vice pres. Axe-Houghton Found., N.Y.C., 1970—. Served to lt. col. USAF, 1951-60. Recipient Superior Accomplishment award USAF, 1954, Outstanding Performance award, 1956. Mem. Speech Assn. Am. Republican. Roman Catholic. Author: (with Oliver and Cartwright) New Training for Effective

Speech, 1946. Planning editor: Bases of International Relations, 1957; Current U.S. Military Strategy, 1959. Co-editor: The North Atlantic Community, 1965. Home: 520 Sunset Rd State College PA 16801 Office: Pa State U Center for Continuing Liberal Edn University Park PA 16801

HAGER, DON JOSEPH, sociologist, educator; b. Dayton, O., Apr. 21, 1951; s. Lorin Maurice and Marie Virginia (Neidhammer) H.; student Ohio Wesleyan U., 1934-35; B.A., Ohio State U., 1941, Ph.D. in Sociology and Anthropology, 1948; m. Hilda Corr, Feb. 28, 1942; childrenMeredith Jane, Loren Michael, Jonathan Corr. Instr. sociology-anthropology Ohio State U., 1946-48; asst. prof. sociology Princeton, 1948-53; dir. research Am. Jewish Congress, 1953-57; prof. sociology-anthropology, chmn. dept. Cal. State Coll. at Los Angeles, 1957-67, chmn. academic senate, 1963-64; also sometime lectr. Columbia, N.Y.U., New Sch. Social Research; research asso. Inst. Human Biology, U. Mich., 1951-52; cons. Cal. regional office Office Econ. Opportunity. Mem. constl. rights sect., adv. bd. Cal. Dept. Justice, 1960-; chmn. com. research So. Cal. Conf. Human Relations, 1960-62. Served with AUS, 1942-45; ETO. Fellow Am. Sociol. Assn.; mem. Soc. Study Social Problems, Soc. Psychol. Study Social Issues, Am. Assn. U. Profs., Sigma Xi. Home: 792 28th St San Pedro CA 90731 Office: Cal State Coll at Los Angeles Los Angeles CA 90032

HAGER, ERIC HILL, lawyer; b. Albany, N.Y., Oct. 5, 1918; s. Herman Edward and Irma Adele (Hill) H.; grad. Phillips Exeter Acad., 1935; A.B. summa cum laude, Princeton, 1939; LL.B., Yale, 1942; m. Jean Dutcher, Apr. 1, 1949 (dec. July 1968); children—George Dutcher, Susan Hill, Bruce Linton. Admitted to N.Y. State bar, 1946, D.C. bar, 1960; law asso. Shearman & Sterling, N.Y.C., 1946-52, partner, 1952-59, 61-; legal adviser Dept. State, 1959-61. Mem. arbitrators panel Internat. Telecommunications Satellite Consortium (Intelsat), 1967-69, adviser U.S. delegation to internat. conf. on definitive arrangements, 1969, dep. chmn. delegation, 1970. Dir. Forbes Inc. Trustee Miriam Osborne Meml. Home Assn., Rye, N.Y. Served to capt. AUS, 1942-46. Decorated Bronze Star medal. Mem. Inter-Am., Am., N.Y. State, Fed. bar assns., Assn. Bar City N.Y., Am. Soc. Internat. Law, Council on Fgn. Relations, Phi Beta Kappa, Order of Coif, Phi Delta Phi. Republican. Episcopalian. Clubs: Links, Princeton, Down Town Assn. (N.Y.C.); Metropolitan (Washington); Belle Haven, Round Hill (Greenwich); University Cottage, Nassau (Princeton). Home: Lake Av Greenwich CT 06830 Office: 53 Wall St New York City NY 10005

HAGER, GEORGE PHILIP, coll. dean; b. Balt., Mar. 16, 1916; s. George Philip and Marie Theresa (Zilch) H.; B.S. in Pharmacy, U. Md., 1938, M.S., 1940, Ph.D., 1941; postgrad. U. Colo., 1938-39; m. Margaret Kathryn League, Dec. 24, 1938; children—Philip, Priscilla, Deborah, Andrew. Postdoctorate fellow Northwestern U., 1941-42; research organic chemist Lilly Research Labs., 1942-45; asst. prof. chemistry U. Md., 1945-48, prof. pharm. chemistry, head dept., 1948-55; sr. sci. Smith Kline & French Labs., 1955-57; dean U. Minn Coll. Pharmacy, 1957-66; dean Sch. Pharmacy, U. N. C. at Chapel Hill, 1966—. Nat. adv. com. selection physicians, dentists and allied specialists/nat. health resources adv. com. SSS; mem. com. on chem. information Nat. Acad. Scis.-NRC, 1961-68, chmn., 1961-66; adv. com. research in biol. and phys. scis. FDA, 1966—; cons. div. physician manpower Bur. Health Manpower, USPHS ednl. facilities br., 1966—, chem. information program office Sci. Information Service NSF, 1965—; pharmacist dir. USPHS, 1967; cons. surg. gen. USAF. Mem. Am. (chmn. sci. sect. 1956-57, trustee 1968-71), N.C. pharm. assns., Am. Chem. Soc. (vice chmn.), Md. Biol. Soc. (pres. 1952), Nat. Acad. Scis. (chmn. com. modern methods handling chem. information), Am. Assn. Colls. Pharmacy (pres.), A.A.A.S., Sci. Research Soc. Am., Acad. Pharm. Scis. (pres.), Sigma Xi, Rho Chi. Editorial adv. bd. Jour. Chem. Documentation. Home: 339 Burlage Circle Chapel Hill NC 27515

HAGER, HELEN LUCILLE, sem. librarian; b. Cape Girardeau, Mo., Apr. 26, 1924; d. Walter Fred and Christine Anne (Keller) Hager; B.S. in Edn., S.E. Mo. State Coll., 1945; B.S. in L.S., U. Ill., 1948. Mem. library staff S.E. Mo. State Coll., Cape Girardeau, 1945-47, 48-52; cataloger Concordia Sem. Library, St. Louis, 1952-67, dir. library, 1967—. Mem. Am. Theol. Library Assn., Am., Mo. library assns. Lutheran. Home: 7203 Sarah St St Louis MO 63143 Office: 801 DeMun St St Louis MO 63105

HAGER, JOHN MANFRED, lawyer, economist; b. Marysville, Mont., Sept. 12, 1889; s. John and Mary C. (Larson) H.; A.B., Leland Stanford U., 1915; student Grad. Sch. Bus Adminstrn., Harvard, 1915-16, Bklyn. Law Sch., 1933-34; LL.B., Washington Coll. Law, 1937; m. Alice M. Rogers, Aug. 3, 1916; children—Carolyn (Mrs. Gregory B. Faith), Helen (Mrs. W. Franklin P. Reid); m. 2d, Pauline Heffleman Thompson. Admitted to D.C. bar, 1939, U.S. Ct. Appeals, 1939, U.S. Supreme Ct., 1943; spl. rep. Harvard Bur. Bus. Research, 1916; dir. corp. sch. Standard Oil Co. Cal., San Francisco, 1916-17; sales mgr. in Orient, Horne Co., Ltd., Tokyo, 1919-20; spl. rep. to Orient and Europe for Japan Advertiser and Trans-Pacific mag., Tokyo, 1920-21; mgmt. counselor John M. Hager, Los Angeles, 1921-24; dir. market surveys, bur. fgn. and domestic commerce Dept. Commerce, 1924-28; asst. to pres. Crucible Steel Co. Am., N.Y.C., 1928-35; exec. asst. to chmn. Fed. Home Loan Bank Bd., 1935-45; dir. U.S. Housing Corps. of Pa., N.Y.C., 1942-45; econ. adviser Dept. State, 1945-46; chmn. gen. rev. bd., mem. adv. council War Assets Adminstrn., 1946-49; dep. chmn. Govt. Patents Bd., 1950-51; v.p., treas. Applied Psychology Corp., 1952-57, dir., 1952-57; trustee Progress Savs. and Loan Assn., Washington, 1953-58. Served as 1st lt. A.S., U.S. Army, World War I. Mem. Am., Fed. bar assns., Phi Delta Phi. Clubs: University (Washington); Harvard, Harvard Business, Stanford, Nat. Lawyers. Author: Commercial Survey of the Southeast. Home: Nokesville VA 22123 also 5169 Dailey Ct La Mesa CA 92041

HAGER, JOHN WILLIAM, mining engr.; b. Corona, Ala., Dec. 6, 1904; s. Charles Jacob and Maggie (Herbert) H.; B.S., U. Ala., 1927; m. Emily Owen, June 17, 1932; 1 son, John William. Engr. Ala. By-Products Corp., 1927-28, sales engr., 1929- 30, mine supt., 1930-40; chief mining engr. Woodward Iron Co. (now Woodward Co. div. of The Mead Company), 1940-52, gen. supt. mines, 1952- 58, v.p. mining, 1958-64, vice pres. basic mfg. and mining, 1964-. Bd. govs. Ala. Mining Inst.; member of Ala. Water Improvement Commission. Recipient of Silver Beaver award Boy Scouts of Am. Registered profl. engr., Ala. Mem. Am. Inst. Mining. Metall. and Petroleum Engrs. (past chmn. sect.), Engrs. Club Birmingham (past pres., dir.), Alabama, Birmingham chambers commerce. Presbyn. Clubs: Vestavia Country, The Club, Downtown (Birmingham). Home: 211 Sheridan Lane Birmingham, AL 35216. Office: Woodward AL 35189

HAGER, JOSEPH ARTHUR, chem. coatings mfg. co. exec.; b. Chgo., Jan. 4, 1900; s. Adam and Wanda (Ehrmann) H.; student Northwestern U., 1919; LL.B., Kent Coll. Law, 1920; m. Margaret Mabel Walbaum, Jan. 5. 1929. Tchr. pub. sch. system, Chgo., 1920; purchasing agt. Great Atlantic & Pacific Tea Co., 1920-21; mfrs. rep., 1921-22; spl. agt. Bradley & Vrooman Co., Chgo., 1922-24; with Grand Rapids Varnish Corp. (Mich.) (now Guardsman Chem. Coatings Inc.), 1924-, v.p., dir. sales, 1944-61, pres., chief exec. officer, 1961-66, chmn. bd. and chief exec. officer, 1966-70, chmn. bd., also dir.; v.p. Grand Rapids Varnish Corp. N.C., 1952-61, pres., chief exec. officer, 1961-; chmn. bd., chief exec. officer Lambert Corp., Houston, 1962-, pres., 1965-; chmn. bd. Lambert Corp. Fla., 1962-; chmn. bd. Schaefer Varnish Co., 1964-, pres., chief exec. officer, 1965-; pres. Alma- Guard Ltd., 1963-69. Cons. paint, varnish and lacquer, sect. chems. bur. WPB, 1942-43, Smaller War Plants, 1943-44. Chmn. bd. trustees Davenport Coll. Bus., Grand Rapids, 1963-. Served with U.S. Army, 1917-19. Recipient George Baugh Heckel award of Paint Industry, 1954; named Ky. col., 1961; recipient Top Mgmt. award Sales and Marketing Execs. Grand Rapids, 1964. Mem. Nat. Paint, Varnish and Lacquer Assn. (dir. 1957-, pres., chmn. bd., chmn. exec. com. 1964-66), Grand Rapids Assn. Furniture Designers, Sales and Marketing Exec. Club Internat., Grand Rapids Sales and Marketing Execs. Club (founder). Elk. Clubs: Blythefield Country (bd. dirs. 1955-58), Peninsular (bd. dirs. 1933-48, pres. 1937-41) (Grand Rapids). Home: 2002 Robinson Rd SE Grand Rapids MI 49506 Office: 1350 Steele Ave SW Grand Rapids MI 49502

HAGER, JOSEPH RICHARD, Jr., road bldg. and truck equipment mfr.; b. Phila., May 30, 1914; s. Joseph Richard and Elizabeth (Young) H.; student Drexel Inst. Tech., 1934-40, 53-55; m. Ann C. Holl, Sept. 10, 1938; childrenJoseph, Ann, Mary, Peter, Elizabeth, Michael. With Baldwin-Lima-Hamilton Corp., 1934-55, works mgr. Eddystone (Pa.) div., 1953-55; v.p., dir. mfg. Gar Wood Industries, Inc., Wayne, Mich. (acquired by Sargent Industries Inc. 1970), 1956-65, pres., 1965—, also dir., mem. exec. com.; v.p. Sargent Industries, Inc., Los Angeles, 1970—. Mem. Am. Welding Soc. Home: 507 Centralia St Dearborn Heights MI 48127. Office: 32500 Van Born Rd Wayne MI 48186

HAGER, LAWRENCE WHITE, Sr., newspaper pub.; b. Louisville, May 28, 1890; s. Samuel Wilber and Bessie Woods (White) H.; A.B., Centre Coll., Danville, Ky., 1909, A.M., 1910; Litt.D., Ky. Wesleyan Coll., 1965; m. Martha Augusta Brown, June 25, 1921; children—Lawrence White, John Stewart. With Owensboro (Ky.) Inquirer 1910—, Consol. Messenger and Inquirer, 1929—, editor and pres. of both; postmaster Owensboro, 1935-41; pres. Owensboro Broadcasting Co., 1938—. Pres. Ky. Press Assn., 1933, Ky. Postmasters Assn., 1935-36; established Good fellows Christmas Club for needy children, 1916, dir. club activities, 1916—. Chmn. County War Finance Com., 1942-45. Mem. Am. Legion Publs. Commn., 1939-50, vice chmn., 1949-50. Del. Democratic Nat. Conv., 1956. Trustee Centre Coll., 1949-50; mem. bd., chmn. finance com. Ky. Wesleyan Coll., 1951-56. Served as officer F.A., U.S. Army, in Argonne offensive, World War I. Mem. C. of C. (charter mem. and dir. 1911), Ky. Hist. Soc. Democrat. Methodist. Mason (K.T.). Clubs: Owensboro Investigators, Rotary (pres. 1922; dist. gov. 1938-39); Filson (Louisville). Home: 1844 Griffith Av Owensboro KY 42301 Office: 1401 Frederica St Owensboro KY 42301

HAGER, LOWELL PAUL, educator, biochemist; b. Girard, Kan., Aug. 30, 1926; s. Paul William and Christine (Selle) H.; A.B., Valparaiso U., 1947; M.A., U. Kan., 1950; Ph.D., U. Ill., 1953; m. Frances Erea, Jan. 22, 1949; childrenPaul, Steven, JoAnn. Postdoctoral fellow Mass. Gen. Hosp., 1953- 55; asst. prof. biochemistry Harvard, 1955-60; Guggenheim fellow Oxford (Eng.) U., also Max Planck Inst. Zellchemie, 1959-60; mem. faculty U. Ill. at Urbana, 1960-, prof. biochemistry, 1965-, head biochem. div., 1967-. Chmn. physiol. chemistry study sect. NIH, 1965-. Served with USAAF, 1945. Mem. Am. Chem. Soc., Am. Soc. Biol. Chemists, Am. Soc. Microbiology (chmn. physiology div. 1967). Editor life scis. Archives Biochemistry and Biophysics, 1966-. Research enzyme mechanisms, intermediary metabolism. Home: 801 W Delaware St Urbana IL 61801*

HAGER, MARTIN KIRK, gas co. exec.; b. Charleston, W.Va., July 30, 1908; s. Joseph Harry and Virginia (Heisley) H.; E.E., U. Cin., 1933; m. Dorothy Jane Kindra, Mar. 4, 1939; children—James Stephen, John Kirk. Engr., Panhandle Eastern Pipe Line Co., Kansas City, 1937-42, v.p., Kansas City, N.Y.C., 1945-60; with WPB, Washington, 1942-45; contract adminstr. Columbia Gas System, Houston, 1960-61; exec. v.p. Consol. Gas Supply Corp., Clarksburgh, W.Va., 1961—; dir. Union Nat. Bank, Clarksburg, Va. Mem. emergency adv. com. for natural gas Dept. Interior, 1964—. Pres., Central W.Va. Vandalia council Boy Scouts Am. Trustee Council for Econ. Edn., W.Va. U. Mem. Am. Gas Assn., Tau Beta Pi, Eta Kappa Nu, Pi Kappa Alpha. Republican. Mem. P.E. Ch. Elk. Club: Clarksburg (W.Va.) Country. Home: 1105 Briercliff Rd Bridgeport, WV 26330. Office: 445 W Main St Clarksburg WV 26301*

HAGERTY, JAMES C., radio-TV exec.; b. Plattsburg, N.Y., May 9, 1909; s. James A. and Katherine S. (Kearney) H.; grad. Blair Acad., 1928; A.B., Columbia, 1934; m. Marjorie Lucas, June 15, 1937; children—Roger C., Bruce C. Mem. staff N.Y. Times, 1934-42, legislative corr., Albany bur. 1938-42; exec. asst. to Gov. Thomas Dewey, 1943-50, sec. to gov., 1950-52; press sec. to the President, 1953-61; v.p. ABC, Mem. Delta Kappa Epsilon. Episcopalian. Home: 7 Rittenhouse Rd Bronxville NY 10708 Office: 1330 Av Americas New York City NY 10019

HAGERTY, WILLIAM WALSH, univ. pres.; b. Holyoke, Minn., June 10, 1916; s. William Walsh and Alice Amanda (Lindberg) H.; B.Sc. in Mech. Engring., U. Minn., 1939; M.S., U. Mich., 1943, Ph.D., 1947; D.Sc., Pa. Coll. Optometry, 1965, Phila. Coll. Textiles and Sci., 1968, Temple U., 1968; m. Mary Elizabeth McKay, Sept. 30, 1939; children—William Walsh III, Catherine Mary, Michael McKay. With pumping sta. operation Gt. Lakes Pipe Line Co., St. Paul, 1935-39; jr. engr. U.S. Gypsum Co., St. Paul, 1939-40, Wright Field, Dayton, O., 1940; instr. mech. engring. Villanova Coll., 1940-41, U. Cin., 1941-42; instr. engring. and mechanics U. Mich., 1942-47, asst. prof., 1947-49, asso. prof., 1949-51, prof., 1951-55; dean U. Del. Sch. Engring., 1955-58; prof., dean Coll. Engring., U. Tex., 1958-63; pres. Drexel U., Phila., 1963—. Dir. Communications Satellite Corp., Central-Penn. Nat. Bank, WHYY, Inc., Phila. Electric Co., Selas Corp., Martin-Marietta Corp.; trustee Hamilton Investment Trust; bd. mgrs. Germantown Savs. Bank. Cons. to adminstr. NASA, 1964-70. Mem. Commn. Presdl. Scholars, 1964-69; chmn. Southeastern Pa. Devel. Fund, 1964-69; mem. Phila. council exec. bd., nat. council Boy Scouts Am.; mem. Nat. Sci. Bd., 1964-70. Trustee Jefferson Med. Coll., 1965-69; bd. visitors Air U., USAF, 1964-67; mem. adv. com. USCG Acad., 1964—, chmn., 1968—. Named Delaware Valley Engr. of Year, 1970; recipient Sesquicentennial award U. Mich., 1967; Outstanding Achievement award U. Minn. Alumni Assn., 1969. Registered profl. engr., Tex. Mem. Am. Soc. M.E., Am. Soc. Engring. Edn., Nat. Soc. Profl. Engrs., Tex. Soc. Profl. Engrs., Sigma Xi, Pi Tau Sigma, Phi Kappa Phi, Tau Beta Pi, Sigma Gamma Tau. Methodist. Clubs: Cosmos (Washington); Aronimink Golf; Union League; Mid-Ocean (Bermuda). Author: (with H. J. Plass, Jr.) Engineering Mechanics, 1967; also articles. Address: Drexel Univ 32d and Chestnut Sts Philadelphia PA 19104

HAGEY, HARRY HOWARD, Jr., investment exec.; b. Chgo., Sept. 11, 1908; s. Harry Howard and Sarah Frances (Graham) H.; Ph.B., U. Chgo., 1929; m. Mary Evelyn Fetterly, Aug. 29, 1936; childrenAnn, Virginia Graham, Harry Robert. Analyst A.G. Becker & Co., investment bankers, 1929-34; cons. Stein, Roe & Farnham, investment counselors, Chgo., 1934-39, partner, 1939—; pres. Stein, Roe & Farnham Balance Fund, Inc., Chgo., 1958—. Mem. Phi Beta Kappa, Chi Psi Club: University (Chgo.). Home: 1150 Lake Shore Dr Chicago, IL 60610. Office: 135 S LaSalle St Chicago IL 60603*

HAGG, BERT, printer; b. Winnipeg, Can., May 6, 1910; s. Alex Bror and Ada Augusta (Sjomark) H.; came to U.S., 1916, derivative citizenship, 1931; student Seattle pub. schs.; m. Helen Kristianna Highland, Dec. 24, 1932. Pressman Lowman & Hanford, 1935-42, asst. mgr., printing salesman, 1942-45, mgr. printing div., 1949-54; with Met. Press, 1945-49; dir. printing U. Wash., 1954—; tchr. Edison Vocational Schs.; graphic arts cons. Mem. Internat. Assn. Printing House Craftsmen (pres.), Seattle Advt. Club, Internat. Printing Pressmen and Offset Workers Union. Mason. Club: Swedish (Seattle). Home: 650 NW 78th St Seattle WA 98107

HAGGARD, PAUL HOMER COUCHMAN, life ins. co. exec.; b. Mexico, Mo., Jan. 11, 1910; s. Frank B. and Carolyn (Couchman) H.; A.B., Williams Coll., 1931; LL.B., U. Conn., 1937; m. Rhoda Powell, Aug. 8, 1934; childrenFrank P., Eleanore (Mrs. David E. Baldwin). With Phoenix Mut. Life Ins. Co., Hartford Conn., 1932- , 2d v.p., 1955-58, v.p., 1958-61, sr. v.p., 1962-, also dir.; dir. Riverside Trust Co., Hartford. Admitted to Conn. bar, 1937. Mem. Williams Coll. Devel. Com., 1958-, chmn. endowment campaign for Conn., 1961-; mem. Charter Oak council Boy Scouts Am., 1958-. Served to lt. (s.g.) USNR, World War II. Mem. Soc. Alumni Williams Coll. (pres. 1958-61), Delta Kappa Epsilon (pres. williams Alumni Soc. of Epsilon chpt. since 1962). Mem. Universalist Ch. (past chmn. trustees, chmn. deacons). Home: 46 Banbury Lane West Hartford CT 06107 Office: 1 American Row Hartford CT 06103

HAGGERTY, BERNARD JOSEPH, banker; b. Alta., Can., Mar. 7, 1925; s. Joseph Patrick and Myrtle (Watts) H.; student Sch. Consumer Banking, 1954, Columbia Grad. Sch. Bus., 1961; m. Dorothy Payne Haggerty, July 6, 1947; children—Joy Elizabeth, Bernard Joseph, John Thomas, Julie Watts. With Va. Nat. Bank, Charlottesville, 1947—, sr. v.p. installment loan dept. Western region, 1963-70, regional exec. officer central region, 1970—. Mem. commn. world service and finance Va. conf. United Methodist Ch. Mayor of Charlottesville, 1962-64. Bd. dirs. Region 18 Community Coll. Served with USNR, 1943-46. Recipient Distinguished Service award Charlottesville Jaycees, 1955, Key Man award, 1956. Mem. Va. Bankers Assn., Charlottesville C. of C., Consumers Bankers Assn. (bd. govs., finance com.). Methodist (trustee). Lion. Clubs: Boar's Head, Redland, Farmington Country (Charlottesville). Home: 2414 Hillwood Pl Charlottesville VA 22901 Office: 300 E Main St Charlottesville VA 22902

HAGGERTY, CORNELIUS J., labor union ofcl.; b. Boston, Jan. 10, 1894. s. Daniel and Nora (Driscoll) H.; m. Margaret Kelleher, June 30, 1920; childrenCornelius J., Donald P. Joined Lathers Union, 1915, bus. mgr. Local 42, Los Angeles, 1928-29; 2d v.p. Internat. Union Wood, Wire and Metal Lathers, 1929-33, 1st v.p., 1958; sec. Los Angeles Bldg. and Constrn. Trades Council, 1933-36; v.p. Cal. Fedn. Labor, 1936, pres., 1937-43; sec.-treas. AFL-CIO, 1943, pres. bldg. and constrn. trades dept., 1960—. Mem. fed. adv. council employment security Dept. Labor, farm placement com. bur. employment security; mem. Gov's Adv. Council, Cal. Dept. Employment; AFL mem. Latin Am. Unit, Internat. Confedn. Free Trade Unions; mem. Joint U.S.-Mex. Trade Union Com.; v.p. Internat. Labor Press Assn., AFL-CIO. Trustee San Francisco Maritime Mus.; mem. nat. council Nat. Planning Assn.; bd. dirs. Nat. Housing Conf. Bd. regents U. Cal. Mem. Am. Legion. Clubs: Commonwealth of California, Union League (San Francisco). Home: 9967 Milburne Dr Sun Valley, CA Office: AFL-CIO Bldg 815 16th St NW Washington DC 20006*

HAGGERTY, LAWRENCE GEORGE, mgmt. cons.; b. Harvey, N.D., Aug. 10, 1916; s. Michael Eugene and Lillian Marie (Evenson) H.; B.M.E., Marquette U., 1940; m. Mary Ellen Sweeney, Oct. 17, 1942; children—Michael Eugene, Catherine Ann (Mrs. James Lenahan), Eileen Mary (Mrs. John Mundy), Patrick Bernard, Margaret Ellen, Sheila Bridget, Maureen Elizabeth, Timothy James, Monica Louise. Successively student engr., mgmt. trainee to mgr. mfg. Indpls. div. RCA Victor Div., 1940-48; gen. mgr. appliance div. and parts mfg. divs. F.L. L. Jacobs Co., Indpls. and Traverse City, Mich., 1948-50; with ITT, 1950-58, successively dir. mfg., v.p. mfg., v.p. and gen. mgr. tech. products div., pres., dir. Capehart- Farnsworth Co., 1950-56; pres. Farnsworth Electronics Co., 1956-58, also dir.; pres., dir., chief exec. officer Warwick Electronics Inc. (formerly Warwick Mfg. Corp.), 1958-66; pres., dir. Lawrence G. Haggerty & Assos., Inc., Northfield, Ill., 1967—; chmn. bd. Resources Management, Inc.; dir. Sci. Holding Co., Godwin Industries, Houseboat Hotels Internat., Medequip Corp. Trustee Marquette U. Mem. Tau Beta Pi, Alpha Sigma Nu, Pi Tau Sigma. Roman Catholic. Clubs: Lyford Cay (New Providence, Bahamas); North Shore Country (Glenview, Ill.); Michigan Shores Club (Wilmette, Ill.); N.Y. Athletic, Metropolitan (N.Y.C.). Home: 850 Alles Rd Winnetka IL 60093 Office: 540 Frontage Rd Northfield IL 60093

HAGGERTY, PATRICK EUGENE, electronics mfr.; b. Harvey, N.D., Mar. 17, 1914; s. Michael Eugene and Lillian (Evenson) H.; B.S. in Elec. Engring., Marquette U., 1936, LL.D., 1960; LL.D., St. Mary's U., San Antonio, 1959, U. Dallas, 1964, Cath. U., 1971; D.Eng., Poly. Inst. Bklyn., 1962; Sc.D. (hon.), N.D. State U., 1967; m. Beatrice E. Menne, Feb. 26, 1938; children—Sheila Margaret, Kathleen Mary, Patrick Eugene, Teresa Ann, Michael Gamble. Asst. gen. mgr. Badger Carton Co., Milw., 1935-42; gen. mgr. lab. and mfg. div. Texas Instruments, Inc. (and predecessors), Dallas, 1945-50, exec. v.p., dir., 1951-58, pres., dir., 1958-66, chmn., chief exec. officer, 1967- 69, chmn. and chief corporate officer, 1969—; mem. internat. adv. com. Chase Manhattan Bank. Mem. Pres.'s Sci. Adv. Com.; mem. Business Council; gov. U.S. Postal Service. Trustee, Rockefeller U.; mem. exec. com., trustee U. Dallas. Served as lt. USNR, 1942-45. Recipient Electronics Industry Assn. medal of honor, 1967; founders award I.E.E.E., 1968; medalist Industrial Research Institute, 1969. Fellow I.E.E.E. (dir. 1960-64, pres. 1962, John Fritz medal 1971), Tex. Acad. Sci.; mem. Nat. Acad. Engring., Nat. Indsl. Conf. Bd., A.A.A.S., Soc. Exploration Geophysicists, Sigma Phi Delta, Tau Beta Pi, Eta Kappa Nu (eminent mem.), Alpha Sigma Nu. Home: 5455 Northbrook Dr Dallas TX 75220 Office: 13500 N Central Expressway PO Box 5474 Dallas TX 75222

HAGGERTY, ROBERT JOHNS, medical educator; b. Saranac Lake, N.Y., Oct. 20, 1925; s. Gordon Abbott and Nina (Johns) H.; A.B., Cornell U., 1946, M.D., 1949; m. Muriel Ethel Protzmann, Oct. 29, 1949; chilren—Robert, Janet, Richard, John. Intern Strong Meml. Hosp., Rochester, N.Y., 1949-51; from resident to chief resident pediatrics Children's Hosp. Med. Center, Boston, 1953-55; med. dir. family health care program Harvard Med. Sch., also asst. prof. pediatrics, 1953-64; prof. pediatrics, chmn. dept. U. Rochester Sch. Medicine, 1964—. Mem. health services research sect. USPHS, 1964-70, chmn., 1968-70; mem. N.Y. State Health Planning Adv. Council. Served to capt. USAF, 1951-53. Markle scholar acad. medicine, 1962-67. Mem. Assn. Med. Sch. Pediatric Dept. Chmn. (pres. 1969-70), Am. Assn. Poison Control Centers (pres. 1962-64), Am. Acad. Pediatrics, Am. Pediatric Soc., Assn. Ambulatory Pediatric Services (chmn. 1963-64), Assn. Am. Med. Colls., Internat.

Epidemiological Assn., Soc. Pediatric Research (v.p. 1970-71), Joint Council Nat. Pediatric Socs., Phi Beta Kappa, Alpha Omega Alpha. Editor: (with M. Green) Ambulatory Pediatrics, 1968. Contbr. articles to med. jours. Home: 2491 Highland Av Rochester NY 14610

HAGGERTY, SANDRA CLARK, (Mrs. Samuel Haggerty, Jr.), columnist; b. Oakley, Kan., July 26, 1939; d. Isaiah and Ruth (Tinsley) Campbell; student U. Denver, 1957-60; B.S., Utah State U., 1961; m. Samuel Haggerty, Jr., Dec. 22, 1961; children—Kendall Gail, Gillian Elaine, Erin Marcell. Research asst. social work dept. U. Cal., Berkeley, 1965-66; columnist Oakland (Cal.) Tribune, 1968—; syndicated columnist Los Angeles Times Syndicate, 1969—; columnist Los Angeles Times, 1969—; substitute tchr., 1961-67; free-lance writer, 1961—. Cons. Narcotics Elimination When Practiced Among Loosers, 1969—; mem. adv. council Laney Coll., 1970.‡

HAGGERTY, WILLIAM J., ednl. cons.; b. Somerville, Mass., Nov. 30, 1908; s. Melvin Everett and Laura C. (Garretson) H.; A.B., U. Minn., 1930; A.M., U. Chgo., 1938, Ph.D., 1943; student Stanford, 1930-31; m. Marjorie Geraldine Hooper, Aug. 22, 1933; children—Susan (Mrs. Douglas Vaughn), Sally (Mrs. C. Baker-Carr), James R. Engaged in research for N. Central Assn. Colls. and Secondary Schs., 1931-33, 34-40; adult edn. program TVA, 1934; research study on regional devel. Nat. Resources Planning Bd., 1935; research President's Commn. on Adminstrn. Management, 1936; dir. student personnel U. Conn., 1940-44; pres. State U. Coll., New Paltz, N.Y., 1944-46; v.p., dir. High-Tor Opera Co., 1963—; on leave as edn. cons. Govt. India, 1952-53, U.S. Tech. Coop. Adminstrn. del. to UNESCO conf., Bombay, 1952; com. on internat. relations Am. Assn. Colls. for Tchr. Edn. (chmn. 1952-59); mem. staff survey N.Y.C. Colls. for Joint Legislative Commn., 1943; mem. staff Md. Commn. Higher Edn., 1946; rep. N.Y. State Tchrs. Assn., World Conf. Teaching Profession, Endicott, N.Y., 1946; cons. Pa. Study on Post-High Sch. Study, 1948; bd. dirs. World Edn., Inc. (pres. 1957-59); chmn. Conf. World Affairs, Inc., 1967—; pres. bd. dirs. Am. Friends of Vidyodaya Girls Sch., Inc.; mem. Am. Overseas Educators Orgn. (pres. 1958-59), Internat. Council Edn. for Teaching (pres. 1958—); adv. com. coll. and univ. pres. Inst. Internat. Edn., 1957-59; edn. com. People to People program; exec. com. Mid-Hudson Sch. Study Council, 1948—; mem. commn. internat. edn. Am. Council Edn., 1964—; pres. Com. on World U., 1965—; vice chmn., dir. Patterns for Progress, Inc., 1966—; mem. edn. com. Asia Soc.; chmn., dir. World Tchr. Project, Inc., 1970—; asso. dir. Ind. Policy Commn. on Post High Sch. Edn.; cons. State U. N.Y., 1967—. Mem. Am. Acad. Polit. and Social Sci., Am. Edn. Research Assn., Sigma Phi Epsilon, Phi Delta Kappa, Kappa Delta Pi. Author: Manual for Instructors for Engineering, Science Management War Training Program, 1944; Purposes of the University of Chicago, 1943; Higher and Professional Education in India, 1970; An Indiana Pattern for Higher Education, 1968. Home: 134 Hawkes Av Ossining NY 10562

HAGIS, PETER, Jr., educator; b. Phila., Jan. 16, 1926; s. Peter and Irene (Supper) H.; B.S., in Edn., Temple U., 1950, M.A. in Math., 1952; Ph.D., U. Pa., 1959; m. Jeanie Clelland MacGregor, Mar. 28, 1953; children—Joann, Peter Scott. Mem. faculty Temple U., 1952—, asso. prof. math., 1963-68, prof., 1968—; cons. Remington Rand Univac, Blue Bell, Pa., 1957-62. Served with USMCR, 1944-46. Mem. Am. Math. Soc., Math. Assn. Am. Presbyn. Contbr. profl. jours. Home: 880 Edison Av Philadelphia PA 19116

HAGLUND, GERHARD OSCAR, mfg. co. exec.; b. St. Paul, Jan. 17, 1916; s. Oscar and Ingeborg (Olson) H.; B.S. in Mech. Engring., U. Minn., 1937, M.S., 1939; m. Mary Elizabeth Vellenga, Nov. 12, 1944; children—Mary Lynn, Gerhard O. Engrs. asst. Allis Chalmers Mfg. Co., 1937-38, asst. engr., 1939-41; engring. instr. and postgrad. student U. Minn., 1938-39; head mech. design sect. Naval Ordance Lab., Washington, 1941-45; mgr. instrument sect. Cornell Aero. Lab., Buffalo, 1945-46; chief engr. aero. research lab. Gen. Mills, Mpls., 1946-47, dir. bus. research, dir. sales, dir. research, 1951-56, dir. planning, 1956-57, dir. nuclear equipment, 1957-61; mgr. engring., physics div. Fredrick Flader, Inc., Buffalo, 1947-51; v.p. Vitro Corp. Am., 1961-63; sr. v.p. Allis Chalmers Mfg. Co., Milw., also dir.; dir. SDS Systems Corp., Nuclear Equipment, Ltd., London, Eng. Active in Jr. Achievement; bd. dirs. United Community Service Greater Milw.; chmn. adv. com. mech. engring. dept. U. Minn. Recipient two citations Dept. Navy; nat. award Am. Soc. M.E., 1937. Profl. engr., Minn. Fellow Am. Inst. Mgmt.; mem. Inst. Aero. Scis., Instrument Soc. Am. (chmn. control elements div., dir.), Am. Nuclear Soc., Am. Soc. M.E., Am. Ordnance Assn., Air Force Assn., U.S. Figure Skating Assn. (governing council), Newcomen Soc. N. Am., Sigma XI. Clubs: Advertising, Executive, Figure Skating (pres.) (Mpls.). Episcopalian (vestryman). Contbr. tech. papers airborne and indsl. instrumentation. Patentee instrumentation and controls. Home: 35245 W Fairview Rd Oconomowoc WI 53066

HAGMAN, HARLAN LAWRENCE, coll. dean; b. DeKalb, Ill., Sept. 8, 1911; s. Gus Carl and Emily Sophia (Peterson) H.; Ed.B., No. Ill. State Tchrs. Coll., 1936; M.A., Northwestern U., 1939, Ph.D., 1947; m. Mary Anna Cassels, May 23, 1943; children William Gordon, Richard Harlan, Jean Cassels, Thomas Lawrence. Formerly tchr. pub. schs., prin. and supt.; instr. Northwestern U., 1940- 41; asso. prof. Drake U., Des Moines, 1947-49, prof. edn., 1949-50, dean coll. edn., 1950-57; prof. edn. Wayne State U., 1957-60, dean adminstrn., 1960-. Moderator fgn. policy radio broadcasts, nat. network. Served as lt. comdr. USNR, World War II. Mem. Am. Assn. Sch. Adminstrs., Nat. Conf. Profts. Ednl. Adminstrn., Am. Edn. Fellowship, Assn. Supervision and Curriculum Devel., Phi Delta Kappa. Author: A Handbook for the Schoolboard Mem., 1941; The Adminstrn. of Am. Public Schools, 1951; Administration in Profile for School Executives (with Alfred Schwartz), 1955; Administration of Elementary Schools, 1956. Editorial cons. McGraw-Hil Book Co., Internat. City Mgrs. Assn. Contbr. to A Dictionary of Education, Ency. of Ednl. Research, ednl. jours. Home: 1017 Kensington Rd Grosse Point Park MI 48236 Office: Wayne State U Detroit MI 48202

HAGNER, ARTHUR FEODOR, geologist; Union City, N.J., May 26, 1911; s. Feodor H.S. and Ernestine (Geggis) H.; A.B., N.Y.U., 1934; Ph.D., Columbia, 1939; m. Dorothy Damon, Aug. 11, 1967; children by previous marriage—Dorothy K. (Mrs. Craig Baker), Thomas P. Instr. to asso. prof. U. Wyo., 1939-47; research asso. U. Chgo., 1947-48; asso. prof. U. Ill., 1948-53, prof. geology, 1953—; geologist U.S. Geol. Survey. Co-dir. NSF Summer Inst. in Geology for Coll. Tchrs., 1957, 58. Mem. Am. Civil Liberties Union, The Pub. Interest, Common Cause, Nat. Parks Assn. Trustee Nat. Hemophilia Found., 1950-67. Nat. Research Council fellow, 1939-39; Columbia U. fellow, 1937-38. Fellow Geol. Soc. Am.; Mineralog. Soc. Am., Geol. Soc. London, A.A.A.S., mem. Nat. Assn. Geology Tchrs. (pres. central sect. 1961-62). Author articles in field. Home: 511 S Russell St Champaign IL 61820 Office: Univ Illinois Urbana IL 61801

HAGNER, DONALD FARLOW, former banker; b. Balt., Dec. 17, 1904; s. Richard A. and Lulu M. (Foster) H.; student Poly. Inst. Balt., also Balt. City Coll., Johns Hopkins; grad. Grad. Sch. Banking, Rutgers U., 1942; m. Christine Sterling League, May 26, 1938; 1 son, Donald R. With Fed. Res. System, 1923—, beginning as clk. transit dept. Fed. Res. Bank of Balt., successively mgr. various depts., asst. cashier, cashier and sec. bd. dirs., 1923-51, v.p. Fed. Res. Bank of Richmond charge Balt. br., 1951-69, sr. vice pres. in charge Balt. branch, 1969-70. Past pres. Hosp. Cost Analysis Service, Inc. Active A.R.C., Community Fund campaigns. Mem. Nat. Assn. Morris Assos., Friends of the Land, Am. Inst. Banking, Balt. Assn. Credit Men (dir. 1950-53), Balt. Assn. Commerce (chmn. gen. edn. com., vice chmn. of the civic development com.). Republican. Protestant Episcopal. Clubs: Rotary (past pres.), Baltimore Country (Balt.). Home: University One 1 E University Pkwy Baltimore MD 21218

HAGOPIAN, LOUIS THOMAS, advt. exec.; b. Pontiac, Mich., June 1, 1925; s. Thomas and Sarah (Uligian) H.; student Northwestern U., 1944; B.A. in Bus. Adminstrn., Mich. State U., 1947; m. Joanne Kelly, Dec. 31, 1955; childrenSusan, Thomas, Matthew. With Pontiac Motor Car Co., 1948-53, beginning as service rep., successively dist. sales mgr., St. Joseph, Mo., Wichita, Kan., Kansas City areas; with Chrysler Corp., 1953-60, mem. exec. staff of gen. sales mgr. Dodge div., 1953-54, merchandising mgr. Dodge div., 1954-55, sales promotion mgr., 1955-56, Eastern new car sales mgr. Dodge div., 1956, dir. advt. and sales promotion Plymouth div., 1956-60; account supr. N. W. Ayer & Son, Inc., 1960-62, v.p., 1962-66, Detroit mgr., 1963-66, exec. v.p., gen. mgr., N.Y. region, 1967-. Active U.S. Treasury Savs. Bond Drive, Mich., 1958; co-chmn. advt. services com. United Fund of Detroit, 1962; chmn. advt. and related services sect. Greater N.Y. Fund Campaign, 1970. Mem. advt. and pub. relations com. Oakland County Republican Com., communications com. N.Y. Urban Coalition. Bd. govs. AAAA, N.Y. Council. Served to lt. (j.g.) USNR, World War II. Mem. Assn. Nat. Advertisers, Adcraft Club Detroit (dir.). Clubs: Detroit Athletic; Wee Burn Country. Home: 5 Meadowbrook Rd Darien CT 06820 Office: 1345 Av of Americas New York City NY 10019

HAGOPIAN, PETER B., psychiatrist, hosp. adminstr.; b. Adana, Turkey, Dec. 25, 1908; s. Sarkis and Maritsa (Kachadoorian) H.; brought to U.S., 1921, naturalized, 1931; B.S., Tufts U., 1935, M.D., 1935; m. Teriz Malootian, Dec. 23, 1951; children-Debby, Peter B., Paul G. Intern Boston City, Carney hosps., Boston, 1935-37; resident psychiatry Danvers State Hosp., Hathorne, Mass., 1937-41, chief staff, 1946-49, supt., med. dir., 1953- ; instr. psychiatry Med. Sch. Tufts U., 1947-49; asst. psychiatry Harvard Med. Sch., 1965-; 1st asst. commr. Mass. Dept. Mental Health, Boston, 1949-53, acting commr., 1950-51, chmn. civil def. com., 1958- ; dir. asso. psychology Mass. Gen. Hosp., 1964-. Served with AUS, 1941- 46. Diplomate Am. Bd. Psychiatry and Neurology. Fellow Am. Psychiat. Assn. (pres. No. New Eng. dist. br. 1959-60); mem. A.M.A., Mass., Essex North Dist. med. socs., New Eng. Soc. Psychiatry (past pres.). Rotarian. Contbr. articles to profl. jours. Address: PO Box 50 Hathorne MA 01937*

HAGOPIAN, ROBERT RONALD, mut. fund exec.; b. North Bergen, N.J., Aug. 22, 1937; s. Joseph and Anna (Melkonian) H.; B.S., Fairleigh Dickinson U., 1960; m. Caroline Jamieson, Aug. 31, 1959; children-Scott, Laura, Amy. With King, Merritt & Co., N.Y.C., 1956-60; with Eastman Dillon, Union Securities, N.Y.C., 1960-62; v.p. charge West Coast mut. fund sales Walston & Co., San Francisco, 1965-66; v.p. Winfield Growth Fund, Inc., San Francisco, 1966- 69; owner Meridian Capital Corp., San Francisco, 1969—; pres. dir. Index Fund, Inc.; dir. Performance Plus Fund, Ltd. Founding mem., dir. Mut. Fund Council. Served with USMCR, 1957-60. Mem. A.I.M. Presbyn. (elder, trustee). Contbr. articles trade mags. Home: 1008 Jackling Dr Hillsborough CA 94010 Office: 120 Montgomery St San Francisco CA 94104

HAGSTRUM, JEAN HOWARD, educator; b. St. Paul, Mar. 26, 1913; s. Andrew and Sadie Gertrude (Fryckberg) H.; A.B. summa cum laude, U. Minn., 1933; M.A., Northwestern U., 1938; Ph.D., Yale, 1941; m. Ruth Pritchett, June 29, 1941; children—Katherine Jeanne, Phyllis Ann. Instr. English and speech N. Park Coll., Chgo., 1934-38; chief allocation sect. U.S. Office Censorship, 1942-44; mem. faculty Northwestern U., 1940-42, 46—, prof. English, 1957—, chmn. dept., 1958-64; lectr. at univs. Copenhagen, Lund, Stockholm, Uppsala, Gothenburg, Aix-en-Provence, Delhi. Spl. research 18th century lit., Romantic lit., lit and psychology, relations of the arts. Trustee Newberry Library, 1964—. Fulbright research fellow, Italy, 1953-54; grantee Am. Philos. Soc., 1952, 59; fellow Newberry Library, Chgo., 1953, 57; sr. fellow Clark Library, U. Cal. at Los Angeles, 1970. Served with AUS, 1944-46. Mem. Modern Lang. Assn. Am., Swedish Pioneer Hist. Soc. Author: Samuel Johnson's Literary Criticism, rev. edit., 1967; The Sister Arts, 1958; William Blake: Poet and Painter, 1964; (with others) A Community of Scholars, 1968. Home: 819 Michigan Av Evanston IL 60202

HAGUE, JAMES EDWARD, assn. exec.; b. Burnley, Lancashire, Eng., Oct. 6, 1914; s. Robert and Ann (Boyle) H.; m. Dorothy Scripture, June 20, 1936; children—Peter, Camille (Mrs. Philip F. Doetsch). Came to U.S., 1924, naturalized, 1932. Reporter, Bridgeport (Conn.) Times-Star, 1933-41; editor A.P., 1941-45; combat corr. USMC, 1943-44; dir. pub. relations Johns Hopkins Hosp., 1945-49; asst. city editor Washington Post, 1949-53; dir. pub. relations Am. Hosp. Assn., 1953-54, exec. editor jour. of assn., 1954-59, trustee Jour. for Governing Bds., 1957-59, asst. dir. assn., 1957-59, asst. sec., 1959-63, asst. dir., 1959-67, editor, 1959—, sec., 1963-67, asso. dir., 1967—. Club: Lake Shore. Home: 834 Lake St Wilmette IL Office: 840 N Lake Shore Dr Chicago IL 60611*

HAGUE, LOU ROSS, business exec.; b. Pitts., Aug. 23, 1920; s. Louis Ross and Edna (Williams) H.; B.S. in Chem. Engring., U. Mich., 1939; S.M. in Chem. Engring., Mass. Inst. Tech., 1940; certificate Japanese lang., U. Minn., 1944; Ph.D. (hon.), U. Tokyo (Japan), 1946; grad. Harvard Bus. Sch., 1960-61; m. Rae M. Ferguson, June 1, 1941; children—Carol L. (Mrs. C.W. Pribus), Gregg Ross. Chem. engr. E.I. duPont De Nemours & Co., 1940-42; asst. engr. Westinghouse Electric Corp., 1942-43; chief research and devel. sect., civil service, C.E., War Dept., Yokohama, Japan, 1946-47; with Westinghouse Electric Corp., 1947-66, dir. bus. systems, 1959-66; prin. in charge S.D. Leidesdorf & Co., N.Y.C., 1966; chmn., pres. Adv. Mgmt., Inc., Greenwich, Conn. until 1970; v.p. computer resources A.S. Hansen, Inc., Lake Bluff, Ill., 1970—. Co-chmn. regional fund raising Harvard Bus. Sch., 1965. Mem. Harvard Found. Advanced Studies; mem. adv. council Mgmt. Scis. Center, U. Pa. Served to maj. AUS, World War II; PTO. Mem. Am. Mgmt. Assn. (v.p. 1964; Distinguished Service award 1965), Harvard Bus. Sch. Assn. Pitts. and N.Y.C., Blackridge Civic Assn. Republican. Presbyn. Clubs: Harvard-Yale- Princeton, Univ. Michigan (N.Y.C.); Burning Tree Country (Greenwich, Conn.); Bath and Tennis (Lake Forest). Author articles in field. Home: 1125 S Oak Knoll Dr Lake Forest IL Office: 1080 Greenbay Rd Lake Bluff IL 60044

HAGUE, RAOUL, sculptor; b. Constantinople, 1905; s. Nazar and Satenig Heukelekian; student Robert Coll. Prep. Sch., Constantinople; student Ia. State Coll., 1921, Beaux-Arts Inst. of Design, N.Y.C., 1926-27, Art Students League, N.Y.C., 1927-28, Courtauld Inst., London, 1950-51. Came to U.S., 1921, naturalized, 1930. Works exhibited in group shows including Mus. Modern Art, 1933, Curt Valentin Gallery, 1945, Whitney Mus. Am. Art, 1945-48, 52, 57, 58, Mus. Modern Art, 1956; represented permanent collection Albright Art Gallery, Mus. Modern Art, Whitney Mus. Am. Art, Miller Co. Recipient Audubon prize, 1945; Kleinert award, 1956; Woodstock Found. grant, 1949; Ford Found. grant, 1959. Served as pvt. AUS, 1941-43. Home: Woodstock NY 12498*

HAGUE, ROBERT WORST, mfg. co. exec.; b. Findlay, O., Apr. 6, 1926; s. Robert W. and Elsie (Ehlenbeck) H.; B.S., Wayne State U., 1949; m. Marguerite Brauer, June 15, 1947; children-Victoria, Jonathan, Tomothy, Philip. Mgr., Ernst & Ernst, C.P.A.'s, Detroit, 1948-64; controller Fed.-Mogul Corp., 1964-69, v.p. finance, 1969—. Pres. Wayne State U. Fund, 1967-68; treas. Lutheran Youth Village, Detroit, 1967-68. Served with AUS, 1944-46. C.P.A., Mich. Mem. Financial Execs. Inst., Am. Inst. C.P.A.'s. Club: Oakland Hills Country (Birmingham). Home: 58 Manor Rd Birmingham MI 48008 Office: PO Box 1966 Detroit MI 48235

HAGUE, WILLIAM EDWARD, Jr., magazine editor; b. Duquesne, Pa., Feb. 2, 1919; s. William Edward and Edith (Osburn) H.; grad. cum laude. Shady Side Acad., Pitts., 1936; A.B., Princeton, 1940; student U. Pitts. Sch. Law, 1940-41; m. Margaret Cleland Anderson, July 22, 1950 (div.). Asso. editor Tide mag., 1947-49; promotion dir. Living for Young Homemakers mag., 1949-50, copy editor, 1951-54, mng. editor, 1954-62; editor Living's Guide to Home Planning mag., 1958-62; editor House & Garden Guides, 1961—, House & Garden Plans Guide, House & Garden Decorating Guide, Remodeling Guide, Building Guide, Kitchen and Bath Guide, Guide to Young Living, Garden Guide, Crafts Guide, Conde Nast Publs., 1962—; asst. account exec. Fitzgerald Advt. Agy., New Orleans, 1950-51. Recipient Dorothy Dawe award for distinguished journalistic coverage in home furnishings field, 1969. Mem. Am. Inst. Interior Designers. Author: How to Decorate With Color, 1964; What You Should Know About Furniture, 1965; Planning Your Vacation Home, 1968; Plan Your Baths for Beauty and Efficiency, 1969; Plan The Kitchen That Suits You, 1969; Making The Most of The One-Room Apartment, 1969. Home: Woodville New Preston CT 06777 Office: 420 Lexington Av New York City NY 10017

HAHN, ARVIN WILLIAM, coll. pres.; b. Milw., May 11, 1923; s. Harry William and Helen (Ewert) H.; B.S. in Edn., Concordia Coll., 1945; M.S., U. Chgo., 1947; Ph.D., Northwestern U., 1952; m. Judith L. Heynem, July 3, 1946; children-Timothy, David, Linda. Tchr., Forest Park (Ill.) elementary schs., 1945-50; prof. geography Concordia Coll., River Forest, Ill., 1952-56; exec. officer Assn. Am. Geographers, 1963-65; dean grad. studies Concordia Coll., 1965-67; pres. Bethany Coll., Lindsberg, Kan., 1967—. Mem. Assn. Am. Geographers, Nat., Luth. edn. assns., Nat. Council Geog. Edn., Sigma Xi. Home: 604 N 3d St Lindsborg KS 67456*

HAHN, AUGUST CHRISTOPHER, former govt. ofcl.; b. Beaumont, Tex., Aug. 17, 1907; s. Tobe and Achsa (Bentley) H.; student Lamar Coll., 1924-26, U. Tex., 1926-27; m. Jesse Juanita Sheffield, July 1, 1931; 1 son, Timothy Christopher. Clk.- carrier Beaumont Post Office, 1926-33, post office insp., 1933-46; exec. dir. Post Office Dept., Bureau Transportation, Washington, 1946-57, deputy asst. Postmaster Gen., 1957-67, spl. asst. to postmaster gen. for policy and planning, 1967-69, exec. asst. to dep. postmaster gen., 1969-70. Served as col., Adj. Gens. Corps. O.R.C., ETO, MTO, 1941-46, USAR ret., 1965. Decorated with Legion of Merit with 2 bronze oak leaf clusters; Officer Order Brit. Empire (Gt. Britain); Medal Militaire (France). Recipient Career Service award, Nat. Civil Service League, 1963; distinguished service award U.S. P.O. Dept., 1970. Home: 1368 4th St SW Washington DC 20024

HAHN, CARL H., automobile co. exec.; b. Chemnitz, Germany, July 1, 1926; s. Carl H. and Maria (Kusel) H.; ed. U. Cologne (Germany). U. Zurich (Switzerland), U. Paris (France), U. Bern (Switzerland); m. Marisa Traina, Apr. 30, 1960; children—Carl Alexander, Pia Louisa, Peter Andreas, Christopher Anthony. Adminstrv. officer OEEC, Paris, 1953; head export sales promotion Volkswagen, 1954-58; exec. v.p., gen. mgr. Volkswagen Am., 1959-64, now vice chmn.; exec. v.p Vorstandmitglied, Volkswagenwerk A.G., Wolfsburg, Germany. 1964—. Served with German Army, 1944-45. Home: 27 Planckstrasse Wolfsburg Germany Office: Volkswagenwerk AG Wolfsburg Germany

HAHN, EDGAR A., lawyer; b. Cleve., Nov. 25, 1882; s. Aaron and Therese (Kalb) H.; LL.B., Western Res. U., 1903; spl. course Columbia, 1903-04; D.H.L., Case Inst. Tech., 1965; L.L.D., Western Res. U., 1967, John Carroll U., 1967; D.H.L., Wilberforce U., 1969; m. Irene Moss, Jan. 10, 1910 (dec. 1939); children—Alice (Mrs. Stanley J. Goodman), Katherine (Mrs. B.S. Bercovici). Admitted to Ohio bar, 1904, since practiced in Cleve.; now sr. partner Hahn, Loeser, Freedheim, Dean & Wellman; dir. several business firms. Mem. 1st charter commn. of Cleve., 1912. Trustee Musical Arts Assn., Cleve. Mus. Art; trustee, pres. Louis D. Beaumont Found. Recipient Fletcher Reed Andrews award Western Res. U., 1964; medal pub. service Cleve. C. of C., 1965; Ursula Lauras medal Ursuline Coll., 1966. Mem. Am., Ohio, Cleve. bar assns., Cleve. C. of C., Soc. Benchers (charter). Clubs: Oakwood, Mid-Day, Rowfant. Home: 1 Bratenahl Pl Bratenahl, OH 44108. Office: Nat City-E 6th Bldg Cleveland OH 44114*

HAHN, EMILY, author; b. St. Louis, Mo., Jan. 14, 1905; d. Isaac Newton and Hannah (Schoen) Hahn; B.S., U. Wis., 1926; student Columbia, 1928- 29, Oxford U., 1934-35; m. Charles R. Boxer, Nov. 28, 1945; children-Carola, Amanda. Mining engr. Deko Oil Co., St. Louis, 1926; courier, Santa Fe, N.M., 1927-28; instr. geology Hunter Coll., N.Y.C., 1929-30; with Red Cross in Belgian Congo, 1930-31; writer of stories and scenarios, N.Y.C. and Hollywood, also travels and newspaper work in England, Continent and N. Africa, 1931-32; instr. English, Customs Coll., Shanghai, and writing in Shanghai, 1935- 38, Chungking, 1940; instr. Customs U., Hong Kong, 1941. Author: several books including Hongkong Holiday, 1946; China A to Z, 1946; Picture Story of China, 1946; Raffles of Singapore, 1946; Miss Jill, 1947; England to Me, 1949; Purple Passage, 1950; Love Conquers Nothing, 1952; Chiang Kai-Shek, 1955; Diamond, 1956; The Tiger House Party, 1959; China Only Yesterday, 1963; China to Me, 1963; Indo, 1964; Africa to Me, 1964; Animal Gardens, 1967; Times and Places, 1970. Interned by the Japanese govt. Dec. 1941; returned to U.S. on Gripsholm Dec. 1943. Address: care Brandt & Brandt 101 Park Av New York City NY 10027

HAHN, ERWIN LOUIS, physicist, educator; b. Sharon, Pa., June 9, 1921; s. Israel and Mary (Weiss) H.; B.S., Juniata Coll., 1943, D.Sc., 1966; M.S., U. Ill., 1947, Ph.D., 1949; m. Marian Ethel Failing, Apr. 8, 1944; children—David L., Deborah A., Katherine L. Asst., Purdue U., 1943- 44; research asso. U. Ill., 1950; NRC fellow Stanford, 1950-51, instr., 1951-52; research physicist Watson IBM Lab., N.Y.C., 1952-55; asso. Columbia, 1952-55; faculty U. Cal., Berkeley, 1955—, prof. physics, 1961—; asso. prof. Miller Inst. for Basic Research, Berkeley, 1958-59, prof., 1966-67. Cons., Office Naval Research, Stanford, 1950-52, U.S. AEC, 1955—; spl. cons. USN, 1959; adv. panel mem. Nat. Bur. Standards, Radio Standards div., 1961-64; mem. Nat. Acad. Scis./NRC com. on basic research, adv. to U.S. Army Research Office, 1967-69. Served with USNR, 1944-46. Guggenheim fellow, 1961-62, 69-70; NSF fellow, 1961-62; vis. fellow Brasenose Coll., Oxford, 1969-70. Fellow Am. Phys. Soc. (past mem. exec. com. div. solid state physics; Oliver E. Buckley prize 1971), Am.

Acad. Arts and Scis. Author: (with T.P. Das) Nuclear Quadrupole Resonance Spectroscopy, 1958. Home: 69 Stevenson Av Berkeley CA 94708 Office: Dept Physics U Cal Berkeley CA 94720

HAHN, FREDERIC HALSTED, investment banker; b. N.Y.C., July 7, 1896; s. William Eugene and Caroline (Watkins) H.; B.S., Wesleyan U., 1919; m. Marylee Nally, Oct. 4, 1919; childrenFrederic Halsted, William N., Lee Ann (Mrs. Neil W. Head), Marylee (Mrs. Kenneth M. Merritt). Salesman, Printers Ink Pub. Co., 1919-22, Curtis Pub. Co., 1922-25; v.p. Percy Gardner Corp., 1925- 27; partner Dewey Bacon & Co., Bacon Stevenson & Co., 1927-34; partner Goodbody & Co., N.Y.C., 1935-70, exec. com., dir. prodn. unit div., 1953-65, spl. partner, 1965-70; dir. Pancake Kitchens, Inc. Treas., bd. dirs. Marcus Goodbody Found., 1952-65; Served as lt. (j.g.), Flying Corps, USN 1917-19 Mem. Dallas Cotton Exchange, Chgo. Bd. Trade, Early and Pioneer Naval Aviators Assn., Psi Upsilon. Episcopalian. Clubs: St. Andrews Golf (Hastings, N.Y.); Am. Yacht (Rye, N.Y.); Bankers of Am., Harbor View (N.Y.C.); Ponte Vedra (Fla.); Country of Fla., Gulf Stream Golf, Gulf Stream Bath and Tennis (Delray Beach). Home: The Scarswold Scarsdale NY (winter) 4115 S Ocean Blvd Delray Beach FL 33444

HAHN, GILBERT, Jr., lawyer, city ofcl.; b. Washington, Sept. 12, 1921; s. Gilbert and Hortense (King) H.; A.B., Princeton, 1943; LL.B., Yale, 1948; m. Margot Hess, June 29, 1950; children— Gilbert III, Amanda B., Polly K. Admitted to bar, 1948; partner firm Amram, Hahn, Sundlun & Sandground, 1954—; dir. W.M. Hahn & Co., U.S. Shoe Corp. Alternate del. Republican Nat. Conv., 1952; pres. Washington Young Rep. Club, 1949; mem. Rep. nat. finance com., 1964-68; chmn. D.C. Rep. Com., 1968-69; chmn. D.C. City Council, 1969—. Pres. bd. dirs. Washington Hosp. Center, 1966-69, Washington Hosp. Center Research Found., 1964-66. Served to 1st lt. AUS, 1942-46; ETO. Decorated Purple Heart. Mem. D.C., Md., U.S. Supreme Ct. bar assns. Clubs: Cannon; Corby Court; Federal City. Address: 3022 University Terrace NW Washington DC 20016

HAHN, HERBERT LEONARD, lawyer; b. Pasadena, Cal., Aug. 23, 1893; s. Benjamin Winfield and Grace Virginia (Gahr) H.; LL.B., Stanford, 1917; m. Lorna Margaret Gailfus, June 20, 1921; children—Richard G., Jean (wife of Dr. J.Y. Watt). Admitted to Cal. bar, 1917, since practiced in Pasadena; mem. firm Hahn & Hahn; lectr. Stanford Law Sch., 1948-58. Trustee emeritus Cal. Inst. Tech.; treas., dir. Cal. Inst. Assos., 1943-55; trustee emeritus Huntington Hosp., Pasadena. Served as 2d lt. inf. U.S. Army, 1918-19. Mem. Am., Cal., Los Angeles, Pasadena bar assns. Mason. Clubs: University, Twilight. Home: 2606 Deodar Circle Pasadena CA 91107 Office: 301 E Colorado Blvd Pasadena CA 91101

HAHN, HERBERT RALPH, broadcasting exec.; b. Boston, June 12, 1924; B.A., Harvard, 1947, M.B.A., 1949; m. Ethelee Bieber, Jan. 31, 1953; children—Licia Rose, Marina Louise, Alexandra, Elena. With Am. Broadcasting Companies, Inc., 1949—, director public relations, 1957—, v.p., 1959—. Mem. Pub. Relations Soc. Am., Commerce and Industry Assn. N.Y. Club: Harvard (N.Y.C.). Home: 55 E 86th St New York City, NY 10028. Office: 1330 Av of Americas New York City NY 10019

HAHN, JACK ALBERT LOUIS, hosp. adminstr.; b. Evansville, Ind., Apr. 24, 1922; s. Albert George and Grace (Osborn) H.; B.A., Evansville Coll., 1943, LL.D., 1958; M.H.A., Northwestern U., 1948; LL.D., De Pawn U., 1970; m. Lois A. Walther, June 13, 1946; children—Susan Louise, Louis Albert, Joan Katheryn. Adminstrv. asst. Chgo. Wesley Meml. Hosp., 1946-47; adminstr. Meml. Hosp., Fremont, O., 1948-52; asst. supt. Meth. Hosp. of Ind., Inc., Indpls., 1952-53, exec. dir., 1954-69, pres., 1969—; vis. lectr., residency preceptor George Washington U., 1949—, Xavier U., 1970—. Cons. AID, 1962, 68; mem. Surgeon Gen.'s Com. Emergency Planning, 1963-70; mem. Certification Council, 1964—, chmn., 1968-70. Mme. bd. Bd. Health and Welfare Ministries, Methodist Ch., 1964—, treas., 1968—. Served to lt. (j.g.) USNR, 1943-46. Fellow Am. Coll. Hosp. Adminstrs. (regent 1964-66); mem. Am. (Ind. del. 1955-60, chmn. council asso. services 1962-65, vice chmn. council adminstrv. practice 1959-62, gen. council 1962-65, 70-72, chmn. 1970, trustee 1965-68, 70-72, pres. 1971), Ind. (pres. 1962-63) hosp. assns., Nat. Assn. Practical Nurse Edn. and Service (dir. 1956-62, chmn. hosp. adv. council 1955-60), Am. Protestant Hosp. Assn. (v.p. 1959, dir., pres. 1965-66), Nat. Health Council (dir. 1967-70), Blue Cross Assn. Ind. (trustee 1961—, past mem. exec. com.). Methodist. Rotarian. Contbr. articles hosp., nursing jours. Home: 4716 Laurel Circle N Dr Indianapolis IN 46226 Office: Methodist Hosp Ind 1604 N Capitol Av Indianapolis IN 46202

HAHN, K. ROBERT, lawyer, mfg. exec.; b. Clear Lake, S.D., Feb. 7, 1921; s. Clement F. and Mildred S. (Hannestad) H.; A.B., Oberlin Coll., 1942; LL.B., Cornell U., 1948; m. Mary L. Crawford, Sept. 25, 1943; children—Marsha, Nancy, Susan. Admitted to D.C. bar, 1948, Mich. bar, 1952; with firm Elmore, Miss & Moore, Washington, 1948-50; v.p., gen. counsel Lake Central Airlines, Indpls., 1950-51; with Lear, Inc. (now Lear Siegler, Inc.), Santa Monica, Cal., 1957—, v.p. sales, 1957-59, exec. v.p., 1959- 65, corporate v.p. charge long-range planning, 1965-66, sr. v.p., 1966-71, exec. v.p., sec., 1971—, also dir. Mem. Am. Inst. Aeros. and Astronautics, Am. Mgmt. Assn. Home: 2 Meadowlark Lane Rolling Hills CA 90274 Office: 3171 S Bundy St Santa Monica CA 90405*

HAHN, LEWIS EDWIN, educator; b. Swenson, Tex., Sept. 26, 1908; s. Edwin D. and Ione (Brewster) H.; B.A., U. Tex., 1929, M.A., 1929; Ph.D., U. Cal., 1939; m. Elizabeth Herring, June 30, 1932; childrenHelen Elizabeth, Mary, Sharon. Teaching fellow U. Cal., 1931-34; instr. philosophy U. Mo., 1936-39, asst. prof., 1939-46, asso. prof., 1946-49; vis. lectr. Princeton, 1947; prof. philosophy Washington U., 1949-63, chmn. dept., 1949-63, asso. dean Grad. Sch. Arts and Scis., 1953-54, dean, 1954-63; research prof. philosophy So. Ill. U., Carbondale, 1963—. Mem. U.S. nat. Commn. UNESCO, 1965-67. Fellow A.A.A.S.; mem. Am. Philos. Assn. (exec. bd. 1950-54, 70—, chmn. com. placement, available personnel, 1951-54; sec.-treas. West div. 1949-51; sec.-treas. 1960- 66), Am. Assn. U. Profs., Am. Soc. Aesthetics, S.W. Philos. Soc. (pres. 1955), Mo. Philos. Assn. (pres. 1949-50), So. Soc. for Philosophy and Psychology (pres. 1958-59), Ill. Philosophy Conf. (pres. 1969-71), Phi Beta Kappa. Author: A Contextualistic Theory of Perception, 1942; (with others) Value: A Cooperative Inquiry, 1949; co-author Guide to the Works of John Dewey, 1970. Contbr. articles to profl. jours. Home: Reed Station Rd Route 2 Carbondale IL 62901

HAHN, MILTON E., educator; b. Galion, Ohio, Oct. 15, 1903; s. Dale Owen and Madge (Linnell) H.; B.A., Hamline U., 1927; M.S., U. Minn., 1938, Ph.D., 1942; m. Margaret Isabel Benson, Mar. 28, 1928; 1 son, Owen Milton. Formerly coordinator vocational orientation U. Minn., then dir. psychol. service center and prof. ednl. psychology Syracuse U.; dean students U. Cal. at Los Angeles, 1948-60, prof. psychology, 1948-; Asia Found. cons. Ministry, Dept. Edn., Ceylon, 1950-60; cons. VA's local hosps., Bur. Medicine. Served from lt. to maj. USMCR. Mem. Am. Psychol. Assn. Home: 1483 La Linda Dr Lake San Marcos CA 92069

HAHN, PHIL, writer; b. Bloomington, Kan., Aug. 21, 1932; s. Joseph W. and Irene (Shaw) H.; B.A. in English, U. Kan., 1955; m. Joanne Dalsass, Sept. 6, 1964. Free-lance writer books and articles, 1958-66; writer TV programs Get Smart, 1967-68, He and She, 1968, That's Debbie, 1969-70, Courtship of Eddie's Father, 1969-70; a creator children's TV show The Banana Splits, 1968-70; script supr. Laugh-In, 1968-69; head writer TV spls. Last Laugh at the 60's, 1970, the Fifth Dimension: An Odyssey in the Cosmic Universe of Peter Max, 1970, America, 1970; co-producer Harper Valley U.S.A., 1970; head writer the Andy Williams Show, 1970-71. Co-author charity ball Thalians Ball, 1968, co-exec. producer, 1969. Served to 1st lt. AUS, 1955-57. Recipient Emmy award, 1968. Mem. Writers Guild Am, (West), A.F.T.R.A., Screen Cartoonists Union, Sigma Nu, Pi Sigma Alpha. Democrat. Co-author: The Great Society Fun and Games Book, 1965; Beastly Rhymes, 1966; The Show-Me Book, 1966; The Adventurers of Captain Klutz, 1967; The Jungle Joke Book, 1966. Address: 4684 White Oak Av Encino CA 91316

HAHN, REUBEN WILLIAM, clergyman; b. Lockport, N.Y., May 20, 1901; s. Edward and Helene (Rosseau) H.; diploma, Concordia Collegiate Inst., Bronxville, N.Y., 1921, Concordia Theol. Sem., 1925; spl. student U. Ala., 1932-34, Northwestern U., 1944-45; D.D., Concordia Sem., St Louis, 1951; m. Alice Richert, Sept. 1, 1925; children—Gloria, Daniel, Natalie. Ordained to ministry Luth. Ch., Aug. 2, 1925; asst. Epiphany Luth. Ch., Detroit. 1923-24; pastor St Paul's, Decatur, Ala.; 1925-29; campus pastor U. Ala., 1929-40; exec. sec. Commn. on Coll. and U. Work, Luth. Ch., Mo. Synod, hdqrs. Chgo., 1940-68, sec. for campus ministry, 1966-68; recruiter Ch. Careers, 1968—. Adviser to Gamma Delta, Internat. Assn. Luth. Students, Beta Sigma Psi, Luth. Collegiate Assn., 1940-68; asso. for coordination religious affairs Luth. Laymen's League, Mem. Religious Edn. Assn. (past pres. Chgo. chpt.). Editor booklets and pamphlets for coll. youth. Contbr. religious jours. Lectr. Home: 849 N Harvey St Oak Park IL 60302

HAHN, SAMUEL WILFRED, educator; b. Columbia, S.C., Mar. 21, 1921; s. Samuel W. and Doris (Becker) H.; A.B., Lenoir Rhyne Coll., Hickory, N.C., 1941; M.A., Duke, 1942, Ph.D., 1948; m. Martha Ann Strowd, June 24, 1947; childrenStephen S., Dale B., Carol C. Vis. instr. math. Duke, 1946-47; instr. U. Mich., 1947-49; asst. prof. math. Wittenberg U., Springfield, O., 1949-51; prof. math., head dept. Winthrop Coll., Rock Hill, S.C., 1951-59; vis. prof. Fla. State U., summer 1960; prof. Hampden- Sydney Coll., 1959-60; prof. math. Wittenberg U., 1960-, chmn. dept., 1961-67, asso. dean, 1963-65. Served to lt. USNR, 1942-46. Fellow Ohio Acad. Sci. (v.p. 1967- 68); mem. Am. Math. Soc., Math. Assn. Am., Am. Assn. U. Profs., Nat. Council Tchrs. Math., Phi Beta Kappa, Sigma Xi. Lutheran. Home: 1019 Redbud Lane Springfield, OH 45504.

HAHN, THOMAS MARSHALL, Jr., coll. pres.; b. Lexington, Ky., Dec. 2, 1926; s. Thomas Marshall and Mary Elizabeth (Boston) H.; B.S. in Physics, U. Ky., 1945; Ph.D., Mass. Inst. Tech., 1950; m. Margaret Louise Lee, Dec. 27, 1948; children—William Marshall, Elizabeth Lee, Anne Dillon. Teaching asst. U. Ky., 1944-45; physicist U.S. Naval Ordnance Lab., 1946-47; research asst. Mass. Inst. Tech., 1947-50; asso. prof. U. Ky., 1950-52, prof., dir. grad. studies physics, also dir. Nuclear Accelerator Labs., 1952- 54; prof. physics, head dept. Va. Poly. Inst., 1954-59, pres., 1962—; dean arts and scis. Kan. State U., 1959-62; physicist N. Am. Phillips Co., summer 1945; staff mem. div. indsl. coop. Mass. Inst. Tech., summer 1950; research participant Oak Ridge Nat. Lab., summer 1951; cons. Reynolds Metals Co., 1958-59, Leeds and Northrup Co., 1958, AEC, 1959. Dir. First Nat. Exchange Bank of Va., Roanoke Electric Steel Corp., Dominion Bankshares Corp., Lane Co. Bd. visitors Ferrum Jr. Coll., Air U., 1966-69; chmn. Va. Met. Area Study Commn., 1966-68. Served with USNR, 1945-46. Named Va.'s Outstanding Citizen, Toastmasters Internat., 1966. Fellow Am. Phys. Soc.; mem. A.A.A.S., Am. Assn. Physics Tchrs., So. Assn. Land-Grant Colls. and State Univs. (pres. 1965-66), Phi Beta Kappa, Sigma Xi, Omicron Delta Kappa, Sigma Pi Sigma, Pi Mu Epsilon. Methodist. Rotarian. Home: Campus Virginia Poly Inst and State U Blacksburg VA 24060

HAHN, WALTER, Jr., city mgr.; b. San Francisco, Apr. 11, 1913; s. Walter and Louise (Stuer) H.; student Sacramento Jr. Coll., 1931-33, U. Cal. at Berkeley, 1935-36; B.S., U. So. Cal., 1961; m. Marian Inscoe, May 12, 1934; childrenKurt, Sharon. Engr., Cal. Div. Hwys., 1936-38; rd. coordinator, planning adviser Solano County, Cal., 1938-45; planning cons. Hahn, Campbell & Assos., Burlingame, Cal., 1945-51; city mgr., Monterey, Cal., 1951-56; chief adminstrv. officer, Inglewood, Cal., 1956-63; asst. city mgr., San Diego, 1963-66, city mgr., 1966—. Home: 3915 Paducah St San Diego CA 92117 Office: City Adminstrn Bldg San Deigo CA 92101

HAHN, WILLIAM DAVID, mfg. exec.; b. Zanesville, O., Dec. 12, 1904; s. William F. and Nellie (Heinle) H.; A.B., U. Toledo, 1927; m. Viola M. Pierce, Oct. 11, 1930; childrenMarilyn M., Elaine M. Instr. U. Toledo, 1927-34; accountant Globe-Wernicke Industries, Inc., Toledo, 1934-38, asst. treas., 1938-46, treas., 1946-54, dir., 1947—, pres., 1954-60, chmn. bd., 1961-67; vice chmn. bd. Sheller-Globe Corp., 1967-; treas. City Machine & Tool Co., 1946-54, pres., 1954-60, also dir.; dir. First Federal Savings and Loan Assn., Ohio Citizens Trust Co.; pres. Toledo Area C. of C., 1965—. Clubs: Toledo, Rotary, Sylvania Country (Toledo). Home: 3441 Bentley Blvd Toldeo OH 43606 Office: 1505 Jefferson Av Toldeo OH 46312

HAHN, WILLIAM EDWARD, educator; b. Pleasant Valley, Md., Apr. 3, 1905; D.D.S., U. Md., 1931; A.B., U. Rochester, 1938; M.S. (Carnegie fellow), 1939; married; 2 children. Intern in oral surgery Md. Gen. Hosp., 1931-32; instr. anatomy Sch. of Dentistry, U. Md., Balt., 1932-36; asst. prof., 1936-37; asso. prof., 1939-41; prof., 1941—; now head dept. anatomy. Fellow Am. Coll. Dentistry; mem. Am. Dental Assn., A.A.A.S. Home: 47 Holmehurst Av Baltimore MD 21228*

HAIEFF, ALEXEI, composer; b. Russia, 1914; mus. edn. in U.S. and abroad. Came to U.S., 1932. Fellow Am. Acad. in Rome, 1947-49, composer in residence, 1952-53, 1958-59; vis. Slee prof. U. Buffalo, 1962, 64-65; Distinguished Vis. Mellon Distinguished Vis. Mellon prof. Carnegie Inst. Tech., 1962-63; vis. prof. Brandeis U., 1965-66. Recipient medal Am. Acad. in Rome, 1942; Lili Boulanger Meml. award, 1943. Guggenheim Fellow, 1946, 49; grant Nat. Acad. Arts and Letters, 1947; N.Y. Music Critics Circle award in orchestral music, 1952; Internat. Recording award UNESCO, 1958. Composer: Symphonies, 1942, 57, 61; (ballet) Divertimento, 1946; (ballet) Zondilda and Her Entourage, 1946; Concerto for Violin, 1948; Piano Concerto, 1950; Eclogne for Harp and String Orch., 1953; Ballet in E, 1955; also chamber and instrumental music and songs. Home: 11 E 53d St New York City NY 10022 Office: care Chappel & Co Inc 609 Fifth Av New York City NY 10017*

HAIG, ALEXANDER MEIGS, Jr., army officer, govt. ofcl.; b. Phila., Dec. 2, 1924; s. Alexander Meigs and Regina Anne (Murphy) H.; student U. Notre Dame, 1943; B.S., U.S. Mil. Acad., 1947; M.A., Georgetown U., 1961; grad. Naval War Coll., 1960, Army War Coll., 1966; m. Patricia Antoinette Fox, May 24, 1950; children—Alexander P., Brian F., Barbara E. Commd. 2d lt. U.S. Army, 1947, advanced through grades to brig. gen., 1969; staff officer Office Dept. Chief of Staff for Operations, Dept. of Army, 1962-64; mil. asst. to Sec. of Army, 1964; dep. spl. asst. to Sec. and Dep. Sec. of Def., 1964-65; bn. and brigade comdr. 1st Inf. Div., Vietnam, 1966-67; regtl. comdr., dep. comdt. U.S. Mil. Acad., 1967-69; mil. asst. to Asst. to the Pres. for Nat. Security Affairs, 1969-70; dept. Asst. to the Pres. for Nat. Security Affairs, Washington, 1970—. Decorated D.S.C., Silver Star with oak leaf cluster, Legion of Merit with 2 oak leaf clusters, D.F.C. with 2 oak leaf clusters, Bronze Star with oak leaf cluster, Air medal with 27 oak leaf clusters, Army Commendation medal, Purple Heart (U.S.); Nat. Order 5th Class, Cross of Gallantry with gold palm (Vietnam). Mem. Soc. of 1st Div. (v.p.). Home: 4622 N 38th St Arlington VA 22207 Office: The White House Washington DC 20500

HAIG, GRAEME THOMSON, lawyer; b. Moose Jaw, Sask., Can., Aug. 7, 1923; s. Gordon Stuart and Catherine Margaret (Thomson) H.; LL.B., Man. Law Sch., 1949; m. Patricia Joyce Jackson, May 28, 1949; children—Gordon, Briony, Margot, Angela. Called to Man. bar, 1949; practice in Winnipeg, 1949-61; spl. counsel Bd. Broadcast Govs. Can., 1960; v.p. R.C. Baxter Ltd., Winnipeg, 1961-64; practice in Winnipeg, 1964—; partner firm D'Arcy, Irving, Haig & Smethurst, 1965—. Dir. Polaris Leasing Co. Ltd. Nat. sec. Young Progressive Conservative Assn. Can., 1951; chmn. provincial policy com. Progressive Conservative Party, 1969—. Bd. dirs. Winnipeg Humane Soc. Served with Canadian Army, 1942-46. Decorated Mil. cross, Can. decoration. Mem. Canadian Bar Assn. (v.p. Man.), Canadian (v.p. Man.), Man. chambers commerce, Canadian Found. Legal Research, Law Sch. Found. Man. Presbyn. Clubs: St. Charles County (St. James, Man.); Manitoba (Winnipeg). Author papers. Home: 1191 Oakdean Blvd St James Assinibola 12 Manitoba Canada Office: 300 286 Smith St Winnipeg 1 Manitoba Canada

HAIG, SID, (Sidney Eddie Mosesian), actor; b. Fresno, Cal., July 14, 1939; s. Haig and Roxie (Mooradian) Mosesian; student Fresno City Coll., 1957-59; grad. Pasadena Playhouse, 1961; m. Patricia Anne Gates, June 27, 1964; children—Phaedra Roxanne, Tate Gavin. Actor, appearing in over 65 television shows, including Mission Impossible, Get Smart, Gunsmoke, Alias Smith & Jones, also TV spls.; motion picture appearances in Diamonds are Forever, The Big Doll House, THX 1138, Che, Point Blank. Home: Canoga Park CA 91304 Office: care Jerry Rosen Agency 8693 Wilshire Blvd Beverly Hills CA 91304

HAIGH, ROBERT WILLIAM, bus. machine co. exec.; b. Phila., Aug. 22, 1926; s. Harry E. and Mildred (Elliott) H.; student Muhlenberg Coll., 1944-45; A.B. cum laude, Bucknell U., 1948; M.B.A. with high distinction, Harvard, 1950, D.C.S., 1953; m. Jane Stanton Sheble, June 19, 1948; children—Cynthia Jane, Anne Sheble, Robert William, Barbara Lynne. Research and teaching faculty Harvard U. Grad Sch. Bus. Adminstrn., 1950-56, asst. prof., 1953-56; asst. to pres. Helmerich & Payne, Inc., Tulsa, 1956, controller and asst. to pres., 1956-57, financial v.p., dir., 1957-61, White Eagle Internat. Oil Co., 1957-60; dir. planning Standard Oil Co. (O.), Cleve., 1961, v.p. planning, 1961-63, v.p. corporate planning and devel., 1963-64, v.p. chems. and plastics bus., 1964-66, Vistron Corp. subsidiary, 1966-67; group v.p., mgr. charge edn. Xerox Corp., 1967—. Served with USNR, 1944-45. Mem. Am. Petroleum Inst., Cleve. C. of C., Cleve. Council World Affairs, Phi Beta Kappa, Phi Lambda Theta. Author: (with John G. McLean) The Growth of Integrated Oil Companies, 1954. Home: 2706 Rocklyn Rd Shaker Heights 22 OH 44122 Office: Midland Bldg Cleveland OH 44115 *

HAIGH, T. ARNOLD, trust co. exec. Chmn. bd. Chittenden Trust Co. Office: 123 Church St Burlington VT 05401*

HAIGHT, CHARLES HARRY, food chain exec.; b. Newark, May 27, 1909; s. Harry Howard and Blanche (Curtis) H.; grad. Pace Inst., 1930; m. Beverly Matthewson, Nov. 1, 1941; 1 dau., Carol Hunting (Mrs. Charles W. Ruess). With Grand Union Co., 1928—, treas., 1960—; treas., dir. Stop and Save Trading Stamp Corp., 1966—, N.Am. Equipment Corp., 1968—. Mem. exec. bd. N. Bergen County council Boy Scouts Am., 1966—. Served with USNR, 1943-45. Home: 762 Schaefer Av Oradell NJ 07649 Office: 100 Broadway E Paterson NJ 07407

HAIGHT, EDWARD ALLEN, lawyer; b. Rockford, Ill., July 2, 1910; s. John T. and Augusta (Granger) H.; B.A., U. Wis., 1931; LL.B., Harvard, 1934; m. Valerie E. Haight, Jan. 1, 1935; childrenEdward Allen, George Ives II, Edith Diane, Stephen Holmes. Admitted to Ill. bar, 1934, since practiced in Chgo.; mem. firm of Haight, Hofeldt & Davis, and predecessor firm, Chgo., 1956—. Served as lt. USNR, 1943-46. Mem. Am., Ill., Chgo., 7th Circuit bar assns., Am., Chgo. patent law assns., Am. Coll. Trial Lawyers. Clubs: Union League (Chgo.); Skokie Country. Home: 159 Abingdon Av Kenilworth IL 60043 Office: 141 W Jackson Blvd Chicago IL 60604

HAIGHT, GILBERT PIERCE, Jr., educator, chemist; b. Seattle June 8, 1922; s. Gilbert Pierce and Ruth (Gazzam) H.; A.B., Stanford, 1943; Ph.D., Princeton, 1946; research fellow Ohio State U., 1946-47; Rhodes scholar, Oxford (Eng.) U., 1947- 48; m. Shirley Myers Grapek, June 30, 1946; children-Jennifer Lea, Loisanne Fox, Charlene Ellen, Charles Pierce, Stephanie Louise, Christopher Warren. Asst. prof. U. Hawaii, 1948-49, George Washington U., 1949-52, U. Kan., 1952-54; asso. prof. Swarthmore Coll., 1954-65; prof. chemistry Tex. A. and M. U., 1965-66, U. Ill. at Urbana, 1966-; vis. scientist Tech. U. Denmark, 1960-61; cons. in field, 1951—. Mem. Rhodes scholar selection com. for Kan., 1965—. Mem. Am. (vis. scientist, program chmn. div. chem. edn.), Danish chem. socs., A.A.A.S. Am. Inst. chemists, Phi Beta Kappa, Sigma Xi, Phi Lambda Upsilon. Author: Introduction to Physical Science, 1964; (with H.B. Gray) Basic Principles of Chemistry, 1967; (with R.E. Dickerson and H.B. Gray) Chemical Principles, 1970; also articles. Home: 108 E Pennsylvania St Urbana, IL 61801.

HAIGHT, GORDON SHERMAN educator; b. Muskegon, Mich., Feb. 6, 1901; s. Louis Pease and Grace (Carpenter) H.; A.B., Yale, 1923, Ph.D., 1933; m. Mary Treat Nettleton, June 24, 1937. Tchr., Kent Sch., 1924, Hotchkiss Sch., 1925-30; mem. faculty Yale, 1933—, prof. English, 1950-66, Emily Sanford prof. English lit., 1966-69, emeritus, 1969—, fellow Calhoun Coll., 1933-49, master Pierson Coll., 1949-53; vis. prof. English, Grad. Sch., Columbia, 1945-46, U. Ore., 1949. Guggenheim fellow, 1946-47, 52-53, 60-61. Fellow Royal Soc. Lit.; corr. fellow Brit. Acad.; mem. Berzelius, Zeta Psi, Torch. Episcopalian. Clubs: Elizabethan (New Haven); Century, Yale (N.Y.C.). Author: Mrs. Sigourney, 1930; George Eliot and John Chapman, 1940; George Eliot: A Biography, 1968 (James Tait Black award, Van Wyck Brooks award, Heinemann award, Nat. Acad. Arts and Letters award). Editor: Miss. Ravenel (J.W. De Forest), 1939, 1955; vols. Classics Club, 1941-42; Yale edit. The George Eliot Letters, 1954- 55, Adam Bede, 1948, Middlemarch, 1955, Mill on the Floss, 1961; A Century of George Eliot Criticism, 1965; Portable Reader of Victorian Prose, 1971. Contbr. articles on Francis Quarles' Emblems, Tennyson, Meredith, Thackeray, Lewes, Dickens, James, Browning; chpt. on Howells, Literary History of the United States, 1948; editorial adviser PMLA, 19th-Century Fiction, Victorian Studies, Studies in English Lit. and Wellesley Index. Home: 145 Peck Hill Rd Woodbridge CT 06525

HAIGHT, J. ROTHERY, hosp. adminstr.; b. Utica, N.Y., Aug. 24, 1907; s. Julius Eugene and Mabel (Spearing) H.; A.B., Colgate U., 1930; M.D., U. Buffalo 1934; m. Margaret Haworth Petty, Apr. 19, 1938; children—Robert Rothery, Jonathan Danner, Donald Haworth. Intern Vassar Bros. Hosp., Poughkeepsie, N.Y., King County Hosp., Bklyn., 1934-35, Harlem Valley State Hosp., Wingdale, N.Y., 1936-38, sr. asst., 1941-45; supr. psychiatrist Creedmoor State Hosp. (N.Y.), 1945-53; asst. dir. Utica (N.Y.) State Hosp., Kings Park State Hosp., 1953-63; dir. St. Lawrence State Hosp., 1963-66, Gowanda State Hosp., 1966—; asst. clin. prof. psychiatry N.Y. Med. Coll., 1956-63, U. Buffalo, 1968—. Served with M.C., AUS, World War II: PTO. Diplomate psychiatry Am. Bd. Psychiatry and Neurology. Mem. A.M.A., N.Y., Erie County med. socs., Am. Psychiat. Assn., Retired Officers Assn. Address: Gowanda State Hosp Helmuth NY 14079

HAIGHT, JAMES THERON, corp. exec., lawyer; b. Racine, Wis., Dec. 10, 1924; s. Walter Lyman and Geraldine (Foley) H.; student U. Neb., 1943-44, U. Bordeaux (France), 1947; diplome d'Etudes, U. Paris (France), 1948; B.A., U. Wis., 1950, LL.B., 1951; m. Patricia Aloe, Apr. 26, 1952; children—Alberta, Barbara, Catherine, Dorothy, Elaine. Admitted to D.C. bar, 1952, also U.S. Supreme Ct.; atty. Covington & Burling, Washington, 1951-56, Goodyear Tire & Rubber Co., Goodyear Internat. Corp., Akron, O., 1956-61; gen. counsel, sec. George J. Meyer Mfg. Co., Milw., 1961-66; sec., chief counsel Thrifty Drug Stores Co. Inc., 1966—. Served with C.E., AUS, 1943-46. Mem. Am. (vice chmn. 1965-67, mem. council internat. and comparative law sect., chmn. nat. inst. on legal aspects of doing business in Europe 1971), Ohio, Wis., Cal., Los Angeles bar assns., Los Angeles Town Hall, Internat. Law Assn., Internat. C. of C., Am. Fgn. Law Assn., Am. Soc. Internat. Law, U. Wis. Alumni Assn., Order of Coif. Author: The Migratory Agricultural Worker in Wisconsin, 1951; A Community Mental Health Services Act for Ohio, 1961; United States Regulation of East-West Trade, 1964; also articles. Home: 1390 Ridge Way Pasadena CA 91106 Office: 5051 Rodeo Rd Los Angeles CA 90016

HAIGNEY, JOHN EUSTACE, corp. exec., lawyer; b. N.Y.C., Feb. 15, 1912; s. John J. and Susan (Lawlor) H.; B.S., N.Y. U., 1933; LL.B., St. John's U., 1936; m. Dorothy Anne Monahan, Aug. 18, 1943; children—Anne, John Eustace, Kathleen, Mark, Paul, Jennifer and Courtney (twins). Admitted to N.Y. bar, 1936, since practiced in N.Y.C.; asso. firm Scandrett, Tuttle & Chalaire, N.Y.C., 1936-42, partner, 1946-49; partner firm Ide & Haigney, 1949—; legal counsel Rheingold Corp., N.Y.C., 1957-67, pres., dir., 1967—, dir. subsidiary corps.; dir. Bischoff Chem. Corp., Clevepak Corp., Glyco Chems., Inc., Chas. L. Huisking & Co. Bd. dirs. Leonard Tingle Found.; pres., dir. Frank L. Huisking Found., N.Y.C.; trustee Fordham U.; mem. lay Council St. John's U. Served to maj. AUS, 1942-46. Mem. Bar Assn. N.Y.C., N.Y. State, N.Y. County bar assns., Nat. Inst. Social Scis. Roman Catholic. Clubs: N.Y. Yacht, Union League (N.Y.C.); Larchmont Yacht. Home: 37 Larchmont Av Larchmont NY 10538 Office: 41 E 42 St New York City NY 10017

HAILE, H. G., educator; b. Brownwood, Tex., July 31, 1931; s. Frank and Nell (Goodson) H.; B.A., U. Ark., 1952, M.A., 1954; Ph.D., U. Ill., 1957; student U. Colgne (Germany), 1955-56; m. Mary Elizabeth Huff, Sept. 1, 1952; childrenJonathan, Christian, Constance. Instr., U. Pa., 1956-57; asst. prof., then asso. prof. Houston, 1957-63; mem. faculty U. Ill. at Urbana, 1963-, prof. German, 1965-, head dept., 1964-. Fulbright fellow, 1955; fellow Am. Council Learned Socs., 1960. Author: Das Faustbuch nach der Wolfenbüttler H Handschrift, 1963; The History of Doctor Johann Faustus, 1965. Home: 1001 W White St Champaign, IL 61820. Office: Dept Germanic Langs Univ Ill Urbana IL 61801

HAILE, JAMES FRANCIS, hosp. adminstr.; b. Shamokin, Pa., Jan. 8, 1920; s. Philip J. and Mary (Brennan) H.; student U. Tenn., 1950-51; m. Betty Jane Kinnaw, May 19, 1943; childrenPatrieia, Peter, Peggy, Pamela, Karen. Finance officer VA hosps. at Thomasville, Ga., Montgomery, Ala. and Memphis, 1945-50; hosp. adminstrn. field rep. VA, Atlanta, 1950-53; adminstr. VA Hosp., Montgomery, 1953-55, Minot, N.D., 1955-58, Hampton, Va., 1958-62, Wadsworth, Kan., 1962-69; dir. VA Hosp., Indpls., 1969—. Bd. dirs. Leavenworth (Kan.) United Fund, 1962- 65. Served to capt. USAAF, 1942-45; ETO. Mem. Am. Acad. Med. Adminstrs. (charter), Am. Legion, Fed. Hosp. Adminstrs. Inst. Alumni Assn. Elk, Rotarian (bd. dirs. Leavenworth 1956-68). Address: Veterans Adminstrn Hosp Indianapolis IN 46202

HAILE, MINASSE, diplomat of Ethiopia; b. Harrar, Ethiopia, Feb. 12, 1930; s. Haile Dibineh and Eleni (Haile) Haile; B.A. in Econs., U. Wis., 1950; LL.B., Columbia, 1954, M.A., 1957, Ph.D., 1961; m. Iris Maxine Robinson, Oct. 8, 1954; children-Suzanne, Daniel and David (twins), Michael. Legal adviser Ministry Fgn. Affairs, 1961; commnr. Civil Service Ethiopia, 1962; minister of state of information, 1965-68; chief polit. affairs. His Imperial Majesty's Pvt. Cabinet, 1962-68; A.E. and P. of Ethiopia to U.S., 1968-. Attended numerous internat. confs. Author: Domestic Jurisdiction: United Nations Consideration of Domestic Questions and of Their International Effects. Home: 2209 Wyoming Av NW Washington, DC 20008. Office: 2134 Kalorma Rd NW Washington DC 20008*

HAILE SELLASSIE, Emperor of Ethiopia; original name Ras Tafari Makonnen; b. July 23, 1892; s. Ras Makonnen; LL.D. Cambridge, Columbia, Howard, McGill, Michigan, Athens, Banaras, Bonn. Laval, D.C.L. Oxford Univs.; m. Wolzero Menen, July 30, 1911; children—Princess Tenagne Worg (wife of Bitwoded Anargachew Masai), Crown Prince Mered Azmach Asfa Wosen (heir apparent), Princess Zannaba Worq (dec. 1933), Princess Tsahai (dec. 1942), Prince Makonnen (dec. 1957), Prince Sahle Sellassie. Proclaimed heir to throne when Zauditu, dau. Menelik II, was nominated Empress and the Queen of Kings of Ethiopia, 1918; proclaimed king, 1928; proclaimed emperor after death of Empress Zauditu, 1930; appeared before League of Nations, Geneva, to appeal against Fascist aggression, 1938; lived in Eng. during war years until 1941; rallied refugee patriots in Kenya and Sudan, and crossed frontier, Jan. 1941; reinstated in Addis Ababa, May 1941; since has reorganized govt., reopened parliament, reinstituted State Bank of Ethiopia, proclaimed new currency, abolished slavery, reorganized army, air force and navy on modern lines, established modern airlines, opened new road, started indsl. and agrl. projects, est. 450 new schs., 4 colls. and a mil. acad., a first-class post, telegraph and telecommunications system, several well-equipped modern hosps., built up system cts. justice, begun codification of laws, entered into diplomatic relations with most of the important nations of the world, secured reintegration of Eritrea, granted full adult suffrage to his people, 1955. Howard, McGill, Michigan, Athens, Banaras, Bonn. Laval, D.C.L. Oxford Univs.; Decorated Grand Cross of Order Legion d'honeur (France); Orders of Annusiata, Leopole (Belgium); Lion dlor de la Maison de Nassau (Lux.); Orange-Nassau (Neth.); Elephant (Den.); San Sebastian Guillaume (Brazil); Azgec Eagle (Mex.); Mil. Merit (Fed. Republic Germ.); Star (Yugo.); Mil. Merit (France); Mohammed Ali (Egypt); Seraphim (Sweden); St. Olaf (Norway); Saviour (Greece). Address: Imperial Palace Addis Ababa Ethiopa*

HAILEY, ARTHUR author; b. Luton, Eng., Apr. 5, 1920; s. George and Elsie (Wright) H.; student pub. schs., Eng.; m. Sheila Dunlop, July 28, 1951; children-Jane, Steven, Diane, (by previous marriage) Roger, John, Mark. Recipient award for most distinguished creative achievement Canadian Council Authors and Artists, 1956, Best Playwright award All-Canadian TV Talent award, 1957, 58; Fiction Gold medal Commonwealth Club Cal., 1969. Mem. Writers Guild Am., Authors League Am., Assn. Canadian Television and Radio Artists (hon. life). Author: (novels) Runway Zero- Eight, (with John Castle) 1958, The Final Diagnosis, 1959, In High Places, 1962 (Doubleday Prize Novel award 1961), Hotel, 1965, Airport, 1968; Wheels, 1971; (collected plays) Close-up on Writing for Television, 1960; motion pictures include Zero Hour, 1956, Time Lock, 1957, The Young Doctors, 1961, Hotel, 1966, Airport, 1969. Address: Lyford Cay New Providence Bahamas also care Maeve Southgate Inc 41 Fifth Av New York City NY 10003

HAILPERIN, HERMAN, rabbi, educator; born at Newark, N.J., Apr. 6, 1899; s. Baer and Sarah (Gutkin) H.; A.B., New York U., 1919; grad. Jewish Theol. Sem. Am., 1922; A.M., U. of Pittsburgh, 1925. Ph.D., 1933; D. D. (honorary). Jewish Theol. Sem. American, 1956; m. Harriet Silverman, July 4, 1922 (dec.); childrenCyrus Baer, Sarah; m. 2d, Celia R. Moss, December 4, 1966. Ordained to the ministry of the Jewish Ch. 1922; rabbi, Tree of Life Congregation, Pitts., 1922-68, emeritus, 1968-; instr. hist. U. Pitts., 1926-27 and 1943; lecturer on Jewish history, Duquesne University, 1937-41, adjunct prof. history and theol., 1965-. Mem. Rabbinical Assembly of Am. (mem. exec. com.) Am. Assn. of University Professors, Phi Beta Kappa (hon. member), Phi Alpha Theta. Author: A Rabbi Teaches, 1939; Nicolas De Lyra and Rashi, 1940; several monographs on The History of Intellectual Relations Between Christians and Jews in Europe; edited magnum opus of J. S. Raisin, Gentile Reactions to Jewish Ideals, 1953; Rashi and the Christian Scholars, 1963; columnist for The Jewish Criterion and American Jewish Outlook. Home: 5048 5th Av Pittsburgh PA 15232 Office: Shady Av Pittsburgh PA 15206

HAILSTONES, THOMAS JOHN, coll. dean; b. Hamilton, Scotland, Apr. 12, 1919; s. James and Mary (Sweeney) H.; came to U.S., 1921, naturalized, 1926; B.S. in Econs. and Bus. Administrn., U. Detroit, 1947; M.A. in Econs., Wayne State U., 1948; Ph.D., St. Louis U., 1951; m. Catherine Paffhausen, Jan. 25, 1944; children—Barbara, William, Patrick. Civilian instr. USAAF and RAF, World War II; instr. U. Detroit, 1947-48, St. Louis U., 1948-51; asst. prof. U. Notre Dame, 1951-52; chmn. dept. econs. Xavier U., Cin., 1952-56, dir. bus. adminstrn. div., 1956-60, dean Coll. Bus. Adminstrn., prof. econs., 1960—; weekly broadcast radio sta. WLW, Cin., 1958-63; panel mem. World Front, sta. WLW-TV, 1958- -; cond. coll. credit program sta. WCET-TV, Cin., 1954. Dir. A. C. Wahl & Assos., Inc., Cin., Clopay Corp. Chmn. Mayor Cin. Full Employment Commn., 1955-61; chmn. adv. bd. Ohio Employment Service, 1961—; mem. adv. com. Cin. region Manpower Devel. and Tng. Program, 1962—; pub. mem. appeals bd. Cin. region Nat. Elec. Contractors Assn., also Internat. Brotherhood Elec. Woekers, 1960—; mem. econ. edn. com. Nat. Invest-in-Am. Council, 1963—. Mem. Am., Cath. (2d v.p. 1964), Midwest econ. assns., Nat. Assn. Bus. Economists. Author: Basic Economics, 3d edit., 1968; (with M. Brennan) Economics: Principles and Applications, 1970; (with B. L. Martin and F. Mastrianna) Contemporary Economic Problems, 2d edit., 1970; also author of weekly column Economic Thoughts, 1955—. Editor: Readings in Economics, 2d edit., 1969. Home: 379 Circlewood Lane Cincinnati OH 45215*

HAIMAN, FRANKLYN SAUL, educator; b. Cleve., June 23, 1921; s. Alfred Wilfred and Stella (Weiss) H.; A.B., Western Res. U., 1942; M.A., Northwestern U., 1946, Ph.D., 1948; m. Louise Josephine Goble, June 11, 1955; children—Mark, Eric. Mem. faculty Northwestern U., 1948—, prof. group communication and urban affairs, chmn. dept. pub. address and group communication, 1965—; cons., lectr. in field. Asso., Nat. Tng. Labs., Inst. Applied Behavioral Scis., 1953—. Chmn. Ill. div. Am. Civil Liberties Union, 1964—, mem. nat. bd. dirs., 1966—, chmn. nat. planning com. 1970—. Served with USAAF, 1942-45. Mem. Am. Psychol. Assn., Speech Communication Assn., Am. Assn. U. Profs. (pres. Northwestern U. chpt. 1961-62). Phi Beta Kappa. Author: Group Leadership and Democratic Action, 1951; Freedom of Speech: Issues and Cases, 1965; co-author: The Dynamics of Discussion, 1960. Home: 824 Ingleside Pl Evanston IL 60201

HAIMAN, ROBERT JAMES, newspaper editor; b. Norwich, Conn., May 6, 1936; s. Albert and Letta (Cone) H.; student U. Conn., 1953-55; B.S., U. Fla., 1957; postgrad. Am. Press Inst. Columbia, 1963; m. Elizabeth Royce Greenlaw, Sept. 26, 1964; 1 son, Robert Greenlaw. Reporter St. Petersburg (Fla.) Times, 1958-60, copy editor, 1962-63, nat. editor, 1964-66, mng. editor, 1966-71; dir. Times Pub. Co., St. Petersburg. Mem. pres. round table Fla. Presbyn. Coll. Served with USMC, 1961. Mem. A.P. Mng. Editors (dir. 1968—), Fla. Soc. Newspaper Editors, Internat. Press Inst. Zurich, Sigma Delta Chi. Democrat. Presbyn. (deacon) Clubs: Racquet, University (St. Petersburg); Bath (Redington Beach, Fla.). Home: 3275 Walnut St NE St Petersburg FL 33734 Office: 490 1st Av S St Petersburg FL 33731

HAIMANN, THEO, educator, author; b. Koblenz, Germany, Nov. 17, 1911; s. Hermann and Auguste (Oppenheimer) H.; Ph.D., U. Bonn (Germany), 1934; M.B.A., Washington U., St. Louis, 1956; m. Ruth G. Treiman, Dec. 31, 1941; children—Carolyn A., Mark H. Came to U.S., 1936, naturalized, 1943. Pres. Lennox Mfg. Co., 1956-57; mem. faculty U. Ariz., 1957-58; mem. faculty St. Louis U., 1958—, Mary Louise Murray prof. mgmt. sci., 1969—. Bd. dirs. St. Mary's Hosp., St. Louis. Mem. Acad. Mgmt., Am. Econ. Assn., Beta Gamma Sigma, Alpha Kappa Psi. Author: Professional Management, 1962; Supervisory Management for Hospitals, 1965; Management in the Modern Organization, 1970. Home: 4 Robin Hill St Louis MO 63124

HAIMO, DEBORAH TEPPER, educator; b. Odessa, Ukraine, July 1, 1921; d. Joseph Meir and Esther (Vodovoz) Tepper; came to U.S., 1931, derivative citizen; A.B. magna cum laude, Radcliffe Coll., 1943, A.M., 1943; Ph.D., Harvard, 1964; m. Franklin Haimo, Feb. 27, 1944; children-Zara Tepper (Mrs. John Allman), Ethan Tepper, Leah Tepper, Nina Tepper, Varda Tepper. Acting head math. dept. Lake Erie Coll., 1943-44; instr. Northeastern U., 1944-45; lectr. Washington U., St. Louis, 1948-61; lectr., asst. prof., asso. prof. So. Ill. U., Edwardsville, 1961-68; prof. math. U. Mo., St. Louis, 1968—, chmn. dept. math., 1969—. Recipient NASA research grant, 1966-69, NSF grants, 1969—. NSF sci. faculty fellow, 1964-65. Mem. Am. Math. Soc., Am. Assn. U. Profs., Phi Beta Kappa. Editor: Orthogonal Expansions and their Continous Analogues, 1968. Contbr. articles profl. jours. Home: 7201 Cornell Av St Louis MO 63130

HAIN, BRUCE VALENTINE, lawyer; b. Selma, Ala., Sept. 3, 1915; s. Jesse Bruce and Ellen May (Moore) H.; A.B., Vanderbilt, 1938; LL.B., U. Ala., 1941; m. Lilla Davenport Anderson, Apr. 20, 1965; 1 stepson, Marvin Williams Goodwyn, Jr. Admitted to Ala. bar, 1941; practice in Selma, 1946—; mem. firm Hobbs & Hain, 1959—; mem. Ala. Ho. of Reps., 1954—. Partner J.B. Hain Co. (farming); trustee J. Bruce Hain Estate. Served to lt. USNR, 1942- 46. Mem. Am., Ala. bar assns., Am. Judicature Soc., Delta Kappa Epislon. Baptist. Home: 109 Hooper Dr Selma AL 36701 Office: 100 Church St Selma AL 36701

HAIN, EDWARD WILES, retired corp. exec.; b. Troy, N.Y., Feb. 14, 1910; s. Andrew Sylvester and Anna (Wiles) H.; student Rensselaer Poly. Inst., 1928-30; m. Marjorie Matthews, July 12, 1944; children—Bruce Wiles, Matthew Edward. Securities analyst Jacob L. Hain & Co., Reading, Pa., 1946-52; sec., treas., dir. Bush Universal, Inc., Bklyn., 1952-71; past dir. Bush Terminal R.R. Co., N.J. Zinc Co., Hamilton Watch Co. Trustee Bloomfield Coll. Served to capt. USAAF, 1942-46. Mem. N.Y. Soc. Security Analysts, Am. Soc. Corp. Secretaries, Bankers Club Am. Lutheran (trustee). Clubs: West Side Tennis (N.Y.C.); Smoke Rise Tennis. Home: 456 Laurel Terrace Smoke Rise Butler NJ 07405

HAIN, JACOB L., mgmt. cons.; b. West Camp, N.Y., 1902; s. Andrew S. and Anna (Wiles) H.; A.B., Johns Hopkins, 1923; m. Mary L. McQuay, July 4, 1946; children—Andrew, John. Dir., mem. exec. com. Am. Bank Note Co., 1952—. Trustee Johns Hopkins, St. Joseph's Hosp., Muhlenberg Coll., Albright Coll. Clubs: Recess (N.Y.C.); Berkshire Country, Wyomissing (Reading). Home: 100 Grandview Blvd Wyomissing Hills PA 19609 Office: 449 Penn St Reading PA 19603

HAINDS, JOHN ROBERT, ednl. cons.; b. Brookfield, Mo., Sept. 10, 1896; s. Frederick Potts and Jennie E. (Jones) H.; student U. Ill., 1918; Ph.B., Shurtleff Coll., 1925; postgrad. U. Mich., summer 1926; M.A., Northwestern U., 1933, Ph.D., 1939; m. Jeannie Armstrong, May 17, 1916; 1 son, James Armstrong. Instr. English and speech Gladstone (Mich.) Sr. High Sch., 1925-27, Davenport (Ia.) Sr. High Sch., 1927-30, J. Sterling Morton High Sch., Cicero, Ill., 1930-33, Morton Jr. Coll., Cicero, 1933-37, Northwestern U., 1937-40; prof. English, No. Ill. U., DeKalb, 1940-66, mem. adminstrv. council, 1945-51, 53-62, acad. v.p., 1959-63, coordinator research grants, 1963-66, dean Grad. Sch., 1951-59, curriculum cons.; dir. No. Ill. U. Found., 1950-67, v.p., 1962-66, emeritus, 1966; prof. English, Friends U., 1967-70; ednl. cons., 1945—. Mem. N.E.A. (life), Ill. Edn. Assn. (pres. Rock River div. 1954-55). Adult Edn. Con. Greater Chgo., Nat. Council Tchrs. English, Phi Beta Kappa, Phi Delta Kappa, Alpha Delta, Sigma Tau Delta. Mason (32, Shriner). Editor: (with others) Bibliogrpahy of the Published Writings of John Stuart Mill, 1945. Contbr. Jour. History of Ideas. Address: PO Box 2201 Tubac AZ 85640

HAINES, CHARLES GROVE, educator; b. Abbottstown, Pa., Dec. 10, 1906; s. Wilbur Emory and Helen Estella (Wolf) H.; A.B., Ursinus Coll., 1927; A.M., Clark U., 1928, Ph.D., 1933; student U. Rome (Italy), 1930-31; m. Frances Elizabeth Marble, June 28, 1928; 1 dau., Frances M. Asst. econs., and govt. Worcester Poly. Inst., 1928-30; mem. faculty Syracuse U., 1931-45, prof. history, 1943-45; dir. area and lang. program, 1943-44; vis. prof. history Columbia, spring 1945; prof. diplomatic history Sch. Advanced Internat. Studies, Johns Hopkins, 1945—, dir. Bologna Center, Johns Hopkins U., (Italy), 1955—. Mem. Fgn. Service Res., research attaché to Milan, Italy and Trieste, 1948-49; cons. Dept. State, 195O-54. Am. Exchange Fellow to Italy, 1930-31. Mem. bd. govs. Middle East Inst., 1946-48. Decorated officer Order of Merit (Italy); Order of the Silver Eagle (Republic Austria). Mem. Am. Hist. Assn., The Burke Soc., Am. Assn. U. Profs., Fgn. Policy Assn., Phi Beta Kappa, Tau Kappa Alpha, Phi Kappa Phi. Democrat. Unitarian. Clubs: Syracuse University (N.Y.); Cosmos. Author: (with W. B. Walsh), The Development of Western Civilization 1941; The Origins and Background of the Second World War (with R. J. S. Hoffman), 1943, 46; Fgn. Policy Assn. Reports on Italian Questions, 1943- 46. Editor: The Threat of Soviet Imperialism; Africa Today, 1955; European Intergration, 1957. Editorial bd Jour. of Modern Hist., 1948-49; editor headline series Fgn. Policy Assn., 1944-45; bd. editor The Middle East Jour., 1946—; dir. The American Review. Contr. articles to jours. Radio broadcaster; public lectr. Home: Via Belmeloro 11 Bologna Italy*

HAINES, CHARLES JAMES, bus. exec.; b. Thomas, Okla., Oct. 6, 1896; s. James and Mary Frances (Spotts) H.; B.S. in Engring., U. of Mo., 1917; m. Marguerite Fralick, Jan. 18, 1936; 1 dau., Heather (Mrs. W. E. Richmond, Jr.). Supt. Am. Cotton Oil Co., Chgo., 1917-20; supt. Electrox Co., Peoria, Ill., 1920-23; exec. Nat. Cylinder Gas Co. (name changed to Chemetron Corp., 1958), Chgo., 1923-, dir., 1934-; pres., 1937-60, chmn. bd., chief exec. officer, 1960-67, chmn. bd. dirs., 1967-70, hon. chmn. bd., 1970—. Fellow Am. Inst. Scientists; mem. Am. Inst. Chem. Engrs., Am. Chem. Soc., Tau Beta Pi, Alpha Chi Sigma, Phi Kappa Psi. Clubs: Chicago, University (Chicago); Exmoor Country (Highland Park, Ill.). Home: 190 E Pearson St Chicago IL 60611 Office: 840 N Michigan Av Chicago IL 60611

HAINES, CHARLES S., II, architect; b. Sabetha, Kan., May 25, 1906; s. Charles S. and Francis (Moon) H.; B.S. in Archtl. Engring., Kan. U., 1929; B. Arch., Columbia, 1930; student Sch. Fine Arts, Fontainebleau, France, 1930; m. Margaret Dinsmore, Feb. 29, 1936; children—Charles Samuel, Ann (Mrs. Dinowitz), Sara (Mrs. Fay), Kate. Architect, Voorhees, Walker, Smith & Smith, N.Y.C., 1932-57; partner Voorhees, Walker, Smith, Smith & Haines, N.Y.C., 1958-64, Smith, Smith, Haines, Lundberg & Waehler, N.Y.C., 1964- 66, Smith, Haines, Lundberg & Waehler, 1966-68, Haines, Lundberg & Waehler, 1968—. Mem. com. on design, constrn. and equipment of labs NRC, 1957-63; mem. exec. com., constrn. sect. Nat. Safety Council, 1951-56; panel mem. Am. Arbitration Assn., 1951—. Trustee Village of Tarrytown, 1946-48, mayor, 1949-51, chmn. planning bd., 1951-52; trustee Citizens Budget Com., 1966—. Dir. Greater N.Y. Safety Council, 1955—; v.p., trustee Scarborough Country Day Sch., 1959-62; mem. engring. council Columbia, 1966—; v.p. Kan. U. Alumni Bd., 1969—. Recipient Distinguished Service citation U. Kan. Registered architect N.Y., 47 other states and territories. Fellow Am. Soc. M.E.; mem. A.I.A. (exec. com. N.Y. chpt. 1959- 62, mem. finance com. 1966-67), Newcomen Soc. N. Am., N.Y. State Assn. Architects, Archtl. League N.Y. (chmn. finance com. 1960-62, treas. 1963-65), Commerce and Industry Assn. N.Y. (membership council 1958—), Am. Soc. Prevention Cruelty to Animals (sr. v.p. 1963—, pres. 1971—), N.Y. Soc. Architects, N.Y. Bldg. Congress (bd. dirs. 1958-65), C. of C. U.S. (constrn. and civic devel. com.), N.Y. Bldg. Congress (pres. 1962-65, life mem.), Tau Beta Pi, Sigma Tau, Phi Delta Theta. Mem. Reformed Ch. Clubs: Pine Valley Golf; Sleepy Hollow Country; Union League (bd. govs.); Edgartown Yacht. Contbr. articles profl. jours. Home: 166 E 63d St New York City NY 10021 Office: 2 Park Av New York City NY 10016

HAINES, EDMUND THOMAS, composer, music educator; b. Ottumwa, Ia., Dec. 15, 1914; s. Verlan J. and Edna May (Waters) H.; student U. Kan., 1933-34; B.M., Kansas City Conservatory of Music, 1936; M.M., Eastman Sch. of Music, U. Rochester, 1938, Ph.D., 1941; m. Joyce Williams, Aug. 27, 1939 (div.); m. 2d, Beatrice Thorne, June 2, 1951 (div.); 1 son, David; m. 3d, Lauren Levey, Mar. 30, 1970. Tchr. piano and theory Conservatory of Kansas City, 1936-37; teaching fellow and grad. student Eastman School, 1938-41; apptd. to faculty U. Mich., 1941, Sarah Lawrence Coll., 1948; Guggenheim fellow, 1956-57, 57-58; Ford Found. orchestral commn., 1958; composer-in- residence La Napoule Art Found., France, 1957-58; Fulbright research grant, Spain, 1965-67. Recipient Pulitzer Prize, 1941. Composer of orchestral, choral, keyboard, ballet chamber music; performed in the U.S. and abroad. Home: 5900 Arlington Av New York City NY 10471

HAINES, HARRY B., newspaper editor; b. Altoona, Pa., Sept. 18, 1892; s. Edward B. and Sarah (Barnette) H.; grad. Paterson (N.J.) High Sch., 1898; m. Helen Brundage, Nov. 12, 1920. Asso. editor first English publ. devoted to automobile users The Horseless Age, 1901-03; sec. Nat Premium Advt. Assn. N.Y.; pres., publ. Paterson (N.J.) Evening News. Mem. Am. Soc. Newspaper Editors. Rotarian, Kiwanian, Optimist. Clubs: New York Athletic, New York Advertising; Preakness Hills Country, Lambs, Lotos. Home: 555 E 27th St Paterson NJ 07514 Office: Paterson News News Plaza Paterson NJ 07505*

HAINES, LEWIS FRANCIS, educator; b. Endicott, N.Y., Oct 28, 1907; s. William Joseph and Teresa Irene (Lewis) H.; A.B., U. Mich., 1930, A.M., 1932, Ph.D., 1941; m. Helen Mary Steere, Sept 1, 1930; 1 son, James Lewis, Instr. English Boys' Tech. High Sch., Milw., 1930-34; teaching fellow English U. Mich., 1935-41, instr. English, summer 1941; acting instr. English U. Fla., 1941-42, asst. prof., 1942-46, prof. humanities, 1946-67, prof. humanities and comprehensive logic, 1967-; editor U. Fla. Press, 1945-67, dir., 1949-67. Mem. Gov's Hwy. Safety Conf. Recipient Rockefeller research grant, summer 1962. Mem. Modern Lang. Assn. Am., S. Atlantic Modern Lang. Assn., Am. Assn. U. Profs., Nat. Council Tchrs. English, Fla. Hist. Soc., Newcomen Soc. N.A., Assn. Am. U. Presses, Am. Book Pubs. Council, Acad. Polit. Sci., Assn. for Latin Am. Studies, Phi Kappa Phi, Kappa Phi Sigma. Contbr. to World Book Ency., Collier's Ency., Appleton's New Century Cyclopedia of Names (cons. specialist), also to scholastic and lit. jours. Home: 23 SW 26th St Gainesville FL 32601 Office: Little Hall U Fla Gainesville FL 32601

HAINES, RALPH EDWARD, Jr., army officer; b. Ft. Mott, N.H., Aug. 21, 1913; s. Ralph Edward and Ethel Lyman (Smith) H.; B.S., U.S. Mil. Acad., 1935; grad. Armed Forces Staff Coll., 1948, Army War Coll., 1951, Nat. War Coll., 1958; LL.D. (hon.), Mary Hardin Baylor Coll., 1967; m. Sally Genevieve Swift, June 11, 1938; children—Palmer Swift, William Lyman. Commd. 2d lt. U.S. Army, 1935, advanced through grades to general, 1967; chief plans J-5, Office Joint Chiefs Staff, 1958-60; asst. div. comdr. 2d Armored Div., 1960-62; comdg. gen. lst Armored Div., 1962-63; dep. asst. chief staff force devel. Dept. Army, 1963-65; comdg. gen. III Corps, also Ft. Hood, Tex., 1965-67; vice chief of staff U.S. Army, 1967-68; comdr.-in-chief U.S. Army Pacific, 1968-70; comdg. gen. U.S. Continental Army Command, 1970—. Cons. Army War Coll., 1959; pres. Army bd. to review army officer schs., 1965-66. Vice pres. Heart O'Tex. council Boy Scouts Am., 1965-67, Aloha council, 1968-70. Decorated Legion of Merit with 2 oak leaf clusters, D.S.M. with oak leaf cluster, Bronze Star medal, Army Commendation medal; recipient Distinguished Eagle Scout award Boy Scouts Am., 1969. Mem. U.S. Armor Assn. (exec. council 1962-68), Assn. U.S. Army. Home: 33 Fenwick Rd Fort Monroe VA 23351 Office: Hdgrs US CONAZC Fort Monroe VA 23351

HAINES, RICHARD CARLETON, archaeol. architect; b. Tabernacle, N.J., Dec. 22, 1904; s. Carleton and Annie (Templeton) H.; B.Arch., Carnegie Inst. Tech., 1928; m. Irene Garwood, June 29, 1940; children-Alice Elizabeth, Richard Carleton. Draftsman in archtl. offices, 1928-30, 45-49; field architect Oriental Inst., U. Chgo., 1930-42, 49-; archaeol. excavations in Turkey, Syria, Iran, Israel, Iraq, 1930-40, 49-65; field dir. Nippur Expdn., 1956-64; mem. faculty U. Chgo., 1959—, asst. prof., 1963-71, emeritus, 1971—. Mem. Soc. Archtl. Historians; corr. mem. Deutsches Archäologisches Inst. Co-author: Soundings at Tell Fakhariyah, 1958; A Byzantine Church at Khirbat al- Karak, 1960; Nippur I, 1968. Home: MR 2 Box 155 Valparaiso, IN 46383. Office: Oriental Inst U Chgo Chicago IL 60637

HAINES, WALTER WELLS, educator; b. Stamford, Conn., Dec. 1, 1918; s. Thomas Kelly Peterson and Carrie Hooker (Williams) H.; B.A., U. Pa., 1940, M.A., 1941; M.A., Harvard, 1942, Ph.D. (Lehman nat. fellow 1941-43), 1943; m. Hazel Ellen Maxwell, Jan. 1, 1945; children—Jennifer Jean, Deborah Lee, Pamela Ann, Christopher Alan, Liseli Ellen, Timothy Maxwell. Instr. econs. Kenyon Coll., 1946-47; mem. faculty N.Y.U., 1947—, prof. econs., 1960—, chmn. dept. Univ. Coll., 1956-68; adminstr. Friends Hosp., Tiriki, Kenya, 1969-70; Fulbright prof. econs. U. Peshawar, Pakistan, 1962-63. Mem. A.A.A.S., Am. Econ. Assn., Am. Assn. U. Profs., Fellowship of Reconciliation. Soc. Internat. Devel., Phi Beta Kappa, Pi Gamma Mu. Mem. Soc. of Friends. Author: Money, Prices and Policy, 1961; also articles. Home: Skyview Acres Pomona NY 10970 Office: Univ Coll NYU Bronx NY 10453

HAINES, WESLEY NORTHRIDGE, coll. pres.; b. Worcester, Mass., Sept. 8, 1914; s. Lester Mascall and Elizabeth (Northridge) H.; A.B., Brown U.,1936; B.D., Colgate Rochester Div. Sch., 1940; Ph.D., Harvard, 1949; m. Catherine Mary Roggie, June 7, 1940; children—Susan Elizabeth (Mrs. John Richard Steidel, Jr.), Averill Catherine, Deborah Caroline, Karen Ina. Ordained to ministry Baptist Ch.; minister First Baptist Ch., Freeport, N.Y., 1944-47; prof. religion Keuka Coll., Keuka Park, N.Y., 1947-51, asst. to pres., 1951-57; dir. devel. Bucknell U., 1957-62, v.p. devel., 1962-64; pres. Franklin Coll. Ind., 1964—; lectr. Program Assos., Inc., Utica, N.Y., 1948—. Vice pres. N.Y. State Baptist Conv., 1956-57; Pa. fund chmn. A.R.C., 1964; mem. Scholarship Commn. Ind., 1965-69; mem. Law Enforcement Tng. Bd. Ind., 1967—. Bd. dirs. Mut. Hosp. Ins., Inc. (Blue Cross), 1971—. Recipient award for distinguished service to coll. and community Keuka Coll.; George Washington Honor award for pub. address Freedoms Found., Valley Forge, 1960; named Sagamore of Wabash, 1967; Outstanding Citizen award Franklin C. of C., 1970. Mem. Newcomen Soc., Phi Beta Kappa, Phi Kappa Delta, Tau Kappa Epsilon. Mason (32; asso. imperial chaplain Shrine of N. Am. 1970). Clubs: Rotary (past dist. gov.); Hillview Country (Franklin); Columbia (Indpls.) Home: 1120 E Adams Dr Franklin IN 46131

HAINES, WILLIAM ELDREDGE, mfg. co. exec.; b. Millville, N.J., Dec 22, 1905; s. Richard R. and Mabel (Hutton) H.; B.S., Rutgers U., 1931, M.Ed., 1932; m. Gladys J. Rice, June 28, 1930 (dec.); 1 dau., Susan Rice; m. 2d, Margaret W. Spencer, June 28, 1948. Tchr., Mt. Holly, N.J., 1929-37; supr. Wilmington (Del.) pub. schs., 1937-41; with WPB, 1941-45, N.A.M., 1945- 47, Hercules Powder Co., 1947-48, U.S. Dept. Commerce, 1952-57; with H. K. Porter Co., Inc., Pitts., 1957—, v.p., 1962—; cons. Crane Co. Pres. Washington Indsl. Round Table. Mem. Am. Ordnance Assn. (pres. Washington 1962, regional v.p. 1965, dir.). Clubs: Burning Tree, Internat. (Washington); Jupiter Hills (Fla.). Home: 4100 Cathedral Av Washington DC 20016 Office: 1001 Connecticut Av NW Washington DC 20036*

HAINES, WILLIAM WISTER, author; b. Des Moines, Sept., 1908; s. Diedrich Jansen and Ella Eustis (Wister) H.; B.S., U. Pa., 1931; m. Frances Tuckerman, Sept., 1934; children William Wister, Laura Tuckerman (Mrs. Murray Belman). Author: Slim, 1934; High Tension, 1938; Command Decision, 1947; The Honorable Rocky Slade, 1957; The Winter War, 1961; Target, 1964; The Image, 1968; also mag. stories, motion picture scripts, play, Command Decision. Commd. 1st lt. AC, AUS, 1942, relieved of active duty as lt. col., 1945. Address: PO Box 401 South Laguna, CA 92677.

HAINEY, RICHARD WILLIS, newspaper editor; b. McCook, Neb., June 1, 1922; s. Conrad Patrick and Esther (Skoog) H.; B. Journalism, Northwestern U., 1945, M. Journalism, 1945; m. Helene Starkey, June 16, 1945; 1 son, Mark F. Mem. staff Chgo. Tribune, 1947-61; exec. editor Chgo. Today, 1961—; lectr. Medill Sch. Journalism, 1947—; pres. City News Bur., Chgo.; v.p. Midwest Press Inst. Mem. Sigma Delta Chi. Home: 6768 Dowagiac Av Chicago IL 60646 Office: 445 N Michigan Av Chicago IL 60611

HAINFELD, FREDERICK, Jr., banker; b. Oyster Bay, N.Y., June 10, 1909; s. Frederick and Margaret (Taylor) H.; student Am. Inst. Banking, also Bankers Inst. Advanced Mgmt., 1952; m. Aletheia Garrison, May 3, 1942; children—Linda Carol, James Frederick. With Corn Exchange Bank & Trust Co., N.Y.C., 1925- 27, State Bank of Sea Cliff, N.Y., 1927-29; with Long Island Trust Co. (formerly Garden City Bank & Trust Co.), 1929-43, 45—, pres., 1954- 68, chief exec. officer, dir., chmn. bd., 1968—; with Southside Bank of Bayshore, L.I., N.Y., 1944-45; trustee Roosevelt Savs. Bank. Mem. com. on pub. library service N.Y. State commr. edn., 1956-57; treas. ann. appeal Salvation Army, Garden City, 1954-59; pres. Tax and Estate Planning Council L.I., 1949; mem., chmn. finance com. Nassau County council Boy Scouts Am., 1957-64, v.p., 1962, exec. bd., 1957—, chmn. trust fund, com., 1968—; treas. Health and Welfare Council Nassau County, 1957-59, now mem.; pres., dir. L.I. Fund Industry, Labor and Commerce for Hosps., Health and Welfare, 1959-66. Trustee Garden City Library, 1956-59; trustee Adelphi U., 1961—, treas., 1962- 65, chmn. finance com., 1964—, vice chmn. bd. 1968; chmn. bd. Adelphi Suffolk Coll., 1963-68. Mem. Garden City trustees, 1965; trustee United Fund L.I., 1965—. Mem. Garden City C. of C. (pres., dir. 1957-58), L.I. (chmn., dir. 1959-61), N.Y. State bankers assns. Mason, Rotarian. Clubs: Garden City Golf, Cherry Valley (Garden City); Lawrence Beach. Home: 20 Cedar Pl Garden City NY 11530 Office: 1401 Franklin Av Garden City NY 11530

HAINS, GASTON, clergyman; b. Drummondville, Que., Canada, Sept. 10, 1921; s. J.H. and Germaine (Gauthier) H.; B.A., U. Montreal, 1941; Lic. P.H, Rome, Italy, 1950; Dr. Sci., Social Politics, Lille, France, 1952. Ordained priest Roman Cath. Ch., 1946; bishop of Amos, Que., 1964—. Home: 450 Principale Amos Abitibi Quebec Canada

HAINSFURTHER, ROBERT M., glass co. exec.; b. Winchester, Ill., Dec. 18, 1908; s. Solomon and Victoria (Sachen) H.; B.S. in Ceramic Engring., U. Ill., 1930; m. Bess Rossan, Dec. 25, 1932; children—Richard Mark, Victoria. With Pitts. Plate Glass Co. (co. name changed to PPG Industries, Inc.), 1930—, gen. mgr. plate glass plants, 1959-60, v.p. prodn. glass div., 1960-62, v.p., asst. gen. mgr. glass div., 1962-66, v.p., gen. mgr. glass div., 1966—. dir., v.p. Inveca Pgh., Venezuela; dir., pres. Pennitalia S.P.A., Italy, S.A. des Glaces de Courcelles, Belgium; dir. Canadian Pgh. Industries, Duplate Can. Ltd. Vice pres. PPG Industries Fund, Mem. Am. Ceramic Soc., Pitts. C. of C., Soc. Automotive Engrs., Keramos (pres. 1930). Mason (Shriner). Home: Washington Plaza Apts 1420 Centre Av Pittsburgh PA 15219 Office: 1 Gateway Center Pittsburgh PA 15222

HAIRE, JOHN RUSSELL, mutual fund exec.; born Newport, R.I., Feb. 11, 1925; s. J. Russell and Pauline (Houghton) H.; grad. St. George's Sch., 1942; student Brown U. 1942-43; LL.B. cum laude, Harvard, 1950; m. Doris J. Buttry, Aug. 26, 1945; childrenElizabeth, Paul, Lynn. Admitted Mass. bar, 1950; asso. Nutter, McClennen & Fish, Boston, 1950-51; legal, exec. asst. to Hon. William H. Vanderbilt, 1951-53; spl. asst. to pres. N.Y. Stock Exchange, 1953-54, sec., 1955-56, v.p. charge relations govtl. agencies and nat. orgns., 1956-59; v.p., sec. Hugh W. Long & Co., Inc., Fundamental Investors, other investment cos., 1959-62; exec. v.p., sec. Anchor Corporation, Fundamental Investors, other investment companies, 1962-64, chmn., 1964—; pres., dir. Fundamental Investors, Inc., Anchor Income Fund, Inc., Anchor Growth Fund, Inc., Westminster Fund, Inc., 1964—. Past pres. Family and Children's Soc., Elizabeth, N.J., Childbirth Edn. Assn. N.J., Inc. Past trustee N.J. Symphony, Pingry Sch.; pres. Elizabeth Gen. Hosp., Internat. Childbirth Edn. Assn., Inc. Served in AUS, 1943-47, ETO, sgt. maj. 18th Mechanized Cav. Squadron 1945-47. Mem. Investment Bankers Assn. Am. (chmn. fed. taxation com. 1963-67), Investment Company Institute (chairman of board 1968). Clubs: Harvard (N.Y.C.); Harbor View (N.Y.); Baltusrol Golf; Metropolitan (Washington). Home: 251 Nottingham Way Hillside NJ 07205 Office: Westminster at Parker Elizabeth NJ 07207

HAIRE, THOMAS BRETT, ret. publisher, pub. cons.; b. Bklyn., Jan. 16, 1913; s. Andrew Joseph and Alice Margaret (O'Sullivan) H.; A.B., Cornell, 1934; m. Virginia Ann McCarty, Oct. 30, 1946; children—Thomas Brett, Virginia Ann, John Edward, Paul Joseph, Janet. Former pub. trade mags. Incentive, Luggage and Leather Goods, Handbags and Accessories, Apparel Mfr., Wire and Wire Products, Product News Internat., Nations, Medical Lab., Gift & Tableware Reporter, also 10 trade directories; with Haire Pub. Co., 1934-70, pres., 1952-70; past chmn. bd. Asso. Bus. Publs.; past dir. Audit Bur. Circulations. Served as maj. USAAF, 1942-45. Decorated Purple Heart, Air Medal with 4 oak leaf clusters, Bronze Star, Presdl. Citation. Mem. Air Force Assn., Friendly Sons St. Patrick, Knights of Malta, Advt. Club of N.Y. Clubs: University, Sailfish (Fla.); Sakonnet Golf, Sakonnet Yacht. Home: 216 Angler Av Palm Beach FL 33480

HAIRSTON, WILLIAM, playwright. Author: (off Broadway) Walk in Darkness, 1962; World of Carlos. Address: care Theatre Guild 27 W 53d St New York City NY 10019*

HAISE, FRED WALLACE, Jr., astronaut; b. Biloxi, Miss., Nov. 14, 1933; s. Fred Wallace and Lucille (Blacksher) H.; A.A., Perkinston Jr. Coll., 1952; B.S. in Aero Engring., U. Okla., 1959; D.Sc. (hon.), Western Mich. U.; m. Mary Griffin Grant, June 4, 1954; children—Mary Margaret, Frederick Thomas, Stephen William, Thomas Jesse. Naval aviation cadet USN, 1952-54; fighter pilot USMC, 1954-56, Air N.G., Okla., Ohio, 1957-63; capt. USAF, 1961-62; research pilot NASA Lewis Research Center, Cleve., 1959-63, NASA Flight Research Center, Edwards AFB, Cal., 1963-66; astronaut NASA Manned Spacecraft Center, Houston, 1966—. Active Indian Guides YMCA, Lancaster, Cal., 1965—. Recipient AB Honts trophy USAF Aerospace Research Pilot Sch., Edwards AFB, 1964; Presdl. Medal Freedom; Miss. Distinguished Civilian Service Medal; Jeff Davis award; Pine Burr award; City Houston Medal Valour. Mem. Soc. Exptl. Test Pilots, Phi Theta Kappa, Tau Beta Pi, Sigma Gamma Tau. NASA Manned Spacecraft Center Houston TX 77058

HAISLIP, WADE HAMPTON, ret. army officer; b. Woodstock, Va., July 9, 1889; s. Reuben Drake and Etta (Heller) H.; B.S., U.S. Mil. Acad., 1912; student Infantry Sch., 1923- 24, Command and General Staff Sch., 1924-25, Ecole Supérieure de Guerre, 1925-27, Army War Coll., 1931-32; m. Alice Jennings Shepherd, July 14, 1932. Commd. lt., June 12, 1912; promoted through grades to general, 1949; served in Vera Cruz, Mexico, 1914; with A.E.F. and Am. Forces in Germany, 1917-21, successively with Gen. Staff, 5th Corps, Div. Machine Gun Officer, 3d Div., Gen. Staff, Am. Forces in Germany; participated in defensive operations in the Vosges, St. Mihiel and Meuse-Argonne operations; instr. U.S. Mil Acad., 1921-23; asst. exec. Office of Asst. Sec. of War, 1928-31; instr. Command and Gen. Staff Sch., 1932-36; with 29th Inf., 1936-38; in Budget and Legislative Planning Branch, War Dept. Gen. Staff, 1938-41, asst. chief of staff for personnel, 1941; commanded 85th Inf. Div. Apr. 1942-Feb. 20, 1943; commanded XV Corps throughout campaigns of Normandy, Northern France, Ardennes, Rhineland, Central Europe; comd. 7th Army, June-Aug., 1945. Pres., Sec. of War's Personnel Bd., Sept. 1945-April 1946; sr. mem. Chief of Staff's adv. group, 1946- 48; dep. chief of staff for adminstrn., 1948-49, vice chief of staff 1949-51; retired from active service, 1951; gov. U.S. Soldiers Home, 1951-66. Awarded Victory medal with 3 bars, Mexican Service medal, D.S.M. with 3 Oak Leaf Clusters, Legion of Merit, Bronze Star with oak leaf cluster, Legion of Honor (grand officer), Croix de Guerre with Palm, other fgn. medals. Clubs: Army and Navy (Washington); Army and Navy Country (Va.). Home: 2101 Connecticut Av NW Washington, DC 20008.

HAIT, JAMES MERRITT, engr.; b. Brooklyn, Apr. 19, 1906; s. James Merritt and Belle (Silvy) H.; M.E., Rensselaer Polytech. Inst., 1928, D. Eng. (hon.), 1962; m. Ruth Hazel Jesmier, May 9, 1931; children—Merritt, Paul. Chief engr. Peerless Pump div. FMC Corp., Los Angeles, 1928-42; mgr. procurement and engring. div. FMC Corp., Los Angeles, 1942-46, v.p., San Jose, Cal., 1946-60, mgr. Ordnance div., 1951-60, dir., 1952—, exec. v.p., 1956-60, pres., 1960-66, chmn. bd., 1966-71; dir. Wells Fargo Bank, Pacific Gas & Electric, Petro-Tex Chem. Corp., Ketchikan Pulp Co., Interpace (Internat. Pipe and Ceramics), Internat. Machinery Corp., Ga.-Pacific Corp., Varian Assos., Arthur D. Little, Inc. Trustee Bay Area Council San Francisco; adv. council Stanford Grad. Sch. Bus.; adv. bd. U. Santa Clara Sch. Bus. Adminstrn.; mem. pres.'s council Cal. Inst. Tech., mgmt. council Bay Area Employment Opportunity, Nat. Indsl. Conf. Bd. Mem. Nat. Acad. Engring., Am. Soc. M.E. Clubs: Union League (N.Y.C.); Sainte Claire and San Jose Country (Cal.); Pacific-Union (San Francisco). Home: 11199 Canon Vista Dr San Jose CA 95127 Office: 1105 Coleman San Jose CA 95106

HAITINK, BERNARD, condr.; b. Amsterdam, Netherlands, 1929. Condr., Netherlands Radio Philharmonic Orch., 1955-61; guest condr. Concertgebouw Orch., Amsterdam, 1956-61, became joint condr., 1961, now sole musical dir.; guest condr. Halle Orch., London (Eng.) Philharmonic Orch., Berlin (Germany) Philharmonic Orch., 1963-64; prin. condr., artistic adviser London Philharmonic Orch., 1967—. Recipient Medal of Honor, Bruckner Soc., 1970. Hon. mem. Internat. Gustav Mahler Soc. Address: care London Philharmonic Orch 53 Welbeck St London W1 England*

HAIZLIP, HENRY HARDIN, Jr., banker; b. Pine Bluff, Ark., Dec. 18, 1913; s. Henry Hardin and Rebecca (Porter) H.; grad. Woodberry Forest Sch., 1932; student Tulane U., 1932- 33; m. Emily Williamson, Feb. 15, 1947; children-Henry Hardin III, Wilson, Jean Hunter, Selden. With W.N. Ballou Cotton Co., Memphis, 1933- 36; with First Nat. Bank Memphis, 1936—, exec. v.p., 1968-70, chmn. exec. com., 1970—; pres. First Memphis Realty Trust, 1970—; dir. MediCenters Am., Inc., Ark. Valley Industries, Inc.; instr. mortgage financing La. State U., Ohio State U. Pres. Memphis Cotton Carnival Assn., 1966, bd. dirs., 1967—; vice chmn. Shelby United Good Neighbors, 1967-68; mem. Chickasaw council Boy Scouts Am. Bd. dirs. Memphis and Shelby County unit Am. Cancer Soc., 1967-68. Served to capt. AUS, 1941- 46. Mem. Am. Bankers Assn., Soc. Residential Appraisers, Kappa Alpha. Episcopalian. Clubs: Memphis Country, University (Memphis); Menasha Hunting and Fishing (Turrell, Ark.). Home: 965 Audubon Dr Memphis TN 38117 Office: 165 Madison Av Memphis TN 38103

HAKEEM, MICHAEL, educator, sociologist; b. Fall River, Mass., Sept. 5, 1916; s. Joseph and Sophia (Daghir) H.; B.S., Ohio State U., 1942, M.A., 1945, Ph.D., 1950; m. Helen Louise Cook, June 8, 1949. Sociologist, Ill. Div. Criminology, 1943-46; instr. State U. Ia., 1946-47; instr., then asst. prof. Ohio State U., 1948-52; mem. faculty U. Wis., 1952-, prof. sociology, 1962-. Fellow Am. Sociol. Assn.; mem. Soc. Study Social Problems (exec. com. 1961-64), Nat. Conf. Delinquency and Crime. Contbr. profl. jours. Home: 517 Caldy Pl Madison, WI 53711.

HAKIM, ALBERT BERNARD, coll. dean; b. Arlington, N.J., Nov. 11, 1919; s. Robert and Susan (Saaty) H.; B.A., B.S., Seton Hall U., 1942; M.A., Fordham U., 1950; Ph.D., Ottawa U., 1954. Ordained priest Roman Cath. Ch., 1946; faculty Seton Hall Prep., South Orange, N.J., 1946-51; faculty dept. philosophy Seton Hall U., 1951-61, chmn., 1959-61, dean Coll. Arts and Scis., 1961-. Contbr. articles, book revs., profl. jours. Home: Seton Hall U South Orange NJ 07079*

HAKIM, GEORGE, univ. adminstr.; b. Tripoli, Lebanon, Apr. 19, 1913; s. John and Victoria (Antakly) H.; B.A., Am. Univ., Beirut, Lebanon, 1932, A.M., 1934; licencie en droit, Universite St. Joseph, Beirut, 1937; m. Laura Belle Zarbock, Oct. 11, 1951; children—John Robert, Nada. Inst. econs. Am. U., 1934-43, adj. prof., 1943-46; counselor legation Lebanon, Washington, 1946-52; mem. Lebanese govt. adv. body Superior Econ. Council, 1945-46; alternate del. of Lebanon to Econ. and Social Council UN, 1946-47, chmn. com. on proposed econ. commn. for Middle East, 1948; chief del. from Lebanon, Internat. Health Conf., 1946, preparatory com. UN Conf. on Trade and Employment, London, 1946, Geneva, 1947, Conf. on Trade and Employment, Havana, 1947-48; minister finance, nat. economy and agr. Lebanon, 1952-53, minister fgn. affairs, 1953, 65-66, 66-68; E.E., M.P. of Lebanon to Fed. Republic of Germany, Bonn, 1955-58, ambassador, 1958-59; ambassador to UN, 1959-65, 66; v.p. Am. U. of Beirut, 1968—. Decorated grand officer Order of Cedars of Lebanon; 1st class Order of Bafidain of Iraq, Order of Ismail of Egypt; chevalier grand cross Order of Merit (Republic of Italy). Contbr. articles on econs. to Econ. Orgn. of Syria and Palestine (2 vols. edited by S. B. Himadeh), 1936, 38. Address: Am Univ PO Box 236 Beirut Lebanon

HAKIMOGLU, AYHAN, electronics co. exec.; b. Erbaa, Turkey, Aug. 19, 1927; s. Mekki and Mediha Hakimoglu; B.S., Robert Coll., Istanbul, 1949; M.S., U. Cin., 1950; m. Meral Cumaoglu, Nov. 21, 1952; children—Betty Z., Rose I., Deborah A. Came to U.S., 1955, naturalized, 1964. Founder, chmn., pres. Dynaplex Corp., Princeton, N.J., 1962-67; gen. mgr. Teledyne Telemetry Co., Los Angeles, 1966-67; founder, chmn., pres. Aydin Corp., Los Angeles, 1967—. Served as lt. Turkish Army, 1951-52. Home: 808 Alpine Dr Beverly Hills CA 90210 Office: 1900 Av of Stars Los Angeles CA 90067

HALABY, NAJEEB E. lawyer, airline exec.; b. Dallas, Nov. 19, 1915; s. Najeeb Elias and Laura (Wilkins) H.; A.B., Stanford, 1937; student U. Mich. Law Sch., 1937-38; LL.B., Yale, 1940; LL.D., Allegheny Coll., 1967, Loyola U., Los Angeles, 1968; m. Doirs Carlquist, Feb. 9, 1946; children—Lisa, Christian, Alexa. Admitted to Cal. bar, 1940, D.C. bar, 1948; practiced in Los Angeles with O'Melveny & Myers, 1940-42; prodn. test pilot Lockheed Aircraft Corp., Burbank, Cal., 1942-43; fgn. affairs adviser to sec. def., 1948-53; dep. asst. sec. def., 1952-54, asso., 1952-54, L. S. Rockefeller and Bros., 1953-56; v.p. Servomechanisms, Inc., 1956-58, exec. v.p., dir., 1959; pres. Am. Tech. Corp.; trustee Aerospace Corp.; v.p. Janss Corp.; faculty lectr. U. Cal. at Los Angeles, also Sch. Bus. Adminstrn., dir. def. studies program, chmn., 1960 disarmament conf.; pvt. law practice, N.Y.C., 1960—; dir. Bank of Am., Chrysler Corp., Viacom, Inc.; Whirlpool; adminstr. FAA, 1961-65; sr. v.p., exec. com., dir. Pan

Am. World Airways, N.Y.C., 1965-68, pres., 1968—, chief exec. officer, 1969—, chmn. bd., 1970—; trustee Aerospace Corp. Vice chmn. White House Aviation Facilities Study Group, 1955-56; mem. N.Y. Urban Coalition, Council Fgn. Relations. Bd. dirs. Planned Parenthood-World Population, Nat. Civil Service League. Trustee The Leelanau Schs., Glen Arbor, Mich., Aspen Inst. Humanistic Studies, Stanford U. Served as naval aviator USN, World War II; asst. chief fighter sect. Naval Air Test Center, Patuxent River, Md. Recipient Arthur Fleming award; Godfrey L. Cabot award; Monsanto Air Safety award. Mem. Fgn. Policy Assn., Am. Arbitration Assn., Am. Inst. Aeros. and Astronautics, Soc. Exptl. Test Pilots, Corbey Ct., Beta Theta Pi, Phi Delta Phi. Clubs: Metropolitan, Chevy Chase, Aviation (Washington); Bohemian, California, Town Hall (Los Angeles); Quiet Birdman; Chevy Chase, Metropolitan (Washington); River Sky (N.Y.C.); Burning Tree (Md.) Home: 1120 Fifth Av New York City NY 10028 Office: Pan Am Bldg New York City NY 10017*

HALAS, GEORGE STANLEY, former profl. football coach; b. Chgo., Feb. 2, 1895; s. Frank and Barbara (Poludna) H.; B.S., U. Ill., 1918; LL.D., St. Joseph's Coll., Ind., 1958; m. Minnie S. Bushing, Feb. 18, 1922; children—Virginia Marion (Mrs. Edward W. McCaskey), George Stanley. With bridge dept. Burlington R.R., 1919-20; played profl. baseball with N.Y. Yankees and St. Paul Club, 1919, profl. football with Chgo., Bears, 1920- 29, coach, 1920-29, 33-42, 46-55, 58-67; pres. Chgo. Bears Football Club, 1920-64, chmn., 1964-68; pres. Halas & Keefe, Inc., Chgo., 1941—. Bd. dirs., Met. Fair Expn. Authority, Crime Detection Inst. Trustee St. Joseph's Coll.; citizens com. U. Ill.; citizens bd. Loyola U. Served as ensign USN, 1918- 19; capt. USNR, 1942-46. Recipient Navy distinguished pub. service award; named Coach of Year, A. P., U.P., Sporting News, 1963; Outstanding Profl. Coach of Year, Washington Touchdown Club, 1963; Acad. Sports Editors award, 1963; J. F. Kennedy Meml. trophy Chgo. Mayor and City Council, 1963; Chicagoan of Year, Chgo. Press Club, Jr. Assn. Commerce and Industry; Alumni Achievement award U. Ill., 1965; Horatio Alger, Jr. award, 1968. Mem. Nat. Profl. Football Hall of Fame (charter mem.), Mil. Order World Wars, Mawan-da, Sachem, Navy League of U.S. (nat. v.p., dir.), Tau Kappa Epsilon, Sigma Tau, Theta Nu Epsilon. Roman Catholic. K.C. Clubs: Athletic, Executives, Mid-America; Athletic (Chgo.); Tavern, Bob O'Link Golf. Contbr. mags. Home: 5555 Sheridan Rd Chicago IL 60640 Office: 173 W Madison St Chicago IL 60602*

HALAS, GEORGE STANLEY, Jr., profl. football exec.; b. Chgo., Sept. 4, 1925; s. George Stanley and Minnie (Bushing) H.; B.S. in Commerce, Loyola U. Chgo., 1950; m. Therese Leona Martin, Apr. 20, 1963; children—Christine, Stephen. Gen. mgr. May- Halas, mail order house, Chgo., 1955-60; treas. Chgo. Bears Football Club, 1953-55, gen. mgr., 1960-63, pres., gen. mgr., 1963—. Served with USNR, 1944- 46. Fellow St. Joseph's Coll., Rensselaer, Ind., 1964—. Roman Cath. Clubs: Mid-America, Ridgemoor Country (Chgo.). Home: 3240 N Lake Shore Dr Chicago IL 60657 Office: Chicago Bears 173 W Madison St Chicago IL 60603

HALASI-KUN, TIBOR, educator, Orientalist; b. Zagreb, Austria-Hungary, Jan. 19, 1914; s. Tibor and Priscilla (Tholt) Halasi-Kun; Ph.D., U. Budapest, 1936; m. Eva Metzger, Jan. 5, 1942; children—Adam, Tibor. Came to U.S., 1952, naturalized, 1961. Research asso. Turkic studies, also Hungarian protohistory U. Budapest, 1936, adj. prof., 1937-42; asso. prof. Hungarian studies Ankara (Turkey) U., 1943-51; prof. Turkic studies Columbia, 1952-66, chmn. dept. Middle East langs. and cultures, 1959-71. Vis. prof. Princeton, 1956; pres. Am. Research Inst. in Turkey, 1963—. Author: Turkish Confession of Gennadios, 1936; Historical Texts of Kazan Turkie, 1949; The Caucasus; An Ethno-Historical Survey, 1962. Editorial bd. Publs. in Near and Middle East Studies, 1960—. Home: 29 Claremont Av New York City NY 10027*

HALASZ, LASZLO, musical director, condr.; b. Debrecen, Hungary, June 6, 1905; s. Ferdinand and Regine (Eichhorn) H.; student and graduate of piano and conducting, Royal Hungarian Conservatory of Music, Budapest, 1924-29. Came to U.S., 1936, became naturalized citizen, June 5, 1943; m. Suzette F. Forgues; children—Georges, Suzanne. Piano soloist with Royal Hungarian Philharmonic Soc., 1928 gave piano concerts and conducted orchestras in Europe, 1928-36; musical and artistic dir. St. Louis Grand Opera Assn., 1937-42; guest condr. Les Concerts Symphoniques, Montreal, Can., Aug. 1940, N.B.C. Symphony, Aug. 1941; musical and artistic dir. Havana Operatic Festivals, Sept. 1940 and 1941; debut as condr. Chgo. Opera in "Falstaff" in English, Nov. 1941, reëngaged for season 1942; musical dir. and condr. Am. Symphony Orch., performing under sponsorship of U.S.O., exclusively for the armed forces at camps, forts and bases, Dec. 1942- July 1943; guest condr. N.Y. Philharmonic Orch., Lewisohn Stadium, 1946, Montreal Festivals, 1946; guest condr. N.B.C. Symphony and Les Concerts Symphoniques, Montreal, June 1952; artistic and music dir. N.Y.C. Opera, 1943-52, also Chgo. Opera Co., 1949-52; recordings for MGM and Remington records; music dir. Remington Records, Inc., 1953-55; music dir. German wing Gran Teatro del Liceo, Barcelona, 1955-59; condr. staff Empire State Festivals, Summer 1957; founder artistic and music dir. Empire State Music Festival Inc., Peabody Art Theatre Balt., Music Festival of L.I., Inc., 1957-65; guest condr. Boston Opera, Royal Philharmonic Orch., London, 1962-63; condr. Eastman Philharmonic Orch. of Rochester, also head conducting dept. Eastman Sch. Music, U. Rochester, 1965-67; dir. music, prof. N.Y. State U. Coll. at Old Westbury, 1968—; guest condr. Budapest State Opera, 1964-66, Teatro Liceo, Barcelona, 1967, 68, 70, 71, Nat. Symphony of Caracas, Venezuela and Lima, Peru, 1969-70; condr. Kodaly Meml. Concerts, Hungary, 1971. Recipient Page One award Newspaper Guild N.Y., 1968; Merit award Nat. Assn. Am. Composers and Conductors. Mem. Central Opera Service. Home: 3 Leeds Dr Port Washington NY 11050 ☆

HALBACH, EDWARD CHRISTIAN, Jr., educator; b. Clinton, Ia., Nov. 11, 1931; s. Edward Christian and Lewella (Sullivan) H. ; B. A., U. Ia., 1953, J.D., 1958; LL.M., Harvard, 1959; m. Janet Elizabeth Bridges, July 25, 1953; childrenKristin Lynn, Edward Christian III, Kathleen Ann, Thomas Elliot, Elaine Diane. Lectr., Coll. Commerce, Ia. U., 1953-54, 56-57, Coll. Law, 1959; asso. prof. Sch. Law, U. Cal. at Berkeley, 1959-62; vis. prof. Harvard Law Sch., 1962-63, U. Chgo. Law Sch., 1964; prof. U. Cal. at Berkeley, 1963—, dean Sch. Law, 1966—; bd. dirs. Cal. Indian Legal Services, 1968-. Served from 2d to 1st lt., USAF, 1954-56. Mem. Am. Bar Assn. (vice chmn. various coms.; chmn. estate and tax planning com. 1967-69, chmn. com. on scope and correlations 1970—; mem. council, sect. real property probate and trust law, 1967—; chmn. com. on coms., sect. on individual rights and responsibilities 1967—), Ia. Bar Assn., American Law Institute, Beta Theta Pi. Democrat. Roman Catholic. Author: (with Eugene F. Scoles) Materials on Decedents' Estates and Trusts, 1965; California Will Drafting, 1965; Reporter, Uniform Probate Code, 1969; also articles in legal publs. Home: 679 San Luis Rd Berkeley, CA 94707

HALBERSTAM, DAVID, author; b. N.Y.C., Apr. 10, 1934; s. Charles A. and Blanche (Levy) H.; A.B. Harvard, 1955; m. Elzbieta Tchizevska, June 13, 1965. Reporter, West Point (Miss.) Daily Times Leader, 1955-56, Nashville Tennessean, 1956-60; mem. staff N.Y. Times, 1960-67, corr., Vietnam, 1962-63, N.Y.C., 1964-65, Warsaw, Poland, 1965-66, expelled, 1966, assigned N.Y.C., 1966-67; contbg. editor Harper's mag., 1967-71. Recipient Pulitzer prize internat. reporting, 1964, George Polk Meml. award, 1964; Louis Lyons award, 1964; Page One award, 1962. Club: Pink Elephant (Warsaw). Author: The Noblest Roman, 1961; The Making of a Quagmire, 1965; One Very Hot Day, 1968; The Unfinished Odyssey of Robert Kennedy, 1969; Ho (Ho Chi Minh), 1971. Home: 130 E 61st St New York City NY 10021

HALBERT, SHERRILL, judge; b. Terra Bella, Cal., Oct. 17, 1901; s. Edward Duffield and Ellen (Rhodes) H.; A.B., U. Cal. at Berkeley, 1924, J.D., 1927; LL.D., McGeorge Coll. Law, 1962; m. Verna Irene Dyer, June 7, 1927; children—Shirley Ellen (Mrs. Herbert M. Hanson, Jr.), Douglas James. Admitted to Cal. bar, 1927; practice of law, Porterville, 1927-41, San Francisco, 1942-44, Modesto, 1944-49; dist. atty. Stanislau County, 1949; judge Superior Ct. of Cal., 1949-54; U.S. dist. judge Eastern Dist. Cal., 1954—. Chmn. bd. advisers McGeorge Sch. Law, Sacramento; regent U. Pacific. Mem. Am. Camellia Soc. (pres. 1971—), Native Sons of Golden West, Nat. Pony Express Centennial Assn. (treas.), Selden Soc., Cal. Hist. Soc., Alpha Chi Rho, Phi Delta Phi. Clubs: Rotary, Ambassador's (Sacramento); Book of California, Commonwealth (San Francisco); Lions (hon.). Contbg. author: Lincoln for the Ages, 1960; Lincoln: A Contemporary Portrait, 1962. Home: 4120 Los Coches Way Sacramento CA 95825 Office: US Courthouse 650 Capital Mall Sacramento CA 95814

HALBOUTY, MICHEL THOMAS geologist, petroleum engr., ind. producer and petroleum operator; b. Beaumont, Tex., June 21, 1909; s. Tom Christian and Sodia (Monnelly) H.; B.S., Tex. A. and M. U., 1930, M.S., 1931, Profl. Degree in Geol. Engring., 1956; D. Eng. (hon.), Mont. Coll. Mineral Sci. and Tech., 1966; m. Fay Renfro, June 22, 1945; 1 dau., Linda Fay. Geologist, petroleum engr. Yount-Lee Oil Co., Beaumont, 1931-33, chief geologist, petroleum engr., 1933-35; v.p., gen. mgr., chief geologist and petroleum engr. Glenn H. McCarthy, Inc., Houston, 1935-37; owner firm of cons. geologists and petroleum engrs. in Houston, 1937—; discoverer numerous oil and gas fields, La. and Tex. Served as lt. col. AUS, 1942-45. Recipient Tex. Mid-Continent Oil & Gas Assn. distinguished service award for an independent, 1965; named engr. of year Tex. Soc. Profl. Engrs. and Engrs. Council, 1968; Distinguished Alumni award Tex. A. and M.U., 1968. Mem. Am. Assn. Petroleum Geologists (hon. mem., pres. 1966-67), Am. Soc. Oceanography, Internat. Assn. of Sedimentology, Inst. Petroleum, London, Am. Petroleum Inst., Am. Inst. Mining and Metall. Engrs., Soc. Paleontologists and Mineralogists, Soc. Econ. Geologists, Mineral. Soc. Am., Geol. Soc. Am., Soc. Exploration Geophysicists, Houston Geol. Soc. (hon.), N.Y. Acad. Scis., Tex. Acad. Scis., A.A.A.S., Am. Inst. Profl. Geologists, Soc. Profl. Engrs., Am. Geol. Inst., Tex. Soc. Profl. Engrs. Episcopalian. Clubs: Ramada, Houston, Petroleum, River Oaks Country (Houston); Dallas Petroleum; New Orleans Petroleum; Cosmos (Washington). Author several books, numerous papers on geology and petroleum engring. Home: 3630 Willowick Rd Houston TX 77019 Office: Halbouty Bldg 5111 Westheimer Rd Houston TX 77027

HALCROW, HAROLD GRAHAM, educator; b. Bowesmont, N.D., Oct. 11, 1911; s. John and Winifred (McIntosh) H.; B.S.A., N.D. State Univ., 1937; M.S. in Agrl. Econs., Mont. State Coll., 1938; Ph.D. in Econs. (Farm Found. fellow 1941- 42), U. Chgo., 1948; m. Eleanor Virginia Fearn, June 14, 1941; children— Meribel, Stephen, Beth, Ronald, Gayle. Instr., then asst. prof. Mont. State Coll., 1938-41, asst. prof., then prof., 1946-49; prof. agrl. economics U. Conn., 1947-57; profl. agrl. economics U. Ill., 1957—, head dept., 1957-70; vis. prof. agrl. econs. Stanford, 1971, U. Cal. at Berkeley, 1971; cons. U.S. Bur. Census, 1956—. Dir. Nat. Bur. Econ. Research, 1956—. Served to lt. USNR, 1943-46. Mem. Phi Kappa Phi, Alpha Zeta, Alpha Phi Sigma, Alpha Gamma Rho. Author: Agricultural Policy of the United States, 1953; Readings in Agricultural Economics, 1955; (with R. J. Saulnier, Neil H. Jacoby) Federal Programs of Lending and Loan Insurance, 1957; also articles. Editor Jour. Farm Economics, 1955-57. Home: 1011 Mayfair Rd Campaign IL 61820

HALDEMAN, HARRY R., (Bob), govt. ofcl.; b. Los Angeles, Oct. 27, 1926; s. Harry F. and Katherine (Robbins) H.; student U. Redlands, 1944-45, U. So. Cal., 1945-46; B.S. in Bus. Adminstrn. U. Cal. at Los Angeles, 1948; m. Jo Horton, Feb. 19, 1949; children-Susan Ward, Harry Horton, Peter Robbins, Ann Kurtz. Account exec. J. Walter Thompson Co., Los Angeles and N.Y.C., 1949-59, v.p., mgr. Los Angeles office, 1960-68; asst. to Pres. U.S., 1969—; dir. Haldeman, Inc., Los Angeles. Chief staff Nixon presdl. campaign, 1968. Bd. regents U. Cal., 1965-67, 68-69; trustee Cal. Inst. Arts, 1966-68, chmn. bd., 1968; chmn. bd. trustees Nixon Found., 1969—; mem. Commn. White House Fellows, 1969—; mem. exec. com., trustee Kennedy Center for Performing Arts, 1970—. Served with USNR, 1944-46. Mem. Beta Theta Pi, Pi Delta Epsilon. Office: The White House Washington DC 20500

HALDEMAN, JACK CARROLL, hosp. orgn. exec.; Downey, Ida., May 18, 1912; s. William O. and Bertie (Fields) H.; A.B., Phillips U., Okla., 1934; B.S., U. Okla., 1935, M.D., 1937; M.P.H., U. Mich., 1943; m. Lorena Spivey, Sept. 15, 1933; children—Jack Carroll, Joe William. Chief epidemiology Alaska Dept. Health, 1938-39; med. dir. Wasco County (Ore.) Health Dept., 1939-41; commd. USPHS, 1941; med. dir. county health dept., Hopkinsville, Ky., 1941-42; gen. med. cons., P.R., 1943-44, New Orleans, 1944-46; exec. officer div. hosp. facilities, Washington, 1946-48; med. officer charge, also founder Arctic Health Research Center, Anchorage, Alaska, 1948-51; chief div. state grants, Washington, 1951-52, asst. chief bur. state services, 1952-54, chief div. gen. health services, 1954-57, asst. chief div. hosp. and med. facilities, 1957-58, chief, 1958-63, asst. surgeon gen., 1958-63; pres. Health and Hospital Planning Council So. N.Y., 1963—. Diplomate Nat. Bd. Med. Examiners. Fellow Am. Pub. Health Assn., N.Y. Acad. Medicine; mem. N.Y. Acad. Scis., Am. Assn. Hosp. Planning, Am. Hosp. Assn., Internat. Hosp. Fedn., N.Y. Acad. Preventive Medicine, Pub. Health Assn. N.Y.C., Am. Coll. Preventive Med., Am. Assn. Pub. Health Physicians, Phi Kappa Phi, Delta Omega. Home: 2 Lake Shore Close North Tarrytown NY 10591 Office: 3 E 54th St New York City NY 10022

HALDEN, CHARLES WILLIAM, stock broker; b. Paterson, N.J., Feb. 6, 1900; s. Charles and Marie (Lorenz) H.; stud. pub. schs.; m. Alice Allen, Oct. 13, 1923; 1 son, Carl Allen. Began brokerage career, 1919, mem. N.Y. Curb Exchange, 1921—, specialist Exchange floor, 1922-47; partner Borg Bros. & Co., 1922-25; sr. partner H. L. Buchanan & Co. 1947-67; sr. partner Halden & Co., N.Y.C., 1955—. Gov., chmn. finance com. Am. Stock Exchange, 1950- 56, vice chmn. exchange, 1953-54, 55-56, trustee gratuity fund, 1969—, bd. dirs. realty commn., 1969—. Mason. Home: 77 Gilbert Rd Ho-Ho-Kus NJ 07423 Office: 74 Trinity Pl New York City NY 10006

HALDENSTEIN, JENNIE WHITEHILL, (Mrs. Herbert W. Hadenstein), assn. exec.; b. Henderson, Ky., Aug. 4, 1907; d. Leon and Celest (Levi) Levy; B.A., Goucher Coll., 1928; m. Clarence K. Whitehill, June 19, 1928; childrenJane, Carol, Richard; m. 2d, Herbert W. Haldenstein. Dir., Whitehill Agy., Inc., N.Y.C., 1935—. Pres. Westchester (N.Y.) Nursery Sch. Council, 1938-43; chmn. child care com. Westchester County War Council, 1943-46; pres. Stuyvesant Neighborhood House, N.Y.C., 1946-49; bd. dirs. Scarsdale Community Service, 1944-45; pres. Child Study Assn. Am., 1955—, chmn. exec. com., 1949-52, chmn. bd., 1952-55, 69—, pres. 1955-69. Mem. adv. com. Fordham Sch. Social Work, 1969-. Trustee Fedn. Jewish Philanthropies, N.Y.C., 1946-49, 60-, chmn. womans div., 1965-68. Home: 21 Split Tree Rd Scarsdale NY 10583 Office: 9 E 89th St New York City NY 10028*

HALDERMAN, JOHN WILLIAM lawyer; born Astoria, Ore., Dec. 5, 1907; s. Charles Walker and Bertha Emily (Hobson) H.; B.S., Univ. of Ore., 1933; LL.B., 1931; graduate study, Princeton University, 1936-37; Natl. War Coll., class of 1951; m. Elenor B. Lonergan, Feb. 4, 1938; 1 s., Charles Reed. Admitted to Ore, bar, 1931 and practiced in Ore., 1931-36; asst. to legal adviser, Dept. of State, 1937-42. International Orgn. Affairs, 1942-50; National War Coll., 1950-51; served in Am. legations at Bonn, Berlin, Casablanca, Colombo, 1951-59; with Bur. Internat. Orgn. Affairs, Dept. State, 1959-60; with Rule of Law Research Center, Sch. of Law, Duke University, Durham, N.C., 1960-. Served in U.S. Army, 1943-45. Mem. secretariat. U.N. Com. of Jurists, Washington, 1945; sec. com. on Internat. Ct. Justice, U.N. Conf. on Internat. Orgn., San Francisco, 1945. Advisor U.S. delegation, U.N. Prep. Commn., London, 1945; 1st session U.N. Gen. Assemly, London, 1946; 9th Internat. Conf. of Am. States, Bogota, 1948; U.N. Palestine Conciliation Commn., 1949. Mem. Phi Beta Kappa, Phi Delta Phi. Author: The United Nations and the Rule of Law, Contbr. legal periodicals. Home: 2216 Elmwood Av Durham NC 27707

HALE, CHARLES RUSSELL, lawyer; b. Talpa, Tex., Oct. 17, 1916; s. Charles L. and Exa (Evans) H.; A.B., Stanford, 1939; J.D., Fordham U., 1950; m. Clementine L. Moore, Jan. 5, 1946; children-Robert R., Norman B. Supr., United Geophys. Co., Pasadena, Cal., 1940-46; admitted to N.Y. bar, 1951. Cal. bar, 1953; mem. patent staff Bell Telephone Labs., N.Y.C., 1947-48, Sperry Gyroscope Co., Great Neck, N.Y., 1948-51; practiced in Pasadena, 1951- 54; mem. firm Christie, Parker & Hale, Pasadena, 1954—. Mem. Am., Los Angeles, Pasadena (v.p. 1960-61) bar assns., Am. Patent Law Assn., I.E.E.E. Clubs: University, Annandale Golf (Pasadena), Rancho Santa Fe (Cal.) Golf. Home: 60 N Golden West Av Arcadia CA 91006 also Avenida de Acaeias Rancho Santa Fe CA 92067Office: 201 S Lake Av Pasadena CA 91101

HALE, CLARENCE BENJAMIN, Sr., educator; b. Lincoln, Vt., Dec. 25, 1905; s. Morton Wilbur and Mable (Purinton) H.; B.A., Wheaton (Ill.) Coll., 1928; M.A., U. Ill., 1929, Ph.D, 1942; m. Florence Suzanne Vouga, Aug. 30, 1932; childrenEverett Austin, Clarence Benjamin. Mem. faculty Wheaton Coll., 1929-, prof. Greek, 1946-, chmn. dept. fgn. langs., 1946-69. Mem. Am. Philol. Assn. (life). Author: Let's Study Greek, 1959; Let's Read Greek, 1968. Home: 515 Scott St Wheaton, IL 60187.

HALE, EZRA ANDREWS, ret. trust co. exec., former publisher; b. Rochester, N.Y., Apr. 6, 1895; s. William Barton and Clara Louise (Andrews) H.; A.B., U. Rochester, 1916; m. Josephine Booth, Oct. 6, 1919; children—William Barton II, Anne Booth (Mrs. Arthur W. Johnson), Andrews Brooks. With Lawyers Coop. Pub. Co., Rochester, N.Y., 1916-60, exec. v.p., 1946-48, pres., treas., 1948-60; dir., treas. Baker-Voorhees Co., Inc., Mt. Kisco, N.Y., 1940-60; dir. Central Trust Co., Rochester, 1930-70, chmn. bd., 1959-66, chmn. exec. com., 1966-70, hon. chmn. bd., 1970—; dir. Bancroft Whitney Co., San Francisco, 1942-52. Bd. dirs. Rochester Gen. Hosp., 1934-65, hon. dir., 1965—, pres. bd., 1944—; trustee Rochester Inst. Tech., 1935-65, lst vice chmn., 1961-65, hon. trustee, 1965—, hon. vice chmn. bd. trustees, 1967—; trustee U. Rochester, 1954-65, hon. trustee, 1965—; trustee Rochester Friendly Home, Bergen Swamp Preservation Soc., 1955-66. Served with U.S. Army, 1917-19; 1st lt. 307th F.A., AEF, 1918. Mem. Rochester C. of C. (dir. 1950-62), U. Rochester Alumni Assn. (past pres.), Am. Legion, V.F.W., Newcomen Soc. N. Am., Delta Kappa Epsilon. Republican. Presbyn. Clubs: University, Rochester Country. Author: (with H.D. Shedd, George Chapman) Co-ops and You, 1945. Home: 61 Douglas Rd Rochester NY 14610 also 910 Lake Rd Webster NY 14580 Office: 67 Chesnut St Rochester NY 14604

HALE, FRANK CONNELL, former govt. ofcl.; b. Madisonville, Tex., Feb. 14, 1906; s. William N. and Florence (Harrison) H.; student John Bronw U., 1924-25, U. Tex., 1925- 26; LL.B., George Washington U., 1933; m. Sue M. Smith, May 31, 1946; childrenSusan Harrison (Mrs. John C. Whitten), Jane Alison. Admitted to Tex. bar, 1935, D.C. bar, 1961; with FTC, 1928-63, 1965-70, dir. bur. deceptive practices, 1968-70, spl. dep. atty. gen. Hawaii, 1963-65. Served as spl. agt., officer CIC, AUS, 1942-45; PTO. Recipient Distinguished Service award FTC, 1963. Mem. State Bar Tex., Fed. Bar Assn. (chmn. antitrust com. 1962-63), Sigma Alpha Epsilon. Methodist. Mason. Clubs: Nat. Lawyers (Washington); Belle Haven Country (Alexandria, Va.). Home: 4217 8th St S Arlington VA 22204

HALE, FRANK J., ballet co. exec.; b. San Francisco, Mar. 26, 1899. Vaudeville dancer; appeared with Dixieland Jazz Vaudeville, Keith-Albee Circuit; prod. Royal Poinciana Playhouse, Palm Beach, Fla.; founder, pres. Palm Beach Ballet Co.; v.p., treas. Internat. Co-Prodns., Inc.; producer films The Princess, Dr. Coppelius; developed Nat. Yeast Corp. (merged with Universal Foods Corp. 1968), now cons. Pres. Am. Soc. Aged. Address: PO Box 231 Palm Beach FL 33480

HALE, GERALD ALBERT, mineral, metal and ore co. exec.; b. Kalamazoo, May 9, 1927; s. Edwin M. and Helen M. (Hinrichs) H.; B.S., Western Mich. U., 1952; m. Emma Jean Hamilton, Aug. 22, 1953; children—Jeffrey, Jeffrey, Kathleen, John. Salesman, Edgar Bros. Co., Metuchen, N.J., 1952-56; with Minerals & Chems. Philipp Corp., and predecessors, 1956—, v.p. sales minerals and chems. div., 1964-66, corp. v.p., 1965-69 (co. merged with Englehard Industries to form Engelhard Minerals & Chems., 1967) exec. v.p. minerals and chems. div., asst. sec., 1967-69, pres. minerals and cchems. div., 1969—, sr. v.p. corp., 1969-70, exec. v.p. corp., mem. exec. com., 1971—, also dir. corp.; pres., dir. Eastern Magnesia Talc Co., Chemstone Corp., Cuyahoga Lime Co., Porocel Corp., Sociét é de la Cournouaille Francaise, Engelhard Minerals Ltd., Engelhard Minerals AG. Trustee, sec., v.p. Paper Tech. Found. of Western Mich. U. Served as meteorologist USAAF, 1945-47. Mem. T.A.P.P.I., Delta Upsilon (dir.). Mason. Clubs: Union League (N.Y.C.); Baltusrol Golf (Springfield, N.J.); Loantaka Skeet (Florham Park, N.J.). Home: 7 Winchester Rd Summit NJ 07901 Office: Engelhard Minerals & Chems Corp Menlo Park Edison NJ 08817

HALE, HAMILTON ORIN, lawyer; b. Crystal Lake, Ill., Sept. 15, 1906; s. Alva Harry and May Gale (Hamilton) H.; B.S., U. Ill., 1928; J.D., Northwestern U., 1931; m. J. Elizabeth Hale, June 29, 1946; childrenJean (Mrs. N. Theodore Sauer, Jr.), Hamilton, and Jamie. Admitted to Ill. bar, 1931, N.Y. bar, 1940; practiced in McHenry County, Ill., 1931; asso. Pruitt & Grealis, Chgo., 1931-40; partner Pruitt, Hale & MacInvre, N.Y.C., 48; founder Hale & Stimson, N.Y.C., 1948, firm now known as Hale, Russel & Stenzel, counsel, 1970—; counsel firm Joslyn & Green, McHenry County, 1970—; served as counsellor and adviser for commercial airlines and related enterprises; rep. Scandinavian, Spanish, Brazilian, Chilean, Israeli air systems in U.S. Mem. CAB adv. com. on procedures and practices,

1951; faculty lectr. on air law at the Northwestern U. Law Sch., 1934-35. Mayor, Village of Roslyn Estates, 1963- 67. Vice pres. bd. trustees Buckley Country Day Sch. Decorated Knight of Order of Saint Olav (Norway). Mem. Am. Bar Assn., Assn. Bar City N.Y., Order of Coif, Theta Chi, Phi Alpha Delta. Republican. Conglist. Clubs: Wings, The Creek, Sky, Nat. Aviation, Woodstock (Ill.) Country. Home: 317 S Valley Hill Rd Woodstock IL 60098 Office: 111 Virginia St Crystal Lake IL 60014

HALE, JAMES CECIL, lawyer; b. Blytheville, Ark., Oct. 9, 1908; s. Edward Augustus and Kate C. (Richards) H.; B.A., U. Ark., 1931, J.D., 1933; m. Jean Allen Robinson, Feb. 6, 1936; children—James Cecil, Ralph Robinson, Jeanie (Mrs. William S. Crain). Admitted to Ark. bar, 1933; practice in West Memphis, 1955—; pros. atty. 2d Jud. Dist., 1945-48; chmn. Supreme Ct. Com. on Profl. Conduct, 1969—. Pres., Crittenden Pub. Co., West Memphis Indsl. Devel. Corp.; dir. Bank of West Memphis, Crittenden Ins. Agy., Superior Supply Co. Mem. Ark. Ho. of Reps., 1939-45; chmn. Democratic Central Com. Crittenden County, 1944—; chmn. Bd. Election Commrs., 1948—. Chmn. bd. govs. Crittenden Meml. Hosp. Named West Memphis Man of Year, 1962. Mem. Am., Ark. (exec. com.), Crittenden County (past pres.) bar assns., Ark. Bar Found. (Lawyer-Citizen award 1962); U. Ark. Alumni Assn. (past nat. pres.), Scabbard and Blade, Sigma Chi, Delta Theta Phi. Mason (32, Shriner), Rotarian. Club: Meadowbrook Country (1st sec. West Memphis). Home: 124 Military Rd Marion AR 72364 Office: Bank of West Memphis Bldg West Memphis AR 72301

HALE, JOHN HAMPTON, aluminum co. exec.; b. London, Eng., July 8, 1924; s. John and Elsie Ledbroke (Coles) H.; student Eton Coll., 1942; B.A. with honours (open scholar math.) in Mech. Sci., Tripos, Magdalene Coll., Cambridge U., 1948; Henry fellow Harvard Grad. Sch. Bus. Adminstrn., 1948-49; m. Linda Jane Hodgson, Dec. 9, 1950; children—Susan, Jonathan, Anne. With Alcan, 1949—, v.p., sec., treas. Aluminum Ltd., Inc., N.Y.C., 1960-62, asst. treas. Aluminum Co. Canada, Ltd., Montreal, 1962-64, successively chief financial officer, asst. mng. dir., mng. dir. Alcan Industries, Ltd., London, Eng. (now Alcan Booth Industries Ltd.), 1964-70, exec. v.p. finance, treas. Alcan Aluminium Ltd., 1970—, also dir.; pres. Alcan Finances Ltd.; dir. major subsidiaries Alcan. Served with R.A.F. and Royal Navy, 1943-46. Clubs: Mount Royal, St. James's (Montreal); Royal Thames Yacht, Hurlingham (London). Home: 3117 Daulac Rd Montreal 218 Quebec Canada Office: 1 Place Ville Marie Montreal 113 Quebec Canada

HALE, JUDSON DRAKE, editor; b. Boston, Mar. 16, 1933; s. Roger Drake and Marian (Sagendorph) H.; grad. Choate Sch., 1951; student Dartmouth, 1951-55; m. Sara Huberlie, Sept. 6, 1958; children—Judson Drake, Daniel, Christopher. Asst. editor Yankee, Inc., Dublin, N.H., 1958-61, asso. editor, 1961-63, mng. editor, 1963-69, editor, v.p., 1969—, also dir.; editor, v.p. Old Farmers Almanac, Cape Cod Compass; dir. Solar Environmental Scis., Inc. Chmn., Dublin Recreation Com., 1971, Dublin Community Ch. Outreach Com., 1970-72. Trustee New Hope Center, R. Sagendorph Trust. Served with AUS, 1955-57. Mem. Phi Kappa Psi. Republican. Episcopalian. Club: Dublin Lake. Editor: That New England, 1968. Home: Valley Rd Dublin NH 03444 Office: Main St Dublin NH 03444

HALE, LESTER LEONARD, univ. ofcl.; b. Rice Lake, Wis., July 6, 1913; s. John Espy and Leona (DeLap) H.; B.A., U. Wis., 1934; M.A., La. State U., 1935, Ph.D., 1942; m. Susannah Evelyn Kent, Sept. 4, 1934; childrenEvelyn Kent, Cynthia Ann, Lester Leonard. Grad. asst. La. State U., 1934-35, 39-41; instr. U. Fla., 1935-37, asst. prof., 1937-39, asso. prof., 1941-45, prof. speech, 1945-, dean men, 1956-60, dean of student affairs, 1960-67, v.p. for student affairs, 1967—; summer vis. prof. Colo. State Tchrs. Coll., 1946, U. Wis., 1947, U. Ala., 1948, Wayne U., 1950, U. Tenn., 1955, Ohio U., 1956-57. Fellow Am. Speech and Hearing Assn.; mem. Speech Assn. Am., So. Speech Assn. (past pres.), Am. Personnel and Guidance Assn., Am. Coll. Personnel Assn. Presbyn. (elder). Kiwanian. Home: 2245 NW 6th Pl Gainesville FL 32601

HALE, LLOYD, machinery mfg. exec.; b. Neosha Falls, Kan., Feb. 21, 1904; A.B., U. Minn., 1927, M.S., 1930, Outstanding Achievement award, 1957; m. Elizabeth S. Adams, Aug. 4, 1928; children-Charles A., Roger L. In constrn. bus., Portland, Ore., 1921-22; mgr. Campus Club, U. Minn., 1924-28; with G. H. Tennant Co., Mpls., 1928—, sec., 1930-36, v.p., 1936-44, pres., dir., 1944-63, chmn. bd., 1963—; dir. E. J. Longyear Co. chmn. citizens' com. for Mpls. Charter Reform, lt. pres. Good Govt. groups; mem. adv. com. floor machinery sect. WPB World War II. Recipient Distinguished Citizen award from Nat. Municipal League, 1959. Mem. Nat. Municipal League (v.p.), Floor Machinery Mfg. Assn. (pres. 1948), Minn. Charter Commn. (v.p.), Asso. Industries (sec.), Mpls. Hosp. Com. (dir.). Conglist. Rotarian. Clubs: Minneapolis, Wayzata Country. Home: 15D Black Oak Lane Wayzata MN 55391 Office: 701 N Lilac Dr Minneapolis MN 55422

HALE, LUCIUS MELVIN, engr., govt. ofcl.; b. Blackfoot, Ida., Mar. 6, 1913; s. Franklin George and Cora E. (Hammond) H.; B.S. in Engring., Utah State U., 1937; postgrad. Purdue U., Northwestern U., Pub. Works Sch., Norfolk, Va., 1942-43; grad. Fed. Exec. Inst., Charlottesville, Va., 1969; m. Lorraine Arnold; children—Joyce Jean, Kathryn Anne. Civil engr. U.S. Dept. Agr. and Utah Expt. Sta., 1936-39, U.S. Army Constrn. Q.M. Corps, 1939-41; airways engr. Fairbanks and Anchorage (Alaska) Civil Aero. Authority, 1941-42; design and contract supt. U.S. Naval Ammunition Depot, Hastings, Neb., 1947-49; civil engr. Arco Idaho Project, AEC, 1949-54; resident engr. St. Lawrence Seaway Devel. Corp., 1954-58, dir. Office Marine and Engring. Operations, 1958-62; dep. dir. engring. AID, State Dept., 1962-71, acting dir., 1965-66, dir. Office Engring., 1971—. Mem. Internat. St. Lawrence River Bd. Control, Can.-U.S. Emergency Planning Com., Internat. Dangerous Cargo Com. Dist. chmn., dist. com. Boy Scouts Am. Served from ensign to comdr., USNR, 1942-47. Recipient meritorious civilian award USN, 1948; citation Govt. of Mexico for Engring. Studies. Registered profl. engr. Mem. Nat. Soc. Profl. Engrs., C. of C. (dir.). Home: 4301 Columbia Pike Arlington VA 22204 Office: New State Dept Bldg Washington DC 20525

HALE, MARK PENDLETON, social worker; b. Salisbury, Mo., Feb. 13, 1912; s. Holly Morgan and Dora Blanche (Pendleton) H.; A.B., Hiram (O.) Coll., 1932; M.A., U. of Mo., 1933; student Sch. of Social Service Administration, University of Chicago, 1941-42, Doctor of Philosophy, 1956; married Allean Lemmon, Dec. 31, 1936; childrenSusanna Lemmon, Mark Pendleton. Supervisor Mo. Nat. Youth Adminstrn., St. Joseph, Mo., 1935; social analyst Mo. State Children's Bur., Jefferson City, Mo., 1935-37, Mo. State Social Security Commn., 1937-41; research asst. and instr. Sch. Social Service Adminstrn., U. of Chicago, 1942, summer 1943, 45; asso. prof. of research Nashville Sch. of Social Work, 1942-43, Tulane Sch. of Social Work, 1943-46, prof. of social economy, 1946-47; prof., chmn., dept. social work U. Mo., 1947-55; prof., dir. sch. of social work State U. Iowa, 1954-62; dir. Jane Addams Grad. Sch. Social Work, U. Ill., 1962-. Mem. accrediting commn., Nat. Council Social Work Edn., 1952; pres. central dist., Mo. Assn. Social Welfare; mem. Social Work Research Group; cons. Tenn. Personnel div., 1943. Recipient Fulbright sr. research scholarship, 1957-58. Mem. Am. Assn. Schs. Social Work (chmn. subcom. on tchg. materials in research since 1947), Am. Assn. Social Workers, Nat. Research Commn. (chapter chmn. New Orleans 1946), Nat. Conf. Social Work, Am. Assn. Univ. Profs., La. Conf. Social Welfare (lst vice-pres. 1946), Mo. Assn. Social Welfare (sec. 1948), Council on Social Work Edn. (chmn. grad. sch. div., chmn. commn. on schs. and depts., 1956, chmn. accreditation commn. 1963-68), Ia. Welfare Assn. (pres. 1961), Nat. Conf. Social Welfare (nat. bd. 1961-62), Am. Pub. Welfare Assn. (nat. bd. 1961-63, lst v.p. 1966-68). Mem. Ch. Disciples of Christ. Home: 22 G H Baker Dr Urbana IL 61801

HALE, MASON ELLSWORTH, Jr., museum curator; b. Winsted, Conn., Sept. 23, 1928; s. Mason Ellsworth and Lillian (Swanson) H.; B.S., Yale, 1950; M.A., U. Wis., 1951, Ph.D., 1953; m. Beatrice Wilde, Apr. 19, 1952; childrenJanet Arlene, Sandra Louise, Robert Alan. Asst. prof. biology U. Wichita, 1953-55, W.Va. U., 1955-57; asso. curator div. cryptogams, dep. botany Mus. Natural History, Smithsonian Institution, Washington, 1957-62, curator, 1962-, chairman dept. botany, 1968-70; field exploration Arctic Can., 1950, Mexico, 1960, Pacific area, 1964-65; spl. research taxonomy and chemistry lichenized fungi. Mem. Am. Soc. Plant Taxonomists, Am. Bryological Soc., Swedish Bot. Soc., Japan Am. Soc., Phi Beta Kappa, Sigma Xi. Author: Lichen Handbook, 1961; Biology of Lichens, 1967; How to Know the Lichens, 1969. Address: Smithsonian Instn Washington DC 20560

HALE, MERLE LEROY, oral surgeon; b. Taylor County, Ia., Dec. 5, 1913; s. John E. and Lulu M. (Pollock) H.; B.A., D.D.S., U. Ia., 1938, M. S., 1948; m. Mary Louise Hackett, July 25, 1939; childrenEdwin Douglas, Marsha Susan, Linda Jane. Gen. practice of dentistry, Ia., 1939-47; practice oral surgery, Iowa City, 1952—; prof. oral surgery, chmn. grad. oral surgery U. Mo. at Kansas City, 1949-52; prof., chmn. oral surgery and anesthesia, Coll. Dentistry and Medicine, U. Ia., 1952—; chief hosp. oral surgery dept. U. Hosps., Iowa City, 1952-; cons. oral surgery VA Hosp., Iowa City, 1952- . Served as maj. Dental Corps, AUS, World War II. Diplomate Am. Bd. Oral Surgery, Fellow Am. Coll. Dentists; mem. Am. Dental Assn., Am. (bd. dirs. 1969—), Midwestern, Ia. socs. oral surgeons, Internat. Assn. Dental Research, Sigma Xi, Omicron Kappa Upsilon, Psi Omega. Home: 1100 N Dubuque St Iowa City IA 52240

HALE, MYRON Q., educator; b. Oakley, Ida., Sept. 17, 1921; B.A., U. Utah, 1947, M.A., 1949; postgrad. Coll. City N.Y., 1954-55; Ph.D., Columbia, 1959; married; 3 children. Lectr. polit. sci. Columbia, 1953-56; instr. U. Tex., 1956-58; asst. prof. Ohio State U., 1959-64, asso. prof., 1964-68; prof., head dept. polit. sci. Purdue U., Lafayette, Ind., 1968—. Served With USNR, 1942-46. Mem. Am. Polit. Sci. Assn. Contbr. articles to profl. jours. Office: Dept Polit Sci Purdue U Lafayette IN 49709*

HALE, NANCY, author; b. Boston, Mass., May 6, 1908; d. Philip L. and Lilian (Westcott) Hale; grad. Winsor Sch., Boston, 1926; student Sch. of Boston Museum of Fine Arts, 1927-28; studied in father's studio number of yrs.; m. Fredson Bowers, Mar. 16, 1942; children (by former marriage)—Mark Hardin, William Wertenbaker. Asst. editor, Vogue, 1928-32, Vanity Fair, 1933-34; news reporter N.Y. Times, 1935; advisery capacity to advt. agy., 1930-35; lectr. short story Bread Loaf Writers Conf., 1957-65. Recipient O. Henry prize for short-short story, 1933; Benjamin Franklin special citation for short story, 1958; Henry H. Bellaman award for lit., 1969. Clubs: Cosmopolitan (N.Y.C.). Author: The Young Die Good, 1932; Never Any More, 1934; The Earliest Dreams, 1936; The Prodigal Women, 1942; Between the Dark and the Daylight, 1943; The Sign of Jonah, 1950; The Empress's Ring, 1955; Heaven and Hardpan Farm, 1957; A New England Girlhood, 1958; Dear Beast, 1959; The Pattern of Perfection (short stories), 1960; The Realities of Fiction (essays), 1962; Black Summer, 1963; New England Discovery (anthology), 1963; The Life In The Studio, 1969; Secrets, 1971. Author short stories which have appeared in over 40 anthologies, including the Foley and O. Henry collections. Contbr. to New Yorker, Harper's Bazaar, Harper's. Home: Route 8 Charlottesville VA 22901

HALE, NEWTON JOHNSTON, merchant; b. San Francisco, Jan. 10, 1902; s. Reuben Brooks and May (Johnston) H.; student Hitchcock Mil. Acad., 1920, Stanford U., 1920- 22, N.Y.U. Sch. Retailing, 1925-26; m. Betty Caughey, July 29, 1922; children—Betty May (Mrs. Edward H. McLaughlin, Jr.), Janet (Mrs. C. E. Havard). With Hale Bros., Inc., 1922; R. H. Macy Co., Franklin Simon, 1925-26; Hale Bros., 1926, dir., 1931, treas., 1934-43, chmn. bd., dir., 1943—; v.p., dir. Hale Bros., Assos., Inc.; sec., dir. O. C. Field Gasoline Corp., 1922-44; dir. Broadway-Hale Stores, Inc.; former pres., dir. Retail Merchants Assn., Retail Dry Goods Assn., Retail Credit Assn., San Francisco, Sigma Alpha Epsilon. Chmn., 1944, Stanford Ann. Conf. Republican. Clubs: Pacific-Union, Bohemian, Burlingame Country, Electric, Commonwealth; Athens (Oakland). Home: 45 Downey Way Hillsborough CA 94010 Office: 601 California St San Francisco CA 94108

HALE, ORON JAMES, educator, historian; b. Goldendale, Wash., July 29, 1902; s. William Robert and Frances Isabella (Putnam) H.; A.B., U. Wash., 1926; A.M., U. Pa., 1928, Ph.D. (George Leib Harrison fellow history 1928-29), 1930; studied in France and Germany, summers 1927, 28; Social Sci. Research Council fellowship in London and Berlin, 1932- 33; Litt. D., Hampden-Sydney Coll., 1958; m. Anette Van Winkle, Aug. 7, 1929 (dec. 1968); m. 2d, Virginia S. Zehmer, July 9, 1970. Instr. history U. Pa., 1926-28; asst. prof. European history U. Va., 1929-38, asso. prof., 1938-46, prof., 1946-65, Corcoran prof. history, 1965—, chmn. dept., 1955-62, dir. Inst. Pub. Affairs, 1942, 53, acting chmn. Woodrow Wilson Sch. Fgn. Affairs, 1947-48; vis. prof. summers Duke, 1934, 38, 39, U. Mo. 1937, U. N.C., 1946, Harvard, 1955; prof. Inst. Advanced Study, Princeton 1963-64. Served to col. AUS, 1942-46; served intelligence div. War Dept. Gen. Staff, 1942-45; mem. War Dept. Gen. Staff Hist. Mission in Germany, 1945; hist. div. War Dept. spl. staff, 1945-46; col., M.I. Res., 1946-62; with U.S. High Commn. for Germany as dep. state commr. for Bavaria, 1950-51; commr., 1951-52. Recipient George Louis Beer prize diplomatic history Am. Hist. Assn., 1931; commdr.'s cross Order of Merit (Federal Republic Germany), 1969; Thomas Jefferson award U. Va., 1969. Mem. Am., So. hist. assns., Soc. Am. Historians, Va. Soc. Sci. Assn., Phi Beta Kappa. Democrat. Presbyn. Club: Colonnade. Author: Germany and the Diplomatic Revolution, 1904-1906, 1931; Publicity and Diplomacy, 1890-1914, 1940; The Captive Press in the Third Reich, 1964 (spl. Polk award 1965); The Great Illusion, 1900-1914, 1971. Contbr. to hist., lit. and mil. periodicals. Home: 1864 Edgewood Lane Charlottesville VA ☆

HALE, PRENTIS CARNES, retired utilities exec.; b. South Haven, Mich., Feb. 27, 1905; s. Channing Ward and Fannie Barbara (Moore) H.; student Pomona Coll., 1925; B.S., Harvard, 1926; grad. student U. So. Cal., U. Cal. at Los Angeles; m. Janet Lindsay Clark, 1933; children—Linda Monroe, Thomas Lindsay. With So. Cal. Edison Co., 1929-70, treas., 1948-70; treas. Asso. So. Investment Co. (formerly Edison Securities Co.), 1948-70; v.p., treas. Electric Systems Co.; treas., controller Guam Power Authority, Agana, Guam. Bd. dirs., dir. financial devel. Met. YMCA, Los Angeles, mem. area bd., nat. bd., mem. internat. com. YMCA, chmn. bd. southwest area YMCA; v.p. nat. council YMCA. Mem. nat. council Pomona Coll. Mem. Hannold Library Soc., C. of C., Pacific Coast Elec. Assn., Nu Alpha Phi. Republican. Presbyn. Clubs: Harvard of So. Cal.; Los Angeles Athletic; Lincoln. Home: 3155 Mesaloa Lane Pasadena CA 91107 Office: 714 W Olympic Blvd Los Angeles CA 90015

HALE PRENTIS COBB, retail store exec.; b. San Francisco, July 30, 1910; s. Prentis Cobb and Linda Hoag (Bryan) H.; A.B., Stanford, 1933, LL.B., 1936; m. Marialice P. King, Sept. 17, 1936; children-Hilary, Prentis Cobb III, Linda, Hamilton Bryan. Admitted to Cal. bar, 1936; with Hale Bros, Stores, Inc., San Francisco, 1936-51, pres. 1948-51; dir. Broadway Dept. Stores, Inc., 1949, chmn. bd. Broadway-Hale Stores, Inc., San Francisco, 1950—; pres. Hale Bros. Assos., Inc., 1950-66, chmn. bd., 1966-; dir. Foremost-McKesson, Inc., Memorex Corp., Rohr Corp., Pacific Lighting Corp., Bank Am., Union Oil Co., A., T. & S. F. Ry., Leslie Salt Co. Pres. San Francisco Opera Assn., 1967—. Trustee Tax Foundation; trustee War Meml. of San Francisco. Served as lt. comdr. USNR, 1941- 45. Mem. Cal. C. of C. (treas.), Cal. Retailers Assn. (dir.), Wine and Food Soc. Clubs: Bohemian, Pacific Union, California (Los Angeles); Burlingame Country; Confrerie des Chevaliers du Tastevin; Circolo Gastronomico Italinao; Villa Taverna; Links (N.Y.C.). Home: 2920 Broadway San Francisco CA 94115 Office: 601 California St San Francisco CA 94108

HALE, RICHARD ERNEST, savs. and loan exec.; b. Boston, Mar. 10, 1917; s. Ernest Alfred and Ruth Tremaine (Mitchell) H.; grad. Country Day Sch., Newton, Mass., 1937; A.B., Brown U., 1941; m. Lewey Elizabeth Appley, July 29, 1944; 1 dau., Judith Barbara (Mrs. Harold F. Drury, Jr.). With 1st Fed. Savs. & Loan Assn., Boston, 1941—, v.p., 1948-55, exec. v.p., 1955-58, pres., 1958—, chmn. bd. dirs., 1967—. Chmn. Carlisle (Mass.) Community Chest, 1966. Chmn. Friends of Library of Brown U., 1963-65. Mem. Mass. Fed. Savs. Council, Inc. (dir., past pres.), Asso. Alumni Brown U. (past dir.), Still Bank Collectors Club Am. (pres.), Fed. Savs. League New Eng. (past pres.), Newcomen Soc. N.A., Carlisle Hist. Soc. (past pres.). Home: Four Corners West St Carlisle MA 01741 Office: PO Box 2276 Boston MA 02107

HALE, RICHARD WALDEN, Jr., archivist; b. Boston, Aug. 5, 1909; s. Richard Walden and Mary (Patterson) H.; A.B., Harvard, 1930, Ph.D., 1937; B.A. with honors in History (Fiske scholar), Cambridge (Eng.) U., 1932; m. Elisabeth Fairbanks, Aug. 9, 1940; childrenPeter, Thomas, Frances, Martha. Instr., Antioch Coll., 1932-33, Princeton, 1935-40; mem. staff Newberry Library, Chgo., 1941-43; head history dept. Roxbury Latin Sch., Boston, 1943-47; lectr. edn. Wellesley Coll., 1948-52; curator Canadian history Harvard Coll. Library, 1953-57; editor Guide to Photocopied Hist. Materials, 1957-60; archivist, Mass., 1961-; acting chmn. Mass. Hist. Commn., 1964—. Pres., Nat. Conf. State Historic Preservation Officers. Soc., Am. Antiquarian Soc., Colonial Soc. Mass., Am. Records Mgmt. Assn., Soc. Am. Archivists, Am., Canadian hist. assns., Brit. Records Assn., Phi Beta Kappa. Clubs: Union (Boston); Century (N.Y.C.); Chgo. Literary; Savile (London). Author: Democratic France, 1870-1940, 1941; Tercentenary History of Roxbury Latin School, 1946; Story of Bar Harbor, 1949; Britain, Her Peoples and the Commonwealth (with Robert Eckles), 1954. Editor: Guide to Photocopied Historical Materials, 1960. Home: 420 Hammond St Chestnut Hill MA 02167 Office: Office of Sec State House Beacon St Boston MA 02133

HALE, ROBERT BEVERLY, art educator; b. Boston, Jan. 29, 1901; s. Herbert Dudley and Margaret Curzon (Marquand) H.; A.B., Columbia, 1923; postgrad. Columbia Sch. Architecture, Fontainebleau, Art Students League; m. Barbara Barnes, Nov. 11, 1941 (div.); m. 2d, Nike Mylonas, Dec. 8, 1962; one son, Alexander Curzon. Asso. editor Art News, 1941-49; asso. curator Am. Art, Met. Mus., N.Y.C., 1949-57, curator Am. painting and sculpture, 1958-66, curator emeritus, 1968—; lectr. artistic anatomy Pa. Acad. Fine Arts, 1968—; instr. drawing, lectr. anatomy Art Students League, 1943—; adj. prof. drawing Columbia, 1945-67. Exhibited one-man show Stamford (Conn.) Mus., 1959, Staempfli Gallery, N.Y.C., 1960; rep. permanent collections Whitney Mus., Met. Mus., U. Ariz., others, many pvt. collections. Pres. Louis Comfort Tiffany Found., 1959-66, trustee, 1966—; v.p. N.Y.C. Art Festival, 1961- -; mem. art com. Chase Manhattan Bank, 1960—. Benjamin Franklin fellow Royal Soc. Arts, 1969. Mem. Mun. Art Soc., Art Students League (v.p. 1941-43; life mem.), Am. Fine Arts Soc. (trustee), Am. Fedn. Arts (internat. com.). Clubs: Columbia University Men's Faculty, Century (N.Y.C.). Author: 100 American Painters of the 20th Century, 1950; Drawing Lessons from The Great Masters, 1964; Showland, 1971. Editor, translator: Anatomie Artistique (Dr. Paul Richer), 1971. Contbr. to New Yorker, mags. of art, article Ency. Brit., 1956. Home: 2 W 67th St New York City NY 10023 Office: Art Students League 215 W 57th St New York City NY 10019

HALE, RUSSELL WILLIAM, economist, govt. ofcl.; b. Syracuse, N.Y., Apr. 17, 1909; s. Harry William and Viola (Lape) H.; student Syracuse U., 1928-29, McGill U., 1929-30; m. Sue Evelyn Galloway, Mar. 21, 1952; 1 son, William Franklin. Buyer John Wanamaker, N.Y. City, 1931-36; merchandise mgr., Joslin Dry Goods Co. (dept. store), located Denver, Colo., 1936-41; regional price exec. (N.Y., N.J., Pa., Md., Del., D.C.), O.P.A., 1942-47; director of trade and services, General Headquarters, Supreme Comdr. for the Allied Powers, Tokyo, Japan, 1947-52; cons. to chmn. NSRB, 1952; advisor on Far East trade to dep. dir. Mut. Def. Assistance Control, FOA, 1952-55; asst. dept. dir. ICA for Mut. Def. Assistance Control, 1955-57, asst. dep. adminstr. Mut. Def. Assistance Control, State Dept., 1958-61, asst. exec. sec. Nat. Aeros. and Space Council, 1961-. Mem. Sigma Chi. Home: 1500 Arlington Blvd Arlington VA 22209 Office: Exec Office of Pres Washington DC 20502

HALE, STANTON GUDMAN, ins. exec.; b. Boise, Ida., July 1, 1910; s. Heber Q. and Bessie (Gudmundson) H.; B.S., U. Ida., 1932; m. Doris Norell, Mar. 10, 1934; children Stanton D., Carole Jean (Mrs. Dabney Coleman), Eleanore (Mrs. William W. Crowell). From agt. to sr. v.p. Mut. Life Ins. Co. N.Y., 1935- 63; pres., dir. Pacific Mut. Life Ins. Co., 1963-; dir. Western Bancorp., So. Cal. Edison Co., United Cal. Bank, Pacific Tel. & Tel. Co., Broadway-Hale Stores, Inc., Olson Bros., Inc. Bd. dirs. Santa Anita (Cal.) Found., Life Ins. Med. Research Fund. Mem. nat. bd. Am. Cancer Soc., Inc.; trustee Com. Econ. Devel., Boys' Clubs Found. So. Cal., Cal. Inst. Tech., Henry E. Huntington Library and Art Gallery; bd. councilors Grad. Sch. Bus. Adminstrn., U. So. Cal.; nat. adv. council U. Ida. Mem. Inst. Life Ins. (dir.), Assn. Cal. Life Ins. Cos. (pres.), Life Ins. Agy. Mgmt. Assn. (past pres.), Newcomen Soc. N. Am., Phi Gamma Delta, Alpha Kappa Psi. Clubs: Links (N.Y.C.); California, Los Angeles Country; Pacific-Union (San Francisco), Pauma Valley Country, San Francisco Golf. Home: 10787 Wilshire Blvd Los Angeles CA 90024 Office: Pacific Mut Bldg 523 W 6th St Los Angeles CA 90014

HALE, WANDA, journalist. Motion picture critic N.Y. Daily News. Office: News Syndicate Co Inc 220 E 42d St New York City NY 10017*

HALE, WILLIAM HARLAN, editor, writer; b. N.Y.C., July 21, 1910; s. William Bayard and Olga (Unger) H.; student Riverdale Country Sch., 1924-27; A.B., Yale, 1931; m. Jean Laughlin Barker, Aug. 19, 1941; childrenKatherine, Jonathan, Elizabeth. Asso. editor Vanity Fair mag., 1932-33; columnist Washington Post, 1933; editorial asso. Fortune mag., 1934-35; free lance writer for various mags., 1935-41; spl. writer Norman Bel Geddes & Co., 1939; with O.W.I., 1941-45, in charge of radio broadcasts to Germany from N.Y., chief of German propaganda operations for O.W.I., London, chief of Radio Luxembourg for psychol. warfare div., supreme hdgrs. A.E.F.; policy adviser, information control div. U.S. Forces European Theater, Bad Homburg, Germany; sr. editor New Republic, 1946-47; sr. writer The Reporter, 1948-49, contbg. editor, 1954-58; apptd. U.S. Fgn. Service Res. Officer, 1950, press attache and chief information br. Office U.S. High Commr. Am. embassy, Vienna, 1st sec., dir. pub. affairs div., 1952-53; mng. editor Horizon mag., N.Y.C., 1958-61, editor, 1961-63, editor Horizon Books, N.Y.C., 1963-67, sr. writer, 1967-68. Democrat. Episcopalian. Club: Century Assn. (N.Y.C.). Author: Challenge to Defeat, 1932; Hannibal Hooker, 1938; The March of Freedom, 1947, Horace Greeley Voice of the People, 1950; Innocence Abroad, 1957; The Horizon Book of Ancient Greece, 1965; The Horizon History of Eating and Drinking Through the Ages, 1968. Editor: The Horizon Book of Ancient Rome, 1966. Contbr. numerous mags. Home: Goodhill Rd Weston CT 06880 *

HALE, WILLIAM HENRI, univ. pres.; b. Krebs, Okla., Aug. 8, 1914; s. George and Carrie (Holmes) H.; B.S., Langston (Okla.) U., 1940; M.A., U. Wis., 1941; Ph.D., U. Chgo., 1949; L.H.D., Okla. Sch. Religion, Langston, 1964; m. Larzette Golden, May 24, 1940; childrenPauline (Mrs. James Jackson), Janis, Gina. Research asst. sociology Fisk U., 1941-42; acting registrar Langston (Okla.) U., 1942-43, pres., 1960—; registrar Bethune-Cookman Coll., 1942- 44, dean-registrar, 1944-46, acting pres., summer 1946; prof. social sci., chmn. dept. Clark Coll., Atlanta, 1948-60. Vis. summer prof. Atlanta U., 1947, 50-52, 55, 59-60, State Tchrs. Coll., Montgomery, Ala., 1948, Hampton Inst., 1949. Nat. adviser pre- alumni group mem. instns. United Negro Coll. Fund, 1958-60; treas. Atlanta Interracial Work Camp, 1956, Atlanta Pan Hellenic Council, 1958- 60; dir. youth activities Atlanta br. N.A.A.C.P., 1949-51; mem. Okla. Commn. on Human Rights; bd. dirs. Atlanta Assn. Mental Health, 1958; mem. Okla. Small Bus. Adv. Council, Okla. Curriculum Improvement Commn; mem. com. edn. center planning Oklahoma City Pub. Schs.; mem. Gov.'s Com. Phys. Fitness, commn. on colls. and univs. North Central Assn. Colls. and Secondary Schs.; mem. exec. com of council of pres.'s Nat. Assn. Land-Grant Coll. and State Univs.; mem. adv. com. U.S. Coast Guard Acad. Named Mason of the Year, 1964. Mem. Am. Sociol. Soc., Assn. Higher Edn. Am. Assn. Sch. Adminstrs., N.E.A., Nat Conf. Christians and Jews, Alpha Phi Alpha (nat. dir. ednl. activities 1957-58, nat. pres. 1961—), Alpha Kappa Delta, Kappa Delta Pi, Phi Delta Kappa. Address: Langston Univ Langston OK 73050*

HALEY, GEORGE H., financial corp. exec.; b. Sewickley, Pa., Mar. 25, 1920; s. James I. and Elizabeth (Helvey) H.; A.B., Catawaba Coll., Salisbury, N.C., 1943; m. Vanja Schard, Sept. 8, 1962; children—Maureen, Kevin, Lilian. Mortgage officer Prudential Ins. Co., Los Angeles, 1946-50; v.p. Glendale Fed. Savs. (Cal.), 1950-54; owner George Haley Co., mortgage broker, Beverly Hills, Cal., 1954-62; sr. v.p. Am. Savs & Loan Assn., San Francisco, 1962-66; gen. mgr. Western Mortgage Corp., Los Angeles and San Francisco, 1966-67; chmn. bd. First Western Savs. & Loan Assn., Las Vegas, 1967—; pres. First Western Financial Corp., Las Vegas, 1967—. Past pres. Los Angeles chpt. Soc. Real Estate Appraisers. Trustee So. Nev. Indsl. Found.; bd. dirs. United Fund Clark County. Served with AUS, 1943-45. Home: 6971 Monta Rosa Las Vegas NV 89109 Office: 118 Las Vegas Blvd Las Vegas NV 89101

HALEY, JACK, actor; b. Boston, 1899; s. John Joseph and Ellen (Curley) H.; LL.D., Stonehill Coll., 1957; m. Florence MacFadden, Feb. 25, 1921; childrenGloria (Mrs. Milan Radovich), Jack. Appeared in numerous motion pictures including Good News, 1928, Follow Through, 1929, Alexander's Ragtime Band, Wake Up and Live, Pigskin Parade, Wizard of Oz; pres. Madera Ranchos, Inc. Served with USO, World War II. Decorated knight of Malta. Mem. Am. Guild Variety Artists (pres.). K.C. (4). Clubs: New York Athletic; Bel-Air Country (Beverly Hills). Home: 1001 N Beverly Dr Beverly Hills CA 90210 Office: 437 S Robertson Blvd Beverly Hills CA 90210*

HALEY, JACK, Jr., (John J., Jr.), director, producer writer; b. Los Angeles, Oct. 25, 1933; s. Jack and Florence (McFadden) H.; B.S. in English, Loyola U., Los Angeles, 1956; postgrad. student U. Cal. at Los Angeles, U. So. Cal., also work in cinema arts. TV actor, 1955-56; joined David L. Wolper to form Wolper Prodns. Inc., 1959; co-producer TV show The Race for Space, 1959; producer-dir. TV spl. Project; Man in Space, 1959, Hollywood: The Golden Years, 1960-61, Hollywood: The Great Stars, 1962, Hollywood: The Fabulous Era, 1962; writer, producer, dir., exec. charge prodn. TV series Hollywood and the Stars (segment won Silver Lion award Venice Film Festival), 1963-64, series Biography (George Foster Peabody Broadcasting award), 1962; producer, dir. And Away We Go, TV spl., 1963-64; exec. producer, dir. The General, TV spl., 1965; producer, dir. The Incredible World of James Bond, TV spl., 1965; prodn. supr. The Legend of Marilyn Monroe, TV spl. 1966; supervising producer Wolper Prodns. Inc. on all Nat. Geog. Spls., 1966; producer, cowriter A Funny Thing Happend on the Way to the White House, 1966; sr. v.p. charge all live entertainment Wolper Prodns., Inc., 1967; writer, producer, dir. TV spl. The Hidden World (Grnad Prix Monte Carlo Internat. TV Festival, Silver Lion award Venice Film Festival, George Foster Peabody Broadcasting award), 1967; exec. producer The Highlights of the Ice Capades, 1967; With Love, Sophia, 1967; producer, co-writer A Funny Thing Happened on the Way to Hollywood, 1967; producer, dir. Movin' With Nancy (Emmy award), 1967; exec. producer Monte Carlo, C'est La Rose, 1968, The Highlights of the Ice Capades, 1968; producer, dir. The Beat of Brass, 1968; exec. producer The Highlights of the Ice Capades, 1969; producer, co-writer-co-dir. Frank Sinatra, Jr...With Family and Friends, 1969; dir. film Norwood, 1969; dir. 1969 Acad. Awards Presentation; four of his documentaries presented by invatation at Moscow Film Festival. Co-founder The Thalians, 1955, bd. dirs., 1955-65; pres. Jack Haley Found., 1962—. Address: 1443 Devlin Dr Los Angeles, CA 90069.

HALEY, JAMES ANDREW, bus. exec., congressman; b. Jacksonville, Ala., Jan. 4, 1899; s. Andrew Jackson and Mary Lee (Steveson) H.; student Ala. U., 1919-22; married Aubrey B. Ringling. Accountant, Sarasota, Florida, 1920-33; general manager John Ringling estate, 1933-43; lst vice president Ringling Circus, 1943-45; pres. and director Ringling Bros. Barnum & Bailey Circus, Sarasota, Fla., 1946-48; member of 83d to 92d Congresses from Seventh Fla. Dist. Elected to Fla. Ho. of Reps., 1948, 50. Served U.S. Army, World War I, Chmn. Dem. exec. com., Sarasota, Fla., 1935-52. Mem. Am. Legion, Vets. Fgn. Wars, S.A.R. Methodist. Mason, Elk. Clubs: Sarasota Yacht, Sun and Surf, 40 and 8; Army and Navy (Washington). Home: Sarasota FL 33578

HALEY JAMES FREDERICK, lawyer, apparel co. exec.; b. Worcester, Mass., Mar. 14, 1926; s. Robert Hutchison and Amelia S. (Kemena) H.; grad. Phillips Exeter Acad., 1944; A.B., Princeton, 1950; LL.B., Harvard, 1953. Admitted to N.Y. bar, 1954, since practiced in N.Y.C.; asso. Sullivan & Cromwell, 1953-57; sec. Cluett, Peabody & Co., Inc., 1957-; dir. Lytton's, Henry C. Lytton & Co., Arrow Inter-Am., Inc. Served with AUS, 1944-45, USAAF, 1945-46. Mem. N.Y., New York County bar assns., Assn. Bar City N.Y. Republican. Episcopalian. Clubs: Racquet and Tennis, Harvard (N.Y.C.). Home: 1136 Fifth Av New York City, NY 10028. Office: 510 Fifth Av New York City NY 10036*

HALEY, JOHN CHARLES, educator, artist; b. Mpls., Sept. 21, 1905; s. John Edward and Clara (Gutzeit) H.; student of Cameron Booth at Mpls. Sch. Art, 1924-27, of Hans Hofmann in Munich, Germany, 1927-28, in Capri, 1927; m. Monica Elizabeth Phares, Apr. 4, 1929. Mem. faculty U. Cal. at Berkeley, 1930- , prof. art, 1946-; mem. Inst. for Creative Arts. 1963-64; exhbns. include San Francisco Art Annuals, 1930-60, Pa. Acad., 1952, also Legion of Honor Winter Invitationals, Internat. Biennial, Sao Paulo, Brazil, U. Ill. Annuals; one man shows Mortimer Levitt Gallery, N.Y.C., 1949, 52, de Young Mus., 1962, U. Cal. at Berkeley, 1962, Chico State Coll., 1963; rep. permanent collections Phillips Meml. Gallery, Washington, Oakland Art Museum, San Francisco Museum of Art, First National Bank Nev., Chico State College, University of California at Berkeley, IBM Corp., Mills Coll. Bd. dirs. San Francisco Art Inst., 1959-62. Served with USNR, 1943- 45. Recipient San Francisco Art Assn. award 1936, 39, 44, 51, 53, 56, Cal. State Fair award, 1950, 51, Richmond Art Center award, 1956, 58, Cal. Watercolor Soc. award, 1956. Mem. Richmond Art Center, San Francisco Art Inst. Home: 771 Ocean Av Richmond CA 94807 Office: Art Dept Univ California Berkeley CA 94720

HALEY, ORA BENJAMIN, Jr., wholesale florist; b. Denver, Dec. 1, 1910; s. Ora Benjamin and Maud (Hunn) H.; student U. Colo; m. Helen Baker, Apr. 23, 1938; children—Ora Benjamin III, Patricia A., William B., James E., Thomas D., Kenneth M., Daniel P., Richard J., Margaret M. With Nat. Cylinder Gas Co., 1934-44; mgr. Junglewood, Inc., greenhouses, Morrison, Colo., 1944-47; mng. dir., sec.-treas. Denver Wholesale Florists Co., 1947—; sec., dir. Dallas Flower Market, Salt Lake Wholesale Florists, D.S. Geddis Jr. Co., St. Louis; dir. Winnipeg Wholesale Florists, Ltd. (Can.), Kansas City Wholesale Florists Co. Pres., Craig Rehab. Hosp., Denver, 1964-65. Mem. Soc. Am. Florists (pres. 1961-63, dir. 1963—), United Floral Industry Colo. (lst pres. 1958), Florists Telegraph Delivery Assn. (dir. 1958-60, chmn. asso. div. 1958-60), Wholesale Commn. Florists Am. (dir. 1951-54, pres. 1956-59), Beta Theta Pi. Rotarian. Home: 3501 S Wadsworth Blvd Morrison CO 80465 Office: PO Box 1138 Denver CO 80201

HALEY, WILLIAM JOHN, former pub. co. exec.; b. Jersey, Eng., May 24, 1901; s. Frank and Marie (Sangan) H.; student Victoria Coll., Jersey; LL.D., U. Cambridge (Eng.), 1951, Dartmouth, 1957, London U. 1963, St. Andrews U., 1965; m. Edith Susie Gibhons, Nov. 2, 1921; children—Anne Claire (Mrs. J.N. Hunt), Donald, Jennifer, David. With Manchester (Eng.) Evening News, 1922-30, mng. editor, 1930; dir. Manchester Guardian & Evening News, Ltd., 1930, joint mng. dir., 1939-43; editor-in-chief BBC, 1943-44, dir.-gen., 1944-52; editor London Times, 1952-66; chmn. Times Newspapers, Ltd., 1967; editor-in-chief Ency. Britannica, Chgo., 1968-69. Decorated knight comdr. Order Sts. Michael and George; chevalier Legion of Honor (France); grand officer Order Orange Nassau (Netherlands). Hon. fellow Jesus Coll., U. Cambridge, 1956. Fellow Royal Soc. Lit. Address: Beau site Gorey Jersey British Isles

HALFAR, EDWIN, educator; b. Alexandria, La., Dec. 10, 1917; s. Vence and Louise (Retek) H.; B.Ed., So. Ill. U., 1939; M.A., U. Ia., 1941, Ph.D., 1947; m. Catherine Ruth Lauber, May 10, 1939; children—Wayne P., Allan C. Asst. mathematician Naval Ordnance Lab., Washington, 1944-45; instr. U. Ia., 1945-47; asst. prof. U. Neb., Lincoln, 1947-55, prof., 1964—, chmn. dept. math., 1964-71. Mem. Am. Math. Soc., Math. Assn. Am., Sigma Xi. Home: 3505 S 37th St Lincoln NB 68506

HALFOND, MURRAY MICHAEL, educator; b. N.Y.C., May 14, 1925; s. Harry and Erna (Abramowitz) H.; B.A. cum laude, Bklyn. Coll., 1948; M.A., Northwestern U., 1949, Ph.D., 1952; m. Jeanne Meltzer, Mar. 21, 1948; 1 son, Jay Aron Harry. Med. speech pathologist Duke U. Hosp., 1951-53; dir.. speech and hearing center Temple U., Phila., 1953-66, chmn. dept. speech, 1965—, prof. speech, 1965—. Cons., Soc. Crippled Children and Adults, Eastern State Sch. and Hosp. Served with AUS, 1943-46. Fellow Am. Speech and Hearing Assn.; mem. Am. Psychol. Assn., Speech Assn. Eastern States, Pa. Speech and Hearing Assn., Pa. Speech Assn. Author: Voice and Articulation Handbook, 1966. Home: 108 N Woodstock St Philadelphia PA 19103

HALFORD, RALPH STANLEY, educator; b. Vallejo, Cal., Apr. 21, 1914; s. John Jefferson and Kathleen (Loftus) H.; B.S., U. Cal., 1935, Ph.D., 1938; m. Marion Kee Glover, Mar. 3, 1939. Instr. chemistry U. Cal., 1938-40; NRC fellow Harvard, 1940-41, instr. chemistry, 1941-43, lectr., 1943-46; asso. prof. Columbia, 1946-51, prof. chemistry, 1952—, vice-provost projects and grants, 1959-67, dean grad. faculties, 1961-67, asst. to pres., 1967, v.p. spl. projects, 1968—; vis. com. chemistry dept. Brookhaven Nat. Lab., 1954-56. Staff OSRD, 1944; NRC adv. com. Office Ordnance Research, 1951-52; nat. selection com. on Fulbright awards to U.K., 1954-56. Trustee Associated Universities, Inc., 1959—. Guggenheim fellow, 1952-53. Fellow Am. Phys. Society; mem. Am. Chem. Soc., N.Y. Acad. Scis., Sigma Xi, Alpha Chi Sigma. Asso. editor Jour. Chem. Physics, 1950-52. Home: 445 Riverside Dr New York City NY 10027

HALFORD, ROBERT LAVELLE, architect; b. El Dorado, Ark., May 13, 1930; s. Robert Bradley and Algie Lee (Shedd) H.; student U. Miss., 1947-49, Fla. State U., 1951-52; B.Arch., U. Tex., 1955-59; m. Jean Elizabeth Hayes, Feb. 25, 1956; 1 dau., Lauren Elizabeth. Project architect Grayson Gill, 1961-65; partner Enslie O. Oblesby Architects, 1968; v.p. The Oglesby Group, Inc. Oglesby, Wiley, Halford, Dallas, 1968—. Mem. Nat. Council Archtl. Registration Bds. Mem. Friends of Dallas Pub. Library, Dallas Mus. Fine Arts, League Ednl. Advancement Dallas. Trustee Episcopal Housing Corp. Served with USNR, 1947-49, USAF, 1951-53. Mem. A.I.A. (commr. Dallas chpt. 1971), Dallas C. of C., Soc. Coll. and Univ. Planners, Council Ednl. Facility Planners. Episcopalian. Home: 9740 Audelia St Dallas TX 75238 Office: 710 N St Paul St Dallas TX 75201

HALGREN, S. ALFRED, food corp. exec.; b. Wahkon, Minn., Dec. 14, 1907; s. Charles Merrit and Margaret (Nunn) H.; A.B., U. Minn., 1930, LL.B., 1932, student Engring. Sch., 3 yrs., accounting extension div. U. Wis., Harvard Bus. Sch.; LL.D., Gonzaga U., 1963; m. Io Peterson, Apr. 8, 1933; children—Jill (Mrs. J. Daniel Cathers), Jack. Admitted to Minn. bar, 1932, Cal. bar, all Fed. Cts., 1952; began practice in Mora, Minn.; atty. Kanabec County (Minn.), 1938; mem. legal dept. Carnation Co., Milw., 1941-44, asst. sec., 1944-50, sec., 1950, v.p., 1954, dir. indsl. relations, 1959-67, sr. v.p., 1967—, mem. exec. and finance com., 1961, dir.; corporate sec. Albers Milling Co.; dir., dep. chmn. Fed. Res. Bank San Francisco. Pres. bd. Carnation Co. Found. Bd. dirs. Los Angeles Council Boy Scouts Am., Nat. 4-H Com., Met. Bd. YMCA. Mem. Cal. Mfrs. Assn. (dir.; v.p. 1960), Phi Alpha Delta, Sigma Phi Epsilon. Mason (past master). Home: 1894 Linda Flora Dr Los Angeles CA 90024 Office: 5045 Wilshire Blvd Los Angeles CA 90036*

HALKIN, SIMON, educator, author; b. Dovsk, Mohilev, Russia, 1899; s. Hillel and Hannah (Paritzky) H.; B.A., N.Y. U., 1926, M.A., 1928; D.H.L., Jewish Inst. Religion, 1948; m. Minnie Levine, Sept. 5, 1932; children—Zefira (Mrs. Amatiza Porat), Hillel. Instr. Hebrew and Hebrew lit. Hebrew Union Sch. For Tchrs., N.Y.C., 1924-32; tchr. Geulah High Sch., Tel Aviv, Israel, 1932-39; lectr. bible, Jewish sociology, modern Hebrew lit. Chgo. Coll. Jewish Studies, 1940-43; prof. Hebrew lit. Jewish Inst. Religion, N.Y.C., 1943-49; prof. Hebrew lit. Hebrew U., Jerusalem, Israel, 1949-68, prof. emeritus, 1969—; vis. prof. U. Cal. at Los Angeles, 1954-55, Jewish Theol. Sem., N.Y.C., 1965-66. Recipient Bialik prize for Lit., 1968. Mem. Acad. Hebrew Lang., Israel P.E.N. Club (pres.). Author: (novel) Yehiel Ha-Hagri, 1928; (essays) Arai Va-Keva, 1943; (novel) Ad Mashber, 1945; (poems) Al Hof Santa Barbara, 1928, Baruch Ben-Neria, 1934, Al Ha-Iy, 1945, Ma-avar Yabbok, 1965; Modern Hebrew Literature: Trends and Values, 1951; La Literature Hebraique Modern, 1957; Literatura Hebrea Moderna, 1968; Collected Literary Essays and Studies, 3 vols., 1970, numerous others; translated numerous books into Hebrew. Home: 5 Redak St Jerusalem Israel

HALL, ALAISTAIR CAMERON, investment banker; b. Edinburgh, Scotland, Jan. 10, 1903; s. William Thomas and Margaret (Cameron) H.; student George Watson's Coll., Edinburgh; m. Consuelo McMicking, June 20, 1930 (dec. 1945); children—Roderick, Ian, Alaistair, Consuelo; m. 2d, Juanita Sudduth, June 19, 1946. Came to U.S., 1953, naturalized, 1956. Mng. partner A. C. Hall & Co., also Hall, Picornell, Origas of Manila, P.I., 1934-53; with Sutro & Co., San Francisco, 1954—, sr. partner, 1959—; mem. N.Y. and the Pacific Coast stock exchanges, 1953—. Past pres. Manila Stock Exchange. Clubs: Cypress Point Golf (Pebble Beach, Cal.); Merchants Exchange, Pacific Union, Golf (San Francisco). Home: 945 Green St San Francisco CA 94133 Office: 460 Montgomery St San Francisco CA 94104*

HALL, ALBERT CARRUTHERS, engring. co. exec.; b. Port Arthur, Tex., June 27, 1914; s. Albert Bright and Eva (Carruthers) H.; B.S., Tex. A. and M. Coll., 1936; Sc.D., Mass. Inst. Tech., 1943; m. Barbara Johnson, July 6, 1941. Asst. elec. engring. Mass. Inst. Tech., 1937-39, instr., 1939-43, asst. prof., 1943- 46, asso. prof., dir. dynamic analysis and control lab., 1946-50; asso. dir research labs. Bendix Aviation Corp., 1950-52, tech. dir., 1953-54, gen. mgr., 1954-57; dir. engring. Denver div., also dir. research Martin Co., 1958-60, v.p. engring., 1960-61, v.p., gen. mgr. space systems div., Balt., 1962-63; dep. for space tech. Office of Dir. Def. Research and Engring., Washington, 1963-65; v.p. advanced tech. Martin Marietta Corp., 1965-67, former v.p. engring., from 1967; engaged in engring. Titan missile. Tech. adv. bd. Bur. Ordnance, Navy Dept., 1950, 57; mem. torpedo study panel com. undersea warfare Nat. Acad. Sci.-NRC, 1963; mem. sci. adv. com. Def. Intelligence Agy.; mem. task group on electronic warfare, mem. arms control bd. Def. Sci. Bd. Chmn. bd. Severn Sch., Severna Park, Md. Recipient certificate of merit Naval Ordnance Dept., 1946; Meritorious Civilian Service award Dept. Def., 1965. Fellow I.E.E.E., Am. Inst. Aeros. and Astronautics (asso.); mem. Sigma Xi, Eta Kappa Nu (Outstanding Young Elec. Engr. award 1947), Tau Beta Pi. Clubs: Cosmos; Annapolis Yacht. Home: Route 2 Box 245 Arnold MD 21012*

HALL, ALBERT LEANDER, Jr., lawyer; b. Chgo., June 17, 1926; s. Albert L. and Orpah (Starratt) H.; grad. Lake Forest Acad., 1944; B.S., U. Ill., 1949, M.S., 1950; J.D., Northwestern U., 1955; m. Catherine Ann Comstock, Sept. 27, 1947; children—Terry Lee, David M., Margaret Ruth, Diane Marie. Tchr. English, journalism Washington Park High Sch., Racine, Wis., 1950-52; admitted to Ill. bar, 1955; asso. mem. firm Hall, Meyer, Fisher, Holmberg, Snook & May, and predecessors, Waukegan, Ill., 1955-58, partner, 1958—. Served with USN, 1944-46. Mem. Lake County, Ill., Am. bar assns., Am. Judicature Soc., Waukegan-North Chicago C. of C. (pres. 1968-69), Delta Tau Delta. Club: City Waukegan (pres.). Home: 2048 Hickory St Waukegan IL 60085 Office: 25 N County St Waukegan IL 60085

HALL, ANDREW DOUGLASS, financial cons.; b. Flushing, N.Y., June 17, 1910; s. Emlen Trenchard and Louisa Frances (Field) H.; grad. Kent (Conn.) Sch., 1928; A.B., Princeton, 1932; m. LeMoyne Noyes, July 31, 1938; childrenAndrew D., Emlen F., Anne D., Linda L., Benjamin T. With Bonbright & Co., 1932-36, Morgan Stanley & Co., 1936-45; with Diamond Match Co., N.Y.C., 1946-59, asst. to pres., 1946-48, v.p., asst. treas., 1949-50, financial v.p., 1950-59, dir., 1952-59; partner Morgan Stanley & Co., 1959-62; v.p., dir. Stauffer Chem. Co., 1962-68; pres., dir. Internat. Knitlock Corp., N.Y.C., 1969-70; chmn. Maran Assos., Inc., 1970—; pres., dir. Homar Internat. Corp., N.Y.C.; dir. Dataram Corp. Trustee Worcester Found. Exptl. Biology. Home: David's Hill Rd Bedford Hills NY 10507 Office: 1133 Av of the Americas New York City NY 10036

HALL, ARNOLD ALEXANDER, aero. mfg. exec.; b. Liverpool, Eng., Apr. 23, 1915; grad. with honors, Clare Coll., Cambridge; married; 3 daus. Mem. staff Royal Aircraft Establishment, 1938-46, dir. Farnborough, 1951-55; Zaharoff prof. aviation U. London, head dept. aero. Imperial Coll. Sci. and Tech., 1946- 51; tech. dir. Hawker Siddeley Group, 1955-58, vice chmn., mng. dir., 1963-67, chmn., mng. dir., 1967—; mng. dir. Bristol Siddeley Engines, Ltd. (merger Bristol Aero-Engines and Armstrong Siddeley Motors 1959), 1958-62, vice chmn., 1963-66. Decorated knight, 1954; recipient Dutch A. G. von Baumhauer medal for contbn. to understanding problems of fatigue in aircraft structures, 1959; Gold medal Royal Aero. Soc., 1962. Fellow Royal Soc., Royal Aero. Soc. (pres. 1958-59, council 1947-66), Inst. Aero-Space Scis. U.K., Am. Inst. Aero. and Astronautics (hon.); mem. Locomotive and Allied Mfrs. Assn. (pres. 1968-69). Address: Hawker Siddeley Group Ltd 18 St James Sq London SW1 England*

HALL, BERNARD, univ. ofcl.; b. N.Y.C., May 7, 1925; B.A., Bklyn. Coll., 1948; Ph.D., U. Cal. at Berkeley, 1955; m. Evelyn Pimentil, Feb. 11, 1954. Teaching asst., then research asst. U. Cal. at Berkely, 1948-53, vis. grad. research economist, summer 1955; asst. prof. econs. Humboldt State Coll., 1953-57; asst. prof. bus. adminstrn. Fresno State Coll., 1958-60, vis. asso. prof., summer 1963; mem. faculty Kent (O.) State U., 1957-58, 60-, prof. econs., 1966-, asso. provost, 1969-. Served with AUS, 1943- 46. Address: Kent State U Kent, OH 44240*

HALL, BRINLEY MORGAN, orgn. exec.; b. Boston, Jan. 4, 1912; s. John Loomer and Dorothy Brinley (Morgan) H.; grad. St. Mark's Sch., 1930; B.A., Yale, 1934; student Corpus Christi Coll., Cambridge, Eng., 1934-35, Harvard Law Sch., 1935- 37; LL.B., Northeastern U., 1947; m. Elizabeth Jaques, June 10, 1939; childrenBrinley Morgan, Dorothy B., Denison M., Robert T. Investment banker Whiting Weeks & Stubbs, Inc. (now F.S. Moseley & Co.), Boston, 1937-42; admitted to Mass. bar, 1947, since practiced in Boston; with Choate, Hall & Stewart, 1947-62, partner, 1951-62, asst. atty. gen.

Commonwealth Mass., 1948-49; exec. dir Com. Central Bus. Dist., 1962-70; v.p., treas. Hubbard Real Estate Investments, 1970—; dir. Amstar Corp., N.Y.; trustee Provident Instn. for Savs., Boston, Treas., exec. com. Episcopal City Mission, Boston; dir. Ellis Meml. and Eldredge House, Boston. Served as maj. USAAF, 1942-46. Member Massachusetts, Boston bar assns. Home: 218 Hart St Beverly Farms MA 01915 Office: 125 High St Boston MA 02110

HALL, BRUCE WOOD, banker; b. Garden City, N.Y., 1912; grad. Yale, 1934. Chmn. bd. Hempstead Bank, (N.Y.). Home: Muttontown Rd Syosset NY 11791 Office: 40 Main St Hempstead NY 11550

HALL, CAMERON PARKER, clergyman; b. Pelham Manor, N.Y., Aug. 30, 1898; s. William Webster and Emily (Parker) H.; grad. Hotchkiss Sch., Lakeville, Conn., 1917; B.A., Williams Coll., Williamstown, Mass., 1921; grad. study, New College, Edinburgh, Scotland, 1921-22, Mansfield Coll., Oxford, Eng., 1922-23, Union Theol. Sem., N.Y.C., 1923-25; D.D., Yale, Chgo. Theol. Sem., 1963, Williams Coll., 1964; m. Margaret Conant, May 18, 1926; 1 son, Alan Conant. Student asst. 1st Presbyn. Ch., N.Y.C., 1923-24; asst. pastor Broome St. Tabernacle, N.Y.C., 1924-26; ordained ministry Presbyn. Ch., 1925; pastor Christ Ch., N.Y.C., 1926-35, Univ. Ch., Madison, Wis., 1935-39; dir. dept. social edn. and action Bd. of Christian Edn., Presbyn. Ch., U.S.A., 1939-46; dir. social edn. Internat. Council of Rel. Edn., 1943-46; exec. sec., dept. ch. and econ. life Fed. Council Schs. Christ in Am., 1946-50; exec. dir. dept. ch. and econ. life Nat. Council Chs. Christ U.S.A., 1951-66, dir. tech. and human values project, 1966-68, dir. lay project, 1968—. Cons., World Council of Churches Assembly, Evanston, Ill., 1954; chmn. youth section World's Sunday School Assn. Conv., Oslo, Norway, 1936; leader World Conf. of Christian Youth, Amsterdam, Holland, 1939. Mem. Sigma Phi, Delta Sigma Rho. Author: Economic Life: A Christian Responsibility, 1947; The Christian at His Daily Work, 1951; Decison Making in Business, 1963; Technology and People, 1969. Editor: On The Job Ethics, 1964; Human Values and Technology, 1967. Home: 117 Kensington Rd Garden City NY 11530 Office: 475 Riverside Dr New York City NY 10027

HALL, CARL WILLIAM, coll. dean, agrl. engr.; b. Tiffin, O., Nov. 16, 1924; s. Lester and Irene (Routzahn) H.; B.S., B.Agrl. Engring. summa cum laude, Ohio State U., 1948; M.M.E., U. Del., 1950; Ph.D., Mich. State U., 1952; m. Mildred Evelyn Wagner, Sept. 5, 1949; 1 dau., Claudia Elizabeth. Instr. U. Del., 1948-50, asst. prof., 1950- 51; asst. prof. Mich. State U., 1951-53, asso. prof., 1953-55, prof., 1955-70, research adviser, 1957-64, chmn. dept. agrl. engring., 1964-70; dean Coll. Engring., prof. mech. engring. Wash. State Coll., Pullman, 1970—; Research cons. U. P.R., 1957, 63; cons. U. Nacional de Colombia, 1960; cons. dairy engring., India, 1961; cons. food engring., China, 1961; Mission to Ecuador, 1966; U. Nigeria, 1967; cons. UNDP/SF project 80, higher edn. Latin Am., 1964-70; cons. Council Grad. Schs., Washington, 1970; with ACA, Inc., cons. engring., 1956-70, pres., 1962-70. Chmn. Nat. Dairy Engring. Conf., 1953-66; mem. U.S. sci. exchange delegation to USSR, 1958. Sec., Tefft Found. for Bible Study, 1960-70. Served with AUS, 1943-46; ETO. Registered profl. engr., Mich., Ohio, Wash. Recipient outstanding tchr. award Alpha Zeta, 1957, 58; Distinguished Faculty award Mich. State U., 1963; Centennial Achievement award Ohio State U., 1970; Wisdom award Honor, 1970. Mem. Am. Soc. M.E. (chmn. central Mich. 1959-60), Am. Soc. Agrl. Engrs. (chmn. electric power and processing div. 1960, div. dir. 1962-64, 67-69; Engr. of Year award Mich. chpt. 1964), Am. Soc. Engring. Edn., A.A.A.S., Am. Inst. Biol. Scis. Nat., Wash. socs. profl. engrs., Internat. Congress Agrl. Engrs. (v.p. 1965-), 99th Inf. Div. Assn., Inst. Food Tech., Sigma Xi, Alpha Zeta, Tau Beta Pi, Phi Kappa Phi, Gamma Sigma Delta, Phi Lambda Tau. Author: Drying Farm Crops, 1957; Agricultural Engineering Index, 1961. Co-author: Drying of Milk and Milk Products, 1966. Co-editor; Agricultural Engineers Handbook, 1960; Processing Equipment for Agricultural Products, 1963, Spanish edit., 1968; Milk Pasteurization, 1968. Editorial bd. Jour. Agr. Engr. Research, Avi Pub. Co., McGraw-Hill Book Co. Contbr. yearbooks, encys., handbooks. Address: Coll Engring Washington State U Pullman WA 99163

HALL, CHARLES FRANCIS, clergyman; b. Dorchester, New Brunswick, Can., April 20, 1908; s. Rev. Edwin A. and Mary Matilda (Blacker-Hamlin) H.; student Palmerton (Pa.) High Sch.; B.S., LL.D., Springfield Coll.; M.Ed., Yale Divinity Sch.; B.D., Episcopal Theol. Sch., 1936; D.D., Tufts U., 1949; L.H.D. (hon.), University of New Hampshire, 1969; m. Constance Lilian Hamilton, June 25, 1938; children—David Hamlin, Tod Latham, Ronald Knight. Deacon 1936, ordained priest, 1937; curate All Saints Ch., Worcester, Mass., 1936-38; rector Grace Ch., Medford, Mass., 1938-45; rector St. Paul's Ch., Concord, N.H., 1945-48; bishop of New Hampshire, 1948. Pres. bd. trustees, Holderness Sch., Plymouth, N.H., St. Mary's-in-the-Mountains, Littleton, N.H.; mem. bd. trustees St. Paul's Sch., Concord, N.H. Mason (33). Home: 122 School St Concord NH 03301

HALL, CHARLES GERSHOM, c. of c. exec.; b. Harwich, Mass., July 7, 1931; s. Gershom D. and Mary E. (Dyke) H.; student Defiance Coll., 1949-51, Syracuse Inst. Organized Mgmt; 1961-65; m. Elaine M. Guerin, Aug. 10, 1953; children—Davis, Dennis, Catherine. Exec. v.p. Raritan Valley C. of C., 1959-63; dir. govtl. affairs Greater Boston C. of C., 1963-65; pres. New Haven C. of C., 1965-69; pres. Greater Newark C. of C., 1969—; mem. urban and regional affairs C. of C. of U.S.; dir. New Haven Savs. & Loan Assn. Mem. Conn. Legislative Reform Commn., 1968; mem. campaign steering commn. for election Lt. Francis W. Sargeant, 1966-68. Bd. dirs. Newark Scholarship Found., Urban Coalition. Mem. Am., New Eng., N.J. assns. c. of c. execs., Civic Assn. Met. N.Y. Rotarian. Home: 255 Boulevard St Mountain Lakes NJ 07046 Office: 1180 Raymond Blvd Newark NJ 07102

HALL, CHARLES W., banker; b. Herkimer, N.Y., July 11, 1899; s. George C. and Margaret C. Hall; grad. Rutgers U. Grad. Sch. Banking; m. Esther E. Adams, Aug. 1, 1925; children—Jane Ann (Mrs. Charles Whitney), Mary Elizabeth (Mrs. Craig Gambee). Chmn. bd. Oneida Nat. Bank & Trust Co. Central N.Y., Munson Mill Machinery Co. Treas. Utica Rescue Mission, Med.-Surg. Care of Utica; chmn. Hosp. Rev. and Planning Council Central N.Y.; pres. Oneida County Indsl. Devel. Treas., trustee Utica YMCA, St. Lukes Meml. Hosp., Utica; trustee Rochester-Colgate Div. Sch., Mohawk Valley Tech. Sch. Mason (Shriner). Baptist. Clubs: Jahnundasis Golf; Ft. Schuyler. Home: 110 Proctor Blvd Utica NY 13501 Office: 268 Genesee St Utica NY 13502

HALL, CHARLES WAYNE, univ. dean; b. Lennoxville, Que., Can., Mar. 1, 1910; s. Charles Loring and Sadie Jane (McMurray) H.; B.A., Bishop's U., 1931, M.A., 1932; m. Grace Elizabeth Hall, July 25, 1936; children—Denis, Mary (Mrs. D. Wells), Jane (Mrs. R. Hilbers), Christopher. Tchr., Sherbrooke High Sch., 1932-34; prin. Coaticook High Sch., 1934-36, St. Francis Coll., 1936-37; insp. Que. Dept. Edn., 1937-40; provincial supr. English, 1940-49; prof. edn. McGill U., 1949-63, dir. Inst. Edn., 1963- 65, dean Faculty Edn., 1965—. Adviser tchr. edn. Fed. Govt. Nigeria, 1960-61; sec. UNESCO Commn. on U. Lagos, 1961; mem. Protestant Central Bd. Examiners, 1955—; mem. Protestant Com. Superior Council Edn., 1965- -. Recipient Order Scholastic Merit award Govt. Que. Fellow Canadian Coll. Tchrs.; mem. Provincial Assn. Protestant Tchrs. (past pres.), Canadian Assn. Profs. Edn. (past pres.), Que. Assn. Tchrs. English (past pres.). Author: Growth Through the Language Arts, rev. edit., 1960; (with others) Four Viewpoints on Teacher Education, 1965. Contbr. profl. jours. Home: 83 St Andrew's Rd Baie d'Urfe Quebec Canada Office: McGill Univ Montreal Quebec Canada

HALL, CHARLES WILLIAM, medical educator; b. Gage, Okla., Feb. 8, 1922; s. Cecil A. and Helen (Greene) H.; A.B., Kan. U., 1950, M.A. in Comparative Anatomy, 1952, M.D., 1956; m. Shirley Anne Thompson, Oct. 20, 1962; children by previous marriage—Daniel C., Kendall W., Gregory A., Patrick C., Conan L. Rotating intern Kan. U. Med. Center, 1956-57, resident surgery, 1957- 62; fellow cardiovascular surgery Baylor U. Sch. Medicine, 1962-64; project dir., artificial heart program Baylor U. Coll. Medicine, 1964- 68, asst. prof. surgery, also asst. prof. physiology, 1964-68; cons. S.W. Research Inst., San Antonio, 1966-68, mgr. artificial organs research dept. bioengring., 1968-70, dir. dept. bioengring., 1970—; clin. asst. prof. surgery U. Tex. Med. Sch. at San Antonio, 1969—. Served with USAAF, 1942-46. Recipient 1st place prize essay contest Houston Surg. Soc., 1963, 64; 1st place prize essay contest S.W. Surg. Soc., 1964; prof. honoris causa Cath. U. Cordoba (Argentina), 1965. Diplomate Am. Bd. Surgery. Fellow Am. Coll. Cardiology, Am. Coll. Chest Physicians; mem. Am. Soc. Artificial Organs, Am. Heart Assn., Assn. Advancement Med. Instrumentation, A.A.A.S., A.M.A., Biomed. Engring. Soc., Tex. Heart Assn., Internat. Cardiovascular Soc., Soc. Surg. Rosario (Argentine), Sigma Xi, Phi Sigma. Home: Welfare TX 78036 Office: PO Drawer 28510 San Antonio TX 78284

HALL, CLARENCE W., editor, author; b. Anna Maria, Fla., Dec. 16, 1902; s. Wilbur Lincoln and Mary Abbie (Bean) H.; student Ga. Sch. Tech., 1925-27, Northwestern U., 1930-31; Litt.D., Neb. Wesleyan U., 1943; LL.D., U. Tampa, 1949; m. Blanche M. Bouterse, July 30, 1925; children—Blanche Barbara, Beverly Carolyn. Reporter, feature writer various newspapers, Fla. and Ga., 1921- 26; asst. editor So. edit. War Cry, 1927-29, asso. editor Central edit., 1930-34; editor-in-chief Salvation Army publs., 1935-39; mng. editor Christian Adv., 1940-42; founder, editor The Link and The Chaplain, wartime publs. interdenominational Service Men's Christian League, 1942- 45; asso. editor Christian Herald, N.Y.C., 1946-47, mng. editor, 1948- 51, exec. editor, 1951-56; sr. editor Reader's Digest, 1956—; editorial dir. Lifetime Living mag.; accredited war corr., participating in mil. and naval engagements, PTO, World War II; spl. lectr. journalism coll. and summer writers assemblies. Mem. President's Com. Employment Physically Handicapped. Mem. Asso. Ch. Press, Overseas Press Am., Am. Soc. Mag. Editors, Mag. Publs. Assn. (chmn. gen. operating com. 1954-56). Republican. Presbyn. Clubs: Dutch Treat (N.Y.C.); Nat. Press (Washington). Author: Out of the Depths: the Life of Henry F. Milans, 1930; Samuel Logan Brengle, Portrait of a Prophet, 1933; Protestant Panorama (with Desider Holisher), 1951; Adventurers for God, 1959. Contbr. secular and religious publs. Home: Deer Run Shore Sherman CT 06784 Office: 200 Park Av New York City NY 10017

HALL, CLEMENT HOWARD, lawyer, former univ. regent; b. Dewitt, Ark., Oct. 3, 1910; s. Merritt Francis and Grace Beatrice (Straight) H.; LL.B., U. Kan., 1933; m. Melba M. Olson, Nov. 28, 1935; children—Roger, Bruce, David. Admitted to Kan. bar, 1933, since practiced in Coffeyville; city atty., Coffeyville, 1935-36: county atty., Montgomery County, 1937-40. Chmn. bd. First Fed. Savs. & Loan Assn., Coffeyville, 1970—. Mem. Kan. Bd. Regents, 1954-68; past mem. Kansas Higher Edn. Facilities Act Commn. Mem. Am. Bar Assn., Phi Alpha Delta. Home: 1208 W 6th St Coffeyville KS 67337 Office: 806 Walnut St Coffeyville KS 67337

HALL, DALE LLOYD, steel foundry exec.; b. Asbury, Mo., Mar. 6, 1912; s. Leslie L. and Pearl (De Vaney) H.; A.B. in Chemistry and Physics, Kan. State Coll., Pittsburg, 1936; m. Annie Marie Lindsay, May 17, 1936; childrenLowell, Gayle. With Okla. Steel Castings Co., Tulsa, 1936-, asst. works mgr., 1946-49, works mgr., 1949-70, gen. mgr., 1970—. Trustee, Foundry Educational Foundation, 1968-. Mem. Am. Foundrymen's Soc. (bd. dirs. 1961-64, pres. 1966-67), Steel Founders Soc. Am. (chmn. tech. and operating com. 1959-62; Tech. and Operating gold medal 1961), Am. Soc. Metals. Home: Rt 2 Box 900 Collinsville OK 74021 Office: 2100 N Peoria St Tulsa OK 74101

HALL, DAVE, mayor; b. Maimisburg, O., July 13, 1906; s. Frank S. and Lillie (Thirkield) H.; ed. pub. schs.; m. Anna Rue Hess, Oct. 19, 1935; children—Sam, Mike, Tony. Pres. Troy Pearl Laundry, 1937, Hall's Laundry, 1940; now pres. Hall Enterprises, real estate holdings, Dayton, O.; city commr. Dayton, 1962-65, mayor, 1966—. Club: Daytonagonis (pres. Dayton 1946). Address: 104 E 3d St Dayton OH

HALL, DAVID, writer, musical adviser; b. New Rochelle, N.Y., Dec. 16, 1916; s. Fairfax and Eleanor (Remy) H.; grad. Philips Exeter Acad., 1935; B.A., Yale, 1939; m. Bernice Dobkin, June 8, 1940; childrenMarion, Jonathan, Peter, Susannah. Internat. editor The Record Book, 1940-48; with advt. dept. Columbia Records, 1940-42, music script div. RCA, 1942-48; mus. dir. classics div. Mercury Records Corp., 1948-56; dir. music center Am.- Scandinavian Found., 1950-57; mus. adviser, N.Y.C., 1957—. Vis. Fulbright scholar U. Copenhagen (Denmark), 1956-57; music editor HiFi-Stereo Rev. mag., 1957-62, contbg. editor, 1962—; pres. Composers Recs., Inc., 1963-67; head Rodgers and Hammerstein Archives Recorded Sound, New York Library, 1967—; free lance lectr., mag. writer. Mem. subcom. Music Sch., Yale, 1963-. Decorated knight Order of Lion (Finland). Mem. Nat. Acad. Rec. Arts and Scis. (gov., trustee 1965-67), Nat. Music Council (chmn. recs. service com.). Author: Records, 1950. Home: 155 Catalpa Rd Wilton, CT 06897. Office: 111 Amsterdam Av New York City NY 10023*

HALL, DAVID GOODSELL, III, medical educator; b. Fayetteville, Ark., June 11, 1927; s. David Goodsell and Pauline (Overholt) H.; M.D., U. Va., 1953; m. Dorothy Anne Hoback, Aug. 25, 1951; children—David Goodsell IV, Susan Elizabeth, Lori Dickenson. Intern U. Va. Sch. Medicine, 1954, resident obstetrics and gynecology, 1954-58; mem. faculty U. Mo. Sch. Medicine, 1958—, prof. obstetrics and gynecology, chmn. dept., 1962—; med. dir. Mid-Mo. Planned Parenthood. Served with M.C. USNR, 1944-46. Diplomate Am. Bd. Obstetrics and Gynecology. Fellow A.C.S., Am. Coll. Obstetricians and Gynecologists, Am. Assn. Obstetricians and Gynecologists; mem. Central Assn. Obstetricians and Gynecologists, Kansas City, St. Louis gynecol. socs., A.A.A.S., Mo. Med. Assn., Boone County Med. Soc., Aircraft Owners and Pilots Assn., So. Med. Soc., Assn. Mil. Surgeons, Sigma Xi, Phi Chi, Sigma Alpha Epsilon. Club: Cent-Travel. Home: 1031 Bourn Av Columbia MO 65201

HALL, DON EMERSON, clergyman; b. North Tonawanda, N.Y., July 21, 1906; s. Emerson D. and Donna Lou (Mitchell) H.; A.B., U. Mich., 1929, M.A., 1930; B.D., San Francisco Theol. Sem., 1944; D.D., Occidental Coll., 1957; LL.D., Grove City Coll., 1969; m. Mildred Lilyquist, Sept. 10, 1937; 1 son, David. With investment firms, Los Angeles, San Francisco, 1930-43; ordained to ministry Presbyn. Ch., 1944; pastor Menlo Park (Cal.) Presbyn. Ch., 1943-58; dir. United Presbyn. Found., N.Y.C., 1958—; mem. Presbytery San Francisco. Home: 750 Kappock St Riverdale NY 10463 Office: 475 Riverside Dr New York City NY 10027

HALL, DONALD, poet, educator; b. New Haven, Sept. 20, 1928; s. Donald Andrew and Lucy (Wells) H.; grad. Philips Exeter Acad., 1947; B.A., Harvard 1951; B. Litt. (Henry fellow), Oxford U., 1953; postgrad. Stanford, 1953-54; m. Kirby Thompson, Sept. 13, 1952 (div. Feb. 1969); children—Andrew, Philippa. Creative writing fellow Stanford, 1953; jr. fellow in Soc. Fellows Harvard, 1954-57; asst. prof. U. Mich., 1957-61, asso. prof., 1961-66, prof., 1966—; poetry editor Paris Review, 1953-61; mem. poetry bd. Wesleyan U. Press, 1958-64; cons. Harper & Row, 1964—; judge Bollingen Prize for Poetry, 1958, 59, Lamont Poetry Competition, 1967-69, Nat. Book awards, 1968. Recipient Lloyd McKim Garrison prize for poetry Harvard, 1951, John Osborne Sergeant prize for Latin translation Harvard, 1951, Newdigate prize for poetry Oxford U., 1952, Lamont Poetry Selection Acad. Am. Poets, 1955, Edna St. Vincent Millay Meml. award Poetry Soc. Am., 1955, Longview Found. award, 1960, Guggenheim fellow, 1963. Mem. Modern Lang. Assn., Am. Assn. U. Profs., Mich Poetry Soc. Author: (poems) Exiles and Marriages, 1955, The Dark Houses, 1958, A Roof of Tiger Lilies, 1963, The Alligator Bride, 1969, The Yellow Room, 1971, American Poetry, 1969, Marianne Moore: The Cage and the Animal, 1970, The Pleasures of Poetry, 1971; (juvenile) Andrew the Lion Farmer, 1959; String Too Short to be Saved, 1961; Henry Moore, 1966; (with David Finn) As the Eye Moves, 1970. Editor: Harvard Adv. Anthology, 1950; (with L. Simpson and R. Pack) The New Poets of England and America, 1957; (with R. Pack) New Poets of England and America, Second Selection, 1962; A Poetry Sampler, 1962; Contemporary American Poetry, 1962; (with W. Taylor) Poetry in English, 1963, 2d edit., 1970; (with S. Spender) A Concise Ency. of English and American Poets and Poetry, 1963; Faber Book of Modern Verse, 1966; The Modern Stylists, 1968; A Choice of Whitman's Verse, 1968; Man and Boy, 1968. Home: 1715 S University Av Ann Arbor MI 48104

HALL, DONALD JOHN, poet; b. Oxford, Eng., 1903; ed. Shrewsbury, Corpus Christi colls., Cambridge (Eng.) U.; m. Isabel Compton; 1 son, 1 dau. Solicitor supreme ct., 1927—; poet, 1932—; writer Fgn. Office Eng., 1939-47. Clubs: Boodles, P.E.N. Author: Enchanted Land, 1932; Romanian Furrow, 1933; No Retreat, 1936; Perilous Sanctuary, 1937; This Other Eden, 1938; The Phoenix Flower: An Epic of 1939-45, 1953; The Seeming Truth, 1954; Eagle Argent, 1956; The Crowd is Silent, 1961. Address: Blorenge House Ashampstead Berkshire England*

HALL, DONALD JOYCE, mfr. greeting cards; b. Kansas City, Mo., July 9, 1928; s. Joyce Clyde and Elizabeth Ann (Dilday) H.; A.B., Dartmouth, 1950; m. Adele Coryell, Nov. 28, 1953; children—Donald Joyce, Margaret Elizabeth, David Earl. With Hallmark Cards, Inc., Kansas City, Mo., 1953—, adminstrv. v.p., 1958-66, pres., chief exec. officer, 1966—, also dir.; dir. Commerce Trust Co., Business Men's Assurance Co., William E. Coutts Co., Ltd. Mem. Civic Council Greater Kansas City. Mem. bd. Am. Royal Assn., Friends of Art, Eisenhower Found., Kansas City Assn. Trusts and Founds., Midwest Research Inst.; trustee Science Pioneers. Served to 1st lt. AUS, 1950-53. Home: 6320 Aberdeen Rd Shawnee Mission KS 66208 Office: Hallmark Cards Inc 25th and McGee Sts Kansas City MO 64141

HALL, DURWARD GORHAM, congressman, physician; b. Cassville, Mo., Sept. 14, 1910; s. Thomas Clemens and Omah Ellen (Neill) H.; A.B., Drury Coll., 1930; M.D., Rush Med. Sch., Chgo., 1934; m. Mary Elizabeth Turner, Sept. 6, 1931; 1 dau., Linda Lea (Mrs. Monty Ross Ellison). Intern St. Elizabeth's Hosp., Washington, 1934-35, Army Inst. Pathology, Walter Reed Gen. Hosp., 1946; surg. resident Roosevelt Hosp., N.Y.C., 1947; with Smith-Glynn-Calloway Clinic, Springfield, Mo., 1936-41; gen. practice of surgery, 1947—; mem. 87th to 92d congresses, 7th Dist. Mo., mem. Armed Services Com., spl. joint com. reorgn. congress. Founder, dir. Springfield Builders, Inc., 1949. Founder 11th regional Red Cross Blood Center, 1947; mem. Ozarks Area council Boy Scouts Am.; founder Springfield Citizens Adv. Council, 1957. Bd. dirs. Springfield Bapt. Hosp., Springfield YMCA; trustee Drury Coll. Served to col., M.C., AUS, 1941-47. Decorated Legion of Honor, Commendation ribbon with 2 palms; recipient Springfieldian award, 1958; Silver Beaver, Silver Antelope awards Boy Scouts Am. Diplomate Am. Bd. Surgery. Fellow A.C.S. (founder S.W. Mo. chpt.), S.W. Surg. Congress (a founder); mem. A.M.A. (ho. dels. 1951-66), Mo. Med. Assn., Springfield (past pres.), U.S. chambers commerce, Am. Humanics Found. (sec., exec. bd.), Conservation Fedn. Mo. Republican. Baptist (past chmn. Christian edn. com., finance bd.). Rotarian (past pres. Springfield). Clubs: Capitol Hill, Army-Navy (Washington); Hickory Hills Country (Springfield). Home: 2442 S Fermont St Springfield MO 65804 Office: Rayburn House Office Bldg Washington DC 20515

HALL, EBEN CLARKE, mfg. and leasing co. exec.; b. Buffalo, Aug. 28, 1916; s. Rodney Dennis and Louise (Clarke) H.; A.B., Princeton, 1939; m. Jane Elizabeth Terhune, Sept. 8, 1945; childrenSusan Medbury, Sarah Elizabeth. With steamship dept. W.R. Grace & Co., Bogota, Colombia, 1939-42; asst. passenger traffic mgr. Grace Line, Inc., N.Y.C., 1946-56; asst. export mgr. materials handling div. Yale & Towne Mfg. Co., N.Y.C., 1957-59; mgr. export sales ACF Industries, Inc., N.Y.C., 1959-63, mgr. internat. licensing, 1963-67, sec., 1967-. Bd. mgrs. Silver Hill Found., New Canaan, Conn. Served to maj., Transp. Corps. AUS, 1942-46. Mem. Am. Soc. Corporate Secs. Republican. Episcopalian. Clubs: Riverside (Conn.) Yacht; Sakonnet Golf (Little Compton, R.I.); Ivy (Princeton, N.J.). Home: 17 Druid Lane Riverside CT 06878 Office: 750 3d Av New York City NY 10017

HALL, EDWARD TUCK, educator; b. Manchester, Mass., Aug. 1, 1918; s. John Loomer and Dorothy Brinley (Morgan) H.; grad. St. Mark's Sch., Southborough, Massachusetts, 1937; A.B., Yale University, 1941, M.A., 1947, M.A. (honorary), 1960; Litt.D. (honorary), Susquehanna University, 1964. Instr. English, Phillips (Andover) Acad., 1941-42; asst. instr. English, asst. chmn. bd. admissions Yale, 1946-47; asst. headmaster, tchr. English St. Mark's Sch., 1947-52; headmaster Hill Sch., 1952-68, St. Mark's School, Southboro, Mass., 1968—. Dir. Brantwood Camp, Peterborough, N.H., 1939- 42, 1946-50, trustee; trustee Harvey Sch. Served as 1st lt. inf., intelligence corps U.S. Army, 1942-46. Mem. New Eng. Assn. Tchrs. English (pres. 1950-51), Aurelian Soc., English-Speaking Union, Skull and Bones, Zeta Psi. Episcopalian. Clubs: Century Association, Elizabethan, Tavern. Address: St Mark's Sch Southboro MA 01772

HALL, EDWARD TWITCHELL, educator, anthropologist; b. Webster Groves, Mo., May 16, 1914; s. Edward Twichell and Jessie Gilroy (Warneke) H.; student Pomona Coll., 1929-30; A.B., U. Denver, 1936; M.A., U. Ariz., 1938; Ph.D., Columbia, 1942; m. Mildred Ellis Reed, Dec. 16, 1946; children—Ellen McCoy, Eric Reed. Asst. staff archeologist Lab. Anthropology, Santa Fe, 1937; staff dendroconologist Peabody Museum Awatovi expdn., 1937-39; dir. Columbia Governador expdn., 1941; field work in Micronesia, 1946, Southwestern U.S., 1933-43, Europe, 1952—; econ. and cultural survey Micronesia, 1946; asso. prof. anthropology, chmn. dept. U.

Denver, 1946-48; faculty Bennington (Vt.) Coll., 1948-51; dir. Point IV tng. program Fgn. Service Inst., State Dept., 1950-55; dir. research and dep. dir. Washington office, Human Relations Area Files, 1955-57; pres. Overseas Tng. and Research, Inc., 1955-60; dir. communications research project Washington Sch. Psychiatry, 1959-63, mem. exec. com., council fellows; prof. anthropology Ill. Inst. Tech., 1963-67; prof. anthropology Northwestern Univ., 1967—. Cons. intercultural relations internat. bus. and govt., 1955—; Leatherbee lectr. Harvard Bus. Sch., 1962; dir. Ansul Corp., Marinette, Wis.; mem. Northeast Ill. Planning Commn.; small grants com. Nat. Inst. Mental Health; bldg. research adv. bd. NRC. Served to capt., C.E., AUS, 1942-46; ETO, PTO. Fellow Am. Anthrop. Assn.; mem. Soc. Applied Anthropology (sec.), Am. Ethnol. Assn., Soc. Am. Archaeology, Tree Ring Soc. Club: Cosmos (Washington). Author: Earl Stockaded Settlements in Governador, N.M., 1942; The Silent La Guage, 1959; The Hidden Dimension, 1966; also articles profl. jours. Home: 1017 Grove St Evanston IL 60201 Office: Northwestern U Evanston IL 60201

HALL, ELEANOR ABELL, nursing educator; b. Naugatuck, Conn., June 14, 1914; d. Edward C. and Anna (Abell) Hall; diploma Presbyn. Hosp. Sch. Nursing, N.Y.C., 1936; B.S., Columbia, 1939, M.A., 1948. Head nurse Presbyn. Hosp., San Juan, P.R., 1936-37; instr. nursing Columbia Coll. Phys. and Surg., 1939-41; asst. dir. nursing Woman's Med. Coll. Hosp. Sch. Nursing, Phila., 1941- 43, Johns Hopkins Hosp. Sch. Nursing, Balt., 1943-47; asst. prof. nursing edn. Yale Sch. Nursing, 1948-53, asst. dean, asso. prof. nursing edn., 1953-57; prof., chmn. dept. nursing U. Rochester, 1957-. Mem. bd. Nurses Ednl. Funds, Inc. Mem. Am. Nurses Assn., Nat. League Nursing, Kappa Delta Pi. Home: 113 Village Lane Rochester NY 14610

HALL, ELISHA ANDERSON, Jr., savs. and loan exec.; b. Lucknow, S.C., Sept. 5, 1927; s. Elisha Anderson and Lois Lynette (Blackwell) H.; B.S., U. S.C., 1954, M.S., 1955; m. Elizabeth Ann Rogers, Nov. 1, 1950; children—Amy Elizabeth, Sara Rogers, Myra Ann. Asst. dean Coll. Bus. Adminstrn., U. S.C., 1953-56; comptroller, treas. S.C. State Hosp., 1956-62; trust officer 1st Nat. Bank S.C., Columbia, 1962-64; pres., dir. Security Fed. Savs. and Loan Assn., Columbia, 1964—; adj. prof. Coll. Bus. Adminstrn., U. S.C., 1970—. Served with AUS, 1946-47, 50-51. Mem. Am. Legion. Methodist (lay speaker 1963—). Mason, Lion (pres. 1967-68). Club: Palmetto (Columbia). Home: 1522 Greenhill Rd Columbia SC 29206 Office: PO Box 11629 Columbia SC 29211

HALL, ERNEST E., retired govt. ofcl.; b. Dayton, Nov. 17, 1901; s. Ozni Hall and Julia (Schlotterbeck) H.; m. Florence M. Byrnes, Oct. 29, 1948; children—Kendra Elizabeth, Kevin Ernest. With Ozni Hall and Co., Dayton, 1917-22; jr. acct. George P. Jackson and Co., 1922-25; asst. sec., treas. Hyde Motor Sales Co., 1925-29; asst. to sec. USDA, Washington, 1929-33; asst. chief div. control U.S. Bur. Pub. Rds., 1933-42; exec. officer Fed. Works Agy., 1942-47; v.p. C.F. Lytle Co., heavy constrn., Sioux City, Ia., 1947-52; asst. adminstr. for operations control services FCDA, Battle Creek, Mich., 1952-55; chief industry asst. br. Office Indsl. Devel. AEC, 1956-59, chief reports and statistics br. Div. Reactor Devel., 1959-64, chief reports staff Office Asst. Gen. Mgr. Reactors, Germantown, Md., 1965-70; retired, 1970. Dir. Am. Cheviot Sheep Soc.; treas. Md. Sheep Breeders Assn. Chmn. Washington Grove Planning Commn., 1957-60, town treas., 1961—. Home: Keymar MD

HALL, ERNEST LEROY, banker; b. Portland, Ore., May 3, 1909; s. Ernest Eugene and Luella (Osgood) H.; B.S., U. Ore., 1930; M.B.A., Harvard, 1932; m. Kathryn Granger Fuller, Dec. 31, 1932; children—Martin L., Michael F. With No. Trust Co., Chgo., 1932—, exec. v.p., 1966—. Pres. Automobile Competition Com. for U.S. FIA, 1969. Mem. Phi Gamma Delta. Home: 2405 Telegraph Rd Deerfield IL 60015 Office: 50 S LaSalle St Chicago IL 60603

HALL, EUGENE RAYMOND, educator, biologist; b. Imes, Kan., May 11, 1902; s. Wilber Downs and Susan Effie (Donovan) H.; A.B., U. Kan., 1924; AM., U. Cal. 1925, Ph.D., 1928; m. Mary Frances Harkey, Aug. 9, 1924; children—William Joel, Hubert Handel, Benjamin Downs. Field biologist U.S. Bur. Biol. Survey, 1924-26; acting in charge Bur. Research, Cal. Dept. Fish and Game, 1927; curator of mammals U. of Cal. Mus. of Vertebrate Zoology, 1927-1944; asst. prof. vertebrate zoology U. Cal., 1930-37, asso. prof., 1937-44; prof. zoology U. Kan., 1944—, chmn. dept. zoology, 1944-61, dir. Mus. Natural History, 1944-67, research asso., 1967—, Summerfield Distinguished prof., 1959- -; dir. Kan. Biol. Survey, 1947-67, sr. biologist, 1967—; state zoologist, 1959-67. Adv. bd. on nat. parks, historic sites, bldgs. and monuments Dept. Interior, 1954-60, cons., 1964—. Guggenheim fellow, 1943; Fulbright research prof., Turkey, 1968. Fellow A.A.A.S. (v.p. and chmn. section zool. scis. 1957), Cal., Wash. acads. sci.; mem. Am. Soc. Mammalogy (hon. mem.; pres. 1944-46), Am. Wildlife Soc., Am. Soc. Systematic Zoology, Defenders of Wildlife (v.p. 1967-71), Cooper Ornith. Club, Am. Ornith. Union, Kan. Acad. Sci. (council 1969—), Am. Assn. Museums, Biol. Soc. Washington, Sigma Xi. (pres. Kan. chpt. 1959-61). Author: The Mammals of North America, 1959; others. Home: 1637 W 9th St Lawrence KS 66044

HALL, FLOYD D., airline co. exec.; b. Lamar, Colo., Apr. 4, 1916; s. Weldon H. and Hattie (Brown) H.; B.S., U. Colo., 1938; grad. student U. Cal. at Los Angeles, U. Mich.; m. Mary Feild, Nov. 5, 1939; children—Nancy Jane (Mrs. George Thomas Morton III), Barbara Jean (Mrs. Harold Stanley Olafson). First officer Trans World Airlines, Inc., 1940-42, capt., 1946, then line check pilot, Los Angeles, supr. flying, Chgo., asst. mgr. flying, Detroit, 1957-58, gen. mgr. U.S. operations, 1958-59, v.p. flight operations, 1959, v.p., gen. transp. mgr., 1959-61, sr. v.p., system gen. mgr., dir., 1961-63; pres., chief exec. officer, dir. Eastern Air Lines, 1963-68, chmn. bd., chief exec. officer, dir., 1968—; dir. S.E. Banking Corp., Miami, N.Y. Telephone Co., Cluett, Peabody & Co., Inc. Bd. dirs. Recordings for Blind, Inc., N.Y.C.; bus. adv. com. Religion in Am. Life; N.Y.C. gen. chmn. campaign Am. Cancer Soc., 1966, now mem. bd. dirs. Served to lt. col. USAAF, 1942-46. Recipient Brotherhood award Nat. Conf. Christians and Jews, 1970. Mem. Nat. Aero. Assn., Fla. Council 100, N.Y.C. C. of C., Internat. Air Transp. Assn. (pres. 1972), Air Transp. Assn. Am. (dir.), N.Y. Urban Coalition, Newcomen Soc. N.Am. Club: Economic (N.Y.C.). Home: 35 Sutton Pl New York City NY 10022 Office: 10 Rockefeller Plaza New York City NY 10020*

HALL, FRANK WILLIAM, advt. exec.; b. N.Y.C., July 2, 1920; s. Frank Lownes and Evelyn (Batchelor) H.; B.A., Dartmouth, 1941; m. Suzanne Louise Riley, Oct. 3, 1943; children—Frank William, Suzanne Louise (Mrs. Chafin), Mary Evelyn. Asst. dir. athletic publicity Dartmouth, 1941-42; with Albert Frank-Guenther Law, Inc., N.Y.C., 1946—, v.p., 1953-70, chmn. exec. com., 1966—, pres., 1970—, also dir. Served with AUS, 1942-45; ETO. Decorated Bronze Star. Mem. N.Y. Financial Advertisers Marketing Assn. (pres. 1965), Bank Marketing Assn. Clubs: Cherry Valley (Garden City); Bankers (N.Y.C.). Home: 121 Meadbrook Rd Garden City NY 11530 Office: 61 Broadway New York City NY 10006

HALL, FREDERICK LEONARD, writer, lectr., conservationist; b. Seneca, Mo., Oct. 30, 1899; s. Frederick Bagby and Corinne (Steele) H.; student Washington U., St. Louis, 1920, LL.D., 1970; student U. Wis., 1921-22; LL.D., Westminster Coll., Fulton, Mo., 1950, Washington U., St. Louis, 1970; m. Virginia Watson, May 28, 1942; 1 son, Frederick Leonard. With Nat. Oats Co., 1926-30, R. R. Donnelley & Sons Co., 1930-45; columnist St. Louis Post Dispatch, 1943-59, St. Louis Globe Democrat, 1959—; conservation lectr. Nat. Audubon Soc., others, 1944—. Chmn. adv. commn. Ozark Nat. Scenic Riverways, 1965-69. Served with USNR, 1917-19. Named Master Conservationist in Mo., 1948; recipient Thomas Stokes award Nieman Fellows of Harvard, 1959; named State Conservationist by Gov. Mo., 1966, appointed to Govs. Acad. Mo. Squires, 1967. Mem. Wilderness Soc., Nat. Audubon Soc., Nat. Parks Assn., (trustee), Am. Forestry Assn., Defenders of Wildlife (dir.), Humane Soc. U.S. (dir.), Mo. Conservation Fedn., Sierra Club, Sigma Delta Chi. Author: Possum Trot Farm, 1948; Country Year, 1958: Stars Upstream, 1962; Ozark Wildflowers, 1969; also numerous articles in nat. mags. Wildlife films: An Ozark Anthology, 1960; Audubon's Wilderness, 1962; Forever Yours, 1966; Birds Over Florida, 1967; Country Year, 1971. Address: Possum Trot Farm Caledonia MO 63631

HALL, FREDERICK WILSON, state justice; b. Pitts., Feb. 22, 1908; s. Peter B. and Rachel (Crispin) H.; Litt.B., Rutgers U., 1928, LL.D., 1960; LL.B. cum laude, Harvard, 1931; m. Jane R. Armstrong, July 18, 1936; 1 son, Peter W. Admitted to N.J. bar, 1932; asso. Arthur T. Vanderbilt, Newark, 1931-41; mem. Wharton & Hall, and successors, Somerville, N.J., 1941-53; judge Superior Ct. of N.J., 1952-58, appellate div. Superior Ct., 1958-59; asso. justice Supreme Ct. of N.J., 1959—. Mem. State Univ. Bicentennial Commn., 1966. Mem. bd. edn., Bound Brook, N.J., 1934-49, pres., 1946-49. Past bd. mgrs. N.J. State Village for Epileptics. Mem. Am., N.J., Somerset County (past pres.) bar assns., Am. Judicature Soc., Am. Law Inst., Inst. Jud. Adminstrn., Phi Beta Kappa, Chi Psi. Democrat. Presbyn. Club: Harvard (N.Y.C.). Home: 261 Metape N Bound Brook NJ 08805 Office: 26 W High St Somerville NJ 08876

HALL, GEORGE EDWARD, former univ. pres.; b. Lindsay, Ont., Can., Oct. 10, 1907; s. George W. and Etta (Brandon) H.; B.S.A., Ont. Agrl. Coll., 1929; M.S.A., U. Toronto, 1931, M.D., 1935, Ph.D., 1936, LL.D., 1959; D.Sc., Laval U., 1951, U. Guelph, 1967; LL.D., U. Windsor, 1954, Madras U., 1957, Queen's Univ., 1958, U. London, 1963; m. Lola Ruth McDonald, June 26, 1937; children—Frances, Burt Ann, Sharon, George Edward II, Elizabeth. Prof. med. research Banting Inst., Toronto, Ont., Can., 1939; dir. med. research Royal Canadian Air Force, 1939-45; dean faculty medicine U. Western Ont., London, Ont., 1945-47, pres., vice chancellor, 1947- 1967; chmn. bd., dir. No. Life Assurance Co. of Can.; dir. IBM (Can). Mem. Ont. Research Council, 1947-53; Nat. Cancer Inst., 1947—, pres., 1950-51; chmn. Canadian Forces Med. Council, 1962-66; mem. Nat. Productivity Council, 1962-64, Ont. Council Health, 1966—. Decorated knight comdr. Order St. Gregory the Gt.; Air Force Cross (Gt. Britain): Legion of Merit (U.S.). Fellow Royal Soc. Can.; mem. Assn. Univs. and Colls. Can. (pres. 1956-57), Assn. Commonwealth Univs. (chmn. 1963- 65). Mem. Ch. of Eng. Clubs: London Hunt and Country, London, Canadian (London). Home: 48 Westchester Dr London Ontario Canada

HALL, GEORGE ELISHA, educator; b. New Haven, July 14, 1917; s. George Elisha and Harriet (Blakeslee) H.; grad. Loomis Sch., 1934; B.S. with highest honors, Yale, 1938, Ph.D., 1942; m. M. Sage Adams, Feb. 5, 1942; children—Elisabeth Adams, John Adams, Stephen Blakeslee, Harriet Blakeslee, Sarah Whitney, Mary Hayden. Research chemist Am. Cyanamid Co., 1941; instr. Yale Summer Sch., 1946; mem. faculty Mt. Holyoke Coll., 1946—, prof. chemistry, 1958—, chmn. dept., 1966—; vis. prof. Cal. Inst. Tech., 1953-54, vis. asso., 1969-70; vis. lectr. U. Bristol (Eng.), 1961-62; mem. grad. faculty U. Mass., 1960—. Served to capt., chem. warfare service, AUS, 1942-45. Decorated Purple Heart; Faculty fellow Fund Advancement Edn., 1953-54; Sci. faculty fellow NSF, 1961-62. Mem. A.A.A.S., Am. Chem. Soc. (chmn. Conn. Valley sect. 1956), Chem. Soc. (London), New Eng. Assn. Chemistry Tchrs., Am. Assn. U. Profs., Phi Beta Kappa, Sigma Xi. Club: Graduate (New Haven). Home: 82 Woodbridge St South Hadley MA 01075

HALL, GEORGE EVERETT, corp. exec., lawyer; b. Charleston, W.Va., Nov. 19; 1925; s. Harry W. and Margaret (Ford) H.; A.B., W.Va. U., 1948; LL.B., Harvard, 1951; m. Helen Babcock. Oct. 6, 1951; children—George Everett. Helen-Elizabeth B., Anne Copen. With firm Sullivan & Cromwell, 1951-58; with Campbell Soup Co., 1958-61; sr. v.p., gen. counsel, sec., dir., mem. exec. com. SCM Corp., N.Y.C. Served with AUS, 1944- 46. Mem. Phi Beta Kappa. Home: 11 St Claire Av Old Greenwich CT 06870 Office: 299 Park New York City NY 10017

HALL, GEORGE HAMILTON, newspaper editor; b. St. Louis, Mar. 29, 1909; s. Louis Tesson and Isabel (von Phul) H.; A.B., Washington U., 1932: B.S., Columbia. 1933; m. Mary Howard Fentress. Feb. 13, 1941; children—Mary Fentress, Louise Tesson. With Midwestern newspapers, 1933-42; reporter St. Louis Post-Dispatch. 1942-45, Washington corr., 1945-59, asst. editor editorial page, 1959-71, editor, 1971—. Roman Catholic. Clubs: University, Noonday (St. Louis), Home: 48 Crestwood Dr Clayton MO 63105 Office: St Louis Post-Dispatch St Louis MO 63101

HALL, GEORGE NAYLOR, architect; b. Pitts., Dec. 22, 1906; s. Harry and Anne E. (Jones) H.; B.A., Cornell U., 1930; postgrad. study and travel, Europe, 1931-32; m. Marion A. Pripps, Oct. 5, 1935; children—Harriet L. (Mrs. Alfred Bloch), George Naylor, Anne Elizabeth (Mrs. Michael Quinn). Architect Kastendieck & Hall, 1935-39, Beine, Hall & Curran, Inc., 1940-66; pres. Beine, Hall, Curran & Kane, Inc., 1966-68, Hall/Kane Assos., Inc., Gary, Ind., 1968—. Mem. Ind. Bd. Registration for Architects, 1945-49; profl. adviser dept. city and regional planning Cornell U. Coll. Arch., Ithaca, N.Y.; dir. Bank of Ind. Pres. Lake Michigan Region Planning Council, 1964-65, Greater Gary Com. 100, 1967; dir. Lake County Community Devel. Council, 1965, Landscapes Ltd. Recipient award Downtown Gary Council, 1960. Fellow A.I.A. (nat. urban design com. 1964-66, award No. Ind. chpt. 1962); mem. Delta Tau Delta. Rotarian (dir. Gary). Prin. works include: Sch. Bus., Ind. U., N.W. Campus, Gary, 1964; Lake County Convalescent Home, Grown Point, Ind., 1959; Gary Main Library, 1966; Extended Care Unit, Meth. Hosp., Gary, 1968; Tech. Center, U.S. Steel, Gary, 1957; others. Home: 1717 W 64th Pl Merrillville IN 46410 Office: 607 Broadway Gary IN 46402

HALL, GEORGE W., lawyer; b. Montreal, Que., Can., Apr. 15, 1909; s. George and Louise Maude (Able) H.; B.A., Bishop's U. (Can.), 1930, M.A., 1931; B.C.L., McGill U. (Can.), 1937; m. Mary Margaret Howe, June 17, 1943; children—Katherine, Alexander, Douglas. Admitted to Que. bar, 1937; now partner firm O'Brien, Home, Hall, Saunders, O'Brien & Smyth, Montreal; lectr. Montreal Ins. Inst., 1946-59. Bd. dirs. United Ch. Montreal Homes for Elderly People. Served with Canadian Army, 1940-45. Mem. Canadian Bar Assn., Canadian Tax Found., Kappa Alpha. Clubs: University; Montreal; Montreal West Curling. Home: 130 Ballantyne Av N Montreal West Quebec Canada Office: 2100 Place du Canada Montreal 101 Quebec Canada*

HALL, HAL OGDEN, govt. ofcl.; b. Springfield, Ill., Nov. 20, 1907; s. Harry Ogden and Pearl Emma (Porter) H.; B.E., So. Ill. U., 1930; M.B.A., Northwestern U., 1934; Ed.D., N.Y.U., 1943; m. Hazel Ann Bouhard, May 28, 1933; children—Hal Stephen, John Michael. Supt. schs., Greenview, Ill., 1930-36; asst. prof., then asso. prof. So. Ill. U., 1936-45; supt. schs., Belleville, Ill., also pres. jr. coll., 1945-57; supt. schs., Villa Park, Ill., 1957-61; civil def. adviser Ill. Dept. Edn., 1961; ednl. adminstrn. adviser AID, State Dept., Indonesia, 1962-65, S.Vietnam, 1965-71, Vietnam Bur., Washington, 1971—; prof. grad. courses in sch. adminstrn. Washington and Ill. univs., 1954-55; lectr. Far East Tech. Center, 1967. Lobbyist (with Ill. Gen. Assembly) for financial assistance for jr. colls., 1948-57. Recipient letters of commendation AID, 1967; Culture and Edn. medal 1st class Minister Edn., 1969. Mem. N.E.A., Am. Assn. Sch. Adminstrs., Ill. Edn. Assn., Fgn. Service Assn., Alumni Assn. U. Ill. Contbr. articles profl. jours. Home: 1200 N Nash Arlington VA 22209 Office: VN/ND/ID/ED Room 606D Rosslyn Plaza AID State Dept Washington DC 20523

HALL, HARRY BENJAMIN, educator, physician; b. Morris, Minn., July 14, 1911; s. Fred W. and Blanche (Wing) H.; B.S., U. Minn., 1935, M.D., 1936; M.S. in Orthopedic Surgery, 1942; m. Betty Jane Smith, Feb. 14, 1942; children—John, Lawrence, Barbara Jean, Elizabeth Jane. Intern Rochester (N.Y.) Gen. Hosp., 1935-36; resident surgery U. Minn. Hosp., 1936-39, resident orthopedic surgery, 1939-42; mem. faculty U. Minn. Sch. Medicine, 1942- -, clin. prof. orthopedic surgery, 1956—, mem. univ. bd. regents, 1968- 69; asso. chief staff Gillette State Hosp., St. Paul, 1958—; mem. staff Project Hope, Saigon, 1962: chief staff Fairview Hosp., Mpls., 1958-59, Fairview Southdale Hosp., Edina, Minn., 1965-67. Chmn. Doctors for Republican Gov. Minn., 1966. Mem. A.M.A. (chmn. spl. exhibit fractures 1963—), Minn. Med. Assn. (1st v.p. 1966), Mpls. Acad. Medicine (pres. 1955-56), Hennepin County Med. Soc. (pres. 1964-65). Home: 4902 Lakeview Dr Edina MN 55424 Office: Southdale Med Bldg Edina MN 55435

HALL, HARRY R., assn. exec.; b. Preston, Md., May 5, 1908; B.S., Temple U., 1931, postgrad., 1937-38; certificate completion Southeastern Inst. for Comml. Orgn. Execs., U. N.C., 1948, Nat. Inst. for Comml. and Trade Orgn. Execs., Northwestern U., 1950; postgrad. Mich. State U., 1963. Program dir. Univ. House, U. Pa., 1933-36; dir. adult edn. and recreation program spl. activities Phila. Bd. Pub. Edn., 1936-39; with Phila. Mut. Life Ins. Co., 1939-41; adminstr. services to armed forces, A.R.C., 1941-46; gen. mgr. Daytona Beach (Fla.) C. of C., 1946-49; exec. v.p. Dayton (O.) Area C. of C., 1949-57; exec. v.p. Mpls. Area C. of C., 1957-60; pres. Mich. C. of C., Lansing, 1960—. Chmn. operating council Inst. Orgn. Mgmt., Mich. State U., 1958; mem. Mich. export com. U.S. Dept. Commerce, 1960-61; chmn. bus. and industry participation Gov. Mich. Anti-Litter Com.; chmn. Mich. Health Facilities Planning Council 1965-66; exec. com. Mich. Human Resources Council; mem. Mich. Gov.'s Commn. Crime, Delinquency and Criminal Adminstrns.; pres. Greater Lansing Urban League, 1967-69; mem. adv. com. for Mich. Sch. Finance Study, 1968; mem. community and regional resource devel. group com. U.S. C. of C., vice chmn. adv. panel on crime prevention and control; mem. exec. com. Mich. Manpower Commn. Chmn. Delta Twp. Republican Finance Com., Lansing, 1962. Bd. regents Inst. Orgn. Mgmt., 1957-60, 62—, chmn. faculty com., 1959; chmn. nat. bd. regents Orgn. Mgmt. Insts., 1967-68; trustee Hillsdale Coll. Mem. U.S. C. of C. (policy com.), Am. C. of C. Execs. (bd. dirs. 1951-58, pres. 1956-57, chmn. standards com. 1960-61, chmn. certification panel), Mich. C. of C. Execs. Presbyn. Clubs: Detroit Economic, Detroit; Lansing City, Lansing Country. Office: Mich State C of C 501 S Capitol Av Lansing MI 48933

HALL, HARVEY, govt. ofcl., physicist; b. Butte, Mont., Aug. 18, 1904; s. Horace Mark and Helen L. (Kirkendall) H.; M.A., U. Cal. at Berkeley, 1930, Ph.D., 1931; A.B., Occidental Coll., 1927; student Cal. Inst. Tech., 1927-28; m. Mary Emily Allen, Sept. 17, 1934; children—William Harvey, John Howland, Mary Suzanne. Instr. Columbia, 1931-34; lectr. N.Y.U., 1934-36; instr., then asst. prof. Coll. City N.Y., 1936-49; asso. prof. U. So. Cal., 1949-51; dir. operational research div. Office Naval Research, Washington, 1951-57; prof., head physics dept. Fla. State U., 1957-62; with U. Cal. Radiation Lab., 1960, NASA, Washington, 1961—. Served from lt. comdr. to comdr., USNR, 1942-46. Fellow Am. Phys. Soc.; sr. mem. I.E.E.E.; mem. Phi Beta Kappa. Club: Cosmos (Washington). Author papers in field. Home: 7207 Park Terrace Dr Alexandria VA 22307 Office: NASA Washington DC 20546

HALL, HOWARD, corp. exec.; b. Onslow, Ia., Dec. 31, 1895; s. Harry Douglas and Margaret (Lamey) H.; m. Margaret Douglas, June 12, 1924. Pres. Iowa Mfg. Co., Ia. Steel & Iron Works; dir. Ia. Nat. Liability Ins. Co., Mchts. Nat. Bank, Ia. Electric Light & Power Co., Square D Co.; chmn. City Nat. Bank of Cedar Rapids, Ia. Founder Hallmar, also founder Margaret and Howard Hall Radiation Center. Clubs: Tavern, Chicago Yacht (Chicago); Com. of 100, Surf (Miami Beach, Fla.). Home: 2160 Linden Dr S E Cedar Rapids IA 52403 Office: Iowa Mfg. Co Cedar Rapids IA 52402

HALL, HOWARD PRATT, lawyer; b. Burlingame, Kan., July 8, 1903; s. Ebert Watson and Artie Lulu (Pratt) H.; A.B., U. Cal. at Los Angeles, 1924; LL.B., U. So. Cal., 1927; m. Jessie Lane, Mar. 27, 1929; children—Barbara Hall (Mrs. Donald Hugh), Howard Lane. Admitted to Cal. bar, 1927; asso. Neil S. McCarthy, 1927-40; West Coast counsel Hughes Tool Co., 1941-48; gen. counsel Hughes Aircraft Co., Culver City, Cal., 1948—, asst. sec., 1948-57, sec., 1957—, v.p., 1957—, also dir. Mem. Cal., Los Angeles bar assns., Phi Delta Phi, Phi Delta Theta. Home: 4627 Perham Rd Corona del Mar CA 92625 Office: Hughes Aircraft Co Florence Av at Teale St Culver City CA 90230*

HALL, J. FRANK, oral surgeon; b. Quaker City, O., Apr. 1, 1899; s. Lewis Walton and Lucretia Margaret (Lowery) H.; student Muskingum Coll., New Concord, O., 1927-28; D.D.S., U. Pitts., 1934, B.S., 1935; Carnegie fellow in pathology, U. Rochester Med. Center, 1935-36; postgrad. in gen. anesthesia, U. Pitts., 1938, in oral surgery, Northwestern U., 1940, oral diagnosis and pathol., Ohio State U., 1946; m. Roberta Cain, Nov. 21, 1927. Dental intern U. Pitts. Med. Center, 1934-35; pvt. practice oral surgery (part time), 1947—; bus. mgr. Jour. Dental Research, 1936-58; instr. oral surgery and anesthesia Med. Coll. Va., 1936-38, asst. prof., 1938-42, asso. prof., 1942; prof. oral surgery Ind. U. Sch. Dentistry, 1942—. Diplomate Am. Bd. Oral Surgery. Mem. Am. Assn. Dental Schs. (chmn. oral surg. sect. 1943- 49), Am. Dental Assn. (organizer council hosp. dental service), Am., Ind., Indpls. Dist. (editor jour. 1955-60) dental socs., Am. Acad. Oral Pathology, Am., Ind., Great Lakes socs. oral surgeons, Am., Ind. socs. anesthesiologists, Internat. Assn. Dental Research, Fauchard Acad., Fedn. Dentaire Internat., Omicron Kappa Epsilon, Psi Omega. Republican. Methodist. Clubs: Columbia, Atheneum (Indpls.). Home: 5750 Carrollton Indianapolis IN 46220 Office: 1122 Shelby St Indianapolis IN 46203

HALL, JACK H., physician, educator; b. Kokomo, Ind., July 28, 1929; s. Sidney G. and Gladys (Huett) H.; A.B., Ind. U., 1951, M.D., 1956; m. Donna Meade, Nov. 26, 1952; children—Pamela, Paula, Jack. Intern Meth. Hosp., Indpls., 1956-57, chief med. resident Grad.

Med. Center, 1959-60, dir. med. edn., 1960—, also dir. cardiovascular lab. and outpatient dept.; fellow in medicine New Eng. Deaconess Hosp., Boston, 1957-58; teaching fellow medicine Harvard Med. Sch., 1958-59; resident cardiology West Roxbury (Mass.) VA Hosp., 1958-59; now in practice medicine, specializing in internal medicine, Indpls.; asso. in medicine Med. Sch. Ind. U., 1960-; mem. staff Robert Long Hosp. Ind. U., Marion County Gen. Hosp., Hendrix County Hosp. Cons. internal medicine (Danville, Ind.); mem. bd. Nat. Intern Matching Program, Nat. Health Forum, Pub. Health Conf.; mem. President's Commn. Health Manpower; v.p. Indpls. Met. Health Council. Bd. dirs., mem. exec. com. Marion County Home Care Agy. Served with Ind. N.G. Diplomate Am. Bd. Internal Medicine. Mem. A.M.A., A.C.P., Am. Coll. Chest Physicians, Am. Fedn. Clin. Research, Am., Ind. (com. chmn.), Marion County (pres. elect) heart assns., Am. Diabetic Soc., N.Y. Acad. Sci., Ind., Marion County med. socs., Am. Hosp. Assn., Assn. Hosp. Med. Edn. (vice pres.), Assn. Ind. Dirs. Med. Edn. (pres.). Contbr. articles med. jours. Home: 5960 Braewick Dr Indianapolis, IN 46226 Office: 1604 N Capitol St Indianapolis IN 46207*

HALL, JACK VERNON, educator; B.A., Central Wash. Coll., 1944; M.A., Colo. State Coll., 1947, Ed. D., 1951. Prof. elementary edn., head elementary grad. program devel. Ore. State U. Address: Dept Elementary Edn Corvallis OR 97330

HALL, JAMES BYRON, univ. provost, author; b. Midland, O., July 21, 1918; s. Harry and Florence (Moon) H.; student Miami U., Oxford, O., 1938-39, U. Hawaii, 1938-40; B.A., State U. Ia., 1947, M.A., 1948, Ph.D., 1953; postgrad. Kenyon Coll., 1949; m. Elizabeth Cushman, Feb. 14, 1946; children—Elinor, Prudence, Kathryn, Millicent, James M.M. Writer-in-residence Miami U., 1948-49, U. N.C., Greensville, 1954, U. B.C., 1955, U. Colo., 1963—; instr. Cornell U., 1952-53; asst. prof. English, U. Ore., 1954-57, asso. prof., 1958-60, prof., 1960-65; prof. English, U. Cal. at Irvine, 1965-68, dir. The Writing Center, 1965-68; provost Coll. V, U. Cal. at Santa Cruz, 1968—. Cons. editor Doubleday & Co., 1960-65; founder Summer Acad. Contemporary Arts, 1959; cultural specialist U.S. Dept. State, 1964. Served with AUS, 1941-46. Recipient Octave Thanet prize, 1950, Ore. Poetry prize, 1958, Emily Clark Balch Fiction prize, 1967, Chapelbrook award, 1967, Inst. Creative Arts award Rockefeller grantee, 1955. Mem. Am. Assn. U. Profs., Am. Civil Liberties Union, Philol. Assn. Pacific Coast, P.E.N. Democrat. Methodist. Author: Not by the Door, 1954; The Short Story, 1955; 15X3, 1957; Racers to the Sun, 1960; Us He Devours, 1964; Realm of Fiction, 1965; Modern Culture and Arts, 1967; Mayo Sergeant, 1967. Contbr. stories, poetry to anthologies. Home: 1100 High St Santa Cruz CA 95060

HALL, JAMES CURTIS, univ. dean; b. Galax, Va., Feb. 12, 1926; s. Alonzo A. and Clara (Crissman) H.; student U. N.C., 1943-44; A.B., Duke, 1947; M.S., Va. Poly. Inst., 1952; Ed.D., Columbia, 1956; m. Mary Anne Jones, Mar. 13, 1954; children—Michael Crissman, Suzanne King. Tchr. Galax High Sch., 1947-50; instr. Va. Poly. Inst., 1951-54, Montclair State Coll., 1955; research asst. Columbia, 1955-56; asst. prof. Va. Poly. Inst., 1956-57; prof. Auburn U., 1957-62; dean Sch. of Bus., Va. Commonwealth U., 1962—; cons. to So. sch. systems; nat. lectr. econ. edn.; pres. Investment Enterprises, Inc. Served with USNR, 1943-46. Mem. Va. Council Econ. Edn. (pres.), Nat. (pres. 1970-71), So. (pres. 1967) bus. edn. assns., Adminstrv. Mgmt. Soc. (pres. Richmond chpt. 1969-70), Phi Beta Kappa, Phi Kappa Phi. Author: (with E.M. Robinson) College Business Organization and Management, 1964; (with others) General Business for Everyday Living, 4th edit., 1972. Home: 10408 Saxony Rd Richmond VA 23235

HALL, JAMES FAY, Jr., mfg. co. exec., lawyer; b. Greenwood, Miss., Aug. 30, 1916; s. James Fay and Lois (Wilson) H.; A.B., U. Miss., 1936; LL.B., Georgetown U., 1945; m. Catherine Keller, May 17, 1941; childrenMarianne Lois, Geraldine Catherine. Admitted to D.C. bar, 1945, Pa. bar, 1958; atty. legal staff Tax Ct. U.S., 1945-48; pvt. practice, Washington, 1948-57; mem. legal staff Rohm and Haas Co., Phila., 1957—, gen. counsel, 1962—, dir., 1963- . Mem. Am., Phila. bar assns. Home: 926 Remington Rd Wynnewood PA 19096 Office: Independence Mall W Philadelphia PA 19105

HALL, JAMES PARKER, financial cons.; b. Chgo., Feb. 26, 1906; s. James Parker and Evelyn H. (Movius) H.; Ph.B., U. Chgo., 1927; M.B.A., Harvard, 1929; m. Frances Ferris, June 8, 1931; children—James Parker, Ferris Minor, Bronson Rumsey. With J. and W. Seligman Co., 1929-33, A. Iselin & Co., 1933-35, Clark Dodge & Co., 1935-46; treas. U. Chgo., 1946-69; dir. Peoples Gas Co., Chgo., 1963-70, Nat. Gas Pipeline Co. Am., 1963-67, Foote, Cone & Belding Communications, Inc., Tchrs. Ins. & Annuity Assn., 1963-70, Am. Steamship Co., Boland & Cornelius Inc., Reiss Steamship Co., Chgo. Title & Trust Co., First Nat. Bank, Highland Park, Ill., 1957-69, Marine Transport Lines, Inc., 1958-70, Marine Nav. Co. Inc., 1958-70, Interstate United Corp., Halsey Stuart & Co., Inc., Thomas Industries, Inc., Common Fund for Nonprofit Orgns., Chgo. Dock & Canal Co., 1953-60. Trustee Elizabeth McCormick Meml. Fund, 1951-61, Chgo. United Charities, La Rabida Childrens Hosp. & Research Center, U. Chgo. Cancer Research Found., Ill. Childrens Home & Aid Soc., 1948-69, Ravinia Festival Assn., 1958-68, Diocesan Found., 1953-58; treas. Bapt. Theol. Union, 1946-69. Mem. bd. edn., Manhasset, N.Y., 1944-46, Highland Park, Ill., 1952-54. Mem. Investment Analyst Soc., Chgo. (pres. 1952-53, dir.), Central Assn. Coll. and U. Bus. Officers (pres. 1957-58), Fgn. Bondholders Protective Council (dir.), Inst. Chartered Financial Analysts, Alpha Delta Phi. Clubs: Exmoor Country (Highland Park); Harvard (N.Y.C.); University, Quadrangle, Mid Day, Executives, Economic, Commercial, Commonwealth, Wayfarers (Chgo.). Home: 2369 Maple Lane Highland Park IL 60035 Office: 111 W Washington St Chicago IL 60602*

HALL, JAMES STANLEY, jazz guitarist, composer; b. Buffalo, Dec. 4, 1930; s. Harold S. and Louella (Cowles) H.; Mus.B., Cleve. Inst. Music, 1955; m. Jane Susan Yuckman, Sept. 9, 1965; 1 dau., Debra Jean. Joined Chico Hamilton, 1955; mem. Jimmy Giuffre Trio, 1957; tour U.S. and Europe with Jazz at Philharmonic, 1958, 59; tour Europe and S.A. with Ella Fitzerald, 1959, 60; featured by Sonny Rollins, 1961-62; formed quartet with Art Farmer, 1962-64; leader own trio, 1962—; performed at White House, 1969; motion picture appearance in Jazz on a Summer's Day, 1958; on Ralph Gleason's TV Show, 1962-63; on BBC, 1964; tour Europe, 1967, 69, Japan, 1970; recording artist for Pacific Jazz, United Artists, Atlantic, Verve, RCA, SABA, Milestone. Recipient award Downbeat Critics Poll, 1963-65, Downbeat Readers Poll, 1965-66; award Jazz mag. poll best performer, 1965-66; Playboy mag. All-Star poll for guitar, 1968, 70. Mem. Broadcast Music, Inc., Nat. Assn. Recording Arts and Scis. Home: 49 W 12th St New York City NY 10011

HALL, JANE HAMILTON, (Mrs. Davis B. Hall), physicist; b. Denver, June 23, 1915;. Jesse E. and Isabelle C. (Carr) Hamilton; student U. Denver, 1932-35; B.S., U. Chgo., 1937, M.S., 1938, Ph.D., 1942; m. David B. Hall, Dec. 30, 1939; childrenMalcolm H., Linda C. Instr. physics U. Denver, 1941-42; with metall. lab. U. Chgo., 1942-44; sr. supr. E. I. DuPont, Hanford, Wash., 1944-45; with Los Alamos (N.M.) Sci. Lab. 1945-55, asst. dir., 1955-7O, cons., 1970—. Mem. gen. adv. com. AEC Washington, 1966-, adv. com. on nuclear materials safeguards, 1967-. Bd. dirs. Santa Fe Opera Assn., 1968-, Internat. Folk Art Found., Santa Fe, 1968—, Espanola Hosp., Espanola, N.M., 1967—. Recipient AEC citation, 1970. Fellow Am. Phys. Soc. Democrat. Home: 400 Circle Dr Santa Fe, NM 87501 Office: PO box 1663 Los Alamos NM 87544

HALL, JEROME, legal educator; b. Chgo., Feb. 4, 1901; s. Herbert and Sarah (Rush) H.; Ph.B., U. Chgo., 1922, J.D., 1923; Jur.Sc.D., Columbia, 1935; S.J.D., Harvard, 1935; LL.D., U. N.D., 1958; m. Marianne Cowan, July 2, 1941; 1 dau., Heather Adele. Admitted to Ill. bar, 1923; with firm Kixmiller & Baar, 1923-26; practice alone, 1926-29; lectr. Ind. U. Extension, Gary, 1924-29; prof. law U. N.D., 1929-32; asst. state's atty. Cook County, Ill., summer 1931; Spl. fellow Columbia Law Sch., 1932-34; Benjamin research fellow Harvard Law Sch., 1934-35; prof. criminal law and criminology La. State U., 1935-39; prof. law Ind. U., 1939-57, distinguished service prof. law, 1957-70; prof. law U. Cal., Hastings Coll. Law, 1970—; Hillman lectr. Coll. Pacific, 1947; Mitchell lectr. U. Buffalo, 1958; Fulbright lectr. U.K., 1954-55, U. Freiburg, Germany, summer 1961; Ford Found. lectr. Mexico and S. Am., 1960; Edward Douglass White lectr. La. State U., 1962; Murray lectr. U. Ia., 1963. U.S. specialist State Dept. program, Far East and India, summers 1954, 68. Recipient Lieber award for distinguished teaching, 1956. Mem. China Acad., Am. Bar Assn., Am. Fgn. Law Assn., Am. Polit. Sci. Assn., Internat. Acad. Comparative Law, Soc. Pub. Tchrs. Law, Am. Soc. Polit. and Legal Philosophy (pres. 1967-69), Am. Soc. Legal History (dir.), Internat. Assn. Legal and Social Philosophy (pres. Am. sect. 1966-68), Latin-Am. Assn. Sociology (hon. pres. 1960). Author: Readings in Jurisprudence, 1938; General Principles of Criminal Law, 2d edit., 1960; Cases and Readings on Criminal Law and Procedure, 2d edit., 1965; Living Law of Democratic Society, 1949; Theft, Law and Society, 2d edit., 1952; Studies in Jurisprudence and Criminal Theory, 1958; Comparative Law and Social Theory, 1963. Editor: 20th Century Legal Philsophy Series, 7 vols. Author articles in field. Home: 198 McAllister St San Francisco CA 94102

HALL, JOHN ALLEN, internat. agy. ofcl.; b. Benton Harbor, Mich., Sept. 22, 1914; s. Maurice John and Dora (Ferry) H.; B.S., Northwestern U., 1936; A.M., Harvard, 1940, Ph.D., 1941; m. Alice Greenidge, June 24, 1939; children—John Allen, Sheila Greenidge. Instr. govt. U. Rochester, 1941-43; adviser U.S. delegation to UN, Dept. State, Washington, 1946, N.Y.C., 1947; chief Office Spl. Projects, AEC, Washington, 1948-52, dir. Office Internat. Affairs, 1952-55, dir. div. internat. affairs, 1955-58, asst. gen. mgr. internat. activities, 1958- 61; dep. dir. gen. Internat. Atomic Energy Agy., 1961-64; asst. gen. mgr. U.S. AEC, Washington, 1964-67; dep. dir. gen. IAEA, Vienna, Austria, 1967—. Joint sec. Combined Devel. Agy., Washington, 1949-55, U.S. mem., 1955; adviser to U.S. rep. UN Tech. Adv. Com., 1955, 58, 59, 60; chief liaison and protocal First Internat. Conf. on Peaceful Uses Atomic Energy, Geneva, Switzerland, 1955; sr. adviser U.S. rep. Conf. on Statute Internat. Atomic Energy Agy., 1956; alternate U.S. rep. Inter-Am. Nuclear Energy Commn., 1959, 60; sr. adviser to chmn. U.S. delegation First Gen. Conf., Internat. Atomic Energy Agy., Vienna, 1957, 2d Conf., 1958, 4th Conf., 1960, 9th Conf., 1965, 10th Conf., 1966; alternate U.S. rep. Am. Nuclear Commn., 1966; U.S. rep. Inter-Am. Sci. Symposium, Brazilia, Brazil, 1960. Served to lt. comdr. USNR, 1943-46. Clubs: Congressional Country, Harvard (Washington). Home: 7 Hasenauerstrasse 1180 Vienna Austria Office: Internat Atomic Energy Agy 11-13 Kaerntnerring 1010 Vienna Austria

HALL, JOHN COX, mortgage banker; b. Carrollton, Ala., Oct. 27, 1905; s. Origin Garrett and Clara Love (Cox) H.; B.S., Ga. Sch. Tech., 1926; m. Elizabeth Denson Mackey, Oct. 22, 1930; 1 son, John Cox. With Jemison Co., Birmingham, Ala., 1926-32; mortgage dept. Metropolitan Life Ins. Co., 1932-37; with Realty Mortgage Co., Birmingham, 1937-46; with Cobbs, Allen & Hall Mortgage Co., Inc., Birmingham, Alabama, 1946—, pres., 1950-64, chmn., pres., 1964—. Recipient Distinguished Service award Mortgage Bankers Assn. Am., 1952. Mem. Birmingham C. of C. (dir. finance div.), Mortgage Bankers Assn. Am. (pres. 1957-58), Birmingham Real Estate Bd. (pres. 1948), Ala. Real Estate Assn. (pres. 1949), Nat. Assn. Real Estate Bds. (dir. 1949), Birmingham Mortgage Bankers Assn. (pres. 1941, 49), Sigma Alpha Epsilon, Delta Sigma Pi. Episcopalian. Clubs: Birmingham Country, Down Town, Birmingham Monday Morning Quarterback, The Club, Redstone, Mountain Brook County, Relay House. Home: 3316 Country Club Rd Mountain Brook Birmingham AL 35213 Office: 2119 6th Av N Birmingham AL 35203

HALL, JOHN FRY, psychologist; b. Phila., Apr. 24, 1919; s. Harry R. and Alta (Herner) H.; B.S., Ohio U., 1946; M.A., Ohio State U., 1947, Ph.D., 1949; m. Jean Midlam, May 14, 1943; 1 son, John. Mem. faculty Pennsylvania State U., University Park, 1949-, prof. psychology, 1958-. Program dir. in psychobiology NSF, Washington, 1966-67; vis. prof. U. Va., 1952, U. Wis., 1954, U. Cal. at Berkeley, 1962, U. Hawaii, 1968. Mem. Am. Psychol. Assn., Psychonomics Soc., A.A.A.S., Sigma Xi. Author: Psychology of Motivation, 1961; Psychology of Learning, 1966; Readings in the Psychology of Learning, 1967; Verbal Learning and Retention, 1971; also articles. Home: 1288 Penfield Rd State College, PA 16801 Office: Pa State U University Park PA 16802

HALL, JOHN GOODALE, mining co. exec.; b. Omaha, Jan. 17, 1917; s. Arthur E. and Cora (Price) H.; m. Dorothy Louise Graham, Apr. 25, 1940; 1 son, John Christopher. With U.S. Smelting, Refining and Mining Co., Utah, 1936-46; gen. supt. Chief Consol. Mining Co., Eureka, Utah, 1946-52; asst. mgr., then mgr. titanium div. Nat. Lead Co., Tahawus, N.Y., 1952-65; with Anaconda Co., N.Y.C., 1965—, pres., 1969-70, vice chmn. bd., 1971—; also dir.; pres., dir. Andes Copper Mining Co., 1969—, Chile Copper Co., 1969—, Chile Exploration Co., 1969—, Chile Steamship Co., Inc., 1969-71, Internat. Smelting & Refining Co., 1969—, pres. Potrerillos Ry. Co., 1969-71. Anaconda Petroleum Corp., 1970—, Golden Reward Mining Co., 1969—; v.p., dir. Andes del Peru, 1968—, Greene Cananea Copper Co., 1967—, Santiago (Chile) Mining Co., 1969-70. v.p. Anaconda Britannia Mines Ltd., 1969-70; dir. Anaconda Australia Inc., Anaconda Aluminum Co., Anaconda Internat. Corp., Anaconda Jamaica, Inc., Anaconda Am. Brass Co., Anaconda Iron Ore (Ont.) Ltd. (Can.), Anaconda Sale Co., Anaconda Wire & Cable Co., Mines Investment Corp., Silesian Holding Co., 1st Nat. City Bank, 1st Nat. City Corp., Washoe Copper Co. Pres. bd. mgrs. Tahawus YMCA, 1955-63. Mem. Am. Inst. Mining Engrs. (dir. and treas. Soc. Mining Engrs. 1962- 65, chmn. mining and exploration div. 1961), Am. Mining Congress (exec. com. of uranium com. 1968), Am. Inst. Mining, Metall. and Petroleum Engrs. (bd. dirs. 1965-66), Am. Mgmt. Assn., Am. Inst. Mgmt., Am. Zinc Inst., Mining and Metall. Soc. Am., Mining Club N.Y.C., Northwest Mining Assn., Phi Delta Theta. Clubs: Clove Valley Rod and Gun (LaGrangeville, N.Y.): Manhasset Bay Yacht, Sands Point Golf (Port Washington N.Y.); Economic (N.Y.C.); University (Salt Lake City). Author articles in field. Home: 14 Bonnie Heights Rd Manhasset NY 11030 Office: 25 Broadway New York City NY 10004

HALL, JOHN LEWIS, lawyer; b. Woodville, Fla., July 26, 1904; s. Thomas Milton and Ola (Page) H.; A.B. in Edn., U. Fla., 1927; m. Martha Buford, Aug. 24, 1927; childrenJohn Lewis, Thomas Munroe. Tchr. pub. schs., Fla., 1927-35; admitted to Fla. bar, 1936, since practiced in Tallahassee; partner firm Hall, Hartwell, Michaels & Hall, 1957—; county atty. Leon County, 1939-66; atty. Fla. Assn. County Commrs., 1941-64. Mem. Fabisinski Com. of Fla., 1956-57, Adv. Commn. Revision Fla. Constn., 1957-59, Fla. Gov.'s Adv. Com. Race Relations, 1957- 58. Bd. dirs. Tallahassee Symphony Assn. Mem. Am., Tallahassee (pres. 1946) bar assns., Fla. Bar (gov. 1954-60, pres. 1959-60), Fla. County Attys. Assn. (pres. 1942), Tallahassee C. of C., Beta Theta Pi, Sigma Delta Chi. Blue Key. Methodist. Mason (grand master Fla. 1958). Clubs: Lions (pres. 1945), Torch (Tallahassee). Home: 1204 Firethorn Lane Tallahassee FL 32303 Office: Midyette-Moor Bldg Tallahassee FL 32301

HALL, JOHN RICHARD, oil co. exec.; b. Dallas, Nov. 30, 1932; s. John W. and Agnes (Sanders) H.; B.Chem. Engring., Vanderbilt U., 1955; m. Ann Leslie McQuiddy, Sept. 24, 1955. Chem. engr. Esso Standard Oil Co., Balt., 1956-58, Ashland Oil Co., Ashland, Ky., 1959-63, coordinator carbon black div., Houston, 1963- 66, adminst. v.p., 1967—, dir., 1968—, sr. v.p., 1970—. Served as 2d lt., Chem. Corps, AUS, 1955-56. Mem. Tau Delta Pi, Sigma Chi, Delta Kappa. Democrat. Home: 2610 Central Pkwy Ashland, KY 41101 Office: 1409 Winchester Ave Ashland KY 41101

HALL, JOHN SCOVILLE, astronomer; b. Old Lyme, Conn., June 20, 1908; s. Nathaniel Conkling and Harriet Rose (Lance) H.; A.B., Amherst Coll., 1930; Ph.D., Yale, 1933; Sc.D. (hon.), Ohio Wesleyan U., 1967; m. Ruth Carolyn Chandler, June 18, 1935; children—Richard Chandler, Carolyn Davison (Mrs. Richard R. Smith). Asst. in astronomy Columbia, 1933-34; instr. Sproul Obs., Swarthmore Coll., 1934- 38; asst. prof., then asso. prof. astronomy Amherst Coll., 1938-48; staff mem. radiation lab. Mass. Inst. Tech., 1942-46; dir. astrometric and astrophys. div. U.S. Naval Obs., 1948-58; dir. Lowell Obs., Flagstaff, Ariz., 1958—; pioneer in photoelectric photometry of stars in infra-red region of spectrum; discover with W. A. Hiltner , polarization of starlight, 1947; initiated, supervised transfer 40-inch Ritchey Chrétien reflector, also 69-inch Perkins reflector to Flagstaff. Mem. adv. panel astronomy NSF, 1958-61, chmn., 1960-61, rep.-at-large AURA bd., 1967-70; chmn. Carnegie Image Tube Com., 1967—; mem. div. phys. scis. NRC-Nat. Acad. scis., 1966-69; mem. lunar and planetary missions bd. NASA, 1967-70. Mem. space sci. bd. Nat. Acad. Scis., 1967-71. Trustee Museum No. Ariz. Recipient Boyden premium Franklin Inst., 1939. Mem. Internat. Astron. Union (pres. sub-commn. 1955-61, commn. 16, 1967-70), Am. Astron. Soc. (councilor 1944-47, 60-62, v.p. 1963-65), Astron. Soc. Pacific (1st v.p. 1963- 65), A.A.A.S. (v.p., chmn. astron. sect. 1967), Phi Beta Kappa, Sigma Xi, Alpha Delta Phi. Editor: Radar Aids to Navigation, 1947; Mars, 1962; Brighter Planets, 1964. Contbr. numerous articles profl. jours. Address: Lowell Observatory Flagstaff AZ 86001*

HALL, JOHN WALTON, educator; b. Burlington, Vt., Dec. 30, 1918; s. Lincoln and Helen (Vose) H.; B.S., U. Mass., 1940; M.S., U. Mass., 1942; Ph.D., U. Ill., 1950; m. Ann Marie Schertiger, Aug. 21, 1950; children—Richard, Elizabeth, Karen. Instr. to prof. botany U. Minn., 1950—; prof. U. Mont., summer 1964. Served with AUS, 1942-46. NATO fellow, Copenhagen, 1960-61. Mem. Bot. Soc. Am. (sec.-treas. paleobot. sect. 1969-71, chmn. 1971-72), Am. Assn. Stratigraphic Palynologists (council mem. 1969), A.A.A.S., Paleontol. Soc., Sigma Xi. Research on fossil plants of Pennsylvanian age, fossil pollen, spores and fossil Azolla from late Cretaceous. Home: 4817 15th Av S Minneapolis MN 55417

HALL, JOSEPH ALBERT, III, banker; b. Bogalusa, La., Jan. 25, 1915; s. Joseph Albert, Jr. and Mabel Inez (McCall) H.; B.S., Ga. Inst. Tech., 1935; m. Menda Coxwell, Apr. 23, 1955; childrenRobert McCall, Joseph Albert IV, John Coxwell, Jack Reeves. With Citizens and So. Nat. Bank, Atlanta, 1935-, comptroller, 1959-, exec. v.p., 1966-; dir. Citizens and So. Holding Co., Jackson Nat. Bank, Farmers & Mchts. Bank, Fayetteville, Citizens and So. Bank, Stone Mountain, Citizens and So. Bank, Tucker. Served to maj. AUS, 1941-45. CBI. Mem. Financial Execs. Inst., Nat. Assn. Bank Auditors and Comptrollers (bd. dirs.), Kappa Sigma. Presbyn. Home: 4100 Conway Valley Rd NW Atlanta GA 30327 Office: P O Box 4799 Atlanta GA 30302*

HALL, JOSEPH ALEXANDER, social welfare adminstr.; b. Chester, W.Va., May 30, 1908; s. Isaac R. and Lottie M. (Poe) H.; B.S., Wilberforce U., 1931; M.S., Western Res. U., 1942; postgrad. Youngstown Coll., 1935-36; m. Marguerite Louise Clemons, Oct. 27, 1933; children—Jo Ann (Mrs. Jon L. Evans), Joseph Andrew. With Family Service Bur. and Trumbull County Welfare Dept., 1933-40; caseworker, supr. Juvenile Ct. Cuyahoga County, Cleve., 1942-45; probation officer Cleve. Urban League, 1945-47; indsl. relations dir. Urban League Greater Cin., 1948—; guest lectr. U. Cin., 1948-68, Central State Coll., 1951-57; cons.-trainer Gen. Electric Co., Cin. Gas & Electric Co., Cin. Bell Telephone Co., Cin. Indsl. Mission. Pres. Ohio Welfare Conf., 1958; bd. dirs., mem. exec. com. Ohio Citizens Council; mem. Ohio Housing Bd., 1961—; chmn. Ohio Vocational Edn. Adv. Council, 1971—; mem. Hamilton County Hosp. Commn., 1965—. Mem. Acad. Certified Social Workers, Nat. Urban League Conf., Nat. Conf. on Social Welfare, Nat. Assn. Social Workers (chmn. Ohio Valley chpt.), Alpha Phi Alpha, Sigma Pi Phi. Methodist. Home: 1351 Burdette Av Cincinnati OH 45206 Office: 2400 Reading Rd Cincinnati OH 45202

HALL, JOSEPH TWICHELL, mining co. exec.; b. N.Y.C., June 13, 1910; s. John Raymond and Louise (Twichell) H.; grad. Hotchkiss Sch., 1928; B.A., Yale, 1932; m. Patricia Plunkett, Apr. 5, 1941; childrenHenry V.S., Joseph Twichell, Jonathan D., Christopher C. Asst. to v.p. John R. Hall Corp., 1932-34; asst. sec., asst. mgr. San Juan Metals Corp. Colo., 1934; asst. v.p. Sunshine Mining Co., 1935-; sec., dir. Callahan Mining Corp., N.Y.C., 1936-37, sec., treas., dir., 1938-40, exec. v.p., dir., 1941, pres., dir., 1946- ; pres., dir. Livengood Placers, Inc., Pinnacle Exploration; past dir. Stewart Lake Iron Mines. Served to maj., F.A., AUS, 1942-45. Mem. Mining and Metall. Soc., Mining Club. Home: 29 Jordan Lane Stamford CT 06903 Office: 277 Park Av New York City NY 10017*

HALL, JOSIAH CALVIN, educator; b. Mentone, Ala., Sept. 22, 1909; s. Josiah Calvin and Mary Walter (Collins) H.; A.B., U. Fla., 1931; M.A., N.Y.U., 1936; Ed.D., Fla. State U., 1955; m. Ella Faye Price, Nov. 16, 1942; childrenJoe and Ed (twins), Mary and Martha (twins), Elizabeth. Prin., tchr., coach Leon High Sch., Tallahassee, 1932-35; supervising prin. Carrabelle (Fla.) Schs., 1935-36; dir. tchr. edn. and certification, health and phys. edn. Fla. Dept. Edn., Tallahassee, 1937-42, dir. div. instrn., 1946-48; dir. instrn. Dade County Pub. Schs., Miami, Fla., 1948-49, asst. supt., 1949-53, asso. supt., 1953-56, supt., 1957-68; prof. edn. U. Miami, Coral Gables, 1968—. Fla. chmn. March of Dimes, 1953; unit v.p. United Fund Campaign, 1967; mem. exec. bd. South Fla. council Boy Scouts Am. Bd. dirs. Dade County Tb Assn., Dade County chpt. A.R.C., Mus. Sci. and Natural History Miami. Served from lt. (j.g.) to lt. comdr., USNR, 1942-46. Mem. Am. Assn. Supervision and Curriculum Devel., Nat. (life), Fla. (chmn. dept. health, phys. edn. and recreation 1939-40, chmn. program, action and resolutions com., pres. 1964-65) edn. assns., A.A.H.P.E.R. (dir. So. div. 1939-42), Everglades Nat. Park Commn., Nat. Conf. Christians and Jews (sec. Fla. region 1955),

P.T.A. (life), U.S. (nat. chmn. youth welfare com.), Fla. (pres. 1940-41, continuing ednl. council) jr. chambers commerce, Am. Legion, U. Fla. Alumni Assn. (v.p.), Fla. State U. Alumni Assn. (dir. 1955), Blue Key, Kappa Delta Pi, Sigma Delta Psi, Pi Kappa Alpha. Kiwanian (pres. Coral Gables 1962). Home: 7830 SW 57 Ct South Miami FL 33143

HALL, JOYCE CLYDE, greeting card publisher; b. David City, Neb., Aug. 29, 1891; s. George N. and Nancy (Dudley) H.; student pub. schs. David City and Norfolk, Neb.; LL.D., U. Mo., 1963, Kan. State U., 1963, U. Neb., 1968; m. Elizabeth Dilday, Mar. 25, 1922; children—Elizabeth Ann, Barbara, Donald. Founder, pres., chmn. bd. Hallmark Cards, Inc., 1910-66, chmn., 1966—; founder, pres., chmn. bd. Hallmark Cards, Gt. Britain, Ltd.; dir. First Nat. Bank of Kansas City. Chmn. exec. com., dir., hon. pres. People-to-People. Bd. dirs. Eisenhower Found., Am. Heritage Found., Midwest Research Inst., also exec. com.; trustee U. Mo. at Kansas City. Decorated knight Order of Leopold; hon. comdr. Order Brit. Empire; recipient Dr. Lee DeForest award Nat. Assn. Better Radio and TV, 1953; Horatio Alger award Am. Schs. and Colls. Assn., 1957; Mr. Kansas City C. of C. award, 1961; Trustees' Sponsors award Nat. Acad. TV Arts and Scis., 1961. Mem. Am. Assn. French Legion Honor. Home: 110th and State Line Kansas City MO 64114 Office: 25th and McGee Kansas City MO 64108*

HALL, KIRK, author. Address: care William Morrow and Co Inc 3207 Washington Blvd St Louis MO 63103*

HALL, LAWRENCE CARL, ins. co. exec.; b. Cambridge, Mass., Sept. 26, 1913; s. Carl D. and Augusta (Peterson) H.; B.S., Mass. Inst. Tech., 1935; m. Elizabeth Gale, Apr. 11, 1942; children—David R., Lawrence Carlton. Engr., N.H. Ins. Co., Manchester, 1944-64, pres., 1964—, also dir.; pres., dir. Granite State Ins. Co., Am. Fidelity Co., Ill. Nat. Ins. Co., Inland Nat. Ins. Co.; chmn. Life Ins. Co. N.H.; dir. Gen. Adjustment Bur., Inc., Am. Internat. Group, Manchester Bank, Amos Keag Industries. Pres. N.H. Bd. Underwriters. Bd. dirs. New Eng. Council; trustee Elliot Hosp. (Manchester). Home: Mont Vernon Rd Amherst NH 03031 Office: 1750 Elm St Manchester NH 03105

HALL, LAWRENCE SARGENT, educator, writer; b. Haverhill, Mass., Apr. 23, 1915; s. Herbert Ivan and Marion (Sargent) H.; B.A., Bowdoin Coll., 1936; Ph.D., Yale, 1941; m. Margaret Mellor, 1938; childrenLawrence Sargent, Marion Mason; m. 2d, Marcia Skillings, October 22, 1954. Member of the faculty of Deerfield (Massachusetts) Academy, 1936-38, Ohio U., 1941-42, Yale, 1946; Carnegie vis. prof. humanities Columbia, 1955-56; mem. faculty Bowdoin Coll., 1946-, prof. English, 1959-, chmn. dept., 1964-67; lectr., cons. lit. and lit. criticism, 1966-. Dir. Me. Citizens Assn. Coop. Planning, 1966-. Served to lt. comdr. USNR, 1942-46. Mem. Modern Lang. Assn., Am. Assn. U. Profs., English Inst., Assn. Depts. English. Author: The Ledge (1st prize O. Henry award), 1960; Stowaway (Faulkner award), 1961; Hawthorne: Critic of Society, 1944; How Thinking is Written, 1963; A Grammar of Literary Criticism, 1965; also articles, short stories. Editor: Seeing and Describing, Uses of English, series, 1966. Home: Bay View Rd Orr's Island, ME 04066 Office: Mass Hall Bowdoin Coll Brunswick ME 04011

HALL, LEE, educator, artist; b. Lexington, N.C., Dec. 15, 1934; d. Robert Lee and Florence (Fitzgerald) H.; B.F.A., U. N.C., 1955; M.A., N.Y.U., 1959, Ph.D., 1965; postgrad. Warburg Inst. U. London, 1965. Asst. prof. N.Y. State U. Coll., Potsdam, 1958-60; asso. prof., chmn. art dept. Keuka Coll.,1960-62; asso. prof. art Winthrop Coll., 1962-65; asst. prof., chmn. art dept. Drew U., Madison, N.J., 1965-67, asso. prof., chmn. art dept., 1967-70, prof., chmn. art dept., 1970—; exhbited group shows in London, N.Y.C., Winston-Salem, Eugene, Ore. and others. Dir. research on Pres. Kennedy's image in recent art, John F. Kennedy Meml. Library. Recipient research grant Am. Philos. Soc., 1965, 68. Mem. Am. Assn. U. Profs., Am. Assn. U. Women, Am. Soc. for Aesthetics, Coll. Art Assn., Pi Lambda Theta. Contbr. articles profl. jours. Home: 31 Ridgedale Av Madison NJ 07940

HALL, LEONARD WOOD, lawyer, former chmn. Republican nat. com.; b. Oyster Bay, N.Y., Oct. 2, 1900; s. Franklyn H. and Mary A. Hall; LL.B., Georgetown U., Washington, 1920; Doctorate, C. W. Post Coll.; m. Gladys Dowsey, May 10, 1934. Admitted to N.Y. bar, 1921; practice in N.Y.C., 1921-27; mem. N.Y. Assembly, 1927-28, 1934-38; sheriff Nassau County, N.Y., 1929-31; chmn. Rep. Com. Town of Oyster Bay; mem. 76th to 82d Congresses, 2d N.Y. Dist.; chmn. Rep. Nat. Com., 1953-57; sr. partner Hall, Casey, Dickler & Howley. Dir. Servo Corp. Am., Beneficial Nat. Life Ins. Co. Chmn. Nassau-Suffolk Regional Planning Bd.; mem. Nassau County Bd. Ethics, N.Y. State Banking Bd.; founder L.I. United Fund. Mem. N.Y. State, Nassau County bar assns. Republican. Episcopalian. Mason, Elk. Clubs: Nassau Country; Internat., Metropolitan (Washington). Home: Feeks Lane Locust Valley NY 11560 Office: 600 Old Country Rd Garden City NY 11530 also 460 Park Ave New York City NY 10022 also Ring Bldg Washington DC 20036

HALL, LINSCOTT ALDIN, ret. air force officer, ednl. adminstr.; b. McAlester, Okla., July 11, 1913; s. William Linscott and May Oscar (Schwab) H.; student Washington U., 1931-33; B.S., U.S. Mil. Acad., 1937; student Columbia, 1946-47, Am. U. of Beirut (Lebanon), 1952; m. Ann Eldredge, Oct. 16, 1937; children—Robin Foster, Kathrine Laurie, Linscott Eldredge. Commd. 2d lt. U.S. Army, 1937, advanced through grades to brig. gen. USAF, 1961; staff Hdqrs. Allied Forces, Algiers, 1943; bn. comdr. 1st Armored Div., Italy, 1944; asst. prof. dept. social scis. U.S. Mil. Acad., 1945-49; student Air War Coll., Maxwell AFB, 1950; joint staff Office Joint Chiefs Staff, Washington, 1952-54; dep. asst. chief of staff-intelligence Hdqrs. USAF, 1957-61; asst. dir. Def. Intelligence Agy., 1961-64; J-2 Hdqrs. U.S. European Command, 1964-66; ret., 1970; bus. mgr. Holton-Arms Sch., Bethesda, Md., 1970—. Decorated Silver Star, Legion of Merit, Bronze Star, Purple Heart (U.S.); Order Brit. Empire; Medhala di Guerra (Brazil); Croix de Guerre (France); Croce di Valore (Italy); Great Star Mil. Merit (Chile). Mem. Archeol. Soc. Md., Air Force Assn., Sigma Chi. Club: Columbia Country. Author: (with Beukema and others) Contemporary Foreign Powers, 1949. Home: 3907 Blackthorn St Chevy Chase MD 20015 Office: Bus Mgr Holton-Arms Sch Bethesda MD 20034

HALL, LIVINGSTON, prof. of law, lawyer; b. Chgo., May 5, 1903; s. James Parker and Evelyn Hallam (Movius) H.; Ph.B., U. Chgo., 1923; LL.B. magna cum laude, Harvard, 1927; m. Elizabeth Blodgett, Sept. 13, 1930; childrenThomas L., Margaret R., Elizabeth C., John K. Admitted to N.Y. bar, 1929, Mass. bar, 1934; law practice with firm, Root, Clark, Buckner, Howland & Ballantine, N.Y.C., 1927-31; asst. U.S. atty., So. Dist. N.Y., 1931-32; asst. prof. law, Harvard, 1932-37, prof. law, 1937-71, vice dean, 1938-58, actg. dean, 1959; regional price and enforcement atty. O.P.A. (on leave from Harvard), Boston, 1942-43. Moderator Town of Weston, 1947-49, Town of Concord, 1957-67. Commd. lt. col. AC, in Manila, P.I., Feb., 1945; served as dep. chief and chief Operations Analysis sects., overseas with 13th and Far East Air Forces, 1943-45, and in Washington, D.C. with 20th Air Force, 1945. Awarded Medal of Freedom, 1946. Mem. Am., Mass. (pres. 1963-64) bar assns., Mass. Jud. Council, Phi Beta Kappa. Republican. Episcopalian. Clubs: Curtis; Social Circle 1782. Author: (with Sheldon Glueck) Cases on Criminal Law and Enforcement, 1958; (with Warren A. Seavey) Cases on Agency, 1956; (with Yale Kamisar, Wayne LaFave, Jerold Israel) Modern Criminal Procedure, 1969. Home: 238 Main St Concord MA 01742 Office: Harvard Law Sch Cambridge MA 02138

HALL, LOUIS HARRISON, Jr., lawyer; b. N.Y.C., Feb. 7, 1909; s. Louis Harrison and Georgia D. (Coyle) H.; grad. Deerfield Acad., 1926; A.B., Amherst Coll., 1931; student Columbia Law Sch., 1931-32; LL.B., Bklyn. Law Sch., 1934; m. Elizabeth Yates Kopf, Aug. 22, 1936; childrenLouis Harrison III, Jeffrey Lyman, Stephen Yates, Timothy Coyle. Admitted to N.Y. bar, 1934, since practiced in N.Y.C.; partner firm Putney, Twombly, Hall & Hirson, 1942—. Dir. Internat. Salt Co., 1949-7O, Akzona, Inc., sec. Botany Mills, 1953-55. Mem. Am., N.Y. State bar assns., Phi Beta Kappa, Psi Upsilon, Phi Delta Phi. Home: 115 Lone Tree Farm Rd New Canaan, CT 06840 Office: 250 Park Av New York City NY 10017

HALL, LYLE GILLIS, mfr.; b. Ridgway, Pa., Nov. 2, 1929; s. Lyle Gillis and Jane (Grube) H.; grad. Phillips Andover Acad., also Yale; grad. Advanced Mgmt. Program, Harvard; m. Lisbeth Jordan; children—Alexander Gillis, Megan Eugenia, Charlotte Grube, Cara Catherine. Treas., dir. Stackpole Carbon Co., St. Marys, Pa., Canadian Stackpole, Ltd. (Toronto); treas., dir. Phin, Inc. (Bloomfield, N.J.), Stackpole Components Co. (Raleigh, N.C. and Farmville, Va.), Stackpole Fibers Co. (Lowell, Mass.); pres., dir. J.K.P. Hall Corp., Ridgway Pub. Co.; vice chmn. bd. Elk County Bank & Trust Co. Pres. Bucktail council Boy Scouts Am.; dir. St. Marys Boys Club. Senator Pa. Legislature, 1963-66. Pres. bd. trustees Elk County Gen. Hosp. Served with USMC, 1951-54. Mem. Am. Legion. Democrat. Episcopalian (trustee Erie Diocese), Elk. Clubs: Elks County Country (Ridgway); St. Marys Country, Valley Hunt, Pennhills (Bradford, Pa.); Yale (N.Y.C.). Home: 602 Hyde Av Ridgway PA 15853 Office: Stackpole Carbon Corp St Marys PA

HALL, MARION TRUFANT, educator; b. Gorman, Tex., Sept. 6, 1920; s. Frank Marion and Nora Gertrude (Wharton) H.; B.S., U. Okla., 1943, M.S., 1947; Ph.D. (Henrietta Heerman scholar 1951), Washington U., St. Louis, 1951; m. Virginia Riddle, Nov. 9, 1944; children—Susan, Alan Lee, John Lane. Ranger, Nat. Park Service, Dept. Interior, 1942; instr. botany U. Okla., 1946-47, curator Bebb Herbarium, 1949; field botanist, instr. Tex. Nature Camp, Nat. Audubon Soc., Kerrville, Tex., 1948; grad. asst. zoology, teaching fellow Washington U., 1948-50, spl. lectr. genetics and evolution Henry Shaw Sch. Botany, 1952; botanist Cranbrook Inst. Sci., Bloomfield Hills, Mich., 1950-56, acting dir., 1955-56; prof., head dept. botany Butler U., 1956-62; vis. prof. botany U. Okla., 1962, dir. Stovall Mus. Sci. and History, 1962-66; dir. Morton Arboretum, Lisle, Ill., 1966—; prof. botany, acting dir. U. Mich. Bot. Gardens, 1963-64; adj. prof. biol. scis. U. Ill., Chgo. Circle Campus; prof. horticulture U. Ill., Urbana; adj. prof. biology No. Ill. U. Cons. Mich. Dept. Conservation, Handbook Biol. Materials for Museums. Served to lt. (j.g.) USNR, 1943-45. Grantee NSF; recipient Alumni award for achievement U. Okla., 1953. Fellow Ind. Acad. Sci.; mem. Am. Soc. Plant Taxonomists, Internat. Assn. Plant Taxonomists, Ecol. Soc. Am., Asa Gray Meml. Assn., Soc. Study Evolution, Mich. Natural Areas Council, Okla. Acad. Sci., Bot. Soc. Am., Mich. Bot. Club (past pres. Detroit), Phi Beta Kappa, Sigma Xi, Phi Sigma. Author numerous research articles. Home: 24 W 276 Pin Oak Lane Naperville IL 60540 Office: Morton Arboretum Lisle IL 60532

HALL, MARSHALL, Jr., educator, mathematician; b. St. Louis, Sept. 17, 1910; s. Marshall and Inez (Bethune) H.; B.A., Yale, 1932, Ph.D., 1936; postgrad. Cambridge (Eng.) U., 1932-33; m. Sarah Ann Clark, June 13, 1942; children—Marshall III, Jonathan Ingersoll. Mem. Inst. Advanced Study, Princeton, 1936-37; instr., then asst. prof. Yale, 1937-46; asso. prof., then prof. Ohio State U., 1946-59; prof. math. Cal. Inst. Tech., Pasadena, 1959—, exec. officer for math., 1966-69. Dir. Summer Inst. Finite Groups, Pasadena, 1960, also several symposia. Served with USNR, 1943-46, 50-52. Henry fellow, 1932-33; Guggenheim fellow, 1955-56, 70-71. Author: Theory of Groups, 1959; Combinatorial Theory, 1967. Home: 2755 E California Blvd Pasadena CA 91107

HALL, MILES LEWIS, Jr., lawyer; b. Ft. Lauderdale, Fla., Aug. 14, 1924; s. Miles Lewis and Mary Frances (Dawson) H.; A.B., Princeton, 1947; LL.B., Harvard, 1950; m. Muriel M. Fisher, Nov. 4, 1950; childrenMiles Lewis III, Don Thomas. Admitted to Fla. bar, 1951, since practiced in Miami; partner Hall & Hedrick, 1953—. Pres. Orange Bowl Com., 1964-65, dir., 1950-71; nat. fund cons. A.R.C., 1963, 66-68; bd. dirs. Coral Gables War Meml. Youth Center, 1967-71, pres., 1969-71; pres. Ransom Sch. Parents Assn., 1966; chmn. S. Fla. Gov.'s Scholarship Ball 1966; exec. bd. South Fla. Council Boy Scouts of Am., 1966-67. Citizens bd. U. Miami, 1961-66; bd. dirs. Salvation Army, Miami, 1968—. Served to 2d lt. USAAF, 1943-45. Mem. Am. (Fla. co-chmn. membership com. sect. corp., banking and bus. law), Dade County (dir. 1964-65, pres. 1967) bar assns., Fla. Bar, Am. Judicature Soc., Miami-Dade County C. of C. (v.p. 1962-64, dir. 1966-68) Harvard Law Sch. Assn. Fla. (dir. 1964-66), Alpha Tau Omega. Methodist (bd. stewards). Clubs: Cottage, Harvard, The Miami, Kiwanis (Miami); Princeton of So. Fla. (past pres., dir.). Author: Titles, Ejectment and Election of Remedies, Vol. VIII, Fla. Law and Practice, 1958. Home: 2907 Alhambra Circle Coral Gables FL 33134 Office: 150 S E 2d St Miami FL 33130

HALL, NANCY JOHNSON, (Mrs. Claris G. Hall), state ofcl.; b. Prescott, Ark., Oct. 5, 1904; d. George Sim and Minnie (Bryan) Johnson; grad. high sch., Little Rock; m. Claris G. Hall, Oct. 5, 1929; 1 dau., Nancy Anne (Mrs. R. Robert Bailey). Head stenographer Ark. Hwy Dept., 1925-30; asst. sec. state State of Ark., Little Rock, 1937-61, sec. state, 1961-63, treas., 1963—. Mem. bd. Employees Retirement System, Hwy. Retirement System, Tchr. Retirement System, Ark. Bd. Finance (sec.), Ark. Rural Endowment Fund, Inc. (sec.-treas.). Mem. Womens C. of C., U.D.C., Daus. of 1812, Bus. and Profl. Womens Club. Democrat. Presbyn. Club: Zonta. Home: 4206 Woodlawn St Little Rock AR 72205 Office: Dept Treasury State Capitol Little Rock AR 72201

HALL, NATHAN I., aircraft engring. exec.; b. Elkins, W.Va., Oct. 24, 1910; s. Nathan I. and Grace (Darlington) H.; B.S., M.S., W.Va. U., 1934, D.Sc., 1956; E.E., Stanford U., 1937; D.Sc., Davis and Elkins Coll., 1959; m.Delores Whitaker, June 28, 1970; children (by previous marriage) Natalia Grace, Leonard Eric. Mem. faculty W.Va. U., 1934-36, Stanford, 1936-37, research engr. Bell Telephone Labs., N.Y.C., 1937-41, project engr. Navy SL radar, 1941-45, electronic telephone switching research engr., 1945-47, sub-dept. head electronic telephone switching 1947; with Hughes Aircraft Co., Culver City, Cal., 1947-, beginning as engr., successively head missile electronics sect., asst. head MX-904 project, asso. head guided missile dept., head guided missile labs., v.p., mem. exec. com., dir. guided missile research and devel., 1947-54, v.p., mem. policy bd., dir. weapon systems devel., 1955- 59, v.p. engring., 1959-65, v.p. product effectiveness, 1965—. Mem. bd. counselors U. So. Cal. Named Nation's Outstanding Young Elec. Engr., Eta Kappa Nu, 1943. Registered engr., Cal., N.Y. Fellow I.E.E.E.; mem. Electronic Industries Assn. (dir.), Sigma Xi, Tau Beta Pi, Eta Kappa Nu. Contbr. tech. publs. Patentee in field. Office: Hughes Aircraft Co Culver City CA 90230

HALL, NEWMAN A, engr.; b. Uniontown, Pa., June 14, 1913; s. (Homer) Maxwell and Susan (Newman) H.; A.B., Marietta (O.) Coll., 1934, D.Sc. (hon.), 1959; Ph.D., Cal. Inst. Tech., 1938; M.A., Yale, 1956; m. Eileen Creevey, Aug. 14, 1938; children—James Creevey, Elizabeth Arnold. Instr. in math. Queens Coll., Flushing, N.Y., 1938-41; engr. Chance Vought div. United Aircraft Corp., Stratford, Conn., 1941-42, supr. engring. personnel, 1942-43; research engr. United Aircraft Corp., Hartford, 1944-47, head analysis sect., research div., 1946-47; prof. mech. engring. and head heat power div., mech. engring. dept. U. Minn., 1947-55; prof. mech. engring., asst. dean charge Grad. Div. Coll. Engring., N.Y.U., 1955-56; prof., chmn. dept. mech. engring. Yale, 1956- 64; exec. dir. Commn. on Engring. Edn., 1962—; cons. on ednl. facilities and adminstrn.; cons. engr. in thermodynamics, fluid dynamics, combustion. Dir. div. engring. scis. Office of Ordnance Research, U.S. Army, 1952-53. Registered profl. engr., N.Y., Conn. Mem. Nat. Soc. Profl. Engrs., Am. Soc. M.E. (chmn. bd. edn., 1959-61), Soc. Automotive Engrs., Inst. Aero. Sci. (asso. fellow), Am. Soc. Engring. Edn. (v.p. 1960-62), Math. Assn. Am., Combustion Inst. (sec., dir.), Phi Beta Kappa, Sigma Xi, Tau Beta Pi. Conglist. Club: Cosmos (Washington). Condr. engring. research in thermodynamics, fluid mechanics, aerodynamics, heat transfer. Author: Thermodynamics of Fluid Flow; (with W. E. Ibele) Engineering Thermodynamics, 1960. Home: 4711 Tilden St NW Washington DC 20016 Office: Nat Acad Engring 2101 Constitution Av Washington DC 20418

HALL, NICHOLS DAWSON, Jr., lawyer; b. New Hope, Ala., May 21, 1907; s. Nicholas Dawson and Lillian (Baker) H.; student McCallie Sch., Washington and Lee U.; m. Owene Lynch, May 25, 1931; children—Dawson James, Owene Philips (Mrs. L. K. Weber, Jr.). Admitted to Tenn. bar, 1930, with firm Hall, Haynes, Lusk & Foster, Chattanooga, 1940—, dir., 1955—; pres. Realty Title Co., Chattanooga; exec. com. Hamilton Nat. Bank of Chattanooga; dir. Chattanooga Gas Co., Ridgedale Bank & Trust Co. of Chattanooga. Served to lt. (s.g.) USNR, World War II. Clubs: Mount City, Fairyland (Chattanooga). Home: 100 James Blvd Signal Mountain TN 37377 Office: Pioneer Bldg Chattanooga TN 37402*

HALL, O. GLEN, coll. dean; b. nr. Irvine, Ky., June 16, 1929; s. Dellie R. and Mattie (Colwell) H.; B.S., Berea Coll., 1951; M.S., U. Ky., 1952; Ph.D., Ia. State U., 1955; m. Doris Swingle, Dec. 31, 1948; childrenDeborah Carol, Martha Lynne, Joel Glenn. Asst. prof. U. Ky., Lexington, 1952; asso. prof. U. Tenn., Knoxville, 1955-65, prof., head dept. agr., Martin, 1965- 67, dean Coll. Agr., Knoxville, 1967-. Mem. Am. Soc. Animal Sci., So. Agrl. Workers Assn., Assn. State U. and Landgrant Colls., Tenn. Farm Bur., Sigma Xi, Phi Kappa Phi, Gamma Sigma Delta, Alpha Zeta. Methodist (adminstry. bd. 1957-). Contbr. articles to profl. jours. Home: 9321 Briarwood Blvd Knoxville TN 37919

HALL, OGDEN HENDERSON, educator; b. Clayton, La., Nov. 8, 1922; s. William A. and Gladys (Denham) H.; B.S., La. State U., 1948, M.B.A., 1961, Ph.D., 1963; m. Barbara Beale, Jan. 9, 1948; children—Michelle, Todd, Jennifer. Office mgr. William Wolf Bakery, Baton Rouge, 1947-50; owner-mgr. Hall-Denham Hardware, Denham Springs, La., 1948-62; asso. prof. bus. Va. Poly. Inst., 1963-68; prof., chmn. dept. mgmt. and marketing La. State U. in New Orleans, 1968—; cons. in field. Pres. Denham Springs C. of C., 1958; bd. dirs. Credit Bur. Baton Rouge, 1959. Served with AUS, 1943-44, USAAF, 1944-46. Mem. Acad. Mgmt., Eastern Acad. Mgmt. (pres.), Am. Inst. Decision Scis., Inst. Gen. Semantics. Home: 1712 Killdeer St New Orleans LA 70122

HALL, PAUL, labor union ofcl.; b. Ala., Aug. 21, 1914; m. Rose Hall; 2 children. Mem. Seafarers Internat. Union N. Am., 1938-, sec.-treas. Atlantic, Gulf, Great Lakes and In Land Waters dists., 1948—, 1st v.p., 1948-57, pres., 1957—; pres. maritime trades dept. AFL-CIO, 1957-, nat. v.p., mem. exec. com., 1962-. Mem. Nat. Com. Immigration, Citizens Com. Free China. Bd. dirs. Am. Immigration and Citizenship Conf.; a founder, mem. nat. council Eleanor Roosevelt Found.; trustee George Meany Found.; sponsor, trustee Coordinating Council Edn. to Disadvantaged; v.p. Civic Center Clinic, N.Y.C. Recipient Humanitarian award Civic Center Clinic; citation of honor Nat. Com. Rural Schs. Address: 675 4th Av Brooklyn, NY 11232.*

HALL, PAYSON, broadcasting co. exec.; b. Oil City, Pa., July 6, 1915; s. Samuel Payson and Marie (Howe) H.; A.B., Cornell U., 1936;M.S., Columbia, 1945; m. Milnore Hoel; son, Samuel. Staff accountant Hurdman & Cranstoun, C.P.A.'s, N.Y.C., 1936-40; financial sec. N.Y. State Vet. Coll., Cornell U., 1940-41; sr. credit analyst Chase Nat. Bank, N.Y.C., 1941-42; exec. accountant U.S. Army Engrs., Iran, 1942-43; chief accountant Bridgeport Brass Co., 1944-45; indsl. engr., mgr. reports and budgets Trans World Airlines, Kansas City, Mo., 1945-47; controller, 1947-50, asst. sec., dir. radio-TV, Meredith Pub. Co., Des Moines, 1947-60, treas., 1953- 60, exec. v.p., 1960-65; v.p. McCall Printing, Inc., 1965; v.p. finance and planning King Broadcasting Co., 1965—, also dir., mem. exec. com., v.p., dir. Cowlitz Cableview Co., 1966—; treas., dir. King Videocable Co., 1966—. Mem. adv. bd. accounting dept. Drake U., 1949-52, sec., 1951-52; mem. TV com. Brotherhood Week, 1947-58, Nat. Conf. Christians and Jews. Mem. Nat. Assn. Cost Accountants (past pres.), Quad-Cities Control Inst. (past pres.), Nat. Assn. Broadcasters (dir.), TV Bur. Advt. (dir.), TV Pioneers (charter), Broadcast Pioneers, Internat. Radio and TV Soc., Financial Execs. Inst. (chmn. corporate accounting procedures and reports 1951-53, chmn. pub. industry conf. 1952), Newcomen Soc., Beta Gamma Sigma. Conglist. Clubs: Rainier (Seattle), Seattle Tennis. Home: 23 Highland Dr Seattle WA 98109 Office: King Broadcasting Co 320 Aurora Av N Seattle WA 98109

HALL, PEIRSON MITCHELL, judge; b. Armour, S.D., July 31, 1894; s. Robert A. and Mary M. (Cripps) H.; student U. So. Cal. Law Sch. 1912-16; m. Kathryn Kyle Black, Nov. 23, 1956; children by previous marriageMary Ellen, Suzanne. Admitted to Cal. bar, 1916; pvt. law practice in Los Angeles until apptd. to bench, 1939; mem. City Council, Los Angeles, 1925-29; U.S. dist. atty. So. Dist. Cal., 1933-37, judge, 1942—; judge Superior Ct. of Los Angeles County, 1939-42. Mason. ‡

HALL, PETER REGINALD FREDERICK, educator, theatre, opera, film dir.; b. Bury St. Edmunds, Suffolk, Eng., Nov. 22, 1930; s. Reginald Edward Arthur Hall and Grace (Pamment) F.; B.A. with honours, St. Catharine's Coll., Cambridge U., 1953, M.A. with honours, 1959, hon. fellow, 1964; Litt.D. (hon.), U. York, 1966; m. Leslie Caron, Aug. 6, 1956 (dissolved 1965); childrenChristopher, Jennifer; m. 2d, Jacqueline Taylor, Oct. 18, 1965; children—Edward Peter, Lucy Marianne. Dir. prodns. Cambridge U. (Eng.), 1950- 53; 1st profl. prodn. Theatre Royal, Windsor, 1953; dir. plays at repertory theatres, 1953-55; dir. Arts Theatre, London, Eng., 1955-56; formed own producing co. Internat. Playwrights Theatre, 1957, produced plays and operas in London, N.Y.C., other cities; mng. dir. Royal Shakespeare Co., 1960-68; dir. films and TV prodns.; asso. prof. drama U. Warwick, 1966-. Decorated comdr. Order British Empire;

recipient London Theatre Critics award for Wars of the Roses, 1963, for Hamlet, 1966, for The Homecoming, 1966; Tony award for The Homecoming, 1967. Address: The Wall House Mangewell Park Wallingford Berles England *

HALL, RAY D., mfg. co. exec.; b. Du Bois, Pa., 1904. Sr. v.p., dir. Fed. Paper Board Co. Mason. Home: 360 Briarly Dr Franklin Lakes, NJ 07417 Office: 24 River Rd Bogota NJ 07603 *

HALL, RAYMOND WILLIAMS, lawyer; born at Weston, Mo., Aug. 15, 1891; s. Charles D and Laura B. (Williams) H.; A.B., U. Mo., 1913, LL.B., 1915; m. Anne Woodroof, June 6, 1924; 1 son, Douglas Jackson. Admitted to Mo. bar, 1915, mem. Hall & Hall, Kansas City, 1915-26; trust officer First Nat. Bank of Kansas City, Mo, 1926-28, v.p., 1928-42; v.p., gen. counsel Fed. Res. Bank of Kansas City, 1950-52, chmn. bd., 1952-62; vice president Hallmark Cards, Inc., 1945- 59; partner firm Hillix, Hall & Hoffhaus, Kansas City, Mo., 1958-69; counsel Hillix, Brewer & Myers, 1969—; dir. Kansas City Life Insurance Company, E.R.C. Corporation, Employers Reins. Corp. Gov. Am. Royal Assn. Mem. Phi Gamma Delta. Clubs: Rotary, Country (Kansas City). Home: 6720 Tomahawk Rd Shawnee Mission KS 66208 Office: Commerce Towers Kansas City MO 64199

HALL, RICHARD DAVID, lawyer; b. Evanston, Ill., Oct. 6, 1916; s. David Francis and Mary (vonGunten) H.; B.A., U. Chgo., 1937, J.D. cum laude, 1939; m. Theresa Ellen Hagan, Mar. 2, 1940; 1 dau., Lynn Ellen. Admitted to Ill. bar, 1939, Colo. bar, 1946; practice in Freeport, Ill., 1939-40, Chgo., 1940- 43, Denver, 1946—; with law firm Burrell & Burrell, 1939-40; with George M. Sundheim, atty., 1940-43; with law firm January & Yegge, 1946- 54; partner Yegge, Hall & Evans and predecessor firm, 1954—; gen. counsel Empire Casualty Co., 1957—. Pres., bd. dirs. Sr. Homes of Colo. Found. Served with AUS, 1943-46. Republican. Conglist (trustee). Club: City (past pres., Denver). Author: Colorado Accident Law Digest, 1950; Colorado Negligence Digest, 1961. Home: 277 S Cherry St Denver CO 80222 Office: Denver Club Bldg Denver CO 80202

HALL, ROBERT ANDERSON, Jr., educator; b. Raleigh, Apr. 4, 1911; s. Robert Anderson and Lolabel (House) H.; A.B., Princeton, 1931; A.M., U. Chgo., 1935; Litt.D., U. Rome, 1934; m. Frances L. Adkins, Aug. 31, 1936; children—Philip Adkins, Diana Katherine (Mrs. William C. Goodall), Caroline Amanda (Mrs. C.M. Erickson). Asst. prof. fgn. langs. U. P.R., 1937-39; instr. modern lang. Princeton, 1939-40; instr. Italian Brown U., Providence, 1940-42, asst. prof., 1942-46; lectr. internat. adminstrn. Columbia, 1943-44; vis. asst. prof. internat. adminstrn. Yale, 1943-44; asso. prof. linguistics Cornell, 1946-50, prof., 1950—; dir. Cornell-Ford English Lang. Program, Rome, 1966-67; Fulbright lectr. linguistics, Rome, 1950-51, 57-58. Guggenheim fellow, 1954, 70. Mem. Linguistic Soc. Am. (v.p. 1961), Am. Assn. Tchrs. Italian (v.p. 1945), Modern Lang. Assn. Am. Conglist. Author: Bibliography of Italian Linguistics, 1941; The Italian Questione della Lingua, 1942; Melanesian Pidgin English, 1943; Hungarian Grammar, 1944; Descriptive Italian Grammar, 1948; Leave Your Language Alone!, 1950; Short History of Italian Literature, 1951; Haitian Creole, 1953; Hands Off Pidgin English, 1955; Italian for Modern Living, 1958; Bibliografia della Linguistica Italiana, 1958; Italian Stories, 1961; Basic Conversational Italian, 1963; Cultural Symbolism in Literature, 1963; Introductory Linguistics, 1964; New Ways to Learn a Foreign Language, 1965; Pidgin and Creole Languages, 1966; Antonio Fogazzaro e la Crisi dell 'Italia Moderna, 1967; An Essay on Language, 1968; English Phrase and Clause Structure, 1969; La Struttura dell' Italiano, 1971. Home: 308 Cayuga Heights Rd Ithaca NY 14850

HALL, ROBERT BRUCE, bishop; b. Wheeling, W.Va., Jan. 27, 1921; s. Kent Bruce and Mary Ellen (Hazlett) H.; B.A., Trinity Coll., Hartford, Conn., 1943, D.D., 1967; S.T.B., Episcopal Theol. Sem., Cambridge, Mass., 1949; D.D., Seabury Western Theol. Sem., 1966, Va. Theol. Sem., 1967, Kenyon Coll., 1969; m. Dorothy Varner Glass, Jan. 26, 1949; children—Ellen Lynn, Kent Bruce II, Elizabeth Hazlett, Anne Louise, Susan Glass. Ordained to ministry Episcopal Ch., 1949; asso. minister, Huntington, W.Va., 1949-53; rector, Huntington, 1953-58, Chgo., 1958-66; bishop coadjutor Episcopal Diocese Va., 1966—. Mem. corp. Seabury Western Theol. Sem., Evanston, Ill., 1964—; trustee Va. Theol. Sem., 1967—, St. Paul's Coll., Lawrenceville, Va., 1968—, Blue Ridge Sch., Dyke, Va., 1968—, United Charities, Chgo., 1965-66. Served with AUS, 1943-46. Fellow Coll. of Preachers; mem. Delta Phi, Pi Gamma Mu. Clubs: Racquet (Chgo.); Rotunda (Richmond, Va.). Home: 11 River Rd Richmond VA 23226 Office: 110 W Franklin St Richmond VA 23220

HALL, ROBERT CARLTON, investment banker; b. Boston, Mar. 13, 1915; s. Francis T. and Lucy (Waterhouse) H.; B.A., Harvard, 1936; Dip. in Econs., Oxford (Eng.) U., 1937; m. Emma Gene Tucker, Nov. 23, 1946. Dist. rep. Guaranty Trust Co. N.Y., 1937-41; partner Bache & Co., 1945-64, treas., 1963—, dir., v.p., mem. exec. com., 1965—, vice chmn. bd., chief financial officer, 1968—, chmn. employee benefit com., 1969—; chmn. Bankhaus Bache; dir. Hume Enterprises, Bache & Co. (over-seas). Mem. Chgo. Bd. Trade. Chmn. finance com. Knickerbocker Hosp. Bd. dirs. Japan Fund, Bache Corp. Found; bd. dirs., treas. H.L. Bache Found.; adv. bd. Pace Coll. Served to lt. comdr. USNR, 1941-45. Mem. Japan Soc., Asian Soc. Clubs: River, Broad Street (N.Y.C.); Achilles (London); Harvard Varsity (Cambridge, Mass.). Home: 130 E 67th St New York City NY 10021 Office: 36 Wall St New York City NY 10005

HALL, ROBERT DAVIDSON, textile co. exec.; b. Belmont, N.C., July 3, 1897; s. Matthews Neagle and Annie (Denny) H.; A.B., Davidson Coll., 1919; LL.D., Phila. Coll. Textiles and Sci., 1962, Belmont Abbey Coll., 1963; m. Mary Howe, Dec. 27, 1935; 1 son, Robert Davidson. Chmn. bd. Belmont Knitting Mills (N.C.); chmn. bd. Belmont Hosiery Mills, 1962—, Climax Spinning Co., 1960—; sec.-treas. Majestic Mfg. Co.; pres. Sterling Spinning Co., Stowe Thread Co.; bd. dirs. Bank of Belmont, Ruddick Corp. Mem. N.C. Employment Security Commn., 1941—. Pres. N.C. Citizens Assn., 1965; trustee St. Andrews Presbyn. Coll.; adv. com. Belmont Abbey Coll. Served to 2d lt. U.S. Army, World War I. Mem. Am. Cotton Mfrs. Inst. (pres. 1961-62), Am. Legion (comdr. N.C. 1940-41), Phi Gamma Delta. Presbyn. Rotarian. Home: 114 W Woodrow Av Belmont NC 28012 Office: N Main St Belmont NC 28012

HALL, ROBERT E. LEE, lawyer, trade assn. exec.; b. Norfolk, Va., Feb. 8, 1910; s. Robert E. Lee and Clyde (Smith) H.; A.B., George Washington U., 1932, LL.B., 1937; student personnel mgmt., U. Colo., 1942; m. Mary Margaret Rovane, Mar. 25, 1938; children—Robert E. Lee, Richard Lee. Admitted to D.C. bar, 1938; atty. Office Gen. Counsel SEC, Washington, 1939-41; personnel exec. Remington Arms Co., Denver, 1941-43; labor relations counsel Mountain States Employers Assn., Denver, 1944-47; Washington counsel, operating subsidiaries maj. oil firms, 1947-49; chief counsel Nat. Coal Assn., 1948-61, dir. govt. relations and gen. counsel, 1961, now exec. v.p.; general counsel Bituminous Coal Inst.; v.p. Peabody Coal Assn. Sec., Fuels Research Council, Washington; instr. labor law Denver U. Law Sch., 1946; instr. labor relations Southeastern U., 1950- 53. Mem. Am. Bar Assn. (past chmn. coal com., also mineral and natural resources law sect.), Fed. Power Bar Assn., Am. Arbitration Assn., Assn. ICC Practitioners, Sigma Alpha Epsilon. Clubs: University; Congressional Country (Washington). Home: 2500 Virginia Av N W Washington DC 20037 Office: Coal Bldg 17th and De Sales St NW Washington DC 20036

HALL, ROBERT KING, educator, cons.; b. Kewanee, Ill., Mar. 13, 1912; s. Nelson and Nellie (Hyer) H.; A.B., Lake Forest Coll. (pres. scholar), 1934, LL.D., 1951; A.M., Harvard, 1935; A.M. in Edn., U. Chgo., 1936; A.M., Columbia, 1944; Ph.D., U. Mich., 1941; M.A., Sch. for Asiatic Studies, 1950; Catedratico Honorario, U. San Marcos, Lima, Peru, 1951; research in Asia, Africa, Europe, Latin Am., Middle East; m. Margaret Wheeler, June 22, 1938; children—Louise Wheeler (Mrs. Chaffin), Margaret Jean, Marshall King. Master in math. Cranbrook Sch., 1936-41 (with leaves); lectr. Inst. Latin Am. Studies, 1939; prof. edn. U. Chile, 1939-40; dir. research and guidance Milw. Country Day Schs., fall 1941; asst. dir. Commn. on English Lang. Studies, Harvard, 1941-44 (with leaves); asst. prof. edn. Tchrs. Coll., Columbia, 1947-50, prof., 1950-55, hon. lectr., 1955-57, asst. dir. tng. Arabian Am. Oil Co., Saudi Arabia, 1955-57, dir., 1957-60; internat. cons., 1961-64; sr. adviser Coll. Petroleum and Minerals, Dhahran, Saudi Arabia, 1964—. Lectr. Latin Am. edn. U. Mich., summer 1941; lectr. Redpath Bur., 1941, A.H. Handley Mgmt., 1942-43; vis. prof. Oxford (Eng.) U., fall term 1951; dir. program evaluation and priorities study YMCA of Greater N.Y., 1962-63; dir, policy study World Service Program of YMCA's of Can. and U.S., 1951-52; ednl. adviser Iranian and Brazilian govts.; cons. various overseas indsl. firms. Served as lt. comdr. in USNR, World War II. Hon. member Associacao Brasileira de Educacaõ; corr. mem. Instituto Nacional de Estudos Pedagógicos; mem. Phi Beta Kappa, Kappa Sigma, Phi Eta Sigma, Sigma Tau Delta, Sigma Pi Sigma, Sigma Eta, Phi Delta Kappa, Phi Kappa Phi (hon.). Pan Am. Airways fellow to Argentina, 1939; Itamarati exchange fellow, 1940; U. of Mich. travel fellow to Brazil, 1940; Guggenheim Fellow (Japanese Edn.), 1946-47, (comparative education), 1953-54; Smith Mundt fellow Brazil, 1949. Co-editor: Report of Workshop of Latin American Studies, 1941; Yearbook of Education (London), 1952-57. Author: (with J. O. Gauntlett) Kokutai No Hongi, 1949; Education for a New Japan, 1949; Shushin: The Ethics of a Defeated Nation, 1949; Education in Crisis, 1950; Problemas de Educaçaõ Rural, 1951; La Edùcación en Crisis, 1954; A Strategy for the Inner City, 1963. Contbr. ednl. and Pan-Am. mags. Address: care College of Petroleum and Minerals Dhahran Saudi Arabia ☆

HALL, ROBERT LATANE, sociologist, educator; b. Atlanta, Feb. 25, 1924; s. James Augustus and Rachel (Rudd) H.; B.S., Yale, 1947; postgrad. U. Stockholm, Sweden, 1947- 48, U. So. Cal., 1950; M.A., U. Minn., 1950, Ph.D., 1953; m. Joyce Engelking Goodwin, July 2, 1957; children—Annalisa, Karen Linda, Jeffrey Beck. Research asst. U. Minn., 1949-52, asst. prof., 1957-60, asso. prof. sociology Office Dean of Students, 1960-62; social psychologist Air Force Personnel and Tng. Research Center, San Antonio, 1952-54, 56- 57, Tampa, Fla., 1954-56; program dir. sociology and social psychology NSF, 1962-65, mem. adv. panel on social sci. traineeships, 1966; asso. prof. sociology and psychology, asst. to dean faculties U. Ill. Chgo. Circle, 1965-66, rof. sociology, head dept., 1966—. Mem. Com. on Sociol. Tng., 1965—. Pres., Hardy Home and Sch. Assn., Washington, 1964-65. Served with USAAF, 1943-45. Decorated D.F.C., Air medal with two oak leaf clusters. Fellow Am. Sociol. Assn.; mem. Am. Psychol. Assn., A.A.A.S., Am. Assn. U. Profs., Am. Vets. Com., Am. Civil Liberties Union. Editorial cons. Sociometry, 1966-70, asso. editor, 1970—. Contbr. articles to profl. jours. Home: 905 Greenleaf Av Wilmette IL 60091 Office: Dept Sociology U Ill at Chgo Circle Box 4348 Chicago IL 60680

HALL, ROBERT LEICESTER, orgn. exec.; b. Taunton, Mass., Aug. 22, 1905; s. Bicknell and Estelle B. (Lane) H.; student Harvard, 1922-24; B.S., U. Mich., 1927; m. Eugenie Zeller, Jan. 1, 1930 (div. Nov. 1937); 1 son, Robert Leicester; m. 2d, Rhoda Halvorsen, Jan. 27, 1938; childrenEdward Christian, Eric Robert Dudley, Benjamin Staples. Aero. engr. Stinson Aircraft Co., Wayne, Mich., 1931-36; with Grumman Aircraft Engring. Corp., 1936-7O, chief engr., 1956, v.p., 1956-7O, ret., 1970; dir. Grumman Allied Industries, Inc.; exec. dir. offshore activities N. Am. Yacht Racing Union, 1969—. Served to lt. (s.g.) USNR, 1938-40. Fellow Am. Inst. Aero. and Astronautics; hon. fellow Soc. Exptl. Test Pilots; mem. Am. Soc. Naval Engrs., Inst. Navigation, Newcomen Soc., Quiet Birdmen, Phi Gamma Delta. Clubs: North American Station of Royal Scandinavian Yacht; N.Y. Yacht; Cruising Am. (ex-commodore); Huntington Yacht (ex-commodore); Storm Trysail (ex-commodore); Off Soundings (ex-commodore); Royal Bermuda Yacht; Seawanhaka Corinthian Yacht (Oyster Bay, N.Y.). Home: 262 Bay Av Huntington NY 11743

HALL, ROBERT MARSHALL, newspaper exec.; b. Providence, Sept. 27, 1909; s. Robert and Ellen Elizabeth (Wood) H.; student Northeastern U. Sch. Law, 1927-30; Ph.B., Brown U., 1934; B.S., Columbia, 1935; m. Ruth Pearl Daniels, Mar. 17, 1936; children—Robert Marshall, Bonnie Ruth. Sales mgr. United Feature Syndicate, 1936-45; pres., past gen. mgr. Publisher's-Hall Syndicate, N.Y.C., 1945—. Clubs: Nat. Press, Nat. Headliners, Overseas Press. Home: 214 Long Neck Point Rd Darien CT 06820 Office: 30 E 42d St New York City NY 10017*

HALL, ROBERT MILTON, mfg. co. exec., inventor; b. Pitts., June 3, 1928; s. DeWitt M. and Virginia (Elig) H.; D.D.S., U. Pitts., 1952; postgrad. U. Tex., Northwestern U.; m. Margaret Ann Heinz, Feb. 7, 1953; children—Bradley Heinz, Jeffrey DeWitt, Barbara Ann. Pvt. practice oral surgery, Pitts., 1957-63; pres. Hall, Inc., surg. systems, Santa Barbara, Cal., 1963—, Hall Air Surgery, Ltd., Zurich, Switzerland, 1963—; dir. Transocean Air Systems Corp. Served to lt. (j.g.) USNR, 1953-55. Recipient Master Design award, 1966; Smithsonian Instn. exhibit award, 1968; nominated for Golden Plate award Am. Acad. Achievement, 1970. Mem. Assn. Advancement Med. Instruments (bd. dirs.), Am. Soc. Oral Surgeons, Internat. Assn. Oral Surgeons, Biomed. Engring. Soc. Rotarian. Club: Explorers (N.Y.C.). Inventor, patentee surg. instruments. Office: 1253 Coast Village Rd Santa Barbara CA 93103

HALL, ROBERT NOEL, physicist; b. New Haven, Dec. 25, 1919; s. Harry V.M. and Clara (Kommers) H.; B.S., Cal. Inst. Tech., 1942, Ph.D., 1948; m. Dora Siechert, Aug. 2, 1941; children—Richard H., Elaine L. Lab. asst., research lab. Gen. Electric Co., 1942-46, physicist, 1948—; spl. research semiconductor laser using gallium arsenide. Recipient David Sarnoff award electronics I.E.E.E., 1963. Fellow Am. Phys. Soc., I.E.E.E.; mem. Electrochem. Soc. Home: 2315 Gurenson Lane Schenectady NY 12309 Office: Gen Electric Research and Devel Center Box 8 Schenectady NY 12301

HALL, ROBERT WILLIAM, educator; b. Arlington, Mass., Apr. 6, 1928; s. Samuel Harry and Agness (Babikian) H.; A.B., Harvard, 1949, M.A., 1951, Ph.D., 1953; m. Mary Alice Starritt, Oct. 25, 1958; children—Christopher Allen, Jonathan Brooks, Pamela Leigh, Timothy Randall. Vis. asst. prof. philosophy Vanderbilt U., 1955-57; vis. asst. prof. philosophy and religion U. Vt., 1957-63, asso. prof., chmn. dept., 1963-67, prof., chmn. dept., 1967—. Served with CIC, AUS, 1953-55. Shedd fellow in religion in higher edn., 1968-69. Mem. Am. Philos. Assn., Soc. Ancient Greek Philosophy (sec.-treas. 1963—), Am. Soc. Aesthetics, Phi Beta Kappa. Author: Plato and the Individual, 1963; Studies in Religious Philosophy, 1969. Editor APEIRON, 1966—. Home: 165 N Prospect St Burlington VT 05401 Office: 481 Main St Burlington VT 05401

HALL, ROY CHARLES, lawyer; b. Seattle, Jan. 28, 1908; s. LeRoy Charles and Stella (Young) H.; A.B., State Coll. Wash., 1929; M.B.A., U. Wash., 1933; postgrad. U. So. Cal., 1942, J.D., U. San Francisco, 1950; children—Elizabeth (Mrs. S. Black), Robert Kilian. Tchr., athletic coach, Centralia (Wash.) 1929-35; tchr., athletic coach, Seattle, 1935- 37; with SouthWestern Pub. Co., 1937-42, 1946-47; dean coll. bus. adminstrn. U. San Francisco, 1947, now lectr. bus. law; sr. partner Hall Buckingham & Cavaguan. Mem. Mayor's Com. on Mental Health. Served with U.S. Army, 1942-46; lt. col. Res. Mem. Cal. bar, San Francisco Bar Assn. (mem. coms. on taxation, continued edn. bar), Am. Bar Assn., Am. Assn. Collegiate Schs. Bus. Adminstrn., Phi Delta Kappa. Republican. Club: Transportation (San Francisco). Pvt. pilot. Writer of miscellaneous articles bus. law. Home: 396 Marietta Dr San Francisco CA 94127 Office: 111 Sutter St San Francisco CA 94104

HALL, ROY MAXWELL, univ. adminstr.; b. Swainsboro, Ga., Mar. 8, 1913; s. Jonah Rayford and Claude Susan (Dozier) H.; student Young Harris Jr. Coll., 1932-34; A.B., Piedmont Coll., 1937; M.Ed., Emory U., 1947; D.Ed., Syracuse U., 1951; m. Leila Carolyn DuPree, Aug. 31, 1939; children—Roy Maxwell, Leila Elizabeth. Prin., supt. Buena Vista (Ga.) pub. schs., 1936-42; supervising prin., Marietta, Ga., 1945-47; research asst., lectr. Syracuse U., 1947-50; asso. dir. Southwestern Coop. Program in Ednl. Adminstrn., prof. ednl. adminstrn., dir. Southwest Sch. Adminstrn. Center, U. Tex., 1950-57; asst. commr. research, dir. div. statistics and research services Office Edn., Dept. Health, Edn. and Welfare, Washington, 1958-61; prof. edn., chmn. dept. curriculum and instrn. U. Tex., 1961-62; dean of edn. U. Del., 1962-68; dean Sch. Edn., Ga. State U., Atlanta, 1968—. Mem. N.E.A., Am. Ednl. Research Assn., Am. Assn. Sch. Adminstrs., Nat. Sch. Bd. Assn., Nat. Soc. Study Edn., Kappa Phi Kappa, Phi Delta Kappa. Address: 33 Gilmer St SE Atlanta GA 30303

HALL, RUFUS GEORGE, educator; b. Sherman, Tex., Dec. 12, 1910; s. Rufus George and Mabel (Skiles) H.; B.A., U. Tex., 1933, M.A., 1935; Ph.D., Harvard, 1948; m. Nancy Joline Furnace, Sept. 20, 1944; children—Nancy Jeanne, Robin James Rufus. Mgr. Rufus G. Hall & Son Ins. Agy., Sherman, 1940-42; instr. polit. sci. U. Okla., 1946-48, asst. prof., 1948-52, asso. prof., 1952-59, prof., 1959—, chmn. dept. govt., 1951-60, asst. dean Coll. Arts and Scis., 1968—, chmn. univ. senate, 1971-72; cons. faculty asso.-in-residence Fgn. Service Inst., Washington, 1967. Bd. dirs., chmn. Wesley Found., Norman. Served with USAAF, 1942-45. Mem. Am. Polit. Sci. Assn., Am. Assn. U. Profs., Southwestern Social Sci. Assn., Internat. Studies Assn., Phi Beta Kappa, Pi Sigma Alpha. Democrat. Methodist. Author: Everthing One Needs to Know About American National Government, 1971. Home: 1031 Grover Lane Norman OK 73069

HALL, RUTH COCHRAN, (Mrs. John E. Hall), educator, assn. exec.; b. Monticello, Ind., Nov. 24, 1916; d. Raymond G. and Helen B. (Graves) Cochran; B.S., Ohio State U., 1947; M.S., Purdue U., 1948, Ph.D., 1956; m. John E. Hall, July 25, 1953; 1 dau., Karen Elizabeth Whitehouse. Asst. instr. Ohio State U., summer 1947, U. Tenn., summer 1948; instr. Mich. State Coll., 1948-49; asst. prof. Okla. A. and M. Coll., 1949-52, U. Colo., 1954-56; prof., dir. Sch. Home Econs., U. Ariz., 1956—. Advisor Nat. Assn. Extension Home Economists, 1970—; mem. nat. adv. bd. Betty Crocker Search for Homemaker of Tomorrow; mem. constrn. teaching facilities for allied health professions rev. com. Health, Edn. and Welfare, 1968-69. Mem. numerous adv. coms. Mem. Am. Home Econs. Assn. (chmn. coll. and univs. sect.; pres. 1964-66; trustee found; vice chmn. West Anniversary fund 1969-70), Ariz. Consumer's Council (exec. bd., v.p. 1966-67), Am. Ednl. Research Assn., Western Regional Home Econs. Research Adminstrs. Council (chmn. 1969-71), Ariz. Home Econs. Assn. (pres. 1963-64), Nat. Council Family Relations, Purdue Alumni Assn. Fellowship, Future Homemakers Am. (hon.), Alpha Lambda Delta, Gamma Sigma Delta, Phi Upsilon Omicron, Omicron Nu. Home econs. authenticator New Standard Ency., Home: 5945 N Piedra Seca Tucson AZ 85718

HALL, SHELDON FRANKLIN, office equipment mfr.; b. Mathews County, Va., July 8, 1914; s. Robert F. and Viola L. (Hudgins) H.; B.S., Va. Poly. Inst., 1936; LL.B., George Washington U., 1946; m. Jess Fisher Holland, July 10, 1937; children—Sheldon Franklin, Kathryn Frances. Salesman, Norfolk (Va.) br. Burroughs Corp., 1936, successively sales promotion, Detroit, asst. to southeastern div. mgr., spl. rep. govtl. affairs, Washington, asst. sec.-treas., Detroit, sec., v.p., 1952- ; v.p., sec., dir. Mittag & Volger, Park Ridge, N.J., Mittag & Methudy, Inc., N.Y.C., Acme Carbon & Ribbon Co., Ltd., Toronto. Patent agt. U.S. Patent Office; mem. office machinery industry adv. com. U.S. Dept. Commerce. Trustee Childrens Hosp., Detroit; bd. dirs. Children Research Center, Detroit. Mem. Office Equipment Mfrs. Inst. (v.p., dir., mem. exec. com.), A.I.M., Am. Soc. Corporate Secs. (pres. Mich. group), Detroit Engring. Soc., Detroit Bd. Commerce, Phi Alpha Delta, Alpha Kappa Psi. Republican. Methodist. Clubs: Recess, Economic (Detroit); Cavalier (Virginia Beach, Va.). Home: 42 Harbor Hill Grosse Pointe MI Office: 6071 Second Av Detroit MI 48202 *

HALL, SPENCER GILBERT, lawyer; b. Harrisburg, Pa., May 13, 1910; s. Francis J. and Harriet Spencer (Gilbert) H.; grad. Lawrenceville (N.J.) Sch., 1928; A.B., Princeton, 1932; LL.B., Dickinson Sch. Law, 1936; m. Josephine McCreight, Jan. 15, 1946; children—Spencer Gilbert, W. Maclay, Harriet G., Josephine McC. Admitted to Pa. bar, 1937; city solicitor, Harrisburg, 1949-68; mem. firm Nauman, Smith, Shissler & Hall, 1937—. Dir. Commonwealth Nat. Bank, 1949—, chmn. exec. com., 1964—; dir. Harrisburg Hotel Co., 1949—, v.p.,, 1963- 67, pres., 1967-71; dir. W.O. Hickok Mfg. Co., Penn- Harris Hotel Co. Trustee Harrisburg Acad., 1952—, past pres.; bd. mgrs. Harrisburg Hosp., 1939—, chmn. med. com. 1948—; trustee Harrisburg State Hosp. Served to lt. comdr. USNR, 1942-46. Mem. Scotch Irish Soc. (past pres.), Delta Psi. Presbyn. (trustee). Rotarian. Clubs: Philadelphia; Harrisburg Country; Ivy (Princeton). Home: Welcome Hall RD 3 Dillsburg PA 17019 Office: Bergner Bldg Harrisburg PA 17108

HALL, STANDISH, finance, trusteeships and warehousing exec.; b. Chgo., Sept. 30, 1891; s. Harry Newbury and Anne (Russell) H.; grad. Hotchkiss Sch., 1912; A.B., Harvard, 1916; m. Helen Brooks, June 5, 1920 (dec. Dec. 1961); children—Brooks, Wolcott (died in service AAF, 1944), Bradford; m. 2d, Margaret Bailey Echols, Dec. 12, 1962. With W. R. Grace & Co., Peru, 1916-17; with credit dept. Union Trust Co., Chgo., 1919-20, mgr. new bus. dept., 1920-21, advt. dir., 1921-22, asst. sec., 1922-23; v.p., dir. Union Nat. Bank, Wichita, 1923-28; v.p., dir. Guarantee Title & Trust Co., 1928-29, pres., dir., 1929-30; pres., dir. Yellow Van & Storage Co., 1931-52, Met. Warehouse Co., 1931—; operator Standish Hall Co., gen. ins. and investment, 1930—; trustee ct. apptd. oil royalty syndicates. Trustee Gerontol. Research Found., St. Louis. Dir. civil def. State of Kan., 1950-54; pres. Nat. Assn. State Civil Def. Dirs., 1951-52. Served from seaman to ensign, USNR, 1917-19, comdr., 1941-46. Awarded Commendation medal. Mem. Kan. Hist. Soc. (dir.), Wichita Art Assn. (trustee), Wichita

Civic Music Assn. (trustee). Republican. Episcopalian. Clubs: University (Chgo.); Army and Navy (Washington). Home and office: Apartado Postal 418 Cuernavaca Morelos Mexico

HALL, THEO ELMER, former fgn. service officer; b. Wichita, Kan., Oct. 12, 1914; s. Orrin Basil and Bessie May (Wilcons) H.; student Wichita U., 1934-35, 36-39, U. Chgo., 1942; A.B., Wichita State, 1970; m. Thayal Flora Roth, Mar. 3, 1938 (div. 1968); children—Terrence Winfield, Sharon Lynn, Judith Ann, Theo Elizabeth; m. 2d, Mary Brannon Shuey, Jan. 9, 1969. Police officer, 1936-39; cons. Pub. Adminstrn. Service, 1939-45; supervising parole ofcr., 1941; chief city police depts., 1941-45; dir. security Metall. Lab., U. Chgo., 1943-44; dep. chief, chief pub. safety br. office Mil. Govt. for Germany, 1945- 49; mem. office U.S. High Commr. for Germany, 1949-53; dir. joint adminstrv. services U.S. Mission, Athens, Greece, 1954-56; fgn. service officer Dept. State, 1956-57; chief pub. safety div. ICA, 1957-60; 1st sec. Am. embassy, Taipei, Taiwan, 1960-62; fgn. service insp., 1962-64; exec. dir. Bur. Edn. and Cultural Affairs, Dept. State, 1964- 66; counselor embassy adminstrv. affairs Am. embassy, New Delhi, India, 1966-68; dep. dir. Pub. Safety Directorate, Saigon, Vietnam, 1968-69; counselor embassy adminstrv. affairs Am. embassy, Saigon, 1969-70; ret. 1970. Address: 1870 Chinook Trail Maitland FL 32751

HALL, THEODORE PARSONS, engr., corp. exec.; b. Wallingford, Conn., Dec. 18, 1898; s. Charles Storrs and Flora (Fordham) H.; E.E., Syacuse U., 1927; M.S., Mass. Inst. Tech., 1928; m. Marion E. Parsons, April 6, 1929; childrenMarguerite Parsons (Mrs. John R. Stitt), Janet C. (Mrs. Harry G. Backer), Theodora P. (Mrs. Robert E. Burton). With Gen. Electric Co., N.Y.C., 1919-22; engr. Thomas-Morse Aircraft Corp., Ithaca, N.Y.; research engr. Cunningham- Hall Aircraft Corp., Rochester, N.Y., 1929-31; chief devel. engr. Consol. Aircraft Corp. (now div. Gen. Dynamics, Inc.), 1931-48; pres., chief engr. T.P. Hall Engring. Corp., San Diego, Cal., 1949—; developed Hall Flying Automobile. Served with U.S. Army, AEF, overseas, 1917-19. Mem. Soc. Automotive Engrs., Inst. Aero. Sci., Acacia, Theta Tau. Mason. Holder patents. Home: 2006 Orizaba Av San Diego CA 92103 Office: Gillespie Field Santee CA 22071

HALL, THOMAS MUNROE, violinist; b. Tallahassee, Fla., Sept. 1, 1943; s. John Lewis and Martha Hauze (Buford) H.; Mus.B. magna cum laude with Honors, Fla. State U., 1964, Mus.M., 1966. With Fla. Symphony Orch., Orlando, 1962-64, Richmond (Va.) Symphony Orch., 1966-69, Cin. Symphony Orch., 1969-70; violinist Chgo. Symphony Orch., 1970—; mem. Meridian String Quartet, 1969—. Served with AUS, 1966-69. Home: 57091 N Sheridan Rd Chicago IL 60660 Office: 220 S Michigan Av Chicago IL 60604

HALL, THOMAS STEELE, educator; born St. Louis, May 4, 1909; s. Frederick Bagby and Corinne (Steele) H.; student Washington U., 1926-28, 32-33; A.B., Yale, 1930, Ph.D., 1940; grad. study Princeton, 1936-38; m. Mary Taussig Tompkins, Oct. 21, 1952; stepchildren—Mary Waterman T., Frederick Kingsbury T. Instructor Lawrenceville School, 1935-41; asst. prof. biol. sci. U. Chicago, 1941-43; asso. prof. biology Purdue U., 1943-45; asso. prof. zoology Washington University, St. Louis, 1945-51, professor zoology, 1951-67, professor of biology, 1967—, chmn. basic coll. program, 1948- 49, dean coll. liberal arts, 1949-61, chmn. commn. undergrad. edn. biol. scis., 1962-66. Mem. com. on edn. policies NRC, 1954-58; adv. bd. on edn. Nat. Acad. Sci.-NRC, 1958-61. Mem. bd. St. Louis Little Symphony Assn., 1951—, music chmn., 1951-56, chmn. bd., 1955, president, 1957- 60. Trustee St. Louis Public Library. Faculty fellow National Science Foundation, 1958-60. Member Missouri State Teachers' Association (president higher education division, 1956-57), A.A.A.S., Am. Soc. Zoologists, Am. Soc. Naturalists, Soc. Hist. Med., Phi Beta Kappa, Sigma Xi. Clubs: University, Town and Gown (St. Louis). Co-author textbook; author hist. papers; author: Ideas of Life and Matter, 1969. Editor: The Source Book of Animal Biology, 1951. Editor, translator: Descarte's Treatise of Man, 1971. Home: 50 Westmoreland Pl St Louis MO 63108

HALL, THOMAS WILLIAM, educator; b. Portis, Kan., Sept. 20, 1921; s. Charles E. and Myrtle (DeWitt) H.; A.B., Kan Wesleyan U., 1943; Th.M., Iliff Sch. Theology, Denver, 1946; Ph.D., Boston U., 1956; m. Ruth Helen Fisher, July 11, 1944, childrenCarolyn Jane, Kristin Elaine, Douglas William. Asst. prof. Kan. Wesleyan U., 1946-48, Pittsburg (Kan.) State Coll., 1950-55; asso. prof., chmn. dept. religion U. Denver, 1956-59; dean religion Stephens Coll., Columbia, Mo., 1959-66; prof., chmn. dept. religion Syracuse U., 1966-. Danforth tchr., 1955-56; grantee Syracuse U. travel and research, summer 1968. Mem. Am. Acad. Religion. Research religious thought Europe and Asia. Home: 139 Lewis Av Syracuse, NY 13224.

HALL, VERNON, educator; born Atlanta, Nov. 30, 1913; s. Vernon and Anne (Webb) H.; student Amherst Coll., 1932-34; A.B., N.Y.U., 1936, M.A., 1937; Ph.D., U. Wis., 1940; M.A. (hon.), Dartmouth, 1950; m. Marie-Louise Michaud, June 17, 1938 (div.); 1 dau., Anne-Marie; m. 2d, Sandra Cox, Sept. 13, 1967. Asst. English, Univ. of Wis., 1937-40; instr. English, Pueblo (Colo.) Jr. Coll., 1940-41, Dartmouth, 1941-46, asst. prof. comparative lit., U. Wis., 1964—, chmn. dept., 1970—; summer tchr. City Coll. N.Y., 1940-41, N.Y.U., 1960, U. Wis. 1961; vis. prof. Univ. of Aix-Marseilles, 1965-66. Publicity dir. Hanover Def. Council, 1942-44. Mem. Am. Assn. U. Profs., Modern Lang. Assn. Modern Humanities Research Assn., Société Académique d'Agen (an honorary member), Psi Upsilon. Author following books: Renaissance Literary Criticism: A Study of Its Social Content, 1945; Life of Julius Caesar Scaliger, 1484-1558, 1950; Byzantine Gold Coins in the Dartmouth Collection (with J.B. Stearns, 1952; Editor: (with O. Cargill and J. Bennett) Studies in English Renaissance Drama, 1959; A Short History of Literary Criticism, 1963; Literary Criticism: Plato Through Johnson, 1970. Asst. editor of Renaissance News, 1948-50; fgn. lang. editor The Explicator, 1948—; editorial advisor Coll. English, 1952-54, 58-60; book reviewer, Herald-Tribune, N.Y.C., 1958-65. Contbr. scholarly publs. Home: 2210 Van Hise Av Madison WI 53205

HALL, WALTER BURNETTE, lawyer; b. Sand Springs, Okla., Oct. 20, 1923; s. Burnette Johnson and Louise (Hixson) H.; B.A., Tex. A. and M. U., 1947; LL.B., Harvard, 1950; m. Mary Carolyn Leicht, Aug. 31, 1946; children—Walter Phillip, Mary Lou. Admitted to Okla. bar, 1951; practice in Tulsa, 1951-52; asst. trial counsel Mid-Continent Petroleum Corp., 1952-56; trial counsel Service Pipe Line Co., 1956-66; sr. partner firm Hall, Estill, Hardwick, Gable & Collingsworth, Tulsa, 1966—; gen. counsel Williams Bros. Co., Tulsa, 1967—; counsel, v.p., dir. Leland Equipment Co., Fleet Finance Co., Barnes Enterprises, Inc., Midwest Gem Co. Vice chmn. Tulsa County Election Bd., 1961-64, Gov. Okla. Spl. Commn. Election Laws, 1965; chmn. Sand Springs Planning Commn., 1955-64, Sand Springs Community Devel. Program, 1962-64, Tulsa County Spl. Commn. Voting Machines, 1965. Served to capt. AUS, 1942-45. Recipient spl. citation Gov. Okla., 1966, 67, City Council Sand Springs, 1967. Mem. Am., Okla. (past pres., sec. adminstrv. law sect.), Tulsa County, Inter-Am. bar assns., Am. Right of Way Assn., Assn. ICC Practitioners, Am. Legion, V.F.W., Harvard Law Sch. Assn. Okla. (pres. 1956). Republican. Presbyn. Mason. Clubs: Tulsa, Southern Hills Country, Cedar Ridge Country, Petroleum, Tex. A. and M. (pres. 1955) (Tulsa); Osage Hills Country (past pres., dir.) (Sand Springs, Okla.) Home: 5809 S Evanston St Tulsa OK 74105 Office: Nat Bank of Tulsa Bldg Tulsa OK 74103

HALL, WARNER LEANDER, clergyman; b. Covington, Tenn., Nov. 9, 1907; s. Warner L. and Leila (Perkins) H.; A.B., Southwestern at Memphis 1929, D.D., 1956; B.D., Louisville Presbyn. Sem., 1932; postgrad. U. Berlin, 1933; Ph.D., U. Edinburgh, 1934; postgrad. U. Zurich, 1964; m. Lucy Hendricks Farrow, Sept. 16, 1929; children—Warner Leander, Nancy Farrow (Mrs. Russell Newell Grimes). Ordained to ministry Presbyn. Ch., 1934; pastor Presbyn. Ch., Leland, Miss., 1934-36, Maxwell St. Presbyn. Ch., Lexington, Ky., 1936-40, First Presbyn. Ch., Tuscaloosa, Ala., 1940-46, Covenant Presbyn. Ch., Charlotte, N.C., 1946—. Mem. bd. world missions Presbyn. Ch. U.S. Chmn. Mayor's Com. on Human Relations, Charlotte, 1965—; chmn. Charlotte-Mecklenburg Community Relations 1965—. Chmn. bd. trustees Davidson Coll.; trustee Union Theol. Sem. Va. Mem. Phi Beta Kappa, Alpha Tau Omega. Democrat. Clubs: Myers Park Country, Charlotte Country, Rotary. Author: Symbols of the Faith, 1965. Home: 727 Queens Rd Charlotte NC 28207 Office: 1000 E Morehead St Charlotte NC 28204

HALL, WARREN ESTERLY, Jr., lawyer; b. Atlanta, Ga., Dec. 22, 1910; s. Warren Esterly and Martha (Haygood) H.; student Ga. Sch. Tech., 1929-30 and 1931-32; LL.B., Atlanta Law Sch., 1938; m. Pauline Lewis, Feb. 3, 1934; children—Martha Anne, Warren Esterly, III (dec.). Engr., B.M. Hall & Sons, Atlanta, 1926-32; various positions including sales, office management and govt., 1932-37; admitted to Ga. bar, 1937, Fla. bar, 1954; labor relations advisor to OPA adminstr., Washington, also atty. and asst. adminstr. Southeastern states, Atlanta, 1942-45; partner Prestwood & Hall, Atlanta, 1937-42, Poole, Pearce & Hall, Atlanta, 1946-61, Hall Sweeny, & Godbee Deland, 1955-60, Adams, Hall, Sweeny & Godbee, Fort Lauderdale, 1958-60, Holland, Bevis, Smith, Kibler & Hall, and predecessors, Bartow and Lakeland, Fla., 1965-68, Holland & Knight, Bartow, Lakeland and Tampa, Fla., 1968—; Gen. solicitor Economic Stablzn. Agy., Washington, 1950-51; legal advisor to under sec. Navy, Washington, 1951; instr., lectr. labor law various law schs. Mem. Fed., Am., Ga., Atlanta, 10th Jud. Circuit bar assns., Am. Judicature Soc., Ga. State Bar, Fla. Bar (del. jud. conf. of 5th circuit, 1964-71, chmn. appellate ct. rules subcom. 1964-67, vice-chmn. Fla. ct. rules committee 1966-67), Am. Arbitration Assn. (nat. panel arbitration), Scribes, Phi Delta Theta. Episcopalian. Clubs: Lawyers (Atlanta); Peace River Country. Bd. editors Fla. Law and Practice. Contbr. articles to legal publs. Home: 1610 S Hibiscus Dr Bartow FL 33830 Office: 245 S Central Av Bartow FL 33830 ☆

HALL, WAYNE CLARK, govt. ofcl.; b. Van Dalia, Mont., Oct. 16, 1919; s. William M. and Gertrude (Clark) H.; B.S., U. Ia., 1941, M.S. in Plant Physiology and Chemistry, 1946, Ph.D., 1948; m. Dorothy R. Holzhauser, Aug. 18, 1941; children—Janice Anne, Randall Clark. Teaching and research asst. State U. Ia., 1938-41, 46-47, research asso., 1948; asst. prof. botany, acting head dept., U. Ky., 1948-49; mem. faculty Tex. A. and M. Coll., 1949—, prof. plant physiology and pathology, head dept., 1958-60, former dean grad. studies, academic v.p., 1964-68; dir. fellowships Nat. Acad. Scis.-NRC, Washington, 1968-71; now v.p. grad. studies and research, prof. biology State U. N.Y. at Binghamton. Vis. lectr. NSF, 1961; project leader plant physiology and radio chemistry Tex. Agrl. Expt. Sta., 1949-61; collaborator for USDA, cotton and cordage fibers research br. and So. utilization research br., 1957-61. Grantee NIH, 1958-61, AEC, 1958-62, Nat. Cotton Council Found., 1960. Recipient 1st faculty Achievement award for research Tex. A. and M. Coll., 1955. Mem. Bot. Soc. Am., Am. Soc. Plant Physiology (pres. So. sect. 1956), Scandinavian Soc. Plant Physiology, Am. Phytopathol. Soc., Am. Inst. Biol. Scis., A.A.A.S., Sigma Xi (past pres. Tex. A. and M. chpt.), Phi Kappa Phi (past pres. Tex. A. and M. chpt.). Author: Laboratory Manual for Plant Physiology, 1958; An Outline of Methods and Procedures Used in Plant Physiological Research, 1958; also numerous articles. Home: 2501 Calvert St NW Washington DC 20008

HALL, WESLEY WHITFIELD, physician; b. Lumberton, Miss., July 11, 1906; s. Wesley William and Carrier (Ellis) H.; A.B., Miss. Coll., 1926; student U. Miss., 1928; M.D., Tulane U., 1930; m. Louise Wilkinson, June 14, 1932 (div. 1944); childrenWesley Whitfield, Susan Caroline; m. 2d, Elise Griffin, Apr. 21, 1945; childrenCaroline Elizabeth, Lee Davis, Margaret Jane. Intern, resident Baroness Erlanger Hosp., Chattanooga, 1933-36; pvt. practice, Reno, 1945-; mem. staff Washoe Med. Center, 1945-, chief surgery, 1953, chief staff, 1955, sr. cons. surgery, orthopedics, gynecology and obstetrics, 1945-; mem. staff St. Mary's Hosp., 1945-, vice chief staff, 1955, chief surgery, 1956. Mem. com. indigent care Council Med. Service, A.M.A., 1956-61, med. adviser, examiner Nev. Boxing and Wrestling Comm., 1960-66; team physician Washoe County High Schs., also athletic teams U. Nev., 1946-. Squadron comdr. Washoe Jeep Squadron, search and rescue unit Civil Air Patrol and Washoe County Sheriffs Office. Fellow A.C.S., Southeastern Surg. Congress; mem. Am. (ho. of dels. 1952-61, trustee 1961-70, chairman of the board of trustees 1966-68, pres.-elect 1970-71), Nev. (sec.-treas. 1948-50) med. assns., Reno Surg. Soc. (a founder, past pres.), Washoe County Med. Soc., Am. Assn. Ry. Surgeons, Kappa Sigma, Theta Kappa Psi. Methodist (steward). Rotarian (past pres. Reno), Mason (Shriner). Clubs: Reno Executives; M (U. Miss.). Office: 607 N Arlington Av Reno NV 89503

HALL, WILBUR CURTIS, lawyer; b. Mountain Gap, Loudoun County, Va., Feb. 5, 1892; s. John W. And Annie E. (Holliday) H.; student Washington and Lee U., 1910-11, 1913- 14; LL.B., Georgetown U., 1915; LL.D., Washington and Lee University, Admitted to Va. bar, 1915, practiced at Leesburg. Chief petty officer U.S. N.R.F., July-Dec. 1918. Mem. Va. Ho. of Dels., 1918-35 (chmn. House Finance com.; chmn. Joint Dem. Caucus); mem. Jud. Council of Va., Commn. of Fisheries; Dem. elector 8th Congl. Dist., Va., 1924; Dem. elector, Va. at large, 1932; chmn. Va. Conservation Commn., 1935-39; mem. exec. com. on Commn. to Reorganize Govt. Va., 1948. Former mem. bd. visitors Coll. William and Mary in Va. Mem. Order Coif, Phi Beta Kappa, Omicorn Delta Kappa, Pi Gamma Mu. Episcopalian. Mason (Shriner), Odd Fellow. Clubs: Rotary (Leesburg); University (Washington). Home: Leesburg VA 22075

HALL, WILFRED MCGREGOR, engring. exec. b. Denver, June 12, 1894; s. Frederick Folsom and Annie L. (Thompson) H.; B.S., U. Colo., 1916; D.Eng., Tufts U., 1955; m. Anne Gertrude Jones, Apr. 4, 1921; children—Fredrick Folsom, Anne (dec.). Engr. hydroelectric constrn. Chas. T. Main Co., 1916-17, engr. hydroelectric investigation and design, 1920-22, with Chas. T. Main, Inc., 1941-, dir., 1943-, v.p., 1953-57, pres., 1957-; engr. Chrisfield Contracting Co., 1919; supt. constrn., engr. U.G.I. Contracting Co., 1922-28; supt. constrn. Electric Bond & Share Co., 1929- 31; cons. engr., 1932-33; engr. charge constrn. TVA, 1933-37; mgr. engring. and constrn., P.R., 1937-41; partner Uhl, Hall & Rich, 1953-62, mng. partner, 1962-; dir. Arkwright-Boston Mfrs. Mut. Ins. Co., Morgan Meml., Inc., Doble Engring. Co. Mem. U.S. Com. Large Dams. Bd. dirs. Mass. Heart Assn. Fellow Am. Soc. C.E.; mem. A.I.M. (fellow pres.'s council 1966), Am. Inst. Cons. Engrs. (past pres. New Eng. sect.), Cons. Engrs. Council New Eng. (dir.), Soc. Mil. Engrs., Newcomen Soc. (trustee, chmn. New Eng. com.), Mass. Soc. Profl Engrs., Alpha Sigma Phi, Sigma Tau, Tau Beta Pi. Clubs: Brae Burn Country (West Newton, Mass.); Algonquin (past dir.), Hamilton Trust (past pres.) (Boston). Home: Longwood Towers Brookline MA 02146 Office: Southeast Tower Prudential Center Boston MA 02199

HALL, WILLIAM BARNETT, banker; b. Windber, Pa., Feb. 9, 1905; s. Arthur S. and Mahala G. (Barnett) H.; B.S., Wayne U., 1926; postgrad. grad. sch. banking Rutgers U., 1949; m. Leah Common, June 20, 1928; childrenBarbara Elayne, Nancy Fay. Cashier, City Indsl. Bank, 1926-29; jr. officer Peoples State Bank, Pontiac, Mich., 1929-33; state auditor Civilian Works Adminstrn., 1933-34; loan examiner R.F.C., 1934-36; mgr. monthly payment loan dept. Detroit Bank (now named The Detroit Bank & Trust Co.), 1936-45, asst. cashier, 1940-43, asst. v.p., 1943-47, v.p., 1947-60, sr. v.p., 1960-64, exec. v.p., 1964-; treas., dir. Mauna Loa Restaurants, Inc.; coordinator Nat. Sales Finance Plan Chgo., 1945-46. Mem. Neighborhood Service Orgn. Bd. govs. Wayne State U., 1964-68, emeritus, 1968-. Trustee Kingswood Hosp. Mem. Detroit Urban League (pres. 1961, dir.), Financial Pub. Relations Assn. (bd. dirs.), Am. Inst. Banking (past pres. Detroit chpt.), Pub. Relations Assn. Detroit, Wayne Alumni Assn. (past. pres.). Presbyn. Clubs: Detroit Athletic; Grosse Pointe Yacht Contbr. profl. mags. and bulls. Home: 1464 N Renaud Grosse Pointe Woods MI 48236 Office: 201 W Fort St Detroit MI 48226 *

HALL, WILLIAM CHARLES, assn. exec.; b. St. Louis, Mar. 21, 1909; s. William Antoine and Grace (Caldwell) H.; student Washington U., St. Louis, 1927; B.S., U.S. Mil. Acad., 1931; M.S. in Civil Engring., U. Cal. at Berkeley, 1938; student Nat. War Coll., 1955-56; m. Elizabeth Pleasants Brooke, Nov. 2, 1940; 1 son, Edward Brooke. Commd. 2d lt. U.S. Army, 1931, advanced through grades to brig. gen., 1959; chief map and photo br. Dept. of Army, 1950- 53; army engr. 2d Army, 1953-55; chief logistics div. Alaskan Command, 1956-59; asst. chief engrs. for personnel Office Chief Engrs. 1959-61, acting chief mil. constrn., 1960-61, dir. research and devel., 1961-62; dep. chief logistics div. European Command, 1962-63; ret., 1963; exec. sec. Soc. Am. Mil. Engrs., Washington, 1965-. Decorated Legion of Merit with oak leaf cluster, Bronze Star medal; Croix de Guerre with palm (France). Registered profl. engr., D.C. Mem. Soc. Am. Mil. Engrs., Permanent Internat. Assn. Navigation Congresses, Assn. of U.S. Army. Clubs: Army- Navy, Army-Navy Country (Washington). Author: A Medal for Horatius, 1955. Contbr. articles tech. mags. Home: 4611 Kenmore Dr NW Washington, DC 20007. Office: 800 17th St NW Washington DC 20006

HALL, WILLIAM DELANEY, accountant; b. Kansas City, Mo., June 16, 1922; s. Thomas N. and Ethel (Delaney) H.; B.S., U. Ill., 1947, M.S., 1948; m. Barbara Doane; children—Laurie E., Thomas D., J. Alexander, Andrew D. With Arthur Andersen & Co., C.P.A.'s, 1948—, partner, 1958—, dir. accounting and audit practice, Europe, 1970—. Served to 1st lt. USAAF, World War II. C.P.A., Ill., 6 other states. Mem. Am. Inst. C.P.A.'s, Ill. Soc. C.P.A.'s, Mich. Assn. C.P.A.'s, Am. Accounting Assn., Alpha Sigma Phi, Beta Alpha Psi, Beta Gamma Sigma. Presbyn. Club: Mid-Day (Chgo.). Home: 10 Stanhope Terrace London W2 England Office: St Alphage House 2 Fore St London EC2 England

HALL, WILLIAM EDWARD, Jr., educator, journalist; b. Weston, W. Va., Mar. 21, 1923; s. William Edward and Olive Marion (McGee) H.; B.A., U. N.M., 1944; M.S., Columbia, 1950; Ph.D., State U. Ia., 1954; m. Lou Ann Jones, Nov. 27, 1946 (div.); childrenSharon Lou, Roberta Ann, William Philip; m. 2d, Carol Ann Cusick, Sept. 1, 1966; children—Kevin Dennis, Kimberlee Marian. Reporter Albuquerque (N.M.) Tribune, 1936-46, sports editor, 1943, 46; dir. alumni relations U. N.M., 1947-52, instr. journalism part-time, 1950-51, asst. to pres., 1953; head dept. journalism, dir. pub. relations Tex. Tech. Coll., 1954-56; prof., dir. Sch. Journalism, U. Neb., 1956-66; prof., dir. Sch. Journalism, Ohio State U., 1966-. Co-ordinator Ia., Internat. Press Inst. flow news study, 1953. Neb. cons. pub. relations, pub. information A.R.C. Served with AUS, World War II; ETO. Winner Printer's Ink Silver Medal award Am. Fedn. Advt., 1964. Mem. Am. Assn. Schs. and Depts. Journalism (pres. 1968-69), Assn. Edn. Journalism, Kappa Tau Alpha, Sigma Delta Chi, Pi Sgma Alpha, Pi Kappa Alpha. Club: Lincoln Advertising (chmn. bd. 1964-65). Home: 2941 Rockford Dr Columbus OH 43220

HALL, WILLIAM HEINLEN, chemist, educator; b. Cairo, W. Va., June 19, 1910; s. Andrew Brown and Jeanette Margaret (Heinlen) H.; A.B., Muskingum Coll., 1932; Ph.D., Ohio State U., 1939; m. Mildred Aileen Walker, Sept. 5, 1937; children-John Brown, James Walker. Instr. chemistry Bowling Green State U., 1936-39, asst. prof., 1939-45, asso. prof., 1945-48, prof., 1948-, chmn. dept. chemistry, 1954-. Fellow A.A.A.S., Ohio Acad. Sci.; mem. Am. Chem. Soc., Nat. Sci. Tchrs. Assn., Am. Soc. Information Sci., Sigma Xi. Home: 152 Troup Av Bowling Green OH 43402

HALL, WILLIAM JACKSON, educator, statistician; b. Beltsville, Md., Nov. 13, 1929; s. Reginald Foster and Lily (Hambleton) H.; A.B., Johns Hopkins, 1950; M.A., U. Mich., 1951; Ph.D., U. N.C., 1955; postgrad. Manchester (Eng.) U., 1953, Cambridge (Eng.), U. 1954; m. Helen Bloxom Cox, Mar. 27, 1954; children-Jacqueline Arden, Rebecca Clayton, Bryan Hambleton, Kay Randall. Statistician, Bell Telephone Labs., N.Y.C., 1954-55; asst. chief Polio Surveillance Unit, Communicable Disease Center, USPHS, Atlanta, 1955-57; lectr. U. Cal. at Berkeley, 1957; asst. prof. U. N.C., 1957-61, asso. prof., 1961-66, prof. statistics, 1966-69; vis. prof. Stanford, 1967-69, U. Cal. at Berkeley, 1969; prof., chmn. dept. statistics U. Rochester 1969—. Fellow A.A.A.S., Am. Statis. Assn., Inst. Math. Statistics; mem. Royal Statis. Soc., Am. Assn. Univ. Profs. Asso. editor Annals of Mathematical Statistics, 1968—. Home: 85 Council Rock Av Rochester NY 14610

HALL, WILLIAM JOEL, educator, cons. engr.; b. Berkeley, Cal., Apr. 13, 1926; s. Eugene Raymond and Mary (Harkey) H.; student U. Cal. at Berkeley, 1943-44; student U.S. Merchant Marine Acad., 1944-45; B.S. in Civil Engring., U. Kan., 1948; M.S., U. Ill., 1951, Ph.D., 1954; m. Elaine Frances Thalman, Dec. 20, 1948; childrenMartha Jane, James Frederick, Carolyn Marie. Teaching asst. U. Kan., 1947-48; engr. Sohio Pipe Line Co., 1948-49; mem. faculty U. Ill. at Urbana, 1949-, prof. civil engring., 1959-, asso. mem. Center Adv. Study, Grad. Coll., 1963-64; cons. structural, seismic, materials to govt. orgns. and industry, 1954—. Mem. adv. com. civil def. Nat. Acad. Sci., 1964-68; participant project HARBOR, 1964, 67; mem. tech. adv. com. high speed ground transp. Dept. Commerce, 1966. Recipient A. Epstein Meml. award U. Ill., 1958. Fellow Am. Soc. C.E. (past chmn. com. plasticity, engring. mechanics div., past chmn. research com. structural div.; pres. Central Ill. sect. 1967-68; Kan. sect. award 1948; Walter L. Huber award 1963); member National Academy of Engineering, American Concrete Institute, Am. Soc. M.E., American Welding Soc. (Adams Meml. membership award 1967), Internat. Assn. Bridge and Structural Engrs., Seismological Soc. Am., Am. Soc. Testing and Materials, Soc. Exptl. Stress Analysis, Am. Soc. Engring, Edn., A.A.A.S., Ill., Nat. socs. profl. engrs., Sigma Xi, Tau Beta Pi, Sigma Tau, Chi Epsilon, Phi Kappa Phi. Author: (with others) Brittle Fracture of Welded Plate, 1967; also articles, chpts. in books, revs. Home: 3105 Valley Brook Dr Champaign, IL 61820. Office: Civil Engring Bldg Univ Ill Urbana IL 61801

HALL, WILLIAM LAYTON, educator; b. Pratt, Kan., Aug. 26, 1912; s. Arthur John and Nellie Maud (Read) H.; A.B., Coll. of Emporia, 1934; M.B.A., Harvard, 1936; m. Grace Vivian Hedlund, June 17, 1939; children—Philip Layton, Richard Hedlund, Walter Randall. Personnel and service exec. Hahne & Co., Newark, 1936-40; dir. placement, lectr. marketing U. Newark (now merged with Rutgers U.), 1940, dir. div. spl. edn. and war tng. 1941-45, coordinator vets. program, dir. div. spl. edn., 1945-47, asso. prof. marketing Sch. Bus. Adminstrn., 1947-50; dean Rutgers U., State U. N.J., Coll. of S. Jersey, 1950-69, prof. econs., community devel. Coll. Agr. and Environmental Sci., 1969—. Mem. Comprehensive Health Planning Agy. So. N.J., Camden County Mosquito Extermination Commn. Bd. dirs. Greater Camden Movement. Trustee West Jersey Hosp., Helene Field Sch. Nursing at West Jersey. Presbyn. (elder). Rotarian. Home: 456 Browning Lane Cherry Hill NJ 08034 Office: 152 Ohio Av Clementon NJ 08021

HALL, WILLIAM LLOYD, surgeon; b. Wichita Falls, Tex., Aug. 25, 1925; s. Lloyd Lorenso and Frankie (Hodges) H.; student N. Tex. State U., 1942-44; M.D., Southwestern Med. Coll., 1947; children—Marc William, Michael Steven, Lisa Merenith, Jay Jonathan. Intern George Washington U. Hosp., 1947-48; resident Great Lakes Naval Hosp., 1948-49, Baylor U. Hosp., 1953-56; practice medicine, specializing in surgery, Dallas, 1956—; mem. staff Methodist Hosp.; chief surgery Kessler Hosp. Served to lt. M.C., U.S. Navy, 1948-53. Diplomate Am. Bd. Surgery. Mem. A.M.A., Tex. Med. Assn., Dallas Surg. Soc., Dallas County Med. Soc. Rotarian. Home: 4509 Crown Knoll Dallas TX 95208 Office: 122 W Colorado St Dallas TX 75208

HALL, WILLIAM O., govt. ofcl.; b. Roswell, N.M., May 2, 1914; s. William O. and Margaret (Barnard) H.; A.B., U. Ore., 1936; postgrad. U. Minn., 1938- 39; m. Jayne Bowerman, Sept. 6, 1939; children—Sarah Booth, William Jay, Robert Barnard. Research asst., field cons., adviser, asst. dir. in charge city hall office, acting dir. and acting exec. sec. Bur. Municipal Research and League of Oregon Cites, 1936-38, 1939-4O; budget examiner, administrative analyst U.S. Bur. Budget, 1940-44, 46; super. Bur. Adminstrv. Mgmt. and Budget, UN, 1946; dir., office budget and planning, and budget officer U.S. State Dept., 1947-50, dir. office Internat. Confs. and Adminstrn. 1950-52; dep. rep. interim com. gen. assembly UN, finance and adminstr. U.S. mission to UN, 1952-56; counselor Am. embassy, London, 1956-58; dep. asst. sec. State, 1958-59; minister counselor, dep. chief of mission Am. embassy, Karachi, Pakistan, 1959-63; asst. admistr. Agy. Internat. Devel., 1963-67; U.S. ambassador to Ethiopia, 1967-71; dir. gen. U.S. Fgn. Service, 1971—. Staff mem. U.S. delegation preparatory commn. UN, 1945-46; asst. exec. sec. for adminstrn., preparatory commn. Internat. Refugee Orgn., 1947; spl. adviser on adminstrv., budgetary and orgnl. aspects, U.S. participation in UN and specialized internat. orgns., State Dept., 1946-47; mem. UN Gen. Assembly adv. com. on adminstrv. and budget questions, 1948-56; del. Geneva Conf. on Peaceful Uses of Atomic Energy, 1955. Served with USNR, 1944-46. Mem. City Mgrs. Assn., Pub. Adminstrn. Soc., Am. Fgn. Service Assn., Phi Beta Kappa. Club: Cosmos (Washington). Home: 2026 Allen Pl NW Washington DC Office: Dept State Washington DC 20025

HALL, WILLIAM PURNELL, business executive; b. Balt., Oct. 19, 1908; s. William Purnell and Lottie W. (Barnes) H.; student Balt. Poly. Inst., 1922-26; B.A., Johns Hopkins, 1930; m. Olga Kalakuka, Apr. 16, 1932. With Md. Shipbldg. & Drydock Co., Balt., 1937-64, successively asst. to pres., v.p., exec. v.p., then pres. and dir.; dir. bus. and indsl. devel. The Rouse Co., Balt., 1964-67; pres. Cadmus Internat., S.A., 1967- -; dir. Black & Decker Mfg. Co. Trustee Goucher Coll., John Hopkins U.; bd. dirs. YMCA. Served as lt. USNR, 1944-46: PTO. Mem. U.S. C. of C. (dir.). Home: 4103 St Paul St Baltimore MD 21218 Office: Cockeysville MD 21030*

HALL, WILLIAM ROGER, textile mill exec.; b. Greenville County, S.C., 1933; grad. Furman U., 1955. Treas. Woodside div. Dan River, Inc., Greenville, S.C. Home: 47 Dameron Av Greenville SC 29607 Office: PO Box 6126 Sta B Greenville SC 29606*

HALL, WILLIAM STONE, mental health ofcl.; b. Wagener, S.C., May 1, 1915; s. Henry F. and Mary (Gantt) H.; M.D., Med. Coll. S.C., 1937; student Sch. Mil. Neuropsychiatry, 1944, Columbia, 1947, U. Chgo., 1959; m. Oxena Elizabeth Gunter, June 29, 1940; children—William Stone, Carol Lynn, Richard F. Intern Columbia (S.C.) Hosp., 1937-38; mem. staff S.C. State Hosp., Columbia, 1938-52, supt., 1952-69; supt. Pineland State Tng. Sch. and Hosp., 1953-66, Palmetto State Hosp., 1963-66; dir. mental health S.C. Dept. Mental Health, 1963-64, commnr. mental health, 1964—; clin. prof. psychiatry Med. Coll. S.C., 1957—. Mem. Presdl. Task Force on Mentally Handicapped, 1970; chmn. planning com. Surg. Gen.'s Conf. State and Ter. Mental Health Program Dirs., 1971. Mem. S.C. Speakers Bur., 1962- -; area chief S.C. Civil Def., 1959—. Bd. dirs. Richland and Lexington counties United Community Services, 1960—; trustee United Community Fund, 1968—. Served as maj., M.C., AUS, 1942-46. Recipient distinguished service plaque S.C. Mental Health Assn., 1960; center intensive treatment, research and edn. at S.C. State Hosp. named William S. Hall Psychiat. Inst. 1964; Orgnl. award S.C. Vocational Rehab. Assn., 1969; Ann. Distinguished Service award S.C. dept. Am. Legion, 1970. Diplomate Am. Bd. Neurology and Psychiatry. Fellow Am. Psychiat. Assn. (editorial bd. publ., staff mag. 1964-70, pres. S.C. dist. br. 1957), Am. Coll. Psychiatrist (charter); mem. Am. Hosp. Assn. (chmn. psychiat. hosp. sect. 1971), A.M.A. (com. on nursing 1966—), Southeastern Soc. Neurology and Psychiatry (pres. 1955), Columbia Med. Soc. (pres. 1958), Assn. Med. Supts. Mental Hosps. (pres. 1964-65), Nat. Assn. State Mental Health Program Dirs. (v.p. 1968-69, pres. 1970-71), S.C. State Employees Assn. (dir. 1968 —). Baptist (deacon). Rotarian. Home: 1427 Summerville Av Columbia SC 29201 Office: 2414 Bull St Columbia SC 29202

HALL, WILSON DUDLEY, journalist; b. Champaign, Ill., Nov. 5, 1922; s. Clarence G. and Marion I. (Hall) H.; B.A., U. Ill., 1943; M.F.A., Yale, 1950; postgrad. N.Y.U., 1951; m. Laurier King, Mar. 17, 1969; 1 dau., Kimberley. Instr. speech U. Ill., 1946-47, Conn. State Tchrs. Coll., 1949-50; corr. NBC in Korea, 1953, bur. chief NBC News in Middle East, Cairo, Egypt, 1953-57, in N.Y.C., 1957-60, Latin Am. bur. chief, 1960-64, assigned N.Y.C., 1964—. Served to 1st lt. AUS, 1943-46, 51-53. Decorated Air Medal, Bronze Star medal. Mem. Sigma Delta Chi. Club: Overseas Press (N.Y.C.). Contbr. books, mags. Office: NBC News Rockefeller Plaza New York City NY 10020*

HALL, WILTON E., former U.S. senator; b. Hall Twp., Anderson County, S.C., Mar 11, 1901; s. Thomas Dean and Sarah (Tucker) H.; ed. Starr High Sch., also Furman U.; m. Mary Elizabeth Lightsey, Feb. 1, 1925; children—Mary Elizabeth, Wilton E., Perry Dean, Sarah Emma. Publisher (founder) Anderson (S.C.) Independent (morning and Sunday), 1924—, Anderson Daily Mail (eve.), 1929—; established radio sta. WAIM, 1935, WAIM-TRV, 1953; mem. adv. com. Columbia Network affiliates for N.C., S.C., Ga., Fla., P.R., 1954; treas. Palmetto Pub. Co.; pub. Nat. Stamp News; apptd. U.S. senator to fill vacancy caused by death of Ellison D. Smith, Nov. 1944. Chmn. Anderson County for S.C. War Finance Adv. Com.; chmn. Hartwell Dam Steering Com. Presdl. elector, 1944, 52, 56. Chmn. Anderson County Democratic Conv., 1936; mem. adv. com. Nat. Dem. Exec. Com., 1954—; del. Dem. Nat. Conv., 1936. Recipient U. Mo. Sch. Journalism silver plaque (for greatest community service in U.S.) from Nat. Editorial Assn., 1941, 44, Man of South award, 1956. Mem. Navy League (chmn.), S.C. Press Assn. (pres. 1946), So. Newspaper Pubs. Assn. (dir.), Nat. Planning Assn., Sigma Delta Chi. Baptist. Elk. Clubs: Nat. Press (Washington); Lions. Home: 229 Boulevard Anderson SC 29621

HALLABA, MOHEB ABDEL SALAM, educator, surgeon; b. Damascus, Syria, Nov. 6, 1929; s. Abdel Salem and Medena (Ezzat) H.; M.B., Ch.B., U. Alexandria (Egypt), 1954; m. Patsy Ruth White, July 2, 1960; children—Sharon, Anthony. Came to U.S., 1956, naturalized, 1965. Intern St. Clare's Hosp., N.Y.C., 1956-57; resident pathology Wesley Med. Center, Wichita, Kan., 1957-58; resident surgery U. Kan. Med. Center, 1958-62; fellow vascular surgery Good Samaritan Hosp., Cin., 1963; instr. surgery Med. Coll. Va., also staff surgeon McGuire VA Hosp., Richmond, 1963-65; chief surgeon, supt. Winfield (Kan.) State Hosp. and Tng. Center, 1965-67; asso. surgery U. Mo., Columbia, 1968—; chief surgery St. John's Med. Center, Joplin, 1971—. Regional med. program dir. Stroke Prevention and Rehab., Joplin, Mo., 1968—. Pres. Jasper County Heart Assn., 1970-71. Fulbright travel grantee, 1956-59; recipient 1st prize Trigeminal Neuralgia essay program, 1957; Gold award for original investigation, mgmt. arterial embolism Ohio State Annual Meeting, 1963. Fellow A.C.S.; mem. Am. Med. Writers Assn., N.Y. Acad. Scis., Southwestern Surg. Congress, Soc. Internat. de Chirurgie, A.M.A. Contbr. articles profl. jours. Home: 808 Hampton Pl Joplin MO 64801 Office: Medical Arts Bldg Joplin MO 64801*

HALLADAY, DANIEL WHITNEY, univ. pres.; b. Santa Ana, Cal., Oct. 13, 1920; s. Harlow Monroe and Marion (Winans) H.; B.A., Pomona Coll., 1942; M.A., Claremont Grad. Sch., 1947; postgrad. U. So. Cal., 1949; Ed.D., Columbia, 1955; m. Elaine Owings, Aug. 21, 1941; childrenWhitney Sue (Mrs. Ernest Whitelaw), Steven Owings. Athletic coach Pomona Coll., 1946-47; asso. prof. phys. edn. and health U. Fla., 1947-51; lectr. health edn. Columbia, 1953-54, asst. provost Tchrs. Coll., 1954-55; prof. of edn. and dean of students U. Ark., 1955-66; pres. E. Tex. State U., 1966—, Pres. Council of Presidents State Sr. Colls., 1967-68; mem. adv. com. on formulas for sr. colls. and univs., coordinating bd. Tex. Coll. and Univ. System; mem. spl. adv. com. to commr. higher edn. State of Tex. Served to capt. AUS, 1942-46; served from capt. to maj., U.S. Army, 1951- 53; lt. col. Res. Decorated Silver Star, Bronze Star with two clusters, Purple Heart with cluster. Mem. East Tex. C. of C. (dir.), Am. Assn. State Colls. and Univs., Tex. Assn. Colls. and Univs. (chmn. commn. on ednl. policy), Kappa Delta Pi, Phi Delta Kappa. Methodist. Kiwanian. Home: Campus East Tex State U Commerce, TX 75428.

HALLADAY, HENRY EARNEST, lawyer; b. Battle Creek, Mich., Mar. 27, 1915; s. Ivor Ronald and Augustine (Earnest) H.; A.B., U. Mich., 1936, J.D., 1937; m. Soramae Greenberg, Oct. 19, 1967. Admitted to Minn. bar, 1937, since practiced in Mpls.; trial and labor relations with firm Dorsey, Marquart, Windhorst, West & Halladay, and predecessors, 1937-. Dir. Asso. Industries Mpls., 1957-. Chmn. Minn. Supreme St. Rules Adv. Com., 1965- , also adv. com. Jury Instrn. Guides. Active Mpls. Community Chest, Minn. Symphony, Mpls.; sponsor Walker Art Inst., Mpls. Mem. Am. Coll. Trial Lawyers, Am. Bar Assn. Home: Route 2 Box 276A Excelsior, MN 55331. Office: First Nat Bank Bldg Minneapolis MN 55402

HALLAUER, CARL S., optics mfg. exec.; b. Rochester, N.Y., Jan. 5, 1894; s. Frank and Hattie Hallauer; ed. Rochester Bus. Inst., Rochester Inst. Tech.; Sc.D., Clarkson Coll. Tech., 1947; LL.D., Alfred U., 1955; m. Florence R. Hallauer, June 22, 1918; 1 dau., Nancy Bausch (Mrs. Arnold L. Johnson). Dir. Bausch & Lomb, Inc., Rochester, N.Y.; dir. Community Savs. Bank Rochester, Lincoln Rochester Trust Co., Rochester Gas & Electric Corp., Garlock, Inc. Dir., past pres. Asso. Industries N.Y. State. Commr. Saratoga Springs Commn.; mem. Nat. Com. Electoral Reform, 1961—. Del. Republican Nat. Conv., 1932—. Trustee Rochester Bus. Inst., Monroe Community Coll., Rochester Inst. Tech., St. John's Home for Aged, Rochester Fire Benevolent Assn., Rochester Community Chest, Salvation Army, Rochester Community Baseball Club; bd. dirs. Saratoga Performing Arts Center; life trustee Clarkson Coll., Rochester Police Benevolent Assn. Recipient Horatio Alger award, 1960. Mem. Am. Ordnance Assn. (past pres., adv. bd.), Am. Chem. Soc., Soc. Naval Engrs., Photographic Soc. Am., Better Vision Inst. (dir.), Sci. Apparatus Makers Assn. (past chmn. bd.), Rochester C. of C., S.A.R., Soc. Cincinnati, Optical Soc. Am. Baptist (trustee). Mason (Shriner), Kiwanian, Elk, Moose. Clubs: Rochester, Oak Hill Country, Genesee Valley, Country, City (Rochester); Capital Hill (Washington). Home: 1600 East Av Rochester NY 14610 Office: 635 St Paul St Rochester NY 14602

HALLBERG, CHARLES WILLIAM, retired educator; b. New Britain, Conn., Nov. 13, 1899; s. John Charles and Ida (Esberg) H.; B.S., Trinity Coll., Hartford, Conn., 1923; M.A., Columbia, 1924, Ph.D. (Univ. scholar). 1931; m. Eleanore R. Kohlhaupt, July 20, 1929; 1 dau., Ingrid (Mrs. F. Whitman Haggerson). Instr. history Purdue U., 1926-28, Syracuse U., 1929-31; professorial lectr. history U. Minn., 1931-32; asst. prof. U. Mo., 1933-34; lectr. history Bklyn. Coll., 1934-37; mem. faculty Queens Coll., 1937—, prof., 1956—, prof. emeritus, 1971—, chmn. dept. history, 1949-64. Mem. Am. Hist. Assn., Internat. Platform Assn., New Eng. Soc. N.Y.C., Delta Phi. Republican. Episcopalian. Club: University (N.Y.C.). Author: The Suez Canal, 1931; Franz Joseph and Napoleon III, 1955. Home: PO Box 113 Little Neck NY 11363

HALLDORSON, CARYL THOMAS, chain store exec.; b. Selden, Neb., Oct. 23, 1906; s. Sveinn Harry and Nellie May (Patch) H.; B.S., U. Denver; m. Virginia Rawles, June 12, 1930; childrenSue (Mrs. Peter Fuller), Caryl Thomas II, James Rawles. With F.W. Woolworth Co., 1929-, asst. sec.-asst. treas., 1952- 62, sec., 1962—. Mem. Am. Soc. Corp. Secs., Am. Soc. Ins. Mgmt. Home: 129 Oakview Av Maplewood NJ 07040 Office: 233 Broadway New York City NY 10007

HALLE, CHISHOLM, retail mcht.; b. Cleve., Apr. 8, 1933; s. Walter M. and Helen (Chisholm) H.; student St. Paul's Sch., 1947-51; grad. Harvard, 1955; m. Ann Gelston King, July 9, 1955; childrenAlvah, Pamela, Samuel, Michael. Asst. buyer, br. dept. mgr., divisional mdse. mgr. Halle Bros. Co., Cleve., 1956-66, pres., 1966—. Pres. bd. Cleve. Opera Assn.; trustee Western Res. Hist. Soc., Blue Coats. Served to 1st lt. AUS, 1955- 57. Home: 7090 Waite Hill Rd Waite Hille Willoughby, OH 44094. Office: 1228 Euclid Av Cleveland OH 44115

HALLE, KATHERINE MURPHY, author; b. Cleve.; d. Samuel Horatio and Blanche (Murphy) Halle; student Smith Coll., also Cleve. Inst. Music. Music commentator on CBS for Cleve. Orch., 1938-40; broadcaster interviews WGAR, Cleve., 1938-42; with OSS, 1942-45; feature writer Cleve. Plain Dealer, 1948—; free- lance mag. writer, 1948—. Chmn. garden com. Blair House Garden, Washington, 1967—. Co-chmn. fine arts com. Womans Nat. Democratic Club, 1967-68. Bd. dirs. Washington Opera Soc. Decorated Order Brit. Empire. Author: Irrepressible Churchill, A Treasury of Winston Churchill's Wit, 1967; Winston Churchill on America and Britain; The Grand Original Portraits of Randolph Churchill by his Friends. Address: 3001 Dent Pl NW Washington DC 20007

HALLE, LOUIS JOSEPH, educator, author; b. N.Y.C., Nov. 17, 1910; s. Louis Joseph and Rita (Sulzbacher) H.; B.S., Harvard, 1932, student Grad. Sch., 1937-38; m. Barbara Mark, Mar. 16, 1946; children—John, Julia, Mark, Robin, Anne. With Internat. Rys. of C.Am. in Guatemala and El Salvador, 1934; with Longmans, Green & Co., pubs., N.Y.C., 1935-36; with Dept. State, 1941-54; asst. chief div. of spl. inter-Am. affairs, 1946-47; spl. asst. for Pan- Am. Corp. Affairs, 1947-50; policy planning adv. Bur. of Inter-Am. Affairs, 1950-51; assigned Nat. War Coll., 1951-52; mem. policy planning staff Dept. of State, 1952-54; research prof. Woodrow Wilson dept. fgn. affairs U. Va., 1954-58; prof. Grad. Inst. Internat. Studies, Geneva, 1956—. Served as pvt. AUS, 1941; commd. lt. (j.g.), USCG Res., 1943; asst. iplomatic adviser UNRRA, 1944. Recipient medal John Burroughs Assn. 1941, for book, Birds Against Men. Clubs: Harvard (N.Y.C.); Cosmos (Washington). Author: Transcaribbean, 1936; Birds Against Men, 1938; River of Ruins, 1941; Spring in Washington 1947; On Facing the World, 1950; Civilization and Foreign Policy, 1955; Choice for Survival, 1958; Dream and Reality, 1959; Men and Nations, 1962; Sedge, 1963; The Society of Man, 1965; The Cold War as History, 1967; The Storm Petrel and the Owl of Athena, 1970; The Nature of Ideological Imagination, 1971. Home: CH 1222 Vésenaz Geneva Switzerland Office: Institut Universitaire de Hautes Etudes Internationales Geneva 21 Switzerland

HALLE, MORRIS, educator, linguist; b. Liepaja, Latvia, July 23, 1923; s. Irving and Lisa (Kahan) H.; student City Coll. N.Y., 1941-43; M.A., U. Chgo., 1948; student Columbia, 1948-49; Ph.D., Harvard, 1955; m. Rosamond Thaxter Strong, July 2, 1955; childrenDavid S., John G., M. Timothy. Mem. faculty Mass. Inst. Tech., 1951-, prof. modern langs. and linguistics, 1961-. Served with AUS, 1943-46. Guggenheim fellow, 1960-61. Mem. Linguistic Soc. Am. Author: (with R. Jakobson and C.G.M. Fant) Preliminaries to Speech Analysis, 1952; The Sound Pattern of Russian, 1959; (with N. Chomsky) The Sound Pattern of English, 1968; (with S.J. Keyser) English Stress: Its Form, Its Growth, and its Use in Verse, 1971. Home: 2O6 Waverley Av Newton MA 02158 Office: Mass Inst Tech Cambridge MA 02139

HALLE, STANLEY JACQUES, investment exec.; b. Hastings-on-Hudson, N.Y., July 6, 1891; s. Jacques Samuel and Hattie (Sidenberg) H.; grad. Phillips Acad., 1908; B.A., Yale, 1912; m. Helen Bernheimer (div. Jan. 1937); children—Anne (Mrs. Seymour), Helen (Mrs. Knothe); m. 2d, Christiane deMilly, Dec. 15, 1937. Hon. chmn. Halle & Stieglitz, Inc., N.Y.C. Mem. N.Y., Am., Midwest stock exchanges, Investment Bankers Assn., Nat. Assn. Securities Dealers. Home: Apple Hill Farm Chappaqua NY 10514 also 1711 Colgate Circle LaJolla CA 92037 Office: 52 Wall St New York City NY 10005

HALLE, WALTER MURPHY, merchant; s. Samuel H. and Blanche (Murphy) H.; student Princeton, 1927; m. Helen Chisholm, Feb. 2, 1929; children-Helen (Mrs. Foster), Chisholm, Kate C. Pres., Halle Bros. Co., Cleve., 1946-66, now chmn. bd.; dir. Basic, Inc., Cleve. Trust Co. Trustee Cleve. Clinic, Oberlin Coll. Served to lt. col., USAAF, 1942-45. Home: Smith Rd Waite Hill Willoughby OH 44O94 Office: 1228 Euclid Av Cleveland OH 44115*

HALLECK, CHARLES A., lawyer; b. De Motte, Ind., Aug. 22, 1900; s. Abraham and Lura I. (Luce) H.; A.B. cum laude, Ind. U., 1922, LL.B., 1924; m. Blance A. White, June 15, 1927; childrenCharles White, Patricia. Admitted to Ind. bar, 1924; engaged in practice at Rensselaer; pros. atty. 30th Jud. Circuit, 5 terms, 1924 to 1934; elected mem. 74th to 90th Congresses, 2d Ind. Dist.; majority leader U.S. Ho. of Reps. 80th and 83d Congresses, minority leader 86th to 88th Congresses. Permanent chmn. Rep. Nat. Conv., 1960. Served Inf., U.S. Army, World War I. Mem. Am. Legion, Beta Theta Pi, Phi Beta Kappa, Phi Delta Phi, Order of the Coif. Republican. Methodist. Club: Columbia (Indpls.). Home: Rensselaer IN 47978 Office: 104 S Nan Rensselaer St Rensselaer IN 47978

HALLECK, CHARLES WHITE, judge; b. Rensselaer, Ind., July 6, 1929; s. Charles Abraham and Blanche (White) H.; A.B., Williams Coll., 1951; J.D., George Washington U., 1957; m. Carolyn L. Wood, Dec. 23, 1950 (div. Oct. 1969); children— Holly Louise, Charles White, Todd Alexander, Heather Leigh, Heidi Lynne, William Hemsley, Hope Leslie; m. 2d, Jeanne Wahl, May 16, 1970. Asst. U.S. atty. for D.C., 1957-59; asso. firm Hogan and Hartson, Washington, 1959-65; judge Superior Ct. D.C., 1965—. Served with USNR, 1951-55; lt. Res. Mem. Beta Theta Pi, Phi Delta Phi. Club: Potomac Hunt. Home: 14211 Turkey Foot Rd Gaithersburg MD 20760 Office: Superior Court DC Washington DC 20409

HALLENBECK, GEORGE AARON, educator, surgeon; b. Rochester, Minn., June 29, 1915; s. Dorr Foster and Bessie (Graham) H.; B.S., Northwestern U., 1936, M.D., 1940; Ph.D. in Physiology, Mayo Found., U. Minn., 1943; m. Marian Mansfield, Dec. 16, 1938; children—John M., George A., Christopher G. (dec.), Linda. Intern Va. Mason Hosp., Seattle, 1939-40; cons. surgeon Mayo Clinic, Rochester, Minn., 1949-60, sect. surg. research, 1961-66, chmn. gen. surgery sects., 1966-68; prof. surgery and physiology Mayo Found., U. Minn., 1960-68; prof. surgery U. Ala. Med. Sch., Birmingham, 1968—. Served to maj., M.C., AUS, 1943-46. Diplomate Am. Bd. Surgery. Fellow A.C.S.; mem. Am., Central, Western surg. assns., Am. Gastroenterol. Assn., Soc. Clin Surgeons, Am. Physiol. Soc., Soc. Exptl. Biology and Medicine, Phi Beta Kappa, Alpha Omega Alpha, Phi Delta Theta, Phi Rho Sigma. Author numerous sci. publs. Home: 2953 Pumphouse Rd Birmingham AL 35243

HALLER, ARCHIBALD ORBEN, educator, sociologist; b. San Diego, Jan. 15, 1926; s. Archie O. and Eleanor (Brizzee) H.; B.A., Hamline U., 1950; M.A., U. Minn., 1951; Ph.D., U. Wis., 1954; m. Hazel Laura Zimmermann, Feb. 15, 1947; children—Elizabeth Ann, Stephanie Lynn, William John. Project asso. U. Wis. 1954-56, prof. rural sociology, also sociology, 1965—, chmn. dept. rural sociology, 1970—; from asso. prof. to prof. sociology Mich. State U., 1956-65; Fulbright prof. Rural U. Brazil, 1962; cons. in field, 1963—. Mem. Mich. Com. Mental Health Policies, 1961-62. Served with USNR, 1943-46. Univ. fellow U. Wis., 1952- 54. Fellow Am. Sociol. Assn., Lutheran Acad. Scholarship; mem. Rural (pres. 1969-70), Am., Western psychol. assns., Sociol. Research Assn., Midwest Sociol. Assn. Internat. Devel., Soc. Psychol. Study Social Issues, A.A.A.S. Author research monographs and tech. articles. Editorial bd. Rural Sociology, 1962—, Jour. Human Resources, 1965—. Contbr. articles profl. jours. Home: 529 Edward St Madison WI 53711

HALLER, CALVIN JOHN, banker; b. Buffalo, July 9, 1925; s. John Martin and Emelia (George) H.; B.S. in Bus. Adminstrn. with distinction, U. Buffalo, 1949; m. Yvette Ann Hogrewe, June 12, 1948; children—Cary John, Darlene Ann. With Buffalo Savs. Bank, 1949—, sr. v.p., 1969—; mem. faculty ednl. programs Nat. Assn. Mut. Savs. Banking, 1966—. Bd. dirs. Niagara Lutheran Home, Cerebral Palsy Assn. Buffalo, Blue Shield Western N.Y., Children's Found. Erie County; chmn. bd. mgrs. YMCA Buffalo and Erie County. Served to lt. (j.g.) USNR, 1943-46. Mem. N.Y. Soc. Security Analysts, Am. Inst.

Banking, Investment Officers Assn. Savs. Banks N.Y. State, U. Buffalo Alumni Assn., Buffalo Area C. of C., Newcomen Soc. N.Am., Beta Gamma Sigma. Lutheran (mem. ch. council). Mason. Clubs: Bond, Buffalo, Mohawk, Equality (Buffalo). Home: 235 Westfall Dr Tonawanda NY 14150 Office: 545 Main St Buffalo NY 14203

HALLER, ELLIS METCALF, editor; b. Carthage, N.Y., Mar. 20, 1915; s. Willis Andrew and Maude E. (Metcalf) H.; A.B., Syracuse U., 1937; m. Dorothy G. Rourke, Nov. 24, 1938; children—Mark Metcalf, Elizabeth Hewitt. Instr. typography Syracuse U., 1936-37; upstate N.Y. corr. Watertown Daily Times, 1933-37; with Wall Street Jour., N.Y.C. and Chgo., 1937-44, chief Chgo. bur., 1943-44, chief Washington bur., 1948-52, indsl. editor, hdqrs. N.Y.C., 1952-56; asso. editor U.S. News & World Report, Washington, 1956- 61, asso. editor and exec. asst. to editor, 1961-63, spl. editor business and finance, 1963-65, gen. editor, nat. staff, 1965-70, asso. exec. editor, 1971—; asso. in journalism Columbia, 1954-56; guest lectr. Am. Press Inst., 1954-56. Mem. dept. information services Episcopal Diocese of Washington. Recipient Free Enterprise Newswriter award Nat. Mgmt. Assn., 1955. Mem. White House Corr. Assn., English Speaking Union, Phi Beta Kappa, Phi Kappa Phi, Sigma Delta Chi. Club: Nat. Press (Washington). Home: 5125 Westpath Way Washington DC 20016 Office: 2300 N St NW Washington DC 20037

HALLER, HENRY EDWIN, Jr., mfg. co. exec.; b. Pitts., Sept. 17, 1913; s. Henry Edwin and Emma (Burns) H.; B.S., U. Pitts., 1936; m. Grace M. Horton, Aug. 15, 1943; children—Henry Edwin III, Marjorie Burns. With Nat. Valve & Mfg. Co., Pitts., 1936—, pres., dir., 1956—; dir. Western Pa. Nat. Bank, Equimark Corp. Bd. dirs. Pa. AAA Fedn., Boys Club Pitts. Served with USNR, 1943-46. Mason. Clubs: Pittsburgh Athletic Assn. (past pres., dir.), West Penn Motor (pres.). Home: 516 Edgerton Pl Pittsburgh PA 15208 Office: 158 49th St Pittsburgh PA 15201

HALLER, JACOB ALEXANDER, Jr., educator, surgeon; b. Pulaski, Va., May 20, 1927; s. Jacob Alexander and Julia (Allison) H.; B.A., Vanderbilt U., 1947; M.D., Johns Hopkins, 1951; m. Emily Merle Simms, June 16, 1951; childrenJulia, Clare Jacob Alexander III, Frederick. Surg. interns Johns Hopkins Hosp., 1951-52; Rotary Found. fellow pathology U. Zurich (Switzerland), 1952-53; sr. asst. surgeon USPHS, 1953-55; asst. resident surgeon Johns Hopkins Hosp., 1955-58, resident surgeon, 1958-59; instr., then asst. prof. surgery U. Louisville Sch. Medicine, 1959-63; vis. asst. prof. surgery U. Pa. Sch. Medicine, 1962-63; surg. fellow organ transplantation and tissue immunity Wistar Inst., Phila., 1962-63; asso. prof. surgery Johns Hopkins Univ. and Hosp., 1963-67, prof. surgery, also Robert Garret prof. pediatric surgery, 1967-; children's surgeon-in-charge Johns Hopkins Hosp., 1965-; mem. active staff Balt. City Hosps., Loch Raven VA Hosp. Sr. asst. surgeon, surg. unit USCGR, 1953-54; sr. asst. surgeon, then clin. asso. NIH, 1954-55. Markle scholar acad. medicine, 1961-66; named Outstanding Clin. Prof., U. Louisville Sch. Medicine, 1961; recipient Eagle Scout award Boy Scouts Am., 1945. Diplomate Am. Bd. Surgery, Nat. Bd. Med. Examiners, Am. Bd. Thoracic Surgery. Fellow A.C.S.; mem. Am. Fedn. Clin. Research, Soc. Univ. Surgeons, So. Soc. Pediatric Research, Southeastern Surg. Congress, So. Surg. Assn., Am. Assn. Thoracic Surgery, Am. Acad. Pediatrics, Internat. Cardiovascular Soc., Soc. Vascular Surgery, Am. Assn. Surgery Trauma. Halsted Soc., Kansas City (Mo.) Surg. Soc., Md. Heart Assn., So. Thoracic Surg. Assn., Phi Beta Kappa, Sigma Xi, Alpha Omega Alpha. Author: Deep Thrombophlebitis: Pathophysiology and Treatment, 1967; The Hospitalized Child and His Family, 1967. Home: Glencoe Rd Glencoe, MD 21070. Office: Johns Hopkins Hosp Baltimore MD 21205

HALLER, JOHN, educator; b. Basel, Switzerland, Mar. 6, 1927; s. Hans and Frieda (Meyer) H.; Ph.D., U. Basel, 1952, venia docendi, 1957; m. Susanna Margaretha Weisskopf, June 4, 1952; children—Daniel Urs, Patrick Renato. Geologist, Lauge Koch's East Greenland Expdns., Greenland Dept., Copenhagen, 1949-62; lectr. U. Basel, 1958-64; vis. lectr. Harvard, 1964-65, asso. prof., 1965-69, prof. geology, 1969—. Fellow Geol. Soc. Am., Arctic Inst. N.Am.; mem. Swiss Mineral. Soc. Author: Geology of the East Greenland Caledonides, 1971. Home: 15 Homer Rd Belmont MA 02178 Office: 24 Oxford St Cambridge MA 02138

HALLERBERG, ARTHUR EDWARD, educator; b. Farmington, Mo., June 9, 1918; s. Herman A. and Laura (Luken) H.; A.B., Ill. Coll., 1940; A.M., U. Ill., 1941; postgrad. U. Chgo., summers 1946-47; Ed.D. in Math., U. Mich., 1957; m. Katherine W. Rausch, June 16, 1947; 1 dau., Gretchen Anne (Mrs. Stephen Dannewitz). Tchr., Bushnell (Ill.) High Sch., 1941-42; instr. Ill. Coll., 1942-44, from asst. prof. to prof., 1946-60, chmn. dept. math., 1957-60; mem. faculty Valparaiso (Ind.) U., 1960- -, prof., chmn. dept. math., 1965-70, dir., instr. NSF summer insts. math., 1961-66, 68-70; vis. lectr. U. Mich., summers 1960, 67; vis. prof. Mich. State U., 1970-71. Served with USNR, 1944-46. Mem. Am. Math. Soc., Math. Assn. Am., Nat. Council Tchrs. Math. (editor Hist. Topics Yearbook), Phi Beta Kappa, Sigma Xi. Democrat. Lutheran. Home: 908 Wood St Valparaiso IN 46383*

HALLETT, CHARLES H., steel co. exec.; b. Hammond, Ind., 1919; B.S. in Bus. Adminstrn., Northwestern U., 1940; married. With Inland Steel Co., 1940-41; plant gen. mgr. Joseph T. Ryerson & Sons Inc., Wallingford, Conn., 1946-59; with Allison Steel Mfg. Co., Phoenix, 1959—, v.p., 1960-62, pres., chief exec. officer, dir., 1962—. Served with USNR, 1942-45. Home: 2 W Northern Av Phoenix AZ 85021 Office: 1841 W Buchanan St Phoenix AZ 85005*

HALLETT, GEORGE HERVEY, Jr., civic sec.; b. Phila., Pa. May 24, 1895; s. George Hervey and Gertrude Amy (Hawkes) H.; A.B., Haverford (Pa.) Coll., 1915; A.M., Harvard, 1916; Ph.D., U. Pa., 1918; m. Mary Spencer Lee, 1922 (div. 1932); children—Arne Lee, Garth Lee; m. 2d, Ruth Dickinson Newton, 1932. Asst. sec. Proportional Representation League, 1919-26; exec. sec., 1926—; asso. sec. Nat. Municipal League, 1932-53; exec. sec. Citizens Union N.Y.C., 1934-67, 70-71, legislative rep., 1934—; mgr. Proportional Representation Campaign Com. (won proportional representation in N.Y.C.), 1936; dir. charter defense campaigns Ashtabula, O., Boulder, Colo.; mem. N.Y. Constl. Conv. Com., 1937-38; prin. drafter of optional county govt. law adopted by N.Y. Legislature, 1937, rev. city home rule law of N.Y. State, 1939, county home rule amendment to N.Y. Constn. adopted 1958, primary law for N.Y. statewide officers 1967; draftsman and tech. adv. Glen Cove (N.Y.) City Charter Commn., 1942-43; drafted city mgr. charters adopted by Long Beach, N.Y., 1943, Poughkeepsie, N.Y., 1949, Rome, N.Y., 1951; research cons. N.Y. State Joint Legislative Com. to Recodify Multiple Dwelling Law, 1944-46; tech. cons. N.Y. State Uniform Co. Laws Commn., 1951-52; mem. Mayor's Com. on Mgmt. Survey, N.Y.C., 1950-53, Mayor's Com. on Port Industry, 1950-51; cons. N.Y. State Com. on Constl. Conv., 1957, mem. N.Y. State Spl. Com. on Constl. Revision, 1958-59; mem. N.Y. State Commns. on Govt. of N.Y.C., 1953-54, 60; research asso. N.Y. State Constl. Conv., 1967; co-dir. Proportional Representation Edn. Project to prepare for community sch. bd. elections, 1969-70; dir. spl. unit to conduct sch. bd. elections N.Y.C. Bd. Elections, 1970; mem. Citizens Com. for Children, N.Y.C. Mem. Haverford Coll. Corp.; founder Robin Hill coop. residential com. Media, Pa., 1926. Parliamentarian N.E.A., 1957-61, Pa. Edn. Assn., 1945-60, N.Y. State Tchrs. Assn., 1968-69. Recipient La Guardia Meml. Assn. award, 1963. Mem. Govtl. Research Assn., Nat. Assn. Civic Secs. (pres. 1957-60), Am. Polit. Sci. Assn., Civic Execs. Conf. Met. N.Y., Pub. Edn. Assn., Citizens Housing and Planning Council N.Y., Am. Soc. Pub. Adminstrn., Friends Com. on Nat. Legislation, N.Y. Friends Com. on Legislation (1st chmn.), Haverford Soc. N.Y., Phi Beta Kappa, Sigma Xi. Club: Snag. Author: Proportional Representation (with C.G. Hoag), 1926; Proportional Representation-The Key to Democracy, 1937, 1947. Editor: Proportional Representation Dept. of Nat. Civic Rev. (formerly Nat. Municipal Rev.), 1932-62; asst. editor and co-editor Proportional Representation Rev., 1919-31. Contbr. articles on govt. to publs. Home: 235 E 22d St New York City NY 10010 Office: Citizens Union 15 Park Row New York City NY 10038

HALLETT, JOHN L., mfg. exec.; b. Seattle, Dec. 5, 1903; s. Fred N. and Adelia (Lindsay) H.; M.E., U. Wash., 1927; m. Alycemarie Page, Apr. 16, 1936; children—Page, Fred, Ann, Katherine, Jacqueline, John. Labour foreman Fegles Constrn. Co., Mpls., 1927-30, project mgr., 1930-34; super. reinforcing steel Grand Coulee Dam project Mason, Walsh, Atkinson & Kier Co., 1934-38; engr., supt. reinforcing steel Grand Coulee Dam, Consol. Builders, Inc., 1938; engring. dept. constrn. cement plant Permanente Cement Co., 1939, super. constrn. sand and gravel conveyor line, Redding, Cal. to Shasta Dam, 1939-40; staff central estimating div. Henry J. Kaiser Co., Oakland, Cal., 1940; gen. supt. Ore. Shipbldg. Corp., Portland, 1941-42, gen. supt. constrn., operations Vancouver yards, 1942-45; plant mgr. Kaiser-Frazer Corp., Long Beach, Cal., 1946, chief engr., works mgr., gen. mgr. Willow Run, Mich., 1946-51, exec. v.p., 1951-54; exec. v.p., gen. mgr. Kaiser Motors, Inc., Willow Run, 1946-53; v.p. charge aircraft prodn. Kaiser Metal Products, Bristol, Pa., 1953-55, v.p. aircraft div., 1955-56; formerly v.p., gen. mgr. Kaiser Engrs. Internat. div. Henry J. Kaiser Co.; formerly v.p. Kaiser Industries. Republican. Episcopalian. Home: 78 Wyngaard Av Piedmont CA 94611*

HALLETT, WILLIAM CHARLES, accountant; b. Los Angeles, Nov. 18, 1923; s. King and Alice (Howley) H.; B.S., U. So. Cal., 1950; m. Sally Lane, Oct. 29, 1948; children-Kirk, Dean. With Ernst & Ernst, C.P.A.'s, 195O—, partner, 1959- , charge Los Angeles office, 1964-. Served with USNR, 1943-46. Mem. Nat. Assn. Accountants (pres. Los Angeles 1963-64, nat. bd. dirs. 1964- 65, nat. v.p. 1966-67), Los Angeles C. of C., Beta Alpha Psi, Beta Gamma Sigma. Clubs: California (Los Angeles); Lakside Golf (N. Hollywood, Cal.). Home: 4972 Calvin St Tarzana, CA 91356. Office: 615 S Flower St Los Angeles CA 90017*

HALLEY, ANDREW STANTON, retired mfg. co. exec.; b. Eureka, Cal., Dec. 18, 1905; s. Andrew William and Margaret (Tydd) H.; A.B., Stanford, 1927, postgrad., 1927-28; m. Martha Eugenia Tucker, Aug. 17, 1940; children—Peter R., Susan M. Successively jr. accountant, sr. accountant, supr., mgr. Price Waterhouse & Co., C.P.A.'s, San Francisco, 1928-49; treas. Fibreboard Corp., San Francisco, 1949-56, v.p., 1951-56, then v.p. finance, then sr. v.p., also dir.; now retired; dir. Di Giorgio Corp. Served to lt. comdr. USNR, 1942-45. Mem. Am. Inst. C.P.A.'s. Clubs: San Francisco Golf, Olymic, Pacific-Union (San Francisco). Home: 1100 Union St San Francisco CA 94109

HALLEY, HARRY LEE STUART, judge; b. Antlers, Okla., Sept. 5, 1894; s. John Henry and Annie Howard (Stuart) H.; A.B., U. Okla., 1915, LL.B., 1917; m. Fredrica Probst, Sept. 6, 1923; 1 dau., Matilda Ann (Mrs. J.R. Rummage). Admitted to Okla. bar June 1916, practiced in Tulsa, 1918-49; asst. city atty., 1922-28, dist. judge Tulsa and Pawnee Counties, Tulsa, 1931-47; justice Supreme Ct. State Okla., 1949—, vice chief justice 1952, 63-65, chief justice, 1953-55, 65-66, supernumerary judge, 1967—. Served with the U.S. Army 1917-18, disch. as capt., Inf.; entered U.S. Army as lt. col., 1942; served N. Africa, Italy, France, 1943-45; disch. to res. as col., Inf., 1945. Mem. Am., Okla., Tulsa County bar assns., Am. Legion, Am. Judicature Soc., Res. Officers Assn., Mil. Order World Wars, Ret. Officers Assn., V.F.W., C. of C., YMCA, Order Coif, Phi Delta Phi, Sigma Chi. Democrat. Methodist (steward). Mason, K.P. Club: High Twelve. Home: Tulsa OK 74101 Office: PO Box 53302 State Capitol Oklahoma City OK 73105

HALLGARTEN, GEORGE WOLFGANG FELIX, educator, historian; b. Munich, Germany, Jan. 3, 1901; s. Robert (b. N.Y.C.) and Constance (Wolff-Arndt) H.; Ph.D., U. Munich, 1925; m. Katherine MacArthur Drew, Feb. 15, 1941. Came to U.S., 1937. Substitute asst. Inst. for Fgn. Politics, Hamburg, Germany, 1925; pvt. research, 1926-34; lectr. Ecole des Hautes Etudes Sociales et Internationales, 1935, grad. div. Bklyn. Coll., 1938; research asso. history U. Cal. at Berkeley, 1940-41; historian, then sr. research analyst Dept. of Army, 1945-49; guest prof. history U. Munich, 1949-50; lectr., author, 1951-; lectr. univs. in India and Japan, 1965, Rome and Munich, 1967; vis. prof. history U. N.M., Albuquerque, 1968-69; Pres.'s scholar and vis. prof. history U. Dayton, 1970-71. Co-founder Am. Com. Study War Documents, 1955. Served with AUS, 1942-45. Research grantee Am. Philos. Soc., 1940-41. Mem. Am. Hist. Assn., Société d'Histoire Moderne, Authors Guild. Author: Imperialismus vor 1914, 2 vols., revised edit., 1963; Why Dictators?the causes and forms of tyrannical rule since 600 B.C., 1954; Däemonen oder Retter?, 1957, English and French edit. 1960; Das Wettrüsten-a short history of the arms race in this century 1968; Als die Schatten Fielen-memoirs, 1969. Home: 4200 Cathedral Av NW Washington DC 20016

HALLIBURTON, GUS GORDON, investment banker; b. Tulsa, Jan. 13, 1911; s. William Hugh and Marie (Gordon) H.; ed. pub. schs., Nashville; m. Mary Rachel Gaston, Nov. 23, 1932; 1 dau., Eleanor Marie (Mrs. W. Gilbert Templeton). With J.C. Bradford & Co., Nashville, 1930-41, Equitable Securities Corp., Nashville, 1941-68; sr. v.p. combined company Equitable Securities, Morton & Co., Inc., 1968—, also dir. Mem. exec. com. Midwest Stock Exchange, 1962, bd. dirs., 1961-63. Active Nashville United Givers Fund, 1945-55. Mem. devel. council George Peabody Coll. Tchrs., 1965—; adv. bd. St. Thomas Hosp., 1969-72, Jr. League Nashville, 1969-71. Mem. Investment Bankers Assn. (v.p., bd. govs. 1967-68), Nat. Assn. Security Dealers (bd. govs. 1962-65, vice chmn. 1965), Nashville Soc. Financial Analysts (a founder, bd. dirs. 1965). Methodist (chmn. endowment trust com.; bd. publs.). Home: 1115 Crater Hill Rd Nashville TN 37215 Office: 404 James Robertson Pkwy Nashville TN 37219

HALLIBURTON, JOHN HOLLOWAY, airline exec.; b. Brownsville, Tenn., May 21, 1906; s. John Holloway and Minnie (McLeskey) H.; grad. Memphis U. Sch., 1924; B.S. in Mech. Engring., U. Tenn., 1929; grad. study Ga. Inst. Tech., 1931-32; m. Mary Redding, Sept. 2, 1934 (dec. 1966); childrenJohn H., David; m. 2d, Dolores Kaemmerer, Apr. 16, 1968. Engring. flight test dept. airplane div. Ford Motor Co., 1929-30; pilot Curtiss Flying Service, 1930-31; with Eastern Airlines, Inc., 1931-, line capt., 1931-41, dir. mil. tng., 1941-43, operations mgr., 1943-57, v.p. flight operations, 1955-58, v.p. operations, 1958-60, exec. v.p. administrative services, 1960-64, vice president for flight operations, 1964-69, v.p. Fla. and Carribean, 1969—; dir. United Way of Am., Inc. Mem. Fla Com. 100; dir. A.R.C., Better Bus. Bur.; pres. Greater Miami Urban Coalition; bd. dirs. Cripples Children's Soc.; chmn. bd. United Fund of Dade County. Trustee Dade Found., Mus. Sci.; sec. Greater Miami Philharmonic Soc. Mem. Miami- Dade County C. of C. (past pres., dir.), Fla. Zool. Soc. (past pres.), Tau Beta Phi, Sigma Chi. Methodist (mem. ofcl. bd.; trustee). Mason, Rotarian. Clubs: Miami; Aviation Executives; Wings Club; Century (director); Riviera Country. Contbr. articles outdoor, sportsmen's mags. Home: 1591 Catalonia Av Coral Gables, FL 33134. Office: Eastern Air Lines Inc Miami International Airport Miami FL 33148

HALLIDAY, RICHARD theatrical producer; b. Denver, Apr. 3, 1905; s. John Craig and Mary (Hope) Hammond; student Washington and Lee U., 1924; m. Mary Martin, May 5, 1940; 1 dau., Mary Heller. Co-producer Broadway prodns. Peter Pan, 1954, The Sound of Music, 1959, Jennie, 1963; producer Broadway prodn. Daughter of Silence, 1961; producer TV prodns. Peter Pan, 1955, 56, 61, 63, 66, Annie Get Your Gun, 1957, Music with Mary Martin, also Magic with Mary Martin, 1959, Mary Martin at Easter, 1966. Mem. Phi Kappa Psi. Author: Fanfare, 1926. Address: 450 E 52d St New York City NY 10022

HALLIDAY, WALTER JOHN, lawyer; b. Bklyn, Feb. 7, 1907; s. Walter and Charlotte Estelle (Kelly) H.; A.B., Harvard, 1928, LL.B., 1931; J.S.D., N.Y.U., 1950; m. Nancy Jane Fowler, Oct. 27, 1927. Admitted to N.Y. bar, 1933; practice in N.Y.C., 1933—; partner firm Nims, Halliday, Whitman, Howes, Collison & Isner, and predecessors, specializing in trademark and unfair competition law, 1945—. Mem. planning bd., Rockville Centre, N.Y., 1937- 43, trustee of village, 1941-43, mayor, 1943-45. Served with AUS, 1943- 44. Mem. Am. (chmn. trademark div. 1957-58), N.Y. State bar assns., Assn. Bar City N.Y., Internat. Patent and Trademark Assn., U.S. Trademark Assn. (dir.; past chmn. lawyers adv. com.), Am. Mgmt. Assn. (lectr. 1968-69), N.Y. Patent Law Assn. (gov. 1957-60), Am. Legion. Republican. Methodist (adminstrv. bd.). Mason. Clubs: Harvard, The 60 East (N.Y.C.); Chancery (Cambridge, Mass.); Rockville Links. Author articles in field. Editor: Trademark Reporter, 1947-52, chmn. editorial bd., 1952-53. Home: 245 Windsor Av Rockville Centre NY 11570 Office: 60 E 42d St New York City NY 10017

HALLIDAY, WILLIAM J., soap products co. exec. Vice pres., also sec. Amway Corp. Office: Amway Corp 7575 E Fulton Rd Ada MI 49301*

HALLIE, PHILIP PAUL, educator, philosopher; b. Chgo. May 4, 1922; s. William I. and Nettie (Leibowitz) H.; B.A., Grinnell Coll., 1936, D.Litt. (hon.), 1968; M.A., Harvard, 1948, Ph.D. (Fulbright scholar), 1951; B.Litt. (Harvard Traveling fellow), Oxford U., 1950; m. Doris Ann Gavriele, Sept. 19, 1954; children—Michelena Louise, Louis Gabriele. Tutor, Trinity Coll., Oxford U., 1950-51; instr. Wesleyan U., Middletown, Conn. 1952-53, Griffin prof. philosophy, 1965—, chmn. philosophy dept., 1965- 67, fellow Center for Advanced Studies, 1963-64, acting dir. Center for Advanced Studies, 1967—, now also dir. Coll. Letters; prof. philosophy Vanderbilt U., 1953-64. Pres. Middletown P.T.A., 1964-65. Am. rep. Internat. Philosophy Congress in Mysore, India, 1959. Served with arty., AUS, 1941-44. Recipient Whitcomb Poetry prize, 1944; Guggenheim fellow, 1959-60; Am. Council Learned Socs. fellow, 1966-67. Author: Maine de Biran-Reformer of Empiricism, 1959; Scepticism, Man and God, 1963; The Scar of Montaigne, 1966; The Paradox of Cruelty, 1969; also articles, chpts. in books. Editorial bd. Am Scholar, 1965—. Home: 79 Lawn Av Middletown CT 06457 Office: Wesleyan U Middletown CT 06457

HALLIGAN, CLAIR WILLIAM, systems engring. and design co. exec.; b. Indpls., Nov. 3, 1902; s. William Wolfskill and Ada (Fessler) H.; B.S. in Elec. Engring., Bucknell U., 1923, M.S., 1924, E.E., 1935; m. Dorothy Arnott Thom, Aug. 20, 1955; children by previous marriage—Susan, Patricia (Mrs. Alastair Bain). Instr. engring. dept. Bucknell U., 1923-26; engr. Am. Tel. & Co., 1926-34; mem. tech. staff Bell Telephone Labs., 1934-42, sub-dept. head, 1949-50, dir. mil. engring., 1950-58, div. chief radio div. Western Electric Co., 1942-50; pres. Mitre Corp., Bedford, Mass., 1958-66, chmn. exec. com. of bd. trustees, 1966-67, dir., 1967-68, dir. lab. electronics, 1968; cons. engr. C.T. Main Co., Boston, 1968-70. Senior member I.E.E.E.; mem. Tau Beta Pi, Kappa Delta Rho. Home: 52 Shaw Dr Wayland MA 01778

HALLIGAN, ROBERT F., electronics co. exec.; b. Chgo., Mar. 22, 1925; s. William J. and Katherine M. (Fletcher) H.; student Notre Dame U., 1942, Northwestern U., 1943-44; B.S., U.S. Mil. Acad., 1947; m. Marilyn Boland, June 14, 1947; childrenRobert F., Judith Lynn, Thomas Michael, Margaret Alice. With Hallicrafters Co., Chgo., 195O—, exec. v.p., 1959-61, pres., 1961—, now chmn. Served with AUS and USAF, 1947-50. Mem. A.F.C.E.A., Inst. Radio Engrs. (sr.), P.G.E.M., Phi Delta Theta. Club: Executives (Chgo.). Home: 545 Thornwood Lane Northfield IL 60093 Office: 4401 W 5th Av Chicago IL 60624

HALLIN, OTIS DONALD, paper co. exec.; b. Cambridge, Minn., Mar. 4, 1907; s. Daniel Ole and Nora (Ossell) H.; grad. Advanced Mgmt. Program, Harvard, 1953; m. Erma Johnson, Mar. 4, 1933; 1 dau., Betty Joan (Mrs. Martin McDougall). With various lumber plywood and paper companies, 1926-33; with Crown Zellerbach Corp., 1933-, v.p. timber 1959-64, sr. v.p. timber operations, 1964-, also dir.; dir. Crown Zellerback Can. Ltd., 1956-57. Past pres., dir. Pacific Logging Congress, 1963-; trustee Am. Forest Products Industries. Club: California Golf (San Francisco) (past pres.). Home: 234 Elm St San Mateo CA 94401 Office: 1 Bush St San Francisco CA 94104

HALLINAN, NANCY, author; b. London, Eng., Feb. 5, 1921 (parents U.S. citizens); d. Charles Thomas and Hazel (Hunkins) Hallinan; B.A., Vasser Coll., 1942; student writing and drama New Sch. Social Research, also Columbia; 1 dau., Rosalind Addison Goethals. Mem. Author League Am., Authors Guild, P.E.N., Am. Mensa. Author: (novels) Rough Winds of May, 1955; A Voice from the Wings, 1965. Contbr. short stories Touchstone mag., Am. Vanguard, Cornhill mag. Home: 276 Riverside Dr New York City NY 10025 Office: care James O Brown Assos 22 E 60th St New York City NY 10022

HALLING, ELIAS JOHN, music educator; b. Valley City, N.D., May 8, 1906; s. Luther M. and Anna (Monson) H.; B.A., Augsburg Coll., Mpls., 1927; B.M., Northwestern U., 1935, M.M., 1939; postgrad. student, U. So. Cal., 1951-52; m. Lydia I. Overby, June 20, 1930; 1 dau., Beverly (Mrs. Ronald Schroer). Music dir. pub. schs., Minn., 1927-36; chmn. dept. music, also chmn. div. fine and applied arts Mankato (Minn.) State Coll., 1936-64, asst. dean School of Arts and Science, 1964-. Mem. Nat., Minn. edn. assns., Nat. Assn. Tchrs. Singing, Music Educators Nat. Conf., Coll. Music Soc., Am. Assn. Higher Edn. Lutheran. Lion. Home: 216 Viola St Mankato MN 56001

HALLMAN, GEORGE HARLAN, educator; b. Moose Lake, Minn., July 8, 1913; s. Henry W. and Antoinette (Hillbrand) H.; B.S., U. Minn., 1934, M.A., 1946, Ph.D., 1957; m. Mildred F. Flint, June 14, 1941; children—Douglas H., Dennis G. Tchr. social studies high schs., Willow River, Minn., 1935-36, Woodlake, Minn., 1936-37, Hoffman, Minn., 1937-39, Mahnomen, Minn., 1939-46; mem. faculty U. Louisville, 1946—, prof. social sci. and sociology, 1963—, chmn. div. social scis., 1965-71, chmn. dept. sociology, 1971—. Mem. bd. social ministry Ind.-Ky. synod Lutheran Ch. Am., 1966—. Served with inf. AUS, 1943-45; ETO. Mem. Am. Sociol. Assn., Nat. Council Social Studies, Am. Acad. Polit. and Social Scis., Am. Assn. U. Profs. (sec. Ky. 1964-66, 70—, pres. U. Louisville chpt. 1962-63), Louisville Urban League, Ky. Civil Liberties Union. Author chpt. in book. Home: 434 Windmere Rd Clarksville IN 47130 Office: Social Sci Annex Univ Louisville Louisville KY 40208

HALLMAN, PAUL W., fgn. service officer; b. Lincolnton, N.C., Aug. 6, 1914; s. Walter C. and Essie P. (Houser) H.; A.B., George Washington U., 1937; m. Ruthine S. Bales, May 2, 1942; childrenPaul W., Brian S., Lorrie Ann. With Dept. State, 1936-, beginning as sect. chief passport div., successively personnel and adminstrv. officer, branch chief, fgn. service officer, 1956-, 1st sec., adminstrv. officer, Bangkok, 1956-61, counselor for adminstrn., 1961; counselor for adminstrn., Cairo, UAR, 1962-65; exec. dir. Office Nr. Eastern and South Asian Affairs, Dept. State, 1965-. Served to lt. comdr. USNR, 1942-46. Home: 6822 N 29th St Arlington VA 22213 Office: Office Nr Eastern and South Asian Affairs Dept State Washington DC 20521

HALLO, WILLIAM WOLFGANG, educator, Assyriologist; b. Kassel, Germany, Mar. 9, 1928; s. Rudolf and Gertrude (Rubensohn) H.; came to U.S., 1940, naturalized, 1946; B.A. magna cum laude, Harvard, 1950; M.A., U. Chgo., 1953, Ph.D., 1955; candidatus Litterarum Semiticarum, U. Leiden (Netherlands), 1951; M.A. (hon.), Yale, 1965; m. Edith Sylvia Pinto, June 22, 1952; children—Ralph Ethan, Jacqueline Louise. Research asst. Oriental Inst., U. Chgo., 1954- 56; from instr. to asst. prof. Bible and Semitic langs. Hebrew Union Coll.-Jewish Inst. Religion, Cin., 1956-62; mem. faculty Yale, 1962—, prof. Assyriology, 1965—, curator Babylonian collection, 1963—. Mem. commn. Jewish edn. Union Am. Hebrew Congregations, 1967—, co-founder, dir., mem. exec. com. Assn. Jewish Studies, 1970-71. Guggenheim fellow, 1965-66; Fulbright scholar, 1950-51. Mem. Am. Oriental Soc. (chmn. Ancient Near East com. 1971—), Soc. Bib. Lit., World Union Jewish Studies, Conf. Jewish Philosophy, Phi Beta Kappa. Club: Harvard Southern Conn. Author: (with J.J.A. van Dijk) The Exaltation of Inanna, 1968; Early Mesopotamian Royal Titles, 2d edit., 1963; (with W.K. Simpson) The Ancient Near East: a History, 1971. Editor: Essays in Memory of E.A. Speiser, 1968. Translator: The Star of Redemption, 1971. Contbr. numerous articles, revs. Assyriology and Bib. archaeology. Asso. editor Am. Oriental Soc., 1965-71; editorial com. Yale Near Eastern Researches, 1967-70, editor, 1970—. Home: 245 Blake Rd Hamden CT 06514 Office: Babylonian Collection Yale Univ New Haven CT 06520

HALLOCK, DONALD HATHAWAY VALENTINE, bishop; b. Menominee, Mich., Apr. 13, 1908; s. Frank Hudson and Anne Walbridge (Brown) H.; student Carleton Coll., 1926-27; B.A., U. Wyo., 1930, M.A., 1933; B.D., Nashotah Theol. Sem., 1935, D.D., 1952; m. Ruth Clayre Graham, Sept. 14, 1930; childrenRichard Graham, Jane Hathaway, Donald Valentine, Peter John, Thomas Michael James. Ordained to ministry P.E. Ch., deacon, 1934, priest, 1935; in charge St. James Ch., West Bend, Wis., 1933-35, Holy Trinity Ch., Platteville, Wis., 1935-40, Trinity Ch., Mineral Point, Wis., 1937-40; also Kemper Meml. Ch., Darlington, Wis., St. Michael's Ch., Shullsburg, Wis.; rector St. John's Ch., Grand Haven, Mich., 1945-49, Grace Ch., Hinsdale, Ill., 1949-52; consecrated bishop 1952. Mem. nat. council Episcopal Ch., 1956-62; chmn. Greater Milw. Conf. Religion and Race. 1963-65. Chmn. St. Luke's Hosp.; Racine, Wis., Kemper Hall, Kenosha, Wis., Nashotah Theol. Sem. Served as capt. to col., Gen. Staff, U.S. Army, 194O-45. Recipient Legion of Merit. Address: 804 E Juneau Av Milwaukee WI 53202

HALLORAN, RICHARD COLBY, newspaper corr.; b. Washington, Mar. 2, 1930; s. Paul James and Catherine (Lenihan) H.; A.B. with distinction, Dartmouth, 1951; M.A., U. Mich., 1957; m. Carol Prins, June 21, 1958; children—Christopher Paul, Laura Colby, Catherine Anne. Staff writer, then asst. fgn. editor Business Week mag., 1957-61; Tokyo (Japan) bur. chief McGraw-Hill World News, 1962-64; mem. staff Washington Post, 1965-69, bur. chief, Tokyo, 1966-68, Washington corr., 1968-69; Washington corr. N.Y. Times, 1969—. Served to 1st lt. AUS, 1952-55. Ford Found. fellow Columbia, 1964-65; recipient citation for interpretation fgn. affairs Overseas Press Club, 1969. Club: Foreign Correspondents (Tokyo). Author: Japan: Images and Realities, 1969. Home: 5809 Wiltshire Dr Washington DC 20016 Office: 1920 L St NW Washington DC 20036

HALLOWELL, ALFRED IRVING, anthropologist; b. Phila., Pa., Dec. 28, 1892; s. Edgar Lloyd and Dorothy (Edsall) H.; B.S., U. Pa., 1914, A.M., 1920, Ph. D., 1924, D.Sc. (honorary), 1963; m. Maude Frame, Oct. 17, 1942. Social worker, Phila., 1914-22; instr. anthropology U. Pa., 1923-28, asst. prof., 1928-36, asso. prof., 1936-39, prof., 1939-44, 47-63, now prof. emeritus; prof. anthropology Northwestern U., 1944-47; prof. anthropology in psychiatry U. Pa. Med. Sch., curator of social anthropology U. Pa. Museum. Guggenheim fellow, 1940-41; Viking medalist in gen. anthropology, 1955. Chmn. div. anthropology and psychology NRC, 1946-49. Mem. Am. Philos. Soc., Internat. Congress Anthrop. and Ethnol. Scis. (mem. permanent council), Am. Folk Lore Soc. (past pres.), Am. Anthrop. Assn. (pres. 1949), Nat. Acad. Sci., Soc. for Personality Assessment (past pres.), Sigma Xi. Club: Cosmos (Washington). Author: The Role of Comjuring in Saulteaux Soc., 1942; Culture and Experience, 1955. Editor: Viking Fund Publications in Anthropology, 1951-56. Home: 401 Woodland Av Wayne PA 19087

HALLOWELL, BURTON CROSBY, univ. pres.; b. Orleans, Mass., May 2, 1915; s. William George and Sarah Frances (Crosby) H.; B.A., Wesleyan U., Middletown, Conn., 1936, M.A., 1938, L.H.D., 1969; Ph.D., Princeton, 1949; L.H.D., Boston U., 1969; m. Pauline Russell, June 7, 1941; 1 son, Robert Crosby. Teller, Windham County Nat. Bank, Danielson, Conn., 1936-37; Social Sci. Research Council pre-doctoral field fellow, 1940-41; instr. econs. Wesleyan U., 1941-42, asst. prof., 1946-50, asso. prof., 1950-56, Andrews prof. econs., 1956-67, v.p. for planning and devel., 1962-65, exec. v.p., 1965-67; research on fed. debt mgmt., Merrill Found. for Advancement Financial Knowledge (on leave), 1956-57; staff mem. N.Y.C. Commn. for Money and Credit (on leave), 1960-61; pres. Tufts U., Medford, Mass., 1967—. Dir. Keystone Custodian Funds, Inc.; trustee Conn. Gen. Mortgage & Realty Investments. Econ. cons. Conn. Gen. Life Ins. Co., 1949-62, Com. Econ. Devel., N.Y.C., Washington, 1953-58. Chmn. Mass. Housing Finance Agy., 1968-71; Mem. exec. com. New Eng. Colls. Fund, 1968— Assn. Ind. Colls and Univs. in Mass., 1968—, Mass. Com. Catholics, Protestants and Jews, 1967—; mem. adv. council Conservation Commn. of Medford, 1971—; mem. corp. Lawrence Meml. Hosp., 1969—. Trustee, Civic Edn. Found. Inc., WGBH Ednl. Found., Inc.; bd. govs. New Eng. Med. Center Hosps.; mem. adminstrv. bd. Tufts-New Eng. Med. Center. With OPA and Office Civilian Supply, 1941, OSS, 1942. Served to capt. AUS, 1942-46. Mem. Am. Assn. U. Profs., Am. Econ. Assn., Am. Finance Assn., Phi Beta Kappa. Clubs: Commercial, Union (Boston); Princeton, University (N.Y.C.). Contbr. articles to profl. jours. Address: Tufts U Medford MA 02155

HALLOWELL, HENRY RICHARDSON, investment banker; b. Phila., Aug. 12, 1898; s. J. Wallace and Bertinia (Essen) H.; B.A., Yale, 1919; m. Dorothy Saylor, June 25, 1919; children—Henry R., Dorothy (Mrs. Peter M. Fetterolf), Bertinia (Mrs. Omar Bailey), J. Wallace III. Agt., George H. McFadden & Bro. 1919-25; propr. Henry R. Hallowell & Son, 1925-31; registered rep. Lee Higginson & Co., 1931-32, Bryan, Penington & Colket, Phila., 1933-36; mgr. investment dept. Eastman Dillon & Co., 1937-45; partner Hallowell, Sulzberger & Co., Phila., 1945-57; sr. partner Hallowell, Sulzberger, Jenks & Co., 1958—; past pres., dir. Exchange Cold Storage Co.; past dir. Allegheny Ventura Corp., Fischer and Porter Co.; dir. Allegheny Air Lines. Asso. mem. N.Y. Stock Exchange; mem. Am. Stock Exchange; asso. mem., gov. Phila.-Balt.-Washington Stock Exchange. Bd. dirs. Merion Civic Assn., pres., 1945-47; pres., dir. Bot. Soc. of Lower Merion. Presbyn. Clubs: Union League, Yale, Penn (pres. 1964-69, dir.), Philadelphia Country. Home: "Berberrie" Greystone and Blancoyd Rds Merion Station PA 19066 Office: Phila Nat Bank Bldg Broad and Chestnut Sts Philadelphia PA 19107

HALLOWELL, HOWARD THOMAS, Jr., mfg. exec.; b. Phila., Mar. 22, 1908; s. Howard Thomas and Blanche (Nice) H.; B.A., Swarthmore Coll., 1929, LL.D., 1969; m. Dorothy Willits, Apr. 16, 1932; children—Howard Thomas III, Anne Miller, Merritt Willits. Machine operator Standard Pressed Steel Co., Jenkintown, Pa., 1929-30, gen. supt., 1930-43, plant mgr., 1943-48, v.p., gen. mgr., 1948-51, pres., 1951-63, president, 1963-71, and chairman of the board, 1963—, active in mgmt. mfg. subsidiaries; pres. Pa. Mfg. Co., 1943-47; dir. Armstrong Cork Company, East Pa. R.R. Company, Cin. Co., Internat. Resistance Co., 1960-68, Phila. Nat. Bank, 1959-71. Mem. precision fastener task com. U.S. Dept. Commerce, 1948-53; chmn. field econ. moblzn. course Armed Services 1953-54; mem. Pres.'s Com. on Safety Award, 1956. Mem. Philadelphia Committee Foreign Relations, Gov.'s Council Bus. and Industry; dir. Fasteners Research Council; dir., pres. Ireland-U.S. Council Commerce & Industry. Mem. Delaware Valley com. Freedoms Found.; mech. engring. vis. com. Carnegie Tech., 1962-66; dir. Abington Meml. Hosp., 1957-62, 64—; trustee, mem. exec. committee Pa., State U.; bd. mgrs. Swarthmore Coll., 1956-68, chmn. centennial fund. Recipient ann. indsl. relations achievement award Nat. Metal Trades Assn., 1943, 2d ann. citation Phila. chpt. Soc. Advancement Mgmt., 1956; Eli Whitney award Am. Soc. Tool and Mfg. Engrs., 1963. Member Am. Standards Assn. (pres. 1956-59), Pa. (dir. 1959-61), Montgomery County (pres. 1960-61) mfrs. assns., N.A.M. (dir. 1958-66), also Franklin Inst. (dir.), Pa. Soc., Newcomen Soc. N.Am., Phila. C. of C. (chmn. mgmt. committee 1953-54, director 1952-53, 61-67, past v.p.), Standards Engineers Society, Society Advancement Mgmt., Phila., Economists Discussion Group, Delta Upsilon, Pi Tau Sigma, Book and Key. Mem. Soc. Friends. Club: Union League (Phila.); York Road Country; Huntingdon Valley Country. Patentee mech. devices. Home: Deerfield Rydal PA 19046 also Woodsmoke Greentown Pike County PA 18426 Office: Standard Pressed Steel Co Jenkintown PA 19046

HALLOWELL, JOHN HAMILTON, educator; b. Spokane, Aug. 19, 1913; s. Harold Atlee and Anna Blanche (Williams) H.; A.B. cum laude, Harvard, 1935; M.A., Duke, 1937; Ph.D., Princeton, 1939; Litt.D., Coll. Holy Cross, 1963; m. Sarah Rebecca Rubin, Jan. 31, 1941; children—Carol Anne (Mrs. Thomas D. Hill), John Hamilton, Katherine Rebecca. Part-time instr. politics Princeton, 1937- 38; instr. polit. sci. U. Cal. at Los Angeles, 1939-42; asso. communications analyst OWI, 1942; mem. faculty Duke, 1942—, prof. polit. sci., 1950—, chmn. dept., 1964-71; vis. prof. Stanford, 1950, U. Ill., 1964, U. Munich (Germany), 1955-56; Charles R. Walgreen Found. lectr. U. Chgo., 1952. Del. Am. Council Learned Socs., 1964-70. Dir. Lilly Endowment Research Program Christianity and Politics, 1957-68. Guggenheim fellow, 1955-56. Mem. Am. (council 1961-64, exec. com. 1963- 64), So. (pres. 1964-65) polit. sci. assns., Am. Soc. Polit. and Legal Philosophy. Democrat. Episcopalian. Clubs: Cosmos (Washington); Harvard (N.Y.C.). Author: Decline of Liberalism as an Ideology, 1943; Main Currents in Modern Political Thought, 1950; The Moral Foundation of Democracy, 1953; also articles.

HALLOWELL, ROBERT EDWARD, educator; b. Charleston, Ill., Aug. 30, 1918; s. Edward Everett and Elizebeth (Stockover) H.; B.S., Eastern Ill. U., 1939, Pd. D., 1965; M.A., U. Ill., 1940, Ph.D., 1942; student U. Geneva (Switzerland), 1946- 47; m. Mirzl Mueller, Aug. 11, 1949; 1 son, Eric Edward. Spl. investigator War Dept., Germany, 1945-46; instr., then asst. prof. French, U. Ill., 1948-60; asso. prof., then prof. French and Italian, U. Wis. at Milw., 1960-68, chmn. dept., 1964-68; prof. French, U. Ill. at Chgo. Circle, 1968—. Served with AUS, 1942-45. Fulbright research scholar, France, 1966-67. Mem. Modern Lang. Assn., Am. Assn. Tchrs. French, Renaissance Soc. Am., Assn. Internat. des Etudes Francaises, Phi Kappa Phi, Kappa Delta Pi, Pi Delta Phi. Author: Ronsard and the Conventional Roman Elegy, 1954; articles in periodicals U.S. and France. French editor: Modern Lang. Jour., 1960-64. Home: 1564 Bowling Green Dr Lake Forest, IL 60045. Office: Univ Hall Univ Ill Chicago IL 60680

HALLOWELL, ROGER HAYDOCK, mfg. exec; b. Milton, Mass., Dec. 7, 1910; s. John White and Marian Hathaway (Ladd) H.; student Milton (Mass.) Acad., 1920-28; A.B., Harvard, 1933; m. Frances Lee Weeks, Feb. 12, 1938; children—Roger Haydock, Beatrice W., Christian. Instr., coach Brooks Sch., N. Andover, Mass., 1933-36; with Incorporated Investors, Boston, 1936-38, Reed & Barton Corp., Taunton, 1938—, personnel dir., 1940-42, v.p., 1947-49, exec. v.p., 1951-53, dir., 1951—, pres., 1953-71, chmn. bd., 1971—; dir. First Bristol County Nat. Bank, Arkwright-Boston Ins. Co. Pres. Boston council Boy Scouts Am., 1941, v.p., 1946- 66, now dir. Annawon council. Trustee Milton Acad. Served with USNR, 1942-46. Decorated Silver Star (2). Mem. N.A.M. (dir. 1957-64, regional v.p. 1961). Clubs: Porcellian, Cruising of America, Ski Hochgebirge (Boston). Home: 585 Gay St Westwood MA 02090 Office: Reed & Barton Corp Taunton MA 02780

HALLOWS, EMERY HAROLD, judge; b. Fond du Lac, Wis., Apr. 20, 1904; s. Hugh B. and Lillian R. (Martin) H.; A.B., Marquette U., 1926; student Columbia, 1926-27; J.D. cum laude, U. Chgo., 193O; LL.D., Mt. Mary Coll., 1951, Marquette U., 1970; m. Mary Vivian Hurley, Feb. 15, 1930; childrenJoseph Hugh, Mary Elizabeth. Admitted to Wis. bar, 1930, practiced law Milw., 1930-58, mem. Hoffman, Hallows & Cannon and predecessors, 1941-58; prof. law Marquette U., 1930-58; justice Wisconsin State Supreme Court, 1958-, chief justice, 1968-. Mem. bd. governors Mount Mary Coll.; past civil com. Marquette U., member advisory council Law School. Past mem. bd. dirs. of Wisconsin region of National Conf. Christians and Jews. Recipient Eagles Civil Service award, 1954, Wis. region award Nat. Conf. of Christians and Jews, 1963: named Wis. Outstanding Cath. Layman, K.C., 1968. Fellow American Bar Foundation; member of the Practising Law Inst. (nat. adv. council), Am. Law Inst., Am. (a Fellow, chmn. appellate judge conf. 1965- 66), Wis. (pres. 1953-54; bd. Found. 1961-65, sec.), Milw. County (pres. 1948-49) bar assns., U. Chgo. Law Rev. Assn., Am. Judicature Soc. (past dir.), Institute Administration Justice, Marquette Univ. Alumni Association, Order of Coif (honorary), Sigma Nu Phi. Roman Catholic. K.C. (4). Clubs: Kiwanis, Serra. Author articles. Home: 703 Moygara Rd Madison, WI 53716. Office: Supreme Ct State Capitol Madison WI 53702

HALL-QUEST, OLGA, author; b. Willis, Tex., Aug. 30, 1899; d. William S. and Mollie (Derrick) Wilbourne; B.S., Columbia, 1933; M.A., N.Y. U., 1934; m. Alfred Lawrence Hall-Quest, June 4, 1931. Tchr. jr. high and elementary schs., San Antonio, 1921-31; tchr. English, Masters Sch., Dobbs Ferry, N.Y., 1943-65; asst. to editor Ednl. Forum, 1935-41. Mem. Authors Guild. Author: How the Pilgrims Came to Plymouth, 1946; Shrine of Liberty, the Alamo, 1948; Jamestown Adventure, 1950; With Stanley in Africa, 1961; Guardians of Liberty, Sam Adams and John Hancock, 1963; The Bell That Rang for Freedom, 1965; From Colony to Nation, 1966; Flames Over New England, 1967; Old New Orleans, the Creole City, 1968; Conquistadors and Pueblos (award best juvenile nonfiction Western Writers Am.), 1969. Address: 104 Charles Rd San Antonio TX 78209

HALLSTEIN, D. WAYNE, mfg. co. exec.; b. Ft. Wayne, Ind., Sept. 7, 1918; s. Walter Philip and Luise (Finck) H.; B.S. in Mech. Engring., Purdue U., 1940, D.Engring. (hon.), 1971; grad. Advanced Mgmt. Program, Harvard, 1965; m. Charlotte E. Little, Mar. 1, 1941; children—Jean L., Thomas W. With Ingersoll-Rand Co., N.Y.C., 1940- -, exec. v.p., 1961-67, pres., 1967—, also dir.; dir. Peoples Trust Co. N.J. Served to maj., F.A., AUS, 1942-46; Decorated Bronze Star, Air medal. Mem. Am. Soc. Tool and Mfg. Engrs., Nat. Indsl. Conf. Bd. (trustee), Am. Mgmt. Assn., Delta Tau Delta. Club: Economic (N.Y.C.). Home: 367 Mountain Av Ridgewood NJ 07450 Office: 11 Broadway New York City NY 10004

HALLSTEIN, WALTER, German statesman; b. Mainz, Germany, Nov. 17, 1901; s. J. and Anna (Geibel) H.; student Bonn U., Muenchen U., 1920-23; LL.D., U. Berlin, 1925, Georgetown U., Washington, U. Padua, Italy, Tufts U., Medford, Mass., Colby Coll., Waterville, Me., Adelphi Coll., Garden City, N.Y., Harvard, John Hopkins University, Univ. of Liege, Belgium, Sussex, Nancy, Louvain, Hamburg Tübingen Bradford Oviedo. Prof. Rostock Univ., 1930-41; prof., dir. Inst. Comparative Law, Frankfurt, 1941-44; rector Frankfurt U., 1946-48; vis. prof. Georgetown U., Washington, 1948-49; chmn. German com. UNESCO activities, 1949-50; head German Schuman Plan delegation, Paris, 1950; state's sec. Fed. Chancellery, 1950, German Fgn. Office, 1951-58; pres. Commn. European Econ. Community, 1958-67, Internat. European Movement, 1968—; mem. parliament, 1969—. Mem. Deutsche UNESCO Commn. Served as lt. German Army, WW II (U.S. prisoner of war 1944); head Camp U., Como, Miss. Recipient Charlemagne prize, 1961; recipient of the Robert-Scuman-Preis, 1969. Mem. Deutsche Gesellschaft für Völkerrecht, Deutsche Gesellschaft für Rechtsvergleichung (pres.), Deutsche Vereinigung für Internationales Recht (pres.), Deutscher Juristentag, Deutsche Parlamentarische Gesellschaft, Presidency Deutsche Gesellschaft für Auswärtige Politik. Author: Die Aktienrechte der Gegenwart, 1931; Die Berichtigung des Gesellschaftskapitals, 1942; Wiederherstellung des Privatrechts, 1946; Wissenschaft und Politik, 1949; United Europe Challenge and Opportunity, 1962; Der Unvollendete Bundesstaat; 1969; also articles in encys. and periodicals. Home: 5439 Rennerod Oberwesterwaldkreis Germany Office: Europa-Buro Oelbergstr 3 53 Bonn Germany

HALMOS, PAUL RICHARD, educator, mathemátician; b. Budapest, Hungary, Mar. 3, 1916; s. Alexander Charles and Paula (Rosenberg) H.; B.S., U. Ill., 1934, M.S., 1935, Ph.D., 1938; m. Virginia Templeton Pritchett, Apr. 7, 1945. Mem. faculty U. Ill., 1938-39, 42-43; asst. Inst. for Advanced Study, Princeton, 1939-42; mem. faculty Syracuse U., 1943-46, U. Chgo., 1946-61; prof. math. U. Mich., 1961-68; prof., chmn. dept. math. U. Hawaii, 1968-69; prof. math. Ind. U., Bloomington, 1970, Distinguished prof., 1970—; with radiation lab. Mass. Inst. Tech., 1945; vis. prof. U. Montevideo, 1951-52, U. Miami, 1965-66. Guggenheim fellow, 1947-48. Mem. Am. Math. Soc. (editor proc. 1956-62, Math. Revs. 1964-69, exec. com. council 1964-66), Math. Assn. Am. (Chauvenet prize for math. expn. 1946, Lester R. Ford award 1970; gov. 1957-60), Assn. Symbolic Logic. Author: Finite dimensional Vector Spaces, 1942; Measure Theory, 1950; Introduction to Hilbert Space, 1951; Naive Set Theory, 1960; Lectures on Ergodic Theory, 1956; Algebraic Logic, 1962; Lectures on Bodeau Algebras, 1968; Hilbert Space Problem Book, 1967. Research in ergodic theory and operator theory in Hilbert space; contbns. to math. expn. and teaching. Home: 9295 Ballantine Rd Bloomington IN 47401

HALOFTIS, TIMOTHY, clergyman; b. Megara, Greece, Sept. 10, 1917; s. George P. and Constantina (Panou) H.; Degree of Theology, U. Athens, 1939; postgrad. (French Govt. scholar), Inst. Catholique of Paris, 1949-51. Ordained deacon and archmandrite Greek Orthodox Ch., 1936; father superior Monastery of Transfiguration of Savior, Karystia, Greece, 1938-40; preacher of Karystia, 1940-41; chancellor Metropolis of Argolis, 1942- 47; mil. chaplain during Italian invasion of Greece, 1940; mil. chaplain of Evelpis, Athens, 1947-49; dir. High Mil. Adminstrn. of Attica and the Islands, 1947-49; presbyter priest Ch. of St. George of Kypseli, Athens, 1947-56; dir. Apostolic Mission of Ch. of Greece, 1951-56; dir. Advance Seminars for Priests of Archdiocese of Athens, 1951-56; prof. advanced seminars Ryzareion Theol. Sem., 1955-56; presbyter priest, Winnipeg, Man., Can., 1956-57; priest Ch. of St. Eleftherios, N.Y.C., 1957-60; chancellor Greek Archdiocese, 1960-62; mem. faculty Holy Cross Orthodox Theol. Sch., Brookline, Mass., 1960; titular bishop of Rodostolon, 1962- , bishop 10th (S.Am.) Diocese, Buenos Aires, Argentina, 1962-63, 9th (Canadian) Diocese, Toronto, Ont., 1963-68, 2d (Midwestern States) Diocese, Chgo., 1968—. Pres., Council Priests 1st Archdiocesan Dist., 1960-62; pres. Inst. for Aged of Greek Archdiocese, Yonkers, N.Y., 1959- 62. Decorated Cross of Holy Sepulchre by Patriarch of Jerusalem; Gold Medal of Byzas, City of Megara. Author: Consultations for Confession, 1953; The Confession of Children, 1954; also numerous articles in Greek and English newspapers and mags. Office: 40 E Burton Pl Chicago IL 60610

HALPER, ALBERT, author; b. Chgo., Aug. 3, 1904; s. Isaac and Rebecca H.; student Northwestern U., 1924-26; m. 2d, Lorna B. Howard; 1 son by previous marriage, Thomas. Writer, 1929—. Guggenheim fellow for creative writing, 1934. Mem. Authors League Am., P.E.N. Author novels including: Union Square, 1933; The Foundry, 1934; On The Shore, 1934; The Chute, 1937; Only an Inch from Glory, 1943; This is Chicago, 1952; The Golden Watch, 1953; Atlantic Avenue, 1956; The Fourth Horseman of Miami Beach, 1966; (memoir) Good-Bye, Union Square, 1970; (non-fiction) Chicago Crime Book, 1967; novels translated into French, Spanish, Swedish, Russian, Danish, Czechoslovakian, Norwegian, Polish, Finnish. Address: Old Route 55 Pawling NY 12564

HALPERIN, VICTOR, univ. dean; b. N.Y.C., Dec. 20, 1915; s. Herman R. and Dora (Cohen) H.; B.A., U. Miss., 1936; B.S., U. Ill., 1939, D.D.S., 1941; m. Anne Emer, Mar. 21, 1945; children—Randi Fay, Mandlebaum, Henry R., Dean. Asst. prof. oral pathology Emory U. Sch. Dentistry, 1953-55; asso. prof. pathology Loyola U. Sch. Dentistry, New Orleans, 1955-60, prof. pathology, 1960-71, dean, 1967-71; prof. oral pathology, head La. State U. Sch. Dentistry, 1967—, asst. dean, 1970—. Served to maj. Dental Corps, USAAF,

1942-46. Diplomate Am. Bd. Oral Pathology. Fellow Am. Acad. Oral Pathology, Am. Coll. Dentists. Home: 853 Martin Behrman Av Metairie LA 70005 Office: 1190 Florida Av New Orleans LA 70122

HALPERN, BENJAMIN, educator; b. Boston, Apr. 10, 1912; s. Solomon Leib and Fannie (Epstein) H.; A.B., Harvard, 1932, Ph.D., 1936; B.J. Ed., Hebrew Tchrs. Coll., 1932; m. Gertrude Elizabeth Gumner, Nov. 26, 1936; children—Elkan Frank, Joseph David. Mng. editor Jewish Frontier, N.Y.C., 1943-49, mem. editorial bd., 1943—; asso. dir. edn. and culture Jewish Agy., N.Y.C., 1949-56; research asso. Harvard Center for Middle East Studies, Cambridge, Mass., 1956—; asso. prof. Near Eastern studies Brandeis U., Waltham, Mass., 1961-66, prof., 1966—. Exec. Jewish Agy., 1968—. Trustee Hebrew Tchrs. Coll.; bd. govs. Tel Aviv U. Sr. fellow Nat. Endowment for Humanities, 1970; Guggenheim fellow, 1961-62. Author: The American Jew, A Zionist Analysis, 1956; The Idea of the Jewish State, 1961; Jews and Blacks, the Classic American Minorities, 1971. Contbg. editor Midstream. Home: 187 Mason Terrace Brookline MA 02146 Office: Golding 115 Brandeis U Waltham MA 02154

HALPERN, BERNARD N., educator, pharmacologist; b. Russia, Nov. 2, 1904; M.D., U. Paris; m. Renée Nysenholz; 3 children. Prof. exptl. medicine College de France. Decorated officer Legion of Honour. Fellow Royal Soc. Medicine (London); mem. Nat. Acad. Scis. (France), N.Y. Acad. Scis., Acad. Medicine (Rome), Royal Acad. Medicine (Belgium), Internat. Assn. Allergology (past pres.). Address: 197 Boulevard Saint-Germain Paris 7e France *

HALPERN, HARRY, clergyman; b. N.Y.C., Feb. 4, 1899; s. David and Dora (Saratchek) H.; B.A., Coll. City N.Y., 1919; student Rabbi Isaac Elchanan Sem., 1920-24; LL.B., Bklyn. Law Sch., 1925, J.D., 1926; M.A., Columbia, 1925; M.H.L., Jewish Theol. Sem., Am., 1929, D.H.L., 1951, D.D., 1958; m. Mollie Singer, Mar. 27, 1941 (dec.); 1 dau., Deborah; m. 2d, Jean Rosenhaus, June 9, 1967. Rabbi, 1929; rabbi Jewish Communal Center of Flatbush, 1919-29, East Midwood Jewish Center, 1929- ; vis. prof. homiletics Jewish Theol. Sem. Am., 1957, now adjunct prof. pastoral psychiatry. President New York Bd. Rabbis, 1961-62. Chmn. bd. edn. Yeshivah of Flatbush; Kings County adv. council N.Y. State Commn. on Discrimination; commr. New York City Commission on Human Rights; chairman Brooklyn div. State of Israel Bonds; exec. com. Bklyn. Cancer Soc. Trustee Jewish Chronic Disease Hosp., Pride of Judea Children's Home, Federation of Jewish Philanthropies; co-chairman National planning committee Jewish Theol. Sem. Fellow Herbert Lehman Institute Ethics; mem. Zionist Organization America (exec. com.), Rabbinical Assembly Am. (pres.). Home: 2107 Av L Brooklyn NY 11210 Office: 1625 Ocean Av Brooklyn NY 11230

HALPERN, JACK, chemist, educator; b. Poland, Jan. 19, 1925; s. Philip and Anna (Sass) H.; B.Sc., McGill U., 1946, Ph.D., 1949; m. Helen Peritz, June 30, 1949; childrenJanice Deborah, Nina Phyllis. Came to U.S., 1962. Postdoctorate overseas fellow NRC, U. Manchester (Eng.), 1949-50; instr. chemistry U. B.C., 1950, prof., 1961-62; Nuffield Found. traveling fellow Cambridge (Eng.) U., 1959-60; prof. chemistry U. Chgo., 1962-; vis. prof. U. Minn., 1962, Harvard, 1966-67, Cal. Inst. Tech., 1968- 69, Princeton, 1970-71; cons. editor Macmillan Co., 1963-65; cons. Am. Oil Co., Monsanto Co. mem. adv. panel chemistry Nat. Sci. Found., 1967-70. Mem. Art Inst. Chgo., 1964—. Trustee Gordon Research Confs., 1968-70. Recipient Young Author's prize Electrochem. Soc., 1953; award in inorganic chemistry Am. Chem. Soc., 1968. Alfred P. Sloan research fellow, 1959-63. Fellow A.A.A.S., Am. Acad. Arts and Scis., Chem. Inst. Can., Chem. Soc. (London, Eng.), N.Y. Acad. Scis.; mem. Am. Chem. Soc. (editorial bd. Advances in Chemistry series 1963-65, chmn. inorganic chemistry div. 1971), Faraday Soc., Sigma Xi. Contbr. Ency. Britannica, research jours. Mem. editorial bd. Jour. Catalysis, Catalysis Revs., Accounts of Chem. Research, Inorganica Chimica Acta Reviews, Jour. Am. Chem. Soc., Jour. Coordination Chemistry. Home: 5630 Dorchester Av Chicago IL 60637

HALPERN, JULIUS JULES, physicist, educator; b. Norfolk, Va., Feb. 4, 1912; s. Jacob and Lena (Kanter) H.; B.S., Carnegie Inst. Tech., 1933, M.S., 1935, Sc.D., 1937; m. Phyllis E. Melnick, Feb. 4, 1940; childrenPaul Joseph, Sydney Ann. Nuclear physics research U. Mich., 1937-40, U. Cal., 1940-41; staff Mass. Inst. Tech., 1941-46, asso. dir. Brit. br. Radiation Lab., tech. advisor USAAF, 1944-45, physics research Research Lab. Electronics, 1946- 47; asst. prof. U. Pa., 1947, asso. prof., 1948-52, prof. since 1952. Sr. postdoctoral fellow Nat. Sci. Found., Paris, France, 1956-57. Recipient Carnegie- Mellon U. Alumnus Merit award, 1970. Fellow Am. Phys. Soc.; mem. Fedn. Am. Scientists (sec. treas. 1951, chmn. 1952, exec. com. 1953), Sigma Xi, Tau Beta Pi, Pi Delta Epsilon, Beta Sigma Rho. Contbr. profl. publs. Home: 243 S 4th St Philadelphia, PA 19106. Office: U Pa Philadelphia PA 19104

HALPERN, MANFRED, educator; b. Mittweida, Germany, Feb. 1, 1924; s. Jacob and Edith (Aron) H.; came to U.S., 1937, naturalized, 1944; B.A., U. Cal. at Los Angeles, 1947; M.A., Sch. Advanced Internat. Studies, Washington, 1948; Ph.D., Johns Hopkins, 1960; m. Betsy Steele, Nov. 5, 1948; children—Jeffrey Kim, Tamara Steele, Katrina Ann, David Nicholas. Research analyst div. research for Europe, Dept. State, 1948, research analyst, 1950-53, spl. asst. to chief div. research for Near East, S. Asia and Africa, 1953-58; prof. politics Princeton, 1958—; mem. faculty Johns Hopkins, 1956, George Washington U., 1951-53; lectr. Nat. War Coll., Fgn. Service Inst., Strategic Intelligence Sch.; cons. Rand Corp., 1958-66, Dept. State, 1963-70. Chmn. chpt. Students for Democratic Action, Washington, 1947-50; mem. nat. bd. Americans for Dem. Action, 1949-50. Served with inf. AUS, 1944-45. Decorated Combat Inf. badge; recipient Meritorious Service award Dept. State, 1952. Fellow Middle East Studies Assn. N.Am. (program chmn.), Middle East Inst., African Studies Assn. (program chmn.), Adlai Stevenson Inst. Internat. Affairs; mem. Am. Polit. Sci. Assn., Am. Soc. Social Psychiatry (council), Phi Beta Kappa. Author: The Politics of Social Change in the Middle East and North Africa, 1963; The Dialectics of Transformation in Politics, Personality and History, 1972. Home: 27 Maclean Circle Princeton NJ 08540

HALPERN, MARTIN, educator, author; b. N.Y.C., Oct. 3, 1929; s. Louis and Edith (Eisinger) H.; B.A., U. Rochester, 1950, M.A., 1953; Ph.D., Harvard, 1959; m. Nancy M. Homer, July 5, 1959; childrenAndrew Homer, Jessica M. Teaching fellow Harvard, 1954-56, 57-59; faculty U. Cal. at Berkeley, 1959-64, U. Mass., 1964-65; faculty Brandeis U., 1965-, asso. prof. theatre arts, 1966-; plays produced by exptl. and regional and univ. theatres in N.Y.C., Cambridge, Mass., Waltham, Mass., San Francisco, Berkeley, Cal. Served with AUS, 1951-53. Fulbright scholar, 1956-57; Howard Found. fellow in writing, 1962-63. Mem. Phi Beta Kappa. Author: Two Sides of an Island and Other Poems, 1963; William Vaughn Moody, 1964; also articles, plays and poems in journals. Home: 14 Waban St Natick, MA 01760. Office: Theatre Arts Dept Brandeis Univ Waltham MA 02154

HALPERN, SEYMOUR, congressman; b. N.Y.C., Nov. 19, 1913; s. Ralph and Anne (Swanton) H.; student Seth Low Coll., Columbia, 1932-34; m. Barbara Olsen, Dec. 27, 1958. Reporter, Long Island Daily Press, 1931-32; feature writer, artist Chgo. Herald-Examiner, 1932-33; asst. to mgr. Fusion Campaign Com., 1933- 37; asst. to pres. Council City N.Y., 1938-40; senator State of N.Y., 1941-54, chmn. com. civil service, 1941-44, com. on pub. instns., 1945, com. on motor vehicles and transp., 1946-47; mem. 86th-87th Congresses, 4th Dist. of N.Y., 88th-91st Congresses, 6th Dist. N.Y., 92d Congress. Impartial chmn. moving and storage industry of N.Y.C., 1955-59; mem. N.Y.C. Commn. on Cts., 1956-58; hon. mem. Mayor's Com. Intergroup Relations; mem. Franklin D. Roosevelt Meml. Commn. Bd. dirs. Queens Mental Health Soc., Queens Hosp. Center, Cancer Research Soc., N. Queens Child Guidance Center; nat. council Fedn. for Jewish Nat. Fund; adv. bd. Nat. Assn. Prevention Juvenile Delinquency, N.Y. Assn. Mental Health; adv. council Nat. Com. on Playgrounds for Young Am.; N.Y. regional adv. bd. Anti-Defamation League; chmn. bd. Nat. Family Council of Drug Addiction; Queens exec. com. Fedn. Jewish Philanthropies; chmn. bd. sponsors Queens Symphony Orch.; bd. dirs. Queens Nat. Conf. Christians and Jews; mem. nat. bd. The Library Presdl. Papers. Recipient Achievement medal V.F.W., 1954, Human Rights award N.Y. chpt., 1964; Pub. Service award N.Y. chpt. Jewish War Vets., 1958; Distinguished Service award Fedn. 213 Housing Co-ops., 1964; 10th Anniversary medal Assembly Captive Nations, 1964. Fellow Am. Geog. Soc., Am. Acad. Polit. and Social Sci.; mem. Internat. Platform Assn., Am. Arbitration Assn. (nat. panel), Nat. Aeros. Assn. (dir.), Zionist Orgn. Am. (nat. exec. council), Assn. Cultural Exchange (dir.), Queens Bot. Soc. (charter), U.S. Capitol Hist. Soc. (charter), N.Y. Soc. in Washington (v.p.), L.I. Art League. Elk; mem. B'nai B'rith (trustee lodge), K.P. Clubs: Canyon Country (Palm Springs); Richmond Hill Republican; Capitol Hill (Washington), Nat. Republican. Contbr. articles, mags. and newspapers. Home: 166-05 Highland Av Jamaica NY 11432 Office: 89-31 161st St Jamaica NY 11432 also House Office Bldg Washington DC 20515*

HALPIN, CLAUDE BERNARD, hosp. adminstr.; b. Calgary, Alta., Can., Dec. 25, 1936; s. Charles Bernard and Kathleen (Detwiller) H.; certificate bus. adminstrn. Mount Royal Jr. Coll., Calgary, 1958; B.S. in Bus. Adminstrn. (Fgn. Student scholar), U. Ore., 1961; diploma hosp. adminstrn. U. Toronto (Ont., Can.), 1963; m. Gail Patricia Lewis, Aug. 24, 1963; children—Kirsten Leigh, Shauna Lynne. Ednl. adviser, field rep. Mount Royal Jr. Coll., 1956-61 (summers); adminstrv. resident Toronto Western Hosp., 1962-63; asst. exec. dir. Glenrose Provincial Gen. Hosp., Edmonton, Alta., 1963-68, Misericordia Hosp., Edmonton, 1968-69; adminstr. Rideau Regional Hosp. Sch., Smiths Falls, Ont., 1969—; lectr. No. Alta. Inst. Tech. and Art, 1966-67, U. Alta., 1965-69, U. Ottawa Sch. Hosp. Adminstrn., 1970-71. Vice chmn. Edmonton Met. div. United Community Fund, 1968, chmn., 1969. Bd. dirs. Edmonton Rehab. Centre for Handicapped (1st v.p. 1968-69). Mem. Am. Coll. Hosp. Adminstrs., Edmonton Met. Hosp. Council (past officer), Edmonton Hosp. Assn. (past officer), Alta. Assn. Remedial Gymnasts (bd. dirs.), Ottawa Valley Hosp. Adminstrs. Conf. (pres. 1971—), Sigma Alpha Epsilon. Mason, Kiwanian. Home: 5 Banting Crescent Kanata Ontario Canada Office: PO Box 2000 Smiths Falls Ontario Canada

HALPRIN, ANN SCHUMAN, (Mrs. Lawrence Halprin), dancer; b. Wilmette, Ill., July 13, 1920; d. Isadore and Ida (Schiff) Schuman; student Bennington Summer Sch. Dance, 1938-39; B.S. in Dance, U. Wis., 1943; m. Lawrence Halprin, Sept. 19, 1940; children—Daria, Rana. Founder, choreographer, dir., performer Dancers' Workshop of San Francisco; appeared in films Four in the Afternoon, The Bed; master tchr. Esalen Inst., U. Cal. at Berkeley, U. Cal. at Los Angeles, U. Ill., Reed Coll., Harvard Sch. Design, Environmental Sch. Design, U. Cal., San Francisco State Coll., U. Mich.; choreographed The Prophetess, The Lonely Ones, Visions, Birds of America or Gardens without Walls, Esposizione, Visage, The Five Legged Stool, Parades and Changes, Apt. 6, The Bath, Myths, Lunch, Look, New Rites of US, New Time Shuffle, Godash, Animal Ritual; (film) Ann, a Portrait. Mem. Regional Bay Area Arts Council; mem. San Francisco Arts Resource Devel. Com.; founder, dir. Marin Dance Coop. Recipient Guggenheim award, 1970-71. Mem. Assn. Am. Dance, Conscientious Artists Am. Founder: Impulse mag. Home: 15 Ravine Way Kentfield CA 94904 Office: 321 Divisadero St San Francisco CA 94117

HALPRIN, LAWRENCE, landscape architect-planner; b. N.Y.C., July 1, 1916; s. Samuel W. and Rose (Luria) H.; B.S. in Plant Scis., Cornell U., 1939; M.S. in Plant Scis., U. Wis., 1941; B. Landscape Architecture, Harvard, 1942; m. Ann Schuman, Sept. 19, 1940; children—Daria, Rana, Sr. asso. Thomas D. Curch & Assos., San Francisco, 1946-49; prin. Lawrence Halprin & Assos., San Francisco, 1949- -; lectr. U. Cal. at Berkeley, 1960-65; vis. lectr. U. B.C. (Can.), 1954, U. N.C., 1955, U. Pa., 1958; dir. Halprin Summer Workshop, 1966, 1968; prin. works include Ghirardelli Sq., San Francisco, Sea Ranch, Cal., Nicollet Mall, Mpls., Old Orchard Shopping Center, Skokie, Ill., Lovejoy Fountain, Petligrove Park, Forecourt Fountain, Portland, Ore., Market St. reconstrn., San Francisco. Panelist White House Conf. Natural Beauty, 1965; mem. bd. urban cons. Bur. Pub. Roads, 1966-67; design cons. Cal. Div. Hwys., 1963-65; landscape architect, urban cons. San Francisco Bay Area Rapid Transit Dist., 1963-66; mem. Gov. Cal. Conf. Cal. Beauty, 1966, Nat. Council Arts, 1966—, Adv. Council Historic Preservation, 1967—. Bd. dirs. San Francisco Planning and Urban Renewal Assn., 1964-65, San Francisco Actors Workshop, 1965-66, San Francisco Dancers Workshop Co., 1950—. Served to lt. (j.g.) USNR, 1943-46. Named One of Leaders of Tomorrow, Time mag., 1953; recipient awards including Allied Professions Gold medal A.I.A., 1964. Fellow Am. Soc. Landscape Architects. Democrat. Jewish religion. Club: Sierra (San Francisco). Author: Cities, 1963; Freeways, 1966; New York, New York, 1968; The RSVP Cycles, 1970; co-author: The Freeway in the City, 1968. Home: 15 Ravine Way Kentfield CA 94904 Office: 1620 Montgomery St San Francisco CA 94111*

HALPRIN, ROSE L., Zionist leader U.S.; b. N.Y.C.; d. Philip and Rebecca (Isaacson) Luria; ed. Washington Irving High Sch., Columbia Tchrs. Coll.; m. Samuel Halprin, Apr. 26, 1914; children—Larry, Ruth. Nat. pres. Hadassah, 1932-34, 47-52, rep. to Actions Com., 1939- 46, chmn., Palestine, 1939-41, polit. chmn., 1941-47, rep. to Am. Zionist Emergency Council, 1942—, mem. Jewish Agy. Exec., 1946-68; vice chmn. Am. Zionist Council, 1953; liaison officer Nat. Bd. Hadassah, Women's Zionist Orgn. of Am. and Hadassah Med. Orgn. in Palestine, 1934-39; mem. legislative council for Zionist affairs between Zionist congresses, 1938; treas. Am. Zionist Emergency Council, 1942, vice chmn., 1945-47; mem. Am. Com. of 8 of World Zionist Orgn., 1946; mem. secretariat for orgn. Am. Jewish Conf., 1946, becoming mem. interim com., exec. com. and chmn. Palestine com.; del. Paris Conf. Jewish Agy. Exec.; co-chmn. World Confedn. Gen. Zionists; chmn. Am. sect. Jewish Agy. for Israel, 1960-68; chmn. Am. sect. World Jewish Congress, 1968-71. Home: 225 E 74th St New York City NY 10021 Office: 65 E 52d St New York City NY 10022

HALPRIN, SOL, pres. Am. Soc. Cinematographers, 1966. Address: 1782 N Orange Dr Hollywood CA 90028 *

HALSEMA, JAMES JULIUS, govt. ofcl.; b. Warren, O., Jan. 1, 1919; s. Eusebius Julius and Marie (Boesel) H.; B.A. with honors in History, Duke, 1940; M.A., Sch. Advanced Internat. Studies, 1949; grad. Nat. War Coll., 1958; m. Alice Cleveland, June 18, 1949; children—J. Wayne, A. Louise, Margaret M., Jane E., Charlotte A., Paul A. Editor, Baguio edition of Manila (Philippines) Daily Bull., 1940-41; interned by Japanese, Baguio, 1941-45; war corr. A.P., 1945-45, fgn. corr. in Philippines and Indonesia, 1945-48; information officer Am. consulate gen., Singapore, 1950-52, Am. embassy, Manila, 1952-54, Am. embassy, Bangkok, Thailand, 1954; spl. asst. to asst. dir. for Far East, USIA, Washington, 1955, dep. asst. dir. for Far East, 1955- 57, planning dir. agy., 1958-61; counselor of embassy for pub. affairs, Cairo, 1961-66; dir. tng. USIA, Washington, 1966-69, chmn. Voice of Am. langs. priority task force, 1969, chief evaluation and spl. studies, 1970, exec. asst. to dir., dept. dir., 1970-71; pub. affairs office Am. embassy, Santiago, Chile, 1971—. Del. of Duke to Japan-Am. student conf., 1940. Recipient Meritorious Service award USIA, 1966. Mem. Am. Fgn. Service Assn. Home: 4701 Berkeley Terrace NW Washington DC 20007 also Glenmoore PA 19343 Office: Santiago State Dept Washington DC 20521

HALSEY, JAMES H., educator; b. Hammond, Ind., May 11 1906; s. Hilary and Gertrude (Herron) H.; A.B., Wabash Coll., 1927, LL.D., 1958; M.A., Columbia, 1939; postgrad. Yale; m. Julia McElhiney Walker, June 18, 1930; children—James Herron, John Easton, George Rogers. Teaching and adminstrv. positions, MacJannet Sch., Paris, France, 1927-30, Hammond (Ind.) High Sch., 1930-33, Morgan Park Mil. Acad., Chgo., 1935-37, Irving Sch., Tarrytown, N.Y., 1937-38; with Jr. Coll. of Conn. (later U. Bridgeport), 1938—, pres. U. Bridgeport, 1946-62, chancellor, 1962—. Dir. Value Line Funds, N.Y.C. State chmn. UN Day, 1954-62; New Eng. regional chmn. UN Day, 1962-65. Sec.-treas. MacJannet Found., Bridgeport, 1968—; Bd. dirs. New Eng. Bd. Higher Edn.; v.p. Conn. Digestive Disease Found., New Haven, 1970—. Past sec. com. on instns. of higher edn. N.E. Assn. of Colls. Conn. Conf. of Jr. Colls. (past pres.), New Eng. Jr. Coll. Council (past pres.). Decorated comdr. Order Acad. Palms (France). Mem. UN Assn. U.S.A. (state pres. 1965-69, hon. pres. 1969—). United Conglst. Clubs: Rotary. University, Brooklawn Country. Contbr. articles to ednl. periodicals. Home: 491 University Av Bridgeport CT 06604

HALSEY, KENNETH STUART, lawyer; b. Detroit, June 27, 1927; s. Elmer F. and Eleanor (Weinand) H.; student Wayne State U., 1944-45, U. Mich., 1945; B.S., U. Neb., 1946; J.D., U. Detroit, 1949; m. Martha Letke, June 27, 1951; children—Debra, Kim, Paul, Kirt. Admitted to Mich. bar, 1949; atty. Davidson Kaess, Detroit, 1947-51; spl. agt. FBI, 1951-53; sr. partner Davison, Gotshall, Halsey & Kohl, Detroit, 1953-69, Halsey, Halsey & McNamara, Detroit and Mt. Clemens, Mich., 1969—. Dir. Am. Silicate Corp., Mid Channel Marine, Alpine Modulars. Chmn. Wayne County Young Republicans, 1949-50. Served with USNR, 1945-46. Mem. Mich. State Bar (bd. dirs. negligence council), Macomb Co. Bar Assn., Am. Bar Assn., Internat. Assn. Ins. Counsel. Home: 1141 N Oxford Rd Grosse Pointe Woods MI 48236 Office: 2 Crocker Blvd Mt Clemens MI 48043

HALSEY, WILLIAM DARRACH, editor; b. Washington, Sept. 17, 1918; s. William D. and Mary Flagg (Price) H.; grad. Loomis Sch., 1936; B.S., Haverford Coll., 1940; m. Frances Murlin, June 27, 1942; m. 2d, Elizabeth Darby, Apr. 11, 1966. Mng. editor Thorndike-Barnhart Comprehensive Desk Dictionary, 1951-, Thorndike-Barnhart Beginning Dictionary, 1952-, Thorndike-Barnhart Jr. Dictionary, 1952-, Thorndike-Barnhart High Sch. Dictionary, 1952-, Thorndike-Barnhart Advanced Jr. Dictionary, 1957-; editorial dir. Collier's Ency., 1960—, Merit Students Ency., 1965—; v.p. Crowell-Collier Pub. Co., N.Y.C., 1962-65, Crowell Collier and Macmillan, Inc., 1965-; pres. Crowell-Collier Ednl. Corp., 1964-. Co- author: New Century Cyclopedia of Names, 1954; New Century Handbook of English Literature, 1956. Home: Rombout Rd RD 3 Poughkeepsie NY 12603 Office: 866 3d Av New York City NY 10022

HALSMAN, PHILLIPPE, photographer, author; b. Riga, Latvia, May 2, 1906; s. Max and Ita (Grintouch) H.; B.A., Vidus Skola, Riga, 1924; student Sch. Engring., Dresden, Germany, 1924-28; m. Yvonne Moser, Apr. 1, 1937; childrenIrene Aline, Jane Ellen. Came to U.S., 1940, naturalized, 1949. Photographer for Vogue, Vu and Voila mags., Paris, France, 1931-40; contbr. photographer to Life, Sat. Eve. Post, Look, other mags., 1941-; portrait photographer Winston Churchill, Dwight Eisenhower, Harold Macmillan, Mrs. Eleanor Roosevelt, Albert Einstein, Andre Gide, Gen. Marshall, others; exhbns. in Paris, N.Y.C., Tokyo; rep. in permanent collections Met. Mus. Art, Mus. Modern Art; dir. motion picture For a Livable America, 1968; faculty mem. Famous Photographers Sch., Westport, Conn., 1969—. Named one of 10 greatest photographers in internat. poll. Popular Photography mag., 1958; recipient of Newhouse award, 1963; Golden Plate award Am. Acad. of Achievement, 1967. Mem. Am. Soc. Mag. Photographers (1st pres.). Clubs: Dutch Treat, Overseas Press (N.Y.C.). Photographer: (books) The Frenchman, 1949, Piccoli, 1953, Dali's Mustache, 1954, Philippe Halsman's Jumpbook, 1959; Halsman on the Creation of Photographic Ideas, 1961. Address: 33 W 67th St New York City NY 10023

HALSTEAD, BRUCE WALTER, biotoxicologist; b. San Francisco, Mar. 28, 1920; s. Walter and Ethel Muriel (Shanks) H.; A.A., San Francisco City Coll., 1941; B.A., U. Cal., Berkeley, 1943; M.D., Loma Linda U., 1948; m. Joy Arloa Mallory, Aug. 3, 1941; children-Linda (Mrs. Robert Baldwin), Sandra, David, Larry, Claudia, Shari. Research asst. in ichthyology Cal. Acad. Scis., 1935-43; instr. Pacific Union Coll., 1943-44; mem. faculty Loma Linda U., 1948- 58, research asso. Lab. Neurol. Research, Sch. Medicine, 1964—; dir. World Life Research Inst., Colton, Cal., 1959—, Internat. Biotoxicological Center; research asso. in ichthyology Los Angeles County Mus., 1964—; instr. Walla Walla Coll., summers 1964—. Cons. to govt. agys., pvt. corps; mem. editorial staff Exerpta Medica, 1959—, Toxicon, 1962—; mem. joint group experts on sci. aspects marine pollution UN; dir. Nat. Assn. Underwater Instrs., Internat. Underwater Enterprises, Internat. Bots., Inc. Fellow A.A.A.S., Internat. Soc. Toxinology (a founder), N.Y. Acad. Scis., Royal Soc. Tropical Medicine and Hygiene; mem. Am. Inst. Biol. Scis., Am. Micros. Soc., Am. Soc. Ichthyologists and Herpetologists, Am. Soc. Limnology and Oceanography, numerous others. Author: Poisonous and Venomous Marine Animals of the World, 3 vols., 1966. Contbr. articles profl. jours. Address: 23000 Grand Terrace Rd Colton CA 92324

HALSTEAD, GEORGIA, educator; b. Lafayette, Ind., July 29, 1915; d. George E. and Alice (Switzer) Halstead; B.S. in Home Econs., Purdue U., 1937; M.S. in Edn., Mich. State U., 1945; Ph.D., Pa. State U., 1954. Tchr., Brook (Ind.) High Sch., 1937-40, Washington Twp. Sch., Logansport, Ind., 1940-44; athletic dir. summer camps, Mich., 1943-44; tchr. Adrian (Mich.) High Sch., 1945-46; instr. Pa. State U., 1947-48; asst. prof. charge home econs. edn. Miami U., 1948-51; head home econs. edn. Winthrop Coll., 1953-58, chmn. home econs. dept., 1955-58, dir. tchr. edn., 1958-59; chmn. dept. home econs. Bowling Green State U., 1959—. Mem. Am. Assn. U. Women, Am. Assn. U. Profs., Am. Home Econs. Assn., Am. Hist. Assn., N.E.A., Am. Vocational Assn., Daus. Am. Revolution, Daus. Am. Colonists, Phi Lambda Theta, Omicron Nu, Kappa Delta Pi, Phi Upsilon Omicron. Club: Purdue Sports Women. Home: 882 Scott Blvd Bowling Green, OH 43402.

HALSTED, ABEL STEVENS, Jr., lawyer; b. Pasadena, Cal., Nov. 22, 1907; s. Abel Stevens and Eleanor (Hall) H.; A.B., Stanford, 1929; LL.B., Harvard, 1932; m. Anne Croftan, July 8, 1931; children—Croftan H. (Mrs. Willis R. Brown), Stevens. Admitted to Cal. bar, 1932, since practiced in Los Angeles; mem. firm Macdonald, Halsted & Layboarne, 1946—; lectr. U. So. Cal. Law Sch., 1952-57. Pres. Town Hall, 1953. Trustee Scripps Coll., Hollenbeck Home; former trustee Poly. Sch ., Westridge Sch. (both Pasadena); bd. dirs., v.p. Legal Aid Found. of Los Angeles. Served to lt. (s.g.) USNR, 1943-45. Mem. State Bar Cal. (bd. govs. 1964-67, pres. 1966-67), Am. Los Angeles County (trustee 1955-62, pres. 1961-62) bar assns., Harvard Law Sch. Assn. So. Cal. (chmn. 1958-60), Am. Judicature Soc. (dir. 1969-71), Phi Beta Kappa. Republican. Episcopalian. Clubs: Chancery, Stock Exchange, Sunset, Twilight, Westerners (Los Angeles); Valley Hunt (Pasadena). Home: 420 Laguna Rd Pasadena CA 91105 Office: 1200 Wilshire Blvd Los Angeles CA 90017

HALSTED, JOHN BURT, educator, historian; b. Antwerp, Belgium, Sept. 17, 1926 (parents Am. citizens); s. Henry Moore and Katharine (Holmes) H.; B.A., Wesleyan U., Middletown, Conn., 1948, M.A., 1949; Ph.D., Columbia, 1954; M.A. (hon.), Amhert Coll., 1966; m. Betty Nilsen, May 14, 1949; childrenMark Nilsen, Brian Whittemore, Lorna Katharine. Instr. humanities Stevens Inst. Tech., 1950-52; mem. faculty Amherst Coll., 1952-, prof. history, 1966- . Served with USNR, 1944-46. Mem. Am. Hist. Assn., Conf. Brit. Studies, Am. Assn. U. Profs. (pres. Amherst 1967-69), Phi Beta Kappa, Psi Upsilon. Democrat. Episcopalian. Editor: Romanticism: Problems in Definition, Explanation and Evaluation, 1965; Romanticism: A Collection of Documents, 1969. Home: 254 Lincoln Av Amherst MA 01002

HALSTED, JOHN MAC HARG, mgmt. cons.; b. Chgo., May 27, 1905; s. Joseph and Mary (Mac Harg) H.; B.A., U. Mich., 1927; m. Nancy Leahy, May 2, 1944; children—Joseph, Ellen, Henry, John Matthew; m. 2d, Dorothy Moore Benson, Dec. 8, 1962; stepchildren—Richard Benson, Virginia Benson, Lynda Benson, Diane Benson. With Colgate-Palmolive Co., 1927-69, dir. purchases, 1958-61, v.p. purchasing, 1961-69, cons., 1969; now mgmt. cons., N. Y.C. Mem. Oil Trades Assn. N.Y. (pres. 1970). Clubs: N.Y. Yacht; Riverside Yacht. Home: 81-18 Courtland Av Stamford CT 06902 Office: 200 Park Av New York City NY 10017

HALTER, EDWIN GEORGE, lawyer; b. Cleve., Jan. 23, 1906; s. Daniel and Ella (Schott) H.; A.B., Western Res. U., 1926, LL.B., 1928; m. Georgia Forbey Wilker, June 20, 1931; children—David Edwin, Nancy Frances (Mrs. Raymond Dacek), Thomas Albert. Admitted to Ohio bar, 1928, since practiced in Cleve.; sr. partner firm Calfee, Halter, Calfee, Griswold & Sommer. Dir. E.F. Hauserman Co., Arthur G. McKee & Co., Western Res. Life Assurance Co. Ohio. Mem. Am., Ohio, Cleve. bar assns., Cleve. C. of C. (past chmn. fed. taxation com.), Phi Gamma Delta, Phi Delta Phi. Club: Union (Cleve.). Home: 29959 Bolingbrook Rd Pepper Pike OH 44124 Office: Central Nat Bank Bldg Cleveland OH 44114

HALTER, HELEN ISABELLE, see Long, Helen Halter

HALTINER, GEORGE JOSEPH, educator; b. St. Paul, Nov. 26, 1918; s. Conrad and Elizabeth (Gardner) H.; B.S. summa cum laude, Coll. St. Thomas, St. Paul, 1940; Ph.M., U. Wis., 1942, Ph.D., 1948; m. Mary B. Wahl, June 21, 1947; children—Mary Louise, Jeffrey Peter, Kathleen Ann, Jean Marie, Michele Marie. Asst. prof. Naval Postgrad. Sch., Annapolis, Md., 1946; mem. faculty Navy Postgrad. Sch., Monterey, Cal., 1948—; prof., 1953—, chmn. dept. meteorology and oceanography, 1964-68, dept. meteorology, 1968—; cons. in field, 1942—. Mem. tech. adv. com. air pollution Monterey and Santa Cruz Counties, 1966—. Served to lt. USNR, 1942-46; capt. Res. Fellow Am. Meteorol. Soc. (council); mem. Japanese, Royal meteorol. socs., Sigma Xi. Author: (with F.L. Martin) Dynamical and Physical Meteorology, 1957; Numerical Weather Prediction, 1971; also numerous articles. Home: 1134 Alta Mesa Rd Monterey CA 93940

HALTOM, ELBERT BERTRAM, Jr., lawyer; b. Florence, Ala., Dec. 26, 1922; s. Elbert Bertram and Elva Mae (Simpson) H.; student Florence State U.; 1940-45; LL.B., U. Ala., 1948; m. Constance Boyd Morris, Aug. 19, 1949; 1 dau., Emily Morris. Admitted to Ala. bar, 1948, since practiced in Florence; mem. firm Bradshaw, Barnett & Haltom, 1948-58; mem. firm Haltom & Patterson, 1959—. Dir. Guardian Savs. Investment Corp. Chmn. Muscle Shoals Mental Health Center, 1968 Mem. Ala. Ho. of Reps., 1954-58; mem. Ala. Senate, 1958-62; candidate lt. gov. Ala., 1962; mem. Ala. Democratic Exec. Com., 1966—. Served with USAAF, 1943-45. Decorated Air medal with four oak leaf clusters. Mem. Florence C. of C. (past pres.), Am. Legion, V.F.W., Phi Gamma Delta, Phi Delta Phi. Methodist. Club: Florence Exchange. Home: 562 Palisade Dr Florence AL 35630 Office: 119 1/2 E Mobile St Florence AL 35630

HALVERSON, ALBERT BENTSEN, ins. co. exec.; b. Kansas City, Kan., June 2, 1913; s. Albert Bentsen and Dora (Moss) H.; student Kansas City Jr. Coll., 1931-33, U. Kan., 1933-34, Kansas City Sch. Law, 1934-36; m. Jean Morgan, June 4, 1939; 1 son, Jeffrey. With Occidental Life Ins. Co. Cal., Los Angeles, 1936-, now exec. v.p. adminstrn. and operations; dir. Occidental Life Ins. . Co., Arbor Life Ins. Co., Dyna-Metric, Inc., Pasadena. Past pres. San Gabriel Valley council Boy Scouts Am., 1960-62. Bd. dirs. Cal. Hosp., Found. Health Care-Cal. State Tchns. Assn., So. Cal. Comprehensive Health Planning Council, Luth, Hosp. Soc. Bd. overseers Cal. Sch. Profl. Psychology. Mem. Town Hall Los Angeles, Phi Alpha Delta. Club: Oakmont Country (Glendale, Cal.). Home: 1615 Pegfair Estates Dr Pasadena, CA 91103. Office: Occidental Life Ind Co Cal Hill and Olive at 12 th St Los Angeles CA 90054

HALVERSON, WALTER STANTON, Jr., mfg. co. exec.; b. Rapid City, S.D., Apr. 14, 1921; s. Walter Stanton and Grace R. (Beardsley) H.; B.A., U. Mont. 1941; student Harvard Bus. Sch., 1942; m. Suzanne Lenoir Kresser, Dec. 14, 1968; children by previous marriage—Hibbard Sherman, Lisa, Stuart. With Don Baxter, Inc., Glendale, Cal., 1941-64; affiliate Pharmaseal Labs., Inc. acquired by Am. Hosp. Supply Corp., 1951, pres., 1959-63, vice chmn. bd., 1964, also pres. McGaw Labs. and Don Baxter, Inc., 1962-64; pres. med. scis. div. Litton Industries, 1964-65; pres. Narco Sci. Industries, Ft. Washington, Pa., 1966—70, chmn., 1970—; dir. Arkay Packaging Co., Ithaca Gun Co. Served to lt. USNR, 1942-46. Mem Am. Mgmt. Assn. (bd. dirs.). Clubs: Phila. Aviation; Manufacturers Golf and Country (Oreland, Pa.). Home: Fox Hill Park Av Wycombe PA 18980 Office: Narco Sci Industries Fort Washington PA 19034

HALVERSON, WENDELL QUELPRUD, coll. pres., clergyman; b. Austin, Minn., July 11, 1916; s. Arthur Benjamin and Emma Josephine (Pederson) H.; B.A., State U. Ia., 1940; B.D., Union Theol. Sem., N.Y.C., 1943; student Grad. Sch. Theology, Oberlin Coll., 1943-49, U. Oslo (Norway), 1949, U. Chgo., 1950; D.D. (hon.), Lake Forest U., 1956; m. Marian Lois Phypers, Aug. 3, 1940; children—Peder Quelprud, Ingrid Maud, Timothy Greenwood. Ordained to ministry Presbyn. Ch., 1943; pastor in Clyde, O., 1943-46, La Grange, Ill., 1949-58; asst. prof. philosophy religion Heidelberg Coll., Tiffin, O., 1946-49; Chgo. corr. Christian Century, 1953; lectr. homiletics McCormick Theol. Sem., Chgo., 1957-58; gen. presbyter Presbytery N.Y., United Presbyn. Ch., 1958-61; pres. Buena Vista Coll., Storm Lake, Ia., 1961—; dir. Ia. State Ednl. Radio and TV Broadcast, 1967-69. Sec. ch. extension bd. N.Y. Presbyn. Found., 1958-61; mem. bd. pensions Presbyn. Ch. U.S.A., 1956-58; pres. Iowans for Better Justice, 1970. Bd. dirs. Ia. Coll. Found. Mem. Ia. Assn. Pvt. Colls. and Univs., Presbyn. Coll. Union. Kiwanian. Club: University (Chgo.). Home: 429 College St Storm Lake IA 50588

HALVERSTADT, ALBERT NAST, former mfg. co. exec.; b. Akron, O., July 11, 1909; s. Hebert and Gertrude (Andrews) H.; B.A., Davidson Coll., 1930; m. Jane Muhlberg, June 29, 1933; children—Albert Nast, Constance (Mrs. John C. Miller II), Linda (Mrs. John W. MacDuffie). With Procter & Gamble Co., Cin., 1930-69, gen. advt. mgr., 1960-62, v.p. advt., 1962-69; ret., 1969. Bd. dirs. Cancer Control Council, Center Family Care; trustee Cin. Boys Club, Christ Hospital. Clubs: Cincinnati Country; Camargo; Hole-In-the-Wall Golf. Home: 12 Peasenhall Lane Cincinnati OH 45208

HALVORSEN, RAYMOND GEORGE, mfg. exec.; b. Manitowoc, Wis., June 15, 1906; s. George J. and Rose P. (Herman) H.; m. Marion Houle, Nov. 17, 1937; children—Morrie E., Brenda Rae. Sales engr. Wiese Mfg. Co., Manitowoc, 1924-29; plant mgr. W. M. Welch Mfg. Co., Manitowoc, 1929-34; dir. sales, lab. equipment div. Hamilton Mfg. Co., Two Rivers, Wis., 1934-42, sales mgr. contract div., 1942-53, v.p. charge sales, 1953-55, exec. v.p., dir., 1955-63, pres., gen. mgr., 1963-66, pres., chief executive officer, 1966-70, chmn., chief exec. officer, 1970—. Member of Association of Home Appliance Manufacturers, Sci. Apparatus Makers Assn. (pres. 1961-62, dir.; recipient sci. award 1966), Manitowoc-Two Rivers (pres., dir.), Wis. State (dir.) chambers of commerce. Mason (32, Shriner), Elk. Clubs: Milwaukee Athletic; Rotary (pres. 1956) (Two Rivers Wis); Manitowoc Branch River Country Home: 3 Horse Shoe Bend Tow Rivers WI 54241 Office: PO Box 75 Two Rivers WI 54241

HALVORSON, HALVOR ORIN, educator; b. River Falls, Wis., Mar. 26, 1897; s. Hallie and Elizabeth (Heyerdahl) H.; B.S., U. Minn., 1921, Chem. E., 1922, Ph.D., 1928; D.Sc. (hon.), St. Olaf Coll., 1948; m. Selma C. Halvorson, Aug. 1922; children—Betty Jean (Mrs. Theodore Caspar), Harlyn, Loren, Gayle Adair (Mrs. John Mosand). Teaching fellow U. Minn., 1922-23, instr., 1923-28, asst. prof., 1928-30, asso. prof., 1930-40, prof., 1940-49; dir. Hormel Inst., 1943-49; prof., head dept. bacteriology U. Ill., 1949-60, dir. Sch. Life Scis., 1959-65; research prof. dept. biochemistry U. Minn., St. Paul, 1965—. Cons. san. engring. and food tech., 1928—. Civilian with Office Sci. Research and Devel., 1943-45, panel mem. Office Naval Research, 1947-51, NIH, 1949-54, mem. council Inst. of Allergy and Infectious Diseases, 1954-58; mem. subcom. food stability NRC, 1955-57. Served as 1st lt. C.A.C., U.S. Army, 1917-19. Named Outstanding Am. Investigator Am. Mfrs. Assn., 194O; recipient Pasteur award, 1960. Mem. Soc. Am. Bacteriologists (past pres.), Am. Acad. Microbiology (chmn. bd. govs. 1956-57), Sigma Xi, Phi Kappa Phi, Phi Lambda Upsilon, Alpha Chi Sigma, Gamma Alpha. Author: Quantitative Bacteriology, 1933; articles sci. jours. Contbg. author: The Chemistry and Technology of Food and Food 1901 E River Rd Minneapolis MN 55414 Office: Dept Biochemistry U Minn St Paul MN 55101*

HALVORSON, HARLYN ODELL, educator; b. Mpls., May 17, 1925; s. Halvor Orin and Selma (Halvorson) H.; B.S. cum laude, U. Minn., 1948, M.S. in Biochemistry, 1950; Ph.D. in Bacteriology, U. Ill., 1952; m. Jean Ericksen, Aug. 26, 1954; children—Lisa, Philip. Instr., then asst. prof. bacteriology U. Mich. Med. Sch., 1952-56; mem. faculty U. Wis., 1956-71, prof. bacteriology, 1962-71, chmn. Lab. Molecular biology, 1966-70; prof. biology, dir. basic med. scis. research center Brandeis U., 1971—; vis. prof. U. Wash., summer 1959; instr. physiology Marine Biol. Sta., Woods Hole, Mass., summers 1962-65, 67; vis. investigator Lab. Enzymology, Central Nat. de Recherche Sci., Gif-sur-Yvette, France, 1965-66; instr. differentiation Hebrew U., Jerusalem, 1965, RNA-DNA hybridization, Naples, Italy, 1966. Mem. adv. bd. Q.M. research Nat. Acad. Scis.-NRC, 1958—; chmn. physiology div. NIH, 1961, mem. biochemistry and nutrition fellowship panel, 1960—, mem. study sect. B microbiology, 1964—; trustee, mem. exec. com. Marine Biol. Lab., Woods Hole; research adv. com. U.S. Dept. Agr.; mem. etiology adv. panel Am. Cancer Soc.; cons, com. mariner sterilization NASA. Mem. Lutheran Student Directing Com., 1957—, Luth. Coll. Bd. Higher Edn., 1964—. Fellow USPHS, 1951-52; Merck sr. postdoctoral fellow Pasteur Inst., Paris, France, 1955-56; NIH career professorship, 1963-71. Mem. Am. Soc. Microbiology (council policy com.), Am. Acad. Microbiology, Am. Chem. Soc., N.Y. Acad. Scis., Soc. Am. Bacteriologists, Nat. Acad. Sci., Am. Inst. Biol. Scis. (cons.), Internat. Research Orgn., Sigma Xi, Alpha Chi Sigma. Author: Microbial Dormancy, 1966; also research papers. Editor: (series) Molecular Biology, 1964; asso. editor Jour. Bacteriology, Accounts of Chem. Research, Analytical Biochemistry, Archives Biochemistry and Biophysics. Home: 101 Loker St Wayland MA 01778

HALVORSON, NEWMAN THORBUS, accountant; b. Blair, Wis., June 16, 1908; s. Thomas Nicholas and Clara (Thorbus) H.; B.A., U. Wis., 1930; m. Virginia Westbrook Markle, Dec. 1, 1934; children—Newman Thorbus, Sigrid (Mrs. L. Richard Freese, Jr.), Karin (Mrs. William A. Hillhouse II). With Ernst & Ernst, C.P.A.'s, 1930—, partner, 1947—. Trustee Cleve. Mus. Natural History, 1960—, treas., 1965—; trustee Musical Arts Assn. Cleve., Hathaway Brown Sch., Cleve., Gates Mills (O.) Hist. Soc., Cleve. Soc. Blind, Cleve. Council Ind. Schs.; v.p. U. Wis. Found. C.P.A., Mich., Ohio. Mem. Am. Inst. C.P.A.'s (accounting principles bd.), Chi Phi. Republican. Episcopalian. Mason. Clubs: Union, Kirtland Country, Chagrin Valley Hunt (Cleve.); Detroit Athletic. Home: Woodstock Rd Gates Mills OH 44040 also Vail CO 81657 Office: Union Commerce Bldg Cleveland OH 44115

HAM, JAMES MILTON, univ. dean; b. Coboconk, Ont., Can., Sept. 21, 1920; s. James Arthur and Harriet Boomer (Gandier) H.; B.A.Sc., U. Toronto, 1943; S.M., Mass. Inst. Tech., 1947, Sc.D., 1952; m. Mary Caroline Augustine, June 4, 1955; children—Peter Stace, Mary Matha, Jane Elizabeth. Lectr., housemaster Ajax div. U. Toronto, 1945-46; research asso. Mass. Inst. Tech., 1949-51, asst. prof. elec. engring., 1951-52; mem. faculty U. Toronto, 1952—, head elec. engring., 1964-66, dean faculty applied sci. and engring., 1966—, fellow New Coll., 1962; vis. scientist U. Cambridge (Eng.) and USSR, 1960-61; indsl. cons., 1950—. Mem. NRC Can.; chmn. com. edn. World Fedn. Engring. Orgns. Bd. govs. George Brown Coll., Toronto. Served with Royal Canadian Navy, 1944-45. Recipient Sci. medal Brit. Assn. Advancement Sci., 1943; Centennial medal Can., 1967; research fellow electronics Mass. Inst. Tech., 1950. Fellow I.E.E.E.; mem. Sigma Xi. Author: (with G.R. Slemon) Scientific Basis of Electrical Engineering, 1961. Home: 135 Glencairn Av Toronto 12 Ontario Canada

HAM, JAMES RICHARD, clergyman; b. Chgo., July 11, 1921; s. James William and Loretta (Freely) H.; B.Ed., Mundelein Maj. Sem., 1940-43; student Maryknoll Sem. at N.Y., 1943-48, D.D. (hon.), 1968. Ordained priest Roman Cath. Ch., 1948; Maryknoll pub. relations work, Chgo., St. Louis, Phila. and Mpls., 1948-58; missionary, Guatemala and El Salvador region, 1958-68; ordained aux. Bishop of Guatemala, 1968; vicar gen. Guatemala, 1968—; rector Asumption Cathedral, 1967-70; pastor Our Lady of Guadalupe, Guatemala, 1970—; dir. Prelature of Esquipulas, Nat. Lay Apostolate, Nat. Maj. Sem. Aux. chaplain mil. ordinariate, Guatemala, 1965-68. K.C. Address: 15 Avenida 18-45 Zona 10 Guatemala Guatemala

HAM, THOMAS HALE, medical educator; b. Oklahoma City, July 19, 1905; s. Thomas C. and Lola M. (Trickey) H.; B.S., Dartmouth, 1927; M.D., Cornell U., 1931; m. Fanny C. Curtis, May 16, 1936; children—Thomas C., Margaret Curtis, Lola Josephine. Asst. resident physician New York Hosp., also instr. in medicine Cornell U. Med. Coll., 1931-34; successively instr., asso., asst. prof., dept. medicine Harvard Med. Sch., 1934-47; asso. physician Thorndike Meml. Lab., 1938-48, asso. dir., 1948-50; jr. vis. physician Boston City Hosp., 1937-48; cons. hematology Cushing VA Hosp., Framingham. Mass.; prof. medicine Western Res. U., Cleve., 1950—, dir. div. research med. edn., 1958—. Diplomate Am. Bd. Internal Medicine. Fellow A.C.P., A.M.A.; mem. Assn. Am. Physicians, Am. Acad. Arts and Scis., Soc. Clin. Investigation. Club: Harvard (Boston). Contbr. med. articles jours. and periodicals. Home: 2961 Broxton Rd Shaker Heights OH 44120

HAM, WILLIAM TAYLOR, Jr., educator; b. Norfolk, Va., Sept. 20, 1908; s. William Taylor and Lucy Goode (Coleman) H.; B.S. in Engring., U. Va., 1931, M.S. in Physics, 1933, Ph.D., 1935; m. Jean Anderson, Oct. 5, 1940; children-Christina Anderson, Elspeth Read. Research asso. U. Va., 1935-36; instr. Columbia, 1936-37; physicist Kendall Mills, Charlotte, N.C., 1937-38; with brokerage firm in Norfolk, Va., 1938-40, OSRD, U. Va., 1940-43; div. head Inst. Textile Tech., Charlottesville, Va., 1946-48; mem. faculty Va. Commonwealth U., 1948—, prof. biophysics, chmn. dept., 1953—; cons. in field. Mem. radiation health study sect. USPHS; panel fellowships NSF, 1955-58; chmn. health physics fellowship bd. AEC, 1966- 67; mem. radiation adv. bd. Commonwealth Va.; chmn. Gordon Conf. Lasers, 1970; mem. standards com. safe use lasers Am. Nat. Standards Inst.; mem. Nat. Council Radiation Protection 1969-73, Electromagnetic Radiation Mgmt. Adv. Council, 1962—. Served to maj. USMCR, 1943-46. Fellow Am. Phys. Soc., A.A.A.S.; mem. Am. Optical Soc., Biophys. Soc., Health Physics Soc. (pres. 1963-64), Va. Acad. Sci. (chmn. research com. 1967- 68), Sigma Xi, Raven Soc. Home: 8653 Cherokee Rd Richmond VA 23235

HAMADY, JACK AMEEN, retail food co. exec.; b. Baakline, Lebanon, May 10, 1909; s. Albert A. and Yamna (Halabee) H.; came to U.S., 1920, naturalized, 1926; student Gen. Motors Inst., Internat. Corr. Schs., LaSalle Extension Bus. U., m. Lily Richany, Feb. 24, 1935; children—Lloyd K., Grant F., Ronald N., Nawal (Mrs. Albert Alley). With Hamady Bros., Flint, Mich., 1920—, sr. v.p., sec., 1959-66, pres., chief exec. officer, 1966-69, chmn. bd. dirs., 1969—. Pres. P.T.A. Council, 1949-50. Bd. dirs. Jr. Achievement, Urban Coalition of Flint, Urban League of Flint; trustee Flint Inst. Music, Flint Community Players, Salvation Army, United Fund Red Feather, Amalgamated Meat Cutters Employer and Employees Pension Fund, Retail Clks. Internat. Assn. Employer and Employees Health and Welfare Fund, Retail Clks. Internat. Assn. Employer and Employees Pension Trust Fund; mem. adv. bd. Coop. Extension Service Genesee County, Mott Adult Edn.; mem. exec. council Boy Scouts Am. Recipient Americanization of Youth award, 1968, Distinguished Sales Achievement award, 1960, Sales Mgmt. Raymond Bill award, 1960. Mem. Asso. Food Dealers Mich. (dir.), Sales and Marketing Exec. Club Flint (past pres.), Super Market Inst., Econ. Club Detroit. Mason (Shriner), Elk, Rotarian. Clubs: Birch Creek Hunt (Carran, Mich.); Flint City; Warwick Hills Golf and Country (Grand Blanc, Mich.). Home: 1009 Woodlawn Park Dr Flint MI 48503 Office: 3301 S Dort Hwy Flint MI 48501

HAMAKER, JOHN CHARLES, Jr., mfg. exec.; b. Canton, O., Apr. 21, 1924; s. John Charles and Lucile F. (Hammersmith) H.; B.S., U. Mich., 1945, M.S., 1947, Ph.D. (Internat. Nickel Co. fellow), 1952; m. Phyllis Lorraine Bourbonnais, June 14, 1947; children—Joanne Cynthia, John Charles III. Plant engr. Stearns-Roger Mfg. Co., Denver, 1951-53; dir. research and engring. VASCO Metals Corp., Latrobe, Pa., 1953-61, v.p., dir., 1961-68; pres. Teledyne Rodney Metals, New Bedford, Mass., 1968-70; group pres. Whittaker Corp., Los Angeles, 1970-71; group exec. Teledyne, Inc., Los Angeles, 1971—, pres. Teledyne Can. Ltd., Toronto, 1971—. Chmn. panels Materials Adv. Bd., Nat. Acad. Scis., 1955—. Served to lt. (j.g.) USNR, World War II. Recipient Outstanding Engring. Alumnus award U. Mich., 1969. Mem. Am. Soc. Metals (nat. trustee 1966-68), Am. Inst. Mining, Metall. Engrs., Soc. Automotive Engrs., Am. Soc. Testing Materials, Soc. Mfg. Engrs., Am. Mgmt. Assn., Aircraft Owners and Pilots Assn., Theta Xi. Presbyn. (elder). Rotarian. Clubs: Wamsutta, New Bedford Yacht, New Bedford Country. Co- author: Metallurgy of Tool Steel, 1958; Tool Steels, 1962. Contbr. articles to profl. jours. Patentee in field. Home: 10820 Savona Rd Los Angeles CA 90024 Office: 528 E Mission Rd San Marcos CA 92069

HAMAND, LAVERN MARSHALL, univ. dean; b. Marshall, Ill., Feb. 16, 1918; s. Charles Wesley and Alice Ruth (Marden) H.; B.S., Ill. Wesleyan U., 1940; M.A., U. Ill., 1947, Ph.D., 1949; m. Martha Elizabeth Tendick, June 9, 1943; childrenMartha Carol, Wendy Faye, Jeffrey Tendick. High sch. instr., Rosiclare, Ill., 1940-42; asst. dean coll. Ark. Poly. Coll., 1949- 57; asst. dean instrn. Eastern Ill. U., 1957-61, dean Grad. Sch., 1961-. Area liaison USAF Acad. County chmn. Cancer Drive; area chmn. Civil War Centenial observance. Served to 2d lt. USAAF, 1943-46; Lt. col. ret. Res. Recipient award of merit Civil War Centennial Comm. Ill. Mem. Am., Miss. Valley, Ill. (dir. 1965-68) hist. socs., Tau Kappa Epsilon. Lion. Editor: (pamphlet) Coles County in the Civil War, 1961. Home: 8 Orchard Dr Charleston IL 61920

HAMARNEH, SAMI KHALAF, museum curator, author; b. Madaba, Jordan, Feb. 2, 1925; s. Kahlaf and Nura A. (Zumut) H.; came to U.S., 1952, naturalized, 1957; B.Sc. in Pharmacy, Syrian U., Damascus, 1948; M.Sc. in Pharm. Chemistry, N.D. State U., Fargo, 1956; Ph.D. in History of Pharmacy, U. Wis. at Madison, 1959; m. Nazha T. Ajaj, July 4, 1948; 1 son, Faris. Curator charge div. med. scis. Mus. History and Tech., U.S. Nat. Mus., Smithsonian Instn., 1959—; vis. asso. prof. history pharmacy George Washington U., 1963-64; vis. prof. history of sci. U. Pa., Phila., 1969; spl. research med. scis. and edn. in medieval Islam. Fluid Research Fund grantee Smithsonian Instn., 1964; grantee Am. Research Center in Egypt, 1967; recipient Star of Jordan medal, 1965; E. Kremers award distinguished pharmaco- hist. writing, 1966. Mem. Am. Assn. History Medicine, Am. Inst. History Pharmacy. Author: (with Glenn Sonnedecker) A Pharmaceutical View of Abulcasis al-Zahrawi in Moorish Spain, 1963; Bibliography of Medicine and Pharmacy in Medieval Islam, 1964; Index of Arabic Manuscripts on Medicine and Pharmacy at the National Library of Cairo, 1967; Index of Manuscripts on Medicine and Pharmacy in the Zahiriyah Library, 1969; also articles. Home: 4631 Massachusetts Av NW Washington DC 20016 Office: Div Med Sciences Smithsonian Instn Washington DC 20560

HAMBLET, JULLA ESTELLE, govt. ofcl.; b. Winchester, Mass., May 12, 1916; d. Abel Martin and Marcia Leavitt (Coburn) Hamblet; A.B., Vassar Coll., 1937; M.S. Ohio State U., 1951. Adminstrv. asst.

USIS, 1937-43; commd. 1st lt. U.S.M.C., 1943, advanced through grades to col., 1953; dir. Marine Corps Women's Res., 1946-48, dir. Women Marines, 1953-59; formerly assigned hdqrs. Allied commdr. in chief for So. Europe, 1959-62; comdg. officer Woman Recruit Tng. Bn., Parris Island, S.C., 1962-65; joined U.S. office Edn., 1965, asso. dir. Nat Right to Read program, 1969—. Decorated Legion of Merit. Recipient Letter of Commendation, Sec. Navy. Clubs: Vassar, Sulgrave (Washington). Home: 2727 29th St NW Washington DC 20008 Office: US Office of Edn 400 Maryland Av SW Washington DC 20202

HAMBLETON, CHALKLEY JAY, banker; b. Chgo., June 22, 1912; s. Chalkley Jay and Elizabeth (McMurray) H.; student Princeton, 1930-33; A.B., U. Chgo., 1934; m. Betty Moore Davis, Feb. 16, 1952; children—Chalkley Jay, Douglas McMurray. With Harris Trust & Savs. Bank, Chgo., 1935—, v.p., 1960-65, sr. v.p., 1965-71, sec., 1962-71, head trust dept., 1963-71, pres., 1971—, also dir.; dir. G.D. Searle & Co. trustee Orchestral Assn. Chgo., 1963—, treas., 1967—; trustee Berkshire Sch., Sheffield, Mass., 1968—, Old Peoples Home City of Chgo.; alternate mem. trustees com. Chgo. Community Trust, 1963—; bd. dirs. Assn. House Chgo., 1936-66, pres. 1949; bd. dirs. Welfare Council Met. Chgo., 1954-66, treas., 1961-66; governing mem. Glenwood Sch. for Boys; trustee Latin Sch., Chgo., 1961-70, pres., 1967-70. Served to lt. comdr. USNR, 1942-46. Mem. Am. Bankers Assn. (exec. com. trust div. 1969—), Ill. Bankers Assn. (pres. trust div. 1968-69), Corp. Fiduciaries Assn. Ill. (pres. 1967-68, exec. com. 1963—), Shedd Aquarium Soc. (treas. 1966—) Clubs: Commercial, Economic, University, Casino, Chicago, Bankers Commonwealth (treas., dir. 1971—) (Chgo.). Home: 70 E Cedar St Chicago IL 60611 Office: 111 W Monroe St Chicago IL 60690

HAMBLETON, HOWARD, banker. Chmn., First Nat. Bank Waco (Tex.). Office: 811 Washington St Waco TX 76703*

HAMBLETON, THOMAS EDWARD, theatrical producer; b. Towson, Md., Feb. 12, 1911; s. Thomas Edward and Adelaide (McAlpin) H.; student St. Paul's Sch., Concord, N.H.; B.A., Yale, 1934; m. Caroline L. Hoysradt, 1936 (dec. 1947); childrenAnne Crawford (dec.), Caroline Lucinda, Susan Sherwood; m. 2d, Merrell You Can't Take It With You, Cock-A-Doodle-Dandy, Harvey, The Criminals, The Persians, The School for Wives, The Trial of the Catonsville Nine, Murderous Angels; managing director Phoenix Theatre, N.Y.C., Hopkins, Feb., 1949; childrenThomas Edward, Mary, Mark. Prod. plays Robin Landing, I Know What I Like, The First Crocus, The Great Campaign, Galileo, Temporary Island, Ballet Ballads, Prides Crossing, The American Bell, Once Upon A Mattress, Saint Joan, Diary of A Scoundrel, The Power and The Glory, The Matchmaker, Man and Superman, War and Peace, Judith, You Can't Take It With You, Cock-A-Doodle-Dandy, Harvey, The Criminals, The Persians, The School for Wives, The Trial of the Catonsville, Murderous Angels; managing director Phoenix Theatre, N.Y.C., 1953-; v.p. Theatre, Inc.; mng. dir. APA-Phoenix, 1964-69; dir. Farrar, Straus & Giroux; dir. Peale Mus., Balt. Served as lt. comdr. USNR, World War II. Mem. A.S.C.A.P. (popular awards panel), Council Living Theatre, League N.Y. Theatres (gov.). Home: Timonium MD Office: Lyceum Theatre 149 W 45th St New York City NY 10036

HAMBLIN, FRANCIS NEWELL, coll. pres.; b. Lexington, Mass., May 3, 1917; s. Stephen Francis and Nellie Jane (Hamblin) N.; A.B., Amherst Coll., 1939; Ed. M., Harvard, 1946, Ed.D., 1954; LL.D. (hon.), Parsons Coll., 1965; m. Alice Frances Cuddeback, June 18, 1946; childrenCheney Jane, Stephen Richard, Amy Schaff. Dioramist, Pitman Art Studio, Cambridge, Mass., 1940-41; tchr. English history Ariz. Desert Sch., Tucson, 1941-42, 46- 47; tchr. LaLoma Feliz and Sch. of Canyons, Santa Barbara, Cal., 1947- 48; registrar U. Vt., 1949-53; exec. dir. U.S. Ednl. Found., Athens, Greece, 1953-55; dean Coll. Edn., Ohio U., 1955-63; dean Sch. Edn., George Washington U., 1963-67; acad. v.p. No. Ariz. U., Flagstaff, 1967- 70; pres. Lock Haven (Pa.) State Coll., 1970—. Cons. internat. edn. Sr. v.p. Center for Advancement Intercultural Studies, Chgo.; 1st v.p. Internat. Council on Edn. for Tchrs., Washington. Bd. dirs. Washington Sch. Psychiatry. Served with C.E., AUS, 1942-45. Mem. Am. Assn. Colls. Tchr. Edn. (past chmn. internat. relations com.), Am. Assn. State Colls. and Univs., Delta Tau Delta, Phi Kappa Phi, Kappa Delta Pi, Phi Delta Kappa. Author profl. reports, articles. Home: 25 W Water St Lock Haven PA 17745

HAMBRICK, GEORGE WALTER, Jr., educator, physician; b. Charlottesville, Va., Dec. 4, 1922; s. George W. and Sallie Anna (McCallum) H.; B.S., Concord Coll., 1944; M.D., U. Va., 1946. Intern State U. Ia., 1946-47; asst. resident dermatology U. Va. Hosp., 1947-48, Columbia-Presbyn. Hosp., N.Y.C., 1950-51; fellow dermatology Duke Hosp., Durham, N.C., 1951-52, asso. dermatology, 1953; instr. Columbia, 1953-55, asso., 1955-57, asst. prof., 1957-62; asso. prof. U. Pa., 1962-66; asso. prof. Johns Hopkins Med. Sch., 1966-69, prof., 1969—, dir. dermatology, 1967—. Served as capt., M.C., AUS, 1948-50. Fellow A.C.P.; mem. Soc. Investigative Dermatology (v.p. 1970-71), Dermatology Found. (trustee), Assn. Profs. of Dermatology, Am. Dermatol. Assn., A.M.A., Am. Acad. Dermatology, Alpha Omega Alpha. Home: 112 Upnor Rd Baltimore MD 21212

HAMBRICK, MARVIN KENNETH, accountant; b. Cin., Oct. 17, 1922; s. Marvin D. and Clara (Christman) H.; B.A., U. Okla., 1948; m. Joan Butell, June 10, 1956; childrenCarol, Steven L. With Arthur Andersen & Co., C.P.A.'s, 1949—, partner, 1958— in charge Oklahoma City, 1958-. Mem. Gov. Okla. Study Commn. Okla. U. Med. Center; mem. Commn. Promotion Efficiency in State Govt. Pres. regents Okla. Colls. Served with AUS, 1942-46, C.P.A., Okla., Tex., N.C., La. Mem. Am. Inst. C.P.A.'s Phi Beta Kappa (pres. Oklahoma City 1966-67). Democrat. Methodist. Home: 1211 Huntington St Oklahoma City OK 73116 Office: Kermac Bldg Oklahoma City OK 73102

HAMBRO, EDVARD ISAK, diplomat of Norway; b. Oslo, Norway, Aug. 22, 1911; s. Carl Joachim and Gudrun (Grieg) H.; LL.B., Oslo U., 1934; Dr. es Scis. Politiques, U. Geneva (Switzerland), 1936; hon. degrees Luther Coll., Seton Hall U., U. Toronto, Wagner Coll.; m. Elisabeth Jacqueline Raverat, June 8, 1940; children Anne Nicoline (Mrs. Egil Alnaes), Carl Joachim, John Christian George, Linda Maragret. Collaborator secretariat League of Nations, 1933; leader internat. relations dept. Christian Michelsens Inst., Bergen. Norway, 1938-40; guest lectr. Northwestern U., 1941; sec. Norwegian Ministry Fgn. Affairs, London, Eng., 1943-45; chief legal sect. UN, 1945-46; registrar Internat. Ct. Justice, 1946-53; lectr., later prof. law Norwegian Sch. Econs. and Bus. Adminstrn., Bergen, 1953 66; vis. lectr. U. Cambridge (Eng.), 1953-54, U. Cal. at Berkeley, 1958; mem. Norwegian Parliament, 1961-66; lectr. Hague Acad. Internat. Law, 1950, 60, also others univs., U.S. and Europe; ambassador, permanent rep. Norway to UN, 1966; chmn. legal com. UN, 1967; pres. gen. assembly UN, 1970—. Dir. first sessions Dag Hammarskjold Sem., The Hague, 1963, 64; head commn. study Chinese refugees in Hong Kong, 1954; mem. appeals bd. Orgn. Econ. Coop. and Devel.; chmn. adminstrv. tribunal Council of Europe, 1966; mem. Permanent Ct. Arbitration, 1965; pres. Permanent Conciliation Commn. Germany and Netherlands, 1965; mem. Franco-German arbitral bd. for Saar; mem. permanent conciliation com. between Finland and U.S., between Norway and Spain, between Portugal and Switzerland. Vice pres. Norwegian Red Cross, 1960-66. Decorated Comdr. Order of St. Olav (Norway); Grand Cross of Order White Rose (Finland); Grand Cross Merite Nat. (Mauritania). Mem. Inst. du Droit Internat. Author: L'Exécution des Sentences Internationales, 1936; Norway and The League of Nations, 1938; The Law of Aliens, 1950; (with L. Goodrich) The Charter of the United Nations, 2d edit., 1949, (with L. Goodrich and P. Simons) 3d. edit., 1969; The Case Law of the International Court, Vol. I, 2d edit., 1958, Vol. II, 1960, Vol. III, 1963, Vol. IV, 1965, (with A. Rovine) Vol. V, 1968; Peaceful Settlement of Disputes, 1956; Choice of Law and Choice of Jurisdiction in Norwegian International Contract Law, 1957; also articles. Home: 10 Gracie Sq New York City NY 10028 also Gimle Terrasse 1 Oslo 2 Norway Office: 825 3d Av New York City NY 10022

HAMBRO, LEONID, pianist; b. Chgo., June 26, 1920; s. Simeon and Dora (Levitan) H.; grad. Julliard Grad. Sch. Music, 1941; m. Crystal Cooper, Apr. 1946 (annulled 1951); m. 2d, Barbara Schnapp, July 25, 1952; children-Aralee, Simeon. Pianist for Joseph Szigeti and Felix Salmond, 1946; staff pianist sta. WQXR, N.Y.C., 1947-; ofcl. pianist N.Y. Philharmonic Symphony Orch., 1948—; asso. in concerts and TV with Victor Borge, 1961—; mem. faculty Julliard Inst. Musical Art, 1949-52; concert pianist, rec. artist Columbia and Victor records; TV and motion picture appearances. Served with USNR, 1942-45. Mem. Am. Guild Musical Artists, Bohemians. Home: 51 Fifth Av New York City, NY 10003. Office: W Colston Leigh Inc 1521 Fifth Av New York City NY 10017

HAMBURG, CARL HEINZ, educator, author; b. Hindenburg, Germany, Mar. 12, 1915; s. Salo H. and Jenny (Lewin) H.; came to U.S., 1938, naturalized, 1944; Diplme d'Etudes Supérieures, U. Bordeaux (France); M.A., Columbia, 1940, Ph.D., 1948; children—Darcy, Toni, Kai. Editorial asst., N.Y.C., 1941-43; mem. faculty Tulane U., 1948—, prof. philosophy, 1960—. Served with AUS, 1943-46. Mem. Am. Philos. Assn., So. Soc. Philosophy and Psychology. Author: Symbol and Reality, 2d edit., 1970; also articles. Home: 1314 Audubon St New Orleans LA 70118

HAMBURG, DAVID A., med. educator; b. Evansville, Ind., 1925; M.D., Ind. U., 1947; Intern, Michael Reese Hosp., Chgo., 1947-48, resident in psychiatry, 1949-50; asst. resident in psychiatry New Haven Hosp., 1948-49; practice medicine, specializing in psychiatry, 1950—; staff psychiatrist Brooke Army Hosp., 1950-52; research psychiatrist Army Med. Service Grad. Sch., 1952-53; asso. dir. Psychosomatic and Psychiat. Inst., Michael Reese Hosp., 1953-56; fellow Center for Advanced Study in Behavioral Scis., Palo Alto, Cal., 1957-58, 67-68; chief Adult Psychiat. br. Nat. Insts. Mental Health, Bethesda, Md., 1958-61; asst. in pathology Ind U., 1946-47; asst. in psychiatry Yale, 1948-49; prof., exec. head dept. psychiatry Stanford U. Med. Sch., 1961—. Served as capt. M.C. AUS, 1950-53. Diplomate in Psychiatry, Am. Bd. Psychiatry and Neurology. Mem. Am. Psychiat. Assn., A.A.A.S., Am. Psychosomatic Soc. Office: Stanford U Med Sch Stanford CA 94305*

HAMBURGER, FERDINAND, Jr., elec. engr.; b. Balt., July 5, 1904; s. Ferdinand and Carrie (Frank) H.; B.Engring., Johns Hopkins, 1924; Eng. D. (Charles A. Coffin fellow, 1930-31), 1931; m. Opal Leavitt, Nov. 25, 1931. With Consol. Gas Elec. Light & Power Co., Balt. 1924-25; research asst. Johns Hopkins, 1928-29, instr. elec. engring., 1931-39, asso. elec. engring., 1939-41, asso. prof. elec. engring., 1941-47, prof. 1947-70, emeritus, 1970—, chmn. dept. elec. engring., 1954-70, dir. centennial planning, 1970—, Carlyle Barton Lab., 1958-70: chief test engr. Bendix Radio div. Bendix Aviation Corp. 1942-45; cons. Nat. Def. Research Com., 1944-45; cons. research and standards sect. Bur. of Ships, Navy Dept., 1945-46; research contract dir., contracts between Dept. Def. and Johns Hopkins, 1945-70; adv. group on electronic warfare Dept. Def., 1960; cons. Nat. Security Agy., 1959-61; cons. May Oil Burner Corp., Adler Safety Control Co., Md. State Police, Radio Sta. W.C.A.O., Bendix Radio div. RCA. Spl. master U.S. Dist. Ct., 1936-37, 39. Active Boy Scouts Am., mem. Balt. area council, 1932—. Fellow I.E.E.E. (dir. 1963-64); mem. Am. Assn. U. Profs., Md. Soc. Profl. Engrs., Sigma Xi, Tau Beta Pi, Eta Kappa Nu. Clubs: Johns Hopkins (gov. 1946-47, pres. 1969-71); Engineers (dir. 1949-50, 52- 53) (Balt.). Contbr. numerous papers on electronics, radio, instrumentation, dielectrics and electromagnetic warfare to profl. jours. Home: 3900 N Charles St Baltimore MD 21218

HAMBURGER, PHILIP (PAUL), writer; b. Wheeling, W. Va., July 2, 1914; s. Harry and Janet (Kraft) H.; B.A., Johns Hopkins, 1935; M.S., Grad. Sch. Journalism, Columbia, 1938; m. Edith Iglauer, Dec. 24, 1942 (div. 1966); children Jay Philip, Richard Shaw; m. 2d, Anna Walling Matson, Oct. 27, 1968. Staff mem. New Yorker mag., 1939—, writer Profiles, Reporter-at- Large articles, letters from fgn. places, music critic, 1948-49, TV critic, 1949-55; on leave from New Yorker as writer Office of Facts and Figures and O.W.I., 1941-43. Past mem. adv. bd. George Foster Peabody Radio and Television Awards. Recipient 50th Anniversary Honors medal Grad. Sch. Journalism, Columbia, 1963. Mem. Authors League Am., P.E.N. Clubs: Nat. Press (Washington); Century Assn., Coffee House (N.Y.C.). Author: The Oblong Blur and Other Odysseys, 1949; J.P. Marquand, Esquire, 1952; Mayor Watching and Other Pleasures, 1958; Our Man Stanley, 1963; An American Notebook, 1965. Home: 151 E 80th St New York City NY 10021 Office: care The New Yorker 125 W 43d St New York City NY 10036

HAMBURGER, ROLF R., advt. agy. exec. Sr. v.p. Compton Advt., Inc., N.Y.C. Office: 625 Madison Av New York City NY 10022*

HAMBURGER, VIKTOR, biologist; born Landeshut, Germany, July 9, 1900; s. Max and Else (Gradenwitz) H.; student U. of Heidelberg, 1919-20, U. of Munich, 1920- 21; Ph.D., U. of Freiburg (Baden), 1924; m. Martha Fricke, July 28, 1928; childrenDoris, Carola. Came to U.S., 1932, naturalized, 1940. Privatdozent, dept. zoology, U. of Freiburg, 1927-32; research fellow, dept. zoology, U. of Chicago, 1932-33, instr., 1933-35; asst. prof. dept. zoology Washington U., St. Louis, 1935-39, asso. prof., 1939-41, professor of zoology, 1941-69, professor emeritus of biology, 1969-, head dept., 1941-66. Fellow American Academy of Arts and Sciences; mem. Am. Assn. Anatomists, Am. Soc. Zoologists (pres. 1955), Nat. Acad. Scis., Soc. Developmental Biology (past pres.), Genetics Soc. Am. Naturalists, Institut International d'Embryologie. Author: Manual of Experimental Embryology, 1960. Home: 740 Trinity Av St Louis MO 63130.

HAMEKA, HENDRIK FREDERIK, educator, chemist; b. Rotterdam, Holland, May 25, 1931; s. Dirk C. and Johanna (Mannebeck) H.; H.Drs., U. Leiden (Netherlands), 1953, D.Sc., 1956; m. Carol E. Carson, Aug. 9, 1958; children—Richard Charles, Christina Laura. Came to U.S., 1960, naturalized, 1963. Research asso. U. Rome, Italy, 1956-57; fellow Carnegie Inst. Tech., 1957-58; research physicist N. V. Phillips Lamps, Eindhoven, Netherlands, 1958-60; asst. prof. chemistry Johns Hopkins, 1960-62; asso. prof. chemistry U. Pa., 1962-67, prof. chemistry, 1967—; mem. editorial bd. Chem. Physics Letters. Alfred P. Sloan Research fellow, 1963—. Mem. Am. Phys. Soc. Author: Advanced Quantum Chemistry, 1965; Introductory Quantum Theory, 1967. Contbr. numerous articles to sci. jours. Research on theory of molecular structure and optical and magnetic properties of molecules; calculations of spin-orbit and spin-spin coupling; theory of resonance optical rotation, magneto-optical rotation and multiple-photon processes. Home: 617 Magill Rd Swarthmore PA 19081 Office: U Pa Dept Chemistry Philadelphia PA 19104

HAMEL, DANA BERTRAND, educator; b. Rumford, Me., Aug. 9,1923; s. Donat H. and Louise (Kenison) H.; A.B., Ashland (O.) Coll., 1951; M.A., Ohio State U., 1952; Ed.D., U Cin., 1962; m. Shirley Elmeree Smith Knavel, Dec. 19, 1945; childrenDana Randolph, Michelle, April. Watchmaker, Thomas J. Apryle & Sons, Johnstown, Pa., 1946; owner Hamels, Jewelers, Conemaugh, Pa., 1946- 48; mem. mgmt. dept. Gen. Motors Inst., Flint, Mich., 1955-57; dean adminstrv. affairs Ohio Coll. Applied Sci. and Ohio Mechanics Inst., Cin., 1957-63, exec. v.p., dean of faculties, 1962-63; dir. Roanoke Tech. Inst., 1963-64; dir. Va. Dept. Tech. Edn., Richmond, 1964-66; chancellor Va. Community Coll. system, Richmond, 1966—. Chmn. subcom.on edn. Appalachia Regional Commn.; mem. Va. Adv. Council Vocational Edn.; adv. bd. Regional Edn. Lab. Carolinas and Va. Served with USAAF, 1942-45. Mem. So. Assn. Schs. and Colls. (exec. com.), Am. Assn. Jr. Colls. (commn. on legislation), Nat. Council State Dirs. (sec.- treas., exec. com.), Va. Acad. Sci., Am. Soc. Engring. Edn., Am. Psychology and Guidance Assn., Nat. Assn. for Gifted Children, Am. Coll. Personnel Assn., Cin. Guidance and Personnel Assn., Phi Delta Kappa, Psi Chi, Iota Lambda Sigma. Mason. Kiwanian. Home: 300 Coalport Rd Richmond VA 23229 Office: Dept Community Colls Richmond VA 23212

HAMEL, WILLIAM ROGERS, electronics co. exec.; b. Erie, Pa., Oct. 18, 1913; s. William V. and Evelyn (Rogers) H.; B.S. in Elec. Engring., Villanova U., 1935; m. Elizabeth C. Murphy, Mar. 2, 1943; childrenMichele, Deirdre, Rogers, Cecily. With Gen. Electric Co., 1936-42; engaged in electronics design Navy Dept., 1946-51; with Raytheon Co., 1951—, gen. mgr. operations, 1959-63, v.p., gen. mgr. submarine signal div., 1963-69, v.p. corp. activities, regional mgr. Eastern dist., Washington, 1969—, Mem. Weekapaug Group. Chmn. Greater Lowell (Mass.) United Fund, 1959; mem. corp. Hosp. Service Corp. R.I., 1962-; mem. Newport Hosp. Assn., 1962- -: Mem. bd. Newport Community Chest, 1961. Served to lt. comdr. USNR, 1942-46. Mem. Am. Ordnance Assn., Nat. Oceanographic Assn. (dir.), Newport C. of C. (dir.), U.S. Navy League, Nat. Security Indsl. Assn., U.S. C. of C. K.C. (4). Home: 10829 Burbank Dr Potomac MD 20854 Office: Raytheon Co Washington DC 20036

HAMELBERG, WILLIAM, educator, physician; b. Chillicothe, O., Dec. 13, 1925; s. William and Dora (Rosenberg) H.; student Ohio State U., 1943-44; B.S. Denison U., 1946; M.D., Ohio State U., 1948; m. Mary Louise Miller, Oct. 1, 1948; children—Lynne Louise, William Robert, Kim Scot, Mark Alan, Carol Leslie, Lisa Krista. Intern U.S. Naval Hosp., Oakland, Cal., 1949-50; resident Ohio State U. Hosp., 1950-52; asst. instr. Ohio State U., 1950-51, instr., 1951-53; asst. prof., 1953-58; prof., chmn. dept. anesthesiology Med. Coll. S.C., 1958-59; prof., dir. div. anesthesia Ohio State U., 1959-68, prof., chmn. dept. anesthesiology, 1968—. Served with USNR, 1943-45. Diplomate Am. Bd. Anesthesiology. Fellow Am. Coll. Anesthesiology; mem. A.M.A., Am. Soc. Anesthesiologists, Internat. Anesthesia Research Soc., Ohio Soc. Anesthesiologists, Columbus Acad. Medicine, Columbus Soc. Anesthesiologists, Am. Coll. Anesthesiologists, Ohio State Med. Assn., Assn. U. Anesthestists, Phi Chi. Home: 3077 Brandon Rd Columbus OH 43221

HAMER, ELIZABETH EDWARDS, (Mrs. Philip May Hamer), librarian; b. Copperhill, Tenn., Jan. 4, 1912; d. John Earl and Fanny Elizabeth (Wallace) Edwards; B.A., U. Tenn., 1933, postgrad. (fellow history), 1933-34; postgrad. history and polit. sci. U. Chgo., Am. U.; m. Philip May Hamer, May 10, 1940. With Survey of Fed. Archives in the States, 1936- 40; various editorial and pub. relations positions Nat. Archives and Records Service, 1942-47, exhibits and information officer, 1947-50, chief exhibits and publs. sect., 1950-51; information and publ. officer Library Congress, Washington, 1951-60, asst. librarian pub. affairs, 1960-63, asst. librarian of Congress, 1963—. Library Congress rep. Nat. Hist. Publns. Com., Am. Revolution Bicentennial Commn.; mem. D.C. com. Nat. Library Week, 1958-66; del. White House Conf. Internat. Coop., 1965, Internat. Congress Archives, Florence, Italy, 1956, Brussels, 1964, Washington, 1966, Madrid, 1968, Internat. Fedn. Library Assns., The Hague, 1966, Copenhagen., 1969; mem. 3d World Congress program com. Agrl. Librarians and Documentalists, 1965; mem. Govt. Liaison Group on Staffing Internat. Orgns., 1964—; mem. pres.'s council Grad. Sch. Arts and Scis., N.Y.U. 1968-71; mem. U.S. com. for Am. Library in Paris. Trustee Greater Washington Ednl. TV Assn. 1960-65, hon. trustee, 1966—. Fellow Library Mass. Hist. Soc.; hon. fellow Harry S Truman Library; mem. Soc. Am. Archivists (a founder; hon. fellow 1960, council 1969-71, chmn. com. archives-library relations 1969—), A.L.A. (program com. 1969—, chmn. com. conf. format 1970—, chmn. joint com. libraries and archives 1971—), Am. Hist. Assn., Manuscript Soc., So. Hist. Assn., S.C. Hist. Soc., Internat. Council Archives, Am. Assn. State and Local History, Phi Kappa Phi. Author govt. brochures. Contbr. articles profl. jours. Home: 6620 River Rd Bethesda MD 20034 Office: Library of Congress 10 First St SE Washington DC 20540

HAMER, FANNIE, mem. Democratic Nat. Com.; married; 1 dau., Dorothy Jean (dec.). Vice chmn. Freedom Democratic Party; mem. Democratic Nat. Com. for Miss., 1968—. Address: 2600 Virginia Av NW Washington DC 20037*

HAMER, ROBERT CALVIN, govt. ofcl.; b. Altoona, Pa., June 18, 1917; s. Michael Calvin and Maude Hicks (Hopkins) H.; B.S., Pa. State U., 1939; m. Miriam Mary Strause, Apr. 11, 1937; children—Sandra (Mrs. Clyde P. Murray), Robert M., John C., David R. Sr. supervisory statistician U.S. Bur. Census, 1948-52; asst. dir. USOM, Jordan, 1952-55; dep. dir. operations, Iran, 1955-58, also provincial dir., chief operations div. AID, Washington, 1958-59, dep. dir., Morocco, 1959-61, dir., Yemen Arab Republic, 1966-67, dir., Guyana, 1967—. Decorated Grand Officer Order of Star Hashamite Kingdom Jordan; recipient silver medal meritorious service Dept. Commerce, 1952, AID meritorious service award, 1959. Fellow Hacettepe Med. Sci. Center U., Ankara, Turkey, 1966. Lutheran (v.p. Md. synod). Home: 13040 Old Cutler Rd Miami FL 33156 Office: USAID Georgetown Dept State Washington DC 20521

HAMER, WALTER JAY, chemist; b. Altoona, Pa., Nov. 5, 1907; s. Jess James and Naomi Gertrude (Roland) H.; B.S., Juniata Coll., 1929, D.Sc., 1966; Ph.D., Yale, 1932; m. Alma Robinson, Mar. 19, 1941; 1 dau., Margaret Jay. Postdoctoral research fellow phys. chemistry Yale, 1932- 34; research asso. phys. chemistry Mass. Inst. Tech., 1934-35; chemist Nat. Bur: Standards, 1935-50, chief electrochemistry sect., 1950-70, cons. electrochemistry, dir. electrolyte center, 1970—; research chemist nat. def. research com. OSRD and Manhattan Project, 1943-44; cons. Dept. Def., 1951-53; lectr. Georgetown U., 1947-50, Cath. U. Am., 1944-45, Grad. Sch. Dept. Agr., 1940-49, Grad. Sch. Nat. Bur. Standards, 1944-45, 52-53. Mem. commn. electrochemistry Internat. Union Pure and Applied Chemistry, 1957-65; U.S. tech. adviser primary batteries Internat.

Electrotech. Commn., 1950-68; adv. council electrochemistry lab. U. Pa., 1962-63. Recipient Certificate of Merit, OSRD, 1945, Manhattan Project, 1945; Dept. Commerce Exceptional Service Gold medal, 1965. Fellow I.E.E.E., N.Y., Washington acads. scis., A.A.A.S.; mem. Electrochem. Soc. (pres. 1963-64), Am. Chem. Soc., Am. Phys. Soc., Internat. Electrochem. Soc., Am. Standards Assn. (chmn. dry cell com. 1950- 68), Sigma Xi, Alpha Chi Sigma. Club: Cosmos (Washington). Editor: The Structure of Electrolytic Solutions, 1959. Compiler: Electrochemical Constants, 1953. Home: 3028 Dogwood St NW Washington DC 20015 Office: Nat Bureau of Standards Washington DC 20234

HAMERMESH, BERNARD, educator; b. Bklyn., Dec. 25, 1919; s. Isidore and Rose (Kornhauser) H.; B.S., Coll. City N.Y., 1940; M.S., N.Y.U., 1942, Ph.D., 1944; m. Sylvia Molberger, Sept. 6, 1941; children—Judith Gay (Mrs. Arthur Springer), Richard George, Kenneth Scott. Tutor physics Coll. City N.Y., 1940-41; grad. asst. N.Y.U., 1941-43, instr., 1943-46; sr. physicist Argonne (Ill.) Nat. Lab., 1948-59; sr. sci. adviser Phys. Research Center, TRW Systems, Redondo Beach, Cal., 1959-68; prof. physics, chmn. dept. Cleve. State U., 1968—; lectr. U. Ill. at Chgo., 1956-57, U. Cal. at Los Angeles, 1964. Mem. Sch. Bd., Sch. Dist. 163, Rich Twp.-Cook County, Ill., 1949-51; sch. trustee Rich Twp., 1951-57. NRC postdoctoral fellow Cal. Inst. Tech., 1946-48. Fellow Am. Phys. Soc.; mem. A.A.A.S., Fedn. Am. Scientists, Sigma Xi, Phi Beta Kappa. Democrat. Jewish religion. Research in cosmic ray neutrons, capture, gamma rays 7.7 meter bent crystal gamma ray spectrometer, micrometeoroid accelerator. Home: 18675 Parkland Dr Shaker Heights OH 44122

HAMERMESH, MORTON, physicist; b. N.Y.C., Dec. 27, 1915; s. Isador J. and Rose (Kornhauser) H.; B.S., Coll. City N.Y., 1936; Ph.D., N.Y.U., 1940; m. Madeline Goldberg, 1941; childrenDaniel S., Deborah R., Lawrence A. Instr. physics Coll. City N.Y., 1941, Stanford, 1941-43; research asso. Radio Research Lab., Harvard, 1943-46; asst. prof. physics N.Y.U., 1946-47, asso. prof., 1947-48; sr. physicist Argonne Nat. Lab., 1948-50, asso. dir. physics dir., 1950-59; dir. physics div., 1959-63, asso. lab. dir. basic research, 1963-65; prof., head Sch. Physics and Astronomy, U. Minn. Mpls., 1965-69, 70—; prof. physics, chmn. dept. physics State U. N.Y., Stony Brook, 1969-70. Fellow Am. Phys. Soc.; mem. Research Soc. Am., Am. Inst. Physics (com. on Russian trans.). Translator: Classical Theory of Fields (by Landau and Lifshitz), 1951. Author: Group Theory, 1962. Author numerous papers in field. Office: Univ Minn Minneapolis MN 55455

HAMEROW, THEODORE STEPHEN, educator; b. Warsaw, Poland, Aug. 24, 1920; s. Haim Schneyer and Bella (Rubinlicht) H.; B.A., Coll. City N.Y., 1942; M.A., Columbia, 1947; Ph.D., Yale, 1951; m. Margarete Lotter, Aug. 16, 1954; childrenJudith Margarete, Helena Francisca. Came to U.S., 1930, naturalized, 1930; Instr., Wellesley Coll., 1950-51, U. Md., 1951-52; instr., asst. prof., then asso. prof. U. Ill, 1952-58; mem. faculty U. Wis., 1958-, prof. history, 1961—; cons. editor Dorsey Press, 1961-71. Served with inf. AUS, 1943-46. Mem. Am. Hist. Assn., Conf. Group Central European History (sec.-treas. 1960-62). Author: Restoration, Revolution, Reaction, 1958; Otto Von Bismarck: A Historical Assessment, 1962; The Social Foundations of German Unification 1858-1871, 1969. Co-author: History of the World, 1960; A History of the Western World, 1969. Editor: Otto von Bismarck, Reflections and Reminiscences, 1968. Mem. editorial bd. Jour. Modern History, 1967-70, Central European History Jour., 1968—. Home: 466 S Segoe Rd Madison, WI 53711.

HAMERSHLAG, ROBERT JOSEPH, stockbroker; b. N.Y.C., Feb. 6, 1894; s. Joseph and Helen (Strouse) H.; ed. Phillips Acad., Andover, Mass., 1910-11, Williams Coll., 1911-13; m. Eleanor Whitney Lloyd. Partner Hamershlag, Borg & Co., mems. N.Y. Stock Exchange. Bd. govs. N.Y. Stock Exchange, 1939-45, trustee Gratuity Fund. Served with inf., U.S. Army, 1917-19; AEF. Decorated knight Order Etoile Noire (France). Mem. Nat. Audubon Soc. (dir. 1952-61, chmn. bd. 1959-61). Home: Kotonah NY 10536 Office: 140 Broadway New York City NY 10004*

HAMID, GEORGE ABOU, circus and entertainment exec.; b. Lebanon, Feb. 4, 1896; s. Joseph A. and Zyne (Asfar) H.; ed. in Lebanon; m. Elizabeth M. Raab, Mar. 17, 1915; children—George Abou, and Zyne Elizabeth. Came to U.S. 1907, naturalized through father. Tumbler, Buffalo Bill Circus, 1907-13, other circuses, 1913-19; propr. booking and importing office for circuses and thrill acts., 1920-55; owner N.J. State Fair Grounds, 1937- -, Steel Pier, Atlantic City, 1945—; operator Hamid Morton Indoor Circus, 1936—. Bd. trustees Am. Guild Variety Artists Welfare Fund; mem. bd. govs. Betty Bacharach Home. Recipient 1st annual Horatie Alger award, 1948; also awards for World War II fund raising. Mem. Nat. Showmens Assn. (founder, pres. emeritus), Miami Showmens Assn. Elk, Mason (Shriner). Author: (autobiography) Circus, 1951. Office: Steel Pier Atlantic City NJ 08404*

HAMID, OSMAN MOHAMED, Sudanese diplomat; b. El-Rahad, Sudan, Feb., 1932; s. Ismail and Makkah Mohamed Hamid; diploma commerce Khartoum Tech. Inst., 1954; B.A., Nottingham (Eng.) U., 1957; postgrad. Columbia, 1962-63. Joined Fgn. Ser. Sudan, 1958; served in Moscow, 1958-61; assigned to Khartoum, 1961-62; rep. to UN, N.Y.C., 1962-66; served in Addis Ababa, Ethiopia, 1966-69, Washington, 1969—. Home: Ministry Fgn Affairs Khartoum Sudan Office: 3421 Massachusetts Av Washington DC 20007

HAMIL, DAVID ALEXANDER, govt. ofcl.; b. Proctor, Colo., Dec. 3, 1908; s. James Newton and Ada Gertrude (Walker) H.; A.B., Hastings Coll., 1930; m. Genevieve Robinson, Dec. 24, 1933; children—Jo Ann, Donald William, Jack Robinson. Mem. Colo. Gen. Assembly, 1938-48, 50-56, speaker Ho. of Reps., 1951-56; adminstr. Rural Electrification Adminstrn., 1956—. Mason (33) (past exalted ruler, past dist. deputy exalted ruler for Colo.). Home: Atwood CO Office: Rural Electrification Administration US Dept of Agriculture Washington DC 20250

HAMIL, HAROLD, assn. exec.; b. Sterling, Colo., Sept. 27, 1906; s. James Newton and Ada Gertrude (Walker) H.; A.B., Hastings Coll., 1928; m. Anna Mabel Keplinger, Sept. 15, 1931; children—James Russell, David William. Reporter, Hastings (Neb.) Tribune, 1928-29, city editor, 1929-30, salesman, 1930-31, mng. editor, 1931-40; feature writer, editor A.P. Feature Service, N.Y.C., 1940-41; dir. U. Neb. Sch. Journalism, 1941-44; editorial writer St. Louis Star-Times, 1944-51; dir. information Farmland Industries, Inc. (formerly Consumers Coop. Assn.), Kansas City, Mo., 1951-61, asst. gen. mgr., 1961-66, sr. v.p., information and pub. relations, 1966—. Mem. Kansas City (Mo.) City Council, 1971—. Mem. Coop. League U.S. (v.p. 1963-65, chmn. bd. 1965-66), Sigma Delta Chi. Club: Kansas City Press. Home: 4314 N Grand Kansas City MO 64116 Office: 3315 N Oak Trafficway Kansas City MO 64116

HAMILL, HAROLD LOUIS, librarian; b. Washington, D.C., Mar. 23, 1908; s. John E. and Minnie (Bell) H.; A.B., George Washington U., 1934; B.L.S., Columbia, 1935; m. Mary Frances Collins, Sept. 3, 1938; childrenJoan Kathryn (Mrs. Anthony F. Trafecanty), Mary Louise (Mrs. Richard Giloth). Circulation assistant, public library, Washington, D.C., 1924-29, order assistant, 1930-34; senior assistant, public library, Mt. Vernon, New York, 1935- 38; assistant librarian, public library, Yonkers, N.Y., 1939; librarian, public library, Schenectady, N.Y., 1940-41; asst. librarian, Enoch Pratt Free Library, Kansas City, Mo., 1943-47; city librarian, Los Angeles Pub. Library, 1947-70; prof. library sci. Sch. Library Sci., U. S Cal., 1970—. State chairman of National Library Week, 1960. Mem. A.L.A. (chmn. fed. relations com. 1942-43, chmn. pub. relations com. 1948-49, chmn. met. area library service com. 1959, pres. pub. library assn. 1961-62), Cal. Library Assn. (pres. pub. libraries sect. 1955, chmn. library devel. and standards com. 1956-57, 61-63, chairman of California public library commission liaison committee, 1958-59), Public Library Executives Assn. So. California. Clubs: Town Hall, Lakeside Golf. Author: Surveys Houston Public Library, Beverly Hills Public Library, Hanford and Kings County Libraries, Whittier Public Library, Memphis and Shelby County Libraries. Contbr. to library publs. Home: 3600 Mound View Av Studio City CA 91604 Office: Sch Library Sci U So Cal Los Angeles CA 90007

HAMILL, ROBERT LYON, engr.; b. Chgo., Apr. 4, 1899; s. Robert W. and Katharine (Lyon) H.; A.B., Yale, 1920; m. Katharine Porter, Oct. 9, 1920; children—Katharine Delano (Mrs. John F. Garde, Jr.), Ann Porter (Mrs. John L. Koehne, Jr.), Joan (Mrs. Robert H. Porter), Robert Lyon. Partner, chmn. bd. Sanderson & Porter, N.Y.; chmn. bd. Lawrence (L.I.)-Cedarhurst Bank, 1933-39; dir. The Liberia Co., Liberian Devel. Corp., Bermuda Properties, Ltd., Pan Am. World Airways; mem. adv. com. The Bank N.Y. Pres. N.Y.C. of C., 1950-52; mem. bus. adv. council N.Y. State Dept. Commerce, 1950-52. Gov., mem. finance and exec. coms. Soc. N.Y. Hosp., 1955-60; pres. bd. trustees Sailors' Snug Harbour, 1950-52. Served as chief boatswains mate, USNRF, 1918; worked on reparations AUS, Japan, 1947, Germany, 1948. Mem. Am. Arbitration Assn., Delta Kappa Epsilon. Clubs: Union, Down Town Assn. (N.Y.C.); Adirondack League (Old Forge, N.Y.); Rockaway Hunting (Cedarhurst); Royal Bermuda Yacht, Mid-Ocean (Bermuda); Lyford Cay (Nassau, Bahamas); Wyandanch Sportsmen's (Smithtown, N.Y.); Sewanhaka Corinthian Yacht (Center Island, N.Y.); Lawrence Beach (Atlantic Beach, L.I.); Cotton Bay (Eleuthera, Bahamas). Home: 700 Park Av New York City NY 10021 also Lawrence NY 11559 Office: 25 Broadway New York City NY 10004

HAMILL, SAMUEL MCCLINTOCK, textile mfr.; b. Schenectady, Mar. 6, 1906; s. Samuel McClintock and Maria Woodward (Baldwin) H.; student Harvard, 1930; m. Margaret LaFarge, Nov. 4, 1937; children-Samuel McClintock, Oliver LaFarge, William H.B. With J.P. Stevens & Co., Inc., textiles, N.Y.C. 1930-, sales exec., 1946—; chmn. Marion Mfg. Co. (N.Y.); dir. Jackson Mills, Welford, S.C., Phila. Carpet Co., Carterville, Ga. Served from lt. to comdr., USNR, 1941-45. Episcopalian. Clubs: Union, Harvard, The Brook (N.Y.C.). Home: R D 3 Carter Rd Princeton NJ 08540 Office: 1460 Broadway New York NY 10018*

HAMILL, SAMUEL WOOD, architect; b. Globe, Ariz., Apr. 27, 1903; s. Joseph H. H. and Flora Isabel (Wood) H.; student San Diego State Coll.; A.B., U. Cal. at Berkeley, 1927; m. Georgette Rousseau, Apr. 11, 1931; children—Georgette Rousseau, Annette Marie. Partner, Requa-Jackson & Hamill, architects, 1928-35, Gill-Johnson-Regua & Hamill, architects San Diego Civic Center, 1934-39, Jackson & Hamill, 1935-40, Hamill, Hope, Lykos, Wheeler & Freeland, architects and engrs., San Diego County Court House, 1956-65; supervising architect San Diego Centre City 1960-65. Chmn. Met. Plans Commn., 1943-45; exec. com. Balboa Park Citizens Com., 1956-60; mem. San Diego Urban Renewal Commn., 1959-60; pres. San Diego Community Chest, 1950-51 vice chmn. San Diego Armed Services, YMCA, 1965—; chmn. San Diego Hist. Sites Bd., 1969-70; co-chmn. Nat. Conf. Christians and Jews, 1969—. Dir. San Diego Bot.-Garden Found., 1966—, Museum of Man, San Diego Fine Arts Soc., Serra Mus.; corp. mem. Save the Children Found. Fellow A.I.A.; mem. San Diego C. of C. (dir. 1940-45), Navy League U.S., San Diego Hist. Soc. (dir.), San Diegans (sec.), Tau Sigma Delta, Delta Epsilon, Epsilon Eta. Contbr. articles to numerous jours. Address: 4467 Ampudia St San Diego CA 92103

HAMILL, WILLIAM HENRY, educator, chemist; b. Oswego, N.Y., June 13, 1908; s. William Henry and Lorena (Brecht) H.; B.S., U. Notre Dame, 1930, M. S., 1931; Ph.D., Columbia, 1936; m. Angela Irma Tobia, Aug. 17, 1934; children—Mary Angela (Mrs. William Walker), Carol Rita, Irma Clare, Ann Therese, Catherine Bridget. Mem. faculty Fordham U., 1931-38; prof. chemistry U. Notre Dame, 1938—. Chmn., Gordon Conf. on Radiation Chemistry, 1958. Mem. Am. Chem. Soc., Faraday Soc., Sigma Xi. Author: (with R.R. Williams, Colin Mackay) Principles of Physical Chemistry, 1959, 2d edit., 1966. Asso. editor Radiation Research, 1961-63; editorial bd. Jour. Am. Chem. Soc., 1957-61. Research, publs. on mechanisms chem. reactions induced by light, radiation; mass spectrometer studies, electrons, ions in irradiated organic solids. Home: 17899 Edgewood Walk South Bend IN 46635

HAMILTON, ALEXANDER DANIEL, forest products co. exec.; b. Westmount, Que., Can., Nov. 13, 1917; s. Daniel Evoy and Isobel (Stewart) H.; B.Eng. in Chem. Engring., McGill U., 1940; m. Frances McLeod, Feb. 25, 1942; children—Joanne, Sandra, Stewart, Kirk, Alex. Groundwood engr. Ont. Paper Co., Thorold, 1946-53, asst. gen. supt., 1953-55, asst. divisional mgr., 1960-61; gen. supt. Que. North Shore Paper Co., 1955-60; v.p. pulp and paper B.C. Forest Products Ltd., Vancouver, 1961-64, pres., 1964-67, pres., chief exec. officer, 1967-68; pres. Domtar Pulp & Paper Products Ltd., Montreal, 1968—. Served RCAF, 1941-45; ETO. Mem. Canadian Pulp and Paper Assn. (chmn. exec. bd.). Home: 3 Murray Av Montreal 217 Quebec Canada Office: PO Box 7211 Montreal 101 Quebec Canada also 395 de Maisonneuve Blvd W Montreal 111 Quebec Canada

HAMILTON, ALLAN CORNING, oil co. exec.; b. Chgo., June 9, 1921; s. Daniel Sprague and Mildred (Corning) H.; B.S. in Econs., Haverford Coll., 1943; m. Edith Johnson, June 3, 1950; children—Kimball C., Scott W., Dean C., Gail W. With Standard Oil Co. (N.J.), 1946-51, Esso Export Corp., 1951-56; treas. Internat. Petroleum Co., Ltd., Coral Gables, Fla., 1956-61, Esso Internat. Inc., 1961-66; with Standard Oil Co. (N.J.), 1966—, treas., prin. financial officer, 1970—. Served to lt. (j.g.) USNR, 1943-46. Home: 181 Parish Rd S New Canaan CT 06840 Office: 30 Rockefeller Plaza New York City NY 10020

HAMILTON, ANTHONY ROBERT, electronics co. exec.; b. North Bergen, N.J., July 14, 1924; s. Anthony J. and Ada (Leeman) H.; student Columbia, 1946-48; m. Theresa Mannarino, Sept. 2, 1942; childrenAnthony, Deborah, Theresa, Sandra, Richard. Dir. purchasing Lear, Inc., Santa Monica, Cal., 1950-57; founder Hamilton Electro Corp. and associated cos., 1957, pres., 1960—; now exec. v.p., dir. Avnet, Inc., N.Y.C. Served with AUS, 1943-45. Mem. Sales and Marketing Execs. Los Angeles, Electronic Reps. Assn. Home: 9142 Cum Laude Av Playa Del Rey CA 93616 Office: 10912 W Washington Blvd Culver City CA 90230 *

HAMILTON, BRYCE LELAND, lawyer; b. Wells County, Ind. Oct. 12, 1902; s. Ira C. and Nora (Beck) H.; Ph.B., U. Chgo., 1923, J.D., 1928; m. Elizabeth B. Millies, Aug. 9, 1930 (dec.); m. 2d, Avonell Conover, June 27, 1936; 1 son, William Marshall. Admitted to Ill. bar, 1928; partner firm Winston, Strawn, Smith & Patterson, Chgo., 1944-; gen. counsel, dir. C.G.W. Ry. Co., 1952-68; lectr. law, U. Chgo., 1957. Mem. Am., Ill., Chgo. bar assns., Delta Theta Phi. Republican. Clubs: Midday, Law, Executives (Chgo.); Hinsdale Golf. Contbr. articles to legal publs. Home: 519 E 7th St Hinsdale IL 60521 Office: 1 First Nat Plaza Chicago IL 60670

HAMILTON, CHARLES HENRY, newspaper exec.; b. Webster Springs, W.Va., Nov. 16, 1903; s. Alfred Patton and Cora Jane (Benedum) H.; grad. Greenbrier Mil. Sch., 1923; A.B., Washington and Lee U., 1926; m. Viola Belle Morrisette, Nov. 3, 1928 (dec. 1963); children—John Alfred, Barbara Morrisette (Mrs. Charles Fraley), Bette (Mrs. Lacey Jacobs, Jr.), Viola Lee; m. 2d, Muriel Marable Butler, 1964. Reporter, Clarksburg Exponent, 1925; sports writer Richmond News Leader, 1926-32, sports editor, 1932- 36, city editor, 1936-51, mng. editor, 1951-69, asst. to pres., 1969—; radio announcer, news commentator, sta. WRVA, Richmond, 1927-34; pres. Dixie Profl. Football League, 1935-36; news commentator sta. WRNL, 1939-42; lectr. Am. Press Inst., Columbia, 1946-51; chmn. Va. Asso. Press Newspapers, 1956-57. Dir. Fed. Home Loan Bank of Greensboro, 1963, chmn. bd., 1970. Chmn. Va. adv. legislative com. unit to rewrite Va. hunting and fishing laws, 1962. Bd. dirs. Richmond Area unit Am. Cancer Soc. Lt. col. AGC, U.S. Army Res., 1949-54. Mem. Am. Soc. Newspaper Editors, Va. Press Assn. (pres. 1959; spl. plaque 1971), A.P. Mng. Editors Assn. (dir. 1955-58), Richmond C. of C. (Congl. action com.), Newcomen Soc. Am., Sigma Delta Chi, Lambda Chi Alpha, Delta Sigma Rho, Pi Delta Epsilon, Omicron Delta Kappa. Methodist. Club: Hermitage Country (pres. 1970—). Contbr. fiction, articles nat. mags., including Reader's Digest, This Week, Sat. Eve. Post. Home: 8207 Tyndale Rd Richmond VA 23227 Office: Richmond Newspapers Inc Richmond VA 23213

HAMILTON, CHARLES HORACE, educator, sociologist; b. McLennan County, Tex., June 10, 1901; s. William Clark and Amy Jane (Whittenberg) H.; A.B., So. Meth. U., 1923; M.S., Tex. A. and M. Coll., 1925; Ph.D., U. N.C., 1932; student U. Chgo., 1925, Harvard, 1930-31; m. Maurine Phifer, Sept. 9, 1928; children—Charles Edward (dec.), Elizabeth Ayers (Mrs. Charles W. Darden), Mary Bellamy (Mrs. Douglas E. Hosler). Prof. edn. Lon Morris Coll., Jacksonville, Tex., 1925-26; asst. rural sociologist Va. Agrl. Expt. Sta., 1927-31; asst. and asso. prof. rural sociology N. C. State Coll., 1931-36; economist in rural life Tex. Agrl. Expt. Sta., 1936-39; sr. social scientist, bur. agrl. econs. U.S. Dept. Agr., Washington, 1939-40; head dept. rural sociology N.C. State Coll., 1940-60, William Neal Reynolds prof. rural sociology, 1960—; vis. prof. U. Wis., 1959-60; vis. prof. sociology and biostatistics, asso. dir. Carolina Population Center, U. N.C., Chapel Hill, 1967—; on leave as dir. sociol. research Commn. on Hosp. Care, Chgo., 1945-46; mng. editor Rural Sociology, Jour. of Rural sociol. Soc., 1940-50; cons. research grants div. NIH, USPHS, 1946-49. Pres. N.C. Conf. for Social Service, 1961-62; sec. rural sub- com. Gov's. Commn. on Hosp. and Medical Care, also chmn. statistics and publs. sub-com.; mem. adv. com. on population 1950 U.S. Census. Recipient Oliver Max Gardner award, 1958; Social Science Research Council fellow, 1930-31. Fellow Am. Statis. Assn.; mem. Am. Rural Sociol. Soc. (pres. 1949-50), Am. Assn. U. Profs., So. Sociol. Soc. (pres. 1957-58), Population Assn. Am. (pres. 1960-61), Internat. Population Union. Author bulls., contbr. to profl. jours. Home: 1515 Duplin Rd Raleigh NC 27607

HAMILTON, CHARLES OWEN, physician; b. Delaware County, Ind., Aug. 27, 1922; s. Mark B. and Lucile E. (Lindsey) H.; B.S., Ind. U., 1943, M.D., 1945; m. Mary L. Fuller, June 29, 1941; childrenKaye, Charles Owen II, Philip F., Lucinda A., Mary Beth. Intern Meml. Hosp., South Bend, Ind., 1945-46, resident, 1948-49; practiced medicine, specializing anesthesiology, South Bend, 1949-. Del. Ind. Republican Conv., 1960. Bd. dirs. South Bend Med. Found., Inc. Served to capt. AUS, 1943-48. Diplomate Am. Bd. Anesthesiology. Mem. Am. Soc. Anesthesiologists (sec. 1963-), Ind. Med. Soc., Ind. Soc. Anesthesiology (pres. 1957-58), A.M.A., Am. Coll. Anesthesiology, South Bend C. of C. Methodist (dir.). Home: 1418 E Washington Av South Bend IN 46617 Office: 622 N Michigan St South Bend IN 46601

HAMILTON, CHARLES STUART, Jr., lawyer; b. Chgo., Nov. 25, 1910; s. Charles Stuart and Frances (King) H.; A.B., Princeton, 1932; LL.B., Yale, 1935; m. Ella Kate Malone, Aug. 15, 1939. Admitted to N.Y. bar, 1936, since practiced in N.Y.C.; mem. Sullivan & Cromwell, 1945-58; v.p., treas., dir. Russell, Burdsall & Ward Bolt and Nut Co., Port Chester, N.Y., 1958-59; v.p. Andrew W. Mellon Found. (Formerly known as Avalon Found.), 1960-61, pres., trustee, 1961-; dir. European-Am. Bank & Trust Co., European-Am. Banking Corp. Past commn. Port N.Y. Authority; mem. Westchester County Park Commn., Westchester County Parkway Authority, 1953-58. Mem. Order of Coif, Phi Beta Kappa. Home: Cross River Rd Katonah NY 10536 Office: 140 E 62d St New York City NY 10021

HAMILTON, CHARLES VERNON, educator; b. Muskogee, Okla., Oct. 19, 1929; s. Owen and Viola (Haynes) H.; B.A., Roosevelt U., Chgo., 1951; J.D., Loyola U., Chgo., 1954; M.A., U. Chgo., 1957, Ph.D., 1964; m. Dona Louise Cooper, Oct. 5, 1956; children—Valli, Carol. Mem. faculty Albany State Coll., 1957-58, Tuskegee Inst., 1958-60, Rutgers U., 1963-64, Lincoln (Pa.) U., 1964-67; prof. polit sci., chmn. dept. Roosevelt U., Chgo., 1967-69; prof. polit. sci. Columbia, 1969—. Served with AUS, 1948-49. Charles Merriam fellow U. Chgo., 1961-62; John Hay Whitney fellow, 1962-63; recipient Lindback Distinguished Teaching award Lincoln U., 1965. Mem. Am. Polit. Sci. Assn., N.A.A.C.P., Congress Racial Equality. Author: Minority Politics in Black Belt Alabama, 1962; (with Stokely Carmichael) Black Power, The Politics of Liberation in America, 1967; also articles. Home: 55 Barnard Rd New Rochelle NY 10801

HAMILTON CHICO see **Hamilton, Foreststorm**

HAMILTON, CYRIL ROBERT PARKE, banker; b. London, Eng., Aug. 4, 1903; s. Alfred Parke and Annie (Frazer) H.; student London U., 1919-23; m. Cissie May Stearn, June 1, 1929 (dec. Apr. 1966); children—Brenda Mary Neville, Clive; m. 2d, Betty Emily Brand, Jan. 6, 1971. With Bank of Eng., 1923-63; dep. chmn. Standard Bank, Ltd., London, 1963—; vice chmn. Standard Chartered Banking Group, 1970—; dir. Bank Orgn. Clubs: Brookes's, Bath, Marylebone Cricket. Home: Peat Moor Harborough Hill Pulborough England Office: Standard Bank 10 Clements Lane London EC 4 England

HAMILTON, DON C., lawyer; b. Westfield, Wis., Nov. 28, 1914; B.E., Central State Tchrs. Coll., 1939; LL.B., U. Wis., 1942. Admitted to Hawaii bar, 1946; now mem. firm Henshaw, Conroy & Hamilton, Honolulu. Mem. Supreme Ct. Standing Com. on Rules of Practice and Procedure, 1962-65. Mem. Am. Bar Assn., Bar Assn. Hawaii. Office: 1st Hawaiian Bank Bldg Honolulu HI 96813*

HAMILTON, DONALD ROSS, physicist; b. Hartford, Vt., Sept. 5, 1914; s. Rollo Albert and May Davina (Ross) H.; A.B., Princeton, 1935; Ph.D., Columbia, 1939; m. Eileen Mary Clare-Patton, Aug. 20, 1938; childrenErica Lynn (Mrs. Richard S. Weeder), Eleanor (Mrs. Stanley Sienkiewicz), David. Jr. fellow Soc. of Fellows, Harvard,

1939-42; staff Mass. Inst. Tech. Radiation Lab., 1940-46; project engr. Sperry Gyroscope Co. Research Labs., Garden City, N.Y., 1941-42, research engr., 1942-45; asst. prof. physics Princeton, 1946-48, asso. prof., 1948-55, prof., 1955-, dean of the graduate school, 1958-65; member of the Inst. for Advanced Study, 1952; vis. sr. physicist Brookhaven Nat. Lab., 1953. Fellow Am. Phys. Soc. Author: Klystrons and Microwave Triodes (with J.B.H. Kuper and J.L. Knipp), 1947. Trustee Princeton U. Press, 1956-, mem. editorial bd., 1956-60. Home: 53 McCosh Circle Princeton, NJ 08540.

HAMILTON, DOUGLAS LELAND, elec. mfg. co. exec.; b. Brookline, Mass., Jan. 1, 1919; s. Edward H. and Johana (Holmes) H.; B.B.A., Northeastern U., 1943, M.B.A., 1957; m. Madelyn P. Congdon, June 28, 1941; children—Douglas P., Stephanie, Mark C. Cost accountant A.C. Lawrence Leather Co., 1939-41; with GTE Sylvania Inc., 1941-51, 53—, controller electronic systems div., Waltham, Mass., 1962-63, corp. v.p. finance, controller, 1963-71, sr. v.p. finance, controller, 1971—; mgmt. cons. McKinsey & Co., Boston, 1951-53. Pres. Genesee County (N.Y.) United Fund, 1961-62; chmn. Ta-Ko-Da dist. council Boy Scouts Am., 1961- 61. Dir.-at-large Nat. Council Northeastern U., 1964—. Bd. govs. White Plains (N.Y.) Hosp. Served to 2d lt. USAAF, 1943-45. Mem. Nat. Assn. Accountants (past chpt. v.p., treas.), Nat. Elec. Mfrs. Assn., Financial Execs. Inst., Bentley Coll. Alumni Assn. (v.p.). Mason, Rotarian. Home: 601 Fort Hill Rd Scarsdale NY 10583 Office: 730 3d Av New York City NY 10017

HAMILTON, EARL F., furniture mfg.; b. Indpls., Dec. 26, 1910; s. B.F. and Nell (Pruitt) H.; ed. pub. schs.; m. Mostella Lee Parham. Vice chmn. Hamilton Cosco, Inc., Columbus, Ind. Bd. dirs. Bartholomew County Hosp. Found. Mem. Columbus C. of C. Republican. Kiwanian. Clubs: Royal Palm Yacht and Country (Boca Raton, Fla.); Harrison Lake Country (Columbus). Home: 429 Alexander Palm Rd Boca Raton FL 33432*

HAMILTON, EARL JEFFERSON, economist, educator; b. Houlka, Miss., May 17, 1899; s. Joseph William and Frances Regina Anne (Williams) H.; B.S., with honors, Miss. State U., 1920; student U. Tex., summers 1922, 23, M.A., 1924; A.M., Harvard, 1926, Ph.D., 1929; Dr. Honoris Causa, U. Paris, 1952, U. Madrid, 1967; LL.D., Duke, 1966; m. Gladys Olive Dallas, June 2, 1923; 1 dau., Sita (Mrs. Joseph Halperin). Athletic dir., football and track coach secondary schs., 1920-24; Thayer fellow econs. Harvard, 1925-26, Frederick Sheldon traveling fellow, 1926-27; asst. prof. econs. Duke, 1927-29, prof., 1929-44, dir. civilian staff Mil. Govt. Fiscal Sch., 1943-44; prof. econs Northwestern U., 1944-47; prof. econs. U. Chgo., 1947-67, emeritus, 1968—; distinguished prof. econ. history State U. N.Y. at Binghampton, 1966-69. Mem. com. on research in econ. history Social Sci. Research Council, 1941-54; rapporteur, com. world regions of Social Sci. Research Council, Am. Council Learned Socs. and NRC, 1943; rapporteur 11th Congress Hist. Scis., Stockholm, Sweden, 1960. Trustee Com. Research in Econ. History, Inc., 1956—. Social Science Research fellow, 1929-30; Guggenheim Meml. fellow, 1937-38; faculty research fellow Ford Found., 1956-57. Fellow Royal Exon. Soc., A.A.A.S., Am. Acad. Arts and Scis.; mem. Am. Econ. Assn. (v.p. 1955), Econ. Hist. Assn. (pres. 1951-52), Am. Hist. Assn., Econ. History Soc. Hispanic Soc. Am. (corr.). Author: American Treasure and the Price Revolution in Spain, 1501-1650, 1934; Money, Prices and Wages in Valencia, Aragon and Navarre, 1351-1500, 1936; War and Prices in Spain, 1651-1800, 1947; El Florecimiento del. Capitalismo y Otros Ensayos, 1948. Mem. bd. editors Jour. Modern History, 1941-43, Jour. Econ. History, 1941-52; editor Jour. Polit. Economy, 1948-54; co-editor: Landmarks in Political Economy, 1962. Contbr. Am., English, French jours. of econs. and history. Home: 1438 Bunker Av Flossmoor IL 60422 Office: Kelly Hall U Chgo Chicago IL 60637

HAMILTON, ELBERT WORK, educator; b. Benkelman, Neb., Mar. 16, 1910; s. Harry Parks and Rebecca Minni (Work) H.; B.A., Tarkie Coll., 1935; M.A., U. Ia., 1947, Ph.D., 1956; m. Edna Almeda Yoder, Dec. 21, 1935; children—Suzanne (Mrs. James A. McCullough), Mary Margaret (Mrs. Harold Baxter). Tchr. pubs. schs., Neb., Ia., Mo., 1935-40; faculty U. No. Ida., Cedar Falls, 1949—, prof. math., head dept., 1963—. Mem. African edn. team Ednl. Services Inc., 1962—. Served with AUS, 1943-45. Mem. Central Assn. Sci. and Math. Tchrs. (pres. 1963-64), Nat. Council Tchrs. Math. Author (with Trimble, et al) Mathematics for General Education, 1963. Contbr. articles to profl. jours. Home: 822 College St Cedar Falls IA 50613

HAMILTON, ERIC LYON, chem. co. exec.; b. Montreal, Que., Can., 1913; B.Commerce, McGill U., 1934, Chartered Accountant, 1935; m. Phyllis Coleby, 1936; children—Robert Arthur, Eric Kenneth. With Canadian Industries, Ltd., Montreal, 1937—, v.p., 1956-68, exec. v.p., 1968-71, pres., 1971—; pres., dir. Canadian Safety Fuse Co., Ltd.; sr. v.p., dir. I.C.I. N.Am., Ltd.; dir. Royal Trust Co., Bapco Paint, Ltd. Bd. govs. Quebec Hosp. Service Assn.; mem. met. adv. bd. Montreal YMCA. Mem. Canadian Inst. Chartered Accountants (hon. sec., mem. exec. com. and council 1968-70), Canadian C. of C. (mem. exec. com. 1964-69). Home: 250 Clarke Av Westmount Quebec Canada Office: CIL House 630 Dorchester Blvd W Montreal Quebec Canada

HAMILTON, FORESTSTORN, (Chico Hamilton), drummer; b. Los Angeles, Sept. 21, 1921; studied drums with Jo Jones. Began musical career as clarinetist; organized band with schoolmates Ernie Royal, C. Mingus, I. Jacquet; with Floyd Ray, Lionel Hampton, 1940, Lorenzo Flennoy, Lester Young, 1941; on tour with Jimmy Munday, Count Basie; drummer Billy Berg's, Hollywood, Cal.; with Lena Horne, 1948-54, 54-55, including European tour; drummer motion picture Road to Bali, Paramount Studios; actor and musician Sweet Smell of Success, 1957; with Charlie Barnet; organized quartet with Gerry Mulligan, 1952; with quintet, concert and club appearances U.S.; recordings include plays South Pacific, Sweet Smell of Success, Bernie's Tune, Chase and Steeple Chase.*

HAMILTON, FOWLER, lawyer; b. Kansas City, May 7, 1911; s. Eugene Paul and Emily Rhodelle (Fowler) H.; B.A., U. Mo., 1931; B.A., B.C.L., M.A. (Rhodes scholar), Oxford U., 1934; m. Helen Katherine Miller, Sept. 15, 1934; children—Helen Dudley, Emily Katherine (Mrs. Valerian L. Puskar), Milo Charles. Admitted to Mo. bar, 1935, D.C. bar, 1945, N.Y. bar, 1947; asso. Watson, Ess, Groner, Barnett & Whittaker, 1935-38; spl. asst. to atty. gen. U.S., 1938-42; dir. war frauds unit Dept. Justice, 1942; with the econ. warfare div. Am. embassy, London, 1943; Fgn. Econ. Adminstrn., 1942-43; chief legal cons. U.S. Dept. Justice, 1945; partner Cleary, Gottlieb, Steen & Hamilton, N.Y.C., 1946-61, 63—; trustee, mem. exec. com. Mut. Life Ins. Co. N.Y.; adminstr. AID, 1961-62; dir., mem. exec. com. N.Y. Telephone Co.; gen. counsel subcom. Air Force, Senate Armed Services Com., 1956. Trustee Am. Schs. Oriental Research, Freedom From Hunger Found. Served with USAAF, 1943-44: CBI. Mem. Am., N. Y. bar assns., Fgn. Policy Assn., Council Fgn. Relations. Democrat, Episcopalian. Clubs: Greenwich (Conn.) Country; Metropolitan, 1925 F Street (Washington); Downtown Assn., Century Assn., The Church (N.Y.C.). Home: 652 Riversville Rd Greenwich CT 06830 Office: 52 Wall St New York City NY 10005*

HAMILTON, FRANK, former banker; b. Liverpool, Eng., Aug. 12, 1903; s. Henry Alfred and Ann Jane (Johnson) H.; came to U.S., 1909, naturalized 1919; student Pratt Inst., 1919-23; m. Elizabeth Small, 1933 (dec. 1965); children-David Peter, Robert Alan (dec.); m. 2d, Rae Myerle Gould, 1969. With Lee, Higginson & Co., N.Y.C., 1920-37, Monnet, Murnane & Co., N.Y.C., 1937-42; mem. staff Combined (U.S.-U.K.-Can.) Prodn. and Resources Bd., Washington, 1942-43; v.p. Nicaro Nickel Co., 1943-47; with Bankers Trust Co., N.Y.C., 1947-69, asst. v.p., v.p., 1949-61, 1st v.p., 1961-69; dir. Consumers Power Co., Jackson, Mich., 1955—, Devel. Credit Corp., Duluth, Minn., 1970—. Episcopalian Clubs: Creek, Union League (N.Y.C.). Home: Chapel Gate Lane Upper Brookville NY 13314

HAMILTON, FRANK STRAWN, folk singer, composer, educator; b. N.Y.C., Aug. 3, 1934; s. Frank Strawn and Gladys (Bley) H.; student Los Angeles City Coll., 1952-53, Chgo. Mus. Coll., 1959-62, Los Angeles Valley Coll., 1963-64; m. Sheila Lofton, Nov. 7, 1954; childrenCameron Auguste, Evan Baird, Liam Christopher, Heather Alexa. Appeared Asheville (N.C.) Folk Festival, 1953, Newport Folk Festival, 1959; organizer, head tech. staff Old Town Sch. Folk Music, Chgo., 1957-62, v.p., 1957-62; house musician folk music nightclub, Gate of Horn, Chgo., 1959-61; mem. folk singing group Weavers, 1962-63; now with dept. humanities U. Cal. at Los Angeles extension; motion picture appearance in Subterraneans, 1958; performances for numerous fund raisings; rec. artist for Folkways, Vanguard records; devel. method annotation folk guitar and 5 string banjo. Recipient award music composition Los Angeles Valley Coll., 1964. Hon. mem. Chgo. Hist. Soc. Unitarian. Composer: (film score) A Time Out of War, 1952; (with others) We Shall Overcome, 1952; (TV score) Survival, 1965. Home: 2002 Navy St Santa Monica, CA 90405. Office: Dept Humanities Extension Div U Cal at Los Angeles Los Angeles CA 90024.*

HAMILTON, GEORGE E., Jr., lawyer; b. Washington, Mar. 29, 1895; s. George E. and Louise (Merrick) H.; student Carlton Acad., 1909-13; A.B., Georgetown U., 1917, LL.B., 1920; m. Marian Hamilton, Oct. 4, 1922. Admitted to D.C. bar, 1920; asso. Hamilton & Hamilton, Washington, 1920-23, mem. since 1923, sr. mem. since 1946; gen. counsel Washington Terminal Co.; local counsel railroads; counsel, dir. Union Trust Co. of D.C.; counsel Eve. Star Newspaper Co., Cath. Archdiocese of Washington, others; director Columbia Planograph Company, Potomac Electric Power Co., Eve. Star Broadcasting Co. Pres. bd. trustees Corcoran Gallery Art. Served as sgt. U.S. Army, 1917-18. Decorated Knight of St. Gregory. Fellow Am. Bar Found.; mem. Am., D.C. bar associations, Society of the Cincinnati, Lawyers Club. Clubs: Chevy Chase (past pres.), Metropolitan (past pres.), Alfalfa (past pres.) Washington); Barristers. Home: 2330 Wyoming Av Washington DC 20008 Office: Union Trust Bldg Washington DC 20005

HAMILTON, GEORGE HEARD, educator, curator; b. Pitts., June 23, 1910; s. Frank Arthur and Georgia (Heard) H.; B.A., Yale, 1932, M.A., 1934, Ph.D., 1942; m. Polly Wiggin, Oct. 20, 1945; children—Richard, Jennett. Research Asso. Walters Art Gallery, Balt., 1934-36; instr. history art Yale, 1936-43, asst. prof., 1943-47, asso. prof., 1947-56, prof., 1956- 66, curator modern art Univ. Art Gallery, 1940-66; Robert Sterling Clark prof. art Williams Coll., Williamstown, Mass., 1963-64, prof. art, 1966—; dir. Sterling and Francine Clark Art Inst., Williamstown, 1966—. Trustee Mus. Modern Art; v.p., trustee Mill-Stead Mus., Farmington, Conn., 1970—. Mem. Coll. Art Assn. Am. (pres. 1966-68), Mass. Council Arts and Humanities, Internat. Assn. Art Critics (pres. Am. sect. 1967-69). Author: Manet and His Critics, 1954; Art and Architecture of Russia, 1954; European Painting and Sculpture 1880-1940, 1967; (with W.C. Agee) Raymond Duchamp Villon, 1967; 19th and 20th Century Art: Painting, Sculpture, Architecture, 1970. Editor: Collection of the Société Anonyme, Yale U. Art Gallery, 1950. Home: Whitman St Williamstown MA 01267*

HAMILTON, GREY, banker; b. Toronto, Ont., Can., Dec. 20, 1929; s. James Grey and Jane (Wilson) H.; ed. Trinity Coll., U. Toronto, 1949; m. Joan Louise Kennedy, June 27, 1953; children—Grey, Elizabeth. Engaged as newspaperman, 1949-58; spl. ast. to Minister of Finance Can., 1958-62; sec. Nat. Energy Bd. Can., 1962-65; dep. sec. Bank of Can. and Indsl. Devel. Bank, 1965-69, sec., 1970—. Bd. dirs. Social Planning Council Ottawa, 1968—; vice chmn. pub. relations United Appeal Ottawa, 1963-67. Home: 737 Island Park Dr Ottawa 3 Ontario Canada Office: 234 Wellington St Ottawa 4 Ontario Canada

HAMILTON, HAROLD PHILIP, coll. pres.; b. High Point, N.C., Apr. 26, 1924; s. Alfred McKinley and Dora Elizabeth (Surratt) H.; student Lehigh U., 1943-44; B.A. cum laude, High Point Coll., 1947, L.H.D., 1965; B.D. (Myers Park scholar), Duke, 1950, Ph.D., 1954; m. Agnes Marie Kametz, Sept. 4, 1944; childrenDawn Elizabeth, Deborah Anne, Harold Philip, Elaine Denise. Asst. prof. philosophy and religion N.C. State Coll., 1953-55; dean of faculty, asso. prof. Christian thought Ky. Wesleyan Coll., 1955-58, dean of coll., prof. 1958-59, dean of coll., acting pres., 1959-60, pres., prof. Christian thought, 1960-70; pres. Central Meth. Coll., 1970—. Pres. Oxford Inst. Meth. Theol. Studies, 1958. Trustee Pop Warner Little Scholars. Served with AUS, World War II. Mem. Am. Renaissance Soc., Central States Faculty Conf. (exec. com.), Am. Soc. Ch. History, Inst. Higher Edn., Fayette C. of C., N.E.A., Newcomen Soc. N.Am., Phi Delta Theta, Phi Alpha Theta, Phi Beta Patron, Omicron Delta Kappa. Methodist (lay leader, ofcl. bd., tchr.). Rotarian (v.p.). Club: Round Table (Fayette). Home: 502 N Linn St Fayette MO 65248

HAMILTON, HERBERT ALFRED, coll. dean; b. Lake Charles, La., July 25, 1913; s. Fuller M. and Lillie Pearl (Litton) H.; B.S., U. Southwestern La., 1932; M.S. (fellow 1932- 33), La. State U., 1933; Ph.D., N.Y.U., 1950; postgrad. student London (Eng.) Sch. Econs., 1956, 64; m. Mary Elizabeth Davies, Dec. 30, 1944. Asst. prin. Lafayette (La.) High Sch., 1934-39; asst. prof. bus. adminstrn. Southeastern La. Coll., 1939-40; asst. prof. bus. adminstrn. Southwestern La. Inst., 1940-42, prof., head dept. econs. and bus. adminstrn., 1946-52, dean adminstrn., 1950-52, dean Coll. Commerce, 1952- ; vis. prof. N.Y.U., 1957. Exec. dir. U. of Southwestern La. Found.; mem. bd. dirs. Mississippi Valley Foundation. Served to lt. comdr. USNR, 1942-45. Fellow economics-in-action U. Wis., 1960. Mem. Seaway Assn. (Chmm. La. coastal commn.), Delta Pi Epsilon (Nat. Research award 1960), Phi Kappa Phi, Phi Delta Kappa. Baptist. Author numerous articles, monographs in field. Home: 507 Laurence Av Lafayette LA 70501

HAMILTON, HERMAN LYNN, Jr., lawyer; b. Prescott, Ark., Feb. 20, 1934; s. Herman Lynn and Esther (Haug) H.; B.A., U. Ark., 1955, LL.B., 1957, J.D., 1969; m. Patricia Alice Walsh, Sept. 4, 1954; children—Herman Lynn III, David Pearson, James A. Admitted to Ark. bar, 1957, since practiced in Hamburg, Ark.; city atty., 1961-62, municipal judge, 1962—. Vice pres. Ashley County Abstract Co.; v.p., treas. AH & S, Inc. Chmn., Ark. Bd. Law Examiners, 1969-70. Pres., Hamburg P.T.A., 1969. Sec., Ashley County Democratic Central Com., 1969-70. Bd. dirs. Ark. Bar Found. Mem. Am., Ark. bar assns., Am. Trial Attys., S.E. Ark. Legal Inst. Mason. Home: 503 S Cherry St Hamburg AR 71646 Office: 110 N Main St Hamburg AR 71646

HAMILTON, HOWARD BRITTON, educator; b. Augusta, Kan., Oct. 28, 1923; s. Silas Howard and Ora (Barker) H.; B.S., U. Okla., 1949; M.S., U. Minn., 1955; Ph.D., Okla. State U., 1962; postgrad. U.S. Army Command and Gen. Staff Coll., 1969; m. Geraldine E. Karr, Jan. 27, 1943; children— Stephen P., Jana L., John V., Christopher H. Engr., Gen. Electric Co., Schenectady, 1949-53; prof., head elec. engring. dept. U. Wichita, 1955-64; unit chief mfg. research Boeing Co., Wichita, 1958-60; chief of party U. Pitts.-U.S. AID at U. Santa Maria, Valparaiso, Chile, 1964-66; prof., head elec. engring. dept. U. Pitts., 1966—; lectr. in power system interconnection, Bogota, Colombia, 1969. Ford Found. cons. U. Santa Maria, 1968. Served to capt. AUS, World War II. Decorated Air medal, Purple Heart. Registered profl. engr., Pa., Kan. Mem. I.E.E.E. (student br. counselor, sec., treas., vice chmn., chmn. Wichita sect., dir. Pitts. sect. 1967-71), Am. Soc. Engring. Edn., Conf. Internat. des Grand Reseaux Electriques, Sigma Xi, Phi Eta Sigma, Eta Kappa Nu, Sigma Tau, Tau Beta Pi. Author: Power Processing (Electric Machinery Analysis), 1970; Economic Control and Operation, Power Systems, 1971. Home: 1422 Oak St Oakmont PA 15139 Office: 348 Benedum Hall U Pitts Pittsburgh PA 15213

HAMILTON, HUBERT EARL, Jr., (Bert), educator; b. Liberty S.C., July 19, 1907; s. Hubert Earl and Cynthia (Riddle) H.; A.B., The Citadel, 1932; M.A., Peabody Coll., 1934, Ed.D., 1954; m. Carolyn Dudney, July 29, 1949; children—Hubert Earl III, Bruce Dudney. Tchr., Walhalla (S.C.) High Sch., 1932-33, Atlanta pub. schs., 1935-53; prin. Vinceland Sch., Easley, S.C., 1933-34; prof. edn., chmn. dept. Mercer U., 1953—, McCommon prof., 1956—. Alderman, Macon, 1959- 63, 67-70; mem. Ga. State Senate, 1970—. Served to maj. AUS, 1941-46; ETO; now lt. col. Res. Member Greater Macon C. of C., Am. Assn. University Profs., Nat., Ga. edn. assns., Assn. Student Teaching, Ga. Council Tchrs. Edn., Am. Legion, Humane Soc., Ga. Conservancy, Phi Delta Kappa, Kappa Delta Pi, Pi Gamma Mu, Kappa Phi Kappa. Mem. Christian Ch. Moose, Eagle. Clubs: Macon Exchange, Touchdown. Home: 464 W Buford Rd Macon GA 31204

HAMILTON, HUGH JAMES, educator; b. Los Angeles, Jan. 17, 1910; s. James Edgar and Ella (Hamilton) H.; A.B., U. Cal. at Los Angeles, 1931; M.S., Brown U., 1933, Ph.D., 1936. Asst. math. U. Cal. at Los Angeles, 1931-32; teaching fellow, part-time instr. Brown U., 1933-36; mem. faculty Pomona Coll., 1936—, prof. math., 1953—. President Cal. br. Humane Soc. U.S., 1967- -; treas. Claremont Friends Meeting, 1951—. Mem. Am. Assn. U. Profs. (chpt. sec.), Am. Civil Liberties Union (chpt. sec.), Phi Beta Kappa, Sigma Xi. Author: A Primer of Complex Variables, 1966. Home: 603 W 8th St Claremont CA 91711

HAMILTON, HUGHBERT CLAYTON, educator, psychologist; b. Cedar Rapids, Ia., Mar. 6, 1903; s. Leslie S. and H. Belle (Clayton) H.; B.A., Cornell Coll., 1925; M.A., Columbia, 1926, Ph.D., 1929; m. Mildred Eckhardt, May 31, 1940. Mem. faculty Temple U., 1928—, prof. psychology, 1946-70, chmn. dept., 1962-70, dir. psychology lab., 1930-70, editor univ. publs., 1945-69, prof. emeritus 1970—. Fellow Am., Pa. psychol. assns., A.A.A.S.; mem. Eastern Psychol. Assn., Psychonomic Soc., Am. Assn. U. Profs., Midwestern Psychol. Assn., Sigma Xi. Contbr. profl. jours. Home: 5720 Wissahickon Av Philadelphia PA 19144

HAMILTON, IALN ELLIS, composer; b. Glasgow, Scotland, June 6, 1922; s. James and Catherine (Ellis) H.; Mus.B., U. London (Eng.), 1950; Mus, D. (hon.), U. Glasgow 1970. Came to U.S., 1961. Engr., 1939-47; lectr. U. London, 1952-60, Morley Coll., London, 1951-60; Mary Duke Biddle prof. music Duke, 1961—, chmn. dept., 1966-67; composer in residence, Tanglewood, Mass., 1962. Chmn. composers Guild Great Britain, 1958; chmn. sect. Inst. Contemporary Arts, London, 1958-60. Recipient Koussevitsky Found. award, 1951; Royal Philharmonic prize, 1951; Arnold Bax gold medal, 1957. Fellow Royal Acad. Music; mem. Internat. Webern Soc. (founding mem.), Am. Soc. Univ. Composers (founding mem.). Composer: (operas) Royal Hunt of the Sun, 1968; Agamemnon, 1961, 68; also symphonies, chamber works and vocal works. Home: 40 Park Av New York City NY 10016

HAMILTON, JAMES ALEXANDER, actuary; b. Kingston, Ont., Can., Sept. 12, 1906; s. John Rennie and Clara (Howlett) H.; B.S., Queens U., 1927; M.S., U. Chgo.; M.A., Pa. State U.; m. Geraldine Lucy Boyce, June 21, 1930; childrenMargaret Lynne, Nancy Lee. Came to U.S., 1927, naturalized, 1940. Instr. math. Pa. State U., 1928-33; research Met. Life Ins. Co., 1933-43; with Wyatt Co., also Wyatt Actuaries, Inc., Washington, 1946—, now cons. actuary, chmn. and dir.; dir. Fidelity Nat. Bank, Arlington, Va. Served to maj. AUS, 1943-46; actuary, then chief life sect., contract ins. br. Offic Chief of Finance. Fellow Soc. Actuaries Conf. Actuaries in Pub. Practice; mem. Fraternal Actuarial Assn., Internat. Assn. Cons. Actuaries (vice chmn.), Internat. Congress Actuaries. Author: (with D.C. Bronson) Pensions. Home: 2370 N Vernon St Arlington, VA 22207. Office: 1629 K St NW Washington DC 20006*

HAMILTON, JAMES BRUCE, anatomist; b. Tarentum, Pa., Apr. 2, 1910; s. James B. and Nellie (Hunger) H.; A.B., Allegheny Coll., 1931, D.Sc. (hon.), 1948; Ph.D., Yale, 1935; m. Ruth Staples, June 30, 1935; childrenPatricia Ruth, Penelope Joan, Margaret Anne, James Bruce. Instr. anatomy, physiology Albany Med. Coll., 1935-37; asst. prof. anatomy Yale Med. Sch., 1937-43; asso. prof. anatomy U. Mo. Med. Sch., 1943-44; prof., chairman dept. anatomy L.I. Coll. Medicine, 1944-50, Med. Center, State U. N.Y., since 1950. Mem. Am. Assn. Anatomists, Am. Physiol. Soc., Am. Assn. Cancer Research, A.A.A.S., Soc. Exptl. Biology and Medicine, Endocrine Soc., Gerontological Soc., N.Y. Acad. Sci., Harvey Soc., Am. Assn. U. Profs., Sigma Xi, Phi Beta Kappa. Lutheran. Author: Role of Testicular Secretions, 1950. Contbr. articles profl. publs. Home: 74 E 39th St Brooklyn NY 11203 Office: 450 Clarkson Av Brooklyn NY 11203

HAMILTON, JAMES BUFORD, ins. com. exec.; b. Vienna, Ga., Sept. 29, 1911; s. James B. and Ollie (Forehand) H.; student Tulane U., 1928-29, Emory U., 1943; LL.B., Atlanta Law Sch., 1933; m. Helen Peek, Oct. 10, 1942; children—Mary Helen, Kathryn, James Buford, Jacqueline. Admitted to Ga. bar, 1933; practice law, Atlanta, 1933-35, 45-47; with Hardware Mut. Casualty Co., Atlanta, 1935-42; with Fed. Mut. Ins. Co., Owatonna, Minn., 1947—, v.p., sec., gen. counsel, 1951—; dir. First Nat. Bank Owatonna, Fed. Acceptance Corp., Fed. Agy. Served with AUS, 1942-45. Mem. Ins. Fedn. Minn. (bd. dirs.), Minn. Mut. Ins. Assn. (bd. dirs.), Am., Ga., Minn. bar assns., Fedn. Ins. Counsel, Internat. Assn. Ins. Counsel, Am. Judicature Soc. Home: 533 Academy St Owatonna MN 55060 Office: 129 E Broadway Owatonna MN 55060

HAMILTON, JAMES LOVE, coal co. cons. b. Leeds, Eng., July 21, 1903; s. William and Clara (Love) H.; student Pa. State Coll.; m. Florence Eloise Barkell, Oct. 23, 1926; children—Ruth E. (dec.), James Love (dec.), Nancy. Safety and mining engr. Youngstown Sheet & Tube Co., 1926-34; mgr. coal mines Republic Steel Corp., 1934-49; v.p. operations Island Creek Coal Co., 1949-56, exec. v.p., dir., 1956-61, pres., dir., mem. exec. com., 1961- 63, chmn. exec. com., chmn. bd., 1963-68, formerly cons., dir.; dir. Occidental Petroleum

Corp. Mem. Am. Inst. Mining, Metall. and Petroleum Engrs., Coal Mining Inst. Am. (past pres.), Am. Mining Congress, Nat. Coal Assn., Nat. Coal Policy Conf., W.Va. Coal Mining Inst. Home: 1 Bratenahl Pl Cleveland OH 44108*

HAMILTON, JOHN ANDREW, educator; b. Columbia, S.C., June 1, 1907; s. John Andrew and Mattie (Wardlaw) H.; A.B., U.S.C., 1928, A.M., 1930; student U. N.C.; A.M., Harvard, 1934, Ph.D., 1937; grad. Nat. War Coll., 1955; m. Elizabeth Pettigrew Verner, Aug. 29, 1931; childrenJohn Andrew, David, Ward, Peter. Coll. instr., prof. Romance langs. Harvard, Bowdoin Coll., Henderson State Coll., Converse Coll., U. S.C., U. N.C., 1930-45; cultural attache Am. embassy, Dominican Republic, 1945-47, Havana, 1947-50; cultural adviser Bur. Inter-Am. Affairs, Dept. State, 1950; asst. dir. program planning staff, dep. asst. dir. policy and plans USIA, 1951-54; pub. affairs adviser U.S. Mission to NATO, Paris, 1955-58; counsellor for pub. affairs U.S. Mission to European 1969-70; prof. Coll. of Charleston, 1970. Mem. U.S. delegation to Berlin Communities, Brussels, 1958-62; USIA mem. Interdepartmental Berlin Task Force, 1962-63; cultural attaché Am. Embassy, Manila, 1963-66; dir. Charleston grad. program U. S. C., 1966-69; pres. Limestone Coll., 1969-70; prof. Coll. of Charleston, 1970—. Conf., 1954, Geneva Conf., 1954. Home: 3 Water St Charleston SC 29401

HAMILTON, JOHN DANIEL MILLER, lawyer; b. Ft. Madison, Ia., Mar. 2, 1892; s. John Daniel Miller and Mary (Rice) H.; grad. Phillips Acad., Andover, Mass., 1913; LL.B., Northwestern U., 1916; LL.D. (hon.), Dickinson Law Sch.; m. Rosamond Kittle. Practiced Kansas City, Mo., 1916-18, Topeka, 1918-40, mem. Pepper, Hamilton and Scheetz. Dir. Glenmede Trust Co. Mem. Kan. Ho. of Reps., 1925-28, speaker, 1927-28. Chmn. Rep. State Central Com., 1930-32; mem. Rep. Nat. Com., 1932-40, chmn., 1936-40. Trustee Robert A. Taft Meml. Found. Mem. Am. Pa., Phila., Shawnee Co. bar assns., Bar Assn. State Kan., Phi Alpha Delta. Mason, Elk. Home: 70 Carlouel Dr Clearwater FL 33515 Office: 123 S Broad St Philadelphia PA 19109

HAMILTON, JOHN DAYTON, former banker; b. Pavilion, N.Y., Aug. 18, 1900; s. John D. and Helen (Ellinwood) H.; A.B., Hamilton Coll., 1922; m. Faith Emerson Mooney, Oct. 5, 1929; children—John Dayton, Hope (Mrs. Robert P. Pettegrew). Asst. cashier State Bank Kenmore (N.Y.), 1923-27; examiner N.Y. State Banking Dept., 1927-32; pres. Ontario County Trust Co., Canadaigua, N.Y., 1934-48; pres. Marine Midland Chautauqua Nat. Bank, and predecessor, Jamestown, 1948-65, chmn. bd., 1965-69; acting pres. Jamestown Community Coll., 1969-70. Trustee Jamestown YMCA; pres. Chautauqua Found., Inc., Gebble Found.; vice chmn., dir. Chautauqua Instn. Served with U.S. Army, 1918. Mem. Jamestown C. of C. Rotarian. Home: 518 Lakeview Av Jamestown NY 14701 Office: Hotel Jamestown Bldg Jamestown NY 14701

HAMILTON, JOHN DRENNAN, physician, educator; b. Revelstoke, B.C., Can., Sept. 22, 1911; s. James Henry and Mary Stearns (Edwards) H.; M.D., U. Toronto, 1935; D.Sc. (hon.), U. Lagos (Nigeria), 1968; m. Doone Constantine, Sept. 6, 1947; children—Suzanne, Douglas, Jane, Doone. Intern Toronto Gen. Hosp., 1935-36; demonstrator pathology U. Toronto, 1936-37, Cambridge (Eng.) U., 1937-39; asst. resident pathology Johns Hopkins Hosp., 1939- 40; asst. prof. McGill U., 1945-46; prof. pathology, head dept. Queen's U., Kingston, Ont., 1946-51; prof. pathology, head dept. U. Toronto, 1951-61, dean medicine, 1961-66, v. p. health sciences, 1966- -; cons. Sick Childrens Hosp., Toronto, 1951-61; pathologist-in-chief Toronto Gen. Hosp., 1951-61. Mem. Canadian Forces Med. Council, 1961—. Served to maj. Royal Canadian Army Med. Corps, 1940-45. Recipient Coronation medal, 1953. Home: 73 Donwoods Dr Toronto 181 Ontario Canada

HAMILTON, JOHN MURRAY, mfg. exec.; b. London, Eng., Aug. 8, 1911 (father U.S. Citizen); s. William I. and Maud (Maitland) H.; grad. Kent Sch., 1929; B.A., Yale, 1933; student Advanced Mgmt. Program, Harvard, 1956; m. Happy Kitchel, Dec. 9, 1933; childrenGayle, John M., William A. With Binney & Smith, Inc. Crayola crayons, N.Y.C., now chmn., chief exec.; chmn. dir. Cosmic Crayon Co., Ltd. (Eng.); chmn. Permanent Pigments, Inco.; pres., dir. Can. Crayon Co., Ltd.; pres. Crayon, Water Color, & Craft Inst.,N.Y.C. Served from It. (j.g.) to lt. comdr., USNR, 1941-45. Episcopalian. Clubs: Yale, Union League (N.Y.C.). Home: 9 Binney Lane Old Greenwich CT 06870 Office: 380 Madison Av New York City NY 10017

HAMILTON, JOHN ROSS, business exec.; b. Winchendon, Mass., Oct. 3, 1924; s. Rollo Albert and May (Ross) H.; student Princeton, 1944-45; B.S., Rensselaer Poly. Inst., 1947; M. B.A., Harvard, 1949; m. Roberta Frances Lowitz, Sept. 17, 1949; childrenHeather Crawford, John Ross, Robert Anson, Hilary Beth. Financial analyst Lever Bros. Co., 1952-54; controller Barnes Engring. Co., Stamford, Conn.; 1954-57; asst. to treas. Colgate- Palmolive Internat., Inc., 1957-60; asst. treas. Lever Bros. Co., 1960- 66; treas. Bulova Watch Co., N.Y.C., 1966-68; dir. financial planning and analysis Crowell Collier & Macmillan, Inc., 1968-69, asst. controller, 1969-70; asst. treas. U.S. Industries, N.Y.C., 1970—; financial cons.; lectr. financial mgmt. Am. Mgmt. Assn. Active Boy Scouts Am. Served as ensign USNR, 1945-46. Mem. Delta Tau Delta. Clubs: Princeton, Harvard Business School (N.Y.C.); Middlesex Swimming (Darien). Republican. Mem. Dutch Reformed Ch. Home: 6 Tanglewood Trail Darien CT 06820 Office: 250 Park Av New York City NY 10017

HAMILTON, JOHN TAYLOR, II, banker; b. Cedar Rapids, Ia., May 26, 1909; s. James E. and Maude Helene (Hazeltine) H.; B.A., Princeton, 1934; m. Consuelo Lippincott Villa, Oct. 10, 1940; children—John Taylor III, Victoria, Helen. Dir., v.p. Mchts. Nat. Bank, Cedar Rapids, 1936-46, pres. 1946-66, chmn. bd., 1966—; dir. Am. Re-Ins. Co., City Nat. Bank Bd. pres. Banks Ia. Inc. Served as maj. USAAF. Republican, Episcopalian. Clubs: Cedar Rapids Country, Racquet and Tennis, Brook (N.Y.C.), Piping Rock. Home: 50 E 77 New York City NY 10021 Office: 222 2d Av SE Cedar Rapids IA 52401

HAMILTON, JOHN WILLIAMSON, oil co. exec., lawyer; b. Picton, Ont., Can., Nov. 17, 1911; s. Harries Alexander and Margaret Beatrice (Williamson) H.; student Royal Mil. Coll., 1930-34, Osgoode Hall, 1934-37; m. Dorothy C. Hogg, June 17, 1939; children—Ian, Peter, Hugh. Called to bar Ont., 1937, created Queen's counsel, 1952; joined Imperial Oil, Ltd., as asst. solicitor, 1938, returned as solicitor, 1945, asst. gen. counsel, 1947, counsel, 1948, general counsel, 1950; sr. v.p., dir. Imperial Oil Ltd.; v.p., dir. Interprovincial Pipe Line Co., dir. Trans Mountain Oil Pipe Line Co., Montreal Pipe Line Co., Portland Pipe Line Co. Bd. dirs. Wellesley Hosp. Joined Royal Canadian Navy, 1939; staff gunnery officer to dir. of warfare and tng., 1944; disch. as lt. comdr., 1945. Mem. Canadian Bar Assn., Ontario Cancer Inst., Alpha Delta Phi. Clubs: York; Toronto; Rosedale Golf. Home: 68 Highland Crescent Willowdale Ontario Canada Office: 111 St Clair Av West Toronto Ontario Canada

HAMILTON, JOSEPH HENRY MICHAEL, Jr., TV producer; b. Los Angeles, Jan. 6, 1929; s. Joseph Henry Michael and Marie (Sullivan) H.; grad. Los Angeles Conservatory Music and Arts, 1951; m. Carol Burnett, May 4, 1963; children—Kathleen, Dana, Joseph Henry Michael III, Jeffrey, Judith, John, Jennifer, Nancy, Carrie, Jody, Erin Kate. Musician and singer, 1948-51; engaged as a writer and asso. TV producer, 1951-57; TV producer, 1957—; prin. prodns. include Gary Moore Show, Julie and Carol at Carnegie Hall, Once Upon a Mattress, Carol and Company, Calamity Jane, Sammy and His Friends, Carol and Company II, Sammy Davis, Jr. Show, The Carol Burnett Show. Recipient Emmy award, 1962, 63. Roman Catholic. Clubs: Bel Air Country; Westchester Country (Rye, N.Y.). Home: 600 N Doheny Rd Beverly Hills CA 90210 Office: 132 S Rodeo Dr Beverly Hills CA 90210*

HAMILTON, LEE HERBERT, congressman; b. Daytona Beach, Fla., Apr. 20, 1931; s. Rev. Frank A. and Myra E. (Jones) H.; A.B. cum laude, DePauw U., 1952; traveling scholar Goethe U., Frankfurt au Main, Germany, 1953; J.D., Ind. U., 1956; m. Nancy Ann Nelson, Aug. 21, 1954; children—Tracy Lynn, Deborah Lee, Douglas Nelson. Admitted to Ind. bar, 1956, Ill. bar, 1957; partner firm Sharpnack & Bigley, Columbus, Ind., 1960-64; mem. 89th-92d Congresses, 9th Dist. Ind.; instr. contracts and negotiables Am. Banking Inst., 1960. Treas. Bartholomew County Young Democrats, 1960-63, pres., 1963-64; chmn. Bayh for Senator Com., 1962, Citizens for Kennedy Com., 1960. Chmn. Mayor's Commn. on Human Relations, 1962-63. Sec., bd. dirs. Columbus Growth, Inc., 1961-64; bd. dirs. Found. for Youth, Columbus Community Sch. Found., 1961-63, Ind. Meth. Home, 1963-64. Recipient Arthur L Trester award Ind. High Sch. Athletic Assn., 1948; Distinguished Service award Jr. C. of C., 1962. Mem. Am., Ind. bar assns., Columbus C. of C. (chmn. comml. redevel. com.). Methodist (ofcl. bd. 1959-64). Rotarian (bd. dirs.). Home: 4216 Peachtree Pl Alexandria VA 22304 Office: Ho of Reps Longworth Bldg Washington DC 20515 *

HAMILTON, LYMAN CRITCHFIELD, Jr., mfg. co. exec.; b. Los Angeles, Aug. 29, 1926; s. Lyman Critchfield and Lorraine (Gluck) H.; B.A., Principia Coll., Elsah, Ill., 1947; student U. Redlands, 1944-45; M.P.A., Harvard, 1949; m. Mary Shepard, June 25, 1949; children—William, Richard, Douglas, David. With Bur. Budget, 1950- 56, U.S. Civil Administrn. of Ryukyu Islands, 1956-60, Internat. Bank Reconstrn. and Devel., also Internat. Finance Corp., 1960-62; with Internat. Tel. & Tel. Corp., 1962—, treas., 1967—, v.p., 1968—, also officer, dir. affiliated companies; dir. Royal Bank Can. Bd. dirs. Internat. Center for N.Y. Served to ensign USNR, 1944-46. Home: 61 Norwood Av Upper Montclair NJ 07043 Office: 320 Park Av New York City NY 10022

HAMILTON, MALCOLM, harpsichordist, organist, educator; b. Victoria, B.C., Can.; student Victoria Coll.; B.A., M.A. in Harpsichord (Nat. Def. Edn. Act fellow 1959-62), U. Wash.; D.M.A. in Harpsichord (Koldofsky Meml. scholar), U. So. Cal. Has concertized extensively in B.C., Wash., Ore., Cal.; appeared with major chamber orchs. on West Coast; faculty U. So. Cal., Cal. State Coll. at Los Angeles, U. Cal. at Los Angeles; resident harpsichordist Los Angeles Chamber Orch.; recordings for Everest, RCA Victor. Licentiate, Royal Schs. Music, London, Eng.; asso. Royal Conservatory, Toronto, Can., Am. Guild Organists. Home: 18118 Coltman Av Gardena CA 90248 Office: U So Cal Los Angeles CA 90007

HAMILTON, MCDONALD KIRKWOOD, educator, oral surgeon; b. Alma, Mich., Feb. 21, 1930; s. Roy W. and Frances (Smith) H.; A.B., Alma Coll., 1952; D.D.S., U. Mich., 1956, postgrad., 1958-60; postgrad U. Md., 1957-58; m. Mary Anne Hafer, Oct. 27, 1956 children-Jean Anne, Karen Leah, McDonald Kirkwood. Mem. faculty U. Md. Sch. Dentistry, 1962—, prof. oral surgery, 1967—, chmn. dept., 1967—; pvt. practice, E. Lansing, Mich., 1965-67. Served to Capt. AUS, 1960-62. Recipient citation Md. Dental Assn., 1963, 65, Am. Dental Assn., 1964. Diplomate Am. Bd. Oral Surgery. Mem. Am. Dental Assn., Am. Soc. Oral Surgeons, Chalmers Lyons Acad. Oral Surgery. Home: 704 Laurel Lane Severna Park MD 21146

HAMILTON, ORRIS LEE, Judge; Prosser, Wash., Nov. 10, 1914; s. G. W. and Nellie J. (Lundquist) H.; LL.B., Am. U., 1940; m. Shirley I. Rosenberg, June 13, 1947; childrenDeea J., Christopher B., Denise L. Admitted to Wash. bar, 1940; atty. U.S. atty. gen.'s office, 1940-42; pvt. practice, Hamilton and Sensney-Prosser, Wash., 1946-48; pros. atty. Benton County, Wash., 1946-48; superior ct. judge Benton-Franklin counties, Wash., 1948-62; justice Supreme Ct. Wash., 1962-. Pres. Superior Ct. Judges Assn. Wash., 1960-61; del. Nat. Conf. Trial Judges, 1961. Mem. Wash. Child Welfare Adv. Com. 1960-62; del. for Wash., Little White House Conf. Children and Youth, 1959-60. Served with inf. AUS, 1942-46. Mem. Am., Wash., Benton-Franklin County bar assns., Am. Judicature Soc., Inst. Jud. Aminstrn., Am. Legion, V.F.W., Sigma Delta Kappa. Mason, Eagle. Home: Route 3 Box 417-A-1 Olympia WA 98501 Office: Temple of Justice Olympia WA 98501 *

HAMILTON, PHILIP BUTLER, paper converter co. exec.; b. Newton, Mass., May 14, 1910; s. Daniel B. and Rene (Green) H.; B.S., Coll. William and Mary, 1931; M.B.A., Harvard, 1933; m. Marion L. Wilson, June 10, 1946; children—Jane L., Ruth A. Dir. Dennison Mfg. Co., Framingham, Mass., 1952—, pres., 1966- -; dir. Dennison Eastman Corp.; dir. Dennison Internat. Co., Dunn Paper Co., Nat. Blank Book Co., State Street Bank & Trust Co., Dennison Mfg. Co. of Can., Ltd. Vice pres., chmn. mfrs. div. Nat. Stationery Office Equipment Assn., 1963-65. Trustee Babson Inst. Bus. Adminstrn.; bd. dirs. Newton YMCA. Served to lt. col. AUS, 1941-46. Decorated Bronze Star medal. Mason. Clubs: Brae Burn Country, Quisset Yacht, Falmouth, (Mass.); Woods Hole (Mass.) Golf.
Home: Newton MA 02158 Office: 300 Howard St Framingham MA 01702

HAMILTON, RAYMOND FOREST, clergyman; b. Muscatine, Ia., Feb. 24, 1905; s. Charles E. and Mary Eva (Wherry) H.; A.B., William Jewell Coll., 1932; D.D., Faith Theol. Sem., Elkins Park, Pa., 1961; m. Katherine Wilma Thomae, June 22, 1929; children—Philip Thomae, Betty Rose (Mrs. Paul Wise), David Bertus. Ordained to ministry Baptist Ch., 1933; student pastor, 1930-32; asst. pastor Central Bapt. Ch., Gary, Ind., 1933-39; pastor First Bapt. Ch., Pana, Ill., 1939-45, Calvary Bapt. Ch., Quincy, Ill., 1945-47, Burholme Bapt. Ch., Phila., 1947-51, Belden Av. Baptist Ch., Chgo., 1951-63; Am. sec. Internat. Council Christian Chs. 1963-68; pastor Temple Bapt. Ch., Portsmouth, O., 1969—. Mem. Council of Fourteen, Gen. Assn. Regular Bapt. Chs., 1935-63, chmn., 1946-48, 59-61. Bd. trustees Bapt. Bible Coll., Clark Summit, Pa., 1949—. Mem. Internat. Council Christian Chs. (treas. 1948-68), Am. Council Christian Chs. (pres. 1961- 63). Home: 1602 Carroll Av Portsmouth OH 45662 Office: 1148 Gallia St Portsmouth OH 45662

HAMILTON, ROBERT EARL, banker; b. Lincoln, Neb., May 25, 1927; s. Earl Smith and Stella (Qualset) H.; B.S., U. Neb., 1949; m. Arlene Noble, Aug. 8, 1948; children—Randall Allen, Janet Kaye, Robert Smith. Instr. agr. Brewster (Neb.) High Sch., 1949-50; sec., mgr. Sandhills Cattle Assn., Valentine, Neb., 1950-54; with Live Stock Nat. Bank (merged to become Central Nat. Bank 1965), Chgo., 1954-64, pres., 1964- 65, also dir., vice chmn.; dir. Central Nat. Chgo. Corp., 1969—. Mayor, Valentine, Neb., 1953-54. Served with USNR, 1945-46. Mem. Robert Morris Assos., Phi Kappa Psi. Mason (Shriner). Club: Union League, Bankers (Chgo.). Home: 906 S Adams St Hinsdale IL 60521 Office: 120 S LaSalle St Chicago IL 60603 *

HAMILTON, ROBERT OTTE, lawyer; b. Marysville, O., July 27, 1927; s. George Robinson and Annette (Ott) H.; A.B., Miami U., Oxford, O., 1950; LL.B., U. Mich., 1953; m. Phyllis Eileen Clark, Dec. 16, 1962; children—Nathan Clark, Scott Robert. Admitted to Ohio bar, 1953, since practiced in Marysville; pros. atty. Union County, O., 1957-67; city atty., Marysville, 1965—. Chpt. chmn. Union County A.R.C., 1968-71; mem. Mental Health and Mental Retardation Bd. Delaware, Morrow and Union Countries. Mem. Union County Republican Exec. Com., 1955-65, sec., 1955-60. Sec. Union County Hosp. Assn., 1968- -; bd. dirs. Union County Hist. Soc., 1958—, pres., 1961-63. Served with USNR, 1945-46. Mem. Ohio Bar Assn. (chmn. jr. bar sect. 1961), Jaycees (pres. 1954). Lutheran. Mason. Home: 432 W 6th St Marysville OH 43040 Office: 116 S Court St Marysville OH 43040

HAMILTON, ROBERT SMITH, railroad ofcl.; b. Benton, Ill., Feb. 7, 1919; s. Earl Raymond and Lela (Smith) H.; B.S. in Indsl. Engring., Ill. Inst. Tech., 1949; m. Mabel Matilda Ayers, Nov. 13, 1941. With Electro-Motive div. Gen. Motors Corp., 1949-52, Arthur Young & Co., 1952-54, N.Y.C. R.R., 1959-60; with So. Ry. Co., 1954-58, 60—, v.p. charge marketing and research, 1962-68, v.p. marketing, 1968-70, exec. v.p. marketing and planning, 1970—; pres. Central of Ga. Motor Transp., So. Region Distributive Services, Inc.; dir. Carolina & Northwestern Ry. Co., Fruit Growers Express, C. of Ga. Ry., G.S.&F. Ry., A.G.S. Ry., C.N.O. & T.P.Ry. Served with AUS, 1943-45. Mem. N.Am. Yacht Racing Union, Tau Beta Pi. Clubs: City Tavern, Internat., Metropolitan (Washington); Annapolis (Md.) Yacht; Fairfax (Va.) Rod and Gun. Home: 4201 Cathedral Av NW Washington DC 20016 Office: So Ry Co 15th and K Sts NW Washington DC 20005

HAMILTON, ROBERT SNYDER, newspaper exec.; b. Springfield, O., Jan. 13, 1912; s. Adelbert and Mary K. (Snyder) H.; B.S. in Edn., Wittenberg U., 1935; m. Marion Kiester, June 24, 1938; 1 dau., Winifred Susan. With Springfield Newspapers, Inc., 1935-, exec. v.p., gen. mgr., 1964-. Trustee Springfield Jr. Achievement, Springfield United Appeal Fund, Springfield Found. Served to lt. USNR, 1943-46. Mem. A.P. Assn., Asso. Newspaper Pub. Assn., Springfield C. of C. (past bd. dirs.). Home: 835 Tanglewood Dr Springfield OH 45504 Office: 202 N Limestone St Springfield OH 45501

HAMILTON, ROBERT WILLIAM, former state justice; b. Nashville, Ark., Mar. 24, 1899; s. Charles Putnam and Eddie (Lassiter) H.; student Alexander Coll., 1916-18; B.A., U. Tex., 1924, law student, 1925-27; m. Lois Rogers, May 4, 1929; childrenRobert William, Emily, Ann. Admitted to Tex. bar, 1927; practiced in Midland, 1935-50; county atty., Martin County, 1929-33; dist. atty., Tex., 1933- 35; dist. judge, Midland and Ector counties, 1950-53; chief justice 8th Ct. of Civil Appears, 1953-59; asso. justice Supreme Ct. of Tex., 1959-71. Mem. sch. bd. Midland, Tex., 1945-51. Democratic chmn. for Smith County, 1927-28, Midland County, 1937-38. Served as pvt. U.S. Army, World War I. Mem. Am., El Paso, Midland bar assns., State Bar of Tex. Episcopalian. Home: 600 W 10th St Austin TX 78701.

HAMILTON, SAMUEL CLINTON, steel co. exec.; b. Trenton, Mo., Aug. 23, 1906; s. Ross R. and Rachel L. (Dixon) H.; B.C.E., Ia. State Coll., 1929; m. Louisa M. Moen, Oct. 3, 1930; children—Samuel Clinton, Paul Robert, David Russell. Field engring. insp. Consoer, Older & Quinlan, cons. engrs., Chgo., 1928; with Chgo. Bridge & Iron Co., 1928—, successively engr. draftsman, constrn. engr., plant engr., dist. sales mgr., Birmingham. Ala., dist. sales mgr., Houston, 1928-57, v.p., gen. mgr. sales, Chgo., 1957-61, sr. v.p. comml., 1961-64, sr. v.p. finance, 1964-70, now dir.; treas., dir. Copeland Process Corp., Oak Brook, Ill., Oceanic Contractors, Inc.; dir. Bank Hinsdale (Ill.), The FluiDyne Engring. Co. (Mpls.), Horton Steel Works, Ltd. (Fort Erie, Can.), Chgo. Bridge & Iron Co., Ltd. (Caracas, Venezuela), Chgo. Bridge Ltd., Eng., Chgo. Bridge (Nederland) N.V., Fabricaciones, Ingernieria y Montajes, S.A., Mexico City, D.F., Chgo. Bridge Philippines; Chgo. Bridge Italiana Montaggi, chmn. bd.; v.p., dir. Walker Process Equipment, Inc., Aurora, Ill. Pres. bd. govs. Ia. State U. Found. Trustee Village of Hinsdale (Ill.). Mem. Am. Welding Soc. (chmn. Houston 1953), Houston, Birmingham jr. chambers commerce, Phi Kappa Phi, Sigma Chi. Presbyn. (elder). Clubs: Chicago, Chicago Golf. Home: 745 Cleveland Rd Hinsdale IL 60521 Office: 901 W 22d St Oak Brook IL 60521 *

HAMILTON, STUART, banker; b. Topeka July 12, 1920; s. Clay and Ernestine (Klein) H.; B.S., Northwestern U., 1946; M.B.A., U. Chgo., 1950; m. Marian Patten, Nov. 7, 1941; childrenMark R., Scott A. With No Trust Co., Chgo., 1946-, asst. auditor, 1957-60, auditor, 1960-63, v.p., auditor, 1963-65, v.p. operations, 1965-67, sr. v.p., 1967-. Served to lt. commdr. USNR, 1941- 46. Decorated Purple Heart, Silver Star. Mem. Nat. Assn. Bank Auditors and Comptrollers, Phi Beta Kappa, Delta Upsilon. Clubs: Executive Program, University (Chgo.); Lake Forest (Ill.). Home: 660 Bent Creek Ridge Deerfield IL 60015 Office: No Trust Co 50 S La Salle St Chicago IL 60690

HAMILTON, T. HERBERT, lawyer; b. Pitts., May 25, 1906; s. T. H. and Alice (Rodgers) H.; A.B., Pa. State U., 1928; LL.B., Duquesne U., 1933; m. Virginia Bowman, Jan. 2, 1937; childrenThomas Herbert III, Patricia B. Admitted to Pa. bar, 1936; with law dept. Koppers Co., Inc., Pitts., 1928-55; gen. counsel, sec. Blaw-Knox Co., Pitts., 1956—, v.p., 1964—; v.p., asst. sec. White Consol. Industries, Inc., 1969—. Home: 374 Fox Chapel Rd Pittsburgh, PA 15238. Office: 1 Oliver Plaza Pittsburgh PA 15222 11770 Berea Rd. Cleveland OH 44111

HAMILTON, THOMAS HALE, estate adviser; b. Marion, Ind., Aug. 4, 1914; s. Burr and Etta (Hale) Hamilton; A.B., DePauw U., 1936, LL.D., 1961; A.M., U. Chgo., 1940, Ph.D., 1947; L.H.D., Alfred U., 1960; LL.D., Rollins Coll., Colgate U., 1961, U. So. Cal., 1967, H.D., Oakland U., 1967; Sc.D., Temple U., 1968; m. Virginia Prindiville, June 1, 1940; children—Thomas P., Ann Hale. Fellow dept. polit. sci. U. Chgo., 1939-40, asst. dean univ. coll., 1946-48; instr. Lawrence Coll., 1940-42, asst. prof. govt., 1942-43, asst. dean, 1941-43; v.p., prof. polit. sci. Chatham Coll., 1948-53; asst. to dean basic coll. Mich. State U., 1954-56, v.p. acad. affairs, 1956-59; pres. State U. of N.Y., 1959-62; pres. U. Hawaii, 1963-68; spl. columnist Honolulu Sunday Star Bull. and Advertiser; adviser to Bishop Estate, 1971—. Dir. Hawaiian Telephone Co., Certified Investments, Far East Finanical Ltd., Pacific Outlets, Ltd.; chmn. bd. Certified Investment Fund. Pres. Hawaii Visitors Bur., 1968-71; mem. staff Commn. on Implications of Armed Services Edn. Programs, 1946-47; cons. to Exploratory Com. on Financing Higher Edn. and Research, 1948; cons. Council for Study Higher Edn. Fla., 1955; commn. instrn. and evaluation Am. Council Edn., 1957-59; adv. bd. coll. presidents Nat. Scholarship Service and Fund Negro Students, 1959-68; mem. exec. com. Gov.'s Adv. Council Indsl. Research and Devel., 1960-63; cons. U. Philippines, 1958- 59; chmn. bd. govs. Kamehameha Schs. Served from ensign to lt., USNR, 1943-46. Recipient Am. Acad. Achievement award in edn., 1965; Paul Bachman award for promotion of understanding in the Pacific and Asia, 1969. Mem. Am. Polit. Sci. Assn., Am. Society Pub. Adminstrn., Am. Assn. U. Profs.,

Am. Studies Assn., Fgn. Policy Assn. (sec. bd. dirs. Pitts. 1950-53), World Affairs Forum (dir. Pitts. 1951-52), Hawaiian Hist. Soc., Am. Council Edn. (dir., past chmn. com. higher edn. and civil def.). Author: The Armed Services and Adult Education (with Houle, Yale and Burr), 1948; The Teaching Profession Comes of Age (with others), 1954; The Basic College of Michigan State (with others), 1955; The Government Study of the University of the Philippines (with others), 1958; The Democracy of Excellence, 1964. Home: 615 Elepaio St Honolulu HI 96816 Office: 33 S King St Honolulu HI 96813

HAMILTON, THOMAS JEFFERSON, newspaper corr.; b. Augusta, Ga., Sept. 20, 1909; s. Thomas Jefferson and Daisy May (Ramsey) H.; A.B. magna cum laude, U. Ga., 1928; M.A. (Rhodes scholar), Oxford U., 1930, student Sch. English Lit., 1931; m. Ethel Mathews, Nov. 3, 1934; children—Anne Elizabeth (Mrs. John K. Jessup, Jr.), Thomas Jefferson, William B. W. Reporter, Atlanta Jour., 1931-34, Washington bur. A.P., 1934-36, London bur., 1936-37; reporter London bur. N.Y. Times, 1937-39, Madrid corr., 1939-41, staff Washington bur., 1941, 45-46, S.A., 1942, chief UN bur., 1946-65, Bonn bur., 1965-67, Geneva bur., 1967—; UN corr. Freedom and Union, 1946-65. Served to lt. USNR, 1942-45. Decorated officer Legion of Honor (France); comdr. Order of Merit (Chile); recipient George Polk Meml. award for outstanding internat. reporting, 1955, 56; co-winner $500 Deadline Club awards for UN coverage, 1962, 63. Mem. UN Corrs. Assn. (chmn. 1947-48, exec. 1948-50, 51-56, pres. 1950-51), Council Fgn. Relations, Soc. Silurians, Phi Beta Kappa, Phi Delta Theta, Sigma Delta Chi. Clubs: Century Assn. (N.Y.C.); Metropolitan (Washington). Author: Appeasement's Child; The France Regime in Spain, 1943. Address: care NY Times Palais des Nations Geneva Switzerland

HAMILTON, THOMAS MACPHERSON, lawyer; b. Winfield, Kan., June 26, 1915; s. Calvin Blythe and Pearl (Heinecken) H.; A.B., Southwestern Coll., Winfield, Kan., 1934; LL.B., Stanford, 1937; m. Charlotte Kuhrts Haughton, Feb. 25, 1955; children—Robert M., Valerie, Scott, Bruce, Timothy. Admitted to Cal. bar, 1937, since practiced in San Diego; partner firm Luce, Forward, Hamilton & Scripps, 1959—. Vice pres. Cohu Electronics, Inc., 1957-59; dir. San Diego Hockey Club; partner San Diego Basketball Club; pres. Del Mar Thoroughbred Club; dir. ESO Co., John Hine Pontiac, Walker-Scott Corp. Mem. San Diego County Med. Instns. Commn., 1961-68. Trustee Scripps Clinic and Research Found.; bd. visitors Stamford, also pres. Law Sch. Fund. Served to lt. comdr. USNR, 1941-45. Decorated Bronze Star (3) with combat V. Mem. Am., San Diego County (pres. 1949) bar assns., Cal. State Bar (chmn. commn. corps. 1966). Home: 2350 6th Av San Diego CA 92101 Office: Charter Oil Bldg San Diego CA 92101

HAMILTON, THOMAS STEWART, hosp. dir.; b. Detroit, June 19, 1911; s. J.T. Stewart and Lucy (Safford) H.; grad. Philips Exeter Acad., 1930; A.B., Williams Coll., 1934, D.Sc., 1969; postgrad. Harvard, 1934-36; M.B., Wayne U., 1938, M.D., 1939; D.Sc. (hon.), Trinity Coll., 1962; m. Amy Washburn, June 30, 1937; childrenAnn Washburn (Mrs. Benjamin E. Cooper), Barbara (Mrs. R. Throop Bergh), Jeanne (Mrs. Arthur W. Frank III). Intern, asst. resident Harper Hosp., Detroit, 1938-40; gen. practice medicine, Truro, Cape Cod, Mass., 1940-41; asst. dir. Mass. Gen. Hosp., Boston, 1941-42, 45-46; dir. Newton-Wellesley Hosp., Newton Lower Falls, Mass., 1946-54; exec. dir. Hartford (Conn.) Hosp., 1954—, pres., 1969—. Trustee Soc. for Savs., 1961-70; dir. Phoenix Mut. Life Ins. Co. Commr. Joint Commn. Accreditation Hosps., 1960-66; mem. cancer 1970; Distinguished Alumnus award Wayne State U. Sch. Medicine, 1970. Fellow Am. Coll. Hosp. Adminstrs. (regent New Eng. 1953-57); control com. USPHS, 1964-70. Regent U. Hartford, 1962-68; trustee McLean Fund, 1968—. Served from capt. to lt. col., M.C., U.S. Army, 1942-45; adj., exec. officer 6th Gen. Hosp. Recipient Distinguished Service awards Am. Hosp. Assn., 1969, 1970; Distinguished Alumnus award Wayne State U. Sch. Medicine, 1970. Fellow Am. Coll. Hosp. Adminstrs. (regent New Eng. 1953-57); mem. A.M.A. (mem. internship rev. com.), Mass., Conn., Hartford County med. assns., Assn. Am. Med. Colls. (sec.-treas. 1968-70), Council Teaching Hosps. (chmn. 1970), Am. (pres., chmn. bd. trustees 1962-63), Conn. (pres. 1966), Mass. (pres. 1951) hosp. assns., Soc. Med. Adminstrs. (pres. 1968-70), Med. Adminstrs. Conf., Marine Hist. Soc. Clubs: Hartford, Hartford Tennis; Williams (N.Y.C.); Masons Island Yacht. Author articles in field. Home: 50 Bayberry Hill Rd Avon, CT 06001. Office: 80 Seymour St Hartford CT 06115

HAMILTON, WILLIAM, Jr., meter co. exec.; b. Phila., 1908. Chmn. Canadian Meter Co., Milton, Ont., Can.; pres., dir. Am. Meter Co. div. Singer Co. Home: 1484 Hunter Rd Rydal PA 19046 Office: 13500 Philmont Av Philadelphia PA 19116 *

HAMILTON, WILLIAM BERRY, Jr., shipping co. exec.; b. Birmingham, Ala., Apr. 4, 1929; s. William Berry and Nettie (Whatley) H.; B.A., Vanderbilt U., 1951; m. Jean Lucile Patteson, Feb. 1, 1951; children—Jean Lucile, Ann Elizabeth, William Berry III. Accountant, Hiwassee Constructors, Chattanooga, 1952; certified pub. accountant O.E. Johnson & Assos., Chattanooga, 1952-54; controller, gen. mgr. Spl. Products Co., Inc., Chattanooga, 1954-59; v.p., controller Ryder Truck Lines, Inc., Jacksonville, Fla., 1959-65; v.p. finance Chgo. Rawhide Mfg. Co., 1965-67; v.p., controller treas. Sea-Land Service Inc., Elizabeth, N.J., 1967-69, exec. v.p. adminstrn., 1969—, also dir.; v.p., treas., asst. sec. McLean Industries, Inc., Elizabeth, 1968—; dir. Gulf Fla. Terminal Co., Inc., Indsl. Opportunity, Inc., Mediterranean Container Service Italia S.p.A., Sea-Land Service-Alaska, Inc., Sea-Land Caribe, Inc., Sea-Land Containerships Ltd., Sea-Land Orient Ltd., Gulf Puerto Rico Lines, Inc., Sea-Land Internat., Inc., Sea-Land Freight, Inc., Donmac Corp., Containership Stevedoring, Inc., Island Terminals, Inc., Mail Express, Inc., Equipment, Inc.; instr. accounting U. Chattanooga, 1953-54. Served with USAF, 1951-52. Recipient Guest Lectr. award U. Fla., 1965. Mem. Am. Inst. C.P.A.'s, Financial Execs. Inst., Am. Trucking Assn. (nat. bd. dirs., chmn. methods and procedures nat. accounting 1959—), Nat. Def. Transp. Assn., Nat. Assn. Accountants (named most valuable mem. Jacksonville 1959-60; chpt. v.p., bd. dirs. 1960-63), Tenn. Soc. C.P.A.'s, Am. Accounting Assn., Nat. Officer Mgmt. Assn., Am. Mgmt. Assn., U.S. Power Squadron, USCG Aux., Phi Delta Theta, Pi Delta Epsilon. Kiwanian. Clubs: Fla. Yacht (Jacksonville); Ponte Vedra (Ponte Vedra Beach, Fla.); Sea Bright (N.J.) Beach; Vanderbilt Alumni (N.Y.C.). Home: 53 Wardell Av Rumson NJ 07760 Office: Sea-Land Service Inc Fleet and Corbin Sts Elizabeth NJ 07207

HAMILTON, WILLIAM COWLES, fgn. service officer; b. New Britain, Conn., July 23, 1922; s. Harold Ernest and Helen Mary (Cowles) H.; B.A., Yale, 1947; M.A., 1949, Ph.D., 1955; m. Jeanne Betty Lawton, June 22, 1946. Instr. polit. sci. N.J. Coll. Women, New Brunswick, 1950-51; intelligence research specialist Dept. State, 1951-57; assigned U.S. Fgn. Service, embassy Burma, 1957-59; dep. spl. asst. internat. affairs Supreme Allied Comdr. Europe, 1960-62; 1st sec., chief polit. sec. embassy, Laos, 1962-64; dep. dir. Far East region Internat. Security Affairs, Dept. Def., 1964- 66; country dir. Laos. Dept. State, 1966-67; counselor of embassy for polit. affairs, Thailand, 1967-70; mem. Sr. Seminar in Fgn. Policy, 1970-71; minister Am. embassy, Philippines, 1971—. Mem. Am. Fgn. Service Assn., Phi Beta Kappa. Home: 4348 N 26th St Arlington VA 22207 Office: care Fgn Service Mail Room Dept State Washington DC 20520

HAMILTON, WILLIAM GORDON, educator; b. Laclede, Mo., Jan. 14, 1910; s. Lee E. and Flossie A. (Rachford) H.; A.B., Am. U., 1930; A.M., Harvard, 1931, Ph.D., 1935; m. Jane Reid Ritchie, Apr. 12, 1941; children—Jane A., William Gordon. Head biology Kemper Sch., 1935-39; instr. biology State U. N.Y. at Geneseo, 1939-47; prof., chmn. scis. State U. N.Y. at Potsdam, 1947-70, prof., chmn. biology, 1971—. Home: RD 2 Potsdam NY 13676

HAMILTON, WILLIAM GRAHAM, Jr., govt. ofcl.; b. Bklyn., Feb. 27, 1925; s. William Graham and Dorothy Adelia (Littlefield) H.; student Cornell U., 1943-44; A.B. in Pub. and Internat. Affairs, Princeton, 1948; postgrad. Am. U., 1949, Bologna Center, Sch. Advanced Internat. Studies, Johns Hopkins, 1962-63; m. Maxine DeWoody Taylor, Feb. 25, 1950; children—Jean Pollock, Ellen Littlefield, Graham Taylor, Carol Newton, Allison Kerr. Information specialist U.S. Bur. Reclamation, Boise, 1949-50; information specialist USIA, Washington, 1952-58, regional affairs officer, 1965-68, policy officer for Western Europe, 1968-70; aid information officer USIS, Djakarata, Indonesia, 1958-62; dep. pub. affairs officer U.S. Mission to European Communities, Brussels, Belgium, 1963-65; counselor for pub. affairs U.S. Mission to NATO, Brussels, 1970—. Mem. personnel com. Internat. Sch., Djakarta, 1960-62; v.p. Montgomery County Assn. for Lang. Handicapped children, 1968-69. Served with USMCR, 1943-46, to capt., 1951-52. Recipient Meritorious Honor award USIA, 1968. Mem. Am. Fgn. Service Assn., Phi Beta Kappa. Office: US Mission to NATO NATO Hdqrs Brussels 1110 Belgium Home: 17 Av de Putdael Brussels 1150 Belgium

HAMILTON, WILLIAM HUGHES, Jr., educator; b. Evanston, Ill., Mar. 9, 1924; s. W.H. and Helen (Anderson) H.; B.A., Oberlin Coll., 1946; B.D., Union Theol. Sem., 1949; Ph.D., U. St. Andrews (Scotland), 1953; m. Mary Jean Golden, June 11, 1949; childrenRoss, Donald, Catherine, Patrick, Jean. Ordained to ministry, 1949; prof. theology Colgate Rochester Div. Sch., 1953-68; prof. religion U. Rochester, 1955-68; prof. religion New Coll., Sarasota, Fla., 1968-70; prof. dean Coll. Arts and Letters, Portland Ore. State U., 1970—. TV writer, producer, broadcaster, 1956—. Served to ensign USNR, 1943-46. Author: The Christian Man, 1957; Modern Readers Guide to the Gospels, 1960; New Essence of Christianity, 1961; Radical Theology and The Death of God (with T.J.J. Altizer), 1966. On Taking God Out of the Dictionary, 1971. Home: 222 SW Harrison Portland OR 97201

HAMILTON, WILLIAM KENNON, physician; b. Guthrie Center, Ia., Dec. 15, 1922; s. Orren G. and Marie (Moberly) H.; B.A., U. Ia., 1943, M.D., 1946; m. Shyrlee Florence Cole, July 14, 1946; children—Douglas Cole, Debra Kay. Intern, St. Luke's Hosp., Duluth, Minn., 1946-47; resident anesthesiology U. Ia. Hosp., 1949-51, clin. instr., 1951-53, asst. prof., 1953-55, asso. prof., 1955- 58, prof., chmn. dept. anesthesia, 1958-67, chief anesthesia Univ. Hosp., 1958-67; prof. chmn. anesthesia U. Cal. Med. Sch., San Francisco, 1967—; practice medicine, specializing anesthesiology, Duluth, 1951; chief anesthesia VA Hosp., Iowa City, 1952-53, cons. VA, 1953—. Mem. adv. bd. Med. Specialities, Inc., 1963-67. Served to capt. AUS, 1947-49. Diplomate Am. Bd. Anesthesiology (bd. dirs.). Mem. Soc. Acad. Anesthesia Chmn., Assn. U. Anethetists, Soc. Exptl. Biology and Medicine, Am. Fedn. Clin. Research, Sigma Xi. Contbr. articles profl. jours. Home: 1 Los Cerros Greenbrae CA 94904 Office: U Cal Med Center San Francisco CA 94122

HAMILTON, WILLIAM L., Jr., fgn. service officer; b. Adrian, Minn., Mar. 26, 1910; s. William L. and Myra (Newton) H.; student Ft. Dodge (Ia.) Jr. Coll.; m. Janey Storer, Nov. 7, 1936; children—William T., Diana S., John A. Desk editor Ft. Dodge (Ia.) Messenger and Chronicle, 1932-44; dir. OWI, Union South Africa, 1945-46; pub. affairs attache Am. legation, Pretoria, Union South Africa, 1946-47; information officer Am. embassy, ndon, 1947-49; internat. affairs officer Brit. Commonwealth div. Dept. State, Washington, 1950-55; 1st sec., consul Am. embassy, Tel Aviv, 1955-58; officer in charge Lebanon-Israel affairs, Washington, 1958-62; counsul gen., Jerusalem. 1962-63, formerly consul gen., Thessaloniki, Greece. Home: 5208 Glenwood Rd Thessaloniki Greece *

HAMILTON, WILLIAM STANLEY, furniture mfr.; b. Indpls., Dec. 25, 1908; s. B. F. and Nell (Pruitt) H.; ed. pub. schs.; m. Mary Elaine Jeffers, Nov. 10, 1934; childrenHarold Philip, Carol Sue (Mrs. Warren M. Pringle), William Stanley. Co-founder Hamilton Cosco, Inc., Columbus, Ind., 1936, chmn. exec. com.; dir. Ind. Gas & Water Co. Trustee Franklin (Ind.) Coll. Mem. Columbus C. of C. (exec. com.). Republican. Clubs: Kiwanis, Columbia (Indpls.); Harrison Lake Country (Columbus). Home: 3210 Sycamore Ct Columbus IN 47201 Office: Hamilton Cosco Inc State and Gladstone Sts Columbus IN 47201 *

HAMILTON, WILLIS BEATTY, stock broker; b. Paris, Ill., Feb. 8, 1916; s. Charles and Elizabeth (Beatty) H.; A.B., U. Ill., 1937; m. Mary Louise, June 17, 1939; children-Sally, James, Stephen, Ann, Michael. Mng. partner A.C. Allyn & Co., Chgo., 1946-63; gen. partner Francis I. du Pont & Co., Chgo., 1963- -. Mem. Chgo. Bd. Trade. Served to lt. col. USAAF, 1941-46. Clubs: Executive Bond, University (Chgo.) Home: 181 Kenmore Av Elmhurst IL 60126 Office: 122 S LaSalle St Chicago IL 60603

HAMITER, JOE BUSBEY, former justice La.; b. Shreveport, La., Nov. 16, 1899; s. Emmett Wyche and Mary (Busbey) H.; LL.B., La. State U., 1923; m. Hattie Wells Courtney, Sept. 21, 1942. Pvt. practice, Shreveport, 1923-35; rep. of Caddo Parish, La. Legislature, 1928-35; judge Ct. Appeal, 2d Circuit La., 1936-42; asso. justice La. Supreme Ct., 1943-70, chief justice, 1970; ret., 1970. Democrat. Baptist. Mem. Am. Legion, 40 and 8, Kappa Alpha, Phi Kappa Phi, Phi Delta Phi. Mason (K.T., Shriner). Home: 344 Edinburgh St Metairie LA 70001

HAMLETT, BARKSDALE, ret. army officer, univ. pres.; b. Hopkinsville, Ky., Dec. 30 1908; student Lindsey Wilson Jr. Coll.; B.S., U.S. Mil. Acad., 1930; grad. F.A. Sch., Ft. Sill, Okla., 1936, Balloon Squadron, 1940; grad. Ecole de Guerre, France, 1946, Nat. War Coll., Washington, 1949; m. Frances Underwood, 1931; one dau., Otilia Crume. Commd. 2d lt. F.A., 1930, advanced through the grades to general, 1962; assigned 12th F.A., Ft. Sam Houston, Tex., 1930-32, 11th F.A., Schofield Barracks, T.H., 1932-35, 18th F.A., Ft. Sill, Okla., 1934, 15th F.A., Ft. Sam Houston, 1939; asst. arty. officer II Corps, 1942-43; asst. G-3 Army Ground Forces, Washington, 1943-44; arty. comdr. 16th Armored Div., 1944-45; comdr. 190th F.A. Group Europe, 1945, asst. arty. officer Arty. Theatre Gen. Bd., 1945; gunnery instr. Arty. Sch., Ft. Sill, 1946, dir. dept. gunnery, 1947, dir. tng., 1947- 48; exec. officer G-4 Sect. Far East Command, 1949-51, chief plans and operations div., 1951, arty. comdr. 24th Inf. Div., Korea, 1951-52; asst. for planning coordination Office Dep. Chief Staff for Plans, Army Hdqrs., 1952-55; arty. comdr. VII Corps, U.S. Army Europe, Heidelberg, Germany, 1955-56; comdg. gen. 10th Inf. Div., 1956-57, U.S. comdr. Berlin, 1957-59; asst. dep. chief of staff for mil. operations Dept. Army, 1959-61, dep. chief of staff, 1961-62, vice chief of staff, 1962- 64, ret.; pres. Norwich U., Northfield, Vt., 1965-. Decorated Bronze Star Medal, Silver Star, Legion of Merit with 2 clusters, D.S.M. Office: Office of Pres Norwich U Northfield VT 05663

HAMLETT, SAMUEL BARKSDALE, educator; b. Farmville, Va., July 23, 1921; s. Samuel Hales and Nell (McCaughan) H.; B.A., U. Tex. at Austin, 1947, M.A., 1949, Ph.D., 1966; m. Ethel Ruth Greer, Mar. 23, 1951; 1 son, Samuel Stephen. Tchr. pub. schs., Alice, Tex., 1948-51, Austin, 1952-56; mem. faculty U. Tex. at Arlington, 1956—, prof. govt., 1969—, chmn. dept., 1966—. Chmn. bd. dirs. Wesley Found., U. Tex. at Arlington, 1968-70. Served with AUS, 1942-45. Decorated Air Medal, Purple Heart. Mem. Am. Polit. Sci. Assn., Southwestern Social Sci. Assn. Author: (with Luther Hagard, Jr. and August Spain) Legislative Redistricting in Texas, 1965. Home: 1304 W Lavender Lane Arlington TX 76013

HAMLEY, FREDERICK GEORGE, U.S. judge; b. Seattle, Oct. 24, 1903; s. Charles E. and Zoe N. (Stetson) H.; LL.B. cum laude, U. Wash., 1932; LL.D. (hon.), Gonzaga U., Spokane, 1967; m. Marjorie E. Wood, Sept. 19, 1932; children—June E., Arlene L. Admitted to Wash. bar, 1932; practice in Seattle, 1932-38; supt. Seattle Water Dept., 1938; asst. dist. counsel Bur. Reclamation, 1938-40; personal legal adviser Gov. Sanglie, 1941; dir. pub. service Wash., 1941- 43; asst. gen. solicitor Nat. Assn. R.R. and Utilities Commrs., Washington, 1943-44, gen. solicitor, 1945-49; judge Wash. Supreme Ct., 1949-56, chief justice, 1955-56; judge U.S. Ct. of Appeals, 9th Circuit, 1956—. Chmn. Gov.'s Statewide Com. on Ednl. TV, 1954-55; chmn. Wash. Jud. Council, 1955-56. Mem. Seattle City Council, 1935- 38. Mem. Am. Bar Assn., Am. Judicature Soc., Inst. Jud. Adminstrn., Phi Beta Kappa, Order Coif, Phi Alpha Delta. Home: 125 Sutro Heights San Francisco CA 94121 Office: US Ct of Appeals 7th and Mission Sts PO Box 547 San Francisco CA 94101

HAMLIN, ARTHUR TENNEY, librarian; b. Haverhill, Mass., Feb. 8, 1913; s. Christopher Robert and Edith (Redman) H.; A.B., Harvard, 1934, grad. work, 1936-37; B.L.S., Columbia, 1939; m. Pauline L. Randolph, Sept. 16, 1939; children—Peter R., Sally R. (Mrs. Richard Price), and Rebecca R. Hamlin. Assistant in Harvard Coll. Library, 1934-36, curator Poetry Room, 1936-38, freshman proctor, adv., 1934-38; asst. gen. reference desk and econs. div. N.Y. Pub. Library, 1939-40; asst.-at-large U. of Pa. Library, 1940- 42, chief service to readers and asst. librarian, 1945-49; exec. sec. Association of College and Reference Libraries, 1949-56; univ. librarian U. Cin., 1956-68, prof. bibliography, 1962-68; dir. libraries, prof. Temple Univ., Phila., 1968—; a founder, dir. Junto, Phila., 1941-42, 45- 48; dir. Midwest Inter-Library Center, 1956-62; Fulbright lectr. U. Pavia, Italy, 1961-62; Fulbright research scholar U. Birmingham, Eng., 1966-67. Bd. dirs. City Charter Com., Cin., 1964-68. Research analyst Office Naval Intelligence, 1942-45. Served as capt. U.S. Army Res., 1949-53. Mem. A.L.A. (chmn. bldg. and equipment sect., 1957-58, chmn. adult services spl. projects com. 1959-60, mem. council 1958-62, 64-68, spl. rep. to flooded Italian libraries, 1967, chmn. spl. com. to aid Italian libraries 1967-69, Ohio Coll. Assn. (pres. libraries sect. 1960- 61), Ohio (chairman development committee, member exec. board; v.p., pres. elect 1965), Pa. (chmn. conf. local arrangements com. 1969-70) library assns., Association College and Reference Libraries (chmn. grants com. 1956-58, 64-66), Bibliog. Soc. Am., Alpha Beta Alpha. Episcopalian. Clubs: Franklin Inn, Harvard (Phila.); Grolier (N.Y.C.). Author: Harvard in Cincinnati, 1969. Contbr. profl. jours. Home: 1250 W Columbia Av Philadelphia PA 19122 Office: Paley Library Temple U Philadelphia PA 19112

HAMLIN, CONDE, mgmt. cons.; b. St. Paul, July 1915; s. Condé and Pearl (Terry) H.; grad. Culver Mil. Acad., 1932; m. Dorothy Armstrong. Nov. 22, 1940; children- Condé III, Jane (Mrs. Richard J. Schulten), William A. Regional sales mgr. Ozalid div. Gen. Aniline & Film Corp., 1946-52; v.p. charge sales DeWalt Inc., Lancaster, Pa., 1952-54, exec. v.p., 1954, pres., dir., 1955-61; pres., dir. Motors Inc., Lancaster, DeWalt Canada Ltd., Guelph, Ont.; mgmt. and marketing cons., 1962-63; v.p. Chgo. Pneumatic Tool Co., 1963-67; pres. Jay V. Hall & Assos., Inc., N.Y.C., 1968-. Served from 2d lt. to lt. col. AUS. 1940-46. Republican. Episcopalian. Club: Army and Navy (Washington). Home: 96 Leroy Av Darien CT 06820 Office: 250 Park Av New York City NY 10017

HAMLIN, JOHN F., real estate broker; b. Chgo., Apr. 30, 1902; s. George J. and Harriet (Eldridge) H.; B.S., Princeton; m. Dorothy Jaeckel, June 21, 1927; 1 son, John F. Architect, 1927-34; real estate broker, N.Y.C., 1934-; now chmn. bd., pres. Douglas L. Elliman & Co.; trustee Empire Savs. Bank. Gov., v.p. Real Estate Bd. N.Y.; dir. Phipps Houses. Home: 45 Sutton Place South New York City NY 10022 Office: 15 E 49th St New York City NY 10017

HAMLIN, RICHARD EUGENE, coll. pres.; b. Royal, Ia., June 2, 1925; s. Fred E. and Nancy Jane (Schuetz) H.; student Drury Coll., 1943; B.S., George Williams Coll., 1949; M.A., U. Omaha, 1952; Ph.D., U. Neb., 1956; m. C. Joan Dahl, Aug. 14, 1949; childrenRobert E., Elizabeth Ann. Asst. camp dir., camp counselor, asst. youth sec. YMCA, 1946-49, exec. sec. South Omaha (Neb.) YMCA, 1949-51, program sec., adult edn. dir., Omaha, 1951-53, asso. dir. research nat. bd., 1953-61; pres. George Williams Coll., 1961-; chmn. bd. dir. Bank of Yorktown, Lombard, Ill. Tchr. summer conf. Am. Youth Found., summer sch. U. Omaha. Mem. Am., N.Y., Ill. psychol. assns., Assn. Secs. YMCA, Alpha Omicron Alpha (past pres.) Conglist. Clubs: University, Economic (Chicago). Author: Hi-Y Today, 1955; A New Look at YMCA Physical Education, 1957. Co-editor: YMCA Yearbook, 1958-61. Address: 555 31st St Downers Grove IL 60515

HAMLIN, ROBERT HENRY, mgmt. cons.; b. Cambridge, Mass., Apr. 2, 1923; s. Howard E. and Margaret E. (Henry) H.; A.B. summa cum laude, Ohio State U., 1944; B.S.M., Northwestern Med. Sch., 1945, B.M., 1946, M.D. with honors, 1947; M.P.H. magna cum laude, Harvard, 1952, LL.B., 1953; m. Beate Kraschewski, Dec. 16, 1960; 1 son, Andrew Werner. Intern, Johns Hopkins Hosp., Balt., 1946-47; cons. Mass. commn. reporting, preparing and promulgating legislation on pub. and mental health and pub. welfare, 1950-53; 1st asst. to commnr. pub. health Mass., 1952-53; asst. prof. legal medicine Harvard Law Sch., 1952-57, lectr. pub. health law and adminstrn. Harvard Sch. Pub. Health, 1952-57, asso. prof. pub. health adminstrn., 1959-62, Roger Irving Lee prof. pub. health, 1962-65, chmn. dept. pub. health practice, 1963-65; v.p. Booz, Allen and Hamilton, mgmt. cons., 1965-67; ind. mgmt. cons., 1968; chmn. bd. MACRO Systems, Inc., N.Y.C., 1969—. Cons., Rockefeller Found., 1959-61; staff dir. spel. commn. Harvard health services 1953-54; mem. U.S. Commn. for UNESCO; dir. pub. health, Brookline, Mass., 1953-57; cons. Hoover Commn. II, 1954-55; asst. to sec. health, edn. and welfare, 1957-59; vis. lectr. pub. health adminstrn. and law Harvard, 1957-59; U.S. del. 10th session gen. conf. UNESCO, Paris, 1958; pub. health adminstrn. cons. to pvt. orgns., state and local govts. Served as apprentice seaman USN, 1943-46, lt. M.C. (j.g.), USNR, 1947-49. Diplomate Am. Bd. Preventive Medicine. Fellow Am. Pub. Health Assn.; mem. Mass. Med. Soc., Mass. Pub. Health Assn., Phi Beta Kappa, Phi Eta Sigma, Alpha Epsilon Delta, Alpha Omega Alpha, Delta Omega. Contbr. articles profl. publs. Office: 135 E 55th St New York City NY 10022*

HAMLIN, WALTER BERGEN, state justice; b. New Orleans, Mar. 13, 1898; s. Charles Hector and Henrietta Mary (Bergen) H.; student Soule Coll., New Orleans, 1914-16; LL.B., Loyola U., New Orleans, 1919; m. Stella Malynn, Apr. 3, 1923. Admitted to La. bar, 1919; gen. practice, New Orleans, 1919-48; judge Civil Dist. Ct., Orleans Parish, 1948-58; asst. city atty. New Orleans, 1943-46; asso. justice Supreme Ct. of La., 1958-. Democratic candidate for atty. gen., La., 1932. served with U.S. Army, World War I.; mem. USNR, 1935-42. Home: 2735 Palmer Av New Orleans LA 70118 Office: 301 Loyola Av New Orleans LA 70112

HAMM, CHARLES, educator, musicologist, composer; b. 1925; ed. U. Va., Princeton; student of Randall Thompson, Martinů, Edward Cone. Former mem. faculty Cin. Conservatory Music, also Newcomb Coll. of Tulane U.; prof. music U. Ill. at Urbana, 1963—. Guggenheim fellow, 1967-68; Fulbright research grant, 1967-68. Author: A Chronology of the Works of Dufay, 1964; Opera, 1966. Composer: six operas; Sinfonia, 1954; Mobile for Piano and Tape; Portrait of John Cage (piano and 3 tape records); Round; Canto; also chamber piano and vocal works. Address: 1214 W Church St Champaign IL 61820*

HAMM, EDWARD FREDERICK, Jr., bus. exec.; b. Chicago, Mar. 27, 1908; s. Edward Frederick and Sarah (Meek) H.; student N. Shore Country Day Sch. Winnetka, Ill., 1926, Dartmouth Coll., 1930; m. Joy Elizabeth Fairman, June 23, 1934; children—Julie Fairman, Thornton Edward, Martha Joy. Pres., treas. Traffic Service Corp. since 1933; pub., Traffic World, Traffic Bull., Daily Traffic World since 1944; president of Coll. of Advanced Traffic, Inc., 1945—; consultant, mag. sect., printing and pub. div. W.P.B., 1944-45; pres. Acad. Advanced Traffic, Traffic Service Corp.; mem. distbn. council U.S. Dept. of Commerce. Apptd. mng. dir. Inter-State Commerce Commn., 1953. Mem. Chicago Bus. Papers Assn. (pres., 1937), Asso. Bus. Papers, Inc. (pres. 1948-49), Advt. Fedn. of Am. (dir., 1948), Am. Soc. of Traffic and Transportation (founder). Republican. Episcopalian. Clubs: Chicago (Chgo.); Metropolitan, Burning Tree, Chevy Chase, Nat. Press (Washington). Home: 2500 Virginia Av NW Washington DC 20037 Office: 815 Washington Bldg Washington DC 20005

HAMM, FRANK COLEMAN, physician, surgeon; b. Belle Plaine, Ia., Sept. 17, 1901; s. John Andrew and Anna (Coleman) H.; student U. Notre Dame; M.D., U. Mich., 1925; M.S., U. Minn., 1931; m. Lisbeth Higgins, June 22, 1935; children—Frank Coleman, Charles John. Intern Kings County Hosp., Bklyn., 1925-27; chief attending urologist Bklyn. Hosp., 1945—; clin. asst. prof. U. State N.Y., 1946—, asso. prof. urology, 1953-56, prof. urology, 1956-63, chmn. dept., 1953-63, chmn. residency rev. com. on urology, 1963-66; surgeon-in-chief Bklyn. Cumberland Med. Center, 1963-66; cons. urologist VA, Maimonides and Lutheran hosps. Served from maj. to lt. col. M.C., AUS, 1942-46. Diplomate, mem. Am. Bd. Urology. Fellow A.C.S.; mem. Am. Assn. Genito-Urinary Surgeons (pres.), Clinical Soc. Genito-Urinary Surgeons, N.Y. Urological Soc., Internat. Soc. Urology, Urosurgeons, Phi Beta Pi. Clubs: MashomacK Fish and Game, Gardiner's Bay Country (Shelter Island, N.Y.); Engineers' (N.Y.C.); The Heights Casino, University (N.Y.C.). Contbr. profl. jours. Home: Gardner's Bay Dr Shelter Island NY 11964 Office: 121 DeKalb Av Brooklyn NY 11201

HAMM, HARRY CHARLES, newspaper editor; b. Wheeling, W.Va., May 26, 1923; s. Harry Lee and Anna (Kirchner) H.; student parochial schs.; m. Mary Elizabeth Haddox, Feb. 14, 1948; children—Marilyn, Harry C., Denise, Mary Heather, Jonathin, Christopher, Kathryn Camille, Robert, Matthew, Gregory, Gretchen, James. City editor Wheeling (W.Va.) News-Register, 1948-51, mng. editor, 1951-56, editor, 1956—; also editor-in- chief Ogden Newspapers, Inc. Sec. Slum Clearance and Redevel. Authority Wheeling, 1954—. Served with inf. AUS, World War II. Decorated Purple Heart with oak leaf cluster; named Citizen of the Month for Wheeling, 1953; recipient ann. award Wheeling Jr. C. of C., 1954. Mem. W.Va. Press Assn., Ohio Valley Press Club (past pres.), UPI Editors W.Va. (past pres.). Club: Civitan. Home: 21 Hamilton Av Wheeling WV 26003 Office: 1500 Main St Wheeling WV 26003

HAMM, IRVING WENDELL, educator; b. Port Washington, N.Y., May 26, 1909; s. Frederick W. and Mary J. (Tate) H.; student Bucknell U., 1926-27; M.E., Cornell U., 1932, M.M.E., 1933; m. Madora I. Rumsey, Oct. 6, 1934; 1 dau., Linda E. With Ritter Dental Co., 1933-34; successively engaged in mfg. engring., personnel and adminstrv. work, war plant design and operations E. I. duPont de Nemours Co., 1934-54; dir. mfg. Carborundum Co., Niagara Falls, N.Y., 1954-61, v.p., 1956-61, v.p., gen. mng. dir. German plants, 1961-64; asso. prof. engring. Bradley U., Peoria, Ill., 1964-67, also dir. grad. program engring. adminstrn., prof. Coll. Bus. Adminstrn., Niagara (N.Y.) U., 1967—; non resident lectr. Cornell U. Active A.R.C., Boy Scouts Am., Girl Scouts Am.; bd. dirs. Niagara Falls Community Chest, chmn., 1959; chmn. Indsl. Devel. Niagara Falls Area. Mem. Am. Soc. M. E., Am. Soc. Advancement Mgmt., Am. Assn. Engring. Edn., Indsl. Relations Research Assn., Am. Mgmt. Assn., Niagara Falls C. of C., Sigma Phi Epsilon, Alpha Kappa Psi, Alpha Pi Omega. Clubs: Rotary, Niagara Falls Country; Youngstown (N.Y.) Yacht; Illinois Valley Yacht and Canoe. Home: Mountain View Dr Lewiston NY 14092 Office: Coll Bus Adminstrn Niagara Univ Niagara NY 14109

HAMM, WILLIAM DOW, petroleum cons.; b. Bentonville, Ark., Sept. 2, 1900; s. William O.C. and Elizabeth Inez (Maxey) H.; B.S., U. Okla., 1922; m. Helen Irene Berry, Oct. 11, 1922; children—William Dow, Richard Berry. With Shell Oil Co., 1922-42, chief geologist, acting mgr. exploration, Houston, 1940-42; with Atlantic Refining Co., Dallas, 1942-67, gen. mgr. domestic and fgn. exploration, 1952-60, v.p., gen. mgr. producing dept., 1960-65, exec. v.p., 1964-67, exec. v.p., mem. exec. com. Atlantic Richfield Co. (merger Atlantic Refining Co. and Richfield Oil Corp.), 1966-67; dir. Arabian Shield Devel. Co., Globe Universal Scis., Inc. Mem. Dallas Citizen's Council, 1960-66, Dallas Crime Commn., 1960-66; pres. Beta Found., 1945-67. Bd. dirs. Dallas Council World Affairs, 1950-71; bd. devel. So. Meth. U., 1963-68; bd. trustees U. Okla. Found., 1950-71. Recipient Distinguished Service citation U. Okla., 1965. Mem. A.A.A.S., Am. Assn. Petroleum Geologists, Am. Petroleum Inst. (hon. dir.), Soc. Exploration Geophysicists, Dallas C. of C., Mid-Continent Oil and Gas Assn., Beta Theta Pi. Presbyn. Clubs: Brook Hollow Golf, Chaparral, Petroleum (Dallas). Home: 4907 DeLoache St Dallas TX 75220 Office: First Nat Bank Bldg Dallas TX 75202

HAMM, WILLIAM GIDEON, surgeon; b. Gainesville, Ga., June 26, 1901; s. Ernest Percy and Theodore (Moreno) Ham; B.S., U. Ga., 1921; M.D., Washington U., 1925; m. Katherine Cathcart, Aug. 28, 1935. Intern, asst. resident, resident surgeon Barnes Hosp., 1925-30, asst. clin. surgery, 1926-30; practice of medicine, specializing in plastic surgery with Dr. Vilray P. Blair, St. Louis, 1930-35, plastic, reconstructive surgery, Atlanta, 1935—; now asst. prof. surgery Emory U. Med. Sch., Atlanta; med. cons. Armed Forces. Served from lt. comdr. to capt., M.C., USNR, 1942-46. Diplomate Am. Bd. Plastic Surgery, Nat. Bd. Med. Examiners. Mem. Am. Soc. Plastic and Reconstructive Surgery (pres. 1955), Fulton County Med. Soc. (pres. 1953), A.C.S., Am., So. surg. assns., Soc. Plastic and Reconstructive Surgery, Am. Assn. Plastic Surgeons, Internat. Surg. Soc., Soc. Univ. Surgeons, Phi Beta Kappa, Phi Delta Theta, Nu Sigma Nu, Alpha Omega Alpha. Rotarian, Kiwanian (hon. Knoxville, Tenn.). Author numerous sci. articles on plastic reconstructive surgery. Home: 202 Valley Rd NW Atlanta GA 30305 Office: 1930 Peachtree St NW Atlanta GA 30309*

HAMMAKER, PAUL M., educator; b. Dayton, O., Jan. 25, 1903; s. Wilbur Emory and Willamine (Weihrauch) H.; B.C.S., U. Ill., 1925, LL.D., MacMurray Coll., 1957; m. Patricia Curry, Sept. 5, 1929 (dec. 1955); children—Robert, John, David; m. 2d, Adrienne V. S. Stokes, June 15, 1956 (dec. 1970). With Marshall Field & Co., 1943-57, divisional v.p., 1948, gen. mdse. mgr., sr. v.p., asst. gen. mgr. Chgo. and suburban stores, until 1957; exec. v.p., gen. mgr. Montgomery Ward, 1957-59, mem. bd. dir., 1958-61, pres., 1959-61; dir. The Fair Store, Montgomery Ward Real Estate Corp., Montgomery Ward Credit Corp., Standard T Chem. Co., Inc. Prof. bus adminstrn. Grad. Sch. Bus. Adminstrn., U. Va., 1962—. Mem. Alpha Tau Omega, Beta Gamma Sigma. Conglist. Clubs: Farmington Country (Charlottesville, Va.); University, Chicago, Economic, Commercial, Mid-Am. (Chgo); Westmoreland Country (Winnetka, Ill.). Home: 15 Farmington Dr Charlottesville VA 22901

HAMMAN, ROBERT L., educator. Prof., head dept. econs. Drexel U., Phila. Office: Drexel U 32d and Chestnut Sts Philadelphia PA 19104*

HAMMAR, LESTER EVERETT, pharm. mfr.; b. Tillamook, Ore., Dec. 15, 1927; s. Leo E. and Harriet L. (Parsons) H.; B.S., Ore. State U., 1950; M.B.A., Washington U., 1964; m. Margrit Steigl, May 9, 1964; children—Lawrence, Thomas, Stephanie. With Montsanto Co., 1952-69, controller Monsanto-Europe, 1966-69; v.p., controller Smith Kline & French Labs., Phila., 1969—; dir. Hammar's Uniforms, Inc. Served to 1st lt., F.A., AUS, 1951-52. Mem. Nat. Assn. Accountants, Financial Execs. Inst. Presbyn. Home: 735 Woodcrest Rd Radnor PA 19087 Office: 1500 Spring Garden St Philadelphia PA 19101

HAMMARSKJOLD, KNUT, assn. exec.; b. Geneva, Switzerland, Jan. 16, 1922; M. Philosophy, Stockholm (Sweden) U.; married; 2 sons. Joined Swedish Fgn. Service, 1946; attache Swedish embassy, Paris, France, 1947-49; assigned Fgn. Office, Stockholm, 1949-51; attache embassy, Vienna, Austria, 1951-52; 2d sec. embassy, Moscow, USSR, 1952-54, 1st sec., 1954-55; 1st sec. Fgn. Office, 1955-57; head fgn. relations dept. Swedish Civil Aero. Bd., 1957- 59; counsellor embassy, Paris, also dep. head Swedish delegation OEEC, 1959-60; dep. sec.-gen. European Free Trade Assn., Geneva, 1960-66; minister plenipotentiary, dir. gen. Internat. Air Transp. Assn., 1966—. Decorated comdr. Order Lion (Finland); Order Falcon (Iceland); comdr. Orange Nassau (Netherlands); Order Black Star (France); grand officer Order Al- Istiqlal (Jordan). Hon. fellow Canadian Aeros. and Space Inst.; hon. academician Mexican Acad. Internat. Law; mem. Inst. Transp. (London). Author articles polit., econ. and aviation topics. Address: 1155 Mansfield St Montreal 113 Quebec Canada also PO Box 315 1215 Geneva 15 Airport Switzerland

HAMMARSTEN, JAMES FRANCIS, educator, physician; b. Grey Eagle, Minn., Mar. 25, 1920; B.S., U. Minn., 1943, M.D., 1944; m. Apr. 15, 1944; three children. Intern U. Okla. Hosps., 1944-45; resident Minn. Hosps., VA Hosp., Mpls., chief med. service VA Hosp., Mpls., 1949-53; chief med. service VA Hosp., Oklahoma City, 1953-62; chief medicine, St. Paul-Ramsey Hosp., 1962-66; vice chmn. medicine dept. U. Okla. Med. Center, 1966-67, head dept., 1967—; asst. prof. medicine U. Minn., 1949-53, prof., 1962-66; from asst. prof. medicine to prof., 1953-62, 1945-49; asst. Carl Puckett prof. medicine, 1966-67, head dept. medicine U. Okla., 1967—. Mem. Nat. Adv. Heart and Lung Council NIH, 1970-72; dir. Am. Bd. Internal Medicine mem. long range planning com. oral exam. com., written exam. com. com. advanced exams. Served with AUS, 1945-47, USAF, 1953. Diplomate Am. Bd. Internal Medicine. Hon. fellow Am. Coll. Chest Physicians; fellow A.C.P.; mem. Am. Fedn. Clin. Research (mem. nat. council 1959, chmn. midwest sect. 1960), Am. Heart Assn. (mem. coms.), Am. Thoracic Soc. (councilor-at-large, pres. 1969-70), Nat. Tb and Respiratory Disease Assn. (dir.), A.A.A.S., Am. Clin. and Climatol. Assn., Soc. Exptl. Biology and Medicine, Okla. State Heart Assn. (dir. 1967-69), Okla. Thoracic Soc. (pres. 1960), So. Soc. Clin. Investigation, Central Soc. Clin. Research (pres. 1967-68), Minn. Soc. Internal Medicine, Alpha Omega Alpha, Sigma Xi. Chmn. med. sch. sect. editorial bd. Jour. Okla. State Med. Soc., 1959-62. Contbr. articles to profl. jours. Address: Med Center and Sch Medicine Univ Okla Oklahoma City OK 73104

HAMMEL, RICHARD FRANK, architect; b. Owatonna, Minn., May 30, 1923; s. Erwin William and Helen (Kasper) H.; B.Arch., U. Minn., 1944; M.Arch., Harvard, 1947; m. Elizabeth Craven Lupton, Nov. 4, 1945 (div. 1964); children—Stephen Jay, Anne Lupton; m. 2d, Bette Jones Munro, July 24, 1970. Draftsman, R.E. Windsch, Honolulu, 1947-50; asst. prof. Sch. Architecture, asst. adv. architect U. Minn., Mpls., 1950-51; cons. architect St. Paul pub. schs., 1951-53; partner Hammel & Green, 1953-56; pres. Hammel, Green & Abrahamson, Inc., St. Paul, 1956-70; partner Hammel, Green & Abrahamson, N.Y.C. Served with USNR, 1944-46. Mem. A.I.A., Minn. Soc. Architects, Tau Beta Pi. Home: 13709 Wood Lane Minnetonka MN 55343 Office: 2675 University Av St Paul MN 55114

HAMMER, ARMAND, petroleum co. exec.; b. N.Y.C., May 21, 1898; s. Julius and Rose (Robinson) H.; B.S., Columbia, 1919, M.D., 1921; m. Frances Barrett, Jan. 26, 1956; 1 son by previous marriage, Julian A. Pres. A. Hammer Pencil Co., Moscow, USSR, 1925-30, Hammer Galleries, Inc., N.Y.C., 1930- -, J.W. Dant Distilling Co., N.Y.C. and Dant, Ky., 1943-54; pres., chmn. bd. MBS, 1957-58; pres., chmn. bd. Occidental Petroleum Corp., Los Angeles, 1957, now chmn., chief exec. officer, dir.; dir. 1st Bank & Trust Co., Perth Amboy, N.J., 1949-61, City Nat. Bank, Beverly Hills, Cal., 1962—. Fla. Nat. Bank of Jacksonville. Chmn., Am. Aid to France, 1947; mem. Citizens Food Com., 1946-47; mem. Cardinal's Com. of Laity for Cath. Charities, N.Y.C., 1946-48. Bd. govs. Monmouth (N.J.) Meml. Hosp., 1946-58, Eleanor Roosevelt Cancer Found., 1960—; trustee Eleanor Roosevelt Meml. Found., 1963—; adv. bd. Inst. Peace, 1950-54. Recipient Humanitarian award Eleanor Roosevelt Cancer Found., 1962. Mem. N.J. Aberdeen Angus Assn. (pres. 1948-49), Alpha Omega Alpha, Mu Sigma, Phi Sigma Delta. Author: Quest of the Romanoff Treasure, 1936. Home: PO Box 107 Colts Neck NJ 07722 Office: 595 Madison Av New York City NY 10022 also 10431 Wyton Dr Los Angeles CA 90024 also 10889 Wilshire Blvd Los Angeles CA 90024*

HAMMER, CARL, Jr., educator; b. Salisbury N.C., Nov. 26, 1910; s. Carl and Carrie (McCanless) H.; B.A. magna cum laude, Catawba Coll., 1934; student U. N.C., 1934-35; M.A., Vanderbilt U., 1936; Ph.D., U. Ill., 1939; student U. Jena (Germany), summer 1938; m. Mae Armes, Nov. 25, 1939; children—Carl III, William Andrew. Teaching asst. German, U. Ill., 1936- 39; instr. German, Vanderbilt U., 1939-45, asst. prof., 1945-47; asso. prof. La. State U., 1947-55, prof., 1955-64; prof. German, chmn. German instrn. Tex. Tech. U., 1964—, chmn. dept., 1967—, Horn prof. German, 1967. Chmn. Goethe Bicentennial celebration La. State U., 1949; guest speaker Goethe Festival, So. Ill. U., 1949, vis. prof., summers 1961, 66; vis. prof. Mont. State U., summers 1962, 67. Rep. for Nashville on Am. Com. Relief German Needy, 1946-47. Recipient Schiller Sesquicentennial medal, 1956; Ford fellow, 1953-54. Mem. Modern Lang. Assn., Am. Assn. Tchrs. German (pres. Tex. 1965-67), South Central Modern Lang. Assn. (asso. editor for German (S. Central) bull. 1955, 59- 63), Phi Beta Kappa, Delta Phi Alpha. Lutheran. Author: Rhinelanders on the Yadkin, rev. edit., 1965; (Longfellow) Golden Legend and Goethe's Faust, 1952; (Goethe) Dichtung and Wahrheit, 1945; also articles. Editor: Goethe After Two Centuries, 1952; Studies in German Literature, 1963. Home: 2123 71st St Lubbock, TX 79412.

HAMMER, CHARLES LAWRENCE, educator; b. Buffalo, N.Y., June 30, 1922; s. Charles L. and Maxine (Burdick) H.; B.A., U. Mich., 1948, M.S., 1950, Ph.D., 1953; m. Hazel Churchill Mills, Aug. 14, 1948; children—David, Alison, Carla, Bonnie. Instr. physics U. Mich., 1953-54; mem. faculty Ia. State U., 1954—, asso. prof., 1959-61, prof., 1961—; cons. Allis Chalmers Mfg. Co., Milw., 1956-68. Mem. Community Theater, Ames, 1964—, Choral Soc., 1966—. Chmn. Ia. Democratic Conf., 1970—. Bd. dirs. Midwestern U. Research Assn., Chgo. Served to 1st lt. USAAF, 1942-45. Decorated D.F.C. with oak leaf cluster, Air Medal with 3 oak leaf clusters; PTO. Fellow Am. Phys. Soc.; mem. Sigma Xi, Phi Beta Kappa, Phi Kappa Phi. Contbr. profl. jours. Home: 1222 Scholl Rd Ames IA 50010

HAMMER, JAN, Jr., jazz pianist, composer; b. Prague, Apr. 17, 1948; s. Jan and Vlasta (Pruchova) H.; student Acad. Arts, Prague, 1966-67. Came to U.S., 1968. Concerts and club dates with own group or as a guest soloist around Europe, 1968, in U.S., 1968—; movie and TV music in Prague. Recipient 2d prize Internat. Competition Jazz, Vienna, 1966. Address: 97 Hemenway St Boston, MA 02115.

HAMMER, PHILIP GIBBON, urban economist; b. Phila., Sept. 18, 1914; s. John Levering and Emma (Gibbon) H.; A.B., U. N.C., 1936; student Grad. Sch. Arts and Scis., Harvard, 1936-37, Littauer Sch. Pub. Adminstrn., 1938-39; m. Jane Amelia Ross, Aug. 27, 1937; children—Philip, Thomas Ross, Michael Levering. With Dept. Agr., 1939-42, State Dept., 1942; asst. to dir.-gen. UNRRA, 1942-45; pres. South Assos., Atlanta, 1945-47; econ. cons. Joseph K. Heyman Co., Atlanta, 1947-50; dir. Atlanta Met. Planning Commn., 1950- 53, Fund for Advancement Edn., 1953; pres. Hammer and Co. Assos., now Hammer, Greene, Siler Assos., 1954—, Urban Design and Devel. Corp., 1971—; v.p. planning and devel. Collaborative Internat., 1970—. Mem. Atlanta Met. Planning Commn., 1956-58; v.p. Potomac Inst., Washington, 1967—; chmn. Nat. Capital Planning Commn., 1968-69; mem. President's Task Force on Suburban Problems, 1967- 68; mem. D.C. Bicentennial Commn., 1969—. Bd. dirs. Atlanta Urban League, 1958-61, Atlanta C. of C., 1958-60, So. Regional Council, 1956-58, Urban Design and Devel. Corp., 1969—, Planning and Devel. Collaborative Internat., 1969—; trustee Clark Coll., Atlanta, 1969—. Mem. Am. Soc. Planning Ofcls. (bd. dirs. 1964-67, pres. 1968-69), Delta Psi. Clubs: Commerce (Atlanta); University (Washington). Home: 5152 Manning Pl NW Washington DC 20016 Office: 1140 Connecticut Av NW Washington DC 20036

HAMMER, PRESTON CLARENCE, computer scientist, educator; b. Rockford, Mich., Oct. 12, 1913; s. Adam and Ada (Zimmerman) H.; A.B. magna cum laude (fellow), Kalamazoo Coll., 1934; A.M. (fellow), U. Mich., 1935; Ph.D., Ohio State U., 1938; m. Hilda Knight, Aug. 6, 1939; children—Phoebe Ann, Frances Jean, Nick Adam, Kathryn Molly, Arthur Stephen. Instr., U. Mich., 1938-40; instr. Ore. State Coll., 1941-42, asst. prof., 1942-44, asso. prof., 1946-47; supr. quality control Lockheed Aircraft Corporation, 1944-45; supr. computing and applied mathematics Los Alamos Sci. Lab., 1947-52; prof. U. Wis., 1952-65, dir. Numerial Analysis Lab., 1952-62, traveling faculty fellow Europe, 1959-60, chmn. dept. computer scis., 1961-65; prof., head computer sci. dept. Pa. State U., 1965—; vis. prof. research U. Cal., 1962-63. Cons. Sandia Corp., Nat. Sci. Found.; Pres. Madison Turners, 1958-60. Fellow A.A.A.S.; mem. Society for Communication, Am. Math. Soc., Math. Assn. Am. (lectr. 1960-), Inst. Math. Statisticians, Assn. Computing Machinery (chmn. com. curriculum in computer sci. 1970—), Soc. Indsl. and Applied Mathematics (lectr. 1962—, council 1962-65), Soc. Symbolic Logic, Am. Assn. U. Profs., Wiskundig Genootshap, Circolo Mathematico di Palermo, Sigma Xi. Baptist. Editor: The Computing Laboratory in the University, 1957; Advances in Mathematical Systems Theory, 1969. Editorial bd. Mathematics of Computation, 1960-63, Communication Jour., 1962—, Math. System Theory Jour. Home: 331 W Fairmount Av State College PA 16801 Office: Computer Sci Dept Pa State U University Park PA 16802

HAMMER, RUTH, publicist; b. Chicago, Aug. 30, 1911; d. Benjamin and Frances (Halbren) Hammer; student Northwestern Sch. Journalism, 1929-30; Licence es lettres, Sorbonne, 1936. Began career as woman's feature writer International News Service, 1931-33, United Press, 1933-35; dir. pub. relations Lord & Taylor, 1940-49; pres., owner Ruth Hammer Assos., 1949- -. Mem. Fashion Group, Shoe Women's Execs. Club (v.p.). Club: Overseas Press. Address: 141 E 33d St New York City NY 10016

HAMMER, SIGMUND IMMANUEL, educator, geophysicist; b. Webster, S.D., Aug. 13, 1901; s. Ludvig E. and Laura (Anderson) H.; B.A., St. Olaf Coll., 1924; Ph.D., U. Minn., 1929; m. Norma Lucille Johnson, Nov. 28, 1925; children—Sigmund L., Laura Blanche (Mrs. William D. Inglis II), John P., Paul L., Kirsten Norma (Mrs. D.E. Gardner), Douglas J., Ludvig E. Geophysicst, Gulf Research & Devel. Co., Pitts., 1929-46, sect. supr., 1946-66, research asso., 1966-67; prof. geology and geophysics dept. geology and geophysics U. Wis., Madison, 1967—; adj. mem. grad. faculty U. Pitts., 1946-67; cons. NSF; chmn. adv. com. Mem. Nat. Acad. Sci.-Nat. Acad. Engring. Joint Adv. Com. to U.S. Coast and Geodetic Survey, 1963-66, adv. com. to Environmental Sci. Services Adminstrn., 1967-70. Mem. Am. Phys. Soc., Phys. Soc. Pitts., A.A.A.S., Pa. Acad. Sci., Am. Assn. Petroleum Geologists, Am. Geophys. Union, Soc. Exploration Geophysicists, Internat. Assn. Geodesy and Geophysics, Am. Geol. Inst., Assn. Mexicana de Geofisicos de Exploration, Geosci. Information Soc., Sigma Xi. Club: Cosmos (Washington). Contbr. articles profl. publs. Developer theories of gravitational field of earth and applications to search for mineral accumulations. Home: 4634 Tokay Blvd Madison WI 53711

HAMMER, THOMAS ALOYSIOUS, Jr., mfr. paper; b. N.Y.C., Sept. 26, 1917; s. Thomas Aloysious and Jeannette (McLaughlin) H.; A.B., Williams Coll., 1939; M.B.A., Harvard, 1941; m. Patricia Fitz Gerald, Apr. 27, 1946; 1 dau., Tricia. With Mead Corp., Dayton, O., 1957—, treas., 1961-69, v.p., 1969—; asst. treas. Ga. Kraft Co., Mead Board Sales Inc.; dir. 1st Nat. Bank of Dayton. Treas. Mead Found. Served with USNR, 1943-46. Mem. N.A.M., Chi Psi. Clubs: Harvard Business School (exec. com.), City (Dayton); Sycamore Creek Country (Springdale, O.). Home: Upper Bellbrook Rd RR 1 Bellbrook OH 45305 Office: 118 W 1st St Dayton OH 45402

HAMMER, THORVALD FREDERICK, mfr. malleable iron and steel; b. Branford, Conn., Dec. 5, 1893; s. Alfred E. and Cornelia (Foster) H.; student Yale, 1918; m. Lucy Taylor, Feb. 19, 1927; 1 dau., Alexandra. Pres., gen. mgr. Malleable Iron Fittings Co., Branford,

Conn., 1935—, chmn. bd.; dir. Branford br. 1st New Haven Nat. Bank, So. Conn. Gas Co.; regional dir. Am. Mut. Ins. Co. Chmn. bd. trustees James Blackstone Meml. Library, Branford; trustee Berkshire Sch., Sheffield, Mass. Home: Cherry Hill Branford CT 06405 Office: Malleable Iron Fittings Co Branford CT 06405*

HAMMER, WILLIAM, educator; b. Kerpen, Germany, Aug. 27, 1909; s. Johann and Thea (Erger) H.; student U. Bonn, 1928-30, U. Paris, 1930-31, U. Cologne, 1931-33; A.M., U. Chgo., 1936, Ph.D., 1937; m. Alma A. Munz, June 15, 1939; 1 dau., Roberta Elise (Mrs. William B. Sellen). Came to U.S., 1935, naturalized, 1940. Instr. German, Ill. Inst. Tech., 1937-42; asso. prof. Evansville (Ind.) Coll., 1945-46; asst. prof. U. Man. (Can.), 1946-49; mem. faculty Carleton Coll., Northfield, Minn., 1949—, prof. German, 1950—, chmn. dept., 1949-60. Fellow U. Chgo., 1936-37. Mem. Renaissance Soc. Am., Am. Soc. Reformation Research, Classical Assn. Can., Bibliog. Soc. Can. Lutheran. Author: Latin and German Ecomia of Cities, 1937; Die Melanchthonforschung im Wandel der Jahrhunderte, 3 vols., 1967-69; also articles. Home: 811 E 2d St Northfield MN 55057

HAMMERSCHMIDT, ANDREW LEWIS, mfg. exec.; b. Medina, O., Oct. 13, 1914; s. W.L. and Pearle (Sellers) H.; B.S. in Elec. Engring., Ohio State U., 1938; m. Hazel Cox, Nov. 28, 1936; children—Sue, Carol, James. Engr. radio sta. WBNS, 1934- 38; tech. supr. Ohio State U. radio sta. WOSU, 1938-41; devel. engr. NBC, N.Y.C., 1941-48, TV operations supr., Cleve., 1948-52, asst. dir. color TV systems devel., N.Y.C., 1952-54, asso. dir. TV tech. operations, 1954-55, v.p., chief engr. NBC, 1955-56, v.p. staff engring. and facilities adminstrn., 1956-61; chief engr. Missile and Surface Radar div. RCA, 1961-64, mgr. program operations, 1964-65, mgr. operations plans Broadcast and Communications Products div., 1965-66, mgr. electronic rec. products dept., 1966-68, div. v.p. broadcast engring. and product mgmt., 1968-70, div. v.p. broadcast systems, 1970—. Mem. exec. bd. Burlington County council Boy Scouts Am. Recipient Distinguished Alumnus award Ohio State U., 1964. Mem. I.E.E.E. (sr.), Eta Kappa Nu. Presbyn. Clubs: Rotary, Moorestown Field. Home: 181 Ramblewood Rd Moorestown NJ 08057 Office: RCA Bldg 15-7 Camden NJ 08101

HAMMERSCHMIDT, JOHN PAUL, congressman; b. Harrison, Ark., May 4, 1922; s. Arthur Paul and Junie (Taylor) H.; student The Citadel, 1938-39, U. Ark., 1940-41, Okla. State U., 1945-46; m. Virginia Sharp, Oct. 11, 1948; 1 son, John Arthur. With Hammerschmidt Lumber Co., Harrison, 1946—, pres., 1959—; dir. Harrison Fed. Savs. & Loan Assn., First Nat. Bank Harrison. Mem. Harrison City Council, 1948, 60, 62; mem. 90th- 92d Congresses, 3d Dist. Ark. Chmn. Ark. Rep. Party, 1964-66; mem. Rep. Nat. Finance Com., 1960-64. Served as pilot USAAF, World War II; CBI. Decorated Air medal with 4 oak leaf clusters, D.F.C. with 3 oak leaf clusters. Mem. Ark. Lumber Dealers Assn. (past pres.), Southwestern Lumbermens Assn. (past pres.), Harrison C. of C. (named Man of year 1965), Am. Legion. Presbyn. (elder). Mason (32, Shriner). Elk, Rotarian (past pres. Harrison). Home: 1701 Kent St Arlington VA 22209 Office: Cannon House Office Bldg Washington DC 20515

HAMMERSCHMIDT, WILLIAM WARNER, nat. affairs analyst, writer; b. Medina, O., May 31, 1916; s. William Louis and Pearle (Sellers) H.; B.A., Ohio State U., 1936, M.A., 1937; Ph.D., Cornell U., 1940; m. Dorothy Lois Daugherty, Sept. 7, 1938. Instr., asst. prof. physics Norwich U., 1941-47; tutor St. John's Coll., 1947-51; sci. warfare adviser Weapons Systems Evaluation Group, Office Sec. Def., 1951- 55; operations analyst Hdqrs. USAF, 1955-58; chief atomic energy div. Office Sec. Def., 1958-62; exec. sec. Def. Sci. Bd. Dept. Def., 1962-70. Served from ensign to lt. (j.g.), USNR, 1944-46. Fellow A.A.A.S.; Am. Phys. Soc., Am. Philos. Assn., N.Y. Acad. Sci., Washington Acad. Sci., Phi Beta Kappa, Phi Kappa Phi, Sigma Pi Sigma. Author: Whitehead's Philosophy of Time, 1947; also articles, studies. Home: 7818 Holmes Run Dr Falls Church VA 22042

HAMMES, GEORGE ALBERT, bishop; b. LaCrosse, Wis., Sept. 11, 1911; s. August Isidore and Caroline (Schumacher) H.; student St. Lawrence Sem., Mt. Calvary, Wis., 1925-31, St. Louis Prep. Sem., 1931-33, Kenrick Sem., St. Louis, 1933- 34, Sulpician Sem., Washington, 1934-37; M.A., Cath. U. Am., 1937; L.H.D. (hon.), Mt. Senario Coll., Ladysmith, Wis., 1969. Ordained priest Roman Cath. Ch., 1937; sec. to Bishop Alexander J. McGavick, LaCrosse, Wis., 1937-43; instr. Latin and religion Aquinas High Sch., LaCrosse, 1937-42; instr. ethics and religion St. Francis Sch. Nursing, LaCrosse, 1937-46; chancellor Diocese of LaCrosse, 1943- 60; pastor Parish of St. Leo the Great, West Salem, Wis., 1957-60; bishop of Superior, Wis., 1960—. Officialis, Diocesan Matrimonial Tribunal, LaCrosse, 1943-60; diocesan dir. Cath. Lawyers' Guild, LaCrosse, 1956-60, pres. Tri-state Interfaith Devel. Enterprise, Superior, 1970—. Adv. bd. Viterbo Coll., LaCrosse, 1954—, Cath. Social Service, La Crosse, 1954-60; trustee Mt. Senario Coll., Wis., 1969—; bd. dirs. Nat. Tech. Assistance Found., Mpls., 1971—. Author article. Home: Gitchinadji Dr Superior WI 54880 Office: 1201 Hughitt Av Superior WI 54880

HAMMES, GORDON G., educator; b. Fond du Lac, Wis., Aug. 10, 1934; s. Jacob and Betty (Sadoff) H.; A.B., Princeton, 1956; Ph.D., U. Wis., 1959; m. Judith Ellen Frank, June 14, 1959; children—Laura Anne, Stephen R., Sharon Lyn. NSF postdoctoral fellow Max Planck Inst. für physikalische Chemie, Göttingen, Germany, 1959-60; from instr. to asso. prof. Mass. Inst. Tech., 1960-65; prof. Cornell U., 1965—, chmn. dept. chemistry, 1970—. Mem. biochemistry tng. grant com. NIH. Mem. Am. Chem. Soc. (award biol. chemistry 1967; editorial bd. jours.), Am. Soc. Biol. Chemists, Phi Beta Kappa, Sigma Xi, Phi Lambda Upsilon. Author: (with I. Amdur) Chemical Kinetics: Principles and Selected Topics; also articles. Asso. editor Biochemistry. Home: 107 Warwick Pl Ithaca NY 14850

HAMMETT, LOUIS PLACK, educator, chemist; b. Wilmington, Del., Apr. 7, 1894; s. Philip Melancthon and Marie Louise (Plack) H.; A.B., Harvard, 1916; student Tech. Hochschule, Zürich, 1916-17; Ph.D., Columbia, 1923, Sc.D. (hon.), 1962; m. Janet Thorpe Marriner, June 4, 1919; children—Philip Marriner, Jane. Civilian chemist Bur. Aircraft Prodn., U.S. Army, 1917-19; comml. research with E. C. Worden, Millburn, N.J., 1919-20; with Columbia, 1920—, successively instr. chemistry, asst. prof., asso. prof., 1935, prof., 1935-60, Mitchill prof. chemistry, 1960-61, emeritus, 1961—; on leave for work on explosives under NDRC, 1941-46; distinguished vis. lectr. U. S.C., 1962; distinguished vis. prof. Pa. State U., 1964, Purdue U., 1964; research dir. Explosives Research Lab., 1943-46. Chmn. div. chemistry and chem tech. NRC, 1946-47. Chmn. Bd. Health, Hampton Township, N.J., 1964. Recipient Wm. H. Nichols medal, 1957; James Flack Norris award in teaching, 1960; Priestly medal, 1961; Willard Gibbs medal, 1961; James Flack Norris award phys. organic chemistry, 1966; Gilbert Newton Lewis medal, 1967; Nat. Medal of Sci., 1968; Charles Frederick Chandler medal, 1968. Hon. fellow Chem. Soc. (London); mem. Am. Chem. Soc. (chmn. N.Y. sect. 1939, bd. dirs. 1956-61, chmn. bd. dirs. 1961), Am. Assn. U. Profs., Nat. Acad. Scis., Phi Beta Kappa, Sigma Xi, Phi Lambda Upsilon, Alpha Chi Sigma. Author: Solutions of Electrolytes, 1929; Physical Organic Chemistry, 1940, 2d edit., 1970; Introduction to the Study of Physical Chemistry 1952. Editorial bd. Internat. Sci. and Tech., 1961-64. Home: RD 4 Box 681 Newton NJ 07860

HAMMETT, RALPH WARNER, architect, educator; b. Mankota, Minn., June 26, 1896; s. William Richard and Nellie Margaret (Russell) H.; B.S., U. Minn., 1919; M. Arch., Harvard, 1923; vis. fellow Am. Acad. in Rome, 1924-26; D.F.A. (hon.), Carthage (Mo.) Coll., 1970; m. Gladys Brouillard, Nov. 10, 1928; children—Eleanore Margaret, Dorothy Jeanne (Mrs. George L. Allen). Asso. prof. architecture U. Wash., 1923-24; chief designer Eric E. Hall, Inc., 1926-31; asso. prof. architecture Armour Inst. Tech., Chgo., 1927- 31; asso. prof. U. Mich., Ann Arbor, 1931-42, prof. architecture, 1942-65, prof. emeritus, 1966—; profl. practice and cons. in architecture, 1936-70. Del. Congress U.I.A., Lisbon, 1953; mem. commn. ch. architecture Lutheran Ch. Am., 1964-70; mem. Ann Arbor Historic Dist. Commn., 1968—. Served to maj. (spl. res. officer), Staff Communications Zone, AUS, 1943-45: ETO. Decorated officier d'Accad. de France with palmes; recipient Gold medal Detroit chpt. A.I.A., 1963. Mem. A.I.A. (centennial com. 1955-57), Am. Assn. U. Profs., Mich. Soc. Architects (dir. 1947-52, 1st v.p. 1950-52). Soc. Archtl. Historians, Lutheran Student Found. (v.p., dir. 1947-53), Acacia, Scarab, Phi Kappa Phi, Tau Sigma Delta, Tau Beta Pi, Alpha Rho Chi (Madsen Key). Republican. Lutheran. Clubs: Exchange, University. Author: The Romanesque of Western Europe, 1927; Architectural History Study Guides, 4th edit., 1948. Contbr. Romanesque Architecture in Collier's Ency., 1951, 57 edits.; also articles profl. jours. Home: 3113 Lake Haven Dr Ann Arbor MI 48105 Office: 231 S Main St Ann Arbor MI 48108

HAMMILL, LEROY RICHARD, coll. pres.; b. Chico, Cal., Dec. 28, 1913; s. John Henry and Lucretia (Fuller) H.; B.Th., Walla Walla Coll., 1936; M.A., Seventh-day Adventist Theol. Sem., 1947; Ph.D., U. Chgo., 1950; m. Dena Tininenko, Sept. 6, 1936; children—Roger, Marcia. Ordained to ministry Seventh-day Adventist Ch., 1945; pastor Wash. State Ch., 1936-40, Danang, Vietnam, 1940-41; tchr. Philippine Union Coll., 1942-43; prisoner of war, 1944-45; prof. religion and philosophy So. Missionary Coll., Tenn., 1946-55; dean, 1952-55; asso. sec. Dept. Edn. Gen. Conf. Seventh-day Adventists, Washington, 1955-63; pres. Andrews U., Berrien Springs, Mich., 1963—. Rotarian. Author: In Full Assurance, 1960. Editor of Jour. True Edn., 1955-63. Contbr. to 7 vol. Bible commentary. Home: 324 Hillcrest Dr Berrien Springs MI 49103

HAMMILL, RICHARD, univ. pres.; b. Chico, Cal., Dec. 28, 1913; s. John Henry and Lucretia (Fuller) H.; B.Th., Walla Walla Coll., 1936; M.A., Andrews U., Berrien Springs, Mich., 1947; Ph.D., U. Chgo., 1950; m. Dena Tininenko, Sept. 6, 1936; children—Roger, Marcia. Ordained to ministry Seventh-day Adventist Ch., 1945; pastor, Wash. State, 1936-40, Danang, Vietnam, 1941; tchr. Philippine Union Coll., 1942-44; tchr. So. Missionary Coll., Collegedale, Tenn., 1946-52, acad. dean, 1952-55; asso sec. Gen. Conf. Seventh-day Adventists, 1955-63; pres. Andres U., 1963—. Rotarian. Home: 324 Hillcrest Dr Berrien Springs MI 49103

HAMMOCK, JOSEPH CULVER, educator, psychologist; b. Cullman County, Ala., Sept. 20, 1926; s. Joseph Emmett and Katie (Taylor) H.; B.S., U. S.C., 1948, M.A., 1950; Ph.D., U. Tenn., 1953; m. Edna Hill Haynes, Sept. 10, 1947; children—Joseph Culver, Baxter Haynes, Margaret Anne. Research psychologist Human Resources Research Office, U.S. Army, 1952-55, dir. research, 1956-59; research psychologist Bell Telephone Labs., Inc., 1959-62; mem. faculty U. Ga., 1955—, prof. psychology, 1962—, head dept., 1962-69, dir. instructional research and devel., 1969—. Served with USNR, 1944-47. Mem. A.A.A.S., Am. Acad. Polit. and Social Sci., Am. (rep. to council), Southeastern (exec. com.), Ga. (pres.) psychol. assns., So. Soc. Philosophy and Psychology, Am. Ednl. Research Assn., Nat. Soc. for Programmed Instrn., Sigma Xi, Sigma Alpha Epsilon, Omicron Delta Kappa. Methodist. Home: 367 Beechwood Dr Athens GA 30601

HAMMON, WILLIAM MCDOWELL, med. research scientist, educator; b. Columbus O., July 20, 1904; s. William Henry and Adaline (McDowell) H.; A.B., Allegheny Coll., 1932, Sc.D. (hon.), 1959; M.D., Harvard, 1936, M.P.H., 1938, Dr. P.H., 1939; Certificate Army Med. Sch., 1943; m. Helen Black, Aug. 3, 1926; children—William M., Barbara Helen. Dir. Med. Dispensary, nr. Shabunda, Belgian Congo, 1926-30; instr. epidemiology School Pub. Health, Harvard, 1939-40; mem. faculty Hooper Found. for Med. Research, U. of Cal., 1940-50, prof. epidemiology, 1947-50, mem. faculty Sch. Pub. Health, 1944-50, prof. epidemiology, 1947-50, lectr. medicine and eurology Sch. Medicine, 1942-50; prof., head dept. epidemiology and microbiology Grad. Sch. Pub. Health, U. Pitts., 1950—; cons., surgeon gen. U.S. Army 1941—; dir. virus infections commn. Armed Forces Epidemiology Bd., 1956-65, dir. tropical medicine commn., 1946, mem. of bd., 1965—; cons. Communicable Disease Center, USPHS, 1948-60; mem. nat. adv. cancer council, 1960-63, adv. com. live poliovirus vaccine Surgeon Gen., 1959- 66; mem. panel viruses and cancer Nat. Cancer Inst., 1959-62; mem. Pacific Sci. Bd., NRC, 1950-56. Recipient Medal of Freedom (Presdl.), 1946; Richard M. Taylor award in arbovirology, 1970. Diplomate Am. Bd. Preventive Medicine and Pub. Health. Fellow Am. Pub. Health Assn. (research and standards com. 1949, chmn. 1950-55), A.A.A.S., N.Y. Acad. Scis., Am. Acad. Microbiology (gov.); mem. Soc. Am. Bacteriologists (pres. 1949), Am. Assn. Immunology, Am. Soc. Tropical Medicine and Hygiene (editorial board 1951- -, pres. 1967-68), Exptl. Biology and Medicine, Soc. Exptl. Pathology, Am. Assn. Physicians, American Epidemiological Soc. (pres. 1962-63), Phi Beta Kappa, Sigma Xi, Alpha Omega Alpha, Delta Omega. Home: 317 Sleepy Hollow Rd Pittsburgh PA 15228

HAMMOND, CALEB DEAN, publisher, cartographer; b. Orange, N.J., June 24, 1915; s. Caleb Dean and Alice (Lindsley) H.; B.S., Worcester Poly. Inst., 1937; m. Patricia Treacy Ehrgott, July 20, 1940; children—Beth Lynn, Wendie Harrison, Caleb Dean 3d. Sales engr. Texas Co., N.Y.C., 1937-39; prodn. mgr. Hammond, Inc. (formerly known as C.S. Hammond & Company), Maplewood, N.J., 1939-42, v.p. charge sales and mgmt., 1945-48, pres., 1948-67, chmn. bd., 1968—; dir. Maplewood Bank & Trust Co. Trustee Orange (N.J.) Med. Center. Served from cadet to engring. lt., USCG, 1942-45. Mem. Assn. Am. Pubs., Am., Royal geog. socs., Phi Gamma Delta. Clubs: Maplewood Country, Maplewood. Home: 61 Woodland Rd Maplewood NJ 07040 Office: 515 Valley St Maplewood NJ 07040

HAMMOND, CHARLES PHILIP, banker; b. Lynn, Mass., July 1, 1916; s. Charles Philip and Mary (Kirk) H.; grad. Philips Acad., Andover, Mass., 1935; B.S., Harvard, 1939; postgrad. Brown U., 1962; m. Nancy Folger, Oct. 25, 1947; children—Philip Kirk, Peter Folger. Mortgage broker, Boston, 1939-40; mortage loan insp. Prudent. Ins. Co., Boston, 1948-50; with Provident Instn. for Savs. in Town of Boston, 1950—, treas., 1968—. Mem. securities com. Savs. Bank Assn. Mass. Bd. dirs. Mass. Purchasing Group, 1962-65. Served to lt. col. USMCR, 1940-46. Mem. Boston C. of C., Am. Inst. Banking, Savs. Banks Officer Assn., Delta Upsilon. Home: 201 Washington St Marblehead MA 01945 Office: 36 Temple Pl Boston MA 02105

HAMMOND, DATUS MILLER, educator; b. Providence, Utah, May 20, 1911; s. Horace E. and Salina (Tibbitts) H.; B.S., Utah Agrl. Coll., 1932; A.M., U. Cal., 1934, Ph.D., 1936; m. Emily Merrill, Dec. 23, 1937; children—Anna Marie, Louise, Betty, Marilyn, Carol. Instr. zoology Utah State U., 1937-40, asst. prof., 1940-41, prof., head dept., 1945—, faculty honor lectr., 1964; asst. protozoölogist, zool. div. Bur. Animal Industry, U.S. Dept. Agr., Beltsville, Md., 1941-42, asso. protozoölogist U.S. regional lab. for animal disease research, Auburn, Ala., 1942-44; guest prof. U. Bonn, 1970. Fulbright research scholar U. Munich, 1955-56. Fellow A.A.A.S.; mem. Utah Acad. Scis., Arts and Letters (v.p. 1971-72), Soc. Protozoologists (sec. 1967—), Am. Soc. Zoölogists, Am. Soc. Parasitol., Am. Micros. Soc., Phi Beta Kappa, Phi Kappa Phi (pres. Utah State chpt. 1963-65), Sigma Xi (pres. Utah State chpt. 1946- 47). Mem. Church of Latter Day Saints. Rotarian. Editorial bd. Jour. Protozoology, Jour. Parasitology, Zeitschrift für Parasitenkunde. Contbr. articles sci. jours. Researcher on coccidia of cattle, other animals. Home: 479 W Center Logan UT 84321

HAMMOND, EDWARD CUYLER, epidemiologist; b. Balt., June 14, 1912; s. Edward and Agnes (Cuyler) H.; student Gilman Country Day Sch., 1929-31; B.S., Yale, 1935, M.A., 1953; Sc.D., Johns Hopkins, 1938; M.D. (hon.), Johannesgutenberg U., Mainz-am-Rhein, 1969; m. Marian E. Thomas, Jan. 3, 1948; children—Thomas Edward, Richard Render, Jonathan Cuyler. Asso. statistician, div. indsl. hygiene NIH, USPHS, 1938-42; cons. med. research sect. Bur. Aeros., U.S. Navy, 1941-42; civilian requirements br. OQMG, 1942; dir. statis. research sect. Am. Cancer Soc., 1946-66, v.p. for epidemiology and statistics, 1966—; clin. prof. community medicine Mt. Sinai Sch. Medicine, 1966—; prof. biometry, dir. grad. studies Yale U., 1953-58, also chmn. univ. exec. com. statistics; lectr. preventive and environmental medicine Albert Einstein Coll. Medicine; cons. dept. biology Brookhaven Nat. Lab. Mem. sci. adv. panel Research to Prevent Blindness, Inc. Served as maj. USAAF, 1942-46; chief statistics dept. Sch. Aviation Medicine, Randolph Field, Tex.; asst. chief statistics div. Office Air Surgeon, Hdqrs. AAF, Washington; nat. lectr. Sigma Xi, 1957-58. Recipient William R. Belknap award for excellence in biol. studies, 1935; Charles Evans Hughes award Riverside Ch., 1967. Fellow Am. Pub. Health Assn.; mem. Am. Statis. Assn., N.Y. Acad. Sci., A.A.A.S. Contbr. articles to profl. jours. Home: 164 E 72d St New York City, NY 10021. Office: 219 E 42d St New York City NY 10017

HAMMOND, FRANKLIN TWEED, Jr., lawyer; b. Cambridge, Mass., Oct. 4, 1901; s. Franklin Tweed and Mabel (McLeod) H.; A.B., Harvard, 1922, LL.B., 1925; m. Catherine Russell Hedge, Oct. 3, 1931; children—John W. II, Henry H., Franklin Tweed III, Catherine R. Admitted to Mass. bar, 1925, since practiced in Boston; asso. firm Gaston, Snow, Motley & Holt, 1925-31, partner, 1931-34, 35- 41, 46—; asst. gen. counsel SEC, 1935; spl. asst. to undersec. war, 1941-44; asst. city solicitor, Cambridge, 1933-34; instr. Boston Coll. Law Sch., 1936-41. Dir. Nat. Shawmut Bank, Boston, Shawmut Assn., Inc.; trustee Suffolk Franklin Savs. Bank. Bd. dirs. Boston Legal Aid Soc.; pres., dir. Cambridge Homes for Aged People; Pres.; trustee Family Service Assn. Greater Boston. Served from maj. to col., AUS, 1942-45; MTO. Decorated Bronze Star medal. Fellow Am. Bar Found.; mem. Am., Mass., Boston bar assns., Am. Law Inst. Republican. Unitarian. Club: Saint Botolph (Boston). Contbr. profl. jours. Home: 17 Traill St Cambridge MA 02138 Office: 82 Devonshire St Boston MA 02109

HAMMOND, GEORGE SIMMS, educator, chemist; b. Auburn, Me., May 22, 1921; s. Oswald Kenric and Marjorie (Thomas) H.; B.S., Bates Coll., 1963; M.S., Ph.D., Harvard, 1947; m. Marian Reese, June 8, 1945; children—Kenric, Janet, Steven, Barbara, Jeremy. Postdoctoral fellow U. Cal. at Los Angeles, 1947-48; mem. faculty Ia. State Coll., 1948-58, prof. chemistry, 1956-58; vis. asso. prof. U. Ill., summer 1953; prof. organic chemistry Cal. Inst. Tech., Pasadena, 1958—, div. chemistry and chem. engring., 1968—, Arthur Amos Noyes prof. chemistry. Mem. chem. adv. panel NSF, 1962-65. Guggenheim fellow; NSF sr. fellow Oxford (Eng.) U. and U. Basel (Switzerland); Cal. Inst. Tech., 1956-57. Mem. Me. N.G., 1944- 45. Recipient James Flack Norris award in phys. organic chemistry, 1968. Mem. Nat. Acad. Scis., Am. Chem. Soc. (award in petroleum chem. 1960), Chemistry Soc. (London), Am. Acad. Arts and Scis., Phi Beta Kappa, Sigma Xi. Author: (with J. S. Fritz) Quantitative Organic Analysis, 1956; (with D.J. Cram) Organic Chemistry, 1958; (with J. Osteryoung, T. Crawford and H. Gray) Models in Chemical Science, 1971. Editor: Advances in Photochemistry, 1961. Editorial bd. Jour. Am. Chem. Soc., 1967—. Home: 1521 E Mountain St Pasadena CA 91104*

HAMMOND, GUYTON BOWERS, educator; b. Birmingham, Ala., Nov. 7, 1930; s. Joseph Langhorne and Fanny (Bowers) H.; B.A., Washington and Lee U., 1951; postgrad. U. Utrecht (Netherlands), 1951-52, So. Baptist Theol. Sem., 192-53; B.S., Yale, 1955; Ph.D., Vanderbilt U., 1962; m. Alice Jean Love, June 27, 1959; children-Bruce Guyton, Mitchell Love. Grad. teaching fellow Vanderbilt U., 1955-57; instr. Va. Polytechnic Inst., 1957-58, asst. prof., 1958-62, asso. prof., 1962-67, prof. philosophy and religion, 1967—. Pres. Council on Human Relations, Montgomery County, Va., 1962- 63. Chmn. bd. advisers Va. Polytechnic Inst. chpt. YMCA, 1966-67. Mem. Am. Acad. Religion (nat. bd. dirs. 1968-69, pres. Southeastern region, 1968-69), Am. Assn. Univ. Profs., Va. Philos. Assn., Lambda Chi Alpha. Baptist. Author: Man in Estrangement, 1965, The Power of Self- Transcendence, 1966. Home: 848 Hutcheson Lane Blacksburg VA 24060

HAMMOND, HALL, judge; b. Balt., May 18, 1902; s. William Saunders and Rosalie Eugenia (Hall) H.; student Balt. City Coll., 1919; A.B., Johns Hopkins, 1923; LL.B., U. Md., 1925; m. Elizabeth Ashton Luck, Oct. 6, 1934 (dec. 1961); m. 2d, Dorothy Nelson, Oct. 27, 1962. Admitted to Md. bar, 1925, since practiced in Balt.; dep. atty gen. Md., 1941-46, acting atty. gen., 1945, atty. gen., 1946-52; judge Ct. Appeals Md., 1952—, chief judge, 1966—. Trustee S. Balt. Gen. Hosp., Pickersgill, Aged Women and Men's Homes. Mem. Am., Md., Baltimore County, Balt. bar assns., Phi Kappa Psi. Democrat. Episcopalian. Home: Stevenson MD Office: Court House Towson MD 21204

HAMMOND, HAROLD FRANCIS, transp. exec.; b. Lynch, Neb., June 1, 1908; s. Edward Francis and Lydia (Kallstrom) H.; student Parsons Coll., Fairfield, Ia., 1926- 27; B.S. in Civil Engring., U. Mich., 1930; M.S., Harvard, 1931; m. Gertrude R. Rouse, Oct. 10, 1931; children—Harold Edward, Susan W. Traffic engr. Gov. Mass. Com. Street and Hwy. Safety, 1931-34; traffic analyst Traffic Audit Bur., N.Y.C., 1934-35; dir. traffic and transp. div. Nat. Conservation Bur., 1935-44; mgr. Washington office Am. Transit Assn., 1944-47; asst. mgr. transp. and communication dept. U.S. C. of C., Washington, 1947- 48. mgr. dept., 1948-55; exec. v.p., dir. Transp. Assn. Am., 1955-62, pres., dir., 1962—; transp. cons. Naval Operating Base, Norfolk, Va., also Office Def. Transportation, 1940-44. Former mem. adv. council fed. reports Bur. of Budget; mem. transp. adv. council Dept. Commerce, 1952. Mem. county council Montgomery County, Md., 1949-53, pres., 1953-54. Registered profl. engr., N.J., D.C. Mem. Nat. Inst. Traffic Engrs. (past pres.). Am. Soc. Traffic and Transp. (founder), Am. Soc. Assn. Execs. Republican. Presbyn. Clubs: Capitol Hill, University, National Aviation, Congressional Country, Metropolitan, Traffic (Washington); Union League, Traffic (Chgo.); Traffic, Harvard (N.Y.C.). Author traffic and transp. manuals.

Co-editor: Traffic Engineering Handbook. Home: 12510 Pennyfield Lock Rd Potomac MD 20854 Office: 1101 17th St NW Washington DC 20036

HAMMOND, JACK, hosp. supt.; b. N.Y.C., Aug. 18, 1916; B.Ac., Dalhousie U., 1935, M.D., C.M., 1939; m. Elizabeth Hammond, Sept. 20, 1941; children—Robert E., Susan G., David A. With N.Y. Dept. Mental Hygiene, 1952; dir. Willowbrook State Sch., Staten Island, N.Y., 1964—, Louis Boehm Diagnostic and Counseling Center, 1966—; attending psychiatrist St. Vincent's Med. Center, Richmond, N.Y., 1964—; clin. prof. pediatrics N.Y.U. Sch. Medicine. Mem. Mayor's Com. Mental Retardation, N.Y.C. Bd. dirs. Staten Island Aid Retarded Children. Served with M.C., USNR, 1941-46. Fellow Am. Assn. Mental Deficiency; mem. Med. Soc. Richmond County, N.Y. Med. Assn. (chmn. subcom. retardation), A.M.A., Am. Psychiat. Assn. Address: Willowbrook State Sch Staten Island NY 10314 *

HAMMOND, JAMES WRIGHT, architect; b. Montclair, N.J., Apr. 12, 1918; s. Robert Stevens and Helen (Johnston) H.; B.S., Ill. Inst. Tech., 1942; m. Katrina Roy Boyden, Feb. 25, 1956 (div. June 1959). Asso. Perkins, Wheeler & Will & Eliel Saarinen Asso. Architects, 1939-40; project mgr., asso. partner, gen. partner Skidmore, Owings & Merrill, Chgo., 1946-61; partner Hammond and Roesch, Chgo., 1961-71; pres. Hammond and Assos., Inc., Chgo., 1971—. Mem. facilities devel. com. Chgo. council Boy Scouts Am., 1958—; mem. Chgo. Crime Commn., 1955—; com. mem. Welfare Council Met. Chgo. Bd. dirs. Chgo. Planetarium Soc.; exec. bd. Auditorium Theatre Council Chgo. Served with AUS, 1942-46. Mem. Chgo. Council Fgn. Relations, A.I.A. (corp. mem., sec.-dir.), Chgo. Commons Assn. (trustee). Bahai religion. Clubs: University, Arts (Chgo.). Home: 860 Lake Shore Dr Chicago IL 60611 Office: 332 S Michigan Av Chicago IL 60604

HAMMOND, JOHN, recording exec.; b. N.Y.C., Dec. 15, 1910; s. John Henry and Emily Vanderbilt (Sloane) H.; grad. Hotchkiss Sch., Lakeville, Conn., 1929; student Yale, 1929-31; m. Jemison McBride, Mar. 13, 1941 (div. 1948); children—John Paul, Jason Hammond; m. 2d, Esmé O'Brien Sarnoff, Sept. 8, 1949. Am. rec. dir. English Columbia & Parlophone Co., Ltd., 1933-36; producer Little Old Boy, Playhouse Theatre, N.Y.C., 1933, Jayhawker, Cort Theatre, N.Y.C., 1935, From Spirituals to Swing, Carnegie Hall, N.Y.C., 1938-39; organizer Benny Goodman Band, 1933-35, Count Basie's Orch., 1936; asso. rec. dir. Columbia Records, 1939-43, 46; co-editor, co-publ. Music and Rhythm, 1942-43; casting dir. Billy Rose prodn. Carmen Jones, 1943; rec. dir. Majestic Records, 1946-47; v.p. Mercury Record Corp., 1946-52; lectr. N.Y. U., 1953-56; pop record dir. Vanguard Record Soc., 1954—; v.p., dir. Newport Jazz Festival, Inst. of Jazz Studies, Horizon Press, N.Y.C., Crisis Publ. Co., N.Y.C. Columnist, Down Beat, 1933-39; critic, columnist Bklyn. Eagle, 1934-36; record critic N.Y. Compass, 1950-52; columnist N.Y. Herald Tribune, 1953-55, Saturday Rev., 1958-59; now dir. talent-acquisition Columbia Records, N.Y.C Second v.p. Profl. Children's Sch., N.Y.C.; bd. dirs. Northside Center Child Devel., N.Y.C., 1950—. Mem. N.A.A.C.P. (v.p.), Nat. Acad. Rec. Arts and Scis. (pres. E. Coast chpt.). Home: 444 E 57th St New York City, NY 10022. Office: Columbia Records 51 W 52d St New York City NY 10019*

HAMMOND, JOHN PAUL, singer, guitarist; b. N.Y.C., Nov. 13, 1942; s. John Henry, Jr.; self-taught musician; m. Dana McDevitt; 1 son, Paul Justin. Singer, plays guitar, harmonica in style based on traditional folk blues; appeared Newport Folk Festival, 1963-64, Village Gate, Village Vanguard, 1964. Carnegie Hall, 1965; toured Eng., 1965; rec. artist Vanguard records, Atlantic records. Composer songs including Lonesome Sundown Blues, Bad Luck Games; recs. include: Southern Fried. Address: 647 Broadway New York City NY 10012*

HAMMOND, JOHN PAYNE, petroleum cons.; b. Okmulgee, Okla., Apr. 19, 1913; s. John Whitten and Grace (Payne) H.; B.S., U. Tulsa, 1936; m. Katharine R. Rees, May 17, 1937; children—Grace (Mrs. Stanley Betzer, Jr.), Patricia (Mrs. Bryan Watt), Sara. With Amerada Petroleum Corp., 1941-69, asst. gen. prodn. supt., 1951-60, v.p., 1960-62, sr. v.p., 1962-67, exec. v.p., 1967-69, dir., mem. exec. com. of bd. dirs.; exec. v.p., dir. Amerada Hess Corp.; pres. Amerada div. Amerada Hess Corp., 1969-71; petroleum cons., 1971—; dir. First Nat. Bank Tulsa. Bd. dirs. Goodwill Industries Tulsa. Mem. Am. Inst. Mining, Metall. and Petroleum Engrs. (past v.p., dir.), Soc. Petroleum Engrs. (past pres.), Am. Petroleum Inst., Mid-Continent Oil and Gas Assn. (bd.dirs.), Petroleum Club Tulsa, Tau Beta Pi, Phi Epsilon Tau. Presbyn. (elder). Clubs: Southern Hills Country; Summit. Home: 2706 S Birmingham Pl Tulsa OK 74114 Office: PO Box 2902 Tulsa OK 74101

HAMMOND, LAURENS, inventor, mfr.; b. Evanston, Ill., Jan. 11, 1895; s. William Andrew and Ida Louise (Strong) H.; M.E., Cornell U., Ithaca, N.Y., 1916; m. Mildred Anton-Smith, Sept. 1, 1924 (dec.); children—Mildred, Margaret; m. 2d, Roxana Scoville, Oct. 25, 1955. Founder, Hammond Organ Co., chmn. bd. to 1960; founder Hammond Clock Co. Inventions include differential mercurial barometer, organ, stereoscopic motion pictures, various stage effects for Ziegfeld, electric clock, parts for guided missiles; cons. U.S. Air Corps, 1940-43. Served as capt., engrs., U.S. Army, 1917-19; AEF in France. Recipient Wetherill medal Franklin Inst., 1940. Holder 110 U.S. patents. Home: Chateau de Champremault Meung-sur-Loire Loizet, France also Mill Reef Club Antigua British West Indies also 166 E 63d St New York City NY 10021 also West Cornwall CT 06753*

HAMMOND, LEWIS MACHEN, educator; b. Wilmington, Del., July 23, 1906; s. Kensey Johns and Caroline (Machen) H.; A.B., U. Va., 1928, A.M., 1929, Ph.D., 1932; German-Am. Exchange fellow U. Hamburg, 1930-31; m. Frances Lile, Jan. 11, 1936; children—Juliet Johns (Mrs. William Barr Hetzel, Jr.), Frances Lile (Mrs. E.C. Deinard). Instr. philosophy U. Va., 1932-36, asst. prof., 1936-42, asso. prof., 1945-48, prof. philosophy, 1948—, asst. dean summer session, 1947-51, dean grad. sch., 1951-60, chmn. philosophy dept., 1962-67; cultural attache Am. embassy, Bonn, Germany, 1960-62; tutor and asst. to pres. St. Johns Coll., 1942-45; sec.-treas. Assn. Grad. Schs.; mem. bd. exec. com. Woodrow Wilson Fellowship Found. Mem. morale div. U.S. Strategic Bombing Survey in Germany, Apr.-Nov. 1945. Mem. Am. Philos. Assn., Assn. for Realistic Philos., Metaphys. Soc. Am., Am. Assn. U. Profs., So. Soc. for Philosophy and Psychology (pres. 1951), So. Soc. for Philosophy of Religion, Episcopal Guild Scholars (pres. 1950), Va. Philos. Assn. (pres. 1949); Phi Beta Kappa, Omicron Delta Kappa, Phi Kappa Sigma, Raven Soc. Democrat. Episcopalian (sr. warden). Translator (with Leckie and Steinhardt); Mathematical Logic from the German of Hilbert and Ackermann, 1950. Contbr. to various books and to Philos. Rev. and Anglican Theol. Rev. (mem. editorial bd., 1941-69). Home: Pavilion 2 East Lawn Charlottesville VA 22903

HAMMOND, MASON, educator; b. Boston, Feb. 14, 1903; s. Samuel and Grace (Learoyd) H.; student St. Mark's Sch., Southborough, Mass., 1916-21; A.B., Harvard, 1925; A.B. (Rhodes Scholar Mass. and Balliol Coll.), Oxford (Eng.) U., 1928, B.Litt., 1930; m. Florence H. Pierson, Aug. 27, 1935; children—Florence, Anstiss, Elizabeth. Instr. Harvard, 1928-34, asst. prof. Greek, Latin and history, 1934-39, asso. prof., 1939-46, prof., 1946—, Pope prof. Latin lang. and lit., 1950—, tutor div. ancient langs., 1928—, master Kirkland House, 1945-55; instr. Radcliffe Coll., 1928-34, asst., then asso. prof., 1934-42; prof. charge classical studies Am. Acad. in Rome, 1937-39, 55-57, prof. summer sch., 1949, prof. classics under Fulbright Act, 1951-52, 63. Trustee Isabella Stewart Gardner Museum, Boston, Mass., Am. Acad. in Rome, St. Mark's Sch. Served to lt. col., USAAF, 1942-45; with Mil. Govt., Italy and Germany, 1943- 45. Fellow Am. Acad. Arts and Scis., mem. Am. Philol. Assn., English Speaking Union (past dir. Boston), Am. Hist. Assn., Am. Archeol. Inst., Mass. Hist. Soc., German Archeol. Inst. (corr.), Phi Beta Kappa. Clubs: Somerset, Tavern (Boston). Author: The Augustan Principate, 1933; City-State and World State, 1952; The Antonine Monarchy, 1959. Co-editor: Plautus' Menaechmi, 1933; Miles Gloriosus, 1963; Aeneas to Augustus, 1962. Home: 153 Brattle St Cambridge MA 02138

HAMMOND, PAUL LYMAN, indsl. banker; b. Egypt, Mass., Dec. 16, 1882; s. William L. and Adelaide (Nowell) H.; grad. Thayer Acad., 1902; student Harvard, 1906; m. Susan R. Sedgewick, Mar. 30, 1929. Sr. partner Hammond, Kennedy & Co., Inc., and predecessors, pvt. indsl. bankers, N.Y.C., 1906-65, chmn. bd., 1965—; dir. Perkin-Elmer Corp., Wall St. Investing Corp.; treas., dir. Sutton Pl. South Corp.; financial cons. hdgrs. financing UN. Adv. com., past treas. U.S. Com. for UN Assn., hon. trustee, mem. corp. com., devel. com. Woods Hole Oceanographic Instn.; mem. overseers com. to visit dept. astronomy Harvard; trustee, dir. Whaling Museum Soc., Cold Spring Harbor, L.I. Served as lt. comdr. U.S. Navy, 1917-18; as capt. USNR, 1940-46. Decorated Bronze Star with citation for devel. anti-U boat weapons and rockets, USN; Order Brit. Empire; Al Merito (Ecuador). Clubs: Seawanhaka Corinthian Yacht (Oyster Bay, L.I.); River, Yacht (N.Y.C.); Harvard Faculty (Cambridge, Mass.); Pilgrims; Royal Yacht Squadron, Royal Naval Sailing Assn., Royal Ocean Racing (Gt. Britain); Real Club de Regatas de Santander (Spain). Home: Syosset NY 11791 also 1 Sutton Pl New York City NY 10022 Office: 230 Park Av New York City NY 10017

HAMMOND, R. PHILIP, govt. ofcl., chem. engr.; b. Creston, Ia., May 28, 1916; s. Robert Hugh and Helen (Williams) H.; B.S. in Chem. Engring., U. So. Cal., 1938; Ph.D. in Phys. and Inorganic Chemistry (Naval Research fellow), U. Chgo., 1947; m. Amy L. Farmer, Feb. 28, 1941; children—Allen L., David M., Jean Phyllis, Stanley W. Chief chemist Lindsay Chem. Co., W. Chicago, Ill., 1938-46; group leader Los Alamos Sci. Lab., 1947-62, asso. div. leader reactor devel. div. 1960-62; dir. nuclear desalination program Oak Ridge Nat. Lab., 1962—. Mem. U.S. delegation Conf. on Peaceful Uses Atomic Energy, Geneva, Switzerland, 1955, 65, 71, Internat. Atomic Energy Agy. Panel on Desalination, Vienna, Austria, 1964, 65, 66, 71; mem. U.S. team to USSR on desalination, 1964. Registered profl. engr., Ill. Mem. Am. Nuclear Soc. (charter), Am. Chem. Soc., Am. Inst. Chem. Engrs., Am. Assn. Cost Engrs., Sigma Xi, Phi Kappa Phi, Phi Lambda Upsilon. Author articles nuclear power reactors, reactor econs., desalting of sea water, energy centers, metallurgy of plutonium and refractory metals, rare earths, radiation chemistry, remote control engring., mech. devices; contbr. Ency. Brit. Patentee in field. Home: 879 West Outer Dr Oak Ridge TN 37830 Office: Oak Ridge Nat Lab PO Box Y Oak Ridge TN 37830

HAMMOND, RICHARD OWEN, airline exec.; b. Des Moines, Sept. 3, 1929; s. George Young and Clarice (Sayers) H.; B.S., U. Cal., Los Angeles, 1952; m. Gloria Kodil, Oct. 4, 1958; children—Steven S., Victoria L. Accountant, Memory, Dukes & Good, C.P.A.'s, Los Angeles, 1953-54; asst. mgr. revenue accounting Western Airlines, Los Angeles, 1954-59, mgr. of ins., 1959-66, asst. treas., 1966-69, treas., 1969—. Served to 2d lt. USAF, 1952-53. Mem. Am. Soc. Ins. Mgmt. Home: 7731 Stewart Av Los Angeles CA 90045 Office: 6060 Avion Dr Los Angeles CA 90009

HAMMOND, T., journalist. Bus. and financial editor Vancouver Sun. Office: Pacific Press Ltd 2250 Granville St Vancouver 9 British Columbia Canada*

HAMMOND, THOMAS L., machinery mfr.; b. Chgo., Feb. 5, 1915; s. Thomas S. and Barbara (Whiting) H.; student U. Ariz.; m. Miriam O'Connell, Aug. 28, 1942; children—Sheila, John, Barbara, Peter, Christopher. With Whiting Corp., Harvey, Ill., 1946—, v.p. gen. sales, 1951, v.p. product div., mgr. trackmobile and gen. products div., 1951-58, chmn., 1958—. Served with Q.M.C., AUS, 1942-46. Home: 233 E Walton Pl Chicago IL 60611 Office: Whiting Corp Harvey IL 60426*

HAMMOND, WILLIAM, physician, editor; b. N.Y.C., Oct. 17, 1900; s. John and Mary (Corbett) H.; M.D., C.M., McGill U., 1927; m. Shirley Louise Blanchard, Aug. 22, 1931; children—Graeme Lord, Mary Rand (Mrs. Arthur W. Ticknor), Melissa Blanchard (Mrs. Donald H. Lang). Postgrad. tng. Royal Victoria Hosp., Montreal, Que., Can., 1927, Mass. Gen. Hosp., Boston, 1928- 29, Johns Hopkins Hosp., 1929-31; pvt. practice internal medicine, Scarsdale, N.Y., 1931—; cons. physician Grasslands Hosp.; vis. physician White Plains Hosp.; med. cons. Westchester County Dept. Welfare, 1942-62, N.Y. State Dept. Social Welfare, 1962—. Mem. Scarsdale Non-Partisan Com., 1960—. Bd. dirs. Physicians Home, N.Y.C., 1963—. Fellow A.C.P., Am. Geriatrics Soc. (pres. 1965; pres. Research Found.), Am. Med. Writers Assn. (pres. Met. chpt. 1964, nat. pres. 1966); mem. N.Y. State (council), Westchester County (historian) med. socs. Clubs: Canadian (N.Y.C.); Shenorock Shore (Rye, N.Y.). Asst. editor N.Y. State Jour. Medicine, 1957-61, editor, 1961—. Home: 36 Crane Rd Scarsdale NY 10583 Office: 750 3d Av New York City NY 10017

HAMMOND, WILLIAM CHURCHILL, Jr., ret. banker; b. Holyoke, Mass., July 4, 1903; s. William Churchill and Fanny (Reed) H.; grad. Groton Sch., 1921; Ph.B., Yale, 1925; M.B.A., Harvard, 1927; m. Gertrude Green, June 24, 1935; children—Diana Churchill, Clarissa Reed, William Churchill. Statistician, J & W Seligman, N.Y.C., 1927-29; research dept. Lehman Corp., 1929-36, Loomis Sayles & Co., Inc., Boston, 1936-42, asst. to pres., 1944-45; exec. asst. to Brig. Gen. Georges F. Doriot, chief research and devel. br. O.Q.M.G., Washington, 1942-43; mng. partner Boston office White, Weld & Co., N.Y.C., 1946-67, ret. ltd. partner, 1968- -. Selectman, Manchester, Mass., 1942. Trustee Pine Manor Jr. Coll., New Eng. Aquarium. Mem. Investment Bankers Assn. Am. (former gov.), Mass. Audubon Soc. (dir. 1947-68), Phi Beta Kappa, Delta Kappa Epsilon, Elihu Club. Mem. Manchester Emmanuel Ch. (trustee). Clubs: Union, Yale, Bond, Somerset (Boston); Yale (N.Y.C.); Singing Beach (Manchester); Myopia Hunt (Hamilton, Mass.). Home: 69 Harbor St West Manchester MA 01944 Office: 125 High St Boston MA 02110

HAMMOND, WILLIAM ROGERS, univ. dean; b. Atlanta, Oct. 19, 1920; s. Charles C. and Edna (Rogers) H.; B.S., Ga. State U., 1941; M.B.A., Harvard, 1943; D.B.A., Ind. U., 1954; m. Frances Estelle Turner, Mar. 22, 1947; children—Claren Charlotte, Alexandra Merlyn. Partner, Brenner & Co., C.P.A.'s, Atlanta, 1946-48; prof. bus. adminstrn., asso. dean Sch. Bus. Adminstrn., Ga. State U., Atlanta, 1948—, dean grad. studies, 1958—. Served to capt. AUS, 1943-46. Decorated Bronze Star medal. C.P.A., Ga. Mem. Am. Inst. C.P.A.'s, Acad. Mgmt., Am. Risk and Ins. Assn. Author accounting mgmt. and ins. books. Home: 1301 Harvard Rd NE Atlanta, GA 30306.

HAMMOND INNES, RALPH, author; b. Horsham, Eng., July 15, 1913; s. William Hammond Innes and Dora Beatrice Crisford; ed. Cranbrook Sch.; m. Dorothy Mary Lang, Aug. 21, 1937. Journalist, Financial News, London, 1934-40. Served to maj., arty., Brit. Army, 1940-46. Author: Trapped, 1940; Attack Alarm, 1942; Fire in the Snow, 1947; Gale Warning, 1947; The Killer Mine, 1947; The Blue Ice, 1948; The Survivors, 1949; The Angry Mountain, 1950; Air Bridge, 1951; Campbell's Kingdom, 1952; The Naked Land, 1954; The Wreck of the Mary Deare, 1956; The Land God Gave to Cain, 1958; Harvest of Journeys, 1960; The Doomed Oasis, 1960; Atlantic Fury, 1962; Scandinavia, 1963; The Strode Venturer, 1965; Sea and Islands, 1967; The Conquistadors, 1969; Levkas Man, 1971. Author films: Snowbound, 1948; Hell Below Zero, 1958; Campbell's Kingdom, 1957; The Wreck of the Mary Deare, 1959. Contbr. Sat. Eve. Post, Holiday mag. Address: Ayres End Kersey Suffolk England

HAMMONDS, OLIVER WENDELL, lawyer; b. DeQueen, Ark., Aug. 4, 1911; s. Oliver Overstreet and Mamie (Scott) H.; A.B., Okla. U., 1932; LL.B., Harvard, 1936; m. Ellen Hewes Flowerree, May 20, 1931; children—Oliver (dec.), Harry Hewes, Patricia, James, John. Admitted to Okla. bar. 1936, U.S. Supreme Ct., 1940, Tex. bar, 1946; atty. office gen. counsel Treas. Dept., Washington, 1936-37; spl. asst. atty. gen., tax div. Dept. Justice, Washington, 1937-42; adv. bd. Southwestern Legal Found., 1954-58; lectr. oil and gas inst., tax inst. N.Y. U. Served as maj. USAAF, 1942-45. Mem. Am., Okla., Dallas County (chmn. com. on ethics 1959-60) bar assns., State Bar Tex., Dallas Council World Affairs (dir., pres. young execs. group 1960, 62), N.Y. Council Fgn. Relations, Phi Delta Phi, Delta Upsilon. Episcopalian. Clubs: Metropolitan, Chevy Chase (Washington); Salesmanship, Imperial, Brook Hollow Golf (Dallas). Contbr. articles legal publs. Home: 5411 Meaders Lane Dallas TX 75211 Office: Two Eleven North Ervay Bldg Dallas TX 75201 *

HAMMONS, PAUL EDWARD, educator; b. Bogalousa, La., June 16, 1925; s. James Clifford and Norma Beatrice (Booty) H.; B.S., Northwestern State Coll., 1949; M.S., U. Ark., 1951; D.D.S., Loyola U., New Orleans, 1954; m. Doris Nell Denham, Sept. 3, 1950; children—Bruce Clifford, Mark Denham. Pvt. practice dentistry, Crossett, Ark., 1954-55; asst. prof. dentistry Sch. Dentistry, U. Ala., Birmingham, 1955-58, asso. prof., 1958-64, prof., 1964—, dir. aux. research, 1963-69, prof., chmn. dept. operative dentistry, 1968—. Cons. VA Hosp., Council on Dental Edn. Am. Dental Assn. Served with AUS, 1943-46. Mem. Am. Assn. Dental Schs., Delta Sigma Delta, Omicron Kappa Upsilon, Beta Beta Beta. Contbr. articles profl. jours. Home: 2220 Pine Crest Dr Birmingham AL 35216

HAMNER, HOMER HOWELL, economist, educator; b. Lamont, Okla., Oct. 22, 1915; s. Homer Hill and Myrtle Susan (Edwards) H.; A.A., Glendale Coll., 1936; A.B., U. So. Cal. (Gen. Achievement scholarship 1936- 37), 1938, J.D., 1941, A.M., 1947, Ph.D., 1949; m. Winnie Elvyn Heafner, May 8, 1943 (dec. Aug. 23, 1946); 1 dau., Jean Lee (Mrs. Richard L. Nicholson); m. 2d, Marjorie Lucille Dittus, Nov. 24, 1947; 1 dau., Elaine. Fellow and teaching asst., dept. econs. U. So. Cal., 1945-49; prof. and chmn. dept. econs. Baylor U., 1949-55, lectr. summer workshop, 1954; prof., chmn. dept. bus. adminstrn. and cons. U. Puget Sound, 1955-58, dir. sch. bus. adminstr. and econs., 1959-63, Edward L. Blaine chair econ. history, 1963—; also occasional lectr. Roman Forums, Ltd., Los Angeles, 1936-40; lectr. Am. Inst. Banking, 1949-50, Southwest Wholesale Credit Assn., 1949, James Connally AFB, 1950; cons. State of Wash. tax adv. council, 1957-58, State Wash. Expenditures Adv. Council, 1960. Served with U.S. Army, 1941-44; discharged as master gunner. Fellow Found. Econ. Edn., Chgo., 1953, Inst. on Freedom, Claremont Men's Coll., 1955. Mem. Am. Assn. U. Profs., Am. Econ. Assn., Southwest Social Sci. Assn. (Tex. chmn. membership com.), Nat. Tax Assn., Am. Finance Assn., Am. Acad. Polit. and Soc. Sci., Waco McLennan County Bar Assn. (hon.), Phi Beta Kappa, Phi Kappa Phi, Order of Artus, Omicron Delta Gamma, Delta Theta Phi, Phi Rho Pi (degree highest achievement 1936). Methodist. Author: Population Change in Metropolitan Waco, 1950. Reviewer, contbr. Jour. of Finance: editor research com. Baylor Business Studies, 1949-55. Home: 4404 N 44th Tacoma WA 98407

HAMON, JAKE LOUIS, oil and gas producer; b. Lawton, Okla., July 24, 1902; s. Jake Louis and Georgia (Perkins) H.; student U. Chgo.; m. Nancy Blackburn, Mar. 28, 1949. Engaged in drilling and producing oil and gas wells in Okla., Tex., Kan., La., Miss. and N.M., 1921—; dir. Employers Casualty Ins. Co., Dallas. Chmn. Nat. Petroleum Council, 1964, 65, chmn. agenda com., 1968—; dir., mem. exec. com. Am. Petroleum Inst., 1938—, chmn. bd., 1954-55, recipient Carl A. Young Meml. award, 1950; dir., mem. exec. com. Ind. Petroleum Assn. Am., 1933—; dir., mem. exec. com. Mid Continent Oil and Gas Assn., 1936—; pres. Nat. Stripper Well Assn., 1937, Dallas Wildcat Com., 1945, Dallas Petroleum Club, 1944, Gen. Mid Continent Oil and Gas Assn., 1950-51; pres. Tex. Mid Continent Oil and Gas Assn., 1937, recipient Distinguished Service award, 1941. Mem. Dallas Athletic Commn. Bd. dirs. Tex. Research League, Tex. Safety Assn., Tex. Good Roads Assn., Dallas C. of C., Dallas Citizens Council, Cotton Bowl Athletic Assn.; trustee So. Methodist U., Southwestern Med. Found., Nat. Safety Council. Recipient Lone Star Steel award, 1956. Home: 4738 Shadywood Lane Dallas TX 75209 Office: Republic Nat Bank Tower Dallas TX 75221

HAMOR, ROBERT BOLTON, ins. exec.; b. Northumberland, Pa., Mar. 3, 1908; s. Robert Fletcher and Mary Eva (Bolton) H.; B.S.C. with honors, Temple U., 1932; m. Hazel May Page, Sept. 26, 1933; 1 dau., Page (Mrs. Lyell D. Henry, Jr.). Began career as a news reporter for Sunbury (Pa.) Daily Item, 1926-28; credit mgr. C.I.T. Corp., 1932-36; Agt. Conn. Gen. Life, Phila., 1936-39, asst. mgr., Buffalo, 1939-48, asst. mgr., Chgo., 1948-52; dir. field services Continental Assurance Co., Chgo., 1952-53; supt. agys., 1953-56, v.p., dir. agys., 1956-66, senior vice president for marketing, 1966-. Served as lt. USNR, World War II; PTO. Mem. Life Ins. Agy. Mgmt. Assn. (bd.; pres. 1966), Sigma Phi Epsilon. Mason (Shriner). Club: Union League (Chgo.). Home: 236 N Hale St Palatine IL 60067 Office: 310 S Michigan Av Chicago IL 60604

HAMOVITCH, WILLIAM, educator; b. Montreal, Que., Can., Sept. 1, 1922; s. Abraham and Tillie (Weisenfeld) H.; B.Com., McGill U., 1943; M.P.A. (Adminstrn. fellow), Harvard, 1945, M.A., 1946, Ph.D., 1949; m. Mitzi Berger, May 30, 1946; children—Alan, Susan. Came to U.S., 1946, naturalized, 1953. Lectr., asst. prof. U. Buffalo, 1946-53; asst. prof., asso. prof., prof. Queens Coll., City U. N.Y., 1953—, chmn. dept. econs., 1965—; research scientist N.Y.C. Temp. Commn. on City Finances, 1965. Chmn. Commn. on Off-Track Betting in Nassau County, 1970. Fellow Royal Econ. Soc.; mem. Am. Econ. Assn. Author: Conflict and Stability in Labor Relations: A Case Study, 1952. Editor: The Federal Deficit: Fiscal Imprudence or Policy Weapon?, 1965; Monetary Policy: The Argument From Keynes' Treatise to Friedman, 1966; Employment and Occupation Projections for Nassau-Suffolk to 1985, 1968. Home: 77 Westminster Rd Great Neck NY 11020 Office: Queens Coll Flushing NY 11367

HAMOWY, EDWIN W., cosmetics co. exec.; b. 1934; B.A., Coll. City N.Y., 1954; postgrad. Columbia, 1955; married. Advt. mgr. internat. div. Shulton Inc., 1961-63, marketing mgr. internat. div., 1963-66; dir. marketing internat. div. Helena Rubinstein, Inc., 1966-67, v.p. fgn. operations, 1967-70, pres., chief operating officer, dir., 1970—. Office: 767 Fifth Av New York City NY 10022*

HAMP, ERIC PRATT, educator, linguist; b. London, Eng., Nov. 16, 1920; s. William Pratt and Edith (McConkey) H.; came to U.S., 1925, naturalized, 1947; B.A., Amherst Coll., 1942; M.A., Harvard, 1948, Ph. D. in Linguistics, 1954; m. Margot Faust, Sept. 29, 1951; children—Juliana Alexander. Chief lend-lease govt. Union South Africa, 1942- 46; mem. faculty U. Chgo., 1950—, prof. linguistics, 1962—, dir. Center Balkan and Slavic Studies, 1965—, chmn. dept. linguistics, 1966- 69. Vis. lectr. U. Mich., 1953, U. Wash., summer 1962; mem. staff Gaelic Dialect Survey, U. Edinburgh (Scotland), 1956, 57, 58; Collitz prof. U. Tex., summer 1960; vis. prof. linguistics U. Beograd (Yugoslavia), 1964, 67, Ind. U., summer 1964, U. Copenhagen (Denmark), 1966; U.S. cultural exchange lectr. Romania, summer 1966; asso. dir. Linguistic Inst. U. Ill., Summer 1968. Chmn. subcom. linguistics Com. Instnl. Coop., 1963-66, mem. com. automatic lang. processing Nat. Acad. Scis.- NRC, 1964—; mem. com. linguistic information Center Applied Linguistics, 1964-68; chmn. com. lang. programs Am. Council Learned Socs., 1963-69; mem. linguistics com. Ind. U. Press, 1965—; chmn. Com. for Ill. Place-Name Survey, 1966—; mem. adv. com. for E. Europe, Com. Internat. Exchange Persons, 1966—. John Woodruff Simpson fellow from Amherst to U. Pa., 1946, to Johns Hopkins, 1947; Sheldon Traveling fellow Harvard, 1949-50; Fulbright Sr. Research scholar U. Athens (Greece), 1955-56; Social Scis. Research Council- Am. Council Learned Socs. grantee in Albanian dialectology, 1960-61; Fulbright-Hays fellow, 1966-67. Fellow A.A.A.S., Am. Anthrop. Assn.; mem. Linguistic Soc. Am. (exec. com. 1954-56, v.p. 1963-70, pres. 1971), Modern Lang. Assn. (sec. Celtic sect. 1954, chmn. 1956), Philol. Soc. (London), Scottish Gaelic Texts Soc., Soc. de Linguistique de Paris, Soc. Linguistica Europaea, Acoustical Soc. Am., Am. Name Soc., Phi Beta Kappa. Author: A Glossary of American Technical Linguistic Usage, 3d rev. edit., 1966. Editor: Readings in Linguistics II, 1966. Adv. editor Foundations of Language, 1964—, Gen. Linguistics, 1966—, Papers in Lang. and Lit., 1965—, Abstracts in Anthropology, 1969—, Jour. Linguistics, 1971—; asso. editor Internat. Jour. Am. Linguistics, 1967—. Contbr. profl. jours. Home: 5200 S Greenwood Av Chicago IL 60615 *

HAMPEL, CHESTER WILLIAM, educator; b. Cohoes, N.Y., May 28, 1906; s. Theodore Sr. and Philomena (Young) H.; A.B., Wesleyan U., 1927, A.M., 1929; Ph.D., Harvard, 1934; m. Helen Frances Campbell, June 15, 1935; childre—David Leonard, John William, Stephen Frederick, Daniel Keith, Jean Elizabeth. Grad. asst. Wesleyan U., 1927-29; teaching fellow Harvard Med. Sch., 1929-34, Austin fellow, 1934-35; adj. prof. physiology Am. U. of Beirut (Lebanon), 1935- 38, asso. prof., 1938-43; vis. prof. physiology Coll. Medicine, N.Y. U., 1942-47, asso. prof., 1947-56; prof. physiology and biophysics Coll. Dentistry, N.Y.U., chmn. dept., 1956-60, prof. physiology and pharmacology, 1960—, chmn. dept., 1960-69. Fellow A.A.A.S., N.Y. Acad. Sci.; mem. Am. Physiol. Soc., Sci. Research Soc. Am. (bd. govs. 1969- -), Soc. Exptl. Biology and Medicine, N.Y. State Soc. Med. Research, Harvey Soc., Sigma Xi, Psi Omega, Omicron Kappa Upsilon. Home: 21 Grant St Yonkers, NY 10704. Office: 421 1st Av New York City NY 10010

HAMPEL, GUNTER, composer, vibist, bass clarinetist, flutist. Appearance in U.S. with Marion Brown's Group; concert tours in U.S.A., Italy, Greece, N.Africa. Recordings include: The Gunter Hampel Group plus Jeanne Lee; The 8th of July 1969; Dances; People Symphony; Ballet Symphony; Espace; Out Of New York; Music From Europe; Heartplants; (with Marion Brown) Le Temps Fou, Sommerhausen, Gesprachsfetzen. Address: Philipp-reis-str 10 34 Gottingen West Germany

HAMPSHIRE, STUART NEWTON, educator; b. Healing, Eng., Oct. 1, 1914; s. G.N. and Marie (West) H.; 1st Class Lit. Hum., Oxford U., 1936; m. Renee Orde-Lees, 1961. Fellow All Souls Coll., lectr. philosophy Oxford U., 1936-40, domestic bursar, research fellow; 1955-60; personal asst. to minister state Fgn. Office, 1945; lectr. philosophy U. Coll, London, 1947-50; fellow New Coll., Oxford, 1950-55; Grote prof. philosophy of mind and logic U. London, 1960-63; formerly prof. philosophy Princeton. Served with Brit. Army, 1940-45. Fellow Brit. Acad., Am. Acad. Arts and Scis. Author: Spinoza, 1951; Thought and Action, 1959; Freedom of the Individual, 1965. Contbr. profl. jours. Home: 70 Western Way Princeton NJ 08540*

HAMPSHIRE, SUSAN, actress; b. London, Eng., 1941; m. Pierre Granier-Deferre; 1 child. Actress; stage Expresso Bongo, Follow That Girl, Ginger Man, She Stoops to Conquer, On Approval, The Sleeping Prince; TV series, Andromeda, The Forsythe Saga, Vanity Fair, The First Churchills; films include During One Night, The Three Lives of Thomasina, Night Must Fall, Wonderful Life, Paris Au Mots d'Aout, The Fighting Prince of Donegal, The Trygon Factor, Monte Carlo or Bust, Rogan, David Copperfield. Winner Emmy award Best Actress in drama series, 1971. Address: National Educational TV 10 Columbus Circle New York City NY 10019*

HAMPTON, AMBROSE GONZALES, newspaper exec.; b. Columbia, S.C., May 17, 1900; s. Frank and Gertrude (Gonzales) H.; B.S., The Citadel, 1921, C.E., 1928, LL.D., 1965; postgrad. N.C. State U., 1939, 51; m. Henriette duBose Dargan, Oct. 10, 1923; children—Henriette Dargan (Mrs. Ben Rankin Morris), Ambrose Gonzales. Resident engr. bridge constrn. S.C. Hwy. Dept., 1921-32; dist. engr. Forest Service Eastern S.C., 1932-36; dist. engr. hwy. and bridge constrn. U.S. Bur. Pub. Rds. in N.C., Raleigh, 1936-42, dist. engr. access rds. to mil. posts, 1942-45, dist. engr. charge design, 1945-55; from asst. to pres. to pres. State-Record Co., Columbia, 1955—; chmn. bd. State-Record Pub. Co. (now Columbia Newspapers, Inc.), 1966-71, Bestway Express, State Printing Co., Gulf Pub. Co., 1968-71; pub. The State, The Columbia Rec., 1963—, Daily Herald, Gulfport-Biloxi, Miss., 1971—; dir. S.C. Nat. Bank, 1963-71. Commr. Richland County Historic Preservation Commn.; former pres., bd. dirs. United Community Services; v.p., trustee Historic Columbia Found. Served with U.S. Army, 1918. Mem. Am. Soc. C.E., Columbia C. of C. (past dir.), Sigma Delta Chi. Episcopalian (vestryman, sr. warden). Clubs: Kosmos, Forest Lake and Palmetto. Home: 5020 Garners Ferry Rd Columbia SC 29209 Office: PO Box 1333 Columbia SC 29202

HAMPTON, BENJAMIN BERTRAM, mfg. co. exec.; b. N.Y.C., Aug. 3, 1925; s. Max and Pauline (Weinberger) H.; B.Aero. Engring., N.Y.U., 1947; certificate mech. engring., Pa. State Coll., 1945; M.B.A., Harvard, 1949; m. Harriet Rodbell, Sept. 8, 1957; 1 son, Roger Neil. Sales mgr. Carew Products, Inc., N.Y.C., 1949- 51; project mgr. Emerson Radio & TV Corp., 1951-52; div. mgr. Paragon Oil Co., Mineola, L.I., 1952-55; mgmt. cons. E.N. Kagan & Co., N.Y.C., 1955-60; exec. asst. to pres. marketing Fed. Pacific Electric Co., Newark, 1960-62; asst. to pres. Seagrave Corp., N.Y.C., 1962-63; v.p. Swingline Inc., Long Island City, N.Y., 1963-68, exec. v.p., 1968—, also dir. Co-chmn. N.Y. State Finance Com. J.F. Kennedy presdl. campaign, 1960. Served with AUS, 1944-46. Mem. Am. Marketing Assn., Pi Lambda Phi. Club: Harvard (N.Y.C.). Home: 120 Central Park South New York City NY 10019 Office: 32-00 Skillman Av Long Island City NY 11101

HAMPTON, COLIN CAMPBELL, ins. co. exec.; b. New Haven, Jan. 4, 1923; s. George W. and Jean (Stuart) H.; B.S. in Bus. Adminstrn., Vanderbilt U., 1948; grad. student N.Y.U., U. Me.; m. Marjorie A. Brown, June 16, 1951; children—Colin Campbell, Carolyn. With Mercantile Commerce Trust Co., St. Louis, 1948-49, McGraw-Hill Co., N.Y.C., 1949-50; bond trader Am. Security Corp., N.Y.C., 1951-52; securities analyst Bankers Trust Co., N.Y.C., 1952-55, Fiduciary Counsel, Inc., N.Y.C., 1955-56; with Union Mut. Life Ins. Co., Portland, Me., 1956—, pres., 1969—; corporator Portland Savs. Bank; trustee Old Stone Mortgage & Realty Trust, Providence. Bd. dirs. Portland Boys Club. Served to 1st lt. USAAF, 1943-45. Fellow Life Office Mgmt. Assn.; mem. Me. (bd. dirs.), Greater Portland (bd. dirs.) chambers commerce. Episcopalian. Clubs: Torch of Western Maine; Portland Country. Home: : Ocean House Rd Cape Elizabeth ME 04107 Office: 2211 Congress St Portland ME 04102

HAMPTON, GEORGE LEO, Jr., ins. co. exec.; b. Monroe City, Mo., Nov. 11, 1909; s. George L. and Carrie (Tooley) H.; student Central Coll., 1926-28, U. Mo., 1931; B.S. in Commerce, Northwestern U., 1933; m. Helen Louise Hess, Aug. 10, 1936; children—George Leo III, Shirley (Mrs. Donald F. Pitcher, Jr.). Spl. agt. Kan. Ins. Co. N.Am., 1935-37; with Phoenix Ins. Co., 1937—, v.p., Chgo., 1948-50, asst. to pres., 1961-65, sr. v.p., Hartford Conn., 1965-67, president, 1967—, also dir.; pres., dir. Equitable Fire & Marine Ins. Co., Providence, Standard Nat. Ins. Co. Served to lt. USNR, 1943-46. Mason. Home: 2 Grennan Rd West Hartford CT 06107. Office: 61 Woodland St Hartford CT 06115

HAMPTON, GORDON FRANCIS, lawyer; b. Fullerton, Cal., July 14, 1912; s. Lorenzo Arnie and Katharine (Twombly) H.; A.B., Stanford, 1935; LL.B., Harvard, 1938; m. Virginia Rivers, Sept. 5, 1943 (dec. Jan. 1968); children—Roger Keith, Katharine Virginia, Wesley Gordon. Admitted to Cal. bar, 1938, since practiced in Los Angeles; partner firm Sheppard, Mullin, Richter & Hampton, and predecessors, 1945—; instr. Loyola U. Law Sch., Los Angeles, 1942-43; lectr. Cal. State Bar Continuing Edn. Program, 1950, 59. Vice chmn. Los Angeles County Republican Central Com., 1947-48; mem. Cal. Rep. Central Com., 1947-48. Fellow Pasadena Art. Mus. Fellow Am. Bar Found.; mem. Am. (chmn. antitrust sect. com. supplementary antitrust sanctions 1964-67, mem. council sect., lectr. Nat. Inst. Antitrust Law 1967, 69, chmn. nat. insts. antitrusts law subcom. 1967-71), Cal., Los Angeles (trustee 1958- 60) bar assns., Am. Judicature Soc., Stanford Alumni Assn. (pres. (1961-62), Phi Beta Kappa. Presbyn. Clubs: Valley Hunt (Pasadena); Chancery, California, University (Los Angeles). Contbr. legal jours. Home: 2665 Wallingford Rd San Marino CA 91108 Office: 458 S Spring St Los Angeles CA 90013

HAMPTON, JAMES C., educator, anatomist; b. Juliaetta, Ida., Sept. 20, 1921; s. Joseph D. and Mary Ruth (Horn) H.; student San Francisco State Coll., 1947-49; B.S., U. Ida., 1951, M.S. in Zoology, 1952; Ph.D. in Anatomy, U. Wash., 1957; m. Erma Dean Law, Mar. 28, 1942; children—Susan Carol, Connie Lou, Joseph Douglas, Walter William. Asso. prof. anatomy, research asso. prof. pathology, med. br. U. Tex., 1961-62; mem. faculty Baylor U. Coll. Medicine, 1959-61, asst. prof. exptl. biology and anatomy, 1960-61; mem. faculty U. Wash., 1957-59 instr. anatomy, 1957-59; prof. anatomy, chmn. dept. Northwestern U. Med. Sch., 1962-69; mgr. cytology sect., dept. biology, Battelle Meml. Inst., Pacific N.W. Lab., Richland, Wash., 1969—. Served with USNR, 1942- 45. Mem. Am. Soc. Cell Biology, A.A.A.S., Am. Assn. Anatomists, Biophys. Soc., Electron Microscope Soc. Am., N.Y. Acad. Sci., Radiation Research Soc., Sigma Xi. Home: 649 Lynnwood Loop Richland WA 99352 Office: Dept Biology Battelle Meml Inst Pacific NW Lab Richland WA 99352

HAMPTON, LIONEL LEO, orch. leader; b. Birmingham, Ala., Apr. 20, 1914; s. Charles and Gertrude (Whitfield) H.; student U. So. Cal., 1934; Mus.D., Allen U., Columbia, S.C.; m. Gladys Riddle, Nov. 11, 1936. Musician Benny Goodman's Orch., 1936-40; organized band, Lionel Hampton Orch., 1940. Mem. Alpha Phi Alpha. Elk (grand band master). Clubs: Friars, Grand Street Boys (N.Y.C.). Home: 337 W 138th St New York City NY 10030 also 3808 W Adams Blvd Los Angeles CA 90018*

HAMPTON, PHILIP, banker; b. Richmond, Ind., Jan. 9, 1907; s. Louis N. and Bertha (Iredell) H.; B.A., Earlham Coll., 1929; m. Margaret McCune Andrew, Aug. 27, 1935 (div. June 1965); children-Philip M., Linda (Mrs. Richard L. Rhodes), Lucy (Mrs. Jacque E. Sohm); m. 2d, Elisabeth Smith, 1965. With Union Trust Co., Cleve., 1929-33; br. mgr. Blair & Co., Columbus, O., 1935-41; v.p. Huntington Nat. Bank, Columbus, 1945-54; pres. Xenia Nat. Bank (O.), 1954-56; investment mgr. State Tchrs. Retirement System, Columbus, 1956-61; v.p. U.S. Trust Co. N.Y., N.Y.C., 1962-66, sr. v.p., 1966-69, exec. v.p., 1969—. Trustee Earlham Found. Served to capt. AUS, 1942-45. Conglist. Mason (32, Shriner). Clubs: Univ., Fifth Av (N.Y.C.) Home: RFD 1 Old Roaring Brook Rd Mt Kisco NY 10549 Office: 45 Wall St New York NY

HAMPTON, ROBERT EDWARD, govt. ofcl.; b. Chattanooga, Sept. 21, 1922; s. Charles Alfred and Mary Lee (Plemons) H.; student U. Tenn., 1946-48; B.A. in Bus. Adminstrn., U. Chattanooga, 1949; m. Geraldyne Ann Stivers, July 12, 1947; children—Adrienne Ann, Jeffrey Scott. Prin., Blackfox Sch., Cleveland, Tenn., 1949-50; vice consul, Munich, Germany, 1950-52; fgn. affairs officer exec. secretariat State Dept., 1952-53, staff asst. to sec. state, 1953-55; asst. dep. manpower, personnel and orgn. Dept. Air Force, 1955-57; spl. asst. to undersec. for adminstrn. State Dept., 1957- 58; spl. asst. for personnel The White House, 1958-61; commr. Civil Service Commn., 1961-69, chmn., 1969—. Vice chmn. bd. trustees Fed. Womens Award Com., 1961—; chmn. Fed. Labor Relations Council, 1970—; mem. President's Commn. on White House Fellows, 1969—, President's Commn. Personnel Interchange, 1969—, President's Commn. Employment Handicapped, 1969—; mem. adv. bd. Internat. Civil Service, 1970—; mem. Cabinet Com. on Opportunity for Spanish Speaking, 1969—; nat. adv. com. Jobs for Vets., 1970—. Served with USAAF, 1942-45; ETO. Named Young Republican of Year, 1960. Home: 10 Savannah Ct Bethesda MD 20034 Office: Civil Service Commn Washington DC 20415

HAMPTON, WADE, packaging co. exec.; b. Yonkers, N.Y., Aug. 14, 1923; s. Samuel Farley and Elsie (Kay) H.; grad. Phillips Exeter Acad., 1942; LL.B., Harvard, 1949; m. Lilly Middleton, May 24, 1948; children—Wade, Samuel Willoughby, Thomas Hayward, Edward Middleton. Admitted to N.Y. bar, 1949; with firm Root, Ballantine, Harlan, Bushby & Palmer, N.Y.C., 1949-54; with Am. Can Co., 1954—, gen. mgr. internat. operations, 1958-63, v.p. internat. operations, N.Y.C., 1963—, also officer, dir. affiliates and subsidiaries. Served to 2d lt., Transp. Corps, AUS, 1942-46. Mem. N.Y. Bar Assn., Nat. Indsl. Conf. Bd., N.A.M., Fgn. Trade Council, Venezuela C. of C. Presbyn. Home: 357 Stanwich Rd Greenwich CT 06830 Office: 100 Park Av New York City NY 10017 *

HAMRE, CHRISTOPHER JOHN, anatomist, educator; b. Madelia, Minn., Jan. 7, 1902; s. Andrew and Ingrie (Fedje) H.; B.A., St. Olaf Coll., 1923; M.S., U. Wis., Ph.D., 1930; m. Dr. Ernestine V. Kandel, Aug. 8, 1935. Instr. zoology St. Olaf Coll., 1923-26; grad. asst., instr. U. Wis., 1926-30; asst. prof. zoology U. Hawaii, 1930-36, asso. prof., 1936-39, prof., 1939-49, chmn. dept. zoology and entomology, 1939-46; asso. prof. anatomy U. Minn., 1946-47; research asso. Mayo Found., 1948-49; prof. anatomy U. N.D., 1949—, head dept., 1949-67, dir. summer session, 1957-63, dean Grad Sch., 1957-67, dir. spl. air force programs, 1961—. Mem. Am. Soc. Zoologists, Am. Assn. Anatomists, Soc. for Exptl. Biology and Medicine, Sigma Xi. Author: Laboratory Manual in Comparative Anatomy, 1948. Contbr. med. jours. Home: 811 Letnes Dr Grand Forks ND 58201

HAMRIC, DARRELL HUGHES, banker; b. nr. Duke, W.Va., Sept. 25, 1909; s. Edwin Lee and Mable (Hughes) H.; B.S., U. Pa. 1931; postgrad. N.Y.U., 1933-35; m. Eleanor M. Sheedy, 1936 (dec. 1955); children—Eleanor S., Darrell Hughes, Bryan D., Joan E.; m. 2d, Jane Denman, Apr. 21, 1961; foster children—Claire D., Shelton, Thomas O. Shelton, Jane M. Shelton. Asst. cashier Bank of Manhattan County, N.Y.C., 1931-42; asst. v.p. Bankers Trust Co,, N.Y.C., 1945-46; sr. v.p. Republic Nat. Bank, Dallas, 1946—, chmn. credit policy com., 1969—; chmn. bd. dirs. Lufkin-Conroe Communications Co.; dir. Gt. Plains Land Co., Pak-A-Sak Service Stores, Inc. Served to maj. USAAF, 1942-45. Mem. Sigma Chi. Clubs: Engineers, Petroleum Engineers, Brook Hollow Golf, Dallas (Dallas). Home: 5570 Nakoma Dr Dallas TX 75209 Office: Republic Nat Bank Dallas PO Box 5961 Dallas TX 75222*

HAMRIC, LOWELL DOW, telephone co. exec.; b. Lexington, Va., Apr. 24, 1933; s. Claud L. and Vera W. (Shelton) H.; B.S., Washington and Lee U., 1955; m. Katherine A. Miller, Nov. 30, 1957; children—Clayton Dow, Janet Miller, Scott Phillip. With Chesapeake & Potomac Telephone Co. Va., Richmond, 1955—, comptroller, 1969—. Mem. finance com. Richmond Area United Givers Fund. Served to 1st lt. AUS, 1957-58. Mem. Adminstrv. Mgmt. Soc. (v.p. 1971-72), Financial Execs. Inst., Phi Beta Kappa, Omicron Delta Kappa, Beta Gamma Sigma. Club: Briar Wood Swim and Racquet (bd. dirs. Richmond 1971). Home: 3017 Kenbury Rd Richmond VA 23235 Office: 703 E Grace St Richmond VA 23219

HAMRICK, EARLE ANTHONY, Jr., textile mfg. exec.; b. Shelby, N.C., June 16, 1920: s. Earle A. and Adele F. (Geier) H.; B.S., The Citadel, 1940; grad. student Wake Forest Coll., 1940-41, N.C. State Coll., 1946-48; Exec. Program in Bus. Adminstrn., Columbia, 1962; m. Germaine Edon Gold, Oct. 16, 1942; children—Germaine Edon (Mrs. Peter G. Kreitler), Celia (Mrs. Barry D. Kole). With Burlington Industries, Incorporated, and predecessor firm of Burlington Mills Corp., N.Y.C., 1948—, asst. to sr. v.p., 1956-58, dir. yarn merchandising, 1958-59, pres. Burlington Yarn Co., div. Burlington Industries, Inc., 1959—, Madison Throwing Co., div. Burlington Industries, Inc., 1970—. Mem. Kappa Alpha, Phi Psi, Sigma Tau Sigma, Phi Kappa Phi. Home: 32 Glen Oaks Av Summit NJ 07901 Office: 1345 Av of Americas New York City NY 10019

HAMRICK, FORREST GAINES, mining co. exec.; b. N.Y.C., Apr. 14, 1910; s. Forrest Gaines and Carrie Jeanette (Thompson) H.; student Lawrenceville (N.J.) Sch.; B.A., Princeton, 1931; M.B.A., Harvard, 1933; m. Marjorie Evelyn Vandill, Apr. 14, 1955. Financial analyst Scudder, Stevens & Clark, Boston, 1934-41; research adviser WPB, Washington, 1941-42; with Am. Smelting & Refining Co., N.Y.C., 1946—, treas., 1957-69, v.p., 1959-71, exec. v.p., 1971—, also dir.; dir. Neptune Gold Mining Co., So. Peru Copper Corp. Trustee, John Simon Guggenheim Found., St. John's Guild. Served from lt. (j.g.) to lt. comdr., USNR, 1942-46. Mem. Am. Inst. Mining, Metall. and Petroleum Engrs., N.Y. Soc. Security Analysts, Phi Beta Kappa. Clubs: Bankers of Am., Union, Down Town Assn. (N.Y.C.); West Side Tennis (Forest Hills, N.Y.); Maidstone (East Hampton, N.Y.). Home: 840 Park Av New York City NY 10021 Office: 120 Broadway New York City NY 10005*

HAMRICK, WILLIAM JARED, life ins. co. exec.; b. Monticello, Fla., Oct. 1, 1906; s. John Leon and Annie (Hawk) H.; student U. Fla., 1926-28; m. Florelle Harrell, June 26, 1927; children—Mary Alyce (Mrs. Stephen Wood), Shirley Anne (Mrs. James E. Smith), Jarrie Elaine (Mrs. Arthur W. Bunch, Jr.). Pub. sch. tchr., 1925-30; with Gulf Life Ins. Co., 1930-65, sr. v.p., 1957-65; hotel and restaurant commnr., Fla., 1965-66; exec. v.p. Equitable Life Ins. Co., 1966-68, pres., 1968—, also dir. Pres. Boys' Home Assn., Jacksonville, Fla., 1963-65; mem. fellowships com. Rotary Internat. Found., 1962-63. Fla., campaign mgr. for Gov. Haydon Burns, 1964. C.L.U., 1947. Mem. C.L.U. Soc., Nat. Life Underwriter Tng. Council (pres. 1962), Life Ins. Agy. Mgmt. Assn. (bd. dirs. 1953-55), Nat. Sales and Marketing Execs. (pres. Jacksonville, Fla. 1952), Washington Bd. Trade, Alpha Kappa Psi. Recipient C.G. Snead Meml. award Fla. Assn. Life Underwriters, 1962. Mem. Order Red Cross of Constantine, Royal Order Scotland Newcomen Soc. Baptist. Mason (33, Shriner), Rotarian (pres. Jacksonville, 1960-61, dist. gov. 1962-63, 64-65). Clubs: University, San Jose Country (Jacksonville); Congressional (Washington). Home: 9012 Cherbourg Dr Potomac MD 20854 Office: 3900 Wisconsin Av NW Washington DC 20016

HAN, PYO-UK, diplomat; b. S. Hamgyong Province, Korea, May 20, 1915; Ph.D., Syracuse U.; Dr. Pol., U. Mich. Ambassador to Geneva, 1966, to Thailand, 1968; Korean permanent observer UN, N.Y.C. Office: Office Permanent Observer Republic Korea to UN 866 UN Plaza 5th Floor New York City NY 10017*

HAN, SUYIN, author, physician; b. Peking, China, Sept. 12, 1917; d. Wei Chou and Marguerite Denis; ed. Yenching U., Peking, 1933-35, Brussels Belgium) U., 1935-38; M.B.B.S. with honours, London (Eng.) U., 1948; m. Paohuang Tang, Oct. 1938 (dec. 1947); 1 dau., Yingmei (Mrs. Sidney Glazier); m. 2d, Leonard F. Comber, Feb. 1952. Practiced as physician in Hong Kong, China, Malaya and Singapore for fifteen years; spl. research on birth control in China; lectr. contemporary Asian lit. Singapore U., 1960-63. Decorated Royal Order Cambodia, 1964. Licentiate Royal Coll. Physicians; mem. Royal Coll. Surgeons. Author: Destination Chungking: A Many-Splendoured Thing; And The Rain My Drink; The Mountain is Young; Four Faces; The Crippled Tree; A Mortal Flower; China in the Year 2001, 1967; Birdless Summer, 1968; also numerous articles on medicine and short stories. Address: care of Jonathan Cape 30 Bedford Square London WC 1 England

HAN, YU-SHAN, educator; b. Peiping, China, May 18, 1899; s. Tai-chong and Jui-lan (Liu) H.; B.A., Yenching U., 1924, B.D., 1926; postgrad. Harvard, 1927- 28; Ph.D., Boston U., 1929; m. Edna Nona Quick, Aug. 2, 1930. Came to U.S., 1941, naturalized, 1953. Prof. history and govt. St. John's U., Shanghai, China, 1933-38; research commr. Central Bank China, Chungking, 1940-41; lectr. history U. Cal., Los Angeles, 1941-47, asso. prof. history, 1947-57, prof., 1957-66, prof. emeritus, 1966—; dir. Art Council, 1954-56. Mem.

council internat. visitors and sister cities, Mayor's Office, City Los Angeles. Mem. Am. Soc. for Legal History, UN Assn. Los Angeles (dir.), Am. Hist. Assn., Assn. for Asian Studies, Am. Assn. U. Profs. Author: Elements of Chinese Historiography, 1955; (with Carl Becker, Sidney Painter) The Past That Lives Today, 1952, rev. edit., 1961. Bd. editors Pacific Hist. Rev. 1953-55. Home: 11672 Rochester Av Los Angeles CA 90025.

HANAFEE, WILLIAM radiologist; b. Louisville, Mar. 21, 1926; s. John F. and Mary (Crist) H.; student Ind. Coll. Pharmacy, 1943-44; B.A., U. Rochester, 1946; M.D., U. Louisville, 1949; m. Constance Gandolph, Nov. 25, 1948; children—William N., Linda, Patrick and Michael (twins). Faculty, U. Cal., Los Angeles, 1953—, prof. radiology Sch. Medicine, 1966—, acting chmn. dept., 1966, chmn. dept., 1967—; attending physician in neuroradiology Wadsworth Gen. Hosp., VA, Los Angeles, 1962—. Cons., Long Beach VA, 1964—, Jules Stein Eye Inst., Los Angeles, 1966—; lectr. San Diego Naval Hosp., 1966. Fellow Am. Coll. Radiology; mem. A.M.A., Nat. Research Council, Los Angeles Soc. Neurology and Psychiatry, Cal., Los Angeles County med. assns., N.Am., Pacific N.W., Cal., Los Angeles radiol. socs., Am. Roentgen Ray Soc., Pan Am. Med. Assn. Devel. new techniques for coronary arteriography, using percutaneous approach through the axilla, as well as new techniques for obtaining contrast of previously unexplored regions of the body, such as cavernous sinus, and the retro-orbital space; contbr. to investigation of trans-jugular cholangiography and controlled selective carotid angiography. Home: 10633 Le Conte Av Los Angeles CA 90024 Office: 405 Hilgard Av Los Angeles CA 90024

HANAHAN, DONALD JAMES, educator, biochemist; b. Springfield, Ill., May 13, 1919; s. James Francis and Clara (Schiller) H.; B.S., U. Ill., 1941, Ph.D., 1944; m. Lillian Marie Larsen, June 21, 1947; children—Douglas A., Laura J., Timothy J., Colleen J., Carolyn M. Research asso. Manhattan Project, 1944-45; postdoctoral fellow U. Cal., Berkeley, 1945-47; faculty U. Wash., Seattle, 1948-67, prof. biochemistry, 1958-67; prof., head dept. biochemistry U. Ariz., Tucson, 1967—. Guggenheim Found. fellow, 1955; NIH spl. fellow, 1965-66. Mem. Am. Chem. Soc., Am. Soc. Biol. Chemists. Author: Lipid Chemistry, 1960. Contbr. articles profl. jours. Home: 90 Calle Primorosa Tucson AZ 85716

HANAN, PATRICK DEWES, educator; b. Morrinsville, N.Z., Jan. 4, 1927; s. Frederick Arthur and Helen (Dewes) H.; B.A., U. N.Z., 1948, M.A., 1949; B.A., U. London, 1953, Ph.D., 1960; m. Anneliese Drube, July 27, 1951; 1 son, Guy. Lectr. Chinese, Sch. Oriental and African Studies U. London, 1953-63; asso. prof. Chinese, Stanford, 1963-66, prof. Chinese, 1966-68; formerly prof. Chinese lit. Harvard. Mem. Assn. Asian Studies, Am. Oriental Soc. Contbr. articles to profl. jours.*

HANAUER, JAMES DONALD, C. of C. exec.; b. Chgo., June 20, 1919; s. Walter C. and Elsie (Stiemert) H.; student U. Rochester, 1937-41; m. Madeleine J. McCoy, Jan. 29, 1944; children—Terry Mack, Jack Scott, Todd Alan. Western indsl. sales mgr. Masonite Corp., Los Angeles, 1940-53; asst. gen. mgr. So. div. E.K. Wood Lumber Co., Los Angeles, 1953-58; sales mgr. Perry Internat. Corp., Inglewood, Cal., 1958-60; gen. mgr. Los Angeles Area C. of C., 1960—. Republican. Rotarian. Club: Jonathan (Los Angeles). Home: 6954 Costello Av Van Nuys CA 91405 Office: 404 S Bixel St Los Angeles CA 90017

HANAWALT, JOSEPH DONALD, educator; b. Royersford, Pa., July 16, 1902; s. Daniel Replogle and Augusta Reid (Preston) H.; student U. Akron, 1920, Juaniata Coll., 1921; A.B., Oberlin Coll., 1924; A.M., U. Wis., 1926, Ph.D., 1929; student U. Mich., 1930, U. Groningen, Holland, 1931; m. Lenore A. Smith, Aug. 20, 1930; children—Philip C., Nancy J., Barbara J. Asst. physics U. Wis., 1924-28, instr. physics, 1928-29; NRC fellow Rockefeller Found., 1929-31; U. Mich. internat. research fellow U. Groningen, 1931; physicist Dow Chem. Co., 1931-34, dir. spectroscopy lab., 1934-40, dir. metall. research, 1940-46, v.p., 1953-62; v.p. Dow Metal Products Co. until 1964, ret.; prof. metall. engring. U. Mich., 1964—. Mem. U.S. Tech. Indsl. Intelligence Com., Germany, 1945; mem. NACA, 1945-56; mem. Nat. Indsl. Res. Rev. Com., 1948-54; chmn. magnesium industry task force NSRB, 1948-54. Mem. nat. council Boy Scouts Am., pres. Paul Bunyan Dist. council, 1956-58; pres. Midland Music Found., 1961-63. Recipient Gold medal Am. Soc. Metals, 1965, Award of Merit, Am. Soc. Testing Materials. Mem. Magnesium Assn. (dir. 1947-63) Am. Chem. Soc., Am. Phys. Soc., A.A.A.S., Am. Soc. Metals, Am. Soc. Testing Materials, Electrochem. Soc., Am. Crystallographic Assn., Am. Inst. Mining Engrs. (Mathewson Gold medalist 1943). Contbr. tech. articles. Patentee in metals field. Home: 745 Heatherway Ann Arbor MI 48104

HANAWAY, WILLIAM LIPPINCOTT, lawyer, corp. exec.; b. Long Branch, N.J., Oct. 26, 1898; s. Joseph E. and Ann (Lippincott) H.; B.Sc., Rutgers U., 1920; postgrad. Harvard, 1922-23; LL.B., George Washington U., 1928; m. Nell Prince, Jan. 23, 1923; children—William Lippincott, Joseph. Asst. chief Bur. Chemistry, Washington, 1924-26; admitted to N.Y. bar, 1929; mem. firm Breed, Abbott & Morgan, N.Y.C., 1936—, sr. partner, 1952-; dir. George C. Frye Co., Leetronics Corp., 40 Fifth Av. Corp., Desert Cactus Land Co.; sec., dir. Lee Spring Corp. Mem. N.Y. State Bar Assn. Home: 40 Fifth Av New York City NY 10011 Office: Breed Abbott & Morgan 1 Chase Manhattan Plaza New York City NY 10005*

HANBERRY, JOHN W., med. educator. Prof. surgery, head div. neurosurgery Stanford U. Med. Sch. Office: Stanford U Med Sch Med Center Stanford CA 94205*

HANBIDGE, ROBERT LEITH lt. gov. Sask.; b. Southampton, Ont., Can.; s. Robert and Frances (Murton) H.; LL.B., Sask. Law Soc.; m. Jane Mitchell, Sept. 8, 1915; cildren—Muriel Jean (Mrs. J.D. Gardiner), Gladys Elaine, Beryl Mitchell (Mrs. C. Lipe), Mildred Bennett (Mrs. F.M. Chisholm), Keith (dec.). Called to Sask. bar, then created King's counsel, 1933; mem. firm Hanbidge, Lewchuk & Mentiplay, Kerrobert, Sask.; mem. Sask. Legislature from Kerrobert Constituency, 1929-34, chief whip, 1929-34; mem. Ho. of Commons, Constituency, 1958—; lt. gov. Sask., 1963—. Del. from Ho. of Commons to NATO Conf., Paris, France, 1958, Commonwealth Parliamentary Assn. Conf., London, Eng., 1961. Former councillor, mayor and chmn. sch. bd. Kerrobert; former chmn. hosp. bd. Kerrobert. Decorated knight of grace Order St. John of Jerusalem, 1963. Sr. life mem. Sask. Law Sch.; mem. Canadian, Sask. bar assns. Mem. United Ch. Can. (chmn. bd. stewards). Mem. Conservative Party. Mason (32), Odd Fellow, Elk. Office: Legislative Bldg Regina Saskatchewan Canada*

HANBURY, UNA, sculptor; b. Eng., Oct. 8, 1909; d. Noel Hardwick and Violet Hilton (Cutbill) Rawnsley; grad. Royal Acad.; studied sculpture Chelsea Poly., painting and drawing La Grande Chaumier, L'Academie Julian (France); m. Anthony H.R.C. Hanbury, Jan., 1926; children—Diana, Jillian (Mrs. Richard A. Poole). Exhibited Royal Acad., London, Salon d'Automne, Paris, Nat. Acad. Design, Nat. Arts Club; retrospective of portraits in bronze Folger Shakespearean Library, 1971; important works include busts of Rachel Carson, Georgia O'Keefe, Andres Segovia; bust of Dato David Sung dedicated in Kuala Lampur, 1971; large sculptures appear on Wilson Blvd., Washington, St. Marks Lutheran Ch., Springfield, Va., also Boston and Cin. Mem. Nat. Sculpture Soc., Am. Fedn. Arts, Sierra Club, Artists Equity (nat. v.p. 1969-70). Club: Santa Fe Downs Jockey. Address: 1108 Calle Catalina St Santa Fe NM 87501

HANCE, WILLIAM ADAMS, economic geographer; b. N.Y.C., Dec. 29, 1916; s. George Clifton and Grace (Adams) H.; A.B., Columbia, 1938, M.S., 1941, Ph.D., 1949; m. Margaret Dorst, Mar. 23, 1940; children—Jean, Bronwen. Mem. faculty Columbia, 1941—, asst. dean coll., 1942-43, 46-49, prof. econ. geography, 1959—, chmn. grad. studies, 1961-64, chairman department geography, 1964—. Field work in Africa, 1951, 52, 56, 1962-63, 65, 69, 70; chairman joint com. African studies Am. Council Learned Societies-Social Sci. Research Council, 1960-62. Bd. mgrs. Uptown br. YMCA, 1949-61. Served to lt. (j.g.) USNR, 1944-46. Founding fellow African Studies Assn. (bd. dirs. 1958-61, exec. sec. 1959-60, vice president 1965-66, president 1966-67); honorary fellow American Geographic Society (mem. council 1968); member of the Royal African Soc., Assn. Am. Geographers, Royal Geog. Soc., Council Fgn. Relations, Phi Beta Kappa. Episcopalian. Author: African Economic Development, 1958, rev. edit., 1967; Location of Export Production in Tropical Africa (map), 1961; The Geography of Modern Africa, 1964; Population, Migration, and Urbanization in Africa, 1970; also articles. Editor, co-author: Southern Africa and the United States, 1968. Home: 106 Morningside Dr New York City NY 10027

HANCHETT, EDWIN LANI, bishop; b. Honolulu, Nov. 2, 1919; s. A. Kaumu and Mary (McGuire) H.; student U. Hawaii, 1947-39; D.D., Ch. Div. Sch. of Pacific, 1969; m. Puanani Akana, June 21, 1941; children-Carolyn (Mrs. Charles Bell), Suzanne (Mrs. William Swartman), Stuart, Tiare. Ordained priest Episcopal Ch., 1952; vicar Ch. of Holy Innocents, Lahaina, Maui, 1952- 59; vicar St. George's Episcopal Ch., Honolulu, 1959-60; rector St. Peter's Episcopal Ch., Honolulu, 1960-67; suffragan bishop Episcopal Ch. in Hawaii, 1967-69, diocesan bishop, 1969—. Rotarian. Home: 949 Kealaolu Pl Honolulu HI Office: St Andrews Cathedral Honolulu HI

HANCHETT, WILLIAM, educator; b. Evanston, Ill., May 25, 1922; s. William Francis and Alice (Trowbridge) H.; student Black Mountain Coll., 1941-42, Roosevelt U., 1946-47; B.A., So. Methodist U., 1948; M.A., U. Cal. at at Berkeley, 1949, Ph.D., 1952; m. Elizabeth Riddle, Sept. 5, 1970; children by previous marriage—Thomas Forster, Emily Porter, Historian, USAF, 1952- 54; acting asst. prof. U. Colo., 1954-55; asst. prof. Colo. State U., 1955-56; mem. faculty San Diego State Coll., 1956—, prof. history, 1965- -, chmn. dept., 1968-71. Served with USAAF, 1942-45. Mem. Am. Hist. Assn., Orgn. Am. Historians. Author: Irish: Charles G. Halpine in Civil War America, 1970; also articles. Home: 5135 63d St San Diego CA 92115

HANCOCK, EDWIN REGINALD, lawyer; b. Maysville, Ga., Dec. 1, 1924; s. Huram Richard and Boyce (Perkins) H.; student N.Ga. Coll., Dahlonega, 1942-43, U.S. Mil. Acad., 1943-44, U. Ga., 1946-50; m. Julianne Singer, Oct. 7, 1950; children—Julie Ann, Shelley Singer. Spl. agt. FBI, Washington, Chgo., Los Angeles, 1950-53; admitted to Ga. bar, 1950; practice in Atlanta, 1953—; gen. atty. NLRB, Atlanta, 1953-57; partner Smith, Currie & Hancock, 1970—. Pres. Stewart County Land Co.; dir. Georgetown Investment Co. Served with USAAF, World War II; ETO. Decorated Air medal. Mem. Am., Ga., Atlanta bar assns., Atlanta Lawyers Club, Soc. Former Spl. Agts. FBI. Kiwanian. Clubs: Cherokee, Capital City Atlanta). Home: 330 Argonne Dr NW Atlanta GA 30318 Office: Fulton Nat Bank Bldg Atlanta GA 30303

HANCOCK, HAROLD BELL, educator; b. Dover, Del., Dec. 5, 1913; s. Harry Richardson and Hazel (Cariss) H.; B.A., Wesleyan. U., Middletown, Conn., 1936; M.A., Harvard, 1938; Ph.D., Ohio State U., 1955. Tchr., Caesar Rodney High Sch., Wyoming, Del., 1938-41, Louisburg (N.C.) Jr. Coll., 1941-42, Brevard (N.C.) Jr. Coll., 1942-44; chmn. dept. history and govt. Otterbein Coll., Westerville, O., 1944—. Trustee Otterbein Coll. Fellow, Am. Philos. Soc., 1958. Mem. Pa., Del. hist. socs. Am. Hist. Assn., Soc. Am. Historians, Phi Beta Kappa. Author: The Delaware Loyalists, 1941; Delaware During the Civil War, 1961; The History of Otterbein College, 1971. Contbr. articles profl. jours. Home: 111 W Park St Westerville OH 43081 Office: Otterbein Coll Westerville OH 43081

HANCOCK, HERBERT JEFFREY, composer, pianist, publisher; b. Chgo., Apr. 12, 1940; s. Wayman Edward and Winnie (Griffin) H.; student Grinnel (Ia.) Coll., 1956-60, Roosevelt U., Chgo., 1960, Manhattan Sch. Music, 1962, New Sch. Social Research, 1967; m. Gudrun Meixner, Aug. 31, 1968. Performed with Chgo. Symphony Orch., 1952, Coleman Hawkins, Chgo., 1960, Donald Byrd, 1960- 63, Miles Davis Quintet, 1963-68; scored film Blow Up, 1966; owner-pub. Hancock Music Co.; pres. Harlem Jazz Music Center, Inc. Recipient citation of achievement Broadcast Music, Inc., 1963; Jay award Jazz mag., 1964; critics poll for talent deserving wider recognition Down Beat mag., 1967, 1st place piano category, 1968, 69, 70, composer award, 1971; All-Star Band New Artist award Record World, 1968. Mem. Nat. Acad. Rec. Arts and Scis., Jazz Musicians Assn., Nat. Acad. TV Arts and Scis., Broadcast Music. Club: Pioneer (Grinnel Coll.). Composer: Watermelon Man, 1962. Address: 202 Riverside Dr New York City NY 10025*

HANCOCK, JOHN COULTER, ednl. adminstr.; b. Martinsville, Ind., Oct. 21, 1929; s. Floyd A. and Katherine (Coulter) H.; B.S. in Elec. Engring., Purdue U., 1951, M.S. in Elec. Engring., 1955, Ph.D., 1957; m. Betty Jane Holden, Feb. 6, 1949; children—Debbie, Dwight, Marilyn, Virginia. Research engr. U.S. Naval Avionics Facility, Indpls., 1951-57; asst. prof. elec. engring. Purdue U., 1957-60, asso. prof., 1960-63, prof., 1963—, head Sch. Elec. Engring., 1965—; dir. Etronics Systems Research Lab., 1964-65, Applied Electronics Research Lab., McClure Research Park, Lafayette, Ind., 1966—; cons. in field. Dir. Sola Basic Industries, 1967—. Sr. co-chmn. Purdue U. United Fund dr., 1969-70; bd. dirs. United Community Services, Lafaytte, 1970-73. Mem. I.E.E.E., Nat. Electronics Conf. (dir. 1966-67), Am. Soc. Engring. Edn. (sec. elec. engring. div. 1970-71), Eta Kappa Nu (nat. pres. 1959-70). Author: An Introduction to the Principles of Communication Theory, 1961; Signal Detection Theory, 1966; An Introduction to Electrical Design, 1970. Home: 105 Drury Lane West Lafaytte IN 47906 Office: Elec Engring Bldg Purdue U Lafayette IN 47907

HANCOCK, JOHN SHONK, banker; b. Syracuse, N.Y., Sept. 28, 1914; s. Clarence E. and Emily (Shonk) H.; B.A., Wesleyan U., Middletown, Conn., 1936; LL.B., Yale, 1939; m. Francis Edwards, Sept. 21, 1946; children—Barbara, Charles, Elizabeth. Admitted to N.Y. bar, 1939, D.C. bar, 1946; asso. Hancock, Dorr, Ryan & Shove, Syracuse, 1939-40, Douglas, Proctor, MacIntyre & Gates, Washington, 1946-47; asst. in Office Sec. Air Force, Washington, 1948-55; trust officer, v.p. First Trust & Deposit Co., Syracuse, 1955- -, now sr. v.p. Mem. Syracuse Airport Adv. Com. Past pres. Onondaga County chpt. A.R.C.; treas., bd. dirs. Community Found. Syracuse and Onondaga County; bd. dirs. Syracuse Boys Club; trustee Manlius-Pebble Hill Sch. Served to maj. USAAF, 1941-46. Mem. N.Y. State, Onondage County bar assns. Republican. Episcopalian. Home: 221 Brattle Rd Syracuse NY 13203 Office: Warren at Washington PO Box 1095 Syracuse NY 13201

HANCOCK, JOHN WALKER, Jr., oil exec.; b. Erie, Kan., Apr. 11, 1909; s. John Walker and Madge (Limbocker) H.; student Long Beach Schs., Long Beach City Coll., 1928- 29, Southwestern U., 1932-33; m. Bernice Wedum, Aug. 12, 1933; children—John Walker III, Richard Wedum, Carol Jean, Linda Lee. In refining dept. Hancock Oil Co. (merged Signal Oil and Gas Co., Los Angeles), Long Beach, Cal., 1924, exec. v.p., 1947-53, pres., 1953-58, dir., 1942-58; pres., dir. John Hancock Devel. Co., Walker Devel. Co., Newport Devel. Co.; dir. Farmers & Mchts. Bank, Long Beach. Headed many coms. including Community Chest, A.R.C., Boy Scouts, U.S.O. drives; dir., mem. exec. com. Long Beach Conv. and Visitors Bur., pres. 1950-51, Internat. Beauty Congress; dir. Long Beach Community Chest, 1944, v.p., 1945- 46; exec. com. Youth Tennis Found. So. Cal.; mem. nat. council, hon. exec. bd. Long Beach Area council Boy Scouts Am. Recipient Silver Beaver award, 1965. Vice chmn. Long Beach State Coll., 1958-70, mem. adv. bd., 1949-70; former mem. adv. bd. St. Mary's Long Beach Hosp. Mem. Cal. Petroleum Safety Bd. (past pres.), Western Oil and Gas Assn. (pres. 1956, dir.), Ind. Petroleum Assn. Am. (dir.), Cal. Natural Gasoline Assn. (dir.), Am. Petroleum Inst., Long Beach C. of C. (dir. 1944-47), Cal. Inst. Assos., Cal. Oil Producers. Mason (past master, 32, K.T., Shriner), Rotarian (v.p. 1943, dir. 1950-51). Clubs: Virginia Country, Pacific Coast, Petroleum, Internat. City (Long Beach); California, Athletic, Petroleum (Los Angeles); Bear River (Brigham City, Utah); Thunderbird Country (Palm Springs); Tuna (Avalon, Catalina Island); Long Beach (Cal.) Yacht. Home: 4681 Virginia Rd Long Beach CA 90807 Office: 4201 N Long Beach Blvd PO Box 7000 Long Beach CA 90807*

HANCOCK, MOFFATT, educator; b. Toronto, Ont., Can., Aug. 19, 1912; s. Ernest William and Eva Pearl (Moffatt) H.; B.A., U. Toronto, 1933; barrister-at-law, Osgood Hall Law Sch., 1935; S.J.D., U. Mich., 1940; m. Catherine Eileen Phinney, Sept. 1, 1949; children-Catherine Phyllis, Graeme Ernest Maxwell. Came to U.S., 1949, naturalized, 1957. Asst. prof. law U. Toronto, 1940; Viscount Bennett prof. law Dalhousie Law Sch., N.S., 1946- 49; prof. law U. So. Cal., 1949-53; prof. law Stanford, 1953-62, Marion Rice Kirkwood prof., 1962—; cons. Canadian Conf. Commrs. on Uniformity of Legislation, 1966-67. Recipient Gold Medal in Law U. Toronto, 1933. Cook fellow U. Mich., 1936-37; Guggenheim fellow, 1965-66. Mem. Selden Soc., Order of Coif, Phi Delta Phi. Episcopalian. Author: Torts in the Conflict of Laws, 1942. Contbr. articles profl. jours. Exhibitor landscape photography Stanford, 1961. Home: 708 Garland Dr Palo Alto CA 94303 Office: Stanford Law Sch Stanford CA 94305

HANCOCK, RALPH LOWELL, author, specialist in Latin Am. affairs; b. Plainville, Ind., Nov. 23, 1903; s. John Hiram and Nancy (Cunningham) H.; ed. Cabool (Mo.) High Sch., Springfield (Mo.) Bus. Coll.; student Washington U., St. Louis, Mo., 1924-27; m. Julia Ellen F. Ross, Dec. 25, 1924 (div.); 1 son, David Lowell (killed in action World War II); married second Frances Fenster Iverson, 1948; children—Nancy Lowell, Bret Hiram. Resident news correspondent covering Latin America 1936-40; organized publicity department Transportes Aereos Centro Americanos Airlines, 1940, dir., 1940-42; sr. economic analyst, specialist on Caribbean Area, Bd. of Economic Warfare, 1942-43; head of economic mission to Latin Am., 1942- 43; Latin Am. adviser on editorial staffs of 3 prominent publishing houses, 1943-49. Vice pres., dir. pub. relations in Latin Am. for Pan- Am. Found., Inc.; pres. Hemisphere Corp. Speaker 7th Annual Conference on Caribbean, U. of Fla., 1956. Author: Handbook of Central America (Bd. of Econ. Warfare); Understanding Central America; Latin America: Land and People; Our Southern Neighbors, 1942; Mexico and Central Am., 1942; Latin America, 1943; Let's Look at Latin America, 1943; Opportunities in Latin America, 1946; Our Latin American Neighbors, 1946; The Rainbow Republics: Central America, 1947; The Magic Land: Mexico, 1948; Fabulous Boulevard, 1949; Caribbean Correspondent, 1951; Douglas Fairbanks: The Fourth Musketeer, 1953; Baja California, 1953; The Forest Lawn Story, 1955; Exploring American Neighbors, 1956; Laughter is a Wonderful Thing, 1956; Blondes, Brunettes and Bullets, 1957; Desert Living, 1958; Puerto Rico: A Success Story, 1960; The Lost Treasure of Cocos Island, 1960; Puerto Rico: A Travellers Guide, 1961; Mexico, 1964; The Compleat Swindler, 1968; authoritative articles on Latin Am. in Ency. Americana and Americana Annual and Book of Knowledge and Annual. Author and photographer of numerous ednl. films on Latin Am. and mag. and newpaper articles. Latin Am. editor of Invitation to Travel series. Editor-in-chief Hemisphere Research. Lectr. Home: 16527 Avenida Florencia Poway CA 92064 Office: PO Box 28012 San Diego CA 92128

HANCOCK, ROBERT SPENCER, educator; b. Lakota, N.D., Nov. 4, 1917; s. Frank and Minnie R. (Stonier) H.; student Cornell Coll., 1936-38; B.S., N. Central Coll., Naperville, Ill., 1947; M.S., U. Ill., 1949, Ph.D. in Econs., 1956; m. Ruth Marie Johnson, June 11, 1949; children—David S., Philip E., Kenneth A. Mem. faculty U. Ill., 1948-50, 53-57, asst. prof., 1956-57; mem. faculty U. Minn., 1957-67, prof. marketing, 1961-67, chmn. dept. bus. functions and management, 1962-64, chairman dept. of marketing, 1964-66; cons., 1957—; dean Sch. Business, So. Ill. U., 1967-70; head dept. marketing U. Ariz., 1970—; director Westminster Foundation Corp.; adviser Mid-Continent Survey, Inc. Served with USAF, 1951-52; lt. col. Res. Mem. Am. Econ. Assn., Am. Marketing Assn. (pres. Minn. 1961-62), Beta Gamma Sigma, Alpha Kappa Psi. Author: (with H.W. Huegy) Credit Problems, rev. edit., 1956; (with R. H. Cole) Consumer and Commercial Credit Management, 1960; (with E. H. Lewis) The Franchise System of Distribution, 1963; (with R. J. Holloway) The Environment of Marketing Behavior, 1964, Marketing in a Changing Environment, 1967; (with Marcus Alexis and R. J. Holloway) Impirical Foundations of Marketing, 1968. Editor: Dynamic Marketing for a Changing World, 1960. Home: 2242 E Seneca Tucson AZ 85719

HANCOCK, THOMAS, mfg. exec.; b. Bloomington, Wis., Aug. 21, 1913; s. Herbert and Helen (Weeks) H.; m. Lena Vogel, Aug. 21, 1942; children—David, Thomas C., Pamela. Asst. to exec. v.p. Trane Co., La Crosse, Wis., 1945-51, v.p. charge sales, 1951-55, exec. v.p., dir., 1955-63, pres., 1963—; dir. Employers Ins. of Wausau (Wis.). Home: 204 S 20th St La Crosse WI 54601 Office: Trane Co La Crosse WI 54601

HANCOCK, WALKER KIRTLAND, sculptor; b. St. Louis, June 28, 1901; s. Walter Scott and Anna (Spencer) H.; student Sch. Fine Arts, Washington U., 1918-20, U. Wis., 1920, Pa. Acad. Fine Arts, 1921-25; fellow Am. Acad. in Rome, 1928; Dr. Fine Arts, Washington U., 1942; m. Saima Esther Natti, Dec. 4, 1943; 1 dau., Saima Deane. Trustee Am. Acad. in Rome, sculptor in residence, 1956-57, 62-63; sculptor in charge Stone Mountain, Ga., 1964; head sculpture dept. Pa. Acad. Fine Arts, 1929- 67. Mem. Nat. Collection Fine Arts Commn. Trustee Saint-Gaudens Meml., Cornish, N.H. Served as capt. AUS, 1942-46. Served as monuments, fine arts, archives officer, overseas 2 yrs. Awarded Widener gold medal, Prix de Rome, 1925; fellowship prize Pa. Acad. Fine Arts, 1931; Helen Foster Barnett prize N.A.D., 1935, Anon. prize sculpture, 1949; Phila. Art Alliance medal of achievement, 1953; acad. medal of honor, Pa. Acad. Fine Arts, 1953; Silver medal Archtl. League, 1955; J. Sanford Saltus medal 1953; Herbert Adams Meml. award, 1954; Thomas R. Proctor prize N.A.D.; Am. Acad. Achievement award, 1971. Academician, N.A.D., 1939, Nat. Inst. of Arts and Letters, 1941; Fellow Nat. Sculpture Soc.; mem. Archtl. League N.Y., Alpha Tau Omega. Episcopalian. Clubs: Peale (Phila); Century Assn. (N.Y.C.); St. Botolph (Boston). Home: Lanesville Gloucester MA 01930

HANCOCK, WALTON MILTON, educator; b. Pitts., Feb. 21, 1929; s. Milton Livingston and Agnes (Jones) L.; B.Engring., Johns Hopkins, 1951, M.S. in Engring., 1952, D.Engring., 1954; m. Charlene Steiger, June 9, 1951; childrenBetsy Joy, Amy Katherine, Robert Laurence. Quality control engr. Lord Baltimore Press, Balt., 1951-54, mgr. indsl. engring. and quality control, 1956- 59; instr. Wittenberg Coll., 1954-56, Johns Hopkins, 1956-59; mem. faculty U. Mich., 1959—, prof. industrial engineering, 1962—, chairman of department, 1963—. Coordinating director of basic research International MTM-Directorate, since 1966. Chmn. tech. adv. com. Mich. Hosp. Assn., 1965—. Served to 1st lt. USAF, 1954-56. Mem. Methods-Time Measurement Assn. (research dir. standards and research 1960—, editor- in-chief jour. 1963-70), Am. Inst. Indsl. Engrs. (dir. operations 1964- 66), Inst. Mgmt. Sci., Sigma Xi, Tau Beta Pi, Alpha Pi Mu. Author monographs prediction human performance. Home: 3440 Cottontail Lane RR 1 Ann Arbor MI 48103

HAND, AVERY CHAPMAN, Jr., banker; b. Mansfield, O., Jan. 17, 1918; s. Avery Chapman and Reba Grace (Ackerman) H.; grad. Asheville (N.C.) Sch., 1937; student Wharton Sch. of U. Pa., 1939; exchange student archaeol. field work, Irish Nat. Museum, Dublin, 1938; m. Mariann Stander, Feb. 23, 1946; children—Jo (Mrs. Jo Lynn Wright) Jill Carla, Heidi Belinda, Holly Anne. With Tracy & Avery Co., wholesale grocers, also Marchand Markets, supermarket chain, 1939-41; v.p. Mansfield Savs. Trust Nat. Bank, 1946-53; with First Nat. Bank Mansfield, 1953—, pres., 1962—, also dir.; v.p., dir. Euclid Coffe Co., Cleve., Tracy & Avery Co., Mansfield; treas., dir. Lynn Realty & Constrn. Co., Inc., Mansfield; dir. United Telephone Co. Ohio, Indsl. & Tech. Sales & Service Co., Shafer Valve Co., Rupp Industries, Inc. (all Manfield); Peoples Nat. Bank (Greenfield, O.), Jos. Bucheit & Sons Co. (Youngstown, O.); v.p., dir. Hugbes Supply Co., Mansfield. Chmn. Ohio sect. U.S. Savs. Bonds, also Richland County Savs. Bond Com. Mem. Mayor Mansfield Com. Human Relations. Pres. bd. trustees Mansfield Gen. Hosp.; bd. dirs. Mansfield Humane Soc.; trustee, pres. Soldiers and Sailors Mansfield Meml. Bldg., State Troopers Ohio; trustee Ashland College, Mansfield Safety Found. adv. bd. Mansfield campus Ohio State U. Served to maj. AUS, 1941-46; ETO. Mem. Ohio (pres., bd. dirs.), Mansfield Area (bd. dirs., past pres.) chambers commerce, U.S. Power Squadron, 12th Army Group Assn., Ohio Geneal. Soc., Richland County Hist. Soc. Conglist. Clubs: Westbrook Country (past pres.), University, Fifty-One, Our (past pres.), Bluecoats (Mansfield); Great Lakes Cruising (Chgo.); Huron (O.) Yacht; Plumbrook Country (Sandusky, O.). Home: 145 S Linden Rd Mansfield OH 44906 Office: 42-44 N Main St Mansfield OH 44901

HAND, CADET HAMMOND, Jr., educator, marine biologist; b. Patchogue, N.Y., Apr. 23, 1920; s. Cadet Hammond and Myra (Wells) H.; B.S., U. Conn., 1946; M.A., U. Cal. at Berkeley, 1948, Ph.D., 1951; m. Winifred Werdelin, June 6, 1942; children—Cadet Hammond III, Gary Alan. Instr., Mills Coll., 1948-50, asst. prof., 1950-51; research biologist Scripps Inst. Oceanography, 1951-53; mem. faculty U. Cal. at Berkeley, 1953—, prof. zoology, 1963- -, dir. Bodega Marine Lab., 1961—; cons. NIH, 1964-66, NSF, 1964-69. NSF Sr. Postdoctoral fellow, 1959-60; Guggenheim fellow, 1967-68. Mem. No. Cal. Malacozool. Soc. (pres. 1963—), Soc. Systemic Zoology, Ecol. Soc. Am., Ray Soc. (Great Britain), Am. Soc. Zoologists, Soc. Limnology and Oceanography. Contbr. profl. jours. Home: Star Route Bogeda Bay CA 94923 Office: Bodega Marine Lab Bodega Bay CA 94923

HAND, CHARLES CONNOR, lawyer; b. Shubuta, Miss., Dec. 6, 1890; s. Robert McLain and Annie Brevard (Case) H.; A.B., Millsaps Coll., 1909; student U. Va., 1910-12; m. Irma Weems, Feb. 23, 1916; children—John Weems, William Brevard, James Albert. Admitted to Miss. bar, 1912, Ala. bar, 1921; practice in Shubuta, Miss. to 1921, Mobile, 1921—, sr. mem. firm Hand, Arendall, Bedsole, Greaves & Johnston, 1940—. Officer, dir. various lumber and investment cos. President, dir. Mitchell Found.; Member of the American, Ala., Mobile (past pres.) bar assns., Am. Counsel Assn., Am. Judicature Soc. Methodist. Mason. Home: 1855 Dauphin St Mobile AL 36606 Office: First Nat Bank Bldg Mobile AL 36602

HAND, DARWIN CLIFFORD, former business exec.; b. Berkeley, Cal., Nov. 24, 1905; s. Clifford Nott and Bertha (Hartshorn) H.; A.B., Pomona Coll., 1926; M.A., Claremont Coll., 1930; m. Pattie Neff, June 21, 1932; childrenLouis Neff, Susan Elizabeth. Indsl. management, 1934-40; factory supt. Colgate-Palmolive- Peet Co. (now Colgate-Palmolive Co.), N.Y.C., 1941-42, dir. indsl. relations, 1942-51, v.p., 1951-70, ret., 1970. Mem. Am. Mgmt. Assn.

HAND, GEORGE HENRY, educator; born Wheeling, W.Va., Feb. 22, 1903; s. George Wesley and Mary (Pietz) H.; A.B., West Virginia U., 1928; Ph.D., Princeton U., 1939; student Columbia, summers 1929, 30, 31; m. Madeline Gladys Randolph, June 10, 1931; children—George Randolph, John Hayhurst. Commercial teacher and athletic coach, Univ. High Sch., West Virginia U., 1928-31; instr. economics, Denison U., 1934-37, asst. prof., 1937-39; asso. prof. economics, Ohio Wesleyan U., 1939-42, prof., 1943-44; chmn. dept. economics, U. of Vt., 1944-45; pres. Fairmont (W.Va.) State Coll., 1945- 52; v.p. business affairs So. Ill. U., 1952-60, chmn. dept. higher edn., 1960-65, prof. econs., 1966-. State price exec. for W.Va., OPA, 1942- 43. Trustee McKendree Coll. Mem. Am. Econ. Assn., Phi Kappa Phi, Phi Sigma Kappa. Rotarian. Home: 19 Hillcrest Dr Carbondale IL 62901

HAND, JOHN ANTHON, banker; b. Rome, Ga., Nov. 18, 1901; s. Thomas Oscar and Berta (Maddox) H.; grad. Sch. Banking, Rutgers U.; student Harvard; m. Eula Elizabeth Gibson, Nov. 1, 1930; children—Barbara Elizabeth, John Anthon. Asst. nat. bank examiner Sixth Fed. Res. Dist., 1924-28; auditor Am. Traders Nat. Bank, Birmingham, Ala., 1928-30; comptroller First Nat. Bank of Birmingham, 1930-38, v.p., 1934-53, exec. v.p., 1953-56, pres., 1956-68, chmn. bd., 1968—, also dir.; dir. Ala. Power Co., Protective Life Ins. Co. Birmingham. Bd. dirs. Community Chest. Methodist. Clubs: Birmingham Country, Rotary (Birmingham). Home: 3822 Cove Dr Birmingham AL 35223 Office: Nat Bank Birmingham AL 35203*

HAND, JOHN WEEMS, engring. exec.; b. Mobile, Ala., Nov. 9, 1922; s. Charles Connor and Irma (Weems) H.; B.S. in Chem. Engring., Auburn U., 1943; m. Mary Louise Pitard, Mar. 8, 1947; children—John Weems, Helen Horn. Chem. engr. Chem. Warfare Service, Pine Bluff (Ark.) Arsenal, 1943-44; with Ideal Cement Co., 1946-65, bus. research dir., 1955-61, v.p. adminstrn., 1961-65; v.p. Cameron & Jones, Inc., Denver, 1965—. Active campaigns Denver Symphony Soc. Served to lt. (j.g.) USNR, 1944-46. Mem. Am. Inst. Chem. Engrs., Inst. Mgmt. Scis., A.A.A.S., Denver C. of C. Methodist. Lion. Home: 305 Kearney St Denver CO 80220 Office: 2150 S Bellaire St Denver CO 80222*

HAND, LEO VINCENT, retired physician; b. Providence, July 25, 1903; s. Bernard and Emma (Doherty) H.; student Holy Cross Coll., 1924-26; A.B., Brown U., 1928; M.D., Temple U., 1933; m. Alice V. Wall, June 23, 1934; chldren—Alice Mae (Mrs. Paul A. Powell), Rose Marie (Mrs. Edward J. Gaffey), Leo Vincent. Intern Rhode Island Hosp., Providence, 1933-35, resident anesthesia, 1935-36; mem. anesthesia staff Lahey Clinic, Boston, 1936-47; dir. dep. anesthesia New Eng. Deaconess Hosp., Boston, 1952-68. Diplomate Am. Bd. Anesthesiology. Mem. Am. (pres. 1959-60), New Eng. (pres 1946-47), Mass. (pres. 1950-51) socs. anesthesiologists. Home: PO Box 345 Waquoit MA 02536

HAND, LLOYD NELSON, lawyer; b. Alton, Ill., Jan. 31, 1929; s. Nelson T. and Robbie Omega (Taylor) H.; B.A., U. Tex., 1952, LL.B., 1957; m. Lucy Ann Donoghue, Feb. 23, 1952; children—Cathy, Lloyd, Susan, Bridget, Thomas Lyndon. Admitted to Tex. bar, 1957; practice in Houston, 1961-63; asst. to Senator Lyndon B. Johnson, 1957-61; partner Allbritton, McGee & Hand, 1963; v.p., dir. Pierce Nat. Life Ins. Co., Los Angeles, 1961-65; chief of protocol U.S., Washington, 1965-66; pres. Worldwide Cons., Inc., 1966- -; partner law firm Wyman, Bautzer, Finell, Rothman and Kuchel, Washington and Paris, France; dir. Continental Air Services, Inc., Continental Air Lines, Inc., U.S. Dir. bd. fgn. Scholarships Dept. State. Del. Dem. Conv., 1965. Served to lt. USNR, 1951-55. Recipient Albert Lee Stevens Achievement award U. So. Cal., 1965. Mem. Los Angeles World Affairs Council (dir.), Phi Kappa Psi, Phi Alpha Delta. Clubs: Bel-Air Country (Los Angeles); Friars Soc. (U. Tex.). Home: 166 Groverton Pl Los Angeles CA 90024 Office: 9454 Wilshire Blvd Beverly Hills CA 90212

HAND, WILLIAM ELI, railroad exec.; b. Pender County, N.C., Dec. 24, 1903; s. William Benjamin and Dorothy Olive (Shivar) H.; ed. pub. schs., N. C.; m. Thelma Webster, Nov. 29, 1924. With Seaboard Coast Line R.R. Co., 1920—, staff asst. to pres., 1946-49, asst. comptroller, 1949, comptroller, 1949-61, v.p., 1961—; v.p. High Point, Thomasville & Denton R.R.; v.p., controller Athens Terminal Co., Gainesville Midland R.R. Co., Southeastern Investment Co., Tampa & Gulf Coast R.R. Co., Tavares & Gulf R.R. Co.; v.p., auditor Balt. Steam Packet Co., Tampa Union Sta. Co.; also comptroller 12 wholly owned or affiliated coms. Mem. Financial Exec. Inst., Assn. Am. Railroads. Mason (33). Clubs: Seminole, River, San Jose Country University (Jacksonville); Ponte Vedra (Fla.). Home: 7204 San Carlos Rd Jacksonville FL 32217 Office: 500 Water St Jacksonville FL 32202

HANDBURY, JOHN D., dept. store exec.; b. Chgo.; B.A., U. Ill.; m. Margarette Handbury; children—John D., Mark, Holly. With Carson Pirie Scott & Co., Chgo., 1934—, now exec. v.p. wholesale div., also dir.; dir. Roxbury Carpet Co., Saxonville, Mass., Coleman Distbrs., Atlanta. Vice pres. bd. govs. DePauw U., Greencastle, Ind. Served to 1st lt. AUS, World War II. Mem. Chgo. Floor Covering Assn., Carpet Trade Golf Assn., Alpha Delta Phi. Clubs: Merchant and Manufacturers (Chgo.); Glen Oak Country. Home: Glen Ellyn IL Office: Carson Pirie Scott & Co Merchandise Mart Chicago IL 60654

HANDEL, ALEXANDER F., social worker; b. St. Joseph, Mo., Dec. 15, 1909; s. Harry G. and Ethel (Krugman) H.; Ph.B., U. Chgo., 1931, A.M., 1950; m. Marguerite A. Wilks, Jan. 15, 1944; children—Richard C., Jeffrey J., Todd D. Case worker Chgo. Relief Adminstrn., 1932-34; dir. health and welfare services UNRRA, U.S. Zone, Austria, 1945-46; dir. rehab. services United Service for New Americans, N.Y.C., 1946-49; dean, prof. social work Sch. Social Work, Adelphi Coll., Garden City, N.Y., 1949-53; cons. community planning Am. Found. for Blind, 1954-58, dir. div. community services, 1958- 66; exec. dir. Nat. Accreditation Council for Agencies Serving the Blind and Visually Handicapped, Inc. Past pres. bd. dirs. Social Work Vocational Bur.; past chmn. Rahway River Assn.; psychiat. social worker, M.C., U.S. Army, 1943-45; dep. chief emergency welfare div., U.S. Citizens Def. Corps. Mich., 1942-43; UNRRA liaison officer with Anglo-Am. Com. of Inquiry on Palestine, 1946. Mem. Nat. Conf. Social Welfare (sec.), Am. Assn. Workers for Blind, Assn. for Edn. of Visually Handicapped, Acad. Certified Social Workers, Nat. Assn. Social Workers, Phi Delta Kappa. Author articles, book reviews various profl. jours. Contbr. to books and Ency. Social Work. Home: 14 Rahway Rd Millburn NJ 08848 Office: 79 Madison Av New York City NY 10016 ☆

HANDELMAN, GEORGE HERMAN, educator; b. Pitts., Mar. 24, 1921; s. Morris and Sophia (Pincus) H.; A.B., Harvard, 1941, A.M., 1942; Ph.D., Brown U., 1946; m. Marcia Lee Mendelson, July 10, 1949; children—Nancy Miriam, Louise Sarah. Asst. prof. engring. Brown U., 1947-48; asst. prof. math. Carnegie Inst. Tech., 1948-51, asso. prof., 1951-55; prof. applied math. Rensselaer Poly. Inst., 1955—, chmn. dept. math., 1960—; spl. research elasticity, plasticity, wave motion, vibrations. Fellow Am. Soc. M.E.; mem. Am. Math. Soc., Soc. Indsl. and Applied Math.,, Am. Assn. U. Profs., Phi Beta Kappa, Sigma Xi. Home: 6 Clinton Pl Troy NY 12180

HANDER, O. BENJAMIN, chem. co. exec.; b. Waco, Tex., Feb. 16, 1918; s. Edwin William and Katherine E. (Munz) H.; B.S. in Mech. Engring., Rice U., 1942; m. Clariece Sego, May 24, 1942; children—Howard Benjamin, Janet Clariece, (Mrs. William G. Quinn, Jr.), Robert William. Chem. engr. Humble Oil Co., 1942-48; mgr. prodn. and control Office Synthetic Rubber, Washington, 1948-51; cons. Exec. Offices Pres. U.S., 1951-52; with Dewey and Almy Chem. Co., 1952-54, asst. to pres., 1953-54; co. merged with W.R. Grace & Co., N.Y.C., 1954, v.p. chem. group, 1962-65, v.p. gen. devel. group, 1965-. Mem. Assn. Corp. Growth and Diversification (officer, dir.), Am. Inst. Chem. Engrs., Am. Soc. M.E. Clubs: Canoe Brook (Summit); Broad Street (N.Y.C.). Home: 30 Colt Rd Summit NJ 07901 Office: 3 Hanover Sq New York City NY 10004

HANDKE, WERNER FREIMUT, German diplomat; b. Breslaw, Germany, Aug. 9, 1920; s. Gustav and Luise (Hirsch) H.; dipl.rer.pol., U. Hamburg, 1949; dr.rer.pol., U. Cologne, 1952; m. Annemarie Kirchner, Dec. 6, 1952; children—Christiane, Annette, Sabine, Amelie Mei-mei. Dep. editor Handelsblatt, Dusseldorf, 1949-53; mem. German Fgn. Service, 1953—; vice consel and consel German Consulate Gen., Hong Kong, 1953-58; sec. German Embassy, Oslo, 1958-62; sec. German Permanent Mission to Orgn. Econ. Coop. and Devel., Paris, 1962-64; counselor Fgn. Office, Bonn, 1964-68; counselor German Embassy, Washington, 1968—. Author: The Economy of Mainland China, 1959. Home: 1423 Ironwood St McLean VA 22101 Office: 4645 Reservoir Rd Washington DC 20007

HANDLER, ELLIOT, toy mfg. corp. exec.; b. 1916. Indsl. designer, 1936-42; owner Elliot Handler Plastics, mfg., 1942-43; partner Elzac Cal. Creations, 1943-44; founder Mattel, Inc., 1944, pres., 1964-1967, now chmn. bd., chief exec. officer, dir. Address: 5150 Rosecrans Av Hawthorne, CA 90250.

HANDLER, MILTON, lawyer; b. N.Y.C., Oct. 8, 1903; s. George and Ray (Friedman) H.; A.B., Columbia, 1924, LL.B., 1926; editor Columbia Law Rev., 1924-26; award Ordronaux prize; LL.D. honoris causa, Hebrew U., 1965; m. Marion W. Kahn, Dec. 21, 1932 (dec.); 1 dau., Carol Enid (Mrs. Peter J. Schoenbach); m. 2d, Miriam Adler, Feb. 3, 1955. Admitted to N.Y. State bar, 1927; on staff Columbia, 1927—, now prof. law; engaged in pvt. practice law, specializing in antitrust and trademark law; partner firm Kaye, Scholer, Fierman, Hays & Handler; pres. N.Y. Majestic Corp., 1937-48. Gen. counsel Nat. Labor Bd., 1933-34; spl. asst. to gen. counsel Treasury Dept., 1938-40; asst. gen. counsel Lend Lease Adminstrn., 1942-43; spl. counsel Fgn. Econ. Adminstrn., 1943-44; asso. pub. mem. Nat. War Labor Bd., 1944; adviser Am. Law Inst. Restatement of Torts and Restatement of Torts second; arbitrator in numerous important labor and comml. disputes; Mitchell lectr. Buffalo Law Sch., 1956-57; lectr. U. Leyden, The Netherlands, 1963. Mem. atty. gen.'s nat. com. to study antitrust laws, 1953-55. Chmn. bd. dirs. Am. Friends of Hebrew U.; dep. chmn., gov. Hebrew U. Recipient bicentennial silver medallion Columbia U., 1954, Scopus award Am. Friends of Hebrew U., 1963. Fellow Am. Coll. Trial Lawyers, Am. Bar Found.; mem. Am. (mem. council antitrust sec. 1961-64). Fed., N.Y. State (chmn. spl. com. to study state antitrust laws 1956-66), N.Y. City bar assns., N.Y. County Lawyers Assn. (dir. 1953-56), Lawyers Club. Democrat. Jewish religion. Clubs: Men's Faculty (Columbia U.); Harmonie. Author books and articles in legal field, including Cases and Materials on Trade Regulation, 4th edit., 1967; Antitrust in Perspective, 1957. Home: 625 Park Av New York City NY 10021 Office: 425 Park Av New York City NY 10022

HANDLER, PAUL, educator; b. Newark, Apr. 24, 1929; s. Jacob and Yetta (Spector) H.; student Ind. U., 1946-48; M.S., Ph.D., U. Chgo., 1954; m. Ellen Oppenheimer, June 22, 1952; children-Ira, Harry, Lilly. Research asso. U. Ill. at Urbana, 1954-56, asst. prof., 1957-60, asso. prof., 1961-64, prof. of physics, 1964—; cons. in semi-conductor physics. Bd. dirs. Champaign-Urbana Planned Parenthood Fedn., 1967—. Guggenheim fellow, 1960-61. Mem. Am. Phys. Soc. Contbr. articles to profl. journals, monographs. Home: 706 W Oregon St Urbana IL 61801

HANDLER, PHILIP, educator; b. N.Y.C., Aug. 13, 1917; s. Jacob and Lena (Heisen) H.; B.S., Coll. City N.Y., 1936; Ph.D., U. Ill., 1939; D.Sc., Case Western Res. U., Carnegie-Mellon U., Colo. State U., U. N.C., Yeshiva U., N.Y. Med. Coll., Hebrew U. Jerusalem; LL.D., Emory U.; m. Lucille P. Marcus, Dec. 6, 1939; children— Mark, Eric Paul. Instr. Duke, 1939-40, asso., 1940-41, asst. prof. physiology, 1941-44, asso. prof. biochemistry and nutrition, 1944-49, prof., 1949-69, chmn. dept. 1950-69, James B. Duke prof. biochemistry, 1961—, dir. AEC fellowship tng. program, 1948-53; pres. Nat. Acad. Scis., Washington, 1969—. Dir. Squibb- Beechnut, Inc., 1966-69. Cons. USPHS, AEC, NRC, VA: chmn. biochem. study sect. NIH, 1956-59, nat. adv. com. research facilities and resources, 1963-67; mem. nat. health adv. council USPHS, 1959-62; mem. biology and medicine research facilities panel NSF, 1958-61, mem. divisional com. for biology and medicine, 1960-62, mem. nat. sci. bd., 1962, chmn. 1966-70; chmn. com. radiation and aging NIH AEC, 1959-62. Mem. President's Sci. Adv. Com., 1964-68, 69—, Pres.'s Commn. on Heart Disease, Cancer and Stroke, 1964-65. Trustee Found. Advanced Edn. Med. Scis., 1964-70, Cold Spring Harbor Lab. Quantitative Biology, 1963-67, Rockefeller U.; bd. visitors Grad. Sch., Yale; vis. com. life scis. Notre Dame U., Johns Hopkins Mem. Unitarian Service Com., Med. Mission to Japan, 1951. Recipient N.C. medal from gov. N.C.; W.O. Atwater medal U.S. Dept. Agr.; Stevens Honor award Stevens Inst. Tech.; Sci. Achievement award A.M.A.; Townsend Harris medal Coll. City N.Y. Mem. Am. Soc. Biol. Chemists (sec. 1953-58, councilor 1958-61, pres. 1962-63), Fedn. Am. Socs. Exptl. Biology (exec. com. 1959- 65, chmn. bd. 1964-65), Nat. Acad. Scis. (chmn. survey com. life scis. 1966-70, council 1968—), Am. Inst. Nutrition, A.A.A.S., Soc. Exptl. Biology and Medicine (pres. S.E. sect. 1953-54), Am. Chem. Soc., Am. Acad. Arts and Scis., N.Y. Acad. Scis., Am. Philos. Soc., Royal Soc. Arts (hon.), Swiss Acad. Sci. (hon.), Sigma Xi. Club: Cosmos (Washington), Author: Principles of Biochemistry (textbook); Biology and the Future of Man; The Life Sciences. also tech. publs. Mem. editorial com. jour. Theoretical Biology, 1961-68, Jour. Comparative Biochemistry and Physiology, 1962-65, Jour Biol. Chemistry, 1964-70, Editor Geriatrics, 1957-65. Home: 2700 Virginia Av Washington DC 20037 Office: 2101 Constitution Av Washington DC 20037

HANDLEY, JACK ALFRED, corp. exec.; b. Kansas City, Mo., Jan. 31, 1910; s. Irvin B. and Cora Lee (Miller) H.; B.S., U. Kan., 1931; m. Marjorie Williams, June 24, 1935; children—John Alexander, Bruce Robert, Susan. Engr., Ford Motor Co., K.C., 1931-41; plant engr. Douglas Aircraft Co., Inc., Long Beach, Cal., 1942-47; plant mgr. Whiting Corp., Los Angeles, 1948-51, exec. v.p., Harvey, Ill., 1951-52, pres., dir., 1952—; pres., dir. Whiting Corp. of Can., Ltd., Welland, Ont.; dir. South Suburban Savs. & Loan Assn., Pullman Trust & Savs. Bank, Ill. Bell Telephone Co. Mem. Sigma Tau, Alpha Tau Omega. Club: Flossmoor (Ill.) Country. Home: 1300 Lake Shore Dr Chicago IL 60610 Office: Whiting Corp Harvey IL 60426

HANDLEY, WILLIAM J., U.S. ambassador; b. Netherlands Guiana, Dec. 17, 1918 (parents Am. citizens); student U. London, 1935-37; B.A., U. Md., 1942, Am. U., 1943-44. Announcer, program writer for broadcasting sta., 1936-39; mgr. import co., Brit. Guiana, 1937-39; priority specialist WPB, 1942-44; analyst Fgn. Econ. Adminstrn., 1944; econ. analyst U.S. Fgn. Service aux., 1944; attache, Cairo, Egypt, 1945, Addis Ababa, Baghdad, Beirut, Damascus, Jerusalem, Jidda and Teheran, 1947; U.S. observer 1st ILO meeting for Near East govts., 1947; assigned State Dept., 1948-49, labor adviser Bur. Near East, S. Asian and African Affairs, 1949-51, Office Asst. Sec. State, 1951; pub. affairs officer, attache, New Delhi, India, 1951-52, planning officer, attache, 1952-53; joined USIA in New Delhi, 1953, dep. chief pub. affairs officer, attache, New Delhi, 1954-55; assigned USIA, Washington, 1955-61, chief Near East policy staff, 1955-56, dep. asst. dir. Near East, S. Asia and Africa, 1956-57, asst. dir., 1957-61; U.S. ambassador to Mali, 1961-64; dep. asst. sec. for Near Eastern affairs Dept. State, 1964-69; U.S. ambassador to Turkey, 1969—. Recipient Superior Service USIA, 1956. Address: State Dept Washington DC 20525 *

HANDLIN, OSCAR, educator; b. Bklyn., Sept. 29, 1915; s. Joseph and Ida (Yanowitz) H.; A.B., Bklyn. Coll., 1934; A.M., Harvard, 1935, Ph.D., 1940; LL.D., Colby Coll., Waterville, Me., 1962; L.H.D., Hebrew Union Coll., 1967, No. Mich. U., 1969; H.H.D., Oakland U., 1968; m. Mary Flug, Sept. 18, 1937; children—Joanna Flug, David Paltiel, Ruth Blume. Instr. history Bklyn. Coll., 1936-38; instr. history Harvard, 1939-44, asst. prof., 1944-48, asso. professor, 1948-54, prof. history, 1954—, dir. center for study of liberty in Am., 1958-66, Winthrop prof. history, 1962- 65, Charles Warren prof. history, 1965—. Vice-chmn. U.S. Bd. Fgn. Scholarships, 1962-65, chmn., 1965-66. Recipient history prize Union League Club, 1934, J.H. Dumning prize Am. History Assn., 1941, award of honor Bklyn. Coll., 1945, Pulitzer prize for history, 1952, Cristopher award, 1958, Brooklyn Coll. alumni award, 1958; Guggenheim fellow, 1954; Brandeis U. fellow, 1965—. Fellow Am. Acad. Arts and Scis.; mem. Am., Miss. Valley hist. assns., Mass. Hist. Soc., Am. Assn. U. Profs., Colonial Soc. Mass., Econ. Hist. Assn., Am. Jewish Hist. Soc. Jewish religion. Author: Boston's Immigrants, 1941; Commonwealth, 1947; This Was America, 1949; The Uprooted, 1951; The American People in the Twentieth Century, 1954; Adventure in Freedom, 1954; Chance or Destiny, 1955; Race and Nationality in American Life, 1956; Readings in American History, rev. edit., 1970; Al Smith and His America, 1958; Immigration as a Factor in American History, 1959; The Newcomers-Negroes and Puerto Ricans in a Changing Metropolis, 1959; American Principles and Issues, 1961; The Dimensions of Liberty, 1961; The Americans, 1963; Fire-Bell in the Night, 1964; Children of the Uprooted, 1966; Popular Sources of Political Authority, 1967; History of the United States, 1967; America, A History, 1968; The American College and American Culture, 1970; Statue of Liberty, 1971; Facing Life-Youth and the Family in American History, 1971. Editor: Library of American Biography; Harvard Guide to American History. Contbr. hist. jours. Home: 18 Agassiz St Cambridge MA 02140

HANDLY, ARTHUR MOORE, govt. ofcl.; b. Malone, N.Y., Mar. 6, 1928; s. Arthur William and Ellen (Lynch) H.; A.B., St. Lawrence U., 1951; student Northwestern Coll. Law, nights 1956-57; M.P.A., Maxwell Sch., Syracuse U., 1952, student, 1968- 69; m. Anne Frenette, Dec. 29, 1951; children—Kevin, Marshall, Brian, Paul. Mgmt. analyst Wis. Dept. Budgets and Accounts, 1952-55; dir. instns. Ore. Bd. Control, 1955-59; dep. commnr. adminstrs., Wis., 1959- 62; with AID, 1962—, dir. mission to Jordan, 1968-70. Served with AUS, 1946-47. Mem. Am. Soc. Pub. Adminstrn., Soc. Internat. Devel., Fgn. Service Assn. Home: 1725 Youngblood St McLean VA 22101 Office: AID Dept of State Washington DC 20523

HANDS, WILLIAM ARTHUR, home products co. exec.; b. Bklyn., July 24, 1917; s. Arthur and Otillie (Muller) H.; B.A., Bklyn. Coll., 1947; M.B.A., Harvard, 1949; m. Grace Rita DeLapp, Aug. 21, 1943; children—James Albert, William Arthur, Bruce Cyril, Brian Thomas, Brent Edward, Carolyn Elizabeth. Asst. to controller Berger Bros. Co., New Haven, 1950-52; cost accountant, cost and inventory supr. Ford div. Ford Motor Co., Boston, 1952-53, Detroit, 1953-57; controller MicroWave and Power Tube div. Raytheon Co., Boston, 1957-61; v.p., treas. Nat. Casket Co., Inc., Boston, 1961-69 with Stanley Home Products, Inc., Westfield, Mass., 1969—, now financial v.p., treas., dir., mem. exec. com. Served with USAAF, 1942-46. Mem. Nat. Assn. Accountants, Financial Execs. Inst., Harvard Bus. Sch. Assn. Boston. Home: Meadowbrook Acres Granville MA 01034 Office: 333 Western Av Westfield MA 01085

HANDSAKER, MORRISON, educator; b. Portland, Ore., Nov. 20, 1907; s. John J. and Alice M. (Smith) H.; A.B., Reed Coll., 1929; Ph.D., U. Chgo., 1939; m. Marjorie Linfield, Aug. 25, 1934; 1 dau., Alice E. (Mrs. David E. Kidder). Code adviser NRA, 1934-36; instr. U. Wash., Seattle, 1937-38; instr. Occidental Coll., Los Angeles, 1938-40, asst. prof., 1940-42, asso. prof., 1942-43; staff Nat. War Labor Bd., 1943-44; personnel rep. Lockheed Aircraft Corp., 1944-45; economist OPA, 1945-46; prof. Lafayette Coll., 1946—, chmn. dept. econs., 1946-70; sr. Fulbright lectr. U. Sheffield (Eng.), 1957-58, Waseda U., Tokyo, and Yokohama (Japan) Nat. U., 1964-65. Mem. emergency bds. under Ry. Labor Act, 1955, 57, 59, 60, 61; serves frequently on labor arbitration cases, apptd. by fed., state and pvt. agys. for cases in both pvt. and pub. sectors; also mediator and fact finder. Mem. Am. Econ. Assn., Internat. Indsl. Relations Assn., Indsl. Relations Research Assn., Am. Assn. U. Profs., Am. Arbitration Assn. (mem. panel), Nat. Acad. Arbitrators (chmn. research and edn. com. 1959-60). Presbyn. (elder). Author: The Chicago Cleaning and Dyeing Industry, 1939; Seasonal Farm Labor in Pennsylvania, 1953; (with Marjorie L. Handsaker) The Submission Agreement in Contract Arbitration (monograph), 1952; Arbitration Decisions. Home: 717 W Lafayette St Easton PA 18042

HANDSCHUMACHER, ALBERT GUSTAVE, mfg. exec.; b. Phila., Oct. 20, 1918; s. Gustave H. and Emma (Streck) H.; B.S., Drexel Inst. Tech., 1940; diploma U. Pitts., 1941, Alexander Hamilton Inst., 1948; m. Bronya C. Inman, Dec. 3, 1962; children—Albert, David W., Megan, Karin, Melissa; m. 2d, Inger W. Jensen, Apr. 11, 1970. Prodn. mgr. Jr. Motors Corp., Phila., 1938-40; sales engr. Westinghouse Electric Co., Pitts., 1941; with Lear, Inc., Grand Rapids, Mich., 1945-57, beginning as sales mgr. central dist., successively asst. to pres., asst. gen. mgr., v.p. and gen. mgr., sr. v.p., dir. sales, pres., dir. Lear, Inc., 1959-62; v.p., gen. mgr. Rheem Mfg. Co., 1957-59; pres., dir. Lear Siegler, Inc., 1965; pres., chmn., chief exec. Aeronica, Inc.; dir. First Exec. Corp. Pacific Am. Industries, Inc., Trans World Financial, Asso. Mfg. Co., Inc. Trustee Drexel U., City of Hope. Recipient 60th Anniversary Alumni award for outstanding achievements and services field of indsl. mgmt. Drexel U., 1951, Outstanding Alumni award, 1971; Man of Year award City of Hope, 1970. Served to maj. USAAF, 1942-45. Mem. Los Angeles C. of C., Am. Mgmt. Assn., Aerospace Industries Assn., N.A.M. (dir.). Clubs: Wings; Jonathan; Bel Air Country; Metropolitan; Union League (Chgo.). Home: 1100 Stone Canyon Rd Bel Air CA 90024 Office: 24751 Crenshaw Blvd Torrance CA 90505

HANDSCHUMACHER, ROBERT EDMUND, pharmacologist; b. Abington, Pa., Oct. 16, 1927; s. Gustav Heinrich and Emma (Streck) H.; B.S., Drexel Inst., 1949; M.S., U. Wis., 1951, Ph.D., 1953; m. Elizabeth Ann Grafly, Sept. 6, 1949; children—Robert Kurt, Mark Davis. Asst. prof. Yale, 1956-59, asso. prof., 1960-64, prof., 1964—, dir. grad. studies in pharmacology, also dir. div. biol. scis. Chmn. bd. Eleanor Roosevelt Internat. Cancer Fellowship Com.; cons. Nat. Cancer Inst.; cancer research cons. Anna Fuller Fund; mem. fellowship commn. Internat. Union Against Cancer. Served with USAAF, 1945-46. Am. Cancer Soc. scholar, 1957-62; Career research prof. Am. Cancer Soc., 1964—. Mem. Am. Soc. Pharmacology and Exptl. Therapeutics, Am. Soc. Biol. Chemistry, Am. Assn. Cancer Research (bd. dirs. 1967-70), Am. Chem. Soc., A.A.A.S., Sigma Xi, Tau Beta Pi. Editorial bd. Cancer Research, 1962-68, Molecular Pharmacology, 1964—. Home: Northford Rd Branford CT 06405 Office: 333 Cedar St New Haven CT 06510

HANDY, JAMISON, film co. exec.; grad. U. Mich.; D.Edn. (hon.), Detroit Inst. Tech. Founder, Jam Handy Orgn., Detroit, 1911, now pres. Recipient Eastman Kodak Gold medal Soc. Motion Picture and TV Engrs., 1970. Office: 2821 E Grand Bldg Detroit MI*

HANDY, JOHN ABNER, Jr., business exec.; b. Mpls., Apr. 19, 1913; s. John Abner and Winnifred (Hammond) H.; A.B., Hamilton Coll., 1935; M.B.A., Harvard, 1937; m. Frances P. Slack, July 4, 1936; children—John Abner, Mary Eugenia. Salesman, Proctor & Gamble Distbg. Co., 1947-40; successively dept. head, gen. office mgr., asst. controller Carborundum Co., Niagara Falls, N.Y., 1940-47; controller, later controller-asst. sec. Deering Milliken & Co., Inc.; sec. Pendleton Fabrics Corp.; controller numerous corps; sec. corp. Joseph E. Seagram & Sons, Inc., 1952-56, also sec. subsidiary corps. Seagram Distillers Corp., Calvert Distilling Co., Carstairs Bros. Distilling Co., Inc., Frankfort Distilleries, Inc., Frankfort Distillers Corp., Gallagher & Burton, Inc., Hunter-Wilson Distilling Co., Inc., Julius Kessler Distilling Co., Inc., Lord Calvert Distilleries, Inc., Paul Jones & Co., Inc., Pharma-Craft Corp., Md. Distillery, Inc., Gen. Distillers Corp.; financial v.p., controller, dir. Chem. Constrn. Corp., subsidiary Electric Bond & Share Co., 1956-66, dir.; v.p., dir. Chem. Constrn. Internat.Del., Chem. Constrn. A. G. Zug (Switzerland); dir. Chem. Constrn. Ltd. (Great Britain), Chem. Construction Ltd. (Can.), Linden Brunswick Corp., 1958-66; exec. v.p., dir. Fabergé, Inc., 1966—. Mem. Financial Execs. Inst., Nat. Assn. Accountants, Am. Mgmt. Assn. (finance council), Nat. Office Mgmt. Assn. (past pres., dir. Buffalo chpt.), Tau Kappa Epsilon, Delta Sigma Rho. Clubs: Harvard (N.Y.C.); Gipsy Trail (Carmel, N.Y.) Contbr. articles profl. publs. Home: Gipsy Trail Club Carmel NY 10512 Office: 1345 Av of Americas New York City NY 10019

HANDY, JOHN RICHARD, III, saxophonist, composer; b. Dallas, Feb. 3, 1933; s. John Richard II and Pauline Elizabeth (Conner) H.; B.A., San Francisco State Coll., 1963; student Coll. City N.Y., 1960; div.; 1 son, John Richard IV. Played with modern jazz groups, also rhythm and blues bands, San Francisco- Oakland (Cal.) area, 1948-58, with Charlie Mingus, Randy Weston, Kenny Dorham, others, 1959-62; concerts with own band Carnegie Recital Hall, 1962, 67, Santa Clara (Cal.) Symphony, 1967, Antibes Jazz Festival, 1967, Newport Jazz Festival, 1967, Hollywood (Cal.) Bowl, 1966, Monterey Jazz Festival, 1964-66; toured Europe, 1961; TV appearances U.S., Can., France; head jazz band San Francisco prodn. opera The Visitation, 1967; guest soloist with maj. symphonies, coll. and univ. symphony orchs., concert bands, stage bands; rec. artist Columbia Records. Tchr., lectr. U. Cal., Berkeley, San Francisco State Coll., San Francisco Conservatory Music, Golden Gate Free U., Stanford, Cal. State Coll. at Haywood, Merritt Coll.; clinics and seminars in jazz and Black music. Mem. San Francisco Interim Arts Adv. Com., 1966-67. Served with AUS. Mem. Jazz Arts Soc. (mus. dir. 1960-61). Composer: The Spanish Lady, Scheme No. 1, If Only We Knew; (for symphony orch.) Concerto for Jazz Soloist and Orchestra, 1970; also composition for symphony band and scores for films. Address: 618 Baker St San Francisco CA 94117 *

HANDY, LYMAN LEE, educator, chemist; b. Payette, Ida., Aug. 4, 1919; s. Clarence Lee and Lillie (Hall) H.; student Western Wash. Coll., 1938-40; B.S., U. Wash., 1942, Ph.D., 1951; m. Lenore E. Ross, Aug. 28, 1948; children—Mark Ross, Gail Eileen. With Chevron Oil Field Research Co., 1951-66; mem. faculty U. So. Cal., 1966—, prof. chem. and petroleum engring., chmn. div. chem. and petroleum engring., 1969—; cons. in field. Served to lt. USNR, 1942-46. Mem. Am. Chem. Soc. (chmn. Orange County sect. 1969), Soc. Petroleum Engrs. (dir. Los Angeles basin sect. 1971), Am. Inst. Chem. Engrs., A.A.A.S., Phi Beta Kappa, Sigma Xi, Phi Lambda Upsilon, Tau Beta Pi. Mem. editorial bd. Trans. Am. Inst. Mining Engrs., 1960, 68, 69. Contbr. articles profl. jours. Home: 1401 Dana Pl Fullerton CA 92631 Office: University Park Los Angeles CA 90007

HANDY, ROBERT THEODORE, ch. historian; b. Rockville, Conn., June 30, 1918; s. William Evans and Sarah (MacDonald) H.; A.B., Brown U., 1940; B.D., Colgate Rochester Div. Sch., 1943; Ph.D., U. Chgo., 1949; m. Barbara Steere Mitchell, Dec. 29, 1941; children—Stephen William, Marilyn Barbara, David Robert. Ordained to ministry Baptist Ch., 1943; pastor South Ch., Mt. Prospect, Ill., 1943-45; instr. Baptist Missionary Tng. Sch., 1948-49, Shimer Coll., 1949-50; instr. ch. history Union Theol. Sem., N.Y.C., 1950-51, asst. prof., 1951-54, asso. prof., 1954-59, prof., 1959—, dir. studies, 1957-63, dean, 1970-71. Mem. Faith and Order Commn. World Council Chs., 1954—. Served from 1st lt. to capt., AUS, 1945-47; PTO. Mem. Am. Soc. Ch. History (past pres.), Am. Baptist Conv. (chmn. adv. bd. theol. studies), Am. Hist. Assn., Am. Acad. Religion, Am. Studies Assn. Author: We Witness Together, 1956; Members One of Another, 1959; (with others) American Christianity, 1960, 63; A Christian America; Protestant Hopes and Historical Realities, 1971. Editor: The Social Gospel in America, 1966; co-editor: Theology and Church in Times of Change, 1970. Home: 20 Holly Lane Cresskill NJ 07626 Office: 3041 Broadway New York City NY 10027

HANDY, ROLLO LEROY, univ. provost; b. Kenyon, Minn., Feb. 20, 1927; s. John R. and Alice (Kispert) H.; B.A., Carleton Coll., Northfield, Minn., 1950; M.A., Sarah Lawrence Coll., 1951; postgrad. U. Minn., 1951-52; Ph.D., U. Buffalo, 1954; m. Toni Scheiner Sept. 17, 1950; children-Jonathan, Ellen, Benjamin. Mem. faculty U. S.D., 1954-60, prof. philosophy, head dept., 1959-60; asso. prof. Union Coll., Schenectady, 1960-61; mem. faculty State U. N.Y. at Buffalo, 1961—, prof. philosophy, 1964—, chmn. dept., 1961-67, chmn. div. philosophy and social scis., 1965-67, provost faculty ednl. studies, 1967—. Served with USNR, 1945-46. Mem. Am. Assn. U. Profl. (chpt. pres. 1964-65), Am. Civil Liberties Union, Am. Philos. Assn., Mind Assn., Philosophy Sci. Assn. Author: Methodology of the Behavioral Sciences, 1964; Value Theory and the Behavioral Sciences, 1969; (with Paul Kurtz) A Current Appraisal of the Behavorial Sciences, 1964. Co-editor: Philosphical Perspectives on Punishment, 1968; The Behavorial Sciences, 1968; The Idea of God, 1968. Home: 185 Oakgrove Dr Williamsville NY 14221

HANEMAN, VINCENT SIERING, retired state justice; b. Bklyn., Apr. 25, 1902; s. Frederick T. and Laura (Siering) H.; LL.B., Syracuse U., 1923; m. Helen Harris, June 17, 1923 (dec. Dec. 1965); children—Vincent Siering, Howard F.; m. 2d, Maxine G. Kimble, July 5, 1967. Admitted N.J. bar, 1924, counsellor, 1927; practice in Atlantic City, 1924-47; city solicitor, Brigantine, N.J., 1925-44; common pleas judge Atlantic County, 1944-47; vice chancellor N.J. Ct. Chancery, 1947-48; judge chancery div. Superior Ct. N.J., 1948-58, appellate div., 1958-60; justice Supreme Ct. of N.J., 1960-71. Mem. bd. edn., Brigantine, 1926-34; counsel N.J. Racing Commn., 1940-44. Mayor, Brigantine, 1934-42; mem. N.J. Gen. Assembly, 1938-44. Mem. Am., N.J., Atlantic County bar assns., Sigma Nu, Phi Delta Phi, Phi Kappa Phi. Mason. Clubs: Atlantic City Tuna; Seaview Country. Home: 464 West Shore Dr Brigantine NJ 08203

HANEMAN, VINCENT SIERING, Jr., cons. engr., educator; b. Orange, N.J., Feb. 19, 1924; s. Vincent Siering and Helen (Harris) H.; S.B., Mass. Inst. Tech., 1947; M.S. in Aero. Engring., U. Mich., 1950, Ph.D., 1956; m. Adelaide Russell, Oct. 3, 1961; children—Vincent Siering III, Charles Frederick, Rosalyn Hobbs, Kay Kovasic. Asst. head flight research Project Meteor, Mass. Inst. Tech., 1947-49; project head automatic wind tunnel data reduction U. Mich., 1949-51; project officer analogue computer research Wright Air Devel. Center, O., 1951-52; asso. prof., asst. dept. head aero. engring. Air Force Inst. Tech., Wright Patterson AFB, O., 1955-59; chief spl. projects div. guidance and control directorate Air Force Ballistic Missile Div., 1959-60; pres., sr. asso. Haneman Assos., Richardson, Tex., 1960-66, 67—; chmn. bd. Haneman Assos., Inc., Richardson, 1961—, exec. v.p., Stillwater, Okla., 1966-67; prof. mech. engring., dir. engring. research, asso. dean Coll. Engring., Okla. State U., 1966—; cons. flight Simulator project U. Mich., 1952-55; cons. Gen. Electric Co., Gen. Dynamics, Space Tech. Labs., Chance Vought Corp., Ling Temco-Vought, others. Mem. Army Sci. Adv. Panel, 1967—. Served to 1st lt. USAAF, 1943-45; MTO; to maj. USAF, 1951-60, now col. Res. Decorated D.F.C. with oak leaf cluster, Air medal with 7 oak leaf clusters, Air Force Commendation medal. Registered profl. engr., Ohio, Okla., Tex. Asso. fellow Am. Inst. Aero. and Astronautics; mem. Am. Soc. Engring. Edn. (past sec. mech. and aero. divs., past nat. chmn. aero. div., past mem. gen. council, mem. exec. com. engring. research council), Am. Astronautical Soc. (sr.), Am. Helicopter Soc., I.E.E.E., Sigma Xi, Tau Beta Pi, Sigma Tau, Pi Epsilon Gamma, Sigma Nu. Contbr. articles on instrumentation, control and guidance, aircraft performance to tech. jours. Home: 1324 N Washington St Stillwater OK 74074 Office: Haneman Assos Inc 1324 N Washington St Stillwater OK 74074 also Coll Engring Okla State U Stillwater OK 74074

HANER, CHARLES FREDERICK, educator, psychologist; b. Kalamazoo, Sept. 26, 1921; s. Frederick Earle and Ruth M. (Fitch) H.; B.A., Kalamazoo Coll., 1943; M.A., U. Ill., 1944; Ph.D., State U. Ia., 1947; m. Martha Louise Howes, Apr. 2, 1947; children—Bruce, Kathryn, Beverly. Formerly mem. faculty Grinnell (Ia.) Coll., prof. psychology, chmn. dept., 1953-60, Austin prof. psychology, dir. research projects under Ford Found., 1959. Dir. research projects for Ia. under Nat. Inst. Mental Health grant, 1962; research cons. to bus., 1954—; mem. Gov. Ia. Mental Health Com., 1957-61. Mem. Am., Midwestern, Ia. (pres. 1956-57, 63-64) psychol. assns., Psychonomic Soc., Sigma Xi. Contbr. profl. jours. Home: 1950 Manor Dr Grinnell IA 50111 *

HANES, FRED WILLIAM, librarian; b. Vandalia, Ill., Aug. 21, 1920; s. Frederick Marion and Mildred (Yost) H.; A.B., Earlham Coll., 1946; M.A., Ind. U., 1951; m. Betty Louise Haines, June 14, 1947; children—Julia Rae, Daniel Bruce, Jennifer Gail. High Sch. tchr., Nevis, Minn., 1947-49; reference and circulation librarian Ind. U. Library, 1951-58; lectr. div. library sci., 1956; bibliographer Am. lit. group Modern Lang. Assn. in preparation publ., Am. Lit. Manuscripts, 1957-58; dir. libraries Ind. State U., 1958-67; librarian Humboldt State Coll., Arcata, Cal., 1967-68; dir. libraries Ind. State U., Terre Haute, 1968- 71, dean library services, 1971—; library dir. Inst. Edn. and Research, U. Punjab, Lahore, W. Pakistan, also prof. library sci., auspices AID, 1961-63. Sec. bd. dirs. Lahore Am. Sch., 1962-63. Served with USAAF, 1943-45. Decorated Belgium Fourragere. Mem. Am., Ind. library assns., Delta Sigma Phi. Home: 1161 Gilchrist Rd Terre Haute IN 47802

HANES, GORDON, hosiery mfr.; b. Winston-Salem, N.C., Mar. 3, 1916; s. James Gordon and Emmie (Drewry) H.; grad. Woodberry Forest Sch., 1928-33; B.A., Yale, 1937; student Pace Inst., 1937-39; H.H.D. (hon.), N.C. State U.; m. Helen Greever Copenhaver, Aug. 30, 1941; children-James Gordon III, Eldridge C., Margaret Drewry. Accountant Hanes Hosiery Mills Co., Winston-Salem, N.C., 1939-41, sec., 1947-48, v.p., 1948- 53, exec. v.p., 1954-57, pres., 1958-65; pres., chief exec. officer Hanes Corp., 1967—, chmn. bd., 1965—; dir. Wachavia Corp., Hunes Dye and Finishing Co., So. Broadcasting Co. State Senator N.C., Forsyth County, 1963-65. Served as adminstrv. officer Ordanance USNR, 1941-45. Mem. Color Assn. U.S. Address: P O Box 1413 Winston-Salem NC 27102

HANES, HORACE ALBERT, air force officer; b. Fayette, Ill., Mar. 1, 1916; s. Albert Lee and Martha (Jones) H.; B.E., Ill. State Normal U., 1937; m. Virginia Ruth Kumler, Aug. 26, 1939; 1 dau., Linda (Mrs. Mark Wisen). Commd. 2d lt. USAF, 1939, advanced through grades to maj. gen., 1964; comdr. 67th Tactical Reconnaissance Group, 1948, 58th Fighter Bomber Wing, 1957-58, 9th Aerospace Def. Div., 1964-66; asst. chief staff operations SHAPE, 1966—. Decorated Silver Star medal, Legion of Merit with oak leaf cluster, D.F.C. with oak leaf cluster, Air medal with five oak leaf clusters; recipient Thompson trophy, 1955; MacKay trophy, 1956. Holder first world supersonic speed record, 1955.‡*

HANES, PLEASANT HUBER, Jr., textile mill exec.; b. Winston-Salem, N.C., Jan. 23, 1915; s. Pleasant Huber and Evelyn (Hazen) H.; grad. Woodberry Forest Sch., 1933; A.B., Duke U., 1937; postgrad: Harvard, 1937-38; m. Jane Knox Hopkins, Aug. 16, 1941; children—Pleasant Huber, Jane Knox, Helen Jamieson, Russell Hopkins. With P.H. Hanes Knitting Co., Winston-Salem, N.C., 1938—, asst. sec., asst. treas., 1946-48, 54, pres., 1954-64, dir., 1938—; dir., mem. exec. com. Hanes Corp.; chmn., dir. West End Properties, Inc., Western Hills Corp., Property Devel. Corp., Hamore Corp.; chmn., dir. Hanes-Millis Sales Corp.; owner, operator Middlebrook Farms, Clemmons, N.C.; dir., mem. exec. com. Wachovia Bank & Trust Co.; dir. Carolina and Northwestern R.R., Hanes Hosiery Mills Co., Blue Bell, Inc., Carolina Capital Corp.; pres., dir. P.H. Hanes Found.; asso. dir. First Nat. Bank, Las Cruces, N.M. Mem. mgmt.-labor textile adv. com. Dept. Commerce; sr. priority specialist textile div. WPB, 1942; mem. U.S. textile tech. mission to investigate German textile industry following German surrender in Europe. Mem. N.C. Recreation Commrs., 1948-49; mem. bd. Forsyth Co. Commnrs., 1952-60. Chmn. bd. United Fund, 1948; bd. dirs. Winston-Salem YMCA, Winston- Salem Found.; v.p., bd. dirs. N.C. Textile Found., N.C. Engring. Found.; trustee Duke U., Inst. Textile Tech., Charlottesville, Va., Winchendon (Mass.) Sch., Pfeiffer Coll.; bd. visitors Davidson Coll., Meml. Coliseum-Dixie Classic Fair. Served as lt. (s.g.), USNR, 1941-46: ETO Received Winston-Salem Jr. C. of C. Distinguished Service Award, 1950. Mem. Am. Textile Mfrs. Inst. (dir.), N.C. Textile Mfrs. Assn. (dir., mem. exec. com), Underwear Inst. (dir.), Research Triangle Inst. N.C. (gov.), So. States Indsl. Council (dir.), N.C. Hereford Breeders Assn. (pres., 1954), Am. Polled Hereford Assn. (past dir.), Am. Legion, Kappa Tau Beta (hon. mem., Man of the Yr. award 1953), Phi Psi, Alpha Tau Omega, Omicron Delta Kappa. Methodist. Clubs: Rotary, Forsyth Country, Old Town. Home: 525 N Hawthorne Rd Winston-Salem NC 27104 Office: P O Box 2935 Winston-Salem NC 27102*

HANES, RALPH PHILIP, mfg. exec.; b. Winston-Salem, N.C., Feb. 22, 1898; s. John Wesley and Anna (Hodgin) H.; grad. Phillips Acad., 1916; B.A., Yale, 1920; m. DeWitt Thurmond Chatham, Apr. 4, 1923; children—Ralph Philip, Martha T. (Mrs. Calder W. Womble), Anna H. (Mrs. Thomas L. Chatham). With Hanes Dye & Finishing Co., Winston-Salem, N.C., 1925—, successively v.p., pres., chmn., now chmn. exec. com.; pres. Central Parking, Inc., 1956- 63, Old Salem, Inc., 1956-58, chmn. bd., 1963—; dir. Chatham Mfg. Co. Executive bd. N.C. Dept. Archives and History; pres. Civic Music Assn. of Winston-Salem; past chmn. bd. Pub. Library of Winston-Salem and Forsyth County. Mem. Nat. Trust for Historic Preservation (vice chmn. bd. trustees), Scroll and Key Soc., Delta Kappa Epsilon. Home: Box 2105 Winston-Salem NC 27104*

HANES, JOHN WESLEY, Jr., investment banker; b. N.Y.C., Mar. 31, 1925; s. John Wesley and Agnes Philips (Mitchel) H.; grad. Deerfield (Mass.) Acad., 1943; B.A., Yale, 1950; m. Lucy Pomeroy Deans, Aug. 19, 1949; children—Lucy Pomeroy, Carol Mitchel, Lindsay Philips, John Wesley III. Econ. specialist with Office of High Commr., Germany, 1950-52, spl. asst. sec. state, Washington, 1953-57; dep. asst. sec. state internat. orgn. affairs, 1957-58; asst. sec. state security and consular affairs, 1958-61; with Wertheim & Co., N.Y.C., 1961- -, partner, 1964—; dir. Squibb-Beechnut, Inc., Olin Corp., Red Food Stores. Mem. delegations to SEATO, London Conf., Bermuda Conf., 1957, UNESCO, 1958; mem. Commn. on Internat. Jud. Procedures, 1959-61; chmn. U.S. sect. Caribbean Commn., 1960-61; vice chmn. Va. Gov.'s Council on Environment, 1970—. Pres., dir. Hanes Found., 1952—; trustee Deerfield Acad. Served from pvt. to capt. AUS, 1943-46. Mem. Nat. Audubon Soc. (trustee), Delta Kappa Epsilon. Republican. Episcopalian. Clubs: Mastigouche Fish and Game (Can.); Capitol Hill, Metropolitan, 1925 F Street (Washington); Links (N.Y.C.). Home: Gunnell's Run Farm Box 64 Great Falls VA 22066 Office: 1 Chase Manhattan Plaza New York City NY 10005

HANES, JOHN WESLEY, Jr., investment banker; b. N.Y.C., Mar. 31, 1925; s. John Wesley and Agnes Philips (Mitchel) H.; grad. Deerfield (Mass.) Acad., 1943; B.A., Yale, 1950; m. Lucy Pomeroy Deans, Aug. 19, 1949; children—Lucy Pomeroy, Carol Mitchel, Lindsay Philips, John Wesley III. Econ. specialist with Office of High Commr., Germany, 1950-52, spl. asst. sec. state, Washington, 1953-57; dep. asst. sec. state internat. orgn. affairs, 1957-58; asst. sec. state security and consular affairs, 1958-61; with Wertheim & Co., N.Y.C., 1961- -, partner, 1964—; dir. Squibb-Beechnut, Inc., Olin Corp., Red Food Stores. Mem. delegations to SEATO, London Conf., Bermuda Conf., 1957, UNESCO, 1958; mem. Commn. on Internat. Jud. Procedures, 1959-61; chmn. U.S. sect. Caribbean Commn., 1960-61; vice chmn. Va. Gov.'s Council on Environment, 1970—. Pres., dir. Hanes Found., 1952—; trustee Deerfield Acad. Served from pvt. to capt. AUS, 1943-46. Mem. Nat. Audubon Soc. (trustee), Delta Kappa Epsilon. Republican. Episcopalian. Clubs: Mastigouche Fish and Game (Can.); Capitol Hill, Metropolitan, 1925 F Street (Washington); Links (N.Y.C.). Home: Gunnell's Run Farm Box 64 Great Falls VA 22066 Office: 1 Chase Manhattan Plaza New York City NY 10005

HANEY, PAUL PRICHARD, journalist; b. Akron, O., July 20, 1928; s. Martin D. and Louise (Berrey) H.; B.A. in Journalism, Kent State U., 1950; grad. student Georgetown U. Law Sch., 1954-55; m. Janet Ann Shrum, Nov. 20, 1967; children—Maura Jeanne, Paul Daniel, Michael Baskett, Megan Elizabeth. Copy boy, reporter Beacon Jour., Akron, 1945-49; teletype attendant A.P., Akron, 1946-49; reporter Erie (Pa.) Times, 1949-50, Comml. Appeal, Memphis, 1952-53; writer Monsanto Chem. Co., St. Louis, 1953-54; copyreader, asst. city editor Evening Star, Washington, 1954-58; pub. affairs officer NASA, Washington and Houston, 1958-69, project information officer Project Mercury, 1958-63, Project Gemini, 1962-66, Project Apollo, 1963-69, astronauts pub. affairs adviser, 1963-69; v.p. Houston Astrodome, 1969-70; exec. v.p. for pub. relations Nat. Assn. Broadcasters, Washington, 1971—. Served with USNR, 1950-52. Roman Cath. Club: Escape Velocity Press (Houston). Home: 13017 Bermuda Dr Galveston TX 77550 Office: Nat Assn Broadcasters 1771 N St NW Washington DC 20036

HANEY, THOMAS MICHAEL, lawyer; b. Bklyn., Aug. 8, 1929; s. Thomas J. and Jean (McCrossan) H.; A.B., Fordham U., 1953; LL.B., St. John's U., 1958; m. Mary N. McCarthy, Oct. 11, 1958; children—Thomas, Elizabeth, Megan, Michael, Judith, Christopher. Admitted to N.Y. bar, 1959; with Shell Oil Co., N.Y.C., 1953-58, Seward & Kissel, N.Y.C., 1959-64; sec., counsel Consol. Cigar Corp., N.Y.C., 1964—. Served with AUS, 1950-52. Mem. Am., N.Y. State bar assns., Assn. Bar City N.Y. Home: 495 E 16th St Brooklyn NY 11226 Office: 1 Gulf and Western Plaza New York City NY 10023

HANFMANN, GEORGE MAXIM ANOSSOV, educator, curator; b. Petersburg, Russia, Nov. 20, 1911; Dr. Phil., U. Berlin, 1934; student U. Jena, Munich U.; Ph.D., Johns Hopkins, 1935; M.A., Harvard, 1949. Came to U.S., 1934, naturalized, 1940. Successively jr. prize fellow, instr., asst. prof. Harvard, 1935-43, asst. prof., 1945-49, asso. prof. fine arts, 1949-56, prof., 1956—, John E. Hudson prof. archeology, 1971—; curator classical art Fogg Art Mus., 1946—; field dir. archeol. exploration, Sardis, 1958—; mem. Inst. Advanced Study, Princeton, 1971-72. Visitor classical dept. Mus. Fine Arts, Boston; mem. mng. com. Am. Sch. Classical Studies in Athens. U.S. editor OWI, 1943-44; chief German sect. ABSIE, 1943-45. Fellow Am. Acad. Arts and Scis., Soc. Antiquaries London (Eng.); mem. Instituto di Studi Etruschi Florence, German Archeol. Inst., Archeol. Inst., Am. Socs. Hellenic and Roman Studies, Am. Schs. Oriental Research, Am. Research Center Egypt, Acad. Mainz, Academie des Inscriptions et Belles Lettres France (corr.), Am. Philos. Soc., Brit. Inst. Persian Studies, Signet Soc., Phi Beta Kappa. Author books, mongraphs, exhbn. catalogues, articles and revs. Asso. editor Am. Jour. Archaeology; editorial bd. Art Bull. Address: Fogg Art Museum Cambridge MA 02138

HANFORD, WILLIAM EDWARD, chemist; b. Bristol, Pa., Dec. 9, 1908; s. Thomas Cook and Irene (Laing) H.; B.S., Phila. Coll. Pharmacy and Sci., 1930, D.Sc., 1956; M.S., U. Ill., 1932, Ph.D., 1935; D.Sc., Alfred U., 1959; m. Lorraine Easom, Sept. 28, 1939; 1 son, William E. Research chemist E. I. duPont de Nemours & Co., Wilnington, Del., 1935-42; dir. research Gen. Aniline & Film Corp., Easton, Pa., 1942-46; v.p., dir. research M.W. Kellogg Co., N.Y.C., 1946-57, also dir.; v.p. research and devel. Olin Corp., Stamford, Conn., 1957—. Trustee Alfred U., Phila. Coll. Pharmacy and Sci. Mem. Am. Inst. Chemists, N.Y. Acad. Sci., Am. Chem. Soc. (regional dir. 1960-70.), A.A.A.S., Soc. Chem. Industry (London, Eng.), Indsl. Research Inst. (pres. 1968), Soc. History of Tech. (dir.), Sci. Research Soc. Am., Phi Beta Kappa, Sigma Xi, Phi Kappa Phi, Phi Lambda Upsilon. Club: Chemists (N.Y.C.). Contbr. to chem. publs. Holder patents. Home: 30 Lost District Dr New Canaan CT 06840 Office: 120 Long Ridge Rd Stamford CT 06902

HANFORD, WILLIAM JAMES, univ. dean; b. Chgo., Mar. 5, 1920; s. Ford Charles and Mary Celeste (Skehan) H.; B.A., U. Notre Dame, 1942; M.A., Wayne State U., 1962, Ph.D., 1965; m. Vera Perry, Sept. 11, 1957; children—Sharon (Mrs. S. Emirbayer), Wendy (Mrs. J. Hohmeyer), William James, Deborah. Ordained priest Roman Catholic Ch., 1946; exec. dir. Del. Ednl. Television Network, 1965-68; prof. art history, dean Coll. Fine Arts, Wis. State U., Stevens Point, 1968—. Bd. dirs. Stevens Point Symphony Orch. Mem. Internat. Council Fine Arts Deans, Nat. Assn. Ednl. Broadcasters, Wis. Acad. Scis., Arts and Letters, Speech Assn. Am. Home: 3188 Dan's Dr Stevens Point WI 54481

HANFT, FRANK WILLIAM, educator; b. Brainerd, Minn., Dec. 21, 1899; s. Frank William and Jennie Maud (Fox) H.; LL.B., U. Minn., 1924, A.B., 1929, LL.M., 1929; S.J.D., Harvard, 1931; completed course, Sch. Mil. Govt., U. Va., 1943; m. Jennie Ensio Wall, Aug. 26, 1924; 1 son, John Wall. Admitted to Minn. bar, 1924; practice in Mpls., 1924-29; staff atty. League Minn. Municipalities, 1929-30; asst. polit. sci. U. Minn., 1928-29, part time instr. in law, 1929-30; asso. prof. law U. N.C., 1931-37, prof. law, 1937-65, Graham Kenan prof. law, 1965—; vis. prof. Duke Law Sch., 1963; asso. utilities commr. N.C., part time, 1934-41, mem. gen. statutes commn., 1946—, chmn. 1961-67. Served with S.A.T.C., U.S. Army, 1918; served to lt. col. AUS, 1943-45; with Ninth Air Force, overseas 20 mos., 1944-45. Decorated Croix de Guerre (France); Bronze Star (U.S.); Fairchild research fellow law railroads and other public utilities Harvard Law School, 1930-31. Mem. N.C. Bar Assn., N.C. State Bar, Phi Beta Kappa, Order of Coif, Delta Sigma Rho, Golden Fleece. Democrat (mem. Minn. Central Com., 1928). Methodist. Author: You Can Believe: A Lawyer's Brief for Christianity, 1952. Presented series pub. lectrs. at U. N.C. on Essentials of Christianity, 1947, 48. Contbr. numerous articles to legal pubs., particularly on adminstrv. and pub. utility law and jurisprudence. Home: Bowling Creek Rd Chapel Hill NC 27514

HANFT, PHILIP MATTHEW, Jr., lawyer; b. Wisconsin Rapids, Wis., June 15, 1916; s. Philip Matthew and Clair E. (Green) H.; student Duluth Jr. Coll., 1934-36, U. Chgo., 1936-37; B.A., Carleton Coll., 1938; LL.B., Harvard, 1942; m. Doris Patricia Chisholm, Sept. 15, 1942; children—Alexandra R. (Mrs. William A. Sivertson), Patricia C. (Mrs. Lee H. Sutton III), Philip Matthew III, Clair E. (Mrs. Gregory R. Oas), Peter B., Sara H. Admitted to Minn. bar, 1943; asso. firm Gillette, Nye, Harries & Montague, Duluth, Minn., 1946-50; partner firm Nye, Montague, Sullivan, Atmore & McMillan, now Sullivan, Hanft, Hastings, Fride & O'Brien), Duluth, 1950—. Dir. First Am. Nat. Bank, Duluth. Bd. dirs. St. Louis County Hist. Soc., 1948-51, Family Service Soc., 1953-54, St. Lukes Hosp., 1965-69; bd. dirs. Duluth Mental Hygiene Clinic, 1961-67, pres. 1963-64. Served to 2d lt., M.I. Corps, AUS, 1942-45. Mem. 11th Jud. Dist., Minn., Am. bar assns., Am. Judicature Soc., Am. Arbitration Assn (panel arbitrators), Am. Inst. Mining Engrs., Harvard Law Sch. Assn., Corp-Counsel Assn. Minn. Rotarian, Mason (Shriner). Clubs: Kitchi Gammi (bd. dirs. 1967, sec. 1969—), Duluth Athletic (Duluth); St. Paul Athletic, Minnesota (St. Paul). Episcopalian. Splist. mining law, natural resources law. Home: 2708 Branch St Duluth MN 55812 Office: Alworth Bldg Duluth MN 55802

HANG, THAM THUY, actress; b. Viet Nam; m. (div.); 1 child. Actress moving pictures, stage, also TV plays, radio; writer advice column Vietnamese newspapers. Movie roles include: The Beautiful Girl of Binh Duong; The Man from the Mountain; No War in Saigon; Saigon to Dien Bien Phu. Address: Saigon, S Viet Nam.*

HANGEN, JOHN, Jr., bus. machines mfg. co. exec.; b. Dayton, O., Feb. 23, 1924; s. Cleo John and Glenna (Welsh) H.; grad. Internat. Accountants Soc., 1950; m. Eleanor Mae Krauss, Mar. 2, 1946; children—Diane, Ronald. With Nat. Cash Register Co., Dayton, 1941—, controller, 1961—, v.p. finance, 1964—, dir., 1965—; dir. Copeland Refrigeration. Mem. Financial Execs. Inst. Home: 7700 Glenbriar Pl Centerville OH 45459 Office: Nat Cash Register Co Main and K Sts Dayton OH 45409*

HANGER, FRANKLIN MCCUE, physician and educator; b. Staunton, Va., Sept. 6, 1894; s. Frank M. and Martha (McDowell) H.; B.S., U. Va., 1916; M.D., Johns Hopkins, 1920; m. Harriet Echols Ewing, Apr. 15, 1942; 1 dau., Harriet Echols. Intern, resident Presbyn. Hosp., N.Y.C., 1920- 26, attending physician, 1945—; asso. in medicine Columbia, 1926-27, asst. prof., 1928-31, asso. prof., 1931-47, prof. medicine, 1947-60, now emeritus; sr. med. cons. Vets. Kingsbridge Hosp., N.Y.C., 1948-61. Emeritus mem. bd. examiners Am. Bd. Internal Medicine. Fellow Am. Coll. Physicians (regent, pres. 1962-63); mem. N.Y. Clin. Soc., Assn. Am. Physicians, Am. Study Liver Diseases (pres. 1954-55), Am. Soc. Clin. Investigation, Am. Assn. Immunologists, Soc. Exptl. Biol. and Med., Harvey Soc., Sigma Xi, Phi Beta Kappa, Alpha Omega Alpha. Democrat. Episcopalian. Club: Century. Contbr. to Nelson System of Medicine, Oxford Loose Leaf of Medicine, Cecil Textbook of Medicine. Originator of cephalin floculation test for disorders of the liver. Home: Cobble Hill Staunton VA 24401 Office: 620 W 168th St New York City NY 10032*

HANGER, WILLIAM ARNOLD, exec. engr., farmer; b. Richmond, Ky., Feb. 5, 1896; s. Harry Baylor and Elizabeth (Arnold H.; grad. Lawrenceville (N.J.) Sch., 1916; wartime certificate Wharton Sch. Finance, U. Pa., 1921; m. Hope Yandell, 1931 (div.); m. 2d, Joanne Glassell, 1942 (div.). Became pres. Silas Mason Co., 1949, Mason & Hanger Co., 1954, since merger of cos. is pres. Mason & Hanger-Silas Mason Co., Inc., heavy constrn., engring., plant constrn., design and operation in fields of explosives and chem. engring.; spl. field testing work for AEC; mng. dir. Arlington Farm, Richmond, Ky., 1925—, Hartland Farm, Versailles, Ky., 1936—, Arlington Ranch, Kenansville, Fla., 1939—; pres. Tri-State Utilities, Richmond, 1927—; dir. Lafayette Hotel Co., Lexington, Ky. Trustee U. Miami, Coral Gables, Fla.; chmn. bd. Lowe Gallery, U. Miami; dir., trustee Keeneland Racing Assn., Lexington Ky.; mem. finance com. N.Y. Infirmary; mem. Ky. Med. Found., U. Ky. Served from ensign to lt. (j.g.) USN, 1917- 19. Mem. Engrs. Club, Am. Ordnance Assn., United Hunts Racing and Steeplechase Assn., V.F.W., Am., Brit. (hon.) legions, U.S. Naval Inst. Am. Democrat. Clubs: Jockey, Brook (N.Y.C.); St. Elmo (U. Pa.); Idle Hour Country, Iriquois Hunt (Lexington, Ky.); Meadowbrook Country (L.I.); La Gorce Country, Indian Creek Country, Surf, Bath, Gun (Miami Beach, Fla.); Phildelphia Gun. Mason, Elk. Home: Arlington Farm Richmond KY 40475 Office: 500 5th Av New York City NY 10036*

HANHAM, HAROLD JOHN, educator; b. Auckland, New Zealand, June 16, 1928; s. John Newman and Ellie (Malone) H.; B.A., Auckland Univ. Coll., 1948, M.A., 1950; Ph.D., Selwyn Coll., Cambridge (Eng.) U., 1954; A.M. (hon.), Harvard, 1960; m. Alison Herbert Foresterr, Oct 9, 1953. Came to U.S., 1968. Asst. to lectr. to sr. lectr. govt. U. Manchester, 1953-63; prof. politics, head dept. U. Edinburgh (Scotland), 1963-68; prof. history Harvard, 1968—; examiner African univs., 1964-69. Mem. Royal Hist. Soc., Hist. Assn., Am. Hist. Assn., Econ. Hist. Soc., Polit. Studies Assn., Royal Commonwealth Soc. Clubs: Oxford and Cambridge Univ. (London); Harvard (N.Y.C.). Author: Elections and Party Management, 1959; The Nineteenth Century Constitution, 1969; Scottish Nationalism, 1969. Home: 21 Gail Rd Weston MA 02193 Office: Widener Library Harvard Univ Cambridge MA 02138

HANIFY, EDWARD BENNO, lawyer; b. Fall River, Mass., Oct. 1, 1912; s. Edward F. and Mary E. (Brodkorb) H.; A.B. summa cum laude, Holy Cross Coll., 1933, S.J.D., 1961; LL.B., Harvard, 1936; LL.D., Tufts U., Bradford Durkee Coll.; J.D., Suffolk U.; D.Sc. (hon.), Lowell Technol. Inst.; m. Jane Elizabeth Dillon, June 17, 1940; children—Edward Benno, Jane Allison Pitt, John Dillon. Admitted to Mass. bar, 1936, since practiced in Boston; now parner Ropes & Gray; dir. State St. Bank & Trust Co., John Hancock, Mut. Life Ins.Co., Am. Tel. & Tel. Co.; dir., mem. exec. com. Boston Edison Co.; trustee Provident Instn. for Savs. Gen. chmn. Community Fund campaign, Greater Boston, 1950; v.p. Boston Dispensary; vice chmn. exec. com. Nat. Cath. Community Services: former mem. Nat. Adv. Council on Edn. Disadvantaged Children: clk., trustee John F. Kennedy Library; chmn. bd. Human Life Found.; former mem. bd. visitors West Point Mil. Acad. Served as lt. USNR, World War II. Mem. Am. Acad. Arts and Scis., Am. Law Inst., Am., Mass., Boston bar assns. Roman Catholic. Clubs: Union, Curtis, Clover (Boston). Home: 30 Clairemont Rd Belmont MA 02178 Office: 225 Franklin St Boston MA 02110

HANIGAN, JOHN LEONARD, corp. exec.; b. N.Y.C., Aug. 15, 1911; s. John P. and Winifred L. (Brennan) H.; student Stevens Inst. Tech., 1930-33; grad. Advanced Mgmt. Program, Harvard, 1944; m. Elsa L. Stelter, Jan. 17, 1953; children by previous marriage—Joan C., John F. With R.H. Macy & Co., N.Y.C., 1933-35; with Corning Glass Works (N.Y.), 1937-62, v.p., 1953-62; pres. Corning Glass Works Can., Ltd., 1957-62; exec. v.p. Dow Corning Corp., 1962-63; pres., dir. mem. exec. com. Brunswick Corp., 1963—, chief exec. officer, 1966—; chmn., dir. Sherwood Med. Industries, Inc., 1967—; dir. The Bunker-Ramo Corp., Martin Marietta Corp., Am. Nat. Bank & Trust Co. Chgo., Allis Chalmers. Served as 1st lt., inf. U.S. Army Res., 1935-37. Mem. Sigma Nu. K.C. Home: 75 South Av Glencoe IL 60022 Office: 69 W Washington St Chicago IL 60602

HANIGAN, THOMAS EDWARD, Jr., shipping co. exec.; b. Schenectady, July 18, 1922; s. Thomas Edward and Jane M. (Fessette) H.; B.A., Union Coll., Schenectady, 1946; m. Olga Emervk, Oct. 19, 1946; children—Ian Thomas, Vitold Michel. With W.R. Grace & Co., N.Y.C., 1946—, beginning as trainee, successively mgr. indsl. dept., asst. treas., asst. v.p., 1946-58, v.p., mem. appropriations com., 1958-69, exec. v.p., 1969—, also dir. Mem. adv. bd. St. Vincent's Hosp., Manhattan, N.Y. Served with AUS, 1943-46. Mem. Nat. Assn. Accountants (dir.), Am. Mgmt. Assn., Psi Upsilon. Club: Pelham Country. Home: 41 Sunnybrook Rd Bronxville NY 10708 Office: 7 Hanover Sq New York City NY 10005*

HANK, LEONARD L., bldg. materials mfr.; b. Cin., Mar. 7, 1904; s. Louis A. and Dora (Randell) H.; student U. Cin., 1922-30; m. Blanche Fiedler, May 4, 1951. Prodn. mgr. various paper cos., 1939-45; prodn. engr. U.S. Gypsum Co., 1945-46; with Nat. Gypsum Co., Buffalo, 1946-, gen. prodn. mgr., 1954-56, v.p. mfg., 1956-58, v.p. operations, 1958-, also dir. Home: 41 Treehaven Lane Elma NY 14059 Office: 325 Delaware Av Buffalo NY 14202*

HANKE, LEWIS ULYSSES, historian; b. Oregon City, Ore., Jan. 2, 1905; s. William U. and Mamie E. (Stevenson) H.; B.S., Northwestern U., 1924, M.A., 1925; Ph.D., Harvard, 1936; Doctor Honoris Causa, Universidade de Bahia (Brazil), Universidad Tomás Frias, Potosí (Bolivia), Universidad de Sevilla (Spain); m. Kate Gilbert, Aug. 12, 1926; children—Jonathan, Peter, Susan, Joanne. Instr. U. Hawaii, 1926-27; adj. prof. Am. U. of Beirut, Syria, 1927-30; instr. Harvard, 1935-39; dir. Hispanic Found., Library of Congress, 1939-51; prof. Latin Am. history, 1951-61, dir. Inst. Latin Am. Studies, U. Tex., 1951-58; prof. Latin Am. history Columbia, 1961-67, U. Cal. at Irvine, 1967-69; Clarence and Helen Haring prof. U. Mass., 1969—. Mem. U.S. nat. com. for UNESCO, 1952-54. Recipient Albert Beveridge Meml. fellowship Am. Hist. Assn., 1947; Amherst Meml. fellow, 1932-33; Archibald Coolidge fellow, 1933-34; Social Science Research Council postdoctoral fellow, 1937-38; Carnegie lectr. in Brazil, 1938; James W. Richard lectr. U. Va., 1948; A.S.W. Rosenbach fellow in bibliography, 1951. Mem. Am. Hist. Assn., Hispanic Soc. Am. (past trustee), Sociedad Peruana de Historia, Real Academia de la Historia (Madrid), Academia Nacional de la Historia, Sociedad de Historia Argentine (both Buenos Aires), Academia Colombiana de Historia (Bogotá), Sociedad de Historia Y Geografía de Guatemala, Instituto Histórico y Geográfica de Uruguay. Author: The First Social Experiments in Am., 1935; The Spanish Struggle for Justice in the Conquest of America, 1949; Bartolomé de Las Casas: Bookman, Scholar, and Propagandist, 1952; Bartolomé de Las Casas: Historian, 1952; Bartolomé de Las Casas, Bibliografía Critíca, 1954; The Imperial City of Potosí, 1956; Aristotle and the American Indians, 1959; Bartolomé Arzáns de Orsúa y Vela's History of Potosí, 1965; Modern Latin America; Continent in Ferment, 2 vols., 1967. Editor: Handbook of Latin- American Studies, 1936-40; Del único modo de atraer todos los pueblos a la verdadera religión (by Bartolomé de Las Casas), 1942; Cuerpo de documentos del siglo XVI sobre los derechos de Espaa en las Indias y las Filipinas, 1943; Relación de Potosí (by Luis Copoche), 1959; (with Gunnar Mendoza) Historia de la Ville Imperial de Potosí, 3 vols., 1965; Readings in Latin American History, 2 vols., 1966; A History of Latin American Civilization, 2 vols., 1967; Hispanic American Historical Review, 1954-60. Home: 65 Echo Hill Rd Amherst MA 01002

HANKE, OSCAR AUGUST, bus. cons.; b. Waterloo, Wis., Mar. 1, 1902; s. Charles Frederick and Bertha Johanna (Schultz) H.; B.S.A., U. Wis., 1926; L.H.D., Carthage Coll., 1954; m. Gertrude Luella Menz, Sept. 21, 1923; children-Robert Warren, Harold Wayne. Exec. v.p., dir. pub. relations P.R. Watt Pub. Co., until 1967; pub. relations, agribusiness cons. Mem. Community High Sch. Bd. of Edn., pres. 1932-49; mem. Mount Morris Recreation Bd., 1938-48; past pres. and treas. Blackhawk area council Boy Scouts Am., Rockford, Ill. (received Silver Beaver and Silver Antelope Awards from Boy Scouts of Am., Lamb award, Nat. Luth. Council on Scouting), mem. relationships com., nat. council, hon. life mem. exec. com. region 7; pres. Ogle County Mental Health Assn., 1968; chmn. Ogle County Community Mental Health Bd.; chmn. pub. relations com. Sinnissippi Mental Health Center Bd. Mem. bd. publ. Luth. Ch. in Am. 1950-62. Trustee Carthage Coll., 1938—, pres. bd., 1943-53. Named Hon. Am. Farmer by Future Farmers of Am., 1947, hon. life mem. Nat. Turkey Fedn.; Man. of Year, Inst. Am. Poultry Industries, 1961; recipient Distinguished Journalism Service award U. Wis., 1969; Community Leader of Am. award. 1969. Mem. Pub. Relations Soc. Am., Am. Agrl. Editors Assn., Poultry Sci. Assn., Assn. Am. Agrl. Coll. Editors, Nat. Council on Family Relations, Agr. Relations Council, Sales and Marketing Execs. Internat., Alpha Zeta, Phi Kappa Phi, Sigma Delta Chi. Mem. Lutheran Ch. Clubs: Nat. Press (Washington); University, Press (Chgo.); Sunset, Kiwanis, Moose (Mount Morris). Contbr. various publs. Address: 302 S Frederick Av Mount Morris IL 61054

HANKE, PAUL ROBERT, clergyman; b. Whitehall, Wis., Nov. 26, 1922; s. Arthur Carl and Clara (Flunker) H.; B.A., Northwestern Coll., Watertown, Wis., 1944; B.A., Wis. Luth. Sem., Mequon, 1947; m. Fern R. Draeger, June 29, 1947; children—David Paul, Steven Paul, Mary Louise. Ordained to ministry Luth. Ch., 1947; parish minister, Saint Peter, Minn., 1947—; sec. Wis. Evang. Luth. Synod, 1962—. Home: 425 W Mulberry St Saint Peter, MN 56082 Office: P O Box 32 Saint Peter MN 56082*

HANKE, PETER STEVENSON, lawyer, co. exec.; b. Beirut, Lebanon, Dec. 8, 1929 (parents Am. citizens); s. Lewis Ulysses and Kate (Gilbert) H.; A.B. cum laude, Harvard, 1951, J.D., 1958; m. Pamela Byrne Knight, Aug. 11, 1957; children—Timothy Lewis, Maria Byrne, Nora Elisabeth, Jennifer Knight. Admitted to D.C. bar, 1959, Mass. bar, 1970; atty. Office Gen. Counsel, Dept. Navy, Phila. and Washington, 1958-62; asst. counsel Pratt & Whitney Aircraft div. United Aircraft Corp., 1962-64, Hamilton Standard div., 1964-65; asst. counsel Emhart Corp., Bloomfield, Conn., 1965-70, asst. sec., 1967-70; sec., corporate counsel Standard Internat. Corp., Andover, Mass., 1970—. Served to lt. (j.g.) USNR, 1951-55. Home: 281 High St Newburyport MA 01950 Office: Elm Sq Andover MA 01810

HANKEY, WILLIAM CAMPBELL, clergyman; b. Bellevue, Pa., May 19, 1911; s. Benjamin Frnaklin and Georgia Fidelia (Campbell) H.; A.B., Thiel Coll., 1932, D.D., 1960; B.D., Lutheran Theol. Sem., Phila., 1936; m. Phyllis Alwilda Shaw, Feb. 3, 1940; children—Benjamin Franklin, Elizabeth Ann. Ordained to ministry Luth. Ch., 1936; pastor in North East, Pa., 1936-40, Arnold, Pa., 1940- 42. Apollo, Pa., 1946-60; pres. Pitts. synod United Luth. Ch. Am. 1960- 62, Western Pa.-W.Va. synod Luth. Ch. Am., 1962—. Served as chaplain AUS, 1942-46; ETO. Home: 230 Crestmont Rd Pittsburgh PA 15237 Office: 9625 Perry Hwy PittsbUrgh PA 15237

HANKIN, BERNARD JACOB, lawyer; b. Ewen, Mich. Apr. 6, 1913; s. Harry and Mae (Chudacoff) H.; A.B., U. Wis., 1934, LL.B., 1937; m. Beatrice Judith Berman, Mar. 17, 1946; children—Janet Ruth, James Alan. Admitted to Wis. bar, 1937, since practiced in Milw.; partner firm Kluwin, Dunphy, Hankin and Hayes, 1958- -. Served with inf. AUS, 1941-45; PTO. Decorated Bronze Star (2), Combat Inf. badge: recipient Vilas medal U. Wis., 1934. Mem. Am., Milw. (pres. 1965-66) bar assns., State Bar Wis., Fedn. Ins. Counsel, Delta Sigma Rho. Jewish religion. Mem. B'nai B'rith. Home: 5814 N Kent Av Milwaukee, WI 53217. Office: 510 E Wisconsin Av Milwaukee WI 53202

HANKINS, JOHN ERSKINE, ret. educator; b. Lake View, S.C., Jan. 2, 1905; s. James Thomas and Roma (McKenzie) H.; B.A., U. S.C., 1924, M.A., 1925; Ph.D., Yale, 1929; m. Nellie Pottle, Aug. 2, 1930; children—Margaret (Mrs. A.E. van Mourik), Thomas Leroy, John David. Adj. prof. English, U. S.C., 1925-26; asst. prof. Ind. State Tchrs. Coll., 1929-30; asst. prof. to prof. U. Kan., 1930-56; prof. U. Me., Orono, 1956-70, emeritus, 1970—, chmn. dept., 1956-66; Fulbright lectr. U. Leyden, 1953-54, U. Frankfurt- am-Main, 1954. Guggenheim fellow, 1949. Mem. Me. Tchrs. Assn., Northeast Folklore Soc., Modern Lang. Assn. Am., Phi Beta Kappa. Episcopalian. Author: (with C.K. Hyder) Selected 19th Century Essays, 1938: Life and Works of George Turberville, 1940; The Character of Hamlet and Other Essays, 1941; Shakespeare's Derived Imagery, 1953; (with H.J. Edwards) Lincoln the Writer, 1962; Source and Meaning in Spenser's Allegory, 1971. Contbr. poems, scholarly articles jours. Home: RR 1 Oxford ME 04270

HANKS, BRYAN CAYCE, lawyer; b. Gatesville, Tex., May 23, 1896; s. William Henry and Lillian (Cayce) H.; grad. Wichita Falls (Tex.) High Sch., 1915; student Rice Inst., 1915-16. Southwestern U., 1917; LL.B., U. Colo. 1922; m. Virginia Margaret Wooding, Sept. 20, 1921; children—Nancy, Larry (dec.). Admitted to N.Y. bar, 1924, Fla. bar, 1929; asso. firm Highes, Rounds, Schurman & Dwight, N.Y.C., 1922-24; legal dept. Electric Bond and Share Co., N.Y.C., 1924-25; head legal dept. Fla. Power & Light Co., Miami, 1925-36, now pres., dir.; pres. Miami Water Power Co., 1933-39, Miami Beach Ry. Co. and Consumers Water Co., 1937-39; mem. law firm Hanks & Preston, 1939-42; pres. Southeastern Electric Exchange, 1938- 39. Served from pvt. to sgt., U.S. Army, 1917-19. Mem. Am. Bar Assn., Am. Legion, Fla. Hist. Soc., Kappa Alpha, Phi Alpha Delta. Democrat. Methodist. Clubs: Lawyers (N.Y.C.); Committee of 100 (Miami Beach); Knife and Fork (Fort Worth); Kiwanis (Miami). Address: 3513 Westridge Av Fort Worth TX 76116

HANKS, JOHN HAROLD, educator, microbiologist; b. Fowlerton, Ind., Sept. 16, 1906; s. John Rufus and Augusta Mae (Smith) H.; B.S., Allegheny Coll., 1928; Ph.D., Yale, 1931; m. Julia King, June 9, 1930; children—John King, James Philip, Juliette Mae, Janet Susan. Fellow NRC, 1931-32; asst. prof., then asso. prof. bacteriology George Washington U. Med. Sch., 1932-39; microbiologist Leonard Wood Meml., 1939—; lectr. bacteriology and immunology Harvard Med. Sch., 1946-59; asso. prof. pathobiology Johns Hopkins Sch. Hygiene, 1959-62, prof., 1962—. Cons. Pan. Am. Health Orgn.; mem. expert com. leprosy, WHO. Mem. Am. Soc. Microbiology, Am. Assn. Immunologists, Soc. Exptl. Biology and Medicine, Internat. Leprosy Assn., Am. Acad. Microbiology. Home: 204 Ridgemede Rd Baltimore, MD 21210.

HANKS, MARION DUFF, retail exec., church ofcl.; b. Salt Lake City, Oct. 13, 1921; s. Stanley A. and Maude (Frame) H.; J.D., U. Utah, 1948; m. Maxine Christensen, Aug. 24, 1949; children—Susan G., Nancy, Ann, Mary, Richard. Missionary, Ch. of Jesus Christ of Latter-day Saints, 1942-44; dir. bur. information Temple Sq., Salt Lake City, 1948-56; v.p. Allen-Duff Assos., advt., Salt Lake City, 1951-57, Gull, Inc., merchandising, Salt Lake City, 1955—; editor Era of Youth mag. Gen. authority Ch. of Jesus Christ of Latter-day Saints, 1953—, mem. Council of Seventy, 1953—. Mem. President's Adv. Com on Fitness Am. Youths; asso. dir. Inst. Religion, U. Utah; bd. dirs. West Sem.; trustee Brigham Young U., Coll. of So. Utah. Served with USNR, 1944-46: PTO. Named Outstanding Young Man of Utah by U.S. Jr. C. of C., 1954. Home: 1399 Butler Av Salt Lake City UT 84102 Office: 47 E South Temple St Salt Lake City UT 84111 *

HANLEY, BRIDGET ANNE ELIZABETH, actress; b. Mpls., Feb. 3, 1943; d. Leland Francis Patrick and Doria Linea (Nihlroos) H.; student San Francisco Coll. Women, 1959-61; B.A. in Drama, U. Wash., 1963; m. E.W. Swackhamer, Apr. 26, 1969; 1 dau., Bronwyn. Actress plays The Crucible, Desire Under the Elms and others in amateur status; roles profl. plays include Private Lives, Under the Yum Yum Tree; TV appearances include Hank, Gidget, The Farmers Daughter, Iron Horse, Second Hundred Years, Bewitched, The Flying Nun, Love on a Rooftop, Occasional Wife, The Outcasts, Love American Style, The Odd Couple, Nanny and the Professor, Cade's Country; star Here Come the Brides, 1968-70. Named Female Star of Yr., 16 mag., 1969. Office: care APA Inc 9000 Sunset Blvd 315 Hollywood CA 90069

HANLEY, CLIFFORD, author; b. Glasgow, Scotland, Oct. 28, 1922; s. Henry and Martha (Griffith) H.; student Eastbank Sch., Glasgow; m. Anna Clark, Jan. 10, 1948; children—Clifford, Jane, Joanna. Newspaper reporter News of the World, 1940-45; sub-editor Scottish Daily Record, 1945-48, later columnist; columnist Daily Record, TV Guide, Glasgow Eve. Citizen; TV critic London Spectator, 1962-63. Mem. Nat. Union Journalists, Screenwriters Guild, Songwriter Guild, P.E.N., Crime Writers Assn., Am. League Authors, Glasgow Lit. and Philol. Soc. (pres. 1962-63). Author: Dancing in the Streets, 1958; Love from Everybody, 1959; The Taste of Too Much, 1960; The System, 1961; It's Different Abroad, 1962; Second Time Round, 1963; A Skinful of Scotch, 1965; The Hot Month, 1967; The Red-haired Bitch, 1969; (pseudonym Henry Calvin) Boka Lives!, 1969; The Italian Gadget, 1965; The DNA Business, 1967; (plays) Durable Element (prod. Dundee and Glasgow), 1961; (musical plays) Saturmacnalia, 1962; Oh for an Island, 1963; Dick MacWhitty, 1964; Oh Glorious Jubilee, 1970. Home: 36 Munro Rd Glasgow Scotland

HANLEY, DEXTER L., univ. pres., clergyman; b. Ft. Worth, June 26, 1919; s. Thomas James, Jr. and Cecelia (Meilleur) H.; A.B., Georgetown U., 1940, LL.B., 1956; Ph.L., Woodstock Coll., 1945, S.T.L., 1952; LL.M., Harvard, 1958. Entered Soc. Jesus, Md. Province, 1940; ordained priest Roman Catholic Ch., 1952; dean Summer Schs., Georgetown U., 1952-53, prof. law, 1959—; dir. Inst. Law, Human Rights and Social Values, 1965—; pres. U. Scranton, Pa., 1970—. U.S. del. ECOSOC, UN, 1967. Mem. Am. (sec. labor law sect. 1967, 70), Fed. (nat. council 1968—) bar assns., Phi Beta Kappa, Delta Mu Delta, Omicron Delta Epsilon, Phi Delta Phi, Phi Delta Kappa. K.C. (4). Address: U Scranton Scranton PA 18510

HANLEY, EDWARD JAMES, steel corp. exec.; b. Whitman, Mass., Feb. 27, 1903; s. Francis J. and Mary Ellen (McGovern) H.; grad. Mass. Inst. Tech., 1924, Harvard Sch. Bus., 1927; D.Sc., Duquesne U., 1951; LL.D., St. Vincent Coll., 1956; m. Dorothy Ward Hanley, 1930. With Gen. Electric Co., 1927-36; sec. Allegheny Ludlum Steel Corp., 1936, treas., 1941, v.p., 1946, dir. 1947—, pres. 1951-67, chief exec. officer, 1951-68, chmn., 1962—; dir. Am. Standard, Inc., NL Industries, Titanium Metals Corp. Am., Duquesne Light Co., Mine Safety Appliances Co., Bell Telephone Co. Pa. Bd. dirs. W. Pa. Safety Council, Pitts. Symphony Soc.; mem. corp. Mass. Inst. Tech., Nat. Fund Med. Edn. Mem. Am. Iron and Steel Inst., Nat. Assn. Accountants, Newcomen Soc. N. Am. Clubs: Union League (N.Y.C.); Duquesne, Rolling Rock, Fox Chapel Golf (Pitts.). Home: 2685 Sunset Lane Oak Hill Farms Allison Park PA 15101 Office: Allegheny Ludlum Steel Corp Oliver Bldg Pittsburgh PA 15222

HANLEY, GEORGE CLEMENT, copper co. exec.; b. N.Y.C., July 10, 1920; s. John Henry and Gertrude (Cullen) H.; B.S., B.B.A., Fordham U., 1948; m. Marie Josephine Flecker, Jan. 23, 1943; children—Mary Anne (Mrs. Michael McCormack), David G., George Clement, John E., Patricia E. Staff accountant Pogson, Peloubet & Co., 1946-48; asst. sec. Anaconda Am. Brass Co., 1958-68; comptroller Anaconda Wire & Cable Co., 1968-69, v.p. finance, dir., 1969—. Vice pres. bd. United Council Fund, Waterbury, Conn., 1960-68; dist. chmn., bd. dirs. Waterbury dist. Boy Scouts Am., 1964-68. Served with USAAF, 1942-46, USAF, 1950-52. Home: 511 Saw Mill Rd Stamford CT 06903 Office: 605 3d Av New York City NY 10016

HANLEY, JAMES ALEXANDER, sign mfg. co. exec.; b. Chgo., Aug. 13, 1931; s. James Alexander and Bernice (Thibeault) H.; B.S., U. Ill., 1953, M.S. 1957; m. D'etta Darlene Dosier, Dec. 27, 1953; children—Michael James, Steven John, Kathleen Marie. Sr. auditor Arthur Anderson & Co., C.P.A.'s, Los Angeles, 1957- 60; successively comptroller, treas., sr. v.p. finance Greyhound Leasing & Financial Corp., Chgo., 1966-68; formerly v.p. finance, treas. Fed. Sign & Signal Corp., Blue Island, Ill. Served as lt. USCGR, 1953-56. C.P.A., Cal. Mem. Financial Execs. Inst., Am. Inst. C.P.A.'s, Delta Tau Delta. Republican. Lutheran. Mason, Elk. Home: 730 S Garfield Av Hinsdale IL 60521 Office: 136th and Western Av Blue Island IL 60406 *

HANLEY, JAMES MICHAEL, congressman; b. Syracuse, N.Y., July 10, 1920; s. Michael Joseph and Alice (Gillick) H.; grad. Saint Lucy's Acad., 1938; LL.D., LeMoyne Coll., Syracuse, 1967; m. Rita Harrington, Aug. 12, 1950; children—Christine Mary, Peter James. Funeral dir., Syracuse, 1939- -; owner Callahan-Hanley-Mooney Funeral Home, Syracuse, 1953—; mem. 89th 92d Congress 35th Dist. N.Y., mem. banking and currency com., post office and civil service com. Mem. President's Council on Voter Registration. Vice chmn. Onondaga County Vets. Adv. Com.; hon. life comdr. Onondaga County Vets. Council. Mem. Onondaga County Democratic Com., also campaign coordinator, 1963. Trustee Maria Regina Coll., Syracuse. Served with AUS, World War II. Mem. Am. Legion (past post comdr.), Holy Name Soc., Ancient Order Hibernians, Regular Vets. Assn. (past N.Y. comdr.), Nat., N.Y., Onondaga County funeral dirs. assns., Syracuse C. of C., Syracuse Liederkranz, Syracuse Police Benevolent Assn., Army and Navy Union, Order of Alhambra (past grand comdr. N Navarre Caravan). K.C. (past grand knight Syracuse Council, Man of Year 1960), Elk. Clubs: Antique Auto, West End Social, All City Veterans, St. Mary's Men (Syracuse). Home: 316 Coleridge Av Syracuse NY 13204 Office: Cannon House Office Bldg Washington DC 20515

HANLEY, JOHN GERALD, clergyman; b. Read, Ont., Can., Feb. 21, 1907; s. Denis and Jessie (Bryson) H.; B.A., U. Toronto, 1927; grad. theology, St. Augustine's Sem., Toronto, 1931. Ordained priest Roman Cath. Ch., 1931; asst. in cathedral, Kingston, Can., 1931-32, Trenton, Can., 1934-41; editor Canadian Register, 1941-70; prof. Jr. Sem., Vancouver, B.C., Can., 1932-34; chaplain Newman Club, Queen's U., Kingston, 1941-58; vicar-gen. Archdiocese Kingston, 1969—; nat. chaplain Canadian Newman Clubs, 1944-45, 52-55. Chmn. Canadian Cath. Press Commn., 1958-67. Recipient Kingston award Queen's U. Alumni Assn., 1970. Mem. Cath. Press Assn. U.S. and Can. (bd. dirs. 1961-64, sec. 1962-64, 65-68), Cath. Bib. Assn. Am. (v.p. 1944-45). Author: Across Canada with Newman, 1957. Address: 279 Johnson St Kingston Ontario Canada

HANLEY, JOHN THOMAS, corp. exec.; b. Chgo., Mar. 26, 1923; s. William C. and Grace (Prindiville) H.; B.S., Dartmouth Coll., 1947, M.S., 1948; Ph.D., U. Ill., 1963; m. Mary Carolyn Duke, Oct. 22, 1945; children—Judith Ellen, Joan Marie, John Thomas, Barbara Brooks, Michael Davies. Served with C.E. corps, USNR, 1948-58, advanced through grades to lt. comdr., 1956; asst. to chief blast br. Armed Forces Spl. Weapons Project, Washington, 1949-52; resident officer in charge constrn. Skiffs Creek Annex, Yorktown, Va., 1952-53; pub. works officer Lake Mead Base, Neb., 1954-56; staff civil engr. hdqrs. Allied Forces Mediterranean, Malta, 1956-58; instr. civil engring., U. Ill., Urbana, 1958-63; asso. head dept. U. Minn., Mpls., 1963-71, dir. undergrad. studies Inst. Tech., 1968-71, prof. Inst. Tech., 1969-71, dir. planning, research and devel. Clark Engring. Co., 1971—; pres., chmn. bd. Environmental Services, Inc., 1971—; cons. Office Civil Def., Washington, 1961-63, Minn. Dept. Civil Def., 1963—, Hart-Carter Co., Mpls., 1964-65, 3M Co., Mpls., 1966—, Oak Ridge Nat. Lab., 1967-69. Vice pres. Minn. Profl. Engrs. Found., 1969-70, pres., 1970-71. Served to signalman 2d class USNR, 1942-45. Ford Found. fellow, 1960-61. Mem. Nat., Minn. (pres. 1971-72) socs. profl. engrs. Home: 5705 Lawndale Lane Hamol MN 55340 Office: 2815 Wayzata Blvd Minneapolis MN 55405

HANLEY, JOHN WELLER, mfg. co. exec.; b. Parkersburg, W.Va., Jan. 11, 1922; s. James P. and Ida May (Ayers) H.; B.S. in Metall. Engring., Pa. State U., 1942; M.B.A., Harvard, 1947; m. Mary Jane Reel, June 26, 1948; children—John Weller, Michael James, Susan Jayne. Metall. engr. Allegheny Ludlum Steel Corp., 1942-43; with Procter & Gamble Co., 1947—, mgr. case soap products, 1961-63, v.p. household soap products div., 1963-67, corp. v.p., group exec., 1967-70, exec. v.p., 1970—, also dir.; dir., Armco Steel Corp. Campaign chmn. United Appeal Greater Cin. Served to lt. (s.g.) USNR, 1943-46; PTO. Home: 2444 Madison Rd Cincinnati OH 45208 Office: P O Box 599 Cincinnati OH 45201

HANLEY, MARSHALL EDWARD, lawyer; b. Muncie, Ind., May 7, 1920; s. Frank A. and Emily (Shirk) H.; student U. Chgo., 1937-39, Princeton, summer 1941; A.B., Indiana U., 1942; J.D., Harvard, 1945; M.A., Ball State U., 1971; m. Elaine Bowers; children—Carol Lee, Marshall Sherman, Mark Anthony. Law clk. for Justice Sherman Minton, U.S. Ct. Appeals, Chgo., 1945-46; partner DeFur, Voran, Hanley, Radcliff & Reed, 1954- -; city atty. City Muncie, 1948-50, 56-63; city controller, 1963; asst. U.S. atty. So. Dist. Ind., 1950-52, U.S. atty., 1953; pres. Marion Finance Co., Ocala, Fla. Dir. Ball State U. Found.; trustee Ft. Wayne State Sch. Pres. Young Democrats of Ind., 1947-49. Mem. Am., Ind., Delaware County bar assns., Beta Theta Pi. Clubs: Rotary, Muncie, (Muncie) Indianapolis Athletic. (Indpls.); Sagamore of Wabash. Home: 11 Wiltshire Rd Muncie IN 47304 Office: Muncie Fed Bldg Muncie IN 47302

HANLEY, PATRICK HENRY, surgeon; b. Lockport, La., Feb. 2, 1909; s. John Patrick and Anna G. (Fleming) H.; M.D., Tulane U., 1933; m. Jeanne C. Roeling, Feb. 17, 1938; children—Jeanne Patricia (Mrs. David F. Hughes). Intern charity Hosp., New Orleans, 1933-34; gen. practice medicine and surgery, Golden Meadow, La., 1934-42; surg. resident Tulane U. unit Charity Hosp., 1945-50, chief surg. resident, 1949-50, surg. dir., 1949-50, now sr. vis. surgeon; mem. staff Ochsner Clinic, New Orleans, 1950—, head dept. colon and rectal surgery, 1961—, also sr. vis. surgeon; prof. clin. surgery Tulane U. Med. Sch., 1959—; pres. Alton Ochsner Found. Hosp., 1966. Bd. dirs. New Orleans Opera House Assn.; mem. adminstrv. bd. physicians Tulane U. Served to lt. comdr. USNR, 1942-45. Diplomate Am. Bd. Colon and Rectal Surgery (pres. 1965-66, sec.-treas. 1968—). Fellow A.C.S., Am. Proctologic Soc. (v.p.); mem. Soc. Surgery Alimentary Tract, A.M.A. (adv. council colon and rectal surgery), La. Med. Soc., La. Surg. Assn., Southeastern Surg. Congress, New Orleans (past pres.), Alton Ochsner (past pres.) surg. socs., Piedmont Proctologic Soc. (pres. 1971), Tulane U. Med. Assn. (sec. 1970), Tulane U. Med. Alumni Assn. (pres. 1968), Alpha Omega Alpha, ALpha Kappa Kappa. Recipient awards N.H., Ohio proctologic socs., also A.C.S. Clubs: New Orleans Opera (pres.), New Orleans Country. Contbr. articles profl. jours. Home: 3501 Napoleon St New Orleans LA 70115

HANLEY, THOMAS F., tax cons.; b. N.Y.C., Dec. 12, 1898; s. Thomas F. and Mary Ann (O'Rourke) H.; B.C.S., N.Y.U., 1928; D.C.S. (hon.), St. John's U.; m. Lillian Marie Griffin, Dec. 27, 1922; children—Thomas F., Rita Marie, Mary Elizabeth, Bernadette Rose, Jeanne F., Corinne G., Daniel J., Therese. Pub. accountant Dept. Finance, N.Y.C., 1917-19, U.S. Treasury Dept., 1919-24; tax cons., partner Thomas F. Hanley & Co., C.P.A.'s, Long Island City, N.Y., 1925- -; fed. receiver, closed Nat. Banks, Queens County, N.Y., 1934-37; v.p., gen. mgr. Hub Industries, Inc., 1941-44; former chmn. R. Hoe & Co., Inc., N.Y.C., now pres., chief exec. officer. Decorated knight of Malta; knight of Holy Sepulchre (Papal). Mem. Queens County, Flushing (v.p.) chambers commerce, N.Y. Soc. C.P.A.'s Execs. Assn., Am. Inst. C.P.A.'s. Democrat. Roman Catholic. Clubs: Catholic, Manhattan, Athletic. Home: 170 Eldersfield Rd Manhasset Long Island NY 11030 Office: C of C Bldg Long Island City NY 11101 *

HANLEY, WILLIAM, author; b. Lorain, O., Oct. 22, 1931; s. William Gerald and Anne (Rodgers) H.; student Cornell U., 1950-51, Am. Acad. Dramatic Arts, 1954- 55; m. Shelley Post, 1956 (div. 1961); m. 2d, Patricia Stanley, Feb. 19, 1962; children-Katherine, Nell. Author: (plays) Mrs. Dally Has a Lover, 1962, Whisper into my Good Ear, 1962, Today is Independence Day, 1963, Slow Dance on the Killing Ground, 1964, Flesh and Blood, 1968, No Answer, 1968; (novel) Blue Dreams, 1971. Served with AUS, 1952-54. Address: 161 W 86th St New York City, NY 10024.

HANLIN, HUGH CAREY, Jr., life ins. co. exec.; b. Chattanooga, Mar. 16, 1925; s. Hugh Carey and Irene (Thompson) H.; student Emory U., 1942-44, 46-47; B.A., U. Mich., 1948; m. Wilma Jean Deal, June 23, 1951; children-Timothy Carey, Chris Allan. With Provident Life & Accident Ins. Co., 1948—, adminstrv, v.p., chief actuary, 1970—; pres. PLA Securites Corp., 1968—. Served to lt. (j.g.) USNR, 1943-46. Fellow Soc. Actuaries; mem. Southeastern Actuaries Club (pres. 1956-57), Chattanooga, C. of C. Home: 7472 Preston Circle Chattanooga TN 37421 Office: Provident Life and Accident Ins Co

HANLON, CYRIL ROLLINS, physician; b. Balt., Feb. 8, 1915; s. Bernard and Harriet (Rollins) H.; A.B., Loyola Coll., Balt., 1934; M.D., Johns Hopkins, 1938; m. Margaret M. Hammond, May 28, 1949; children—Philip, Paul Richard, Christine Thomas, Mary, Martha, Sarah. Intern John Hopkins Hosp., 1939- 40, W. S. Halsted Fellow in surgery, 1939-40, instr. surgery, 1946-48, asst. prof., 1948-50; asst. resident, resident in surgery Cin. Gen. Hosp., 1940-41, 43-44; exchange fellow surgery U. Cal., 1941-42; prof. surgery, chmn. dept. St. Louis U., 1950-69; prof. surgery Northwestern U. Med. Sch., 1969—. Chmn. surgery study sect. NIH, 1965-66. Served to lt. (j.g.). M.C., USNR, 1944-46; CBI Recipient Fleur-de-lis award St. Louis U., 1968. Diplomate Am. Bd. Surgery (chmn. 1966-67); founder group Am. Bd. Thoracic Surgery, 1949. Fellow A.C.S. (gov., regent 1967-69, bd. dirs. 1969—); mem. Am. Heart Assn. (surgery research study com. 1966- 68), Internat. Cardiovascular Soc. (pres. N. Am. chpt.), A.M.A., Am. (sec. 1968-69) Western surg. assns., Am. Assn. Thoracic Surgery (treas.), Soc. U. Surgeons (pres.), St. Louis Surg. Soc., Alpha Omega Alpha. Roman Catholic. Club: Serra (1st v.p.) (St. Louis). Contbr. articles profl. jours. Address: 55 E Erie St Chicago IL 60611

HANLON, JOHN JOSEPH, pub. health adminstr.; b. Boston, May 7, 1912; s. John Joseph and Florence (Livingston) H.; B.S., Mass. Inst. Tech., 1933, M.S., 1934; spl. student Harvard Sch. Pub. Health, 1934; M.B., Wayne U., 1940, M.D., 1941; M.P.H. Johns Hopkins, 1942; m. Frances E. Pizzo, June 24, 1939; children—Jon Jerrold, Donald Livingston, Asst. sanitary engr. Eaton County, Mich., 1934; asst. epidemiologist, statistician Detroit Dept. Health, 1935-40; staff Harper Hosp., Detroit, 1940-41; health officer Bradley County, Tenn., 1941; dir. nutrition Tenn. Pub. Health, 1942-43; asso. prof. pub. health adminstrn. U. N.C., 1943-44; lect. preventive medicine Duke U., 1943-44; asso. prof. U. Mich., 1944-49, prof. pub. health, 1951-52; chief health Mission, Inst. Inter-Am. Affairs, Bolivia, 1949-51; med. dir. USPHS, Chief pub. health div. U.S. Fgn. Aid Program, 1952-57; dir. pub. health services City of Phila., 1957-64; prof., chmn. dept. preventive medicine and pub. health Temple U. Sch. Medicine, 1957-64; pub. health dir. Detroit and Wayne County; adjunct prof. pub. health adminstrn. U. Michigan; prof., chmn. dept. community medicine Wayne State U. Sch. Medicine, 1964- 68; asst. surgeon gen. Pub. Health Service, Washington, 1968—. Mem. U.S. delegation to World Health Assembly, 1953, 54, 56. Decorated Order of Condor (Bolivia), 1951. Diplomate Am. Bd. Preventive Medicine and Pub. Health. Fellow Am. Pub. Health Assn. (pres. 1967-68); mem. A.M.A., Alpha Omega Alpha, Sigma Xi, Delta Omega; hon. mem. Sociedad Boliviana de Salud Publica, Hellenic Pub. Health Soc. Author: (with Beeuwkes) Nutrition and Public Health, 1945, 47; Principles of Public Health Adminstration, 1950, 55, 60, 64, 69; Principios de Salud Publica, 1956, 63; Design for Health, 1963, 71; Guias Para La Salud de la Comunidad, 1967; (with others) A Strategy for a Livable Environment, 1967; also articles, bulls. Home: 9805 Canal Rd Montgomery Village Gaithersburg MD 20760 Office: 5600 Fishers Lane Rockville MD 20852

HANLON, JOHN W., tobacco co. ofcl.; b. N.Y.C., Aug. 11, 1910; s. William J. and Julia L. (McDonnell) H.; student Fordham U.; m. Blanche Gaulin, June 14, 1936; children—John W., Robert L. Asst. sec. Am. Brands, Inc. Tobacco Co. formerly Am., Yonkers, N.Y., 1939-46, sec., 1946—; sec., dir. Am. Tobacco Co. Orient, Inc., Golden Belt Mfg. Co., Hatheway-Steane Corp. Mem. Am. Soc. Corporate Secs. Home: 75 Borcher Av Yonkers NY 10704 Office: 111 5th Av New York City NY 10003

HANN, ROBERT HENRY, steel co. exec.; b. Hornell, N.Y., June 19, 1907; s. Charles William and Gertrude (Ingalls) H.; LL.B., Rutgers U., 1940; m. Pauline E. Pierce, May 3, 1930. Admitted to N.J. bar, 1941, Ohio bar, 1942; pvt. sec. Judge John C. Barbour, circuit ct. judge N.J., 1938-41; atty. Erie R.R. Co., 1942-44, asst. gen. atty., 1944-46, gen. atty., 1946-52, corporate sec., 1952—, sec. treas., 1964-66 (co. now Erie-Lackawanna R.R. Co.), also dir. several subsidiaries; sec. Wean Industries, Youngstown, O., 1966—, Wean Engring. Co. Can. Ltd., Hamilton, 1967—; asst. sec. Wean United, Inc., Pitts., 1968; mem. finance com. Trailer Train, Inc.; treas. Buffalo Creek R.R. Chmn. R.R. Community Com., Cleve., 1961; chief warden Civil Def., 1949-52. Pres. West Hill Colony, Inc. Mem. U.S., Ohio, Youngstown chambers commerce, Am. Soc. Corporate Secs. (past pres.), Rutgers U. Alumni Assn., Delta Theta Phi. (past dean). Episcopalian. Mason. Club: Mayfield Country; Trumbull Country. Home: 543 Butler Rd NE Warren OH 44483 Office: 3805 Henricks Rd Youngstown OH 44501

HANNA, ALFRED JACKSON, educator, historian; b. Tampa, Fla., May 5, 1893; s. Josiah Calvin and Sarah Emily (Jackson) H.; A.B., Rollins Coll., 1917, L.H.D., 1945; grad. study U. Madrid (Spain), 1931, U. Mex., 1934; m. Kathryn T. Abbey, July 5, 1941 (dec. Apr. 1967). Successively adminstrv. officer, instr., asst. prof., asso. prof. and prof. history Rollins Coll., 1917-70, also dir. Inter-Am. studies, 1942-65, Weddell prof. history, 1946-70, v.p., 1951-70. Served with

USNRF, 1918-19. Decorated officer d'Academie, Palmes Universitaires (France), 1935; Social Sci. Research Council-Am. Philos. Soc. research grantee, France, 1952. Mem. Am., So., Va. hist. assns., Hispanic Inst. Fla. (pres. 1933-40), Fla. Acad. Scis., Fla. Audubon Soc. (past pres.), Kappa Alpha. Episcopalian. Republican. Clubs: Cosmos (Washington); University (Winter Park). Author: Fort Maitland, 1935; Founding of Rollins College, 1936; Flight Into Oblivion, 1938; (with Branch Cabell) The St. Johns River (in Rivers of Am. series), 1943; A Prince in Their Midst, 1946; (with Kathryn Abbey Hanna) Lake Okeechobee (Am. Lake series), 1948, Florida's Golden Sands, 1950, Confederate Exiles in Venezuela (Confederate Centennial series), 1960, Napoleon III and Mexico: American Triumph over Monarchy, 1971. Editor: Rollins Alumni Record, 1925-32; Recommended Readings for the Florida Centennial, 1945. Contbr. hist. articles mags., also Dictionary Am. Biography, Dictionary Am. History, Ency. Americana, Ency. Brit. Home: 235 Sterling Av Winter Park FL 32789

HANNA, ARCHIBALD, Jr., librarian; b. Worcester, Mass., Sept. 24, 1916; s. Archibald and Rachel Sutherland (Knight) H.; A.B., Clark U., 1939; M.A., Yale, 1946, Ph.D., 1951; M.S. Columbia, 1949; m. Edith Sue Mensch, June 1, 1940; children—Stewart Billings, Jean, James Diener. Sr. cataloger Yale U. Library, 1949-52, William Robertson Coe librarian Yale Collection Western Am. and Benjamin Franklin Collection, 1952—, Fellow Ezra Stiles Coll. Ordained deacon Protestant Episcopal Church, 1961. Served with USMCR, 1942-46; col. Res. ret. Mem. Bibliog. Soc. Am., Am. Antiquarian Soc. Clubs: Grolier, St. Botolph. Home: 6 Damascus Rd Branford CT 06405

HANNA, GORDON, newspaperman; b. Jack County, Tex., Feb. 22, 1920; s. John Grey and Ethyl (Wood) H.; student Tex. Technol. Coll., 1936-39; m. Annie Lou Guidry, Apr. 22, 1941; children—Judith, Harriet. Reporter Port Arthur (Tex.) News, 1939-42; reporter Houston Press, 1943-44, reporter, legislative corr., 1946-48, city editor, 1949-54; mng. editor Comml. Appeal, Memphis, 1954-59; editor Evansville (Ind.) Press, 1959-68, Comml. Appeal, Memphis, 1969—. Served with USAAF, 1944-45. Mem. Am. Soc. Newspaper Editors. Rotarian. Home: 5450 Valleybrook Cove Memphis TN 38117 Office: 495 Union Av Memphis TN 38101

HANNA, JANE FIQUET, cons., ret. govt. ofcl.; b. Buenos Aires, Argentina, Nov. 23, 1916 (parents U.S. citizens); d. Louis Albert and Mary (Perry) Fiquet; student U. Mo., 1934- 35; m. Frank S. Hanna, Apr. 4, 1936 (div. 1961); children—Frank F., Fiquet. Chmn. civil def. volunteer office, St. Joseph, Mo., 1941-45; asst. dir. civil def., St. Joseph, 1951-54; spl. asst. to asst. sec. def. Office Civil Def., Dept. Def., 1962-64; dep. dir. civil def. Office Sec. Army, 1964-69; now cons. Mem. adv. bd. Nat. Bank Washington. Mem. adv. council Family and Childrens Bur., St. Joseph, 1943-44; dir., sec., v.p. Community Chest, St. Joseph, 1943-45, 50-53; sec. Council Social Agys., St. Joseph, 1945-46; mem. bd. Green Acres Pension Home, St. Joseph, 1952-54; v.p. Varner Ednl. Found., St. Joseph, 1958-62; pres. Jr. League St. Joseph, 1944-46; bd. dirs. Assn. Jr. Leagues Am., 1954-56, pres., 1956-58; mem. com. volunteer services Nat. Social Welfare Assembly, 1963-67; nat. pub. relations com. Girl Scouts U.S.A., 1966-69; mem. membership and budget com. Greater Washington Health and Welfare Council. Mem. Adult Edn., Assn., Am. Acad. Polit. and Social Sci., Jr. League Washington, Pi Beta Phi. Home: 5101 River Rd Chevy Chase MD 20016

HANNA, JOHN PAUL, lawyer; b. N.Y.C., July 12, 1932; s. Paul Robert and Jean (Shuman) H.; grad. Phillips Acad., Andover, Mass., 1950; B.A., Stanford, 1954, J.D., 1959; m. Joyce Adams, June 18, 1955; children—Kristine, Katherine. Admitted to Cal. bar, 1959, since practiced in Palo Alto; partner firm Thoits, Lehman & Hanna, and predecessors, 1961—. Mem. Santa Clara County Estate Planning Council, 1963-65; mem. Peninsula Estate Planning Council, 1962-65, chmn. com. new legislation, 1963-65. Vice pres. Univ. and Crescent Park Assn., 1967; sec. Palo Alto chpt. United Fund, 1966-68; founding mem. Palo Altans Town Hall, 1966; mem. Mayor's Com. Planning in the Foothills, 1964—. Mem. Cal. Republican Central Com., 1971—. Served to 1st lt. AUS, 1954-56. Named Young Man of Year in Palo Alto, 1964; named one of Five Outstanding Young Men Cal., 1967. Mem. Am., Palo Alto, Santa Clara County bar assns., State Bar Cal., Am., Cal. trial lawyers assns., Palo Alto C. of C. (v.p. 1967-68), Delta Tau Delta, Phi Delta Phi. Methodist. Elk, Kiwanian (pres. Palo Alto 1968), Club: Menlo Circus (Menlo Park, Cal.). Author: Teenagers and the Law, 1967. Editor, co-author: Youth and the Law, 1963. Home: 6 Phillips Rd Palo Alto CA 94303 Office: Palo Alto Office Center Palo Alto CA 94302

HANNA, KEITH LAZELL, hotel exec.; b. Promise City, Ia., Dec. 8, 1908; s. Harry Clyde and True (Townsend) H.; B.S.C., U. Ia., 1932; LL.B., Ind. U., 1940; m. Virginia V. Poston, July 20, 1935; children—Vicki Ann, Keith Lawrence, Mary Jane. With Dept. Agr., 1936-51, chief div. budgetary and financial reporting Office Budget and Finance, 1946-51; dir. Office Budget and Finance, Small Def. Plants Adminstrn., 1951-53; with Small Bus. Adminstrn., 1953- 66, asst. adminstr. for adminstrn., 1963-66; adminstrv. dir. Frontier Hotel, Las Vegas, 1967-70; mng. dir. Castaways Hotel & Casino, 1970—; dir. First Western Savings & Loan Assn. mem. Salvation Army Adv. Bd. Mem. Nev. Gov.'s Gaming Task Force, 1968. Recipient Superior Service award Small Bus. Adminstrn., 1964, 66. Mem. Fed. Govt. Accountants Assn., Order Artus, Beta Gamma Sigma, Sigma Delta Kappa. Mem. Christian Ch. Home: 1096 Tam O'Shanter Dr Las Vegas NV 89109 Office: 3120 Las Vegas Blvd S Las Vegas NV 89109

HANNA, PAUL JOHNSTON, banker; b. Canonsburg, Pa., Sept. 26, 1915; s. George J. and Ethel (Lyon) H.; B.S., U. Pitts., 1939; postgrad. Rutgers U., 1950, Dartmouth Grad. Sch. Credit and Financial Mgmt., 1955; m. Grace M. Gillen, June 22, 1946; children—Paul Johnston II, Lee E. With Citizen's Trust Co., Canonsburg, 1939-41; sr. v.p. nat. div. Mfrs. Hanover Trust Co., N.Y.C., 1946—; dir. 2d Nat. Bank Orange (N.J.), Govt. Employees Life Ins. Co., Govt. Employees Ins. Co., Govt. Employees Corp., Govt. Employees Financial Corp., Govt. Employees Life Ins. Co., Criterion Ins. Co. Trustee Rider Coll., Pingry Sch., Elizabeth, N.J. Served to lt. col. AUS, 1941-45. Decorated Bronze Star. Mem. Am., N.Y. State (adminstrv. bd.) bankers assns., Assn. Res. City Bankers. Presbyn. (elder). Clubs: Baltusrol Golf (Springfield, N.J.); Racquet (Phila.). Home: 219 Oak Ridge Av Summit NJ 07901 Office: 350 Park Av New York City NY 10022

HANNA, RICHARD THOMAS, congressman; b. Kemmerer, Wyo., June 9, 1914; s. Robert Alexander and Martha Jane (Thomas) H.; B.A., U. Cal. at Los Angeles, 1937, LL.B., 1952; m. Doris Muriel Jenks, Apr. 1, 1945; children—Pamela, Alexander Harris, Kimberly Grace. Newspaper reporter, Sweetwater (Tex.) Reporter, 1937-38; recreation suptr. WPA, W. Tex., 1938-41, Cal., 1946; admitted to Cal. bar, 1952; gen. practice, Orange County, 1952—; sr. partner with the firm of Launer, Chaffee & Hanna, 1958—; member of the California Legislature 75th Dist., 1956-62, chmn. rules and edn. com.; mem. 88th-92d Congresses, 34th Dist. Cal. Dir., sec. Spectra-Strip Wire Cable Corp., Garden Grove, Cal., 1955—. Area dir. W. Orange County chpt. A.R.C., 1956-67; city-county area dir. United Fund Fullerton, 1962. Bd. dirs. Gemco Scholarship Found. Served with Air Corps, USNR, 1941-45. Mem. Am., Cal., Orange County bar assns., Westminster C. of C. (past pres.), Phi Delta Phi, Lambda Chi Alpha. Democrat. Mem. Ch. of Jesus Christ of Latter-Day Saints. Elk, Lion (past pres.). Home: 17071 Westport Dr Huntington Beach CA also 9124 River Rd Potomac MD 20854 Office 1695 Crescent Av Anaheim CA 92801 also Cannon Bldg Washington DC 20006

HANNA, ROBERT THOMAS, dairy exec.; b. Shelby County, Ky., Dec. 30, 1909; s. Robert Price and Edmonia (Brown) H.; B.S. in Agr., U. Ky., 1937; m. Andrea Skinner, Apr. 24, 1936; children—Jane (Mrs. Robert Bender), Barbara. With Sealtest Foods, now div. Nat. Dairy Products Corp., 1936—, dist. gen. mgr., Louisville, 1958-64, v.p., 1964—. Mem. Tenn. (past pres.), Ky. (bd. dirs.) dairy products assns., Am. Dairy Assn. (bd. dirs. Ky.), So. Assn. Ice Cream Mfrs. (bd. dirs.), Nashville Jr. C. of C. (past pres.). Home: 887 Forest Hill Rd Lake Forest IL 60045 Office: 455 E Grand Av Chicago IL 60601

HANNA, ROLAND PEMBROOK, pianist; b. Detroit, Feb. 10, 1932; s. Timothy Elisha and Bernice Louise (Smith) H.; student Juilliard Sch. Music, 1960; m. Ramona Ruth Woodard, Feb. 3, 1954; children—Michael Curtis, Christopher Roland. Performed in Germany, France, Austria, 1958-60, in Germany, Belgium, Sweden, Switzerland, 1960; tour of Australia and New Zealand, 1964; commd. to write and perform in first Japanese musical, Tokyo, 1964; night club, concert, musical and TV appearances throughout U.S., 1950-; mem. N.Y. Jazz Sextet, 1965—, Thad-Jones-Mel Lewis Jazz Orch., 1965—. Served with AUS, 1950-52. Composer: Sonata for Piano and Cello, 1959; (jazz work to bassist) MusesDedicated to Richard Davis, 1963; (jazz composition) Midtown, 1963.

HANNA, STANLEY SWEET, physicist, educator; b. Sagaing, Burma, May 17, 1920 (parents Am. citizens); s. Alexander Carson and Hazel (Ames) H.; A.B., Denison U., 1941 D.Sc., 1970; Ph.D., Johns Hopkins, 1947; m. Jane Reeves Martin, Dec. 27, 1942; childrenDavid Stanley, Peter Alexander, Susan Lee. Mem. faculty Johns Hopkins, 1943-55, asst. prof. physics, 1948-55; asso. physicist Argonne Nat. Lab., 1955-60, sr. physicist, 1960-63, cons., 1963—; prof. physics Stanford, 1963—; cons. Los Alamos Sci. Lab., 1967—. Served with AUS, 1945-46. Guggenheim fellow, 1958-59. Fellow Am. Phys. Soc. (exec. com. div. nuclear physics 1967-68), mem. Phi Beta Kappa, Sigma Xi, Omicron Delta Kappa. Spl. research nuclear structure, polarizations of nuclear radiations, lifetimes of nuclear states, resonance absorption, analogue states, g-factor measurements, Mössbauer effect. Home: 784 Mayfield St Stanford, CA 94305.

HANNA, THOMAS LOUIS, educator, author; b. Waco, Tex., Nov. 21; s. John Dwight and Winifred (Beaumier) H.; B.A., Tex. Christian U., 1949; B.B., U. Chgo., 1954, Ph.D., 1958; m. Susan Taff, May 12, 1950; children—Mary Alice, Michael John, Wendell France. Dir. Jean de Beauvais Club, U. Paris (France), 1951-52; chmn. dept. philos. and religious through Hollins Coll., also dir. Hollins Abroad, Paris, 1961-62; writer-in-residene Duke, 1964-65; prof., chmn. dept. philosophy U. Fla., 1965—. Fellow Am. Council Learned Socs.,1968-69. Mem. Am. Philos. Assn., Assn. Humanistic Psychology, Modern Lang. Assn. Author: Bodies in Revolt: A Primer in Somatic Thinking, 1970; The Thought and Art of Albert Camus, 1958; The Bergsonian Heritage, 1963; The Lyrical Existentialists, 1963. Home: 518 NE 4th Av Gainesville FL 32601

HANNA, WILLIAM DENBY, animated cartoon producer; b. Melrose, N.M., July 14, 1910; s. William John and Avice Joyce (Denby) H.; m. Violet B. Wogatzke, Aug. 7, 1936; children—David William, Bonnie Janna (Mrs. Sidney Williams). Mem. story dept., also lyricist and composer Harman-Ising Studios, 1930-37; with Metro-Goldwyn-Meyer, 1937-57, created with Joseph Barbere, Tom and Jerry series; dir.-producer, pres. Hanna-Barbere Prodns., Inc., Hollywood, Cal., 1957—; created series TV, Ruff & Reddy, Huckelberry Hound, Yogi Bear, The Flintstones, Top Cat, Jetsons, Wally Gator, Touche Turtle, Lippy the Lion, Jonny Quest, Quick Draw McGraw; also producer for theatrical release Loopy de Loop. Recipient 7 Acad. awards for Tom and Jerry series. Home: 4123 Mary Ellen Av North Hollywood CA 91604 Office: Cahuenga Bldg Hollywood CA 90028*

HANNAFEY, FRANCIS J., banker. Asst. v.p., also auditor People's Savs. Bank of Bridgeport. Office: Main and State Sts Box 1580 Bridgeport CT 06602*

HANNAH, ARCHIBALD DOUGLAS, corporate exec.; b. Pitts., Jan. 31, 1909; s. Thomas and Grace (Hood) H.; B.S. in Mech. Engring., Princeton, 1930; m. Margaret A. Patton, Sept. 5, 1942; children—Katharine Mills (Mrs. Edward A. Servick), Annette Todd, Douglas Patton. Sec.; treas. Frozen Carbonic Corp., Pitts., 1935-40; mgr. coal loading dept. Pitts. Coke & Chem. Co., Pitts., 1940-41; chief gray iron castings sect., steel div. WPB, Washington, 1941-45; v.p. Fidelity Trust Co., Pitts., 1945-55; v.p., treas., dir. Hillman Co., Pitts., 1955, now exec. v.p.; v.p., dir. Hillman Barge & Constrn. Co., Hillman Transp. Co.; chmn. bd. Western Ky. Gas Co.; dir. Grant Bldg., Inc., Nichols-Homeshield, Inc., Kollmorgen Corp., Green Giant Co., Pitts. Nat. Bank, Pitts. Coke & Chem. Co., Global Marine, Inc. Trustee Chatham Coll.; dir. Hillman Found., Inc. Clubs: Duquesne, Pitts. Golf, Rolling Rock, Harvard-Yale- Princeton (Pitts.). Home: 5030 Castleman St Pittsburgh PA 15232 Office: Grant Bldg Pittsburgh PA 15219

HANNAH, HARVEY HORATIO, lawyer; b. Atlanta, July 26, 1912; s. Gerald G. and Clio (Stocks) H.; B.S., Georgia Institute of Technology, 1933; LL.B., University of Tennessee, 1937; m. Sidney June Ingram, Aug. 23, 1940; children—Jeryl Ann (Mrs. Robert K. Stone), Rebecca (Mrs. Andrew W. Greene), Harriett Phyllis (Mrs. Anthony J. Bonanno), Carolyn Candace. Admitted to Tenn. bar, 1937, Ky., bar, 1940; pvt. practice in Tenn. and Ky., 1937-41; with FTC, Washington, 1941-62, dir. bur. textiles and furs, 1946-62; dep. gen. counsel Post Office Dept., Washington, 1962-69, special Asst. Gen. counsel, 1969-70, ret., 1970. Recipient Distinguished Service award FTC, 1953, 62, Ofcl. commendation, 1960; citation Nat. Civil Service League, 1957; Distinguished Service award P.O. Dept., 1968. Mem. Textile Roundtable, Phi Delta Phi, Sigma Nu. Club: Belle Haven Country (past bd. dirs.) (Alexandria). Home: 2502 Turbridge Lane Alexandria VA 22308

HANNAH, JOHN ALFRED, govt. ofcl.; b. Grand Rapids, Mich., Oct. 9, 1902; s. Wilfred Steele and Mary Ellen (Malone) H.; student Grand Rapids Jr. Coll., 1919-21, U. Mich., 1921-22; B.S., Mich. State U., 1923, D. Agr. (hon.), 1941; LL.D., U. Mich., 1944, Central Mich. U., 1955, U. R.I., 1954, Albion Coll., 1954, U. Conn., 1960, Colo. State U., 1963, Alma Coll., 1964, U. Me., 1965, Ariz. State U., 1966, Howard U., 1966, Tuskegee Inst., 1967, Kalamazoo Coll., 1967, U. S.D., 1967, Tri-State Coll., 1967, Western Mich. U., 1967, Akron U., 1970, Hope Coll., 1970, U. Notre Dame, 1970; H.H.D., U. Ryukus, 1952; L.H.D., U. Fla., 1953, U. Md., 1966, Ohio U., 1969, U. Am., 1970; D.Sc., Mich. Coll. Sci. and Tech., 1953, U. Nigeria, 1961; Litt. D., Grand Valley State College, 1968, No. Mich. U., 1957; m. Sarah May Shaw, June 22, 1938; children—Mary Elisabeth, Robert W., Thomas A., David H. Extension specialist in poultry husbandry Mich. State U., 1923-33; mng. agt. Fed. Hatchery Co-ordinating Com., Kansas City, Mo., 1933-35; sec. bd. trustees Mich. State U., 1935-41; pres. Mich. State U., 1941-69; adminstr. AID, 1969—; mem. internat. devel. adv. bd. Point IV, 1950-52; asst. sec. def. for manpower, 1953-54; hon. prof. Sch. Bus., Sao Paulo. Chmn. U.S. sect. Permanent Joint Bd. on Def. Can. and U.S., 1954-63; chmn. U.S. Commn. Civil Rights, 1957-69; mem. President's Council Equal Opportunity, Ednl. Policies Commn., Nat. Com. Immigration Reform. Del. Mich. Constl. Conv., 1961-62. Gov. nat. A.R.C., 1953-54; mem. Nat. Service Com. on 4-H; trustee Found. European Ednl. Centers; bd. judges Paul Gray Hoffman award Automotive Safety Found.; trustee Edn. and World Affairs, Intern-Am. Social Devel. Inst.; chmn. bd. Overseas Pvt. Investment Corp., 1970. Recipient Medal of Freedom, 1954. Mem. Nat. Assn. State Univs. and Land-Grant Colls. (pres. 1948-49, chmn. exec. com. 1949-51), Am. Council Edn. (chmn. 1967-68), Newcomen Soc., Phi Beta Kappa, Beta Sigma Sigma, Phi Eta Sigma, Alpha Phi Omega, Phi Kappa Phi, Sigma Delta Chi, Pi Kappa Delta, Alpha Zeta. Mason. Home: 2801 New Mexico Av Washington DC Office: State Dept Washington DC 20037

HANNAH, JOHN DONALD, accountant; b. Spokane, Oct. 18, 1920; s. Dan and Margaret (Hindley) H.; B.A., U. Wash., 1942; m. Mary King, Dec. 8, 1945; children—Dan, Richard. With Price Waterhouse & Co., C.P.A.'s, 1946—, partner, 1962—, opened new office in Sacramento, then Mpls. Served with AUS, 1942-45. Decorated Bronze Star medal. Mem. Mpls. C. of C., Minn. Soc. C.P.A.'s, Am. Inst. C.P.A.'s, Inst. Internal Auditors, Am. Accounting Assn. Kiwanian. Home: Route 3 Box 558 Excelsior MN 55331 Office: First Nat Bank Bldg Minneapolis MN 55402

HANNAH, NORMAN BRITTON, fgn. service officer; b. Mattoon, Ill., Dec. 1, 1919; s. Harry Ingalls and Vivian (Britton) H.; B.A. with honors, U. Ill., 1941; M.A., La. State U., 1942; postgrad. U. Minn., 1946-47; m. Edna McCoy, Feb. 20, 1943; children—Norman Britton, Harry Ingalls II. Instr. polit. sci. U. Minn., 1946-47; with Dept. of State, 1947—, beginning as vice consul Am. consulate gen., Shanghai, China, successively 2d sec., consul Am. embassy, Bangkok, Thailand, consul, prin. officer Am. consulate, Tabriz, Iran, 2d sec., consul Am. embassy, Tehran, Iran, 1947-55, officer charge Iranian affairs, Washington, 1955-57; spl. asst. to dep. under-sec. of state, 1957-58; assigned Nat. War Coll., 1958-59; dep. chief mission Am. embassy, Kabul, Afghanistan, 1959-62; dep. dir. S.E. Asian affairs, 1962-64; polit. adviser to comdr.-in-chief Pacific, Honolulu, 1964-66; U.S. minister Am. embassy, Bangkok, 1966-70; diplomat-in-residence, vis. prof. polit. sci. Haverford Coll., 1970-71; consul gen., Sydney, Australia, 1971—. Served to lt. USNR, 1942-46; PTO. Mem. Delta Phi. Editorial bd. Fgn. Service jour., 1955-58. Home: 3113 Western Av Mattoon IL 61939 Office: Dept of State Washington DC 20025

HANNAH, PAUL FRANCIS, lawyer; b. Berlin, N.H., Nov. 11, 1905; s. Frank C. and Mary M. (McKenna) H.; B.S., Dartmouth, 1927; LL.B., George Washington U., 1933; m. Elizabeth Wingfield Jackson, Dec. 26, 1933; children—Paul F., Richard J. Asst. editor Nature mag., Washington, 1928-32; admitted to D.C. bar, 1931, Mass. bar, 1946, also U.S. Supreme Ct.; asso. firm Morris, Kix Miller & Baar, Washington, 1932-36. jr. partner, 1936-41; gen. counsel Raytheon Co., Waltham, Mass., 1946-63, sec. 1947-61, v.p., 1960-63; dir., mem. exec. com. Waltham Fed. Savs. and Loan Assn.; partner firm Gadsby & Hannah, Boston. Served from maj. to col., Signal Corps, AUS, 1941-46. Decorated Legion of Merit, Bronze Star. Mem. Am. (ho. of dels.), Mass., Fed., Boston bar assns. Assn. Gen. Counsel, Phi Delta Phi, Order of Coif. Unitarian. Clubs: Barristers (Washington); Chevy Chase (Md.); Brae Burn Country (Newton, Mass.); Union (Boston); Metropolitan (Washington). Home: 44 Hubbard Rd Weston MA 02193 Office: 75 Federal St Boston MA 02110

HANNAN, FRANK P., life ins. co. exec.; b. Council Bluffs, Ia., Oct. 15, 1914; B.A., Creighton U., 1936, LL.B., 1939. Sec.-treas. Companion Life Ins. Co. N.Y., 1949-50; with United Benefit Life Ins. Co., 1942-59, sec., 1952, v.p., sec., 1965—. Mem. presidents council Coll. St. Mary. Mem. Neb. Inst. Life Ins., Inst. Home Office Underwriters. Home: 8010 Woolworth St Omaha NB 68124 Office: United Benefit Life Ins Co 33d and Farnam Sts Omaha NB 68131

HANNAN, JAMES MACCLYMONT, automotive supply co. exec.; b. Lincoln, Neb., Dec. 1, 1908; s. William Everett and Janet (MacClymont) H.; A.B., Yale, 1933; m. Mary Luther, June 24, 1950; 1 dau., Mary Elizabeth (Mrs. George H. Glover, Jr.). Dept. mgr. R.H. Macy & Co., N.Y.C., 1933-40; sales exec. J.S. Blank & Co., N.Y.C., 1940, 46-47; gen. sales mgr. Standard Products Co., Cleve., 1948-57; exec. v.p. Automotive Materials Corp., Detroit, 1957-62, pres., 1962-66; pres. Am. Safey Equipment Corp. Mich., 1966-68; exec. v.p., dir., 1968—. Chmn. U.S. Naval Sea Cadet Corps, 1966-67. Trustee Bloomfield Village, Mich.; bd. mgrs. St. Joseph Mercy Hosp., Pontiac, Mich. Served to comdr. USNR, 1941-46; PTO. Decorated Bronze Star medal with Combat V; recipient Distinguished Pub. Service award Sec. Navy, 1966. Mem. Cum Laude Soc., Navy League of U.S. (dir. Detroit council, nat. pres.), Beta Theta Pi. Democrat. Episcopalian. Clubs: Orchard Lake (Mich.) Country; Recess, Detroit, one hundred (Detroit); Huron River Hunting and Fishing (Farmington, Mich.); Yale (N.Y.C.); Army and Navy (Washington). Home: 344 Yarmouth Rd Birmingham MI 48009 Office: Fisher Bldg Detroit MI 48202

HANNAN, JOSEPH ARTHUR, Jr., banker; b. Rye, N.Y., June 12, 1904; s. Joseph Arthur and Mary Agnes (Hayes) H.; ed. pub. schs.; m. Rosemary Edwards, Apr. 9, 1928; children—Joseph Arthur 3d, Geraldine, Myles, Michael, Susan. With Bank of N.Y., 1922—, v.p. 1953-60, exec. v.p., 1960—; dir. Mangel Stores Corp., Elizabeth Arden Sales Corp. Mem. exec. com., bd. dirs., v.p. Fifth Av. Assn. Mem. cardinal's com. of laity Roman Cath. Archdiocese N.Y. Clubs: Union League, Fifth Avenue (N.Y.C.). Home: 200 E 66th St New York City, NY 10021 Office: 48 Wall St New York City NY 10005 *

HANNAN, KENNETH HERON, retired corp. exec.; b. Lincoln, Neb., Jan. 25, 1911; s. William E. and Janet (MacClymont) H.; A.B., Yale, 1933, LL.B., 1936; m. Anne Berdell, Feb. 22, 1939; children—Kenneth, Theodore, Anne. Member law dept. Union Carbide Corp., N.Y.C., 1936, asst. treas., 1948, sec. 1949, treas., 1952, v.p., dir., 1954-56, exec. v.p., 1956-69, vice chmn. bd., dir., 1969-71; dir. N.Y. Life Ins. Co. Bd. govs. Soc. New York Hosp., 1957—, pres., 1966. Served from ensign to lt. comdr., USNR, 1941-45. Clubs: Blind Brook (Port Chester, N.Y.); Links Golf (Roslyn, N.Y.); Links, Racquet and Tennis, Madison Square Garden (N.Y.C.); Laurel Valley Golf (Ligonier, Pa.); Augusta Nat. Golf. Home: Canoe Hill Rd New Canaan CT 06840

HANNAN, PHILIP MATTHEW, bishop; b. Washington, May 20, 1913; s. Patrick Francis and Lillian Louise (Keefe) H.; student St. Charles Coll., 1931-33; A.B., Catholic U., 1935, M.A., 1936, J.C.D., 1949; student North Am. Coll., 1936-40; S.T.B., S.T.L., Gregorian U., Rome, 1940. Ordained priest Roman Cath. Ch., 1939; clerical appointment St. Thomas Aquinas Ch., Balt., 1940-42; student Cath. U., 1946-49, vice chancellor, 1948-51, chancellor, 1951- 62, vicar gen., 1960—; adminstr. St. Patrick's Ch., Washington, 1951-56, pastor, 1956-65; aux. bishop Archdiocese Washington, 1956-65; archbishop of New Orleans, 1965-; editor-in-chief Catholic Standard, 1956-65. Mem. goals com. Met. Area Com. New Orleans; mem. White House Conf. on Children and Youth, 1970—; mem. exec. bd.

New Orleans council Boy Scouts Am., 1970—; mem. bd., chmn. interfaith com. United Fund New Orleans, 1970—. Served as chaplain USAAF, 1942-46. Address: 7887 Walmsley Av New Orleans, LA 70125.

HANNAN, WILLIAM KELLEY, optical co. exec.; b. Council Bluffs, Ia., Oct. 16, 1917; s. Charles R. and Lucile (Kelley) H.; B.S. in Engring., Ia. State U., 1939; m. Alison Walbridge, Nov. 13, 1943; children—Alison, William Kelley, Sarah. Trainee, Eastman Kodak Co., Rochester, N.Y., 1939-41; various positions Am. Optical Co., Buffalo, 1941-48, spl. asst. to pres., Southbridge, Mass., 1948-53, mgr. Keene (N.H.) plant, 1953-55, gen. mgr. instrument div., Buffalo, v.p., Southbridge, Mass., 1957- 65, formerly exec. v.p., dir.; dir. Warner Lambert Co. Mem. Optical Soc. Am. Episcopalian. Home: 43 Windsor Av Buffalo NY 14209

HANNAY, ALLEN BURROUGHS, judge; b. Hempstead, Tex., Feb. 14, 1892; s. Robert Edwards and Katherine Donaldson (Allen) H.; student Agrl. and Mech. Coll. Tex., 1907-09; LL.B., U. Tex., 1913; m. Frances Edna Johnson, July 16, 1918; children—Helen Johnson, Allen Burroughs. Admitted to Tex. bar, 1913; practiced law, Hempstead and Houston, Tex., 1913- 30; Waller County judge, 1915-17, dist. judge 113th Dist. of Tex., 1930; U.S. dist. judge, Houston, 1942—. Served with U.S.Army, 1917-19. Mem. Am., Houston bar assns., Tex. State Bar, Phi Delta Phi, Delta Sigma Phi. Mason (32, Shriner), Elk (past pres. Tex. chpt.). Club: River Oaks Country (Houston). Home: 4001 Ella Lee Lane Houston, TX 77027. Office: Fed Bldg 515 Rusk Av Houston TX 77002*

HANNEKEN, CLEMENS B., educator, mathematician; b. Ramsey, Ill., Oct. 10, 1923; s. Bernard H. and Mary Hanneken, B.S., Eastern Ill. State U., 1945; M.S., U. Ill., 1946, Ph.D., 1952; m. Mary Elizabeth Hanneken, June 30, 1955; children—Anne, Mark, Jane, John, David, Joan, Sally. Prof. math. Marquette U., Milw., 1953—. Mem. Am. Math. Soc., Math. Assn. Am. Author: Introduction to Abstract Algebra, 1968. Contbr. articles profl. jours. Home: 1902 N 49th St Milwaukee WI 53208

HANNELLY, ROBERT JEFFREY, educator; born Creston, Ia., Apr. 30, 1901; s. Robert and Rachel (Jeffrey) H.; A.B., Grinnell Coll., 1923; M.S., State U. Ia. 1926; Ph.D., U. Colo., 1939; m. Eugenie Rutherford, Nov. 25, 1925; children—Robert Eugene, Mary (Mrs. Merle Noble), Thomas Rutherford. Tchr. math. Iowa City High Sch., 1923-27; chmn. math. dept. Phoenix Coll., 1927-47, dean, 1947-63; president Maricopa County Junior Colleges, 1963-68, president emeritus, 1968—. Chairman Defense Advisory Committee Edn. for Armed Forces, 1959-60; mem. Gov. Ariz. Com. Aging, 1960—; workshop leader Peabody Coll. and U. Colo., 1950, 60; mem. Jr. Coll. Survey Com. for Ariz., 1959-60; spl. adviser Ariz. Bd. Dirs. Jr. Colls., 1961. Mem. Am. Assn. Jr. Colls. (chmn. commn. instruction, director, 1965-66), Council North Central Junior Colleges (past board of directors), Arizona Education Assn. (past pres.), Ariz. Adult Edn. Assn. (past pres.), N. Central Assn. (exec. bd. Commn. Colls. and Univ). Conglist. Kiwanian. Club: Dons (past pres.) (Phoenix). Author elementary textbook in meteorology and trigonometry. Home: 1637 E Osborn Rd Phoenix AZ 85016

HANNOCH, HERBERT J., lawyer; b. Newark, 1890; LL.B., N.Y. U., 1911. Admitted to N.J. bar, 1911; mem. firm Hannoch, Weisman, Stern and Besser, Newark. Chmn. Legislative Commn. for Revision of Eminent Domain Law, 1962—. Mem. Am. (mem. coms. municipal law and eminent domain 1959—), N.J. State, Essex County (pres. 1934) bar assns. Office: 744 Broad St Newark NJ 07102*

HANNON, JOHN WILLIAM, Jr., banker; b. N.Y.C., Apr. 22, 1922; s. John William and Leonora (King) H.; A.B., St. Lawrence U., 1946; m. Vivien Gardner, July 26, 1944; children—Bruce, Elizabeth, Christine. With Comml. Nat. Bank, N.Y.C., 1946-51; with Bankers Trust Co., N.Y.C., 1951—, adminstrv. v.p., 1970—. Treas., chmn. finance com. local A.R.C.; mem. finance com. Community Blood Council. Trustee, treas. St. Lawrence U. Served as officer USAAF, 1942-45. Decorated Air medal. Home: 17 Warfield St Upper Montclair NJ 07043 Office: 280 Park Av New York City NY 10017

HANNON, THOMAS EUGENE, govt. ofcl.; b. Lowell, Mass., Apr. 7, 1921; s. Thomas J. and Ellen (Hunt) H.; B.B.A. cum laude, Northeastern U., 1956. Regional personnel officer Gen. Services Adminstrn., Boston, 1949-62, dep. regional adminstr., Boston, 1962-63, regional adminstr., San Francisco, 1963—. Mem. Los Angeles Fed. Exec. Bd., 1963—, Honolulu Federal Exec. Bd., 1966—, San Francisco Fed. Exec. Bd., 1967—, Regional Civil Def. Mblzn. Bd., Santa Rosa, 1963—; mem. regional preparedness com. Office Emergency Planning, Santa Rosa, 1963—. Mem. Honolulu Civic Center Policy Com., 1964—. Served with USNR, 1942-45. Recipient Distinguished Service medal Gen. Services Adminstrn., 1963. Home: 17539 Garland Ct Castro Valley, CA 94546 Office: 49 4th St San Francisco CA 94102

HANNON, WILLIAM AMBROSE, reins. co. exec.; b. Leavenworth, Kan., Jan. 8, 1901; s. William Ambrose and Susan (Lynch) H.; J.D., U. Mo. at Kansas City, 1927; m. Marjory Elizabeth Thompson, Sept. 7, 1935; children—Dorothy Sue, Marcia Ann. Admitted to Mo. bar, 1926, Kan. bar, 1938; with Employers Reins. Corp., Kansas City, Mo., 1931-68, v.p., 1952-68, also dir., atty., mem. exec. com.; consul of The Netherlands in Kansas City, 1930—. Mem. Kansas City Crime Commn. Hon. trustee Kansas City Art Inst. Decorated officer Order Orange Nassau (Netherlands). Mem. Am., Mo. bar assns., Kansas City C. of C., Casualty and Surety Underwriters Assn., Delta Theta Phi. Clubs: Kansas City, Internat. Trade (Kansas City, Mo.). Home: 6534 Summit St Kansas City MO 64113 Office: 21 W 10th St Kansas City MO 64105

HANNON, WILLIAM MURRAY, mfg. co. exec.; b. Cleve., May 13, 1919; s. Clarence William and Nora Marie (Murray) H.; student U. Notre Dame, 1939-42; m. Jane Carol Powell, Oct. 17, 1957; children—Thomas Murray, John Clarence, Daniel Neil, Chistopher Taylor, Robert Caperton. With Murray Ohio Mfg. Co., Lawrenceburg, Tenn., 1946- -, asst. to pres., 1954-55, exec. v.p., 1956-62, pres., 1962—, chief exec. officer, 1966—, also dir.; dir. Third Nat. Bank, Nashville. Mem. Tenn. Mfrs. Assn., Nashville Area C. of C. Home: 4410 Gerald Pl Nashville TN 37205 Office: 635 Thompson Lane Nashville TN 37204*

HANNUM, CLIFFORD PERSHING, army officer; b. Lyons, Ind., Dec. 7, 1919; s. William Morton and Grace (Fordyce) H.; B.S.M., Ind. U., 1949; grad Command and Gen. Staff Coll., 1953, Armed Forces Staff Coll., 1956, Nat. War Coll., 1961; m. Jane Merriwether Price, Sept. 28, 1956; 1 dau, Annette Currie. Commd. 2d lt. U.S. Army, 1941, advanced through grades to brig. gen., 1968; assigned 32d Inf. Div., Pacific, 1941-45, 17th Airborne Div., then 2d Inf. Div. and Hdqrs. Dept. Army, 1946-53; battalion and regtl. comdr. 5th Inf. Div., Europe, 1953-56; dep. G-3, Mil. Dist. Washington, then G-3 KMAG, Seoul, Korea, 1956-60; assigned 2d Inf. Div., Ft. Benning, Ga., 1961-63, U.S. Strike Command, MacDill AFB, Fla., 1963-66; Vietnam, 1966-67; assigned successively Joint Chiefs Staff, The Pentagon, then dir. R.O.T.C. affairs Dept. Personnel, Dept. Army, 1967-70; asst. div. comdr. 2d Inf. Div., Korea, 1970—. Decorated D.S.M. Silver Star, Legion of Merit with oak leaf cluster, Bronze Star with 2 oak leaf clusters, Air medal with oak leaf cluster, Army Commendation medal with oak leaf cluster, Combat Inf. badge, Parachutist's badge. Home: 6320 Mori St McLean VA 22101 Office: Asst Div Comdr 2d Inf Div APO San Francisco CA 96224

HANNUM, ERWIN CHARLES, govt. ofcl.; b. Syracuse, N.Y., Aug. 4, 1908; s. Ralph Charles and Coral Louise (Snyder) H.; B.S. in Civil Engring., Syracuse U., 1932, M.S. in Pub. Adminstrn. 1935; grad. student Coll. Pub. Law, Columbia, 1936-39; m. Cynthia Wentworth, Jan. 28, 1939; children—Patricia (Mrs. Robert Vietro), Julia (Mrs. Frank T. Rose), Harcourt. Municipal govt. research Works Progress Adminstrn., Washington, 1933-35; faculty grad. course, pub. works adminstrn. Sch. Tech. Coll. City N.Y., 1936-39; orgn., procedures staff U.S. Housing Authority, Fed. Works Agy., Washington, 1939-41; adminstrv. analyst, budget exam. adminstrv. mgmt. and estimates divs., Buf. Budget, Washington, 1941-47; exec. asst. to chmn., fgn. operating com. Petroleum Adminstrn. War, Washington, 1945-46; program coordinator Bonneville Power Adminstrn., Portland, Ore., 1947-53; acting country dir. U.S.-ICA mission to Egypt, then dep. dir., Cairo, 1953-55; exec. dir. Libyan-Am. Recontrn. Commn., Tripoli, Libya, 1955-58; loan officer Africa, Development Loan Fund, Washington, 1958-60; Brazil desk officer ICA, ash., D.C., 1960-62; dir. Office Indsl. Equipment, Bus. and Def. Services Adminstrn., Dept. Commerce, 1962-67, water resources coordinator, 1967—. Mem. Am. Society Public Administration, American Foreign Service Association. Home: 9815 Indian Queen Point Rd Ft Foote MD also P O Washington DC 20022 Office: Dept Commerce 2001 Wisconsin Av NW Washington DC 20230

HANNUM, JOHN BERNE, U.S. judge; b. Chester, Pa., Mar. 19, 1915; s. John Berne and Helen (Weaver) H.; grad. Lawrenceville (Pa.) Sch., 1934; student Princeton, 1934-37, Franklin and Marshall Coll., 1937-38; LL.B., Dickinson U., 1941; m. Nancy Penn Smith, Dec. 21, 1940; children—John Berne, Richard P.S., Carol A. Admitted to Pa. bar; partner firm Pepper, Hamilton & Scheetz, Phila., 1955-68; judge Superior Ct. Pa., 1968-69, U.S. Dist. Ct. Eastern Pa., 1969—. Mem. commissary, past advocate Episcopal Diocese Pa. Mem. Chester County (Pa.) Republican Com., 1962-64; del. Pa. Constl. Conv., 1967-68, Rep. Nat. Conv., 1960. Trustee Dickinson Sch. Law, Lincoln U., Phila. Div. Sch.; bd. mgrs. Chester County Hosp. Served to lt. USNR, 1941-45. Mem. Am., Pa., Chester County bar assns. Mason. Home: Unionville PA 19375 Office: US Courthouse 9th and Market Sts Philadelphia PA 19107

HANOLD, TERRANCE, lawyer, food products exec.; b. Mpls., June 22, 1912; s. Robert Arter and Dena (Tillotson) H.; A.B., U. Minn., 1934, LL.B., 1936; m. Ruth Lorraine Evarts, June 17, 1939; children—Ruth Lorraine, John Terrence, Robert Evarts, Dena Gail, Thomas Tillotson, David Comstock, Lee, Dennis. Admitted to Minn. bar, 1936; law sec. to chief justice Minn. Supreme Ct., 1936-38; pvt. practice law, Mpls., 1938-44; legal counsel Mpls. Star & Tribune Co., 1944-46; with Pillsbury Co., Mpls., 1946—, atty., asst. sec., treas., asst. gen. counsel, 1946-56, treas., 1956-59, treas., prin. finance officer, 1959—, v.p. finance, 1960-63, exec. v.p. and gen. mgr. internat. operations, 1963-65, exec. v.p., treas., 1965- 67, pres., 1967—, also dir. Bd. dirs. Mpls. Symphony, Inst. Ecumenical and Cultural Study. Clubs: Minakahda, Minneapolis. Home: 4835 Queen Av S Minneapolis MN 55410 Office: Pillsbury Co Minneapolis MN 55402*

HANRAHAN, EDWARD V., state ofcl.; b. Cocoanut Grove, Fla., Mar. 11, 1921; s. Edward J. and Kathleen (Walsh) H.; B.Sc., U. Notre Dame, 1943; LL.B., Harvard, 1948; m. Geraldine Tyrell. Asst. corp. counsel City Chgo., 1955-60; asst. atty. gen. Ill., 1961-62, 1st asst. atty. gen., 1962-64; formerly U.S. atty. No. Dist. Ill.; now state atty. Cook County, Chgo. Served with AUS, 1943-46. Democrat. Home: 1840 N Nagle Av Chicago IL 60635*

HANRAHAN, JOHN VINCENT, (Jack), comedy writer; b. Cleve., Jan. 16, 1933; s. George Anthony and Mary A. (McGlynn) H.; B.S. in Social Studies, John Carroll U., 1962; m. Rosemarie T. Donovan, Apr. 7, 1956; children—Maribeth, John Vincent, James D., Katie, Bridget, Mary George. Co-writer TV prodns. including Mike Douglas Show, 1956, Jackie Gleason Show, 1965-66, He and She, 1967-68, Las Vegas Show, 1967, Get Smart, 1967-68, The Banana Splits, 1967-69; co-script supr. Rowan and Martin's Laugh-In, 1967—; co-writer TV animations Hanna- Barbere Prodns., 1966-67, The Impossibles, 1966-67, Abbott and Costello, 1967, The Fantastic Four, 1967-68, Birdman and The Galaxy Trio, 1967-68; lectr. in field. Active funds for handicapped children. Served with AUS, 1955-57. Recipient Emmy award, 1968. Mem. Writers Guild West, Motion Picture Screen Cartoonists, Nat. Acad. TV Arts and Scis., A.F.T.R.A. Republican. Co-author: The Great Society Fun and Games Book, 1964; The Jungle Joke Book, 1965; Beastly Rhymes, 1965; The Show Me Book, 1965; Captain Klutz, 1965; The What Do You Get Book, 1968; also articles. Home: 4922 Escobedo Dr West Hills, CA 91364 Office: 4425 Lakeside St Burbank CA 91505

HANS, ROBERT JOHN, mfg. co. exec.; b. Cin., Nov. 20, 1917; s. Clarence L., Sr., and Martha. H. (Dornette) H.; A.B., Miami U., Oxford, O., 1939; student U. Cin., 1952-58; m. Betty Lou Abel, May 25, 1957; children—Robert John, Sandra Lee. With Cin. Milacron Inc., formerly Cin. Milling Machine Co., 1940—, asst. sec., 1963-70, sec., 1970—; sec. Cin. Lathe & Tool Co., 1961-70; asst. sec. Cin. Milling & Grinding Machines, Inc., 1961-70; sec. Cin. Milacron Co., Cin. Milacron Chems. Inc. Mem. Bd. Edn. of Greenhills Forest-Park City Sch. Dist., 1962-67, pres., 1964. Served with USAAF, 1942-45. Decorated Air Medal. Mem. Sigma Chi, Alpha Sigma Lambda. Presbyn. (elder). Club: Greenhills Country (Cin.). Home: 10360 Lochcrest Dr Cincinnati OH 45231 Office: 4701 Marburg Av Cincinnati OH 45209

HANSBERGER, ROBERT VAIL, lumber co. exec.; b. Worthington, Minn., June 1, 1920; s. Floyd L. and Edythe (Vail) H.; A.A. Worthington Jr. Coll., 1940; B.M.E. with distinction, U. Minn., 1942; M.B.A. with high distinction, Harvard, 1947; LL.D., Seattle U., 1963, U. Ida., Lewis and Clark Coll., Gonzaga U.; m. Klara K. Kille, Mar. 27, 1942; children—Roberta Ann, Carol Ann. Asst. to exec. v.p. Container Corp. Am., 1947-50, div. chief engr., 1950-53, budget dir., 1953-54; exec. v.p., dir. Western Kraft Corp., Portland Ore., 1954- 56; dir., mem. exec. com. Western Corrugated, Inc., 1955-56; pres., dir. Western Sales Co., 1956; dir. Boise Payette Lumber Co. (Ida.), 1956-57; pres., dir., chmn. bd. Boise Cascade Corp. (Ida.); dir. Albertson's Inc., First Charter Financial Corp., 1st Security, Gould, Inc., USI Corp., Ida. Power Co., ABC, Western Pacific R.R. Co., Mfrs. Hanover Trust; trustee Penn. Mut. Life Ins. Co. Exec. com. Business Council. Trustee St. Luke's Hosp., Aspen Inst. Humanistic Studies, Cal. Inst. Tech., Coll. Ida. Served to ensign USNR, 1945-46. Mem. Tau Beta Pi, Pi Tau Sigma. Home: 1305 Harrison Blvd Boise ID 83702 Office: PO Box 200 Boise ID 83701

HANSCH, CORWIN HERMAN, educator; b. Kenmare, N.D., Oct. 6, 1918; s. Herman William and Rachel (Corwine) H.; B.S., U. Ill., 1940; Ph.D., N.Y.U., 1944; m. Gloria J. Tomasulo, Jan. 8, 1944; children—Clifford, Carol. Research chemist Manhattan project E.I. du Pont de Nemours & Co., Inc., 1944-45, research chemist, 1945-46; prof. chemistry Pomona Coll., 1946—; spl. research relationship chem. structure and drug action. Guggenheim fellow Fed. Inst. Tech., Zurich, Switzerland, 1952-53; Pomona Coll., 1966-67; Petroleum Research Fund fellow U. Munich (Germany), 1959-60. Home: 4070 Olive Knoll Pl Claremont, CA 91711.

HANSELL, HERBERT JOSEPH, lawyer; b. Pitts., Nov. 16, 1925; s. Abraham and Bess (Weiner) H.; B.S., Mass. Inst. Tech., 1946; LL.B., Yale, 1949; m. Jeanne Louise Harris, Apr. 7, 1951; children—David, James, Linda. Admitted to N.Y. bar, 1950, Ohio bar, 1949; asso. firm Cravath, Swaine & Moore, N.Y.C., 1949-51; atty. NSF, 1951-52, asst. gen. counsel, 1952-53; asso. firm Jones, Day, Cockley & Reavis, Cleve., 1953-60, partner, 1960—. Sec. Weatherhead Co., 1968—. Mem. bd. edn., Shaker Heights, O., 1966—, v.p., 1970; pres. Legal Aid Soc. Cleve., 1963-65; v.p. Cleve. Council World Affairs, 1965-66; mem. exec. com. Yale Alumni Bd., 1969-70. Served with USNR, 1944-46. Mem. Am., Cleve. (trustee 1967-70), Ohio bar assns., Cleve. Bar Found. (trustee, v.p 1968—), Yale Law Sch. Assn. (pres. 1966-68, chmn. exec. com. 1968-70). Mass. Inst. Tech. Alumni Assn. (adv. council 1968—), Sigma Xi, Tau Beta Pi. Home: 2854 Winthrop Rd Shaker Heights OH 44120 Office: Union Commerce Bldg Cleveland OH 44115

HANSEN, ALBERT MARTIN, ins. co. exec.; b. Maxwell, Neb., June 30, 1917; s. Alfred Malone and Stella (Grandstaff) H.; A.B., Midland Lutheran Coll., 1939; LL.B., Creighton U., 1942; m. DeLoris A. Norvell, July 28, 1939; children—Allan Marshall, Thomas Dean, Susan Rae. With claims dept. Mut. of Omaha Health & Accident Assn., 1942-43, underwriter, 1943-49, mgr. underwriting dept., 1949-53, chief underwriter, 1953-56; asst. v.p. Mut. of Omaha, 1956-58, 2d v.p., 1958-62, v.p., 1962-65, exec. v.p., 1965-69, sr. exec. v.p., 1969-; dir. Cass County Bank, Plattsmouth, Neb. Past pres. Bd. Edn., Plattsmouth, King Korn Karnival. Pres. bd. dirs. Tabitha Home, Lincoln, Neb. Mem. Fed., Neb. bar assns., Health Ins. Assn. Am. (com. chmn.), Plattsmouth C. of C. (hon. life), P.T.A., Servientes Ad Legem, Gamma Eta Gamma. Contbr. articles profl. jours. Home: RFD 2 Plattsmouth, NB 68048 Office: Mut of Omaha 33d and Farnham Omaha NB 68101 518 Lakeview Av Jamestown NY 14701

HANSEN, ALVIN HARVEY, educator; b. Viborg, S.D., Aug. 23, 1887; s. Niels and Bergita Mary (Nielsen) H.; B.A., Yankton (S.D.) Coll., 1910, LL.D., 1936; M.A., U. Wis., 1915, Ph.D., 1918; m. Mabel Lewis, Aug. 25, 1916; children—Marian Grace, Mildred Jean. Prin. high sch., Lake Preston, S.D., 1910-12, supt., 1912-13; asst. instr. econs. U. Wis., 1915-16, Brown U., 1916-19; asso. prof. econs. U. Minn., 1919-23, prof., 1923-37; Lucius N. Littauer prof. polit. economy Harvard, 1937, now emeritus; vis. prof. U. Bombay (India), 1957-58; William Allan Nielson research Smith Coll., 1960; dir. research, sec. Commn. of Inquiry on Nat. Policy in Internat. Econ. Relations, 1933-34; economist Dept. State, 1934-35; econ. adviser Prairie Provinces before Canadian Royal Commn. in Dominiton-Provincial Relations, 1937-38. Mem. Adv. Council on Social Security, 1937-38; chmn. econ. adv. council Nat. Indsl. Conf. Bd., 1938-39; chmn. U.S.-Can. joint Econ. Coms., 1941-43; spl. econ. adviser Fed. Res. Bd., 1940-45. Guggenheim fellow, 1928-29; recipient Francis A. Wolher medal Am. Econ. Assn., 1967. Mem. Am. Econ. Assn. (pres. 1938), Am. Statis. Assn. (v.p. 1937), Royal Econ. Soc., Econometric Soc., Social Sci. Research Council. Author numerous books including: Economic Policy and Full Employment, 1947; (with Paul Samuelson) Economic Analysis of Guaranteed Wages, 1947; Monetary Theory and Fiscal Policy, 1948; Business Cycle and National Income, 1951; A Guide to Keynes, 1953; The American Economy, 1957; Economic Issues of the 1960's, 1960; The Dollar and the International Monetary System, 1965. Asso. editor Econometrics, 1933-38; bd. editors Quar. Jour. Econs., 1937-48, Review Econ. Statistics, 1938—, Inter-Am Econ. Affairs, 1947; Kylos, 1947—. Home: 56 Juniper Rd Belmont MA 02178

HANSEN, ANKER KARL ANDREAS, Danish diplomat; b. Copenhagen, Denmark, Oct. 18, 1908; s. Andreas C.H. and Johanne (Pedersen) H.; B.A., Copenhagen U., 1928; M.Sc., Denmark Tech. U., 1932; grad. advanced mgmt. program Harvard, 1951; m. Ingeborg Astrup, June 13, 1936; children—Søren, Inger, Lars, Anne Lise. Chem. engr. Danish Oil Mills, Esbjerg, Denmark, 1932-34, Copenhagen Power Sta., 1934-39; factory mgr. Galle-Jessen Chocolate Works, Copenhagen, 1940-47; indsl. attache Danish Consulate Gen., N.Y.C., 1948-62; sci. adviser Danish Permanent Mission to UN, N.Y.C., 1956-62; sci. counselor Danish Embassy, Washington, 1962—. Decorated knight's cross Order of Dannebrog 1st class. Mem. Soc. Danish Engrs., Am. Chem. Soc., Am. Soc. Danish Engrs. (pres. 1957-61), Am. Scandinavian Found., Am. Mgmt. Assn., Nat. Indsl. Conf. Bd., A.A.A.S. Club: International (Washington). Home: 2944 Garfield Terrace NW Washington DC 20008 Office: 3200 Whitehaven St NW Washington DC 20008

HANSEN, ARTHUR, bldg. corp. exec.; b. N.Y.C., Apr. 22, 1917; s. Herman Charles and Jessie (Evans) H.; student N.Y.U.; m. Eleanor Green, Oct. 16, 1938; children—Wayne, Carol, Pamela. Clk. Nat. City Bank N.Y., 1935-37; personnel mgr., chief paymaster Brewster Aero. Co., 1937-42; factory mgr. Bulova Watch Co., 1942-54; v.p., gen. mgr., dir. Roller-Smith Corp., Bethlehem, Pa., 1954-55; exec. v.p. Gruen Industries, Cin., also exec. v.p., dir. Gruen Precision Labs., Inc. and Gruen Nat. Watch Case Co., Inc., 1955-58; plant mgr. J. I. Case Co., Churubusco, Ind., 1958-60; v.p. mfg. Cherry Burrell Corp., Cedar Rapids, Ia., 1960-68; v.p. Continential Builders & Developers, Inc., Golden, Colo., 1969-70; pres. Home Research and Devel. Corp., Scottsdale, Ariz., 1970—; v.p., dir. Total Wall Systems, Inc., Los Angeles, 1971—. Mem. Am. Soc. Tool Engrs., Am. Mgmt. Assn. Home: 5490 W Geddes Av Littleton CO 80120

HANSEN ARTHUR GENE, univ. pres.; b. Sturgeon Bay, Wis., Feb. 28, 1925; s. Henry A. and Ruth (Anderson) H.; B.S. in Elec. Engring., Purdue U., 1946, M.S., 1948. D.Eng., 1970; Ph.D., Case Inst. Tech., 1959. Research scientist NASA, 1948-49, 50-58; tchr. U. Md., 1949-50; sect. head Cornell Aero. Lab., Buffalo, 1958-59; mem. faculty mech. engring. U. Mich., 1959-66; dean Ga. Inst. Tech., 1966-69, pres., 1969-71; pres. Purdue U., 1971—; prof. mech. engring. Tuskegee Inst., 1965; sr. research engr. Douglas Aircraft Co., 1964; curriculum cons. Gen. Motors Inst., 1965; cons. to industry, 1961—. Mem. Atlanta Civic Design Commn., 1967- 69, Ga. Sci. and Tech. Commn., 1968—, Ga. Ocean Sci. Center of Atlantic Commn., Atlanta, 1968—; mem. adv. council Skidaway Oceanographic Inst. for Univ. System Ga., 1968—. Served with USMCR, 1943-46. Registered profl. engr., Ga. Mem. Ga. Engrs. and Architects Soc., Ga. Soc. Profl. Engrs., Am. Soc. M.E., Am. Inst. Aeros. and Astronautics, Am. Soc. Engring. Edn., Sigma Xi, Eta Kappa Nu, Pi Tau Sigma, Tau Beta Pi. Author: Similarity Analyses of Boundary Layer Problems in Engineering, 1964; Fluid Mechanics, 1967. Home: West Lafayette IN

HANSEN, CARL NORMAN, telephone co. exec.; b. New Haven, Dec. 20, 1916; s. Hans J. and Margaret (Wright) H.; student Conn. Coll. Commerce, New Haven, 1934-36, Bklyn. Coll., 1942-43, So. Conn. State Coll., 1948, U. Bridgeport, Conn., 1948-50; B.S., Quinnipiac Coll., 1952; m. Emilie Neumann, Dec. 18, 1943; children—Ranald David, Roderick Peter. Cashier, Coca-Cola Bottling Co. of Conn., New Haven, 1936-37; with So. New Eng. Telephone Co., New Haven, 1937—, v.p. area operations, 1962-65, v.p., comptroller, 1965-70, v.p. finance, dir., 1970—; mem. adv. com. Conn. Bank & Trust Co. Mem. Commn. for Higher Edn. Task Force, 1970-71, Conn. Revenue Task Force, 1969-71; chmn. New Haven chpt. A.R.C., 1957-59. Pres. New Haven Council Chs.; chmn. bd. trustees Quinnipiac Coll., Hamden, Conn. Served with USCGR, 1942-45. Recipient Spl. award of recognition to a non-Catholic for outstanding contbn. to ecumenical movement New Haven Cath. Telephone Employees Soc., 1966. Mem. Conn. Bus. and Industry Assn. (dir., mem. exec. com.), Financial Execs. Inst. (dir. So. Conn. chpt., nat. edn. com.), Alumni Assn. Quinnipiac Coll. (Alumni Achievement Gold Key plaque), Conn. C. of C. (past pres., chmn. bd.). Clubs: Graduate Club Assn., Quinnipiac (New Haven). Home: 420 Longmeadow Rd Orange CT 06477 Office: 227 Church St New Haven CT 06506

HANSEN, CHARLES, corp. exec.; b. Jersey City, May 23, 1926; s. Charles Henry and Katherine (Bensch) H.; B.S., U. Mich., 1946; J.D., Mich. Law Sch., 1950; m. Carolyn P. Smith, Sept. 26, 1953; children—Mark, Melissa. Engr., Westinghouse Electric Co., 1946; admitted to N.Y. bar, 1951, Wis. bar, 1961; asso. Mudge, Stern, Williams & Tucker, 1950-53; chief labor counsel, div. counsel Sylvania Electric Products, 1953-61; sec., gen. counsel Trane Co., La Crosse, Wis., 1961-69, exec. v.p., 1968—; dir. State Bank La Crosse. Trustee Adolph Gunderson Med. Found. Served to lt. (j.g.) USNR, 1943-46. Mem. Am., Wis. bar assns., Bar Assn. City N.Y., Order of Coif, Tau Beta Phi. Home: 218 S 14th St La Crosse WI 54601 Office: Trane Co 3600 Pammel Creek Rd La Crosse WI 54601

HANSEN, CHRIS ANTHONY, univ. ofcl.; b. Guelph, N.D., Sept. 17, 1915; s. John A. and Marie (Mohr) H.; student Normal and Indsl. Coll., Ellendale, N.D., 1933-34; B.S. in Civil Engring., N.D. State Coll., 1937; M.S. in San. Engring., U. N.C., 1942; m. Mary Elizabeth Runice, July 5, 1938; children—Jeanne Elizabeth, Kristie Ann. County mapping engr., Dickey County, N.D., 1937-38; pub. health engr. Ga. Health Dept., Atlanta, 1938-41; asst. chief, then chief engring. div. malaria control in war areas USPHS, Atlanta, 1942-52, exec officer, asst. officer charge Communicable Disease Center, 1952-56; dir. Div. Research Services, NIH, Bethesda, Md., 1956- 68; commr. environmental control adminstrn. USPHS, 1968-70; v.p. Georgetown U., 1970—. Diplomate Am. Acad. San. Engring. Mem. Nat., Md. socs. profl. engrs., Am. Soc. C.E., Sci. Research Soc. Am., Am. Pub. Health Assn., Sigma Xi, Tau Beta Pi. Address: 5614 Marengo Rd Washington DC 20016

HANSEN, CLIFFORD PETER, U.S. senator; b. Zenith, Wyo., Oct. 16, 1912; s. Peter Christofferson and Sylvia Irene (Wood) H.; B.S., U. Wyo., 1934, LL.D., 1965; m. Martha Elizabeth Close, Sept. 24, 1934; children—Mary Elizabeth, Peter Arthur. Vice pres. Jackson State Bank, 1953—; gov. of Wyo., 1963-67; U.S. senator from Wyo., 1967—. Mem. exec. com. Nat., Western govs. confs., 1965- 71; regional dir. Assn. Govt. Bds. State Univ. and Allied Instns., 1956; chmn. adv. com. on livestock research and marketing to sec. of agr.; v.p. Northwest Devel. Assn., also mem. com. for Wyo. on Snake River Compact, 1947-50; mem. Can. for Wyo. Columbia Interstate Compact, 1950—; exec. com. Efficiency in Conservation Inter-state Oil Compact Commn., 1963-67. Mem. Wyo. Community Coll. Commn. Del. Republican Nat. Conv., 1960, 64, 68. Trustee U. Wyo., 1946—, pres. bd., 1956-63; pres. bd. trustees St. John's Hosp., Jackson, Wyo., 1957-67. Mem. Wyo. Stock Growers Assn. (pres. 1953-55), Am. Nat. Cattlemen's Assn. (sec., v.p. 1956-57), Am. Soc. Range Mgmt., Sigma Nu, Phi Kappa Phi, Delta Sigma Rho, Alpha Zeta. Episcopalian. Mason (Shriner), Rotarian. Home: Jackson WY 83001 Office: Senate Office Bldg Washington DC 20510

HANSEN, ELWOOD LESLIE, savs. and loan exec.; b. San Francisco, 1917. Pres., mgr. Bay View Fed. Savs. & Loan Assn., San Francisco. Mason (Shriner). Home: 340 El Portal Hillsborough CA 94010 Office: 2601 Mission St San Francisco CA 94110*

HANSEN, ERIC RICHARD, trust co. exec.; b. N.Y.C., Aug. 12, 1918; s. Curt Eric and Elvine (Richard) H.; grad. Pomfret (Conn.) Sch., 1937; ed. Yale, 1941; m. Susan Mayne Kelsey, Apr. 9, 1941; 1 son, Eric Richard. With Bankers Comml. Corp., N.Y.C., 1945-64, treas., 1958-64, pres., 1960-64, also dir.; chmn. bd. Mt. Beacon Ins. Co., N.Y.C., 1960-64; v.p. Pacific Finance Corp., Los Angeles, 1961-64; v.p. Union Trust Co., Stamford, Conn., 1964- 66, exec. v.p., 1966—. Trustee Pomfret Sch. Served to lt. comdr. USNR, 1940-45; comdr. Res. Club: Yale (N.Y.C.). Home: 31 Arrowhead Way Darien CT 06820 Office: 300 Main St Stamford CT 06901

HANSEN, ERNEST R., banker; b. Perth Amboy, N.J., May 16, 1909; s. Niels P. and Hilda (Yonson) H.; student Rutgers U., 1945-46; m. Frances M. Tucker, Sept. 20, 1941; children—Warren T., John B. Asst. treas. Perth Amboy Savs. Instn., 1940-51, treas., 1951-58, exec. v.p., 1958-63, pres., 1963—; dir. Nat. State Bank, Elizabeth, N.J. Pres., Perth Amboy Gen. Hosp. Bd. dirs. Arthritis Found. N.J. Mem. Savs. Banks Assn. N.J. (past pres.). Home: 14 Home St Metuchen NJ 08840 Office: 210 Smith St Perth Amboy NJ 08862

HANSEN, FRANCIS EUGENE, clergyman; b. Underwood, Ia., Oct. 30, 1925; s. John Alexander and Annie (Rasmussen) H.; student Biarritz (France) Am. U., 1946; A.A., Graceland Coll., Lamoni, Ia., 1948; B.S., U. Kan., 1950; m. Wanda Ann Hoss, Aug. 20, 1949; children—Blair, Cheryl. Claim service rep. Mut. of Omaha, 1950- 54; ordained to ministry Deorganized Ch. of Jesus Christ of Latter-day Saints, 1943, ordained bishop, 1956; asst. to Presiding Bishopric, World Hdqrs. Reorganized Ch. of Jesus Christ of Latter-day Saints, Independence, Mo., 1954-56, counselor to presiding bishop, 1966—; bishop Los Angeles Stake and Hawaii Dist., Los Angeles, 1956-66. Vice pres., mem. bd. publs. Herald Pub. House. Mem. Good Govt. League, 1969- -. Mem. community adv. com. to Councilman John Cassidy, Los Angeles City Council, 1966—. Treas., trustee Independence Sanitarium and Hosp., 1966- -; bd. dirs. Mound Grove Cemetery, Social Service Center. Served with AUS, 1944-46; ETO. Decorated Combat Inf. badge, Purple Heart. Mem. Order of Bishops, Lambda Delta Sigma, Beta Gamma Sigma. Home: 3321 S Crane St Independence MO 64055 Office: The Auditorium River at Walnut Independence MO 64051

HANSEN, GEORGE, merchandising exec.; b. Boston, Jan. 15, 1899; s. Henry and Elizabeth (McGrath) H.; B.C.S., LL.B., Northeastern U., LL.D., 1953; m. Virginia Bain, Apr. 16, 1923; children—Virginia L., George, Norman E. Pres. Conrad & Chandler Inc., Boston. Home: 8 Whittier Pl Boston MA 02114 Office: 27 Winter St Boston MA 02108

HANSEN, GEORGE VERNON, legislator; b. Tetonia, Ida., Sept. 14, 1930; s. Dean Erlease and Elmoyne Bendicta (Brewer) H.; A.B. in History and Russian with honors, Ricks Coll., Rexburg, Ida., 1956; grad. Grimms Bus. Coll., 1958; postgrad. edn. Ida. State U., 1932-63; m. Constance Sue Camp, Sept. 19, 1952; children—Steven, James, Patricia, William Joanne. Tchr. math. secondary pub. sch., 1956-58; guest lectr. ins. and estate planning colls. and high schs.; spl. agt. N.Y. Life Ins. Co., 1958-65; mayor, Alameda, Ida., 1961-62, city merged with Pocatello, Ida., 1962, mem. city commn., 1962-65; mem. 89th-90th Congresses, 2d Dist. Ida.; formerly dep. under-sec. agr. for congl. relations; now dep. adminstr. for state and county operations. Chmn. Bannock County Heart Assn., 1962-64. Served with USAF, 1951-54. Recipient Distinguished Service award Pocatella Jr. C. of C., 1961. Mem. Ida. Municipal League (bd. dirs. 1961-63), Pocatello C. of C., Am. Legion, Ida. Farm Bur., Life Ins. Underwriter Assn. Republican. Mem. ch. of Jesus Christ of Latter-Day Saints. Clubs: Kiwanis (past dir. Pocatello), Pocatello 20-30 (past pres.). Home: 1129 Meadowbrook La Pocatello ID 83201 also 2792 N Quebec St Arlington VA 22207 Office: Adminstrn Bldg Jefferson Dr between 12th and 14th Sts SW Washington DC

HANSEN, GRANT LEWIS, govt. ofcl.; b. Bancroft, Ida., Nov. 5, 1921; s. Paul Ezra and Leona Sarah (Lewis) H.; B.S. in Elec. Engring., Ill. Inst. Tech., 1948; postgrad. engring. and mgmt., U. Cal. at Los Angeles, Cal. Inst. Tech.; m. Iris Rose Heyden, Apr. 21, 1945; children—Alan Lee, Brian Craig, Carol Margaret, David James, Ellen Diane. With Douglas Aircraft Co., 1948-65, v.p., program dir. for Centaur, Convair div., 1960-65; v.p. launch vehicle programs Convair div. Gen. Dynamics Corp., 1965-69; asst. sec. air force for research and devel., 1969—. U.S. del. NATO, Adv. Group for Aerospace Research and Devel., 1969—; U.S. mem. sci. com. for nat. reps. SHAPE Tech. Center, The Hague, Netherlands, 1969—; mem. research and tech. adv. council NASA, 1971—. Served with USNR, World War II. Decorated Purple Heart; recipient Pub. Service award NASA, 1966; Alumni Recognition award Ill. Inst. Tech., 1967. Asso. fellow Am. Inst. Aeros. and Astronautics; sr. mem. I.E.E.E.; mem. Eta Kappa Nu, Tau Beta Pi. Home: 3608 N 36th Rd Arlington VA 22207 Office: The Pentagon Washington DC 20330

HANSEN, HAROLD LOUIS, indsl. exec.; b. North Loup, Neb., May 4, 1906; s. Sofus Viggo and Petrea Emile (Due) H.; A.B. with high distinction, Neb. Wesleyan U., 1928; M.S., Northwestern U., 1929, Ph.D., 1932; m. Esther Kelly, Sept. 1, 1929; children—Steven Valdemar, Arnold Eric. Instr. chemistry Northwestern U., 1929-32, asst. prof., 1932-38; sec. council on dental therapeutics Am. Dental Assn., 1938-42; asst. to pres. Winthrop Labs., 1942-47, v.p., 1947-56; v.p. Sterling Drug, Inc., N.Y.C., 1956-71; gen. mgr. Hilton-Davis Chem. Co., Cin., 1956-71. Chmn. Air Pollution Control League Greater Cin. Area. Foreman spl. grand jury investigating crime and polit. corruption N.Y. State, 1951-53. Trustee Children's Dental Care Found. Fellow A.A.A.S., Am. Inst. Chemists; mem. Am. Chem. Soc., Internat. Assn. Dental Research, Sigma Xi, Phi Kappa Phi, Pi Gamma Mu, Phi Lambda Upsilon. Editor; Accepted Dental Remedies, 1941. Contbr. profl. jours. Home: 6205 S Clippinger Dr Cincinnati OH 45243

HANSEN, HARRY, editor; b. Davenport, Ia., Dec. 26, 1884; s. Hans and Christine (Jochims) H.; Ph.B., U. Chgo., 1909; m. Ruth McLernon, Apr. 29, 1914; children—Ruth Eleanor, Marian Hope. Alumni sec., 1909-11; war corr. Chgo. Daily News with German, Belgian, French and Austrian armies and in Baltic zone, 1914-16, corr. at Paris Peace Conf., 1919, lit. editor, 1920-26, New York World, 1926-31, New York World-Telegram, 1931-48; reviewer for Harper's Mag., 1923-39, Redbook, 1940-50, for Survey, 1940-52; lectr. on reviewing Columbia Univ., 1928-33, on biography, etc., 1939-41, U. Colo., 1940; v.p. Hastings House, Pubs., Inc., N.Y.C., 1965—. Mem. edit. bd. Armed Services Editions; book bd. East and West Assn.; judge MGM and Nat. Book (novel) award. Mem. Soc. Am. Historians, Ill. Hist. Soc., Hist. Soc. Ia., Sigma Alpha Epsilon. Clubs: Dutch Treat, Coffee House, Overseas Press (N.Y.C.); Tavern (Chgo.). Author: The Adventures of the Fourteen Points, 1919; Midwest Portraits, 1923; Carl Sandburg, the Man and His Poetry, 1924; Your Life Lies Before You, 1935; The Chicago (Rivers of America), 1942; North of Manhattan, 1950; Scarsdale: From Colonial Manor to Modern Community, 1954; The Fighting Constitution, 1955; The Story of Illinois, 1956; The Civil War, 1961; The Boston Massacre, 1969. Co-author: Writing Up the News, 1940; Journalism in Wartime, 1943; The Aspirin Age, 1949; also essays, magazine articles. Contbr. Ency. Britannica, Universal Jewish Ency. Translator: A Peace Congress of Intrigue (by F. Freksa), 1918; Faber (by Jacob Wassermann), 1925. Editor: O. Henry Prize Stories, 1933-40, World Almanac, 1949-65; The Stories of O. Henry, 1968; California, 1967; New England Legends and Folklore, 1967; Texas, 1969; All Quiet on the Western Front, 1969; Colorado, 1970; Louisiana, 1971. Office: 10 E 40th St New York City NY 10016

HANSEN, HARRY JAMES, naval officer; b. Freesoil, Mich., Mar. 24, 1888; s. Harry and Myrtina (Hanson) H.; student Naval War Coll., 1924-25; m. Mary Jane Hunt, Apr. 28, 1909 (div. 1934); 1 dau., Madeleine Dorothy; m. 2d, Edna Bartzen, Mar. 23, 1935 (dec. Oct. 1951); 1 son, Harry James (USN); m. 3d, Nona Ann Bartzen, Dec. 28, 1952. Enlisted in U.S. Navy, 1905, commd. ensign, 1917, promoted through grades to rear adm.; served with Amphibious Forces, Western Pacific to end of War with Japan. Awarded Bailey medal, 1905, Mexican Service medal, World War I medal and campaign medals Cuba, Hayti and Santo Domingo, Am. Def., Am. sector, Asiatic sector, Philippine Liberation, World War II Occupation, Bronze Medal. Mem. Naval Inst. Elk, Moose. Club: Commonwealth of Cal. Contbr. verse and articles on govt., economy, social welfare and profl. mil. subjects to mags. Home: 1548 Irving Av Glendale CA 91201

HANSEN, HARRY LOUIS, educator; b. N.Y.C., Oct. 21, 1911; s. Louis and Florence Caroline (Ernest) H.; B.S, Haverford Coll., 1933; M.B.A., Harvard, 1935, D.C.S., 1939; Dr. Ed. in Bus. Adminstrn. (hon.), De La Salle Coll., Philippines, 1967; m. Carolyn Guptill, June 22, 1940; children—Jeffrey Northedge, Carolyn Oakes. Mem. faculty Harvard, 1935—, research asst., 1935-36, instr. sales mgmt., 1936-39, asst. dean, 1939-42, asst. prof. marketing, 1939-45, asso. prof. bus. adminstrn., 1945-49, prof. bus. adminstrn., 1949-65, dir. div. internat. activities, 1963-65, program adviser for Harvard to Indian Inst. Mgmt., Ahmedabad, 1964-69, Malcolm P. McNair prof. marketing, 1965—. Dir. Multinat. Bus. Assos., Quincy Market and Cold Storage Warehouse, Co.; cons. to bus. and founds. Spl. cons. to comdg. gen. USAAF, 1942-45; mem. original faculty USAAF Statis. Officers Candidate Sch., 1942-45; co-dir. USAAF War Adjustment Program, Harvard, 1944-45; sci. cons. Office Field Services, Office Sci. Research and Devel., 1945. Mem. adv. bd. Instituto de Estudios Superiores de la Empresa, Barcelona, Spain, 1965—. Recipient Silver All-American award Sports Illus., 1957. Author: (with M.P. McNair) Problems in Marketing, 1949; Marketing— Text, Cases and Reading, 1956; Marketing—Text, Techniques and Cases, 1961, 67. Editor: (with M.P. McNair) Readings in Marketing, 1949. Home: 41 Woodland Rd Lexington MA 02173

HANSEN, HENRY PAUL, educator; b. La Crosse, Wis., Apr. 28, 1907; s. Andrew and Emma (Petersen) H.; Ph.B., U. Wis., 1930, M.S., 1931; Ph.D., U. Wash., 1937; m. Helen S. Rivedal, Oct. 21, 1939; children—Sigurd P., Karen A., David H., Kristin H. Fellow U. Wash., 1935-37, research asso., 1938-39; instr. U. Wyo., 1937-38; instr. Ore. State Coll., 1939-42, asst. prof., 1942- 45, asso. prof., 1945-47, prof. botany since 1947, dean grad. sch. since 1949. Guggenheim Fellow 1943-44, 1947-48; Fulbright research fellow U. of Oslo, Norway, 1962; research asso. U. Oslo, Norway, 1969-70. Mem. Bot. Soc. Am., Ecol. Soc. Am., A.A.A.S. (pres. Pacific div. 1960), Arctic Inst. N. Am., N.W. Sci. Assn. (pres. 1953), Ore. Acad. Sci. (pres. 1965), Torrey Bot. Club, Sigma Xi, Phi Sigma, Phi Kappa Phi. Contbr. profl. jours. Home: 1121 SW Sunset Dr Corvallis OR 97330

HANSEN, HOBART GARFIELD, hosp. supt.; b. Hancock, N.Y., Aug. 10, 1923; s. Hobart Garfield and Dorothy (Nielsen) H.; A.B., Columbia, 1945, M.A., 1946; M.D., U. Va., 1957; m. Archer Ellis, Sept. 3, 1949; children—Christian Stowe, Margaret Ellis. Intern research psychology N.Y. State Psychiat. Inst. and Hosp., 1945-46; intern clin. psychology N.Y. State Dept. Mental Hygiene, 1946- 47; clin. psychologist Elmira (N.Y.) Reception Center and Elmira Reformatory, 1947-51; chief psychologist Western State Hosp., Staunton, Va., 1951-53; med. intern U. Va. Hosp., 1957-58; staff physician Western State Hosp., 1958-60; resident psychiatry St. Elizabeth's Hosp., Washington, 1960-63; clin. dir. Western State Hosp., 1963-65, asst. supt., 1965-67, supt., 1967—; clin. asst. prof. psychiatry U. Va. Sch. Medicine, 1965—. Mem. Am. Psychiat. Assn., A.M.A., Am. Hosp. Assn., Assn. Med. Supts, Mental Hosps. Home: 743 Opie St Staunton VA 24401 Office: Box 1080 Staunton VA 24401

HANSEN, HOWARD JAMES, cons. engr., author; b. Chgo., Mar. 12, 1909; s. Harry John and Selma (Fick) H.; B.S. in C.E., Purdue U., 1930, C.E., Tulane U., 1939; m. L.H. O'Neill, Sept. 16, 1931; children—Jennifer Ann, Gretchen. Project engr. Ind. Hwy. Commn., 1930-31; instr. Tulane U., 1941-42; chief research tech. plywoods, 1942-43; cons. engr. Lockwood-Andrews, 1942- 43; asso. prof. A. and M. Coll. of Tex., 1942-46; asso. prof. U. Fla., 1946-47, prof. engring. mechanics, acting head indsl. engring. dept., 1947-49; mgr. framed structures br. U.S. Naval Civil Engring. Lab., Solomns, Md., 1949-50, head structures research dept., Port Hueneme, 1950; pres. Howard Hansen, Inc., tech. publs.; structural engr. Prestressed Concrete Products Co., Mandeville, La. Served to lt. USN, 1943-46; officer Res. Mem. Am. Soc. C.E., Fla. Engring. Soc. Episcopalian. Author: Modern Timber Design, 1943, 48; Timber Engineers Handbook, 1948; also army manuals. Home: PO Box 243 Covington LA 70433 Office: 325 E Galena Blvd Aurora IL 60505 ☆

HANSEN, HUGH JUSTIN, publisher; b. Thief River Falls, Minn., Mar. 30, 1923; s. Oscar Edward and Othelia C. (Olen) H.; B.S. in Agrl. Engring., N.D. State U., 1951; M.S., Cornell U., 1952; m. JoAnne Skeim, Aug. 28, 1949; children—Susan Marie, Christopher Hugh, Mark Alexander. Asst. prof. agrl. engring., Purdue U., 1952-55; with Reuben H. Donnelley Corp., N.Y.C., 1955-71, publisher, 1962-71; with Dun-Donnelly Pub. Corp., N.Y.C., 1971—. Served with USMCR, 1942-46. Mem. Am. Soc. Agrl. Engrs. (bd. dirs. 1964-66, pres. 1971-72), Am. Soc. Engring. Edn., Am. Agrl. Editors Assn. Home: 2 Maple Hill Rd Valhalla NY 10595 Office: 466 Lexington Av New York City NY 10017

HANSEN, IRA BOWERS, educator; b. Floral Park, N.Y., May 13, 1907; s. Frederick Hans and Hannah Esther (Bowers) H.; B.S., Wesleyan U., Middletown, Conn, 1928, M.A., 1929; Ph.D., U. Chgo., 1932; m. Rachel Louise Wilcox, Dec. 28, 1931; children—Nancy Louise (Mrs. James Marchbank), Elizabeth Louise (Mrs. E. Kent Cockerham). Instr. biology Wesleyan U., 1929- 30; instr. bklyn. Coll., 1932-33, Union Coll., Schenectady, 1933-35; faculty zoology George Washington U., 1935-, prof., 1944-, exec. officer dept., 1939-69; splty. embryology. Mem. Am. Soc. Zoologists, Washington Acad. Scis., Soc. Study Devel. and Growth, A.A.A.S., Phi Beta Kappa, Sigma Xi. Home: 7812 Custer Rd Bethesda, MD 20014. Office: Dept Biol Scis George Washington U Washington DC 20006

HANSEN, IRWIN ROY, mfg. exec.; b. Osceola, Wis., Aug. 16, 1913; s. Lindsley T. and Florence (Koch) H.; Ph.B., U. Wis., 1936; m. Ruth Mac Kay, June 25, 1937. With Haskins & Sells, C.P.A.'s, 1936-44; with Minn. Mining & Mfg. Co., St. Paul, 1944—, gen. auditor, 1944-50, asst. controller, 1950-54, asst. treas., 1954-57, treas., 1957-63, v.p. finance, 1963—, also dir.; treas. Big Rock Stone & Material Co., Prehler Elec. Insulation Co.; dir. First Nat. Bank St. Paul, 3M Bus. Products Sales, Inc. Mem. Am. Inst. C.P.A.'s, Tax Execs. Inst. (past pres. St. Paul chpt.), Financial Execs. Inst. (past dir. St. Paul; mem. various nat. coms.). Mason (Jester). Clubs: Minnesota, St. Paul Athletic, White Bear Yacht, Pool and Yacht. Home: 44 Evergreen Rd St Paul MN 55115 Office: 3M Center St Paul MN 55101

HANSEN, JAMES ROGER, musician; b. Joliet, Ill., Sept. 22, 1908; s. James and Minnie (Petersen) H.; Mus.B., Cosmopolitan Sch. Music (Chgo.), 1952; Mus.M., Chgo. Conservatory Music, 1955; student Loyola U. at Chgo.; m. Rita Ellen Williams, Aug. 29, 1947; children—Jane, Susan, Mary Joan. Violinist, Kansas City Philharmonic Orch., 1935-42, Pitts. Symphony Orch., 1945-46, Chgo. Symphony Orch., 1946—; chmn. Chgo. Symphony Orch. mems'. com., 1970-71, 71-72; faculty Chgo. Conservatory Music. Served with USAAF, 1942-45. Mem. Chgo. Fedn. Musicians (shopsteward 1970-71, 71-72). Club: Cliff Dwellers (Chicago). Home: 2232 Bryant Av Evanston IL 60201 Office: 228 S Michigan Av Chicago IL 60604

HANSEN, JOHN ROBERT, retired state ofcl.; b. Manning, Ia., Aug. 24, 1901; s. Herman P. and Laura (Karstens) H.; student State U. Ia.; m. Mary Louise Osthoff, June 21, 1929 (dec. 1967); children—Robert, Jack; m. 2d, Dorothy Meyer, May 19, 1969. Majority owner, operator Dultmeier Mfg. Co., Manning, 1932-62; gen. mgr. Dultmeier Sales Co., Omaha, 1934-57, prin. owner, 1934-64; Western Ia. area mgr., savs. bond div. Treasury Dept., 1962-64; mem. 89th Congress 7th Dist. Ia.; commr. Ia. Hwy. Commn., 1967-69. Mem. Ia. Bd. Control State Instns., 1957-60; mem. exec. council Gov. Ia. Commn. Alcoholism, 1958-60; mem. Ia. Commn. Interstate Coop., 1958, Ia. div. Nat. Council on Crime and Delinquency. Mem. S.W. Ia. council Boy Scouts Am., 1944-50; mem. Carroll County com. A.R.C., 1942-48, Ia. Mental Health Assn., 1958-62. Mem. Carroll County Democratic Central Com., 1932-52, chmn., 1944-52; chmn. 6th Dist. Ia., Dem. Party, also mem. Ia. Central Dem. Com., 1952-57; alternate del. Dem. Nat. Conv., 1944, 64, del., 1948, 68; Dem. nominee lt. gov. Ia., 1960. Mem. bd., past pres. Manning Gen. Hosp.; trustee Osteopathic Coll. Medicine and Surgery, Des Moines. Mem. Nat. Farm Equipment Mfrs. Assn., Former Members of Congress, Izaak Walton League. Presbyn. (elder). Rotarian (past pres. Manning). Mason (Shriner), Lion (past pres. Manning); mem Order Eastern Star. Address: 69 Lane St Winterset IA 50273

HANSEN, JULIA BUTLER, congresswoman; b. Portland, Ore., June 14, 1907; d. Don C. and Maude (Kimball) Butler; student Ore. State Coll., 1924-26; A.B., U. Wash., 1930; m. Henry A. Hansen, July 15, 1939; 1 son, David Kimball. Mem. Wash. Ho. of Reps., 1939-60, minority leader, 1953-55, speaker pro tem, 1955-60, chmn. hwys. com.; chmn. Joint Fact Finding Hwy. Com., 1949-53; mem. Eleven Western State Hwy. Policy Com., 1949-60, chmn., 1951-60; mem. Nat. Rivers and Harbors Congress; mem. 87th-92d Congresses 3d Dist. Wash. Mem. Democratic Com. Wash., 1936—. Mem. Ore. Hist. Soc., P.T.A., Delta Kappa Gamma (hon.). Author: Singing Paddles, 1935; also poetry, feature articles. Home: Cathlamet WA 98612 Office: Cannon Bldg Washington DC 20515

HANSEN, JULIUS PAUL, mcht.; b. N.Y.C., May 7, 1907; s. Julius and Clara (Wagner) H.; B.A., U. Wash., 1928; m. Gladys Van Dyke, Nov. 26, 1936; children—Linda, Michael, Buyer, Bloomingdale Bros., N.Y.C., 1930-35, mdse. mgr., 1936-41; mdse. mgr. Frederick Loeser, Bklyn., 1941-45, gen. mgr., v.p. 1946-51; gen. mgr., v.p. Oppenheim Collins, N.Y.C., 1951-52, exec. head, 1952-54; exec. v.p. The Fair,

Chgo., 1954-56, pres., 1956-64; pres., chief exec. officer Lit Bros., Phila., 1964—; v.p., dir. City Stores Co., N.Y.C. Mem. Sigma Phi Epsilon. Home: 611 Glendale Rd Newtown Square PA 19073 Office: Lit Bros 8th and Market Sts Philadelphia PA 19107

HANSEN, KERMIT READ, banker; b. Omaha, Feb. 26, 1917; s. Axel T. and Mary (Sarman) H.; A.B., U. Neb., 1939; grad. Sch. Financial Pub. Relations, Chgo., 1962; m. Mary Rosborough, June 6, 1945; children—Kurt, Eric, Kristin, Lauren, Announcer radio sta. KOWH, Omaha, 1939-41; engaged in advt. sales and as editorial columnist Omaha World-Herald, 1946-50, asst. bus. mgr., 1951- 53; with Gardner Advt., Washington, 1950-51; partner Allen & Reynolds Advt., Omaha, 1953-59; with U.S. Nat. Bank Omaha, 1959—, exec. v.p., 1967—; instr., trustee Basic Sch. Banking, 1964-68, pres., instr. Intermediate Sch. Banking, 1968—; dir. Northwest Computer Services Inc., Mpls., Component Concepts Corp., Omaha. Pres. Omaha Symphony, 1956-62, United Community Services, 1969-71; 1st v.p., mem. exec. bd. Mid-Am. council Boy Scouts Am., 1959-68; pres. Omaha Safety Council, 1959-61, chmn., 1961-62. Bd. regents U. Neb., 1971—. Served to col. AUS, World War II. Deocrated Silver Star, Bronze Star with 2 oak leaf clusters, Purple Heart, Combat Inf. Badge; recipient Silver Beaver award Boy Scouts Am., 1965; named Man of Year, Omaha Jr. C. of C., 1948, Omaha Order Eagles, 1949; recipient Safety award Neb. B'nai B'rith, 1964. Mem. U.S., Neb. (v.p., treas. 1963-65), Omaha chambers commerce, Bank Pub. Relations and Marketing Association (bd. dirs. 1964-67), Ak-Sar-Ben (councilor 1968—). Beta Theta Pi. Clubs: Omaha, Omaha Country. Home: 10604 Frances St Omaha NB 68124 Office: 1919 Douglas St Omaha NB 68103

HANSEN, LEROY C., elec. mfg. co. exec.; b. Ft. Pierre, S.D., Mar. 4, 1917; s. Roy C. and Julia (Freeze) H.; B.S., U. Ia., 1941; m. Irene Kathryn Hefte, Sept. 13, 1941; children—Robert Chris, Elaine Kathryn (Mrs. Monroe James Warren), Kristie Ann. Test engr. Gen. Electric Co., Pittsfield, Mass., 1941-42, test engr. engring. dept., 1942-46, transformer specialist, 1946-47; sales engr. A.B. Chance Co., Centralia, Mo., 1947-48, asst. to sales mgr., 1948-49, gen. sales mgr., 1949-56, dir. marketing, 1956-57, v.p. marketing, 1957-60, v.p. gen. mgr., 1960-68, exec. v.p., 1968—, also dir.; dir. A.B. Chance Co. of Can., A.B. Chance de Mexico S.A. Trustee, Chance Found.; bd. visitors, Mo. Mil. Acad., Mexico. Mem. Eta Kappa Nu. Mason. Home: 448 S Jefferson St Centralia MO 65240 Office: 210 N Allen St Centralia MO 65240

HANSEN, MARC FREDERICK, med. educator, pediatrician; b. Marshfield, Wis., Sept. 19, 1930; s. Marc A. and Lorette (Broecker) H.; A.B., Harvard, 1952, M.D., 1956; m. Alice Leone Orvedahl, Dec. 20, 1955; children—Marc Frederick, Christine Elizabeth. Intern Boston City Hosp., 1956-57; resident pediatrics U. Wis., 1957-59, postdoctoral fellow Inst. Enzyme Research, 1961-63, mem. faculty univ., 1963—, asst. prof. pediatrics, 1963-69, asso. prof., 1968—, dir. Univ. Child Health Service, 1966-69, asst. dean, 1970—. Served to capt., M.C., AUS, 1959-61. Recipient Lederle Med. Faculty award, 1966-69. Mem. Am. Acad. Pediatrics, A.M.A., Midwest Soc. Pediatric Research, Soc. Tchrs. Family Medicine, Assn. Am. Med. Colls. Lutheran. Home: 4201 Wanetah Trail Madison, WI 53711.

HANSEN, MILLARD WINCHESTER, educator; b. Grand Island, Neb., June 1, 1912; s. Thorwald Jorgensen and Bertha (Winchester) H.; B.A., Grinnell Coll., 1933; M.A., State U. Ia., 1936, Ph.D., 1939; m. Esther Valines, Jan. 23, 1964. Asst. prof. history No. State Tchrs. Coll. (S.D.), 1940-44; hist. specialist War Dept., 1944-45; asst. prof. history U. Chgo., 1945-49; asso. prof. social sci. U. P.R., Rio Piedras, 1949-56, prof., 1956—, dir. Social Sci. Research Center, 1949-64. Mem. P.R. Minimum Wage Com., 1956; mem. adv. com. on population P.R. Planning Bd., 1957-61, mem. adv. com. on statis. coordination, 1958-59; curriculum cons. P.R. Dept. Edn., 1966; exec. dir., ad hoc adv. group for Presidential Vote for P.R., 1970—. Mem. Gov.'s Food Adv. Commn., 1953; pres. Comite Pro San Juan, 1959-62. Mem. Am. Hist. Assn., Assn. U. Profs. (chpt. pres. 1953-54). Editor: Social Change and Public Policy, 1968. Co-editor: The People Shall Judge, 1949; Puerto Rico: A Study in Democratic Development, 1953. Home: Box 22572 University Sta Rio Piedras PR 00931

HANSEN, ORVAL, congressman; b. Firth, Ida., Aug. 3, 1926; s. Farrel L. and Lily (Wahlquist) H.; B.A., U. Ida., 1950; J.D., George Washington U., 1954; m. June Duncan, Dec. 31, 1955; children—Margaret, Elizabeth, James, Katherine, John, Mary, Sarah. Admitted to Ida. bar, 1954; practice law, Idaho Falls, 1956-68; staff asst. to Senator Henry Dworshak, 1950-54; mem. Ida. Ho. of Reps., 1956-62, 64-66, house majority leader, 1961-62; mem. Ida. Senate, 1966-68, chmn. manpower adv. com., 1963-68; mem. 91st-92d Congresses 2d Dist. Ida. Mem. Eastern Ida. Nuclear Indsl. Council, 1968—. Served with USNR, 1944-46. Rotary Found. fellow U. London (Eng.) Sch. Econs., 1954-55. Mem. Am., Ida. bar assns., Am. Legion, V.F.W., Ida. C. of C., Phi Beta Kappa, Sigma Chi, Phi Alpha Delta, Sigma Delta Chi. Republican. Mem. Ch. Jesus Christ Latter Day Saints. Rotarian. Home: 4405 33d Rd N Arlington, VA 22207. Office: House Office Bldg Washington DC 20515

HANSEN, PETER SIJER, educator, pianist; b. Hayward, Cal., Feb. 5, 1911; s. Peter and Anna (Christoffersen) H.; A.B., U. Cal., 1931; M.Music, Eastman Sch. Music, 1934; Ph.D., U. N.C., 1939; exchange student U. Munich (Germany), 1937- 39; m. Doris L. Ballard, Dec. 30, 1942. Pianist-accompanist, N.Y.C. and touring, 1945-46; head music dept. Stephens Coll., Columbia, Mo., 1946- 53; prof., head music dept. Newcomb Coll., also chmn dept. music Tulane U., 1953—; prof. in charge Tulane-Newcomb Jr. Year Abroad, 1962-63; weekly series lecture recitals on ednl. TV, WYES, New Orleans. Served to lt. (s.g.) USNR. 1942-45. Fulbright research fellow, Paris, 1951-52. Mem. Nat., La., New Orleans music tchrs. assns., Am. Musicol Soc., Coll. Music Soc. Author: An Introduction to Twentieth Century Music, 1960, 3d rev. edit., 1971. Home: 1331 Louisiana Av New Orleans LA 70115

HANSEN, PHIL LAMARR, lawyer; b. Park City, Utah, Sept. 5, 1923; s. Henry and Hazel Marie (Sharp) H.; student Carroll Coll., Helena, Mont., 1943-44, Mont. State Sch. Mines, 1944-45; J.D., U. Utah, 1949; div.; children—Jane Marie, Steven LaMarr, David Alan. Admitted to Utah bar, 1950; engaged as trial lawyer, 1956-65, 69—; prosecutor Murray City, Utah, 1951; judge, Murray City, 1951-56; atty. gen. Utah, 1965-69. Pres. Utah League to Abolish Capital Punishment, 1962. Served with USNR, World War II. Mem. Am., Utah, Salt Lake County bar assns., Murray Jr. (charter), Murray (pres. 1956) chambers commerce, Am. Legion, V.F.W., Nat. Assn. Attys. Gen. Nat. Assn. Dist. Attys., Phi Alpha Delta. Mem. Ch. of Jesus Christ of Latter day Saints. Democrat, Elk, Eagle. Home: 1205 E South Temple St Office: Empire Bldg Salt Lake City UT 84111

HANSEN, PREBEN, architect; b. Copenhagen, Denmark, Mar. 7, 1908; s. Gustav Nikolaj and Jennny Marie (Marcussen) H.; grad. Royal Acad. Fine Arts, 1933; m. Ruth Langeback, Jan 27, 1939; children—Peter Preben, Jesper Preben. Pvt. archtl. practice, Copenhagen, 1937—; apptd. Royal Govt. Architect, 1958; prof. architecture Royal Acad. Fine Arts; works include Am. Builds exhibit, Aalborg Hall, Akvavit Distilleries, Danish Atomic Energy Commn., Cherry Heering Distillery, Copenhagen U., Tuborg Breweries, European Space Research and Tech. Center (Netherlands), Danish Embassy (Paris), WIVEX Restaurants, Tivoli. Recipient gold medal Acad. Fine Arts, 1933, 43, prize City of Copenhagen, 1970; decorated Ridder of Danneborg (Denmark) Officier de l'ordre national du merite (France). Fellow A.I.A.; mem. Royal Inst. Brit. Architects (hon.). Club: Copenhagen Rotary (past pres.). Home: 67 Nyhavn Copenhagen K Denmark Office: 29 Amagertorv Copenhagen K Denmark

HANSEN, RICHARD ALAN, automotive parts co. exec.; b. Berwyn, Ill., July 10, 1931; s. Melvin Alfred and Dorothy Lucille (Richey) H.; B.A., DePauw U., 1953; M.B.A., Ind. U., 1956; m. Joan Katherine Lacey, Sept. 10, 1955; children—Debra Ann, Richard Alan, David Andrew. With Ernst & Ernst, C.P.A.'s, Indpls., 1956-59; with Booyer Test Mgmt. Service, Indpls., 1959-62; sec., treas. Gen. Automotive Parts Corp., Dallas, 1962—. Served with U.S. Army, 1953-55. Mem. Am. Inst. C.P.A.'s, Tex., Ind. socs. C.P.A.'s. Episcopalian. Rotarian. Home: 4640 Allencrest Lane Dallas TX 75234 Office: 4600 Hines Blvd Dallas TX 75235

HANSEN, RICHARD MARDON, business exec.; b. Albany, N.Y., Jan. 30, 1912; s. Nils Richard and Magda (Tonnesen) H.; M.E., Rensselaer Poly. Inst., 1934; grad. Advanced Mgmt. Program, Harvard, 1957; m. Edith Hawkins, Dec. 21, 1947; 1 son, Richard Nils. With the Halliburton Co. (formerly the Halliburton Oil Well Commenting Co.), Duncan, Okla., 1936—, coordinator of mfg., engring. and materials, 1950-55, v.p. mfg., 1955- 65, v.p. planning, 1965—. Home: 6569 Crestpoint Dallas TX 75240. Office: Halliburton Co 3211 Southland Center Dallas TX 75201

HANSEN, ROBERT JOSEPH, educator; b. Tacoma, May 27, 1918; s. Joseph and Olaug (Axness) H.; B.S., U. Wash., 1940; Sc.D., Mass. Inst. Tech., 1948; m. Eleanor Swaim Welch, Dec. 26, 1948; children—Eric Charles, Karen Welch. Research engr. NRC, 1940-43; Princeton, 1943-45, Arthur D. Little Co., Cambridge, Mass., 1945; NRC postdoctoral fellow, 1946-47; research asso. Mass. Inst. Tech., 1947-48, mem. faculty, 1948—, prof. civil engring., 1957—, dep. dir. Project Transp., 1964-67; partner Hansen, Holley & Biggs, cons. engrs., Cambridge, 1955—, Newmark, Hansen & Assos., Cambridge and Urbana, Ill., 1958—; cons. biomechanics Mass. Gen. Hosp., 1956—. Mem. security resources panel Exec. Office of Pres., 1957; mem. sr. adv. panel Air Force Ballistic Div., USAF, 1958-60; mem. exec. com. Adv. Com. Civil Def., Nat. Acad. Scis., 1959—. Recipient Army-Navy certificate appreciation, 1948; Distinguished Service citation Dept. Def., 1969. Fellow Am. Soc. C.E.; mem. Am. Concrete Inst., Soc. Exptl. Stress Analysis, Boston Soc. Civil Engrs., Sigma Xi, Tau Beta Pi. Author: (with others) Structural Design for Dynamic Loads, 1959; also articles, chpts. in books. Editor: Seismic Design for Nuclear Power Plants, 1970. Home: 25 Cambridge St Winchester, MA 01890. Office: Mass Inst Tech Cambridge MA 02139

HANSEN, ROBERT SUTTLE, chemist, educator; b. Salt Lake City, June 17, 1918; s. Charles Andrew and Bessie (Suttle) H.; B.S., U. Mich., 1940, M.S., 1941, Ph.D., 1948; m. Gilda Cappannari, Apr. 8, 1939; 1 son, Edward Charles. Asst. prof. chemistry dept. Ia. State U., Ames, 1948-51, asso. prof., 1951-55, prof., 1955—, chmn., 1965-68, distinguished prof., 1967—; asso. chemist Ames Lab. AEC, 1948-55, sr. chemist, 1955—, chief chemistry div., 1965-68, dir., 1968—; cons. Union Carbide Corp., Procter & Gamble Co. Fellow A.A.A.S.; mem. Am. Chem. Soc. (past sec.-treas. Colloid div.; Kendall Co. award Colloid Chemistry 1966), Am. Phys. Soc., Am. Assn. U. Profs., Phi Beta Kappa, Sigma Xi, Phi Kappa Phi. Home: 2030 McCarthy Rd Ames, IA 50010.

HANSEN, ROGER GAURTH, biochemist; b. Smithfield, Utah, Aug. 18, 1920; s. Willard Alton and Syble (Toolson) H.; student Utah State U., 1938-41; B.S., U. Wis., 1944, M.S., 1946, Ph.D., 1948; m. Anna Lou Rees, Aug. 14, 1943; children—Roger, Ted, Lars Peter. Asst. prof. biochemistry U. Utah, 1948- 50; asso. prof. biochem. agr. U. Ill., 1950-55, prof., 1955-57; prof., head agrl. chemistry dept. Mich. State U., 1957-61, prof., chmn. biochemistry dept., 1961-68; prof. chemistry, provost Utah State U., Logan, 1968—. Recipient Borden award Am. Inst. Nutrition, 1960. Mem. Am. Inst. Nutrition, Am. Soc. Biol. Chemists, Am. Chem. Soc., Soc. Exptl. Biology, Sigma Xi, Gamma Alpha. Home: 1676E 1030N Logan UT 84321 Office: Utah State U Logan UT 84321

HANSEN, VICTOR RUSSELL, lawyer; b. Mpls., Mar. 12, 1904; s. Hans A. and Gina (Ericksen) H.; student U. Cal. at Los Angeles, 1923-25; J.D., U. So. Calif., 1928; grad. Command and Gen. Staff Sch., 1943; m. Lillian Clausen, May 7, 1932; children—Marlene Adrianne, Victor Russell, Robert Arthur. Admitted to Calif. bar, 1928, since practiced in Los Angeles; partner Hansen & Sweeney, 1931-51; judge Superior Ct., 1951-56; asst. atty. gen. U.S. charge antitrust div. Dept. Justice, 1956-59; partner firm Hansen & Dolle, Los Angeles until 1970; now in pvt. practice. Adj. gen. of Cal., 1944-46; brig. gen. Cal. N.G., 1944—. Regent U. Cal., 1946-62; v.p., dir. Braille Inst. Am. Mem. Recipient Dickson Alumni award U. Cal. at Los Angeles, 1950, Medal of Merit State Cal., 1952. Res. Officers Assn. (past pres. Los Angeles), Am., Los Angeles, Cal. bar assns., Phi Delta Theta, Phi Delta Phi. Mason (32, Shriner). Clubs: Pacific Coast, Los Angeles Athletic, Riviera Country, Sertoma, Lincoln. Author: History of State Guard of California, 1946; Tort-uous Path of a Fiduciary; Preparation of Condemnation Cases for Trial; The Antitrust Laws in a Changing Economy. Home: 1734 Earlmont Av La Canada CA 91011

HANSEN, WALTER, educator; b. Cordova, Neb., Apr. 23, 1899; s. Frederick Christian and Margarite Katrina (Hansen) H.; A.B., Neb. Wesleyan U., 1925; A.M., U. Neb., 1927, Ph.D., 1934; m. Elsie Marie Anderson, June 16, 1926; children—Shirley Carol (Mrs. Lawrence Fields), Walter Neal (dec.), Elsie Darlene (Mrs. Dudley Doyle). Instr. geography Oberlin Coll., 1926-29; prof. geography State Tchrs. Coll., Conway, Ark., 1930-31, State Tchrs. Coll., Dickinson, N.D., 1931-32, Neb. Wesleyan U., 1932-33, State Tchrs. Coll., Minot, N.D., 1934-35; faculty N. Tex. State U., 1935—, prof. geography, 1935—, dir. dept., 1941-; summer tchr. State Tchrs. Coll., Ypsilanti, Mich., Berea Coll., State Tchrs. Coll., Emporia, Kan. Mem. Assn. Am. Geographers, Southwestern Social Sci. Assn., Am. Assn. U. Profs., Tex. Assn. Coll. Tchrs., Denton Forum, Sigma Xi, Phi Delta Kappa. Methodist. Contbr. articles profl. jours. Home: 1206 Egan St Denton TX 76201

HANSEN, WILLIAM SCOTT, mcht.; b. La Junta, Colo., July 4, 1921; s. Niels Svoger and Botilda Katherine (Scott) H.; student U. Wash., 1945-46; m. Kathryn Zileen Walsh, Aug. 4, 1942; children—Karen (Mrs. David Erickson), Kristin (Mrs. F. Keenan Behrle), Tria, Marka, Brita, Rundi. With Bon Marche, Seattle, 1946-53; with Buffums, Long Beach, Cal., 1953-57, 70— pres., 1970—; with J.W. Robinson, Los Angeles, 1957-64, mdse. mgr., 1957-64, mdse. mgr. Meier & Frank, Portland, Ore., 1964-66; with Julius Garfunckel & Co., Washington, 1966-70, pres., 1968-70. Served with USNR, 1942-45. Clubs: Pacific Coast (Long Beach); Los Angeles Athletic. Office: Buffums 127 Pine Av Long Beach CA 90802 Home: 6918 Crest Rd Palos Verdes CA 90274

HANSEN, ZENON CLAYTON RAYMOND, truck mfr.; b. Hibbing, Minn., July 23, 1909; s. N. C. M. and Ivah Delle (Raymond) H.; student pub. schs., Sioux City, Ia., H.H.D., Salem College, Salem, W.Va., 1959; LL.D., Linfield College, McMinnvill, Oregon, PMC Colls., Chester, Pa., St. Michaels Coll., Winooskie, Vt.; m. Juanita Kellog, December 2, 1954; one son, Zeonon Raymond Mauritz. With Internat. Harvest Co., also Internat. Harvester Export Co., Europe and North Africa, 1927-44, asst. dist. mgr. Internat. Harvester Co., Portland, Ore., 1941-44; v.p., dir., mgr. Automotive Equipment Co., Portland, 1944-53; v.p., dir. sales Diamond T Motor Car Co., Chgo., 1953- 55, exec. v.p., 1955-56, pres., 1956-58; pres., dir. Diamond T Motor Truck Co.; exec. vice pres., dir. White Motor Co. Cleve., 1958-65; pres., chief exec. officer, dir. Mack Trucks, Inc., 1965-67, chmn. bd., pres., 1967—; v.p., dir., mem. exec. com. Signal Cos., Inc., Los Angeles, 1968—; chmn., dir. Hayes Mfg. Co., Ltd., Vancouver, B.C., Can.; dir. Dartnell Corp., Cherry-Burrell Corporation, Indsl. Valley Bank, Buehler Corp. Chmn. Gov's. Com. of 100,000 Pennsylvanians for Econ. Growth, 1968-70. Pres. Portland area council Boy Scouts Am., 1949- 51, vice chmn. region 11, 1952-53, mem. region 7, exec. com., 1956—, chmn., 1959-62, mem. nat. exec. bd., 1959—, mem. exec. bd. Chgo. council, 1957—, chmn. nst. explorer com., 1962—, chmn. nat. finance com. 1967—, nat. treas., 1967—. Pres. American Humanics Founds., 1956- 58, chmn. adminstrv. committee, 1959-69, patron, honorary life member, chairman board, 1968-69; bd. trustees Mo. Valley Coll., Marshall, Mo.; dir. Salem Coll.; bd. assos. Muhlenberg Coll., Cedar Crest Coll. Recipient Silver Beaver, Silver Antelope, Silver Buffalo awards Boys Scouts Am., also Distinguished Eagle Scout, 1969; St. George award, 1969; fellowship of Christian Athletes; Distinguished Service award, Latin C. of C. Mem. Soc. Automotive Engrs. (Ore., chmn. 1942-43), Am. Ordnance Assn. (life mem.; v.p. Chgo. 1956-63, v.p. Mich. 1963-), Soc. Am. Mil. Engrs. (life), Navy League U.S. (life), Allentown C. of C. (dir.), Automotive Old Timers (life), Newcomen Soc. N.Am., Alpha Phi Omega (nat. exec. bd.). Presbyn. Mason (32, Shriner, Jester), Moose, Elk; mem. Order Eastern Star. Clubs: University (N.Y.); Lehigh Valley, Lehigh Country, Livingston (Allentown, Pa.); Giant Schnauzer Club Am. Inc. (Lansing, Mich.); Chicago, Union League (Chgo.); Oregon Boxer (pres. 1948) (Portland, Ore.). Home: RD 1 Macungie PA 18062 Office: Mack Trucks Inc Box M Allentown PA 18105

HANSER, RICHARD FREDERICK, writer; b. Buffalo, Dec. 15, 1909; s. Adolf T. and Caroline (Feiertag) H.; student Concordia Lutheran Collegiate Inst., Bronxville, N.Y., 1923- 29; m. Anne Golcar, Nov. 29, 1931; 1 son, David Karl. Reporter, feature writer Buffalo Times, 1929-33; reporter, rewrite man Cleve. Press, 1933- 34; feature writer, columnist Buffalo Times, 1934-36; editor, asst. to mng. editor Fawcett Publs., Inc., 1936-41; city editor PM newspaper, 1941-42; psychol. warfare specialist OWI, London, Eng., 1942-43; attached Psychol. Warfare Detachment, 12th Army Group, ETO, 1944-45; documentary script writer RKO Pathe, Inc., 1946-51; script writer NBC TV, 1952—, chief writer Project 20, 1959-70; prodns. include Meet Mr. Lincoln, Mark Twain's America. The Coming of Christ, The Island Called Ellis, others; free-lance contbr. mags., periodicals U.S. and abroad. Recipient Robert E. Sherwood award for Meet Mr. Lincoln, 1959; Writers Guild Am. award for Mark Twain's America, 1961; nominee Acad. TV Arts and Scis., 1960-63. Mem. N.Y. Acad. TV Arts and Scis., Writers Guild Am. East Soc. Mag. Writers. Club: Overseas Press (N.Y.C.). Author: (with Henry Salomon) Victory at Sea, 1959; (with Donald B. Hyatt) Meet Mr. Lincoln, 1960; True Tales of Hitler's Reich, 1962; Putsch! How Hitler Made Revolution, 1970. Translator: (from German) Aftermath, 1947; Walk in Darkness, 1948; The Sword of Satan, 1952. Editorial bd. Television Quar., 1963-71; editorial asso. Am.-German Rev., 1965-71. Home: 1815 Palmer Av Larchmont NY 10538

HANSFORD, BYRON WISEMAN, educator; b. Longwood, Mo., Mar. 18, 1920; s. George M. and Adah (Wiseman) H.; B.S in Edn., S.W. Mo. State Coll., 1941; M.Ed., U. Mo., 1947, Ed.D, 1954; m. Sue Gilliam, Aug. 17, 1941; children—Robert Byron, Carol Sue, Joyce Anne. Tchr.-prin. Pilot Grove (Mo.) High Sch., 1947-48; supt. schs., Gower, Mo., 1948-51, Higginsville, Mo., 1951-55; prof. ednl. adminstrn. Mich. State U., 1955-59; dep. supt. pub. instrn. Mich., 1959-60; commr. edn. Colo., 1960-62, 1969—. Served with AUS, 1942-46; ETO. Author: Guidebook for School Principals, 1961. Home: 6970 W 5th Av Denver CO 80226 Office: State Office Bldg Denver CO 80202

HANSHAW, ARMAND ALAN, lawyer; b. Kankakee, Ill., June 23, 1926; s. Armand E. and Deborah (Sanborn) H.; student U.S. Merchant Marine Acad., 1944-46, Northwestern U., 1946-47, Beloit Coll., 1948-49; B.S., U. Ariz., 1951, LL.B., 1955; m. Emma Hernandez, Sept. 1, 1951 children-Mark Alan, John Wallis, David Matthew, Deborah Leah, Alan Andrew Admitted to Ariz. Bar, 1955, also U.S. Supreme Ct.; law clk.Ariz. Supreme Ct., 1955-56; asst. city atty., Tucson, 1956-58; mem. firm Goddard, Gin, Hanshaw & Gianas, Tucson, 1958- 69; gen.counsel U.S. Virgin Is. Corp., 1964-65. Pres. Com. Econ. Opportunity, Tucson, 1966-68; mem. Ariz. Bd. Pardons and Paroles, 1966- 69; Bd. dirs. Pima County San. Dist., 1961-64. Mem. Am., Fed., Pima County (exec. com. 1970—) bar assns., State Bar Ariz., Am. Judicature Soc., Phi Kappa Sigma, Delta Sigma Pi. Beta Gamma Sigma, Phi Delta Phi. Episcopalian. Rotarian. Club: Mission Bay (San Diego) Home: 802 N Corinth Av Tucson AZ 85710 Office: 4400 E Broadway Tucson AZ 85711

HANSMANN, RALPH EMIL, investment exec.; b. Utica, N.Y., May 25, 1918; s. Emil C. and Friedericka (Fuchs) H.; A.B., Hamilton Coll., 1940; M.B.A., Harvard, 1942; m. Doris Macdonald, Oct. 16, 1943; children—Robert E., Jane C. Investment asso. Harold F. Linder, William T. Golden, N.Y.C., 1945-48, 53—; staff Gen. Am. Investors Co., Inc., 1949-52; dir. Federated Devel. Co., Internat. Holdings Corp., Henry St. Settlement, Julius Wile Sons & Co., Inc., CMI Investment Corp., Group Health Ins., Inc., N.Y.C., TV Communications Corp., Standard Shares, Inc. Trustee, treas. Inst. Advanced Study, Princeton, N.J.; trustee Hamilton Coll., Clinton, N.Y. Served as lt. USNR, 1942-45. Mem. Phi Beta Kappa. Clubs: Fort Schuyler (Utica, N.Y.); Wall Street (N.Y.C.). Home: 385 Manchester Rd Ridgewood NJ 07450 Office: 40 Wall St New York City NY 10005

HANSON, ALVIN WALTER, educator, physicist; b. Alta, Ia., Dec. 14, 1904; s. Christain and Marie (Hansen) H.; B.A., Buena Vista Coll., 1927; student U. Chgo., 1928; M.S., U. Ia., 1933, Ph.D., 1934; m. Florence Andrews, June 2, 1935; children—Meta (Mrs. William Mason), Harriet, Frances (Mrs. Eugene Fischer), Alvin Walter, Tchr., Am. Sch., Shanghai, China, 1928-31, Miss. Coll., 1934-37; mem. faculty the Citadel, 1937-70, prof.. physics, 1960-70, head dept., 1966-70, prof. math., chmn. dept. Baptist Coll., Charleston, S.C., 1970—. Pres. Edgewater Park Civic Club, 1960. Fellow A.A.A.S.; mem. Am. Phys. Soc., Am. Assn. Physics Tchrs., Sigma Xi. Baptist (deacon). Research on elastic properties of zinc single crystals. Home: 1332 N Edgewater Dr Charleston SC 29407

HANSON, ANGUS ALEXANDER, geneticist; b. Chilliwack, B.C., Can., Jan. 1, 1922; s. Francis George and Orpha (McKenzie) H.; B.S.A., U. B.C., 1944; M.S., McGill U., 1946; postgrad. Va. Poly. Inst., summer 1947; Ph.D., Pa. State U., 1951; m. Helen Gertrude Crook,

July 3, 1948; children—Bruce. Alexander, Brian Ernest, Margot Ruth. Grad. asst. agronomy dept. Macdonald Coll., Quebec, Can. 1944-46, lectr., 1946-48, asst. prof., 1948-49; agt. U.S. Regional Pasture Research Lab., University Park, Pa., 1949-52; research leader, grass and turf investigations, crops research div. Agrl. Research, Research Service, U.S. Dept. Agr., 1953-65, chief forage and range br., crops research div., 1965-. Trustee Hillandale Elementary sch. Recipient Superior Service award Dept. Agr., 1961. Fellow Am. Soc. Agronomy; mem. Agrl. Inst. Can., A.A.A.S., Am. Genetics Assn., Am. Soc. Agronomy, Crop Sci. Soc. Am. (pres.), Am. Soc. Range Mgmt., Sigms Xi. Home: 10411 Sweetbriar Pkwy Silver Spring MD 20903 Office: US Dept Agr Forage and Range Research Br Beltsville MD 20705

HANSON, ARNOLD JULIAN, civil engr.; b. Great Falls, Mont., Nov. 23, 1912; s. John E. and Emma (Grorud) H.; B.S., Mont. State Coll., 1934; m. Rose M. Mathern, Aug. 2, 1935; children—Wayne A., Marcia M. (Mrs. Hajdukovich), Robert M., Dale M. Engring. foreman Glacier Nat. Park, Mont., 1934; engring. aide to asso. engr. C.E., Ft. Peck, Mont., 1934-44; project engr. Birch M-K Aleutian Islands, 1944-45; project engr. Birch-Lytle-Green, Fairbanks, Alaska, 1946-49; chief engr., v.p. Reed & Martin, Inc., Fairbanks and Honolulu, 1949—; sr. v.p. Reed & Martin, Inc., Honolulu; project mgr. Martin-Zachry and joint venture constructing facilities on Kwajalein for A.B.M. Test Facilities, 1968—. Mem. Fairbanks Municipal Utilities Bd., 1955-59; bd. dirs. Fairbanks YMCA, 1954-60. Registered profl. engr., Alaska. Mem. Am. Soc. C.E., Tau Beta Pi, Phi Kappa Phi. Home: PO Box 943 APO San Francisco CA 96555 Office: PO Box 3316 Honolulu HI 96811

HANSON, ARTHUR BRIGGS, lawyer; b. Washington, Dec. 8, 1916; s. Elisha and Beatrice Marie (Kurtz) H.; student Episcopal High Sch., Alexandria, Va., 1930-34, Cornell U., 1934-36; A.B., Coll. William and Mary, 1939, B.C.L., 1940; m. Jane Harden, Jan. 23, 1943; children—Clara Miskimen, Jane Dimmick. Admitted to Va. bar, 1940, Md. bar, 1946, D.C. bar, 1947; sr. partner Hanson, O'Brien, Birney & Stickle, and predecessor firms, Washington, 1947—; gen. counsel Am. Newspaper Pubs. Assn. Nat. Geog. Soc., Am. Chem. Soc., Am. Pharm. Assn., U.S. Capitol Hist. Soc.; Civil counsel Smithsonian Instn.; counsel Washington div. Safeway Stores, Inc. Mem. Marine Corps Res. Policy Bd., 1954-57, pres., 1971. Chmn. bd. govs. Nat. Cathedral Sch., 1964-69; trustee Episcopal High Sch., 1953-54; mem. alumni bd. Coll. William and Mary, 1949-52, mem. endowment bd., 1970—; pres. Marine Corps War Meml. Found., 1959—; trustee Nat. Geographic Soc., U.S. Capitol Hist. Soc. Served to maj. USMCR, 1941-46; PTO; maj. gen. Res. Decorated Bronze Star (3); recipient Alumni medallion Coll. William and Mary, 1955. Mem. Am. D.C., Md., Va. bar assns., Am. Law Inst., The Barristers, Old Boys Assn. Episcopal High Sch. (pres. 1952-54), William and Mary Law Sch. Assn. (pres. 1961-62), Marine Corps Res. Officers Assn. (pres. 1964-66, chmn. bd. 1967—), Phi Delta Phi (hon.), Republican. Episcopalian. Clubs: University (Washington); Chevy Chase (Md.); Gibson Island (Md.); Potomac Hunt (Md.); City Tavern (D.C.). Home: 10 Stanmore Ct Potomac MD 20854 Office: 888 17th St NW Washington DC 20006

HANSON, CARL ARNOLD, coll. pres.; b. Akron, O., Apr. 24, 1913; s. Charles and Alma (Carlson) H.; A.B., U. Akron, 1939; student U. Chgo., 1939-41; Ph.D., Cornell U., 1948; m. Jean Landefeld, Mar. 2, 1946; children—Barbara, Carl Arnold Adviser of men U. Akron, 1939; asst. dir. adult edn. Cornell U., 1940- 42, prof., dir. resident instrn. Sch. Indsl. and Labor Relations, 1948- 61, also dean univ. faculty; pres. Gettysburg Coll., 1961—. Chmn., sec. of Air Force's R.O.T.C. Adv. Panel. Trustee Luth. Theol. Sem. Nat. Luth. Campus Ministry. Served with USNR, 1942-45. Mem. Theta Chi, Omicron Delta Kappa, Phi Kappa Phi. Home: 243 W Broadway Gettysburg PA 17325

HANSON, CARL RAYMOND, diversified mfg. co. exec.; b. Mpls., Apr. 12, 1931; s. Carl Benman and Ida Louise (Wilson) H.; B.A. in Accounting, U. Minn., 1955; m. Barbara Jean Harstad, Mar. 23, 1953; children—Naomi Rae, Gustav Carl, Matthew David, Timothy Charles, Bambi Elizabeth, Benman Curtis. Salesman Gamble Skogmo, Mpls., 1949-51; prodn. control clk. Mpls. Moline, Mpls., 1951-53; cost accountant Archer Daniels Midland, Mpls., 1954-55; with Apache Corp., Mpls., 1955—, asst. treas., 1955-59, chief accounting officer, 1960-66, treas., 1966—; dir. Goals, Inc., Lanesboro, Minn. Served with USAF, 1951-52. Mem. Mpls. C. of C., Beta Alpha Psi, Alpha Kappa Psi. Conglist. Club: Mpls. Athletic. Home: 17323 Bay Circle Wayzata MN 55391 Office: 1800 Foshay Tower Minneapolis MN 55402

HANSON, CHARLES STUART, state justice; b. Howard, S.D., Apr. 14, 1911; s. Theodore and Lillian (Sylvester) H.; student Gen. Beadle Tchrs. Coll., 1929-31; LL.B. magna cum laude, U. S.D., 1934; m. Lois Braskamp, 1939 (dec. May 1964); children—Suzanne, Dan; m. 2d, Loretta C. Bowers, 1965. Admitted to S.D. bar, 1934; practice in Canton and Howard, S.D., 1934-42; judge Circuit Ct. S.D., 1948-56, Supreme Ct., 1956—. Served from lt. (j.g.) to lt. comdr., USNR, 1943-46. Mem. Am., S.D. (commr. uniform laws) bar assns. Episcopalian. Home: Howard SD 57349 Office: State Capitol Pierre SD 57501

HANSON, CLARENCE BLOODWORTH, Jr., publisher; b. Augusta, Ga., Nov. 7, 1908; s. Clarence Bloodworth and Harriet (Pinkham) H.; student Richmond Acad., Augusta, Ga., 1921-25; B.S., U. Va., 1930; m. Elizabeth Fontaine Fletcher, Sept. 9, 1929; 1 son, Victor Henry II. Advt. dept. Indpls. Star, 1929- 30; advt. dept. Birmingham (Ala.) News, 1930-34, nat. advt. mgr., 1934-37, asst. advt. dir., 1937-42, pub., 1945—; pres., dir., mem. exec. com. The Birmingham News Co. (pubs. Birmingham News, Huntsville Times Agent, Birmingham Post-Herald); v.p., dir. Mercury Express, Inc.; dir., mem. exec. com. First Nat. Bank of Birmingham, Hayes Internat. Corp.; dir. chmn. exec. com. Royal Crown Cola Co. Bd. dirs. Birmingham Mus. of Art; trustee Ala. Mus. Natural History, Eye Found. Hosp. Served to maj. USAAF, 1942-45. Mem. Asso. Press (v.p. 1952-56), American Newspapers Publishers Assn., Southern Newspaper Pubs. Assn. (pres. 1950), Ala. Press Assn. (pres. 1951), Newcomen Soc. N. Am., Phi Gamma Delta. Mem. Episcopalian Ch. Clubs: Mountain Brook Country, Birmingham Country, Relay House (Birmingham); Grolier (N.Y.C.). Home: 4055 Old Leeds Rd Mountain Brook AL 35213 Office: 2200 4th Av N Birmingham AL 35203

HANSON, DICK VINCENT, magazine editor; b. Bode, Ia., Sept. 15, 1925; s. Lawrence Herman and Pearl (Watnem) H.; B.S., Ia., State U., 1948; m. Marilyn Louise Taylor, Apr. 23, 1949; children—Dirk Taylor, Kimberly Ann, Richard Elliott. Mem. editorial staff Successful Farming mag., Des Moines, 1949—, exec. editor, 1955-57, editor, 1957—; mem. journalism curriculum com. U. Ill. at Urbana, 1969—. Mem. Gov. Ia. Com. Outdoor Recreation, 1965-67; adv. com. to council rural health A.M.A., 1963-65; chmn. Nat. Farm Inst., 1963. Mem. Am. Agrl. Editors Assn. (past pres.), Am. Assn. Agrl. Coll. Editors, Nat. Wildlife Fedn., Wilderness Soc., Outdoor Writers Assn. Am., Sigma Delta Chi, Gamma Sigma Delta, Alpha Zeta, Delta Upsilon. Home: 4702 SW 15th St Des Moines IA 50315 Office: 1716 Locust St Des Moines IA 50313

HANSON, 'DONALD NORMAN, educator, chem. engr.; b. Minooka, Ill., Aug. 3, 1918; s. Charles M. and Nellie K. (Pope) H.; B.S., U. Ill., 1940; M.S., U. Wis., 1941, Ph.D., 1943; m. Sarah L. Hartman, Nov. 6, 1943; children—Charl Hartman, David Frederick, Kristin Ann. Mem. faculty U. Wis., 1943-44, Kan. State U., 1946; with Shell Devel. Co., 1944-46; mem. faculty U. Cal. at Berkeley, 1947—, prof. chem. engring., 1958—, chmn. dept., 1963-67; vis. prof. U. Philippines, 1956-58. Mem. Am. Inst. Chem. Engrs., Am. Chem. Soc., Sigma Xi, Delta Sigma Phi, Alpha Chi Sigma, Tau Beta Pi. Author: (with others) Computation of Multistage Separation Processes, 1961. Home: 522 Moraga Way Orinda CA 94563 Office: Chem Engring Dept Univ California Berkeley CA 94720

HANSON, DURWIN MELFORD, educator; b. Decorah, Ia., Dec. 29, 1915; s. Melvin C. and Nickolena (Rasmusen) H.; B.S., Ia. State U., 1939, M.S., 1949, Ph.D., 1956; m. Margorie Nell Kennard May 15, 1937. Tchr. pub. schs., Storm Lake, Ia., 1939-41, Melvindale, Mich., 1941-42; tng. facilities officer VA, Des Moines, 1946-49; mem. faculty Ia. State U., Ames, 1949- 60, asso. prof. vocational edn., 1949-55, prof., 1955-60; prof., head dept., N.C. State U. Raleigh, 1960—. Chmn. United Fund, N.C. State U., 1968-69, chmn. adv. com., 1970—. Served with USNR, 1942-46. Mem. Am. Vocational Assn. (tech., indsl. planning com. 1967-69, publs. com., 1968—), Am. Soc. Engring. Edn., Nat. Assn. Indsl. Tech. Tchr. Educators (pres. 1969-70), So. Assn. Colls. and Schs. (vice chmn. implementation com., com. on occupational edn.), N.E.A., Raleigh Bowling Assn. (sec. treas.), Southeastern Bowling Conf. (bd. dirs.), Phi Kappa Phi, Psi Chi, Phi Delta Kappa. Home: 4513 Pamlico Dr Raleigh NC 27609

HANSON, EARL DORCHESTER, educator; b. Shahjahanpur, India, Feb. 15, 1927 (parents Am. citizens) s. Harry Albert and Jean (Dorchester) H.; A.B., Bowdoin Coll., 1949; Ph.D., Ind. U., 1954; m. Carlota Ferne Kinzie, June 10, 1948; children—Mardi Jean, Stanley Royce, Kenric Mark. Teaching fellow Ind. U., summer 1954; from instr. to asst. prof. Yale, 1954-60; asso. prof. Wesleyan U., Middletown, Conn., 1960-63, prof. biology, 1963—. Mem. Commn. Undergrad. Edn. in Biol. Scis., 1962-67, chmn., 1965-67; mem. regional bd. examiners Woodrow Wilson Fellowships, 1964-65. Served with USMCR, 1945-46. Recipient Harbison award for distinguished teaching, 1970. Fulbright fellow, 1960-61; Guggenheim fellow, 1960-61. Mem. Am. Assn. U. Profs., A.A.A.S., Am. Inst. Biol. Scis. (bd. govs. 1970—), Genetics Soc. Am., Soc. Protozoologists. Author: Animal Diversity, 2d edit., 1964. Editor: (with others) The Lower Metazoa, 1963. Home: Millbrook Rd Middletown, CT 06457.

HANSON, EARL PARKER, engr., geographer; b. Berlin, Germany (parents U.S. citizens), Mar. 16, 1899; s. Albert Parker and Lida (Siboni) H.; B.S., U. Wis., 1922; grad. study U. Chgo., 1933; m. Dorothy Lane, Feb. 4, 1933; 1 son, John Parker; m. 2d, Charlotte Leeper, Oct. 1, 1938; children—David Parker, Nancy Leeper, (dec.). Engr., Chuquicamata, Chile, 1922-25; editor tech. publs., N.Y.C., 1926; ind. exploratory research in Iceland, 1927; editor in N.Y.C., 1928-29; exploratory research in subarctic Can., 1929; writer on geog. subjects, 1929-31, exec. sec. Explorers' Club, 1931; expdn. to Amazon and Orinoco basins for Carnegie Instn. of Wash., to study fluctuations of earth's magnetic field, 1931-33; research technician for Nat. Resources Com., Washington, 1934-35; planning cons., mem. exec. bd. P.R. Reconstrn. Adminstrn., San Juan, 1935-36; cons. O.Q.-M.G., U.S. Army, on clothing and equipment for jungle warfare, 1942-44; adviser, mem. U.S. Army Engineers' expdn. to Rio Orinoco and Rio Negro, 1943; cons. USAAF, 1944; spl. rep. of F.E.A. in Liberia, spl. asst. to U.S. Minister in Liberia, and spl. agt. of U.S. Comml Co., 1944-46; cons. com. on geophysics and geography Nat. Research and Devel. Bd., 1949-51; vis. lectr. geography U. Md., spring 1948; prof. geography, chmn. dept. geography and geology U. Del., 1949-56; organized areas study course in P.R., 1952; conducted courses in geography U.S. Navy War Coll., Newport, R.I., 1952; cons. econ. devel., Monagas, Venezuela, 1955; cons. Dept. of State, Commonwealth of P.R., 1956-69, Commonwealth of P.R. Planning Bd., 1958; weekly columnist on world affairs, Island Times, San Juan, 1955-64; survey econ. devel. Peruvian Amazon, 1965; lectr. sci. subjects. Decorated knight ofcl. Liberian Humane Order of African Redemption 1946; knight order Icelandic Falcon, 1953. Fellow Am. Geog. Society. Club: Explorers (N.Y.C.). Author: Journey to Manaos, 1938; Highroad to Adventure, 1941; Chile, Land of Progesss, 1941; Stefansson, Prophet of the North, 1941; New Worlds Emerging, 1949; Tranformation, The Story of Modern Puerto Rico; The Amazon, A New Frontier, 1944; Puerto Rico, 1956; Chile, 1957; Bolivia, 1959; Puerto Rico, Land of Wonders, 1960; Puerto Rico, Ally for Progress, 1962; South from the Spanish Main, 1967. Editor: New World Guides to Latin America; Index to Millionth Map of Hispanic America, 1942-43. Contbr. mags. Home: 3 Atlantic Pl Santurce PR 00911

HANSON, EUGENE NELSON, univ. dean.; b. Iola, Wis., Sept. 27, 1917; s. Harris Gilbert and Delia (Nelson) H.; B.A., Luther Coll., Decorah, Ia., 1939; M.A., U. Wis., 1940, J.D., 1946; LL.M., U. Mich., 1948; m. Katie Lou Craft, June 29, 1950; children—P. Louise (Mrs. Ronald F. Gossard), Jennifer Lou. Admitted to Wis. bar, 1946, Ohio bar, 1954; asst. prof. law, Ohio No. U., Ada, 1947-51, asso. prof., 1951-54, prof., 1954—, dean, 1958—; Fulbright prof., U. Iceland, 1960; mem. fellowship rev. panel, Dept. Health, Edn. and Welfare, NSF panel. Pres. Village Council, 1960-61. Sec. Nat. Lutheran Campus Ministry, Luth. Ch. Am., 1964-67, mem. exec. bd., Ohio Synod, 1969—. Recipient Distinguished Service award Luther Coll., 1966. Mem. Am., Ohio, Hardin County (pres.) bar assns. Democrat. Home: 604 Merrie Mont Lane Ada OH 45810

HANSON, GEORGE FULFORD, geologist; b. Schenectady, N.Y. 14, 1916; s. George F. and Barbara (Taylor) H.; student Oxford U., 1935; B.S., Union Coll., 1943; M.S., U. Wis., 1952; m. Marguerite Gardner, Apr. 19, 1948; children—Hollis, Tracy, Lindley. Asst. geologist Union Coll., 1940-43, instr., 1946-47; state geologist, Wis. and dir. Wis. Geol. and Natural History Survey, U. Wis., 1953—. Mem. U.S. Maritime Service, 1943-45. Fellow Royal Geog. Soc., Geol. Soc. Am., mem. A.A.A.S., Assn. Am. State Geologists, Wis. Acad. Sic., Am. Inst. Profl. Geologists, Am. Water Resources Assn., Phi Beta Kappa, Sigma Xi. Home: 1102 Lincoln St Madison WI 53711

HANSON, HAROLD PALMER, educator, physicist; b. Virginia, Minn., Dec. 27, 1921; s. Martin Bernhard and Elvida Elaine (Paulsen) H.; B.S., Superior (Wis.) State Coll., 1942; M.S., U. Wis., 1944, Ph.D., 1948; m. Mary Jean Stevenson, June 22, 1944; children—Steven Bernard, Barbara Jean. Mem. faculty U. Fla., 1948-54, dean grad. sch., 1969-71, v.p. acad. affairs, 1971—; mem. faculty U. Tex., Austin, 1954-69, prof. physics, 1961-69, chmn. dept., 1962-69; summer research physicist Lincoln Labs., Mass. Inst. Tech., 1953, Gen. Atomic Co., San Diego, 1964; summer vis. lectr. U. Wis., 1957; Fulbright research scholar, Norway, 1960-61. Fellow Am. Phys. Soc.; mem. Sigma Xi, Sigma Pi Sigma. Club: Town and Gown (Austin). Office: Grad Sch U Fla Gainesville FL 32601

HANSON, HARRY GLENYS, sanitary engr.; b. Crookston, Minn., Nov. 26, 1909; s. Edward Thron and Agnetta (Backlund) H.; B.S., N.D. State U., 1935; grad. study U. Minn., 1937; M.S., Harvard, 1940; m. Dorothy Ruth Greenland, July 1, 1939; children—Harry Glenys, Karl Edward, John Robert. Successively gen. san. engring. work, asst. dir., dir. div. san. engring., N.D. State Dept. Health, 1936-42; exec. officer malaria control war areas U.S.P.H.S., Atlanta, 1942-48, exec. officer to Surgeon Gen., 1948-52, asst. chief san. engring. officer Office of Surgeon Gen., Washington, 1952-54; dir. Robert A. Taft San. Engring. Center, Cin., 1954-58, appointed asst. surgeon gen. USPHS, 1958—, asso. chief Bur. State Services for Environmental Health, 1960-66; regional adviser Pan Am. Health Orgn., 1966—. Advisor to U.S. Mem. exec. bd. WHO, Geneva, Switzerland 1950-53; chmn. first export com. on water pollution control WHO, Geneva, 1964. Registered profl. engr., N.D. Mem. Conf. Fed. Sanitary Engrs., Am. Pub. Health Assn., Am. Water Works Assn., Inter-Am. Assn. San. Engrs., Fedn. Water Pollution Control; Fed. Water Quality Conf. State San. Engrs., Am. Acad. Environmental Engrs., Nat. Soc. Profl. Engrs. Home: 11824 Charen La Rockville MD 20854 Office: Pan Am Health Orgn Washington DC 20203

HANSON, HOWARD, composer, comdr., educator; b. Wahoo, Neb., Oct. 28, 1896; s. Hans and Hilma (Eckstrom) H.; student Luther Coll., Wahoo; U. Neb., sch. of music; Inst. Musical Art, N.Y. City; Mus. B., Northwestern U., 1916; Mus.D., Honoris causa, Northwestern U., Syracuse U., Horner Inst., Augustana Coll. and Theol. Sem., U. Neb., Am. Conservatory Mus., Columbia, Capital U.; Shurtleff Coll., Hartt Coll., of Music, New Eng. Conservatory, Temple U., Newcomb Coll. of Tulane U., U. Mich., N.Y. State U., Mus. Fund Soc. Phila., N.Y.; LL.D., U. Ky., Ill. Wesleyan U., Coll. of the Pacific, Ball State Teachers Coll., Litt.D., Keuka Coll., Wooster Coll.; L.H.D., Drury Coll., Valparaiso U.; Mus. D. (hon.), Boston U., 1964; D.F.A., Drake U., 1966, U. Portland, 1968; L.H.D., Midland Luth. Coll., 1967; D.Sacred Music, Kenyon Coll., Youngstown U.; m. Margaret Elizabeth Nelson, July 24, 1946. Mem. staff theory dept. Coll. of the Pacific, San Jose, Calif., 1916, dean Conservatory Fine Arts, 1919-21, dir. Eastman Sch. Mus., U. Rochester, 1924-64, dir. Inst., of Am. Music, 1964—; Phi Beta Kappa visiting scholar, 1964-65. Cons. U.S. Dept. of State; adv. com. arts Nat. Cultural Center, Washington; mem. exec. com. of UN-ESCO. Served as guest condr. major cities both U.S. and fgn.; works have been performed by major fgn. and U.S. orchestras and bands. Bd. regents U. Ariz., Gustavus Adolphus Coll., Boston U. Winner several awards 1921—, including Pulitzer Prize, 1944. George Foster Peabody Award, 1946, Huntington Hartford Found. award, 1959, and several others. F. Am. Acad. Rome, 1921-24, Royal Acad. Music in Sweden, 1938; mem. N.Y. State Council Arts (concert adv. panel), Am. Acad. Arts and Scis., Am. Philosophical Soc. Newcomen Soc., Phi Beta Kappa. Lutheran. Composer wide variety musical compositions, including symphonic poems, symphonie operas, mixed choruses, male choruses, instrumental selections for particular instruments, including among many others: Two Yule-tide Pieces, Opus 19; Concerto in G Major, Opus 36 for piano and orchestra; "Vermeland" from Scandinavia Suite, Opus 13, for organ; Concerto for organ, strings and harp. Opus 22; also Harmonic Materials of Modern Music Clubs: University, Rochester, Century Association, Torch, The Bohemians (N.Y.C.). Home: 362 Oakdale Dr Rochester NY 14618

HANSON, HOWARD GRANT, educator, physicist; b. Douglas County, Minn., Jan. 22, 1920; s. Alfred C. and Emma (Olson) H.; B.S., St. Cloud (Minn.) State Coll., 1943; Ph.D., U. Wis., 1948; m. Agnes Eleanor Johnson, June 19, 1945; children—Grant Peter, Catherine Marie, Bruce Howard, Jean Elizabeth. Mem. faculty U. Minn. at Duluth, 1947—, prof. physics, 1959—, chmn. dept., 1952-; research scientist Oak Ridge Nat. Lab., summers 1958, 59; sci. cons. Holloman AFB, summer 1960; research physicist Lawrence Radiation Lab., summer 1961-62; prin. investigator Office Naval Research summers 1964, 65, 66, 68, 69. Observer Scandinavian Summer Inst. Physics, NSF, 1959. NSF sci. fellow, Sweden, 1963. Mem. Minn. Area Assn. Physics Tchrs. (pres. 1951-52, 62-63), Am. Assn. Physics Tchrs. (mem. nat. council 1966—), Am. Phys. Soc., A.A.A.S., Sigma Xi. Author research papers. Home: 5120 Crosley Av Duluth MN 55804

HANSON, JACK, dept. store exec.; b. 1915; B.B.A., City Coll. N.Y., 1936; married. With R.H. Macy & Co., Inc., 1946—, sr. v.p. control and finance, now v.p., treas. C.P.A., N.Y. Address: 151 W 34th St New York City NY 10001*

HANSON, JOHN BERNARD, educator, plant physiologist; b. Denver, Mar. 24, 1918; s. Bernard and Emily (Vogt) H.; B.A. in Botany magna cum laude, U. Colo., 1948; Ph.D. in Botany, Wash. State U., 1952; m. Rebecca Elizabeth Hanson, Jan. 30, 1943; children—Emily Frances, Elizabeth Louise, Lois Rebecca. NRC postdoctoral fellow Cal. Inst. Tech., 1952-53; mem. faculty U. Ill. at Urbana, 1953—, prof. botany, 1960—, head dept., 1967—. Served with AUS, 1940-45. Fulbright research scholar Waite Ag. Research Inst., Australia, 1959-60; NATO sr. fellow, summer 1968, U. E. Anglia, Norwich, Eng. Mem. Am. Soc. Plant Physiologists (exec. bd. 1968-), Am. Soc. Agronomy (Crop Sci. award 1965), Am. Soc. Cell Biology, Sigma Xi. Conglist. Asso. editor Plant Physiology, 1964-69, Crop Sci., 1963-66, Weed Sci., 1963-67. Home: 610 Burkwood St Urbana IL 61801

HANSON, JOHN MARTIN, mfr. ladies apparel; b. Evanston, Ill., June 28, 1919; s. Wilbur Martin and Ethel Marion (Hale) H.; B.S. in Edn., U. So. Cal., 1940; m. Sally Jean Conlin, Feb. 2, 1958. Opened Jax Dress Shop. Beverly Hills, Cal., 1944, subsequently opened branches in N.Y.C., Chgo., San Francisco, Palm Beach, Fla; Southampton, L.I., Westwood, Cal., Balboa Island; now pres. parent company Jax of Cal.; designer womens clothes, 1944—; pub. Cinema mag., 1964—; propr. The Daisy, pvt. club, Beverly Hills, 1964—. Served with USAAF, 1942-44. Mem. Sigma Nu. Home: 610 N Beverly Dr Beverly Hills CA Office: 9667 Wilshire Blvd Beverly Hills CA 90212

HANSON, KERMIT OSMOND, univ. dean; b. Troy Twp., Ia., May 14, 1916; s. Gerhard Severin and Suniva Fosmark (Borge) H.; A.B. cum laude, Luther Coll., Decorah, Ia., 1938; M.S., Ia. State U., 1940, Ph.D., 1950; m. Jane Elizabeth Haugen, Aug. 17, 1940; children—James Stephen, Katherine Jane, Paul Richard, Daniel Gerhard. Operations analyst Fed. Land Bank, Omaha, 1941-43; chief statis service sect. VA br. office, Seattle, 1946-47; mem. faculty Sch. Bus. Adminstrn., U. Wash., Seattle, 1948—, prof. accounting, finance and statistics, 1954—, chmn. dept. accounting, finance and statistics, 1955- 60, asso. dean, 1959-64, dean Grad. Sch. Bus. Adminstrn., 1964—; instr., ednl. adminstr. Pacific Coast Banking Sch., 1949—, also bd. dirs. Dir. Leckenby Co., Syncro Growth Fund, Washington Fed. Savs. & Loan Assn.; cons. P.O. Dept., 1969—, Gen. Accounting Office, 1970—. Mem. exec. bd. Chief Seattle council Boy Scouts Am., 1958—, pres., 1967- 69, mem. Nat. council, 1961—, recipient Silver Beaver award, 1963. Bd. dirs. Journey for Perspective Found., 1964—. Served to lt. USNR, 1943- 46. Mem. Am. Assn.. Collegiate Schs. Bus. (pres. 1971—), Am. Accounting Assn., Am. Finance Assn., Am. Statis. Assn., Financial Execs. Inst., Beta Gamma Sigma, Beta Alpha Psi, Alpha Kappa Psi. Lutheran. Author: Managerial Statistics, 1955; (with G. Brabb) Managerial Statistics, 2d edit., 1961. Home: 17760 14th Av NW Seattle WA 98177

HANSON, KITTY, newspaperwoman; b. Chgo.; d. T. Nagle and Selma (Sittig) Baile; student Ind. State Tchrs. Coll., also Denver U.; m. Hal Golden, Apr. 27, 1957. Reporter, feature writer Gary (Ind.) Post-Tribune, 1949-54, N.Y. Daily News, 1954—. Recipient 6 major awards for nursing home expose, 1962, including George Polk Meml.

award, Soc. Silurians award. Mem. Newspaper Women's Club N.Y. (treas. 1961-62, pres. 1962-63; awards outstanding series and features 1955, 59, 62, 66, 67, 69). Author: (with husban) Special Events, 1960, Working with the Working Press, 1962; Rebels in the Streets, 1964; For Richer, for Poorer, 1968. Writer documentary films. Office: NY Daily News 220 E 42d St New York City NY 10017

HANSON, KURTZ MCROBERTS, business exec.; b. Washington, Dec. 18, 1913; s. Elisha and Beatrice (Kurtz) H.; student Cornell U., 1933-34; m. Helen Louise Davis, July 7, 1936; 1 dau., Helen Louise. Staff Nat. Geog. Soc., 1934-42, asst. sec., 1946-54; dir. Champion-Internat. Co., 1946—, v.p., 1948-50, pres., 1950- 58; dir., pres. Lanston Industries, Inc., Phila., 1959-60; pres. Photon, Inc., Cambridge, Mass., 1960-64, chmn., 1964—; dir., pres. Monotype Co., Can., Companhia Lanston do Brasil; dir. Western Elec., New England Transp. Co.; pres. Champion-Internat. Co.; incorporator Broadway Savs. Bank; dir., mem. exec. com. Mass. Bus. Development Corp. Dir. Mass. Higher Edn. Assistance Corp.; chmn. Mass. Payroll Savs. Com.; dir. World Trade Center of New England, Inc.; member National Assn. Boys Clubs Am. Served as maj. USMC, 1942-46, ret. col. Reserves. Mem. Asso. Industries Mass. (pres., 1955-57, mem. exec. com.), C. of C. (dir.), N.A.M. (dir.). Clubs: Chevy Chase; Everglades, Beach (Palm Beach, Fla.). Home: 369 S Lake Dr Palm Beach FL 33480

HANSON, LESTER EUGENE, educator; b. Willmar, Minn., Mar. 31, 1912; s. Edwin William and Esther Dorothea (Lundquist) H.; B.S. with distinction U. Minn. 1936; M.S., Cornell U., 1937, Ph.D., 1940; m. Gladys Diessner Aug. 21, 1937; children—Bruce E., Ronald L., Karen. Grad. asst. Cornell U., 1936-37, 38- 40; fellow Am.-Scandinavian Found., study in Denmark, 1937-38; instr., then asst. prof., asso. prof., prof. dept. animal husbandry U. Neb., 1940-50; prof. dept. animal husbandry U. Minn., 1950—, head dept., 1956- 66, prof. dept. animal sci., 1966—. Recipient award for research swine nutrition and mgmt. Am. Feed Mfrs. Assn., 1955; named Distinguished Nutritionist, Distillers Research Council, 1964. Mem. A.A.A.S., Am. Assn. U. Profs., Am. Soc. Animal Sci. (v.p. 1961-62, pres. 1962-63, dir. 1963-64), Am. Dairy Sci. Assn., Metric Assn., Am. Inst. Biol. Scis., Am. Inst. Nutrition, Sigma Xi, Phi Kappa Phi, Gamma Sigma Delta, Alpha Zeta, Farm-House, Phi Zeta. Lutheran. Home: 1413 W Idaho Av St Paul MN 55108

HANSON, LYLE EUGENE, educator, veterinarian; b. Sarona, Wis., Oct. 2, 1920; s. Fred S. and Marion (Bergquist) H.; Ph.B., Northland Coll., Ashland, Wis., 1942; D.V.M., Mich. State Coll., 1950; M.S., U. Ill., 1953, Ph.D., 1957; m. Ruth Allee Magruder, June 18, 1945; children—Bruce Lloyd, Karen Ruth, Craig Lyle, Jane Eileen. Veterinarian, Wis. Dept. Agr., 1950; mem. faculty U. Ill. at Urbana, 1950-, prof., 1961-, head dept. vet. pathology and hygiene, 1967—. Served with AUS, 1942-46. Mem. Am., Ill. vet. med. assns., Am. Assn. Avian Pathologists, Am. Soc. Microbiology, Am. Pub. Health Assn., Am. Coll. Vet. Microbiology, A.A.A.S., U.S. Livestock San. Assn., Sigma Xi, Phi Zeta, Gamma Sigma Delta. Home: RR 2 Urbana IL 61801

HANSON, NORMAN, lawyer; b. Roy, Mont., Feb. 12, 1916; B.A., U. Mont., 1937, J.D., 1940. Admitted to Mont. bar, 1940; now mem. firm Crowley, Kilbourne, Hayghey, Hanson & Gallagher, Billings, Mont. Trustee, Rocky Mountain Mineral Law Found. Mem. Yellowstone County Bar Assn., Phi Delta Phi. Editor Mont. Law Review, 1940. Office: Electric Bldg Billings MT 59101*

HANSON, ROGER WAYNE, educator; b. Frost, Minn., Sept. 3, 1922; s. Maynard P. and Hazel B. (Lund) H.; B.A., U. Ia., 1946, M.A. in Protozoology, 1948; Ph.D. in Zoology and Physiology, U. Cal. at Los Angeles, 1952; m. Bette Ruth Johnson, Dec. 27, 1948; children—Heidi, Eric. Lectr. biology U. Cal. at Santa Barbara, 1952-53; NSF postdoctoral fellow U. Ala., 1953-54, pharmacology fellow U. Ala., Birmingham, 1954-55, NIH fellow, 1955-57, instr., 1957-59, asst. prof., 1959-62, asso. prof., 1962-66, prof., 1966—; prof. pharmacology U. Ala. Med. Center, 1967, prof. biology, chmn. div. natural scis. and math., 1966—. Mem. Ala. Council Human Relations, 1954-64, Ala. bd. Am. Civil Liberties Union, 1968—, Ala. adv. council U.S. Civil Rights Commn., 1968—, Equal Employment Adv. Council for Transp. Dept. FAA, 1969—. Served with AUS, 1943-46. Fellow A.A.A.S.; mem. Am. Physiol. Soc. (v.p. 1957-58), Ala. Acad. Sci. (chmn. med. sect. 1960-61), Am. Assn. U. Profs., Nat. Sci. Tchrs. Assn., Am. Inst. Biol. Scis., Sigma Xi. Contbr. articles profl. jours. Home: 1734 Woodbine Dr Birmingham AL 35216

HANSON, VICTOR HENRY II, newpapers exec.; b. Augusta, Ga., Aug. 17, 1930; s. Clarence Bloodworth, Jr. and Elizabeth (Fletcher) H.; grad. Choate Sch., 1949; student U. Va., 1949-51; B.A., U. Ala., 1954; m. Elizabeth Stallworth, Dec. 29, 1953; children—Clarence Bloodworth III, Victor Henry III, Elizabeth Mickel, Mary Fletcher, Robert Stallworth. With Birmingham (Ala.) News & Post Herald, 1946-54, 57—, gen. mgr., 1963—; with advt. and prodn. dept. WAPI-TV, Birmingham, 1954-55; v.p. Birmingham News Co., 1960—; dir. City Fed. Savs. & Loan Assn. Bd. dirs. Jefferson County United Appeal. Served to 1st lt. USAAF, 1955-57. Mem. Birmingham C. of C., Kappa Alpha. Presbyn. Rotarian. Clubs: Birmingham Country, Downtown, Mountain Brook, The Club, Relay House (Birmingham). Home: 3557 River Bend Rd Birmingham AL 35243 Office: 2200 4th Av N Birmingham AL 35203

HANSON, WALTER EDWARD, accountant; b. Adelphia, N.J., Oct. 17, 1925; s. Samuel and Ida (Clayton) H.; A.B., Lafayette Coll., 1949; postgrad. Lehigh U., summer 1949, U. Minn., 1951-52; m. Frances Barber, Aug. 24, 1946; children—Katharine, Elizabeth, Barbara. Sr. accountant Haskins & Sells, N.Y.C., 1949, Mpls., 1949-55; v.p., comptroller M. & St. L. R.R., 1955- 57; partner Peat, Marwick, Mitchell & Co., N.Y.C., 1957-61, partner in charge N.Y.C. office, 1961-65, sr. partner, 1965—. Mem. adv. council Stamford U. Grad. Sch. Bus. Trustee Lafayette Coll., Am. Health Found.; bd. govs., exec. com. UN Assn. U.S. Served with USNR, 1943-45. C.P.A., N.Y., 15 other states. Mem. Am. Inst. C.P.A.'s (treas., dir.) , N.Y. State Soc. C.P.A.'s, N.Y. State Bar Assn. Joint Practice Com. of Lawyers and Accountants, Internat. C. of C. (dep. treas., trustee, exec. com. U.S. council) , Beta Alpha Psi. Clubs: Downtown Assn., N.Y. Yacht, Board Room (N.Y.C.); Wee Burn Country (Darien, Conn.); Noroton Yacht. Home: 21 Butlers Island Rd Darien CT 06820. Office: 345 Park Av New York City NY 10022

HANSTEEN, HENRY B., educator; b. nr. Bklyn., Apr. 28, 1904; s. Henry and Elise (Baatz) H.; E.E., Polytech. Inst. Bklyn., 1924; A.M., Columbia, 1929, Ph.D., 1942; m. Emma Burkat, Dec. 29, 1930; children—Robert Henry, Beatrice Anna. With Westinghouse Elec. Corp., 1924-26, Bklyn. Edison Co., 1926-28, Bell Telephone Lab., 1929-30; mem. faculty Polytechnic Inst. Bklyn., 1930-37, City Coll. N.Y., 1937-46, Cornell U., 1946-50; prof. elec. engring. City U. N.Y., 1950- 67, prof. emeritus elec. engring., 1967—, chmn. dept. elec. engring., 1952-55; ednl. cons. on leave Internat. Atomic Energy Agy., Vienna, Austria, 1960-63; sr. engr. Brookhaven Nat. Lab., 1967—. Fellow Am. Inst. E.E.; mem. Am. Phys. Soc., Am. Soc. Engring. Edn., Am. Assn. U. Profs., Fedn. Am. Scientists, Sigma Xi, Eta Kappa Nu, Tau Beta Pi, Epsilon Chi. Home: Edinburg-Northville NY 12134 Office: Brookhaven Nat Lab Upton NY 11973

HANTZ, HAROLD DONOVAN, educator; b. Thermopolis, Wyo., June 17, 1911; s. Hosea Marsh and Margaret Grace (Kirby) H.; A.B. magna cum laude, U. Colo., 1932, A.M., 1933; Ph.D., Columbia, 1939; m. Katharine Lucile Clark, Oct. 3, 1941; children—Edwin Charlton, David Kenneth. Legislative research asst. U.S. Senate Library, Washington, 1934-37; asst. prof. philosophy and acting chmn. dept. U. Miss., 1939-43; asso. prof. philosophy Okla. State U., 1946-48, chmn. dept., 1947-48; prof. philosophy U. Ark., 1948—, chmn. dept., 1948-54, co-ordinator of honors, 1958- -; vis. prof. philosophy Columbia, summer 1949, U. Colo., summer 1953, 66; Ford faculty fellowship study, Columbia U., 1952-53. Served to 1st lt. AUS, 1943-46. Mem. A.A.A.S., Am. Philos. Assn., Am. Assn. Profs., Nat. Collegiate Honors Council, Phi Beta Kappa, Phi Kappa Psi. Author: Index of Congressional Committee Hearings (with James D. Preston and Robert L. Baldridge), 1935, supplement, 1937; The Biological Motivation in Aristotle, 1939; (with Harry Girvetz, George Geiger, Bertram Morris) Science, Folklore, and Philosophy, 1966. Home: 855 Fairview St Fayetteville AR 72701

HANWAY, JOHN, II, mfg. co. exec.; b. Mt. Vernon, N.Y., Oct. 23, 1924; s. John Howard and Marie Theresa (Fenlon) H.; grad. Hill Sch., 1942; B.A., Yale, 1948; m. Elena Gracia, May 8, 1950; children—John III, David Howard, Robert William, Linda, Thomas Edward. With A.D. McKelvy Co., also Prince Matchabelli, Inc., 1948-53, Robert Heller & Assos., 1953-63; with Internat. Tel. & Tel. Corp., 1963-, v.p. adminstrn., 1964-, also sr. v.p., 1964—. Served to 1st lt., pilot USAAF, 1942-45; PTO. Home: 34 Helena Av Larchmont, NY 10538. Office: 320 Park Av New York City NY 10022

HANZEN, WILLIAM ERWIN, lawyer; b. Moscow, Ida., Aug. 6, 1914; s. Erwin Alfred and Viola (Reed) H.; J.D., Willamette U., 1940; m. Rhaecilla E. Morse, Dec. 7, 1962; children—Cheryl Lee (Mrs. Kenneth Chipman), William Gary, Linda Lou. Admitted to Wash. bar, 1940, Ore. bar, 1940, also U.S. Dist. Cts. Ore.- Wash., U.S. Supreme Ct., U.S. Ct. Mil. Appeals; practice in Pendleton, Ore., 1946—; partner Isaminger & Hanzen, 1956—. Chmn. Ore. All Star E-W Shrine Football Game, Pendelton, 1956-61. Ore. presidential elector, 1956; Eastern Ore. Republican nat. del., 1960. Trustee, Eastern Ore. Episcopal Found. Served to capt., M.I., AUS, 1942-46; eol-Res Recipient certificate of merit Ore. State Bar, 1969. Mem. Ore. (past bd. govs.), Wash., 6th Judicial Dist. (past pres.) bar assns., Am. Trial Lawyers Assn., Ore. Jr. (past v.p.), Pendleton (past dir.) chambers commerce. Mason (Shriner, Jester), Elk, Kiwanian. Home: Box 7 Meacham OR 97859 Office: 123 SE Court Av Pendelton OR 97801

HAPALA, MILAN ERNEST, educator; b. Hranice, Czechoslovakia, Sept. 19, 1919; s. Vladimir and Marie (Micochova) H.; came to U.S., 1938, naturalized, 1943; A.B., Beloit Coll., 1940; A.M., Neb. U., 1941; Ph.D. in Polit. Sci., Duke, 1956; m. Adelaide E. Hamilton, Sept. 6, 1947; children—Milan Ernest, Mary Elizabeth. Mem. faculty Sweet Briar Coll., 1947—, asso. prof. govt., chmn. div. social studies, 1956-60, 7O—, prof. govt., 1960—, Carter Glass prof., 1962—, chmn. dept., 1952-63, 65-68; instr. Lynchburg (Va.) br. Am. Inst. Banking, 1955-59; vis. lectr. Lynchburg Coll., 1951; vis. prof. U. Va., 1967-68; dir. faculty seminar in India U.S. office edn., Summer 1970. Served with USAAF, 1942-45. Fgn. lang. (Hindi-Urdu) fellow Nat. Def. Fgn. Lang., U. Pa., 1964-65. Mem. Am. Polit. Sci. Assn., Assn. Asian Studies, Am. Soc. Internat. Law, Am. Assn. Advancement Slavic Studies, Am. Assn. U. Profs., Czechoslovakian Soc. Arts and Scis., Va. Soc. Sci. (mem. bd. 1966-69), Phi Beta Kappa. Rotarian (pres. Amherst 1955). Author articles, book revs. Home: Waugh's Ferry Rd Amherst VA 24521 Office: Box S Sweet Briar VA 24595

HAPGOOD, CYRUS STOW, lawyer; b. Lynn, Mass., Apr. 21, 1912; s. Cyrus Howard and Edith (Dow) H.; B.E., Mass. Inst. Tech., 1933; LL.B., Fordham U., 1936; m. Mildred Mennen, Mar. 14, 1942; children—Cyrus Stow, Candra, Gay. Admitted to N.Y. bar, 1936, since practiced in N.Y.C; partner firm Davis, Hoxie, Faithfull & Hapgood, 1945—. Served with USNR, 1942-45. Decorated Navy Commendation ribbon. Mem. Am., N.Y. (pres. 1962-63) patent law assns., Bar Assn. City N.Y. Home: Indian Point La Riverside CT 06878 Office: 30 Broad St New York City NY 10004

HAPKE, DANIEL SUPER, banker, lawyer; b. St. Louis, Oct. 5, 1916; s. Arthur Andrew and Mary (Super) H.; LL.B., St. Louis U., 1939; m. Nancy Conway Anderson, May 12, 1941; children—Charles Arthur, Margaret (Mrs. Lloyd James), Daniel Super. Admitted to Mo. bar, 1939; pvt. practice, St. Louis, 1939-47; with Bank of St. Louis, 1948—, gen. counsel, 1958—, sr. v.p., 1965—; v.p. sec., gen. counsel Gen. Bancshares Corp., 1858—; chmn. bd. First Bank and Trust Co., Cairo, Ill., 1962—; dir. Comml. & Indsl. Bank, Memphis. Trustee Gen. Bancshares Charitable Trust. Served with U.S. Merchant Marine, 1943-45. Mem. Mo. Bar Assn., Bar Assn. St. Louis, Delta Theta Phi (gold key for scholarship award 1938). Mason. Home: 702 Edgewood Pl Kirkwood MO 63122 Office: 901 Washington Av St Louis MO 63101

HAPPEL, HENRY WILLIAM, lawyer; b. Bklyn., Dec. 4, 1911; s. Henry W. and Ottilee (Kieselbach) H.; A.B. magna cum laude, Williams Coll., 1933; LL.B. (editor Law Rev.), Harvard, 1936; m. Alice M. Hicks, Sept. 14, 1935; 1 son, Henry William III. Admitted to N.Y. bar, 1937; with Gen. Counsel's Office, Navy Dept., 1944-45; with firm Brown, Wood, Fuller, Caldwell & Ivey, and predecessor, N.Y.C., 1936—, partner, 1943—. Sec. Nichols Engring. & Research Corp. Sec. Charles E. Merrill Trust; trustee Nichols Found., Yorkshire Fund; bd. dirs. Spence- Chapin Adoption Agy. Mem. Am., N.Y. State bar assns., Bar Assn. City N.Y., Phi Beta Kappa. Clubs: West Side Tennis (bd. govs. 1942-44, 55-56, sec. 1959-61) (Forest Hills, N.Y.); Eastern Lawn Tennis Assn. (L.I. del.- at-large) (N.Y.C.); Quogue (N.Y.) Field (bd. govs., sec. 1950-60). Home: 115 Hampton Rd Garden City NY 11530 Office: 70 Pine St New York City NY 10005

HAPPEL, JOHN, chem. engr., educator; b. Bklyn., Apr. 1, 1908; s. John and Emilie (Weinkauf) H.; B.S., Mass. Inst. Tech., 1929, M.S., 1930; D.Ch.E., Poly. Inst. Bklyn., 1948; m. Dorothy Merriam, 1951; children—Jill, George, Ruth. With Socony Vacuum Oil Co., 1930-48; prof. chem. engring., chmn. dept. N.Y.U., 1949—; cons. to various cos. on petro. chems.; chmn. bd. Methacet Chem. Corp., Plaswax Corp. Mem. petroleum industry war council, 1942-45; mem. tech. com. charge constrn. and operation world's largest butadiene plant for synthetic rubber, 1942-47. Recipient Certificate of Distinction, Poly. Inst. Bklyn.; Tyler award N.Y. sect. Am. Inst. Chem. Engrs. Registered profl. engr., N.Y. Fellow N.Y. Acad. Scis.; mem. Am. Chem. Soc. (honor scroll), Am. Inst. Chem. Engrs., Sigma Xi, Alpha Chi Sigma Phi Lambda Upsilon, Tau Beta Pi. Episcopalian. Club: Chemists (N.Y.C.). Contbr. tech. books and jours. Author: Chemical Process Economics, 1958; (with Howard Brenner) Low Reynolds Number Hydrodynamics, 1965. Translator: (with M.F. Delleo, Jr., G. Dembinski, A.H. Weiss) Catalysis by Non-Metals (from Russian by O.V. Krylov), 1970. Patentee in field. Home: 69 Tompkins Av Hastings-on-Hudson NY 10706 Office: NY U University Heights New York City NY 10453

HARA, EIKICHI, Japanese diplomat; b. Tokyo, Japan, June 11, 1919; s. Kichibei and Aki (Tomita) H.; ed. law dept. Tokyo U: m. Taeko Kano, Apr. 15, 1945; children—Hisako, Satoshi. Consul, N.Y.C., 1952-53, Hong Kong, 1953-54; counsellor of embassy, Belgrade, Yugoslavia, 1958-61; dir. in charge of Middle East, Fgn. Office, 1961-64, dep. dir. gen. in charge of Europe, 1964-65; minister of embassy, Taipei, 1965-68, Saigon, Vietnam, 1968-69; consul gen. of Japan, San Francisco, 1970—. Home: 801 El Camino Del Mar San Francisco CA 94121 Office: 1601 Post St San Francisco CA 94121

HARA, JAMES ELLSWORTH, oil co. exec.; b. Cleve., June 19, 1918; s. Arch and Elizabeth (Cowan) H.; B.B.A. with honors (scholar, award Am. Bankers Assn. 1940), Miami U., 1940; LL.B., U. Tex., 1947; m. Margaret Sue Parker, June 12, 1943; children—James Paul, Susan Margaret. Admitted to Tex. bar, 1947, Okla. bar, 1948; asso. atty. firm Critz & Kuykendall, Austin, Tex., 1947-48; with Skelly Oil Co., Tulsa, 1948—, v.p., asst. to pres., 1960-63, exec. v.p., 1963—, also dir.; exec. v.p., dir. Skelly Oil Co., Iran; pres., dir. Skelly Mozambigue Oil Co., Skelly Oil of Great Britain, Ltd.; dir. Skelly Oil Co. Libya, Skelly Internat. Oil Co., Skelly Pipe Line Co., Hawkeye Chem. Co., Nuclear Fuel Services, Inc., Skelly Leasing Co., Skelly Oil Can. Ltd., Boulder Bank & Trust Co. Bd. dirs. Tulsa Community Chest; adv. bd. Tulsa Salvation Army; trustee Tulsa Charity Horse Show, Hillcrest Med. Center; adv. bd. Indian Nat. Council Boy Scouts Am. Served as aviator USNR, 1941-45; PTO. Decorated D.F.C. with gold star, Navy Air medal with 3 gold stars. Mem. Am., Okla., Tex. bar assns., Ind. Petroleum Assn. Am. (dir.), Nat. Petroleum Refiners Assn. (dir.), Internat. Petroleum Expn. (dir.), Tulsa C. of C. (dir.), Phi Beta Kappa, Phi Delta Phi, Delta Sigma Pi. Club: Southern Hills Country. Home: 4432 S Atlanta Pl Tulsa OK 74105 Office: PO Box 1650 Tulsa OK 74102

HARALDSON, WESLEY CLIFFORD, govt. official; b. Aneta, N.D., Aug. 16, 1910; s. Henry and Caroline (Lang) H.; A.B., Jamestown (N.D.) Coll., 1935, LL.D., 1955; A.M., U. of Iowa, 1940; student U. Minn., 1940-43; m. Catherine Nashold, May 28, 1935; 1 dau., Ann Kristin. Economist, Fed. Res. Bank, N.Y. City, 1944, Fed. Reserve Bd., Washington, 1944-45, Dept. of State, Paris and Berlin, 1945-48; fgn. service officer since 1948, dir. finance and economic Free Ty. of Trieste 1949-52; first sec. U.S. Embassy, Tokyo, 1953; assigned Nat. War Coll., 1954; spl. asst. Dept. of State, Washington, 1955; counselor of embassy and dep. dir. U.S. Operations Mission. Saigon. Vietnam, 1956-58; dir. U.S. Mutual Security Mission, China, 1958-63, spl. asst. Dept. State, Washington, 1963-65; dir. U.S. AID Mission Philippines, Am. Embassy, Manila, 1965-70. Address: 10618 N Sundown Dr Scottsdale AZ

HARBAGE, ALFRED BENNETT, ret. educator; author; b. Phila., July 18, 1901; s. John and Elizabeth (Young) H.; A.B., U. Pa., 1924, A.M., 1926, Ph.D., 1929, Litt.D., 1954; m. Eliza Price Finnesey, Sept. 7, 1926; children—Diana (Mrs. Allen Baker), Klara (Mrs. David Manzella), Alfred, John. From instr. to asso. prof. English, U. Pa., 1924-42, prof. and grad. chmn., 1942-47; prof. English and comparative lit. Columbia, 1947-52; prof. Harvard, 1952-60, Cabot prof. English lit., 1960-70, emeritus, 1970—. Guggenheim fellow, 1953-54, 65-66. Del. Shakespeare Conf. England, 1947; Alexander lectr. U. Toronto, 1954-55; Brit. Acad. Shakespeare lectr., 1969. Mem. Shakespeare Assn., Modern Lang. Assn., Am. Acad. Arts and Scis., Am. Philos. Soc., Elizabethan Club, Phi Beta Kappa. Author: Shakespeare's Audience, 1941; As They Liked It; on Shakespeare and Morality, 1947; Shakespeare and the Rival Traditions, 1952; Theatre for Shakespeare, 1955; William Shakespeare: A Reader's Guide, 1963; Conceptions of Shakespeare, 1966; Shakespeare's Songs, 1970. Gen. editor Pelican edit. Shakespeare. Contbr. jours. Home: 52 Grant Av Cherry Hill NJ 08034

HARBAGE, MARY, educator, editor; b. Madison, O.; d. Arnett and Helen (Postle) Harbage; student Ohio Wesleyan U., 1927-29; B.A. with honors and distinction, Ohio State U., 1931, M.A., 1949; Ed.D., Columbia Tchrs. Coll., 1963. Tchr. elementary schs., Ohio, 1931-43; recreation dir., club dir. A.R.C., Norwich, Eng., 1943-46; asst. prof. Miami U., Oxford, O., 1946- 49; dir. elementary edn. City of Akron, O., 1949-56; chmn. Am. Edn. Mission to Korea, 1952-53; dir. research elementary div. Scholastic mags., N.Y.C., 1956-63, editor Explorer mag., 1957-63, News Trails mag., 1960-63, Vacation Fun mag., 1961-63, editorial and curriculum cons., elementary div., 1957-65, contbr. elementary sect. Scholastic Tchr., 1963—; head elementary edn. dept. U. Ark., 1963-65; prof. edn. Wright State U., Dayton, O., 1965—. Mem. Assn. Childhood Edn. (v.p.), N.E.A., Assn. Supervision and Curriculum Devel., Nat. Council Tchrs. English, Phi Beta Kappa, Pi Lambda Theta, Phi Alpha Theta, Delta Kappa Gamma, Kappa Delta Pi. Contbg. author: Creativity in Teaching, 1961. Address: Coll Edn Wright State U Colonel Glenn Rd Dayton OH 45431

HARBAUGH, CHARLES WILLIAM, assn. exec.; b. Port Huron, Mich., May 9, 1914; s. Clayton Dane and Nellie (Crull) H.; B.S., Purdue, 1936, postgrad., 1937-38; m. Charlotte Cooper, Jan. 25, 1952; 1 son, William S. Tchr. pub. schs., Lafayette, Ind., 1936-41; exec. v.p. Connersville (Ind.) C. of C., 1946-47; sec., mgr. Anderson (Ind.) C. of C., 1947-50; exec. v.p. The Am. Guard Co., Anderson, 1950-52; adminstrv. staff U.S. C. of C., Washington, 1952—, gen. mgr. communications and marketing, 1964-70, exec. mgr., 1970—; lectr. in field, 1948—, Bd. dirs. Nat. Center Vol. Action. Served with USAAF, 1941-45. Decorated Bronze Star; recipient Distinguished Service medal Jr. C. of C., 1951. Mem. Am. C. of C. Execs. Assn., Am. Soc. Assn. Execs. Clubs: Army-Navy (Washington); Kenwood Country (Kenwood, Md.). Home: 6128 Overlea Rd Washington DC 20016 Office: 1615 H St NW Washington DC 20036

HARBAUGH, JANE WORTH, univ. dean; b. Balt., Apr. 24, 1930; d. Vernon Leslie and Charlotte (Kirby) Harbaugh; A.B., Tufts Coll., 1952; M.A., Fletcher Sch. Law and Diplomacy, 1953, Ph.D., 1957. Instr. history, polit. sci. U. Chattanooga, 1957-59, asst. prof., 1959-62, asso. prof., 1962-65, prof., chmn. dept. history, 1965-69, now dean Coll. Arts and Scis., U. Tenn. at Chattanooga, 1969—. Rockefeller Found. research grantee, 1956; recipient Evans Found. award, 1963; fellow Center E. Asian Studies, Harvard, 1960-61. Mem. ad hoc com. Adv. Editorial Bd., U. State N.Y., 1965-66; v.p. Adult Edn. Council Chattanooga Area, 1962-64, dir., 1958-60; bd. dirs. Allied Arts Council of Chattanooga, 1970-71. Mem. Assn. for Asian Studies (chmn. com. on undergrad. edn. 1966-68). Democrat. Home: 720 Maryland Circle Chattanooga TN 37412

HARBAUGH, JOHN WARVELLE, educator; b. Madison, Wis., Aug. 6, 1926; s. Marion Dwight and Marjorie (Warvelle) H.; student Denison U., 1944-45; B.S., U. Kan., 1948, M.S., 1950; Ph.D., U. Wis., 1955; m. Josephine Taylor, Nov. 24, 1951; children-Robert, Dwight, Richard. Geologist U.S. Geol. Survey, Denver, 1950, Carter Oil Co., Shreveport, La. and Tulsa, 1951-53; asst. prof. Stanford, 1955-61, asso. prof., 1961-66, prof., chmn. dept. geology, 1966—, faculty athletic rep., 1970—; cons. in field. Served with USNR, 1944-46. Recipient U. Kan. Haworth distinguished alumni award, 1968. Fellow Geol. Soc. Am.; mem. Am. Assn. Petroleum Geologists (recipient A.I. Levorsen award 1970). Author: with Daniel F. Merriam) Computer Applications in Stratigraphic Analysis, 1968; Stratigraphy and Geologic Time, 1968; (with Graeme Bonham-Carter) Computer Simulation in Geology, 1970. Home: 683 Salvatierra St Stanford CA 94305

HARBAUGH, WILLIAM HENRY, educator, historian; b. Newark, Jan. 16, 1920; s. William K. and Emily (Wright) H.; A.B., U. Ala., 1942; M.A., Columbia, 1947; Ph.D., Northwestern U., 1954; m. Virginia Wayne Talbot, Aug. 15, 1953; children—Emelyn Hartridge, William Talbot, Henry Richmond. Instr., U. Conn., 1946-49, 53-56, asst. prof., 1956-61; instr. U. Md., 1952-53; vis. asso. prof. Rutgers U., 1961-62; prof., chmn. dept. history Bucknell U., Lewisburg, Pa., 1962-66; prof. U. Va., 1966—. Served to capt. AUS, 1942-45; ETO. Decorated Croix de Guerre with gold star. sr. fellow Yale Law Sch., 1960-61. Mem. Am. Civil Liberties Union, Phi Beta Kappa (hon.), Chi Phi. Democrat. Unitarian. Club: Keswick. Author: Power and Responsibility: Life and Times of Theodore Roosevelt, 1961, rev. as The Life and Times of Theodore Roosevelt, 1963. Home: 1930 Thomson Rd Charlottesville VA 22903

HARBELL, JOHN B., educator. Prof., chmn. dept. econs. and bus. San Francisco State Coll. Office: San Francisco State Coll San Francisco CA 94132*

HARBER, WINFORD ELMER, banker; b. Pineville, Ark., July 3, 1892; s. Thomas W. and Cynthia (Franks) H.; ed. pub. schs., Seminole, Okla.; m. Mauda Stroud, Feb. 1, 1936. With First Nat. Bank, Seminole, 1911—, pres., 1921-70, chmn. bd., 1970—; pres. Am. Nat. Bank & Trust Co., 1935-70, chmn. bd., 1970—; dir., chmn. bd. R.F.C., Washington, 1950; dir. Liberty Nat. Bank, Oklahoma City. Bd. regents Okla. A. and M. Coll. 1945-64; mem. sch. bd., Shawnee, Okla., 1944. Served with U.S. Army, World War I. Mem. Shawnee C. of C. (bd. dirs.), Okla. C. of C. Democrat (nat. committeeman from Okla. 1948). Presbyn. Mason. Clubs: Oklahoma (Oklahoma City); Country (Shawnee). Home: 2403 E Highland Shawnee OK 74801 Office: American Nat Bank and Trust Co Shawnee OK 74801

HARBERGER, ARNOLD CARL, economist; b. Newark, July 27, 1924; s. Ferdinand C. and Martha (Bucher) H.; student Johns Hopkins, 1941-43; M.A., U. Chgo., 1947, Ph.D., 1950; m. Ana Beatriz Valjalo, Mar. 15, 1958; children—Paul Vincent, Carl David. Asst. prof. polit. economy Johns Hopkins, 1949-53; asso. prof. econs. U. Chgo., 1953-59, prof., 1959—; chmn. dept., 1964—, dir. Center Latin Am. Econ. Studies, 1965—; vis. prof. Mass. Inst. Tech., Center Internat. Studies, New Delhi, 1961-62; vis. prof. Econ. Devel. Inst., Internat. Bank Reconstrn. and Devel., 1965; cons. Internat. Monetary Fund, 1950, Pres' Materials Policy Commn., 1951- 52, U.S. Treasury Dept., 1961—, Com. Econ. Devel., 1961—, Planning Commn. India, 1961-62, Pan Am. Union, 1962—, Dept. State, 1962—, Planning Dept., Panama. Ford Found., 1967—. Served with AUS,1943- 46. Guggenheim fellow, Fulbright scholar; faculty research fellow Social Sci. Research Council; Ford Found. faculty research fellow, 1968-69. Fellow Econometric Soc.; mem. Am. Econ. Assn. (mem. exec. Com. 1970—), Royal Econ. Soc., Phi Beta Kappa. Editor: Demand for Durable Goods, 1960; The Taxation of Income from Capital, 1968; Key Problems of Ecomix Policy In Latin America, 1970. Contbr. sci. papers profl. jours. govt. publs. Home: 4840 S Greenwood Av Chicago IL 60615

HARBERT, FREDERICK, ret. educator, otolaryngologist; b. Detroit, Jan. 27. 1905; s. Frederick and Albertina (Burksthal) H.; A.B., M.B., Wayne State U., 1928, M.D., 1929; M.S. in Medicine, U. Pa., 1940, D.Sc. in Otolaryngology, 1942; m. Frances M. Clark, Jan. 8, 1927; children—E. Lorraine, Winifred L., Barbara E., Mary J., Carol Ann, E. Jean. Commd. lt. (j.g.) M.C., USN, 1928, advanced through grades to capt.; intern U.S. Naval Hosp., Phila., 1928-29; mem. eye, ear, nose and throat staff Naval Hosp., Newport, R.I., 1931-33, Washington, 1934-35, Naval Hosp., Phila., 1938-40, U.S.S. Relief, 1940-42; resident in ophthalmology Ill. Eye and Ear Infirmary, 1943; chief eye, ear, nose and throat dept. Naval Hosp., Phila., 1945-51, 52-54, Bethesda, Md., 1951-52; ret., 1954; cons. U.S. Naval Hosp., Phila., VA Hosp., Wilmington, Del., Phila. Gen. Hosp.; guest lectr. ophthalmology Grad. Sch. Medicine U. Pa., 1946-48, asso. prof., 1948-51, vis. lectr., 1953-64; prof. otolaryngology, head dept. Jefferson Med. Coll., Phila., 1954-70. Prin. investigator NIH grants, 1959-70 adv. group VA 1965-70. Recipient Distinguished Service citation, Wayne State Med. Coll., Wayne State Alumn. Assn., Am. Acad. Otolaryngology, Am. Acad, Facial Plastic and Reconstructive Surgery. Diplomate Am. Bd. Otolaryngology, Bd. Ophthalmology. Fellow Am., Internat. colls. surgeons, Am. Otorhinologic Soc. for Plastic Surgery (pres. 1964), Acad. Facial Plastic and Reconstructive Surgery, Am. Laryngological, Rhinological and Otological Soc. (v.p. 1968), Am. Otological Soc; mem. Am. Acoustical Soc., Otosclerosis Study Group, Am., Pa. (v.p. 1965) acads. opthalmology and otolaryngology. Phila. Art Alliance, Am. Council Otolaryngology, N.Y. Acad. Scis., Alpha Omega Alpha, sigma Xio Contbr. articles to profl. jours. Home: Worton MD 21678

HARBESON, JOHN FREDERICK, architect; b. Phila., July 30, 1888; s. James Page and Fredericka (Krauter) H.; M.S. in Architecture, U. Pa., 1911; m. Georgiana Newcomb Brown, Oct. 5, 1916 (div. 1929); children—John Frederick (dec.), Paul Cret. Began practice at Phila., 1911; instr. in perspective Pa. Acad. Fine Arts, 1916-55; asso. prof. archtl. design Sch. Fine Arts, U. Pa., 1919-48; sometime chmn. dept. architecture; partner of Paul P. Cret, 1919-45; now Harbeson, Hough, Livingston & Larson, architects, consultants to Am. Battle Monuments Commn. and to architect of U.S. Capitol, Washington; cons. architect Nat. Monument Commn., Corregidor Bataan Meml. Commn.; prin. works: include Pioneer Mother Monument (with Charles Grafly, sculptor), 1916; Mallory Meml. Fountain, Phila., 1917; Whitfield Meml. (with R. Tait McKenzie, sculptor); restoration of Senate and House chambers U.S. Capitol, 1948; Normandy Am. War Meml.; interior design Pa. R.R., Senator and Congl. trains. Pres. Carpenters' Co. of Carpenters Hall, 1965. Recipient Arthur Spayde Brooke gold medal in design U. Pa., 1910: Walter Cope meml. prize Phila. chpt. A.I.A. and T Square Club, 1913; Henry Hering Meml. medal, 1960; Benjamin Franklin fellow Royal Soc. Arts, 1960; John Howard Benson award Am. Inst. Commemorative Art, 1961, Medal of Honor, Nat. Sculpture Soc., 1964. Fellow A.I.A, N.A.D. (pres. 1959-62); mem. Nat. Sculpture Soc. (v.p. 1964-65), Soc. Archtl. Historians, Nat. Trust Historic Preservation, Sigma Xi. Presbyn. Clubs: Century, Salmagundi (N.Y.C.); Cosmos (Washington); Philobiblon, University, Art Alliance, Franklin Chess (Phila.). Author: The Study of Architectural Design, 1926. Home: 2105 Delancey St Philadelphia PA 19103 Office: Architects Bldg Philadelphia PA 19103

HARBIN, JOHN PICKENS, service co. exec.; b. Waxahachie, Tex., July 17, 1917; s. E.P. and Mary Joy (Beale) H.; B.B.A., U. Tex., 1939; m. Dorothy Lee Middleton, Oct. 18, 1943; 1 dau., Linda Ann. Accounting tng. program Carter Oil Co. (Standard Oil of N.J.), Tulsa, 1939-40; accountant Creole Petroleum Corp., Venezuela, 1940-42, 45-47; became controller, asst. sec. Halliburton Co., 1948, now sr. v.p. finance, dir.; dir. Otis Engring. Corp., Jet Research Center, Halliburton Co. (Can.), Halliburton Ltd. (Eng.), Brown & Root, Life Ins. Co. of S.W., Highlands Ins. Co., Harlan Inc. Served as lt. USNR, 1943-45. Mem. Ind. Petroleum Assn. of Am., Financial Execs. Inst., Am. Petroleum Inst., C. Of of C., Delta Tau Delta, Beta Alpha Psi. Clubs: Dallas Petroleum, Chaparrel, Brook Hollow Golf. Home: 5125 Springmeadow Dr Dallas TX 75229 Office: 3211 Southland Center Dallas TX 75201

HARBIN, WAYNE DEWITT, mfg. co. exec.; b. Donna, Tex., Apr. 29, 1925; s. Jesse Matthews and Lela Pearl (Betts) H.; B.B.A., U. Tex., 1949; A.M.P., Harvard, 1962; m. Elinor Victoria Telish, Apr. 17, 1946; children—Kenneth Wayne, Richard Wayne. Accounting mgr. Arthur Young & Co., N.Y.C., 1949-58, partner, Houston, 1958-68; chmn., pres. Marathon Mfg. Co., Houston, 1968—; vice-chmn. bd. Crutcher Resources Corp., Houston, 1968—; chmn. bd. R.G. Letourneau Inc., Metallic Bldg. Co., Carey-McFall Co., Mineral Oil Refining Co., George Franke Sons Co., Marathon Battery Co.; dir. Service corp. Internat. Mem. adv. council U. Tex. Served with USNR, 1942-46. C.P.A., N.Y., Tex. Mem. Am. Inst. C.P.A.s, N.Y., Tex. socs. C.P.A.s. Mason. Clubs: Houston, River Oaks Country, Coronada (Houston). Home: 3994 Inverness St Houston TX 77019 Office: 801 Houston Natural Gas Bldg Houston TX 77002

HARBISON, FREDERICK HARRIS, labor economist; b. Sewickley, Pa., Dec. 18, 1912; s. Ralph Warner and Helen (Harris) H.; A.B., Princeton, 1934, Ph.D., 1940; m. Josephine Koppelman, Jan. 17, 1941; children—Ralph W., William A., Henry H. Research asst. indsl. relations sect. Princeton, 1938-40 and internat. affairs, 1955—, Straus prof. of human relations, since 1967—; instr. econs. U. Chgo., 1940-41, prof. econs., exec. officer indsl. relations center, 1945-55. Labor, Manpower cons. WPB, War Labor Bd., ASF, Petroleum Adminstrn. for War, 1941-45. Trustee Am. U. Cairo. Mem. Am. Econ. Assn., Nat. Acad. Arbitrators, Indsl. Relations Research Assn., Am. Philos. Soc. , Nat. Acad. on Edn. Author: Seniority Policies and Procedures as Developed Through Collective Bargaining, 1941 (with Robert Dublin) Patterns of Union-Management Relations, 1947; (with John Coleman) Goals and Strategy in Collective Bargaining, 1951; Human Resources for Egyptian Enterprise, 1959; Management in Industrial Society (with Charles A. Myers), 1959, Education, Manpower and Economic Growth, 1963. Author articles on collective bargaining, mgmt., edn., unions. Home: 159 Hartley Av Princeton NJ 08540

HARBISON, HERBERT WATSON, utility co. exec.; b. St. Louis, Aor. 25, 1907; s. Herbert Watson and Cora (Scott) H.; LL.B., Coll. City St. Louis, 1941; m. Louis Cowgill, Aug. 30, 1930; 1 dau., Janice C. With Union Electric Co., St. Louis 1929—, successively accountant, asst. claims agt., asst. treas., now treas. Mason (trustee 1960—; Shriner). Home: 4022 Utah St St Louis MO 63116 Office: 1 Memorial Dr St Louis MO 63133

HARBISON, MCCLARTY, investment exec.; b. Shelbyville, Ky., Oct. 7, 1895; s. Howard and Anna Pennebaker (McClarty) H.; A.B., U. Ky., 1917; m. Frances Dudley Geisel, Nov. 19, 1919; children—Edward McClarty, Frances Dudley. Real estate business, Lexington, Ky., 1919-21; partner Dunk Harbison & Co., Los Angeles, 1923- 43, Harbison & Gregory, 1943-48, Harbison & Henderson, 1948-64; pres. Los Angeles Stock Exchange, 1932-45, chmn., 1946—; former vice chmn., bd. govs. Pacific Coast Stock Exchange; v.p. McDonnell & Co., Inc., mems. N.Y. Stock Exchange, 1964-69. Mem. city council, San Marino, 1954-64. Past chmn. San Marino Pub. Library. Served as 1st lt. U.S. Army, 1917-19; AEF. Mem. U.S., Cal., Los Angeles chambers commerce. Clubs: Amnandale Country (Pasadena, Cal.); Los Angeles Stock Exchange, Los Angeles Bond. Address: 1045 Roanoke Rd San Marino CA 91108

HARBISON, SAMUEL POLLOCK, II, surgeon; b. Sewickley, Pa., Mar. 15, 1909; s. Ralph Warner and Helen (Harris) H.; A.B., Princeton, 1931; M.D., Cornell, 1936; m. Mary Jane Bierman, July 13, 1949; 1 son, Samuel Pollock III. Intern Barnes Hosp., St. Louis, 1937, resident surgeon, 1940-41, instr. surgery, 1941-46; chmn. dept. surgery Sch. Medicine, U. Pitts., 1950-63, asso. dean, 1963- -, prof. surgery, 1950—. Served 1t. col. M.C., AUS, 1942- 46. Decorated Legion of Merit. Diplomate Am. Bd. Surgery. Fellow A.C.S. (sec. 1962-68, 1st v.p. 1971); mem. Excelsior Surg. Soc., Am., Central surg. assns., Soc. U. Surgeons. Home: 840 Canterbury La Pittsburgh PA 15232 Office: Sch Medicine Scaife Hall Pittsburgh PA 15213

HARBISON, WINFRED AUDLF, educator; b. Montgomery County, Ind., Mar. 8, 1904; s. Alvin Turner and Eva Florence (Grimes) H.: A.B., Wabash Coll., 1924; M.A., U. of Ill., 1926, Ph.D., 1930; m. Ocie Burnice Kelly, Nov. 24, 1927; 1 son, Stanley Lincoln. Asst. instr. in history U. of Ill., 1927-29; instr. in history Wayne State U., 1929-33, asst. prof., 1933-42, asso. prof., 1942-47, prof., 1947—, asso. dean adminstrn., 1952-53, chmn. dept. history, 1951-53, acting dean grad. sch., 1954-56, v.p. academic adminstrn., 1953-70; Fulbright lectr. Am. history, U. Aberdeen, Scotland, 1953-54. Served as lt. comdr., USNR, 1943-46. Mem. Miss. Valley, So. hist. assns., Mich., Ind., Detroit, Disciples (trustee) historical societies, also U.S. Naval Inst., Detroit Lincoln Group, Phi Beta Kappa. Mem. Christian Ch. Author: (with Alfred H. Kelly) The American Constitution; Its Origins and Development, 1948, 70; also articles on Abraham Lincoln and edn. Home: 8549 Marygrove Dr Detroit MI 48221

HARBOURT, CYRUS OSCAR, educator; b. Baton Rouge, June 1, 1931; s. John Leslie and Marie (Berthelot) H.; B.S. in Elec. Engring., La. State U., 1952; M.S., Mass. Inst. Tech., 1955; Ph.D., Syracuse U., 1961; m. Mary Josephine Heuvel, Dec. 27, 1952; children—Ellen Catherine, Joan Carol, Cyrus David, Anna Marie, Mary Alice. Instr., La. State U., 1954-55, Syracuse (N.Y.) U., 1957-61; asst. prof., then asso. prof. U. Tex. at Austin, 1961-67; prof. elec. engring., chmn. dept. U. Mo. at Columbia, 1967—. Asso. prin. engr. Radiation, Inc., Melbourne, Fla., summer 1965; cons. to industry. Served with AUS, 1955-57. Recipient Engring. Teaching Excellence award Gen. Dynamics Co.-U. Tex. 1963. Mem. I.E.E.E., Am. Soc. Engring. Edn., Sigma Xi, Tau Beta Pi, Phi Kappa Phi, Omicron Delta Kappa. Roman Catholic. Co-author: Network Computer Analysis, 1969. Home: 2306 Ridgefield Rd Columbia MO 65201

HARBRECHT, PAUL PETER, educator; b. Detroit, Apr. 17, 1923; s. Paul Peter and Josephine (Rettinger) H.; student Xavier U., Cin., 1941-44; A.B., Loyola U., Chgo., 1945; LL.B., Georgetown U., 1950; S.J.D., Columbia Univ., 1958; m. Wanda (Farris) Aileen Harbrecht. Entered the Society of Jesus, 1941; ordained priest Roman Cath. Ch., 1955; vis. scholar Columbia, 1956-57; mem. Inst. Social Order, Nat. Jesuit Social Sci. Center, 1957-63; research project dir. 20th Century Fund, 1958, 61-64; asst. prof. law St. Louis U., 1958-59; asst. prof: of law U. of Detroit School of Law, 1960-68, dean, 1965-68; sr. program asso. Nat. Inst. Pub. Affairs, 1968—; prof. law Osgoode Hall, York U., 1969—; cons. Fund for Republic, 1960—; admitted D.C. bar, 1951, Mich. bar, 1967, U.S. Ct. Appeals, Mem. exec. com. Inst. for Internat. and Fgn. Trade Law, Georgetown U. Law Center; vice chmn. Mich. State Housing and Devel. Authority. Chmn. bd. dirs. Georgetown U. Mem. Am. Bar Assn., Phi Alpha Delta. Author: Pension Funds and Economic Power, 1959; (with A. A. Berle, Jr.) Toward the Paraproprietal Society, 1960. Office: 1825 K St NW Washington DC 20006

HARBURG, EDGAR Y., lyricist, librettist, author; b. N.Y.C., Apr. 8, 1898; s. Lewis and Mary (Ricing) H.; B.S., City Coll. N.Y., 1918; m. Alice Richmond, Feb.23, 1923; children—Marjorie, Ernest; m. 2d, Edelaine Roden, Jan. 16, 1943. Propr. elec. appliance co., 1921-29; contbr. light verse newspapers, mags., 1916-29; lyricist theatrical prodns. Earl Carroll's Sketchbook, 1929; The Garrick Gaieties, 3d edit., 1930; Earl Carroll's Vanities, 8th edit., 1930; Shoot the Works, 1931; Ballyhoo of 1932, 1932; Americana, 3d edit., 1932; Walk a Little Faster, 1932; Ziegfield Follies, 1934; Life Begins at 8:40, 1934; Hooray for What, 1937; Hold on to Your Hats, 1940; Bloomer Girl, 1944; lyricist, co-libretist theatrical prodns. Finian's Rainbow, 1947; Flahooley, 1951; Jamaica, 1957; The Happiest Girl in the World, 1961, Darling of the Day, 1969; numerous lyrics for films, 1930—, latest being Wizard of Oz, 1937, Day at the Circus, 1939, Cabin in the Sky, 1940, Kismet, 1944; Can't Help Singing, 1944; Centennial Summer, 1946; State Struck, 1946; California, 1946; Gay Purree, 1961. Oscar award for Over the Rainbow, Acad. Motion Picture Arts and Scis., 1937, also citations for Brother Can You Spare a Dime?, Happiness is a Thing Called Joe, Cabin in the Sky, More and More; Townsend Harris award outstanding alumni Coll. City N.Y., 1950; Henderson award for best mus. comedy Finian's Rainbow, 1947-48. Mem. A.S.C.A.P., Dramatists Guild, Am. Guild Authors and Composers, Authors League Am, Screen Writers Guild, Acad. Motion Picture Arts and Scis., Am. Civil Liberties Union, N.A.A.C.P. Home: 262 Central Park W New York City NY 10024 Office: 551 Fifth Av New York City NY 10017

HARBURY, HENRY ALEXANDER, educator, biochemist; b. The Hague, Netherlands, Dec. 11, 1927; s. Lawrence and Josephine (Elion) H.; B.A., Cornell U., 1947; Ph.D., Johns Hopkins U., 1953; m. Dorothy Ann Harley, Dec. 20, 1947; children—Katharine Edith, Jennifer Kristina, Olin Laurence, Alexander Robert. Naturalized, 1945. Instr. biochemistry Yale, 1953-55, asst. prof., 1955-60, 1956-61, asso. prof. 1960-67; prof. biochemistry, chmn. sect. biochemistry and molecular biology U. Cal. at Santa Barbara, 1967—, chmn. dept. biol. scis., 1969—. Markle Scholar med. sci., 1956-61; recipient Francis Gilman Blake award, 1964. Mem. Am. Soc. Biol. Chemists, Biophys. Soc., Am. Chem. Soc., A.A.A.S., Sigma Xi. Research structure and function of proteins; oxidative enzymes. Home: 4005 Ramitas Rd Santa Barbara CA 93110

HARBY, JACK DELAMOTTE, sci. products co. exec.; b. Sumter, S.C., May 6, 1916; s. Arthur Sydney and Ella (Dils) H.; student U. Rochester, 1933-35; B.S., U.S. Naval Acad., 1939; m. Josephine Conklin Sutton, June 8, 1939; children—Diana (Mrs. Roger E. VanDuzer), Stephen, John. With Bausch & Lomb, Rochester, N.Y., 1940—, marketing exec. v.p., 1963-65, v.p., gen. mgr., 1965-67, exec. v.p., dir., now pres. Trustee Rochester Inst. Tech., Eastman Dental Center. Mem. Rochester C. of C., Indsl. Mgmt. Council, Psi Upsilon. Clubs: Monroe Golf (Pittsford); Rochester. Home: 40 Oak Manor Pittsford NY 14534 Office: 635 St Paul St Rochester NY 14602

HARCHA, HOWARD HENRY, Jr., lawyer; b. Portsmouth, O., Jan. 22, 1927; s. Howard Henry and Edith (Redwine) H.; LL.B., Ohio State U., 1952; m. Mary Lee White, Apr. 10, 1955; children-Howard Henry III, Michele. Admitted to Ohio bar, 1952; practice in Portsmouth, 1953—; asst. prosecuting atty., 1955-62; mem. firm Kimble, Schapiro, Stevens, Harcha & Young, 1959—. Dir. Nat. Bank of Portsmouth. Mem. Methodist Ohio Conf. Pastoral Care and Counseling Commn., 1965—. Pres. Child Welfare Bd., A.R.C., United Fund Bd., Portsmouth City Health Board; mem. Portsmouth Library Bd. Served with USNR, 1945-46, U.S. Army, 1951-53. Mem. Ohio, Portsmouth bar assns., Ohio Acad. Trial Lawyers Assn. (trustee), Am. Trial Lawyers Assn., Portsmouth C. of C. (past dir.), Am. Legion, Ohio State U. Alumni Assn., Delta Tau Delta, Phi Delta Phi. Republican. Mason, Kiwanian, Elk. Home: 2809 Willow Way Portsmouth OH 45662 Office: Nat Bank Bldg Portsmouth OH 45662

HARCHAR, HARRY A., assn. exec.; b. Bethlehem, Pa., June 3, 1912; s. Andrew and Julia (Skultety) H.; student Lehigh U., 1935-39; m. Helen Cylmer, Aug. 9, 1939; 1 dau., Helen C. (Mrs. Bryant). Asst. dir. health and safety service Boy Scouts Am., 1939-40, field scout exec., Omaha, 1940-41, asst. dir. scouting services, 1947-51, circulation mgr. Boys' Life mag., 1951, exec. editor, 1951-52, editor, 1952-64, editor Scouting mag., also nat. dir. editorial service Boy Scouts Am., 1964-71, nat. coordinator XIII World Jamboree, Japan, 1971, scout exec. Far E. council, 1971—. Officer-in-charge editions Stars and Stripes, ETO, also writer column Hash Marks. 1941-45; exec. officer orientation br. information and edn. div., Gen. Staff, War Dept., 1945-46. Mem. Pa. Soc. Pi Delta Epsilon, Sigma Delta Chi, Alpha Phi Omega. Clubs: Overseas Press, Army-Navy (N.Y.C.); American (Tokyo). Editor: Boys Life Treasury. Home: 216 Maxwell Av Hightstown NJ 08520 Office: Boy Scouts Am APO San Francisco CA 96323

HARCLEROAD, FRED FARLEY, educator; born Cheyenne, Wyo., Nov. 22, 1918; s. Fred Farley and Ina Mary (Livermore) H.; A.B., Colo. State Coll. Edn., 1939, M.A., 1942; Ph.D., Stanford, 1948; m. Moyne Payne, Dec. 20, 1942; children—Patricia Irene, Fred Douglass. Tchr., coach Ault (Colo.) High School, 1939-42, prin., 1942-43; tchr., coach, counselor Menlo Sch. and Jr. Coll., 1943- 46; asst., acting instr. Stanford, summers 1944, 45; staff San Diego State Coll., 1946-52, coordinator audio-visual service, 1947-50, coordinator secondary edn., 1949-51, chmn. div. edn., 1951-52; dean instrn. San Jose State Coll. 1952-57, dean of the college, 1957-59; pres. California State Coll. at Hayward, 1959-68; prof. higher edn. U. Ia., Iowa City, 1968—. Pres. Am. Coll Testing Program, 1967—. Pres.-elect Am. Assn. State Colls. and Univs., bd. dirs., 1965-68, chmn, com. internat. edn., 1966-69, chmn. or mem.. com. on purposes and policies, 1966-71. Mem. Am. Council Edn (mem. Pacific coast com, 1955-58), Western Coll. Assn. (dir. 1963-67), N.E.A. (dept. audio visual instrn. com. on profl. edn. 1951- 53, mem. adv. bd. ednl. policies commission 1961-63, 65-68, Cal. Audio- Visual Edn. Assn., (pres. So. sect. 1950-51, sec. 1951-52), Cal. Council Tchr. Edn.(chmn. ednl. TV com.), Phi Delta Kappa, Phi Alpha Theta, Kappa Delta Pi, Phi Kappa Phi, Phi Mu Alpha, Sinfonia, Blue Key. Club: Commonwealth. Co-author: International Education in the Developing State Colleges and Universities, 1966; co-author: Audio-Visual Instruction: Media and Methods, 1959, rev. edits., 1964, 69; sr. author: The Developing State Colleges and Universities: Historical Background, Current Status, and Future Plans, 1969. Editor: Audio Visual Administration (with William Allen), 1951; The Education of the Audio Visual Communication Specialist, 1960; Learning Resources in Colleges and Universities, 1964; Issues of the Seventies: The Future of Higher Education, 1970. Audio-Visual editor Cal. Jour. Secondary Edn., 1952- 55. Author mag. articles edn., also textbooks. Home: Iowa City, IA 52240.

HARCOURT, WILLIAM EDWARD, (2d Viscount), banker; b. London, Eng., Oct. 5, 1908; s. Lewis (1st Viscount) and Mary (Burns) H.; student Eton Coll., 1922-26; B.A., Christ Ch., Oxford, 1930, M.A., 1954; m. Hon. Elizabeth Grosvenor, 1931; children—Elizabeth Ann (Mrs. Crispin Gascoigne), Penelope Mary (Mrs. Antony David Motion), Virginia Vernon (Mrs. Julian Wells); m. 2d, Elizabeth Sonia Snagge, 1946 (dec. 1959). With Morgan Grenfell & Co., Ltd., mcht. bankers, at London, 1931—, mng. dir., 1938—, chmn., 1968; minister econ. Brit. Embassy, head U.K. Treas. Del., Washington, 1954-57; U.K. exec. dir. Internat. Monetary Fund, 1954-57. Internat. Bank for Reconstrn. and Development 1954-57; chmn Legal & Gen. Assurance Soc., Ltd., British Commonwealth Ins. Co., Ltd., Gresham Life Assurance Soc., Ltd., Gresham Fire & Accident Ins. Soc., Ltd., Mem. Departmental (Radcliffe) Com. Monetary and Credit Policy, 1957-59. Trustee Rhodes Trust: chmn. trustees London Mus.; chmn. bd. of govs. Museum of London; hon. fellow St. Antony's Coll., Oxford,

Eng. Served Brit. Army, 1939-45 (lt. col.). Decorated officer Order Brit. Empire, Knight Comdr. St. Michael and St. George. Clubs: Whites, Pratt's (London); Metropolitan (Washington). Home: Stanton Harcourt Oxford England Office: 23 Great Winchester St London EC 2 England

HARCUM, EUGENE RAE, educator; b. Cambridge, Md., Mar. 1, 1927; s. Eugene Payten and Myrtle (Larmore) H.; B.S., Coll. William and Mary, 1950; M.A., Johns Hopkins, 1952; Ph.D., U. Mich., 1955; m. Phoebe Carroll Martin, Aug. 30, 1952; children—Sarah Lois, James Payten. Jr. instr., then research asst. Johns Hopkins, 1950-52; with U. Mich., 1952-58, research asso., 1957-58; mem. faculty Coll. William and Mary, 1958—, prof. psychology, 1965—; vis. scholar U. Cal. at Berkeley, 1967-68. Mem. com. vision Nat. Acad. Sci.-NRC, 1960-71. Bd. dirs. Wesley Found., Williamsburg Methodist Ch., 1950; mem. commn. coll. religious life Va. Conf. Meth. Ch., 1965—. Served with USNR, 1945-46. Recipient J. Shelton Horsley award Va. Acad. Sci., 1964. Fellow A.A.A.S.; mem. Va. Acad. Sci., Am., Eastern, Southeastern psychol. assns., Phi Beta Kappa, Sigma Xi, Pi Tau Chi, Psi Chi. Author: Reproduction of Linear Visual Patterns Tachistoscopically Exposed in Various Orientations, 1964. Asso. editor Perceptual and Motor Skills, 1964. Home: 103 Plantation Dr Williamsburg VA 23185

HARD, WALTER LEON, anatomist; b. E. Lansing, Mich., Feb. 8, 1912; s. Leon Delos and Josephine (Nelson) H.; A.B., Albion (Mich.) Coll., 1934; Ph.D., Duke, 1937; m. Harriette Violette Pollard. June 15, 1938 (div. 1965); children—Frank Delos, Walter Carl; m. 2d, Rita Swisher Haye, 1966 (div. 1970); m. 3d, Harriette V. Pollard, Sept. 3, 1970. Teaching fellow, Duke, dept. zoology, 1934-37; instr., dept. zoology, Univ. Md., 1937, asst. prof., 1938-40, asst. prof., dept. microscopic anatomy, sch. of medicine, 1941-44; asst. prof., dept. anatomy, Med. Coll., State of S.C., 1944-45, asso. prof., 1946; prof. and chmn. dept. anatomy, Univ. S.D., 1946-66, acting dean, School of Medicine, 1951, dean, 1952-66; prof., vice chmn. dept. anatomy U. Neb., 1966—. Mem. Volunteer Coast Guard Res., Baltimore, 1942-44. Mem. Am. Assn. Anatomists, Am. Soc. Zoologists, Soc. Exptl. Biology and Med., A.A. A.S., Sigma Xi. Independent Republican. Methodist. Contbr. articles in scientific and med. jours. on anatomy. Research in histology, crytology, histochemistry and cytogenetics. Home: 6020 Nebraska Av Omaha NB 68104

HARDACRE, PAUL HOSWELL, educator; b. Los Angeles, Aug. 25, 1915; s. Ralph Beldam and Edith (Hoswell) H.; A.B., Stanford, 1937; M.A., U. Cal. at Los Angeles, 1940, Ph.D., 1947; m. Gracia Louise Manspeaker, July 24, 1947; children-Helen, Alan Godfrey. Mem. faculty Vanderbilt U., 1947—, prof. history, chmn. dept., 1967-70. Served to maj. AUS, 1941-46. Fulbright research scholar, 1950-51; Guggenheim fellow, 1956-57. Decorated Bronze Star. Mem. Am., So. hist. assns., Conf. Brit. Studies, Phi Gamma Delta. Conglist. Author: The Royalists During the Puritan Revolution, 1956. Contbr. articles hist. jours. Home: 6205 Bresslyn Rd Nashville TN 37205

HARDART, THOMAS R., corp. exec.; b. 1918; grad. Notre Dame U., Columbia Law Sch. With The Horn & Hardart Co., 1938—, treas., 1953-60, v.p., 1960-67, pres., chief exec. officer, 1967—, also dir. Served as lt. (j.g.) USN, World War II. Address: 600 W 50th St New York City NY 10019*

HARDAWAY, ELLIOTT, librarian; b. Nashville, Jan. 1, 1913; s. Owen and Della (Holloway) H.; B.A., Vanderbilt U., 1935, M.A., 1936; B.S. in L.S., U. Ill., 1938, M.S., 1940; m. Sylvia Shaver, July 7, 1937; 1 dau., Sylvia Jean. Jr. librarian U. Ill., 1937-41; asst. librarian E. Carolina Tchrs. Coll., 1941-42; subject cataloger Library Congress, 1942-44; librarian N.D. Agr. Coll., 1944-47; asst. chief Information Service br., Tokyo, Japan, 1947-50; chief tech. procs. La. State U., 1950-53, asso. dir., 1953-55; asst. dir. U. Fla., 1955-57; dir. libraries U. South Fla., 1957-64, dean instructional services, 1965-67, dean adminstrn., 1967, v.p. for adminstrn., 1967-71; dir. Clearwater (Fla.) Pub. Library, 1971—. Mem. A.L.A., Southeastern, Fla. library assns. Home: 11337 Oakleaf Av Tampa FL 33612

HARDAWAY, ROBERT MORRIS, III, physician, army officer; b. Camp John Hay, P.I., Jan. 9, 1916; s. Robert Morris and Olive (Gray) H.; A.B., U. Denver, 1936; postgrad. U. Colo. Med. Sch., 1935-37; M.D., Washington U., St. Louis, 1939; m. Lee H. Harkey, June 12, 1939; children—Robert Morris IV, Elizabeth J., Thomas G.II, Christopher. Commd. 1st 1t., M.C., U.S. Army, 1939, advanced through grades to brig. gen., 1970; ward officer, surg. service Fitzsimons Gen. Hosp., Denver, 1940-41, N. Sector Gen. Hosp., Hawaii, 1941-43; tchr. Med. Field Service Sch., Carlyle Barracks, Pa., 1943-45; surg. trainee Nichols Gen. Hosp., Louisville, 1945-46; resident surgery Madigan Gen. Hosp., Tacoma, 1946-47, Fitzsimons Gen. Hosp., 1949-50; chief surg. service 34th Gen. Hosp., Korea, 1947-49, Sta. Hosp., Ft. Belvoir, Va., 1950-54, 97th Gen. Hosp., Frankfurt, Germany, 1954-58, Martin Army Hosp., Ft. Benning, Ga., 1958-60; dir. div. surgery Walter Reed Army Inst. Research, Washington, 1960-67; comdg. officer 97th Gen. Hosp., Frankfurt, Germany, 1967-70; comdg. gen. Wm. Beaumont Gen. Hosp., El Paso, Tex., 1970—. Decorate Army Commendation medal with oak leaf cluster; decorated Legion of Merit with oak leaf cluster; recipient 2d prize for exhibit A.M.A.,1964; Silver award exhibit Am. Soc. Clin. Pathologists- Coll. Am. Pathologists, 1964, certificate of outstanding achievement U.S. Army Sci. Conf., 1964. Diplomate Am. Bd. Surgery. Fellow A.C.S., Am. Coll. Angiology, Am. Assn. for Surgery Trauma, Microcirculation Assn.; mem. Assn. Mil. Surgeons U.S., A.M.A., Alpha Omega Alpha. Episcopalian. Author: Syndromes of Disseminated Intravascular Coagulation, 1966; Clinical Management of Shock, Surgical and Medical, 1968. Contbr. articles on intravascular coagulation and hemorrhagic shock to jours. and books. Office: Comdg Gen William Beaumont Gen Hosp El Paso TX 79920

HARDBECK, GEORGE WILLIAM, coll. dean; b. Edwardsville, Ill., Dec. 18, 1925; s. George Fred and Clara (Stahlhut) H.; B.S., U. Ill., 1954, M.S., 1956, Ph.D. in Labor Econs., 1958; m. Grete Olga Zipser, Apr. 17, 1947; 1 dau., Gail Leontine. Supr. Vienna Area Command Engr. Depot, U.S. War Dept., 1946-47; with Shell Oil Refinery, Wood River, Ill., 1947-49; teaching asst. U. Ill. at Urbana, 1955-58; asso. prof. econs. La. Poly. Inst., 1958- 59; asst. prof. econs. St. Louis U., 1959-61; asso. prof. Kan. State U., Manhattan, 1961-64; resident dir. grad. program bus. U. Mo., 1964-66; prof. econs. Creighton U., 1966-71, asso. dean, 1966-68, dean Coll. Bus. Adminstrn., 1968-71; prof. econs., dean Coll. Bus. and Econs., U. Nev., 1971—; cons. in field, 1960—. Served with AUS, 1944-46; ETO. Decorated Purple Heart, Combat Inf. badge; H.B. Earhart fellow, 1957-58; fellow econs. U. Ill., summer 1956. Mem. Am., Midwest econ. assns., Internat. Econ. Assn., Indsl. Relations Research Assn., Am. Arbitration Assn., Order Artus, Alpha Kappa Psi, Beta Gamma Sigma. Author monographs and articles. Home: 3659 Descanso St Las Vegas NV 89109

HARDBERGER, PHILLIP DUANE, lawyer, journalist; b. Morton, Tex., July 27, 1934; s. Homer Reeves and Bess (Scott) H.; B.A., Baylor U., 1955; M.S., Columbia, 1960; LL.B., Georgetown U., 1965; m. Linda Morgan, May 1968. Reporter, Waco (Tex.) News Tribune 1952-54; press rep. Tex. Baptist Conv., 1958-59; asso. editor Mil. Pub. Inst., N.Y.C., 1961; exec. sec. Peace Corps, 1962-66; spl. asst. to dir. Office Econ. Opportunity, 1967- 68; trial lawyer, 1968—. Served to capt. USAF,1955-58. Contbr. articles. Home: 331 Arcadia San Antonio TX 78209 Office: 119 Villita San Antonio TX 78205

HARDEE, WILLIAM COVINGTON, lawyer; b. Florence, S.C., Mar. 2, 1919; s. Abram Lindsay and Cornelia (Covington) H.; A.B., Emory U., 1940; LL.B. magna cum laude, Harvard, 1943; m. Georgina Hazeltine, Sept. 5, 1942 (div. 1955); 1 dau., Pamela Graves (Mrs. F.G. Jackson, Jr.); m. 2d, Joan Chappell Lamont, May 14, 1955; stepchildren—Thrae (Mrs. William L. Harris), Robin Lamont, John E. Lamont; children—Felicity, Meredith, Nell. William. Admitted to Mass. bar, 1947, N.Y. bar, 1955; practiced in Boston, 1947-54, N.Y.C., 1955—; asso. firm Ropes & Gray, 1947-50; asst. prof., then prof. law Harvard Law Sch., 1950-55; asso. firm Clark, Carr & Ellis, 1954-69, partner. 1957-69; gen. counsel U.P.R.R. Co., 1967-68; partner Kelley, Drye, Warren, Clark, Carr & Ellis, N.Y.C., 1969-71, Hardee, Barovick, Konecky & Gaines, N.Y.C., 1971—. Dir., mem. exec. com. Diner's Club Inc.; trustee Lincoln Savs. Bank; mem. consultative bd. Companhia Petroquimica Brasileira, Sao Paulo, Brazil. Mem. U.S. R.R Trade Mission to Brazil for Dept. Commerce, 1967. Trustee Wykeham Rise Sch., Washington, Conn.; trustee, v.p. Bklyn. Inst. Arts and Scis.; chmn. governing com. Bklyn. Mus. Served to lt. comdr. USNR, 1942-46. Mem. Am., N.Y. State, N.Y.C. (past com. chmn.) bar assns., Am. Arbitration Assn., Phi Beta Kappa, Omicron Delta Kappa, Kappa Alpha. Episcopalian. Clubs: Union League (N.Y.C.); Metropolitan (Washington); Rembrandt (Bklyn.). Editor: (with R. Amory, Jr.) Materials on Accounting, 1953. Home: 14 Remsen St Brooklyn NY 11201 also Goose Hill Farm Mallory Brook Rd Washington CT 06793 Office: 300 Park Av New York City NY 10005

HARDEEN, THEODORE, Jr., lawyer; b. London, Eng., Dec. 20, 1905 (parents Am. citizens); s. Theodore and Elsie (Parsons) H.; LL.B., U. Va., 1930; m. Elizabeth Brett, Nov. 1, 1952; 1 son, Theodore Brett. Admitted to Ill. bar, 1930, Va. Bar, 1964; practiced in Chgo., 1930-53; adminstr. Def. Air Transp., Dept. Commerce, Washington, 1953-64; gen. counsel Va. Trailways, 1964-67; v.p. Western Sales, Ltd., Geneva, 1967-70, counsel Export- Import Bank U.S., Washington, 1970—. U.S. rep. NATO Civil Aviation delegation, 1958, 59, 60, 61, 62. Dir. Universal Motor Co., Universal Foundry Co., Lantana Aero Corp., Dr. Peter Fahrney & Sons Co., Palm Beach Aero Corp. Vice Pres. Chgo. Blackhawk Hockey Team. Serves as maj. Air Transport Command, USAAF, 1942-45. Decorated Air medal, Commendation medal. Mem. Chgo. Bar Assn., Phi Sigma Kappa. Clubs: Everglades (Palm Beach, Fla.); Tavern (Chgo.); Farmington Country, Farmington Hunt, Boar's Head (Charlottesville, Va.); University (Washington). Address: care Expert-Import Bank of US 811 Vermont Av NW Washington DC 20571

HARDEMAN, BEN, U.S. atty.; b. 1903; B.S., LL.B., U. Ala. Admitted to bar, 1926; formerly U.S. atty. middle Dist. Ala. Address: 1435 Finley Curve Montgomery AL 36106*

HARDEMAN, WILLIAM D., geologist; b. Nashville, Mar. 4, 1915; s. William D. and Nannie (Overton) H.; A.B., Vanderbilt U., 1937, M.S. in Geology, 1941; m. Helene Barry Groves, Apr. 4, 1947; children—Linda Helene (Mrs. Harold L. Moses), Fredrick Charles, Jackson Overton, Barbara Ann (Mrs. Joseph M. Balthrop). Geologic aide Tenn. Div. Geology, 1941; asst. geologist Nashville Dist. Corps Engrs., U.S. Army, 1941-42; with Tenn. Div. Geology, 1946—, state geologist, 1952-69; chief geologic br. Tenn. Valley Authority, 1969-70; liaison officer Tenn. U.S. Bur. Mines, 1970—. Served with USNR, 1942-45. Mem. Am. Inst. Profl. Geologists, Am. Assn. Petroleum Geologists, Geol. Soc. Am., Am. Assn. State Geologists, Am. Inst. Mining and Metall. Engrs. Author: Mineral Resources and Mineral Industries of Tennessee, 1959; Geologic Map of Tennessee, 1966. Home: Route 1 Box 404 Old Hickory TN 37138 Office: State Office Bldg Nashville TN 37219

HARDEN, CECIL MURRAY, (Mrs. Frost R. Harden), mem. Republican Nat. Com.; b. Covington, Ind.; d. Timothy and Jennie (Clotfelter) Murray; ed. Ind. U.; m. Frost R. Harden, Dec. 22, 1914; 1 son, Murray Harden. Mem. Republican Nat. Com. for Ind., 1964—; mem. 81st-86th congresses. Mem. D.A.R.; charter mem. Bus. and Profl. Women's Club. Home: 302 5th St Covington, IN 47932. Office: Republican Nat Hdqrs 1625 Eye St NW Washington DC 20006

HARDEN, EDGAR LAWRENCE, corp. exec.; b. Montezuma, Ia., Oct. 31, 1907; s. Charles B. and Marian (Curry) H.; B.A., Ia. State Tchrs. Coll., 1930; M.A., State U. Ia., 1937; Ed.D., Wayne U., 1950; LL.D., Northwood Inst., 1965, Alma Coll., 1966; m. Elizabeth I, Craver, May 18, 1929; children—Donald Fred, Pamela Kay. Tchr., Ia. Schs., 1930-38; prin. high sch., dean jr. coll., Independence, Ia., 1938-41; prin. Charleston (Ill.) High Sch., 1941-43, Galesburg, Ill., 1943-45, Battle Creek, Mich., 1945-46; asso. prof. Inst. Counseling, Testing and Guidance, Mich. State Coll., 1946-50, dir. continuing edn. service, 1950-53, dean continuing edn. service, 1953-56; exec. v.p. Drop Forging Assn., Lansing, Mich., 1955-56; pres. No. Mich. U., Marquette, Mich., 1956-67; chmn. bd. Lake Superior & Ishpeming R.R., Marquette, Mich.; dir. Win Schuler's Restaurants, Inc., Marshall, Mich.; pres. Story, Inc., 1967—. Mem. bd. Mich. Welfare League, Mich. Med. Service, Mich. United Fund, Sparrow Hosp., Lansing Symphony; chmn. Mich. Week; mem. Mich. Health Council, Mich. YMCA Com. Higher Edn., Mich.-Ohio Regional Ednl. Lab., Upper Midwest Research and Devel. Council. Mem. Am. Assn. Sch. Adminstrs., Nat., Mich. edn. assns., Phi Delta Kappa. Methodist. Co-author: A Basic Text for Guidance Workers, 1947; How to Organize Your Guidance Program, 1950. Asso. editor mag. Personnel and Guidance. Contbr. articles in field. Home: 1018 Wildwood Dr., East Lansing, MI 48912

HARDEN, JOHN WILLIAM, publicist; b. Graham, N.C., Aug. 22, 1903; s. Peter Ray and Nettie Cayce (Abbott) H.; A.B., U. N.C., 1927; m. Josephine Holt, June 13, 1928 (dec. Dec. 1951); children—Glenn Abbott (Mrs. Fred Springer-Miller), John William; m. 2d, Sarah Plexico, Oct. 5, 1953; children—Holmes Plexico and Mark Michael (twins), Jonathan Holder. Circulation mgr., advt. mgr. Burlington (N.C.) Daily Times-News, 1922, also editor Graham news dept., classified advt. mgr. Raleigh News and Observer, 1923; with U. N.C. News Bur., 1923-28; reporter, columnist Charlotte (N.C.) News, 1928-37; news editor Salisbury Evening Post., 1937-44, Greensboro Daily News, 1944; pvt. sec. Gov. R. Gregg Cherry, 1945-48; mem. campaign staff U.S. Senator William B. Umstead, 1948; dir. pub. relations Burlington Industries, 1948-58, asst. v.p., 1948, v.p., 1949-58; pub. relations counsellor and cons. John Harden Assos., Greensboro, 1958—. Mem. N.C. Indsl. Devel. Found., Inc.; mem. N.C. council Nat. Council Crime and Delinquency. Mem. exec. bd. Greensboro council Boy Scouts Am.; mem. vis. com. Guilford Coll.; dirs. Penick Meml. Home, United Health Services of N.C., Inc., N.C. Bus. Found., Inc. Mem. Greensboro C. of C. (dir., pres.) N.C. Soc. Preservation Antiquities, N.C. Press Assn., Gen. Alumni Assn. U. N.C. (pres. 1955), Pub. Relations Soc. Am. (N.C. chmn. eligibility com.). Democrat. Episcopalian (chmn. 1958 every mem. canvass; vestryman, sr. warden). Clubs: Merchants and Manufacturers, Rotary (dir., pres., dist. gov.), Greensboro Country, Carolina Motor (dir.), Grandfather Golf and Country (dir., chmn. membership com.), Lake of Grandfather Mountain (dir.). Author: Alamance County: Economic and Social 1928; The Devil's Tramping Ground and Other North Carolina Mystery Stories, 1949; Tar Heel Ghosts, 1954; North Carolina Roads and Their Builders, 1966. Contbr. trade publs. Home: 2700 Twin Lakes Dr Greensboro NC 27407 Office: 100 E Lake Dr Greensboro NC 27403

HARDEN, KOMURIA ALBERT, physician, former coll. dean; b. Bessemer, Ala., Aug. 20, 1905; s. Albert and Lilly (Taylor) H.; student Wayne State U., 1923-26; B.A., U. Mich., 1927, M.D., 1931; m. Julia Woodhouse, Dec. 27, 1934; 1 dau., Katharine Judith (Mrs. Paul Fairley). Intern, Freedmen's Hosp., Washington, 1931- 32, chief div. chronic pulmonary diseases, 1958-65; practice medicine, specializing in internal medicine, Detroit, 1933-34, Catonsville, Md., 1935-40; asso. physician Henryton (Md.) Sanatorium, 1939-40; instr. medicine Coll. Medicine, Howard U., 1941, asst. prof. medicine, 1945-47, asso. prof., 1947-58, prof., 1958—, vice dean Coll. Medicine, 1960-65, acting dean, 1965-66, dean, 1966-70; research fellow chest service Bellevue Hosp. Columbia div., N.Y.C., 1944-45. Diplomate Am. Bd. Internal Medicine. Fellow A.C.P., Am. Acad. Tb Physicians, Am. Pub. Health Assn.; mem. A.M.A., Nat. Med. Assn., A.A.A.S., Am., D.C. (past pres.) thoracic socs., D.C. Tb Assn. (pres., dir.), Medico-Chirur. Soc. D.C., Am. Cancer Soc. (trustee), Am. Heart Assn., Sigma Xi, Alpha Omega Alpha. Contbr. profl. jours. Home: 4629 Blagden Terrace N.W., Washington. DC 20011. Office: 520 W St NW Washington DC 20001

HARDENBROOK, HARRY JUNIOR, educator; b. Cope, Colo., Nov. 18, 1917; s. Harry Herbert and Della Pauline (Barger) H.; D.V.M., Colo. State U., 1940; M.S., U. Ill., 1944, Ph.D., 1953; m. Lois Jeanette Burke, Feb. 17, 1944; 1 son, Harry Herbert. Pvt. practice vet. medicine, Denver, 1940-41; with meat insp. div. U.S. Dept. Agr., Omaha, 1941-42; mem. faculty U. Ill., 1942—, prof. vet. clin. medicine, 1945—; instr. large animal vet. surgery. Dir. Bernbrook Co., Berwyn, Ill. Mem. Am., Ill. vet. med. assns., Am. Equine Practice Assn., Am. Vet. Radiology Soc., Am. Vet. Soc. for Study of Breeding Soundness, Sigma Xi, Phi Sigma, Gamma Sigma Delta. Co-inventor cold-pressure bandage. Research on reproductive problems in domestic animals, healing of wounds, blood changes as result of exercise, tissue changes under application of cold. Home: 1203 Foothill Dr Champaign IL 61820 Office: Large Animal Clinic Univ Illinois Urbana IL 61801

HARDER, A.D., life ins. co. exec.; b. 1902; B.S. in Econs., U. Okla., 1925; married. With Southwestern Life Ins. Co., 1925—, chmn. bd., dir., 1967—. Address: P.O. Box 2699, Dallas, TX 75221*

HARDER, F. WILLIAM, investment banker; b. Delhi, N.Y., Aug. 16, 1904; s. William Henry and Alice L (Every) H.; student Del. Acad., 1921, Central City Bus. Sch., Syracuse, N.Y, 1922; m. Myrtle P. Gerst, Feb. 28, 1925 (div.); children—Betty (Mrs. Donald M. McClellan), Phyllis Mae (Mrs. Richard Reininger), Alice Joanne (Mrs. Albert N. Drake); m. 2d, Lois M. Chillingworth, May 16, 1952. Security trader E.G. Childs & Co., Inc., Syracuse, 1922-30, Eschleman-Harder Co., Inc., 1930-32, Harder- Mengarelli, Inc., 1932-36, Harder & Co., Inc., N.Y.C., 1936-38; with Allen & Co., Inc., 1938—, exec. asso., 1964-66, pres., dir., 1966-67, dir., chmn. exec. com., 1967—; dir. AMBAC Industries, Inc., Garden City, L.I.; dir. Airborne Freight Corp., Seattle, Arts-Way Mfg. Co., Armstrong, Ia., Bunker-Ramo Corp., N.Y.C., Allied Supermarkets, Detroit; dir., mem. exec. com. Ogden Corp., N.Y.C. Trustee Nat. Mus. Racing, Saratoga Springs, N.Y., Skidmore Coll., Saratoga Springs, N.Y.; vice chmn. devel. com. Inst. of Living, Hartford, Conn. Mem. Thoroughbred Owners and Breeders Assn. (trustee Jamaica, N.Y.). Assn. N.Y.C. Clubs: Saratoga Golf and Polo (bd. mem.) (Saratoga Springs); Turf and Field (gov.), Bankers of Am., Harbor View, N.Y. Athletic (N.Y.C.); Garden City (N.Y.) Golf; Indian Creek Country (Indian Creek Village, Fla.); Seaview Country (Absecon, N.J.). Home: 50 Sutton Pl S New York City NY 10022 Office: 30 Broad St New York City NY 10004

HARDER, FREDERICK EUGENE JOHN, assn. exec.; b. Clinton, Mo., Feb. 28, 1916; s. John C. and Anna (Oblander) H.; B.A., Andrews U., Berrien Springs, Mich., 1940; M.A., Seventh-day Adventist Theol. Sem., 1951; Ph.D., N.Y.U., 1960; m. Marjorie Myrtle Harris, June 5, 1939; children—Frederick Lee, Caludette Lucille (Mrs. Merlin D. Tuttle). Tchr. elementary sch., Macon, Ga., 1940-41; pres. Middle East Coll., Beirut, Leanon, 1945-50; supt. edn. Seventh-day Adventist Sch., N.Y. State, 1956-58; chmn. div. edn. Atlantic Union Coll., 1958-59; mem. faculty Andrews U., 1959-71, prof. edn., chmn. dept., 1962-69, dean Sch. Grad. Studies, 1969-71; exec. sec. Bd. Higher Edn., N.Am. div. Gen. Conf. Seventh Day Adventists, 1971—. Guest lectr. Mich. State U., 1967, Newbold Coll., 1967, Seminaire Adventiste, France, 1970. Mem. exec. com. Greater N.Y. Conf. Seventh Day Adventists, 1951-58; mem. Berrien Springs Dist. Sch. Bd., 1963-67. Mem. Berrien County Democratic Com., 1966—. Trustee Bagdad (Irag) Hosp., 1945-50, Greater N.Y. Acad., New York City, 1951-58. Mem. Am. Assn. Sch. Adminstrs., Am. Assn. Higher Edn., Am. Acad. Polit. and Social Scis., Am. Acad. Religion, Soc. Bib. Lit., Mich. Acad. Sci., Arts and Letters, Am. Assn. U. Profs., Religious Edn. Assn. Author: Giants of Faith, 1962; Bible for Today, 1963; The Church of Yesterday, 1964; Revelation, a Source of Knowledge, as Conceived by Ellen G. White, 1960. Home: 9039 Sligo Creek Pkwy Silver Spring MD 20901

HARDER, HOWARD CHARLES, food products mfr.; b. Mart, Tex. May 15, 1916; s. Henry Charles and Eula Wilkenson (Lawrence) H.; student U. Tex., 1933-37; advanced mgmt. program Harvard, 1947; m. Julia Johns, Aug. 31, 1940; children—Nancy Johns, Beverly Ann. With Corn Products Refining Co. (name changed to Corn Products Co. 1958), N.Y.C., 1937—, successively accountant, asst. treas., asst. comptroller exec. asst. to exec. v.p., 1937-57, treas., 1957-58, comptroller, 1958—, v.p. finance, 1959-61, sr. v.p., 1961-64, exec. v.p., adminstrn., 1964-65, pres., 1965-68, pres., chief exec. officer, 1968-69, co. name changed to CPC Internat. Inc., 1969, chmn. and chief exec. officer, 1969—, also dir.; dir. Carrier Corp., Peoples Trust N.J., Otis Elevator Co, Lord & Taylor, Asso. Dry Goods Corp. Trustee Nutrition Found., Nat. 4-H Club Found. Served to capt. Ordance Dept., AUS, 1942-46. Mem. N.A.M. (dir.), Kappa Alpha. Mason (32). Clubs: Mountain Lakes (N.J.); Fifth Avenue (treas.), Metropolitan (N.Y.C.); Knickerbocker County (Tenafly, N.J.). Home: 4 Deer Hill Rd Alpine NJ 07620 Office: Internat Plaza Englewood Cliffs NJ 07632

HARDER, HUDSON ORLAN, petroleum exec.; b. Wilburton, Indian Ty., Aug. 18, 1905; s. David O. and Cora (Strong) H.; A.B., U. Okla., 1927; m. Lucille Roby, Dec. 14, 1929; 1 dau., Hope. Petroleum engr. Cities Service Co., 1927-34, supt. prodn. Indian Ty. Illuminating Oil Co. (Cities Service), 1934-41, supt. prodn., 1941-45; gen. supt. prodn. Sunray Oil Corp., 1945-49, v.p., mgr. prodn., 1949-52, v.p., mgr. exploration, 1952-58; v.p., mgr. exploration Sunray Mid-Continent Oil Co., 1958-62, v.p., dir., 1962-66; exec. v.p. directing exploration and prodn. Sunray DX Oil Co., 1963-66; dir., mem. exec. com. Western Diversified Industries, Inc. Pres. U. Okla. Found., Inc.; bd. dirs. Okla. U. Research Inst. Mem. Landman Assn., Am. Inst. Mining and Metall. Engrs., Ind. Petroleum Assn. Am., Sigma Tau, Pi Epsilon Tau, Phi Kappa Sigma, Beta Gamma Sigma. Republican. Mem. Ch. Jesus Christ of Latter Day Saints

(Reorganized). Mason (32, K.T.). Club: Petroleum. Home: 3914 S Delaware Pl Tulsa OK 74105 Office: Mid-Continent Bldg Tulsa OK 74103

HARDER, KELSIE BROWN, educator; b. Pope, Tenn., Aug. 23, 1922; s. Prince William and Belle (MaGee) H.; B.A. magna cum laude, Vanderbilt U., 1950, M.A., 1951; Ph.D., U. Fla., 1954; m. Louise Maron, Oct. 9, 1960; children—Gerald William, Dennis Prince, Frank Maron, Thomas Brown. Asst. prof. English, Youngstown U., 1954-58, asso. prof., 1958-60, prof., 1960-64; Fulbright lectr., India, 1962-63, prof., chmn. dept. English and drama State U. Coll., Potsdam, N.Y., 1964—; Fulbright vis. prof. U. Lodz (Poland), 1971-72; cons. Office Edn., Washington, summers 1966, 67, Random House Dictionary of the English Lang. Served with AUS, 1944-46. Mem. Am. Name Soc. (exec. sec.-treas.), Modern Lang. Assn., Ohio Folklore Soc. (past pres.), Am. Assn. U. Profs., Renaissance Soc. Am., Phi Beta Kappa, Sigma Phi Epsilon, Eta Sigma Phi, Sigma Delta Pi, Phi Kappa Phi. Editor: Names, 1966-68. Mem. adv. bd. American Speech, 1960- 61. Contbr. articles profl. jours. Home: 5 Lawrence Av Potsdam NY 13676

HARDER, LEWIS BRADLEY, business exec.; b. N.Y.C., July 23, 1918; s. Lewis Francis and Gertrude Burbank (Harris) H.; grad. St. Mark's Sch., Southboro, Mass., 1937; B.A., Harvard, 1941; m. Dorot Dyer Butler, Sept. 7, 1941; children—Deirdre Butler, Diana. Analyst, Morgan Stanley & Co., N.Y.C., 1941; customers man Harris Upham & Co., 1945-51, partner, 1951-54; pres. South Am. Gold & Platinum, 1954-63, dir., 1952-63; pres., dir. Colamer Co., Pacific Met Co., Colamerican Metals Corp., Pagas Corp.; chmn. bd., chief exec. officer Internat. Mining Corp.; chmn. bd. Frontino Gold Mines, Ltd., Molybdenum Corp. Am.; exec. com., dir. Marchant Mines, Ltd., Broulan Reef Mines, East Malartic Gold Mines, Ltd., Panam. Capitol Corp., Pato Consol. Gold Dredging. Ltd., Madison Fund, Canton Corp., Fresnillo Co., Pitts. and W.Va. Ry. Co.; dir. Kawecki Berylco Industries, Brassan Ltd., Foote Mineral, Indian Head, Bancroft Fund. Served to lt. USNR, 1942-45. Decorated D.F.C. Roman Catholic. Clubs: Nat. Golf Links Am.; Brook (N.Y.C.); Bedford Golf and Tennis; Stamwich, Seminole. Home: Harris Rd Bedford Hills NY Office: 280 Park Av New York City NY 10017

HARDER, MARTHA BROWN, univ. dean; b. Linden, Tenn., Dec. 31, 1933; d. Edmund Green and Bonnie (Kirk) Harder; B.S., George Peabody Coll. Tchrs., 1955; M.A., Austin Peay State Coll., Clarksville Tenn., 1958. Tchr., Clarksville city schs., 1955-58, Cumberland Coll., Lebanon, Tenn., 1958-63; dean students Lander Coll., Greenwood, S.C., 1963-66; dean women Va. Poly. Inst. Blacksburg, 1966-68, dean for men's and women's programs, 1968—. Mem. Nat., Regional assns. women deans and counselors, So. Coll. Personnel Assn. (sec. 1966-68), Delta Kappa Gamma. Home: Carlton Scott Apts Blacksburg VA 24060

HARDER, PHILIP M., banker; b. N.Y.C., 1920. Sr. v.p., exec. officer, dir. 1st Nat. Bank Mpls. Home: 127 S Ferndale Av Wayzata MN 55391 Office: 120 S 6th St Minneapolis MN 55402*

HARDER, WILLIAM HARTMAN, banker; b. Buffalo, Sept. 13, 1908; s. Edwin Partridge and Cordelia (Cousins) H.; A.B., Cornel U., 1930; postgrad. N.Y.U., 1931-34; m. Jane Torrence, Sept. 21, 1935; children—William H., Luella R., Torrence C., Sarah Jane. Clk., First Nat. Bank, Boston, 1930-32; clk. First Boston Corp., 1932-37, mgr. Buffalo office, 1937-46; mgr. bond dept. Buffalo Savs. Bank, 1946-48, v.p., 1948-61, trustee, 1954—, pres., 1961—; pres. Instl. Inves Mut. Fund, Inc., 1958-60; dir. Savs. Banks Trust Co., Nat. Fuel Gas Co., Mfrs. & Traders Trust Co. (Buffalo). Active Boy Scouts Am.; chmn. United Fund of Erie County, 1967. Mem. adv. council D'Youvil Coll. Trustee Children's Found. of Erie County, pres. 1961—; trustee Millard Fillmore Hosp. Mem. Buffalo C. of C. (dir.), Investment Officers Assn. Savs. Banks State N.Y. (pres., 1954-55). Fedn. Cornell Mens Clubs (pres. 1957-59). Clubs: Midday, Buffalo, Buffalo Country (Buffalo). Home: 1088 Delaware Av Buffalo NY 14209 Office: 545 Main St Buffalo NY 14203

HARDESTY, CHARLES HOWARD, Jr., lawyer, coal co. exec.; Fairmont, W.Va., Jan. 18, 1922; s. Charles Howard and Elizabeth (Miller) H.; grad. Mercersberg (Pa.) Acad., 1939; B.S., Duke, 1943; LL.B., W.Va. U., 1949; m. Doris Wilson, Apr. 24, 1946; children—Sarah Elizabeth, Charles Howard III. Admitted to W.Va. bar, 1949, since practiced in Fairmont as partner firm Furbee & Hardesty; tax commr. W.Va., 1961-62; gen. counsel Consol. Coal Co., 1963-66, exec. v.p., 1967-68; sr. v.p. Continental Oil Co., 1968—. Mem. Am., W.Va. (pres. 1964), Va. bar assns., Am. Judicature Soc. Home: Parsonage Rd Greenwich CT 06830 Office: 30 Rockefeller Plaza New York City NY 10020

HARDESTY, DONALD HOWE, airlines exec.; b. Watertown, Minn., June 20, 1907; s. William H. and Nellie Ann (Cunningham) H.; student U. Minn.; m. Marion P. Caldwell, Sept. 6, 1935. With Harris Upham & Co., 1929-43; with Northwest Airlines, Inc., 1943—, treas., 1960—, v.p. finance, 1961—; pres., dir. Mont. Enterprises, Inc., Billings, 1960—; dir. Aero. Radio, Inc., ARINC Research Corp., Washington Airways, Inc. (all Washington). Bd. dirs. Louise Whitbeck Fraser Sch., Mpls. Home: 2401 Maple Av Bloomington MN 55431 Office: Minneapolis-St Paul Internat Airport St Paul MN 55111

HARDESTY, HIRAM HAINES, physician, educator; b. Paulding, O., Jan. 16, 1914; s. Eugene and Ida (Underwood) H.; A.B., Miami U., Oxford, O., 1936; M.D., Western Res. U., 1940; m. Mary Le Bill, June 12, 1940; children—Susan (Mrs. William R. Corcoran), Thomas Haines, John Lee. Intern St. Vincent Charity Hosp., Cleve., 1940-41, Grad. Sch. U. Pa., 1945-46; resident ophthalmology Univ. Hosps., Cleve., 1946-48, mem. teaching staff, 1948—, asst. clin. prof., 1960—. Active local United Appeal. Served with USAAF. 1941-45. Diplomate Am. Bd. Ophthalmology. Fellow Am. Acad. Ophthalmology and Otolaryngology; mem. Cleve. Ophthalmology Club (past pres.), Innominatum Soc. (past pres.), Aesculapian Soc. (past pres.), Ohio Soc. Prevention Blindness (bd. dirs.). Contbr. profl. jours. Home: 1490 Burlington Rd Cleveland Heights OH 44118 Office: Severance Med Arts Bldg 5 Severance Circle Cleveland OH 44118

HARDIE, ROBERT HOWLE, astronomer; b. Lachine, Que., Can., Dec. 5, 1923; s. Robert Howie and Catherine (Campbell) H.; B.Sc., McGill U., 1945, M.Sc., 1946; Ph.D., U. Chgo., 1950; m. Frances Harriet Isley, Aug. 23, 1950; children—James Alexander, Robert Stephen. Came to U.S., 1946, naturalized, 1960. Vis. asst. prof. Ohio State U., 1951-53; astronomer Lowell Obs., Flagstaff Ariz., 1953-55; mem. faculty Vanderbilt U., 1955—, prof. astronomy, 1963—, dir. Dyer Obs., 1961—; spl. research stellar photometry, astron. instrumentation. Mem. Am., Royal astron. socs., Astron. Soc. Pacific, Am. Soc. Tool and Mfg. Engrs. Home: Oman Dr Brentwood TN 37027 Office: Dyer Observatory Vanderbilt U Nashville TN 37203

HARDIE, THORNTON, Jr., lawyer; b. El Paso, Tex., Dec. 2, 1917; s. Thornton and Mabelle (Bryan) H.; LL.B., U. Tex., 1947; m. Mary Elizabeth Whitaker, Dec. 26, 1942; children—Mary Adele, Ann Elizabeth, Thornton III. Admitted to Tex. bar, 1947, since practiced in Midland; partner firm Turpin, Smith, Dyer, Hardie & Harman, 1947—. Dir. Western State Bank Midland. Past county chmn. Midland Democratic Party. Past trustee Midland Ind. Sch. Dist. Served to lt. USNR, 1942-45. Fellow Internat. Acad. Trial Lawyers; mem. Am., Midland County (past pres.) bar assns., State Bar Tex., Midland C. of C. (pres. 1967—). Presbyn. (elder). Home: 1908 North St Midland TX Office: First Nat Bank Bldg Midland TX 79701

HARDIMAN, MILTON GORDON, ednl. adminstr.; b. California, Mo., July 22, 1906; s. Lewis Dexter and Emma Gertrude (Short) H.; A.B., Lincoln U., 1927; M.A., U. Ia., 1931, Ph.D., 1945; m. Ruth Naomi Roberts, June 5, 1932; children—Patsy Ruth (Mrs. James Long, Jr.), Barbara Anne (Mrs. Allen Chandler). Tchr., adminstr. Coleman Coll., Gibsland, La., 1927-30; faculty Lincoln U., Jefferson City, Mo., 1930—, head dept. modern fgn. langs., 1951—, dir. summer session, 1965—. Guest prof. Fla. A. and M. U., 1951, Tex. So. U., summer 1954. Pres., Community Center Assn., Jefferson City, 1958-68; v.p. social planning com. United Community Fund, 1962-64. Recipient Merit award Kiwanis Club Jefferson City, 1965; named Outstanding Alumnus in Edn. St. Louis Alumni, 1967. Mem. Coll. Lang. Assn. (pres. 1965-67), Phi Delta Iota, Kappa Alpha Psi. Baptist (chmn. ofcl. bd. 1958-69). Mason (Merit award 1968). Home: 810 Lafayette Jefferson City MO 65101

HARDIN, ADLAI STEVENSON, sculptor; b. Mpls., Sept. 23, 1901; s. Martin D. and Julia (Stevenson) H.; A.B., Princeton, 1923; m. Carol Moore, Feb. 22, 1934; children—Carol J., Adlai Stevenson. With Quaker Oats Co., 1923-25, Z.L. Potter Co., 1925-33; v.p. Wm. Esty Co., 1933-60; rep. permanent collections Pa. Acad. Fine Arts, New Britain (Conn.) Mus. Am. Art, IBM Collection of Sculpture of Western Hemisphere, McMaster Div. Coll., McMaster U., Interchurch Center, N.Y.C., Seamen's Bank for Savs., N.Y.C., Princeton. Winner Ecclesiastical Competition, Nat. Sculpture Soc., 1950, Lindsey Morris Meml. prize, 1956; recipient Saltus medal N.A.D., 1945, Avery prize Archtl. League, 1940, Daniel Chester French medal N.A.D., 1968. N.A. Fellow Nat. Sculpture Soc. (pres. 1957-59; Mrs. Louis Bennett prize 1965). Club: Century Assn. (N.Y.C.). Address: Cove Rd Lyme CT 06320

HARDIN, CHARLES ROE, Jr., lawyer; b. Newark, June 18, 1921; s. Charles Roe and Emma (Downer) H.; grad. Phillips Exeter Acad., 1938; A.B., Princeton, 1942; LL.B., Columbia, 1948; m. Jean Sherrill, May 19, 1951; children—Katharine, Andrew S. Admitted to N.J. bar, 1949, since practiced in Newark; partner firm Pitney, Hardin & Kipp, 1958—; law clk. N.J. Superior Ct., 1949-50. Candidate for N.J. Assembly, 1951; mem. Essex County (N.J.) Democratic Com., 1953-54; mem. Chester Twp. Planning Bd., 1969—, chmn., 1970—. Trustee Babies Hosp., Newark, 1952-57, sec. 1957; trustee Florence Critenton League Newark, 1952-57, 63-66. Served to lt. USNR, 1942-46. Mem. Am., N.J., Essex County, Morris County bar assns., Am. Geog. Soc. Episcopalian. Clubs: Princeton (N.Y.C.); Essex (bd. govs.) (Newark); Essex Hunt (Peapack, N.J.). Home: Old Gladstone Rd Chester NJ 07930 Office: 570 Broad St Newark NJ 07102 also 310 South St Morristown NJ 07960

HARDIN, CLIFFORD MORRIS, government ofcl.; b. Knightstown, Ind., Oct. 9, 1915; s. James Alvin and Mabel (Macy) H.; B.S., Purdue U., 1937, M.S., 1939, Ph.D., 1941, D.Sc. (hon.), 1952; student U. Chgo., 1939-40; LL.D., Creighton U., 1956; Ph.D. (hon.), Nat. U. Colombia, 1968; D.Sc. Mich. State U., 1969, N.D. State U., 1969; m. Martha Love Wood, June 28, 1939; children—Susan Carol (Mrs. L.W. Wood), Clifford Wood, Cynthia (Mrs. Robert Milligan), Nancy Ann (Mrs. Douglas L. Rogers), James. Grad. asst. Purdue U., Lafayette, 1937-39, 40-41; instr. U. Wis., 1941-42, asst. prof. agrl. econs., 1942-44; asso. prof. agrl. economics Mich. State Coll., 1944-46, prof., chmn. agrl. econs. dept., 1946-48, asst. dir. agrl. expt. sta., 1948, dir., 1949-53, dean agr., 1953-54; chancellor U. Neb., 1954-69; sec. Agr. Washington, 1969—; dir. Fed. Res. Bank of Kansas City (Omaha br.), 1961-67, chmn., 1962-67; bd. dirs. Behlen Mfg. Co., Columbus Neb.; trustee Bankers Life Ins. Co. of Neb., 1958. Mem. ednl. adv. com. W.K. Kellogg Found, 1960; trustee Rockefeller Found.; Farm. found. fellow U. Chgo., 1939-40, U.S. del. Internat. Conf. Agrl. Economists, Eng., 1947; mem. Pres.'s Com. to Strengthen Security Free World, 1963. Mem. Nat. Sci. Bd., 1966—. Bd. dirs. F.C.A. of St. Paul, 1950-51. Mem. Assn. State Univs. and Land-Grant Colls. (pres. 1960, chmn. exec. com. 1961), Am. Council Edn. (dir. 1963- 65), Phi Kappa Phi, Sigma Xi, Alpha Zeta, Alpha Gamma Rho, Gamma Sigma Delta Rotarian. Editor: Overcoming World Hunger, 1968. Home: 5930 Norman Av Lincoln NB 68512 Office: Dept Agr Washington DC 20515

HARDIN, DALE WAYNE, govt. ofcl.; b. Peoria, Ill., Sept. 9, 1922; s. James P. and Lucille Center; H.; student Bradley U., 1941, 46-47; A.A., A.B., George Washington U., 1949, J.D., 1951; m. Virginia Phillips, Apr. 21, 1946; children—Bradley James, Rebecca May. Admitted to Va. and D.C. bars, 1951; pvt. practice, 1951; spl. agt. FBI, 1951-54; legislative atty., Congl. liaison officer ICC, 1954-63; sec., counsel Transp. Assn. Am., 1959; mgr. transp. and communication dept. U.S. C. of C., 1963-66; v.p. Overmeyer Co., Washington, 1966-67; spl. counsel Am. Trucking Assn., 1967; commr. ICC, 1967—, vice chmn., 1970—; mem. council of Adminstrv. Conf. U.S., 1971—. Served with USMCR, 1942-46. Mem. Fed., Va., D.C. bar assns., Soc. Former FBI Agts., Phi Delta Phi. Club: Congressional Country, Nat. Lawyers (Washington). Bus. sec. George Washington Law Rev., 1950. Home: 1011 Emerald Dr Alexandria VA 22308 Office: Interstate Commerce Commn Washington DC 20423

HARDIN, GEORGE CECIL, Jr., petroleum exec.; b. Oakwood, Tex., Oct. 6, 1920; s. George Cecil and Pearl (Moore) H.; B.S. in Geology and Petroleum Engring., Tex. A. and M. U., 1941; Ph.D. in Geology (Van Hise fellow 1941), U. Wis., 1942; m. Virginia Howard, Nov. 21, 1942; children—George Howard, Susan. Mining engr. Victory Fluorspar Mine, Cave In Rock, Ill., 1942; geologist U.S. Geol. Survey, 1942-45, party chief, 1944-45; geologist Carter Gragg Oil Co., Palestine, Tex., 1945-46; geologist, petroleum engr. M.T. Halbouty Cons Firm, Houston, 1946-51; exploration and prodn. mgr. M.T. Halbouty Oil and Gas Interests, Houston, 1951-59, gen. mgr., 1959-61; exec. v.p., dir. Halbouty Alaska Oil Co., 1957-61; partner Hardin and Hardin, cons. geologists, Houston, 1961-65; mgr. oil and gas expln. Kerr- McGee Oil Ind., Inc., 1964-65; v.p. N.Am. Oil & Gas Exploration, 1965-67, v.p. oil, gas and minerals exploration, 1967-68, group v.p. exploration, 1968; v.p. Kerr-McGee Argentina, 1967-68, Kerr- McGee Can., Ltd., 1967-68, Kerr-McGee Australia, Ltd., 1967-68; pres. Royal Resources Corp., 1968-70, Ada Oil Exploration Corp., 1970—; dir. Continental Bank & Trust Co., Houston, 1956—, mem. exec. com., 1956-62, chmn. auditing com., 1962-65; owner Poverty Ridge Farm, Cedar Lane, Tex., Quail Ridge Farm Okla. City. Registered engr., Tex., Okla. Fellow Geol. Soc. Am., A.A.A.S., mem. Houston Geol. Soc. (pres. 1961- 62), Soc. Econ. Paleontologists and Mineralogists, New Orleans, S. Tex. geol. socs., Gulf Coast Assn. Geol. Socs. (pres. 1959), Am. Assn. Petroleum Geologist (sec.-treas. 1964-66), Assn. Mexicana de Geologos Petroleros, Soc. Exploration Geophysicists Am. Inst. Profl. Geologists. Clubs: Petroleum (bd. dirs. 1956-58), Terra (bd. dirs. 1958- 59), Lakeside Country (Houston); Brazos River Hunting and Fishing (bd. dirs. 1961-64) (W. Columbia, Tex.). Author articles in field. Home: 204 Arborway Houston TX 77027 Office: Adams Petroleum Center Bldg 6910 Fannin St Houston TX 77025

HARDIN, HERBERT OLIVER, govt. ofcl.; b. Kansas City, Mo., Aug. 5, 1919; s. Evan Ellis and Greetah Bernadette (Sudduth) H.; B.A., U. Cal. at Berkeley, 1948; certificate Carnegie Inst. Tech., 1944; postgrad. U.N.M., 1939-41; m. Alice Bunting Darbee, July 27, 1957; 1 son, Matthew. Law enforcement adminstrn. Bernalillo County, Albuquerque, 1936-40; spl. Indian officer Bur. Indian Affairs, Albuquerque, 1941-42, 45-46; municipal police adminstrn., Albuquerque, 1948-57; chief Latin Am. Region Office Pub. Safety, ICA-AID, Dept State, Washington, 1957-64; chief pub. safety adviser AID, Am. embassy, Colombia, 1964-69, Guatemala, 1969—. Chmn. Unitarian Fellowship, Bogota, Colombia, 1965-66. Served with AUS, 1942-45. Decorated Silver Star award, Order Commendador (Colombia). Mem. Internat. Assn. Chiefs Police, Am. Fgn. Service Assn., Am. Assn. Guatemala, Am. Employees Assn. (pres. Colombia chpt. 1966-68). Unitarian (trustee). Address: AID Mission Am Embassy Guatemala City Guatemala

HARDIN, LENARD EDWARD, oil co. exec.; b. Calhoun City, Miss., July 28, 1909; s. Zollie Kay and Katherine (Landreth) H.; student Miss. Coll., 1926-28; m. Margaret Elizabeth Davis, July 27, 1935. Accountant, Black Gold Refinery, Oklahoma City, 1936-39; gen. sal mgr. Mecury Oil Refining Co., Oklahoma City, 1939-42, 46-54; mgr. gen. office sales, then v.p. sales Champlin Oil & Refining Co., Ft. Worth, 1954-65; pres. Bell Oil & Gas Co., Tulsa, 1965-. Served to lt. col. AUS, 1942-46. Mem. Am. Petroleum Inst., Nat. Petroleum Refiners Assn. (bd. dirs. 1965—), 25-year Petroleum Club, Chgo. Oil Mens Club. Democrat. Baptist. Mason (32, Shriner). Clubs: Tulsa; Hillcrest Country (Bartlesville). Home: 1026 Johnstone St Bartlesville OK 74003 Office: Box 1492 Bartlesville OK 74003

HARDIN, LOUIS SAMUEL, lawyer; b. Charleston, Ill., Feb. 28, 1895; s. A.L. and Mary Jane (Wyeth) H.; A.B., Yale, 1917; J.D., U. Chgo., 1921; m. Mary Anthony Drake, June 28, 1930 (div. 1948); children—Edith Drake (Mrs. Charles Seymour), Carol Hardin Henderson; m. 2d, Shirley Garnett, August 19, 1950. Admitted to Ill. State Bar, 1921, practiced in Chicago since 1921; asso. with Cutting, Moore & Sidley, 1921-24, with Wilson & McIlvaine, 1924-28; asso. with Pam, Hurd & Reichmann, 1928-33, partner, 1933—; firm reorganized as Schiff, Hardin, Waite, Dorschel & Britton. Director Bliss & Laughlin, Inc., Community Pub. Service Co. Dir. Ill. Inst. Tech., Armour Research Found. Mem. Am., Ill., Chgo. bar assns., Chgo. Law Club. Legal Club. Clubs: Rqcquet, Chicago (Chgo.). Home: 1335 Astor St Chicago IL 60610 Office: 231 S LaSalle St Chicago IL 60604

HARDIN, LOWELL STEWART, educator; b. nr. Knightstown, Ind., Nov. 16, 1917; s. J. Fred and Mildred (Stewart) H.; B.S., Purdue U., 1939; Ph.D., Cornell U., 1943; m. Mary J. Cooley, Sept. 21, 1940; children—Thomas Stewart, Joyce Ann, Peter Lowell. Grad. asst., instr. Cornell U., 1939-43; instr., asst. and asso. prof., prof. Purdue U., 1943-65, adj . prof. agrl. econs., 1965—, acting head dept. agrl. econs., 1954-57, head dept., 1957-65, also dir. Purdue Work Simplification Lab.; program adviser agr. Ford Found., 1965- 66, program officer agr., 1966—. Mem. Am. Farm Econ. Assn. (pres. 1963- 64), Internat. Assn. Agrl. Economists, Sigma Xi, Alpha Gamma Rho, Phi Kappa Phi, Alpha Zeta, Sigma Delta Chi. Presbyn. Author: (with L.M. Vaughan) Farm Work Simplification, 1949. Home: 520 E 77th St New York City NY 10021 Office: 320 E 43d St New York City NY 10014

HARDIN, MARION MOODY, mining exec.; b. Kileen, Tex., Mar. 26, 1904; s. Ernest Lynwood and Mary Belle (Smith) H.; A.B., Southwestern U., 1927; m. Jeanne Campbell, Nov. 17, 1932 (dec. May 1966); 1 dau., Helen Eugenia (Mrs. Henry M. Jackson); m. 2d, Mary Stanley Smith, Jan. 1, 1967. Sales work Internat. Harvester Co., Amarillo, Tex., 1928-34; owner Hardin Truck & Supply Co., Hobbs, N.M., 1934-43; partner Hardin & Coggins, Albuquerque, 1943- 48; owner Border Machinery Co., El Paso, Tex., 1948-52; partner La Salle Mining Co., Grand Junction, Colo., 1948—; pres., dir. Am. Gypsum Co., Alburquerque, 1959-62, chmn. bd., dir., 1962; dir., past pres. S.W. Sun Country, Inc.; dir. Kennecott Copper Corp., Braden Copper Co. of Chile, Albuquerque Fed. Savs. & Loan Assn., Treesdale Labs. Mem. N.M. State Authority Commn., Gov.'s Indsl. Adv. Com. Chmn. bd. N.M. State Hosp., 1946-47; state dir. Arthritis and Rheumatism Found., 1954-55; dir. Albuquerque Civic Symphony, Gypsum Assn. (treas.), Albuquerque Mus. Assn., Opera Guild Assn. N.M. Mem. N.A.M. (dir.). Educational Research Assn. chmn. bd.), Albuquerque Petroleum Club, Newcomen Soc. N.Am., Albuquerque C. of C. (v.p., dir.), Nat. Council Crime and Delinquency (dir.), Navy League N.M. (dir.), Kappa Alpha. Democrat. Methodist. Mason. Clubs: Rotary (dir. 1946-47), Albuquerque Country (pres., dir. 1959). Address: Park Plaza Apts 1331 Park Av S W Albuquerque NM 87102

HARDIN, PAUL, III, coll. pres.; b. Charlotte, N.C., June 11, 1931; s. Paul and Dorothy (Reel) H.; A.B., Duke, 1952; J.D., 1954; L.H.D., Clemson U., 1970; m. Barbara Russell, June 8, 1954; children—Paul Russell, Sandra Stone, Dorothy Ruth. Admitted to Ala. bar, 1954; practice law, Birmingham, Ala., 1954, 56-58; asst. prof. Duke Law Sch., 1958-61, asso. prof., 1961-63, prof., 1963-68, univ. trustee, 1969—; pres. Wofford Coll., Spartanburg, S.C., 1968—. Vis. prof. U. Tex., summer 1960, U. Pa., 1962- 63. Chmn., Human Relations Com., Durham, N.C., 1961-62; mem. gen. conf. United Meth. Ch., 1968, chmn. jud. com., 1968. Trustee Lake Junaluska Assembly. Served with CIC, AUS, 1954-56. Mem. Spartanburg C. of C. (dir.), Phi Beta Kappa, Order of Coif. Author: (with Sullivan, others) The Administration of Criminal Justice, 1966; (with Sullivan) Evidence, Cases and Materials, 1968. Contbr. articles to profl. jours. law revs. Home: 148 Wofford Campus Spartanburg SC 29301

HARDIN, PAUL, Jr., bishop; b. Joanna, S.C., Nov. 7, 1903; s. Paul and Harriet (Wannamaker) H.; A.B., Wofford Coll., 1924, D.D., 1950; B.D., Emory U., 1927; D. D. Birmingham-So. Coll., 1950; m. Dorothy Elizabeth Reel, Oct. 18, 1927; children—Betsy Reel (Mrs. Arthur Utley, Jr.), Paul III, Edward Reel. Ordained to ministry Methodist Ch., 1927; pastor, N.C., 1927-49, First Meth. Ch., Birmingham, Ala., 1949-60; bishop, Columbia, S.C., 1960- -. Pres. elect Council of Bishops, U.S. Meth. Ch., pres. Council on World Serv ice and Finance. Chmn. bd. trustees Emory U.; vice chmn. bd . trustees Lake Junalaska Assemly. Home: 3600 Chateau Dr Columbia SC 29204 Office: 1420 Lady St Columbia SC 29204

HARDIN, RICHARD LYNN, educator; b. Oskaloosa, Ia., June 19, 1923; s. James O. and Marie (Ensor) H.; B.A., Washington U., St. Louis, 1948; Ph.D., Ind. U., 1952; m. Mildred Musick, Sept. 14, 1944; children—Judith, Richard, Jill, Randolph. Instr. biochemistry, U. Louisville, 1952-54; asst. prof., Med. Coll. Va., 1954-56; prof. chemistry, Lomar State Coll. Tech., Beaumont, Tex., 1956-60; prof., head dept. chemistry, Western Ill. U., Macomb, 1960—. Served with USMCR, 1941-45. Mem. Am. Chem. Soc. Home: RR 2 Macomb IL 61455

HARDIN, ROBERT CALVIN, univ. dean, physician; b. Portland, Ore., Mar. 25, 1913; s. Calvin Esau and Ruth Alice (Clark) H.; B.S., U. Ia., 1935, M.D., 1937; m. Velma Eleanor Holets, Dec. 27, 1939;

children-Margaret Ann, John Thomas. Intern, State U. Ia. Hosps., 1937-38, asst. resident, 1938-39, resident internal medicine, 1939-40, asst. physician dept. medicine, 1940-41; instr. dept. medicine U. Ia., 1945-46, asst. prof., 1946-49, asso. prof. internal medicine, 1950-53, prof. internal medicine, 1953-, asst. dean Coll. Medicine, 1950-52, dean Coll. Medicine, 1962-69, v. p. med. services, 1964-69, v.p., dean for health services, 1969-70, vice provost, dean for health affairs, 1970—; past mem. staff of dept. anethesia. Hartford (Conn.) Hosp.; cons. internist St. Francis Hosp., Hartford, 1949-50; cons. Manchester (Conn.) Community Hosp., VA hosps., Des Moines and Iowa City. Med. dir. Conn. regional blood program Am. Nat. Red. Cross, 1949-50, also cons. nat. blood program; expert cons. pathology and allied scis. Office Surg. Gen. U.S. Army. Served from capt. to lt. col. M.C., AUS, 1941-45; sr. cons. transfusion and shock ETOUSA, 1943-45. Decorated Legion of Merit. Diplomate Am. Bd. Internal Medicine. Fellow A.C.P.; mem. Ia. (chmn. com. emergency med. service), Johnson County (sec. 1947-49, pres. 1954) med. socs., Ia. Interprofl. Assn. (chmn. com. emergency med. service), A.M.A., Central Soc. Clin. Research, Central Clin. Research Club, Soc. Med. Cons. Armed Forces, A.A.A.S., Ia. Clin. Med. Soc., Am. Heart Assn., Am. Diabetes Assn. (mem. council; pres. 1969), Am. Soc. for Study Arteriosclerosis, N.Y. Acad. Sci., Royal Soc. Medicine, Horsehoe Club, Hawley Club, Central Interurban Club, Sigma Xi. Home: 9 Ridgewood Lane Iowa City IA 52240

HARDIN, THURMAN CRAIG, educator; b. Sheffield, Ala., June 7, 1923; s. Thomas Covie and Della (Richardson) H.; B.S. in Mech. Engring., U. Tenn., 1946; M.S., Va. Poly. Inst., 1950; Ph.D. (Ford Found. fellow), Ga. Inst. Tech., 1965; m. Mary Gladys Mason, May 10, 1946; children—James Craig, Juliann. Engring. draftsman TVA, Wilson Dam, Ala., 1941-42; asst. prof. U. Tenn., Knoxville, 1946-51; project engr. E.I. duPont de Nemours & Co., Inc., Wilmington, Del., 1951-54; asso. prof. mech. engring. Tenn. Tech. U., Cookeville, 1954-61, also head dept.; head mech. engring. dept. Clemson (S.C.) U., 1965-70, prof., 1970—. Cons. U.S. Naval Research Lab., Washington, 1956-57. Mem. Am. Soc. M.E., Hist. Soc. Pendleton, S.C., Sigma Xi, Tau Beta Pi, Scarabbean Soc. Baptist (deacon 1958-61). Research in freeze drying and energy conversion. Home: 506 Shorecrest Dr Clemson SC 29631

HARDIN, WILLIAM DOWNER, lawyer; b. Newark, Sept. 27, 1926 s. Charles R. and Emma (Downer) H.; A.B., Princeton, 1948; LL.B., Columbia, 1951; m. Rosemarie Koellhoffer, Jan. 19, 1952; children—William Downer, David Gerth, Peter Roe. Law clk. N.J. Superior Ct. Judge John O. Bigelow, 1951-52; admitted to N.J. bar, 1951, since practiced in Newark; mem. firm Pitney, Hardin & Kipp, Newark, 1957—. Mem. N.J. Bd. Bar Examiners, 1964-68, chmn., 1968; mem. local draft bd. SSS, 1953—, chmn., 1970—. Mem. Family Service Bur. Newark, 1953—, pres., 1960-66; mem. membership com. Family Service Assn. Am., 1965—, dir., 1971—, mem. Nat. Budget and Consultation Com., 1966—. Trustee Newark Acad., 1952—. Served with USNR, 1944-46. Mem. Am., N.J., Essex County bar assns. Episcopalian (vestry). Clubs: Essex (Newark); Princeton (N.Y.). Home: 15 Gap View Rd Short Hills NJ 07078 Office: 570 Broad St Newark NJ 07102

HARDING, BERTRAND MORRISON, govt. ofcl.; b. Ft. Worth, Feb. 19, 1919; s. Bertrand Morrison and Martha (Duncan) H.; A.B. in Econs., Antioch Coll., 1941; student pub. adminstrn. U. Minn., 1941-42; grad. Nat. Inst. Pub. Affairs, 1942; m. Isobel Ames, Sept. 14, 1941; children-Bertrand Morrison, Jeffrey A. Orgn. and methods examiner VA, 1946-50; analyst atomic weapons programs AEC, 1950-53; asst. to dep. commnr. Internal Revenue Service, 1953-54. asst. dir. collection div., 1955-58, asst. commr. planning and research, 1958-61, dep. commr. Internal Revenue Service 1961-66; dep. dir. Office Econ. Opportunity, 1966-68, acting dir., 1968-69; v.p. Fry Cons. Inc., 1969-70; asso. adminstr. FAA, Washington, 1970—. Served with USAAF, 1943-46. Mem. Am. Soc. Pub. Adminstrn. Home: 7206 Park Terrace Dr Alexandria VA 22307 Office: 800 Independence Av NW Washington DC

HARDING, DONALD FREDERICK, investment counsel; b. Newtonville, Mass., Jan. 25, 1906; s. Frederick W. and Laura (Restall) H.; A.B., Harvard, 1927; m. Charlotte Boyer Bent, Dec. 1, 1955; stepchildren—Edward S. Bent, Julia Bent. With Scudder, Stevens & Clark, Boston, 1927-42, 45—, partner, 1953—. With China Def. Supplies Agy., Washington and New Delhi, India, 1942-45, FEA, 1945. Trustee James Jackson Putnam Children's Center, Roxbury, Mass., 1957-65, treas., 1958, 61-62, pres., 1958; trustee New Eng. Conservatory Music, 1970—. Mem. Harvard Alumni Assn. (bd. dirs. 1963-65). Clubs: Country (Brookline); Nantucket (Mass.) Yacht. Home: 97 Laurel Rd Chestnut Hill MA 02167 Office: 10 Post Office Sq Boston MA 02109

HARDING, HAROLD FRIEND, educator; b. Niagara Falls, N.Y., July 30, 1903; s. Robert and Florence Alice (Friend) H.; A.B., Hamilton Coll., 1925, L.H.D., 1962; A.M., Cornell U., 1929, Ph.D., 1937; student summers 1930, 33, Eng. and France; grad. Command and Gen. Staff Sch., 1944; m. Eliza A. Reeves, Sept. 4, 1935; children—Daniel, Robert and Susan (twins). Instr. pub. speaking Ia. State Coll., 1925-27; asst. in English, Harvard Coll., 1928; instr. pub. speaking Cornell U., 1928- 31, asst. prof., 1931-38, asso. prof., 1938-44, prof., 1944-46; Chauncey M. Depew prof. and exec. officer, dept. of speech George Washington U., 1946; prof. speech Ohio State U. 1946-66; vis. prof. speech U. Cal., Santa Barbara, 1965-66; Benedict prof. U. Tex. at El Paso, 1966—; cons. for Battelle Meml. Inst., 1960—. Mem. ednl. survey commn. Command and Gen. Staff Coll., 1956. Active duty as capt. 57th C.A., 1941; advanced through grades to maj. gen. U.S. Army Res., 1960, chief of staff for replacement tng. command, Pacific Ocean areas, Sept. 1944-45, 43 mos. in PTO; inactive status, 1946; comdt. Ft. Hayes Army Res. Sch., 1950- 57; div. arty. comdr. 83d Inf. Div., 1957-60, div. comdr., 1960-64; active duty, C. & G.S.C., Ft. Leavenworth, Kan., summers, 1948-55. Decorated Bronze Star medal, Legion of Merit with oak leaf cluster. Rockefeller Found. post-war fellow in the humanities, 1946. Mem. A.A.A.S., Speech Assn. Am., Am. Assn. U. Profs., Inst. Strategic Studies (London), Delta Kappa Epsilon, Delta Sigma Rho (nat. treas. 1937- 41, trustee 1948-53), Pi Delta Epsilon. Editor: Quar. Jour. Speech, 1948-51; Eastern Public Speaking Conf., 1940; The Age of Danger, Major Speeches on American Problems, 1952; A Source Book for Creative Thinking, 1962; Lectures on Rhetoric and Belles Lettres, 1965. Contbr. to ednl. jours. Specialist in English rhetorical theory. Home: 60 Sutton Pl., El Paso, TX 79912

HARDING, HENRY WILFORD, aircraft engine mfg. co. exec.; b. Detroit, Dec. 10, 1910; s. Henry W. and Agnes L. Harding; A.B., Hamilton Coll., 1934; m. Agnes Bundy Burke, Aug. 29, 1936; children—Mary (Mrs. Joseph S. Nye, Jr.), Agnes Bundy (Mrs. Robert S. Boit), Anne (Mrs. Demetrius P. Lalas), Henry Wilford, Coleman Burke. With Gen. Electric Co., 1934-40; pres. Mfrs. Chem. Co., Berkeley Heights, N.J., 1940-47; sales dir. Koppers Co., 1947-49; pres. Stewart Hartshorn Co., Oswego, N.Y., 1949-52, Vulcan Rubber Co., Bklyn., 1952- 53, Tech.-Art Plastics Co., Morristown, N.J., 1953-60; pres., dir. Lab. for Electronics, Inc., Boston, 1956-68; chmn., dir. Charisma Internat. Corp., Boston, 1969—; chmn., chief exec. officer, dir. Allied Aero Industries, Inc., Syracuse, N.Y., Fanklin Engine Co., Syracuse; dir. Mohawk Airlines, Inc. Mem. corp. Boston Museum Sci., Univ. Hosp.; adv. com. Internat. Marketing Inst., Harvard Sch. Bus. Adminstrn.; trustee Boston U. Med. Center; incorporator Wentworth Inst. Mem. N.A.M. (dir.), Boston C. of C. (dir., v.p.), Chi Psi. Home: 300 Woodland Rd Chestnut Hill MA 02167 Office: Old Liverpool Rd Syracuse NY

HARDING, JAMES GORDON, hosp. adminstr.; b. Warsaw, Ind., June 12, 1921; s. Claude A. and Mabel (James) H.; B.S., Wayne State U., 1949; M.Hosp. Adminstrn., Washington U., St. Louis, 1951; m. Phyllis Meyer, June 14, 1947; children—Susan M., James M., Phillip A., Thomas D. Adminstrv. resident Aultman Hosp., Canton, O., 1950-51; asst. supt. St. Luke's Hosp., Cleve., 1951-52; adminstr. Cleve. Clinic Hosp., 1953-71; pres. Wilmington (Del.) Med. Center, 1971—. Mem. Bd. of Council and League for Nursing, Cleve.; chmn. Com. Regional Med. Program; mem. Blue Cross of N.E. Ohio Adv. Com. Served with AUS, 1942-45. Fellow Am. Coll. Hosp. Adminstrs.; mem. Am. (del.), Ohio (pres., dir.) hosp. assns., Nat. League Nursing. Home: 400 Foulk Rd Wilmington DE 19803 Office: PO Box 1668 Wilmington DE 19899

HARDING, JAMES WARREN, finance co. exec.; b. Montoursville, Pa., Nov. 9, 1918; s. James John and Alda (Edkin) H.; B.A., Lycoming Coll., 1937-38; M.A., U. Chgo., 1940; m. Emily Sue Landes, Mar. 22, 1941; 1 dau., Connie Sue (Mrs. Richard E. Fisher). With Kemper Cos., Chgo., 1940—, accountant, 1940-50, comptroller, 1960-68, exec. v.p., 1969, chmn. bd. Bank of Chgo., 1969—, pres. Tower Finance, Mercury Acceptance, Am. Underwriting Corp., Central Mortgage Co., Nat. Agts. Service Co., 1969—, also dir.; dir. Extel Corp., Hogan & Farwell, Kemperco Reinsurance Co. Pres. Park Ridge (Ill.) Community Assn., 1962-63; finance chmn. Crusade of Mercy, Chgo., 1964-65. Trustee James S. Kemper Found. Served with USNR, 1943-44. Recipient Hardy award Ins. Inst., 1946. Mem. Am. Mgmt. Assn., Econ Club, Financial Execs. Inst., Ins. Statis Assn., Phi Kappa Sigma. Republican. Methodist. Club: Univeristy (Chgo.). Contbr. articles to ins., trade mags. Home: 2455 Farrell Park Ridge IL 60068 Office: 4750 Sheridan Rd Chicago IL 60640

HARDING, JOHN FRANCIS, lawyer, pub. co. exec.; b. Pittsfield, Mass., Apr. 25, 1908; s. Clark J. and Clara (Decker) H.; A.B. magna cum laude, Harvard, 1930; LL.B., 1934; m. Anita M. Hutchinson, Sept. 2, 1934; 1 dau., Deborah Ann. Admitted to Mass. bar, 1934, N.Y. bar, 1935, also U.S. Supreme Ct.; asso. atty. firm Cravath de Gersdorff, Swaine & Wood, 1934-44; gen. counsel, dir. Cowles Communications, Inc., broadcasting and publishing, 1944—, sec., 1947—, v.p., 1953-65, exec. v.p., 1965—; v.p., dir. Cowles Fla. Broadcasting, Inc., Travelventures, Inc., Cowles Tenn. Radio Properties, Inc. Trustee Arts Trust Fund, Cowles Charitable Trust. Mem. Am., Fed. (N.Y., N.J., Conn.) bar assns., Assn. Bar City N.Y., Phi Beta Kappa, Delta Sigma Rho. Clubs: Harvard, University (N.Y.C.). Home: 136 E 56th St New York City NY 10022 also Danbury CT 06810 Office: 488 Madison Av New York City NY 10022

HARDING, THOMAS SPENCER, librarian; b. Gaines, N.Y., Feb. 24, 1910; s. Harrison Herbert and Jessie Louise (Call) H.; B.A. summa cum laude, U. Buffalo, 1933, B.S. in L.S., 1937; M.A., U. Chgo., 1939, Ph.D., 1957. Library asst. U. Buffalo, 1930-36; librarian Univ. Coll., Northwestern U., 1937-42, Mo. Valley Coll., 1946-48, Evansville (Ind.) Coll., 1948-66, Washburn U., Topeka, 1966—. Served with USNR, 1942-45. Mem. A.L.A., Am. Assn. U. Profs., Phi Kappa Phi, Pi Gamma Mu. Mem. Unitarian-Universalist Assn. Mason. Author articles. Home: 2120 High Av., Topeka KS 66611

HARDING, VICTOR MATHEWS, Jr., lawyer; b. Chgo., July 23, 1908; s. Victor Mathews and Mary M. (Boak) H.; grad. Phillip Exeter Acad., 1927; A.B. cum laude, Harvard, 1931, LL.B., 1935; Harvard scholar, Emmanuel Coll., Cambridge U., 1931-32; m. Julia Burley, May 25, 1940; children—Julia (Mrs. Richard L. Weidman), Mary Elizabeth, Katherine DeBlois, Victor Clark, Nancy Jane, Burley. Admitted to Ill. bar, 1935, Wis. bar, 1944; practiced in Chgo., 1935-42, Milw., 1944—; with firm Bell, Boyd & Marshall, 1935-42; trial atty. for solicitor U.S. Dept. Labor, 1942-44; mem. firm Whyte, Hirschboeck, Minahan, Harding & Harland, 1944—. Dir. Milw. Machine Products Co., Milmac Corp., Remus Catering Co., Tower Ranch. Mem. bd. appeals and bd. health, Village River Hills, 1948-65; mem. sch. bd. Nicolet High Sch., 1952-57, Mapledale Elementary Sch., 1950-56; mem. Com. Ct. Reorgn. Milwaukee County Bd. Suprs., 1959-60; mem. Joint Com. Bench and Bar to revise rules Circuit Ct. Milwaukee County, 1951-53. Trustee Milw. U. Sch., 1955-63. Mem. Am., Fed., Wis., Milw. bar assns., Am. Judicature Soc., Legal Club Chgo. Clubs: Milwaukee Athletic, Town, Wis. Harvard. Home: 7730 N. River Rd Milwaukee, WI 53217. Office: 2100 Marine Plaza Milwaukee WI 53202

HARDING, VINCENT, historian, educator; b. N.Y.C., July 25, 1931; B.A., City Coll. N.Y., 1952; M.S. in Journalism, Columbia, 1953; M.A. in History, U. Chgo., 1956, postgrad., 1965; m. Rosemarie Freeney, Aug. 1960; children—Rachel, Jonathan. Supply pastor 7th-day Adventist Ch., Chgo., 1955-57; lay asso. pastor Woodlawn Mennonite Ch. Chgo., 1957-61; So. rep. service com. Mennonite Central Com., Atlanta, 1961-64; asst. prof. history, chmn. dept. history and social scis. Spelman Coll., Atlanta, 1965—, dir. Martin Luther King, Jr. Library Project, 1968-70, Inst. of Black World. Kent fellow Soc. Religion in Higher Edn. Author: Must Walls Divide?, 1965, also chpts. to books. Contbg. editor, mem. editorial bd. Concern, Christianity and Crisis, Christian Century, others. Contbr. articles, poems, short stories, sermons to profl. publs. Home: 1592 Mayflower St SW Atlanta GA 30314

HARDING, WARREN GAMALIEL, hosp. adminstr., univ. adminstr.; b. Texico, N.M., May 15, 1922; s. Nath R. and Ethel (McQuatters) H.; B.A., Eastern N.M. U., 1943; M.Ed., Tex. Technol. U., Lubbock, 1950; m. Dorothy Llewellyn Paul, Mar. 12, 1949; children—Paula Joan (Mrs. Vernon R. Long), Robert Warren, Evelyn Ann, LaDenna Kaye. Jr. high sch. math tchr., Texico, 1946- 48; asst. registrar Tex. Technol. U., 1949-56; registrar U. Tex. Med. Br., Galveston, 1956-58; asso. dean medicine, 1958-65, v.p., 1965-70; adminstr. Bexar County Hosp. Dist. and asso. dean U. Tex. Med. Sch., San Antonio, 1970—; cons. hosp. adv. com USPHS Hosp., Galveston; lectr. Trinity U. Sch. Hosp. Adminstrn., San Antonio. Dir. Univ. Nat. Bank, Galveston. Pres. Galveston County Civic Music Assn., 1968-70; mem. Family Service Bd., 1968-69. Served to lt. (j.g.) USNR, 1943-46; PTO. Mem. Am., Tex. hosp. assns., San Antonio C. of C. Democrat. Baptist. Mason, Rotarian. Home: 10206 Kings Grant Dr San Antonio TX 78230 Office: 4502 Medical Dr San Antonio TX 78229

HARDINGE, HARLOWE, mfr.; b. Denver, Mar. 17, 1894; s. Hal Williams and Bertha (Wilson) H.; student Collegiate Sch., N.Y.C., 1906-10, Tome Sch., Port Deposit, Md., 1910-12; M.E., Cornell U., 1916; m. Florence Donnelly, Mar. 22, 1929; children—Byron Cantine, Harlowe De Forest. With Hardinge Conical Mill Co., N.Y.C., 1916-23; v.p., gen. mgr. Hardinge Co., Inc., York, Pa., 1923-39, pres., 1939-68, chmn., 1964—, also chief exec. officer; dir. Nat. Central Bank Pa.; cons. Hardinge Co. of Koppers Co., Inc., 1965-67. Trustee York Coll. Pa.; mem. council, former mem. alumni bd. Cornell U. Served as capt., Signal Corps, AUS, 1917-19. Registered profl. engr., Pa. Mem. Am. Inst. Mining and Metall. Engrs. (Legion Honor), York Mfrs. Assn. (past pres.) Pa. C. of C. (bd. dirs.), Canadian Inst. Mining and Metallurgy, Mining and Metall. Soc. Am., York Art Assn., Hist. Soc. York County, Laurel Fish and Game Assn., Sigma Xi, Phi Kappa Sigma. Republican. Clubs: Rotary, Lafayette, York Country; Chapleau (Que.); Monterey Peninsula Country (Pebble Beach, Cal.). Contbg. author: Taggart's Handbook of Mineral Dressing; Liddell Handbook of Plant Engineering; Zimmerman and Lavine Handbook of Engineering Costs. Home: 556 Country Club Rd York PA 17403 Office: PO Box 867 York PA 17404

HARDINGE, MERVYN GILBERT, univ. dean; b. Calcutta, India, July 29, 1914; s. Eustace Gilbert and Constance (Wilson) H.; B.S., Pacific Union Coll., 1939; M.D., Coll. Med. Evangelists (now Loma Linda U.), 1942; M.P.H., Harvard, 1949, D.P.H., 1952; M.A. in Pharmacology, Stanford, 1953, Ph.D., 1956; m. Margaret Olive Feldkamp, Aug. 31, 1939; children—Fred Gilbert, Jeanne Ann. Came to U.S., 1936, naturalized, 1951. Gen. surgery resident Coll. Med. Evangelists, 1942-43; mem. faculty Loma Linda (Cal.) U., 1943—, prof. pharmacology, chmn. dept., 1957-67, dir. div. pub. health, 1966-67, dean Sch. Pub. Health, 1967—. Diplomate Nat. Bd. Med. Examiners; licentiate Med. Council Can. Fellow Am. Heart Assn.; mem. Sigma Xi, Delta Omega, Alpha Omega Alpha. Editor: Life and Health, 1972. Contbr. articles to profl. jours. Home: 25139 Huron St Loma Linda CA 92354

HARDIS, STEPHEN ROGER, mfg. co. exec.; b. N.Y.C., July 13, 1935; s. Abraham I. and Ethel (Krinsky) H.; B.A. with distinction, Cornell U., 1956; M.P.A. in Economics, Woodrow Wilson Sch. of Pub. and Internat. Affairs, Princeton, 1960; m. Sondra Joyce Rolbin, Sept. 15, 1957; children—Julia Faye, Andrew Martin, Joanne Halley. Asst. to controller Gen. Dynamics, 1960-61; financial analyst Pfaudler Permutit Inc., 1961-64; staff asst. to controller 1964; mgr. corp. long-range planning Ritter Pfaudler Corp., 1965-68, dir. corporate planning, 1968; treas. Sybron Corp., Rochester, N.Y., 1969—, v.p. finance, 1970—; dir. Security Trust Co., OPIC Corp., Richardson Corp. Bd. dirs. Meml. Art Gallery, Genesee Hosp., United Negro Coll. Fund. Served with USNR, 1956-58. Mem. Rochester Soc. Security Analysts (pres.), Phi Beta Kappa. Home: 591 Winton Rd South Rochester NY 14618 Office: 1100 Midtown Tower Rochester NY 14604

HARDISON, OSBORNE BENNETT, Jr., educator; b. San Diego, Oct. 22, 1928; s. Osborne Bennett and Ruth (Morgan) H.; B.A., U. N.C., 1949, M.A. in English lit., 1950; Ph.D., U. Wis., 1956; m. Marifrances Fitzgibbon, Dec. 23, 1950; children—Charity Ruth, Sarah Frances, Laura Fitzgibbon, Agnes Margaret, Osborne Bennett, Mathew Fitzgibbon. Teaching asst. U. Wis., 1950-53; instr. English, U. Tenn., 1954-56, Princeton, 1956-57; mem. faculty U. N.C. at Chapel Hill, 1957-69, prof. English and comparative lit., 1967-69; dir. Folger Shakespeare Library, Washington, 1969—. Chmn. Southeastern Inst. Medieval and Renaissance Studies, 1965, co-chmn., 1966. Trustee U. Detroit, 1970—. Fulbright fellow, Rome, Italy, 1953-54; Folger Library fellow, summer, 1958; Guggenheim fellow, 1963-64; recipient Haskins medal Medieval Acad. Am., 1967. Fellow Am. Acad. Arts and Scis.; mem. Modern Lang. Assn. (exec. council 1968- -), Renaissance Soc. Am., Phi Beta Kappa. Author: Lyrics and Elegies, 1958; Modern Continental Literary Criticism, 1962; The Enduring Monument, 1962; English Literary Criticism: The Renaissance, 1964; Christain Rite and Christian Drama in the Middle Ages, 1965; Practical Rhetoric, 1966; (with Leon Golden) Aristotle's Poetics: A Translation and Commentary for Students of Literature, 1968. Editor (with others) The Encyclopedia of Poetry and Poetics, 1965; Medieval and Renaissance Studies, 1966; The Quest for Imagination, 1971; (with others) Film Scripts I-IV 1971. Editor Studies in Philology, 1966—; also series editor for book pubs. Office: Folger Library 2d and E Capitol Sts Washington DC 20005

HARDMAN, LAMARTINE GRIFFIN, Jr., textile mfr., banker; b. Commerce, Ga., July 5, 1908; s. Lamartine Griffin and Emma (Griffin) H.; student Ga. Mil. Acad.; B.S., U. Ga., 1930; m. Dorothy Shell, Oct. 16, 1934; children—Lamartine Griffin III, John, Shell (Mrs. Wyck A. Knox, Jr.). Chmn. bd. dirs. First Nat. Bank, Commerce; pres., treas. Harmony Grove Mills, Inc., Commerce; dir. Citizens & So. Nat. Bank, Savannah, Ga. Power Co., Bibb Mfg. Co., Macon, Ga. Past trustee Mercer U., Macon, Truett-McConnell Jr. Coll., Cleveland, Ga. Mem. Cotton Mfg. Assn. Ga. (past pres.), Am. Cotton Mfg. Inst. (past pres.), Phi Delta Theta. Democrat. Baptist. Clubs: Kiwanis, Capital City, Piedmont Driving (Atlanta). Home: Commerce GA 30529 Office: Harmony Grove Mills Inc Commerce GA 30529

HARDRE, JACQUES, educator; b. Dinan, France, Jan. 10, 1915; s. Rene S. and Berthe (Lefevre) H.; came to U.S., 1945, naturalized, 1956; B.A., Guilford (N.C.) Coll., 1937; M.A., U. N.C., 1942, Ph.D., 1948. Instr. French and German, Guilford Coll., 1937-39; teaching fellow U. N.C., Chapel Hill., 1939, instr. French, 1941-42, 45-49, asst. prof., 1949-53, asso. prof., 1953-57, prof., 1957-71, Kenan prof. French, 1971—, chmn. dept. Romance langs., 1964—, chmn. div. humanities, 1965-68; instr. Sewanee (Tenn.) French House, U. of South, summers 1960-61, N.C. U., Durham, 1961. Served to lt. French Army, 1939-40, 42-45. Decorated Croix de Guerre, Medaille de la France Libre, Medaille des Combattants Volontaires, chevalier Ordre des Palmes Academiques, chevalier Lēgion d'Honneur. Mem. Am. Assn. Tchrs. French (past pres.), Modern Lang. Assn. (past chmn. nat. com), S. Atlantic Modern Lang. Assn. (past. sect. chmn.), Modern Humanities Research Assn., Fédération Internationale des Professeurs de Français (exec. council 1969—), Société des Professeurs Français en Amerique, Alliance Francaise Chapel Hill (hon. pres.). Author: Letters of Louvois, 1949; La France et sa civilisation, 1969. Editor: (with G.B. Daniel). Huis-Clos, 1962, Le Malentendu, 1963; Les Enfants terribles, 1969; editor-in-chief The French Rev., 1968—. Contbr. profl. jours. Home: PO Box 771 Chapel Hill NC 27514

HARDWICK, ELIZABETH, (Mrs. Robert Lowell), author; b. Lexington, Ky., July 27, 1916; d. Eugene Allen and Mary (Ramsey) Hardwick; A.B., U. Ky., 1938, M.A., 1939; postgrad. Columbia, 1939-41; m. Robert Lowell, July 28, 1949; 1 dau., Harriet. Adj. asso. prof. Barnard Coll. Guggenheim fellow, 1947; recipient George Jean Nathan award, dramatic criticism, 1966. Author: (novels) The Ghostly Lover, 1945, The Simple Truth, 1955; (essays) A View of My Own, 1962. Editor: The Selected Letters of William James, 1960; adv. editor N.Y. Rev. Books. Contbr. Partisan Rev., New Yorker, Harpers. Home: 15 W 67th St New York City NY 10023

HARDWICK, JOHN HAROLD, banker; b. Stanton, Ky., Jan. 12, 1910; s. John Hudson and Ella (Grigsby) H.; A.B., Washington and Lee U., 1931; M.B.A., Harvard, 1933; m. June Lankford Warden, May 21, 1938; children—John Harold, Robert Duncan, Wayne Clay. With Guaranty Trust Co., N.Y.C., 1933-34; with Louisville Trust Co., 1934—, pres., 1962-67, chmn. bd., 1967—, also dir.; dir. Porter Paint Co., Commonwealth Life Ins. Co. Bd. dirs. Lexington Theol. Sem., Meth. Evang. Hosp., Blue Cross Plan. Mem. Ky. Bankers Assn., Assn. Res. City Bankers, Louisville C. of C., Phi Beta Kappa, Phi Delta

Theta, Omicron Delta Kappa. Republican. Mem. Christian Ch. Home: 2531 Tophill Rd Louisville KY 40206 Office: Louisville Trust Co 5th and Market Sts Louisville KY 40201

HARDY, ALEXANDER GEORGE, bus. exec., lawyer; b. Medford, Mass., Mar. 22, 1920; s. William and Grace A. (Mellen) H.; student bus. adminstrn., Boston U., 1945-46; LL.B., Suffolk U., 1941; m. Elisabeth M. Stewart, Aug. 5, 1947; children—Michael Stewart, Alexander George, Robin. Admitted to Mass. bar, 1942, D.C. bar, 1955, Fed. bar, 1945, FCC bar, 1954; atty. Evarts & Gallagher, Boston, 1945-46; exec. counsel Nuremberg War Crime Trials, 1946-49; pub. counsel CAB, 1949- 51; br. counsel OPS, 1951; exec. asst. to pres. Nat. Airlines, Washington, 1951-53, asst. v.p., 1953-54, v.p., 1954-55, sr. v.p., 1955- 60, sr. v.p., corporate sec., Miami Fla., 1960-63; asst. to chmn. bd. Automatic Canteen Co. Am., 1963, exec. v.p., 1963-65; dir. AVEMCO Corp., 1960—, pres., chmn. bd., 1965—; dir. Union Trust Co. Md. Mem. Nat. Def. Exec. Res. Served with Office Naval Intelligence, USNR, 1942-45; CBI. Recipient Horatio Alger award, 1971. Mem. Bar Assn. D.C., Air Force Assn. Clubs: Nat. Aviation (gov. 1958-60, pres. 1967-68), Congressional Country (Washington); Palm Bay (Miami, Fla.). Author: Hitler's Secret Weapon, 1968. Home: 9030 River Rd Potomac MD 20854 Office: 7979 Old Georgetown Rd Bethesda MD 20014

HARDY, ALLAN FRASER, Jr., mfg. co. exec.; b. Worcester, Mass., Apr. 13, 1913; s. Allan Fraser and Lillian Caroline (Dahiquist) H.; B.S., Worcester Poly. Inst., 1935; grad. Advanced Mgmt. Program, Harvard, 1945; m. Mildred I. Sears, Nov. 26, 1938; children—Pamela S., Allan Fraser III, Bruce Robert, Christopher Douglas. With Norton Co., Worcester, 1935—, now group v.p., also dir.; v.p., pres., dir. National Research Corporation, Newton, Mass., 1965—; incorporator Worcester Mechanics Savs. Bank. Gen. campaign chmn. Worcester Community Chest, 1961-62, Worcester A.R.C., 1955-56. Bd. dirs. Holden (Mass.) Dist. Hosp., Worcester Community Services, Baptist. Clubs: Worcester Country, Kiwanis (past pres., dir.), Economic (Worcester). Home: 127 Highland St Holden MA 01520 Office: Nat Research Corp Charlemont St Newton MA 02169

HARDY, ALLSTER CLAVERLING, zoologist, educator; b. Nottingham, Eng., Feb. 10, 1896; s. Richard Hardy; ed. Oundle Sch., Exeter Coll., Oxford; M.A., Oxford U., D.Sc.; LL.D., U. Aberdeen; D.Sc Southampton, Hull; m. Sylvia Lucy Garstang, 1927; 1 son, 1 dau. Christopher Welch biol. research scholar, 1920; Oxford biol. scholar Stazione Zoologica, Naples, Italy, 1920; asst. naturalist fisheries dept. Ministry Agr. and Fisheries, 1921-24; chief zoologist Discovery Expdn., 1924-28; prof. zoology and oceanography Univ. Coll., Hull, Eng., 1928-42; Regius prof. natural history U. Aberdeen, 1942-45 Gifford lectr., 1963-65; Linacre prof. zoology Oxford U., 1946-61, now prof. emeritus, hon. fellow Merton Coll. Created knight, 1957. Recipient Sci. medal Zool. Soc., 1939. Fellow Royal Soc. Author: The Open Sea, Part I, The World of Plankton, 1956, Part II, Fish and Fisheries, 1958; Memoirs on Biological Oceanography; The Living Stream, 1965; The Divine Flame, 1966; Great Waters, 1967. Joint editor Bulls. Marine Ecology. Club: Athenaeum. Address: 7 Capel Close Oxford England

HARDY, ARTHUR C., physicist; b. Worcester, Mass., Dec. 2, 1895; s. Charles Clough and Helen Estelle (Cobb) H.; A.B., U. Cal., 1917, A.M., 1919; Sc.D., St. Lawrence U., 1938; LL.D., U. Cal. at Berkeley, 1967; m. Charlotte Lansing, 1920; 1 son, Robert Lansing (dec.). Asst. in physics Mass. Inst. Tech., 1917, instr. physics, 1919; with Kodak Research Labs., 1920-22; asst. prof. optics and photography Mass. Inst. Tech., 1922-28, asso. prof., 1928-33, prof., 1933-61, prof. emeritus, 1961—. Served as comdg. officer 23d Photog. Sect., U.S. Army, with AEF, 1918; lt. comdr. USNR, 1936-40; NDRC sect. chief, World War II. Recipient Longstreth medal Franklin Inst., 1939; Presdl. Certificate of Merit, 1948; Modern Pioneer award, 1940; Frederic Ives medal Optical Soc. Am., 1957; Progress Medal award Soc. Motion Picture and Television Engineers, 1963. Fellow Photo. Soc. Am., Am. Acad. Arts and Scis., Soc. Motion Picture Engrs., Distinguished Serv. Found. of Optometry; mem. Optical Soc. Am. (pres. 1935-37, sec. 1940-57), Am. Assn. Physics Teachers, Sigma Xi. Inventor recording spectrophotometer. Author of books and scientific papers on light and color. Home: 15 Kenilworth Rd Wellesley MA 02181

HARDY, CLYDE THOMAS, educator; b. Fremont, O., Apr. 23, 1921; s. Clyde Harold and Nellie Mae (Capper) H.; B.A., Ohio State U., 1943, M.S., 1948, Ph.D., 1949. Asst. prof. Utah State U., Logan, 1950-53, asso. prof., 1954-66, prof., head dept. geology, 1967—. Vis. asso. prof. Ohio State U., summer 1957. Served to 1st lt. USAAF, 1943-46. Fellow Geol. Soc. Am., Meteoritical Soc.; mem. Am. Assn. Petroleum Geologists, Am. Geophys. Union. Home: 543 N 4th East Logan UT 84321

HARDY, CORNELIUS EDWARD, office equipment co. exec.; b. Rosboro, Ark., Dec. 8, 1924; s. Jennings Bryan and Essie (McDonnell) H.; A.B. in Commerce, Chico State Coll., 1951; m. Mary Elizabeth Tedford, Aug. 27, 1950; children—Heather Jeannett Colin Edward, Craig Tedford, Meaghan Elizabeth. Staff accountant Peat. Marwick, Mitchell & Co., San Francisco, 1951-58; staff accountant Friden, Inc., San Leandro, Cal., 1958-63, controller marketing, 1963-69, treas., 1964-69; controller Arcata Data Mgmt. (formerly Butler Data Systems), Hawthorne, 1969-70, v.p., 1971—. Served with USNR, 1943-46. C.P.A., Cal. Mem. Inst. C.P.A.'s, Financial Execs. Inst. Presbyn. (elder). Home: 4191 Silliman Dr Huntington Beach CA 92647 Office: 12911 Cerise Av Hawthorne CA 90250

HARDY, D. ELMO, educator; b. Lehi, Utah, Sept. 3, 1914; s. Horace P. and Ivy (Allred) H.; B.S., Brigham Young U., 1937; posgrad Utah State U., 1938; Ph.D., U. Kan., 1941; m. Agnes Thomas, Sept. 6, 1935; children—Patricia-Jane (Mrs. Willard C. Swiger), Joan (Mrs. J.P. Layton), Cheryl (Mrs. Marlon S. Maloy), Dee Elmo. Instr. entomology U. Kan., 1938-41; asst. entomologist Kan. Entomol. Com., 1941-42; asst. prof. Ia. State U., 1945-48; sr. prof. entomology U. Hawaii, 1948—, chmn. dept., 1958- 68; field research, New Guinea, summer 1957; asso. B.P. Bishop Mus., Honolulu, 1950—; field research, Southeast Asia, 1968; research in European Museums, 1954, 60-61, 68. Dir. research projects sponsored by NIH, also NSF; participant Internat. Congresses Entomology and Sci., Vienna, Austria, 1960, London, Eng., 1964, Honolulu, 1961, Tokyo, Japan, 1966. Mem. Hawaii Natural Areas Res. Commn., 197O—. Served to maj. AUS, 1942-45; CBI. Decorated Bronze Star; recipient award for outstanding research U. Hawaii, 1968. Fellow Orgn. European Econ. Devel., U. Vienna, 1960-61. Fellow A.A.A.S., Am., Hawaiian (past pres.) entomol. socs., Sigma Xi (past pres. U. Hawaii). Author: Diptera: Nematocera and Brachycera, Insects of Hawaii, Vol. 10, 1960, Diptera Brachycera II-Cyclorrhapha I. Vol. 11, 1964, Diptera: Cyclorrhap. II, family Drosophilidae, Vol. 12, 1965 Contbr. numerous articles to profl. jours Bd. editors Beltrage Zur Entomologie, Berlin, Germany, 1964—, Tropical Insects, New Delhi, India, 1971—. Home: 2238 Seaview Av Honolulu HI 96822

HARDY, DAVID, mfg. co. exec., lawyer; b. Los Angeles, May 15, 1924; s. Rex Giffen and Dorothy Field (Simpson) H.; student U. Cal. at Los Angeles, 1942-44, 46- 47, at Berkeley, 1947-50; B.A., LL.B., m. Constance Parrette, (div. 1969); children—Francesca, David Kimberley, Robert Paul; m. 2d, Charlotte Barkar Solomons, Feb. 28, 1969; stepchildren—Karen Lee, Varda; 1 dau., Crystine. Admitted to Cal. bar, 1951; v.p., sec., counsel Kaiser Steel Corp., 1969—; v.p., sec. Kaiser Resources, Ltd., Vancouver, B.C., 1969—. Served to lt. (j.g.) USNR, 1943-46 Mem. Am. Bar Assn., State Bar Cal., Order of Coif. Home: 2684 Green St San Francisco CA 94123 Office: 300 Lakeside Dr Oakland CA 94604

HARDY, DAVID ROSS, lawyer; b. Versailles, Mo., Aug. 4, 1917; s. David Crockett and Jana Ross (Witten) H.; student Westminister Coll., Fulton, Mo., 1934-36; LL.B., U. Mo., 1939; m. Eleanor Louise Kincaid, June 8, 1940; children—David Kincaid, Sarah Elizabeth. Admitted to Mo. bar, 1939; asso. firm Sebree, Sebree & Shook, Kansas City, 1939-42; partner Shook, Hardy, Ottman, Mitchell & Bacon and predecessors, 1942—. Lawyer-mem. 16th Circuit Jud. Selection Com., 1956-61; chmn. 16th Circuit Bar Disciplinary Com., 1956-60, 63—. Dir. Commerce Bank of Tipton, Fidelity Security Life Ins. Co., Myron Green Cafeterias, Myron Green Bldg. Co., Wornall Bank. Chmn., Mayor's Commn. on civil Disorders, 1969. Trustee, pres. U. Mo. Law Sch. Found., 1959-60; trustee Mo. Sch. Religion, 1958-61; bd. dirs. Nat. Edn. Found, Served to capt., Corps Mil. Police, AUS, 1942-46. Mem. Am., Mo., Kansas City (pres. 1959-60) bar assns, Kansas City (Mo.) Claims Assn. (pres. 1958), Am. Coll. Trial Lawyers, Internat. Soc. Barristers, Nat. Assn. Railroad Trial Lawyers, Internat. Assn. Ins. Counsel, Fedn. Ins. Counsel, Kappa Alpha, Phi Delta Phi. Democrat. Mem. Christian Ch. Mason. Clubs: University, Mission Hills Country (Kansas City, Mo.). Home: 1246 W 62d St Kansas City KA 64113 Office: 915 Grand Av Kansas City MO 64106

HARDY, EDWARD ROCHIE, clergyman, educator; b. N.Y., June 17, 1908; s. Edward R. and Sarah (Belcher) H.; grad. Friends Sem., N.Y.C., 1920; A.B., Columbia, 1923, M.A., 1924, Ph.D., 1931; grad. Gen. Theol. Sem., N.Y.C., 1929, S.T.B., 1933, S.T.M., 1934; S.T.D., 1956; S.T.M., Union Theol. Sem., N.Y.C., 1932; M.A., Cambridge U., 1969; m. Marion Dunlap, Sept. 14, 1939; 1 son, Stephen Minear. Ordained to ministry P.E. Ch. as deacon, 1929, priest, 1932; asst. pastor St. Paul's Ch., Spring Valley, also St. Stephen's Ch., Pearl River, N.Y., 1930-31, St. Andrew's Ch., Astoria, L.I., N.Y., 1932-36; fellow and tutor Gen. Theol. Sem., 1929-44, instr. Hebrew 1940-44; asso. prof. ch. history Berkeley Div. Sch., New Haven, 1945-47, prof., 1947-69; Univ. lecturer, Cambridge, 1969-; World Council of Churches del. to Near East, 1947, 55; mem. Joint Commn. Ecumenical Relations (Episcopal Church), 1955-61, 64-70; mem. World Council of Chs. Commn. on Faith and Order, 1961—. Author: The Large Estates of Byzentine Egypt, 1931; Militant in Earth: Twenty Centuries of the Spread of Christianity, 1940; Christian Egypt: Church and People, 1952; Faithful Witnesses; Records of Early Christian Martyrs, 1959; (with Eugene Fairweather) The Voice of the Church: The Ecumenical Council, 1962; others. Editor: Orthodox Statements on Anglican Orders, 1946; (with W.N. Pittenger) This Holy Fellowship: The Ancient Faith in the Modern Parish, 1939; Christology of the Later Fathers, 1954, others. Home: 12 St Mark's Ct Cambridge England Office: Div Sch St John's St Cambridge England

HARDY, GLENN W., educator; A.B., M.S., Kan. State Coll.; Ph.D., Kan. State U. Now prof. agronomy, dean Coll. Agr. and Home Econs., U. Ark. Address: Coll Agr and Home Econs U Ark Fayetteville AR 72701

HARDY, GORDON ALFRED, educator; b. Hudson, Ind., Aug. 18, 1918; s. Carl Alfred and Gayle (Pike) H.; B.A., B.Mus., U. Mich., 1941, M.Mus., 1946; B.S., Juilliard Sch. Music, 1952; m. Lillian Studebaker, May 19, 1945; children—Gordon Alfred, John Studebaker, Christopher Bartlett, Susan, Jeffrey Pike. Teaching fellow Juilliard Sch. Music, 1952-53, teaching asst., 1953-54, mem. faculty lit. and materials of music dept., 1954—, asso. dean, 1963- 69, dean students, 1970—; dean Aspen (Colo.) Music Sch., 1963—. Served to lt. USNR, 1942-45. Mem. Theta Chi. Author: (with Arnold Fish) Music Literature-A Workbook for Analysis, vol. I, Homophony, 1963, vol. II, Polyphony, 1966. Home: 149 E 73 St New York City NY 10021

HARDY, JAMES DANIEL, educator; b. Georgetown, Tex., Aug. 11, 1904; s. James Chappel and Lulu (Daniel) H.; B.A., U. Miss., 1924, M.A., 1925; Ph.D., Johns Hopkins, 1930; M.A. (hon.), Yale, 1961; D.Sc, Kansas City Coll. Osteopathy and Surgery, 1966, Southwestern U., 1967; honoris causa U. Lyon (France), 1970; m. Augusta Ewing Haugh, June 8, 1928; children—James Daniel, George Frederick. Asst. prof. math., physics and astronomy U. Miss., 1925-27; NRC fellow physics U. Mich., 1930-32; research fellow Russell Sage Inst. Pathology, Cornell U., 1932-41, asst. prof. physiology Cornell U., 1941-53; prof. physiology U. Pa., 1953-61; prof. physiology Yale Sch. Medicine, dir. John B. Pierce Found. Lab., New Haven, 1961—. George Phillips Graves lectr. U. Ind., 1960; Rowe-Smith Meml. lectr., 1961; Kennon Meml. lectr. U. Miss., 1956; mem. man in space com., space sci. bd. NRC, 1958-60; chmn. Com. on Naval Med. Research, 1964-69. Served to comdr. USNR, 1941-45; ETO; rear adm. Res. Decorated Legion of Merit, Purple Heart; recipient Meritorious Civilian Service award U.S. Navy, 1961. Fellow Am. Phys. Soc., Aerospace Med. Assn. (Eric Liljencrantz medal 1960), Nat. Acad. Scis., Am. Acad. Arts and Scis.; mem. Am. Physiol. Soc., Harvey Soc., Soc. Exptl. Biology and Medicine, John Morgan Soc., Biophysics Soc., Am. Soc. Heating, Refrigeration and Air-Conditioning Engrs., Internat. Inst. Bioclimatology, A.A.A.S., Naval Res. Assn., Res. Officers Assn. Conglist. Clubs: Yale (N.Y.C.); Cosmos (Washington). Editor: Temperature, Its Measurement and Control in Science and Industry, 3d edit., 1962; Pain Sensations and Reactions, 1952; Physiological Problems in Space Exploration, 1963; Physiological and Behavioral Temperature Regulation, 1970. Home: 1127 Racebrook Rd Woodbridge CT 06519

HARDY, JAMES DANIEL, surgeon; b. Birmingham, Ala., May 14, 1918; s. Fred Henry and Julia Ann (Poynor) H.; B.A., U. Ala., 1938; M.D., U. Pa., 1942, M.S., 1951; m. Louise Scott Sams, July 1, 1949; children—Louise Scott, Julia Ann, Bettie Winn, Katherine Poynor. Intern Hosp. of U. Pa., 1942-43, med. residency, 1943-44, surg. residency, 1946-51; asst. instr. medicine U.Pa. Sch. Medicine, 1943-44, asst. instr. surgery, 1946-49, instr. surgery, 1949-51; asso. prof. surgery, dir. surg. labs. U. Tenn. Sch. Medicine, 1951-55; prof., chmn. dept. surgery, dir. surg. research U. Miss. Sch. Medicine, 1955—; surgeon-in-chief Hosp. of U. Miss., 1955—; chief surg. cons. VA Hosp., Jackson, Miss., Miss. Tb Sanatorium, 1955—. Served as capt., M.C., AUS, 1944-46. Diplomate Am. Bd. Surgery (mem. bd.), Am. Board Thoracic Surgery. Mem. Internat. Surg. Group (founder mem.), Am., So. surg. assns., Soc. Univ. Surgeons (pres. 1961), A.C.S., A.M.A., Am. Assn. Thoracic Surgery, Am. Coll. Cardiology, Surg. Biology Club (founder mem.), Central Med. Soc., Miss., So. med. assns., Transplanation Soc., Sigma Xi, Pi Kappa Alpha, Alpha Omega Alpha, Phi Chi. Presbyn. Author: Surgery of the Endocrine System, 1952; Fluid Therapy, 1954; surgical physiology of the Adrenal Cortex, 1955; Pathophysiology in surgery, 1958; Total Surgical Management, 1959; (with others) Biopsy Manual, 1959; Surgery of the Aorta and Its Branches, 1960. Editor: (with C.P. Artz) Complications in Surgery and Their Management, 1960; (with others) Manual on Preoperative and Postoperative Care of the American College of Surgeons, 1967; Human Organ Support and Replacement: Transplantation and Artificial Prostheses, 1971; Critical Surgical Illness, 1971. Editorial bd. Am. Jour. Surgery, Jour. Surg. Research, Surgery. Home: 2531 Eastover Jackson MS 39211

HARDY, JEROME SPILMAN, financial exec.; b. Manhattan, Kan., Jan. 2, 1918; s. Cleo Clinton and Irene (Johnson) Hardy; B.S., U. Md., 1939; m. Betty St. Clair, Dec. 13, 1946; children—Martha, James, Douglas, Gordon, Quentin. Mem. hwy. edn. bd. Automotive Safety Found., 1939-43; partner Harris & Hardy, S.A., pub. relations firm, 1946; exec. Doubleday & Co., N.Y.C., 1947-59, v.p. for advt. 1956-59; dir. Life Book div. Time, Inc., N.Y.C., 1959-60, pub. Book div., 1961, also v.p. corp.; pub. Life mag., 1964-70; exec. v.p. Dreyfus Corp., 1970, pres., 1970—. Bd. dirs. Salk Inst., Nat. Book Com., Project Hope. Served from pvt. to 1st lt. USAAF, 1943-46. Mem. Nat. Library Assn. (bd. dirs), Franklin Book Programs). Clubs: Country of Darien (Conn.); University (N.Y.C.); Stanwich Country, Augusta Nat. Golf, Pine Valley Golf, Nat. Golf Links Am., Mid-Ocean, Bermuda, New Canaan Field. Home: 19 Fable Farm Rd New Canaan CT 06840 Office: Rockefeller Center New York City NY 10020

HARDY, JOHN EDWARD, educator, author; b. Baton Rouge, Apr. 3, 1922; s. Roger Barlow and Mary (McCoy) H.; B.A., La. State U., 1944; M.A., State U. Ia., 1946; Ph.D., Johns Hopkins, 1956; m. Marie Elam, Dec. 30, 1942 (div.); children—Margot (Mrs. Timm Ferguson); Leonore (Mrs. David Dvorkin), Catherine (Mrs. Joseph Yahr), Laura, Anne, Eve; m. 2d, Willene Schaefer, June 25, 1969. Mem. English faculties U. Detroit, 1945-46, Yale, 1946- 48, U. Okla., 1948-52, Johns Hopkins, 1952-54; mem. faculty U. Notre Dame, 1954-66, prof. English, 1964-66, mem. acad. council, 1963-66, grad. council, 1963-66; prof. English, chmn. dept. U. South Ala., 1966- 69; prof. English, U. Colo., Boulder, 1969-70; prof. English, chmn. dept. U. Mo., ST. Lowis, 1970—, spl. research modern English and Am. lit.; Fulbright prof. Am. lit. U. Munich (Germany), 1959-61. Ford Faculty Study fellow, 1952-53; Rockefeller fellow poetry, 1954. Mem. Modern Lang. Assn., Am. Assn. U. Profs., Phi Beta Kappa. Author: (with Cleanth Brooks) Poems of Mr. John Milton, 1951; The Curious Frame, 1962; Man in the Modern Novel, 1964; Certain Poems, 1958. Editor: The Modern Talent, 1964; (Seymour L. Gross) Images of the Negro in American Literature, 1966. Office: Dept of English Univ of Missouri St Louis MO 63121

HARDY, JOHN FORSTER, ret. oil co. exec.; b. Carnegie, Pa., Dec. 31, 1895; s. George and Lillian (Forster) H.; grad. Kiskiminetas Prep. Sch., 1915; M.E., Lehigh U., 1919; m. Grace Lucille Borgerding, June 17, 1955. With sales dept. Cadillac Motor Co., 1919-20; engr. Jones & Laughlin Steel Co., Pitts., 1920-23; mgr. New Eng. office Pitts. Water Heater Co., Boston, 1923-26; asst. to pres. Benedum-Trees Oil, Pitts., 1926-54; dir., gen. mgr. Central Leduc Oils, Ltd., also Del Rio Producers, 1954, following their merger became v.p., dir., gen. mgr. Central-Del Rio Oils Ltd., later pres. and chmn.; pres., gen mgr., dir. Central-Del Rio Oils, Inc., U.S.; v.p., dir. Minerals Ltd. Served to 2d lt. as pilot USAC, World War I; col. USAAF, 1942-44. Mem. Can. Petroleum Assn. (former gov., dir. exec. com. Alta. div.), Order Daedalians, Alpha Iota Epsilon, Delta Tau Delta. Republican. Episcopalian. Mason (32 Shriner). Clubs: Aero, Chartiers Country (Pitts.); Calgary Golf and Country, Ranchmen's, Calgary Petroleum (Calgary). Home: 728 Crescent Blvd SW Calgary 6 Alberta Canada

HARDY, JOHN SPENCER, retired air force officer; b. Logansport, La., May 7, 1913; s. John Spencer and Addie (Hunt) H.; student Baylor U., 1930-31, La. Poly. Inst., 1931-32, U. Tex., 1932-33; A.B., Centenary Coll., 1938; m. Virginia Elizabeth Doyle, Sept. 21, 1940; children—Elizabeth, John Spencer, George. Commd. 2d lt. AC, U.S. Army, advanced through grades to lt. gen. USAF, 1966; pilot tng. Randolph and Kelly fields, San Antonio, 1935-36; flying, staff assignments, March Field, Cal., Barksdale Field, La., also Savannah, Ga., to World War II; chief operations 8th Air Force, Eng., North Africa, Italy, then chief operations AAF, Mediterranean Theater, World War II; bomb wing, div. comdr. Strategic Air Command, 1951-53; dep. dir. mil. personnel hdqrs. USAF, 1953-57; dep. chief staff for plans and operations Pacific Air Forces and Pacific Comd., 1957-60; comdr. Keesler Tech. Tng. Center, Biloxi, Miss., 1960-64; chief mil. assistance adv. group U.K., 1964-65, comdr. 3d Air Force USAF, Europe; comdr. Allied Air Forces So. Europe, 1966-68; comdt. Indsl. Coll. Armed Forces, 1967-70, ret., 1970; now cons. Decorated D.S.M. Trustee Centenary Coll. La. with oak leaf cluster, Legion of Merit with two oak leaf clusters, Croix de Guerre with Palm (Belgium), Air Force D.S.M.; Royal Order King George I (Greece); Comdr. with Merit of Italian Republic. Mem. Air Force Assn. Baptist. Address: 508 Wilder Pl Shreveport LA 71104

HARDY, JOSEPH, actor; b. Arlington, Mass., Aug. 10, 1918; s. James Joseph and Nora (Curtin) H.; m. Lynne Emery, August 17, 1966. Appeared on the Major Bowes Radio Amateur Hour, 1942; appeared on the Arthur Godfrey Radio Talent Show, 1947; night club mimic act, 1945—; Broadway appearances include Tempest, 1945, Detective Story, 1950, Small Hours, 1951, Male Animal, 1952, Mr. Roberts, 1956; Cut of the Axe, 1960, The Freaking Out of Stephanie Blake, 1967; motion picture appearances include Middle of the Night, 1959, Tell Me in The Sunlight, 1963, Husbands, 1969; The Arrangement, 1969; toured in The Front Page, Fla.-Can. tour, 1970; appeared with wife in Never Too Late, 1970, Masque of St. George and the Dragon, Actor's Studio, 1970. Mem. Screen Actors Guild, Actors Equity Assn., A.F.T.R.A. Democrat. Roman Catholic. Office: Box 238 Radio City Station New York City NY 10019

HARDY, L. MARTIN, physician; b. Riverside, Ia., Sept. 8, 1906; s. Alva B. and Fannie May (Fessler) H.; student Arkansas City Jr. Coll., 1924-26, U. Chgo., 1927- 29; B.M., Northwestern U., 1933, M.D., 1934; m. Margaret Rothfus, Sept. 19, 1929; children—Catherine (Mrs. Robert Ream), Ann (Mrs. Peter Janss). Intern Passavant Meml. Hosp., Chgo., 1932-33, resident, 1933-34; resident Children's Meml. Hosp., Chgo., 1934-35, 36, Municipal Contagious Disease Hosp., Chgo., 1935-36; practice pediatrics, Chgo., 1936—; chmn. pediatrics Passavant Meml. Hosp., 1940—, Chgo.. Wesley Meml. Hosp., 1961-71; med. dir. outpatient dept., attending physician Children's Meml. Hosp., 1949—; Abt fellow pediatrics Northwestern U. Med. Sch., 1936-42, asso. prof. pediatrics, 1954—. Mem. med. adv. bd. Vis. Nurse Assn. Chgo., 1963-66. Trustee Ill. Children's Home and Air Soc. Diplomate Nat. Bd. Med. Examiners. Mem. A.M.A., Ill., Chgo. med. socs., Am. Acad. Pediatrics, Chgo. Pediatric Soc., Inst. Medicine Chgo., Alpha Kappa Kappa, Phi Delta Theta. Contbr. profl. jours. Home: 2230 Lincoln Park W Chicago IL 60614 Office: 700 N Michigan Av Chicago IL 60611

HARDY, ROBERT MACDONALD, univ. dean; b. Winnipeg, Man., Can., Sept. 25, 1906; s. Robert and Winifred (Paterson) H.; B.Sc. in Civil Engring., U. Man., 1929, D.Sc., 1957; M.Sc., McGill U., 1930; m. France de Savoye, Aug. 23, 1939; children—Robert Alexander, John Antony. Mem. faculty U. Alta., Edmonton, 1930-59, prof. civil engring., 1946-59, dean faculty engring., 1946-59, 63—; cons. engr. field found. engring. and earth structures, Edmonton, 1959—; pres. R.M. Hardy & Assos., Ltd., Edmonton, 1950-, Materials Testing Labs., Ltd., Edmonton, 1950—. Mem. Borden Royal Commn. on Energy, 1958-59; tech. adviser Manning Royal Commn. on location Pine Point Ry., 1959-60; mem. Alta. Research Council, 1959—. Mem. Alta. Hotel Assn. Scholarship Com. Recipient citation Canadian

Good Roads Assn., 1962. Fellow Royal Soc. Can., Engring. Inst. Can.; mem. Am. Soc. C.E., Am. Soc. Engring. Edn., Assn. Profl. Engrs. Alta. and Man. Unitarian. Mason, Rotarian. Contbr. articles engring. and edn. profl. jours. Home: 11615 Edinboro Rd Edmonton Alberta Canada

HARDY, RONALD, author; b. London, Eng., Nov. 16, 1919; s. Harold Frederick and Elsie Alice (Wheeldon) H.; student Bec Sch., London, 1931-36; m. Joyce Margaret Cook, Sept. 30, 1946; children—Christopher Julian, Christine. Practice as certified pub. accountant, 1950-60; writer 1960—. Served with Royal Corps Signals, 1939-45. Asso. mem. Assn. Certified and Corp. Accountants. Author: The Place of Jackals, 1954; A Name Like Herod, 1955; Kampong, 1957; The Men From the Bush, 1959; Act of Destruction (James Tait Black Meml. Book prize 1962), 1962; The Iron Snake, 1965; The Savages, 1967 (Putnam award); also four radio and TV plays. Address: Bridle Path Cottage Ralliwood Rd Ashtead Surrey England

HARDY, ROYCE ALLER, mining engr.; b. Reno, May 20, 1921; s. Roy A. and Bonnie (Thoma) H.; B.S., U. Nev., 1946; student U. Arizona, Stanford University; m. Joan E. Eldredge; children—Helen (Mrs. M.E. Mills), Susan Leslie, Royce Aller III. Gen. supt. Getchell Mine, Inc., Humboldt County, Nev., 1946-56; v.p., gen. mgr. Manganese, Inc., Henderson, Nev., 1956-57; asst. sec. for mineral resources Dept. Interior, 1957-61; cons. engr., 1961; devel. dir. Duval Corp., 1961-67, v.p., 1967—. Served with AUS, 1943-46. Mem. Nat. Soc. Profl. Engrs., Am. Inst. Mining, Metall. and Petroleum Engrs., Mining and Metall. Soc. Am. Republican. Mason (Shriner, 32). Clubs: Mining (N.Y.). Home: 6745 Tivani Dr Tucson AZ 85715 Office: 4715 Fort Lowell Rd Tucson AZ 85716

HARDY, WILLIAM GEORGE, educator; b. Cleve., Oct. 7, 1910; s. Edward Clyde and Elizabeth (Kuhl) H.; Ph.B., Brown U., 1931; A.M., N.Y.U., 1933; Ph.D., Cornell U., 1943; m. Miriam Dorothy Pauls, Aug. 3, 1960; children by previous marriage— Robert Clyde, Mary Virginia (Mrs. Lonnie J. Wall, Jr.), John Andrew. Asst. instr. speech Brown U., 1931-32; instr. speech U. N.Y. at Albany, 1935-40, Cornell U., 1940-43; prof. environmental medicine, asso. prof. otolaryngology, also dir. hearing and speech Johns Hopkins Med. Instns., 1947—; cons. in field, 1947—. Chmn. med. adv. bd. United Cerebral Palsy Greater Balt., 1963—. Served to lt. USNR, 1944-46. Mem. Am. Speech and Hearing Assn. (pres. 1966, mem. exec. council 1965-67), Alexander Graham Bell Assn. for Deaf (1st v.p. 1967), Sigma Xi, Phi Kappa Phi. Author numerous articles, chpts. in books. Home: 2533 Pickwick Rd Baltimore MD 21207

HARDY, J. E., steel corp. exec. Vice pres., treas. Continental Steel Corp. Office: 1109 S Main St Kokomo IN 46901*

HARE, CHANNING, portrait painter; b. N.Y.C.; s. William I. and Florence Angela (Monk) H.; student Art Students League; also with Robert Henri and George Bellows; m. Josephine Whitney Brooks, July 29, 1929. One man shows; various private galleries; exhbns. at Worcester Mus. Art, Balt. Mus. Art, John Herron Art Inst., Carnegie Inst., U. Ill., Met. Mus. Art, others; represented in permanent collections Boston Mus. Art, Pa. Acad. Fine Arts, Colo. Springs Mus., Davenport (Ia.) Municipal Art Gallery, IBM collection, Va. Hist. Soc., pvt. collections. Mem. Soc. Four Arts (life mem.; bd. dirs.). Clubs: Everglades, Bath and Tennis (Palm Beach, Fla.). Home: 220 Worth Av Palm Beach FL 33480 also Meeting House Ogunquit ME 03997 also Son Juliá Lluchmayor Mallorca Spain

HARE, CLARENCE CLIFTON, physician; b. nr. Pitts.; July 12, 1901; s. William and Pamelia (Brooks) H.; Ph.G., U. Pitts.; 1921, B.Sc., 1926, M.D., 1928; Sc.M., Coll. Phys. and Surgs., Columbia, 1930, Sc.D., 1931; m. Margaret E. McGeary, June 12, 1935; children—Betsy Jane, Polly Anne, Daniel Aber. Interne St. Francis Hosp., Pitts.; 1928-30; resident in neurology at Neurol. Inst., N.Y.; 1930-32; pvt. practice of medicine specializing in neurology and psychiatry, N.Y.C.; 1930-70. Comdr., USNR, 1942—; active duty, 1942-45 as pres. Spl. Bd. of Med. Examiners. Mem. Am. Neurol. Assn., Am. Acad. Neurology, Assn. for Research in Nervous and Mental Diseases, A.M.A.; State Med. Soc.; Neurol. Soc. N.Y. Republican. Presbyn. Contbr. numerous articles on neurol. subjects in med. publs. Home: 880 Painted Bunting Lane Vero Beach FL 32960

HARE, EMLEN WALN, investment exec.; b. Villanova, Pa., July 21, 1910; s. Emlen Spencer and Ann Hutchinson (Waln) H.; student U. Va., 1935; m. Jean Gibbs, Sept. 28, 1935; children—Emlen Gibbs, Nixon Waln. Vice pres., dir. Hare's Ltd., N.Y.C., 1934-50; v.p. sales Nat. Securities & Research Corp., N.Y.C., 1950-60; v.p., dir. Waddell & Reed, Inc., Kansas City, Mo., 1960- 64; v.p. Channing Financial Corp.; sales v.p. Channing Co., Inc., 1964- -. Mem. Delta Psi. Clubs: Bedens Brook, Racquet and Tennis. Home: Pheasant Hill Rd Princeton NJ 08540 Office: 280 Park Av New York City NY 10017

HARE, FRANCIS HUTCHESON, lawyer; b. Lower Peach Tree, Ala., Aug. 13, 1904; s. Crosland C. and Sallie (Morrissette) H.; student Auburn U., 1921-22, U.S. Naval Acad., 1922-23; LL.B., U. Ala., 1927; m. Isabelle Corr, Jan. 25, 19 1930: children—Lucille (Mrs. Clarence L. Moss), Francis Hutcheson. Admitted to Ala. bar, 1927, since practiced in Birmingham; sr. mem. firm Hare, Wynn, Newell and Newton, 1944—; asso. justice Spl. Supreme Ct. Ala., 1967. Chmn. Jefferson County Civil Service Bd., 1951-52. Medalist Law Sci. Acad. Fellow Am. Bar Found.; mem. Am., Ala. (pres. 1950), Birmingham (pres. 1943) bar assns., Internat. Acad. Trial Lawyers (pres. 1967), Kappa Alpha, Phi Delta Phi. Methodist. Trial lawyer, legal author, lectr. Home: 3827 Forest Glen Dr Birmingham AL 35213 Office: City Federal Bldg Birmingham AL 35203

HARE, FREDERICK KENNETH, educator; b. Wylye, Eng., Feb. 5, 1919; s. Frederick Eli and Irene (Smith) H.; B.S. 1st class honors; U. London, 1939; Ph.D., U. Montreal, 1950; LL.D., Queens U. 1964, U. Western Ont., 1968; D.Sc., McGill U., 1969; m. Suzanne Alice Bates, Aug. 23, 1941 (div. 1952); 1 son, Christopher John; m. 2d, Helen Nielson Morrill, Dec. 26, 1953; children—Elissa Beatrice, Robin Gilbert. Asst. prof. geography McGill U., 1945-49, prof., chmn. dept. geography, 1950-62, chmn. social studies and commerce group, 1958-62, prof. geography and meterology, dean faculy arts and scis., 1962-64; dir. Arctic Meteorology Research Group, McGill Sub-Arctic Research Lab.; prof. geography King's Coll., U. London, 1964-66, master of Birkbeck Coll., U. London, 1966-68; pres. U. B.C., Vancouver, Can., 1968-69 prof. geography and physics U. Toronto, Ont., Can., 1969—. Mem. NRC (Can.), 1962-64; mem. Natural Environment Research Council (U.K.), 1965-68. Served as meteorologist Brit. Air Ministry, 1941- 43; flight lt., meteorol. br. R.A.F.V.R., Gt. Britain, 1943-45. Fellow King's Coll., 1967. Fellow Meteorol. Soc., Royal, Am. (hon., councillor) geog. socs., Arctic Inst. N.Am. (past chmn.), Royal Soc. Can., Am. Meteorol. Soc.; mem. Geologists Assn., Inst. Brit. Geographers, Canadian Assn. Geographers (past pres.), Assn. Am. Geographers (hon. pres. 1963-64), Author: The Restless Atmosphere, 1953; On University Freedom, 1968; author papers sci. subjects. Office: Univ of Toronto Toronto 181 Ontario Canada

HARE, GORDON B., educator; B.A., Columbia Union Coll., 1951; M.S., U. Colo. 1954, Ph.D., 1964. Prof., chmn. dept. math. Walla Walla Coll., College Place, Wash. Office: Dept Math Walla Walla Coll College Place WA 99324*

HARE, RAYMOND ARTHUR, govt. ofcl.; b. Martinsburg, W.Va., Apr. 3, 1901; A.B., Grinnell Coll., 1924, LL.D., 1957; children—Raymond Arthur, Paul Julian. Instr. Robert Coll., Constantinople, 1924-27; exec. sec. Am. C. of C. for the Levant, 1926-27; clerk Am. consulate gen. Constantinople, 1927, later becoming vice consul; lang. officer, Paris 1929, vice consul, 1931; vice consul, Cairo, 1931, Beirut, 1932; 3d sec., vice consul, Teheran, 1933, consul, 1935, with additional duties as 3d sec.; 2d sec., Cairo, 1939, consul, 1940; 2d sec., Jidda, 1940-44, in addition to consular duties Cairo; 2d sec., consul, London, 1944, 1st sec. and consul, 1944; area adviser U.S. group, Dumbarton Oaks Conversations on Internat. Orgn., 1944; liaison officer Chgo. Aviation Conf., 1944; polit. adviser U.S. delegation, 1st Assembly UN, London, 1946; sec. to Am. delegation Paris Conf., 1946; assigned Nat. War Coll., 1946-47; mem. Spl. Mission to Nepal, 1947; chief div. Middle Eastern and Indian affairs State Dept., 1947, chief div. So. Asian affairs, 1947, then dep. dir. Office of Near Eastern and African Affairs; dep. asst. sec. of state for Near Eastern, S. Asian and African affairs; A.E. and P. to Kingdon of Saudi Arabia; E.E. and P., Kingdom of Yemen, 1950; ambassador to Lebanon, 1953; dir. gen. U.S. Fgn. Service, 1954-56; A.E. and P. to Egypt, 1956-58, to UAR, 1958-60; E.E. and M.P. to Yemen, 1959-60; dep. under sec. state, 1960-61; ambassador to Turkey, 1961-65; asst. sec. for Nr. Eastern and South Asian affairs, Dept. State, 1965-66; pres. Middle East Inst., Washington, 1966-69, nat. chmn., 1969—. Recipient Distinguished Service award, 1964. Home: 3214 39th St NW Washington DC 20016

HARE, ROBERT YATES, educator; b. McGrann, Pa., June 14, 1921; s. Robert Deemar and Beulah (Yates) H.; Mus.B., U. Detroit, 1948; M.A., Wayne State U., 1950; Ph.D., U. Ia., 1959; m. Constance King Rutherford, Mar. 31, 1948; children—Stephen, Beverly, Madeleine. French Horn recitals Carnegie Music Hall, Pitts., 1940, 42; French hornist Pitts. Symphony Orch., 1941-43, 44-45, Buffalo Philharmonic, 1943-44, Cin. Summer Opera Co., 1945, Indpls. Symphony Orch., 1945-46, San Antonio Symphony Orch., 1947-49; orchestrator San Antonio Symphony Orch., 1947-49; instr. Marietta (O.) Coll., 1949-51, Del Mar Coll., Corpus Christi, Tex., 1951-55; prof., chmn. grad. studies San Jose (Cal.) State Coll., 1956-65, condr. coll. symphony band, 1956-63; condr. San Jose Youth Symphony, 1957-59; prof., dean Eastern Ill. U. Music, Muxic, 1965—, condr. univ. symphony, 1968—; cons. in field. Mem. council music edn. in higher edn. Ill. Music Educators Assn., 1969—; mem. com. grad. and profl. edn. in arts and humanities Ill. State Bd. Higher Edn., 1969-70, commissioned mem. performing arts commn. Ill. Sesquicentennial, 1967. Recipient Profl. Promise scholarship Carnegie Inst. Tech., 1939. Mem. Music Educators Nat. Conf. (publns. planning com. 1970—), Mus. Teachers Nat. Assn., Am. Musicol. Soc., Phi Mu Alpha, Sinfonia (hon.). Mason (Shriner). Contbr. articles profl. jours. Home: 40 Circle Dr Charleston IL 61920

HARE, WILLIAM VARNER, physician, educator; b. Evansville, Ind., Dec. 12, 1919; s. John Herbert and Imogen (Varner) H.; A.B., Ind. U., 1941, M.D., 1944; m. Mary Nell Stewart (div. 1957); m. 2d, Virginia Sue Boatman, 1960; 1 son, Jeff Varner. Intern St. Vincent's Hosp., Indpls., 1944-45; grad. student Meml. Hosp., N.Y.C., 1945-46; resident pathology U. Tenn., 1945, instr. pathology, 1946-48; asst. med. dir. W. Tenn. Cancer Clinic, Memphis, 1946-48; spl. research fellow Nat. Cancer Inst., Bethesda, Md., 1948-49, cons. pathology sect., 1949—; chmn. dept. pathology U. Miss., 1949-59, now clin. prof. pathology, med. sch., dir. Univ. Tumor Clinic, 1955-60; pathologist Miss. Bapt. Hosp., Jackson, 1963—; apptd. coordinator undergrad. cancer teaching by Nat. Cancer Inst., 1950. Cons. VA Hosp., 1955—, dept. animal husbandry and nutrition Ala. Poly. Inst., Auburn. Diplomate Am. Bd. Pathology. Mem. A.M.A., Central Med. Soc., Coll. Am. Pathologists, Miss. Med. Assn., Miss. Assn. Pathologists, Phi Gamma Delta, Phi Beta Pi. Methodist. Contbr. med. articles to profl. jours. Home: 4108 N State St Jackson, MS 39206. Office: 1190 N State St Jackson MS 39201

HARE, WOODROW WILSON, educator, plant pathologist; b. nr. Scooba, Miss., Aug. 10, 1915; s. William Henry and Madie (Daws) H.; A.A., E. Miss. Jr. Coll., 1934; B.S., Miss. State U., 1937, M.S., 1940; Ph.D., U. Wis., 1943; m. Mary Louise Eckles, June 23, 1940; children—Marjorie Jane (Mrs. William Lester Self Andrews), Julia Katherine (Mrs. Alney Austin Baham). Instr. plant pathology and agronomy U. Wis., 1943-45, asst. prof., 1945-48; asso. prof. plant pathology Miss. State U., State College, 1948-57, prof. plant pathology, 1957-64, head plant pathology and weed sci., 1964—. Vice pres., dir. Harson Growers, Inc., Wiggins, Miss. Served from ensign to lt. (j.g.), USNR, 1944-46. Mem. Bot. Soc. Am., A.A.A.S., Am. Phytopathological Soc. (pres. So. div. 1957, nat. council 1958-59, editorial bd. Phytopathology, 1969—), Sigma Xi, Beta Beta Beta, Kappa Mu Epsilon, Gamma Sigma Delta, Phi Kappa Phi. Contbr. articles profl. jours. Home: Route 3 Box 317 Starkville MS 39759 Office: Drawer PG State College MS 39762

HARELICK, NORMAN ROBERT, county ofcl.; b. N.Y.C., June 29, 1913; s. Abraham and Rebecca (Zteitlin) H.; B.B.A., St. John's U., 1936, LL.B., 1938; m. Evelyn Deborah Kertez, Jan. 18, 1941; children—Dale Andrea, Judy Ellen. Admitted to N.Y. bar, 1939; with Platt & Munk, N.Y.C., 1942-69, dir. prodn. and new products devel., 1951-68, v.p., dir. prodn., 1968-69; dir. spl. mfg. services Am. Book-Stratford Press, 1969-70; purchasing supr. graphic arts County of Nassau, L.I., N.Y., 1970—. Served USAAF, 1943-45. Decorated Purple Heart. Mem. Am. Bar Assn. Jewish religion. Home: 148 Hamilton Rd., Rockville Centre New York City, NY 11570. Office: 140 Old Country Rd Minecola NY 11501

HAREWOOD, EARL OF, (George Henry Hubert Lascelles), musical adminstr.; b. London, Eng., Feb. 7, 1923; s. Henry George Charles (6th Earl of Harewood) and Her Royal Highness Princess Mary; M.A., King's Coll., Cambridge U., 1948; LL.D. (hon.) Leeds University, 1959, Aberdeen, 1965; Mus.D. (hon.), Hull U., 1962; m. Stein, Maria Donata, Sept. 29, 1949 (div. July 1967); children—David, James, Jeremy; m. 2d, Patricia Elizabeth Tuckwell, 1967; 1 son, Mark. Aide de camp to Earl of Athlone in Can., 1945-46; editor Opera mag., 1950-53; a dir. Royal Opera House, Covent Garden, London, 1951-53, 69—, an adminstr., 1953-61; artistic dir. Edinburgh (Scotland) Internat. Festival, 1961-65, Leeds Triennial Festival, 1958—; artistic adviser New Philharmonia Orch., London, 1966—; overseas dir. Australian Opera. Chmn. music adv. com. British Council, 1956-66; chmn. music adv. com. British Council, 1956-66; chmn. music panel Arts Council Eng., 1966—; chmn. B.B.C. Central Music Adv. Council. Dir. British Bank Commerce Ltd., British Inst. Recorded Sound Ltd. Pres. Royal Manchester Coll. Music, 1945—, Leeds United Football Club, 1961—, English Football Assn., 1964-71. Served to capt., Grenadier Guards, British Army, 1939-45; prisoner of war, 1944-45. Editor, revisor: Kobbe's Complete Opera Book, 1954. Home: Harewood House Leeds Yorkshire England

HARFINGER, FREDERICK JOSEPH, II, navy officer; b. Albany, N.Y., Sept. 14, 1913; s. August B. and Marie Ann (Berben) H.; B.S., U.S., Naval Acad., 1935; grad. Submarine Sch., 1947, Advanced Undersea Warfare Sch., 1950, Armed Forces Staff Coll., 1952, Indsl. Coll. Armed Forces, 1955; m. Francis Clarke Blance, Apr. 2, 1939; children—Frances Marie (Mrs. Gary G. Hyde), Dorothy May (Mrs. Robert T. Beidleman), Frederick Joseph III, Clarke August. Commd. ensign U.S. Navy, 1935, advanced through grades to vice adm., 1971; assigned U.S.S. Ariz., 1935-37, U.S.S. Ramapo, 1938, U.S.S. S-38, 1938-40, U.S.S. Trout, 1940-42, U.S.S. Whale, 1942-43; comdg. officer U.S.S. S-32, 1943-44, U.S.S. Trigger, 1944-45, U.S.S. Sirago, 1945-47; staff Submarine Squadron 4, 1950-51; comdr. Submarine Div. 43, 1951-52; assigned Office Chief Naval Operations, 1953-54; naval attache, Bonn, Germany, 1955-57; comdg. officer U.S.S. Mauna Loa, 1957-58; comdr. Submarine Squadron 12, 1958-59; assigned Submarine Office Chief Naval Operations, 1959-62, Submarine Flotilla 1, 1963-64; dir. collection Def. Intelligence Agy., 1964-67; comdr. S. Atlantic Force, U.S. Atlantic Fleet, 1967-68; asst. chief naval operations intelligence, 1968-71; dir. command support programs Office CNO, 1971—. Dir. Washington Investors Network. Trustee Woodrow Wilson Found; bd. dirs. USO, San Juan, P.R., Navy Marine Coast Guard Residence Found., Armed Services Relief and Benefit Assn., Naval Hist. Found. Decorated Navy Cross, Silver Star with 2 gold stars, Legion of Merit, Bronze Star with combat V, Commendation medal with combat V, also numerous unit and area ribbons; Commander's Cross (West Germany); Brazilian Order Naval Merit; Venezuelan Order Naval Merit, 2d class; Colombian Naval decoration. Home: Quarters 10 Arlington Service Center 8th and S Court House Rd Arlington VA 22204 Office: Dept Navy Washington DC 20350

HARFORD, JAMES JOSEPH, assn. exec.; b. Jersey City, Aug. 19, 1924; s. Thomas William and Jane Hume (Henderson) H.; B.S. in Mech. Engring., Yale, 1945; m. Mildred Rita Waters, Apr. 19, 1952; children—Susan Gately, James Joseph, Peter Benedict (dec.), Jennifer, Christopher. Sales engr. Worthington Corp., 1946-49; asso. editor Modern Industry, 1950-52; free- lance writer, Europe, 1952-53; exec. sec. Am. Rocket Soc., 1953-63, Am. Inst. Aeros. and Astronautics, 1963—. Pres. Thomas More Found. Served as ensign USNR, 1945-46. Fellow Am. Inst. Aeros. and Astronautics, A.A.A.S., Brit. Interplanetary Soc., Royal Aero. Soc. (asso.). Home: 32 Mason Dr Princeton NJ 08540 Office: 1290 6th Av New York City NY 10019

HARGIS, WILLIAM JENNINGS, Jr., coll. dean; b. Lebannon, Va., Nov. 24, 1923; B.A., U. Richmond, 1950, M.A., 1951; Ph.D., Fla. State U., 1954; m. Dolores E. Martin; children—Laura Anne, Thomas Jonathan, Susan Combs, Emily Martin. Asst. prof. biology and chemistry The Citadel, 1954-55; asso. biologist Va. Inst. Marine Sci., 1955-59, dir., 1959—; lectr. Coll. William and Mary, 1955-59, prof. marine sci., 1959-61, dean Sch. Marine Sci., prof., 1961—; prof., chmn. dept. marine sci. U. Va., 1963—. Pres. Mariners Mus., Newport News, Va. Served with USAAF, 1943-45. Fellow A.A.A.S.; mem. Am. Inst. Biol. Sci., Am. Soc. Paristologists, Am. Micros. Soc., Atlantic Estuarine Soc. (past pres.), Soc. Exploration Atlantic Shelf (chmn.), Chesapeake Research Council (past chmn.), Va. Acad. Sci., Assn. Southeastern Biologists, Am. Soc. Limnology and Oceanography, Helminthological Soc. Washington; Nat. Shell fisheries Assn., Gloucester C. of C. (past dir.), Va. C. of C., Sigma Xi. Beta Beta Beta. Home: Windward House Gloucester Point VA 23062 Office: Va Inst Marine Sci Gloucester Point VA 23062

HARGRAVE, ALEXANDER DAVIDSON, banker; b. Canadaigua, N.Y., Mar. 17, 1920; s. Thomas J. and Catherine (Davidson) H.; grad. cum laude Phillips Exeter Acad., 1937; A.B., Princeton, 1941; LL.B. cum laude, Harvard, 1948; m. Betty Ryder Crouch, Mar. 14, 1944; children—Susan (Mrs. Bertram Hopeman), Alexander MacKenzie, Charles Crouch, Margaret Davidson. Admitted to N.Y. bar, 1948; with firm Nixon, Hargrave, Devans & Doyle, Rochester, N.Y., 1948—, partner firm, 1953—; exec. v.p. Lincoln Rochester Trust Co., 1963-68, pres., 1968—, chief exec. officer, 1970—, also dir.; v.p., sec., treas. Lincoln 1st Banks Inc., 1967—, also dir.; dir. Taylor Wine Co., Inc., Sybron Corp., Gleason Works, Rochester Telephone Corp. Mem. Republican Finance Com. Monroe County, N.Y. Rep. State Finance Com. Past Pres., dir. Community Chest Rochester and Monroe County; pres., George Eastmen House; trustee, past pres. Highland Hosp., Rochester; trustee Rochester Inst. Tech. Served to lt. comdr. USNR, 1941-45; PTO. Mem. N.Y. State Bar Assn. Clubs: Country of Rochester, Rochester, Princeton, Genesee Valley (Rochester). Home: 800 Allens Creek Rd Rochester NY 14618 Office: 183 E Main St Rochester NY 14604

HARGRAVE, VICTORIA ELIZABETH, librarian; b. Ripon, Wis., Aug. 22, 1913; d. Alexander Walter and Estelle Winifred (Swanson) Hargrave; A.B., Ripon Coll., 1934; library diploma, U. Wis., 1938; M.A., U. Chgo., 1947; postgrad. U. Cal. at Los Angeles, 1970. Tchr., Brandon (Wis.) High Sch., 1934-37; extension librarian Ia. State Coll. Library, 1938-44; librarian Ripon Coll., 1944-46, MacMurray Coll., 1947—. Mem. adv. council librarians U. Ill. Grad. Sch. Library Sci., 1962-64. Mem. A.L.A., N.E.A., Am. Assn. U. Women, League Women Voters. Home: 1017 W College Av Jacksonville IL 62650

HARGRAVE, WILLIAM LOFTIN, clergyman; b. Wilson, N.C., Nov. 10, 1903; s. Benjamin Worthington and Frances (Daniel) H.; LL.B., Atlanta Law Sch., 1924; B.D., Va. Theol. Sem., 1932, D.D., 1962; S.T.M., U. of South, 1952, D.D., 1962; m. Minnie Frances Whittington, Feb. 13, 1939; children—Frances, Elizabeth, Sarah, William. Admitted to Ga. bar, 1925; asst. trust officer Miami Bank & Trust Co. (Fla.), 1924-26; asso. firm Shutts & Bowen, Miami, 1926-27; ordained to ministry Episcopalian Ch., 1932; rector in Cocoa, Fla., 1932- 43, Ft. Pierce, Fla., 1943-45, Holy Comforter Ch., Miami, 1945-48, Holy Communion Ch., Charleston, S.C., 1948-53; exec. sec. Diocese of South Fla., Winter Park, 1953-61; consecrated bishop Diocese of South Fla., 1961-70; bishop of S.W. Fla., 1970—; pres. Wuesthoff Hosp., Cocoa, Fla., 1941-43, Porter Mil. Acad., Charleston, 1952. Pres. Fla. Council Chs., 1957-58, Fla. Migrant Ministry, 1963-66; mem. gen. bd. Nat. Council Chs. Christ, 1964—; mem. Lambeth Conf., London, Eng., 1968. Club: St. Petersburg Yacht. Home: 1701 Brightwater Blvd NE St Petersburg FL 33074 Office: PO Box 4043 St Petersburg FL 33731

HARGREAVES, ROBERT, educator, orch. conductor; b. Baxenden, Lancashire, Eng., Aug. 20, 1914; s. William and Mary Elizabeth (Hankinson); brought to U.S., 1923, naturalized, 1938; A.B. summa cum laude, Albion Coll., 1936, Mus. D. honoris causa, 1969; M.Mus., Eastman Sch. Music, U. Rochester, 1939, Ph.D., 1941; student Ecole Monteux, summers 1951-52; m. Katherine Elizabeth Benedict, Apr. 11, 1938; children—Hall Robert, Daniel Dewhurst, Mary LeValley. Supr. music pub. schs., Chelsea, Mich., 1936-38; teaching fellow Eastman Sch. Music, 1938-41; dir. grad. studies Ill. Wesleyan U., 1941-45; guest lectr. Drake U. Coll. Fine Arts, 1942; founder Bloomington-Normal Symphony Orch., 1944, Nat. Orch. Arrangers' Festival, 1944; head sch. music Ball State U., 1945—; founder Muncie Symphony Orch., 1949; guest prof. U. Tex. Coll. Fine Arts, 1953; guest condr. String Symphony, Am. Symphony Orch. League, 1954, premiere season French Lick Music Festival, 1957, Indianapolis Philharmonic Orchestra, 1963, Nashville Symphony and Chamber

Orch., 1967; conductor of tours Am. Allegro Ballet Co., 1958-66; condr. premiere performances Indpls. Civic Ballet, 1959; conductor N.E. Regional Festival Ballet Gala (7 cos.), 1967; columnist The Indiana Musicator. Recipient awards Rockefeller Found., Kulas Found., A.S.C. A.P., Am. Symphony Orch. League for study of conducting with Eugene Ormandy, Alfred Wallenstein, and George Szell; Outstanding Young Man award Muncie Jr. C. of C. Examiner for Nat. Commn. Accreditation Tchr. Edn. Nat. Assn. Schs. of Music. Mem. Nat. Assn. Schs. Music (regional v.p. 1956-57, chmn. com. research 1959-63, chmn. grad. commn., 1965; pres. 1966-70), Internat. Platform Assn., Ind. Music Educators Assn. (bd. dirs.), Am. String Tchrs. Assn. (pres. Ind. div. 1948-53), N.E.A., Symphony Orch. League, Nat. Sch. Orch. Assn., Music Tchrs. Nat. Assn., Nat. Music Council (bd. dirs. 1969—), Tau Kappa Epsilon, Phi Mu Alpha Sinfonia (province gov. 1949-51, nat. hon. mem.), Pi Kappa Lambda, Phi Beta (nat. hon. patron 1962). Author: The Teaching of Brass Instruments in School Music Supervisors Training Courses, 1952; Survey of Available Data on the Violin Vibrato. Editorial asso. Jour. of Research in Music Edn. Editorial com. Music for Everybody. Contbr. articles music, edn. publs. Home: 601 N Hawthorn Dr Muncie IN 47304

HARGROVE, JAMES WARD, govt. ofcl.; b. Shreveport, La., Oct. 31, 1922; s. Reginald H. and Hallie (Ward) H.; grad. Sewanee Mil. Acad., 1939; B.A., Rice Inst., 1943; m. Marion Elizabeth Smith, Aug. 25, 1942; children—James W., Florence, Thomas M., William H. Sec., treas. Caddo Abstract Co., 1946- 47; with Tex. Eastern Transmission Corp., 1947-69, successively office mgr., asst. sec., asst. treas., sec., treas., 1947-54, v.p., sec., 1954- 58, v.p. finance, 1958-67, sec., 1958-63, sr. v.p., 1967-69; asst. postmaster gen. finance and adminstrn. U.S. Postal Service, Washington, 1969-71, sr. asst. postmaster gen. support, 1971—. Gov.-advisor Rice U., mem. bd. World Missions Presbyn. Ch. U.S.A. Mem. Phi Beta Kappa. Home: 60 Tiel Way Houston TX also 2409 49th St NW Washington DC 20007 Office: US Postal Service Washington DC 20260

HARGROVE, MERWIN MATTHEW, univ. dean; b. Enid, Okla., Jan. 22, 1910; s. Frank Kirk and Effie (Matthews) H.; A.B., U. Omaha, 1932; A.M., State U. Ia., 1934; LL.D., Phillips U., 1951; m. Jane Eleanor Marshall, Sept. 2, 1933; children—Linda Jean, Charles Marshall. Auditor, Woodman of the World Life Ins. Co., 1932-33; instr. bus. adminstrn. U. of Omaha, 1934; registrar Lincoln Coll., 1935-37; successively instr., asst. prof., asso. prof., prof., asst. dean, dean Coll. Bus. Adminstrn., Tulsa, 1937—, now Trustees' prof.; cons. accounting and personnel. Dir. Nat. Equity Life Ins. Co. Mem. Mid-Continent Research and Devel. Council. Bd. trustees Found. Consumer Credit, Met. Tulsa Transit Authority; vice chmn., trustee Phillips U. Dir. Tulsa Community Chest; pres. Council Social Agys.; head 75th Coll. Tng. Detachment, U. Tulsa, World War II; mem. Adv. Council, U. Tulsa. Hon. mem. Okla. Soc. of C.P.A.'s, Tulsa Soc. of C.P.A.'s; mem. So. Case Writers Assn. (pres.), Tulsa Real Estate Bd., Nat. Assn. Accountants (nat. edn. dir.), United Bus. Edn. Assn., Okla. Acad. Sci., S.W. Social Sci. Assn., Am. Mgmt. Assn., Financial Execs. Assn., Lambda Chi Alpha, Delta Sigma Pi, Pi Gamma Mu, Beta Gamma Sigma. Republican. Mem. Christian Ch. Rotarian. Co-editor: Business Policy Cases (textbook) 1969. Home: 1725 S Evanston St Tulsa OK 74104

HARGROVE, WILLIAM RICHARD, coll. dean; b. Port Arthur, Tex., Feb. 4, 1928; s. William Richard and Etta (Clark) H.; B.S., N. Tex. State U., 1950, M. Ed., 1951; Ed.D., George Peabody Coll., 1957; m. Robbie Fletcher, May 26, 1968; children—Linda, Diana, Lisa. Tchr., Appalachian State Tchrs. Coll., Boone, N.C., 1953-57, U. Okla., 1957-59; tchr. edn., dean Sch. Edn., Tex. Woman's U., 1959-64; dean Sch. Edn., Lamar State Coll. Tech., 1964- -. Recipient Sullivan award George Peabody Coll., 1952; Peabody Living Endowment scholarship, 1951-52; Jessie Jones scholar, 1952-53. Mem. Am. Ednl. Research Assn., A.A.A.S., N.E.A., Phi Delta Kappa. Home: 1210 Longfellow, Beaumont, TX 77706

HARGROVES, VERNON CARNEY, clergyman; b. Nansemond County, Va., Sept. 4, 1900; s. Robert Tatem and Emily Martha (Carney) H.; A.B., Princeton, 1922, M.A., 1927; Th.G., So. Baptist Theol. Sem., 1925; D.D., U. Richmond, 1941; LL.D., Temple U., 1955; m. Narcissa Bruce Daniel, Dec. 1, 1928; children—Narcissa Daniel, Emily Carney, Jeannette Snead. Instr. Am. Sch., Kuling, China, 1922-23; pastor Princeton (N.J.) Baptist Ch., 1925-27, Weatherford Meml. Ch., Richmond, Va., 1928-32, 2d Bapt. Ch. of Germantown, Phila., 1932-71; preaching mission to Russia, 1955, 58, Czechoslovakia and Hungary, 1964; fellowship mission to Romania and Yugoslavia, 1966, to Russia, 1971. Trustee, past moderator Phila. Bapt. Assn.; dir., past pres. Phila. Council Chs.; pres. Am. Bapt. Conv., 1954-55; v.p. Bapt. World Alliance, 1960-65, pres., 1970—; chmn. N. Am. Bapt. Fellowship, 1966-68; Chmn. Phila. Medal Honor Award Com., 1954-55, 66-70. Past dir. Community Chest of Phila. Mem. Phi Kappa Sigma, Phi Alpha, Phi Beta Kappa (alumnus mem.). Rotarian. Club: Morgan Edwards (Phila.). Contbr. to various publs., nat. and denominational. Chmn. editorial com. The Secret Place, 1950-54. Home: 7806 Linden Rd Philadelphia PA 19118

HARHOFF, GEORG FREDERIK KROGH, Danish diplomat; b. Copenhagen, Denmark, Apr. 16, 1919; s. G.F.K. and Maria Alba (Pollak) H.; Dr. Law, U. Copenhagen, 1945; m. Marie Louise Countess Moltke, Apr. 29, 1958; children—Anne Charlotte, Georg Frederik Krogh, Adam Christian. Asst. dist. atty., Copenhagen, 1945; joined Danish Ministry Fgn. Affairs, 1945; sec. embassy, Paris, France, 1949- 56; charge d'affaires, Djakarta, Indonesia, 1956-59; ambassador to Morrocco, 1959-61, to Tunis, 1961-62, to Libya, 1962-63 ambassador on spl. mission at independence of Algeria, 1963, of Togo, 1960, of Senegal, 1961, of Malta, 1963; consul gen. of Denmark, N.Y.C., 1964—. Council pres. Danish Seamen's Ch. in N.Y.C. Decorated commander Order Dannebrog, Order Red Cross (Denmark); knight Order Wasa 1st degree (Sweden); knight Legion of Honor (France); grand cross Aisa, Alao uite (Morocco); grand cross Ordre de la Republique (Tunisia). Home: 857 Fifth Av New York City NY 10017

HARING, ELLEN STONE, (Mrs. E.S. Haring), educator; b. Los Angeles, Dec. 1921; d. Earl E. and Eleanor (Pritchard) Strone; B.A., Bryn Mawr Coll., 1942; M.A., Radcliffe Coll., 1943, Ph.D. (Am. Assn. U. Women fellow), 1959; m. Philip S. Haring, Dec. 1942 (div. June 1951). Adminstrv. worker A.R.C., Boston, 1943; mem. faculty Wheaton Coll., Norton, Mass., 1944-45; mem. faculty Wellesley Coll., 1945—, asso. prof., 1958-64, prof. philosophy, 1964—. Mem. Am. Philos. Assn., Assn. Realistic Philosophy, Metaphys. Soc. Am. Home: 73 Eliot St., South Natick, MA 01760. Office: Dept of Philosophy Wellesley Coll Wellesley MA 02181

HARING, JOSEPH EMERICK, educator, economist; b. Mansfield, O., July 19, 1931; s. Joseph and Kathryn (Woerner) H.; B.S., Ohio State U., 1952; Ph.D., Columbia, 1959; m. Loreen Carolyn Stuber, June 2, 1956; children-Crystal Janine, Arianne Denise, Elisa Jo, Peter Joseph Andre. Instr. econs. Columbia, 1958-59; mem. faculty Occidental Coll., Los Angeles, 1959—, Richard W. Miller prof. econs. and finance, 1965—, chmn. dept. econs., 1962—; Brookings Nat. research prof. econs. S.E. Asia, 1961-62; cons. Govt. Thailand, 1963-64. Mem. steering com. So. Cal. Research Council, 1959—; moderator TV series Inside Business, 1970. Served with AUS, 1953-55. Mem. Am., Western, So. Cal. (past pres.) econs. assns., Western Finance Assn., Econometric Soc., Royal Econ. Soc. Author: Migration and the Southern California Economy, 1964; The New Economics of Regulated Industries, 1968; Urban and Regional Economics 1971, Asso. editor Jour. Financial and Quantitative Analysis, 1965-68. Contbr. profl. jours. Office: 1600 Campus s Rd Los Angeles CA 90041

HARITHAS, JAMES, museum dir.; b. Lewiston, Me., Dec. 1, 1932; s. Nicholaus and Terspichore (Seferlis) H.; A.B. in History, U. Me., 1961; M.A. in Fine Arts, U. Pa., 1962; m. Christiana Bacas, Nov. 25, 1958; children—Jean, Terry, Lea. With Program Young Am. Culture, Helsinki, Finland, 1962; curator DeCordova Mus., 1962-63, Phoenix Art Mus., 1963-65; mem. staff Corcoran Gallery Art 1965—, dir., 1968—. Bd. dirs. ednl. TV sta. WETA. Served with AUS, 1955-57. Recipient Outstanding Sr. award U. Me., 1961; fellow U. Pa., 1962. Mem. Nat. Soc. Arts and Letters (adv. council Washington). Author articles, catalogues; responsible for spl. exhbns. Home: 1215 Fort Myer Dr., Arlington, VA 22209. Office: Corcoran Gallery of Art 17th and New York Av NW Washington DC 20006

HARJU, ONNI RUDOLPH, paper co. exec.; b. Bessemer, Mich., Oct. 28, 1918; s. V. Hjalmar and Selma (Karjala) H.; B.A., U. Wis., 1940; m. Dorothea W. Berndt, 1952. Accountant Wis. Electric Power Co., Milw., 1940-42; systems mgr. Marathon Corp., Menasha, Wis., 1946-50; systems mgr. Trackson Co., Milw., 1951- 53; treas. Consol. Papers, Inc., Wisconsin Rapids, Wis., 1953—; treas., dir. Consoweld Corp., Mead Realty Corp.; treas. Newaygo Timber Co., Ltd., Barcon, Inc.; dir. Marshfield Airways, Inc. Chmn. So. Wood County chpt. A.R.C., 1963-64, dir., 1963—, program chmn. Wis. State Conv., 1964, dir. So. Wood County Sheltered Workshop, 1964—; adviser Jr. Achievement, Milw., 1952; mem. Wis. Gov.'s Com. on Bus. Practices, 1960-61; treas. Wis. Paper Industry Information Service, 1964-65; mem. Wis. Tax Commrs. Adv. Com., 1966—. Served to maj. AUS, 1942-46. Decorated Bronze Star medal; Medalha de Gue (Brazil). Mem. Am. Vets. World War II, Tax Execs. Inst. (nat. dir., past pres. Wis. chpt.), Wisconsin Rapids C. of C. Elk. Home: 730 4th St S Wisconsin Rapids WI 54494 Office: 231 1st Av N Wisconsin Rapids WI 54494

HARKARVY, BENJAMIN, ballet master, choreographer; b. N.Y.C., Dec. 16, 1930; s. Irving and Sonia (Shapiro) Goldfarb; student New Sch., Sch. Am. Ballet, also ballet schs. of Mme. Anderson-Nantzova, Edward Caton, George Chaffee. Dir. Benjamin Harkarvy Ballet Sch. and Co., N.Y.C., 1954-57; artistic dir. Royal Winnipeg (Can.) Ballet, 1957-58; ballet master Netherlands Nat. Ballet, 1958-59; founder, artistic dir., ballet master Netherlands Dance Theatre, 1955—; artistic dir. Harkness Ballet, 1969-70; choreographer Canadian Broadcasting Co.-TV, 1957-58. Mem. com. awarding choreographic commns. Ministry Arts and Scis. Holland, 1967—. Created ballets: Septet; Recital for Cello and Eight Dancers; Aswingto; Madrigalesco; Grand Pas Espagnol; Visage; Double Duet; Quartet. Home: 4 E 75th St New York City NY 10011

HARKAVY, OSCAR, found. exec.; b. N.Y.C., May 28, 1923; s. Jacob and Anna (Schultz) H.; grad. Ethical Culture Schs., N.Y.C., 1940; A.B., Columbia, 1944; student Amherst Coll., 1943-44, Harvard, also Mass. Inst. Tech., 1945; M.B.A., Syracuse U., 1948, Ph.D., 1952; m. Frances Hoffman, Dec. 23, 1950; children—Stephen James, John Brooks. From instr. to asso. prof. Coll. Bus. Adminstrn., Syracuse U., 1946-53; asst. to dir. Program Econ. Devel. and Adminstrn., Ford Found., 1953-55, program asso., 1955-61, asso. dir., 1961-63, dir. population program, 1963-66, program officer in charge population office, 1966—. Cons. to Dept. Health, Edn. and Welfare, AID. Served to 1st lt. USAAF, 1943-46. Fellow A.A.A.S., mem. Am. Econ. Assn., Am. Finance Assn., Population Assn. Am., Phi Beta Kappa, Beta Gamma Sigma. Author: Leadership for Life Insurance, 1955; also articles. Home: 15 Split Rock Lane New Rochelle NY 10804 Office: 320 E 43d St New York City NY 10017

HARKEN, DWIGHT EMARY, surgeon; b. Osceola, Ia., June 5, 1910; s. Conreid Rex and Edna (Emary) H.; A.B., Harvard, 1931, M.D., 1936; Licentiate Medicine and Surgery, Soc. Apothecaries, London, Eng., 1939; Sc.D. (hon.), Suffolk U., Boston, 1964; m. Anne Louise Hood, Aug. 29, 1934; children—Alden Hood, Anne Louise. Intern, house surgeon, adult, childrens' surg. service Bellevue Hosp., N.Y.C., 1936-38; Alexander Cochrane-Bowen-Harlow Brooks fellow N.Y. Acad. Medicine, resident surg. officer Brompton Hosp., London, 1939-40; asst. resident, resident Harvard surg. service Boston City Hosp., 1940-42; asso. prof. clin. surgery Tufts U. Med. Sch., 1946-48; asso. prof., prof. surgery Harvard Med. Sch., 1948- 70, prof. emeritus, 1970—; chief dept. thoracic surgery Peter Bent Brigham Hosp., Boston, 1948-70, emeritus chief dept. thoracic surgery, 1970—, surgeon, 1948—; surgeon, chief dept. thoracic surgery Mt. Auburn Hosp., Cambridge, Mass., 1946—, Malden (Mass.) Hosp., 1949—; vis. surgeon Waltham, Boston Lying-In hosps; cons. VA, U.S. Naval hosps.; special work cardiac and thoracic surg. operations, design surg. instruments, heart-lung machines, artificial heart valves. Served to lt. col., M.C., AUS, 1942-46; ETO. Decorate Legion of Merit; recipient Joseph Strickland Meml. lecture cardiology medal, London, 1945; Susan and Theodore Cummings humanitarian award, 1963, 64, 65, 66, Argentine Ordende Mayo. Deplomate Am. Bd. Surgery, Am. Bd. Thoracic Surgery. Fellow Am. Coll. Cardiology (pres. 1964), A.C.S., Am. Coll. Chest Physicians; mem. Am. Assn. Thoracic Surgery, Am. Heart Assn., Am., Pan Am. med. assns., Soc. Vascular Surgery, Internat. Cardiovascular Soc., Royal Soc. Medicine, Internat. Soc. Cardiology, Assn. Advancement Med. Instrumentation (pres.), Assn. Am. Med. Colls., Am. Thoracic Soc., Soc. Thoracic Surgeons, New Eng. Surg. Soc., Pan-Pacific Surg. Assn., Soc. Colombiana de Cirujanos, Soc. Chilena de Cardiologia, Soc. de Cirujanos de Chile, Soc. Medica de Valparaiso, Soc. Argentina de Cardiologia, Japanese Med. Soc., Japanese Soc. Artificial Organ Aesculapian Club, Sociedad Uruguaya de Cardiologia (hon.), Sigma Xi, Alpha Omega Alpha, Delta Upsilon, Nu Sigma Nu. Clubs: Harvard Faculty; Harvard (Boston). Contbr. profl. jours. Home: 4 Lowell St Cambridge, MA 02138. Office: 67 Bay State Rd Boston MA 02115

HARKER, DAVID, scientist; b. San Francisco, Oct. 19, 1906; s. George Asa and Harriette (Buttler) H.; B.S. U. Cal., 1928; Ph.D., Cal. Inst. Tech., 1936; m. Katherine deSavich, July 1, 1930; children—Tatiana, Liudmila. Research asst. Atmospheric Nitrogen Corp., Solvay, N.Y., 1930-33; instr. chemistry Johns Hopkins, 1936, asso. chemistry, 1939-41; asso. Research Lab. Gen. Elec. Co., Schenectady, 1941-49, head crystallography div., 1949-50, cons. X-ray diffraction to X-ray dept., Milw., 1953—; cons. X-ray diffraction Carborundum Co., 1962—; dir. The Protein Structure Project, Polytech., Inst. Bklyn., 1950-59, adj. prof. physics, 1953-56, prof. crystallography, 1956-59; dir. biophysics Roswell Park Meml. Inst., Buffalo, 1959—, dir. Center for Crystallographic Research, 1965—; research prof. biophysics Grad. Sch., State U. N.Y. at Buffalo, 1960—; adj. prof. physics State Univ. Coll. at Buffalo; 1966—, professorial lectr. physics dept., 1959—; vis. prof. biophysics U. Rochester, 1965—; research prof. Grad. Faculty, Niagara U., Niagara Falls, N.Y., 1968—; vis. prof., cons. Centre Nat. de la Rescherche Sci., Bellevue, France, 1969-70; asso. prof. faculty sci. U. Bordeaux, Talence, France, 1970. Mem. U.S. nat. com. on crystallography NRC, 1951-56, 58-70, chmn., 1954-55; mem. adv. bd. on Russian translations Am. Inst. Physics, 1958—; mem. vis. com. for chemistry Brookhaven Nat. Lab., 1950- 53, chmn., 1953; chief U.S. del. to Internat. Congress on X-Ray Crystallography London, 1946; U.S. del. Assembly Internat. Union of Crystallography, Montreal, 1957, Moscow, 1966. Recipient Sigma Xi award for meritorious service to sci., 1967; Buffalo Eve. News Outstanding Citizen award, 1968; Schoellkopf award Western N.Y. sect. Am. Chem. Soc., 1969. Fellow N.Y. Acad. Scis., Am. Phys. Soc., Am. Inst. Mining and Metall. Engrs., Am. Inst. Chemists; mem. A.A.A.S., Am. Crystallographic Assn., Societe Francaise de Mineralogie et de Crystallographie, Biophys. Soc., Si Xi. Clubs: Cosmos (Washington); Saturn (Buffalo). Contbr. papers sci. publs. Adv. editor Soviet Physics-Crystallography, 1958-69. Patentee in field. Home: 23 High St Buffalo NY 14203 Office: Roswell Park Meml Inst Buffalo NY 14203

HARKER, HAYES EUGENE, govt. ofcl.; b. Platteville, Wis., July 30, 1909; s. Hayes Edward and Kathryn (Yeager) H.; student Cornell Coll., Mt. Vernon, Ia., 1932, Am. U., Washington, 1940-42; B.C.S., Benjamin Franklin U., Washington, 1941; m. Esther Elizabeth Weber, Dec. 24, 1938. Actor, Lyceum and Chautauqua Circuits, 1931-36; actor resident stock co., 1936-37; with Fed. Crop Ins. Corp., Dept. Agr., Washington, 1938—, now dir. adminstrv. mgmt. div. Nat. dir. Credit Union Nat. Orgn.; dir. D.C. Credit Union League; treas., bd. dirs. Agr. Fed. Credit Union Washington. Served with USAAF, World War II. Methodist. Mason (Shriner). Home: 5323 Massachusetts Av NW Washington DC 20016 Office: Fed Crop Ins Corp US Dept Agr Washington DC 20250

HARKER, JOHN STANLEY, clergyman, coll. pres.; b. Wrightstown, N.J., Dec. 12, 1903; s. Stephen Douglas and Ella (Johnson) H.; A.B., Grove City Coll., 1925, D.D., 1941; B.D., McCormick Sem., M.A., U. Pitts., 1935, Ph.D., 1951; LL.D., Cedarville Coll., 1952; m. Helen Calderwood, July 18, 1928; children—Ruth Calderwood (Mrs. William James Mills), Dorothy Jean (Mrs. Charles Robert Jansen), Anne Elizabeth (Mrs. David M. Dayton). Ordained to ministry Presbyn. Ch., 1928; minister First Ch., Prattsburg, N.Y., 1928-30, Saltsburg, Pa., 1930-35, Martins Ferry, O., 1935-39, Hamilton, O., 1939-51; pres. Alma (Mich.) Coll., 1951-56, Grove City (Pa.) Coll., 1956—. Republican. Mason, Rotarian. Home: 350 Memorial Av Grove City PA 16127

HARKEY, IRA BROWN, Jr., journalist; b. New Orleans, Jan 15, 1918; s. Ira Brown and Flora Broad (Lewis) H.; B.A., Tulane U., 1941; postgrad. U. Fla., 1960-61; M.A., Ohio State U., postgrad., 1970; m. Marie Ella Gore, 1939 (separated 1959); children—Ira Brown III, Marie Ella (Mrs. Loren E. Bosarge), Erik G., Lewis, Amelie (Mrs. Rex Foster), William Millsaps; m. 2d, Marion Marks Drake, Dec. 10, 1963. Reporter, feature writer Times-Picayune, New Orleans, 1939-42, 46-49; editor, pub., pres. The Chronicle, Pascagoula, Miss., 1949-63; pres. Gulf Coast Times, Ocean Springs, Miss., Advertiser Printing Inc., Pascagoula, 1949-63; mem. faculty Ohio State U., 1965-66; Carnegie vis. prof. U. Alaska, 1968-69; profl. lectr. journalism U. Mont., 1970. Sec., treas., dir. Okla. Coca-Cola Bottling Co., Inc., Oklahoma City; dir. Cushing Coca-Cola Bottling Co. (Okla). Served to lt. USNR, 1942- 46. Recipient Pulitzer prize for distinguished editorial writing, 1963; Sidney Hillman Found. award, 1963; Sigma Delta Chi award for distinguished pub. service in newspaper journalism, 1963, Media award Nat. Conf. Christians and Jews, 1963. Mem. Am. Assn. U. Profs., Assn. Edn. Journalism, Am. Polit. Sci. Assn., Phi Beta Kappa, Delta Kappa Epsilon, Sigma Delta Chi. Clubs: Louisiana, Boston (New Orleans). Author: The Smell of Burning Crosses, 1967. Contbr. articles to mags. Address: Lurton Blassingame 60 E 42d St New York City NY

HARKEY, JOHN NORMAN, lawyer; b. Russellville, Ark., Feb. 25, 1933; s. Olga John and Margaret (Fleming) H.; A.S., Marion (Ala.) Inst., 1952; LL.B., U. Ark., 1959, B.S., 1959, J.D., 1969; m. Willa Moreau Charlton, May 24, 1959; children-John Adam, Sarah Leigh. Admitted to Ark. bar, 1959, since practiced in Batesville; pros. atty. 3d Jud. Dist. Ark., 1961-65. Ins. commnr. Ark., 1967-68; chmn. Ark. Commerce Commn., 1968-69. Served to 1st lt. USMCR, Korea. Mem. Am., Ark. bar assns., Am. Assn. Trial Lawyers, Am. Judicature Soc., Am. Civil Liberties Union, Ark. Council Human Relations, U.S. Marine Corps League, Delta Theta Phi. Home: 110 Ridgecrest St Batesville AR 72501 Office: P O Box 710 Batesville AR 72501

HARKINS, GEORGE FREDERICK, clergyman; b. Phila., Feb. 28, 1913; s. John and Jennie (Waters) H.; A.B., Gettysburg Coll., 1937, L.H.D., 1969; B.D., Gettysburg Sem., 1940; D.D. Muhlenberg Coll., 1954; Th.D., Midland Lutheran Coll., 1967; S.T.D., Thiel Coll., 1970; m. Janet I. Earhart, June 18, 1940; children—John Edgar, Paul Frederick. Ordained to ministry Luth. Ch., 1941; pastor in Penbrook-Harrisburg, Pa., 1941-49; asst. to pres. United Luth. Ch., 1949-60, sec., 1960-62; asst. to pres. Luth. Ch. in Am., 1962-68, sec., 1968—; v.p. Nat. Luth. Council, 1962-65, pres., 1965-66. Mem. Luth. Resettlement Com., 1951-54, chmn., 1953-54; mem. Joint Commn. on Luth. Unity; pres. U.S.A. nat. com. Luth. World Fedn., 1966-70; mem. commn. on world service, 1970—; mem. gen. bd., exec. com. Nat. Council Chs. Christ U.S.A.; v.p. Luth. Council in U.S.A., 1970—; bd. dirs. Religion in Am. Life, 1969—. Named Young Man of Year, Harrisburg, Pa., 1948. Mem. Alpha Kappa Alpha, Kappa Phi Kappa, Kappa Delta Rho. Author: The Church and Her Work, 1960; Handbook for Committees, 1966. Contbr. Luth. Ency., religious periodicals. Home: 437 Meer Av Wyckoff NJ 07481 Office: 231 Madison Av New York City NY 10016

HARKINS, JOHN STEVEN, mfg. co. exec.; b. Phila., Sept. 7, 1926; s. John Lawrence and Mabel Lillian (Snyder) H.; A.B., U. Pa., 1950; B.S., LaSalle Coll., 1955; m. Elizabeth G. Watson, Aug. 31, 1944; children—Robert, Gloria (Mrs. James Lynch), Gerald, Steven. With Raytheon Co., Lexington, Mass., 1959-67; dir. mgmt. information systems Lorillard Corp., N.Y.C., 1967-69; gen. controller Borden, Inc., N.Y.C., 1969—. C.P.A., Pa. Mem. Financial Execs. Inst., Am. Inst. C.P.A.'s. Club: Pinnacle (N.Y.C.). Home: 10 Rockford Dr West Nyack NY 10994 Office: Borden Inc 277 Park Av New York City NY 10017

HARKINS, PAUL WILLIAM, educator, author; b. N.Y.C., June 17, 1911; s. James C. and Mary (Clune) H.; A.B., Ph.L., Fordham U., 1937, M.A., 1942; M.A., U. Mich., 1943, Ph.D., 1948; LL.D. (hon.), St. Ambrose Coll., 1960; m. Rhea Margaret Hopler, Feb. 22, 1941; children—Eileen (Mrs. Henry L. Horstman), Kathleen (Mrs. Gerald F. Wesselkamper), Patrick, Mary Ellen (Mrs. Arthur L. Masson), James, Michael, Paul, Marguerite, Peter. Asst. prof. Loyola Coll., Balt., 1937- 39, Sacred Heart Sem., Detroit, 1940-46, Mt. St. Joseph-on-the-Ohio, Cin., 1946-49; from asst. prof. to prof. Classical langs. Xavier U., Cin., 1949—; prof. Cath. U. Am., 1969- 70; lectr. Mem. Am. Philol. Assn., Ohio Classical Conf., Classical Assn., Midwest and South, Internat. Conf. Patristic Studies, Assn. Internat. de Papyrologes, Phi Beta Kappa. Author: St. John Chrysostom; Baptismal Instructions, 1963; Galen: On the Passions and Errors of the Soul, 1964. Contbr. articles encys. and jours. Home: 820 Yorkhaven Rd Cincinnati OH 45240

HARKINS, WILLIAM BLAKE, educator, physician; b. Macomb, Ill., Nov. 17, 1910; s. Claude Howard and Katherine May (Blake) H.; A.B., U. Ill., 1935; M.D., Johns Hopkins., 1936; m. Katherine Phelps, Oct. 3, 1950. Intern St. Luke's Hosp., St. Louis, 1935-36; asst. otolaryngology St. Louis U. Sch. Medicine, 1936-41, mem. faculty, 1941—, prof. otolaryngology, 1962—. chmn. dept., 1968—; cons. Crippled Children's Service, U. Mo., 1949-66, asso., 1966—. Served with M.C., USNR, 1942-47. Diplomate Am. Bd. Otolaryngology. Fellow A.C.S.; mem. St. Louis Med. Soc., Am., Mo. med. assns., Am. Acad. Ophthalmology and Otolaryngology, Am. Laryngol., Rhinol. and Otol. Soc., Eye, Ear, Nose and Throat Club St. Louis (pres. 1959-60). Author articles in field. Home: 7 Kingsbury Pl St Louis MO 63112

HARKINS, WILLIAM EDWARD, educator; b. State College, Pa., Nov. 10, 1921; s. John F. and Mary K. (Wagner) H.; B.A., Pa. State U., 1942; M.A., Columbia, 1946, Ph.D., 1950. Instr. Slavic langs. U. Pa., 1948-49; mem. faculty Columbia, 1949- -, prof. Slavic langs., 1964—, chmn. dept., 1964-71. Pres., Masaryk Inst., 1970—. Served as officer USNR. 1942-45. Guggenheim fellow, 1958-59. Author: Dictionary of Russian Literature, 1956; Karel Capek, 1962. Home: 100 LaSalle St New York City NY 10027

HARKINS, WILLIAM G., librarian; b. Macon, Miss., Mar. 28; 1911; s. Samuel Walter and Mattie (Dillard) H.; A.B., U. Ala., 1932; B.S. in L.S., U. Ill., 1933; M.A. in L.S., U. Mich., 1940; postgrad. U. Chgo., 1948-50; Carnegie fellow Rutgers U., 1958; m. Nina Elizabeth Markette, May 27, 1936 (dec.); m. 2d, Jean B. Foerster, Nov. 25, 1969; 1 son, Barrett Foerster. Med. librarian, cataloger U. Miss., 1933-36, asst. librarian, 1937; asst. reclassification U. Mich., 1936-37; asst. librarian U. Ala., 1937-40; librarian U. Miami, 1940-51, Coll. William and Mary, 1951-57; asso. dir. libraries U. Fla., 1957-62; Univ. librarian U. of South, 1962—. Mem. Tenn., Southeastern library assns., Phi Sigma Kappa. Methodist. Home: Sewanee TN 37375

HARKNESS, ALBERT, architect; b. Hamilton, N.Y., Nov. 8, 1886; s. Albert G. and Katherine M. (Beebee) H.; A.B., Brown U., 1909; B.S., Mass. Inst. Tech., 1912; m. Sara Arden Cheesman, Aug. 29, 1914; children—Albert, John Cheesman, Livingston Arden (dec.); m. 2d, Mrs. Thomas Ives Hare Powel, Sept. 2, 1954. Employed in archtl. offices Delano & Aldrich; H. Van Buren Magonigle; McKim, Mead & White, 1912-18; in pvt. practice, Providence, 1919—; asso. of Peter Geddes, 1948—. Dir. Providence Athenaeum, 1930-32, 38-46; mem. R.I. Bd. of Exam. and Registration of Architects, 1936, 40-54, 59-64. Ofcl. in mfr. of munitions Gorham Mfg. Co., 1943-44. A.I.A. rep. to U.S. Com. for UNESCO, 1947-48. Mem. Providence Redevel. Agy., 1947-66, vice chmn., 1947-54. Fellow A.I.A. (dir. 1937-39, pres. R.I. chpt. 1933-34, 45-46); asso. N.A.D.; mem. Alpha Delta Phi. Republican. Baptist. Clubs: Century Assn. (N.Y.C.); Hope, Art (Providence). Home: 5 Cooke St Providence RI 02906 Office: 274 Weybosset St Providence RI 02903

HARKNESS, ALBERT, Jr., govt. ofcl.; b. Providence, May 29, 1915; s. Albert and Sara Arden (Cheesman) H.; A.B., Harvard, 1938; Ph.D., Brown U., 1949; student Nat. War Coll., 1956-57; m. Mary Le Grand Howell, Sept. 14, 1940; children—Albert III, Frances, Judith. Tchr., Ruston Acad., Havana, 1938- 39; dir. Chile-U.S. Cultural Inst., Santiago, Chile, 1942-44; pub. affairs officer USIS, Am. embassy, San Jose, Costa Rica, 1949-51; cultural affairs afficer Am. embassy, Caracas, Venezuela, 1951-54; pub. affairs officer Am. embassy, Santiago, 1954-56; asst. dir. USIA, Washington, also dir. Information Center Service, 1958-60, chmn. Bd. Examiners, 1959-60; dir. USIS, Athens, Greece, 1960- 63, Lima, Peru, 1963-64; counselor for pub. affairs Am. embassy, Mexico, 1964-69, Madrid, Spain, 1969-71; sr. Murrow fellow Fletcher Sch. Law and Diplomacy, 1971—. Served to lt. USNR, 1944-47. Decorated comdr. Order Civil Merit (Spain). Mem. Soc. Cincinnati. Author articles, revs. on Latin Am. and history. Home: 257 Post Rd Wakefield RI 02879 Office: Tufts Univ Medford MA

HARKNESS, BRUCE, univ. dean; b. Beaver Dam, Wis., Apr. 16, 1923; s. Reuben Ellmore Ernest and Ruth (Thomas) H.; student Kalamazoo Coll., 1941-42, Swarthmore Coll., 1942-43; M.A. in English, U. Chgo., 1948, Ph.D., 1950; m. Barbara McNutt White, Oct. 29, 1967; children by previous marriage—Stephen W., Marguerite, Laura C., Jonathan C., Michael B. From instr. English to prof. U. Ill., 1950-63, 64-66, asso. dean liberal arts and scis., 1964- 66; prof. English, chmn. dept. So. Ill. U., 1963-64; dean arts and scis. Kent (O.) State U., 1966—. Served with USAAF, 1943-45. Carnegie fellow, 1949-50; Guggenheim fellow, 1957-58. Mem. Modern Lang. Assn. (exec. bd. Midwest sect. 1961), Nat. Council Tchrs. English (dir. at large 1964- 68), Bibliog. Soc. Va. Author: Bibliography and Novelistic Fallacy, 1959; Secret of the Secret Sharer, 1965. Editor: (Conrad) Heart of Darkness, 1960; (Conrad) Secret Sharer, 1962. adv. editor: College English, 1964-70. Home: 1295 Lake Martin Dr Kent OH 44240

HARKNESS, EARL, banker; b. Danbury, Conn., May 21, 1898; s. Alexander Harkness and Alicia (Hughes) H.; B.C.S., N.Y.U., 1924; m. Millicent Pierce, Feb. 11, 1937. Dep. supt. of banks N.Y. State Banking Dept., 1934-35; comptroller, exec. v.p., Jamaica Savs. Bank, N.Y., 1935-43; chmn. bd., pres., trustee Greenwich Savs. Bank, N.Y.C., 1943-69, chmn. bd., chief exec. officer, trustee, 1969—; trustee Savs. Banks Retirement System. Dir. Citizens Tax Council, Inc.; investment adv. com. Comptroller City N.Y.; treas., dir. Citizens Budget Commn. Bd. dirs. Soc. Prevention Crime, N.Y.C., Av. of Americas Assn. Served as seaman, USN, 1918. Recipient Madden Meml. award, 1957. Mem. Newcomen Soc., New Eng. Soc. Clubs: Economic, Quaker Hill Golf and Country. Home: 200 E 66th St New York City NY 10021 also Quaker Hill Pawling NY 12564 Office: Greenwich Savs Bank 1356 Broadway New York City NY 10018

HARKNESS, GEORGIA ELMA, author; b. Harkness, N.Y.; d. J. Warren and Lillie (Merrill) Harkness; A.B., Cornell U., 1912; M.A. (univ. fellow), Boston U., 1920, M.R.E., 1920, Ph.D., 1923, hon. Litt.D., 1938; student Harvard, 1926, Yale (Sterling fellow), 1928-29, Union Theol. Sem., 1936-37; Litt.D., MacMurray Coll., 1943, Elmira (N.Y.) Coll. 1962; D.D., Wilson Coll., 1943, Pacific Sch. Religion, 1961; LL.D., Mills Coll., Oakland, Cal., 1958. Tchr. Latin high sch., Schuylerville, N.Y., 1912-14, Scotia, N.Y., 1915-18; instr. English Bible, Boston U. Sch. Religious Edn., 1919-20; asst. prof. religious edn. Elmira (N.Y.) Coll., 1922, asso. prof. philosophy, 1923, prof. philosophy, 1926-37; ordained to ministry Meth. Ch., 1926; asso. prof. religion Mt. Holyoke Coll., 1937-39; prof. applied theology Garrett Theol. Sem., 1939-50, Pacific Sch. Religion at Berkeley 1950-61; prof. Christianity, Japan Internat. Christian U., 1956-57. Del. Oxford Conf. on Life and Work, 1937, Madras Conf. Internat. Missionary Council, 1938, Amsterdam Conf. of World Council Chs., 1948, Lund, 1952, Evanston, 1954. Recipient Scroll of Honor award Gen. Fedn. Women's Clubs for pioneer work in religion, 1941; $7,500 prize as co-winner Abingdon-Cokesbury award for book ms., 1947. Mem. Am. Philos. Assn., Am. Acad. Religion, Phi Beta Kappa. Author several books including Understanding the Christian Faith, 1947; Prayer and the Common Life, 1948; The Gospel and Our World, 1949; Through Christ Our Lord, 1950; The Modern Rival of Christian Faith, 1952; Toward Understanding the Bible, 1952; Be Still and Know, 1953; The Sources of Western Morality, 1954; Foundations of Christian Knowledge, 1955; Christian Ethics, 1957; The Providence of God, 1960; The Church and Its Laity, 1962; Our Christian Hope, 1964; The Fellowship of the Holy Spirit, 1966; Disciplines of the Christian Life, 1967; A Devotional Treasury from the Early Church, 1968; Stability Amid Change, 1969; Grace Abounding, 1969; The Ministry of Reconciliation, 1971. Home: 1377 Via Zurita Claremont CA 91711

HARKNESS, JOHN CHEESMAN, architect; b. N.Y.C., Nov. 30, 1916; s. Albert and Sara (Cheesman) H.; A.B. cum laude, Harvard, 1938, B.Arch., 1941, M.Arch., 1941; m. Sarah Pillsbury, June 14, 1941; children—Sara (Mrs. Super), Joan (Mrs. Edwin Hantz), Nell (Mrs. Christopher Huvos), Timothy, Alice, Frederick, John P. Founding partner firm The Architects Collaborative, Cambridge, Mass., 1946—; mem. archtl. faculty Grad. Sch. Design, Harvard, 1946-50; vis. lectr. Mass. Inst. Tech., 1950, also Tulane U., Va. Poly. Inst., U. Pa., others. Active Boston Arts Festival. Served with Am. Field Service, 1943-44, AUS, 1944-45. Recipient 7 design awards Am. Assn. Sch. Adminstrs. Fellow A.I.A.; mem. Boston Soc. Architects (bd. dirs.), Nat. Acad. Design, Art League N.Y., Harvard Alumni Assn. (bd. dirs. 1965). Projects include Children's Hosp. Med. Center Boston (Nat. award A.I.A.); various bldgs. Harvard; U. Tunis, Tunisia; Nat. Shawmut Bank, Boston; pub. schs. Home: 34 Moon Hill Rd Lexington MA 02173 Office: 46 Brattle St Cambridge MA 02173

HARKNESS, REBEKAH WEST, composer, philanthropist, found. exec.; b. St. Louis Apr. 17, 1915; d. Allen T. and Rebekah (Semple) West; composition student with Nadia Boulanger, Fontainebleau, France; student of Fred Werele, Mannes Coll. Music, Dalcroze Sch., Geneva, Switzerland; studied orchestration with Lee Holby; D.F.A., Franklin Pierce Coll., Rindge, N.H., 1968; Hum.D., Lycoming Coll., 1970; m. Dickson Pierce, 1938; children—Allen West, Anne Terry; m. 2d, William Hale Harkness, 1947; 1 dau., Edith Hale. Founder, Rebekah Harkness Found., sponsors ballet and dance programs throughout U.S., pres., 1959- -; founder Harkness Ballet, 1964, pres., 1964—, artistic dir., 1970 —; opened Harkness House for Ballet Arts, 1965; pres., dir. William Hale Harkness Found., supporting med. research. Bd. dirs. Soc. More Beautiful Nat. Capitol, President's Council Youth Opportunity. Recipient bronze medal appreciation N.Y.C., 1965; Marguis de Cuevas prize U. de la Dance, Paris, France, 1965; Congl. Record citation, 1965-66; Handel award N.Y.C., 1967; Shield award Am. Indian and Eskimo Cultural Found., 1967; citations White House, 1968, D.C. Dept. Correction, 1969. Named officer Merite Cultural and Artistique (France), 1966. Clubs: River, Colony (N.Y.C.). Composer: (tone poem) Safari, 1955; Mediterranean Suite, 1957; Musical Chairs, 1958; (ballet) Journey to Love, 1958; Barcelona Suite, 1958; Gift to the Magi, 1959; Letters to Japan, 1961; Elements, 1965; (orch. suite) Macumba, 1965; orchestrated Six Etudes in the Form of a Canon (Schumann), 1964, Suite 1 (Rachmaninoff), 1967, Variations in B Flat (Schubert), 1967, Adantino Varie and Two Marches (Schubert), 1967; 'Cello Sonata (Rachmaninoff), 1969. Address; 4 E 75th St New York City NY 10021

HARKNESS, RICHARD LONG, radio and television news commentator, journalist; b. Artesian, S.D., Sept. 29, 1907; s. Rev. Samuel Dacke and Anne Marie (Long) H.; A.B., U. Kan., 1928; Litt.D., Keuka Coll., 1946; m. Gladys Estelle Suiter, Feb. 6, 1934; children—Richard Long, Peter Anthony, Christopher Rollin. White House corr. United Press Assns., 1936-37; Washington Bur. Phila. Inquirer, 1937-42, Congl. corr., covering Am. fgn. policy debate in U.S. Senate; Washington corr. N.B.C. since 1943, covering Roosevelt-Churchill war confs., Que., United Nat. Orgn. sessions, San Francisco, Security Council meetings, N.Y.C. and Paris, France, North Atlantic Treaty meeting, Rome, E.T.O., assigned nat. polit. convs. and campaigns since 1936; originated N.B.C.'s 1st network TV news program from Washington, Story of the Week. Mem. Delta Chi, Sigma Delta Chi. Clubs: Nat. Press Overseas Writers, Gridiron (Washington). Home: 3035 Dumbarton Av Washington DC 20007 Office: NBC Washington DC 20013

HARKNESS, SARAH P., (Mrs. John C. Harkness), architect; b. Swampscott, Mass., July 8, 1914; d. Samuel H. and Helen (Watters) Pillsbury; certificate M.Arch., Smith Coll.; m. John C. Harkness, June 14, 1941; children—Sara, Joan, Nell, Timothy, Alice, Frederick, John Pillsbury. Designer office Eleanor Raymond, architect, Boston, 1938-39; draughtsman Peter & Stubbins, architects, Boston, 1939- 40; agt. for Artek-Pascoe, under name Pillsbury and Vaughan, Boston, 1940-41; designer Dan Cooper, Inc., N.Y.C., 1941-43; designer circulation exhbns. Mus. Modern Art, 1943-44; partner Architects Collaborative, Inc., Cambridge, Mass., 1946-. Home: 34 Moon Hill Rd Lexington MA 02173 Office: 46 Brattle St Cambridge MA 02138

HARKRADER, CARLETON ALLEN, lawyer; b. Bristol, Va., Dec. 17, 1917; s. Charles Johnston and Elva Louise (Moorman) H.; A.B., Va. Mil. Inst., 1940; LL.B., Yale, 1953; m. Julia Visetti, Jan. 1946 (div. 1949); 1 son, Richard; m. 2d, Doris Newman, Feb. 3, 1951; children—Carol, Elva, Deborah. Mailer, reporter, editorial writer Bristol Va. Herald Courier, 1934-41; corr. Newsweek mag., Rome (with Newbold Noyes Jr. interviewed Pope Pius XII on Vatican reaction to atomic bomb), 1945-46; also corr. in Middle East and France, 1945; exec. editor and pub. Bristol Herald Courier and News Bull., 1946-51; appellate atty., legal adviser FTC, 1957-61; partner law firm Wlad, Harkrader, Nicholson & Ross and predecessor firm, Washington, 1961—. Served from 2d lt. to maj., AUS, 1941-42; with II Corps on North African landing; served in Allied Force Hdqrs. in North Africa and Italy. Decorated Bronze Star. Recipient Lee Editorial award Va. Press Assn. and Lee Sch. of Journalism, Washington and Lee U. for distinguished editorial writing, 1941. Mem. Am., Fed., Va., D.C. bar assns., Sigma Delta Chi, Phi Delta Phi. Democrat. Clubs: Metropolitan (Washington); River Bend Country. Home: 905 Chinquapin Rd McLean VA 22101 Office: 1320 19th St NW Washington DC 20036

HARKRADER, CHARLES JOHNSTON, editor, banking exec.; b. Blountville, Tenn., Sept. 13, 1885; s. Fletcher Lloyd and Susan M. (White) Harkrader; ed. pub. schs.; studied law, 1904-05; m. Louise Moorman, Nov. 27, 1908; children—Harriett (Mrs. R.P. London, Jr.), Charles Johnson (M.D.), Carlton Allen, Elva (Mrs. W. E. Latture). Newspaper reporter until 1913; pub. Bristol Herald Courier, 1919-50, established Johnson City (Tenn.) Press (daily newspaper), 1924, which in Jan. 1935 absorbed its two rival newspapers; pres. Robert Porterfield's Barter Theatre of Va., Inc.; dir. First Nat. Bank of Sullivan County, H.p. King Co. Chmn. Va. A.P. membership, 1930; mem. Va. War Bond Com.; covered San Francisco UN Conf., 1945; regional dir. civilian def. for 14 counties in western Va., also set up rationing and selective service bds. in these counties, 1941. Chmn., Bristol chpt. A.R.C. Mem. Va. Senate, 1936-40, mem. roads and gen. laws com., active for enlarged hwy. program; del. Dem. Nat. Conv., 1932, 36, 40. Mem. Va. Press Assn., Soc. Am. Newspaper Editors, Asso. Press., So. Newspaper Pubs. Assn. (editorial com.), Am. Newspaper Pubs. Assn. Methodist. Mason (Shriner). Clubs: Rotary (hon.), Bristol Country. Covered as a reporter every Dem. Nat. Conv., 1920—. Author: Witness to an Epoch, 1965. Home: 916 Prospect Av Bristol VA 24201

HARKRIDER, LESTER DORE, bus. exec.; b. Hoopeston, Ill., Jan 13, 1898; s. A.L. and Anna Belle (Boyd) H.; ed. pub. sch.; m. Lola Brown, Mar. 6, 1920; 1 dau., Lois June. Began with Verillion Malleable Iron Co., Hoopeston, 1916; successively with Inland Malleable & Steel Co., Terre Haute, Ind.; Samson Tractor Co. div. Gen. Motors Corp., Janesville, Wis.; now chmn., treas. Gen. Casting Corp., Waukesha; dir. Hein-Werner Motor Parts Corp., Waukesha Motor Co., Indsl. Bldg. & Loan Assn., Waukesha, Wis. Mem. Am. Foundrymens Assn., Wis. Mfrs. Assn. (bd. dirs.). Republican. Clubs: Kiwanis, Elks (Waukesha); University (Milw.). Home: 315 E College Av Waukesha WI 53186 Office: 706 E Main St Waukesha WI 53186

HARLAN, CAMPBELL ALLEN, elec. engr.; b. Columbia, Tenn., May 31, 1907; s. Alexander and Ellagreen (Pickard) C.; student coll. engring. U. Tenn., 1926-28; D.Sc. (hon.), U. of Detroit; m. Ivabell Campbell, June 29, 1932; children—John Marshall, Campbell Allen, Joyce Lily, James Gregory, Joseph Duncan, Jay Scott, Jean Marie. Engr., estimator Turner Engring. Co., Detroit, 1929-35, mgr., 1935-40; chmn. bd. Harlan Electric Co., v.p., dir. subsidiary and affiliated cos.; dir. Power Piping Co., Pitts., Liberty Mut. Co. City National Bank Detroit, Detroit Mortgage & Realty Co.; pres. Univ. House-Holiday Inn, Morgantown W.Va. Bd. dirs. Community Health Assn., Maryglade Coll.; vice chmn. Detroit com. Nat. Jewish Hosp.; mem. alumni bd. govs. U. Tenn.; v.p. dir. exec. com. United Found.; bd. dirs., past pres. Ednl. TV Found; trustee Burton Mercy Hosp., Bethany Coll., Fisk U., Hampton Inst.; trustee emeritus Mich. State U.; fellow Brandeis U.; hon. trustee Brandeis U. Assos. Served as lt. USNR, 1944-45. Mem. Engring. Soc. Detroit, Navy League U.S. (Detroit Council), Mich. Soc. Architects (hon.), Am. Assn. UN (bd. mem.), Detroit Bd. Commerce, Nat. Elec. Contractors Assn., Detroit Elec. Assn. (past pres.). Met Art Assn., Tau Beta Pi. Clubs: Detroit Athletic, Recess, Economic (dir.) (Detroit). Home: 3535 N Adams Rd Bloomfield Hills MI 48013 Office: 24000 Telegraph Rd Southfield MI 48075

HARLAN, JACK RODNEY, geneticist; b. Washington, June 7, 1917; s. Harry Vaughn and Augusta (Griffing) H.; B.S. in Botany with distinction, George Washington U., 1938; Ph.D. in Genetics, U. Cal. at Berkeley, 1942; m. Jean Yocum, Aug. 4, 1939; children—Sue (Mrs. Robert Hughes), Harry, Sherry, Richard Edwin. Research asst. Tela R.R. Co., Honduras, 1942; geneticist Dept. Agr., Woodward, Okla., 1942-51, Stillwater, Okla., 1951-61; prof. agronomy Okla. State U., 1951-66; prof. gentics U. Ill. at Urbana, 1966—; botanist Dept. of Agr. plant exploration and introduction, Turkey, Syria and Iraq, 1948, Iran, Afghanistan, Pakistan, India and Ethiopia, 1960; sr. staff mem. Iranian prehistoric project, Oriental Inst. U. Chgo., 1960, Turkish prehistoric project, 1964. Fellow A.A.A.S., Am. Soc. Agronomy; men. Crop Sci. Soc. Am. (pres. 1966), Am. Inst. Biol. Scientists (gov. bd.), Bot. Soc. Am., Am. Soc. Range Mgmt. (charter), Am. Soc. Agronomy (exec. com.), Phi Beta Kappa, Sigma Xi. Presbyn. (elder). Contbr. profl. jours. Home: 1822 Crescent Dr Champaign IL 61820 Office: Crop Evolution Lab Agronomy Dept U Ill Urbana IL 61801

HARLAN, JOHN FREDERICK, Jr., hosp. adminstr.; b. Charlottesville, Va., Dec. 18, 1925; s. John Frederick and Myrtle (Clarke) H.; B.A., U. Va., 1950; grad. Med. Coll. Va. Sch. Hosp. Adminstrn., 1952; m. Dorothy Reedy Koontz, Sept. 6, 1950; children—Patricia Ann, John Frederick III, Dorothy Karol and Barbara Ellen (twins), Douglas Allen. Adminstrv. asst. U. Va. Hosp., Charlottesville, 1952-54; asst. dir., 1954-58, asso. dir., 1958-65, dir., 1965—. Dir. Va. Nat. Bank. Chmn. community drive Nat. Found. Infantile Paralysis, 1958. Mem. Charlottesville Sch. Bd., 1963-66; mem. Albemarle Dem. Com., 1956-60. Pres. U. Va. Hosp. Employees Credit Union; bd. dirs. United Givers Fund, U. Va. Student Aid Found., Blue Cross/Blue Shield of Va. Served with AUS, 1944-46. Decorated Bronze Star. Recipient Key Man award Jaycees, 1959. Mem. Med. Coll. Va. Sch. Hosp. Adminstrn. Alumni Assn. (pres. elect), U. Va. Alumni Assn., Albemarle County Med. Soc., Charlottesville-Albemarle Jr. C. of C. (past pres.), Va. Hosp. Assn. (past pres.). Methodist (bd. dirs.). Lion (past pres.). Home: 1628 Keith Valley Rd Charlottesville VA 22901 Office: U Va Hosp Charlottesville VA 22901

HARLAN, JOHN GRAYDON, Jr., chem. co. exec.; b. Pitts., Apr. 30, 1918; s. John Graydon and Anna M. (Durning) H.; student George Washington U., U.S. Dept. Agr. Grad. Sch., 1936-41; m. Margaret Fenwick Wetmore, June 15, 1940. Served with Fed. Govt., 1937-69, with Treasury Dept., 1937-48, in Fgn. Aid Program, 1948-57; chief indsl. productivity and exec. officer AID Mission to Austria, 1950-53; dep. dir. indsl. tech. assistance FOA, 1953- 54; asst. dir. Office Indsl. Resources ICA, 1954-57; mgmt. officer Office Adminstr. Gen. Services Adminstrn., 1957-58, dep. commr. Def. Materials Service, 1958-66, commr., 1966, commr. Property Mgmt. and Disposal Service, 1966-69; v.p. Engelhard Minerals & Chem. Corp., 1969—, exec. v.p. Engelhard Industies div., Newark, 1969-70, exec. v.p., 1970—. Rep., Pres. Com. on Econ. Impact Def. and Disarmament; project mgr. President's Spl. Task Force on Use Surplus Property to Meet Critical Urban Needs for Housing; mem. Ind. Study Bd. to examine effects govt. policies on regional econ. levels. Served to lt. USCGR, 1942-45. Recipient Meritorious Service award FOA, 1955, Meritorious Service award, 1960, Distinguished Service award Gen. Services Adminstrn., 1965. Mem. Sigma Chi. Home: 19 Oakes Rd Rumson NJ 07760 Office: 430 Mountain Av Murray Hills NJ 07974

HARLAN, NEIL EUGENE, mgmt. cons.; b. Cherry Valley, Ark., June 2, 1921; s. William and Mary Nina (Ellis) H.; student U. Edinburgh (Scotland), 1946; B.S., U. Ark., 1947, LL.D., 1969; M.B.A., Harvard, 1950, D.B.A., 1956; m. Martha Almlov, Sept. 27, 1952; children—Lindsey Beth, Neil Eugene, Sarah Ellis. With Homer K. Jones & Co., Memphis, 1947-48; asst. ednl. dir. Am. Inst. C.P.A.'s, N.Y.C., 1950-51; mem. faculty Grad. Sch. Bus. Adminstrn. Harvard, 1951-62, asst. prof., 1954-58, asso. prof., 1958-61, prof., 1962; asst. sec. air force, Washington, 1962-64; v.p., chief financial officer, dir. Anderson, Clayton & Co., 1964-66, exec. v.p., 1966-67; dir. McKinsey & Co., Inc., 1967—. Trustee D.C. Inst. Mental Hygiene, Doctors Hosp. Found., Washington. Served with AUS, 1943-46. Mem. Am. Inst. C.P.A.'s Author: Management Control in Air Frame Subcontrating, 1956; (with R.H. Hassler) Cases in Controllership, 1958; (with R.F. Vancil) Cases in Accounting Policy, 1961; (with Christenson and Vancil) Managerial Economics, 1962. Home: 11 Stanmore Ct Potomac MD 20854 Office: 1700 Pennsylvania Av NW Washington DC 20006

HARLAN, W. GLEN, lawyer; b. Stuart, Ia., Oct. 14, 1912; s. Wilber George and Lillian (Russell) H.; A.B., Simpson Coll., 1936; J.D., State U. Ia., 1939; m. Esther Wadleigh, Mar. 15, 1941; children—Michael (dec.), Esther E. Admitted to Ia. bar, 1939, Ga. bar, 1942, N.Y. bar, 1961; law clk. to Wiley Rutledge, asso. justice U.S. Ct. Appeals, D.C., 1939-41; asso. Gambrell & White, Atlanta, 1941-47; partner Gambrell, Harlan, Russell & Moye, and predecessors, 1948-67; v.p. legal affairs Eastern Air Lines, Inc., 1967-69, sr. v.p. legal affairs, 1969—; dir. Dorado Beach Hotel Corp., Dorado Beach Devel., Inc., Dorado Beach Estates, Inc., Eastern Air Lines, S.A., Eastern Pacific, Inc. Mem. labor relations com. Council of State C.'s of C. Mem. Am. (ho. of dels. 1956-58), Fed., Ga., Atlanta, N.Y. State, N.Y.C. bar assns., Am. Judicature Soc., Lawyers Club, Internat. Air Transport Assn. (legal com.), Legal Aid Soc., Newcomen Soc. N.Am., Order of Coif, Pi Kappa Delta. Methodist. Clubs: Siwanoy Country

(Bronxville, N.Y.); Rotary: Pinetree Country; Cherokee Town and Country. Home: 47 Valley Rd Bronxville NY 10708 Office: 10 Rockefeller Plaza New York City NY 10020

HARLAN, WILLIAM MORRISON, Jr., banker; b. Farmington, Mo., Nov. 23, 1911; s. William Morrison and Helen Bell (Montgomery) H.; A.B., Westminster Coll., 1933; m. Lauralee Woolley, Sept. 2, 1934; children—George Woolley, William Morrison III. With Manchester Bank of St. Louis, 1933—, asst. cashier, 1940-44, v.p., 1944-48, pres., dir. 1948—; dir. James R. Kearney Corp., Hill- Hentschel Co. Trustee Westminster Coll., Presbyn. Home for Children of Mo., Bethesda Gen. Hosp., Presbyn. Homelife for Sr. Citizens. Mem. St. Louis C. of C. (dir.), Beta Theta Pi. Presbyn. (elder). Clubs: University, Racquet, Algonquin Golf (St. Louis). Home: 119 S Gore Av Webster Groves MO 63119 Office: 4019 Chouteau Av St Louis MO 63110

HARLAND, JAMES PENROSE, educator, archaeologist; b. Wenonah, N.J., Feb. 5, 1891; s. James and Catherine (Welsh) H.; student William Penn Charter Sch., 1904-09; A.B., Princeton, 1913, A.M., 1915, Ph.D., 1917; student U. Bonn am Rhein, 1913- 14, Am. Sch., Athens, Greece, 1914; m. Agnes Westerlund, Feb. 2, 1924 (dec. Aug. 1959). Instr. Greek, U. Mich., 1921-22; asst. prof. classics U. N.C., 1922-23; asst. prof. archaeology and Greek, U. Cin., 1923-26; asso. prof. archaeology U. N.C., 1927-29, prof., 1929—; excavated at Nemea, Zygouries and other sites; archaeol. study, Greece, U. Uppsala, Sweden, 1939; visited museums eleven countries, Norway to Turkey, 1939. Mem. Town Planning Bd. Chapel Hill. Mem. mng. com. Am. Sch. at Athens, 1959—. Served from seaman to ensign, communications officer USN, 1917-19. Fellow Archaeol. Inst., Am. Sch., Athens, Greece, 1920-21; Guggenheim fellow, 1926-27. Mem. Archaeol. Inst. Am. (recorder 1946-47, lectr.; pres. Carolina soc.), Am. Schs. Oriental Research, Am. Philol. Assn., Princeton Alumni Assn. of Eastern N.C. (pres.), Am. Research Center in Egypt, Phi Beta Kappa. Presbyn. Club: Archaeological. Author: Peloponnesos in The Bronze Age, 1923; Prehistoric Aigina, 1925; Date of Hellenic Alphabet, 1945; Archaeological Excavations, 1946; Sodom and Gommorah, 1961. Contbr. articles to Biblical Archaeologist, Ency. Brit., Jr., Collier's Ency., Interpreter's Dictionary of the Bible, profl. jours. Home: 700 Laurel Hill Rd Chapel Hill NC 27514

HARLAND, LEWIS E., corp. exec.; b. Chgo., Jan. 8, 1905; s. George E. and Carrie D. (Dana) H.; B.S., U. Ill., 1926; m. Isabell C. Ioas, May 14, 1927. Bond salesman for Harris Trust & Savs. Bank, Chgo., 1926-27; salesman, mgr. tabulating dept. Remington Rand Co., 1927-32; office mgr. B.N. Anderson & Co., ins. agy., 1932-43; with Wm. Wrigley Jr. Co., 1943- -, now exec. v.p.; dir. Ariz. Biltmore Hotel, Phoenix, Santa Catalina Island Co., Avalon, Cal. Home: 4045 Grand Av Western Springs IL 60558 Office: 410 N Michigan Av Chicago IL 60611

HARLAND, ROBERT P., lawyer; b. Milw., 1910; B.M.E., Marquette U., 1932, J.D. cum laude, 1935. Admitted to Wis. bar, 1935, U.S. Supreme Ct. bar; now partner firm Whyte, Hirschboeck, Minahan, Harding & Harland, Milw. Mem. Am., Milw. bar assns., State Bar Wis. Editor-in-chief Marquette Law Rev., 1935. Office: 2100 Marine Plaza Milwaukee WI 53202*

HARLEM, GUDMUND, Norwegian govt. ofcl., physician; b. Oslo, Norway, July 24, 1917; s. Gudmund and Olga (Haug) H.; M.D., U. Oslo, 1946; m. Inga Brynolf, Oct. 3, 1938. House physician Inst. Hygiene, Oslo, 1946-48; physician State Rehab. Center, Oslo, 1946-53, med. dir., 1953-55; UN expert on rehab., Egypt, 1954, Greece and Italy, 1955; chmn. Com. Invalid Care, 1953-55, Rehab. Council Norway, 1955-57; minister health and social affairs, 1955- 61, minister def., 1961-65; resident Oslo U. Hosp., 1965-66; dir. State Rehab. Inst. in Oslo, 1966—. Mem. Norwegian Research Council Sci. and Humanities, 1949-57; pres. Internat. Soc. for Rehab. of Disabled, 1966-69. Pres. Norwegian Students Assn., 1945; mem. Oslo Town Council, 1946-47; exec. com. Labor Party Youth Orgn., 1946-49; offcr. Internat. Union Socialist Youth, 1496-51; dep. chmn. Oslo Labor Party, 1952-57. Recipient Albert Lasker award in medicine, 1960. Home: Sigbjörn Obsffelders vei 2 Oslo 3 Norway Office: State Rehab Inst in Oslo Sinsenvn 76 Refstad Oslo 5 Norway

HARLEMAN, DONALD ROBERT FERGUSSON, educator; b. Palmerton, Pa., Dec. 5, 1922; s. Robert Roy and Nora (Curry) H.; B.S. in C.E., Pa. State U., 1943; M.S., Mass. Inst. Tech., 1947, D.Sc., 1950; m. Martha Havens, Oct. 21, 1950; children—Kathleen T., Robert I.H., Anne C. Design engr. Curtiss-Wright Corp., Columbus, O., 1944-45; research asst., research asso. Hydrodynamics Lab., Mass. Inst. Tech., 1945-50, asst. prof. hydraulics, 1950-56, asso. prof. hydraulics, 1956-62, prof. civil engring., 1963—; vis. prof. Cal. Inst. Tech., 1962-63; sr. visitor applied math. and theoretical physics U. Cambridge (Eng.), 1968-69. Mem. Water Pollution Control Fedn.; mem. U.S. Nat. Com. Internat. Assn. Water Pollution Research. Recipient Desmond Fitzgerald medal Boston Soc. Civil Engrs., 1967; Guggenheim fellow, 1968-69. Mem. Am. Soc. C.E..(research prize 1960), Am. Geophys. Union, Internat. Assn. for Hydraulic Research, Am. Soc. Limnology and Oceanography. Bd. editors Jour. Hydraulic Research. Research in fluid transport process and water quality control. Home: 16 Bloomfield St Lexington MA 02173 Office: 335 Parsons Lab for Water Resources and Hydrodynamics Mass Inst Tech Cambridge MA 02139

HARLESTON, BERNARD WARREN, educator; b. N.Y.C., Jan. 22, 1930; s. Henry Mitchell and Anna (Tobin) H.; B.S., Howard U., 1951; Ph.D., U. Rochester, 1955; m. Marie AnnLombard, June 19, 1954; children-David Warren, Jeffrey Stuart. Instr. U. Rochester, 1954-55, asst. prof., 1955-56, research asso., 1956; asst. prof. psychology Tufts U., 1956-61, asso. prof., 1961-68, prof. psychology, dean Faculty Arts and Scis., 1970—; provost, prof. psychology Lincoln (Pa.) U., 1968-70; research fellow Stanford, 1963-64; vis. asst. prof. N.Y.U., summer 1959. Mem. profl. adv. com. Nat. Inst. Mental Health, 1966-68; dir. West Medford (Mass.) Community Center, 1966- 68; chmn. Winchester (Mass.) Council Community Action, 1967-68, Trustee Cambridge Friends Sch.; mem. adv. council bd. trustees U. Rochester, Exptl. and Spl. Tng. Review Com. U.S. Dept. Health, Edn. and Welfare, 1969—. Fellow Mass. Psychol. Assn.; mem. Am. Psychol. Assn., Am. Assn. U. Profs., A.A.A.S., Phi Beta Kappa, Sigma Xi. Contbr. articles profl. jours. Producer TV series Principles of Behavior, Boston. Home: 22 Lawrence Lane Lexington MA 02173 Office: Ballou Hall Tufts U Medford MA 02155

HARLEY, CHARLES RICHARD, govt. ofcl.; b. Charleston, Mo., Dec. 3, 1912; s. John Duncan and Sarah (Howland) H.; B.A., Coll. Wooster (O.), 1935; M.A., Fletcher Sch. Law and Diplomacy, 1939; student sr. seminar, Fgn. Service Sch., 1962-63; m. Constance Knickerbocker, Aug. 16, 1940; children—Charles K., Katherine H., Peter C. With Dunlop Tire and Rubber Co., Buffalo, 1935-38; bd. govs. Fed. Res. System, 1941-48; with Treasury Dept., 1948—, dir. office internat. financial policy coordination and operations, 1964-70; U.S. alternate exec. dir. IMF, 1970—. Mem. Phi Beta Kappa. Presbyn. Home: 5016 Hampden Lane Bethesda MD 20014 Office: Treasury Dept 15th and Pennsylvania Av NW Washington DC 20220

HARLEY, ROBISON DOOLING, educator, physician; b. Pleasantville, N.J., Feb. 27, 1911; s. Halvor L. and Alice (Robison) H.; B.Sc., Rutgers U., 1932; M.D., U. Pa., 1936; Ph.D., U. Minn., 1949; m. Loyde Hazel Gochnauer, Dec. 18, 1944; children—Robison Dooling, Ardee R. and Heather L. (twins), Halvor L. II, William W. Intern, Phila. Gen. Hosp., 1936-38; fellowship Mayo Clinic, Rochester, Minn., 1938-41, jr. staff cons., 1941-42; pvt. practice as ophthalmologist and ophthalmic surgeon, Atlantic City and Phila., 1947—; attending surgeon St. Christopher's Hosp. for Children, Phila., 1958—; chief surgeon Atlantic City Hosp., 1950—; cons. Shore Meml. Hosp., Somers Point, 1958—; attending surgeon Temple U. Hosp., Phila., 1947—, also Wills Eye Hosp. and Research Inst.; cons. Betty Bacharach Home for Children and Children's Seashore Home, 1955—; attending surgeon, dir. dept. pediatrics and motility; prof. ophthalmology Temple U. Sch. Medicine, Phila. Mem. exec. bd. Atlantic area council Boy Scouts Am., 1949—; bd. dirs. YMCA, 1957—. Served from lt. to lt. col., AUS, 1942-47. Decorated Legion of Merit from Panama (Vasco Nunez de Balboa). Diplomate Am. Bd. Ophthalmology. Fellow A.C.S. (gov. 1959-62), Am. Acad. Ophthalmology and Otolaryngology (asso. sec. continuing edn.); mem. Assn. Research Ophthalmology, Pan-Am. Congress Ophthalmology, Am. Ophthal. Soc., Phi Beta Kappa, Sigma Xi. Clubs: Explorers N.Y.C.; Brigantine (N.J.) Yacht (commodore); Cricket, Union League (Phila.). Author: (with G.G. Gibson) Sensorimotor Anomalies of Extrinsic Ocular Muscles, 1965; Anomalies of Binoc. Pos., Visual Perception and Ocular Motility, 1966. Home: Alden Park Kenilworth Philadelphia PA 19144 Office: 1601 Spring Garden St Philadelphia PA 19136

HARLIN, MAXEY BARLOW, lawyer; b. Bowling Green, Ky., Oct. 13, 1915; s. Max B. and Margaret (Franklin) H.; LL.B., U. Louisville, 1938; m. Nancy Moore, Aug. 24, 1935; children—Maxey B. III, John Moore, Nancy Elizabeth. Admitted to Ky. bar, 1937; practiced in Bowling Green since 1938, mem. firm Harlin, Parker & Ricketts, Luca and English. Mem. Constn. Revision Assembly, 1964-66. Mem. bd. regents Western Ky. U. Mem. Ky. Bar Assn. (pres. 1952-53) Home: 1508 Chestnut St Bowling Green KY 42101 Office: 519 10th St Bowling Green KY 42101

HARLLEE, ELLA FULMORE, assn. exec., radio-TV producer; b. Washington; d. William Curry and Ella (Fulmore) Harllee; B.A., Am. U., 1938; M.A. Columbia, 1939; student summers U. Brazil, 1940, U. Mich., 1941, U. So. Cal., 1946, N.Y.U., 1951, Birmingham U. (Eng.), 1952, Brit. Film Inst. (Glasgow), 1952. Dir. Studio of Speech, Washington, 1941-46; speech instr. St. Mary's Jr. Coll., 1942; asst. prof. speech Am. U., 1946-52; dir. radio-TV dept. D.C. Council Chs., Washington, 1953-60. Dir. Belize (Brit. Honduras) E.C.A. Audio-Visual Edn. Project, 1971—; sec. Internat. Christian Com. for Brussels World's Fair; nat. pub. relations chmn. Ch. Women United, 1956-59, mem. Com. of 100. Mem. women's plan com. Japanese Internat. Christian U. Named Church Woman of Year, Religious Heritage Am. Assn., 1962; Golden Mike award McCall's mag., 1964. Mem. Am. Women Radio-TV, Press Club, Washington, Am. Newspaper Women's Club, Soc. Women Geographers (pres. 1962-63), First Families Va., Colonial Dames Am., Religious Pub. Relations Council, Washington Bd. Trade, Am. Assn. U. Women, Ednl. Communication Assn. (pres.), Faith Media, Inc. (pres.). Club: Columbia U. (N.Y.C.). Author: Pronunciation Drills in English. Home: 1200 N Nash St Arlington VA 22209 Office: Nat Press Bldg Washington DC 20004

HARLLEE, JOHN, mgmt. cons.; b. Washington, Jan. 2, 1914; s. William Curry and Ella Florence (Fulmore) H.; B.S., U.S. Naval Acad., 1934; grad. Naval War Coll., 1950; m. Jo-Beth Carden, Sept. 10, 1937; 1 son, John. Commd. ensign U.S. Navy, 1934, advanced through grades to rear adm.; comdr. motor torpedo squadron 12, 1943-44; mem. Naval Congl. Liaison Unit, 1948- 49; comdr. destroyer U.S.S. Dyess, 1949-50, U.S.S. Rankin, 1958; ret., 1959; v.p. Edward I. Farley & Co., Inc., investments, N.Y.C., 1960-61; prodn. planner Ampex Corp., Redwood City, Cal., 1960; cons. under sec. commerce for transp., 1961; mem. Fed. Martime Commn., and predecessor, 1961-69, chmn., 1963-69; now mgmt. cons. shipping. Dir., past v.p. Peter Tare, Inc. Trustee Am. Mcht. Marine Library Assn. Chmn. Citizens for Kennedy and Johnson, No. Cal., 1960. Decorated Silver Star, Legion of Merit with combat V, Commendation ribbon with combat V, Presdl. Unit citation with bronze star. Mem. Sons Republic Tex., Tex. Soc. Washington, Peter Tare (1st v.p., bd. dirs.). Clubs: Tex. Breakfast (charter); Chevy Chase (Md.); Metropolitan, Army Navy, Propeller (Washington); N.Y. Yacht. Contbr. articles profl. jours. Home: Oakley Front Royal VA 22630 Office: 2000 K St NW Washington DC 20006

HARLOR, JOHN CLAYTON, lawyer; b. Worthington, O., Aug. 27, 1898; s. John David and Alice (McLeod) H.; A.B., Ohio State U., 1920, J.D., 1922; m. Inez J. Turner, Sept. 24, 1930; children—John T., Douglas M. Admitted to Ohio bar, 1922, since practiced in Columbus; mem. firm Wright, Harlor, Morris & Arnold, 1926—. Dir. various corps. Mem. city council, Bexley, O., 1936-56, pres. council, 1953-56. Mem. Am., Ohio, Columbus (past pres.) bar assns., Am. Judicature Soc., Chi Phi, Phi Delta Phi. Clubs: Kit Kat (past pres.), Wheaton (past pres.), University, Rocky Fork Hunt and Country (past pres.), Rocky Fork Beagle (Columbus). Home: 2859 Powell Av Columbus OH 43209 Office: 37 W Broad St Columbus OH 43215

HARLOW, BRYCE NATHANIEL, mfg. co. exec.; b. Oklahoma City, Aug. 11, 1916; s. Victor Gertrude (Gindling) b.; B.A., U. Okla., 1936, M. A., 1942; postgrad. U. Tex., 1936-37; m. Elizabeth Larimore, Sept. 25, 1940; children—Margery Gindling, Trudy Paxton, Bryce Larimore. Grad. asst. U. Tex., 1937; asst. librarian Ho. Reps., 1938-40, profl. staff Com. Armed Services, 1947-49, chief clk., 1950-51; sec. Mem. Congress, 1940-41; advt. mgr. Harlow Pub. Corp., Oklahoma City, 1946, v.p., 1951-52; spl. asst. White House Staff, adminstrv. asst., spl. asst., dep. asst. to Pres., 1953-61; dir. govtl. relations Procter and Gamble Mfg. Co., Washington, 1961-68, v.p., 1971—; asst. to Pres. U.S., 1969, counsellor to Pres., 1969-70. Served lt. to lt. col. U.S. Army, 1941-46. Decorated Legion Merit. Mem. Okla. Hist. Assn., Oklahoma City Jr. C. of C., Phi Beta Kappa, Phi Delta Theta. Clubs: Capitol Hill, Army-Navy Country (Washington); Nat. Press, Carlton, Metropolitan. Home: 3744 30th Rd N Arlington VA 22207 Office: Procter & Gamble Mfg Co Washington DC 20013

HARLOW, H. GILBERT, educator; b. Plymouth, Mass., Apr. 27, 1914; s. Elmer R. and Florence (Nightingale) H.; B.S., Tufts Coll., 1937; M.S., Harvard, 1940; m. Jeannette Martin, Sept. 4, 1940; children—Priscilla, Sally, Susan, Bradford, Heidi. Engr. Asso. Factory Mut. Fire Ins. Cos., 1937-39; instr. civil engring. Union Coll., 1940-43, asst. prof., 1943-47, asso. prof., 1947-50, prof. civil engring., 1951—, chmn. engring. div., 1954-56, 62-66. Dir. nat. test program for begonias Men's Garden Clubs of Am. Mem. Am. Soc. C.E. (pres. Mohawk-Hudson sect), Am. Assn. U. Profs., Am. Soc. E.E., Sigma Xi, Tau Beta Pi. Club: Men's Garden (pres. Schenectady). Home: 17 Front St Schenectady NY 12305

HARLOW, HAROLD EUGENE, newspaper editor; b. Miami, Fla., Nov. 28, 1925; s. Eugene L. and Hattye (Tygrett) H.; student Western Ky. State U., 1946-47; B.S. in Journalism, U. Tenn., 1950; m. Lela Mae Brenan, Sept. 1, 1950; children-Eugene Brenan, Mary Lee, Harold Alan, Carol Ann. Copy editor Knoxville (Tenn.) News-Sentinel, 1949-59, asst. news editor, 1959-67, news editor, 1967- 69, mng. editor, 1969—. Served with USAAF, 1943-46 Mem. Sigma Delta Chi. Home: 11545 Nassau Dr Concord TN 37720 Office: 204 W Church Av Knoxville TN 37901

HARLOW, HARRY F., univ. prof.; b. Fairfield, Ia., Oct. 31, 1905; s. Lon H. and Mable (Rock) Israel; student Reed Coll., 1923-24; A.B., Stanford, 1927, Ph.D., 1930; m. Clara Mears, 1932 (div. 1946); children—Robert M., Richard F.; m. 2d, Margaret Kuenne, 1948 (dec. 1971); children—Pamela Ann, Jonathan. Asst. prof. psychology U. Wis., 1930-38, asso. prof., 1938-44, prof., 1944-50, 1952-56, George Cary Comstock prof. psychology, dir. primate lab., 1956- -. dir. regional primate center, 1961-71. Chief human resources research U.S. Army, 1950-52; chmn. d.v. anthropology and psychology NCR, 1954-56. Recipient Nat. Medal of Sci., 1967. Fellow Am. Acad. Arts and Scis.; mem. Am. (pres. div. exptl. psychology 1950-51, pres. 1957-58), Midwest (pres. 1947-48) psychol. assns., Am. Philos. Soc., Nat. Acad. Scis., Gamma Alpha, Sigma Xi. Editor Jour. Comparative and Physiological Psychology, 1951-63. Home: 2005 Jefferson St Madison WI 53711

HARLOW, JAMES GINDLING, univ. pres., pub.; b. Okla. City, June 11, 1912; s. Victor Emmanuel and Gertrude (Gindling) H.; student Oklahoma City U., 1926-28; A.B., U. Okla., 1931. M.S., 1933; grad. student Central State Coll., Edmond, Okla., 1933-35, U. Okla., 1937-41, 41-42; grad. student U. Chgo., 1951, Ph.D., 1954; m. Adalene Agnes Rae, Aug. 15, 1932; children—James Gindling, Mary Adalene, Dan Rae. Tchr. high sch., jr. high sch., Hobart, Okla., 1932-33, Seminole, 1933-34, Classen High, Oklahoma City, 1934-37; sci. tchr., head dept. Northeast High, Oklahoma City, 1937-41; editor Harlow Pub. Corp., Oklahoma City, 1934-41, 46-48, now chmn. bd. dirs., pres.; dir. high sch. sci. service, instr. physics U. Okla., 1948-51, asso. dean Univ. Coll., asst. prof. physics, 1951-53, dean coll. Arts and Scis., 1952-53, prof., dean Coll. Edn., 1958-67; pres. W.Va. U., 1967—; research asso. U. Chgo., 1953-54, asso. prof. edn., 1954- 57. Exec. v.p. Frontiers of Sci. Found. of Okla., 1957-67. Served from lt. (j.g.) to lt. comdr., USNR, 1942-46; comdr. ret. Fellow Okla. Acad. Sci. (editor proc. 1949-53); mem. A.A.A.S., Am. Phys. Soc., Nat. Sci. Tchrs. Assn. (dir. 1951-53, chmn. policies com.), N.E.A., Am. Assn. Sch. Adminstrs., Am. Acad. Polit. and Social Sci., Mid-Continent Regional Ednl. Soc. (mem. exec. com.), Am. Edn. Research Assn., Okla. Edn. Assn., N.Y. Acad. Sci., John Dewey Soc., Oklahoma City C. of C. (dir.), Phi Beta Kappa, Sigma Pi Sigma, Kappa Delta Pi, Phi Delta Kappa. Clubs: Quadrangle (Chgo.): Mens Dinner, Tower (Oklahoma City); University (Washington). Author numerous articles in jours., encys. Home: 948 Riverview Dr Morgantown WV 26505

HARLOW, JAMES GINDLING, Jr., utility exec.; b. Oklahoma City, May 29, 1934; s. James Gindling and Adalene (Rae) H.; B.S., U. Okla., 1957, postgrad., 1959-61; m. Jane Marriott Bienfang, Jan. 30, 1957; children—James Gindling III, David Ralph. Research analyst Okla. Gas and Electric Co., Oklahoma City, 1961- 63, div. auditor, 1963-65, adminstrv. asst., 1965-66, asst. treas., 1966- 68, treas., 1968-69, sec.-treas., 1969-70, v.p., treas., dir., 1970—; dir. Village Bank, Oklahoma City, Fidelity Bank N.A. Treas., Oklahoma County Red Cross, 1969; vice chmn. bd. Frontiers of Sci. Found., Inc. Bd. dirs. Salvation Army, Community Council Central Okla.; bd. visitors U. Okla. Coll. Bus. Served with USNR, 1957-59. Mem. Okla. Soc. Security Analysts, Petroleum Club. Clubs: Oklahoma City Golf and Country, Men's Dinner (Oklahoma City). Home: 1713 Pennington Way Oklahoma City OK 73116 Office: PO Box 321 Oklahoma City OK 73101

HARLOW, NEAL, librarian; b. Columbus, Ind., June 11, 1908; s. Robert William and Ora May (Rotan) H.; Ed.B., U. Cal. at Los Angeles, 1932, certificate librarianship, at Berkeley, 1933, M.A. 1949; L.H.D. (hon.), Moravian Coll., Pa., 1967; m. Marian Gardner, Sept. 12, 1936; children—Mary Diane Killou, Eleanor Lucille Klapmuts. Asst. Bancroft Library, U. Cal. at Berkeley, 1934-38; asst. Cal. sect. Cal. State Library, 1938-45; head dept. spl. collections, asst. librarian U. Cal. at Los Angeles, 1945-51; univ. librarian U. B.C., Vancouver, Can., 1951-61; dean, prof. Grad. Sch. Library Service, Rutgers U., 1961-69; cons. edn. for librarianship, library bldgs. Mem. drafting com. Commn. Nat. Plan Library Edn., 1959-63; mem. steering com. Nat. Library Week; mem. biomed. communications study sect. NIH, 1966-70; bd. dirs. U.S. Book Exchange, 1966-70; chmn. bd. mgrs. Pacific N.W. Bibliographic Center, 1954-57; mem. com. sci. information Nat. Research Council Can., 1958-61; mem. library survey com. Nat. Conf. Canadian Univs. and Colls., 1959- 61; mem. B.C. Bd. Examiners Profl. Librarians, 1959-61; sec. projects com. Leon and Thea Koerner Found., Vancouver, 1956-61. Bd. dirs. Community Arts Council, Vancouver, 1956-61. Mem. Am. (council 1952-64, exec. bd. 1959-63), Canadian (council 1953-56, pres., 1960-61), N.J. (exec. bd. 1961-69) library assns., Assn. Coll. and Research Libraries (dir., pres. 1963-64), Am. Assn. U. Profs., Canadian Bibliog. Soc. Club: Rounce and Coffin (Los Angeles). Author: The Maps of San Francisco Bay from the Spanish Discovery to the American Occupation, 1950. Editor Cal. Library Bull., 1957-59. Contbr. profl. and hist. jours. Address: PO Box 26101 Los Angeles CA 90026

HARLOW, REX FRANCIS, author, editor and publisher; b. Winfield, Mo., June 19, 1892; s. James and Mary Adeline (Davis) H.; B.S., Central State Tchrs. Coll., Edmond, Okla., 1934; A.M., U. Tex., 1935; Ed.D., Stanford, 1937; m. Ruby Esther Wilson, Jan. 22, 1920; children—William (dec.), Esther Frances, Benjamin LeRoy (dec.). Business mgr. Harlow's Weekly, 1912-15; sec.-treas. Harlow Pub. Co., 1915-24, v.p., 1924-36; instr. edn. Stanford, 1937-38, asst. prof. edn., 1938-40, asso. prof. pub. relations, 1940-44; founder, pres. Pub. Relations Inst. of West, 1948—; editor, pub. The Social Sci. Reporter, 1952—, also Pub. Relations Research Rev., 1958—. Dir. Stanford School-Press Relations Investigation, 1938-39; organized, 1939, pres. Am. Council Pub. Relations, 1939-47. Del. World Conf. of Allied Ex-Service Men of First World War, London, 1924. Served with 61st F.A. Brigade, 36th Div., U.S. Army, 1918; A.E.F.; maj., 45th Div., Okla. N.G. Mem. Pub. Relations Soc. Am. (bd. dirs. 1947-52, Ann. Profl. award 1952, 69, named one of 12 leading pub. relations profls. of century, 1970). Author: Public Relations in War and Peace, 1942; The Daily Newspaper and Higher Education, 1939; Social Science in Public Relations, 1957; also 38 other books. Co-author: Practical Public Relations, rev. edit., 1952. Editor Harper Series of Public Relations Books, 1939-65, Public Relations Jour., 1945-47. Contbr. to nat. periodicals, Ency. Americana. Home: 850 Webster St Palo Alto CA 94301

HARM, DUANE ROLLO, broadcasting exec.; b. Chgo., Feb. 23, 1939; s. Frederick George and Gertrude Cora (Pfeil) H.; B.S., U. Wis., 1960; m. Susan Galley Rathburn, Mar. 25, 1961; children—Kelly Susan, Wendy Lynn. Sales service ABC-TV Network, Chgo., 1960-61; sales account exec. Avery Knodel, Chgo., 1961-62, John Blair Co., Chgo., 1962-65; sales mgr. WJRT-TV, Flint, Mich., 1965-66, gen. mgr., 1966-68; v.p., gen. mgr. Pacific & So. CO KHON-TV, NBC, Honolulu, 1968—. Radio, tv chmn. Honolulu United Aloha Fund, 1968-71; mem. steering com. Honolulu Media Council, 1970—. Clubs: Waialae Country; Outrigger Canoe. Home: 4639 Waipahee St Honolulu HI Office: 1170 Auahi Honolulu HI

HARM, RAY, artist; b. Randolph County, W.Va., 1926; student Cooper Sch. Comml. Art, Cleve.; hon. doctorate Centre Coll., 1967, Pikeville Coll., 1967, Davis and Elkins Coll., 1969; m. Mildred Anne Atkins, Aug. 12, 1969. Cowhand, pilot, rodeo rider, western U.S.; staff artist Ky. Ornithol. Soc.; artist wildlife; conservation lectr.; writer, illustrator Louisville Times; contbg. editor Fla. Naturalist mag.; now artist-in-residence U. Ky. Cons. C.E. Buckley wildlife sanctuary, Versailles, Ky. Mem. Nat., Louisville, Buckley Hills (Ky.) Audubon socs., Am. Ornithology Union, Ky. Ornithology Soc., Soc. Animal Artists, Wilson Club. Author: The Ray Harm Nature Sketchbook. Home: Chenoa KY 40925

HARMAN, ARCHER, Jr., headmaster; b. Orange, N.J., May 25, 1923; s. Archer and Lillien Adele (Cox) H.; grad. St. Paul's Sch., Concord, N.H., 1941; B.A., Yale, 1944; Ed.M., Harvard, 1950; m. Mari Alice Brainerd, Feb. 26, 1944; children—Jane (Mrs. Brewer), Archer III, David Brainerd, John William. Tchr. math. Westminster Sch., Simsbury, Conn., 1946-48, St. Paul's Sch., 1948-54; headmaster Peck Sch., Morristown, N.J., 1954-61, St. George's Sch., Newport, R.I., 1961—. Served to lt. (j.g.) USNR, 1943-46. Address: St George's Sch Newport RI 02840

HARMAN, AVRAHAM, Israeli diplomat; b. London, Eng., 1914; B.A., Oxford, 1936; married; 3 children. With Zionist Fedn. S. Africa, 1939-40, Jewish Information Dept. Agy., 1940-48; dep. dir. Israel Govt. Press Office, 1948-49; consul gen., Montreal, P.Q., 1949-50; dir. Israel Office Information, counselor Israel Del. UN, 1950-53; consul gen., N.Y.C., 1953-55; asst. dir. gen. Ministry Fgn. Affairs, Jerusalem, 1955-56; ambassador to U.S., 1959-68; pres. Hebrew U., Jerusalem, 1968—; mem. exec. Jewish Agy., 1956-59. Address: Hebrew U Jerusalem Israel

HARMAN, CHARLES LEE, clergyman, coll. pres.; b. Gallatin, Mo., June 19, 1906; s. Pearly T. and Etta T. (Hahn) H.; B.S. cum laude, Lynchburg Coll., 1929; postgrad. U. Va., 1929-30; M.S., Ga. Sch. Tech., 1931; Th.B., Th.M., So. Bapt. Theol. Sem., 1939; LL.D., Lynchburg Coll., 1953; m. Ossie Katherine West, Sept. 1, 1932; children—Charles Lee (dec.), John Roger. Ordained to ministry Bapt. Ch., 1935; grad. instr. chemistry U. Va., 1929-30, Ga. Sch. Tech., 1930-31; chmn. depts. math. and physics, dean of men Lynchburg (Va.) Coll., 1932-36; research chemist, Lynchburg, Va., 1932-36; Protestant pastor Louisville and Jefferson Co. Children's Home, 1938-39; pastor First Bapt. Ch., Narrows, Va., 1939- 41, Starling Av. Ch., Martinsville, Va., 1941-46; pres. Bluefield (Va.) Coll., 1946—. Moderator Blue Ridge, New Lebanon (Va.) Bapt. assns.; Va. chmn. edn. commn. So. Bapt. Conv.; pres. So. Assn. Jr. Colls., 1955-56 Am. Assn. Jr. Coll., 1962; Southeastern Jr. Coll. Athletic Assn., 1954-55; pres. Bapt. Gen. Assn. Va., 1955-56; mem. Nat. Commn. on Accrediting, 1963-65; mem. accrediting commn. So. Assn. Colls. and Secondary Schs., 1957- 61, pres., 1959-60; mem. So. regional group President's Commn. Edn. High Sch., 1957-61; pres. Industries Inc., 1957—. Mem. Martinsville Sch. Bd. Mem. Narrows Jr. C. of C. (pres. 1940), Am. Chem. Soc., N.E.A., Tau Kappa Alpha, Alpha Chi Sigma. Mason. Club: Kiwanis (local pres. 1946). Home: Bluefield College Bluefield VA 24605

HARMAN, JOHN ROYDEN, lawyer; b. Elkhart, Ind., June 30, 1921; s. James Lewis and Bessie Bell (Mountjoy) H.; B.S., U. Ill., 1943; J.D., Ind. U., 1949; m. Elizabeth Rae Crosier, Dec. 12, 1943; 1 son, James Richard. Admitted to Ind. bar, 1949, since practiced in Elkhart; asso. firm Proctor & Proctor, 1949-52; pvt. practice, 1952-60; partner firm Cawley & Harman, 1960-65; partner firm Thornburg, McGill, Deahl, Harman, Carey & Murray, 1965—. City atty., Elkhart, 1952-60. State del. Republican Party, 1962—. Pres., bd. dirs. Crippled Childrens Soc.; bd. dirs. United Community Services Elkhart County. Served to 1st lt. F.A., AUS, 1943-46; PTO. Mem. Am., Ind., Elkhart County, Elkhart (pres. 1970) bar assns., Elkhart C. of C., Phi Kappa Psi, Alpha Kappa Psi, Phi Delta Phi. Presbyn. Rotarian, Elk. Clubs: Elcona Country, Indiana (South Bend). Home: 3725 Shorelane W Elkhart IN 46514 Office: First Nat Bank Bldg Elkhart IN 46514

HARMAN, STETSON BROMLEY, banker; b. Oak Park, Ill., Dec. 13, 1912; s. Francis Lynde Stetson and Mary Adelaide (Millington) H.; grad. Phillips Exeter Acad., 1931, Am. Inst. Banking, 1939; student Pomona Coll., 1931-33; m. Barbra Cleland, Oct. 11, 1935; children—Lorna Cochran, Ellen Millington. With Bank of Am. Nat. Trust & Savs. Assn., Los Angeles, 1933-36; joined First Trust & Savs. Bank of Pasadena (Cal.), 1936, trust officer, 1943-54, asst. sec., 1948-54; asst. v.p., trust officer First Nat. Bank Ore., Portland, 1954-58, v.p., trust officer, 1960-64, sr. v.p., exec. trust officer, 1964—, also mgr. trust dept. Regent Grad. Sch. Banking, Rutgers U, 1952-54, Nat. Trust Sch., 1959-63; trustee Found. for Edn. in Econs., Med. Research Found. Ore.; life trustee Lewis and Clark Coll., Portland. Mem. Am. Inst. Banking (life mem.; v.p. 1952-53, pres. 1953-54, mem. nat. exec. council, 1949-52, pres. Pasadena chpt. 1942-44), Pasadena Tournament of Roses Assn., Portland C. of C., Am. (exec. council 1952-54, 63-68, chmn. banking edn. com. 1963-68, chmn. trust div. exec. com. 1970-71 Ore. (pres. trust div. 1963, exec. council) bankers assns., Phi Delta. Presbyn. Mason. Clubs: University, Arlington, Waverley Country, Portland City (pres. 1965-66). Home: 7620 SW Brentwood St Portland OR 97225 Office: First Nat Bank of Oregon Portland OR 97208

HARMEL, MEREL HILBER, anesthesiologist, educator; b. Cleve., May 19, 1917; s. Louis and Hermine (Greenbaum) H.; B.A., Johns Hopkins, 1938, M.D., 1943; m. Armide Chilcoat, July 2, 1944; children—Nancy Armide, Ruth Courtney, Priscilla Gover, Mary Louise. Practice medicine, specializing in anesthesiology, Bklyn., 1952-68, Chgo., 1968-71; anesthesiologist-in-chief, State U. Kings County Med. Center, 1952-68, pres. med. bd., 1958-62, chmn. exec. com., 1964-65; cons. L.I. Jewish, St. Albans Naval, Maimonides, St. John's Episcopal, VA hosps.; prof., chmn. dept. anesthesiology, State U. N.Y. Downstate Med. Center, 1952-68; prof., chmn. dept. anesthesiology, Pritzker Sch. Medicine, U. Chgo., 1968-71, Duke Med. Center, 1971—. Commonwealth fellow Oxford U., 1961-62. Diplomate Am. Bd. Anesthesiology. Fellow Am. Coll. Anesthesiology; mem. A.M.A., Am. Soc. Anesthesiologists. Contbr. articles profl. jours. Office: Dept Anesthesiology Duke U Med Center Durham NC 27706

HARMON, ALBERT JOHN, urban renewal adminstr.; b. Sedan, Kan., Aug. 29, 1914; s. Robert L. and Sallie (Dyer) H.; A.B., U. Kan., 1935, LL.B., 1937; m. Sally Jane Martin, Dec. 21, 1937 (div. Aug. 1961); children—Sallie Lee, Robert M. Admitted to Kan. bar, 1937; jr. atty. legal div. Fed. Home Loan Bank, 1937-39; atty. legal div. Pub. Housing Adminstrn., and predecessor, 1939- 43, 46-50; area counsel Urban Renewal Adminstrn., Washington, 1950-53; exec. dir., counsel Land Clearance for Redevel. Authority, Kansas City, Mo., 1953—; exec. dir. Housing Authority, Kansas City, 1959-65. Dir. Des Marteau Investment Co., Kansas City, Mo., Metropolitan National Bank, Kansas City. Served to lt. USNR, 1943-46; PTO. Mem. Nat. Assn. Housing and Redevel. Ofcls. (pres. S.W. regional council 1959- 60, nat. pres. 1961-63), Nat. Housing Conf., Am. Legion, Phi Gamma Delta. Rotarian. Home: 1233 Romany Rd Kansas City MO 64113 Office: 306 E 12th St Kansas City MO 64106

HARMON, ERNEST N., former univ. pres., ret. army officer; b. Lowell, Mass., Feb. 26, 1894; s. Ernest Josiah and Junietta (Spaulding) H.; student Norwich U., 1912-13, hon. S.M., 1931, Dr.Engring. (hon.), 1965; B.S., U.S. Mil. Acad., 1917; student Command and Gen. Staff Coll., 1931-33, Army War Coll., 1934; LL.D., Middlebury Coll., 1952, St. Michael's, 1955, U. Vt., 1966; m. Leona Tuxbury, Aug. 15, 1917; children—Barbara Ruth (Mrs. Sylvester Roll), Halsey W., Robert S., Ernest N., Jeane L. (Mrs. Oliver). Commd. 2d lt. U.S. Army, Apr. 20, 1917, advanced through grades to maj. gen., 1942; served in France, 1918-19; assigned to 2d cav., Ft. Riley, Kan., 1919-20, Cav. Sch., 1920-21; instr. U.S. Mil. Acad., 1921-25; with 6th cav., Ft. Oglethorpe, Ga., 1925-27; prof. mil. sci. and tactics, Norwich Univ., 1927-31; comdr. squadron 8th cav., Ft. Bliss, Tex., 1934-35; served on War Dept. Gen. Staff, Washington, 1935-39; asst. chief of staff for supply armored forces, later chief of staff of armored Force, Ft. Knox, Ky., 1939-41; comdg. gen. 2d armored div., 1942; on loan as dep. corps comdr., battle of Kasserine Pass, Feb. 1943; comdr. 1st armored div., Tunisian campaign, Cassino and Anzio, Italy, 1943-44; comdg. gen. 2d armored div., Belgium, Battle of Bulge, 1944-45; comdr. XXII Army Corps, France, 1945; 1st mil. gov. of Rhine province, 1945 and comdr. U.S. Army of occupation, Czechoslovakia, 1945; comdr. U.S. Constabulary, Germany, 1946-47; dep. comdr. ground forces, U.S., 1947; ret. from active duty, Mar. 1, 1948; pres. Norwich U., 1950-65, ret. Awarded D.S.C., D.S.M. (3), Legion of Merit (3), Silver Star, Bronze Star, Air medal, Purple Heart; decorated Comdt., Legion of Honor and Croix de Guerre (France), Order of Bath (Gt. Britain), Star of Ouissam (Morocco), grand officer, Order of Orange Nassau with swords (Netherlands), Order of Red Banner (Russia), Order of St. Maurice and Lazarus and Silver Star (Italy), Comdr., Order of Leopold I (Belgium), Order of White Lion 2d class and War Cross (Czechoslovakia), Croix de Guerre and Fouragier (Belgium). Author: Combat Commander, 1970. Home: 2939 Markridge Sarasota FL 33581

HARMON, FRANCIS STUART, editor, lawyer; b. Paulding, Miss., Jan. 3, 1895; s. Rev. Gus Shaw and Jessie Bruce (Banks) H.; B.A., U. Va., 1916, M.A., 1917; LL.B., Harvard Univ., 1922; LL.D., Millsaps Coll., Jackson, Miss., 1936; m. Lucile Waverley Harwood, Apr. 16, 1927; children—Virginia Blackwell (Mrs. John F. Jameson II), Francis Stuart. Began practice of law with Wells, Stevens & Jones, Jackson, Miss., 1922; asst. atty. gen., Miss., 1924, 25; candidate for Dem. nomination for Congress, 1926; editor, pub. Hattiesburg (Miss.) American, 1926-33, pres., 1928-60. Pres. Nat. Council Y.M.C.A.'s of U.S., 1929-31; gen. sec. Internat. Com. Y.M.C.A.'s of U.S. and Can., 1932-37; dir. N.Y.C. Y.M.C.A. Mem. exec. staff Motion Picture Producers and Distributors of Am., Inc., 1937-41, v.p, 1945-51; v.p. Motion Picture Export Assn., Inc., 1945-51; exec. v. chmn. and industry coordination, war activities com., Motion Picture Industry, 1942-45. Trustee State U. and Colls. of Miss., 1926-29; v.p., Nat. Council Chs. of Christ in U.S.A., 1958-60; v.p., trustee The Interchurch Center, N.Y.C., 1957—; trustee Mohonk Trust, 1963—. Served as 2d lt. F.A., AUS, World War I; in action at St. Mihiel and Meuse-Argonne, France. Mem. Am. Bar Assn., Kappa Sigma, Phi Beta Kappa. Author: The Command Is Forward, 1944; A Good Inheritance, 1960; Adam's Eves, 1965. Home: 464 Riverside Dr New York City NY 10027 Office: 475 Riverside Dr New York City NY 10027

HARMON, GARY LEE, educator; b. Aurora, Neb., Aug. 16, 1935; s. Vyrle Martin and Esther (Koberstein) Uehling; B.A., Hastings Coll., 1956; M.A. M.A.T., Ind. U., 1960, Ph.D., 1966; postgrad., U. Mich., 1962-63, Mich. State U., 1963-64; m. Susanna Marie Pollock, Dec. 27, 1960; children—Thomas Thorburn, James Matthias. Instr. English Flint (Mich.) Community Coll., 1960-64; asso prof., chmn. div. lang. and lit., dir. grad. English program Morehead (Ky.) State U., 1966-67; chmn. div. lang., lit., philosophy, chmn. English dept. Stephens Coll., Columbia, Mo., 1967-71; prof. English, chmn. dept. langs. and lit. U. North Fla., Jacksonville, 1971—. Ind. U. fellow, 1964-66; faculty research grantee Stephens Coll., 1971. Mem. Mod. Lang. Assn., Popular Culture Assn., Nat. Council Tchrs. English, Am. Studies Assn., Assn. for Am. Higher Edn. Author; (with R.F. Dickinson) Write Now, 1971; (with Peter Parshall) Short Fiction; Man's Ultimate Concerns, 1972. Office: U North Fla Jacksonville FL 32211

HARMON, GEORGE DEWEY, historian; b. Pittsboro, N.C., Aug. 23, 1896; s. Joseph Carson and Cynthia Jane (Petty) H.; A.B., Trinity Coll. (now Duke U., 1921, A.M., 1923; Ph.D., U. Pa., 1930; m. Gertrude Elizabeth Mckay, Oct. 21, 1926; 1 dau., Patricia Laura (Mrs. Joseph Wilbur Davis). Asst. instr. Am. history U. Pa., 1922-24, asst. instr. English history, 1924-25; instr. polit. sci. Lehigh U., 1925-27, asst. Prof. Am. history, 1927-31, asso. Prof., 1931-42, prof. Am. history, 1942-64, acting head dept. history and govt., June- Oct. 1946, head dept., 1946-62, head dept. history, 1962-63, prof. Am. history, 1963-64; prof. history Millersville State Coll., 1964-65, 71—; prof. history East Stroudsburg State Coll., 1965-71, acting head dept. polit. sci., 1970-71; summer session instr. Wake Forest Coll., 1925, Duke U., 1926, 30, 34, 37, Pa. State Coll., 1935; lectr. Moravian Coll., 1944-46. Commd. 2d lt. Inf., U.S. Army, 1918. Awarded Philadelphia Inquirer prize for essay on George Washington, 1936. Mem. Am., Pa. (mem. council) hist. assns., Phi Beta Kappa, Phi Alpha Theta, Tau Kappa Alpha, Pi Kappa Alpha. Republican. Presbyn. Author: Sixty Years of Indian Affairs, Political, Economic, and diPlomatic, 1789-1850, 1941; Aspects of Slavery and Expansion, 1845-1860, 1929; Principles and Functions of Government in the United States (with others), 1948; Political Aspects of Slavery and the Civil War, 1952. Contbr. Dictionary Am. History, 5 vols., 1940, Ency. Brit. Contbr. articles and revs. on Am. history in several hist. publs. Mem. editorial bd. The Historian, 1942-49. Specialist Nineteenth Century Am. history. Home: 415 N New St Bethlehem PA 18018

HARMON, GEORGE THOMAS, III, architect; b. Starr, S.C., Sept. 15, 1908; s. George Thomas and Mary Virginia (Sullivan) H.; student Ala. Polytech. Inst., 1927-29, Ga. Sch. Tech., 1929-31, Ecole Des Beaux Arts, 1931; m. Sara Rembert Williamson, May 24, 1941; children—George Thomas IV, Sally W., Roberta Hall. Engaged in pvt. practice architecture, Columbia, S.C., 1932—; designer Fairfield County Ct. House, Williamsburg County Ct. House, S.C. Archives Bldg., U. S.C. Men's Residence Hall, St. Joseph's Catholic Ch., Columbia. Dirs. Columbia Planning Commn., 1954—; mem. S.C. Bd. Archtl. Examiners, 1952—; chmn. A.I.A.-Nat. Soc. Profl. Engrs., 1952-54. Bd. dirs. Columbia Art Mus. Served as lt. USNR, 1943-46. Fellow A.I.A. (pres. S.C. 1939-41; exec. com. nat. bd. dirs. 1954; organizer first S. Atlantic regional conf. 1952); mem. Columbia C. of C. (bd. dir.), Agrl. and Mech. Soc. S.C., Newcomen Soc. N.A., S.A.R., Phi Delta Theta. Clubs: (charter), Forum, Forest Lake Country, Alumni Phi Delta Theta (pres.) (Columbia). Home: 19 Heathwood Circle Columbia SC 29205 Office: 3350 Millwood Av Columbia SC 29205

HARMON, HARRY WILLIAM, architect; b. San Francisco, Feb. 8, 1918; s. Harry A. and Isabel (Quagelli) H.; B.Arch., U. So. Cal., 1941; m. Lois Anna Holtin, July 28, 1953; children—Bruce Gregory, Mark Brian, Patricia Andree. Draftsman, Kaufmann, Lippincott & Eggers, architects, Los Angeles, 1945-48; project architect U. Cal., Los Angeles, 1948-50, sr. architect, 1952-62; chief coll. facilities planning Cal. State Colls., Inglewood, Cal., 1962-67, asst. vice chancellor, Los Angeles, 1967-69, vice chancellor phys. planning, devel., 1969—; spl. cons. FAO. Mem. Nat. Panel Arbitrators. Served to lt. USNR, 1942-45, to lt. comdr., 1950-51. Fellow A.I.A.; mem. Assn. U. Architects, Am. Arbitration Assn., U. So. Cal. Alumni Assn., Blue Key, Alpha Rho Chi. Home: 3307 Scadlock Lane Sherman Oaks CA 91403 Office: 5670 Wilshire Blvd Los Angeles CA 90036

HARMON, LINDSEY RICHARD, psychologist; b. Spokane, Mar. 22, 1914; s. Ralph LaVerne and May (Hamilton) H.; B.A., U. Minn., 1935, M.S. 1938, Ph.D., 1952; m. Janet Bruce Burwell, Sept. 5, 1937 (div. 1968); children—Bruce, Joan, Douglas, William; m. 2d, Eloise Goade Wilner, Nov. 29, 1969. Psychologist with A.R.C., St. Louis, 1937-41; research asst., teaching asst., instr. psychology dept. U. Minn., 1941-43; chief advisement and guidance sect. VA Regional Office, Mpls., 1943-46, asst. chief advisement and guidance div. VA Br. Office, Mpls., 1946-49; spl. examiner U.S. Civil Service Commn., St. Paul, 1950; research psychologist personnel research br. Adj. Gen. Office, U.S. Army, Washington, 1950-51, chief leadership and personality research unit, 1951-53, chief performance sect. 1953-54; dir. research Office Sci. Personnel, Nat. Acad. Scis.-NRC, Washington, 1954—. Mem. Am. Psychol. Assn., Phi Beta Kappa. Unitarian. Home: 1201 N Illinois St Arlington VA 22205 Office: 2101 Constitution Av Washington DC 20037

HARMON, MARTIN M., textile co. exec.; b. N.Y.C., Oct. 8, 1915; s. David and Aline (Levy) Hertzog; B.C.S., N.Y.U., 1936; m. Rose Igstaedter, June 11, 1939; children—Ona (Mrs. Philip Wexler), Douglas A. Vice pres. Majestic Factors Corp., 1936-42; sr. accountant S.D. Leidesdorf & Co., 1942-46; comptroller M. Lowenstein & Sons, Inc., N.Y.C., 1946—; lectr. City U. N.Y., 1947-62. C.P.A., N.Y. Mem. Financial Execs. Inst., N.Y. State Soc. C.P.A.'s. Jewish religion. Club: Alpine (N.J.) Country. Home: 2055 Center Av Fort Lee NJ 07024 Office: 1430 Broadway New York City NY 10018

HARMON, MONT JUDD, univ. dean; b. Tremonton, Utah, Aug. 7, 1917; s. Mont and Alice (Judd) H.; B.S., Utah State U., 1948; M.S., U. Wis., 1951, Ph.D., 1953; m. Helen Gleave, Dec. 28, 1936; children—Judd Scott, Michael Mont. Instr. polit. sci. Utah State U., Logan, 1951-53, asst. prof., 1954-57, asso. prof., 1958-62, prof., 1962—, head dept. polit. sci., 1963-67, dean Coll. Social Scis., 1967-69, dean Coll. Humanities, Arts and Social Scis., 1970—. Served with USNR, 1944-46. Mem. Am. Assn. U. Profs., Am., Western Polit. sci. assns., Utah Acad. Scis., Arts and Letters, Phi Kappa Phi, Pi Sigma Alpha. Author: Political Thought: From Plato to the Present, 1964. Contbg. editor: Dictionary of Political Science, 1964; Handbook of World History, 1967. Home: 1252 Sumac Dr Logan UT 84321

HARMON, MYRA RUTH FREED, corp. exec.; b. Danville, Ind., June 7, 1917; d. John Elbert and Myra (Bartoo) Freed; B.A., De Pauw U., 1939; m. Russell H. Harmon, Sept. 2, 1967 (dec. 1969); 1 stepdau., Mrs. Charles L. Vogt. Jr. Asst. office and credit mgr. Firestone Stores, Lafeyette, Ind., 1939-41, office and credit mgr., 1947-68; sec.-treas. Monticello Tire Mart (Ind.), 1963—. Trustee Bus. and Profl. Womens Found. Mem. Nat. (pres. 1969-70), Ind. (pres. 1961-62), Lafayette (pres. 1944-45; Lady of Year award 1966) bus. and profl. womens clubs. Greater Lafayette C. of C., Lafayette Altrusa Club (bd. dirs. 1955-56, corr. sec. 1956-57), Delta Chi Sigma (pres. 1952-53). Home: PO Box 444 Brookston IN 47923 Office: PO Box 308 Lafayette IN 47902

HARMON, NOLAN BAILEY, bishop; b. Meridian, Miss., July 14, 1892; s. Nolan Bailey and Juliet (Howe) H.; A.B., Millsaps Coll., Jackson, Miss., 1914, D.D., 1929; D.H.L., Mt. Union Coll., 1946; D.D., Duke, 1959; D.Litt., Am, U., 1946, Western Md. Coll. 1947, Hamline U., 1947; student Emory U. Sch. Theology, 1916-17, D.D., 1958; LL.D., Wofford Coll., Spartanburg, S.C., 1961; M.A., Princeton, 1920; m. Rebecca Barry Lamar, June 20, 1923; children—Nolan Bailey III, George Lamar. Camp pastor Walter Reed Gen. Hosp., Washington, 1918-19; ordained to ministry M.E. Ch., South, 1918; pastor chs. in Md., Va., 1920-33; pastor Greene Meml. Meth. Ch., Roanoke, Va., 1933-40; book editor Meth. Ch., 1940-56; bishop Meth. Ch., 1956—; resident bishop Western N.C.Conf., 1956-64; supt. bishop KY. Conf., 1960, North Ala. Conf., 1961-64; vis. prof. practical theology Emory U., 1964, Candler Sch. Mem. book com. M.E. Ch. S., 1930- 40; mem. Joint Commn. on Meth. Hymnal, 1930-34; mem. Hymnal Commn., 1960-64; mem. Meth. Sesquicentennial Commn., Commn. on Course of Study for Conf. Undergrads., M.E. Ch. S., 1934-38; mem. Gen. Conf. M.E. Chs., 1930, 34, 38; mem. Uniting Conf. of Methodism, 1939; mem. gen. conf., Meth. Ch. 1940, 44, 48, 52, 56; mem. exec. com. Fed. Council Chs., 1944-48; dir. Save The Children Fedn., 1940-48; mem. United Bd. for Christian Colls. in China; mem. Curriculum Com. of Meth. Ch., also mem. Commn. on Ministerial Training and Commn. on Church Union, on Worship, 1940-56; mem. Bd. Edn., Meth. Ch., 1956-64, mem. Board of Temperance. Trustee Emory U., Ga., Drew U., N.J., 1940-56, High Point Coll., N.C., 1957-64, Wesley Theol. Sem., Am. U., 1964-68. Attended Chaplains' Tng. Camp, Louisville, Ky., Oct.-Dec. 1918; 1st lt. and chaplain O.R.C. Mem. Kappa Sigma. Mason. Clubs: University, Sigma Chi (N.Y.C.). Author several books including; Ministerial Etiquette, 1928; The Famous Case of Myna Clark Gaines, 1946; The Organization of the Methodist Church, 1948. Editor Abingdon-Cokesbury Press, 1940-56; Methodist Book of Discipline, 1940, 44, 48, 52, 56; Religion in Life (quar.). 1940-56; Ency. of World Methodism. Contbr. to ch. publs. Address: 998 Springdale Rd NE Atlanta GA ☆

HARMON, PATRICK, newspaperman; b. St. Louis, Sept. 2, 1916; s. Jack and Laura (Duchesne) H.; A.B., U. Ill., 1939; m. Anne M. Worland, Aug. 29, 1940; children—Michael, Timothy, Kathleen, Daniel, John, Sheila, Peggy, Brigid, Keven, Teresa, Christopher. Sports Editor News-Gazette, Champaign, Ill., 1942-47, Gazette, Cedar Rapids, Ia., 1947-51, Post & Times-Star, Cin., 1951—; sports commentator sta. WCPO-TV, Cin., 1953- 56, radio sta. WKRC, Cin, 1958, sta. WLW-TV, Cin., 1958-68. Contbg. sports editor World Book, 1959—; regional sports editor Illustrated Ency. of Sports, 1960—. Recipient Fred Hutchinson Meml. award for community service, 1969. Home: 19 Walnut St Wyoming OH 45215 Office: 800 Broadway Cincinnati OH 45202

HARMON, REGINALD CARL, charitable found, exec., ret. air force officer; b. Olney, Ill., Feb. 5, 1900; s. Frank and Mary (Persoon) H.; J.D., U. Ill., 1927; LL.D., George Washington U., 1951; m. Doris Evangeline Vance, June 19, 1937; 1 dau., Susan Diane. Admitted to Ill. bar. 1928, also U.S. supreme Ct.; gen. practice, Urbana, Ill., 1928-40; mayor, Urbana, 1929-33; commd. 2d lt. (Res.) U.S. Army, 1926, advanced through grades to maj. gen. USAF, 1948; maj., Wright Field, O., 1940; charge legal representation U.S. Govt. indsl. expansion program to meet need USAAF, World War II; judge advocate Air Material Command, Wright Field, 1945; commd. Regular Army, 1946; transferred to USAF, 1948; judge advocate gen. USAF, 1952, 56; retired, 1960; pres. United Services Security Corp., 1960-65; dir. Air Force Aid Soc., 1966—. Decorated D.S.M., Legion of Merit, Army Commendation ribbon. Mem. Phi Delta Phi. Presbyn. (councel Nat. Presbyn. Ch. and Center). Mason (K.T., Shriner). Clubs: Army and Navy (Washngton); Army-Navy Country (Arlington, Va.); Exchange (pres. Ill.). Home: 2709 N Norwood St Arlington VA 22207 Office: Hdgrs Air Force Aid Soc 117 N 19th St Arlington VA 22209

HARMON, REUEL DURKEE, publishing co. exec.; b. St. Paul, Feb. 6, 1904; s. Albert Hiram and Carolyn (Durkee) H.; A.B., Harvard, 1926; m. Catharine Grey Beattie, Apr. 14, 1928 (dec. Oct. 1968); 1 dau., Ann (Mrs. A.W. Clapp III); m. 2d, Margaret L. Weyerhaeuser, Mar. 30, 1971. With Webb Publishing Co., St. Paul, 1926—, pres., dir., 1952-69, chmn. bd., 1969—; dir. Soo Line R.R., St. Paul Ins. Cos., First Nat. Bank, St. Paul, Torit Corp., St. Paul. Trustee Carleton Coll., Northfield, Minn., St. Thomas Coll., St. Paul. Served to maj. AUS, 1943-45. Home: 722 Linwood Av St Paul MI 55105 Office: 1999 Shepard Rd St Paul MN 55116

HARMS, JOHN W., clergyman, ch. exec.; b. Blue Springs, Neb., Sept. 22, 1902; s. Eilert W. and Mary Rebecca (West) H.; grad. Enid Bus. Coll., 1922; A.B., Phillips U., Enid, OKla., 1931, LL.D., 1952; postgrad. Auburn Sem., 1933-34; postgrad. U. Chgo., 1936-37, 40, M.A., 1952; D.D., Christian Theol. Sem., 1960; m. Pearl Ella Goddard, May 1, 1926; children—John Goddard (dec.), Dorothea Mae (Mrs. James A. Jewell), Mary Frances (Mrs. Louis G. Freeman). Surveyor, dept. of endowments, bd. of edn. Disciples of Christ, 1925-26; bus. mgr. Central Christian Ch., Enid, 1926-29; ordained to ministry Christian Ch. Disciples of Christ, 1931; dir. religious edn. Eastern area United Christian Missionary Soc. (Disciples of Christ), N.Y.C., 1931-34; state dir. religious edn. Ind., 1934-38; exec. sec. Council of Churches and Christian Edn. of Md.-Del., Inc., 1938-42; pres. Assn. Council Secs., 1941-42; exec. v.p. Ch. Fedn. of Greater Chicago, 1943- 60; exec. minister Christian Ch. (Disciples of Christ) in Ind., 1960-70, mem. com. on restructure Christian Chs., 1965-69. Internat. Council Religious Edn., 1938-50; mem. war services com. Internat. Conv., Disciples of Christ, 1942-46; mem. bd. World Council Christian Edn., 1940-47; mem. Disciples of Christ delegation to 1st Assembly World Council Chs., Amsterdam, Holland, 1948; mem. council Nat. Council Chs. of Christ in U.S.A., 1950-54; mem. study com. U.S. Conf. for World Council Chs., 1948-54; chmn. Action Com. for Freedom of Religious Expression, 1956-60; mem. gen. bd. Christian Ch. (Disciples of Christ), 1969-70. Trustee Disciples Div. House, U. Chgo., 1955-64, Christian Theol. Sem., 1965-71, Christian Chs. in Ind. (Disciples of Christ), 1960-; mem. com. on Mem. Pi Kappa Delta. Author: Prayer in the Market Place, 1958. Contbr. to religious jours. Home: 310 s Butler Av Indianapolis IN 46219

HARMSEN, TYRUS GEORGE, librarian; b. Pomona, Cal., July 24, 1924; s. Fred H. and Hazel (Weigle) H.; A.B., Stanford, 1947, M.A., 1950; A.B. in L.S., U. Mich., 1948; m. Lois Spaulding, Apr. 15, 1955; children—Mark Spaulding, Caroline Lora. Cataloguer dept. manuscripts Henry E. Huntington Library, San Marino, Cal., 1948-49, 50-59; librarian Occidental Coll., Los Angeles, 1959—; vis. lectr. Sch. Library Sci., U. So. Cal., 1958, 68. Served with AUS, 1943-46. Council on Library Resources fellow, 1969. Mem. Cal. Library Assn. Presbyn. Clubs: Zamorano, Rounce and Coffin (treas. 1956—) (Los Angeles). Author: The Plantin Press of Saul and Lillian Marks, 1960. Home: 1300 Medford Rd Pasadena CA 91107 Office: Occidental Coll Library Los Angeles CA 90041

HARMSWORTH, ESMOND CECIL, see Rothermere, Viscount

HARMSWORTH, HARRY CLAYTON, ret. educator; b. Aurora, Mo., May 4, 1902; s. Charles William and Mary Lavina (Clayton) H.; A.B., Colo. State Coll. Edn., 1928, M.A., 1932; Ph.D., U. So. Cal., 1943; m. Ruth Viola Lane, June 1, 1927; children—Clayton Lane, Donald Kemp. Tchr. Colo. pub. schs., 1925-35; asst. prof. sociology and econs. Southwestern State Tchrs. Coll., Weatherford, Okla., 1935-39; asst. prof. sociology Tex. Western Coll., 1941-44; asso. prof. sociology U. Ida., 1944-54, prof., chmn. dept., 1954-67, prof. emeritus, 1967—; later prof. sociology Winona (Minn.) State Coll. Pres. Pacific Northwest Conf. Family Relations, 1960-61; mem. Gov.'s Conf. on Problems of Older Citizens, 1956. Fellow Inst. Social Gerontology, Am. Sociol. Assn.; mem. Pacific Sociol. Soc., Nat. Council Family Relations, Population Assn. Am., Alpha Kappa Belta, Phi Delta Kappa. Author: Sixty Years of population Growth in Idaho, 1980-1950, 1952; A Survey of the Alcohol and Narcotics Problem in Idaho, 1954; Population Trends in Idaho, 1950-60, 1965. Editorial bd. N.W. Science, 1950-56. Home: 1435 Chinook St Moscow ID 83843

HARNACK, ROBERT VICTOR, educator; b. Milan, Italy, July 29, 1927; s. Harold Henry and Anna Joy (Peshak) H.; student Westmar Coll., 1946-47; B.A., State Coll. Ia., 1950; M.A., U. Okla., 1951; Ph.D., Northwestern U., 1954; m. Martha Jane Beebe, June 6, 1948; children—Douglas Hall, Harold James. Instr. speech U. Okla., 1951-52; asst. prof. speech U. Colo., 1954-60, asso. prof. 1960-64; prof. chmn. dept. speech and theatre U. Ill. at Chgo. Circle, 1964—; cons. N.Am. Air Def. Command, 1955—. Mem. Boulder Civic Opera, 1956—. Ednl. cons. Colo. Dem. Party, 1960- -. Served with USNR, 1945-46. Mem. Speech Assn. Am., Central States Speech Assn., Nat. Soc. for Study Communication, Am. Assn. U. Profs., Ill. Speech Assn., Delta Sigma Rho, Tau Kappa Alpha. Author: (with Thorrel B. Fest) Group Discussion: Theory and Technique, 1964. Contbr. articles profl. jours. Home: 1737 S Brookview Lane Palatine IL 60067 Office: U Ill Chgo Circle 601 S Morgan St Chicago IL 60680

HARNED, DAVID BAILY, educator; b. Allentown, Pa., June 5, 1932; s. William Biechele and Mary (Baily) H.; B.A., Yale, 1954, B.D., 1957, M.A., 1959, Ph.D., 1963; postgrad. New Coll. Edinburgh U. (Scotland), 1954-55; m. Elaine Paula Heydenreich, July 1, 1961; children—Christopher Baily, Timothy Heydenreich. Ordained to ministry Lutheran Ch., 1961; instr. Williams Coll., 1960-61, Yale, 1962-63; asst. prof. religion Smith Coll., 1963- 67, asso. prof., 1967; prof. religious studies, chmn. dept. U. Va., 1967- -; vis. research prof. religious studies Punjabi U., Patiala, India, 1970; chmn. bd. selection post-doctoral fellowships for Cross- Disciplinary Study. Pres. League Winant Vols., 1951. Nat. Endowment for Humanities Jr. Humanist, 1970-71; fellow Soc. Religion in Higher Edn., Kent fellow, 1957-60, Rockefeller doctoral fellow, 1959-60. Democrat. Lutheran. Author: Theology and the Arts, 1966; The Ambiguity of Religion, 1968, 69; Grace and Common Life, 1970. Editor (with J.F. Childress) Secularization and the Protestant Prospect, 1970, 71. Editorial bd. Jour. of Religious Studies, India, 1969—. Home: 1853 Fendall Av Charlottesville VA 22903

HARNED, MALCOLM STUART, aircraft co. exec.; b. Wichita, Kan., June 11, 1921; s. Frank Simpson and Ada (Sleeth) H.; B.S., U. Kan., 1943; M.S., Cal. Inst. Tech., 1948; m. Jo Ann Glatt, Mar. 16, 1953; children—Douglas Stuart, Holly Ann. Instr. math U. Kan., 1943; structures engr., project engr. N.Am. Aviation, Los Angeles, 1943-50; chief tech. engr., asst. chief engr. Marquardt Corp., Van Nuys, Cal., 1950-55; project mgr. Aircraft Nuclear Propulsion Dept., Gen. Electric Co., Cin., 1955-59; v.p. engring aircraft div. Hughes Tool Co., Culver City Cal., 1959-64, v.p. operations, 1964-67; exec. v.p., gen. mgr. aircraft div. Lear Jet Industries, Wichita, 1967-70; group v.p. Cessua Aircraft Co., Wichita, 1970—; dir. Kansas State Bank & Trust Co. Fellow Am. Inst. Aeros. and Astronautics (asso.); mem. Wichita C. of C., Am. Helicopter Soc. (dir.); Soc. Automotive Engrs. (tech. bd.), Tau Beta Pi, Sigma Tau, Theta Tau. Club: Wichita Country. Home: 8325 Tipperary St Wichita KS 67206 Office: PO Box 1521 Wichita KS 67201

HARNED, ROBERT VAN HORN, securities broker; b. Allentown, Pa., June 12, 1909; s. William C. and Hilda (Blechele) H.; Ph.B., Muhlenberg Coll., 1928; m. Estelle V. deJourno, Dec. 27, 1932 (dec. 1955); children—R. Victor, Sarah Elizabeth (Mrs. Robert Dover); m. 2d, Mae Cawley, 1957. With Warren W. York & Co., Inc., Allentown, Pa., 1928-, partner, 1932-46, exec. v.p., 1946-48, Pres., 1948—; chmn. bd. Zollinger-Harned Co.; dir., exec. com. Gen. Acceptance Corp.; dir., mem. finance com., exec. com. Stuyvesant Ins. Co.; dir. Glen gery Shale Brick Co., Reading, Pa. Vice Pres., bd. govs. Phila.-Balt. Stock Exchange. Active Lehigh County United Fund. Trustee Sacred Heart Hosp. Served to lt. USNR, 1943-45. Mem. Nat. Assn. Securities Dealers (gov.). Roman Catholic. Home: Lehigh Pkwy N Allentown PA 18103 Office: York Commonwealth Bldg Allentown PA 18101

HARNER, PAUL B., gray iron foundry exec.; b. Kutztown, Pa., Oct. 30, 1909; s. John Z. and Katie (Breitensteine) H.; B.A., Franklin and Marshall Coll., 1931; M.B.A., U. Pa., 1932; m. Flora A. Schoenley, Nov. 26, 1936; children—Carl J., Mary A. (Mrs. Jamieson Brown). With Union Mfg. Co., Inc., Boyertown, Pa., 1932-68, pres., 1963-68; with Fashion Hosiery Mills, Inc., Boyertown, 1936-68, pres., 1965-68; pres., dir. Berkmont Industries, Boyertown, 1968—. Bd. dirs., past chmn. indsl. com. United Chest Bovertown. Mem. Nat. Gray and Ductile Iron Soc. (bd. dirs., past sec.; citation for service 1968), Am. Foundrymen's Soc. (bd. dirs. Phila. 1971-72); Gray and Ductile Iron Founders Soc. (bd. dirs. 1971-73, sec. 1967-68, treas. 1971-72). Rotarian (past pres. Boyertown). Home: 600 Highland St Boyertown PA 19512 Office: Berkmont Industries 6th and Washington Sts Boyertown PA 19512

HARNESS, DON KENNETH, patent lawyer; b. Detroit, Apr. 24, 1921; s. J. King and Vera (Gregory) H.; Student U. Mich. Engring. Coll., 1939-41; J.D., Wayne U., 1947; m. Florence Eurich, July 13, 1941; children—Jay K., Linda J. With engring. dept. Chrysler Corp., 1941-44; admitted to Mich. bar, 1947; with firm Harness, Dickey & Pierce, 1947—, partner, 1949—. Bd. dirs. Children's Center of Wayne County, 1953-60, 67-70, pres., 1957-59; bd. dirs. Cranbrook Sch. 1966—, Mich. Assn. Emotionally Disturbed Children, bd. dirs. Boys' Republic, 1954-69, pres., 1959-60; trustee Straith Meml. Hosp., pres., 1971—. Served from pvt. to 1st lt., Inf., AUS, 1944-46. Recipient Distinguished Service award U.S. Jr. C. of C., 1954. Mem. Am. Patent Law Assn., Am., Mich., Detroit bar assns., Delta Tau Delta, Delta Theta Phi. Lutheran. Clubs: Rotary (pres. Detroit 1956-57); Orchard Lake Country (pres. 1966); The Recess (gov. 1967—); Metamora. Home: 6000 Snowshoe Circle Birmingham MI 48010 Office: Fisher Bldg Detroit MI 48202

HARNESS, EDWARD GRANVILLE, soap products mfr.; b. Marietta, O., Dec. 17, 1918; s. Lewis Nye and Mary (McKinney) H.; A.B., Marietta Coll., 1940; m. Mary McCrady Chaney, Aug. 7, 1943; children—Frances Ann (Mrs. Daniel J. Jones), Edward Granville, Robert R. With Procter & Gamble Co., Cin., 1940—, v.p. paper products div., 1963-66, v.p.-group exec., dir., 1966-70, exec. v.p., 1970—. Dir. Cin. A.R.C. Trustee Marietta Coll., Ohio Found. Ind. Colls., Cin. Children's Home. Served with USAAF, 1942-46. Clubs: Carmargo, Queen City, Commonwealth (Cin.). Office: 301 E 6th St Cincinnati OH 45202

HARNEST, GRANT HOPKINS, educator, chemist; b. Carthage, Ill., Nov. 23, 1916; s. Waldo Wright and Goldie (Hopkins) H.; A.B., Knox Coll., 1939; M.S., Middlebury (Vt.) Coll., 1941; Ph.D., U. Va., 1945; m. Kathryn Irene Hampson, June 24, 1945. Mem. faculty Middlebury Coll., 1943-45, 46—, prof. chemistry, 1956—, chmn. dept., 1953-70, John G. McCullough prof., 1964-68, Old Dominion prof., 1968-69, chmn. div. natural scis., 1966—; research asst. OSRD, U. Va., 1945-46. Recipient Bd. Visitors prize U. Va., 1947; grantee Research Corp., 1948. Mem. Am. Chem. Soc. (pres. W. Vt. sect. 1949-50, nat. councilor 1960-66), Sigma Xi, Alpha Chi Sigma (pres. U. Va. chpt. 1942-43). Contbr. Articles. Home: 125 S Main St Middlebury VT 05753

HARNETT, JOSEPH DURHAM, oil co. exec.; b. Paterson, N.J., Aug. 23, 1917; s. James Harold and EMily (Steele) H.; B.S., Purdue U., 1939; m. Wilhelmina Nordstrom, June 21, 1941 (dec. July 1958); children—Gordon D., Linda C., Ralph H., David S.; m. Nancy Beam. With Consol. Edison Co., N.Y.C., 1939, Worthington Pump & Machinery Corp., 1940; with Standard Oil Co. (O.), 1941—, v.p., 1957-68, sr. v.p., 1968-70, exec. v.p., 1970—, also dir.;pres., dir. Fleet-Wing Corp.; v.p. dir. Mountaineer Carbon Co., Boron Oil Co., Sohio Petroleum Co., dir. Cardinal Vending Co., Hospitality Motor Inns, Inc., Vistron Corp., Atlas Supply Co. Mem. Am. Petroleum Inst. Presbyn. Clubs: Athletic, Mentor Harbor Yacht, Country, Pepper Pike (Cleve.); University (N.Y.C.). Home: Hunting Trail Chagrin Falls OH 44022 Office: Midland Bldg Cleveland OH 44115

HARNEY, JOHN PHILIP, advt. agy. exec.; b. Peoria, Ill., Nov. 23, 1924; s. Harry Edward and Mary (Code) H.; B.S., U. Ill., 1949; m. Kathleen Theresa Waugh, Jan. 36, 1952; children—Colleen Ann, John Philip, Mary Beth, Brian, Timothy, Maureen Theresa, Kathleen Ann, Robert Joseph. Account exec. Ruthrauff & Ryan, Inc., Chgo., 1949-54; v.p., sec., treas. Hall, Haerr, Peterson & Harney, Inc., Peoria, 1954, now pres., dir. Bd. dirs. Cabrini Hall, Peoria. Served with USAAF,1943-45. Decorated D.F.C., Air Medal with five silver oak leaf clusters. Mem. Delta Upsilon. Clubs: Chicago Athletic; Creve Coeur; Willow Knolls Country (Peoria). Roman Catholic. K.C. (4). Home: 1218 W Oakglen Dr Peoria IL 60614 Office: Lehmann Bldg Peoria IL 60612

HARNICK, SHELDON MAYER, lyricist; b. Chgo., Apr. 30, 1924; s. Harry M. and Esther (Kanter) H.; Mus.B., Northwestern U., 1949; m. Mary Boatner, Aug. 29, 1950 (annulled); m. 2d, Elaine May, Mar. 25, 1962; m. 3d, Margery Gray. Writer light verse, songs; contbr. songs Northwestern U. ann. musical Waa-Mu Show. 1946-50; contbr. songs to Broadway, off-Broadway shows, New Faces of 1952; Two's Company, 1953; John Murray Anderson's Almanac, 1954, The Shoestring Revue 1955, The Littlest Revue 1956, Shoestring '57, 1957; lyricist (with composer Jerry Rock) Body Beautiful, 1958, Fiorello, 1959, Tenderloin, 1960, (with composer David Baker) Smiling the Boy Fell Dead, 1961; Broadway show, Fiddler on the Roof, 1964 (Tony award), The Rothchilds, 1970; appeared in Apple Tree, 1966. Served with Signal Corps, AUS, 1943-46. Recipient Pulitzer prize for lyrics Fiorello, 1959. Mem. Broadcast Music inc., Am. Guild Authors and Composers, Dramatists Guild. Office: care David J Cogan 350 Fifth Av New York City NY 10001

HARNIK, GEORGE WILLIAM, packaging co. exec.; b. Budapest, Hungary, Apr. 14, 1921; s. William and Charlotte (Ferri) H.; came to U.S., 1939, naturalized, 1943; B.S. in Food Tech., Ore. State Coll., 1943, M.S., 1948; m. Merrilee Caryl Will, Sept. 8, 1946; children—Peter Louis, Victoria Marie. With Am. Can. Co., 1947—, asst. to gen. mgr. internat. div., N.Y.C., 1958-64, v.p. Eastern hemisphere operations internat. div., Tokyo, Japan, 1964—; exec. v.p., rep. dir. Nihon-Dixie Co. Ltd., Tokyo, 1964-68, pres. rep. dir., 1968—. Served to 1st lt. AUS, 1943-46. Mem. Soc. Am. Bacteriologists, Inst. Food Technologists. Presbyn. (elder). Home: 502 Shiba Shirokane Sanko-Cho Minato-Ku Tokyo Japan Office: Nihon Dixie Co Ltd 16 No 10 8-Chome Akaska Minanto-Ku Tokyo Japan

HARNISCHFEGER, HENRY, bldg. constrn. exec.; b. Milw., 1923. Pres., dir. Harnischfeger Homes, Inc., Milw.; chmn. bd. Harnischfeger Corp., Milw., 1970—; dir. Maritime Steel & Foundries, Ltd. Home: 2635 N Terrace Av Milwaukee WI 53211 Office: 4400 W National Av Milwaukee WI 53214*

HARNISH, JAMES LESTER, educator; b. LeQuille, Annapolis County, N.S., Can., Aug. 24, 1913; s. James Reed and Florence Annie (Todd) H.; came to U.S., 1925, naturalized, 1941; B.A., Wheaton (Ill.) Coll., 1935, D.D., 1952; B.D., Eastern Baptist Theol. Sem., 1938, M.Th., 1945; D.D., Cal. Bapt. Theol. Sem., 1952; m. Elizabeth Stockton, Aug. 20, 1936; children—Judith Elizabeth (Mrs. Richard Harpel), James Stockton, Jonathan Todd. Ordained to ministry Am. Bapt. Conv., 1938; pastor in Bklyn., 1938-43, Phila., 1943- 48, Detroit, 1948-51, Los Angeles, 1951-59, First Bapt. Ch., Portland, Ore., 1959-68; pres. Eastern Bapt. Theol. Sem., Eastern Bapt. Coll., 1968—. Mem. N.Am. Bapt. Fellowship, com. Bapt. World Alliance. Chmn. bd. mgrs. Am. Bapt. Home Mission Soc., 1960, 61; pres. Am. Bapt. Conv., 1964-65; bd. dirs. Harvest Fund of Presbyn Ministers fund, Phila. Recipient Alumni Achievement award Eastern Bapt. Theol. Sem., 1956, Spl. citation, 1965. Rotarian. Club: City (Portland). Co-author: We Prepare and Preach, 1959; author The Harvest of the Spirit, 1965. Contbr. articles. Contbg. editor Seek, 1940—, Secret Place, 1950—, Christianity Today, 1956—. Home: 905 Cooperstown Rd Bryn Mawr PA 19010 Office: City LIne and Lancaster Av Philadelphia PA 19151

HARNISH, JAY DEWEY, architect; b. Lancaster, Pa., May 21, 1898; s. Jacob Martin and Emma (Herr) H.; B.Arch., U. Cal. at Berkeley, 1924; m. Jerene C. Reaver, Feb. 1, 1938. With art dept. MGM, 1936-37; sole practitioner, Ontario, Cal., 1940-60; pres. firm Harnish, Morgan & Causey, architects, Ontario, 1960—. Sec., dir. Ontario Savs. & Loan Assn., 1960—. Mem. Cal. Bd. Archtl. Examiners, 1962-70, pres., 1964. Served with C.E., U.S. Army, 1916-17. Fellow A.I.A.; mem. U. So. Cal. Archtl. Guild. Club: Balboa Bay Newport Beach, Cal. Project included San Antonio Community Hosp., Upland (recipient Hosp. of Month award Modern Hosp. 1966), HMC Bldg., Ontario (award for creative use concrete Portland Cement Assn. 1969), Ontario High Sch. (Merit award A.I.A. 1969), Lockheed Engring. Bldg., Ontario (Merit award A.I.A. 1970), Ontario Internat. Airport. Home: Uplander Hotel 81 W Foothill Blvd Upland CA 91786 Office: 500 East E St Ontario CA 91764

HARNISH, WILLIAM MAX, naval officer; b. Bradford, Ill., Nov. 1, 1919; s. Wilber E. and Bess (Davidson) H.; student U. Ill., 1937-39; B.S., U.S. Naval Acad., 1942, U.S. Navy Postgrad. Sch., 1950; M.S., Mass. Inst. Tech., 1951; grad. Naval War Coll., 1958; m. June Markert, July 22, 1944; children—Karen E., Leslie S. Commd. ensign U.S. Navy, 1942, advanced through grades to rear adm., 1968; assigned battleship S. Pacific, 1942-44; naval aviator, 1945; fighter and attack squadron duties, grad. edn. and tech. duties in aircraft weapons and Polaris devel., 1946-59; navigator, exec. officer, comdg. officer various aircraft carriers, 1959-66; nuclear propulsion tng. AEC, 1960; dep. dir. systems analysis div. Office Chief Naval Operations, 1966-67; dir. Office Program Appraisal for sec. navy, 1967-69; comdr. Carrier Div. 6, 1969-70, dep. comptroller of navy, 1970—. Decorated Legion of Merit (2), D.F.C., Air medal (3), Navy Commendation medal (2). Mem. Phi Gamma Delta. Home: 718 S Lynn St Champaign IL 61820 Office: Deputy Comptroller of Navy Navy Dept Washington DC 20310

HARNONCOURT, NIKOLAUS, musician; b. Berlin, Germany, Dec. 6, 1929; s. Eberhard and Ladislaja (Meran) d'H.; student Music Acad. Vienna, 1948-52; m. Alice Hoffelner, June 27, 1953; children—Elisabeth, Philipp, Eberhard, Franz. Mem. Vienna Symphony Orch., 1952-69; mem. Found. of Concentus Musicus, ensemble for ancient music with original instruments, 1954-69; tchr. performance practice; editor ancient operas for performances in our time. Recipient numerous internat. awards for records including Grand Prix du Disque Paris, 1966, 68, Deutscher Schallplattenpreis, 1968, 69, Prix Mondial, Montreux D'or, 1969. Composer new score of Ritorno d'Ulisse and Poppea by Monteverdi, 1968-70; new editions of H-Moll Messe, Johannespassion und Matthäuspassion by Bach, 1965, 67, 70. Home: 38 Piaristengasse A 1080 Vienna Austria

HARNUM, EWART JOHN ARLINGTON, lt. gov. Province Newfoundland and Labrador; b. Sound Island, Newfoundland, Oct. 13, 1910; s. Louis John and Maude (Dawe) H.; student Bishop Feild Coll., St. John's, Newfoundland, 1918-28; m. Phyllis Mary Dowden, July 29, 1936; children—Jacqueline (Mrs. Rayner Lamb), Patricia (Mrs. Robert L. Reid), Linda (Mrs. I. David Butler). Ins. clk. Dale & Co., Ltd., 1928-30; clk. Bowring Bros. Ltd., St. John's, 1930-35, ins. mgr., 1935-48; life ins. agt. Mut. Life of Can., 1949-50; gen. agt., partner firm W.U. Knowling, 1950-58; pres. Harnum Ins. Agys. Ltd., 1958— (all St. John's); lt. gov. Province Newfoundland and Labrador, St. John's 1969—. Created Knight Order St. John Jerusalem, 1969. Mem. Newfoundland C. of C., Newfoundland Bd. Ins. Underwriters (past pres.), Ins. Inst. Newfoundland (past pres.), Newfoundland Ins. Agents Assn. (past pres.). Dist. grand master Grand Lodge Scotland, 1964-69; provincial grand master Royal Order Scotland, 1971—. Address: Government House St John's Newfoundland Canada

HARNWELL, GAYLORD P., educator, bus. exec.; b. Evanston, Ill., Sept. 29, 1903; s. Frederick William and Anna Jane (Wilcox) H.; B.S., Haverford Coll., 1924; student Cambridge U. (Eng.), 1924-25; M.A., Princeton, Ph.D., 1927, LL.D., 1955; LL.D., U. Pa., 1953, Ursinus Coll., 1954, Dropsie Coll., 1955, U. Pitts. and Columbia U., 1957; D.Sc., Temple U., Haverford Coll., Hahnemann Med. Coll., 1954, Franklin and Marshall Coll., 1956, U. So. Cal., 1959, Drexel Inst., 1961; LL.D., Washington Coll., 1957, Northwestern U., 1958; Brown U., 1959, Swarthmore, 1959, Coll. William and Mary, 1960, Duke, St. Andrews (Scotland), 1963, U. Cal. at Los Angeles, Occidental Coll., 1964, Harvard, 1965, Hahnemann Med. Coll., Yale, Pahlavi U. (Iran), 1970; Pd.D., LaSalle Coll., 1957; C.L.D., The Div. Sch. in Phila., 1957; Sc.Ped.D., Elizabethtown Coll., 1959; L.H.D., Wilkes Coll., 1965, Jewish Theol. Sem. Am., 1965, Yeshiva U., 1966, Loyola U. Chgo., 1970; A.H.D., St. Joseph's Coll.; m. Mary Louise Rowland, June 18, 1927; children—Mary Jane (Mrs. Frederick Wallace), Ann Wheeler (Mrs. John Ashmead), Robert Gaylord. NRC fellow Cal. Inst. Tech., 1927-28, Princeton, 1928-29; asst. prof. of physics, Princeton, 1929-36, asso. prof., 1936-38; prof. physics, chmn. dept. and dir. Randal Morgan Lab., U. Pa., 1938-53, pres., 1953-70, pres. emeritus, univ. prof. physics, 1970—; leave absence, 1942-46, to act as dir. U. Cal. div. war research, U.S. Navy Radio and Sound Lab., San Diego, Cal.; chmn. bd. Penn Central Co., 1970, now dir.; dir. Rorer-Amchem Co., First Pa. Banking & Trust Co., PEN JERDEL; chmn. bd. West Phila. Corp. Mem. com. undersea warfare NRC. Bd. dirs. University City Sci. Center, University City Sci., Inst.; bd. dirs. United Fund of Phila., 1954—, Greater Phila. Movement. Awarded medal for Merit. Fellow Am. Phys. Soc., Accoustical Soc.; mem. Am. Philos. Soc., Newcomen Soc. N.Am., Am. Council on Edn. (chmn. 1959-60), Sigma Xi, Phi Beta Kappa, Sigma Pi Sigma, Alpha Epsilon Delta, Alpha Phi Omega. Clubs: Century Assn. (N.Y.C.); Union League, Cricket, Rittenhouse (Phila.); Cosmos (Washington). Cons. editor, Internat. Series in Physics, McGraw-Hill Book Co., 1946-53. Author: Principles of Electricity and Electromagnetism, 1929; Experimental Atomic Physics (with John J. Livingood), 1939; Atomic

Physics, (with W.E. Stephens) 1955; Russian Diary, 1960; Educational Voyaging in Iran, 1962. Home: 126 Grays Lane Haverford PA 19041

HARO, JOHN CALVIN, architect; b. East Chicago, Ind., June, 18, 1928; s. John Henry and Lydia (Lind) H.; student Mich. Technol. U., 1945-47; B.Arch., U. Mich., 1950; M.Arch., Harvard, 1955; m. Elizabeth Alison Smith, Dec. 26, 1954; children—John Stephen, Alexander James, Alison Margaret. Designer, draftsman firm Sanders & Malsin, Architects, Ann Arbor, Mich., 1950- 51, firm Minoru Yamasaki & Assos., Detroit, 1952-54; with Albert Kann Assos., Inc., Architects & Engrs., Detroit, 1955—, asso., 1959-63, v.p., chief archtl. designer, 1963—, also dir.; instr. Boston Archtl. Center, 1954; vis. critic Coll. Architecture and Design, U. Mich., 1961. Mem. Detroit Inst. Arts, 1965—, Art. Assn. Birmingham, Mich., 1965—; mem. planning bd. City of Birmingham, 1971—. Bd. dirs. Detroit Archtl. Found. Served to lt. (j.g.) USNR, 1951-52. Wheelwright Traveling fellow Harvard, 1960. Fellow A.I.A. (mem. nat. com. on commerce and industry); Mem. Engring. Soc. Detroit. Unitarian. Project include physics and astronomy bldg., 1963, office and classroom bldg., 1971, both U. Mich.; Air Terminal Bldg., City Detroit, 1966; die and engring facility Gen. Motors Corp., Flint, Mich., 1968, also adminstrv. office bldg., Saginaw, Mich., 1969; southeastern br. facilities Avon Products, Inc., Atlanta, 1970; Children's Hosp. of Mich., Detroit, 1971; office and publishing facilities The Washington Post, Washington, 1971. Home: 837 Shepardbush Rd Birmingham MI 48008 Office: New Center Bldg Detroit MI 48202

HAROLD, RAYMOND PAGET, savs. and loan exec.; b. Worcester, Mass., July 12, 1898; s. George S. and Sarah (Whittum) H.; student Mass. Inst. Tech., Carnegie Inst. Tech.; LL.D., Assumption Coll., 1959; D.C.S. (hon), Holy Cross Coll. 1966; m. Myrtle S. Harold Rice, 1921; children—Charlote I. (Mrs. John D. Druce), Dorothy A. (Mrs. Lester C. Conner, Jr.), Ruth L. (Mrs. Robert M. Zollinger, Jr.), Asst. trust officer Pa. Trust Co., Pitts.; staff fgn. dept. First Nat. Bank of Boston; bank examiner, Mass.; treas. Worcester Coop. Bank, 1928; pres. Mass. Coop. Bank League, 1932; dir., organizer Mass. Coop. Central Bank, Coop. Share Ins. Fund, 1933; pres. Fed. Savs. League of New Eng., 1943-44, Nat. League Insured Savs. Assns., 1946-47; pres. Worcester Fed. Savs. and Loan Assn., 1937—, chmn., 1958—; pres. Spruce Point Inn, Boothbay Harbor, Me., Green Pastures Farms, West Boylston, Mass.; dir. Harbor Nat. Bank, Boston, Investors Mortgage Ins. Co. Pres., study housing and capital needs in Peru, ICA, 1959; mem. adv. com. on housing and urban devel. AID, State Dept.; mem. Fed. Home Loan Bank Bd., Boston, 1932-48. Chmn. Worcester Housing Authority, 1946-54, Worcester Redevel. Authority. Bd. dirs. Worcester chpt. A.R.C., Hahnemann Hosp., Mass. Heart Assn.; adv. com. Worcester YWCA; trustee New Eng. Bapt. Hosp., St. Vincent Hosp.; former chmn. com. doctors, dentists and nurses Mass. Scholarship Found. Served with Engrs. Corps, U.S. Army, World War I. Recipient distinguished service award Am. Cancer Soc., 1951, award Worcester Vets. Council, 1951, Freedoms Found. award, 1951, Worcester AmVets, 1955, Am. Heart Assn., 1959; Isaiah Tomas award Worcester Advt. Club; comdr. Order of Merit, Peru, 1960. Mem. Am. Legion, Newcomen Soc. N.Am., Internat. Benjamin Franklin Soc., Royal Soc. Arts (London). Clubs: Economic (past pres.) (Worcester): N.Y. Athletic; Boothbay Harbor Yacht; Johathan (Los Angeles); Key Biscayne Yacht; Conn. Valley Hereford Cattle, Am. Jersey Cattle. Office: 22 Elm St Worcester MA 01608

HARP, ELMER, Jr., educator; b. Cleve., Apr. 13, 1913; s. Elmer and Bertha (Treiber) H.; B.S., Harvard, 1938, M.A., 1947, Ph.D., 1953; student Case Inst. Tech., 1939-40; m. Elaine Garland Groves, June 3, 1939; children—John G., Geoffrey G., Victoria G., Douglas G. Methods engr. Lincoln Electric Co., Cleve., 1939-43; curator anthropology Dartmouth Mus., 1947-52, mem. faculty, 1951—, prof. anthropology, 1957—, chmn. dept., 1961—, dir. mus., 1961-68; archaeol. expdns. to Yukon Ty., N.W. Tys. Ungava, Labrador, Nfld. Served to lt. (j.g.) USNR, MTO, PTO. Fulbright sr. research fellow, Denmark, 1959-60. Fellow Am. Anthrop. Assn., Arctic Inst. N.Am., A.A.A.S.; mem. Soc. Am. Archaeology, Current Anthropology. Author: Archaeology fo the Lower and Middle Thelon, N.W. Territories, 1961; Cultural Affinities of the Newfoundland Dorset Eskimo, 1964. Research air photo interpretation archaeology and settlement patterns. Home: 28 Maple St Hanover NH 03755

HARP, RENO SHEFFER, Jr., clergyman; b. Frederick, Md., Sept. 20, 1905; s. Reno Sheffer and Bessie Dell (Zentz) H.; A.B., Johns Hopkins, 1926; B.D., Union Theol. Sem., N.Y.C., 1929; D.D., U. Richmond, 1955; m. Ruth Maynard Cline, Sept, 5, 1929; 1 son, Reno Sheffer III. Ordained to ministry P.E. Ch as deacon, 1929, priest, 1930; rector Christ Church, West River, Md., Richmond, Va., 1946-Trinity Ch., Washington. 1936-46, St. Stephen's Ch. Richmond. Va., 1946- -. Mem. exec. council Diocese of Washington, 1940-46, chmn. dept. missions, 1943-46, also dep, also dep. to Provincial Synod: dep. Diocese of Va. to Provincial Synod, 1951; examining chaplain Diocese of Va. , also mem. standing com., 1961-63, chmn., 1963. Trustee Church Schs. of Va.; mem. bd. St Catherine's. Mem. Kappa Sigma. Home: 4912 Cary St Rd Richomnd VA 23226 Office: 6004 Three Chopt Rd Richmond VA 23226

HARPER, ALFRED EDWIN, educator; b. Lethbridge, Alta., Can., Aug. 14, 1922; s. Alexander and Frances (Bradley) H.; came to U.S., 1952, naturalized, 1957; B.Sc., U. Alta., 1945, M.Sc., 1947; Ph.D., U. Wis.-Madison, 1953; research asso., U. Cambridge (Eng.), 1955-56; m. Naila Evelyn Jwaideh, Apr. 17, 1948; children—Shareen Frances, Gwendolyn Ann. Lectr., then asst. prof. biochemistry U. Alta., 1948-54; asst., then asso. prof. biochemistry U. Wis.-Madison, 1954-61; prof. nutrition Mass. Inst. Tech., 1961-65; prof. biochemistry U. Wis-Madison, 1965—, chmn. dept. nutritional scis., 1968—. Mem. exec. com. Food and Nutrition Bd., NRC-Nat. Acad. Scis., 1968—; chmn. nutrition tng. com. Nat. Inst. Gen. Med. Scis., 1968—; sci. adv. com. Nutrition Found. and Am. Inst. Baking. Fellow NRC, 1955-56. Fellow A.A.A.S.; mem. Am. Inst. Nutrition (council 1966-70, pres. 1970—; Borden award 1965), Am. Physiol. Soc., Am. Soc. Biol. Chemists, Sigma Xi. Democrat. Unitarian. Author numerous papers in field. Asso. editor Canadian Jour. Biochemistry; editorial bd. Am. Jour. Physiology. Home: 3447 Edgehill Pky Madison WI 53705

HARPER, ALLEN DREW, ins. exec.; b. East St. Louis, ILL., July 2, 1911; s. Lon and Helen (Allen) H.; A.B., Westminster Coll., 1932; M.B.A., Harvard, 1934; m. Jane Barnes, May 1, 1937; children—Ann, Katherine, Drew. With securities dept. Gen. Am. Life Ins. Co., St. Louis, 1934-41; with securities dept. Pacific Mut. Life Ins. Co., Los Angeles 1941—, v.p., 1951 —: dir. Continental Telephone Co. Cal., Dominguez Water Co. , Southwest Water Co., Suburban Water Co. Trustee Westminster Coll. Mem. C. of C., Beta Theta Pi, Zeta Tau Delta. Presbyn. Club: Los Angeles Stock Exchange. Home: 3343 San Pasqual Pasadena CA 91107 Office: 523 W 6th St Los Angeles CA 90014

HARPER, ASHBY TAYLOR, educator; b. Washington's Crossing, N.J., Oct. 1, 1916; s. Frank Williamson and Roberta Ashby (Taylor) H.; grad. Blair Acad., Blairstown, N.J., 1935; A.B., Princeton, 1939, postgrad., 1945-47; postgrad. Middlebury (Vt.) Coll., 1940; m. Madge Lorene Palmer, Mar. 25, 1944; children—Frederick, Richard, David, Margery. Asst. dir. athletics Princeton, 1939-40; tchr., coach Mt. Hermon (Mass.) Sch., 1940-41; dir. Colegio Americano de Quito, Ecuador, 1947-51; headmaster Am. Sch., Lima, Peru, 1951-53, St. Louis Country Day Sch., 1953-62, Albuquerque Acad., 1964—; dir. Peace Corps program in Guatemala, 1962-64. Served to lt. (s.g.), aviator, USNR, 1941-45; PTO. Decorated D.F.C., Air medal (4). Mem. Headmasters Assn., Country Day Sch. Headmasters Assn., Inter-Am. Edn. Assn. (founding dir.), Am. Assn. Tchrs. Spanish and Portuguese. Rotarian. Home: 7816 Harwood St NE Albuquerque NM 87110 Office: 6400 N Wyoming Blvd Albuquerque NM 87109

HARPER, BERCHEL HAROLD, gas co. exec.; b. Cumberland, Ia., May 18, 1907; s. Earl Leslie and Bertha (Madden) H.; extension student U. Neb., 1928-30; m. Alice Wilma Dale, June 7, 1931. Cashier, Neb. Treas. Office, Lincoln, 1928-30; asst. cashier, clk., asst. sec., sec. No. Natural Gas Co., Omaha, 1931-59, corp. sec., 1959—. Mem. Task Force on Paperwork Mgmt., Second Hoover Commn., 1954-58. Dir., past pres. Omaha Symphony Assn. Mem. Am. Soc. Corporate Secs. (pres., dir.), Am. Gas. Assn., Ind. Natural Gas Assn. Am. Clubs: Omaha, Omaha Country. Home: 9955 Bloomfield Dr Omaha NB 68114 Office: 2223 Dodge St Omaha NB 68102

HARPER, DICKINSON COATES, investment banker; b. Seattle, June 22, 1905; s. Paul Coates and Alice (Dickinson) H.; Ph.B., Yale, 1927; student Harvard Bus. Sch., 1927-28; m. Helena Robbins, June 20, 1940; children—Alice D., Robbins D., Paul C. Statistician, Seaboard Nat. Bank, N.Y., 1928; rep. First of Boston Corp., N.Y.C., 1929; v.p., sec. Willim P. Harper & Son & Co., Seattle, 1930—; pres. 15-0-4 3d Av. Inc., 1939—. Mem. Investment Bankers Assn. Am. (pres. N.W. group 1964, nat. bd. gobs. 1965-67). Clubs: University, Golf, Tennis, Wash. Athletic (Seattle). Home: 3707 E Highland Dr Seattle WA 98102 Office: 1504 3d Av Seattle WA 98101

HARPER, EDWARD J., clergyman; b. Bklyn., July 23, 1910; s. John Edward and Josephine (Realånder) H.; student St. Marys Coll., North East, Pa., 1928-33, St. Mary's Coll., Annapolis, 1933-34, Mt. St. Alphonsus Maj. Sem., 1934-40. Ordained priest Roman Catholic Ch., 1939; missionary, P.R., 1941-46, Dominican Republic, 1946-50; dean Mayaguez, P.R., 1950-56; superior Vice Province of San Juan Redemptorist Fathers, 1956-60; prelate V.I., 1960, bishop, 1960—. Pres. Citizens for Drug Edn., Inc., 1968—, Cath. Community Conscious Corp. K.C. (chatter). Address: Estate Elizabeth 9 St Thomas VI 00801

HARPER, GEORGE MILLS, educator; b. Linn Creek, Mo., Nov. 5, 1914; s. Charles Avery and Grace (Shipman) H.; A.B., Culver-Stockton Coll., 1940; M.A., U. Fla., 1947; Ph.D., U. N.C., 1951; m. Mary Jane Hughes, June 15, 1944; children—Margaret Mills, Ann Christian. From instr. to prof. English, U. N.C.,1950-66, asso. dean arts and scis., 1955-60, chmn. English dept., 1962-66, chmn. faculty, 1961-64, chmn. humanities, 1962-65; prof., chmn. English dept. U. Fla., 1966-69; dean arts and scis. Va. Poly. Inst., 1969-70; chmn. English dept. Fla. State U., Tallahassee, 1970— cons. U.S. Office Edn., 1967, 68, 69; lectr. Yeats Internat. Summer Sch., Ireland, 1964, 65, 68, Internat. Congress Comparative Lit., Fribourg, Switzerland, 1964. Pres. Chapel Hill (N.C.) C. of C., 1965. Bd. govs. Chapel Hill Pub. Library, 1959-65. Served to lt. comdr. USNR, 1942-46; comdr. Res. Mem. Modern Lang. Assn. (chmn. Celtic group 1967), Comparative Lit. Assn. Democrat. Methodist. Author: Neoplatonism of William Blake, 1961; Yeats's Quest for Eden, 1966. Contbr. articles. Editor; (with Kathleen Raine) Thomas Taylor the Platonist, 1969. Home: 407 Plantation Rd Tallahassee FL 32303

HARPER, GORDON KEITH, ins. co. exec.; b. Chgo., May 17, 1907; s. John and Lila Jean (Smith) H.; ed. U. Ill., 1929; m. Elizabeth Louise Watson, June 30, 1934; children-Martha Watson (Mrs. Olav Redi), Sara Jane (dec.), Nancy Keith (Mrs. Philip Ehrensatt). With Phoenix Mut. Life Ins. Co., 1931—, sr. v.p. sales, 1967—, also dir. Served to comdr. USNR, 43-45. C.L.U., 1940 Mem. Beta Theta Pi. Club: Hartford Golf. Home: 1101 Mountain Rd Bloomfield CN 06002 Office: Phoenix Mut Life Ins Co 1 American Row Hartford CN 06115

HARPER, HAROLD, lawyer; b. N.Y.C., Nov. 22, 1885; s. James Alsop and Emma Louise (Hageman) H.; A.B., Columbia, 1905, A.M., LL.B., 1907; m. Elizabeth Roop, June 9, 1923; children—James Albert, Mary (Mrs. Mary Harper Hutchins). Admitted to N.Y. bar, 1907, U.S. Supreme ct., 1910, D.C. bar, 1920; practiced law N.Y.C. 1907 asso. Davies, Auerbach & Cornell, 1909-13; mem. Harper & Matthews and predecessors, 1920—; asst. U.S. atty., 1913-20; spl. asst. to U.S. atty. gen., 1920; chmn. com. which drafted unified rules U.S. Dist. Cts., So. and Eastern N.Y. adopted 1952, chmn. standing com. rules So. Dist. N.Y.; lectr. N.Y.U. Sch. Law, 1949-52, Practising Law Inst., 1939- 46; pub. mem. Joint Industry Bd., Elec. Contracting Industry. Mem. Selective Service Bd., 1941-45, Fellow Am. Coll. Trial Lawyers; mem. N.Y. County Lawyers Assn. Bd., 1943-48, chmn. com. fed. cts. 1938-53, mem. com. on discipline 1964-70, Assn. Bar City N.Y. mem. com. municipal aaffairs, 1949-52), N.Y., Am. bar assns., Seventh Regt. Vets. Assn. (past mem. bd. mgt.), Alpha Chi Rho (nat. v.p., 1925-26). Democrat. Presbyn. Clubs: University, Columbia, Lawyers (N.Y.C.). Author monograph Civil Practice in Federal Courts. Home: 145 E 74th St New York City NY 10021 Office: 60 Wall St New York City NY 10005

HARPER, HAROLD ANTHONY, univ. dean; b. San Francisco, Sept. 22, 1911; s. Gustavus David and Regina Teresa (Pistolesi) H.; B.Sc., U. San Francisco, 1933; student U. Cal. at Los Angeles, 1933-34; Ph.D., U. So. Cal., 1941. From instr. to asst. prof. biol. scis. Loyola U., Los Angeles, 1933-41; asso. prof., then prof. biology U. San Francisco, 1941-42, 46-53; mem. faculty U. Cal. Sch. Medicine, San Francisco, 1953—, prof. biochemistry, 1959—, dean Grad. Div., U. Cal. at San Francisco, 1961—, vice chancellor grad. studies and research, 1966—; cons. to U.S. Naval Hosp., Oakland, Cal. Bd. dirs., past pres. San Francisco br. Am. Cancer Soc., also bd. dirs Cal. div.; chmn. nutrition adv. com. Cal. Dept. Pub. Health. Bd. regents Coll. Notre Dame, Belmont, Cal. Served to capt., med. dept., AUS, 1942-46. Decorated Army Commendation ribbon exceptional service citation Surgeon Gen. U.S. Navy, 1962; citation patriotic civilian service Dept. Army, 1961; meritorious pub. service citation Navy Dept., 1967. Diplomate Am. Bd. Nutrition, Am.Bd. Clin. Chemistry. Fellow Cal. Acad. Scis., A.A.A.S., Am. Soc. Clin. Chemists; mem. Am. Chem. Soc., Am. Soc. Biol. Chemists, Soc. Exptl. Biology and Medicine, Sigma Xi. Author: Review of Physiological Chemistry, 12th edit., 1969 (also in French, Spanish, Italian, Japanese, Portuguese). Editor: Enzymes in Health and Disease, 1960.

HARPER, HARRY HALSTED, Jr., editor; b. Chgo., Dec. 2, 1910; s. Harry Halsted and Eugenia (MacLaurin) H.; grad. Berkshire Sch., Sheffield, Mass., 1929; B.A., Yale, 1934; m. Mary H. Jopling, Sept. 28, 1934; children—Jean (Mrs. Armin S. Lindenmeyer), Jonathan. With Reader's Digest, 1934-42, 46—, exec. editor, v.p., 1961—. Served with AUS, 1942-44; to 1st lt. USMCR, 1944- 46. Decorated Legion of Merit. Clubs: Coffee House (N.Y.C.); Lake Zurich Golf; Norwalk (Conn.) Yacht. Home: PO Box 236 Katonah NY 10536 Office: Reader's Digest Pleasantville NY 10570

HARPER, HERBERT E., corp. exec.; b. 1901; grad. Drexel Inst. Tech.; married. With Pub. Service Coordinated Transp., 1922—, now pres., chief exec. officer, dir. Address: 180 Boyden Av Maplewood, NJ 07040.•

HARPER, HOWARD HOLDFORD, govt. ofcl.; b. Zebulon, N.C., July 22, 1920; s. James Madison and Susie (Norment) (Mc Ger) H.; B.S. in Agrl. Edn., N.C. State U., 1947; m. Dorothy Cecile Thonnesen, Sept. 15, 1947; children—Dorothy E. (Mrs. J. Timothy Smith), Howard Holdford, Sara June, Derward B., Michael D. Tchr. vocational agr. Accadia High Sch., 1947-48; with Brit. Am. Tobacco Co., Costa Rica, Nicaragua, El Salvador, 1948-56; farmer, Island Omotape, Lake Nicaragua, 1956-57; agronomist ICA-AID, Vietnam, 1957-61; dep. food and agr. officer, Iran, 1961-62, officer, 1962-64; food and agr. officer, Dominican Republic, 1964-70; rural devel. officer, Bogota, Colombia, 1970—. Served with USMC, 1941-44. Decorated Order Christopher Columbus Knight Dominican Republic. Mem. Phi Kappa Phi. Republican. Episcopalian. Home: Little Switzerland NC Office: AID Bogota Colombia

HARPER, HOWARD VINCENT, clergyman, author; b. Kenton, O., June 1, 1904; s. Earl Vincent and Grace (Howard) H.; Ph.B., Kenyon Coll., 1927, D.D. (hon.), 1953; B.D. cum laude, Bexley Hall, Gambier, O., 1930; m. Elizabeth Lane, Dec. 2, 1935 (dec. May 1968); m. 2d, Josephine Montgomery Williams, June 7, 1969. Ordained to ministry Episcopal Ch., 1931; served as pastor In Cleve., 1931—33, Hudson, O., 1933-35, Waycross, Ga., 1935-40, The Plains, Va., 1940-42, Jackson, Mich., 1942-53; asst. to bishop of Mich., 1952-53; nat. dir. laymen's work Episcopal Ch., 1953-68; hon. canon st. Paul's Cathedral, Detroit, 1952—; founder, 1st pres. Nat. Diocesan Press, 1938. Mem. religious adv. com. Nat. Safety Council, 1961. Bd. dirs. N. Conway Inst. Alcoholics and Alcoholism, Boston, 1960- 67. Mem. Psi Upsilon. Author: Days and Customs of All Faiths, 1957; Customs and Holidays Around the World, 1963; The Vestryman's Manual, 1964; Profiles of Protestant Saints, 1967; also numerous articles, tracts and syndicated column Days and Customs of All Faiths, 1952—. Asso. editor So. Churchman, 1940-42. Address: 859 Robin Ct Marco Island FL 33937

HARPER, JENE, oil equipment supply co. exec.; b. Sapulpa, Okla., Dec. 27, 1910; s. Jacob P. and Myrtle (Ham) H.; student U. Nev., 1929-30; m. June Aleff, Apr. 16, 1955; children—Paul, Ronald, Teresa, Debra. Chmn. Roosevelt Oil Co., Mt. Pleasant, Mich., 1930-33; with Franklin Supply Co., Denver, 1933—, chmn. bd. dirs., 1962—; dir. Lark Oil Co., Colo. Nat. Bank (both Denver), Franklin Pipe & Supply Ltd., Calgary, Alta., Can., Red Top Valley Ditch Co., Granby, Colo., Mt. States Pipe & Supply Co., Colorado Springs, Colo. Pres. bd. trustees Graland Country Day Sch. Mem. Rocky Mountain Oil and Gas Assn. (dir. 1968—), Chicago Oil Men's Club, Petroleum Equipment Suppliers Assn. (dir. 1933-62), Indsl. Petroleum Assn. Am. (dir. 1965—). Clubs: Denver (bd dirs.), Cherry Hills Country (bd. dirs.) (Denver). Home: 225 S Clermont St Denver CO 80222 Office: Denver Club Bldg Denver CO 80202

HARPER, JOHN DICKSON, aluminum mfg. co. exec.; b. Louisville, Tenn., Apr. 6, 1910; s. Lafayette Rodgers and Mary Alice (Collier) H.; B.S., U. Tenn., 1933; D.Eng., Maryville Coll., 1964, Lehigh U., Rensselaer Poly. Inst.; LL.D., U. Evansville; Sc.D., Clarkson Coll. Tech.; m. Samma Lucille McCrary, Oct. 21, 1937; children—Rodger McCrary, John Dickson, Thomas William. With Aluminum Co. of Am., 1933—, successively elec. engr., Alcoa, Tenn., asst. dist. power mgr., works mgr., Rockdale, Tex., gen. mgr. smelting div., Pitts., asst. prodn. mgr., 1933-60, v.p., 1960, v.p. prodn., 1962, exec. v.p., 1962-63, pres. 1963—, chief exec. officer, chmn. exec. com., 1965—, chmn. bd., 1970 —; dir. Mellon Nat. Bank & Trust Co., Pitts., Goodyear Tire & Rubber Co., Akron, O., Met. Life Ins. Co. Mem. nat. council Boy Scouts; mem. Com. Econ. Devel., Bus. Council, Bus. Com. for Arts, Inc., Nat. Safety Council, Automotive Safety Found., Radio Free Europe, Nat. Alliance Businessmen; exec. com. Nat. Indsl. Conf. Bd. Life trustee Carnegie-Mellon U.; mem. devel. bd. U. Tenn.; bus. adv. council Stanford Grad. Sch. Bus.; bd. dirs. Pitts. Regional Indsl. Devel. Corp. Recipient Silver Quill award Am. Bus. Press, Inc. Fellow Am. Soc. M.E., I.E.E.E. (past v.p.); mem. Newcomen Soc., Aluminum Assn. (chmn. bd.), Am. Soc. for Metals, Tex. Chem. Council (past pres.), Tau Beta Pi, Eta Kappa Nu. Clubs: Headliners (award 1960) (Austin, Tex.); Duquesne, University, Allegheny, Fox Chapel, St. Clair Country (Pitts.); Laurel Valley Golf, Rolling Rock (Ligonier, Pa.); Internat. (Washington); Links, Racquet and Tennis (N.Y.C.); Tres Vidas (Acapulco, Mexico); Burning Tree (Bethesda, Md.). Home: 880 Old Hickory Rd Pittsburgh PA 15243 Office: Alcoa Bldg Pittsburgh PA 15219

HARPER, JOHN LESLIE, mfg. co. exec.; b. LaGrange, Ill., Aug. 22, 1910; s. John and Lila Jean (Smith) H.; B.S., U. Ill., 1931; m. F. Marjorie Peacock, July 1, 1933; children—Jean (Mrs. Michael Artin), Robert, Gordon, James. With Eastman Kodak Co., 1931—, comptroller, 1963—. Pres. bd. trustees Rochester Gen. Hosp., 1967—; bd. dirs. Rochester Regional Health and Hosp. Council, 1967—. Mem. Financial Execs. Inst. (past pres. Rochester), Chi Phi. Republican. Presbyn. Home: 860 Rock Beach Rd Rochester NY 14617 Office: 343 State St Rochester NY 14617

HARPER, LAURA JANE, nutritionist; b. Jackson, Miss; Aug 18, 1914; d. William Pinkney and Elnora (Collins) Harper; B.S., Belhaven (Miss.) Coll., 1934; student Miss. So. U., 1935; M.S.U. Tenn., 1948; Psotgrad. Cornell U., 1951; Ph.D. , Mich. State U., 1955. Mem. faculty Va. Poly. Inst., 1949—, prof. home econs., 1956- -, chmn. dept., 1958-60, dean Coll. Home Econs., 1960 —, asst. dir. research div., 1967—. Sec. So. regional nutrition' research tech. com. State Expt. Stas., 1960-62, chmn., 1962-63; mem. com. of 9 U.S. Dept. Agr., 1969—. Recipient All Star Key award Va. 4-H, 1962, Distinguished Alumni award, 1964, 68; hon. mem. Young Homemakers Va., 1964. Mem. Am. (vice chmn. foods and nutrition sect. 1957-59), Va. (chmn. research sect. 1958, pres. 1964- 66) home econ. assns., Am., Va. dietetic Assns., Assn. State Univs. and Land Grant Colls. (sec. interregional nutrition research com. 1959, chmn. So. region home econ. adminstrs. 1959-61, chmn. research sect. home econs. div. 1962-63, sec. home econs. div. 1963-64, mem. home econs. comm. 1965-66, chmn. Assn. of Adminstrs. home econs. 1969-70), Inst. Food Technologists, Va. Acad. Scis., A.A.A.S., Am. Assn. U. Women, N.E.A., Sigma Xi, Omicron Nu, Phi Upsilon Omicron, Phi Sigma, Phi Tau Sigma, Phi Kappa Phi. Contbr. profl. jours. Home: 100 Sunset Blvd Blacksburg VA 24060.

HARPER, LAWRENCE AVERELL, lawyer, educator; b. Oakland, Cal., May 18, 1901; s. Fred Fogg Gale and Elizabeth Sarah (Averell) H.; A.B., U. Cal., 1922 , A.M., 1924, J.D., 1925; student King's Coll. U. London, 1925-26; Ph.D., Columbia, 1939; m. Anna Virginia McCune, July 7, 1925; children—Lawrence Vernon, Virginia Ann, Robert Gale. Admitted To Cal. bar, 1927; mem. firm Harper & Harper, specializing in customs law, 1928-45, Lawrence, Tuttle & Harper, 1945-54; instr. history U. Cal. at Berkeley, 1928-39, asst. prof., 1939-43, asso. prof., 1943-47, prof. 1947-68, prof. emeritus, 1968—. Mem. council Inst. Early Am. History and Culture, 1969-71. Guggenheim fellow, 1944-45. Mem. Am. Hist. Assn., Am. Soc. Information Sci., Am. Econ. History Assn., Am. Soc. for Legal History (v.p. 1960, dir.), Phi Beta Kappa, Delta Theta Phi. Club:

Berkeley Tennis. Author: The English Navigation Laws 1939; The Effect of the Navigation Acts on the Thirteen Colonies, in The Era of the American Revolution, 1939; Charts and Outlines for United States History (2 vols., syllabus series), 1943, 55; also contbr. to hist. and legal publs. Editor: (with F.F.G. Harper) Harper's Customs Tariff, 1930; mem. editorial bd. Am. Jour. Legal History. Home: 52 Oakwood Rd Orinda CA 94563 Office: U Cal Berkeley CA 94720

HARPER, MARION, Jr., advt. exec.; b. Oklahoma City, May 14, 1916; s. Marion and Lotus (Alexander) H.; student Phillips Acad., 1932-34; A.B., Yale, 1938; m. Virginia Epes, Apr. 4, 1942; children—Stephen Henry, Chilton Epes, Francis Marion, Reid M.; m. 2d, Valerie Feit, Nov. 8, 1963; 1 dau., Victoria. Trainee McCann-Erickson, Inc., 1939, mgr. copy research, 1942- 44, asso. dir. research, 1944-45, v.p. in charge research and merchandising, 1945-48, dir., 1946—, asst. to pres., 1947- 48, pres., 1948-69, chmn. bd., 1958-69; chmn. bd., pres. Interpublic Group of Cos., 1961-68; chmn. exec. com. Interpublic, Inc., 1968-71; dir. Franklin Corp. Mem. alumni council Phillips Acad., Andover, Mass. Decorated Cruzeiro do Sul, 1955; recipient Distinguished Service award Young Men's Bd. Trade Inc., Parlin Meml. award. Mem. Nat. Distbn. Council, Nat. Outdoor Advt. Bur. (dir.), Am. Assn. Advt. Agys. (chmn. bd. 1961-62). Clubs: Lotos, Metropolitan, Yale, Pinnacle (N.Y.C.); Ardsley Country. Author: Getting Results from Advertising, 1948; contbg. author Public Relations Handbook, 1950; author articles on radio-TV, copy research. Home: Ridge Acres Langdon Av Irvington-on-Hudson NY 10533

HARPER, PAUL ALVA, physician, educator; b. Watertown, Conn., Sept. 18, 1904; s. George A. and Alice (Beach) H.; A.B., Dartmouth, 1926; M.D., Yale, 1931; M.P.H., Johns Hopkins (Rockefeller fellow), 1947; m. Cornelia Esther Edwards, Apr. 29, 1938; children—Cornelia, Paul, Eugenia. Intern. asst. resident, resident pediatrics New Haven Hosp., 1931-35 ; pvt. practice in pediatrics, Conn., 1935-42; instr., s.in. instr. pediatrics Yale, 1935-42; asso. prof. pub. health adminstrn. div. maternal and child health Johns Hopkins. 1947-51, prof. pub. health adminstrn., 1951- 63, prof., head dept. maternal and child health, 1963- 65, assoc. prof. pediatrics, 1951—. prof., chmn. dept. maternal and child health and population dynamics, 1965—. Served with AUS, 1942-46. Mem. A.M.A., Balt. City Med. Soc., Am. Acad. Pediatrics, Am. Pediatric Soc. Author: Preventive Pediatrics, 1962. Contbr. health and med. jours. Home: 21 Elmwood Rd Baltimore MD 21210 Office 615 N Wolfe St Baltimore MD 21205

HARPER, PAUL CHURCH, Jr., advt. exec.; b. Coblenz, Germany, Dec. 16, 1920 (parents Am. Citizens); s. Paul Church and Anne Lindsay (White) H.; B.A., Yale, 1942; m. Eleanor Emery, Jan. 3, 1947; children—Diana, Jessica, William, Lindsay, Samuel, Charles. With Needham, Harper & Steers, Inc., Chgo., 1946—, exec. v.p., 1958-60, pres., 1960-67, chmn. bd., N.Y.C., 1967—, also chief exec. officer. Trustee Beloit Coll. Served as maj. USMCR, 1942-45. Decorated Bronze Star. Mem. Am. Assn. Advt. Agys. (dir. 1960- 61, past chmn. Central region). Clubs: Knickerbocker, 5th Avenue, Yale (N.Y.C.); Belle Haven (Greenwich, Conn.); Chgo. Home: 1107 Fifth Av New York City NY 10028 Office: 909 3d Av New York City NY 10022

HARPER, RAYMOND LAWRENCE, oil field supply exec.; b. Sapulpa, Okla., June 29, 1915; s. Jacob P. and Myrtle (Harris) H.; divorced; children—Michael, Sally, Dana, Melissa. Pres., dir. Franklin Supply Co., Houston, 1939—; pres., dir. Franklin Pipe & Supply, Ltd. (Calgary, Alta.); dir. Lark Oil Co. (Denver). Served to maj. AUS, 1941-45. Decorated Bronze Star with oak leaf cluster. Mem. Petroleum Equipment Supply Assn. (dir.), Am. Petroleum Inst., Ind. Petroleum Assn., So. Gas Assn., Mid Continent Oil and Gas Assn., Houston C. of C., Houston Petroleum Club. Club: River Oaks Country. Home: 502 S Post Oak Lane Houston TX 77027 Office: Americana Bldg Houston TX 77002

HARPER, ROBERT ALEXANDER, educator; b. Chgo., Apr. 16, 1924; s. Robert Haskell and May Isabelle (Wilsdon) H.; student DePauw U., 1941-42; Ph.B., U. Chgo., 1946, S.B., 1947, S.M. 1948, Ph.D., 1950; m. Sarah Ann Lofgren, Sept. 38, 1944; children—Carol Leslie, Judith Lynn, Robert Willard. Research asso. geography, then home study dept. U. Chgo., 1948-50; mem. faculty So. Ill. U., Carbondale, 1950-67, prof. geography, 1959-67, chmn. dept., 1959-66; vis. scientist Assn. Am. Geographers, 1965-66; prof. head dept. geography U. Md., 1967—; exchange lectr. Sch. Geography, U. Manchester (Eng.), 1961-62. Mem. research tech. adv. com. Wabash Valley Bi-State Commn., 1961-65. Served to 2d lt., navigator, USAAF, 1943-45. Decorated Air medal with oak leaf cluster; recipient Profl. Achievement award U. Chgo. Alumni Assn., 1971. Mem. Assn. Am. Geographers (exec. council 1967-70), Nat. Council Geog. Edn. (pres. 1970-71), Nat. Council Soc. Scis., Sigma Xi, Phi Gamma Delta. Author: (with C.W.Sorensen) Europe and North America, 1955, Economic Geography, 1955; (with Sorensen and R.E. Crist) Learning About Latin America, 1961. Editor: (with Jean Gottmann) Metropolis on the Move, 1967. Home: 13705 Creekside Dr Silver Spring MD 20904

HARPER, ROBERT ALLAN, cons. psychologist; b. Dayton, O., Apr. 25, 1915; s. Earl Paull and Mary (Belden) H.; student U. Dayton, 1934-36; B.A., Ohio State U., 1938, M.A., 1939, Ph.D., 1942; m. Flora Mie Bridges; children—Robert Belden, John Paull. Instr. Kent State U., 1942-43; analyst War Manpower Commn., 1943; asso. prof. Wagner Coll., 1943-45; psychiat. social worker U.S. Army, 1945-46; asst. prof. Ohio State U., 1946-50, dir. marriage counseling clinic, 1949-50; chmn. family life dept., dir. marriage counseling service Merrill-Palmer Sch., Detroit, 1950-53; pvt. practice psychotheraphy and marriage counseling, Washington, 1953—. Fellow Am. Psychol. Assn., Am. Assn. Marriage Counselors (sec. 1954-58, pres. 1960- 62), Nat. Council Family Relations (dir. 1951-55), Am. Acad. Psycholtherapists (pres. 1961-63), Am. Group Psychotheraphy Assn., Eastern, D.C. psychol. assns., Washington Social Hygiene Soc. (bd. 1957- 60); mem. Psychologists in Pvt. Practice (exec. com.), Soc. Sci. Study Sex, Interam. Soc. Psychologists, Am. Soc. Group Psychotherapy and Psychodrama, Internat. Council Psycholgists (exec. bd. 1971—), N.Y. Acad. Sci., Internat. Soc. Gen. Semantics, Inst. Rational Living (bd.), Am. Civil Liberties Union, Washington Soc. Clin. Psychologists (exec. com. 1968—), Phi Beta Kappa. Author: (with John F. Cuber) Problems of American Society, 1948; Marriage, 1949; Psychoanalysis and Psychotherapy: 36 Systems, 1959; (with Albert Ellis) Creative Marriage, 1961, A Guide to Rational Living, 1961; (with Walter R. Stokes) 45 Levels to Sexual Understanding and Enjoyment, 1971. Home: 4903 Potomac Av NW Washington DC 20007 Office: 3000 Connecticut Av NW Washington DC 20008

HARPER, ROBERT DONALD, educator; b. Grand Junction, Colo., July 6, 1913; s. Sinclair Ollason and Mabel Esta (Roberts) H.; B.A., U. Denver, 1935; M.A., U. Chgo., 1939, Ph.D., 1949; m. Rhoda Ann Bendry, July 24, 1942. Surveyor, mathematician Bur. Reclamation, 1935-37; instr. English, Mich. Coll. Mining and Tech., 1940-42, U. Chgo., 1946-48; mem. faculty U. Neb., Omaha, 1948—, prof. English, 1957—, dean arts and scis., 1960-70. Served to lt. USNR, 1942-45; PTO. Mem. Am. Studies Assn., Am. Assn. U. Profs., Modern Lang. Assn., English Speaking Union Am. (pres. Omaha 1961-62), Neb. Arts Council (bd. dirs.), Lambda Chi Alpha, Omicron Delta Kappa. Author articles on Am. poetry, drama, theatre. Home: 8515 Indian Hills Dr Omaha NB 68114

HARPER, ROY W., judge; b. Gibson, Mo., July 26, 1905; s. Marvin H. and Minnie (Brooks) H.; A.B., U. Mo., 1929; L.L.B., 1929; m. Ruth Butt, July 30, 1941; children—Katherine Brooks, Arthur Murray. Admitted to Mo. bar, 1929; mem. tax ins. claims dep. dept. Shell Petroleum Corp., St. Louis, 1929-30; pvt. practice law, Steele, Mo., 1931-34; mem. firm Ward & Reeves, Caruthersville, 1934-47; U.S. dist. judge of Mo., Eastern and Western dists. of Mo., 1947—; chief judge Eastern Dist. Mo., 1959-70. sr. judge Eastern and Western Dists. Mo., 1971—. Enlisted Air Corps, U.S. Army, 1942; apptd. 2d lt., Sept. 1942; served with 35th Fighter Group, Southwest Pacific, 1942-; col. Air Corps Res., 1945. Mem. Am., Mo., Pemiscot County bar assns., Order of Coif, Delta Theta Phi. Democrat chmn. Mo. state com. 1946-47). Mason (32, Shriner). Home: 3 Woodcliffe Lane Clayton MO 63105 Office: US Sourt House and Custom House ST Louis MO 63101

HARPER, TERRELL RAY, architect; b. Ft. Worth, Oct. 30, 1908; s. John Thomas and Rachel (Evans) H.; student Tex. A. and M. Coll., 1925-27, Internat. Corr. Schs., 1940-42; m. Susie Mae Huckaba, June 13, 1931; children—Patricia Lois (Mrs. James Weaver Leftwich), Barbara Jeanne (Mrs. James Lowell McAlpin). Draftsman, constrn. inspector John M. Marriott, Architect, San Antonio, 1927-30; constrn. inspector, architect U.S. War Dept., C.Q.M., Tex. and Okla., 1930-34; constrn. inspector, office engr. U.S. PWA, Okla. and Tex., 1935-40; draftsman, specifications writer, asso. charge office George L. Dahl, Architect- Engr., Dallas, 1940-54; propr. Terrell R. Harper, Architect, Dallas, 1954-55; partner Harper & Kemp, Architects, Dallas, 1955—. Bd. dirs. Dallas County Community Chest, 1958-60, Dallas County United Fund. 1968-70. Fellow Constrn. Specifications Inst. (past pres. Dallas chpt., inst. pres. 1964-65), A.I.A. (past pres., dir. Dallas chpt.); mem. Tex. Soc. Architects (past dir.). Methodist (chmn. adminstrv. bd. 1971-72). Home: 9920 Strait Lane Dallas TX 75229 Office: 2020 Live Oak St Dallas TX 75201

HARPER, THOMAS, lawyer, mem. Democratic Nat. Com.; b. Greenwood, Ark., Nov. 23, 1908; s. Robert Atlas and Merton (Othella) H.; student U. Ill., 1927-28; m. Vivien W. Tatum, Jan. 16, 1939 (dec.); children—Thomas, Granville T., Blake, Kay Nelson. Admitted to Ark. bar, 1930; practice in Greenwood, 1930-39, Ft. Smith, 1939—. Sec., v.p., dir., gen. counsel Ark.-Best Freight System, Inc.; v.p., dir., gen. counsel Ark. Best Corp.; dir. gen. counsel City Nat. Bank. Chmn. Ark. Dem. Com., 1954-64; del. Dem. nat. conv., 1956, 60, 64, 68, chmn. delegation, 1960, 64; mem. Dem. Nat. Com. for Ark., 1964—. Bd. dirs. Ft. Smith Boys Club. Served to lt. (j.g.) USNR, 1944-45. Mem. Am. Coll. Trial Lawyers, Am., Ark., Sebastian County bar assns., Motor Carrier Lawyers Assn., Ft. Smith C. of C. Methodist. Club: Hardscrabble County (past pres.). Home: 5001 S Cliff Dr Ft Smith AR 72901 Office: Kelley Bldg Ft Smith AR 72901

HARPER, TOMMY, profl. baseball player; b. Oak Grove, La., Oct. 14, 1940; s. Ulysses and Louetta (Weir) H.; student Santa Rosa Jr. Coll., 1958-59; m. Bonnie Jean Williams, Oct. 6, 1962. Outfielder, Cin. Reds, 1963-67, Cleve. Indians, 1968, Seattle Pilots, 1969, Milw. Brewers, 1970—. Modern Am. League record for stolen bases, 1969. Home: 1324 67th St Berkeley CA 94702

HARPER, VERNE LESTER, educator, forester; b. Monroe, S.D., Aug. 13, 1902; s. Charles Leverett and Eva Luceta (Gamble) H.; B.S., U. Cal., 1926, M.S., 1927; Ph.D., Duke U., 1943; D.Sc., N.C. State U., 1967; m. Elizabeth Owen, Oct. 33, 1927; 1 son, William Lester. Forest research in S.E., U.S. Forest Service, 1927-34, chief div. forest mgmt. research so So. Forest Expt. Sta., New Orleans, 1935-36, forest service, Washington, 1937-44, dir. Northeastern Forest Expt. Sta., Upper Darby, Pa., 1945-50, dep. chief Forest Service in charge research, Washington, 1951-65; prof. forestry U. Fla., 1966—. Mem. U.S. delgation Conf. UN FAO, 51,53,57,59,65, chmn. Latin Am. Forestry Research Com., 1958-61; mem. organizing com. V World Forestry Congress, Seattle, 1960, chmn. exec. com., vice chmn. U.S. delegation 6th World Congress, Madrid, 1966; Mem. permanent com. Internat. Union Forest Research O., 1956-62, v.p., 1962-67; chmn. forestry alumni adv. com. Duke, 1955-65, Recipient Distinguished Service award U.S. Dept. Agr., 1961; Fernow award for distinguished service to internat. forestry, 1965; award for contbns. to forestry Forest Farmers Assn., 1968. Fellow Soc. Am. Foresters (chmn. internat. relations com. 1956-67; mem. Internat. Union Socs. of Foresters (pres. 1966—), soil Conservation Soc. Am., Soc. Foresters Finland (hon.), Sigma Xi, Phi Sigma, Xi Sigma Pi, Alpha Zeta. Club: Cosmos (Washington). Mem. editorial bd. Forest Sci., 1955-65, Agrl. Sci. Rev., 1963-65. Home: 1812 SW 6th Terrace Gainesville FL 32601

HARPER, A. M., lawyer; b. Vancouver, B.C., Can., Feb. 17, 1914; B.A., U. B.C., 1934; LL.B., Vancouver Law Sch. Admitted to B.C. bar, 1937; partner firm Harper, Gilmour, Grey & Co., Vancouver. Mem. Canadian, Vancouver bar assns., Law Soc. B.C. (treas. 1968-69), Psi Upsilon. Office: 409 Granville St Vancouver 2 British Columbia Canada*

HARR, KARL GOTTLIEB, Jr., lawyer; b. South Orange, N.J., Aug. 3, 1922; s. Karl Gottlieb and Mildred (Reid) H.; A.B., Princeton, 1943; LL.B., Yale, 1948; D.Phil. (Rhodes scholar), Oxford U., 1950; m. Patricia Stratton Adams, Oct. 11, 1947; children—Timothy Adams, Karl Gottlieb III, Catherine Anne, Amy. Admitted to N.Y. bar, 1951; asso. Sullivan & Cromwell, N.Y.C., 1950-54; spl. asst. to under-sec. state for adminstrn., staff dir. sec. state's pub. com. on personnel, 1954-55; dir. spl. project Richardson Found., 1955; dep. asst. sec. def. Nat. Security Council Affairs and Plans, alternate def. mem. Nat. Security Council Planning Bd., 1956-57; spl. asst. to Pres. U.S., vice chmn. Operations Coordinating Bd., adviser Nat. Security Council Planning Bd., 1958-61; counsel to Rogers, Hoge, Holls, N.Y.C., 1961-63; pres. Aerospace Industries Assn. Am., Inc., Washington, 1963—; dir. Union Trust Co., Washington. Mem. council Def. and Space Industry Assns.; chmn. Nat. Aero. Noise Abatement bd. dirs. Expt. in Internat. Living, 1967. Alumni Trustee Princeton, 1968—. Served with AUS, 1943-46. Mem. Am. Bar Assn., Phi Beta Kappa, Phi Delta Phi. Home: 6 W Kirke St Chevy Chase MD 20015 Office: 1725 Desales St Washington DC 20036

HARR, LUTHER ARMSTRONG, computer cons.; b. Phila., Sept. 11, 1920; s. Luther Armstrong and Kathryn (Cressman) H.; grad. William Penn Charter Sch., Phila., 1937; B.S., Bowdoin Coll., 1941; M.B.A., Temple U., 1948; m. Eileen Connor, Jan. 2, 1948. Sales mgr. Sperry Rand Corp., N.Y.C., 1948-56, br. mgr., 1957-61; mgr. Peat, Marwick Mitchell & Co., C.P.A.'s, N.Y.C., 1956; dir. UNIVAC tabulating operations Sperry Rand Internat. Corp., Lausanne, Switzerland, 1961-63; asst. to chmn. bd. Teleregister Corp., Stamford, Conn., 1963 (consol. with Bunker-Ramo Corp. 1964); v.p., gen. mgr. bus. and industry div. Bunker-Ramo Corp., 1964-66, exec. v.p., dir., 1966-68; sr. v.p., dir. Translux Corp., N.Y.C., 1968-69; pres. Luther Harr Assos., Inc., Lansdale, Pa., 1969—. Mem. Assn. Computing Machinery, Sigma Nu. Home and Office: 319 Palm Ct Indialantic FL 32903

HARRAR, ELLWOOD SCOTT, educator; born Pitts., Jan. 18, 1905; s. Ellwood Scott and Lucetta Elsie (Sterner) H.; student Oberlin Coll., 1922-24; B.S., N.Y. State Coll. Forestry, 1927, M.S., 1928, Ph.D., 1936; Sc.D. (hon.), Syracuse U. 1961; m Marion Green, Sept. 10, 1927; children—Joanne, Carolyn. Asst. dendrology and wood tech. N.Y. State Coll. Forestry, Syracuse, 1926-28; instr. forest products U. Wash., Seattle, 1928-32, asst. prof., 1933-36; research asso. West Coast Lumbermen's Assn., 1928- 32; project coordinator Civilian Conservation Corps in N.J., 1933; asso. prof. wood technology Duke, 1936-45, prof. wood tech., 1945-67, dean Sch. Forestry, 1957-67, James B. Duke prof. wood sci., 1967—; chief materials and process labs. airplane div. Curtiss-Wright Corp., Louisville, 1942-43, chief adminstrv. engr., 1943-45; veneer, plywood cons. C.E. U.S. Army, Southeastern div., Atlanta, G., 1952-65; cons. U.S. Army Biological Lab., Ft. Detrick, Fredrick, Md., 1961-68. Mem. forest products task force President's Bipartisan Commn. for Increased Use Agr. Products, 1956-58; mem. Gov's Adv. Com. Forestry for N.C. Recipient G.'s citation for outstanding contbns. to forestry N.C., 1966. Fellow Soc. Am. Foresters (com. for standardization tree names 1945-50); mem. Internat. Soc. Tropical Foresters, Internat. Assn. Wood Anatomists (sec.-treas. 1938-45), Forest Products Research Soc. (chmn. pro tem Carolinas-Chesapeake sect. 1948, sec.-treas. 195O-53; v.p. 1957-58, pres. 1959-60), N.C. Forestry Council (pres. 1958-59), N.C. Forestry Assn. (adv. com. furniture, plywood, veneer council 1957-57), Phi Kappa Phi, Alpha Xi Sigma, Xi Sigma Pi, Lambda Chi Alpha. Presbyn. Clubs: Rotary, Torch (Durham). Author: (with C.J. Hogue) Douglas Fir Use Book, 1930; Forest Dendrology, 1933; (with J.G. Harrar) Guide to Southern Trees, 1946, rev. edit., 1962; (with others) Forest Products, 1950; (with W.M. Harlow) Textbook of Dendrology, rev. edit., 1968; Hough Encyclopedia of American Woods, Vols. I-VII, 1957—. Contbr. Ency. Brit., also sci. and profl. jours. Home: 2228 Cranford Rd Durham NC 27706

HARRAR, HELEN JOANNE, librarian; b. Seattle, May 9, 1935; d. Ellwood Scott and Marion (Green) Harrar; B.A. Oberlin Coll., 1957; M.L.S., Rutgers—The State U., 1960, Ph.D., 1962. Student asst. Duke Univ. Library, summers 1951-55, Oberlin Coll. Library, 1953-57; asst. Duke U. library, 1957-58; research asst., then instr. library service Grad. Sch. Library Service, Rutgers—The State U., 1958-60, research asso., 1960-61; research asst., then asst. to dir. Columbia U. Library, 1961-63; librarian, prof. library sci. Winthrop Coll., Rock Hill, S.C., 1963-71; asso. dir. libraries U. Ga., Athens, 1971—. Mem. adv. com. on library research and tng. projects U.S. Office of Edn., 1968-71. Mem. Am., S.C., N.C., Southeastern library assns., Am. Assn. U. Women, Beta Phi Mu. Republican. Home: 620 Hill St Athens GA 30601

HARRAR, J. GEORGE, found. exec.; b. Painesville, O., Dec. 2, 1906; s. F.S. and Lucetta (Sterner) H.; A.B. Oberlin Coll.; 1928, LL.D. (hon.), 1962, M.S., Ia. State Coll., 1929; Ph.D., U. Minn., 1935; LL.D., U. Cal., 1963, U. Neb., 1969; D.Sc., U. Fla., 1964, W.Va. U., 1964, Ohio State U., 1964, Emory U., 1966, Clemson (S.C.) U., 1967, U. Ill., 1968, U. Ariz., 1968, U. State U., 1971, Columbia, 1971; D.Sc., Rockefeller U., 1968, Washington U., 1969; Dr. honoris causa, Central U., Quito, 1966, U. Andes, Colombia, 1966; m. Georgetta Steese, Jan. 193O; children—Cynthia Ann (Mrs. Alvin Wilson) Georgetta Louise (Mrs. David T. Denhardt). Prof. botany Coll. of Agr., U. P.R. 1929-3O, chmn. dept., 1930-33; instr. plant pathology U. Minn., 1934-35; prof. biology Va. Polytech. Inst., 1935-41; chmn. dept. plant pathology Wash. State Coll., 1941-42; dep. dir. agr. div. natural sciences and agr. Rockefeller Found., 1952-55, dir. for agr., 1955-59, v.p., 1959-61, pres., 1961—. Dir. Campbell Soup Co., Internat. Flavors & Fragrances, Inc. Trustee Gen. Edn. Bd., 1960-61, pres., 1961; mem. Pres.'s Gen. Adv. Com. on Fgn. Assistance, 1965-69. Pub. trustee Nutrition Found., N.Y.C.; bd. trustees The Found. Center, 1969—; nat. adv. council Monell Chem. Senses Center, U.Pa., 1968—; vis. com. Harvard Med. Sch. and Sch. Dental Medicine, 1967—; trustee Oberlin Coll. Recipient Certificate of Merit for service to agr. U. Fla., 1950; Medal Agrl. Merit, Coll. Agr., Saltillo, Mexico; Medal Agrl. Merit, Govt. Mex., 1952; Cruz de Boyaca, Govt. Republic Colombia, 1954; Chilean Order of Merit, 1958; Pub. Welfare medal Nat. Acad. Scis., 1963; Order Golden Heart (Govt. Philippines), 1964; Outstanding Achievement award U. Minn., 1953, Elvin Charles Stakman award, 1969; Citation of Merit, U. Ariz., 1960; citations from several Latin Am. govts.; Distinguished Achievement citation Ia. State U., 1970; Edward A. Browning award Am. Soc. Agronomy, 1971. Fellow A.A.A.S., Am. Phytopath. Soc.; mem. Am. Mycol. Soc., Am. Acad. Arts and Scis., Nat. Acad. Scis, (com. Sci. and pub. policy 1967—), Am. Philos. Soc., Italian Nat. Acad. of Agr. Clubs: Westchester Country; Century Assn. (N.Y.C.); Cosmos (Washington). Author: (with E.S. Harrar) Guide to Southern Trees, 1945; (with E. C. Stakman) Principles of Plant Pathology, 1957; Strategy for the Conquest of Hunger, rev. edit., 1967. Editorial adv. bd. Ency. Britannica Sci. yearbook, 1967- 71. Contbr. publs. in fields phytopathology and mycology. Home: 125 Puritan Dr Scarsdale NY 10583 Office: 111 W 50th St New York City NY 10020

HARRELL, BEN. army officer; b. Medford, Ore., Mar. 15, 1911; s. Joe E. and Mamie Bell (McClain) H.; B.S., U.S. Mil. Acad., 1933; grad. Inf. Sch., 1940, Nat. War Coll., 1952; m. Harriet Campbell, Sept. 6, 1933; children—Hunter C., Charles J. Commd 2d lt. U.S. Army, 1933, advanced through grades to gen., 1968; comdr. inf. combat troops, war operations planner MTO, ETO, World War II; asst. dir. tng., acad. dept. Inf. Sch., Ft. Benning, Ga., 1945-46, dir. combat requirements sect., 1946, comdg. Officer 37th Inf. Regt., 1946-47, chief, then chmn. operations tng. com., gen. subjects sect., 1947-48, 49; asst. chief staff Hdqrs. 11th Airborne Div., Ft. Campbell, Ky., 1949; comdg. officer 511th Airbone Div., 1949- 50; chief staff 11th Airbone Div., 1950-51; operations and tng. officer SHAPE, Marley, France, 1952-53; comdg. officer 6th Inf. Regt., Europe, 1953-54; chief staff U.S. Comdr., Berlin, 1954-55; exec. officer Office Sec. Army, Washington, 1955-56; chief inf. br., career mgmt. div. Office Adj. Gen., Washington, 1956-58, officers assignment div., 1958; asst. div. combr. 7th Inf. Div., comdg. gen 7th Inf. Brigade, Korea, 1958-59; asst. dep. chief staff for operations, plans and tng. Hdqrs. U.S. Continental Army Command, Ft. Monroe, Va., 1959-60, dep. chief staff, 1960; comdg. gen. 101st Airborne Div., Ft. Campbell, Ky., 1960-61; comdg. gen. Inf. Center, Benning, Ga., 1961-63; asst. chief staff for force devel. Dept. Army, 1963-65; comdg. gen. U.S. Army Combat Devel. Command, 1965-67; comdg. gen. 6th U.S. Army, 1967- 68; comdr. Allied Land Forces Southeastern Europe, 1968—. Decorated D.S.M. with cluster, Legion Merit with two clusters, Silver Star, Bronze Star with cluster (U.S.); Golden Cross of Merit with swords (Poland); Croix de Guerre (France); Fourragere; Cross of Italy, Crown of Italy; Order Brit. Empire; War Medal (Brazil). Home: 879 Mithat Pasa Izmir Turkey Office: Army Element Allied Land Forces Southeastern Europe APO NY 09224

HARRELL, DAVID EDWIN, Jr., educator; b. Jacksonville, Fla., Feb. 22, 1930; s. David Edwin and Marilyn Mildred (Lee) H.; B.A., David Lipscomb Coll., 1954; M.A., Vanderbilt U., 1958, Ph.D., 1962; m. Adelia Francis Roberts, Sept. 5, 1955; children—Mildred Susan, David Edwin III, Elinor Elizabeth, Marilyn Lee, Harold Robert. Asst. prof. E. Tenn. State U., 1961-64, asso, prof., 1964-66; asso. prof. U. Okla., 1966-67; asso. prof. U. Ga., 1967-70; prof., chmn. dept. history U. Ala. at Birmingham, 1970—. Recipient author's awards for best articles E. Tenn. Hist. Soc., 1966, Mo. Hist. Soc., 1969. Mem. Am.

Hist. Assn., Orgn. Am. Historians, So. Hist. Assn., Am. Soc. Church History, Disciples of Christ Hist. Soc. (trustee), Am. Studies Assn., Cath. Hist. Soc. Author: Quest for a Christian America, 1966; White Sects and Black Men in the Recent South, 1971. Contbr. articles profl. jours. Home: 4225 Old Leeds Lane Birmingham AL 35213

HARRELL, EVANS MALOTT, investment cons.; b. Indpls., Aug. 20, 1926; s. Samuel Runnels and Mary Robertson (Evans) H.; grad. Groton Sch., 1944; A.B., U. Pa., 1948; m. Mary Edith Guckes, Feb. 7, 1948; children—Margaret Scott, Evans Malott II, Martha Wilder, Mary Runnels. With Acme-Evans Co., Indpls., 1947-58, Cleve. Grain Co., Inc., Indpls., 1947-58, Acme-Goodrich, Inc., Indpls., 1947-58; with Early & Daniel Co., Cin., 1958-68, exec. v.p., 1960-63, sec.-treas., 1960-63, pres., treas., 1963-68; pres. Gt. Southeast Corp., Atlanta, 1968-71, also dir.; dir. Dextra Corp.; chmn. bd. dir. Gen. Grain, Inc., Indpls.; dir. Wainwright Bank & Trust Co., Noblesville, Ind. Former mem. Indpls., Cin. and Chgo. boards of trade. Served with USNR, 1944-47. Mem. Am. Legion (past post comdr.), Nat. Thistle Class Assn. (past pres.), Am. Feed Mfrs. Assn., Grain and Feed Dealers Nat. Assn., Young President's Orgn., Delta Tau Delta. Episcopalian. Mason (Shriner). Clubs: Indpls. Athletic, Players, Dramatic (Indpls.); Cowan Lake Sailing Assn. (past commodore), Queen City (Cin.), Lake Lanier Sailing. Home: 2836 Ridgewood Rd NW Atlanta GA 30327 Office: First Fed Bldg Atlanta GA 30303

HARRELL, EVERETT RICHARD, Jr., physician; b. Checotah, Okla., Apr. 5, 1922; s. Everett Richard and Golden (Duncan) H.; student Ohio Wesleyan U., summer 1942; M.D., Duke, 1946; m. Ann McSwain, Oct. 17, 1947; children—Katherine R., Patricia A., Carolyn L., Na cy W. Intern Duke U. Hosp., 1946-47; resident dermatology U. Mich. Med. Center, 1949-52, instr. dermatology, 1952-53, asst. prof., 1953-56, asso. prof., 1956-60, prof., 1960-67, prof., chmn. dept. dermatology, 1967—; practice medicine, specializing in dermatology, Ann Arbor, Mich., 1952—. Served to lt. USNR, 1947-49. Mem. Am. Acad. Darmatology (bd. dirs.) A.M.A. (sec. sect. on dermatology), Detroit Dermatol. Soc. (pres.), Sigma Xi, Alpha Omega Alpha, Sigma Alpha Epsilon, Phi Chi. Contbr. articles profl. jours. Home: 3076 Geddes Av Ann Arbor MI 48104

HARRELL, GEORGE FOSTER, architect; b. Norfolk, Va., Aug. 29, 1906; B.Arch., Ga. Inst. Tech., 1930; M.Arch. (Paul Cret fellow 1930), U. Pa., 1931. Practice as George F. Harrell, N.Y.C. and Dallas, later Gill & Harrell, Dallas; with Harrel & Hamilton, Dallas, 1956—; prin. works include U.S. Steel Bldg., N.Y. World's Fair, 1939, Ouachita Nat. Bank&Parking Structure, Monroe, La., 1958, Temco Gen. Office Bldg.&Eng. Center, Garland, Tex., 1958, Petroleum Bldg., Am. Center, Beaumont, 1959, Republic Nat. Motor Bank, Dallas, 1960, 2300 Riverside Apts., Tulsa, 1961, Am. Nat. Bank, Beaumont, 1961, Republic Nat. Bank Tower, 1964, North-Park Shopping Center, Dallas, 1965. Mem. Dallas Rehab. Com.; dir. Greater DAllas Plan Council. Trustee Dallas Mus. Fine Arts. Served with USNR, 1942-45. Recipient div. prizes Libby-Owens-Ford Modernize Main Street competition; award Tex. Soc. Architects, 1950, 63, 64, A.I.A., 1963. Fellow A.I.A. (pres. 1958 Dallas, regional dir. 1966-69); mem. Tex. Soc. Architects (dir. 1961-63, pres. 1965); Tex. Research League (dir.). Home: 3840 Turtle Creek Dr Dallas TX 75219 Office: Republic Bank Bldg TX 75201

HARRELL, GEORGE THOMAS, Jr., physician; b. Washington, June 16, 1908; s. George Thomas and Anna (Muhlenberg) H.; A.B., Duke, 1932, M.D., 1936; student tropical medicine Army Med. Sch., 1943; m. Janet Elliott Griffin, June 18, 1937; children— George Thomas III, Robert Griffin. Intern medicine and pathology, asst. resident and resident medicine Duke Hosp., 1936-41; with Bowman Gray Sch. Medicine, 1941-54; dean Coll. Medicine, prof. medicine U. Fla. Med. Sch., 1954-64; dean Coll. Medicine, Pa. State U., dir. Hershey Med. Center, 1964—. Mem. Phi Beta Kappa, Alpha Omega Alpha. Episcopalian Editorial bd. Medicine, 1947—. Home: 1141 Cocoa Av Hershey PA 17033 Office: Hershey Med Center Hershey PA 17033

HARRELL, JAMES, textile mfg. exec.; b. San Saba, Tex., Sept. 29, 1911; s. Joab B. and Zula A. (Brazil) H.; B.S., Tex. Technol. Coll., 1935; m. Margaret Tillotson, Oct. 8, 1937; children—Katherine Tillotson, James, Margaret. Joined J.P. Stevens & Co., Inc., 1947; v.p., 1949-68, dir., 1961—, mem. exec. com., 1962—, vice chmn., 1964, officer in charge cotton div., 1961-68, exec. v.p. in charge mfg., 1968—, chmn. mfg. adv. com., 1967—; gen bd. dirs., adv. bd. dirs. Greenville br. Citizens & So. Nat. Bank S.C. Trustee J.E. Sirrine Found. Mem. S.C. Textile Mfrs. Assn. (pres. 1965-66, dir., exec. com.), Nat. Phi Psi. Methodist. Home: 215 McDaniel Av Greenville SC 29601 Office: Daniel Bldg Greenville SC 29602 also 1185 Av of Ams New York City NY

HARRELL, MORRIS, lawyer; b. Grandview, Tex., Apr. 16, 1920; s. Oscar Martin and Mozelle (Morris) H.; B.B.A., LL.B., Baylor U., 1942; m. Rhoda Burks Baylor, Dec. 5, 1943; children—James Byron, Julia Marye, Rhoda Baylor. Admitted to Tex. bar, 1942; pvt. practice, Dallas, 1946-47; asst. U.S. atty. No. Dist. Tex., 1947-51; pvt. practice, Dallas, 1951-55; trial atty. firm Thompson, Knight, Wright & Simmons, Dallas, 1955-65; trial atty., partner Rain, Harrell & Emery, 1965—. Research fellow Southwestern Legal Found. Served to lt. USNR, 1942-46; PTO. Fellow Tex. Bar Found. (dir.); mem. Am., Dallas (pres. 1962) bar assns., State Bar Tex. (dir.), Am. 6629 Golf Dr Dallas TX 75205 Office: Republic Nat Bank Tower Dallas TX 75201

HARRELL, SAMUEL RUNNELS; b. Noblesville, Ind., Nov. 25, 1897; s. Samuel and Vivian (Voss) H.; B.S. in Econ., U. Pa., 1919; LL.B., Yale Law Sch., 1924; m. Mary Robertson Evans, Oct. 10, 1925; children—Evans Malott, Mary Eleanor, Samuel Macy. With Land Title & Trust Co., Phila.; admitted to Ind. bar, 1922; chmn exec. com., chmn. bd. Gen. Grain, Inc.; pres. Acme Evans Co., Inc. 1945-49, chmn. bd., 1954—; pres. Acme Goodrich, Inc., 1947-52, chmn. bd., chmn. exec. com., 1952-58; chmn. exec. com., dir. Early & Daniel Co., Cin., 1946—, also chmn. bd.; dir. Cleve. Grain Co., 1950-58, pres., chmn. bd., 1955-58; pres., chmn. bd., dir. Tidewater Grain Co. Phila., dir. Pa. and Del. corps.; dir. Nat. Terminal Elevator Assn., Indpls. Union Ry. Co.; adv. com. Union Fed. Savs. & Loan Assn. Chmn. bd. Indpls. Bd. Trade; mem. citizens com. Hoover Commn. chmn. Ind. Adv. Com. on Commerce, Industry, Agr. Pub. Relations; mem. adv. com. U.S. Banking and Currency Com. Trustee, chmn. Nat. Found. for Edn., Nat. Found. for Edn. in Am. Citizenship; trustee U. Pa., 1940-50, Wharton Sch. Finance and Commerce, 1940-54; mem. vis. com. Harvard Grad. Sch. Edn., 1941-56; exec. council, nat. treas. Am. Heart Assn., 1947-48; founder Ind. Heart Found., Sagamores of Wabash. Mem. Ind. Millers Assn. (pres.), Am. Bar Assn., Am. Econ. Assn., Am. Polit. Sci. Assn., Acad. Polit. Sci., Am. Acad. Polit. and Social Sci., Am. Soc. Pub. Adminstrn., S.R., S.A.R., Delta Tau Delta, Phi Delta Phi. Presbyn. Mason (32). Clubs: Racquet (Phila.); Harvard Faculty (Cambridge); University (Chgo., N.Y.C.); Contemporary, Athletic, Lawyers, Literary, Pioneer, Pennsylvania, Yale (Indpls.); Queen City (Cin.); Pendennis (Louisville, Ky.). Chmn., editor Nat. Found. Press. Publisher: Fundamental American Principles. Home: 5850 Sunset Lane Indianapolis IN 46208 Office: Valley Forge Farms Route 4 Noblesville IN 46060

HARRELL, THOMAS WILLARD, psychologist, educator; b. nr. West Point, Ga., Sept. 8, 1911; s. Thomas Gordon and Lura (Wallace) H.; A.B., U. Ga., 1932, M.S., 1933; Ph.D., Johns Hopkins, 1936; m. Margaret Louise Strong, May 30, 1941; children—Susan (Mrs. Kress), Thomas Strong. Successively instr., asst. prof., asso. prof. U. Ill., 1936-52; prof. applied psychology Stanford, 1952—; advt. research Roche-Williams & Cunnyngham, 1939-40; cons. behavior patterns for mgmt. potential. Mem. Cal. Psychology Exam. Com., 1959-67. Served from 2d lt. to lt. col., AUS, 1942-46. Fellow indsl. psychology Ga. Engring. Expt. Sta., 1937; Ford Found. faculty research fellow bus. and econs., 1958-59. Mem. Am., Western psychol. assns., Am. Assn. U. Profs., Phi Beta Kappa. Clubs: University (Palo Alto); Stanford University Faculty. Democrat. Author: Industrial Psychology, rev. ed., 1958; Managers' Performance and Personality, 1961; (with Rusmore) Casebook in Personnel and Industrial Psychology, 1958; (with others) The Accounting Process: A Program of Self-Instruction, 1963. Home: 466 La Prenda Rd Los Altos CA 94022 Office: Stanford U Stanford CA 94305

HARRELL, WILLIAM BURRUSS, ret. ednl. adminstr.; b. Hyde County, N.C., June 2, 1897; s. Lafayette and Alice Maude (Mathias) H.; B.A., U. N.C., 1921; M.A., U. Chgo., 1925; m. Valeria Smith, May 26, 1927. Instr. econs. U. N.C., 1922-24; asst. comptroller U. Chgo., 1925-28; sec., comptroller Julius Rosenwald Fund, 1928-29; asst. to bus. mgr. U. Chgo., 1929-33, asst. bus. mgr., 1933-38, bus. mgr., 1938-53, v.p. bus. affairs, 1953-62, v.p. spl. projects, 1962- 68, v.p. emeritus, 1968—. Served with U.S. Army, 1918-19. Club: Quadrangle (Chgo.). Home: 5801 Dorchester Av Chicago IL 60637 Office: 5801 S Ellis Av Chicago IL 60637

HARRELSON, ALLEN MCRAE, Jr., corp. exec.; b. St. Louis, Apr. 14, 1913; s. Allen McRae and Margie (McAllum) H.; A.B. in English cum laude, Washington and Lee U., 1935; m. Caroline F. Costello, Oct. 28, 1944; children—Sandra Lee, Marcia McAllum (Mrs. Dale Dietz), Joanne McRae, Allen McRae III, Gordon McAllum, David Lee. With Haskins & Sells, C.P.A.'s, Cin., 1936-42; supr. Peat, Marwick Mitchell & Co., C.P.A.'s, Pitts., 1947-51; controller Scaife Co., Oakmont, Pa., 1951-56; financial v.p., treas. H.K. Porter Co., Pitts., 1956-59; treas., chief financial officer Crane Co., N.Y.C., 1959-65; v.p. Bendix Corp, 1965-66, v.p., treas., 1966, v.p. finance, dir., 1966-69, exec. v.p. finance, 1969-71, also dir.; sr. v.p. finance Midland-Ross Corp., Cleve., 1971—. Served to lt. comdr. USNR, 1942-47. C.P.A., Ohio, Pa. Mem. Financial Execs. Inst., Am. Inst. C.P.A.'s, Am. Mgmt. Assn., Phi Beta Kappa, Delta Tau Delta. Presbyn. Clubs: Oakland Hills country; Economic (Detroit); Recess; Canadian (N.Y.C.). Home: 1585 Lone Pine Rd Bloomfield Hills MI 48013 Office: 55 Public Sq Cleveland OH 44113

HARRELSON, WALTER JOSEPH, educator, clergyman; b. Winnabow, N.C., Nov. 28, 1919; s. Isham Danvis and Mae (Rich) H.; student Mars Hill (N.C.) Coll., 1940-41; A.B., U. N.C., 1947; B.D., Union Theol. Sem., 1949, Th.D., 1953; postgrad. U. Basel (Switzerland), 1950-51, Harvard, 1951-53; m. Idella Aydlett, Sept. 20, 1942; children—Marianne, David Aydlett, Robert Joseph. Instr. philosophy U. N.C., 1947; ordained to ministry Baptist Ch., 1949; tutor asst., instr. Union Theol. Sem., 1949-50; prof. O.T., Andover Newton Theol. Sch., 1951-55; dean, asso. prof. O.T., U. Chgo. Div. Sch., 1955-60; prof. O.T., Div. Sch., Vanderbilt U., 1961—, chmn. grad. dept. religion, 1962-67, dean Divinity Sch., 1967—. Traveling fellow Union Theol. Sem., 1949; fellow Am. Council Learned Socs., 1950-51; exchange fellow U. Basel, 195O- 51; Fulbright research scholar, Rome, 1962-63. Mem. Nat. Council Religion in Higher Edn., Soc. Bibl. Lit., Am. Schs. Oriental Research, Chgo. Soc. Bibl. Research, Phi Beta Kappa. Author: Jeremiah, Prophet to the Nations, 1959; Interpreting the Old Testament, 1964; From Fertility Cult to Worship, 1969. Co-author, editor Teaching the Biblical Languages, 1967. Editor, contbr. Israel's Prophetic Heritage, 1962. Home: 305 Bowling Av Nashville TN 37205

HARRELSON, WILLIAM LOUIS, state ofcl.; b. Mullins, S.C., July 25, 1913; s. Maxey Clarence and Dora (Page) H.; student The Citadel, 1931-32; LL.B., U. S.C., 1937; m. Grace Hough, Mar. 29, 1956; children—Cynthia Page, William Louis. Admitted to S.C. bar; farmer, Mullins, 1932—; dir. Davis Nat. Bank, Mullins and Marion Broadcasting Co.; mem. S.C. Ho. of Reps., 1941-42, State Senate, 1953-55; commr. agr. State of S.C., 1956—. Chmn., S.C. Marketing Commn. Past pres. So. Assn. State Depts. Agr.; bd. dirs. Nat. Assn. State Depts. Agr., rep. So. region, 1971. Served with USCGR, 1942. Mem. S.C. Crop Improvement Assn., Farm Bur., Blue Key, Phi Delta Phi, Gamma Sigma Delta. Democrat. Presbyn. (elder). Mason. Home: 306 Wine St Mullins SC 29514 Office: Wade Hampton Bldg Columbia SC 29202

HARRER, GUSTAVE ADOLPHUS, librarian; b. Durham, N.C., Dec. 30, 1924; s. Gustave Adolphus and Florence Caroline (Wagner) H.; A.B., U. N.C., 1948, M.A., 1950, Ph.D. in Germanic Langs., 1953; M.S. in L.S., U. Ill., 1954; m. Elizabeth Varnado, Sept. 3, 1948; children—Elizabeth Ida, Kathryn Florence, Hugh, Thomas. Asst. prof. German and Latin, Millsaps Coll., 1949-51; asst. order librarian U. Tenn. Libraries, 1954-55, asso. order librarian, 1955-57; chief acquisition librarian Stanford Libraries, 1957-58, asst. dir. for central services, 1958-60; dir. libraries Boston U., 1960-68; chmn. dept. library sci., dir. libraries U. Fla., Gainesville, 1968—. Served with AUS, 1943-45. Faculty fellow Fund for Advancement Edn., 1951-52; Katherine L. Sharp fellow U. Ill. Library Sch., 1953-54; fellow Carnegie Project Advanced Library Adminstrn., Rutgers U., 1958. Mem. A.L.A. Contbr. articles to profl. jours. Home: 2815 NW 29th St Gainesville FL 32601 Office: Library West U Fla Gainesville FL 32601

HARRER, HEINRICH, geographer, author; b. Austria, July 6, 1912; s. Josef and Johanna (Penker) H.; student U. Graz, Austria, 1938; m. Charlotte Wegener, Dec. 24, 1938 (div. 1942); 1 son, Peter; m. 2d, Margaretta Truxa, Dec. 19, 1953; m. 3d, Katharina Haarhaus, Aug. 10, 1962. Member expdn. in first ascent of north wall of Ogre, Switzerland, 1938; mem. Himalayan Expdn., 1939; interned Brit. Internment Camp, India 1939; tutor to Dalai Lama, Lhasa, Tibet, 1944-51; mem. Himalayan Expdn., 1951, 64, Andes Expdn., 1953, Alaska Expdn., 1954, Belgian Congo, 1957, Netherlands, New Guinea, 1962, Malo Grono, 1967, Bushurproes of Surinam, 1967. Author: 7 Years in Tibet, 1952 (colour movie story shown Internat. Film Festival, Cannes and Edinburgh); The White Spider; Tibet is My Country, 1960; I Come from the Stone Age, 1964; Huka-Huka. Nat. amateur golf champion of Austria, 1958. Names prof. by pres. Austrian Republic, 1964. Home: Kitzbuhel Austria Office: Liechtenstein Verlag Vaduz Liechtenstein

HARRIES, LYNDON PRITCHARD, educator; b. Port Talbot, South Wales, Jan. 11, 1909; s. Harry Pritchard and Gwendolen (Hill) H.; M.A., St. Catherine's Coll., Oxford (Eng.) U., 1930; student Ely Theol. Coll., Cambridge, Eng., 1930-32; m. Jeanette Johnson, 1969. Came to U.S., 1964. Ordained to ministry, 1932; priest-missionary Univs. Mission Central Africa, 1935- 45; research tonal structure Kikuyu, Kenya, 1945-47; lectr. Sch. Oriental and African Studies, U. London, 1948-64; prof. African langs. and lit. U. Wis., 1964—, chmn. dept., 1967-70. Author: Survey of African Marriage and Family Life, 1958; Swahili Poetry, 1962; Swahili Prose Texts, 1963; Poems from Kenya, 1965. Home: 2238 Eton Ridge Madison WI 53705

HARRIFORD, WILLIE LLOYD, Jr., archivist; b. Kansas City, Kan., Jan. 19, 1935; s. Willie Lloyd and Thelma (Jones) H.; B.A., U. Kan., 1957; Archival certificate, Am. U., 1968; m. Fosteen Ward, June 1, 1961; 1 son, Willie Lloyd III. Archivist, Harry S. Truman Library, Independence, Mo., 1957-68; archivist Martin Luther King Library Documentation Project, Atlanta, 1968-69, asst. dir., 1969-70, acting dir., 1970—; lectr. Ga. State Archives, Fisk Inst. on Archivies. Served with U.S. Army, 1957-59. Ga. State Archivist. Mem. Soc. Am. Archivists, Alpha Phi Alpha. Home: 2843 Monica Ct SW Atlanta GA 30311 Office: 671 Beckwith St Atlanta GA 30314

HARRIGAN, ALICE ANNA, mem. Democrat Nat. Com.; b. Orwigsburg, Pa., Dec. 2, 1909; d. Clarence B. and Myrtle (Newhard) Brown; student Beckley Comml. Tchrs. Coll., 1929; B.A., Pa. State Coll., 1931; m. James F. Harrigan, Aug. 7, 1933; children—Alice Ann (Mrs. Charles Stedman), Patricia (Mrs. James Gallian), James Joseph. Comml. tchr., West Hazleton, Pa., 1929-33; tchr. Mt. Edgecumbe Vocational Sch., Sitka, Alaska, 1939-41; now pub. relations rep. Alaska Airlines. Active Dem. Party, 1933—; mem. Dem. Nat. Com. for Alaska, 1939—. Mem. exec. com. Alaska Centennial Commn.; mem. Gov.'s Adv. Com. Alaska Centennial; exec. sec. Alaska Day Festival Com.; bd. dirs. Sitka Visitor's Bur.; mem. Alaska Travel Adv. Bd. Club: Sitka Emblem (past pres.). Address: Cathedral Apts Sitka AK 99835

HARRIGAN, CORNELIUS HERBERT, Jr., journalist; b. Norristown, Pa., July 1, 1921; s. Cornelius Herbert and Bertha Lukens (McCurdy) H.; A.B., Dartmouth, 1943; M.S., Columbia, 1947; postgrad. Brown U., 1949, Richmond (Va.) Profl. Inst. 1951-52; m. Margaret Rowan, Apr. 19, 1950; stepchildren—Barbara Ann (Mrs. Donald Barton), Bruce D. Robinson, Carol Joanne (Mrs. David Alexander). Copy editor, editorial writer Providence Jour., 1947-54, Richmond News Leader, 1954-56; copy editor Phila. Inquirer, 1956-62, editorial writer, 1962—; lectr. journalism U. Pa., 1958-62. Served with AUS, World War II. Decorated Air medal with three oak leaf clusters; recipient Merit plaque Freedoms Found., 1967, 1969. Mem. Dartmouth Edn. Assn., Phila. Press Assn., Nat. Conf. Editorial Writers. Presbyn. Clubs: Pen and Pencil, Dartmouth (Phila.). Home: 629 Strath Haven Av Swarthmore PA 19081 Office: 400N Broad St Philadelphia PA 19101

HARRILL, ERNEST EUGENE, educator; b. Forest City, N.C., Aug. 14, 1917; s. Buron and Viola (Davis) H.; A.A., Mars Hill Jr. Coll., 1936; A.B., U. N.C., 1947, M.A., 1949, Ph.D., 1958; m. Mary Bell Clark, Dec. 18, 1949; children—David Lawson, Alice Gibbon. Claims examiner N.C. Unemployment Compensation Commn., 1937-41; asst. prof. polit. sci. Furman U., Greenville, S.C., 1949-58, asso. prof., 1958-61, prof., 1961—, former dean students. Pres. Summit Drive P.T.A. Mem. county exec. com. Democratic Party, Greenville. Served with USAAF, 1942-45. Mem. Phi Beta Kappa. Baptist. Club: Western Carolina Torch (pres.). Home: 112 Broughton Dr Greenville SC 29609

HARRIMAN, E. ROLAND, 0banker; b NYC Dec 24 1895; s. Edward Henry and Mary W. (Averell) H; grad. Groton Sch., 1913; A.B., Yale, 1917, LL.D., 1960; LL.D., Columbia U., 1955; m. Gladys C.C. Fries, Apr. 12, 1917; children—Elizabeth (dec.) Phyllis. Banking bus. N.Y.C., 1922—, partner Brown Brothers Harriman & Co.; chmn bd. U.P. R.R., 1946-69, hon. chmn., 1969—; hon. chmn. Union Pacific Corp.; dir. Centennial Ins. Co.; trustee Atlantic Mut. Ins. Co., Mut. Life Ins. Co. N.Y. Chmn. Am. Nat. Red Cross; chmn. Boys Club N.Y.; hon. trustee Am. Mus. Natural History; corp. mem. Presbyn. Hosp., N.Y. Served as lt. Ordnance Dept., World War I. Republican. Episcopalian. Clubs: Yale, University, Racquet and Tennis, Links, Tuxedo. Home: NY 10910 Office: 59 Wall St New York City NY 10005

HARRIMAN, EDWARD EUGENE, govt. ofcl.; b. Berwick, Me., June 14, 1921; s. Kirk Eugene and Annie (McKay) H.; B.S. in Mech. Engring., U. N.H., 1944; postgrad. student Cath. U. Am., 1947-56; M.S., U. N.H., 1950; M.S. in Indsl. Mgmt. (Sloan fellow), Mass. Inst. Tech., 1957; m. Jean C. Buescher, June 11, 1949; children—Linda Lee, Robert Kirk. Engr. research and devel. labs., Ft. Belvoir, Va., 1946-50; engr. research and development div. Bur. Ordnance, U.S. Navy Dept., 1950-58; sci. adviser to dir. guided missles, exec. sec. to sci. adv. com. officer Sec. Def., 1958-59; chief satellite br., advanced research projects agy. Office of Sec. Def., 1959-61; dir. Office of Research and Engring., Post Office Dept., 1961-66; dir. tech. service Housing and Urban Devel., 1966-67; dir. policy devel. Dept. Health, Edn. and Welfare, 1967—. Active civil orgns. Served with C.E., AUS, 1943-46. Recipient Superior Accomplishment award U.S. Govt., 1956. Registered profl. engr., Me., D.C. Mem. Assn. Engrs. and Scis. Bur. Ordnance, Am. Rocket Soc., Am. Soc. M.E., Citizens Assn. Wellington Heights. Home: 7613 Holiday Dr Wellington Heights Alexandria VA 22308 Office: Dept Health Edn and Welfare Washington DC 20202

HARRIMAN, SIR GEORGE WILLIAM, industralist; b. Coventry, Eng., Mar. 3, 1908. With Austin Motor Co., 1940-52, dep. chmn. bd. 1952; with Brit. Motor Corp., 1952—, dep chmn., joint mng. dir., 1956-58, chmn., mng. dir., 1961-66; chmn. Brit. Motor Holdings, Ltd., 1966-68; chmn., pres. Brit. Leyland Motor Corp., Ltd., 1968—. Decorated companion Order Brit. Empire. Home: The Dial House Heronfield Knolle Solihull Warickshire England Office: Brit Leyland Motor Corp Ltd Lonebridge Birmingham England

HARRIMAN, GERALD EUGENE, educator; b. Dell Rapids, S.D., May 30, 1924; s. Roy L. and Margaret (Schrantz) H.; B.S., U. Notre Dame, 1947; A.M., U. S.D., 1949; Ph.D., U. Cin., 1957; m. Eileen Bernadine Bensman, June 10, 1950; children—G. Peter, Mary K., Margaret C., Elizabeth A. Expediter, Minn. Mining & Mfg. Co., 1947-48; from instr. to asst. dean, chmn. dept. bus. adminstrn. and finance Xavier U., 1949-66; prof. bus. adminstrn., chmn. div. bus. and econs. Ind. U., South Bend, 1966—. Vis. prof. finance U. S.D., 1962; cons. in field. Mem. citizens adv. council long range financial planning Council of City Cin., 1963. Served with USNR, 1942-45. Mem. Am. Econs. Assn., Am. Finance Assn. Home: 16600 Gerald St Granger IN 46530 Office: 1825 Northside Blvd South Bend IN 46615

HARRIMAN, JOHN WALTER, economist, educator; b. Providence, July 8, 1898; s. John W. and Mary (Jones) H.; Ph.B., Brown U., 1920; M.B.A., Harvard, 1925, D.C.S., 1932; M.A., Dartmouth, 1938; m. Ingeborg Sophie Rathe, Oct. 12, 1945; children—Mary (Mrs. Robert C. Young), Joan (Mrs. John C. Watson). Mem. faculty Grinnell Coll., also U. Rochester, 1925-28; head research dept. Russell, Berg & Co., Boston, also instr. bank mgmt. Harvard Bus. Sch., 1928-32; prof. finance Dartmouth, 1932-46; prof. bus. adminstrn. Syracuse U., 1946-53, dean Bus. Sch., 1950, Grad. Sch., 1952; prof. finance N.Y. U. Grad. Sch. Bus. Adminstrn., 1953-64, prof. emeritus, 1964—, vice dean, 1953—; research cons. J.R. Williston & Co., 1955-57; economist Union Service Corp. (Tri-Continental Corp. and Union Service Funds), 1958-68; dir. Atlantic Bank N.Y., Guardian Park Fund; cons. Whitney Goadby, Robert

Smith, Inc. Head priorities specialist OPM and WPB, Washington, 1941-42; fgn. service officer ECA and Mut. Security Adminstrn., Washington, Paris, London, Belgrade, 1949-52, dep. chief mission to U.K., 1950-51. Served from capt. to col. USAAF, SHAEF, 1942-46. Mem. Am. Finance Assn., N.Y. Soc. Security Analysts, Phi Beta Kappa, Delta Upsilon, Beta Gamma Sigma. Conglist. Club: N.Y. University. Home: 37 Washington Sq W New York City NY 10011 Office: 100 Trinity Pl New York City NY 10006

HARRIMAN, LEWIS GILDERSLEEVE, banker; b. Windsor, Conn., Mar. 24, 1889; s. Frederick W. and Cora Elizabeth (Jarvis) H.; B.S., Trinity Coll., 1909, M.S., 1917, sr. fellow; spl. courses N.Y.U.; LL.D., Trinity Coll., 1954, Alfred U., 1960; m. Grace Bastline, June 24, 1915; children—Lewis G., William B., John H., Thomas J., Elizabeth; m. 2d, Louise children—Joan Oct. 11, 1939; children-Joan B., Ann L. Engr., Am. Creosoting Co., Louisville, 1909-11; engr., elec. Am. Real Estate Co., N.Y.C., 1912-15; with Coggeshall & Hicks, and Merrill, Lynch & Co., both mems. N.Y. Stock Exchange, later asst. trust officer and investment trust officer Guaranty Trust Co., N.Y.C., until 1919; v.p. Fidelty Trust Co. of Buffalo, 1919-23, pres., 1924-25; pres. Mfrs. and Traders Trust Co., 1925-54, chmn. bd., 1954-64, hon. chmn., 1964—; hon. chmn. M. & T. Discount Corp.; vice chmn. Morgan N.Y. State Corp.; dir. Buffalo City Cemetery, 1929-64, pres., 1958- 64, hon. dir., 1964—; mem. adv. com. N.Y. Agy. R.F.C., 1932-54. Mem. Victory Fund Com. and War Finance Com., 2d Fed. Res. Dist.; chmn. Victory Fund Com., Group I; co-chmn. War Finance Com., Group I; mem. Buffalo War Council. Mem. 9th C.A., N.Y. N.G., 1917-18. Lectr. on finance N.Y.U. Sch. of Commerce, 1917, 18. Pres. Buffalo Clearing House, 1926, 30, 32, 34, 36, 38, 43, 45, 48, 51, Buffalo C. of C., 1927, 28; a founder, v.p. Nat. Better Bus. Bur., 1926-29, Buffalo Better Bus. Bur., 1923-34; treas. Buffalo chpt. A.R.C., 1924-41, chmn., 1941-45; Buffalo treas. U.S.O.; mem. Buffalo Council on World Affairs; a founder Citizens Appeal Rev. Com., chmn., 1955-58. Republican presdl. elector for N.Y., 1956. Chmn. U. Buffalo Found., 1962-64; mem. citizens bd. U. Miami; trustee Trinity Coll., 1927-31, Buffalo Sem., 1925-27; trustee U. Buffalo, 1943-62, vice chmn., 1955-62; trustee Nichols Sch., 1928-48, Joint Charities and Community Fund; chmn. United War and Community Fund, 1942-44; an original incorporator Community Chest of Buffalo, Erie County; fellow in perpetuating Buffalo Fine Arts Acad.; bd. dirs. Buffalo Hist. Soc., Buffalo Philharmonic Orch., 1943-48, Buffalo Conv. and Tourist Bur. (founder), Niagara Frontier Planning Assn.; governing com. Buffalo Found. Named Man of Year, U. Buffalo Sch. Bus., 1954; recipient 4th Ann. Brotherhood citation Nat. Conf. Christians and Jews, 1956, Walter P. Cooke award U. Buffalo. Mem. Buffalo Soc. Natural Scis. (hon. life), Res. City Bankers Assn., Soc. Mayflower Descs., S.R., Newcomen Soc., Cult of White Buffalo (hon.), Psi Upsilon. Republican. Episcopalian (mem. exec. council Diocese N.Y. 1924-26, 32-34). Mason (33). Clubs: Buffalo (pres. 1933); Buffalo Country Thursday (Buffalo); Cherry Hill Golf, University (N.Y.C.); Riviera Country (Coral Gables). Home: 5400 SW 98th Terrace Miami FL 33156 Office: Mfrs & Trader Trust Co Buffalo NY 14202

HARRIMAN, RAYMOND DAVIS, educator; b. Grinnell. Ia., June 6, 1888; s. Augustus Chase and Kate Miles (Davis) H.; A.B., Grinnell Coll., 1909, L.H.D., 1959; A.M., U. Wis., 1914. Ph.D., 1914; fellow Am. Acad. in Rome, 1915-16; m. Mary Ruth Martin, Sept. 11, 1918; children— John Martin, Joan Martin. Tchr., Muscatine (Ia.) High Sch., 1909-12; fellow in Latin, U. Wis., 1913-14, asst. in ancient history, 1914-15; instr. ancient langs. U. Utah, 1917-22, asst. prof., 1922-28, asso. prof., 1926-28, also acting dean men; vis. lectr. ancient history U. Wis., 1926; vis. asso. prof. Latin, U. Chgo., summer 1927; asso. prof. classics Stanford, 1928-34, prof., 1934-53, emeritus, 1953—, exec. head dept., 1937-53, chmn. Sch. Letters, 1940-42, chmn. Sch. Humanities, 1941-42, acting dean, 1947-48; vis. prof. classics U. Wash., 1953-54; civilian edn. adviser, spl. tng. and reclassification Unit 3903, 1943 (also coordinator Army spl. tng. unit 3905); also coordinator mil. programs, 1946. Mem. Am. Philol. Assn., Philol. Assn. Pacific Coast (pres. 1945,), Classical Assn. Pacific Coast (pres. 1931), Am. Assn. U. Profs., Phi Beta Kappa, Phi Kappa Phi, Alpha Kappa Lambda. Home: 135 Riviera Dr Los Gatos CA 95030

HARRIMAN, WILLIAM AVERELL, former govt. ofcl.; b. Nov. 15, 1891; s. Edward Henry and Mary (Averell) H.; B.A., Yale, 1913; m. Kitty Lanier Lawrence, Sept. 21, 1915; children—Mary (Mrs. Shirley C. Fisk), Kathleen (Mrs. Stanley C. Mortimer, Jr.); m. 2d, Mrs. Marie Norton Whitney, Feb. 21, 1930 (dec. Sept. 1970). Vice Pres. purchase and supplies Union Pacific R.R., 1915- 17; chmn. bd., 1932-46; chmn. bd. Mcht. Shipbldg. Corp., 1917-25, W.A. Harriman & Co., Inc., 1920-31; partner Brown Bros. Harriman & Co. (merger), 1931-46, ltd. partner, 1946—; chmn. exec. com. Ill. Central R.R. Co., 1931-42, dir. 1915-46. Adminstr. Div. II, N.R.A. 1934, spl. asst. adminstr., 1934, adminstrv. officer, 1934-35; mem. bus. adv. council Dept. Commerce, 1933, chmn., 1937-39; chief materials br. prodn. div., O.P.M., 1941; spl. rep. of Pres. in Gt. Britain with rank of minister, 1941, to USSR (chmn. mission), rank of ambassador, 1941; apptd. rep.in London of Combined Shipping Adjustment Bd., 1942; apptd. mem. London Combined Prodn. and Resources Bd., 1942; U.S. ambassador to Russia, 1943-46, to Gt. Britain, 1946; sec. of commerce, 1946-48; U.S. rep. in Europe under Econ. Coop. Act of 1948, rank of A.E. and P., 1948-50; spl. asst. to Pres., 1950-51; Am. rep. on com. to study Western def. plans NATO, 1951; dir. Mut. Security Agy., 1951-53; gov. N.Y., 1955-58; ambassador-at- large, 1961, 65-68; asst. sec. of state for Far Eastern affairs, 1961-63; under sec. of state polit. affairs, 1963-65; personal rep. of Pres. to conversations on Vietnam in Paris, 1968-69. Author: Peace with Russia?, 1959; America and Russia in a Changing World, 1971. Home: 3038 N St Washington DC 20007

HARRINGTON, CURTIS, motion picture dir.; b. Los Angeles, Sept. 17, 1928; s. Raymond Stephen and Isabel (Dorum) H.; B.A., U. So. Cal., 1947; postgrad. U. Cal. at Los Angeles, 1948-49. Asso. producer Jerry Wald Prodns., 20th Century Fox Corp., 1958-62; prodns. include Hound Dog Man, 1959, Return to Peyton Place, 1962, The Stripper, 1963; dir., author original screen play Night Tide, 1963; USIA documentary The Four Elements, 1965; co- author original story, dir. Games, 1967; short exptl. films include Fragment of Seeking, 1946, Picnic, 1948, On the Edge, 1949, The Assignation, 1953, The Wormwood Star, 1957. Mem. Count Dracula Soc. (dir.), Acad. Motion Picture Arts and Scis., Dirs. Guild Am. Democrat. Episcopalian. Author: An Index to the Films of Josef Von Sternberg, 1948. Office: care Universal Pictures Universal City CA 91608

HARRINGTON, DONALD DECOURSEY, investment co. exec.; b. Edinburg, Ill., Sept. 26, 1899; s. James R. and Gertrude (Brownback) H.; B.A., Washington U., St. Louis, 1917; m. Sybil Buckingham, Dec. 7, 1935; 1 dau., Sally (Mrs. Robert Goldwater). With Standard Oil Co., N.J., 1919-22, Marland Oil Co., 1922-26; sr. partner Harrington & Marsh, Amarillo, Tex., 1926—; dir. Am. Marine Corp., Ins. Securities Inc., Sea Drilling Corp., Southwestern Pub. Service Co. Chmn. Don and Sybil Harrington Found.; co-chmn. Amarillo Area Found. Clubs: Brook (N.Y.C.); Travellers (Paris, France). Home: 1600 Polk St Amarillo TX 79102 Office: First Nat Bank Bldg Amarillo TX 79101

HARRINGTON, EMMETT STEPHEN, accountant; b. Stevensville, Mont., Dec. 19, 1908; s. Jeremiah P. and Anna (O'Neill) H.; B.A., U. Wash., 1930; m. Lillian Alvestad, Sept. 7, 1940; children—Patricia A. (Mrs. Ronald M. Chuka), Therese M. Partner Haskins & Sells, C.P.A.'s, N.Y.C. Mem. Accounting Principles Bd. Served to lt. comdr. USNR. 1942-46. Clubs: Spyglass Hill Golf (Pebble Beach, Cal.); Harbor View, Metropolitan (N.Y.C.); Rainier, Seattle Golf (Seattle); Greenwich Country, Stanwich (Greenwich, Conn.). Home: Dingletown Rd Greenwich CT 06830 Office: 2 Broadway New York City NY 10004

HARRINGTON, FRANK GOODWIN, ins. co. exec.; b. Baldwinsville, N.Y., Dec. 31, 1913; s. Frank Goodwin and Florence (Kendrick) H.; student U. Buffalo, 1933-37; m. Jeanne M. Higgins, Apr. 30, 1941; children—Michael Goodwin, Richard Beaudoin. With Flack Advt. Agy., Syracuse, N.Y., 1937-40; sales promotion mgr. Sta. WSYR, Syracuse, 1940-42; with Curtis Pub. Co., Phila., 1945-51; sr. v.p. Ins. Co. N.Am., Phila., 1951—; v.p. INA Corp., 1969—. Chmn. Ins. Information Inst., N.Y.C., 1969-70. Pres., bd. dirs. Nat. Council on Alcoholism; Mem. Gov.'s Blue Ribbon Ins. Com., 1969—, mem. Gov.'s Adv. Council on Alcoholism, 1969—; mem. Dist. Atty's com. on Alcoholism and Drug Addiction, 1969—. Bd. dirs., trustee Boy Scouts Am., Vol. Service for Blind, CARE, Inc., United Fund Phila., U. Buffalo Found. Served with USMCR, 1942-45. Roman Catholic. Home: 323 West Av Wayne PA 19087 Office: 1600 Arch St Philadelphia PA 19101

HARRINGTON, FRANK LEIGHTON, ret ins. exec.; b. Worcester, Mass., Jan. 17, 1902; s. Frank Chester and Leora (Leighton) H.; grad. Phillips Exeter Acad., 1920; A.B., Dartmouth, 1924, M.A. (hon.); J.D., Harvard, 1927; LL.D., Assumption Coll., 1968; m. Louise Cronin, July 9, 1927; children— Frank Leighton, Roxanna (Mrs. John M. Stevenson), Thomas Barth, George Chester. With Mass. Protective Assn., Inc., 1927-66, also Paul Revere Life Ins. Co., Worcester, 1930-68, successively claim examiner, asst. sec., asst. counsel, counsel, v.p., 1929-45, pres., 1945-66, chmn. bd., 1966-68, dir.; pres. Paul Revere Variable Annuity Ins. Co., 1965-66, chmn. bd., 1966-68, also dir.; dir. Paul Revere Corp., Guaranty Bank & Trust Co.; trustee Worcester Five Cents Savs. Bank (now Consumers Savs. Bank). Pres. Health and Accident Underwriters Conf., 1949-50. Trustee Worcester Hahnemann Hosp., 1951-69; life trustee Dartmouth; bd. dirs. Legal Aid Soc., Salisbury Mansion Assos., Student Achievement Inst.; incorporator Worcester Art Mus. Mem. Ins. Econs. Soc. Am. (pres. 1951-52), Health Ins. Assn. Am. (bd. dirs. 1956-61), Newcomen Soc. N.Am., Am., Worcester County bar assns., Am. Antiquarian Soc. (council), Acacia, Phi Beta Kappa. Mason (33). Clubs: Webhannet Golf; Tatnuck Country, Worcester Country, Worcester, Kiwanis, Dartmouth (Worcester); Harvard (N.Y.C.). Home: 98 William St Worcester MA 01609 Office: 18 Chestnut St Worcester MA 01608

HARRINGTON, FRANK LEIGHTON, Jr., ins. co. exec.; b. Cambridge, Mass., May 26, 1928; s. Frank L. and Louise (Cronin) H.; grad. Phillips Acad., Andover, Mass., 1946; B.A., Dartmouth, 1950; M.B.A., Harvard, 1952; m. Sara G. Heathman, May 29, 1954; children—Frank Leighton III, Brooks Chester, Andrew Heathman. With Paul Revere Life Ins. Co., Worcester, Mass., 1954-69, v.p. adminstrn., 1964-66, pres., 1966-69; pres. Paul Revere Variable Annuity Ins Co., Worcester, 1966-69; v.p., group exec. ins., dir. Avco Corp., N.Y.C., 1967-69; v.p., dir. Paul Revere Corp., Worcester, 1967-69; bd. incorporators Peoples Savs. Bank Worcester. Chmn. Harrington Center Com., Worcester YMCA, 1962-67; chmn. advance gifts div. team Golden Rule, Worcester, 1965-67; pres. Dartmouth Class of 1950, 1960-65; pres. Dartmouth Class Chmn. and President's Assn., 1964-65, 67-68. Trustee Shepherd Knapp Sch. Boylston, Mass., New Eng. Aquarium, Boston, Pine Manor Jr. Coll., Chestnut Hill, Mass.; bd. incorporators Children's Friends Soc., Worcester, Hahnemann Hosp., Worcester, St. Vincent Hosp., Worcester; bd. dirs. Worcester Orch. Soc., Worcester Housing Devel. Corp. Served to 1st lt. USAF, 1952-54. Mem. Am. Soc. C.L.U.'s (dir. Worcester chpt.), Kappa Sigma. Mason (Shriner). Clubs: Worcester Country, Worcester (dir.), Tatnuck Country (Worcester). Home: 22 Brookshire Rd Worcester MA 01609

HARRINGTON, FRED HARVEY, educator; b. Watertown, N.Y., June 24, 1912; s. Arthur William and Elsie (Sutton) H.; A.B. with honors, Cornell U., 1933; A.M., N.Y.U. (Frederic Courtland Penfield fellow 1933-36), 1934, Ph.D., 1937, LL.D., 1963; LL.D., U. Cal., 1965, Drake U., 1969, Loyola U., Chgo., 1970; L.H.D., U. Me., 1966, DePaul U., 1966, Miami U., 1967, Northland Coll., 1969; Litt.D., U. Ife (Nigeria), 1969; m. Nancy Howes, Oct. 19, 1935; children—Heather (Mrs. Robert Monroe), Holly (Mrs. Frank L. Jackson), Hilary (Mrs. Noel Phillips), Helise, Harvey Haynes. Instr. history Washington Square Coll., N.Y.U., 1936-37; instr. history U. Wis., 1937-39, asst. prof., 1939-40; prof. history and polit. sci., chmn. dept. U. Ark., 1940-44; asso. prof. history U. Wis., 1944-47, prof. 1947-70, chmn. dept. 1952-55, spl. asst. to pres., 1956-58, v.p. acad. affairs, 1958-62, v.p. univ., 1962, pres., 1962-70, William F. Vilas research prof. history, 1970—; program adviser in India for Ford Found., 1971—; vis. prof. U. W.Va., 1942, Cornell U., 1944, U. Pa., 1949. U. Colo., 1951, Oxford U. 1955; Am. studies sem. U. Kyoto, Japan, 1962. Dir. Carnegie study of role of univ. in adult edn., chmn. com. on instnl. coop. Big Ten and Chgo., 1960-62; bd. vis. Air Acad., 1961-64; Wis. chmn. Brotherhood Week, Nat. Conf. Christians and Jews, 1965; mem. bd. Found. Library Center, Am. Univs. Field Staff; trustee Johnson Found.; pres. Nat. Assn. State Univs. and Land Grant Colls., 1968-69; mem. Army Adv. Panel on ROTC Affairs, 1963- 68. Fellow Guggenheim Meml. Found., 1943-44; Ford Faculty fellow, 1955-56. Mem. Am. Hist. Assn., Am. Council Edn. (chmn. commn. acad. affairs 1962-65, bd. dirs. 1966-69), Fgn. Policy Assn. (bd. dirs. 1966-68), Nat. Commn. Accrediting (pres. 1966-68), Nat. Assn. Ednl. Broadcasters (bd. dirs. 1965-68), Assn. Am. Historians (exec. com. 1944-48), Wis. Hist. Soc. Edn. Commn. States (v.p. 1966-68), Phi Beta Kappa, Phi Kappa Phi. Author: God, Mammon and the Japanese: Dr. Horace N. Allen and Korean-American Relations (1884-1905), 1944; Fighting Politician: Mayor General N. P. Banks, 1948; An American History (2 vols.) (with M. Curti, R. H. Shryock, T.C. Cochran), 1950: Hanging Judge, 1951: History of American Civilization (with Curti, Shryock, Cochran), 1953. Address: Van Hise Hall U Wis Madison WI 53706

HARRINGTON, GEORGE WILLIAM, educator; b. N.Y.C., Nov. 13, 1929; s. George Washington and Hedwig Louise (Sommer) H.; B.A., N.Y. U., 1954, Ph.D., 1959; m. Patricia Miller, June 4, 1955; children—Steven George, Cathy Louise. Project engr. Philco Corp. (Lansdale Tube Co.), 1959; prof. chemistry Temple U., Phila., 1959—, asso. dean Coll. Liberal Arts, 1968—. Research contractor AEC, 1959-62, Campbell Soup Co., 1963-65. Served with AUS, 1948-52; Korea. Recipient Founders Day award N.Y. U., 1969. Fellow Am. Inst. Chemists (sr. medal 1955)); mem. Am. Chem. Soc. (chmn. phys. sect. Phila. 1969), Am. Assn. Univ. Profs., Sigma Xi. Research and publication in electroanalytical chemistry, non-aqueous chemistry (molten salt systems). Home: 1208 Duncan Dr Dresher PA 19025 Office: Dept of Chemistry Temple Univ Philadelphia PA 19121

HARRINGTON, HAROLD ERNEST, physicist, educator; b. Rhinelander, Wis., Sept. 18, 1902; s. Ernest Gideon and Mary Hill (Carncross) H.; student Tex. A. and M. Coll., 1920- 22, Sam Houston State Coll., 1923; B.S., Okla. State U., 1926, M.S., 1928; Ph.D., U. Tex., 1938; m. Leafy Rickstrew, July 28, 1926; 1 dau., Mary Elizabeth (Mrs. Dale W. Curry). High sch. tchr., Tex., 1923-25; mem. faculty Okla. State U., 1929-42, 46-68, prof. physics, 1947-68, dir. electronics lab., 1947-53, chmn. physics dept., dir. research electronics lab. Research Found., 1953-68, prof. and head emeritus physics, 1968—; prof., chmn. physics dept. Hardin-Simmons U., Abilene, Tex. 1968—. Regional counselor physics for Okla., 1961-63; research physicist Naval Research Lab., 1943-46. Mem. Am. Assn. Physics Tchrs., Sigma Xi, Sigma Pi Sigma. Home: 1502 Sylvan Dr Abilene TX 79605

HARRINGTON, HARRY FRANCIS, ret. banker; b. St. Louis, Feb. 6, 1900; s. Edward H. and Nellie T. (Riley) H.; grad. Sch. Banking, Rutgers U., 1941; m. Edwina G. Daly, Feb. 5, 1940. With Boatmen's Nat. Bank of St. Louis, 1915-70, beginning as asst. auditor, successively auditor, v.p., 1915-54, pres., 1954-61, chmn. bd., pres., 1961-65, chmn. bd., 1965-70, dir., 1947—. Mem. St. Louis Crime Commn.; commr. Bi-State Devel. Agy., Mo.-Ill. Met. Dist., 1957-63, treas., 1962-63. Bd. dirs., mem. exec. com. United Fund Greater St. Louis (treas. 1958-59, campaign chmn. 1963-64, pres. 1967-68); v.p., bd. dirs. Civic Progress, Inc., St. Louis Bicentennial Corp.; v.p., trustee Jefferson Nat. Expansion Meml. Assn.; bd. dirs. Municipal Theater Assn. St. Louis (treas. 1957-63), St. Louis Symphony Soc., Better Bus. Bur.; exec. bd. St. Louis Area council Boy Scouts Am.; bd. dirs., pres. Cath. Charities St. Louis, 1966-67; bd. dirs. Downtown St. Louis Inc., pres. 1966-67; trustee St. Louis Regional Open Space Found., Govtl. Research Inst., Jr. Achievement Miss. Valley, Inc.; mem. pres.'s council St. Louis U. Named knight of Malta; recipient Brotherhood citation Nat. Conf. Christians and Jews; Silver Beaver award Boy Scouts Am. Mem. Am. (chmn. fed. agy. relations com. 1963-67), Mo. bankers assns., Assn. Res. City Bankers (bd. dirs. 1963-66), St. Louis Clearing House Assn. (pres. 1960-61), Financial Execs. Inst., C. of C. Met. St. Louis. Clubs: Bellerive, Mo. Athletic, Saint Louis. Home: 57 Briarcliff St Louis MO 63124

HARRINGTON, HOLLIS E., banker; b. Preston Hollow, N.Y., Sept 23, 1908; s. Elmer and Mary C. (Hulbert) H.; ed. high sch.; L.H.D. (hon.), Siena Coll., 1968; m. Elizabeth A. Hewlett, Aug. 5, 1931; 1 son, Hollis E. With State Bank of Albany (N.Y.), 1926—, pres., dir., 1957—; dir. Turbonetics, Inc. Mem. N.Y. State Banking Bd., 1963-69. Mem. Bus. Adv. Council Urban Devel. Corp. Mem. bd. govs. Albany Med. Center Hosp.; trustee, treas. Albany Med. Coll.; trustee Russell Sage Coll.; chmn. bd. trustees Siena Coll.; bd. dirs., treas. Green Mountain Coll.; bd. dirs. Saratoga Performing Arts Center. Mem. Am. (mem. state legislative com. 1965-66), N.Y. State (pres. 1965-66) bankers assns. Republican. Methodist. Mason. Clubs: Fort Orange, Albany Country (Albany); Union League (N.Y.C.). Home: 68 Fernbank Av Delmar NY 12054 Office: 69 State St Albany NY 12201

HARRINGTON, HOWARD DEWITT, orch. cons.; b. Andover, Mass., Dec. 19, 1907; s. Virgil DeWitt and Alice (Howard) H.; student Phillips Andover Acad., 1927; student Boston U., 1928-32, New Eng. Conservatory Music, 1932-38; m. Edna Grace Merritt, Sept. 2, 1936; children—Faith (Mrs. John Frederick Jones), Jonathan Brooke. Profl. tenor to 1941; mgr. Indpls. Symphony Orch., 1941-51; gen. mgr. Detroit Symphony Orch., 1951-71; cons. Am. Symphony Orch. League, 1971—. Mem. Mich. Council Arts; bd. dirs. Am. Symphony Orch. League. Home: 10 Elm St Thomaston ME 04861

HARRINGTON, J. ERIC, bus. exec.; b. Montreal, Que., Can., Aug. 28, 1914; s. C.D. and Muriel (Featherstonhaugh) H.; student Selwyn House Sch., Trinity Coll., Port Hope, Ont., Instn. Silling, Switzerland, Royal Mil. Coll., Kingston, Ont.; m. Hazel P. Hastings, Nov. 2, 1939; 3 daus. Pres., chief exec. officer Canadian Vickers Ltd.; pres., dir. Vickers-Krebs, Ltd. Vice pres. Montreal Bd. Trade. Councillor, City of Montreal, 1950-54. Bd. mgmt. Montreal Children's Hosp. Served as lt. comdr. Royal Canadian Naval Vol. Res., 1939-45. Mem. Canadian Constrn. Assn. (past pres.), Engring. Inst. Can. Mem. Ch. of Eng. Clubs: Saint James, Laurentian Golf and Country, Mount Bruno Country. Address: 3030 Trafalgar Av Montreal Quebec Canada *

HARRINGTON, JEREMY THOMAS, clergyman, editor; b. Lafayette, Ind., Oct. 7, 1932; s. William and Ellen (Cain) H.; B.A., Duns Scotus Coll., 1955; postgrad. U. Detroit, 1955, Marquette U., 1961; M.A., Xavier U., Cin., 1965; M.S. in Journalism, Northwestern U., 1966. Joined Order Friars Minor, 1950; ordained priest Roman Catholic Ch., 1959; tchr. Roger Bacon High Sch., Cin., 1960- 64; asso. editor St. Anthony Messenger, Cin., 1964-66, editor, 1966—; mem. bd. Franciscan Province Cin. Mem. Cath. Press Assn. (dir.), Cin. Editors Assn., Kappa Tau Alpha. Editor: Conscience in Today's World, 1970. Home: 1615 Vine St Cincinnati OH 45210 Office: 1615 Republic St Cincinnati OH 45210

HARRINGTON, JOHN VINCENT, educator, elec. engr.; b. N.Y.C., May, 9, 1919; s. John J. and Dorothy (Neisel) H.; B.E.E., Cooper Union, 1940; M.E.E., Poly. Inst. Bklyn., 1948; Sc.D., Mass. Inst. Tech., 1958; m. Frances Cullinane, Jan. 23, 1943; children—John F., Nancy J., Jeffrey, Richard L., Brian T. Student engr. Consol. Edison Co. N.Y., 1940-41; asst. engr. Am. Gas & Electric Co., 1941-42; electronics engr. Air Force Cambridge (Mass.) Research Center, 1946-51; leader data transmission group Lincoln Lab., Mass. Inst. Tech., 1951-55, asso. div. head radio physics div., 1955-58, head radio physics div., 1958-63, prof. aero. and astronautics, prof. elec. engring., also dir. Center Space Research, 1963—. Standing com. sci. and tech. Greater Boston C. of C., 1964—; mem. Gov.'s Com. on Sci. and Tech., 1966—. Dir. Epsco, Inc., Westwood, Mass., County Bank N.A., Cambridge. Recipient Exceptional Civilian Service medal USAF, 1952. Fellow I.E.E.E. (dir. New Eng. regional meeting 1964-66); mem. Am. Phys. Soc., A.A.A.S., Am. Geophys. Union, Am. Inst. Aeros. and Astronautics, Sigma Xi, Tau Beta Pi. Home: 10 Loring Rd Lexington MA 02173 Office: Center Space Research Mass Inst Tech Cambridge MA 02139

HARRINGTON, MICHAEL, author; b. St. Louis, Feb. 24, 1928 s. Edward Michael and Catherine (Fitzgibbon) H.; A.B., Holy Cross Coll., 1947; student Yale Law Sch., 1947-48; M.A., U. Chgo., 1949; D.H.L., Bard Coll., 1966; m. Stephanie Gervis, May 30, 1963. Asso. editor Catholic Worker, 1951-52; orgn. sec. Workers Def. League, 1953; cons. Fund for Republic, 1954—; editor New America, 1961-62; organizer March on the Convs. Movement, 1960; chmn. bd. League Indsl. Democracy, 1964—. Mem. nat. exec. com. Socialist Party, 1960—, also nat. chmn.; del. exec. com. Internat. Union Socialist Youth, Berlin, Germany, 1959; del. Congress Socialist Internat., Amsterdam, Holland, 1963. Bd. dirs. Workers Def. League, Am. Civil Liberties Union, A. Phillip Randolph Inst. Recipient George Polk award, 1963, Sidney Hillman award, 1963, Riordan award D.C. Newspaper Guild, 1964. Author: The Other America, 1963; The Retail Clerks, 1963; The Accidental Century, 1965; Toward a Democratic Left, 1968. Editor: (with Paul Jacobs) Labor in a Free Society, 1959. Office: 1182 Broadway New York City NY 10001

HARRINGTON, MICHAEL JOSEPH, congressman; b. Salem, Mass., Sept. 2, 1936; s. Joseph B. and Elizabeth (Kenneally) H.; B.A. in History with honors, Harvard, 1958, LL.B., 1961, grad. student Grad. Sch. Pub. Adminstrn., 1963; m. Dorothy M. Leahy, Sept. 12, 1959; children—Leslie, Mark, Keith, Alison, Michael Justin. Admitted to Mass. bar, 1961; mem. Salem (Mass.) City Council, 1960-63, Mass. Ho. of Reps., 1964-69; mem. 91st Congress 6th dist. Mass.; partner firm Ronan and Harrington, Salem, 1962—. Bd. corporators Salem Hosp. Democrat Home: Bay View Av Beverly MA 01915 Office: Longworth House Office Bldg Washington DC 20515

HARRINGTON, MILTON ELREE, tobacco exec.; b. Winterville, N.C., Sept. 19, 1908; s. James Frank and Edith Agatha (Tucker) H.; A.B., Duke, 1931; m. Bonnie Windham, July 19, 1937; 1 son, John Milton (killed in action). With Ligget & Myers Tobacco Co., Durham, N.C., 1934—, successively factory mgr., leaf buyer, leaf supr., mgr. leaf dept., v.p. leaf, exec. officer charge Durham operations, exec. v.p., 1963, pres., chief exec. officer, 1964—. Dir., mem. exec. com. Tobacco Inst. Served as pfc. AUS, 1944. Mem. Grocery Mfrs. Am. (dir.). Home: Pelham Manor NY 10803 Office: 630 Fifth Av New York City NY 10020

HARRINGTON, ROBERT WARREN, educator; b. Morrison, Ill., May 21, 1923; s. Loyd Weaver and Anna (Mundt) H.; B.S., Ill. State U., 1947; M.A., U. Ia., 1948, Ph.D., 1952; postgrad. U. Wis., summer 1954, U. Cambridge (Eng.), 1963. Instr., Central Coll., Pella, Ia., 1948-50; from asst. to asso. prof. Wis. State Coll., Superior, 1951-56; prof. Ind. State U., Terre Haute, 1956-68; prof., dir. bus. and econs. Ill. Wesleyan U., Bloomington, 1968—. Served with USNR, 1943-46. Mem. Am., Midwest econs. assns., Pi Omega Pi, Alpha Kappa Psi, Omicron Delta Kappa. Home: 703 Jersey Av Bloomington IL 61701

HARRINGTON, RUSSELL PAUL, educator, engr.; b. Akron, O., Oct. 22, 1905; s. Melvin Whinton and Emma Alice (Reiker) H.: B.S.E., U. Mich., 1930, M.S.E., 1931, D.Sc., 1936; m. Emogene Dyson, Sept. 14, 1929 (dec.); children—Marigene (Mrs. Daniel K. Butler), Julia (Mrs. Gordon M. Kiby), Cynthia (Mrs. Enest Symes); m. 2d, Babette D. Marshall, Dec. 27, 1966. Instr. Poly. Inst. Bklyn., 1934-36, asst. prof., 1936-39, asso. prof., 1939-41, prof., head dept. aero. engrng. and applied mechanics, 1941-50; prof., head dept. aero. engrng. Rensselaer Poly. Inst., Troy, N.Y., 1950-56, prof., 1958-60; dir. tng. center for exptl. aerodynamics NATO, Brussels, 1956- 58; prof. head dept. aerospace engrng. U. Cin., 1960—, dir. Inst. Space Scis., 1963—. Sheehan scholar, 1930-31, Guggenheim fellow, 1932-34. Decorated Croix de Chevalier de L'Ordre Leopold (Belgium). Asso. fellow Am. Inst. Aeros. and Astronautics (dir.), Royal Aero. Soc.; mem. Am. Soc. Engrng. Edn. (chmn. aerospace div. 1967-68), Engrng. Council for Profl. Devel. (exec. com.), A.A.A.S., Tau Beta Pi, Phi Kappa Phi, Sigma Xi, Iota Alpha. Home: 1717 Neeb Rd Cincinnati OH 45238

HARRINGTON, TIMOTHY J., bishop. Ordained priest Roman Catholic Ch., 1946; aux. bishop Worcester, Mass. and titular bishop Rusuca, 1968—. Address: 11 Sycamore St Worcester MA 01608 *

HARRINGTON, WILLIAM FIELDS, educator, biochemist; b. Seattle, Sept. 25, 1920; s. Ira Francis and Jessie Blanche (Fields) H.; B.S., U. Cal. at Berkeley, 1948, Ph.D., 1952; m. Ingeborg Leuschner, Feb. 24, 1947; children—Susan, Eric, Peter, Robert, David. Research chemist virus lab. U. Cal. at Berkeley, 1952-53; Nat. Found. Infantile Paralysis postdoctoral fellow Cambridge (Eng.) U., 1953-54; Nat. Cancer Inst. postdoctoral fellow Carlsberg Lab., Copenhagen, Denmark, 1954-55; asst. prof. chemistry Ia. State U., 1955- 56; biochemist Nat. Heart Inst., 1956-60; prof. biology Johns Hopkins, 1960—; vis. scientist Wiezmann Inst., Rehovot, Israel, 1959, vis. prof., 1970; vis. prof. Oxford U., 1970. Mem. adv. panel physiol. chemistry NIH, 1962-66, adv. panel biophys. chemistry study sect., 1968—; bd. sci. councillors Nat. Inst. Arthritis and Metabolic Diseases, 1968—; sci. adv. bd. New Eng. Inst. Med. Research; mem. vis. com. for biology Brookhaven. Nat. Lab., 1969—. Mem. Soc., Soc. Biol. Chemists, Sigma Xi. Bd. editors Jour. Biol. Chemistry, 1963-68, Mechanochemistry and Motility, 1970—, Biochemistry, 1971—. Home: 2210 W Rogers Av Baltimore MD 21209

HARRIS, AARON, library mgr.; b. Birmingham, Ala., Oct. 27, 1930; s. Moses and Fannie (Williams) H.; B.A., Talladega Coll., 1952; M.S., Columbia, 1959; postgrad. Princeton, 1961; m. Edna Mabel Turner, May 13, 1954; children—Kevin Brian, Edwin Maurice. Trainee Bklyn. Pub. Library, 1956-59; asst. librarian Burroughs Wellcome Co., Tuckahoe, N.Y., 1959-64; asso. librarian IBM Corp., East Fishkill, N.Y., 1964-66; library mgr. IBM Research Lab., San Jose, Cal., 1966—; cons.; instr. San Jose City Coll. Pres., dir. Youth Care Centers, Inc.; gen. chmn. Citizens Com. on Schs., San Jose, 1969-71; dir. Opportunities Indslzn. Center. Candidate San Jose Sch. Bd., 1969. Served with AUS, 1952-55. Recipient citizen of the year award Omega Psi Phi, 1970. Mem. Spl. Libraries Assn., Am. Soc. Information Sci., Omega Psi Phi. Mem. A.M.E. Ch. (trustee). Home: 2777 Thrasher Lane San Jose CA 95125 Office: IBM Monterey and Cottle Rds San Jose CA 95114

HARRIS, AL, coll. pres.; b. Altus, Okla., Dec. 15, 1909; s. Francis M. and Aggie (Fourmentin) H.; B.S., Southwestern State Coll., Weatherford, Okla., 1931, B.A., 1934; M.A., George Peabody Tchrs. Coll., 1938; Ed.D., Okla. State U., 1955; m. Joe de Bob Dickerson, June 26, 1938; 1 dau., Ruth F. (Mrs. Ruth Harris Teasley). Tchr. sci. and math Custer (Okla.) schs., 1931-33, supt. schs., 1933-39; supt. schs., Watonga, Okla., 1939-47, Clinton, Okla., 1947-60; pres. Southwestern State Coll., 1960—. Pres. Okla. Tchr. Edn. and Certification Commn., 1954-55; mem. Commn. Improvement Ednl. Adminstrn, Okla., 1951-60, Okla. Curriculum Improvement Commn., 1960—; state liaison rep. Am. Assn. Colls. Tchr. Edn., 1969-71. Mem. Nat., Okla. edn. assns., Am., Okla. assns. sch. adminstrs., Clinton C. of C. (bd. dirs. 1950), Phi Delta Kappa. Methodist. Mason, Rotarian (pres. Clinton 1948-49.) Home: 815 N Custer St Weatherford OK 73096

HARRIS, ALFRED, educator, anthropologist; b. Abington, Pa., July 26, 1919; s. Henry S. and Margaret (Britton) H.; B.A., U. Chgo., 1941, M.A., 1952; postgrad. Oxford (Eng.) U., 1949-50; Ph.D., Cambridge (Eng.) U., 1958; m. Grace Louise Gredys, Oct. 16, 1948. Cartographer, 1942-47; teaching asst. U. Chgo., 1947-49; Colonial Social Sci. Research Council studentship and fellowship, 1949-53; instr., then lectr. Smith Coll., 1957-59, 59-60; vis. asst. prof. Brandeis U., 1960-61; mem. faculty U. Rochester, 1961- -, asso. prof. anthropology, 1964—, chmn. dept. anthropology, 1964-71; cons. in field, 1958—. Fellow Am. Anthrop. Assn., African Studies Assn., Royal Anthrop. Inst., Assn. Social Anthropologists (U.K.); mem. Internat. African Inst. Editorial staff Am. Sociol. Rev., 1957-60. Office: Harkness Hall Univ Rochester Rochester NY 14627

HARRIS, ARTHUR L., lawyer; b. Atlanta, Feb. 28, 1910; s. Arthur I. and Irma (Liebmann) H.; student Philips Andover Acad.; A.B., Yale, 1931; LL.B., Harvard, 1934; m. Liliane Langlois; children—Arthur III, Alexander, Jill. Admitted to Ga. bar, 1934; with Hirsch & Smith, Atlanta, 1934-36; v.p., gen. mgr. Atlanta Paper Co., 1936-42, 45-47, pres., 1947-59; pres. Mead Packaging Internat., Inc., pres. Mead packaging div.; dir. Mead Corp., Dayton, O., 1948-68; v.p., dir. Packagemaster, Ltd., Toronto, 1948-68; pres., chief exec. officer Scripto, Inc., 1968-71, dir., 1968—; of counsel Coudert-Freres, Paris, France; dir. Mead Corp., Spruce Co., Dallas, Lames, Inc., Atlanta. Asst. chief bur. priorities WPB, 1942. Past pres. Jr. Achievement of Ga., Inc.; bd. dirs. Atlanta Symphony Guild; trustee Atlanta Art Assn.; hon. S.E. regional dir. Jr. Achievement; mem. nat. com. Whitney Mus. Served to maj. AUS, 1942- 45. Decorated Legion of Merit (U.S.); Merite de l'Economie Nationale, Ordre National de la Legion d'Honneur (France). Mem. Paperboard Packaging Council (bd. dirs.), Nat. Folding Box Assn. (nat. bd. dirs.), Atlanta Freight Bur. (bd. dirs., past pres.). Home: 1130 W Conway Dr NW Atlanta GA 30327 also Paris France

HARRIS, BARBARA, actress; b. Evanston, Ill., 1935; d. Oscar and Natalie (Densmoor) Harris; m. Paul Sills (div.). Appeared with Second City Co., Chgo., 1960-61, with Second City Co. in From the Second City, N.Y.C., 1961-62, Oh Dad, Poor Dad, Mama's Hung You in the Closet and I'm Feelin' So Sad, N.Y.C., 1962, Mother Courage and Her Children, N.Y.C., 1963, Dynamite Tonight (off-Broadway), On a Clear Day You Can See Forever, 1965; appeared in film version Oh Dad, Poor Dad, also movie A Thousand Clowns. Recipient N.Y. Drama Critics award for most promising new actress, Variety Poll, 1961, 62; Off-Broadway award Village Voice, 1962.

HARRIS, BRICE, educator; b. Troy, Tenn., Aug. 20, 1900; s. Robert Sidney and Margaret (Brice) H.; A.B., Erskine Coll., Due West, S.C., 1921; A.M., Vanderbilt U., 1925; Ph.D., Harvard, 1932; postgrad. summer sch., U. Chgo., 1925; m. Loring Smith, Sept. 10, 1926; 1 son, Brice. Instr. English, Clemson Coll., 1923-24, Tex. A. and M. Coll., 1925-26, Cornell U., 1930-37; teaching fellow Vanderbilt U., 1924-25, asst. prof. English, The Citadel, 1926-27; asst. in English, U. Wis., 1927-28; mem. faculty U. Ill., 1937-47, asso. prof., 1945-47., prof. English lit. Pa. State U., 1947-62, chmn. dept., 1947-57; prof. English, Ariz. State U., 1962—; vis. prof. N.M. Highlands U., summer 1941, U. Zaragoza (Spain), 1957, Alaska Methodist U., Anchorage, summers 1965, 66; vis. lectr. Ohio State U., summer 1947. Grant-in-aid Am. Council Learned Soc., 1934; research fellow Huntington Library, 1936-37. Mem. Am. Assn. U. Profs., Modern Lang. Assn. Am., Coll. English Assn., Nat. Council Tchrs. English (pres. 1958). Republican. Club: Harvard (Phoenix). Author and editor books, latest being Restoration Plays, 1953. Editor: Humours and Conversations of the Town (by James Wright), 1961. Home: 1020 E Laguna Dr Tempe AZ 85282 ☆

HARRIS, BRUNO, educator, mathematician; b. Ploesti, Romania, Mar. 1, 1932; s. Marc and Adele (Iacovici) H.; came to U.S., 1946, naturalized, 1953; B.S., Cal. Inst. Tech., 1952; M.A., Yale, 1954, Ph.D., 1956; m. Janet Laura Bloch, Mar. 25, 1956; children—Ruth, Joel, Abigail, Susan. NSF postdoctoral fellow Yale, 1956-57; instr., then asst. prof. Northwestern U., 1957-60; asso. Air Force Office Sci. Research, Princeton, 1960-61; mem. faculty Brown U., 1961—, prof. math., 1965—, chmn. dept., 1968-69. Mem. Am. Math. Soc. Contbr. articles algebra and algebraic topology. Home: 19 Brenton St Providence RI 02906

HARRIS, BYRON P., accountant; b. Atlantic City, Jan. 11, 1904; s. Harry G. and Hattie W. Harris; ed. pub. schs., Atlantic City, also La-Salle U. extension course, 1925; m. Dena Lewis, June 1, 1929; children—Arthur F.M., Buron L. Accountant, Shaner & Knauer, Atlantic City, 1920-25; partner Arthur F. Morton & Co., C.P.A.'s, 1927-55; partner A.M. Pullen & Co., pub. accountants, Atlanta, 1955—; lectr. numerous tax forums. Mem. budget com. Community Services, 1958—, admissions com., 1964; treas. Atlantic Art Assn., 1960-64, exec. com., 1960-64; mem. exec. com. Estate Planning Council; past pres. Atlanta Estate Planning Council. Treas., dir. Atlanta Florence Crittenton Home; bd. sponsors High Museum Art, Atlanta Symphony Orch.; trustee Ga. Tax Research Found. C.P.A., Ga., N.C., Va., Pa., N.Y. Mem. Am. Inst. C.P.A.'s (past chmn. social security com., council taxation sect.), Nat. Assn. Accountants, Ga. Soc. C.P.A.'s (past pres., chmn. various coms., 1945—, trustee, 1938—), Nat. Soc. Accounts Coops., Am. Arbitration Assn., Ga. (chmn. taxation and spending council 1960—, area adviser 1956—), Atlanta chambers commerce, Asso. Industries Ga., S.A.R. Episcopalian (past vestyman, sec., treas.). Clubs: Peachtree, Commerce, Kiwanis, Atlanta Athletic, Chattahoochee, Capital City. Home: 1820 W Paces Ferry Rd NW Atlanta GA 30327 Office: Candler Bldg Atlanta GA 30303

HARRIS, CARL VERNON, educator; b. Morganton, N.C., Dec. 29, 1922; s. Asbury David and Laura (Clark) H.; A.A., Mars Hill (N.C.) Coll., 1942; A.B., Wake Forest U., 1944; B.D., Yale, 1946, S.T.M., 1947; Ph.D., Duke, 1952; m. Ida Lucille Sawyer, Aug. 6, 1955. Tchr., Mars Hill Coll., 1947-50; with Va. Dept. Welfare and Instns., 1952-53; tchr. E. Carolina U., Greenville, N.C., 1953-54; faculty U. Dubuque, Ia., 1954-56; tchr. Wake Forest U., Winston-Salem, N.C., 1956—, now prof. classical langs. and lit. Mem. Am. Acad. Religion, N.C. Council Human Relations, Am. Soc. Ch. History, Am. Classical League, Classical Assn. Middle West and South, N.C. Classical Assn., Am. Assn. U. Profs., Phi Beta Kappa, Eta Sigma Phi, Delta Kappa Alpha. Author: Origen of Alexandria's Interpretation of the Teacher's Function in the Early Christian Hierarchy and Community, 1967. Address: PO Box 7402 Reynolda Sta Winston Salem NC 27109

HARRIS, CARLETON, state justice; b. Pine Bluff, Ark., Dec. 31, 1909; s. Frank A. and Ada (Rodgers) H.; student Union U., Jackson, Tenn., 1929-31; LL.B., Cumberland U., 1932; LL.D., Quachita Baptist Coll., 1960; m. Marjorie Wilson, Apr. 20, 1934; 1 son, Eugene Starke. Admitted to Ark. bar, 1932; practice in Pine Bluff, 1932-48; pros. atty., Pine Bluff, 1947-48; judge 4th Chancery Dist. Ark., 1949-57, Supreme Ct., 1957—. Pres. Ark. Jud. Council, 1955. Mem. Ark. Ho. of Reps., 1933-38. Bd. dirs. nat. council Boy Scouts Am.; disaster relief chmn. Jefferson County A.R.C., 1943—; past v.p. Jefferson County Men of Chs. Mem. Am., Ark., Jefferson County (pres. 1942) bar assns., Conf. Chief Justices (nat. chmn. 1966-67), Central States Shrine Assn. (past pres.). Democrat. Baptist (mem. exec. com. So. Bapt. Conv. 1967—). Mason (past grand lodge orator; Shriner, past potentate). Lion (pres. Pine Bluff 1936). Home: 2005 Laurel St Pine Bluff AR 71601 also Plaza Towers Little Rock AR 72205 Office: Justice Bldg Little Rock AR 72201

HARRIS, CHARLES, union exec.; b. Sulligent, Ala., Feb. 15, 1926; s. Charles and Annie Mae (Holliday) H.; student U. Ala., 1947; m. Doris Eleanor Ketring, Feb. 14, 1948; children—Blake James, Blaine Charles. Profl. baseball player various teams including Phila. Athletics, 1948-51; profl. baseball mgr., West Palm Beach, Fla., 1951-52, Cleve. Indians, 1952-53; bus. mgr. Internat. Brotherhood Elec. Workers, West Palm Beach, 1956-63; pres. Fla. State Elec. Workers, West Palm Beach, 1962-63, Fla. AFL-CIO, Miami, 1963—. Bd. dirs. Variety Childrens Hosp., Miami. Served with USNR, 1944-46. Democrat. Baptist. Elk. Home: 4730 Maine St Lake Worth FL 33460 Office: 1400 36th St Miami FL 33142

HARRIS, CHARLES DAVID, judge; b. Balt., Dec. 11, 1906; s. Carlton D. and Katharine (Matthaei) H.; A.B., Johns Hopkins, 1928, J.D., U. Md., 1933; m. Janet B. Jeffery, Oct. 17, 1933; children—Susanne (dec.), Charles David (dec.), Janet, Judith. Admitted to Md. bar, 1933; practice in Balt., 1933- 62; partner France, Rouzer, Mundy & Harris, 1941-62; judge Supreme Bench of Baltimore City, 1962—; staff Balt. Sun, 1937-40; gen. counsel Pub. Service Commn Md., 1948-55; spl. hearing officer U.S. Dept. Justice, 1948-62. Mem. Employment Security Bd. Md., 1955-56; chmn. Md. Commn. to Revise Bus Taxes, 1959-61. Trustee Prisoners Aid Assn. Fellow Md. Bar Found.; mem. Am., Md. (v.p. 1960-61), Balt. (pres. 1958-59) bar assns. Clubs: Elkridge, Johns Hopkins (Balt.). Home: 5222 Springlake Way Baltimore MD 21212 Office: Court House Baltimore MD 21202

HARRIS, CHARLES ELMER, lawyer; b. Williamsburg, Ia., Nov. 6, 1922; s. Charles Elmer and Loreto (Judge) H.; student St. Ambrose Coll., 1940-42; B.S.C., U. Ia., 1946; J.D., 1949; m. Marjorie Clark, July 9, 1949 (div. June 1969); children-Martha Ann, Julie Ann, Charles Elmer III. Admitted to Ia. bar, 1949; mem. firm Brody, Parker, Roberts, Thoma & Harris, Des Moines, 1949- 66, Herrick, Langdon, Belin & Harris, Des Moines, 1966—; lectr. tax schs., meetings 1951, 55, 67, 69. Bd. dirs. Nat. Conf. Christians and Jews, 1964-67, Polk County Mental Health Center Bd., 1966—. Served to lt. (j.g.) USNR, 1943-46. Mem. Ia., Polk County (v.p. 1970-71) bar assns., Polk County Jr. Bar Assn. (pres. 1952-53), Order of Coif, Sigma Chi, Delta Theta Phi. Roman Catholic. Comments editor Ia. Law Rev., 1948- 49. Home: 5141 Robertson Dr Des Moines IA 50312 Office: Home Fed Bldg Des Moines IA 50309

HARRIS, CHARLES OVERTON, engrng. educator; b. Altamont, Ill., June 22, 1909; s. William and Laura Ann (Parks) H.; student James Millikin U., 1926-28; S.B., U. Ill., 1930, M.S., 1932; D.Sc., U. Mich., 1941; m. Mary Louise Henebry, Dec. 26, 1934; children—Judith Anne, William Overton, Carolyn Louise, Susan Ruth. Research asst. U. Ill., 1930-32; instr., then prof. Ill. Inst. Tech., 1934-46; prof. engrng. mechanics, head dept. U. Notre Dame, 1946-49; head dept. civil engrng. Mich. State Univ., 1949- 51, head dept. applied mechanics, 1951-62; dir. faculty devel. Gen. Motors Inst., Flint, Mich., 1962—. Mem. Am. Soc. M.E., Am. Soc. Engrng. Edn., Sigma Alpha Epsilon, Triangle, Sigma Xi, Tau Beta Pi, Sigma Tau, Pi Tau Sigma, Chi Epsilon, Tau Omega. Author: Slide Rule Simplified, 1943; Elementary Engineering Mechanics, 1947; Strength of Materials, 1949; Introduction to Structural Design, 1951; Introduction to Stress Analysis, 1959; also tech. papers. Home: 1151 Clearview Dr Flushing MI 48433 Office: Gen Motors Inst Flint MI 48502

HARRIS, CHARLES UPCHURCH, sem. pres.; b. Raleigh, N.C., May 2, 1914; s. Charles Upchurch and Saidee (Robbins) H.; B.A., Wake Forest Coll., 1935; B.D., Va. Theol. Sem., 1938, D.D. (hon.), 1958; postgrad. Union Theol. Sem., 1939-40; m. Janet Jeffrey Carlile, June 17, 1940; children—John C., Diana Jeffrey (Mrs. Melvin). Ordained deacon P.E. Ch., 1938, priest, 1939; rector All Saints Ch., Roanoke Rapids, N.C. 1938-39; asst. rector St. Bartholomew's Ch., N.Y.C., 1939-40; rector Trinity Ch., Roslyn, L.I., 1940-46, Trinity Ch., Highland Park, Ill., 1946-57; pres., dean faculty Seabury-Western Theol. Sem., Evanston, Ill., 1957—; dean Lake Shore Deanery; founder St. Gregory's Ch., Deerfield, Ill. Chmn bd. exam. chaplains, dept. Christian edn. Armed Forces Commn.; mem. joint commn. theol. edn. Episcopal Ch.; chmn. exam. chaplains 5th and 6th provinces Episcopal Ch., cons. nat. dept. Christian edn.; pres. Chgo. Theol. Inst.; v.p. Chgo. Inst. Advanced Theol. Studies. Bd. dirs. Central House of Deaconesses. Mem. Am. Theol. Soc., Am. Acad. Sci. and Religion, Am. Acad. Polit. and Social Sci., Soc. Colonial Warriors, S.A.R. Editorial bd. Anglican Theol. Rev., now acting editor. Contbr. Viewpoints; Confirmations: History, Doctrine and Practice. Clubs: University, Executives (Chgo.); University (Evanston); Burt Lake Yacht, Columbus Beach (Indian River, Mich.); Glen View (Golf, Ill.); Columbus (O.) Country. Home: 625 Garrett Pl Evanston IL 60201

HARRIS, CHARLES WAYNE, lawyer; b. Cushing, Okla., Feb. 11, 1937; s. Charles C. and Ruth Alice (Wilson) H.; B.B.A., U. Okla., 1959, LL.B., 1962; m. Emma Mae Brooks, May 22, 1965; 1 son, Mark Wayne. With land dept. Skelly Oil Co., Midland, Tex., 1962; admitted to Okla. bar, 1962, Ark. bar, 1966; since practiced in Ft. Smith; trial atty. Warner, Warner, Ragon & Smith, 1966—. Served to capt. Judge Adv. Gen. Corps, AUS, 1962-66. Mem. Okla., Ark., Sebastian County bar assns., Phi Alpha Delta, Omicron Delta Kappa. Home: 4421 Victoria Dr Fort Smith AR 72901 Office: 214 N 6th St Fort Smith AR 72901

HARRIS, CHAUNCY DENNISON, geographer; b. Logan, Utah, Jan. 31, 1914; s. Franklin Stewart and Estella (Spilsbury) H.: A.B., Brigham Young U., 1933; B.A., Oxford Univ. (Rhodes scholar, 1934-36), 1936, M.A., 1943; student London Sch. Econs., 1936-37; Ph.D., U. Chgo., 1940; D.Econ. (honoris causa), Catholic U., Chile, 1956; m. Edith Young, Sept. 5, 1940; 1 dau., Margaret. Instr. in geography Ind. U., 1939-41; asst. prof. geography U. Neb., 1941-43; asst. prof. geography U. Chgo., 1943-46, asso. prof., 1946-47, prof., 1947—, dean social scis., 1955-60, dir. Center for Internat. Studies, 1966—, chmn. dept. geography, 1967-69, Samuel N. Harper prof., 1969—. Del. Internat. Geog. Congress, Lisbon, 1949, Washington, 1952, Rio de Janeiro, 1956, Stockholm, 1960, London, 1964, New Delhi, 1968; v.p. Internat. Geog. Union, 1956-64, sec.-treas., 1968—; v.p. U.S. Com., 1949—. Mem. Assn. Am. Geographers (sec. 1946-48, v.p. 1956, pres. 1957), Am. Geog. Soc. (council 1962—, v.p. 1969—), Am. Assn. Advancement Slavic Studies (pres. 1962), Regional Sci. Assn. (v.p. 1963-64), Social Sci. Research Council (dir. 1959-70, vice chmn. 1963-65, exec. com. 1967-70), Nat. Acad. Scis. (adv. com. for internat. orgns. and programs 1969—), Internat. Council Sci. Unions (exec. com. 1969—), Internat. Research and Exchanges Bd. (exec. com. 1968-71). hon. mem. Royal Geog. Soc., geog. societies of Berlin, Frankfurt, Rome, Florence, Paris, Warsaw. Club: Quadrangle. Author: Cities of the Soviet Union, 1970. Editor: Economic Geography of the U.S.S.R., 1949, Internat. List of Geog. Serials, 1960, 71; Soviet Geography: Accomplishments and Tasks, 1962. Contbg. editor The Geog. Rev., 1960—. Contbr. profl. jours. Home: 5649 S Blackstone Av Chicago IL 60637

HARRIS, CLIFFORD WRIGHT, banker; b. Nottingham, Eng., 1908. Vice pres., sec. Bank of Montreal; pres., dir. St. James Land Co. Ltd.; sec., dir. Bankmont Realty Co., Ltd.; dir. Monroy Holdings, Ltd. Address: 129 St James St W Montreal 1 Quebec Canada *

HARRIS, CYRIL MANTON, educator, physicist, acoustical engr.; b. Detroit, June 20, 1917; s. Bernard O. and Ida (Moss) H.; B.A., U. Cal. at Los Angeles, 1938, M.A., 1940; Ph.D., Mass. Inst. Tech., 1945; m. Ann Schakne, July 12, 1949; children—Nicholas Bennett, Katherine Anne. Teaching asst. U. Cal. at Los Angeles, 1939-40; research fellow Mass. Inst. Tech., 1940, war research OSRD, 1941-44, teaching fellow, 1943-45; war research Carnegie Instn. Washington, 1941; mem. staff Bell Telephone Labs., 1945-51; cons. Office Naval Research, London, Eng., 1951; Fulbright lectr. Tech. U., Delft, Holland, 1951-52; now prof. elec. engrng. and architecture Columbia; vis. Fulbright prof. U. Tokyo (Japan), 1960; acoustical cons. Met. Opera House, N.Y.C., John F. Kennedy Center for Performing Arts, Washington, Krannert Center for Performing Arts, U. Ill., Powell Symphony Hall, St. Louis, Nat. Acad. Scis. Auditorium, Washington. Past dir. U.S. Inst. Theatre; tech. mem. subcom. aircraft noise NACA, 1955-57; mem. noise control group, com. undersea warfare NRC,

1955-57; mem. council hearing and bio-acoustics Armed Forces-NRC, 1953-55; mem. NRC adv. panel 213 to Nat. Bur. Standards, 1966-69, chmn., 1969-71. Fellow Acoustical Soc. Am. (exec. council 1954-57, v.p. 1960-61, pres. 1964-65, asso. editor jour. 1959-70), I.E.E.E. (chmn. profl. group ultrasonic engring. 1957-58, profl. group audio 1961-62), Audio Engring. Soc.; mem. Am. Inst. Physics (governing bd. 1965-66), ANTA (bd. standards, planning). Am. Standards Assn. (supr. com. Z-24, 1953-57), Am. Soc. Testing Materials (v.p. com. C-20, 1949-56), Sigma Xi, Tau Beta Pi. Author: (with V.O. Knudsen) Acoustical Designing in Architecture, 1950; Handbook of Noise Control, 1957; (with C.E. Crede) Shock and Vibration Handbook, 1961. Contbr. articles profl. jours. Editorial adv. bd. Physics Today, 1955-66. Office: Columbia U New York City NY 10027

HARRIS, DALE BENNER, psychologist; b. Elkhart, Ind., June 28, 1914; s. Ward Manning and Lillian (Benner) H.; A.B. with high distinction (Rector scholar), DePauw U., 1935; M.A., U. Minn., 1937, Ph.D., 1941; m. Elizabeth Saltmarsh, July 17, 1935; children—Ruthann E., James S., David B., Geoffrey M. Ednl. dir. Minn. Tng. Sch. for Boys, 1936-38; staff Inst. Child Welfare U. Minn., 1939-59, prof., 1939-59, dir., 1954-59; prof. psychology Pa. State U., 1959—, chmn. dept. psychology, 1962- 67; Fulbright vis. prof. Ochanomizu U., Tokyo, 1968-69. Mem. Mpls. Citizens Com. on Pub. Edn., 1946-59, Gov.'s Adv. Com. on Children and Youth, 1950-55, on Exceptional Children, 1956-59; mem. bd. Children's Home Soc. Minn., 1954-59; mem. adv. com. young workers Bur. Labor Standards. Dept. Labor, 1955-59; mem. adv. com. Clearing House for Research Relating to Children, U.S. Children's Bur., 1962-68; mem. exec. bd. Joint Commn. Correctional Manpower and Tng., 1965-69; mem. task force Joint Commn. Mental Health Children, 1966-69; research adv. com. Commonwealth Mental Health Research Found. Fellow Am. Psychol. Assn. (past pres. div. developmental psychology), A.A.A.S. (governing council 1962—, v.p., sect. chmn. 1972, sec. 1957-61, cons. editor monographs); mem. Am. Statis. Assn., Nat. Soc. Study Edn., Am. Assn. U. Profs., Am. Edn. Research Assn. (v.p. 1964), Phi Beta Kappa, Sigma Xi, Psi Chi, Phi Delta Kappa. Author: Children's Drawings as Measures of Intellectual Maturity, 1963; co-author: Child Care and Training, 8th edit., 1958. Editor: The Concept of Development, 1957; Child Development Abstracts, 1964—; editorial com. Ann. Rev. of Psychology, 1956-62. Contbr. profl. jours. Home: 317 W Ridge Av State College PA 16801

HARRIS, DAVID JOHN, investment banker; b. Chgo., June 13, 1913; s. David John and Harriet (Aurelius) H.; B.A., U. Chgo., 1935; m. Evelyn Carr, Dec. 19, 1936; children—Carol Ann, Glenn Carr, John Corydon. Sales positions Sills, Minton & Co., investment bankers, 1935-43; chief cost accountant United Drill & Tool, 1943; pres. Sills, Fairman & Harris, Inc., 1944-56; asso. N.Y. Stock Exchange, 1949—; resident partner Bache & Co., 1956-64; pres. Chgo. Corp., 1964-69, chmn., chief exec. officer, 1969—; dir. Liberty Loan Corp., St. Louis, Sentry Ins., Stevens Point, Wis. Gov. Midwest Stock Exchange, 1959—, chmn. exec. com., 1962-63, chmn., 1963-65, mem., 1964—; mem. Am. Stock Exchange, 1966—. Mem. Sch. Bd., Lake County, Ill., 1954-57; chmn. Highland Park Community Chest, 1958. Trustee Highland Park Hosp., 1970—. Mem. Investment Bankers Assn. (chmn. Central States group 1955, gov. 1956- 59, v.p. 1960-63, pres. 1963-64), Assn. Stock Exchange Firms (gov.), Chgo. Bd. Trade, Delta Kappa Epsilon. Clubs: University, Chicago, Attic (Chgo.); Exmoor Country (gov. 1957-59, pres. 1969-71) (Highland Park). Home: 142 Central Av Highland Park IL 60035 Office: 208 S LaSalle St Chicago IL 60604

HARRIS, DAVID TAYLOR, banker; b. N.Y.C., Mar. 1, 1923; s. Victor and Catherine (Richardson) H.; A.B., Princeton, 1944; m. Susie Skidmore, July 9, 1949; children—David Taylor Jr., Catherine. With U.S. Trust Co., N.Y.C., 1947—, asst. sec., 1955- 57, asst. v.p., 1957-60, v.p., 1960-66, sr. v.p., 1966—. Chmn. devel. com. Am. Field Service, N.Y.C.; mem. Retirement Bd., Greenwich, Conn., 1970—. Trustee Am. Acad. Rome, Am. Field Serivce. Served to lt. j.g. USNR, 1943-46. Mem. Nat. Inst. Social Scis. Republican. Episcopalian. Clubs: Field, Round Hill (Greenwich); India House, University, Pilgrims of U.S. (N.Y.C.). Home: Quail Rd Greenwich CT 06830 Office: 45 Wall St New York City NY 10005

HARRIS, DAVID WILLIAM, petroleum exec.; b. Machen, Ga., Sept. 7, 1891; s. Nathaniel Edwin (ex- gov. of Ga.) and Fannie (Burke) H.; B.S. in E.E., Ga. Sch. Tech., 1912; m. Mildred Stoutenborough, July 2, 1914; children—Walter Alexander, Holton Edwin. Engr., Denver Gas & Electric Co., 1912-13; dir. budget, asst. treas. Cities Service Co., 1913-23; treas. Empire Gas & Fuel Co., 1923-27; v.p. Ind. Ty. Ill. Oil Co., 1927-28; v.p., gen. mgr. Ark. Natural Gas Corp. and subsidiary cos., pres. Ark. Natural Gas Corp., 1944-45, Orange State Oil Co., 1939- 45; v.p., dir. Cities Service Def. Corp., 1941-45; pres., chief exec. officer Universal Oil Products Co., 1945-60; chmn. David W. Harris & Assos., cons., 1962—; dir. Harrel, Inc. Mem. Mid-Continent Oil and Gas Assn. (exec. com., past pres. La.-Ark. div.), Am. Gas Assn. (dir. 1941-45), Bartlesville (Okla.) C. of C., Western Soc. Engrs., Newcomen Soc. N.Am., Chi Phi. Recipient Alumni Distinguished Service award Ga. Inst. Tech., 1954. Methodist. Mason (32, K.T., Shriner). Clubs: Chicago; Glen View; Westmoreland, McGraw Wildlife Found. Home: 2305 Central Park Av Evanston IL 60201 Office: Golf Mill Profl Bldg Niles IL 60648

HARRIS, EARL EDWARD, Jr., hosp. adminstr.; b. Hopkinsville, Ky., Sept. 26, 1936; s. Earl Edward and Mary Elizabeth (Gresham) H.; B.S., Murray (Ky.) State U., 1959; m. Peggy Joyce Lowry, June 11, 1961; 1 son, James Richard. Sanitarian, Christian County (Ky.) Health Dept., 1960-62; asst. adminstr. Western State Hosp., Hopkinsville, 1962-66; adminstr. Outwood State Hosp., Dawson Springs, Ky., 1966—. Pres. Elect Twin Lakes Hosp. Conf., 1969. Served with AUS, 1959-60. Mem. Ky. Hosp. Assn., Hopkinsville Jr. C. of C. Mason. Home: 313 Roney Dr Hopkinsville KY 44240 Office: Outwood State Hosp Dawson Springs KY 44208

HARRIS, EDDIE, saxophonist; b. Chgo., Oct. 20, 1934; s. Walter and Alice (Nolan) H.; student U. Ill., Roosevelt U., also in Paris; m. Sara Turner, May 22, 1961; children—Lolita M., Yvonne M. Player with big bands, 1948—; now working on playing trumpet with reed mouthpiece; saxophonist with 2 octaves above written range; recording artist for Atlantic Records. Recipient Cash Box Top Record award, 1961, Jazz Poll award, 1968. Home: 8010 S Cottage Grove Chicago IL 60619 Office: 200 W 57th St New York City NY 10019

HARRIS, EDWARD, lawyer; b. Rochester, N.Y., Sept. 24, 1912; A.B., Princeton, 1935; LL.B., Cornell U., 1938. Admitted to N.Y. bar, 1939; mem. firm Harris, Beach, & Wilcox, Rochester. Trustee Rochester Savs. Bank; dir. Security Trust Co. Rochester. Trustee Columbia Sch., 1947-50, Allendale Sch., 1950-53, Auburn at Union Theol. Sem., 1959-62, Springfield Coll., 1964—. Mem. Am., Rochester, Monroe County bar assns., U.S. Combined Tng. Assn. (pres. 1966-68), Phi Delta Phi. Office: 5 S Fitzhugh St Rochester NY 14614*

HARRIS, EDWARD ARNOLD, writer, newspaperman. b. St. Louis, Oct. 20, 1910; s. Nathan and Rose (Goldman) H.; A.B., Washington U., St. Louis, 1933; M.S. in Journalism, U. Cal. at Los Angeles, 1958; m. Miriam Sima Levy, Oct. 5, 1938; children—Linda Gail, Mark Geoffrey, Robert Nathaniel. Campus corr. Washington U. for St. Louis Star-Times, 1931-33; columnist, gen. reporter Star-Times, 1933-40; city hall reporter St. Louis Post-Dispatch, 1940, reporter, local polit. writer, 1940-43, Washington corr., 1943-54; St. Louis corr. Fortune, Life and Time, 1936- 43; chief West Coast bur. St. Louis Post-Dispatch, 1954-58; syndicated columnist, 1960-63; pres. Edward A. Harris & Assos., 1963—. Recipient Pulitzer prize for distinguished nat. correspondence, 1946; journalism award in behalf of Post-Dispatch Washington bur. Fontbonne Coll., St. Louis, 1947; co-recipient Heywood Broun runner-up award, 1951; Alumni citation Washington U., 1957; Agrl. writers award, 1961. Author: (with J.T. Salter, editor) Public Men, In and Out of Office, 1946; Love Thy Neighbor, 1958. Contbr. articles on nat. affairs to mags. Home: Jordan River Farm Huntley VA 22640

HARRIS, EDWARD GEORGE, clergyman; b. Boston, Apr. 30, 1917; s. Ulysses Sylvester and Lillian (Dennett) H.; diploma Boston Latin Sch., 1934; B.A., Harvard, 1938; B.D., Episcopal Theol. Sch., 1941; S.T.M., Union Theol. Sem., 1942; D.D. (hon.), U. Pa., 1961; m. Shirley Lucille Barlow, June 21, 1941; children—David Barlow, Jennifer Dennett, Geoffrey Pollitt. Ordained deacon P.E. Ch., 1941, priest, 1941; asst. minister Ch. of Ascension, N.Y.C., 1941-44; rector St. Mark's Episcopal Ch., Southborough, Mass., 1946-50; tchr. sacred studies St. Mark's Sch., Southborough, 1947-50; examining chaplain Episcopal Diocese of Mass. 1948-50; tutor Episcopal Theol. Sch., Cambridge, Mass., 1949-50; chaplain U. Pa., 1950-61; dean, prof. Div. Sch. P.E. Ch. Phila., 1961—; rector St. James Summer Chapel, Burkehaven, N.H., 1952-63. Mem. Corp. for Christian Work Ednl. Instns., Diocese Pa., 1951-70; mem. Diocesan Council, Diocese Pa., 1968—; dep. gen. conv. Episcopal Ch., 1967, 69, 70; mem. Phila. Commn. on Alcoholism, 1956-70. Served as chaplain U.S. Army, 1944-46. Recipient citation Nat. Conf. Christians and Jews. Mem. Soc. Bibl. Lit., Alpha Epsilon Delta, Alpha Phi Omega, Sphinx Sr. Soc. Clubs: Faculty (U. Pa.); Harvard (Phila.). Author: The Physician, The Clergyman, and the Patient in Terminal Illness; The Valley of Decision; Mission to Mankind; God and Our Daily Work; Ethics in Ferment; Doubt and Faith; A Study in Existentialism; The Urgency of Ethics; Prayers for a University, 1961. Home: 4243 Spruce St Philadelphia PA 19104 Office: 4205 Spruce St Philadelphia PA 19104

HARRIS, EDWARD MONROE, Jr., office equipment co. exec.; b. Phila., June 5, 1923; s. Edward Monroe and Grace (Wilson) H.; B.A., Yale, 1943; LL.B., U. Pa., 1949; m. Marion Hoyt Stevens, Sept. 16, 1950; children—Edward Monroe III, Marion Olney, Peter Duncan. Admitted to N.Y. bar, 1949; with firm Sullivan and Cromwell, N.Y.C., 1949-57; asso. counsel Kennecott Copper Corp., 1957- 62; corp. counsel, sec. Crowell Collier and MacMillan Inc., N.Y.C., 1963-67; sec., gen. counsel Pitney-Bowes, Inc., Stamford, Conn., 1967—, v.p., 1969—. Mem. nat. com. self devel. of people United Presbyn. Ch. U.S.A., 1970—. Mem. Darian (Conn.) Bd. Edn., 1965-68, chmn., 1966-68. Served to 1st lt. USMCR, 1943-46. Mem. Am. Bar Assn., Assn. Bar City N.Y. Republican. Club: Wee Burn Country (Darien). Home: 337 Hollow Tree Ridge Rd Darien CT 06820 Office: Pitney-Bowes Inc Darien CT 06820

HARRIS, ELLEN GANDY, (Mrs. J. Ramsay Harris), civic worker; b. Spokane, Wash., Jan. 9, 1910; d. Lloyd Edward and Helen (George) Gandy; student U. Wash.; grad. Smith Coll., 1930; m. J. Ramsay Harris, Jan. 20, 1936; children—Sue Ellen, Hayden Henry. Mem. U.S. com. UNICEF, 1948-66; mem. Def. Adv. Com. Women in Service, 1951-54; nat.-co- chmn. Citizens for Eisenhower, 1953-54; Rep. candidate U.S. Congress from Denver, 1954; mem. Internat. Devel. Adv. Bd., 1955- 57; nat. co. chmn. Com. Internat. Econ. Growth, 1958-60; regional chmn. Met. Opera Council, 1958-66; mem. Gov. Colo.'s Local Affairs Commn., 1963-66; pres. Colo. Consumers Council, 1965-67; dir. Nat. Safety Council, 1958-60; mem. Nat. Adv. Council on Nurse Tng., U.S. Dept. Health, Edn. and Welfare, 1969—; mem. The Park People, 1971—. Trustee Nat. Fund Grad. Nurse Edn., Central City Opera, Denver Symphony Soc. Staff writer Denver Post. Mem. Assn. Jr. Leagues Am. (bd. dirs. 1947-50). Episcopalian. Home: 1077 Race St Denver CO 80206

HARRIS, ERROL EUSTACE, educator; b. Kimberley, S. Africa, Feb. 19, 1908; s. S.J. and Dora (Gross) H.; B.A., Rhodes Coll., Grahamstown, S. Africa, 1927, M.A., 1929; B.Litt., Magdalen Coll., Oxford U. (Eng.), 1933; D.Litt., Witwatersrand U., Johannesburg, S. Africa, 1951; m. Sylvia Mundahl, July 11, 1946; children—Jonathan, Nigel, Hermione, Martin. Came to U.S., 1956. Lectr. philosophy Ft. Hare (S. Africa) Univ. Coll., 1930; edn. officer British Colonial Service in Basutoland and Zanzibar, 1937-42; from lectr. to prof. philosophy, head dept. U. Witwatersrand, 1946-56; vis. lectr. Yale, 1956-57, Terry lectr., 1957; prof. philosophy Conn. Coll., 1956-62; acting head dept. logic nd metaphys. Edinburgh U. (Scotland), 1959-60; Roy Roberts distinguished prof. philosphy U. Kan., 1962-66; prof. philosophy Northwestern U., 1966—. Served with British Army, 1942-46. Alfred Belt scholar Rhodes Univ. Coll., 1928; Queen Victoria scholar U. Oxford, 1931-33; Hugh Le May research fellow Rhodes U., 1949; Bollingen research fellow, 1960-62; Ford Found. research fellow, 1964. Mem. Metaphys. Soc. Am. (pres. 1968-69). Author: The Survival of Political Man, 1950; Nature, Mind and Modern Science, 1954; Revelation Through Reason, 1958; Foundations of Metaphysics in Science, 1965; White Civilization, 1952; South African Survey, 1947; Annihilation and Utopia, 1966; Fundamentals of Philosophy 1969; Hypothesis and Perception, 1970. also numerous articles, revs. Editor: (H. H. Joachim) Descartes's Rules for the Direction of the Mind, 1957. Home: 452 Oak Av Evanston IL 60201

HARRIS, EVERETTE BAGBY, exchange exec.; b. Norris City, Ill., Apr. 19, 1913; s. George N. and Maud (Bagby) H.; A.B., U. Ill., 1935; M.B.A., U. Chgo., 1945; m. Marguerite Anita Solberg, May 14, 1939; children—Scott Scott Walden, Dale Alan. Staff soil conservation service Dept. Agr., 1935-38; economist Dept. Labor, 1938-46; tchr. econs. evening schs. De Paul U., U. Chgo., 1943-45; dir. personnel, supt. non-selling depts. Mandel Bros., Chgo., 1946-49; exec. sec. Chgo. Bd. Trade, 1949-53; pres. Chgo. Merc. Exchange, 1953—. Mem. exec. and steering coms. Chgo. chpt. Nat. Found.; exec. bd. Chgo. council Boy Scouts Am.; Ill. chmn., mem. nat. council U.S.O., 1956-57. Mem. Am. Statis. Assn., Am. Marketing Assn., Young Presidents Assn. Presbyn. Mason (32, Shriner), Elk. Clubs: University (Park Ridge, Ill.); Union League, Economic, Executives, Lions (Chgo.); Kenwood Country. Author: Earnings and Hours in Book and Job Printing, 1942; also chpt. Am. Peoples Ency. Home: 524 Parkwood Park Ridge IL 60068 Office: 110 N Franklin St Chicago IL 60606

HARRIS, FRANK EPHRAIM, educator, chemist; b. Boston, Aug. 26, 1929; s. Frank Ephraim and Wilhelmina (Sellers) H.; A.B., Harvard, 1951; Ph.D., U. Cal. at Berkeley, 1954. Instr. chemistry Harvard, 1953-56; asst. prof. chemistry U. Cal. at Berkeley, 1956-59; faculty Stanford, 1959-68, asso. prof. chemistry, 1961-68; prof. chemistry and physics U. Utah, Salt Lake City, 1968—; cons. Lawrence Radiation Lab. U. Cal., United Aircraft Research Labs.; lectr. Internat. Summer Inst. in Quantum Chemistry; acting dir. Quantum Chemistry group Uppsala U. (Sweden), 1963-64; mem. adv. editorial bd. Internat. Jour. of Quantum Chemistry, also Quantum Theory of Matter. A.P. Sloan fellow, 1957-59. Author: Principles of Chemistry, 1963-65. Research, publs. in theoretical chemistry; theory of orientation of molecules in an electric field; dimensions and charge distbn. in charged polymer molecules; devel. of methods for the calculation of the distbn. of electrons in atoms and molecules, especially for use on large-scale digital computers. Office: Dept Physics U Utah Salt Lake City UT 84112

HARRIS, FRED EARL, coll. dean; b. Washington, June 8, 1917; s. James Riley and Elizabeth Annette (Schoolfield) H.; B.S., Ind. State U., Terre Haute, 1940; M.S., 1942; Ed.D., Ind. U., 1950; m. Frances Bandy, Dec. 24, 1938; children—Susan, Nancy. Dir. grad. studies elementary edn., prof. edn. U. Ky., 1950-57; specialist fundamental edn. ICA, Egypt, 1954-55; cons. edn. ICA, Kabul, Afghanistan, 1959; dean coll. Baldwin-Wallace Coll., 1957-69, also vice pres. acad. affairs, 1964-69; v.p. acad. affairs U. Evansville, 1969—. Mem. Nat. Edn. Study Team, Viet Nam, 1967, 70; cons. AID, Uganda, Tanzania, Kenya, 1969. Recipient Distinguished Alumni award Ind. State U., 1965. Mem. Assn. Higher Edn., N.E.A., Nat. Conf. Research English, Am. Assn. U. Profs., Nat. Soc. Study Edn., Comparative Edn. Soc., Phi Delta Kappa. Methodist. Contbr. articles profl. jours. Office: U Evansville Evansville IN 47701

HARRIS, FRED JOSEPH, jurist, fgn. service officer; b. Chgo., Nov. 19, 1908; s. Frank Harris and Anna (Smith) H.; student Morton Jr. Coll., Cicero, Ill., 1928-31; LL.B., Chgo. Kent Coll. of Law, 1934; m. Carolyn Wood, Oct. 4, 1940; children—JoAnne, Frank X., Fred J., John W., J. Peter. Admitted to Ill. bar, 1934; gen. practice of law, 1934-41; dist. judge, Regensburg, U.S. Mil. Govt. for Germany, 1946-49; presiding judge, Regensburg, U.S. High Commn. for Germany, 1949-53; justice U.S. Ct. of Restitution Appeals, Nürnberg, U.S. High Commn. for Germany, 1955, justice Supreme Restitution Ct., 3d Div., Nurnberg, 1955, justice Supreme Restitution Ct. for Berlin, 1959—, justice U.S. Embassy, Bonn, Germany. Served from private to capt., AUS, 1941-46. Home: 321 S Gilbert Av LaGrange IL 60525 Office: care American Embassy Bonn Germany

HARRIS, FRED ORIN, retired educator; b. Sumpter, Ore., Jan. 24, 1901; s. Orin and Mary Ellen (Murphy) H.; B.F.A., U. Wash., 1924; M.F.A., N.Y.U., 1939; m. Mary Caroline Blaisdell, July 26, 1931. Play prodn. in community, univ. group and studio theatres including U. Ore., Padua Hills, Cal., Portland (Ore.) Civic Theatre, Peterborough, (N.H.) Players, Maria Ouspenskaya Studio, N.Y.C., 1925-40; tchr. dramatic art U. Cal., 1941-51, prof. 1951-68, chmn. dept., 1944-60, asst. dean Coll. Letters and Sci., 1964-68. Club: Bohemian (San Francisco). Home: 1622 Spruce St Berkeley CA 94709

HARRIS, FRED R., U.S. senator; b. Walters, Okla., Nov. 13, 1930; s. Fred Byron and Alene (Person) H.; B.A. in Polit. Sci., U. Okla., 1952, LL.B. with distinction, 1954; m. LaDonna Crawford, Apr. 8, 1949; children—Kathryn, Byron, Laura. Admitted to Okla. bar, 1954; founder, sr. partner firm Harris, Newcombe, Redman & Doolin, Lawton, Okla., 1954-64; mem. Okla Senate, 1956-64; mem. U.S. Senate from Okla., 1964—, former chmn. senate subcom. govt. research, mem. senate finance and govt. operations coms. Mem. Nat. Adv. Commn. Civil Disorders, 1967-68. Chmn., Democratic Nat. Com., 1969-70. Mem.. Order of Coif, Phi Beta Kappa. Democrat. Author: Alarms and Hopes, 1969; Now Is The Time, 1971. Home: 1120 Cherry St Lawton OK 73501 also 1104 Waverly Way McLean VA Office: Old Senate Office Bldg Washington DC 20510

HARRIS, FREDERICK GEORGE, publishing co. exec.; b. Niles, O., Apr. 12, 1922; s. William H. and Nell H. (Zempkey) H.; B.S. in Bus. Adminstrn., Ohio State U., 1948; m. Marjorie E. Bork, Sept. 10, 1950; children—Frederick, David, Joyce. Staff accountant Lybrand, Ross Bros. & Montgomery, 1948-56; with Dow Jones & Co., Inc., 1956—, comptroller-asst. sec., 1970—; trustee Trenton Lutheran Housing Corp., 1969—. Chmn. local troop Boy Scouts Am., 1965-67, sec., 1967-69. Served with USAAF, 1942-45. Mem. Financial Execs. Inst. (chmn. orgn. planning com. N.Y. chpt. 1963-64), Nat. Assn. Accountants (asso. dir. N.Y. chpt. 1959-61), Inst. Newspaper Controllers and Finance Officers (bd. dirs. 1964—, chmn. budget and finance com. 1965-66, chmn. steering com. 1968-69, pres. 1970-71; Walter F. Carley award), Delta Sigma Pi. Lutheran (v.p. 1967-68, council 1965—). Home: 113 Lewis Brook Rd Pennington NJ 08534 Office: PO Box 300 Princeton NJ 08540

HARRIS, GEORGE BERNARD, judge; b. San Francisco, Calif., Aug. 16, 1901; s. Bernard Dugan and Gertrude (Howard) H.; grad. Sacred Heart Coll., 1919; LL.D., U. San Francisco, 1926; m. Aileen Adele Duffy, July 22, 1930; 1 dau., Gail Sheridan. Admitted to Calif. state bar 1926; judge Calif. State Cts., 1941, U.S. Dist. Ct., 1946—, now sr. judge. Mem. Soc. Cal. Pioneers. Democrat. Roman Catholic. Clubs: Bohemian (San Francisco); The Family; St. Francis Yacht. Home: 1812 Broadway San Francisco CA 94109 Office: Fed Bldg and US Courthouse San Francisco CA 94102

HARRIS, GEORGE GORDON, lawyer; b. Smithton, Mo., Feb. 13, 1883; s. John Vaughn and Margaret (Summerville) H.; LL.B., U. Mo., 1908; m. Laurine Shireman, Sept. 7, 1930. Admitted to Mo. bar, 1908, Cal. bar, 1908, Wash. bar, 1908, Mont. bar, 1912; mem. firm Church, Harris, Johnson & Williams, Great Falls, Monts., 1941—. Dir. Great Falls Fed. Savs. & Loan Assn. Chmn. State Bd. Pub. Welfare, Helena, 1940-44. Served with U.S. Army, World War I. Mem. Great Falls C. of C. (dir.), Am. Legion, Phi Delta Phi. Mason. Clubs: Pivitan, Meadow Lark Country (dir.) (Great Falls). Home: 311 3d Av N Great Falls MT 59401 Office: Great Falls Bank Bldg Great Falls MT 59401

HARRIS, GEORGE S., corp. exec.; b. St. Louis, 1898. Pres., dir. Chgo. Met. Mut. Assurance Co., Chgo.; owner George S. Harris Real Estate; pres Parkway Amusement Corp.; v.p., dir. Silvart Corp.; dir. Freeway Mortgage Co., Tuesday Publs., Inc. Home: 9327 S Michigan Av Chicago IL 60619 Office: 4455 South Pkwy Chicago IL 60653

HARRIS, GEORGE TAYLOR, educator; b. Waterloo, Ia., Mar. 15, 1917; s. Orlie Burley and Elvia (Taylor) H.; student Monmouth Coll., 1936-38; B.A., Ia. State Tchrs. Coll., 1947; M.A., State U. Ia., 1950, Ph.D., 1953; m. Dorothy Eleanor Clark, Oct. 6, 1944; children—Susan Elizabeth, Carolyn Jean, George Clark. Office supr., clk., salesman Rath Packing Co., Waterloo, 1935- 36, 38- 47; instr. Tama (Ia.) High Sch., 1947-48; instr. econs. State U. Ia., 1948-53; asst. prof. finance Ind. U., 1953-55; asso. prof. bus. adminstrn. U. Neb. at Omaha, 1955-58, prof. bus. adminstr., 1958—, Frederick W. Kayser prof. finance, 1964—, acting dean Coll. Bus. Adminstrn., 1971—; instr. Am. Savs. and Loan Inst., 1956-63. Mem. citizens adv. com. Omaha Sch. Bd., 1960-63. Mem. Am. Assn. U. Profs., Omaha Assn. Credit Mgmt., Am., Midwest (pres. 1968-69) finance assns., Nat. Fedn. Financial Analysts, Am., Midwest econ. assns., Omaha-Lincoln Financial Analysts, Kappa Delta Pi, Pi Gamma Mu, Omicron Delta Epsilon. Mason. Home: 5020 Eastridge Dr Omaha NB 68134

HARRIS, GEORGE THOMAS, Jr., lawyer; b. Henryetta, Okla., Sept. 12, 1922; s. George Thomas and Gertrude V. (Smith) H.; LL.B., U. N.M., 1950; m. Martha J. Henry, Aug. 8, 1941; children—George Thomas III, Ronald G., Debra Lyn. Admitted to N.M. bar, 1950; asso. firm Modrall, Sperling, Roehl, Harris & Sisk, Albuquerque, 1950—, partner firm, 1956—. Dir. Ruidoso (N.M.) State Bank. Mem. N.M.

Bd. Bar Commrs. Served to 1st lt. USAAF, 1943-45; MTO. Mem. Albuquerque Bar Assn. (past pres.), N.M. Attys.' Assn. (past pres.) Home: 2615 Schell Ct NE Albuquerque NM 87112 Office: Pub Service Bldg PO Box 2168 Albuquerque MN 87103

HARRIS, GORDON MCLEOD, educator; b. Chungking, China, July 23, 1913; s. George Gordon and Agnes (McLeod) H.; B.Sc., U. Saskatchewan, Can., 1939; M.Sc., 1940; A.M., Harvard, 1942, Ph.D., 1943; m. Justyn Lee Montgomery, June 10, 1943; children—David, Deborah, Matthew. Came to U.S., 1953, naturalized, 1958. Research chemist NRC of Can., Ottawa, 1944-45; asst. prof. chemistry U. Saskatchewan, 1945-48; sr. lectr. phys. chemistry U. Melbourne, Australia, 1948-52; asso. prof. chemistry State U. N.Y. at Buffalo, 1953-55, prof., 1955-56, chmn. dept. chemistry, 1956-69, Larkin prof. chemistry, 1961—; hon. research asso. University Coll., London, 1961; vis. prof. Australian Nat. U., 1969. Served as operational research officer RCAF, 1943-44. Fellow Am. Inst. Chemists; mem. Am. Chem. Soc., A.A.A.S., Chem. Soc. (London), Sigma Xi. Home: 128 Crosby Blvd Eggertsville NY 14226 Office: State U N Y Buffalo NY 14214

HARRIS, GRADY DEWITT, Jr., banker; b. Alex, Okla., June 27, 1926; s. Grady DeWitt and Robena H. (Dellinger) H.; A.B., U. Okla., 1945, LL.B., 1949, postgrad. Coll. Bus. Adminstrn.; m. Alice June Hunter, Aug. 23, 1947; children—Barbara Jean, Grady Hunter. Various positions Liberty Nat. Bank & Trust Co., Oklahoma City, 1950-59, sr. v.p., chmn. loan com., dir., mem. exec. com., 1956-59; pres. Fidelity Nat. Bank & Trust Co., Oklahoma City, 1960—; chmn. First Nat. Bank, Alex, Okla., First State Bank, Blanchard, Okla.; dir. Capitol Hill State Bank & Trust Co., Kerr-McGee Oil Industries, Inc., Am. Fidelity Assurance Co. (all Oklahoma City); adv. dir. Community Nat. Bank of Warr Acres, Okla. Past pres. Travelers Aid Soc., Oklahoma City; past co-chmn. United Fund-Red Cross campaign of Oklahoma City; pres. Downtown Action, Inc., Oklahoma City; treas. Santa Claus Commn. Okla.; dir. Sunbeam Home and Family Service, Oklahoma County chpt. A.R.C., Better Bus., Oklahoma City; past dir. Okla. Heart Assn.; trustee U. Okla. Found., Inc.; bd. regents Okla. Coll. for Women. Served as lt. USNR, World War II. Recipient Outstanding Young Man of Year award, Oklahoma City, 1959; Distinguished Service award, Okla., 1960. Mem. Young President's Orgn., Assn. Res. City Bankers, Beta Gamma Sigma, Phi Delta Theta. Presbyn. (elder). Club: Economic of Okla. (past pres.). Home: 7317 Lancet La Oklahoma City OK 73120 Office: PO Box 24128 Oklahoma City OK 73124

HARRIS, GRANT ANDERSON, educator; b. Logan, Utah, July 13, 1914; s. Joseph Smith and Hilda (Anderson) H.; B.S., Utah State U., 1939, Ph.D., 1965; M.S., U. Ida., 1941; m. Jennabee Ballif, Oct. 18, 1939; children—Judith (Mrs. Gaylon Sanford Campbell), Patricia Florence (Mrs. Harold Davis Oak), Joseph Ballif, Halli H. Supt., Vigilante exptl. range U.S. Forest Service Research Br., Alder, Mont., 1941-48; project leader Upper Columbia Research Center, Spokane, Wash., 1948-51; asst. prof., extension forester, research Utah State U., 1951-56; asso. prof., research forester Wash. State U., Pullman, 1956-67, prof., chmn. dept. forestry and range mgmt., 1967—. Mem. adv. council Pacific N.W. Forest and Range Expt. Sta.; cons. W. Pakistan Agrl. U. Active Boy Scouts Am. Served to lt. (j.g.) USNR, 1944-46. Fellow A.A.A.S.; mem. Am. Soc. Range Mgmt. (Pacific N.W. sect. pres. 1964), Soc. Am. Foresters, Am. Forestry Assn., N.W. Sci. Assn., Wash. Farm Forestry Assn., Wash. State Forestry Conf. (trustee). Mem. Ch. of Jesus Christ of Latter-day Saints (bishop Pullman ward 1965—). Editorial bd. N.W. Science. Contbr. articles profl. jours. Home: 1401 Upper Dr Pullman WA 99163

HARRIS, GRANVILLE LIPSCOMB, transp. exec.; b. Tenn., Sept. 6, 1898; s. Joseph Henry and Lula (Franklin) H.; m. Jane Gonzales Strickland, Sept. 18, 1954; 1 son; Granville Reed. With Celotex Corp., Chgo., 1923-31; with Yellow Cab Co., San Francisco, 1933—, now exec. v.p., also dir. asso. cos. Bd. dirs. Conv. Bur. San Fransisco, Employers Council San Francisco. Mason (Shriner), Rotarian. Club: Commonwealth (San Francisco). Home: 305 Moseley Rd Hillsborough CA 94010 Office: 695 8th St San Francisco CA 94102

HARRIS, HARWELL HAMILTON, educator, architect; b. Redlands, Cal., July 2, 1903; s. Frederick Thomas and May Julia (Hamilton) H.; student Pomona Coll., 1921-23, Otis Art Inst., 1923-25; m. Jean Murray Bangs, Feb. 23, 1937. Sculptor, 1926- 29; practice architecture with Richard Neutra, 1929-32; pvt. practice, 1933—, in Los Angeles 1933-51, Austin, Tex., 1951-56, as Harris & Sherwood, Ft. Worth, 1956-57; architect with office in Dallas, 1958-62; lectr. U. So. Cal., 1945, 1946; vis. critic Columbia, 1943, Yale, 1950, 52; design cons. to Nat. Orange Show, 1950—; grad. design critic Columbia, 1960-61; prof. architecture N.C. State U., 1962—; dir. Sch. Architecture, U. Tex. 1951-55; prin. works include Lowe House, 1934, Fellowship Park House, 1935, Havens House, 1941, Birtcher House, 1942, Johnson House, 1947, English House, 1950, Chadwick School, 1951, Texas State Fair House, 1954, J. Lee Johnson House, 1956, Am. Embassy, Helsinki, 1957, Havens Meml. Plaza, Berkeley, Cal., 1961, Greenwood Mausoleum, 1959, Dallas Unitarian Ch., 1964, others; prin. projects include Segmental House for Revere Cooper & Brass Co., 1942, Pottenger Hosp., 1946, Palos Verdes Coll., 1947, Homestyle Found. House for S. West, 1956. Recipient 1st prize Pitts. Glass Inst., 1937, 38. Fellow A.I.A.; mem. Congress Internationaux d'Architecture Moderne (sec. Am. chpt. 1932, chpt. for relief and postwar planning, 1944), Tau Sigma Delta. Home: 124 Cox Av Raleigh NC Office: 122 Cox Av Raleigh NC 27605

HARRIS, HENRY HITER, Jr., banker; b. Richmond, Va., Aug. 16, 1922; s. Henry Hiter and Mary (Murdoch) H.; grad Woodberry Forest Sch., 1941; A.B., Princeton, 1946; postgrad. N.Y.U., 1946-48; m. Elizabeth Spalding Trueheart, Apr. 16, 1955; children—Mary Lawrence, Elizabeth Robinson, Henry Hiter III. Comml. credit analyst Chem. Bank N.Y. Trust Co., N.Y.C., 1946-50; asst. treas., asst. v.p. Chase Manhattan Bank, N.Y.C., 1950-55; v.p. Colonial-Am. Nat. Bank, Roanoke, Va., 1955-59; v.p., dir. So. Bank & Trust Co., Richmond, 1959-61; pres., dir., 1961-66, chmn. bd., pres., 1966—; chmn. bd., pres. So. Bankshares, Inc., Richmond, 1970—; dir. Williamsburg Nat. Bank (Va.), 1971—; dir. Central Va. Ednl. TV Corp., 1964—, mem. exec. com., 1968—, v.p., 1970—; dir. Va. Indsl. Devel. Corp., Richmond, 1961—. Mem. Va. Commn. Local Debt, 1962—, chmn., 1971—. Mem. Richmond City Sch. Bd., 1966-70. Trustee, mem. investment com. U. Richmond, 1969—; bd. dirs., past pres. Childrens Home Soc. Va.; bd. dirs., chmn. finance com. Crippled Childrens Hosp.; bd. dirs. Richmond Meml. Hosp.; trustee, exec. com. Mary Baldwin Coll., Staunton, Va., 1968—; trustee Va.-Md. Bankers Schs., 1968—. Served to 1st lt. USAFF, 1943-45. Mem. Soc. Colonial Wars, Va. Hist. Soc., Richmond C. of C. Presbyn. (elder). Clubs: Commonwealth, Country of Va., Forum (Richmond); University (N.Y.C.). Home: 4206 Sulgrave Rd Richmond VA 23221 Office: So Bank and Trust Co Grace St at 2d Richmond VA 23219

HARRIS, HENRY UPHAM, investment banker; b. Chgo., Apr. 27, 1900; s. John F. and Gertrude (Upham) H.; A.B., Harvard, 1923; m. Mary M. Webster, Oct. 3, 1925; children—Henry Upham, Joan (Mrs. Harold W. Hawkey), Evelyn G. (Mrs. Lawrence B. Van Ingen, Jr.), Mary A. (now Mrs. John H. Livens), David W. With firm Harris, Upham & Co., Inc. (and predessor firms), N.Y.C., 1923—, gen. partner, 1925-65, inc., 1965, pres., 1965-67, chmn., chief exec. officer, 1967-70, chmn., 1970—, also dir.; chmn. bd. Marineland of the Pacific, Inc.; dir. So. Pacific Co., Texaco, Inc., Stone & Webster, Inc. Trustee emeritus Fay Sch., Southborough, Mass. Home: Brookville Glen Head NY 11545 Office: 120 Broadway New York City NY 10005

HARRIS, HENRY UPHAM, Jr., pres. Harris, Upham and Co. Address: 120 Broadway New York City NY 10005*

HARRIS, HENRY W., banker; b. 1907; grad. Hampden-Sydney Coll., also Rutgers U. Grad Sch. Banking; married. With Wachovia Bank and Trust Co. N.A., 193O—, treas., 1954—. Address: PO Box 3099 Winston-Salem NC 27102

HARRIS, HENRY WILLIAM, physician; b. Catawba, N.C., Jan. 6, 1919; s. Henry William and Katie (Coulter) H.; B.A., U.N.C., 1940; M.D. cum laude, Harvard, 1943; m. Margaret Ann Roberts, Nov. 29, 1950; children—Henry William, John R., James P. Intern Harvard Med. Service, Boston City Hosp., 1944-45, asst. resident medicine, 1945-46; resident fellow Thorndike Meml. Lab., 1944, 46; resident chest service Bellevue Hosp., N.Y.C., 1947; staff physician Gunderson Clinic, LaCrosse, Wis., 1948-53; asst. prof. medicine U. Utah Coll. Medicine, 1955-59, asso. prof., 1959-60; chief pulmonary disease service VA Hosp., Salt Lake City, 1955-60; prof. chmn. dept. medicine Woman's Med. Coll. of Pa., 1960-67; chmn. dept. medicine Cath. Med. Center Bklyn. and Queens, 1967-70, prof. clin. medicine, 1970—; asso. prof. clin. medicine N.Y.U. Sch. Medicine, 1969-70; attending med. services Hosp. Cath. Med. Center; vis. physician Bellevue Hosp., N.Y.C., Queens Gen. Hosp., Jamaica, N.Y. Cons. surgeon gen. U.S. Army. Bd. dris., Nat. Tb Assn., Bklyn. Tb and Heath Assn. Served to capt., M.C., AUS, 1953-55; chief non-Tb pulmonary disease service, asst. chief pulmonary disease service Fitzsimons Army Hosp., Denver. Diplomate Am. Bd. Internal Medicine, 1951. Fellow A.C.P.; mem. Am. Thoracic Soc. (pres. 1962- 63), Western Soc. Clin. Research, N.Y. Acad. Sci. Am. Fedn. Clin. Research, A.A.A.S., N.Y. Acad. Medicine. Contbr. articles publs. Home: 14 Seabury Rd Garden City NY 11530 Office: Chest Service Bellevue Hosp 1st Av and 27th St New York City NY 10016

HARRIS, HERMAN KARDD, II, educator; b. Heath Springs, S.C., Apr. 8, 1940; s. Roby and Carrie Roxana (Harris) H.; A.A., Friendship Jr. Coll., 1960; B.S., Morris Coll., 1963. Instr. phys. edn. Friendship Jr. Coll., Rock Hill, 1965-71, basketball coach, 1965-71, baseball coach, 1965-71. Recreation dir., City of Rock Hill, 1965-70. Mem. Mt. Meriya Assn. (v.p. 1961-62), Modern Poets Am., Palmetto Bowling Assn. Contbr. to Longview Jour. Modern Poets, Spectrum, Friendship Jr. Coll. Chronicle. Home: 423 Allen St Rockhill SC 29730 Office: Friendship Jr Coll Rockhill SC 29730

HARRIS, HUGH PATE, ret. army officer; b. Anderson, Ala., June 15, 1909; s. Leo C. and Maude Ethel (Alsup) H.; B.S., U.S. Mil. Acad., 1931; student Inf. Sch., 1938, Armed Forces Staff Coll., 1946, Command and Staff Coll., 1948, Nat. War Coll., 1950; m. Jane Boyd, Aug. 24, 1934 (dec. 1958); 1 dau., Beverly Boyd; m. 2d, Kathleen Burns, 1961; 1 adopted dau., Betsy. Commd. 2d lt. U.S. Army, 1931, advanced through grades to gen.; unit comdr. 22d Inf., 1931-34, Hawaiian Div., 1934-37, 5th Inf. Div., 1940-41; assigned airborne units, Ft. Benning, Ga. and Ft. Bragg, N.C., 1942-46; instr. Army Staff Coll., 1948; chief staff U.S. 13th Airborne Div., 1944-46, 18th Airborne Corps, 1951-52, 2d Army, 1953-55; liason with Canadian Army, Joint Chiefs Staff, 1948; regt. comdr. 224th Inf., 40th Div., Korea, 1952; dep. chief staff for operations 8th Army, Korean War, 1953; comdg. gen., Berlin, 1955; div. comdr. 11th Airborne Div., Germany, 1956; dep. chief of staff for operations, plans and tng. G3, U.S. Continental Army Command, Fort Monroe, Va., 1958-60; comdt. U.S. Army Inf. School and comdg. gen. U.S. Army Inf. Center, Ft. Benning, 1960; comdg. gen. I Corps. (Group), Korea, 1961, 7th Army, 1962, Continental Army Command, 1964; comdr.-in-chief Army Strike Forces, 1964; pres. The Citadel, Charleston, S.C., 1965-70. Mem. S.C. Wildlife Commn., S.C. Atomic Energy Commn. Decorated D.S.M. with cluster, Silver Star, Legion Merit with clusters (U.S); D.S.M. with cluster (Korea). Mem. Assn. Grads. U.S. Mil. Acad. (trustee). Mason (32). Club: Optimist. Assisted preparation airborne lit. for U.S. Army tng. system. Home: Box 774 Route 1 Bonneau SC

HARRIS, HUNTER, Jr., air force officer; b. San Antonio, Nov. 27, 1909; s. Hunter and Lula B. (Allen) H.; student Va. Mil. Inst., 1926-27, U. Ga., 1928; B.S., U.S. Mil. Acad., 1928-32; m. Margaret Stratton McCurdy Bostic, Sept. 25, 1937; children—Margaret Hunter (dec.), Hunter III. Commd. 2d lt. USAAF, 1932, advanced through grades to gen. USAF, 1964; pilot, 1933, command pilot, 1943, tech. observer, 1945; various assignments U.S. and overseas, 1933-41; asst. operations officer War Dept. Gen. Staff, 1941- 52; group comdr. Harris Provisional Group, 1942; group comdr. 447th Bomb Group, 1942-44, 13th Combat Bomb Wing, 1944-45; dep. chief staff operations 3d Bomb Div., 1945; comdr. 92d Combat Bomb Wing, 1945; chief officers br. mil. personnel, dept. chief mil. personnel div. Hdqrs. USAAF, 1945-47; student Air Wall Coll., 1947-48; chief plans div., dep. comdr. Sandia Base, 1948-49; comdr. 509th Bomb Wing, 1950-51; comdg. gen. 47th Air Div., 1951-52; chief war plans div. dep. chief staff operations Hdqrs. USAF, 1952-53; air force mem. joint stategic plans com. Joint Chiefs Staff, dep. dir. plans, dep. chief staff operations Hdqrs. USAF, 1953-55; dep. for operations Hdqrs. Far East Air Force, Tokyo, Japan, 1955-57; dep. chief staff for plans and operations CINCPAC, Honolulu, 1957-58; dep. comdr. 8th Air Force, Westover AFB, Mass., 1958-61, comdr., 1961-62; vice comdr. in chief Strategic Air Command, 1962-64; comdr.-in-chief Pacific Air Forces, 1964-67; cons. Northrop Corp., Trans World Airlines, Mut. of Omaha; dir. Hawaii Nat. Bank. Decorated D.S.M. (USAF), D.S.M. (Army), Silver Star, Legion of Merit, D.F.C. with oak leaf cluster, Air Medal with 5 clusters, Purple Heart (U.S.); Croix de Guerre with Palm (France); D.F.C. (Eng.); Order of Cloud and Banner (China); Order of Mil. Merit Taeguk (Korea); Order of White Elephant, Order of Crown (Thailand). Mem. Kappa Alpha. Home: Hilton Lagoon Apts 2003 Kalia Rd Honolulu HI 96815

HARRIS, HUNTINGTON, corp. exec.; b. N.Y.C., May 15, 1914; s. Hayden Bartlett and Lina (Small) H.; student U. Chgo., 1931-37; B.S., Am. U., Washington, 1939; Ph.D., Columbia, 1950; m. Mary Winifred Hutchinson, Oct. 9, 1943; children—Susan V., Henry J.H. Export witness Dept. Justice, 1940; chief press sect. Office Facts and Figures, 1941; agt., chief agt. OSS, 1941- 45; founder Press Intelligence, Inc., Washington, 1946. pres., 1946-66; treas. Quadri-Sci., Inc.; chmn. Farrington Mfg. Co., 1959-63, Adrema, Ltd., 1960-63; dir. Cybertronic Inc., Harris Trust & Savs. Bank. Nat. fund vice chmn.-at-large A.R.C., 1960-61, bd. govs., 1961-68; v.p. No. Va. Ednl. TV Assn.; pres. Nat. Cathedral Assn. Trustee, pres. Ashville Sch.; trustee Syracuse U., Brooking Instn. Recipient Medal of Freedom. Mem. Royal Soc. Arts (London). Clubs: University (Washington and N.Y.C.); Metropolitan, Nat. Press (Washington); Chicago. Home: R D 1 Leesburg VA 22075 Office: 1028 Connecticut Av NW Washington DC 20036

HARRIS, IRVING BROOKS, business exec.; b. St. Paul, Aug. 4, 1910; s. William and Mildred (Brooks) H.; A.B., Yale, 1931; m. Rosetta Wolpert, Dec. 20, 1932; children—Roxanne, Virginia, William. Exec. in finance business, 1931-42, aircraft part bus., 1944-46; exec. Toni Home Permanent Co., 1946—; sold stockholdings in Toni Co. to Gillette Safety Razor Co., 1948; dir. Gillette Safety Razor Co. 1948-60; exec. v.p. Toni Co., 1946-52; chmn. bd. Sci. Research Assos., 1953-58; pres. Michael Reese Hosp. and Med. Center, Chgo., 1958-61; pres. R.J. Levy, Harris, Inc., 1959—; pres., dir. Standard Shares; chmn. bd. Pittway Corp.; chmn., dir. Cypress Communications. Served with Bd. Econ. Warfare, OPA, 1942-44. Trustee U. Chgo., Michael Reese Hosp.; pres. Chgo. Inst. for Early Childhood Edn., Chicago Ednl. TV Assn., Erikson Inst. Early Edn., Three Prong TV Assn., Chgo. Inst. Psychoanalysis. Clubs: Standard, Lake Shore Country, Midday, Downtown (Chgo.). Home: 244 Woodbridge Lane Highland Park IL 60035 Office: 1 First National Plaza Chicago IL 60670

HARRIS, JAMES B., film producer; b. N.Y.C., Aug. 3, 1928; ed. Julliard Sch. With Realart Pictures, 1948; formed Flamingo films, 1949, Harris-Kubrick Prodns., 1954, James B. Harris Prods., Inc., 1963; pictures include: The Killing, Path of Glory, Lolita, The Bedford Incident. Office: care Columbia Pictures Corp 71 Fifth Av New York City NY 10022*

HARRIS, JAMES COSGROVE, banker; b. Mpls., Sept. 10, 1920; s. George Henry and Myrtle (Cosgrove) H.; B.A., Macalester Coll., St. Paul, 1942; M.B.A., U. Minn., 1947; m. Elizabeth Fulton, Mar. 31, 1943; 1 dau., Margaret Susan. With Northwestern Nat. Bank, Mpls., 1947—, v.p., 1957-66, sr. v.p., adminstrv. trust officer, 1966-67, sr. v.p., exec, trust officer, 1967- 69, exec. v.p., 1969—; dir. E.F. Johnson Co., Waseca, Minn., Blandin Paper Co., Grand Rapids, Minn., Farmhand, Inc., Hopkins, Minn. Trustee Macalester Coll. Served to lt. comdr. USNR, 1942- 46. Mem. Twin Cities Soc. Security Analysts (past pres.), Nat. Assn. Bus. Economists, Financial Analysts Fedn. (dir.). Home: 500 Prospect Av Minneapolis MN 55419 Office: 7th and Marquette Sts Minneapolis MN 55440

HARRIS, JAMES THEODORE, Jr., orgn. exec.; b. Phila., July 11, 1923; B.A., LaSalle Coll., 1948, LL.D., 1965; certificate U. Geneva, 1950-51; M.A. in Pub. Affairs, Princeton, 1953; Ford Fellow, U. Cairo, 1953-55; married; 4 children. Pres. U.S. Nat. Student Assn., Madison, Wis., 1948-49; asst. sec. gen. World Univ. Service, Geneva, 1949-51; dir. fgn. student leadership program U.S. Nat. Student Assn., Phila., 1955-57; asst. exec. dir. Am. Soc. Study African Culture, 1957-61; sec.-gen. Nat. Sch. Law and Adminstrn., Kinshassa, Democratic Republic of Congo, 1961-63; program asso., overseas devel. program Middle East and Africa, Ford Found., 1963-64; dir. edn. and tng. Corning Glass Works, 1964-66, cons., 1966—; mem. President's Spl. Adv. Council Vocational Edn., 1966-68; v.p. African-Am. Inst., 1966-68; exec. dir. Nat. Cath. Conf. Interacial Justice, 1968—. Founder-dir. So. Tier Employment Council; mem. Cath. Commn. Intellectual and Cultural Affairs. Bd. dirs. Scholarship; Racial Equality, Friends of Touliline, Africa Service Inst.; mem. adv. com. U.S. Com. World Festival of Negro Arts; trustee Newton Coll., Boston. Served with AUS, 1943-46. Recipient D.A.R. medal for good citizenship, also scholarship LaSalle Coll., 1941, John Meshain award, 1948; James Hooey award, 1959; LaSalle Centennial award, 1965. John Hay Whitney fellow, 1951; fellow, class 1928, Princeton, 1952. Mem. Nat. Assn. Tng. Dirs., N.A.A.C.P., Am. Soc. African Culture, Am. Arbitration Assn. (bd.). Author articles in field. Home: 4811 S Kimbark Av Chicago IL 60615 Office: 1307 S Wabash St Chicago IL 60605

HARRIS, JED, theatrical producer; b. Vienna, Austria, Feb. 25, 1900; s. Meyer W. and Esther (Schurtz) Howowitz; brought to U.S., 1901; student Yale, 1917- 20; m. Anita Green (div. 1928); m. 2d, Louise Platt (div. 1944); 1 dau., Abigail; m. 3d, Bebe Allan, Apr. 1, 1957 (div. 1962). Theatrical reporter with The Clipper, 1921; editor, press agt., co. mgr., 1921-26; producer, 1926—; producer plays Broadway, 1926, Coquette, 1927, The Front Page, 1926, The Royal Family, 1928, Uncle Vanya, 1930, The Green Bay Tree, 1933, Our Town, 1938, One-Man Show, 1945, The Heiress, 1945, Red Gloves, 1949, Child of Fortune, 1956. Co-author: Operation Mad Ball.

HARRIS, JEROME SYLVAN, educator, physician; b. N.Y.C., Feb. 27, 1909; s. Mark and Mary (Marcus) H.; A.B. summa cum laude, Dartmouth, 1929; M.D. cum laude, Harvard, 1933; m. Jacqueline Cato Hijmans, Oct. 23, 1958. Intern U. Chgo. Clinics, 1934; resident Boston Children's Hosp., 1935-36; mem. faculty Duke Sch. Medicine, 1937—, J. Buren Sidbury prof. pediatrics, also asso. prof. biochemistry, 1950—; chmn. dept. pediatrics Duke Med. Center, 1954-68. Cons. Nat. Bd. Med. Examiners, 1956-60; mem. human embryology and devel. study sect. NIH, 1959-63. Bd. dirs. Durham Child Guidance Clinic, 1950-54. Served to lt. col., M.C., AUS, 1942-46. Mem. Am. Soc. Clin. Investigation, Soc. Pediatric Research, Am. Acad. Pediatrics, Am. Pediatrics Soc., So. Soc. Pediatric Research, Phi Beta Kappa, Sigma Xi, Alpha Omega Alpha. Contbr. profl. jours. Home: 2907 Hope Valley Rd Durham NC 27707

HARRIS, JESSE GRAHAM, Jr., educator, psychologist; b. Jacksonville, Fla., Jan. 5, 1926; s. Jesse Graham and Mona (Woods) H.; B.A., Harvard, 1946; Ph.D., Duke, 1955; m. Julia Patricia McNamee, Sept. 5, 1953; children—Julia Kathleen, Cecilia Anne. Asst. prof. psychology U. Conn., 1958-60; asso. prof., dir. psychology, dept. psychiatry U. Ky. Med. Center, 1960-63; prof. psychology U. Ky., 1963—, chmn. dept., 1963-67, dir. clin. tng. U. Ky., 1963-67, 69—; vis. lectr. U. Hawaii, 1968; cons. USPHS Hosp., Lexington, 1961—, VA hosps. in Ky. and Ohio, 1962—, Peace Corps, 1968— (field selection officer 1968-70, tng. devel. officer, cons. in research 1970—). Vice chmn. Ky. Mental Health Manpower Commn.; mem. Ky. Bd. Examiners of Psychologists, 1966—, chmn. bd., 1970—. Dir., v.p. mem. artists com. Central Ky. Concert and Lecture Series, 1960—. Served to lt. USNR, 1955-58. Diplomate Am. Bd. Examiners Profl. Psychology. Fellow Am. Psychol. Assn.; mem. Southeastern, Ky., Central Ky. (pres. 1962), Western Fla. (pres. 1957), Midwestern psychol. assns., So. Soc. Philosophy and Psychology, Am. Assn. U. Profs., Phi Beta Kappa, Sigma Xi. Adv. editor Jour. Consulting and Clin. Psychology, 1970— Contbr. profl. jours., chpt. to book. Home: 3356 Bellefonte Dr Lexington KY 40502

HARRIS, JOHN BLACK, corp. exec.; b. Bklyn., Apr. 17, 1918; s. John Black and Helen (Woodman) H.; A.B., Bard Coll., 1939; postgrad in econs. Columbia, 1939- 42; m. Elizabeth Moody, Nov. 29, 1941; children—Pamela Preston, Lee Woodman, Holly Stetson, John Black. Financial, research staff Chase Nat. Bank, 1939-42, fgn. credit depts., 1946-50; asst. to treas. W.R. Grace & Co., N.Y.C., 1950-51, asst. to pres., 1951-52, asst. project mgr. chem. devel., 1951-52, dir. personnel, 1953-55, v.p. mgmt. orgn. and planning, 1955-56, v.p., gen. mgr. operations West Coast S. Am. and C. Am., 1956-61; v.p. indsl. operations United Fruit Co., 1961-64; v.p. United Fruit & Food Corp. (now Liana, Inc.), 1961-64; v.p. gen. devel. div. W.R. Grace & Co., 1964-68, v.p. frozen foods div., 1969—. Trustee, treas. Bard Coll., 1946-49. Served as maj. USAAF, 1942-46. Home: 122 Asbury St St Simons Island GA 31561 Office: Box 667 St Simons Island GA 31561

HARRIS, JOHN EDWARD, physician, educator; b. Toledo, Dec. 27, 1913; s. Byron Acacia and Gladys Irene (Turner) H.; B.S., U. Toledo, 1935; Ph.D., State U. Ia., 1940; M.D., U. Ore., 1950; m. Bessie Hatherly, June 4, 1938; children—Michael Hatherly, John Dennis, Gregory Byron. Research asso. State U. Ia., 1940-41; fellow NRC, U. Pa., 1941-42; research asso. U. Ore., 1946-51; intern Walter Reed Army Hosp., Washington, 1950-51; from asst. prof. to asso. prof. ophthalmology U. Ore., 1951-58; prof. ophthalmology, chmn. dept. U. Minn., 1958—. Mem. Nat. Adv. Neurol. Diseases and Blindness Council, 1967-69; mem. Nat. Adv. Eye Council, 1969—; mem. bd. Nat. Assn. for Prevention Blindness, 1970—; cons. surgeon gen. U.S. Served to maj. USAAF, 1942-46. Mem. Am. Ophthalmology Soc., A.M.A. (asso. editor Archives Ophthalmology 1952-55), Assn. Research in Ophthalmology (trustee 1958-64, chmn. 1964), Am. Acad. Ophthalmology and Otolaryngology, Sigma Xi, Alpha Omega Alpha. Author, co-author numerous research papers. Mem. editorial bd. Investigative Ophthalmology. Home: 2177 Rosewood Lane N St Paul MN 55113 Office: Mayo Meml Minneapolis MN 55414

HARRIS, JOHN WILLIAM, physician, educator; b. Boston, Mar. 30, 1920; s. Ulysses Sylvester and Lillian (Dennett) H.; B.S., Trinity Coll., Hartford, Conn., 1941; M.D., Harvard, 1944; m. Stephanie Jean Bunting, Apr. 7, 1951; children—Wendy Alexandra, Alison Dennett, Stephen Bunting. Intern, Boston City Hosp., 1944-45, resident, 1947-48; research fellow medicine Thorndike Meml. Lab., Harvard Med. Sch., 1948-51, research asso., 1951-52; sr. instr. medicine Western Res. U., Cleve., 1952-54, asst. prof., 1954-57, asso. prof., 1957-62, prof., 1962—; hematologist, vis. physician Cleve. Met. Gen. Hosp., 1952—, asso. dir. dept. medicine, 1967—; attending physician VA Hosp., Cleve., 1953-58, sr. attending physician hematology, 1959—; cons. staff Luth. Hosp., 1965—; mem. hematology study sect. NIH, 1962-66; mem. com. blood and transfusion Nat. Acad. Scis.-NRC, 1963-65. Served to capt. U.S. Army, 1945-47. Recipient USPHS Research Career award, 1962. Alfred Stengel Research fellow A.C.P., 1951- 52, Markle scholar in medicine, 1955-60. Mem. Am. Fedn. Clin. Research, Am. Soc. Clin. Investigation (past v.p.), Central Soc. Clin. Research Soc. Exptl. Biology and Medicine, Am. Soc. Hematology, A.C.P., A.M.A., Acad. Medicine Cleve., Assn. Am. Physicians, Phi Beta Kappa, Alpha Omega Alpha. Home: 3080 Coleridge Rd Cleveland Heights OH 44118 Office: 3395 Scranton Rd Cleveland OH 44109

HARRIS, JOHN WILLIAM, paper co. exec.; b. Wadeville, N.C., Dec. 12, 1912; s. James Atlas and Lena (Hadley) H.; A.A., Wingate (N.C.) Jr. Coll., 1932; B.S. in Chem. Engring., N.C. State Coll., 1936; grad. Advanced Mgmt. Program, Harvard, 1959; m. Billie Francis, Jan. 31, 1936; children—Francis Leanna (Mrs. Michael Grove Rees), Phillip Hadley. With Champion Papers, Inc., Hamilton, O., 1933—, successively cost accountant Carolina div., Canton, N.C., div. controller, co-ordinator budgetary control, Hamilton, O., asst. corp. controller, 1933-61, corp. controller, 1961-67, operations comptroller for U.S. Plywood-Champion Papers, Inc., 1967-71, controller, 1971—; dir., mng. officer Clyde Bldg. & Loan Assn. (N.C.), 1940-49. Mem. council, Town of Clyde, 1942-43, mayor, 1944-46. C.P.A., Ohio. Mem. Financial Execs. Inst., Ohio Soc. C.P.A.'s. Democrat. Presbyn. Home: 832 Elizabeth Dr Hamilton OH 45013 Office: US Plywood-Champion Papers Inc Knightsbride Hamilton OH 45011

HARRIS, JOSEPH, ins. exec.; b. Toronto, Can., 1892; grad. U. Toronto, 1915. With Harris Abattoir, packing firm, 1915-51, merged to become Canada Packers, Ltd., 1927, successively in charge mgmt., v.p., dir.; pres. Great-West Life Assurance Co., 1951-59, chmn. bd. dirs., 1959-69; hon. dir. Royal Trust Co. Home: 60 Osborne ST N Winnipeg Manitoba Canada

HARRIS, JOSEPH DAVID, educator, physicist; b. Evansville, Ind., Jan. 16, 1934; s. Benjamin Manuel and Anne (Bredenkamp) H.; B.S., Purdue U., 1951, Ph.D., 1955; student U. Chgo., 1951-52, Marine Biol. Lab., Woods Hole, Mass., 1953-54; m. Paulanne Trepanier, Oct. 26, 1951; children—David Lawrence, Jed Alan, Anne Trepanier, Paul Andre. Research asso. Max Planck Inst. for Physics Göttingen, Germany, 1956-57; physicist Aerial Measurements Lab., Evanston, Ill., 1957-58; asst. prof. Utah State U., 1958-59; mem. faculty Dartmouth, 1959—, prof. physics, since 1968—; lectr. biochemistry Dartmouth Med. Sch., 1960—; cons., tchr. Danforth Found. Recipient E. Harris Harbison award distinguished teaching Dartmouth, 1966. Mem. Am. Phys. Soc., Biophys. Soc., Soc. Gen. Physiologists, Soc. Religion in Higher Edn., Sigma Xi. Episcopalian (vestry). Author articles in field. Home: Elm St Norwich VT 05055 Office: Dartmouth Coll Hanover NH 03755

HARRIS, JOSEPH PRATT, educator; b. Sulphur Springs, N.C., Feb. 18, 1896; s. John C. and Otelia (Emerson) H.; student U. N.C., 1914-15; A.B., U. Kan., 1918; Ph.D., U. Chgo., 1923; m. Polly Margaret Smith, Jan. 12, 1918; 1 son, Willard Emerson (dec.). Instr. polit. sci. U. Wis., 1923-25; dir. research, com. on public adminstrn. Social Science Research Council, 1935-39; prof. polit. sci. U.Cal., 1939-40, 41-64, prof. emeritus, 1964—; prof. polit. sci. Northwestern U., 1940-41; prof. pub. adminstrn. U. Bologna, (Italy), 1956; cons. editor McGraw Hill Book Co., 1940—; cons. Nat. Def. Adv. Commn., 1940-41. Mem. President's Com. on Selective Service, 1940-41; chmn. exec. com. Cal. Legislative Internship Program, 1957-64; mem. Adv. Constl. Revision Commn. Wash., 1934; lectr. Am. U., 1937-39. Social Science Research Council fellow, 1926-27; Fulbright fellow, Gt. Britain, 1956-57; Guggenheim fellow, 1957. Served as 2d lt., Air Service, U.S. Army, World War I; col., U.S. Army, mem. faculty, dir. of pub. adminstrn., Sch. Mil. Govt., Charlottesville, Va., 1942-44; dir. Personnel and Tng., U.N.R.R.A., 1944-45. Mem. Am. Polit. Sci. Assn., Am. Soc. Pub. Adminstrn., Polit. Sci. Assn. (Gt. Britain), Internat. City Mgrs. Assn., Phi Beta Kappa, Pi Sigma Alpha. Author books including: A Model Direct Primary Election System, 1950; The Advice and Consent of the Senate, 1953; California Politics, 1955; Congressional Control of Adminstration, 1964; co-author: America Prepares for Tomorrow, 1941; The President and Congress, 1963; Public Adminstrator in Modern Society, 1963. Contbr. articles on polit. sci. and pub. adminstrn. to profl. jours. Home: 1020 Lassen St Berkeley CA 94707 ☆

HARRIS, JULIAN EARLE, educator; b. Henderson, N.C., Sept. 3, 1896; s. Samuel Rogers and Rosalie (Hicks) H.; A.B., U. N.C., 1917; A.M., Columbia, 1920, Ph.D., 1930; postgrad. Sorbonne (Am. Field Service fellow), 1922-24, U. Madrid (summer), 1922, Eleve titulaire de l'Ecole des Hautes Etudes, 1923; m. Elizabeth Marshall, 1928; 1 dau., Ann (Mrs. Mitsuru Yasuhara). Instr. extension Columbia, 1920-22, asst., 1921-22; instr. Romance langs. U. Wis., 1924-29; summer sessions Duke, 1925, Chautauqua, 1928; asst. prof. French, U. Wis., 1929-42, asso. prof., 1942, prof., 1944-67, prof. emeritus, 1967—, chmn. dept. French and Italian, 1943-59, chmn. div. of humanities, 1946-49, prof. Inst. Research in Humanities, 1964-65. Pres. French House, Inc. Organized instrn. in French for A.S.T.P. and C.A.T.P. students, World War II (method used for civilian instruction, 1944—). Served in France, World War I. Decorated officier de la Legion d'Honneur (France); elected Hall of Fame, Nat. Fedn. Modern Lang. Assns., 1962. Mem. Modern Lang. Assn. Am., Mediaeval Acad. Am., Am. Assn. U. Profs., Am. Assn. Tchrs. French (pres. 1950-54), Wis. Ednl. Assn., Société des Anciens Textes Francais, Phi Beta Kappa, Phi Delta Theta, Sinfonia, Sigma Upsilon. Episcopalian. Mason. Clubs: University, Madison Literary. Author: Marie de France; The Lays Gugemar, Lanval and a fragment of Yonec (with a study of the life and work of author), 1930; French Reader for Beginners, 1940; Recueil de chansons de France (with Marguerite Treille), 1927; Conversational French (with André Lévque), 1946; the same recorded on vinylite disks, 1948; French Reader for Colleges, 1949; The Humanities: an Appraisal, 1950; Basic Conversational French (with André Lévque), 1953, rev. with tape recordings and film strips, 1958, adapted for German, 1968, Spanish, 1970; Petites Conversations (for 10 yr. olds) (with HeleEe Monod- Cassidy), 1956; Basic French Reader (with André Lévque), 1956; Intermediate Conversational French (with André Lévque). 1960; Nouvelles Conversations (with Helene Monod-Cassidy), 1961; Conversationes d'aujourd'hui, 1962. Editor of 5 Knapp lectures on Devel. of the Am. Way of Life, 1952. Editor-in-chief French Rev., 1953-62. Contbr. profl. jours. Home: 1309 Edgehill Dr Madison WI 53705

HARRIS, JULIAN HOKE, sculptor; b. Carrollton, Ga., Aug. 22, 1906; s. Joseph H. and Margaret Myra (Kennedy) H.; B.S. in Architecture, Ga. Inst. Tech., 1928; studied sculpture Pa. Acad. Fine Arts, 1930-33; m. Jean Sawyer Fambrough, Dec. 18, 1938; children—Jean Olivia (Mrs. Ward Wright III), Judy Ann. Draftsman, Henz, Adler and Shutze, Atlanta, 1928-29; asst. designer Marye, Alger & Vinour, 1929; free lance sculptor, Atlanta, art dir. Fed. Theatre, Atlanta, 1936-37; lectr., prof. of architecture Ga. Inst. Tech., 1936—; prof. Atlanta Art Inst., 1946-52; designed and executed sculpture numerous pub. bldgs., including Grant Park Zoo, Grady Hosp., State Agrl. Bldg., Commerce Bldg., Atlanta, Speech and Hearing Center, Nashville, also meml., portrait commns., including heroic bronze of John Wesley, Buckhannon, W.Va., U.Va. Sesquicentennial, Sidney Lanier medallion for Hall of Fame, N.Y.U., Joel C. Harris for Soc. Medalists; one man shows Atlanta Art Center; works exhibited Jewish Mus., N.Y.C., Pa. Acad. Fine Arts, Mus. Modern Art, Rockefeller Center, N.Y. World's Fair, Nat. Sculpture Soc. Bas Relief Exhbn. Served from 1st lt. to maj. USAAF, 1942-46. Recipient Edgar Tobin award So. States Art League, 1939; 1st prize sculpture Tri-County Exhbn., Atlanta, 1940; Nat. Art Week in Ga., 1951; Fine Arts medal A.I.A., 1954; Ivan Allen award Ga. chpt. A.I.A., 1961; and others; winner nat. competition for medallion to commemorate 40th Anniversary of Soc. Medalists, 1970. Licensed architect, Ga. Fellow Nat. Sculpture Soc.; mem. A.I.A. Atlanta Art Assn. (v.p. 1952-55), Studio Club Atlanta (pres. 1939-41), Assn. Ga. Artists (pres. 1935-36). Clubs: Piedmont Driving, Rotary, Breakfast. Home: 177 5th St NW Atlanta GA 30313

HARRIS, JULIE, actress; b. Grosse Pointe Park, Mich., Dec. 2, 1925; d. William Pickett and Elsie (Smith) Harris; student Perry Mansfield Theatre Work Shop, 1941-43, Yale Drama Sch., 1945; m. Jay I. Julien, Aug. 12, 1946; m. 2d, Manning Gurian, Oct. 21, 1954; 1 son, Peter. Appeared in plays Sundown Beach, 1948; The Young and Fair, 1948-49; Magnolia Alley, 1949; Montserrat, 1949; The Member of the Wedding, 1950-51; I Am a Camera, 1951-52, film, 1956; The Lark, 1956; Little Moon of Alban, 1960; A Shot in the Dark, 1961; Marathon 33, 1964; Ready When You Are, C.B.!, 1964; tour, Broadway, The Warm Peninsula; appeared in Skyscraper, 1965; Harper, 1966; motion pictures Poacher's Daughter, 1960, The Haunting, The Moving Target. Recipient Antoinette Perry award for East of Eden, 1956; Antoinette Perry award as best actress in Forty Carats, 1969. Address: care Actors Equity 226 W 47th St New York City NY 10019

HARRIS, L. JULIAN, lawyer; b. Omaha, Apr. 13, 1901, Ph.B., U. Chgo., 1923, J.D., 1924. Admitted to Ill. bar, 1925; practice of law, Chgo.; mem. firm D'Ancona, Pflaum, Wyatt & Riskind. Mem. Am., Ill., Chgo. bar assns. Office: 33 N LaSalle St Chicago IL 60602

HARRIS, LAWRENCE WILKINSON, Jr., forest products exec.; b. San Francisco, July 23, 1911; s. Lawrence W. and Lucie (King) H.; A.B., Stanford, 1932; m. Jane W. Beebe, Sept. 2, 1939; children—Lawrence Wilkinson III, Caroline V., Edwin B., Kenneth J., Maria Louise. Sales and merchandising Emporium Dept. Store, San Francisco, 1932-33; sales and prodn. Ames Harris Neville Co., Portland, Ore., 1933-42, asst. mgr., 1946-52, v.p., 1952-55, exec. v.p., San Francisco, 1955-60; nat. sales dir. Boise Cascade Corp. (Ida.), 1960- 62, dir. corp. relations, 1962-67, sec., 1968—; dir. Yosemite Park & Curry Co., Beebe Co., Portland. Bd. dirs. Yosemite Nat. Park, Cal. Served with AUS, 1942-46. Home: 1925 Montclair Dr Boise ID 83702 Office: PO Box 200 Boise ID 83707

HARRIS, LEE BERTHOLD, found. exec.; b. Boston, Jan. 2, 1915; s. Isaac and Emma (Lewis) H.; A.B., Yale, 1936; M.B.A., Harvard, 1939; m. Leah Jacobsen, Mar. 11, 1948; children—Alona, Ori, Ronald. Asst. to v.p. R.H. Macy & Co., N.Y.C., 1939-41; v.p. Palestine Econ. Corp., N.Y.C. and Israel, 1947- 55; sr. mgmt. cons. Ford, Bacon & Davis, N.Y.C. and Bolivia, 1956; v.p. adminstrn., sec. Carnegie Endowment Internat. Peace, N.Y.C., 1956—. Served to lt. comdr. USNR, 1941-46. Decorated Commendation medal. Mem. Internat. City Mgrs. Assn., Am. Polit. Sci. Assn., Am. Acad. Polit. and Social Sci., V.F.W., Res. Officers Assn., Phi Beta Kappa. Clubs: Yale, Harvard Business School (N.Y.C.). Home: 18 Clover Pl Davenport Neck New Rochelle NY 10805 Office: 345 E 46th St New York City NY 10017

HARRIS, LEONARD R., publishing co. exec.; b. N.Y.C., 1922. Formerly dir. promotion, mem. editorial bd. Prenrtice Hall, Inc., then dir. new products Banrtam Books, officer Book Club Guild and Channel Press, Inc., also cons. new publishing projects N.Y. Times; with Ency. Britannica, Chgo., 1965-69; exec. v.p., pub. World Pub. Co., 1969—. Address: 110 E 59th St New York City NY 10022*

HARRIS, LLOYD O., Jr., cotton mills exec. Pres., Fulton Cotton Mills div. Allied Products Corp., Atlanta. Office: PO Box 1726 Atlanta GA 30301*

HARRIS, LLOYD WEBB, mfg. co. exec.; b. Marietta, Ga., July 22, 1922; s. William Lloyd and Fannie (Webb) H.; student Ga. Tech., 1939-40, Emory U., 1940-41; m. Harriet Hanson, Aug. 16, 1947; children—Carl L., Eric W., Freya E. With Lockheed-Ga Co., 1951-68, JetStar dist. mgr., 1964-68; pres., chief exec. officer Hawker Siddeley Internat., Inc., 1968—. Bd. dirs. Atlanta Com. Internat. Visitors, 1967-68, Atlanta Com. Fgn. Relations, 1967-68. Served with USNR, 1944. Mem. British-Am. C. of C. (bd. dirs.). Unitarian. Clubs: Royal Aero (London, Eng.); American, Wings (N.Y.C.); Cherokee Town and Country (Atlanta). Home: 1050 Park Av New York City NY 10028 Office: care Hawker Siddeley Internat Inc Marine Air Terminal LaGuardia Airport Flushing NY 11371

HARRIS, LOUIS, pub. opinion analyst, columnist; b. New Haven, Jan. 6, 1921; s. Harry and Frances (Smith) H.; A.B. in Econs., U. N.C., 1942; m. Florence Yard, June 16, 1943; children—Susan (Mrs. Eric Robertson), Peter, Richard. With Elmo Roper and Assos., 1946-56, partner, 1954- 56; propr. Louis Harris and Assos., Inc., marketing and pub. opinion research, N.Y.C., 1956—; cons. CBS News, 1962-68, ABC News Nat. Polling Day, 1971—; columnist Washington Post, also Newsweek mag., 1963-68; columnist Chgo. Tribune-N.Y. Daily News Syndicate, 1969—; dir. Time mag.-Harris Poll, 1969—; dir. Life Poll, 1969—; faculty asso. Columbia, N.Y.C., 1953- 64; adj. prof. polit. sci. U. N.C., 1964—; v.p., dir. Donaldson, Lufkin & Jenrette, N.Y.C., 1971—. Trustee Riverdale Country Sch. Bd. dirs., treas. Asso. Councils of Arts. Served as officer USNR, World War II Mem. Am. Assn. Pub. Opinion (dir.), Am. Sociol. Assn., Am. Statis. Assn., Am. Mgmt. Assn., Am. Marketing Assn., Am. Polit. Sci. Assn. Author: Is There a Republican Majority, 1954; (with William Brink) The Negro Revolution in America, 1964, Black and White, 1967; also numerous articles. Home: New York City NY Office: 1270 Av Americas New York City NY 10020

HARRIS, LOUIS CARL, newspaper editor; b. Montgomery, Ala., Feb. 20, 1912; s. Augustus J. and Florence (Hirsch) H.; student pub. schs.; m. Margaret M. Brown, Aug. 9, 1944; children—Jeffrey Peden, Louis Carl, William McCollough. Carrier, Montgomery Advertiset, 1931-32; asst. circulation mgr. Augusta (Ga.) Chronicle, 1932-34, reporter, telegraph editor, 1934-38; reporter Pontiac (Mich.) Daily Press, 1938-40, telegraph editor, 1946-47; news editor Columbus (Ga.) Ledger, 1947—, Augusta Chronicle and Herald, 1947—, editor, 1959—; v.p. Augusta Chronicle and Herald; v.p. Southeastern Newspapers Corp., 1966—. Dir. Richmond Assos., Inc. Bd. dirs. Augusta United Fund, 1952-58. Served to capt. USAAF, 1940-45. Decorated Bronze Star. Nieman travel fellow, Japan, 1956. Mem. Ga. Asso. Press News Council (pres. 1950, 52), Am. Soc. Newspaper Editors, Augusta C. of C. (v.p.), Ga. Press Assn. (pres. 1967-68). Presbyn. (deacon). Kiwanian (dir. Augusta 1950). Home: 618 Oberlin Rd Augusta GA 30904 Office: 725 Broad St Augusta GA 30902

HARRIS, LOUIS KENNETH, educator; b. St. Clairsville, O., Mar. 3, 1923; s. Silas I. and Sara (Stewart) H.; A.B., Ohio State U., 1945, M.A., 1946; Ph.D., U. Cal., Los Angeles, 1956; m. Martha Lee Wolfe, Mar. 30, 1946; children—Cassandra Lou Arnold, Jeffrey Lee, Javier Gomez. Instr., prof. Kent (O.) State U., 1947-66, chmn. dept. polit. sci., 1966-68, v.p., provost, 1968-69, dir. winter program U. Ams., Mexico, also distinguished prof.; prof., cons. U. Panama, 1962-63; vis. Fulbright prof. U. Mexico, 1964. Mem. Am. Polit. Sci. Assn., Latin Am. Studies Assn., Pi Sigma Alpha. Author: (with B. Burnett and K. Johnson) Political Forces in Latin America, 1968. Home: 3566 Dayton Av Kent OH 44240

HARRIS, LOYD ERVIN, coll. dean; b. Ryan, Okla., Sept. 21, 1900; s. Howard Luther and Necie Emma (Culwell) H.; B.S. in Pharmacy, U. Okla., 1922, M.S., 1924; Ph.D. (Marshall fellow 1925-26), U. Wis., 1926; m. Maurine Dill, June 19, 1923; children—Lorene Anne (Mrs. Glenn J. Reid), Ronald David. Mem. faculty U. Okla., 1919-46, 63—, prof. pharmacy, dean Coll. Pharmacy, 1963-70, dean, prof. emeritus, 1970—; mem. faculty Ohio State U., 1946-63, prof. pharmacy, 1946-63, acting dean coll. Pharmacy, 1955-56. Mem. Grandview Heights (O.) Bd. Health, 1953-63, pres., 1957-63. Bd. dirs. Okla. Med. Research Found. Served to col. Chem. Corps, AUS, 1942-46, 52-53. Mem. Am., Okla. pharm. assns., Am. Chem. Soc., Phi Beta Kappa, Sigma Xi, Rho Chi, Lambda Chi Alpha. Presbyn. Lion. Contbr. Jour. Pharm. Scis. Home: 2514 S Pickard Av Norman OK 73069

HARRIS, LUMAN, baseball mgr.; b. Birmingham, Ala., Jan. 17, 1915; s. Chalmer Lee and Lula Jane (Taylor) H.; grad. high sch.; m. Margaret Reynolds, Feb. 15, 1936; children—Pat (Mrs. Charles M. Renta), Phil, Johnny. Pitcher, Phila. Athletics, 1941-46, Washington Senators, 1947, Buffalo, 1948-49, Balt., 1950; coach Chgo. White Sox, 1951-55; coach Balt. Orioles, 1955-61, mgr., 1961; head coach Houston Astros, 1961-64, mgr., 1964; now mgr. Atlanta Braves, Inc., mgr. Caracas (Venezula) Baseball Club, 1958, San Juan (P.R.) club, winter, 1961. Served with USNR. Home: 810 Piedmont St Sugar Land TX 77478

HARRIS, MARK, author; b. Mt. Vernon, N.Y., Nov. 19, 1922; s. Carlyle and Ruth (Klausner) Finkelstein; B.A., Denver, 1950, M.A., 1951; Ph.D., U. Minn., 1956; m. Josephine Horen, Mar. 17, 1946; children—Hester Jill, Anthony Wynn, Henry Adam. Reporter, Port Chester (N.Y.) Item, 1944, PM, N.Y.C., 1945, I.N.S., St. Louis, 1944-46; prof. English, San Francisco State Coll., 1954—. Served with AUS, 1943- 44. Recipient award Nat. Inst. Arts and Letters, 1961. Fulbright prof., Japan, 1957; Ford grantee, 1960. Author: Trumpet to the World, 1946; City of Discontent, 1952; The Southpaw, 1953; Bang the Drum Slowly, 1956; Something About a Soldier, 1957; A Ticket for a Seamstitch, 1957; Wake Up, Stupid, 1959; (play) Friedman & Son, 1962; Mark the Glove Boy, 1964; Twenty One Twice: A Journal, 1966. Writer, producer The Redwoods (Acad. award for best short documentary 1968). Address: 1800 Pacific Av San Francisco CA 94109

HARRIS, MARQUIS LAFAYETTE, bishop; b. Armstrong, Ala., Mar. 8, 1907; s. William Eugene and Estelle Marie (Glenn) H.; B.S., Clark U., Atlanta, 1928, LL.D., 1959; B.D., Gammon Theol. Sem., Atlanta, Ga., 1929, D.D., 1941; student Harvard, 1929-30; S.T.M., Boston U., 1930; Ph.D., Ohio State U., 1933; L.H.D., Southwestern Coll., 1960; m. Geneva Nelson, Sept. 6, 1931; 1 son, M. LaFayette. Instr. phys., chem., math. Clark U., 1927-29; ordained to ministry M.E. Ch., 1928; coach and instr. physics and religion Claflin Coll., 1930-31; pastor Pa. Avenue M.E. Ch., Columbus, O., 1931-33; dean, prof. of sociology, Samuel Houston Coll., Austin, Tex., 1933-36; 1933; Philander Smith Coll., Little Rock, Ark., 1936-60; became bishop of Meth. Ch. 1960—; resident bishop of Atlantic Coast Area; dir. Security Life Ins. Co., Citizens Trust Bank (Atlanta). Mem. World Meth. Conference, 1956; mem. gen. conf. Meth. Ch. 1940, 44, 48, 52, 56, mem. gen. bd. edn.; mem. exec. com. Gen. Br. Edn., Meth. Ch., 1956-60, mem. exec. com. Commn. on Higher Edn., 1956-60; trustee, 1952-56. Trustee Urban League, Little Rock; mem. Fed. Council of Chs. of Christ Am.; bd. dirs. of Colored Work, Southwestern southwestern region; mem. Meth. Ecumenical Conf. Oxford, Eng., 1951, General Conf. com. on rules, 1952; chmn. com. on Edn., Jurisdictional Conf., 1952, 56. Chmn. bd. trustees Clark Coll., Gammon Theol. Sem., Bethune Cookman Coll., Claflin Coll. Mem. Am. Philos. Assn., So. Soc. for Philosophy and Psychology, Southwestern Philos. Conf., Am. Acad. of Social and Polit. Sci., Ministerial Assn. of Little Rock (mem. exec. com.) Alpha Delta Alpha, Alpha Pi Alpha, Beta Kappa Chi, Alpha Kappa Mu, Sigma Pi Phi. Mason, Elk. Author: The Voice in the Wilderness, 1941; Our Tomorrow's World, 1945; A Syllabus on Freshman Orientation, 1948; To Magnify Thy Power, 1948; Life Can Be Meaningful, 1951. Home: 25 Patrick Rd Westport CT 06880

HARRIS, MARTIN, lawyer; b. El Paso, Tex., May 16, 1921; s. Jesse Martin and Rose (Thomason) H.; B.A., U. Tex., 1942, LL.B., 1947; m. Faye Hoefgen, Apr. 25, 1942; children—Nancy (Mrs. Cowan), Judith Ann, Faye Davis. Admitted to Tex. bar, 1947; asst. atty. gen. Tex., 1947-48; partner firm Manager, Clark, Thomas, Harris, Denius & Winters, Austin, 1948—. Served to lt. USNR, 1942-45. Mem. Am., Travis County bar assns., State Bar Tex., Phi Delta Phi, Kappa Alpha. Episcopalian (vestry). Home: 4612 Ridge Oak Dr Austin TX 78731 Office: Capital Nat Bank Bldg Austin TX 78701

HARRIS, MARVIN, educator, author; b. Bklyn., Aug. 18, 1927; s. Irving and Sadie (Newman) H.; A.B., Columbia, 1949, Ph.D., 1953; m. Madeline Grove, Jan. 25, 1953; children—Robert Eric, Susan Lynn. Mem. faculty Columbia, 1952—, now prof. anthropology, chmn. dept., 1963-66; tech. adviser Ministry Edn. Brazil, 1953; exec. sec. Columbia-Cornell-Harvard-Ill. summer field studies program,

1960-66. Served with AUS, 1945-47. Mem. Am. Anthrop. Assn., A.A.A.S. Author: Town and Country in Brazil, 1956; (with Charles Wagley) Minorities in the New World, 1958; Patterns of Race in the Americas, 1964; The Nature of Cultural Things, 1964; The Rise of Anthropological Theory, 1968; Culture, Man and Nature, 1971. Home: 174 Park Av Leonia NJ 07605 Office: Dept Anthropology Columbia U New York City NY 10727

HARRIS, MAURICE COLENAN, physician; b. Albany, N.Y., Feb. 15, 1899; s. Joseph and Rose (Coleman) H.; M.D., Tufts U., 1923. Intern Flower Hosp., N.Y.C., 1923-24, resident, 1924; vis. physician allergy clinic Roosevelt Hosp., N.Y.C., 1929-33; vis. physician, chief allergy N.Y. Dispensary, 1927-41, San Francisco Polyclinic Hosp. and Post-Grad. Coll., 1954-62; attending physician internal medicine (allergy) Mary's Help Hosp., also head allergy clinic Mary's Help Hosp. Clinics, San Francisco, 1962—; pvt. practice, San Francisco; lectr. phys. diagnosis N.Y. Med. Coll., 1925-30; adj. prof. medicine (allergy), chief allergy clinic N.Y. Polyclinic Hosp. and Postgrad. Med. Sch., 1933-45; asst. clin. prof. medicine (allergy) Loma Linda U. Sch. Medicine, 1946-48, asso. prof., 1948-51. Chmn. bd. govs. Allergy Found. No. Cal., 1955-56, 62-63, pres., 1952—. Served with U.S. Army, 1918; to comdr. USNR, 1942-45. Fellow A.C.P., Coll. Allergy (regent 1959-61, pres. 1965), Am. Acad. Allergy, Internat. Coll. Chest Physicians, Internat. Assn. Allergology, Am. Med. Authors; mem. A.M.A., Cal. (chmn. allergy sect. 1952), Pan Am. (v.p. allergy sect. 1962—) med. assns., Internat., Am., Cal., San Francisco socs. internal medicine, Allergy Assn. No. Cal. (pres. 1962), Cal. Soc. Allergy (pres. 1952), Am. Med. Editors and Authors Assn., West Coast Allergy Soc. (pres. 1963), Brit. Assn. Allergists, Royal Soc. Medicine, Tufts U. Med. Alumni Assn. Cal. (pres. 1957-58). Author: Normal Facts in Diagnosis, 1930; Practical Allergy, 1957; Sensitivity Chest Diseases, 1964. Editor: Annals of Allergy; editor in chief Clin. Allergy and Immunology; editor allergy Cal. Medicine; cons. editor allergy The New Physician. Contbr. chpts. on allergy to books, numerous articles profl. publs. Home: 1000 North Point San Francisco CA 94109 Office: 450 Sutter St San Francisco CA 94108

HARRIS, MICHAEL MARCUS-MYERS, architect; b. Newark, Sept. 8, 1907; s. Bernhardt and Josephine (Myers) H.; B.Arch., Cornell U., 1930; m. Rosalind Wright, Mar. 8, 1946; children—Alison, Peter Quincy. Mem. staff Office John Russell Pope, 1935-39; designer Office Alfred Easton Poor, 1939- 40; asst. project designer Shreve, Lamb & Harmon, 1941-42; architect Harrison & Abramovitz, N.Y.C., 1942—, partner, 1962—; adj. prof. architecture Columbia, 1965—. Vice pres. N.Y. Bldg. Congress, 1968—; mem. adv. com. constrn. N.Y.C. Bd. Edn., 1964-69. Fellow A.I.A. (treas. N.Y. chpt. 1961-64, exec. com. 1960-65); mem. Nat. Inst. Archtl. Edn. (bd. dirs.), Century Assn. Principal works include asst. dir. planning UN Hdqrs., 1950; partner-in-charge UN Library, 1962, Time and Life Bldg., 1963, McGraw-Hill World Hdqrs., 1969, Celanese Corp. Bldg., 1970, Standard Oil of N.J., 1968 (all N.Y.C.). Home: 130 E 67th St New York City NY 10021 Office: Harrison & Abramovitz 630 5th Av New York City NY 10020

HARRIS, MICHAEL SAUL, publisher; born Boston, July 15, 1916; s. Bert Martin and Bessie (Cogan) H.; ed. pub. schs. of Phila.; m. Marjorie Helen Kipp, February 9, 1940; children—Susan Virginia, Katherine Kipp. Field rep. Steelworkers Organizing Com., C.I.O., Berwick, Pa., 1937, sub-regional dir., Phila., 1938-41, dist. dir. and mem. Internat. exec. bd., United Steelworkers of Am. Phila., 1942-48; chief, labor div., E.C.A. Spl. Mission to France, 1948; chief, E.C.A. Spl. Mission to Sweden, 1949-51, to Germany, 1951-53; U.S. rep. to finance and econs. com. Allied High Com. for Germany, 1951-54; apptd. U.S. Minister, 1954; chief U.S. Operations Mission to Germany, 1953-54, dir. 1954-55; rep. Ford Found. for Indonesia, 1955-61, with office in N.Y.C., 1961-63; dep. sec.-gen. Orgn. Econ. Coop. and Devel., Paris, 1963-67; pres., dir. Franklin Book Programs, Inc., N.Y.C., 1967-69; v.p. John A. Wiley & Sons, Inc., N.Y.C., 1969—. Pres. Phila. Indsl. Union Council, 1943-48. Bd. dirs. Iran Found., N.Y. Served with AUS, 1944-46. Mem. Regional War Labor Bd., 3d Region, 1942-43. Mem. Am. Acad. Polit. and Social Sci., Nat. Planning Assn., Assn. for Asian Studies, Am. Vets. Com., Asia Soc. (chmn. Indonesian council), Standing Com. Secs.-Gen. (chmn.). Club: Players (N.Y.C.). Home: 25 Partrick Rd Westport CT 06880 Office: 605 3d Av S New York City NY

HARRIS, MILTON, chemist; b. Los Angeles, Mar. 21, 1906; s. Louis and Naomi (Granish) H.; B.Sc., Ore. State Coll., 1926; Ph.D., Yale, 1929; Dr. Textile Sci., Phila. Textile Inst., 1955; m. Carolyn Wolf, Mar. 30, 1934; children—Barney Dreyfuss (adopted), John. Research asso. Am. Assn. Textile Chemists and Colorists, Nat. Bur. Standards, 1931-39, dir. research Textile Found., 1939-45; pres. and founder Harris Research Labs., 1945-61; dir. research Gillette Co., its subsidiaries, 1956-66, v.p. corp., 1957-66; chmn. exec. com. Sealectro Corp.; dir. Warner Lambert Co.; adv. bd. Jour. Polymer Sci.; asso. editor Textile Research Jour.; cons. Exec. Office of Pres., Office Sci. and Technology, 1962-65. Adv. bd., cons. O.Q.M.G., World War II; chmn. com. on textiles and cordage, tropical deterioration project Nat. Def. Research Com.; sec. com. on clothing NRC, World War II; chmn. Wool Conservation Bd., World War II; mem. panel on clothing Research and Devel. Bd., World War II; mem. Yale Council, 1964-69, Yale Devel. Bd., 1964-67; exec. bd. Yale Grad. Sch. Assn., 1965—; mem. Nat. Bur. Standards Adv. Com., 1971—; mem. sub-com. Food and Agrl. Orgn. UN; mem. Utilization research and devel. adv. com. U.S. Dept. Agr., 1966—; mem. adv. com. planning NSF, 1968—; mem. Pres.'s Sci. Adv. Com. Panel on Environment, 1968—; observer-cons. Task Group Nat. Systems Sci. and Tech. Information, Fed. Council Sci. and Tech., 1968—. Trustee Phila. Textile Inst., 1956-60, Dermatology Found., Textile Research Inst.; bd. dirs. Sci. Service. Recipient award Wash. Acad. Sci., 1943, Olney medal for textile chemistry research, 1945; honor award Am. Inst. Chemists, 1957, Harold DeWitt Smith Meml. medal, 1966, Distinguished Service award Ore. State U., 1967, Perkin Medal award Soc. Chem. Industry, 1970. Fellow Textile Inst., N.Y. Acad. Sci.; mem. Am. Assn. Textile Tech., Yale Chemists Assn. (past pres.), Am. Assn. Biol. Chemists, Am. Inst. Chemists (pres. 1960-61), N.A.M., Textile Research Inst., Am. Assn. Textile Colorists and Chemists, Am. Oil Chemists Soc., Soc. Cosmetic Chemists, Fiber Soc. (hon.) Am. Chem. Soc. (chmn. bd. dirs. 1966-70, dir-at-large), A.A.A.S. (editorial bd. publ. Sci. 1968-70), Soc. Chem. Industry, Wash. Acad. Sci., Sigma Xi, Tau Beta Pi, Phi Lambda Upsilon, Phi Kappa Phi, Gamma Alpha. Clubs: Cosmos (Washington); Chemists (N.Y.C.). Contbr. articles to tech. jours. Editor: Harris' Handbook of Textile Fibers; Natural and Synthetic Fibers. Home: 4101 Linnean Av Washington DC 20008 Office: 3300 Whitehaven St NW Washington DC 20007

HARRIS, MILTON M., distbg. co. exec.; b. San Francisco, Sept. 6, 1916; s. A.H. and Rebecca (Harris) H.; ed. pub. schs.; m. Lorraine D. Love, July 3, 1938; 1 son, Jerrold B. With Braun-Knecht-Heimann Co., San Francisco, 1933-60, v.p., 1951-60; co. acquired by Van Waters & Rogers, Inc. (now VWR United Corp.), San Francisco, 1960, sr. v.p., gen. mgr. 1960-61, pres., 1962- 66, chmn., 1966-70, vice chmn., 1970—, also dir. Clubs: Rotary, Cercle de l'Union, Olympic, Lakeside Country (San Francisco); Raineer, Bermuda Dunes Country. Home: 1345 San Raymundo Rd Hillsborough CA 94010 Office: PO Box 3200 San Francisco CA 94119

HARRIS, MORGAN, educator; b. St. Anthony, Ida., May 25, 1916; s. Archibald Overton and Augusta Pearl (Lewelling) H.; A.B. with highest honors, U. Cal. at Berkeley, 1938, Ph.D., 1941; George Leib Harrison postdoctoral research fellow U. Pa., 1941-42; Merck sr. postdoctoral fellow U. Paris, 1953-54; m. Marjorie Ruth Mason, Aug. 10, 1940; children—Roger Mason, Ronald Morgan. Teaching asst. dept. zoology U. Cal. at Berkeley, 1938-41, instr. zoology, 1945-46, asst. prof., 1946-50, asso. prof., 1950-56, prof., 1956—, vice chmn. zoology, 1952-57, chmn., 1957-63, Miller research prof., 1963-65; research asst. dept. biology Stanford, 1942-44; instr. zoology U. Wash., 1944-45. Research aviation physiology OSRD, 1942-44; mem. cell biology study sect., div. research grants NIH, 1958- 60, 61-63, mem. nat. adv. gen. med. scis. council, 1963-65. Guggenheim fellow, Cambridge, Eng., 1960-61. Mem. Tissue Culture Assn. (pres. 1958-60), Soc. Gen. Physiologists, Internat. Soc. Cell Biology (exec. com. 1964—, treas. 1968—), Am. Soc. Cell Biology (mem. exec. council 1964-68), Soc. for Growth and Devel., Am. Soc. Zoologists, Phi Beta Kappa, Sigma Xi, Phi Sigma (Scholarship medal 1937-38). Clubs: American Alpine (N.Y.C.); Sierra (Cal.). Author: Cell Culture and Somatic Variation, 1964; also research papers. Home: 605 Plateau Dr Berkeley CA 94708

HARRIS, NEISON, corp. exec.; b. St. Paul, Jan. 24, 1915; s. William and Mildred (Brooks) H.; grad. Phillips Exetor Acad.; A.B., Yale, 1936; m. Bette Deutsch, Jan. 25, 1939; children—Katherine, King, Toni. Founder Toni Co.; pres. Toni Co. div. Gillette Co., dir. Paper Mate div., to 1950; Pres., dir. Pittway Corp.; chmn. exec. com., dir. Standard Shares, Inc.; pres. U.S. Bowling Lanes, Inc.; dir. Dickson Electronics, Inc., Old Orchard Bank & Trust Co. Bd. dirs. Skokie Valley Community Hosp. Named 1 of 10 outstanding young men U.S. Jr. C. of C., 1948. Clubs: Standard, Lake Shore Country (Chgo.); Boca Rio Country; La Quinta Country. Home: 225 N Deere Park Dr E Highland Park IL 60035 Office: PO Box 602 601 Skokie Blvd Northbrook IL 60062

HARRIS, NELL, pub. relation, real estate exec; b. Palestine, Tex.; d. Thomas Jefferson and Nellis (Hester) Harris, A.B., Rice U.; student Baylor U. Coll. Medicine, 1943-45; postgrad. Mayo Clinic, U. Minn., 1945; certificate phys. therapy, U. Tex., 1947; student hosp. adminstrn., U. Chgo. 1948, 50; m. Charles Y. Swartz (div. Mar. 1947); children—Charles Harris, Mary Nell (Mrs. Charles E. Richards Jr.), Thomas Byrne; m. 2d, Bruce Stone, Jan. 12, 1952 (div. May 1963). Formerly engaged in rehab. handicapped children; established Hedgecroft Clinic for complete treatment polio victims, Houston, 1942, owner, 1942-48, incorporated as non-profit corp., 1948, chmn. bd., dir., 1948-51, exec. dir., trustee 1951-58, dir., trustee 1958-62 (center gen. rehab.); cons. orgn. and operation health and hosp. facilities, 1962-64; free-lance counselor pub. relations and advt., 1964—; pres. Hosp. Adv. Services, Inc., 1962—; pres. Nell Harris Assos., Inc., theatre and concert mgmt. Trustee Hedgecroft Hosp; sponsor Houston Horse Show. Past pres. Houston Hosp. Council. Elected nominee Am. Coll. Hosp. Adminstrs. Mem. Advt. Fedn. Am., Am. Women in Radio and TV, Achievement Rewards for Coll. Scientists Found. Episcopalian. Clubs: Advertising, Altrusa (Houston); Farm and Ranch; College Women's; Scribbler's; Junior League Luncheon. Contbr. articles profl. publs. Address: 1300 Woodhollow Dr Houston TX 77027

HARRIS, OREN, U.S. judge; b. Belton, Ark. Dec. 20, 1903; s. Homer and Bettie (Bullock) H.; A.B., Henderson State Coll., Arkadelphia, Ark., 1929; LL.B., Cumberland U., 1930; m. Ruth Ross, May 9, 1934; children—Carolyn Marie, James Edward. Admitted to Ark. bar, 1930, since in practice of law; admitted to U.S. Supreme Ct. bar, 1943; dep. pros. atty., Union County, Ark., 1933-36; pros. atty. 13th Jud. Circuit, 1936-40; mem. 77th-89th Congresses, 4th Dist.; now U.S. judge Western Dist. Ark. Mem. Am., Ark. bar assns. Lion (dist. gov. Ark. 1939-40). Democrat. Baptist. Mason (32, Shriner), K.P. Home: 1110 W Main St El Dorado AR 71730 Office: Federal Bldg El Dorado AR 71730

HARRIS, PATRICIA ROBERTS, lawyer, educator; b. Mattoon, Ill., May 31, 1924; d. Bert Fitzgerald and Hildren Brodie (Johnson) Roberts; A.B., Howard U., 1945; J.D. (with honor); George Washington U., 1960; postgrad. U. Chgo., 1945-47, Am. U., 1949-50; LL.D., Lindenwood Coll., Morgan State Coll., 1967, Russell Sage Coll.; Tufts U., Dartmouth Coll., 1970; D.H.L., Miami U.; 1967; D.C.L., Beaver Coll., 1968; m. William Beasley Harris, Sept. 1, 1955. Program dir. YWCA, Chgo., 1946-49; asst. dir. Am. Council Human Rights, 1949-53; exec. dir. Delta Sigma Theta, 1953-59; research asso. George Washington U. Sch. Law, 1959-60; admitted to D.C. bar, 1960, also U.S. Supreme Ct.; trial atty. Dept. Justice, 1960-61; asso. dean students, lectr. law Howard U., 1961-63, prof. law, 1963-69, dean Sch. of Law, 1969; partner Strasser, Spiegelberg, Fried, Frank & Kampelman, 1970—; mem. U.S.-P.R. Commn. Status P.R., 1964-66; U.S. ambassador to Luxembourg, 1965-67. Alternate del. of U.S. to 21st Gen. Assembly of UN, 1966. Dir. Nat. Bank Washington. Mem. Exec. com. Nat. Citizens Com. Community Relations, 1964-65; co-chmn. Nat. Womens Com. Civil Rights, 1963-64; vice chmn. Nat. Capitol Area Civil Liberties Union, 1962-65; exec. bd. D.C. chpt. N.A.A.C.P., 1963-65, bd. dirs. Legal Defense Fund, since 1967—; chmn. welfare com. Urban League D.C., 1961-65. Del. Dem. Nat. Conv., 1964; presdl. elector, D.C., 1964. Bd. dirs. Am. Civil Liberties Union, 1964-65, YWCA of U.S., 1958- 60, Am. Council Human Rights, 1953-58, Nat. Capitol area YWCA, 1963-65, Family and Child Services D.C., 1963-65, Home Rule Com. D.C., 1965-66, Com. on Admissions and Grievances U.S. Dist. Ct. for D.C., 1970—; adminstrv. conf. U.S., 1968—; nat. adv. com. Reform Fed. Criminal Laws, 1967—; Nat. Com. on Causes and Prevention Violence, 1968-69; Carnegie Commn. on Future Higher Edn., 1969—. Bd. dirs. Georgetown U; trustee Twentieth Century Fund; bd. govs. Atlantic Inst.; bd. dirs. Un Assn.; vice chmn. Greater Washington Ednl. TV. Decorated Order of Oaken Crown (Luxembourg). Mem. Am., Fed. bar assns., Phi Beta Kappa, Order of Coif, Delta Sigma Theta, Kappa Beta Pi. Address: 1742 Holly St NW Washington DC 20012 Office: 1700 K St NW Washington DC 20006

HARRIS, PAUL, sculptor; b. Orlando, Fla., Nov. 5, 1925; student U. N.M., New Sch. Social Research, Hans Hofmann Sch. Fine Arts. Fulbright prof. sculpture Universidad Catolica de Chile, 1961-62, mem. faculty architecture, 1962; later faculty San Francisco Art Inst., Cal. Coll. Arts and Crafts, Oakland; exhibited group shows Mus. Modern Art, N.Y.C., 1958, 63, N.Y. World's Fair, 1965, Art Inst. Chgo., 1965, Md. Inst. Art, 1966, Mus. Contemporary Crafts, 1966, Sao Paulo Bienal, 1967, Smithsonian Instn. Traveling Exhbn., 1969, also Phila. Inst. Art, San Francisco Mus. Art, N.J. State Mus., Los Angeles County Mus., Brandeis U.; exhibited one- man show Poindexter Gallery, N.Y.C., 1957, 60, 63, 67, 70, Lanyon Gallery, 1965, Berkeley Gallery, 1965, William Sawyer Gallery, San Francisco, 1969, 71, Galerie Thelen, Essen, 1970. Recipient Longview Found. grant, 1960, Neallie Sullivan award, 1967; Tamarind fellow, 1969-70. Contbr. Art News, Art in Am. Address: Box 214 Bolinas CA 94924

HARRIS, PAUL STEWART, art historian; b. Orange, Mass., Mar. 7, 1906; s. Carl Chester and Elizabeth (Stewart) H.; B.S., Antioch Coll., 1928; S.B. in Art History, Harvard, 1932; part-time student Grad. Sch. of Fine Arts, N.Y. U., 1933-38; student art history in Europe, 3 summers; m. Jean Lida Morrill, Jan. 28, 1944; children—Andrew Morrill, Alexandra Morrill (Mrs. Alexander W. Fraser, Jr.). Curatorial asst. and asst. curator decorative arts dept. Met. Mus. Art, N.Y.C., 1933, dept. mediaeval art and The Cloisters, 1934-38; dir., sec. Des Moines Assn. of Fine Arts, 1938-40; sr. curator Mpls. Inst. Arts, 1941-42, 46; dir., curator J.B. Speed Art Mus., 1946-62; dep. dir. Winterthur Mus., 1962-67; dir. collections Henry Ford Mus., 1967-71; lectr. history Am. painting U. Minn., 1946; adviser to bldg. com. Satterwhite Wing, Louisville, 1953-54. Served from lt. to lt. comdr., USNR, World War II. Mem. Am. Fedn. Arts (trustee), Am. Assn. Museums, Soc. Colonial Wars, Coll. Art Assn. Conglist. Mason, Rotarian. Club: Harvard (N.Y.C.). Author: Fourteen Seasons of Art Accessions in Kentucky, 1947-60, 1960; also articles on art history and catalogues for mus. publs. Home: RFD Chesham Marlborough NH 03455

HARRIS, PHILIP BREWER, banker; b. Mpls., June 28, 1911; s. Walter Stewart and Jeannette (Brewer) H.; student U. Minn., 1930-34; m. Marian Ardene Berg, Nov. 9, 1940; children—Philip Brewer, Daniel Stewart, Timothy Jenkins, Thomas Vincent. Vice pres. Charles W. Sexton Co., Mpls., 1934-42, 45-52; civilian chief USAAF Material Command Ins. div., Dayton, O., 1942-45; exec. v.p., dir. Northwestern Nat. Bank, Mpls., 1952-69, pres., 1969—, also dir.; dir. Gen. Mills. Inc., Gt. No. Ins. Co., Chubb Corp., Upper Midwest Research & Devel. Corp. Trustee Abbott Hosp. Mem. Res. City Bankers Assn., Mpls. C. of C. (past pres.). Presbyn. (trustee). Clubs: Minneapolis, Woodhill, Minikahda. Home: 985 Edgewood Hill Rd Wayzata MN 55391 Office: 620 Marquette Av Minneapolis MN 55440

HARRIS, REED, writer, govt. ofcl.; b. N.Y.C., Nov. 5, 1909; s. Tudor Reed and Lois Estella (Jones) H.; student Staunton (Va.) Mil. Acad., 1928, Columbia. 1932, George Washington U., 1947; m. Martha Margaret Tellier, Aug. 2, 1931 (dec. 1966); children—Robert Reed, Ann Shapleigh, Donald Reed; m. 2d, Mary Mateer West, Dec. 27, 1966. With Washington County Post, Cambridge, N.Y., 1925-27; editor Columbia U. Daily Spectator, 1932; circulation dept. N.Y. Times, 1931-32; reporter N.Y. Jour., 1932; free lance reporter Newspaper Enterprise Assn., N.A. Newspaper Alliance, King Features Syndicate and others, 1932-33; advt. Robert Mack, Inc. and Badger, Browning & Hersey, Inc., N.Y.C., 1933- 34; exec. editor Fed. Emergency Relief Adminstrn., WPA, Washington, 1934-38; travel book editor Europe on Wheels, Inc., N.Y.C., 1938-39; N.Y. State dir., then regional supr. Nat. Emergency Council, Office Govt. Reports, O.W.I., 1939-42; chief mgmt. planning O.W.I., Washington, 1942-44; chief div. of communications and records U.S. Dept. of State, 1945-48, chief pubs. div., 1949-50, dep. adminstr. U.S. Internat. Information Adminstrn. 1950-53; pres. Publ. Services, Inc., 1953-61, Reinforced Learning, Inc., 1958-62; exec. asst. to dir. USIA, Washington, 1961-64, asst. dir. Information Centers, 1964-66, agy. asst. dir. for policy and plans, 1966- 68, agy. spl. asst. for research and assessment, 1969—. Mem. Army-State Dept. survey mission to Germany, 1948; dir. Nat. Self Govt. Com., Inc. Served USAAF, 1944-45. Recipient Edward R. Murrow award pub. diplomacy Tufts U., 1966; Silver Helmet award, civil servant of yr. Amvets., 1968. Mem. Am. Fgn. Service Assn., Amvets (mem. Nat. Americanism Council 1958-61, D.C. dept. comdr. 1959-60, nat. exec. com. 1960-62), Nat. Soc. Srs., Inc. (pres. 1946—), Phi Gamma Delta. Democrat. Methodist. Mason. Club: Internat. (dir.) Washington). Author: King Football, 1932; Travelers' Windfall (with J.S. Robbins), 1938; (with Lewis Robins) Living Method Typing Course, 1958, Rider FCC Code Course, 1958, Instant French, 1959, Instant Russian, 1960, also other langs. Contbg. editor: Concerning Govt. Benefits, 1935; Am. Guide Series, 1935-38; Aging in the Modern World, 1958; New Frontiers of Knowledge, 1958. Home: 4905 Berkley St Crestview MD 20016 Office: 1750 Pennsylvania Av NW Washington DC 20547

HARRIS, REESE HARVEY, Jr., retired banker; b. LaPlume, Pa., Apr. 28, 1911; s. Reese Harvey and Christine (Richards) H.; grad. Phillips Exeter Acad., 1929; A.B., Princeton, 1933; LL.B., Harvard, 1936; m. Dorothy Lois Ripple, June 16, 1934; children—Reese Harvey III, Ezra R. Admitted to Conn. bar, 1937; practice in Hartford, 1937-44, 46-50; dir., retired chmn. trust com. Mfrs. Hanover Trust Co.; trustee Soc. for Savings; dir. Connecticut Gen. Life Ins. Co., Aetna Ins. Co., Phelps Dodge Corp., Simmons Co., Weeden & Co. Served with USNR, 1944-46. Mem. Phi Beta Kappa. Home: Foxboro Point Saw Mill Lane Essex CT 06426

HARRIS, RICHARD ST. JOHN, actor; b. Limerick, Eire, Oct. 1, 1933; s. Ivan Harris; student London Acad. Music and Dramatic Arts; m. Joan Elizabeth Rees-Williams, Feb. 9, 1957; 3 sons. Dir. off-West End prodn. The Country Girl, 1956; appeared on stage with Joan Littlewood's Theatre Workshop, London, Eng.; film appearances include A Terrible Beauty, Mutiny on the Bounty, This Sporting Life (best actor award Cannes Film Festival 1963), The Red Desert, Major Dundee, The Heroes of Telemark, The Bible, Hawaii; also appeared on TV and stage in The Ginger Man and Diary of a Madman. Recipient Golden Globe award for best mus.-comedy actor Camelot, 1967. Mem. Socialist Party. Roman Catholic. Home: Allen House Allen St London W8 England Office: care Asso Brit Picture Corp Ltd Elstree Studios Boreham Wood Hertfordshire England

HARRIS, ROBERT ADRIAN, textile co. exec.; b. N.C., Aug. 9, 1918; s. Robert Ivory and Myrtle (Wemyss) H.; student Campbell Coll., Buie's Creek, N.C., also U. N.C.; m. Elizabeth W. Everett, Mar. 21, 1948; children—Robert Shields, Justus Everett, Elizabeth Wemyss. Trainee, U.S. Steel Co., 1939-42; successively cost accountant, mill mgr., sec.-treas., sr. v.p. mfg., sec. Fieldcrest Mills, Inc., Spray, N.C., 1946—. Served to lt. USNR, 1942- 46. Mem. Phi Beta Kappa. Baptist. Rotarian. Home: 420 Greenway St Spray NC 27288 Office: Fieldcrest Mills Inc Eden NC 27288

HARRIS, ROBERT CRONLEY, lawyer; b. San Francisco, Oct. 27, 1916; s. Lawrence W. and Lucie (King) H.; A.B., Stanford, 1937; LL.B., Harvard, 1940; m. Nancy Gray, Feb. 22, 1941; children—Lucie S., Robert Cronley, William G. Admitted to Cal. bar, 1941; partner Heller, Ehrman, White & McAuliffe, San Francisco, 1950—. Vis. lectr. law U. Cal. Law Sch. Mem. Republican County Central Com., San Francisco, 1948, vice chmn., 1954-59. Sec., trustee San Francisco Mus. Art; bd. dirs., chmn. Town Sch. for Boys; bd. dirs. Travelers Aid Soc., San Francisco. Served as lt. comdr. USNR, World War II. Mem. Am., Cal., San Francisco (past dir.) bar assns. Clubs: Family; Burlingame Country. Home: 25 Sixth Av San Francisco CA 94118 Office: 14 Montgomery St San Francisco CA 94104

HARRIS, ROBERT EDWARD GEORGE, educator, writer; b. Bloomington, Ind., Apr. 3, 1903; s. C. Edward and Frances (Whiteley) H.; A.B., Ind. U., 1925, M.A., 1926; grad. student Yale, 1926-27; m. Edna Welton, Aug. 8, 1925; 1 dau., Nancy W. (Mrs. Robert R. Kirsch). Instr. journalism and pub. affairs Los Angeles City and State colls., 1929-42; chief editorial writer Los Angeles Daily News, 1945-49; editorial columnist Los Angeles Times, 1949-52; prof. journalism dept. U. Cal. at Los Angeles, 1950-70; guest prof. Institut für Publizistik U. Vienna, 1970-71; editor-in-chief Capricorn TV Enterprises, 1962. Exec. com. Cal. Congl. Reorgn. Plan, 1956—; mem. Gov. planning com. Mental Health in Cal., 1949. Served as lt. USNR, 1942-44. Recipient Am. Specialist Grant, Dept. State, Turkey and Iran, 1959; Del Amo fellow, Spain, 1960. Mem. Am. Assn. U. Profs., Sigma Delta Chi. Democrat. Methodist. Author: The Press in an Authoritarian State, 1964; Spain's Mass Cultural Communications Media, 1966; Spain's Move Toward Freedom of the Press, 1966; The Spanish Press in Transition, 1967. Editor: Poster Propaganda of the Spanish Civil War, 1970. Home: 1413 Thayer Av Los Angeles CA 90024

HARRIS, ROBERT JENNINGS, educator, polit. scientist; b. Wilson County, Tenn., Oct. 25, 1907; s. Robert Jennings and Lucy (Talley) H.; A.B. magna cum laude, Vanderbilt U., 1930; A.M. (polit. sci. scholar), U. Ill., 1931; Ph.D., Princeton, 1934; m. Martha Dashiel Baxter, June 10, 1937. Asst. and fellow in politics Princeton, 1931-34; instr. polit. sci. U. Cin., 1934-36; asst. prof. govt. La. State U., 1936-38, asso. prof. 1938-43, prof., 1943-54, chmn. dept., 1941-54; prof. polit. sci. Vanderbilt U., 1954- 63, chmn. dept., 1962-63; prof. polit. sci., dean faculty arts and sci. U. Va., 1963-68, James Hart prof. govt., prof. history, 1968—; vis. prof. Vanderbilt U., summer 1946, U. Minn., summer 1947, U. N.C., summer 1948, Columbia, 1957-58; Edward Douglass White lectr. La. State U., 1959; spl. staff Library of Congress, 1950. Mem. Am. Assn. U. Profs. (nat. council 1961-64), Am. (v.p. 1950), So. (pres. 1947) polit. sci. assns., Phi Beta Kappa. Clubs: Colonnade; Cosmos (Washington). Author: The Judicial Power of the United States, 1940; The Quest for Equality: The Constitution, Congress and the Supreme Court, 1960; (with others) Continuing Crisis in American Politics, 1963; also articles, book reviews in profl. journals. Bd. editors jour. Politics, 1945-48, editor, 1939-45; asso. editor Am. Polit. Sci. Rev., 1951-53; adv. bd. editors Va. Quar. Rev., 1964—. Collaborator: Constitution of the United States: Analysis and Interpretation, 1953. Home: Pavilion IX West Lawn Charlottesville VA 22903

HARRIS, ROBERT MARK, educator; b. N.Y.C., Aug. 6, 1931; s. Leo and Ella (Newman) H.; B.A., Columbia, 1952; M.F.A., Princeton, 1955, Ph.D., 1960; m. Anabell Thornton, July 15, 1958; children—Robin, Mark. Mem. faculty Smith Coll., 1957—, prof. history of art, 1967—, also now chmn. dept. Fulbright grantee, Paris, France, 1955-56, Warburg Inst., London, Eng., 1961-62; Herodotus fellow Sch. Hist. Studies, Inst. Advanced Study, 1965; Procter fellow Princeton, 1956-57. Mem. Coll. Art Assn. Am., Mediaeval Acad. Am., Phi Beta Kappa. Home: 33 Washington Av Northampton MA 01060

HARRIS, ROBERT SAMUEL, educator; b. Brookline, Mass., May 10, 1904; s. William and Ann Ellen (Bell) H.; B.S., Mass. Inst. Tech., 1928, Ph.D., 1935; hon. degree, U. Havana, 1953; children—Richard, Donald. Research asst. Mass. Inst. Tech., 1928-31, research asso., 1931-37, asst. prof., 1937-41, asso. prof., 1941-46, prof. nutritional biochemistry, 1946-70, emeritus, 1970—, dir. oral sci. research lab.; guest prof. U. Minn., 1970-71, U. Cal. at Los Angeles, 1970-71; field rep. Pan-Am. San. Bur., 1943-52; sci. dir. Nat. Inst. Nutrition, Ecuador, 1950-54, Laboratorios FIM de Nutricion, Havana, 1952-58; hon. prof. U. Havana. Expert nutrition cons. to sec. war, 1943-46, Bd. Econ. Warfare, 1943-46; mem. sci. adv. com. Inst. Nutrition C.Am. and Panama, 1946-54; spl. cons. to sec. of health and assistance, Mexico, 1943-47; mem. com. NRC, 1942- 46; mem. grants com. NIH. Trustee Gordon Research Confs. Decorated by presidents Ecuador, Cuba, Guatemala. Fellow A.A.A.S. (v.p. 1969). Am. Acad. Dentists, Am. Pub. Health Assn., N.Y. Acad. Sci.; mem. Internat. Soc. Dental Research, Am. Inst. Nutrition, Brit. Nutrition Soc., Am. Chem. Soc., Am. Gerontol. Soc., Acad. Phys. Med., Am. Oil Chem. Soc., Am. Dental Assn. (asso.), Sigma Xi, Delta Omega, Theta Delta Chi, Omicron Kappa Upsilon. Author: The Vitamins (7 vols.), 2d edit., 1968; Nutritional Evaluation of Food Processing, 1960; also numerous articles. Editor: Vitamins and Hormones, vols. I-XVII. Home: 32 Dwhinda Rd Newton MA 02168

HARRIS, ROBERT TAYLOR, educator, philosopher; b. Joliet, Ill., Mar. 18, 1912; s. Eugene Nelson and Bess (Hutchinson) H.; Ph.B., Northwestern U., 1937; M.A., Harvard, 1948, Ph.D., 1949; m. Mary Margaret Simmons, Mar. 30, 1946; children—Paul, Peter, Eugene and John (twins). Mem. faculty U. Utah, 1949-52, So. Ill. U., 1952-55, Bradley U., 1955-58; prof. philosophy, Miami U., Oxford, O., 1958—, chmn. dept., 1958-69; vis. prof. philosophy Simmons Coll., 1970-71. Served with USMCR, 1942-45. Author: (J. Jarrett) Language and Informal Logic, 1956; Social Ethics, 1962. Home: 74 Babcock St Brookline MA 02146

HARRIS, ROGER I., business exec.; b. 1910; A.B., U. Pitts., 1931, LL.B., 1934; married. Admitted to Pa. bar, 1935; pvt. practice law, Pitts., 1934-42; spl. asst. to chief real estate, chief engrs. U.S. Army, 1942-43; dep. gen. counsel AEC, 1943-52; with Gen. Dynamics Corp., N.Y.C., 1952—, v.p., chief counsel, 1957—. Office: One Rockefeller Plaza New York City NY 10020*

HARRIS, ROSEMARY ANN, actress; b. Ashby, Eng.; d. Stafford Berkley and Enid (Campion) H.; Theatrical appearances include Climate of Eden, N.Y.C., 1952, Seven Year Itch, London, 1953, Bristol Old Vic, 1954, London Old Vic, 1955-56, Interlock, N.Y.C., 1957, Group 20, Wellesley, Mass., 1958, 59, The Disenchanted, N.Y.C., 1958, The Tumbler, N.Y.C., 1960, Assn. Producing Artists Repertory Company, N.Y.C., 1960-63, 63-64, 65-67, Chichester (Eng.) Festival, 1963, 64, Brit. Nat. Theatre, 1964-65; appeared in films Beau Brummell, The Shiralle. Recipient Antoinette Perry award, 1966, Vernon Rice award, 1962, Theatre World award, 1952, Drama League award, 1967, Obie award, 1962, Whitbread award, 1965-67.

HARRIS, ROY ELLSWORTH, composer; b. Lincoln County, Okla., Feb. 12, 1898; s. Elmer Ellsworth and Laura (Broddle) H.; student U. Cal., 1919-20; Mus.D. (hon.), Rutgers U., 1941, U. Rochester, 1946; student of music under mother, Arthur Farwell and Nadia Boulanger; m. Beula Duffey, Oct. 10, 1936; 3 children. Composer since 1926; has composed 6 symphonies, music for schools, bands, orchestras, choruses; 3 string quartets, string and piano quintets, choral compositions and piano solos. Guggenheim fellow, 1928-30; creative fellowship Pasadena Music and Art Assn., 1930-33. Composer in residence Cornell U., 1941-42, Colo. Coll., Colorado Springs, 1942-48, Utah State Agrl. Coll., 1948-67, U. Cal. at Los Angeles, 1967—. Served with U.S. Army, 1918; mus. dir. with Office of War Information , 1945. Awarded 1st honors for most important score (Folk Song Symphony), 1940, by Committee for Appreciation of Am. Music; certificate of honor for outstanding contbns. to Am. Music by Nat. Assn. for Composers and Conductors, 1940; Coolidge medal for eminent contbn. to chamber music, Library of Congress, 1942. Fellow Nat. Inst. Arts and Letters; mem. Am. Soc. Composers, Authors and Publishers, Am. Composers Assn., Nat. Assn. Composers and Conductors, Nat. Composers Congress (dir. 1944-45), Fellowship Am. Composers (pres. 1946-50), Sinfonia; hon. life mem. Pitts. Musicians Club, Phi Mu Gamma, Phi Mu Alpha. Clubs: Clef (Cornell); Lotos (N.Y.C.); El Paso (Colorado Springs). Editor: Singing Through the Ages, 2 vols., 1940. Contbr. articles to Scribner's N.Y. Times, Twice a Year, Mus. Quar., Modern Music, Music News, etc. Folk Song Symphony (No. 4 and 5) recorded by U.S. Govt. for distribution in allied camps. Sixth (Lincoln) Symphony premiere, Boston Symphony, 1944. Home: 1200 Tellem Dr Pacific Palisades CA 90272

HARRIS, RUFUS CARROLLTON, univ. pres.; b. Monroe, Ga., 1897; s. Virgil Vascar and Jessie (Green) H.; grad. Gordon Inst., Barnesville, Ga., 1915; A.B., Mercer U., 1917, LL.D., 1931; LL.B., Yale, 1923, J.D., 1924; LL.D., U. Ala., 1941, William Jewell Coll., 1943, U. Me., 1953, U. Chattanooga, 1953, Northwestern U., 1958, La. State U., 1960, Tulane U., 1965; Litt.D., Birmingham So. U., 1950, U. Miami, 1958; D.C.L., U. Hawaii, 1952; prof. honoris causa, U. Pueblo, 1956; L.H.D., Samford U., 1961, Stetson U., 1962, Jacksonville U., 1964; m. Mary Louise Walker, June 23, 1918; children—Rufus Carrollton, Joseph Henry Walker, Louie Kontz. Prof. law Mercer U. Law Sch., 1923-27, dean, 1925-27; dean, prof. law Tulane U., 1927-37, pres., 1937-60; pres. Mercer U., Macon, Ga., 1960—. Dir. U.S. Fed. Res. Bank, Atlanta, 1938-56, chmn. bd. dirs., 1954-56. Pres., So. Assn. Colls. and Secondary Schs., 1958, Council So. Univs., 1956-57, So. U. Conf., 1941-43; mem. La. Bd. of Edn., 1940-49; mem. Commn. on Colls., 1957—; mem. Nat. Commn. on Uniform State Laws, 1925-27, Joint Army- Navy Bd. on Tng. Unit Contracts, 1943-45; mem. adv. com. VA, Washington, 1943-69, chmn. 1958-69; mem. U.S. Adv. Commn. on Internat. Ednl. and Cultural Affairs, 1965-69; mem. adv. panel So. Regional Office Coll. Entrance Exam. Bd., 1969—; chmn. So. Region Marshall Scholarship Com., 1956—; mem. Ga. Higher Edn. Facilities Commn., 1964—. Trustee Eisenhower Exchange Fellowships, Inc., 1953—, Inst. for Def. Analyses, 1956—, Nutrition Found., 1946-50; mem. bd. Carnegie Found. for Advancement of Teaching, 1945—, chmn., 1955; Served with inf. U.S. Army, 1917-19. Decorated Chevalier of French Legion of Honor, Confrerie des Chevaliers du Tastevin; Most Excellent Order Brit. Empire, 1970; Distinguished Civilian Service award Navy Dept., World War II. Mem. Am., La., Ga., New Orleans bar assns., Nat. Planning Assn. (trustee, chmn. com. on So. devel.), Assn. Am. Law Schs. (sec. 1931-35, pres. 1935), Order of Coif, Phi Beta Kappa, Omicron Delta Kappa, Phi Delta Theta. Baptist. Democrat. Mason. Clubs: Boston, Round Table, New Orleans Country, Capital City, Commerce (Atlanta); Century Assn. (N.Y.C.). Home: 1309 Adams St Macon GA 31201

HARRIS, RUTH MIRIAM, sch. adminstr.; b. Cin., Aug. 15, 1898; d. Rev. Henry Howell and Zelia M. (Ward) Harris; Ph.B. cum laude, U. Chgo., 1921; A.M., Columbia, 1929, Ph.D. 1940. Tchr. pub. elementary schs., St. Louis 1919-23, pub. high schs., 1924-25, Sumner Normal Sch., 1925-26; instr., dean of women, registrar Stowe Tchrs. Coll., St. Louis, 1926-40, pres., 1940-54; dir. edn. Bd. Edn. St. Louis, 1954; asst. supt. St. Louis pub. schs., 1962—. Mem. Mayor's Race Commn., St. Louis, 1945—. Named Woman of Achievement, St. Louis Globe Democrat, 1964. Mem. Alpha Kappa Alpha, Kappa Delta Pi, Pi Lambda Theta (nat. v.p.). Christian Scientist. Author: Teachers' Social Attitudes, 1940; Harriet Beecher Stowe Teachers' College and Her Predecessors, 1968. Home: 7495 Ahern Ct University City MO 63130

HARRIS, S. HERSCHEL, business exec.; b. Carroll, Ga., 1898; grad. Ga. Inst. Tech., 1921. Chmn., dir. Standard-Coosa-Thatcher Co. Home: 111 Robin Hood Rd Lookout Mountain TN 37350 Office: 18th and Watkins Sts Chattanooga TN 37404*

HARRIS, SEYMOUR EDWIN, economist; b. N.Y.C., Sept. 8, 1897; s. Henry and Augusta (Kulick) H.; A.B., Harvard, 1920, Ph.D., 1926; LL.D., U. Mass., Monmouth Coll.; Ruth Black, Sept 3, 1923 (dec.); m. 2d, Dorothy Marshall, April 27, 1968. Instr., Princeton, 1920-22; instr., Harvard, 1922, lectr., 1927, asst. prof. 1933, asso. prof., 1936, prof. 1945-64, Lucius N. Littauer prof. of polit. economy, 1957-64; chmn. dept. econs. Harvard and U. Cal., San Diego, 1964—; vis. 1948; editor Rev. of Econ. and Statistics, 1943-64, asso. editor Quarterly Jour. of Econs., 1947—; sr. cons. to sec. of treas., 1961-68. Mem. bd. Econ. Warfare Policy com., 1942; com. on postwar comml. policy, Sec. of State, 1943; advisor Latin Am. countries on econ. stabilization, 1943; economic adviser to vice chmn. W.P.B., 1944-45; mem. adv. bd. C.C.C., 1949-53; mem. Agrl. Mblzn. Policy Bd., 1951-53. Dir. office export-import price control, O.P.A., 1942-43; adviser to N.R.S.B., 1946-47; cons. to President's Council of Econ. Advs., 1950-51. Chmn. New England Gov.'s Textile Com., 1955-60; mem. pub. adv. com. Area Redevel. Adminstrn., 1964—. Trustee John F. Kennedy Library. Adviser Dem. Nat. Com. Served as pvt., U.S. Army, 1918. Awarded David A. Wells Prize, Harvard, 1927; ¾00 1st Prize, Greater Boston Metropolitan Contest (co-winner), 1944; Alexander Hamilton prize, sec. treasury, 1967. Member Am. Econ. Assn. (exe . com., v.p. 1945-48), Am. Acad. Arts and Scis. Club: Harvard (N.Y.). Author books including: How Shall We Pay for Education, 1948; Stabilization Subsidies, 1948; Foreign Economic Relations of the United States, 1948; European Recovery Program, 1948; Saving American Capitalism, 1948; Economics of Planning; Market for College Graduates, 1949; Inflation and Anti-Inflationary Policies of American States, 1950; Economics of Mobilization and Inflation, 1951; Economics of New England, 1952; Keynes' Economist and Policy Maker, 1955; Interregional and International Economics, 1958; More Resources for Education, 1960; Higher Education in the United States: The Economic Problems, 1960; The Dollar in Crisis, 1961; The Economics of the Political Parties, 1962; Higher Education: Resources and Finance, 1962; Economics of American Medicine, 1964; Economics of the Kennedy Years, 1964; Economic Aspects of Higher Education, 1964; Economics of American Medicine, 1964; The Economics of Harvard; Education and Public Policy; Challenge and Change in American Education. Editor publications including: Schumpeter, Social Scientist, 1951. Home: 9036 La Jolla Shores Dr La Jolla CA 92037 Office: U Cal at San Diego La Jolla CA 92037

HARRIS, SHEARON, utility exec.; b. Middleburg, N.C., Sept. 12, 1917; s. Joseph Pegues and Lucy (Shearon) H.; A.B., Wake Forest Coll., 1936, LL.B., 1938; m. Helen Morgan, June 27, 1942; children—Sarah Helen, Jennie Grace, Susan Finch. Admitted to N.C. bar, 1938; practice in Albemarle, 1939-57, Charlotte, 1946-57; sr. partner firm Harris & Coble, Albemarle, 1955-57; with Carolina Power & Light Co., Raleigh, 1957—, v.p., 1960-63, gen. counsel, 1962-63, pres., 1963—, chief exec. officer, 1968—, chmn. bd., 1970—, also dir.; dir. Durham Life Ins. Co., Wachovia Bank & Trust Co. N.A. Parliamentarian, N. C. Bapt. Conv., 1957-62. Prin. clk. N.C. Ho. of Reps., 1941-43; mem. N.C. Ho. of Reps. from Stanly County, 1955; mem. N.C. Commn. Reorgn. State Govt., 1957-59. Chmn. S.E. Regional Adv. Commn. to Fed. Power Commn., 1968—; pres. N.C. Indsl. Council 1968. Trustee Wake Forest Coll., 1955-59; bd. dirs. N.C. Found. Ch. Related Colls., 1962—, N.C. Bapt. Found., 1961-66, N.C. Citizens Assn., 1966—, (pres. 1970); bd. dirs. N.C. Ednl. Council on Nat. Purposes Inc., 1964—, pres., 1966; chmn. bd. trustees Meredith Coll.; bd. dirs. Edison Electric Inst., 1968—, vice chmn., 1970, chmn., 1971. Served with AUS, 1943-45. Decorated Legion of Merit, Bronze Star. Mem. Am., N.C. bar assns., U.S. C. of C. (policy com.), Nat. Assn. Electric Cos. (chmn. bd. dirs. 1969). Democrat. Home: 2516 Wake Dr Raleigh NC 27608 Office: 336 Fayetteville St Raleigh NC 27602

HARRIS, STANLEY EDWARD, Jr., educator, geologist; b. Basking Ridge, N.J., Mar. 5, 1918; s. Stanley Edwards and Margaret (Roberts) H.; A.B. in Geology magna cum laude, Princeton, 1940; M.S., State U. Ia., 1942, Ph.D., 1947; m. Jane Morgan Powers, June 29, 1940; children—Barbara Morgan (Mrs. Edward Zinn), Carolyn Roberts (Mrs. Leonard Horecker), Janet Elizabeth, David Stanley. Jr. geologist Ia. Geol. Survey, 1942-48; vis. asst. prof. U. Mo., 1948- 49; mem. faculty So. Ill. U., 1949—, prof. geology, 1963—, chmn. dept., 1955-66, acting chmn., 1969-70; with Ill. Geol. Survey, summers 1950-57; vis. prof. Geologisches Staatsinstitut, U. Hamburg (W. Germany), 1957-58; with Ia. Geol. Survey, 1961-63; cons. hwy. geology and limestone, 1955—; asso. dir. NSF Earth Sci. Summer Inst., 1968, dir. In-Service Inst. for Secondary Sch. Tchrs., 1970-71. Mem. Geol. Soc. Am., Am. Assn. Petroleum Geologists, Ill. Acad. Sci., Ill. Geol. Soc., Sigma Xi, Phi Kappa Phi. Presbyn. Spl. research geology of environment, earth sci. teaching. Home: 805 W Cherry St Carbondale IL 62901

HARRIS, STANLEY GALE, Jr., banker; b. Chgo., June 19, 1918; s. Stanley Gale and Muriel (Bent) H.; student Yale, 1936-38; certificate in indsl. adminstrn., Harvard Grad. Sch. Bus. Adminstrn., 1943; m. Marian Short, Jan. 28, 1939; children—John Trumbull, Thomas Bartlett. With Nat. Bank Commerce, Seattle, 1939-42, Carnegie-Ill. Steel Corp., 1943-44; with Harris Trust & Savs. Bank, Chgo., 1944—, now vice chmn. bd., dir.; dir. Snap-On Tools Corp, Kenosha, Wis. Trustee Ill. Children's Home and Aid Soc., U. Chgo., Rush-Presbyn.-St. Luke's Med. Center. Mem. Reserve City Bankers Assn. Clubs: Chicago, Tavern, Attic, Economic, Yale, Harvard Business, Bankers (Chgo.); Skokie Country. Home: 390 Grove St Glencoe IL 60022 Office: Harris Trust & Savs Bank 111 W Monroe St Chicago IL 60690

HARRIS, SYDNEY JUSTIN, newspaper columnist; b. London, Eng., Sept. 14, 1917; student U. of Chgo. and Central Coll., Chgo.; m. Grace Miller (div. 1951); m. 2d, Patricia Roche, 1953; children—Carolyn, Michael, Barbara, David, Lindsay. Employed in various positions with the Chicago Herald and Examiner 1934-35, Chicago Daily Times, 1936; editor Beacon Mag., Chicago, 1937-38; with public relations dept., legal div., City of Chicago, 1939-41; with Chicago Daily News since 1941; now drama critic and writer of column, Strictly Personal, syndicated in U.S. and Canada by Pubs.-Hall syndicate, 1944—, appearing in more than 150 newspapers; mem. faculty U. Coll., U. Chgo., 1946—. Vice pres. Assos. of Inst. for Psychoanalysis in Chgo. Trustee Francis W. Parker Sch., Chgo. Recipient Ferguson award Friends of Lit., 1958; Brotherhood award Nat. Conf. Christians and Jews, 1968. Mem. Sigma Delta Chi. Clubs: Arts, Headline, Press. Author: Strictly Personal, 1953; A Majority of One, 1957; Last Things First, 1961; On the Contrary, 1964; Leaving the Surface, 1968. Office: 401 N Wabash Av Chicago IL 60611

HARRIS, T. GEORGE, editor; b. Simpson County, Ky., Oct. 4, 1924; s. Garland and Luna (Byrum) H.; student U. Ky., 1946; B.A., Yale, 1949; m. Sheila Hawkins, Oct.31, 1953; children—Amos, Anne, Crane, Gardiner. Reporter, Clarksville (Tenn.) Leaf-Chronicle, 1942; corr. Time Inc., 1949-55, Midwest bur. chief, 1955-58; contbg. editor Time, N.Y.C., 1958-60, N.W. bur. chief, 1960-62; sr. editor Look mag., 1962- 64, 64-68; editor Psychology Today mag., 1969—. Vis. com. on humanities U. Chgo.; mem. scholastic grants jury Nat. Endowment on Humanities. Served to 1st lt., F.A., AUS, World War II. Decorated Bronze Star, Air Medal with cluster; named Outstanding Young Man of Chgo., 1955; named Ky. col., to U. Ky. Hall of Fame; recipient prize mag. journalism U. Mo. Mem. Am. Acad. Polit. and Social Sci., Am. Acad. Arts and Sci., Phi Beta Kappa. Clubs: Yale (N.Y.C.); Chicago. Home: 203 via Del Norte La Jolla CA 92037 Office: Psychology Today Mag Del Mar CA 92014

HARRIS, THEODORE EDWARD, educator, mathematician; b. Phila., Jan. 11, 1919; s. Julius and Hazel (Rosenfield) H.; student So. Meth. U., 1935-37; B.A., U. Tex., 1939; M.A., Princeton, 1946, Ph.D., 1947; m. Constance Ruth Feder, June 29, 1947; children—Stephen Joel, Marcia Faye. with Rand Corp., 1947-66, chmn. dept. math., 1959-66; prof. math. U. So. Cal., 1966—; vis. asst. prof. U. Cal. at Los Angeles, 1949-50; vis. asso. prof. Columbia, 1953; vis. prof. Stanford, 1963. Served to maj. USAAF, 1942-45. Mem. Am. Math. Soc., Inst. Math. Statistics (pres. 1966-67), Am.A.A.S. Jewish religion. Author: The Theory of Branching Processes, 1963. Editor Annals of Math. Statistics, 1955-58. Home: 422 S Clark Dr Beverly Hills CA 90211 Office: Dept Math Univ Southern California Los Angeles CA 90007

HARRIS, THOMAS EVERETT, lawyer, labor union ofcl.; b. Little Rock, May 25, 1912; s. Marvin and Ina (Thomas) H.; B.A., U. Ark., 1932; LL.B., Columbia, 1935; m. Lucille Hassell, 1935 (div. 1944); children—Marvin Bryan, Ruffin Kirby; m. 2d, Margaret Samson, Aug. 14, 1944; 1 son, Thomas Everett. Admitted to N.Y., D.C. bars; law clk. to Justice Stone, 1935-36; asso. firm Covington & Burling, Washington, 1936-37; with Dept. Justice, 1937-41, assigned Office Solicitor Gen., 1939-41; asso. gen. counsel FCC, 1941-42, OPA, 1942-43; with Bd. Econ. Warfare, 1943; asso. firm Cahill, Gordon, Zachry & Parlin, N.Y.C., 1943-45; with U.S. Mil. Govt. in Germany, 1945-46; partner firm Alvord & Alvord, Washington, 1946-47; spl. asst. to atty. gen., alien property div. Dept. Justice, 1947-48; asso. gen. counsel CIO, 1948-55, AFL-CIO, 1955—. Mem. Nat. Labor Mgmt. Panel, 1963-67. Democrat. Home: 1201 Key Dr Alexandria VA 22302 Office: 815 16th St NW Washington DC 20006

HARRIS, THOMAS LEWIS, surgeon; b. Hedgeville, W.Va., Feb. 28, 1889; s. James Trone and Ruth Lewis (Martin) H.; B.S., W.Va. U., 1910, D.Sc. (hon.), 1960; M.D., Jefferson Med. Coll., Phila., 1912; Sc.D. (hon.), Marietta (O.) Coll., 1942; m. Caroline M. Neal, June 28, 1922 (dec.); children—Caroline (Mrs. William A. Goebel), Ruth Neal (Mrs. Frank L. Gillis); m. 2d, Elizabeth W. Moran, Apr. 17, 1948. Resident surgery Pa., Children's hosps., Phila., 1912-15; chief resident Louisville City Hosp., 1915-16; chief surgeon St. Joseph's Hosp., Parkersburg, W.Va.; pres. Wood Co. Home Corp.; dir. Consol. Natural Gas Co., N.Y.C. Mem. President's Com. Employment Handicapped; mem. Emergency Resource Planning Com., Com. Higher Edn. W.Va., Gov.'s Com. Phys. Rehab.; mem. Pres.' Com. Crime and Delinquency Bd. dirs. Boys' Clubs Am.; bd. govs. W.Va U. Served as surgeon U.S. Army, 1917-19. Diplomate Am. Bd. Surgeons (founders group). Fellow A.C.S., Internat. Coll. Surgeons; mem. World Med. Assn. (U.S. com.); Med. Rehab. Assn.; Pan Am. Med. Assn., Southeastern, So Surg. socs., Acad. Polit. Sci., N.Y. Acad. Sci., Am. Assn. R.R. Surgeons, Am. Assn. Trauma, A.M.A., Newcomen Soc. London, W.Va. Med. Assn. (pres. 1940-41, 45-46), W.Va. Hosp. Assn. (pres. 1938-39), Va., N.C., S.C. hosp. assns. (pres. 1940-41), Beta Theta Phi, Phi Rho Sigma. Elk, Mason (32, Shriner). Clubs: Parkersburg Country, Williams Country (Weirton, W.Va.); Everglades, Bath and Tennis (Palm Beach, Fla.). Contbr. tech., articles surg. jours. Home: 1109 Ann St Parkersburg WV 26101 Office: 610 Market St Parkersburg WV 26101

HARRIS, THOMAS P., ins. co. exec.; b. Columbus, Miss., Dec. 16, 1898; B.A., Fisk U., 1922; J.D., U. Chgo., 1929. Engaged in ins., Ark., 1922-24; asst. mgr. Little Rock dist., 1924-26; admitted to Ill. bar, 1929; formerly asst. atty. for receivership Binga State Bank, then asso. mem. firm Edward H. Morris and James B. Cashin, Chgo.; legal adviser Chgo. Met. Mut. Assurance Co., 1932-34, v.p., gen. counsel, 1934-56, pres., 1956-61, chmn. bd. dirs. 1961—; dir. Drexel Nat. Bank. Mem. Nat. Ins. Assn. (pres. 1959, chmn. bd. 1960-61), Am., Nat., Cook County bar assns., A.I.M. (asso.), Chgo. C. of C., Nat. Assn. Real Estate Brokers, Cosmopolitan C. of C., Royal Coterie

Snakes, Chgo. Urban League, Chgo. Assembly, Frontiers of Am., Dearborn Real Estate Bd., N.A.A.C.P., Alpha Phi Alpha. Address: 4455 Dr Martin Luther King Jr Dr Chicago IL 60653*

HARRIS, THOMAS WILLIAM, banker; b. Peoria, Ill., Oct. 17, 1912; s. Alfred Wilson and Mary (Black) H.; C.P.A., Western Res. U., 1947; grad. Rutgers U. Grad. Sch. Banking, 1953; m. Martha Olive Owen, Sept. 13, 1936; children—Judith Owen (Mrs. Aldo Ajello), Nancy Elaine (Mrs. William M. Newbury II). With Central Nat. Bank Cleve., 1936—, sr. v.p., 1961—. Active local United Appeal, Anti-Tb League. Mem. Financial Execs. Inst. (dir. 1965—), Nat. Assn. Bank Auditors and Controllers (speaker 1956-), Am. Inst. Bankers. Home: 28810 Wolf Rd Bay Village OH 44140 Office: 123 W Prospect St Cleveland OH 44101

HARRIS, VICTOR, educator; b. Newport News, Va., July 11, 1910; s. Aaron and Eva (Fisher) H.; B.S., U. Va., 1930, M.S., 1932; Ph.D., U. Chgo., 1945; m. Sarah Michie, Aug. 14, 1938 (dec. Sept. 1959); children—Susan Dena, Halli Ann. Instr. English, U. Chgo., 1937-43; from asst. prof. to prof. English, U. Ia., 1945-61, chmn. humanities, 1953-61; prof. English, Brandeis U., 1961—, former chmn. dept. English and Sch. Humanities; mem. faculty Bread Loaf Sch. English, summer 1963. Fellow Ford Fund Advancement Edn., 1951-52, Yaddo Corp., 1965; Huntington Library fellow, 1961. Mem. Am. Assn. U. Profs., Renaissance Soc., Phi Beta Kappa. Author: All Coherence Gone, 1949; English Prose, 1600-1660, 1965. Home: 1000 Memorial Dr Cambridge MA 02138 Office: Brandeis Univ Waltham MA 02154

HARRIS, VINCENT CROCKETT, educator; b. Mpls., Jan. 26, 1913; s. Jesse Brownell and Virginia Case (Crockett) H.; B.A., Northwestern U., 1933, M.A., 1935, Ph.D., 1950; postgrad. U. Wis., 1935-38, U. Minn., summers 1932, 37, U. Kan., summer 1957; m. Blanche Peterson Hanson, Jan. 3, 1945; children—Jacqueline (Mrs. Thomas Hardeman Jones), Diane (Mrs. Charles M. Gill). Accountant, Wells Lamont Corp., 1938-41; instr. Northwestern U., 1946-50; asst. prof., asso. prof., prof. San Diego State Coll., 1950—. Summer faculty Ariz. State U., 1961, U. Mo., 1962, Northwestern U., 1963. Served to lt. USNR, 1942-46; PTO. Mem. Math. Assn. Am. (chmn. So. Cal. sect. 1966-67), Math. Assn. (Eng.), Phi Beta Kappa. Sigma Chi. Republican. Methodist. Home: 5054 55th St San Diego CA 92115

HARRIS, VINCENT MADELEY, bishop; b. Conroe, Tex., Oct. 14, 1913; s. George Malcolm and Margaret (Madeley) H.; student St. Mary's Sem., La Porte, Tex., 1934; S.T.B., N. Am. Coll., Rome, Italy, 1936, J.C.B., 1939; J.C.L., Cath. U. Am., 1940. Ordained priest Roman Cath. Ch., 1938; prof. St. Mary's Sem., 1940-51; chancellor Diocese Galveston-Houston, 1948-66, diocesan consultor, 1951- 66; domestic prelate, 1956; bishop of Beaumont, Tex., 1966-71; coadjuter bishop of Austin, Tex., 1971—. Decorated knight comdr. with star Equestrian Order Holy Sepulchre Jerusalem. K.C. (chaplain Tex. 1967-69). Home: 4007 Balcones Dr Austin TX 78731 Office: PO Box 1828 Austin TX 78767

HARRIS, WHITNEY ROBSON, lawyer; b. Seattle, Aug. 12, 1912; s. Olin Whitney and Lily (Robson) H.; A.B. magna cum laude, U. Wash., 1933; J.D., U. Cal., 1936; m. Jane Freund Foster, Feb. 14, 1964; 1 son, Eugene Whitney. Admitted to Cal. bar, 1936, U.S. Supreme Ct. bar, 1945, Tex. bar, 1953, Mo. bar, 1964; gen. law practice in Los Angeles, 1937-42; chief legal advice br. U.S. Mil. Govt. for Germany, 1946-48; prof. law So. Meth. U., 1948-54; staff dir. legal service and proc. Com. Orgn. Exec. Br. Govt., 1954; exec. dir. Am. Bar Assn., 1954-55; solicitor for Tex., Southwestern Bell Telephone Co., Dallas, 1955-63, gen. solicitor, St. Louis, 1963-65; practice law, of counsel Sumner, Hanlon & Sumner, St. Louis. Pres., St. Louis Civic Ballet, 1970-71. Served from ensign to lt. comdr., USNR, 1942-46; trial counsel U.S. Chief Counsel, Nuremberg, 1945-46; capt. Res. ret. Decorated Legion of Merit. Mem. Inter-Am., Am. (chmn. internat. law sect. 1953-54, chmn. adminstrv. law sect. 1960-61) bar assns., State Bar Tex. (chmn. adminstrv. law com. 1952-54, internat. law com. 1961-62), Phi Beta Kappa, Order Coif, Phi Kappa Psi, Delta Theta Phi. Author: Family Law, 1953; Tyranny On Trial, 1954; Legal Services and Procedure, 1955. Contbr. Ency. Brit., also mags. and legal periodicals. Home: 2 Glen Creek Lane St Louis MO 63124

HARRIS, WILLIAM, flower importer; b. N.Y.C., July 5, 1904; s. Leopold and Jenny (Hillman) H.; A.B., Columbia, 1924, A.M., 1925; m. Thelma Sacks, Oct. 1929 (div. 1939); children—Paul Richard, Steven Peter. Pres., treas. M. Goldfarb-My Florist, Inc., N.Y.C., Arcadian Gardens, Inc.; William Harris & Sons, Inc. Mem. adv. com., chmn. com. vocational tng. N.Y.C. Bd. Edn. Decorated Chevalier du Merité (France), 1953. Club: Columbia University. Author: Seventy and Seven, 1947; Beating the Great Rap, 1949; Interviews on Judgement Day, 1950. Home: 10 E 85th St New York City NY 10028 Office: 888 Madison Av New York City NY 10021

HARRIS, WILLIAM ALLEN, retired army officer; b. Ilo Ilo, Philippines, Feb. 3, 1911 (parents U.S. citizens); s. Hunter and Lula (Allen) H.; student Va. Mil. Inst., 1927- 28; B.S., U.S. Mil. Acad., 1933; grad. F.A. Sch., 1937, 38, Command and Gen. Staff Coll., 1943, Army War Coll., 1952; m. Harriet Deland Smith, Dec. 15, 1933; children—Harriet Kendall, Elizabeth Allen. Commd. 2d lt. U.S. Army, 1933, advanced through grades to maj. gen., 1962; various arty. assignments, 1933-43; with G-3 sect. U.S. Army Hdqrs. ETO, 1943, First and Twelfth U.S. Army Group, 1944-45; assigned Joint Chiefs Staff, 1945-46, plans and operations div. War Dept. Gen. Staff, 1946-47, U.S. Army Gen. Staff, 1947-48; with 271st F.A., Japan, 1948-49, 77th F.A. Battalion, Japan and Korea, 1949-50, 7th Cav. Regt., Korea, 1950- 5l; spl. asst. to chief staff SHAPE, Paris, France 1955-56; comdg. gen. 3d Inf. Div. Arty., Ft. Benning, Ga., 1956-57, XIII Airborne Corps Arty., Ft. Bragg, N.C., 1957-60, V Corps Arty., Darmstadt, Germany, 1960-61, 7th Army Arty., Stuttgart Vaihingen, Germany, 1961-62, 7th Army Support Command, Mannheim Kaefertal, Germany, 1962-64; dep. comdg. gen. 4th U.S. Army, Ft. Sam Houston, also comdg. gen. Ft. Sam Houston, 1964-66; now vice chmn. Mil. Retirement Communities, Inc. Decorated D.S.M., D.S.C. Silver Star, Legion of Merit with oak leaf cluster, Air medal, Army Commendation ribbon; Croix de Guerre with star (France); Croix de Guerre with palm (Belgium); cross Royal Order Phoenix (Greece). Mem. 12th Army Group Assn., 1st Cav. Div. Assn., Assn. U.S. Army, SHAPE Officers Assn., Legion of Valor, Kappa Alpha. Club: Argyle. Home: 7711 Broadway San Antonio TX 78209 Office: Alamo Nat Bank Bldg San Antonio TX 78205

HARRIS, WILLIAM CRANFIELD, investment broker; b. Toronto, Ont., Can., Dec. 26, 1900; s. William T. and Ruth (Beesley) H.; B.Commerce, U. Toronto, 1925; m. Ethel M. Bowles, Sept. 18, 1926; 1 son, William B. Chmn. Harris & Partners, Ltd., Toronto, Harris & Partners, Inc., N.Y.C., Harris & Partners Securities, Ltd., Toronto; dir. Bank of N.S., Brascan, Ltd., Canadian Gen. Electric Co. Ltd., Ralston Purina of Can., Ltd., Imperial Life Assurance Co. of Can., Ltd. Home: 59 Old Forest Hill Rd Toronto 7 Ontario Canada Office: 11 King St W Toronto 1 Ontario Canada

HARRIS, WILLIAM JAMES, Jr., research adminstr.; b. South Bend, Ind., June 17, 1918; s. William James and Elizabeth M. (Scott) H.; B.S. in Chem. Engring., M.S. in Engring., Purdue U., 1940; Sc.D., Mass. Inst. Tech., 1948; m. Ruth Clara Laubinger, Aug. 26, 1944; children—June Elizabeth, William James III. Head ferrous alloys br. metallurgy div. Naval Research Lab., 1947- 51; exec. sec. materials adv. bd. Nat. Acad. Sci.-NRC, 1951-54, exec. dir., 1957-60, asst. sec., planning div. engring., 1960-62; asst. to dir. Battelle Meml. Inst., 1954-57, asst. to v.p., 1962-67, asst. dir. tech. Columbus Labs., 1967-69; v.p. research and test dept. Assn. Am. Railroads,1970—. Pres., chmn. bd. Piscataway Co., Accokeek, Md., 1958-63. Mem. nat. materials adv. bd. Nat. Acad. Sci., 1967—, chmn., 1969-70; sec. Pres.'s Com. on Hwy. Safety, 1969. Pres. Moyoane Assn., 1951-53, 58; pres., chmn. bd. Alice Ferguson Found., 1966-68. Served to lt. comdr. USNR, 1941-45. Decorated Naval Letter of Commendation. Recipient Distinguished Alumnus award Purdue U., 1965. Fellow Metall. Soc. (pres. 1970); mem. Am. Inst. Mining, Metall. and Petroleum Engrs., treas. 1964-69, v.p., 1964—; vice chmn. inst. metals div. 1960, dir. assn. 1962—, v.p. 1964-65; Mathewson medal 1950), Engrs. Joint Council (bd. dirs. 1965—, pres. 1968-70), Engring. Found. (chmn. research conf. com. 1964-67, bd. dir. 1968-70), Am. Ordnance Assn. (chmn. materials div. 1966- 68), Nat. Security Indsl. Assn. (chmn. exec. planning com. 1965-67, chmn. research and devel. adv. com. 1967-69), Sigma Xi, Tau Beta Pi, Phi Lambda Upsilon, Sigma Delta Chi. Author tech. papers. Editor: (with others) Perspectives in Materials Research, 1963. Home: Route 1 Box 665 Accokeek MD 20607 Office: 1920 L St NW Washington DC 20036

HARRIS, WILLIAM ROBERT, retail exec.; b. Fayetteville, Ga., Aug. 16, 1914; s. Leonard A. and Millie L. (Boyd) H.; grad. Young Harris Coll., 1935; m. Gertrude Goss, Nov. 30, 1942; children-Sally S. (Mrs. S.D. Alford), William Robert. With F.W. Woolworth Co., 1935-42, 45—, v.p., N.Y.C., 1965-70, exec. v.p., 1970—, dir., mem. exec. com., 1967—; dir. Kinney Shoe Corp., Richmond Bros. Co., F.W. Woolworth Co., Ltd., Can. Served with Q.M.C., AUS, 1942-45. Mem. Sales Exec. Club N.Y. Methodist. Clubs: Greenwich (Conn.) Country: Seaview Country (Absecon, N.J.). Home: Aiken Rd Greenwich CT 06830 Office: 233 Broadway New York NY 10007

HARRIS, ZELLIG SABBETAI, educator; b. Balta, Russia, Oct. 12, 1909; s. Hyman and Rachel (Selenger) H.; brought to U.S., 1913, naturalized, 1921; A.B., U. Pa., 1930, A.M., 1932, Ph.D., 1934. Instr., U. of Pa., 1931-38, asst. prof., 1938-42, asso. prof. 1943, prof. linguistic analysis, 1947-67, Benjamin Franklin prof., 1967—; lectr. Linguistic Inst., U. Mich., summer 1937. Guggenheim Meml. Found. fellow, 1939-40; research asso. Am. Philos. Soc., 1945-47; liaison fellow Am. Anthrop. Assn. Mem. Joint Com. Am. Native Langs. Fellow Am. Acad. Arts and Scis.; mem. Linguistic Soc. Am. (pres. 1955), Am. Oriental Soc. (editor 1941-48), Am. Philos. Soc., Phi Beta Kappa. Club: Research (Phila.). Author: Development of the Canaanite Dialects, 1939; Methods in Structural Linguistics, 1951; String Analysis of Sentence Structure, 1962; Discourse Analysis Reprints, 1963; Mathematical Structures of Language, 1968; Papers in Structural and Transformational Linguistics, 1970; also sci. monographs. Contbr. to tech. jours. Research in math. linguistics, descriptive linguistic structure, culture, lang. Office: U Pa Box 12 Philadelphia PA 19104

HARRIS, E. R., Jr., banker. Pres., Fidelity Nat. Bank, Lynchburg, Va. Office: 901 Main St Lynchburg VA 24505*

HARRIS, L. G., bus. exec.; b. Regina, Sask., Can., 1911; ed. U. B.C. (Can.). Exec. v.p. MacMillan Bloedel Ltd., Vancouver, B.C.; dir. Burnaby Paperboard Ltd., MacMillan Bloedel Industries Ltd., Martin Paper Products, Powell River-Alberni Sales Ltd., Export Sales Ltd. Home: 6275 St Georges Crescent W Vancouver British Columbia Canada Office: 1199 W Pender St Vancouver British Columbia Canada*

HARRIS, R. W., gas co. exec.; b. 1910; married. With El Paso Natural Gas Co., 1930—, v.p., mgr. Rocky Mountain region, 1960-66, sr. v.p., 1966—. Office: PO Box 1492 El Paso TX 79999*

HARRISON, ADA MARGERY, educator; b. Sask., Can.; d. Lewis Douglas and Florence Gladys (Ryan) Harrison; came to U.S., 1921, naturalized, 1941; B.A. in Econs., State Coll. Wash., 1941; Ph.D. in Econs., Radcliffe Coll., 1952. With price div. OPA, Denver and Washington, 1943-46; faculty Carleton Coll., 1948—, prof. econs., 1958—, also former chmn. dept. Research fellow Brookings Instn., 1957-58. Mem. Am., Midwest econs. assns., Phi Beta Kappa. Home: 304 1/2 E 5th St Northfield MN 55057

HARRISON, ALBERTIS SYDNEY, Jr., judge, ex-gov. Va.; b. nr. Alberta, Va., Jan. 11, 1907; s. Albertis S. and Lizzie (Goodrich) H.; LL.B., U. Va., 1928; m. Lacey Virginia Barkley, May 8, 1930; children—Albertis Sydney, Antoinette B. Admitted to Va. bar, 1928; commonwealth's atty., Brunswick County, 1932-48; gen. counsel Farmers & Merchants Bank, 1932-58; atty. gen. of Va., 1958-62; gov. Va., 1962-66; justice Supreme Ct. of Appeals Va, 1967—. Mem. Jud. Conf. Va., 1958-60. Chmn. Gov.'s Adv. Bd. on Indsl. Devel.; chmn. So. Regional Edn. Bd., 1963-65. Mem. Va. Senate, 1948-58; chmn. Commn. to Revise Constn. of Va., 1968. Bd. visitors U. Va. Fellow Am. Coll. Trial Lawyers, Am. Inst. Trial Lawyers, Am. Bar Found.; mem. Commonwealth's Attys. Assn. Va. (pres. 1943), Va. (v.p.), Am. bar assns., Va. State Bar (council 1955- 58), Order of Coif, Omicron Delta Kappa, Delta Sigma Phi, Phi Delta Phi. Democrat. Episcopalian. Home: Saddletree Farm Lawrenceville VA 23868 Office: Va Nat Bank Bldg Lawrenceville VA 23868

HARRISON, ALFRED CARLISLE, adj. gen. Ala.; b. Opelika, Ala., July 2, 1912; s. A. Claude and Lucy (Carlisle) H.; B.S., Auburn U., 1933; m. Erin Underwood, July 9, 1935; children—Katherine, George. Owner, Opelika (Ala.) Mop Co., 1946—; pres. Lee County TV Cable Co., Opelika, 1959-63; v.p. Gulf Video, Inc., Eglin AFB, Fla.; adj. gen. Ala., Montgomery, 1963—. Dir. 1st Nat. Bank, Ft. Rucker, Ala. Served with AUS, 1942-46. Mem. U.S., Ala. N.G. assns. Home: 704 6th Av Opelika AL 36801 Office: 1720 Federal Dr Montgomery AL 36102

HARRISON, ANNA JANE, chemist, educator; b. Benton City, Mo., Dec. 23, 1912; d. Albert S.J. and Mary (Jones) Harrison; student Lindenwood Coll., 1929-31; A.B., U. Mo., 1933, B.S., 1935, M.A., 1937, Ph.D., 1940. Instr. chemistry Newcomb Coll., 1940-44; asst. prof. chemistry Mt. Holyoke Coll., 1945-47, asso. prof., 1947-50, prof., 1950—, chmn. dept., 1960-66. Recipient Frank Forrest award Am. Ceramic Soc., 1948; Sarah Berliner fellow Cambridge U., Eng., 1952-53, Petroleum Research Fund Internat. fellow NRC of Can. Am. Chem. Soc., 1959-60; recipient Coll. Chemistry Tchr. award Mfg. Chemists Assn., 1969. Mem. Am. Chem. Soc., Sigma Xi Contbr. articles to profl. jours. Address: Dept Chemistry Mount Holyoke Coll South Hadley MA 01075

HARRISON, ARTHUR DUDLEY, retired utilities exec.; b. Harrow, Eng., Feb. 28, 1905; s. Arthur James and Ethel (John) H.; came to U.S., 1920, naturalized, 1932; M.E., Stevens Inst. Tech., 1926; m. Elizabeth Underhill Powell, June 27, 1931; children—Arthur Dudley, Thomas Dudley. Cadet engr. Stone & Webster, Inc., Boston, 1926-27; engr. Chgo., Wilmington & Franklin Coal Co., 1927-28; with Bklyn. Union Gas Co., 1928-70, asst. chief engr., 1951-53, sr. v.p., 1964-70; now ret.; dir. Gas Energy, Inc., 1965-70. Mem. emergency adv. com. for natural gas Dept. Interior, 1962-70. Recipient Engring. award, Am. Soc. M.E., 1965, Kings County Profl. Engrs. award, 1966. Mem. Soc. Gas Lighting (treas.), Tau Beta Pi, Chi Psi. Club: Garden City Country. Patentee in field. Home: 62 Whitehall Blvd Garden City NY 11530

HARRISON, BAYA M., Jr., lawyer; b. Tampa, Fla., Sept. 14, 1912; LL.B., U. Fla., 1935. Admitted to Fla. bar, 1935; practice in St. Petersburg; mem. Harrison, Greene, Mann, Davenport, Rowe & Stanton and predecessor firm; lectr. law trial and appeal practice John B. Stetson U. Fellow Am. Coll. Trial Lawyers; mem. Am., St. Petersburg, Tampa, Hillsborough County bar assns., Fla. Bar (pres. 1957-58), Fed. Communications Bar Assn., Internat. Assn. Ins. Counsel, Phi Delta Phi. Address: First Federal Bldg St Petersburg FL 33701 *

HARRISON, BENJAMIN FRANKLIN, Jr., mfg. foundry exec.; b. Eufaula, Ala., Feb. 27, 1924; s. Benjamin F. and Clyde (Edwards) H.; B.S., U. Ala., 1948; LL.B., Jones Law Sch., Montgomery, Ala., 1954; m. Margaret Erline Smith, Jan. 14, 1945; children—Margaret Joan, Brenda Jill. With Internal Revenue Service, 1949- 58; with U.S. Pipe and Foundry Co., 1958—, asst. auditor, 1960-62, controller, 1962-64, treas., 1964-69, v.p., 1964-69, sr. v.p., 1969-70, pres., chief exec. officer, 1970—; vice chmn. Lorch, Inc.; dir. Rockwin Corp., Jim Walter Corp., 1970—, (v.p. 1971—), Central Bank and Trust Co., Birmingham, Ala. C.P.A., Ala. Mem. Financial Execs. Inst., Ala. Soc. C.P.A.'s, Beta Alpha Psi. Home: 2116 Viking Circle Birmingham AL 35216 Office: 3300 1st Av N Birmingham AL 35222

HARRISON, BERTRAM COWGILL, ret. air force officer; b. Phila., Mar. 19, 1917; s. Benjamin George and Ellen (Cowgill) H.; B.S., U.S. Mil. Acad., 1938; grad. Pilot Tng. Sch., 1939, Army Command and Staff Sch., 1946, Joint Staff Coll., 1949, Advanced Mgmt. Program, Harvard, 1962; m. Janet Fauntleroy Harrison, Sept. 2, 1939; children—Mary Arthur (Mrs. Charles B. Jackson), Bertram Cowgill, Janet F. Commd. 2d lt. U.S. Army, 1938, advanced through grades to lt. gen., USAF, 1963; comdr. or dep. comdr. groups, wings or divs., U.S. and overseas, 1942-57; dir. or dep. dir. Oklahoma City Air Material Area, 1957-63; dep. insp. gen. USAF, 1963-65; dir. manpower and orgn. Hdqrs. USAF, 1965-68; comdr. 6 Allied Tactical Air Force, Izmir, Turkey, (NATO), 1969, ret.; owner Harrison Properties, gen. real estate firm, 1969—. Decorated Silver Star, D.S.M., Legion of Merit with 3 oak leaf clusters, D.F.C. with 1 oak leaf cluster, Air medal with 4 oak leaf clusters; Croix de Guerre with palm (France). Home: Limestone Quarter Leesburg VA 22075

HARRISON, BERTRAND FEREDAY, botanist; b. Springville, Utah, Feb. 20, 1908; s. Winfred Homer and Martha (Fereday) H.; B.S., Brigham Young U., 1930, M.S., 1931; Ph.D., U. Chgo., 1937; m. Lorna Jensen, Sept. 17, 1931; children—Bertrand Kent, Linnaea, Leon Christen, Philip Alan. Ranger naturalist Yellowstone Park, 1931; instr. in botany Brigham Young U., 1931-35, asst. prof., 1935-37, asso prof., 1937-38, prof. botany, 1938—, chmn. botany dept., 1937-58, 61-64; teaching asst. U. Chgo., 1936-37; research asso. Am. Smelting & Refining Co., Agrl. Research Lab., Salt Lake City, 1943-44. Mem. Bot. Soc. Am., Am. Soc. Plant Physiologists, Utah Acad. Sci. (fellow; past pres.), Sigma Xi. Home: 655 N 1130 East Provo UT 84601

HARRISON, BURR POWELL, former congressman; b. Winchester, Va., July 2, 1904; s. Thomas Walter and Nellie (Cover) H.; student Woodberry Forest Sch., 1918-20, Va. Mil. Inst., 1920-21, Hampden-Sydney Coll., 1921-22, U. Va., 1922-23, Georgetown U., 1923-26; LL.D., Hampden-Sydney Coll., 1949; m. Dorothy W. Green. Admitted to Va. bar, 1926, to practice before Supreme Ct. of Appeals of Va., 1928, Supreme Ct. of U.S., 1937; gen. law practice, Winchester, Va., 1926-42, 1946—; mem. firm Harrison & Johnston; atty. for Commonwealth, Frederick County, Va., 1932-40; mem. Va. Senate, 1940-42; judge 17th Jud. Circuit, 1942- 46; mem. 79th to 87th Congresses, 7th Dist. Va.; mem. Va. Commn. on Constl. Govt., 1963. Bd. visitors Madison Coll., Harrisonburg, Va. Home: Winchester VA 22601 Office: Graichen Bldg Winchester VA 22601

HARRISON, C. BENNETT, banker; b. Memphis, May 10, 1918; s. Caldwell and Nell (Fuqua) H.; B.S., Davidson Coll., 1940; student Vanderbilt U. Grad. Sch., 1940-41; m. Hunter Wright, Sept. 16, 1950; children—C. Bennett, James. With credit dept. Chmn. Bank N.Y. Trust Co., 1946; v.p. First Nat. Bank, Miami, Fla., 1948-65; chmn. bd. Union Planters, Nat. Bank, Memphis, 1965—; dir. Fed. Co., Holiday Inns Am. Active Shelby United Neighbors. Trustee So. Coll. Optometry, William R. Moore Sch. Tech. Served to maj., inf., AUS, 1941-46. Decorated Bronze Star. Mem. Robert Morris Assos. (dir.), Assn. Res. City Bankers, Sigma Alpha Epsilon, Omicron Delta Kappa, Scabbard and Blade. Home: 155 Grove Dale Memphis TN 38117 Office: 67 Madison Av Memphis TN 38103

HARRISON, CARTER RIDGELY, merchandising exec.; b. Kansas City, Mo., June 7, 1918; s. John Scott and Norma (Freyschlag) H.; A.B., Williams Coll., 1940; m. Joan Fitts, July 22, 1944; children—Sallie Dix, Carter Ridgely, Susan Marie, Cynthia Norma, John Scott. With Puritan Compressed Gas Corp., 1940-41; with Fitts Dry Goods Co., Kansas City, Mo., 1945—, successively buyer, asst. sec., v.p., 1945-60, pres., 1960—. Served as officer USAAF, 1942- 45. Decorated Air Medal with 3 oak leaf clusters. Trustee Pembroke Country Day Sch., 1953-59, sec., 1957-59. Mem. Nat. Assn. Textile and Apparel Wholesalers (dir. 1957, 1st v.p. 1961, pres. 1963), Williams Coll. Alumni (pres. Kansas City br.), Kansas City C. of C., Chi Psi. Presbyn. Clubs: Rotary, Kansas City, Textile, Mission Hills Country (Kansas City). Home: 428 W 57th Terrace Kansas City MO 64113 Office: 407 W 8th St Kansas City MO 64105

HARRISON, CHARLES HENRY, advt. exec.; b. Far Rockaway, N.Y., June 29, 1916; s. Meyer and Anna (Brand) H.; student Columbia, 1933, extension student, 1934; m. Esther Stein, July 26, 1940; children—Lynn (Mrs. Joseph Halperin), Katherine. With Henry J. Kaufan Advt. Agy., Washington, 1937-46; with Lester Harrison Advt., Inc., N.Y.C., 1947—, pres., 1965—, now chmn. exec. com. Bishopric, Lieberman, Harrison & Felden, Inc.; creative promotion cons. to charities and polit. parties. Bd. dirs. Five Towns Community Chest, 1960, 61. Club: Friars (N.Y.C.). Home: 1119 E Broadway Hewlett NY 11557 Office: 825 3d Av New York City NY 10022

HARRISON, CHARLES TRAWICK, educator; b. Union Springs, Ala., July 23, 1903; s. William Robert and Eva (Trawick) H.; A.B., U. Ala., 1923; A.M., Harvard, 1925, Ph.D., 1932; m. Eleanor Brownfield, Sept. 4, 1928. Instr. English, Hobart Coll., 1925- 27; asst. prof. English, U. Ala., 1927-28, Boston U., 1929-34; mem. faculty Coll. William and Mary, 1934-47, prof. English, 1939-47; prof. English, U. of South, 1947—, dean Coll. Arts and Scis., 1952-57, Jesse Spalding prof. English lit., chmn. dept. English, 1956—, trustee univ., 1957-62. Mem. Phi Beta Kappa, Phi Kappa Sigma. Democrat. Episcopalian. Contbr. articles, revs. profl. jours. Home: Sewanee TN 37375

HARRISON, DAVID KENT, educator, mathematician; b. Dorchester, Mass., Apr. 6, 1931; s. George Russell and Florence Bartram (Kent) H.; grad. Phillips Andover Acad., 1949; B.A.,

Williams Coll., 1953; Ph.D., Princeton, 1956; m. Priscilla Ann Hill, May 21, 1955; children—Jo Ellen, Michael. Instr. Princeton, 1953-56; asst. prof. Brown U., 1956-58, Haverford Coll., 1958- 59; asst. prof. then asso. prof. U. Pa. at Phila., 1959-62; vis. asso. prof. N.M. State U., 1962-63; mem. faculty U. Ore., Eugene, 1963—, now prof. math. Guggenheim fellow, 1963- 64; NSF postdoctoral fellow, 1965-66. Mem. Am. Math. Soc., Math. Assn. Am. Home: 2362 Malabar Dr Eugene OR 97403

HARRISON, DEAN WILLARD, lawyer, banker; b. Boston, May 2, 1931; s. Lester W. and Hazel O. (Eldridge) H.; grad. Phillips Exeter Acad., 1950; A.B., Princeton, 1954; LL.B., Columbia, 1959; m. Nancy J. Barrows, Dec. 21, 1957; children—Jennifer, Dean Willard. Admitted to Mass. bar, 1959, Conn. bar, 1960, Cal. bar, 1963, also U.S. Supreme Ct.; with firm Heselron & Tisdale, Greenfield, Mass., 1959-60; atty. Travelers Ins. Co., 1960-61; v.p., counsel Bankers Leasing Corp., 1961-62; asst. gen. counsel Pacific Finance Corp., Los Angeles, 1962-67; sec., gen. counsel First Western Bank and Trust Co., Los Angeles, 1957—. Treas. Financial Lawyers Conf., 1968; mem. Cal. Bank Law Adv. Com., 1968. Vice pres. Friends of Library, Monterey Park, Cal. Served with AUS, 1953-56. Mem. Am., Cal., Los Angeles bar assns., Columbia U. Law Sch. Alumni Assn. (treas. So. Cal. 1968). Democrat. Episcopalian (vestry). Clubs: Nassau, University Cottage (Princeton, N.J.); Los Angeles Athletic. Home: 2016 Alamo Dr Monterey Park CA 91754 Office: 548 S Spring St Los Angeles CA 90013

HARRISON, DESALES, sales exec.; b. Atlanta, July 13, 1899; s. James Lawrence and Kathleen (Mecaslin) H.; student Marist Coll., 1913-16; Oglethorpe U., 1917-18; m. Virginia Wyatt Pegram, June 6, 1923; children—DeSales, Virginia (Mrs. Jack Friling), Robert Pegram, Nancy Knight (Mrs. Keith S. Latimore). Salesman various cos., 1919-20; head advt. dept. The Coca-Cola Co., Atlanta, 1925-30, regional mgr. Southeastern Region, New Orleans, 1930- 33, v.p. Central Region, Chgo., 1933-34, v.p. in charge of Fountain Sales Div. U.S., 1934-41; chmn. adv. com., dir. Coca-Cola Bottling Co. (Thomas), Inc.; dir. other cos., The Alabama Gt. So. R.R. Interstate Life & Accident Ins. Co., Am. Nat. Bank & Trust Co. Pres. YMCA Chmn. Bd. dirs. Meml. Hosp., Community Found. Greater Chattanooga, Inc.; trustee Benwood Found., Inc. Served to comdr. USNR, 1942-45, H.I., Okinawa. Mem. Am. Soc. Sales Execs., Newcomen Soc. N. Am., Kappa Alpha. Episcopalian. Clubs: Nine O'Clocks, The Fifty Club, Piedmont Driving (Atlanta); Mountain City, Lookout Mountain-Fairyland. Rotary (Chattanooga). Home: 101 East Brow Road Lookout Mountain TN 37350 Office: Am Nat Bank Bldg Chattanooga TN 37402

HARRISON, EARL LEONARD, clergyman; b. Alto, Tex., Jan. 23, 1891; student Butler Coll., 1912-13; B.Th., Bishop Coll., 1915-19; student Union Theol. Sem., 1935-37; m. Eula Mae Anderson, Jan. 10, 1910 (dec. 1945); children—Earlene Jane (Mrs. Frederick George Sampson), Eldene Catherine (Mrs. Eugene W. James II), Earl Leonard; m. 2d, Ella B. Snell, June 13, 1948. Ordained to ministry Baptist Ch., 1911; pastor in Tex., 1910-36; pres. Bishop Coll., Dallas, 1951-52; pastor Shiloh Bapt. Ch., Washington, 1936—. Pres. Tex. Bapt. Fgn. Mission Conv., 1928-30, Bapt. Conv. D.C. and vicinity, 1943-44, Progressive Nat. Bapt. Conv. D.C., 1970-71; mem. Nat. Bapt. Conv. U.S. A., Inc., 1912-62. Dir. Indsl. Bank, Washington. Pres. Nannie H. Burrough's Sch., Inc., Washington, 1968-69; chmn. bd. trustees Bapt. Sem., Washington; trustee Bishop Coll., 1929-63; bd. dirs. Interdenominational Theol. Center, Atlanta; organizer, chmn. Washington Inst. Employment Tng., 1965-71. Home: 1743 Webster St NW Washington DC 20011 Office: 1500 9th St NW Washington DC 20001

HARRISON, EARLE, county ofcl.; b. Rainsville, Ala., May 20, 1905; s. Robert Lee and Sarepta Ophelia (Hansard) H.; A.B., Northwestern U., 1929, postgrad. in bus. adminstrn., 1942; LL.B., Chgo.-Kent Coll. Law, 1935; m. Joan Mary Jackson, Jan. 24, 1942. With Marshall Field & Co., Chgo., 1929—, div. operating mgr. customer accounts and services div., 1958-60, v.p. operations, 1960-64, v.p., treas., 1964-68; bd. dirs. Credit Bur. Cook County, 1949-69, pres., 1958-69; mem. bd. suprs., chmn. planning and zoning com. Lake County, Ill., 1970—. Commr., Northwestern Ill. Planning Commn., 1970—. Pres., bd. dirs. Family Financial Counseling Service Greater Chgo. Mem. Phi Delta Phi. Episcopalian. Club: Chicago Athletic Assn. Home: Greenbriar Farm 740 N St Mary's Rd Libertyville IL 60098

HARRISON, EDWARD JAMES, lawyer, corp. exec.; b. Streator, Ill., June 21, 1926; s. Frank J. and Nell (Webb) H.; B.S., U. Ill., 1950, J.D., 1952; m. Roberta I. Roberts, June 18, 1948; children—Victoria Beth, Cynthia Ann. Admitted to Ill. bar, 1951, U.S. Supreme Ct.; trainee small appliance div. Gen. Electric Co., Bridgeport, Conn., 1952-54, asst. to trade regulation counsel legal dept., N.Y.C., 1954-55; atty. anti-trust div. Dept. Justice, Wshington, 1955-60; atty. law dept. Westinghouse Electric Corp., N.Y.C., 1960-66, chief counsel internat. sect., 1966, chief counsel N.Y. Office, 1966-69; v.p., sec., gen. counsel J.I. Case Co., Racine Wis., 1969—. Mem. Wis. Gov.'s Com. on Spl. Learning. Bd. dirs. Wustum Mus. Fine Arts, Racine United Community Services. Served with USAAF, 1944-46. Named Alumni of Month, U. Ill. Mem. Am., Fed. bar assns., Constrn. Industry Mfrs. Assn., Farm and Indsl. Equipment Inst. Home: 3340 Michigan Blvd Racine WI 53402 Office: 700 State St Racine WI 53404

HARRISON, EDWARD ROBERT, educator, physicist; b. London, Eng., Jan. 8, 1919; s. Robert and Daisy (White) H.; student Sir John Cass Coll., London U., 1937-40; m. Photeni Marangas, June 23, 1945; children—John Peter, June Zoe. Came to U.S., 1965. With Atomic Energy Research Establishment, Harwell, Eng., 1948-64; vis. scientist CERN, Geneva, 1959-60; prin. scientist Rutherford High Energy Lab., Harwell, 1964-65; Nat. Acad. Sci. sr. research asso., Washington., 1965-66; prof. dept. physics and astronomy U. Mass., Amherst, 1966—. Fellow Inst. Physics, Royal Astron. Soc.; mem. A.A.A.S., Internat. Astron. Union, Am. Astron. Soc., Am. Phys. Soc., Sigma Xi. Contbr. articles profl. jours. Home: 73 Butterfield Terrace Amherst MA 01002

HARRISON, EDWIN DAVIES, corp. exec.; b. Evadale, Ark., Jan. 8, 1916; s. William Franklin and Anna Elizabeth (Williams) H.; B.S., U.S. Naval Acad., 1939; M.S., Va. Poly. Inst., 1948; Ph.D., Purdue U., 1952, D.Eng. (hon.), 1962; D.Sc. (hon.), Jacksonville U., 1960; D.Eng. (hon.), U. Toledo, 1961; m. Dorothy Estelle Manyon, May 25, 1940; children—Robert W., Richard M. Instr. physics and chemistry Randles Prep. Sch., 1939-42; asst. prof. Va. Poly. Inst., 1946-50, asst. dean engring. and architecture, 1952- 55; dean Coll. Engring., U. Toledo, 1955-57; pres. Ga. Inst. Tech., Atlanta, 1957-69; research Purdue Research Found., Va. Engring. Expt. Sta.; exec. v.p. J.P. Stevens & Co., Inc., N.Y.C., 1969—; dir. Gen. Electric Co., 1962-69, J.P. Stevens and Co., Inc. Mem. bd. visitors U.S. Mil. Acad., 1961-63, Air U., 1963-65, U.S. Naval Acad., 1965-70. Served with USNR, 1942-46; capt. Res. Registered profl. mech. engr., Va.; profl. engr., Ga. Mem. Am. Soc. Engring. Edn., Am. Soc. M.E., Sigma Xi, Tau Beta Pi, Pi Tau Sigma, Phi Kappa Phi, Omicron Delta Kappa. Presbyn. Address: 1185 Av Americas New York City NY 10036

HARRISON, EVELYN BYRD, educator, archaeologist; b. Charlottesville, Va., June 5, 1920; d. William Byrd and Eva (Detamore) Harrison; A.B., Barnard Coll., 1941; A.M., Columbia, 1943, Ph.D., 1952; postgrad. Bryn Mawr Coll., 1942-43. Instr. classics U. Cin., 1951-53; asst. prof. fine arts and archaeology Columbia, 1955-59, asso. prof., 1959-67, prof., 1967-70; prof. art and archaeology Princeton, 1970—. Mem. Archaeol. Inst. Am., Soc. Promotion Hellenic Studies, German Archaeol. Inst. (corr. mem.). Author: The Athenian Agora, I, Portrait Sculpture, 1953; XI, Archaic and Archaistic Sculpture, 1965. Contbr. articles to Hesperia, Am. Jour. Archaeology. Home: 84 Western Way Princeton NJ 08540

HARRISON, FRANCIS M., govt. ofcl.; b. Calhoun County, Ark., Mar. 17, 1918; s. Marion Randolph and Myrtle (Vaughan) H.; B.S. in Bus. Adminstrn., Miss. State U., 1942; m. Frieda Dolan, Oct. 22, 1943; children—John, Kathleen, Nancy. With Fisher Aircraft Co., Memphis, 1942, Phelps Dodge Copper Products Corp., 1946-50; auditor gen. USAF, 1950-51; with audit agy. Dept. Army, 1951- 59, ICA mission, India, 1959-61, AID mission, Spain, 1961-63, chief internal audit AID, Dept. State, Wash., 1964-66, dept. chief audit div., 1966-70; area auditor gen. East Asia (Manila), AID, 1970—. Served to 1st lt. AUS, 1942-46; ETO. Mem. Fedn. Govt. Accounts Assn. (bd. dirs. Los Angeles 1956-58, Washington 1958-59), Inst. Internal Auditors. Home: 4913 Tarheel Way Annandale VA 22003 Office: AID Dept State Washington DC 20523

HARRISON, FRANK, univ. pres.; b. Dallas, Nov. 21, 1913; s. Frank and Ruby (Davison) H.; B.S., So. Methodist U., 1935; M.S., Northwestern U., 1936, Ph.D., 1938; M.D., U. Tex. Southwestern Med. Sch., 1956; m. Elsie Claire Redfearn, June 26, 1946; children—Frank, Susan Claire, James Redfearn. Mem. faculty U. Tenn. med. units, Memphis, 1938-51, prof., 1946-51, chief div. anatomy, 1946-51; prof. anatomy U. Tex. Southwestern Med. Sch., Dallas, 1952-68, asso. dean, 1956-68; asso. dean grad. studies U. Tex. at Arlington, 1965-68, acting pres., 1968-69, pres., 1969—. Trustee Tarrant County United Fund. Named Distinguished Alumnus, So. Meth. U., 1971. Mem. Am. Assn. Anatomists, Am. Physiol. Soc., Tex. Philos. Soc., Biophys. Soc., I.E.E.E., Soc. Exptl. Biology and Medicine, Arlington C. of C. (bd. dirs.), Phi Beta Kappa, Alpha Omega Alpha, Kappa Sigma, Alpha Kappa Kappa. Home: 4165 Shady Valley Arlington TX 76013

HARRISON, GEORGE, musician, vocalist; b. Liverpool, Eng., Feb. 25, 1943: s. Harold and Louise H.; student Liverpool Inst.; m. Patricia Anne Boyd, January 21, 1966. Mem. sch. skiffle group, The Quarrymen, 1958; played with John Lennon and Paul McCartney as trio, The Moondogs, 1959; toured Scotland with them and Stu Sutcliffe as The Silver Beatles; made 1st ofcl. appearance as the Beatles at Litherland Town Hall, nr. Liverpool, 1960; appeared as mem. Beatles in Sweden, 1963, at Royal Variety performance Prince of Wales Theatre, London, 1963, in Paris, Denmark, Hong Kong, Australia, New Zealand, 1964; made appearances on Ed Sullivan TV show, U.S., 1964, coast-to-coast tour, 1964; appeared in France, Italy, Spain, U.S., 1965; appeared with other Beatles in films A Hard Day's Night, 1964, Help! 1965, Yellow Submarine, 1968; co-filmer TV spectacular Shindig. Composer songs including Don't Bother Me, The Inner Light, Within You Without You, Northern Song, Blue Jay Way, I Want To Tell You, Love You To, Think For Yourself, If I Needed Someone, Something, My Sweet Lord, All Things Must Pass (album); composer film soundtrack for Wonderwall, 1967. Decorated Order Brit. Empire. Recipient (with other Beatles) Grammy awards in best performance by vocal group and best new artist of 1964 categories Nat. Acad. Rec. Arts and Scis. (U.S.), 1965; silver medal and ribbon from Queen Elizabeth, 1965; recipient Pop Album of Year award, 1967. Address: Apple Corps 3 Savile Row London W1 England

HARRISON, GEORGE BAGSHAWE, retired educator, author; b. Hove, Eng., July 14, 1894; s. Walter and Ada Louisa (Bagshaw) H.; student Brighton Coll., 1907-13, Queens' Coll., Cambridge U., 1913-14, 19-20, B.A., 1920, M.A., 1923; Ph.D., London U., 1928; Litt.D., Villanova U., 1960, Holy Cross Coll., 1961, Marquette U., 1963; LL.D., Assumption Coll., 1962; m. Dorothy Agnes Barker, Apr. 9, 1919. Came to U.S., 1949. Asst. lectr. King's Coll., U. London, 1924-27, lectr. 1927-28, reader in English and lit., 1928-43; prof., head dept. English, Queen's U., Kingston, Can., 1943-49; prof. English, U. Mich., 1949-64, prof. emeritus, 1964—. Mem. Internat. Com for English in the Liturgy, 1965—. Served with Brit. Inf., in India and Mesopotamia (mentioned in despatches), 1914-19; served with Royal Army Service Corps, Intelligence and War Office, 1940-43. Recipient Campion medal, 1970. Author books including: The Elizabethan Journals, 1591-1603, 3 vols., 1928-33; The Jacobean Journal 1603-06, 1941; The Day before Yesterday, 1938; Shakespeare's Tragedies, 1951; A Second Jacobean Journal, 1607-1610, 1958; Profession of English, 1962; The Fires of Arcadia, 1965. Editor works including: A Companion to Shakespeare Studies (with Harley Granville-Barker), 1934; Shakespeare: The Complete Works, 1952; contbr. to The Road to Damascus, 1949. Home: 532 Halemaumau St Honolulu HI 96821

HARRISON, GILBERT A., editor; b. Detroit, May 8, 1915; s. Samuel Louis and Mabel (Wolfe) H.; A.B., U. Cal., 1937; student Balliol Coll., Oxford, 1948; m. Anne Blaine, Oct. 13, 1951; children—David, James, Joel, Eleanor Anne. Mem. Univ. Religious Conf., Los Angeles, 1937-41; staff Office Civilian Def., Washington, 1941-42; nat. chmn. Am. Vets. Com., 1948-49; assisted founding World Vets. Fedn., Paris, France, 1950; rep. Found. for Unified and Dem. Germany in United Europe, Germany, 1951; editor in chief, New Republic Mag.; chmn. bd. Liveright Pub. Co. Pilot tng. with R.A.F., 1942; with A.A.C., 1942- 45. Recipient George Polk Meml. award, 1963. Clubs: Century (N.Y.C.). Editor: Gertrude Stein's America, 1965. Home: 3556 Macomb St NW Washington DC 20016 Office: 1244 19th St NW Washington DC 20036

HARRISON, GREGORY ALEXANDER, lawyer; b. San Francisco, Sept. 9, 1896; s. Edward Charles and Mary Gertrude (Bodkin) H.; B.S., U. Cal., 1917; LL.B., Hastings Coll. of Law, 1921; m. Christine Finnell Wheeler, October 29, 1966; children—Gregory Alexander, Patricia H. (Mrs. J.W. Brown, Jr.), Michael B., Elizabeth R., Barbara Ann. Admitted to Cal. bar, 1920, since practiced in San Francisco; partner Brobeck, Phleger & Harrison, 1931—. Dir. Pacific Power & Light Co. Trustee War Meml. of San Francisco Acad. Scis. Mem. Am. Coll. Trial Lawyers. Home: 3701 Jackson St San Francisco CA 94118 Office: Brobeek Phleger & Harrison 111 Sutter St San Francisco CA 94104

HARRISON, GUY FRASER, conductor; b. Gildford, Surrey, Eng., Nov. 6, 1894. Formerly conductor Oklahoma City Symphony; now condr. Rochester (N.Y.) Civic Orch. and Rochester Civic Chorus, also asso. condr. Rochester Philharmonic; guest condr. Mpls. Symphony Orch., St. Paul Opera Co. Address: care Rochester Civic Orchestra Rochester NY 14604 •

HARRISON, HAROLD EDWARD, physician; b. New Haven, July 23, 1908; s. Abraham and Rose (Chaikind) H.; B.S., Yale, 1928, M.D., 1931; m. Helen Miriam Coplan, Aug. 2, 1936; children—Stephen Coplan, Richard Gerald. Intern, resident pediatrics New Haven Hosp., 1931-35; instr. pediatrics Yale Sch. Medicine, 1935-38, asst. prof. pathology, 1942-45; asst. prof. pediatrics Med. Coll. Cornell U., 1938-42; investigator com. war gas casualties OSRD, 1942- 45; pediatrician-in-chief Balt. City Hosps., 1945 ; asso prof. pediatrics Sch: Medicine Johns Hopkins, 1945-65, prof., 1965. Mem. nutrition study sect. NIH, 1958-63; mem. food and nutrition bd. Nat. Acad. Sci., NRC. Recipient (with Helen C. Harrison) E. Mead Johnson award for research in pediatrics, 1941, Borden award Am. Acad. Pediatrics, 1960. Mem. Soc. For Pediatric Research (past pres.), Am. Pediatric Soc., Soc. Clin. Investigation, Endocrine Soc., Am. Inst. Nutrition, Sigma Xi, Alpha Omega Alpha. Mem. editorial bd. Clin. Pediatrics, 1962 . Contbr. to articles profl. jours. Home: 5500 N Charles St Baltimore MD 21210 Office: 4940 Eastern Av Baltimore MD 21224

HARRISON, HENRY STUART, iron exec.; b. Cleve., Nov. 25, 1909; s. Henry Thomas and Regina (Troler) H.; A.B., Yale, 1932; LL.D., Mich. Tech. U., 1964, No. Mich. U., 1967; m. Suzanne Brookhart, Oct. 30, 1943; children—Mary (Mrs. John T. Lansing), Henry Stuart, Virginia Foster. With Corrigan McKinney Steel Co., 1932-33; trust dept. Central Hanover Bank & Trust Co., 1933-36; with Lionel D. Edie & Co., investment counsel, 1936-37; with Cleveland-Cliffs Iron Co., 1937—, asst. treas., 1940- 45, treas. 1945, v.p., treas., 1952, v.p. finance, 1954-58, exec. v.p., 1958-60, pres., 1960—, chief exec. officer, 1961—, dir., 1957—; pres., dir. Cliffs of Can., Ltd., Albanel Minerals, Ltd., Marquette Iron Mining Co., Mesaba-Cliffs Mining, Negaunee Mine Co., Empire Mining Co., Arctic Iron Co., Humboldt Mining Co., Cliffs Internat., Inc.; chmn., dir. Cleve.-Cliffs S.S.; dir. Medusa Portland Cement Co., Cleve. Trust Co., White Motor Co., Northwestern Mut. Life Ins. Co., Weatherhead Co., Midland Ross Corp. Trustee Cleve. Inst. Art, Univ. Sch., Cleve. Play House, Cleve. Found., U. Hosps. Mem. Am. Iron and Steel Inst. (dir.), Am. Mining Congress (dir.), Greater Cleve. Growth Assn. (bd. dir.), Phi Beta Kappa. Republican. Presbyn. Clubs: Union, Tavern, Chagrin Valley Hunt, Kirtland; Duquesne (Pitts.); Laurel Valley (Ligonier, Pa.); Ottawa (Fremont, O.). Home: 22089 Shaker Blvd Shaker Heights OH 44122 Office: Union Commerce Bldg Cleveland OH 44115

HARRISON, HORACE HAWES, banker; b. Richmond, Va., Nov. 8, 1924; s. A.E. Willson and Anne Sterling (Hawes) H.; B.A., Yale, 1948; grad. Stonier Grad. Sch., Banking, 1956, Mgmt. Program, U. Va. Grad. Sch. Bus., 1958; m. Sallie M. Labouisse, Feb. 18, 1949; children—Sally Cameron, Ann Hawes. With United Va. Bank/State Planters, and predecessors, Richmond, 1948—, pres. UVB Service Corp., 1971—. Mem. Richmond Tax Study Commn. Bd. dirs. Richmond Symphony; pres. Family and Children's Service Richmond, 1967- 68; trustee Va. Council Health and Med. Care, 1969-71. Served to 1st lt. AUS, 1942-46. Mem. Bank Adminstrn. Inst. (dir.-at-large 1969-71), Va. Bankers Assn., Soc. Colonial Wars, The Richmond German, Soc. Va. Creepers, Delta Kappa Epsilon, Berzelius. Clubs: Country of Va., Commonwealth (Richmond); Linville (N.C.) Golf. Home: 403 Harlan Circle Richmond VA 23226 Office: 900 E Main St Richmond VA 23219

HARRISON, J. FRANK, business exec.; b. 1931; B.A., U. Chattanooga, 1954; married. With Chattanooga Glass Co. Inc., 1953-63; with Dorsey Corp., Chattanooga, 1963—, now chmn. bd., dir.; dir. Am. Nat. Bank & Trust Co. Chattanooga. Office: 400 W 45th St Chattanooga TN 37410*

HARRISON, JAMES LERLIE, assn. ofcl.; b. Greer, S.C., June 3, 1906; s. John D. and Sallie (Pitts.) H.; ed. pub. schs., N.C.; m. Margaret Scott, Dec. 31, 1960; 1 dau., Joan (Mrs. Albert D. Silbaugh). Engaged in wholesale and retail food bus., 1927-33; with Bur. Census, 1934-42; liaison officer at Capitol, OPA, 1942-47; staff dir. Joint Congl. Com. Printing, 1949-61; pub. printer of U.S., 1961-70; dir. Washington & Lee Bldg. Assn. No. Va. Mem. Wash. and Chgo. Printing House Craftsmen, Graphic Arts Assn. Execs. Mem. Christian Ch. Clubs: Litho (Washington and Chgo.). Author: Biographical Directory of American Congress-1774-1949, 1950. Editor, compiler Congl. Directory, 1949-61; Govt. Printing and Binding Regulations, 1949-61; Govt. Paper Specification Standards, 1959-61. Home: 4000 Massachusetts Av NW Washington DC 20016

HARRISON, JAMES MERRITT, Canadian govt. ofcl.; b. Regina, Sask., Can., Sept. 20, 1915; s. Roland O. and Vera (Merritt) H.; B.Sc., U. Man., 1935, D. Sc. (hon.), 1965; M.A., Queen's U., 1941, Ph.D., 1943, LL.D., 1967; D.U.C., U. Calgary (Alta.), 1967; D.Sc. (hon.), McMaster U., 1967; m. Herta Boehmer Sliter, May 5, 1944; 1 stepson, Norman. Engaged as chemist, 1936-38; with Geol. Survey Can., 1943-64, dir., 1956-64; asst. dep. minister for research Canadian Dept. Mines and Tech. Surveys, 1964-66, asst. dep. minister sci. and tech. Dept. Energy, Mines and Resources, 1966- -; spl. lectr. Queen's U., 1949-50. Recipient Kemp medal Columbia, 1963; Gold medal pub. service to Can., Profl. Inst. Can., 1966; Outstanding Achievement award pub. service, 1970. Fellow Royal Soc. Can. (past pres.), Geol. Assn. Can. (past pres.), Royal Canadian Geog. Soc. (bd. dirs.); mem. Internat. Union Geol. Scis. (pres. 1961- 64), Internat. Council Sci. Unions (pres. 1966-68), Canadian Inst. Mining and Metallurgy (pres. 1969-70; Blaylock medal 1966), Soc. Econ. Geologists (v.p.), Arctic Inst. N. Am., A.A.A.S., Sci. Council Can.; fgn. asso. mem. Nat. Acad. Scis. Home: 4 Kippewa Dr Ottawa kis 364 Ontario Canada Office: 588 Booth St Ottawa Kia OE4 Ontario Canada

HARRISON, JAMES RADFORD, hosp. adminstr.; b. Commerce, Tex., Sept. 2, 1914; s. William R. and Georgia Mae (Henderson) H.; A.B., E. Tex. State U., 1935; m. Amber C. Darnall, July 23, 1939; children—Ginger (Mrs. Mason Scott Foote, Jr.), William E. Harrison. Clk., Gen. Foods Sales Co., 1936-40; with Office Sec. War, 1941-44; personnel dir. VA Hosp., Temple, Tex., 1946-51; asst. dir. VA Hosp., Spokane, 1951-55; asst. dir. VA Hosp., Reno, 1956-61, dir., 1961-67; dir. VA Hosp., Portland, Ore., 1967. Vice pres. Reno United Fund, 1966-67; chmn. citizens adv. com. to pres. U. Nev., 1966- 67. Served with AUS, World War II. Recipient Exceptional Service award VA, 1958, Am. Coll. Hosp. Adminstrs., Am., Ore. hosp. assns., Council Teaching Hosps. Rotarian (past pres. N. Spokane), Elk, Mason. Club: Oswego Lake (Ore.) Country. Home: Quarters 7 Sam Jackson Park Portland OR 97207 Office: VA Hosp Sam Jackson Park Portland OR 97207

HARRISON, JAMES THOMAS, state judge; b. Hankinson, N.D., Apr. 4, 1903; s. Edward Charles and Karen Marie (Andersen) H.; LL.B., St. Paul Coll. Law, 1926; LL.D. (hon.), Montana Sch. Mines, 1962; LL.D., William Mitchell Coll. Law, 1967; m. Leah Lambert, August 26, 1926; children—Beverly Ann (Mrs. Stanely J. Hould), Barbara Louise (Mrs. R. J. Losleben, Jr.), James Thomas. Admitted to Minn. and N.D. bars, 1927, Mont. bar, 1930; practice of law, Minot, N.D., 1927-28, Malta, Mont., 1938-57; reporter, Glasgow, Mont., 1929-38; city atty. Malta, 1940-48; county atty. Phillips County, 1948-52; chief justice Supreme Ct. of Mont., 1957- -. Chmn. Pardon Bd. of Mont., 1955-56. Candidate for Congl. nomination from Mont., 1954. Methodist. Mason (grand master Mont. 1958-59). Home: 1616 Highland St Helena MT 59601 Office: Supreme Court Helena MT 59601

HARRISON, JAY SMOLENS, music critic, educator; b. N.Y.C., Jan. 25, 1927; s. Abraham and Stella (Fleischman) Smolens; student Columbia Prep. Sch., 1940-44; A.B., N.Y.U., 1948; music student Philip James; m. Jane King Cohan, May 15, 1954 (div.); children—Paige Julie, Troy Nedda. Network radio actor, 1936- 44; oboist, symphony orchs., 1940-45; instr. music N.Y.U., 1948-55, asst. prof. music, 1955-56; asso. producer Met. Opera broadcasts, 1954- 56, quizmaster, 1957-58, panelist 1958—; TV and radio writer, 1954—; writer, master of ceremonies History of Opera, NBC- TV; music cons. Cultural Presentation Program U.S. State Dept., 1955—, N.Y. State Council of Arts, 1957—; guest critic N.Y. Herald Tribune, 1948-52, asso. critic, 1952, music editor, 1952-60; exec. editor Music mag., 1960-61; music interviewer, NBC monitor week-end radio series; dir. Reader's Digest Music, Inc., 1961-63; with Roving Critic program, WOR radio sta., 1962—; editor Musical Am., 1963- 64; dir. editorial services Columbia Records, 1965-67; asso. prof. music Queens Coll. City U. N.Y., 1968-70; adj. prof. Fordham U., 1970-71. Mem. N.Y. Music Critics' Circle, Am. Newspaper Guild, Am. Musicol. Soc., Nat. Council Govt. and Arts, Phi Beta Kappa. Contbr. profl. publs., Book of the Month periodicals on Great Music. Address: 741 West End Av New York City NY 10025

HARRISON, JOAN, producer; b. Guildford, Eng., June 20, 1909; d. Walter and Amelia (Muir) Harrison; ed. Sorbonne, Paris, France, also St. Hugh's Coll., Oxford U.; m. Eric Ambler, Oct. 11, 1958. Author screenplays in Eng., The Girl Was Young, 1937, Jamaica Inn, 1938; author screenplays in U.S., Rebecca, 1940, Foreign Correspondent, 1941, Suspicion, 1943; producer motion pictures Phantom Lady, 1945, Uncle Harry, 1946, They Won't Believe Me, 1947, Ride the Pink Horse, 1948; producer TV program Alfred Hitchcock Presents, 1953-64; owner Tarantula Prodns., 1964—; exec. producer TV series Journey to the Unknown. Home: 10640 Taranto Way Los Angeles CA 90024 Office: Tarantula Prodns Box 1065 Studio City CA 91604

HARRISON, JOHN ARMSTRONG, univ. dean, historian; b. Johnstown, N.Y., July 4, 1915; s. Joseph Oliver and Rosalind (Rogers) H.; B.A., Columbia, 1941; Ph.D., U. Cal. at Berkeley, 1949; m. Clarice Troth, Jan, 18, 1943. Mem. faculty U. Fla., 1949-65, prof. history, 1956-65, chmn. dept., 1962-65, chmn. high honors studies, 1961-65; dean U. Miami Grad. Sch., Coral Gables, Fla., 1965—. Mem. U.S. delegation Internat. Congress Orientalists, Moscow, USSR, 1961, New Delhi, India, 1964; mem. com. lang. and area studies So. Regional Edn. Bd., 1963—. Served to lt. (s.g.) USNR, 1942-46; PTO. Mem. Assn. Asian Studies (bd. dirs.). Author books, articles history N.E. Asia. Editor Jour. of Asian Studies, 1969—. Home: 1408 Dorado Av Coral Gables FL 33146

HARRISON, JOHN CONWAY, state justice; b. Grand Rapids, Minn., Apr. 28, 1913; s. Francis Randall and Ethelyn (Conway) H.; student Mont. State Coll., 1931-34, U. Mont., 1936-37; LL.B., George Washington U., 1940; m. Virginia Flanagan, Aug. 28, 1941; children—Nina Lyn, Robert Charles, Molly McKinlay, John Conway, Frank Randall, Virginia Lee. Admitted to Mont. bar, 1947; city atty., E. Helena, 1951-60; county atty. Lewis and Clark County, 1955-60; gen. counsel Ft. Belknap Indian Community, 1952-60, Mont. Tb Assn., 1948-62; asso. justice Mont. Supreme Ct., 1961—. Bd. dirs. Nat. Tb and Respiratory Disease Assn., 1948—, pres. elect, 1971-72; pres. Mont. Tb Assn., 1951, Western Tb Assn., 1953. Served to lt. col. AUS, World War II; mem. Res. Decorated Bronze Star; Croix de Guerre with star (France). Mem. Am., Mont. (sec.- treas.) bar assns., Am. Judicature Soc., Am. Legion (past post comdr.), Res. Officers Assn., Sigma Chi. Episcopalian. Kiwanian (past pres. Helena). Home: 516 N Park St Helena MT 59601 Office: Supreme Court Bldg Helena MT 59601

HARRISON, JOHN FLETCHER CLEWS, educator; b. Leicester, Eng., Feb. 28, 1921; s. William and Mary (Fletcher) H.; M.A., Cambridge (Eng.) U., 1946; Ph.D., Leeds (Eng.) U., 1955; m. Margaret Ruth Marsh, Dec. 12, 1945; children—Richard John, Elizabeth Ruth. Came to U.S., 1961. Lectr., U. Leeds, 1947-58, dep. dir. extra mural studies and adult edn., 1958-61; prof. history U. Wis., 1961-71. Served to capt. Brit. Army, 1941-45. Scholar, prizeman Selwyn Coll., Cambridge U., 1946. Author: History of the Working Men's College, 1854-1954, 1954; Learning and Living, 1790-1960, 1961; Society and Politics in England, 1780-1960, 1965; Robert Owen and the Owenites, 1968, Utopaism and Education, 1968; Quest for the New Moral World, 1969. Address: 13 Woodlands Barrowfield Dr Hove Sussex England

HARRISON, JOHN HARTWELL, surgeon, educator; b. Clarksville, Va., Feb. 16, 1909; s. Isaac Carrington and Rosalie (Smith) H.; B.S., U. Va., 1929, M.D., 1932; M.A. (hon.), Harvard; m. Gertrude Chisholm, June 16, 1934 (dec. Feb. 1965); children—John Hartwell, Robert C. II, Cornelia, Jeffrey; m. 2d, Mary Louise Harding, July 16, 1965. Intern Lakeside Hosp., Cleve., 1932-33; intern Peter Bent Brigham Hosp., Boston, also resident urology, asst. resident surgery, 1933-38, Harvey Cushing fellow surgery, 1939, sr. asso. urology, chief of service, 1940-45, urologic surgeon, chief of service, 1945—, acting surgeon in chief, 1967; asst. genito-urinary surgery Harvard Med. Sch., 1935-37, instr. surgery, 1938-39, instr. genito-urinary surgery, 1939-41, asso. 1941-46, asst. prof., 1946-48, asso. clin. prof., 1948-54, clin. prof., 1954-65, Elliott Carr Cutler prof. surgery, 1965—; Edgar Burns vis. prof. urology Tulane U., 1961; Clyde Deming vis. prof. Yale Sch. Medicine, 1968; cons. urology Mass. Hosp. Sch. Crippled Children, Children's Med. Center, Boston Lying-In Hosp., VA Hosp., West Roxbury, Mass., Lemuel Shattuck Hosp., Jamaica Plain, Mass.; vis. prof. urology Ohio State U., 1964, U. Mo., 1968, Johns Hopkins, 1969, U. Va., 1970; mem. vis. faculty Mayo Clinic, 1965; cons. to surgeon gen. USAF. Trustee Boston Med. Library. Served to lt. col., M.C., AUS, 1942-45; PTO. Recipient Amory prize Am. Acad. Arts and Scis.; Ferdinand C. Valentine award N.Y. Acad. Medicine, 1970; Purkyne medal Czechoslovakian Med. Soc., 1971. Diplomate Am. Bd. Surgery, Am. Bd. Urology (examiner 1966—). Fellow A.C.S. (gov. 1961- 65); mem. Am. Acad. Arts Scis., Am. Urol. Assn. (exec. com. 1961-62; Ramon Guiteras award 1965); Am. Urological Assn. (pres. N.E. sec. 1953), Boston (v.p. 1958, pres. elect 1971), N.E. surgery socs., Am. Surg. Assn. (1st v.p. 1970-71), Am. Assn. Genito-Urinary Surgeons, Clin. Soc. Genito-Urinary Surgeons (pres. 1964-65), Urologic Forum Clin. Investigation, A.M.A. Author: Urology, 1970. Adv. bd. Am. Jour. Surgery, Jour. Surgery. Home: 25 Glenridge Rd Dedham MA 02026 Office: 721 Huntington Av Boston MA 02115

HARRISON, JOHN RAYMOND, newspaper exec.; b. Des Moines, June 8, 1933; s. Alfred and Dorothy (Stout) Cohen; grad. Phillips Exeter Acad., 1951; A.B., Harvard, 1955, postgrad. Bus. Sch., 1955-56; m. Lois Cowles, June 24, 1955; children—Gardner Mark, Kent Alfred, John Patrick, Lois Eleanor. Vice pres., dir. N.Y. Times Media Corp.; pres., dir. Gainesville (Fla.) Pub. Co., Lakeland (Fla.) Pub. Co., Leesburg (Fla.) Daily Comml. Pub. Co., Ocala Star-Banner Pub. Co., The Palatka (Fla.) Daily News Pub. Co. Pulitzer Prize juror, 1967, 68. Trustee Fla. Ednl. TV System, Robert H. Anderson Found.; bd. dirs. Ft. Pierce-St. Lucie County Indsl. Devel. Council, 1959-62, Ft. Pierce Meml. Hosp., 1959-62, Lincoln Park Child Care Center, 1959-62, Gainesville United Fund, 1965. Boys Club, Gainesville, 1965, U. Fla. Found.; chmn bd. dirs. Ft. Pierce Art Gallery, 1965. Recipient Pulitzer prize for editorial writing, 1965. Mem. Lakeland C. of C. (bd. dirs.), Sigma Delta Chi. Clubs: Lakeland Yacht and Country, Lone Palm Country, Imperial University (Lakeland); Gainesville Golf and Country; Pelican Yacht (Ft. Pierce); Rotary. Home: 2311 Nevada Rd Lakeland FL 32802 Office: Box 408 Lakeland FL 32802

HARRISON, JOHN ROBERT, educator; b. Washington, Oct. 11, 1923; s. William Henry and Edna Elizabeth (Rother) H.; B.A., Am. U., 1948; M.A., Johns Hopkins, 1949; Ph.D., U. Minn., 1951; m. Muriel Ruth Adams, Sept. 26, 1946; children—William, Ellen. With dept. zoology Miami U., Oxford, O., 1951-65, chmn. dept., 1958-61, research prof., 1961-65; chmn. dept. biology Washington and Jefferson Coll., 1965-68; chmn. dept. biology State U. N.Y. at Oswego, 1968-70, chmn. dept. zoology, 1970—; cons. in field. Served with USAAF, 1942-45. Mem. A.A.A.S., Am. Soc. Zoologists (mem. edn. com. 1961-69; chmn. 1964-67, 69), Soc. Developmental Biology, Nat. Assn. Biology Tchrs., Sigma Xi. Mason. Contbr. articles profl. jours. Home: RD 3 Brown Dr Oswego NY 13126

HARRISON, JOHN SIDNEY, aluminum co. exec.; b. Coraopolis, Pa., Feb. 10, 1911; s. George S. and Hilda (Sutherland) H.; B.S. in Metall. Engring., Lehigh U., 1931; m. Anne Tomb, June 11, 1947; children—John Sidney, Douglas Tomb. With Aluminum Co. Am., 1931—, gen. mgr. personnel and indsl. relations, 1956- 60, v.p. personnel and indsl. relations, 1960-63, exec. v.p., dir., 1963- -. Mem. Indsl. Hygiene Bd., Community Chest Bd., Jr. Achievement S.W. Pa. Bd., Magee Womens Hosp. Bd., Hosp. Planning Assn. Bd. Mem. Chi Psi. Mason (Shriner). Clubs: University, Duquesne (Pitts.); Oakmont (Pa.) Country; Laurel Valley Country, Rolling Rock. Home: 1020 Hulton Rd Oakmont PA 15139 Office: Alcoa Bldg Pittsburgh PA 15219

HARRISON, JOSEPH, judge; b. Shreveport, La., June 10, 1904; s. Leon and Charlotte (Rosenberg) H.; B.S., Tufts Coll., 1926; LL.B., Harvard, 1929; m. Amy Harvey, Aug. 13, 1938 (dec. 1961); children—Joseph Leon, George Harvey; m. 2d, Frances Boehm Ginsberg, 1967. Admitted to N.J. bar, 1930, since practiced in Newark; state dep. atty. gen., assigned Bd. Pub. Utility Commrs., 1947-52, spl. counsel, pub. utility, railroad rate matters; partner firm Harrison and Jacobs, 1960-70; judge Essex County Ct., 1970—. Dep. state rationing adminst. for OPA, 1941-42, state rationing atty., 1942-44; sec. N.J. Com. for Constl. Revision, 1944-47; mem. Montclair Civil Rights Commn., 1952-65; mem. N.J. Supreme Ct. adv. com. profl. ethics; co-chmn. N.J. Com. Fair Representation; mem. Gov.'s Com. Legal Services Poor; chmn. N.J. Law Enforcement Council, 1957; counsel Gov.'s Transition Com., 1969-70; chmn. N.J. Election Law Revision Com., 1970; commr. from N.J. Nat. Conf. Commrs. Uniform State Laws, 1954-56; lectr. Rutgers Law Sch., 1956-59; mem. adv. com. profl. ethics N.J. Supreme Ct. Mem. Am. (chmn. standing com. Bill of Rights 1958-59, exec. com. world peace through law 1962-63, council sect. individual rights and responsibilities 1966-70), N.J., Essex County, Montclair bar assns., Am. Assn. UN (N.J. pres. 1960-62), Am. Judicature Soc. (bd. dirs.), Phi Beta Kappa. Republican. Mem. B'nai B'rith. Editor N.J. Law Jour., 1937-42, 51-70. Contbr. articles legal jours. Home: 62 Havenwood Dr Livingston NJ 07039 Office: Chambers Essex County Cts Bldg Newark NJ 07102

HARRISON, JOSEPH GRAHAM, journalist, writer; b. Port Dickinson, N.Y., Aug. 29, 1912; s. Roland R. and Hortense (Long) H.; student Williams Coll., 1931-32, U. Geneva (Switzerland), 1932-33, Sorbonne, Paris, 1933, Harvard, 1933-35, Boston U., 1933-35. m. Marzee Garnand, May 20, 1938; 1 dau., Susan A. Mem. staff Christian Science Monitor, Boston, 1935—, assigned State Dept., 1940-42, war corr. British 8th Army and U.S. 5th Army, 1942-45, assigned Middle East, 1943-44, Greek Civil War, 1944-45, Yugoslavia, 1945, Central Europe and Balkans, 1945-46, opened UN bur., 1946, head Mediterranean news bur., 1946-49, fgn. news editor, 1949-61, managing editor, 1961-65, chief editorial writer, 1965—; editor gen. publs. Christian Sci. Pub. Soc., 1971—. Decorated Gold Cross Order Phoenix (Greece), Knight Order of Merit (Italy). Christian Scientist. Author: (with others) The World at Mid Century, 1951. Contbr. articles, essays. Home: 9 Taylor Rd Wellesley Hills MA 02181 also Snow Shore Rd Orleans MA 02653 Office: 1 Norway St Boston MA 02115

HARRISON, KENNETH STEVENS, govt. ofcl.; b. Templeville, Md., Apr. 19, 1900; s. William S. and Clara B. (Stevens) H.; student St. John's Coll., Annapolis, Md., 1918- 19; LL.B., Georgetown Univ., 1922, LL.M., 1923; A.B., Nat. Univ., 1927; m. Anita B. Bales, Dec. 15, 1953. Atty. office chief of finance and office of the q.m. gen., War Dept., 1923-30; spl. atty. and asst. to gen. counsel, Bur. of Customs, Treasury Dept., 1930- 38; chief counsel, USCG, Washington, 1938-69, asst. to commdt. for special projects, 1969-70, ret. Served as private with U.S. Army, World War I; capt., USCG, World War II; rear adm. USCGR, 1956. Awarded spl. Commendation Ribbon, Sec. of Navy. Mem. Fed. Bar Assn. Methodist. Mason. Club: Propeller of U.S. Home: 3403 Valley Dr Parkfairfax Alexandria VA 22302

HARRISON, LAWRENCE ELLIOT, govt. ofcl.; b. Brookline, Mass., Mar. 11, 1932; s. David Albert and Jennie (Levin) H.; A.B, Dartmouth, 1953; M.P.A., Harvard, 1960; m. Polly Jane Fortier, Jan. 30, 1954; children—Julia, Beth, Amy. Planner Office Sec. Def., Washington, 1957-62; program officer AID, Washington, 1962-63; program officer mission, Costa Rica, 1964-65, dep. dir. mission, Dominican Republic, 1966-68, dir., Costa Rica, 1969-70; spl. asst. to Dep. U.S. Coordinator Alliance for Progress, Washington, 1971—. Serve to lt. USNR, 1954-57. Decorated Order Durate, Sanchez and Mella (Dominican Republic). Mem. Soc. Internat. Devel., Am. Fgn. Service Assn. Home: 3253 Worthington St NW Washington DC 20015 Office: Office Dep US Coordinator Alliance for Progress Dept State Washington DC 20523

HARRISON, LOU, composer; b. Portland, Ore., 1917; student of Henry Cowell, San Francisco, of Arnold Schoenberg, Los Angeles. Formerly music critic N.Y. Herald Tribune, also tchr. Mills. Coll., Black Mountain Coll.; playwriter, mus. instrument maker, dancer; composer numerous works percussion ensemble, including Doubles, in collaboration with John Cage and The Canticles.

HARRISON, MARK, educator, physicist; b. Paris, Mo., Nov. 21, 1919; s. Marvin Evans and Lula (Smith) H.; B.S., N.E. Mo. State Coll., 1942; Ph.D., Cath. U. Am., 1952; m. Mary Frances Davis, Oct. 5, 1942; children—David Mark, Sally Page. Research scientist Columbia, 1942-45; head research br. David Taylor Model Basin, 1945-52; cons. Navy Dept., 1952-60; prof. physics, chmn. dept. Am. U., Washington, 1960—. Cons. in field. Mem. Met. Bd. Trade. Bd. dirs. Washington Planetarium. Fellow Am. Phys. Soc., Acoustical Soc. Am.; mem. Philos. Soc. Washington (gov. bd.), Sigma Xi. Contbr. articles to profl. jours. Home: 2325 42d St NW Washington DC 20007

HARRISON, MARK, newspaper editor; b. Warsaw, Poland, Aug. 10, 1924; s. Harry A. and Sonia (Doduck) H.; A.B., U. Toronto, 1948, postgrad., 1949; m. Isabel Clifton Hay-Roe, Feb. 24, 1950; children—Steven Paul, Timothy Jon, Judith Ann, Nancy Ellen. With Toronto Daily Star, 1949, exec. editor, 1969—. Bd. dirs. Canadian Inst. Pub. Affairs. Served with RCAF, 1943-46. Home: 33 Apple Orchard Path Thornill Ontario Canada Office: 80 King St W Toronto Ontario Canada

HARRISON, MARK ISAAC, lawyer; b. Pitts., Oct. 17, 1934; s. Coleman and Myrtle (Seidenman) H.; A.B., Antioch Coll., 1957; LL.B., Harvard, 1960; m. Ellen R. Gier, June 15, 1958; children-Lisa, Jill. Law clk. to justices Ariz. Supreme Ct., 1960-61; admitted to Ariz. bar, 1961, since practiced in Phoenix; partner firm Harrison, Strick, Myers & Singer, 1966—. Bd. dirs. Careers for Youth, 1964-67, pres., 1966-67. Vice chmn. Maricopa County Democratic Central Com., 1967-68, Ariz. Dem. Party, 1969-70; legal counsel 1970—; del. Dem. Nat. Conv., 1968. Mem. Am., Maricopa County (pres. 1970) bar assns., Am., Phoenix (bd. dirs. 1964-67) trial lawyers assns., Phoenix Assn. Def. Counsel, Am. Bd. Trial Advocates, State Bar Ariz., Am. Judicature Soc., Ariz. Civil Liberties Union. Co-author: Arizona Appellate Practice, 1966. Home: 326 E Kaler Dr Phoenix AZ 85020 Office: 111 W Monroe St Phoenix AZ 85003

HARRISON, MARTIN LEIGH, lawyer, univ. prof.; b. Opelika, Ala., Apr. 4, 1907; s. William Robert and Eva (Trawick) H.; A.B., U. Ala., 1927, LL.B., 1929, LL.D., 1959; LL.M., Harvard, 1935; m. Barbara Sinclair, Dec. 24, 1935; children—Barbara Ann, William Robert. Admitted to Ala. bar, 1929; practiced in Birmingham, 1929-34; instr. law So. Meth. U., 1935-38; asst. prof. law U. of Ala., 1938-40, prof., 1944-66, Warner prof. law, 1966—, also dean Law Sch., 1950-66. Mem. Ala. Bd. Bar Examiners, Ala. Bar Assn., Phi Beta Kappa, Omicron Delta Kappa, Phi Delta Phi, Phi Kappa Sigma. Democrat. Episcopalian. Editor: Cases on Alabama and Common Law Pleading, 1941; Alabama Cases on Equity Pleading, 1948. Contbr. articles to law revs. Home: 29 Beech Hills Tuscaloosa, AL 35401. Office: Box 1474 University AL 35486

HARRISON, MELVIN W., trust co. exec.; b. Balt. 1913; LL.B., U. Balt. Vice pres., sec. Equitable Trust Co. Bd. dirs., trustee Silver Cross Home and Hosp. Home: 302 Felton Rd Lutherville MD 21093 Office: Equitable Trust Co. Calvert and Fayette Sts Baltimore MD 21202*

HARRISON, MICHAEL JAY, educator; b. Chgo., Aug. 20, 1932; s. Nathan J. and Mae (Nathan) H.; A.B., Harvard, 1954; M.S., U. Chgo., 1956, Ph.D., 1960; m. Ann Tukey, Sept. 1, 1970. Fulbright fellow and H. Van Loon fellow in theoretical physics U. Leiden, Netherlands, 1954-55; NSF fellow U. Chgo., 1957-59; research fellow math. physics U. Birmingham, Eng., 1959-61; asst. prof. Mich. State U., East Lansing, 1961-63, asso. prof., 1963-68, prof., 1968—; with Air Force Cambridge Research Center, summer 1953, Mass. Inst Tech. Lincoln Lab., summer 1954, RCA Sarnoff Lab., summers 1961-63; cons. RCA Lab., 1961-64, United Aircraft Co., 1964-66. Am. Council on Edn. fellow U. Cal., Los Angeles, 1970-71. Mem. Am. Phys. Soc. Jewish religion. Club: Harvard of Central Michigan. Office: Physics Dept Mich State U East Lansing MI 48823

HARRISON, MILTON M., educator; b. Gibsland, La., Oct. 15, 1915; s. John J. and Grace (Moore) H.; B.A., La. Poly Inst., 1935; LL.B., La. State U., 1941; m. Eugenia Taylor, Feb. 14, 1946; children—Kay, Jane, John T. Tchr. high sch., 1935-38; admitted to La. bar; reporter, asst. coordinator revised statutes project La. State Law Inst., 1946-48; lectr. law La. State U., 1946-47, asst. prof., asst. to dean Law Sch., 1948-50, asst. to pres., asst. prof. law, 1950-57, dean, prof. law, 1957-59, v.p., dean acad. affairs La. State U., 1959-62, asso. dean, prof. law, 1962-71, prof. law, 1971—. Bd. dirs. Baton Rouge Speech and Hearing Found., 1960—, pres., 1962. Served to capt. USAAF, 1941-46. Mem. La. Bar Assn. (gov. 1958), La. Law Inst., Omicron Delta Kappa, Phi Kappa Phi, Order of Coif. Home: 2335 Olive St Baton Rouge LA 70806

HARRISON, PAUL MELVIN DALE, electronics co. exec.; b. Mt. Pleasant, Mich., Aug. 4, 1926; s. William Arthur and Lanora (Keiser) H.; A.B., U. Mich., 1948, J.D., 1951; m. Georgia Ann Thompson, July 23, 1960; children—Robert Bruce, Paula Dale. Admitted to Mich. bar, 1951, Ind. bar, 1960; with firm Hill, Lewis, Anrews, Granse & Adams, 1953-59; asst. sec. P.R. Mallory & Co., Inc., Indpls., 1960-62, sec., resident counsel, 1962-67, v.p., sec., 1967—; dir. Fed. Screw Works. Served with USAF, 1951-53. Mem. Am., Ind., Indpls. bar assns., Tax Execs. Inst., Am. Soc. Corp. Secs. Sigma Chi, Delta Theta Phi. Presbyn. Clubs: Indpls. Athletic, Meridian Hills Country (Indpls.); University (N.Y.C.). Home: 7322 Glenview Dr W Indianapolis IN 46250 Office: 3029 E Washington St Indianapolis IN 46206

HARRISON, PRESTON ERSHELL, physician; b. Bryans Mill, Tex., Aug. 26, 1911; s. Alonzo Louis and Ola (Henson) H.; B.S., E. Tex. State Coll., 1932; M.A., U. Tex., 1936; M.D., Baylor U., 1941; Ph.D. (Mary Strong Sheldon fellow), U. Chgo., 1946; m. Elizabeth Badgett, Jan. 17, 1970; children—Preston Ershell, Robert. Instr., Baylor U., Houston, 1941-43, asst. prof., 1943-46, asso. prof., 1946-48, prof., 1948-49; intern Baylor U. Hosp., 1942-43; resident. Menninger Found., 1957-58; gen. practice medicine, Maud, Tex., 1949-53; clin. dir. Big Spring (Tex.) State Hosp., 1953-57, acting supr., 1957- 58, supt., 1958—; research asso., instr. U. Chgo., 1945-46. Fellow A.A.A.S.; mem. A.M.A., Am. Psychiat. Assn., Am. Hosp. Assn., Am. Soc. Clin. Hypnosis, soc. clin and exptl. hypnosis, Sigma Xi, Alpha Omega Alpha. Home: PO Box 231 Big Spring TX 79721

HARRISON, REX CAREY, actor, producer; b. Eng., Mar. 5, 1908; s. William Reginald and Edith (Carey) H.; ed. Birkdale Prep. Sch. and Liverpool Coll.; m. Marjorie Noel Collette Thomas, 1934; 1 son; m. 2d, Lilli Palmer, 1943 (div.); 1 son. Carey; m. 3d, Kay Kendall, June 23, 1957 (dec. 1959); m. 4th, Rachel Roberts, Mar. 1961 (div.). On legitimate stage, 1924—, in films, 1929- -; London stage deubt. 1930, N.Y.C., 1936; appeared as star numerous plays in London; in role of Henry VIII, Anne of the Thousand Days, N.Y.C., 1948-49, The Cocktail Party, 1950, My Fair Lady, 1956-59, Techekos Platonov for English Stage Co., Royal Court Theatre, 1960, French Without Tears, Design for Living, Venus Observed, The Loves of Four Colonels; actor, producer Bell, Book and Candle, 1954; producer Nina, 1955; starred in Films including Storm in a Teacup, Night Train, Major Barbara, Blithe Spirit, Anna and the King of Siam, The Foxes of Harrow, The Agony and the Ecstasy, The Honey Pot, Dr. Honey Pot, Dr. Doolittle, A Flea In Her Ear; films Notorious Gentleman, Night Train, Reluctant Debutant, 1958, Midnight Lace, 1960, The Yellow Rolls-Royce, Escape, Unfaithfully Yours, King Richard and the Crusaders, The Constant Husband; played Caesar in Cleopatra, 1961-62. Prof. Higgins in My Fair Lady, 1963; also appeared on radio in Berkley Square; Served with RAF Vol. Res., World War II. Recipient Tony award as best actor, 1948-49, for mus. star, 1956-57; Evening Standard award as best actor of year for appearances in Platinov, 1960; Acad. award as best actor year for appearances in Platinov award, 1965; Golden Glove, 1965; David di Donatello award, 1965; named to world box office stars, 1966.

HARRISON, RICHARD AHRNELL, assn. exec.; b. Indpls., Aug. 19, 1914; s. H.W. and Ruth K. (Hunter) H.; m. Jane Louise Cline, Nov. 26, 1942 (div. 1965); 1 dau., Margaret Ann; m. 2d, Emeleen Tyler Ramage, Jan. 29, 1965. With U.S. Lines Co., 1930- 40; commd. ensign Supply Corps, USNR, 1939, advanced through grades to capt., 1957; active duty, 1940-47, 49-54; engaged in packing industry,

1954-62; exec. dir. Navy League U.S., 1962-65, dir. Chgo. council, 1958-62; exec. v.p. Nat. Def. Assn., 1966- -. Mem. Naval Res. Officers Assn., Ill. Commandery Naval Order. Home: 6120 Long Meadow Rd McLean VA 22101

HARRISON, RICHARD DONALD, food co. exec.; b. Salt Lake City, May 19, 1923; s. William Z. and Mary Frances (Sappington) H.; B.A., Stanford, 1946; LL.B., U. Mich., 1949; m. Marilyn Fleming, Aug. 30, 1953; children—Amy Virginia, Leslie Lynn, Julie, Susan Elizabeth, Alyse, Richard. Admitted to D.C. bar, 1950, Mich. bar, 1950, Utah bar, 1950, Wash. bar, 1952, also U.S. Supreme Ct., other fed. cts.; spl. asst. to atty. tax div., appellate sect. Dept. Justice, 1950-52; pvt. practice, Seattle, 1952-54; with Fleming Co., Topeka, 1954—, v.p., 1957-64, dir. planning, 1963-64, pres., 1964- -, chief exec. officer, 1966—, also dir.; dir. First Nat. Bank, Quaker Oats Co., Mid-Continent Life Ins., First Nat. Bank Topeka. Chmn. bd. Ind. Grocers Alliance; pres. Supermarket Inst. Bd. dirs. Okla. Sci. and Arts Found., Oklahoma City YMCA; trustee Okla. Christian Coll. Mem. Nat. Am. Wholesale Grocers (bd. govs., exec. com.), Topeka C. of C. (bd. dirs.), Sigma Chi, Phi Delta Phi. Presbyn. Clubs: River (Kansas City, Mo.); Beacon, Oklahoma City Golf and Country (Oklahoma City). Home: 1508 Guilford Lane Oklahoma City OK 73120 Office: 3545 NW 58th Oklahoma City OK 73112

HARRISON, RICHARD EDES, cartographer; b. Balt. Mar. 11, 1901; s. Ross Granville and Ida (Lange) H.; B.A., Yale, 1923, B.F.A., 1930; m. Elizabeth Hamilton Briggs, Aug. 22, 1933; children—Nancy H. (dec.), Ross Granville III, Samuel. Sci. illustrator, draftsman and designer James Gamble Rogers, Cass Gilbert, Henry K. Murphy, architects, 1923-27; designer S.P.R. galleries, 1929-32; free-lance in cartography and design. 1933-35; cartographer Time mag., 1933-38, Fortune, 1936-38; independent cartographer, 1939—; map cons. to State Dept., OSS, Fortune and Life mags., Geol. Survey, USAF, NBC, com. geography and geophysics Research and Devel. Bd., com. on globes NRC; vis lectr. Clark U., Columbia, Carleton Coll., U. Va.; lectr. Syracuse U., 1945-49, U. Pitts., 1959-60. Chmn. Save Central Park Com. Candidate N.Y. State Assembly, Liberal Party, 1960. Recipient citation for meritorious contbn. Am. Assn. Geographers, 1967; honors award Spl. Libraries Assn., 1968; O.M. Miller medal cartography Am. Geog. Soc., 1968. Fellow Royal Geog. Soc., Am. Geog. Soc., A.A.A.S.; mem. Am. Congress of Surveying and Mapping, Assn. Am. Geographers (chmn. N.Y. met. sect. 1951-52, map editor 1958- -), Linnaean Soc. N.Y. (v.p. 1957-59, pres. 1959-60), Municipal Art Soc., Darwin Anniversary Com. (exec. sec. 1957-60). Club: Coffee House (N.Y.C.). Illustrator: Woodruff's Foundation of Biology, other zool. works. Cartographer for numerous books in field of geology, polit. geography and mil. history, also for General Marshall's 3d Biennial Report, Fortune mag., Life mag.; designer maps for New Ginn Geographics, 1957; designer map murals N.Y. Times lobby, Time-Life Bldg., N.Y.C. Author: Maps and How to Understand Them, 1943; Look at the World, 1944; also numerous tech. papers. Co-editor: Compass of the World, 1944; New Compass of the World, 1949. Contbr. book revs., N.Y. Herald Tribune, Sat. Rev. Lit., N.Y. Times. Specialist in perspective map techniques. Originator of nomographic methods in constrn. of map projections. Address 313 E 51st St New York City NY 10022

HARRISON, RICHARD HOLMES, mfg. co. exec.; b. Seattle, Nov. 29, 1907; s. Max and Kate Turner (Homes) H.; student U. Wash., 1925-27; B.S., U.S. Mil. Acad., 1931; grad. Arty. Sch., 1939, Command and Gen. Staff Coll., 1946, Armed Forces Staff Coll., 1947, Army War Coll., 1952; m. Patricia Donahue, June 12, 1931; 1 dau., Patricia Jean. Commd. 2d lt. U.S. Army, 1931, advanced through grades to brig. gen., 1955; assigned ETO, 1944-45, Korea, 1950- 51; comdg. gen. 11th Airborne Arty., 1955-56; chief army sect. JUSMAG Greece, 1956-58; dep. chief Def. Atomic Support Agy., also chief Joint Atomic Information Exchange Group, 1958-61; ret., 1961; asst. to v.p. Babcock & Wilcox Co., 1961-62, gen. mgr. atomic energy div., 1962-63, v.p. charge atomic energy div., 1963-68, vice pres. in charge Washington office, 1969—. Decorated Legion of Merit with oak leaf cluster, Bronze Star medal, Air medal, Army Commendation ribbon with metal pendant; Korean Presdl. citation. Mem. Atomic Indsl. Forum, Newcomen Soc. N. Am., Assn. U.S. Army, Am. Mgmt. Assn., Soc. Naval Architects and Marine Engrs., N.A.M., Phi Gamma Delta. Clubs: University, Chemists, Cloud (N.Y.C.); Boonsboro Country (Lynchburg); Army and Navy (Washington). Home: 3901 Peakland Pl Lynchburg VA 24503 Office: 1725 K St NW Washington DC 20006

HARRISON, ROBERT DREW, dept. store exec.; b. Des Moines, May 17, 1923; s. Roland T. and Grace M. (Drew) H.; S.B., Harvard, 1945, M.B.A., 1948; m. Evelyn Colonna Berkley, June 5, 1948; children—Nancy Berkley, Evelyn Lee, Roberta Drew, Adrienne Tipp. Mem. faculty Harvard Grad. Sch. Bus. Administrn., 1948- 49; with John Wanamaker, Phila., 1949—, pres., 1968—; dir. Provident Nat. Bank, Phila., Phila. Electric Co., Fidelity Mut. Life Ins. Co., Phila. Savs. Fund Soc. Bd. dirs. Paoli (Pa.) Meml. Hosp. Served to lt (j.g.) USNR, 1943-46. Clubs: Union League, Racquet (Phila); Merion (Pa.) Golf; Millrose Athletic Assn. (bd. dirs.) (N.Y.C.); Merior Cricket (Haverford). Home: 326 Grays Lane Haverford PA 19041 Office: 1300 Market St Philadelphia PA 19101

HARRISON, S. DAVID, lawyer; b. N.Y.C., Jan. 29, 1930; s. Louis and Molly (Ginsburg) H.; A.B., Harvard, 1951, LL.B., 1954; LL.M., N.Y.U., 1959; m. Joan S. Horowitz, Mar. 23, 1958; children—Andrew L., Rachel E. Admitted to N.J. bar, 1955, N.Y. bar, 1968; law sec. N.J. Supreme Ct. Justice Brennan, Jr., 1954-55; asso., then partner firm Platoff, Platoff & Heftler, Union City, N.J., 1955-65; corp. counsel Beaunit Corp., N.Y.C. 1965-71, corp. sec., 1966-71; asst. sec. Tyrex, Inc., 1969-71; dir. Man-Made Fibers Producers Assn., 1970-71; mem. firm Harrison & Baker, N.Y.C., 1971—. Mem. Am. Bar Assn., N.Y. State Bar Assn., Nat. Panel Arbitrators, Am. Arbitration Assn., Lawyers Assn. Textile Industry. Jewish religion. Mason. Home: 2 Oxford Rd Hastings-on-Hudson NY 10706 Office: 261 Madison Av New York City NY 10016

HARRISON, SELIG SEIDENMAN, journalist; b. Wilkinsburg, Pa., Mar. 19, 1927; s. Coleman and Myrtle (Seidenman) H.; A.B., Harvard, 1948, Nieman fellow, 1954-55; m. Barbara Johnston, Oct. 10, 1951; children—Coleman Peter, Kathreen Grosvenor. With Detroit bur. A.P., 1949-50, fgn. desk, N.Y.C., 1951, 55, fgn. corr., New Delhi, India, 1951-54; asso. editor New Republic, 1956-60, mng. editor, 1960-62; S. Asia corr. Washington Post, 1962-65, mem. editorial staff, 1966-67; sr. fellow charge Asian studies Brookings Instn., 1967-68; chief N.E. Asia bur. Washington Post, Tokyo, 1968—. Research asso. Lang. and Communication Research Center, Columbia, 1955; cons. Center S. Asia Studies, U. Cal. at Berkeley, 1955-56. Mem. Am. Polit. Sci. Assn. Clubs: Overseas Writers, Nat. Press (Washington). Author: India: The Most Dangerous Decades, 1960; also articles. Editor: India and the United States, 1961. Home: 3611 Spring St Chevy Chase MD 20015 Office: Washington Post 1515 L St NW Washington DC 20005

HARRISON, T. FELTON, coll. pres.; b. Sandersville, Ga., Sept. 25, 1918; s. John Felton and Laura (Alford) H.; B.A. in Edn., U. Fla., 1948, M.A. in Edn., 1950; Ed.D., U. Miss., 1960; m. Mary Ruth Stevens, Dec. 7, 1941; children—T. Felton, Ruthann, Laura. Formerly instr. history and sci. McKee Tng. Sch.; instr. history, econs. and polit. sci. Western Carolina Coll., 1950-55; mem. faculty Pensacola (Fla.) Jr. Coll., 1955—, dean instrn., 1962-63, v.p. for degree program, 1964, pres., 1964—. Cons. Fellows Meml. Fund; counselor Kappa Delta Pi; mem. Inter-Visitation and Self Study Program. Served with AUS, 1943-46. Mem. Nat., Fla., Escambia edn. assns., So. Assn. Colls. and Schs., Fla. Assn. Pub. Jr. Colls., Assn. Higher Edn., Phi Kappa Phi, Phi Delta Kappa, Kappa Delta Pi, Phi Alpha Theta. Methodist (mem. bd). Lion. Home: 711 Dunwoody Dr Pensacola FL 32504

HARRISON, THOMAS GALBRAITH, grocery exec.; b. Mpls., July 8, 1895; s. Perry and Miriam (Thomas) H.; student Hotchkiss Prep. Sch., 1911-12, Blake Sch., Mpls., 1913-14; m. Gladys Baldwin, June 23, 1920; children—Edith (Mrs. Randolph Herman), Thomas G. (dec.), Miriam (Mrs. William Sigrist). With Winston, Harper, Fisher Co. (now Super Valu Stores, Inc.), Mpls., 1919—, successively asst. sales mgr., asst. treas., exec. v.p., 1919-44, pres., 1944-58, chmn. bd. Served as capt. U.S. Army, 1918. Home: RD 3 Box 240 Wayzata MN 55391

HARRISON, THOMAS WADE, lawyer; b. Palmetto, Fla., Feb. 6, 1904; s. M.O. and Evie (Mason) H.; LL.B., U. Fla., 1930; m. Lois Chandler, Sept. 21, 1935; 1 dau., Nancy Evelyn. Admitted to Fla. bar, 1930, U.S. Supreme Ct. bar, 1934; practiced law, Tampa, Fla., 1930-34; with Home Loan Bank Bd., Washington, 1934—, asst. gen. counsel, 1942-49, asso. gen. counsel, 1949-51, gen. counsel, 1951-54; counsel U.S. Savs. and Loan League, 1955-56; pres. 1st Fed. Savs. Loan Assn., Gainesville, Fla., 1956—. Served with USNR, 1943-46. Mem. Am., Fed. bar assns., Phi Delta Theta. Bapt. Mason (Shriner). Elk. Home: 1743 NW 14th Av Gainesville FL 32601 Office: 249 W University Av Gainesville FL 32601

HARRISON, W BENTON graphic arts exec.; b. Atlanta, Aug. 25, 1907; s. Wallace Benton and Bertha (Arden) H.; A.B., Birmingham-So. Coll., 1926; M.A., U. Mich., 1927; m. Mildren R. Pierson, June 29, 1929; children—Sigrid, Barbara, Wallace Benton III. Asst. sales mgr. Halsey, Stuart & Co., N.Y.C., 1927-32; corr. Guaranty Trust Co., 1932-36; asst. mgr. J. & W. Seligman & Co., 1936-40; analyst Kidder, Peabody & Co., 1940-42; asst. to treas. Gen. Aniline & Film Corp., 1942-43, asst. treas., 1943-47, treas., 1947- 51; treas. Sylvania Electric Products, Inc., 1951-53, v.p. finance, 1953- 58, sr. v.p., 1958-60; exec. v.p., dir. Ryder System, Inc., 1960-63, vice chmn., 1962-63; v.p. corporate devel. Harris Intertype Corp., 1963-66, v.p. finance and corporate devel., 1966-67; sr. v.p. Monogram Industries, Inc., Los Angeles, 1967-70. Council financial execs. Nat. Indsl. Bd., N.Y. Home: 3015 Emathla St Miami FL 33133

HARRISON, W. EARL, banker; b. Ellis County, Tex.; s. Robert E. and Lucretia (Vestal) H.; law degree under pvt. tutordship, 1936; grad. Rutgers U. Sch. Banking, 1939; m. Minnie Louise Howell, June 1, 1926; 1 son, William Earl. Admitted to Tex. bar, 1935; with First Nat. Bank Waco, Tex., 1926—, pres., 1965—, vice chmn., 1970—, also dir.; dir. Bickholts State Bank (Tex.), Waco Hardware Co., Haven Manor, Golden Triangle Corp., Texland Corp., Baylor Stadium Corp., Baylor Bear Club. Bd. dirs. Waco Research Devel. Corp., Tex. Good Roads Assn; trustee Baylor U., Council for Instl. Devel.; trustee McLennan Community Coll.; past pres., dir. Waco YMCA, Waco Library. Served to lt. USNR, World War II. Mason (Shriner); Lion (past pres., bd. dirs. Waco). Club: Ridgewood Country (Waco). Home: 3111 Austin Av Waco TX 76710 Office: 811 Washington Av Waco TX 76701

HARRISON, W SPENCER, corp. executive; b. Yorktown, Ind., Apr. 30, 1917; s. William Henry and Myrtle (Decker) H.; A.B., Ind. U., 1939, LL.B., 1941; m. Margie Leonard, Apr. 25, 1950. Admitted to N.Y. bar, 1947; joined C.B.S. TV, 1942, sr. atty., 1951-52, v.p., 1952, later v.p., bus. mgr. talent and contract properties; v.p. Ashley Famous Agy., Inc., 1962-69; exec. v.p. Warner Bros. Inc., 1969—; dir. Kinney Nat. Service, Inc. Home: 1375 Beverly Estate Dr Beverly Hills CA 90210 Office: Warner Bros Inc 4000 Warner Blvd Burbank CA 91505

HARRISON, WALDO MAURICE, retired elec. engr.; b. Pawnee, Okla., Feb. 12, 1904; s. Howard and Rose Belle (Norris) H.; E.E., U. Cin., 1929; m. Madge Violet Curtis, June 15, 1935; 1 dau., Sally Madge. Indsl. sales engr. Pa. Power & Light Co., Allentown, 1929-41; elec. engr. Atlas Powder Co., Wilmington, Del., 1941- 43; with Cummins Engine Co., Inc., Columbus, Ind., 1943-69, successively asst. to sales mgr., materials controller, asst. controller and material mgr., treas. and controller, 1943-48, v.p., sec.-treas., 1954-61, v.p. finance, 1961-64, v.p., sec., 1966-69, v.p., also dir.; ret., 1969; dir. Arkwright Boston Mut. Ins. Co., 1952-69, Mut. Boiler & Machinery Co., Boston, 1959-69; mem. Ind. adv. bd. Liberty Mut. Ins. Cos., Boston, 1965-69. Registered profl. engr., Pa. Mem. U.S. C. of C. (mem. spl. adv. panel fgn. trade policy), Phi Delta Theta, Tau Pi, Eta Kappa Nu. Republican. Presbyn. (elder). Clubs: Rotary (Columbus); Columbia (Indpls.). Home: 2885 Franklin Dr Columbus IN 47201 Office: 432 Washington St Columbus IN 47201

HARRISON, WALLACE KIRKMAN; architect; b. Worcester, Mass., Sept. 28, 1895; s. James Henry and Rachel (Kirkman) H.; L.H.D., Dartmouth, 1950; A.F.D., Rollins Coll., Oberlin Coll., New Sch. Social Research; LL.D., Harvard, 1958, Clark U., 1960; LL.D., U. Mich., 1968; m. Ellen Milton, Feb. 13, 1926; 1 dau., Sarah Moore. Co-architect Rockefeller Center; architect Met. Opera Lincoln Center, Albany (N.Y.) Mall, Museum of Sci. N.Y.; dir. planning hdqrs. UN; former dir. Office Inter-Am. Affairs. Recipient gold medal A.I.A., 1967. Episcopalian. Clubs: Century Assn., Knickerbocker (N.Y.C.). Home: 834 Fifth Av New York City NY 10021 Office: 630 Fifth Av New York City NY 10020

HARRISON, WALTER ASHLEY, educator, physicist; b. Flushing, N.Y., Apr. 26, 1930; s. Charles Allison and Gertrude (Ashley) H.; B.Engring. physics, Cornell U., 1953; M.S., U. Ill., 1954, Ph.D., 1956; m. Lucille Prince Carley, July 17, 1954; children—Richard Knight, John Carley, William Ashley, Robert Walter. Physicist, Gen. Elec. Research Labs., Schenectady, 1956-65; prof. applied physics Stanford, 1965—. Guggenheim fellow, 1970- 71; vis. fellow Clare Hall, Cambridge U., 1970-71. Fellow Am. Phys. Soc.; mem. Am. Assn. Univ. Profs. Author: Pseudopotentials in the Theory of Metals, 1966; Solid State Theory, 1970. Editor: The Fermi Surface, 1960. Home: 817 San Francisco Ct Stanford CA 94305

HARRISON, WARD DUNCAN, paper mfr.; b. Blue Earth, Minn., Sept. 15, 1909; s. Charles H. and Grace (Putney) H.; B.S., Ia. State Coll., 1932; M.S., Inst. Paper Chemistry, Appleton, Wis., 1934, Ph.D., 1936; m. Martha Jentz, Sept. 5, 1936; children—Frederick, Martha Ann, Lynn. Chem. engr. Riegel Paper Corp., Milford, N.J., 1936-41, asst. to exec. v.p., N.Y.C., 1948-49. v.p., Milford, 1949-55, N.Y.C., 1955-58, dir., 1950-58; pres. Allied Paper Corp. (now Allied Paper Inc. div. SCM Corp.), 1958-64, chmn. bd., 1964-70, chief exec. officer, 1964-70, also dir.; v.p., dir. SCM Corp., 1968-70, asst. to exec. v.p., 1971—; asst. gen. mgr. Ecusta Paper Corp., Psigah Forest, N.C., 1941-48. Registered engr., N.C. Mem. T.A.P.P.I. (pres. 1957-58), Paper Industry Mgmt. Assn. Presbyn. Club: Union League (N.Y.C.). Contbr. articles profl. publs. Home: 1150 Long Rd Kalamazoo MI 49001 Office: 1608 Lake St Kalamazoo MI 49001

HARRISON, WILLIAM HENRY, journalist; b. Charlestown, Ireland, Apr. 21, 1910; (parents Am. citizens); s. John Joseph and Anna (Johnston) H.; student Niagra U., 1927-29; Litt. B., Columbia, 1932; m. Mary Killian Quigley, Apr. 21, 1939; children—Mary Killian (Mrs. Gregory Justin Perry), James Quigley. Entertainment critic Radio-Keith-Orpheum Corp., N.Y.C., 1932; asso., acting editor Hornell (N.Y.) Tribune, 1932-34; editorial exec. Providence Jour. and Eve. Bull. 1934-36, editorial writer, 1940-43; editor Pathfinder mag., Washington, 1936-40; editorial writer Washington Evening and Sunday Star, 1943-70. Recipient Editorial award Freedoms Found., 1962. Mem. Nat. Conf. Editorial Writers, Overseas Writers, Nat. Aviation Club, Sigma Delta Chi. Clubs: Nat. Press, Internat. (Washington). Home: 2029 Connecticut Av Washington DC 20008

HARRISON, WILLIAM HENRY, banker; b. Cape Girardeau, Mo., Aug. 1, 1910; s. Charles Luce and Maude (Rozier) H.; B.A., U. Mo., 1932, M.A., 1933; m. Mina Mary Cohan, June 30, 1945; children—Mary Rozier (Mrs. John H. Hayward, Jr.), William Henry, John Valle, Robert Sverdrup. Vice pres., sec. Housing Service, Inc., 1935-40; owner William H. Harrison, realtor, St. Louis, 1946-60; with First Nat Bank St. Louis, 1960—, exec. v.p., 1969—, also sec. bd. dirs. Mem. City Plan Commn. St. Louis, 1955-65, vice chmn., 1959-61, chmn., 1961-65; mem., treas. Bd. Police Commnrs. Met. St. Louis, v.p., dir. Downtown St. Louis, 1961—; chmn. Mayor St. Louis Community Adv. Com., 1965-67; mem. army gen. staff com. Army Res. and N.G. Affairs, 1957-62; mem. forces res. policy bd. Dept. Def., 1960-63. Trustee Jefferson Nat. Expension Meml. Assn.; bd. dirs., dist. chmn. St. Louis council Boy Scouts Am.; bd. dirs. St. Louis Bi-State chpt. A.R.C., St. Louis council U.S.O. Served to col. AUS, 1940-46; maj.-gen. Res. Decorated Legion of Merit with oak leaf cluster (U.S.); Croix de Guerre (France); Order Leopold, Croix de Guerre (Belgium). Mem. St. Louis Met. C. of C. (dir.), St. Louis Real Estate Bd., Am. Inst. Real Estate Appraisers, Soc. Indsl. Realtors, Am. Bankers Assn., Mil. Order World Wars, Phi Delta Theta. K.C. Clubs: Rotary, Bellerive Country, Noonday, Racquet, Stadium (St. Louis); Wings of St. Albans. Home: 51 Kingsbur Pl St Louis MO 63112 Office: 510 Locust St St Louis MO 63101

HARRISON, WILLIAM HENRY, architect; b. Richmond, Ind., Jan. 2, 1897; s. Thomas H. and Claribel (Barrett) H.; B.Arch., Cornell U., 1921; m. Josephine A. Lewis, Dec. 22, 1922; children—Martha Jo (Hubbard), William Lewis (dec.). Draftsman, Starrett & Van Vleck, N.Y.C., 1921; designer Bass-Knowlton Co., Indpls., 1921-25; with Robert Frost Daggett, Indpls., 1925-26; archtl. practice under own name, Los Angeles, 1930—. Governing bd. Nat. Sch. Facilities Council; pres. Whittier Area Beautiful, Whittier Area Edn. Study Council. Recipient 1st prize two residential competitions, 1923, 31; co-winner 1st prize Lehigh Airport competition, 1929; award of merit for sch. design, 1952, 54. Fellow A.I.A. (certificates of merit So. Cal. 1938); mem. Cornell U. Alumni Assn. So. Cal. (gov. bd.), U.S., Cal. chambers commerce, Los Angeles Planning Congress. Mem. Soc. of Friends. Club: University (Los Angeles). Archtl. work illustrated in profl. publs. Home: 6554 S Friends Av Whittier CA 90601 Office: 1052 W 6th St Los Angeles CA 90017

HARRISON, WILLIAM HENRY, communications co. exec.; b. Winston Salem, N.C., Sept. 5, 1924; s. William Henry and Kathryn (Hagerty) H.; B.S. in Econs., Wharton Sch. of U. Pa., 1948; m. Jane Jones, June 2, 1948; children—Sally Jane, William Henry, Nancy Jean. With Arthur Andersen & Co., C.P.A.'s, N.Y.C., 1948- 58, mgr., 1953-58; comptroller, asst. treas. Metro-Goldwyn-Mayer, Inc., 1958-64; v.p., controller Gen. Telephone & Electronics Corp., N.Y.C., 1964—. C.P.A., N.Y. Mem. Am. Inst. C.P.A.'s, N.Y. State Soc. C.P.A.'s. Home: 211 Homestead Lane Fairfield CT 06430 Office: 730 3d Av New York City NY 10017

HARRISON, WILLIAM HENRY, ex-congressman; b. Terre Haute, Ind., Aug. 10, 1896; s. Russell Benjamin and Mary A. (Saunders) H.; student Friends Sch., Wash., also U. Neb.; LL.D., Vincennes U.; m. Mary E. Newton, Oct. 19, 1920; children—Mary Elizabeth, William Henry. Admitted to Ind. bar, 1925, Wyo. bar. 1937; practice in Indpls., also Sheridan, Wyo.; mem. Ind. Ho. of Reps., 1927. Wyo. Ho. of Reps., 1945, 47, 49; member-at-large for Wyo., mem. 82d-83d, 87th-88th, 90th Congresses. Mem. Renegotiation Bd., 1968. County chmn. Wyo. Republican Com., 1948-50, state committeeman, 1946-48; Mem. U.S. Jr. (past exec. v.p.), Sheridan (past pres.) chambers commerce, V.F.W., Am. Legion, Sigma Chi, Sigma Delta Kappa. Mason (33, Shriner) Rotarian. Home: Sheridan WY 82801 Office: Box 6046 Sheridan WY 82801

HARRISON, WILLIAM HENRY, Jr., elec. utility exec.; b. Washington, Dec. 30, 1916; s. William Henry and Edna E. (Rothery) H.; B.C.S., Southeastern U., 1940, LL.B., 1937, LL.M., 1941; m. Virginia Darcey, June 22, 1940; children—Pamela V., Patricia L., William Henry III. Admitted to D.C. bar, 1937; asst. to comptroller Potomac Elec. Power Co., Washington, 1937-53; controller Tex. Elec. Service Com., Ft. Worth, 1953-63; now v.p., treas. Tex. Utilities Co., Dallas. Served from ensign to lt. comdr., USNR, 1942-45. C.P.A., Tex., Va. Mem. Financial Execs. Inst., Am. Inst. C.P.A.'s. Republican. Methodist. Home: 4234 Irvin Simmons Dallas, TX 75229 Office: 1506 Commerce St Dallas TX 75201

HARRISON, WILLIAM J., freight co. exec.; b. 1907; student N.Y.U. With U.S. Freight Co., 1922- -, asst. treas., 1951-67, treas., 1967—. Address: 711 3d Av New York City NY 10017

HARRISON, WILLIAM WRIGHT, banker; b. Kingston, N.Y., Aug. 6, 1915; s. James Burwell and Isabella (Clarke) H.; student U. Va., 1933-34; m. Janet Phillips, Apr. 6, 1940; children—Janet P. (Mrs. Richard Rea Hinch), Susan F. (Mrs. Glassell Slaughter Fitz-Hugh, Jr.), William Wright. With Va. Nat. Bank (formerly Peoples Nat. Bank Charlottesville), 1942—, chmn., chief exec. officer, 1969—; pres., dir. Crozet Cold Storage Corp.; vice chmn. Allied Bank Internat., dir. Shenandoah Life Ins. Co., Roanoke, Va., Royster Co., Norfolk, Jefferson Cable Corp., Charlottesville, Atlantic States Bankcard Assn. Chmn. Mun. Bond Commn., Norfolk. Bd. dirs. Gen. Hosp. Virginia Beach; Norfolk Acad.; trustee Norfolk Found., Eastern Va. Med. Sch. Found.; bd. visitors U. Va. Mem. Norfolk C. of C. (pres. 1971). Episcopalian. Clubs: Boar's Head Inn, Farmington Country; Norfolk Yacht and Country; Princess Anne Country; Harbor. Home: 1104 Wythe Lane Virginia Beach VA 23451 Office: 1 Commercial Pl Norfolk VA 23510

HARRISS, JULIUS WELCH, mfg. co. exec.; b. High Point, N.C., Oct. 26, 1905; s. Julius Ward and Florence (Welch) H.; A.B., Duke, 1927. With Harriss & Covington Hosiery Mills, Inc., 1927—, pres., 1928—; pres., dir. Harco, Inc.; dir. High Point br. 1st Union Nat. Bank of N.C. Mem. Research Triangle Inst. Corp. Mem. Edenton (N.C.) Hist Commn. Bd. dirs. High Point (N.C.) Hist. Museum; trustee Duke; mem. bd. visitors Duke Library; ex-trustee N.C. Central U., Durham; mem. Meth. Coll. Found. of N.C., Inc.; trustee Harriss Found. Served to lt. comdr. USNR, World War II. Mem. Nat. Planning Assn. (nat. council), N. C. Art Soc. (former bd. dirs.), N.C. Lit. and Hist. Assn. (life), Alpha Tau Omega. Methodist (steward). Clubs: Rotary (past pres.), Emerywood Country (sr. bd. dirs.), Quadrille, String and Splinter, Executives. Home: 900 Rockford Rd High Point NC 27260 Office: 2525 E Green Dr High Point NC 27261

HARRISS, LLOYD JOHN, food processing exec.; b. Mt. Sterling, Ill., July 24, 1898; s. Cicero and Sarah (Dunn) H.; student public schs.; m. Josephine Allen, Oct. 28, 1925; children—Joanne P., George A., Lloyd J. Partner Harriss Bros., 1921-25; mgr. Pie Bakers of Am., Detroit, 1925-26, Sunkist Pie Co., Chgo., 1926-35; with Lloyd J. Harris Pie Co., Chgo., 1935—, now mgr., and pres.; mgr. Food Industries Am., Inc., Mich., 1951—, pres., dir., 1961—; mgr. Douglas Cold Storage Co., 1951—, pres., dir., 1959-69, chmn., and pres., 1969—; president, also dir. Mich. Lloyd J. Harriss Pie Co. Patentee food processing and freezing, bakery equipment and machinery. Home: Saugatuck MI 49453 Office: 1751 W Hubbard St Chicago IL 60622

HARRISS, LYNN MERRIAM FROEBEL, govt. ofcl.; b. Hanford, Cal., Apr. 21, 1907; s. Walter Hiram and Nellie Goldsmith (Scott) H.; student Pomona Coll., 1924-26; B.S. in Landscape Arch., U. Ill., 1931; M. Landscape Arch., Ia. State U., 1940; m. Elizabeth Rogan Neal, Feb. 14, 1941. Teaching fellow landscape architecture Ia. State U., 1932-33; asst. landscape architect Blue Ridge Pkwy., Nat. Park Service, 1933-40; pvt. practice landscape architecture, Marin County, Cal., 1945-47; asst. supt. parks, Oakland, Cal., 1947-59; mem. Am. Soc. Landscape Architects, 1938-45, 56—, field sec., 1960, exec. dir., 1960- 67; with U.S. Dept. Housing Urban Devel., 1968—. Served to maj. AUS. 1940-45. Fellow Lake Forest Found. Architecture and Landscape Architecture, 1931. Fellow Am. Soc. Landscape Architects; mem. Cal. Council Landscape Architects (exec. sec. 1955-59, honor award 1959), Cal. Bd. Landscape Architects (pres. 1957-58), Am. Soc. Assn. Execs., Internat. Shade Tree Conf. (pres. Western chpt. 1954-55), Cal. Hort. Soc. (pres. 1956-57), Alpha Kappa Lambda. Club: University (Washington). Home: 4831 Sedgwick St NW Washington DC 20016 Office: 451 7th St SW Washington DC 20413

HARRITON, ABRAHAM, artist; b. Bucharest, Rumania, Feb. 16, 1893; s. Joseph and Ghizella (Scheiner) H.; brought to U.S., 1900, naturalized, 1906; student Nat. Acad. Design (Hallgarten prize figure painting, 1911, compositon 1913, painting 1915, Suydam bronze medal still life, 2d Baldwin prize etching 1911. Baldwin prize etching 1913, 15), 1908-15; m. Estelle Safron, Mar. 9, 1919; children—Charles Francis, Maria Louise. Exhbns. include Panama-Pacific World's Fair, 1915, Nat. Acad. Design, 1914-20, 41, 45, 47-48, Whitney Mus., 1936, 37, 39, 40, 41, N.Y. World's Fair 1939, Carnegie Inst., 1941, 43, 44, 45, 46, Corcoran Gallery 1941, Met. Mus. Art, 1942, Goodwill Exhbn. Am. Art in N.Y.C., London, Scotland, 1945, also Bklyn. Mus., St. Louis City Art Mus., Pa. Acad. Fine Arts, Art Inst. Chgo., Mus. Modern Art, others; rep. permanent collections Whitney Mus. Am. Art, Newark Mus., Oakland (Cal.) Art Mus., Addison Gallery Art, Tel Aviv and Ain Harod Museums, Israel, Living Arts Found., N.Y.C., other pub. and pvt. collections. Recipient Patrons prize 2d ann. exhbn. Nat. Soc. Painters in Casein, 1956, Marine award 14th New England Exhibition Silvermine Guild of Artists, 1963; Marjorie Peabody Waite award Nat. Inst. Arts and Letters, 1968. Served with U.S. Army, World War I. Mem. Audubon Arts (bd. dirs., first hon. mention 1960), Artists Equity Assn. Spl. work on theory and practice of underpainting and glazing. Abraham Harriton Manuscript Collection at Syracuse U. in Library Archives. Address: 66 W 9th St New York City NY 10011

HARROD, SIR ROY FORBES, economist; b. London Eng., Feb. 13, 1900; s. Henry Dawes and Frances Marie Desirée (Forbes-Roberson) H.; M.A., New Coll., Oxford, 1922; LL.D., U. Poitiers, Aberdeen U., U. Pa.; D.Litt., U. Glasgow, U. Warwick; m. Wilhelmine Margaret Eve Crosswell, Jan. 8, 1938; children—Henry Mark, Dominick Roy. Lectr., Christ Ch., Oxford, 1922- 24, mem. governing bd., tutor, 1924-67, jr. censor, 1927-29, sr. censor, 1930-31; lectr. for faculty philosophy, politics and econs. Oxford, 1923—, mem. hebdomadal council, 1929-35, mem. commn. library provision, 1930-31; served on pvt. statis. br. of Mr. Churchill as first lord of admiralty, 1940, as prime minister, 1940-42; statis. advisor to fifth sea lord of admiralty, 1943-45; personal adviser to sec. Dept. Overseas Trade, 1943-45; temporary mem. Internat. Monetary Fund, 1952; joint editor Econ. Jour., 1945- 61. Served as 2d lt. Royal Arty., 1918-19. Recipient Bernard Harms prize, 1966. Pres. sect. F, Brit. Assn., 1938. Fellow Brit. Acad.; mem. Royal Econ. Soc. (past pres.). Clubs: Beefsteak, Atheneum (London); Norfolk (Norwich). Author books including: International Economics, 1933, rev. edit., 1957; Trade Cycle, 1936; Are These Hardships Necessary? 1947; Towards a Dynamic Economics, 1948; And So It Goes On, 1951; Life of J.M. Keynes, 1951; Economic Essays, 1952; The Dollar, 1953; Foundations of Inductive Logic, 1956; Policy Against Inflation, 1958; The Prof., 1959; Topical Comment, 1961; The British Economy, 1963; Reforming the World's Money, 1965; Towards a New Economic Policy, 1967; Money, 1969. Contributor to professional jours. Home: The Old Rectory Holt Norfolk England Office: 51 Campden Hill Sq London W 8 England ☆

HARROD, SCOTT, mfg. exec.; b. Sandwich, Ill., Aug. 11, 1910; s. Fred and Hattie (Scott) H.; A.B. magna cum laude, Knox Coll., 1933; m. Doris Shearer, Sept. 10, 1938; children—Scott B., Frederick S. Tchr. math. Galva (Ill.) High Sch., 1933-36; investment analyst Lawrence Stern & Co., Chgo., 1936-38; asst. treas. Spiegel, Inc., Chgo., 1938-43; asst. treas. Bell & Howell Co., Chgo., 1946-49, treas., 1949-50, sec.- treas., 1950-55, dir.; sec.-treas. Bell & Howell Can., 1954, Three Dimension Co., Chgo., 1954-55; sec. DeVry Corp., Chgo., 1955; v.p. DITTO, Inc., Chgo., 1955-57, exec. v.p., gen. mgr., 1957-58, pres., chief exec. officer, 1958-64, also dir.; exec. v.p., dir. H.M. Harper Co., 1965-66, pres., chief exec. officer, 1966-71; pres., dir. ITT Harper Inc., 1971—; dir. H.M. Harper Co., Ltd., Anti Corrosive Metal Products Co., The Seng Co., Chgo. Rawhide Co.; treas., dir. Nat. Lecture Bur., Inc., 1950-55; dir., v.p. Bell & Howell Co., 1962-64. Pres. Park Ridge (Ill.) Sch. Bd., 1953-56. Served with USNR, 1943-46. Men. Financial Execs. Inst., Chgo. Assn. Commerce and Industry, Phi Beta Kappa, Beta Theta Pi. Clubs: University, Economic, Executives (Chgo.). Contbr. articles profl. publs. Home: Middleton Dr RR2 Long Grove IL 60047 Office: 8200 N Lehigh Av Morton Grove IL 60053

HARROLD, BERNARD, lawyer; b. Wells County, Ind., Feb. 5, 1925; s. James Delmer and Marie (Mounsey) H.; student Biarritz Am. U., 1945; A.B., Ind. U., 1949, LL.B., 1951; m. Kathleen Walker, Nov. 26, 1952; children—Bernard James, Camilla Ruth, Renata Jane. Admitted to Ill. bar, 1951, since practiced in Chgo.; mem. firm Kirkland, Ellis, Hodson, Chaffetz & Masters, 1951-67; sr. partner Wildman, Harrold, Allen & Dixon, 1967—. Mem. Winnetka Caucus Com., 1967-68. Served with AUS, 1944-46; ETO. Mem. Internat., Am., Ill. (chmn. evidence program 1970), Chgo. bar assns., Soc. Trial Lawyers, Order of Coif, Phi Beta Kappa, Phi Eta Sigma. Clubs: Chicago Curling; Univ. Club of Chicago; North Shore Duplicate Bridge (Winnetka). Note editor Ind. Law Jour., 1950-51. Home: 809 Locust St Winnetka IL 60093 Office: 6 N Michigan Av Chicago IL 60602

HARROLD, ORVILLE GOODWIN, Jr., mathematician, educator; b. Chgo., Sept. 2, 1909; s. Orville Goodwin and Estelle (Pancake) H.; A.B. with great distinction, Stanford, 1931, M.A. 1932, Ph.D., 1936; NRC fellow U. Va., 1939-40; m. Gladys Buell, June 30, 1934; children—Philip, Jeffrey. Lectr., Mich. Topology Conf., 1940, Princeton, 1946-47; prof. math. U. Tenn., 1947-64, head dept., 1961-64; prof. math., head dept. Fla. State U., 1964—; mem. Set-Theoretic Topology Inst., U. Mich., 1955, Three-Dimensional Topology Inst., U. Ga., 1961; cons. Union Carbide Corp., Oak Ridge, 1949-61. Mem. regional selection com. Woodrow Wilson Fellowship Bd.; regional devel. com. NRC. Recipient Research award Oak Ridge Inst. Nuclear Studies, 1949. Guggenheim fellow Oxford (Eng.) U., 1958. Mem. Soc. Indsl. and Applied Math., Am. Math. Soc. (asso. sec.), Math. Assn. Am., Phi Beta Kappa, Sigma Xi. Home: 1101 Lothian Dr Tallahassee FL 32303

HARRON, MARION JANET, judge; b. San Francisco, Sept. 3, 1903; d. Charles Merrill and Minnie Jane (Little) Harron; A.B., U. Cal., 1924, J.D., 1926. Teaching fellow, U. Cal., 1924-26; staff Cal. Minimum Wage Commn., 1925; admitted to Cal. bar, 1926, U.S. Supreme Ct. bar, 1938; dir. Survey of Labor Laws in N.Y. State, Nat. Indsl. Conf. Bd., N.Y.C., 1926-27; mem. faculty Inst. of Law, Johns Hopkins, 1928; gen. practice of law, 1929-33; asst. counsel NRA, Washington, 1933-35; regional custodian of rehab. corps. Resettlement Adminstrn., Berkeley, Cal., 1936; judge U.S. Tax Ct., 1936—. Mem. Fed. Bar Assn., Bar Assn. San Francisco, Internat. Fedn. Women Lawyers, Nat. Lawyers Club, Am. Assn. U. Women, Nat. Assn. Women Lawyers, Woman's Nat. Dem. Club, Phi Beta Kappa, Delta Sigma Tho, Phi Delta Delta. Democrat. Conglist. Author: Current Research in Law (1928-29), 1929. Address: US Tax Court Washington DC 20044

HARROP, WILLIAM CALDWELL, fgn. service officer; b. Balt., Feb. 19, 1929; s. George A. and Esther (Caldwell) H.; A.B., Harvard, 1950; postgrad. Grad. Sch. Journalism U. Mo., 1953-54; fellow Woodrow Wilson Sch., Princeton, 1968-69; m. Ann G. Delavan, Aug. 22, 1953; children—Mark D., Caldwell, Scott N., George H. Fgn. service officer, 1954—; vice consul, Palermo, 1954-55; 2d sec., Rome, 1955-58; internat. relations officer Dept. State, 1958-63; 1st sec., Brussels, 1963-66; consul, Lubumbashi, Congo, 1966-68; dir. Office Research for Africa, Dept. State, Washington, 1969—. Chmn., Am. Fgn. Service Assn., 1971—. Served with USMCR, 1951-52. Recipient State Dept. Merit Service award, 1968. Mem. Am. Fgn. Service Assn. (dir.). Clubs: Harvard Varsity, Fly (Cambridge Mass.); Metropolitan (Washington); Royal Leopold (Brussels). Home: 3615 49th St NW Washington DC 20016 Office: Am Fgn Service Assn 2101 E St NW Washington DC 20520

HARROWER, LEONTINE LYLE, mem. Republican Nat. Com.; b. N.Y.C., Feb. 12, 1926; d. William Gordon and Leontine (de Sable) Lyle; grad. Miss Hewitt's Sch., 1944; m. Norman Harrower, Jr., Sept. 1, 1945; children—Harriet Greeley, Norman III, Mary Stuart. Co-chmn. Conn. Vols. for Nixon-Lodge, 1960; mem. campaign staff mayoralty, congl. and senatorial candidates, Conn., 1961-62; co-chmn. Conn. for Scranton for Pres. Com., 1964; alternate del. Rep. Nat. Conv., 1964, del., 1968, mem. arrangements, platforms coms., 1968; mem. exec. bd. Young Rep. Nat. Fedn.; mem. Rep. Nat. Com. for Conn., 1964—. Address: 144 Edgehill Rd New Haven CT 06511

HARROWER, MOLLY, psychologist; b. Johannesburg, S. Africa, Jan. 25, 1906; d. James and Ina Mary (White) H.; student Godolphin Sch., Salisbury, Eng., 1918- 24; U. of London, 1924-27; Ph.D., Smith, Northampton, Mass., 1932; m. Mortimer Lahm, 1955 (dec. Mar. 1967). Came to U.S., 1928, naturalized, 1944. Asso. editor Psyche, 1927-28; research asso. Research Lab., Smith Coll., Northampton, Mass., 1928-30, 1931-32, 33-34; instr. psychology Wells Coll., N.Y., 1930-31; sr. lectr. psychology Bedford Coll., U. London (Eng.), 1932-33; dir. students New Jersey Coll. for Women, New Brunswick, 1934-37; clin. psychol. Montreal Neurol. Inst., 1937-41; research asso., dept. neuropsychiatry U. of Wis., 1942-45; research and psychol., pvt. practice, N.Y.C., 1945; prof. research clin. psychology, dept. of psychiatry Temple Univ. Med. Center, Phila.; now prof. psychology New Sch. Social Research, N.Y.C.; research dir. Ct. Intake Project, Manhattan Children's Court, 1952-54; vis. lectr. psychiatry, U. Tex., Medical Br. Galveston, Tex., 1953-55; vis. prof. psychology New Sch. Social Research, N.Y., 1962-67, U. Fla., 1968—; psychol. cons. Dept. of State, Washington, 1947; vice chmn. exec. com., bd. govs., Internat. Com. for Mental Health, 1947; cons., mem. tech. adv. com. Air Surgeon Gen.'s Office, 1948-51; cons. in psychology U.S. Army; chmn. adv. council in psychology State Ed. Dept., U. N.Y.; editor Am. Lecture Series in Psychology 1946—; adv. bd., Am. Soc. for Research in Psychosomatic Problems, 1947. Fellow Rorschach Inst. (past pres.). Mem. Am., British, Canadian psychol. Assns., Nat. Com. for Mental Hygiene, New York Acad. Scis. Democrat. Church of England. Author books including: Time to Squander, Time to Reap, 1946; Appraising Personality, 1952; Personality Change and Development, 1959; The Practice of Clinical Psychology, 1961; Psychodiagnostic Testing; An Empirical Approach, 1965. Address: Sound Rd Greenport NY 11944 ☆

HARRY, K.J., gas co. exec. Comptroller, Consumers' Gas Co., Toronto, Ont., Can. Office: 19 Toronto St Toronto 1 Ontario Canada*

HARRY, ROBERT LEE, A.R.C. exec.; b. Sharon, Pa., Mar. 27, 1918, s. Fred L. and Lorena (Heile) H.; student Pa. State U. extension, 1939-40, A.R.C. Mgmt. Devel. Sch., 1955, pub. relations Am. U., 1958; m. Donna M. Smith, Sept. 27, 1941; children—Dianne, Robert. With Pa. Dept. Unemployment Compensation, 1937-38, Pa. Dept. Pub. Assistance, 1939-41; with A.R.C., 1942—, dir. fund raising Eastern area, 1955-57, asst. dir. nat. fund raising, 1957-59, nat. dir. fund raising, 1959—. Home: 2000 Basset St Alexandria VA 22308 Office: Am Nat Red Cross 17th and E Sts Washington DC 20006

HARSCH, JOSEPH C., journalist; b. Toledo, May 25, 1905; s. Paul Arthur and Leila Kathrine (Close) H.; A.B., Williams Coll., 1927, M.A. (hon.); B.A., Corpus Christi Coll., Cambridge (Eng.) U., 1929; m. Anne Elizabeth Wood, Dec. 11, 1932; children—J. William Wood, Jonathan Hannum, Paul Arthur, III. With Christian Sci. Monitor, 1929—, corr. Wash. bur., 1931- 39, corr. Rome, then Berlin, 1939-41, fgn. affairs columnist, 1952—, chief editorial writer, 1971—; asst. dir. Intergovtl. Com. (on leave from Monitor), 1939; news commentator CBS, 1943-49; news commentator NBC, 1953-67, sr. European corr., 1957-65, diplomatic corr., 1965-67; commentator ABC, 1967-71. Decorated comdr. Order Brit. Empire. Mem. Chi Psi. Christian Scientist. Clubs: Nat. Press, Metropolitan (Washington); Century (N.Y.C.); Garrick, St. James (London). Author: Pattern of Conquest, 1941; The Curtain Isn't Iron, 1950. Address: Highland Dr Jamestown RI 02835

HARSH, DAVID NEWBY, lawyer, banker; b. Gallatin, Tenn., Sept. 30, 1897; s. George and Thankful (Barry) H.; LL.B., Cumberland U., 1917; m. Helen Russ Westervelt, Oct. 15, 1919; children—Jane (Mrs. Edward Vieh, Jr.), David Newby, George Westervelt, Ruth (Mrs. Lukin Taylor Gilliland). Admitted to Tenn. bar, 1917; practice in Memphis, 1917-56; partner firm Harsh & Harsh, 1917-27, Harsh, Harsh & Harsh, 1927-43, Harsh, Pierce, Cochran, Rickey & Carey, 1943-56; chmn., commr. finance, purchases, personnel Shelby County (Tenn.) Commn., 1956-62, ret., 1962; now spl. counsel Harsh, Harsh & Crawford, Memphis. Co-owner, v.p., dir. Georgian Woods, Inc., Desoto Land Co.; dir. First Nat. Bank of Upper Keys (Fla.), mem. loan com., 1969—. Mem. Tenn. Def. Commn., 1940-42; chmn. Memphis Bd. Adjustment, 1939-55; mem. Memphis Planning Commn., 1939-55; chmn. Shelby County Planning Commn., 1939-55; chmn. Shelby County Bd. Adjustment, 1965—. Vice pres. bd. Heart Assn. Upper Keys (Miami). Served to 2d lt., F.A., U.S. Army, 1918. Mem. Am. Legion (past mem. exec. com. from Tenn.), Nat. Assn. Real Estate Bds., S.A.R., Isaac Walton League. Conglist. Mason (Shriner). Clubs: Rivermont (Memphis), Islamorada Fishing (pres., bd. dirs.); Ocean Reef (North Key Largo, Fla.). Author: Private Acts of Shelby County, 1960. Initiated before U.S. Supreme Ct. case requiring all states to reapportion their legislatures. Home: Route 1 Box 40F Islamoradar FL 33036 Office: Chamber Commerce Bldg Islamorader FL 33036 also Commerce Title Bldg Memphis TN 38103

HARSHA, WAYNE, trade jour. editor; b. Ellenboro, W.Va., May 2, 1905; s. Arthur V. and Nellie Mae (Lightner) H.; A.B., Otterbein Coll., 1927; M.A., Ohio State U., 1941. Mng. editor U.S. Printer and Pub., 1927-32, Nat. Printer-Journalist, 1932-38, The Printing Industry, 1935-38, also asst. plant supt. Williamson Press (all Springfield, Ill.); faculty mem. Sch. Journalism, adviser to student publs. Ohio State U., 1939-51; editor Inland Printer Am. Lithographer, Chgo., 1951—. Alumni adv. council Sch. Journalism, Ohio State U. Mem. Internat. Assn. Printing House Craftsmen, Soc. Typographic Arts, Internat. Graphic Arts Edn. Assn., Typocrafters, Tech. Assn. Graphic Arts, Ohio State U. Assn., N. Side (Chgo.) Printers Guild, Am. Bus. Press, Inc., Am. Soc. Bus. Press Editors, Indsl. Editors Assn. Chgo., Assn. Edn. in Journalism, Otterbein Coll. Alumni Assn., Chgo. Bus. Publs. Assn., Kappa Tau Alpha, Sigma Delta Chi, Alpha Delta Sigma, Phi Alpha Theta, Alpha Phi Omega. Republican. Methodist. Clubs: Chicago Printing House Craftsmen, Calumet Ben Franklin, Paper of Chicago, Chicago Press, Lithographers-of Chicago, Chicago Headline. Home: 2811 W Tennyson Pl Hazel Crest IL 60429 Office: 300 W Adams St Chicago IL 60606

HARSHA, WILLIAM HOWARD, congressman; b. Portsmouth, O., Jan. 1, 1921; s. William Howard and Imogene (Matthews) H.; A.B., Kenyon Coll., 1943; LL.B., Western Res. U., 1947; m. Rosemary Spellerberg, Sept. 28, 1946; children—Bill, Mark, Bruce, Brian. Admitted to Ohio bar, 1947; asst. city solicitor, Portsmouth, 1947-51; prosecutor Scioto County, 1951-55; practice in Portsmouth, 1947-61; mem. 87th-92d Congresses, 6th Ohio Congl. Dist. Chmn. Portsmouth Charity Horse Show, 1960, Scioto County Tb and Health Assn., 1948-49. Bd. dirs. Scioto County Cancer Soc., 1958-59, Portsmouth chpt. A.R.C., 1956—. Served with USMCR, World War II. Recipient Outstanding Citizenship award Portsmouth Community Chest, 1959. Mem. Farm Bur., Scioto Valley Grange, Scioto County Agrl. Assn., Portsmouth Bar Assn., Amateur Trapshooting Assn. (life), Bus. and Profl. Mens Club Portsmouth, Am. Legion, 40 and 8, D.A.V. Republican. Mason, Odd Fellow, Elk. Club: Portsmouth Exchange. Home: 2021 Sunrise Av Portsmouth OH 45662 also 1102 Delf Dr McLean VA 22101 Office: House Office Bldg Washington DC 20515

HARSHA, WILLIAM NEWCOMB, Jr., food products mfg. exec.; b. Haskell, Okla., Nov. 16, 1917; s. William N. and Florastine H.; grad. U. Cal. at Los Angeles, 1939, Adv. Mgmt. Program, Harvard, 1960; m. Mary Jo Needham, Nov. 1, 1940; children—Carol Lynne, Constance Louise, Kristen Elizabeth. Salesman, Campbell Soup Co., 1939-40; sales and marketing positions Pet Milk Co., 1940-51, regional sales mgr., 1951-56, mng. dir. Pet Milk Can., Ltd., 1956-58; gen. mgr. frozen foods div., 1958- 59, gen. product mgr. milk products div., 1959-60, v.p., asst. to pres., 1960-62, pres. milk products div., 1962-64, pres. snack foods div., 1964- 65; now dir., group v.p. Pet, Inc., 1965-67, exec. v.p. operations, mem. exec. com., 1968—, dir., 1967—; dir. Stuckey's, Inc., Matutano y Petmilk, S.A., Spain, AB Estrella, Sweden. Served with AUS, 1943-46. Republican. Episcopalian. Mason. Clubs: Bellerive Country, University (St. Louis); Jonathan (Los Angeles); Harvard Business School. Home: 40 Portland Dr St Louis MO 63131 Office: Pet Plaza 400 S 4th St St Louis MO 63166

HARSHAW, DAVID HARE, bus. exec.; b. Phila., March 6, 1904; s. Edward and Margaret Lyons (Jamison) H.; B.S., in Econs., U. Pa., 1926; postgrad. Temple U. Law Sch., 1927-28; D.Sc., Stetson U., 1955; m. Frances Darlington Drewes, 1930; children—David Hare, Adele Drewes Smith. With U.G.I. Contracting Co., 1926-29, United Engrs. and Constrn. Co., 1929-35; with John B. Stetson Co., 1935—, sec. and treas., 1931, asst. treas., 1939, v.p. and treas., 1945, pres., dir., 1947-66, vice chmn., 1966—; dir. North City Corp., Phila. Employment Devel. Corp., John B. Stetson Co. of Can., Ltd., 1st Pa. Corp., 1st Pa. Banking & Trust Co., Am. Mut. Ins. Cos. Bd. dirs. St. Luke's and Children's Med. Center, Phila., Greater Phila. Movement; chmn. Citizens Budget Com.; past pres. YMCA, Phila.; bd. dirs. West Park Hosp., Phila.; trustee Stetson U., Deland, Fla. Mem. Pa. C. of C. (past pres.), Phi Kappa Tau. Republican. Mem. Plymouth Brethren Meeting. Clubs: Union League, Philadelphia Country (Phila.). Home: 537 Brookfield Rd Drexel Hill PA 19026 Office: 5th St and Montgomery Av Philadelphia PA 19111

HARSHAW, MARGARET, opera singer; b. Phila.; d. David and Mary Ann (Rogers) H.; grad. Juilliard Sch. Music; pupil Mme. Schoen-Rene; m. Oskar Eichna; children—Oskar, Margaret. Debut as contralto as second Norn, Goetterdaemmerung, Met. Opera, N.Y.C., 1942; as contralto sang Amneris, Azucena, Erda, Ortrud, Herodias, and several other roles; sang with San Francisco, Mexico Nacional, Cin. opera cos.; appeared with Paris Grand Opera, 1948; debut as soprano Met. Opera, 1950, Senta in The Flying Dutchman; currently appears as the three Brunnhildes in Die Walküre, Siegfried, Goetterdaemmerung; Sieglinde in Die Walküre; Isolde in Tristan and Isolde; Elisabeth in Tannhäuser Kundre in Parsifal; Donna Anna in Don Giovanni; regular concert tours throughout U.S.; has performed various music festivals; mem. faculty Sch. Music, Ind. Sigma Alpha Iota. Office: 147 W 39th St New York City NY 10018

HARSHBARGER, BOYD, educator; b. Weyers Cave, Va., Feb. 15, 1906; s. John A. and Eugenia (Tutwiler) H.; A.B., Bridgewater Coll., 1928, D. Sc., 1955; M.S., Va. Poly. Inst., 1931; A.M., U. Ill., 1935; Ph.D. (Rockefeller fellow 1939- 41), George Washington U., 1943; postgrad. U. N.C., 1940, Ia. State Coll., 1941-42; m. Isabelle Hoge, Sept. 5, 1935; children—John Hoge, Barbara Hume (Mrs. Charles Church). Instr. Miller (Va.) Sch. 1929-30; instr. Va. Poly. Inst., 1931-37, asst. prof. math., 1937-39, prof. statistics, 1941- 48, head dept. statistics, dir. statis. lab., 1948—; statistician Va. Agrl. Expt. Sta., Blacksburg, 1941-48; tchr. quality control courses Princeton, U. N.C., Va. Poly. Inst., 1941-43; cons. ordnance dept. U.S. Army, 1949—; cons. U.S. Army Hercules, Inc., Poly Sci. Co., Pocahontas Coal Co. Mem. Denny Commn. Edn. Va., 1944. Recipient J. Shelton Horsely research award for meritorious research, 1946, Ivey F. Lewis Distinguished Service award Va. Acad. Sci., 1966. NATO sr. fellow, 1969. Fellow Am. Statis. Assn. (mem. council 1956-58); mem. Inst. Math. Statistics, Biometric Soc. (pres. 1957), Va. Acad. Sci. (pres. 1949-50), A.A.A.S., Va. Edn. Assn., Am. Assn. U. Profs., Sigma Xi. Author (booklet); Rectangular Lattices, Memoir No. L, 1947. Editor-in- chief, founder Va. Jour. Sci., 1950-55. Contbr. articles profl. jours. Home: 213 Country Club Dr SE Blacksburg VA 24060

HARSHBARGER, HENRY CLAY, educator; born Quimby, Ia., July 23, 1900; s. Charles Clay and Annie (Ford) H.; B.A., Grinnell Coll., 1922; M.A., Columbia, 1925; Ph.D., Cornell U., 1929; m. Gretchen

Fischer, Sept. 1, 1928; children—Frederick, Karl. Instr. Grinnell Coll., 1922-24, Ia. State Coll., 1925-26; successively asst. prof., asso. prof., prof. and chmn. dept. speech and dramatic art U. of Ia., 1929-68, prof. emeritus, 1968- -, asst. dean Coll. Liberal Arts, 1950-63 asso. dean, 1963-68; dean Cottey Coll., 1968-70. Recipient Lydia Roberts fellow, 1925-26, Rockefeller fellow, 1937, Ford fellow, 1952. Mem. Speech Assn. Am., Central States Speech Assn.; Am. Ednl. Theatre Assn., Phi Beta Kappa, Delta Sigma Rho. Kiwanian. Author: Television Techniques (with Samuel Becker), 1958. Address: Route 6 6 Longview Knoll Iowa City IA 52240

HARSHMAN, RICHARD RENVILLE, investment banker; b. Los Angeles, Aug. 21, 1926; s. Harry Charles and Marcelle (Dreyfus) H.; student Philips Andover Acad., 1939-43; B.A., Harvard, 1947, M.B.A., 1949; m. Mary Ashley Cooper Hewitt, Sept. 16, 1950; children—Edward Jay, Cecily Cooper, Thomas Ringwood. Trainee, J.P. Morgan & Co., Inc., N.Y.C., 1949-50; asst. to pres. W. India Comml. Co., Ltd., N.Y.C., 1950-51; asso. G.L. Ohrstrom & Co., N.Y.C., 1952-54, ltd. partner, 1954-55, gen. partner, 1956—; sec. Carlisle Corp.; dir. Tensolite Insulated Wire Co., Inc., Tarrytown, N.Y., Internat. Wire Products, Inc., Midland Park, N.J., Lockwood Mfg. Co., Cin., Leigh Products, Inc., Coopersville, Mich., Korth Furniture Industries, Warsaw, Ind., Subscription TV, Inc., Los Angeles, Leach Corp., Los Angeles, Vistan Corp., San Leandro, Cal., Jasper Cabinet Co. (Ind.), Trustee Cooper Union for Advancement Sci. and Art, N.Y.C. Office: 540 Madison Av New York City NY 10022

HART, ALBERT GALLORD, economist; b. Oak Park, Ill., Mar. 9, 1909; s. Hastings Hornell and Josephine (Newton) H.; B.A. in Economics, summa cum laude, Harvard, 1930; grad. study. U. Chgo. 1931-36, Ph.D., 1936; studed in Vienna and Germany, 1930-31, London, 1934-35; m. Ann Elizabeth Webster, July 27, 1936; children—Josephine W. (Mrs. Melvin Bristol), Mary Gailord (Mrs. Robert Lewis), Stephen Albert. Sheldon travelling fellow Harvard, 1930-31; asso. prof. econs. Ia. State Coll., 1939-42, prof., 1942-45; research econ. Com. Econ. Devel., 1945-46; vis. prof. econ. Columbia, 1946-47, prof., 1947—, chmn. econs. dept., 1958-61, Ford faculty research fellow, 1956-57; cons. expert U.S. Treasury 1943-53, 61—; adviser to minister of finance, Santiago, Chile, 1961-62; tax expert Mexico, Orgn. Am. States, 1963; adviser Consejo Nacionale de Desarrollo, Argentina, 1964; research dir. econ. stablzn. project, 20th Century Fund, 1949-52; research asso. Inst. de Science Economique Appliquee, Paris, 1952-53; draftsman proposals, Ways and Means Com., May 1941, by 178 economists; presented proposals in conjuntion with S. E. Harris, advocating taxing at source; presented further version of proposals on behalf of research economists in War Finance Study, Ia. State Coll., Mar. 1942. Fulbright prof. Germany, 1967, Uruguay, 1968. Fellow of the Royal Econ. Soc.; mem. Am. Econ. Assn., Am. Assn. U. Profs., Econmetric Soc., Century Assn., Phi Beta Kappa. Author books including: Money, Debt and Econ. Activity, 1948, 53, 61, 69; Defense Without Inflation, 1951; Financing Defense (with E. C. Brown), 1951; Defense and the Dollar, 1953; pamphlets. Co- author publs. inc.: Jobs and Markets in the Transition, 1946; Social Framework of the American Economy, 1945, 55; Economic Order, 1958; International Compensation for Fluctuations in Commodity Trade, 1961. Contbr. articles and revs. Home: 54 Morningside New York City NY 10025 Office: Fayerweather Hall Columbia U New York City NY 10027 ☆

HART, ALBERT MOSES, telephone co. exec.; b. N.Y.C., Mar. 15, 1919; s. Sydney Moses and Antoinette (Hart) H.; A.B., U. Cal. at Los Angeles, 1940; LL.B., Stanford, 1947; m. Dorothy (Judy) Saye, May 11, 1947. Admitted to Cal. bar, 1948; adjudicator VA, Oakland, Cal., 1948-49; with Gen. Telephone Co. Cal., Santa Monica, 1949—, sec., gen. atty., 1957-67, v.p., gen. counsel, sec., 1967—, also dir.; dir. Western Cal. Telephone Co. Served to comdr. USNR, 1941-45, 51-52. Mem. Am., Cal. bar assns., Conf. Cal. Pub. Utility Counsel (chmn. 1964), Am. Soc. Corp. Secs., Town Hall Los Angeles. Club: Jonathan (Los Angeles). Home: 972 Norman Pl Los Angeles CA 90049 Office: 2020 Santa Monica Blvd Santa Monica CA 90406

HART, ALEXANDER HENDRY, railroad ofcl.; b. Regina, Sask., Can., July 17, 1918; s. Alexander and Mary (Davidson) H.; B.Sc., Dalhousie U., 1939, LL.B., 1947; m. Janet MacMillan Mackay, June 5, 1948; children—Mary, Colin, Sandy, John. Called to N.S. bar, 1947; with C.N. Ry. Co., 1949—. v.p. traffic, 1960, v.p. sales, 1960-67, v.p. for marketing, 1967-71, sr. v.p., 1971—; dir. Duluth, Winnipeg & Pacific R.R. Served to maj. Royal Canadian Arty., 1939-45. Mem. Canadian Bar Assn., N.S. Barristers Soc., Montreal Traffic Club, Canadian Ry. Club. Nat. Freight Traffic Assn., Newcomen Soc. N.Am., Phi Kappa Pi. Presbyn. Clubs: Shaughnessy Golf & Country; Pine Valley Golf; Union of Victoria; Mount Royal; Royal Montreal Golf; Laurentian Lodge. Home: 3676 Pine Crescent Vancouver British Columbia Canada Office: Suite 2000 777 Hornby St Vancouver 1 British Columbia Canada

HART, BUDDY WARREN, lawyer; b. Promise City, Ia., Mar. 19, 1923; s. Harry Henry and Alfreda (DeBolt) H.; B.A., State U. Ia., 1946; LL.B., Harvard, 1950; m. Beverly Ann Brynjolfson, June 19, 948; children—Linda Jo, Dianne Adair, Patricia Ann, Barbara Bryn, Blake Warren. Admitted to Minn. bar, 1950; law clk. Chief Justice Minn. Supreme Ct., St. Paul, 1950; partner Moore, Costello & Hart, St. Paul, 1951—; instr. trust law Wm. Mitchell Coll. Law, 1954-55; atty. City of West St. Paul, 1959-60; mem. Minn. Supreme Ct. Lawyers Adv. Com., 1966-67; chmn. Ramsey County Ct. rules and procedures com., 1967-68; mem. lawyers adv. com. U. Minn. Law Sch., 1966- 67; lectr. Engring. Inst. on Constrn. Contracts and Specifications, U. Wis., 1966, Plant Engring. and Maintenance and Indsl. Bldg. Conf., Phila., 1968, Constrn Specifications Inst., Denver, 1968, fidelity and surety law com., sect. of ins., negligence and compensation law Am. Bar Assn., St. Louis, 1970. Mem. Mayor's Com. on Drug Abuse, 1969-70; mem. St. Paul Urban Coalition Housing Task Force, 1969—. Chmn. Ramsey County Elmer L. Anderson Gubernatorial campaign, 1960; chmn. campaigns all Republican candidates Minn. Constl. Offices, 1962. Bd. dirs. St. Paul Community Chest, St. Croix Valley council Girl Scouts Am.; mem. exec. com. Indianhead council Boy Scouts Am. Served to capt., inf., AUS, 1942- 46; ETO. Decorated Bronze Star medal, Purple Heart with oak leaf cluster; recipient Distinguished Service award St. Paul Jr. C. of C., 1956; named Outstanding Chpt. Pres., Minn. Jr. C. of C., 1957. Mem. St. Paul Jr. C. of C. (past pres.), Am. Judicature Soc., Am., Minn., Ramsey County bar assns., Am. Arbitration Assn., Law-Sci. Acad., Am. Legion, Phi Beta Kappa, Delta Sigma Rho. Presbyn. (trustee). Home: 188 Amherst St St Paul MN 55105 Office: Northwestern Nat Bank Bldg St Paul MN 55101

HART, C ALAN, Jr., lawyer; b. St. Paul, Oct. 7, 1909; A.B., Stanford, 1931; LL.B., Yale, 1934. Admitted to Ore. bar, 1934, U.S. Supreme Ct. bar, 1939; instr. Yale Law Sch., 1934-35; asst. U.S. atty., Ore., 1936-38; spl. asst. to U.S. atty. gen., U.S. Dept. Justice, Washington, 1938-39; gen counsel Bonnevile Power Adminstrn., 1939-42; now mem. firm Lindsay, Nahstoll, Hart, Duncan, Dafoe & Krause, Portland, Ore. Mem. Am., Multnomah County bar assns., Ore. State Bar. Office: Loyalty Bldg 317 SW Alder St Portland OR 97204*

HART, CHARLES EDWARD, ret. army officer; b. Ft. Washington, Md., June 17, 1900; s. James William and Grace Louise (Duncan) H.; B.S., U.S. Mil. Acad., 1924; grad. F.A. Sch., Ft. Sill, Okla., 1931, Command and Gen. Staff Sch., Ft. Leavenworth, Kan., 1942; grad. Nat. War Coll., Washington, 1947; m. Virginia Byrd Hereford, Jan. 7, 1925; children—Virginia Byrd Ramsey, Susie Jane Forman, Sally Anne Adams. Commnd. 2d lt., Field Arty., U.S. Army, 1924, advanced through grades to lt. gen., 1954; asst. arty. officer, later arty. officer, II Corps, 1942-43, participated in North African invasion and campaigns in Tunisia and Sicily; arty. officer, First U.S. Army in Normandy invasion, continental operations, and redeployment to Pacific Theater, 1944-45; deputy chief of staff (operations) Hdqrs. First Army, 1945-47; asst. comdt., anti-air-craft and guided missile br., The Arty. Sch., Fort Bliss, Tex., 1947-48; comdg. gen. 1st Inf. Div. Arty., 1949-50; arty. comdr. Seventh Army, 1950-51; chief Joint U.S. Mil. Aid Group Greece 1951-53; condg. gen. Arty. Center, comdt. arty. sch., Ft. Sill, Okla., 1954; comdg. gen. V corps, Europe, 1954-56; comdg. gen. Second Army, 1956-57; comdg. gen. USARADCOM, 1957-60, ret. 1960; dir. armed forces dept. Harris, Upham & Co., Inc., 1961-65, v.p., 1965-71. Decorated Commednation Ribbon with metal pendant, the European Theatre ribbon with arrowhead and eight battle stars, Pacific Theater ribbon, Distinguished Service medal with oak leaf cluster, Legion of Merit with oak leaf cluster (U.S.); Legion of Honor, Croix de Guerre with palm (France); Order of Zuvorov II Class (Russia); Order de la Couronne de Chene, Comdr., Croix de Guerre (Luxembourg). Clubs: Army and Navy, Army- Navy Country (Washington). Home: 1701 Oak Lane McLean VA 22101

HART, CONSTANCE GRAY, assn. exec.; b. Bklyn., Feb. 28, 1896; d. Percy R. and Emma (King) Gray; grad. Bklyn. Heights Sem., 1914; student Child Edn. Found., Montessori Normal, 1916-18; m. Jes Jessen Dall, Jr., Nov. 24, 1917 (dec. June 1942); children—Jes Jessen III, Joan (Mrs. Edward C. Patton); m. 2d, Merwin K. Hart, Dec. 9, 1961 (dec. Nov. 1962). Asst. tchr. Montessori dept. Bklyn. Heights Sem., 1915; prodn. control Sperry Gyroscope Co., 1943-44, buyer, 1944-46; with Nat. Econ. Council, Inc., 1946-68, v.p., dir., 1951-58, exec. v.p., 1958-68, dir., 1968—. Dir. emergency com. German Protestantism, N.Y.C. Bd. dirs., v.p. Ithaca (N.Y.) Community Chest, Girl Scouts Am., other civic groups, 1927-42. Republican. Episcopalian. Clubs: Women's National Republican (nat. council); Quantuck Beach; Westhampton Beach. Home: 200 E 66th St New York City NY 10021

HART, CYRIL SPEARING, ins. cons.; b. Port Washington, L.I., N.Y., May 1, 1916; s. Frederick Charles and Margaret Amy (Brown) H.; student Monmouth Jr. Coll., 1933- 34, Boston U., 1934-35; m. Anna Muriel Alcott, Dec. 22, 1939; children—Cynthia Ann, Frederick Charles. With Employers' Liability Assurance Corp., Boston, 1935-41, Gen. Accident Fire & Life Assurance Corp., Ltd., 1941-50; casualty prodn. mgr. Boston Old Colony Ins. Co., 1950-53, asst. to pres., 1953-54, asst. sec., 1954-55, pres., 1955-67, now dir. trustee Boston Five Cents Savs. Bank. Vice pres., trustee New Eng. Bapt. Hosp.; trustee Gordon Coll. Home: 82 Country Club Dr Yarmouth Port MA 02675

HART, D. JACK, mfg. co. exec.; b. 1916; B.S., Northwestern U., 1938; married. With Joslyn Mfg. and Supply Co., Chgo., 1939—, now treas., asst. sec., dir. Address: 155 N Wacker Dr Chicago IL 60606

HART, DON LEROY, mfg. co. exec.; b. Anaheim, Cal., Nov. 26, 1928; s. C.L. and Evelyn (Swank) H.; student Chgo. Coll. Physio Therapy, 1951; m. Wanda Beghtel, Feb. 28, 1946; children—Jon Kelly, Steven Eric, Jeri Lynn. Nat. sales dir. Richardson Homes Corp., Elkhart, Ind., 1951-61; exec. v.p. Elcona Homes Corp., Elkhart, 1961-62; pres. Monarch Industries, Middlebury, Ind., 1962—, Regent Homes Corp., Middlebury, 1964—; owner Diamondd D Industries, Elkhart, 1962—. Sec. bd. govs. Mobile Homes Mfrs. Assn., 1965; mem. Legislative and Transp. Nat. Com., 1964—. Active Elkhart (Ind.) Crippled Childrens Center; past adviser Jr. Achievement Am. Served with AUS, 1946-49. Mem. Nat. Assn. Accountants, Sales and Advt. Execs. Assn. Am. Elk. Home: 168 Gage St Elkhart IN 46515 Office: Box 441 Middlebury IN 46540

HART, DONALD JOHN, coll. pres.; b. Milw., Aug. 9, 1917; s. Edward William and Minnie Marie (Keller) H.; A.B., Lake Forest (Ill.) Coll., 1938; M.A., U. Wis., 1941, Ph.D., 1951; m. Margaret Ellen Thorpe, June 22, 1940; children—Roger, Susan (Mrs. Stephen R. Johnston), Charles, Mary. Dir. publicity Lake Forest Coll., 1938-40; grad. asst. econs. U. Wis., 1940-41, 1946-47; chief priorities clk. purchasing dept., Allis-Chalmers Mfg. Co., Milw., 1941; asst. bus. mgr. Ia. State Coll., 1942-43; asso. prof. econs. Carroll Coll., 1947-50; dean sch. bus. adminstrn. U. Ida., 1950-56, U. Fla., 1956-68; prof. mgmt. Va. Poly. Inst., 1968-69; pres. St. Andrews Presbyn. Coll., Laurinburg, N.C., 1969—. Vice pres. Ida. Inst. Christian Edn., 1952-56. Pub. mem., chmn. adv. council Employment Security Agy., Ida., 1950-56. Trustee Fla. Presbyn. Coll., 1961-65. Served as lt. supply corps USNR, 1943-46. Mem. So. Econ. Assn., Laurinburg C. of C. (bd. dirs.), Am. Assn. Collegiate Schs. Bus. (exec. com., sec.-treas. 1965-66, pres. 1967-68), President's Assn. (deans' adv. council), Am. Acad. Mgmt. Presbyn. (ruling elder). Rotarian. Author: Business in a Dynamic Society, 1963; Introduction to Business in a Dynamic Society, 1970. Contbr. Ency. Britannica Book of Year, 1948-65. Home: 612 S Main St Laurinburg NC 28352

HART, DWIGHT HOWARD, Jr., hotel exec.; b. Los Angeles, Sept. 10, 1921; s. Dwight Howard and Mable Sophie (Runge) H.; student Harvard Mil. Sch., 1932-38; B.S., A.B., U. So. Cal., 1938-42; 1 dau., Rosslyn Diane (Mrs. Harry L. Whitaker, Jr.). Vice pres., dir. Allied Properties (owners Clift Hotels, San Francisco, Santa Barbara Biltmore Hotel); gen. mgr. Clift Hotel. Mem. Am. (dir.), Cal. (past pres.) hotel assns., Hotel Greeters Am., Phi Kappa Alpha. Mason (Shriner). Clubs: Burlingame (Cal.) Country; Bohemian, Pacific Union, Olympia (San Francisco). Office: Clift Hotel Geary and Taylor Sts San Francisco CA 94101

HART, EDWIN JAMES, chemist; b. Port Angeles, Wash., Feb. 7, 1910; s. Fitch James and Josie Anna Elizabeth (Blater) H.; B.S., M.S., Wash. State Coll.; Ph.D., Brown U., 1934; m. Rozella Patricia Clark, June 17, 1939; children—Fitch J., Ann E., John P. With L.I. Biol. Lab., 1934-36, U.S. Rubber Co., 1936-48; sr. chemist Argonne Nat. Lab., 1948—; Brit. Empire Cancer Campaign fellow Mt. Vernon Hosp., Eng., 1961-62. Vis. prof. Hebrew U., Israel, fall 1967. Mem. quartermaster dosimetry panel Nat. Acad. Sci., 1955-58, radiobiology com., 1958-64, food irradiation com., 1963—; del. 2d UN Internat. Conf. on Peaceful Uses Atomic Energy, Geneva, 1958; mem. Internat. Com. on Radiol. Units, 1960-63; cons. Danish Atomic Energy Commn., 1967—; Internat. Atomic Energy Agy. cons. to Bhabha Atomic Research Centre, Trombay, India, winter 1970; mem. scientific staff U.S. Atoms in Action Program, Tehran, Iran, 1967; vis. prof. Hebrew U., Israel, 1967. Mem. Am. Chem. Soc., A.A.A.S., Radiation Research Soc., Faraday Soc., Research Soc. Am., Phi Beta Kappa, Sigam Xi, Phi Kappa Phi, Phi Lambda Upsilon. Author (with M. Anbar) The Hydrated Electron, 1970. Home: 740 S Bodin St Hinsdale IL 60521 Office: 9700 S Cass Av Argonne IL 60439

HART, ERIC MULLINS, corp. exec.; born Clanton, Ala., May 6, 1925; s. Eric and Myrtle (Mullins) H.; B.S., U. Ala., 1946; m. Joy Porter, May 16, 1953; children—Anne Porter, Eric Mullins. With Internat. Paper Co., 1946-69, asst. to v.p.-treas., 1962-64, comptroller, 1964-69; treas. Red River Paper Mill, Inc., 1964-69; financial v.p., dir. Lever Bros. Co., 1969—. Mem. Sigma Alpha Epsilon. Home: 95 Pembroke Rd Darien CT 06280 Office: 390 Park Av New York City NY 10022

HART, FREDERICK DONALD, assn. exec.; b. N.Y.C., May 12, 1915; s. Lewis T. and Charlotte (Hyde) H.; M.E., Cornell U., 1936, M.M.E., 1937; m. Ann Wright, Apr. 18, 1942; children—Anne, Charlotte, Jane. Mgmt. engr. E.I. duPont de Nemours Co., 1937-44; exec. v.p. Temco, Inc., Nashville, 1944-57, pres., 1957-64; pres. Lear Siegler Internat., 1964-66; adminstrv. dir. Am. Gas Assn., N.Y.C., 1966-68, mng. dir., 1968-71, pres., 1971—; dir. 1st Am. Nat. Bank, Indusmin Ltd., Clarendon Trust Co. Past pres. Inst. Appliance Mfrs., Gas Appliance Mfrs. Assn. Mem. Am. Ordnance Assn. (v.p. 1958-63), N.A.M. (v.p. 1960-65), Nashville C. of C. (past pres.), Cornell U. Council, Am. Nat. Standards Inst. (mem. bd.). Clubs: Belle Meade Country (Nashville); Cornell, Union League, Pinnacle (N.Y.C.). Home: 1001 Wilson Blvd Arlington VA 22209 Office: 1515 Wilson Blvd Arlington VA 22209

HART, GEORGE A., Jr., lawyer; b. Los Angeles, Jan. 19, 1914; s. George A. and Lillian (York) H.; A.B., U. So. Cal. 1935, LL.B., 1938; m. Beatrice Green, Sept. 28, 1938; children—Patricia (Mrs. Michael Bradbury), George A. III. Admitted to Cal. bar, 1938; asso. firm Denio, Taubman, Hart & Simpson, Long Beach, 1938-41; chief leasing and disposal br., div. engring. War Dept., Los Angeles, 1942-45; partner firm Ball, Hunt, Hart & Brown, Long Beach, 1945—. A founder, chmn. bd. Bank of Long Beach, N.A.; co-owner, developer Pacific Holiday Tower Apts., Long Beach. Pres. bd. dirs. Tichenor Orhopedic Clinic, Long Beach; bd. dirs., officer Long Beach Heart Assn., Long Beach Community Chest; past pres. Community Vol. Office, Long Beach; bd. dirs. Long Beach Meml. Hosp. Mem. Am., Cal., Los Angeles, Long Beach bar assns., Phi Kappa Tau, Phi Alpha Delta. Clubs: Alamits Bay Yacht (past commodore); Los Angeles Yacht; Catalina Tuna. Home: 5670 Camp Walk Long Beach CA 90803 Office: 120 Linden Av Long Beach CA 90802

HART, GEORGE ARNOLD REEVE, banker; b. Toronto, Can., Apr. 2, 1913; s. George S. and Laura M. (Harrison) H.; student high sch., Toronto; LL.D., U. Sask., 1961, U. Montreal, 1962; D.C.L., Bishop's Univ., 1963, Acadia U., 1970; D.Comml. Sci. (hon.), U. Sherbrooke, 1965; m. Jean C. Gilbert, Sept. 2, 1939 (dec. 1960); 1 dau., Diane (Mrs. J.M. Hodgkin); m. 2d, Patricia I. Plant, Dec. 8, 1961. With Bank Montreal, Toronto, 1931—, various positions brs. in Toronto, Western Can., N.Y. Agy., successivly supt. head office, asst. gen. mgr., dep. gen. mgr., gen. mgr., 1931-58, v.p., dir., 1958-59, pres., 1959-67, chief exec. officer, 1959—, chmn. bd., exec. com., 1964—; dir., mem. exec. com. Consol-Bathurst, Ltd., Sun Life Assurance Co. Can. Internat. Nickel Co. of Can., Ltd.; dir. C.P. Ry. Co., Canadian Investment Fund, Ltd., Canadian Fund, Inc., Uniroyal Inc., Cominco, Ltd., United Aircraft Can. Ltd., Royal London & Lancashire Canadian Adv. Bd., Western Brit. Am. Assurance Cos. Group. Bd. dirs., Met. YMCA, Montreal; hon. v.p. St. John Ambulance, Que. council; bd. dirs. Canadian Exec. Service Overseas; hon. mem. nat. council, hon. v.p. Montreal region Boy Scouts Can.; Gov. Institut de Cardiologie de Montreal, McGill U.; mem. adv. bd. Sir George Williams U.; bd. dirs. Federated Appeal Greater Montreal; bd. mgmt. Montreal Neurol. Hosp. Served as maj. Canadian Army, World War II. Decorated Order Brit. Empire. Mem. Canadian Export Assn. (bd. govs.), Nat. Indsl. Conf. Bd., Canadian Trade Com., Canadian Assn. Latin Am. (gov.), La Chambre de Commerce des Jeunes du Dist. de Montreal (bd. govs.). Mem. Anglican Ch. Clubs: St. James's, Mt. Royal, Royal Montreal Golf, Forest and Stream, St. Denis (Montreal); Ranchmen's (Calgary); Royal Canadian Yacht, Toronto (Toronto); Laval-sur-le Lac; Mount Bruno Country (St. Bruno); Metroplitan (N.Y.C.). Home: 1700 McGregor St Montreal 109 Quebec Canada Office: 129 St James St W Montreal 126 Quebec Canada

HART, GEORGE DAVID, business exec.; b. San Francisco, Jan. 25, 1908; s. George Edward and Nettie (Hynes) H.; A.B., Stanford, 1931; grad. Q.M. Sch., 1943, Brit.-Am. Staff Sch., 1943, Command and Gen. Staff Coll., 1949; m. Jessica Wilbur Ely, June 6, 1946; children—George David, Margaret, Bruce, Douglas. Admitted to practice ICC; pres. George D. Hart, Inc., Farnsworth & Ruggles, Inc., Inglewood Realty Corp.; chmn. Asso. Investors No. Cal.; dir. Boston Mfrs. Mut. Ins. Co., Bank of San Rafael, 1st Nat. Bank San Rafael, Mut. Boiler Ins. Co., Liberty Mut. Fire Ins. Co., Liberty Mut. Ins. Co. Bd. govs. San Francisco Employers Council. Pres. Library Commn., 1947-53; mem. Art Commn. (City and County of San Francisco). Bd. dirs., v.p. San Francisco Art Assn.; bd. mem. Salvation Army, Columbia Park Boys Club; trustee Cal. State Coll. Commd. 2d lt., Q.M.U.S.A.R., 1931, dep. q.m., Normandy Base, 1944-45, active duty lt. to Col., 1945-46. Awarded Letter of Commendation, Certificate of Merit, Battle Participation Star, Bronze Star with oak leaf cluster, Mem. Am. Soc. Traffic and Transp. (founder mem.), Stanford Alumni Assn., Stanford Assos. (sec. 1935), V.F.W., Am. Legion (vice comdr. 1949), Res. Officers Assn. U.S. (pres. San Francisco chpt. 1946-47), Q.M. Assn. (pres. N. Cal. 1947-48), English Speaking Union U.S. (v.p., dir. 1948). Clubs: Bohemian, Family, Rotary, Commonwealth, Olympic (San Francisco); Athenian-Nile (Oakland); University (N.Y.C.); Commercial, Merchants (Boston); Duxbury (Mass.) Yacht. Home: PO Box 156 Ross CA 94957 Office: 111 Sutter St San Francisco CA 94104

HART, GEORGE JOSEPH, Jr., electronic co. exec.; b. Chgo., Mar. 15, 1918; s. George and Irene (Tobin) H.; student Ill. Inst. Tech., 1943; m. Annette Verdico, July 12, 1945; children—Georgeann, Richard, William. With Cinch Mfg. Co., Chgo., 1939—, pres., 1964—; exec. v.p. United Carr Inc., Boston, 1965—, also dir. Pres. Inst. Printed Circuits, 1966—. Home: 665 Cedar Elmhurst IL 60126 Office: 1500 Morse Av Elk Grove Village IL 60007

HART, GEORGE LUZERNE, Jr., U.S. judge; b. Roanoke Va., July 14, 1905; s. George Luzeren and Lavela (Slicer) H.; A.B., Va. Mil. Inst., 1927; LL.B., Harvard, 1930; m. Louise Neller, Oct. 12, 1935; 1 son. George Luzerne III. Admitted to D.C. bar, 1930, Va. bar, 1936; practice law with firm Lambert & Hart, 1930-40, Lambert, Hart & Northrop, 1946-58; judge U.S. Dist. Ct. D.C., 1958—. Home: 3901 Jenifer St NW Washington DC 20015 Office: US Courthouse Washington DC 20544

HART, HENRY, writer, editor; b. Phila., Sept. 14, 1903; s. Henry Gideon and Henrietta (Lehman) H.; student pub. schs., Phila.; m. Marian Ansbacher, 1935 (div. 1944); m. 2d, Elspeth Burke, 1953 (div. 1967); children—Henry, John. Reporter, Phila. Record, 1922-28; publicity dir. Charles Scribner's Sons, 1930-33; editor-in-chief G.P. Putnam's Sons, 1934-36; reader-cons. Macmillan Co., 1937-60; contbg. editor Time mag., 1943; asso. editor Fortune mag., 1944-46; editor Films in Review 1950—; treas. Nat. Bd. Rev. Motion Pictures, Inc., 1946—. Mem. Vets. of 7th Regt. Author: The Great One, 1934; Dr. Barnes of Merion, 1963. Editor: The American Writers Congress,

1935; The Writer in a Changing World, 1937. Home: 308 Pennsylvania Av Spring Lake NJ 07762 Office: 210 E 68th St New York City NY 10021

HART, HENRY COWLES, educator; b. Lucknow, India, Nov. 17, 1916; s. Henry G. and Helene B. (Baker) H.; came to U.S., 1926; B.A., Vanderbilt U., 1936; M.A., U. Wis., then Ph.D., 1950; m. Virginia L. Baily, Aug. 21, 1939; children—Nancy, Benjamin. Messenger to tng. specialist TVA, Knoxville, 1936-43; from instr. to prof. polit. sci. U. Wis., Madison, 1950—, chmn. dept. Indian studies, 1966-69; sr. specialist East- West Center U. Hawaii, 1966. Served to 2d lt., inf., AUS, 1943-46, Fulbright lectr., India, 1952-53. Mem. Am. Inst. Indian Studies (trustee, past sec.), Am. Polit. Sci. Assn., Am. Soc. Pub. Adminstrn., Assn. Asian Studies, Phi Beta Kappa. Author: New India's Rivers, 1956; The Dark Missouri, 1957; Campus India, 1961; The Village and Development Administration, 1967. Home: 1825 Summit Av Madison WI 53705

HART, J. EUGENE, Jr., advt. agy. exec. Sr. v.p., dir. promotion and marketings services Young and Rubicam, Inc., N.Y.C. Office: 285 Madison Av New York City NY 10017*

HART, JACK, lawyer; b. N.Y.C., Jan. 13, 1909; s. Harry and Clara (Mersack) H.; B.A., Coll. City N.Y., 1930; LL.B., Columbia, 1933; m. Rose Ratner, Aug. 15, 1937; children-William, Jane. Admitted to N.Y. bar, 1934; practice in N.Y.C., 1933—; asso. George Z. Medalie, 1933-38; pvt. practice, 1938- 50; partner Hart & Hume and predecessor firms, 1950—. Bd. dirs. Navy Yard Boys Club. Mem. Am. Bar Assn., N.Y. County Lawyers Assn. Club: Columbia University (N.Y.C.). Home: 400 E 56th St New York NY 10022 Office: 10 E 40th St New York NY 10016

HART, JAMES AUSTIN, coll. dean; b. Des Moines, Oct. 20, 1914; s. James F. and Anna (Canavan) H.; B.S., Fordham U., 1936, M.A., 1937, Ph.D., 1940; LL.B., Georgetown U., 1946; m. Marie Kelleher, Dec. 27, 1939; children—James, Elizabeth, Maureen, Denise, Patrick, Laurence, Margaret, Daniel, Vincent. Economist, mem. faculty Manhattan Coll., 1937-38; economist, mem. faculty DePaul U., 1938-40, dean Coll. Commerce, 1958—; economist, mem. faculty Fordham U., 1940-42, Creighton U., 1946-55; admitted to Neb. bar, 1947, also bars of Ill., N.Y., D.C., Iowa; law practice in Omaha, 1947-55; dean Sch. Bus. Adminstrn., Seton Hall U., 1955-57; practiced law, N.Y.C., 1957-58; lectr. fgn. bus. Dir. First Comml. Bank of Chgo. Democratic candidate for Congress, Neb. 2d Dist., 1952, 54. Bd. dirs. Arthur Schmitt Found., Chgo., Chgo. Council Fgn. Relations. Served lt. (j.g.) USNR, 1943-46. Mem. Assn. Edn. Internat. Bus. (pres. 1965-66), Assn. for Social Econs. (pres. 1963-64), Am. Mgmt. Assn., Am. Marketing Assn., Chgo. Assn. Commerce and Industry. Club: Chicago Athletic. Home: 294 Central Av Highland Park IL 60035 Office: 25 E Jackson Blvd Chicago IL 60604

HART, JAMES DAVID, educator; b. San Francisco, Apr. 18, 1911; s. Julien and Helen Louise (Neustadter) H.; A.B., Stanford, 1932; M.A., Harvard, 1933, Ph.D., 1936; m. Ruth Arnstein, June 14, 1938; children—Carol Helen (Mrs. John L. Field), Peter David. Instr., English, U. Cal. at Berkeley, 1936-41, asst. prof., 1941-47, asso. prof., 1947-51, prof., 1951—, chmn. dept., 1955-57, 65-69, vice chancellor, 1957-60; acting dir. Bancroft Library, 1961-62, dir., 1969—; vis. prof. Harvard, 1964. Chmn. Marshall Scholarship Com. Western U.S., 1959-63. Trustee Mills Coll., Oakland Museum Assn., Anna Head Sch. Decorated comdr. Order Brit. Empire. Fellow Am. Antiquarian Soc., Am. Acad. Arts and Scis.; mem. Modern Lang. Assn., Philol. Assn. Pacific Coast, Book Club of Cal. (pres. 1956-60). Clubs: Bohemian, Grolier, Faculty (Berkeley). Author: The Oxford Companion Am. Lit., 1941, rev. edits.; The Popular Book, 1950, 61; America's Literature (with C. Gohdes), 1955; American Images of Spanish California, 1960; The Private Press Ventures of Samuel Lloyd Osbourne and R.L.S., 1966. Editor: My First Publication, 1961; The Oregon Trail (Francis Parkman), 1963; From Scotland to Sliverado (Robert Louis Stevenson), 1966; A Novelist in the Making (Frank Norris), 1970. Contbr. articles to mags., revs. Home: 740 San Luis Rd Berkeley CA 94707

HART, JAMES KAULL, investment co. exec.; b. Newport, R.I., Aug. 8, 1913; s. Simon and Lena M. (Kaull) H.; B.A., Harvard, 1935, M.B.A., 1942; m. Virginia Hall, Dec. 24, 1936; children—Barbara (Mrs. George Corey), Suzanne (Mrs. Thomas Barnett), Virginia K. Asst. prof. Harvard Grad. Sch. Bus., 1942-50; asst. cashier Middlesex County Nat. Bank, 1950-53; asst. v.p. Bankers Trust Co., 1953-61; formerly exec. v.p., dir. Lehman Corp.; partner Lehman Bros., 1966. Home: 125 McKinley Av New Haven CT 06515

HART, JAMES WIRTH, mfg., ins. co. exec.; b. Trenton, N.J., July 31, 1933; s. Earle Russell and Mildred (Barnes) H.; B.S., Drexel U., 1955; M.B.A., U. Pitts., 1965; P.M.D., Harvard, 1965; m. N. Joanne Weber, Mar. 28, 1953; children—James Wirth, Steven Weber, Douglas Barnes, Jennifer Joanne Rife. Sr. staff and operating positions Westinghouse Electric Corp., Pitts., 1955-66; exec. asst. to chmn. and chief exec. officer Bendix Corp., Detroit, 1966-67; asst. office pres. ITT, N.Y.C., 1967-69; pres. Laird Enterprises, N.Y.C., 1969-71; chief operating officer Equity Corp., N.Y.C., 1971—; Mem. Am. Inst. Indsl. Engrs. (sr.), Theta Chi. Clubs: Racquet and Tennis, Union League, New York Athletic (N.Y.C.). Home: 12 Sherry Lane Darien CT 06820 Office: Equity Corp 299 Park Av New York City NY 10017

HART, JEFFREY, educator, author; b. N.Y.C., Feb. 24, 1930; s. Clifforf Francis and Cladys (Reith) H.; B.A., Columbia, 1952, Ph.D., 1962; M.A., Boston U., 1956; m. Stephanie Wiley Woods, Dec. 26, 1954; children—Benjamin, Emily, Rosemary, Matthew. Instr., then asst. prof. Columbia, 1956-63; faculty Dartmouth, 1963—, now prof. English; asso. editor Burke Newsletter; sr. editor Nat. Review; columnist King Features Syndicate, 1970—. Advisor to Gov. Reagan, 1968, Pres. Nixon, 1968. Bd. dirs. Am. Conservative Union, 1966—. Served to lt. USNR, 1953-56. Mem. Am. Assn. U. Profs. Author: Political Writers of 18th Centruy England; Viscount Bolingbroke: Tory Humanist, 1966; The American Dissent, 1966. Contbr. articles to profl. jours. Home: Pompanoosuc Norwich VT 05055 Office: Sanborn Hall Dartmouth Coll Hanover NH 03755

HART, JOHN FRASER, educator; b. Staunton, Va., Apr. 5, 1924; s. Freeman H. and Jean. B. (Fraser) H.; A.B., Emory U., 1943; M.A., Northwestern U., 1949, Ph.D., 1950; m. Meredith A. Davis, Feb. 5, 1949; children—Richard L., Meredith A. Asst., then asso. prof. U. Ga., 1949-55; from asst. prof. to prof. Ind. U., 1955-67; exec. sec. Assn. Am. Geographers, 1965-66; prof. geography U. Minn., Mpls., 1967—. Served with USNR, 1943-46. Recipient medaille de l'Université de Liège, 1960; Platinum Plow, U. Minn. geography grad. students, 1971. Fellow Am., Royal, Royal Scottish geog. socs.; mem. Assn. Am. Geographers (editor annals 1970—, citation for meritorious contbns. 1969), Pierce County Geog. Assn. (sec.), Inst. Brit. Geographers, Nat. Council Geog. Edn. Contbr. monographs, articles to profl. lit. Home: 4505 Drexel Av S Edina MN 55424 Office: Geography Dept U Minn Minneapolis MN 55455

HART, JOHN LATHROP JEROME, lawyer; b. Denver, Aug. 15, 1904; s. Richard Huson and Elizabeth (Jerome) H.; A.B., Harvard, 1925; B.A. in Jurisprudence (Rhodes scholar), Oxford U., Eng., 1927, B.C.L., 1928, M.A., 1932; m. Jane Kelsey, Oct. 19, 1935; children—Katherine (Mrs. Paul L. Zimmerman), Sally (Mrs. David V. Whiting), John. Trust dept. Colo. Nat. Bank, Denver, 1929-35; atty. RFC, Washington, 1935-37, Bur. Internal Revenue, Washington, 1937; admitted to Colo. bar, 1929. D.C. bar, 1937; asso. Henry McAllister in gen. practice of law, 1938-48; sr. partner Holland & Hart, Denver, 1948—. Various positions in reorganizing M.P. R.R., D. & R.G.W. R.R., others, 1942-61; gen. counsel Nat. Center Atmospheric Research; dir. Humphreys Engrng. Co., Robinson Brick & Tile Co., Boettcher Realty Co., Cement Investors, Inc., Gen. Securities Co.; adv. bd. United Bank of Denver. Mem. Assn. Bar City N.Y., Asso. Harvard Clubs (pres. 1960-61). Clubs: Denver Athletic, Denver Country; Harvard, Am. Alpine (pres. 1971—), Century Assn. (N.Y.C.); Alpine (London); Colo. Mountain (hon.), Colo. White Water; Bohemian (San Francisco). Author: Fourteen Thousand Feet, rev. edit., 1931. Home: 650 S Monroe Way Denver CO 80209 Office: Equitable Bldg Denver CO 80202

HART, JOHN LEWIS, cartoonist; b. Endicott, N.Y., Feb. 18, 1931: s. Irwin James and Grace Ann (Brown) H.; ed. pub. schs.; m. Bobby Ann Hatcher, Apr. 26, 1952; children—Patti Sue, Perri Ann. First nationally pub. cartoon appeared in Sat. Eve. Post, 1954; comic strip B.C. nat. syndicated, 1958—, The Wizard of Id, 1964—. Served with USAF, 1950-53; Korea. Recipient award for best humor strip Nat. Cartoonists Soc., 1967; named outstanding cartoonist of year, 1968. Mem. Nat. Comics Council, Nat. Cartoonists Soc. Author: Hey! B.C., 1959; Back to B.C., 1960; B.C. Strikes Back, 1961; The Sunday Best of B.C., 1964; What's New B.C.?; B.C. Big Wheel; B.C. Is Alive and Well; The King Is A Fink. Address: 639 Elm St Endicott NY 13762

HART, JOHN NATHANIEL, rubber co. exec.; b. Chesterhill, O., Nov. 30, 1909; s. Hiram and Lucy (Hambleton) H.; B.S., Ohio State U., 1931, M.A., 1932; m. Gertrude Fox, Oct. 21, 1933; children—Benson, Hannah, Sarah, John. Instr. Ohio State U., 1933-43; dir. research Ohio Dept. Taxation, 1933-43; economist B.F. Goodrich Co., Akron, O., 1945-52, dir. personnel Akron operations, 1952- 53, dir. employee relations, 1953-57, controller, 1957—, v.p., 1960-70, group v.p. finance, 1970—; dir. B. F. Goodrich Can., Ltd., Goodrich Co., Ltd., Ameripol, Inc., B. F. Goodrich Internat. Finance Co., Akron Nat. Bank & Trust Co. Trustee Akron Gen. Hosp. Served to lt. USNR, 1943-45. Mem. Financial Execs. Inst., Am. Econ. Assn., Child Welfare League Am. (trustee), Delta Tau Delta. Clubs: Akron City, Portage Country (Akron). Home: 157 Hudson St Hudson OH 44236 Office: 500 Main St Akron OH 44311

HART, LORING EDWARD, coll. adminstr.; b. Bath, Me., Sept. 22, 1924; s. Joseph Edward and Elizabeth (Hayes) H.; B.A., Bowdoin Coll., 1948; M.A., U. Miami (Fla.), 1951; Ph.D., Harvard, 1961; m. Marilyn Louise Cummings, Jan. 7, 1950; children—Ellen Louise, Matthew Cummings. Teaching fellow Harvard, 1954-56; instr. English, U. Ky., 1956-57; from asst. prof. to prof. English, Norwich U., Northfield, Vt., 1956—, head dept. English, 1961-68, dean of faculty, 1968-69, v.p., dean, 1969—. Mem. Bd. Civil Authority, Northfield, 1969—. Bd. dirs. Vt. Philharmonic Orch. Served with Armored Inf., AUS, World War II; ETO. Decorated Bronze Star, Combat Inf. badge. Mem. Phi Beta Kappa, Sigma Nu. Home: 27 Slate Av Northfield VT 05663

HART, NORMAN, banker; b. Denver, Jan. 6, 1930; s. Horace H. and Eva (Saville) H.; B.A., Colo. Coll., 1951; postgrad. Colo. Sch. Banking, 1958-60; m. Wilma Jean Shadley, Sept. 17, 1952; children—Linda Lea, Patricia Sue, David Bruce. Sales trainee U.S. Rubber Co., 1953; exec. trainee United Bank of Denver, N.A., 1954-56, asst. operations mgr., 1956-58, asst. cashier, 1958- 61; asst. sec. United Banks Colo., Inc., 1962-66, asst. sec. bd. dirs., 1966—, v.p. operations, 1965-69, sr. v.p. personal banking div., 1969, sr. v.p., trust officer, 1969—; dir. United Bank of Lakewood, N.A. Mem. exec. council, finance com. St. Joseph Hosp., Denver, 1969—. Trustee Founders Fund of Beta Theta Pi; chmn. bd. trustees Colo. Sch. Banking. Served to capt. USMCR, 1951-53. Named Denver Met. Exec. of Year, Denver chpt. Nat. Secs. Assn., 1968. Mem. Bank Adminstrn. Inst. (research council), Colo. Bankers Assn. (chmn. finance com.), Adminstrv. Mgmt. Soc. (past pres. Denver chpt.), Beta Theta Pi. Republican. Rotarian. Home: 2560 Van Gordon Dr Lakewood CO 80215 Office: PO Box 5247 Denver CO 80217

HART, PARKER THOMPSON, ednl. exec.; b. Medford, Mass., Sept. 28, 1910; s. William Parker and Ella Louisa (Thompson) H.; A.B., Dartmouth Coll., 1933; A.M., Harvard, 1935; diplome Institut Universitaire de Hautes Etudes Internationales, Geneva, Switzerland, 1936; m. Jane Constance Smiley, Apr. 23, 1949; children—Margaret, Judith. Translator of French, Dept. State, 1937-38; U.S. fgn. service officer, 1938-69; vice consul, Vienna, 1938-39, Para, Brazil, 1940-43; 3d sec. and vice consul, Cairo, 1944, Jidda, 1944; as vice consul opened consulate, Dhahran, Saudi Arabia, 1944, consul, 1945; with Div. Fgn. Serivce Planning, Dept. State, 1947-49; mem. selection bd. for promotion Jr. Fgn. Service officers, 1949; consul gen., Dhahran, 1949; detailed as student Nat. War Coll., 1951-52; dir. Office Near Eastern Affairs, Dept. State, 1952- 55; dep. chief mission and counselor Am. embassy, Cairo, Egypt, 1955-58; named A.E. and P. to Jordan, Feb. 1958, canceled because of union between Jordan and Iraq; consul gen., Damascus, Mar.-Sept. 1958; dep. asst. sec. state Near East and South Asia Affairs, 1958- 61; minister to Yemen, 1961-62; ambassador to Kuwait, 1962-63, to Saudi Arabia, 1961-65, to Turkey, 1965-68; asst. sec. state for Nr. Eastern and South Asian affairs, Washington, 1968-69; dir. Fgn. Service Inst., 1969, ret., 1969; pres. Middle East Inst., Washington, 1969—. Mem. vis. com. on Middle East civilizations Harvard; mem. bd. visitors Air U., Maxwell Field, Ala.; mem. adv. bd. Indsl. Coll. Armed Forces, Am. Security & Trust Co. Chmn. bd. fgn. promotion Service Officers Class 2, 1964. Recipient Meritorious Service award, Nat. Civil Service League, 1957. Mem. Middle East Inst., Am. Fgn. Service Assn., Council Fgn. Relations, Washington Inst. Fgn. Affairs, Am. Turkish Soc. N.Y.C. (co-pres.), Am. Turkish Assn. Washington, Royal Central Asian Soc. Methodist. Clubs: Cosmos (Washington); Harvard (N.Y.C.). Home: 4705 Berkeley Terrace NW Washington DC 20007 Office: Middle East Inst 1761 N St NW Washington DC 20036

HART, PHILIP A., United States senator; b. Bryn Mawr, Pa., Dec. 10, 1912; s. Philip A. and Ann (Clyde) H.; A.B., Georgetown U., 1934; J.D., U. Mich., 1937; m. Jane Briggs, June 19, 1943; children—Ann Clyde, Jane Cameron, Walter Briggs, James Cox, Michael Patrick, Clyde William, Mary Catherine, Laura Elizabeth. Admitted to Mich. bar, 1938, practiced in Detroit until entering pub. office. Mich. Corp. and Securities commr., 1949-51; dir. Mich. OPS, 1951-52; U.S. atty. Eastern Dist. of Mich., 1952-53; lt. gov. of Mich., 1955-59; U.S. senator from Mich., 1959—. Legal adviser to Gov. G. Mennen Williams, 1953-54. Served to lt. col., 4th Inf. Div. AUS until 1946. Decorated Bronze Star, Purple Heart (U.S.); Croix de Guerre (France). Democrat. Home: Mackinac Island MI 49757 Office: Senate Office Bldg Washington DC 20510

HART, RALPH ALBERT, oil co. exec.; b. Cleve., Feb. 20, 1913; s. Albert Ernst and Adeline (Quere) H.; A.B., Ohio U., 1934; J.D., Cleve. Law Sch., 1939; m. Lorna Kydd, Sept. 3, 1938; children—James, Charles, Valerie. Admitted to Ohio bar, 1939; with Standard Oil Co. (Ohio), 1934—, asst. to pres., 1957- 62, v.p., 1962-64, adminstrv. v.p., 1964-66, sr. vice pres., dir., 1966—; dir. Sohio Petroleum Co., Boron Oil Co., Hospitality Motor Inns, Inc., Vistron Crop., Old Ben Coal Corp., BP Oil Corp. Bd. dirs. Goodwill Industries, Better Bus. Bur., Ohio Pub. Expenditures Council. Mem. Govtl. Research Inst., Am. Bar Assn., Am. Mgmt. Assn., Fgn. Affairs Council. Home: 1055 Nicholson Av Lakewood OH 44107 Office: 1750 Midland Bldg Cleveland OH 44115

HART, RALPH ALBERT MILLET, mfg. exec.; b. Boise, Ida., May 28, 1904; s. Edward and Sophie Elvira (Johnson) H.; m. Laura M.E. Purdy, Aug. 15, 1936; 1 dau., Jacqueline Gay, (Mrs. Stanley N. Gaines). With Colgate-Palmolive Co., 1932-61, exec. v.p., 1957-61; pres. Colgate-Palmolive Internat., 1957-61; pres., dir. Heublein, Inc., 1961-66, chmn. chief exec. officer, 1964-68, chmn., 1968—; dir. Cal. Sports, Inc., Emhart Corp., Econs. Lab., Inc., Internat. Distillers & Vintners, London. Mason. Clubs: Baltusrol Golf (Springfield, N.J.); American (Toronto, Ont.); Canadian (N.Y.C.); Pine Valley (N.J.) Golf; Wampanoag Country (West Hartford); Hartford (Conn.) Golf; Tryall (Jamaica). Home: 500 Simsbury Rd Bloomfield CT 06002 Office: 330 New Park Av Hartford CT 06101

HART, RAY LEE, educator; b. Hereford, Tex., Mar. 22, 1929; s. Albert Mann and Ruby Douglas (Bracken) H.; B.A., U. Tex., 1949; B.D., So. Methodist U., 1953; Ph.D., Yale, 1959; m. Juanita Fern Morgan, Sept. 8, 1951; children—Douglas Morgan, Stuart Bracken. Instr., then asst. prof. Drew U. Theol. Sch., 1956-63; asso. prof. philos. and systematic theology Vanderbilt U. Div. Sch., 1963-69; prof., chmn. dept. religious studies U. Mont., 1969—. Mayor, Polebridge, Mont., 1969-70. Mem. Am. Acad. Religion (editor jour. 1970—), Metaphysical Soc. Am., Soc. Sci. Study Religion, Soc. Religion in Higher Edn. Author: Unfinished Man and the Imagination, 1968. Editor: Selections from Thomas Aquinas (trans. into Chinese), 1966. Home: 16 Carriage Way Missoula MT 59801

HART, ROBERT MAYES, oil co. exec.; b. Tulsa, Aug. 27, 1925; s. James Eben and Marthel (Mayes) H.; A.B., Harvard, 1946, M.B.A., 1947; LL.B., U. Okla., 1949; LL.M., N.Y. U., 1957; m. Joanne Krusen, Dec. 23, 1948; children—Robert Mayes, Susan, Nancy, Steven. Admitted to Okla. bar, 1949, N.Y. bar, 1953; clk. U.S. dist. judge, 1949-50; atty. Shell Oil Co., 1950-62, treas., 1962-63, gen. mgr. transp. and supplies, 1966-67, v.p. transp. and supplies, 1967-68, exec. v.p., Houston, Tex., 1968—, also dir.; gen. mgr. Shell Chem. Co., 1963-66. C.P.A., Okla. Mem. Order of Coif, Phi Beta Kappa, Sigma Alpha Epsilon, Phi Delta Phi. Home: 421 Buckingham Dr Houston TX 77024 Office: Shell Oil Co One Shell Plaza PO Box 2463 Houston TX 77001

HART, SAMUEL LEO, educator; b. Mszance, Austria, May 13, 1900; s. Schewach and Clara (Appel) H.; Ph.D., U. Vienna (Austria), 1923; m. Ann Marie Schwoner, May 26, 1946. Came to U.S., 1939, naturalized, 1944. Owner, dir. preparatory sch. of philosophy for coll. students, Vienna, Austria, 1923-28; asst. prof. philosophy Sampson (N.Y.) Coll., 1947-49, Champlain Coll., 1949- 53; mem. faculty Fairleigh Dickinson U., 1953—, prof. philosophy, chmn. dept., 1961—. Mem. Am. Philos. Assn., Mind Assn., Am. Soc. Aesthetics, Am. Assn. U. Profs. Author: Treatise on Values, 1949; Ethics, the Quest for the Good Life, 1963, (with others) New Frontiers of Social Science, 1957; contbr. articles to profl. jours. Home: 573 Grenville Av Teaneck NJ 07666 Office: Fairleigh Dickinson U Teaneck NJ 07666

HART, STANLEY, business exec.; b. Chgo., 1897; married; 2 children. Chmn. bd. dirs. Allied Thermal Corp.; chmn. exec. com., dir. Hart & Cooley Mfg. Co.; mem. exec. com., dir. Fafnir Bearing Co.; dir. Goss & DeLeeuw Machine Co., Savs. Bank of New Britain; trustee New Britain Trust Co. Bd. dirs. YMCA, New Britain Gen. Hosp. Home: Andrews St Southington CT 06489 Office: New Britain CT 06050

HART, STEPHEN HARDING, lawyer; b. Denver, Apr. 13, 1908; s. Richard Huson and Elizabeth (Jerome) H.; A.B., Yale, 1929; student Harvard Law Sch., 1929-30; A.B. (Juris), New Coll., Oxford (Eng.) U., 1932, A.M., 1938; LL.B., Denver U., 1933; m. Lorna Rogers, Dec. 30, 1937; children—Richard Huson, James Grafton Rogers, Georgina (Mrs. Dudley Tyler Smith, Jr.). Instr. Denver Law Sch., 1933-35; asst. solicitor Dept. Interior, Washington, 1935-36; admitted to Colo. bar, 1933, since practiced in Denver; partner Holland & Hart, 1947—; dir. United Bank Denver, United Banks Colo., Empire State Oil Co., Grassy Creek Coal Co., Ideal Basic Industries Inc., Gano-Downs Clothing Co. Mem. Downtown Denver Master Planning Com., 1959-66, Gov.'s Local Affairs Study Commn., 1964-66, Gov.'s Sci. Adv. Com., 1965-66; Colo. rep. U.S. Pub. Land Law Rev. Commn., 1965-70. Mem. Colo. Ho. of Reps., 1937-39. State Senate, 1939-43. Trustee Frederick G. Bonfils Found., 1960-67, Helen G. Bonfils Found., 1961-69, Denver Country Day Sch., 1958-66. Mem. Colo. Hist. Soc. (trustee 1938—, pres., 1960-70), Colo. Cattlemen' Assn. (hon.). Clubs: University (pres. 1952-53), Denver Country (Denver); Am. Alpine (v.p. 1956-58); Brit. Alpine; Metropolitan (Washington); Yale, Century (N.Y.C.). Author numerous articles on fed. income and estate taxes with respect to livestock. Editor: Zebulon Pike's Arkansas Journal, 1932. Home: 4001 E Ellsworth Av Denver CO 80222 Office: Equitable Bldg Denver CO 80202

HART, THOMAS, lawyer; b. Phila., Nov. 24, 1894; s. Charles Byerly and Ida Virginia (Hill) H.; A.B., U. Pa., 1916, LL.B., 1929; m. Margaret Newbold Smith, May 15, 1918 (dec. 1959); children—Margaret Newbold (Mrs. John Kapp Clark, M.D.) (dec.), Thomas (dec.); m. 2d, Virginia Dilkes Harrison, June 25, 1960. With J. B. Lippincott Co., Phila., Phila. Trust Co., Cadbury, Ellis & Haines, bankers, Phila., 1916- 24; dir. Houston Hall, U. Pa., 1924-29; gen. practice law, 1929—; formerly sr. partner Hart, Childs, Hepburn, Ross & Putnam, now counsel; chmn. bd. dirs. Charles F. Kellom & Co. Bd. dirs. Inst. for Cancer Research, Inc.; bd. mgrs. Ludwick Inst.: trustee Young Man's Inst.; v.p., bd. mgrs. Spring Garden Coll.; past pres., bd. dirs. Athenaeum of Phila.; v.p., trustee Am. Oncologic Hosp., Lankenau Hosp.; trustee emeritus, past pres. Episcopal Acad.; pres. Magee Meml. Hosp. for Convalescents; bd. mgrs., past pres. Preston Maternity Hosp.; pres. Independence Hall Assn.; bd. dirs., past pres. Phila. Charity Ball, Inc. Served with U.S. Army, World War I; ensign to lt. (j.g.) USCGR, 1942-44. Hon. mem. 1st Troop Phila. City Cav., Pa. N.G. Mem. Swedish Colonial Soc., Am., Pa., Phila. bar assns., Juristic Soc., Colonial Soc. Pa. (council, past gov.), S.R. (past pres., hon. pres. Pa.), Soc. War of 1812 (v.p.), Mil. Order of Loyal Legion U.S. (hon.), Soc. Colonial Wars (council, past gov. Pa.), Sons of Copper Beeches, Baker Street Irregulars, Delta Psi. Republican. Episcopalian. Clubs: Sharswood Law, Socialegal, Mask and Wig (past pres.) (U. Pa.); Philadelphia, Racquet, Franklin Inn, Penn (past pres. Saint Anthony (Phila.); The Rabbit State-in Schuylkill, Corinthian Yacht (charter) (Cape May); Rittenhouse. Author: A Record of the Hart Family of Philadelphia (1735-1920), pub. privately, 1920; Vol. 2, A History of the Schuylkill Fishing Company of the State-in-Schuylkill, 1888-1932, pub. privately, 1932. Home: 271 Hathaway Lane Wynnewood PA 19096 Office: Penn Center Plaza Philadelphia PA 19102 Inc., cons. engrs., N.Y.C., 1928, pres., 1938-67, chmn., chief exec. officer, dir. Security Nat. Bank; trustee N.Y. Savs. Bank. Asst. to sec. navy, 1944-45; mem. Manhattan Coll. Council, 1959—, mem. N.Y.C.

HART, THOMAS A., educator, fgn. service officer; b. Buenos Aires, Argentina, Aug. 18, 1905 (parents Am. citizens); s. Joseph Lancaster and Tennessee (Hamilton) H.; B.S., William and Mary Coll., 1930; M.A., Emory U., 1933, M.S., 1937; Ph.D., U. Chgo., 1941; m. Jeanelle Mitchell Hardy, Dec. 2O, 1934. Prof., chmn. dept. sci. West Ga. Coll., 1933- 42; prof. biology, dean Sch. Arts and Scis., Roosevelt Coll., 1947- 51; cons. North-Strong Corp., Bethesda, Md., 1950-51; vis. lectr. San Simon, U., Bolivia, summer 1950; cons. to surgeon gen. U.S. Army, 1951; chief Saudi Arabia-Yemen br. Tech. Cooperation Adminstrn., Dept. State, 1951-53; chief edn. div. U.S. Operations Mission to Bolivia, 1953- 57, to Brazil, 1957-59, to Haiti, 1959-61; chmn. manpower devel. div. USAID, Venezuela, 1961-63, cons., 1969, 70, 71; prof. edn. U. Pitts., 1964-71, prof. emeritus, 1971—. Mem. Contract Group, Quito, Ecuador, 1964-68; dir. Brazilian-Am. Edn. Commn., 1957-58; co- pres. Haitian-Am. Devel. Orgn., 1960-61; bd. dirs. Pub. Health Center, Cochabamba, 1945-46; pres. bd. La Paz Community Theatre, 1955; del. several Latin-Am. confs. on edn., 1954-55; U.S. del., adviser U.S. delegation III Inter-Am. Indian Congress, La Paz. Bolivia, 1954; U.S. del. 2d Conf. Latin-Am. Ministers Edn., Lima, Peru, 1956. Served wtih USMC, 1922-25; lt. col. San Corps, AUS, 1942-46: S.W. Pacific area and Bolivia; chief malaria control sect. and sec. army's com. for insect and rodent control Office of Surgeon Gen., Washington, 1945; del. 1st regional Inter-Am. Conf. San. Engrs., Rio de Janeiro Brazil, 1946. Decorated Bronze Star medal for spl. work in Scrub Typhus Control on Goodenough Island; recipient Gold medal Nat. Confedn. Bolivian Farmers for work in rural edn., 1955: Rosenwald Fund fellow, 1938-39. Fellow Am. Pub. Health Asso.; mem. Pan- Am. Bd. Edn. (Chgo.), Sociedad Boliviana de Salud Publica, Am. Assn. U. Profs., Am. Edn. Assn., Sigma Xi. Co-author: Compendium I and II de Biologia General, I, 1965, II, 1967. Founder tech. jour. Anales del Laboratorio Central, and edn. jour. Educacion Boliviana. Contbr. profl. jours. Address: U Pitts Social Sci Bldg Box 4 IDEP Pittsburgh PA 15213

HART, WILLIAM FORRIS, educator; b. Hopewell, N.J., Jan. 8, 1906; s. Warren F. and Annie E. (Chick) H.; A.B., Lafayette Coll., 1927; M.A., Princeton, 1928; Ph.D., N.Y. U., 1936; m. Helen B. Lentz, June 14, 1930 (dec. Feb. 1944); 1 dau., Caryl Elaine (Mrs. Allyn R. Von Neida); m. 2d, Hilda F. Schug, June 18, 1946. Research chemist Reed & Carnrick, Jersey City, 1929-35, Endo Products, Inc., N.Y.C., 1935-37; mem. faculty Lafayette Coll., Easton, Pa., 1937—, prof. chemistry, 1954-71, J.D. and F.H. Larkin prof., 1957-71, chmn. dept., 1957-69, prof. emeritus chemistry, 1971—. Mem. Am. Chem. Soc. (past sec., chmn. Lehigh Valley sect.) Am. Assn. U. Profs., Phi Beta Kappa, Sigma Xi, Alpha Chi Sigma, Kappa Phi Kappa, Kappa Sigma. Presbyn. (elder). Contbr. articles to profl. jours. Home: 732 Burke St Easton PA 18042

HART, WILLIAM MILTON, ophthalmologist; b. St. Clair County, Mo., June 28, 1913; s. Ruben V. and Harriet (Hoskins) H.; A.B., S.E. Mo. State Tchrs. Coll., 1937; M.S., U. Ia., 1939; Ph.D., U. Minn., 1941; M.D., Temple U., 1948; m. Ethelwyn Featherstun Stevens, Apr. 14, 1938; children—Juliet Katheryn, William Milton, Sarah Stevens, Ethelwyn Featherstun. Mayo Found. fellow physiology Mayo Clinic, 1939-41; research asso. ophthalmology U. Ia., 1941-42; asso. physiology Jefferson Med. Coll., 1942-44, asst. prof. ophthalmology, 1952-53; asst. prof. biochemistry, clin. asst. ophthalmology Temple U., 1944-49, research asso. prof. ophthalmology, 1949-52; chief br. ophthalmology Nat. Inst. Neurol. Diseases and Blindness, 1953-54; clin. prof. neuro-ophthalmology U. Md.; now chmn., Roy E. Mason Distinguished prof. ophthalmology, U. Mo.; surgeon USPHS, 1953-57. Pres., Eye Research Found., Bethesda. Recipient prize ophthalmology Assn. for Research, 1941; Zentmayer award ophthalmology Coll. Physicians of Phila., 1946. Diplomate Am. Bd. Ophthalmology. Mem. Aerospace Med. Assn., Am. Acad. Ophthalmology and Otolaryngology, A.M.A., Med. Sec. D.C., Am. Physiol. Soc., Am. Chem. Soc., Assn. Research in Ophthalmology, Am. Fedn. Clin. Research, A.A.A.S., Assn. Am. Med. Colls., A.C.S., Sigma Xi, Alpha Omega Alpha. Republican. Methodist. Kiwanian. Home: 109 Sappington Dr Columbia MO 65201

HART, AUGUSTIN SNOW, Jr., cereal mfr.; b. Bklyn., Aug. 5, 1915; s. Augustin Snow and Alice (O'Conner) H.; A.B., Princeton, 1937; m. Margaret Stuart, Apr. 11, 1942; children—Augustin Snow III, Kathryn Stuart, Douglas Stuart, Harriet Heather, Robert Dixon. With The Quaker Oats Co., N.Y.C., 1937- -, now exec. v.p. internat., dir.; pres. Quaker Oats Internat., Inc., Quaker Oats Pan-Am., Inc.; trustee U.S. Trust Co. of N.Y. Bd. dirs. Union Theol. Sem. Served as lt. col. AUS, World War II. Home: 1200 N Green Bay Rd Lake Forest IL 60045 Office: Mdse Mart Plaza Chicago IL 60654

HARTE, EDWARD HOLMEAD, newspaper pub.; b. Pilot Grove, Mo., Dec. 5, 1922; s. Houston and Isabel (McCutcheon) H.; B.A., Dartmouth, 1947; m. Janet Frey, Feb. 8, 1947; children—Christopher, Elizabeth, William, Julia. With Kansas City Star, 1948-50; editor, co-owner Synder (Tex.) Daily News, 1950-52; pres. San Angelo (Tex.) Standard-Times, 1952-56; v.p. Corpus Christi Caller Times, 1956-62, pub., pres., 1962—. Home: 222 Ohio St Corpus Christi TX 78404 Office: 820 Lower Broadway Corpus Christi TX 78401

HARTE, HOUSTON, newspaper pub.; b. Knobnoster, Mo., Jan. 12, 1893; s. Edward Stettinius and Elizabeth (Houston) H.; student U. So. Cal., 1912-13; B.J., U. Mo., 1915; LL.D., Austin Coll., 1950, Tex. Tech. Coll., 1958; m. Caroline Isabel McCutcheon, Mar. 26, 1921; children—Edward Holmead, Houston Harriman. Reporter, Los Angeles Examiner, 1912- 13: pub. Knobnoster Gem, 1914; bus. mgr. Mo. Republican, Boonville, 1915, editor and pub., 1916-20; pub. San Angelo (Tex.) Evening Standard, 1920-62, San Angelo Standard-Times, 1928-62; mem. Harte, Hanks & Co., pubs. San Angelo Standard-Times, Abilene Reporter-News, Corpus Christi Caller-Times, Paris Evening News, Big Spring Herald, Marshall News-Messenger, Denison Herald, Greenville Herald-Banner, San Antonio Express-News, dir. Times Pub. Co., Wichita Falls, Bryan Daily Eagle, Corsicana Daily Sun, Commerce Jour., Huntsville Item. Mem. Texas Indsl. Commn. Pres. Concho Valley council Boy Scouts Am., 1932- 35; mem. Tex. Relief Commn., 1933-35; v.p. Asso. Press, 1935-36, dir. 1937-43, 1st v.p., 1943-46. Bd. dirs. Tex. Technol. Coll., 1926-33. Served from 2d lt. to capt. inf., U.S. Army, 1918-19. Awarded medal of honor Sch. Journalism, U. Mo., 1931. Democrat. Mem. Tex. Pubs. Assn., Inc. (pres.), West Tex. C. of C. (pres. 1931), Alpha Delta Sigma, Sigma Delta Chi, Delta Upsilon. Presbyn. Clubs: San Angelo Country, San Angelo, River. Editor: In Our Image. Home: 925 Montecito Dr San Angelo TX 76901 Office: Standard-Times San Angelo TX 76901

HARTE, HOUSTON HARRIMAN, newspaper-TV exec.; b. San Angelo, Tex., Feb. 15, 1927; s. Houston and Caroline Isabel (McCutcheon) H.; B.A., Washington and Lee U., 1950; m. Carolyn Esther Hardig, June 17, 1950; children—Houston Ritchie, David Harriman, Sarah Elizabeth. Partner, Snyder (Tex.) Daily News, 1950-52, editor, 1952-54; promotion with Des Moines Register and Tribune, 1954-56; pres. San Angelo (Tex.) Standard, Inc., 1956-62; v.p. Express Pub. Co., San Antonio, 1962-66, pres., 1966—; v.p., chmn. bd. Harte-Hanks Newspapers, Inc., 1971—. Pres. bd. San Angelo Symphony, 1950; v.p. Concho Valley council Boy Scouts Am., 1960-62. Bd. visitors USAF Acad., 1965-69; bd. regents East Tex. State U., 1970—. Served with USNR, 1945-46. Democrat. Presbyn. Rotarian. Home: 2207 Camelback St San Antonio TX 78209 Office: PO Box 2171 San Antonio TX 78297

HARTE, JOSEPH MEAKIN, bishop; b. Springfield, O., July 28, 1914; s. Charles Edward and Ruth Elizabeth (Weisenstein) H.; A.B., Washington and Jefferson Coll., 1936, D.D., 1954, U. South, 1955; S.T.B., Gen. Theol. Sem., 1939, S.T.D., 1955; m. Alice Eleanor Taylor, Oct. 14, 1941; children—Victoria Ruth, Joseph Meakin, Judith Alice. Ordained deacon and priest Protestant Episcopal Ch., 1939; rector All Saints Ch., Miami, Okla., 1939-40; asst. Trinity Ch., Tulsa, 1940-42; rector St. George's Ch., Rochester, N.Y., 1942-43, All Saints Ch., chaplain Episcopal students U. Tex., Austin, 1943-51; dean St. Paul's Cathedral, Erie, Pa., 1951-54; suffragan bishop Dallas, 1954-62; bishop of Ariz., 1962—. Dep., Gen. Conv. P.E. Ch., 1952. Pres. bd. St. Luke's Hosp. Med. Center, Phoenix, St. Luke's in Desert Hosp., Tucson, 1962—; pres. Pacific Province 1967-68. Mem. Am. Legion, Beta Theta Pi. Mason. Author: Some Sources of Common Prayer, 1944; The Language of the Book of Common Prayer, 1945; The Title Page of the Book of Common Prayer, 1946; The Church's Name, 1958; The Elizabethan Prayer Book, 1959; The 1662 Prayer Book, 1962. Home: 815 E Orangewood Phoenix AZ 85020 Office: 110 W Roosevelt St Phoenix AZ 85003

HARTE, ROBERT ADOLPH, biochemist, assn. exec.; b. N.Y.C., July 28, 1911; s. Edward A. and Sadie (Martin) H.; B.S., Coll. City N.Y., 1931; m. Florence Rhea Powell, Sept. 2, 1934; 1 dau., Janet (Mrs. Robert C. Abbe) (dec.). Asst. Rockefeller Inst., N.Y.C., 1932-42; chief research chemist Arlington Chem. Co., Yonkers, N.Y., 1942-49; research adminstr. Sharp & Dohme, Inc., Glendolden and W. Point, Pa., 1949-53; coordinator sci. information Merck & Co., Inc., West Point, Pa., 1953-61; exec. officer Am. Soc. Biol. Chemists, also mgr. Jour. Biol. Chemistry, Washington, 1961—. Exec. sec. 6th Internat. Congress Biochemistry, 1964; chmn. 31st Internat. Congress Fedn. Internat. Documentation, 1965; mem. U.S. Nat. com. Internat. Union Biochemistry, Nat. Acad. Scis.-NRC, 1957-60: mem. U.S. nat. com. Internat. Fedn. Documentation, 1961-69, chmn., 1968-69, councillor, 1967—; dir. Phila. Sci. Council, 1955-61: chmn. Gordon Research Conf. on Food and Nutrition, 1956, Gordon Research Conf. Sci. Information Problems in Research, 1961, 69; mem. adv. com. sci. publs. USPHS, 1962-65. Fellow A.A.A.S., N.Y. Acad. Sci.; mem. Am. Soc. Biol. Chemists, Am. Inst. Nutrition, Council Biology Editors (chmn. 1970), Am. Chem. Soc., Sigma Xi. Club: Cosmos. Contbr. articles in field. Home: Meredith Dr Derwood MD 20855 Office: 9650 Rockville Pike Bethesda MD 20014

HARTECK, PAUL, educator, research chemist; b. Vienna, Austria, July 20, 1902; s. Josef and Gabriele (Schattenfroh) H.; student U. Vienna, 1921-23; Ph.D., U. Berlin (Germany), 1925; D.Natural Sci. (hon.), U. Bonn (Germany), 1966; m. Marcella Piccino-Hay, Sept. 27, 1948; children—Claudia, Christian Wolfgang, Lawrence Paul. Came to U.S., 1951, naturalized, 1957. Asst. to Prof. Eucken, U. Breslau (Germany), 1926-28; asst. to Geheimrat Haber, Kaiser Villhelm Inst., 1928-33; Rockefeller fellow Cavendish Lab., Cambridge, Eng., 1933-34; prof., dir. Inst. Phys. Chemistry, Hamburg, Germany, 1934-51; rector U. Hamburg, 1948-50; Distinguished Research prof. phys. chemistry Rensselaer Poly. Inst., 1941—. Recipient Jean Servaois Stas medal Soc. Chimique de Belgique, 1957; Wilhelm Exner medal Vienna, Oester. Gewerbeverein, 1961. Mem. Joachim-Jungius Gesellschaft der Wissenschaften (v.p. 1949); fgn. sci. mem. Max Planck Soc.; hon. mem. Soc. Chimique de Belgique. Research on ortho-para hydrogen-photo- chemistry-nuclear physics. Deuterium-Deuterium reaction producing Tritium and Helium III. Home: Brunswick Hills Troy NY 12180

HARTER, BENEDICT THOMAS, mfg. co. exec.; b. Irvington, N.J., 1917; B.S., Fordham U., 1939; LL.B., Georgetown U., 1949; 6 children. Vice pres. finance, treas., dir. Becton, Dickinson & Co. Trustee Marymount Coll., Tarrytown, Y.Y., Overlook Hosp., Summit, N.J., Fordham Bus. Inst., N.Y.C. Home: 619 Ocean Av Sea Girt NJ 08750 Office: Becton Dickinson & Co Rutherford NJ 07070

HARTER, DONALD ROBERT, lawyer; b. Moravia, N.Y., Nov. 17, 1917; s. Ralph Amanzo and Mabel B. (Hull) H.; B.A. magna cum laude, Hobart Coll., 1939; LL.B., with distinction, Cornell U., 1942; m. Ruth Marion Ashdown, Sept. 6, 1941; children—Ralph M., Geoffrey J., Laurie Susan. Admitted to N.Y. bar, 1942; asso. firm Wiser, Shaw, Freeman, Ickes & Williams and predecessor, Rochester, 1942-50, mem. firm, 1950-65; sr. partner Wiser, Shaw, Freeman, VanGraafeiland, Harter & Secrest, 1965—. Dir. H. L. Baughman, Inc., H. L. Baughman Equipment Corp., Inc., H. L. Baughman Transit-Mix Corp., Inc., Rochester, Hickson Electric Co. Commr., N.Y. Commn. to Revise Laws of Estates. 1963-64. Pres. Penfield High Sch. P.T.A., 1963-64; bd. dirs. Otetiana council Boy Scouts Am., 1963-70, Monroe County Fair Assn., Monroe br. YMCA; pres., bd. dirs. Estate Planning Council Rochester, 1966. Mem. finance com. Monroe County Rep. Party, 1950—. Bd. dirs. Rochester Maternal and Adoption Service, 1958-65, Rochester Orthoptic Center; trustee Hobart and William Smith Colls., Clifton Springs Hosp., 1968-69; sec. bd. dirs. Ch. Home Rochester; adv. council Cornell U. Law Sch.; mem. corp. Rochester Community Chest. chancellor Episcopal Diocese Rochester. Served to 1st lt. AUS, 1943-46. Fellow Am. Coll. Probate Counsel; mem. Am., N.Y., Monroe County bar assns., Hobart Coll. Alumni Assn. (pres.), Order of Coif, Phi Phi Delta Alumni Assn., Phi Beta Kappa. Episcopalian. Clubs: Oak Hill Country, Genesee Valley (Rochester). Mng. editor Cornell Law Quar., 1941-42; editor-in-chief Echo of the Seneca, 1939. Home: 86 Highledge Dr Penfield NY 14526 Office: 16 Main St W Rochester NY 14614

HARTER, LAFAYETTE GEORGE, Jr., educator; b. Des Moines, May 28, 1918; s. Lafayette George and Helen Elizabeth (Ives) H.; B.A. in Bus. Adminstrn., Antioch Coll., 1941; M.A. in Econs., Stanford, 1948, Ph.D., 1960; m. Charlotte Mary Toshach, Aug. 23, 1950; children—Lafayette George III, James Toshach, Charlotte Helen. Instr. Menlo Coll., Menlo Park, Cal., 1948-50; instr. Coll. of Marin, Kentfield, Cal., 1950-60; prof. econs., chmn. dept. Ore. State U., 1960—; mem. panel arbitrators Fed. Mediation and Conciliation Service, 1965—, Ore. Conciliation Service, 1967—. Asso. campaign chmn. Benton United Good Neighbor Fund, 1970-71. Bd. dirs. Ore. Council Econ. Edn., 1971—. Served to lt. comdr. USNR, 1941-46. Mem. Am. Arbitration Assn. (mem. pub. employment disputes panel 1970—), Am., Western econ. assns., Indsl. Relations Research Assn., Am. Assn. U. Profs., Ore. State Employees Assn. Democrat. Mem. United Ch. of Christ. Author: John R. Commons: His Assault on Laissez-faire, 1962; Labor in America, 1957; Economic Responses to a Changing World, 1972. Home: 3755 N W Van Buren St Corvallis OR 97330

HARTFELDER, HERBERT EDWARD, food co. exec.; b. Kansas City, Kan., Jan. 8, 1914; s. George and Christine (Rollwagen) H.; student Kansas City Jr. Coll., So. Methodist U.; m. Ruby Akins, May 7, 1939; childrenJack Fryar, Patricia Anne (Mrs. Haberman), Orra Christine (Mrs. Simpson), Mary Lee (Mrs. Wilder). With Oak Farms Dairies, 1936-60, pres., 1953-; pres. Midwest Dairies, Spreckles Dairies, Cabell Dairies, Velda Dairies, Embassy Dairies, Cooper Farms Dairies, Harbison Dairies, Adohr Dairies; dir. Oak Cliff Bank & Trust Co.,; pres. The Southland Corp. Bd. Milk Industry Found. Mem. Nat. Assn. Accountants (past pres. Dallas chpt., Dairy Products Inst. Tex. (past pres.), Nat. Diary Council (bd. dirs., v.p.), Internat. Assn. Ice Cream Mfrs. (bd. dirs.), Ice Cream Mdse. Inst. (bd. dirs.), So. Assn. Food Processors. Methodist (steward). Clubs: Dallas, Petroleum, Northwood Country, Dallas Athletic. Home: 9300 Hathaway St Dallas TX 75220 Office: 2928 N Haskell St Dallas TX 75204

HARTFORD, ELLIS FORD, educator; b. Fordsville, Ky., Mar. 13, 1905; s. Ellis Casnor and Attella (Ford) H.; A.B., U. Ky., 1930, A.M., 1934; Ed.D., Harvard (Rosenwald fellow, Univ. scholar), 1942; m. Alma Jane Barker, Dec. 23, 1939; children—Jane Barker, Ellis Ford. Prin., Williamstown (Ky.) High Sch., 1930-33; supt. Williamstown pub. schs., 1933-35; chmn. social studies dept., duPont Manual High Sch., and mem. curriculum com., Louisville (Ky.) pub. schs., 1935-39; specialist in instructional materials TVA, 1939-42; dir.. Univ. schs., prof. of edn. and chmn. div. of found. U. Ky., 1946-64, on leave, head Bur. Instrn. Ky. Dept. Edn., Jan. to Sept, 1956; exec. sec. Ky. Council on Pub. Higher Edn., 1962-64; dean Community Coll. system, U. Ky., 1964-70, v.p. com. colls., 1970, prof. edn., 1970—. Vis. prof. N.M. Western Coll., summers 1955- 58, U. Me., summers, 1953, 57, 61; cons. Ky. Dept. Edn., 1956-58; pres. Ky. Council Social Studies, 1936-38; coordinating agt. Com. Curricular Problems and Research, So. Assn. Colls. and Secondary Schs., 1946-49; pres. Ky. Assn. Colls., Secondary and Elementary Sch., 1959-60. Trustee, Lincoln Found., Ky. Adv. Council for Vocational Edn. Served from lt. to lt. comdr., USNR, 1943-46; vis. expert Civil Information and Edn., G.H.Q., S.C.A.P., Tokyo, Japan, Feb.-May, 1949. Mem. John Dewey Soc., History Edn. Soc., Nat. Council for Social Studies, N.E.A., Kappa Delta Pi, Phi Delta Kappa. Author: Our Common Mooring, 1941; Emphasizing Moral and Spiritual Values in a Kentucky High School, 1952; Moral Values in Public Education, 1958; Planning A Teaching Career, 1958; Education in These United States, 1964; (with others) Citizenship Problems for Young Americans, 1938; Emphasizing Values in Five Kentucky Schools, 1954; A Plan Book for Future Teachers, 1961. Editor: The Public Schools, Religion, and Values, 1956. Home: 401 Holliday Rd Lexington KY 40502 ☆

HARTFORD, HUNTINGTON, financier, art patron; b. N.Y.C., Apr. 18, 1911; s. Edward Vassallo and Henrietta (Guerard) H.; grad. St. Paul's Sch., 1930; A.B., Harvard, 1934; m. Mary Lee Epling (div. 1939); m. 2d, Marjorie Steele, Sept. 10, 1949 (div. 1961); children—Catherine, John; m. 3d, Diane Brown, Oct. 6, 1962 (div. 1970); 1 dau., Cynara Juliet. Co-chmn. Oil Shale Corp., N.Y.C. Patron Lincoln Center for performing Arts; founder, bd. dirs. Gallery Modern Art (now N.Y. Cultural Center), 1964; founder Huntington Hartford Found., 1949, Huntington Hartford Theatre, Cal., 1954; owner, developer Paradise Island, Nassau; editor-in-chief Show mag. Apptd. mem. Nat. Council on Arts, 1969; mem adv. council dept. art history and archaeology Columbia; mem. U.S. People's Fund for UN. Served as lt. USCGR, 1942-45. Named Art Man of Year, Nat. Art Materials Trade Assn., 1962; recipient Broadway Assn. Man of Year award; Orgn. of Am. States award, 1966. Hon. fellow Nat. Sculpture Soc., 1960. Author: (play) Jane Eyre, 1958; Art or Anarchy, 1964. Pub. Show mag. Office: 420 Lexington Av New York City NY 10017

HARTGEN, VINCENT ANDREW, educator, museum dir., artist; b. Reading, Pa., Jan. 10, 1914; s. William J. and Jane (Hadfield) H.; B.F.A., U. Pa., 1940, M.F.A. (fellow), 1941; m. Frances Caroline Lubanda, July 6, 1940; children—David Thomas, Stephen Anthony. Traveling curator Anna Hyatt Huntington Exhbn. of Sculptures, 1937-39; dir. U. Me. Art Gallery, also prof., head art dept. U. Me., 1946, John H. Huddilston prof. art, 1962—; works in collections including Boston Mus. Fine Arts, Brooks Meml. Mus., Memphis, Howard U. Collection, State Tchrs. Coll., Kutztown, Pa., Everhart Mus., Scranton, Pa., U. Me. Art Collection, Wadsworth Atheneum (Hartford), Smith, Colby colls., Reading (Pa.) Mus., Phoenix Art Mus., Internat. Tel & Tel. Collection, Brandeis U., Elvejhem (Wis.) Mus.; one-man exhibits including Binet Gallery, N.Y.C., Md. Inst., Howard U., Howard Everhart Mus., Claflin U., Coll. of Pacific, U. Ida., Bermuda Art Assn., Chase Gallery N.Y., Weeden Gallery, Boston. Art adviser Cultural Olympics, U. Pa., 1939-41; mem. Gov.'s Commn. Arts and Humanities, 1966-70. Trustee Haystack Mountain Sch. of Crafts, Liberty, Me., 1953-55. Recipient BAID Award, 1935, Soldier Art Award, 1945; Audubon Artists Award, 1950; Audubon Artists medal for creative aquarelle, 1965; Distinguished Faculty award, 1965; State Me. (Gov.'s) art award, 1967. Mem. Am. Assn. U. Profs., (Coll., Cath. art assns., Audubon Artists, Am. Watercolor Soc., Canadian Soc. Painters, Etchers and Engravers (hon.), Phi Kappa Phi. Home: 109 Forest Av Orono ME 04473

HARTGRAVES, RUTH, physician; b. Norse, Tex., Oct. 24, 1901; d. Frank and Mary Adeline (Collier) Hartgraves; B.A., 1925, M.D., 1932. Intern New Eng. Hosp. Women and Children, Boston, 1932-33; resident obstetrics and gynecology N.Y. Infirmary Women and Children, N.Y.C., 1933-34; practice medicine, specializing obstetrics and gynecology, Houston, 1935—; active staff, attending obstetrics and gynecology Meth. Hosp., 1936-, sec. staff, 1943—. 1947—; asst. prof. obstetrics and gynecology Baylor Med. Coll., 1943—. Mem. Postgrad. Med. Assembly of South Tex., Mus. Fine Arts of Houston, Houston Opera Soc., Symphony Soc. Houston, Tex. Obstet. and Gynecol. Assn., Am. Med. Women's Assn. (pres. 1963, past br. v.p., pres.), A.M.A., Harris County Med. Soc., Chi Omega. Methodist (ofcl. bd.). Clubs: Altrusa (pres. 1937-39), Lakeside Country (Houston). Address: Medical Towers Houston TX 77025

HARTH, PHILLIP, educator; b. Sioux City, Ia., Feb. 1, 1926; s. John Baptiste and Grace (Conlon) H.; A.B., Trinity Coll., 1946; student Univ. Coll., London (Eng.) U., 1954-56; M.A., U. Chgo., 1949, Ph.D., 1958; m. Sydney Joan Jacobs, Dec. 19, 1953; children—David James, Margaret Rosalind, Rebecca Joan. From instr. to asso. prof. English, Northwestern U., 1953-54, 56-65; prof. English, U. Wis., 1965—. Served with AUS, 1946-48. Fulbright grantee, 1954-55, 55-56; Guggenheim fellow, 1962-63; sr. fellow Humanities Research Center, Reed Coll., 1966-67. Mem. Am. Assn. U. Profs., Internat. Assn. Univ. Profs. English, Modern Lang. Assn., Bibliog. Soc. (London), Oxford Bibliog. Soc., Cambridge Bibliog. Soc., Johnson Soc., Am. Soc. for 18th Century Studies. Author: Swift and Anglican Rationalism, 1961; Contexts of Dryden's Thought, 1968; Editor: The Fable of the Bees, 1970. also articles. Home: 749 Miami Pass Madison WI 53711

HARTH, SIDNEY, musician; b. Cleve., Oct. 5, 1929; s. Leonard and Anne (Dunnire) H.; Mus.B., Cleve. Inst. Music, 1947; studied with Joseph Knitzer, Mishel Piastro, Georges Enesco; m. Teresa Testa, July 7, 1949; children—Laura, Robert. Exchange artist Les Jeungesses Musicales de France, 1952; internat. tours, France, Corsica, North Africa, State Dept. tour Germany, 1952; with Mrs. Harth nat. tour 1952; concertmaster Louisville Orch., 1953-58, Chgo. Symphony, 1959—62 asso. prof. U. Louisville, 1953-58; faculty DePaul U., 1959-62; chmn. dept. music. A.W. Mellon distinguished prof. Carnegie-Mellon U., Pitts., 1963—; Condr., Evanston (Ill.) Orch., 1960- 62; mem. faculty Aspen (Colo.) Music Festival, 1963—; laureate Wienlanske competition Poland, 1957; Yugoslavia, ann. internat. tours including Yugoslavia, Poland, Belgium, Austria, Eng.; USSR, Poland, Czechoslavakia Romania, Switzerland, Holland. Recs.

for Vanguard, Iramac, Concert Hall Soc. Recipient Ysaye medal; Wieniawske medal. Contbr. articles for nat. mags. Home: 1081 Shady Av Pittsburgh PA 15232

HARTHUN, LUTHER ARTHUR, lawyer; b. Lansing, Ill., Apr. 25, 1935; s. Herbert A. and Mildred (Loeber) H.; student Thornton Jr. Coll., 1953-55; B.A., Valparaiso (Ind.) U., 1957; J.D., U. Chgo., 1960; LL.M., U. Cal. at Berkeley, 1961; m. Ann Elizabeth Brose, Sept. 24, 1961; children—Matthew James, Nancy Lynn, Jill Marie, Laura Ann. Admitted to Cal. bar, 1961, Ill. bar, 1961; practiced in Chgo., 1961-66; asso. Hopkins, Sutter, Owen, Mulroy & Davis, 1961-66; gen. counsel, sec. A-T-O, Inc., Cleve., 1966-70, v.p., gen. counsel, Willoughby, O., 1970—. Mem. Am., Ill., Cal. bar assns., Am. Soc. Corporate Secs. Lutheran. Home: Cottage Hill Farm Chardon Rd Kirtland OH 44094 Office: 4420 Sherwin Rd Willoughby OH 44094

HARTIGAN, GRACE, artist; b. Newark, Mar. 28, 1922; d. Matthew A. and Grace (Orvis) Hartigan; student pvt. art classes; m. Robert L. Jachens, May 1941 (dic. 1948); 1 son, Jeffrey A.; m. 2d, Robert Keene, Dec. 14, 1959 (div. 1960); m. 3d, Winston H. Price, Dec. 24, 1960. One man shows Tibor de Nagy Gallery, N.Y.C., 1951-55, 57-59, Vassar Coll. Art Gallery, 1954. Robert Keene Gallery, Southampton, N.Y., 1957-59, Gres Gallery, Washington, 1960, Martha Jackson Gallery, 1962, 64, U. Minn., 1963; exhibited in numerous group shows including Modern Art in U.S., 1955-56, 3d Internat. Contemporary Art Exhbn., 1957, 4th Internat. Art Exhbn., Japan, 1957, IV Biennial, Sao Paulo, 1957, New Am. Painting Show, Europe, 1958-59, World's Fair, Brussels, 1958, The Figure Since Picasso, Mus. Ghent (Belgium); collections Mus. Modern Art, N.Y.C., Walker Art Center, Whitney Mus., Chgo. Art Inst., Met. Mus., Raleigh Mus., Providence Mus., Bklyn. Mus., Mpls. Mus., Albright Gallery, Buffalo, others. Address: 112 S Calvert St Baltimore MD 21202

HARTIN, JOHN SYKES, librarian; b. Columbus, Miss., Oct. 26, 1916; s. Jesse Sykes and Mattie Aura (Williams) H.; B.A., U. of Miss., 1939; A.B. in Library Sci., University of Mich., 1940, A.M. in Library Sci., 1942, A.M. in English Language and Literature, 1953, Doctor of Philosophy, 1956; married Rita Mae Miller, Oct. 26, 1943; children—Martha Elizabeth, John Sykes, and Paul Francis. Student assistant gen. library U. Miss., 1935-39; asst. gen. library U. of Mich., 1940-42, librarian Sch. of Music Library, 1942-45; chief pub. services Swarthmore Coll. Library, 1945-47; dir. of libraries U. of Miss. since 1947. Pres. U. of Mich. Assn. of Library Sci. Alumni, 1945-46; mem. exec. com. and planning com. Miss. Library Survey, 1949. Member Am., Miss. and Southeastern library assns., Beta Phi Mu, Phi Eta Sigma, Phi Kappa Phi. Democrat. Methodist. Contbr. profl. periodicals. Home: 20 Faculty Row University MS 38677

HARTJE, ROBERT GEORGE, educator; b. Conway, Ark., Aug. 8, 1922; s. Henry Cornelius and Perlin (Thayer) H.; student Ark. State Tchrs. Coll., 1940-42, Amherst Coll., 1943-44; B.A., Vanderbilt U., 1948, M.A., 1950, Ph.D., 1955; m. Martha Elizabeth Feldkircher, June 20, 1946; children—John, Tom, James, Philip, Paul, Elizabeth Anne. Dir. U. Ga. Center, Augusta, 1952-53, Columbus, 1953-56; mem. faculty Wittenberg U., Springfield, O., 1956—, prof. history, 1963—, chmn. dept., 1958-64, 66-70, (on leave); dir. bicentennial project Am. Assn. For State and Local History, Nashville, 1970—; Danforth asso. post-doctoral fellow Yale, 1964-65; mem. faculty U. Neb., summer 1965, Ohio State U., spring 1968; dir. Lutheran Summer Camp, Gun Lake, Mich., summers 1957-61. Served to 1st lt. AUS, 1942-46, 51-52. Mem. So. Hist. Assn., Ohio Acad. History. Author: Van Dorn: The Life and Times of a Confederate General, 1967; also articles, book reviews. Home: 110 E 1st St Springfield OH also 1315 8th Av S Nashville TN 37203

HARTKE, GILBERT VINCENT clergyman, educator; b. Chicago, Jan. 16, 1907; s. Emil and Lillian (Ward) H.; grad. Loyola Acad., 1925; A.B., Providence Coll., 1929; A.M., Cath. U. Am., 1938; grad. work Northwestern, 1941; LL.D. (hon.), Notre Dame, 1951; D.F.A., Providence Coll., 1968; L.H.D., Georgetown U., 1971. Mem. Order of Preachers since 1929; ordained Dominican priest, 1936; head grad. drama dept. Cath. U. Am. Since 1937. Trustee Players, Inc.; a founder Chicago Loyola Community Theatre, 1927; mem. drama panel U.S. Fine Arts Com., 1959-60; mem. nat. com. UNESCO, 1959- 60; nat. com. U.S.O., 1959-60. Vice chmn. Ford's Theatre Soc. Mem. Am. Ednl. Theatre Assn. (chmn. vets. committee 1950-52; member advisory council; pres. 1955), American National Theatre and Acad. (corporate mem.), Am. Soc. Aesthetics, Am. Assn. U. Profs., Speech Assn. Am., Cath. Theatre Conf. Appeared in Army Chaplain, RKO series short subjects This Is America during World War II. Home: 487 Michigan Av NE Washington DC 20017

HARTKE, VANCE, United States senator; b. Stendal, Ind., May 31, 1919; s. Hugo and Ida Hartke; A.B., Evansville Coll., 1941; J.D., Ind. U., 1948; LL.D., 7 children—Sandra Larry Schott), Jan, Wayne, Keith, Paul, Anita, Nadine. Admitted to the Indiana State bar, 1948, practiced in Evansville, until 1948; deputy prosecuting attorney, Vanderburgh County, Ind.; U.S. senator from Ind., 1958—, mem. commerce com., finance com., special committee on aging, chmn. com. on Vets. affairs, chmn. subcom. on surface transp. Chmn. Vanderburgh County Democratic Central Com., 1952-58; mayor, Evansville, 1956-58. Past chmn. Democratic Senatorial Campaign Com.; member of Democratic Steering Committee. Served as lt. USCGR, USNR, World War II. Mem. Nat. Assn. Claimants Compensation Attys., Ind. Soc. Washington, Evansville Jr. C. of C., Fed., Am., Ind. bar assns., Evansville Central Turners. Lutheran. Clubs: Indianapolis Athletic, Press, Exchange (Evansville); National Capitol Democratic. Author: Inside the New Frontier, The American Crisis in Vietnam; You and Your Senator. Editor: Indiana Law Review, Indiana Law Jour., The Barker (Jr. Chamber of Commerce publ.). Home: 850 S Dexter Av Evansville IN 47714 also: 6500 Kerns Ct Falls Church VA 22044 Office: Senate Office Bldg Washington DC 20510

HARTKEMEIER, HARRY PELLE, statistician; b. Louisville, May 23, 1904; s. John Fred and Mathilda (Reichenbacher) H.; B.S., U. of Louisville (awarded univ. scholarship, James B. Speed scholarship), 1927; A.M., Harvard (awarded univ. scholarship), 1928; Ph.D., U. of Chicago, 1930; m. Mona McKittrick, Dec. 23, 1930; 1 son, Leonard Douglas. Instr. in econ. statistics U. Chgo., 1929; asst. prof. econs. U. of Mo., 1930, asso. prof. accounting and statistics, 1934, asso. prof. bus. statistics, 1935, prof. bus. statistics, 1941-59, dir. Statis. Lab., 1946-59, principle research statistician Nat. Safety Council, Jan.-Aug. 1956; engr. AA, Data Reduction Analysis & Quality Control, Missile Test Project, Patrick Air Force Base, Aug. 1956-Jan. 1957 (while on leave absence U. Mo.); research asso. Research Center, Stanford University, Stanford, Cal., 1957-58; staff member, electronic data processing dept. Sandia Corporation, Sandia Base, Albuquerque, N.M., 1958-59; staff engr., information processing Lockheed Aircraft Corp., Sunnyvale, Cal., 1959- 62; sr. staff engr. Lockheed Missiles & Space Co., 1962-69, ret.; prof. statis. analysis and electronic computer data processing Santa Clara (Cal.) U., 1960-70. Served as spl. agt. U.S. Census Bureau; sr. statistician U.S. Dept. of Agr.; cons. to bus. orgns. With U.S. Office of Edn. and Office of Prodn. Research and Development, W.P.B., giving special instruction on use of statis. methods and sampling to control quality of war prodn., 1944. Fulbright lectr., Coll. Commerce & Econs., Baghdag, 1953-54. Mem. Am. Statis Assn., Econometric Soc., Am. Econ. Assn., Am. Assn. U. Profs., Legion of Honor, Beta Gamma Sigma, Pi Gamma Mu. Author books including: Business Statistics, 1946, rev. edit., 1947; Elementary Statistical Analysis, 1952; Punch Card Methods, 1952; Data Processing, 1966; Fortran Programming of Electronic Computers, 1966; Introduction to Statistical Analysis, 1967; Applied Statistical Analysis, and Workbook, 1968. Contbr. articles to profl. jours. Home: 638 Tomi Lea St Los Altos CA 94022

HARTL, ALBERT VICTOR, utility exec.; b. New Rockford, N.D., Oct. 21, 1911; s. William R. and Frances (Dusek) H.; B.S.C., U. N.D., 1932; m. Ruth A. Stenquist, June 25, 1935; children—Marlene (Mrs. Robert Kools), Claudeen (Mrs. A. Kenneth Boyd), Kathleen (Mrs. Dennis Faltynski), Mary (Mrs. F. Joseph Pettit), Patricia (Mrs. Joseph Doyle), Albert V. Chief income div. N.D. Tax Commn., 1933-36; chief accountant N.D. Pub. Service Commn., 1935-41; with Ottertail Power Co., Fergus Falls, Minn., 1946—, pres., 1961—, also dir.; dir. Security State Bank, Pioneer Mut. Life Ins., Co., Fargo, N.D. Regent U. Minn., 1965-71, St. John's U., 1963—. Served to col. AUS, 1941-46. Decorated Bronze Star medal with 2 oak leaf clusters, Silver Star medal with oak leaf cluster; recipient Silver Beaver award Boy Scouts Am., 1956, Silver Antelope award, 1966; St. George award Cath. Ch., 1962; named knight St. Gregory, 1965. Mem. Am. Mgmt. Assn., Pres.'s Assn., Financial Execs. Inst., Nat. Assn. Elec. Cos. (dir.), Electric Heating Assn., N. Central Electric Assn., Fergus C. of C., Delta Sigma Pi, Beta Gamma Sigma. Republican. Roman Catholic. K.C. Clubs: Kiwanis (Fergus Falls); Minneapolis. Home: 950 Summit Av W Fergus Falls MN 56537 Office: 215 S Cascade St Fergus Falls MN 56537

HARTL, LEON, artist; b. Paris, France, Jan. 31, 1889; s. Joseph and Marie (Blard) H.; ed. in Paris; m. Fannie Engle, June 30, 1954. Came to U.S., 1921, naturalized, 1922. One man exhbns. include Whitney Studio Club, N.Y.C., 1925-26, Brummer Gallery, N.Y.C., 1934, 38, Valentine Gallery, N.Y.C., 1936, Peridot Gallery, N.Y.C., 1954, 55, 58, 60, 62, Zabriskie Gallery, N.Y.C., 1967; group exhbns. include Independent Artists, 1915, 22, Pa. Acad., 1936, 62, Corcoran Gallery, 1938, Whitney Mus., 1949, Peridot Gallery, 1954, 55, 56, Palazzo del Parco, Bordighera, Italy, 1955, Carnegie Inst., 1955, Korman Gallery, N.Y.C., 1955, Chgo. Art Inst., 1957, 61, U. Neb., 1958, 56, Art U.S.A., 1959, U. Colo., 1960, Butler Inst. Am. Art, 1961, U. Wis., 1956, Am. Fedn. Arts, 1963, Parke-Benet Galleries, N.Y.C., 1962-63, Kansas City (Mo.) Art Inst., 1962-63, Zabriskie Gallery, 1964, 66, Byron Gallery, N.Y.C., 1965, Weeden Gallery, Boston, 1965; rep. permanent collections Wadsworth Atheneum, Soc. N.Y. Hosp., Corcoran Gallery, Whitney Mus., Phillips Collection, Newman Collections, Joseph Brummer Collection, Valentine-Dudensing Collection, U. Neb. Art Galleries, Mus. Modern Art, Joseph Hirshhorn Collection. Recipient Marjorie Peabody Waite award Nat. Inst. Arts and Letters, 1959; purchase prize Butler Inst. Am. Art, 1960, Hallmark Cards, 1960. Yaddo fellow, 1960, 61, 63; McDowell fellow 1957, 58, 59, 60, 61; Ingram Merrill Found. award, 1968. Address: 56 7th Av New York City NY 10011

HARTLE, ROBERT WYMAN, educator; b. Kongmoon, China, Sept. 1, 1921, (parents Am. citizens); s. Jacob Everett and Margaret (Wyman) H.; B.A., U. Tex. 1947, M.A., 1947; A.M., Princeton, 1949, Ph.D., 1951; m. Huguette Clemen'con, Sept. 17, 1958; children by previous marriage—Shirley Shirley Ann (Mrs. Thomas Seawell), John Wyman. Instr. French, Princeton, 1950-53, asst. prof., 1953-60; asst. prof. Romance langs., Queens Coll., N.Y.C., 1960-61, prof., chmn. dept. Romance and Slavic langs., 1963-66, asso. dean faculty, 1963-66, dean faculty, 1966-70, dir. Ph.D. program in France, City U. N.Y., 1970—. Bd. dirs. Council on Internat. Ednl. Exchange, Am. Center for Students and Artists. Served with AUS, 1944-46; PTO. Decorated chevalier l'Ordre des Palmes Academiques; Knight Order of Merit (Italy). Mem. Am. Assn. U. Profs., Modern Lang. Assn. Am. Author: Index du vocabulaire du théatre classique, 8 vols., 1956-64. Translator: Tartuffe (Molière), 1963. Home: 4 rue Gaston Couté Paris XVIII France Office: Office of Dean of Faculty Queens Coll Flushing NY 11367

HARTLEY, EDWARD NEAL, educator; b. Lowell, Mass., Sept. 15, 1914; s. Richard Herbert and Beatrice (Cauchon-White) H.; A.B., Harvard, 1941, A.M., 1942; m. Charlotte Dexter Corlew, Sept. 10, 1942. Instr., Cushing Acad., Ashburnham, Mass., 1942; mem. faculty Mass. Inst. Tech., 1946—, prof. history, 1966—, inst. archivist, 1966—, sec. faculty, 1966-71, acting head history sect., 1967-68; research historian Saugus (Mass.) Ironworks Restoration, 1949-54. Trustee New Eng. Coll., Henniker, N.H., 1954-70. Served to lt. USNR, 1942-46. Mem. Am. Hist. Assn., Soc. Am. Archivists, Newcomen Soc. N.Am., Colonial Soc. Mass., First Ironworks Assn., Concord Antiquarian Soc., Phi Beta Kappa. Unitarian. Club: St. Botolph (Boston). Author: Ironworks on the Saugus. Home: 65 Park Lane Concord MA 01742 Office: Mass Inst Tech Cambridge MA 01239

HARTLEY, EUGENE BOYKIN, express co. exec.; b. Washington, Jan. 30, 1909; s. Eugene Fuller and Celeste (Boykin) H.; M.E., Stevens Inst. Tech., 1933; m. Iris Lenke Jakobb, June 28, 1934; children—Eugene Davis, Laurence Arpad, Eric Boykin, Alf Edwin. Sales engr. IBM Corp., 1934-39; tech. expert bituminous coal div. U.S. Dept. Interior, 1939-41, asst. dir., 1941-43, asst. dep. adminstr. solid fuels for war, 1943-47, asso. dir. surplus property div., 1947-48, spl. asst. sec. interior on reconstrn. in P.R., rehab. of V.I., establishment civilian govts. Guam and U.S. Trust Ty., 1948-50; asst. to v.p. United Parcel Service, 1950-52; asst. to pres. REA Express, 1952-55, dir. purchasing 1955-58, v.p. traffic, 1958-62, v.p. sales, 1962-65; cons. Fast Service Shipping Terminals, Inc., 1965- -. Served as lt. USNR, 1943-46. Mem. Soc. Advancement Mgmt., Marine Hist. Assn., S.S. Hist. Soc. Am., Branford Elec. Ry. Assn., Internat. Oceanographic Found., Am. Soc. Traffic and Transp., Nat. Def. Transp. Assn. Clubs: Rockefeller Center Luncheon (N.Y.C.); Indian Harbor Yacht (Greenwich, Conn.); Boca Raton; Antique Auto Am. Home: 1003 Hwy A-1-A Hillsboro Beach FL 33062

HARTLEY, EUGENE LEONARD, educator, psychologist; b. N.Y.C., Jan. 16, 1912; s. Max Horowitz and Bella (Steiner) H.; A.B., Columbia U., 1932, A.M., 1933, Ph.D., 1936; m. Ruth E. Shuchowsky, May 24, 1935; children—Sue Ann (Mrs. Evan Alderson), Wendy Ellen. With Bklyn. Child Guidance Centre, 1932-35; asst. psychology dept. Columbia U., 1932-36; asst. state supr. N.Y. WPA nursery sch. and parent Edn. project, 1936-37, state supr., 1937-38; research grant, Pi Lambda Phi Found., Columbia U., 1938-39; instr., psychology Coll. City N.Y., 1939-47, asst. prof., 1948, asso. prof., 1949-53, prof., 1953-69, prof. emeritus, 1969—; dean Coll. Community Scis., prof. psychology U. Wis.-Green Bay, 1968-70, dean ednl. devel., prof. community scis., 1970—. Scholar in residence Inst. Advanced Projects, East West Center, U. Hawaii, 1963-64; cons. editor Doubleday Publns., 1953-55; vis. research asso. Columbia U., 1951- 52; spl. cons. Div. Pub. Health Edn., USPHS, 1952-62; Erskine vis. fellow U. Canterbury, N.Z., 1967; cons. to Gunnar Myrdal, Carnegie Corp. study, The Negro in America, 1939-40; collaborator R. M. MacIver. Rockefeller Found. project on intergroup relations, 1946; research exec. Research Inst. in Am. Jewish Edn., Am. Jewish Com., 1947-48; pres. Com. for Certification of Psychologists in N.Y. State, Inc., 1955- 58. Served with Office War Information, 1942-44; Brown U., Nat. Def. Research Com., 1944-45, U.S. Strategic Bombing Survey, E.T.O.U.S.A., 1945. Social Sci. Research Council fellow, 1935- 36. Mem. Am. Psychol. Assn., Soc. Psychol. Study Social Issues (pres. 1954), New Eng., Midwestern, East, Wis. psychol. assns., Am. Anthrop. Assn., Am. Public Health Assn., Am. Sociol. Assn., Am. Assn. Pub. Opinion Research, Sigma Xi. Club: Border Terrier Am. Author: Problems in Prejudice, 1946; (with R.E. Hartley) Fundamentals of Social Psychology, 1952. Editor Readings in Soc. Psychology (with T. M. Newcomb), 1947, rev., 1952; (with R. E. Hartley) Readings in Psychology, 1950, rev. 1957, 63; Casebook in Social Processes (with G.D. Wiebe), 1960. Contbr. jours. Home: 3511 Delahaut St Green Bay WI 54301 Office: Office Ednl Devel Univ Wisconsin Green Bay WI 54302

HARTLEY, FREDERICK LEWIS mfg. exec.; b. Lima, O., Apr. 1, 1932; B.S., U. San Francisco, 1954; M.S., Stanford University, 1956; m. Rosemarie Lois Brown, May 15, 1955; 1 son, Anthony Robinson. Sales rep. Ames-Brockton Fabricated Products, Akron, O., 1956-58, sales mgr. Coshocton, Ohio, 1959-61, gen. manager plant, 1961-68, v.p. sales, 1968--. Instr. bus. Cosyhoscton Jr. College, 1968-69. Secretary Coshocton YMCA, 1960-61; active Boy Scouts of America. Trustee Coshocton Animal Welfare League, Curry Home for the Aged. Named Man of Year, Coshocton Junior Chamber of Commerce, 1968. Mem. Coshocton C. of C. (vice president 1967-68, pres. 1969-70), English Speaking Union, Coshocton Sertoma Club, Nat. Assn. Mfrs., Sales Executives Institute, Phi Beta Kappa, Sigma Chi, Phi Mu. Democrat. Mem. Christian Ch. (lay leader). Mason (32, Shriner). Clubs: Coshocton Country, Coshocton City, Running Deer Country. Home: 2d Av Coshocton OH Office: 3d Av Coshocton OH

HARTLEY, GEORGE MORGAN, metall. engr.; b. N.Y.C., July 12, 1922; s. George LeRoy and Hilda Marie (Karlsson) H.; B.S. in Metall. Engring., Renselaer Poly. Inst., 1942; m. M. Louise Anderson, Mar. 26, 1946; children—Donna J., Linda M., JoAnne, Paul D., Diane L. With Gen. Electric Co., 1946-61, marketing mgr. metall. products dept., Detroit, 1961; pres., mng. dir. Castolin S.A., Switzerland, 1961-63; mng. dir. Copper Devel. Assn., Inc., N.Y.C., 1963- 67, pres., now mng. dir. Dir. U.S.A. Standards Inst. Served to lt. USNR, 1943-46; PTO. Mem. Am. Soc. Metals, Am. Mgmt. Assn., Metall. Soc. of Am. Inst. Mining, Metall. and Petroleum Engrs., Delta Tau Delta. Presbyn. Clubs: Burning Tree Country (Greenwich, Conn.); Cloud (N.Y.C.). Home: Turtleback Rd New Canaan CT 06840 Office: 405 Lexington Av New York City NY 10017

HARTLEY, HAROLD WILLIAM, ins. co. exec.; b. Mpls., July 31, 1923; s. Leonard A. and Catherine L. (Cass) H.; B.A., Hamline U., 1949; postgrad. U. Minn., 1950-52; m. Arlene F. Swanson, Dec. 27, 1947; children—Thomas D., Paricia L., James W. Analyst, Minn. Mut. Life Ins. Co., St. Paul, 1949-55; analyst Investors Diversified Services, Inc., Mpls., 1955-61; analyst Republic Nat. Bank Dallas, 1961-65; securities officer Southwestern Life Ins. Co., Dallas, 1965-67, 2d v.p., 1967-69, v.p., treas., 1969-70, sr. v.p. finance, 1970—; pres., dir. Southwestern Mgmt. & Research Corp. Served with USCG, 1943-46. Mem. Dallas Assn. Investment Analysts (past pres.). Lutheran. Home: 5711 Ridgetown Circle Dallas TX 75230 Office: 1807 Ross Av Dallas TX 75201

HARTLEY, HERBERT LEE, med. editor; b. Centerdale, Ia., Mar. 25, 1900; s. Harry P. and Alda Ball (Pownall) H.; student Ia. State Coll., 1916-18, 22-23; M.D., State U. Ia., 1928; m. Margaret Hulbert Weeks, May 9, 1958. Intern Lakeside Hosp., Cleve., 1928-29; resident surgery Cleve. Clinic Hosp., 1929-32; pvt. practice, Seattle, 1932-60; asst. to editor Northwest Medicine mag., 1936-52, editor, 1952—, full time, 1960—; asso. clin. practice U. Wash. Sch. Medicine. Trustee Wash. Hosp. Service Assn. (Blue Cross), 1954-65. Served to comdr. USNR, 1942-46. Mem. Am., Wash. State med. assns., Nat. Assn. Standard Med. Vocabulary (council of editors), Am. Med. Writers Assn., King County Med. Soc., Seattle Surg. Soc., Alpha Omega Alpha. Cons. editor Nutrition Today, 1966—. Home: 5115 108th Av NE Kirkland, WA 98033. Office: 500 Wall St Seattle WA 98121

HARTLEY, JOSEPH ROBERT, univ. adminstr.; b. Portland, Ind., June 25, 1931; s. Alton H. and Josephine (Norris) H.; student Ball State U., 1949-50; B.S. with highest distinction, Ind. U., 1953; M.B.A. (Earhart fellow), 1954, D.B.A. with highest distinction, 1957; m. Louise Evelyn Logan, July 22, 1951; children—Karen Louise, Lynn Marie, Gregory Alton. Faculty, Ind. U. Grad Sch. Bus., Bloomington, 1957—, asso. prof., 1959-63, prof. bus. adminstrn., 1963—, asso dean faculties, 1965-68, v.p., dean faculties, 1968, v.p., dean for academic affairs, 1969—; transport economist Magdalena Valley Devel. Planning Group, Colombia, S. Am., 1959; asso. research dir. Ind. Higher Edn. Study, Commn., 1962; research dir. Ford Found. study U. Pitts., 1965-66. Cons. economist Tenn-Tombig Waterway Devel. Authority, 1961—; dir. Bloomington Nat. Bank. Mem. Edn. Bd. Bus. Horizons, 1959-64. Bd. mgrs. Eastern Ind. Center, Earlham Coll. Served to 1st lt. USAF, 1956-57. Recipient Nat. Ben Franklin award U.S. Savs. and Loan League, 1953. Mem. Am. Assn. U. Profs., Am. Econ. Assn., Soc. for Internat. Devel., Regional Sci. Assn., Am. Soc. Traffic and Transp., Ind. Soc. Chgo., Ind. Acad. Social Scis. Phi Beta Kappa, Beta Gamma Sigma, Alpha Kappa Psi. Democrat. Methodist (ofcl. bd. 1960-63). Club: Columbia (Indpls.). Author: Effects of the St. Lawrence Seaway, 1957; (with others) Programma de Desarrollo Economico del Valle del Magdalena y Norte de Colombia, 1960; Problems and Needs of Indiana Higher Education, 1963; Economic Feasiblity of Tennessee-Tombigbee Canal, 1963, The University of Pittsburgh: A Selective Review with Proposals for Future Paths, 1966; Airports and Air Service in Indiana, 1960. Home: 2714 Pine Lane Rural Route 3 Box 30 Bloomington IN 47401

HARTLEY, LESLIE POLES, novelist; b. Whittlesea, Eng., Dec. 30, 1895; s. Harry Bark and Mary (Thompson) H.; student Harrow Sch., 1910-15, Balliol Coll., 1919-22; B.A., Oxon, 1922. Author: Night Fears (short stories), 1924; Simonetta Perkins, 1925; The Killing Bottle (short stories), 1932; The Shrimp and the Anemone, 1944; The Sixth Heaven,1946; Eustace and Hilda, 1947; The Boat, 1949; The Travelling Grave (short stories), 1951; My Fellow Devils, 1951; The Go- Between, 1953; The White Wand (short stories), 1954; A Perfect Woman, 1955; The Hireling, 1958; Facial Justice, 1960; Two for the River, 1961; The Brickfield, 1964; The Betrayal, 1966; Poor Clare, 1968; The Collected Short Stories of L.P. Hartley, 1968; The Love-Adept, 1969. Served in Brit. Army, 1916-18. Deocrated comdr. Order Brit. Empire. Recipient James Tait Black Meml. prize, 1948; W. H. Heineman Found. award Royal Soc. Lit., 1954. Fellow Royal Soc. Lit. Clubs: Athenaeum; Beefsteak. Home: Avondale Bathford Bath England Office: 53 Rutland Gate London SW England

HARTLEY, LODWICK CHARLES, educator, writer; b. Batesburg, S.C., June 12, 1906; s. Lodwick Chappell and Nannie (Kneece) H.; A.B., Furman U., 1927, Litt.D., 1954; A.M., Columbia, 1928; Ph.D., Princeton, 1937. Instr., Columbia (S.C.) High Sch., 1928-29; instr. N.C. State Coll., 1929-30, asst. prof., 1930-32; tutor The Hun Sch., Princeton, N.J., 1932-34; asst. prof. N.C. State Coll., 1934-38, asso. prof., 1938-40, prof. 1940—, head English dept., 1940-71. Vis. prof. U. N.C., summers 1940, 50, U. Va. 1954, Duke U., 1970. Served as lt. to lt. comdr., 1942-45. Mem. Modern Lang. Assn. Am., Coll. English Assn., South Atlantic Modern Lang. Assn., Internat. Assn. U.

Profs. English, Am. Soc. 18th Century Studies, N.C. Lit. and Hist. Soc., Blue Key, Phi Kappa Phi. Democrat. Episcopalian. Author books including: Patterns in Modern Drama (with Arthur Ladu), 1948; short story "Mr. Henig's Wall," included in O. Henry prize stories of 1948; Bibliography of William Cowper, 1950; William Cowper: The Continuing Revaluation, 1960; Laurence Sterne in the Twentieth Century, 1966; Laurence Sterne: A Biographical Essay, 1968; Katherine Anne Porter: A Critical Symposium (with George Core), 1969. Contbr. articles to lit. jours. Home: 812 Fairall Dr Raleigh NC 27607 ☆

HARTLEY, RICHARD GLENDALE, c. of c. exec.; b. Bennet, Neb., Feb. 16, 1926; s. Charles Lynn and Hazel Myra (Williams) H.; student U. Neb., 1945-46, Hastings (Neb.) Coll., 1947-48; m. Wynona Elaine Smutz, Oct. 27, 1962; 1 dau., Patricia Ann. Mgr., Mt. Pleasant (Ia.) C. of C., 1959-62; mgr. Kearney (Neb.) C. of C., 1962-67; mgr. membership Greater Kansas City (Mo.) C. of C., 1967-68; exec. v.p. Kansas City (Kan.) Area C. of C., 1968—. Mem. exec. com. Starlight Theatre, Kansas City, Mo.; bd. govs. Am. Royal, Kansas City, Mo. Served with AUS, 1944-45, 53-56. Mem. Am., Kan. C. of C. execs. assns. Revised, edited jour. Evaluating Chamber Management Opportunities, 1966. Home: 8704 Lafayette Ct Kansas City KS 66109 Office: P O Box 1310 Kansas City KS 66117

HARTLEY, WILLIAM HARRISON, educator; b. Lewistown, Pa., Sept. 19, 1906; s. Charles Milton and Mary Ellen (Baughman) H.; B.S., Springfield Coll., 1931; M.A., Columbia Tchrs. Coll., 1932, Ed.D., 1940; m. Elizabeth Catherine Judge, July 1, 1931; 1 dau., Elizabeth Ellen (Mrs. William L. Kreller). Tchr., Ellis Coll., Newton Sq., Pa., 1932-36, Patterson (N.J.) State Coll., 1938-41, Albany (N.Y.) State Coll., 1941-42; mem. faculty Towson (Md.) State Coll., 1942-67, prof. edn., 1960-67; lectr. Columbia Tchrs. Coll., 1937- 47, Johns Hopkins, 1945-70. Program cons. WMPB-ITV, 1969-71. Mem. Nat. (pres. 1965), Middle States (pres. 1957) councils social studies, N.E.A., Am. Assn. U. Profs., Md. Tchrs. Assn., Md. History Tchrs. Assn. (pres. 1945), Md. Audio-Visual Assn. (pres. 1947), Phi Delta Kappa. Author: Selected Films for American History and Problems, 1950; Guide to Audio-Visual Materials for Elementary Social Studies, 1950; Story of American Nation, 1962; (with others) Conservation and Citizenship, 1940, The World Around Us, 1965; American Civics, 1967; America: Its People and Values, 1971. Audio-visual editor Social Edn. mag., 1940-70. Home: Route 3 Box 353A Severna Park MD 21146

HARTLIEB, GORDON WESLEY, banker; b. Ravenna, O., July 4, 1920; s. George Wesley and Mildred (Arteno) H.; B.A., Kent (O.) State U., 1949; J.D., Ohio State U., 1953; children—Raymond Meyer, Georges Wesley, Lynda Mae. Admitted to Ohio bar, 1953, Alaska bar, 1953; U.S. commr., Anchorage, 1954-55; partner firm Hartlieb, Groh & Rader, Anchorage, 1955-63; founder First Fed. Savs. & Loan Assn., Anchorage, 1956, pres., chmn. bd., atty., 1968—, also dir.; founder, 1965, since dir. Security Title & Trust Co. Alaska; dir., mem. exec. com. Nat. Bank Alaska, 1961—; instr. bus. law U. Alaska, 1954—. Councilman, Anchorage, 1968—, mayor pro-tem, 1970. Chmn. adv. com. to bd. regents U. Alaska. Served with USNR, 1943-46. Mem. Am., Ohio, Alaska, Anchorage bar assns., Am. Trial Lawyers Assn., A.I.M. (pres. council), U.S. Savs. and Loan League, Alaskan League Insured Savs. and Loan Assns. (charter), Ohio State U. Alumni Assn., Model A Restorers Club Am. Republican. Methodist. Elk. Club: Petroleum (Anchorage). Home: 601 E 15th Terrace 25 Anchorage AK 99501 Office: 305 5th Av Anchorage AK 99501

HARTLINE, ANN CATHERINE HURLEY, ecologist; b. Chgo., Dec. 6, 1946; d. John James and Dorothy (Sauber) Hurley; A.B., Stanford, 1967; m. Peter H. Hartline, July 1969. Participant as aquanaut-scientist Tektite II underseas habitat program, 1970. Recipient Conservation award Dept. Interior. Mem. Am. Ecol. Soc., Am. Soc. Limnology and Oceanography, Western Soc. Naturalists. Home: 2526 Via Pisa Del Mar CA 92104 Office: Scripps Instn Oceanography La Jolla CA 92037

HARTLINE, HALDAN KEFFER, educator, physiologist; b. Bloomsburg, Pa., Dec. 22, 1903; s. Daniel Schollenberger and Harriet Franklin (Keffer) H.; B.S., Lafayette Coll., Easton, Pa., 1923, D.Sc., 1959; M.D., Johns Hopkins, 1927, LL.D., 1969; Eldridge Johnson traveling research scholar U. Leipzig and Munich, 1929-31; m. Mary Elizabeth Kraus, Apr. 11, 1936; children—Daniel Keffer, Peter Haldan, Frederick Flanders. Nat. Research fellow med. scis. Johns Hopkins, 1927-29; fellow in med. physics Eldridge Johnson Research Found., U. Pa., 1931-36, asst. prof. biophysics, 1936-40, 41-42, asso. prof. biophysics, 1943-48, prof., 1948-49; asso. prof. physiology Cornell Univ. Med. Coll., N.Y.C., 1940-41; prof. biophysics, chmn. dept. Johns Hopkins U., Balt., 1949-53; prof. Rockefeller Univ., N.Y.C., 1953—. Recipient William H. Howell award physiology, 1927; Howard Crosby Warren medal exptl. psychology, 1948; A.A. Michelson award Case Inst., 1964; Nobel prize in physiology and medicine, 1967. Mem. Nat. Acad. Scis., Am. Physiol. Soc., Am. Philos. Soc., Am. Acad. Arts and Scis., Royal Soc. (London), Biophys. Soc., Optical Soc. Am., Phi Beta Kappa, Sigma Xi. Address: Rockefeller U 66th St and York Av New York City NY 10021

HARTMAN, ALEXANDER PAUL, educator; b. Grosschoenau, Germany, Sept. 17, 1910; s. Paul Richard and Fortuna (Boden) H.; student U. Tuebingen (Germany), 1930-32, U. Geneva, 1935; Ph.D., U. Leipzig, 1937; student Middlebury Coll., summer 1946; m. Ota Elisabeth Fox, Aug. 20, 1946. Came to U.S. 1939, naturalized 1943. Asst., Romance Inst., U. Leipzig, 1936; instr. Royal Sch., Armagh, No. Ireland 1938-39; lectr., asst. prof. French and German, U. S.D., Vermillion, 1939-42, asso. prof. French and German, 1946-47, prof., head French dept. 1947-49, head modern fgn. lang. dept., 1949—. Served with AUS, 1943-45. Mem. Am. Assn. Tchrs. French, Am. Assn. Tchrs. German, Romance Lang. Honor Soc., Phi Sigma Iota. Author: C. F. Ramuz, Mensch, Werk und Landschaft, 1937. Contbr. articles to mags. and newspapers. Home: 101 S Pine St Vermillion SD 57069

HARTMAN, CLINTON W., elec. equipment mfg. co. exec.; b. Elkhart, Ind., 1916; postgrad. Purdue U., 1939. Pres., chief exec. officer, dir. CTS Corp., Elkhart. Home: 1939 Rainbow Bend Blvd Elkhart IN 46514 Office: 905 N West Blvd Elkhart IN 46514

HARTMAN, DAVID DOWNS, actor; b. Pawtucket, R.I., May 19, 1935; s. Cyril Balxin and Fannie Rodman (Downs) H.; B.A. in Econs., Duke, 1956; grad. Am. Acad. Dramatic Arts, 1961. Actor, appearing with Belafonte Singers, 1961, My Fair Lady, 1962-63, original cast of Hello Dolly, Broadway, 1963-65, original cast The Yearling, 1965; films include Feminist and the Fuzz, Ballad of Josie, Nobody's Perfect; appeared on NBC-TV in regular running role in The Virginian, 1968-69; appearing on TV in The Bold Ones, NBC-TV, 1969—. Served with USAF, 1956-59. Vice pres. Muscular Dystrophy Assns. Am., 1970—. Address: care Trascott Alyson & Craig Inc 179 Cedar Lane Teaneck NJ 07666

HARTMAN, GEOFFREY H., educator; b. Germany, Aug. 11, 1929; s. Albert and Agnes (Heumann) H.; came to U.S., 1946, naturalized, 1946; B.A., Queens Coll., 1949; Ph.D., Yale, 1953; Fulbright fellow U. Dijon (France), 1951-52; m. Renee Gross, Oct. 21, 1956; children—David, Elizabeth. Mem. faculty Yale, 1955-62, prof. English and comparative lit., 1967—, U. Ia., 1962-65, Cornell U., Ithaca, N.Y., 1965-67. Vis. lectr. and/or prof. U. Chgo., U. Washington, Hebrew U., Jerusalem, U. Zürich (Switzerland), Princeton U. Mem. bd. visitors arts faculty State U. N.Y. at Buffalo, 1968—. Served with AUS, 1953-55. Recipient Christian Gauss prize, 1965; study fellow Am. Council Learned Socs., 1963; Gauss seminarist Princeton, 1968; Guggenheim fellow, 1969. Author: The Unmediated Vision, 1954; Andre Malraux, 1960; Wordsworth's Poetry, 1964; Beyond Formalism, 1970. Home: 260 Everit St New Haven CT 06511

HARTMAN, GEORGE EITEL, architect; b. Ft. Hancock, N.J., May 7, 1936; s. George Eitel and Evelyn (Ritchie) H.; B.A., Princeton, 1957, M.F.A., 1960; m. Ann Burdick, May 22, 1965. Pvt. practice architecture, 1964-65; partner Hartman-Cox Architects, Washington, 1965—; design critic Cath. U. Am., 1964-69; works include master plan, dormitory and chapel Mt. Vernon Coll., EURAM office bldg. (Washington), Brewer residence (Chevy Chase, Md.). Served to 2d lt. F.A., AUS, 1957. Recipient nat. honor awards, A.I.A., 1970, 71. Mem. A.I.A. (dir. at large Washington met. chpt. 1969-71, treas. 1972). Club: Cosmos (Washington). Home: 2236 Decatur Pl NW Washington DC 20008 Office: 1071 Thomas Jefferson St NW Washington DC 20007

HARTMAN, GERHARD, hosp. adminstr.; b. Buffalo, Apr. 21, 1911; s. Frederick and Pauline (Woiwode) H.; A.B. (Berta Ribble scholar), U. Buffalo, 1932, M.B.A., 1935; Ph.D. (Rosenwald fellow), U. Chgo., 1942; m. Fern Tittle, Apr. 27, 1940; 1 son, Gerhard Daniel. Adminstrv. statistician Presbyn. Hosp., N.Y.C., 1932-33; exec. sec. Am. Coll. Hosp. Adminstrn., 1937-42, also asso. dir. grad. program hosp. adminstrn. U. Chgo.; dir. Newton Wellesley Hosp., Newton Lower Falls, Mass., 1942-46; dir. State U. Ia. Hosps., also prof. hosp. adminstrn. Coll. Medicine, State U. Ia., 1946—. Mem. joint commn. edn. Am. Hosp. Assn. and Am. Coll. Hosp. Adminstrs., 1944; vice chmn. hosp. adv. council Ia. Hosp. Survey and Constrn. Program, 1946-55; cons. hosp. adminstrn. chief med. service Office Surgeon Gen., U.S. Army, 1952-55; mem. Fed. Health Manpower Council, 1968—. Trustee Upper Midwest Hosp. Conf., Mpls., 1948-51. Fellow Am. Coll. Hosp. Adminstrs.; mem. Am., Ia. (pres. 1947) hosp. assns., Assn. U. Programs Hosp. Adminstrn. (pres. 1961-62), Univ. Hosp. Execs. Council (gen. chmn. 1954-55), Am. Assn. Hosp. Cons., Am. Soc. Pub. Adminstrn., Ia. Pub. Health Assn., Am. Soc. Polit. Sci., Am. Assn. U. Profs. Author: Problems and References in Hospital Administration, 1939; (with Arthur C. Bachmeyer), The Hospital in Modern Society, 1943, Hospital Trends and Developments, 1940-46, 1948. Home: 306 Lee St Iowa City IA 52240 Office: U Ia Hosps Iowa City IA 52240

HARTMAN, GLEN JUNIOR, steel co. exec.; b. Shelby, O., Mar. 29, 1919; s. Glen Arvine and Alma (Sprague) H.; B.A., Ashland (O.) Coll., 1941; m. Maurine Fulmer, Apr. 19, 1942; children—Marilyn (Mrs. W.B. Sutton), Daniel, Douglas. With Ohio Steel Tube div. Copperweld Steel Co., Shelby, 1941—, v.p., gen. mgr., 1969—, also dir.; dir. Shelby Bldg. & Loan Co., First Nat. Bank Shelby. Dist. chmn. Boy Scouts Am., 1968-72; pres. Shelby United Fund. Recipient Silver Beaver award Boy Scouts Am., 1967. Mem. Am. Iron and Steel Inst., Am. Iron and Steel Engrs., Welded Steel Tube Inst., Am. Ordnance Assn., Ohio, Shelby chambers commerce. Rotarian. Home: RD 1 E Smiley St Shelby OH 44875 Office: 132-140 W Main St Shelby OH 44875

HARTMAN, HOWARD CARL, newspaperman; b. Morris Twp., N.J., Jan. 9, 1917; s. Dennis and Ruth (Shavelson) H.; student George Washington U., 1932-33; A.B., Princeton, 1936; M.A. in Journalism, Columbia, 1942; m. Josephine M. Troxell, Aug. 25, 1942; 1 dau., Jessica A. Engaged in gold mining, Cal., 1936-37; translator, publicity, copy boy, reporter various newspapers, 1937-40; fgn. editor Puerto Rico World-Jour., San Juan, P.R., 1940-41; reporter, rewrite man N.Y.C. News Assn., 1941; Washington corr. Jewish Telegraphic Agy., also Overseas News Agy., 1942-44; city editor Puerto Rico World-Jour., 1944; with Asso. Press, 1944—. assigned N.Y.C., Madrid, Paris, Washington, Vienna, 1944-57, corr., Budapest, Hungary, 1957-59, staff mem., Frankfurt, 1959, corr., Berlin, 1959-63; corr. Bonn and European Econ. Affairs, 1963-67, corr. Common Market and NATO, Brussels, 1967—. Alternate Pulitzer travelling fellow, 1942. Mem. Berlin Fgn. Press Assn. (pres. 1960-61), Anglo-Am. Press Assn. Paris (dir. 1951, 56), Phi Beta Kappa. Clubs: Nat. Press (Washington); Overseas Press (N.Y.C.). Office: care Asso Press 50 Rockefeller Plaza New York City NY 10020 also care Asso. Press 4 rue Treurenberg Brussels Belgium

HARTMAN, HOWARD LEVI, univ. dean; b. Indpls., Aug. 7, 1924; s. Howard Levi and Catherine (Miller) H.; student Colo. Sch. Mines, 1942-44; B.S. in Mining Engring., Pa. State U., 1946, M.S., 1947; Ph.D., U. Minn., 1953; m. Bonnie Lee Sherrill, June 8, 1947; children—Sherilyn, Greg Alan. Mining engr. Phelps Dodge Corp., Bisbee, Ariz., 1948-49; mine dust engr. for Ariz., Phoenix, 1949-50; instr. U. Minn., 1950-54; asst. prof., then asso. prof. Colo. Sch. Mines, 1954-57; prof. mining engring., head dept. Pa. State U., 1957-63, asso. dean engring., acting dean, 1963-67; dean engring. Sacramento (Cal.) State Coll., 1967-71; dean engring. Vanderbilt U., Nashville, Tenn., 1971—. Cons., Minn. Tax Commn., summers 1951-54, Colo. Dept. Hwys., 1955, Anaconda Co., summer 1956, Dept. Justice, 1955-57, U.S. Steel Corp., 1960, Standard Oil Co., N.J., 1960-65, H. E. Fletcher Co., 1961- 65, Ingersoll-Rand Co., 1963-66, Martin Co., 1966-67, gen. Aerojet-Corp., 1969-70; chmn. Fed. Metal and Nonmetallic Mine Safety Bd. Rev., 1971—. Served to ensign USNR, 1942-44. Mem. Am. Inst. Mining, Metall. and Petroleum Engrs. (Mineral Industries Edn. award 1965), Am. Soc. Engring. Edn., Nat. Soc. Profl. Engrs., Sigma Xi, Sigma Gamma Epsilon, Kappa Sigma. Democrat. Presbyn. (elder). Author: Mine Ventilation and Air Conditioning, 1961; also articles. Editor Case Studies in Surface Mining, 1969; asso. editor Surface Mining, 1968. Home: 907 Forest Acres Ct Nashville TN 37220

HARTMAN, JOHN ADAMS, Jr., communications cons.; b. Windber, Pa., July 10, 1911, s. John Adams and Fanny (Shook) H.; A.B., Dickinson Coll., 1932; LL.B., George Washington U., 1936; m. Denise Cary, Aug. 19, 1958 (dec.); m. 2d, Thora Lawson, Sept. 13, 1961. Admitted to D.C. bar, 1935; atty. FCC, 1936-41, Am. Cable & Radio Corp., 1946-57, v.p., gen. counsel, 1957—, dir., 1961—; dir. All Am. Cables & Radio, Inc., Comml. Cable Co., Press Wireless, Inc., ITT World Communications, Inc., now cons., 1971—; dir. Globe Wireless, Ltd.; sr. counsel ITT Communications Operations, now cons. Served to lt. col. USAAF, 1942-46. Mem. Am. Bar Assn., U.S. Supreme Ct. Bar Assn., Phi Kappa Sigma, Phi Delta Phi. Mem. Dutch Ref. Ch. Address: 243 W Louther St Carlisle PA 17013

HARTMAN, JOHN JACOB, educator; b. Kansas City, Mo., June 5, 1931; s. Jacob Benjamine and Helen Elizabeth (Jones) H.; B.S. Ed. in Sociology, S.W. Mo. State Coll., 1961; M.S. in Sociology, U. Mo., 1962, Ph.D., 1966; m. Norma Jean Coffman, Mar. 8, 1953. Instr., U. Mo., 1964-65; asst. prof. Ia. State U., 1965-68; prof. sociology, chmn. dept. Wichita (Kan.) State U., 1968—. Cons., tchr. Urban Tchr. Edn. Program. Bd. dirs. Edgerton Research Found. Served with USNR, 1951-55. Mem. Am. Sociol. Assn., Midwest (sec.), Rural sociol. socs., S.W. Social Sci. Assn., Alpha Kappa Delta, Gamma Sigma Delta, Alpha Phi Zeta. Home: 1110 Lawrence Ct Wichita KS 67206

HARTMAN, JOHN WHEELER, publisher; b. Detroit, June 3, 1922; s. Hubert Ezra and Margaret Mary (Martin) H.; student Colgate U., 1939, Duke, 1943; post grad. Columbia, 1943; m. Esther Kelly Bill, Nov. 8, 1947; children—Kelly Martin Bill, Raymond Bill. Exec. v.p., partner Bacon, Hartman & Vollbrecht, Inc., advt. agy., 1946-69; dir. sales Sales Mgmt. mag., 1951—, pres., 1957—; pres. Bill Bros. Pub. Corp. (name changed to Bill Communications, Inc.), 1953-70, chmn. bd., 1970—; pres. Brewster Handcraft Industries, 1957—; dir. Market Publs., Inc. Served as lt. (j.g.) USNR, 1943-45; ETO: founder, pub. U.S. Navy newspaper. Mem. Mag. Pubs. Assn. (pres.), Young Pres. Orgn. (dir., pres. 1963—), Nat. Sales Execs., Nat. Indsl. Advertisers Assn., Am. Bus. Press (dir.) Sigma Alpha Epsilon. Clubs: Wee Burn Country (Darien, Conn.); Bonnie Briar Country (Larchmont, N.Y.); Sky, Pinnacle (N.Y.C.); Campfire (Chappaqua, N.Y.); New Canaan (Conn.) Field; Old Lyme (Conn.) Country. Home: 364 Laurel Rd New Canaan CT 06840 Office: 630 3d Av New York City NY 10017

HARTMAN, KENATH, hosp. adminstr.; b. St. Louis, Feb. 1, 1920; s. Saul Boyce and Sadie (Slavick) H.; M.S.H. in Hosp. Adminstrn., Northwestern U., 1953; m. Lorene Chow, Mar. 20, 1948; children—Neill, Kim, Gary. Adminstrv. asst. Mt. Sinai Hosp., Chgo., 1947-48; asst. supt. Chgo. Wesley Meml. Hosp., 1948- 60, supt., 1960-70, exec. v.p., 1970—, also trustee; instr., co-ordinator program hosp. adminstrn. Northwestern U., 1953-60. Bd. dirs. Chgo. Hosp. Council, 1961-67, Tri- State Hosp. Assembly, 1965—, Council on Community Nursing, Chgo., 1971; treas. Nat. Assn. Meth. Homes and Hosps., 1966-69; cons. to trustees Northwest Community Hosp., Arlington Heights, Ill., 1952-57, founder, sec. bd. trustees, 1953-57; mem. Chgo. Conf. No. Ill. Trustee Northwestern U., 1960—; exec. council Spiritual Frontiers Friendship, 1958-65, treas., 1961-63; bd. health and welfare ministry United Meth. Ch., 1964-69, treas., 1967-69. Served with USAAF, 1941-47. Decorated Award of Merit. Fellow Inst. Medicine Chgo. (acad.), Am. Coll. Hosp. Adminstrs.; mem. Am., Ill. hosp. assns., Assn. Am. Med. Colls., Alumni Assn. Northwestern U. (pres. program hosp. adminstrn. 1961). Home: 1730 Wilmette Av Wilmette IL 60091 Office: 250 E Superior St Chicago IL 60611

HARTMAN, LOUIS FRANCIS, educator; N.Y.C., Jan. 17, 1901; s. Louis Francis and Josephine (Grennan) H.; student Mt. St. Alphonsus Sem., Esopus, N.Y., 1922-28; Licentiate Sacred Scripture, Pontifical Bibl. Inst., Rome, Italy, 1932, Licentiate Oriental Langs., 1936. Entered Congregation Most Holy Redeemer, 1922; prof. sacred scripture Redemptorist Sem., Esopus, 1932-34, 1936-48; asst. prof. semitics Cath. Univ., 1948-52, asso. prof., 1952-62, prof., 1962-70, head Semitic dept., 1964-67; exec. sec. Cath. Bibl. Assn. Am., 1948-70; ann. prof. Am. Schs. Oriental Research in Jerusalem, 1959-60. Chmn. editorial bd. new translation Cath. Bible in English, 1948-68; chmn. com. for nat. observance 400th anniversary Gutenberg Bible, 1952. Mem. Am. Oriental Soc., Am. Schs. Oriental Research, Soc. Bib. Lit. Author: Encyclopedic Dictionary of the Bible, 1963. Staff editor New Cath. Ency., 1962-66; editorial staff New Am. Bible, 1968- 70. Contbr. articles profl. jours. Home: 3112 7th St NE Washington DC 20017 Died Aug 22 1970

HARTMAN, PAUL WILLIAM, actor; b. San Francisco, Mar. 1, 1904; s. Ferris Luce and Josephine (Davies) H.; student U. Cal. at Berkeley, 1922; m. Grace Adelaide Barrett, Nov. 14, 1922; 1 son, Ferris Luce III. Dancer, actor until 1922; vaudeville headliner, 1926; dance satirist, 1932-47; comedian, 1936-56; Broadway appearances include Red, Hot and Blue, 1937, You Never Know, 1942, Top Notchers, 1942, Keep 'Em Laughing, 1942, Angel in the Wings, 1948, All For Love, 1949, Tickets Please, 1950, Of Thee I Sing, 1952, The Pajama Game, 1955, Show Boat, 1956; films include Sunny, The Man on a Tightrope, The Thrill of it All, Inherit the Wind, Soldiers in the Rain, How to Succeed in Business Without Really Trying, Luv; TV appearances, 1956—, including Bell Telephone Hour, Ben Casey, Lucy Show, Chrysler Theatre, Andy Griffith Show, Mayberry R.F.D., Petticoat Junction, others. Recipient Stage Palm award, 1937, Tony award, 1948, Donaldson award, 1948, Page One award, 1942, Lambs award, 1957, N.Y. Daily Mirror award, 1939, Critics award, 1947, Variety Poll award, 1948. Author: Much Love, Pop, 1945. Address: care Agency for Performing Arts Inc 9000 Sunset Blvd Los Angeles CA 90069

HARTMAN, PHILIP, educator; b. Balt., May 16, 1915; s. Joseph and Anna (Wiener) H.; student U. Md., 1930-31; A.B., Johns Hopkins, 1934, Ph.D., 1938; m. Sylvia Mazer, June 12, 1949; children—Judith B., Marilyn D. Instr. Queen's Coll., N.Y.C., 1938-41; mem. faculty Johns Hopkins U., 1946—, prof. math., 1952—, chmn. dept. math., 1965-69. Vis. prof. U. Cal. at Los Angeles, 1957-58. John Simon Guggenheim Meml. Found. fellow, 1950-51. Served with F.A., AUS, 1941- 43; capt. USAAF, 1943-46. Mem. Am. Math. Soc. (mem. council 1970—), Phi Beta Kappa, Sigma Xi. Asso. editor Am. Jour. Mathematics, 1946-57, editor, 1958—. Office: Dept Math Johns Hopkins U Baltimore MD 21205

HARTMAN, ROBERT S., paper co. exec.; b. Chgo., Oct. 7, 1914; s. Edward A. and Blanche S. (Straus) H.; student Northwestern U., 1933-34; m. Betty Regenstein, Oct. 25, 1941; children—Ann (Mrs. Chalres H. Arrington III), Ruth. Br. mgr. Draper & Kramer, Inc., 1937-41; pres. Arvey Corp., Chgo., 1941—. Vice pres., bd. dirs. Chgo. Boys Clubs. Served with AUS, 1943-46. Mem. Chgo. Envelope Mfg. Assn. (pres. 1949-51), Envelope Mfg. Assn. Am. (dir. 1950-54). Clubs: Mid-America (Chgo.); Lake Shore Country (Glencoe, Ill.). Home: 900 Mt Pleasant St Winnetka IL 60093 Office: 3450 N Kimball St Chicago IL 60618

HARTMAN, ROBERT S., former educator; b. Berlin, Germany, Jan. 27, 1910; student German Coll. Polit. Sci., 1926-27, U. Paris (France), 1927-28, London Sch. Econs. and Polit. Sci., 1928-29; LL.B., U. Berlin, 1932, U. Mexico, 1941; Ph.D., Northwestern U., 1946; m. Rita Emanuel, Aug. 30, 1936; 1 son, Jan Alfred. Asst. to faculty law U. Berlin, 1932-33; referendar (asst. judge), Dist. Court Berlin, Charlottenburg, 1932-33; rep. for Walt Disney Prodns. in Scandinavia, Mexico, C.A., 1934-41; master Lake Forest (Ill.) Acad., 1942-45; instr., asst. prof. The Coll. of Wooster (O.), 1945-48; asso. prof. Ohio State U., 1948-56; exchange prof. Center Philos. Studies, Nat. U. Mexico, 1956-57, research prof., 1957- -. Vis. prof. Mass. Inst. Tech., 1955-56, Yale U., 1966, U. Tenn., 1968, 69; organizing chmn. of the Council of Profit Sharing Industries, 1947, exec. sec., 1947-49; co-founder Institut fur Sozialwirtschaftliche Betriebsberatung, Dusseldorf, Germany, 1952; cons. Mexican Govt. Profit-Sharing Commn., 1963. Mem. Allgemeine Gesellschaft Für Philosophie in Deutschland, Am. Philos. Assn., Am. Assn. U. Profs., Nat. Edn. Assn., Am. Assn. Humanistic Psychology (founding sponsor), Am. Soc. Value Inquiry (pres. 1971), Delta Phi Alpha (hon.). Contbr. chpt. and articles to philos. and econ. publs. Translator publs. including: Hegel, Introduction to the Philosophy of History, 1953; Kant, Logic, 1971. Author: Profit Sharing Manual, 1948; The Partnership of Capital and Labor: Theory and Practice of a New Economic System, 1958; The Structure of Value & Foundations of Scientific Axiology, 1959, rev. 1969; The Knowledge of Good, 1965; The Hartman Value

Inventory, 1966. Co-author: The Language of Value, 1957; New Knowledge In Human Values, 1958; Chronique de Philosophie, 1958. Cons. editor Kantstudien, 1952—, Rev. Humanistic Psychology, 1963—. Address: Apartado 422 Cuernavaca Morelos Mexico ☆

HARTMAN, WILLIAM ELLIS, educator, sociologist; b. Meadville, Pa., Feb. 17, 1919; s. Hartley J. and Janet A. (Ellis) H.; student N.Y.U., 1937-41, Centenary Coll., 1943; A.B., U. So. Cal., 1947, M.A., 1948, Ph.D., 1950; m. Iva R. Decker, June 30, 1944; children—Carol, William Ellis, Donald, Paul, Beverly, Stephen, Lawrence. Instr. sociology and psychology El Camino (Cal.) Coll., 1950- 51; mem. faculty Long Beach State Coll., 1951-, prof. sociology, 1961- -, chmn. dept. sociology and social welfare, 1960-63; pvt. practice as marriage counselor, Los Angeles and Long Beach, 1959—. Dir. Center for Marital and Sexual Studies, Long Beach, Cal. Mem. Am., So. Cal. assns. marriage counselors, Am. Sociol. Assn., Nat. Council Family Relations. Home: 5199 E Pacific Coast Hwy Long Beach CA 90804

HARTMAN, WILLIAM RALPH, mfg. co. exec.; b. Cleve., Dec. 3, 1928; s. Vaughn L. and Williamina (Ralph) H.; A.B., Western Res. U., 1951; m. Claire Landgrebe, Aug. 24, 1951; children—Marian, Margaret, Claire, William Ralph. With Republic Steel Corp., Cleve., 1951-56; with Robert Heller & Assos., 1957-63; pres. William Hartman & Co., Cleve., 1963-66; dir. orgn. and planning Internat. Tel. & Tel. Corp., N.Y.C., 1966-69, dep. group exec. indsl. products group, 1969, v.p., 1966-70; pres., chief exec. officer, dir., mem. exec. com. Grinnell Corp., Providence, 1970—; dir. Flowstream Internat., Ltd., U.K.; dir. Indsl. Nat. Corp., Providence. Served with Signal Corps, U.S. Army, 1947-48. Clubs: Univeristy (N.Y.C.), Quidnessett Country (North Kingstown, R.I.). Home: 30 Downing St East Greenwich RI 02818 Office: 260 W Exchange St Providence RI 02901

HARTMANIS, JURIS, mathematician, educator; b. Riga, Latvia, July 5, 1928; s. Martins and Irma (Liepins) H.; came to U.S., 1950, naturalized, 1956; student U. Marburg, 1947-49; M.A., U. Kansas City, 1951; Ph.D., Cal. Inst. Tech., 1955; m. Ellymaria Rehwald, May 16, 1959; children—Reneta, Martin, Audrey. Instr., Cornell U., Ithaca, N.Y., 1955-57, prof., chmn. dept. computer sci., 1965—; asst. prof. Ohio State U., 1957-58; research mathematician Gen. Electric Research & Devel. Center, Schenectady, 1957- 65. Mem. Am. Math. Soc., Math. Assn. Am., Assn. Computing Machinery, Sigma Xi. Author: (with R.E. Stearns) Algebraic Structure Theory For Sequential Machines, 1966. Asso. editor: Jour. Computer and Systems Scis., 1966—; Jour. Math. Systems Theory, 1966—. Mem. editorial bd. SIAM Jour. Applied Mathematics, 1970. Home: 324 Brookfield Rd Ithaca NY 14850

HARTMANN, EDWARD GEORGE, educator, historian; b. Wilkes-Barre, Pa., May 3, 1912; s. Louis and Catherine (Jones-Davis) H.; A.B., Bucknell U., 1937, A.M., 1938; Ph.D., Columbia, 1947, B.S. in L.S., 1948. Instr. history Ann-Reno Inst., N.Y.C., 1942-43; asst. prof. Wilkes Coll., 1946-47; fellow in library, lectr. history City Coll. N.Y., 1947-48; mem. faculty Suffolk U., Boston, 1948-, prof. history, 1956—. Served with AUS, 1943-46; ETO; maj. USAF Res. Mem. Am. Hist. Assn., Soc. Am. Historians, Hon. Soc. of Cymmrodorion (London, Eng.), Welsh Soc. Phila. (gold medallion 1966), St. David's Soc. N.Y. State (Hopkins medal 1970), Nat. Gymanfa Ganu Assn., 90th Div. Assn., Soc. King's Chapel (Boston), Immigration History Group, Phi Beta Kappa. Author: The Movement to Americanize the Immigrant, 1948; A History of American Immigration, 1967; Americans from Wales, 1967; also articles. Editor: Tough 'Ombres, The Story of the 90th Infantry Division, 1944; A Short History of the 357th Infantry Regiment, 1945; Centennial History of the Welsh Baptist Association of Pennsylvania, 1955; History of the Welsh Congregational Church of the City of New York, 1801-1951, 1969. Home: 69 Hancock St Boston MA 02114 Office: Suffolk U. Beacon Hill Boston MA 02114

HARTMANN, F. NORMAN, paper mfg. co. exec.; b. Toledo, July 2, 1906; s. Charles and Laura (Blanchet) H.; B.S. in Econs., U. Pa., 1928; m. Elizabeth A. Bellwoar, Apr. 7, 1928; children—Polly (Mrs. Albert D. Purvis, Jr.), Charles B., Norene (Mrs. Jerry F. Haislip). Salesman sales mgr., v.p. Butler Paper Products Co., Toledo, 1928-52, pres., 1952-53; asst. to pres. Lily-Tulip Cup Corp., N.Y.C., 1953-56, v.p. planning and devel., 1956-62, pres., 1962-68; gen. mgr. Lily-Tulip div., group v.p. Owens-Ill., Inc., 1968-70, ret. Home: 105 Bayberry Circle Sea Palms St Simons Island GA 31522

HARTMANN, FREDERICK HOWARD, educator; b. N.Y.C., July 6, 1922; s. Frederick Herman and Grace (MacNamara) H.; A.B., U. Cal. at Berkeley, 1943; M.A., Princeton, 1948, Ph.D., 1949; student Grad. Inst. Internat. Studies, U. Geneva (Switzerland), 1947; m. Regina Lou Kiracofe, Dec. 26, 1943; children—Lynne Merry, Vicky Carol, Peter Howard. Instr. politics Princeton, 1947; from asst. prof. to prof. polit. sci. U. Fla., 1948-66, dir. Inst. Internat. Relations, 1963-66; Alfred Thayer Mahan prof. maritime strategy and spl. academic adviser to pres. U.S. Naval War Coll., 1966—; vis. prof. Wheaton (Mass.) Coll., part-time, 1966-69, Brown U., part-time, 1968-69, U.R.I., part-time, 1970-71; lectr., cons. in field, 1955—. U. Fla. rep. Fla. Bd. Control Com. Academic Freedom, 1961-62; mem. Fulbright Nat. Selection Com., 1954-56; U.S. del. 4th Conf. Naval War Colls. Am., 1966, 6th Conf., 1970. Served to lt. (j.g.) USNR, 1943-46; capt. Res. Fulbright research prof. U. Bonn (Germany), 1953-54; Rockefeller grantee, 1959. Mem. Am. Assn. U. Profs. (pres. U. Fla. chpt. 1959-60, mem. nat. council 1963-66), Am. Polit. Sci. Assn., Internat. Studies Assn., Inst. Strategic Studies (london), Blue Key, Pi Sigma Alpha, Delta Phi Epsilon. Author: The Relations of Nations, 3d edit., 1967; The Swiss Press and Swiss Foreign Affairs, 1960; Germany Between East and West, 1965; The New Age of American Foreign Policy, 1970. Editor: Basic Documents of International Relations, 1951; Readings in International Relations, 1952; World in Crisis, 3d edit., 1967. Home: 22 Chartier Circle Newport RI 02840 Office: US Naval War Coll Newport RI 02840

HARTMANN, GREGORY KEMENYI, govt. ofcl.; b. Buffalo, May 25, 1911; s. Arthur and Claire Marie (Tucker) H.; B.S. in Physics, Cal. Inst. Tech., 1933; B.A. (Rhodes scholar 1933-36), Oxford (Eng.) U., 1936, M.A., 1943; Ph.D. in Physics, Brown U., 1939; m. Harriet Marie Johnston, July 2, 1939; children—George Cole, Karen Elizabeth, John Warner, Joan Teresa. Asst. physics Brown U., 1936-39; asst. prof. physics U. N.H., 1939-41; cons. Bur. Ordnance, Navy Dept., 1941-43, chief applied explosives, 1943-46, dir. group at Bikini, 1946, chief explosives div., also dir. research Naval Ordnance Lab., 1947-55, tech. dir. lab., 1955-. Mem., 1st chmn. Undersea Warfare Research and Devel. Planning Council, 1959—; sr. vis. dept. applied math. and theoretical physics Cambridge (Eng.) U., 1964-65. Recipient Navy Distinguished Civilian Service award, 1945, Distinguished Civilian Service award Dept. Def., 1958, Nat. Civil Service League award, 1963. Fellow Washington Acad. Sci., Acoustical Soc. Am.; mem. Fed. Profl. Assn. (a founder; pres. 1964), Am. Phys. Soc., Philos. Soc. Washington, Sigma Xi, Tau Beta Pi. Club: Cosmos (Washington). Contbr. articles profl. jours., editor tech. proc. Home: 10701 Keswick St Garrett Park MD 20766 Office: Naval Ordnance Lab White Oak Silver Spring MD 20910

HARTMANN, HENRIK ANTON, educator, physician; b. Sandar, Norway, Mar. 20, 1920; s. Henrik Anton and Elvira Kathinka (Erlandsen) H.; M.D., U. Oslo, 1947; m. Ann Smith, Sept. 17, 1952; children—Lisa, Tony, Jeni, Arne, Signe. Came to U.S., 1950, naturalized, 1955. Intern, Ullevaal Hosp., Oslo, Norway; resident Rikshospitalet, Oslo; faculty U. Wis. Med. Sch., Madison, 1954—, prof. pathology, 1965—. Cons. Mendota State Hosp. Served with Norwegian Allied Army, 1944-45. Diplomate Am. Bd. Pathology. Grantee USPHS, 1954. Mem. Am. Assn. Neuropathologists, Am. Assn. Pathology and Bacteriology, Am. Soc. Exptl. Pathology. Contbr. articles to profl. jours. Home: 10 S Kenosha Dr Madison WI 53705

HARTMANN, JOHN JOSEPH, financial cons.; b. San Jose, Cal., Oct. 15, 1918; s. John Joseph and Bertrande (Cauhape) H.; B.S., U. Santa Clara (Cal.), 1940; M.B.A., Stanford, 1947; C.P.A., Cal., 1947; m. Barbara Hyland, June 15, 1940; children—Anne Elizabeth, Catherine Marie. With Haskins & Sells, C.P.A.'s, San Francisco, 1947-54, Kern County Land Co., San Francisco, 1954-68, v.p., 1961-68; gen. partner J. Barth & Co., investment bankers, San Francisco, 1968-70; dir. Genesys Systems, Inc., Watkins-Johnson Co., Daconics Corp. Mem. adv. com. Santa Clara U. Sch. of Bus., 1971—. Pres. San Francisco Citizens League, 1969—. Served with Q.M.C., AUS, 1942-46. 51. Home: 98 Larch Dr Atherton CA 94025

HARTMANN, PAUL ELLSWORTH, fgn. commerce cons., former naval officer; b. Ashland, Mass., Sept. 13, 1914; s. Max and Margaret (Daly) H.; student Bowdoin Coll., 1931-33; B.S., U.S. Naval Acad., 1937; m. Margaret Philips Moore, Aug. 3, 1940; children—Robin P., Margaret P. (Mrs. Larry L. Coy), Mary E. (Mrs. Robert I. Money), Martha D., Paul K. Commd. ensign U.S. Navy, 1937, designated aviator, 1940, advanced through grades to rear adm., 1964; operations officer 7th Fleet, 1959-60; comdr. U.S.S. Antietam, 1960-61; operations officer Atlantic Fleet, 1961-63; comdr. Fleet Air, Western Pacific, 1963-66, Carrier Div. 20, 1966-67; dir. logistics plans div. Navy Dept., 1967-68; asst. vice chief naval operations Dir. Naval Adminstrn., Washington, 1968-70, ret.; pres. Global Enterprises, Inc., cons. fgn. commerce, Arlington, Va., 1971—. Decorated Bronze Star medal (3): Third Order of Rising Sun (Japan), Legion Merit medal. Mem. Naval Inst., Naval Hist. Soc., Theta Delta Chi. Home: 1701 Albemarle St McLean VA 22101 Office: 1815 Fort Meyer Dr Arlington VA 22209

HARTMANN, ROBERT CARL, educator, physician; b. Everett, Wash., July 23, 1919; s. Rudolf and Eugene (Kaiser) H.; A.B., Johns Hopkins, 1941, M.D., 1944; m. Margaretta O'Sullivan, Mar. 16, 1946; children—Kathleen, Robert Carl, David, Richard, Margaret, Ellen. Rotating intern Pa. Hosp., 1944-45, resident medicine, 1945-46; fellow medicine Johns Hopkins Sch. Medicine, 1948-49, 50-52; faculty Vanderbilt U. Sch. Medicine, Nashville, 1962—, prof. medicine, 1963—, dir. div. hematology, 1952—. Cons. nat. nutrition survey USPHS, anemia and nutrition survey Inst. Nutrition for Central Am. and Panama, Guatemala, 1965-68; mem. hematology study sect., sub-com. platelet-glass- adhesion Internat. Commn. Haemostasis and Thrombosis, 1967-71. Bd. dirs. Pan-Am. Assn. Tenn., Cath. Youth Orgn., Nashville. Served with AUS, 1946-48. Mem. So. Soc. Clin. Research, Am. Soc. Clin. Investigation, Am., Internat. socs. hematology, Am. Assn. Physicians, Johns Hopkins Alumni Assn. (pres. Tenn. chpt. 1967). Contbr. papers to profl. lit. Home: 6315 Brownlee St Nashville TN 37205

HARTMANN, ROBERT TROWBRIDGE, govt. ofcl.; b. Rapid City, S.D., Apr. 8, 1917; s. Miner Louis and Elizabeth (Trowbridge) H.; A.B., Stanford, 1938; m. Roberta Sankey, Jan. 17, 1943; children—Roberta T. (Mrs. Charles F. Brake), Robert S. Reporter Los Angeles Times, 1939-41, 45-48, editorial and spl. writer, 1948-54, chief Washington bur., 1954-63; chief Mediterranean and Middle East Bur., 1963-64; FAO information adviser, Washington, 1964-65; editor Republican Conf. U.S. Ho. Reps., 1966-69; minority Sgt.-at-arms U.S. Ho. Reps., 1969—. Asst. to permanent chmn. Rep. Nat. Conv. 1968. Served from ensign to lt. comdr., USNR, 1941-45; PTO now capt. Res. Recipient Sigma Delta Chi Distinguished Service award for Washington Corrs., 1957; Better Understanding citation English Speaking Union of U.S., 1958; Vigilant Patriot award, 1960; Overseas Press Club citation for best articles on Latin Am., 1961; Freedoms Found. citation, 1963. Reid Found. fellow in Middle East, 1951. Mem. Delta Chi, Sigma Delta Chi, Delta Sigma Rho, Hammer and Coffin Soc. Mem. Ch. of Christ. Clubs: Nat. Press, Internat., Capitol Hill (Washington); Mil. Order of the Carabao; Pelican Cove (St. Croix, V.I.). Home: 5001 Baltimore Av Westgate MD 20016 Office: US Capitol Washington DC 20510

HARTMANN, SVEN R., educator; b. N.Y.C., Feb. 22, 1932; s. Fred Valdemar and Hertha (Palme) H.; B.S., Union Coll., 1954; Ph.D., U. Cal., 1961; m. Helen Catherine Gellhorn, Dec. 24, 1954. Research asso. U. Cal., 1961-62; asst. prof. physics Columbia, 1962-65, asso. prof., 1965-68, prof., dir. Columbia Radiation Lab., 1968—. Served as lt., USAF, 1955-57. Sloan research fellow, 1963-67. Fellow Am. Phys. Soc.; mem. Sigma Xi. Research on nuclear double resonance, magnetic resonance in the demagnetized state, photon echoes. Home: 2 Summit Terrace Dobbs Ferry NY 10522 Office: Columbia Univ New York City NY 10027

HARTMANN, WILLIAM EDWARD, architect; b. Springfield, N.J., May 6, 1916; B.Arch., Mass. Inst. Tech., 1938; D.H.L. (hon.), Lake Forest Coll., 1968. With George Howe & Oskar Stonorov, 1940-41, Skidmore, Owings & Merrill, Chgo., also N.Y.C., Portland, Ore., San Francisco, 1945—, gen. partner, 1951—. Trustee, Art Inst. Chgo., Ill. Inst. Tech., Com. for Econ. Devel.; bd. dirs. Ill. Arts Council; bd. govs. U. Chgo. Internat. House; mem. corp. Mass. Inst. Tech. Served to lt. col. AUS, 1941-45. Rotch Traveling Scholar, 1939. Fellow A.I.A.; mem. Lambda Alpha, Mus. Contemporary Art, Chgo. Hist. Soc. (life). Clubs: Century Assn. (N.Y.C.); Commercial; Wayfarers; Commonwealth; Chicago, Attic, Midday, Quadrangle, Tavern, Casino. Home: 175 E Delaware Pl Chicago IL 60611 Office: 30 W Monroe St Chicago IL 60603

HARTMEYER, JOHN, meat packer; b. Madison, Wis., Sept. 21, 1907; s. John and Margaret (Hoven) H.; ed. U. Wis., 1928; m. Betty Lenore Warriner, Mar. 1, 1938; children—John Warriner, Jane Ann (Mrs. Frederick Ginther), Andrea Hoven, Elizabeth Ellen. Br. mgr. Oscar Mayer, Milw., 1932-35, sales mgr., Chgo., 1935-40; nat. service sales mgr. Armour & Co., 1940-45; exec. v.p. Marhoefer Packing Co., Muncie, Ind., 1945, chmn. bd. dirs., 1962—; pres., dir. Consumer Lumber Co.; sec.-treas., dir. Ind. Refrigerator Lines, Ind. Leasing Corp.; dir. Central Ind. R.R.; pres., treas. Command Helicopter (Medford, Ore.). Mem. Beta Theta Pi. K.C., Elk, Moose. Clubs: Delaware Country, Muncie (Muncie). Home: 11 Oak Rd Muncie IN 47303 Office: 109 E Main St Muncie IN 47305

HARTNACK, CARL EDWARD, banker; b. Los Angeles, Apr. 9, 1916; s. Johannes C. and Kate (Schoneman) H.; grad. Pacific Coast Banking Sch., Seattle, 1950; grad. honor certificate Am. Inst. Banking, 1949; m. Roberta DeLuce, Sept. 6, 1939; children—Richard, Robert, Gretchen. With Security Pacific Nat. Bank, Los Angeles, 1934—, sr. v.p., 1961-69, pres., 1969—, also dir.; dir. San Diego Gas & Electric Co.; trustee Continental Mortgage Investors. Mem. exec. com. Central City Assn., Los Angeles. Mem. Navy League U.S. Clubs: Town Hall, Stock Exchange, Los Angeles Country, California (Los Angeles); Bankers of San Francisco. Home: 5240 Los Grandes Way Los Angeles CA 90027 Office: 561 Spring St Los Angeles CA 90054

HARTNELL, NORMAN, couturier; b. Streatham, London, Eng., June 12, 1901; student Magdalene Coll. Cambridge U., 1921. Began dressmaking bus., London, 1923; commanded to design women's uniforms Brit. Ministry Supply, World War II; dressmaker by appointment to the Queen and to the Queen Mother. Decorated Officier d'Academie, France, 1939; recipient Nieman-Marcus award for distinguished service field of fashion, 1947; mem. Royal Victorian Order (H.M. Queen Elizabeth II). Office: 26 Bruton St London W 1 England

HARTNETT, JAMES PATRICK, engring. educator; b. Lynn, Mass., Mar. 19, 1924; s. James Patrick and Anna Elizabeth (Ryan) H.; B.S. in Mech. Engring., Ill. Inst. Tech., 1947; M.S., Mass. Inst. Tech., 1948; Ph.D., U. Cal. at Berkeley, 1954; m. Shirley Germaine Carlson, July 14, 1945 (div. 1969); children- -James, David, Paul, Carla, Dennis. Engr. gas turbine div. Gen. Electric Co., 1948-49; research engr. U. Cal. at Berkeley, 1949-54; from asst. prof. to prof. mech. engring. U. Minn., 1954-61; Guggenheim fellow, vis. prof. U. Tokyo (Japan), 1960; cons. ICA, Seoul, Korea, 1960; Fulbright lectr., cons. mech. engring. U. Alexandria (Egypt), 1961; H. Fletcher Brown prof. mech. engring., chmn. dept. U. Del., 1961-65; engring. cons., 1954-65; prof., head dept. energy engrings., U. Ill., Chgo. Circle, 1965— Mem. Am. Soc. M.E., Am. Inst. Aero. and Astronautics, Am. Soc. Engring. Edn., Am. Assn. U. Profs., A.A.A.S., Sigma Xi, Tau Beta Pi, Pi Tau Sigma. Author papers heat transfer, fluid mechanics. Editor: Recent Advances in Heat and Mass Transfer, 1961; co-editor International Journal Heat and Mass Transfer, 1960-; Advances in Heat Transfer, 1963. Gen. editor (with T.F. Irvine, Jr.) Pergamon Unified Engring. Series, 1966-; co-editor Heat Transfer-Soviet Research, 1969- -. Home: 409 Custer Evanston IL 60202

HARTNETT, ROBERT CLINTON, clergyman, educator; b. Escanabe, Mich., Dec. 7, 1904; s. John M. and Mary Winifred (Killian) H.; A.B., Loyola U., Chgo., 1927; A.M., St. Louis U., 1932; S.T.L., Heythrop Coll., Eng., 1939; Ph.D., Fordham U., 1945. Entered Soc. of Jesus, 1927, ordained priest Roman Catholic Ch., 1938; instr. English, U. Detroit, 1932-35; instr. religion and sociology Xavier U., Cin., 1940-41; summer editor America, 1943, 47, editor-in-chief America and Catholic Mind, pres. America Press, N.Y.C., 1948-55; asso. prof., prof. polit. sci. U. Detroit, 1956; dean Coll. Arts and Scis., Loyola U., Chgo., 1956-58, asso. prof. polit. sci., 1958-60, prof. polit. sci., lectr. Sch. of Law, 1960-64; lectr. polit. philosophy Fordham, 1945; dir. dept. polit. sci. U. Detroit, 1946-48; lectr. polit. sci. Fordham U. Grad. Sch., fall 1948; lectr. on current affairs affecting religion, 1940—. Mem. Am. Polit. Sci. Assn. Author booklets: Equal Rights for Children, 1947; Federal Aid to Education, 1950; The State and Religious Education, 1952. Address: 5625 Sheridan Rd Chicago IL 60626

HARTRANFT, JOSEPH BECKWITH, Jr., assn. exec.; b. Buffalo, May 24, 1915; s. Joseph Beckwith and Leila Cooledge (Sherman) H.; B.A., Wharton Sch. of U. Pa., 1937; m. Dorothy Mae DuQuoin, Dec. 31, 1937; m. 2d, Evelyn Lapariere Melby, July 3, 1948 (dec. Feb. 1964); 1 dau., Diane Lynn. Mem. staff Aircraft Owners and Pilots Assn., 1939—, pres., 1952—; pres. Aircraft Owners and Pilots Found., 1951—, Aircraft Owners and Pilots Service Corp., 1953—, Internat. Council Aircraft Owners and Pilots Assns., 1961—; dir. Avemco Corp. Sec. Interdeptl. Air Traffic Control Bd., War Aviation Com.; mem. bd. Aviation Devel. Adv. Com., Joint Mil.- Civilian Air Def. Com; founder U.S. Air Guard, 1940; adv. bd. Nat. Intercollegiate Flying Assn.; mem. Radio Tech. Commn. for Aero. Trustee Bates Found. Aero. Edn. Served to lt. col. USAAF, World War II. Mem. S.R., Royal Aero Club (hon.), Washington Air Derby Assn. (hon.), Nat. Citizens Commn. Internat. Coop., Nat. Aviation Club, Aero Club Washington. Clubs: Rotary (Chevy Chase, Md.); Pacific; U. Pa. (Washington); Nantucket (Mass.) Yacht; Executives (Chgo.); Columbia Country (Chevy Chase, Md.); Annapolis Yacht (Md.). Home: 4405 East West Hwy Bethesda MD 20014 Office: Aircraft Owners and Pilots Assn PO Box 5800 Washington DC 20014 also: PO Box 7550 Schiphol-Central Netherlands also 44 Washington St Nantucket MA 02554

HARTRIDGE, ALFRED LAMAR, civil engr.; b. Seattle, May 20, 1909; s. Alfred Lamar and Frances Alice (Hickox) H.; student Phillips Exeter Acad.; A.B., Harvard, 1931; m. Nell Elizabeth Bryan, Jan. 20, 1934; 1 dau., Sharon (Mrs. George Hamilton Fettus III). Field engr. Stone & Webster Engring. Corp., 1931-33, office engr., resident engr., supt. constrn., 1939-45, asst. mgr. bus. studies and reports, 1945, personnel mgr., 1946-53, treas., 1954-60, v.p., 1954-59, exec. asst. to pres., 1955-59, financial v.p., 1959-60, exec. v.p., 1950-65, pres., 1966-69, also dir.; asst. trust adminstr. Irving Trust Co., 1933-37; resident engr., office engr. Ulen & Co., 1937-39; pres., dir. Stone & Webster Internat., Inc., Stone & Webster Constrn. Co., Stone & Webster India Corp., Stone & Webster, Mich., Inc.; dir. Mass. Blue Cross, Inc. Mem. Am. Soc. M.E., Nat. Soc. Profl. Engrs. Clubs: Union, Algonquin (Boston); Brae Burn. Home: Black Banks St Simons Island GA 31522 Office: 226 Franklin St Boston MA 02107

HARTROFT, WALTER STANLEY, pathologist; b. Calgary, Alta., Can., Aug. 5, 1916; s. Samuel Munroe and Myrtle Pearl (Coons) H.; B.S., M.D., U. Alta., 1941, LL.D., 1961; Ph.D., U. Toronto, 1949; m. Phyllis Merritt, Sept. 30, 1950. Came to U.S., 1954, naturalized, 1958, returned to Can., 1964. Research asst. dept. histology U. Western Ont., 1941-43; resident pathology Toronto Gen. Hosp., 1943; research asso. Banting and Best Dept. Med. Research, U. Toronto, 1946-47, asst. prof., 1947-49, asso. prof., 1949-52, prof., 1952, asso. dept. pathology, 1952; chmn. pathology sect. Acad. Medicine, Toronto, 1951-52; Emmerling-Stewart Meml. lectr. U. Pitts., 1953; chmn. dept. pathology Washington U. Sch. Medicine, 1954-61; dir. research inst. Hosp. for Sick Children, Toronto, 1961-70; prof. physiology U. Toronto, 1961-70; prof. pathology U. Hawaii Sch. Medicine, 1970—. Served as maj., pathologist M.C., Royal Canadian Army, 1944-46. Recipient research prize Royal Coll. Physicians and Surgeons of Can., 1949. Diplomate in human nutrition Am. Bd. Nutrition. Fellow Royal Soc. Can., Royal Coll. Physicians and Surgeons Can.; mem. Am. Soc. Clin. Nutrition (pres. 1969-70), Am. Assn. Pathologists and Bacteriologists, Gerontol. Soc., Inc., Canadian Assn. Pathologists, Coll. Physicians and Surgeons of Ont., Ont. Assn. Pathologists, Mo. Soc. Pathologists, Soc. Exptl. Biology and Medicine, Am. Assn. Study Liver Diseases (pres. 1960- 61). Home: 5677 Kalanianaole Honolulu HI 96821 Office: 512 Biomed Scis Bldg U Hawaii Sch Medicine 1960 East West Rd Honolulu HI 96822

HARTSHORN, HERBERT HADLEY, coll. dean; b. St. Joseph, Mo., Apr. 25, 1909; s. Andrew and Mabel (Alexander) H.; B.S., Lincoln U., Jefferson City, Mo., 1930; A.M., U. Minn., 1940, Ph.D., 1948; m. Goldie Reid, Aug. 20, 1934; children—Gail Patricia, Hadley Reid. Sec., YMCA, St. Joseph, 1930-31; dean St. Philip's Jr. Coll., San Antonio, Tex., 1931-32; dir. extension schs. Samuel Huston Coll., Austin, Tex., 1932-33; social worker, St. Louis, 1935-36; tchr. Lab. High Sch., Lincoln U., 1936-40; prin., 1940-48; asst. prof. edn., Lincoln U., 1940-48, prof. edn., 1948, dean of students, 1948-50; dean

Coll. Arts and Scis., Tex. So. U., Houston, 1950—, acad. v.p., 1968-70, v.p., 1970—. Mem. Coll. Personnel Assn., Tex. Tchrs. Assn., Psi Chi, Phi Delta Kappa. Episcopalian. Home: 3934 Roseneath Dr Houston TX 77021

HARTSHORN, JOHN ELDEN, refractories co. exec.; b. Washington, Jan. 1, 1924; s. Hosmer and Naomi (Haller) H.; A.B., Dartmouth, 1947; LL.B., Yale, 1950; m. Avonne Allen, July 6, 1946; children—Dana, Amy, Laura, John Allen. Admitted to D.C. bar, 1950; with firm Cummings, Stanley, Truitt & Cross, Washington, 1950- 56; with Gen. Refractories Co., Phila., 1956—, exec. v.p., 1966—, also dir. Served with USAAF, 1943-46. Home: 296 S Aberdeen Av Wayne PA 19087 Office: 1520 Locust St Philadelphia PA 19102

HARTSHORN, JOSEPH HAROLD, educator, geologist; b. Cleve., June 23, 1922; s. Humphrey and Ella (Krise) H.; S.B., Harvard, 1947, M.A., 1950, Ph.D., 1955; m. Eleanor Clover Johnson, Dec. 13, 1942; children—John Edward, Jo Ann (Mrs. Norman James Morrisson III). With U.S. Geol. Survey, 1950-67, asst. to br. chief, 1961-67; part-time geologist, 1967—; vis. prof. U. Mich., Ann Arbor, 1963; asso. prof. geology U. Mass., Amherst, 1967-70, prof., head dept., 1970—. Mem. sch. com. Town of Boxborough, Mass., 1954-68, Acton-Boxborough Regional Sch. Com., 1955-68. Mem. Gov.'s Commn. Preservation Commonwealth Heritages, 1960—. Served with RCAF, 1941-44; to maj. USAAF, 1944-46; ETO. Decorated D.F.C., Air medal with 4 oak leaf clusters; D.F.C. (Great Britain). Fellow A.A.A.S., Geol. Soc. Am., Glaciological Soc. Am., Arctic Inst. N. Am., Sigma Xi; mem. Am. Polar Soc., Nat. Assn. Geology Tchrs., Geol. Soc. Boston, Mass. Archeol. Soc., Am. Quaternary Assn. Home: 1150 Bay Rd Amherst MA 01002

HARTSHORN, MERRILL FRANCIS, educator; b. Taunton, Mass., Dec. 31, 1909; s. Harry Lister and Lena May (Hall) H.; diploma Oxford Sch. Bus. Adminstrn., Cambridge, Mass., 1931; Adj. in Arts, Harvard, 1941, M.A. in Teaching, 1942; m. Sibyl McCarley, Jan. 1, 1949. Asst. prof. bus. adminstrn. Oxford Sch. Bus. Adminstrn., 1943-41; univ. fellow, Harvard, 1941-42, asst. dir. Harvard Workshop in Edn., summers 1942-43; asst. prof. social scis. Northland Coll., Ashland, Wis., 1942-43; exec. sec. Nat. Council Social Studies, Washington, 1943—; workshop dir. U. Toronto (Ont., Can.), summer 1945, tchr. summer sch. Am. U., 1947-48, 49; cons. HICOG U.S. Zone, 1950; summer faculty various univs. and colls. Mem. N.E.A., Am. Hist. Assn., Am. Polit. Sci. Assn., Nat. Council for Social Studies, Nat. Council Geog. Tchrs., Pi Gamma Mu (hon.). Contbr. articles to ednl. jours. Home: 3501 Perry St Fairfax VA 22030 Office: 1201 16th St Washington DC 20036

HARTSHORNE, CHARLES, educator; b. Kittanning, Pa., June 5, 1897; s. Francis Cope and Marguerite (Haughton) H.; student Haverford Coll., 1915-17; A.B., Harvard, 1921, A.M., 1922, Ph.D., 1923; postgrad. U. Frieburg (Germany) 1923- 25, U. Marburg, 1925; L.H.D., Haverford Coll., 1967; Litt.D. (hon.), Emory U., 1969; m. Dorothy Eleanore Cooper, Dec. 22, 1928; 1 dau., Emily Lawrence (Mrs. Nicolas D. Goodman). Sheldon travelling fellow Harvard U., 1923-25, instr., research fellow, 1925-28; mem. faculty U. Chgo. 1928-55, mem. federated theol. faculty 1943-55, prof. philosophy, 1949-55; prof. pholosophy, Emory U., Ga., 1955-62; prof. philosophy U. Tex., Austin, 1962-63, Ashbel Smith prof. philosophy, 1963- -. Vis. asso. prof. Stanford U., 1937, New Sch. Social Research, 1941-42, Johann Wolfgang Goethe U., Frankfurt, Germany, 1948- 49, U. Wash., 1958; Terry lectr. Yale, 1947; Fulbright lectr. Melbourne, 1952, Kyoto, Japan, 1958, 66; Dudleian lectr. Harvard, 1963; Morse lectr. Union Theol. Sem., 1964. Served as pvt., hosp. orderly, U.S. Army, 1917-19. Mem. Am. Philos. Assn. (pres. western div. 1948-49), Internat. Phenomenological Soc., Metaphys. Soc. Am. (pres. 1954-55), Charles Pierce Soc. (pres. 1950-51), Am. Ornithol. Union, Soc. Philosophy Religion (pres. 1963-64), So. Soc. Philosophy and Psychology (pres. 1964-65), Phi Beta Kappa. Author: The Philosophy and Psychology of Sensation, 1934; Beyond Humanism, 1937; Man's Vision of God, 1941; The Divine Relativity, 1948; Reality as Social Process, 1953; (with Wm. Reese) Philosophers Speak of God, 1953; The Logic of Perfection, 1962 (Lecomte du Noüy award 1963); Anselm's Discovery, 1965; A Natural Theology for Our Time, 1967; Creative Synthesis and Philosophic Method, 1970; articles professional jours. Editor: The Collected Papers of Charles S. Peirce, 1931-35. Home: 724 Sparks Av Austin TX 78705 Office: Waggener Hall Univ Tex Austin TX 78712

HARTSHORNE, MARION HOLMES, educator; b. Englewood, N.J., Jan. 11, 1910; s. Edward C. and Marian (Holmes) H.; student Mass. Inst. Tech., 1928-30; B.A., Williams Coll., 1933, M.A., 1934; B.D., Union Theol. Sem., N.Y.C., 1936, Th.D., 1938; m. Ruth Scotford, Jan. 13, 1939; children—Jonathan E., Richard A., Timothy S., Sarah M., William H. Becker. Ordained to ministry Presbyn. Ch., 1936; pastor in Wilmington, Vt., 1938-40, at Olivet Coll., 1940-42, Doane Coll., 1942-46; mem. faculty Colgate U., 1946—, prof. philosophy and religion, 1955—, chmn. dept., 1963-70. Mem. Soc. Religion in Higher Edn., Phi Beta Kappa, Phi Kappa Tau. Author: The Promise of Science and the Power of Faith, 1958; The Faith to Doubt, 1963. Home: 17 Hamilton St Hamilton NY 13346

HARTSHORNE, RICHARD, educator; b. Kittanning, Pa., Dec. 12, 1899; s. Francis Cope and Marguerite (Haughton) H.; student Yeates Sch., Lancaster, Pa., 1912-16; B.S., Princeton, 1916-20; Ph.D. U. Chgo., 1924; LL.D., Clark U., 1971; m. Lois Huntington Wilde, June 8, 1928; children—Judith Ann, Marguerite Wilde, Harriet Huntington. Instr. geography, U. Minn., 1924-27, asst. prof., 1927-37, asso. prof., 1937-40; asso. prof., U. Wis., Madison, 1940-41, prof., 1941—, chmn. dept., 1950-54. Vis. prof. Pa. State U., 1965; on leave with OSS as chief geog. div., then asst. chief, research dir. research and analysis br. OSS, Washington, 1941-45; mem. civilian faculty Nat. War Coll., 1949. Served as pvt. U.S. Army, 1918. Social Sci. Research Council fellow, 1931-32. Mem. Assn. Am. Geographers (council 1937-40, pres. 1949), NRC (vice chmn. for geography, div. geography 1940-42), Am. Assn. U. Profs. (nat. council 1948-50), Phi Beta Kappa, Gamma Alpha. Unitarian. Clubs: Campus; University (Madison). Author: The Nature of Geography, 1939; Perspective on the Nature of Geography, 1959; The Academic Citizen, 1970; also reviews and articles. Home: 3218 Topping Rd Shorewood Hills Madison WI 53705

HARTSON, NELSON THOMAS, lawyer; b. Spokane, Wash., Nov. 26, 1887; s. Millard T. and Margaret S. (Roberson) H.; LL.B., U. Wash., 1912; m. Vera C. Bibbitt, Mar. 5, 1925 (dec. Nov. 1960); m. 2d, Elizabeth Robinson de Sibour, July 9, 1963. Practice law, Seattle, Wash., 1912; asst. corp. counsel City Seattle, 1919-22; apptd. asst. solicitor Internal Revenue, Washington, 1922, solicitor, 1923-25; now sr. partner Hogan & Hartson; gen. counsel, dir. Riggs Nat. Bank, 1944-68; adv. dir. Woodward and Lothrop; gen. counsel D.C. Bankers Assn., 1944-59; counsel Washington, D.C. Clearing House Assn., 1944-59; prof. taxation Georgetown U. Law Sch., 1934-36. Pres. U. Washington Alumni Assn., 1920-21. Gov., Menninger Found., Topeka; now mem. exec. com., dir. D.C. chpt. A.R.C., chmn. Washington regional blood program, 1960-61. Trustee, v.p. D.C. Pub. Library, 1947- 66, Washington Hosp. Center (hon.); hon. mem. chpt. Protestant Episcopal Cathedral Found., Washington. Entered first O.T.C. at the Presidio, San Francisco, May 12, 1917; commd. 2d lt. and assigned to machine gun co. 363d Inf., 91st Div.; served with A.E.F. in France; advanced to capt. and adj. 316th Ammunition Train; hon. discharged, May 26, 1919. Fellow Am. Bar Found.; mem. Am., D.C. bar assns., Washington Inst. Fgn. Affairs, S.A.R., Columbia Hist. Soc., Phi Delta Phi, Sigma Delta Chi, Phi Delta Theta. Republican. Episcopalian. Clubs: Metropolitan (president 1960-62), Alibi, Alfalfa (pres. 1957-58), National Press, Lawyers (pres. 1958-59). Rotary (Washington); Bohemian (San Francisco). Home: 2029 Connecticut Av Washington DC 20008 Office: 815 Connecticut Av Washington DC 20006

HARTSTEIN, JACOB I., educator; b. Stary Sambor, Austria, Sept. 10, 1912; s. Nathan B. and Lea (Harris) H.; ed. Talmudical Acad.; A.B., Yeshiva Coll., 1932, L.H.D., 1962; M.S., N.Y. City Coll., 1933; M.A., Columbia, 1936; Ph.D., N.Y. U., 1945; m. Florence Waldman, Aug. 16, 1942; children—Kalman, Norman Bernard. Came to U.S., 1920, naturalized, 1922. Sec., Rabbi Elchanan Theol. Sem. Tchrs. Inst., 1929-37; instr. social scis. Talmudical Acad., 1932-36; acting registrar Yeshiva Coll., 1935-36, registrar, 1936-44, sec. faculty, 1938-43, instr. edn., 1939-41, asst. prof. edn., 1941-44, dir., asst. prof. edn. Bernard Revel Grad. Sch., 1944-45; prof. edn., dir. Grad. Schs., Yeshiva U., 1945-50, dean, 1950-53, also dean Sch. Edn. and Community Adminstrn. 1948-53; lectr. edn. L.I. U., 1938-41, also psychology, 1939-41, asst. prof. edn. and psychology, 1941-45, acting head dept., 1944-45, prof., head dept., 1945-60, chmn. grad. div., 1949-51, dir. Grad. Sch., 1951-52, dean, 1953-60, dean sch. edn., 1960- 64; pres. Kingsborough Community Coll., 1964-69; prof. City U. N.Y., 1964- -. Supt. of schs., bd. secular edn. The United Yeshivos, 1945-48; research cons. Human Engring. div. U.S. Navy; cons. U.S. Office Edn.; dir. ednl. survey Jewish Community Portland, Me.; vice chmn. Mayor's Com. on Scholastic Achievement, N.Y.C., 1954-66, Gov.'s Com. on Scholastic Achievement, 1966—, on state, city, regional edn. coms.; bd. dirs., v.p. Council Higher Ednl. Instns. in N.Y.C. Gov., Jewish Acad. Arts and Scis.; mem. acad. adv. council, trustee Bar-Ilan U., Israel; mem. Met. N.Y. Commn. Tchr. Edn. and Profl. Standards, Community Planning Bd. 4, Borough Bklyn., Bklyn. citizens adv. bd. N.Y. State Constl. Conv.; mem. acad. adv. council Ferkauf Grad. Sch. Edn., Yeshiva U. Recipient Abraham Freeda award; Yeshiva Flatbush award; Yeshiva Coll. Alumni Assn. Bernard Revel Meml. award in arts and scis.; Outstanding Grad. Alumnus award L.I. U. Bklyn. Educator of Yr., 1964; Chief Rath Isaac Haleoi Herzog fellow, Gold medal award, 1965; Yeshiva U. Distinguished Service award, 1970. Fellow A.A.A.S., Nat. Assn. Jewish Day Sch. Prins. (pres.); mem. N.Y. Acad. Pub. Edn., Am. Ednl. Research Assn., Am. Assn. Sch. Adminstrs., Am. Assn. U. Profs., N.Y., Am., Eastern, Bklyn, (chmn. com. profl. ethics; exec. com.) psychol. assns., Eastern Assn. Coll. Deans (exec. com., dir.), Nat. Council Jewish Edn., N.E.A., Nat. Soc. Coll. Tchrs. Edn., N.Y. Counsellors Assn., Religious Edn. Assn. U.S., Soc. Advancement Edn., Phi Delta Kappa, Phi Alpha Theta. Jewish Orthodox religion. Mason. Author: Jewish Education in New York City; State Regulatory and Supervisory Control of Higher Education in New York. Co- author: A Model Program for the Talmud Torah; The Jews in American HistoryA Resource Book for Teachers of American History and Social Studies. Editor: Guide to General Psychology. Contbr. on ednl. history and problems to tech. and trade jours. Home: 1125 Virginia St Far Rockaway NY 11691 Office: City Coll UNY Convent Av at 136th St New York City NY 10031

HARTT, FREDERICK, educator; b. Boston, May 22, 1914; s. Rollin Lynde and Jessie Clark (Knight) H.; B.A., Columbia, 1935; postgrad. Princeton, 1935-36; M.A., N.Y. U., 1937, Ph.D., 1949; m. Margaret DeWitt Veeder, Mar. 11, 1943 (div. July 1960). Asst., Yale Art Gallery, 1941-42; vis. lectr. art, acting dir. art mus. Smith Coll., 1946-47; lectr. fine arts N.Y. U., 1948-49; from asst. prof. history art to prof. Washington U., St. Louis, 1949-60; prof. history art U. Pa., 1960-67, chmn. dept. art, 1960-65; McIntire prof. history art, chmn. dept. art U. Va., Charlottesville, 1967—. Vis. art historian Harvard Renaissance Center, Florence, Italy, 1965-66; mem. exec. com. Com. to Rescue Italian Art, 1966—. Bd. dirs. Am. Com. Restoration Italian Monuments, 1946-49. Guggenheim fellow, 1948-49, 54-55; Fulbright research grants, 1954-55, 65-66; Am. Council Learned Socs. fellow, 1965-66. Served to 1st lt. USAAF, 1942-46. Decorated Bronze Star medal; knight's Cross Crown of Italy; knight Officer Order Merit, Italian Republic; hon. academician Acad. Arts Design, Florence, 1970; named hon. citizen Florence, 1946. Mem. Coll. Art Assn. Am. (dir. 1959-62), Am. Assn. U. Profs., Renaissance Soc. Am. (council 1970). Episcopalian. Author: Florentine Art Under Fire, 1949; Botticelli, 1952; Giulio Romano, 2 vols., 1958; (with Kennedy and Corti) The Chapel of the Cardinal of Portugal, 1964; Love in Baroque Art, 1964; The Paintings of Michelangelo, 1964; Michelangelo, the Complete Sculpture, 1969; History of Italian Renaissance Art, 1969; Michelangelo's Drawings, 1971; also numerous articles. Home: Old Ordinary Route 7 Box 164 Charlottesville VA 22901

HARTT, JULIAN NORRIS, educator; b. Selby, S.D., June 13, 1911; s. Albert and Laura (Beals) H.; A.B., Dakota Wesleyan, 1932, D.Litt., 1959; B.D., Garrett Bibl. Inst., 1937; M.A., Northwestern U., 1938; Ph.D., Yale, 1940; m. Neva Beverly Leonard, June 16, 1935; children—Beverly Ann, Susan Laura, Julian Norris. Asso. prof. philosophy and religion Berea Coll., 1940-43; Noah Porter prof. philos. theology Yale, 1943—, chmn. dept. religion, 1956- 64, dir. grad. studies, dept. religious studies, 1964-67, chairman department of religious studies, 1967—. Recipient Fulbright fellow, 1963-64, Guggenheim fellow, 1963-64. Mem. Am. Philos. Assn., American Theological Association, National Council Religion in Higher Edn. Co- author: Humanism vs Theism, Towards A Theology of Evangelism; Being Known and Being Revealed; The Lost Image of Man, 1963; A Christian Criticism of American Culture. Author: Theology and the Church in the University, 1969. Home: 71 Swarthmore St Hamden CT 06517 Office: 409 Prospect St New Haven CT 06510

HARTUNG, ALBERT FERDINAND, labor leader; b. Catract, Wis., June 18, 1897; s. Ernest and Minnie (Jessica) H.; student pub. schs., Catract; m. Farris Chapman, Aug. 5, 1922; 3 children; m. 2d, Nina Calhoun, Sept. 5, 1953; 1 child. Began as logger, Ore., 1915; pres. local 5-37, Internat. Woodworkers of Am., Vernonia, Ore, 1935, Columbia River Dist. Council 5, 1936-41; asst. dir. orgn. Internat. Woodworkers Am., 1941-42; regional dir. State of Ore., C.I.O., 1942-47; 1st v.p. Internat. Woodworkers. 1947-51, pres., 1951-55; pres. Internat. Woodworkers Am; v.p. indsl. union AFL-CIO, 1955—. Mem. exec. bd. Ore. United Appeal. Served with WPB, lumber div. OPA, war bond com. and West Coast Lumber Commn. of War Labor Bd., World War II. Recipient citation from former Gov. Sprague Ore., for serving on first fire prevention com. State of Ore.; also citations War Manpower Commn., Treasury Dept., War Labor Bd. Democrat. Mason (32, Shriner). Home: 735 SW St Clair Av Portland OR 97205 Office: 1622 N Lombard St Portland OR 97217

HARTUNG, ERNEST WILLIAM, Jr., univ. president; b. N.Y.C., Jan. 20, 1917; s. Ernest W. and Marie (Drescher) H.; A.B., Dartmouth, 1938; A.M., Harvard, 1940, Ph.D., 1942; m. Mary W. Dennen, June 17, 1944; children—John W., Katharine D., Ernest D. Teaching fellow Harvard, also Radcliffe Coll., 1940-42; instr. to asst. prof. U. Vt., 1946-48; vis. lectr. Harvard, 1947, asst. prof. summers, 1948-52; asst. prof., then v.p. U.R.I., 1948—, chmn. dept. zoology, 1953-60, dean Grad. Sch., coordinator research, 1960-65; president University of Idaho, Moscow, Ida., 1965—. Trustee Knox Sch., 1949-53. Served from 2d lt. to capt., USAAF, 1942-45. Cramer fellow, Dartmouth, 1938-39; grantee cancer research USPHS-Am. Cancer Soc. Fellow N.Y. Acad. Scis.; mem. R.I. Heart Assn., Am. Soc. Zoologists, Soc. Study Devel. and Growth, Am. Inst. Biol. Scis., Am. Assn. U. Profs., Am. Genetic Assn., N.E.A., Sigma Xi, Phi Kappa Phi, Phi Sigma, Sigma Alpha Epsilon. Unitarian (chmn. bd. trustees). Home: 1026 Nez Perce Dr Moscow ID 83843

HARTUNG, HANS HEINRICH ERNST, artist; b. Leipzig, Sept. 21, 1904; s. Curt and Margarete (Nakonz) H.; student Lycee, Dresden, also Acad. Beaux Arts, Leipzig U.; m. Anna-Eva Bergman, Feb. 20, 1957. Abstract painter, 1922—; one man shows, Dresden, 1931, Oslo, 1932, Paris, 1939, 47, Basle, 1952, Brussels, 1954, Paris, 1956, 61, 62, 64, Germany, 1957, traveling exhbn., N.Y.C., 1957, internat. exhbns., Venice, Turin, Sao Paulo, Pitts., London, N.Y.C., Tokyo, Berlin, Zurich, Vienna, Düsseldorf, Brussels, Amsterdam; rep. permanent collections Mus. Modern Art, Paris, also Germany. Served with Fgn. Legion, 1939-41, 43-45. Decorated officer Legion of Honor, Croix de Guerre, First Internat. Painting Prize, 30th Venise Beinnale, 1960. Mem. Acad. Fine Arts Berlin, Acad. Fine Arts Munich. Address: Musée National d'Art Moderne 2 rue de Manutention 75 Paris 16e France

HARTUNG, WALTER MAGNUS, educator; b. N.Y.C., Aug. 10, 1907; s. Magnus and Amelia (Bradtke) H.; B.S. in Mech. Engring., N.Y.U., 1928, Aero. Engr., 1936, M.A., 1957, Ph.D., 1960; m. Emily M. Stasse, Oct. 19, 1935; 1 dau., Gale Anne (Mrs. Baldwin). Airplane designer Aeromarine-Klemm Corp., 1928-29; asst. chief engr. Aircraft Improvement Corp., 1929-31; dean aero. engring. Beckley Coll., Pa., 1931-32; aero engr. Granville Aircraft Corp., 1932-33; chief engring. instrn. Casey Jones Sch. Aeros., 1933-43; exec. v.p., dean Acad. Aeros., Flushing, N.Y., 1946-63, pres., 1964—. Mem. Queens adv. bd. Mfrs. Hanover Trust Co., 1970—. Chmn. U.S. Tech. Edn. Delegation to USSR, 1961. Chmn. planning bd., Tenafly, N.J., 1961- 63; mem. adv. com. on accreditation and instnl. eligibility Office Edn. Dept. Health, Edn. and Welfare, 1969—. Mayor Borough Tenafly, N.J., 1970—. Trustee Bergen Community Coll. Served from capt. to col., USAAF, 1943-46. Decorated Bronze Star medal with oak leaf cluster. Registered profl. engr., N.Y. Fellow Am. Inst. Aeros. and Astronautics; mem. Am. Soc. Engring. Edn. (v.p., chmn. tech. inst. council 1964-66, mem. ethics and legal phases com. 1968—), Nat. Council Tech. Schs. (pres. 1958- 60, trustee), N.Y.U. Alumni Fedn. (pres. 1964-66), Air Force Assn., Engrs. Council Profl. Devel. (chmn. engring. tech. com. 1966-68, engring. edn. and engring. accreditation and engring. tech. joint com. 1969—; bd. dirs. (1968-70), Nat. Indsl. Conf. Bd. (exec. com. 1968—), Nat. Soc. Profl. Engrs. (chmn. engring. tech. com. 1969-70), Delta Chi. Presbyn. Clubs: Knickerbocker Country (Tenafly); Englewood (Englewood, N.J.) Field; Lake Placid (N.Y.); Nat. Aviation (Washington); Wings (mem. council, 1965—, pres. 1967-68), Kiwanis, N.Y. University (gov. 1965-68) (N.Y.C.). Home: 145 E Clinton Av Tenafly NJ 07670 Office: LaGuardia Airport Flushing NY 11371

HARTWELL, ROBERT WELLINGTON, utility exec.; b. Detroit, Aug. 9, 1917; s. Everard George and Della (Johnston) H.; B.S. in Mech. Engring., U. Mich., 1939, M.B.A., 1940; m. Helene Walker, June 12, 1947; 1 son, Kenneth W. With Detroit Edison Co., 1940—, controller, 1968—, also exec. v.p. Served as officer USNR, 1941- 46, USN, 1952-53. Recipient Distinguished Profl. Achievement award U. Mich. Coll. Engring., 1968. Registered profl. engr., Mich. Mem. Am. Nuclear Soc., Detroit Nuclear Council, Am. Soc. M.E., Am. Soc. Engring. Edn., Engring. Soc. Detroit. Mem. industry com. U. Mich. Coll. Engring. Home: 30050 Bayview Dr Grosse Ile MI 48138 Office: 2000 2d Av Detroit MI 48226

HARTWELL, STEPHEN, investment co. exec.; b. Phila., Apr. 10, 1916; s. Stephen Warren and Elizabeth (Thompson) H.; B.S. in Adminstrv. Engring., Lafayette Coll., 1936; m. Elizabeth van Laer Speer, Feb. 21, 1946; children—Stephen Warren II, Robert van Laer. Investment analyst Pa. Co. Banking & Trusts, 1936-41; procurement officer electronic equipment CAA, 1947-48; indsl. specialist AEC, 1948-49, chief progress and statistics sect., prodn. div., 1949-51, chief constr. engring. reports br., 1951-54; exec. v.p. Steadman Security Corp. and predecessor cos., 1954-68; v.p. Washington Mut. Investors Fund, Inc., 1968—; chmn. adv. bd. Woodlawn Nat. Bank, Alexandria, Va., 1966—; director Ohmart Corp., Cin., Colchester Corp., Woodbridge, Va. Mem. Fairfax County (Va.) Planning Commission, 1961-67, chairman, 1964-66; member of Northern Virginia Regional Planning and Economic Devel. Commn., 1963-64. Mem. of Fairfax County Republican Com., 1955-61, 66-. Bd. trustees Washington chpt. Nat. Multiple Sclerosis Soc., 1959—; bd. govs. Gunston Hall Sch. (Virginia), 1963—. Served to maj. AUS, 1941-46. Decorated Commendation ribbon. Mem. Washington Society Investment Analysts, National Association of Securities Dealers (dist. 10 com. 1968-71), Zeta Psi. Club: Metropolitan (Washington). Home: 5929 River Dr Lorton VA 22079 Office: Southern Building Washington DC 20005

HARTWICK, ELBERT STUART, investor; b. Fargo, N.D., Dec. 7, 1903; s. Louis B. and Roberta Frances (Stuart) H.; A.B., U. Minn., 1930, J.D., 1930; m. Margaret Smith, Dec. 29, 1930; 1 son, Ronald Stuart. Admitted to Ill. bar, 1931, Minn. bar, 1931; atty. Theodore, Gary & Co., Chgo., 1930-33; atty., sec. Carnation Co., Los Angeles, 1933-44, v.p., dir. 1944-67, sr. v.p., 1967- 70; past pres., dir. Dairy Foods, Inc., Carnaco Equipment Co.; dir. Olson Farms, Inc., Cal. Bankers Trust Co., pres., dir. Bus. Investments Co., Rialto Center Co., Corporate Investments, Inc., Del Rosa Bldg. Co. Mem. Cal. Rep. State Central Com. Trustee U. Redlands. Mem. Am., Ill., Minn. bar assns., Acacia, Gray Friar, Alpha Delta Sigma, Pi Delta Epsilon, Phi Alpha Delta. Republican. Episcopalian. Mason (Shriner), Rotarian. Clubs: Los Angeles Country, Bel Air Bay; Thunderbird Country. Home: 436 Loring Av Los Angeles CA 90024 Office: 10889 Wilshire Blvd Los Angeles CA 90024

HARTWIG, CLEO, sculptor; b. Webberville, Mich., Oct. 20, 1911; d. Albert and Julia (Klunzinger) Hartwig; A.B., Western Mich. U., 1932; student Internat. Sch. Art, Europe, 1935; m. Vincent Glinsky, 1951; 1 son, Albert. Tchr. pvt. schs., N.Y.C., 1935-42; instr. Cooper Union, 1945-46; sculpture instr. Montclair (N.J.) Art Mus., 1945-71. First one man show, 1943; included group exhbns. Nat. Acad., Pa. Acad., Detroit Inst. Arts, Chgo. Art Inst., Met. Mus., Phila. Mus., Whitney Mus., others; traveling one- man show, Can., U.S.; represented in permanent collections Newark Mus., Detroit Inst. Arts, Pa. Acad., Montclair Art Mus., Mt. Holyoke Coll., Western Mich. U., Oswego (N.Y.) Univ., Norfolk (Va.) Museum. Recipient Kamperman Haass prize Mich. Artists Assn., 1943; Anna Hyatt Huntington prize for sculpture, 1945, L. Reusch & Co. prize N.Y. Soc. Ceramic Arts, 1946; Nat. Assn. Women Artists 1st prize for sculpture, 1951; Audubon Artists prize for sculpture, 1952; award mural and sculpture competition Munson-Williams-Proctor Inst., 1958; Feist Meml. prize Nat. Assn. Women Artists, 1968; Silver medal Nat. Sculpture Soc., 1969. Mem. Audubon Artists, Sculptors Guild, Nat.

Sculpture Soc., Nat. Assn. Women Artists (medal of honor 1967), Soc. Animal Artists, Nat. Acad. Design. Home: 9 Patchin Pl New York City NY 10011 Studio: 5 W 16th St New York City NY 10011

HARTWIG, HELLMUT ARTHUR ALBIN, educator; b. Berlin, Germany, July 10, 1910; s. Charles F. and Antonie (Tessel) H.; came to U.S., 1925, naturalized in 1929; A.S., Crane Jr. Coll., Chgo., 1932; B.A., U. Ill., 1936; M.A., La. State U., 1937; Ph.D., U. Ill., 1943; m. Anna Beata Erickson, Sept. 3, 1940; children—Charles Walter, Richard Eric, Frederic York (dec.). Teaching fellow La. State U., 1936-37, asst. German, 1937-39; asst. German, Ind. U., 1941; asst. prof. German and Spanish, Lindenwood Coll., St. Charles, Mo., 1941-42; asst. prof. German and Spanish, U. Kansas City, 1946, Union Coll., Schenectady, 1946-48; asso. prof. German, So. Ill. U., 1948-57, prof., 1957—, chmn. dept. fgn. langs., 1967—; dir. Nat. Def. Edn. Act, German Insts.; Fulbright exchangee Bismarckshule, Hannover and U. Goettingen, (West Germany), 1954-55. Bd. dirs. Carbondale YMCA, 1950-53, Carbondale Community Council, 1951-54. Served as capt., AUS 1942-46; ETO. Decorated Croix de Guerre (France). Mem. Am. Assn. U. Profs. (founder, past pres. Ill.), Ill. Modern Lang. Tchrs. Assn. (pres. 1959-60), Modern Lang. Assn., Am. Assn. Tchrs. German, Jean Paul Gesellschaft, Assn. Fgn. Lang. Depts., Am. Council Fgn. Langs., Internat. Germanistic Lang. and Lit. Assn. Contbr. articles rev. profl. jours. Editor: Southern Illinois Goethe Bicentennial Celebration, 2d edit., 1951. Translator: (with others) Henry George's Progress and Poverty (into German). Home: 103 S Parrish Lane Carbondale IL 62901

HARTWIG, LAWRENCE EDWARD, lawyer; b. Escanaba, Mich., Oct. 21, 1906; s. Frank and Bertha (Luecke) H.; A.B., U. Mich., 1931, J.D., 1934; fellow Carnegie Endowment for Internat. Peace, Cambridge U., Eng., 1936-37. Admitted to N.Y. bar, 1936; with firm Mudge, Stern, Williams & Tucker, N.Y.C., 1934- 36; asst. in law U. Mich., 1937-38; asst. prof. law, U. Ore. Sch. Law, 1938-42; atty. OPA, Washington, 1942-43; atty. gen. counsel's office Treasury Dept., 1943-45; mem. Appeal Bd. office contract settlement, 1945, chmn. bd. 1945-51; mem. The Renegotiation Bd., 1951—, chmn., 1961—. Mem. Fed., Am. bar assns., Am. Judicature Soc., Phi Beta Kappa, Phi Kappa Phi, Delta Sigma Rho. Home: 3520 39th St NW Washington DC 20016 Office: 1910 K St NW Washington DC 20006

HARTY, HARRY LAFAYETTE, Jr., naval officer; b. Grays Point, Mo., July 25, 1917; s. Harry Lafayette and Terzah (Mechin) H.; B.S., U.S. Naval Acad., 1939; postgrad. Indsl. Coll. Armed Forces, 1957-58; M.B.A., George Washington U., 1958; m. Frances Joan Brown, Mar. 10, 1942; children—Frances S. (Mrs. Elton C. O'Byrne), Terzah G. (Mrs. James E. Doyle), Marie J. (Mrs. R.W. Ewing), Melissa H. Commd. ensign USN, 1939, advanced through grades to vice adm., 1971; officer U.S.S. Saratoga, 1939-42; navigator comdr. patrol squadrons, also comdr. Hdqrs. Squadron 5, World War II; aide, flag lt. Air Force, U.S. Atlantic Fleet, 1945-46, Carrier Div. 1 (U.S.S. Midway and U.S.S. Roosevelt), 1946-47; navigator U.S.S. Roosevelt, 1951-52; comdg. officer U.S.S. Greenwich Bay, 1961-62, U.S.S. Randolph, 1962-63, aide, later operation and plans officer naval air stas. at Quonset, R.I. and Pensacola, Fla., 1947-51, Jacksonville, Fla., 1952-55; staff Field Marshall Montgomery SHAPE, Paris, France, 1955-57; mem. staff Joint Chiefs of Staff, 1959- 61; asst. dir. Office Navy Program Appraisal, Washington, 1963-66, dep. asst. chief plans and programs Bur. Naval Personnel, Washington, 1966; comdr. anti-submarine warfare group 3, Vietnam, 1966-67; dep. asst. chief staff plans and policy SHAPE, Brussels. 1967-70, asst. vice chief naval operations, 1970-71; vice chmn. UN Mil. Staff Com., 1971—. Active local civic affairs. Decorated D.S.M., Legion of Merit, Armed Forces Expeditionary medal Cuba (missile crisis 1962); Nat. Order Vietnam 5th class, Gallantry Cross with palm (Vietnam); numerous campaign and service medals. Rotarian. Clubs: Army/Navy Country (Arlington, Va.). Home: PO Box 130 Sikeston MO 63801 Office: 799 UN Plaza New York City NY 10017

HARTZ, LOUIS, educator; b. Youngstown, O., Apr. 7, 1919; s. Max and Fannie (Plotkin) H.; B.S. summa cum laude, Harvard, 1940, Sheldon traveling fellow, 1940- 41, Ph.D., 1946; m. Stella Feinberg, July 3, 1943; 1 son, Steven. Writer, Council for Democracy, 1941; instr. govt. Harvard, 1945-47, asst. prof., 1947-50, asso. prof., 1940-56, prof., 1956—, chmn. com. Am. Civilization, 1955-58; lectr. U. London, 1962; Walker-Ames vis. prof. U. Wash., 1963; Edward Douglass White lectr. La. State U., 1965; Centennial prof. U. Toronto, 1967. Recipient Woodrow Wilson prize Am. Polit. Sci. Assn. 1956. Mem. Am. Acad. Arts and Scis., Am. Polit. Sci. Assn. Author: Economic Policy and Democratic Thought, 1948; the Liberal Tradition in America, 1955; The Founding of New Societies, 1964. Contbr. articles polit. sci., hist. periodicals. Home: 10 Chenery Terrace Belmont MA 02178 Office: Littauer Center Harvard U Cambridge MA 02139

HARTZ, PAUL FERDINAND, automotive parts co. exec.; b. Denmark, Aug. 20, 1921; s. Ernest Ferdinand and Clara (Folden) H.; B.C., U. Toronto (Can.), 1949; C.P.A., 1953; m. Stella Duncanson, Dec. 16, 1943; children—Jo Ann, Peter. Naturalized, 1970. With Fram Can. Ltd., 1953-64, pres., 1960-64, now chmn. bd., dir.; exec. v.p. Fram Corp., 1964- 66, pres., chief exec. officer, 1966—, chmn. bd., 1970—, also dir.; dir. Bendix Corp., Detroit, R.I. Hosp. Trust Nat. Bank, Outlet Co., Providence, Jamesburg Corp., Worcester, Mass. Served as flight lt., pilot, RCAF, World War II. Mem. Young Presidents Orgn., N.A.M. (dir.). Home: 32 Nayatt Rd Barrington RI 02890 Office: 105 Pawtucket Av East Providence RI 02916

HARTZELL, FRANKLIN MACVEAGH, lawyer; b. Carthage, Ill., Aug. 24, 1923; s. Franklin MacVeagh and Mary (Ferris) H.; B.S., U. Ill., 1948, LL.B., 1950; m. Eleonore Gaebe, May 18, 1946; children—Susan L., Thomas F., Phoebe M. Admitted to Ill. bar, 1950; practice in Carthage, 1952—; asso. Homer H. Williams, 1952-55; partner Williams & Hartzell, 1955-65; pvt. practice law, 1966; partner Hartzell & Glidden, 1967—; city atty. Carthage, 1955-69. Sec., dir. Pioneer Lumber Co., Dallas City, Ill.; v.p., dir. Colchester Savs. & Loan Assn.; dir. Marine Trust Co. of Carthage. Bd. dirs. Meml. Hosp. Assn. Carthage, Hancock County Nursing Home Assn. Served with AUS, 1943-46, to 1st lt., 1950-52. Mem. Am., Ill., Hancock County bar assns., Soc. Hosp. Attys., Delta Kappa Epsilon, Phi Delta Phi. Democrat. Presbyn. Mason. Home: 306 S Madison St Carthage IL 62321 Office: 608 Wabash St Carthage IL 62321

HARTZELL, KARL DREW, former educator; b. Chgo., Jan. 17, 1906; s. Morton Culver and Bertha Vincent (Drew) H.; Ph.B. (cum laude), Wesleyan U., 1927; A.M., Harvard, 1928, Ph.D., 1934; m. Anna Carolyn Lomas, Sept. 7, 1935; children—Karl Drew, Richard Lomas, Julian Crane. Instr. history Carleton (Pa.) Coll., 1930-31; asst. history Harvard, 1934-35; asso. prof. econs., social sci. Ga. Sch. Tech., 1935-40; asso. prof. history Emory U., summers 1937-38; asst. prof. social studies State Tchrs. Coll., Geneseo, N.Y., 1940-45, 46-47; dir. div. records, historian N.Y. State War Council, 1945-46; adminstrv. officer Brookhaven Nat. Lab., 1947-49; in charge ednl. services Asso. Univs., Inc., 1949-52; dean Cornell Coll., 1952-56, Bucknell (Pa.) U., 1956-62; exec. dean State U. N.Y. at Stony Brook, 1962-65, adminstrv. officer, 1965-71, ret. Historian, Livingston County (N.Y.), 1943-46; mem. exec. com. Council Protestant Colls. and Univs., 1961-62; mem. commn. on religion in higher edn. Assn. Am. Colls., 1963-67, v.p., 1966-67; mem. Suffolk Indsl. Commn., 1964—; mem. Suffolk County Planning Commn., 1965-69; mem. Suffolk chpt. A.R.C., 1965—. Bd. dirs. John T. Mather Meml. Hosp. Mem. N.Y. Assn. County Historians (sec. 1944-46), Am. Hist. Assn., Assn. Am. Archivists, A.A.A.S., Am. Soc. Christian Ethics, Am. Acad. Religion, Phi Beta Kappa, Beta Theta Pi. Republican. Methodist. Author: The Empire State at War: World War II, 1949; Opportunities in Atomic Energy, 1950. Joint editor The Study of Religion on the Campus Today, 1967. Home: Box 826 Setauket LI NY 11733

HARTZELL, WILLIAM HENRICK, mfg. co. exec.; b. Middletown, O., Apr. 9, 1926; s. Omer and Marguerite (Ferguson) A.; B.S. in Bus. Adminstrn., Ohio State U., 1950; C.P.A., Ill., 1951; m. Anna Marie Kramer, May 17, 1958. With Price Waterhouse Co., C.P.A.'s, Chgo., 1950-54, Ekco Products Co., Chgo., 1954-65; with H.K. Porter Co., Inc., Pitts., 1965—, treas., 1967—. Home: 247 Tech Rd Thornburg Pittsburgh PA 15205 Office: 601 Grant St Pittsburgh PA 15219

HARTZMAN, CARL EDWIN, shipyard exec.; b. Kiowa, Kan., Jan. 1, 1913; s. Carl Theodore and Fannie Warder (Dunn) H.; B.S. in Mech. Engring., U. Minn., 1935; m. Claire Juanita Creech, Oct. 1, 1938; 1 son, Carl Davis. Marine sales engr. Fairbank Morse Co., 1935-41; with Avondale Shipyards, Inc., New Orleans, 1941—, v.p. engring., 1961-68, exec. v.p., 1968—. Mem. central tech. com. Am. Bur. Shipping, 1969—. Mem. hosp. bd. So. Baptist Conv., 1945—, pres., 1958. Trustee Baptist Hosp., New Orleans. Mem. New Orleans C. of C., Soc. Naval Architects and Marine Engrs. (chpt. chmn. 1963), La. Engring. Soc., Tau Beta Pi. Club: Propeller (New Orleans). Home: 1138 Washington Av New Orleans LA 70130 Office: PO Box 50280 New Orleans LA 70150

HARTZOG, GEORGE BENJAMIN, Jr., govt. ofcl.; b. Colleton County, S.C., Mar. 17, 1920; s. George Benjamin and Mazell (Steedly) H.; student Wofford Coll., Spartanburg, S.C., 1937; B.S. in Bus. Adminstrn., Am. U., 1953; LL.D. (hon.), Wash. U., St. Louis, 1971; m. Helen Carlson, June 28, 1947; children—George, Nancy, Edward. With Bur. Land Mgmt. and Nat. Park Service, Dept. Interior, 1946-62; exec. dir. Downtown St. Louis, Inc., 1962-63; asso. dir. Nat. Park Service, 1963-64, dir., 1964—; trustee John F. Kennedy Center Performing Arts, 1964—, mem. exec. com.; admitted to S.C. bar, 1942, Mo. bar, 1963, Supreme Ct. U.S. bar; 1949; U.S. Dist. Ct. D.C.; 1970. Mem. Zoning Commn. D.C., Nat Capital Planning Commn. Trustee, chmn. property mgmt. com. Nat. Trust for Historic Preservation; Com. Preservation White House; exec. dir. Pres.'s Adv. Council Historic Preservation; sec. Nat. Park Found.; bd. dirs. White House Hist. Assn. Mem. Nat. Recreation and Park Assn. (trustee), Washington Nat. Monument Soc. (sec.) Home: 1643 Chain Bridge McLean VA 22101 Office: Interior Bldg Washington DC 20240

HARVARD, WILLIAM CLYDE, Jr., educator; b. Canton, Miss., Sept. 26, 1923; s. William Clyde and Wilhelmenia L. (McCraine) H.; B.A., La. State U., 1943, M.A., 1947; Ph.D., U. London Sch. Econs., 1956; m. Sylvia G. Woodley, May 12, 1945; children—Deborah May, Valerie Lee. Asst. prof. Northwestern State Coll., 1949-52; asst. prof. La. State U., 1952-53, asso. prof., 1957-60, prof., 1960-64, chmn. dept. govt., 1961-64; prof., head dept. also V.O. Key prof. govt. U. Mass., Amherst, 1964-70; dean Coll. Arts and Scis. Va. Poly. Inst. and State U., 1970—, U. prof., 1971—; asst. prof. U. Fla., 1953-56, asso. prof., 1956-57, dir. Pub. Adminstrn. Clearing Service, 1954-57; vis. prof. U. Munich, Germany, Amherst Coll., Mt. Holyoke Coll., Lake Forest Coll. Temporary research dir. Fla. Constl. Adv. Commn., 1955; chmn. review com. Baton Rouge Plan of Govt., 1959-60; research asso. La. Law Inst., 1946-47, La. Legislative Council, 1953, 58. Served to 1st lt. AUS, 1943-46. Fellow So. Fellowships Fund, 1955-56; sr. Fulbright grantee, 1960-61. Mem. Am., New Eng. (pres. 1967-68), So. (exec. com. 1962-65) polit. sci. assns., Am. Soc. Legal and Polit. Philosophy, Am. Assn. U. Profs., Phi Beta Kappa, Pi Sigma Alpha, Tau Kappa Alpha, Delta Chi, Phi Eta Sigma. Author: The Government of Louisiana, 1958; Henry Sidgwick and Later Utilitarian Political Philosophy, 1959; (with Loren P. Beth) The Politics of Mis-Representation, 1962; (with Rudolph Heberle and Perry Howard) The Louisiana Elections of 1960, 1963; (with Floyd L. Corty) Rural-Urban Consolidation, 1964; The Government and Politics of the United States, 1965; (with Peter Odegard and Hans Baerwald) Peter Odegard's The American Republic, 2d edition, 1969. Editor: (with David Mayhew) Institutions and Practices of American Government, 1968. Editorial bd. Polity, 1968—. Home: 601 Rainbow Ridge Dr Blacksburg VA 24060

HARVELL, QUENTIN LINCOLN, assn. exec.; b. Flushing, N.Y., May 22, 1931; s. Thomas Lincoln and Sarah (Healy) H.; B.A. in Econs., Iona Coll., New Rochelle, N.Y., 1952; B.S. in Fgn. Trade, Georgetown U., 1956; m. Sandra J. Merriam, Apr. 4, 1956; children—Richard Morgan, Michael, Laurie Ann, Timothy Lee. Reporter-salesman F.W. Dodge Corp., 1956-58; mgr. advt. and sales promotion, feed supply div. Borden Co., 1958-61; dir. research Indian Jute Mills Assn., N.Y.C., 1961-62; v.p. Advt. Fedn. Am., 1962-63; chief staff exec. Pub. Relations Soc. Am., 1964-70; chief exec. officer Vol. Group Services, N.Y.C.; 1970—; lectr. on pub. relations, 1964. Active fund drive N.Y.C. council Boy Scouts Am., 1965-66. Served with AUS, 1952-54. Mem. Am. Soc. Assn. Execs. Club: Canadian (N.Y.C.). Author articles; contbr. Ency. Britiannica. Home: 280 Millwood Rd Chappagua NY 10514 Office: 845 3d Av New York City NY 10022

HARVEY, ABNER MCGEHEE, prof. medicine; b. Little Rock, Ark., July 30, 1911; s. George S. and Jenette (McGehee) H.; A.B., Washington and Lee U., 1930, D.Sc., 1949; M.D., Johns Hopkins, 1934; Sc.D. (honorary), University of Arkansas, 1951; m. Elizabeth Baker Treide, June 21, 1941; children—Jenette, Elizabeth, Joan, George. Intern, Johns Hopkins Hosp., 1934-35, asst. resident phys., 1935-37; research fellow, Nat. Inst. Med. Research, London, 1937-39: fellow, Johnson Foundation for Biophysics, U. of Pa., 1939-4O; resident physician, Johns Hopkins Hosp., 194O-41; asst. prof. medicine, Vanderbilt U. Med. Sch., 1941-42; prof. medicine, Johns Hopkins U. Med. School, physician-in-chief, Johns Hopkins Hosp. since 1946. Commd. capt., M.C., U.S. Army, 1942, advanced through grades to lt. col., 1945. Awarded battle stars. New Guinea Campaign and Southern P.I. Campaign. Mem. American Rheumatism Assn., Assn. of American Physicians (pres. 1968), American Soc. for Clin. Investigation, Physiol. Soc. of Gt. Britian, Interurban Clin. Club, Am. Physiol. Soc., Am. Clin. and Climatolog. Assn., American College Physicians, Medical and Chirurgical Faculty of Md., Baltimore City Med. Soc., Am. Society for Pharm. and Exptl. Therap., Phi Beta Kappa, Alpha Omega Alpha, Nu Sigma Nu, Sigma Chi. Author. (with J. Bordley III) Differential Diagnosis, 1969. Editor: The Principles and Practice of Medicine; (with others) The Principles and Practice of Medicine, 1968. Home: 4201 St Paul St Baltimore MD 21218 Office: Johns Hopkins Hosp Baltimore MD 21205

HARVEY, ALEXANDER, II, judge; b. Balt., May 3, 1923; s. Fred B. and Rose (Hopkins) H.; B.A., Yale, 1947; LL.B., Columbia, 1950; m. Mary E. Williams, Feb. 24, 1951; children—Elizabeth H., Alexander IV. Admitted to Md. bar, 1950; asso. firm Ober, William, Grimes & Stinson, Balt., 1950-66, partner, 1953-66; asst. atty. gen. Md., 1957-58; judge U.S. Dist. Ct. for Md., 1966—. Mem. Gov. Md. Com. to Study Blue Sky Law of Md., 1961; mem. character com. Ct. Appeals Md. 8th Jud. Circuit. Bd. dirs. Balt. Symphony Assn., 1966-68; pres., dir. Balt. Opera Guild, 1960; bd. dirs. Balt. Council Social Agys., 1957-63; trustee Ch. Home and Hosp., Balt., 1952- 71. Served to 1st lt. AUS, World War II: ETO. Mem. Am., Md., Balt. bar assns., Phi Beta Kappa. Episcopalian (vestry 1967-70). Home: Brightside Rd Baltimore MD 21212 Office: Post Office Bldg Baltimore MD 21202

HARVEY, ALEXANDER MILLER, clergyman: b. Topeka, July 20, 1907; s. Alexander Miller and Isabelle (Cone) H.: A.B., St Mary's Coll., 1932: M.A., Catholic U., 1932: S.T.L., Gregorian U., Rome, 1936. Ordained priest Roman Catholic Ch., 1935; priest Archdiocese of Kansas City, Kan.; 1935; chancellor; 1940- 52: pastor Old Cathedral of Immaculate Conception; Leavenworth, Kan., 1953—, formerly vicar gen. archdiocese. Pres. Immaculata High Sch. Address: 709 N 5th St Leavenworth KS 66048

HARVEY, BARTLETT, govt. ofcl.; b. Brookline, Mass., Dec. 24, 1919; s. Elbert A. and Lucile H. (Stimson) H.; grad. Deerfield Acad., 1938; B.A., Amherst Coll., 1942; M.A., Harvard, 1947, M.P.A., 1948; m. Margaret J. Brown, Oct. 17, 1942; children—Bartlett, Joan C., Elizabeth M. (Mrs. Kilbreth), David S. Intern, Nat. Inst. Pub. Affairs, 1942; program economist ECA, Paris, France, 1949-50, The Hague, 1950-52, chief program officer, Rome, 1952-55; asst. chief internat. div. Bur. of Budget, 1955-60; dep. asst. adminstr. for program A.I.D., 1961-66, spl. asst. to adminstr., 1966-67, dep. dir., Turkey, 1967-69, dir., Afghanistan, 1970—. Chmn. Brazil study group Nat. Security Council, 1969- 70. Treas. Overseas Sch., Rome, 1953-55. Served to 1st lt., AUS, 1943-46. Mem. Am. Econ. Assn., Soc. Internat. Devel. Home: 902 Turkey Run Rd McLean VA 22101 Office: Kabul (ID) Dept State Washington DC 20521

HARVEY, CHARLES DAGGETT, restaurant exec.: b. Chgo., Nov. 24, 1906: s. Byron Schermerhorn and Helen (Daggett) H.: grad. St Mark's Sch., A.B., Yale, 1928; J.D., Northwestern U., 1933: m. Jean Wilhelm, June 22, 1935 (dec.); children—Jean (Mrs. Alfred G. Vanderbilt), Daggett, Melissa. Admitted to Ill. bar, 1933; asso. Sidley, McPherson, Austin & Burgess, Chgo., 1933- 42: v.p. Fred Harvey, Inc., Chgo., 1946-55, vice chmn., 1955-65, chmn., 1965—; dir. Amfac, Inc., Baxter Labs. Adv. com. internat. bus. problems U.S. State Dept. Dir. Chgo. Crime Commn.; mem. Ill Arts Council, Chgo. Commn. on Human Relations. Bd. dirs., chmn. Chgo. Maternity Center; bd. dirs. Gt. Books Found., Women's Hosp. and Maternity Center of Chgo., Inst. for Philos. Research, Lincoln Park Zool. Soc., Adlai E. Stevenson Inst. Internat. Affairs; chmn. Lyric Opera Chgo.; trustee Northwestern U., Chgo. Orchestral Assn., Lake Forest Coll., Shedd Aquarium Served as lt. comdr. USNR, 1942-45. Decorated chevalier French Legion of Honor. Mem. Chgo. Council Fgn. Relations, Art Inst. Chgo., Chgo. Bar Assn. Episcopalian. Clubs: Confrerie des Chevaliers du Tastevin, Commonwealth, Law, Commercial, Wayfarers, Chicago, Caxton, Mid-Am., Tavern, Saddle and Cycle (Chgo.). Home: 2430 Lake View Av Chicago IL 60614 Office: 80 E Jackson Blvd Chicago IL 60604

HARVEY, DONALD JOSEPH, educator; b. N.Y.C., Oct. 4, 1922; s. William Harold and Helen (Chiampou) H.; B.A. cum laude, Princeton, 1943; M.A., Columbia, 1948, Ph.D., 1953; postgrad. U. Paris, 1950- 51; m. Jacqueline Rozendaal, June 11, 1955; 1 dau., Nanett. Instr., Hunter Coll., City U. N.Y., 1951-56, asst. prof., 1956-60, asso. prof., 1960-67, prof. history, 1967—, chmn. dept. history, 1968—; reader/cons. Univ. presses of Yale, Cornell, State U. N.Y. Served to capt., arty., AUS, 1943-46; ETO. Ford Found. fellow, 1954-55; Fulbright alternate, 1959-60. Mem. Am. Hist. Assn., Soc. for French Hist. Studies, Am. Assn. U. Profs., Phi Alpha Theta. Author: (with E.M. Earle) Modern France, 1951; France Since the Revolution, 1968. Contbr. articles profl. jours. Home: 279 Park Av Manhasset NY 11030 Office: 695 Park Av New York City NY 10021

HARVEY, EDWARD, educator: B. Lewiston, Me., Mar. 14, 1917; s. John Edward and Eva (Langelier) H.: B.A., Bates Coll., 1937; M.A., Middlebury Coll., 1946; M.A., Harvard, 1946, Ph.D., 1952; m. Alice Savina Wilson, Aug. 30, 1939; childrenDiane (Mrs. Gerald M. Clarke), Janet (Mrs. William Graddick), and James. Fellow Institute of International Education, Lycee, Angers, France, 1937-38; tchr. French, chmn. dept. langs. Rochester (N.H.) High Sch., 1938-42; teaching fellow Harvard, 1944-48; Samuel Mather prof. French, Kenyon Coll., 1948—; vis. prof. Colby Coll., 1962, 66; Colo. Coll., 1963, Ohio State U., 1965; prof.-in-charge Jr. Year in France, Sweet Briar Coll., 1966-67. Mem. Coms. advanced placement program Coll. Entrance Exam. Bd., 1952-61. Central committeeman Knox County Democratic Party, 1956—, chmn., 1964; mem. Ohio Democratic Platform Com., 1958, 60. Mem. Central States Modern Lang. Assn., (v.p. 1962), Am. Assn. Tchrs. French, Modern Lang. Assn. Am., Phi Beta Kappa. Contbr. profl. jours. Asst. mng. editor Modern Lang. Jour., 1964-70. Home: Box 123 Gambier OH 43022

HARVEY, FREDERICK BARTON, Jr., investment banker; b. Balt., June 22, 1921; s. Frederick Barton and Rose (Hopkins) H.; grad. Hill Sch., 1939; A.B., Harvard, 1943; m. Grace Locke, Jan. 25, 1946; children—Grace Walker, Frederick Barton III, John Locke, Rose Hopkins. Mng. partner Alex Brown & Sons. Balt., 1946—; dir. So. Airways, Inc., Am. Fidelity Life Ins. Co., P.A. & S. Small Co., Balt. & Annapolis Railroad, Canton Co., Commercial Credit Co., Savs. Bank Balt. Gov. N.Y. Stock Exchange. Bd. dirs. Greater Balt. Med. Center, Family and Childrens Soc., Home for Incurables Balt. City, Community Chest Balt.; trustee Hill Sch. Served to capt. USMCR, World War II. Decorated Navy Cross, Purple Heart; named Outstanding Young Man of Year Balt.. Jr. Assn. Commerce, 1956, 57. Mem. Investment Bankers Assn. Am., Assn. Stock Exchange Firms, Met. Balt. C. of C. (dir.). Episcopalian. Clubs: Elkridge, Merchants Home: 2 Lindsay Lane Baltimore MD 21212 Office: 135 E Baltimore St Baltimore MD 21202

HARVEY, GEORGE B., corp. exec.; b. 1931; B.S., U. Pa., 1954; postgrad. student, U. Md., N.Y. U.; married. With Pitney-Bowes, Inc., 1957—, treas., 1968—. Served with AUS, 1954-56. Address: Pitney-Bowes Inc Walnut and Pacific Sts Stamford CT 06903*

HARVEY, GEORGE GRAHAM, physicist; b. St. Louis, Jan. 25, 1908; s. William Augustus and Pauline Virginia (Graham) H.; A.B., Washington U., 1928, M. Sc., 193O, Ph.D., 1932; M. Dorothy Evelyn Howe, Mar. 27, 1954. Asst. physics Washington U., 1928-3O; Nat. Research Council fellow, U. Chgo., 1932-34; instr. physics Mass. Inst. Tech., 1934-37, asst. professor physics, 1938-43, associate professor physics, 1943-61, professor physics, 1961—; staff radiation laboratory, 1942-46; asst. dir. research lab. electronics, 1950-52, asso. dir., 1952—, exec. officer dept. physics, 1952-70, academic officer, 1970—. Cons. office field service OSRD, 1944-45. Fellow A.A.A.S., Am. Phys. Soc., Inst. Physics (London), Phys. Soc. London, Am. Acad. Arts and Scis.; mem. Am. Assn. Physics Tchrs., Am., Edinburgh, London mathematical societies, American Ordnance Association, Math. Assn. Am., Optical Society of Am., Air Force Assn., Sigma Xi, Phi Beta Kappa, Pi Mu Epsilon, Phi Beta Kappa Assos. Home: 12 Washington St Belmont MA 02178 Office: Mass Inst Tech Cambridge MA 02139

HARVEY, H.D., business exec.; b. Orange, N.J., 1902; married. Partner, Hammond, Harvey & Braxton, mortgage brokers, 1932-52; with Uris Bros., 1952-60; with Uris Bldgs. Corp., N.Y.C., 1960—, now v.p., chmn. finance com., dir.; trustee Union Sq. Savs. Bank, N.Y.C. Trustee Midtown Hosp. Office: 850 3d Av New York City NY 10022*

HARVEY, HOLMAN, writer; b. Washington, Aug. 5, 1894; s. Frederick L. and Pamela D. (Holman) H., Jr.; student George Washington U., 1912; m. Marie Baylor 1917 (dec.); 1 dau., Barbara H. (Mrs. Morgan Greenwood); m. 2d, Dorothy Hoffman, 1920 (dec.); children—Frederick H., Dean H. (dec.); m. 3d, Phoebe A. Guthrie, Nov 15, 1941. Reporter, Washington Times, 1913-15; Washington corr. United Press, 1915-18; dir. information FTC, 1919; U.S. editor in chief Cross-Atlantic Newspaper Service, 192O; reporter Phila. Enquirer, 1922; roving reporter N.Y. Evening Mail, 1922-23; nat. dir. publicity Hearst mags., N.Y.C., 1925-30; publishers rep., N.Y.C., 1931- 34; nat. dir. Mark Twain Centennial Com., 1935; nat. mag. writer, 1936- 44; staff writer Readers Digest, 1944—; assignments to Africa, Mediterranean, Europe, 1951-52, to Italy, 1964-65. Mem. Acad. Polit. Sci. Episcopalian. Clubs: Nat. Press (Washington); Overseas Press (N.Y.C.); Press (London, Eng.). Contbr. articles mags. Address: 20 State St Charleston SC 29401

HARVEY, JAMES, congressman; b. Iron Mountain, Mich., July 4, 1922; s. Martin and Agnes (Thomas) H.; LL.B., U. Mich., 1948; m. June Elizabeth Collins, Apr. 1, 1948; children—Diane E., Thomas M. Admitted to Mich. bar, 1948; asst. city atty., Saginaw, Mich., 1949-53; with firm Smith, Brooker & Harvey, Saginaw, 1953-61; mem. 87th-92d Congresses from 8th District of Michigan. Served to 1st lt. USAAF, 1942-45. Named one of five outstanding young men of Mich., 1957. Mem Am., Mich. bar assns., Saginaw Jr. C. of C. (pres.; chmn. safety com). Republican. Presbyn. Home: 2746 W Genesee Saginaw MI 48602 Office: House Office Bldg Washington DC 20515

HARVEY, JAMES DOUGLAS, hosp. adminstr.; b. Yankton, S.D., Jan. 19, 1929; s. Guy Hazelton and Edythe (Canon) H.; B.A., U.S.D., 1950; M.H.A., U. Minn., 1952; m. Inadoll Cruickshank, Sept. 9, 1950; children—Stuart James, Barbara Beth, Scot Wallace. Asst. adminstr. Hillcrest Med. Center, Tulsa, 1955-61, adminstr., 1961—; instr. hosp. adminstrn. Okla. Baptist U., 1959-60; vis. lectr. Washington U., St. Louis, 1963—. Served with Med. Service Corps, USAF, 1952-54; Korea. Fellow Am. Coll. Hosp. Adminstrs. (council regents 1964-70, gov. 1970—); mem. Am. (chmn. com. personnel 1965- 66, council on finance 1971—), Okla. (treas. 1958-59, 60-61, pres. 1961-62, 63-64) hosp. Assns., Tulsa Hosp. Council (pres. 1961-62), Tulsa Execs. Assn., Midwest Hosp. Assn. Rotarian (pres. Will Rogers club 1962). Home: 2207 Terwilleger Tulsa OK 74114 Office: 1120 S Utica Av Tulsa OK 74104

HARVEY, JASPER ELLIOTT, educator; b. Sweetwater, Tex., July 15, 1924; s. Wiley James and Julia Mae (Nolen) H.; B.A., U. Tex., 1950, M.Ed., 1952, Ph.D., 1959; m. Kathryn McDaniel, Nov. 27, 1947; children—Laurel, Leigh. Dir. spl. edn., Texas City, Tex., 1952-53; spl. edn. tchr. disturbed and retarded, Austin, Tex., 1953-54; dir. Variety Sch. Exceptional Children, Las Vegas, 1954- 57, lectr. spl. edn. U. Tex., summer 1954, advanced grad. student, research asso. ednl. psychology, 1957-59, lectr. ednl. psychology, summers 1958, 59; chmn. dept. spl. edn. U. Ala., 1959-69, prof., 1963- 69: prof., chmn. dept. spl. edn. Coll. Edn., U. Tex., 1969—; cons. in field, 1963—. Mem. adv. bd. handicapped children project So. Regional Edn. Bd., 1964-68; Ala. rep. Am. Assn. Mental Deficiency, 1966-69: field reader U.S. Office Edn., 1966—; mem. exec. com. Ala. Gov.'s Com. Statewide Plan Vocational Rehab., 1966-69; gov. bd. Council Exceptional Children Washington, 1967-69; interim com. Reorgn. Ala. Dept. Edn., 1967- 69; chmn. med. profl. adv. and evaluation bd. United Cerebral Palsy Ala., 1966-69; adv. bd. mental retardation Ala. Bd. Mental Health, 1967-69; rep. White House Conf. Mental Retardation, 1963; spl. edn. communications systems task force Bur. Edn. for Handicapped. Served with AUS, 1944- 46. Decorated Combat Med. badge. Mem. Council Exceptional Children, Am. Assn. Mental Deficiency, Am. Psychol. Assn., Am. Speech and Hearing Assn., Am. Acad. Cerebral Palsy of A.M.A., Phi Kappa Phi. Episcopalian. Author reports in field. Home: 1122 Colorado St Austin TX 78701

HARVEY, JEAN CHARLES, writer, journalist; b. Murray Bay, Que., Can., Nov. 10, 1891; s. John and Mina (Trudell) H.; student Chicoutimi Coll. 1905-08, Jesuit's Coll., Montreal, 1908-14; B.A., Laval U., Montreal, 1914; m. Eve Pelland; children—Carmen, Claire (Mrs. F. M. Trentham), Jeanne (Mrs. Thola Theilhaber), Charles M., Claude E., Marcel, F. Axel. Reporter La Patrie, daily, Montreal, Que., 1915, La Press, daily, 1916-18; publicity mgr. Nat. Farming Machinery, Montmagny, 1919-21; reporter, asst. chief editor, parliamentary corr., le Soleil, Quebec City, 1922-27, chief, 1928-34; chief statistician, P.Q., 1934-37; founder, editor Le Jour, polit. and lit. weekly, Montreal, 1937-46; radio producer, commentator, Canadian Broadcasting Corp., CKAC, Montreal, 1946-53; editor Le Petit Jour. Photo-Jour., weeklies, Montreal, 1953-66. Decorated Officier d'Academie (France). Clubs: Twenty, Men's Press. Author: Marcel Faure, 1922; Pages de Critque, 1926; L'Homme qui Va. . . , 1929; Les Demi- Civilises, 1934; Sebastian Pierre, 1935; Art et Combat, 1938; Eternal Struggle, 1943: Les Paradis de Sable, 1953; La Fille du Silence (poems), 1958, Pourquoi je suis antisparatiste, 1962; Visages du Quebec, 19665; Des Champs, des bois, des bettes, 1965. Home: 4780 Cote-des-Neiges Montreal Quebec Canada Office: 5460 Royalmount Av Montreal Quebec Canada

HARVEY, JOHN COLLINS, physician; b. Youngstown, O., Sept. 11, 1923; s. Joseph Paul and Mary J. (Collins) H.; grad. Phillips Exeter Acad., 1941; B.S., Yale, 1944; M.D., 10 children—Elizab Viola, John Collins, William Charles II, Amy Lavinia Ryan, Margaret Julia Bingham. House officer, asst. resident physician, resident Johns Hopkins Hosp., 1947-53, physician, 1953—; research in muscle diseases, practice of internal medicine, Balt., 1953—; dir. out patient services Johns Hopkins Hosp., 1962—; A. Blaine Brower traveling fellow to Guy's Hosp., London, Eng., 1956; instr., asst. prof. medicine Johns Hopkins, 1952-57, then asso. prof., now prof. Served as capt., M.C., AUS, 1949- 51. Diplomate Am. Bd. Internal Medicine. Fellow A.C.P.; mem. Am. Fedn. Clin. Research, A.M.A., Biophys. Soc., S.A.R., N.Y. Acad. Sci., Am. Clin. and Climatological Assn., Am. Assn. U. Profs., A.A.A.S., Phi Beta Kappa, Sigma Xi, Alpha Omega Alpha. Republican. Roman Catholic. Author: articles in field. Editor: Tice's Practice of Medicine, 1961. Home: 410 Northway Baltimore MD 21218 Office: 725 N Wolfe St Baltimore MD 21205

HARVEY, JOHN FRANCIS, publisher; b. Jefferson City, Mo., Aug. 1, 1922; s. William Walter and Exie Marie (Lindley) H.; S.B., Harvard, 1943, M.B.A., 1947; m. Mary Jane Shaw, Jan. 24, 1959; children—Mary Lindley, Laura Treat, Thomas Shaw. With Time Inc., 1947—, comptroller, 1957-71, v.p.; 1965—, Sec., 1967-71; asst. to pres.; 1971—; dir. Time-Life Broadcast, Inc., Printing Devels., Inc., N.Y. Graphic Soc. Ltd., Gen. Learning Corp. Mem. adv. com. Cardinal Spellman of N.Y. Spl. Edn. Program, 1965-69; mem. Cardinals Com. on Edn.; 1970—; exec. council Harvard Bus. Sch. Assn., 1967-70. Served with AUS, 1944-46. Mem. Internat. Golf Assn. (sec.-treas.), Financial Execs. Inst. Clubs: Harvard (N.Y.C.); Sleepy Hollow Country (Scarborough-on-Hudson N.Y.); Bedford Golf and Tennis (Bedford, N.Y.). Home: 1192 Park Av New York City NY 10028 also Bedford NY 10506 Office: Time-Life Bldg Rockefeller Center New York City NY 10020

HARVEY, JOHN FREDERICK, librarian; b. Maryville, Mo., Aug. 24, 1921; s. Abraham Frederick and Lois Ernestine (Glenn) H.; A.B., Dartmouth, 1943; B.S. in Library Sci., U. Ill., 1944; Ph.D. (John Crerar Library scholar 1945-47, U. Chgo. Divisional scholar 1947-49), U. Chgo., 1949. Dean, Grad. Sch. Library Sci., Drexel U., Phila., 1958-67, dir. libraries, 1958-63; prof. dept. library sci. Coll. Edn., U. Tehran, 1967-71, chmn. dept., 1967-68; founder, tech. dir. Iranian Documentation Centre and Tehran Book Processing Centre, 1968—. Recipient Library Binding Inst. Silver Book award, 1965. Fulbright grantee, 1967-71. Mem. A.L.A., Assn. Coll. and Research Libraries. Am. Assn. Univ. Profs., Iran Am. Soc., Ianian Library Assn. (hon. life), Ch. and Synagogue Library Assn. (hon. life), Library Pub. Relations Assn. (hon. life). Club: Philobiblon. Author monographs, articles profl. periodicals. Editor: The Library-College, 1966; Data Processing in Public and University Libraries, 1966. Home: 1517 N Barton St Arlington VA 22201

HARVEY, JOHN HENRY, arts critic; b. New Prague, Minn., Oct. 27, 1911; s. William Lemuel and Eleonora (Holub) H.; B.A., Yale, 1933; m. Irene Forsyth Gorman, Aug. 21, 1939; children—Eleonora H. (Mrs. Edward F. D'Arms, Jr.), William Lemuel, John Henry. Reporter, St. Paul Dispatch and Pioneer Press, 1934-45, music and art critic, 1945—, drama critic, 1947—; program annotator Minn. Orch., 1960-63. Mem. Music Critics Assn. Clubs: University, Minnesota (St Paul). Home: 445 Summit Av St Paul MN 55102 Office: 55 E 4th St St Paul MN 55101

HARVEY, JOHN STEWART, former restaurant exec.; b. Chgo., June 2, 1905; s. Byron Schermerhorn and Helen (Daggett) H.; grad. St Mark's Sch.; grad. Yale, 1928; m. Laura Cornell, Sept. 2, 1931; children—John Stewart, Frederick Huckel, William Cornell. Apprentice food operations Palmer House, Chgo., 1927; with Fred Harvey, Inc., Chgo., 1928-70, beginning as dining car steward, successively dir., 1936-70, v.p., 1938-55, vice chmn., 1955-67, corp. dir., 1968, ret., 1969; dir. Santa Fe Downs Racetrack bd. dirs. Mem. Soc. Colonial Wars. Episcopalian. Club: Santa Fe Country. Address: PO Box 2344 Santa Fe MN 87501

HARVEY, LASHLEY GREY, govt. cons.; b. Cal., Mo., Dec. 18, 1900; s. Alexander N. and Ella (Inglish) H.; A.B., William Jewell Co., Liberty, Mo., 1925; A.M., Stanford, 1930; Ph.D., Harvard, 1942; m. Ernestine Dow, Aug. 7, 1926; 1 son, David Dow. Exec. sec. Bur. Govt. Research, asst. prof. govt. U. N.H., 1938-42; asst. prof. govt. Boston U., 1946-47, Maxwell prof. govt., citizenship, chmn. dept. govt., 1948, 56, dir. Bur. Pub. Adminstrn., 1948-67, prof. govt., 1946-67. Fulbright scholar, vis. prof. London Sch. Econs. and Polit. Sci., 1951-52; vis. prof. Coll. Holy Cross, Worcester, Mass., 1968- 69; vis. scholar Norfolk (Va.) State Coll., 1968; lectr. Royal Inst. Internat. Affairs Chatham House, London, 1952; cons. Mass. Com. on Structure State Govt., 1950; U.N. expert, Inst. Pub. Adminstrn. for Turkey and Middle East, Ankara, 1953-54. Served as lt. to lt. comdr. USNR, 1942-45. Mem. Am. Polit. Sci. Assn., Am. Assn. U. Profs., Phi Gamma Delta. Democrat. Episcopalian. Author: A Guide to Governmental Procurement Techniques, 1965; Water: Modern Methods of Use and Conservation, 1966. Contbr. articles polit. sci. prof. publs. Address: 1516 Westwood Rd Charlottesville VA 22901

HARVEY, LAURENCE, actor; b. Yonishkis, Lithuania, Oct. 1, 1928; s. Ber Skikne and Ella Zotnickaita; studied schs. of Johannesburg, South Africa; student Royal Academy of Dramatic Art, London, England, 1946; m. Joan Perry Cohn, 1968. Came to U.S., 1952. Appeared various plays, theatre in Manchester, Eng., 1947-51; actor As You Like It, Coriolanus, MacBeth, Volpone, Stratford-on-Avon, 1952-54, Romeo and Juliet, also Troilus and Cressida, 1954; appeared in The Rivals, London, 1955, Island of Goats, N.Y.C., 1956, The Country Wife, London and N.Y.C., 1957, toured U.S. with Old Vic in Henry V, 1959, Dial "M" for Murder, 1968; television roles in England include Othello, in 1949, As You Like It, 1953, The Small Servant, 1955, Violent Years, 1959; motion picture films House of Darkness, Man From Yesterday, Cairo Road, Black Rose Scarlet Thread, Wall of Death, Gathering Storm, Innocents of Paris, Romeo and Juliet, Good Die Young, Three Men in a Boat, Silent Enemy, Room at the Top, Expresso Bongo, The Alamo, Butterfield 8, Wonderful World of Brothers Grimm, Tamiko, The Long, The Short, and The Tall, The Manchurian Candidate, The Running Man, The Ceremony, of Human Bondage, The Outrage, Darling, 1965, Life at the Top, 1965, Dandy in Aspic, 1968, Struggle for Rome, 1968, She and He, 1969, Hall of Mirrors, 1969, The Magic Christian, 1969, Child's Play, 1971, others; stage appearances Camelot, 1964, The Winters Tale, 1968; Starred in Arms And The Man at Chichester Festival Theatre; starred on TV in Arms and the Man. Dir. play entitled Simply Heavenly, 1958. Served So. African Armed Forces. Named Most Promising Actor of Yr. N.Y Theater, 1955; nominated for performances in Room at the Top and Expresso Bongo, Brit. Film Acad., 1959-60; named best actor of year Variety Clubs of Great Britain, 1960; nominated best actor for Room at the Top, Am. Acad award, 1960; nominated one of Filmdom's Famous 5's, 1960. Office: care Romulus Films Ltd Brook House Park Lane London W1 England

HARVEY, LAWRENCE A., aluminum co. exec.; b. Ontario, Cal., 1912; B.S., U. So. Cal., 1931, J.D., 1934; M.B.A., Harvard, 1936; married. With Harvey Aluminum Inc., 1938—, pres., chief exec. officer, 1962—, also dir.; pres., dir. Consol. Pacific Investment Co.; pres. Harcraft Co.; Compagnie des bauxites de Guinee; chmn. Signal Ins. Co.; chmn. Alnor, Budget Industries Inc. Home: 10761 Bellagio Rd Los Angeles CA 90024 Office: 417 S Hill Los Angeles CA 90013

HARVEY, LAWRENCE ELLIOT, educator; b. Denver, Feb. 13, 1925; s. Elliot McNary and Marguerite (Dolan) H.; B.A., Western Res. U., 1948; certificate U. Paris (France), 1949; M.A., Harvard, 1951, Ph.D., 1955; student U. Turin (Italy), 1951- 52; m. Sheila Madden Shea, June 23, 1951; children—John L., Katherine D., Elizabeth D., Edmund S. Teaching fellow Harvard, 1950-51, 52-55; cultural affairs officer USIS, Turin (Italy), 1951-52; mem. faculty Dartmouth, Hanover, N.H., 1955—, prof. Romance langs. and comparative lit., 1963—, dir. fgn. study program, 1959-62, chmn. comparative lit. program, 1966-68, chmn. div. humanities, 1967-68, asso. dean faculty, 1967- 70, dean faculty, 1970-71; Served with AUS, World War II: ETO. Rotary Internat. fellow, 1948-49; Harvard Faculty Arts and Scis. fellow, 1954-55; Guggenheim fellow, 1961-62; grantee Am. Council Learned Socs., 1961-62; Dartmouth Faculty fellow, 1964-65; Fulbright sr. research scholar, 1968-69. Mem. Modern Lang. Assn. (chmn. French 3 sect. 1963), Am. Assn. Tchrs. French, Am. Assn. U. Profs., Phi Beta Kappa, Phi Gamma Delta. Author: The Aesthetics of the Renaissance Love Sonnet, 1962; Samuel Beckett; Poet and Critic, 1970; also articles, essays. Home: 3 Tyler Rd Hanover NH 03755

HARVEY, LEO M., aluminum co. exec.; b. 1886; married. Founder Harvey Machinery Co., 1913, Harvey Machinery Co. Inc., 1942; formerly chmn. bd. successor co. Harvey Aluminum Inc. Address: 19200 S Western Av Torrance CA 90509

HARVEY, LESTER SCHLEY, fire ins. exec.; b. Manchester, N.H., July 3, 1898; s. Frank H. and Anna E. (Power) H.; ed. pub. schs.; m. Harriet N. Jenkins, June 1, 1925; children—Phyllis (Mrs. John R. Wood), Frank L. Pres., dir. N.H. Fire Ins. Company, Manchester, 1950-69, chairman, 1969—; pres., dir. Mchts. Nat. Bank, Mchts. Savs. Bank, Manchester. Trustee emeritus Colby Jr. College. Served with U.S. Army, World War I. Republican. Mason. Club: Manchester Country. Home: 784 Maple St Manchester NH 03104 Office: 1750 Elm St Manchester NH 03104

HARVEY, M.J., pipe mfg. co. exec.; b. Center, Tex., 1898; married. With Tyler Pipe Industries, Inc., Tyler, Tex., 1935—, pres., chmn. bd., 1937-65, chmn. bd., 1965—, also dir.; dir. Tyler Bank & Trust Co., Tyler Corp. Home: 2030 S Chilton Tyler TX 75701 Office: PO Box 2027 Tyler TX 75701*

HARVEY, MOSE LOFLEY, educator; b. Friendship, Ga., Nov. 25, 1910; s. Mose Lofley and Pearl (Wells) H.; Ph.B., Emory U., 1930, M.A., 1931; Ph.D., U. Cal., 1938; m. Mary Ruth Vaughn, Aug. 11, 1931; 1 son, Dodd Lofley. Grad. fellow Social Sci. Research Council, 1932-33, grant for research USSR, 1939; spl. Rockefeller fellow for advanced research USSR, 1941-42; asst. prof. history Emory U., 1933-41; research sec. Council Fgn. Relations, 1941-42; chief economist WPB, 1942-43, dep. dir. fgn. div., 1943-46; dir. Bur. Internat. Supply, Civilian Prodn. Adminstrn., 1946-47; dir. U.S. staff, dep. U.S. mem. Combined Prodn. Resources Bd., 1946; cons. Soviet affairs Dept. State, 1947-48, chief div. research and intelligence USSR and Eastern Europe. 1948-50, cons. and sec. in Diplomatic Service, 1955; assigned as instr. Nat. War Coll., 1955, dir. polit. affairs div., 1956-57; mem. policy planning staff Dept. of State, 1957; dep. chief mission and counselor of embassy, American embassy, Helsinki, Finland, 1957-59; dep. U.S. rep. Internat. Atomic Energy Agy., 1959-64; prof. history, dir. Center Advanced Internat. Studies, U. Miami (Fla.), 1964—. Cons. to adminstr. NASA, 1965—, policy planning council U.S. Dept. State, 1964-70. Lectr. on Soviet history Johns Hopkins, 1947-48, Soviet affairs Sch. Advanced Internat. Studies, 1951-57; guest lectr. Nat. War Coll., Indsl. War Coll., 1951; commentator internat. affairs radio sta. WSB, Atlanta, 1940- 42. Mem. Am. Hist. Assn., Phi Beta Kappa, Omicron Delta Kappa. Methodist. Author: Focus on the Soviet Challenge, 1963; East-West Trade and United States Policy, 1966; also articles in field of internat. affairs. Chmn. bd. editors Jour. Inter-Am. Studies, 1968—. Home: 8195 SW 69th Terrace Miami FL 33143 Office: Univ Miami Coral Gables FL 33124

HARVEY, PAUL, news analyst, author, columnist; b. Tulsa, Sept. 4, 1918; s. Harry Harrison and Anna Dagmar (Christiansen) Aurandt; Litt.D. (hon.), Culver- Stockton Coll., 1952, St. Bonaventure U., 1953; LL.D., John Brown U., Siloam Springs, Ark., 1959, Parsons Coll., Fairfield, Ia., 1968; H.H.D., Wayland Bapt. Coll., 1960, Union Coll., 1962; m. Lynne Cooper, June 4, 1940; 1 son, Paul Harvey. Announcer radio sta. KVOO, Tulsa; sta. mgr., Salina, Kan.; spl. events dir. radio sta. KXOK, St. Louis; program dir. radio sta. WKZO, 1941-43; dir. news and information O.W.I., Mich., Ind., 1941-43; news analyst and commentator ABC, 1944—; syndicated columnist Gen. Features Corp., 1954—; TV Commentator, 1968. Recipient citation D.A.V., 1949; Freedoms Found. award, 1952, 53, 62, 64, 65, 67, 68; received radio award Am. Legion, 1952, citation of merit, 1955, 57; certificate of merit V.F.W., 1953; Bronze Christopher's award, 1953; award of honor Sumter Guards, 1955; elected to Okla. Hall of Fame, 1955; nat. pub. welfare services trophy Colo. Am. Legion, 1957; named Top Commentator of Year, Radio-TV Daily, 1962; Great Am. KSEL award, 1962. Mem. Washington Radio and Television Corrs. Assn., Aircraft Owners and Pilots Assn. Club: Chicago Press. Author: Remember These Things, 1952; Autumn of Liberty, 1954; The Rest of the Story, 1956. Album recordings: Yesterday's Voices, 1959; Testing Time, 1960; Uncommon Man, 1962. Home: 1035 Park Av River Forest IL 60305 Office: 360 N Michigan Av Chicago IL 60601

HARVEY, PAUL CASPAR, profl. painter; b. Gallatin, Mo., Nov. 25, 1889; s. Wiley Wesley Wesley and Cora Fredrica (Caspar) H.; A.B., William Jewell Coll., Liberty, Mo., 1910, A.M., 1911; studied Kansas City Sch. of Law, 1911-12, U. Chgo., 1914; m. Victoria Adelaide Unruh, June 11, 1919. Tchr. English and journalism, high sch., Leavenworth, Kan., 1912-14; head dept. English, Fort Hays (Kan.) State Normal Sch.; 1914-20, dir. pub. service div., 1919-20, Fort Hays (Kan.) State Normal Sch.; prof. English composition William Jewell Coll., Liberty, Mo. 1920-58, prof. emeritus, 1958—, debate debate coach, 1920-30, dir. publicity, 1928-35, became dir. pub. relations, 1939, dir. forensics, 1936-48, mng. editor coll. bulls., dir. Living Endowment; profl. painter of oil portraits and Living Endowment; profl. painter of oil portraits and abstractions of personalities, 1958—; tchr. pub. speaking Huff Coll., Kansas City, Mo., 1938-40. Mgr. Liberty C. of C., 1961-65; mem. various civic coms. and orgns., 1917—. Pres. Bd. pres. Bd. Pub. Works, Liberty, 1950-59; mem. City Council, Liberty, 1965—. Mem. profl. and academic assns. Republican. Baptist. Mason (K.T., Shriner). Clubs: Rotary, Claycrest, Golf. Author several books, Episcopalian. Clubs: Archons of Colophon, New York

HARVEY, PAUL HENRY, educator; b. St. Paul, Neb., Aug. 2, 1911; s. William and Ella Mae (Roe) H.; B.S. in Agr., U. Neb., 1934, Ph.D. in Genetics, Ia. State U., 1938; m. Ethel Marie Larson, June 8, 1938; children—Ann (Mrs. Herbert P. Scott), Lois Kay (Mrs. Robert Morin), David Paul. Graduate assistant in genetics Iowa State University, 1934-38; member of faculty N.C. State University at Raleigh, 1938—, prof. agronomy, 1945-56, William Neal Reynolds prof., 1955—, head dept. crop sci., 1956—; on leave as agrl. adminstr. Coop. State Research Service U.S. Dept. Agr., Washington, 1970-71. Mem. Gov. N.C. Sci. Adv. Com. Mem. Am. Soc. Agronomy, Crop Science Society of America, also mem. Sigma Xi, Phi Kappa Phi, Gamma Sigma Delta (nat. award distinguished service agr. 1956), Farm House Frat. Kiwanian (pres. 1969). Home: 1311 Mayfair Rd Raleigh NC 27608

HARVEY, PETER ROBERT, mfr.; b. Chgo., Dec. 11, 1934; s. John J. and Dolores H. (Goss) H.; grad. Loyola Acad., 1957; B.A., U. Fla., 1961; m. Jean Marie Schroeder, Aug. 24, 1968; children—Robert Alan, Lisa Jean. Pres. El-Tronics, Inc., N.Y.C., 1969—, also dir.; pres., vice chmn. bd. Balt. Paint & Chem. Corp.; dir. B.S.F. Co., TelePro Industries, Inc., Mercantile Nat. Bank of Chgo.; pres. Lori Corp. (Chgo.). Mem. Kappa Sigma. Home: 77 Williamsburg Rd Evanston IL 60203 Office: 200 Park Av New York City NY 10017

HARVEY, RAYMOND, sch. supt.; b. Osborne, Kan., Aug. 31, 1896; s. C.A. and Jane (Canfield) H.; B.S., Southeastern State Coll., 1931; M.A., Okla. State U.; postgrad. Colo. State Coll., 1937, Okla. U., 1938; m. Jennie Moran, Dec. 8, 1920; 1 dau., Bobbie Jean (Mrs. Eugene Hainze). Supt. schs., Bixby, Okla., 1936-56, Vinita, Okla., 1956-58; asst. supt. Star Spencer Schs., Oklahoma City Schs., 1958-63; supt. Oklahoma County Schs., 1963—. Mem. Okla. State Legislature, 1929. Mem. State Sch. Adminstrs. (past v.p.). Democrat. Home: 8601 NE 47th St Oklahoma City OK 73084 Office: Courthouse Oklahoma City OK 73102

HARVEY, REJANE MARCELLE, physician; b. Brattleboro, Vt., Aug. 24, 1917; d. John N. and Juliette (Archambault) Harvey; A.B., Vassar Coll., 1939; M.D., Columbia, 1943; m. John R. West, III, Mar. 12, 1943. Intern Bellevue Hosp., N.Y.C., 1943-44, resident 1944-45; prof. medicine Coll. Phys. and Surg., 1968—; vis. physician Harlem Hosp. Recipient research career award, USPHS, 1963. Mem. Am. Soc. Clin. Investigation, N.Y. Acad. Medicine, Am. Physiol Soc., Harvey Soc., N.Y. Heart Assn. (dir.). Research in cardiopulmonary disease. Home: 200 E 66th St New York City NY 10021 Office: Harlem Hospital 136th St and Lenox Av New York City NY 10037

HARVEY, ROBERT DIXON HOPKINS, banker; b. Balt., July 10, 1920; s. F. Barton and Rose (Hopkins) H.; grad. cum laude, Hill Sch., 1938; A.B. summa cum laude, Princeton, 1942; B.S. in Bus., Johns Hopkins, 1953; grad. Rutgers U. Grad. Sch. Banking; m. Nancy Criswell Gross, Feb. 7, 1953; children—Nancy Criswell, Ellen Dixon, Robert Dixon Hopkins, Jane Whitthorne. Assistant secretary, assistant treasurer Maryland Trust Co., Balt., 1948-50, asst. v.p., 1950- 53, v.p., 1954-59, pres., 1959-60; Maryland Trust Co. and Fidelity-Balt. Nat. Bank consolidated and now known as Md. Nat. Bank, 1960, vice chmn. bd. dirs., 1960-66, chmn. bd. dirs., 1966—, also chief exec. officer; ofcl. U.S. Gov., Washington, 1951-54; dir. Noxell Corp., Arundel Corp., Balt. Life Ins. Co., Finance Co. of Am., Md. Title Guarantee Co., Eutaw Savings Bank of Balt., U.S. Fidelity & Guaranty Co., Balt., Noxell Corp., Reliable Stores Corp. Sec.-treas., trustee Union Meml. Hosp.; treas., dir. Md. Hosp. Service, Inc. (Blue Cross); chairman of board of trustees Johns Hopkins University; director Greater Baltimore Committee, Maryland Sch. for Blind; trustee Md. Acad. Scis., Peabody Inst. Served from 2d lt. to capt., AUS, 1942-46. Decorated Bronze Star; Breast Order of Yun-Hui (China). Mem. Res. City Bankers, Balt. Assn. Commerce (bd. dirs.), Phi Beta Kappa. Home: Brightside Rd and Lindsay Lane Baltimore MD 21212 Office: Md Nat Bank Baltimore MD 21202

HARVEY, ROBERT DUNCAN, librarian; b. Bklyn., Feb. 9, 1919; s. John L. and Edith L. (Bligh) H.; B.A., Wesleyan U., Middletown, Conn., 1941; M.S. in L.S., Columbia, 1950; m. Mary Jane Hatfield, May 14, 1945; 1 son, Spencer Gordon. Head pub. services U. Vt. library, 1950-56; chief reference and spl. services Northwestern U. Library, 1956-59; head librarian, prof. library sci. Southwest Mo. State Coll., Springfield, 1959—. Served to 1st lt. USAAF, 1942-45. Mem. Am., Mo. library assns., Am. Assn. U. Profs., Mo. Assn. Coll. and Research Libraries (pres. 1968-69). Home: 821 E Delmar St Springfield MO 65804

HARVEY, ROBERT EDWIN, corp. exec., accountant, lawyer; b. Washington, Sept. 12, 1910; s. John William and Ida Ann (Allen) H.; student George Washington U., 1930-36, LL.B., LL.M.; B.C.S., Strayer Coll., 1940; m. Mildred Ida Battle, Nov. 24, 1937; children—Shirley Battle, Robert Edwin, Evelyn Ida. Miscellaneous accounting, 1928-42; head accountant and auditor Cost Inspection Service, USN, 1942-45; chief accountant, tech. staff on fiscal mgmt. CCC, 1945-48; asst. sec.-treas., div. controller Todd Shipyards Corp., 1948-50; v.p., comptroller Capital Transit Co., 1951- 54; exec. v.p., gen. mgr., dir., exec. com. Newport Steel Corp. (KY.), 1954-55; exec. v.p. Merritt-Chapman & Scott Corp., 1955-56, dir., 1955—, mem. exec. com., 1956—, sr. exec. v.p., 1956-59, pres., 1959- 61; v.p., dir., mem. exec. com. N.Y. Shipbuilding Corp., 1955-61, pres., chmn., 1961—; v.p., dir. Devoe & Raynolds, Inc., 1955-61, dir., 1951—; v.p., dir., mem. exec. com. Tenn. Products & Chem. Corp., 1955-61, dir., 1961—; chmn. bd. Higgins, Inc., 1961—. Mem. bar U.S. Cts. D.C., U.S. Tax Ct. Mem. Financial Execs. Inst., Assn. ICC Practitioners, Phi Eta Sigma, Sigma Eta Sigma, Phi Sigma Kappa. Methodist. Clubs: Tavistock Country (Haddonfield, N.J.); Nat. Lawyers (Washington); India House, Pinnacle (N.Y.C.). ‡

HARVEY, ROBERT OTTO, univ. dean; b. Bloomington, Ind., Dec. 12, 1923; s. Paul and Amy (Arnett) H.; B.S., Ind. U., 1947, M.B.A., 1949, D.B.A., 1951; m. Margaret Johnson, Aug. 28, 1948; children—David W., Robert Otto (dec.), John P. Asst. prof. real estate Ind. U., 1948-52; vis. lectr. U. Cal. at Berkeley, 1952-53; mem. faculty U. Ill., 1953-63, prof. finance, 1959- 63, dir. exec. devel. center, 1961-63; dean Sch. Bus. Adminstrn., U. Conn., 1963—. Dir. 1st Fed. Savs. & Loan East Hartford (Conn.), Trans World Life Ins. Co. N.Y., Spencer Hayden Co. Trustee Heitman mortgage investor. Sec. Loeb Awards Adv. Bd., 1964—. Mem. Indsl. Devel. Commn., Town of Mansfield, Connecticut. Served to 1st lt., inf., AUS, 1943-46. Member Hartford Sales and Marketing Execs. Club, Am. Savs. and Loan Inst. (hon.); Beta Gamma Sigma (national v.p. 1970-71) Lambda Alpha, Delta Sigma Pi, Omicron Delta Kappa, Sigma Iota Epsilon, Sigma Alpha Epsilon, Tau Kappa Alpha; Theta Alpha Phi. Author: Land Uses in Bloomington, Indiana, 1818-1950, 1951. Home: 22 Eastwood Rd Storrs CT 06268

HARVEY, ROBERT WILSON, editor; b. Washington, Mar. 18, 1920; s. Robert Porter and Margaret (Posey) W.; B.A., Dartmouth, 1941; postgrad. U. Stockholm, 1946-47; m. Barbara Ann Landon, Sept. 3, 1941; children—Michael L., Martha E., Sara M. Reporter Washington Post, 1941-43; asst. mng. editor The Nation, N.Y.C., 1945-46; free-lance corr., Stockholm, 1946-47; asst. mng. editor The Reporter, Washington, 1948; staff editor Changing Times, Washington, 1948-51, asst. mng. editor, 1951-58, mng. editor, 1958-64, editor, 1964—; dir. Kinliner Washington Editors, Inc., 1965—. Bd. dirs. D.C. Heart Assn., 1964-68, Council for Family Financial Edn., 1969—; gov. D.C. Amateur Athletic Assn., 1962-64. Served with USMC, 1943-45. Episcopalian. Clubs: Nat. Press Internat., Dartmouth (Washington); Washington Golf and Country (Arlington, Va.). Home: 4513 N 40th St Arlington VA 22207 Office: 1729 H St NW Washington DC 20006

HARVEY, ROGER ALLEN, physician, radiologist; b. Binghamton, N.Y., Mar. 7, 1910; s. Zina Austin and Alice (Finch) H.; B.S., Hamilton Coll., 1933; M.S., U. Rochester, 1938, M.D., 1939; m. Marjorie Harding, June 20, 1940; children—Carol Eileen, Jean Emily. Intern, U. Chgo. Clinics 1939- 40; resident radiology U. Rochester, 1940-42, instr. radiology, 1942- 45, asst. prof., 1945-46; research asso. Manhattan Project, 1943-46; cons. AEC, Rochester project, 1946-49; prof. radiology U. Ill. Coll. Medicine, 1946-70, chmn. dept., 1946-70, acting dean coll., 1953-54; radiologist-in-chief, U. Ill. Hosps., 1946-70, acting med. dir., 1953-54; cons. Armed Forces Center, Chgo., USPHS, Hines (Ill.) VA Hosp.; dir. med. Betatron project U. Ill.; med. adviser to state dir. SSS, 1949-62; dir. Tb Inst. Chgo. and Cook County, 1958- 71; mem. radiation protection adv. council Ill. Dept. Pub. Health, chmn., 1960-70; mem. Ill. Legislative Commn. on Atomic Energy, 1969-71. Fellow Chgo. Roentgen Soc. (pres. 1953), Assn. U. Radiologists (pres. 1957-58), Am. Cancer Soc. (nat. pres. 1967-68, dir.; pres., dir. Ill.; chmn. Region IV 1958), Am. Coll. Radiology; mem. A.M.A., Chgo., Ill. med. socs. Am. Roentgen Ray Soc., Radiation Research Soc., Radiol. Soc. N.Am., Sigma Xi, A.A.A.S., Delta Upsilon, Pi Kappa Epsilon, Alpha Kappa Kappa. Mem. Hinsdale Union Ch. Contbr. articles to profl. jours. Address: 1489 Forest Canyon Dr Ponderosa Hills Parker CO 80134

HARVEY, THOMAS WILLIAM, govt. ofcl.; b. Huntington, W.Va., June 4, 1918; s. Thomas William and Helen (Brandebury) H.; A.B., Marshall Coll., 1939; LL.B., Duke, 1941; m. Fann Danaher Downey, Aug. 15, 1942; children—Thomas Danaher, William Brandebury, John Wilson. Admitted to W.Va. bar, 1941; practice in Huntington, 1945-61; chief counsel Area Redevl. Adminstrn. 1961-65; dir. Office Appalachian Assistance, 1965-66; dep. adminstr. Econ. Devel. Adminstrn., Dept. Commerce, Washington, 1966-69, also dep. asst. sec. commerce, asso. chief counsel, 1969—. Pres. bd. Family Service, Huntington, 1955. Del. Democratic Nat. Conv., 1952; condidate for Congress, 4th Dist. W.Va., 1958. Served to capt. USAAF, 1942-45: PTO. Decorated Air Medal with 5 oak leaf clusters. Mem. Fed. Bar Assn., W.Va. State Bar (chmn. 5 dist. grievance com. 1959- 61). Home: 4110 Thornapple St Chevy Chase MD 20015 Office: Main Commerce Bldg Washington DC 20230

HARVEY, VIRGINIA LEE, educator; b. Indpls., Nov. 20, 1913; d. Philip Cranston and Marie Ruth (Unversaw) Harvey; B.S., Russell Sage Coll., 1935; A.M., U. Pitts., 1942. Dir. phys. edn. for girls Roeliff Jansen Central Sch., Hillsdale, N.Y., 1935-44; instr. phys. edn. Russell Sage Coll., 1944-45, asst. prof., 1945-52, asso. prof., 1952-58, prof., 1958-69, dean freshmen, 1954-56, asso. dean 1955- 59, dean, 1959-68, trustee, 1968—; tchr. English, Sandwich (Mass.) High Sch., 1968-70; prof. English Cape Cod Community Coll., W. Barnstable, Mass., 1970—. Mem. Am. Assn. U. Profs., N.E.A., Am. Assn. Univ. Women, Assn. for Higher Edn. Home: East Sandwich MA 02537 Office: Cape Cod Community Coll West Barnstable MA 02668

HARVEY, WATKINS PROCTOR, physician, educator; b. Lynchburg, Va., Apr. 19, 1918; s. William Cochrane and Caroline (Proctor) H.; A.B., Lynchburg Coll., 1939; M.D., Duke, 1943; m. Irma M. Burns, Apr. 30, 1949; children—Watkins Proctor, Janet Carolyn, Blair Burns (dec.). Intern medicine Peter Bent Brigham Hosp., Boston, 1943-44; fellow medicine Harvard Med. Sch., 1946-48; sr. asst. resident medicine Peter Bent Brigham Hosp., 1948-49, chief resident medicine, 1949-50; mem. faculty Georgetown U. Sch. Medicine, 1950—, prof. medicine, 1960—; dir. div. cardiology Georgetown U. Hosp., 1950—; cons. Walter Reed Army, VA, U.S. Naval, Andrews AFB hosps., NIH, FAA. Fellow A.C.P., Am. Coll. Cardiology; mem. Am. (fellow council clin. cardiology; pres. 1969-70), Washington (pres. 1962-64) heart assns., Assn. U. Cardiologists (sec.-treas. 1967-69, v.p. 1969-70, pres. 1970-71), Assn. Am. Physicians, Clin. and Climatological Assn., Am. Fedn. Clin. Research, A.M.A., D.C. Med. Soc., So. Soc. Clin. Research, Clinico- Pathol. Soc. D.C., Alpha Omega Alpha. Co-author; Clinical Auscultation of the Heart, rev. edit., 1959. Co-editor: Year Book Series on Cardiovascular Disease, 1962—; mem. editorial bd. Am. Heart Jour. Home: Overlook Dr Woodside McLean VA

HARVEY, WILLIAM BARTLETT, publisher; b. Pitts., Aug. 27, 1914; s. Walter B. and Aurelia (Bartlett) H.; A.B., U. Pitts., 1936; m. Dorothy Colvin, Aug. 14, 1943; children—Walter B. II, George C., Claudia. Mng. editor Macmillan Co., 1948-55; asst. dir. U. Chgo. Press, 1955-58; dir. N.Y. Univ. Press, 1958-67, U. Fla. Press, Gainesville, 1967—. Served from pvt. to capt., F.A., AUS, 1941-45. Decorated Bronze Star medal, Purple Heart with oak leaf cluster. Mem. Assn. Am. U. Presses (treas. 1964-66, v.p. 1969, pres. 1971—). Delta Tau Delta, Omicron Delta Kappa. Home: 2911 NW 13th Ct Gainesville FL 32601 Office: 15 NW 15th St Gainesville FL 32601

HARVEY, WILLIAM BURNETT, educator; b. Greenville, S.C., Sept. 4, 1922; s. Charles Hugh and Emma (Ballenger) H.; A.B., Wake Forest Coll., 1943; J.D., U. Mich., 1948; student U. Heidelberg (Germany), 1955-56; m. Mary Louise Geleide, Mar. 28, 1945; children—Anne Constance, David Kent. Admitted to D.C. bar, 1949; with firm Hogan and Hartson, Washington, 1949-51: prof. law U. Mich., 1951-66; prof. law, dean faculty law U. Ghana, 1962- 64; prof. law and polit. sci., dean faculty law, Ind. U., Bloomington, 1966—, on leave as vis. prof. law U. Nairobi (Kenya), 1971—. Served to lt. USNR, 1943-46. Fellow African Studies Assn.; mem. Am. Bar Assn. Democrat. Episcopalian. Contbr. profl. jours. Home: Ridgewood Dr Bloomington IN 47401

HARVEY, WILLIAM JAMES, III, clergyman; b. Oklahoma City, June 18, 1912; s. William James and L. Mae (Johnson) H.; B.A., Fisk U., 1935; B.D., Chgo. Theol. Sem., 1938; m. Jean Nelson, Apr. 5, 1946; children—Janice Faith, William James IV. Ordained to ministry Baptist Ch., 1939; pastor in Phila., 1939-50, Oklahoma City, 1950-53, Pitts., 1954-66; guest preacher Va. Union U., 1946, 48, Fisk U., 1949, Cheyney State Tchrs. Coll., 1949, Hampton U., 1950, Prairie View State Coll., 1951, 52, Okla. State U., 1953; mem. exec. bd., fgn. mission bd. Nat. Bapt. Conv., 1946-50, exec. sec., 1961- -; prof. homiletics and ch. history Sch. Religion, Langston, Okla., 1951- 53. Auditor Pa. Bapt. Conv., 1945-50; v.p. Phila. Bapt. Ministers Conf., 1950; pres. Oklahoma City Ministers Alliance, 1953; v.p. Pitts. Bapt. Ministers Conf., 1961; treas. Allegheny Union Bapt. Assn., 1961-62; del. constl. convening Conv. Nat. Council Chs., 1951, Nat. Bapt. Conv. to World Bapt. Alliance, London, Eng., 1955; preinvestigation editor World Bapt. Alliance, Rio de Janeiro, Brazil, 1959. Mem. Alpha Phi Alpha, Sigma Pi Phi. Mason. Author: Baptist Fundamentals in an Emerging Age of Freedom, 1958; also articles. Asso. editor Mission Herald, 1954-50. Office: 701 S 19th St Philadelphia PA 19146

HARVEY, XEN WORDEN, mag. editor; b. Grant County, Ind., May 30, 1922; s. John Milton and Forest (Edwards) H.; A.B., Marion (Ind.) Coll., 1950; m. Beatrice Olive Haisley, July 25, 1947; children—Judith Ann, John Russel. Recorded as minister Soc. of Friends, 1948; pastor in Grant County, Ind., 1945-49, Fairmount, Ind., 1949-64; formerly editor Quaker Life mag., Richmond, Ind.; pastor Friends Meml. Ch., Muncie, Ind., 1968—. Mem. Friends World Com. for Consultation, Phila., 1961—, Friends Com. Nat. Legislation, Washington, 1964—; mem. bd. Christian edn. Five Years Meeting of Friends, 1961-64, chmn. youth dept., 1961-64, mem. exec. council, 1961-64; co-leader Quaker Internat. Youth Pilgrimage to N.W. Eng., W. Germany and Holland, 1961; dir. Nat. High Sch. Young Friends Conf., 1962. Lion. Home: 901 Northwest B St Richmond IN 47374 Office: 101 Quaker Hill Dr Richmond IN 47374

HARVIE, DONALD SOUTHAM, oil co. exec.; b. Calgary, Alta., Can., Mar. 16, 1924; s. Eric and Dorothy (Southam) H.; B.Sc. in Chem. Engring., U. Alta., 1945; M.B.A., Harvard, 1949; m. Mary Soper, Sept. 10, 1949; children—Janet, Ian, Patrick, Mary Ann. With Western Leaseholds Ltd., 1949-63, pres., 1961- 62; pres. Canadian Western Natural Gas Co. Ltd., 1963-65; dep. chmn. Petrofina Can. Ltd., Bank of Montreal, Fina Oil Ltd., 1965—; dir. Petrofina Can. Ltd., Bank of Montreal, Molson Industries, Ltd. Vice pres. Calgary United Fund. Bd. dirs. Heritage Park Soc., Glenbow-Alta. Inst. Served with Royal Canadian Engrs., 1945-46. Home: 4119 Crestview Rd Calgary Alberta Canada Office: 736 8th Av Sw Calgary Alberta Canada

HARVIE, ERIC LAFFERTY, barrister; b. Orillia, Ont., Can., Apr. 2, 1892; s. William McLeod and Cecile Elizabeth (Lafferty) H.; LL.B., Osgoode Hall and U. Alta., 1914; LL.D., U. Alberta, 1957; Dr. of U. Calgary, 1967; m. Dorothy Jean Southam, Sept. 29, 1919; children—Margaret Joy (Mrs. Donald Maclaren), Donald Southam, Frederick Neil Southam. Admitted to Alta. (Can.) bar, 1915, since practiced law in Calgary; created Kings Counsel, 1939; chmn., dir. Glenbow Found., Glenbow Investments, Ltd., Mgrs., Ltd., Ace Found., Luxton Museum Ltd., Riveredge Found., Western Minerals Ltd.; pres., chmn., dir. Harvie Found; v.p., dir. Belvedere Securities Ltd. and Belvedere Found.; hon. chmn. Fathers Confedn. Bldgs. Trust; Fathers Confn. Meml. Citizens Found.; dir. Glenbow Ranching Ltd., Riske Creek Ranching, Ltd., Royal Can. Geog. Soc. Mem. nat. council Duke Edinburgh's Award Com.; hon. dir. Calgary YMCA; adv. mem. nat. council Boy Scouts Can., hon. patron Calgary Regional council, Heritage Park Soc. Adv. com. U. Western Ont. Sch. Bus. Adminstrn.; trustee Banff Found.; hon. chmn. Glenbow-Alberta Inst.; patron Calgary Zool. Soc. Served as lt. inf., Canadian Army, 1915-17, capt. Royal Flying Corps, R.A.F., 1917-19. Decorated Comdr. Bro. Order St. John Jerusalem. Recipient medal of Service Order Can., 1967. Fellow Royal Soc. Arts (Eng.), Patent Inst. Can.; mem. Canadian, Calgary bar assns., Law Soc. Alta, Presbyn. Clubs: Ranchmen's, Calgary, Calgary Golf and Country. Home: 303 36th Av SW Calgary 6 Alberta Canada Office: 901 10th Av SW Calgary 3 Alberta Canada

HARVILL, RICHARD ANDERSON, economist, former univ. pres.; b. Centerville, Tenn., Aug. 29, 1905; s. Young Fletcher and Fannie Madiera (Williams) H.; S.B. with distinction, Miss. State Coll., 1926; A.M. in Econs., Duke, 1927, LL.D., 1959; student U. Chgo., summers 1929, 33, 35; Ph.D. in Econs., Northwestern U., 1932; Dr. Honoris Causa, Universidade Fed. do Ceará, 1966; m. George Lee Garner, Aug. 12, 1936. Instr. history and econs. Miss. State Coll., 1927-28; instr. econs. Duke, 1928-30, 32-34; research and teaching asst. Northwestern U., 1930-32; asst. prof. U. Ariz., 1934-39. asso. prof., 1939-42, prof. econs., dean Grad. Coll., 1946-47, dean Coll. Liberal Arts, 1947-51, pres. univ., 1951-71, ret. Vis. asst. prof. econs. U. Buffalo, 1937-38; asst. dist. price exec. OPA, Phoenix, 1942-43, dist. price exec., 1943-46; mem. Ariz. Bd. Edn., 1951-64, 70-71; vice chmn. Western Interstate Commn. on Higher Edn., 1958-59, chmn., 1959-60, sec. Ariz. commn., 1956—; council of pres.'s Nat. Assn. State Univs. and Land-Grant Colls. 1951-71, exec. com., 1962-65, 69-71, pres., 1970. Mem. adv. bd. Ariz.-Sonora Desert Mus., 1954-65, Tucson chpt. A.R.C., 1951-56; mem. Catalina council Boy Scouts Am., 1953-67; adv. bd. Inst. World Affairs, 1951-68; bd. dirs. S.W. Research Inst., 1951-71, Ariz. Cardio-Pulmonary Research Found., 1958-61; chmn. Arizona com. of Selection for Rhodes Scholarships, 1951-61, 65-66; hon. mem. Tucson Fine Arts Assn., 1960-69; nat. council Atlantic Union Com., 1959-71; sponsor Atlantic Council; nat. trustee Am. Inst. Fgn. Trade, 1961-68; adv. com. univ. relations Agy. Internat. Devel., 1970-71; bd. dirs. Devel. Authority for Tucson's Expansion, 1967-71; mem. Nat. Commn. Accrediting, 1956-61; cons. adv. com. econ. and manpower studies NSF, 1964-68; civilian liaison group of comdg. gen. U.S. Army Electronic Proving Ground, Ft. Huachuca, 1961—; mem. Ariz. adv. bd. U.S. Bur. Land Mgmt., 1962-66; hon. bd. Phoenix Fine Arts Assn., 1958—; mem. acad. adv. com. Prescott Coll., 1962-65, lay adv. bd. St. Mary's Hosp., Tucson, 1959-67; nat. adv. council health research facilities USPHS, 1963-66; bd. dirs. Def. Orientation Conf. Assn., 1960-62, 66-67; mem. higher edn. adv. com. Edn. Commn. States, 1966-67; bd. dirs. Hosp. Planning Council Greater Tucson, Inc., 1964-67; mem. council presidents Western Athletic Conf., 1962-71; U.S. Army adv. panel R.O.T.C. affairs, 1964-67; nat. adv. gen. med. sci. council NIH, 1968-72; v.p. Baird Found., 1967-70, pres., 1970—; bd. visitors Air U., 1970—. Fellow Royal Econ. Soc.; mem. Assn. Am. Colls. (commn. coll. adminstrn. 1966- 69), U.S. sect. Mexico-U.S. com. 1961—, mem. internat. affairs com. 1969—), Tucson (dir. 1951—) chambers commerce, Am., Western econ. assns., Western Coll. Assn., Canadian Polit. Sci. Assn., Nat. Assn. State Univs. (exec. com. 1958-61, del. to Am. Council on Edn. 1958-60), Newcomen Soc., Ariz. Acad. Pub. Affairs (dir.), Blue Key, Phi Kappa Phi, Phi Eta Sigma, Alpha Kappa Psi, Beta Gamma Sigma, Kappa Kappa Psi, Pi Gamma Mu. Clubs: Kiwanis, Old Pueblo, Skyline Country (Tucson); University (N.Y.C.); Concha (Phoenix). Contbr. to econ. and ednl. jours. Address: 2925 E Hawthorne St Tucson AZ 85716

HARVIN, LUCIUS HERMAN, Jr., retail mcht.; b. Manning, S.C., July 27, 1914; s. Lucius Herman and Katharine (Susong) H.; B.S. in Elec. Engring., Clemson Coll., 1934; M.B.A., Harvard, 1939; m. Jessie Myrick Rose, Mar. 8, 1939; children—Lucius Herman III, Paul Rose (dec.), George Myrick, Jessie Rose, Emma Katharine. Stockboy, floorman, asst. buyer Rose's Stores. Henderson, N.C., 1943-36, sec., 1946-53, v.p., 1953, v.p., treas., 1954-56, exec. v.p., treas., 1956-63, pres., treas., 1963- 69, pres., 1969—, also dir.; merchandise mgr. Rose Merchandise warehouse; exec. v.p., gen. mgr. The Paul H. Rose Corp., Norfolk, Va., 1944-53, now chmn.; dir. Wachovia Bank & Trust Co., Winston- Salem; N.C., Citizens Bank & Trust Co., Henderson, N.C., Carolina Power & Light Co., 1958—, Durham Life Ins. Co., Raleigh, N.C., Jewel Box Stores Corp., Greensboro, N.C. Bd. dirs. St. Andrews Coll., Kittrell Coll. Served with AUS, 1941-42. Presbyn. (elder). Mason (Shriner), Rotarian (pres. Henderson 1959). Home: 935 Hargrove St Henderson NC 27536 Office Rose's Stores Inc Henderson NC 27536

HARVUOT, CLIFFORD, opera and concert singer; b. Norwood, O., Sept. 10, 1912; s. Clifford T. and Esther (Bishop) H.; student Cin. Conservatory Music, 1930-38; certificate (fellow). Juilliard Grad. Sch., N.Y.C., 1942; m. Nellis DeLay, June 4, 1943; children—Susan Glenn, Clifford Allen. Winner Met. Opera Auditions of the Air, 1942; with Met. Opera Assn., N.Y.C., 1947—. Mem. Am. Guild Mus. Artists (gov.). Home: Nanuet NY 10954

HARWARD, VERNON JUDSON, Jr., educator; b. Durham, N.C., Dec. 1, 1922; s. Vernon Judson and Mozelle (Newton) H.; A.B., U. N.C., 1943; A.M., Columbia, 1948, Ph.D., 1953; m. Marion Lippincott, Dec. 18, 1945; children—Vernon Judson III, Alma Lippincott. Instr., then asst. prof. City Coll. N.Y., 1948-62; mem. faculty Smith Coll., 1962—, prof. English, chmn. dept., 1966-70; vis. asso. prof. grad. dept. English, Columbia, 1965. Served to lt. (j.g.) USNR, 1943-46; PTO. Sr. Fulbright research fellow, also Guggenheim fellow, 1960-62. Author: The Dwarfs of Arthurian Romance and Celtic Tradition, 1958. Home: 55 Dryads Green Northampton MA 01060

HARWELL, COLEMAN, ret. publisher; b. Nashville, June 13, 1905; s. Samuel Knox and Lelia (McClure) H.; student Peabody Demonstration Sch., 1917-23; B.S., U. of South, 1926; postgrad. Columbia, 1926-27; m. Ann McLemore, Mar. 29, 1932; children—Ann McClure (Mrs. Charles E. Wells), Carolyn Briggs (Mrs. Julian S. Carr, Jr.). Reporter, mng. editor The Tennessean, Nashville, 1927-31, v.p., editor, 1937-59; with N.Y. World-Telegram, 1931-37; editor and pub. Herald and Citizen, Cookeville, Tenn., 1959-69; pub. Sparta (Tenn.) Expositor, 1963-71; exec. v.p. Tenn. Bot. Gardens and Fine Arts Center, Nashville, 1969-71. Pres., Community Chest, 1945-47. Trustee George Peabody Coll. for Tchrs. Served to capt. AUS, with Allied Mil. Govt., World War II. Mem. A.P. Mng. Editors Assn. (pres. 1957-58). Kappa Alpha. Democrat. Presbyn. Clubs: Rotary (pres. 1940-41), Meade Country, Round Table. Home: 703 Lynwood Blvd Nashville TN 37205

HARWELL, KENNETH, lawyer; b. Lenora, Okla., Sept. 13, 1911; s. Edward and Donna (McCool) H.; LL.B., Cumberland U., 1938; m. Virginia Sanders, Sept. 9, 1945; 1 son, Kenneth Sanders. Admitted to Tenn. bar, 1939; practice in Nashville, 1939-61, 64—; mem. firm Williams, Harwell, Howser & Thomas, 1945-61; U.S. atty. Middle Dist. Tenn., 1961-64. Home: 269 Cumberland Circle Donelson TN 37214 Office: 1418 Parkway Towers Nashville TN 37219

HARWELL, RICHARD BARKSDALE, librarian; b. Washington, Ga., June 6, 1915; s. Davis Gray and Helen (Barksdale) H.; A.B., Emory U., 1937, B.L.S., 1938; D. Litt., New Eng. Coll., 1966. Asst. Flowers collection Duke U. Library, 1938-40; staff Emory U. Library, 1940-54, asst. librarian, 1948-54; dir. Southeastern Interlibrary Research Facility, 1954-56; dir. publs. Va. State Library, 1956-57; exec. sec. Assn. Coll. and Research Libraries, 1957-61, also asso. exec. dir. Am. Library Assn. 1958-61; librarian Bowdoin Coll., Brunswick, Me., 1961-68, Smith Coll., Northampton, Mass., 1968- -70; dir. libraries Ga. So. Coll., Statesboro, 1970—. Bibliog. cons. U. Va. Library, 1953, Boston Athenaeum, 1953; adv. bd. Civil War Centennial Commn.; cons. U. Jordan library, 1966. Bd. dirs. Kittredge Found. Served from seaman to lt., USNR, 1943-46. Fellow Henry E. Huntington Library, 1951, 67. Mem. Ga. (curator 1954-56), Atlanta (dir. 1955-56), So. hist. socs., Am., Southeastern (exec. sec. 1952-54), Ga. library assns., Am. Antiquarian Soc., Bibl. Soc. U. Va., Phi Beta Kappa, Sigma Alpha Epsilon. Clubs: Grolier (N.Y.C.); Forest Hills (Statsboro, Ga.). Author: Confederate Belles-Lettres, 1941; Confederate Music, 1950; Songs of the Confederacy, 1951; Cornerstones of Confederate Collecting, 1953; The Confederate Reader, 1957; More Confederate Imprints, 1957; The Union Reader, 1958; The Alma College Library (with R.L. Talmadge), 1957; The Arizona State University Library (with E.T. Moore), 1959; The War They Fought, 1960; Confederate Imprints in the University of Georgia, 1964; The Confederate Hundred, 1964; Hawthorne and Longfellow, 1966. Editor Stonewall Jackson and the Old Stonewall Brigade (J. E. Cooke), 1954; Destruction and Reconstruction (Richard Taylor), 1955; The Committees of Safety of Westmoreland and Fincastle, 1956; Cities and Camps of the Confederate States (FitzGerald Ross), 1958; Kate: The Journal of a Confederate Nurse (Kate Cumming), 1959; Outlines from the Outpost (J. E. Cooke), 1961; Lee (1 vol. abridgement of D. S. Freeman's R.E. Lee), 1961; The Colorado Volunteer's in New Mexico, 1862 (O. J. Hollister), 1962; A Confederate Marine, 1963; The Uniform and Dress of the Army and Navy of the Conferate States, 1960; Hardtack and Coffee (John D. Billings), 1960; Two Views of Gettysburg (Sir A.J.L. Fremantle and Frank Haskell), 1964; Washington (1 vol. abridgement D.S. Freeman's George Washington), 1969. Asso. editor Emory Sources and Reprints series, 1948-54; editor: College & Research Libraries, 1962-63. Editorial bd. Emory U. Quar., 1946-54, Civil War History, 1954-59. Contbr. Conf. Imprints, 1955; The Lasting South, 1957; Lincoln for the Ages, 1960, also articles, revs. in history, library publs. Home: 204 N Edgewood Dr Statesboro GA 30458 Office Ga So Coll Library Statesboro GA 30458

HARWICK, JOHN WILLIAM, bus. adminstr.; b. Rochester, Minn., Dec. 22, 1912; s. Harry John and Margaret (Graham) H.; student Phillips Exeter Acad., 1929-31; A.B., Dartmouth, 1935; m. Linda Rollins, Aug. 27, 1935; children—Hannah, Elizabeth, Prudence, Harry John II, Peter R. Chmn. dept. adminstrn. Mayo Clinic, also vice chmn. bd. trustees Mayo Found.; mem. bd. govs. of Mayo Clinic; dir. Kahler Corp., 1st Nat. Bank Mpls., Rochester Airport Co., Northwestern Nat. Life Ins. Co. Trustee, Rochester Found. Mem. Dragon, Psi Upsilon. Conglist. Clubs: University (Rochester); Minneapolis (Mpls.). Home: 1021 10th Street SW Rochester MN 55901 Office 200 1st St SW Rochester MN 55901

HARWOOD, DOUGLAS AMEND, govt. ofcl.; b. N.Y.C., June 17, 1912; s. Brunn and Elsie Amelia (Amend) H.; B.A., Yale, 1932; postgrad. Columbia, 1934; m. Laura Lucille Turner, Apr. 16, 1952; 1 son, Douglas Turner. Welding industry sales engr., 1935-41; exec. asst., liaison officer to Maritime Commn., WPB, 1941-42; regional mgr., asst. dir. devel. N.A.M., 1946-51; cons. Office Civilian Requirements, dir. Program planning staff NPA, 1951-52; dir. sales promotion, fleet div. Chrysler Corp., 1952-54; with Mut. Security Program and Fgn. Aid Program, 1955-64, dir. in East Pakistan, 1958-60, in Mali, Guinea and Equatorial Africa, 1961-64; sr. market devel. officer, dir. marketing activities Bur. Internat. Commerce, Dept. Commerce, 1964-68, nat. export sales mgr., dir. global marketing campaigns, dir. program coordination staff, export devel. activities program, 1968—. Served to 1st lt. AUS, 1942-46; PTO. Club: Yale (N.Y.C.). Home: 1021 Arlington Blvd Arlington VA 22209 Office Bur Internat Commerce Dept of Commerce Washington DC 20230

HARWOOD, EDWARD CROSBY, economist; b. Cliftondale, Mass., Oct. 28, 1900; s. Edward T. and Mary Howe (Pinney) H.; B.S., U.S. Mil. Acad., 1920; C.E., Rensselaer Poly. Inst., 1922; M.C.E., 1930, M.B.A., 1931; m. Harriet Haynes, Sept. 3, 1921; children—Marjorie H., Edward L., Richard F.; m. 2d, Helen L. Fowle, Oct. 29, 1938; children—William F., Eve C., Frederick C., Katherine S. Commd. 2d lt. U.S. Army, 1920, advanced through ranks to col., 1933, ret. 1937; returned to active duty, U.S. Army, 1940; exec. engr. service ETO, 1942-43; chief mobilization div. War Dept., 1943; Corps Engr. XI Corps, 1943-44; chief of staff Army Service Command, S.W. Pacific Theater, 1944; ret. as col., 1946; asso. prof. mil. sci. Mass. Inst. Tech., 1930-34, 1940-42; exec. U.S. dist. engr. Boston, in charge Cape Cod Canal Improvement Program, 1934-36; in charge flood control Surveys of N.E., 1936. Dir., trustee Am. Inst. for Econ. Research, 1934—; mem. Behavioral Research Council for Sci. Inquiry into Problems of Men in Society; treas. Behavioral Research Council; trustee Progress Found. Henry George Sch. of Social Sci.; dir. Econ. Edn. League; mem. Economists Nat. Com. on Monetary Policy; treas., trustee Am. Inst. Counselors, Inc. Decorated Legion of Merit, Bronze Star. Mem. A.A.A.S., Sigma Xi. Author: Cause and Control of the Business Cycle, 1932; Current Economic Delusions, 1938; What will Inflation and Devaluation Mean to You, 1934; Life Insurance from the Buyer's Point of View, 1935; Reconstruction of economics, 1955; Useful Economics, 1956; Twentieth-Century Common Sense, 1958; also articles profl. jours., 1923—. Home: Great Barrington MA 02130

HARWOOD, JAMES EDWARD, tobacco products mfg. exec.; b. Nashville, Nov. 2, 1902; s. James Eugene and Katharine (Murray) H.; LL.B., U. Memphis, 1927; m. Katharine D. Butler, Feb. 27, 1933; children—James Edward III, Katharine B. With Am. Snuff Co., Memphis, 1924—, v.p., 1949-59, exec. v.p., 1959—, also dir.; dir. Taylor Bros. Tobacco Co., Hot-Shot Quality Products Co., Blevins Popcorn Co., Harvell-Kilgore Corporation. Member Delta Theta Phi. Roman Catholic. Clubs: Memphis Country (past pres.), Memphis Hunt and Polo. Home: 2875 Arawata Lane Memphis TN 38111 Office: 701 N Main St Memphis TN 38103

HARWOOD, JEROME, advt. exec.; b. Jersey City, June 19, 1926; s. Louis and Dorothy (Cohen) Horowitz; B.A. cum laude, L.I. U., 1949; M.A., N.Y. U., 1953; m. Ruthella Zimmerman, June 25, 1950; children—Robin Jill, Dean Brook. Tech. instr. U.S. Bur. Census, 1950-51; tchr. Roselle and Jersey City, 1951-58; account exec. Martin E. Segal, pension and welfare cons., N.Y.C., 1958-60; sr. project dir. W.R. Simmons Research Co., N.Y.C., 1960-62; v.p., asso. research dir. Kenyon & Eckhardt Advt., N.Y.C., 1962-66; sr. v.p., dir. research Needham, Harper & Steers Advt., N.Y.C., 1966—. Mem. research com. Am. Assn. Advt. Agys., Consumer Research Inst. Grocery Mfrs. Am.; mem. bd. N.Y. Inst. Consumer Edn. Bd. dirs. Mus. Black History and Culture. Served with USAAF, 1944-46. Mem. Am. (founder Advt. Effectiveness Awards Program, N.Y.C. chpt., pres. N.Y.C. 1970-71), Nat. Am. (bd. dirs.), marketing assns., Am. Sociol. Assn., Am. Acad. Polit. and Social Sci., Am. Assn. Pub. Opinion Research, Am. Psychol. Assn. Jewish religion (trustee temple). Mem. B'nai B'rith. Club: Short Hills Community (bd. dirs.). Home: 22 Athens Rd Short Hills NJ 07078 Office: 909 3d Av New York City NY 10022

HARWOOD, JOHN HENRY, steel fabricating co. exec.; b. Milw., Apr. 3, 1919; s. Paisley B. and Sylvia (Rehm) H.; B.S., U. Mich., 1941, M.B.A., 1942; m. Betty Ann Cattell, Feb. 10, 1942; children—John C., Nevin R., James C., Christopher R. Sales rep. Metal Goods Corp., St. Louis, 1947-51, personnel dir., 1951-59, sec.-treas., 1959-68, v.p. finance, 1968-69, dir., 1960-69; asst. to pres. Miss. Valley Structural Steel Co., Chgo., 1969-70, v.p. finance and adminstrn, 1970—. Mem. Am. Soc. Corp. Secs., Financial Execs. Inst. Home: 57 Berry Rd Park St Louis MO 63122 Office: 500 Northwest Plaza St Ann MO 63074

HARWOOD, KENNETH, educator; b. Chgo., July 12, 1924; s. Robert Samuel and Lilian (Feuerlicht) H.; student U. Mo., 1941-43; A.B., U. So. Cal., 1947, A.M., 1948, Ph.D., 1950; m. Arlette Mary Bartley, Jan. 28, 1949. Asst. prof., asso. prof., prof. dept. radio and TV, U. Ala., 1950-54, chmn. dept., 1951-54; asso. prof. U. So. Cal., 1954-57, prof., 1957-68, chmn. dept. telecommunications, 1954-68; dean Sch. Communication and Theater, Temple U., 1968—. Chmn., dir. Oak Knoll Broadcasting Co., Pasadena, Cal., 1964—. Dir. Brooks Found., Santa Barbara, Cal., 1963-68; dir., chmn. Broadcast Found. Cal., Pasadena, 1964—; trustee Telecommunications Found., Los Angeles, 1965-68. Served with AUS, 1943-45. Fellow Am. Sociol. Assn.; mem. Am. Psychol. Assn., Internat. Communication Assn. (pres. 1956), Assn. Profl. Broadcasting Edn. (pres. 1957-58), Am. Statis. Assn., Am. Marketing Assn., Speech Communication Assn., Am. Assn. U. Profs. (pres. U. So. Cal. chpt. 1960, pres. So. Cal. conf. 1961-62, mem. nat. council 1963-66, chmn. assembly state and regional confs. 1963-65), Western Ednl. Soc. For Telecommunication (dir., v.p. 1955-69), Nat. Assn. Ednl. Broadcasters (dir. 1959-60), Nat. Assn. Broadcasters (dir. 1966-68), Alpha Epsilon Rho (dir. 1959-63), Sigma Delta Chi, Blue Key. Home: Valley Forge PA 19481 Office: Sch Communications and Theater Temple Univ Philadelphia PA 19122

HARWOOD, RAYMOND CHARLES, publisher; b. Bklyn., June 10, 1906; s. Charles Edwin and Josephine C. (Bangel) H.; B.C.S., N.Y. U., 1926; m. Joan B. Underwood, June 4, 1938; children—Ann Macrae, Joan Underwood. Pub. accountant Martin Kortjohn & Co., 1926-30; asst. treas. Harper & Bros., N.Y. City, 1930- 42, treas., 1942-45, sec., treas. and gen. mgr., 1945-50, exec. v.p., 1950-55 dir., mem. exec. com., 1943-68, treas., pres., 1955-62; chmn. bd. Harper & Row, Pubs., Inc., 1967-68, ret., 1968; cons., bd. dirs. Book-of-the-Month Club; chmn. bd. Franklin Book Programs, Inc. Mem. council Hofstra U., nat. adv. council Hampshire Coll., pres., mem. finance com., president board of trustees Princeton U. Press. C.P.A., N.Y. Mem. Am. Arbitration Assn., 1957; The Players, Publishers Lunch (N.Y.C.); The Creek (Locust Valley, L.I., N.Y.). Home: 31 Intervale Roslyn Estates Roslyn NY 11576 Ret.

HARWOOD, RICHARD LEE, journalist; b. Chilton, Wis., Mar. 29, 1925; s. Luther Milton and Ruby (Heath) H.; A.B., Vanderbilt U., 1950; m. Beatrice Bottrell Mosby, Dec. 18, 1950; children—Helen, John, Richard, David. Reporter, Nashville Tennessean, 1947-52, Louisville Courier- Jour. and Times, 1952-61, Washington corr., 1961-65; nat. corr. Washington Post, 1966-68, nat. editor, 1968-70, asst. mng. editor, 1970—. Served with USMCR, 1942-46: PTO. Nieman fellow Journalism Harvard, 1955-56; Carnegie fellow journalism Columbia, 1965-66; Recipient citation Nat. Edn. Writers Assn., 1957; George Polk Meml. award L.I. U., 1967; Distinguished Service medal Sigma Delta Chi, 1967. Mem. Soc. Nieman Fellows (dir. So. chpt. 1959-61), Am. Civil Liberties Union (dir. Ky. 1959-61). Am. Polit. Sci. Assn. (citation 1960). Democrat. Clubs: Nat. Press, Fed. City (Washington). Contbr. nat. mags. Home: 4521 Drummond Av Chevy Chase MD 20015 Office: 1515 L St Washington DC 20005

HARWOOD, RICHARD ROBERTS, Jr., mfg. co. exec.; b. Balt., May 1, 1921; s. Richard Roberts and Willyhyde (Hart) H.; A.B., Princeton, 1948; m. Marion Virginia Smith, Feb. 23, 1946; children—Richard Roberts III, Edward Smith, William Whittingham. With Mfrs. Record Pub. Co., Balt., 1947-55; v.p. Fleet McGinley Balt., 1955-56; asst. to pres. Young & Selden Co., Balt., 1956-57, exec. v.p., 1957-58, pres., dir., 1958-62; pres., dir. Master Power Corp., Solon, O., 1962-64, chmn. bd., dir., 1964-66; v.p. adminstrn. Black & Decker Mfg. Co., Towson, Md., 1963-66; adminstrv. v.p. Arundel Corp., 1966-69; pres., chief exec. officer Barton-Cotton, Inc., Balt., 1969—; director Monumental-Security Storage Co., Balt. Trustee, Commn. Govt. Efficiency and Economy Inc., Balt., 1954-57, 63—, mem. exec. com., 1963- -; chmn. downtown div. A.R.C. campaign, 1954. Bd. dirs. Keswick Home; trustee St. Paul's Sch. for Boys; founding trustee St. Paul's Sch. for Girls, treas., 1958-63. Served with USAAF, 1942-43. Mem. Balt. Jr. Assn. Commerce (pres. 1953-54). Republican. Episcopalian (vestryman, diocesan treas. 1964-). Home: 303 Club Rd Baltimore MD 21210 Office: 2604 Sisson St Baltimore MD 21211

HARWOOD, ROBERT BERNARD, state justic; b. Eutaw, Ala., June 4, 1902; s. Bernard and Helene (Braune) H.; A.B., LL.B., U. Ala.; LL.M., Harvard; m. Mary Lee Leach, Sept. 11, 1926; children—Eve Minturn, Robert Bernard. Admitted to Ala. bar, mem. firm Harwood & McQueen, Tuscaloosa, 1926-27; pvt. practice, 1927-32; asst. U.S. atty. No. Dist. Ala., 1933-35; asso. prof. law U. Ala., 1935-36, prof., 1936-37, asst. to dean, 1937; atty. gen. Ala., 1945; judge Ct. Appeals, 1945-63; now asso. justice Supreme Ct. Ala. Commr. Uniform State Laws, 1940. Mem Ala. Legislature, 1927-31. Served from capt. to maj., AUS, 1942-45. Mem. Am., Ala. bar assns., Delta Kappa Epsilon, Phi Delta Phi, Omicron Delta Kappa. Democrat. Episcopalian. Club: Montgomery Country. Author books; contbr. law jours. Home: 36 Haardt Dr Montgomery AL 36105 Office: Judicial Bldg Montgomery AL 36102

HARWOOD, THEODORE HENRY, ednl. adminstr.; b. Dorset, Vt., Apr. 28, 1911; s. Elmer D. and Emma (Maranville) H.; A.B., Hamilton Coll., 1932; M.D., U. Vt., 1936; m. Laura Jean Lathrop, Oct. 8, 1936; children—Judith A., Theodore Henry, William L. Intern Mary Fletcher Hosp., Burlington, Vt., 1936-37, resident medicine, 1939-40, attending physician, 1943-53; fellow Lahey Clinic, 1937-38; asst. resident medicine Royal Victoria Hosp., Montreal, 1938-39; vis. physician Bishop de Goes Briand Hosp., Burlington; asst. prof. medicine sch. medicine U. Vt., 1940-46, asso. prof., 1946-53, asst. dean sch. medicine, 1950 ' 53; dir. student health service U. Vt., 1940-48, Burlington Free Dispensary, 1940-53, Durfee Meml. Clinic, Burlington, 1952-53; contact surgeon ASTP U. Vt., 1941-45; dean sch. medicine U. N.D., 1953—; vis. physician Deaconess and St. Michael's hosps., Grand Forks, N.D., 1953—; dir. N. D. State Med. Center, 1962—. Chief examiner SSS, Chittenden County, Vt., 1940-45; dir. Vt.-N.H. Blue Cross-Blue Shield, 1946-53; dir. N. D. Blue Cross, 1958; patron Grand Forks Symphony. Dir. Dakota Med. Found., 1962. Diplomate of Am. Bd. of Internal Medicine. Fellow American Coll. of Physicians; mem. A.M.A. (ho. dels. 1947-49), N.D., Med. Soc., Vt. Hist. Soc., Am. Heart Assn. (dir.), Alpha Omega Alpha. Presbyn. Clubs: Rotary, Franklin. Home: 2704 Belmont Rd Grand Forks ND 58201

HASBUN, JUDET ABRAHAN, Dominican Republic diplomat; b. Santo Domingo, Dominican Republic, Dec. 30, 1929; s. Domingo Amado and Eva Maria (Espinal) H.; Dr. of Law, Universidad Autonoma de Santo Domingo, 1956; m. Carmen Montas, Dec. 30, 1959; children—Yudex, Cesar. Fiscal treas. Mecanografo en la Secretaria de Agricultura; justice of peace; gen. dir. of sports; counselor, gen. consul Dominican Embassy, Washington, 1969—; adj. prof. social and polit. sci. U. Pedro Henriquez Urena. Juridical counsel of some Dominican cos. Mem. Revolutionary Social Christian Party; treas. Democratic Christian Party, also gen. sec., candidate for dep., 1966, candidate for senator, 1970. Mem. Coll. of Lawyers of Dominican Republic. Home: 3611 39th St Washington DC 20016 Office: 1715 22d St Washington DC 20008

HASELDEN, CLYDE LEROY, librarian; b. Latta, S.C., Aug. 26, 1914; s. Hampton Berry and Mary Beulah (Allen) H.; B.A. Furman U., 1938; B.S. in L.S., Columbia, 1939; M.A., U. Chgo., 1948; m. Erva Lee Buchanan, Dec. 3, 1940; 1 dau., Janice Charlotte. Fellow reference dept. City Coll. N.Y., 1938-39; reference asst. U. Ark., 1939-43; assignee Civilian Pub. Service, 1943-46; librarian Parsons Coll., Fairfield, Ia., 1947-50, Baldwin-Wallace Coll., 1950-59, Lafayette Coll., 1959—. Coll. and univ. library bldg. cons. Mem. A.L.A., Ohio Coll. Assn. (pres. 1954-56), Pa. Library Assn., Assn. Coll. and Research Libraries (pres. Phila. 1965-67), Am. Assn. U. Profs., Phi Kappa Phi. Contbr. articles to profl. jour. Home: 1018 Cattell St Easton PA 18042

HASELMAYER, LOUIS AUGUST, coll. pres.; b. Newark, June 4, 1911; s. Louis A. and Helen (Kaufhold) H.; B.A., Williams Coll., 1933; Ph.D., Yale, 1937; S.T.B., Gen. Theol. Sem., 1941; postgrad. Oxford U., 1952, U. Paris, 1955, Goethe Inst., Munich, 1956, U. Florence, 1960, U. Salzburg, 1961, 65. Instr., U. Minn., 1936-38, Gen. Theol. Sem., N.Y.C., 1938-41; ch. work, 1941-49; dean Cathedral Sch., Dallas, 1949-50; prof. Daniel Baker Coll., Tex., 1950-51; head dept. English, Ia. Wesleyan Coll., Mt. Pleasant, 1952—, chmn. div. humanities, 1954, pres., 1970—, also dir. Archives. Lit. critic Burlington Hawk-Eye. Pres. Community Concert Assn., 1959-64. Mem. Modern. Lang. Assn., Nat. Council Tchrs. English, Coll. English Assn., Ch. Hist. Soc., Phi Beta Kappa, Alpha Psi Omega, Sigma Tau Delta, Lambda Chi Alpha. Rotarian. Author: Lambeth and Unity, 1948; Christmas Past and Christmas Present (poem), 1965; The 125th Anniversary History of Iowa Wesleyan College 1842-1967, 1967. Founder, editor: Design mag., 1954. Editor: Iowa Wesleyan Faculty Lecture Series, 1959-69. Asso. editor: Anglican Theol. Rev., 1948—; Lyrical Iowa, 1959- 69; Iowa English Yearbook, 1959-63. Contbr. articles and poems profl. jours. Home: 611 E Washington St Mount Pleasant IA 52641

HASELTINE, BENJAMIN WARREN, II, educator; b. Pitts., Jan. 17, 1909; s. Nathan Stone and Mary Anna (Pilgram) H.; A.B., Franklin and Marshall Coll., 1931; M.A., U. Pitts., 1939, Ph.D., 1949; m. Lucile Long, June 10, 1938. Tchr., counselor Swissvale High Sch., Pa., 1931-43; instr. to asso. prof. French lang. and lit. U. Pitts., 1946-53, head dept. modern langs., 1952-59, prof. French lang. and lit., 1954—. Decorated Ordre des Palmes Académiques (France). Mem. Modern Lang. Assn. (past pres. Pitts.), Am. Assn. U. Profs., Sigma Kappa Phi, Phi Kappa Sigma, Phi Epsilon Delta. Presbyn. Mason. Home: 130 Glenfield Dr Pittsburgh PA 15235

HASELTON, WALLACE MEREDITH, banker; b. Worcester, Mass May 3, 1922; s. Edgar C. and Emma E. (Desaultels) H.; student Boston U., 1940-41, 45-46, Rutgers U. Grad. Sch. Banking, 1952-53; m. Eleanor Pestana, June 16, 1943; children—Gloria, Lee Ellen, Amy. Employed with the National Shawmut Bank, Boston, Massachusetts, 1940-42, 46-48; with Merrimack Valley Nat. Bank, and predecessor, Andover, Mass., 1948-64, pres., 1960-64; pres. Depositors Trust Co., Augusta, Me., 1964-68, chmn. bd., 1968—; pres. Depositors Corp., 1967—. Mem. Augusta Devel. Corp., 1954-65; Small Bus. Adminstrn. Adv. Council, 1964—, Governor's Council of Economic Advisers; pres. Econ. Devel. Corp. Augusta, 1964—; adv. council Me. Dept. Econ. Devel.; mem. Me. Secs. Approval Bd.; vice chmn. Me. Planning Council. Pres. Depositors Foundation. Served to lt. USNR, 1942-45, 51-52. Decorated Air medal (3), Commendation ribbon. Club: Augusta Country. Home Tallwood Rd Augusta ME Office: 286 Water St Augusta ME 04330

HASELTON, WILLIAM RAYMOND, paper co. exec.; b. Glens Falls, N.Y., Jan. 11, 1925; s. Raymond R. and Mary (Vanderwerker) H.; B.S. in Chem. Engring., Rensselaer Poly. Inst., 1949; M.S. in Chemistry, Lawrence Coll., 1951, Ph.D., 1953; m. Frances C. Crooks, July 10, 1948; children—Susan, Judith, June. With Rhinelander Paper Co. div. St. Regis Paper Co., Rhinelander, Wis., 1954-61, v.p., gen. mgr., 1958-1961; v.p. St. Regis Paper Co., Tacoma, Wash., 1961-69, sr. v.p., 1969-71, exec. v.p., 1971—; pres., dir. R.W. Paper Co., Longview, Wash., 1962—; dir. Nat. Bank Wash. Served with USNR, 1943-46. Recipient Westbrook Steele award Inst. Paper Chemistry, 1953. Home: 16 Shagbark Rd Darien CT 06820 Office: 150 E 42d St New York City NY 10017

HASELWOOD, WILLIS EADS, metal working co. exec.; b. Edina, Mo., July 9, 1908; s. Ralph W. and Gertrude (Cottey) H.; B.E.E., U. Ill., 1929; m. Irma G. Tockwitz, Aug. 23, 1930 (dec. Oct. 1961); children—Patricia Ann (Mrs. William E. Smith), Donald E., James E.; m. 2d, Ruth Weir Willer, Sept. 15, 1962; 1 foster son, Grouner Leon Willer. Exptl. engr. Cutler Hammer Co., 1929; asst. chief engr. Chgo. Telephone Supply Co., 1930-40; owner, mgr. Edwood Co., 1939-41; chief engr. Taylor Sales Engrs., 1941-45, v.p., 1946-56; pres. Taylor Mfg. Co., 1945-46; v.p. Taylor Products, Inc., Elkhart, Ind., 1956-64; v.p. Tecumseh Products Co. (Mich.), 1960-64, pres., dir., 1964-66, chmn. bd., 1966-70, mem. exec. council, 1958-70; owner pres. Central Tube Products Co., Brooklyn, Mich., 1970—; Mich. adv. bd. Liberty Mut. Ins. Co.; dir. Lenawee County Bank, Adrian, Mich., 1964-71. Trustee Citizens Research Council Mich. Mem. Newcomen Soc. N.Am., Mich. C. of C. (dir. 1968—, vice chmn. 1970-71), Soc. Automotive Engrs., Pi Kappa Phi. Republican. Methodist (trustee). Clubs: Rotary; Eagle Lake (Mich.) Yacht (commodore 1954, 63); Lenawee Country (Adrian, Mich.). Home: 1021 Red Mill Dr Tecumseh MI 49286 Office: Central Tube Products Co Brooklyn MI 49230

HASHIDA, CHIKATARO, Japanese diplomat; b. Ehime Prefecture, Japan, July 17, 1907; s. Yoji and Mine (Takeda) H.; ed. Wakayama (Japan) Comml. Coll., 1930; m. Sumako Takahira, Nov. 30, 1936; children—Miyako (Mrs. Toshiaka Takagi), Yotaro. Joined Fgn. Ministry of Japan, 1931, mem. staff Japanese Embassy, USSR, 1937-38, Poland, 1938-39, France, Germany; consul Consulate Gen. of Japan in Singapore, 1952-54; mem. staff Econ. Bur., 1954-59; first sec. Japanese Embassy in Greece, 1959-65; chief fgn. affairs sect. Secretariat of the Ho. of Reps., 1965-69; consul gen. of Japan, New Orleans, 1969—. Mem. Fgn. Relations Assn., Japan Soc. New Orleans, Consulat Corps New Orleans, New Orleans C. of C. (fgn. trade com.), Internat. Trade Mart, Internat. House. Club: Plimsoll. Home: 6565 Oakland Dr New Orleans LA 70118 Office: Consul Gen of Japan Internat Trade Mart New Orleans LA 70130

HASKAYNE, R.F., oil and gas co. exec. Vice pres., treas. Hudson's Bay Oil & Gas Corp., Ltd. Office: 320 7th Av SW Calgary 2 Alberta Canada*

HASKEL, BENJAMIN, economist, fgn. service officer; b. N.Y.C., Aug. 9, 1910; s. Max and Ida (Heimowitz) H.; B.S., Coll. City N.Y., 1929, student Sch. Edn., 1929-30; A.M., Columbia, 1930; grad. faculty New Sch. Social Research, 1933-34; m. Doris Reich, Jan. 30, 1943; children—Peter, Ellen. Research asst. Am. Labor Yearbook, 1929-30, Am. Assn. Social Security, 1930-31, 33-34; instr. history Bklyn. Coll., 1932-39; labor economist NLRB, Social Security Bd., U.S. Office Edn., WPB, 1939-44; dir. research United Textile Workers Am., 1944-52; economist ODM, Def. Prodn. Adminstrn., 1952-54; economist ICA, 1954—, dep. dir. labor-manpower div. USRO, Paris, 1957-60, labor economist Near Eastern and South Asian Affairs, Washington, 1960—. Editor The Textile Challenger, 1944-52. Contributor articles to various professional jours. Home: 8402 Whitman Dr Bethesda MD 20034 Office: Agy Internat Devel Nr East-S Asia Bur Washington DC 20523

HASKEL, MERWIN R., business exec.; b. N.Y.C., 1900. Pres., dir. Clearwater Mfg. Co.; dir. Cohn-Hall-Marx Co., N.Y.C.; pres., dir. Davis Mills Corp., Seminole Mills, So. Textile Chem. Co., United Mchts. Sales Corp.; v.p., dir. Ashland Corp., Jewett City, Conn.; chmn., chief exec. officer United Mchts. & Mfrs., Inc., Wilmington, Del.; asst. treas., dir. United Factors Corp.; dir. Asso. Textiles of Can., Ltd. Home: 7 Richbell Close Scarsdale NY 10583 *

HASKELL, BRODERICK, business exec.; b. Grand Rapids, Mich., Aug. 22, 1899; s. Broderick and Mollie (Dunleby) H.; grad. Phillips Andover Acad., 1918; B.S. in Chem. Engring., Mass. Inst. Tech., 1922; m. Josephine M. Heathcote, June 27, 1925 (div. June 1948); m. 2d, Ruth Harvey Stead, Oct. 8, 1949. Devel. engr. Franklin Ry. Supply Co., N.Y.C., 1923-26; buying dept. J.W. Seligman & Co., investment banking, N.Y.C., 1926- 30, Guaranty Co. of N.Y.C., 1930-34; asst. treas. Guaranty Trust Co. of N.Y.C., 1934-36, 2d v.p., 1936-37, v.p., 1937-53, dir., 1944-56; vice chmn. Combustion Engring., Inc., 1953-56; dir. investments Internat. Finance Corp. (affiliate World Bank), Washington, 1956-61; partner Bache & Co., Inc., 1962-65, v.p., 1965- 71; dir. Foote Mineral Co., Cummings Properties, Ltd.; trustee, chmn. exec. com. Mut. Income Found., Columbus, O. Dir. Atomic Indsl. Forum, 1954-57. Served USNR, 1918. Civilian cons. USN, World War II. Mem. Council on Fgn. Relations, Phi Gamma Delta. Republican. Episcopalian (vestryman; trustee). Clubs: Links, University, Recess (N.Y.C.); Metropolitan (Washington); Fairfield (Conn.) Country. Co- author The American Individual Enterprise System, 1947. Home: 39 E 79th St New York City NY 10021 Office: 36 Wall St New York City NY 10005

HASKELL, CHARLES A., lawyer; b. Silver Cliff, Colo., Sept. 19, 1905; s. Charles W. and Mary E. (Mulhall) H.; LL.B., U. Notre Dame, 1929; m. Irene M. Conway, July 14, 1934; children—Roger W., Charles A. II, Russell K., Dana Marie, Jenean, Daniel Mark. Admitted to Colo. bar; practicing atty., Denver, Colorado, 1929—; senior member of the firm of Haskell & Crandell, Denver, Colo.; Former dir. Cherry Creek Sch. Bd. Former Republican state chmn. of Colo. Mem. Am., Colo., Denver bar assns. Home: 3938 E Evans Denver CO 80210 Office: Majestic Bldg Denver CO 80202

HASKELL, CLIFFORD T., corp. exec.; b. Riverside, Cal., 1913. Formerly pres., dir. Alpha Beta Acme Markets, Inc.; dir. Greater Cal. Capital Corp.; mem. Anaheim main adv. bd. Bank of Am. Office: 777 S Harbor Blvd La Habra CA 90631 *

HASKELL, DOUGLAS, editor; b. Monastir, Turkey, June 27, 1899 (parents Am. citizens); s. Rev. Edward Bell and Martha (Miller) H.; A.B., Oberlin Coll., 1923, D.F.A. (hon.), 1961; m. Helen Lacey, Aug. 22, 1924. Asst. editor Creative Art mag., 1928; asst. editor, contbr., sr. asso. editor Archtl. Record, 1929-49; archtl. editor Archtl. Forum, 1949- 51, editorial chmn., 1952-54, editor, 1955-64; lectr. Pratt Inst., 1950- 51; adj. prof. Columbia Sch. of Architecture, 1960-63; mem. President's Council on Pennsylvania Av.; vis. lectr., critic at archtl. schs. various univs. and colls. vice chmn. archtl. adv. com. Pub. Housing Adminstrn., 1949-50. Decorated Order of So. Cross (Brazil). Fellow A.I.A.; mem. Soc. Archtl. Historians, N.Y. Archtl. League, Assn. Collegiate Schs. of Architecture, N.Y. Bldg. Congress, Nat. Assn. Housing and Redevel. Ofcls., Nat. Council Chs. (archtl. adv. com.), Citizens Union N.Y. (bd.). Clubs: Nat. Arts (bd.), University. Editor: Rehousing Urban America (Henry Wright), 1935; Building U.S.A., 1957. Contbr. articles to archtl. publs., popular mags. Address: 1 Lexington Av New York City NY 10010

HASKELL, DUANE HEDRICK, music educator; b. St. Louis, Sept. 8, 1905; s. Dr. Claude D. and Mabel L. (Hedrick) H.; Mus.B., Ill. Wesleyan U., 1926; Mus.M., Eastman Sch. Music, 1945; Ph.D., Ind.U., 1951; spl. violin study with William Kritch, Louis Siegel; m. Laura A. Kerr, Dec. 21, 1932; children—James C., Ellen S. Recital appearances central Ill., 1922-26; mem. Bloomington (Ill.) Philharmonic, Rochester Philharmonic, 1926-31; faculty Rochester pub. schs., 1929-45, dir. instrumental music East High Sch., Rochester, 1930-45; head music dept. No. Mich. Coll., Marquette, 1945-49; teaching fellow, vis. prof. Ind. U., 1949-51; chmn. grad. and undergrad. music edn. dept. Chgo. Musical Coll., 1951-53, also dean summer sch.; dean Coll. Fine Arts Ark. State Univ., 1965-. Founder, condr. Northern Tri- City Symphony, Marquette, Mich., 1947-49. Mem. Am. String Tchrs. Assn. (founder, 1st pres. 1947-50; Distinguished Service award 1969), Music Tchrs. Nat. Assn. (pres. 1957-59), Phi Delta Kappa, Phi Mu Alpha. Mem. Christian Ch. Mason (Shriner). Home: 302 E Aggie Rd Jonesboro AR 72401 Office: Arkansas State College State College AR 72032

HASKELL, HAL, mayor of Wilmington, Del. Address: City Hall Wilmington DE 19801

HASKELL, JOHN HENRY FARRELL, financial exec., ret. army officer; b. Fort Leavenworth, Kan., Dec. 5, 1903; s. Lt. Gen. William Nafew and Winifred (Farrell) H.; student Polytechnic Sch., Bklyn., 1917-19; student Sainte-Croix, France, 1919-20; B.S., U.S. Mil. Acad., 1925; grad. Army Command and Gen. Staff Sch., 1941; m. Paulette Heger, May 8, 1931; children—John H.F., Paul Heger. With domestic and fgn. depts. Nat. City Co., N.Y.C., 1925-31; v.p. N.Y. Stock Exchange, 1939-55, ret.; def. adviser to NATO, U.S. rep. N. Atlantic and Mediterranean areas, 1955-60; rep. Bankers Trust Co., Paris, 1960-68, ret.; now dir. Haskell Assos., N.Y.C. Chief ECA mission to Sweden, 1948-49. Bd. dirs. Belgian Am. Ednl. Found., N.Y.C.; trustee Hoover Found., Brussels. Served as 2d lt. C.E., U.S. Army, 1925, resigned from regular army; served in N.Y.N.G., 1925-40; chief of staff 27th div. in Pacific, 1942; acting dir. civil affairs div. War Dept., 1942-43; with OSS in Middle East, Russia, Italy, ETO, 1943-44; comdg. officer T force, 12th army group, 1944-45; wounded in action Germany, 1945, ret. from army, 1946. Decorated Legion of Merit, Bronze Star, Purple Heart; chevalier Legion of Honor, Croix de Guerre (France); Czechoslovakian 1939 War Cross; Order Brit. Empire. Roman Catholic. Clubs: Chevy Chase, Army-Navy (Washington); Century Assn. (N.Y.C.). Home: 510 Av Louise Brussels 1050 Belgium

HASKELL, JOSEPH FARRELL, mgmt. cons.; b. Ft. Omaha, Neb., July 1, 1908; s. Gen. William Nafew and Winifred (Farrell) H.; B.S., U.S. Mil. Acad., 1930; grad. Command and Gen. Staff Sch., 1940; m. Elizabeth Weld Brott, 1962; children by former marriage—William N., Julia (Mrs. Hugh E. Paine, Jr.), Janet (Mrs. Charles Spalding). Commd. 2d lt. U.S. Army, 1930, advanced through grades to col., 1946; assigned posts in U.S., Philippines, 1930-41; asst. chief of staff for intelligence 7th Corps, 1941-42; staff COSSAC, London, Eng., 1943; chief secret operations OSS, London, 1943; comdr. CC B, 7th Armored Div., 1944-45; asst. chief of staff Hdqrs. Army Forces Middle Pacific, 1945-46; assigned War Dept. Gen. Staff, 1946; retired, 1946; with Nat. Distillers & Chem. Corp., N.Y.C., 1946-63, v.p. indsl. relations, 1957-63; vice pres. Rogers Slade & Hill, N.Y.C., 1964-69; pres. Haskell Assos., Inc., N.Y.C., 1969—. Decorated Silver Star, Legion of Merit, Bronze Star medal with cluster (U.S.); Legion of Honor, Croix de Guerre with palm (France); King Christian X's Medal of Liberation (Denmark). Roman Catholic. Clubs: Army and Navy, Army and Navy Country (Washington); Union (N.Y.C.) Home: 136 E 64th St New York City NY 10021 Office: 230 Park Av New York City NY 10017

HASKELL, RICHARD BYRON, banker; b. Holyoke, Mass., June 29, 1912; s. Clayton William and Ella (Guy) H.; B.A., Duke, 1933; m. Kathleen Phyllis Renison, May 15, 1939; children—Richard Bruce, Linda May, Robert Scott. Clk. Union Trust Co., Springfield, Mass., 1933-35; sales rep. Kidder, Peabody & Co., Boston, also Springfield, 1935-38; clk. Woronoco Savs. Bank, Westfield, Mass., 1938-39, asst. treas., 1939-40, treas., 1940-45, pres., 1945-47; v.p., asst. treas. dir. Mechanics Savs. Bank, Hartford, Conn., 1948-51, v.p., treas., 1951-54, exec. v.p., treas., 1954-55, pres., treas. 1955-56, pres., 1956—, also dir., mem. exec. com.; dir., mem. exec. com. Nat. Fire Ins. Co., Hartford, Phoenix Mut. Life Ins. Co., N.E. Utilities Co.; dir. Transcontinental Insurance Company, New York, Coca-Cola Bottling Co. So. New Eng., Phoenix Fund, Inc.; corporator Mt. McKinley Mut. Savs. Bank, Fairbanks, Alaska, Alaska Mut. Savs. Bank, Anchorage; dir. Mut. Investment Fund Conn., Inc., 1957-61, 65-71, v.p., 1965-71. Mem. joint com. urban problems of Savs. Bank and Savs. and Loan Industries, 1968-70. Regent, U. Hartford. Dir. Greater Hartford Community Chest, 1963-69, pres., 1966-68; trustee Greater Hartford YMCA; dir. Good- Will Boys Club, Mt. Sinai Hosp., 1960-69 (2d v.p. 1965-66), St. Francis Hosp., former dir. Greater Hartford Tb Soc., Govtl. Research Inst.; adv. com. capital Region, 1965-70; mem. com. for Hartford, 1958-70, chmn. 1959-60; corporator Hartford Hosp., 1955—, Am. Sch. for Deaf, 1957-66; asso. trustee St. Joseph Coll., 1961-68; corporator, dir. Inst. Living, 1957—, Conn. Inst. for Blind, 1959-67; former trustee Kingswood Sch.; bd. advisors Rensselaer Poly. Inst. Conn. Served from 2d lt. to capt., USAF 1942-45. Decorated Bronze Star; named Boss of Yr. Jr. C. of C., 1960; Citizen of Yr. Greater Hartford Community Chest, 1968. Mem. Greater Hartford C. of C. (dir. 1965-61, 63-68, pres. 1957- 59; Charter Oak Leadership medal 1961), Nat. Assn. Mut. Savs. Banks (dir. 1961—; mem. com. relationship with fed. agys.; pres. 1969-70), Am. Bankers Assn. (state v.p. 1955; past chmn. conventional mortgage com.; past mem. exec. com. savs. and mortgage div.), Savs. Banks Assn. Conn. (pres. 1961-62), mem. legislative com. 1967—, Newcomen Soc. N.Am., Clubs: Hartford, Hartford Golf; Economic, Twentieth Century (N.Y.C.). Home: 32 Uplands Dr West Hartford CT 06107 Office: 80 Pearl St Hartford CT 06101

HASKELL, ROBERT NELSON, bus. exec.; b. Bangor, Me., Aug. 24, 1903; s. Hiram S. and Maude M. (Gulliver) H.; S.B. in Elec. Engring., U. Me., 1925. Design engr. Bangor Hydro- Electric Co. (Me.), 1925, field engr., 1926-27, v.p., comml. mgr., 1928-34, v.p., gen. mgr., 1935-58, pres., 1958—; pres., dir. East Br. Improvement Co.; chmn bd. Mchts. Nat. Bank, Bangor; dir. Diamond Internat. Corp. Mem. Me. Ho. of Reps., 1945-46; mem. Me. Senate, 1947-53, pres. senate, 1955-59; gov. of Me., Jan. 2-Jan. 8, 1959. Trustee, U. Me. Mem. N.A.M. Me. Publicity Bur., Me. C. of C. (dir.), Electric Council of N.E. (dir.), Phi Gamma Delta. Republican. Mason. Home: 645 Hammond St Bangor ME 04401 Office: 33 State St Bangor ME 04401

HASKEW, LAURENCE DEFEE, educator; b. Perote, Ala., Oct. 4, 1907; s. Daniel Walter and Leila (Gavin) H.; B.Ph., Emory Univ., 1926; A.M., Univ. of Chicago, 1934; Ph.D., University of Georgia, 1941; LL.D., Southwestern University, 1962; m. Rose Sheridan, Aug. 8, 1929; children—Rose Mary, Laurence DeFee. Prin. Thomaston (Ga.) High Sch., 1926-28, at Greensboro, Ga., 1928-31; prin. and supt. schs., Monroe, Ga., 1931-41; dir. teacher edn. Emory U. and Agnes Scott Coll., 1941-47; dean coll. of edn. U. Tex., 1947-62, also v.p. Univ., 1954-60, vice chancellor Univ. of Texas System, 1961-67, prof. ednl. adminstrn., 1967—; cons. pres. commn. on higher edn., 1947; chmn. Nat. Adv. Council on Education Professions Development, 1967-70. Consultant Gilmer-Akin Com. on Education, Texas, 1947-48. Mem. Educational Policies Commn. U.S. (exec. com. on teacher edn.), Am. Council on Edn., Am. Assn. Colleges for Tchr. Edn. (pres. 1955), Ga. Assn. Sch. Adminstrs. (pres. 1939), Ga. Edl. Assn. (pres. 1942-43), N.E.A., Nat. Soc. Coll. Teachers of Edn., Nat. Assn. Colleges and Depts. of Edn. (v.p. 1947), Am. Assn. Sch. Adminstrs., Assn. Tex. Colls. and Univs. (pres. 1967-68), Phi Beta Kappa, Kappa Phi Kappa, Phi Delta Kappa. Methodist. Consultant state and local sch. surveys. Author books and monographs. Contbr. ednl. periodicals. Lecturer. Address: U Tex Austin TX 78712

HASKIN, DAVIS, lawyer; b. Frankfort, Kan., Mar. 16, 1905; LL.B., U. Kan., 1930. Admitted to Mo. bar, 1930, Kan. bar, 1930; mem. firm Thompson, Mitchell, Douglas, Neill & Guerri, St. Louis. Mem. Bar Assn. Met. St. Louis, Mo. Bar, Am. Bar Assn. Office: 705 Olive St St Louis MO 63101*

HASKIN, LARRY ALLEN, educator; b. Olathe, Kan., Aug. 17, 1934; s. Harvard Glenn and Mary Virginia (Callaway) H.; B.A., Baker U., 1955; Ph.D., U. Kan., 1960; m. Mary Anita Gehl, Dec. 21, 1963; children—Dierk Allen, Rachel Lee, Jean Marie. Asst. prof. Ga. Inst. Tech., 1959-60; instr. U. Wis., Madison, 1960-61, asst. prof., 1961-65, asso. prof., 1965-68, prof. chemistry, 1968—; cons. NASA, 1970—, Argonne Nat. Lab., 1960-68; mem. mercury rev. panel Nat. Acad. Scis., 1970-71. Guggenheim fellow Max Planck Inst. for Nuclear Physics, Heidelberg, Germany, 1966-67. Mem. Am. Chem. Soc., Geochem. Soc., Am. Geophys. Union, A.A.A.S., Phi Beta Kappa, Sigma Xi. Research on trace inorganic elements in meteoritic, lunar and terrestrial matter. Home: 5810 Idledale Circle Madison WI 53711

HASKINS, ARTHUR LYMAN, educator, physician; b. Phila., Mar. 31, 1917; s. Arthur Lyman and Julia (Ingersol) H.; B.A., U. Rochester, 1938, M.D., 1943; m. Kathryn S. Burke, Mar. 22, 1943; children—Arthur Lyman III, Donald, Mark, Kathy Ann. Intern U.S. Naval Hosp., Bklyn., 1943; intern, then resident obstetrics and gynecology St. Louis Maternity Hosp., also Barnes Hosp., St. Louis, 1947-52; mem. faculty Washington U. Sch. Medicine, St. Louis, 1953-55; prof. obstetrics and gynecology, chmn. dept. U. Md. Sch. Medicine, 1955—. Served to lt., M.C., USN, 1943-47. Mem. Am., So. med. assns., Am. Coll. Obstetricians and Gynecologists, Am. Assn. Obstetricians and Gynecologists, Endocrine Soc., Fertility Soc., A.C.S., Soc. Gynecol. Investigation, Alpha Omega Alpha, Delta Upsilon. Research on endocrinology of reprodn. Home: 7000 Copeleigh Rd Baltimore MD 21212

HASKINS, CARYL PARKER, educator, research scientist; b. Schenectady, Aug. 12, 1908; s. Caryl Davis and Frances Julia (Parker) H.; Ph.B., Yale, 1930; Ph.D., Harvard, 1935; D.Sc., Tufts Coll., 1951, Union Coll., 1955, Northeastern U., 1955, Yale, 1958, Hamilton Coll., 1959, George Washington U., 1963 LL.D., Carnegie Inst. Tech., 1960, U. Cin., 1960, Boston Coll., 1960, Washington and Jefferson Coll., 1961, U. Del., 1965; m. Edna Ferrell, July 12, 1940. Staff mem. research lab. Gen. Electric Co., Schenectady, 1931-35; research asso. Mass. Inst. Tech. 1935-45; pres., research dir. Haskins Labs., Inc., 1935-55, dir., 1935—, chmn. bd., 1970—; pres. Carnegie Instn. of Washington, 1956-71, also trustee. Dir. E.I. duPont de Nemours & Co. Asst. liaison officer OSRD. 1941-42, sr. liaison officer, 1942-43; exec. asst. to chmn. NDRC, 1943- 44, dep. exec. officer, 1944-45; sci. adv. bd. Policy Council, Research and Devel. Bd. of Army and Navy, 1947-48; cons. Research and Develop. Bd., 1947-51, to sec. of def., 1950-60, to sec. of state 1950-60; mem. President's Sci. Adv. Com., 1955-58, cons., 1959—; mem. President's Nat. Adv. Commn. on Libraries, 1966-67; mem. Joint U.S.- Japan Com. on Sci. Coop., 1961-67, cons., 1967—, Internat. Conf. Insect Physiology and Entomology; panel advisers Bur. East Asian and Pacific Affairs, Dept. of State, 1966-68. Trustee Carnegie Corp. N.Y., 1955—, Rand Corp., 1955-65, 66—; fellow Yale Corp., 1962—; regent Smithsonian Instn., 1956—; bd. dirs. Council Fgn. Relations, 1961—, Population Council, Ednl. Testing Service, Center for Advanced Study in Behavioral Scis., Inst. Current World Affairs, Arctic Inst. N.Am., Schenectady Trust Co., Woods Hole Oceanographic Instn., Nat. Geog. Soc., Franklin Book Programs, 1953-58, Council on Library Resources, Pacific Sci. Center Found., Asia Found., Marlboro Coll. Mem. vis. coms. Harvard Overseers Com., Johns Hopkins U.; bd. visitors, Tulane U. Recipient Certificate of Merit (U.S.), 1948, Kings Medal for Service in Cause of Freedom (Gt. Britain), 1948. Fellow Am. Phys. Soc., A.A.A.S. (dir.), Am. Acad. Arts and Scis., N.Y. Zool. Soc., Pierpont Morgan Library, Royal Entomol. Soc. (Gt. Britain), Entomol. Soc. Am.; mem. Washington Acad. Scis., Royal Soc. Arts (Benjamin Franklin fellow), Faraday Soc., Met. Mus. Art, Am. Mus. Natural History, Am. Philos. Soc., Brit. Assn. Advancement Sci., Audubon Soc., Save-the-Redwoods League, West Australian Naturalist Soc., Biophys. Soc. Nat. Acad. Sci. N.Y. Acad. Scis., N.Y. Bot. Garden, P.E.N., Pilgrims, Sigma Xi (nat. pres. 1967-69), Delta Sigma Rho, Omicron Delta Kappa, Phi Beta Kappa. Episcopalian. Clubs: Century, Coffee House (N.Y.C.); Mohawk (Schenectady); Metropolitan, Cosmos, Chevey Chase, Federal City, University (Washington). Author: Of Ants and Men, 1939; The Amazon, 1943; Of Societies and Men, 1950; The Scientific Revolution and World Politics, 1964; contbr. to anthologies and tech. papers. Editor: The Search for Understanding, 1967; (with others): Am. Scientist, 1971—. Home: 1545 18th St NW Washington DC 20036 Office: 2100 M St NW Washington DC 20037 also: 22 Green Acre Lane Westport CT 06880

HASKINS, GEORGE LEE, lawyer, educator; b. Cambridge, Mass., Feb. 13, 1915; s. Charles Homer and Clare (Allen) H.; Classical Diploma, Phillips Exeter Acad., 1931; A.B. summa cum laude, Harvard, 1935, LL.B., 1942; Henry fellow, Merton Coll., Oxford U., 1935-36; m. Anstiss Crowninshield Boyden, July 15, 1944. Jr. fellow Soc. of Fellows, Harvard, 1936-42, lectr. dept. sociology, 1937-38; Lowell lectr., Boston, 1938; asso. Herrick Smith, Donald & Farley, Boston, 1942; admitted bar of Mass., 1943, Pa., 1952, Me. 1968, U.S. Supreme Ct., 1952, other fed. cts.; ofcl. observer and War Dept. rep. U.S. delegation to UN Conf., San Francisco, 1945; with office of spl. asst. to sec. of state, 1946; asst. prof. law U. Pa., 1946-48, asso. prof., 1948-49, prof., 1949-; spl. atty. legal dept. Pa. R.R., 1951-54, apptd by Pres. Eisenhower to Permanent Com. on Oliver Wendell Holmes Devise, 1956; asst. reporter for Supreme and Superior Cts. Pa., 1970—. Permanent mem. Jud. Conf. U.S. Third Circuit. Dir. Pa. Mut. Fund, N.Y.C. Served from pvt. to cpl. U.S. C.A.C., 1942-43; lst. lt. to capt. War Dept. Gen. Staff, 1944-45, Gen. Staff Corps, 1945. Decorated Army Commendation medal with oak leaf clusters, 1946; Demoblzn. Award, Social Sci. Research Council, 1946; elected Consejero del Instituto Internacional para Unificación del Derecho Publico, 1956; John Simon Guggenheim fellow, 1957. Fellow Royal Hist. Soc.; mem. Am., Mass., Me., Pa., Phila. bar assns., Assn. Bar City of N.Y., Swedish Colonial Soc., Am. Judicature Soc., Am. Arbitration Assn. (nat. panel arbitrators 1968—), Societe Internationale de l'Histoire du Droit (council 1970), Am. Soc. for Legal History (pres. 1970), Antiquarian Soc. Internat. Law Soc., Soc. Colonial Wars, Am. Acad. Polit. Sci., Am. Hist. Assn., Am. Law Inst., Assn. ICC Practitioners, Juristic Soc., Brit. Records Assn., Mediaeval Acad. Am., Soc. Comparative Legislation, Colonial Soc. Mass., Mass. (corr. mem.), Me., Va. hist. socs., Colonial Soc. Pa., Art Alliance Phila., Selden Soc., Am. Geneal. Soc., Geneal. Soc. Pa., Inst. Early Am. History and Culture (mem. council, editorial bd.), S.R., Order of Coif, Soc. War 1812, Phi Beta Kappa. Clubs: Somerset (Boston); Rittenhouse, Racquet, Harvard (Phila.): Metropolitan (Washington). Author: The Statute of York and the Interest of the Commons, 1935; The Growth of English Representative Government, 1948; American Law of Property (with others), 1952; Pennsylvania Fiduciary Guide (with M.P. Smith), 1957; Law and Authority in Early Massachusetts, 1960; also numerous articles in U.S. and fgn. periodicals; mem. panel of authors preparing History of U.S. Supreme Court authorized by Congress, 1958. Editor: Death of a Republic (John Dickinson), 1963; Phi Beta Kappa series, 1934-37. Adv. bd. editors Speculum, 1949-69; bd. editors William and Mary Quar., Papers of John Marshall, Williamsburg, Va. Box 760 Paoli PA 19301 Office: 3400 Chestnut St Philadelphia PA 19104

HASKINS, JACK BURTON, educator; b. Macon, Ga., Mar. 20, 1922; s. DeForest Algood and Fleeta (Ward) H.; A.B., U. Ga., 1949; M.A., Emory U., 1951; Ph.D., U. Minn., 1959; 1 son, Casey Reed. News editor Gainesville (Ga.) News, 1949-50; instr., asst. research dir. Sch. Journalism, U. Minn., 1951-56; sr. research exec. Curtis Pub. Co., Phila., 1956-61; advt. research mgr. Ford div., Dearborn Mich., 1961-63; prof., chmn. mass communications Ind. U., 1963-66; John Ben Snow research prof. Syracuse (N.Y.) U., 1966-, also dir. Newspaper Research Program. Mem. mass communications com. Nat. Safety Council, 1964-. Served with USNR, 1943-46, 52-54. Mem. Am. Psychol. Assn., Am. Assn. Pub. Opinion Research, Assn. for Edn. in Journalism, Council on Newspaper Research and Devel., Am. Marketing Assn., Phi Beta Kappa. Author: How to Evaluate Mass Communication, 1968; Advertising Research and Testing, 1969. Contbr. articles profl. jours. Home: 40 Lakeview Circle Skaneateles NY 13152 Office: Syracuse U Syracuse NY 13210

HASKINS, JOHN CHRISTOPHER, music critic; b. St. Joseph, Mo., Sept. 2, 1918; s. Aaron Benjamin and Margaret (Feld) H.; B.Mus., Catholic U. Am., 1950, M.A., 1952; m. Margaret Varda, Sept. 20, 1945; 1 dau., Maria Caterina. Contbg. music critic Washington Post, 1954-59; program specialist Pan Am. Union, 1955; contract script writer Voice of Am. USIA, 1957-59, 61-65; cultural attache U.S. Embassy, Ottawa, Ont., Can., 1959-61; contbg. music critic Washington Evening Star, 1961-65; instr. music dept. George Washington U., 1964-65; music editor Kansas City (Mo.) Star, 1965—; instr. Conservatory Music, U. Mo. at Kansas City, 1954—; music critic Washington Times-Herald, 1952-54; music dir. radio sta. WGMS, Washington, 1956-57. Served with USNR, 1942-46; PTO. Member Music Critics Association (secretary), National Press Club. Contributor articles profl. publs. Home: 5841 McGee St Kansas City MO 67113 Office: 1729 Grand Av Kansas City MO 64108

HASKINS, RALPH STUART, biochemist, med. technologist; b. Dalton, Neb., June 14, 1920; s. Homer L. and Winnie H. (Knight) H.; B.A., U. Neb., 1949; B.S., 1954; M.S. in Biochemistry, U.Ark., 1964; m. Carol Ellen Rule, Aug. 1, 1948; children—Teresa Ellen, Laurin Dale, Thomas Gregg, Holly Ann. Med. Technician Lincoln (Neb.) Clinic, 1949, Lincoln VA Hosp., 1950-54; successively biochemist, clin. lab. supr., instr. med. tech. VA Hosp., Little Rock, 1954-65, clin. chemist research and spl. chemistry, 1965- 69, clin. chemist, chief research and development section, clinical laboratory, 1969—. Member of board of dirs. Accrediting Bur. Med. Tech. Schs., 1963-65; del. confs. Dept. Labor and Dept. Health, Edn. and Welfare, 1966, Nat. Health Conf., 1966. District chairman of Boy Scouts of Am., 1967-70 Served with AUS, 1942-46. Recipient Superior Performance award VA Hosp., Little Rock, 1960; Distinguished Achievement award Am. Med. Technologists, 1961, Exceptional Meritorious award, 1963; Order Golden Microscope, Am. Med. Technologists, 1969. Mem. Am. Med. Technologists Assn. (bd. dirs. 1963—, pres. 1965-67), Am. Chem. Soc., Am. Assn. Clin. Chemists, Assn. Advancement Biology and Medicine. Methodist (past mem. ofcl. bd.). Mason (32). Author articles. Home: 8400 Stanton Rd Little Rock AR 72209 Office: 300 E Roosevelt Rd Little Rock AR 72206

HASLAM, JAMES YARNELL, oil co. exec.; b. Arnett, Okla., May 9, 1912; s. Earl James and Sydney (Robbins) H.; B.S. in Mech. Engring., Okla. A. and M. Coll., 1933; m. Kathryn Lorene Bricker, July 30, 1938 (dec. 1965); children—Sydney Jo, John Hoyt; m. 2d, Dorothy L. Greenwood Roper, Dec. 14, 1968; 1 stepson, W.E. Roper. With Skelly Oil Co., 1933—, mgr. tech. services, 1961-65, v.p. engring and construction, 1965-69, vice president of project development, 1969—; vice president, director Hawkeye Chem. Co., Clinton, Ia., 1962—; v.p. Complex Constrn. Corp., Wilmington, Del., 1965—; v.p., dir. Vanply Inc., Vanply Liberia, Liberia, Africa; dir. Nuclear Fuel Services Inc., Wheaton, Maryland, Vancouver Plywood Co. Inc. La.; dir. Chembond Corp.; mem. policy com. Chemplex Co. Registered profl. engr., Ia., N.M., Okla. Mem. Am. Petroleum Assn., Nat. Gasoline Producers Assn., Ind. Petroleum Assn. Am., Pi Tau Sigma, Sigma Tau. Member of Christian Church. Club: Petroleum (Tulsa). Home: 2807 E 36th Pl Tulsa OK 74105 Office: PO Box 1650 Tulsa OK 74102

HASLANGER, ROBERT UREY, oil and gas co. exec.; b. Menominee, Mich., Jan. 4, 1914; s. Harry Leroy and Vesta (Urey) H.; B.S. in Chemistry, U. Wis., 1935; grad. Advanced Mgmt. Program, Harvard, 1947; m. Anne Clarke, Dec. 30, 1942; children—Mary (Mrs. Richard Kortegast), Paul A., Robert C., Sally. Engr., Marathon Paper Co., 1936-37, Burgess Cellulose Co., 1937-40; with Monsanto Chem. Co., 1940-54, dir. marketing Tex. div., 1950-54; v.p. sales Stauffer Chem. Co., 1954-55; pres. Escambia Chem. Corp., 1955-63; exec. v.p. United Gas Corp., Shreveport, La., 1963-68; exec. v.p., dir. Pennzoil United Inc., 1968; exec. v.p., dir. Pennzoil-United Inc.; pres., dir. United Gas Pipe Line Co.; dir. Duval Corp., Atlas Processing Co. Trustee La. State Fair, Centenary Coll., Shreveport, Inst. Gas Tech. Am. Gas Assn., Ind. Natural Gas Assn. Am. (dir.), Home: 12415 Overcup Dr Houston TX 77024 Office: 1500 Southwest Tower Houston TX 77018

HASLER, ARTHUR DAVIS, educator; b. Lehi, Utah, Jan. 5, 1908; s. Walter Thalmann and Ada (Broomhead) H.; B.A., Brigham Young U., 1932; Ph.D., U. Wis., 1937; D.Sc., U. Nfld., 1967; m. Hanna Prusse, Sept. 6, 1932 (dec.); children—Sylvia (Mrs. Gilbert Thatcher), A. Frederick, Mark, Bruce, Galen, Karl. Aquatic biologist U.S. Fish and Wildlife Service, 1935-37; instr., prof. U. Wis., Madison, 1937—, chmn. dept. zoology, 1953, 55-57, dir. Lab. Limnology, 1963—; chmn. com. freshwater productivity internat. biol. program, 1964—, Nat. Acad. Sci.-NRC, 1963—, chmn. nat. com. Internat. Union Biol. Scis., 1965-69, chmn. com. ecology, 1966—. Chmn., Internat. Congress Limnology, 1962; pres. Internat. Assn. Ecology, 1962—; trustee The Inst. Ecology, 1971—. French horn player, mem. exec. com. Madison Civic Music Assn., 1937-65; chmn. Lake Mendota Problems Com., 1965—. Fulbright research scholar, Germany, 1955, Finland, 1963. Fellow Societas Zoologica Botanica Fennica Finland, Phila. Acad. Sci.; mem. Am. Behavioral Soc., A.A.A.S. (past v.p. div. F), Am. Soc. Limnology and Oceanography (past pres.), Ecol. Soc. Am. (past pres.), Am. Fisheries Soc., Am. Soc. Naturalists (past v.p.), Am. Soc. Zooligists (pres. 1971), U.S. Nat. Acad. Scis., Internat. Assn. Limnology, Phi Kappa Phi (hon.). Mem. Ch. of Jesus Christ of Latter-day Saints. Author: Underwater Guideposts, 1966. Contbr. articles to profl. jours. Home: 205 Lathrop St Madison WI 53705

HASLER, FREDERICK EDWARD, former banker; b. Wethersfield, Essex, Eng., Feb. 27, 1882; s. Thomas and Jane Chatterson (Banyard) H.; ed. pvt. schs., Eng.; M.A. (hon.), Bowdoin Coll., 1943; LL.D., Columbia, 1955, Trinity Coll., Conn., 1957; m. Marguerite Isabel Messent, Sept. 5, 1912; children—Audrey, Shirley, Marjory. Came to U.S., 1901, naturalized, 1919. Began as clk., London, 1899: chartering clk. J.H. Winchester & Co., N.Y.C., 1903-06; mgr. Am. Smelters S.S. Co., 1906-08; asst. to pres. Chesapeake & Ohio Coal & Coke Co., 1908-09; sr. partner Hasler Bros., 1909-23; v.p. Bank of Am., 1923-36; pres. Internat. Trust Co., 1929-31; chmn. exec. com. Continental Bank & Trust Co., 1931, chmn. bd., 1941-48; chmn. U.S. bd. N. Brit. & Merc. Ins. Co. Ltd. and subsidiaries, 1946-61; cons., former mem. adv. com. of bd., mem. Lower Manhattan adv. bd. Chem. Bank N.Y. Trust Co., now ret.; chmn. Haytian Am. Sugar Co., S.A., 1938-67, now dir.; chmn., dir. Signet Fund (Bermuda) Ltd., 1957-68, Hermes Enterprises, Ltd. (Bermuda); dir. La Plantation Dauphin, S.A., Haiti West Indies Co., ECL Industries, Ltd., Haitian Am. Devel. Corp., S.A.; incorporator Litchfield Savs. Soc. Trustee Sch. Indsl. Relations, Cornell U., 1943-45, Leake and Watts Children's Home, St. Margaret's Sch. and others; hon. dir. Americas Found.; bd. dirs. Inter-Am. Literacy Found. others. Decorated Honneur et Merite (Haiti); Orden Nacional del Merito de Carlos Manuel de Cespedes, Orden del Merito Comercial (Cuba); Orden del Libertador Bolivar (Venezuela); Orden Nacional do Cruzeiro do Sul (Brazil); Sul Orden Mexicana del Aguila Azteca (Mexico); Orden al Merito (Ecuador); Orden del Condor de los Andes (Bolivia); Orden de Cristobal Colon, Orden del Merito Juan Pablo Duarte (Dominican Republic); Orden de Vasco Nunex de Balboa (Panama); Orden de Ruben Dario (Nicaragua), others. Mem. N.Y. C. of C. (pres. 1942-44, hon. life mem.), Pan Am. Soc. U.S. (pres. 1940-46, now hon. pres., dir.). Episcopalian. Clubs: Pilgrims, University (N.Y.C.) Home: Church Hill Washington Depot CT 06794 also 715 Park Av New York City NY 10021

HASLUCK, PAUL MEERNAA CAEDWALLA, Australian diplomat; b. Fremantle, Western Australia, Apr. 1, 1905; s. E. M. and Patience (Wooler) H.; M.A., U. Western Australia; m. Alix Darker, Apr. 14, 1932; children—Rollo, Nicolas. Editorial staff Western Australian; lectr. history U. Western Australia; staff Dept. External Affairs, Canberra, 1941-47, officer-in-charge Postwar Sect., 1942, dir. Post-Hostilities div., 1944-46, counsellor-in-charge Australian Mission to UN, 1946, acting rep. Australia on security council and atomic energy commn., 1946-47; reader in history U. Western Australia, 1948; minister for territories, 1951-63, for def., 1963-64, for external affairs, 1964-69; gov. gen. of Australia, 1969—, minister for external affairs, 1969—. Apptd. mem. Her Majesty's Privy Council, 1966. Adviser to Australian del. UN Conf., San Francisco, UN Prep. Commn. (Australian rep. on exec. com.), London, 1945, alternate del. to UN Prep. Commn. and Gen. Assembly, London, del. to Gen. Assembly, New York, 1946; elected to Australian Parliament, 1949. Author: Black Australians, 1942; Workshop of Security, 1948; The Government and the People, 1951; Native Welfare in Australia, 1954. Hist. research, 1947—. Home: 2 Adams Rd Claremont Western Australia Address: Parliament House Canberra ACT Australia

HASS, FIRMAN HENRY, accountant; b. New Holstein, Wis., July 27, 1902; s. Peter M. and Lily (Pieper) H.; B.A., U. Wis., 1925; m. Althea Louise Wacker, June 24, 1925; children—David Peter, Barbara (Mrs. Peter Hoadley). With Ernst & Ernst, C.P.A.'s, 1926-29, 40-67, charge Mich. dist., Detroit, 1955-67; with Walter P. Chrysler, N.Y.C., 1929-40. Bd. dirs., mem. exec. com. Detroit United Found., 1960-67. C.P.A., Mich., numerous other states. Mem. Am. Inst. C.P.A.'s (council 1962-64), Mich. Assn. C.P.A.'s (pres. 1961-62), Nat. Assn. Accountants (pres. 1966-67, exec. com. 1961-69), Phi Kappa Phi, Beta Gamma Sigma, Beta Alpha Psi, Delta Sigma Pi. Clubs: Detroit Athletic, Economic, Detroit Golf (pres. 1967-68) (Detroit). Home: 15903 Rosemont Rd Detroit MI 48223 Office: Buhl Bldg Detroit MI 48226

HASS, GEORGE MARVIN, physician; b. Tingley, Ia., Apr. 29, 1907; s. Albert R. and Edna (Hall) H.; M.D., Harvard, 1929; m. Ruth Virginia Hoskins, Oct. 10, 1942; children—George Michael, Barbara Ruth, Nancy Sue, Martha C., Elizabeth Ro., Susan V. Intern, Peter Bent Brigham Hosp., Boston, 1929-30, resident, 1932-34, Childrens Hosp., 1930-32; med. research and edn., Chgo., 1946—; chmn. dept. pathology Presbyn. Hosp., Chgo., 1946- 59, Presbyn.-St. Luke's Hospital (now Rush-Presbyn.-St. Luke's Med. Center), 1959—; medical faculty Harvard, 1932- 38, Cornell U., 1938-46, U. Ill., 1946-71, Rush Med. Coll., Chgo., 1971—. Cons., surgeon gen. USAF, USPHS. Served from capt. to lt. col., M.C., USAAF, 1942-46. Mem. Soc. Fellows Harvard. Home: 53 S Lombard St Lombard IL 60148 Office: 1753 W Congress St Chicago IL 60612

HASS, MARC, transp. co. exec.; b. Cin., Mar. 16, 1908; s. Marc and Alice (White) H.; grad. Horace Mann Sch., 1925, princeton, 1929; m. Helen Hotze, Feb. 3, 1951. Partner, Emanuel & Co., mems. N.Y. Stock Exchange, 1933-42; dept. dir. Office Def. Transp., Washington, 1942-45; asso. Allen & Co., N.Y.C., 1945-55; pres. Am. Transp. Enterprises, Inc., N.Y.C., 1955—; pres. Am. Diversified Enterprises, Inc.; dir. Lehigh Valley Transit, Omaha Transit, Cin., New Port and Covington Transit, Va. Transit, Nashville Transit, Oceanographic Devel. Co., So. Coach, Harrisburg Rys., Wilkes Barre Transit, Tishman Realty, Golden Cycle Co. Mem. Am. Transit Assn. Episcopalian. Clubs: Princeton (N.Y.C.); Long Island Country (Eastport, L.I.); Bel Air (Cal.) Country. Home: 14 E 75th St New York NY 10021 Office: 30 Broad St New York NY

HASS, PETER STIBOLT, corp. exec.; b. Davenport, Ia., Aug. 26, 1916; s. Leon H. and Otie B. (Stibolt) H.; B.S. in Chemistry summa cum laude, Stanford, 1938; m. Harriet Shepherdson, Oct. 22, 1938; children—Stephen P., Michael S., Eric S., Susan A. With Firestone Tire & Rubber Co., San Jose, Cal.; photog. paper devel. and research Eastman Kodak Co., Rochester, N.Y., 1938-47, supr. photog. paper melting dept., 1945-47; with Permanente Cement Co., Los Altos, Cal., 1947—, exec. v.p., 1959-64, pres., chief exec. officer, 1964—, also dir. (co. name changed to Kaiser Cement & Gypsum Corp. 1964); dir. Ryukyu Cement Co. Ltd. Clubs: Los Altos Country (past pres.); Orinda (Cal.) Country; Claremont Country (Oakland, Cal.). Home: 5708 Glenbrook Dr Oakland CA 94618 Office: Kaiser Center 300 Lakeside Dr Oakland CA 94612

HASSAN, IHAB HABIB, lit. critic, educator; b. Cairo, Egypt, Oct. 17, 1925; s. Habib and Faika (Hamdi) H.; came to U.S., 1946, naturalized, 1956; B.Sc. with highest honors, U. Cairo, 1946; M.S., U. Pa., 1948, M.A., 1950, Ph.D., 1953; m. Sarah Margaret Greene, 1966; 1 son by previous marriage, Geoffrey. Instr. English, Rensselaer Poly. Inst., 1952-54; mem. faculty Wesleyan U., Middletown, Conn., 1954-70, Benjamin L. Waite prof. English, 1962-70, chmn. dept. English, 1963-64, 68-69, dir. Coll. Letters, 1964- 66, dir. Center for Humanities, 1969-70; Vilas research prof. U. Wis., Milw., 1970—. Mem. editorial bd. Am. Quar., 1965-67, Wesleyan U. Press, 1963-66; tutor Salzburg Seminars Am. Studies, summer, 1965; Fulbright lectr. to France, 1966-67; Guggenheim fellow, 1958-59, 62-63; fellow Sch. Letters, Ind. U., 1964. Mem. Sigma Xi. Author: Radical Innocence: Studies in Contemporary American Novel, 1961; Crise du Héros Américain Contemporain, 1963; The Literature of Silence; Henry Miller and Samuel Becket, 1967; The Dismemberment of Orpheus: Toward a Postmodern Literature, 1971. Editor Liberations: New Essays on the Humanities in Revolution, 1971. Home: 2137 N Terrace Av Milwaukee WI 53202

HASSANEIN, SALAH M., married; 5 children. Exec. v.p., dir. United Artists Theatre Circuit, Inc.; pres. United Artists Eastern Theatres, Inc., The Todd-AO Corp. Mem. Nat. Assn. Theatre Owners. Office: 1700 Broadway New York NY 10019

HASSAN II, KING OF MOROCCO, (Moulay Hassan); b. Rabat, Morocco, July 9, 1929; s. King Mohammed V; ed. Imperial Coll. at Rabat; licentiate in law U. Bordeaux; m. Lalla Litifa, 1961; children—Lalla Mariam, Sidi Mohammed. Tng. course French Navy, served aboard battleship Jeanne d'Arc; with royal family exiled by French govt. to Island of Corsica, then Madagascar, 1954-55; participated negotiations on treaty granting independence to Morocco, 1955-56; became chief dep. to father; comdr. in chief Royal Moroccan Army, 1957; became minister of def., vice premier, 1960, became King Hassan II of Morocco, 1961; wrote democratic constitution providing for elected parliament, 1962. Address: Royal Palace Rabat Morocco*

HASSE, WILLIAM FREDERICK, former banker; b. New Haven, May 10, 1906; s. William Frederick and Lillie (Ammann) H.; grad. Am. Inst. Banking, 1930; student Rutgers U., 1944; m. Helen Scholz, Sept. 20, 1930; children—William Frederick III, Robert G. Auditor, New Haven Bank, 1945-57, comptroller, 1951-57; comptroller 1st New Haven Nat. Bank, 1957-69, v.p., 1964-70, ret.; instr. Am. Inst. Banking, 1945-67, Waterbury chpt., 1946-49; instr. Quinnipiack Coll., 1945-57, Stone's Coll., 1950-; mem. Conn. State Bank Examining Com., 1964—. Treas. Town of East Haven, 1946-48; asst. treas. USO, 1942-46. Dir., sec., treas. New Haven Safety Council, 1959-62; chmn. Housing Authority East Haven, 1969; auditor Old Stone Ch., Womens Seamens Soc. Pres., bd. dirs. East Lawn Cemetery; bd. dirs. Stone Coll. Mem. Am. Inst. Banking (past pres. local chpt.), Bank Auditors and Comptrollers (past pres. local chpt.), Conn. Bankers Assn., Financial Execs. Inst. Author: History of Banking in New Haven, 1946: History of Money and Banking in Connecticut, 1957. Home: Mansfield Rd East Haven CT 06512

HASSEL, MILTON JOHN, coll. pres.; b. Harlan County, Neb., Apr. 22, 1916; s. Carl Arvid and Anna Hildur (Carlson) H.; B.S., Kearney State Coll., 1941; M.A., U. Neb., 1947, Ph.D., 1957; m. Lou Forre, Jan. 18, 1944; children—Jane, Dian. Faculty Wayne (Neb.) State Tchrs. Coll., 1947-57., dean students, 1954-57, interim pres., 1956-57; acad. dean Mankato (Minn.) State Coll., 1957-61; pres. Kearney (Neb.) State Coll., 1961—. Dir., Platte Valley State Bank. Bd. dirs. United Fund, A.R.C. Mem. Neb. Edn. Commn. States; chmn. Neb. Council on Econ. Edn.; mem. commn. N. Centra Assn. Recipient Medallion of Service award Luther Coll., Wahoo, Neb., 1962; Midland Coll. Achievement award, 1965. Mem. Nat., Neb. edn. assns., Assn. Higher Edn., Am. Assn. Sch. Adminstrs., Am. Assn. State Colls. and Univs. (mem. nat. com.), Neb. Schoolmasters Club, Kearney C. of C. (dir.), Phi Delta Kappa. Kiwanian. Home: 3116 9th Av Kearney NB 68847

HASSEL, ODD, chemist; b. Oslo, Norway, May 17, 1897; s. Ernst A. and Mathilde (Kaveness) H.; Candireal., U. Oslo, 1920; Dr.phil., Berlin U., 1924; Dr.phil.h.c., Copenhagen (Denmark) U., 1950; Fildr.h.c., Stockholm (Sweden) U., 1960. Faculty Oslo U., 1925—, prof., dir. phys. chemistry dept., 1934-64. Decorated knight Order of St. Olav, recipient Gunnerus medal; Guldberg-Waage medal; co-recipient Nobel Prize in chemistry, 1969. Hon. fellow Chem. Soc. (London), Norwegian Chem. Soc. (past chmn.). Mem. Norwegian council for Scis. and Humanities, acads. scis. of Oslo, Trondheim, Stockholm, Uppsala, Gothenberg, Copenhagen. Author: Kristallchemie, 1934; also numerous articles. Norwegian editor Acta Chemica Scandinavica, 1947-57. Research, numerous publs. on crystal and molecular structures using X-ray and electron diffraction methods and measurement of electric dipole moments, stereochemistry connected with 6-membered rings and conformational analysis, atomic arrangement in weak complexes formed by electron transfer from donor to acceptor molecules. Home: 10 Holsteinveien Oslo 8 Norway

HASSELBLAD, OLIVER WILLIAM, physician, clergyman, missionary; b. Beresford, S.D., Feb. 7, 1909; s. Carl and Ada (Tingleaf) H.; B.A., U. Omaha, 1931; M.D., U. Neb., 1936; m. Norma Bornschlegel, Aug. 29, 1933; children—Marva Elaine, Wyva Louise, Carl Douglas. Ordained to ministry Bapt. Ch., 1934; intern, surg. resident Mo. Bapt. Hosp., St. Louis, also Peru, Ind., 1936-38; med. missionary, chief med. officer Christian Hosp., Jorhat Assam, India, 1938-57; pres. Am. Leprosy Missions, Inc., N.Y.C., 1959—. Recipient Kaisar-i-Hind medal for humanitarian services to India, King George VI, 1947. Mem. A.M.A., Mo. Med. Assn., Am., N.Y. socs. tropical medicine, Internat. Soc. Tropical Dermatology, Internat. Leprosy Assn., Internat. Soc. for Rehab. of Disabled, Phi Chi. Home: 470 W 24th St New York City NY 10011 Office: 297 Park Av S New York City NY 10010

HASSELGREN, HARRY R., union ofcl. Sec., Internat. Longshoremen's Assn. AFL-CIO. Office: 17 Battery Pl New York City NY 10004*

HASSELL, ANDREW PIERSON, Jr., govt. ofcl.; b. Takamatsu, Japan, May 2, 1916 (parents Am. citizens); s. Andrew Pierson and Barbara (Savage) H.; B.S. in Physics and Math., Davidson Coll., 1936; grad. Fed. Exec. Inst., 1968; m. Mary Harrison Benson, June 22, 1940; children—Mary Benson (Mrs. Don Stuart Whisonant), Barbara Amelia (Mrs. Richard Thomas Duemler). With Agrl. Stablzn. and Conservation Service, USDA, 1936—, div. chief state office, Raleigh, N.C., 1949-61, state exec. dir., 1961-66, dep. dir. budget div., Washington, 1966-68, dir., 1968—; dir. Budget Commodity Credit Corp., Washington, 1968—. Recipient Superior Service award USDA, 1961. Mem. Orgn. Profl. Employees USDA, Nat. Agrl. Stabilization and Conservation Service County Employees Assn., Fed. Exec. Inst. Alumni Assn., Sigma Phi Epsilon. Democrat. Presbyn. (elder). Home: 1327 Rand Dr Raleigh NC 27608 also Hunting Towers Alexandria VA 22314 Office: 6605 South Agr Bldg 14th and Independence Av Washington DC 20250

HASSELQUIST, SHIRLEY ELAINE, orgn. ofcl.; b. Omaha, May 27, 1929; d. Verner F. and Alice (Melotz) Hasselquist; A.B., Neb. Christian Coll., 1952; B.S. in Edn., U. Omaha, 1962. Asst. instr. Greek, Neb. Christian Coll., 1951-52; Christian edn. missionary McKinely Indian Mission, Toppenish, Wash., 1952-58; pub. sch. tchr., Omaha, 1960-66; nat. gen. sec. of Loyal Temperance Legion, Women Christian Temperance Union, 1966—. Mem. Kappa Delta Pi. Republican. Mem. Christian Ch. Address: 1730 Chicago Av Evanston IL 60201

HASSIALIS, MENELAOS DIMITRI educator, engr.; b. N.Y.C., Dec. 25, 1909; s. Dimitri A. and Marie (Mantsalis) H.; A.B., Columbia, 1931; D.Sc. (hon.), Bard Coll., Annandale-on- Hudson, N.Y., 1953; m. Ruth Elizabeth Arnold, June 17, 1931; children—Joan Illeana (Mrs. Dieter C. Bucher), Peter John. Engaged research Columbia U., 1934-37; mem. faculty Columbia Sch. Mines, 1937—, prof., 1951—, exec. officer, mem. exec. com. senate, 1969—, chmn. investment policy com., 1970; pres. Pacific Uranium Mines Co., 1959-61; v.p. Tech. Investors Corp., 1961-62, Tech. Investors Mgmt. Co., 1961-63; pres., dir. T.I.C. Mining Co., 1969—; dir. Ambrosia Lakes Uranium Corp., Tudor Industries Corp., Sandvik Steel Co., Karmac Nuclear Fuels Corp. Cons. fields ore dressing, petroleum engring., surface chemistry; dir. Columbia Mineral Benefication Lab. operated for AEC, 1951-58; mem. adminstrv. bd. Lamont Geol. Obs., 1965—; mem. and vice chmn. adminstrv. board Inst. for Study of Sci. in Human Affairs 1967-70; mem. Council for Atomic Age Studies; chmn. phosphate slimes panel, minerals and metals adv. bd. Nat. Acad. Scis., NRC, Am. del. to Geneva Conf. on Peaceful Uses of Atomic Engergy, 1955, 58; Am. rep. to Paris meeting on atomic energy UNESCO. Vice pres., trustee Valley Hosp., Ridgewood, N.J. Recipient Great Tchrs. award, 1957; 1st encumbent of Harry Krumb chair in mining Columbia, 1959. Mem. Am. Inst. Mining, Metall. and Petroleum Engrs. (regional vice chmn., beneficiation div.), Am. Chem. Soc., Am. Inst. Mining Engrs., A.A.A.S., Sigma Xi, Tau Beta Pi. Clubs: Marshall Chess (N.Y.C.); Ridgewood (N.J.) Bridge. Contbg. author Handbook of Mineral Dressing (by A.F. Taggart). Contbr. articles pubs. Am. Inst. Mining Engrs. since 1936. Home: 122 Phelps Rd Ridgewood NJ 07450 Office: Columbia Sch Mines New York City NY 10027

HASSID, SAMI, educator, architect; b. Cairo, Egypt, Apr. 19, 1912; s. Joseph S. and Isabelle (Israel) H.; diploma in architecture with distinction, Sch. Engring., Giza, Egypt, 1932; B.A. in Architecture with honors, U. London (Eng.), 1935; M.Arch., U. Cairo, 1943; Ph.D. in Architecture, Harvard, 1956; m. Juliette Mizrahi, June 29, 1941; children—Fred, Muriel. Came to U.S., 1957, naturalized, 1962. Tchr., Alexandria (Egypt) Tech. Sch., 1932-34; successively tchr., lectr., asst. prof. U. Cairo, 1934-56; prof. architectural theory and design U. Ein-Shams, Cairo, 1957; mem. faculty U. Cal. at Berkeley, 1957—, prof. architecture, 1964-; archtl. practice, Cairo, 1932-57, Berkeley, 1957-; from draftsman to sr. designer office Ali Labib Gabr, architect, Cairo, 1935-47; partner Sami Hassid and Youssef Shafik, Cairo, 1947-57, Hassid and Kelemen, Berkeley, 1963-65, prin. works include Hill House, student hostel Am. U. Cairo, 1952. Commnr. Cal. Bd. Archtl. Examiners, 1961—. Fulbright grentee, 1954-56; recipient First prize Al-Chams Competition, Cairo, 1947, San Francisco A.I.A. Hdqrs. Competition, 1963. Mem. A.I.A., Bldg. Research Inst., Assn. Collegiate Schs. Architecture. Democrat. Jewish religion (pres. temple; v.p. East Bay synagogue council 1970-71). Author: The Sultan's Turrets, 1939; Architectural Construction Details, 1954; Development and Application of a System for Recording Critical Evaluations of Architectural Works, 1964; Architectural Education U.S.A., 1967; Surface Materials in Architecture, 1970. Home: 976 Oxford St Berkeley CA 94707

HASSINGER, HAROLD BERTRAM, banker; b. Pitts., June 30, 1911; s. Walter B. and Ethel (Fischer) H.; student U. Pitts., 1934-41; grad. Stonier Sch. Banking, Rutgers U., 1951; m. Virginia Clarke Means, June 30, 1939; children—Robert, Ann, Richard, Norman. Messenger, then bookkeeper Continental Trust Co., Pitts., 1926-28; with Pitts. Nat. Bank, 1928-47, successively bookkeeper, teller, bookkeeping supr., audit clk., clerical asst. to comptroller, asst. comptroller, 1928-46, auditor, 1946-47; auditor First Nat. Bank of Boston, 1947-55, asst. v.p., 1955, v.p. charge br. div., 1955-60, v.p. charge brs., installment loans and deposit operations, 1960-63, v.p. charge brs., installment loans, deposit operations and data processing, 1963-64, sr. v.p. charge brs., installment loans, deposit operations, systems research, data processing, E.D.P. planning and trust operations, 1964-65, exec. v.p. deposit operations, systems research, data processing, E.D.P. planning and trust operations, 1966- 69, exec. v.p. charge deposit operations, systems research, data processing, E.D.P. planning, corporate trust operations, mut. funds, 1969-70; v.p. Old Colony Trust Co., 1964-69; pres., chief exec. officer Interbank Card Assn., 1970—. Mason (32, Shriner). Home: PO Box 1392 Oak Bluffs MA 02557 Office: 110 E 59th St New York City NY 10022

HASSLEIN, GEORGE JOHANN, coll. dean; b. Los Angeles, Aug. 31, 1917; s. August Theodore and Lena (Matranga) H.; B.Arch., U. So. Cal., 1945; m. Neva B. Henderson, Oct. 13, 1945 (dec. Dec. 1963); children—Vaughn, Tracey; m. 2d, Marilyn L. Collins, Sept. 10, 1966 (dec. Dec. 1967); m. 3d, Betty Sanders, June 24, 1970. Archtl. designer firm Welton Becket, architect, Los Angeles, 1948-50; mem. faculty Cal. State Poly. Coll., Obispo, 1949—, prof., head dept. archtl. engring., 1952-68, dean Sch. Architecture and Environmental Design, 1968—. Archtl. adviser bd. trustees Cal. State Colls., 1961—. Chmn. Indsl. Survey Com. San Luis Obispo, 1955, Traffic Survey Com., 1956; chmn. Bldg. Appeals Bd. San Luis Obispo, 1963-65; mem. Am. Arbitration Assn., 1960—. Served with C.E., AUS, 1942-44. Fellow A.I.A.; mem. Scarab, Delta Phi Delta, Tau Sigma. Home: 2333 Helena St San Luis Obispo CA 93401

HASSLER, FRANCIS JEFFERSON, educator, agrl. engr.; b. Cooper Hill, Mo., Aug. 2, 1921; s. Millard Franklin and Etta (Jett) H.; B.S. in Agrl. Engring., U. Mo., 1946; M.S., Mich. State U., 1948, Ph.D., 1950; m. Oneta Marceline Miller, Aug. 5, 1942; children—Olivia Ann, Reginald Robert, Gregory, Rodney, Melanie. Mem. faculty N.C. State U. at Raleigh, 1950—, prof. agrl. engring., 1954—, head dept. agrl. engring., 1961-65, head dept. biol. and agrl. engring., 1965—, William Neal Reynolds prof., 1961—, charge tobacco curing research, 1952-61. Served to 1st lt. AUS, 1943-46. Named Tarheel of Week, News and Observer, Raleigh, 1960. Mem. Am. Soc. Agrl. Engrs., Am. Soc. Engring. Edn., A.A.A.S., Sigma Xi, Tau Beta Pi, Pi Mu Epsilon, Sigma Pi Sigma, Phi Kappa Phi, Gamma Sigma Delta. Rotarian. Patentee in field. Home: 1404 Eden Lane Raleigh NC 27608

HASSLER, HOWARD EDWARD, retail co. exec.; b. N.Y.C., June 29, 1929; s. Milton C. and Madeline (Form) H.; B.S. in Accounting, L.I. U., 1951; student N.Y. U. Grad. Sch. Bus. Adminstrn.; m. Virginia A. Diviny, Dec. 26, 1953; children—Susan, Barbara, Robert, Craig. Mgr. Ernst & Ernst, C.P.A.'s, N.Y.C., 1953-65; with Allied Stores Corp., 1965—, treas., 1968—, v.p. finance, 1970—; v.p., dir. Allied Stores Credit Corp., 1969—, v.p., dir. Alstores Realty Corp., 1969. Treas. Laymen's Nat. Bible Com., 1966, bd. dirs., 1967—. Served with AUS, 1951-53. C.P.A., N.Y. Mem. Am. Inst. C.P.A.'s, N.Y. State Soc. C.P.A.'s, Nat. Assn. Accountants, Financial Pub. Relations Assn. Home: 161 Hampshire Rd Bronxville NY 10708 Office: 401 Fifth Av New York City NY 10016

HASSLER, WILLIAM WOODS, educator; b. Clearfield, Pa., Sept. 6, 1917; s. John W. and Clara (Woods) H.; B.S., Juniata Coll., 1939; M.S., U. Pa., 1941, Ph.D., 1951; m. Mary Ellen Jackson, June 12, 1941; children—Virginia (Mrs. Norman Lathbury), Thomas, Martha (Mrs. James Chapman). Research chemist Rohm & Haas, 1942-46; prof. chemistry Drexel U., 1946-51; chmn. dept. chemistry and physics Beaver Coll., Glenside, Pa., 1951-63; dean Sch. Arts and Scis., Indiana U. of Pa., 1963-69, pres., 1969—; tech. cons. Dir. Farmers Bank. Pres. Commn. Pub. Univs. and Colls. Pa., 1969-70. Active YMCA bldg. drive, 1970. Bd. dirs. Upper Moreland Pub. Library, regional council Boy Scouts Am., Indiana County Hosp. Recipient Bronze Plaque award Lincoln Civil War Soc. Phila., 1965, Freedoms. Found. Essay award, 1968. Fellow Co. Mil. Historians, Am. Inst. Chemists; mem. Am. Chem. Soc., Pa. Assn. Colls. and Univs. (mem. exec com.), Indsl. Mgmt. Club (pres.), Alpha Chi Sigma, Phi Alpha Theta, Phi Delta Kappa, Alpha Phi Omega. Republican. Episcopalian. Contbr. articles profl. jours. Home: 255 S 7th St Indiana PA 15701

HASSLOCHER, MARCEL DEZON COSTA, Brazilian govt. ofcl.; b. Rio de Janeiro, Brazil, Dec. 9, 1928; s. Alfredo Egon and Maria Luiza (Costa) H.; LL.B., Cath. U. Rio de Janeiro, 1951; postgrad. Instituto Rio Branco, 1954; m. Lais Carneiro, Sept. 12, 1964; children—Alfredo, Ciro, Marcel. Sec. to minister of justice, Rio de Janeiro, 1955-56, with Brazilian embassies, Montevideo, Uruguay, 1956-57, La Paz, Bolivia, 1957-59, Paris, France, 1961-62; sec. to minister finance, Rio de Janeiro, 1963; counselor Brazilian embassy, Washington, 1966-71; sec., counselor Brazilian embassy, Bonn, Germany, 1971—. Mem. Interam. Law Assn. (sr.). Clubs: Jockey (Rio de Janeiro); Golf (Brasilia); American Embassy (Bonn.). Home: 42 Rolandstrasse Bonn-Badgodesberg Germany

HASSO, SIGNE ELEONORA CECILIA, actress; b. Stockholm, Sweden, Aug. 15, 1915; d. Kefas Johannes and Helfrid Elisabet (Lindstrom) Larsson; ed. Royal Acad. Dramatic Arts; div.; 1 son, Henry (dec.). Actress, Royal Dramatic Theatre of Sweden, 1926—; appeared in plays in Scandinavia, Eng., Scotland, U.S., Can.; appeared in films, Europe and U.S.; appeared on television, Europe and U.S.; writer, corr., lyricist. Recipient Swedish Oscar, 1937; Gösta Ekman Scandinavian theatrical award, 1939; Le Grand Prix Edison award for lyrics of album Scandinavian Folksongs—Sung and Swung, 1965. Home: 215 W 90th St New York City NY 10024

HASTERLIK, ROBERT JOSEPH, physician, educator; b. Chgo., Mar. 17, 1915; s. Henry and Antonia (Epstein) H.; S.B., U. Chgo., 1934, M.D., 1938. Mem. faculty U. Chgo., 1948-70, asso. dir. Argonne Cancer Research Hosp., 1951-63, prof. medicine, 1960-70; clin. prof. medicine U. Cal. at San Diego, 1970—; v.p. Enviro-Med, Inc., 1970—. Mem. sci. com. 14 Nat. Council Radiation Protection, 1955—, mem., 1971—; mem. expert adv. panel radiation WHO, 1960-65; mem. U.S. mem. Ill. Legislative Commn. on Atomic Energy, 1955, co-chmn. 1967—; mem. Ill. Radiation Protection Adv. Council, 1960- 70; cons. subcom. toxicity internal emitters, com. path. effects atomic radiation Nat. Acad. Scis.-NRC, 1958-65; mem. ofcl. sci. mission to S. Am., AEC-State Dept., 1956, 57; mem. Internat. Coop. Year Com. Peaceful Uses Atomic Energy; fellow Acad. Policy Study, U. Chgo., 1965-70. Served to lt. comdr., M.C. USNR, 1942-46. Diplomate Am. Bd. Internal Medicine. Mem. Central Soc. Clin. Research, Inst. Medicine Chgo., Health Physics Soc., A.A.A.S., A.C.P., Radiol. Soc. N.Am., Phi Beta Kappa, Alpha Omega Alpha. Clubs: Quadrangle, Arts (Chgo.). Author articles in field. Home: 7722 Ludington Pl La Jolla CA 92037 Office: Enviro-Med Inc 7765 Girard Av La Jolla CA 92037

HASTIE, REID WILLIAM, educator; b. Donora Pa., Feb. 14, 1916; s. William and Ellen (Reid) H.; B.S., State Tchrs. Coll., Edinboro, Pa., 1936; M.A., U. W.Va., 1940; Ph.D., U. Pitts., 1953; student Carnegie Inst. Tech., Harvard, U. Minn.; m. Olivia Kendrick, Aug. 8, 1941; children—Reid Reid K., Bruce C. Art supr., Monongalie County Schs., W.Va., 1936-38; art tchr. Pitts. pub. schs., 1938-40; instr. dept. fine arts U. Pitts., 1940-41, 46-49; asst. prof., asso. prof., then prof. dept. art edn. U. Minn., 1949—; mem. fine arts staff Carnegie Inst., Pitts., 1939-40, 46-49; prof. Tex. Tech. Coll., Lubbock, 1969—. Cons. Central Midwestern Regional Ednl. Lab., Inc.; exhibited paintings Carnegie Inst., St. Paul Gallery, Mpls. Inst. Arts, Walker Art Center, U. Minn.; water color exhibit Minn State Fair. Served to lt. USNR, 1941-46. Mem. Nat. Art Edn. Assn. (pies.), Western Arts Assn., Asso. Artists, St. Paul Painters and Sculpture Assn., N.E.A., Nat. Soc. Study Edn., Phi Delta Kappa, Delta Phi Delta, Omicron Delta Kappa. Author: (with Christian Schmidt) Encounter with Art, 1969. Editor: Art Education, 1965. Home: 2114 65th Pl Lubbock TX 79412 Office: Tex Tech U Lubbock TX 79409

HASTIE, WILLIAM HENRY, judge; b. Knoxville, Tenn., Nov. 17, 1904; s. William Henry and Roberta (Child) H.; A.B., Amherst Coll., 1925, A.M. (hon.), 1940, LL.D., 1960; LL.B., Harvard, 1930, S.J.D., 1933; LL.D. Hampton Inst., 1946, Va. State Coll., 1947, Lincoln U., 1950, Ohio Wesleyan, 1951, Knoxville Coll., 1952, Rutgers U., 1953, Howard U., 1955, Yale, 1957, Central State Coll., 1959, Temple U., 1961, U. Pa., Atlanta U., 1964; m. Beryl Lockhart, Dec. 25, 1943; children—Karen Roberta, William Henry. Admitted to bar, 1930; practiced law, 1930-33; asst. solicitor Dept. of Interior, 1933-37; judge Dist. Ct. V.I., 1937-39; dean Howard U. Sch. of Law, 1939-46; civilian aide to the sec. of war, 1940-42; gov. of V.I., 1946-49; judge 3d U.S. Circuit Ct. of Appeals, 1949-71. Mem. Caribbean Commn., 1947-51. Trustee Amherst Coll. Fellow Am. Acad. Arts and Scis; mem. Phi Beta Kappa, Omega Psi Phi. Mason. Home: 804 W Sedgwick St Philadelphia PA 19119

HASTIN, KENNETH NEIL, lawyer, b. Bakersfield, Cal., Sept. 28, 1920; s. Rheu A. and Rae (Carpenter) H.; B.A., U. of Pacific, 1942; J.D., U. Cal. at Berkeley, 1949; m. Iris Elaine Davis, Oct. 31, 1943; children—Thomas Edward, Steven Roger, Anne Marie. Admitted to Cal. bar, 1950, since practiced in Bakersfield; partner firm DiGiorgio, Davis, Hastin & Klein, 1968—. Pres. Bakersfield Civic Light Opera Assn., 1961-66, exec. producer, 1966-68; bd. dirs. Kern Philharmonic Soc., 1968—, v.p., 1970. Served to lt. USNR, 1942-45. Decorated Commendation medal. Mem. Kern County Bar Assn. (sec., dir. 1970). Mem. Disciples of Christ Ch. Kiwanian (pres. Kern club 1959, lt. gov. 1967). Home: 1724 Camino Promavera Bakersfield CA 93306 Office: 1000 Truxtun Av Bakersfield CA 93301

HASTING, MARTIN FRANKLIN, coll. dean; b. Denver, Oct. 12, 1913; s. Martin Henry and Caroline Mary (Sendelbach) H.; student Regis Coll., Denver, 1931-34; A.B., St. Louis U., 1938, Ph. Licentiate, 1940, M.A., 1941, S.T.L., 1948; Ph.D., U. Cal. at Berkeley, 1952. Joined Soc. of Jesus, 1934, ordained priest Roman Cath. Ch., 1946; instr. Am. history and govt. Marquette U. High Sch., Milw., 1941-43; lectr. Am. history Regis Coll., 1947; asst. prof. history St. Louis U., now asso. prof. history, dean Coll. Arts and Scis., dir. summer sessions, 1958—, dir. Am. studies, 1966—; chaplain Boys Indsl. Sch., Topeka, Kan., 1946-47, U.S. Penitentiary, Alcatraz Island, 1951-52, Municipal Jail, St. Louis, 1954-59. Bd. dirs. Harry S Truman Library, Am. div. Jesuit Hist. Inst. Mem. Am., Cath., Miss. Valley, Am. Jesuit (chmn.) hist. assns., Hist. Soc. Mo., Am. Studies Assn. (bd. editors jour. Central Miss. Valley), North Central Assn., Nat. Cath., Jesuit ednl. assns., Delta Sigma Phi, Phi Alpha Theta. Mng. editor Hist. Bull., 1938-40. Address: 221 N Grand Blvd St Louis MO 63103

HASTINGS, ALBERT BAIRD, researcher; b. Dayton, Ky., Nov. 20, 1895; s. Otis Luther and Elizabeth (Henry) H.; B.S., U. Mich., 1917; Ph.D., Columbia, 1921; Sc.D., U. Mich., 1941, Oxford, 1952, Boston U., 1956; M.A., Harvard, 1942, Sc.D., 1945; Sc.D., St. Louis U., 1965, Columbia, 1967; m. Margaret Anne Johnson, 1918; 1 son, Alan Baird. Chemist USPHS, 1917-21; prof. physiol. chemistry U. Chgo., 1926-28, prof. biochemistry Lasker Found. for Med. Research, 1928-35; Hamilton Kuhn prof. biol. chem. Harvard Med. Sch., 1935-59, emeritus, 1959—; head lab. metabolic research Scripps Clinic and Research Found., La Jolla, Cal., 1959-66, mem. emeritus, 1966—; hon. prof. U. San Marcos, 1957; research asso. U. Cal. at San Diego, 1960—. Vis. prof. Pahlavi Univ., Shiraz, Iran, 1967; syndic Harvard Univ. Press; Fulbright lectr. Oxford U., 1952, mem. sr. common room Trinity Coll., 1953—. Trustee Brookhaven Nat. Lab., Asso. Univs., 1948-51; cons. Com. on Biology and Medicine, U.S. AEC, 1947-63; cons. USPHS Nat. Adv. Arthritis and Metabolic Diseases, 1956-60, adviser Heart Council, 1960-64; cons. sci. adv. bd. Walter Reed Army Inst. Research, 1956-62; mem. vis. com. Brookhaven Nat. Lab., 1956—, chmn., 1962-63; nat. sci. adv. com. Okla. Med. Research Found. and Inst. Mem. Com. on Med. Research, OSRD, 1941-46, Nat. Adv. Cancer Commn., 1942, Research Bd. for Nat. Security, 1945. Mem. Sci. Adv. Com., The Nutrition Found., 1947-61; adv. bd. Biochem. Preparations, 1945—; adv. council Life Ins. Med. Research Fund, 1946-50; nat. adv. com. to White House Conf. on Aging, 1971. Recipient Distinguished Service award Med. Alumni Assn. U. Chgo., 1961; Banting medal Am. Diabetes Assn., 1962; A.C.P. award, 1964; USPHS citation, 1964; Modern Medicine Distinguished Achievement award, 1965. Mem. Assn. Am. Physicians, Nat. Acad. Scis., A.A.A.S., Royal Danish Acad. Sci. and Letters, Am. Acad. Arts and Scis., Am. Chem. Soc., Am. Soc. Biol. Chemists (pres. 1945), Am. Philos. Soc., Am. Physiol. Soc., Soc. Exptl. Biol. Medicine (pres. 1945), Harvey Soc., Sinfonia (Phi Mu Alpha), Alpha Chi Sigma, Sigma Xi, Alpha Omega Alpha. Clubs: Harvard (N.Y.C.); Cosmos (Washington); Chicago Literary; Century Assn. (N.Y.); Cuyamaca (San Diego). Writer various articles. Editor: Jour. Biol. chemistry, 1941- 54, 55-59, Am. Jour. Physiology, 1956-63, Endocrinology, 1963—. Home: 5912 Bellevue La Jolla CA 92037

HASTINGS, ALICE TURNER, librarian; b. Albany, N.Y., June 10, 1917; d. Harry Worthington and Louise (Clement) Hastings; A.B., Radcliffe Coll., 1938; M.A., B.S. in L.S., N.Y. State Coll. Tchrs., 1940; M.S., Columbia, 1956; m. Sherman A. Murphy, Jr., Apr. 17, 1971. Librarian, F.D. Roosevelt High Sch., Hyde Park, N.Y., 1940-43; young adult librarian Albany (N.Y.) Pub. Library, 1943-45; campus sch. librarian State Tchrs. Coll., Oneonta, N.Y., 1946-47; asst. librarian State U. N.Y. at Albany, 1948-56, univ. librarian, 1956-64, director of libraries of the university, 1964-70; coll. librarian Smith Coll., Northampton, Mass., 1970-71; instr. Library Sch., 1960-61; instr. Am. lit. Oneonta State Tchrs. Coll., summer 1947, Pres. Hudson-Mohawk Library Assn., 1959-60; chmn. State U. N.Y. Librarians Conf., 1960-61, mem. library devel. com., 1960-68; pres. State U. N.Y. Albany Library Sch. Alumni, 1961-62; chmn. Librarians Grad. Centers Capital Dist., 1962-67. Mem. Am., N.Y. library assns., Assn. Coll. and Research Librarians, Am. Assn. U. Profs., English Speaking Union, N.Y. State Tchrs. Assn., Jr. League Albany (sec. 1952-54, v.p. 1954-56). Club: Albany University. Home: 53 Roweland Av Delmar NY 12054

HASTINGS, DONALD WILSON, educator, psychiatrist; b. Madison, Wis., June 4, 1910; s. William Alexander and Minnetta (Littlewood) H.; A.B., U. Wis., 1931, A.M., 1932, M.D., 1923; Rockefeller fellow in psychiatry, 1936-38; m. Jane Wenban, Aug. 22, 1936; children—Jan, Donald, Mary Lindsay. Intern, Phila. Gen. Hosp., 1934-36; psychiatrist Harvard, 1938-39; clin. dir. Pa. Hosp., Phila., 1939-42; prof. psychiatry and neurology U. Minn. Med. Sch., 1946—, head dept., 1946-69. Chmn. Gov.'s Adv. Council on Mental Health; psychiat. cons. Surgeon Gen. Army and USPHS, 1946—; sci. adv. bd. USAF, 1952—; med. research and devel. com. Dept. Def. Served with USAAF, 1942-45; chief psychiatrist 8th A.F., chief psychiatrist AAF, Washington. Mem. A.M.A., Am. Psychiat. Assn., Group for Advancement of Psychiatry, Central Neuropsychiatry Soc., Hennepin County Med. Soc., Nu Sigma Nu, Chi Phi, Alpha Omega Alpha. Presbyn. Home: 1525 E River Rd Minneapolis MN 55414

HASTINGS, EDWIN KILPATRICK, hotel exec.; b. Bklyn., Feb. 13, 1903; s. Thomas G. and Florence (Kilpatrick) H.; student Richmond Hill (N.Y.) Bus. Coll.; m. Nancy W. Stahlman, June 1, 1942. Cruise dir. Hamburg-Am. Line, 1926-34; cruise dir., Western mgr. Raymond-Whitcomb, 1934-40; mgr., v.p. The Waldorf-Astoria Hotel, N.Y.C., 1940-55; v.p. hotels Matson Nav. Co., Honolulu, 1955-60; gen. mgr. The Barkley and Park Lane Hotels, N.Y.C., 1960; v.p. Pacific, Hilton Hotels Internat., v.p., gen. mgr. Hilton Hawaiian Village, Honolulu, 1961—; exec. v.p. Hilton- Burns Hotel Co., Inc., 1965—; sr. v.p. Hawaiian div. Hilton Hotels Corp., 1966—. Bd. dirs. Hawaii Visitor's Bur. Served from 1st lt. to lt. col. USAAF, 1942- 46; CBI. Mem. Am. Soc. Travel Agts. (chmn. Am. hotel com.), Am. Hotel Assn., Mil. Order World Wars, Am. Legion, Hawaii Hotel Assn. (dir.). Clubs: Skal, Waialae Country, Pacific. Address: 2003 Kalia Rd Honolulu HI 96815

HASTINGS, ELIZABETH THOMSON, coll. dean; b. Providence, Sept. 27, 1913; d. William Thomson and Hester Jane (Mercer) Hastings; A.B., Pembroke Coll. of Brown U., 1934, A.M., 1935; Ph.D., Yale, 1939. Instr. Illinois Coll., 1939-42, asst. prof., 1942-44, prof., co-chmn. dept. English, 1944-51; prof. English, dean Flora Stone Mather Coll. of Case-Western Res. U., 1951—. Mem. Modern Lang. Assn., Am. Assn. U. Profs., Am. Assn. U. Women, Nat., Ohio assns. deans women, Coll. English Assn., Am. Studies Assn., League Women Voters, Phi Beta Kappa. Unitarian. Home: 2419 Queenston Rd Cleveland OH 44118

HASTINGS, JAMES FRED, congressman; b. Olean, N.Y., Apr. 10, 1926; s. Glenn Tracy and Ruth Elizabeth (Trail) H.; ed. pub. schs., Allegany, N.Y.; m. Barbara Louise Gaylor, Sept. 24, 1947; children—Linda A., Karen D., James R., David M., Tracy E. Mgr., v.p. radio sta. WHDL, Olean, N.Y., 1952-66; nat. advt. mgr. Olean Times Herald, 1964-66; v.p. Hastings & Jewell, real estate and ins., Allegany, N.Y., 1966-68; police justice, Allegany, 1958-63; mem. N.Y. State Assembly, 1963-65, Senate, 1965-68; mem. 91st-92d Congress 38th Dist. N.Y. Served with USNR, 1943-46. Mem. Am. Legion. Republican. Methodist. Mason. Home: 124 N 2d St Allegany NY 14706 Office: Cannon House Office Bldg Washington DC 20515

HASTINGS, JOHN SIMPSON, judge; b. Washington, Ind., June 30, 1898; s. Elmer Ellsworth and Bertha Jane (Garten) H.; B.S., U.S. Mil. Acad., West Point, 1920; LL.B., Ind. U., 1924, LL.D., 1959; LL.D., Northwestern U., 1961; married Mary Esther Smiley, June 2, 1925; twin sons, William Elmer and James Roland. Admitted to Ind. bar, 1924, practiced in Washington, Ind.; mem. Hastings, Allen & Hastings, 1924-57; judge U.S. Ct. of Appeals, 7th Circuit, Chgo., 1957—, chief judge, 1959-68, sr. judge, 1969—. Hon. dir. Ind. U. Found., v.p., 1951; trustee Ind. U., 1936-59, pres. bd., 1950-59; mem. Ind. State Bd. Law Examiners, 1949-54, pres., 1951. Gov. Riley Hosp. Crippled Children, Indianapolis, Indiana. Member of American, Illinois, Indiana (past governor), Chgo. bar assns., 7th Circuit Bar Association, Chicago Law Club, Ind. U. Alumni Assn. (past pres.), Am. Legion, Am. Law Inst., Am. Judicature Soc., Chgo. West Point Soc., Order of the Coif, Phi Beta Kappa, Phi Delta Phi, Sigma Delta Chi, Phi Gamma Delta. Republican. Presbyn. Mason, Rotarian (hon.). Clubs: Union League, Legal, Standard. Home: 860 N DeWitt Pl Chicago IL 60611 Office: 219 S Dearborn St Chicago IL 60604

HASTINGS, JOHN THOMAS, educator; b. Louisville, Mar. 16, 1911; s. Walter H. and Laura (Keirstead) H.; B.A., Ball State U., 1934; M.A., U. Chgo., 1940, Ph.D., 1943; m. Maxine E. Hazelrigg, Dec. 22, 1935; children—J. Christopher, C. Nicholas. Math. and sci. tchr. Union City (Ind.) pub. schs., 1934-35; math. tchr., Muncie (Ind.) pub. schs., 1935-39; research asst. U. Chgo., 1939-42; personnel cons. Willet Trucking Co., Chgo., 1940-42; mem. faculty U. Ill. at Urbana, 1942—, prof. ednl. psychology, 1953—, high sch. testing bur., unit on evaluation, edn. testing office Center Instructional Research and Curriculum Evaluation, 1942-48, 48-57, 57- 63, 63—. Asst. dir. Am. Council Edn. study edn. experience in armed services, 1943-44; specialist cons. SCAP, Tokyo, Japan, 1950; pres. Nat. Council Measurement in Edn., 1968-69. Pres. Council Community Integration, Urbana, Ill., 1956-57; exec. com. Urban League, Champaign County, 1961-68; treas. Univ. YMCA, 1957-64. Trustee Wesley Found., Urbana, 1965-71. Recipient Kiwanis award, 1934; Rosenblum research award for research U. Chgo., 1943. Mem. Am. Ednl. Research Assn. (v.p. div. 1966-68), Assn. Am. Geographers (commn. on coll. geography 1964—), Am. Psychol. Assn., Nat. Council Measurement in Edn., A.A.A.S., Phi Delta Kappa. Home: 203 E Mumford Dr Urbana IL 61801

HASTINGS, JOHN WOODLAND, educator, biologist; b. Salisbury, Md., Mar. 24, 1927; s. Vaughan Archelaus and Kathrine (Stevens) H.; B.A., Swarthmore Coll., 1947; M.A., Princeton, 1950, Ph.D., 1951, Harvard, 1966; m. Hanna Machlup, June 6, 1953; children—Jennifer, David, Laura, Karen. AEC postdoctoral fellow Johns Hopkins, 1951-53; instr. to asst. prof. biol. scis. Northwestern U., 1953-57; from asst. prof. to prof. biochemistry U. Ill. at Urbana, 1957-66; prof. biology Harvard, 1966—; summer research participant Oak Ridge Nat. Lab., 1958; vis. lectr. biochemistry Sheffield (Eng.) U., 1961-62; instr. physiology Marine Biol. Lab., Woods Hole, Mass., 1961-66, dir., 1962-66; guest investigator Rockefeller U., 1965-66. Mem. panel molecular biology NSF, 1963-66; com. postdoctoral fellowships chemistry Nat. Acad. Scis., 1965-67, com. photobiology, 1965- -; mem. Commn. Undergrad. Edn. in Biol. Scis., 1965-66; space biology com. NASA 1966-71; biochemistry tng. com. Nat. Inst. Gen. Med. Scis., 1968—. Mem. corp. Marine Biol. Lab., Woods Hole, Mass., 1961—, trustee, 1966—. Served with USNR, 1944-45. Guggenheim fellow, 1965- 66. Mem. A.A.A.S., Am. Assn. U. Profs., Am. Soc. Biol. Chemists, Am. Soc. Zoologists, Biochem. Soc., Biophys. Soc., Soc. Am. Microbiologists, Soc. Gen. Physiology (pres. 1963-65). Contbr. profl. jours. Home: 405 Commonwealth Av Newton MA 02159 Office: 16 Divinity Av Cambridge MA 02138

HASTINGS, LAWRENCE VAETH, physician, lawyer, b. Flushing, N.Y., Nov. 23, 1919; s. Henry Luftman and Lillian (Vaeth) H.; student Columbia, 1939-40, Columbia U. Law Sch., 1949-50, U. Mich. Engring. Sch., 1942-43, Washington U., 1943-44, U. Vt., 1943; M.D., Johns Hopkins, 1948; LL.B., U. Miami, 1953; m. Jean Heck, Feb. 29, 1950 (div.); 1 son, Lance Clifford; m. 2d, Wilhelmina Tegeder, Apr. 16, 1955; children—Wilhelmina Streeton and Laura Thynne (twins). Intern U.S. Marine Hosp., S.I., N.Y., 1948-49; asst. surgeon, sr. asst. surgeon USPHS, 1949-52; asst. resident surgery Bellevue Hosp. Med. Center, 1951; med. legal cons., trial atty., Miami, Fla., 1953—; sr. partner Hastings, Thomas & Sheppard, attys., 1955-60, Green & Hastings, 1960—. to Asst. prof. medicine U. Miami, 1964—, lectr.

law, 1966—. Admitted Fla. bar, 1954, U.S. Supreme Ct. bar, 1960. Served with AUS, 1943-46. Certified Am. Bd. Legal Medicine. Fellow Acad. Fla. Trial Lawyers, Law- Sci. Acad. Found. Am.; mem. Am. Acad. Forensic Scis., Fla. Bar (vice chmn. med. legal com. 1957, vice chmn. trial tactics com. 1963-65, chmn. steering com. trial tactics and demonstrative evidence seminars), American, Florida State, and Dade County medical assns., Assn. Mil. Surgeons, U. Miami Alumni Assn. (pres. 1967), Am., Dade County bar assns., Acad. Psychomatic Medicine, Com. of 100 Miami Beach, Alpha Delta Phi, Phi Eta Sigma, Phi Alpha Delta. Roman Catholic. Clubs: Coral Gables Country, Riviera Country, LaGorce Country, Surf, Palm Bay, Indian Creek Country, River of Jacksonville; Bath; Jockey; University, Jacksonville Country; N.Y. Athletic. Contbr. to profl. publs. Home: 335 Navarre Av Coral Gables FL 33134 Office: Biscayne Bldg 19 W Flagler St Miami FL 33130

HASTINGS, PHILIP KAY, educator; b. Worcester, Mass., Aug. 27, 1922; s. Rowland and Eunice (Leach) H.; B.A., Williams Coll., 1943; M.A., Princeton, 1949, Ph.D., 1950; m. Elizabeth Frances Hann, Mar. 11, 1950; children—Pamela Dillenback, Elizabeth Leach, Ann Upton, Mary Florence. Instr. psychology Williams Coll., 1946-48, lectr., asst. prof., asso. prof., 1951-61, prof. psychology and polit. sci., 1961—; instr. psychology Princeton, 1950-51; dir. Roper Pub. Opinion Research Center, 1957—; research asso. Psychol. Corp. N.Y., cons. Am. Tel. & Tel. Co., 1944-58. Served to lt. (j.g.) USNR, 1944-46. Fellow Am. Psychol. Assn., American Sociol. Assn.; mem. World (pres. 1970—), Am. assns. pub. opinion research, Sigma Xi. Contbr. articles to profl. jours. Home: Bulkley St Williamstown MA 02167

HASTINGS, RICHARD HOMER, lawyer; b. Two Harbors, Minn., May 17, 1916; s. Warren Erwin and Hattie (Falk) H.; student U. Minn., 1937-38; J.S.D., U. Wis., 1941; m. Helen C. Dicks, Apr. 6, 1954 (dec.); children—Helene (Mrs. Joseh Oreck), John J.; m. 2d, Iris Heinz, Dec. 24, 1970. Admitted to Wis. and Minn. bars, 1941; individual practice law, Hibbing, Minn., 1946-48; partner firm Sullivan, Hanft, Hastings, Fride & O'Brien, Duluth, Minn., 1948—; counsel Minn. Iron Mining Industry, 1955—. Served to capt. USAAF, 1942-46. Mem. Delta Kappa Epsilon. Clubs: Kitchi Gammi, Northland Country (Duluth); Minnesota (St. Paul). Home: 100 Elizabeth St Duluth MN 55803 Office: Alworth Bldg Duluth MN 55802

HASTINGS, ROBERT FRANK, architect; b. Kenosha, Wis., Dec. 20, 1914; s. John Frank and Bernice (Stretch) H.; student U. Wis., 1932-33, 34-35; B.S. in Archtl. Engring. with high honors, U. Ill., 1937; D. Arch. (hon.), Lawrence Inst. Tech., 1967; m. LaVerne Helen Wegner, Sept. 7, 1937; children—Carlyn (Mrs. Richard F. Venus), Cynthia Ann (Mrs. Robert S. Wagner). With Smith, Hinchman & Grylls Assos., Inc., Detroit, 1937—, exec. v.p., treas., 1959-60, pres., 1960—; prin. works include guided missile plant, Bristol, Tenn. for Navy Bur. Yards and Docks, 1954, mgmt. services in Korea for ICA, 1960, Yonsei U. Med. Sch., Seoul, 1963, (with Saarinen) Gen. Motors Tech. Center, Warren, Mich., 1954, Mercury assembly plant Ford Motor Co., Rosemead, Cal., 1957. Mem. adv. bd. dept. architecture U. Detroit; adv. com. dept. architecture U. Ill.; cons. Bd. Registration Architects Mich., 1947-56. Co-chmn. bldg. industry United Found., 1961-64; mem. Mich. Week Com., 1963, Detroit Met. Com. Aging, 1955-65, Mich. Gov.'s Adv. Com. White House Conf. Aging, 1960-61; mem. United Bd. Christian Higher Edn. in Asia, 1958, dir., past pres. Presbyn. Village Detroit, 1954—. Adv. com. and trustee Alma Coll.; cooperating com. Sch. Architecture Syracuse U.; selection com. Pitts. Plate Glass Found.; bd. dirs. McCormick Theol. Sem., 1964-68, Children's Center Wayne County, 1965-70, Bldg. Research Inst.; trustee Producers Council Ednl. Found.; mem. devel. com. Riverside Civic Fund, Inc. 1963-67. Mem. A.I.A. (pres. Detroit 1956-59, nat. treas. 1963-64, nat. pres. 1970-71); mem. Mich. Soc. Profl. Engrs., Am. Soc. C.E., Engring. Soc. Detroit (chmn. profl. activities bd.; bd. dirs.). Clubs: Detroit, Detroit Athletic, Golf, One Hundred (Detroit). Mem. panel editorial cons. Archtl. Record mag. Home: 1052 W Lincoln Birmingham MI 48009 Office: 3107 W Grand Blvd Detroit MI 48202

HASTINGS, ROBERT PUSEY, lawyer; b. Los Angeles, May 23, 1910; s. Hill and Mary Garvin (Brown) H.; B.A., Yale, 1933; LL.B., Harvard, 1936; m. Susan S. Schriber, July 9, 1938; 1 dau., Susan Hastings Mallory. Admitted to Cal. bar, 1936, since practiced in Los Angeles; counsel Motion Picture div. Office Coordinator Inter-Am. Affairs, 1942-43; partner Paul, Hastings, Janofsky & Walker, 1946—. Chmn. Cal. campaign USO, 1956-57; pres., chmn. bd. Los Angeles Civic Light Opera Assn., 1959-65, now trustee; sec., trustee Music Center Operating Co., 1961-65; vice chmn. bd. Harvey Mudd Coll. Sci. and Engring.; trustee Thacher Sch., 1965-70, now trustee; v.p., trustee The Friends of the Claremont Colls.; chmn. bd. trustees Friends Huntington Library and Art Gallery, 1953-61, Churchill Found. Served to lt. USNR, 1943-45. Decorated Bronze Star Medal. Member American, California, Los Angeles County bar associations, Los Angeles Stock Exchange Club, Southern Cal. Harvard Law School Association (trustee, chairman 1967-69), Delta Kappa Epsilon. Republican. Episcopalian (vestryman 1968-69). Clubs: Chancery, California, Los Angeles Stock Exchange, Sunset (past sec., pres.), Zamorano, Lincoln (Los Angeles). Home: 855 Rosalind Rd Pasadena CA 91108 Office: 510 S Spring St Los Angeles CA 90013

HASTINGS, WILMOT REED, govt. ofcl.; b. Salem, Mass., May 29, 1935; s. Abner Horace and Florence (Hylan) H.; A.B. magna cum laude, Harvard, 1957, LL.B. magna cum laude, 1961; postgrad. Universite de Paris (France), 1957-58; m. Joan Amory Loomis, Aug. 30, 1958; children—W. Reed, Jr., Melissa H., Claire A. Admitted to Mass. bar, 1961; law clk. Chief Justice Raymond S. Wilkins, Boston, 1961-62; asso. firm Bingham, Dana & Gould, Boston, 1962-68; 1st asst. and dep. atty. gen. Mass., 1968-69; spl. asst. and exec. asst. to undersec. state, 1969-70; gen. counsel Dept. Health, Edn. and Welfare, 1970—. Bd. dirs. Cambridge (Mass.) Civic Assn., 1964- 69, mem. exec. com., 1967-69. Mem. Harvard Law Sch. Assn. Republican. Home: 905 Turkey Run Rd McLean VA 22101 Office: Dept HEW 330 Independence Av Washington DC 20201

HASTORF, ALBERT HERMAN, educator; b. N.Y.C., Nov. 26, 1920; s. Albert Herman and Hilda (Menke) H.; A.B., Amherst Coll., 1942; Ph.D., Princeton, 1949; Doctor of Humane Letters, Amherst College, 1967; m. Barbara E. Reck, Oct. 4, 1943; children—Elizabeth C., Christine A. Instr. psychology Princeton, 1947- 48; with dept. psychology Dartmouth, 1948-61; successively instr., asst. prof., 1948-55, prof., chmn. dept., 1955-61; prof. dept. psychology and Grad. Sch. Business Stanford University, 1961—, also exec. head dept. psychology, dean humanities and scis., 1970—. Bd. examiners of psychologists State of N.H., 1956-60. Member of bd. trustees of Mills College, 1967—. Served from pvt. to sgt., USAAF, 1942-46. Recipient fellowship Center for Advanced Study in Behavioral Scis., Palo Alto, Cal. Fellow Am. Psychol. Assn. Contbr. articles profl. publs. Address: 571 Foothill Rd Stanford CA 94305

HASTRICH, JEROME JOSEPH, clergyman; b. Milw., Nov. 13, 1914; s. George Peter and Clara (Dettlaff) H.; student Marquette U., 1933-35; B.A., St. Francis Major Sem., Milw., 1940, M.A., 1941; student Cath. U. Am., 1947. Ordained priest Roman Cath. Ch., 1941; chancellor Diocese Madison, Wis., 1952-53, vicar gen., 1953—, aux. bishop, 1963-67; pastor St. Raphael Cathedral, Madison, 1967-69; bishop, Gallup, N.M., 1969—. Diocesan dir. Confraternity Christian Doctorine, 1946—, St. Martin Guild, 1947—; pres. Latin Am. Mission Program; sec. Am. Bd. Cath. Missions; vice chmn. Bishop's Com. for Spanish Speaking. Mem. Gov. Wis. Commn. Migratory Labor, 1964—. Home: 201 E Wilson St Gallup NM 86301

HASWELL, HAROLD ALANSON, Jr., govt. ofcl.; b. Joplin, Mo., Mar. 23, 1912; s. Harold A. and Kannah Elizabeth (Marcum) H.; A.A., S.W. Bapt. Coll., 1933; B.S., S.W. Mo. State Coll., 1940; A.M., U. Mo., 1943, Ph.D., 1951; m. Mildred Irene Liles, June 5, 1932; 1 son, Edward Alanson. Elementary tchr. Wright County, Mansfield, Mo., 1933-38; elementary prin., Hartville, Mo., 1938-40; high sch. prin., Camdenton, 1941; high sch. supt., Linn Creek, 1942; audio-visual aids dir. and high sch. instr., Kirkwood, Mo., 1943-45; dean S.W. Bapt. Coll., Bolivar 1946-49; asst. dean Coll. Arts and Sci., U. Mo., 1947; dean Ouachita Coll., Arkadelphia, Ark., 1950-51; pres. Ouachita Bapt. Coll., 1952-53; exec. coordinator Tex. Bapt. Edn. Commn. 1953-59; dir. higher edn. programs br., div. higher edn. U.S. Office Edn., 1959-64, dir. Ednl. Research Information Center div. ednl. research, 1964-67, dir. ednl. research region VII, Dallas, 1967—. Mem. Am. Acad. Polit. Sci., N.E.A., Alpha Pi Zeta. Author: Anglo-American Relations, 1892-1902; The Public Life of Richard Parks Bland; Self-Survey Manual for Texas Bapt. Colls.; Higher Education in the United States; co-author Academic Degrees, Curriculum Patterns in Higher Education, Baptist Higher Education of Alabama, Summer Sessions in Colleges and Universities of the United States. Editor: Standard Accounting Manual for Texas Baptist Colls. Home: 7646 Alto Caro Dr Dallas TX 75240 Office: Office of Edn US Dept of Health Edn and Welfare 1114 Commerce St Dallas TX 75202

HATAM, DJAMAL, Iranian diplomat; b. Teheran, Iran, Apr. 1, 1924; s. Hossein and Hatamalmolouk (Hatam); student Am. U., Beirut, 1944-45, U. Geneva (Switzerland), 1946-47; law degree, U. Teheran, 1950; m. Ilse Berger, Sept. 11, 1963. Consul, Hamburg, Germany, 1954; 1st sec. embassy, Belgrade, Yugoslavia, 1955-58; consul embassy, Ottawa, 1958-60; head adminstrn., Teheran, 1960-62, head passport, 1962-63; chief protocol of prime minister of Iran, 1963-65; adviser govt. hospitality, Teheran, 1965-66; head confs., Teheran, 1966; dir. adminstrn. and security, Teheran, 1966-69; consul gen. of Iran, Chgo., 1969—. Decorated Homayoun 5, Homayoun and Decoration 3. Home: 199 E Lake Shore Dr Chicago IL 60611 Office: 875 N Michigan Av Chicago IL 60611

HATCH, ALDEN, author, journalist, historian; b. N.Y. City, Sept. 26, 1898; s. Frederic Horace and May Palmer (Daly) H.; student Horace Mann Sch., 1912-13, U. Chicago extension, 1918-20, Blackstone Inst., 1919-21; m. Ruth Brown, Dec. 28, 1932; 1 son, Alden Denison; m. 2d, Allene Pomeroy Gaty, Sept. 9, 1950. Author (novels): Gaming Lady, 1931; Glass Walls, 1933; Bridlewise, 1941; (biographies) Glenn Curtiss, 1942; Heroes of Annapolis, 1943; Young Willkie, 1944; General Ike, 1944, revised and enlarged edit. 1952; Franklin D. Roosevelt, 1947; Woodrow Wilson, 1948; General Patton, 1950; Red Carpet for Mamie, 1954; (histories): American Express, 1950; Full Tilt (with Foxhall P. Keene), 1938; Son of the Smoky Sea, Back to the Smoky Sea (with Nutchuck), 1941; Ambassador Extraordinary (Clara Boothe Luce), 1956; Remington Arms in American History, 1956; Crown of Glory (with Seamus Walshe), 1957; For the Life of Me (with Robert Briscoe), 1958; The Wadsworths of the Genesee, 1959; The Miracle of the Mountain, 1959; The Circus Kings (with Henry Ringling North), 1960; The DeGaul Nobody Knows, 1960; First Lady Extraordinary: Edith Bolling Wilson, 1961; Bernhard, Prince of the Netherlands, 1962; A Man Named John: Pope John XXIII, 1963; The Mountbattens, 1965; Apostle on the Move: Pope Paul VI, 1966; (with Krishna Nehru Hertheesing) We Nehrus, 1967; The Byrds of Virginia, 1969. Editor: Thank You Twice, 1941. Contbr. articles polit., mil., naval and sporting events and personalities to national magazines. Member of the P.E.N. Ind. Republican. Episcopalian. Clubs: Rockaway Hunting (Cedarhurst, L.I.); Field (Sarasota, Fla.); Overseas Press. Home: 1312 S Orange Av Sarasota FL 33579

HATCH, ARTHUR JOEL, elec. equipment mfr.; b. Toledo, Sept. 26, 1910; s. Arthur Joel and Mary (Voelker) H.; B.S. in Engring., U. Toledo, 1934; m. Helen M. Bellows, June 5, 1936; children—Arthur W., David R. With Strong Electric Corp. subsidiary Holophane Co., Inc., 1935—, elec. engr., v.p., 1947-56, pres., 1956—. Registered profl. engr., Ohio. Fellow Soc. Motion Picture and TV Engrs.; mem. Am. Ordnance Assn., Solar Energy, Soc., Nat. Soc. Profl. Engrs., Tech. Assn. Graphic Arts, Theater Equipment and Supply Mfrs. Assn. (dir.), Newcomen Soc., Western Lake Erie Cruiser Assn. Rotarian. Clubs: Tower; Put-In-Bay Yacht; Bay View Yacht (Toledo). Home: 3426 Bentley Blvd Toledo OH 43606 Office: 87 City Park Av Toledo OH 43601

HATCH, EASTMAN NIBLEY, educator, physicist; b. Salt Lake City, June 14, 1927; s. Joseph Eastman and Florence (Nibley) H.; student U. Utah, 1946-48, 51-52; B.S., Stanford, 1950; Ph.D., Cal. Inst. Tech., 1956; m. Anne Clawson, June 21, 1952; children—Joseph Eastman II, Richard Clawson, Anne Florence. Postdoctoral fellow in physics Cal. Inst. Tech., 1956-57; research asso. physics Brookhaven Nat. Lab., Upton, N.Y., 1957-58; sci. liaison with USN in Frankfurt/Main, Germany, 1958-60; guest physicist Heidelberg U., Germany, 1960-61; asso. prof. physics Ia. State U., 1961-66, prof. physics, 1966-69, asst. dean Grad. Coll., 1967-69, physicist Ames Lab., 1961-66, sr. physicist, 1966-69; prof. physics Utah State U., Logan, 1969—; vis. research asso. Los Alamos Sci. Lab., 1971—. Served with USNR, 1945-46. Fellow Am. Phys. Soc., Phi Beta Kappa, Sigma Xi. Home: 1795 Country Club Dr Logan UT 84321

HATCH, EDWIN IRBY, utility exec.; b. Uniontown, Ala., Mar. 21, 1913; s. Benjamin Francis and Helen (Earle) Irby; A.B., U. of South, 1933; LL.B., U. Ala., 1936; m. Helen Richardson Hume, Nov. 29, 1939; children—Helen (Mrs. Richard K. Means), Edwin Irby, Carolyn Tayloe. Admitted to Ala. bar, 1936; practiced in Birmingham and Montgomery, 1936-38, 38-55; mem. firm Martin, Blakey & Hatch, and predecessor, Montgomery, 1943-55; v.p. Ala. Power Co., Birmingham, 1955-58, exec. v.p., 1958-62; sr. v.p. Ga. Power Co., Atlanta, 1962-63, pres., 1963—, also dir.; chmn. SCL Industries, Inc., Fed. Res. Bank Atlanta; dir. S.C.L. R.R. Co., City Investing Co., So. Electric Generating Co., So. Co., Found. Life Ins. Co., Founders Financial Corp., Home Ins. Co., Citizens & So. Realty Investors. Bd. dirs. Atlanta chpt. A.R.C. Mem. Newcomen Soc. (trustee), Asso. Electric Illuminating Cos., N.A.M., Atlanta Arts Alliance, Ga. State C.of C., Alpha Tau Omega, Omicron Delta Kappa, Phi Delta Phi, Blue Key. Episcopalian. Rotarian. Clubs: Piedmont Driving, Capital City, Peachtree Golf, Sewanee, Commerce (dir.) (Atlanta); Augusta National Golf, Pinnacle (Augusta, Ga.). Home: 3425 Wood Valley Rd NW Atlanta GA 30327 Office: 270 Peachtree St Atlanta GA 30302

HATCH, GEORGE CLINTON, TV exec.; b. Erie, Pa., Dec. 16, 1919; s. Charles Milton and Blanche (Beecher) H.; B.A., Occidental Coll., 1940; M.A., Claremont Coll., 1941; m. Wilda Gene Glasmann, Dec. 24, 1940; children—Michael Gene (Mrs. Berton Zbar), Diane Glasmann (Mrs. Michael Orr), Jeffrey Beecher, Randall Clinton, Deborah Lynne. Chmn. bd. Intermountain Network, Inc., Salt Lake City, 1941—, Nat. Tecofilm Assos., Inc., 1971—; pres. Communications Investment Corp., 1945—, KUTV-TV, Inc., Salt Lake City, 1956—, Gem State Broadcasting Corp., Boise, Ida., 1962—, Cooper Broadcasting Co., Billings, Mont., 1963—, The Orpheum Corp.; v.p. Community Tele-Communications, Inc., Denver, 1964—, Galaxy Outdoor Advt., Inc., Salt Lake City, 1965—, Western Tele-Communications, Inc., Denver, 1965—, Pacific Broadcasting Co., Inc., Honolulu, 1965—, Corp., Tele-Communications, Inc.; treas. TeleMation, Inc., 1969; mem. Salt Lake adv. bd. First Security Bank Utah; dir. Rocky Mountain Pub. Broadcasting Corp. Chmn. bd. govs. Am. Information Radio Network; bd. govs. NBC-TV Affiliates. Past pres. Salt Lake Com. on Fgn. Relations. Mem. Utah Joint Com. on Ednl. TV. Mem. Utah State Bd. Higher Edn., 1969; mem. nat. adv. council Hampshire Coll. Bd. dirs. Salt Lake County Civic Auditorium Bd. Recipient Service to Journalism award U. Utah, 1966, Silver Medal award Salt Lake Advt. Club, 1969. Mem. Fedn. Rocky Mountain States (sec.), Nat. Assn. Broadcasters (past pres. radio bd. dirs.), Utah Broadcasters Assn. (past pres., Mgmt. award, 1964), Phi Beta Kappa, Phi Rho Pi (life). Rotarian. Clubs: University; Ft. Douglas. Home: 1100 S 15th E Salt Lake City UT 84105 Office: 179 Social Hall Av Salt Lake City UT 84111

HATCH, HAROLD A., mfr.; b. Brooklyn, Conn., 1876; grad. Yale, 1898. Vice pres., asst. treas., dir. Deering Milliken, Inc.; pres. Dutchess Bleachery, N.Y.C., Milline Advt., Inc. Home: Sharon CT 06069 Office: 1045 6th Av New York City NY 10018

HATCH, HENRY CLIFFORD, beverage co. exec.; b. Toronto, Ont., Can., Apr. 30, 1916; s. Harry C. and Elizabeth (Carr) H.; student St. Michael's Coll. Sch., Toronto; m. Joan Ferriss, May 1, 1940; children—Henry Clifford, Gail Elizabeth, Sheila Mary, Richard Ferriss. Salesman, T.G. Bright & Co., Ltd., Niagara Falls., Ont., 1933-37; merchandising staff Hiram Walker, Inc., Walkerville, 1937; dir. Hiram Walker & Sons., Ltd., 1938—, asst. to v.p. in charge sales, 1936—, v.p., 1946—; v.p., dir. Hiram Walker-Gooderham & Worts, Ltd., Walkerville, 1955-61, exec. v.p., 1961-64, pres., 1964—; dir. T.G. Bright & Co., Ltd., Niagara Falls, Ont., H. Corby Distillery Ltd., Montreal, Que., Toronto- Dominion Bank. Served as comdr. Royal Canadian Navy, 1940-45, in command HMCS Drummondville, Ville de Que. Clubs: Rosedale Golf (Toronto); Essex Golf, Windsor Curling (Windsor, Ont.); Detroit Athletic. Home: 7130 Riverside Dr E Windsor Ontario Canada Office: 2072 Riverside Dr E Walkerville Ontario Canada

HATCH, JOHN DAVIS, museum cons., historian; b. Oakland Cal., June 14, 1907; s. John Davis and Gethel (Gregg) H.; student U. Cal., 1926-28; student Oriental Studies, Harvard, 1932, Near East Studies, Princeton, 1938, Yale, 1940; m. Olivia Phelps Stokes, Oct. 14, 1939; children— John Davis III, Daniel Lindley, James Stokes, Sarah Stokes. Landscape architect, Santa Barbara, Cal., 1925, Seattle, 1928; exec. sec. Seattle Art Museum, 1928-29, dir., 1929- 31; v.p. Western Assn. Art Museums, 1930-31; surveyed facilities and materials for Far Eastern studies in U.S. and Can., 1932-35, Am. studies in U.S. colls. and univs. for Am. Council Learned Socs., 1938-39, traveling exhibits for Carnegie Corp., 1936- 37; dir. U.S. art projects in New Eng., 1933-34; had pioneer exhibit The Negro Artist Comes of Age, 1945; mem. McDowell Colony, 1938; asst. dir. Isabella Stewart Gardner Mus., Boston, 1935-36; founder, adviser So. Negro Colls. Coop. Exhibits Group, 1936-41; founder Am. Artist Depository, 1938, Am. Drawing Ann., 1940, Commn. on Art Studies, 1941. Dir. Albany Inst. History and Art 1940-48; vis. prof. U. Ore., 1948-49, U. Cal., summer 1949; dir. Norfolk Mus. Arts and Scis., 1950-59; pres. Phelps Stokes Corp., 1959- 62; coordinating adviser, acting chmn. fine arts div. Spelman Coll., Ga., 1964-70; v.p. Nevada Co. Former trustee Lenox Sch., Hoosac Sch. Mem Master Drawing Assn. (trustee, founder 1962), Am. Drawing Soc. (adv. bd.), Berkshire County Hist. Soc. (treas., trustee), Stockbridge Bowl Assn. (past pres., trustee), Albany N.E. conf. 1941, S.E. conf. 1951), Abacadabra. Episcopalian. Rotarian. Club: Grolier (N.Y.C.). Author: American sect. Great All Times, 1962. Co-compiler works, including: Historic Church Silver in the Southern Diocese of Virginia, 1952; Historic Survey of Painting in Canada. Editor: Albany County Hist. Assn. Record, 1941-48, Parnassus, 1937-39, Early Am. Industries Chronicle, 1942-49. Address: Lenox MA 01240 ☆

HATCH, LEWIS FREDERICK, ednl. adminstr.; b. Puyallup, Wash., Aug. 21, 1912; s. Lewis Miles and Mary (Brayton) H.; B.S., Wash. State U., 1933; M.S., Purdue U., 1934, Ph.D., 1937; m. Marie Shultz Bailey, June 12, 1959; children—Carna Mary, Christine Ann (Mrs. Christine H. Jones). Research chemist Shell Devel. Co., Emeryville, Cal., 1937-40; from instr. to prof. chemistry U. Tex. at Austin, 1940-67; prof. chemistry, dean sci. U. Tex. at El Paso, 1967-71, v.p. acad. affairs, 1971—. Vis. prof. Philipps U., Marburg, Germany, 1966; cons. petrochem. industry, 1955—; Fulbright cons. petrochems. Nat. Research Centre, Cairo, Egypt, 1960-61. Fellow Am. Inst. Chemists, Tex. Acad. Sci., Chem. Soc. (London); mem. Am. Chem. Soc., A.A.A.S., Sigma Xi, Alpha Chi Sigma, Alpha Kappa Lambda. Author books and articles in field; also patentee. Home: 524 Satellite Dr El Paso TX 79912

HATCH, ROBERT LITTLEFIELD, mag. editor; b. N.Y.C., Aug. 21, 1910; s. Robert L. and Grace (Rockwell) H.; A.B. cum laude, Princeton, 1933; m. Ruth E. Bower, Nov. 7, 1939; children—Peter, Gillian. Publicity dir. Viking Press, 1933-43; editor Voir, London and Paris, also Heute, Munich, Germany, for OWI, 1944-45; lit. editor New Republic, 1946-54; asso. editor Sci. Am., 1955; lit. editor The Nation, 1965-64, mng. editor, 1964-67, exec. editor, 1967—, film critic, 1955—; drama critic Horizon mag., 1962-63. Office: 333 6th Av New York City NY 10014

HATCH, ROBERT MCCONNELL, former clergyman; b. Bklyn., July 6, 1910; s. William Henry Paine and Marion Louise (Townsend) H.; A.B., Harvard, 1933; A.M., Columbia, 1935; B.D., Episcopal Theol. Sch., 1939; D.D., Trinity Coll., 1951; S.T.D., Berkeley Div. Sch., 1951; Litt. D., Norwich U., 1963; m. Helen Crocker Addison, June 15, 1940; children—Martha Addison, Louise Townsend. Ordained to ministry P.E. Ch., 1939; curate Trinity Ch., Boston, 1939- 41; rector St. John's Ch., Arlington, Mass., 1941-45; dean St. John's Cathedral, Wilmington, Del., 1945-48; rector St. John's Ch., Waterbury, Conn., 1948-51; Suffragan bishop of Conn., 1951-57; bishop of Western Mass., 1957-70, ret., 1970. Sponsor Hawk Mountain Sanctuary. Author pamphlets and articles on religious subjects and conservation. Home: Randolph NH 03593

HATCH, SINCLAIR, lawyer; b. Chgo., Dec. 7, 1906; s. Samuel G. and Mattie (Sinclair) H.; adopted George A. and Lucy (Sinclair) Kingsley; A.B., Princeton, 1928; LL.B., Harvard, 1931; m. Laura Lea Robertson, Feb. 11, 1933; children—Robertson, George Kingsley, Sinclair. Admitted to N.Y. bar, 1932; with Davis, Polk, Wardwell, Gardiner & Reed, 1931-34, 35-41; mem. Hatch, McLean, Root & Hinch, 1941-42, Hatch, Root & Barrett, and successor firms, 1946-55, Graustein, Hatch & Kormendi, 1956, Pell, Butler, Hatch, Curtis & LeViness, 1957-60, Milbank, Tweed, Hadley McCloy, 1960—. Dir. Barnes & Noble, Inc. Mem. staff, securities div. FTC and SEC, 1934-35; regional dir. O.C.D., 1943. Bd. dirs. Blue Hill Found., Inc., 1941-71; trustee Emma Clark Meml. Library, Setauket, N.Y., 1948-68, pres., 1958-68. Commd. lt. comdr. USNR, 1944; asst., indsl. readjustment br. in charge contract termination Navy Dept.,

Washington, 1944-45. Recipient Legion of Merit. Fellow Am. Bar Found. Mem. Am., Fed, N.Y. State bar assns., Assn. Bar City of N.Y., N.Y. County Lawyers Assn., Am. Judicature Soc., Am. Law Inst., Phi Beta Kappa Assos. Democrat. Episcopalian. Clubs: University, Century, Down Town Assn., Church (trustee). Home: Setauket NY 11733 Office: 1 Chase Manhattan Plaza New York City NY 10005

HATCH, VINCENT JOSEPH, lawyer; b. East St. Louis, Ill., Dec. 26, 1917; s. Charles and Ellen (Desmond) H.; B.S., St. Louis U., 1940; certificate in Meteorology, U. Cal., Los Angeles, 1943; J.D., Washington U., St. Louis, 1946; m. Frances Dennis, Feb. 18, 1950; children—Ann, Vincent Joseph, Dennis, Claire, Ellen. Admitted to Ill. bar, 1947, since practiced in Belleville; partner Hatch and Hatch 1947-55 partner Brady, Donovan & Hatch, 1955—; spl. asst. to U.S. atty. gen. in conscientious objector cases, 1954-55. Candidate for County Bd. Assessors, 1948. Served to 2d lt. USAAF, 1943-44. Mem. Am., Ill., St. Clair County, East St. Louis (past pres.) bar assns. Republican. Roman Catholic (trustee). Club: St. Clair Country (Belleville). Home: 32 S 87th St Belleville IL 62223 Office: 8 E Washington St Belleville IL 62220

HATCH, WILLIAM EDWARD, financial cons.; b. San Francisco, Oct. 16, 1917; s. William Sherman and Sophie (Disteli) H.; A.B., Stanford, 1939; M.B.A., Harvard, 1947; m. Dorothy A. LeBaker, June 22, 1941; children—Dorothea Lee, William Edward. With Firemans Fund Ins. Co., San Francisco, 1939, L.H. Penney & Co., C.P.A.'s, San Francisco, 1939-40; comml. audit mgr. Arthur Andersen & Co., C.P.A.'s, N.Y.C., 1947-54; with Ted Bates & Co., Inc., N.Y.C., 1954-69, sr. v.p., treas., 1959-68, sr. v.p. finance, treas., 1968-69, also dir. ind. financial and mgmt. cons., 1971—; v.p. finance Norton Simon Communications, Inc., N.Y.C. Served to lt. col. USAAF, 1940-46; lt. col. Res. C.P.A., N.Y. Mem. Am. Inst. C.P.A.'s, N.Y. State Soc. C.P.A.'s, N.Y. Credit and Financial Mgmt. Assn. (pres. advt. agy. group 1962-64), Newcomen Soc. N.Am., Am. Assn. Advt. Agys. (chmn. spl. com. fiscal control 1962-64), Delta Chi. Mason. Club: Harvard Business School. (N.Y.C.). Home: 153 Kensington Rd Garden City NY 11530 Office: 666 Fifth Av New York City NY 10019

HATCH, WINSLOW ROPER, educator; b. Lexington, Mass., Mar. 1, 1908; s. Roy Winthrop and Bertha May (Roper) H.; A.B., Dartmouth, 1930; Ph.D., Johns Hopkins, 1934; m. Dita Alvarado Keith, June 30, 1937; children—Robert Winslow, John Keith, Rosita Alvarado. Instr. botany Johns Hopkins, 1934-35; instr., dir. Ross Garey Biol. Field Sta., Johns Hopkins, summer 1935; Nat. Research fellow in botany Harvard, 1935-36; instr. botany Dartmouth, 1936-39; asst. prof., head dept. botany State Coll. Wash., 1939, asso. prof., 1941, prof., 1945, chmn. div. of biol. scis., 1949, asso. dean Coll. of Scis. and Art, 1953-55; dean Coll. Gen. Edn., Boston U., 1955-57; formerly dir. clearing house of studies on higher edn. Office Edn., Dept. Health, Edn., Welfare, Washington, editor New Dimensions in Higher Education; collector Johns Hopkins Expdn. to Am. Tropics, 1932-34. Mem. Am. Mycol. Soc., Bot. Soc. Am., A.A.A.S., Sigma Xi, Phi Kappa Phi, Phi Gamma Delta, Phi Beta Kappa. Editor: Northwest Sci., 1944-55; nat. editorial adv. bd. Improving College and Univ. Teaching. Author: Inquiry (series 7 articles improving coll. and univ. teaching); contbr. articles to sci. publs. Home: 6800 Churchill Rd McLean VA 22101

HATCHER, ANNA GRANVILLE, educator; b. Balt., Aug., 1905; d. Eldridge Burwell and Anna Granville (Denson) Hatcher; B.A., Blue Mountain Coll., Miss., 1925; M.A., U. Va., 1927; Ph.D., Johns Hopkins, 1934. Acad. dean Harcum Jr. Coll., Bryn Mawr, Pa., 1934-38; faculty Johns Hopkins, 1939-67, prof. Romance langs., 1958-67; prof. French and Italian, Ind. U., Bloomington, 1967-70, Distinguished prof., 1970—. Guggenheim fellow, 1953-54. Mem. Modern Lang. Assn. Author: Modern English Word Formation and Neo-Latin, 1951; Reflexive Verbs: Latin, Old French, Modern French, 1948; Theme and Underlying Questions, 1956. Co-editor: Essays in Historical Semantics, 1942; Studia Philologica et litteraria in honorem L. Spitzer, 1958. Editor: Essays in English and Am. Lit., 1962; Classical and Christian Ideas of World Harmony, 1963. Home: 430 S Dunn St Bloomington IN 47401

HATCHER, HARLAN HENTHORNE, author, univ. pres. emeritus; b. Ironton, O., Sept. 9, 1898; s. Robert Elison and Linda (Lesley) H.; A.B., Ohio State U., 1922, A.M., 1923, PH.D., 1927, LL.D., 1952; postgrad. U. Chgo., 1925, Europe, 1928; Litt.D., Miami U., 1947, U. Toledo, 1952, Albion Coll., 1952, U. Ky., U. Pitts., 1955, Waseda U., Tokyo, 1962, Pa. Mil. Coll., 1963, No. Mich. U., 1964; LL.D., Bowling Green State U., 1948, U. Mich., 1951, U. Cin., 1952, Ohio Wesleyan U., 1953, U. of Akron, 1953, Mich. State Coll., 1955, Butler U., 1955, N.D., 1956, Northwestern U., 1956, Kalamazoo Coll., 1958, U. Cal., 1966; L.H.D., Coll. Wooster, 1954, N.Y.U., 1956, Lawrence Inst. Tech., 1958; Ed.D., Hillsdale Coll., 1961, So. Ill. U., 1966; m. Frank Wilson Colfax, Dec. 29, 1922 (dec.); m. 2d, Anne Gregory Vance, Apr. 3, 1942; children—Robert Leslie, Anne Linda. Instr. English, Ohio State U., 1922-28, asst. prof., 1928-32, prof., 1932-44, dean Coll. Arts and Scis., 1944-48, v.p., 1948-51; pres. U. Mich., 1951- 67, pres. emeritus, 1967—; pres. Developing Great Lakes Megalopolis Research Project, Inc., Ann Arbor, 1968—; lectr. U. So. Cal., summer 1951; dir. Ann Arbor Bank, Detroit Edison Co., Tecumseh Products Co. Trustee Inst. Def. Analyses; mem. Ford Found. Fellowship Adv. Bd., 1961- 65; past dir. Council Financial Aid Edn. Coordinator War Accelerated Program, Ohio State U., 1942; lectr. State U. Ia., 1932. Served as pvt. U.S. Army, 1918; lt. USNR, 1942-44. Decorated comdr. Netherlands Order of Orange-Nassau; companion Most Exalted Order White Elephant, Thailand; Ky. Col.; Star Italian Solidarity; 2d Order Merit with Middle Cordon of Rising Sun (Japan); Wolverine Frontiersman Award. Mem. Modern Lang. Assn. Am., Assn. Am. Univs. (pres.), Am. Assn. Univ. Profs., Nat. Council Tchrs. English, The Great Lakes Hist. Soc., Am. Hist. Soc., Phi Beta Kappa. Clubs: Century (N.Y.C.); Economic of Detroit (dir.), Detroit, Detroit Athletic; Rotary; Newcomen Soc. Author: The Versification of Robert Browning, 1928; Tunnel Hill, 1931; Patterns of Wolfpen, 1934; Creating the Modern American Novel, 1935; Central Standard Time, 1937; The Buckeye Country: A Pageant of Ohio, 1940; The History of Ohio, Vol. VI (with others), 1943. Modern Dramas, Shorter Edition, 1944, The Great Lakes, 1944, Lake Erie (Great Lakes Series), 1945; The Western Reserve: The Story of New Connecticut in Ohio, 1949; A Century of Iron and Men, 1950. Editor: The Ohio Guide, 1940; Modern Continental, British, and American Dramas (with critical introductions) 3 vols., 1941; A Modern Repertory, 1953; Giant from the Wilderness, 1955; A Pictorial History of the Great Lakes, 1963. Contbr. many profl. articles and fiction to mags. State dir. Fed. Writers Project in Ohio, 1937-39. Book critic The Columbus Citizen, 1938-44; editorial advisor Coll. English, 1938-48. Home: 631 Oxford Rd Ann Arbor MI 48104

HATCHER, KENNETH MACKENZIE, food co. exec.; b. N.Y.C., July 21, 1915; s. Arthur B. and Sarah (Pangburn) H.; grad. Hotchkiss Sch., 1933; A.B., Williams Coll., 1937; M.B.A., Harvard, 1939; m. Ruth Cronk, June 10, 1940; children—Kenneth, Harriet, Stuart. With Arthur Andersen & Co., C.P.A.'s, N.Y.C., 1939-46; with Nabisco, Inc., N.Y.C., 1946—, asst. treas., 1955-60, sec.- treas., 1960-71, sec., 1971—. Mem. task force subsistance services 2d Hoover Commn., 1953-55. C.P.A., N.Y. Mem. Harvard Advanced Mgmt. Assn., Am. Soc. Corp. Secs. Home: 5 Crown Top Rd Manhasset NY 11030 Office: 425 Park Av New York City NY 10022

HATCHER, LLOYD BROWER, investment banker; b. Atlanta, Jan. 14, 1907; s. Clifford Cicero and Imogen (Brower) H.; A.B., Va. Mil. Inst., 1929; M.B.A., Harvard, 1931; m. Barbara Holdsworth, June 1, 1935; children—Barbara H. van Marx, Lloyd Brower. With Guaranty Co. of N.Y., 1931-33, Edward B. Smith & Co., N.Y.C., 1933-35; v.p. Trust Co. of Ga., Atlanta, 1935-53, mgr. bond dept., 1943-53; gen. partner, mem. exec. com. White, Weld & Co., N.Y.C., 1953—. Vice pres. Investment Bankers Assn. Am., 1963-65, mem. exec. com., 1963, also past chmn. N.Y. group. Served with USMCR, 1943-46; maj. Res. Mem. Sigma Alpha Epsilon. Clubs: Bond, Municipal Bond, Municipal Forum, University, Wall Street (N.Y.C.); Piedmont Driving (Atlanta); Huntington (N.Y.) Country. Home: 1220 Park Av New York City NY 10028 Office: 20 Broad St New York City NY 10005

HATCHER, PAUL GILLIAM, coll. dean; b. Sylvia, Tenn., July 1, 1922; s. William Thomas and Maggie (Singleton) H.; B.S., Peabody Coll., 1942; A.M., U. Mich., 1946, Ph.D. in Romance Langs., 1956; postgrad. Vanderbilt U., 1947; m. Ernestine Graham, June 27, 1946; 1 son, Paul Graham. Instr. modern fgn. langs. Delta State Tchrs. Coll., Miss., 1946-47; asso. prof. King Coll., Tenn., 1947-49; tchr. Spanish and French, Detroit U. Sch., 1951-52; asst. prof. Furman U., Greenville, S.C., 1952-56; asso. prof. Carson- Newman Coll., Jefferson City, Tenn., 1956-59, acting head dept. fgn. langs., 1958- 59; prof. Spanish, head dept. fgn. langs. Western Ky, U. Bowling Green, 1959-67, dean Coll. Liberal Arts, 1965—. Served with USNR, 1942-45. Mem. Am. Assn. Tchrs. Spanish and Portugese, South Atlantic Modern Lang. Assn., Ky. Edn. Assn., Pi Delta Phi, Kappa Phi Kappa, Sigma Delta Pi, Alpha Psi Omega. Baptist. Mason. Contbr. articles profl. jours. Home: 2311 Hemlock Heights Bowling Green KY 42101

HATCHER, RICHARD G., mayor; b. Michigan City, Ind., July 10, 1933; s. Carlton and Catherine Hatcher; B.A., Ind. U.; LL.B., Valparaiso U. Admitted to Ind. bar, practiced in East Chicago; formerly dep. prosecutor Lake County, Ind.; councilman- at- large Gary City Council, 1963-66; mayor of Gary, 1967—. Mem. U.S. Conf. Mayors; mem. steering com. on human resources devel. Nat. League Cities. A founder Muigwithania, social and civic club, now v.p.; mem. Nat. Com. of Inquiry; chmn. edn. subcom. Ind. adv. com. to U.S. Commn. Civil Rights; mem. exec. com. Nat. Urban Coalition. Mem. Ind. exec. bd. N.A.A.C.P., legal adviser Gary chpt.; bd. dirs. Greater Gary United Fund; trustee, mem. adv. com. Gary Urban League. Mem. Am., Ind., Gary (exec. com.) bar assns., Gary Jaycees. Democrat. Address: 2009 Broadway Gary IN 46407*

HATCHER, ROBERT DOUGLAS, educator, physicist; b. St. John's, Nfld., Can., June 26, 1924; s. Charles W. and Lillian (Nichols) H.; B.Sc., Dalhousie U., Halifax, N.S., Can., 1945, M.Sc., 1947; M.S., Yale, 1948, Ph.D., 1949; m. Helen Charlotte Schober, June 16, 1951; children—Robert, Brian, Peter, Christopher. Came to U.S., 1947, naturalized, 1952. From instr. to asso. prof. N.Y.U., 1949-62; mem. faculty Queens Coll., City U. N.Y., 1962-, prof. physics, 1962—, chmn. dept. physics, 1965-67. Cons. Brookhaven Nat. Lab. 1958—. Fellow N.Y. Acad. Scis., Am. Phys. Soc.; mem. Am. Assn. Physics Tchrs., Am. Assn. U. Profs. Spl. research radiation defects in ionic crystals, phys. properties pure ionic crystals. Home: 8 Winchester Lane Halesite NY 11743 Office: Physics Dept Queens Coll Flushing NY 11367

HATCHETT, STEPHEN PINCKNEY, govt. ofcl.; b. Mogollon, N.M., June 30, 1915; s. Samuel Pinckney and Annie Margaret (Huther) H.; A.B., Am. U., 1937; A.M., U. Mich., 1938, Ph.D., 1943; m. Dorothy Belle Chandler, July 16, 1945; children—Stephen Pinckney, Anne Elizabeth. Prof. biology Presbyn. Coll., S.C., 1946-47; asst. prof. biology Am. U., 1947-48, asso. prof., 1948-50, prof., 1950- 55, chmn. dept. biology, 1947-55, chmn. div. natural sci., 1948-53; asst. chief career devel. rev. br. NIH Div. Research Grants, Bethesda, Md., 1955-58, chief, 1958-63, dep. dir. div. research grants, 1963-69, dir. div. research grants, 1969—. Fellow A.A.A.S.; mem. Soc. Systemic Zoology, Am. Micros. Soc., Nat. Assn. Biology Tchrs., Sigma Xi, Beta Beta Beta, Phi Kappa Phi, Phi Sigma, Alpha Sigma Phi. Home: 4804 Crescent St Bethesda MD 20016

HATFIELD, ALVIN KEYSER, ins. co. exec.; b. Phila., Mar. 27, 1914; s. Alvin Bossert and Estella (Keyser) H.; grad. Peirce Sch. Bus. Adminstrn., Phila., 1934; m. Grace Elizabeth Herde, Sept. 10, 1950; children—John, Robert, George. Sr. accountant Joseph Froggatt & Co., Phila., 1939-48; v.p., controller Govt. Employees Ins. Cos., Washington, 1948-55; v.p., treas. Nat. Union Ins. Cos., Pitts., 1955-69; v.p. Am. Internat. Underwriters, Inc., 1968—; v.p.-comptroller Am. Home Assurance Group and Nat. Union Ins. Cos., 1970—. Served to capt. USAAF, 1941-45; PTO. Mem. Ins. Accountants Assn. Home: Queenstown MD 21658 Office: 102 Maiden Lane New York City NY 10004

HATFIELD, DAVID UNDERHILL, artist; b. Plainfield, N.J., July 16, 1940; s. Richard Pearson and Margaret (Weldon) H.; B.F.A., Miami U., Oxford, O., 1962; postgrad. Art Students League, 1964, Sch. Visual Arts, 1963. Exhibited in one-man show at Grand Central Art Gallery, N.Y.C., 1972; exhibited in group shows at Nat. Acad. Galleries, N.Y.C., 1968, 71, Nat. Arts Club, N.Y.C., 1970. Recipient 1st prize Washington Sq. Outdoor Art Exhibit, 1969-70, Julius Hallgarten prize Nat. Acad. Design, 1970. Mem. Grand Central Art Galleries, Am. Artists Profl. League, Allied Artists Am. Hudson Valley Art Assn. Club: Salmagundi (N.Y.C.). Address: 311 E 75th St New York City NY 10021

HATFIELD, HENRY CARAWAY, educator; b. Evanston, Ill., June 3, 1912; s. James Taft and Estelle (Caraway) H.; A.B., Harvard, 1933; A.M., Columbia, 1938, Ph.D., 1942; m. Jane Stauff, Mar. 15, 1937; children—Robert Allan, Barbara. Instr. Williams Coll., 1938-42, asst. prof., 1942-46; asst. prof. Columbia, 1946-48, asso. prof., 1948-54; asso. prof. Harvard, 1954-56, prof. German, 1956-67, Kuno Francke prof. German art, culture, 1967—, chmn. dept. Germanic lang. and lit., 1957-59; vis. prof. Free U. Berlin, 1961. With O.W.I., London, 1944-45. Recipient Guggenheim and Fulbright fellowships, 1952-53; Am. Council Learned Socs. award, 1962. Mem. Modern Lang. Assn. Am. (exec. com. 1956-59), Am. Acad. of Arts and Scis., Am. Assn. for Tchrs. German, Am. Civil Liberties Union, Ams. for Dem. Action. Author: Winckelmann and His German Critics, 1943; Thomas Mann, 1951, rev. 1962; (with J.M. Stein) Schnitzler, Kafka, Mann, 1953; (with F.H. Mautner) The Lichtenberg Reader, 1959; Goethe: A Critical Introduction, 1963; Aesthetic Paganism in General Literature, 1964; Thomas Mann, A Critical Anthology, 1964; Modern German Literature, 1967; Crisis and Continuity in Modern German Fiction, 1969. Gen. editor Germanic Rev., 1947-53; editorial bd. PMLA, 1951-56. Home: 7 Avon St Cambridge MA 02138

HATFIELD, JOSEPH WHARTON, business forms co. exec.; b. Xenia, O., May 26, 1905; s. Joseph Ryan and Edna (Wharton) H.; student U. Dayton, 1927-31; children (by previous marriage)—Dale N., Larry; m. 2d, Thelma Bryant, Dec. 21, 1964; step children—Susan Alice, Elizabetn Gail. Admitted to Ohio bar, 1932; practice law in Xenia; with Standard Register Co., Dayton, O., 1936—, asst. sec., 1957-66, sec., 1966-69, v.p.-sec., 1969—, also dir. Mem. Am. Bar Assn. Home: Rt 3 Lytle Rd Box 388 Waynesville OH 44688 Office: Standard Register Co Dayton OH 45401

HATFIELD, MARK, U.S. senator; b. Dallas, Ore., July 12, 1922; s. Charles Dolen and Dovie (Odom) H.; A.B., Willamette U., 1943, LL.D., 1958; A.M., Stanford U., 1948; recipient numerous hon. degrees; m. Antoinette Kuzmanich, July 8, 1958; children—Mark, Elizabeth, Theresa, Charles. Resident asst. Stanford (Cal.) U., 1947-49; instr. Willamette U., 1949, dean students, asso. prof. polit. sci., 1950-56; sec. State of Ore., 1957-59, gov., 1959-67; U.S. senator from Ore., 1967—. Mem. Ore. Ho. of Reps., 1951- 55, Ore. Senate, 1955-57; del. Republican Nat. Conv., 1952, 56, 60, 64, 68. Served from ensign to lt. (j.g.), USNR, 1943-46. Baptist. Mason (Shriner). Office: Senate Office Bldg Washington DC 20510

HATFIELD, ROBERT M., mech. engr.; b. Evanston, Ill., Nov. 18, 1907; s. Robert Marcus and Edith Pearl (Winterrowd) H.; B.S., Purdue, 1932, M.E., 1940; m. Ruth Victoria Bursley, June 2, 1934; 1 dau., Linda Ruth. With Combustion Engring., Inc., N.Y.C., 1934-68, gen. mgr. Western div., 1949-52, v.p. corp., 1952-56, v.p. mfg. 1957-59, v.p., gen. sales mgr., 1960-68; power cons. to Govt. India, 1968; now dir. bus. devel. power div. Ralph M. Parsons Co., N.Y.C. vice chmn. for govt. agys. and exec. asst. to chmn. Munitions Bd., Dept. Def., 1951. Served as dep. vice chmn. for prodn. W.P.B., World War II; lt. (j.g.) USNR, 1944-45. Registered profl. engr., Ohio and Cal. Mem. Am. Soc. M.E., Holland Soc. N.Y., Sigma Chi. Club: Engineers (N.Y.C.). Home: 415 E 52d St New York City NY Office: 26 Broadway New York City NY 10004

HATFIELD, ROBERT SHERMAN, can mfg. co. exec.; b. Utica, N.Y., Jan. 16, 1916; s. Albert R. and Mary (Sherman) H.; student Cornell U., 1937; LL.B., Fordham U., 1945; grad. Advanced Mgmt. Program, Harvard, 1954; m. Roberta Sullivan, May 8, 1937; children—Roberta A. (Mrs. A.M. Williamson), Suzanne S. (Mrs. John A. Miele), Molly J., Robert Sherman. Vice pres., gen. mgr. Eastern div. Continental Can Co., 1961- 62, exec. v.p., gen. mgr. metal div., 1962-69, sr. exec. v.p., chief operating officer, 1969—, also dir. Clubs: Chicago; Pinnacle (N.Y.C.); Greenwich Country; Blind Brook; Pine Valley Golf. Home: 480 North St Greenwich CT 06830 Office: 633 3d Av New York City NY 10017

HATFIELD, THEO NOEL, educator; b. Bunkie, La., Apr. 5, 1905; s. Charles Rushing and Anna Lou (Glaze) H.; B.S. in Math., La. State U., 1929, M.S. in Chemistry, 1932; Ph.D. in Physics, U. Tex., 1940; m. Beryl Dyson, June 4, 1932; children—Charles Rushing, Bruce Glen. From instr. to asso. prof. physics La. State U., 1932-46; asso. prof. physics U. Tex., 1946-51; M.D. Anderson prof. physics, chmn. dept. U. Houston, 1952-60, M.D. Anderson prof. physics, 1960—; cons. Sandia Corp., 1950-55; dir. Electro- Mechanics Co., Austin, Tex. Mem. Am. Assn. Physics Tchrs. (pres. Tex. 1956-58), Houston Phys. Soc. (pres. 1958-59), Am. Phys. Soc., Am. Geophys. Union, Soc. Exploration Geophysicists, Sigma Xi, Phi Kappa Phi. Home: 2914 Sunset Blvd Houston TX 77005

HATHAWAY, BAXTER LEVERING, educator; b. Cin., Dec. 4, 1909; s. William B. and Etta (Fee) H.; A.B., Kalamazoo Coll., 1935; M.A., U. Mich., 1936, Ph.D., 1940; m. Sherry W. Kitchen, June 37, 1936; children—Hannah E. (Mrs. Alan H. Colen), William K., James B. Tchr., U. Mich., 1936-40, U. Mont., 1940- 44, 45-46, U. Wis., 1944-45; mem. faculty Cornell U., 1946—, prof. English, 1962—; vis. prof. U. Padua (Italy), 1957-58. Ednl. adviser Am. Coll., Paris, France, 1963—; dir. Asso. Writing Programs, 1967—. Mem. Modern Lang. Assn. Author: The Stubborn Way (novel), 1937; Writing Mature Prose, 1951; The Age of Criticism, 1962; A Transformational Syntax, 1967; Marvels and Commonplaces, 1969. Editor: Epoch, 1947—. Home: 419 Wyckoff Av Ithaca NY 14850

HATHAWAY, CALVIN SUTLIFF, museum curator; b. Lockport, N.Y.; s. Rev. Harry St. Clair and Jean (Groo) H.; grad. Episcopal Acad., 1925; A.B., Princeton, 1930; grad. student Harvard, 1930-31, N.Y.U., 1933-34. Asst. Phila. Mus. Art, 1930, sec. to dir., editor, 1931-32, charge dept. decorative arts and editor, 1932-33; asst. curator Cooper Union Mus., N.Y.C., 1933-34, asso. curator, 1934-42, curator, 1946-51, dir., 1951-63; R. Wistar Harvey curator decorative arts Phila. Museum of Art, 1964—; research asso. Henry Francis du Pont Winterthur Mus., 1964-68. Mem. fine arts com. for the White House, 1961-68. Served from pvt. to capt. AUS, 1942-46, mil. govt. monuments, fine arts and archives sect., 1943-46. Decorated Delaware Medal (Sweden), 1938; Bronze Star medal (U.S.), 1945; recipient traveling fellowship Am.- Scandinavian Found., 1935. Mem. Mil. Order Loyal Legion, Am. Assn. Museums, Internat. Inst. Conservation of Historic and Artistic Works, Inter-Soc. Color Council, S.R., Centre International d'Etude des Textiles Anciens (v.p.; Am. corr.); Benjamin Franklin fellow Royal Soc. Arts (London). Club: Century Association (N.Y.C.). Home: 2601 Parkway Philadelphia PA 19130 Office: PO Box 7646 Philadelphia PA 19101

HATHAWAY, CARL EMIL, trust co. exec.; b. Boston, Aug. 12, 1933; s. Carl Barbour and Tekla (Neumaier) H.; B.A., Harvard, 1955; M.B.A., Cornell U., 1959; m. Gail Humphries Oglee, Dec. 6, 1959; children—Brian Kent, Carl Nichols, Andrew Oglee. With Morgan Guaranty Trust Co. N.Y., 1959—, sr. v.p. pension investments, trust and investments div., 1969—. Served to lt. (j.g.) USNR, 1955-57. Clubs: Woodway Country (Darien, Conn.); Harvard (Fairfield County, Conn.); Fairfield Country. Home: Homewood Lane Darien CT 06820 Office: 23 Wall St New York City NY 10015

HATHAWAY, DALE ERNEST, educator; b. Decatur, Mich., June 28, 1925; s. Roy C. and Ruth (Cooper) H.; B.A. in Econs., Mich. State U., 1947, M.A., 1948; D.P.A., Harvard, 1952; m. Helen Gene Pollock; children—Anne Lee, Linda Marie, Roy Randal, Kathy. Mem. faculty Mich. State U., 1947—, prof. agrl. econs., 1958—, chmn. dept., 1969—; sr. staff mem. Council Econ. Advisers, Exec. Office of Pres., 1955-56; vis. prof. econs. U. Chgo., 1961-62. Cons. joint econ. com. U.S. Congress, 1960, Dept. Agr., 1961-66, Council Econ. Adviser, 1961-62, Pres.'s Sci. Adv. Com., 1966-67; mem. Nat. Manpower Adv. Com., 1970—. Served to ensign USNR, 1944-46. Recipient Distinguished Faculty award Mich. State U. 1965. Mem. Am. Agrl. Econs. Assn. (pres, 1969-70, v.p. 1960-61, Best Published Research award 1956, 58). Author: Government and Agriculture, 1963; Problems of Progress in the Agricultural Economy, 1964; (with others) The People of Rural America, 1967. Home: 345 Whitehills Dr East Lansing MI 48823

HATHAWAY, EARL BURTON, rubber products mfg.; b. Hot Springs, Ark., Feb. 11, 1903; s. Burt Wallace and Blanche Leona (Kearney) H.; B.S., Northwestern U., 1927; m. Margaret Steel Moinet, Oct. 8, 1932; children—Alden Moinet, Earl Burton, Margaret Anne. With Firestone Tire & Rubber Co., Akron, O., 1927—, v.p. charge all sales, 1959-62, exec. v.p., 1962-64, pres., 1964-70, now dir. Mem. Nat. Motor Vehicle Safety Adv. Council. Trustee Western Res. Acad. Mem. Delta Upsilon. Episcopalian (vestryman). Clubs: New York Athletic; Detroit Athletic; Portage

Country (Akron); Sharon Country; Firestone Country; Rolling Rock. Home: 482 St Andrews Dr Akron OH 44307 Office: Firestone Tire & Rubber Co Akron OH 44308

HATHAWAY, EDWARD WINSLOW, headmaster; b. Montclair, N.J., Feb. 16, 1916; s. Joseph Wood and Sarah (Vaughan) H.; B.A., Bates Coll., 1938; M.A., N.J. State Coll., Montclair, 1948; m. Dorcas Davis, June 8, 1940; children—Dorcas, Evelyn. Tchr., Somerset Hills Sch., Far Hills, N.J., 1938-41, Columbia Grammar Sch., N.Y.C., 1941-42; tchr., coach, guidance, asso. dir. summer session Pingry Sch., Elizabeth, N.J., 1942-50; registrar, bus. dir., dir. summer sch. Montclair Acad., 1950-52; headmaster Adelphi Acad., Bklyn., 1952-65, Vail-Deane Sch., Elizabeth, 1965—. Mem. N.Y. Assn. Tchrs. Ind. Schs., Nat. Assn. Secondary Sch. Prins., Am. Philatelic Soc. Conglist. Mason, Rotarian. Club: Rembrandt (Bklyn.). Home: 235 Bradford Rd Hillside NJ 07205 Office: 618 Salem Av Elizabeth NJ 07207

HATHAWAY, H. WINSTON, lawyer; b. Muskegon, Mich., Dec. 21, 1908; A.B., U. Mich., 1930, J.D., 1933. Admitted to Mich. bar, 1933, U.S. Supreme Ct. bar; mem. firm Landman, Hathaway, Latimer, Clink & Robb, Muskegon, Mem. Com. Visitors U. Mich. Law Sch., 1963—. Mem. Am., Muskegon County (pres. 1947-48) bar assns., State Bar Mich. (mem. judiciary com. 1949—, negligence law sect.), Assn. Ins. Attys., Internat. Assn. Ins. Counsel. Contbr. articles to profl. jours. Office: 500 Hackley Union Nat Bank Bldg Muskegon MI 49443*

HATHAWAY, KENNETH A., business exec.; b. Pontiac, Mich., 1918; grad. Mich. State U., 1942; married. With Redman Industries, Inc., Dallas, 1956—, now exec. v.p., dir. Mason. Home: 7127 Oak Bluff Dr Dallas TX 75240 Office: 7800 Carpenter Freeway Dallas TX 75247*

HATHAWAY, STANLEY K., gov. Wyo.; b. Osceola, Neb., July 19, 1924; s. Franklin E. and Velam (Holbrook) H.; student U. Wyo., 1942-43; A.B., U. Neb., 1948, LL.B., 1950; m. Roberta Harley, Nov. 25, 1948; children—Susan, Sandra. Admitted to Wyo. bar; pros. atty. Goshen County, Wyo., 1954-62; gov. of Wyo., 1967—. Nat. committeeman Young Republican Fedn., 1958-60; committeeman Wyo. Rep. Party, 1960-62, chmn., sec., 1962-64; chmn. Goshen County Rep. Party, 1962-64. Served with USAAF, 1943-45; ETO. Decorated Air medal (5). Mem. Am., Wyo. bar assns., Wyo. County Attys. Assn. (pres. 1961), Am. Legion, V.F.W., Delta Theta Phi, Sigma Chi. Episcopalian. Lion, Mason, Elk, Moose. Address: 219 Linda Vista Torrington WY 82240 *

HATHAWAY, STARKE ROSECRANS, clin. psychologist; b. Central Lake, Mich., Aug. 22, 1903; s. Martin Walter and Bertha Bell (Rosecrans) H.; A.B., Ohio U., 1927, L.H.D., 1966; A.M., Ohio State U., 1928; Ph.D., U. Minn., 1932; m. (Mary) Virginia Riddle, Aug. 25, 1928. Prof. dir. div. clin. psychology U. Minn., 1951-70, prof. emeritus, 1970—; vis. prof., Thomas Wilton research fellow Stanford, 1952-53. Served as expert, Adj. Gen. Office, 1943-45; cons. in psychology VA, St. Paul. Fulbright prof., Nat. U. of Mexico, 1964-65. Diplomate in clin. psychology Am. Bd. Examiners in Profl. Psychology. Fellow Am. Psychol. Assn. (sci. contbn. award 1959); mem. Phi Beta Kappa, Sigma Xi. Author books including: (with P.E. Meehl) Atlas for the Clinical Use of the MMPI, 1951; (with E.D. Monachesi) Adolescent Personality and Behavior, 1963: Home: 222 Melbourne St Minneapolis MN 55414

HATHAWAY, WILLIAM DODD, congressman; b. Cambridge, Mass., Feb. 21, 1924; s. James F. and Charlotte A. (Dodd) H.; A.B. cum laude, Harvard, 1949, LL.B., 1953; m. Mary Lee Bird, Aug. 21, 1945; children—Susan Louise, Fred William. Admitted to Mass. bar, 1953, Me. bar, 1954; practice, Lewiston, Me., 1953—; mem. 89th-92d Congresses 2d Dist. Me. Bd. dirs. Lewiston-Auburn chpt. A.R.C., Lewiston-Auburn Assn. Retarded Children. Served to capt., navigator, USAAF, World War II. Mem. Am., Me., Androscoggin County bar assns., Me. Med.-Legal Soc. Democrat. Home: 80 Orchard St Auburn ME 04210 Office: Canon House Office Bldg Washington DC 20515

HATHEWAY, JOHN HARRIS, advt. exec.; b. Waterbury, Conn., Aug. 9, 1926; s. Fred Whipple and Louise (Wood) H.; A.B., Dartmouth, 1948, M.B.A., Amos Tuck Sch. Bus. Adminstrn., 1950; m Patricia Mary Flaherty, Sept. 24, 1955; children—John Harris, Geoffrey Mills, Sara Wood. With Young and Rubicam Inc., N.Y.C., 1950—. sr. v.p., mgmt. supr., 1968—; bd. overseers Hanover Inn (N.H.), 1968—. Mem Council of Alumni Dartmouth, 1968—. Served with AUS, 1945-46. Mem. Phi Beta Kappa. Episcopalian (vestry). Clubs: New Castle Town (Chappaqua, N.Y.), Dartmouth Coll. of New York (pres. 1965-66, bd. dirs. 1958-64, 67-70). Home: Hoffman Rd RFD 1 Mount Kisco NY 10549 Office: 285 Madison Av New York City NY 10017

HATHHORN, JAMES ROBERT, univ. dean; b. Cambridge, Ida., Jan. 19, 1925; s. Harry Homer and Nina (VandenBroeck) H.; B.S., U. Ida., 1951, M.S.; m. Marian May Booth, July 13, 1945; children—Maureen K. (Mrs. Rodney A. Cole). Michael J., Debra A., David A. Dir. guidance Power County (Ida.) Pub. Schs., 1951- 53; counselor Oregon City (Ore.) Pub. Sch., 1953-60; counselor U. Nev., 1960-62, dean of men. 1962—. Bd. dirs. Tchrs. Credit Union, 1962-64, sec., 1964-66; pres. Oregon City Classroom Tchrs. Assn., 1956-57. Served with USMCR, 1942-46. Mem. Am. Personnel and Guidance Assn., Nat. Assn. Student Personnel Adminstrs. Elk. Mason. Home: 200 Devere Way Sparks NV 89431 Office: U Nev Reno NV 89705

HATHORN, RICHMOND YANCEY, educator; b. Alexandria, La., July 31, 1917; s. John Wesley and Aimee Aileen (Sleet) H.; B.A., ga. Coll., 1937; M.A., La. State U., 1940; Ph.D., Columbia, 1950; m. Isabel Voelker, May 23, 1947; children—Isabel Voelker, Richmond Yancy, Emily Montgomery. Lectr. classics Columbia, 1947-53; prof. Northwestern State Coll. La.,1953-61; asso. prof. La. State U., 1961-62; prof. classics, chmn. dept. U. Ky., 1962-66; prof. European langs. and lit. Am. U. Beirut, 1966-69; prof., chmn. dept. classics State U. N.Y., Stony Brook, 1969—; vis. prof. U. Mich., 1959. Mem. Am. Philol. Assn., Am. Assn. U. Profs., Classical Assn. Middle West and South, Vergilian Soc. Am. Author: Tragedy, Myth and Mystery, 1962; Handbook of Classical Drama, 1967. Address: Dept Classics State U NY Stony Brook NY

HATHWAY, CLIFFORD NEWTON, machinery mfg. co. exec.; b. Waukesha, Wis., Mar. 12, 1918; s. Clifford W. and Maude (Birkenheier) H.; ed. pub. schs., Waukesha; m. Ruth Hammond, June 1, 1940; children—Stephen Dallas, John Hammond, Michael Wilson, Deborah Nell, Clifford Newton. With Caterpillar Tractor Co., Peoria, Ill., 1935—, gen. mgr. domestic plants, 1963-64, v.p., 1964—. Bd. dirs., past pres. Creve Coeur council Boy Scouts Am.; bd. dirs. Silver Cross Hosp., Joliet, Ill., 1957-63, Central Ill. Jr. Achievement, 1963—, Nat. Safety Council, Lakeview Center Arts; trustee, past chmn. bd. Eureka Coll. Mem. Ill., Peoria chambers commerce, Navy League. Club: Peoria Country. Home: 507 W Northgate Rd Peoria IL 61614 Office: 100 NE Adams St Peoria IL 61602

HATIE, GEORGE DANIEL, lawyer; b. Detroit, Mar. 11, 1910; s. George Leon and Mildred Belle (Edwards) H.; J.D., U. Detroit, 1933. Admitted to Mich. bar, 1933, since practiced in Detroit; mem. firm Cross, Wrock, Miller & Vieson, 1936—, partner, 1945—. Bd. govs. Am. Numis. Assn., 1967—, legal counsel, 1965-69; bd. dirs. Mich. Humane Soc., 1953—, pres., 1957-63; bd. dirs. Mich. Kidney Found., 1969—, bd. dirs. Girl Scouts Met. Detroit, 1970—. Mem. Am., Mich. (pres. 1964), Detroit (pres. 1964), Grosse Pointe (pres. 1960), Central States (pres. 1970—) numismatic socs., Token and Medal Soc. (pres. 1970—), Soc. Paper Money Collectors (gov. 1964-66), Am. Humane Soc. (hon. v.p. 1959-63), Am., Detroit bar assns., State Bar Mich. Republican. Roman Catholic. Home: 1126 Whittier Rd Grosse Pointe Park MI 48230 Office: Penobscot Bldg Detroit MI 48226

HATLEY, OWEN P., hosp. adminstr.; b. St. Marie's, Ida., Oct. 14, 1918; s. Olaf and Johanna (Wick) H.; ed. U. Ida., 1939, U. Minn., 1952-54; m. Betty Lee, Jan. 31, 1943; children—Ann Lee, Mary Margaret, Sr. sanitarian N. Central dist. Lewiston (Ida.) Health Dept., 1944-50; dir. hosp. and med. facilities Ida. Dept. Pub. Health, 1950-57; asst. adminstr. Charles T. Miller Hosp., St. Paul, 1957-60; adminstr. Community Meml. Hosp. of San Buenaventura, Ventura, Cal., 1960-67, Kern County Hosp. System, Bakersfield, Cal., 1967—. Sec.-treas. Ida. Hosp. Assn., 1954-57; bd. dirs. Hosp. Council So. Cal., 1965-67; chmn. adv. com. Ventura Coll. Sch. Nursing, 1964-67; chmn. Ventura County Hosp. Planning, 1960-67. Served to maj. USMCR, 1942-46. Home: 5225 Ojai St Bakersfield CA 93306 Office: 1830 Flower St Bakersfield CA 93305

HATMAKER, GEORGE EDWARD, life ins. co. exec.; b. St. Louis, Dec. 1, 1910; s. John Edward and Eulalia M. (Milligan) H.; ed. pub. schs.; m. Lucile Brem, Apr. 20, 1943; 1 dau., Lucy Ann. With Franklin Life Ins. Co., Springfield, Ill., 1928- -, v.p., sec. 1953-56, exec. asst. to pres., 1956-61, exec. v. p., 1961-64, pres., 1964—, chief exec. officer, 1969—, chmn. bd., 1970—, also dir.; pres., dir. Franklin United Life Ins. Co., Ill. Power Co., 1st Nat. Bank Springfield. Mem. Springfield Met. Exposition and Auditorium Authority. Served to capt. with AUS, 1942- 46. Clubs: Union League, Tavern (Chgo.); Sangamo (Springfield); Illini Country. Home: 2500 W Lakeshore Dr Springfield IL 62702 Office: Franklin Sq Springfield IL 62702

HATT, ROBERT TORRENS, museum cons.; b. Lafayette, Ind., July 17, 1902; s. William Kendrick and Josie Belle (Appleby) H.; student Purdue U., 1919-20; B.Sc., U. Mich., 1923; A.M., Columbia, 1925, Ph.D., 1932; m. Marcelle Roigneau, Mar. 30, 1929 (dec. 1951); children—Richard R., Peter K.; m. 2d, Suzannah Beck Vaillant, Jan. 10, 1953. Instr. biology N.Y. U., 1923-28; asst. curator mammals Am. Mus. Natural History, 1928-35; dir. Cranbrook Inst. Sci., Bloomfield Hills, Mich., 1935-67, trustee, 1967-71, trustee emeritus, 1971—; research collaborator mus. zoology U. Mich., 1937—; cons. museums Iraq, Pakistan, Can., U.S.; expdns. to Michoacan, Yucatan, Iraq, Rhodesia. Mem. com. to visit Mus. Comparative Zoology, Harvard, 1946-50. Trustee Eskimo Art, Inc.; pres. bd. trustees Cranbrook Inst. Sci. Fellow Rochester Mus. and Sci. Center, A.A.A.S., N.Y. Zool. Soc., Zool. Soc. London, Atlantica Found., Am. Mus. Natural History; mem. Detroit Acad. Natural Sci. (pres. 1940-41), Am. Assn. Museums (council 1940-61; v.p. 1955-60), Midwest Mus. Conf. (pres. 1944-46), Internat. Council Museums (chmn. sci. sect. 1947, mem. U.S. nat. com. 1952-62, 65—, chmn. 1959-60), Museums Assn. (Eng.), Am. Soc. Mammalogists, Am. Soc. Naturalists, Am. Soc. of Zoologists, Mich. Acad. Sci. (pres. 1962- 63), Pakistan Museum Assn. Nature Conservancy, Sigma Xi. Clubs: Explorers; The Century Association (N.Y.C.); Cosmos (Washington). Author: Island Life in Lake Michigan, 1948; Mammals of Iraq, 1959. Contbr. profl. jours. Address: Rt 1 Box 75 Littleton NH 03561

HATTEN, FREDA MARIE WESTENSEE, librarian; b. Bartlett, N.D., Oct. 7, 1905; d. William Frederic and Anna (Kunkel) Wdstensee; student U. Minn., 1926; B.A., State Coll., Mayville, N.D., 1928; M.A. in Librarianship, U. Wash., 1963; m. William Clarence Hatten, Oct. 9, 1930; children—JoAnn Clora (Mrs. Thomas Laurie Swinland), William Forrest. Asst. librarian Mayville State Coll., 1926-29; librarian Pub. Library, Kalispell, Mont., 1930; tchr. elementary and secondary schs.; field librarian, cons. State Library Commn., Bismarck, N.D., 1960-65, dir., 1965; former dir. State Library Commn., Lincoln, Neb. Bd. dirs. N.D. Hist. Soc. Mem. A.L.A., Am. Assn. State Librarians, Mountain-Plains, N.D. library assns., Zonta Internat., Nat. Fedn. Bus. and Profl. Women. Lutheran.

HATTEN, WILLIAM SEWARD, mfg. co. exec.; b. Chgo., Apr. 7, 1917; s. William Seward and Margaret (Ahearn) H.; B.A., Lawrence Coll., 1939; M.B.A., Northwestern U., 1944; m. Marjorie Popp, Dec. 29, 1939; 1 dau., Patricia Marie (Mrs. Dudley D. Pendleton III). Indsl. engr. Sears, Roebuck & Co., 1940-43; mgr. control div. Chgo. Ordnance Dist., 1943-45; owner Eskimo Ice Cream Co., Tucson, 1945-50; gen. mgr. Utica Knitting Co. (N.Y.), 1950-54; cons. Worden & Risberg, Phila., 1954-64; pres., chief exec. officer, dir. Clayton Mark & Co., Evanston, Ill., 1964-67; chmn. bd. Ken-Ray Brass Products, Inc., Vermont, Ill., 1964-67; pres., chief exec. officer, dir. Harper-Wyman Co., Hinsdale, Ill., 1967-69; exec. v.p. Warner Electric Brake & Clutch Co., Beloit, Wis., 1969—; dir. Beaver Precision Products, Inc., Troy, Mich., Martin Cantine Co., Saugerties, N.Y. Mem. Ill. C. of C., Chgo. Assn. Commerce and Industry, Am. Ordance Assn., N.A.M., Northwestern U. Grad. Bus. Alumni Assn., Am. Inst. Mgmt., Phi Delta Theta. Episcopalian. Clubs: Golf, University (Evanston); Union League, Executives (Chgo.). Home: 6906 Kinnikinnick Rd The Ledges Roscoe IL 61073 Office: Beloit WI 53511

HATZFELD, HELMUT ANTHONY, educator; b. Bad Duerkheim, Germany, Nov. 4, 1892; s. Conrad and Hortense (Maas) H.; B.A., Gymnasium Neustadt, 1911; Ph.D., U. Munich, 1915; Dr.h.c., U. Grenoble, 1959; L.H.D., Assumption Coll., 1959, LaSalle Coll., 1960, Cath. U. Am., 1964, U. Notre Dame, 1966, Marquette, 1967, George Washington U., 1968; m. Herta Scheitel, Aug. 6, 1924. Came U.S., 1940, naturalized, 1945. Privatdozent U. Frankfurt, 1922, extraordinary prof., 1923-32; substitute for ordinary prof. U. Königsberg (Germany), 1928-29; prof. Romance langs. U. Heidelberg (Germany), 1932-35; vis. prof. Louvain U., 1939-40, Cath. U. Am., Washington 1940-42, prof. Romance langs., 1942-68; cons. comparative lit., 1949-70, Revue de Littérature Comparée, 1958—. Recipient awards Academie Francaise, 1961, Institut des Inscriptions et Belles Lettres, 1962; Oxford award Modern Lang. Assn., 1949. Mem. Am. Assn. Tchrs. French, Am. Assn. Tchrs. Italian, Am. Assn. Tchrs. Spanish and Portuguese, Hispanic Soc. Am. (corr.), Bavarian Acad. Scis. (corr.). Author: Der Don Quijote als Wortkunstwork, 1927; Literature through Art, 1952; Trends and Styles in Twentieth Century French Literature, 1957. Bibliographie Critique de la Nouvelle Stylistique, 1961; Saggi di Stilistica Romanza, vol. I, 1967, vol. II, 1971; Estudios Sobre el Barroco, 1968; Santa Teresa, 1969. Home: 2401 Calvert St NW Washington DC 20008

HAUBERG, JOHN HENRY, lumber co. exec.; b. Rock Island, Ill., June 24, 1916; s. John Henry and Suzanne Christine (Denkmann) H.; grad. Hotchkiss Sch., 1935; student Princeton, 1939; B.S. in Forestry, U. Wash., 1949; m. Anne Westbrook Gould, June 9, 1941; children—Fay Westbrook, Sue Bradford. Pres. Pacific Denkmann Co., Seattle, 1953—; dir. Weyerhaeuser Co., Equity Fund, Inc., Seattle, Standard Ins. Co., Portland. Mem. platform com. Republican Nat. Conv., 1960. Trustee Reed Coll., Portland; trustee, past pres. bd. Helen Bush Sch.; trustee U. Puget Sound, Seattle Found.; pres. Found. for Handicapped Children; trustee, pres. Victoria Ranch, Inc. Mem. Northwest Hardwoods Assn. (founder, trustee), Soc. Am. Foresters, Phi Beta Kappa, Phi Sigma, Xi Sigma Pi. Presbyn. (vestryman). Home: 1101 McGilvra Blvd Seattle WA 98102 Office: Washington Bldg Seattle WA 98101

HAUBERG, ROBERT ENGELBRECHT, U.S. dist. atty.; b. Brookhaven, Miss., Nov. 20, 1910; s. Frederick and Wilhelmina (Mortensen) H.; student Millsaps Coll., 1928-30; LL.B., Jackson (Miss.) Sch. Law, 1932; m. Robbie Mae Bowen, Dec. 11, 1940; 1 son, Robert Engelbrecht. Admitted to Miss. bar, 1932, since practiced in Jackson; prof. law Jackson Sch. Law, 1933-64, registrar, vice-dean and dean, 1938-54; asst. city pros. atty., Jackson, 1932-37; asst. U.S. atty., 1944-54; U.S. dist. atty. for So. Dist. Miss., 1954—. Mem. Miss. Senate from 12th senatorial dist., 1940-44. Treas. Hinds County chpt. A.R.C., 1937-46; bd. dirs. Miss. Assn. on Crime and Delinquency, 1941; mem. Jackson Juvenile Council; mem. Council Social Agys., 1939-43. Mem. Fed., Am., Miss., Hinds County bar assns., Jackson Jr. C. of C. (charter mem., pres. 1935), Alpha Omega, Sigma Delta Kappa. Methodist. Club: Knife and Fork. Home: 1045 Claiborne St Jackson MS 39209 Office: Post Office Bldg Jackson MS 39205

HAUBIEL, CHARLES, composer-pianist; b. Delta, O., Jan. 30, 1892; s. Edward Marion Pratt and Mary Matilda (Haubiel) Pratt; student Berlin and Leipzig, 1909-13, Paris, 1919; grad. David Mannes Coll. of Music, 1919- 24; pupil of Rudolph Ganz, Josef and Rosina Lhevinne in piano, Rosario Scalero in composition; Mus. D., Southwestern Conservatory; m. Mary Rice Storke. Concert pianist, 1912-13; tchr. piano Kingfisher Coll., 1913-15, Musical Art Inst., Oklahoma City, 1915-17, Inst. of Musical Art of Juilliard Found., 1922-30; prof. composition N.Y.U., 1923-47; pres. The Composers Press, 1935-67. Composer Berta (Mexican Folk opera), 1950; recorded compositions include: New Music for the Piano Teacher, Albums 1-2, 1960- 62; Portraits (for symphony orch.); Pioneers (symphonic saga); In the French Manner (trio flute, cello, piano); Sonata for Cello and Piano; Gothic Variations and Nuances for Violas and Piano; Solati for Piano. Prize works include: Karma (Of Human Destiny) (Schubert Centennial award 1928); Ritratti, Swift Symphonic contest, 1935; The Plane Beyond, N.Y. Philharmonic Symphony Soc. contest, 1938; Distinguished Service to Music award, Internat. Piano Tchrs. Assn., 1953; Martha Kinney Cooper citation Ohioana Library Assn., 1953, Pegasus award, outstanding cultural contbns., 1967; Double Three Star award of merit Nat. Fedn. Music Clubs, 1963, Special Two Star award of merit, 1965. Served as 2d lt., bandmaster, 1917-19. Mem. Am. Soc. Composers, Authors and Publishers, Nat. Assn. for Am. Composers and Condrs. Republican. Episcopalian. Clubs: Bohemians, Musicians (N.Y.C.). Recording artist So. Music Co. Home: 4941 Ambrose Av Los Angeles CA 90027

HAUCK, CHARLES FRANCIS, mfg. and engring. co. exec.; b. Cleve., Sept. 26, 1912; s. William C. and Nell (Terwoord) H.; B.S., John Carroll U., 1940; m. Lillian B. Nocar, Aug. 19, 1940; children—Nancy, Judy, Terry, William. Plant engr. Atlas Powder Co., 1940-45; sr. staff design engr. Hagan Chem. & Control Co., 1946-51; mgr., v.p. sales chem. plants div. Blaw-Knox Co., Pitts., 1952-64, v.p., gen. mgr. chem. plants div., 1964-67, sr. v.p., 1967, pres., 1967—, chief exec. officer, 1968- -; v.p., dir. White Consol. Industries, Inc., 1968—. Mem. Pitts. C. of C., Am. Inst. Chem. Engrs. (exec. council past chmn. Pitts.), Am. Petroleum Inst., Am. Iron and Steel Inst., Nat. Soc. Profl. Engrs., Am. Arbitration Assn. Clubs: Duquesne, Field (Pitts.); Laurel Valley Golf (Ligonier, Pa.). Office: 1 Oliver Plaza Pittsburgh PA 15222

HAUCK, HERMAN JOHN, ednl. adminstr.; b. Cliffside, N.J., Dec. 11, 1911; s. Charles and Frances (Greubel) H.; A.B., Gonzaga U., 1935, M.A., 1936; S.T.L., 1950. Mem. Soc. of Jesus (The Jesuits), 1929—; instr. English, Santa Clara (Cal.) U., 1936-38, asst. prof. theology, 1942-43, pres., 1951-58; regional dir. studies Cal. Jesuit Univs., 1958—; asso. prof. English, U. San Francisco, 1949-51. Superior summer sch. Loyola U., 1949; rector Mission Santa Clara, 1951-58; sec.-treas. Conf. Religious Dirs. Edn., 1968—; chmn. Jesuit Assn. Personnel Edn., 1970—; commr. State of Cal. Scholarship Program, 1955-67, vice chmn., 1959-61, chmn., 1962-67. Mem. Jesuit Edn. Assn. (mem. exec. com., 1958-64) Am. Council Edn. (mem. Pacific Coast Com. 1956- 58), Nat. Cath. Edn. Assn. (chmn. S.W. region, coll. div. 1954-55, vice chmn. 1964-66, chmn. 1966-67), Western Coll. Assn. (v.p. 1954-55, pres., 1955-56), Cal. Ind. Found. (v.p. 1956- 57), Western Assn. Schs. and Colls. (sr. commn. 1965-70). Contbr. articles profl. jours. Lectr. Address: PO Box 519 Los Gatos CA 95030

HAUCK, HUBERT HOWARD, banker; b. Dayton, O., June 6, 1917; s. Arthur A. and Gladys (Hubert) H.; A.B., Harvard, 1938; m. Eleanor Elaine Letson, June 1, 1940; children—Thomas A., Bruce A., John A., Asso. advt. Gannett Pub. Co., 1938-41; treas., sec. Eastern Marine Products Co., Me. Sea Products Corp., Me. Marine Products, Inc., 1946-60; exec. v.p. First Portland Nat. Bank, 1959-60; pres. Me. Nat. Bank, Portland, 1960-69, chmn., chief exec-officer, 1969—; bd. corporators Portland Savs. Bank; dir. Central Me. Power Co., Coca-Cola Bottling Plants, Inc. (Me.), Me. Bonding and Casualty Co. Chmn. Portland dist. Boy Scouts Am., 1952-54, Greater Portland Community Chest drive, 1953; pres. Portland YMCA, 1952-53; exec. com. Me. Council for Econ. Edn., 1969—; mem. Portland Planning Bd. Bd. dirs., United Fund (pres. 1957-58), Falmouth Sch.; pres. Greater Portland Area Devel. Council; trustee Westbrook Coll., Me. Med. Center (pres. 1969—), Northeast Research Found., U. Me.; v.p., trustee U. Me. Found., 1961-67; trustee M. Maine Devel. Council. Served with USNR, 1944-45. Recipient civic award U.S. Jr. C. of C., 1952, Distinguished Service award Kiwanis Club, 1964. Mem. Am. Bankers Assn. (nat. chmn. edn. in econs. 1965-70, chmn. exec. com. nat. bank div. 1970-71; trustee Found. Edn. in Econs.), New Eng. Lawn Tennis Assn. (exec. com.), Portland C. of C. (past treas.), Me. Bankers Assn. (pres. 1965-66). Conglist. Mason (32, Shriner), Rotarian. Clubs: Cumberland, Portland Country, Harvard. Home: Longmeadow Rd Cumberland Foreside ME 04021 Office: 400 Congress St Portland ME 04111

HAUCK, JOHN CHRISTIAN, utility exec.; b. Philipsburg, Mont., Dec. 22, 1910; s. Lawrence and Dora (Kroger) H.; B.A., U. Mont., 1934, J.D., 1934; m. Elizabeth Carman, Nov. 7, 1957; children—John Christian II, Robert L., Thomas C., Mary T. Admitted to Mont. bar, 1934; atty. The Montana Power Co., Butte, 1936—, sr. counsel, 1966—, sec., 1969—, v.p., 1971—. Mem. Am., Mont. bar assns. Kiwanian. Home: 845 W Galena St Butte MT 59701 Office: 40 E Broadway Butte MT 59701

HAUCK, JOHN JOSEPH, labor union exec.; b. Phila., Nov. 26, 1902; s. John C. and Carrie (Kirk) H.; ed. pub. and night schs.; m. Alice Victoria Whitt, Oct. 21, 1925; 1 son, John E. Mem. Operative Plasterers and Cement Masons Internat. Assn. U.S. and Can., 1919—, internat. v.p., 1941-43, 1st v.p., 1943-54, gen. sec.-treas., 1954—. Mem. Am. Concrete Inst. Club: Touchdown (Washington). Home: 8700 Fallen Oak Dr Bethesda MD 20034 Office: 1125 17th St NW Washington DC 20036

HAUDEREVSKI, KEVIN mfg. exec.; b. Lima, O., Apr. 1, 1932; B.S., U. San Francisco, 1954; M.S., Stanford University, 1956; m. Rosemarie Lois Brown, May 15, 1955; 1 son, Anthony Robinson. Sales rep. Ames-Brockton Fabricated Products, Akron, O., 1956-58, sales mgr. Coshocton, Ohio, 1959-61, gen. manager plant, 1961-68, v.p. sales, 1968--. Instr. bus. Coshocton Jr. College, 1968-69. Secretary Coshocton YMCA, 1960-61; active Boy Scouts of America. Named Man of Year, Coshocton Junior Chamber of Commerce, 1968. Mem. Coshocton C. of C. (vice president 1967-68, pres. 1969-70), English Speaking Union, Coshocton Sertoma Club, Nat. Assn. Mfrs., Sales Executives Institute, Phi Beta Kappa, Sigma Chi, Phi Mu. Democrat. Mem. Christian Ch. (lay leader). Mason (32, Shriner). Clubs: Coshocton Country, Coshocton City, Running Deer Country. Home: 2d Av Coshocton OH Office: 3d Av Coshocton OH

HAUER, R.J., food co. exec.; b. 1911; ed. U. Notre Dame. 1934; married. Auditor, Lamperrt Yards Inc., St. Paul, 1934-39; with income tax div., Minn., 1939-45; with Pillsbury Co., 1945—, sec., asst. treas., 1962—. Address: 608 2d Av S Minneapolis MN 55402*

HAUF, HAROLD DANA, educator; born Utica, N.Y., June 27, 1905; s. Martin J. and Helena (Dana) H.; B.S. in A.E., U. Mich., 1927; M.S., Yale, 1932; m. Dorothy A. Nix, April 14, 1928; 1 dau., Carolyn Dana. Instr. civil engring. Yale, 1929-32, asst. prof. archtl. engring., 1933-39, asso. prof., 1939- 46, prof., 1947-49, chmn. dept. architecture, 1947-49; cons. archtl. engring., New Haven, 1929-49; became editor Archtl. Record, 1949. Cons. examiner Conn. Architecture Registration Bd., 1935-41; spl. cons. to Conn. State Comptroller on Reorgn. of State Pub. Works Div., 1947; dir. tech. br. Nat. Housing Agy., Washington, in connection with Vets Emergency Housing Program; research asso. Yale, 1952-53, also mng. engr. Yale's Edwards St. Lab.; dir. profl. relations A.I.A., 1953-54; head dept. architecture and chmn. archtl. group Rensselaer Poly. Inst., 1954-57, dean Sch. Architecture, 1957-61; v.p., dir. architecture Charles Luckman Assos., N.Y.C. and Los Angeles, 1961-63; prof. architecture U. So. Cal., Los Angeles, 1964-70. Past chmn. bldg. research adv. bd. NCR. Served to comdr. Civil Engr. Corps USNR, 1941- 45, 51-52. Registered architect, Ariz., N.Y., Cal.; registered engr., Ariz. N.Y., Cal. Fellow A.I.A., Am. Soc. C.E.; mem. Bldg. Research Inst. (gov. 1959-61), Nat Acad. Sci., Sigma Xi. Author: Design of Steel Buildings, 1932; Building Contracts for Design and Construction, 1968. Home: 13224 108th Dr Sun City AZ 85351

HAUG, CLARENCE CARL, ret. army officer; b. Spillville, Ia., Aug. 17, 1910; s. Carl R. and Louise (Fisher) H.; student U. Ia., 1928-31; B.S., U.S. Mil. Acad., 1935; M.S. in Engring., Cornell U., 1938; grad. Army Engr. Sch., 1939, Naval War Coll., 1949; m. Carolyn Hester Meyers, Nov. 18, 1936; children—Louise Ann (Mrs. Charles A. Mays), Mary Catherine, Robert C. Commd. 2d. Lt. U.S. Army, 1935, advanced through grades to maj. gen., 1960; various assignments in U.S. and ETO, 1935-46; exec. officer, dir. mil. constrn. Office Chief Engrs., 1946-48; comdg. officer Yuma (Ariz.) Test Br., 1949; dist. engr. Sacramento Engrs. Dist., 1950-53; comdg. officer 19th Engr. Group, Korea, 1953-54; dep. engr. 8th U.S. Army, Korea, 1954; comdg. officer 2d Amphibious Support Brigade, Japan, 1954- 55; chief properties and installations Office Asst. Sec. Army, 1955-58; chief engr. office Hdqrs. Army Ordnance Missile Command, Redstone Arsenal, Ala., 1958-61; dep. dir. mil. constrn. Office Chief Engrs., 1961-62; dir. installations and services Hdqrs. Army Material Command, 1962, chief Mut. Security Office, 1962-65; spl. asst. to comdg. gen. U.S. Army, Ryuku Islands, 1965; comdg. gen. 2d Logistical Command, Okinawa, 1965-68; div. engr. U.S. Army Engr. Div., Southwestern, Dallas, 1968-69, ret., 1969; gen. mgr. Acres Internat. (Overseas) Ltd., 1969—; gen. cons. East Pakistan Water and Power Devel. Authority, Dacca, 1969—. Decorated D.S.M. with oak leaf cluster, Legion of Merit with 2 oak leaf clusters, Army Commendation medal. Mem. Theta Xi, Theta Tau, Tau Beta Pi, Chi Epsilon. Home: Spillville IA 52168 Office: Acres Internat (Overseas) Ltd Epwapda Bldg PO Box 160 Dacca 2 East Pakistan

HAUGAN, RANDOLPH EDGAR, publisher; b.Martel, Wis., July 31, 1902; s. Torgier H. and Hilda (Ehrhardt) H.; A.B., St. Olaf Coll., Northfield, Minn. 1924; LL.D., Luther Coll., Decorah, Ia., 1944; m. Mildred Kathryn Knudson, Aug. 5, 19; children—James, Mary. Gen. mgr. Augsburg Pub. House, Mpls., 1929-70; dir. Marquette Nat. Bank, Mpls., Luth. Brotherhood (Legal Res. Life Ins.), Mpls., 1947-59; v.p. Graphic Arts Industry, Mpls. 1939-54; nat. pres. Pubs. Adv. Sect. of Internat. Council Religious Edn., 1941-42; mem. Charter Commn., Mpls. 1944. Chmn. bd. trustees St. Olaf Coll., 1950-54. Bd. mem. United Hosp. Fund, Minn. Coll. Fund Assn. Mem. Selective Service Bd., Hennepin County; state chmn. Am. Relief for Norway. Dir. First Fed. Savs. and Loan Assn. (Mpls.); v.p. bd. dirs. Fairview Hosp., Mpls., mem. joint polity and orgn. com. formation Am-Luth. Ch.; bd. mem. bd. Protestant Ch.-Owner Pubs. Assn., 1952—; exec. dir. div. publs. Am. Luth. Ch., 1961-70. Mem. joint polity and orgn. com. formation Evang. Luth. Church of Canada. Decorated Knight, First Class, Royal Order of St. Olaf (Norway), 1948. Mem. Am. Inst. Mgmt. (pres.'s council), Am. Inst. Graphic Arts; Mpls. Community Research Council, Inc. (dir.), Minn. Poll (adv. bd), Nat. Luth. Council (councilor 1945-54, 61—). Republican. Kiwanian. Clubs: Minneapolis, Minneapolis Athletic. Editor: Christmas in Many Lands, Vols. 1-3, 1936-38; Yuletide in Many Lands, Vols. 4-7, 1939-42. Editor of "Christmas, An American Annual." Home: 133 W 50th St Minneapolis MN 55410 Office: 426 S Fifth St Minneapolis MN 55415

HAUGE, GABRIEL, trust co. exec. b. Hawley, Minn., Mar. 7, 1914; s. Soren Gabrielson and Anna B. (Thompson) H.; A.B., Concordia Coll., Moorhead, Minn., 1935, LL.D., 1957; George Christian fellow, Harvard, 1936-38, M.A., 1938, Social Sci. Research Council fellow, 1946, Ph.D., 1947; LL.D., Bryant Coll. 1958, Muhlenberg Coll., 1959, Gettysburg Coll., 1960; m. Helen Landsdowne Resor, Nov. 6, 1948; children—Ann Bayliss, Stephen Burnet, John Resor (twins), Barbara, Susan, Elizabeth, Caroline. Asst. dean of men, coach forensics Concordia Coll., 1935-36; budget examiner Office Commr. Budget, State of Minn., 1938; instr. econs. Harvard, 1938-40; sr. statistician Fed. Res. Bank of N.Y., 1939; instr. econs. Princeton, 1940-42; chief div. research and statistics, N.Y. State Banking Dept., 1947-50; mem. tech. commn. Joint N.Y. Legislative Com. on Interstate Cooperation, 1949-50; editor Trend editorial, Bus. Week Mag., asst. chmn. exec. com. McGraw-Hill Pub. Co., Inc., 1950-52; research dir. Citizens for Eisenhower, 1951-52; research dir. personal campaign staff Dwight D. Eisenhower, 1952; adminstrv. asst. to Pres. of U.S. for econ. affairs, 1953-56, spl. asst. to Pres. of U.S. for econ. affairs, 1956-58; dir., chmn. finance com. Mfrs. Trust Co., N.Y.C., 1958-61; vice chmn. bd. Mfrs. Hanover Trust Co., 1961-63, pres., now chmn. bd.; dir. N.Y. Life Ins. Co., Am. Metal Climax, Inc.; dir. or trustee Harlem Savs. Bank, Mfrs. Hanover Internat. Finance Corp., Mfrs. Hanover Internat. Banking Corp., Am. Home Products Corp., 950 Park Av. Corp., Religion Am. Life, Inc.; dir. Greater N.Y. Fund, Bklyn., Union Gas Co., Trustee Juilliard Mus. Found.; trustee or dir. Nat. Bur. Econ. Research, Carnegie Endowment Internat. Peace, Com. for Econ. Devel.; vis. com. to dept. econs. Harvard. Served from ensign to lt. comdr., USNR, 1942-46.; lt. comdr. Res. Mem. Council Fgn. Relations (dir.) N.Y.C., Assn. Res. City Bankers, Pilgrims U.S., Am. Econs. Assn., U.S. Naval Inst., N.Y. Young Republican Club. Lutheran. Clubs: Economic, University, Links, Recess, Century Assn. (N.Y.C.). Home: 950 Park Av New York City NY 10028 Office: 350 Park Av New York City NY 10022

HAUGEN, EINAR INGVALD, educator; b. Sioux City, Ia., Apr. 19, 1906; s. John and Kristine (Gorset) H.; student Morningside Coll., Sioux City, 1924-27; B.A., St. Olaf Coll., 1928, D.H.L. (hon.), 1958; M.A., U. Ill., 1929, Ph.D., 1931; Litt.D., U. Mich., 1953; M.A. (hon.), Harvard, 1960; Ph.D. honoris causa, U. Oslo (Norway), 1961; m. Eva Lund, June 18, 1932; children—Anne Margaret, Camilla Christine. Asst. prof. Scandinavian langs., U. Wis., 1931-36, asso. prof., 1936-38, Thompson prof. Scandinavian langs., 1938-62, Vilas research prof. Scandinavian lang. and linguistics, 1962-64, Victor S. Thomas prof., Harvard, 1964—; dir. Linguistic Inst., 1943-1944; tchr. army specialized tng. program, 1943-44; cultural relations officer (attaché) Am. embassy, Oslo, 1945-46. Guest lectr. U. Oslo, 1938, Fulbright research prof., 1951-52; instr. summers U. Minn., 1948, 1958, U. Mich., 1949, Georgetown U., 1954, Ind. U., 1964; cons. Eng. Lang. Exploratory Com., Tokyo, Japan, summer 1958, 1st sem. 1959-60. Guggenheim fellow, 1942-43; spl. State Dept. lectr. U. Iceland, Reykjavik, and other Scandinavian univs., 1955-56; pres. IX Internat. Congress Linguists, pres., 1966—. Bd. dirs. Center for Applied Linguistics. Decorated Order of St. Olaf, 1st class (Norway); Order of North Star (Sweden). Recipient fellow Center Advanced Study Behavioral Studies, 1963-64; sr. fellow Nat. Endowment for Humanities, 1967-68. Mem. Am. Acad. Arts and Scis., Icelandic, Norwegian, Swedish acads. sci., Royal Norwegian Sci. Soc., Am. Dialect Soc. (pres. 1965), Modern Lang. Assn., Linguistic Soc. Am. (pres. 1950), Norwegian-Am. Hist. Assn. (bd. editors), others. Author: Beginning Norwegian, 1937; Norsk i Amerika (Oslo), 1939; Reading Norwegian, 1940; Norwegian Word Studies, 2 vols., 1941; Voyages to Finland, 1941, 42; Spoken Norwegian, 1946 (with K.G. Chapman rev. edit. 1964); First Grammatical Treatise, 1950, rev. edit., 1971; Norwegian Language in America: A Study in Bilingual Behavior, 1953, rev. edit., 1969; Bilingualism in the Americas: A Guide to Research, 1957, 2d edit., 1964; Norwegian-English Dictionary, 1965; Language Conflict and Language Planning: The Case of Modern Norwegian, 1966; Riksspråk og folkemal, 1969. Translated Beyer's History of Norwegian Lit., 1956; Fire and Ice, Three Icelandic Plays, 1967; The Norwegians in America, 1967. Contbr. to publs. Home: 45 Larch Circle Belmont MA 02178 Office: Boylston Hall Harvard U Cambridge MA 02138

HAUGERUD, HOWARD EDWARD, govt. ofcl.; b. Harmony, Minn., Aug. 22, 1924; s. Sherman Allen and Anna (Armstrong) H.; B.A., U. Minn., 1955; m. Mary E. Stafford, Apr. 2, 1946; children—Mark, James Sherman, Kent, Lisa. Asst. to U.S. Senator Humphrey, 1956-59; profl. staff mem., subcom. nat. policy machinery U.S. Senate Com. Govt. Operations, 1959-61; dep. undersec. army for internat. affairs, 1961-63; asst. sec. state, dep. insp. gen. fgn. assistance, 1963-69; chmn. Nat. Interdepartmental Seminar, 1969—; Pres. U.S. Senate staff, 1956-58, Pres. bd. McClellan Meml. Fund, 1958—, Capitol Hill Symphony Soc., 1964-66. Served as pilot USAAF, 1942- 45, 48-53. Recipient Exceptional Civilian Service medal Army Dept., 1963; award for saving a life A.R.C. Mem. Army Aviation Asso. (v.p. 1957-61), Sigma Delta Chi. Club: International (Washington). Home: 2609 S Hayes St Arlington VA 22202 Office: Dept of State Washington DC 20520

HAUGH, ROBERT DARRELL, coll. pres.; b. Venice, Cal., July 26, 1914; s. Byron Darrell and Maude Sally (Dingman) H.; A.B., U. So. Cal., 1935, M.S. in Edn., 1949, Ed.D., 1956; m. Helen W. Osterhage, Nov. 18, 1939; children—Judy Lou, Nancy Lee. Tchr. social sci., varsity baseball Paso Robles (Cal.) High Sch., 1939-41; tchr. history El Monte (Cal.) High Sch., 1941-42; edn. and rehab. officer VA, 1946-47; counselor Pasadena (Cal.) City Coll., 1947- 48, dean men, 1948-52, dean student activities, 1952-59; pres. Glendale (Cal.) Coll., 1959-67, Citrus Coll., Azusa, Cal., 1967—. Mem. exec. com. Bank of Am. jr. coll. awards, adv. council U. So. Cal. Sch. Relations, chmn. alumni scholarship com. Bd. dirs. Monrovia (Cal.) Family Service Assn., Glendale chpt. A.R.C. Served to lt. (s.g.) USNR, 1942-45. Named Man of Yr., Sigma Sigma, 1970. Mem. N.E.A., Cal. Tchrs. Assn., Am. Assn. Jr. Colls., Cal. Jr. Coll. Assn., So. Cal. Jr. Coll. Deans Assn. (pres. 1959), P.T.A. (hon. life), Glendale C. of C., Educare, Blue Key, Skull and Dagger, Phi Delta Kappa, Delta Epsilon, Kappa Sigma (pres.). Baptist (past chmn. deacons). Kiwanian. Home: 180 Stedman Pl Monrovia CA 91016 Office: Citrus Coll 18824 E Foothill Blvd Azusa CA 91702

HAUGH, ROBERT JAMES, ins. co. exec.; b. Milw., Jan. 19, 1926; s. John Joseph and Adeline Margaret (Bolmes) H.; J.D., Marquette U., 1948; m. Mary Jane Botsch, Oct. 15, 1949; children—Robert James, Jane Elizabeth, William R., Nancy Ann. Admitted to Wis. bar, 1948; practiced law, Milw., 1948-60; claims mgr. St. Paul Ins. Cos., Milw., 1948-60, gen. adjuster, St. Paul, 1960-62, asst. sec., 1962-67, sec., 1967-69, asst. v.p., treas., 1969—. Mem. Sigma Nu Phi. Roman Catholic. Club: St. Paul Athletic. Home: 643 Sunset Lane St Paul MN 55118 Office: St Paul Fire and Marine Insurance Co 385 Washington St St Paul MN 55102

HAUGHEY, JAMES MCCREA, lawyer, artist; b. Courtland, Kan., July 8, 1914; s. Leo Eugene and Elizabeth (Stephens) H.; LL.B., U. Kan., 1939; m. Katherine Hurd, Sept. 8, 1938; children—Katherine (Mrs. Lester B. Loo), Bruce Stephens, John Caldwell. Admitted to Kan. bar, 1939, Mont. bar, 1943; landman Carter Oil Co., 1939-43; practice in Billings, Mont., 1943—; partner firm Crowley, Kilbourne, Haughey, Hanson & Gallagher, 1957—; one man exhbns. include U. Kan., U. Mont., Mont. State U., Concordia Coll., C.M. Russell Gallery, Great Falls, Mont., Boise Mus. Art, Mont. State Mus., Helena, also numerous group shows. Pres., Rocky Mountain Mineral Law Found., 1957- 58, trustee, 1955—; pres. Mont. Inst. Arts Found., 1965-67, Yellowstone Art Center Found., 1969—. Mem. Mont. Ho. of Reps., 1960-64, Mont. Senate, 1966-70; senate minority leader, 1969-70. Fellow Mont. Inst. Arts (Permanent Collection award 1960); mem. Am., Yellowstone County (pres. 1960-61) bar assns., Am., Northwest watercolor socs., Am. Judicature Soc., Am. Artists Profl. League. Republican. Episcopalian. Home: 2205 Tree Lane Billings MT 59102 Office: Electric Bldg Billings MT 59101

HAUGHEY, ROGER E., lawyer; b. Normal, Ill., Apr. 28, 1928; s. Daniel Max and Berta (Ross) H.; B.A., Ill. State Normal U., 1948; J.D., U. Ill., 1951; m. Frances Isabelle Willet, June 29, 1952; children—Bruce William, Douglas Roger, Jeffrey Thomas. Admitted to Ill. bar; practice in Champaign; partner firm Thomas, Mallikan & Mamer, 1964—; assoc. counsel to Revise Ill. Civil Practice Act Pres. McKinley YMCA; chmn. Champaign County Cancer Soc.; chmn. Champaign Plan Commn. Served with AUS, 1951-53. Mem. Am., Ill., Champaign County bar assns., Am. Judicature Soc., Phi Alpha Delta. Republican. Presbyn. Kiwanian. Home: 1510 Waverly St Champaign IL 61820 Office: 30 Main St Champaign IL 61820

HAUGHTON, DANIEL JEREMIAH, aerospace mfg. exec.; b. nr. Dora, Ala., Sept. 7, 1911; s. Gayle, Sr., and Mattie (Davis) H.; B.S., U. Ala., 1933, also LL.D.; LL.D. (hon.), George Washington U.; m. Martha Jean Oliver, Sept. 28, 1935. Cost accountant Consol. Aircraft Corp., San Diego, 1936-39; with Lockheed Aircraft Corp., or its subsidiaries, 1939—, beginning as systems analyst, successively coordinator, asst. to v.p. Vega Airplane Co., asst. gen. works mgr. and asst. to v.p. Lockheed Aircraft Corp., pres. Airquipment Co. and Aerol Co., Inc., asst. gen. mgr. Ga. div. Lockheed Aircraft Corp., gen. mgr., v.p., gen. mgr., 1952-56; exec. v.p. Lockheed Aircraft Corp., 1956-61, pres., 1961-67, chmn., 1967- -, dir. subsidiares; dir. United Cal. Bank, So. Cal. Edison Co. Pres. Nat. Multiple Sclerosis Soc. Mem. Nat. Def. Transp. Assn., Aerospace Industries Assn. (gov.). Clubs: California (Los Angeles); Captial City (Atlanta). Home: 12956 Blairwood Dr Studio City CA 91604 Office: Lockheed Aircraft Corp Burbank CA 91503

HAUGHTON, JAMES GRAY, municipal health ofcl.; b. Panama, Republic Panama, Mar. 20, 1925; s. Johnathan A. and Alice E. (Gray) H.; came to U.S., 1942, naturalized, 1953; student Pacific Union Coll., 1942-45, B.A., 1947; M.D., Loma Linda, U., 1950; M.P.H., Columbia, 1962; D.Sc. (hon.), U. Health Scis./Chgo. Med. Sch., 1971; m. Odessa L. Owens, July 2, 1950 (div. 1971); children—James Gray, Paula. Intern Unity Hosp., Bklyn., 1949-50; resident pub. health adminstrn. N.Y.C. Health Dept., 1960-62; pvt. practice, N.Y.C., 1952-66; dir. med. care N.Y.C. Health Dept., 1962-65, exec. dir. med. care services, 1965-66; 1st dep. commr. N.Y.C. Dept. Hosps., 1966; 1st dep. adminstr. Health Services Adminstrn. N.Y.C., 1966- 70; exec. dir. Health and Hosps. Governing Commn. Cook County, dir. Cook County Hosp., 1970—; adj. asst. prof. adminstrv. medicine Columbia Sch. Pub. Health, 1965- -. Bd. dirs. N.Y.C. Pub. Health Assn., Nat. Accreditation Com. Services to Blind; profl. services com. Chgo. Hosp. Council, 1971—; tech. adv. bd. Milbamk Meml. Fund, 1971. Served to lt. comdr., M.C., USNR, 1956-58. Recipient Merit award N.Y.C. Pub. Health Assn., 1964; Achievement award as outstanding naturalized citizen Travelers Aid Soc., Immigrants Service League. Diplomate Am. Bd. Preventive Medicine. Fellow Am. Pub. Health Assn. (gov. council), Am. Geriatric Soc., Am. Coll. Preventive Medicine, N.Y. Acad. Medicine, Inst. Medicine, Chgo.; mem. Royal Soc. Health (Gt. Britain). Contbr. profl. jours. Office: Health and Hosps Governing Commn Cook County 1900 W Polk St Chicago IL 60612

HAUGHTON, RONALD WARING, educator, arbitrator; b. Toronto, Can., July 20, 1916; s. Herbert J. and Lilian J. (Strachan) H.; brought to U.S., 1927; naturalized, 1927; B.A., U. Wash., 1937; M.A., U. Wis., 1938; m. Anne Fletcher, Feb. 23, 1952; children—Jan, Patricia, Leslie, John. Assembly worker Gen. Electric Co., 1936-37; chief contested claims Wash. State Unemployment Compensation Div., 1938-40; Rockefeller research grant, 1940; tech. adviser U.S. Social Security Bd., 1941-42; successively disputes dir. Detroit Regional War Labor Bd., dir. strike div. Nat. War Labor Bd., 1942-45; spl. asst. dir. Inst. Indsl. Relations, U. Cal. at Berkeley, 1947-50; impartial arbitrator Ford Motor Co. and United Automobile Workers, 1950- 55; prof. mgmt., co-dir. Inst. Labor and Indsl. Relations, U. Mich., Wayne State U., 1956—; pres. Bd Mediation for community disputes, N.Y.C., 1970-71; permanent arbitrator labor disputes bus. firms and unions. Chmn. Ford Motor Co.-United Autor Workers Joint Pension Bd.; cons. to Sec. of Labor, 1960, 63, to USAF, 1961, to govt. agys., 1960-62, to UN, Minsk, Russia, 1964. Mem. adv. com. on Pres.'s Com. Equal Employment Opportunity; chmn. Presdl. Fact Finding Bds. in maritime, r.r. and airline industries, 1962- 64; fact finder for govs. Mich., Cal., 1966—; lectr. U. Stockholm, Sweden, 1966; mem. Detroit Indsl. Mission. Mem. Am. Arbitration Assn. (dir.), Nat. Acad. Arbitrators (past sec.), Indsl. Relations Research Assn., Am. Econ. Assn. Club: Economic (Detroit). Mem. Soc. of Friends. Home: 269 Cloverly Rd Grosse Pointe Farms MI 48236 Office: Wayne State U Detroit MI 48202

HAUGLAND, JOHN CLARENCE, univ. dean; b. Superior, Wis., Nov. 29, 1929; s. Christ R. and Molla (Haugen) H.; B.S., Wis. State U., Superior, 1954; postgrad. U. Wis., 1955; M.A., U. Minn., 1958, Ph.D., 1961; m. Joan C. Palm, Sept. 23, 1950; children—Debra Ann, Gregg John. Tchr. pub. schs., Manitowoc, Wis., 1954-56; with J.C. Penney Co., Sioux City, Ia., 1956-57; adminstrv. fellow, faculty U. Minn., 1957-61, tchr., asst. grad. dean, 1963-65; faculty Wis. State U., Superior, 1961-63, 66—, dean letters and sci., 1966-67, v.p. acad. affairs, dean of faculty, 1967—; postdoctoral acad. adminstrn. internship Am. Council Edn., U. Md., 1965-66. Mem. Douglas County Overall Econ. Devel. Plan Com., 1968—. Alderman, Superior City Council, 1971—. Bd. dirs. Wis. Community Devel. Inst., Superior YMCA, Catholic Charities Bur. Served with U.S. Army, 1948-50, 50-51. Recipient U. Minn. Grad. Sch. grant, 1960, Wis. State U.- Superior research grant, 1962. Mem. Am. Assn. U. Profs., Minn. Hist. Soc., Orgn. Am. Historians, Assn. Wis. State U. Faculties, Superior C. of C. Rotarian. Contbr. articles profl. jours. Home: 1717 Ogden Av Superior WI 54880

HAUK, A. ANDREW, judge; b. Denver, Dec. 29, 1912; s. A.A. and Pearl (Woods) H.; A.B., Regis Coll., 1935; LL.B., Cath. Univ. Am., 1938; J.S.D., Yale, 1942; m. Jean Nicolay, Aug. 30, 1941; 1 dau., Susan. Admitted to Cal. bar, Colo. bar, D.C. bar; spl. asst. to atty. gen., counsel for govt. antitrust div. U.S. Dept Justice, Los Angeles, Pacific Coast, Denver, 1939-41; asst. U.S. dist. atty., Los Angeles, 1941-42; with firm Adams, Duque & Hazeltine, Los Angeles, 1946-52; individual practice law, Los Angeles, 1952-64; asst. counsel Union Oil Co., Los Angeles, 1952-64; judge Superior Ct., Los Angeles County, 1964-66; U.S. dist. judge Central Dist. Cal., 1966—; lectr. U. So. Cal. Law Sch., 1947-56. Vice chmn. Cal. Olympic Com., 1958-62; ofcl. VIII Olympic Winter Games, Squaw Valley, 1960. Served from lt. to lt. comdr., USNR, 1942-46. Mem. Los Angeles Town Hall, World Affairs Council, Los Angeles County Bar Assn., Cal. State Bar, Am., Fed. bar assns., Lawyers Club Los Angeles, Am. Judicature Soc., Am. Legion, Navy League, U.S. Lawn Tennis Assn., So. Cal. Tennis Patrons Assn. (bd. govs.), Far West Ski Assn., Yale Law Sch. Assn. So. Cal. (dir., past pres.) Clubs: Yale of Southern Cal.; Newman; Valley Hunt (Pasadena); Jonathan (Los Angeles). Home: 1408 Ridge Way Pasadena CA 91106 Office: US Court House 312 N Spring St Los Angeles CA 90012

HAUKE, WILLIAM J., ins. co. exec.; b. Newark; A.B., U. Mich., M.A., 1951; married. With Pan Am. Life Ins. Co., 1951-53, with Continental Assurance Co., Chgo., 1953—, v.p. group dept., 1965-69, sr. v.p., 1969—. Served with USNR, 1943-46. Home: 182 W Elm St Wheaton IL 60187 Office: 310 S Michigan Av Chicago IL 60604

HAUN, HARRY THURMAN, film critic; b. Greenville, Tex., Aug. 24, 1940; s. John Thurman and Stella (Waddle) H.; B.A., So. Methodist U., 1962; m. Helen Lee Thornberry, Sept. 1, 1962. With Nashville Tennessean, 1963—, movie editor, critic, 1963—; critic judge 1st ann. USA Film Festival, Dallas, 1971; free-lance writer, 1956—; numerous appearances on local TV and radio. Mem. Sigma Delta Chi. Democrat. Home: 1719 Temple Av Nashville TN 37215 Office: 1100 Broadway Nashville TN 37215

HAUN, JAMES WILLIAM, food co. exec.; b. Birmingham, Ala., Sept. 8, 1924; s. James Cecil and Eva (Walker) H.; B.S. in Chem. Engring., U. Tex., 1946, M.S., 1948, Ph.D. (Humble Oil & Refining Co. fellow 1949-51), 1950; grad. Advanced Mgmt. Program, Harvard, 1961; m. Lucia Land, Sept. 6, 1946; children—James William, Lucy Margaret, Daniel Victor, Robert Paul. Instr. chem. engring. U. Tex., 1948-49; successively research engr., sr. research engr. and research group leader plastics div. Monsanto Chem. Co., 1950-56; with Gen.

Mills, Inc., Mpls., 1956—, dir. corp. engring., 1960- 63, v.p., 1963—; dir. Kenner Co., Cin., Parker Bros. Co., Salem, Mass., Craftmaster Corp. Nat. adv. council air pollution research Environmental Protection Agy. citizens adv. com. N. Hennepin State Jr. Coll. Served with USMCR, 1942- 46. Mem. Am. Inst. Chem. Engrs., N.A.M., Sigma Xi, Omega Chi Epsilon, Phi Lambda Upsilon. Home: 6912 E Fish Lake Rd Rt 2 Osseo MN 55369 Office: Gen Mills Inc Minneapolis MN 55440

HAUNSCHILD, OTHO HAROLD, shipbuilding co. exec.; b. Lockwood, Mo., Mar. 7, 1916; s. Walter Fred and Gertrude (Haubein) H.; student Tex. Coll. Arts and Industries; m. Helen Norsworthy, June 14, 1946; children—Harold Edward, Ann Elizabeth. With Levingston Shipbuilding Co., Orange, Tex., 1941—, v.p. prodn. 1967, pres., 1967—, also dir. Bd. dirs. A.R.C., Orange. Mem. Shipbuilders Council (v.p.), Soc. Naval Architects and Marine Engrs., Tex. Mfrs. Assn. (v.p. state affairs), Am. Waterways Operators Assn., Propeller Club U.S., C. of C. Orange. Lutheran (chmn. bd. stewardship). Lion (past pres.). Home: 1903 W Link St Orange TX 77630 Office: PO Box 968 91 Front St Orange TX 77630

HAUNZ, EDGAR ALFRED, physician; b. London, Eng., Dec. 12, 1910; s. Charles F. and Caroline (Weissenberger) H.; brought to U.S., 1916, naturalized, 1921; M.D., U. Buffalo, 1943; M.S. in Medicine, U. Minn., 1947; m. Millicent Arnold, Mar. 19, 1948; children—Barbara Jane, William Edgar. Intern Buffalo Gen. Hosp., 1943-44; resident fellow medicine Mayo Found., Mayo Clinic and Affiliated Hosps., Rochester, Minn., 1944-47; practice medicine, specializing in internal medicine and endocrinology, Grand Forks, N.D., 1947—; mem. staff St. Michael's Hosp., Deaconess Hosp., Grand Forks, chief of staff, 1968-69; prof., chmn. dept. medicine U. N.D. Sch. Medicine, 1960—. Spl. cons. in diabetes USPHS, 1952-60; founder Diabetic Children's Camp Sioux, 1952; lectr. on diabetes and endrocrinology, 1947—. Chmn., Greater Grand Forks chpt. A.R.C., 1956- 57; mem. Grand Forks Bd. Edn., 1955-64, pres., 1962-64; mem. Grand Forks Symphony Orch., mem. Nat. Med. Adv. Bd. on Ednl. Film Prodn. Bd. dirs. Medic-Alert, 1963. Recipient N.D. Gov.'s award for service to handicapped, 1966, Service to Mankind award Sertoma Club, 1963. Fellow A.C.P.; mem. Am. (dir., past chmn. bd. govs., asst. treas. 1968-70), N.D. (exec. sec.-treas.) diabetes assns., Pan Am., N.D. med, assns., Grand Forks Dist. Med. Soc. (past pres.), Am. Soc. Internal Medicine, Newcomen Soc. North Am., Sigma Xi. Kiwanian (hon. life, Distinguished Service award 1962), Rotarian (past dir. Grand Forks). Editorial bd. Jour. Clin. Medicine, 1950—, Jour. Lancet, 1955-68, Jour. Cardiovascular Diseases. Contbr. articles med. jours. and textbooks. Home: 1029 Lincoln Dr Grand Forks ND 58201 Office: Grand Forks Clinic 221 R 4th St Grand Forks ND 58201

HAUPERT, RAYMOND SAMUEL, bank cons; b. Watertown, Wis., Mar. 9, 1902; s. Albert Peter and Maria Louise (Moehrke) H.; A.B., Moravian Coll., 1922; B.D., Moravian Theol. Sem., 1924; M.A., U. Pa., 1926, Ph.D., 1931; D.Sc. in Edn., Lafayette Coll., 1950; LL.D., Lehigh U., 1951; L.H.D., Seton Hill Coll., Greensburg, Pa., 1965, Allentown Coll. of St. Francis, 1971; m. Esteele Hege McCanless, July 30, 1932; children—Albert Peter, William Hege (dec.), Thomas John, Stephen Andrew. Ordained to ministry Moravian Ch. in Am., 1924; instr. Bible, Lafayette Coll., 1924-26; asst. prof. Bibl. lit. and langs. Moravian Coll. and Theol. Sem., 1924-31, prof. 1931-44, pres., 1944-69, pres. emeritus, 1969—, also pres. Moravian Sem. and Coll. for Women, 1953—, following merger of two schs. became pres. merged corp. Moravian Coll., pres. emeritus, 1969—; dir. First Nat. Bank and Trust Co., Bethlehem; tng. cons. First Valley Bank, 1969—. Chmn. Christian edn. bd., Moravian Ch. in Am., No. Province, 1936-41; Joseph Henry Thayer fellow Am. Sch. Oriental Research, Jerusalem, Palestine, 1930-31. Vice chmn. bd. dirs. Hosp. Service Plan of Lehigh Valley; past chmn. bd. trustees St. Luke's Hosp., Bethlehem, Pa.; past dir. Bethlehem Library; past pres., dir. Historic Bethlehem, Inc. Trustee Moravian Music Found. Mem. Pa. Assn. Colls. and Univs. (pres. 1960-61, past chmn. commn. ind. colls. and univs.), Am. Oriental Soc., Archaeol. Inst. Am., Soc. Bibl. Lit. and Exegesis (asso. in council, treas. 1938-41). Nat. Assn. Bibl. Instrs., Assn. Am. Colls. (commn. on religion higher edn.), Council Protestant Colls. and Univs. (past dir., treas.), Fgn. Policy Assn. (Lehigh Valley br., past pres.), Newcomen Soc., Phi Beta Kappa. Clubs: Oriental (pres. 1944-45) (Phila.); Torch (pres. 1946-47) (Lehigh Valley, Pa.); Rotary (pres. 1947-48) (Bethlehem, Pa.). Author: The Transcription Theory of the Septuagint, 1934; The Lachish Letters, 1938; The Relation of Codex Vaticanus and the Lucianic Text in the Books of the Kings from the Viewpoint of the Old Latin and the Ethiopic Versions, 1931; Exploring the Jordan and Dead Sea with the U.S. Navy, 1945; Lachish Letters, The Biblical Archaeologist, 1939, Pioneers in Moravian Education, 1954. Home: 1841 Main St Bethlehem PA 18018 Office: Moravian Coll Bethlehem PA 18018

HAUPT, ENID ANNENBERG, mag. pub. and editor; b. Chgo.; d. Moses Louis and Friedman Annenberg; student Mt. Ida Sem., Newton, Mass.; m. Ira Haupt, Aug. 11, 1936. Spl. corr. Phila. Inquirer, 1942-53, asst. to pub., 1953-54; pub., editor in chief Seventeen mag., N.Y.C., 1954—. Recipient awards for work with young people. Author: The Seventeen Book of Young Living, 1957; The Seventeen Book of Etiquette and Entertaining, 1963; The Seventeen Guide to Your Widening World, 1965; column Young Living, 1958-65. Office: 320 Park Av New York City NY 10022

HAUPT, GEORGE EDWARD, Jr., lawyer; b. Omaha, Sept. 8, 1925; s. George Edward and Gladys Marie (Larson) H.; student Harvard, 1943; A.B. magna cum laude Marietta Coll., 1949; J.D., U. Cin., 1950; m. Ruth Elizabeth Williams, Apr. 4, 1947; children—Lorrayne Marie, Bruce William, Janet Louise, Jennifer Lynne; m. 2d Ruth Echols McKinney, Feb. 27, 1969. Admitted to Ohio bar, 1950, since practiced in Marietta; asso. William M. Summers, 1950-54; partner Summers, Haupt & Theisen, 1954—, now sr. partner; lectr. Marietta Coll., 1950-67. Mem. Bd. Edn. Muskingum Sch. Dist., 1955-58, pres., 1958; county chmn. Ohio Information Com., 1969—. Pres., trustee Marietta YMCA. Served with AUS, 1943-46. Mem. Am., Ohio, Washington County (past chmn.) bar assns., Am. Judicature Soc., Fedn. Ins. Counsel, Assn. Ins. Attys., Ohio Def. Assn., Def. Research Inst., Marietta C. of C., Marietta Coll. Alumni Assn. (past pres.), Order of Coif, Lambda Chi Alpha, Phi Delta Phi, Tau Pi Phi, Omicron Delta Kappa. Republican. Methodist. Mason (Shriner). Kiwanian. Home: 113 Hillcrest Dr Marietta OH 45750 Office: Peoples Bank Bldg Marietta OH 45750

HAUROWITZ, FELIX, educator, biochemist; b. Prague, Czechoslovakia, Mar. 1, 1896; s. Rudolf and Emilie (Russ) H.; M.D., German U., Prague, 1922, Sc.D., 1923; m. Gina Perutz, June 23, 1925. Came to U.S., 1948, naturalized, 1952. Asst. prof. physiol. chemistry Med. Sch. German U., Prague, 1952-30, asso. prof., 1930-39; head dept. biol. chemistry, also prof. Med. Sch. U. Istanbul (Turkey), 1939-48; prof. chemistry Ind. U., 1948—, Distinguished prof., 1958—; spl. research protein chemistry and immunochemistry. Recipient Paul Ehrlich prize and gold plaquette Paul Ehrlich Found., Frankfurt, Germany, 1960. Fellow Am. Acad. Arts and Sci.; mem. Am. Chem. Soc. (chmn. div. biol. chemistry 1962-63), Leopoldina Acad. Scis., Am. Soc. Biol. Chemists, Am. Assn. Immunologists, Societe Philomathique. Author: Biochemistry, 1955; Progress in Biochemistry since 1949, 1959; Chemistry and Function of Proteins, 1963; Immunochemistry and the Biosynthesis of Antibodies, 1968. Home: 417 S Henderson St Bloomington IN 47401

HAURWITZ, BERNHARD, educator; b. Glogau, Germany, Aug. 14, 1905; s. Paul and Betty (Cohn) H.; Ph.D., U. of Leipzig, 1927; m. Eva Schick, May 11, 1934 (div. Nov. 1946); 1 son, Francis David; m. 2d, Marion B. Wood, Jan. 16, 1961. Came to the U.S., 1941, naturalized, 1946. Privatdozent U. of Leipzig, 1931-32; research asso. Harvard, 1932-35; lectr. U. Toronto, 1935-37; meteorologist Dominion Can., 1937-41; asso. prof. meteorology, Mass. Inst. Tech., 1941-47; asso. Woods Hole Oceanographic Inst., 1947- 59; prof., chmn. dept. meteorology and oceanography N.Y.U., 1947-59; prof. astrogeophysics U. Colo., 1959-64, prof. geophysics, 1960; with Nat. Center Atmospheric Research, Boulder, Colo., 1964—, dir. advanced study program, 1968-69; prof. U. Tex., 1966-68. Recipient Rossby award Am. Meteorol. Soc., 1962. Mem. Nat. Acad. Sci., Deutsche Akademie der Naturforscher Leopoldina, Royal, Am. meteorol. socs., Am. Geophys. Union (Bowie award 1970), Am. Civil Liberties Union, Sigma Xi. Contbr. tech. articles numerous publs. Office: Nat Center Atmospheric Research Boulder CO 80302

HAURY, EMIL WALTER, educator, archaeologist; b. Newton, Kan., May 2, 1904; s. Gustav A. and Clara K. (Ruth) H.; student Bethel Coll., Newton, Kan., 1923-25; A.B., U. Ariz., 1927, A.M., 1928; Ph.D., Harvard, 1934; LL.D., U. N.M., 1959; m. Hulda E. Penner, June 7, 1928; children—Allan Gene, Loren Richard. Instr., U. Ariz., 1928-29, research asst. in dendrochronology, 1929-30, asst. dir. Gila Pueblo, Globe, Ariz., 1930-37, prof. anthropology U. Ariz., 1937-70, Fred A. Riecker Distinguished prof. anthropology, 1970—, head dept., 1937-64; dir. Ariz. State Mus., 1938-64. Guggenheim fellow, 1949- 50. Chmn. div. anthropology and psychology NRC, 1960-62; mem. Adv. Bd. Nat. Parks, Historic Sites, Bldgs. and Monuments, 1964-70, chmn., 1968-70. Viking Fund medalist in anthropology, 1950; recipient Alumni Achievement award U. Ariz., 1957; Salgo-Noren Found. award for teaching excellence, 1967. Mem. Nat. Council Humanities, Am. Philos. Soc., Am. Acad. Arts and Scis., Nat. Speleological Soc. (hon. life mem.), Soc. for Am. Archaeology, Am. Anthrop. Assn. (pres. 1956), Nat. Acad. Scis., Tree-Ring Soc., A.A.A.S., Sigma Xi, Phi Kappa Phi. Author publs. including: The Excavations of Los Muertos and Neighboring Ruins in the Salt River Valley, Southern Arizona, Peabody Museum Papers, Vol. XXIV. No. 1, 1945; (with others) The Stratigraphy and Archaeology of Ventana Cave, 1950. Home: 2749 E 4th St Box 4366 Tucson AZ 85717 ☆

HAUS, HERMANN ANTON, educator; b. Ljubljana, Yugoslavia, Aug. 8, 1925; s. Otto Maxmilian and Helene (Hynek) H.; student Technische Hochschule, Graz, 1946-48, Technische Hochschule, Vienna, 1948; B.S., Union Coll., 1949; M.S., Rensselaer Poly. Inst., 1951; Sc.D., Mass. Inst. Tech., 1954; m. Eleanor Laggis, Jan. 24, 1953; children—William Peter, Stephen Christopher, Cristina Ann, Mary Ellen. Came to U.S., 1948, naturalized, 1956. Asst. prof. Mass. Inst. Tech., Cambridge, 1954-58, asso. prof., 1958-62, prof. elec. engring., 1962—. Vis. prof. Technische Hochschule, Vienna, 1959- 60; vis. MacKay prof. U. Cal. at Berkeley, summer 1968; cons. Raytheon Co., 1956—, Lincoln Labs., 1963—; mem. Nat. Acad. Scis. adv. panel, Radio Propagation Lab. Nat. Bur. Standards, 1965-67. Guggenheim fellow, 1959-60. Fellow I.E.E.E.; mem. Am. Phys. Soc., Sigma Xi, Eta Kappa Nu. Tau Beta Pi, Phi Delta Theta. Author: (with R.B. Adler) Circuit Theory of Linear Noisy Networks, 1959; (with L.D. Smullin) Noise in Electron Devices. 1959; (with P. Penfield, Jr.) Electrodynamics of Moving Media, 1967. Mem. editorial bd. Jour. Applied Physics, 1960-63, Electronics Letters, 1965—. Home: 3 Jeffrey Terrace Lexington MA 02139 Office: 77 Massachusetts Av Cambridge MA 02139

HAUSCHLER, FREDERICK JON chemist, educator; b. Chicago, 1928; B.S. in Physics, Yale, 1950; Ph.D. in Chemistry, Harvard, 1956; m. Sally Ann Jones, July 5, 1957; children--Kenneth J., Nancy A. Chemist, Acme Chem. Co., Blue Island, Ill., 1950-51; director of Research Lab., Indsl. Chemicals Corp., Cambridge, Mass., 1956-60; project coordinator environmental sect. Steinmetz Assos., Chgo., 1960-61; v.p. for research Bauer Bros. Chem. Co., Inc., Memphis, 1961-64; asst. prof. chemistry Washington U., St. Louis, 1964-66, asso. prof., 1966-70, prof., 1970--, head of chemistry dept., 1970-71. Vis. prof. So. Ill. U., summer 1967, U. of Ore., 1969. Scoutmaster, Boy Scouts America, University City, Mo., 1968-70. Bd. dirs. Rest Haven Home for Elderly, 1960-61; trustee of the Lutheran Hosp., 1965-71. Served from lt. to capt., AUS, 1951-53. Mem. Am. Chem. Soc., Sci. Research Soc. Am. (chpt. treas. 1967), American Instititute Chemists, Ecological Soc. Am. (chpt. sec.), Sigma Xi. Author: (with others) Basic Inorganic Chemistry, 1971. Contbr. articles to profl. jours., encys., also chpts. to books. Home: Fairfax Apts 7291 Windermere Dr University City MO 63105 Office: Dept Chemistry Washington University St Louis MO 63130

HAUSEMAN, DAVID NATHANIEL, steel corp. exec.; b. Pottstown, Pa., Mar. 4, 1895; s. Morris Edward and Sallie (Rudy) H.; B.S., U. Pa., 1918; B.S. in Mech. Engring., Mass. Inst. Tech., 1928; M.B.S., Sch. Bus. Adminstrn., Harvard, 1935; grad. F.A. Sch., Ft. Knox, 1922, Army Indsl. Coll., 1939; D.Sc., Temple U., 1944; m. Rosa Rowan Pegues, June 13, 1920; 1 son, David Pegues. Enlisted as pvt., Ordnance U.S. Army, 1917; commd. 2d 1t., Ordnance, 1918, advancing through the grades to brig. gen., 1944; ret. 1946. Vice pres. Temple U., 1946-48; pres., dir. Research Inst., 1947-48; pres., dir. Houdry Process Corp., 1948-52; chmn. bd. Catalytic Constrn. Co., 1948-52; v.p. Davison Chem. Corp., div. of W.R. Grace Co., 1952-62; pres., dir. North Am. Steel, Lakeland, Fla., 1962-65, chmn., dir., 1966—; chmn. Hattras Indsl. Corp., New Bern, N.C., 1966; pres., dir. Fla. Phosphate Terminal Corp., 1964; dir. Lakeland Fed. Savs. & Loan Assn., Oliver B. Cannon and Son, Inc., Phila. Trustee, Temple U., 1949-52. Chief Philadelphia Ordnance District. 1940-43; dir. readjustment div., hdgrs. Army Service Forces, Washington, 1943-46, in charge gen. staff supervision of settling terminated war contracts and disposal of surplus property for Army Service Forces and Army Air Forces. Decorated Legion of Merit. D.S.M.; John C. Jones medal. Mem. Army Ordnance Assn. Episcopalian (vestryman). Mason. Clubs: Racquet (Phila.); Army-Navy (Washington); Harvard (N.Y.); Maryland (Balt.); Lakeland Yacht, Lone Palm Golf (Lakeland, Fla.). Home: 2611 Jonila Lakeland FL 33803 Office: PO Box 2463 Lakeland FL 33803

HAUSER, ALFRED HOLL, former banker; b. St. Paul, May 21, 1904; s. Paul and Clara (Holl) H.; B.S., Harvard, 1926; m. Helen P. Bassett, Dec. 24, 1926; children—Joan Holl (Mrs. Robert J. Daeschler), Mary Preston (Mrs. Donald A. Macrae), Edward Bassett. Former exec. v.p. Chem. Bank N. Y. Trust Co., ret., 1969; chmn., dir. Colonial Industries, Inc., dir. Tandy Corp., Granisle Copper Co., Ltd., Comml. Trust Co. N.J., Granby Mining Co., Ltd.; trustee Empire Savs. Bank. Bd. mgrs. Am. Bible Soc.; treas. Am. U. Beirut; trustee Am. Coll. Madura; chmn. investment com. Bd. dirs. Homeland Ministries of United Ch. Christ. Mem. Am. Finance Assn. Conglist. Clubs: Bond, Harvard (N.Y.C.); Short Hills (N.J.); Baltusrol Golf (Springfield, N.J.). Home: 87 Old Hollow Rd Short Hills NJ 07078

HAUSER, CRANE CHESHIRE, lawyer; b. Newark, Jan. 8, 1923; s. Simeon Floyd and Jessie Walrath (Crane) H.; A.B., Franklin and Marshall Coll., 1946; J.D., Northwestern U., 1950 C.P.A., U. Ill., 1953; m. Mary Corliss Kosovinc, May 29, 1949; 1 son, Stephen Crane. Admitted to Ill. bar, 1950; asso. firm Winston, Stawn, Black & Towner, Chgo., 1950-54; partner firm Winston Strawn Smith & Patterson, Chgo., 1954-61, 63—; chief counsel Internal Revenue Service, also asst. gen. counsel Treasury Dept., 1961-63. Mem. Ill. Bd. Examiners Accountancy, 1966-69. Served with AUS, 1943-46. Mem. Am., Fed., Ill., Chgo. bar assns., Ill. Soc. C.P.A.'s (Gold medal 1953), Chgo. Fed. Tax Fornum, NOrthwestern U. Law Sch. Alumni Assn. (bd. dirs. 1961—). Presbyn. (elder). Clubs: National Lawyers (Washington); Mid-Day (Chgo.). Home: 1440 Lake Shore Dr Chicago IL 60610 Office: One First National Plaza Chicago IL 60670

HAUSER, EMIL DANIEL WILLIAM, orthopedic surgeon; b. Freeland, Pa., Feb. 22, 1897; s. Karl and Wilhelmina (Volkert) H.; student Concordia Coll., St. Paul, 1911-15; B.S., U. Minn., 1918, M.S., 1921, M.D., 1922; M.S. in Orthopedic Surgevy, Surgery, Found., 1927; m. Mary Frances Thomas, July 28, 1930; children—Joan Thomas (Mrs. Michael Gately), Emil David William, Constance, Mary, Kevin. Postgrad. study Stockholm, Copenhagen, Berlin, Vienna, Hannover, Paris, London, others; asso. Dr. H.B. Thomas, Chgo., 1927-29; staff med. sch. Northwestern U., 1930—, asso. prof. bone and joint surgery, 1949—, med. dir. course in phys. therapy, 1950- 54, also Poliomyelitis Epidemic Aid Unit, 1945-53; attending orthopedic surgeon (pres. med. staff 1959-60) Passavant Meml. Hosp., Chgo.; dir. Winnetka Med. Center. Served as hosp. apprentice, U.S. Navy, World War I. Diplomate Am. Bd. Orthopedic Surgeons. Mem. Am. Acad. Orthopedic Surgeons, Am. Orthopedic Assn., A.C.S., A.M.A., Clin. Orthopedic Assn., Chgo. Orthopedic Soc., Ill. Med. Soc., Am. Assn. Railway Surgs., Inst. Medicine Chgo., Societe Internationale de Chirurgie Orthopedique et de Traumatologie, also mem. Societe Belge d'Orthopedic et de Chirurgie de l'Appariel Moteur, Sociedad Latino- Americana de Ortopedia Y Traumatologia, Pan-American Med. Assn., Inc., Alpha Sigma Phi, Nu Sigma Nu. Republican. Lutheran. Clubs: Med-Am. (Chgo.); Indian Hill (Winnetka, Ill. Author: Diseases of the Foot; Curvatures of the Spine, 1962; Congenital Clubfoot, 1966. Contbg. author Surgical Treatment of the Motor Skeletal System. Contbr. articles to med. jours. Home: 1410 Sheridan Rd Chicago IL 60093 Office: 60 Green Bay Rd Winnetka IL 60093

HAUSER, HARRY RAYMOND, lawyer; b. N.Y.C., July 12, 1931; s. Milton I. and Lillian (Perlman) H.; A.B., Brown U., 1953; J.D., Columbia, 1959; m. Deborah Marlowe, Aug. 6, 1954; children—Mark Jeffrey, Joshua Brook, Bradford John, Matthew Milton. Admitted to N.Y. bar, 1959, Mass. bar, 1963; practice in N.Y.C., 1959-61, Boston, 1962—; atty. Sperry Rand Corp., 1959-61, Hotel Corp. Am., N.Y.C., 1961-62, asst. sec., counsel, Boston, 1962-65, sec., counsel, 1965-67, sec., gen. counsel, 1967-68, v.p., sec., gen. counsel, 1968-70; with firm Gadsby & Hannah, Boston, 1970—. Guest lectr. Am. Mgmt. Assn. Served to lt. comdr. USNR, 1954-47. Mem. Am., N.Y., Boston bar assns., Am. Soc. Corp. Secs., Asso. Alumni Brown U. (dir.). Club: Brown University (v.p., dir.) (Boston). Home: 9 Channing Rd Newton Centre MA 02159 Office: 75 Federal St Boston MA 02110

HAUSER, JON WILLIAM, indsl. designer; b. Sault Ste. Marie, Mich., June 8, 1916; s. Kenneth and Arlie (Hershey) H.; m. Jean MacCallum, Aug. 30, 1939; 1 son, Jon William II. Designer, Gen. Motors Corp., 1936-41, Chrysler Corp., 1941-43; dir. design Sears, Roebuck & Co., 1943-45; designer with Dave Chapman, Chgo., 1945-46, Barnes & Reinecke, Chgo., 1946-49; asso. Reinecke Assos., Chgo., 1949-52; pres. Jon W. Hauser, Inc., St. Charles, Ill., 1952—. Two designs included in Best 100 Designs in History, 1959. Del. Internat. Council Socs. Indsl. Design, Paris, 1963, Vienna, 1965, Montreal, 1967. Fellow Indsl. Designers Inst., (Design award 1956; exec. v.p. 1961-62, pres. 1962-64, chmn. bd. 1964), Indsl. Designers Soc. Am. (chmn. bd. 1967-68, dir.). Mason (Shriner). Clubs: St. Charles Country; Quiet Birdmen (Chgo.). Home: Route 3 Box 471 St Charles IL 60174 Office: 10 E State Av St Charles IL 60174

HAUSER, MAXWELL, banker; b. Austria, 1902; ed. U. Frankfurt/Main (Germany). Sr. v.p. Trade Bank & Trust Co., N.Y.C. Home: 211 Central Park W New York City NY 10024 Office: Fifth Av at 48th St New York City NY 10036*

HAUSER, MILTON STANGE, former oil co. exec.; b. Charles City, Ia., May 27, 1904; s. Christian and Elsbeth (Stange) H.; B.A., State U. Ia., 1926; grad. Advanced Mgmt. Program, Harvard, 1955; m. Theodora Esther Morning, Sept. 15, 1930; 1 son, T. Stephen. With Marathon Oil Co., Findlay, O., 1930-70, asst. mgr. retail sales, 1945-47, mgr. pub. relations div., 1947-70, ret. Mem. oil information com. Am. Petroleum Inst., 1947-59, chmn. com., 1957, mem, pub. relations adv. com., 1959-70; pres. N.W. Ohio chpt., Pub. Relations Soc. Am., 1964, nat. sec., bd. dirs., 1964—, recipient Silver Anvil award, 1962. Bd. dirs., sec., v.p. Cloister Del Mar Assn., Boca Raton, Fla., 1970-71. Trustee Marathon Oil Found. Mem. Findlay Area C. of C. (bd. dirs. 1951-53, pres. 1952), Delta Tau Delta. Mason (Shriner), Elk. Clubs: Findlay Country (trustee 1951-59, pres. 1958-59), Boca Raton H; Del Ray Beach. Home: 1180 Ocean Blvd Boca Raton FL 33432

HAUSER, NORBERT, educator; b. Poland, Aug. 13, 1924; s. Morris and Debora (Griminger) H.; came to U.S., 1940, naturalized, 1945; B.Mech.Engring., Cooper Union, 1950; M.I.E., N.Y. U., 1955, Engr. Sci.D., 1962. Quality Control engr. Gen. Electric Co., 1950-55; from instr. to asso. prof. indsl. engring. and operations research N.Y. U., 1955-65; vis. asso. prof., mem. NSF project on use of computers in engring. edn. U. Mich., 1965; prof. indsl. engring. and mgmt. sci., head dept. operations research and system analysis Bklyn. Poly. Inst., 1966—; cons. in field, 1955—. Served with AUS, 1943-46. Mem. Am. Inst. Indsl. Engring. (sr.), Operations Research Soc. Am., Inst. Mgmt. Scis., Assn. Computing Machinery, Am. Soc. Engring. Edn., Am. Soc. U. Profs., Sigma Xi, Tau Beta Pi, Alpha Pi Mu, Pi Tau Sigma. Contbr. profl. jours. Home: 21 Pomander Walk New York City NY 10025 Office: 333 Jay St Brooklyn NY 11201

HAUSER, PHILIP MORRIS, educator; b. Chgo., Sept. 27, 1909; s. Morris and Ann (Diamond) H.; Ph.B., U. Chgo., 1929, M.A., 1933, Ph.D., 1938; L.H.D., Roosevelt U., Chgo., 1967; LL.D., Loyola U., Chgo., 1969; m. Zelda B. Abrams, Nov. 27, 1935; children—William Barry, Martha Ann, Instr. in sociology, U. Chgo., 1932-37, now prof. sociology dir. Population Research Center and dir. Chgo. Community Inventory, chmn. dept. sociology, 1956-65; chief labor inventory sect., F.E.R.A. and W.P.A., 1935-37; asst. to dir., Study of Social Aspects of Depression, Social Sci. Research Council, 1937; asst. chief statistician, Nat. Unemployment Census, 1937-38; asst. chief statistician for population, Bur. of Census, 1938-42, asst. dir., 1942-47, dep. dir., 1947-48, acting dir. of U.S. Census, 1950; asst. sec. Dept. of Commerce, 1945-47; U.S. Rep., Population Commn., UN 1947-51; statis. adviser to Govt. Union of Burma, UN Tech. Assistance, 1951-52; expert cons. to sec. of nat. def. Research and Devel. Bd.; Statis. adviser to govt. Thailand, 1955-56; Walker- Ames prof. U. Wash., 1958; vis. Ford prof. Ind. U., 1960, U. Wash., 1961, 62. Mem. bd. of dirs. Selected Am. Shares, Inc. Mem. bd. govs. Met. Planning and Housing Council, Chgo.; cons., or mem. various coms. re population and vital statistics reporting. Former dir. Social Sci. Research Council; chmn. Adv. Panel on Integration Chgo. Pub. Schs., 1963-64; mem. Ill. Am. Negro Emancipation Commn., 1963-65; dir. Task Force on Edn., White House Conf. to Fulfill These Rights, 1966; bd. dirs. Nat. Assembly for Soc. Policy and Devel.; mem. exec. com. S.E. Asia Devel. Adv. Group. Fellow Am. Statis. Assn. (pres. 1962- -), A.A.A.S. (sect. v.p. 1959), Am. Assn. for Pub. Opinion Research (chmn. standards com. 1948); mem. Am. Assn. U. Profs., Population Assn. Am. (pres. 1951), Am. Sociol. Assn. (pres. 1967- 68), Internat. Statis. Inst., Inst. Math. Statistics, Soc. Social Research, Sociol. Research Assn. (pres. 1961), Am. Philos. Soc., Internat. Union for Sci. Study Population, Phi Beta Kappa, Lambda Alpha, Pi Gamma Mu. Author: Government Statistics for Business Use (with W.R. Leonard), 1946, rev., 1956; Workers on Relief in U.S., 2 vols., 1939; Movies, Delinquency and Crime (with Herbert Blumer), 1933; Population and World Politics, 1958; Urbanization in Asia and the Far East, 1958; A Study of Population; An Inventory & Appraisal (editor with O.D. Duncan), 1959; Population Perspectives, 1960; Housing; A Metropolis- Chicago (with Beverly Duncan). 1960; Urbanization in Latin America, 1961; The Population Dilemma, 1963, 2d edit., 1969; The Study of Urbanization, 1965. Asso. editor Jour. Am. Statis. Assn., 1945-49, Am. Jour. Sociology. Editor: Handbook for Social Research in Urban Areas, 1965. Contbr. jours. Home: 5729 S Kimbark Av Chicago IL 60637

HAUSERMAN, FREDRIC MARTIN, mfg. exec.; b. Cleve., Aug. 11, 1909; s. Earl Fredric and Mary (Martin) H.; M.E., Cornell U., 1931; student Harvard Bus. Sch., 1931-32; m. Margaret Kenny, Sept. 9, 1935; children—Rinda Kenny (Mrs. Lewis A. Burleigh III), Jane Kenny (Mrs. William M. Hogan III), Mark Kenny. Engr. E.F. Hauserman Co., Cleve., 1932-39, sec., 1939-43, pres., 1943-69, chmn., 1969-70; dir. Central Nat. Bank, Cleve., Ohio Bell Telephone Co. Pres. Cath. Charities, 1956-59, Welfare Fedn. Cleve., 1962-63; v.p. Community Action for Youth, 1963. Decorated Knight of St. Gregory, 1963, Knight Malta, 1971; recipient Outstanding Service award Welfare Fedn., 1963; Distinguished Service award United Appeal, 1964; U. Sch. Grad. award, 1969. Mem. Producers' Council, Inc. (pres. 1957-58), Bldg. Research Inst. (pres. 1954-55), Young Presidents Orgn. (chmn. Cleve. chpt. 1953, area v.p. 1955). Office: 5711 Grant Av Cleveland OH 44105

HAUSERMAN, WILLIAM FOLEY, mfg. co. exec.; b. Cleve., Nov. 2, 1919; s. Earl Frederic and Mary (Martin) H.; B.S., Lehigh U., 1941; m. Diane DuBois, Jan. 26, 1946; children—Joan (Mrs. Frederick C. Collignon), Pamela, Mary Holland, William F., Terrance, Cynthia, Patricia, David. With The E.F. Hauserman Co., Cleve., 1946—, exec. v.p., 1968-69, pres., 1969—, also chmn. bd.; pres., dir. Fostoria Mfg. Co.(O.), subsidiary E.F. Hauserman Co., 1955—, Hauserman, Ltd. (Can.), Rexdale, 1961—; pres., dir. Hauserman, Inc., Cleve., 1970—. Team capt. United Appeal Cleve., 1960-63; chmn. adv. bd. Hudson (O.) Boys' Sch., 1966-67; mem. adv. bd. Univ. Sch., Cleve., 1967—; mem. spl. repair com. Welfare Fedn. Cleve., 1962-67. 8d. dirs. Jr. Achievement Greater Cleve.; trustee Soc. Crippled Children, Cleve. Served to lt. comdr. USNR, 1941-45. Mem. Chief Execs. Forum, Young Pres.'s Orgn. Home: 33200 Fairmount Blvd Pepper Pike OH 44121 Office: 5711 Grant Av Cleveland OH 44105

HAUSMAN, ARTHUR HERBERT, electronics co. exec.; b. Chgo., Nov. 24, 1923; s. Samuel Louis and Sarah (Elin) H.; B.S. in Elec. Engring., U. Tex., 1944; S.M., Harvard, 1948; m. Helen Mandelowitz, May 19, 1946; children—Susan Lois, Kenneth Louis, Catherine Ellen, Electronics engr. Engring. Research Assos., St. Paul, 1946-47; supervisory electronics scientist U.S. Dept. Def., Washington, 1948-60, now cons.; v.p., dir. research Ampex Corp., Redwood City, Cal., 1960-63, v.p. operations, 1963-65, group v.p., 1965-67, exec. v.p., 1967-71, exec. v.p., chief operating officer, 1971—, also dir. Trustee United Bay Area Crusade. Served with USNR, 1944-54. Recipient Meritorious Civilian Service award Dept. Def. Mem. I.E.E.E., Army Ordnance Assn. (dir. chpt. 1969—). Club: Commonwealth Cal. Home: 55 Flood Circle Atherton CA 94025 Office: 401 Broadway Redwood City CA 94063

HAUSMAN, JACK, textile mfr.; b. Austria, Jan. 4, 1902; s. Morris and Bertha (Hoffman) H.; m. Ethel Hoffman, Dec. 11, 1927; children—Richard Demaret, Peter, Michael Paul. Came to U.S., 1906, naturalized, 1912. Vice chmn. bd., Belding Hausman Fabrics, Inc.; dir. ABC. Chmn. bd. United Cerebral Palsy, N.Y.C., 1959—; vice chmn. United Cerebral Palsy Assn., 1955; chmn. bd. United Cerebral Palsy Research and Ednl. Found., 1960; trustee North Shore Hosp., Manhasset, N.Y. Clubs: City Athletic (N.Y.C.); Fresh Meadow Country (Great Neck, N.Y.); Deepdale Country (Manhasset). Home: 247 Kings Point Rd Kings Point NY 11024 Office: 10 E 32d St New York City NY 10022

HAUSMAN, JEROME JOSEPH, educator; b. N.Y.C., May 4, 1925; s. Benjamin and Etta (Kobak) H.; student Pratt Inst., 1942-43; A.B., Cornell U., 1946; student Columbia, 1947-48, Art Students League, 1948; M.A., N.Y.U., 1951, Ed.D., 1954; m. Flora Siman, June 20, 1948; children—Sandra Ellen, Madelynn, Leah Ann. Free-lance artist, N.Y.C., 1946-47; analytical chemist Lederle Labs., Pearl River, N.Y., 1947; art tchr. pub. schs., Elizabeth, N.J., 1949- 53; vis. lectr. Sch. Art, Syracuse U., 1957; vis. prof. art edn. dept. Pa. State U., 1958; asso. prof. Sch. Fine and Applied Arts, Ohio State U., 1953-68, acting dir. Sch. Fine and Applied Arts, 1958-59, dir., 1959- 68; prof. div. creative arts N.Y. U., 1968—. Mem. arts and humanities panel U.S. Office Edn., 1964-70. Cons. John D. Rockefeller III Fund, 1969—. Served USNR, 1943-46. Mem. Nat. Art Edn. Assn. (chmn. research com., adv. research bd.), Nat. Commn. Art Edn. (chmn.), Art Students League, Am. Soc. Aesthetics, Western Arts Assn., Inst. for Study Art in Edn. (pres.). Editor: Research in Art Edn., yearbook Nat. Art Edn. Assn., 1959; Studies in Art Edn. Jour. Issues and Research; editorial bd. Jour. Aesthetic Edn., 1968- -. Contbr. articles profl. jours. Home: 212 Rock Creek Lane Scarsdale NY 10583 Office: Div Creative Arts NY U New York City NY 10003

HAUSMAN, LOUIS, govt. ofcl.; b. N.Y.C.; Oct. 25, 1906; s. Louis and Estelle (Samuels) H.; A.B. cum laude, Columbia, 1927; m. Theodora Berger, July 15, 1930, Asso. advt. mgr., Am. Safety Razor Corp., Bklyn., 1937; dir. advt. and sales promotion gen. shaver div. Remington Rand Co., Bridgeport, Conn., 1938-39; with CBS, N.Y.C., 1940-66, asso. dir., 1947-49, dir., 1949-50, v.p. in charge advt. and sales-promotion, 1950-51, adminstrv. v.p. CBS Radio, 1951, v.p. CBS-Columbia, 1952-55, v.p. CBS, Inc., 1955-57; dir. television information NBC, Inc., 1957-62, v.p. gen. exec., 1962- 66; formerly asst. to U.S. commr. edn., Washington. Treas. Brand Names Found., 1952-58. Cons. Office Facts and Figures, 1952. OWI, 1942-44, War Dept. Spl. Services Div., 1942; various industry coms. Contbr. trade jours. Home: 419 33d St NW Washington DC 20013

HAUSMAN, SAMUEL, utilities exec.; b. Austria, Nov. 14, 1897; s. Morris and Bertha (Hoffman) H.; m. Vera Kuttler, May 4, 1924; children—Bruce Alan, Merna (Mrs. Richard Miller), Alice (Mrs. Morton Davidson). Chmn. Belding- Hausman Fabrics, Inc.; chmn. bd., chmn. exec. com. and dir. Belding Hemingway Co., Inc.; dir. L.I. Lighting Co., Interstate Dept. Stores. Mem. bus. adv. council Urban Devel. Corp.; chmn. bd. govs. Brotherhood in Action; chmn. United Jewish Appeal; 1st v.p. bd. Beth Israel Hosp., Martin Found., trustee Fedn. Jewish Philanthropies; bd. dirs. Am. Jewish Com.; former trustee N.Y. State U.; bd. sponsors Met. Adv. Council Internat. Recreation, Culture and Lifelong Edn.; mem. N.Y. State Manpower Advt. Council. Mem. Am. Arbitration Assn. Clubs: City Athletic (N.Y.C.); Fresh Meadow Country (Great Neck, N.Y.); Capitol Hill (Washington) Home: 930 Fifth Av New York City NY 10021 Office: 10 E 32d St New York City NY 10016

HAUSMAN, WILLIAM, physician, educator; b. Bklyn., July 25, 1925; s. Jacob Henry and Tillie (Hoffman) H.; student Washington U., 1942-43, M.D., 1947; student Miami U., 1943; m. Lillien Margaret Fuerst, June 12, 1947; children—Steven, Linda, Peter, Clifford. Intern, Coney Island Hosp., Bklyn., 1947-48; resident Worcester (Mass.) State Hosp., 1948-49, Inst. Pa. Hosp., Phila. 1949-52; commd. 1st lt. M.C., U.S. Army, 1949, advanced through grades to col., 1964; chief Med. Research Project, U.S. Army Hosp., West Point, N.Y., 1953- 58; asst. chief dept. neuropsychiatry Letterman Gen. Hosp., San Francisco, 1958-62, chief consultation service, 1958-61, chief psychiatry service and acting chief dept., 1961-62; chief behavioral scis. research br. Hdqrs. Med. Research and Devel. Command, OTSG, U.S. Army, 1962-65; dep. dir. div. neuropsychiatry Walter Reed Army Inst. Research, WRAMC, Washington, 1965-66; ret., 1966; asso. prof. psychiatry, psychiatrist-in-charge Student Mental Health Service, Johns Hopkins Sch. Medicine, 1966-69; prof., head dept. psychiatry U. Minn. Med. Sch., Mpls., 1969—; faculty Washington Sch. Psychiatry, 1966—. Bd. dirs. A.K. Rice Inst., Washington Sch. Psychiatry. Decorated Legion of Merit, Bronze Star medal. Diplomate Am. Bd. Psychiatry and Neurology. Fellow Am. Psychiat. Assn.; mem. A.A.A.S., N.Y. Acad. Sci. Home: 212 Parkview Terrace Minneapolis MN 55416 Office: Box 393 Mayo Hosp Minneapolis MN 55455

HAUSMANN, EMIL JOHN, securities broker; b. Bklyn., May 27, 1902; s. Henry and Sophia (Selig) H.; B.S. in Accounting, St. John's U., 1947, LL.B., 1949; m. Edna Anna Maier, June 29, 1924; 1 son, Donald George. Accountant, Mfrs. Trust Co., N.Y.C., 1916-18, First Nat. City Bank N.Y., 1918-23; self employed, Jamaica, N.Y., 1923-28; accountant, controller Baker, Weeks & Co., N.Y.C., 1929—, gen. partner, 1957-69; admitted to N.Y. bar, 1955. Mem. N.Y. Securities Panel arbitration com. N.Y. Stock Exchange; bd. govs. accounting sect. Assn. Stock Exchange Firms; former gov. Am. Stock Exchange; mem. exec. com., past chmn. Brokers and Dealers Taxation, N.Y.C.; tax and budget com. N.Y. Bd. Trade Adv. council St. John's U. Mem. local bd. SSS. Trustee Borough Queens, N.Y.C. Library System, 1946-52. Mem. Am., Queens County bar assns., Phi Delta Phi, Zeta Sigma Pi, Beta Gamma Sigma. Club: Lawyers (N.Y.C.). Home: 2905 Harbor Rd Merrick LI NY 11566 Office: Battery Park Plaza New York City NY 10004

HAUSMANN, FRANK WILLIAM, Jr., banker; b. Chgo., May 18, 1914; s. Frank William and Laurette I. (Bresnen) H.; A.B., Loyola U., Chgo., 1936, J.D., 1940; postgrad. in commerce, Northwestern U., 1941; m. Mary Frances Sullivan, Nov. 26, 1938; children—John Francis, Regina Denise, Mary Loretta. Ins. broker 1934-37; asst. sec. No. Trust Co., Chgo., 1937-53; admitted to Ill. bar, 1940; with Nat. Bank of Detroit, 1953—, sr. v.p., 1969—; dir. Nationwide Corp. (Columbus, Ohio). Bd. dirs., exec. com., chmn. finance com. Mich. Diabetes Assn., 1969—. Served to 1st lt. USAAF, 1943-46. Chartered financial analyst. Mem. N.Y. Soc. Security Analysts, Financial Analysts Soc. Detroit (past pres.), Econ. Club Detroit, Greater Detroit Bd. Commerce, Financial Analysts Fedn. (dir. chmn. corp. information com. 1969—), Delta Theta Phi. Clubs: Boat, Athletic, Detroit (all Detroit). Asso. editor: Financial Analysts Jour., 1964—. Home: 361 McMillan Rd Grosse Pointe Farms MI 48236 Office: Nat Bank of Detroit Detroit MI 48232

HAUSNER, GIDEON MAKS, lawyer; b. Lwow, Poland, Sept. 26, 1915; s. Bernard and Ema (Lande) H.; advocate, Hebrew Coll., Tel Aviv, Israel, 1933; student Hebrew U., Jerusalem, 1941; grad. govt. law classes, Jerusalem, 1943; m. Yehudith Liphshitz, Dec. 19, 1944; children—Tamar, Amos-Dov. Migrated to Palestine, 1927. Admitted to bar, 1943; legal practice in Jerusalem, 1943-47, 49-60, 63—; atty. gen. Israel, 1960-63; chief prosecutor in Eichmann trial, 1961-62; lectr. Hebrew U., 1956-60. Mem. Central Com. Bar Assn. and Law Council, 1954-60; del. Zionist Congress, 1954, 56, 64. Mem. Israeli Parliament, 1965—; chmn. Parliamentary group Ind. Liberal Party Israel, 1968—; chmn. Yad Vashem, Nat. Authority to Commemorate Victims World War II, 1969—. Mem. Jewish def. orgn. Hapana, 1932-48; served with Israeli Army, 1947-49. Mem. Polit. Sci. Assn., Israel Assn. for Human Rights (chmn.). Rotarian, Mem. B'nai B'rith. Author: Justice in Jerusalem; also articles, papers. Address: 6 Bartanura St Jerusalem Israel

HAUSNER, HENRY H., educator, cons. engr.; b. Vienna, Austria, June 1, 1901; s. Hans and Helene (Tritsch) H.; E.E., Technische Hochschule, Vienna, 1925; D.Eng., U. Vienna, 1938; m. Elizabeth Wallner, July 30, 1927 (dec.); m. 2d, Hedda M. John, Nov., 1962 (dec.); m. 3d, Ada Berger, May, 1970. Came to U.S. 1940, naturalized, 1946. Supervising engr. Elin A.G., Vienna, 1925-38; dir. research Elin Gluehlampenfabrik, Vienna, 1938-40; successively research engr., chief research engr. Am. Electro Metal Corp., Yonkers, N.Y., Gen. Ceramics & Steatite Corp., Keasbey, N.J., 1940-45, cons. engr.; research asso. N. Y. U., 1946-48, adj. prof., 1947-48; research cons. Rutgers U., 1946; sect. head metall. research lab. Sylvania Electric Products, Inc., Bayside, L.I., 1948-51, mgr. engring., atomic energy div., 1951-55; adj. prof. Bklyn. Poly. Inst., 1951—; mgr. sci. information services Franklin Inst. Research Labs., 1970—; prof. Max Plauck Inst., Germany, 1971; v.p. Penn-Texas Corp., N.Y.C., 1956-58. Research scientist Rensselaer Poly. Inst.; vis. prof. U. Cal. at Los Angeles, 1962—; prof. Olivetti Technol. Inst., Ivrea, Italy, 1967—. Recipient Powder Metall. Achievement award Stevens Inst. Tech., 1956. Registered profl. engr., N.Y. Fellow, N.Y. Acad. Scis., mem. Am. Inst. Mining and Metall. Engrs. (chmn. powder metall. com. 1954-55, 62-63), Internat. Plansee Soc. Powder Metall., Am. Soc. Metals, Inst. Metals London, German Soc. Metals, Swedish Powder Metall. Assn., Soc. Applied Spectroscopy (treas. 1945), Powder Metall. Tech. Assn. Japan, A.A.A.S., Am. Nuclear Soc., Atomic Indsl. Forum, Sigma Xi. Club: Metal Science (N.Y.C.). Author: Powder Metallurgy, 1947; (with W.E. Kingston, others) The Physics of Powder Metallurgy, 1951; (with others) Human Engineering, 1951; (with S.B. Roboff) Materials for Nuclear Power Reactors, 1955; (with others) Metal Beryllium, 1955; (with others) Metallurgy of Zirconium, 1955; (with others) Problems in Nuclear Engineering, 1957; (with others) Vacuum Metallurgy, 1958; (with others) Metals for Supersonic Aircraft and Missiles, 1958; (with C.R. Tipton, Jr., others) Reactor Handbook, vol. 1, Materials, 2d edit., 1960; Powder Metallurgy in Nuclear Reactor Construction, 1961; New Types of Metal Powders, 1964; Modern Developments in Powder Metallurgy, 1966; Fundamentals of Refractory Compounds, vol. 1-4, 1968-71; also edits. of sci. books. Editor: Internat. Jour. Powder Metallurgy, 1965—, Powder Metallurgy Science and Technology, 1969—. Contbr. articles to sci. jours. Home: 549 W 123d St New York City NY 10027 Office: 730 Fifth Av New York City NY 10019

HAUSSER, ROBERT LOUIS, lawyer; b. Cin., Apr. 3, 1914; s. Oscar and Alma J. (Ebel) H.; A.B., DePauw U., Greencastle, Ind., 1936; LL.B., Columbia, 1939; m. Dorothy Ann Oakes, Aug. 17, 1940; children-George Louis, Robert Oakes, Julia Janet and Joel Severin (twins). Admitted to Ohio bar, 1939, N.Y. bar, 1940; practice in N.Y.C., 1939-41, Marietta, O., 1941—; asso. Baldwin, Todd & Young, 1939-41; pvt. practice, 1941—. Vice pres., dir. Ohio Bar Title Ins. Co., Dayton; trustee Dime Savs. Soc., Marietta. Librarian Washington County Law Library. Judge, Marietta Police Ct., 1946-57; pres. Marietta Bd. Edn., 1963; mem. Mariietta Civil Service Commn., 1967- -. Served with AUS, 1944-45. Decorated Purple Heart with oak leaf cluster. Mem. Ohio Bar Assn. (sect. chmn., past mem. exec. com.), Am. Legion, Phi Beta Kappa. Democrat. Presbyn. Lion. Club: Marietta Country. Author: Ohio Real Property, 5 vols., 1952-58; (with William R. Van Aken) Ohio Real Estate Transactions, 3 vols., 1964; (with Allen B. Diefenbach) Ohio Estate Planning and Probate Administration, 2 vols., 1969. Editor: Title Topics, monthly jour. Ohio Land Title Assn., 1967—. Home: 409 Warren St Marietta OH 45750 Office: First Nat Bank Bldg Marietta OH 45750

HAUSSERMANN, ARTHUR H., mut. fund exec.; b. Bklyn., 1914; grad. Harvard, 1938, LL.B., 1941. Sr. v.p., sec., treas., dir. Vance, Sanders & Co., Inc., Boston; treas., clk. Depositors Fund of Boston, Inc. Asst. to pres. Boston Fund, Inc., Boston Common Stock Fund, Inc.; treas., clk. Capital Exchange Fund, Inc., Diversification Fund, Inc., Exchange Fund of Boston, Inc., Fiduciary Exchange Fund, Inc., Leverage Fund of Boston, Inc., 2d Fiduciary Exchange Fund, Inc.; v.p., treas. Vance, Sanders Spl. Fund, Inc., Vance, Sanders & Co. Can. Ltd. Home: 22 Allen Rd Wellesley Hills MA 02182 Office: Depositors Fund of Boston Inc 111 Devonshire St Boston MA 02109*

HAUSSERMANN, OSCAR WILLIAM, lawyer; b. Indpls., June 13, 1888; s. Christian John and Caroline (Burkhardt) H.; grad. Phillips Exeter Acad., 1908; A.B. Harvard, 1912, LL.B., 1916; J.D. (hon.), Suffolk U., 1966; D.C.L. (hon.), Franklin Pierce Coll., 1967; m. Eleanor Rodman Drinker, Jan. 28, 1918; children—Oscar William, Caroline. Practiced law, Boston, 1916—; admitted to Mass. bar, 1919; partner Ropes, Gray, Boyden & Perkins, 1930-39, Haussermann, Davison & Shattuck, 1939—; lectr. on bus. law Mass. Inst. Tech., 1921-30. Past v.p. Mass. UN Assn.; former chmn. Warrant Com. Town of Milton; gen. chmn. Greater Boston Emergency Campaign, 1935; former v.p., dir. Community Fedn. of Boston; former pres. New Eng. Alumni Assn. Phillips-Exeter Acad., Nat. Alumni Assn. Phillips-Exeter Acad., Boston C. of C.; hon. dir. Am. Research and Devel. Corp.; dir. Income and Capital Shares, Inc.; trustee Charity of Edward Hopkins (Harvard), The Chase Fund of Boston, Shareholders' Trust of Boston. Commd. 2d lt. Plattsbury (N.Y.) Training Camp., 1917; 1st lt. 301st Machine Gun Batt., 76th Div.; personnel, later actg. adj. 1st Div. Machine Gun Regt. A.E.F., World War I Mem. Am., Mass., Boston bar assns., Am. Bar Found., Mass. Com. Catholics, Protestants and Jews (past chmn.). Republican. Clubs: DU, Hasty Pudding (Harvard); Somerset, Harvard, Union (Boston). Contbr. legal articles. Home: 42 Dudley Lane Milton MA 02186 Office: 15 State St Boston MA 02109 ☆

HAUSSLER, ARTHUR GLENN, univ. adminstr.; b. Milw., Sept. 29, 1899; s. Arthur August and Mae (Reinhart) H.; LL.B., Ill. Wesleyan U., 1923, LL.D., 1954; B.E., Ill. State Normal U., 1939; M.A., N.Y. U., 1941; student U. Chgo., Northwestern U., U. Wis., So. Meth. U., U. Ill.; m. Helen Bentley, June 22, 1926. Tchr., athletic dir. Twp. High Sch., Pontiac, Ill., 1923-25, Community High Sch., Pekin, Ill., 1925-41, prin., 1941-45, West High Sch., Aurora, Ill., 1945-50; exec. v.p., sec. trustee Bradley U., Peoria, 1950-68, exec. sec. univ., 1968—, also dir. devel. Mem. Olympic Canoe Com.; mem. scholarship com. Nat. Assn. Tobacco Distbrs. Named to Ill. Athletes Hall of Fame. Mem. Ill. Assn. Health and Phys. Edn. (pres. 1945), No. Ill. High Sch. Conf. (pres. 1949), Am. Arbitration Assn., Assn. Commerce, Alpha Phi Omega, Phi Delta Kappa, Omicron Delta Kappa, Sigma Chi, Phi Delta Phi, Pi Kappa Delta. Mason. Clubs: Pekin Country, Town and Gown, Creve Coeur. Contbr. feature articles Chgo. Daily News, 1935-41. Home: 807 N Glenwood Av Peoria IL 61606

HAUTY, GEORGE THOMAS, educator; b. Remer, Minn., Jan. 7, 1919; s. Charles T. and Lola E. (Eckland) H.; B.A., Stanford, 1947, M.A., 1948; Ph.D., U. Rochester, 1950; m. Catherine E. Dougan, Dec. 26, 1949; children—Michael, Kathleen, Andrew, Christopher. Research psychologist USAF Sch. Aerospace Medicine, San Antonio, 1951-56, asso. prof., 1957-60, asst. chief div. space medicine, 1960—; chief psychology br. Civil Aeromed. Research Inst., Oklahoma City, 1960-65; chmn. dept. psychology U. Del., Newark, 1965—. Served with AUS, 1942-46. Fellow Aerospace Med. Assn. (recipient Longacre award 1962), Am. Psychol. Assn.; mem. Del. Psychol. Assn. (pres. 1968-69), Internat. Soc. for Biol. Rhythms, Psychonomics, Sigma Xi. Contbr. articles to profl. jours. Home: 220 Cheltenham Rd Newark DE 19711

HAVAS, PETER, éducator, physicist; b. Budapest, Hungary, Mar. 29, 1916; s. George G. and Irene (Harmos) H.; Absolutorium, Technische Hochschule, Vienna, Austria, 1938; Ph.D., Columbia, 1944; m. Helga Francis Hollering; children—Eva Catherine, Stephen Walter. Came to U.S., 1941, naturalized, 1948. Research asst. in mass spectroscopy U. Vienna, 1937-38; research fellow Institut de Physique Atomique, Lyon, France, 1938-41; lectr. in physics Columbia, N.Y.C., 1941-45; instr. physics Cornell U., 1945-46; asst. prof. physics Lehigh U., Bethlehem, Pa., 1946-49, asso. prof., 1949-54, prof., 1954-65; mem. Inst. for Advanced Study, Princeton, N.J., 1953-54; prof. physics Temple U., Phila., 1965—. Guggenheim fellow, 1953-54. Research on classical and quantum theories of radiation, theory of relativity, especially equations of motion of interacting elementary particles, foundation problems. Home: 240 Berkeley Rd Glenside PA 19038 Office: Temple U Dept Physics Philadelphia PA 19122

HAVEL, VACLAV, playwright; b. Prague, Oct. 5, 1936; s. Václav and Bozena (Vavreckova) H.; grad. Acad. Dramatic Arts, 1967; m. Olga Splichalova, July 11, 1933. Served with Ceske Budejovice. 1957-59. Recipient Austrian State prize for European lit., 1968. Mem. Union Czech Writers. Author: The Garden Party, 1963; The Memorandum, 1965; The Increasing Difficulty of Concentration, 1968; also essays and poetry. Address: 78 Engelsovo nabr 78 Prague 2 Czechoslovakia

HAVELOCK, ERIC A., educator, author; b. London, Eng., June 3, 1903; s. Alfred Henry and Annie Louise (William) H.; educated at Leys School; B.A., Emmanuel Coll. (scholar), Cambridge U., 1926, M.A., 1929; m. Ellen Parkinson; children—Joan Ellen, John Eric, Ronald Geoffrey; m. 2d, Christine Mitchell. Came to U.S., 1946, naturalized, 1955. Assistant, later asso. prof. classics Acadia, U., Wolfville, N.S., 1926-29; asso. prof. classics Victoria Coll., Toronto, Ont., 1929-47; vis. lectr. Harvard, 1946-47, asso. prof., 1947-51, prof. Greek and Latin, 1951-63, chmn. classics dept., 1955-60, acting chmn., 1962, lectr. gen. edn., 1949-63, sr. tutor Leverett House, 1947-50, chmn. bd. tutors, classical dept., 1949; Sterling prof. classics, chmn. dept. Yale University, 1963-68; sr. fellow Nat. Endowment for Humanities, 1968- 69; vis. prof. Princeton, 1960, 62; Vanier lectr. U. Ottawa (Can.), 1971; Semple lectr. U. Cin., 1970. Candidate for election Ontario provincial election, South Wellington, 1945. Trustee Radcliffe, Coll., 1959-63. Guggenheim fellow, 1941-42, 43; sr. fellow Center for Hellenic Studies, 1965—. Mem. Am. Philos. Assn., Am.

Philol. Assn. Can. Classical assn. (founder, 1st pres.), Am. Acad. Arts and Scis. Author: Lyric Genius of Catullus, 1939; Crucifixion of Intellectual Man, 1950; The Liberal Temper in Greek Politics, published 1957; Preface to Plato, 1963; also numerous articles profl. jours. Sr. editor Prentice-Hall Greek Drama Series, 1969—. Co-founder, asso. editor The Phoenix; asso. editor Canadian Forum, 1936-38. Home: Merryall Rd New Milford CT 06460

HAVELOCK-ALLAN, ANTHONY, film producer, dir.; b. Darlington County, Durham, Eng., 1905; ed. Charterhouse, Switzerland, Chmn., Constellation Films Ltd. Pictures include From the Four Corners, Unpublished Story, In Which We Serve, This Happy Breed, Blithe Spirit, Brief Encounter, Great Expectations, Take My Life, Blanche Fury, The Small Voice, Interrupted Journey, Shadow of the Eagle, Never Take No For an Answer, Meet Me Tonight, Young Lovers, Orders to Kill, The Square Fellow, Evening with the Royal Ballet, others. Mem. Cinematograph Films Council, 1948-50, Nat. Film Prodn. Council; chmn. council Soc. Film and TV Arts, 1962. Address: care Lloyd Bank Ltd Berkeley Sq House Berkeley Sq London England

HAVEMANN, JOEL, journalist. Edn. editor Chgo. Sun Times. Office: Chgo Sun Times 401 N Wabash Chicago IL 60611*

HAVEMEYER, HARRY WALDRON, sugar refinery exec.; b. N.Y.C., Nov. 23, 1929; s. Horace and Doris (Dick) H.; grad. St. Paul's Sch., Concord, N.H., 1948; B.A., Yale, 1952; m. Eugenie Aiguier, Nov. 23, 1951; children—Linden, Ann, Adaline, Eugenie Waldron, Catherine Deliverance. Chmn. bd. Bklyn. Eastern Dist. Terminal, 1959-62; v.p. Nat. Sugar Refining Co., 1962-64, exec. v.p., treas., dir., 1964-68. Mem. Yale Devel. Bd., 1964—; trustee Chapin Sch., 1966-, pres. bd. trustees, 1969—; trustee Juilliard Sch., 1969—. Served with arty. AUS, 1952-54. Decorated Bronze Star medal. Mem. S.R., N.Y. Hist. Soc. (trustee 1969—). Club: Yale (N.Y.C.). Home: 860 Park Av New York City NY 10021 Office: 350 Fifth Av New York City NY 10001

HAVEMEYER, HORACE, Jr., former sugar refining exec.; b. Islip, N.Y., July 14, 1914; s. Horace and Doris (Dick) H.; grad. Choate Sch., 1932, Yale, 1936; m. Rosalind Everdell, Sept. 1939; children—Horace, Rosalind, William, Christian. Exec. v.p. Nat. Sugar Refining Co., N.Y.C., 1942-48, pres., 1948-66, chmn. bd., 1966-68, dir. 1943-68. Home: 380 Deer Park Av Dix Hills NY 11746

HAVEN, FRANK P., newspaper editor; b. Buffalo. Mar. 31, 1913; s. Roland D. and Belle (Hopkins) H.; grad. Silver City (N.M.) High Sch., 1928; m. Margaret Brewster, May 26, 1935 (dec. 1956); children—Marjean (Mrs. Tom Walsh), Francene (Mrs. Michael Chapman), Suz; m. 2d, Dorothy Leding Porterfield, Mar. 28, 1958; children—Margaret (Mrs. Paul Richards), Susan L. Porterfield. Successively reporter, news editor, sports editor San Diego Sun, 1930-38; reporter, news editor San Diego Union- Tribune, 1939-40; with Los Angeles Times, 1941—, news editor, 1945-60, mng. editor, 1960—; lectr. journalism U. Cal. at Los Angeles, 1957-58. Mem. Sigma Delta Chi. Office: Times Mirror Sq Los Angeles CA 90053

HAVEN, GRANVILLE JAMES, electric utility exec.; b. Barnhart, Mo., Nov. 15, 1927; s. David F. and Matilda (Oberfeld) H.; B.S. in Indsl. Engring., Washington U., St. Louis. 1952, M.B.A., 1957; m. Joyce M. Alsmeyer, Apr. 5, 1952; children—Joy Anita, Grant Gilbert. With Union Electric Co. St. Louis. 1952—, sec., treas., 1964—, dir. regional operations, 1967-69, v.p. regional operations, 1969—. Pres. St. Louis Jr. C. of C., 1958; chmn. St. Louis County Bus. and Indsl. Devel. Commn., 1966-67; chmn. econ. devel. council Mo. C. of C., 1968. Served with AUS, 1946-48. Registered profl. engr., Mo. Mem. Kappa Alpha. Presbyn. Home: 822 Mason Wood Dr St Louis MO 63141 Office: 1901 Gratiot St St Louis MO 63166

HAVEN, THOMAS KENNETH, bus. exec.; b. Muskegon, Mich., June 27, 1906; s. Ole B. and Minnie B. (Larson) H.; A.B., U. Mich., 1928, M.B.A., 1929, Ph.D., 1940; m. Marion L. Reading, Dec. 11, 1935; children—Carl, Donna Jean, Madge, Daniel. Research asso. Bus. Adminstrn. Sch., U. Mich., 1929-36, grad. teaching staff, summer 1940; with Watling, Lerchen & Co., investment bankers, Detroit, 1936-42; rep. bd. dirs. Wabash Portland Cement Co., Dayton, O., 1940-44; v.p. charge finance Reichhold Chems., Inc., Detroit, 1942-47, dir., 1946-54, exec. v.p., 1947-54; v.p., dir. Detrex Corp., 1954-58; pres., dir. Pioneer Finance Co., Mobile Homes Life Ins. Co., 1958-66; v.p., dir. Beaver Precision Products, Inc., 1957-65; founding dir., v.p. Med. Center Devel. Corp., 1961-65; adv. dir. Detroit Bank and Trust Co., Ferndale br., 1958-66; dir. Seibert Oxidermo Co., Vac-Hyd Co., Detrex Chem. Industries, Inc. Prof. finance Sch. Bus. Adminstrn. U. Mich., 1970, 71. Financial advisor Malaya, 1966, Financiera Dominicana S.A. Dominican Republic, 1968—. Past pres., trustee Grace Hosp.; treas., trustee Cranbrook, Kingswood, Brookside schs. Mem. Delta Sigma Pi. Clubs: Circumnavigators, Bloomfield Hills Country, Detroit, Edgewood Country. Author: Investment Banking Under the Securities and Exchange Commission, 1940. Home: 3675 Ward Point Dr Orchard Lake MI 48033

HAVENS, GEORGE REMINGTON, educator; b. Shelter Island Heights, N.Y., Aug. 25, 1890; s. George R. and Elizabeth (Jennings) H.; B.A., Amherst, 1913; Ph.D., Johns Hopkins, 1917; European travel and study periodically; Guggenheim fellow, 1929-30; L.H.D., U. Mich., 1959, Ohio State U., 1964; m. Louise Curtiss, July 18, 1917. Tchr. Riverview Mil. Acad., Poughkeepsie, N.Y., 1913-14, Mt. Vernon Collegiate Inst., Balt., 1914-16; instr. in French, Ind. U., 1917-18; asst. prof. French, Ohio State U., 1919-21, prof., 1921-61, emeritus; tchr. summers, Johns Hopkins, U. Chgo., U. Cal., U. Pa., Columbia. Mem. Modern Lang. Assn. Am., Phi Beta Kappa, Delta Tau Delta. Author: The Abbé Prévost and English Literature, 1921; The Age of Ideas, 1955, rev. 1962; Frederick J. Waugh, American Marine Painter, 1969. Editor lit. works: Selections from Voltaire, 1925, rev., 1969; (with Olin H. Moore) Selected Stories from Guy de Maupassant, 1928; Voltaire's Marginalia on Rousseau, 1933; Voltaire's Candide, 1934, rev., 1969; J.J. Rousseau, Discours sur les Sciences et les Arts. 1946; A Critical Bibliography of French Literature, Vol. IV, The 18th Century (with Cabeen and Bond, others), 1951; (with Norman L. Torrey) Voltaire's Catalogue of His Library at Ferney, 1959. Contbr. to learned and profl. jours. Home: 415 Glen Echo Circle Columbus OH 43202

HAVENS, PAUL SWAIN, coll. pres.; b. Lawrenceville, N.J., Sept. 19, 1903; s. Henry Clay and Anne Elizabeth (Swain) H.; student Lawrenceville (N.J.) Sch., 1916-21; A.B., Princeton, 1925; Rhodes Scholar, Oxford U. (Eng.). 1925-28, B.Litt., 1928. M.A., 1932; LL.D., Washington and Jefferson Coll., 1936, Dickinson Coll., 1946, Lafayette Coll., 1963; L.H.D., Moore Coll., 1962; Litt. D., Wilson Coll., 1970; m. Lorraine Elizabeth Hamilton, Aug. 20, 1930; children—Anne Elizabeth. Mary Hamilton, Thomas Robert Hamilton. Instr. English, Princeton, 1928-30; dept. of English. summer session George Washington U., 1930; asst. prof. of English Scripps Coll., 1930-36; pres. of Wilson Coll., Chambersburg, Pa., 1936-70, emeritus, 1970—; mem. Grad. faculty, Claremont Colls., 1930-36. sec. English Grad. faculty, 1933-34. Mem. bd. Christian Edn., Presbyn. Ch. U.S.A., 1947-50. Mem. adv. com. on edn. Pa. State Council on Def. Chmn. Franklin County Chpt., A.R.C., 1941-52. Mem. Victory Fund Com. of Franklin County. Pa. Mem. Wartime Edn. Com. on Acceleration and Pre-profl. Accreditation, Pa. Dept. of Pub. Instrn.; mem. spl. commn. on liberal edn. Assn. of Am. Coll. Pres. Dept. of Higher Edn., Pa. State Edn. Assn., 1942; pres. Assn. Coll. Pres. of Pa., 1943-45, v.p., 1942-43; pres., Presbyn. Coll. Union. 1944; mem. Gov's Adv. Com. on Higher Edn., 1946; pres. exec. com. Found Ind. Colls., Inc. Pa. Trustee Templeton Christian U. Decorated Frihedsmedaille of King Christian X, Denmark. Mem. Pa. C. of C. (chmn. edn. com. 1957-59), Assn. Am. Rhodes Scholars (dir.), Modern Lang. Assn. Am., Kittochtinny Hist. Soc., Phi Beta Kappa. Presbyn. Clubs: Rotary, Princeton (N.Y.C.); Harvard-Yale- Princeton (Pitts.). Editor: The American Oxonian 1949-55. Address: Wilson College Chambersburg PA 17201

HAVENS, RALPH MURRAY, educator; b. Mound City, Kan., June 10, 1904; s. Harry S. and Elizabeth (Marrs) H.; A.B., Baker U., 1927; M.B.A., U. Kan., 1933; Ph.D., Duke, 1941; m. Catherine Clark, June 10, 1931; children—Murray Clark, Harry Stewart. Tchr., sr. high sch., Exira. Ia., 1928-31, Little Rock, 1931- 36; asst. prof. State Tchrs. Coll., Valley City, N.D., 1937-38; instr. Duke, 1938-41; asst. prof. Baldwin-Wallace Coll., 1941-43; prof. econs. U. Ala., 1946—, chmn. dept., 1954-68, asso. dean for internat. relations, 1968-69; vis. Fulbright lectr. Univ. Coll., Dublin, Ireland, 1959. Economist, OPA, 1943; econ. analyst Marshall Plan, Paris, France. 1948-49, Washington, 1951-52. Served to capt. AUS, 1943-46; ETO. Mem. Am., So. econ. assns., Royal Econ. Soc., Am. Assn. U. Profs., Phi Beta Kappa, Beta Gamma Sigma. Author: (with D.L. Cramer and J.S. Henderson) Economics: Principles of Income, Prices and Growth, 1966. Home: 2008 14th St E Tuscaloosa AL 35401 Office: Bidgood Hall University AL 35486

HAVENS, RICHARD WOODRUFF, banker; b. Phila., July 7, 1920; s. Earle A. and Gertrude (Wick) H.; grad. Episcopal Acad., 1938; B.S. in Econs., Wharton Sch. of U. Pa., 1942, M.B.A., 1948; m. Carolyn L. Jameson, Nov. 28, 1942 (dec.); children—R. Wick, Peter J., C. Louise, Anne, Peggy, Jane; m. 2d, Sally Atwater Bettle, Oct. 12th, 1963; 1 son, David Atwater. Administrv. asst. Fed. Res. Bank Phila., 1946-49; account exec. Lionel D. Edie & Co., Phila., 1949-52; staff economist Electric Storage Battery Co., 1952-53; pres. Indsl. Valley Bank and Trust Co., Phila., 1953—, also dir.; pres., dir. Indsl. Valley Title Ins. Co., Nat. Express Co.; dir. Central Mortgage Co., Central Mortgage of N.J., G.A. Bisler, Inc. Trustee Episcopal Acad.; trustee Pa. Coll. Podiatry, St. Joseph's Hosp. Served with USMCR, 1942-46. Home: 1324 Youngsford Rd Gladwyne PA 19035 Office: Indsl Valley Bank & Trust Co York Rd and West Av Jenkintown PA 19046

HAVENS, WILLIAM WESTERFIELD, Jr., physicist; b. N.Y.C., Mar. 31, 1920; s. William Westerfield and Elsie (Medl) H.; B.S., City Coll. N.Y., 1939; M.A., Columbia U., 1941, Ph.D., 1946; m. Aldine V. Morris, Oct. 22, 1944; children—Nancy E., Cynthia (Mrs. John M. Gosline). Asst. in physics Columbia, 1940, research scientist Manhattan Project, 1941-45, instr. physics 1945-47, asst. prof., 1947-50, asso. prof., 1950-55, prof., 1955—, dir. div. nuclear sci. and engrng., 1961—. Chmn. European Am. Nuclear Data Com., 1970—; mem. nuclear cross sect. adv. com. AEC; mem. adv. com. I.A.E.A. Anglo-Am. Hellenic Bur. Edn. Mem. Am. Phys. Soc. (exec. sec. 1966—), A.A.A.S. (v.p. 1967-68), Am. Inst. Physics (exec. com., gov. bd.) Contbr. numerous articles neutron spectroscopy to sci. jours. Home: 219 Palisade Av Dobbs Ferry NY 10522 Office: 520 W 120th St New York City NY 10027

HAVERKAMP, HAROLD JUDSON, coll. dean; b. Monroe, S.D., July 29, 1912; s. Anthony and Jennie (Lubbers) H.; B.A., Central Coll. Ia., 1935; M.A., State U. Ia., 1940, Ph.D., 1951; m. Ruth Leona Boot, Aug. 37, 1940; children—Larry Jon, Judson Paul, James Anthony, Beth Elaine, Kirk David, Jennifer Ann. Instr., Cornell Coll., Ia., 1940-42; asst. prof., dir. counseling Hope Coll., 1946-52; dean coll. Central Coll., 1952-62; acad. dean Hanover (Ind.) Coll., 1962—. Pres. Ia. Bd. for Internat. Edn. 1952; mem. Jefferson County (Ind.) Youth Commn., 1963—. Served to lt. USNR, 1943- 46; PTO. Mem. Am. Psychol. Assn., Am. Assn. for Higher Edn., Sigma Xi, Phi Delta Kappa. Presbyn. Address: Hanover Coll Hanover IN 47243

HAVERTY, RAWSON, retail mcht.; b. Atlanta, Nov. 26, 1920; s. Clarence and Elizabeth (Rawson) H.; B.A., U. Ga., 1941; m. Margaret Middleton Munnerlyn, Aug. 25, 1951; children—Margaret Elizabeth, Jane Middleton, James Rawson, Mary Elizabeth, Ben Munnerlyn. With Haverty Furniture Co., 1941-42, Haverty Furniture Cos., Inc., Atlanta, 1946—, pres., 1955—, also dir.; dir. J.M. Tull Industries, Inc. Instr. credit and collection So. Retail Furniture Assn. Sch. for Execs., U. N.C., 1950, instr. credits, collections, market anlayses, 1951; instr. br. stores Nat. Retail Furniture Sch. for Exec. U. Chgo., 1957—; dir. Fulton Nat. Bank, Central Atlantic Progress, Southwestern Life Ins. Co. Former chmn. Met. Atlanta Rapid Transit Authority. Mem. adv. bd. St. Joseph's infirmary; bd. dirs. U. Ga. Alumni, chmn. loyalty fund, 1969-70, 70-71; past pres. bd. trustees St. Joseph's Village; trustee Atlanta Arts Alliance, Westminster Sch., Atlanta, U. Ga. Found.; past pres. bd. sponsors Atlanta Art Sch. Former mem. Fulton Indsl. Authority. Served as maj. AUS, 1942-46. Decorated Bronze Star medal; Order of Leopold, Croix de Guerre with palms (Belgium); named All Am. Mcht. in retail furniture industry, 1958. Mem. Atlanta Retail Mchts. Assn. (past pres., dir.), Nat. Home Furnishings Assn. (past v.p., dir.), Am. Retail Fedn., Atlanta Jr. C. of C. (hon. life), Assn. U.S. Army (past pres., adv. bd.), Atlanta C. of C. (dir., past pres.), Sigma Alpha Epsilon. Roman Catholic. Kiwanian. Clubs: Piedmont Driving, Capital City (Atlanta); Lake Shore (Chgo.); Ponte Vedra (Fla.). Home: 3740 Paces Valley Rd NW Atlanta GA 30327 Office: 22 Edgewood Av NE Atlanta GA 30303

HAVICE, CHARLES WILLIAM, educator; b. Oil City, Pa., Dec. 24, 1901; s. Frank Davis and Edna May (Carrington) H.; A.B., Allegheny Coll., 1924, D.D., 1951; M.A., Boston U., 1926, S.T.B., 1927, Ph.D., 1937; student London U., summer 1930, Mansfield Coll., Oxford U., summer 1969-71; m. Edith Ann Gray, July 7, 1921; children—John Carrington, Ann Gray. Ordained to ministry Meth. Ch.; pastor West Abington M.E. Ch., 1926- 39, First Meth. Ch., South Braintree, 1939-42, Acton Congl. Ch., 1942-45, First Congl. Ch., Belmont, Mass.; instr. social sci. Northeastern U., 1927-29, asst. prof., 1929-32, asso. prof. sociology, 1932-35, prof. and head dept. sociology 1937-60, dean chapel, 1941—, head dept. philosophy and religion, 1960- 65, sr. prof., 1965—; dir. Gen. Theol. Library Bd. dirs. Washington Hosp.; mem. corp. N.E. Deaconess Hosp.; mem. exec. com. N.E. region Nat. Conf. Christians and Jews; bd. dirs. Russell B. Stearns Research Project. Recipient citation Nat. Conf. Christians and Jews. Mem. Religious Edn. Assn., Am. Philos. Assn., Soc. Sci. Study Religion, Fellowship of Reconciliation, Nat. Assn. Coll. and U. Chaplains (chmn. editorial bd., assn. pres.), Assn. Coordination U. Religious Affairs, Acad. Religion and Mental Health, ReHazen Asso. Com. on Religion in Higher Edn., Religious Research Assn., Am. Acad. of Religion, Nat. Campus Ministers Assn., Phi Beta Alpha, Alpha Chi Rho, Kappa Phi Kappa, Pi Delta Epsilon. Mason. Editor Campus Values. Contbr. articles profl. jours. Home: 178 Goden St Belmont MA 02178 Office: 360 Huntington Av Boston MA 02115

HAVIGHURST, ALFRED FREEMAN, educator; b. Mt. Pleasant, Ia., Sept. 30, 1904; s. Freeman Alfred and Winifred (Weter) H.; A.B., Ohio Wesleyan U., 1925; A.M., U. Chgo., 1928; Ph.D., Harvard, 1936; A.M. (hon.), Amherst Coll., 1954; m. Mildred Linscott Porter, Nov. 23, 1966. Instr. history Holmes High Sch., Covington, Ky., 1925-27; prof. history and polit. sci. Pacific U., 1928- 29; asst. history Harvard, 1930-31; mem. faculty Amherst Coll., 1931—, prof. history, 1954-70, prof. emeritus, 1970—; vis. asst. prof. Mt. Holyoke Coll., 1942. Mem. exec. com. Anglo-Am. Assos. Served to 2d lt. AUS, 1942-46; ETO. Mem. Am. Assn. U. Profs., Am. Hist. Assn., Conf. Brit. Studies, Hist. Assn. (Eng.), Brit. Records Assn., Phi Delta Theta. Methodist. Author: Twentieth Century Britain, 2d edit., 1966; also articles profl. jours. Editor: The Pirenne Thesis: Analysis, Criticism and Revision, 1958. Contbr. World Book Ency. Home: 11 Blake Field Amherst MA 01002

HAVIGHURST, HAROLD CANFIELD, law educator; b. Findlay, O., Dec. 24, 1897; s. Christian R(udolph) and Emilie (Canfield) H.; A.B., Ohio Wesleyan U., 1919, LL.D., 1950; A.M., Harvard, 1922, LL.B., 1926; m. Marion Perryman, July 23, 1927; children—Clark Canfield, Virginia Morgan. Practiced law with firm of Miller, Otis Farr, N.Y. C., 1926-28; asso. prof. law, W. Va. U., 1928- 30; asso. prof. law Northwestern U., 1930-32, prof., 1932-66, dean, 1948- 57; vis. prof. Cornell U., 1957-58; Ford Distinguished vis. prof. Howard U., 1966-67; prof. law Ariz. State U., 1967—. Mem. Nat. Conf. of Commrs. on Uniform State Laws, v.p., 1959-63; legal cons. office Fgn. Relief and Rehab. Operations, Dept. of State, 1943. Chmn. bd. mgrs. Ill. Law Review. 1932-45. Spl. asst. to atty. gen. of the U.S., 1939-40. Mem. Am., Chgo. bar assns., Phi Beta Kappa, Phi Delta Theta, Delta Sigma Rho, Pi Delta Epsilon, Order of Coif. Democrat. Presbyn. Club: Tavern (Chicago). Author: Cases on Contracts, 1934, rev. edit. 1950; The Nature of Private Contract, 1961; contbr. various legal periodicals. Home: 728 Noyes St Evanston IL 60201

HAVIGHURST, ROBERT J., educator; b. DePere, Wis., June 5, 1900; s. Freeman Alfred and Winifred (Weter) H.; A.B., Ohio Wesleyan Univ., 1921; Ph.D., Ohio State U., 1924; m. Edythe McNeely, June 21, 1930; children—Helen S., Ruth L., Dorothy C., James P., Walter M. NRC fellow in physics, Harvard, 1924-26; asst. prof. chemistry Miami U., Oxford, O., 1927-28; asst. prof. physics, adviser in exptl. coll. U. Wis., 1928-32; asso. prof. sci. edn. Ohio State U., Columbus, 1932-34; asst. dir. for gen. edn., Gen. Edn. Bd. (Rockefeller Found.), 1934-37; dir. for gen. edn., 1937-41; prof. edn. U. Chgo., 1941—. Co-dir., Brazil Govt. Center Ednl. Research, 1956-58. Mem. Soc. Research in Child Devel., A.A.A.S., Am. Psychol. Assn., Am. Sociol. Assn., Am. Ednl. Research Assn., Am. Assn. U. Profs., Nat. Acad. Edn., Gerontol. Soc., Nat. Soc. Study Edn., Phi Beta Kappa, Sigma Xi, Phi Delta Theta. Co-author; Who Shall be Educated, 1944; Father of the Man, 1947; Adolescent Character and Personality, 1949; Personal Adjustment in Old Age, 1949; Social History of a War Boom Community, 1951; The American Veteran Back Home. 1951; Intelligence and Cultural Differences, 1951; Older People, 1953; The Meaning of Work and Retirement, 1954; American Indian and White Children 1954; Educating Gifted Children, 1957; Society and Education, 1967; Psychology of Moral Character, 1960; Growing Up in River City, 1962; Society and Education in Brazil, 1965; Brazillian Secondary Education and Socioeconomic Development, 1969; 400 Losers, 1971; Adjustment to Retirement, 1970; Cross-National Research: Social Psychological Methods and Problems, 1971. Author: Developmental Tasks and Education, 1948; Human Development and Education, 1953; American Higher Education in the 1960's, 1960; Sociedad y Educacion en America Latina, 1962; The Public Schools of Chicago, 1964; The Educational Mission of the Church, 1965; Education in Metropolitan Areas, 1971; Comparative Perspectives on Education, 1968; Contbr. articles in field. Address: Judd Hall U Chgo Chicago IL 60637

HAVIGHURST, WALTER, author, educator; b. Appleton, Wis., Nov. 28, 1901; s. Freeman Alfred and Winifred Aurelia (Weter) H.; student Ohio Wesleyan U., 1919-21; A.B., U. Denver, 1924; S.T.B., Boston U., 1926; student Kings Coll., U. London (Eng.), 1926-27; A.M., Columbia, 1928; Litt. D., Lawrence Coll., 1947, Ohio Wesleyan U., 1947, Marietta Coll., 1959; L.H.D., Miami U., 1959; m. Marion Boyd, Dec. 22, 1930. Asst. prof. of English, Miami U., Oxford, O., 1928-37, asso. prof., 1937- 42, prof., 1942-50, research prof., 1950-67, regents prof., 1967-69, prof. emeritus, 1969—; lectr. English U. of Cin., 1935-37. Trustee Ohioana Library Assn. Mem. Authors League of Am., Am. Assn. U. Profs., Phi Delta Theta, Phi Beta Kappa (hon.). Author books including: Land of Promise, 1946 (awarded annual prize by Friends of Am. Writers); Song of the Pines (with Marion Havighurst), 1949; Signature of Time, 1949; Climb a Lofty Ladder (with Marion Havighurst), 1951; George Rogers Clark: Soldier in the West, 1952; Annie Oakley of the Wild West, 1954; Wilderness for Sale, 1956; The Miami Years, 1959; Vein of Iron, 1959; Land of the Long Horizons, 1960; The Heartland, 1962; Voices on the River, 1964; Three Flags at the Straits, 1966; Alexander Spotswood; Portrait of a Governor, 1967; River to the West, 1970. Bd. editors Ohio Hist. Soc. Recipient Ohioana Writers award, 1947-48. Compiled works including: Masters of the Modern Short Story, 1945; The Great Lakes Reader, 1966. Home: Shadowy Hills Dr Oxford OH 45056 ☆

HAVILAND, FRED RUSS, Jr., brewing co. exec.; b. Tampa, Fla., Mar. 24, 1915; s. Fred Russ and Louise M. (Kerns) H.; B.A., Carleton Coll., 1938; M.B.A., Northwestern U., 1941; m. Barbara Roland Moses, May 20, 1943; children—Sarah Keith (Mrs. Peter Michael Brewer), Susan Holmes (Mrs. Richard David Clayborne), Fred Russ III. Sr. Asso., part owner Stewart, Dougall & Assos., N.Y.C., 1946-51; dir. market devel., chmn. long range planning com. Mpls.-Honeywell Regulator Co., 1951-56; dir. bus. planning Anheuser-Busch, Inc., 1956-59; with Jos. Schlitz Brewing Co., 1959—, v.p. marketing and corp. planning, 1963-64, exec. v.p., 1964—. Mem. exec. devel. program adv. com. Mgmt. Inst., U. Wis., 1964- -. Served to maj. USAAF, 1941-45. Mem. Inst. Mgmt. Scis., Am. Mgmt. Assn. (Outstanding Contbn. to Marketing award 1948), A.A.A.S., Assn. Nat. Advertisers. Author: Changing Perspectives in Marketing, 1951. Home: 7945 N Fairchild Rd Milwaukee WI 53217 Office: 235 W Galena St Milwaukee WI 53201

HAVILAND, HENRY FIELD, Jr., polit. scientist; b. Summit, N.J., Sept. 7, 1919; s. Henry Field and Laura (Cole) H.; A.B., Harvard, 1941, M.A., 1948, Ph.D., 1949; m. Barbara Briggs, June 2, 1947; children—Deborah Mark, Stewart. With Bd. Econ. Warfare, 1942-43; cons. Hoover Commn. Task Force Fgn. Policy, 1948- 49; prof. internat. relations Haverford Coll., 1949-58; cons. Brookings Instn., 1950-51, 54-56, sr. staff mem. fgn. policy studies program, 1956- 68, dir. program, 1960-68; prof. internat. politics, dir. research Fletcher Sch. Law and Diplomacy, Tufts U., 1968—. Mem. conf. bd. Asso. Research Councils, Com. Internat. Exchange Persons, 1958-68; mem. Commn. Study Orgn. of Peace, 1958—; vice chmn. Am. Council Learned Socs., 1967—. Served with USNR, 1943-46. Mem. Internat. Studies Assn. (pres., 1967-68), Social Sci. Research Council (dir.), Council Fgn. Relations, Am. Polit. Sci. Assn. (council, exec. com.), Am. Soc. Internat. Law, Am. Soc. Pub. Adminstrn. Author: The Political Role of the General Assembly, 1951; co-author American Foreign Policy and the Separation of Powers, 1952; Organizing For Peace, 1954; Administrative Aspects of U.S. Foreign Assistance Programs, 1957; Formulation and Administration of U.S. Foreign Policy, 1960; Vietnam After the War: Peacekeeping and

Rehabilitation, 1968. Bd. editors Internat. Orgn., 1954—. Home: 105 Coolidge Hill Cambridge MA 02138 Office: Fletcher Sch Law and Diplomacy Tufts U Medford MA 02155

HAVILAND, JAMES WEST, physician; b. Glens Falls, N.Y., July 18, 1911; s. Morrison LeRoy and Mabel Eva (West) H.; A.B., Union Coll., Schenectady, 1932; M.D., Johns Hopkins, 1936; m. Marion Cranston Bertram, Oct. 23, 1943; children—James Marshall, Elizabeth Bullard, Donald Sherman, Martha Adams. Intern medicine Johns Hopkins Hosp., 1936-37, intern, asst. resident, chief outpatient dept. pediatrics, 1937-38, asst. resident medicine, 1939- 40, New Haven Hosp., 1938-39; instr. medicine Yale Med. Sch., 1938-39, Johns Hopkins Sch. Medicine, 1939-40; chief services crippled children Wash. Dept. Social Security, also Dept. Health, 1940- 42; lectr. medicine U. Wash. Sch. Nursing, 1946-60; practice medicine, Seattle, 1946—; clin. asst. prof., to clin. prof. U. Wash. Sch. Medicine, 1947—, asst. dean, 1949-53, 1954-59, acting dean, 1953- 54. Trustee, Seattle Artificial Kidney Center, Seattle Symphony Orch. Served as lt. comdr., M.C., USNR, 1942-46. Fellow Am. Geog. Soc. N.Y., Am. Heart Assn.; mem. Wash. State Med. Assn. (sec.-treas. 1948-51), Seattle Acad. Internal Medicine (pres. 1952-53), King County Med. Soc. (pres. 1962), A.M.A. (council med. edn. 1966—), Pacific Interurban Clin. Club, A.A.A.S., Am. Fed. Med. Research, Western Soc. Clin. Research, North Pacific Soc. Internat. Medicine, A.C.P. (pres. 1970), Am. Clin. and Climatol. Assn., Am. Assn. History Medicine, Phi Beta Kappa, Sigma Xi, Alpha Omega Alpha, Kappa Alpha. Home: 8207 SE 29th St Mercer Island WA 98040 Office: 721 Minor Av Seattle WA 98104

HAVILAND, JOHN KENNETH, educator; b. Mt. Kisco, N.Y., Jan. 19, 1921; s. John Kenneth and Phyllis (Aldridge) H.; B.Sc., London U. (Eng.), 1946; Ph.D., Mass. Inst. Tech., 1962; m. Eleanor Valerie Baker, July 23, 1943; children—Susan, David, Peter, Laurence Beckton, Julia. Structural engr. Bristol Aeroplane Co., Eng., 1946-47; sci. officer Nat. Research Council, Ottawa, Can., 1948; project engr. Canadair, Ltd., Montreal, 1948-51; dynamics supr., mgr. structures and materials LTV Aerospace, Dallas, 1951-67; prof. aerospace engrng. U. Va., 1967—; cons. Served as flight lt. R.A.F., 1939-45. Decorated D.F.C. Mem. Am. Inst. Aeros. and Astronautics. Home: Ardwood Earlysville VA 22936 Office: Univ Virginia Charlottesville VA 22901

HAVILAND, PETER ROBBINS, hosp. exec.; b. Pitts., Sept. 6, 1930; s. Harris G. and Frances (Miller) H.; A.B., Haverford Coll., 1952; M.H.A., U. Minn., 1957; m. Deborah Wisner Phillips, June 26, 1954; children—Rebecca, Sarah, Andrew, Matthew. Adminstrv. resident U. Kan. Med. Center, 1956-57; adminstrv. asst., asst. adminstr. Ia. Luth. Hosp., Des Moines, 1957-61; asst. adminstr. Presbyn. unit United Hosps. of Newark (N.J.), 1961-64, adminstr. crippled children's unit, 1964-68, asso. dir., 1968-69, dir., 1970—. Mem. Am. Coll. Hosp. Adminstrs., Am., N.J. hosp. assns., Am. Pub. Health Assn. Mem. Soc. of Friends. Home: 52 Division Av Summit NJ 07901 Office: 15 S 9th St Newark NJ 07107

HAVLICEK, JOHN, athlete; b. Martins Ferry, O., Apr. 8, 1940; grad. Ohio State U., 1962; m.; 1 son. With Boston Celtics, 1962—, capt. Mem. All-Star game Nat. Basketball Assn., 5 times, All-Defensive team, 3 yrs. Address: Boston Celtics North Station Boston MA 02114*

HAWA, ALBERT NICOLAS, steel co. exec.; b. Boston, Nov. 5, 1920; s. Nicolas and Nora (Shamieh) H.; B.B.A., Coll. City N.Y., 1941; m. Inge Jeanne Lederer, May 14, 1955; children—Albert Nicolas, Gregory David. With Colo. Fuel & Iron Corp. (name changed to CF&I Steel Corp.). N.Y.C., 1946-, asst. to financial v.p., 1960-62, treas., 1962-69, v.p., treas., 1969—; treas. Colo. & Wyo. R.R. Co., dir., treas. Colo. Bus. Devel. Corp., CF&I Fabricators, Inc.; dir. Ferro Processing Corp., Met. Nat. Bank. Sec.-treas. CF and I Roebling Found. C.P.A., N.Y. Mem. Am. Inst. C.P.A.'s, Financial Execs. Inst. (dir. Rocky Mountain chpt.), Am. Iron and Steel Inst., Denver C. of C., Am. Mgmt. Assn. Mason. Clubs: Columbine Country, Denver. Home: 3205 S Gregg St Denver CO 80201 Office: 11951 E Yale Ct Denver CO 80232

HAWETT, MARSHALL KENNETH educator, biologist; b. Ames, Ia.; B.A., Ia. State U., 1936, M.A., 1937, Ph.D. with honors, 1940. Instr., Ia. State U., 1946-47; asst. prof. biology Johns Hopkins, 1947-50, asso. prof., 1950-62, prof., 1962--, chmn. dept., 1963-69; vis. lectr. Stanford, 1970-71. Active Boy Scouts Am., 4-H Club. Served with AUS, 1940-46. Mem. Am. Soc. Biologists, Md. Soc. Cell Biologists, Am. Soc. Exptl. Biology, Internat. Union Biologists, A.A.A.S., Am. Acad. Arts and Scis., Phi Beta Kappa. Home: 48936 W Hancock Blvd Baltimore MD 20206

HAWES, HARDIN HOUGHTON, bank exec.; b. Atlanta, Ill., Apr. 27, 1903; s. Burt Hardin and Nora Casandra (Houghton) H.; B.S., Northwestern U., 1925; student Harvard Law Sch., 1925-26; m. Virginia Boteler Millet, Apr. 27, 1929; children—Carol, Julian Millet. With Harris Trust and Savs. Bank, Chgo., 1926—, exec. v.p. 1967—. Mem. adv. com. monetary affairs U.S. treas.; chmn. spl. adv. com. U.S. comptroller. Trustee Northwestern U. Recipient Northwestern U. Alumni Service award. Mem. Northwestern U. Alumni Assn. (pres. 1947-48, dir. 1935—), Phi Gamma Delta, Phi Kappa Psi. Clubs: Municipal Bond (pres. and dir. 1947-48), Bond (pres.), University, Mid-Day (Chgo.). Home: 1311 Holly Lane Winnetka IL 60093 Office: 111 W Monroe St Chicago IL 60603

HAWES, LILLA KENNERLY MILLS, (Mrs. Foreman McConnell Hawes), librarian, soc. exec.; b. Camden, S.C., Feb. 1, 1908; d. Laurens Tenney and Margaret (Johnstone) Mills; A.B., Agnes Scott Coll., 1928; B.S. in L.S., George Peabody Coll. Tchrs., 1939; certificate preservation and adminstrn. archives, Am. U., 1948; m. Foreman McConnell Hawes, May 29, 1936. Sec. chemistry dept. Ga. Inst. Tech., 1930-36; gen. asst. Savannah (Ga.) Pub. Library, 1937-40, reference asst., 1941-43, br. librarian, 1943-48; dir. Ga. Hist. Soc., Savannah, 1948—. Sec. Savannah-Chatham County Hist. Site and Mounument Commn., 1955-66. Bd. dirs. Youth Mus. Savannah, Inc., 1954-66, rec. sec., 1954-56, corr. sec., 1962-64; bd. dirs. Historic Savannah Found., Inc., 1955-62. Recipient Merit award Lachlan McIntosh chpt. D.A.R. 1956, Merit award Historic Savannah Found., 1966. Mem. Ga., Southeastern library assns., Soc. Am. Archivists, Am. Assn. for State and Local History, So. Hist. Assn., Ga. Hist. Soc., Savannah Hist. Research Assn. (pres. 1946-48), Am. Assn. U. Women (sec. Ga. chpt. 1943-45), Telfair Acad. Arts and Scis., League Women Voters, Nat. Soc. Colonial Dames Am. In State Ga., Victorian Soc. Savannah, Pi Gamma Mu, Delta Kappa Gamma. Presbyn. Editor: Collections of the Georgia Historical Society, Vols. X-XIV, 1952-64; Lachlan McIntosh Papers in the U. Ga. Libraries, 1968. Home: 1134 E 49th St Savannah GA 31404 Office: 501 Whitaker St Savannah GA 31401

HAWKANSON, ROBERT OSCAR, steel co. exec.; b. Red Wing, Minn., Nov. 19, 1915; s. Oscar L. and Esther A. (Nelson) H.; B.B.A., U. Minn., 1937; m. Jane Elizabeth Crosby, Oct. 10, 1940; children—James Crosby, David Robert. With U.S. Steel Co., 1938—, dir. personnel, Pitts., 1962, asst. to v.p. personnel, 1963, v.p., pub. relations, 1964—. Mem. Duluth Civil Service Commn., 1957-61; mem. adv. com. Pa. Selective Service Commn., 1961-64. Bd. dirs. Duluth Community Chest, Minn. Arrowhead Assn., St. Louis County Tb and Health Assn., Jr. Achievement Western Pa. Mem. adv. com. econ. edn. N.Y.C. Bd. Edn. Trustee Nat. Joint Council Econ. Edn., Miller Meml. Hosp. Served to lt. (j.g.) USNR, 1943-46. Mem. Am. Iron and Steel Inst., Pub. Relations Soc. Am., Pitts. C. of C. (bd. dirs). Republican. Episcopalian. Clubs: Kitchi Gammi (Duluth); Duquesne, Pittsburgh Press; Fox Chapel Racquet. Home: 144 North Dr Pittsburgh PA 15238 Office: 600 Grant St Pittsburgh PA 15230

HAWKE, JOHN HOWARD, corp. exec.; b. St. Catharines, Ont., Can., Apr. 14, 1926; s. Charles W. and Edith (Magee) H.; B.A., U. Toronto, 1949; m. Aileen Gwendolyn Demont, Jan. 29, 1960; children—Laurein, Martha, Charles, Gordon, Kelly. With Glengair Group Ltd., Toronto, and predecessor, 1949—, pres., 1969—; chmn. bd. Atlantic Sugar Refineries Co. Ltd., Can. Brick Co., St. Lawrence Brick Co. Ltd., Redi-Set Business Forms Ltd., Tancord Industries Ltd., Allanson Mfg. Corp. Ltd.,; v.p., dir. I.T.L. Industries Ltd.; dir. Acadia Pulp and Paper Ltd., Atlantic Fish Processors Co. Ltd., Canadian Tuna Co. (1965) Ltd., Canadian Gas & Energy Fund Ltd., CSM Japan Fund Ltd., Canadian Security Growth Fund Ltd., Canadian Security Mgmt. Ltd., Exquisite Form Brassiere (Can.) Ltd., Internat. Tools Ltd., Jefferson Lake Petrochems. Can. Ltd. Lyman Tube & Supply Co., Ltd., No. Tar, Chem. and Wood, Ltd., Orangeroof Can. Ltd., Sonco Steel Tube Ltd., Venpower Ltd. Bd. govs. St. Andrew's Coll., Aurora, Ont. Served as sub-lt. Royal Canadian Naval Vol. Res., 1944-45. Mem. Delta Upsilon. Clubs: Ontario, Rosedale, Empire of Canada, Lambton Golf and Country, Granite (Toronto); Marco Polo (N.Y.C.). Home: 34 Whitney Av Toronto 5 Ontario Canada Office: Box 53 Toronto Dominion Centre Toronto 1 Ontario Canada

HAWKES, ELDEN EARL, newspaper pub.; b. Preston, Ida., Jan. 8, 1908; s. Earl and Margaret (Geddes) H.; B.S., Utah State U., 1929; m. Editha Emiline Rich, Nov. 16, 1930; 1 son, Earl Rich. With Burroughs Adding Machine Co., 1929-30; with Gen. Motors Acceptance Corp., 1930-32; with Farm Credit Adminstrn., 1932- 36; with Hearst Newspapers, 1936-64, gen. mgr. Boston Record Am.-Sunday Advertiser, 1960-64; exec. v.p., gen. mgr., pub. Deseret News Pub. Co., Salt Lake City, 1964-67, exec. v.p., publisher, 1967—; v.p., sec., dir. Newspaper Agy. Corp.; dir. Prudential Fed. Savs. & Loan Co. Mem. Downtown Planning Assn., Salt Lake City, 1964—. Bd. dirs. Utah Assn. Mental Health, Utah Symphony, Salt Lake City dist. Boy Scouts Am., Radio Free Europe; mem. exec. com. Pro-Utah Orgn. Served to 1st lt. AUS, 1943-45. Mem. Salt Lake City C. of C. (gov.), Alpha Kappa Psi, Phi Kappa Phi, Sigma Delta Chi. Mem. Ch. of Jesus Christ of Latter-day Saints. Clubs: Bonneville Knife and Fork, Country, Timpanogas, Rotary, Alta. Home: 746 16th Av Salt Lake City UT 84103 Office: Deseret News Pub Co Salt Lake City UT 84101

HAWKES, JOHN, author, educator; b. Stamford, Conn., Aug. 17, 1925; s. John C. B. and Helen (Ziefle) H.; A.B., Harvard, 1949; A.M. (hon.), Brown U., 1962; m. Sophie Goode Tazewell, Sept. 5, 1947; children—John Clendennin Burne III, Sophie Tazewell, Calvert Tazewell, Richard Urquhart. Asst. to prodn. mgr. Harvard U. Press. 1949-55; vis. lectr. English, Harvard, 1955-56, instr. English, 1956-58; asst. prof. Brown U., 1958-62, asso. prof. English, 1962-67, prof. English, 1967; spl. guest of the Aspen (Colo.) Inst. Humanistic Studies, summer 1962; mem. staff Utah Writers Conf., summer 1962, Bread Loaf Writers Conf., summer 1963; vis. lectr. Stanford, 1966-67. Served with Am. Field Service, Italy and Germany, 1944-45. Recipient grant in lit. Nat. Inst. Arts and Letters, 1962; Guggenheim fellow, 1962-63; Ford Found. fellow poets and fiction writers, 1964; Rockefeller Found. grant, 1966. Author: (novels) The Cannibal, 1949; The Beetle Leg, 1951; The Goose on the Grave and The Owl (one vol.), 1954; The Lime Twig, 1961; Second Skin, 1964; (4 short plays) The Innocent Party, 1966; (shorter fiction) Lunar Landscapes, 1969; The Blood Oranges, 1971. Home: 18 Everett Av Providence RI 02906

HAWKES, LESTER LLTCHFIELD, educator; b. Brimfield, Ill., Dec. 18, 1905; s. Arthur John and Mae (Litchfield) H.; student Monmouth Coll., 1927, Carnegie Inst. Tech., summer 1934; B.S., Stout State U., 1943; Ph.M., U. Wis., 1945; m. Lydia Alvina Stindt, Feb. 27, 1932; children—Dennis L., Judith (Mrs. Patrick Pagel) and Jeanne (Mrs. David Hoffmann) (twins). Co-editor Sheldon (Ill.) Jour., 1923-27; editor The Stoutonia, 1929-30; mgr. Campus Pub. Co., Madison, Wis., 1944-48; instr. U. Wis., Madison, 1944-48, prof., 1959—, asst. dir. Journalism, 1967—, exec. sec. student publs., 1952—; tchr. Madison Adult Edn. Sch., 1930-44. Recipient Distinguished Service award Wis. Press Assn., 1962. Mem. Assn. for Edn. Journalism, Wis. Press Assn., Author: (with Carl Zielke) Your Front Page, 1949; Survey of Wisconsin House Publications, 1951; Sixteen Year Study of the Community Press of Wisconsin, 1971. Home: 4610 Tokay Blvd Madison WI 53711

HAWKES, STUART ZEH, surgeon; b. Newark, Sept. 30, 1905; s. Edward Zeh and Mary (Hawley) H.; B.A., Union Coll., Schenectady, 1926; M.D., Johns Hopkins, 1930; D.M.S., N.Y.U., 1937; m. Marion Murray, Oct. 12, 1946; children—Edward Zeh II, Dudley Farrand, Richard Champenois (dec.). Intern Newark City Hosp., 1930-32; pvt. practice, specializing in surgery, Newark, 1937-42, 46- -; instr. surgery N.Y.U., 1937-46; prof. surgery, chmn. dept. Essex Coll. Medicine and Surgery, 1946-48; attending surgeon Presbyn. Hosp., St. James Hosp., Newark, Harrison Martland Med. Center, Newark; cons. in surgery Eye and Ear Infirmary, Newark, VA and East Orange Gen. hosps., East Orange, N.J., St. Clare's, Riverside hosps., Boonton, N.J., Newton (N.J.) Meml. Hosp., St. James Hosp., Newark; clin. prof. surgery N.J. Coll. Medicine and Dentistry; med. dir. United Hosps. Newark, 1959- 66; past pres. med. bd. Newark City Hosp. Chmn. Newark Council Social Agys.; gov. Union U., Newark Boys Club; chmn. trustees Newark Acad. Served as lt. col. USAF, 1942-45. Recipient Alumni award Union Coll., 1955; Silver Beaver award, Boy Scouts Am. Diplomate Am. Bd. Surgery, Internat. Bd. Surgery. Fellow Pan Am. Med. Assn., Internat. Coll. Surgeons, A.C.S. (gov. 1961-67); mem. Assn. Mil. Surgeons, Soc. Surgeons N.J., N.J. Acad. Med. (past pres.), N.J. Diabetes Assn., Union Coll. Alumni Assn. (past pres.), Newcomen Soc. Contbr. med. jours. Home: RD 2 Box 38 Boonton NJ 07005 Office: 161 Roseville Av Newark NJ 07107

HAWKINS, ARTHUR HANSON, III, advt. exec.; b. N.Y.C., Mar. 11, 1930; s. Arthur Hanson and Patricia (LaPorte) H.; student U. Va., 1951; children by previous marriage— Jesse, Linda; m. 2d, Kathleen Hogan Walsh, Jan. 3, 1966; children—Matthew, Arthur Hanson IV. With McCann-Erickson, 1953-57, J. Walter Thompson Ltd., 1957-59, Young & Rubicam, 1959-60; v.p., co-creative dir. Marschalk Co., 1959-64; v.p., asso. creative dir. Grey Advt., 1964-66; sr. v.p., creative dir., mem. bd. West, Weir & Bartel, 1966-68; sr. v.p., corp. creative dir. Ketchum, MacCleod & Grove, 1968—; speaker, writer in field, judge advt. awards exhbns. Served to 1st lt. AUS, 1951-53. Recipient 52 nat. advt. awards. Mem. Alpha Tau Omega. Home: 445 E 80th St New York City, NY 10021. Office: 90 Park Av New York City NY 10016

HAWKINS, ASHTON, business exec.; b. Carlsbad, N.M., 1895; ed. Yale. Sec., dir. Merc. Stores Co., Inc.; with Kidder Peabody & Co. Home: Syosset NY 11791 Office: Kidder Peabody & Co 20 Exchange Pl New York City NY 10005*

HAWKINS, AUGUSTUS FREEMAN, congressman; b. Shreveport, Aug. 31, 1907; s. Nvanza and Hattie H. (Freeman) H.; A.B. in Econs., U. Cal. at Los Angeles, 1931; m. Pegga A. Smith, Aug. 28, 1945 (dec. Aug. 1966). Engaged in real estate and retail bus., Los Angeles, 1945—; mem. Cal. Assembly from Los Angeles County, 1935-62, chmn. rules com., 1961-62; mem. 88th to 92d Congresses from 21st dist. Cal. Democrat. Methodist. Mason. Home: 4251 / Avalon Blvd Los Angeles CA 90011 Office: House Office Bldg Washington DC 20515

HAWKINS, DONALD MERTON, lawyer; b. Manhattan, Kan., June 19, 1921; s. Floyd and Madge (Thompson) H., student U. Mich., 1943; A.B., U. Chgo., 1946, J.D., 1947; m. Lucille Bilsborough, Dec. 25, 1942; children-Frances Elizabeth (Mrs. Donald L. Lossing), Shirley Lorraine (Mrs. David J. Lowe), Richard Henry, Rebecca Susan. Admitted to Ill. bar, 1947, Ohio bar, 1948; partner firm Fuller, Seney, Henry & Hodge, and predecessors, Toledo, 1952—. Pres. Toledo Area Council Chs., 1968-69, Toledo Dist. Methodist Union, 1966-70. Trustee Goodwill Industries Toledo, 1957—, sec., 1963-68, v.p., 1968—. Served to 1st lt. USAAF, 1943-46. Mem. Am., Ohio, Toledo bar assns., Am. Judicature Soc., Order of Coif, Kappa Sigma. Clubs: Toledo; Inverness (Toledo). Home: 2227 Innisbrook Rd Toledo OH 43606 Office: 300 Madison Av Toledo OH 43604

HAWKINS, EARLE TAYLOR, educator; b. Harford County, Md., Mar. 5, 1903; s. Philip Hopkins and Laura Bell (Taylor) H.; A.B., summa cum laude, Western Md. Coll., 1923; A.M., Columbia, 1928; Ph.D., Yale, 1942; LL.D., Western Md. Coll., 1948, Coll. Notre Dame Md., 1966; m. Juanita Maxine Greer, June 16, 1951. Various ednl. positions in Md., 1924-38; supr. high schs. Md. Dept. Edn., 1938- 45, dir. div. instr., 1945-47; summer inst. U. Md., 1938, 1943, Johns Hopkins U., 1944-71); pres. Towson State Coll., Balt., 1947-69, pres. emeritus, 1969—. Mem. gen. com. and exec. com. Coop. Study of Secondary Sch. Standards, 1940-68; chmn. Econ. Edn. Council Md., 1963-69; organizer, dir., state program curriculum revision, 1945-47; chmn. nat. confs. on citizenship, 1946-49; chmn. dept. research and edn. Md. Bd. Natural Resources, 1948-61; adv. com. Automobile Club Md.; mem. state library survey com. Md. Planning Commn.; mem. Nat. Commn. on Accrediting, 1961-66; bd. mgrs. Md. Tng. Sch. Boys, 1959-65. Recipient Distinguished Service to Youth medal Central Atlantic Area council Y.M.C.A., 1946; Outstanding Services medallion Montgomery Coll., 1970. Mem. Middle States Assn. Colls and Secondary Schs. (commn. on higher edn. 1950-55, exec. com. 1956-59), Nat. Congress Parents and Tchrs. (hon. life), Am. Assn. State Colls. and Univs. (pres. 1965-66, chmn. legislative com. 1967-69), Council Cooperation in Tchr. Edn. (joint com. on tchr. recruitment 1943-45), Am. Assn. Colls. Tchr. Edn. (com. on legislation), Y.M.C.A. (chmn. youth and govt.), Presbyn. Social Union of Md. (pres. 1947-49), Ruling Elders Assn. of Presbytery of Balt. (pres. 1940-41), N.E.A. (v.p. 1947-49), Nat. Assn. Secondary Sch. Prins. (state coordinator 1941-47; exec. com. 1945-48; chmn. planning com., 1948-49). Nat. Council Tchrs. English (com. on supervision 1944-50), Greater Towson C. of C. (pres. 1964-66), Md. Assn. Higher Edn., Md. Tchrs. Assn. (exec. com. 1949-51, pres. 1951-52), Md. Hist. Soc. (chmn. com. on history in schs.), Md. Library Assn. (planning com.), Ednl. Soc. Balt. (v.p. 1948-49). Phi Delta Kappa, Kappa Delta Pi, Alpha Phi Omega Presbyn. Rotarian. Club: Baltimore Music. Author: Reliability of Secondary Sch. Evaluations; contbr. to ednl. jours. Mem. team ednl. survey, Philippines Sch. System, 1959-60, Pakistan, 1964. Address: 3902 Canterbury Rd Baltimore MD 21218

HAWKINS, EDLER GARNETT, clergyman; b. N.Y.C., June 13, 1908; s. Albert and Annie (Lee) H.; B.A., Bloomfield Coll., 1935, D.D., 1960; B.D., Union Theol. Sem., N.Y.C., 1938; m. Thelma Burnett, Jan. 30, 1944; children—Renee, Ellen. Ordained to ministry Presbyn. Ch., 1938; pastor St. Augustine Presbyn. Ch., Bronx, N.Y., 1938-70; moderator Presbytery N.Y., 1958-60; vice moderator Gen. Assembly United Presbyn. Ch. U.S.A., 1960-61, moderator, 1964-65, mem. bd. Christian edn., 1959—; prof. practical theology Princeton. Mem. Nat. Urban Coalition, N.Y. Urban Coalition; pres. bd. Forest House, Bronx; adv. com. Bronx Community Coll. Home: Princeton Theol Sem 38 Alexander St Princeton NJ 08540

HAWKINS, EUGENE PALMER, corp. exec.; b. St. Louis, Mar. 18, 1904; s. Eugene Palmer and Sarah F. (Anderson) H.; B.S. in Mech. Engring., Washington U., 1925; m. Rachel E. Heppenstall, July 18, 1935 (dec. June 1970); 1 dau., Eleanor Forman (Mrs. John D. Durno); m. 2d, Jean McKiggen, Jan. 2, 1971. Served as account exec. with Goldman Sachs & Co., 1928-42; gen. mgr. subsidiary cos. Callaway Mills, 1945-50; asst. to v.p. Revere Copper & Brass, Inc., Detroit, 1950-52, asst. gen. mgr., 1952-55, v.p., exec. head Mich. div., 1955-69; v.p. Revere Jamica Alumina Ltd., 1969—; dir. Indsl. Towel & Uniform Co., Houston. Bd. dirs. Jr. Achievement, Employer's Assn. Detroit, Traffic Safety Assn. Council of Detroit. Served to lt. comdr. USNR, 1942-45. Mem. Detroit Bd. Trade, Newcomen Soc. N. Am., Tau Beta Pi. Clubs: Country of Detroit, Rotary (Detroit). Home: 91 Touraine Rd Grosse Pointe Farms MI 48236

HAWKINS, EVERETT WILLIAM chemist, educator; b. Chicago, 1928; B.S. in Physics, Yale, 1950; Ph.D. in Chemistry, Harvard, 1956; m. Sally Ann Jones, July 5, 1957; children--Kenneth J., Nancy A. Chemist, Acme Chem. Co., Blue Island, Ill., 1950-51; director of Research Lab., Indsl. Chemicals Corp., Cambrige, Mass., 1956-60; project coordinator environmental sect. Steinmetz Assos., Chgo., 1960-61; v.p. for research Bauer Bros. Chem. Co., Inc., Memphis, 1961-64; asst. prof. chemistry Washington U., St. Louis, 1964-66, asso. prof., 1966-70, prof., 1970--, head of chemistry dept., 1970-71. Vis. prof. So. Ill. U., summer 1967, U. of Ore., 1969. Bd. dirs. Rest Haven Home for Elderly, 1960-61; trustee of the Lutheran Hosp., 1965-71. Served from lt. to capt., AUS, 1951-53. Mem. Am. Chem. Soc., Sci. Research Soc. Am. (chpt. treas. 1967), Sigma Xi. Author: (with others) Basic Inorganic Chemistry, 1971. Home: Fairfax Apts 7291 Windermere Dr University City MO 63105 Office: Dept Chemistry Washington University St Louis MO 63130

HAWKINS, FRANK NELSON, newspaperman; b. Griffin, Ga., Aug. 3, 1911; s. Ralph Walter and Mary Elizabeth (Hankinson) H.; A.B., U. Ga., 1933; m. Lottie Norton, Apr. 22, 1939; children—Frank Nelson, William E., John C. Reporter Macon (Ga.) Telegraph, 1933-39; mng. editor Macon News, 1939-41, Augusta (Ga.) Chronicle, 1941-43; reporter N.Y. Herald Tribune, 1943-44; editorial writer Atlanta Jour., 1944-46; chief editorial writer Pitts. Post-Gazette, 1946—, asso. editor, 1947-65, editor, 1965—; instr. evening sch. U. Pitts; Reid Found. fellowship for study in Western Europe, 1952. Dir. pub. schs., pub. library, Sewickley, Pa.; trustee Allegheny County Community Coll., also Pitts. Child Guidance Center. Mem. gov. com. Edn. in Pa., 1960; chmn State Council Higher Edn. Pa.; mem. Gov.'s Adv. Com. Pub. TV, 1967 Mem. Pa. State Bd. Edn. Dir. Allegheny County Bd. Pub. Assistance. Mem. Pa., Am. socs.

newspaper editors, Kappa Alpha, Sigma Delta Chi. Presbyn. Clubs: Pittsburgh Press, Edgeworth Home: 227 Thorn St Sewickley PA 15143 Office: 50 Blvd of Allies Pittsburgh PA 15222

HAWKINS, GEORGE ANDREW, educator, engr.; b. Denver, Dec. 11, 1907; s. George Herbert and Pauline Katherine (Erbshauser) H.; B.S. in Mech. Engring., Purdue U., 1930, M.S. in Mech. Engring., 1932, Ph.D., 1935; m. Alma Mae Williams, Aug. 15, 1931; 1 son, James Edward. Asst. applied mechanics Purdue U., 1930-32. instr., 1932-36, asst. prof. mech. engring., 1936- 38, asso. prof., 1938-42, prof. 1942-43, prof. thermodynamics, 1943—, research asst. Engring. Exptl. Sta., 1932-36, research asso., 1936-44, Westinghouse Research prof. heat transfer, 1944-53, asst. dean Grad. Sch., 1947-50, acting dean, 1948-49. Research dir. small arms div. U.S. Army Ordnance Exptl. Stat., 1941-51; vis. prof. engring. U. Cal., 1949-50; asso. dir. Engring Expt. Sta. Purdue U., 1950-53, dir., 1953-61, dean engring. Purdue U., 1953-67, v.p. acad. affairs, 1967—. Recipient certificate appreciation War Dept., 1945, gold medal Pi Tau Sigma, 1940. Fellow Am. Soc. M.E.; mem. Am. Inst. Chem. Engrs., Nat. Soc. Profl. Engrs., Am. Phy. Soc., Am. Soc. Engring. Edn. (pres. 1970-71), Nat. Acad. Engring. Math., Army Ordnance Assn., Scabbard and Blade, Sigma Xi, Phi Kappa Phi, Tau Beta Pi, Pi Tau Sigma, Sigma Pi Sigma, Phi Eta Sigma. Mason. Elk. Author and co-author books including: Thermodynamics, 1950; Elements of Heat Transfer, 1957; Engineering Thermodynamics, 1960; Multilinear Analysis for Students in Engineering and Science, 1963; Editor: Student's Engineering Manual, 1968. Home: 701 Crestview Pl West Lafayette IN 47906 ☆

HAWKINS, GERALD STANLEY, educator; b. Great Yarmouth, Eng., Apr. 20, 1928; s. Frederick A. and Annie L. (Nichols) H.; B.S., Nottingham U., 1949; Ph. D., Manchester U., 1952, D.S., 1963; m. Dorothy Zoe Barnes, July 15, 1955; children—Lisette Carole, Carina Geraldine. Came to U.S., 1954, naturalized, 1964. Electronic engr. Ferranti, Ltd., Manchester, 1952-54; research asso. Harvard Coll. Obs., Cambridge, Mass., 1954-69; astronomer Smithsonian Astrophys. Obs., Cambridge, 1962—; asst. prof. Boston U., 1957-61, asso. prof., 1961- 64, prof., 1964-69, chmn. dept. astronomy, 1966-69; dean of Coll., Dickinson Coll., 1969-71; coordinator radiometeor research Smithsonian, 1965-68. Fellow Am. Meteoritical Soc.; mem. Am. Astronomy Soc., Am. Geophys Union, A.A.A.S., Phi Beta Kappa, Sigma Xi. Club: Boston Authors. Author: Splendor in the Sky, 1961; Meteors, Comets, Meteorites, 1964; (with John B. White) Stonehenge Decoded, 1965. Contbr. articles profl. jours. Address: Fairfields Horstead Norwich NOR 66Y England

HAWKINS, HAROLD L., ins. co. exec.; b. 1906; A.B., LL.B., U. Wash.; married. With United Pacific Ins. Co., Inc., Tacoma, 1945—, sec., legal counsel, 1965—. Office: 728 St Helens Av Tacoma WA 98402*

HAWKINS, HOWARD GRESHAM, Jr., corp. exec., lawyer; b. Terre Haute, Ind., June 6, 1916; s. Howard Gresham and Margaret Josephine (Smith) H.; student Mich. State U., 1934- 37; A.B., U. Chgo., 1939, J.D., 1941, M.B.A., 1953; m. Gloria Althea Olson, July 22, 1950; (dec. Apr. 1966); children—Howard Gresham III, Susan Alison, Lawrence Arthur. Admitted to Ill. bar, 1941, N.Y. bar, 1942, Cal. bar, 1954; practiced in N.Y.C., 1941-42, Chgo., 1946-52, San Francisco, 1952—; sec. Kern County Land Co., 1955-68; v.p., sec., gen. counsel Dean Witter & Co., Inc., San Francisco, 1968—. Served to 2d lt., CIC, also OSRD, AUS, 1942- 46. Mem. Am. Bar Assn., Am. Soc. Corp. Secs. (dir.). Republican. Episcopalian. Club: Stock Exchange (San Francisco). Home: 70 Country Club Dr Hillsborough CA 94010 Office: 45 Montgomery St San Francisco CA 94106

HAWKINS, HOWARD ROBERT, telephone and telegraph co. exec.; b. Star City, Ind., Feb. 11, 1916; s. Martin A. and Mary (deVaney) H.; B.S., U. Ind., 1938, J.D. with distinction, 1941; m. Helen Foley, Oct. 26, 1946; children—Katherine, Howard, Rosemary, Suzanne. Spl. agent FBI, 1941-46; asst. gen. atty. RCA Global Communications, Inc. (formerly RCA Communications, Inc.), N.Y.C., 1946-48, gen. atty., 1948-65, v.p., 1951-64, exec. v.p., dir., 1964-66, pres., dir., 1966—; pres., dir. RCA Philippines Communications Corp., Marconi Telegraph-Cable Co., RCA Alaska Communications, Inc., 1969—. Admitted to bar N.Y., Ind. Mem. Armed Forces Communications and Electronics Assn., (pres. N.Y. chpt. 1969-70), Soc. Former Spl. Agts. FBI Inc., Assn. Bar City N.Y., Am., Fed. Communications bar assns., Order of Coif, Phi Delta Phi, Phi Delta Theta. Home: 33 Meadow Croft Lane Greenwich CT 06830 Office: 60 Broad St New York City NY 10004

HAWKINS, JACK, actor, producer; b. London, Eng., Sept. 14, 1910; s. Thomas George and Phoebe (Goodman) H.; ed. Trinity County Sch., Middlesex, Eng.; m. Jessica Tandy, 1932 (div. 1940); 1 dau., Susan (Mrs. John Tettemer); m. 2d, Doreen Lawrence, 1947; 3 children. Actor, 1924—; made debut on legitimate stage in St. Joan, London, 1924, films The Lodger, 1932; appeared on stage and in films, London and N.Y.C., 1924-39, 47—; more recent films include The Cruel Sea, The Intruder, Front Page Story, Bridge on the River Kwai, Ben Hur, League of Gentlemen, The Spinster, Lawrence of Arabia, Judith, Great Catherine, 1967, Shalako, 1968, Battle of Waterloo, 1969. Decorated comdr. Order Brit. Empire. Joined Royal Welch Fusillers, 1940; served in India and Burma until 1946. Home: The Penthouse 3A Ennismore Gardens London SW 7 England

HAWKINS, JAMES VICTOR, banker; b. Coeur d'Alene, Ida., Sept. 28, 1936; s. William Stark and Agnes M. (Ramstedt) H.; B.S., U. Ida., 1959; postgrad. Am. Savs. and Loan Inst., 1960-67, Pacific Coast Banking Sch., 1970—; m. Gail Ruth Guernsey, June 19, 1959; children-John William, Nancy Clare. Mgmt. trainee Gen. Telephone Co. of N.W., Coeur d'Alene, 1959-60; asst. mgr. First Fed. Savs. & Loan Assn., Coeur d'Alene, 1960-67; v.p., gen. mgr. Ida. S.W. Devel. Co., Boise, 1967-68; v.p., trust officer First Security Bank of Ida., N.A., Boise, 1968—. Bd. dirs. Boise United Fund, Boise Art Assn. Named Outstanding Young Idahoan, Ida. Jr. C. of C., 1967. Eagle Scout. Mem. Am. Inst. Banking, Boise C. of C., Boise Estate Planning Council, U. Ida. Alumni Assn. (mem. exec. bd.), Phi Gamma Delta. Episcopalian. Elk, Lion. Club: Crane Creek Country (Boise). Home: 1019 N 17th St Boise ID 83702 Office: PO Box 7069 Boise ID 83707

HAWKINS, JOHN BERNARR, banker; b. Salt Lake City, May 27, 1924; s. John Buchwalter and Lydia (Osguthorpe) H.; B.A., Columbia 1949, M.S., 1950; m. Florence Williams, Sept. 30, 1951; children—Cheryl, Lydia. With First Nat. Bank Ariz., Phoenix, 1950—, chief examiner, 1958—; tchr. Bank Adminstrn. Inst., 1952—. Served with inf. AUS, 1942-46; ETO. Decorated Bronze Star. Mem. Phi Kappa Psi (pres. Ariz. alumni assn. 1966). Home: 3418 W Rona Av Phoenix AZ 85017 Office: 411 N Central Av Phoenix AZ 85004

HAWKINS, JOHN CLINTON, YMCA exec.; b. St. Louis, Sept. 25, 1903; s. Charles O. and Alretta (Hardinger) H.; L.H.D., Central Coll., Fayette, Mo.; LL.D., George Williams Coll., 1963; m. Marguerite L. Hartman, Jan. 2, 1926; children—Barbara (Mrs. A.A. Angel), Jane (Mrs. C.G. Gerard), Marjorie (Mrs. Dard H. Schmidt). Chmn. bd. mgrs. Northside YMCA, St. Louis, 1947- 51; pres. West Central Area Council YMCA's (Colo., Kan., Mo., Neb., Wyo.), 1951, chmn., 1952-56; v.p. met. bd. dirs. YMCA's of St. Louis, St. Louis County, 1956—; nat. program chmn. YMCA's, 1956-57; pres. Nat. Council YMCA'S of U.S., 1958, 59; chmn. Nat. Bd. YMCA'S U.S., 1960-65; mem. exec. com. World Alliance of YMCA's Geneva, Switzerland; mem. internat. com., YMCA, 1956—, World Council, Kassel, Germany, 1957, Geneva, Switzerland, 1961, Tozanzo, Japan, 1965, Nottingham, Eng., 1969; chmn. Nat. Conv. YMCA's U.S.A., St Louis, 1969. Mgr. Wheeling Corrugating Co., St. Louis; exec. com. dir. Meth. Pub. House. Lay leader St. Louis Conf., Meth. Ch., 1948-58, mem. Gen. Confs., 1948, 52, 56, 60, 64, 66, 68, 70, lay leader Mo. E. Conf.; chmn. lay activities. South Central jurisdiction, 1952-56, 56-64; del. 4th Assembly World Council of Chs., Sweden, 1968; exec. dir. Mo. United Meth. Found., Inc., 1968—. Recipeint Ch. Lay Leadership award Religious Heritage of Am., 1967. Mem. United Churchmen Am. (nat. pres. 1954-57), Ill. Corrugated Steel Pipe Assn. (pres. 1967—). Home: 7421 Warwick Dr St Louis MO 63121

HAWKINS, MERRILL MORRIS, univ. dean; b. Maben, Miss., Mar. 19, 1914; s. Edgar Preston and Viola (Monts) H.; student Wood Jr. Coll., 1934-36; B.S., Miss. State U., 1944, M.S., 1950; Ed.D., U. Miss., 1960; m. Carrie Lee Brabham, Dec. 21, 1946; children—Jane, Merrill Morris. Supt. schs., Centreville, Miss., 1953-56; critic tchr. Univ. High Sch., U. Miss., 1956-57; instr. edn. U. Miss., 1956-57; prof. dept. elementary and secondary edn. Miss. State U., State College, 1965-66, asst. dean Coll. Edn., 1966-68, dean Coll. Edn., dir. tchr. edn., 1970—; asst. supt. schs., Vicksburg, Miss., 1957-60, supt., 1960-65. Served with AUS, 1941-43. Mem. Miss. Assn. Sch. Adminstrs. (past pres.), Starkville C. of C., Phi Delta Kappa, Kappa Delta Pi, Phi Kappa Phi, Blue Key. Methodist. Mason; mem. Order Eastern Star. Home: Tally-ho Dr Starkville MS 39759 Office: PO Box 5365 State College MS 39762

HAWKINS, ORWILL VAN WICKLE, lawyer; b. Freneau, N.J., Jan. 14, 1891; s. James Magee and Marion Eliza (Pullen) H.; Ph.B., Bucknell U., 1913, D.C.L. (hon.), 1959; LL.B., N.Y. Law Sch., 1917; m. Marian Katrina Harman, Sept. 17, 1917; children—Harman, Glenn Alan. Admitted to N.Y. State bar, 1918, since practiced in N.Y.C.; formerly mem. firm Duer, Strong & Whitehead. Trustee Bucknell U.; bd. govs., v.p. Sigma Chi Found. Mem. Am. Bar Assn., N.Y. County Lawyers Assn., Sigma Chi. Republican, Baptist. Clubs: Broad Street, University (N.Y.C.). Specialist in mgmt. of estates and financial interest, taxation and corp. practice. Home: Lloyd Neck Huntington NY 11743 Office: 20 Exchange Pl New York City NY 10005

HAWKINS, OSLE PENMAN, Jr., opera and concert singer; b. Phenix City, Ala., Aug. 16, 1913; s. Osie Penman and Eula Myrtle (Brown) H.; pvt. vocal studies with Margaret Hecht, Frederich Schorr, Renato Cellini, Samuel Margolis. Choir soloist First Presbyn. Ch., also Temple Israel, Columbus, Ga., 1930-42; Wagnerian baritone Met. Opera Co., N.Y.C., 1941—, exec. stage mgr., 1963—; leading baritone appearing roles Central City (Colo.) Opera House Assn., singer with Cin. Zoo Summer Opera; concert, radio, TV and oratorio singer; European tour, summer and fall 1954. Appearances on Ed Sullivan Show, Omnibus and 1st closed circuit theater TV-Carmen. Opera recordings RCA Victor, Met. Opera Book-of-the-Month Recordings. Mem. Am. Guild Mus. Artists (gov.), Am. Fedn. TV and Radio Artists, Ala. (hon.), Ga. (hon.) fedns. music clubs, Phenix City Jr. C. of C. Baptist. Club: Orpheus (Columbus). Home: 904 19th St Phenix City AL 36867 Office: Met Opera Lincoln Center Plaza New York City NY 10023

HAWKINS, PAULA, mem. Republican Nat. Com.; b. Salt Lake City. Jan. 24, 1927; d. Paul B. and Leoan (Staley) Fickes; student Utah State U., 1944-47; m. Walter Eugene Hawkins, Sept. 5, 1947; children—Genean, Kevin Brent, Kelley Ann. Rep. precinct committeewoman Orange County. Fla., 1965—; speakers chmn. Rep. Exec. Com. Fla., 1967—; mem. Fla. Rep. Nat. Conv., 1968; mem. Nat. Fedn. Rep. Women, 1965—, bd. dirs., 1968—; mem. Rep. Nat. Com. for Fla., 1968—. Mem. Maitland Civic Center. 1965—; charter mem. bd. dirs. Fla. Americans Constl. Action Com. of 100, 1966- -, sec.-treas., 1966—; mem. Central Fla. Museum Speakers Bur., 1967—; mem. Fla. Gov.'s Commn. Status Women, 1968-71. Recipient citation for service Fla. Rep. Party, 1966-67; Above and Beyond award as outstanding woman in Fla. politics, 1968; nominated Orange County Woman of Year, Maitland Womans Club, 1969. Mem. Maitland C. of C. (chmn. congl. action com.) Mem. Ch. of Jesus Christ of Latter-day Saints (pres. Relief Soc., Orlando Stake 1964-64, Sunday sch. tchr. 1964—). Clubs: Winter Park (Fla.) Racquet; Maitland Woman's. Home: 241 Dommerich Dr Maitland FL 32751 Office: care Republican Nat Com Washington DC 20025

HAWKINS, REBECCA BOWLES, lawyer, state ofcl.; b. Tenn.; d. Ernest Bethel and Estelle (Pierce) Bowles; student Brenau Coll., Gainesville; LL.B., U. Fla., 1935; m. Herbert S. Marks, Apr. 12, 1942 (div. 1946); 1 son, Jonathan Bowles; m. 2d, N. Hawthorne Hawkins, Jr., Mar. 19, 1960 (dec. Mar. 1967). Admitted to Fla. bar, 1935, Ala. bar, 1963; engaged in law practice in Bradenton, Fla., 1935-37; with TVA, 1938-41, OPM and WPB, 1941-43; asst. atty. gen. Fla., 1946-49, 69—; research asst. Fla. Supreme Ct., 1949-60; mem. firm Hawkins & Hawkins, Birmingham, Ala. and Shalimar, Fla., 1962-67. Mem. Am. (ho. of dels. 1961-63), Ala., Birmingham bar assns., Nat. (pres. 1960-61), Fla. (pres. 1953-54) assns. women lawyers, Fla. Bar, Internat. Fedn. Women Lawyers, Phi Kappa Phi, Phi Delta Delta. Home: 1026 McClendon Dr Tallahassee FL 32303

HAWKINS, RICHARD HAYS, Jr., former fgn. service officer; b. Pitts., Mar. 22, 1913; s. Richard H. and Ada M. (McCrea) H.; student St. Paul's Sch., Concord, N.H., 1925-30; B.A., Yale, 1934; diploma Ecole Lebre des Sciences Politiques, Paris, France, 1936; m. Christina Ekengren, Apr. 23, 1938; children—Ada McCrea (Mrs. Corwith Cramer, Jr.), William Ekengren, Richard Hays III. Vice consul U.S., Vancouver, Can., 1939-40, Brisbane, Australia, 1940-41, Sydney, 1941-45; temp. vice consul Melbourne, Australia, 1941, Noumea, New Caledonia, 1945; asst. chief, div. Dept. State, Washington, 1946-49; 1st sec. embassy, Lima, Peru, 1949-52; consul, Singapore, 1952-54, Bilbao, Spain, 1955-56; counselor embassy, Madrid, Spain, 1956-59, Jidda, Saudi, Arabia, 1959-62, assigned Dept. State, Washington, 1962-64; U.S. antarctic observer, 1964; consul gen., Montreal, Que., Can. 1964-70; ret. Served as ensign USNR, 1934-40. Fellow Am. Geog. Soc. N.Y.; mem. Am. Acad. Polit. and Social Sci., Am. Fgn. Service Assn. Club: Elizabethan. Address: 2829 Woodland Dr NW Washington DC 20008

HAWKINS, THOMAS FRANCIS, univ. adminstr.; b. Chgo., June 12, 1914; s. Thomas Francis and Hazel Josephine (Barry) H.; diploma in commerce Northwestern U., 1944; student Loyola U., Chgo., 1944, U. Omaha, 1951-53; m. Irene Ellen Murphy, May 6, 1939; children—Kathleen (Mrs. Dimitris N. Triantafillou), Thomas Francis, John Joseph, Joan (Mrs. John A. Pioake), Robert Michael. With Arthur Young & Co., C.P.A.'s, Chgo., 1932-36; asst. sec., asst. treas. H.A. Brassert & Co., N.Y.C., Chgo. and Pitts, 1936-41; asst. controller Esquire, Inc., Chgo., 1941-45; treas., controller Nachman Corp., Chgo., 1945-51; bus. mgr. Loyola U., Chgo, 1951—, v.p., 1956-68, v.p. finance, 1968—; dir. Chgo. Fed. Savs. and Loan Assn. Mem. adv. bd. grad. edn. Ill. Commn. Higher Edn., 1957—; mem. nat. council, nat. coms. Boy Scouts Am., 1954—, mem. nat. exec. bd., 1971—, exec. com. Region 7, 1958—, exec. bd. Thatcher Woods area council, 1954—, mem., vice chmn. Nat. Cath. Com. Scouting, 1961-70; mem. bd. lay advisers Sisters of St. Joseph, La Grange Park, Ill. Recipient Silver Beaver award, Silver Antelope award, Distinguished Eagle Scout award, Boy Scouts Am.; St. George award Cath. com. scouting Boy Scouts Am. C.P.A., Ill. Mem. Am. Inst. C.P.A.'s, Ill. Soc. C.P.A.'s, Am. Accounting Assn., Financial Execs. Inst., Nat. Assn. Accountants, Am. Mgmt. Assn., Nat. Assn. Coll. and Univ. Bus. Officers, Blue Key, Delta Sigma Pi, Pi Gamma Mu, Beta Alpha Psi. Clubs: Union League, Economic (Chgo.). Home: 19W062 Av Barbizon N Oak Brook IL 60521 Office: 6525 Sheridan Rd Chicago IL 60626

HAWKINS, THOMAS JEROME, sportscaster; b. Winston-Salem, N.C., Dec. 22, 1936; s. John Simpson and Juanita (Morgan) H.; B.A. in Sociology, U. Notre Dame, 1959; m. Doris Anne Shropshear, Jan. 16, 1959; children—Kevin, Karel, Traci, David. Forward Los Angeles Lakers, 1959-62, Cin. Royals, 1962-66; player rep., 1959-69; sportscaster NBC-TV, Burbank, Cal., 1969—; v.p. Bishop Hawkins & Assos., pub. relations and advt., Beverly Hills, Cal., 1967-68. Chmn. youth activities div. Los Angeles Urban Coalition, 1968-69; mem. adv. bd. Los Angeles Municipal Sports, 1969—. Recipient God and Country award Congregation Mushkan Yicheskel, Los Angeles City Resolution award Los Angeles City Council, Red Rose award Hosp. Charities, all Los Angeles, 1968; Russwurm award Nat. Newspaper Pubs., N.Y.C., 1968; Am. Freedoms award Past Comdrs. Club Cal.-Am. Legion, Los Angeles, 1969. Mem. Nat. Basketball Assn., Player Assn. (labor negotiation team 1967-69), Athletes for a Better Am. (founder 1965, pres. 1965—). Office: NBC-TV 3000 Alameda Blvd Burbank CA 91505

HAWKINS, THOMAS LAWRENCE, Jr., hosp. exec.; b. Orange, N.J., Feb. 19, 1927; s. Thomas L. and Margaret (Wheeler) H.; student Union Coll., 1947-49; M.D., Albany Med. Coll., 1953; m. Helen Audrey Taylor, Jan. 1, 1952; children—William Gregg, Thomas Scott, Robert Kent, Margaret Lynn. Intern Albany (N.Y.) Med. Center Hosp., 1953-54, resident, 1954-56; practice medicine, Albany, 1960— asst. prof. medicine Albany Med. Coll., 1960-62; asst. dir. Albany Med. Center Hosp., 1962-66, dir., 1966-68, exec. v.p., dir., 1968- -; chmn. med. adv. com. Northeastern N.Y. Blood Program. Vice chmn. Albany Area chpt. A.R.C., 1967. Served with USNR, 1945-46. Mem. A.M.A., Hosp. Assn. N.Y. State (com. chmn.). Home: 1141 New Scotland Av Albany NY 12208 Office: Albany Med Center Hosp Albany NY 12208

HAWKINS, WALTER LINCOLN, engr.; b. Washington, Mar. 21, 1911; s. William Langston and Catherine Elizabeth (Johnson) H.; Chem.E., Rensselaer Poly. Inst., Troy, N.Y., 1932; M.S., Howard U., Washington, 1934; Ph.D., McGill U., Montreal, Que., 1938; m. Lilyan Varina Bobo, Aug. 19, 1939; children—W. Gordon, Philip L. Sessional lectr. McGill U., 1938-41; NRC fellow Columbia, 1941-42; with Bell Telephone Labs., Inc., Murray Hill, N.J., 1942—. Chmn. bd. trustees Montclair State Coll.; trustee Mountainside Hosp., Montclair; mem. exec. com. Eagle Rock council Boy Scouts Am. Recipient Honor scroll Am. Inst. Chemists, 1970. Editor: Polymer Stabilization. Contbr. articles profl. jours., chpts. to books. Patentee in field. Home: 26 High St Montclair NJ 07042 Office: Bell Telephone Labs Murray Hill NJ 07971

HAWKINS, WILLIAM LYCETT, c. of c. exec.; b. Bridgeport, Conn., May 12, 1915; s. William Joseph and Irene (Burns) H.; grad. Boston Latin Sch., 1933; A.B., Tufts U., 1937; postgrad. U. Va.; m. Marion G. Sullivan, Sept. 27, 1947; children—Sally, Elizabeth, William, Jane. With Census Bur. of U.S. Dept. Commerce, 1946-50; exec. v.p. Bridgeport Area C. of C., 1950—. Chmn. Trumbull Indsl. Devel. Commn., 1957-59; treas. Greater Bridgeport Symphony Soc. Mem. bd. assos. U. Bridgeport, 1960—. Served to col., USMC, 1940-46. Decorated Legion of Merit, Silver Star. Mem. New Eng. (pres. 1965), Conn. (pres. 1963-64) assns. C. of C. execs. Club: Algonquin (Bridgeport). Home: 21 Woodcrest Av Trumbull CT 06611 Office: 1 Chapel St Bridgeport CT 06603

HAWKINS, WILLIAM STARK, lawyer; b. St. Joe, Ida., Aug. 4, 1910; s. James Victor and Ora Betsy (Stark) H.; LL.B., U. Ida., 1932, LL.D.; m. Agnes Matilda Ramstedt, Nov. 11, 1934; children—James Victor, Ruthanna, Willa Mae. Admitted to Ida. bar, 1932, since practiced in Coeur d'Alene, Ida.; served as pros. atty., Kootenia County, Ida., 1937-44; dist. judge 8th Jud. Dist. of Ida., 1945-46. Grand exalted ruler Benevolent and Protective Order of Elks, 1959-60; mem. nat. council Boy Scouts Am. Del. Democratic Nat. Conv., 1936, 4O, 44; presdl. elector, 1960. Served with USNR, 1944-45. Fellow Am. Coll. Trial Lawyers, Am. Coll. Probate Counsel; mem. Am., Internat. bar assns., Internat. Barristers, S.A.R. (president Ida.), World Peace Through Law Ct., Am. Judicature Soc., Am. Legion, V.F.W., Phi Alpha Delta, Tau Kappa Epsilon. Mason (Shriner), Eagle. Home: 627 Government Way Coeur d'Alene ID 83814

HAWKINS, WILLIS MOORE, Jr., aircraft co. exec. b. Kansas City, Mo., Dec. 1, 1913; s. Willis Moore and Elizabeth (Daniels) H.; student Ill. Coll., 1932-34; B.S. in Aero. Engring., U. Mich., 1937, D.Eng., 1964; D.Sc., Ill. Coll., 1966; m. Anita E. Stanfil, June 22, 1940; children—Nancy Gay, Willis Moore III, James Walter, Engr. trainee Grumman Aircraft Co., 1936- 37; with Lockheed Aircraft Co., 1937-54, dir. advanced design, 1942-54; with Lockheed Missiles and Space Div., Sunnyvale, Cal., 1954-63, asst. gen. mgr., 1957-61, v.p., gen. mgr. space systems, 1961-62, corporate v.p. engring., 1962-63; lectr. aerospace scis. and mgmt. U. Cal. at Los Angeles, 1954-55; asst. sec. army for research and devel., 1963-66; v.p. sci. and engring. Lockheed Aircraft Corp., Burbank, Cal., 1966-70, sr. v.p., 1970—. Mem. Army Sci. Adv. Panel, 1957—; adviser NACA, 1952- 54. Recipient Distinguished Pub. Service medal for contbns. to Polaris fleet ballistic missile system, Navy Dept., 1961; Distinguished Civilian Service medal, 1965, with laurel, 1966. Fellow Am. Inst. Aeros. and Astronautics, Royal Aero. Soc.; mem. Nat. Acad. Engring., Tau Beta Pi. Home: 4249 Empress Av Encino CA 91316 Office: Lockheed Aircraft Corp Burbank CA 91503

HAWKINSON, JOHN, investment mgmt. co. exec.; b. Walker, Ia., May 26, 1912; s. Theodore W. and Gertrude (Nietert) H.; A.B., U. Ia., 1936; m. Florence Mallaire, Oct. 12, 1946; children—Diane, Judith. With Halsey, Stuart & Co., Inc., Chgo., 1936-49; v.p., treas., dir. Central Life Assurance Co., Des Moines, 1950-62; pres., dir. Supervised Investors Services, Inc., Chgo., 1962—; pres., dir. Tech. Fund, Inc., 1963—, Balanced Income Fund, Inc., Supervised Investors Growth Fund, Inc.; dir. Supervised Investors Summit Fund, Gen. Growth Properties, Home Fed. Savs. & Loan Assn. of Des Moines, Ia.- Kemper Mut. Ins. Co., Mapco, Inc., Berkley & Co., Kemperco, Inc., Kansas City So. Industries , Kansas City So. Ry., La. & Ark. Ry., Studebaker Worthington, Inc., Am. Motorists Ins. Co. Bd. dirs. Investment Co. Inst. Mem. Ill. Securities Adv. Commn. Mem. Nat. Fedn. Financial Analysts. Clubs: Des Moines, Wakonda (Des Moines); Chicago, Attic, Economic (Chgo.). Home: 10 Rolling Ridge Rd Northfield IL 60093 Office: 120 S LaSalle St Chicago IL 60603

HAWKINSON, ROBERT WAYNE, mfg. co. exec.; b. Chgo., Jan. 12, 1920; s. Frank W. and Esther (Hallgren) H.; student Wright City Coll., 1941-42, Ill. Inst. Tech., 1949-50; certificate exec. program U.

Chgo., 1954; m. Janet Ristow, Dec. 16, 1944; children—Robert Wayne, John A., Barbara J. With Belden Mfg. Co., Chgo., 1945—, asst. to the pres., 1962-63, pres., 1963—, chief exec. officer, 1965- -, also dir.; dir. Union Spl. Machine Co., Nat. Can Corp. (both Chgo.). Mem. Chgo. Crime Commn. Mem. Glen Ellyn (Ill.) Dist. 41 Sch. Bd., 1964- 70. Bd. dirs. Central DuPage Hosp., Winfield, Ill., 1964—. Served to capt. USAAF, 1942-45. Decorated D.F.C., Air medal, Purple Heart; recipient Horatio Alger award, 1966. Mem. Ill. C. of C., Nat. Elec. Mfrs. Assn. (bd. govs.), Am. Assn. Indsl. Mgmt. (dir. Midwest div.), Elec. Mfrs. Club, Ill. Mfrs. Assn., Am. Mgmt. Assn., Am. Soc. Testing and Materials, Armed Forces Communications and Electronics Assn. Lutheran. Clubs: Union League (Chgo.); Glen Oak Country. Home: 284 Maple St Glen Ellyn IL 60137 Office: 415 S Kilpatrick Av Chicago IL 60644

HAWKLAND, WILLIAM DENNIS, educator; b. Willmer, Minn., Nov. 25, 1920; s. Douglas F. and Lola (Johnston) H.; B.S., U. Minn., 1942, J.D., 1947; LL.M., Columbia, 1949; m. Rosemary Neal, Aug. 27, 1949; children—William Dennis, Stephen D. Admitted to Minn. bar, 1947, Ill. bar, 1961, N.Y. bar, 1970; asst. prof. U. Tenn. Law Sch., 1949-50; from asst. prof. to prof. Temple U. Law Sch., 1950-56; vis. prof. U. Cal. at Los Angeles Law Sch., 1956; prof. Rutgers U. Law Sch., 1956-60; vis. summer lectr. N.Y. U., 1957, Tex. Law Sch., 1961; Internat. Faculty Comparative Law. Strasburg, France, 1970; prof. U. Ill. Law Sch., 1960-64; 70—; dean, prof. State U.N.Y. at Buffalo Law Sch., 1964-67, prof., provost, 1968-70. Bd. dirs. Am. Arbitration Assn., John Howard Soc. Vice chmn. Republican Com. to Elect Senator Kenneth Keating, 1964. Served to lt. USNR, 1942-46. Mem. Am., N.Y. State, Minn., Ill. Erie County bar assns., Am. Law Inst., Order of Coif. Author: (with George Bogert and William Britton) Sales and Security, 1962; A Transactional Guide to the Commercial Code, 1964; Commercial Paper and Bank Deposits and Collections, 1966; Bills and Notes, 1956; Sales and Bulk Sales Under The Uniform Commercial Code, 2d edit., 1959; also articles. Editorial bd. Unification Commercial Code. Home: 1402 Prospect Av Champaign IL 61820

HAWKS, HOWARD WINCHESTER, film director; b. Goshen, Ind., May 30, 1896; student Phillips Exeter Acad., Cornell U.; m. Nancy Roe Gross (div.); m. 2d, Dee Hartford (div.). Began career as profl. racing car driver; producer, film industry, 1922—, directed first film Road to Glory, 1926; other films include Dawn Patrol, Scarface, Ceiling Zero, Bringing Up Baby, Only Angels Have Wings, Sergeant York, Red River, Gentlemen Prefer Blondes, Rio Bravo, Hatari, Red Line 5000, El Dorado. Served as 2d lt. AAC, World War I. Address: 1225 Beverly Estates Dr Beverly Hills CA 90210 *

HAWKS, THOMAS HARRIS, banker; b. Rochester, N.Y., Feb. 15, 1916; s. George H. and Mary (Harris) H.; grad. Choate Sch., 1935; A.B., Cornell U., 1939; M.B.A., Harvard, 1941; m. Marion LaDue Jones, June 23, 1939; children—Devlin C., Sandra A., Lucinda M. Trustee Rochester Savs. Bank, 1949—, pres., 1951-70; chmn. bd.; 1970—; dir. Instl. Securities Corp., Savings Banks Trust Co.; N.Y.C. Dir.; treas. Rochester Jobs; Inc. Rochester Community Chest, also Colgate-Rochester Div. Sch., Genesee Hosp.; trustee Rochester Episcopal Diocese Investment Trust Fund, Rochester Area Ednl. TV Assn., Colgate Rochester Divinity Sch., Bexley Hall, Rochester Center; bd. regents St. John Fisher Coll. Mem. C. of C., Savs. Banks Assn. N. Y. State (past pres.). Episcopalian (vestryman, treas.). Home: 167 Council Rock Av Rochester NY 14610 Office: 40 Franklin St Rochester NY 14604

HAWLEY, ALEXANDER, banker; b. Bridgeport, Conn., Sept. 29, 1917; s. Samuel M. and Cornelia (Hincks) H.; B.A., Yale, 1940; m. Barbara King, Nov. 15, 1940; children—James M., Alexandra, Bronson K. With Conn. Nat. Bank, Bridgeport, 1940—, exec. v.p., 1964-68, pres., 1968—, also dir.; dir. Acme Shear Co., Chessco Industries, Inc. Chmn. central bus. dist. com. Citizens Action Com. Bridgeport; co-chmn. Community Relations Com. Urban Coalition; mem. regional adv. com. First Nat. Bank Region; mem. Bridgeport Narcotics Control Commn., Bridgeport Mayor's Action Com. Mem. exec. bd. Pomperaug council Boy Scouts Am.; treas. Conn. chpt. United Negro Coll. Fund. Trustee Museum Art, Sci. and Industry, Sacred Heart U., United Fund Eastern Fairfield County, Conn. Pub. Expenditure Council; bd. dirs. Goodwill Industries Western Conn.; pres. adv. bd. St. Vincent's Hosp., Bridgeport. Served as officer USNR, World War II. Mem. Bridgeport C. of C. (dir.), Conn. Bankers Assn., U.S., C. of C. Newcomen Soc. Clubs: Algonquin, Brooklawn Country, Rotary, University (Bridgeport); Country of Fairfield; Pequot Yacht (Southport, Conn.); Potatuck (Waterbury, Conn.); Yale (N.Y.C.). Home: 43 Hickory Lane Fairfield CT 06430 Office: 888 Main St Bridgeport CT 06602

HAWLEY, AMOS HENRY, educator; b. St. Louis, Dec. 5, 1910; s. Amos H. and Margaret Belle (Holtzclaw) H.; student Miami U., 1929-30; A.B., U. Cin., 1936; A.M., U. Mich., 1938, Ph.D., 1941; m. Gretchen Haller, Sept. 5, 1937; children—Steven Amos, Margie Lynne, Susan Esther, Patrice Ann. Instr. U. Mich., 1941-44, asst. prof., 1944-47, asso. prof., 1947-51, prof., 1951-66, chmn. dept. sociology, 1952-61, dir. social sci. research project; prof. sociology U. N.C., Chapel Hill, 1966—, Kenan prof. sociology, 1971—. Demographic adviser Govt. of Thailand, 1964-65; research asso. Scripps Found. Population Research, 1950-52; vis. prof. U. Philippines, 1953-54; Fulbright research scholar U. Naples (Italy), 1959; sr. cons., operations research office, Dept. Army, 1949-54, human relations research inst. Dept. of Air Force 1951—. Fellow A.A.A.S.; mem. Population Assn. Am. (pres. 1971—), Am. Sociol. Soc., Am. Assn. U. Profs., Phi Kappa Phi, Delta Kappa Epsilon. Author: The Population of Michigan, 1840 to 1960; An Analysis of Growth, Distribution and Composition, 1949; Human Ecology, 1950; (with R. Freedman, W. Landecker, H. Miner) Principles of Sociology, 1952; Demography and Public Administration, 1954; Population Redistribution with Metropolitan Areas, 1900-1950, 1955; R.D. McKenzie and Human Ecology, 1967; (with B. Zimmer) Metropolitan Community, 1970; Urban Society: An Ecological Approach, 1971. Contbr. articles profl. pubs. Home: 407 Brookside Dr Chapel Hill NC 27514

HAWLEY, CLAUDE EDWARD, educator; b. Milw., Nov. 11, 1914; s. William James and Myrtle (Holub) H.; A.B., U. Chgo.; 1935, Ph.D., 1939. Instr. bus. and pub. adminstrn. U. Mo., 1939-40; mem. faculty U. Fla., 1940-46; asso. prof. polit. sci., pub. adminstrn. U. So. Cal.; 1946-48; vis. prof. polit. sci. summers Northwestern U., 1946, 47, Am. U., 1963, Georgetown U., 1963; field sec. to mayor of Los Angeles, 1947-48; chief social scis. U.S. Office Edn., Washington, 1948-51; chief for edn. and research office human resources NSRB, 1951-52, cons. U.S. govt., 1952-55; dep. dir. information center service U.S. Information Agy., 1955-60, Nat. Security Council, 1960; chmn. bd. Investment Brokerage, N.Y.C., 1955-63; asso. dean grad. studies City U. N.Y., 1963- 66, prof. polit. sci., 1963—, dean grad. studies John Jay Coll. Criminal Justice, 1967-69, dean Coll.; 1969-71, v.p., 1971—. Trustee, Inst. for Am. Univs., Aix-au-Provence, France; pres. Am. Peace Soc.; 1967-69; pres. Helen Dwight Reid Ednl. Found. Served with AUS, 1942-46. Decorated Legion of Merit. Mem. Nat. Assn. Schs. Pub. Affairs and Adminstrn. (pres. elect 1971-72), Am. Polit. Sci. Assn., Am. Soc. Pub. Adminstrn., Phi Kappa Sigma, Delta Sigma Rho, Pi Sigma Alpha (nat. pres. 1958-60), Alpha Pi Zeta. Author or co-author books and articles on govt. and edn. Home: 5 Tudor City Pl New York City NY 10017

HAWLEY, EDMUND SUMMERS, lawyer, investment exec.; b. Bridgeport, Conn., Nov. 25, 1891; s. Charles Wilson and Katharine (Beardsley) H.; grad. Hotchkiss Sch., 1909; A.B., Yale, 1913; J.D., Harvard, 1916; spl. course Sorbonne, U., Paris, France, 1919; m. Dagmar Perkins, Sept. 12, 1922 (dec.); m. 2d, Marguerite Kalt Treadway, June 23, 1947; 1 son, Edmund Blair. Admitted to Conn. bar, 1916, N.Y. bar, 1920; asso. Kirlin, Woolsey & Hickox, N.Y.C., 1916-17; atty. Gen. Motors Corp., N.Y.C., 1919-20, Am. Tel. & Tel. Co., N.Y.C. 1920-56; v.p., dir. Inst. World Affairs, 1954—; v.p.; 1954-69; chmn. exec. com., 1962-67; mem. of adv. com. Internat. Missionary Council, 1952-55; mem.-at-large Protestant Council, 1953-59; chmn. Labor Temple, 1956-57; bd. mgrs. Am. Bible Soc., 1946-66; adviser Inter-Am. Radio Conf., Mexico City, 1924, Internat. Radio Conf., Washington, 1941; industry rep. Internat. Telecommunications Conf., Atlantic City, 1947. Bd. dirs. Samaritan Home for Aged, 1959—, v.p., 1961—; dir., pres. Youth Found. 1967—. Served to lt., C.E., U.S. Army, 1918-19; AEF in France. Recipient Honor award Wisdom Soc., 1970. Mem. N.Y. Soc. Founders and Patriots Am. (gov. 1955-58), New Eng. Soc., Nat. Inst. Social Scis., N.Y. Hist. Soc., Bar Assn. City N.Y., Mil. Order Fgn. Wars, N.Y. Soc. Mil. and Naval Officers World Wars, Soc. Colonial Wars, Huguenot Soc. (sec. 1957-59, pres. 1959-60), Pilgrims Soc., S.A.R., Revolution, St. Nicholas Soc., Phi Beta Kappa, Sigma Xi. Presbyn. (bd. elders 1955-61). Clubs: Union, Metropolitan Opera (N.Y.C.); Everglades (Palm Beach); Woodstock (Vt.) Country. Home: 850 Park Av New York City NY 10021

HAWLEY, JEAN GANNETT, publishing co. exec.; b. Augusta, Me., Jan. 16, 1924; d. Guy Patterson and Anne (Macomber) Gannett; student Masters Sch., Dobbs Ferry, N.Y., 1939-41, Bradford (Mass.) Jr. Coll., 1942-43; H.H.D., Nasson Coll., D.Bus. Adminstrn., Portland U.; L.H.D., Colby Coll., 1959; m. Roger Chilton Williams, Oct. 12, 1945 (div. 1952); children—Roger C., Guy G., Timothy A.; m. 2d, J. Richard Arnzen, June 16, 1962 (div. 1970); m. 3d, Sumner A. Hawley, Dec. 21, 1970. Pres., pub. Gannett Broadcasting Services, 1954—. Pres., Guy P. Gannet Found. Home: 37 Western Av Bath ME 04530 Office: 390 Congress St Portland ME 04111

HAWLEY, JOHN BLACKSTOCK, Jr., corp. exec.; b. Ft. Worth, July 11, 1899; s. John Blackstock and Sue Anna (Terrell) H.; student Tex. Christian U., Colo. Coll., U. Tex.; C.E., Cornell U., 1920; D. Sc., Colo. Coll., 1970; m. Helen Winston Thurston, 1925; children—Terrell Thurston, John Blackstock III; m. 2d, Anne McGill, May 30, 1937; children—McGill Joseph, Michael Augustine; m. 3d, Rosita Hofmeister, Mar. 30, 1946; children—MacDonald S., James, Lisa, Lane H. Gen. mgr. Anaconda Gravel Co., Ft. Worth, 1921-22; cons. engr. John B. Hawley, Ft. Worth, as chief designer on work covering water supply and san. engring., 1922-23; inventor mech. devices, specializing in perfection of oil well pumping devices; became constrn. engr. and v.p. No. Pump Co., 1928, now pres., gen. mgr. Recipient Navy Distinguished Pub. Service award. Mem. Am. Soc. C.E. (life mem.), Delta Kappa Epsilon. Clubs: Woodhill Country (Lake Minnetonka); Wayzata (Minn.) Country. Patentee in field. Home: 555 Bushaway Wayzata MN 55391 Office: 1915 57th Av N Brooklyn Center MN 55412

HAWLEY, LANGSTON THACKER, educator; b. Houston, Nov. 17, 1909; s. Willard Scott and May Elizabeth (Thacker) H.; B.S., U. Ala., 1932, M.S., 1933; Ph.D., U. N.C., 1946; m. Marion House Scholl, Jan. 28, 1933. Instr. commerce U. Ala., 1932-36; chief div. research Ala. Unemployment Compensation Commn., 1937; statistician U. Ala. Bur. Bus. Research, 1938; instr. econs. U. N.C., 1939-42; Ala. price exec. OPA, 1942-43; mem. faculty U. Ala., 1946—, prof. mgmt., 1950—, chmn. dept., 1966-71. Tech. adviser Ala. Indsl. Devel. Bd., 1938-39; research asso. Com. South, Nat. Planning Assn., 1951-52; research coordinator Ala. Bus. Research Council, 1954-55; arbitrator labor disputes, 1947—. Bd. dirs. Ala. Heart Assn., 1960-63, Am. Heart Assn., 1966-69. Served to lt. USNR, 1943-45: PTO. Recipient Nat. Distinguished Service award Pi Kappa Phi, 1954; Teaching Service award Alpha Kappa Psi, 1957. Mem. Nat. Acad. Arbitrators, Indsl. Relations Research Assn. (charter), So. Econ. Assn. (past v.p., bd. editors), So. Mgmt. Assn. Author: (with others) Human Relations Factors in Air Force Maintenance Work Units, 1952; Negro Employment in the Birmingham Metropolitan Area, 1954. Home: 267 Woodland Hills Tuscaloosa AL 35401 Office: Bridgood Hall University AL 35486

HAWLEY, NEWTON, educator. Prof. math. Stanford. Office: Math Dept Stanford U Stanford CA 94305*

HAWLEY, WHEELER, educator; b. Hartford, Conn., Sept. 20, 1904; s. Frank Wheeler and Julia (Bunnell) H.; A.B., Trinity Coll., Hartford, Conn., 1924; M.A., Harvard, 1925, postgrad. 1924-26, 34-35; postgrad. U. Minn., 1926-28; Ph.D. in Romance Langs., U. Tex., 1948; student Sorbonne, Paris, France, summer 1927; m. Esther D. Carrier, Sept. 4, 1926 (dec. 1950); children—Diana Grace (Mrs. Van H. Foster); m. 2d, Armina H. Schenck, Dec. 21, 1951; children—Jan Michael, Carol Ann, Julia Laurel. Mem. faculty U. Minn., 1926-28, Blake Sch., Mpls., 1928-29, Trinity Coll., 1929-30, U. Buffalo, 1930-31, McBurney Sch., N.Y.C., 1931-34; ednl. rep. G. & C. Merriam Co. in S.W., 1938-45; instr. Romance langs. U. Tex., 1945-48; asst. prof., then asso. prof. Tex. Christian U., 1948-52; mem. faculty Samford U., Birmingham, Ala., 1952—, prof. Romance langs., 1956, chmn. dept. fgn. langs., 1962—, chmn. div. humanities, 1966-69; part-time evening tchr. U. Ala. in Birmingham, 1957-67. Russell fellow, 1924-26. Mem. Am. Assn. Tchrs. French, Modern Lang. Assn., South Atlantic Modern Lang. Assn., Ala. Edn. Assn., Phi Beta Kappa, Pi Delta Phi, Sigma Delta Pi. Baptist. Lion. Home: 219 Dixon Av Homewood AL 35209

HAWN, CHARLES F., oil exec., ranching, real estate exec.; b. Athens, Tex.; s. William Arthur and Edna Rebecca (Leopard) H.; m. Ollie Jo Bowen; children—Charles A., Jo Anne. Pres., Hawn Lumber Co., Inc., Athens, Tex., 1960; dir. Southland Life Ins. Co., Dallas, Tex. Power & Light Co., Dallas, Tyler Bank & Trust Co. (Tex.), Mem. Tex. Hwy. Commn., 1957-63. Bd. dirs. Tex. Meth. Found. Served to lt. comdr. USNR, 1942-46. Mem. Tex. Good Roads Assn. (pres. 1968-70), East Tex. C. of C. (pres. 1955-56). Home: 704 Mulberry Dr Athens TX 75751 Office: PO Box 549 Athens TX 75751

HAWN, GOLDIE (Mrs. Gus Trikonis), actress; b. Washington, Nov. 21, 1945; d. Edward and Laura (Steinhoff) Btudlendgehawn; ed. pub. schs.; m. Gus Trinkonis, May 16, 1969. Profl. dancer, 1965; 1st profl. acting in Good Morning World, 1967-68; mem. company Laugh-In 1968—; film Cactus Flower, 1969. Address: 3604 Alma Av Manhattan Beach, CA 90266.

HAWORTH, DONALD ROBERT, educator; b. Steubenville, O., Jan. 26, 1928; s. Henry L. and Mary Etta (Morton) H.; B.S. in Mech. Engring., Purdue U., 1952, M.S., 1955; Ph.D., Okla. State U., 1961; m. Miriam Anna Pletcher, Mar. 24, 1951; children—Merry Jayne, Melodie Susan, Donald Robert. Designer- draftsman Bell Helicopter Corp., Ft. Worth, 1952-54; instr. Purdue U., 1954-56; propulsion engr. Chance Vought Aircraft Co., Dallas, 1956-58; asst. prof. Okla. State U., 1958-61, asso. prof., 1962-66; sr. scientist LTV Research, Dallas, 1961-62; prof. mech. engring., chmn. dept. U. Neb., Lincoln, 1966—; engring. cons., 1962—. Served with AUS, 1946-48. Registered profl. engr., Okla. Mem. Profl. Engrs. Neb. (sec. 1970-71, dir. 1971—), Am. Inst. Indsl. Engrs., Am. Soc. Engring. Edn., Am. Soc. M.E. (chmn. mech. engring. dept. heads region VII 1968-70, nat. vice chmn. dept. 1968-69, chmn. 1969-70), Nat. Soc. Profl. Engrs., Sigma Xi, Pi Tau Sigma (nat. v.p. 1963-68, nat. pres 1968-71), Tau Beta Pi, Phi Kappa Phi, Sigma Tau. Contbr. articles in field to profl. jours. Club: University Flying (pres. 1968) (U. Neb.). Home: 421 Sycamore Dr Lincoln NB 68510

HAWORTH, LELAND JOHN, sci. adminstr.; b. Flint, Mich.; July 11, 1904; s. Paul Leland and Martha (Ackerman) H.; A.B., Ind. U., 1925, A.M., 1926, D.Sc., 1961; Ph.D., U. Wis., 1931, D.Sc., 1962; D.Sc., Bucknell U., 1961; Engring. D., Stevens Inst. Tech., 1961; D.C.L., Union Coll., 1964; D.Sc., Columbia, 1965, U. Ill., 1965; LL.D., Rider Coll., 1964, Del. State Coll., 1965, L.I.U., 1965; m. Barbara Mottier, July 2, 1927 (dec. 1961); children—Barbara Jane (Mrs. Charles Beck), John; m. 2d, Irene Benik, May 15, 1963. High sch. tchr., Indpls., 1926-28; instr. physics U. Wis., 1930-37; Lalor F. phys. chemistry Mass. Inst. Tech., 1937-38; asso. physics U. Ill., 1938-39, asst. prof. physics, 1939-44, prof. physics, 1944-47; staff mem. Mass. Inst. Tech., 1941-46, group leader, 1942-43, div. head, 1943-46; asst. dir. projects Brookhaven Nat. Lab., 1947-48, dir. 1948-61; v.p. Asso. Univs., Inc., 1951-60, pres. 1960-61; mem. U.S. AEC, 1961-63, dir. NSF; Washington, 1963- 69; spl. asst. to pres. Asso. Univs., Inc., Upton, N.Y., 1969—. Former chmn. exec. com. Nat. Sci. Bd.; past chmn. com. on acad. sci. and engring. Fed. Council Sci. and Tech.; mem. or officer other govt. adv. groups. Recipient certificate of merit from Pres. U.S. Fellow Am. Nuclear Soc. (dir. 1955-60, pres. 1957-58), Am. Phys. Soc.; mem. Nat. Acad. Scis.; Am. Philos. Soc.; Am. Acad. Arts and Scis., Phi Beta Kappa, Sigma Xi, Gamma Alpha, Lambda Chi Alpha. Club: Cosmos. Author numerous articles for profl. sci. jours., also several chpts. Radiation Lab. Tech. Series. Home: Cliff Rd Belle Terre Port Jefferson NY 11777 Office: Brookhaven Nat Lab Asso Univs Inc Upton NY 11973

HAWORTH, MARY, (see Young, Mary Elizabeth Reardon)

HAWORTH, MICHAEL ELLIOTT, Jr., aerospace co. exec.; b. Pitts., Dec. 18, 1928; s. Michael E. and Margarett (Thomas) H.; student U. Ala., 1946-50; B.S., Samford U., 1958; m. Elizabeth Jean Evans, Dec. 20, 1949; children—Michael Elliott III, Jean Evans. Gen. mgr. Haworth Engring. & Mfg. Co., Birmingham, Ala., 1954-56; chief contract negotiator U.S. Army Ordnance, Birmingham, 1956-61; dir. procurement Kennedy Space Center NASA, 1961-67; v.p., sec. Hayes Internat. Corp., Birmingham, 1967—, also dir. Served with Quartermaster Corps, AUS, 1952-54. Mem. Nat. Contract Mgmt. Assn., Am. Ordnance Assn. (life, chpt. pres. 1969-71), Nat. Aerospace Services Assn. (dir. 1971-72), Birmingham Urban League (bd. dirs.). Phi Gamma Delta. Presbyn. Clubs: Birmingham Country, The Club, Downtown (Birmingham). Home: 3724 Rockhill Rd Birmingham AL 35223 Office: PO Box 2287 Birmingham AL 35201

HAWTHORN, HORACE BOLES, sociologist; b. Castana, Ia., Dec. 4, 1889; s. William Franklin and Annie (Masters) H.; student State U. Ia., 1907; B.S., Ia. State Coll., 1914, M.S., 1915; Ph.D., U. Wis. (fellow in econs. 1920), 1922; m. Hazel Waples, Sept. 21, 1916; children—Miriam (Mrs. Carl Baker), Clarice (Mrs. Donald Watson), Horace Duane. Asst. prof. sociology Ia. State Coll., 1921-26; asso. prof. sociology, Municipal U. Akron, 1926-30; prof. Sociology, Morningside Coll., Sioux City, Ia., 1931-58, prof. emeritus and research sociologist, 1958—; rural sociologist, Ia. Agrl. Expt. Sta., 1925-26; research sociologist Better Akron Fedn., 1926-30; lectr. Civic and Welfare Assn., 1928. Mem. Am. Sociol. Soc.; Am. Assn. U. Profs., Nat. Writers Club, Alpha Kapps Delta, Phi Kappa Phi, Delta Sigma Rho, Gamma Sigma Delta, Pi Gamma Mu. Methodist. Author: Outlines of Sociology, 1923; Sociology of Rural Life, 1926; Sociology of the World Crisis, 1947; Efficiency of Akron Welfare Agencies Board, 1928; Sociology of the United Nations World, 1952; Culture of Sioux City Youth, bull.; 1936; Sociology of Personality Functioning, 1954; The Immortal Survival of the Human Personality, 1959, enlarged edit., 1967; A Case Study of Iowa School Reorganization, 1966; Social Factors In a Scholastic Writing Career, 1968. Research in personality adjustment in rural and urban communities. Home: 825 S Mulberry Sioux City IA 51106

HAWTHORNE, BETTY EILEEN, educator; b. Seattle, Nov. 22, 1920; d. Harry Albert and Marcia (Thompson) Hawthorne; B.S., U. Wash., 1941, M.S., 1944; Ph.D., Mich. State U., 1954. Field nutritionist Pacific area A.R.C., Wash., 1943-44; instr., asst. prof. Ore. State U., Corvallis, 1946-55, asso. prof. foods and nutrition dept., 1955-62, prof., 1962—, dean Sch. Home Econs., 1965- -. Bd. dirs. Good Samaritan Hosp., Corvallis. Served from ensign to lt. (j.g.), Supply Corps, USNR, 1944-46. Mem. Am., Ore. (past pres.) dietetic assns., Am. Chem. Soc., Am. Home Econs. Assn. (sect. chmn.) Am. Assn. U. Women, A.A.A.S., Altrusa Internat., N.W. Assn. Secondary and Higher Schs. (mem. commn. higher schs.), Phi Beta Kappa, Sigma Xi, Phi Kappa Phi, Omicron Nu, Iota Sugma Pi. Home: 144 NW 29th St Corvallis OR 97330

HAWTHORNE, BOWER, newspaper editor; b. Granville, Ill., Mar. 27, 1913; s. Lawrence and Charlotte (Bower) H.; student U. Minn.; m. Jane Speakes, Sept. 14, 1939; children—Susan (Mrs. William B. Plank), Sarah (Mrs. Douglas R. Jones), Priscilla (Mrs. Steven C. Williams), Prudence. Reporter, Mpls. Star, 1935-42, asst. city editor, 1942-45; city editor Mpls. Tribune, 1945-52, news editor, 1952-55; exec. asst. Mpls. Star and Tribune, 1955, asst. exec. editor, 1956-60, exec. news editor, 1960-67; exec. editor Mpls. Tribune, 1967-69, editor, 1969—. Clk. Village of Edina, Minn., 1943-52. Mem. Am. Soc. Newspaper Editors, Sigma Delta Chi. Conglist. Clubs: Minneapolis; Edina (Minn.) Country. Home: 5301 Minnehaha Blvd Edina MN 55424 Office: 425 Portland Av Minneapolis MN 55415

HAWTHORNE, EDWARD WILLIAM, educator, physiologist; b. Port Gibson, Miss., Nov. 30, 1921; s. Edward W. and Charlotte (Killian) H.; B.S., Howard U., 1941, M.D., 1946; M.S., U. Ill., 1949, Ph.D. (Life Ins. Med. Research fellow physiology 1949- 51), 1951; m. Eula Roberts, June 18, 1948; children—Coral, Dayle, Hilary, Leigh, Edward William. Asst. in physiology Howard U. Coll. Medicine, 1942-44, U. Ill.; 1948-49; intern Freedmen's Hosp., Washington, 1946-47; mem. faculty Howard U. Coll. Medicine, 1951—, head dept. physiology, 1951—, prof. physiology, 1958—; asso. dean, 1969—. Spl. cons. edocrine sect. Nat. Inst. Arthritis and Metabolic Diseases, 1954-57; med. adviser SSS, 1960—. Diplomate Nat. Bd Med. Examiners. Fellow Am. Coll. Cardiology; mem. Am. Orthopedic Assn., Am. (del. assembly 1960—), Washington heart assns., Council High Blood Pressure Research, Am. Assn. U. Profs., A.A.A.S., Physiol. Soc. Phila., Medico-Chirugical Soc., Am., Nat. med. assn., N.Y. Acad. Scis., Washington Soc. Pathologists, Washington Acad. Scis., Am. Physiol. Soc., Sigma Xi. Author numerous articles in field. Home: 1414 Ingraham St NW Washington DC 20011

HAWTHORNE, FRANK HOWARD, lawyer; b. Hope Hull, Ala., Sept. 16, 1923; s. William Blackwell and Bessie Louise (Greene) H.; student Vanderbilt U., 1943-44; B.S., Auburn U., 1946; LL.B., U. Ala., 1949; m. Esther Rae Wille, Feb. 26, 1952; children—Frank Howard, Raymond James, Mary Jule. Instr. Auburn U., 1946, U. Ala., 1946-49; admitted to Ala. bar, 1949; partner firm Balch, Bingham, Baker, Hawthorne & Williams, Birmingham and Montgomery, Ala., head Montgomery office, 1955—. Dir. New Southland Nat. Ins. Co. Chmn. adv. bd. Salvation Army, 1968-70; past chpt. chmn. Nat. Found. Served to 2d lt. USAAF, 1943-45; 1st lt. USAAF, 1951-52. Mem. Am. (mem. resolutions com. 1959-60), Ala. (grievance com. 1961-62), Montgomery County bar assns., Jr. C. of C. (dir. 1950), Auburn U. Alumni Assn. (exec. com. 1957-59), Newcomen Soc. N.Am., Pioneers of Montgomery, The Thirteen, Omicron Delta Kappa, Pi Tau Chi, Pi Kappa Phi (nat. historian 1954-56, nat. chancellor, mem. nat. council; bd. dirs., pres. Pi Kappa Phi Properties 1966—), Phi Alpha Delta. Episcopalian. Kiwanian. Clubs: Capital City, Men of Montgomery (bd. of control 1968-71) (Montgomery); Montgomery Country; Beauvoir Country. Home: 3382 Thomas Av Montgomery AL 36111 Office: 600 N 18th St Birmingham AL 35203 also 1st Nat Bank Bldg Montgomery AL 36101

HAWTHORNE, MARION FREDERICK, educator; b. Ft. Scott, Kan., Aug. 24, 1928; s. Fred Elmer and Colleen (Webb) H.; B.A., Pomona Coll., 1949; Ph.D. (AEC fellow), U. Cal. at Los Angeles, 1953; m. Beverly Dawn Rempe, Oct. 30, 1951; children—Cynthia Lee, Candace Lee. Research asso. Ia. State Coll., 1953-54; research chemist Rohm & Haas Co., Huntsville, Al., 1954-56, group leader, 1956-60, lab. head, Phila., 1961; vis. lectr. Harvard, 1960, 68, Queen Mary Coll., U. London, 1963; prof. chemistry U. Cal. at Riverside, 1962-68, U. Cal. at Los Angeles, 1968—. Recipient Chancelors award, 1968; Sloan Found. fellow, 1963-65. Mem. Aircraft Owners and Pilots Assn., Sigma Xi, Alpha Chi Sigma, Sigma Nu. Editor: Inorganic Chemistry, 1969—. Editorial bd. Progress in Solid State Chemistry, 1971—, Inorganic Syntheses, 1966—, Organometellics in Chemical Synthesis, 1969—, Synthesis in Inorganic and Metalorganic Chemistry, 1970—. Home: 2512 Pesquera Dr Los Angeles CA 90049

HAWTHORNE, WILLIAM REDE, engr.; b. Newcastle-on-Tyne, Eng., May 22, 1913; s. William and Elizabeth (Greenfield) H.; student Westminister Sch., London, 1926-31; A.B., Trinity Coll., Cambridge, Eng., 1934; Sc.D., Mass. Inst. Tech., 1939; m. Barbara Runkle, Apr. 29, 1939; children—Alexander, Joanna Temple, Elizabeth Grenville. Came to U.S., 1935. Student engr. Babcock & Wilcox, Ltd., Renfrew, Scotland, 1934, devel. engr., 1937-39; research and devel. in gas turbine aero-engines Royal Aircraft Establishment, Farnborough, Hants, Eng., 1940-44; tech. liaison officer Brit. Air Commn., Washington, 1944; dep. dir. aero-engine research Brit. Ministry of Supply, London, 1945; asso. prof. mech. engring. Mass. Inst. Tech., 1946-48, George Westinghouse prof. mech. engring., 1948-51; Hopkinson and Imperial Chem. Industries prof. applied thermo-dynamics Cambridge U., Eng., 1951—, head engring. dept., 1968—, master Churchill Coll., 1968; vis. prof. Mass. Inst. Tech., 1962-68. Mem. Mass. Inst. Tech. Corp., 1968—. Recipient Medal of Freedom, 1947. Fellow Royal Soc., Royal Aero. Soc. London; mem. Inst. Mech. Engrs., Inst. Aero. Scis., U.S. Nat. Acad. Scis. (fgn. asso.). Home: Tideacres Cedar St Duxbury MA 02332 also Churchill Coll Cambridge England Office: Mass Inst Tech Cambridge MA 02139

HAXO, FRANCIS THEODORE, educator, biologist; b. Grand Forks, N.D., Mar. 9, 1921; s. Henry Emile and Florence (Shull) H.; B.A., U. N.D., 1941; Ph.D., Stanford, 1947; m. Judith Morgan McLaughlin, Apr. 15, 1961; children—John Frederick, Barbara, Philip, Francis Theodore, Aileen. Teaching, research asst. Stanford, 1941-44, acting instr., 1943; research asst. Cal. Inst. Tech., 1946; research asso. Hopkins Marine Sta., Pacific Grove. Cal., 1946-47; from instr. to asst. prof. plant physiology Johns Hopkins, 1947-52; mem. faculty U. Cal. Scripps Inst. Oceanography, La Jolla, 1952—, prof. biology, 1963—, chmn. marine biology dept., 1960-65; instr. marine botany Marine Biol. Lab., Woods Hole, Mass., 1949-52, 70; mem. vis. faculty botany U. Cal. at Berkeley, 1957, U. Wash. Marine Lab., Friday Harbor, 1963; spl. research photosynthesis, plant pigments, physiology of algae Corp. mem. Marine Biol. Lab. Abraham Rosenberg fellow Stanford, 1945. Fellow A.A.A.S., San Diego Zool. Soc.; mem. Bot. Soc. Am., Am. Soc. Plant Physiologists, Phycological Soc. Am., Soc. Gen. Physiologists, Western Soc. Naturalists, Internat. Phycological Soc., Phi Beta Kappa, Sigma Xi. Home: 6381 Castejon Dr La Jolla CA 92037

HAY, CHARLES C., oil co. exec.; b. Kingston, Ont., Can., June 28, 1902; s. Donald James and Jessie (Craig) H.; B. Applied Sci., U. Sask., 1925, postgrad., 1926, 27, LL.D., 1965; m. Florence Miller, 1928; children—James, Donna Joan, William. With Canadian Pacific Ry., Gibbs Bros., 1927-31; mem. founder group Hi-Way Refineries, Ltd., Sask., Can., 1931, mgr. refinery, Saskatoon, 1932-41, charge refining operations, 1941-44, gen. mgr., Regina, 1944-46, v.p., 1946, pres., 1947-54; v.p., dir. Royalite Oil Co., Ltd. (purchaser Hi-Way Refineries, Ltd.), Calgary, Alta., 1955, exec. v.p., 1956-58, pres., 1958-64, chmn. bd., 1964—; dir. Gulf Oil Can., Ltd. (formerly Brit. Am. Oil Co. Ltd.); dir. Bank of N.S., Shawinigan Chems., Ltd. Dir. Nat. Indsl. Conf. Bd. Can.; mem. export adv. com. Dept. Trade and Commerce. Chmn. campaign adv. bd. Nat. Crusade Can.'s Mentally Retarded. Mem. Ind. Petroleum Assn. (past pres.), Engring. Inst. Can., Assn. Profl. Engrs. Ont. Mem. United Ch. Mason (Shriner). Clubs: Ranchem's, York, Toronto, Toronto Cricket, Skating and Curling; Canadian (N.Y.C.). Home: 19 York Ridge Rd Willowdale Ontario Canada Office: 800 Bay St Toronto 5 Ontario Canada

HAY, DAVID OSBORNE, Australian govt. ofcl.; b. Corowa, Australia, Nov. 29, 1916; s. Harry Algernon and Marjory (Osborne) H.; B.A., Oxford (Eng.) U., 1938, Melbourne (Australia) U., 1939; m. Alison Marion Parker Adams, Jan. 25, 1944; children—Andrew Osborne, David William Parker. Joined Australian Dept. External Affairs, 1939; ofcl. sec., later counsellor Australian High Commn., Ottawa, Can., 1950-52; del. UN Gen. Assembly, 1949-50; del. UN Trusteeship Council, 1950; assigned Dept. External Affairs, 1952-53, Imperial Def. Coll., London, Eng., 1954; minister, later ambassador embassy, Bangkok, Thailand, 1955-57; asst. sec. Dept. External Affairs, 1957-61; Australian high commr., Ottawa, 1961-63; Australian permanent rep. to UN, 1963-65; first asst. sec. Dept. External Affairs, 1965-67; adminstr. Ty. Papua and New Guinea, 1967-70; now sec. Dept. External Ters., Canberra, Australia. Served with Australian Inf., 1940-46. Decorated comdr. Order Brit. Empire; Distinguished Service Order (Australia). Address: 10 Hotham Crescent Deakin ACT Australia

HAY, ELIZABETH DEXTER, educator, physician; b. St. Augustine, Fla., Apr. 2, 1927; d. Isaac Morris and Lucille (Lynn) Hay; A.B., Smith Coll., 1948; M.D., Johns Hopkins, 1952; M.S., Harvard, 1964. Intern Johns Hopkins Hosp., 1952-53; instr. Johns Hopkins Med. Sch., 1953-56, asst. prof., 1956-57; asst. prof. Cornell Med. Coll., 1957-60; asst. prof. Harvard Med. Sch., 1960-64, Louise Foote Pfeiffer asso. prof. embryology, 1964-70, Louise Foote Pfeiffer prof. embryology, 1970—; cons. NIH. Mem. Am. Assn. Anatomists, Am. Assn. Zoologists, Internat. Inst. Embryology, Soc. Developmental Biology, Soc. Cell Biology, Phi Beta Kappa, Sigma Xi, Alpha Omega Alpha. Home: 14 Aberdeen Rd Weston MA 02193 Office: Harvard Med Sch 25 Shattuck St Boston MA 02115

HAY, GEORGE EDWARD, mathematician; b. Durham, Ont., Can., June 11, 1914; s. Edward Alexander and Frances Annetta (Scarr) H.; B.A., U. Toronto, 1935, M.A., 1936, Ph.D., 1939; m. Lillian Edith Parker, May 28, 1943; children—Edward James, John Robert, Kathryn Ann. Instr. Armour Inst. Tech., 1939-40; instr. U. Mich., 1940-42, asst. prof., 1942-47, asso. prof., 1947-56, prof., 1956—, chmn. dept. math., 1957-67, asso. dean Grad. Sch. 1967—, research asso. OSRD, 1944-45. Mem. Am., London math. socs., Math. Assn. Am., Soc. Indsl. and Applied Math., Sigma Xi. Home: 1714 Morton Av Ann Arbor MI 48104

HAY, ISAAC KLINE, ex-govt. ofcl.; b. Covington, Ga., Feb. 26, 1905; s. Samuel Martin and Medora (Peek) H.; LL.B., U. Ga., 1928; m. Florice Caldwell, Sept. 6, 1935; 1 son, Isaac Kline. Admitted to Ga. bar, 1928; partner firm King & Hay, Covington, 1928-31; sec. Exec. Dept. Ga., 1931-33; asso. state counsel HOLC, 1933-34; lst asst. U.S. dist. atty., Atlanta, 1934-39; with ICC, 1939-68, asso. gen. counsel, 1951-63, dep. gen. counsel 1963- 68; now transp. cons. Pres. Atlanta Fed. Bus. Assn., 1936-38; bd. dirs. Atlanta Jr. C. of C., 1935-39. Sec. Ga. Bd. Electors, 1931-33. Served to lt. col. AUS, 1942-46. Mem. Am., Fed. bar assn., Judge Adv. Assn., Sigma Delta Kappa (pres. Atlanta 1935-36; nat. v.p. 1937). Baptist. Mason. Clubs: Atlanta Lawyers; Sphinx, Blue Key, Gridiron Honor (U. Ga.); Kenwood Country (Washington); University. Author, dir. radio series, Uncle Sam at Work, 1936-37, Jaycess Highway Safety Campaign, 1935. Home: 3209 Legion Dr Covington GA 30209

HAY, JESS THOMAS, corp. exec.; b. Forney, Tex., Jan. 22, 1931; s. George and Myrtle (Roddy) H.; B.B.A., So. Methodist U., 1953, J.D., 1955; m. Betty Jo Peacock, Aug. 3, 1951; children—Deborah Anne, Patricia Lynn. Admitted to Tex. bar, 1955; practice in Dallas, 1955-65; chmn. bd., chief exec. officer Lomas & Nettleton Financial Corp., Dallas, 1965—, also dir.; chmn. bd., chief exec. officer Lomas & Nettleton Mortgage Investors, 1969—; dir. Dallas Airmotive, Inc., Trinity Industries, Lomas & Nettleton Co., Mercantile Nat. Bank Dallas, CMI Investment Corp., Continental Mortgage Ins., Inc., NCS. Computing Corp., Braewood Devel. Corp. Mem. bd. visitors So. Meth. U. Mem. Am., Tex., Dallas bar assns., Am. Judicature Soc., So. Meth. U. Law Alumni Assn. (pres. 1965-66, dir. 1964-70), Phi Alpha Delta, Order of Woolsack. Home: 7236 Lupton Circle Dallas TX 75225 Office: Hartford Bldg Dallas TX 75201

HAY, JOHN, author; b. Ipswich, Mass., Aug. 31, 1915; s. Clarence Leonard and Alice (Appleton) H.; grad. St. Paul's Sch. Concord, N.H., 1934; A.B., Harvard, 1938; m. Kristi Putnam, Feb. 14, 1942; children—Susan, Katherine, Rebecca (dec.), Charles. Washington corr. Charleston (S.C.) News and Courier, 1939-40; engaged as writer, 1946—. Pres. bd. Cape Cod Museum Natural History, Brewster, Mass., 1956—; chmn. Brewster Conservation Commn., 1964-71. Served with AUS, World War II. Named Phi Beta Kappa Poet Harvard, 1963; named Conservationist of Year, Mass. Wildlife Fedn., 1970; named hon. mem. Phi Beta Kappa. Episcopalian. Author: (poems) A Private History, 1947; The Run, 1959; Nature's Year, 1961; (with Arlene Strong) A Sense of Nature, 1962; The Great Beach (John Burroughs medal 1964), 1963; (with Peter Farb) The Atlantic Shore, 1966; In Defense of Nature, 1969; The Primal Alliance: Earth and Ocean, 1971; also articles, poems, book revs. Address: Brewster MA 02631

HAY, JOHN HANCOCK, Jr., army officer; b. Thief River Falls, Minn., Oct. 2, 1917; s. John Hancock and Elsabeth (Robbecke) H.; B.S., U. Mont., 1940; postgrad. Harvard, 1962; m. Helen Hoerning, Oct. 18, 1941; 1 dau., Susan Elsabeth (Mrs. Peter Hamilton Ward). Commd. 2d lt. U.S. Army, 1939, advanced through grades to lt. gen., 1966; comdt. Mountain Tng. Center Austria, 1952-53; G-3 Tactical Command, Austria, 1953-54; instr. Command and Gen. Staff Coll., Ft. Leavenworth, Kan., 1955-58; student Canadian Def. Col., Kingston, 1958-59; battle group comdr. 101st Airborne Div., Ft. Campbell, Ky., 1959-60, chief of staff, 1960-61; dep. G-3, 8th Army, Korea, 1961-62; with Weapons Systems Evaluation Group, Pentagon, Washington, 1962-64; comdg. gen. Berlin Brigage, 1964-66; comdg. gen. 1st Inf. Div., Vietnam, 1967-68; dep. comdg. gen. II Field Force, Vietnam, 1968, command and gen. staff coll., 1968-71; comdg. gen. XVIII Airborne Corps, Ft. Bragg, N.C., 1971—. Decorated D.S.C., D.S.M., Silver Star medal with three oak leaf clusters, D.F.C. with three oak leaf clusters, Legion of Merit with oak leaf cluster, Bronze Star with two oak leaf clusters, Air medal with 27 oak leaf clusters, Army Commendation medal, combat Inf. badge. Mem. Assn. U.S. Army, Phi Delta Theta. Mason (Shriner), Rotarian. Home: 2733 S Milwaukee Denver CO Office: Office Comdg Gen XVIII Abn Corps Ft Bragg NC 28307

HAY, JOHN THOMAS, c. of c. exec.; b. Lincoln, Neb., Jan. 30, 1921; s. Ronald Harding and Luella (Sands) H.; student U. Neb., 1942, Harvard, 1942; m. Mable Margaret Secund, May 26, 1942; children—Susan Diane, Sally Lynn, John Thomas. Sec., Colby (Kan.) C. of C., 1946; mgr. Columbus (Neb.) C. of C., 1947-51; asst. mgr. Greater Muskegon (Mich.) C. of C., 1951-52, mgr., 1952-59; exec. v.p. St. Paul Area C. of C., 1959-67; exec. v.p. Cal. C. of C., Sacramento, 1967—. Organizer, Mich. C. of C., 1958-59; v.p. for Mich.-Gt. Lakes States Indsl. Devel. Council, 1958-59; chmn. Gov.'s Blue Ribbon Com., Summer Youth Campaign, 1968-69; chmn. Inst. for C. of C. Execs., U. Colo., 1965. bd. regents, 1960-66, instr., 1960-67. Served to capt., Q.M.C., AUS, 1942-46. Recipient Distinguished Service award as Greater Muskegon's. Outstanding Young Man of Year, 1954, F.O.Y.M. award as one of five outstanding young men of Mich., 1955, Outstanding U.S. Chamber Program of Work award, Muskegon, 1958, St. Paul, 1960, 62; Accreditation award St. Paul C. of C., 1962. Mem. Am. (past dir.), Minn, (past pres.) Chamber of Commerce execs. Home: 1316 San Augustine Way Sacramento CA 95831 Office: 455 Capitol Mall Sacramento CA 95814

HAY, STEPHEN JOHN, ins. co. exec.; b. Dallas, Apr. 4, 1899; s. Stephen John and Mary (Randle) H.; B.A., So. Meth. U., 1919; LL.D., Daniel Baker Coll., Brownwood, Tex. 1951; m. Avella Winn, Jan. 17, 1924 (dec. Feb. 1958); children—Stephen John, William Winn; m. 2d, Nadine de Puisieux, Feb. 23, 1961. Clk., Am. Life Reins. Co., Dallas, 1919-21; with United Fidelity Life Ins. Co., Dallas, 1921-27, asst. sec., 1924-27, dir., 1925- 27; organizer Gt. Nat. Life Ins. Co., Dallas, 1928, pres. 1928-58, chmn. bd., 1958-68; chmn. bd. Hesse Envelope Co., Dallas, 1954—; dir. Tex. Utilities Co., Am. Savs. Assn. Dallas. Founder, dir., exec. com. Tex. Research League, 1953—, chmn., 1967. Mem. exec. com. region 9, Boy Scouts Am. Commr., University Park, Tex., 1932-38. Trustee So. Meth. Univ. founder, 1st pres. Inst. Ins. Marketing, bd. dirs. Univ. Found. for Sci. and Engring.; trustee Southwestern Med. Found.; trustee exec. com. St. Mark's Sch. Tex., 1946-56; bd. dirs. Family Service Dallas, 1934-49, pres. 1947- 49. Recipient Silver Antelope award Boy Scouts Am., 1951; Distinguished Alumnus award So. Meth. U., 1952. Mem. Am. (exec. com. 1944-51, pres. 1949-50), Tex. (pres. 1942-43) life convs. Methodist. Mason, Kiwanian (pres. Dallas Downtown club 1949). Home: 5526 Stonegate Rd Dallas TX 75209 Office: 5526 Stonegate Rd Dallas TX 75209

HAY, WILLIAM HENRY, educator; b. Washington, June 9, 1917; s. Edward Northup and Doris (Drain) H.; A.B., Haverford Coll., 1938; A.M., Brown U., 1939; Ph.D., U. Ill., 1943; m. Joan Leigh Parrish, Feb. 13, 1943 (dec. Sept. 1960); 1 dau., Miranda; m. 2d Helen Card Clements, July 6, 1961. Instr. philosophy U. Ill., 1946, State U. Ia., 1946-47; asst. prof. philosophy U. Wis., 1947-52, asso. prof. 1952-59, prof., 1959—, chmn. dept., 1958- 63, research prof. Humanities Research Inst., 1965-66. Served to lt. (s.g.) USNR, 1942-46. Recipient fellowship for original work Western div. Am. Philos. Assn., 1957-58. Mem. Am. Philos. Assn. (sec.-treas. div. 1951-53, nat. sec.-treas. 1954-57, chmn. nat. com. philosophy and edn. 1965—), Amateur Chamber Music Players, Phi Beta Kappa. Co-editor: Reason and Common Good, 1963. Home: 39 Bagley Ct Madison WI 53705

HAY, WILLIAM WALTER, educator; b. Bay City, Mich., Dec. 10, 1908; s. William K. and Addilade Belle (Kyler) W.; B.S., Carnegie Inst. Tech., 1931, mgmt. engr., 1948; M.S., U. Ill., 1948, Ph.D., 1956; m. Mary Clark Hubley, Feb. 20, 1943; children—William Walter, Mary Elizabeth. Railroad constrn. and maintenance supr. and engring. with various rys., 1934-43; project engr. Reading R.R. Co., 1946-47; asst. to prof. ry. civil engring. U. Ill., Urbana, 1947—. Ry. cons. for city planning; project engr. Alaska R.R. 1948; mem. bd. cons. evaluating proposed ry. routes in Mocambique and So. Rhodesia, 1950; cons. Fed. R.R. Adminstrn. Task Force on R.R. Safety, 1970—; mem.-at-large NRC div. engring. and indsl. research, 1963-66; mem. com. sci. and tech. in the ry. industry Nat. Acad. Sci., 1963-64; mem. task force com. govt. policy transp. research and devel. C. of C. U.S., 1965-66; chmn. com. qualification for registration Nat. Council Engring. Examiners, 1969-70; mem. sub.-com. chmn. panel high speed ground transp. U.S. Dept. Commerce, 1966-67. Served from lt. to lt. col., Mil. Ry. Service, AUS, 1943-46: ETO, PTO; chief engr. Korean Rys. for U.S. Mil. Govt., 1945-46. Mem. Ill. Profl. Engrs. (mem. exam. com. 1959-60, 61-63), Nat. Council State Bd. Engring. Examiners. Am. Ry. Engring. Assn. (chmn. area com. 24, dir. 1957-58, 58-61), Roadmasters and Maintenance Way Assn. Am., Am. Soc. Engring. Edn., Sigma Xi, Chi Epsilon, Tau Beta Pi. Presbyn. Mason (Shriner). Author: Railroad Engineering, Vol. I, 1953; TM 5-370 Railroad Construction in the Theater of Operations, 1954; An Introduction to Transportation Engineering, 1961. Home: 801 Kirby Av Champaign IL 61820 Office: Engring Hall U Ill Urbana IL 61801

HAY, WILLIAM WINN, educator; b. Dallas, Oct. 12, 1934; s. Stephen John and Avella (Winn) H.; student Universitaet Muencheon, Germany, 1953-54; B.S., So. Methodist U., 1955; postgrad. Universitaet Zuerich, Switzerland, 1955-56; M.S., U. Ill., 1958; Ph.D., Leland Stanford Jr. U., 1960. NSF postdoctoral fellow Universitaet Basel, Switzerland, 1959-60; asst. prof. U. Ill., Urbana, 1960-63, asso. prof., 1963-68, prof., 1968—; adj. prof. Inst. Marine Scis., U. Miami, Fla., 1966-68, prof. Rosenstiel Sch. Marine and Atmospheric Scis., 1968—; mem. Joides Planning Com.; chmn. SEPM Research Symposium, 1970; hon. research fellow U. Coll., U. London (Eng.). Dir. Hesse Envelope Co. Fellow Geol. Soc. Am.; mem. A.A.A.S., Am. Assn. Petroleum Geologist, Geol. Vereinigung, Paleontol. Instn., Soc. Econ. Paleontologists and Mineralogists, Paleontol. Soc., Schweiz. Geol. Ges., Schweiz. Paleontol. Ges., Soc. Geol. Mexicana, Soc. Geol. France, Soc. Study Evolution, Soc. Protozoologists, Phi Beta Kappa, Sigma Xi, Phi Eta Sigma, Delta Phi Alpha. Home: 508 S Mattis Av Champaign IL 61820 also 2451 Brickell Av Miami FL 33129 Office: Natural History Bldg U Ill Urbana IL 61801 also 10 Rickenbacher Causeway Miami FL 33149

HAYAKAWA, SAMUEL ICHIYE, coll. pres., writer; b. Vancouver, B.C., Can., July 18, 1906; s. Ichiro and Tora (Isono) H.; B.A., U. Man., 1927; M.A., McGill U., 1928; Ph.D., U. Wis., 1935; D.F.A. (hon.), Cal. Coll. Arts and Crafts, 1956; D.Litt. (honoris causa), Grinnell Coll., 1967; m. Margedant Peters, May 27, 1937; children—Alan Romer, Mark, Wynne. Fellow English, U. Wis., 1929-30, asst., 1930-36, instr. English extension div., 1936-39; instr. English, Armour Inst. Tech., 1939-40; asst. prof. English, Ill. Inst. Tech., 1940-42, asso. prof., 1942-47; lectr. univ. coll. U. Chgo., 1950-55; prof. English, San Francisco State Coll., 1955-68, acting pres., 1968-69, pres., 1969—; Alfred P. Sloan vis. prof. Menninger Sch. Psychiatry, 1961. Recipient Claude Bernard Medal Exptl. Medicine and Surgery, U. Montreal, 1959. Fellow A.A.A.S., Am. Psychol. Assn., Am. Sociol. Assn.; mem. Modern Lang. Assn., Internat. Soc. for Gen. Semantics (pres. 1949-50), Am. Anthrop. Assn., Consumers Union U.S. (dir. 1953-55), Inst. Jazz Studies (dir.). Clubs: Press San Francisco; Pannonia Athletic. Author: Oliver Wendell Holmes (with Howard M. Jones), 1939; Language in Action (Book-of- the-Month Club selection), 1941; Language in Thought and Action, 1949; Language, Meaning and Maturity, 1954; Our Language and Our World, 1959; Symbol, Status and Personality, 1963. Columnist Chgo. Defender, 1942-47; reviewer Chgo. Sun Book Week. Editor: ETC.; A Review of General Semantics, 1943-70. Editor: Funk & Wagnalls Modern Guide to Synonyms, 1968; supr. editorial bd. Funk & Wagnalls Standard Dicts. Contbr. to Middle English Dict., U. Mich., 1933-38. Home: 225 Eldridge Mill Valley CA 94941 Office: 1600 Holloway San Francisco CA 94132

HAYAKAWA, SESSUE, (Kintaro Hayakawa), Japanese film actor; b. Naaura Twp., Honshu, Japan, June 10, 1890; s. Yoichoro and Kane Hayakawa; grad. Naval Prep. Sch. (Tokyo), 1908; grad. polit. sci. U. Chgo., 1913; m. Tsura Aoki, May 1, 1914 (dec. Oct. 1961); children—Yukio, Yoshiko, Fujiko. Actor, dir. Japanese theatre; 1913; motion picture debut in Hollywood prodn. Typhoon, 1914, other roles in Wrath of Gods, 1914, Hashimura Togo, City of Dim Faces, Call of the East, Hidden Faces; formed Haworth Corp., 1918, merged with Roberts & Cole, 1920; producer motion pictures The Swamp, Vermilion Pencil, Daughter of the Dragon, 1931; actor motion pictures Yoshiwara (France), 1937, Tokyo Joe, 1949, Three Came Home, 1950, Bridge Over the River Kwai, 1957, Geisha Boy, 1958; actor on stage in the Love City, Bandit Prince (vaudeville), Honorable Mr. Wong (Tokyo), role of Claudius in Hamlet (Tokyo), 1934; prod. play Life of Buddha, Tokyo, 1949; appeared TV prodns. Judge Internat. Film Festival, Venice, 1947. Ordained Zen Buddhist priest. Recipient Golden Globe award Hollywood Fgn. Press Assn., 1957; nominated best supporting actor Acad. Award, 1957. Author: The Bandit Prince. Address: Hotel Edison 228 W 47th St New York City NY 10036

HAYASHI, TERU, educator, zoologist; b. Atlantic City, Feb. 12, 1914; s. Andrew Tetsuji and Shizuka Hayashi; B.S., Ursinus Coll., 1938; student U. Pa., 1939; Ph.D., U. Mo., 1943; m. Sarah Darlington Rexon, Sept. 22, 1943; children—Curt, Tesa, Tomi, Tuck; m. 2d, Sarah Dixon Browne, May 15, 1970. Instr. physics USAAF-ASTP program, 1943- 44; instr. zoology U. Mo., 1944-45, research asso. zoology, 1945-46; mem. faculty Columbia, 1946-67, prof. zoology, 1958-67 chmn. dept. zoology, 1963-67; prof., chmn. dept. biology Ill. Inst. Tech., Chgo., 1967—, Mem. NRC. Trustee Marine Biol. Lab., Woods Hole, Mass., 1968—, Fulbright and Guggenheim fellow, Denmark, 1954-55. Mem. Soc. Gen. Physiologists (pres. 1962-63), Am. Inst. Biol. Scis., Am. Physiol. Soc., Harvey Soc., Am. Soc. Cell

Biology. Author articles in field. Editor: Molecular Architecture in Cell Physiology; Subcellular Particles. Address: 3100 S Michigan Av Chicago IL 60616

HAYASHI, TERUO TERRY, educator, physician; b. Sacramento, Cal., July 23, 1921; s. Jinnosuke and Koto (Watanabe) H.; student U. Cal. at Berkeley, 1939-42, Temple U., 1943-44; M.D., Temple U., 1948; m. Ursula M. Promann, Nov. 29, 1953; children—William Promann, Peter John, James Douglas, Ann Koto, Robert Terry. Intern, Temple U. Hosp., 1949, resident, 1951-54; instr. Temple U. Med. Sch., 1954-59, asst. prof., 1960-62, asso.prof., 1963-65; prof. obstetrics and gynecology U. Pitts., 1965—; study sect. human embryology and devel. NIH, 1964-68, now mem. com. perinatal biology and infant mortality br. Served with AUS, 1949-51. Mem. Am. Coll. Obstetrics and Gynecology, Soc. Gynecol. Investigation, Am. Gynecol. Soc., Sigma Xi. Home: 146 Woodshire Dr Pittsburgh PA 15215

HAYCRAFT, HOWARD, publisher, author; b. Madelia, Minn., July 24, 1905; s. Julius E. and Marie (Stelzer) H.; A.B., U. Minn., 1928; m. Molly Randolph Costain, Oct. 9, 1942. Staff, U. Minn. Press, 1928; with H.W. Wilson Co., N.Y.C. 1929—, v.p., 1940-52, pres., 1953-67, chmn. bd., 1967—; dir. Forest Press, 1951-68, pres., 1961-62 Specialist War Dept., 1942. Mem. Pres.'s Com. Employment of Handicapped, 1963—, chmn. A.L.A. Round Table Services to blind, 1968-69. Served from capt. to maj., U.S. Army Service Forces, 1942-46. Recipient of U. Minn. Outstanding Achievement award, 1954; Campbell medal and citation A.L.A., 1966, Mem. Mystery Writers Am. (pres. 1963), Kappa Sigma. Clubs: Players, Dutch Treat (N.Y.C.). Author, editor, or joint editor: Authors Today and Yesterday, 1933; Junior Book of Authors, 1934; Boys' Sherlock Holmes, 1936; British Authors of the Nineteenth Century, 1936; Boys' Book of Great Detective Stories, 1938; American Authors: 1600-1900, 1938; Boys' Second Book of Great Detective Stories, 1940; Murder for Pleasure; The Life and Times of the Detective Story, 1941; Crime Club Encore, 1942; Twentieth Century Authors, 1942; Art of the Mystery Story, 1946; Fourteen Great Detective Stories, 1949; British Authors Before 1800, 1952; Treasury of Great Mysteries, 1957; Ten Great Mysteries, 1959; Five Spy Novels, 1962; Three Times Three, Mystery Omnibus, 1964; Books for the Blind: A Postscript and an Appreciation, 1968. Contbr. to lit. publs. Office: 950 University Av Bronx NY 10452

HAYDEN, AUSTIN JOSEPH, food processing co. exec.; b. Le Sueur, Minn., Mar. 16, 1922; s. Henry James and Mary (White) H.; B.S, U. Minn., 1947, M.S., 1948; m. Marilyn Jean Griffin, June 16, 1947; children—Gail, Gregory, Gary, Geralyn. Chem. lab. worker Green Giant Co., Le Sueur, part time 1940-43, insect control coordinator, Montgomery, Minn., summer 1948, agrl. supt., Glencoe, Minn., 1948-49, Montgomery, 1949-51, spl. agrl. asst. Minn.-Ia. div., Le Sueur, 1951-52, agrl. mgr., 1952-55, prodn. supt., 1955-60, dir. agrl. products, U.S., Can., 1960-63, dir. prodn., U.S., Can., 1963-66, v.p. U.S. prodn., Le Sueur, 1966-70, sr. v.p., 1971—. Mem. Minn. Gov.'s Tech. Services Adv. Com., 1966—; mem. Gov.'s Commn. to Minn. Dept. Econ. Devel., 1967—, chmn. transp. com., 1968—. Bd. dirs. Geen Giant Found. Served to capt., A.C., USMCR, 1944-46; PTO. Mem. Nat. Canners Assn. (chmn. agr. com. 1966-67), Minn. Farm Mgrs. Assn. (past pres.), Am. Soc. Farm Mgrs. and Rural Appraisers, N.A.M., Nat. Assn. Frozen Food Packers (dir.). Roman Catholic. Home: 217 Snow Ridge Le Sueur MN 56058 Office: 1200 Commerce St Le Sueur MN 56058

HAYDEN, CARL (TRUMBULL), former U.S. senator; b. Hayden's Ferry, now Tempe, Ariz., Oct. 2, 1877; s. Charles Trumbull and Sallie Calvert (Davis) H.; grad. Normal Sch. of Ariz., Tempe, 1896; attended Leland Stanford U., 1896-1900; LL.D., U. Ariz., 1948, Ariz. State U., 1959; m. Nan Downing, Feb. 14, 1908 (dec.). Mem. Tempe Town Council, 1902-04; treas. Maricopa County, 1904- 06, sheriff, 1907-12; maj. inf., U.S.N.A., 1918; mem. Congress from Ariz. 1912-69; U.S. senator from Ariz. 1927- 69, pres. pro tempore, 1957-69; specialized on legislation relating to irrigation of arid lands and fed. aid for hwys.; chmn. state com. on appropriations; mem. interior and insular affairs. com. Democrat. Mason. Home: 3049 S Country Club Way Tempe AZ 85281

HAYDEN, CARLOS KEITH, educator; b. Newark, O., Mar. 27, 1917; s. Alva Maguire and Vera Murl (Gilmore) H.; B.S. in Edn., Ohio State U., 1941, M.A., 1946, Ph.D., 1950; m. Marguerite Christina Lind, Jan. 4, 1942; children—Carlos Keith, Beth Ann. With Newark Hatchery, 1935-36, Newark Stove Co., 1936- 37, tchr. bus., chmn. dept. Central High Sch., Piqua, O., 1946-48; instr. Ohio State U., 1948-50; mem. faculty U. Houston, 1950—, prof. bus. edn., 1952—, chmn. dept. bus. edn. and office adminstrn., 1950- 64, asso. dean Coll. Bus. Adminstrn., 1964-65, program coordinator bus. edn., 1965-69, chmn. bus. tech., 1969—. Dean, Inst. Certifying Secs., 1961-63. Served to capt., F.A., AUS, 1941-45. Decorated Silver Star medal with oak leaf cluster, Bronze Star medal. Purple Heart. Mem. Nat. Bus. Edn. Assn., Res. Officers Assn., Nat. Secs. Assn. (hon.), Phi Kappa Phi, Pi Omega Pi, Delta Pi Epsilon. Author: Principles and Problems of Business Education, 3d edit., 1967. Home: 6039 Yarwell Houston TX 77035

HAYDEN, DONALD EUGENE, educator; b. Blairstown, Mo., Aug. 28, 1915; s. Frank Langston and Georgia May (Jefferson) H.; B.A., U. Mo., 1936, M.A., 1937; Ph.D., Syracuse U., 1946; m. Mary Frances Dick, Sept. 12, 1939; children— Donald Eugene, Elizabeth Ann. Instr. English, Syracuse U., 1937-42; head English dept. Westbrook Jr. Coll., Portland, Me., 1942-47; asst. prof. English, U. Tulsa, 1947-51, asso. prof., 1951-56, prof. English 1956, asst. dean liberal arts 1956-57, dean, 1957-70. Chmn. Tulsa Com. for UN, 1956-58; chmn. Tulsa Community Relations Commn. 1961- 64; Tulsa v.p. Nat. Conf. of Christians and Jews, 1968-70. Pres. Tulsa Psychiat. Found., 1959-64. Mem. Am. Assn. U. Profs., Okla. Univ. and Coll. Deans Assn. (pres. 1965-66), Desc. of the Mayflower, south Central Modern Lang. Assn., Phi Beta Kappa, Phi Gamma Kappa, Phi Eta Sigma, Omicron Delta Kappa Mem. Disciples of Christ Ch. (elder; pres. ofcl. bd. 1954-57). Author: After Conflict; Quiet-A Study of Wordsworth, 1951; (with E. Paul Alworth) A Semantics Workbook, 1956; Classics in Semantics, 1964; His Firm Estate, 1967; Classics in Linguistics, 1967; Classics in Composition, 1969, The Creative Process: Introspection, 1971. Home: 3626 S Birmingham Av Tulsa OK 74105

HAYDEN, HAROLD WALTER, librarian; b. Creston, Ia., Dec. 26, 1905; s. Walter L. and Katherine (Wiedman) H.; A.B., Neb. State Coll., 1927; B.S. in L.S., U. Ill., 1929; A.M., U. Mich., 1938; m. Margaret Deane Murray, Aug. 10, 1931; children— Helen Arlene, Carolyn Marie. Asst., Neb. State Tchrs. Coll. Library, 1926-28; sr. asst. U. N.D., 1929-31; supt. serial and exchange U. Ia., 1931-34, supr. dept. libraries, 1934-37; librarian Bucknell U., 1938-65, Lycoming Coll., 1965-71; ret. 1971. Mem. Gov.'s Commn. on Pub. Library Devel. in Pa., 1958-60. Mem. Pa. Library Assn. (pres. 1957-58). Republican. Methodist. Home: 550 Harding Av Williamsport PA 17701

HAYDEN, J. FRANCIS, lawyer; b. Paterson, N.J., May 9, 1907; s. William J. and Catherine (Braun) H.; LL.B., Fordham U., 1928; student spl. courses Columbia, 1929- 30; m. Katharine Greene McCabe, Apr. 20, 1940; children—Dolores Mari, Gregory. Admitted to N.Y. bar, 1929; asso., later partner Murray, Kissam & Hayden, and predecessors, N.Y.C., 1929-45; spl. asst. to atty. gen. U.S., 1945-50; mem. Stickles, Hayden, Kennedy, Hort & Van Steenburgh; pres. James King & Son, constrn. contractors, N.Y.C., 1949-55; chmn. AFA Protective Systems, Inc., N.Y.C., 1968-69. Served as lt., U.S. Coast Guard Res., 1943- 45. Recipient Commendation, U.S. Coast Guard and U.S. Coal Mine Adminstrn., Dept. of Interior. Mem. Assn. Bar City of N.Y., Am., Fed., N.Y. State bar assns. Clubs: Canadian (N.Y.C.). Home: 55 Atherstone Rd Scarsdale NY 10583 Office: 36 W 44th St New York City NY 10036

HAYDEN, MARTIN SCHOLL, newspaperman; b. Detroit, May 21, 1912; s. Jay G. and Marguerite (Scholl) H.; grad. Culver Mil. Acad., 1929; A.B., U. Mich., 1934; L.H.D., Detroit Coll. Law, 1967; m. Elizabeth Dodds, July 26, 1938; children—Jay G. II, John D., Martin Scholl. Reporter Kansas City (Mo.) Star, 1929-30; mem. staff Detroit News, 1930—, Ann Arbor (Mich.) corr., 1930-34, gen. reporter, 1934-37, city and state polit. writer, 1938-47, Washington corr., 1948-58; fgn. assignments include: Japan, China, Philippines, 1936, Berlin fgn. ministers meeting, 1954, Geneva Conf. and Poland, 1955, Hungarian and Polish uprising, 1956, Bermuda Conf., 1957; asso. editor Detroit News, 1958, editor-in-chief, 1959—; dir. A.P. Trustee Cranbrook Sch. (bd. pres. 1963-67; trustee Harper Hosp.; Sec. Leader Dogs for Blind; exec. com. Greater Detroit Area Hosp. Council. Served from 2d lt. to lt. col., AUS, 1942- 45; ETO, D-Day. Decorated Normandy Beach arrowhead. Newspaper Editors, Sigma Chi. Clubs: Chevy Chase, Gridiron, Nat. Press, Overseas Writers (Washington); Detroit, Country of Detroit Home: 218 Merriweather Rd Grosse Pointe Farms MI 48236 Office: Detroit News Detroit MI 48231

HAYDEN, MELISSA, (Mildred Herman), ballerina; b. Toronto, Ont., Can., Apr. 25, 1928; d. Jacob and Kate (Weinberg) Herman; student Boris Volkoff Ballet Sch., Sch. Am. Ballet, Vilzak- Shollar; m. Donald Hugh Coleman, Jr., Feb. 1954; children—Stuart H., Jennifer H. Canadian citizen. Mem. corps de Ballet, Radio City, N.Y.C., 1945, then soloist Ballet Theatre, tours U.S. and Europe, 1946-55, prima ballerina on tour, 1953; toured S.A. with Ballet Alicia Alonso; with N.Y. City Ballet, 1949-53, 55—; appeared in ballets Pas de Trois, The Cage, The Duel, Illuminations, Firebird, Ivesiana, Agon, Copelia, Swan Lake, Medea; appeared in motion picture Limelight; appeared as prima ballerina with Royal Ballet, London, Eng., Nat. Ballet Can., Chgo. Opera Ballet. Recipient merit award Mademoiselle, 1952, Albert Einstein Woman of Achievement award. Mem. scholarship com. Ford Found.; mem. N.Y. State's Arts Council Com. Address: care NY City Ballet 130 W 56th St New York City NY 10019

HAYDEN, MERRILL A., corp. exec.; b. New Albany, Ind., Jan. 16, 1913; s. Roy A. and Josephine (Warth) H.; B.E.E., U. Detroit, 1935; m. Evelyn M. Bradford, Oct. 10, 1936; children—Merrill A., Kathleen, Susan. With Vickers, Inc., 1935- 68, successively engr., various engring., sales, mgmt. positions, 1935- 55, gen. mgr. Waterbury div., 1955-57, Machinery Hydraulics div., 1957- 64, v.p., 1957-64; pres. Vickers, Inc., div. Sperry Rand Corp., Detroit, 1964-68; exec. v.p. Sperry Rand Corp., N.Y.C., 1968—, Mem. Soc. Automotive Engrs., Am. Soc. Naval Engrs., Soc. Naval Architects and Marine Engrs., Nat. Sales Execs., Sales Execs. Club of Waterbury (pres. 1956). Clubs: Detroit Golf. Home: 6926 Valley Spring Dr Birmingham MI 48010 Office: 1290 Av of Americas New York City NY 10019

HAYDEN, MURIE MARTIN, state ofcl.; b. Elmdale, Kan., Nov. 6, 1903; s. Charles and Ida C. (Vetter-Hayden) H.; B.S. in Edn., Kan. State Tchrs. Coll., 1925, M.S., 1935; postgrad. Northwestern U.; m. Emma Adel Wilson, May 24, 1927. Tchr., Talmage (Kan.) High Sch., 1925-26, supt. schs., 1926-33; prin. Lincoln (Kan.) High Sch., 1933-35; rural high sch. prin., Beverly, Kan., 1935-40; supt. schs., Lincoln, 1940-60; with Kan. Dept. Pub. Instrn., 1960-69; acting commnr. edn. Kan. State Dept. Edn., 1969; exec. dir. Kans. State Adv. Council Vocational Edn., 1969—. Mem. Lincoln and Dickinson County Tchrs. Assn. (pres. 1932), Kan. Tchrs. Assn. (v.p. 1941, dir. 1947- 53, chmn. bd. dirs. 1953), Solomon Valley and N. Kan. Leagues (pres. 1939), Kan. Assn. Sch. Adminstrs. (pres., dir. 1960, Kan. State Tchrs. Coll. Alumni Assn., Native Sons and Daus. Kan. (life), Am. Assn. Sch. Adminstrs., Am. Soc. Pub. Adminstrn., Kan. Educators Club, Kan. Adult Edn. Assn., Phi Delta Kappa. Author: Kansas Adult Education, 1961; School Laws of Kansas, 2d edit., 1965. Home: 1605 W 27th St Topeka KS 66611

HAYDEN, RALPH FREDERICK, pub. accountant, corp. exec.; b. N.Y.C., Jan. 15, 1922; s. Fred T. and Thrya (Ohlson) H.; B.B.A., Pace Coll., 1951; student Coll. City N.Y., C.W. Post Coll., N.Y.C.; m. Gloria McCormick, Feb. 27, 1943; children Craig, Glen. Sr. Partner Hayden & Hayden, pub. accountants, Williston Park and Northport, N.Y., 1941—, controller, sec., dir. King Kullen Grocery Co., Inc., 1948—; chmn. bd. dirs., chief exec. officer Browne's Bus. Sch., Inc., 1967-71. Dir., v.p. County Devel. Corp. Past pres., treas., dir. Old Chester Hills Civic Assn., Bellerose Commonwealth Civic Assn.; mem. county exec. com., past chmn., vice chmn. Suffolk County 4-H; local leader, area leader, project leader Greenlawn Friendship 4-H Club; dir. L.I. Com. for Crime Control, Inc.; treas., Elwood Scholarship Fund; v.p. Elwood Community Council; dir. at large Suffolk County Extension Service. Suffolk County Republican County committeeman. Served with USCGR, 1942-45. Mem. Empire State Assn. Pub. Accountants, Nat. Soc. Pub. Accountants, C.W. Post Tax Inst. Kiwanian (past pres.) Home: 22 Bunkerhill Dr Huntington Long Island NY 11743 Office: 374 Hillside Ave Williston Park NY 11596 also 11 Bayview Av Northport NY 11768

HAYDEN, RICHARD HAMILTON, banker; b. Newton, Mass., July 6, 1923; s. Thomas and Carrie L. (Sears) H.; A.B., Amherst Coll., 1945; LL.B., Boston U., 1949; postgrad. Rutgers U., 1956; m. Joan Shelby Eldredge, July 24, 1943; children—Jonathan B., Shelby H. Trust officer, legal officer Nat. Shawmut Bank, Boston, 1949- 61; v.p., trust officer Canal Nat. Bank, Portland, Me., 1961-65, exec. v.p., 1965-67, pres., 1967—. Chmn. Community Leadership Seminar, Portland, 1967-68; vice chmn. advance gifts Portland United Fund Campaign, 1968. Bd. dirs. Home for Aged. Served with AUS, 1943-46. Mem. Mass., Me. bar assns., Theta Delta Chi. Clubs: Portland Country, Cumberland (Portland). Home: 16 Portland St Yarmouth ME 04096 Office: Box 231 Pearl St Sta Portland ME 04112

HAYDEN, ROBERT EARL, educator, poet; b. Aug. 4, 1913; ed. Wayne State U., U. Mich. Teaching fellow U. Mich., Ann Arbor, 1944-46; asso. prof. English, Fisk U., Nashville, 1946—. Recipient Jules and Avery Hopwood award for poetry U. Mich., 1942. Rosenwald fellow in creative writing, 1947-48; Ford Found. fellow for writing, travel in Mexico, 1954-55. Mem. Phi Kappa Phi. Author: (with Myron O'Higgins) The Lion and the Archer (poems); Figures of Time (poems). Contbr. anthologies: The Poetry of the Negro: American Sampler; Cross Section; Negro Carvan; also mags. Home: 1804 Hermosa St Nashville TN 37208 *

HAYDEN, SHERMAN STRONG, educator; b. Cleve., Feb 9, 1908; s. Warren Sherman and Elizabeth (Strong) H.; A.B., Harvard, 1930, L.L.B., 1933; M.A., Columbia, 1936, Ph.D., 1942; m. Marjorie Kearsley Mallett, July 5, 1932; children— Clare H. (Mrs. Stephen T. White), Lorna H. (Mrs. John F. Power Jr.), Christopher Mallett. Admitted to Ohio bar, 1934; with firm Squire, Sanders & Dempsey, Cleve., 1933-35; instr. Columbia, 1938-42; asst. to pres. Fgn. Policy Assn., N.Y.C., 1942-44; mem. faculty Clark U., 1946—, prof. internat. relations, 1956—, chmn. dept., 1962-69. chmn. Worcester Fgn. Policy Assn., 1950-55; pres. Worcester Area Mental health Assn., 1958- 60. Served to lt. (s.g.) USNR, 1944-46. Mem. Am. Polit. Sci. Assn., Acad. Polit. Sci., Am. Soc. Internat. Law, Internat. Law Assn. Democrat. Episcopalian. Author: International Protection of Wildlife, 1942; also articles. Home: Newell Rd Holden MA 01520

HAYDN, HIRAM, editor, author; b. Cleve., Nov. 3, 1907; s. Howell Merriman and Mary (Olmstead) H.; A.B., Amherst Coll., 1928; A.M., Western Res. U., 1938, Litt. D., 1963; Ph.D., Columbia, 1942; m. Rachel Hutchinson Norris, Sept. 14, 1935; 1 dau., Mary Rachel; m. 2d, Mary Wescott Tuttle, June 5, 1945; children—Michael Wescott, Jonathan Olmstead, Miranda Merriman. Instr. Hawken Sch., Cleve., 1928-41; lectr. in English, Cleve. Coll., Western Res. U., 1939-41; asst. prof. English, Woman's Coll., U. N.C., 1942-43, asso. prof., 1943-44; exec. sec. United Chpts. Phi Beta Kappa, 1944-45; asso. editor Crown Publishers, 1945, editor-in-chief, 1948-50; N.Y. editor Bobbs-Merrill Co., 1950-54; sr. editor Random House, 1955-56, editor-in-chief, 1956-59; mem. exec. com. Atheneum Pubs., 1959-64; co-pub. Harcourt, Brace Javanovich Inc., Phila., 1964—. With New Sch. for Social Research, 1947-60; vis. prof. communications U. Pa., 1965-66, prof. communications, Annenberg Sch. Communications, 1966—. Fellow Center Advanced Studies, Wesleyan U., 1964. Lang. Assn., Am. Assn. U. Profs., Phi Beta Kappa, Alpha Delta Phi. Editor: the Am. Scholar, 1944—; co- editor: Explorations in Living: a record of the democratic spirit, 1941; A World of Great Stories, 1947; The Makers of the American Tradition series, 1953—; A Renaissance Treasury, 1954; The Papers of Christian Gauss, 1957; also The American Scholar Reader, 1960. Editor: The Portable Elizabethan Reader, 1946; The Twentieth Century Library series, 1946—. Author: By Nature Free, 1943; Manhattan Furlough, 1945; The Time Is Noon, 1948; The Counter Renaissance, 1950; The Hands of Esau, 1962; Report from the Red Windmill, 1967. Home: 3317 Baring St Philadelphia PA 19104 Office: U Pa 3620 Walnut St Philadelphia PA 19104

HAYDN, RICHARD, actor, director. Appeared in movies Charley's Aunt, And Then There Were None, Cluny Brown, Forever Amber; other films include The Green Years, The Late George Apley, Foxes of Harrow, Mr. Music, Dear Wife, Merry Widow, You Belong to Me, Her Twelve Men, Toy Tiger, Please Don't Eat The Daisies, Mutiny On the Bounty, Sound of Music. Writer under pseudonym Edwin Carp.*

HAYDOCK, THOMAS CARMICHAEL, investment counsel; b. Cin., Aug. 3, 1904; s. George Sewell and Ellen (Carmichael) H.; grad. Taft Sch., 1922; B.S., Yale, 1926; children—George Sewell II, Thomas Carmichael, Nancy Ross (Mrs. James M. Detmer). Partner Scudder, Stevens & Clark, Cin., 1959—. Clubs: Camargo, (Cin.); Country Florida (Delray Beach); Cotton Bay (Bahamas). Home: 8905 Shawnee Run Rd Cincinnati OH 45243 Office: Carew Tower Cincinnati OH 45202

HAYDON, ALVAH EDISON, Jr., banker; b. Irvington, Va., Feb. 28, 1916; s. Alvah Edison and Lucy (McDaniel) H.; B.S., in Bus. Adminstrn., U. Richmond, 1937; comml. certificate, Rutgers U. Grad. Sch. Banking, 1956; m. Mary Nuckols, Oct. 6, 1951; children—Michael E., Stephen N. Asst. cashier Lancaster Nat. Bank, Irvington, 1937-39, Bank of Powhatan (Va.), 1939-41; with United Va. Bank/State-Planters, Richmond, 1946—, sr. v.p., 1967—. Served to lt. USNR, 1941-46. Mem. Va. Bankers Assn. (bd. dirs.), Va. C. of C. (bd. dirs.), Phi Gamma Delta. Democrat. Baptist. Clubs: Windmill Point (Va.) Yacht; Downtown (Richmond). Home: 206 Wood Rd Richmond VA 23229 Office: 900 E Main St Richmond VA 23214

HAYDON, EVERETT PENN, former life ins. co. exec.; b. Frankfort, Ky., Dec. 19, 1905; s. Fount T. and Elizabeth (Flynn) H.; A.B., U. Louisville, 1928; m. Edith Nell Mann, Oct. 5, 1929; children—Everett P., George W., Robert F. Actuary, State N.C., 1936-38; actuary Continental Life Ins. Co., 1938-50, dir., 1948- 50; with Southland Life Ins. Co., 1950—, actuary, 1957-61, asst. v.p., 1961-63, v.p., 1963-70, ret. Home: 3003 Stanford St Dallas TX 75225

HAYDON, HAROLD EMERSON, educator, artist; b. Ft. William, Ont., Can., Apr. 22, 1909; s. Albert Eustace and Edith Elizabeth (Jones) H.; came to U.S., 1918, naturalized, 1942; Ph.B., U. Chgo., 1930, M.A. in Philosophy, 1931; student Sch. Art Inst. Chgo., 1932-33; m. Virginia Elnore Sherwood, July 4, 1937. Artist in residence Pickering Coll., Newmarket, Ont., 1933-34; from instr. to asst. prof. arts George Williams Coll., Chgo., 1934-44; asst., then asso. prof. art U. Chgo., 1944—, dean students in coll., 1957-59, marshal of univ., 1962-67, dir. Midway Studios, 1963—; art critic Chgo. Sun-Times, 1963—; exhbt. paintings U.S. and Can., 1933—, mobile sculpture, 1948—; murals and paintings permanent collections Pickering Coll., tapestry ark cover Temple Beth Am, Chgo., 1958, mosaic mural, 1968; mosaic murals Temple Beth El, Gary, Ind., 1959-60, ceramic murals Sonia Shankman Orthogenic Sch., Chgo., 1961, 66, mosaic St. Francis Assisi in St. Cletus Roman Cath. Ch., La Grange, Ill., 1963. Mem. cultural adv. com. Mayor Chgo. Com. Econ. and Cultural Devel., 1963—. Recipient prize for excellence in teaching U. Chgo., 1945. Mem. Artists League Midwest (pres. 1947-50), Artists Equity Assn. (pres. Chgo. 1950-52, 55-57), Chgo. Soc. Artists (pres. 1959-61), Renaissance Soc. U. Chgo. (pres. 1956-67), Nat. Soc. Mural Painters, Am. Assn. U. Profs., Japan-Am. Soc. Chgo., Guild for Religious Architecture, Phi Beta Kappa, Psi Upsilon, Order of C. Author: Great Art Treasures in America's Smaller Museum, 1967. Home: 5009 Greenwood Av Chicago IL 60615

HAYDON, JOHN MORSE, Jr., govt. ofcl.; b. Billings, Mont., Jan. 27, 1920; s. John Morse and Harriet U. (Rossiter) H.; student U. Wash., 1945-47; m. Jean Parker, July 3, 1941; children—Mrs. Conner Gray, Mrs. Don Ackelson, John Robert, Molly. Mem. staff Port of Seattle, 1949-52; pub. relations dir. Bardahl Internat. Corp., 1952-56; owner Marine Digest, 1956—; gov. Am. Samoa, 1969—. Mem. Seattle Port Commn., 1960-69; chmn. Oceanograph. Commn. Wash., 1967-69; pres. Oceanograph. Inst. Wash., 1967-69. Past mem. Gov. Wash. Adv. Com. in Dept. Commerce and Econ. Devel., Gov. Wash. Com. for State Dept. Fisheries; bd. dirs., exec. com. Wash. Internat. Trade Fair, Seattle Traffic Assn., Pacific Coast Assn. Port Authorities, also past pres., Seattle Mayor's Maritime Adv. Bd., Curriculum Adv. Mem. bd. Shoreline Community Coll., Seattle Community Coll. Named Maritime Man of Year, Puget Sound Maritime Press Assn., 1970. Address: Government House Pago Pago American Samoa

HAYEK, FRIEDRICH AUGUST VON, see von Hayek, Fredrich August.

HAYES, ALBERT MCHARG, educator; b. Milw., Dec. 14, 1909; s. Floyd Tomkins and Grace (McHarg) H.; A.B. summa cum laude, Dartmouth, 1930; Ph. D., Princeton U., 1933; m. Elizabeth Knox Irwin, Aug. 12, 1935; children—Judith McHarg (Mrs. William M.

Weir), Philip Knox. Mem. faculty Williston Acad., Easthampton, Mass., 1933-34, Duquesne U., 1934-38, Bowling Green State U., 1938-43; prof. humanities and English, U. Chgo., 1943—, asst. dean coll., 1959-65, coll. examiner, 1963-67, registrar, 1969—; Fulbright lectr. U. Philippines, 1955-56. Sec. Midwest Unitarian Universalist Found., 1963—, Harper Court Found., 1966—. Mem. Modern Lang. assn. Am., Phi Beta Kappa. Unitarian. Contbr. profl. jours. Home: 5515 S Woodlawn Av Chicago IL 60637

HAYES, ALFRED, banker; b. Ithaca, N.Y., July 4, 1910; s. Alfred and Christine Grace (Robertson) H.; grad. Milton (Mass.) Acad., 1926; student Harvard, 1926- 27, Harvard Grad. Sch. Bus. Adminstrn., 1930-31; B.A., Yale, 1930; B.Litt. (Rhodes scholar), New Coll., Oxford, Eng., 1933; m. Vilma F. Chalmers, Dec. 30, 1937; children—Anita Robertson (Mrs. Henry Weare Gratwick), Thomas Chalmers. Investment analyst City Bank Farmers Trust Co., N.Y.C., 1933-40; bond dept. Nat. City Bank of N.Y., N.Y.C., 1940-42; ast. sec. investment div. N.Y. Trust Co., 1942-47, asst. v.p. fgn. div., 1947-49, v.p. charge fgn. div., 1949-56; pres. Fed. Res. Bank of N.Y., 1956—. Vice chmn. Fed. Open Market Com., 1956—. Pres. bd. trustees Lignan U., Canton, China, 1947-54; mem. Yale Univ. Council. Served from lt. (j.g.) to lt., USNR, 1944-46. Mem. Council Fgn. Relations, Pilgrims U.S., Canadian Soc., Phi Beta Kappa, Sigma Xi, Phi Alpha Kappa, Alpha Delta Phi. Clubs: Economic (pres. 1965-66), Century Assn., University (N.Y.C.); Country (New Canaan, Conn.). Home: Brushy Ridge Rd New Canaan CT 06840 Office: care Fed Res Bank of NY 33 Liberty St New York City NY 10045

HAYES, ALFRED, author Edn of Me, 1968; Just Before the Divorce, 1968; Temptation of Don Volpi. Address: 5060 Gloria St Encino CA 91316

HAYES, ALFRED SOROKER, educator, linguist; b. Boston, Apr. 18, 1914; s. Saul Soroker and Lucy (Asher) H.; A.B., Bowdoin Coll., 1934; A.M., Harvard, 1936; postgrad. U. Wis., Ind. U., U. Cal.; m. Bernice Rogan, May 23, 1942; children— Barbara Nan (Mrs. Alan Hofstein), David Alan, Gary. Instr. Beloit Coll., 1936-39. U. Wis. at Beloit, 1938-40; teaching asst. U. Wis., 1940-42, instr. radio, 1942-44, charge German instrn. extension, 1944-45; asst. prof. to asso. prof., chmn. dept. Germanic and Slavic langs. La. State U., 1945-53; research linguist U. Cal., 1953-54; engring. sales mgr. Thomas Tenney Music, Berkeley, Cal., 1954-60; contractor, cons. lang. research U.S. Office Edn., 1960-63; head research and spl. projects Center Applied Linguistics, Washington, 1962—, dir. lang. in edn. program, 1964—; cons., lectr. lang. colls. and univs., govt., instns.; dir. N.E. Conf. Teaching of Fgn. Langs., 1963-65, chmn., 1964. Grantee Am. Council Learned Soc., 1952; Am. specialist U.S. Dept. State, 1964; Ford Found. travel and study grant, 1968; Nat. Distinguished Service award N.Y. State Fedn. Fgn. Lang. Tchrs., 1968. Mem. Modern Lang. Assn. Am., N.E.A., Linguistic Soc. Am., Nat. Council Tchrs. of English, Internat. Reading Assn., Phi Beta Kappa. Tau Kappa Epsilon. Democrat. Jewish religion. Author: Language Laboratory Facilities, 1963. Editor: (with others) Approaches to Semiotics, 1964; mem. editorial bd. Internat. Rev. Applied Linguistics in Lang. Teaching, 1963—. Contbr. articles profl. jours. Home: 715 Gilbert St Takoma Park MD 20012 Office: 1717 Massachusetts Av NW Washington DC 20036

HAYES, BARTLETT HARDING, Jr., art mus. dir.; b. Andover, Mass., Aug. 5, 1904; s. Barlett Harding and Marjorie (Scull) H.; grad. Phillips Acad., 1922; A.B., Harvard Coll., 1926; m. Clare Wadleigh, Sept. 15, 1932; children—Bridget, Deborah, Hilary, Delia-Maria. Studied art U.S., 1927-29, Europe, 1927-33; instr. art, Phillips Acad., 1933—, asst. curator Addison Gallery Am. Art, 1934-40, dir., 1940-69. Guggenheim fellow, 1955; Fulbright Grantee (Germany), 1956. Resigned as 2d lt., F.A. Res., 1926. Trustee Am. Fed. of Arts, 1940-70, Boston Art Festival, 1952-65, Mus. Fine Arts, Boston, 1949-71, St. Gaudens Meml., Cornish, N.H., 1967—, Amon Carter Mus., Ft. Worth, 1968—, Inst. Contemporary Art, Boston; mem. vis. com. Dept. Edn., Met. Mus., N.Y.C., chmn. commn. to survey role of arts Mass. Inst. Tech., 1952-54, 69-70; mem. Art Commn. Smithsonian Inst., 1954—; bd. dirs. Print Council Am., 1957-63; lectr. in fine arts, research asso. Grad. Sch. Edn., Harvard, 1964-68; dir. Am. Acad. Rome, 1969—; mem. art adv. com. Internal Revenue Service, 1970—; mem. exec. com. Art in Am. Embassies Program, Dept. State, 1965—; bd. dirs. Council Pub. Schs.; trustee Old Sturbridge Village, 1950-70, Coll. Art Assn., 1946-50, 57-65, sec., 1959-64. Fellow Am. Acad. Arts and Scis.; mem. Colonial Soc. Mass. Clubs: Century (N.Y.); Tavern (Boston). Author: The Naked Truth and Personal Vision, 1954; The American Line, 1959; TV series (N.E.T.) Intent of Art; American Drawings, 1965. Co- author: Layman's Guide to Modern Art, 1949; Artist or Advocate, 1969. Contbr. to mags. Mem. editorial bd. Art in America, 1944-69. Bd. editors John Harvard Library, 1957- 61; editor serveral monographs. Home: Am Acad in Rome 5 via A Masina Rome 00153 Italy

HAYES, CHARLES AMOS, Jr., educator; b. Winnipeg, Man., Can., Apr. 9, 1916; s. Charles Amos and Amy (Noblett) H.; A.B., U. Cal. at Berkeley, 1937, M.A., 1938, Ph.D., 1942; m. Lola Thelma Valente, June 21, 1942; children—Rodney C., Laura L. Instr. math. U. Cal., 1946-47, asst. to asso. prof., U. Cal. at Davis, 1947- 59, prof. math., 1959—, chmn. dept. 1959-64. Served to 1st lt. USAAF, 1942-46. Mem. Am. Math. Soc., Math. Assn. Am., Phi Beta Kappa, Sigma Xi, Pi Mu Epsilon. Author: Concepts of Real Analysis, 1964; (with C.Y. Pauc) Derivation and Martingales, 1970. Contbr. articles profl. jours. Home: 302 E 11th St Davis CA 95616

HAYES, CHARLES LEONARD, coll. pres.; b. Baton Rouge, Dec. 16, 1921; s. Charles and Amelia (Lewis) H.; A.B., Leland Coll., 1947; Ed.M., Loyola U., Chgo., 1949; Ed.D., U. No. Colo., 1958; m. Bette Harris, Nov. 26, 1949; children—Charles Jerome, Jaime Howard. Elementary sch. tchr., Chgo., 1948-49; instr. N.C. A. and T. State U., 1949-52, asst. prof., 1952-58, prof. psychology, 1958-61, chmn. dept. edn., dir. tchr. edn., 1961-66; Am. Council Edn. fellow acad. adminstrn. George Washington U., 1966-67; chief developing instns. br., div. coll. support Bur. Higher Edn., U.S. Office Edn., Dept. Health, Edn. and Welfare, 1967-69; pres. Albany (Ga.) State Coll., 1969—; asso. prof. Barber-Scotia Coll., Concord, N.C., 1960-64; supr. practicum internship NDEA Counseling and Guidance Inst., Va. State Coll., Petersburg, summer 1963. Bd. dirs. Nat. Conf. Christians and Jews, 1960-67. Served with USNR, 1942-46. Mem. Am. Assn. U. Profs. (adv. council), Assn. Higher Edn., N.E.A. (life), N.C. Tchrs. Assn., Am. Personnel and Guidance Assn., Am. Coll. Personnel Assn., Assn. Counselor Educators and Suprs., N.C. Psychol. Assn., Am. Council on Edn. (adv. council), Asso. Orgn. for Tchr. Edn. (adv. council), Greensboro C. of C. Democrat. Contbr. articles profl. jours. Home: President's Home Albany State Coll Albany GA 31705

HAYES, CHARLES WILLARD, lawyer; b. Washington, Sept. 11, 1902; s. Charles Willard and Rosa (Paige) H.; Ph.B., Brown U., 1925; LL.B., Georgetown U., 1929; m. Annie Graham Hume, June 13, 1929; children—Sally Cox (Mrs. Carl Sydney Dorn), Charles Willard III. Admitted to D.C. bar, 1928; with Cushman, Bryant & Darby, patent law, Washington, 1927-29, partner successor firm Cushamn, Darby & Cushman, 1942—. Mem. Am. (ho. of dels. 1959-61), D.C. bar assns., Am. Patent Law Assn. (chmn. laws and rules com. 1952-54, pres. 1957-58), Nat. Council Patent Law Assns. (chmn. legislative com. 1955-56, chmn. council 1958-59), Psi Upsilon. Clubs: University (Washington); Chevy Chase. Home: 3519 Chevy Chase Lake Dr Chevy Chase MD 20015 Office: 730 15th St Washington DC 20005

HAYES, DAVID VINCENT, sculptor; b. Hartford, Conn., Mar. 15, 1931; s. David Vincent and Adelaide (Brown) H.; A.B., U. Notre Dame, 1953; M.F.A., Ind. U., 1955; m. Julia Moriarty, June 22, 1957; children—David Matthew, Brian James, Mary Judith, John Mark. One man shows include U. Ind., 1955, Wesleyan U., Middletown, Conn., 1958, Mus. Modern Art, 1959, Willard Gallery, N.Y.C., 1961-64, 66, 69, 71, U. Notre Dame-Ind. U., 1963, Root Art Center, Hamilton, N.Y. 1963, Galerie David Anderson, Paris, France, 1966, others; numerous group shows, 1959—; rep. permanent collections Mus. Modern Art, Guggenheim Mus., Carnegie Inst., Joseph Hirschorn Found., N.Y.C., U. Notre Dame, Dallas Mus., Mus. Fine Arts, Houston, Wadsworth Anthenaeum, Addison Gallery Am. Art, Andover, Mass., Currier Gallery Art, Manchester, N.H., others. Recipient Logan medal Art Inst. Chgo., 1960. Fulbright research grantee, 1961; Guggenheim fellow, 1961; grantee Nat. Inst. Arts and Letters, 1965. Address: Box 109 Coventry CT 06238

HAYES, DOROTHY TOOHEY, educator; b. Milw., Oct. 24, 1905; d. Michael Henry and Margaret (Hake) Toohey; B.A., U. Wis., 1926; M.A., U. Chgo., 1935, Ph.D., 1950; m. Birchard Platt Hayes, June 24, 1927 (dec. 1958); children—Jonathan, Carolyn (Mrs. Charles Pangborn), Margaret (Mrs. Malcolm Taylor), Richard, Libby (Mrs. Chester Sass), James Birchard. Elementary and secondary tchr., West Bend, Wis., Clearwater, Fla., 1926-30; faculty U. Chgo., 1931-42; guidance dir., Western Springs, Ill., 1943-46; dir. early childhood edn. Syracuse U., 1946-48; prof., dir. early childhood edn. State U. Coll., Oswego, N.Y., 1948-50; prof., dir. edn., chmn. div. edn., dir. Mental Health Workstudy Program, State U. Coll., New Paltz, N.Y., 1950—; mem. Middle States Evaluation Teams, N.Y. State Congress Parents and Tchrs. Mem. Foster Parents Plan, 1966—; dir. Nursing Edn. Workshop, WHO, Taiwan, 1952. Mem. N.E.A., Assn. for Higher Edn., N.Y. State Assn. Tchr. Educators, Assn. for Supervision and Curriculum Devel., N.Y. State Assn. for Childhood Edn. (pres. 1952-54), Council for Children (chmn. 1955), Pi Lambda Theta, Delta Kappa Gamma, Kappa Delta Pi. Contbr. articles profl. jours. Home: PO Box 584 New Paltz NY 12561

HAYES, DOUGLAS ANDERSON, educator; b Highland Park, Mich., Feb. 27, 1918; s. Edward N. and Lillian (Anderson) H.; A.B., U. Mich., 1939, M. B.A., 1940, Ph.D., 1949; m. Anne Martin, Dec. 7, 1940; children—Douglas M., Randall B., Susan A. Research asso. Investment Council, Inc., Detroit, 1940-42; faculty U. Mich., 1946—, prof. finance, 1955—, dir. Sch. Banking, 1952—; cons. economist Treasury Dept., 1951-53; ednl. cons. Mich. Bankers Assn., 1952—. Dir. Security Bank of Lincoln Park. Mem. Bd. of Pensions, United Presbyn. Ch. of U.S. Served with USNR, 1943-45. Mem. Financial Analysts Soc. Detroit., Am. Finance Assn. (v.p. 1966—), Am. Econs. Assn., Inst. of Chartered Financial Analysts (trustee 1968-70), Phi Beta Kappa, Sigma Phi, Beta Gamma Sigma. Presbyn. (past trustee). Author: Business Confidence and Business Activity, 1951; Appraisal and Management of Securities, 1956; Investments. Analysis and Management, 1961, 2d edit., 1966; Bank Lending Policies; Issues and Practices. Home: 2200 Belmont Ann Arbor MI 48104

HAYES, EARL THOMAS, govt. ofcl.; b. Wallace, Ida., Apr. 1, 1912; s. Charles and Hazel (Bathurst) H.; B.S. in Metall. Engring., U. Ida., 1935, M.S., 1936; Ph.D. in Chem. Engring., U. Md., 1940; m. Carlene Smith, Dec. 28, 1935; children—David C., Donna C. (Mrs. James Stueve), Linda (Mrs. Roger Bookhultz). Mine operator, Mullan, Ida., 1936-38; research metallurgist U.S. Bur. Mines, College Park, Md., 1938-40, Salt Lake City, 1940-48, Albany, Ore., 1948- 56, asst. chief metallurgist, Washington, 1956-57, chief metallurgist, 1957-62, sci. adviser, 1966-67, dep. dir., 1967-70, acting dir., 1968-70, chief scientist, 1970—; asst. dir. materials Dept. Def., Washington, 1962-66. Guest lectr. internat. meetings including Sao Paulo, Brazil, 1969. Mem. Am. Inst. Metall. Engrs., Am. Soc. Metals, Phi Kappa Phi, Sigma Gamma Epsilon. Mehtodist. Club: Cosmos (Washington). Author: Metallurgy of Hafnium, 1960. Contbr. articles profl. Jours. Home: 517 Gilmoure Av Silver Spring MD 20901 Office: Dept Interior 18th and C Sts NW Washington DC 20240

HAYES, EDWARD BEAN, lawyer; b. Blue Hill, Me., Dec. 30, 1896; s. Edward Cary and Annie Lee (Bean) H.; A.B., U. Ill., 1918; LL.B., Harvard, 1921; LL.D., John Marshall Law Sch., 1949; m. Helen Frances Walker, July 2, 1932; children—Edward Cary, Mary Lee (Mrs. Daniel Orr). Admitted to Ill. bar, 1921; partner firm Nortrup, Nortrup and Hayes, Havana, Ill., 1921-25; asst. atty. gen. Ill., 1924-25; asso. firm Scott, Bancroft, Martin & Macleish, Chgo., 1925-30, Cutting, Moore & Sidley, Chgo., 1930-32; partner firm Kremer Branand & Hayes, Chgo., 1932-43, Lord, Bissell & Brook, and predecessor firms, Chgo., 1943—; lectr. constnl. and maritime law; founder, 1st dir. admiralty and maritime law div. Grad. Inst. John Marshall Law Sch. Served with USN, World War I. Mem. Am., Ill., Chgo. (1st chmn. admiralty and maritime sect.), Inter-Am. bar assns., Maritime Law Assn. U.S., Phi Beta Kappa, Delta Upsilon. Clubs: Traffic, Legal, Law; Drug and Chemical (N.Y.C.). Home: 4737 Elm St Downers Grove IL 60515 Office: 135 S LaSalle St Chicago IL 60603

HAYES, EDWIN SPENCER, educator; b. Bryson, Tex., June 28, 1909; s. James and Mattie Lou (Price) H.; B.S., N. Tex. State Tchrs. Coll., 1929; Ph.D., U. Tex., 1933; m. Dorothy Faye Wier, May 30, 1937; children—James Wier, Thomas Morton. Prof. biology Edinburg (Tex.) Coll. 1933-42, Lamar Coll., 1942- 51; prof. biology, dean Sch. Scis., Lamar State Coll. Tech., 1951—. Pres., Beaumont Tb Assn. Bd. dirs. Tex. div. Am. Cancer Soc., Beaumont Assn. for Mental Health, Beaumont Council Alcoholism, Services Unlimited, S.E. Tex. Heart Assn., Beaumont chpt. A.R.C., Trinity-Neches council Boy Scouts Am. Recipient Silver Beaver award Boy Scouts Am., 1959. Mem. Am. Assn. U. Profs. (pres. Lamar State Coll. chpt. 1956), Tex. Assn. Coll. Tchrs., Tex. Acad. Sci. Club: South Park Rotary (past pres.). Home: 1387 Pipkin St Beaumont TX 77705

HAYES, GEORGE JOSEPH, Jr., army officer; b. Washington, July 10, 1918; s. George J. and Joanna (Lawler) H.; B.S., Catholic U. Am., 1940; M.D., Johns Hopkins U., 1943; m. Catherine Conger, July 7, 1945; children—Timothy, Patrick, Joseph, Kathleen, Monica, Christopher, Steven, Martin, Brendan. Commd. 1st lt., M.C., U.S. Army, 1946, advanced through grades to brig. gen., 1966; resident Lahey Clinic, Boston, 1944-46; fellow Duke Hosp., 1949-50, Georgetown U., 1951; chief neurosurgery service Walter Reed Army Hosp., Washington, 1947-51; comdg. officer 160th Neurosurgical Detachment, Korea, 1952-53, 46th Surg. Hosp., Korea, 1952-53; chief neurosurg. service Brooke Gen. Hosp., San Antonio, 1953-55, Walter Reed Gen. Hosp., 1955-66; dir. profl. services Office Surgeon Gen., 1966-68; comdg. gen. med. command, Tokyo, Japan, 1968-69; dir. staff Office Dep. Sec. Def. for Health Affairs, Washington, 1969-70; prin. dep. asst. sec. def. for health and environment, 1970—; clin. prof. neurosurgery George Washington U., Washington 1968—. Decorated Medal Honor, World Assn. Mil. Surgeons, Legion Merit; recipient Alumni Achievement award for medicine Catholic U. Am., 1965, Mem. A.M.A., A.C.S., Am. Assn. Neurol. Surgeons. Assn. Mil. Surgeons, Internat. Coll. Surgeons, Soc. Neurol. Surgeons. Contbr. profl. jours. Home: 303 Skyhill Rd Alexandria VA 22314 Office: The Pentagon Washington DC 20301

HAYES, GEORGE NICHOLAS, lawyer; b. Alliance O., Sept. 30, 1928; s. Nicholas J. and Mary (Fanaday) H.; B.A., U. Akron, 1950; M.A., Western Res. U., 1952, LL.B., 1955. Admitted to Ohio bar, 1955, Alaska bar, 1958; asst. prosecutor Portage County, Ravenna, O., 1955-57; prosecutor City of Ravenna, 1955-57; atty. Village of Mantua, O., 1956-57; asst. U.S. atty., Fairbanks, Alaska, 1957-58, Anchorage, 1958-59; dist. atty. 3d Jud. Dist., State of Alaska, Anchorage, 1960-62; atty. gen. Alaska, Juneau, 1962-64; partner law firm Delaney, Wiles, Moore & Hayes, Anchorage, 1962—; spl. counsel to gov. Alaska. 1964-66. Bd. dirs. Alaska Housing Authority, 1965-66. Mem. Am., Alaska, Ohio bar assns. Home: 521 3d Av Anchorage AK 99501 Office: 360 K St Anchorage AK 99501

HAYES, HAROLD THOMAS PACE, editor; b. Elkin, N.C., Apr. 18, 1926; s. James M. and Aline (Pace) H.; B.S., Wake Forest Coll., 1948; m. Susan Meredith, Apr. 7, 1955; children—Thomas Pace, Carrie Meredith. With So. Bell Telephone Co., Atlanta, 1948-49; with U.P.I., Atlanta, 1949-50; asst. editor Pageant mag., N.Y.C., 1952, asso. editor, 1953; asso. editor Tempo mag., 1953; editor Picture Week mag., 1954; asst. to pub. Esquire mag., N.Y.C., 1955-59, articles editor, 1959-62, mng. editor, 1962-63, editor, 1963—; instr. mag. journalism New Sch. for Social Research, N.Y.C., 1961-63. Served with USNR, 1943-45; to lst lt. USMCR, 1950-52. Nieman fellow Harvard, 1958-59. Recipient Distinguished Alumni award Wake Forest U., 1968. Mem. Am. Soc. Mag. Editors (chmn. exec. com. 1969). Office: 488 Madison Av New York City NY 10022

HAYES, HARRISON C., accountant; b. West Shefford, Que., Can., Aug. 1, 1904; s. Peter Monroe and Addie Melvina (Newell) H.; B.Commerce, McGill U., 1925; m. Anna Muriel Webb, May 23, 1928; children—Michael John, Anne Marjorie. With Donald, Currie & Co., chartered accountants, Montreal, 1928—; partner Coopers & Lybrand, chartered accountants, Montreal, 1957—; chmn. bd. Urwick, Currie Ltd., 1965—, also dir. Bd. dirs., gov. Que. Hosp. Service Assn., Que. Mut. Assurance Co. Pres. Montreal Jr. Bd. Trade, 1935-36, Montreal Bd. Trade, 1958-59, Canadian Jr. C. of C., 1937-38. Chartered accountant, 1927. Mem. Inst. Chartered Accountants Que.(past pres.). Home: 3468 Drummond St Montreal 25 Quebec Canada Office: 630 Dorchester Blvd W Montreal 2 Quebec Canada

HAYES, HELEN, (Mrs. Charles MacArthur), actress; b. Washington, Oct. 10, 1900; d. Francis Van Arnum and Catherine Estell (Hayes) Brown; grad. Sacred Heart Acad., Washington, 1917; L.H.D., Hamilton Coll., Clinton, N.Y., 1939, Smith Coll., 1940; L.H.D., Elmira (N.Y.) Coll.; Litt.D., Columbia, 1949, U. Denver, 1952; D.F.A., Princeton, St. Mary's Coll.; m. charles McArthur, Aug. 17, 1928 (dec. Apr. 1956); 1 son, James. First appeared on stage at age of 6; mem. Columbia Players, Washington, 4 seasons; later toured with Lew Fields and John Drew; played in Old Dutch, Prodigal Husband, Pollyanna, Penrod; appeared with William Gillette in Dear Brutus; appeared in Clarence, Bab, To the Ladies, We Moderns, Dancing Mothers, Caesar and Cleopatra, What Every Woman Knows, Coquette, Mr. Gilhooley, Mary of Scotland, 1934, Victoria Regina, 1937-38, Ladies and Gentlemen, 1939-40, Twelfth Night, 1940-41, Candle in the Wind, 1941-42, Harriet, 1943-45, Happy Birthday, The Glass Menagerie, London, 1948, Farewell to Arms, Vanessa, The Wisteria Trees, 1950, Mrs. McThing, 1952, Mainstreet to Broadway, 1953, Skin of Our Teeth, Europe and U.S., 1955, Harvey, others; appeared in motion pictures The Sin of Madelon Claudet, Arrowsmith, My Son John, 1951, Anastasia, Airport (Acad. award as best supporting actress 1971, others; Mrs. Derth in TV revival of Barrie's Dear Brutus, 1956; mem. A.P.A. Phoenix Repertory Co., 1966—. Awarded gold statuette Motion Picture Acad. Arts and Sciences, 1932, as outstanding actress in The Sin of Madelon Claudet; Emmy award, 1954; Antoinette Perry award for best actress in Time Remembered, 1958. Hon. pres. Am. Theatre Wing; pres. Am. Nat. Theatre and Acad. Chmn. Women's activities Nat. Found. for Infantile Paralysis. Republican. Roman Catholic. Author: A Gift of Joy, 1965. Home: Nyack NY 10960 also Cuernavca Mexico Mailing address:

HAYES, JACK DABNEY, Jr., chem. co. exec.; b. Atlanta, Jan. 5, 1913; s. Jack Dabney and Annie (Muse) H.; A.B. in Chemistry, Emory U., 1936, M.S. in Organic Chemistry, 1937; grad. Advanced Mgmt. Program, Harvard, 1954; m. Florine Douglas Huger, June 7, 1941; 1 son, Stephen D. With Hercules Inc., 1937—, gen. mgr. explosives and chem. propulsion dept., 1960-66, v. p., 1966—, dir. co., 1963—. Chmn. budget com. United Community Fund. No. Del., 1963-65. Mem. Am. Inst. Mining and Metall. Engrs., Am. Ordnance Assn., Assn. U.S. Army, Am. Inst. Aero. and Astronautics. Home: 3 Carriage Rd Greenville DE 19807 Office: 910 Market St Wilmington DE 19899

HAYES, JAMES LEO, advt. exec.; b. Chgo., July 25, 1895; s. Thomas S. and Katherine (Covdierre) H.; A.B., St. Mary's (Kan.) Coll., 1917; m. Edna E. Eischen, Oct. 27, 1934; 1 son, James Leo. Advt. rep. Curtis Pub. Co., 1919-25; asst. to pres. Richfield Oil Co., 1925-32; v.p. Minn. Mining & Mfg. Co. 1941—; pres. Midland Rubber Corp., 1949—, also dir.; v.p., gen. mgr. Nat. Advt. Co., Waukesha, Wis., 1951-53, pres., 1953—, also dir. (latter firms subsidiaries Minn. Mining & Mfg. Co.); dir. First Nat. Bank of Barrington, MBS, Inc., Washington Park Jockey Club. Clubs: Mid-Dy, Tavern (Chgo.); Rescess (Detroit); Minnesota (St. Paul); Everglades, Bath and Tennis (Palm Beach, Fla.). Home: 210 Via Linda Palm Beach FL 33480 Office: 6850 S Harlem Bedford Park IL 60638

HAYES, JAMES LOUIS, assn. exec.; b. Binghamton, N.Y., Sept. 25, 1914; s. James C. and Margaret (Sullivan) H.; A.B., St. Bernard's Coll. and Sem., 1936; M.A., St. Bonaventure U., 1937; postgrad. Columbia, 1938; D.Bus. Adminstrn. (hon.), Theil Coll.; m. Pauline Jacobus, Sept. 1, 1941; children—Elizabeh, James C. With St. Bonaventure U., 1936-59, successively instr. social sci. 1936-38, prof. econs., 1941-59, head dept. bus. adinstrn., 1941-59, coordinator vet. affairs, dir. guidance, 1946-59; dean Duquesne U. Sch. Bus. Adminstrn., Pitts., 1959-70; exec. v.p. devel. Am. Mgmt. Assn., N.Y.C., 1970-71, pres., chief exec. officer, 1971—, also mem. exec. com.; chmn. bd. affiliate Internat. Mgmt. Assn.; vice chmn., trustee affiliate Am. Found. Mgmt. Research; dir. affiliate Supervisory Mgmt. Assn., affiliate Thunderbird Grad Sch. Internat. Mgmt.; dir. Western Pa. Nat. Bank, Levinson Steel Corp., Pitts. Instr. Am. Inst. Banking, 1941-59; ednl. cons. Clark Bros. Co., Olean, N.Y., Dresser Industries, Dallas; prin. lectr. Am. Mgmt. Assn., N.Y.C., 1956—; hon. faculty mem. Army Mgmt. Sch., 1959-70 faculty Stonier Grad. Sch. of Banking, Rutgers U., 1961—, Va.-Md. Sch. Bankers U. Va., 1965—; lectr. Presidents Assn., N.Y.C., 1960—. Commr. Pitts. Commn. Human Relations; mem. Pitts. Mayor's Com. Econ. Devel. Trustee St. Joseph Coll., Emmitsburg, Md. Recipient Bronze Pelican award Cath. Com. Scouting, Silver Beaver award, also St. George award Boy Scouts Am. Fellow Am. Mgmt. Assn.; mem. Nat. Assn. Credit Mgmt., Financial Execs. Inst., Am. Risk and Ins. Assn., Nat. Sales Execs., Am. Econ. Assn., A.I.M., Cath. Bus. Edn. Assn., Am. Bus. Writing Assn., Fgn.

Policy Assn., Cath. Econ. Assn., Soc. Advancement Mgmt., Olean C. of C. (pres. 1962-63), Delta Sigma Pi, Beta Gamma Sigma. Kiwanian (past lt. gov.). Editor: Cath. Bus. Edn. Rev., 1956-62. Contbr. articles to profl. jours. Home: 400 E 56th St New York City NY 10022

HAYES, JAMES MARTIN, archbishop; b. Halifax, N.S., Can., May 27, 1924; s. Leonard J. and Rita (Bates) H.; student St. Mary's U., Halifax, 1939-43; B.A., Holy Heart Sem., Halifax, 1947; J.C.D., Angelicum, Rome, 1957; Litt. D. (hon.), St. Anne's U., Church Pt., N.S., 1966; S.T.D. (hon.), Kings Coll., Halifax, 1967. Ordained priest Roman Cath. Ch., 1947; chancellor Archdiocese Halifax, 1957-63; rector St. Mary's Basilica, Halifax, 1963-66; aux. bishop Halifax, 1965-67; archbishop Halifax, 1967—. Home: 6541 Coburg Rd Halifax Nova Scotia Canada Office: PO Box 1527 Halifax Nova Scotia Canada

HAYES, JAMES T.G., archbishop; b. N.Y.C., Feb. 11, 1889; s. John and Elizabeth (Gibbons) H.; prep. edn. St. Stephen's Sch. and St. Francis Xavier Coll., New York; entered Soc. of Jesus, 1907; studied Poughkeepsie, N.Y.; A.B., Woodstock Coll., 1920, A.M., 1923; student at Trochiennes, Belgium. Instr., Regis High Sch., N.Y., 1914-18; prof. Boston Coll., 1918- 19; ordained priest Roman Catholic Ch., 1921; dean of discipline Fordham U., 1923-25; missionary superior of Jesuits, Mindanao, P.I., 1927-30; superior of Jesuits entire P.I., 1930-33; first bishop of Cagayan, Mindanao, 1933-51, first archbishop of Cagayan, 1951-71; ret. 1971. Address: Cagayon de Ora City Philippines

HAYES, JOHN CORNELIUS, lawyer, educator; b. Chgo., Sept. 5, 1909; s. John Christopher and Mary Catherine (Ryan) H.; A.B., Georgetown U., 1931; J.D., Loyola U., Chgo., 1937; Litt. D., Aquinas Coll., Grand Rapids, 1961; LL.D., St. John's U., 1963, Loras Coll., 1964. Admitted to Ill. bar, 1938; instr. Loyola Acad., Chgo., 1931-39; lectr. history Loyola U., Chgo., 1935-37, asst. prof. law 1938-42, prof., 1942—, dean law, 1959-67; atty. Office Alien Property Custodian, Washington, 1946. Cons., Ill. Legislative Nonpub. Elementary and Secondary Schs. Study Commn., 1970-71; lectr. Nat. Trust Sch., Am. Bankers Assn.; bd. dirs. Better Govt. Assn., 1965-71. Served to capt., USAAF, 1942-46. Mem. Am., Ill., Chgo. bar assns., Nat. Council Cath. Men (pres. 1959-61, dir. 1952—), Pi Gamma Mu, Phi Alpha Delta. Home: 301 Sheridan Rd Wilmette IL 60091 Office: 41 E Pearson St Chicago IL 60611

HAYES, JOHN NEWTON, govt. ofcl.; b. Hensonville, N.Y., June 21, 1904; s. John H. and Nellie (Ennis) H.; B.S., N.Y. State Coll., 1924; M.A., Columbia, 1934; postgrad. N.Y. U., summer 1941, U. Geneva, Switzerland, 1949; m. Joan Eames, Sept. 7, 1964; 1 son, Richard E.; stepchildren—Thomas C. Wilson, Steven M. David, Anthony P. David, Deborah (Mrs. Steuart Dewar). Prin. pub. schs., Valley Falls and North Creek, N.Y., 1924-29; chmn. math. dept. Saratoga Springs (N.Y.) High Sch., 1929-30; prin. pub. schs., Corinth, N.Y., 1930-34; supt. city schs., Mechanicville, N.Y., 1934-42; div. chief Richmond (Va.) br. office VA, 1946-47; attache for vets. affairs Dept. State, Geneva, Switzerland, 1947-51, sect., br. and div. chiefs Internat. Ednl. Exchange Service, 1951-56, asst. dir., 1957-58, dep. dir., 1958-60, Office Cultural Exchange, 1960-62, dept. dir. Office U.S. Programs and Services, 1962-67, dir., 1967; dir. Honolulu Reception Center, 1968—. Served from capt. to col., AUS, 1942- 46. Decorated Legion of Merit, Bronze Star medal; Luxembourg Couronne de Chene; French Croix de Guerre. Mem. Am. Fgn. Service Assn., Am. Legion. Rotarian. Home: 1561 Kanunu St Honolulu HI 96814 Office: 2227 A Kalakaua Av Honolulu HI 96815

HAYES, JOHN PATRICK, mfg. co. exec.; b. Manistee, Mich., May 9, 1921; s. John David and Daisy (Davis) H.; student U. Detroit, 1939-42, 46-47; m. Margaret Barbara Butler, Apr. 12, 1947; children—John Patrick, Timothy Michael. With Nat. Gypsum Co., 1947—, group v.p., 1970—, pres. bldg. products div., 1969—, also dir. Served to 1st lt. AUS, 1942-45. Mem. Gypsum Assn. (pres.). Clubs: Buffalo; Park Country (Williamsville, N.Y.). Home: 63 Ruskin Rd Eggertsville NY 14226 Office: 325 Delaware Av Buffalo NY 14202

HAYES, JOHN RICHARD, educator; b. Toronto, Ont., Can., Oct. 29, 1929; s. James Victor and Kathleen Marie (Denroche) H.; A.B., Harvard, 1951; Ph.D., Mass. Inst. Tech., 1956; m. Barbara Wright, June 8, 1951; children—Elizabeth, Caroline, Marian. Teaching asst. psychology Mass. Inst. Tech., 1954-55; psychologist Bell Telephone Labs., Murray Hill, N.J., 1956-57; psychologist U.S. Naval Research Lab., 1957-61; lectr. psychology George Washington U., 1960-61, psychologist decision scis. lab., 1961-64, research fellow Center Cognitive Studies, 1964-65; dean Carnegie-Mellon U., 1968-71, asso. prof., 1965—. Mem. Am. Psychol. Assn., Research Soc. Am. Contbr. to book. Home: 660 Foxhurst Dr Pittsburgh PA 15238

HAYES, JOHN S., former ambassador; b. Phila., Aug. 21, 1910; A.B., U. Pa., 1931; m. Donna Gough; children—Jonatan S., Rhea Anne, Ellen Laurie, Peter Ogle. Pres. Post-Newsweek Stas.; exec. v.p. Washington Post Co., 1947-66, also dir.; U.S. ambassador, Switzerland, 1966-69. Pres. United Community Funds Am., 1962-64; mem. U.S. delegation Internat. Conf. on Communication Satellits, 1969. Mem. Fed. City Council, Washington, 1963-66. Pres. Meridian House Found., Washington, 1970—; trustee Radio Liberty Com., Springfield Coll. Nat. Urban League; dir. Washington Performing Arts Soc. Lt. col., U.S. Army, 1941-46, comdg. officer Am. Forces Radio Newtwork ETO. Decorated Bronze Star; Order of Brit. Empire; Croix de Guerre. Clubs: 1925 F Street, Federal City, Georgetown. Author: (with Horace Gardiner) Both side of the Microphone, 1940. Address: 4625 Garfield St NW Washington DC 20007

HAYES, JOHN W., osteopathic surgeon, hosp. adminstr.; b. Chillicothe, O.; grad. Kirksville Coll. Osteopathy and Surgery, 1928; married; 1 dau. Began practice osteo. medicine, 1928; chief staff, chmn. dept. surgery, adminstr. East Liverpool (O.) Osteo. Hosp., also pres. bd. trustees. Mem. adv. bd. Am. Profl. Practice Assn., 1967—. Dir. Potters Bank and Trust Co., East Liverpool. Trustee Eastern O. chpt. Am. Heart Assn. Diplomate Am. Osteo. Bd. Surgery. Fellow Am. Coll. Osteo. Surgeons; mem. Am. Osteo. Assn. (pres. 1966-67, chmn. chpt. bus. affairs; chmn. bur. comprehensive health planning 1967-69), Ohio Osteo. Assn. Phys. and Surg. (trustee, past pres.; mem. ho. dels.), Columbiana County Mental Health Assn. (pres. 1968-69), C. of C., Psi Sigma Alpha (exec. sec.- treas.). Methodist. Mason (32 K.T. Shriner), Elk. Home: 3101 St Clare Av East Liverpool OH 43920 Office: 203 W 5th St Box 654 East Liverpool OH 43920

HAYES, JOSEPH, author; b. Indpls., Aug. 2, 1918; s. Harold J. and Pearl (Arnold) H.; student Ind. U., 1941, D.H.L., 1970; m. Marrijane Johnston, Feb. 18, 1938; children—Gregory J., Jason H., Daniel D. Asst. editor Samuel French Plays, 1941- 43; free-lance writer, 1943—; chmn. Sarasota (Fla.) Theatre Performing Arts, 1962—. Chmn. Sarasota chpt. Am. Civil Liberties Union, 1963—. Co-producer-dir. play, The Happiest Millionaire, 1956. Author: (play) Leaf and Bough, 1949; (book, play, motion picture) The Desperate Hours (Lit. Guild, Readers Digest book clubs) selection; Antoinette Perry award 1954-55), 1954; (play) The Midnight Sun, 1959; (novel) The Hours After Midnight, 1959; (play) Calculated Risk, 1962; (novel) Don't Go Away Mad, 1963; (novel) The Third Day, 1964; (novel) The Deep End, 1967; (novel) Like Any Other Fugitive, 1971; numerous screen plays. Co-author 18 pub. plays with wife, also Bon Voyage, 1956. Contbr. short stoies nat mags. Home: 1168 Westway Dr Sarasota FL 33577 also Obtuse Hill Brookfield Center CT 06805 Office: Joseph Hayes Productions Inc 18 W 55th St New York City NY 10019

HAYES, JOSEPH CLAUDE, educator; b. Ozark, Ala., June 15, 1904; s. Henry Joseph and Martha Emma (Dean) H.; B.S., U. Ala., 1928, A.M., 1931; Ph.D., N.Y. U., 1938; student U. Heidelberg, 1938-39; m. Claudia Jordan, Jan. 3, 1933; 1 son, Henry Joseph. Asst. in German, N.Y. U., 1933-36; instr. in German, U. Ala., 1928-33, 1936-37, asst. prof., 1937-46, asso. prof., 1946-47, prof. German, 1947—, head dept. German, 1949—. Mem. Am. Assn. Tchrs. German, Modern Lang. Assn. Am., S. Atlantic Modern Lang. Assn. (exec. com. 1952-54; sec. German sect. 1952, chmn. 1953), Ala. Hist. Assn., Gamma Sigma Epsilon, Kappa Delta Pi, Phi Delta Kappa. Methodist. Author: Laurence Sterne and Jean Paul, 1942. Translator: Seven Months in the Rebel States, During the North American War, 1863, by Captain Justus Scheibert, 1958. Contbr. to jours. Home: 3127 Freemont Dr Tuscaloosa AL 35404

HAYES, LAWRENCE JOSEPH, lawyer; b. Evanston, Ill., Sept. 10, 1926; s. Lawrence Wilfred and Katherine (Bott) H.; B.S., J.D., Loyola U., Chgo.; m. Marcella Ann McGee, June 21, 1952; children—Lawrence Joseph, Maryann, James, Susan, Matthew, Patrick, Katie, Sally, Michael. Admitted to Ill. bar, 1950, Minn. bar, 1960; asso. firm Ryan, Condon & Livingston, Chgo., 1950-56; partner firm Groble, O'Flaherty & Hayes, Chgo., 1956-60; asso. firm Maun, Hazel & Busch, St. Paul, 1960-61; partner Green, Jayes, Simon & Aretz, 1961—. Chmn. St. Paul Housing and Redevel. Authority, 1967-70; mem. exec. bd. Indianhead council Boy Scouts Am., 1967—; bd. dirs. St. Paul Winter Carnival, 1968-71, prime minister, 1964. Exec. dir. United Democrats for Humphrey, Washington, 1968. Served with USNR, 1944-46. Mem. Serra Internat. (v.p. 1970—). Roman Catholic (mem. adv. council U.S. Cath. conf. 1968-). Home: 378 N Mississippi River Blvd St Paul MN 55104 Office: Hamm Bldg St Paul MN 55102

HAYES, MARIAN educator; b. Grand Rapids, Mich., May 23, 1905; d. Charles Washington and Margaret (Thompson) Hayes; student Rockford Coll., 1921-23; B.A., Mt. Holyoke Coll., 1925; M.A., (Univ. fellow), N.Y. U. Inst. Fine Arts, 1929, (Carnegie Corp. scholar), Radcliffe Coll., 1930, Ph.D., 1944; postgrad. U. Wis., summer 1926, Ecole de Chartes, Sorbonne, Paris, France, 1930, Western Mich. State Tchrs. Coll., 1931-32. Asst. dept. art Mt. Holyoke Coll., 1925-28, instr. 1932-37, asst. prof., 1937-44, asso. prof., 1944-54, prof., 1954-70, prof. emeritus, 1970—; chmn. art dept., 1948-60. Vis. prof. Sweet Briar Coll., 1971. Chmn. Mt. Holyoke Friends of Art, 1937-48, 65-66. Ford grantee, 1964-65. Mem. Am. Assn. U. Profs., Coll. Art Assn., Soc. Archtl. Historians, Mediaeval Acad. Am., Conn. Antiquarian and Landmarks Soc., Phi Beta Kappa. Home: 106 Woodbridge St South Hadley MA 01075

HAYES, MARK ALLAN, educator, surgeon; b. Bay City, Mich., Oct. 19, 1914; s. Howard Mark and Mildred Marian (Anderson) H.; A.B., U. MIch., 1937, M.D. cum laude, 1940, Ph.D., 1948, M.S., 1951; M.A. (hon.), Yale, 1961; m. Margaret Mary Rupff, June 23, 1948; 1 son, Mark Allan. Intern U. Mich. Hosp., 1940-41, asst. resident surgery, 1941-42, resident surgery, 1942-43, 48-49, demonstrator anatomy, 1942-43, Kellogg fellow anatomy, 1946-47; mem. faculty U. Mich. Med. Sch., 1947-52, asst. prof. sugery, 1951-52; mem. faculty Yale Med. Sch., 1952—, dir. Samuel C. Harvey Metabolic Unit, 1952-54, asso. prof. surgery, 1952-61, prof. surgery, 1961—. Served to lt. comdr., M.C., USNR, 1942-46. Diplomate Am. Bd. Surgery. Fellow A.C.S.; mem. Am. Surg. Assn., Am. Gastroenterol. Assn., Frederick A. Coller, New Eng. surg. socs., Soc. Univ. Surgeons, Endocrine Soc., Collegium Internationale Chirurgiae Digestivae, Pan Am. Med. Assn., Societe Internationale de Chirurgie, Soc. Surgery Alimentary Tract (a founder), Sigma Xi, Alpha Omega Alpha. Home: 163 Ridgewood Av Hamden CT 06514 Office: 333 Cedar St New Haven CT 06510

HAYES, MARVIN LEROY, petroleum co. exec.; b. Jamesport, Mo., Aug. 4, 1921; s. Roy H. and Mattie (McCoy) H.; B.S., Washington U., St. Louis, 1948, M.B.A., 1949; postgrad. Harvard, 1966; m. Sarah Jeanne Gardner, Jan. 22, 1943; children—Richard G., Shelley S. With Standard Oil Co. (Ind.), Chgo., 1940-61, supr. banking, 1955-57, asst. to sec., 1957-58, adminstrv. asst. to chmn., pres., 1958-61; mgr. auditing Am. Oil Co. (Md.), Chgo., 1961-62, asst. treas., 1962-63, treas., 1963-65, comptroller, 1965—; dir. Amoco Enterprises, Inc., Petroleum Heat & Power Co., So. Towing Co. Mem. Bd. Edn. High Sch. Dist. 87, 1968—. Served with USNR, 1942-45. Mem. Financial Execs. Inst., Am. Petroleum Inst., Ill. C. of C., Artus, Beta Gamma Sigma. Home: 590 Riford Rd Glen Ellyn IL 60137 Office: 910 S Michigan Av Chicago IL 60605

HAYES, MILTON JOHN, banker; b. Chgo., July 14, 1906; s. Frederick Stephen and Catherine (Fielding) H.; Ph.B., U. Chgo., 1928; postgrad. Northwestern U., 1933- 35. Investment analyst Continental-Ill. Nat. Bank & Trust Co., Chgo., 1929-34; with Am. Nat. Bank & Trust Co., Chgo., 1935-71, asst. cashier, 1940-48, asst. v.p., 1948-53, v.p., 1953-67, sr. v.p., 1967-71, exec. officer, 1966-71; chmn. exec. com., dir. Mid-Am. Nat. Bank, Chgo., 1971—. Staff lectr. Wis. U. Sch. Banking, 1956—. Served to lt. col. USAAF, 1942-46. Mem. Mil. Order World Wars, Kappa Sigma. Clubs: Attic, University, Mid-America (Chgo.). Home: 1130 S Michigan Av Chicago IL 60605 Office: Prudential Plaza Chicago IL 60601

HAYES, NATHANIEL PERKLINSON, steel fabricator; b. Wise, N.C., Sept. 29, 1901; s. Malvern Hill and Olivia (Perkinson) H.; A.B., U. N.C., 1921, B.S., 1922; m. Louise Elizabeth Hull, Nov. 24, 1927; 1 son, Nathaniel Perkison. Engr. McClintic-Marshall Co., Pitts., 1922-26; engr. Carolina Steel Corp; Greensboro, 1926-30, sales mgr., 1930—, dir., 1941—, now chmn. bd.; chmn. bd. Salem Steel Co., Greenville Steel & Foundry Co. (S.C.); dir., mem. exec. com. Home Fed. Savs. & Loan Assn.; dir. N.C. Nat. Bank, Pomona Corp. Pres. Greensboro Industries, Inc., 1953, Greensboro Tb Assn., 1949. Dir. Am. Inst. Steel Constrn., Inc., 1946-69; 2d v.p., 1952, 1st v.p. 1954-56, pres., 1956-58. Pres. Bus. Found. of N.C., Inc., 1958-60. Trustee, Moses H. Cone Meml. Hosp., Inc., Oak Ridge Found., Inc. (Oak Ridge Mil. Inst.) 1965—, N.C. Found. Ch.-Related Colls.; bd. visitors St. Andrews Presbyn. Coll., Campbell Coll., Guiford Coll.; bd. dirs. N.C. Engring. Found.; mem. adv. bd. U. N.C. Press; Chapel Hill; N.C. Fellow Am. Soc. C.E.; mem. C. of C. (pres. 1951), N.A.M. (dir. 1969). Presbyn. (ruling elder). Kiwanian. Home: 2109 Lafayette Av Greensboro NC 27408 Office: 1457 S Elm St Greensboro NC 27406

HAYES, NEVIN WILLIAM, clergyman; b. Chgo., Feb. 17, 1922; s. James Timothy and Ella Mary (Williams) H.; Ph.B., Mt. Carmel Coll., 1943; postgrad. Whitefriars Hall, Washington, 1943-47, Cath. U., 1944-50. Joined Carmelite Order, 1939, ordained priest Roman Catholic Ch., 1946; instr. Romance langs., Carmelite Sem., Hamilton, Mass., 1947-51; pastor Lima, Peru, 1951-59; prelate nullius, Sicuani, Peru, 1959-70; bishop, Sicuani, 1965-70; aux. bishop, Chgo., 1971—. Co-founder Instituto de Pastoral Andino, Cuzco, Peru, 1969, bd. dirs., 1969-71; pres. Comite Episcopal de Religiosos, Lima, 1967-70, Comite Episcopal para Laicos, Lima, 1970-71. Address: 211 E Chicago Av Chicago IL 60611

HAYES, PETER LIND, actor; b. San Francisco, June 25, 1915; s. Joseph Conrad and Grace Dolores (Hayes) L.; student parochial schs., Cairo, Ill.; m. Mary Healy, Dec. 19, 1940; children—Peter Michael, Cathy Lind. Debut Palace Theatre, N.Y.C., 1932; worked with mother, Grace Hayes, 1932-42, with wife, Mary Healy, 1946—. movies: Once You Kiss A Stranger, The Ying and Yang of Dr. Go; The Senator was Indiscreet, The 5000 Fingers of Dr. T., producer Movies from 1939, Million Dollar Legs, All Women Have Secrets, These Glamour Girls, 1940, Seventeen, Dancing on a Dime, Playmates, Seven Days Leave; appeared in TV series; Inside U.S.A., The Peter & Mary Show, The Stork Clubs, Star of the Family, Arthur Godfreys replacment on CBS radio and TV; writer, producer Columbia Discovers America. Served as tech. sgt., USAAF, 1942-46, PTO. Decorated 2 Battle and 1 Bronze Star. Roman Catholic. Club: Pelham Country. Author: Twenty-five Minutes from Broadway, 1961. Home: 3538 Pueblo Way Las Vegas NV 89109

HAYES, RALPH, business exec.; b. Crestline, O.; A.B., Case-Western Res. U. Sec. City Club, Cleve., 1915-16; pvt. sec. to sec. of war, 1916-18; asst. to sec. war, 1920; asst. to pres. Cleve. Trust Co., 1920-22; asst. to pres., Motion Picture Producers & Distbrs. of Am. 1922-23; v.p. Chatham Phenix Nat. Bank & Trust Co., 1927-29; 2d v.p. Press Pub. Co (N. Y. World), 1929-30; former exec. dir. N.Y. Community Trust and Community Funds Inc.; N.Y.C.; formerly sec., treas. Coca-Cola Co., and dir. Coca-Cola Internat. Exec. com. Community Blood Council, N.Y.C.; dir. exec. com. Nat. Information Bur., N.Y.C. Past chmn. James Found., St. James, Mo. Exec. com. Nat. War Fund, 1943-46. Pvt. 11th Div. U.S.Army, 1918; commd. lt., Ligny, France, 1918. Mem. Phi Beta Kappa (ex-pres. Alpha of Ohio), Delta Sigma Rho, Alpha Delta Phi (ex-treas.), Phi Delta Phi. Clubs: City (past treas., past. sec., past dir.) (Cleve.); Wilmington, Wilmington Country; Century, Univeristy, Sky (N.Y.C.). Home: Hotel du Pont Wilmington DE 19899

HAYES, RAY HOGAN, hosp. supt., psychiatrist; b. Elizabethtown, Ky., Oct. 14, 1919; s. John Howard and Wilma (Hogan) H.; B.S., Georgetown U., 1946, M.D., 1950; widower; children—Kristen Suzanne, Armand Christopher. Intern Providence Hosp., Washington, 1950-51; resident chest diseases Glenn Dale Tb Hosp., 1951-54, resident chest diseases Springfield State Hosp., Sykesville, Md., 1954-55, resident psychiatry, 1954-55; resident psychiatry U. Louisville Sch. Medicine, 1955-57; dist. psychiatrist Eastern region Ky. Dept. Mental Health, 1957-61; chief psychiat. service USPHS Hosp., Lexington, Ky., 1961-62, clin. dir., 1962-65; supt. Central State Hosp., Louisville, 1965—; instr. psychiatry U. Louisville Sch. Medicine, 1957-62, clin. asst. prof. psychiatry, 1965— adj. prof. pastoral care Coll. of Bible, Lexington, 1957-62; instr., then clin. asst. prof. psychiatry U. Ky. Sch. Medicine, 1961-65. Diplomate Am. Bd. Psychiatry and Neurology. Mem. A.M.A., Am. Pub. Health Assn., Am., Ky. psychiat. assns., Am. Group Psychotheraphy Assn., Tri-State Group Psychotheraphy Assn., A.A.A.S., Assn. Med. Supts. Mental Hosps. Contbr. profl. jours. Home: 7313 Boxwood Rd Louisville KY 40222 Office: Central State Hosp Louisville KY 40223

HAYES, ROBERT BRUCE, coll. dean; b. Clarksburg, W.Va., Nov. 15, 1925; s. Bruce and Ruby (Hitt) H.; student Fairmont (W.Va.) State Coll.; B.A., Asbury Coll., Wilmore, Ky., 1950; M. Ed., U. Kan., 1956, Ed. D., 1960; m. Ruth Harrison, July 19, 1947; children—Steven, Ruthann, Mark. Tchr., prin. elementary and secondary schs. Kan., 1951-57; chmn. dept. edn. and psychology Asbury Coll., Willmore, Ky., 1957- 59; dir. tchr. edn. Taylor U., Upland, Ind., 1959-65; dean Tchrs. Coll., Marshall U., Huntington, W.Va., 1965—. Mem. W.Va. Adv. Com. Tchr. Edn., 1965-71; mem. exec. com. Assn. Tchr. Educators 1968—; adviser to W. Va. Sch. Bds. Assn., State rep. Am. Assn. Colls. for Tchr. Edn., 1969—. Mem. Huntington Council Mentally Retarded, 1965-69. Chmn. bd. Huntington Day Care Nursery. Served with USMCR, 1944- 46. Mem. Nat., W.Va. edn. assns., Assn. Higher Edn., Assn. Tchr. Educators; Coll. Tchrs. Edn. Assn., Phi Delta Kappa, Kappa Delta Pi, Pi Omega Pi. Methodist. Kiwanain. Editor, contbr. 1966 Yearbook of Assn. Student Teaching. Home: 180 S Edgemont Rd Huntington WV 25701

HAYES, ROBERT MAYO, educator; b. N.Y.C., Dec. 3, 1926; s. Dudley Lyman and Myra Wilhelmina (Lane) H.; B.A., U. Cal. at Los Angeles, 1947, M.A., 1949, Ph.D., 1952; m. Alice Peters, Sept. 2, 1952; 1 son, Robert Dendrou. Mathematician, Nat. Bur. Standards, Wash. and Los Angeles, 1949-52; mem. tech. staff Hughes Aircraft Co., 1952-54; head applications group Nat. Cash Register Co., 1954-55; head bus. systems group Magnavox Co., 1955- 60; pres. Advanced Infomrations Systems, Inc., Los Angeles, 1960-64; v.p., sci. dir. Electrada Corp., Los Angeles, 1960-64; lectr. Sch. Library Sci., also dept. math. U. Cal. at Los Angeles, 1952-64, prof., 1964—, dir. Inst. Library Research, 1965-70, vis. lectr. Am. Univ., 1959, U. Wash., 1960-62; v.p. Becker & Hayes, Inc., 1969—. Mem. A.L.A. (pres. information sci. and automation div. 1969), Am. Soc. Information Sci. (pres. 1962-63), Am. Math. Soc., Assn. Computing Machinery (asso. editor jour. 1959-69), Soc. Indsl. and Applied Math., Phi Beta Kappa, Sigma Xi, Co-author: Indtroduction to Information Storage and Retrieval: Tools, Elements, Theory, 1963; Handbook of Data Processing for Libraries, 1970. U.S. regional editor Problems in Information Storage and Retrieval, 1959-63. Home. 3943 Woodfield Dr Sherman Oaks CA 91403 Office: U Cal Westwood CA 96137 also 10835 Santa Monica Blvd Westwood CA 96137

HAYES, ROBERT SAMUEL, naval officer; b. Columbus, O., July 5, 1922; s. Earl Raymond and Arlene (Wise) H.; B.S., U.S. Naval Acad., 1944; M.A., Boston U., 1959; certificate communications U.S. Naval Postgrad. Sch., 1951; m. Betty Redfern, June 8, 1946; children—Ronald R., Stephen B., Elizabeth A. Commd. ensign U.S. Navy, 1944, advanced through grades to capt., 1965; assigned U.S.S. Santa Fe, 1944-46, U.S.S. Perry, 1948-50; mem. staff ComBatCruPac, 1946-48, SACLANT, 1951-54; assigned U.S.S. New, 1954-56; comdg. officer U.S.S. Hemminger, 1956-57, U.S.S. Power, 1961-63, U.S.S. Jouett, 1966-68; mem. staff Naval War Coll., 1957-59, ComPhibGru 4, 1959-61; head fgn. lang. dept. U.S. Naval Acad., 1964-66; head spl. studies and objectives div. Office Program Appraisal, Navy Dept., Washington 1969—. Mem. U.S. Naval Inst. Home: 8013 Lynnfield Dr Alexandria VA 22306 Office: Office Program Appraisal Navy Dept Washington DC 20350

HAYES, ROLAND, tenor; b. Curryville, Ga., June 3, 1887; s. William and Fanny H.; student Fisk U.; extension course, Harvard; pupil W. Arthur Calhoun 2 yrs., Jennie A. Robinson, Fisk U., 4 yrs., Arthur J. Hubbard, 2 yrs.; also studied in Europe, 1920, under Ira Aldridge, Victor Beigel, Sir George Henschel, Dr. Theo Leierbammer; Mus.D., Fisk U., 1932, Ohio Wesleyan U., 1939, Boston U., 1948, Howard U., 1950, Temple U., 1956, New Eng. Conservatory Music, 1961; H.H.D., W.Va. State Coll., 1944; LL.D., Morehouse Coll.; L.H.D., Va. Union U., 1951; m. Helen A. Mann; 1 dau., Africa Fanzada. Conducted own concert tour U.S., 1916—; studying and conducting concert tours, Europe, 1921; command performances before George V of Eng., 1920, Queen Mother Maria Christina of Spain, 1925; sung with Orch. Collonne, Paris, Orch. Mengelberg, Amsterdam, Vienna and Berlin, other mus. centers of Europe; toured U.S., singing with Boston, Phila., Detroit and N.Y. symphony orchs. Recognized for interpretation of classics and traditional Negro melodies. Recipient Spingarn medal for most outstanding achievement among colored people, 1925; Purple Ribbon award for services to French music (France), 1949 Fellow Am. Acad, Arts and Scis. Address: 58 Allerton St Brookline MA 02146

HAYES, SAMUEL BANKS, Jr., former telephone co. exec.; b. Troy, Tenn., June 28, 1906; s. Samuel Banks and Besse Eudora (Crockett) H.; A.B., Presbyn. Coll., Clinton, S.C., 1925; M.A., Duke, 1928; m. Priscilla Alden Bailey, July 6, 1935; children— Samuel Banks III, Alden Vance. Tchr., North Charleston (S.C.) High Sch., 1925-26, Durham (N.C.) High Sch., 1927-29; with N.J. Bell Telephone Co., 1929-71, gen. traffic mgr., 1955-60, v.p. personnel, 1960-71, ret. Clubs: Essex, Down Town (Newark). Home: 146 Phelps Rd Ridgewood NJ 07450 Office: NJ Bell Telephone Co 540 Broad St Newark NJ 07102

HAYES, SAMUEL PERKINS, social scientist; b. South Hadley, Mass., Jan. 28, 1910; s. Samuel Perkins and Agnes Hayes (Stone) H.; A.B., Amherst Coll., 1931, L.H.D., 1966; Ph.D., Yale, 1934; postgrad. (fellow Social Sci. Research Council) U. Chgo., 1937-38; m. Alice Mary Cable, Mar. 25, 1937; children—Susan, Jonathan. Asst. psychology Yale U. Inst. Human Relations, 1931-34; instr. psychology Mt. Holyoke Coll., 1934-37; faculty dept. econs. Sarah Lawrence Coll., 1938-40; market research Young & Rubicam, Inc., N.Y.C., 1940-42; various positions U.S. govt. in Washington, Algiers, London, Scandinavia, mainly for Fgn. Econ. Adminstrn. and State Dept., 1942-45, 48-51; asso. dir. marketing and research div. Dun & Bradstreet, Inc., N.Y.C., 1945- 48; chief Spl. Tech. and Econ. Mission, Indonesia, 1951-52; asst. dir. Mut. Security Agy., Far East, 1952-53; dir. Found. for Research on Human Behavior, 1953-60; lectr. econs. U. Mich., 1955-57, prof. econs., 1959-62, dir. Center for Research on Econ. Devel., 1961-62; cons. President's Task Force on Fgn. Econ. Assistance, 1961, Peace Corps, 1961-62; pres. Fgn. Policy Assn., 1962—. Sr. specialist E.-W. Center, Honolulu, 1968. Fellow A.A.A.S., Am. Statis. Assn., Am. Psycho. Assn.; mem. Soc. Internat. Devel., Am. Econ. Assn., Council Fgn. Relations, Amateur Chamber Music Players (nat. chmn.), Am. Assn. Pub. Opinion Research, Phi Beta Kappa, Sigma Xi, Chi Phi. Democrat. Clubs: Cosmos; Pilgrims; Century, Yale (N.Y.C.). Author: Measuring the Results of Development Projects, 1959; An International Peace Corps, 1961; Evaluating Development Projects, 1966; The Beginning of American Aid to Southeast Asia, 1971. Editor: (with others) Some Applications of Behavioral Research, 1957. Contbg. author books, articles profl. publs. Home: West Shefield Rd Great Barington MA 01230 and 468 Riverside Dr New York City NY 10027 Office: 345 E 46th St New York City NY 10017

HAYES, THOMAS JAY, III, constrn. and engring. co. exec.; b. Omaha, Aug. 26, 1914; s. Thomas Jay and Mary (Ringwalt) H.; B.S., U.S. Mil. Acad., 1936; M.S., Mass. Inst. Tech., 1939; grad. Engr. Sch., 1940, Command and Gen. Staff Coll., 1944, Indsl. Coll. Armed Forces, 1958; m. Jean Jocelyn Pedley, Nov. 20, 1942; children—Thomas Jay IV (dec.), Mary Helen (Mrs. Roy Attride), Barbara Jean (Mrs. David Basham). Commnd. 2d lt., C.E., U.S. Army, 1936, advanced through grades to maj. gen., 1965; various assignments U.S., Greenland, Bahamas, Can. and Alaska, 1936-43; mem. faculty, asst. commdt. Engr. Sch., Fort Belvoir, Va., 1944-45; engr. liaison officer, asst. mil. attache, London, Eng., 1946-49; asst. engr. commr. govt., Washington, 1949-52; dist. engr., Little Rock, 1952-53, Omaha, 1953-57; engr. I Corps, Korea, 1958- 59; chief Los Angeles Field Office, Office Chief Engrs., 1959-60; vice comdr., then comdr. C.E. Ballistic Missile Constrn. Office, Los Angeles, 1960-62; asst. chief engrs. NASA support, also dep. dir. mil. constrn. for space programs Office Chief Engrs., 1962-64, dir. topography and mil. engring., 1964-67; div. engr. South Atlantic div. C.E., Atlanta, 1967-69; ret., 1969; pres. Internat. Engring. Co., Inc., San Francisco, also Cal. Internacional de Ingeniera, Santiago, Chile, 1969—; v.p. Morrison-Knudsen Co., Inc., Boise, Ida., 1971—. Mem. Fed. Exec. Bd., Bd. Engrs. for Rivers and Harbors, also Coastal Engring. Research Bd., 1967-69; vice chmn. S.E. Basin Inter Agy. Commn., 1967-69. Decorated D.S.M. with oak leaf cluster, Legion of merit with 2 oak leaf clusters. Registered Profl. engr., D.C., Alaska. Mem. Am. Soc. C.E.s, Soc. Am. Mil. Engrs. (pres. Little Rock 1952, Omaha 1954, Korea 1958, Washington 1964; George W. Goethals medal 1961), Permanent Internat. Assn. Navigation Congresses, Nat. Geog. Soc., U.S. Com. Large Dams, Am. Pub. Works Assn., Assn. U.S. Army, San Francisco C. of C. Episcopalian (past vestryman, lay reader). Clubs: Bankers; World Trade (San Francisco); Army-Navy (Washington); Royal Engineer Yacht (hon.) (London); Belvedere Tennis (Tiburon, Cal.). Contbr. articles profl. jours. Home: 2646 Chestnut St San Francisco CA 94123 Office: 220 Montgomery St San Francisco CA 94104

HAYES, WALLACE DEAN, educator; b. Peking, China, Sept. 4, 1918; s. Jesse Earnest and Grace Raymond (Helmick) H.; B.S. with honor, Cal. Inst. Tech., 1941, Aero. Engr., 1943, Ph.D. magna cum laude, 1947; Frank B. Jewett fellow Princeton, 1947-48; m. Laura Louise Merriman, Sept. 11, 1948; children— Carolyn Grace, Judith Louise, Barbara Dean. Various positions aircraft industry, 1939-45; cons. aircraft-missile industry in highspeed aerodynamics, 1946—; asst. prof. applied mathematics Brown U., 1948-49, asso. prof., 1949-51; Fulbright vis. lectr. Delft Tech. U., 1951-52; sci. liaison officer Office Naval Research, London, Eng., 1952-54; asso. prof. aero. engring. Princeton, 1954-57, prof., 1957—. Devised supersonic area rule for use in design supersonic aircraft; mem. subcon. fluid mechanics NACA, 1955-58. Fellow Am. Inst. Aeros. and Astronautics; mem. Am. Phys. Soc., Sigma Xi, Tau Beta Pi, Pi Kappa Delta. Club: Sierra (San Francisco). Author: (with Ronald F. Probstein) Hypersonic Flow Theory, 1959, 2d edit. vol. 1, Inviscid Flows, 1966. Mailing address:

HAYES, WAYLAND JACKSON, Jr., educator, toxicologist; b. Charlottesville, Va., Apr. 29, 1917; s. Wayland Jackson and Mary Lula (Turner) H.; B.S., U. Va., 1938, M.D., 1946; M.A., U. Wis., 1940, Ph.D., 1942; m. Barnita Donkle, Feb. 1, 1942; children—Marie, Maryetta (Mrs. Charles Andrew Hacskaylo), Lula, Wayland, Roche del. Chief vector-transmission investigations USPHS, Savannah, Ga., 1947-48, chief toxicology sect., 1949-67, Atlanta, 1960-67, chief toxicologist, 1967-68; prof. biochemistry Vanderbilt U. Sch. Medicine, Nashville, 1968—. Vol. asso. prof. pharmacology Emory U., Atlanta, 1962-68; cons. WHO, 1950—, Nat. Acad. Scis.-NRC, 1964—. Served with AUS, 1943-46. Recipient Meritorious Service medal USPHS, 1964. Mem. Soc. Toxicology (charter, pres. 1971-72), Am. Soc. Pharmacology and Exptl. Therapeutics, Am. Soc. Tropical Medicine and Hygiene Am. Conf. Govtl. Indsl. Hygienists. Author: Clinical Handbook on Economic Poisons, 1963. Mem. editorial bds. Jour. Pharmacology and Exptl. Therapeutics, 1962-64, Archives Environmental Health, 1965—, Food and Cosmetics Toxicology, 1967—. Contbr. sci. papers to profl. lit. Home: 2317 Golf Club Lane Nashville TN 37215

HAYES, WILLIAM ALOYSIUS, educator; b. Chgo., June 25, 1920; s. John and Stella (Ahern) H.; A.B., DePaul U., 1942; M.A., Cath. U. Am., 1948, Ph.D., 1952; m. Joan Leahy, Aug. 22, 1953; children—Mary, Joseph, William, Anne, Partick, Margaret, John, Teresa. Instr. econs., asst. prof., asso. prof. DePaul U., Chgo., 1950-60, prof. econs., 1960—, chmn. dept., 1959-67. Exec. bd. Nat. Cath. Social Action Conf.; bd. dirs. Adult Edn. Centers, Chgo. Mem. Am., Cath. (exec. council, pres. 1968) econ. assns., Am. Assn. U. Profs., Blue Key, Beta Gamma Sigma, Pi Gamma Mu. Home: 10600 S Leavitt St Chicago IL 60643

HAYHURST, NORMAL CLIFTON, savs. and loan assn. exec.; b. Berryville, Ark., Jan. 23, 1893; s. Michael M. and Dorothy (Martin) H.; B.S., U. Ariz., 1915; M.A., U. So. Cal., 1934; m. Margaret Ewell, 1967. Dir. athletics Glendale (Cal.) High Sch., 1919-29; vice prin. Hoover High Sch., Glendale, 1929- 37, prin., 1937-55; dep. supt. schs., Glendale, 1945-47, supt., 1947-55; pres. Fidelity Fed. Savs. & Loan Assn., Glendale, 1940-71, pres.-mgr., chmn. bd., 1960-71. Mem. Cal. Citizens Adv. Com. Pub. Edn. System. Bd. dirs. Los Angeles Met. Water Bd. Mem. Kappa Sigma, Phi Delta Kappa. Mason, Elk, Kiwanian. Home: 1641 Highland Av Glendale CA 91202

HAYMAN, TELFORD, Brit. diplomat; b. Deal, Eng., June 14, 1914; s. Charles Henry Telford and Hilda (Waite-Browne) H.; B.A., Worcester Coll., Oxford, (Eng.) U., 1936; m. Rosemary Eardley Blomefield, June 6, 1942; children—Virginia Rosemary, Christopher Wilmot Avdon. Asst. prin. Home Office, also Ministry of Home Security, 1937-41; pvt. sect. to home sec., 1941- 42; asst. sec. Ministry of Def., 1949-52; mem. U.K. delegation to NATO, 1952-54; counsellor Brit. embassy, Belgrade, Yugoslavia, 1955-58; counsellor Brit. embassy, Baghdad, 1959-61; dir. gen. Brit. Information Sers., N.Y.C., 1961-64; minister, Berlin, 1964-66; asst. under sec. state Fgn. Office, 1966-69; dep. under sec. state Fgn. and Commonwealth Office, 1969-70; high commr. in Can., Ottawa, Ont., 1970—. Served with Brit. Army, 1942-45; Italy, Balkans. Decorated knight comdr. Order St. Michael and St. George; mem. Order Brit. Empire; comdr. Royal Victorian Order. Clubs: Travellers, Marylebone Cricket (London); Pilgrims (N.Y.C.); Rideau (Ottawa); Mt. Royal (Montreal). Home: Ernscliffe Ottawa Ontario Canada also: Uxmore House Checkendon Oxfordshire England Office: Brit High Commn Ottawa Ontario Canada

HAYMES, HARMON HAYDEN, educator, economist; b. Lynchburg, Va., June 8, 1927; s. Joseph Albert and Reba (Hayden) H.; B.A. magna cum laude, Lynchburg Coll., 1954; M.A., U. Va., 1956, Ph.D., 1959; m. Beatrice Ann Mason, Nov. 26, 1952; children—Ann Elizabeth, William Hayden. Acting asst. prof. Lynchburg Coll., 1956-57; instr. U. Va., 1957-59; asst. prof. Smith Coll., 1959-61, Washington and Lee U., 1961-64; asst. v.p. Fed. Res. Bank of Richmond, 1964-68; prof., chmn. dept. econs. Va. Commonwealth U., 1968—, also acting dir. Bur. Bus. and Econ. Research. Mem. Gov.'s Adv. Com. for Urban Incentive Fund, 1970-73; mem. adv. bd. RCAP Youth Econ. Devel. Program, 1970-71; trustee Planning for Econ. Progress, 1968-70. Served with AUS, 1950-52. Recipient McKinsey award Bus. Horizons, 1962; duPont fellow, 1954; John Y. Mason fellow, 1955; Virginia Mason Davidge fellow, 1955. Mem. Am. Econ. Assn., So. Econ. Assn., Omicron Delta Epsilon. Editor Va. Social Sci. Jour., 1970—. Contbr. articles profl. jours. Home: 7516 Rockfalls Dr Richmond VA 23225

HAYMES, ROBERT C., physicist; b. N.Y.C., July 3, 1931; s. Michael and Winifred (Koenig) H.; B.A., N.Y.U., 1952, M.S., 1953, Ph.D., 1959; m. Jamie Buswell, Jan. 22, 1965; children—Douglas Fletcher, Lisa Melanie. Research asso. N.Y., 1955-59, asst. prof. physics, 1959-62; resident research fellow Jet Propulsion Lab., Cal. Inst. Tech., 1962-64; asst. prof. space sci. Rice U., Houston, 1964-66, asso. prof., 1966—; cons. in field. Mem. Am. Phys. Soc., Am. Geophys. Union, Am. Astron. Soc., Sigma Xi, Sigma Pi Sigma. Space scientist who calculated Gemini 7's time slowdown; research gamma-ray astronomy, cosmic rays, planetary magnetism. Home: 10611 Candlewood Dr Houston TX 77042

HAYMES, STEPHEN DENIS, investment co. exec.; b. N.Y.C., Mar. 2, 1937; s. Morice and Beatrice (Glick) H.; B.S., Wharton Sch. Finance and Commerce, U. Pa., 1957; LL.B., Harvard, 1960; m. Gail Lowe, June 20, 1965; 1 son, Evan. Admitted to N.Y. bar, 1960; practiced in N.Y.C., 1960-61; v.p., prin. Morice Haymes & Co., N.Y.C., 1961-64; v.p. Investors Funding Corp., N.Y.C. 1964—, also dir.; pres., dir. P. Ballantine & Sons, Newark, 1969—. Trustee Essex County Blood Bank, East Orange, N.J. Recipient Distinguished Service awards United Negro Coll. Fund, 1970, Jr. C. of C., 1970, JFK Library for Minorities, N.Y.C., 1970. Mem. Am., N.Y. bar assns., Young Pres.'s Orgn. Jewish religion (dir. mens club). Mason. Clubs: Harvard, Lone Star Boat (N.Y.C.). Home: 945 Fifth Av New York City NY 10021 Office: 57 Freeman St Newark NJ 07101

HAYMOND, FRANK CRUISE, judge; b. Fairmont, W. Va., Apr. 13, 1887; s. William Stanley and Agnes (Cruise) H.; grad. Fairmont State Normal Sch., 1906; A.B. cum laude, Harvard Coll., 1910; student Harvard Law Sch., 1910-12; LL.D., Morris Harvey Coll., W. Va. U., 1963; m. Susan Watson Arnett, Jan. 25, 1922; children—William Stanley II, Thomas Arnett. Admitted to W. Va. bar, 1912; in gen. practice, specializing in corp. and trial work until 1939; apptd. judge 16th Jud. Circuit of W. Va., 1939, elected 1940, 44, resigned 1945; apptd. judge Supreme Court of Appeals of W. Va., 1945, elected since, present term ends 1976. Mem. Ho. Dels. W. Va. Legislature, 1916-18; mem. W. Va. Commn. on Constl. Revision. Served from pvt. to capt. U.S. Army, 1918, AEF 1918-19. Mem. Am. (mem. bd. govts. 1943-46, 67-68, past chmn. ways and means com.; state del.; chmn. spl. com. to cooperate with A.M.A. 1957-62), W. Va. (pres. 1934-35), Marion County (pres. 1929) bar assns.; mem. W. Va. Council 1935-60; chmn. 1948-60; also mem. several other profl. assns. and vet. orgns.; pres. W. Va. Supreme Ct. Appeals, 1949, 53, 58, 61, 64; mem. Conf. Chief Justices, 1949, 53, 58, 61, 64; past pres. W. Va. Jud. Assn. Democrat. Roman Catholic. Elk, K.C. Clubs: Army-Navy (Charleston, W. Va.); Press; Harvard (Boston). Lectr. on ins. law, W.Va. U., 1935- 39. Home: 227 Jefferson St Fairmont WV 26554 also 114 Bradford Street Charleston WV 25301 Office: State Capitol Charleston WV 23305 ☆

HAYNES, DOUGLAS MARTIN, physician, educator; b. N.Y.C., Jan. 25, 1922; s. Daniel Hagood and Courtenay (Collins) H.; B.A., B.S., So. Meth. U., 1943; M.D., Southwestern Med. Coll., 1946; m. Elizabeth B. Johnson, June 17, 1961; children—Douglas Marshall, Lewis D. Intern in pathology Parkland Meml. Hosp., Dallas, 1946-47, resident obstetrics and gynecology, 1949-52; asst. prof. obstetrics and gynecology U. Tex. Southwestern Med Sch., 1952-55; asso. prof. obstetrics and gynecology U. Louisville Sch. Medicine, 1955-57, prof., chmn. dept., 1957—, interim dean Sch. of Medicine, 1969-70, dean, 1970—. Served to capt., M. C., AUS, 1947-49. Diplomate Am. Bd. Obstetrics and Gynecology. Fellow A.M.A., Am. Assn. Obstetricians and Gynecologists; mem. Am. Coll. Obstetricians and Gynecologists, A.C.S., Central Assn. Obstetricians and Gynecologists, So. Obstet. and Gynecol. Soc., So. Med. Assn., Phi Beta Kappa, Phi Chi, Delta Chi, Alpha Omega Alpha. Democrat. Presbyn. Author: Medical Complications During Pregnancy, 1969. Contbr. articles med. jours. Home: 5204 Tomahawk Rd Louisville KY 40207

HAYNES, F. BOYKIN, banker; b. Union Springs, Ala., Oct. 22, 1907; s. Frank B. and Eva (Caldwell) H.; m. Florence Rainer, Aug. 16, 1952. Cashier, Am. Nat. Bank, Union Springs, 1928-38; examiner FDIC, 1938-47; with Birmingham Trust Nat. Bank (Ala.), 1947—, now sr. v.p. Served with AUS, 1942-46. Home: 3800 N Woodridge Rd Birmingham AL 35223 Office: 112 N 20th St Birmingham AL 35202

HAYNES, FRED ELMORE, Jr., marine corps officer; b. Dallas, Jan. 5, 1921; s. Fred Elmore and Louise Ernestine (Schimelpfenig) H.; B.S., So. Methodist U., 1941; postgrad. Marine Corps Amphibious Warfare Sch., 1952-53, Fgn. Service Inst., 1957-58, Air War Coll., 1961-62; M.A., George Washington U., 1963; m. Frances Corinne Lane, Aug. 8, 1942; children—Karen Frances, Fred Elmore III, William Lane. Commd. 2d lt. U.S. Marine Corps, 1942, advanced throuh grades to brig. gen., 1968; operations officer 28th Marine Regt. that seized Mt. Suribachi, Iwo Jima, 1945; exec. officer 2d Bn., 1st Marines, Korea, 1954; naval attache, Turkey, 1958-61; comdg. officer 5th Marines, Vietnam, 1966-67; G-3 III Marine Amphibious Force, Vietnam, 1967; mil. sec. to comdt. Marine Corps, 1968, legislative asst., 1968—. Various adult leadership positions Boy Scouts Am., 1937-62. Decorated Legion of Merit with combat U and 2 gold stars, Bronze Star with combat V, RVN Army Distinguished Service Order, RVN Cross of Gallantry with palm, RVN unit citation Cross of Gallantry with palm; recipient Silver Beaver award Boy Scouts Am., 1960. Mem. Council on Fgn. Relations N.Y., Middle East Inst., Washington. Contbr. articles profl. jours. Home: 1011 Langley Hill Dr McLean VA 22101 Office: Hdqrs US Marine Corps Washington DC 20380

HAYNES, GEORGE, mfg. co. exec.; b. Lemsford, Eng., Apr. 28, 1911; s. Charles Edward and Edith (Bashford) H.; student St. Paul's Sch., West Kensington, London, 1924-28; m. Joan Mary Ireland, July 13, 1937; children-John Charles, Diana Sybil (Mrs. Peter Trainor), Edward George, Catherine Sylvia. Joined Nat. Cash Register Co., Ltd., London, 1929; supr. Far Eastern activities Nat. Cash Register Co., Dayton, O., 1949-61, v.p. internat. operations, 1961-64, v.p., group exec. internat. operations, 1964—, also dir. Bd. dirs. Nat. Fgn. Trade Council, Far East Am. Council Commerce and Industry, Inc., Internat. Golf Assn. Served with Hong Kong Vol. Def. Corps., 1941-46. Clubs: Moraine Country, Rotary (Dayton); Devonshire (London); Hong Kong; American (Tokyo); Phlis Court (Henley-on-Thames, Eng.). Home: 3371 Southdale Dr Dayton OH 45409 Office: Nat Cash Register Co Main and K Sts Dayton OH 45409

HAYNES, GILMAN BALLARD, Jr., banker; b. Los Angles, May 24, 1923; s. Gilman Ballard and Mildred E. (Eirick) H.; B.S., U. Cal. at Berkeley, 1948; m. Ruth A. Wood, June 30, 1949; children—Geoffrey, David. With Wells Fargo Bank, 1955—, v.p. valley div., 1962-67, sr. v.p., 1967—. Trustee Robert Louis Stevenson Sch., Pebble Beach, Cal. Served to capt. AUS, 1943-46, 50-51. Mem. San Francisco C. of C., Sacramento-San Joaquin Wine and Food Soc., Psi Upsilon. Clubs: Bohemian; Peninsula Tennis (Burlingame); Commonwealth (San Francisco). Home: 2179 Pacific Av San Francisco CA 94115 Office: 464 California St San Francisco CA 94104

HAYNES, HAROLD JEAN, oil co. exec.; b. Ft. Worth Sept. 29, 1925; s. Jean Calvin and Hallie May (Badgett) H.; B.S. in Civil Engring., Tex. A. and M. U., 1947; m. Reta Kathryn Adams, Mar. 14, 1945; children-Sharon, Karen, Toya. Engr., Cal. Co., 1947-58; v.p. Richmond Exploration Co., 1958-60; v.p. Standard Oil Co. Cal., Western Operations, Inc., 1963-65, pres., 1965-66; v.p., dir. Standard Oil Co. of Cal., 1966-69, pres., 1969—. Bd. dirs. Am. Petroleum Inst. Trustee World Affairs Council No. Cal. Served with USNR, 1944-46. Clubs: University (N.Y.C.); California (Los Angeles); Stock Exchange, World Trade (San Francisco); Burlingame (Cal.) Country; Meadow (Fairfax, Cal.). Home: 51 Blue Ridge Rd Kentfield CA 94904 Office: 225 Bush St San Francisco, CA 94120

HAYNES, HAROLD WALTER, aircraft mfr.; b. Snoqualmie, Wash., Jan. 23, 1923; s. Ralph and Bertha (Sewell) H.; B.A., U. Wash., 1948; m. Barbara J. Tatham, Oct. 11, 1943; children—Christine, Steven, Kevin. With Touche, Ross, Bailey & Smart, C.P.A.'s, Seattle, 1948-54, Boeing Co., Seattle, 1954—, v.p. finance, 1960-70, sr. v.p. finance, 1970—, also dir.; dir. United Pacific Ins. Co., Pacific Nat. Bank Wash., Bank for Investment and Credit, Berne, Switzerland. Served as pilot USMCR, 1942-45. C.P.A., Wash. Mem. Financial Execs. Inst., Wash. State Soc. C.P.A.'s. Home: 2 Holly Lane Mercer Island WA 98040 Office: P O Box 3707 10-14 Seattle WA 98124

HAYNES, JOHN CREPIN, Jr., lawyer; b. Tucson, Nov. 17, 1922; s. John Crepin and Edith Virgil (Failor) H.; LL.B., U. Ariz., 1947; m. Patsy Hargitt, Dec. 15, 1944. Admitted to Ariz. bar, 1947, also U.S. Supreme Ct., Ariz. Supreme Ct., U.S. Ct. Mil. Appeals; practice in Tucson., 1947—. Pres. Family Service Agy., 1959. Served with USAAF, World War II; Maj. Res. Decorated Air medal. Mem. Am., Pima County bar assns., State Bar Ariz. (gov. 1958- 64; pres. 1962-63), Air Force Assn., Ariz. Pioneers Hist. Soc., Am. Legion, Sigma Alpha Epsilon, Phi Delta Phi. Rotarian (dir. Tucson; pres. Tucson 1966-67), Clubs: Tucson Kennel; Old Pueblo Dog Training. Home: 3100 N Craycroft Rd Tucson AZ 85712 Office: 127 N Stone Av Tucson AZ 85701

HAYNES, JOHN JACKSON, educator, civil engr.; b. Dallas, Sept. 13, 1925; s. Frank Hooker and Annie Laurie (Richardson) H.; B.S. in Civil Engring., Tex. Tech. Coll., 1949; M.A., Tex. A. and M. U., 1959, Ph.D., 1964; m. Louise Elizabeth Vaughn, June 5, 1948. Asst. resident engr. Tex. Hwy. Dept., 1949-51; city engr., Arlington, Tex., 1952; design engr. tex. Hwy. Dept., 1953- 55; asso. prof. Arlington State Coll., 1955-58; prof. civil engr., chmn. dept. U. Tex. at Arlington, 1959—. Chmn. regional codes com. N. Central Tex. Council Govts., 1967-70. Served with USNR, 1943-46. Registered profl. engr., Tex. Mem. Am. Soc. C.E., Am. Soc. Engring. Edn., Inst. Traffic Engrs., Nat. Soc. Profl. Engrs., Sigma Xi, Tau Beta Pi, Chi Epsilon. Home: 1200 Windmill Ct Arlington TX 76013

HAYNES, SAMUEL LLOYD, actor; b. South Bend, Ind., Oct. 19, 1934; s. Alfred Lloyd and Loquette Ruth (Thompson) H.; student San Jose State Coll., 1960, Ind. U.; m. Saundra Madariage, June 12, 1971; stepchildren—Tammy, Michael. Actor TV series Room 222. Served with USMCR, 1962-66. Mem. Baha'i faith. Office: care Landsman and Frank 9350 Wilshire Blvd Beverly Hills CA 90212

HAYNES, SHERWOOD KIMBALL, educator; b. Boston, Apr. 7, 1910; s. John and Jessie M. (Bailey) H.; A.B., Williams Coll., 1932; Ph.D., Cal. Inst. Tech., 1936; m. Pauline J. McBride, 1943; children—Charles, Margaret E., Sherwood K. II, Jessie. Instr., Williams Coll., 1936-39; asst. prof. Brown U., 1940-42; instr. elec. communications Radar Sch., Mass. Inst. Tech., 1942-44, asst. dir. Radar Sch., 1944-45; asso. prof. Vanderbilt U., 1945-51, prof., 1951-58; head dept. physics and astronomy Mich. State U., 1957-66, chmn. dept. physics, 1966-69, prof. physics, 1969—, vis. scientist Am. Inst. Physics, 1963—. Cons.-examiner North Central Assn. Colls. and Secondary Schs., 1964—; vis. physicist IKO, Amsterdam, 1965; cons. Fulbright selection com., 1955, Midwest planning com., 1959. French sci. fellow Inst. Internat. Edn., 1939-40; Fulbright lectr., Paris, France, 1954-55. Fellow Am. Phys. Soc. (v.p. Southeastern sect. 1953-54). Home: 2821 E Mt Hope Rd Okemos MI 48864 Office: Michigan State U East Lansing MI 48823

HAYNES-DIXON, MARGARET RUMER, Godden, Rumer.

HAYNIE, HUGH, editorial cartoonist; b. Reedville, Va., Feb. 6, 1927; s. Raymond Lee and Margaret Virginia (Smith) H.; A.B., Coll. William and Mary, 1950; L.H.D., U. Louisville, 1968; m. Lois Ann Cooper, Dec. 5, 1953; 1 son, Hugh Smith. Cartoonist, Richmond (Va.) Times-Dispatch, 1950-53, Greensboro (N.C.) Daily News, 1953-55, 56-58, Atlanta Jours., 1955-56; with Louisville Courier Jour., 1958—, now editorial cartoonist; syndicated by Los Angeles Times; dir. Haynie Products Balt. Served to lt. USCGR, 1944-46, 51-52; PTO. Named One of Ten Outstanding Young Men, U.S. Jr. C. of C., 1962; recipient Headliner award, 1966; Freedoms Found. award, 1966. Mem. Soc. Alumni Coll. William and Mary (dir.), Phi Beta Kappa, Omicron Delta Kappa, Pi Kappa Alpha. Democrat. Episcopalian. Clubs: Windmill Point, Yacht (Foxwells, Va.). Home: Indian Hills Trail and Tribal Rd Louisville KY 40207 Office: Courier-Jour 525 W Broadway Louisville KY 40202

HAYNIE, ROSCOE GEORGE, food co. exec.; b. Belgrade, Neb., Apr. 17, 1910; s. Ralph John and Flora Blanche (Gardner) H.; B.S., Cotner Coll., Lincoln, Neb., 1932; postgrad. Creighton U., 1932; m. Delpha Christine Porr, July 3, 1931; children—Kenneth Harlan, Linda Lee. Laborer, Dold Packing Co., Omaha, 1932-33, foreman, 1933-38; asst. mgr. beef div. Wilson & Co., Inc., Omaha, 1938-39, mgr. grading div., Chgo., 1939-43, mgr. beef div., 1943-46, v.p. in charge beef, lamb and veal operations, 1946-55, v.p. charge meat div., 1955-60, pres., 1960-67, chief exec. officer, 1963-68, chmn. bd., 1967-68, dir. 1960—; chmn. exec. com. Ling-Temco-Vought, Inc., 1968-70, dir., 1968—; vice chmn. bd. Jones & Laughlin Steel Corp., 1971—, dir., 1968—; chmn. bd. Wilson Sporting Goods Co., River Grove, Ill., 1963-68, dir., 1960-70; chmn., chief exec. officer Wilson Pharm. & Chem. Corp., 1967-68, dir., 1967-70; dir. LTV Aerospace Corp., LTV Electrosystems, Inc., 1967-71, LTV Ling-Altec, Inc., 1967-71, Okonite Co., 1968-71, Braniff Internat., 1968-70, Nat. Car Rental System, Inc., 1968-69, Jones & Laughlin Industries, Inc., 1969—, Computer Tech., Inc. Chmn. beef industry adv. com. OPA, 1944-46. Trustee Wesley Meml. Hosp., 1964-68. Mem. Am. Meat Inst. (chmn. 1964-67), Am. Iron and Steel Inst. Methodist. Clubs: Chicago, Mid-America, Economic, Executives (Chgo.); Midlothian (Ill.) Country (pres. 1964-66); Lost Tree (West Palm Beach, Fla.); Northwood, Preston Trail Golf (Dallas); Tres V Das (Acapulco); Laurel Valley Golf (Ligonier, Pa.); Duquesne (Pitts.). Home: 5135 Royal Crest Dr Dallas TX 75229 Office: Ling-Temco-Vought Inc LTV Tower Dallas TX 75230

HAYNSWORTH, CLEMENT FURMAN, Jr., fed. judge; b. Greenville, S.C., Oct. 30, 1912; s. Clement Furman and Elsie (Hall) H.; ed. Darlington Sch., Rome, Ga.; A.B., Furman U., 1933; LL.B., Harvard, 1936; LL.D., Furman U., 1964; m. Dorothy Merry Barkley, 1946. Admitted S.C. bar, 1936; mem. firm Haynsworth, Perry, Bryant, Marion & Jonstone, Greenville, until 1957; judge U.S. Ct. Appeals 4th Circuit, 1957-64, chief judge, 1964—; chief judge 4th Jud. Circuit U.S., 1964—. Adv. council Furman U. Mem. Am., S.C., Greenville bar assns., Am. Law Inst., Am. Judicature Soc. Episcopalian. Clubs: Poinsett (Greenville, S.C.); Commonwealth (Richmond, Va.). Home: 415 Crescent Av Greenville SC 29605 Office: Fed Bldg Greenville SC 29603

HAYNSWORTH, HUGH CHARLES, Jr., corp. exec.; b. Sumter, S.C., Feb. 10, 1910; s. H. C. and Emilie E. (Beattie) H.; B.S., U.S. Naval acad., 1930; m. Marguerite T. Cuttino, Dec. 30, 1930; children—Hugh Charles III, Marguerite Allan. Commd. ensign USN, 1930, advanced through grades to rear adm., 1956; assigned aircraft carriers, Battleship Pennsylvania, Destroyer Zane; staff Dept. Navy, 1937-39; comdg. officer Navy Finance Center, Cleve., 1947-49; Supply Center, Norfolk, Va., 1959-63, Oakland, Cal., 1963-64; ret., 1964; pres. Surface Preparation-Va., Inc., Norfolk, 1964—. Decorated Legion of Merit. Mem. Nat. Def. Transp. Assn. Clubs: Army-Navy (Washington); Army Navy Country (Arlington, Va.). Home: 7623 Argyle Av Norfolk VA 23505 Office: 2710 Church St Norfolk VA 23504

HAYS, ANNA MAE VIOLET, army officer; b. Buffalo, Feb. 16, 1920; d. Daniel Joseph and Matie (Humphrey) McCabe; R.N., Allentown (Pa.) Hosp. Sch. Nursing, 1941; B.S. in Nursing Edn., Columbia, 1958; M.S. in Nursing, Cath. U. Am., 1968; m. William Anstead Hays, July 14, 1956 (dec. Nov. 1962). Commd. 2d 1st., 1942, advanced through ranks to brig. gen., 1970; operating room nurse, staff nurse, head nurse, supr., asst. chief, then chief Army Nurse Corps; served Clairborne, La., India, Ft. Dix, N.J., Valley Forge, Pa., Japan, Indiantown Gap, Pa., Ft. Sam Houston, Tex., Walter Reed Gen. Hosp. and Office Surgeon Gen., Washington; Decorated Legion of Merit with oak leaf cluster, Army Commendation medal. Mem. Am. Nurses Assn., Nat. League Nursing, Am. Assn. U. Women, Assn. U.S. Army, Kappa Delta Pi, Pi Lambda Theta, Sigma Theta Tau. Home: 1200 N Nash St Arlington VA 22209 Office: 1000 Independence Av SW Washington DC 20314

HAYS, BROOKS, former congressman, lawyer, educator; b. Russellville, Ark., Aug. 9, 1898; s. Adelbert Steele and Sallie (Butler) H.; A.B., U. Ark., 1919; J.D., George Washington U., 1922; LL.D., Coll. of Ozarks, Clarksville, Ark., Salem (W.Va.) Coll.; hon. degrees Mercer U., William Jewell Coll., Coll. of Pacific, Stetson U., and others; m. Marian Prather, Feb. 2, 1922; children—Betty Brooks (Mrs. William E. Bell), Marion Steele. Admitted to Ark. bar, 1922; mem. Hays, Priddy & Hays, Russellville, 1922-25; asst. atty. gen. Ark., 1925-27; mem. Hays & Turner, Little Rock, 1928-33. Mem. Democratic Nat. Com., 1932-39. Directed surveys, chmn. Ark. Rural Ch. Commn., 1928-29, Pulaski County Hosp. Com., 1929-30; apptd. labor compliance officer for Ark., NRA, 1934, spl. asst. to adminstr. of resettlement, 1935; later asst. dir. rural rehab. Farm Security Adminstrn., resigned 1942 to become congrl. candidate; mem. 78th-85th Congresses, 5th Dist. Ark.; bd. dirs. TVA, 1959-60; asst. sec. state for congl. relations. Dept. State, 1961; spl. asst. to Pres. of U.S., 1961-63; presdl. cons., 1963-66; Arthur T. Vanderbilt prof. pub. affairs, Rutgers U., 1963-65; vis. prof. pub. affairs U. Mass., 1966; dir. Ecumenical Inst., Wake Forest U., 1969—. Chmn. Good Neighbor Council N.C., 1970—. U.S. del. to 10th gen. assembly UN, 1955. Bd. dirs. Ark. Tb Assn., Ark. Children's Home and Hosp., pres. 1928-29; pres. Ark. State Conf. Social Work, 1932-35. Trustee George Peabody Coll., George Washington U. Recipient Silver Buffalo award, Boy Scouts Am. Mem. Am. Bar Assn., Phi Beta Kappa, Sigma Chi, Phi Alpha Delta, Tau Kappa Alpha, Omicron Delta Kappa. Baptist. Mason (33). Author: This World: A Christian's Workship; A Southern Moderate Speaks; (with John E. Steely) The Baptist Way of Life; Hotbed of Tranquility, 1968. Home: 314 2d St SE Washington DC 20003 Office: PO Box 12525 Raleigh NC 27605

HAYS, CORNELIUS LANSING, Jr., lawyer; b. Lake Pleasant, N.Y., Aug. 27, 1915; s. Cornelius Lansing and Mary Pratt (Love) H.; A.B., Williams Coll., 1936; LL.B., Columbia, 1939; m. Nathalie B. Spencer, June 7, 1941; children—Cornelius Lansing III, Spencer B., Priscilla B., Stephen H. Admitted to N.Y. bar, 1940, since practiced in N.Y.C.; partner firm Hecht, Hadfield, Hays and McAlpin, and predecessors, 1946—. Vice pres., dir. Pacwest Realty Corp.; dir., gen. counsel Getty Oil Co., Mission Devel. Co., Spartan Aircraft co.; dir. Pacific Western-Iran Ltd., Minnehoma Financial Co., Minnehoma Ins. Co., Minnehoma Life Ins. Co. Trustee Williston Acad., Easthampton, Mass. Served to lt. comdr. USNR, 1941-46. Mem. Am. Bar Assn., Assn. Bar City N.Y. Home: Leeward Lane Riverside CT 06878 Office: 11 Broadway New York City NY 10004

HAYS, DAVID ARTHUR, stage designer; b. N.Y.C., June 2, 1930; s. Mortimer and Sarah (Reich) H.; A.B. magna cum laude, Harvard, 1952; M.A. (teaching fellow), Boston U., 1955; student Yale Drama Sch., 1953-54; m. Lenore Landau, Dec. 28, 1954; children—Julia Carrie, Daniel Edward. Apprentice, Brattle Theatre, Cambridge, Mass., 1949-52; designer stock theatres, Green Mansions, N.Y. 1954, Tanglewood, Mass., 1955; designer off-Broadway prodns. The Iceman Cometh, 1956, Cradle Song, 1955, Children of Darkness, 1958, Endgame, 1958, The Quare Fellow, 1958, Our Town, 1959, The Balcony, 1960, Desire Under the Elms, 1963; designer Broadway prodns. including Night Circus, 1951, The Innkeepers, 1956, Long Day's Journey into Night, 1956, Tenth Man, 1959, Roman Candle, 1960, All the Way Home, 1960, Love and Libel, 1960, Sunday in New York, 1961, Gideon, 1961, Strange Interlude, 1963, A Family Affair, 1962, Look, We've Come Through, 1961, No Strings, 1962, In the Counting House, 1962, Lorenzo, 1963, A Murderer Among Us, 1964, Marco Millions, 1964, The Last Analysis, 1964, The Changeling, 1964, Tartuffe, 1964, Peterpat, 1964, Hughie, 1964, The Diamond Orchid, 1965, Drat the Cat, 1965, Mrs. Dally, 1965, UTBU, 1966, Dinner at Eight, 1966, We Have Always Lived in the Castle, 1966, Yerma, 1966, The Goodbye People, 1968, The Miser, 1969, Two By Two, 1970, The Gingerbread Lady, 1970, Scarlett (Tokyo), 1970; designer N.Y.C. Opera prodns. St. Joan, 1959, The Cradle Will Rock, 1960; tech. supr. Met. Opera prodn. Wozzeck, 1959, Susannah, 1965, La Boheme, 1966, N.Y.C. Ballet prodn. Divertimento No. 15, 1966; co-designer Mummers Theatre, Oklahoma City; designer Shakespeare Festival prodns. Hamlet, Stratford, Conn., 1958, A Mid-Summer Night's Dream, 1958, Romeo and Juliet, 1959, A Winter's Tale, 1958; designer N.Y.C. Ballet prodns. Pastorale, 1958, The Masquers, 1957, Stars and Stripes, 1959, Native Dancers, 1959, episodes, 1959, Panamerica, 1960, Liebeslieder Waltzer, 1960, Electronics, 1961, Midsummer Night's Dream, 1962, Bugaku, 1963, The Chase, 1963, Irish Fantasy, 1964; staff designer Vivian Beaumont Theatre, Lincoln Center; also The Miser at Lincoln Center, 1968, A Cry of Players, 1969; dir., bd. dirs. stage designer, mng. dir. Nat. Theatre of Deaf; tchr. stage designing N.Y. U., 1961-62, Boston U., 1963; asst. prof. Columbia. Vice pres., trustee Eugene O'Neill Meml. Theatre Found., Waterford, Conn.; tech. adviser Kabuki tour U.S., Japan, 1960; vis. com. on performing arts Harvard bd. overseers. Fulbright grantee to Old Vic, London, Eng., 1952-53; Ford Found. grantee to design an ideal theatre, 1959-61; recipient Obie awards for The Quare Fellow, 1958, The Balcony, 1960; Critic's poll best designer award for No Strings, 1962; ann. award New Eng. Theater Conf., 1967. Mem. Phi Beta Kappa. Club: White's Point Yacht. Editorial bd. U.S. Inst. Theatre Tech. Holder passage record for small boat sailing from Africa to N.Y., 1963. Address: 118 E 64th St New York City NY 10021

HAYS, DONALD C., lawyer; b. N.Y.C., Apr. 30, 1911; s. Walter E. and Mary (Lansing) H.; B.A., U. Colo., 1932, LL.B., 1935; 1 dau., Viviane J. Admitted to N.Y. bar, 1937, since practiced in N.Y.C.; partner firm Gifford, Woody, Carter & Hays, 1942—. Sec., dir. Am. Talc Co., Inc., Imperial Products Co., Inc., Arthur H. Lee & Jofa Inc., Charles Mathieu, Inc., John J. McMullen Assos., Inc., Resource Processors, Inc.; asst. sec., dir. Met. Talc Co., Inc. Served with AUS, 1943-46. Mem. Assn. Bar City N.Y., Am. Bar Assn., N.Y. County Lawyers Assn., N.Y. C. of C., judge Advvocate Gen. Assn., Phi Delta Phi, Phi Delta Theta (sec. N.Y.C.). Republican. Presbyn. Clubs: Players, New York York Athletic, Downtown Assn., Lawyers (N.Y.C.). Home: 501 E 79th St New York City NY 10021 Office: 1 Wall St New York City NY 10005

HAYS, DONALD OSBORNE, govt. ofcl.; b. New Braintree, Mass., June 5, 1907; s. Edward Christopher and Grace Theresa (Osborne) H.; grad. Mt. Hermon Prep. Sch., 1925; student Middlebury Coll., 1925-27; B.A. Colo. U., 1929; M.A. Columbia, 1937, grad. student, 1942; grad. study Am. U., 1951; m. Mary Katherine Jackson Oliver, Aug. 3O, 1937. Tchr. English, head dept. English, pub. schs. of Colo., Pa., 1929-38; head English dept. sr. master Woodmere (L.I.) Acad., 1938-42; mgmt. analyst, asst. dir., mgmt. and planning staff Spl. Services, VA, 1946-51; asst. dir. budget and mgmt. div. NPA, 1951-53; asst. dist. commr. for adminstrn. Internal Revenue Service, Balt., 1953, asst. regional commr. for adminstrn., Boston, 1953- 54, Phila., 1954-57; asst. to dir. Bur. Fgn. Commerce, Dept. Commerce, Washington, 1957-61, Bur. Internat. Commerce, 1961-63; dir. overseas personnel div. Office Fgn. Comml. Services, Dept. Commerce, 1963-68, dir. performance evaluation div., 1968-70, dir. performance evaluation Fgn. Comml. Services Staff, 1970—. Dept. of Commerce mem. 13th and 16th Fgn. Service Officer Selection Bd. Dept. of State, 1959, 62, dep. examiner Bd. Fgn. Service Examiners, 1960—. Served from lt. (j.g.) to lt. comdr., USNR, 1942-46; staff Comdr. Fourth Fleet, Recife, Brazil, 1943-44; contact negotiator, electronics div. Bur. Ships, also staff Navy Manpower Survey Bd., 1944- 46. Mem. Cum Laude Soc., S.A.R., Alpha Sigma Phi, Kappa Phi Kappa. Episcopalian (jr. warden). Clubs: Metropolitan (D.C.); Dacor. Home: 4000 Massachusetts Av Washington DC 20016 Office: Dept of Commerce Washington DC 20230

HAYS, HERBERT ANDREWS, banker; b. Howell, Mich., July 11, 1919; s. James Grant and Bessie L. (Andrews) H.; B.A., Mich. State U., 1941; m. Jean C. Widick, June 8, 1941; children—Andrea (Mrs. R. Bruce Laidlaw), John J., Janice. With Am. Bank & Trust Co., Lansing, Mich., 1946—, personnel officer, 1949-51, v.p., comml. loan officer, 1951-61, pres., 1966—, also dir.; dir. Capital Advt., Inc. Bd. dirs. Real Estate Investment Trust Lansing. Served to maj. AUS, 1941-45. Decorated Silver Star, Bronze Star, Purple Heart with 2 oak leaf clusters. Mem. Mich. Bankers Assn. (pres. 1969-70). Home: 6314 Skyline Dr East Lansing MI 48823 Office: 101 S Washington Av Lansing MI 48933

HAYS, JACK D.H., justice; b. Lund, Nev., Feb. 17, 1917; s. Charles Harold and Thelma (Savage) H.; grad. So. Meth. U., 1941; children (by previous marriage)—Eugene Harrington, Rory Cochrane, Bruce Harvey, Victoria Wakeling; m. 2d, Dorothy M. Taylor, Sept. 4, 1971. Admitted to Ariz. bar, 1946, since practiced in Phoenix; asst. city atty., Phoenix, 1949-52; U.S. atty. dist. Ariz., 1953-60; superior ct. judge Maricopa County, 1960-69; justice Ariz. Supreme Ct., 1969—. Mem. 21st Ariz. Legislature, 1952; mem. Young Republican Exec. Com., 1948-50, Rep. State Central Com., 1948-53; vice chmn. Maricopa Rep. Com., 1949-53; Ariz. chmn. Eisenhower for Pres., 1952. Mem. adv. bd. Roosevelt council Boy Scouts Am. Bd. dirs. Maricopa Legal Aid Soc.; pres. bd. Phoenix Jr. Coll. Found. Served as maj. F.A., AUS, 1941-46. Mem. Am. Judicature Soc., Fed., Am., Inter-Am. bar assns., Ariz. Judges Assn. (pres. 1965-66), Ariz. Acad., Lambda Chi Alpha, Phi Alpha Delta. Episcopalian. Rotarian. Home: 727 W Palo Verde Dr Phoenix AZ 85013 Office: 1700 W Washington Phoenix AZ 85007

HAYS, PAUL R., judge; b. Des Moines, Apr. 2, 1903; s. Everett Hollingsworth and Fae Susan (Hatch) H.; A.B., Columbia, 1925, M.A., 1927, LL.B., 1933; m. Eleanor W. Hays, Feb. 1, 1924 (div. Dec. 1943); 1 son, Rhys Williams; m. 2d, Elinor Rice, November 19, 1949. Instr. Greek and Latin, Columbia, 1926-32; associated with law firm, Cravath, de Gersdorff, Swaine & Wood, N.Y.C., 1933-34, 1935-36; counsel Nat. Recovery adminstrn., Resettlement Adminstrn., Washington. 1934-35; asst. prof. law, Columbia, 1936-38, asso. prof. law, 1938-43, prof. law, 1943-57, 61-71, Nash prof. law, 1957-61; U.S. Circuit judge, second circuit, 1961—. Mem. N.Y. State Bd, Mediation, 1940-44, U.S. Bd. Legal Examiners, 1941-44; legal cons. N.Y. State Banking Dept., 1936-37, N.Y. State Law Revision Com., 1937, 45, U.S. Dept. Justice, 1944, 45, labor arbitrator and impartial chmn. many industries, 1940-61; mem. N.Y.C. Bd. Health, 1954-60. Chmn. gov.'s com. on welfare funds, 1957-60. Chmn. Liberal Party, 1960-61; presidential elector, 1960. Member American (secretary of the section on labor relations law 1959-60), N.Y. State bar assns., Assn. of Bar of City of N.Y., N.Y. County Lawyers assn., Phi Beta Kappa. Club: Century. Author: The Judicial Function in Federal Administrative Agencies (with Jos. P. Chamberlain and Noel T. Dowling), 1942, 2d edit., 1970; Cases and Materials on Civil Procedure, 1947; Cases on Labor Law (with Milton Handler), 1950, rev. edit., 1963; Labor Arbitration: A Dissenting View, 1966; also articles in periodicals. Home: 276 Riverside Dr New York City NY 10025

HAYS, ROBERT L., corp. exec.; b. Cleve., June 28, 1903; s. Louis Henry and Jessie (Feiss) H.; A.B. Cornell, Ithaca, N.Y., 1924; m. Lois Mendelson, Feb. 1, 1938; children—Michael Louis, Mary. Pres., treas. Kaynee Co., Cleve., 1937-54; with McDonald & Co., Cleve., 1955—, partner, 1958—; dir. Imperial Paper Co., Cleve., Myers Industries, Akron, J. M. Smucker Co., Orrville, O. Clubs: Cornell (N.Y.C., Cleve.); Oakwood (Cleve.). Home: 3139 Courtland Blvd Cleveland OH 44122 Office: Central Nat Bank Bldg Cleveland OH 44115

HAYS, SAMUEL PFRIMMER, educator; b. Corydon, Ind., Apr. 5, 1921; s. Clay Blaine and Clara Ridley (Pfrimmer) H.; B.A., Swarthmore Coll., 1948; M.A., Harvard, 1949, Ph.D., 1953; m. Barbara Darrow, June 11, 1948; children—Peter Darrow, Mary Elizabeth, Michael Pfrimmer, Rebecca deSchweinitz. Instr. history U. Ill., 1952-53; asst. prof., then asso. prof. history U. Ia., 1953-60; prof. history, chmn. dept. U. Pitts., 1960—. Mem. exec. com. Inter- Univ. Com. Superior Student, 1957-60. Bd. dirs. Harry S. Truman Library Inst., 1958-70., Social Sci. Research Council, 1967—. Mem. Am. Hist. Assn., Orgn. Am. Historians, Am. Assn. U. Profs. Mem. Soc. of Friends. Author: The Response to Industrialism, 1957; Conservation and the Gospel of Efficiency, 1959. Home: 1421 Wightman St Pittsburgh PA 15217

HAYS, STEELE, judge; b. Little Rock, Mar. 25, 1925; s. L. Brooks and Marion (Prather) H.; B.A., U. Ark., 1948; J.D., George Washington U., 1951; m. Sarah Brown, Nov. 1, 1952; children—Andrew Steel, Melissa Louise, Sarah Anne. Admitted to Ark. bar, 1951; adminstrv. asst. to Congressman Brooks Hays, 1951-53; practice in Little Rock 1953-70; mem. firm Spitzberg, Mitchell & Hays, 1954-70; circuit judge 6th Jud. Circuit Ark., Little Rock, 1970—. Mem. Bd. Law Examiners Ark. Supreme Ct., 1968-70; mem. Ark. com. U.S. Civil Rights Commn. Del., Presbyn. Ch. Consultation on Ch. Union, 1968-70. Trustee Presbyn. Found. Mem. Am., Ark. (past sec.-treas.) bar assns., Am. Judicature Soc., Am. Trial Lawyers Assn., Sigma Chi, Delta Theta Phi. Home: 5424 S Wood Rd Little Rock AR 72205 Office: Pulaski County Court House Little Rock AR 72201

HAYS, THOMAS ALVIN, retail co. exec.; b. Cleve., Dec. 2, 1932; s. Oren Everett and Gertrude (Whiteman) H.; A.B. in Econs., Wabash Coll., 1955; m. Martha L. Pearson, Aug. 21, 1954; children—Jonathan, Elizabeth, James, Elaine. Supr., Touche, Ross, Bailey & Smart, C.P.A.'s, Detroit, 1957-63, mgr., N.Y.C., 1963-65; with Diners Club, Inc., 1965-68, exec. v.p., 1967-68, vice chmn. bd. dirs., 1967-68; v.p. finance, dir. stores Venture Stores Inc., St. Ann, Mo., 1969—. Served to 1st lt. USMCR, 1955-57. C.P.A., Mich. Mem. Am. Assn. C.P.A.'s, Am. Inst. C.P.A.'s, Beta Theta Pi (treas.). Home: 148 Wyckcliffe Pl St Louis MO 63141 Office: 615 Northwest Plaza St Ann MO 63074

HAYS, WAYNE LEVERE, congressman; b. Bannock, O., May 13, 1911; s. Walter Lee and Bertha Mae (Taylor) H.; B.S., Ohio State U., 1933; postgrad. Duke U., 1935; LL.D., Ohio U., 1966, Coll. Steubenville, 1968; m. Martha Judkins, June 3, 1937; 1 dau., Martha Brigitte. Mayor, Flushing, O., 1939-45; state senator from 20th-22d Ohio Dist., 1941-42; commr. Belmont County, 1945-49; mem. 81st-92d Congresses, 18th Dist. Ohio; chmn. bd. dirs. Citizens Nat. Bank, Flushing, O. Owner Red Gate Farms, Belmont, O.; breeder Angus cattle and Tenn. walking horses. Pres. NATO Parliamentary Conf. in Paris, 1956; pres. N. Atlantic Assembly, 1969-70, permanent rep. U.S. to standing com. Recipient Caritas medal, 1969. Democrat. Presbyn. Club: Rotary. Home: Flushing OH 43977 Office: Rayburn House Office Bldg Washington DC 20515

HAYT, WILLIAM HART, Jr., ednl. adminstr.; b. Wilmette, Ill., July 1, 1920; s. William Hart and Gertrude (Seelbach) H.; B.S. in Elec. Engring., Purdue U., 1942, M.S., 1948; Ph.D., U. Ill., 1954; m. Mary Lewis Phillips, July 18, 1946; children—Margaret Ann, Thomas William, David Walter. Field service engr. Sperry Gyroscope Co., Great Neck, N.Y., 1942-46; mem. faculty Purdue U., Lafayette, Ind., 1946—, prof. elec. engring., 1958—, head Sch. Elec. Engring., 1962-65, asst. (for TV) to v.p. acad. affairs, 1965—, rep. Interuniv. Communications Council, 1966—; chmn. State Univ. Telecommunications Coordinating Council, 1967—. Dir. Duncan Electric Co., Lafayette, 1962—; mem. tech. adv. com. Wabash Magnetics Co., West Lafayette, 1963-64; cons. to govt. and industry, 1957—. Mem. Harrison Trails exec. council Boy Scouts Am., 1964—. Fellow I.E.E.E. (bd. dirs. Central Ind. sect. 1964-66), Am. Soc. Engring. Edn., Nat. Assn. Ednl. Broadcasters, Sigma Xi, Beta Theta Pi. Rotarian. Author: Engineering Electromagnetics, 1958, 2d edit., 1967; (with J.E. Kemmerly) Engineering Circuit Analysis, 1962, 2d edit., 1971; (with G.E. Hughes) Introduction to Electrical Engineering, 1968. Home: 705 Sugar Hill Dr West Lafayette IN 47906 Office: Elec Engring Sch Purdue U Lafayette IN 47907

HAYTER, EARL WILEY, historian; b. Ridgeway, O., Feb. 25, 1901; s. Amner Z. and Luella E. (Garner) H.; student Grand Island (Neb.) Coll., 1922-26; A.B., U. Neb., 1927; M.A., U. N.D., 1931; Ph.D., Northwestern U., 1934; m. Beulah Overman, June 3, 1927; children—Donna Jean (Mrs. Thomas Sheeley), Mary Overman (Mrs. Edmund Harmon). Telegraph operator C.B. & O Ry., Crow Agy., Mont., 1919-22; instr. pub. schs., N. D., 1927-30; chmn. history dept. McKendree Coll., 1934-36; summer faculty Tex. Sch. Mines and Metallurgy, El Paso, 1935; staff social sci. dept. No. Ill. U., 1936-59, prof. history, 1959—, co-dir. European Seminar to Oxford, summers 1959, 62, acting chmn. history dept., 1963-64. DeKalb County chmn. independents for reelection Sen. Paul Douglas, 1954; DeKalb County co-dir. inds. for election Adlai Stevenson, 1956. Social Sci. Research Council grantee, 1940, 46. Mem. Agrl. Hist. Soc. (exec. com. 1960), Am. Philos. Soc. (grantee 1962), Brit. Agrl. History Soc., Am. Hist. Assn., Orgn. Am. Historians, Am. Fedn. Tchrs., Am. Econ. Hist. Assn., Am. Assn. U. Profs., Am. Civil Liberties Union, Council Basic Edn., Workers Def. League, Sigma Xi, Pi Kappa Delta, Alpha Chi Sigma, Phi Alpha Theta. Author: The Troubled Farmer, 1968. Research in agrl. history. Home: 560 Normal Rd DeKalb IL 60115

HAYTHORNE, ROBERT E., lawyer; b. Moose Jaw, Sask., Can., Oct. 24, 1915; s. Percy B. and Catherine (Eckles) H.; came to U.S., 1915, naturalized, 1948; A.B., U. Chgo., 1936, J.D., 1938; m. Alice Hudelson, Nov. 8, 1947; children—Robert E., Catherine Elizabeth. Admitted to Ill. bar, 1938, N.Y. bar, 1940; practice in Chgo., 1938; mem. legal staff SEC, Washington, 1938-40; practice in N.Y.C., 1940-41; grad. U.S. Army Command and Gen. Staff Sch., 1944; atty., U.S. Chief of Counsel, Nuremburg War Crime Trials, 1945; asst. gen. counsel Fgn. Liquidation Commn., U.S. Dept. of State, 1946; with firm Seyfarth, Shaw & Fairweather Chgo., 1946-53, Milliken, Vollers & Parsons, Chgo., 1955-57; v.p., gen. counsel Am.-Maritetta Co., Chgo., 1957-61; partner Kirkland, Ellis, Hodson, Chaffetz & Masters, Chgo., 1963—. Served to maj. AUS, 1941-46; lt. col. Res. Mem. Am., Ill., Chgo. bar assns., Phi Alpha Delta. Home: 207 S 5th St Geneva IL 60134 Office: Prudential Plaza Chicago, IL

HAYTON, JACOB WILLIAM, lawyer; b. Carterville, Ill., Mar. 17, 1926; s. James Wesley and Zella (West) H.; B.A., U. Chgo., 1946, J.D., 1950; m. Beata Mueller, Mar. 17, 1962; 1 son, James Wesley. Admitted to Ill. bar, 1950, since practiced in Chgo.; partner firm Bell, Boyd, Lloyd, Haddad & Burns, 1965—. Treas., Beacon Neighborhood House, 1952-64, Chgo. Fedn. Settlements, 1959- 62. Mem. Chgo. Am., bar assns., Phi Beta Kappa. Order of Coif. Unitarian. Clubs: University, Legal. Home: 404 Greenwood Av Evanston IL 60201 Office: 135 S LaSalle St Chicago IL 60603

HAYWARD, CHARLES LYNN, educator; b. Paris, Ida., July 16, 1903; s. William Gammon and Ellen (Neibaur) H.; B.S., Brigham Young U., 1927, M.S., 1931; Ph.D., U. Ill., 1942; m. Elizabeth Cook, Aug. 6, 1930; children—Margaret (Mrs. Bruce J. Taylor), Gerald Lynn. With Brigham Young U., 1930—, prof. zoology, 1954- -, chmn. dept., 1958-62. Mem. A.A.A.S., Ecol. Soc. Am., Utah acad. Scis. Arts and Letters, Am. Soc. Mammalogists. Mem. Ch. of Jesus Christ of Latter-day Saints. Author numerous sci. papers, articles. Home: 949 Cedar Av Provo UT

HAYWARD, EDWARD BEARDSLEY, librarian; b. Rutland, Vt., Jan. 21 1916; s. James E. and Rita (Beardsley) H.; B.S., Middlebury Coll., 1938; postgrad. Columbia, 1939; M.A., Bread Loaf Sch. of Eng., 1940; B.L.S., Ill. U., 1947; m. Ruth Kelley, Aug. 15, 1940; children—James Kelley, John Linn, Dana Beardsley. Inst. library sci. U. Wis., 1950; asst. librarian Racine (Wis.) Pub. Library, 1951-53; dir. Hammond (Ind.) Pub. Library, 1953—. Served with CIC, AUS, 1943-46. Mem. Ind. Library Assn., A.L.A., Hammond C. of C., Sigma Phi Epsilon. Kiwanian. Home: 6708 Madison Av Hammond IN 46324 Office: 564 State St Hammond IN 45320

HAYWARD, HENRY SYDNEY, fgn. corr.; b. Cumberland, Md., Aug. 23, 1915; s. Henry S. and Ruth (Perdew) H.; A.B., Harvard, 1939; m. Ferne J. Martin, Feb. 24, 1945 (dec. 1961): children—Holly Susan, Stephen Henry; m. 2d, Elizabeth Warner Howe, July 28, 1962. Mem. staff Christian Sci. Monitor, 1939—, chief Far East corr., Tokyo, Japan, 1951-54, chief London bur., 1954-61, overseas news editor, 1961-70, Far East corr., Hong Kong, 1970—. Served with USNR, 1942-45. Address: 1 Norway St Boston MA 02115

HAYWARD, JAMES PARKER, electric utility exec.; b. Barrow-in-Furness, Eng., May 11, 1908; s. Simeon and Edith Bell (Parker) H.; came to U.S., 1909, naturalized, 1914; diploma elec. engring., Internat. Corr. Schs., 1935; grad. mgmt. course Am. Mgmt. Assn., 1958. With Atlantic City Electric Co. (N.J.), 1925—, v.p. comml., 1958-59, exec. v.p., 1959-61, pres., 1961—, chief exec. officer, 1962—, also dir.; v.p., dir. subsidiary Deepwater Operating Co., 1960—, pres., dir. subsidiary Overland Realty, Inc.; dir. Pa.-Reading Seashore Line, N.J. Mfrs. Ins. Co. Dir. Phila. chpt. Ams. for Competitive Enterprise System, Inc.; trustee Atlantic City Conv. and Publicity Bur.; mem. N.J. Civil Def. Corps; trustee So. N.J. Devel. Council, Atlantic City YMCA, Atlantic Hosp, Hosp. Children's Seashore House, Richard Stockston State Coll.; chmn. Atlantic County Improvement Authority; Mem. N.J. Utilities Assn. (pres., dir. 1960-61), Atlantic City, N.J. (dir.) chambers commerce; Engring. Soc. So. N.J. (asso.). Methodist. Clubs: Rotary (pres. 1965), Seaview Country, Atlantic City Country (Atlantic City). Home: 132 Coolidge Av Absecon NJ 08201 Office: 1600 Pacific Av Atlantic City NJ 08401

HAYWARD, JOHN FRANK, educator; b. Peabody, Mass., May 8, 1918; s. J. Frank and Catherine (Everest) H.; A.B., Harvard, 1940; B.D., Meadville Theol. Sch., 1943, D.D., 1968; Ph.D., U. Chgo., 1949; m. Muriel Fay Sternglanz, Mar. 29, 1943; children—Peter Brian, Steven Bruce, Miriam Ruth, David Michael. Ordained to ministry Unitarian Ch., 1943; minister First Unitarian Ch., Columbus, O., 1948-51; asst. prof. religion and art Federated Theol. Faculty, U. Chgo., 1951-60; prof. theology Meadville Theol. Sch., 1960-68; religious studies dir., prof. philosophy So. Ill. U., 1968—; dir. First Unitarian Ch. Chgo. Center for the Study of Theology and the Scis., Chgo., 1964-68. Served with USNR, 1943-46. Mem. Am. Acad. Religion, Soc. Sci. Study Religion, Unitarian Universalist Ministers Assn., Am. Soc. for Ch. Architecture. Author: Existentialism and Religious Liberalism, 1962. Home: Route 4 Union Hill Carbondale IL 62901

HAYWARD, JOHN HOPKINS, investment banker; b. St. Louis, Apr. 28, 1904; s. Louis J. and Clara (Hopkins) H.; B.A., Yale, 1928; m. Cynthia Polk, Feb. 4, 1931; children—Cynthia (Mrs. Allen), John Hopkins. Trader with Knight, Dysart & Gamble, 1928-32; partner H.H. Knight & Co., 1932-42; with Reinholdt & Gardner, St. Louis, 1946—, partner, 1948—; dir. Ocean Drilling & Exploration Co., K-V Pharm. Co. Bd. dirs. Washington U., St. Louis. Served as maj., USAAF, 1942-46. Mem. St. Louis C. of C. (dir., exec. com.). Home: 3 Edgewood Rd St Louis MO 63124 Office: 506 Olive St St Louis MO 63102

HAYWARD, JOHN LEDORSETT, brewery exec.; b. St. Louis, July 9, 1927; s. John D. and Lucille (Meador) H.; B.S. in Bus. Adminstrn., Washington U., St. Louis, 1950, J.D., 1953; m. Judy Crawford, Sept. 8, 1951; children—Ellyn, Lucy, Suzanne. Admitted to Mo. bar, 1953; adjuster-investigator Transit Casualty Co., St. Louis, 1953-55; asst. pros. atty. St. Louis County, 1955-57; with Anheuser-Busch, Inc., 1957—, asst. sec., 1959-68, asst. treas. 1962-68, treas., 1969—, also sec., 1968—; also provisional police judge, Kirkwood, Mo., 1960-62. Mem. bd. adjustment, Kirkwood, 1965—. Served with USNR, 1945-46. Mem. Am., Mo., St. Louis bar assns., Am. Soc. Corp. Secs., Phi Delta Theta, Phi Delta Phi. Home: 8 Orchard Way Kirkwood, MO 63122 Office: 721 Pestalozzi St St Louis MO 63118

HAYWARD, JOHN TUCKER, aerospace exec.; b. N.Y.C., Nov. 15, 1910; s. Charles Brian and Rosa (Valdetaro) H.; B.S., U.S. Naval Acad., 1930; student U. Pa., U.N.M., U. Cal., Stanford, Cal. Inst. Tech.; D.Sc., U. Portland, 1965; LL.D., Providence Coll., 1968; m. Leila Marion Hyer, Oct. 14, 1932; children—Mary Shelley, Leila Marion, Victoria, Jenny, John T. Commd. ensign USN, 1930, advanced through grades to vice adm., 1959, designated naval aviator, 1931; various assignments ships and naval stas., 1931-40; with RAF, Eng., 1940-41; comdg. officer Bombin 106, Pacific, 1942-44; assigned Manhattan Project, Los Alamos Sci. Lab., exptl. officer rocket ordnance and weaponry, Inyokern, 1944- 47; plans and operations for atomic weapons and warfare Armed Forces Spl. Weapons Base, Sandia, 1947-51; head weapons research, div. mil. applications AEC, 1951-53; with Task Group 95, Yellow Sea, 1953-54; dir. Naval Ordnance Lab., 1954-56; comdg. officer U.S.S. Franklin Roosevelt, 1956-57; spl. asst. to dir. strategic plans div., DCNO, Navy Dept., 1957-59, DCNO, 1959-62; comdr. Carrier div. 2, 1962-63; comdr. anti-submarine warfare force, Honolulu, 1963-66; pres. Naval War Coll., Newport, R.I., 1966-68; v.p. Gen. Dynamics Corp., Pierre La Clede, Mo., 1968—. Decorated Silver Star, D.F.C. with three oak leaf clusters, Air medal (5), Bronze Star medal, Legion of Merit, D.S.M. with oak leaf cluster, Congressional medal for life saving (U.S.), Order Brit. Empire; Order So. Cross (Brazil); Order Taegu (Korea); Legion of Honor (France); knight comdr. Order Merit (Italy). Fellow Am. Inst. Aeros. and Astronautics; mem. Am. Phys. Soc., Am. Rocket Soc. (sr.), Am. Inst. Physics, A.A.A.S., Newcomen Soc. Home: 9725 Conway Dr Ladue MO Office: Gen Dynamics Corp Pierre La Clede St Louis MO 63105

HAYWARD, SUSAN, motion picture actress; b. Bklyn., June 30, 1919; d. Walter and Ellen (Pearson) Marrener; student pub. schs., Bklyn; m. Jesse Thomas Barker, 1944 (div.); children—Timothy and Gregory (twins); m. 2d Floyd Eaton Chalkley, 1957. Photographer's model, 1937-38; under contract Warner Bros., 1939, Paramount Pictures, 1939-45, Walter Wangner, 1945-49, 20th Century Fox 1949—; first motion picture appearance Beau Geste, 1939, other pictures include Hit Parade of 1943, Young and Willing, Fighting Seabees, 1944, And Now Tomorrow, Canyon Passage, Deadline at Dawn, 1946, The Lost Moment, 1946, Smash-Up, Tap Roots, Tulsa, 1949, House of Strangers, My Foolish Heart, David and Bathsheba, With a Song in My Heart, 1952, Snows of Kilimanjaro, 1952; I'll Cry Tomorrow, 1956; Conqueror, 1956; Top Secret Affair, 1957, I Want to Live, 1958; Thunder in the Sun, Women Obsessed, 1959; Marriage-Go-Around, 1961, Demetrius and the Gladiators, Garden of Evil, Untamed, Soldier of Fortune, The Conquered, Ada, Back Street, I Thank a Fool, Honey Pot. Named as one of two most popular motion picture stars, Foreign Press Assn. of Hollywood, 1952; Cannes Film Festival award, 1956; New York Film Critics award, best actress of year, 1958; Motion Picture Acad. award for best actress of 1959 for picture I Want to Live.

HAYWOOD, ALILEA, food processing co. exec.; b. Fort Worth, Tex., Oct. 12, 1921; d. William Franklin and Ophelia (Ferrell) H.; B.A., U. Mich., 1943. Adminstrv. asst., civilian in charge Signal Office, Stockton (Cal.) Ordnance Depot, 1943-47; sec. to v.p., treas. Tillie Lewis Foods, Inc., Stockton, 1947-59, sec. to pres., adminstrv. supr., 1961—, sec., 1965—. Mem. Citizens Com. to Study Area-Wide Jr. Coll., 1961-62, World Affairs Council, 1971—, League Women Voters, 1971—, Friends Pub. Library, 1971—. Mem. Am. Assn. U. Women (past pres.), Assn. Women in Pub. Office (past Cal. chmn.), Bus. Profl. Women's Club (named bus. woman of yr. 1965; chmn. Cal. pub. relations com. 1963-64). Methodist (trustee). Mem. Order Eastern Star. Home: 1665 W Flora St Stockton CA 95203 Office: Tillie Lewis Foods Inc Stockton CA 95201

HAYWOOD, BRUCE, ednl. adminstr.; b. York, Eng., Sept. 30, 1925; s. Joseph Edgar and Eva (Street) H.; student U. Leeds (Eng.), 1947-48; B.A., McGill U., 1950, M.A., 1951; Ph.D., Harvard, 1956; m. Isona Gretchen Shelley, June 21, 1947; children—Anne Margaret, Elizabeth Shelley. Came to U.S., 1951, naturalized, 1957. Mem. faculty Kenyon Coll., 1954, prof. German lit., 1960-63, dean coll., 1963-67, provost, 1967—. Served with Brit. Army, 1943-47. Mem. Am. Assn. Tchrs. of German. Author: Novalis; The Veil of Imagery, 1959. Home: Box 402 Gambier OH 43022

HAYWOOD, CHARLES, musicologist; b. Grodno, Russia, Dec. 20, 1904; s. Nathan and Dora (Blume) H.; came to U.S., 1916, naturalized, 1922; B.S., City Coll. N.Y., 1926; artist diploma, Inst. Mus. Art, 1930; diploma Juilliard Grad. Sch. Music, 1935; M.A., Columbia, 1940, Ph.D., 1949; m. Frances Dillon, May 24, 1928 (dec.); 1 son, John. Lectr., Juilliard Sch. Music, 1939- 52; prof. music Queens Coll., City U. N.Y., 1939—; vis. prof. Hunter Coll., 1958-59, U. Minn., 1959, Ind. U., 1960, U. Cal. at Los Angeles, 1961; opera singer, concert artist, soloist symphony orchs., also radio and TV appearances, 1930—; lectr. Harvard, Columbia; founder, co-dir. Dici Sch. Performing Arts, L.I., 1930-38. Pres. U.S. nat. com. Internat. Folk Music Council, 1962—; ednl. coordinator, program dir. U.S.O., 1940- 45; Juilliard grad. fellow, 1930-35; Folger Shakespeare fellow, 1951; Henry F. Huntington fellow, 1952-53; Fulbright Research grantee, Austria, 1961-62, 67-68. Mem. Nat. Folk Festival Assn. (mem. exec. bd.), Am. Musicol. Soc., Am. Folklore Soc., Ethnomusicol. Soc. (mem. council), Shakespeare Soc., N.Y. Folklore Soc., Friends of Bodeian Library, Phi Beta Kappa. Author: James A. Bland: His Life and Songs, 1946; Modern Russian Art Songs, 1947; Cervantes and Music, 1948; Masterpieces of Scared Songs, 1958; A Bibliography of North American Folklore and Folksong, rev. and enlarged edit., 2 vols., 1961; Folk Songs of the World, 1966; Negro Minstrelsy and Shakespearean Burlesque, 1966; Latin American Music in the college Curriculum: Problems and Prospects, 1966; Maretzek's Revelations of an Opera Manager, 1968; George Bernard Shaw on Incidental Music in the Shakespearean Theater, 1969; also numerous articles. Editor: Yearbook Internat. Folk Music Council. Home: 145 E 92d St New York City NY 10028

HAYWOOD, CHARLES FOSTER, coll. dean; b. Ludlow, Ky., Apr. 7, 1927; s. Charles Adam and Julia (Strode) H.; A.B., Berea Coll., 1949; A.M., Duke, 1950; Ph.D., U. Cal. at Berkeley, 1955; m. Josephine Richards, June 15, 1948; children—Julia Elizabeth, Mary Josephine, Charles Ransome, John Watson. Econ. analyst Am. Bankers Assn., 1954-55; asst. prof. Tulane U., 1955-57; economist Bank of Am., 1957-58, dir. econ. research, 1963-65; prof. banking U. Miss., 1958-60, provost, 1960-63; dean Coll. Bus. and Econs., U. Ky., Lexington, 1965—; on leave with Am. Bankers Assn., 1969-70; chmn. bd. Carter H. Golembe Assos., Inc., Washington, 1967- 71. Mem. Ky. Econ. Devel. Commn., 1965—; adv. mem. research council Am. Bankers Assn., 1955-57, 59-61, 63-69; chmn. Ky. Council Econ. Advisers, 1971—. Served with U.S. Mcht. Marines, 1945, AUS, 1946-48. Mem. Am., So. econ. assns., Council of So. Mountains. Democrat. Mem. Christian Ch. Author: The Regulation of Deposit Interest Rates, 1968; The Pledging of Bank Assets, 1967; The Expansion of Bank Funds in the 1970's, 1969; Regulation and Monetery Policy, 1971. Home: 3309 Overbrook Dr Lexington KY 40502

HAYWOOD, CLARENCE ROBERT, univ. ofcl.; b. Fowler, Kan., Aug. 27, 1921; s. C.O. and Elsie (Long) H.; A.B., Kan. U., 1947, M.A., 1948; Ph.D., U. N.C., 1956; m. Louise Marie Stephenson, Jan. 2, 1943; children—Sandra (Mrs. Phillip Jarvis), Robert Alan, Ray. Mem. faculty Southwestern Coll., Winfield, Kan., 1948- 66, dean coll., 1956-66; dean Coll. Arts and Scis., Millikin U., 1966- 69; v.p. acad. affairs Washburn U., Topeka, 1969—. Served with USNR, 1942- 45. Mem. So. Hist. Soc., Orgn. Am. Historians, Am. Conf. Acad. Deans. Democrat. Methodist. Contbr. profl. jours. Home: 2001 Oakley Av Topeka KS 66604

HAYWOOD, EGBERT LYNCH, lawyer; b. Durham, N.C., June 4, 1911; s. Charles Lewis and Zoa Lee (Rigsbee) H.; A.B., U. N.C., 1931; LL.B., Harvard, 1934; m. Margaret Davis, June 21, 1938; children—Egbert Lynch, John Davis. Admitted to N.C. bar, 1934, since practiced in Durham; sr. partner firm Haywood, Denny and Miller; asst. city atty., Durham, 1946-56. Dir. Citizens Nat. Bank, 1946-59, N.C. Nat. Bank, 1959—; pres. Arden Properties, Inc., 1956—. Served to lt. comdr. USNR, 1942-45. Mem. Am. (mem. Ho. of Dels. 1953—, gov. 1959-62, adv. bd. jour. 1962-66), N.C., Durham County bar assns., Internat. Assn. Ins. Counsel (exec. com., pres. 1967-68), Am. Judicature Soc. (dir.), N.C. Harvard Law Assn. (pres.), Harvard Law Sch. Assn., Am. Legion (past post comdr.), Durham Jr. C. of C. (past pres.), Jud. Conf. U.S. (com. on evidence), Chi Phi. Baptist (deacon). Clubs: Kiwanis (past pres.), Torch, Cotillion (Durham), Hope Valley Country, ToBac (Durham). Home: 28 Oak Dr Durham NC 27707 Office: 111 Corcoran St Durham NC 27701

HAYWOOD, LEMUEL JULIAN, educator, physician; b. Reidsville, N.C., Apr. 13, 1927; s. Thomas Woodly and Louise Viola (Hayley) H.; B.S., Hampton Inst., 1948; M.D., Howard U., 1952; m. Virginia Elizabeth Paige, Dec. 3, 1953; 1 son, Julian Anthony. Intern St. Mary's Hosp., Rochester, N.Y., 1952-53; resident Los Angeles County Hosp., 1956-58; fellow cardiology White Meml. Hosp., 1959-61; instr. medicine Loma Linda (Cal.) U., 1960-61, asst. prof., 1961—; asst. prof. medicine U. So. Cal., 1963-68, asso. prof., 1968—; dir. coronary care unit Los Angeles County-U. So. Cal. Med. Center; dir. physicians tng. program Regional Med. Programs. Cons. Indsl. Accident Bd. Cal., Health Care Tech. Div., USPHS. Bd. dirs. Sickle Cell Disease Research Found. Served with M.C., USNR, 1954-56. Recipient award of merit Los Angeles County Heart Assn., 1968, 69. Fellow A.C.P., Am. Coll. Cardiology, Am. Heart Assn. (council on clin. cardiology); mem. Am. Fedn. Clin. Research, A.A.A.S., Western Soc. Clin. Research, Assn. Advancement Med. Instrumentation, A.M.A., Nat. Med. Assn. (Charles Drew Med. Soc.), N.Y. Acad. Scis., Hampton Inst. Alumni Assn. (past pres. Los Angeles chpt.), Med. Faculty Assn. U. So. Cal. Sch. Medicine (sec.-treas.), Los Angeles Soc. Internal Medicine (sec.-treas.). Contbr. articles profl. jours. Home: 3551 Lowry Rd Los Angeles CA 90027 Office: 1200 N State St Los Angeles CA 90033

HAYWOOD, LORNA, soprano; b. England; grad. Royal Coll. Music, London, 1961; grad. Julliard Sch. Music, 1965. Operatic appearances include Covent Garden, London, Eng., Cleve. Orch., Washington Opera Soc., Chgo. Lyric Opera, Mpls. Symphony Orch., Denver Symphony Orch., Ft. Worth Opera Company, Chgo. Symphony Orch., Sadlers Wells Opera, London, Eng., Tanglewood Music Festival, Dallas Civic Opera, San Diego Opera, Atlanta Symphony, Toronto Symphony, Cin. Symphony; soloist Robert Shaw Chorale. Address: 740 West End Av New York City NY

HAYWOOD, OLIVER GARFIELD, electronics mfg. co. exec.; b. Highland Mills, N.Y., Nov. 29, 1911; s. Oliver Garfield and A. Olive (Wiggins) H.; B.S., U.S. Mil. Acad., 1936; M.S., Harvard, 1940; D.Sc., Mass. Inst. Tech., 1940; grad. Air War Coll., 1950; m. Helen Elizabeth Salisbury, June 12, 1936; children—Barbara Ann (Mrs. Robert A. List), Betty Jean (Mrs. Lynn B. Moon), Richard William, Robert Carroll. Commd. 2d lt., C.E., U.S. Army, 1936, advanced through grades to col., 1947; served to col. USAF, 1947-53, resigned, 1953; mgr. missile systems lab. Sylvania Electrics Products, Inc., Whitestone, N.Y., 1953-54, lab. mgr. electronic systems div., Waltham, Mass., 1955-56; v.p. Emerson Electric Mfg. Co., St. Louis, 1957-58; v.p. Huyck Corp., Stamford, Conn., 1958-65, pres., chief exec. officer, 1966—, also dir.; dir. Dynalectron Corp., 1969—; trustee MITRE Corp., 1960-70. Vice chmn. sci. adv. group Office Aerospace Research, 1963-67. Decorated Legion of Merit with oak leaf cluster. Bd. dirs. Univ. Me. Pulp and Paper Found., 1971—. Mem. T.A.P.P.I., Paper Industry Mgmt. Assn. Hudson Inst., N.Y. Acad. Scis., Council on Fgn. Relations. Clubs: Woodway Country (Darien, Conn.); Field (New Canaan); Army-Navy Country (Arlington, Va.); Board Room (N.Y.C.). Home: 13 Woodridge Circle New Canaan CT 06840 Office: 733 Summer St Stamford CT 06902

HAYWOOD, RICHARD MANSFIELD, educator; b. Lynn, Mass., June 12, 1905; s. Charles Edward and Annie (Moulton) H.; A.B., Dartmouth, 1926; Ph.D., Johns Hopkins, 1932; m. Margaret Rider Mowbray, Sept. 6, 1930; children-Richard Mowbray, Anne Mowbray, Mary Coale (Mrs. Donald L. Metz). Tchr., Johns Hopkins, 1932- 44, Hotchkiss Sch., 1944-50; mem. faucity N.Y.U., 1950—, prof. Classics, 1960—. Guggenheim fellow, 1939-40; Fulbright research fellow Italy, 1960-61. Mem. Phi Beta Kappa. Author: Studies on Scipio Africanus, 1933; Roman Africa, 1938; The Myth of Rome's Fall, 1958; Ancient Greece and the Near East, 1964; Ancient Rome, 1967; The Ancient World, 1971. Home: 16 E 8th St New York NY 10003

HAYWOOD, THEODORE JOSEPH, physician, educator; b. Monroe, N.C., Feb. 33, 1929; s. Jesse Beman and Mary (McDonald) H.; B.S., The Citadel, 1948; M.D., Vanderbilt U., 1952; m. Nancy Hume Ferguson, Dec. 21, 1959; children—Elizabeth Linscott, Keene McDonald. Pvt. practice allergy, Houston, 1958—; chief pediatric allergy clinic Tex. Children's Hosp., 1958—; mem. faculty Baylor U. Coll. Medicine, 1958—, clin. asst. prof. microbiology and pediatrics, 1967—; mem. faculty U. Tex. Grad. Sch. Biomed. Scis., 1960—, asso. prof. allergy, 1969—. Served with M.C., AUS, 1955-57. Fellow Am. Coll. Allergists, Am. Acad. Allergy, Am. Acad. Pediatrics, Sigma Xi. Republican. Episcopalian. Club: River Oaks Country (Houston). Home: 3257 Reba Dr Houston, TX 77019. Office: 6655 Travis St Houston TX 77025

HAYWORTH, DON, former congressman, educator; b. Toledo, Ia., Jan. 13, 1898; s. Charles LeRoy and Mae Estelle (Wilkinson) H.; A.B., Grinnell Coll., 1918; M.A., U. Chgo., 1921; Ph.D., U. Wis., 1928; m. Frances Margaret Knight, June 17, 1934; children—Donna Lou, Francene Mae, Barbara. High sch. tchr., Oskaloosa, Ia., 1921-23; head speech dept. Penn Coll., 1923-27; head speech dept. U. Akron, 1928-37; head speech dept. Mich. State Coll., 1937-42, prof. speech, 1944-54, 57- 63; consultant to U.S. Dept. Agr., 1963-64; mem. 84th Congress, 6th Dist. Mich. In charge of speakers' activities Office Civilian Def., Washington, 1942- 43; promotion of speakers' activities for fund raising campaign A.R.C, Washington, 1944; in charge of relations with states on fuel conservation Dept. of Interior, 1944-46; chmn. Mich. Victory Speakers Bureau, 1941-42; cons. Social Security Adminstrn., 1965-67; mem. nat. com. Am. Friends of Vietnam. Mem. Speech Assn. Am., Am. Assn. U. Profs., N.A.A.C.P., Pi Kappa Delta. Democrat. Kiwanian. Club: Torch. Author: Oral Argument (with Robert Capel), 1933; Public Speaking, 1935; Introduction to Public Speaking, 1940; A Research into the Teaching of Public Speaking (mimeographed), 1941. Contbr. to profl. jours. and lit. mags. Home: 1311 Delaware Av SW Washington DC 20024

HAYWORTH, RITA, (Margarita Carmen Cansino), actress; b. N.Y.C., Oct. 17, 1918; d. Eduardo and Volga (Haworth) Cansino; ed. high sch., Los Angeles; m. Edward C. Judson, 1936 (div. 1942); m. 2d. Orson Welles, Sept. 7, 1943 (div. 1942); 1 dau., Rebecca; m. 3d, Ali Shah Khan, 1949 (div. 1953); 1 dau., Yasmin; m. 4th, Dick Haymes (div. 1955); m. 5th, James Hill, Feb. 2, 1958. Stage debut in sch. play at age 11; profl. debut in stage prologue to motion picture Back Street, Carthay Circle Theatre, Los Angeles; with father as partner, appeared as dancer, night clubs and resorts; motion picture actress, 1935—, films include Loves of Carmen, Miss Sadie Thompson, Happy Thieves, Cover Girl, 1944, Tonight and Every Night, 1945, Gilda,

1946, Down to Earth, 1947. Lady from Shanghai, 1948, Affair in Trinidad, 1952, Salome, 1953, Fire Down Below, 1957, Pal Joey, 1957. Separate Tables, 1958, They Came to Condura, 1959; Story on Page One, 1960; Money Trap, The Poppy is also a Flower, 1966. Address: 202 N Canon Dr Beverly Hills CA 90210

HAZAM, LOUIS JOSEPH, TV producer; b. Norwich, Conn., Jan. 3, 1911; s. George John and Afifi (Habeeb) H.; B.A. in Journalism, Columbia, 1933; m. Ruby Gene Hymer, Oct. 30, 1939; children—Nancy Lynn, Chad Thomas. Script writer U.S. Dept. Interior, 1938-45; freelance writer for radio and TV, 1945-59; TV producer, writer NBC News, Washington, 1959—. Mem. adv. bd. Council Internat. Nontheatrical Events, Washington. Recipient Christopher award, 1960, George Foster Peabody award, 1961, Bronze award Venice Film Festival, 1962, 1st place documentary, 1963, Golden Gate award San Francisco Internat. Film Festival, 1963, 64, 66. Mem. Acad. TV Arts and Scis., Radio and TV Corrs. Assn., Writers Guild. Club: Nat. Press (Washington). Producer, writer: Way of the Cross, 1960; Vincent Van Gogh, 1961; US #1, 1962; River Nile, 1963; Shakespeare: Soul of an Age, 1963; Greece: The Golden Age, 1964; Michelangelo, The Last Giant (Part I), 1965, (Part II), 1966; The National Gallery of Art, 1967; The Art Game, 1968; Sahara, La Caravane Du Sel, 1969. Office: 4001 Nebraska Av NW Washington DC 20016

HAZARD, ELLISON LOCKWOOD, corp. exec.; b. Redlands, Cal., Aug. 6, 1911; s. George Irving and Lucy May (Lockwood) H.; student U. Cal., 1928-32, Advanced Mgmt. Program Harvard Bus. Sch., 1953; m. Helen Hammill, Nov. 24, 1935; children—Lawrence, James. With Continental Can Co., 1934—, Plant mgr., Los Angeles, 1948-51, mgr. mfg. Pacific metal div., 1951-54, gen. mgr. Northeastern dist., 1954-56, dir. staff metal operations group, 1956-58, v.p. central metal div., Chgo., 1958-62; dir. and exec. v.p. plastics and closures, 1962-63, pres., 1963-71, chmn. bd., chief exec. officer 1968-71, now chmn. exec. com.; dir. Kennecott Copper Corp., Goodyear Tire & Rubber Co. Vice chmn bd. Nat. Center for Solid Waste Disposal, Washington; mem. Bus. Council, Washington; vice chmn. Nat. Indsl. Pollution Control Council Commerce Dept., Washington; trustee Conf. Bd.; trustee Com. Econ. Devel. Recipient award for outstanding leadership supervisory devel. Los Angeles Mchts. and Mfrs. Assn., 1951. Registered profl. mech. engr., Cal. Mem. Harvard Bus. Sch. Assn. (exec. com.). Republican. Episcopalian. Mason (Shriner). Clubs: Wee Burn Country (Darien, Conn.); Chicago; Pinnacle, Sky, Economic, Links, Blind Brook (N.Y.C.); Commonwealth of Cal. Patentee in field. Home: 31 Farm Bd Darien CT 06820 Office: 633 3d Av New York City NY 10017

HAZARD, GEOFFREY CORNELL, Jr., educator; b. Cleve., Sept. 18, 1929; s. Geoffrey Cornell and Virginia (Perry) H.; B.A., Swarthmore Coll., 1953; LL.B., Columbia, 1954; m. Barbara Wade Jackson, Apr. 30, 1951; children—James G., Katherine W., Robin P. Admitted to Ore. bar, 1954, Cal. bar, 1960; asso. firm Hart, Spencer, McCulloch, Rockwood & Davies, Portland, Ore., 1954-57; exec. sec. Ore. Legislative Interim Com. Jud. Adminstrn. 1957-58; asso. prof. law, then prof. U. Cal. at Berkeley, 1958-64; prof. law U. Chgo., 1964-71, Yale U., 1971—. Exec. dir. Am. Bar Found., Chgo., 1964-70; reporter Am. Bar Assn. Commn. on Standards of Jud. Adminstrn., 1971—; mem. Adminstrv. Conf., U.S., 1971—. Served with USAF, 1948-49. Mem. Am., Ore., Cal. bar assns., Assn. Bar City N.Y., Am. Polit. Sci. Assn., Am. Assn. U. Profs., Phi Beta Kappa Episcopalian. Author: (with David W. Louisell) Pleading and Procedure, 1962; Research in Civil Procedure, 1963; also articles. Editor Law in a Changing America, 1968. Home: 112 Huntington St New Haven CT 06511

HAZARD, JOHN BEACH, physician; b. White Horse, Pa., Jan. 7, 1905; s. Frank Birdsall and Blanche Darrah (Stong) H.; B.S., U. Fla., 1924, M.S., 1925; M.D., Harvard, 1930; m. Etta Mae Holly, Sept. 3, 1931. Intern, resident, asst. in pathology Mallory Inst. Pathology, Boston City Hosp., 1930-34; practice medicine, specializing in pathology, Boston, 1934-46, Cleve., 1946—; dir. pathology Faulkner Hosp., 1935-46; cons. pathology Robert B. Brigham Hosp., 1937-46; head dept. tissue pathology Cleve. Clinic Found., 1946-70, chmn. div. pathology, 1957-70, emeritus cons., 1970—, acting dir. div. research, 1966- 67, vice chmn., 1967-70 instr. pathology Sch. Medicine, Boston U., 1931-32; instr., asst. prof. pathology Med. Sch. Tufts Coll., 1932-46; asso. pathology to clin. prof. pathology Sch. Medicine Case Western Res. U., 1952-70, emeritus clin. prof., 1970—; mem. pathology study sect. USPHS, 1962- 65. Bd. dirs. Cleve. chpt. A.R.C., Blue Cross N.E. Ohio. Served from maj. to col., M.C., AUS, 1942-46. Mem. A.M.A. (sec. pathology), Am. Assn. Pathologists and Bacteriologists, Am. Soc. Clin. Pathologists (past dir.), Am. Thyroid Assn. (past v.p.), Coll. Am. Pathologists, Internat. Acad. Pathology (past pres.), N.Y. Acad. Sci., A.A.A.S., Am. Soc. Cytology, Royal Soc. Medicine. Author, editor chpt. The Thyroid, 1964. Home: 1 Ocean Lane Dr Key Biscayne FL 33149 Office: 2020 E 93d St Cleveland OH 44106

HAZARD, JOHN NEWBOLD, prof. pub. law; b. Syracuse, N.Y., Jan. 5, 1909; s. John Gibson and Ada Bosarte (DeKalb) H.; ed. The Hill Sch., 1926; A.B., Yale, 1930; LL.B., Harvard, 1934; certificate Moscow Juridical Inst., 1937; J.S.D. U. Chgo., 1939; LL.D., U. Freiburg, 1969, Lehigh U., 1970; m. Susan Lawrence, March 8, 1941; children—John Gibson, William Lawrence, Nancy, Barbara Peace. Fellow Inst. of Current World Affairs (student of Soviet law), 1934-39; asso. with law firm, Baldwin, Todd & Young, N.Y.C., 1939-41; dep. dir., U.S.S.R. br., Fgn. Econ. Adminstrn. (and predecessor agys.), 1941-45; adviser on state trading, Dept. of State, 1945-46; prof. pub. law, Columbia, since 1946; spl. asst. to V.P. Henry Wallace on mission to U.S.S.R. and China, 1944; adviser on Soviet law to U.S. chief of counsel for prosecution of Axis criminality, 1945; lectr. on Soviet law, U. Chgo., 1938-39, on Soviet polit. instns., Columbia, 1940-41, on internat. politics, Fgn. Service Ednl. Found., 1944-46, on Soviet govt. and law, U. Minn., summer 1947, Claremont Coll., summer, 1948, Stanford, summer, 1951, 53, vis. prof. of law Yale, spring 1949, 50, 52, 54, 56; vis. Fulbright prof. U. Cambridge, London Sch. Econs., 1952-53; vis. prof. U. Tokyo, summer 1956, Grad. Sch. Internat. Studies, Geneva, 1959-60; prof. Luxembourg Comparative Law Faculty, summers 1958-60; prof. Strasbourg Comparative Law Faculty, summers 1962-71; vis. prof. U. Teheran, fall 1966; sr. specialist East-West Center Hawaii, spring 1967; fellow Center for Advanced Study in the Behavioral Scis., 1961-62. Dir. and sec. Am. Assn. for the Advancement of Slavic Studies, 1948-60, treas., 1961-65. Recipient Pres.'s Certificate of Merit, 1947. Mem. U.S. Supreme Ct. and N.Y. Bars, Am. (vice chmn. internat. and comparative law 1951-58), N.Y. state bar assns., Assn. Bar City of N.Y. (chmn. com. on fgn. law, 1947-50), Am. Polit. Sci. Assn., Am. Soc. Internat. Law (exec. council, 1946-49, 51- 54), Am. br. of Internat. Law Assn. (chmn. exec. com. 1958- 59), Internat. Acad. Comparative Law, Internat. Assn. Legal Sci. (pres. 1968-70), Phi Alpha Delta, Alpha Delta Phi. Democrat. Episcopalian. Clubs: Authors (London); Century (N.Y.); University (Washington), Wolf's Head. Author: Soviet Housing Law, 1939; (with M.L. Weisberg) Cases and Readings on Soviet Law, 1950; Law and Social Change in the USSR, 1953; The Soviet System of Government, 1957; Settling Disputes in Soviet Society, 1960; (with I. Shapiro) The Soviet Legal System, 1962; Communists and Their Law, 1969. Editor: Soviet Legal Philosophy, 1951. Bd. of editors Am. Slavic and East European Rev. (mng. editor, 1951-59), Am. Polit. Sci. Rev., 1950, Am. Jour. Internat. Law, 1956—, Am. Jour. Comparative Law, 1952—. Home: 20 E 94th St New York City NY 10028 Office: 435 W 116th St New York City NY 10027

HAZARD, LELAND, lawyer; b. Kansas City, Mo., July 7, 1893; s. Henry E. and Lucinda (Holderbaum) H.; student William Jewell Coll., Liberty, Mo., 1911-12; A.B., U. of Mo., 1916; student, law sch., Harvard, 1919-20 U. Chgo., 1926; LL.D., Carnegie Mellon U., 1970; m. Mary Chorn, Dec. 22, 1923. Admitted to Mo. bar, 1920, Pa. bar, 1940; practiced law Kansas City, Mo., 1920-38; counsel PPG Industries, Inc. (formerly Pitts. Plate Glass Co.), 1938-39, gen. counsel, v.p., dir., 1940-58, dir.- cons, 1959-65, cons., 1965-68; prof. indsl. adminstrn. and law, Carnegie-Mellon U., 1959-61, prof. emeritus, lectr., 1961—; hon. chmn. Met. Pitts. Ednl. TV Sta. (WQED). Served First O.T.C., commd. 2d lt., F.A., U.S. Army; promoted maj., Adj. Gen.'s Dept.; with 89th Div., A.E.F., in France and Germany during World War 1. Dir. Pitts. Symphony Soc. (hon.); trustee Archeol. Inst. Am.; bd. mem. Council Pub. Schs., 1962-67; pres. Community Chest, Pitts., 1949-50; bd. mem. Pitts. Regional Indsl. Devel. Corp., Allegheny County Port Authority; cons. Ford Found. Indian Program, 1963-65; chmn. Gov.'s Com. Transp., 1966-70; bd. dirs. Pitts. Urban Transit Council; trustee O.W. Holmes Assn. Mem. Am. Arbitration Assn. (dir.). Nat. Planning Assn. (trustee, mem. steering com., 1959-67), Am., Pa., Mo., Allegheny County bar assns., Am. Legion, Sigma Nu, Phi Alpha Delta, Omicron Delta Kappa. Clubs: Century Association (N.Y.C.); Duquesne, University (Pitts.), Rolling Rock. Contbr. to Atlantic Monthly, Harvard Bus. Rev.; also to manuals and publs. Home: 5023 Frew Av Pittsburgh PA 15213

HAZARD, ROWLAND KEOUGH, lawyer; b. North Kingstown R.I., Mar. 7, 1913; s. Rowland T. and Margaret (Keough) H.; A.B. magna cum laude, Holy Cross Coll., 1934; J.D. Georgetown U., 1940. Admitted to D.C. bar, 1942, C.Z. bar, 1953, U.S. Ct. Appeals D.C., U.S. Ct. Appeals 5th Circuit, U.S. Ct. Mil. Appeals; clk. 2d Dist. Ct. R.I., 1935-36; practice law C. Z. since 1948; formerly sp. inspections U.S. div., immigration and naturalization service Dept. Justice; asst. U.S. atty. C. Z., 1948-52, U.S. atty., 1952, 70; now asst. to asst. gen. counsel marketing, regulatory laws, research and operations Dept. Agr., Washington. Served with CIC, U.S. Army, 1943-45. Papal Knight Order St. Gregory the Great. Roman Catholic. Home: 1600 S Joyce St Arlington VA 22203 Office: Office Gen Counsel South Bldg Washington DC

HAZEL, JAMES FREDERIC, educator; b. Carrollton, Mo., Oct. 2, 1905; s. James Frederic and Erdeen Wynona (Zartman) H.; A.B., U. Kan., 1928; Ph.D., U. Wis., 1931; m. Margaret V. Paden, Apr. 11, 1929; children—James Frederic III, Karl Erlend. Instr. chemistry U. Wis., 1931-37; asst. prof. U. Pa., Phila., 1937-44, asso. prof., 1944-54, prof. colloid and inorganic chemistry, 1954—, dir. NSF Insts. for High Sch. Tchrs. Sci. and Math., 1959-70. Cons. in field. Mem. Am. Electrochem. Soc. (sec., chmn. sect. 1944-49), Am. Chem. Soc., A.A.A.S., Am. Soc. Engring. Edn., Sigma Xi, Phi Lambda Upsilon, Alpha Chi Sigma. Contbr. articles to profl. jours. Patentee in field. Home: 214 Kathmere Rd Havertown PA 19083 Office: 215 S 34th St Philadelphia PA 19104

HAZEL, LEWIS FREDERICK, banker; b. Waterport, N.Y., Feb. 6, 1921; s. George Robert and Lizzie (Grimes) H.; Certificate, Am. Inst. Banking, 1959; m. Anna Narice Clark, Sept. 5, 1943; 1 son, James Robert. Accountant Socony Mobil Oil Co., Inc., Buffalo, 1946-48; with Marine Midland Bank-Western, Buffalo, 1948—, asst. sec., 1963-68, sec., 1968—. Treas. Children's Found. Erie County, 1963—. Recipient Buffalo Clearing House Assn. scholarship award, 1959. Mem. Am. Inst. Banking, C. of C. Methodist (trustee). Home: 292 Northwood Dr Kenmore NY 14223 Office: 241 Main St Buffalo NY 14203

HAZEL, MICHAEL F., steel co. exec.; b. Bellefonte, Pa., July 24, 1908 s. Michael F. and Susann Elizabeth Hazel; B.S. in Mech. Engring., Pa. State U., 1930; m. Sara K. Bracken, Aug. 19, 1967; children—J. Patrick, Michael V., John S. With Oilwell div. U.S. Steel Corp., 1930—, exec. v.p., 1961, pres., Dallas, 1961—. Served with USNR, 1943- 46. Mem. Am. Petroleum Inst. (dir.), Petroleum Equipment Suppliers Assn. (pres. 1965-66), Mid Continent Oil and Gas Assn., Dallas Petroleum Club (pres. 1962). Clubs: Dallas Country, Texas (Dallas). Home: 3624 Lovers Lane Dallas TX 75225 Office: 2001 N Lamar St Dallas TX 75202

HAZEL, RONALD SPRAGUE, lawyer; b. Spring Valley, Minn., Sept. 14, 1908; s. Roy W. and Theodosia (Sprague) H.; student Hamline U., St. Paul, 1925-27; LL.B., St. Paul Coll. Law, 1933; m. Mina R. Danielson, Apr. 2, 1931; children—Karen Jean (Mrs. Raymond Gerst), Lee Allison (Mrs. Leonard Burt). Admitted to Minn. bar, 1933; law clk. to Judge John B. Sanborn, U.S. Circuit Ct. of Appeals, 1934-37; asso., partner Bundlie, Kelley & Maun, St. Paul, 1937-38, 43-59; asso. atty., asst. gen. counsel The Panama Canal, 1938-43; partner Maun, Hazel, Green, Hayes, Simon & Aretz, St. Paul, 1959—. Chmn. bd. Minn. Heart Assn., 1965-66. Served with inf., AUS, 1945-46. Mem. Am., Minn. bar assns., Am. Judicature Soc. Mason (32). Home: Route 1 Osceola WI 54016 Office: Hamm Bldg St Paul MN 55102

HAZELET, CRAIG POTTER, cons. engr.; b. O'Neill, Neb., Sept. 19, 1892; s. George C. and Harriet Sherman (Potter) H.; B.S., U. Wash., 1915; grad. student Mass. Inst. Tech., 1918: m. Frances Gillam, Nov. 12, 1920; children—Suzanne (Mrs. John H. Clark.), Sally Potter (Mrs. F. Weichel Drummond). Surveyor Copper River and Northwestern Ry., Alaska, 1911; field engr. Kennecott (Alaska) Copper Corp., 1912-14; designer mill constrn., Kennecott, 1915-17; designer B. & A., R.R., Fay, Spofford & Thorndyke, Boston, 1919, Smith Hinchman & Grylls, and Ford Motor Co., Det., 1920, U. Ill., Urban, 1920-22; chief engr., gen. mgr. Scherzer Rolling Lift Bridge Co., Chgo., 1922-31, pres., dir., 1931-36; mem. cons. firm Hazelet & Erdal since 1936; co-designer Internat. Bridge, Tientsin, China Chukiang Bridge, Canton, China, San Teimo bridge, Seville, Spain, Ill. Waterway Bridges, Joliet, Queenston Rd., Bridge, Can., Mississippi River Bridge, East St. Louis, Ill., Edsel Ford Expressway, Det., Columbia Expressway, Cin., Ohio Turnpike, Cleve. sec. Ind. Toll Rd., Ky. Turnpike, Ohio River bridge, Parkersburg, W. Va., Bay St. Louis and Pascagoula Miss. bridges; now designing 5 maj. bridges over Ohio River; designer Green River Ordnance Plant, 1942, static test lab. Air Corps, Wright Field, O., 1943; cons. design of marine equipment Transp. Corps, U.S. Army, 1944. Served as lt. C.E., U.S. Army, 1918. Awarded first prize internat. competition for elevated highway, Am. Inst. Steel Constrn., 1938, also ann. award for design LaFayette Av. Bridge, Bay City, Mich., 1938, award for design of Sherman-Minton Bridge over Ohio River, also the John F. Kennedy bridge over Ohio River, Interstate Bridge over Miss. River. Bd. overseers U. Louisville; bd. govs. J.B. Speed Art Mus. Mem. Am. Inst. Cons. Engrs. (councilor), Am. Soc. C.E. (dir. 1957-60; sec. Ill. sect. 1940-41, pres. Ky. sect. 1951), Phi Gamma Delta. Republican. Presbyn. Clubs: Union League (Chgo.); Pendennis, Harmnoy Landing Country (Louisville); Country of Fla. Home: Old Stone Lane Louisville KY 40207 Office: Commerce Bldg Louisville KY 40202

HAZELL, WILLIAM, coll. dean; b. Plainfield, N.J., July 9, 1908; s. William and Ella (Frentz) H.; B.S., Newark Coll. Engring., 1930, M.S., 1960; grad. student N.Y. U.; Litt.D., Jersey City State Coll.; m. Gwendolyn Bressan, May 3, 1935; children—Patience Ann (Mrs. N.G. Anderson), Timothy Scott, Priscilla Jane (Mrs. D.B. Stephens), Deborah Joan. Instr. physics Newark Coll. Engring., 1933-39, asst. prof., 1939-45, asso. dean, dir. admissions, 1945-50, dean adminstrn., 1950-59, dean, v.p., 1959-70, pres., 1970—; head dept. physics Newark Tech. Sch., 1939-45. Membership com. Coll. Entrance Exam. Bd.; N.J. com. Community Colls. and Tech. Insts.; mem. state com. on articulation between colls. and secondary schs. Past pres. Watchung area council Boy Scouts Am. Mem. Engrs. Joint Council (chmn. engring. manpower commn.), Am. Assn. Higher Edn., Am. Assn. Acad. Deans, Am. Soc. Engring. Edn., Sigma Pi, Tau Beta Pi, Omicron Delta Kappa. Presbyn. (bd. of elders). Author: (with F.N. Entwisle) Introduction to Physics, 1938; Laboratory Experimentation, 1939. Home: 742 Hillside Av Plainfield NJ 07060 Office: 323 High St Newark NJ 07102

HAZELTINE, HERBERT SAMUEL, Jr., lawyer; b. Westminister, Cal., Dec. 12, 1908; s. Herbert S. and Emma (Phelps) H.; A.B., Stanford, 1931; LL.B., Harvard, 1934; m. Frances Sue Coffin, July 5, 1936; children—Susan, Ann, Lynn. Admitted to Cal. bar, 1935; partner Adams, Duque & Hazeltine, Los Angeles, 1945—; pres. La Bolsa Tile Co.; dir. Norris Industries Inc.; sec. Hoffman Electronics Corp., Los Angeles. Sec., gen. counsel Boys Club Found. So. Cal.; dir. Los Angeles chpt. A.R.C. Served as lt. comdr. USNR, 1942-45. Mem. Am. Bar Assn., Am. Soc. Corp. Secs. Clubs: California; Valley (Montecito, Cal.); Annandale Golf. Home: 495 Orange Grove Circle Pasadena CA 91105 Office: 523 W 6th St Los Angeles CA 90014

HAZELTINE, JOHN, banker; b. Prescott, Ariz., May 8, 1928; s. Bonsall and Norma (Keech) H.; B.S. in Botany, U. Ariz., 1952; grad. Pacific Coast Banking Sch., 1966; m. Sandra Woodbridge, May 29, 1962; children—John B., Christopher, Toble, With First Nat. Bank Ariz., Phoenix, 1952—, v.p., 1964—, comptroller, 1964—; mem. faculty Pacific Coast Sch. Banking, 1965-66, now Am. Inst. Banking. Mgr. Tucson Clearing House, 1962; mem. bd. Phoenix Clearing House, 1964- -, pres., 1970. Pres. Jr. Achievement Met. Phoenix, 1967-68. Bd. dirs. Jane Wayland Child Guidance Center, 1965—, pres., 1970—. Served with USMC, World War II. Mem. Am. Inst. Banking (pres. Tucson chpt. 1962), Bank Adminstr. Inst., Financial Execs. Inst. Home: 5517 N 3d St Phoenix AZ 85012 Office: 411 N Central Av Phoenix AZ 85002

HAZELTINE, SHERMAN, banker; b. Prescott, Ariz., Aug. 13, 1907; s. Moses B. and Anna (Criley) H.; A.B., Stanford, 1929; m. Mary Temple Favour, Sept. 24, 1932; children—Mary Favour, Cynthia Criley. With Bank of Ariz., Prescott, 1929- 57, pres., 1948-57, merged First Nat. Bank of Ariz., Phoenix, 1957, pres., 1957-58, chmn., chief exec. officer, 1958—; dir. Sperry Rand Corp., Inspiration Consol. Copper Co., N.Y.C., Western Bancorp., Los Angeles br. Fed. Res. Bank of San Francisco; pres. Phoenix Clearing House, 1958. Bd. dirs. Ariz. State Hosp. Bd. Control, 1951-52, chmn., 1953-55. Trustee Good Samaritan Hosp.; bd. dirs. Phoenix Symphony Assn., Heard Mus., Ariz. State U. Found., Ariz. Hist. Found.; mem. U. Ariz. Found. Mem. Am. Bankers Assn. (exec. council, adminstrv. com., pres. nat. band div. 1965, chmn. legislative com. 1955-56, research council 1956-59, mem. econ. policy com. 1969-71), Ariz. Bankers Assn. (sec. 1937-45, pres, 1946, chmn. legislative com. 1947- 55), Phoenix C. of C. (dir., pres. 1961-62), Ariz. Tax Research Assn. (dir., pres.), Newcomen Soc., Central Ariz. Project Assn., Thunderbird Grad. Sch. Internat. Mgmt. Kiwanian. Clubs: Press, Arizona, Phoenix Country, Paradise Valley (Phoenix); Metropolitan (N.Y.C.). Home: 2921 W Manor Dr Phoenix AZ 85014 Office: 411 N Central Av Phoenix AZ 85004

HAZELTON, PAUL VERNON, educator; b. Biddleford, Me., July 22, 1919; s. Charles Bernard and Jessie (Sands) H.; B.S., Bowdoin Coll., 1942; postgrad. Yale, 1947-48; Ed. M., Harvard, 1958; m. Jane O'Connell Desaulniers, Nov. 14, 1942; children—Stephen, Mary, Anne. Tchr., English pub. and pvt. schs., Me., Va., Conn., 1944-48; admissions officer, instr. English Bowdoin Coll., Brunswick, Me., 1948-57, prof. edn., 1957—; tchr. Colby Coll., 1963, U. Me., 1964, 70. Mem. Me. State Bd. Edn., 1968—. Served with AUS, 1942-43. Mem. Comparative Edn. Soc., N.E.A., Am. Assn. U. Profs. Democrat. Home: 33 Elm St Topsham ME 04086 Office: Sills Hall Bowdoin Coll Brunswick ME 04011

HAZELTON, ROGER, educator, clergymen; b. Chgo., Nov. 11, 1909; s. Purdy William and Esther May (Palmer) H.; B.A., Amherst Coll., 1931, D.D., 1951; B.D., Chgo. Theol. Sem., 1934, D.D., 1960; A.M., U. Chgo., 1934; Ph.D., Yale, 1937; L.H.D., Findlay Coll., 1965; m. Bonnie Jean Hanvey, Aug. 17, 1935; children—David Roger, Daniel Robert, Mark William. Tutor religion Olivet (Mich.) Coll., 1936-39; dean chapel Colo. Coll., 1939-45; prof. philosophy of religion Andover Newton Theol. Sch., 1945-51, Abbot prof. Christian theology, 1951-57, 65—; Clark lectr. Pomona Coll., 1950, McLean prof. religion, 1957-60; Alden-Tuthill lectr. Chgo. Theol. Sem., 1953; Taylor lectr. Yale, 1955; McLean prof. religion Claremont Grad. Sch., 1957-60; Swander lectr. Lancaster Theol. Sem., 1958; dean Grad. Sch. Theology, Oberlin Coll., 1960-65; lectr. Doshisha U., Kyoto, Japan, 1964, others. Fulbright research prof. U. Paris, 1951-52; vis. prof. Pontifical Gregorian U., Rome, 1971-72; frat. del. Gen. Synod Evang. Ch., Berlin, Germany, 1959; vice chmn. message com. Nat. Council Chs., 1957. Trustee emeritus Internat. Coll., Beirut, Lebanon. Fellow Nat. Council Religion in Higher Edn.; mem. Am. Theol. Soc. (pres. 1971-72). Author, 1943—, latest books: New Accents in Contemporary Theology, 1960; Christ and Ourselves, 1965; God; The Creator and Governor, 1966; A Theological Approach to Art, 1967; Knowing The Living God, 1968. Home: 125 Herrick Circle Newton Centre MA 02159

HAZELTON, RUTH ARDELLE, librarian; b. Oakland, Me., Oct. 7, 1912; d. Carl Dorsey and Ardelle (Robinson) Hazelton; B.S., Simmons Coll., 1934. Asst. Meriden (conn.) Pub. Library, 1935-37; cataloger Yale Law Library, 1937-42; children's librarian Waterville (Me.) Pub. Library, 1942-45; br. librarian, Newton, Mass., 1945-50; head librarian, Belmont, Mass., 1950-58; librarian Me. State Library, 1958—. Mem Am., Me. (pres. 1959-60), New Eng. (dir. 1959-60) library assns., Am. Assn. U. Women. Club: Zonta. Home: 1 Sewall St Augusta ME 04330 Office: Maine State Library Augusta ME 04330

HAZEN, ALLEN TRACY, educator; b. Portland, Conn., Nov. 4, 1904; s. Rev. Carleton and Julia (Trask) H.; A.B., Yale, 1927, Ph.D., 1935; A.M., Harvard, 1932; m. Edith Patterson; 1 son. Tutor Am. Coll., Tarsus, Turkey, 1927-30; master, Romford Sch., Washington, Conn., 1930-31; instr. in English, Yale, 1935-40; bibliographer and cataloguer, Yale Library, 1940-42; instr. in English, Hunter Coll., N.Y.C., 1942-45; cons. in bibliography, Library of Congress, summer, 1942; asso. prof. of English and bibliographer U. Library Chgo., 1945-47, prof. of English and dir. of U. Library, 1947-48; Prof. English, Columbia, 1948-71, prof. emeritus, 1971—; Guggenheim fellow, 1952-53. Mem. Modern Lang. Assn., Bibliog. Soc. (London), Am. Library Assn., Bibliog. Soc. Am., Phi Beta Kappa. Selden fellow in English Yale, 1933-34. Conglist. Author: Samuel Johnson's Prefaces and Dedications, 1937; (with R.W. Chapman) Johnsonian

Bibliography, a supplement to Courtney, 1939; Bibliography of the Strawberry Hill Press, 1942; Bibliography of Horace Walpole, 1948; Catalogue of Walpole's Library, 3 volumes, 1969. Compiler: (with E.L. McAdam) Catalogue of Exhibition of books by Johnson in Yale Library, 1935. Asst. in ann. bibliography, "English lit., 1660-1800," Philological Quarterly, 1939-41. Contbr. of short articles on literary and bibliog. problems to various publs. Gen. editor Yale edition of Samuel Johnson's Works, 1958-66. Home: 460 Riverside Dr New York City NY 10027

HAZEN, ARLON GIBERSON, coll. dean; b. Stillwater, Okla., Feb. 25, 1920; s. Leslie Eugene and Ella V. (Brooks) H.; B.S. in Agrl. Engring., Okla. State U., 1940; M.S., La. State U., 1941; m. Betty Mae Sewell, June 3, 1940; children— Leslie Ray, Gale Arlon. Instr. agrl. engring. U. Ark., 1941-42; supt. Williston (N.D.) Br. Expt. Sta., 1946-51; asst. to dir. Agrl. Expt. Sta. N.D. State U., 1951-56, dean Coll. Agr., also dir. Agrl. Expt. Sta., 1956—. Served to lt. col., C.E., AUS, 1942-46; ETO. Mem. Am. Soc. Agrl. Engrs., Alpha Zeta. Home: 905 15th St S Fargo ND 58102

HAZEN, DAVID COMSTOCK, educator; b. Greenburg, N.Y., July 3, 1927; B.S. in Engring., Princeton, 1948, M.S., 1949; married; 3 children. From instr. to prof. aero. engring. Princeton, 1949—. Mem. Am. Inst. Aeros. nd Astronautics. Office: Sayre Hall Forrestral Campus Princeton U Princeton NJ 08540*

HAZEN, EDWARD GATES, banker; b. Thomaston, Conn., June 8, 1906; s. Robert and Helen (Gates) H.; student Lawrence Acad., 1922-24; A.B., Amherst Coll., 1928; LL.B., U. Conn., 1938; m. Virginia May Robert, Sept. 10, 1938; children-Edward Gates, Robert Dana. Clk., Waterbury Savs. Bank (Conn.), 1929; trainee Scovill Mfg. Co., 1930-32; clk. Colonial Bank & Trust Co., 1933-46, trust officer, 1946-55, v.p., trust officer, 1955-65, sr. v.p., 1965-67, exec. v.p., 1967-69 exec. v.p., chmn. trust com., 1969—; dir. Hallden Machine Co., Waterbury Screw Machine Products Co., Am. Fastener Co.; dir., corporator Thomaston Savs. Bank. Mem. Conn. Bankers Trust Com., 1966—. Mem. bd. finance Town of Thomaston, 1946-48; trustee, treas. Waterbury Found., Inc.; mem. Watertown Sch. Bldg. Com. 1956-59, chmn. 1958-59. Trustee Waterbury chpt. A.R.C., 1961-63. Served with USAAF, 1943-45. Clubs: Litchfield County University (Watertown); Waterbury. Home: 99 North St Watertown CT 06795 Office: 81 W Main St Waterbury CT 06720

HAZEN, HAROLD LOCKE, educator; b. Philo, Ill., Aug. 1, 1901; s. Wirt Mandeville and Elta Belle (Brewer) H.; S.B., Mass. Inst. Tech., 1924, S.M., 1929, Sc.D., 1931; m. Katherine Pharis Salisbury, Sept. 5, 1928; children—Stanley Seamans, Martha Locke (Mrs. William Liller), Nathan Lord, Anne Webb (Mrs. John G. Bowen). With Mass. Inst. Tech., 1925—, research asst. in elec. engring., 1925-26, instr., 1926-31, asst. prof., 1931-35, asso. prof., 1935-38, prof., head dept. elec. engring., 1938-52, dean Grad. Sch., 1952-67, fgn. study adviser, 1967—; mem. adv. council dept. elec. engring. Princeton, 1948-56; chief div. 7. Nat. Def. Research Comm., 1942-46, exchange prof. elec. engring. Ohio State U., 1934-35; cons. on engring. edn. Robert Coll. Istanbul, 1955, interim pres., 1961; cons. engring. edn. Am. U. Beirut, 1957, Ministry of Edn., Iceland, 1958. Mem. U.S. Naval Weapons Lab. adv. council, 1953-65; chmn. edn. com. Engrs. Council for Profl. Devel., 1954-56, exec. com., 1954-58; chmn. Engring Edn. Mission to Japan, 1951, cons. engring. edn. UN Mission to U. Brasilia, 1962. Trustee Robert Coll. Bebek, Istanbul, Turkey, Coll. of Petroleum and Minerals, Dhahran, Saudi-Arabia. Awarded Levy medal of Franklin Inst., 1935; Lamme Gold medal Am. Soc. Engring. Edn., 1962; Presdl. Certificate of Merit, 1948. Served as 2d lt. Air Service, 1924-29; lt. comdr. USNR, 1936-49. Fellow I.E.E.E., Am. Acad. Arts and Scis. (council); mem. Franklin Inst., Am. Soc. Engring. Edn. (chmn. com. devel. engring. faculties), Inst. Elec. Engrs. Japan (hon.) Sigma Xi, Tau Beta Pi, Eta Kappa Nu. Contbr. articles on instrumental calculation, automatic control devices, engring. edn., accreditation. Home: 81 Clark St Belmont MA 02178 Office: Mass Inst Tech Cambridge MA 02139

HAZEN, JOSEPH CHALMERS, Jr., publishing co. exec.; b. Janesville, Wis., Feb. 13, 1912; s. Joseph Chalmers and Ruth (Burchard) H.; B.A., Princeton, 1935; m. Helen C. Stevens, Mar. 6, 1939; children—Libby M. (Mrs. Michael W. McCarthy), Joseph Chalmers III. With Archtl. Forum mag., 1938-64, asso. pub., 1961- 63, pub., 1963-64; gen. mgr. Time-Life Books div. Time, Inc., 1964-67, 68-70; dep. adminstr. Multi-Media group Time Inc., 1970—, gen. mgr. Gen. Learning Corp., 1967-68. Chmn. planning bd., Summit, N.J., 1958-70; mem. adv. council Princeton Sch. Arch., 1960-68; trustee Summit Art Center. Served to lt. col., F.A., AUS, 1942- 45. Mem. A.I.A. Home: 37 Lenox Rd Summit NJ 07901 Office: Time and Life Bldg Rockefeller Center New York City NY 10020

HAZEN, STANLEY PHILLIP, educator; b. Alexandria, Minn., Aug. 29, 1924; s. Ray and Edith (Packard) H.; B.A., Macalester Coll., 1949; D.D.S., U. Minn., 1953; M.S., U. Rochester, 1960; certificate Eastman Dental Center, 1960; m. Evelyn Joyce Edwards, Aug. 21, 1948; children—Jean, Elizabeth, Robert, Patricia, James, Anne, Suzanne. Asso., dept. periodontology Eastman Dental Center, Rochester, N.Y., 1960-63; asso. prof., chmn. dept. periodontology State U. N.Y. at Buffalo, 1963-67; prof., dir. grad. and postgrad. studies Temple U. Dental Sch., Phila., 1967-70; prof., head dept. periodontology U. Conn. Dental Sch., Hartford, 1970—. Served with USNR, 1942-46, 53-57. Postdoctoral research fellow NIH, 1957-60. Mem. Am. Dental Assn., Am. Academy Periodontology, Am. Assn. Dental Schs., Internat. Assn. Dental Research, A.A.A.S., Conn. Dental Soc., Hartford Dental Soc., Omicron Kappa Upsilon. Home: 2 Candlewood Lane Farmington CT 06032 Office: 2 Holcomb St Hartford CT 06105

HAZEN, WILLIAM HARRIS, investment co. exec.; b. Salem, Mass., Jan. 6, 1931; s. Julius Elijah Dorothy (Harris) H.; A.B., Bowdoin Coll., 1952; LL.B., Harvard, 1958; m. Judith Ettl, Feb. 22, 1959; children—Cordelia, Alexes. Admitted to N.Y. bar, 1959; with firm Pell, Butler, Hatch, Curtis & LeViness, N.Y.C., 1959- 61; exec. asst. to N.Y. supt. banks, 1962-64; with J.W. Weligman & Co., N.Y.C., 1964-68, partner, 1969—; v.p., dir. Union Capital Fund, Inc.; v.p. Tri-Continental Corp., N.Y.C., 1969—, Broad St. Investing Corp., 1969—, Nat. Investors Corp., 1969—, Whitehall Fund, Inc., 1969—. Adv. mem. Joint Legislative Com. Revise Banking Laws, N.Y. State, 1964. Vice pres., bd. govs. N.Y.C. Young Republican Club, 1962-64, adv. com., 1965—. Served to lt. USNR, 1952-55: Korea. Mem. Am., N.Y. bar assns., Bar Assn. City N.Y., Zeta Psi. Conglist. (trustee). Club: Bedens Brook (Princeton, N.J.). Home: 55 Remsen St Brooklyn Heights NY 11201 Office: 65 Broadway New York City NY 10006

HAZLEHURST, FRANKLIN HAMILTON, educator; b. Spartanburg, S.C., Nov. 6, 1925; s. Robert Purviance and Lottie Lee (Nicholls) H.; B.A., Princeton, 1949, M.F.A., 1952, Ph.D. (Charlotte Elizabeth Proctor fellow), 1956; m. Carol Foord, Aug. 26, 1950; children—Franklin Hamilton, Robert Purviance II, Mary Hadley, Abigail Norris. Instr., Princeton, 1954-56; lectr. Frick Collection, lectr. Princeton Theol. Sem., 1956-57; asst. prof., asso. prof. U. Ga., 1957-63; prof., chmn. dept. fine arts Vanderbilt U., Nashville, 1963—. Mem. adv. bd. Tenn. Arts. Council. Served with AUS, 1944-46. Fulbright fellow, 1953-54; Sarah H. Moss fellow U. Ga., 1961-62; summer grantee Am. Council Learned Socs., 1967, Am. Philos. Soc., 1967-68. Mem. Coll. Art Assn. Am., Soc. Archtl. Historians, La Société de l'histoire de l'art francais. Author: Jacques Boyceau and the French Formal Garden, 1966. Contbr. articles to profl. jours. Home: 4430 Shepard Pl Nashville TN 37205

HAZLEHURST, ROBERT PURVIANCE, Jr., lawyer; b. Spartanburg, S.C., Jan. 7, 1919; s. Robert Purviance and Lottie Lee (Nicholls) H.; grad. Hill Sch., Pottstown, Pa., 1936; A.B., Princeton, 1940; LL.B., Yale, 1947; m. Mary Kierulff, Feb. 20, 1947 (dec. July 1971); children—Ellen, Charlotte, Anna; m. 2d, Dorothy Wilson Desmer, Jan. 7, 1972. Admitted to N.J. bar, 1947, since practiced in Newark; partner Pitney, Hardin & Kipp, 1952—. Dir. Driver-Harris Co., Harrison, N.J. Bd. dirs. Princeton Fund, 1966-71, chmn. ann. giving campaign, 1967-68. Pres., trustee United Hosps., Newark; sec., trustee Greater Newark Hosp. Devel. Fund; trustee Kent Pl. Sch., Summit N.J., 1960-70; trustee, exec. com. Silver Hill Found., New Canaan, Conn. Served to capt. USAAF. 1942-45. Mem. Am., N.J., Essex County bar assns. Clubs: Essex (Newark); Short Hills (N.J.). Home: 12 Hillside Av Short Hills NJ 07078 Office: 570 Broad St Newark NJ 07102

HAZLET, STEWART EMERSON, organic chemist, educator; b. Freeport, Ill., Feb. 4, 1910; s. Luther A. and Veretta M. (Voorhees) H.; A.B., U. Dubuque, 1931; M.S., U. Ia., 1933, Ph.D., 1935; m. Ann Louise Crow, Dec. 26, 1936; children—Ruth (Mrs. William Kirk), Stewart (dec.), William. Instr. math. U. Dubuque, summer 1931; grad. asst. chem., U. Ia., 1931-35; instr. chemistry, George Washington U., 1935-36; instr. organic chemistry U. Ill., summer 1936; instr. chemistry Wash. State U., 1936-41, asst. prof., 1941-45, asso. prof., 1945-47, prof. chemistry, dean grad. sch., 1947-60, prof. organic chemistry, 1960—; vis. asso. chemistry Cal. Inst. Tech., 1960- 61; vis. scholar U. Cal. at Los Angeles, 1960-61; guest Mass. Inst. Tech., summer 1971. Bd. dirs. Wash. Div. Am. Cancer Soc., 1948—, v.p., 1958, mem. exec. com., 1961-70, chairman public education committee, 1961-68. Fellow Ia. Acad. Sci., Am. Inst. Chemists, A.A.A.S.; mem. Am. Chem. Soc. (past chmn. and councilor, Wash.-Ida. border sect.), N.W. Sci. Assn. (past chmn. math.-physics-chem. sect.), Internat. Platform Assn., Sigma Xi, Alpha Chi Sigma, Phi Lambda Upsilon, Pi Kappa Delta. Contbr. articles in sci. and chem. jours. Specializes in organic chem. with spl. reference to aromatic compounds. Home: 102 Anthony Pullman WA 99163

HAZLETT, CHARLES BROWN, banking exec.; b. Moscow, Md., Aug. 18, 1909; s. Eugene and Mame (Brown) H.; A.B., Akron U., 1932; m. Virginia Wigley, Apr. 21, 1936 (dec.); children—Temmy (Mrs. William Caine), Jan (Mrs. William Gaskill), Ann; m. 2d, Sally M. Orrison, 1969. With Am. Bank of Commerce, formerly known as Evans Savings Assn., Akron, Ohio, 1932—, pres., 1959—, also chief exec. officer; trustee Summit Properties, Inc. Past treas. West Akron Kiwanis Found.; trustee Akron Gen. Hosp., Akron Family Service Soc., Akron YWCA, McAlonan Found.; mem. adv. bd. Akron Child Welfare Bd. Mem. Ohio (exec. com., past pres.), Summit County (past pres.) savs. and loan leagues, Akron, Ohio chambers commerce, Akron Real Estate Bd., Home Builders Assn., Bank Pub. Relations and Marketing Assn., Ohio Jr. C. of C. (past pres.), Akron U. Hilltoppers, Soc. Residential Appraisers. Mason (Shriner, Jester). Clubs: City (past trustee), Portage Country (Akron). Home: 751 Delaware Av Akron OH 44303 Office: 157 S Main St Akron OH 44308

HAZLETT, JAMES ARTHUR, govt. ofcl.; b. Kansas City, Mo., May 26, 1917; s. Arthur J. and Clara E. (Quackenbush) H.; B.S., Kansas City Tchrs. Coll., 1937; M.A., U. Kansas City, 1943, postgrad. U. Mo., U. Kan.; LL.D., Park Coll., 1958; m. Mary Quinn Pope, July 3, 1937; 1 son, Stephen. Tchr. Kansas City Pub. Schs., 1938-45, elementary sch. prin., 1945-51, dir. research, 1951-55, supt. schs., 1955-69; adminstrv. dir. Nat. Assessment Program Edn. Commn. States, Denver, 1969—; lectr. edn., prin. Summer Demonstration Sch., U. Kansas City, 1950-55. Mem. bd. Kansas City Mus., Philharmonic Assn.; area council Boy Scouts; treas. Mid-Continent Regional Edn. Lab., 1966- 68. Chmn. Pres.'s Nat. Adv. Council Supplementary Centers and Services, 1968-70. Recipient of Nat. Human Relations award from the Nat. Conf. Christians and Jews, 1962. Mem. Am. Assn. Sch. Adminstrs. (chmn. resolutions com. 1967), Mo. Tchrs. Assn. (past pres.), Nat. Congress Parents and Tchrs. (bd. mgrs. 1968-71), N.E.A., Native Sons Kansas City, Phi Delta Kappa. Methodist (bd.). Rotarian. Home: 818 Logan Denver CO 80203 Office: Lincoln Tower Bldg Denver CO

HAZLETT, MCCREA, coll. ofcl.; b. Tarentum, Pa., Feb. 24, 1916; s. Elmer Emerson and Mertie Mae (Love) H.; B.A., Westminster Coll., 1937; student U. Pitts., summer 1936, Northwestern U. summer 1934; M.A., U. Chgo., 1938, Ph.D., 1951; m. Doris Elizabeth Hill, Aug. 31, 1940; children—William McCrea, Alec Emerson, Janet Mae. Instr. English Westminster Coll. 1938-40; research analyst Office Chief Signal Officer, War Dept., 1942-45; instr. English, U. Chgo., 1946-48, asst. dean students, asst. prof. English, 1948-52, asst. dir. admissions, 1952-55, dir. admissions, 1955-56, dean students 1956-57; dean students U. Rochester, 1957-58, dean Coll. Arts and Scis., 1958-61, provost of univ., acting pres., 1961-62, provost, 1963, v.p., provost, 1964-68, v.p. for spl. acad. activities, 1968-69, v.p. for pub. affairs, 1969—, dir. South Asian Lang. and Area Study Center, 1965-67; dir. Am. Inst. Indian Studies, Poona, India, 1963-64. Bd. mgrs. Rochester Meml. Art Gallery; bd. trustees Highland Hosp., Rochester. Served with AUS, 1945-46. Mem. Am. Inst. Indian Studies (exec. com., chmn. bd. 1970-71), Assn. Asian Studies. Episcopalian. Clubs: Pundit, Genesee Valley (Rochester). Home: 10 Hawthorne St Rochester NY 14610

HAZLETT, ROBERT CUMMINS, banker; b. Wheeling, W.Va., June 7, 1910; s. Robert and Anne (Cummins) H.; grad. Linsly Mil. Inst., Wheeling, 1927; C.E., Cornell U., 1931; m. Susan Arbenz, Oct. 17, 1936; children—Robert Cummins, John A., James B., George S., Thomas McK. With Wheeling Dollar Savs. & Trust Co., 1931—, successively clk., asst. trust officer, trust officer, v.p. charge trusts, 1931-58, pres., 1958—; dir. Scott Lumber Co., Wheeling, Weirton Savs. & Loan Assn. (W.Va.). Mem. Ohio County Bd. Ed., 1952-68; past pres. Community Chest. Pres., dir. Greenwood Cemetery Assn., Wheeling; pres., treas. trustees Linsly Mil. Inst.; trustee Ohio Valley General Hosp. (Wheeling), Reynolds Meml. Hosp. (Glendale, W.Va.). Named Citizen of Year, Wheeling, 1952. Mem. W.Va. Bankers Assn. (pres. 1968-69), Symposhiarchs, Phi Kappa Sigma. Presbyn.(trustee). Elk. Club: Fort Henry (Wheeling). Home: 6 Echo Point Circle 26003 Office: 315 Market St Wheeling WV 26003

HAZLITT, HENRY, editor, author; b. Phila., Nov. 28, 1894; s. Stuart Clark and Bertha (Zauner) H.; student Coll. City of N.Y., 1912; Litt. D., Grove City Coll., Pa., 1958; LL.D., Bethany Coll., 1961; m. Frances S. Kanes, 1936. Mem. staff Wall St. Journal, 1913-16, financial staff, N.Y. Evening Post, 1916-18; wrote monthly financial letter of Mechanics and Metals Nat. Bank, N.Y.C., 1919-20; financial editor N.Y. Evening Mail, 1921-23; editorial writer N.Y. Herald, 1923-24, The Sun, 1924-25; lit. editor The Sun, 1925-29; lit. editor The Nation, 1930-33; editor Am. Mercury, 1933-34; on editorial staff of N.Y. Times, 1934-46; asso. Newsweek, writer column Bus. Tides, 1946-66; nationally syndicated columnist, 1966-69; co-editor The Freeman, 1950-52, editor-in-chief, 1953. In A.S., U.S. Army, World War. Recipient honor medal Freedoms Found., 1950, 60, 62. Mem. Mont Pelerin Soc. Clubs: Authors (London, Eng.); Dutch Treat, Century, Overseas Press (N.Y.C.). Author: Thinking as a Science, 1916; The Anatomy of Criticism, 1933; A New Constitution Now, 1942; Economics in One Lesson, 1946; Will Dollars Save The World?, 1947; The Great Idea, 1951, rev. edit. titled, Time Will Run Back, 1966; The Free Man's Library, 1956; The Failure of the New Economics; An Analysis of the Keynesian Fallacies, 1959; What You Should Know About Inflation, 1960; The Foundations of Morality, 1964; Man vs. The Welfare State, 1970. Editor: A Practical Program for America, 1932; The Critics of Keynesian Economics, 1960. Home: 65 Drum Hill Rd Wilton CT 06897

HAZUMI, TAKAYUKI, banker; b. Nagoya, Japan, Apr. 1, 1927; s. Koji and Yuki (Shibata) H.; B.A. in Econs., Nagoya U., 1951; postgrad. dept. econs. Harvard Sch. Arts and Scis., 1956-57; m. Kazuko Patricia Makita, Sept. 24, 1959. With Sumitomo Bank, Ltd., Osaka, Japan, 1951-63, asst. mgr. Tokyo econs. dept., 1963, asst., mgr. Ikebukuro br., 1964, asst. mgr. Tokyo fgn. dept., 1965, v.p., sec. Sumitomo Bank Cal., San Francisco, 1966-69, v.p., cashier, 1969—. Mem. World Trade Club, Japan Soc. Home: 8101 Geary Blvd San Francisco CA 944121 Office: 365 California St San Francisco CA 94119

HAZZARD, LOWELL BRESTEL, clergyman; b. Peoria, Ill., Feb. 6, 1898; s. William and Lona Rebecca (Evans) H.; student Bradley Poly. Inst., 1911-17; B.A., Ohio Wesleyan U., 1919; B.D., Garrett Bibl. Inst., 1922, D.D., 1943; Ph.D., U. Edinburgh (Scotland), 1927; m. Stella M. Tombaugh, July 30, 1926; children—Joseph William, Mary Ellen, Robert Tombaugh. Pastor Grace Meth. Ch., Peoria, 1923-26; asst. prof. English Bible, Ohio Wesleyan U., 1927- 30; pastor Meth. Ch., Pittsfield, Ill., 1930-35, Union Meth. Ch., Quincy, Ill., 1935-41; prof. religion Ill. Wesleyan U., 1941-50; prof. O. T. Westminster Theol. Sem., 1951-57, Wesley Theol. Sem., 1958-70, prof. emeritus, 1970—. Mem. S.A.T.C., 1918. Lectr., writer ch. sch. curriculum. Meth. Ch. Mem. Phi Beta Kappa, Pi Gamma Mu. Phi Kappa Phi, Author: A Pocket Book of Methodist Beliefs. Address: 215 E Washington St Pontiac IL 61764

HAZZARD, SHIRLEY, author; b. Sydney, Australia, Jan. 30, 1931; d. Reginald and Catherine (Stein) Hazzard; ed. Queenwood Sch., Sydney until 1946; m. Francis Steegmuller, Dec. 22, 1963. With Combined Services Intelligence, Hong Kong, 1947-48, U.K. High Commnrs. Office, Wellington, New Zealand, 1949- 51, UN (Gen. Service Category), N.Y.C., 1952- 62. Recipient grant in lit. Nat. Inst. Arts and Letters, 1966. Author: Cliffs of Fall and Other Stories, 1963; (novel) The Evening of the Holiday, 1966; (fiction) People in Glass Houses, 1967, (novel) The Bay of Noon, 1970; contbr. short stories to New Yorker mag. Address: 200 E 66th St New York City NY 10021

HEABERLIN, FRED S., editor; b. St. Paul, Sept. 4, 1904; s. Freeman E. and Emma M. (Stuth) H.; A.B., U. Minn., 1926; m. Florence E. Miller, July 3, 1937; children—Janet, Jean. With St. Paul Pioneer Press and St. Paul Dispatch since 1926, city editor, 1940-43, asst. mng. editor, 1943-45, mng. editor, 1945-57, exec. editor, 1957-70, dir. Ridder News Service, 1970—. Home: 1218 Edgcumbe Rd St Paul MN 55105 Office: 55 E 4th St St Paul MN 55101

HEACOCK, JOE DAVIS, educator; b. Birmingham, Ala., Sept. 12, 1906; s. Joseph Davis and Ida (Waldrop) H.; A.B., Howard Coll., Birmingham, Ala., 1928, L.H.D. (hon.), 1960; M.R.E., South-Western Bapt. Theol. Sem., 1939, D.R.E., 1950; spl. student Peabody Coll., Columbia; m. Nell Marbury Russell, May 30, 1932; 1 dau., Charlene. Minister edn. Coll. Av Bapt. Ch., Ft. Worth, 1936-37, Olivet Bapt. Ch., Oklahoma City, 1937-42; dir. assn. tng. union work So. Bapt. Conv., 1942-44; minister edn. Poly. Bapt. Ch., Connell Bapt. Ch., Univ. Bapt. Ch., Ft. Worth, 1944-52; prof. Southwestern Bapt. Theol. Sem., 1944—, dean Sch. Religious Edn., 1956- -; guest prof. Hong Kong Bapt. Sem. and Japan Bapt. Theol. Sem., 1964. Pres. Ala. Bapt. Young People's Union Conv., 1929-31, Okla. Bapt. Tng. Union Conv., 1940-41, Southwestern Bapt. Religious Edn. Assn., 1948; nat. chmn. Allied Youth, 1933-34, also mem. nat. sponsoring com. Mem. Religious Edn. Assn., Southeastern, Southwestern (pres. 1948), So. (pres. 1966- 67) Bapt. religious edn. assns., Sigma Nu.‡

HEAD, C. J., lawyer; b. El Dorado, Ark., Sept. 17, 1927; s. J. C. and Agnes (Kastner) H.; student N.M. Mil. Inst., 1942-47; B.A., St. Marys Coll., Cal., 1949; J.D., U. Chgo., 1952; m. Elizabeth Bonner, Dec. 30, 1950; 1 dau., Alison Elizabeth. Admitted to Ill. bar, 1952, Cal. bar, 1955, N.Y. bar, 1958; practice in San Francisco, 1955-57, N.Y.C., 1957—; law clk. Hon. Walter L. Pope, U.S. Circuit judge 9th Circuit, 1954-55; asso. Chickering & Gregory, 1955-57; asso. Hecht, Hadfield, Hays, Landsman & Head and precessor firms, 1957-59, partner, 1959—. Dir. Mission Corp., Skelly Oil Co., Benilite Corp. of Am. Served to 1st lt., Judge Adv. Gen. Corps, U.S. Army, 1952-54. Mem. Am. Bar Assn., Assn. Bar City N.Y., State Bar Cal., Am. Judicature Soc. Home: 410 E 57th St New York NY 10022 Office: 11 Broadway New York NY 10004

HEAD, DOUGLAS M., atty. gen. Minn.; b. Mpls., Apr. 14, 1930; grad. Phillips Exeter Acad., 1948; B.A., in Polit. Sci., Yale, 1952; LL.B. (asso. editor law rev.), U. Minn., 1956. Admitted to Minn. bar, 1956; practice in Mpls., 1957-66; mem. Minn. Ho. of Reps., 1960-64; atty. gen. Minn., 1966—. Named one of two outstanding first term legislators, 1961. Mem. Order of Coif. Republican. Address: State Capitol Bldg St Paul MN 55101*

HEAD, EDITH, costume designer; b. Los Angeles; A.B., U. Cal.; M.A., Stanford; student Otis Art Sch., Chouinard Art Sch. (Los Angeles). Began as tchr. French, Spanish and art, Hollywood Sch. for Girls, and Bishop's Sch. (La Jolla); chief designer Paramount Pictures Corp., now with Universal City Studios. Recipient (with Gile Steele) Acad. Award for black and white costume design (The Heiress), 1949, Acad. Award (in collaboration) (All About Eve), 1950, (Samson and Delilah), 1951; award for costume design (Place in the Sun), 1952, (Roman Holiday), 1954; Acad. Award black and white costume design (Sabrina), 1954, (The Facts of Life), 1960. Author: The Dress Doctor; How to Dress for Success. Address: care Universal Studios Universal City CA 91608

HEAD, HOWARD, mfr. and designer skis; b. Phila., July 31, 1914; s. Joseph and Annie (Wilkinson) H.; grad. William Penn Charter Sch., Phila., 1928-32; A.B. in Engring. Scis., Harvard, 1936; m. Joan Johnson, June 11, 1968; 1 dau. by previous marriage, Nancy Stratton. Journalist, writer, motion picture editor, 1937-38; mem. engring. dept. Glenn L. Martin Co., Balt., 1939-47; cons., designer engring. and physics research depts. Johns Hopkins, 1948-51; organizer, 1952-70, pres., chmn. bd., treas. Head Ski Co. Inc., Timonium, Md. A founder Ski Industries Am., pres., dir., 1958-59; chmn. industry fund raising U.S. Olympic Ski Team, 1961-62. Democrat. Clubs: Harvard, Baltimore County, Ski (Balt.) conceived, designed, developed ski derived from metal sandwich aircraft constrn. Home: 21 Blythewood Rd Baltimore MD 21210

HEAD, JACK DAVIS, lawyer, corp. exec.; b. Ft. Worth, Tex., June 18, 1915; s. Charles William and Hazel (Walker) H.; LL.B., Washington and Lee U., 1939; m. Jane Arnold, May 3, 1942; children—Jane Lanham, Julia Arnold, Anne Elizabeth, John Davis, Joseph Arnold. Admitted to Tex. bar; with firm Vinson, Elkins, Weems & Searls, 1940-58, partner, 1952-58; v.p., gen. counsel Tex. Eastern Transmission Corp., Houston, 1958—. Trustee Bertner Found. Served with USN, World War II. Mem. Am., Tex. bar assns. Clubs: Houston Country, Ramada (Houston). Home: 3652 Chevy Chase St Houston TX 77019 Office: So Nat Bank Bldg Houston TX 77002 also PO Box 2521 Houston TX 77001

HEAD, JAMES DEAN, newspaper editor; b. Independence, Kan., Mar. 11, 1926; s. James Edward and Ruby (Brown) E.; student Washburn U., 1944-45; B.S., Kan. U., 1949; m. Gladys Corel Dunkley, Aug. 28, 1948; children—Laura, Lynn, Kathleen, Michael. City editor Lawrence (Kan.) Jour.-World, 1949-54; state editor Miami (Fla.) Herald, 1954-59, Miami News, 1959-62; asst. new editor N.Y. Herald Tribune, 1962-63; exec. sports editor Detroit Free Press, 1963-66; exec. editor Today, newspaper, Cape Kennedy, Fla., 1966-68, Hartford (Conn.) Times, 1968-70, Westchester-Rockland Newspapers, White Plains, N.Y., 1970—. Served with USNR, 1944-46. Mem. Asso. Press Mng. Editors, Internat. Press Inst., Sigma Delta Chi. Home: 50 Cross Ridge Rd Chappaqua NY 10514 Office: 8 Church St White Plains NY 10602

HEAD, JAMES ROBERT, lawyer; b. Springfield, Mo., Oct. 16, 1928; s. James Earl and Clara (Mengerhausen) H.; B.S., Okla. A. and M. U., 1951; LL.B., U. Tulsa, 1957; m. Ruth Ann Schult, Jan. 5, 1952; children—James Stephen, John Richard, Jane Elizabeth, Justin Randolph. Admitted to Okla. bar, 1957; practice in Tulsa, 1958—; with patent dept. Pan Am. Petroleum Corp., 1953-58; partner Paul H. Johnson, 1960—. Mem. Am. Bar Assn., Am. Patent Law Assn. Republican. Rotarian. Home: 2637 E 69th St Tulsa OK 74105 Office: Beacon Bldg Tulsa OK 74103

HEAD, ROBERT FRANCIS, theologian, author; b. Providence, Ky., May 6, 1918; s. Volney Burean and Flora (Lane) H.; B.A., Oakland City (Ind.) Coll., 1954; B.D., So. Sem., Louisville, 1958; grad. student Ind. U., Ind. State U.; m. Anna Lucille Rheinheimer, Oct. 26, 1940; 1 son, Robert Noel. With Dearborn (Mich.) Press, 1940-42, Abee Press, Detroit, 1946-50; ordained to ministry Bapt. Ch., 1952., pastor in Ft. Branch, Ind., 1958-59; tchr. Bible and Theology Oakland City Coll., 1959—, chmn. philosophy and Bible div., 1966—. Pres. Ministerial Alliance Ft. Branch, 1960; moderator Nat. Conv. Gen. Baptists, 1964. Served with U.S. Navy, 1936-40, 42-45. Mem. Phi Delta Kappa, Alpha Phi Gamma, Mu Tau Kappa. Mason. Author: Evangelism, 1962; Theology of General Baptists, 1963; Essentials of Church Administration, 1966. Editor: Christian Education in the Local Church, 1964. Home: 631 Sherman St Oakland City IN 47560

HEAD, ROBERT J., retail store co. exec.; b. Tallapoosa, Ga., Sept. 20, 1919; s. Iverson and Ruth (Hubbard) H.; B.C.S., Ga. State Coll., 1947; m. Anne E. Mallinson, June 15, 1940; children-Robert J., Mary C., Charles W., Margie A., Dorothy M. Sr. accountant Fisher body div. Gen. Motors Corp., 1940-50; with Winn-Dixie Stores, Inc., 1950—, controller, 1955—. Bd. dirs. Jacksonville (Fla.) Jr. Achievement, 1964-67. Served with USAAF, 1944-45. Mem. Financial Execs. Inst. (bd. dirs. Fla. chpt. 1967-68; pres. N. Fla. chpt., 1969-70). Clubs: Sertoma Breakfast (pres. 1968-69); Timuquana Country (Jacksonville); Ponte Verda (Ponte Verda Beach, Fla.). Home: 5735 Salerno Rd Jacksonville FL 32210 Office: 5050 Edgewood Ct Jacksonville FL 32203

HEAD, WALTON O., ins. co. exec.; b. Stephenville, Tex., June 5, 1909; s. William Burres and Lulu Rose (O'Hara) H.; B.A. cum laude, Dartmouth, 1929; LL.B. with highest honors, U. Tex., 1932. Admitted to Tex. bar, 1932; asso. Worsham, Rollins, Burford, Ryburn & Hincks, Dallas, 1932-36; with Employers Casualty Co., 1936—, dir., 1938—, pres., 1962—, chmn. bd., 1967—; with Employers Nat. Inc. Co., 1954—, dir., 1954—, pres., 1962- -, chmn. bd., 1967—; dir. Employers Nat. Life Ins. Co., 1961—, pres., 1963—, chmn. bd., 1967—; with Tex. Employers' Ins. Assn., 1936—, dir., 1956—, pres., 1962—, chmn. bd., 1967—. Served to lt. col. USAAF, 1942-46. Decorated Legion of Merit. Mem. Am. Judicature Soc., Am. Inst. Property and Liability Underwriters, Am., Tex., Dallas bar assns., Internat. Assn. Ins. Counsel. Home: 4215 Lakeside Dr Dallas TX 75214 Office: Employers Insurance Bldg Dallas TX 75202

HEADLEE, RICHARD HAROLD, investment co. exec.; b. Ft. Dodge, Ia., May 15, 1930; s. William Clarke and Violet Rebecca (Lunn) H.; B.A., Utah State U., 1953; m. Mary E. Mendenhall, Oct. 21, 1948; children—Mike, Douglas, Kathy, Bruce, Natalie, Carolyn, Laura, Howard, Elaine. Account exec. Burroughs Corp., Detroit, 1957-66; pres. Morbark Industries, Winn, Mich., 1968-69; pres. Hamilton Internat. Devel. Co., 1970—; engaged as cons. and field dir. Romney Assos. Pres. Bountiful (Utah) Jr. C. of C., 1960, Utah Jr. C. of C., 1962; bd. dirs. U.S. Jr. C. of C., 1961-65, v.p., 1962-63, pres., 1963-64, chmn. bd., 1964-65, life mem., senator; bd. dirs. U.S. C. of C., 1964—. Asst. campaign chmn. gov. Mich., 1966; chmn. Citizens for Romney; nat. chmn. Young Civic Leaders for Nixon-Agnew, 1968. Chmn. S. Davis United Fund, 1960; mem. steering com. Am. Landmarks Com., 1963-66; a founder S. Davis Welfare Com., 1960, Bountiful Community Concerts Assn., 1961; bd. dirs. Nat. Multiple Sclerosis Soc., 1963-65, Nat. Mental Health Adv. Bd., 1963- -; adv. bd. Small Bus. Administrn.; exec. com. United Republican Fund. Served to 1st lt. AUS, 1953-56. Recipient Outstanding Alumnus award Utah State U., 1964; Distinguished Service award Bountiful, 1960. Mem. Blue Key, Sigma Nu. Mem. Ch. Jesus Christ Latter-Day Saints (bishop 1969). Bd. editors Outstanding Young Men of America, 1964- 66. Home: 26129 Hidden Valley Farmington MI 48024 Office: Hamilton Internat Devel Co Farmington MI 48024

HEADLEY, HERROLD EUGENE, educator, condr.; b. Athens, O., Jan. 22, 1919; s. Ross Wyattand Pearl Belle (Robinson) H.; B.Sc. in Edn., Ohio State U., 1942; M.M., Ind. U., 1947; Ph.D., North Tex. State U., 1959; m. Ellen Romette Shoemaker, July 26, 1942; children—Erin Jean, Janis Romette. Asst prof. music Tex. Wesleyan Coll., 1947-51, U. Ark., 1951-55; instr. music North Tex. State U., 1955-58; asso. prof. music So. Ill. U., Edwardsville, 1958-63, acting head fine arts div., 1960-61; Adelbert Wells Sprague prof. music, head dept. music U. Me., 1963-67; chmn. dept. music U. R.I., Kingston, 1967-71; chmn. dept. fine arts and humanities Albany (Ga.) Jr. Coll., 1971—; dir. music festivals, 1951—. Organizer, dir. Southwestern Ill. Chorophonic Soc., 1959-63; mem. cultural affairs com. Southwestern Ill. Area Study Commn., 1962-63. Served to 1st lt., F.A., AUS, 1942-45. Mem. Music Tchrs. Nat. Assn., Music Educators Nat. Conf., Me. Music Educators Assn., Am. Assn. U. Profs., Pi Kappa Lambda, Phi Mu Alpha. Episcopalian. Rotarian. Office: Dept Fine Arts Albany Jr Coll Albany GA 31705

HEADLEY, RUSSELL ALBERT, coll. dean; b. New Kensington, Pa., June 20, 1901; s. Nathan Albert and Blanche (Davis) H., A.B. (univ. scholar. 1920-24), U.Pa., 1924, A.M., 1936, Ph.D., 1955: m. Ellen Louise Miller, Dec. 25, 1934; children —Nathan, Ellen, Ruth. Tchr. history Wesley Collegiate Inst., Dover, Del., 1924-25; tchr. English, Punxsutawney (Pa.) High sch., 1925-30; chmn. social studies dept. Jenkintown (Pa.) High Sch., 1930-46; instr. econs. U. Pa., 1946-49; faculty Bucknell U., 1949—, prof. econs., 1955- -, chmn. dept. econs. and bus. adminstrn., 1958—, Christian R. Lindback prof., 1959—, dean Coll. Bus. Adminstrn., 1961—. Mem. bd. sch. dirs. Jenkintown, 1947-49. Mem. Conf. Pa. Economists (exec. com. 1958-59), Pi Gamma Mu, Delta Mu Delta, Tau Kappa Epsilon, Omicron Delta Epsilon. Baptist. Home: College Park Lewisburg PA 17837

HEADLY, JOHN FREDERICK, lawyer; b. West Grove, Pa., Sept. 22, 1903; s. James D. and Margaret (Lynch) H.; A.B., Haverford Coll., 1924; LL.B., U. Pa., 1927; m. Dorothy F. Irwin, Aug. 22, 1928; children—Jonathan I., Elizabeth A. (Mrs. Bruce R. Joyce), Peter D. (dec.), Sarah Mary (Mrs. Peter Maxwell). Admitted to Pa. bar, 1927, and since practiced in Phila.; partner Montgomery, McCracken, Walker & Rhoads, 1940—. Dir. FML Equity Income Fund, Inc., FML Growth Fund, Inc., Keystone Portland Cement Co., Budd Co., Fidelity Mut. Life Ins. Co., Oestereichisch-Ameri Kanische Magnesit, A.G., Rorer-Amchem. Mem. Am., Pa., Phila. bar assns. Home: 1814 Delancey Pl Philadelphia PA 19103 Office: Three Pkwy Philadelphia PA 19102

HEADY, EARL OREL, educator; b. Chase County, Neb., Jan. 25, 1916; s. Orel C. and Jessie (Banks) H.; B.S., U. Neb., 1939, M.S., 1940, D.Sc. (hon.), 1960; Ph.D., State U., 1945; postgrad. U. Chgo., 1941; D.Sc. (honoris causa), U. Uppsala, 1965; m. Marian R. Hoppert, Mar. 1, 1941; children-Marilyn (Mrs. Timothy Kling), Stephen, Barbara. Faculty State U., Ames, 1940—, prof. econs., 1949—, Curtis Distinguished prof., 1956—, dir. Center for Agrl. and Econ. Devel., 1958—; vis. prof. U. Ill., 195O, N.C. State Coll., 1952, Harvard, 1956. Cons. TVA, 1950—, Dept. of Agr., 1953- -, Ministry Food and Agr. Govt. India, 1959, Orgn. for European Econ. Cooperation, AID, Ministry Agr. Kingdom Thailand, 1971, Ministry Agr. and Water Kingdom Saudi Arabia, 1970; chief cons. to Govt. of Greece on nat. research program, 1963, 64; permanent chmn. East-West Conf. Agrl. Economists; cons. Ford Fund.; mem. White House Com. on Domestic Affairs; mem. research and adv. com. AID U.S. Dept. State, 1971—; mem. Commn. on Human Settlements, 1969-70; adv. panel to Nat. Water Commn., 1970-71 Recipient Social Sci. Research Council Faculty award, 1951; fellow Center Advanced Studies Behavioral Scis., 1960-63; recipient distinguished service award Am. Agrl. Editor's Assn. Fellow Am. Statis. Assn., A.A.A.S., Econometric Soc., Am., Western econ. socs.; mem. Can. Agrl. Econ. Soc., Am., Western econ. assns., Econometrica, Am. Farm Econs. Assn. (v.p., editorial council; research and publ. award 1949, 53, 56, 59), Canadian (v.p.), Internat. agr. econs. assns., Hungarian Acad. Sci. (hon.), Phi Kappa Phi, Alpha Zeta, Gamma Sigma Delta (Distinguished Service award). Rotarian. Author books including: Linear Programming Methods, 1958; Agricultural Production Functions, 1960; Resource Demand and Industry structure; Farm Management Economics; Records and Accounting; Agricultural Policy Under Economic Development; Economics of Agricultural Producation and Resource Use: Roots of the Farm Problem; Problems and Policies of Agriculture in Developed Countries; Food, Agriculture and Economic Policy; Economic Models and Quantitative Methods for Decisions and Planning of Agriculture, 1971; Studies in Farm Policies, 1971. Contbr. numerous papers and bulls. in field to profl. jours. Home: 919 Gaskill St Ames IA 50010

HEADY, FERREL, univ. pres.; b. Ferrelview, Mo., Feb. 14, 1916; s. Chester Ferrel and Loren (Wightman) H.; A.B., Washington U., St. Louis, 1937, A.M., 1938, Ph.D., 1940; research fellow adminstrn. law, Brookings Instn., 1940-41; m. Charlotte Audrey McDougall, Feb. 12, 1942; children—Judith Lillian, Richard Ferrel, Margaret Loren, Thomas McDougall. Jr. adminstrv. technician, also adminstrv. asst. Office Dir. Personnel, Dept. Agr., 1941-42; vis. lectr. polit. sci. U. Kansas City, 1946; faculty U. Mich., 1946-67, prof. polit. sci., 1957-67, dir. Inst. Pub. Adminstrn., 1960- 67; acad. v.p. U. N.M., Albuquerque, 1967-68, pres., 1968—. Asst. to commr. Com. Orgn. Exec. Br. of Govt., 1947-49; dir., chief adviser Inst. Pub. Adminstrn., U. Philippines, 1953-54; mem. U.S. delegation Internat. Congress Adminstrn. Scis., Spain, 1956, Germany, 1959, Austria, 1962; exec. bd. Inter-Univ. Case Program, 1956-67; sr. specialist in residence East-West Center, U. Hawaii, 1965; mem. Conf. on Pub. Service, 1965—. Chmn. state affairs com. Ann Arbor (Mich.) Citizens Council, 1949-52; mem. exec. com. Mich. Meml.-Phoenix Project and Inst. Social Research, 1960-66; mem. Gov. Mich. Constl. Revision Study Commn., 1960-62; schs. and univs. adv. bd. Citizens Com. for Hoover Report, 1949-52, 54-58; cons. to Ford Found., 1962; chmn. Council on Grad. Edn. in Pub. Adminstrn., 1966; mem., vice chmn. N.M. Gov.'s Com. on Reorgn. of State Govt., 1967-70. Served to lt. (s.g.) USNR, 1942-46. Mem. Am., Internat. polit. sci. assns., Am. Soc. Pub. Adminstrn. (pres. 1969- 70), Internat. Inst. Adminstrv. Scis., Pub. Personnel Assn., Nat. Municipal League, N.E.A., Am. Assn. Higher Edn., Am. Assn. U. Profs. (chmn. com. T 1957-61), Am. Council Edn. (mem. commn. on fed. relations 1969—), Phi Beta Kappa, Phi Kappa Phi. Presbyn. Author: Administrative Procedure Legislation in the States, 1952; (with Robert H. Pealy) The Michigan Department of Administration, 1956; (with Sybil L. Stokes) Comparative Public Administration: A Selective Annotated Bibliography, 1960; Papers in Comparative Public Administration, 1962; State Constitutions: The Structure of Administration, 1961; Public Administration: A Comparative Perspective, 1966. Contbr. profl. jours. Home: 1901 Roma Av NE Albuquerque NM 87106

HEADY, HAROLD FRANKLIN, ecologist; b. Buhl, Ida., Mar. 29, 1916; s. Orah E. and Edith A. (Philbrick) H.; B.S., U. Ida., 1938; M.S., N.Y. State Coll. Forestry, 1940; postgrad. U. Minn., 1940-41; Ph.D., U. Neb., 1949; m. E. Eleanor Butler, June 12, 1940; children—Carol Marie, Kent Arthur. Range conservationist U.S. Soil Consveration Service, White Salmon, Wash., 1941; asst. prof. N.Y. State Coll. Forestry, Syracuse, 1942; asst. prof. Mont. State U., Bozeman, 1942-47; asso. prof. Tex. A. and M. U., College Station, 1947-51; faculty U. Cal. at Berkeley, 1951—, prof. forestry, 1962—. Pasture cons. FAO, Saudi Arabia, 1962-63. Fulbright Research scholar, East Africa, 1958-59, Australia, 1966; Guggenheim fellow, 1958- 59. Mem. Ecol. Soc. Am., Am Soc. Range Mgmt. Research and numerous publs. on ecol. relationships and methods sampling grasslands and deserts, influence of domestic and wild animals on vegetation, range mgmt. Home: 1864 Capistrano Av Berkeley CA 94707

HEALD, D.F., dairy products exec. Sec., treas. Consol. Dairy Products Co., Seattle. Office: 635 Elliott Av W Seattle WA 98121*

HEALD, HENRY TOWNLEY, consultant; b. Lincoln, Neb., Nov. 8, 1904; s. Frederick De Forest and Nellie (Townley) H.; B.S., State Coll., Wash., 1923; M.S., U. Ill., 1925; D.Eng., Rose Poly. Inst., 1942, Clarkson Coll. Tech., 1948; LL.D., Northwestern U., 1942, Rutgers U., 1952, Columbia, 1954, Hofstra Coll., 1955, Fairleigh Dickinson Coll., 1955, Princeton, U. Pitts., 1956, U. N.Y., 1962, U. Ill., 1963, Ill. Inst. Tech., 1966; D.C.L., N.Y. U., 1956, Case Western Res. U., 1968; L.H.D., Rollins Coll., 1953, Pacific Luth. U., 1966, Brandeis U., 1966, Coll. Wooster, 1966; D.Sc. (hon.) Pratt Inst., 1954, Newark Coll. Engring., 1954, Union Coll., 1956; D.H.L., Cornell Coll., 1967; m. Muriel Starcher, Aug. 4, 1928. Asst. prof. to pres. Armour Inst. Tech., 1927-40; pres. Ill. Inst. Tech., Armour Research Found., Inst. Gas Tech., 1940-52; chancellor N.Y. U., 1952-56; pres., trustee The Ford Found., N.Y.C., 1956-65; partner Heald, Hobson & Assocs., N.Y.C., 1965-67; chmn. Heald, Hobson & Assos., Inc., 1967-71; dir. Lever Brothers Co. Bd. trustees Rollins Coll., Winter Park, Fla. Recipient distinguished service awards Chgo. Jr. Assn. Commerce, 1940, Ill. Jr. C. of C., 1940; Navy award for distinguished civilian service, 1945; Washington award, 1952; Nat. Inst. Social Sci. medal, 1956; Hoover medal 1959; Distinguished Alumni Award Wash. State U., 1962; Alumni Honor award Coll. Engring. U. Ill., 1966; Albert Gallatin award N.Y. U., 1969. Chmn. Mayor's Com. (to reform) Chgo. Bd. Edn., 1946; trustee John Crerar Library, 1945-52; commr., vice chmn. Chgo. Land Clearance Commn., 1947- 52; chmn. South Side Planning Bd., Chgo., 1946-52; trustee Town Hall, Inc., 1952-56; vice chmn. Mayor's Com. for Better Housing, N.Y.C., 1954- 56; commr. Nat. Commn. on Accrediting, 1950-56; chmn. N.Y. State Com. on Higher Edn., 1960. Mem. Am. Soc. Engring. Edn. (pres. 1942-43), A.A.A.S. (v.p. 1946-47), Am. Pub. Works Assn., Am. Soc. C.E., Am. Soc. M.E., Western Soc. Engrs. (pres. 1945-46), Nat. Acad. Engring., Tau Beta Pi, Sigma Tau, Phi Kappa Phi, Chi Epsilon, Theta Xi; also several hon. affiliations. Clubs: Century, University (N.Y.C.); Commercial, Wayfarers Home: 35 Trismen Terrace Winter Park FL 32789

HEALD, JAMES EUDEAN, univ. dean; b. Moscow Station, Mo., Jan. 3, 1929; s. James Wilfred and Elsie Clare (Smith) H.; B.S., Ill. State U., 1951, M.S., 1952; Ph.D. (Univ. fellow), Northwestern U., 1957; m. Phyllis Anita Kosir, Sept. 9, 1951; children—Paul Justin, Laura Kay. Tchr., Evanston (Ill.) Twp. High Sch., 1954-59; asst. prin. Shorewood (Wis.) High Sch., 1959-61; asst. to supt. Ladue (Mo.) Pub. Schs., 1961-63; prof. ednl. adminstrn. Mich. State U., 1963-70; dean Coll. Edn., No. Ill. U., DeKalb, 1970—; mem. faculty U. Wis., 1960-61, Northwestern U., 1958; cons. Nat. Insts. Mental Health, Dept. Def., Collegio Americano de Guatemala. Regional pres. Mich. Edn. Assn., 1967-68. Served with U.S. Army, 1952-54. Recipient U.S. Office Edn. grants, 1969, 70. Mem. Am. Ednl. Research Assn., Am. Assn. Sch. Adminstrs., Nat. Soc. for Study Edn., Phi Delta Kappa. Mem. Christian Ch. (deacon). Author: (with Samuel A. Moore III) The Teacher and Administrative Relationships in School Systems, 1968; (with Louis Romano and Nicholas Georgiady) Selected Readings on General Supervision, 1970. Home: 6 Greenwood Ct De Kalb IL 60115

HEALD, MARK AIKEN, educator, physicist; b. Princeton, N.J., Jan. 27, 1929; s. Mark Mortimer and June (Kilts) H.; B.A., Oberlin Coll., 1950; M.S., Yale, 1951, Ph.D., 1954; m. Jane Dewey, Mar. 19, 1931; children—Kathryn, John S., Charles K. Mem. research staff Project Matterhorn, Princeton, 1954-59; mem. faculty Swarthmore Coll., 1959—, prof. physics, 1970—. U.S. tech. del. UN Conf. Peaceful Uses Atomic Energy, 1958. NSF sci. faculty fellow Culham Lab., U.K. AEA, 1963-64, Plasma Physics Lab., Princeton, 1969-70. Mem. Phi Beta Kappa, Sigma Xi. Author: (with C.B. Wharton) Plasma Diagnostics with Microwaves, 1965; (with W.C. Elmore) Physics of Waves, 1969. Home: 420 Rutgers Av Swarthmore PA 19081

HEALD, MORRELL, educator; b. Oak Park, Ill., July 16, 1922; s. Howard Leslie and Helen (Morrell) H.; A.B., Yale, 1946, A.M., 1947, Ph.D., 1951; m. Barbara Legg, June 25, 1949; children—David M., Seth G., Sarah H. Instr. history Yale, 1950-53; mem. faculty Case Inst. Tech., 1953-68, asso. prof. history, 1958-68, chmn. dept. humanities and social studies, 1959-62; prof. of Am. studies Case Western Res. U., 1968—, chmn. div. spl. interdisciplinary studies, 1971—; vis. prof. Am. history Indian Inst. Tech., Kanpur, 1966-67. Vice pres. Cleveland Heights Your Schools Com., 1962, pres. 1965. Pres. of the First Ward Democratic Club, Cleveland Heights, 1962. Served with AUS, 1943-45; ETO. Mem. Soc. History Tech., Am. Soc. Engring. Edn. (v.p. humanities and Social sci. sect. 1962-63), Am. Hist. Assn., Am. Studies Assn., Ohio Acad. History, Phi Beta Kappa. Episcopalian. Author: The Social Responsibilities of Business: Company and Community, 1900-1960, 1970. Co-editor: The Aims and Organization of Liberal Studies, 1966. Home: 2219 Demington Dr Cleveland Heights OH 44106 Office: 10900 Euclid Cleveland OH 44106

HEALEY, DENIS WINSTON, British polit. ofcl.; b. Mottingham, Kent, Eng., Aug. 30, 1917; s. William and Winifred (Powell) H.; M.A., with 1st class honours in moderns, Balliol Coll., Oxford U., 1938, Jenkyns Exhbn., 1939, Harmsworth sr. scholar, 1940, B.A., 1940, M.A. with 1st class honours in lit. humaniores, 1945; m. Edna May Edmunds, Dec. 21, 1945; three children. Sec. internat. dept. Labour Party, 1945-52; mem. Parliament for S.E. Leeds, 1952-55, for Leeds E., 1955—; sec. of state for def., 1964-70; shadow fgn. sec. in labour opposition, 1970—. Councillor Royal Inst. Internat. Affairs, 1948-60, Inst. Strategic Studies, 1958-61; mem. Brit. delegation Commonwealth Relations Conf., Can., 1949; Brit. del. Consulative Assembly, Council of Europe, 1952-54, Internat. Parliamentary Union Conf., Washington, 1953, Western European Union and Council of Europe, 1963-65. Served to maj., Brit. Army, 1939-45; N. Africa, Italy. Mem. Order Brit. Empire. Mem. Fabian Soc. (exec. com. 1954-61). Author: The Curtain Falls, 1951; New Fabian Essays, 1952; Neutralism, 1955; Fabian International Essays, 1956; A Neutral Belt in Europe, 1958; NATO and American Security, 1959; The Race Against the H Bomb, 1960; Labour Britain and the World, 1963. Office: House of Commons London NW 1 England

HEALEY, GEORGE, lawyer; b. Lincoln. Neb., July 7, 1905; s. Thomas Martin and Wilhemina (Simon) H.; LL.B., U. Neb., 1929; m. Rose M. Gerhold, Feb. 5, 1930; children-Patrick W., Janet (Mrs. David P. Weber), Susan Rose (Mrs. Edward Fitzgerald, Jr.). Admitted to Neb. bar, 1929, since practiced in Lincoln; now mem. law firm Healey, Healey, Brown & Burchard. Mem. bd. examiners Neb. Bar Commn., 1942—. Mem. Am. Coll. of Trial Lawyers, Am. Nebr. (pres. 1962-63; mem. ho. of dels. 1954-55, jud. council 1954-57), Lincoln (pres. 1946-47) bar assns., Nat. Conf. Bar Examiners (sec. 1952-53), Internat. Assn. Ins. Counsel, Assn. Ins. Attys., Phi Delta Phi, Delta Sigma Rho. Republican. Roman Catholic. Home: 3434 Grimsby Lane Lincoln NB 68502 Office: Profl Arts Bldg Lincoln NB 68508

HEALEY, HARRY JOSEPH, educator, endodontist; b. Indpls., Nov. 28, 1906; s. Maurice Francis and Louise (McNally) H.; A.B., Butler U., 1931; D.D.S., Ind. U., 1931, M.S.D., 1958; m. Elizabeth Ann Samsa, Dec. 17, 1945; children—George Michael, Kenneth Raymond. Mem. faculty Ind. U. Sch. Dentistry, 1931—, prof. endodontics, chmn. dept., 1967—, cons. VA, 1967-. Served to comdr. USNR, 1943-46. Diplomate Am. Bd. Endodontics. Fellow Am. Coll. Dentists; mem. Am. Assn. Endodontists (pres. 1955), Ind. U. Sch. Dentistry Alumni Assn. (pres. 1957; Distinguished faculty mem. award 1970), Ind. Dental Assn. (pres. 1967), Indpls. Dist. Denta Soc. (pres. 1956), A.A.A.S., Omicron Kappa Upsilon. Author: Endodontics, 1960; also monograph and articles. Home: 3243 W 29th St Indianapolis IN 46222

HEALEY, JAMES FRANCIS, corp. exec.; b. Cambridge, Mass., Jan. 13, 1920; s. Hugh Henry and Mary Elizabeth (Seifen) H.; B.S., Mass. Inst. Tech., 1941, M.S., 1948; m. Madelon Kathryn O'Brien, Oct. 11, 1942; children—James J., John M. Commd. 2d lt. USAAF, 1941, advanced through grades to col. USAF, 1955; various research and devel. assignments in field aircraft and missiles; ret., 1955; dir. research and planning Mpls.-Honeywell, St. Petersburg, Fla., 1957-61, v.p., gen. mgr. aero. div., 1961-66; group exec. def. space group Internat. Tel. & Tel. Co., N.Y.C., 1966-67; pres., dir., chief operating officer KMS Industries, Inc., 1967—. Mem. USAF Sci. Adv. Bd., 1958—. Asso. fellow Am. Inst. Aeros. and Astronautics; mem. Fla. Council of 100, Air Force Assn., Navy League. Club: St. Petersburg Yacht. Home: 1361 Snell Harbor Dr St Petersburg FL 33704 Office: 220 E Huron St Ann Arbor MI 48108

HEALEY, JAMES STEWART, librarian; b. Chgo. July 14, 1931; s. James Alfred and Bernice (Stewart) H.; A.B., Stonehill Coll., 1955; M.S., Simmons Coll., 1958; m. Evelyn J. Murphy, Aug. 10, 1958; children-James F., Siobhan E., Kathleen E. Reference asst. Boston Pub. Library, 1955-56; librarian, Stonehan, Mass., 1956-61; city librarian, New Bedford, Mass., 1961-67; chief div. library extension services Dept. State Library Services R.I. Providence, 1967-68; asst. prof. Grad. Library Sch., U. R.I., 1968—; library cons. Somerset, Mass., also Cumberland and Woonsocket, R.I. pub. libraries, Swain Sch. Design, New Bedford, No. R.I. Regional Library, Lincoln, R.I.; teaching asst. Columbia U., 1970-71, chmn. Restoration Ball Com., New Bedford, 1962-63; chmn. New Bedford Summer Festival, 1963; chmn. Nat. Library Week Com. R.I., 1967—. Mem. New Bedford Port Soc., Old Dartmouth Hist. Soc., Waterfront Historic Area league. Recipient U.S. Title II B fellowship, 1969-70. Mem. Am., New Eng., R.I. library assns. Home: 30 Carriage Hill Rd North Kingstown RI 02852 Office: Grad Library Sch U RI Kingston RI 02852

HEALEY, JOSEPH PETER, banker; b. Cambridge, Mass., Nov. 29, 1915; s. Hugh Henry and Mary Elizabeth (Seifen) H.; A.B., Harvard, 1938, M.B.A., 1942, LL.B., 1945; m. Irene Wilson, Oct. 31, 1943; 1 son, Peter Wilson. Law clk. to U.S. dist. judge, 1945-46; practice in Boston, 1947-57; asso. prof. law Boston Coll. Law, 1949-52, lectr. law, 1952—; exec. dir. Mass. Spl. Comm. Taxation, 1953-57; partner firm Hemenway & Barnes, Boston, 1953-58; v.p., gen. counsel Boston Edison Co., 1959-63, now dir.; pres., dir. Middlesex Bank, N.A., Everett, Mass., since 1963; Boston Mut. Life Ins. Co.; trustee Charleston Savs. Bank. Mem. gov. council Adminstrv. Conf. U.S., 1961-63. Commnr. trust fund, Town of Arlington, Mass. Trustee U. Mass., 1959—. Served with Q.M.C., AUS, 1942- 43. Mem. Am., Boston bar assns. Clubs: Algonquin (Boston); Winchester Country. Home: 14 Winchester Rd Arlington MA 02174 Office: 431 Broadway Everett MA 02149

HEALEY, VINCENT PATRICK, naval officer; b. N.Y.C., Mar. 13, 1918; s. John William and Katherine Mary (Clancy) H.; student Fordham U.; B.S., U.S. Naval Acad., 1940; M.S., Mass. Inst. Tech., 1949; m. Helen Marie Clarke, Oct. 27, 1945; children—Dominic Mark, John Stephen, Mary Helen, Jane Marie, Peter Joseph. Commd. ensign USN, 1940, advanced through grades to rear adm., 1966; active duty during World War II included participation in Philippine Liberation; various staff and command posts, 1949-52; with Bur. of Ordnance, Dept. of Navy, Washington, 1952-55; staff officer, exec. officer ship service including U.S.S. Northampton, 1955-59; asst. plans officer Office Asst. Chief for Research, Devel., Test and Evaluation, 1959-63; comdr. Destroyer Squadron 3, Viet Nam coast, 1963- 65; dep. mgr. Anti-Submarine Warfare Systems Project, 1965-67; comdr. Cruiser Destroyer Flotilla 6, also comdr. in 6th Fleet, Mediterranean, 1967-69; dir. undersea and strategic warfare devel. div. Office Chief Naval Operations, 1969—. Decorated Bronze Star. Mem. Sigma Xi. Home: 1259 Delaware Av Washington DC 20024 Office: Chief of Naval Operations Pentagon Washington DC 20350

HEALY, ARTHUR KELLY DAVID, artist, author, educator, architect; b. N.Y.C., Oct. 15, 1902; s. Thomas and Elizabeth (Kelly) H.; A.B., Princeton, 1924, M.F.A., 1926; student Fontainebleau (France) Summer Sch. Fine Arts, 1925; fellow Am. art, U. Pa., 1945; m. Troy Tapp, Sept. 2, 1944; children—Sophia Warner, Arthur Kelly David. Practice architecture, N.Y.C. and Rutland, Vt., 1957; supr. PWA, 1938-40; archtl. engr. Portsmouth (Vt.) Navy Yard, 1941-43; mem. faculty Middlebury (Vt.) Coll., 1943-, prof. dept. fine arts, 1958-68, prof. emeritus, 1968; numerous exhbns. paintings through Italy, Eng., U.S.; 10 one man exhbns., Boston, N.Y.C.; works rep. Harvard, Canajoharie (N.Y.), Mus., New Britain (Conn.) Mus., Kansas City (Mo.) Mus., Boston Mus. Fine Arts, Fleming Mus., Burlington, Vt., Portland (Me.) Mus., Addison Gallery Am. Art, Andover, Mass., Bennington (Vt.) Mus., Middlebury Coll. (Vt.), Norwich U., Northfield, Vt., also pvt. collections; illustrator comml. jours. Pres. Motion Picture Operation Symphony Theatre, Inc., N.Y.C., 1944—. Former Democratic candidate for Vt. senator, also town rep. Middlebury. Chmn. planning com., trustee Yaddo Corp., Saratoga Springs, N.Y., 1956-; chmn. bd. Sheldon Mus., Middlebury; mem. Vt. Bd. of Historic Sites, 1967; chmn. Champlain Celebration, 1960; mem. bd. Mt. Independence Assos. Recipient prizes for water color painting Am. Water Color Soc., Audubon Artists, Boston Soc. Ind. Artists, Boston Soc. Water Color Painters, No., Mid. and So. Vt. Artists, Springfield (Mass.) Art Assn., Stockbridge (Mass.) Art Assn. Vt. Profl. Artists, Exhbn. Vt. Artists Norwich U., 1968, 69, 7O, others. Mem. N.Y.C., Washington water color clubs, Am., Phila. water color socs., Audubon Artists, Springfield Art Assn., Boston Festival Fine Arts, College de Pataphysique (Paris), Club di Rigalio (Rome, Italy), Irish Georgian Soc. Author: (with Alfred Frankenstein) Two Journeymen Painters; also numerous articles. Home: R D 3 Middlebury VT 05753

HEALY, DANIEL J., union ofcl. Dir. Region 4 Dept. Orgn. AFL-CIO. Office: 1025 Transportation Bldg 608 S Dearborn Chicago IL 60605*

HEALY, GEORGE ROBERT, ednl. adminstr.; b. Milw., May 31, 1923; s. Russell Kerfoot and Elmina (Hodgson) H.; B.A., Oberlin Coll., 1948; M.A., U. Minn., 1950, Ph.D., 1956; m. Dorothy Ann Kohli, Aug. 14, 1948; children—David George, Thomas Robert, Roger Knowles. Instr. history U. Minn., 1951-52; instr., then asst. prof. history Mass. Inst. Tech., 1952-57; asso. prof. cultural heritage and history Bates Coll., 1957-62, chmn. dept. cultural heritage, 1958-62, dean faculty, 1962-71, provost, 1970-71; v.p. for academic affairs Coll. William and Mary, 1971—, vis. prof., summer 1960. Served with USAAF, 1943-45. Mem. Am. Hist. Assn., Soc. French Hist. Studies, Conf. Acad. Deans. Contbr. profl. jours. Editor, translator: (Montesquieu) Lettres persanes, 1964. Home: 298 E Queen's Dr Williamsburg VA 23185

HEALY, GEORGE WILLIAM, Jr., editor; b. Natchez, Miss., Sept. 22, 1905; s. George William and Rosa Lee (Longmire) H.; A.B., U. Miss., 1926; m. Margaret Hoy Alford, Sept. 22, 1927; children—George William III, Floyd Alford (dec.). Began as corr. for A.P., and several newspapers while at coll.; reporter Knoxville (Tenn.) Sentinel, 1926; with The Times-Picayune, New Orleans, since 1926, as reporter, then city editor, 1931, mng. editor, 1936, editor, 1952—; exec. editor The Times-Picayune-New Orleans States- Item, 1964-69; treas. Times-Picayune Pub. Corp., 1939, v.p., 1942—, dir., 1948—; dir. A.P., 1957-66, v.p., 1965-66; lectr.(part time), Tulane U., 1946-52; dir. domestic branch. O.W.I. on leave from the Times-Picayune, 1944; cons. on domestic problems O.W.I., 1945. Trustee Jefferson Mil. Coll. 1950-62; bd. dirs. The Adv. Council, Inc., 1954-60. Decorated Caballero de Order de Cristobal Colon (Domincan Republic) 1946; Order Leopole II (Belgium), 1956; Star of Solidarity (Italy), 1958. Chmn. New Orleans chpt. A.R.C., 1956-58. Mem. A.P. Mng. Editors Assn. (chmn. 1943-46). Am. Soc. Newspaper Editors (pres. 1958-59), Inter Am. Press Assn. (dir. 1950-58), S.A.R. (pres. La. 1951), Sigma Nu, Sigma Delta Chi (pres. 1946), Omicron Delta Kappa. Democrat. Methodist. Mason. Clubs: Recess (pres. 1947-48), Southern Yacht, Boston, Louisiana, Internat. House (v.p. 1964-67) (New Orleans); Circumnavigators (N.Y.C.); National Press (Washington); Mount Kenya Safari (East Africa) Home: 2110 State St New Orleans LA 70118 Office: 3800 Howard Av New Orleans LA 70140

HEALY, HAROLD HARRIS, Jr., lawyer; b. Denver, Aug. 27, 1921; s. Harold Harris and Lorena (Isom) H.; A.B., Yale, 1943, LL.B., 1949; m. Elizabeth A. Debevoise, May 24, 1952; 1 son, Harold Harris III. Admitted to N.Y. bar, 1949; now mem. firm Debevoise, Plimpton, Lyons & Gates, N.Y.C., resident partner European office, Paris, 1964-66; exec. asst. to U.S. atty. gen., 1957-58. Bd. dirs. Legal Aid Soc., 1968—, treas., 1970—. Served from 2d lt. to capt. F.A., AUS, 1943-46; ETO. Decorated Bronze Star medal. Mem. Am., N.Y. State bar assns., Assn. Bar City N.Y. (sec.) 1959-61), Order of Coif, Am. Soc. Internat. Law, France-Am. Soc., Pilgrims U.S., Phi Beta Kappa, Zeta Psi, Phi Delta Phi. Republican. Episcopalian. Clubs: University, Century Assn. (N.Y.C.); Travellers, Nouveau Cercle (Paris); Metropolitan (Washington). Home: 1170 Fifth Av New York City NY 10029 Office: 320 Park Av New York City NY 10022

HEALY, JOSEPH JOHN, airline exec.; b. Caldwell, N.J., Aug. 24, 1926; s. Thomas P. and Agnes (O'Dowd) H.; student Montclair Acad., 1946-47; m. Audrey Barton, Sept. 6, 1952; children—John Thomas, Bridget Ann, Patrick, Timothy, James, Shaun Michael. With Flying Tiger Line, Inc., Newark, Los Angeles, 1948—, dir. ground operations, 1956-63, v.p., 1963-70, sr. v.p., gen. mgr. terminals, 1970—, dir., 1971—; chmn. Bradley Facilities, Inc. Mem. traffic adv. com. Internat. Air Transport Assn. Bd. dirs. Nat. Com. on Internat. Trade Documentation; mem. com. for continuing edn. Grad. Sch. Mgmt., U. Cal. at Los Angeles, bd. dirs. Exec. Program Alumni Assn. Served with USNR, 1944-46. Home: 7248 W 88th Pl Los Angeles CA 90045 Office: 7401 World Way West Los Angeles CA 90009

HEALY, KENT TENNEY, educator; b. Chgo., Feb. 2, 1902; s. William and Mary Sylvia (Tenney) H.; A.B., Harvard, 1921, student Law Sch., 1923-24; B.S. in E.E., Mass. Inst. of Tech., 1923; M.A., Yale, 1945; m. Ruth Emily Allen, Nov. 3, 1928; children—Ruth Tenney, William Kent, Kent Allen, Sylvia Kent. Switchboard operator, N.Y., N.H. and H.R.R., 1922, insp., 1924-25, cost engr., 1925-26; studying transp. in Europe, 1926- 27; asst. prof. transp. Yale, 1928-35, asst. prof. econs., 1935-40, asso. prof., 1940-45, T. DeWitt Cuyler Prof. transp., 1945, chmn. com. on transp. 1943-69, chmn. econs. dept., 1945-51, dir. div. social scis., 1956-59; cons. Conn. Commn. on Reorgn. of State Depts., 1935; transp. cons. Nat. Resources Planning Bd., 1940, Bituminous Coal Div., Dept. of Interior, 1941; to adminstr. of Land-Lease, 1942-44, F.E.A., 1944-45; also at various times to pvt. transp. agys.; mem. Conn. Hwy. Adv. Commn., 1943-45; chmn. Conn. Savs. Bank R.R. Investment Com., 1945-64; mem. Reorgn. Com., dir. N.Y. H.H. and H. R.R. Co., 1947-48; dir. Conn. Co. 1947-64; mem. Transp. Council for Dept. of Commerce, 1952-57. Chmn. bd. finance, Killingworth, Conn. 1959-65, chmn. planning and zoning commn., 1965-68; mem. Conn. Estuary Regional Planning Agy., 1970—. Mem. Am. Econ. Assn., Royal Econ. Soc., Am. Econ. Hist. Assn., Sigma Xi, Delta Psi. Club: Graduate (New Haven, Conn.). Author: Steam Railroad Electrification, 1929; Economics of Transportation in America, 1940; The Effects of Scale in the Railroad Industry, 1961. Home: Chestnut Hill Rd Killingsworth CT 06520 Office: Strathcona Hall Yale U New Haven CT 06520

HEALY, MARY, (Mary Healy Hayes), singer, actress; b. New Orleans, Apr. 14, 1918; d. John Joseph and Viola (Armbruster) Healy; student parochial schs., New Orleans; m. Peter Lind Hayes, Dec. 19, 1940; children—Peter Michael, Cathy Lind. With 20th Century Fox, Hollywood, Cal.; pictures: Second Fiddle, Stardust, 20,000 Men a Year, and others, 1937-40; Broadway prodns. Count Me In, Common Ground, Around the World, 1943-46; TV series with husband Inside U.S.A., Peter and Mary Show, Stork Club, Star of the Family and Peter Lind Hayes Radio show, CBS, 1954-57; Broadway prodn. Who Was That Lady, 1957-58; Peter Lind Hayes show, ABC-TV, 1958-59; Peter and Mary, ABC-Radio, 1959—; Peter and Mary in Las Vegas TV-film; appeared with husband at Supper Clubs; Star WOR radio show, 6 yrs. Recent film: The 5000 Fingers of Dr. T., 1953. Appeared in: Peter Loves Mary, 1960. Club: Pelham Country. Roman Catholic. Home: 3538 Pueblo Way Las Vegas NV 89109

HEALY, NICHOLAS JOSEPH, lawyer; b. N.Y.C., Jan. 4, 1910; s. Nicholas Joseph and Frances Cecilia (McCarthy) H.; A.B., Holy Cross Coll., 1931; J.D., Harvard, 1934; m. Margaret Marie Ferry, Mar. 29, 1937; children-Nicholas, Margaret, Rosemary (Mrs. James F. Bell 3d), Mary Louise (Mrs. William R. White), Donall, Kathleen. Admitted to N.Y. bar, 1935; pvt. practice, N.Y.C., 1935-42, 48—; mem. Healy & Baillie and predecessor law firms, 1948— ; special assistant to atty. gen. U.S., 1945-48; tchr. admiralty law N.Y.U. Sch. Law, 1947—, adj. prof., 1960—. Chmn. USCG industry adv. com. on Rules of the Road. Served to lt. (s.g.) USNR, 1942-45. Mem. Maritime Law Assn. U.S. (pres. 1964-66), Assn. Average Adjusters U.S. (chmn. 1959- 60), Am. (ho. dels. 1964-66), N.Y. State bar assns., Comité Maritime Internat. (hon. v.p. 27th conf. 1965), Assn. Bar City N.Y., Soc. Friendly Sons St. Patrick. Democrat. Roman Cath. Clubs: Harvard, India House, Downtown Athletic (N.Y.C.). Contbr. chpts. on admiralty to Annual Survey Am. Law, 1948—. Author (with Sprague) Cases on Admiralty, 1950; (with Currie) Cases and Materials on Admiralty, 1965. Home: 132 Tullamore Rd Garden City NY 11530 Office: 29 Broadway New York City NY 10006

HEALY, PATRICK, assn. executive; b. Los Angeles, Apr. 30, 1910; s. Patrick and Mary (Sedwick) H.; A.B., Amherst Coll., 1932; postgrad. Syracuse U., 1932- 33; m. Ruth Potter Snagg, May 26, 1934 (dec. Jan. 1955); 1 son, Patrick IV; m. 2d, Martha Ann Dumke, June 3, 1957; children—Edmund, Nancy Lee. Field cons. League Va. Municipalities, 1933-34; exec. dir. N.C. League Municipalities, 1934-42; editor-pub. Southern City, 1937-42; owner-mgr. Pepsi-Cola Bottling Co., Odgen, Utah, 1946-55; chmn. Utah Tax Commn., 1950-54; exec. v.p. Nat. League of Cities, Washington, 1954—; editor Nation's Cities, 1963—; pres. Am. Inst. for Municipal Research, Edn. and Tng., Inc., 1958—, League Cities-Conf. Mayors, Inc., 1969—; sec. Urban Studies, Inc. 1960—. U.S. del. Internat. Congress Local Authorities, Rome, 1955, The Hague, 1957, Berlin, 1959, Tel Aviv, 1960, Brussels, 1963, Inter-Am. Municipal Congress, San Juan, 1954, Panama, 1956, Rio de Janeiro, 1958, San Diego, 1960, Punta del Este, 1962, Caracas, 1966; v.p. Internat. Union Local Authorites, The Hague, 1971—; mem. U.S. Census Adv. Com. on State and Local Govt. Statistics, 1956—; Mem. dept. urban transp. planning Hwy. Research Bd., Nat. Acad. Scis., 1962—; adv. council on police tng. Internat. Assn. Chiefs of Police, 1964—; mem. Pres.'s Com. on Employment of Handicapped, 1963—, Pres.'s Nat. Adv. Council on Extension and Continuing Edn., 1966-69. Chmn. Weber County (Utah) Republican Central Com., 1946- 50, chmn. 1st Utah Congl. Dist. Rep. Com., 1946-50; del. Rep. Nat. Conv., 1948; candidate for mayor of Ogden, 1947. Bd. dirs. Internat. Eye Found., Govtl. Affairs Inst., Washington 1971—; trustee Pub. Adminstrn. Service, Chgo., 1955—. Served to lt. comdr. USNR, World War II; comdr. Res. Recipient Order of Municipal Merit, Inter-Am. Municipal Orgn., 1968. Mem. U.S. C. of C. (co-chmn. nat. urban leadership adv. council 1968—), Am. Soc. Pub. Adminstrn., Internat. City Mgrs. Assn. (hon.), Am. Soc. Assn. Execs., Internat. Municipal Parking Congress, Nat. Trust for Historic Preservation, Psi Upsilon. Episcopalian. Mason (Shriner). Clubs: Weber (Ogden, Utah); Chevy Chase, Internat., Columbia Country, Nat. Capital Trap and Skeet, Army and Navy, Nat. Press (Washington). Author reports. Home: 2500 Calvert St NW Washington DC 20008 Office: 1612 K St NW Washington DC 20006

HEALY, PAUL FRANCIS, newspaperman; b. Chgo., Mar. 1, 1915; s. Waldo and Julia (Henzie) H.; Ph.B., Loyola U., Chgo., 1938; m. Constance Maas, Jan. 2, 1943 (div.); children—Kevin, Julie, Monica, Jane, Kathleen. Reporter, Chgo. Tribune, 1938-43; asso ed editor Popular Mechanics mag., 1943-45; mem. Chgo. bur. Time, Inc., 1945; civilian information officer War Dept., 1945; Washington corr., polit. columnist N.Y. Daily News, 1945—. Roman Cath. Club: Nat. Press (Washington). Author: (with B. K. Wheeler) Yankee From The West, 1962; Cissy, A Biography of Eleanor M. Patterson, 1966. Contbr. nat. periodicals, Office: Nat Press Bldg Washington DC 20004

HEALY, ROBERT EDWARD, bus. exec.; b. Bklyn., Aug. 15, 1904; s. Walter F. and Florence D. (Davis) H.; grad. Dwight Prep. Sch., N.Y.C., Pace Inst., N.Y.C.; D.C.S (hon.), Pace Coll.; m. Lilie Rose, Aug. 3, 1927 (div. Jan. 1957); children—Lilie Jane, Patricia Anne, Robert Edward (dec.); m. 2d, Wayne Clark, Jan. 11, 1957; 2 sons, Edward Walter, James Davis. Asst. to v.p. in charge sales promotion Johns-Manville Co., 1928-33; mgr. prodn. sect., advt. dept. Colgate-Palmolive Co., 1934-36, asst. advt. mgr., 1936-39, brand advt. mgr., 1939-42, gen. advt. mgr., 1942-46, became v.p. in charge advt., 1946; dir., v.p., treas. McCann-Erickson, Inc., 1952-53, gen. mgr. N.Y. office, 1954, exec. v.p. charge N.Y. office, 1955-58, mem. finance com., 1956-62, vice chmn. bd., 1958-61; chmn. McCann Erickson Corp. (Internat.), 1956-58; pres. Inter-public, S.A., Geneva, Switzerland, 1962-65; exec. v.p. Interpub. Group of Cos., Inc., 1965-67, pres., chief exec., mem. exec. com., 1967-72, chmn. bd., 1968—. Clubs: N.Y. Athletic (N.Y.C.); Ocean Reef, Miami,; Rod and Reel. Home: Plantation Key FL 33314 Office: 1271 Av of Americas New York City NY 10020

HEALY, ROY, space program exec.; b. N.Y.C., Jan. 1, 1915; s. Morgan Joseph and Grace (Mulholland) H.; student aero. engring. Casey Jones Tech. Sch., 1934-39; m. Gloria Corey, Dec. 23, 1940; children—Joy, Adele, Lee, Lyn. Experimenter rocket Propulsion, 1927—; active worker Am. Rocket Soc. (affiliate Am. Soc. M.E.) during the group's pioneering period developing and testing liquid propellant rocket devices, 1932-41; pres. Am. Rocket Soc., 1942, 47, then dir. Project engr. for devel. of air craft rocket projectiles and launching devices, Air Material Command, U.S.A.A.F., Wright Field, World War II; conducted combat service tests of secret rocket weapons, CBI 1944; assisted in orgn. U.S.A.A.F. rocket devel. center, Dover, Del., 1944-46; chief test and preliminary design M.W. Kellogg Co., 1946-53; staff N. Am. Aviation, Inc., Rocketdyne div. program mgr. Jupiter and Army 1.5 million LB engines, 1958; asst. program mgr. Saturn S II Stage, Space div. N.AM. Rockwell Corp., 1962—. Lectr. in field. Fellow Am. Inst. Aeros. and Astronautics. Contbr. numerous articles on rocket and jet propulsion research to profl. jours.

HEALY, SARAH LUTES, univ. dean; b. Richmond, Mich.; d. Charles Burton and Ella (Mills) Lutes; student Ward Belmont Jr. Coll., 1826-27; A.B., U. Mich., 1930; student Cornell U., summers 1930-31, Syracuse U., 1932-34; LL.D., U. Ala., 1971; m. Harry T. Healy, July 25, 1940. Residence hall social dir. U. Mich., 1930- 32, asso. dean women, 1949-54; dir. residence system Syracuse U., 1934-35; asst. dean women, dir. residence U. Ariz., 1935-39; dean women So. br. U. Ida., 1939-40; dean women U. Ala., 1954—. Mem. Am. Personnel and Guidance Assn., Ala. Edn. Assn., Nat. Assn. Women Deans and Counselors (univ. chmn. 1961-63), Nat. Vocational Guidance Assn., So. Personnel Assn., Am. Assn. U. Women, League Women Voters, N.E.A., Alpha Lambda Delta (mem. nat. council; dir. 1954—; nat. v.p. 1962—), Delta Delta Delta, Mortar Board. Democrat. Episcopalian. Home: 2200 S Ocean Blvd Delray Beach FL 33444

HEALY, THOMAS MORRIS, govt. ofcl.; b. New Orleans, Feb. 19, 1901; s. Thomas M. and Mary Ann (Carroll) H.; student pub. schs.; m. Olga Marie Adams, Sept. 5, 1923; children—Thomas M. (USMC), Donald J., Elaine M., Miriam M. (Mrs. Richard G. Gibson), Gerald P., James D., Louis D., Doris A. (Mrs. David L. Schneider), Eileen (Mrs. Thomas Smith), Kathleen. Messenger S.P. Co., New Orleans, 1915-20, sec. to v.p. and gen. mgr., 1920- 23; traffic dept. Ill. Central System, 1923-24, Southern Pine Assn., 1924-25; successivley field sec. Assn. Am. R.R.'s, mem. Southeast Shippers' Adv. Bd., car service agt., dist. mgr., 1925-55; mgmt. mem. R.R. Retirement Bd., 1955—. Recipient certificate award for handling mil. traffic, World war II, War Dept.; testimonial for contbns. to transportation Southeast Shippers Adv. Bd. Home: 205 Ridge Rd Wilmette IL 60091 Office: 844 Rush St Chicago IL 60611

HEALY, WILLIAM J., brewery exec.; b. St. Louis, 1914; ed. St. Louis U. With Falstaff Brewing Corp., 1936—, chief accountant, 1951-54, asst. treas., 1954-55, asst. sec., asst. treas., 1955-60, treas., 1960-64, treas., controller, 1964-68, v.p., treas., 1968—. Served with AUS, 1943-45. Home: 5 Chaminade Dr Creve Coeur, MO 63141. Office: 5050 Oakland St Louis MO 63110

HEALY, J. W., lawyer; b. Toronto, Ont., Can., Oct. 12, 1917; grad. St. Michael's Coll. (Can.); LL.B., Osgoode Hall (Can.). Admitted to Ont. bar, 1948; partner firm Miller, Thomson, Hicks, Sedgewock, Lewis & Healy, Toronto. Office: 21 King St W Toronto 1 Ontario Canada*

HEAMAN, WILLIAM MCPHERSON, engring co. exec.; former naval officer; b. White Salmon, Wash., Apr. 2, 1910; s. Bertram M. and Harriet (McPherson) H.; B.S. in Civil Engring., U. Wash., 1935; grad. Armed Forces Staff Coll., 1947; postgrad. George Washington U., 1961; m. Mildred Coe, Oct. 8, 1937; children—Patricia Louise (Mrs. L. Murphy), Richard Coe. Engr. with Nat. Tank and Pipe Co., Portland, Ore., 1935-41; commd. lt. (j.g.) Civil Engr. Corps, U.S. Navy, 1941, advanced through grades to rear adm., 1965; assigned Pearl Harbor, 1941-44, Newport, R.I., 1944-47; mem. staff Fleet Marine Force, Pacific, 1947-50; assigned Seabee Center, Pt. Hueneme, Cal., 1950- 51, Bur. Yards and Docks, Washington, 1951-55; pub. works officer Naval Air Sta., Alameda, Cal., 1955-59; officer charge constrn., Philippines, 1959-60; asst. chief Bur. Yards and Docks, 1960-61; comdr. Seabees, Atlantic Fleet, 1962-63; dir. S.E. div. Bur. Yards and Docks, 1963-65; officer charge constrn., Vietnam, 1965; comdr. Pacific div. Naval Facilities Engring. Command, 1965-69; pres. Heaman Engring. Co., 1970—. Registered profl. engr., Ore., Fla., Hawaii. Mem. Soc. Am. Mil. Engrs., Nat. Soc. Profl. Engrs., Nat. Rifle Assn., Sigma Chi. Office: Box 6355 Honolulu HI 96818

HEANEY, GERALD WILLIAM, U.S. judge; b. Goodhue, Minn., Jan. 29, 1918; s. William J. and Johanna (Ryan) H.; student St. Thomas Coll., 1935-37; B.S.L., U. Minn., 1939. LL.B., 1941; m.

Eleanor R. Schmitt, Dec. 1, 1945; children—William M., Carol J. Admitted to Minn. bar, 1941; lawyer securities div. Dept. of Commerce Minn., 1941-42; mem. firm Lewis. Hammer, Heaney, Weyl & Halverson, Duluth, 1946-69; judge 8th Jud. Circuit, U.S. Court Appeals, 1969—. Mem. Dem. Nat. Com. from Minn., 1955. Bd. regents U. Minn., 1964-65. Served from pvt. to capt., AUS, 1942-46. Mem. Am., Minn. bar assns. Roman Catholic. Home: 235 Pike Lake Duluth MN 55802 Office: US Court of Appeals Duluth MN 55802

HEANEY, ROBERT CECIL CURTIS, lawyer; b. Big Rapids, Mich., Jan. 22, 1906; s. Herbert Melville and Harriet Irene (Emmons) H.; student Grand Rapids Jr. Coll., 1924-26; A.B., J.D., U. Mich., 1930; m. Barbara Helen Patton, Feb. 14, 1931; children—Robert Daniel, Brian Richard, Marilyn Jean. Admitted to Mich. bar, 1930, Ariz. bar, 1971; since practiced Grand Rapids; mem. McCobb and Heaney, Van & Hof, 1936—; officer, dir. several Mich. corps. Treas. Mich. Republican State Central Com., 1949-57. Bd. dirs. YMCA, Arthritis and Rheumatism Found., pres. Mich. chpt. Mem. Am. Judicature Soc., Am., Mich., Grand Rapids bar assns., State Bar Ariz., Phi Sigma Kappa, Phi Alpha Delta. Conglist. (trustee; dir. League to uphold Congl. principles). Clubs: Peninsular, University Mich. Alumni (past pres.), Rotary (Grand Rapids); Tucson Nat. Golf. Home: 645 Cardinal Dr SE East Grand Rapids MI 49506 Office: Union Bank Bldg Grand Rapids MI 49502

HEANEY, ROBERT PROULX, med. educator; b. Omaha, Nov. 10, 1927; s. Clarence Earl and Lorraine (Proulx) H.; B.S., Creighton U., 1947, M.D., 1951; m. Barbara Rose Reardon, July 12, 1952; children—Robert Michael, Marian Ghislaine, Barbara Lorraine, Rachel Ann, Margaret Reardon, Christopher Joseph, Elizabeth Joan. Intern St. Louis City Hosp., 1951-52, asst. resident internal medicine, 1952-53; clin. fellow Okla. Med. Research Hosp., Oklahoma City, 1953-55; clin. asso. NIH, 1955-57; mem. faculty Creighton U. Sch. Medicine, 1957—, prof. medicine, chmn. dept., 1961-69, v.p. health scis., 1971—. Mem. dental tng. com. NIH, 1962-66, gen. medicine B study sect., 1966-71; orth tng. com., 1971—; chmn. Gordon Research Conf. Bones and Teeth, 1966. Served with USPHS, 1955-57. Fellow A.C.P.; mem. Am. Soc. Clin. Investigation, Central Soc. Clin. Research (council 1966-69), Endocrine Soc., A.A.A.S., N.Y. Acad. Sci., Am. Fedn. Clin. Research. Roman Catholic. Mem. editorial bd. Calcified Tissue Research, 1967—, Jour. Clin. Endocrinology and Metabolism, 1968- 70. Home: 5210 Burt St Omaha NB 68132

HEAPS, ALVIN EUGENE, labor union exec.; b. Royalton, Ill., Dec. 4, 1919; s. John and Susie (Sprouse) H.; m. Evelyn M. Lassa, May 22, 1941 (div. Feb. 1968); 1 dau., Melody M.; m. 2d, Jo Anne C. Gibilaro, Mar. 10, 1968. Mem. Retail, Wholesale and Dept. Store Union, 1941—, pres. Chgo. joint bd., 1946-48, internat. sec.-treas., 1948—, also chmn. bd. trustees union industry pension fund and union industry health and welfare fund; mem. exec. bd., indsl. union dept., mem. gen. bd. AFL-CIO. Mem. Ill. Retail Industry Minimum Wage Bd., 1946-47; labor mem. Dept. Labor com. fair labor standards to P.R., 1963; mem. Labor Dept. exchange program to Japan, 1964; mem. exec. com. Internat. Fedn. Comml., Clerical and Tech. Employees. Served with inf. AUS, 1943-45; ETO. Decorated Silver Star with oak leaf cluster, Purple Heart. Home: 251 E 32d St New York City NY 10016 Office: 101 W 31st St New York City NY 10001

HEAPS, MARVIN DALE, food services co. exec.; b. Boone, Ia., June 26, 1932; s. Donald and Mary Isabel (Robson) H.; B.A. in Econs., Whitworth Coll., 1953; postgrad., George Washington U., 1957; M.B.A. (Achievement scholar), U. Pa., 1959; m. Martha Coleman Davis, July 4, 1957; children—Mitchell, Matthew, Martha. Asso., McKinsey & Co., mgmt. cons., Washington, Geneva, Switzerland, N.Y.C., 1960-66; dir. service systems engring. Automatic Retailers of Am., Phila., 1967, v.p., 1968; sr. v.p. ARA Services, Inc., Phila., 1969-71; pres. ARA Food Services Co., 1971—. Cons. to Office Edn., Dept. Health, Edn. and Welfare; mem. food service industry adv. com. Exec. Office of Pres., 1969—. Bd. dirs. Young Life Campaign, Haven House Teen Center. Served to lt. USNR, 1955-59. Mem. Am. Mgmt. Assn., Soc. Personnel Adminstrn., Assn. Internat. Devel., Nat. Automatic Mdse. Assn. (bd. dirs.), Wharton MBA Alumni Club. Republican. Presbyn. (elder). Club: Metropolitan (Washington); Union League (Phila.). Home: 301 Elm Av Swarthmore PA 19081 Office: Independence Sq W Philadelphia PA 19106

HEARD, GEORGE ALEXANDER, educator; b. Savannah, Ga., Mar. 14, 1917; s. Richard Willis and Virginia Lord (Nisbet) H.; A.B., U. N.C., 1938, LL.D., 1968; M.A., Columbia, 1948, Ph.D., 1951, LL.D., 1965; L.H.D., Pepperdine Coll., 1968; D.Sc., U. Chattanooga, 1969; m. Laura Jean Keller, June 17, 1949; children—Stephen Keller, Christopher Cadek, Francis Muir, Cornelia Lord. U.S. govt. Service in Depts. Interior, War and State, 1939-43; research asso. bur. pub. adminstrn. U. Ala., 1946-49; asso. prof. polit. sci., research asso. Inst. Research in Social Sci., U. N.C., 1950-51, prof. polit. sci., 1952-63, dean Grad. Sch., 1958-63; prof. polit. sci., chancellor Vanderbilt U., 1963—. Dir. Time, Inc. Chmn. Pres.'s Commn. on Campaign Costs, 1961-62; Spl. advisor to Pres. U.S. on campus affairs, 1970. Del. county, state Dem. convs., 1952-62; mem. State Dem. Congl. Dist. Exec. Com., 1954-56. Pres., bd. dirs. Citizens' Research Found., mem. U.S. Adv. Commn. Intergovtl. Relations, 1967-69. Trustee Ford Found. Served from ensign to lt. USNR, 1943-46. Mem. Internat., Am. (v.p. 1962-63), So. (pres. 1961-62) polit. sci. assns., Am. Assn. U. Profs., Am. Acad. Arts and Scis., Phi Beta Kappa, Sigma Alpha Epsilon. Episcopalian. Clubs: Nat. Capitol Democratic, Cosmos (Washington); Belle Meade Country (Nashville); Century Assn. (N.Y.C.). Author: (asst. to V. O. Key, Jr.) Southern Politics in State and Nation, 1949; (with Donald S. Strong) Southern Primaries and Elections, 1950; A Two-Party South?, 1952; The Costs of Democracy, 1960. Office: Kirkland Hall Vanderbilt U Nashville TN 37203

HEARD, GERALD, author; b. London, Eng., Oct. 6, 1889; s. Henry James and Maud (Bannatyne) H.; student Cambridge U., 1908-13 (grad. with honors in history). Came to U.S., 1937. Worked in Ireland with founder of Agrl. Co-op. Movement, 1919-23; in Eng. with same work, 1923-27; author and lectr., 1927—; radio lectr., 1930—; commentator on sci. BBC, 1930-34; lectr. South Place Ethical Soc., 1932-34; lectr., Oxford U., London, 1929-31; lectr. New Sch. of Social Research, N.Y.C. Haskell lectr. Oberlin Coll., 1958; Macliesh lectr. Rockford Coll., 1958. Two-year fellowship, Bolingen Found., N.Y.C., 1954. Mem. council Psychol. Research Soc. Eng., 1933-44. Author books: Ayer Found, lecture, The Eternal Gospel, 1946; Dopplegangers, 1947; Is God In History?, 1949; Is Another World Watching, 1951; The Five Ages of Man; The Perennial Praxis; A Journey Into Consciousness; Training for a Life of Growth. Editor of Realist, London, 1929. Home: 322 E Rustic Rd Santa Monica CA 90402 ☆

HEARD, HAROLD RAY, furnace mfr.; b. St. Paul, Dec. 25, 1915; s. Charles George and Amanda J. (Bowen) H.; grad. Anderson Coll., 1940; student Butler U., 1942, Ind. U. Extension, 1943; m. Murl Evelyn Montgomery, May 19, 1938; children—Carol Evelyn, Harold Roberick, Barbara Rae. Accountant, O.L.D. Forwarding Corp., 1938-42; accountant RCA, Indpls., 1942-45, Bloomington, Ind., 1945-46, div. accountant. Camden N.J., 1946-47; asst. controller woolen div. Deering Milliken and Co. Inc., 1948-54; controller Spencer Kellog and Sons, Inc., 1954-61; pres. Salem Corp., 1961—, dir., 1962—. Soc. Buffalo control Financial Execs. Inst., 1961. Vice pres. Hamburg Sch. Bd., 1961. Mem. U.S. Jr. C. of C. (pres. Greenwood chpt. 1953). Methodist (elder). Home: Club Rd Rosslyn Farms PA 15106 Office: PO Box 2222 Pittsburgh PA 15230

HEARD, MARSTON, banker; b. Manchester, N.H., Dec. 2, 1897; s. Arthur M. and Ora B. (Farrar) H.; student Phillips Andover Acad., 1916; A.B., Harvard, 1920; m. Doris F. Fellows, Apr. 30, 1924; children—Mary (Mrs. Thomas Johnson), Joan (Mrs. Kenneth B. White, Jr.), Arthur, Elizabeth (Mrs. Chauncey F. Lufkin, Jr.). Asst. Nat. Bank Examiner, 1922-24; asst. cashier Amoskeag Nat. Bank, Manchester, 1924-38, v.p., 1938-50, pres., 1950- 67, chmn. bd., 1967—, also dir.; pres., dir. Amoskeag Trust Co., 1931—; dir. N.H. Ins. Co., Amoskeag Industries, Inc., N.H. Pub. Service Co.; trustee Amoskeag Savs. Bank. Trustee Currier Gallery of Art. Home: 2366 Elm St Manchester NH 03104 Office: 875 Elm St Manchester NH 03101

HEARD, NATHAN CLIFF, author, musician; b. Newark, Nov. 7, 1936; s. Nathan E. and Gladys (Pruitt) H.; ed. pub. schs.; m. Nina Heard; children—Melvin, Cliff DeNina. Player drums with various bands, 1961—; tchr. Fresno State Coll., 1969—; asst. prof. Rutgers U., New Brunswick, N.J., 1970—. Served with USAF, 1952-54. Author: (novels) Howard St., 1968, To Reach a Dream, 1967; (songs) When Our Tomorrow Comes, 1968, Sweeting, 1969; (poem) The American Slumflower, 1971. Playwrite (musical drama) Bubi, 1970. Home: 35 Warwick St East Orange NJ 07017

HEARD, RALPH DENNIS, clergyman; b. Coal Hill, Ark., Nov. 10, 1918; s. Grover Cleveland and Emily Lucinda (Ketcherside) H.; student pub. schs. of Cal.; D.D., So. Bible Coll., Houston; m. Edith Mildred Shaffer; children—Alice C. (Mrs. C. Leon Thacker), Mildred Elizabeth. With Title Ins. and Trust Co., Los Angeles; escrow and loan officer Security-First Nat. Bank of Los Angeles; ordained to ministry, Pentecostal Ch. of God of Am., 1942; pastor, Los Angeles and Bakersfield, Cal.; youth div. officer Pentecostal Young People's Assn., So. Cal., 1938-42, dist. pres. 1942-43, internat. pres., 1946-49; editor P.Y. P.A. Challenger, 1942-46; dist. sec. treas. So. Cal. Dist., Pentecostal Ch. of God, 1944-46; chmn. Kern County Inter-Pentecostal Fellowship; gen. supt. Pentecostal Ch. of God Am., 1953—. Hon. lt. col. a.d.c. Gov. of Ala. Ky. Col. Mem. Nat. Assn. Evangelicals (sec. commn. on chaplains and service to mil. personnel), Internat. Platform Assn. Author: Patterns for Abundant Living, 1965. Home: 1313 W 17th St Joplin MO 64801 Office: 312-316 Joplin St Joplin MO 64801

HEARD, WILBUR WRIGHT, lawyer; b. New Orleans, Jan. 29, 1905; s. William Wright and Isabelle (Manning) H.; LL.B., Tulane U., 1926; postgrad. Harvard, 1952; m. Agnes Peyton Marshall, June 22, 1931; children—Anne Marshal, Courtenay (Mrs. Charles B. Tetrick), William Wright. Agnes Elizabeth. Admitted to La. bar, 1926, Okla. bar, 1941; practice in New Orleans, 1926-36, Tulsa, 1936—; atty. Pan. Am. Petroleum Corp., Tulsa, 1936-50, gen. atty., 1950- 61, gen. counsel, 1961-70, also dir. Regional counsel Region 5 Office Emergency Petroleum and Gas Adminstrn., Dept. Interior, ret. 1970. Mem. Am., La., Okla. bar assns. Episcopalian. Home: 1325 E 31st St Tulsa OK 74105 Office: Pan Am North Bldg Tulsa OK 74102

HEARD, WINIFRED OSBORNE, civic and welfare worker; b. Waverly, Ill., May 15, 1898; d. William Wallace and Nydia May (Walters) Osborne; student Emerson Coll., Boston, Mass., 1916-18; A.B., U. Cal. at Berkeley, 1920; m. Bartlett Bradford Heard, May 26, 1921; children—Bartlett Bradford, Helen Maie. Cons. UN Conf., San Francisco for Women's Action Com. Bd.; v.p., dir. Heard Mus., Phoenix. Vis. expert on women's affair in Germany, Office of the High Commr. for Germany, Dept. of State, 1950. Awarded citation War Dept., 1946. Mem. Corp. U.S.O., also v.p. of Bay Area; chmn. Asilomar Found. Bd., 1953-60; v.p. at large YWCA of U.S. 1949-52, mem. World Council, 1949, del. World Council, China, 1947, Lebanon, 1951, Eng., 1955; com. revision of constn. World YWCA; chmn. 1952 conv. com.; mem. Recreation Commn., State of Cal., 1947-61; mem. Delinquency Prevention Com. Alameda County; trustee mem. nat. bd. YWCA, 1936-64, chmn. Western region, 1940-46, hon. mem. nat. bd., 1965; bd. dirs. Travelers Aid Assn. of Am.; mem. Comprehensive Health Planning Council Alameda County; mem. bd. Internat. Hospitality Center, San Francisco; bd. dirs. Bay Area Soc. Planning Council; mem. bd. dirs. Internat. House U. Cal.; trustee Alta Bates Hosp.; hon. mem. bd. dirs. Mus. Internat. Folk Art, Santa Fe; mem. bd. Nat. Social Welfare Assembly. Mem. Prytannean Honor Soc., Chi Kappa Rho, Theta Sigma Phi. Conglist. Clubs: Women's Faculty; Women's Athletic (Oakland, Cal.). Cosmopolitan (N.Y.C.). Home: 565 Bellevue Av Oakland CA 94610

HEARE, CLAYTON, lawyer; b. Henrietta, Tex., Oct. 14, 1897; s. Lewis Cass and Martha (Karr) H.; B.A., U. Tex., 1918, LL.B., 1922; m. Jean Ragsdale, July 27, 1935; 1 dau., Marnelle (Mrs. John L. Gafford). Admitted to Tex. bar, 1922; gen. practice, Austin, 1922-26, Shamrock, Tex., 1927-43; asso. justice Ct. Civil Appeals, Amarillo, Tex., 1943-45; partner firm Underwood, Wilson, Sutton, Heare and Berry, Amarillo, 1945—. Dir. Amarillo Savs. Assn., 1954—. Pres. Am. Bus. Club, 1948, mem. nat. scholarship com., 1963-67. Bd. dirs. Cal Farley's Boys Ranch, Amarillo, 1955—; bd. regents Tex. State Sr. Colls., 1963-69. Served with USMC, 1918-19; AEF in France and Germany. Democrat. Presbyn. Mason (32). Home: 5301 Everett St Amarillo TX 79106 Office: Amarillo Nat Bank Bldg Amarillo TX 79101

HEARIN, ROBERT MATLOCK, banker; b. Demopolis, Ala., Dec. 10, 1916; s. Jesse Bethea and Johnnie (Kennedy) H.; B.A., U. Ala., 1939; m. Annie Laurie Swain, June 27, 1940; children—Anne Laurie, Robert Matlock. Land man United Gas Co., 1939-53, mgr. transmission and prodn. facilities, Miss., Ala., Fla., 1953-56; vice chmn. First Nat. Bank of Jackson, Miss., 1956-58, pres., 1958-69, chmn. bd. 1969—; pres. First Capital Corp.; chmn. bd., dir. Intersystems, Inc.; dir. South Central Bell Telephone Co., Miss. Power and Light Co., Lamar Life Ins. Co., First Miss. Corp., Miss. Valley Title Ins. Co., Amerada Hess Corp. Pres. Miss. Arts Center, Inc. Bd. dirs., Piney Woods Sch. Mem. U.S. C. of C. (dir.), Mid-Continent Oil and Gas Assn., Sigma Alpha Epsilon. Home: 139 Woodland Dr Jackson MS 39216 Office: PO Box 291 Jackson MS 39205

HEARN, EDELL MIDGETT, educator; b. Watertown, Tenn., Oct. 3, 1929; s. Will Ray and Verna Tillie (Midgett) H.; A.A., Tenn. Wesleyan Coll.; B.S., Middle Tenn. State Coll., 1952; M.A., U. Tenn., 1953, Ed.D., 1959; m. Jeanette Weaver, Apr. 19, 1952; children—Janna, Valerie Elizabeth, Kaydell. Tchr., Central High Sch., Murfreesboro, Tenn., 1952-53, South High Sch., Knoxville, Tenn., 1955- 57, Knoxville Adult High Sch., 1956-57; instr. U. Tenn., 1958-59, asso. prof., dir. student teaching Martin br., 1958-61; vis. prof. Tenn. Technol. U., Cookeville, summer 1958, prof. edn., 1961—, chmn. dept., 1961-62, dean Coll. Edn., 1963—. Bd. dirs. Tenn. Joint Council Econ. Edn., 1961—; mem. Tenn. Tchr. Edn. and Profl. Standards Com., 1964—, chmn., 1967—; mem., chmn. State Adv. Com. on Certification and Tchr. Edn.; mem. evaluation bd. Nat. Council for Accreditation of Tchr. Edn., 1971—. Served with AUS, 1953-55. Mem. Nat., Tenn. edn. assns., Am. Personnel and Guidance Assn., Nat. Vocational Guidance Assn., Assn. Supervision Curriculum Devel., Am. Assn. U. Profs., Assn. Higher Edn., Assn. Student Teaching, Nat. P.T.A., Phi Delta Kappa, Kappa Delta Pi, Phi Kappa Phi, Theta Sigma Chi. Methodist. Mason (32), Lion. Author: Test in Tennessee History and Government, Forms A and B, 1957; Public Educational Changes in Tennessee Through Legislation, 1959; Planning Effective Meetings, 1964; Simulated Behavioral Teaching Situations, 1971; also articles. Home: 1235 E 9th St Cookeville TN 38501

HEARN, GEORGE HENRY, govt. ofcl.; b. Bklyn., July 4, 1927; s. Henry G. and Grace A. (Flaherty) H.; B.A., St. Francis Coll., 1950; student Fordham U. Sch. Bus. Adminstrn., 1948; LL.B., St. John's U., 1954; m. Cecelia Anne Philbin, June 28, 1952; children—Annemarie Jude, Margaret Mary, George Henry. Admitted to N.Y. bar, 1955, also U.S. Supreme Ct.; with firm Haight, Gardner, Poor and Havens, specializing admiralty matters, N.Y.C., 1954-61; mem. CAB, 1961-64; commr. Fed. Maritime Commn., 1964—. Dist. commr. Boy Scouts Am., 1958—. Mem. N.Y.C. Council, 1958-61; chmn. Kings County speakers com. for 1960 presdl. election; vice chmn. com. nationalists and intergroup relations N.Y. State Democratic Com., 1960—. Served with USNR, World War II; PTO. Recipient Distinguished Service award U.S. Jr. C. of C., 1958. Mem. St. Patrick's Soc. Bklyn. (past pres.), Am. Com. Italian Migration (recording sec. Bklyn. div.). K.C. Home: 423 Bay Ridge Pkwy Brooklyn NY 11209 also 1414 Dilston Rd Silver Spring MD 20903 Office: 1321 H St NW Washington DC 20573

HEARN, GEORGE J., N.G. officer; m. Nell Potts, Sept. 18, 1929; 1 son, George J. III. Owner, Hearn Hardware Co., Monroe, Ga.; joined Ga. N.G., 1925; commd. 2d lt., 1932, advanced through grades to maj. gen., 1952; active duty Army Res. N.G., 1940-46, Korean War; Ga. adj. gen., dir. civil def. Ga. Past mayor, Monroe Bd. dirs. Walton (Ga.) County Hosp. Mem. Am. Legion (past dep. comdr. Ga.), Atlanta Consistory, V.F.W., 40 and 8, U.S.A., Ga. N.G. assns. Mem. Christian Ch. (elder). Mason. Address: Mil Dept Ga 959 E Confederate Av SE Atlanta GA 30312

HEARN, WILFRED ASQUITH, ret. naval officer; b. Memphis, Dec. 23, 1906; s. Wilfred and Evelyn Rutherford (Asquith) H.; student U. Md., 1925-27; LL.B., George Washington U., 1931; grad. Judge Adv. Gen. Sch., 1956; m. Katherine Elizabeth Roller, Mar. 7, 1944; 1 son, Wilfred Asquith. Admitted to D.C. bar, 1931, Tenn. bar, 1936; mgr. br. office HOLC, 1931-36; pvt. practice law, Memphis, 1936-42; commd. lt. USNR, 1942, advanced through grades to rear adm. USN, 1964; assigned Naval Air Sta., San Juan, P.R., 1942-44, Naval Air Sta., Memphis, 1944, Bur. Aero., 1945-46; designated law specialist, 1946; chief tax officer Dept. Navy, 1948- 50; dist. legal officer 14th Naval Dist., 1950-52; successively dir. gen. law div., dir. adminstrv. div., dir. internat. law div. Office Judge Adv. Gen., 1952-58; asst. judge adv. gen. Navy Dept., 1958-60; comdg. officer U.S. Justice Sch., 1960-64; judge adv. gen. Navy Dept., 1964-68; spl. rep. dept. defense for law the sea, 1968—. Mem. U.S. delegation UN Conf. Law of Sea, 1958, 60; guest lectr. Naval War Coll. Mem. Am., Fed. bar assns., Judge Adv. Assn., Am. Soc. Internat. Law, Phi Alpha Delta, Sigma Nu. Episcopalian.Club: Army-Navy Country (Arlington, Va.). Home: 1116 Beverly Dr Alexandria VA 22302

HEARNE, JOSEPH FREDERIC, musician; b. Lorain, O., Aug. 20, 1942; s. Wayne and Meta (Loose) H.; student Juilliard Sch. Music, 1960-62, New Eng. Conservatory Music, 1962-64; m. Myra Ruzsits, Mar. 29, 1965; children—Michelle, Sean. Mem., Portland (Ore.) Symphony Orch., 1959-60, Aspen (Colo.) Festival Orch., 1961, Boston Symphony Orch., 1962—; asst. prin. double-bass Boston Pops Orch., 1962—; prin. double-bass Boston Opera Co., 1967; artist-in-residence Boston Conservatory Music, 1968-69. Recipient award Ore. Com. Mus. Arts, 1960; Am. Fedn. Musicians' Internat. Congress of Strings fellow, 1960; Eleanor Morgan Satterlee Meml. scholar Juilliard, 1961-62. Home: 44 Mill St Westwood MA 02090 Office: Symphony Hall Boston MA 02090*

HEARNES, WARREN EASTMAN, gov. of Mo.; b. Moline, Ill., July 23, 1923; s. Earle B. and Edna May (Eastman) H.; B.S., U.S. Mil. Acad., 1946; A.B., U. Mo., 1952, LL.B., 1952; m. Betty Sue Cooper, July 2, 1948; children—Lynn, Leigh, Julia B. Served as enlisted man, inf., AUS, World War II; commd. 2d lt. U.S. Army, 1946, advanced through grades to 1st lt., 1947; resigned, 1949; mem. Mo. Ho. of Reps. from Mississippi County, 1950-60, majority floor leader, 1957, 59; admitted to Mo. bar, 1952; sec. of State Mo., 1960-64; gov. Mo., 1964—. Bd. dirs. Mo. Assn. Mental Health. Mem. Mo. Bar Assn., V.F.W., Phi Delta Theta, Phi Delta Phi. Democrat. Baptist. Mason (Shriner), Elk, Lion, Eagle. Home: Executive Mansion Jefferson City MO 65101 Office: Executive Office Capitol Bldg Jefferson City MO 65101

HEARST, DAVID WHITMIRE, pub. exec.; b. N.Y.C., Dec. 2, 1915; s. William Randolph and Millicent (Willson) H.; student St. Bernard's, N.Y.C., 1927-30, St. George's, Newport, R.I., 1931-33, Princeton, 1933-36; m. Hope Chandler, Mar. 23, 1938; children—Millicent, David. Began as reporter N.Y. Journal-Am.; later with Balt. News-Post as asst. advt. dir., then city editor; classified and display advt., Los Angeles Evening Herald-Express, 1938-44, bus. mgr., 1944-45, gen. mgr., 1945-47, exec. pub., 1947-50, pub., 1950-60; v.p., dir. Hearst Corp. Bd. dirs. Los Angeles County Mus. Clubs: California, Jonathan, Wilshire Country (Los Angeles); El Dorado Country (Palm Desert). Home: 719 N Beverly Dr Beverly Hills CA 90210 Office: Hearst Corp 404 N Roxbury Dr Beverly Hills CA 90210

HEARST, GEORGE RANDOLPH, Sr., newspaper exec.; b. Washington, Apr. 23, 1904; s. William Randolph and Millicent (Willson) H.; grad. St John's Mil. Sch.; student U. Cal. at Berkeley; m. Blanche Wilbut, June 19, 1923 (div. 1930); children—George R. and Phoebe M. (twins); m. 2d, Rosalie Winn, 1960. Pub. San Francisco Examiner, 1924-27; v.p. Los Angeles Examiner, 1929-53, now v.p., dir. bd. trustees Hearst Corp., N.Y.C. Pres. Hearst Found. Home: 701 Panorama Rd Palm Springs CA 92262 Office: Hearst Bldg 959 8th Av New York City NY 10019 also 404 N Roxbury Dr Beverly Hills CA 90210

HEARST, GEORGE RANDOLPH, Jr., newspaper exec.; b. San Francisco, July 13, 1927; s. George and Blanche (Wilbur) H.; m. Mary Thompson, Apr. 23, 1951 (dec. Dec. 1969); children—Mary, George Randolph III, Stephen T., Erin; m. 2d, Patricia Ann Bell, Nov. 30, 1969. Pvt. bus., 1946-48; staff Los Angeles Examiner, 1948-50. San Francisco Examiner, 1954-56; with Los Angeles Evening Herald-Express, 1956—, bus. mgr., 1957—, pub., 1960—; pub. Los Angeles Herald-Examiner, 1962—; dir. Hearst Corp. Trustee Hearst Found. Served with USNR, 1945-46; with AUS, 1950-54. Mem. V.F.W. Clubs: Burlingame Country, Jonathan, Riviera. Home: 318 N Rockingham Av Los Angeles CA 90049 Office: 1111 S Broadway Los Angeles CA 90015

HEARST, JOSEPH ALBERT, Jr., coll. dean; b. Leavenworth, Wash., Apr. 16, 1917; s. Joseph Albert and Lou (Risk) H.; B.S., U. Wash., 1940, M.A., 1948; Ph.D., Columbia, 1959; m. Priscilla D. Fox, June 23, 1949; children—Jonena M., Alice L., Joseph Albert III, Melissa A. Grad. asst. dept. history U. Wash., 1946, research fellow

Bur. Govtl. Research and Services, 1947, Univ. fellow dept. polit. sci., 1947, spl. research asso. Inst. Pub. Affairs, 1948; tutor Columbia, 1948-50; instr. dept. polit. sci. Whitman Coll,, Walla Walla, Wash., 1950-53; lectr. govt. Barnard Coll., also Columbia, 1952-56; prof. govt. Ida. State U., Pocatello, 1956-65, asst. dean Coll. Liberal Arts, 1965-67, dean, 1967—. Served to capt., inf., AUS, 1950-45. Decorated Bronze Star. Mem. Am., Western (past mem. exec. bd.) polit. sci. assns., Am. Soc. Internat. Law, Pi Sigma Alpha. Contbr. articles profl. jours. Home: Johnny Creek Rd Pocatello ID 83201

HEARST, JOSEPH FRANCIS, journalist; b. St. Joseph, Mo., Nov. 27, 1901; s. Loren Andrew and Frances (Dunn) H.; grad. high sch.; m. Susan E. Gogerty, Feb. 6, 1932. Former reporter St. Joseph News Press, Kansas City (Mo.) Star, Internat. News Service, U.P.I.; mem. staff Chgo. Tribune, 1943—, corr. Washington Bur. Chgo. Tribune Press Service, 1944—. Mem. White House Corrs. Assn. Roman Catholic. Club: Nat. Press (Washington). Home: 4301 Columbia Pike Arlington VA 22204 Office: 1750 Pennsylvania Av NW Washington DC 20006

HEARST, MRS. RANDOLPH A., mem. bd. regents U. Cal. Address: 233 W Santa Inez Av Hillsborough CA 94010*

HEARST, RANDOLPH APPERSON, pub. exec.; b. N.Y.C., Dec. 2, 1915; s. William Randolph and Millicent (Willson) H.; student Harvard, 1933-34; m. Catherine Campbell, Jan. 12, 1938; children—Catherine, Virginia, Patricia, Anne, Victoria. Asst. to editor Atlanta Georgian, 1934-38; asst. to pub. San Francisco Call- Bull., 1938-41, exec. editor, 1946—, pub., 1950-53; pres., dir., chief exec. officer Hearst Consol. Publs., Inc.; pres. Hearst Pub. Co., Inc., 1953-64; The Hearst Corp., 1965—; trustee Hearst Found. Served as capt., Air Transport Command, USAAF, 1942-45. Roman Catholic. Clubs: Piedmont Driving (Atlanta), Burlingame Country; Pacific Union; Press (San Francisco). Home: 233 W Santa Inez Av Hillsborough CA 94010 Office: Hearst Bldg San Francisco CA 94103

HEARST, WILLIAM RANDOLPH, Jr., editor; b. N.Y.C., Jan. 27, 1908; s. William Randolph and Millicent Veronica (Willson) H.; student U. Cal. 1925-27; m. 3d, Austine McDonnell, July 29, 1948; children—W.R. Hearst III, John Augustine Chilton. Began career with N.Y. Am., N.Y.C., 1928, as reporter, asst. to city editor, pub., 1936-37; pub. N.Y. Jour.-Am., N.Y.C., 1937-56, The Am. Weekly and The Comic Weekly Puck, 1945-56; served as war corr., 1943-45; now chmn., dir. Hearst Corp.; dir. 20th Century Fox Film Corp., U.P.I., San Luis Mining Co. Recipient Pulitzer prize, 1956; Overseas Press Club award, 1958. Mem. Sigma Delta Chi, Phi Delta Theta. Clubs: Brook, Madison Square Garden, Marco Polo (N.Y.C.); Pacific Union Club; Metropolitan, Nat. Press, F. Street, Sulgrave, Burning Tree (Washington); Bohemian (San Francisco). Home: 810 Fifth Av New York City NY 10021 Office: 959 8th Av New York City NY 10019

HEARTT, PHILIP BREWSTER, found. exec.; b. St. Joseph, Mich., Feb. 16, 1896; s. Lincoln and Ella Gertrude (Pride) H.; ed. U. Mich; m. Mathilda Hutzel, Feb. 25, 1922; 1 son, Stephen. Dir. Angier B. Duke Meml., Inc., 1951—; trustee Duke Endowment, 1951—; trustee several personal trusts. Club: New Canaan Country. Home: Canoe Hill New Canaan CT 06840 Office: 30 Rockefeller Plaza New York City NY 10020

HEARTWELL, CHARLES MONROE, Jr., educator; b. Lawrenceville, Va., Aug. 27, 1908; s. Charles M. and Elva (Dortch) H.; student Hampden Sidney Coll., 1925-27, U. Va., 1927-28; D.D.S., Med. Coll. Va., 1932; m. Marjorie Coleman Elmore, June 24, 1933; 1 son, Charles Monroe III. Practice dentistry, South Hill, Va., 1932-40; joined Dental Corps, USNR, 1940, commd., advanced through grades to capt., 1955; stationed at Norfolk, Va., 1940-44, New London Conn., 1946- 49, Naval Amphibious Base, Little Creek, Va., 1952-55; service in U.S.S. Clytie, 1944-46, U.S.S. Shenandoah; mem. staff U.S. Naval Hosp. Bethesda, Md., 1949-50, U.S. Navy Dental Sch., Bethesda, 1955-57, U.S. Naval Hosp., Yokosuka, Japan 1957-61; ret., 1961; prof. prosthodontics Med. Coll. Va. Sch. Dentistry, 1961—, cons. dept. onocology Hosp., 1967—, also dir. maxilofacial prosthodontics, 1967- -. Diplomate Am. Bd. Prothodontics. Fellow Am. Coll. Dentistry; mem. Am., Va. dental assns., Richmond (Va.) Dental Soc., McGee Dental Study Club, Am. Prosthodontics Soc., Carl Boucher Prosthetic Conf., Southeastern Acad. Prosthodontics, Navy League, Theta Chi, Psi Omega, Omicron Kappa Upsilon. Methodist. Author: Syllabus of Complete Dentures, 1968. Contbr. articles profl. jours. Home: 16 Ralston Rd Richmond VA 23229

HEARTZ, DANIEL LEONARD, educator; b. Exeter, N.H., Oct. 5, 1930; s. Harold Francis and Katherine (McEnhill) H.; A.B., U. N.H., 1950; A.M., Harvard, 1951, Ph.D. (Sheldon fellow), 1957. Instr. U. Chgo., 1957-58, asst. prof., 1958-60; asst. prof. U. Cal. at Berkeley, 1960-65, asso. prof., 1965-67, prof., 1967—, chmn. music dept., 1969—. Humanities Research fellow, Princeton, 1963-64; Guggenheim fellow, 1967-68. Mem. Am. Musicological Soc. (council 1960-62, 66-68, Kinkedy Award, 1971), Royal Mus. Assn. (Dent medal 1970), Société Française de Musicologie. Author: Pierre Attaingnant, Royal Printer of Music, 1969. Editor: Preludes, Chansons and Dances for Lute, 1964; (with Alfred Mann) Theorie-und Kompositions studien bei Mozart (Thomas Attwood) 1964-1969; Idomeneo (Mozart), 1972. Home: 1098 Keith Av Berkeley CA 94708

HEATH, DONALD R., former ambassador; b. Topeka, Aug. 12, 1894; s. Hubert A. and Estelle (Read) H.; ed. Washburn Coll., U. de Montpellier, France; LL.D., Washburn U.; m. Sue Louise Bell, Oct. 10, 1920; children—Sue Louise, Donald. White House corr. United Press, 1920; vice consul at Bucharest, 1921-23; consul, Warsaw, 1923-25, Berne, Switzerland, 1925-29; chargé d'affaires ad interim, Port au Prince, 1929-30, consul and 2d sec., 1932-33; detailed to State Dept., asst. chief Div. Latin-Am. Affairs, 1933-37; first sec. Am. embassy, Berlin, 1938-41; counselor Am. embassy, Santiago, Chile, 1941-44; chief Div. North and West Coast Affairs, State Dept., Aug.-Nov. 1944; counselor to U.S. polit. adviser for Germany; dir. polit. affairs Office of Mil. Gov. for Germany (U.S.), Nov. 1944; U.S. minister to Bulgaria, 1947-50; U.S. minister to Asso. States of Cambodia, Laos and Vietnam; U.S. ambassador to Cambodia and Vietnam, 1952; U.S. ambassador to Lebanon, 1955, to Saudi Arabia, 1958-61; v.p. Fgn. Bondholders Protective Council, 1961- 69, pres.; 1969—; Regents prof. U. Cal at Los Angeles, 1962-63. Served with U.S. Army, 1917-19, with AEF, 1918-19, disch. as 1st lt. inf. Mem. Council Fgn. Relations, Phi Delta Theta. Clubs: Bonnie Briar Country (Larchmont, N.Y.); Metropolitan; University (N.Y.C.). Lectr. fgn. affairs. Home: 1120 Park Av New York City NY 10028 Office: 1775 Broadway New York City NY 10019

HEATH, DOUGLAS HAMILTON, educator; b. Woodbury, N.J., Oct. 1, 1925; s. Russell M. and Eleanor H. (Conrow) H.; student Swarthmore Coll., 1941-42; A.B. summa cum laude, Amherst Coll., 1949; A.M., Harvard, 1952, Ph.D., 1954; m. Harriet Elizabeth Frye, June 15, 1952; children—Russell, Wendilee, Anne Marie. Instr. grad. sch. edn. Harvard, 1953-54; asst. Haverford (Pa.) Coll., 1954-59, asso. prof., chmn. psychology dept., 1959-65, 67-68, prof., 1965—. Nat. Sci. Faculty fellow U. Mich., 1957; Fulbright Research scholar, 1965-66; research cons. Acad. Religion and Mental Health. Served with AUS, 1942-44. Mem. Am. Psychol. Assn., Soc. for Personality Assessment. Mem. Soc. of Friends. Author: Explorations of Maturity, 1965; Growing Up In College: Liberal Education and Maturity, 1968; Humanizing Schools: New Directions, New Decisions, 1971. Home: 21 Matlack Lane Villanova PA 19085 Office: Haverford Coll Haverford PA 19041

HEATH, EDWARD CHARLES, biochemist, educator; b. St. Louis, Mar. 29, 1926; s. Glenn Garrison and Edna M. (Fluchel) H.; B.S., St. Louis U., 1949; A.M., U. Mo., 1951; Ph.D., Purdue U., 1955; m. Patricia L. Nolan, Jan. 29, 1947; children—Justin P., Paula J., Dana J. Instr. to asso. prof. microbiology U. Mich., 1957-63; asso. prof. physiol. chemistry Sch. Medicine Johns Hopkins, Balt., 1963-66, prof., 1966-71; prof., chmn. dept. biochemistry U. Pitts. Sch. Medicine, 1971—; cons. USPHS; mem. biochemistry tng. com. NIH. Served with USNR, 1944-46. Mem. Am. Soc. Biol. Chemists, Am. Soc. Microbiology, Sigma Xi, Phi Lambda Upsilon. Editorial bd. Jour. Biol. Chemistry, Analytical Biochemistry. Contbr. articles sci. jours. Home: 5436 Albermarle Av Pittsburgh PA 15217

HEATH, EDWARD RICHARD GEORGE, Brit. prime minister; b. Broadstairs, Kent, Eng., July 9, 1916; s. William George and Edith Anne (Pantony) H.; M.A. (scholar), Balliol Coll., Oxford U., 1939. With Civil Service, 1946-47; mem. Parliament for Bexley, 1950—; asst. Conservative whip, 1951; lord commr. Treasury, 1951; joint dep. govt. chief whip, 1952, dep. govt. chief whip, 1953-55; Parliamentary sec. Treasury, also govt. chief whip, 1955-59; minister of Labour, 1959-60; Lord Privy Seal with Fgn. Office responsibilities, 1960- 63; sec. state for industry, trade, regional devel., also pres. Bd. Trade, 1963-64; leader of the Opposition, 1965-70, leader of Conservative Party, 1965—; prime minister, 1st Lord Treasury, 1970—. Pres. Oxford U. Conservative Assn., 1937, Fedn. U. Conservative Assn., 1938, 59—, Oxford Union, 1939. Past dir. Brown Shipley and Co. Ltd., mcht. bankers. Mem. council Royal Coll. Music, 1961, also hon. fellow. Served to lt. co. Brit. Army, 1940-46; ETO. Vis. fellow Nuffield Coll., Oxford U., 1963; recipient Charlemagne prize Aachen, W. Germany, 1963. Hon. fellow Royal Coll. Organists, Co- author: One Nation-a Tory approach to social problems, 1950; Old World, New Horizons, 1970. Clubs: Buck's, Carlton (London). Office: 10 Downing St Whitehall London SW 1 England

HEATH, GLORIA WHITTON, aviation cons.; b. N.Y.C., May 7, 1922; d. Royal Vale and Lillian (Hart) H.; grad. The Putney Sch., 1939; A.B., Smith Coll., 1943. Operations analyst engring. dept. Am. Export Airlines, N.Y.C., 1943; service pilot Woman's Air Force, (WASP), 1943-44; dir. summer aviation program Conn. Coll., 1945; spl. asst. to chief engr. loss prevention Aero Ins. Underwriters, N.Y.C. 1945-48; with Flight Safety Found., N.Y.C., 1948-65, as spl. asst. to managing dir., dir. pvt. flying, dir. spl. affairs; asst. dir. Cornell-Guggenheim Aviation Safety Center, N.Y.C., 1965-68; prin. dir. SAR-ASSIST, Inc., 1968—. Women's adv. com. to FAA, 1967-70. Bd. govs. Flight Safety Found. Recipient Lady Hay Drummond-Hay trophy, 1955; Amelia Earhart award, 1957, Laura Taber Barbour Air Safety award, 1965. Asso. fellow Am. Inst. Aeros and Astronautics; mem. Nat. Pilots Assn. (nat. sec. 1966), Am. Astronaut Soc. (nat. sec. 1962-65; chmn. safety com. 1969—), Aviation Space Writers Assn., Ninety-Nines, Internat. Acad. Astronautics (mem. space rescue studies com. 1968—), Aerospace Med. Assn. (hon. mem. wives wing). Home: Island Lane Greenwich CT 06830

HEATH, HOWARD DAVIS, ins. co. exec.; b. Eagle, Alaska, Mar. 29, 1904; s. Archie Lee and Agnes (Windblad) H.; student U. Wash., 1925; m. Myra Helen Webber, June 11, 1930; 1 dau., Jane Ann (Mrs. Douglas M. Stuart). With Unigard Mut. Ins. Co., Seattle, 1923—, v.p., 1960-61, pres., 1961-69, also dir.; pres., dir. Unigard Ins. Co., Seattle, 1961-69, Cream City Mut. Ins. Co., Milw., 1961-65, Unigard Service Corp., Seattle, 1961-69, Unigard Inc., Seattle, 1961-69; dir., mem. exec. com. Am. Mut. Ins. Alliance, Chgo., Olympic Nat. Life Ins. Co., Seattle; mem. governing bd., v.p. Mut. Loss Research Bur., Chgo., 1963-66; governing bd. Improved Risk Muts., N.Y.; dir. Unigard Security Ins. Co. Tex. Trustee, past pres. Wash. State Indsl. Conf. Bd. Mem. Seattle C. of C., Phi Sigma Kappa. Republican. Lutheran. Rotarian. Clubs: Washington Athletic, Rainier, Broadmoor Golf (Seattle). Home: 2502 Canterbury Lane E Seattle WA 98102 Office: 217 Pine St Seattle WA 98101

HEATH, JOHN CLOVIS, packing co. exec.; b. Sibley, Ia., July 14, 1939; s. Harold Edwin and Ann (Sokol) H.; B.S., Ia. State U., 1961; M.B.A., Wharton Sch. U. Pa., 1967; m. Judith Ann Morgan, Dec. 9, 1961; children—Christopher James, Deborah Anne. With Needham Packing Co., Inc., Sioux City, Ia., 1967-70, treas., asst. sec., dir. finance and control, 1968-70; treas. Illini Beef Packers, Inc., Geneseo, Ill., 1970—. Instr. econs. U. Pa., 1967. Served to lt. USNR, 1961-65. Decorated Letter of Commendation. Mem. Geneseo Jr. C. of C. (dir.). Beta Gamma Sigma, Phi Delta Theta, Alpha Kappa Psi. Presbyn. Home: Rural Rt 2 Geneseo IL 61254 Office: PO Box 245 Geneseo IL 61254

HEATH, PERCY LEROY, Jr., musician; b. Wilmington, N.C., Apr. 30, 1923; s. Percy Leroy and Arlethia (Wall) H.; m. June Ellen Jones, Mar. 31, 1950; children—Percy Leroy III, Jason, Stewart. Founder mem. Modern Jazz Quartet, treas., 1955—, string bass player, 1951—; bass player 2d Internat. Jazz Festival, ensemble of Howard McGhee, 1948; played at Maggio Musicale, Florence, Italy, 1959, Contemporary Music Festival, Donaueschingen, Germany, 1957; played with Miles Davis, J. J. Johnson, Dizzy Gillespie; faculty Sch. of Jazz, Lenox, Mass. Served with 99th Pursuit Squadron, AUS, 1943-45. Home: 175-02 139 Rd Springfield Gardens Queens NY 11413 Office: care Monte Kay 200 W 57th St New York City NY 10019

HEATH, PETER LAUCHLAN, educator; b. Milan, Italy, May 9, 1922; s. Philip George and Olga (Sinclair) H.; ed. Shrewsbury Sch., 1936-40; B.A. with honors, Magdalen Coll. Oxford U., 1942. Came to U.S., 1962. Lectr. moral philosophy U. Edinburgh (Scotland), 1946-58; sr. lectr. in logic and metaphysics U. St. Andrews (Scotland), 1958-62; prof. philosophy U. Va., 1962—. Served with Brit. Army, 1942-45. Mem. Am., Va. philos. assns., Aristotelian Soc., So. Soc. Philosophy. Editor On the Syllogism, 1966. Translator works from German. Home: 808 Winston Terrace Charlottesville VA 22903

HEATH, PRESTON ELLSWORTH, ins. co. exec.; b. Denver, Aug. 30, 1908; s. Thomas Sumner and Leita (Berry) H.; B.S., Ill. Inst. Tech., 1930; m. Eleanor Kinney Smith, Dec. 29, 1930; 1 dau., Margaret Eleanor. Engr. Mt. States Inspn. Bur., Denver, 1930-35; field rep. Cole.-N.M., Wyo., Ohio Scottish Union Nat. Ins. Co. of Hartford, 1935-54; v.p., sec. Nat. Union Ins. Cos., Pitts., 1954—, Am. Home Group, 1969—; sec. Am. Internat. Group, Inc., N.Y.C., 1968—. Served to lt. comdr. USNR, 1942-46. Mem. Am. Soc. Corp. Secs., Soc. Fire Protection Engrs., Theta Xi. Presbyn. Mason (Shriner). Clubs: University of Pitts. Home: 377 S Harrison St East Orange NJ 07018 Office: 102 Maiden Lane New York City NY 10005

HEATH, RICHARD RAYMOND, govt. ofcl.; b. La Junta, Colo., June 22, 1929; s. Perry Stanford and Genevieve Anabelle (Whitney) H.; B.A. in Econs., U. Colo., 1951, LL.B., 1954; m. Arlene Newbrow, Nov. 3, 1961. Admitted to Colo. bar, 1954, Cal. bar, 1957; mem. firm Neyhart & Grodin, San Francisco, 1957-66; dep. Peace Corps dir., Ivory Coast, 1966-68, dir., 1968-69; Peace Corps dir., Mali, 1969—. Del., Conf. State Bar Dels. Sponsoring mem. San Francisco Democratic County Central Com., 1964-66; mem. San Francisco Dem. Forum, 1963-66. Served to 1st lt. USAF, 1955-57. Mem. State Bar Cal., San Francisco Bar Assn. (past chmn. indsl. accident com.), San Francisco Lawyers Club, Am., Cal. trial lawyers assns., Am. Civil Liberties Union, San Francisco Planning and Urban Renewal Assn., Nat. Parks Assn., Cal. Applicants Attys. Assn. (v.p.). Club: Sierra (San Francisco). Address: B P 85 Bamako Mali

HEATH, ROBERT GALBRAITH, physician, educator; b. Pitts., May 9, 1915; s. Robert Malcolm and Minnie Coleman (Galbraith) H.; B.S., U. Pitts., 1937, M.D., 1938; D.M.Sc., Columbia, 1949; m. Eleanor Bugher Wright, Sept. 7, 1940; children—Anne, Shari, Barbara, Carol, Robert Galbraith. Intern Mercy Hosp., Pitts., 1939; instr. medicine U. Pitts., 1939-40; asst., chief resident neurology Neurol. Inst., N.Y., 1940-42, asst. attending neurologist, 1946-49; psychiatrist Pa. Hosp. Nervous and Mental Diseases, also demonstrator neurology Jefferson Med. Coll., 1942-43; instr. neurology Columbia, 1946-49, attending psychoanalyst Psychoanalytic Clinic, 1951-56; prof., chmn. dept. psychiatry and neurology Tulane U., 1949—; cons. psychiatrist Knickerbocker Hosp., N.Y., also N.J. State Hosp., 1947-49; sr. vis. physician Charity Hosp.; cons. VA Hosp., New Orleans, Southeast La. State Hosp., East La. State Hosp.; med. staff DePaul Hosp., Touro Infirmary; chief med. officer Mcht. Marine Rest Center, U.S. Marine Hosp.; chief psychiatrist U.S. Penitentiary, Lewisburg, Pa. 1943-46. Pres. Inst. Mental Hygiene of New Orleans, med. dirs., 1965—. Med. adviser to La. dir. SSS; USPHS coms. psychosurgery and tng. grants; com. med. edn. Am. Psychiat. Assn. U.S. rep. Internat. Symposium on Biol. and Clin. Aspects Central Nervous Systems, Basle, Switzerland. Fellow Am., So. psychiat. assns., Am. Coll. Neuropsychopharmacology (charter), Am. Acad. Neurology, N.Y. Acad. Medicine, A.C.P.; mem. Am. Neurol. Assn., Am. Assn. Psychonalytic Medicine, A.M.A., Soc. Research Psychosomatic Problems, Soc. Biol. Psychiatry (v.p. 1967-68, pres. 1968-69), Assn. Research Nervous and Mental Disease, A.A.A.S., Group for Advancement of Psychiatry, New Orleans Soc. Neurology and Psychiatry, Orleans Parish Med. Soc., So. Soc. for Clin. Research, Am. Acad. Psychoanalysis (trustee), La. Pyschiatric Assn. (pres. 1960-61), Sigma Xi. Author: Selective Partial Ablation of the Frontal Cortex (ed. F. A. Mettler), 1949. Editor: Studies in Schizophrenia, 1954; Serological Fractions in Schizophrenia, 1963; The Role of Pleasure in Behavior, 1964. Asso. editor: Internat. Rev. Neurobiology. Mem. editorial Com. Jour. Biol. Psychiatry, Behavioral Neuropsychiatry. Address: 1430 Tulane Av New Orleans LA 70112

HEATH, WILLIAM CLARENCE, corp. exec.; b. N.Y.C., Sept. 20, 1900; s. Horace Washington and Margaret Helen (Langenhadder) H.; student Alexander Hamilton Inst., 1919- 22; student civil engring. Marine Corps Inst., 1928-40; student Cal. Inst. Tech., 1938, San Diego Evening Coll., 1939-40; m. Ragnhild Viola Nelson, Dec. 12, 1923; children—William Clarence, Dorothy H. (Mrs. W. H. Wilkinson, Jr.), Arthur N., Barbara J. (Mrs. John C. Sebastian). Overseer, United Fruit Co., Gutamela, 1922-26; survey, engr. Rochester Gas and Electric Co. (N.Y.), 1926-29, 34-35; constrn. engr. A. W. Hopeman and Sons, Rochester, 1929-33; with Allan Iron and Welding Works, Rochester, 1936; engr. to asst. chief engr. Solar Aircraft Co., San Diego, 1937-42, chief engr., 1942-55, sales and mgmt., 1955-62; sr. requirements engr., marketing Gen. Dynamics/Convair, San Diego, 1962-64; product devel. mgr. NTH Products, Inc., subsidiary of Carpenter Steel Co., El Cajon, Cal., 1964- -; owner, gen. mgr. Modular Display Engring. Co., San Diego, 1965—. Sci. cons. tech. indsl. intelligence com. Joint Chiefs of Staff, investigating German mil. aircraft devels. Served with USMC, 1918-22. Fellow Am. Soc. M.E. (v.p., mem. council, gen. co-chmn. 1960-61); asso. fellow Inst. Aero. Scis. (chmn. San Diego 1951-52); mem. Am. Ordnance Assn. (dir. San Diego 1958-59), San Diego C. of C., Soc. Automotive Engrs. (chmn. San Diego 1950-51, 55-56, v.p., mem. nat. council 1959). Patentee aircraft engines, related equipment. Home: 8428 Lemon Av La Mesa CA 92041 Office: 8 S 21st St San Diego CA 92113

HEATH, WILLIAM RUSSELL, forge co. exec.; b. Buffalo, Feb. 22, 1900; s. Byron H. and Mayme J. (Doyle) H.; M.E., Cornell U., 1922; m. Elizabeth N. Webster, Dec. 15, 1926; (dec. Sept. 1966); children—William W., M. Virginia; m. 2d, M. Patricia Hammond, Dec. 28, 1967. With Buffalo Forge Co., 1922—, successively engr., chief engr., dir. mfg., v.p. mfg., 1948-55, exec. v.p., 1955-58, pres., 1958-66, dir., 1951-70, chmn. bd., 1966-70, chmn. emeritus, 1970—; dir. Marine Trust Co. Western N.Y., 1963-68, mem. sr. adv. bd., 1968—. Mem. Am. Soc. Heating and Air Conditioning Engrs. (past pres. Western N.Y.). Mason. Clubs: Gyro (past pres.), Buffalo (past pres.) (Buffalo). Home: 18 Audley End Eggertsville NY 10021 Office: 490 Broadway Buffalo NY 14204

HEATH, WILLIAM WEBSTER, educator; b. Buffalo, July 1, 1929; s. William Russell and Elizabeth (Webster) H.; B.A., Amherst Coll., 1951; M.A., Columbia, 1952; Ph.D., U. Wis., 1956; m. Mary Louise Townsend, June 21, 1952; children-Elizabeth Townsend, Emily Byron. Teaching asst. English U. Wis., 1952-56; instr. English, Amherst Coll., 1956-59, asst. prof., 1959-64, asso. prof., 1964- 69, prof., 1969—; vis. prof. English, U. Mass., summers 1962, 64, 65, 66, 67, 68, 70; coordinator English Tchr.'s Inst., Amherst, 1969. Mem. Modern Land Assn., New U. Conf. Democrat. Author: Elizabeth Bowen: An Introduction to Her Novels, 1961. Editor: Wordsworth and Colerdige: A Study of Their Literary Relations, 1801-02, 1970. Home: 76 North East St Amherst MA 01002

HEATH, WILLIAM WOMACK, lawyer, former ambassador; b. Normangee, Tex., Dec. 7, 1903; s. John Al and Runie (Hill) H.; student Tex. Christian U., U. Tex. Law Sch.; m. Mavis Barnett, July 14, 1927; children—Cynthia (Mrs. D. G. Ray) and Linda (Mrs. Dean Hester). Admitted to Tex. bar, 1924; practiced in Anderson, Tex. 1924-33, in Austin, 1933-67, 69—; county atty. Grimes County, 1925-29; county judge Grimes County, 1931-32; asst. atty. gen. Tex., 1935-37; dir. Nat. Old Line Ins. Co., Pub. Savs. Life Ins. Co., gen. counsel or Tex. counsel numerous ins. cos.; U.S. ambassador to Sweden, Stockholm, 1967-69; dir. Dillard Stores, Braniff Airways, Inc., Capital Nat. Bank, Austin; rancher, 1950—. Chmn. Tex. Bd. for Hosps. and Spl. Schs., 1957-59; vice chmn. bd. lease U. Tex. lands, 1959-61; mem. bd. regents U. Tex., 1959-67, vice chmn. bd. regents, 1961-62, chmn., 1962-66; exec. com. gov. bds. Tex. State Supported Colls. and Univs., 1959-62. Gen. chmn. Gov. of Tex. inauguration, 1961, co-chmn., 1965. Del.-at-large Nat. Democratic Conv., 1960, 64. Mem. Tex. Tax Adv. Commn.; past pres. Tex. Youth and Law Enforcement Found. Sec. of state, Tex., 1933-35. Recipient U. Tex. Distinguished Alumnus award Pepperdine U., 1968; Distinguished Citizen Yr. award. Mem. Am. Bar Assn., State Bar Tex., Tex. Bar Found., Am. Judicature Soc. Methodist. Clubs: Austin, Headliners, Forty Acres, Citadel. Home: 1808 Vance Circle Austin TX 78701 Office: Perry Brooks Bldg Austin TX 78701

HEATHCOTE, LESLEY MURIEL, librarian; b. Edmonton, Alta., Can., May 12, 1904; d. Henry Walter and Annie Selina (Hilton) Heathcote; B.A., U. Alta., 1924, M.A., 1928; B.S. in L.S., U. Wash., 1929, postgrad. history, 1938-51. Came to U.S., 1928, naturalized, 1934. Asst. to registrar U. Alta., 1924-28; serials librarian U. Wash., 1929-44; research asst. ILO, 1945-46; gen. librarian Mont. State U. Library, Bozeman, 1946-47, head librarian, 1947- 65, dir. of libraries, 1965-70, prof. of library sci., 1952-70, prof. emeritus, 1970; editor Mont. Library Quar., 1955-63, compiled 8 yr. index, 1955-60; compiled 20 year index Mont. libraries, 1946-66. Second flutist Mont. State U. Civic Symphony Orch., 1958-70; sec. Bozeman Symphony Soc., 1967- 70. Bd. dirs. Mercer Island Environmental Council, 1971—. Recipient gold medal in French, Le Club Verendrye, 1924, silver medal Italian Club, 1930. Life mem. Am. (chmn. serials sect. 1938-40), Pacific Northwest (pres. 1951-52), Mont. (pres. 1953-54) library assns., Am. Assn. U. Profs. (v.p. Mont. State U. 1954-56), Agrl. History Soc., Phi Alpha Theta. Compiler 5 year indexes to PNLA Quar., 1951-56, 56-61, 61- 65. Author chpts. in books. Editor: Books Are Friends, 1962. Contbr. profl. jours. Home: 9236 SE 33d Mercer Island WA 98040

HEATHER, GEORGE GAIL coll. dean; b. LaPlata, Mo., May 9, 1917; s. George and Mary Katherine (Jones) H.; B.S., S.W. Mo. State Coll., 1938; A.M., State U. Ia., 1942, Ph.D., 1946; m. Mary Caroline Stewart, Apr. 15, 1946; children—Robert Marshall, Georgia Michelle, Patricia Lizabeth, John Gilbert, James Stewart. Comml. tchr., coach Cincinnati (Ia.) High Sch., 1938-39; comml. tchr. Ritenour High Sch., St. Louis, 1939-42; instr. State U. Ia., 1942-45; asst. prof. econs. and bus. adminstrn., Ft. Hays (Kan.) State Coll., 1946; asso. prof. econs., dir. curriculum coll. bus. adminstrn., U. Denver, 1946-47; chmn. dept. commerce Fla. State U., 1947-50; dean bus. adminstrn. Tex. Tech. Coll., Lubbock; 1950-69, dir. evening program, 1950-55; prof. bus. adminstrn., dean Coll. Bus. Adminstrn., U. Neb., Omaha, 1969—. Mem. Southwestern Social Sci. Assn., Midwest Bus. Adminstrn. Assn., Omaha Execs. Assn., Omaha C. of C., Sigma Tau Gamma, Alpha Kappa Psi, Pi Gamma Nu, Phi Alpha Kappa, Beta Gamma Sigma, Beta Alpha Psi, Pi Omega Pi. Mason (32, Shriner), Rotarian. Contbr. articles in univ. bulls. Home: 5181 Jackson St Omaha NB 68106

HEATHERINGTON, J. SCOTT, osteopathic physician and surgeon; b. Athol, Kan., Apr. 22, 1919; s. Clarence Linder and Nora B. (Scott) H.; B.S., York Coll., 1943; D.O., Still Coll. Osteopathy and Surgery, 1944; m. Geraldine Virginia Greene, Feb. 20, 1944; children—Jeffrey Scott, Douglas Linder, Marc Filbert. Intern Detroit Osteopathic Hosp., 1944-45; pvt. practice, Medford, Ore., 1945-57, Gladstone, Ore., 1957—; guest lectr. Coll. Osteopathic Medicine and Surgery, Des Moines, Phila. Coll. Osteopathic Medicine; pres. staff Portland (Ore.) Osteopathic Hosp., 1963-64. Mem. Ore. Meth. Conf. Finance Commn., 1956-60. Trustee Coll. Osteopathic Medicine and Surgery, 1967—, Medford Salvation Army, 1954-57, Rouge River Valley Manor, 1951-57, Nat. Osteopathic Found., 1960-69. Mem. Am. (ho. dels. 1954-63, trustee 1959-68, exec. com. 1964-71, pres. elect 1968- 69, pres. 1969-70), Ore. (trustee 1949-63, pres. 1952-53, 60-61) osteopathic assns., So. Ore. Osteopathic Soc. (pres. 1949), Ore. Tri-City C. of C. (bd. dirs. 1960- 62), Am. Coll. Gen. Practitioner in Osteopathic Medicine and Surgery, Sigma Sigma Phi (hon.). Republican. Rotarian (pres. Oregon City 1961-62). Clubs: Oswego Lake (Ore.) Country; Clackamas County Knife and Fork (pres. 1962-63) (Milwaukie, Ore.). Home: 995 S Skyland Dr Lake Oswego OR 97034 Office: 1550 McLoughlin Blvd Gladstone OR 97027

HEATHERTON, JOEY, actress; d. Ray Heatherton. Appeared in movies Where Love Has Gone, Twilight of Horror, My Blood Runs Cold; formerly appeared on TV show Hulabaloo, in TV play Of Mice and Men, 1968. Address: care of Sidney J Gittler 9777 Wilshire Blvd Beverly Hills CA 90212*

HEATON, CULVER, architect; b. Los Angeles, Jan. 3, 1912; B.Arch., U. So. Cal., 1936. With Culver Heaton & Assos., Pasadena, Cal., 1941—; prin. works include Van Nuys Savs. & Loan Assn., La Habra Civic Center, Muir High Sch., Pasadena, 300 ch. projects, including Covenant Presbyn. Ch., Long Beach, St. Peter's By The Sea Presbyn. Ch., Portuguese Bend. Fellow A.I.A. (pres. Pasadena 1951; dir. 1952; treas. Cal. council 1952, dir. 1958); mem. Ch. Archtl. Guild Am., Guild Religious Architecture (western regional dir. 1969-70). Address: 774 N Lake Av Pasadena CA 91104

HEATON, KENNETH LOUIS, indsl. psychologist; b. Bloomington, Ind., May 26, 1902; s. Thomas and Hessie (Edwards) H.; A.B., Ind. U., 1924; A.M., Boston U., 1926; Ph.D., U. Chgo., 1929; m. E. Allison Bolitho, Aug. 11, 1926; children—Elizabeth (Mrs David C. Skinner), Janet (Mrs. Gerard P. Thomas). Dir. Mich. Bur. Research, 1933-41; chief tng. officer, liaison officer with Republic of Mexico, U.S. Office Civilian Def., Washington, 1942-44; chief program devel. and research, civilian personnel and tng. div. Office Sec. War, 1944-46, also research cons. U.S. Strategic Bombing Survey, chmn. postwar planning com. on civilian personnel Sec. War; dean adminstrn. Boston U., 1946-50; v.p. Richardson, Bellows, Henry & Co., 1950-56; partner Heaton, Floyd & Watson, mgmt. cons., Phila., 1956—. Cons. Nat. Security Resources Bd., 1952-53; dir. evaluation Mut. Security Program, 1952-53; cons. Dept. Def., 1948—; cons. domestic, fgn. industries. Fellow A.A.A.S.; mem. Am. Edn. Research Assn., Phi Beta Kappa, Phi Delta Kappa. Republican. Conglist. Clubs: Cosmos (Washington); Urban (Philadelphia); St. Botolph (Boston). Author: Identifying the Worker in Need of Training, 1945; Guide for Industrial Managers, 1958; Personnel Manuals (fgn. industries), 1960, 61; Audit Guide for Industrial Managers, 1964; Overseas Management and the Local Community, 1964; also of profl. articles, and studies of fgn. industries. Co-author: Curriculum Based on Functional Needs of Students, 1937; Examining Personnel for Civilian Employment, 1946. Home: School House Lane and Wissahickon Av Philadelphia PA 19144 Office: The Cambridge Philadelphia PA 19144

HEATON, LEONARD DUDLEY, retired army surgeon gen.; b. Parkersburg, W. Va., Nov. 18, 1902; s. George and Emma Gertrude (Dudley) H.; student Denison U., 1919-22, D.Sc., 1959; M.D., U. Louisville, 1926, D.Sc., 1959; D.Sc., W.Va. U., 1962; L.H.D., Brandeis U., 1964; m. Sara Hill Richardson, June 30, 1926; 1 dau., Sara Dudley (Mrs. Preston B. Magson Jr.). Intern, Letterman Gen. Hosp., San Francisco, 1926-28; entered M.C., U.S. Army, 1926, commd. 1st lt., 1927, advanced through grades to lt. gen., 1959; asst. to chief surg. services William Beaumont Gen. Hosp., El Paso, Tex., 1929-30, Tripler Gen. Hosp., Honolulu, 1930-32, Brooke Gen. Hosp., San Antonio, 1932-37; chief surg. services, Ft. Warren, Wyo., 1937-40, N. Sector Gen. Hosp., Hawaii, 1940-42; exec. officer Woodrow Wilson Gen. Hosp., Staunton, Va., 1942- 44; comd. 160th Gen. Hosp. and 802d Hosp. Center, Blandford, Eng., 1944- 45; comdg. gen. Letterman Gen. Hosp., 1946-53; comdg. gen. Walter Reed Army Med. Center, Washington, 1953-59; surgeon gen. Dept. of Army, 1959-70, retired, 1970. Decorated Legion of Merit with 2 oak leaf clusters, D.S.M. with 3 oak leaf clusters. Diplomate Am. Bd. Surgery. Fellow A.C.S., Am., So. surg. assns., Royal Coll. Surgeons Eng. (hon.); mem. Internat. Soc. Surgery, Halstead Soc., A.M.A., Pacific Coast Surg. Assn., Alpha Omega Alpha, also mil. orgns. Baptist. Home: Linden Rd Pinehurst NC 28374

HEATON, RICHARD HARRY, mfg. co. exec.; b. Ashland, Mass., Aug. 28, 1919; s. Charles Dean and Mabel (Messom) H.; B.S. in Bus. Adminstrn., Boston U., 1941; m. Bernice E. Marble, May 13, 1942; children—Richard, Donald, Beverly, Nancy. With Gillette Co., 1955—, controller, 1962-66, controller, v.p., 1966- 68, treas., v.p., 1968—. Mem. bd. visitors Boston U. Coll. Bus. Adminstrn., 1964—. Served to 1st lt. AUS, 1943-46. C.P.A., Mass. Mem. Am. Inst. C.P.A.'s, Financial Execs. Inst. Home: 43 Cutler Dr Ashland MA 01721 Office: Gilette Park Boston MA 02127

HEAVNER, THEODORE JAMES CHOPARD, fgn. service officer; b. Canton, O., Jan. 3, 1929; s. Homer Clyde and Irene (Chopard) H.; A.B., Western Res. U., 1951; postgrad. State U. Ia., 1951-52, Harvard, 1952- 53, Cornell U., 1957-58; m. Jean Louise Schupp, Aug. 27, 1950 (div.); 1 dau., Sandra Lynn; m. 2d, Penelope Fay Robertson, Dec. 8, 1970. Fgn. service officer Dept. State, 1955—, consul, Hue, Viet Nam, 1958-60, Medan, Indonesia, 1964-66; 1st sec. Am. embassy, Saigon, 1966-69; dep. chief of mission Am. embassy, Georgetown, Guyana, 1969—. Served with AUS, 1953-55. Recipient Superior Honor award Dept. State, 1965. Home: 731 Terrace Av NW Canton OH 44708 Office: Am Embassy Georgetown Guyana

HEAZEL, FRANCIS JAMES, lawyer; b. Shenandoah, Va., Dec. 10, 1891; s. James F. and Catherine (Morrisey) H.; student Mt. St. Mary's Coll., 1909-10; LL.B., Washington and Lee U., 1912; m. Anna L. Flanagan, Apr. 28, 1914; children—Gertrude (Mrs. John J. Vogel, Jr.), Francis James, Catherine (Mrs. P. F. Clark). Admitted to Va. bar, 1912, Tenn. bar, 1916, N.C. bar, 1922; city atty., Kingsport, Tenn., 1918-19; dir. Forman Realty Corp., Chgo., Bismark Hotel Corp., (Chgo.); dir. sec. Madison Sq. Garden Corp. N.Y.C., 1956-59. Mem. of Buncombe Co. Sinking Fund Com., 1933-54; N.C. Nat. Park, Pkwy. and Forest Devel. Com., 1947-53. Mem. Am., N.C., Buncombe bar assns., C. of C. (pres. 1947), Ashville Indsl. Council (pres. 1947-48). Democrat. Roman Catholic. K.C. (dir.; past nat. treas.). Home: 175 Stratford Rd Asheville NC 28804 Office: Jackson Bldg PO Box 7437 Asheville NC 28807

HEBALD, MILTON, sculptor; b. N.Y.C., May 24, 1917; s. Nathan and Eva (Elting) H.; student Nat. Acad. Design, Beaux Arts Sch., Art Students League; m. Cecile Rosner, June 10, 1958; 1 dau., Margo. Commns. include facade Equador Pavilion, N.Y. World's Fair, 1939, trophy Rep. Aviation Co., 1942, Turtle Tent, play sculpture, Phila., 1954, Isla Verdi Aeroport, San Juan, P.R., 1954, 16 foot bronze group East Bronx (N.Y.) Tb Hosp., 1954, portrait bust of Archibald MacLeish, Am. Acad. Arts and Letters, 1957, bronze relief Zodiac, Pan Am. Terminal, Kennedy Airport, 1957-58, Ackland Meml., U. N.C., 1961; one-man exhbns. include ACA Gallery, N.Y.C., 1937, 40, Grand Central Moderns, N.Y.C., 1950, 54, Schneider Gallery, Rome, Italy, 1957, Nordness Gallery, N.Y.C., 1959-71; represented permanent collections N.Y. Acad. Arts and Letters, Notre Dame U. (N.J.), Phila. Mus., Whitney Mus. Am. Art, Yale, U. Ariz., U. N.C., Ackland Meml., Ein. Harrod, Israel, Joyce Mus., Dublin, Joyce Meml., Zurich, Switzerland; tchr. Am. Artist Sch., 1940-41, Cooper Union, 1945-53, Bklyn. Mus. Art Sch., 1946-52, Skowhegan Art Sch., 1951-53, U. Minn., 1949, Long Beach (Cal.) State, 1968. Recipient 2d prize Social Security Competition, U.S. Govt. relief in Post Office, Toms River, N.J., 1940; 2d prize Wings for Victory, 1942, 1st prize Bklyn. Mus., 1950, 2d prize Pa. Acad., 1951, 1st prize N.Y.C. Dept. Pub. Works for East Bronx Tb Hosp., 1953, Prix de Rome in Sculpture, 1955-58. Fellow Am. Acad. in Rome. Home: Viale Trastevere 60 Office: Studio Via Orti D'Alibert 7A Rome Italy

HEBARD, FRANKLIN A., ret. banker; b. Sturbridge, Mass., 1897; grad. Middlebury Coll., 1919; LL.B., Northeastern U., 1924. Past chmn. bd. Salem Five Cents Savs. Bank (Mass.); dir. Holyoke Mut. Fire Ins. Co., Naumkeag Trust Co. Home: 33 Chestnut St Salem MA 01970

HEBB, DONALD OLDING, psychologist, educator; b. Chester, N.S., Can., July 22, 1904; s. Arthur Morrison and Mary Clara (Olding) H.; B.A., Dalhousie U., 1925; M.A., McGill U., 1932; Ph.D., Harvard, 1936; D.Sc. (hon.), U. Chgo., 1961, McMaster U., 1967; LL.D., Queen's U., 1967; m. Marion Isabel Clark, Dec. 20, 1931 (dec. 1933); m. 2d, Elizabeth Nichols Donovan, June 19, 1937 (dec. 1962); children—Jane, Mary; m. 3d, Margaret Doreen Williamson, Aug. 31, 1966. High sch. tchr., elementary sch. prin., 1925-34; tchr. Queen's U., Kingston, Ont., 1939-42; prof. McGill U., 1947—, chmn. dept. psychology, 1948-58; research Montreal Neurol. Inst., 1937-39, Yerkes Labs., Orange Park, Fla., 1942-47. Bd. sci. counsellors NIH, 1965—, chmn., 1967-68. Hon. fellow Brit. Psychol. Soc.; mem. Am. (dir. 1955-58, pres. div. 3, 1954, pres. 1960), Canadian (pres. 1953) psychol. assns., A.A.A.S., Sigma Xi. Author: Organization of Behavior, 1949; Textbook of Psychology, 1958

HEBB, FURMAN HELVESTON, pub. co. exec.; b. Sarasota, Fla., Feb. 25, 1930; s. Homer Lincoln and Mabel Stuart (Helveston) H.; B.A., U. Fla., 1952; m. Jean Arnold McIntosh, June 7, 1952; children—Carol Grace, Stuart Furman, Kathryn Elizabeth. Supr., Dan River Mills, 1952-53; dept. mgr. Lord and Taylor, N.Y.C., 1953-54; salesman Audio Exchange, Jamaica, L.I., N.Y., 1954-57; with Ziff-Davis Pub. Co., 1957—, feature editor Popular Electronics mag., 1958-60, editor HiFi/Stereo Rev., 1960-65, asst. to pres. of co., 1965-68, adminstrv. v.p., 1968—. Home: 359 W 22d St New York City NY 10011 Office: 1 Park Av New York City NY 10016

HEBB, MALCOLM HAYDEN, physicist; b. Marquette, Mich., July 21, 1910; s. Thomas Carlyle and Evelyn Shewell (Hayden) H.; B.A., U. B.C., 1931, D.Sc., 1963; postgrad. U. Wis., 1931-34; Ph.D., Harvard, 1936; m. Marion Elizabeth Evers, May 8, 1943. Instr. physics Harvard, 1936-37, Harvard travelling fellow to U. Utrecht, 1937-38; instr. physics Duke U., 1938-42; anti- submarine devices Harvard Underwater Sound Lab., Nat. Def. Research Com., 1942-45; physicist research lab. Sharples Corp., 1945-49; research asso. Gen. Electric Co., 1949-51, mgr. gen. physics research dept., 1951-68, physicist, 1968—. Vis. com. physics Tufts U., 1967; vis. com. elec. engering. Princeton, 1959—. Recipient Gov. Gen. Medal (B.C.), 1931. Fellow Am. Phys. Soc.; mem. of Netherlands Phys. Soc., Sigma Xi. Clubs: Mohawk, Mohawk Golf. Home: 2012 Lexington Pkwy Schenectady NY 12309 Office: Research Lab Gen Electric Co Schenectady NY 12301

HEBBARD, FREDERICK WORTHMAN, educator; b. Eureka, Utah, Aug. 6, 1923; s. Frederick Archibald and Betty (Metscher) H.; B.S., U. Cal. at Berkeley, 1949, M.S., 1951, Ph.D., 1957. Apprentice patternmaker Mare Is. (Cal.) Shipyard, 1941-43, patternmaker, 1943-45; teaching asst. optometry U. Cal. at Berkeley, 1949-50, clin. instr., 1950-57; mem. faculty Ohio State U., 1957—, prof. optics and optometry, 1967—, dir. Sch. Optometry, 1966-68, dean Coll. Optometry, 1968—. Bd. dirs. Nat. Bd. Examiners in Optometry, 1964- -; cons. div. hosp. and med. facilities, edn. facilities br. USPHS, 1966—. Named Alumnus of Year, U. Cal. Coll. Optometry, 1956. Fellow Am. Acad. Optometry; mem. Optical Soc. Am., A.A.A.S., U. Cal. Alumni Assn., (bd. dirs. 1953-56), U. Cal. Optometric Alumni Assn. (pres. 1952- 55), Phi Beta Kappa, Sigma Xi, Epsilon Psi Epsilon, Beta Sigma Kappa. Republican. Lutheran. Author articles in field. Home: 2100 Haverford Rd Columbus OH 43220

HEBBARD, WILLIAM LAWRENCE, internat. financial ofcl.; b. Ishpeming, Mich., Mar. 18, 1912; s. William J. and Louise (Hicks) H.; B.S., No. Mich. U., 1934; M.A. in Econs.; U. Mich., 1935, postgrad., 1935-38, 39-40; postgrad. Grad. Inst. Internat. Studies, Geneva, Switzerland, 1938-39; m. Ethel Frances Mikulich, May 3, 1945; children-Barbara L., Patricia J., Bruce L. Asst. to chmn. Geneva Research Centre, 1938-39; with Office Internat. Finance, Treasury Dpt., 1940-54, U.S. Treasury rep., London, 1948-50, asst. dir., 1950-54; with exchange restrictions dept. Internat. Monetary Fund, Washington, 1954-64, dep. sec., 1964-67, sec., 1967—. Recipient Distinguished Alumnus award No. Mich. U., 1968. Traveling fellow Social Sci. Research Council, 1938-39. Unitarian. Home: 4300 Glenridge St Kensington MD 20795 Office: Internat Monetary Fund 19th and H Sts NW Washington DC 20431

HEBBEL, ROBERT, medical educator; b. Windom, Minn., Sept. 23, 1906; s. Henry and Christine (Mensen) H.; B.S., U. Minn., M.B., 1932, M.D., 1933, M.S., 1939, Ph.D., 1942; m. Beulah Agre, Mar. 13, 1942; children—Robert Peter, Elizabeth Agre. Intern Mpls. Gen. Hosp., 1933; resident pathology U. Minn. Hosp., 1937-41; instr. pathology U. Minn. Med. Sch., Mpls., 1941-45, asst. prof., 1945-47, asso. prof., 1947-51, prof. pathology, 1951—. Served with M.C., AUS, 1942-45. Decorated Bronze Star. Mem. Hennepin County Med. Soc., Minn. Med. Assn., Am. Assn. Pathologists and Bacteriologists, A.M.A., Am. Soc. Clin. Pathologists, Coll. Am. Pathologists, Am. Assn. Cancer Research, Internat. Acad. Pathology, Alpha Omega Alpha, Phi Delta Theta, Nu Sigma Nu. Office: Home: 1510 Grantham St St Paul MN 55108

HEBDEN, CHARLES STEWART, chem. co. exec.; b. Phila., June 18, 1920; s. Joseph Stewart and Mae Irene (Batty) H.; A.B. in Bus. Adminstrn., Ursinus Coll., 1945; m. Evelyn D. DeVore, July 7, 1945; children—Ronald S., Carolyn L., Roger S. With Phila. Nat. Bank, 1938-42; with Rohm & Haas Co., Phila., 1946—, asst. treas., 1954-63, treas., 1963—, v.p., dir., 1971—; dir. subsidiaries Warren-Teed Products Co., Sauquoit Fibers Co.; dir. Benjamin Franklin Hotel Co., Phila. Served with USNR, 1942-46. Clubs: St. Davids (Pa.) Golf; Down Town, Rittenhouse (Phila.). Home: 1110 Wyndon Rd Rosemont PA 19010 Office: Independence Mall W Philadelphia PA 19130

HEBDEN, J.R., business exec. Comptroller, Delco Moraine div. Gen. Motors Corp., Dayton, O. Office: 1420 Wisconsin Blvd Dayton OH*

HEBEL, ANTHONY JEROME, advt. agy. exec.; b. LaSalle, Ill., Mar. 2, 1928; s. Anthony Joseph and Minerva (Maher) H.; B.A., U. Ill., 1951; m. Lynn DeBiasio, June 16, 1951; children—Thomas, Richard and William (twins). Account supr. McCann- Erickson, Inc., Chgo., 1951-59; v.p. Post & Morr. Inc., Chgo., 1959-61; sr. v.p. Post & Moor, Inc., Chgo., 1959-61; sr. v.p. Post, Moor & Gardner, Inc., 1961-63; exec. v.p., dir., chmn. operations com., chmn. profit sharing trust fund com. Post-Keyes-Gardner, Inc., Chgo., 1963—; dir. PKG-Brunning, Inc., London, Brunning Group of Cos., Ltd., London. Active Chgo. Crusade of Mercy and United Settlement Appeal campaign drives, 1964-71. Served with USNR, 1946-48. Mem. Chgo. Assn. Commerce and Industry, John Henry Newman Honor Soc., Wilderness Soc., Isaac Walton League, Nat. Parks Assn., Lincoln Park Zool. Soc., Am. Field Service Art Inst., Alpha Delta Sigma. Home: 1037 Warrington Rd Deerfield IL 60015 Office: 875 N Michigan Av Chicago IL 60611

HEBERT, F. EDWARD editor, congressman; b. New Orleans, Oct. 12, 1901; s. Felix Joseph and Lea (Naquin) H.; student Tulane U., 1920-24; m. Gladys Bofill, Aug. 1, 1934; 1 dau., Dawn Marie (Mrs. John Malcolm Duhe, Jr.). Sports reporter The New Orleans Times-Picayune, 1919-20, asst. sports editor, 1920-25; asst. sports editor New Orleans States, 1925-26, polit. editor and columnist, 1929-37, city editor, 1937-40, when paper broke "Louisiana Scandals," 1939, resulting in overthrow of Huey Long polit. machine (paper subsequently awarded Delta Sigma Chi plaque for "courage in journalism"); dir. publicity Loyola U., New Orleans, 1926-29; dir. Central Homestead Assn. Mem. 77th-92d Congresses, 1st La. Dist., chmn. house armed Services com. Pres. Young Men's Bus. Club New Orleans, 1932. Mem. Delta Sigma Phi (nat. v.p. 1937-49). Democrat. Roman Catholic. Author: I Went, I Saw, I Heard. Home: 5367 Canal Blvd New Orleans LA 70124 Office: House Office Bldg Washington DC 20515

HEBERT, LOUIS, chmn., pres. Banque Canadienne Nationale, Montreal, Que., Can.; dir. Wabasso Ltd., Sun Life Assurance Co. Can., Compagnie Immobilière BCN Ltée, RoyNat Ltd., RoyNat Leasing Ltd., Noranda Mines Ltd., la Compagnie des Ciments du St-Laurent. Address: 500 Place d'Armes Montreal 126 Quebec Canada

HEBERT, PAUL MACARIUS, univ. dean; b. Baton Rouge, Nov. 1, 1907; s. Paul Armand and Annie (Byrne) H.; A.B., La. State U., 1929, LL.B., 1929; J.S.D., Yale, 1930; LL.D., Loyola U., New Orleans, 1968; m. Estelle Le Jeune, May 18, 1926; children—Barbara Clare, Mary Sunshine, Paul Macarius. Admitted to La. bar, 1929; prof. law Loyola U., New Orleans, 1930-31, prof., dean Law Sch., 1932-36; asst. prof. law La. State U., 1931-32, prof. law, dean adminstrn., 1936-37, dean Law Sch., prof. law, 1937-39, acting pres., 1939-41, dean law, 1941-49, dean univ., prof. law, 1949-51, dean law, 1952-57, 59—; mem. firm Breazeale, Sachse, Wilson & Hebert, 1951- 52, 57-59; spl. asst. atty. gen. La. for La. Coast Line Litigation, 1965-67. Atty., La. Legislative Bur., 1932, 34, 36, 38; sec., mem. council La. State Law Inst., 1938—; mem. La. Ednl. Survey Commn., 1940-42; mem. gen. com. to draft new constn. State of La., 1946—; civilian judge U.S. Mil. Tribunals, Nurnberg, Germany, 1947-48; mem. panel Fed. Mediation and Conciliation Service; mem. loyalty rev. bd. U.S. Civil Service Commn., 1948-53; chmn. La. Labor Mediation Bd., 1953-67; mem. La. Labor-Mgmt. Commn. Inquiry, 1967—. Served from capt. to lt. col., AUS, 1942-45. Decorated Legion of Merit. Mem. Am. Arbitration Assn. (panel), Nat. Acad. Arbitrators (panel), Am., La. (bd. govs. 1946-47, 53), Assn. Am. Law Schs. (chmn. com. inter-Am. coop. 1945-47, exec. com. 1946-47), Order Coif, Delta Kappa Epsilon, Phi Delta Phi, Phi Kappa Phi, Omicron Delta Kappa. Democrat. Roman Catholic. K.C. Home: 2331 Kleinert Av Baton Rouge LA 70806

HEBNER, PAUL CHESTER, oil co. exec.; b. Warren, Pa., Dec. 29, 1919; s. Henry G. and Mabel (Gross) H.; student Ohio State U.; grad. Bliss Coll., 1940; m. Dorothy Farrell, Feb. 16, 1943; children—Richard P., Kathleen D., Susan M., Christine L., Elizabeth A., Jeannie M. Accountant, adminstrv. asst. Altman-Coady Co., Columbus, O., 1940-41; mgr. accounting, exec. adminstr. T & T Oil Co. and asso. cos., Los Angeles, 1954-57; with Occidental Petroleum Corp., Los Angeles, 1957—, sec.-treas., 1958-68, v.p., sec., 1968—, dir., 1960—; officer, dir. subsidiary cos. Served to maj. USAAF, 1942-45. Mem. Am. Soc. Corporate Secs., Petroleum Accountants Assn. Home: 30484 Ambersky Dr Palos Verdes Peninsula CA 90274 Office: 10889 Wilshire Blvd Los Angeles CA 90024

HECHENBLEIKNER, LOUIS, artist; b. Innsbruck, Tyrol, Austria, Oct. 29, 1893; s. Jakob and Magdalene (Fischler) H.; student Royal Acad. Art, Duesseldorf, Germany, 1913-14, Akademie der Bildenden Kunste, Munich, Germany, 1919-22; m. Christl Ritter, Aug. 26, 1926. Came to U.S. 1923, naturalized, 1930. Engaged in advt. design, 1923-30; graphic artist, tchr., 1930—; tchr. N.Y. Evening Sch. Indsl. Arts, 1930-39; formerly prof. of graphic art Queens Coll., Flushing; woodcut, lithographic exhbns. Boston Mus., Bklyn. Mus., Cin. Art. Mus., Rochester Meml. Art Gallery, Library of Congress, De Cordova Mus., others; rep. print collections Met. Mus., Phila. Mus., Cin. Art Mus., Library of Congress; wood engravings for Winston edit. Brothers Karamazov, 1949, Colophon, Quar. for Bookmen, 1934, 38. Recipient Purchase prize Library of Congress, 1943, 48, 54, 57, 62, Phila. Print Club, 1946, 43d exhbn. S.A.G.A.-IBM Galleries, 1960; also hon. mentions A.N.A.; mem. Boston Printmakers, Phila. Print Club, Soc. Am. Graphic Artists, Yaddo Corp. Home: 1181 Madison Av New York City NY 10028

HECHINGER, FRED MICHAEL, newspaper editor; b. Nuremberg, Germany, July 7, 1920; s. Dr. Julius and Lilly (Niedermaier) H.; A.B., Coll. City N.Y., 1943; student N.Y.U., 1937-38; postgrad. U. London, 1945; LL.D., Kenyon Coll., 1955, Bates Coll., 1963, U. Notre Dame, 1963, Knox Coll., 1966; L.H.D., Bard Coll., 1956, Wash. Coll., 1965, Wilkes Coll., 1968, St. Joseph's Coll., 1970; m. Grace Bernstein; children—Paul David, John Edward. Came to U.S., 1937, naturalized, 1943. Corr. for the London Times Ednl. Supplement, 1946-47; ednl. columnist Washington Post, 1947-50; edn. editor, fgn. corr., cons. to pub. Sunday Herald, Bridgeport, Conn., 1947-50; fgn. corr. Overseas News Agy., 1948-50; spl. writer This Week mag., 1946-59; edn. editor N.Y. Herald Tribune, 1950-56; asso. pub. The Sunday Herald, Bridgeport, Conn., 1956-59; edn. editor, The N. Y. Times, N.Y.C., 1959-69, mem. editorial bd., 1969—. Cons. edn. and cultural relations div. U.S. Mil. Govt., summers 1948, 49. Served with Office Mil. Attache, Am. Embassy, London, also with Brit. War Office, 1944-46. Recipient Brit. Empire Medal, George Polk Meml. Award, 1950, 51, Fairbanks Award, 1952, Townsend Harris medal, 1968. Mem. Am. Pub. Relations Assn. (recipient award 1952), Edn. Writers Assn. (pres. 1956; awards 1948, 49, 52, 64), Phi Beta Kappa. Clubs: Coffee House, Century Assn. Author: An Adventure in Education, 1956; New Approaches, 1955; Worrying About College, 1958; The Big Red Schoolhouse, 1959; (with Grace Hechinger) Teen-age Tyranny, 1963; The New York Times Guide to N.Y.C. Pvt. Schools, 1968; Pre-School Education Today, 1966. Education editor Parents' Mag., 1957-59. Contbr. to Harper's mag., The Reporter mag., Sat. Rev. Lit., McCall's mag. Home: 40 E 88th St New York City NY 10028 Office: 229 W 43d St New York City NY 10036

HECHLER, KEN, congressman; b. Roslyn, N.Y., Sept. 20, 1914; s. Charles Henry and Catherine Elizabeth (Hauhart) H.; A.B., Swarthmore Coll., 1935; A.M., Columbia, 1936, Ph.D., 1940. Lectr. govt., Columbia, Barnard Coll., 1937- 41; research asst. Judge Samuel I. Rosenman, on Pres. Roosevelt's pub. papers, 1939-50; sect. chief Bur. Census, 1940; personnel technician Office Emergency Mgmt., 1941; adminstrv. analyst Bur. Budget, 1941-42, 46-47; spl. asst. Pres. Truman, White House, 1949-53; research dir. Stevenson-Kefauver campaign, 1956; adminstrv. aid U.S. Senator Carroll of Colo., summer 1957; mem. of 86th-92d Congresses, 4th District West Virginia, chmn. sub-com. on advanced research and tech. Ho. Com. on Sci. and Astronautics. Asst. prof. politics Princeton, 1947-49; asso. prof. polit. sci., Marshall U., 1957; radio, TV commentator WHTN, Huntington, W.Va., 1957-58. Del.-at-large from W.Va. to Democratic Nat. Convs., 1964, 68. Served from pvt. to major AUS, 1942-46; combat historian, 1944. Mem. Am. Polit. Sci. Assn. (asso. dir. 1953-56), Am. Legion, V.F.W., D.A.V. Democrat. Episcopalian. Elk Club: Civitan (Huntington). Author: Insurgency: Personalities and Policies of the Taft Era, 1940; The Bridge at Remagen, 1957-(tech. adviser for motion picture by Wolper Prodns. for United Artists, 1969); West Virginia Memories of President Kennedy, 1965. Home: 917 5th Av Huntington WV 25701 Office: Cannon Office Bldg Washington DC 20515

HECHT, ABRAHAM BERL, clergyman, educator; b. Bklyn., Apr. 5, 1922; s. Samuel and Sadie (Auster) H.; B. Religious Edn., Yeshivah U., 1959, B.A., 1960, M.S., 1961; D.D., Philathea Coll., Ont., Can., 1960; m. Lillian Greenhut, June 4, 1944; children—Naomi, Esther, Eli, Joseph Isaac, Rachel, Shoshana, Samuel, Aaron, Israel. Ordained rabbi, 1942; founder All Day Yeshivah schs. in Dorchester and Worcester, Mass., also Newark and Buffalo, 1943- 44; rabbi Bnei Magen David Congregation, Bklyn., 1946-50, Magen David Community Center, Bklyn., 1950-57, Shaare Zion Congregation, Bklyn., 1957—; prin. Shaare Zion Talmud Torah, 1960—, Shaare Zion Girls Sch., 1958—; instr. Bible and Jewish philosophy Yeshiva U. High Sch., Bklyn., 1964—. Hon. chmn., leader ann. dinner State Israel Bond Orgn., 1961- -; hon. chmn ann. dinner United Jewish Appeal, 1964—. Recipient Honor award Israel Bond Orgn., 1959, 62; Honor award Yeshivah Magen David, 1960. Mem. Rabbinical Alliance Am. (pres. 1964-67), Rabbinical Bd. Flatbush (v.p. 1962-65, pres. 1963—), Hebrew Prins. Assn. Author: Spiritual Horizons, 1964. Home: 2110 Ocean Pkwy Brooklyn NY 11223 Office: 2030 Ocean Pkwy Brooklyn NY 11223

HECHT, ADOLPH, botanist, educator; b. Chgo., July 25, 1914; s. Mannassa and Bertha (Friedmann) H.; B.S., U. Chgo., 1936, M.S., 1937; Ph.D., Ind. U., 1942; m. Edith Goldstein, July 19, 1942; children—Anton Louis, Julia Ann. Field asst. U.S. Forest and Range Expt. Sta., Missoula, Mont., 1937-38; grad. teaching, research asst. Ind. U., 1938-42; instr. botany U. Chgo., 1946-47; asst. prof., then prof. botany Wash. State U., 1947—, chmn. dept., 1955-70. Mem. Commn. on Undergrad. Edn. in Biol. Scis., 1966-69. Served from pvt. to capt., USAAF, 1942-46, lt. col. Res., ret. Fellow A.A.A.S. (pres. Pacific div. 1966-67); mem. Bot. Soc. Am. (chmn. Pacific sect. 1955-56), Am. Genetic Assn., Genetics Soc. Am., N.W. Sci. Assn. (pres. 1965-66; hon. life mem., hon. trustee), Western Soc. Naturalists, Phi Beta Kappa, Sigma Xi. Editor: Plant Sci. Bull., 1965-71; Guide to Graduate Study in Botany for the United States, 1966. Home: 306 Derby St Pullman WA 99163

HECHT, ALAN DANNENBERG, ins. exec.; b. Balt., Aug. 31, 1918; s. Lee I. and Miriam (Dannenberg) H.; B.S., Johns Hopkins, 1940; m. Margaret R. Moses, June 27, 1943; children—Stephen Lee, Nancy H., Elizabeth Ann. Solicitor, Travelers Ins. Co., 1945-60; partner Hecht-Schoenfeld Ins. Agy., 1960-62; merged and formed Wolman-Hecht-Schoenfeld, Inc., 1962, v.p., 1962-64; v.p. Wolman-Hecht, Inc., 1964-70, pres., 1971—; formed Alan D. Hecht & Co., 1964, inc., 1966, now pres.; gen. agt. Sun Life Ins. Co. Am., Balt., 1960—. Mem. Balt. Estate Planning Council. Tchr. C.L.U. econs. and finance Johns Hopkins, 1954—; bd. graders Am. Coll. Life Underwriters. Bd. dirs. Balt. chpt. Am. Jewish Com., pres., 1958-60, now mem. nat. exec. bd.; mem. bd. trustees Sinai Hosp. of Balt., 1959-68. Served to 1st lt. AUS, 1941-45. Recipient Nat. Quality award Nat. Assn. Life Underwriters; Nat. Sales Achievement award, 1966, 67. C.L.U. Mem. Am. Soc. C.L.U. (bd. dirs. 1957—; nat. sec. 1962-63; pres. 1964-65), Omicron Delta Kappa, Pi Delta Epsilon. Jewish religion (pres. congregation 1968-70, past dir.). Home: 23 Hamill Rd Baltimore MD 21210 Office: 819 Fidelity Bldg Baltimore MD 21201

HECHT, ANTHONY EVAN, poet; b. N.Y.C., Jan. 16, 1923; s. Melvyn Hahlo and Dorothea (Holzman) H.; B.A., Bard Coll., 1944; M.A., Columbia, 1950; m. Patricia Harris, Feb. 27, 1954 (div. 1961); children—Jason, Adam; m. 2d, Helen D'Alessandro, June 12, 1971. Tchr., Kenyon Coll., 1947, State U. Ia., 1948, N.Y. U., 1949, Smith Coll., 1956-59; asso. prof. English, Bard Coll., 1961; faculty U. Rochester, 1967; Hurst prof. Wash. U., fall 1971. Recipient Prix de Rome, 1950, Brandeis U. Creative Arts award, 1965; Guggenheim fellow, 1954, 59; Ford Found. fellow, 1960; Hudson Rev. fellow, 1958; Rockefeller Found. fellow, 1967. Fellow Acad. Am. Poets (chancellor 1971); mem. Nat. Inst. Arts and Letters. Author: A Summoning of Stones, 1954; The Seven Deadly Sins, 1958; A Bestiary, 1960; The Hard Hours (Brit. Poetry Book Soc. choice, 1967; Miles Poetry award Wayne U.; Pultizer Prize 1968; Russell Loines award Nat. Inst. Arts and Letters), 1968. Co- author, co-editor Jiggery Pokery, 1967. Home: 240 E 82d St New York City NY 10028

HECHT, GEORGE ANTHONY, bookseller; b. N.Y.C., July 27, 1910; s. George and Helen Mary (Lenny) H.; student Columbia, 1928, 29; m. Dorothea Rallings Ackermann, July 23, 1937 (div. 1955), remarried Nov. 6, 1964; children—Karen, Dorothea; m. 2d, Elaine Ann Kelly, Nov. 17, 1956 (div. 1964); 1 son, George Anthony. Clk. for Doubleday Page Book Shops, N.Y.C., 1925-29; pub. rep., Doubleday Doran Co., 1930-37; asst. gen. mgr. Doubleday, Doran Book Shops, 1937-40, gen. mgr. Doubleday Book Shops, N.Y.C., since 1940; v.p. Doubleday Co., since 1948; pres. The Old Corner Book Store, Inc. since 1950. Dir. Council on Books in Wartime, 1941-46, Armed Services Editions, 1941-46. Treas. Overseas Edits., 1944-46. Mem. Am. Book Travellers (pres. 1937), Am. Booksellers Assn. (pres. 1946-47; chmn. bd. 1948). Democrat. Episcopalian. Author: Notes on a Modern Bookshop, 1941. Home: 3 Washington Sq Village New York City NY 10012 Office: 673 Fifth Av New York City NY 10022

HECHT, GEORGE JOSEPH, publisher; b. N.Y.C., Nov. 1, 1895; s. Meyer and Gella (Stern) H.; Ethical Culture Sch., N.Y.C., 1902-13; A.B., Cornell U., 1917; L.H.D., Temple U., 1956; m. Freda Epstein, Jan. 6, 1930; children—Susan (Mrs. Cramer), George M. Founder, Better Times Mag., 1919, N.Y.C., editor until 1931; and sec., dir. Welfare Council N.Y.C., 1926-45; a founder Greater N.Y. Fund, Inc., sec., 1938-44; founder, pub. Parents' Mag. since 1926; pub. Expecting, Baby Care Manual, Your New Baby, Children's Digest, Young Miss, Humpty Dumpty's Mag.; chmn. bd. dirs. The Parents' Mag. Enterprises, Inc., F.A.O. Schwarz; pres. Internat. Fedn. Periodical Press, 1963-65, now hon. chmn. Chmn. Am. Parents Com., Inc. Pres., Hecht-Parents Mag. Found. for Child Welfare, Inc. Vice pres. Child Welfare League Am.; pres. Assn. for Two Child Families, Basic Esperanto Assn. Head U.S. Govt. Bur. Cartoons, U.S. Com. Pub. Information, World War I. Served in statis. div. Gen. Staff, U.S. Army, World War I. Decorated Palmes Academique (France). Mem. Ethical Culture Soc. Club: Sunningdale Country. Editor and compiler: Above Cayuga's Waters, 1916; The War in Cartoons, 1921. Chmn. Nat. Com. Observance Mother's Day. Home: 730 Park Av New York City NY 10021 also 339 Underhill Rd Scarsdale NY 10584 Office: 52 Vanderbilt Av New York City NY 10017

HECHT, HAROLD, motion picture producer; b. N.Y.C., June 1, 1907; s. Joseph and Rose (Lowey) H.; student Am. Lab. Theatre; m. Gloria J. Buzzell, Nov. 1, 1947; children—Steven, Duffy, Alma Virginia; m. 2d, Margaret Truefitt, 1962; 1 son, Harold W. Asst. to Richard Boleslavky; actor in N.Y. Theatre, 1923-30; dancer, choreographer, N.Y.C., 1926-31; motion picture dance dir. Paramount Pictures, Warner Bros., MGM, Los Angeles, 1931-36; established literary agy., Goldstone Agy., later Hecht-Rantz Agy., Hollywood, Cal., 1938-41; partner with Burt Lancaster, Norma Prodns., 1945-53; pres. Hecht-Lancaster Cos., 1954—. Recipient of year award Look mag., 1955; recipient Acad. Award for prodn. Marty, 1955. Mem. Screen Producers Guild, Acad. Motion Picture Arts and Scis. Home: 1967 Coldwater Canyon Dr Beverly Hills CA 90210 Office: 1438 N Gower St Hollywood CA 90028

HECHT, JOSEPH H., business exec. Pres., Drug King, Inc., Hollywood, Cal. Office: 6290 Hollywood Blvd Hollywood CA 90028*

HECHT, MAX KNOBLER, educator, biologist; b. N.Y.C., Feb. 15, 1925; s. Julius and Eva (Knobler) H.; B.S., Cornell U., 1944, M.S., 1947, Ph.D., 1953; m. Bessie Matalas, Feb. 13, 1947; children—Suzanne, Matthew, Jason. Lectr. biology Hunter Coll., 1949-52; mem. faculty Queens Coll., 1953—, now prof. biology; research asso. Am. Mus. Natural History, 1954—. Served with AUS, 1944-46. Sci. faculty fellow NSF, 1966-67. Co-editor: Evolutionary Biology, 1967. Home: 63-19 137th St New York City NY 11367 Office: Queens Coll Flushing NY 11367

HECHT, MORTON ROBERT, wholesale trade co. exec.; b. Galveston, Tex., Dec. 16, 1934; s. Edmund M. and Mae (Leitner) H.; student U. Tex., 1950-52, U. Houston, 1952-55, Baylor U., 1955-58; m. Shirley Miller, Dec. 29, 1956; children—Michael Robert, Kathryn Ann. Owner, Hecht Ins. Agy., Houston, 1957; pres. Keystone Homes, Inc., 1958-65; exec. v.p. Mortgage Co. of Am., 1965-68, also dir.; chmn. bd. MCA Financial Corp., A Delaware Corp., 1968-69, also dir.; chmn. bd. Peden Industries, Inc., Houston, 1969—, also dir.; dir. Am. Mchts. Life Ins. Co., Oak Forest Bank. Gen. chmn. Houston Appeal for Human Relations, 1969, United Jewish Campaign of Houston, 1971-72; v.p. Jewish Family Service, Jewish Community Council, Am. Jewish Com. Recipient Ben Susholtz Leadership award, 1971. Jewish religion (v.p. congregation). Mason (32). Clubs: Houston, University, Westwood Country (bd. govs. Houston). Home: 514 Timberwilde St Houston TX 77024 Office: One Shell Plaza Houston TX 77002

HECHT, WILBUR HUDSON, lawyer; b. N.Y.C., Apr. 25, 1905; s. Adolph and Charlotte (Tressel) H.; A.B., Colgate U., 1927; LL.B., Fordham U., 1930; m. Helen Willis, June 5, 1933; 1 dau., Barbara. Admitted N.Y. bar, 1930, since practiced in N.Y.C.; partner firm Mendes & Mount, and predecessor, 1945—. Titular mem. Comite Maritime Internacional. Mem. Maritime Law Assn. U.S. (sec. 1954-56, v.p. 1958-60, pres. 1962-64), Am. Bar Assn. (ho. dels. 1962-64, chmn. standing com. admiralty and maritime law 1964-67), Internat. Assn. Ins. Counsel, Lambda Chi Alpha. Club: Down Town Assn. (N.Y.C.). Home: 35 Huntington Rd Garden City NY 11530 Office: 27 William St New York City NY 10005

HECHTMAN, ROBERT AARON, educator, structural engr.; b. Spokane, Apr. 22, 1911; s. Abe and Maren (Olson) H.; B.S. in Civil Engr., U. Wash., 1938, M.S. in Civil Engring., 1939; student Lehigh U., 1939-41; Ph.D., U. Ill., 1948; m. Sarajane Furman; children—Geoffrey Kier, Paul Randall. With Dravo Corp., 1941-44, adminstr. asst., 1944-45; research engr. civil engring. U. Ill., 1945- 49; asso. prof. structural research U. Wash., 1949-53, prof., 1953-55; prof. civil engring. George Washington U., 1955-64, chmn. dept. 1955-62; vis. prof. U. Chile, 1959; pres. Planning, Analysis & Design Corp., Kensington, Md., 1964-65; pres. R.A. Hechtman & Assos., 1966- -; adj. prof. civil engring. Howard U., 1967—. Cons. engr. pressure vessels, failure ship and land structures, heavy machinery, shell structures. Column Research Council, 1951—, project dir., 1963-64; mem. Nat. Bur. Standards, 1959-69, chmn. adv. panel to bldg. research div., 1964-69. Mem. Nat. Commn. on Fire Prevention and Control, 1970—. Fellow Am. Soc. C.E.; mem. Soc. Naval Architects and Marines Engrs., Am. Concrete Inst., Soc. Exptl. Stress Analysis, Sigma Xi, Tau Beta Pi. Author research publs., reports. Address: 11453 Washington Plaza W Reston VA 22070

HECK, FRANK HOPKINS, educator; b. Racine, Wis., Oct. 18, 1904; s. Victor and Ruth Alice (Perham) H.; A.B., Lawrence Coll., 1925; M.A., U. Minn., 1929, Ph.D., 1938; m. Edna Drill, Oct. 3, 1945; 1 son, Edward V. Tchr. high sch., Rice Lake, Wis., 1926-27, Faribault, Minn., 1928-29; asst. prof. history Neb. State Tchrs. Coll., Peru, 1929-33, asso. prof., 1933-38; asst. prof. Miami U., Oxford, O., 1938-46, asso. prof., chmn. integrated studies, 1946-48; prof. of history at Centre Coll., Danville, Ky., 1948—, dean, 1955-65. Served to capt. AUS, 1942-46. Mem. Am., So. hist. assns., Orgn. Am. Historians, Phi Beta Kappa, Beta Theta Pi. Democrat. Episcopalian. Author: The Civil War Veteran in Minnesota Life and Politics, 1941. Home: 614 E Main St Danville KY 40422

HECK, HAROLD JOSEPH, economist; b. Brusly, La., Jan. 7, 1906; s. Henry Jean B. and Hortense (Dupont) H.; B.A., La. State U., 1926, M.A., 1931; M.B.A., Wharton Sch., U. Pa., 1933; D.C.S., N.Y. U., 1939; m. L. Suzanne Holt, Sept. 16, 1935; children—Peter M., Henry d'A., Thomas F. With La. Nat. Bank, Baton Rouge, 1926-32, Bank of N.Y., 1933-36; instr. finance U. Notre Dame, 1937-38; asst. sec. Robert Morris Assos., Phila., 1938-41; lectr. Georgetown U., 1941-45; prof. econs. Loyola U. of South, 1946-47; prof. bus. adminstrn. Tulane U., 1947-59; comml. attaché Am. embassy, Paris, France, 1957-62; dir. internat. trade analysis div. U.S. Dept. Commerce, Washington, 1962-64; prof., chmn. dept. internat. trade and transp. Sch. Fgn. Service, Georgetown U., 1964-71; ret., 1971; vis. prof. econs. Waseda U. Tokyo, Japan, 1952-53, Helsinki (Finland) Sch. Econs., 1971. Mem. Am. Econ. Assn. Club: Cosmos (Washington). Author: Foreign Commerce, 1953; International Business Environment, 1969; International Trade—A Management Guide, 1971. Home: Bozman MD 21612

HECK, JAMES BAKER, univ. dean; b. Columbus, O.,, Aug. 26, 1930; s. Arch O. and Frances (Agnew) H.; B.S., Ohio State U., 1953, M.A., (Nat. Def. Edn. Act fellow), 1961. Ph.D., 1967; m. Jo Ann Gatton, Nov. 18, 1950; children—Janice M., Judith L., J. Jeffrey. Comml. sales engr. Ohio Bell Telephone Co., Dayton, 1955-57; tchr. Ohio Pub. Schs., Dayton, 1957-59, sch. counselor, 1959-60; instr. Ohio State U., 1960-63, asst. to dean Coll. Edn., 1963-66, asst. dean faculties, research asso., 1966-67, asso. dean faculties, asst. prof. edn., 1967-68; asst. state supr. for guidance service Dept. Edn. Ohio. 1962-63; Am. Council on Edn. fellow in academic adminstrn. U. Ill., 1965-66; prof. dean Coll. Edn., U. Del., Newark, 1968—; chmn. Ad Hoc Planning Com. on Occupational Edn. for State of Del.; pres. bd. dirs. Research for Better Schs., Inc., 1970-71. Served with USAF, 1953-55. Mem. Nat. Assn. Land Grant Colls. and State Univs., Am. Assn. Sch. Adminstrs. Am. Ednl. Research Assn., Am. Assn. Higher Edn., Del. Assn. Sch. Adminstrs., Am. Assn. Instl. and State Colls. Tchr. Edn., Phi Delta Kappa. Co-author: Counseling; Selected Readings, 1962; Educational Administration: Selected Readings, 1965; Analysis of Educational Changes in Ohio Public Schools, 1968. Home: 111 Country Club Dr Newark DE 19711

HECK, THEODORE, clergyman, educator; b. Chariton, Ia., Jan. 16, 1901; s. Henry and Margaret (Steinbach) H.; A.B., St. Meinrad Coll., 1925; M.A., Cath. U. Am., 1933, Ph.D., 1935. Ordained priest Roman Cath. Ch., 1929; tchr. Cath. high schs., 1929-32; mem. faculty St. Meinrad Sem., 1935-56, pres., 1956-66; prior St. Meinrad Archabbey, 1966-69, sec. bd., 1969—. Mem. Am. Benedictine Acad. (past pres.). Author: The Curriculum of the Major Seminary in Relation to Contemporary Conditions, 1935; also booklets. Home: St Meinrad Sem St Meinrad IN 47577

HECK, THOMAS W., clergyman; b. Newark, Sept. 30, 1928; s. Joseph and Jane (Murray) H.; A.B., Seton Hall U., 1952; postgrad. Immaculate Conception Sem. Ordained priest Roman Cath. Ch., 1957; asst. pastor Our Lady of All Souls Ch., East Orange, N.J., 1957-58; missionary Puerto Rico, 1958-69; asst. pastor St. Patricks Ch., Newark, 1960-69; episcopal vicar Apostolate of Spanish Speaking, Newark, 1970—. Mem. Interdiocesan Coordinating Com. Spanish N.Y. Met. Region; organizer Spanish Family Life Program, Newark. Home: 25 Thomas St Newark NJ 07114 Office: 23 Pennsylvania Av Newark NJ 07114

HECKART, EILEEN, actress; b. Columbus, O., Mar. 29, 1919; d. Leo Herbert and Esther (Stark) Purcell; B.A., Ohio State U., 1942; student Am. Theatre Wing, 1944-48; m. John Harrison Yankee, Jr., June 26, 1943; children—Mark Kelly, Philip, Craig, Luke, Brian. Actress Broadway plays, Voice of the Turtle, 1944, Brighten the Corner, 1946, They Knew What They Wanted, 1948, Stars Weep, 1949, The Traitor, 1950, Hilda Crane, 1951, In Any Language, 1953, Picnic, 1953, Bad Seed, 1955, A View From the Bridge, 1956, Dark at the Top of the Stairs, 1958, Invitation to a March, 1960, Everybody Loves Opal, 1961, Family Affair, 1962, Too True To Be Good, 1963, And Things That Go Bump in the Night, 1965, Barefoot in the Park, 1965-66, You Know I Can't Hear You When the Water's Running, 1967, The Mother Lover, 1968, Butterflies Are Free, 1969; movies Miracle in the Rain, Bad Seed, Somebody Up There Likes Me, Bus Stop, Hot Spell, Heller in Pink Tights, My Six Loves, 1962, Up the Down Staircase, 1966, No Way To Treat A Lady; TV actress, 1947—. Recipient Outer Circle award, 1953, Daniel Blum award, 1953, Sylvania TV award, 1954, Donaldson award, 1955, Oscar nomination, 1956, Hollywood Fgn. Press award, 1956, Film Daily citation, 1956, Variety Poll of N.Y. Drama Critics award, 1958; N.Y. Emmy for Save Me A Place at Forest Lawn, 1967; March Dimes award, 1970; Azgis award, 1970; Ohio State U. Centennial award, 1970. Mem. Pi Beta Phi. Home: 135 Comstock Hill Rd New Canaan CT 06840 Office: care Internat Famous Artists 1301 Av of Americas New York City NY 10019

HECKEL, CHARLES WILLARD, univ. dean; b. Bloomfield, N.J., May 1, 1913; s. Charles Otto and Edith Mae (Decker) H.; A.B., Dartmouth, 1935; M.A., Columbia, 1936; LL.B., U. Newark, 1940. Admitted to N.J. bar, 1941; mem. law dept., Montclair, N.J., 1941-42; formerly prof. law, dean faculty Rutgers U. Law Sch. Chmn. Mayor Newark Commn. Human Relations, 1955-56, Newark Citizens Com. Municipal Govt., 1952-54; pres. Newark chpt. Am. Assn. UN, 1961-63; hon. chmn. N.J., Am. Dem. Action, 1962—; moderator Presbytery Newark, United Presbyn. Ch. U.S.A., 1962-63. Bd. dirs. Bloomfield Coll., 1962—. Mem. Am. Bar Assn., Am. Assn. U. Profs. Home: 375 Mt Prospect Av Newark NJ 07104

HECKER, ARTHUR ORR, physician, hosp. supt.; b. Pitts., Aug. 14, 1910; s. Arthur Walter and Carrie (Orr) H.; M.D., U. Pitts., 1933; m. Sarah Johnson, Feb. 22, 1936; children—Carolyn Ann, Sarah Atlanta, Deborah Lee; m. 2d, Eleanore Reidell Wright, Feb. 11, 1956; children—Eleanor Helen Wickersham Wright, Curtis Wright IV (foster children). Intern U. Pitts. Med. Center, 1933- 34; resident C. H. Buhl Hosp., Sharon, Pa., 1934-35; practice medicine, specializing in psychiatry, Downington, Pa., 1953-54; staff psychiatrist Pa. State Hosp. System, 1935-41; chief profl. services, dir. profl. tng. VA Hosp., Coatesville, Pa., 1945-53; clin. dir. Friends Hosp., Phila., 1954-55;

supt. Embreeville (Pa.) State Hosp., 1955-70, ret. Served from capt. to col., M.C., AUS, 1941-45; ETO. Decorated Bronze Star medal. Fellow A.C.P., Am. Psychiat. Assn.; mem. Chester County Med. Soc. (past pres.), Phila. Psychiat. Soc. (past pres.). Address: Embreeville State Hosp Coatesville PA 19320

HECKER, JOHN CHALMERS, chemist, bus. exec.; b. New Brighton, Pa., Apr. 27, 1908; s. Oliver A. and Armida M. (Miller) H.; B.S., Geneva Coll., 1930; Ph.D., Yale, 1933; m. Ruth R. Abbott, June 25, 1934. Research chemist Eastman Kodak Co., 1933-37; with Distillation Products, Inc., 1937-43, works mgr., 1946-52, v.p. charge tech. operations, 1952-57, v.p., gen. mgr. distillation products, 1957-65, pres., gen. mgr., 1965—; prodn. mgr. Clinton Engring. Works, Oak Ridge, Tenn., 1943-46. Mem. Am. Chem. Soc., Am. Inst. Chemists, Sigma Xi. Home: 189 E Parkway Rochester NY 14617. Office: 1100 Ridgway Av Rochester NY 14615

HECKER, LEWIS J., corp. exec.; b. N.Y.C., Feb. 2, 1934; s. Charles E. and Fannie (Goldfinger) H.; B.A., Coll. City N.Y., 1957; M.A., N.Y. U., 1959, LL.B., 1963; m. Miriam Panich, Feb. 8, 1959; children—Charles Eli, Judith Bryna. Admitted to N.Y. bar, 1963; pvt. practice, N.Y.C., 1963-68; v.p., gen. counsel Bangor Punta Operations, Inc., 1968-69, group v.p. leisure time group, 1969—, also dir. Served with AUS, 1954-56. Mem. Queens County Bar Assn., Order of Coif. Home: Stamford CT 06903 Office: 1 Greenwich Plaza Greenwich CT 06830 Mailing Address:

HECKER, ROBERT LEVI, lawyer; b. Kansas City, Mo., June 19, 1905; s. Alvin and Emma (Vanhook) H.; LL.B., U. Mo., 1927; m. Frances M. Alexander, July 1, 1933; 1 son, James Alexander. Admitted to Mo. bar, 1927; asso. Morrison, Nugent, Wylder & Berger (now Morrison, Hecker, Cozad, Morrison & Curtis), 1927, 35, partner, 1935—. City atty., Mission Hills, Kan. Bd. dirs. Spofford Home; trustee Nettleton Home. Fellow Am. Bar Found.; mem. Am. (ho. dels. 1948-56), Mo., Kansas City bar assns., Lawyers Assn. Kansas City, Kappa Sigma, Phi Delta Phi. Methodist (ch. trustee). Clubs: Kansas City, University, Mission Hills. Home: 2105 W 49th St Shawnee Mission, KS 66205. Office: Bryant Bldg Kansas City MO 64106

HECKER, WILLIAM FRANTZ, lawyer; b. Detroit, Aug. 19, 1900; s. Albert Hopkins and Eleanor (McDermott) H.; A.B., Western Res. U., 1922, LL.B., 1924; m. Hannah Elizabeth Kagy, Oct. 10, 1925. Admitted to Ohio bar, 1924, since practiced law in Cleve. Pres. Cleve. Crime Commn., 1949-51, Euclid (O.) Bd. Edn., 1941-42, Euclid Pub. Library Bd., 1960-67; area chmn. United Appeal Greater Cleve. Met. div., 1958-62; mem. Euclid Charter Commn., 1950-51, chmn., 1962-63. Trustee Euclid Gen. Hosp., Blue Cross of Northeast Ohio. Served to maj. with USAAF, 1942-45; ETO. Mem. Am., Ohio, Cleve. (pres. 1961-62) bar assns., Am. Judicature Soc., Greater Cleve. Growth Assn., Delta Tau Delta, Phi Delta Phi. Club: Mayfield Country (South Euclid). Home: 21211 Edgecliff Dr Euclid OH 44123 Office: Williamson Bldg Cleveland OH 44114

HECKERT, JOSIAH BROOKS, educator, accountant; b. Tescott, Kan., Jan. 22, 1893; s. Uriah E. and Nancy Jane (Roy) H.; A.B., Kan. Wesleyan U., 1916, D.C.S. (hon.), 1941; postgrad. U. Kan., 1916-17; A.M., U. Chgo., 1923; LL.D. (hon.), Simpson Coll., 1950; m. Marie Hood, June 5, 1918. Prof. econs. Simpson Coll., 1920-25; asso. prof. accounting Ohio State U., 1925-45, prof. since 1945; dir. indsl. and financial corps.; pres. Columbus Blank Book Mfg. Co.; v.p. Dollar Fed. Savs. & Loan Assn., Avis Rent-a- Car System, Inc. Served as 1st lt., U.S. Army, 1917-19; with A.E.F., 1 yr. C.P.A., Ohio. Mem. Am. Inst. Accountants, Nat. Assn. Cost Accountants (past nat. dir., pres. 1952-53), Beta Gamma Sigma, Beta Alpha Psi, Lambda Chi Alpha. Author: Accounting Systems—Design and Installation 1936; Distribution Costs—Analysis and Control, 1940; Business Budgeting and Control, 1946; Wholesale Accounting and Control (with I. J. Stone), 1935; Drugstore Accounting (with W. E. Dickerson), 1943; Controllership (with J. D. Wilson), 1952. Contbg. editor to Accountants Handbook, 1943; Cost Accounting Handbook, 1944. Home: 2451 Brixton Rd Columbus OH 43221

HECKLER, GEORGE EARL, educator, chemist; b. Marietta, O., Dec. 20, 1920; s. Charles Davis and Georgia (Hendershott) H.; B.A., Marietta Coll., 1947; Ph.D., U. Wis., 1952; m. Hilde Unterleitner, Aug. 11, 1945; children—Mary, William, Jane, John. Research chemist E.I. duPont de Nemours & Co., 1952-56; mem. faculty Ida. State U., 1956—, prof. chemistry, 1964—, chmn. dept., 1961—. Served with USAAF, 1942-45. Decorated Air medal with 4 oak leaf clusters. Mem. Am. Chem. Soc., A.A.A.S., Am. Civil Liberties Union, Am. Assn. U. Prof. (nat. council 1967-70), Phi Beta Kappa, Sigma Xi. Contbr. profl. jours. Home: 525 S 7th Av Pocatello ID 83201

HECKLER, MARGARET MARY, (Mrs. John M. Heckler), congresswoman; b. Flushing, N.Y., June 21, 1931; d. John and Bridget (McKeon) O'Shaughnessy; B.A., Albertus Magnus Coll., 1953; LL.B., Boston Coll., 1956; student U. Leiden, Holland, 1952; hon. degrees Northeastern U., Stonehill Coll., Emmanuel Coll., Regis Coll.; m. John M. Heckler, Aug. 29, 1953; children—Belinda West, Alison Anne, John M. Admitted to Mass. bar, 1956, also U.S. Supreme Ct.; practice in Boston, 1956-66; mem. 90th to 92d Congresses, 10th Dist. Mass.; mem. Mass. Gov.'s Council, 1962-66; lectr. Univ. Speakers Bur., Republican Nat. Com. Alternate del. Rep. Nat. Conv., 1964; speaker Nat. Rep. Womens Fedn. Conv., 1967. Named Outstanding Young Woman Am., 1965. Mem. Mass. Womens Rep. Clubs, Boston Coll. Law Sch. Young Rep. Club (past dir.), Cath. Womens Coll. Alumnae Assn. (past pres.), 90th Club U.S. Congress (v.p.), Bus. and Profl. Womans Club. Home: Wellesley MA 02181 Office: House Office Bldg Washington DC 20515

HECKMAN, DONALD JOSEPH, critic, composer; b. Reading, Pa., Dec. 18, 1932; s. Lawrence H. and Leda Cecelia (Ponzoli) H.; B.A., Fla. State U., 1957; M.A., Coll. City N.Y., 1971. Music critic, 1960—; contbg. editor Stereo Rev., 1968—; jazz editor Am. Record Guide, 1964- -; rec. editor, pop critic N.Y. Times, 1971—; composer music for TV programs, films and theatrical prodns.; record producer Blood, Sweat and Tears; rec. artist for Ictus, Avant-Garde, Decca, Caedmon records. Lectr. City Coll. N.Y., 1970—. Mem. Nat. Assn. Rec. Arts and Scis. Address: 113 Christopher St New York City NY 10014

HECKMAN, SISTER EILEEN MARIE, ednl. adminstr.; b. Sterling, Ill., May 4, 1904; d. Adam L. and Elizabeth E. (Hamblock) Heckman; A.B., Loretto Heights Coll., Denver, 1932; M.S., U. Notre Dame, 1941; postgrad. U. Minn., Cath. U. Am. Joined Order Sisters Loretto, 1922; tchr. elementary and secondary schs., 1924- 43; dean women, prof. chemistry Loretto Heights Coll., 1943-51, dean coll., 1951-57, pres. coll., 1964-67, alumni coordinator, 1969—; provincial superior, Sacred Heart Province, 1957-64; counselor Holy Family High Sch., Denver, 1967-69. Ednl. cons. Colo. Bd. Nurse Examiners. Trustee Colo. Assn. Ind. Colls. and Univs.; bd. dirs. People-to-People Corp., Denver. Mem. Asso. Colls. Colo., Nat. Cath. Ednl. Assn. North Central Assn., Am. Personnel and Guidance Assn., Am. Coll. Personnel Assn., Am. Assn. Coll. Tchr. Edn., Nat. Council Accreditation Tchr. Edn., Nat. Assn. Deans Women. Home: 4000 S Wadsworth Blvd Littleton CO 80123

HECKMAN, JAMES WILLIAM, telephone co. exec.; b. St. Louis, Oct. 18, 1910; s. George Talbot and Helen (Fallis) H.; A.B., U. Denver, 1932; m. Virginia Shannon, Oct. 16, 1937; children—James William, Judith Ann. With Mountain States Tel. & Tel. Co., 1934-58, 60—, v.p. revenue requirements and bus. research, 1960—; asst. treas., then asst. v.p. Am. Tel. & Tel. Co., 1958-60; dir. Continental Nat. Bank, Englewood, Colo., Key Savs. and Loan. Mem. Kappa Sigma. Republican. Episcopalian. Clubs: Denver Athletic, Cherry Hills Country (Denver). Home: 5443 S Franklin Lane Littleton CO 80120 Office: 931 14th St Denver CO 80202

HECKMAN, JOHN DRIES, banker; b. Reading, Pa., May 18, 1907; s. Charles Ellsworth and Candace M. (Dries) H.; student Wharton Sch. of U. Pa., 1927; grad. Am. Inst. Banking, 1937; m. Emily F. Schmeck, Feb. 12, 1930 (dec. Mar. 1971); 1 son, J. Bruce; m. 2d, Olla M. Rothermel. With City Bank & Trust Co., Reading, 1934-60, v.p., 1942-45, pres., 1945-60; pres. Bank Pa. (formerly Peoples Trust City Bank), Reading, 1960—, vice chmn. bd., 1966-69; dir., chmn. finance com. Security Am. Life Ins. Co., 1963-70; dir. Standard Paper Box Mfg. Co., 1962-70, Standard Offset Printing Co., 1962-70, UAG Investment Corp., Maiers Bakery Co., Croll & Keck Co. Mem. investment com. Home for Widows and Single Women, Reading; pres. United Fund Berks County, 1962-64; pres. Wyomissing Bd. Edn., 1950-52, Wyomissing Recreation Bd., 1953. Bd. dirs. Greater Berks Devel. Fund, 1963-69; dir., treas. Salvation Army Berks County. Mem. Am., Pa. bankers assns. Lutheran (past chmn. finance com.). Mason, Lion. Club: Wyomissing. Author: A Manual of Leading Procedures, 1962. Home: 1333 Monroe Av Wyomissing PA 19610 Office: 50 N 5th St Reading PA 19601

HECKMAN, JOHN F., Jr., ins. co. exec.; b. Providence, Dec. 19, 1914; grad. Phillips Exeter Acad., 1932; A.B., Brown U., 1936. Clk. actuarial div. Aetna Life Ins. Co., Hartford, Conn., 1936-44, asst. actuary, 1944-53, asso. actuary, 1953-58, asst. v.p., actuary, 1960-61, v.p., 1961-63, sr. v.p., corporate actuary, 1969—. Mem. City of Hartford Pension Commn., 1948-69, chmn., 1950-69. Fellow Soc. of Actuaries (past mem. exam. com.). Unitarian (trustee). Home: Bushnell Plaza Hartford CT 06114 Office: 151 Farmington Av Hartford CT 06115*

HECKMAN, RUSSELL FREDERICK, educator, chem. engr.; b. West Carrolton, O., Oct. 16, 1907; s. Elmer F. and Bessie May (Mueller) H.; B.Chem. Engring., U. Minn., 1931; M.S., U. Colo., 1949, Ph.D., 1951; m. Dorothy Merrill, Mar. 10, 1930; 1 dau., Karin Johanna (Mrs. David Schneider). Asst. chemistry Mason City (Ia.) Jr. Coll., 1922-25; research asst. to I.M. Kolthoff, Sch. Chemistry, U. Minn., 1928-31; chem. engr. S.W. Shattuck Chem. Co., Denver, 1931-32, Am. Crystal Sugar Co., Denver, 1932-43, 1947-48; v.p., chief engr. Ingwersen Mfg. Co., Denver, 1943-47; instr. engring. U. Colo., 1948-51, dir. chem. engring. labs., 1950-53, asst. prof., 1952-53; prof. chem. engring. S.D. Sch. Mines and Tech., Rapid City, 1952—, head dept., 1953—; cons. to industry, 1932—. Musical dir. Denver Choral Soc., 1932-47, Rapid City Choral Club, 1955- 69. Fellow A.A.A.S., Am. Inst. Chemists; mem. Am. Inst. Chem. Engrs., Am. Chem. Soc., Electrochem. Soc., Am. Soc. Engring. Edn., Soc. Rheology, S.D. Acad. Sci., Rapid City Astron. Soc. (bd. dirs. 1955—), Sigma Xi, Alpha Chi Sigma, Sigma Tau. Registered profl. engr., S.D., Colo. Baptist (dir. music 1954—). Author: (with B.E. Lauer) Chemical Engineering Techniques, 1952. Home: 1619 Morningside Dr Rapid City SD 57701

HECKMAN, WILLIAM ROBERT, aerospace co. exec.; b. Greensburg, Pa., Jan. 16, 1921; s. Harry Leslie and Mary Cecilia (Coffman) H.; B.S. in Bus. Adminstrn., U. Pitts., 1946; postgrad. Exec. Mgmt. Program, Pa. State U., 1957; m. Jane Woods Lewis, July 8, 1943; children—William Robert, Harry Leslie. Spl. agt. FBI, 1947-52; various exec. positions in personnel adminstrn. Internat. Tel. & Tel., Ft. Wayne, Ind., Nutley, N.J., N.Y.C., 1952-69, dir. adminstrn. def.-space group, 1966-69; v.p. adminstrn. Aerojet-Gen. Corp., El Monte, Cal., 1969—; dir. Watts Mfg. Co. Served to 1st lt. USMCR, 1942-45. Mem. Delta Tau Delta. Clubs: San Gabriel (Cal.) Country, Jonathan (Los Angeles). Home: 20 Mill Canyon Rd San Marino CA 91108 Office: 9100 E Flair Dr El Monte CA 91734

HECKMANN, IRVIN LEE, coll. dean; b. Omaha, Apr. 25, 1925; s. Irvin Lee and Kathryn Pauline Heckmann; B.S. in Commerce, Creighton U., 1950; M.B.A., U. Wis., 1951, Ph.D. (fellow econ. edn. 1954), 1955; m. Phyllis Marie Calabrese, June 20, 1953; children—Kathryn Anne, Peter James. From instr. to asso. prof. mgmt. U. Ill., 1954-63, acting head dept. mgmt., 1961-63; prof. mgmt., dean Coll. Bus. Adminstrn., Creighton U., 1963-68; dean Coll. Bus. Adminstrn., prof. mgmt. U. Ill., Chgo., 1968—; cons. exec. devel., labor arbitrator. Dir. Man-Tec Systems, Inc., Kapri Fashions, Inc., Met. State Equipment Co., Mgmt. Resources, Inc. Trustee Ill. Council Econ. Edn. Served with AUS, 1942-46. Mem. Acad. Mgmt., Indsl. Relations Research Assn., Am. Econ. Assn., Am. Mgmt. Assn., Beta Gamma Sigma. Co-author: Human Relations in Management, 1972; Management of the Personnel Function, 1962. Contbr.: Ency. Mgmt., 1972; Critical Incidents in Management, 1963. Home: 92 Old Mill Ct Barrington IL 60010 Office: Coll Bus Adminstrn U Ill at Chgo Circle Chicago IL 60680

HECKSCHER, AUGUST, journalist, author, city ofcl.; b. Huntington, N.Y., Sept. 16, 1913; s. Gustave and Louise (Vanderhoef) H.; student St. Paul's Sch., Concord, N.H., 1927-32; B.A., Yale, 1936; M.A., Harvard, 1939; LL.D., Fairleigh Dickinson U., 1962; L.H.D., State U. N.Y., 1952; Litt. D., C.W. Post Coll., 1963, Adelphi Coll., 1963; L.H.D., Temple U., 1964, Brandeis U., 1964; m. Claude Chevreus, Mar. 19, 1941; children—Stephen August, Philip Hofer, Charles Chevreux. Instr. govt. Yale, 1939-41; ed. Auburn (N.Y.) Citizen-Advertiser, 1946-48; chief editorial writer N.Y. Herald Tribune, 1948-56; dir. The Twentieth Century Fund, until 1967; adminstr. recreation and cultural affairs, commr. of parks, N.Y.C., 1967- -; also apptd by Pres. Kennedy as spl. cons. on arts, 1962- 63. Art commr. City of N.Y., 1957-62; chmn. bd. Internat. Council Mus. of Modern Art, 1958-63; mem. bd. trustees St. Paul's School; mem. N.Y. State Council on Arts; v.p. Municipal Art Soc., 1965; chmn. Nat. Repertory Theatre Found.; vice chmn. bd. Urban Am.; mem. Nat. Com. New Whitney Mus.; past chmn. New Sch. Social Research; past pres. Am. Council Nationalities Service. Fellow Jonathan Edwards Coll., Yale; former pres. Woodrow Wilson Found. Served with OSS, 1941-45. Decorated Chevalier French Legion of Honor; Officer Moroccan order of Ouissam Alouit. Fellow Am. Acad. of Arts and Scis.; mem. A. I. A. (hon. mem.), Am. Craftsmen's Council (mem. bd. dirs.), Century Assn., Council Fgn. Relations, Am. Civil Liberties Union (mem. bd.), Phi Beta Kappa. Author: These Are the Days, 1936; A Pattern of Politics, 1947; The Politics of Woodrow Wilson, 1956; (with Raymond Aron) Diversity of Worlds, 1957; The Public Happiness, 1962. Editorial bd. The Am. Scholar; governing bd. Yale U. Press. Home: 159 E 94th St New York City NY 10021 Office: 830 Fifth Av New York City NY 10021

HECKSCHER, MAURICE, lawyer; b. Phila., May 24, 1907; s. Stevens and Henrietta A. (Brown) H.; grad. Hill Sch., 1924; A.B. cum laude, Harvard, 1928, postgrad. Law Sch., 1928-30; m. Constance Antelo Butcher, June 24, 1929; children— Stevens, Constance (Mrs. H. Curtis Wood III), Martin A. Admitted to Pa. bar, 1932; asso. firm Duane, Morris & Heckscher, Phila., 1931-35, partner, 1935—; dir. Laurel Hill Cementery Co., West Laurel Hill Cemetery Co., Equitable Life Assurance Soc. of U.S. Served as prin. atty. OPM; asst. gen. counsel WPB, 1941-44. Trustee Dolfinger- McMahon Found., Phila. Served as lt. USNR, 1944-45. Recipient citation Sec. Navy. Mem. Am. Philos. Soc., Am., Pa., Phila. bar assns., Zool. Soc. Phila (dir.). Episcopalian. Clubs: Philadelphia, Sunnybrook Golf, Harvard. Home: Sheaff Rd Fort Washington PA 19034 Office: Land Title Bldg Broad and Sansom Sts Philadelphia PA 19110

HECKSCHER, WILLIAM SEBASTIAN, art historian; b. Hamburg, Germany, Dec. 14, 1904; s. Siegfried and Hulda (Foerster) H.; Ph.D., U. Hamburg, 1935; student N.Y.U., also Oxford U.; m. Mary Dixon Leitch, Aug. 30, 1943; children—Diana, Katherine. Naturalized Canadian citizen. Tchr. univs. Sask., Man., State U. Ia., 1947-55; chmn. dir. Iconological Inst., U. Utrecht (Netherlands), 1955-66; chmn. dept. art Duke, 1966-69; dir. Duke U. Art Mus., 1970—; one man exhbn. Allied Arts Gallery, Durham, N.C., 1967, mem. Inst. Advanced Study, Princeton, 1936-40, 52-53. Recipient Festschrift, Netherlands Yearbook History Art, 1964. Fellow Folger Shakespeare Library; Benjamin Franklin fellow Royal Soc. Arts, London; corr. mem. Soc. Indexers (London). Author publs. in field. Home: 6605 College Station Durham NC 27708

HECTOR, LOUIS JULIUS, lawyer; b. Ft. Lauderdale, Fla., Dec. 11, 1915; s. Harry Howard and Grace (Kellerstrass) H.; grad. Phillips Andover Acad., 1933; B.A., Williams Coll., 1938; student Christ Church, Oxford, Eng., 1939; LL.B., Yale, 1942; m. Dorothy Anne Dooley, Aug. 12, 1950; children—Denis Howard, Dorothy Anne, William Frederic, Louis Julius. Admitted to D.C. bar, 1942, Fla. bar, 1946; atty. U.S. Dept. Justice, Washington, 1942- 43; asst. to under sec. state, 1944; pvt. practice law, Miami, Fla., 1946-47; pres. Hector Supply Co., Miami, 1948-55; mem. firm Hector, Faircloth & Davis, Miami, 1956-57, 59-66, McCarthy, Steel, Hector & Davis, 1966—; dir. First Nat. Bank Miami; dir., chmn. exec. com. S.E. Banking Corp. Mem. Civil Aero. Bd., 1957-59. Trustee U. Miami; mem. bd. cons. Portsmouth Abbey Sch.; mem. council Yale. Served with OSS in China, 1945. Clubs: Century Assn. (N.Y.C.); Metropolitan (D.C.). Home: 3507 St Gaudens Rd Coconut Grove FL 33133 Office: 1st Nat Bank Bldg Miami FL 33131

HEDBERG, HOLLIS DOW, geologist, educator; b. Falun, Kan., May 29, 1903; s. Carl A. and Zada M. (Dow) H.; A.B., U. Kan., 1925; M.S., Cornell U., 1926; Ph.D., Stanford, 1937; m. Helen F. Murray, Nov. 8, 1932; children—Ronald M., James D., William H., Franklin A., Mary F. Asst. Kan. Geol. Survey, 1924- 25; petrographer Lago Petroleum Corp., Venezuela, 1926-28; stratigrapher, dir. geol. lab. Mene Grande Oil Co., Venezuela, 1928-39, asst. chief geologist, 1939-46; chief geologist fgn. prodn. div. Gulf Oil Corp., 1946-51, exploration mgr., 1951-52, chief geologist Pitts., 1952-53, exploration coordinator, 1953-57, v.p., 1957-64, exploration adviser, 1964—. Prof. geology Princeton, 1959—. Mem. Am. Com. Stratigraphic Nomenclature, 1946-60, chmn., 1950-52; pres. Internat. Com. Stratigraphic Terminologyy, 1952—; v.p. Internat. Commn. Stratigraphy, 1968—; chmn. Consortium Exploration Adv. Group, Iran, 1965—; chmn. tech. subcom. petroleum resources of ocean floor Nat. Petroleum Council, 1968—; chmn. coordinating panel Internat. Geol. Correl. Program, 1969—; chmn. JOIDES Panel Pollution Prevention and Safety, 1970. Bd. dirs. Cushman Found. Foraminiferal Research, 1951-63; Decorated Medalla de Honor de la Instruction Publica (Venezuela). Recipient Sidney Powers medal Am. Assn. Petroleum Geologists, 1963; Distinguished Service award U. Kan., 1963. Mem. Geol. Soc. Am. (pres. 1959-60; asso. editor bull. 1962-68), Nat. Acad. Sci., Am. Assn. Petroleum Geologists (asso. editor bull. 1937—; pres. Eastern sect. 1948-49), A.A.A.S., Am. Petroleum Inst., Am. Geophys. Union, Paleontol. Soc. Am. (v.p. 1952), Soc. Econ. Paleontology and Minerology, Swiss Geol. Soc., Soc. Exptl. Geophys., Am. Inst. Mining, Metall. and Petroleum Engrs., Am. Geol. Inst. (pres. 1962-63), Internat. Union Geol. Scis. (chmn. U.S. nat. com. on geology 1965-66), Am. Inst. Profl. Geologists, Geol. Soc. Stockholm (hon. corr.), Assn. Venezolana Geol. Mining Petroleum (hon.), U.S. Nat. Com. World Petroleum Congresses, Geol. Soc. London (fgn.), Danish Royal Acad. Sci., Phi Beta Kappa, Sigma Xi, Phi Kappa Phi, Sigma Gamma Epsilon. Clubs: Cosmos (Washington); Nassau (Princeton); Duquesne (Pitts.); Mining (N.Y.C.). Contbr. articles profl. jours. Home: 118 Library Pl Princeton NJ 08540

HEDBERG, ROBERT DANIEL, investment counselor; b. Portland, Ore., Mar. 14, 1922; s. John and Emma Sophia (Gronberg) H.; A.B. in Math., U. Pa., 1946, M.S. in Banking and Finance, 1947; m. Martha Jane Carr, Oct. 27, 1945; children—Hanna, John, Sarah. Chmn. Hedberg & Gordon, Inc., investment counselors, Paoli, Pa., 1964—; chmn., dir. Hedberg and Gordon Fund, Inc., Paoli, 1964—; chmn., dir. Patrician Paper Co., N.Y.C., 1963—; dir. financial counsel Betz Labs., Inc., 1960—. Cons. corp. financial planning, 1948—; lectr. investments Wharton Grad. div. U. Pa., 1960. Home: 208 N Ship Rd Exton, PA 19341. Office: 1 Station Sq Paoli PA 19301

HEDBLOM, FREDERICK L., radio mfg. co. exec.; b. Evanston, Ill.; student Northwestern U. Journeyman die-maker, later chief engr. Accurate Spring Mfg. Co.; with Shure Bros., Chgo., until 1939; tool and die-maker, 1939-40; chief mech. engr. Comar Electric Co., 1940-41; with Zenith Radio Corp., Chgo., 1941- -, successively die insp., chief tool insp., tool room supt., asst. supt. mfg., gen. supt. mfg., factory mgr. main plant, Chgo., 1941-52, gen. works mgr., 1952-62, v.p., works mgr., 1962-69, v.p. prodn., 1969- -. Office: 1900 N Austin Blvd Chicago IL 60636

HEDDING, J. FRED, business exec.; b. Tyrone, Pa., July 4, 1901; student Pa. State Coll.; m. Margaret Overholt, Oct. 8, 1925 (dec. 1957); children—J. Fred, Williamson. Pres., dir. Financial Cons., Inc., Pitts. Clubs: Duguesne, University, Harvard-Yale-Princeton (Pitts.); Belham River Valley Golf (Montserrat, W.I.). Office: Oliver Bldg 535 Smithfield Pittsburgh PA 15222

HEDE, HENRY THOMAS, broadcasting co. exec.; b. Bklyn., Sept. 28, 1910; s. Henry Thomas and Mary (Carhart) H.; m. Hilda Spierling, Aug. 16, 1936. With Blue Network Co., Inc. and ABC, divs. Am. Broadcasting Cos., Inc., N.Y.C., 1942- -, bus. mgr. TV network, sales dept., 1952-57, v.p. sales adminstrn., TV network sales dept., 1958—. Mem. Broadcast Pioneers, Radio and TV Exec. Soc. Home: 440 Kinderkamack Rd River Edge NJ 07661 Office: 1330 Av of Americas New York City NY 10019

HEDEEN, NATHANAEL EVERETT, church ofcl.; b. Bklyn., Sept. 6, 1906; s. Erik Nathanael and Ida Louise (Larson) H.; student U. Cal. at Berkeley, 1925-27; A.B., Gustavus Adolphus Coll., 1929; B.D., Augustana Theol. Sem., 1932, D.D., 1954; m. Esther Mathilda Holm, June 22, 1932; children—Everett Nathanael, Mary Louise (Mrs. David High Clark), John Erik. Ordained to ministry Lutheran Ch., 1932; pastor, Palo Alto, Cal., 1932-36, Council Bluffs, Ia., 1936-39, Essex, Ia., 1939-42, Kansas City, Mo., 1945-54; mem. bd. finance Augustana Luth. Ch., 1947-50, pres. West Central Conf., 1950-62, mem. bd. am. missions, 1954-62, pres., 1959-62; pres. Central States Synod, 1962-70, pres. bd. Am. missions Luth. Ch. in Am., 1962-66; now mission developer Bd. Am. Missions Luth. Ch. Del. gen.

assembly Nat. Council Chs. Christ U.S., 1960, 63; mem. div. Am. missions Nat. Luth. Council. Bd. dirs. Central Theol. Sem., Fremont, Neb., Bethany Coll., Lindsborg, Kan., 1949—, Trinity Luth. Hosp., Kansas City, Mo., 1945-54. Mem. Kansas City Council Chs. (exec. com. 1947-52; bd. dirs.). Home: 6760 S Depew St Littleton CO

HEDERMAN, THOMAS MARTIN, Jr., newspaper editor; b. Jackson, Miss., May 23, 1911; s. Thomas Martin and Pearl (Smith) H.; B.A., Miss. Coll., 1932, LL.D. (hon.), 1967, grad. student Columbia, 1932-33; m. Bernice Flowers, May 11, 1938; children—Thomas Martin III (dec. USAF), Bernice. Asso. editor of the Clarion-Ledger, Jackson, Miss., 1948, editor, co-pub., 1948—; v.p. Miss. Publs. Corp.; pres. Capitol Broadcasting Co., owners WJTV and WSLI; chmn. bd. Magnolia Fed. Savs. & Loan Assn., Jackson. Pres. bd. trustees Miss. Coll. Mem. exec. com. Miss. Research and Devel. Commn. Named Outstanding Alumnus of Year, Miss. Coll.; recipient Silver EM award, Miss. Scholastic Press Assn. and Miss. Journalism Assn., 1970. Mem. Miss. Press Assn. (pres.), Am. Soc. Newspaper Editors, So. Newspaper Pubs. Assn. (dir. 1947-49). Home: 1331 Belvoir Pl Jackson MS 39202 Office: 311 E Pearl St Jackson MS 39201

HEDGECOCK, WILLIAM ANSON, utilities exec.; b. Bloomington, Ill., Aug. 27, 1913; s. William LeRoy and Elizabeth (Noel) H.; A.S., Flint Jr. Coll., 1933; student U. Mich., 1934-35, 38-39, Gen. Motors Inst., 1937-39, Mass. Inst. Tech., 1964; m. Wealtha J. Haley, Aug. 24, 1935; children—Wealtha Ann (Mrs. David Rea), William Anson. With Consumers Power Co., 1936—, div. mgr., Saginaw, Mich., 1962-64, gen. exec. divs., Jackson, Mich., 1964-65, v.p. divs. and customer service, 1965—, also chmn. electric forecasting com., gas forecasting com., alternate finance, budget control com., adminstr. contbn. and membership programs. Div. chmn. Jackson County United Fund drive, 1965. Bd. dirs. Mich. United Fund, Detroit Met. Fund. Home: 1206 Hampton Dr Jackson MI 49203 Office: Consumers Power Co 212 W Michigan St Jackson MI 49201

HEDGES, DONALD W., lawyer; b. Kansas City, Mo., May 24, 1921; s. Byron C. and Irma (McCleary) H.; student Principia Coll., 1939-40; B.S., Wharton Sch., U. Pa., 1943, LL.B., 1947; m. Mary Elizabeth Mancill, Jan. 29, 1944 (div.); children—Judith Elizabeth, Donna Louise, Byron C. III, Steven M.; m. 2d, Diane Scheid, Jan. 15, 1965; children—Scott Andrew, Hillary Carson. Admitted to Phila. bar, Supreme Ct. of Pa., 1948, U.S. Circuit Ct. Appeals, 1949, Dist. Ct. Eastern Dist. Pa., 1949; admitted to practice Treasury dept.; law clk., Chief Justice Pa. Supreme Ct., 1948-49; mem. firm Mancill, Cooney, Semans & Hedges, 1949-64; partner Wolf, Block, Schorr & Solis Cohen, Phila., 1965—. Dir. Investment Annuity, Inc., First Investment Annuity Co. of Am., Materials Tech., Inc., Servotronics, Inc. Served as lt. (j.g.), Air Force, USNR, 1943-46. Decorated Distinguished Flying Cross, Air medal. Mem. C. of C. Greater Phila. (dir. economics and taxation council), Newcomen Soc. Eng. in N.Am., Am., Pa., Phila. bar assns., Juristic Soc. Phila., Beta Theta Pi. Episcopalian. Clubs: Union League (Phila.); Sharswood Law (U. Pa.); Merion Golf; Lake Placid; Merion Cricket. Home: 1026 Rock Creek Rd Bryn Mawr PA 19010 Office: Packard Bldg Philadelphia PA 19102

HEDGES, HARRY GEORGE, educator; b. Lansing, Mich., Oct. 7, 1923; s. Charles William and Elsie (Frost) H.; B.S., Mich. State U., 1949, Ph.D., 1960; M.S., U. Mich., 1954; m. Dorellen Lyons, Aug. 30, 1968; children—Richard, Patrick, Kevin Rastall, Susan Hedges, Kay, Guy, George Jenkins, Martha Hedges. Electronics engr. USAF Wright Air Devel. Center, Dayton, O., 1949-51; research asso. U. Mich., 1951-54; instr. Mich. State U., East Lansing, 1954-60, asst. prof., 1960-63, asso. prof., 1963-69, prof., chmn. dept. computer sci., 1969—. Dir. Nat. Electronics Conf., Inc., 1968—. Mem. Selective Service Bd. 264, Lansing, 1970—. Served with AUS, 1943-46; PTO. NSF sci. faculty fellow, 1960. Mem. Am. Soc. Engring. Edn. (chmn. N.Central sect. 1968-69), I.E.E.E. (dir. 1967-69, treas. 1969—, Southeastern Mich. sect.). Tech. editor Analysis of Discrete Physical Systems, 1967. Home: 610 Dunbar Ct East Lansing MI 48823

HEDGES, JOHN LELAND, fgn. service officer; b. Chgo., Feb. 5, 1927; s. Leland Gilleland and Ethelyn Blanche (MacMillan) H.; A.B., Harvard, 1948; M.S., George Washington U., 1967; postgrad. Air War Coll., 1967; m. Margaret Houser, Aug. 20, 1946; children—Jeffrey Leland, John Arthur. Free-lance writer, Paris, France, 1948; adminstrv. officer information div. Marshall Plan European Hdqrs., Paris, 1949-50; asst. information officer Spl. and Tech. Mission to Indochina, Saigon, 1950-51; overseas operations officer information div. ECA/Mut. Security Agy., Washington, 1951-53; gen. mgr. Congl. Quar. Newsfeatures, Washington, 1953-54; pub. affairs officer for Western France, Tours, 1954-56; labor information officer, Paris, 1956-57; pub. affairs officer So. France, Marseille, 1957-59; press attache Am. embassy, Paris, 1959-62; country pub. affairs officer, Brazzaville, Congo, 1962-63; dep. country pub. affairs officer, Rabat, Morocco, 1963-66; policy officer for Africa, USIA, 1967-69; country pub. affairs officer 1st sec., Beirut, Lebanon, 1969-71; counselor embassy for pub. affairs, Bangkok, Thailand, 1971—; alternate U.S. delegate Cannes Internat. Film Festivals, 1958-59; press officer U.S. delegation UNESCO Gen. Conf., Paris, 1958. Served with USNR, 1945-46. Mem. Am. Fgn. Service Assn. Clubs: Nat. Press (Washington); Harvard (N.Y.C.); Royal Bangkok Sports. Home: 139 Grafton St Chevy Chase MD 20015 Office: Am Embassy Bangkok Thailand

HEDGES, WILLIAM LEONARD, educator; b. Arlington, Mass., Feb. 16, 1923; s. James B. and Nina (Leonard) H.; B.A., Haverford Coll., 1946; Ph.D., Harvard, 1954; m. Elaine Catherine Ryan, June 28, 1956; children—Marietta, James Leonard. Teaching fellow Harvard, 1950-53; instr. U. Wis., 1953-56; mem. faculty Goucher Coll., 1956-57, 58—, prof. English, 1967—; vis. asst. prof. U. Cal. at Berkeley, 1957-58. Served with AUS, 1943-45. Decorated Purple Heart, Fulbright fellow, France, 1949-50; fellow Am. Council Learned Socs., 1963-64. Mem. Modern Lang. Assn., Am. Assn. U. Profs., Phi Beta Kappa. Author: Washington Irving: An American Study, 1965. Co-author and co-editor: Major Writers of America, 1962. Mem. editorial bd. Early American Lit., 1971—. Home: 6309 Pinehurst Rd Baltimore, MD 21212.

HEDIN, SVEN FREDRIK, Swedish govt. ofcl.; b. Sunne, Sweden, Nov. 6, 1923; s. Josef Nathanael and Anna Gabriella (Palm) H.; student U. Stockholm, 1951; m. Britt-Marie Huss, Dec. 23, 1951; children—Jockum and Cecilia (twins). Joined Swedish Fgn. Service, 1949; attache legation, Madrid, Spain, 1951-53; attache, later 2d sec. embassy, Oslo, Norway, 1953-55; assigned Ministry Fgn. Affairs, 1955-58; 1st sec. embassy, Rio de Janeiro, Brazil, 1958-62; 1st sec. embassy Permanent Mission Sweden to UN, 1963-65, dep. permanent rep. Sweden, counsellor embassy, 1964-65; head div. Ministry Fgn. Affairs, Stockholm, Sweden, 1965-68; Swedish ambassador to Tanzania, 1968—, ambassador to Somalia, 1971—. Recipient decorations from Brazil, Norway, Spain, and Finland. Home: 29 Msasani Rd Oyster Bay Dar es Salaam Tanzania Office: Royal Swedish Embassy Dar es Salaam Tanzania

HEDLUND, EARL CLIFFORD, air force officer; b. Valparaiso, Neb., July 16, 1916; s. Claus Oscar and Hulda (Lundquist) H.; B.S., U. Neb., 1938; M.S., U. Ill., 1939, Ph.D., 1948; grad. USAAF Flying Sch., 1942, Naval War Coll., 1953; m. Eleanor Ruth Neff, Oct. 10, 1948; children—Robert Kent, John William, Steven Earl, Richard Carl, Roger Ellis, Karen Ann. Grad. ROTC, 1938, commd. 2d lt. USAAF, 1938, advanced through grades to lt. gen. USAF, 1967; successively fighter pilot, squadron comdr., group comdr. PTO and ETO, 1942-47; prisoner of war, 1945; escaped, 1945; assigned Joint Chiefs Staff, 1948-50, Hdqrs. USAF, 1950-52; dir. transp. Far East Air Forces, Tokyo, Japan, 1953-56; dep., then dir. transp. Hdqrs. USAF, 1956- 61; dep. comdr. Ogden Air Material Area, Utah, 1961-63; comdr. Warner Robbins Air Material Area, Ga., 1963-66; dep. dir. Def. Supply Agency, Dept. Def., 1966-67, dir., 1967—. Decorated D.S.C., D.S.M., Legion of Merit with cluster, D.F.C. with cluster, Purple Heart with cluster, Air Medal with 19 clusters; D.F.C. (Eng.); Croix de Guerre with star (France); Fourragere (Belgium). Mem. Air Force Assn., Nat. Def. Transp. Assn., Am. Soc. Traffic and Transp., Def. Supply Assn., Armed Forces Mgmt. Assn., Am. Acad. Polit. and Social Sci., Alpha Zeta, Gamma Sigma Delta. Lutheran. Club: Army-Navy Country (Arlington, Va.). Author: Transportation Economics of the Soybean Processing Industry, 1952. Home: 3613 Sprucedale Dr Annandale VA 22003 Office: US Element Cento Am embassy APO New York City NY 09245

HEDLUND, FLOYD FREDERICK, govt. ofcl.; b. Valparaiso, Neb., July 4, 1911; s. Claus Oscar and Hulda (Lundquist) H.; B.S., U. Neb. 1933; Ph.D., Cornell U., 1937; m. Delia M. Roth, May 18, 1963. Asso. with the Dept. Agr., Marketing Adminstrn. and Agrl. Marketing Service, 1946-61, now dir. of the fruit and vegetable div. of the Consumer and Marketing Service, 1961—. Served to maj. USAAF, 1942-46; lt. col. Res. Mem. Am. Agrl. Econs. Assn., Internat. Assn. Agrl. Economists, Nat. Assn. Marketing Ofcl., Farm House Frat., Neb. U. Alumni Assn., Alpha Zeta, Gamma Sigma Delta, Phi Kappa Phi. Lutheran. Clubs: Cornell, Congressional Country (Washington); Palmetto Dunes Golf (Hiltonhead, S.C.). Home: 4101 Cathedral Av N W Washington, DC 20016 Office: Dept of Agriculture Washington DC 20250

HEDLUND, GLENN WILBER, agrl. economist; b. Raymond, Neb., June 11, 1909; s. Claus Oscar and Huldah (Lundquist) H.; B.S., U. Neb., 1930, Ph. D., Cornell, 1936; m. Helen Howard, July 5, 1939; children—James Howard, Jean Helen, Mary Beth. Asst. Cornell, 1930-33, instr., 1933-36, asst. prof., 1937-41, prof. agrl. economics, 1946—, acting head dept., 1952-54, head dept., 1954-68; prof. U. Nanking, China, 1936-37; prof., head dept. agrl. econs. Pa. State University, 1941-46; vis. prof. U. Philippines, 1956-57; cons. Govt. Bermuda, 1939, Farm Credit Adminstrn., 1944-46, Ford Foundation, India, 1964. Trustee Am. Inst. Coop. Mem. Am. Agrl. Econs. Assn., Internat. Assn. Agrl. Economists, Sigma Xi, Alpha Zeta, Gamma Sigma Delta, Phi Kappa Phi. Home: 110 Homestead Rd Ithaca NY 14850

HEDLUND, GUSTAV ARNOLD, educator; b. Somerville, Mass., May 7, 1904; s. Mauritz Theodor and Thekla Maria (Starck) H.; A.B., Harvard, 1925, Ph.D., 1930; A.M., Columbia, 1927; m. Frances Denton Hutcheson, Jan. 24, 1931; children—Marianna, Gustav William. Instr. math. Hunter Coll., 1925-27; part-time instr. math. Harvard 1927-30; instr. math. Radcliffe Coll., 1928-30; asso. math. Bryn Mawr Coll., 1930-34, asso. prof., 1934-39; NRC fellow Princeton Inst. Advanced Study, 1933-34, mem., 1938-39, 53-54; prof. math. U. Va., 1939-48, Yale, 1948—; research mathematician communications research div. Inst. Def. Analyses, 1959-60, dir., 1962- 63. Research Mathematician OSRD, applied math. group Columbia, 1944-45. Mem. Am. Math. Soc. (councilor 1937-39, colloquium speaker 1948, v.p. 1951), Math. Assn. Am., A.A.A.S. (v.p. 1958), Conn. Acad. Arts and Scis., Sigma Xi. Presbyn. Home: 309 McKinley Av New Haven CT 06512

HEDMEG, ANDREW, state ofcl.; b. Bratislava, Czechoslovakia; s. John and Susan (Hutnik) H.; came to U.S., 1912, naturalized, 1922; A.B., Ohio State U., 1931, M.D., 1936; M.P.H., Johns Hopkins, 1941; m. Jennie Katonak, May 21, 1932; 1 dau., Andra (Mrs. Francis Ledet). County health officer Miss. Bd. Health, 1937-52; dir. preventative medicine div., local health services div. La. Bd. Health, 1952-66, pres. La. Bd. Health, state health officer, 1966—. Clin. prof. pub. health adminstrn. La. State U. Sch. Medicine, 1953—; adj. prof. Tulane U. Sch. Tropical Medicine and Pub. Health, New Orleans, 1953—. Served with AUS, 1942-46. Recipient C.B. White Meml. award La. Pub. Health Assn., 1964, Outstanding Service award So. br. Am. Pub. Health Assn., 1966. Diplomate Am. Bd. Preventive Medicine. Life fellow Am. Pub. Health Assn.; mem. La. State, Orleans Parish med. socs., British Royal Soc. Health. Home: 900 Robert E Lee Blvd New Orleans LA 70124 Office: PO Box 60630 New Orleans LA 70160

HEDREN, TIPPI, (Nathalie Kay Hedren), actress; b. New Ulm, Minn., Jan. 19, 1935; d. Bernard Carl and Dorothea Henrietta (Eckhardt) H.; ed. Pasadena City Coll., acting studies with Claudia Franck and Gertrude Fogler; m. Noel Marshall, Sept. 27, 1964; 1 dau. by previous marriage—Melanie. High fashion model with Eileen Ford, N.Y.C., 1952-60; appeared in numerous television commls.; actress appearing in motion pictures, summer theatre, television; film credits include The Birds, Marnie, Countess of Hong Kong; hosted television talk show New Yorkers; summer theatre plays include Hatful of Rain, Black Comedy; mem. U.S.O. tours to Vietnam. Dir. Women's Council of Channel 28, Ednl. TV. Spl. guest speaker March of Dimes; active Multiple Sclerosis, internat. orphans. Home: 4156 Knobhill Dr Sherman Oaks CA 91403 Office: care Noel Marshall Mgmt 4156 Knobhill Dr Sherman Oaks CA 91403

HEDRICH, KENNETH, photographer; recipient Fine Arts medal A.I.A. Address: care A I A 1735 New York Av N W Washington DC 20006

HEDRICK, FRANK EDGAR, aircraft co. exec.; b. Paola, Kan., June 20, 1910; s. Melvin Earl and Hulda Catherine (Mellor) H.; ed. pub. schs., also extension courses; m. Harriet Elizabeth Miller, Sept. 17, 1949. Sales Mgr. E.S. Cowie Electric Co., Wichita, Kan., 1935-40, v.p., dir., 1952—; v.p., coordinator Beech Aircraft Corp., Wichita, 1940-60, exec. v.p., 1960-68, pres., 1968—, also dir.; pres., dir. Beech Acceptance Corp., Wichita, 1956—; Vice chmn. bd. Beechcraft-Hawker Corp., 1969—; dir. Southwest Petro-Chem., Inc., Battenfeld Grease and Oil Corp. (Kansas City, Mo.). Bd. dirs. Gen. Aviation Mfrs. Assn. Active Air Force Acad. Found., Wichita YMCA. Mem. Wichita (past dir.), Kan. chambers commerce, Am. Mgmt. Assn., N.A.M. Clubs: Kiwanis (Past dir. Wichita Downtown), Wichita Country (past dir.), Wichita Shocker, Century (Wichita); Burning Tree (Bethesda, Md.); Cherry Hills Country (Denver). Home: 644 Brookfield St Wichita KS 67206 Office: Beechcraft Aircraft Corp Wichita KS 67206

HEDRICK, FREDERIC CLEVELAND, Jr., lawyer; b. Jacksonville, Fla., July 18, 1911; s. Frederic Cleveland and Edith (Warrington) H.; B.S., U. Fla., 1936, LL.B., 1938; m. Rosalie Sutton, May 10, 1939; children—Frederic Cleveland III, Meredith, Charles Warrington. Admitted to Fla. bar, 1938, D.C. bar, 1944; practice in Washington, 1945—; spl. asst. antitrust div. U.S. Atty. Gen., 1938-41; mem. firm Pierson & Ball, 1946-52; pvt. practice, 1952-55; sr. partner Hedrick & Lane, 1955—. Past pres. Ocean Mews, Delray Beach, Fla. Past trustee Fauquier Ednl. Found. Served from 1st lt. to lt. col. AUS, 1941-45. Recipient Legion of Merit award for work with SSS, 1945. Fellow Am. Bar Found.; mem. Am. (mem. ho. dels. 1970—), D.C. (past sect. chmn., dir.), bar assns., Tax Inst. Am. (past pres.), Am. Law Inst., Am. Judicature Soc., U. Fla. Alumni Assn. (past pres. Washington chpt.), Blue Key, Alpha Tau Omega, Phi Delta Phi. Episcopalian (vestry). Clubs: Army and Navy, Metropolitan (Washington); Chevy Chase (Md.); Metropolitan (N.Y.C.); Ocean (Fla.). Home: 5215 Cammack Dr Washington DC 20016 also The Oceans Mews 6845 N Ocean Blvd Delray Beach FL 33444 Office: 1001 Connecticut Av NW Washington DC 20036

HEDRICK, IRA GRANT, aircraft engring. co. exec.; b. Kansas City, Mo., Feb. 10, 1913; s. Ira Grant and Adaline (Luther) H.; student U. Ill., 1929-30, U. Wash., 1931-32; B.S., U. Ark., 1936; C.E., Princeton, 1937; m. Shirley Poythress, Aug. 24, 1934; children—Ira Grant, John Karl. Designer, Waddell & Hardesty, N.Y.C., 1937-42; chief structural engr. U.S. Engring. Dept., Cairo, Egypt, 1943; v.p. Grumman Aerospace Corp., Bethpage, N.Y., 1943-70, sr. v.p., 1970—. Fellow Am. Inst. Aeros. and Astronautics. Home: 250 Mount Joy Av Freeport NY 11520 Office: S Oyster Bay Rd Bethpage NY 11714

HEDRICK, JAY ELDRED, chem. engr.; b. Meredosia, Ill., July 17, 1909; s. Commodore P. and Kathrn (Pfenninger) H.; A.B., Ill. Coll. 1931; M.S., State U.Ia., 1932, Ph.D., 1934; m. Mary Ellen Love, Feb. 4, 1937 (dec. 1957); children—Peter Jay, Mary Susan, Katherine Ann, Sara Ellen; m. 2d, Elizabeth Cook, Oct. 15, 1960; 1 dau., Carol Elizabeth. Asst. chemist Ia. Pub. Health Dept., 1934-36; instr. chem. engring., Kan. State Coll. 1936-41; sr. technologist, Shell Oil Co., Martinez, Cal., 1941-42; sr. engr., Shell Devel. Co., San Francisco, 1942-45; cons. WPB, 1944-45; exec. asst., Shell Chem. Corp., San Francisco and N.Y.C. 1945-49; prof. chem. engring., Cornell U., since 1949, asst. dean engring., 1953-57, dir. engring. placement, 1968—. Fellow Am. Inst. Chemists; mem. Am. Inst. Chem. Engrs., Am. Chem. Soc., Tau Beta Pi, Alpha Chi Sigma, Phi Lambda Upsilon, Sigma Xi. Licensed profl. engr., N.Y. State. Unitarian. Home: 715 The Parkway Ithaca NY 14850

HEDRICK, WALTER RUSSELL, Jr., ret. air force officer; b. Hawley, Tex., Aug. 2, 1921; s. Walter Russell and Mary (James) H.; B.S. in Physics, U. Md., 1941, M.S., 1952; m. Betty Ben Sanford, Jan. 17, 1941; children—Walter Russell III, Robert Douglas. Commd. 2d lt. USAAF, 1941, advanced through grades to brig. gen. USAF, 1966; with 86th Fighter-Bomber Group, World War II; assigned 10th Air Force, Brooks Field, Tex., 1947-48, 14th Air Force, Orlando AFB. Fla., 1948-49; project officer sec. air force, 1949-51; with test br. Air Force Office Atomic Energy, 195255; chief tech. operations div. Air Force Spl. Weapons Center, Kirtland AFB, N.M., 1955-57; comdr. 4951st Suppost Squadron, Eniwetok, 1957-58; asst. to group comdr., later air comdr. 4925th Test Group, Kirtland AFB, 1958-60; assigned Space Systems Office, Air Force Ballistic Missile Div., Los Angeles, 1960-65; dep. comdr. for space Air Force Systems Command, 1966-67; dir. space, dep. chief staff research and devel., 1967-70, ret., 1970; v.p. Itek Corp., 1970—. Decorated Legion of Merit, Air medal with 4 oak leaf clusters, Air Force Commendation medal. Home: Carlisle MA 01741 Office: Itek Corp 10 Maguire Rd Lexington MA 02173

HEEBE, FREDERICK JACOB REGAN, U.S. dist. judge; b. Gretna, La., Aug. 25, 1922; s. Bernhardt and Marguerite (Reagan) H.; B.A., Tulane U., 1943, LL.B., 1949; m. Willie Dee Barnes, Aug. 29, 1947; children—Frederick Riley, Adrea Dee. Admitted to La. bar, 1949; practice in Gretna, 1949-60; dist. judge div. B, 24th Jud. Dist. Ct., Jefferson Parish, La., 1961-66; U.S. dist. judge Eastern Dist. La., 1966—: Charter mem. Community Welfare Council Jefferson Parish, 1957—; chmn. Jefferson Parish Bd. Pub. Welfare, 1953- 55. Mem. Jefferson Parish Council, 1958-60, vice chmn., 1958-60. Bd. dirs. Social Welfare Planning Council New Orleans, New Orleans Regional Mental Center and Clinic, W. Bank Assn. for Retarded. Served to capt., inf., AUS, World War II. Decorated Purple Heart, Bronze Star. Mem. Am., La., New Orleans, Fed. bar assns., Am. Judicature Soc., Phi Beta Kappa. Home: 1407 Whitney Av Gretna LA 70053 Office: 400 Royal St New Orleans LA 70130

HEEDY, HENRY GLEN, Jr., synthetic fibers co. exec.; b. Youngstown, O., May 5, 1914; s. Henry Glen and Cecelia (Stambaugh) H.; grad. Asheville Sch., 1933; A.B., Yale, 1937; m. Elizabeth Adele Orr, June 24, 1941; children—Elisabeth Glen (Mrs. James Curwen), Kathleen (Mrs. Ray P. Ballard), Cecelia Eileen (Mrs. Michael Latta), Henry Glen III, Michael Andrew. With Sharon Steel Corp. (Pa.) 1937-39; instr. Asheville (N.C.) Sch., 1939-42; with Am. Enka Co. (N.C.), 1946—, plant mgr., 1959-63, v.p. gen. mgr. staple fiber div., 1963-68 v.p., 1968—. Trustee Asheville Sch. Served to lt. USNR, 1942- 46. Decorated Bronze Star medal. Mem. Am. Mgmt. Assn., Am. Textile Mgr. Assn., Newcomen Soc. N.Am. Clubs: Asheville City, Biltmore Forest Country (Asheville); Morristown (Tenn.) Country. Home: 9 Forest Rd Asheville NC 28803 Office: Am Enka Co Enka NC 28728

HEEKIN, JAMES R., advt. exec.; b. Cin., 1926; ed. Williams Coll., 1948. Formerly pres., dir. Ogilvy & Mather, Inc. Home: 139 Turrell Av South Orange NJ 07079

HEER, RALPH WALDO, found. exec.; b. Silver City, Ida., Dec. 3, 1903; s. Frank and Catherine (Fannin) H.; B.B.A., U. Wash., 1927; m. Doris Vivian Finch, July 10, 1936; 1 dau., Judith. With Price Waterhouse & Co., 1934-39; with Superior Oil Co., 1939-65, comptroller, 1957-63, treas., 1963-65; sec. W.M. Keck Found., Los Angeles, 1965—. C.P.A., Cal. Home: 2222A Via Puerta Laguna Hills CA 92653 Office: 1801 Av of Stars Los Angeles CA 90067

HEESCHEN, DAVID SUTPHIN, astronomer; b. Davenport, Ia., Mar. 12, 1926; s. Richard George and Emily (Sutphin) H.; B.S., U. Ill., 1949, M.S., 1951; Ph.D., Harvard, 1954; m. Eloise St. Claire, June 11, 1950; children—Lisa Clair, David William, Richard Mark. Instr., Wesleyan U., Middletown, Conn., 1954-55; lectr., research asso. Harvard, 1955-56; scientist Nat. Radio Astronomy Obs., 1956—, dir., 1962—; G.R. Agassiz fellow Harvard Obs., 1953-54. Cons. NASA, 1960-61, 68—. Mem. Am. Astron. Soc. (v.p.) 1969-71), Internat. Astron. Union (v.p. commn. 40, 1967-70, pres. 1970—), Internat Sci. Radio Union, Sigma Xi. Contbr. sci. jours. Home: 1930 Barracks Rd Charlottesville VA 22903 Office: NRAO Edgemont Rd Charlottesville VA 22901

HEEZEN, BRUCE CHARLES, oceanographer, geologist; b. Vinton, Ia., Apr. 11, 1924; s. Charles Christian and Esther (Schirding) H.; B.A., State U. Ia., 1948; M.A., Columbia, 1952, Ph.D., 1957. Geologist Woods Hole (Mass.) Oceanographic Inst., 1947-48; fellow in geology Columbia, 1948-51, asst. in geology, 1951-53, lectr., 1953-55, research asso., 1955-57; sr. research scientist Lamont Geol. Obs., Palisades, N.Y., 1957-60, mem. academic staff, 1960—; asst. prof. geology Columbia, 1960-64, asso. prof., 1964- -; cons. U.S. Naval Oceanographic Office: 1968—. Pres. Internat. Commn. Marine Geology; chmn. Internat. Commn. World Rift System. Recipient Henry Bryant Biglow medal, prize in oceanography for contbn. to marine sci. Fellow A.A.A.S., Am. Geog. Soc., Geol. Soc. Am., Ia.

Acad. Sci., Marine Biol. Assn. of U.K., Royal Astron. Soc.; mem. Am. Assn. Petroleum Geologists, Am. Geophys. Union, Am. Soc. Limnology and Oceanography, Geochem. Soc., N.Y. Acad. Scis., Seismol. Soc. Am., Soc. Exploration Geophysicists, Socitea Limnologae Internalis, Sigma Xi, Sigma Chi. Unitarian. Author: The Floors of the Oceans; The Face of the Deep. Contbr. numerous articles to profl. jours. Home: 747 River Rd Piermont NY 10968 Office: Torrey Cliff Lamont Geol Observatory Palisades NY 10964

HEFFELFINGER, TOTTON PEAVEY, business exec.; b. Mpls., Jan. 23, 1899; s. Frank Totton and Lucia L. (Peavey) H.; student Thacher Sch., Yale, ex-1921 war class; m. Mildred Virginia Kidder, Jan. 3, 1922 (dec. July 1931); children— Frank Totton, Marcus Willard, Lila K. Coleman; m. 2d, Elsmore G. Anderson, Jan. 31, 1933; children—John Christopher B. Grain buyer Brit. Am. Elevator Co., Ltd., 1921; mgr. commn. dept. No. Elevator Co., Ltd., 1923, asst. mgr., 1926; asso. mgr. Security Elevator Co., Ltd., 1927; treas. Van Dusen Harrington Co. (merger with Peavey Co.), Mpls., 1928, v.p., 1932-45, exec. v.p., 1945, pres. 1946—; pres. Occidental Fuel Co., Ltd., 1924-28; chmn. bd. Peavey Co. (formerly F.H. Peavey & Co.) , 1965—; dir. First Bank System, Trico Oil & Gas Co. Served from lt. to comdr. USNR, 1942-45; USN Preflight Sch., St. Marys Coll., Cal.; exec. officer Naval Air Sta., Honolulu. Mem. U.S. Golf Assn. (pres. 1952-53), Am. Legion (past dept. comdr. Can.) . Clubs: Minneapolis, Minnikahda, Woodhill Country (Mpls.); Hazeltine Nat. Golf (Chaska, Minn.). Home: Route 1 Box 124-3 Chaska MN 53318 Office: Grain Exchange Minneapolis MN 55415

HEFFELFINGER, WILLIAM STEWART, corp. exec., govt. ofcl.; b. Effingham, Kan., Jan. 31, 1925; s. William Stewart and Nora (Estell) H.; m. Dorothy M. Shockley, Sept. 24, 1944; children—William Stewart III, Sharon A., Lee S. With Sweet Hotel System, 1942-43; bus. mgr. Eleemosynary Instns., Kans., 1946-53; sec., trustee A. J. Rice Estates, 1948—; dir. Olney facility FCDA, 1953-54, dir. adminstrv. operations office, 1955-56, asst. adminstr. for gen. adminstrn., 1956-58; adv. com. Gen. Services Adminstrn., 1956-62; dir. adminstrn. Exec. Office of President U.S., 1958-62; reviewing officer Bd. of Surveys, 1956-62; chmn. bd. U.S. Civil Service Examiners, 1955- 62; dir. program rev. Martin-Marietta Corp., 1962-69; spl. asst. to asst. sec. water and power devel. Dept. Interior, 1969; dep. asst. sec. Dept. Transp., Washington, 1969-70, asst. sec., 1970—. Mem. Joint Task Force Seven in Operation Redwing, 1956. Served with AUS, 1943-46. Recipient Wm. A. Jump Meml. Found. Meritorious award, 1960. Mem. Am. Soc. Pub. Adminstrn., Am. Legion. Mason. Home: 1708 Wolfram Ct McLean VA 22101 Office: Dept Transp 400 7th St Washington DC

HEFFERLINE, RALPH FRANKLIN, psychologist; b. Muncie, Ind., Feb. 15, 1910; s. Samuel Thomas and Blanche (Cecil) H.; B.S., Columbia, 1941, M.A., 1942, Ph.D., 1947; m. Dorothy Halliday, Aug. 25, 1939. Faculty, Columbia, N.Y.C., 1948—, prof., 1967—, pre-med. adviser, 1949-54, chmn. dept. psychology, 1965-68. Fellow Am. Psychol. Assn., A.A.A.S., N.Y. Acad. Scis.; mem. Psychonomic Soc., Eastern Psychol. Assn., Soc. for Gen. Systems Research, Soc. Psychophysiol., Bio-Feedback Soc., Soc. Neuroscis.; affiliate mem. Royal Soc. Medicine (London). Research. Author: (with F.S. Peris and P. Goodman) Gestalt Therapy, 1950. Research on significance of patterns of muscular tension for psychoneurosis and anxiety, electromyographic study of very small responses as behavioral counterpart of mental processes. Home: 549 W 123d St New York City NY 10027

HEFFERNAN, JAMES D., banker; b. Fabius, N.Y., Feb. 27, 1910; s. Daniel J. and Ella (Sheaban) H.; B.A., Syracuse U.; m. Geraldine Allen, Sept. 9, 1939; children—James D., Joseph C., Patricia R., Geraldine M. Pres., chief exec. officer Lincoln Bank, Syracuse, N.Y., also dir.; chmn. bd. Lincoln First Banks, Inc.; mem. exec. com., dir. Unity Life Ins. Co. Bd. dirs. Le Moyne Coll., Community Gen. Hosp., Met. Devel. Assn. Mem. Am., N.Y. State bankers assns., Robert Morris Assos. Home: 38 Lynacres Blvd Fayetteville NY 13066 Office: 1 Mony Plaza Syracuse NY 13201

HEFFERNAN, JOHN BAPTIST, ret. naval officer; b. Washington, Ind., Oct. 21, 1894; s. William and Ellen (Sullivan) H.; B.S., U.S. Naval Acad., 1917; student Naval War Coll., Army-Navy Staff Coll.; m. Patricia Grattan Esmonde (d. late Sir Thomas Grattan Esmonde, Bart., M.P., of Ballynastragh, Gorey, Co. Wexford, Ireland), Nov. 18, 1927; children—Patricia Grattan, Henry Grattan, Eithne Mary Grattan (Mrs. Thomas M. Hartnett), Kathleen Barbara Grattan (Mrs. R. J. Wach). Instr. history U.S. Naval Acad., 1932-35, 38-40; chief of staff 7th Naval Dist., 1946; dir. naval history, 1946-56. Served in destroyers, Europe, 1917-18; comd. destroyer div., Atlantic, 1940-41, destroyer squadron, Atlantic, 1942; comd. U.S.S. Tenn. in battle for Leyte Gulf, 1944, at Iwo Jima and Okinawa, 1945; ret. with rank of rear adm. USN. Decorated Legion of Merit, Bronze Star medal (4), Commendation ribbon (2). Mem. Naval Hist. Found. (trustee and v.p., sec.). Naval Inst., Am., Am. Irish, Am. Cath. hist. assns., Ind. Hist. Soc., Soc. Nautical Research (London), Mil. Hist. Soc. Ireland. Club: Army and Navy (Washington). Roman Catholic. Naval editor Ency. Brit. Home: 3029 Que St N W Washington DC 20007 Office: Naval Hist Found Navy Dept Washington DC 20360

HEFFERNAN, JOHN WILLIAM, journalist; b. Stockbridge, Enq., Oct. 21, 1910; s. John and Alice Ann (Edwards) H.; student Clark's Coll., Putney, Eng., 1926; m. Lea Arney, Aug. 6, 1938; m. 2d, Edith Curry, Dec. 10, 1948; 1 stepson, Anthony E. Heffernan. Came to U.S., 1946. Editorial asst. Central News Ltd., London, Eng., 1929-34; sub-editor Press Assn., London, 1934-36, sports reporter, 1936-39, news desk editor, 1939-41; with Reuters, 1946—, chief corr. at UN, 1952-57, chief corr. in Washington, 1957—. Pres. UN Corr. Assn., 1956. Served to maj. Brit. Army, 1941-46; C.B.I. Decorated officer Order Brit. Empire, comdr. Order British Empire. Clubs: Nat. Press (bd. govs. 1964—69), Internat. (Washington); Overseas Press (N.Y.C.). Home: 2852 Arizona Av NW Washington DC 20016 Office: Nat Press Bldg Washington DC 20004

HEFFERNAN, JOSEPH VICTOR, lawyer, corp. exec.; b. Washington, Ind., Dec. 23, 1905; s. William and Ellen (Sullivan) H.; A.B., St. Louis U., 1928; J.D., Ind. U., 1930; LL.M., Columbia, 1935; m. Marion Cahill, 1942; 1 son, William C. Admitted to N.Y. bar, 1936; with Cahill, Gordon, Reindel & Ohl, N.Y.C., 1935-40; v.p., head law dept. RCA Corp., 1945-57; financial v.p. NBC, 1957-58; partner Hecht, Hadfield, Farbach & McAlpin, N.Y.C., 1958-65; counsel, head law dept. Reynolds Metals Co., 1965-68; dep. chmn. Brit. Aluminium Co., Ltd., London, 1968-71. Bd. visitors Ind. U. Sch. of Law, 1964-68; nat. chmn. Ind. U. Annual Giving Campaign, 1964. Served to lt. USNR, World War II. Recipient distinguished alumni award Ind. U., 1956. Contbr. articles profl. jours. Home: 10 Gracie Sq New York City NY 10028

HEFFERNAN, NATHAN STEWART, justice Wis. Supreme Ct.; b. Frederic, Wis., Aug. 6, 1920; s. Jesse Eugene and Pearl Eva (Kaump) H.; B.A., U. Wis., 1942, LL.B., 1948; student Harvard Bus. Sch., 1943-44; m. Dorothy Hillemann, Apr. 27, 1946; children—Katie, Michael, Thomas. Admitted to Wis. bar, 1948; asso. firm Schubring, Ryan, Peterson & Sutherland, Madison, 1948-49; practice in Sheboygan, 1949-59, partner firm Buchen & Heffernan, 1951-59; counsel Wis. League Municipalities, 1949; research asst. to gov. Wis., 1949; asst. dist. atty. Sheboygan County, 1951-53, city atty., 1953-59; dep. atty. gen. Wis., 1959-62; U.S. atty. Western Dist. Wis., 1962-64; justice Wis. Supreme Ct., 1964—; lectr. municipal corps. U. Wis. Law Sch., 1961-64, lectr. appellate procedure and practice, 1971. Wis. chmn. Nat. Conf. Christians and Jews. Pres. City Attys. Assn., 1958-59. Gen. chmn. Wis. Democratic Conv., 1960, 61. Bd. visitors U. Wis. Law Sch., 1970—; trustee Wis. Meml. Union, Wis. State Library. Served to lt. (s.g.) USNR, 1942-46. Recipient distinguished service award Nat. Conf. Christians and Jews, 1968. Mem. Am. Law Inst., Inst. Jud. Adminstrn., Am., Fed., Wis., Dane County, Sheboygan County bar assns., Am. Judicature Soc., Order of Coif, Iron Cross, Phi Delta Phi. Conglist. Home: 17 Thorstein Veblen Pl Madison WI 53705 Office: State Capitol Madison WI 53702

HEFFERNAN, PAUL MALCOLM, architect, educator; b. Decorah, Ia., Jan. 23, 1909; s. Walter A. and Laura D. (Bethuram) H.; B.S. in Archtl. Engring., Ia. State Coll., 1929, M.S. Archtl. Engring., 1931; M. Arch., Harvard, 1935; student Ecole des Beaux Arts, Paris, France, 1935-38. Instr., Ia. State Coll., 1933-35; mem. faculty Sch. Architecture, Ga. Inst. Tech., Atlanta, 1938—, prof., 1944—, dir. sch., 1956—; designer Bush-Brown, Gailey and Heffernan, which conducted master plan and bldg. plans for Ga. Inst. Tech., 1944- 54; cons. archtl. edn. So. Regional Edn. Bd., 1953; cons. architect Ga. Inst. Tech., 1956-64, local firms; cons. design PHA, Washington; mem. archtl. award juries. Pres. Ga. Bd. Exam. and Registration of Architects, 1967-69. Summer fellow Found. Architecture and Landscape Architecture, Lake Forest, Ill., 1929; Condé-Nast fellow Am. architecture, 1929-30; Sheldon fellow, also Appleton fellow Harvard, 1935; recipient Eugene Dodd medal Harvard, 1934; 28th Paris prize Soc. Beaux-Arts Architects, N.Y.C., also certificate Beaux-Arts Inst. Design, N.Y.C., 1935; citation for effective teaching archtl. design Coll. Fellows A.I.A., 1955; hon. mention for West Stands Ga. Inst. Tech., Progressive Architecture mag., 1948; award for Price Gilbert Library A.I.A., 1952; citation N.Ga. chpt. A.I.A., 1965. Fellow A.I.A. (com. scholarships and awards 1956-58); life fellow Internat. Inst. Arts and Letters, Lindau, Germany; mem. Theta Delta Chi, Tau Beta Pi, Phi Kappa Phi, Tau Sigma Delta. Home: 166 5th St N W Atlanta GA 30313

HEFFERNAN, PHILLIP THOMAS, Jr., publisher; b. Natick, Mass., July 2, 1922; s. Phillip Thomas and Hazel (Toner) H.; B.S., Northeastern U., 1947; m. Mildred Brock Lippitt, Aug. 27, 1949; children—Phillip Thomas III, John, Lisa, Caroline. With Gage Pub. Co., N.Y.C. and Chgo., 1947-58, bus. mgr., 1956-58; sales mgr. Conover Mast Publs., N.Y.C., 1958-60; v.p., pub., dir. Ziff Davis Pub. Co., pubs. of Popular Electronics, Stereo Rev., Electronics World mags., 1960—. Pres. Park Forest (Ill.) Playhouse, 1952-53. Served to capt. USMCR, 1942-45. Decorated D.F.C., Air medal, Silver Star, Bronze Star. Mem. Sigma Soc. Clubs: Pelham (N.Y.) Country; Shorehaven Golf (East Norwalk, Conn.) Home: 12 Meadow Av Bronxville NY 10708 Office: 1 Park Av New York City NY 10016

HEFFNER, GROVER CHESTER, naval officer; b. Seattle, Mar. 25, 1919; s. Grover C. and Ida (Bevan) H.; B.S., U. Wash., 1940; M.B.A., Stanford, 1950; grad. Nat. War Coll., 1964; m. Jane Ellen Bender, Apr. 18, 1942; children—Jann Kathryn, Grayson Chester. Commd. ensign USN, 1940; advanced through grades to rear adm., 1967; assigned U.S.S. Altair, 1941, Naval Supply Depot, Brisbane, Australia, 1943-44, U.S.S. Euryale, 1944-46; inventory mgmt. Office Naval Material, 1950-53; comdg. officer Naval Supply Facility, C.Z., 1953-55; force supply officer Cruiser/Destroyer Pacific Fleet, 1955-57; dir. Supply Corps personnel, 1957-60; dir. supply Puget Sound Naval Shipyard, 1960-63; comdg. officer Naval Supply Center, Long Beach, Cal., 1965-66; insp. Gen. Def. Supply Agy., 1966-67; comdr. Def. Indsl. Supply Center, Phila., 1967-70; comdr. Def. Constrn. Supply Center, Columbus, O. Bd. dirs. United Funds; exec. bd. Goodwill Industries. Decorated Joint Commendation medal, Navy Distinguished Service medal. Mem. Def. Supply Assn., C. of C. (mil. affairs com., problems inner city com.), Sigma Alpha Epsilon. Mason (K.T.), Rotarian. Presbyn. Club: Stanford (Phila.). Home: Qtrs 120 3990 E Broad St Columbus OH 43215

HEFFNER, HUBERT CROUSE, educator; b. Maiden, N.C., Feb. 22, 1901; s. Sylvanus Lafayette and Lily (Crouse) H.; A.B. with honors in Lang. and Lit., U. N.C., 1921, M.A., 1922; student U. Chgo., 1930-34, 44; L.H.D., Ill. Wesleyan U., 1964; Litt.D., U. N.C., 1969; m. Ruth Penny, Apr. 8, 1922; 1 son, Hubert Heffner. Instr. English, dir. dramatics U. Wyo., 1922- 23; instr. English, dir. dramatics U. Ariz., 1923-26; asst. prof. English, asso. dir. The Carolina Playmakers, U. N.C., 1926-30; prof. dramatic lit. Northwestern U., 1930-39; prof. dramatic lit., exec. head dept. speech and drama, Stanford, 1939-54; Rockefeller grant in aid for research and study in France and Eng., 1951-52; Folger Shakespeare Library grant in aid, 1952; Fulbright award, 1954-55; prof. speech, theatre, and dramatic lit. Ind. U., 1954-61, Distinguished Service prof. dramatic lit., 1961—, chmn. div. theatre, 1970-71; vis. prof. summers Northwestern U., 1930, Stanford, 1937, U. Cal., 1939, Cornell U., 1948, U. Colo., 1950, 65, U. Denver, 1962; Carnegie vis. prof. drama U. Hawaii, 1958, U. Bristol, 1954-55, U. Denver, summer 1962, U. Colo., summer 1965. Commd. capt., Spl. Res., U.S. Army, 1943; grad. Sch. of Mil. Govt., U. Va., 1943; inactive status in charge of mil. govt. instrn. Civil Affairs Training Sch., Stanford, 1943-44; research project Provost Marshal Gen's. Office, 1944; head Theatre and Radio Arts Br., chief Fine Arts sect. Biarritz Am. U., 1945-46. Fellow Am. Edn. Theatre Assn. (pres. 1949, editor Jour. 1955-56); mem. Am. Assn. U. Profs., Speech Assn. Am., Modern Lang. Assn., Nat. Theatre Conf., ANTA (bd. dirs. 1953-56, 60—). Author several publs. Editor: (with Isaac Goldberg) Davy Crockett and Other Plays, 1940. Asso. editor Quarterly Jour. of Speech, 1947-50; dir. number of theatrical prodns. for U. Wyo., U. Ariz., The Carolina Playmakers, Northwestern U. and Stanford. Home: 1310 Hunter Av Bloomington IN 47401

HEFFNER, RAY LORENZO, Jr., univ. adminstr.; b. Durham, N.C., Mar. 7, 1925; s. Ray Lorenzo and Gladys Lillian (Gordy) H.; A.B., Yale, 1948, M.A., 1950, Ph.D., 1953; m. Ruth Adele Cline, June 16, 1951; children—David, Christopher. Instr. English, U. Ky., 1950-51; mem. faculty Ind. U., 1953-63, asso. prof. English, 1960-63, asso. dean faculties, 1962-63, v.p., dean of faculties, 1964-66; prof. English, v.p. instrn., dean faculties U. Ia., 1963-64; pres. Brown U., Providence, 1966-69; provost U. Ia., 1969—. Served with USNR, 1943- 46; PTO. Guggenheim fellow, 1960. Mem. Am. Assn. U. Profs., Modern Lang. Assn., Renaissance Soc. Am., Shakespeare Assn. Am., Phi Beta Kappa. Home: 523 Templin Rd Iowa City IA 52240

HEFFNER, RICHARD DOUGLAS, educator, communications cons.; b. N.Y.C., Aug. 5, 1925; s. Albert Simon and Cely (Bender) H.; A.B., Columbia, 1946, M.A. (Mitchell fellow), 1947; m. Anne de la Vergne, Dec. 14, 1946; m. 2d, Elaine Segal, July 30, 1950; children—Daniel Jason, Charles Andrew. Teaching asst. history U. Cal. at Berkeley, 1947-48; instr. Am. history Rutgers U., 1948-50, U. prof. communications, pub. policy, 1964—; lectr. history Columbia, 1950- 52; prof. history Sarah Lawrence Coll., 1952-53; dir. pub. affairs WNBC- TV, N.Y.C., 1955-57; dir. programs Met. Ednl. TV Assn., N.Y.C., 1957-59; producer-moderator The Open Mind NBC-TV, 1956-59; editorial cons. CBS, Inc.; mem. editorial bd., dir. spl. projects CBS-TV Network, 1959-61; v.p., gen. mgr. ednl. TV Channel 13 WNET, N.Y.C., 1961-63; moderator-host Nat. Ednl. TV series People and Politics, 1964; pres. Richard Heffner Assos., Inc., N.Y.C., 1964—. Dir. commn. on campaign costs Twentieth Century Fund, 1968-69; dir. Ford Found. study on TV's environmental messages, 1970—. Mem. A.A.A.S., Am. Hist. Assn., Nat. Assn. Ednl. Broadcasters, Phi Beta Kappa. Author: A Documentary History of the United States, 1952. Editor: Democracy in America, 1956. Home: 90 Riverside Dr New York City NY 10024 Office: 100 Riverside Dr New York City NY 10024

HEFLEBOWER, RICHARD BROOKS, economist; b. Milliken, Colo., Oct. 4, 1903; s. Ernest and Etna Tabitha (Brooks) H.; student Fresno State Coll., 1921-23; A.B., U. Cal., 1925, Ph.D., 1929; m. Velma Harris, June 2, 1926; children—Ellen, Louise, Jean, Linda. Instr. econs. U. Ida., 1928- 29; asst. prof. econs. State Coll. of Wash., 1929-34, asso. prof., 1934-36, prof. and dean Sch. Bus. Adminstrn., 1936-45. various positions, including Econ. Adviser to dep. adminstr. OPA, 1943-46; economist Brookings Instn., Washington, 1946-49; prof. econs. Northwestern U., 1949—, chmn. dept., 1951-59; vis. prof. Harvard, 1962-63. Mem. Midwest Econs. Assn. (pres. 1967-68), Am. Econ. Assn., Royal Econ. Soc. Author: (with E. F. Dummeier and T. Norman) Economics with Applications to Agriculture, 1934; also articles. Asso. editor of Jour. Indsl. Econs., 1952—. Home: 418 Central St Wilmette IL 60091

HEFLER, RICHARD JAMES, chem. mfg. exec.; b. Boston, July 1, 1912; s. Clarence S. and Alice (Henderson) H.; A.B., Dartmouth, 1936; student Fordham U. Law Sch., 1937- 39; M.B.A., U. So. Cal., 1954; m. Edith A. Timmins, Oct. 26, 1946; children—Olivia Catherine, Richard James. Financial analyst Hanover Bank, N.Y.C., 1936-41; spl. studies analyst E. I. duPont de Nemours Co., 1941-42; controller Royal Heaters, Inc., Alhambra, Cal., 1946-47; with Am. Potash & Chem. Corp., Los Angeles, 1948—, sec., 1953-57, now v.p. adminstrn., dir., 1959—; v.p., dir. San Antonio Chems., Inc. Mem. Dartmouth Coll. Alumni Council. Served with USNR, World War II; comdr. Res. Mem. Phi Beta Kappa. Clubs: California (Los Angeles); Union League (N.Y.C.). Home: 10450 Charing Cross Rd Los Angeles CA 90024 Office: 3000 W 6th St Los Angeles CA 90054

HEFLIN, AUBREY NEWBILL, banker; b. Fredericksburg, Va., Sept. 21, 1912; s. Joseph Granville and Garnett Addie (Newbill) H.; B.A., U. Richmond, 1933; LL.B., U. Va., 1936; grad. Rutgers U. Grad. Sch. Banking, 1951; m. Ellen Virginia Simmerman, May 28, 1939; children—Ellen N., Joseph G. Admitted to Va. bar, 1936; asso. atty. firm Parrish, Butcher & Parrish, Richmond, 1936- 41; with Fed. Res. Bank Richmond, 1941-42, 46—, v.p., gen. counsel, 1953-61, 1st v.p., 1961-68, pres., 1968—. Mem. bd. Christian edn. Presbyn. Ch. U.S., 1960—, internat. com. YMCA U.S. and Can., 1961—, met. bd. Richmond YMCA, 1956—; capt. Richmond United Givers Fund, 1961-62. Trustee Richmond Eye Hosp., Union Theol. Sem., Richmond, Va., U. Richmond. Served to lt. (s.g.) USNR, 1942-45. Mem. Am., Va. bar assns. Club: Country Va. (dir.). Home: 1705 Park Av Richmond VA 23220 Office: 100 N 9th St Richmond VA 23219

HEFLIN, HOWELL THOMAS, chief justice Supreme Ct. Ala.; b. Poulan, Ga., June 19, 1921 s. Marvin Rutledge and Louise D. (Strudwick) H.; A.B., Birmingham So. Coll., 1942; J.D., U. Ala., 1948; m. Elizabeth Ann Carmichael, Feb. 23, 1952; 1 son, Howell Thomas. Admitted to Ala. bar, 1948, practiced in Tuscumbia; now chief justice Supreme Ct. Ala. Bd. dirs. Meth. Pub. House, 1952-64; lectr. U. Ala., 1946-48; lectr. Florence State Tchrs. Coll., 1949-52. Mem. Ala. Edn. Commn., 1957-58, 68-69; chmn. Colbert County A.R.C., 1950; Ala. field dir. Crusade for Children, 1948; pres. Ala. Com. Better Schs., 1958-59, Tuscumbia Bd. Edn., 1954-64; chmn. Ala. Tenure Commn., 1959-64; pres. U. Ala. Law Sch. Found., 1964- 66; co-chmn. Nat. Conf. Christians and Jews, Tri-Cities area; chmn. Brotherhood Week. Served to maj. USMCR, 1942-46. Decorated Silver Star, Purple Heart. Fellow Internat. Acad. of Law and Scis., Internat. Acad. Trial Lawyers, Internat. Soc. Barristers, Am. Coll. Trial Lawyers; mem. Ala. Law Inst. (v.p.), Am., Ala. (pres. 1965-66), Colbert County (past pres.) bar assns., Ala. Bar Found. (pres.), Am. Judicature Soc., Ala. Law Sch. Alumni Assn. (pres.), Ala. Plaintiff Lawyers Assn. (pres.), V.F.W., Am. Legion, 40 and 8, Disabled Am. Vets., Third Marine Div. Assn., C. of C., Omicron Delta Kappa, Phi Delta Phi, Tau Kappa Alpha, Lambda Chi Alpha. Methodist. Clubs: Elks, The Club (Birmingham), Turtle Point Yacht and Country, Tennessee Valley Country, Tri-Cities Quarterback, Kiwanis. Home: 311 E 6th St Tuscumbra AL 35674 Office: Supreme Ct Bldg Montgomery AL 36101

HEFNER, FRANK KARL, inst. adminstr.; b. Vienna, Austria, Nov. 10, 1917; s. Frank and Leopoldina (Koziste) H.; brought to U.S., 1921, naturalized, 1936; B.A., Westminster Coll., Fulton, Mo., 1939; M.A., U. Mo., 1942; postgrad. Yale; m. Annadell Pegram, Nov. 10, 1939; children—Cynthia Lee, Paul Douglas. Instr. Fulton (Mo.) High Sch., 1939-42, Conn. Coll. Pharmacy, New Haven, 1942-44; indsl. engring. staff Winchester Repeating Arms Co., New Haven, 1942-44; budget examiner Bur. Budget, Exec. Office of the Pres., Washington, 1944-49; mgmt. analyst, budget staff sec. commerce, Washington, 1949-50; fgn. mgmt. analyst bur. European affairs Dept. State, 1950-52, exec. dir. bur. German affairs, 1952-54; dep. exec. dir. U.S. High Commn. for Germany, Bonn, 1954-55, exec. dir., 1955- 56; consul, sec. Diplomatic Service, 1955; counselor for adminstrn. Am. embassy, Bonn, Germany, 1956-57; dir. exec. staff bur. econ. affairs Dept. State, 1957-59, chief econ. devel. div., 1959-60, dep. dir. Office Internat. Financial and Devel. Affairs, 1960-61, dep. dir. Office Internat. Adminstrn., 1961-62, dir., 1962-63; dep. U.S. rep. Internat. AEC, Vienna, Austria, 1963-66; dir. mgmt. reports staff Dept. State, 1966-68; adminstr. Crowell Collier Inst., Arlington, Va., 1968—. Mem. Fgn. Service Assn., Am. Soc. Pub. Adminstrn., Am. Acad. Polit. and Social Sci. Home: Neck Rd Old Lyme CT 06371

HEFNER, HARRY SIMON, educator, painter; b. Kalamazoo, Nov. 20, 1911; s. Charles R. and Clara Belle (Heiney) H.; B.A., Western Mich. U., 1936; M.A., Columbia, 1939; m. Leona Dorothea Adolf, Sept. 1, 1946; children—Holly, Lynne. Tchr., Muskegon (Mich.) pub. schs., 1937-38, Cranbrook (Mich.) Boys Sch., summers 1937-39, Skidmore (N.Y.) Coll., 1939, U. Vt., summers 1954-56, Harvard, summer 1941; mem. faculty Western Mich. U., Kalamazoo, 1940—, prof. watercolor and design, 1956-, head art dept., 1963-66; exhbns, include Mich. Water Color Soc., 1963-65, N.Y. Water Color Soc., 1963, Detroit Inst. Arts, 1963-64, Muskegon Inst. Arts, 1965-66, Kalamazoo Inst. Arts, 1963-66, Battle Creek (Mich.) Inst. Arts, 1966, Grand Rapids (Mich.) Inst. Arts, 1964-65, South Bend (Ind.) Inst. Arts, 1964-66, Dow Meml. Library, Midland, Mich., 1964-65; represented permanent collections Kalamazoo Coll., South Bend Art Center, Albion (Mich.) Coll., Western Mich. U. Served with inf. AUS, World War II. Mem. Mich. Water Color Soc., Mich. Art Edn. Assn. Home: 1415 Sutherland St Kalamazoo MI 49007

HEFNER, HUGH MARSTON, mag. pub.; b. Chgo., Apr. 9, 1926; s. Glenn L. and Grace (Swanson) H.; B.S., U. Ill., 1949; m. Mildred M. Williams, June 25, 1949 (div.); children—Christie A., David P. Subscription promotion writer Esquire mag., 1951; promotion mgr. Pubs. Devel. Corp., 1952; circulation mgr. Children's Activities mag., 1953; pres. HMH Pub. Co. Inc., (now Playboy Enterprises, Inc.), 1953—, editor, pub. Playboy mag., 1953—; pres. Playboy Clubs

Internat., Inc., 1959—; editor, pub. VIP mag., 1963—. Served with AUS, 1944-46. Home: 1340 N State Pkwy Chicago IL 60610 Office: 919 N Michigan Av Chicago IL 60611

HEFT, ARNOLD ABRAHAM, constrn. co. exec., profl. basketball exec.; b. Balt., May 29, 1919; s. Harry and Rose (Taransky) H.; student Washington and Lee U., 1937; m. Sylvia E. Abramson, Aug. 25, 1940; children—Gwendolyn (Mrs. Carl H. Oppenheim), Harriet M. (Mrs. Martin Feldman), Barbara D. Profl. baseball player, 1938-42; with Md. Drydock & Shipbuilders, Balt., 1943; asso. with parents in retail meat bus., Wash., 1947-55; officated basketball in So. Conf., Atlantic Coast Conf., Eastern Collegiate Athletic Conf., Basketball Assn. Am., later Nat. Basketball Assn., 1946-61; asso. part-time Swesnik & Blum, Inc., Wash., 1956-61; engaged in syndicating and bldg. comml. projects, Washington, 1961—; part owner Balt. Bullets Basktball Club, 1964—. Served with USNR, 1944-46. Mem. Washington Real Estate Bd., Inst. Real Estate Mgmt. Builders and Owners Mgmt. Assn., Suburban Md. Builders Assn., Internat. Assn. Approved Basketball Ofcls. Mason. Club: Home Plate (past pres.) (Washington). Home: 11700 Old Columbia Pike Silver Spring MD 20904 Office: 2400 Queens Chapel Rd Hyattsville MD 20782

HEFT, CARROLL RAHN, lawyer; b. Iron Mountain, Mich., Oct. 1, 1900; s. Charles G. and Ella (Rahn) H.; B.A., Lawrence Coll., 1922; LL.B., U. Wis., 1923; m. Arleen Klug, Dec. 26, 1925; children—Barbara (Mrs. Edmund Warren), C. James. Admitted to Wis. bar, 1923, since in pvt. practice; partner Lawrence H. Smith, 1929-41, Heft & Coates, Racine, 1941-64; sr. partner Heft, Coates, Heft, Henzl & Bichler. Dir. Motor Specialty, Inc., First Fed. Savs. & Loan Assn., Klug & Smith Co., Empress Dilene Co., Wis. Rubber Products, Inc., others. Pres. Family Service, 1941-43. Fellow Internat. Acad. Trial and Appellate Lawyers, Am. Coll. Probate Counsel, Am. Bar Found.; mem. Internat. Acad. Ins. Counsel, Assn. Ins. Attys., Fedn. Ins. Counsel (pres., bd. govs.), Am. Bar Assn. (chmn. publs.), State Bar Wis. (chmn. ins. sect.), Racine County Bar Assn. (pres.), Wis. Law Alumni Assn. (dir.), Bencher's Soc., Scribes. Mason (33). Clubs: Cedar Lake Yacht; Racine Country (pres.); Milwaukee Athletic. Author articles and books in field. Home: 3101 Michigan Blvd Racine WI 53402 Office: 827 Main St Racine WI 53403

HEFTI, NEAL PAUL, composer, music pub.; b. Hastings, Neb., Oct. 29, 1922; s. John Henry and Norma (Conway) H.; grad. high sch.; m. Chiarina Francesca Bertocci, Nov. 3, 1945; children—Marguerita Christina, Paul Anthony. Trumpet player with Woody Herman, Harry James orchs., 1942-50; leader own orch., 1950-60; condr. Arthur Godfrey Show CBS-TV, 1954, Kate Smith Show CBS- TV, 1960, ABC Network, 1957, NBC Bandstand, 1957; operator music pub. cos., 1950—; composer scores for motion pictures, 1964—, including Sex and the Single Girl, 1964, How to Murder Your Wife, 1964, Synanon, 1965, Harlow, 1965, Boeing-Boeing, 1965, Lord Love A Duck, 1965, Batman TV Theme, 1966, Duel at Diablo, 1966, Oh Dad Poor Dad, 1966, Barefoot in the Park, 1967, P.J., 1967, The Odd Couple, 1967; musical dir. The Fred Astaire Show, NBC-TV Spl., 1968 (recipient Emmy award), The Odd Couple TV series, 1970; pres. Neal Hefti Music, Inc., Marguerita Music Corp., Encino Music Co. Mem. A.S.C.A.P., Nat. Acad. Recording Arts and Scis. (past bd. govs.), Composers and Lyricists Guild Am. Roman Catholic. Composer: Coral Reef, 1951; Lil Darlin, (' Don't Dream of Anybody But Me '), 1958; Cute, 1958; I Must Know, 1964; Lonely Girl, 1965; Girl Talk, 1965; Batman Theme, 1966; Barefoot in the Park, 1967; Fred, 1968; The Odd Couple, theme 1968; Gotham City Municipal Swing Band, 1966. Home: 15917 Valley Vista Encino CA 91316 Office: PO Box 101 Encino CA 91316

HEFTLER, GEORGE, lawyer; b. N.Y.C., Apr. 11, 1910; s. Harry and Edith (Aswal) H.; B.A., Rutgers U., 1931; J.D., Fordham U., 1934; m. Frances Haynig, Apr. 19, 1935; 1 son, Thomas E. Admitted to N.J. bar, 1935, since practiced in Union City; mem. firm Platoff, Heftler & Harker, 1952—; mem. ethics and grievance com. Hudson County, N.J., 1957-60. Dir. Lomas & Nettleton Financial Corp., Beaunit Corp., Meadowland Nat. Bank North Bergen. Chmn. Bd. Adjustment, Teaneck, N.J., 1968; chmn. Twp. Teaneck Redevel. Agy., 1969—. Bd. dirs. Jewish Hosp. and Rehab. Center N.J. Mem. Am., N.J., Hudson, Bergen County bar assns., Phi Beta Kappa. Jewish religion (temple trustee). Home: 1206 Sussex Rd West Englewood NJ 07666 Office: 400 38th St Union City NJ 07087

HEGELMANN, JULIUS, advt. exec.; b. N.Y.C., Oct. 19, 1921; s. Julius and Augusta (Schubert) H.; B.S. in Pharmacy, Rutgers U., 1943; m. Marjorie Scallon, May 30, 1943; children—Marjorie Ann (Mrs. Gerome Thompson), Jill Marie. Prodn. mgr. Ebilhuber Inc., 1939-50; v.p., sales mgr., dir. Knoll Pharm. Co., 1950-62; with Hegelmann & Bartolone Inc., N.Y.C., 1962-70, chmn. bd., 1962-70; pres. J. Hegelmann Assos., Inc., Franklin Lakes, N.J., 1970—. Pres. Orange (N.J.) C. of C., 1956. Served with AUS, 1943-46. Mem. Am. Mgmt. Assn., Am. Pharm. Assn., Pharm. Advt. Club. Rotarian (pres. Orange 1956). Home and office: 263 Arbor Rd Franklin Lakes NJ 07417

HEGG, WILLIAM G., savs. and loan assn. exec. Pres., mgr. Sacramento Savs. and Loan Assn. Office: 424 L St Sacramento CA 95804•

HEGGEN, ROBERT LEWIS, cement co. exec.; b. Estherville, Ia., June 9, 1934; s. Lewis C. and Elizabeth (Jensen) H.; B.S.C., U. Ia., 1959, J.D., 1961; m. Carol Vise, June 11, 1958; 1 dau., Linda Jean. Admitted to Ia. bar, 1961; instr. Coll. Bus. Adminstrn., U. Ia., 1960-61; trial atty. div. mergers FTC, 1961-66; gen. counsel Am. Cement Corp., 1966-70, V.p., sec., gen. counsel, 1970—. Served with USNR, 1954- 56. Mem. Am., Fed., Ia. bar assns. Home: 7029 Teesdale Av North Hollywood CA 91605 Office: 2404 Wilshire Blvd Los Angeles CA 90057

HEGGIE, ROBERT, chemist; b. Glasgow, Scotland, Jan. 19, 1909; s. Robert Heron and Agnes Russell (Lawrie) H.; S.B., Mass. Inst. Tech., 1933, Ph.D., 1936; m. Florence Sokovich, Nov. 25, 1939; children—Patricia (Mrs. M. J. Festino), Frances. Research asso. Mass. Inst. Tech., 1936-39; chemist Am. Chicle Co., Long Island City, N.Y., 1939-44, head research and devel., 1944, dir. research, 1944-56, v.p., 1956-61; exec. v.p. research Am. Chicle Co. div. Warner-Lambert Pharm. Co., 1961-65; v.p. consumer products research Warner-Lambert Research Inst., 1965-68; v.p. consumer products group Warner-Lambert Pharm. Co., Morris Plains, N.J., 1969—. Mem. Soc. Chem. Industry (hon. sec. 1946-49, hon. comptroller). Mem. Am. Chem. Soc., Am. Inst. Chemists, A.I.M., A.A.A.S., Assn. Research Dirs., Chem. Soc., N. Y. Acad. Scis., Internat. Acad. Law and Sci., Burns Soc., St. Andrews Soc., Sigma Xi. Presbyn. Clubs: Chemists, Cherry Valley, St. Botolph, M.I.T. (N.Y.C.). Home: Mt Pleasant Village Morris Plains NJ 07950 Office: 201 Tabor Rd Morris Plains NJ 07950

HEGGIE, ROBERT JAMES, steel co. exec.; b. Gary, Ind., Dec. 27, 1913; s. Robert Bruce and Persis (Hart) H.; student U. Ill., 1931-33; m. Maxine Dixon, Apr. 30, 1959; children—Frank Anderson, Robert Heggie (dec.), Karen Armstrong, Jane Major, Janet Anderson. With A.M. Castle & Co., Franklin Park, Ill., 1934—, pres., 1961—, also dir.; dir. Fansteel Inc., Oakley Steel Products Co., Amforge Inc., Mem. Am. Iron and Steel Inst., Steel Service Center Inst. (pres. 1961—, bd. dirs. 1953-70), Copper and Brass Wholesale Assn. (bd. dirs. 1965-70) Republican. Presbyn. Club: Chicago. Home: 2326 Elmwood St Wilmette IL 60091 Office: 3400 N Wolf Rd Franklin Park IL 60131

HEGMANN, EDWARD HENRY, cons.; b. Pitts., Nov. 24, 1907; s. William H. and Mary (Kemper) H.; B.S., U. Pitts., 1930; m. Mary Louise Haddock, Mar. 28, 1932; children—Nann H. (Mrs. Alfred F. Cooke III), Edward Henry II. Treas. Duquesne Light Co., Pitts., 1963-70, ret.; cons., dir. Beaver Valley Alloy Foundry Co., Monaca, Pa. Home: 112 Woodhaven Lane Pittsburgh PA 15237

HEGNER, CASPER FORMAN, architect; b. Cin., June 30, 1909; s. Casper Frank and Rose (Forman) H.; A.B., Princeton, 1930, M.F.A., 1933; B.F.A., Yale, 1932; m. Nancy Lee, June 22, 1935; children—Casper Frank 2d, Archibald Allen Lee, Christopher. Jr. engr. Bur. Reclamation, 1935-37; architect T. H. Buell & Co., Denver, 1937-41, Gieb, Laroche, Dahl and Chappell, Texarkana, Ark., 1941-42; partner Smith & Hegner, Denver, 1946-62; mgr. operations Office Constrn., VA, 1962-65, tech. asst., 1966-68, dir. archtl. service, 1969—; commr. Pub. Bldgs. Service, Gen. Services Adminstrn., 1965-66. Mem. Colo. Bd. Examiners Architects, 1957- 61; mem. Denver Bd. Adjustment Zoning, 1953-57; mem. Nat. Capitol Planning Commn., 1965-66; prin. works include United Fund bldg., Thomas Jefferson High Sch., Ross Br. Library, Westridge Homes (all Denver); also residential bldgs. at Clayton Coll., Denver and Bradley, Gilpin and Univ. Park schs. (all Denver). Pres. Met. Council for Community Service, Denver, 1958-60; chmn. Fed. Fire Council, 1965-66. Mem. adv. bd. Sch. Architecture, U. Colo., 1950-59; trustee Mile High United Fund, Denver, 1959-62; mem. gov. bd. Nat. Sch. Facilities Council, 1957- 59. Served with USMCR, World War II and Korea. Mem. A.I.A. (pres. Colo. 1961), Am., Internat. hosp. assns. Clubs: Denver Country, Mile High (Denver); Princeton (Washington). Home: 5315 Blackistone Rd Washington DC 20016 Office: Office Constrn Vets Adminstrn Washington DC 20420

HEGNER, HERMAN H., educator; b. Chgo., Sept. 12, 1902; s. Herman Frederick and Bertha (Hofer) H.; student U. of Ill., 1920-22, U. of Chicago, 1922-1923, 1928- 35; Ph.B., U. Wis., 1925; m. Irma Rowe, Sept. 12, 1925; children—Herman H., Jr., James Rowe, Michael Stanton. Tchr., Pestalozzi Froebel Tchrs. Coll., Chgo., 1925-36, pres. and trustee, 1936-66, formerly chmn. bd. trustees. Mem. Kappa Sigma. Club: University (Chgo.).

HEGSTED, DAVID MARK, biochemist; b. Rexburg, Ida., Mar. 25, 1914; s. John and Edna Margaret (Porter) H.; B.S., U. Ida., 1936; M.S., U. Wis., 1938, Ph.D., 1940; A.M. (hon.), Harvard, 1962; m. Maxine Scow, May 26, 1941; children—Christina, Eric John. Research asst. U. Wis., 1936-41; research chemist Abbott Labs., 1941-42; asso. nutrition Harvard Schs. of Medicine and Pub. Health, 1942-43, asst. prof., 1943-48, asso. prof., 1948-62, prof., 1962—. Cons. nutrition to Colombian Govt., 1946; nutritionist Inst. Inter-Am. Affairs, Peru, 1950- 51; adviser to nutrition program of Peru, 1951-57; U.S. rep. Conf. Nutrition Problems of Latin Am., UN FAO, Caracas, 1954, Guatemala, 1958; cons. UN FAO, Chile, 1956, Rome, 1961, 69; cons. WHO, 1962, 70, NIH, 1958—; mem. food and nutrition bd. NRC, 1955, chmn. food and nutrition bd., 1968—. Mem. Am. Inst. of Nutrition (Osborne Mendel award 1965), Am. Chem. Soc., Am. Pub. Health Assn., N.Y. Acad. Scis., Peruvian Pub. Health Soc., A.M.A. (council foods and nutrition 1960-68), Sigma Xi, Alpha Chi Sigma, Sigma Alpha Epsilon. Club: Cosmos. Editor: Nutrition Revs., 1968—. Contbr. articles, chpts. profl. jours. and books. Home: 58 Boulder Rd Wellesley Hills MA 02181

HEGYI, JULIUS, condr., musician; b. N.Y.C., Feb. 2, 1923; s. Francois and Rose (Konye) H.; B.A., Juilliard Sch. Music, 1943; pupil violin Sascha Jacobsen, Jacques Gordon, Eddy Brown; pupil composition Vittoria Giannini; pupil conducting Dimitri Mitropoulos; m. Charlotte Ann Barrier, Aug. 27, 1953; 1 dau., Lisa. Condr. Wagner Coll. Symphony, 1941-43; asso. condr. San Antonio Symphony, 1948-51; condr. San Antonio Little Orch., 1949-51, Abilene (Tex.) Symphony, 1952-55, Southwestern Symphony Center, 1951-56, Chattanooga Symphony, 1955-65; founder-dir. Sewanee Summer Music Center, 1958; founder-condr. Carlatti Orch., 1964; debut violinist Town Hall, N.Y., 1945; chamber music concerts, solo recitals U.S., Mexico; founder Hegyi and Amati string quartets, 1941, Music in the Round series, 1951; mem. Gordon, Am. string quartets, N.Y. Philharmonic, City Center Ballet, RCA Victor Symphony, N.Y. Little Orch. Soc.; performer complete Beethoven String Quartet cycle Bershire Quartet, 1970; with music faculty Williams Coll., 1965—, lectr. music, condr. and violinist in residence, 1971—; mem. Williams Trio, dir. chamber music activities; music dir., condr. Albany (N.Y.) Symphony, 1966—, Berkshire Symphony, 1966—. Recipient Frank Damrosch Scholarship, 1941, Alice Ditson award service, 1957, nat. condr. recognition award Am. Symphony League, 1959. Home: Northwest Hill Rd Williamstown MA 01267

HEHEMANN, ROBERT FREDERICK, educator; b. Cin., Feb. 10, 1921; s. Fred H. and Edna (Timberman) H.; B.S. in Engring., U. Mich., 1943; M.S., Case Inst. Tech., 1949, Ph.D., 1953; m. Ruth Louise Graham, Sept. 8, 1945; children—David G., Elizabeth A. Mem. faculty Case Western Res. U., 1946—, prof. metall. engring., 1959—, acting head dept. of metallurgy, 1967-69; research asso. Argonne Nat. Lab., summer 1965. Served to capt. AUS, 1943-46. Mem. Am. Soc. Metals (Bradley Stoughton award 1958), Am. Inst. M.E., Am. Nuclear Soc., Sigma Xi, Tau Beta Pi, Iota Alpha, Phi Eta Sigma, Sigma Alpha Epsilon, Scabbard and Blade. Contbr. profl. jours. Home: 20100 Green Oak Dr Euclid OH 44117 Office: Case Western Res U Univ Circle Cleveland OH 44106

HEHMEYER, ALEXANDER, corp. exec., lawyer; b. N.Y.C., Oct. 20, 1910; s. Frederick William and Catherine Enole (Schrader) H.; grad. Montclair (N.J.) Acad., 1928; B.S., Yale, 1932; LL.B., Columbia, 1935; m. Florence Isobel Millar, Oct. 10, 1936 (dec. 1967); children—Alexander Millar, Christine McKesson; m. 2d, Sheila Mary Vought, 1968. Admitted to N.Y. bar, 1936, Ill. bar, 1968; with firm Cravath, Swaine & Moore, N.Y.C., 1935-40, 44-46; partner Paul, Weiss, Rifkind, Wharton & Garrison, N.Y.C., 1946-67; asst. to chmn. Time, Inc., 1940-43; exec. v.p., gen. counsel, dir., mem. exec. com. Field Enterprises, Inc.; v.p., dir. Field Creations, Inc.; dir., mem. exec. com. Field Communications Corp., Field Enterprises Ednl. Corp.; dir. Field Ednl. Publs., Inc., A.J. Nystrom Co., FSC Paper Corp., Manistique Pulp & Paper Co., Met. Printing Co., World Book Ednl. Ins. Co., Field Enterprises Charitable Corp.; mem. mgmt. bd. Pubs.-Hall Syndicate, N.Y.C. Legal, econ. cons. Fgn. Econ. Adminstrn., 1943-44; cons. U.S. Econ. Missions, West Berlin, 1952, Gold Coast, 1954. Trustee Kent (Conn.) Sch., Chgo. Sun-Times/Daily News Charity Trust. Mem. Fed., Am., Chgo. bar assns., Bar Assn. City N.Y., Chgo. Council Fgn. Relations (dir.). Republican. Episcopalian. Clubs: Yale, University (N.Y.C.); Chicago, Racquet, Saddle and Cycle, Tavern (Chgo.). Author: Time for Change, 1943. Home: 179 E Lake Shore Dr Chicago Il 60611 also 57 Owenoke Park Westport CT 06880 Office: 401 N Wabash Av Chicago IL 60611

HEIDEGGER, MARTIN, philosopher; b. 1889. Prof. philosophy, Marburg U., 1923-28; prof. Freiburg i. Br. U., 1928, rector, 1933, emeritus, 1951—. Author numerous publs., among latest being: Holzwege, 1950; Der Feldweg, 1953; Was heisst Denken, 1954; Was ist Philosophie, 1956; Zur Seinsfrage, 1956; Der Sata vom Grund, 1957; J.P. Hebel, 1957; Umterwegs zur Sprache, 1959; Nietzsche, 1961; Die Frage nach dem Ding, 1962; Kants These über das Sein, 1963: Die Technik und die Kehre, 1963; What is Philosophy, 1964; What is a Thing, 1966; Discourse on Thinking, 1966. Address: Rotebuckweg 47 Freiburg i Br German Federal Republic *

HEIDELBERGER, CHARLES, educator; b. N.Y.C., Dec. 23, 1920; s. Michael and Nina (Tachau) H.; S.B., Harvard, 1942, M.S., 1944, Ph.D., 1946; m. Judith Werble, Dec. 22, 1943; children—Nina, Philip, Lisa. Instr. chemistry Harvard, 1946; research chemist Radiation Lab., U. Cal. at Berkeley, 1946-84; mem. faculty U. Wis., 1948—, prof., 1958—, Am. Cancer Soc. prof. oncology, 1960—; cons. Nat. Cancer Inst., 1958—. Recipient Teplitz award cancer research Langer Meml. Fund, 1958; award of merit Am. Cancer Soc., 1965; Lucy Wortham James award James Ewing Soc., 1969; G.H.A. Clowes award, Am. Assn. Cancer Research, 1970. Mem. Am. Chem. Soc., Am. Soc. Biol. Chemists, Am. Assn. Cancer Research (bd. dirs. 1960-62, 66-68), British Biochem. Soc. Synthesired, devel. tumor inhibitory drug 5-fluorouracil, 1956; pioneered studies chem. carcinogenesis in tissue culture. Home: 118 Vaughn Ct Madison WI 53705

HEIDELBERGER, MICHAEL, chemist; b. N.Y.C., Apr. 29, 1888; s. David and Fannie (Campe) H.; student Ethical Culture Schs., New York, 1900-05; B.S., Columbia U., 1908, A.M., 1910, PhD., 1911; student Federal Poly. Inst., Zurich, Switzerland, 1911-12; Dr. (hon.) Faculty of Medicine, U. Bordeaux, 1947, U. Oslo, 1956; Dr. Faculty Pharmacy, U. Paris, 1949; Faculty Philosophy, U. Upsala, Sweden, 1950; Faculty Pharmacy, U. Strasbourg, 1952; Dr. (hon.). Faculty of Scis., U. Aix-Marseille, 1959; Dr. (hon.), Faculty of Pharmacy, U. Nancy, 1960; D.Sc., Rutgers U., 1961, N.Y. Med. Coll., 1968, Thomas Jefferson U., Phila., 1970; m. Nina Tachau, June 29, 1916 (dec. July 1946); 1 son, Charles; m. 2d, Charlotte Rosen, June 23, 1956. Asst. in qualitative analysis, supplementary term, Stevens Inst., Hoboken, N. J., 1909; fellow to asso. mem. Rockefeller Inst. Med. Research, 1912-27; chemist Mt. Sinai Hosp., N.Y., 1927-28; successively chemist to Med. Service and chemist to Presbyn. Hosp., N.Y.C., 1928- 55; asso. prof. medicine, Coll. Physicians and Surgeons, Columbia U., 1928-29, asso. prof. biochemistry, 1929-45, prof. biochemistry, 1945-48, prof. immunochemistry, 1948-56, prof. emeritus, 1956—; vis. prof. immunochemistry Inst. of Microbiology Rutgers U., 1955-64; adj. prof. pathology N.Y.U. Sch. Medicine, 1964—; cons. to Sec. War, 1941-46; cons. WHO, 1965—. Served as 1st lt., San. Corps, AUS, 1918-19. Awarded A. Cressy Morrison prize (with F. E. Kendall), N.Y. Acad. Scis., 1929; Ehrlich silver medal, 1933; Albert Lasker award, 1953; share in reward for cure of African sleeping sickness, Belgian Govt.; officer Order Leopold II, 1953; John Simon Guggenheim Meml. fellow, 1934, 36; Behring prize, 1954; Pasteur medal Swedish Medical Soc., 1960; T. Duckett Jones Meml. award Whitney Found., 1964; Nat. Medal Sci., 1967; medal N.Y. Acad. Med., 1968; von Pirquet medal, 1971. Chmn. research council N.Y.C. Pub. Health Research Inst., 1952-56; mem. biochem. panel Am. Inst. Biol. Scis. for Office Naval Research, 1950-52. Fellow Am. Acad Microbiology; member Nat. Acad. Scis., Am. Chem. Soc., A.A.A.S., Soc. Am. Biochemists, Soc. Am. Bacteriologists, Am. Assn. Immunologists (pres. 1946, 49), Harvey Soc. (pres. 1952-53), Royal Danish Acad. Sci. (corr.), Microbiol. Soc. France (hon.), Soc. de Biologie, British Soc. Immunologists, Accademia dei Lincei (fgn. mem.), Am. Philos. Soc., Mexican Soc. Allergy and Immunology, Sigma Xi. U.S. del. 50th Anniversary of death of Pasteur, Paris and Caen (France), 1946. Author textbook and collection of lectures. Home: 333 Central Park W New York City NY 10025 ☆

HEIDELBERGER, RICHARD JOHN, architect; b. N.Y.C., Oct. 5, 1907; s. Walter Charles and Wilhelmina (Burck) H.; student Cornell U. Coll. Architecture, 1928-32, Columbia Coll. Architecture, 1932-34; m. Lillian Alice Knorr, Aug. 7, 1937; children—Richard Christopher, Jonathan. Govt. facilities mgr. Republic Aviation Corp., 1941-46; mem. firm Jagow & Heidelberger, architects, 1946- 60; propr. Richard J. Heidelberger & Assos., architects, Hempstead, N.Y., 1961—. Mem. N.Y. State Bd. Examiners Architects, 1954-64, chmn., 1964-65. mem. Nat. Council Archtl. Registration N.Y., 1958—. Fellow A.I.A. (pres. L.I. chpt. Bds., 1954—; architect-mem. Nassau County Civil Def. Orgn., 1953—, Archtl. Rev. Bd., Bellport, 1948-50; award of merit 1940); mem. N.Y. State Assn. Architects (bd. dirs. 1948-50), Sigma Phi. Clubs: Cornell (Nassau County, N.Y.); Bellport Bay Yacht (trustee); Cherry Valley (Garden City). Home: 90 4th St Garden City NY 11530 Office: 658 Fulton Av Hempstead NY 11550

HEIDEMAN, GEORGE JOHN, tool co. exec.; b. Union, Ill., Apr. 9, 1912; s. George E. and Mathilda (Schmidt) H.; B.S., U. Ill., 1934; postgrad. Yale, 1934-36; m. Sarah Elizabeth Blake, May 20, 1944. Instr. accounting Yale, New Haven, Conn., 1934-36; pub. accountant firm Arthur Andersen & Co., N.Y.C., Detroit, Cleve., 1936-55, mgr. adminstrv. services, 1951-55; treas. Kennametal Inc., Latrobe, Pa., 1955—, v.p. finance, 1968—; dir. treas. Kennametal Co. Ohio, Kennametal Internat., S.A., Kenroc Tools Ltd., Kenroc Western Ltd.; treas. Kennametal Holdings Ltd. (Can.); dir. Kennametal Holdings Ltd. (Eng.). Served with AUS, 1941-42, to comdr. USNR, 1942-46. C.P.A., N.Y., Ohio. Mem. Am. Inst. C.P.A.'s, Am. Accounting Assn., Beta Gamma Sigma, Alpha Kappa Lambda. Republican. Mem. Evangelical and Reformed Ch. Clubs: Ligonier Country; Latrobe Country. Home: 2 Franklin Rd Ligonier PA 15658 Office: 1 Lloyd Av Latrobe PA 15650

HEIDENHEIM, ROGER STEWART, mfg. co. exec.; b. Phila., Oct. 5, 1909; s. Samuel and Rose (Sadler) H.; ed. pub. schools of Pa. and Cal.; 1 son, Taylor. Mem. staff sales dept. McQuay Norris Mfg. Co., St. Louis, 1929-42, dist. sales mgr., 1946-54, nat. sales mgr., 1954-59, exec. v.p., 1960-68, pres., 1968—, also dir.; pres. Am. Automotive Products Co., Advt. Distributors, Inc.; v.p., dir. Dura Bond Bearing Co., Palo Alto, Cal.; dir. McQuay Norris Mfg. Co., Toronto, Can. Bd. dirs. Nat. Standard Parts Assn., Chgo., 1957-58, Automotive Service Industry Assn., 1961-64; chmn. Automotive Engine Rebuilders Assn. Affiliate Council, 1964-66; pres. Piston and Pin Mfg. Group, 1965-66; pres. Piston Ring Mfg. Group, 1967-68. Served as maj. AUS, 1942-46. Mem. Nat. Sales Execs. Club. Club: Algonquin Country (Webster Groves, Mo.). Home: 9 Old Westbury Lane Webster Groves MO 63119 Office: 2320 Marconi Av St Louis MO 63110

HEIDER, FREDRICK, TV producer, writer; b. Milw., Apr. 9, 1917; s. Fred and Ida (Ristow) H.; student Notre Dame U., 1932-33; B.D.A., Goodman Theatre of Art Inst. Chgo., 1936. Producer TV prodns. Miss Am. Pageant, 1954-56, Voice of Firestone, 1955-59, 63-64, Life Is Worth Living, 1956-57, Music for A Summer Night, 1960-61, Bell Telephone Hour, 1961-63; writer-producer TV Show, 1953, Martha Wright Show, 1954, others; TV writer Warner Bros.; pres. Peter Pretzel prodns. Recipient Christopher award, 1956, 59, 60, Peabody award, 1959, Best Music Show award Radio and TV Critics Am., 1964. Mem. A.S.C.A.P. Office: 9507 Santa Monica Blvd Beverly Hills CA 90210

HEIDRICH, ROBERT WESLEY, metal products co. exec.; b. Chgo., Aug. 1, 1927; s. Carl G. and Harriette B. (Butzlaff) H.; student U. Wis., 1944-45, 47-48; J.D., DePaul U., 1951; m. Lennice L. Hubenbecker, June 19, 1948; children—John G., Robert G., Kimberly L. Admitted to Ill. bar, 1951; atty. Brunswick Corp., 1953-60, 65-69; v.p. Brunswick AG (Switzerland), 1960-61; dir. Brunswick Internat. Finance AG (Switzerland), 1962-65; sec., corp. counsel Nat. Can Corp., Chgo., 1969—. Founding pres. Frederick Law Olmsted Soc., 1967-69; bd. dirs. Am. Internat. Sch. of Zurich, Switzerland, 1964-65. Served with CAC, AUS, 1945-47. Mem. Am. Soc. Corporate Secs. (chmn. Jr. Achievement com. 1970—), Ill., Chgo. bar assns. Home: 165 Longcommon Rd Riverside IL 60546 Office: 5959 S Cicero Av Chicago IL 60638

HEIDT, LAWRENCE JOSEPH, phys. chemist; b. Portage, Wis., Apr. 5, 1904; s. Frank and Barbara Cecilia (Ehr) H.; A.B., U. Wis., 1927, M.S., 1928, duPont fellow, 1929- 30, Ph.D., 1930; m. Agnes Grace Kiley, June 26, 1933; children—Marianne, David, Barbara. Teaching fellow U. Wis., 1927-29; research asso. photochemistry, Harvard, 1930-35; instr. Mass. Inst. Tech., 1935-40, mem. faculty with professorial rank, 1940—; Distinguished Univ. prof. Emmanuel Coll., 1969—; vis. prof. Islamabad U., Pakistan with Ford Found. support, 1970; cons. several orgns.; Guggenheim fellow study in Japan, Australia, 1962-63. Mem. several spl. phys. and inorganic chem. coms. Recipient Guggenheim fellow, 1962- 63. Fellow Am. Acad. Arts and Sci., A.A.A.S.; mem. Am. Chem. Soc. (chmn. northeastern sect. 1964-65, councillor nat. soc. 1963- -), N.Y. Acad. Arts and Scis., Am. Assn. U. Profs., Sigma Xi, Phi Lambda Upsilon, Alpha Chi Sigma, Gamma Alpha. Roman Catholic. Co- editor: Photochemistry of Liquid and Solid States, 1960; hon. editor Jour. Photochem. and Photobiology, 1961—. Contbr. profl. publs. Patentee sugar solutions intravenous feeding, voltage stabilized polyolefin dielectrics and thermally stabilized ozone. Home: 46 Bailey Rd Arlington MA 02174 Office: 77 Massachusetts Av Cambridge MA also 400 The Fenway Boston MA 02115

HEIFETZ, BENAR, cellist; b. Moghilew, Russia, Dec. 11, 1899; s. Efim Heifetz; studied with pvt. tchrs.; student Conservatory of Music, Leningrad; m. Olga Band, July 7, 1937; 1 dau., Susanne Florence. First concert, Petersburg, Leningrad, 1915; other concerts Russia, Poland, Germany, Austria, France, Holland, Belgium, Egypt, N.A.M., S.A.M., Honolulu, T.H. and P.R.: mem. Kolisch String Quartet, 1927-39; solo cellist Phila. Orch., 1939-43; cellist NBC Symphony, also mem. Albeneri Trio, 1944—; internat. concert tours, 1957-58; nomination vis. prof. cello and chamber music U. Ind., 1957-58. Address: 30 Deepdale Dr Great Neck NY 11021

HEIFETZ, JASCHA, violinist; b. Vilna, Russia, Feb. 2, 1901 (Jan. 20, Russian calendar); began learning violin at age of 3; entered Royal Sch. of Music, Vilna, at 5, grad. at 9; was taken immediately to St. Petersburg and became pupil of Prof. Leopold Auer; Mus.D. (hon.), Northwestern U., 1949; m. Florence Vidor, movie star, Aug. 20, 1928; children—Josepha, Robert; m. 2d, Frances Spiegelberg, Jan. 1947 (div.); 1 son, Joseph. Made first pub. appearance at 5 years; played Mendelssohn Concerto at 7, first recital in St. Petersburg at 9, and engaged for solo with Symphony Orch., Pavlovsk, playing before audience of 5,000; later appeared in leading cities of the world; New York debut, Carnegie Hall, Oct. 27, 1917. Donor of concert hall at Tel- Aviv, Palestine, 1926. Decorated comdr. Legion of Honor (France), 1957. Home: 1520 Gilcrest Dr Beverly Hills CA 90210

HEIGES, DONALD RUSSEL, clergyman, educator; b. Biglerville, Pa., June 25, 1910; s. Edmund Dale and Elsie (Slaybaugh) H.; B.A., Gettysburg Coll., 1931, D.D., 1955; B.D., Luth. Theol. Sem., Gettysburg, 1934; M.A., Union Theol. Sem. and Columbia, 1941; D.D., Concordia Coll., Moorhead, Minn., 1954; m. Mary Susannah Kump, June 1, 1935; children—Carol Sue (Mrs. Kenneth Reinhardt), Joan Christiana (Mrs. David Blythe). Ordained to ministry Luth. Ch., 1935; mem. faculty, chaplain Gettysburg Coll., 1934-44; Luth. pastor to students, counselor Columbia, 1944-50; exec. sec. div. coll. and univ. work Nat. Luth. Council, 1950-58; dean Chgo. Luth. Theol. Sem., 1958-62; pres. Luth. Theol. Sem. at Gettysburg, 1962—, Luth. Theol. Sem. at Phila., 1964-70. Bd. dirs. Nat. Luth. Campus Ministry; mem. directing com., div. ednl. services Luth. Council U.S. Mem. Phi Beta Kappa, Eta Sigma Phi, Phi Sigma Kappa. Republican. Author: The Christian's Calling, 1958. Address: Seminary Ridge Gettysburg PA 17325

HEIGES, JESSE GIBSON, lawyer; b. nr. Shippensburg, Pa., Sept. 19, 1914; s. Jesse Shearer and Susan (Fickes) H.; A.B., Ursinus Coll., 1935; LL.B., U. Pa., 1938; m. Virginia M. Rodgers, Apr. 20, 1957. Admitted to N.Y. bar, 1939; atty. Mudge, Stern, Williams & Tucker, N.Y.C., 1939-43, 46-50; atty. Pfizer Inc. (formerly Charles Pfizer & Co., Inc.), 1950-56, sec., 1956-69, gen. counsel, 1956—, v.p., 1967—, dir., 1960—; dir. U.S. Life Corp., U.S. Life Ins. Co. Served as lt. USNR, 1943-46. Mem. Am., N.Y. bar assns., Assn. Bar City N.Y., Pa. Soc. N.Y. Clubs: River of New York; University (N.Y.C.); West Side Tennis of Forest Hills (gov. 1955-62); Maidstone (East Hampton). Home: 440 E 56th St New York City NY 10022 Office: 235 E 42d St New York City NY 10017

HEIGES, RALPH EBY, ednl. adviser; b. Shippensburg, Pa., Apr. 20, 1905; s. Jesse S. and Susan (Fickes) H.; A.B., Ursinus College, 1925, LL.D., 1960; A.M., Columbia 1928, Ph.D., 1933; m. Ruth Bretz, May 1930; 1 son, Richard. Tchr., prin. Royersford (Pa.) High Sch., 1925-27; instr. govt. Findlay Coll., 1929-34; instr. social studies Clarion (Pa.) State Tchrs. Coll., 1934-36; asso. prof. social studies Ind. (Pa.) State Tchrs. Coll., 1936-39, head div. secondary edn., 1939-42, dean, 1942-55; dean instrn. Shippensburg State Coll., 1955-56, pres., 1956-70; ednl. adviser Charles Morris Price Sch., 1970—. Dir. First Nat. Bank, Shippensburg. Treas. Tressler Luth. Home. Mem. Am. Polit. Sci. Assn., Pa. Edn. Assn. (past pres. dept. higher edn.), Phi Delta Kappa, Kappa Delta Pi, Phi Sigma Pi. Lutheran. Mason (33, Shriner; past master), Rotarian. Home: 624 Glen St Shippensburg PA 17257

HEIGES, RICHARD FICKES, educator; b. Findlay, O., Jan. 22, 1931; s. Ralph Eby and Ruth (Bretz) H.; student Swarthmore Coll., 1949-50; B.S., Indiana (Pa.) U., 1953; M.A., Ohio State U., 1955, Ph.D., 1959; m. Betty Ann Kummer, June 12, 1955; children—Susan, Nancy, Linda, Richard. Faculty polit. sci. dept. Ohio State U., 1956, 58-60; tchr. South High Sch., Columbus, O., 1956-58; research asso. Ohio Legislative Service Commn., 1960-61; prof. Indiana U., 1961—, chmn. polit. sci. dept., 1966—. Served with U.S. Army, 1953-55. Presbyn. (elder). Kiwanian. Home: 660 Diamond Av Indiana PA 15701

HEIGHT, DOROTHY, pres. Nat. Council Negro Women. Address: 1346 Connecticut Av Washington DC*

HEIKENEN, HARRY WILBUR, fgn. service officer; b. Kettle River, Minn., July 19, 1918; s. Charles and Anna (Sippa) H.; B.B.A., U. Minn., 1946. Expediter aircraft firm; sales rep. Johnson & Johnson, 1946-50; joined U.S. Fgn. Service, 1950; vice consul, polit. officer, Munich, Germany, 1950-52; econ. officer, Singapore, 1953-55; consul, 2d sec. Am. embassy, Helsinki, 1955-58; internat. economist Bur. Econ. Affairs, Dept. State, Washington, 1958- 60, asst. coordinator comml. activities, 1960-63; consul, dep. dir. U.S. Trade Center, Milan, Italy, 1964-68; 1st sec. Am. embassy, dir. U.S. Trade Center, London, Eng.; now economist comml. office, Rome, Italy. Served to 1st lt. USAAF, 1942-45; capt. Res. Decorated D.F.C., Air medal; recipient award Silver Spur Hon. Soc., U. Minn. Mem. Fgn. Service Assn., Delta Upsilon. Address: care Dept State Washington DC 20525

HEIKOFF, JOSEPH MEYER, educator; b. Bklyn., Nov. 18, 1917; s. Reuben and Rose (Dubin) H.; B.S., City Coll. N.Y., 1938; B.Landscape Arch., Harvard, 1943, M.P.A., 1957; M.A., U. Chgo., 1953, Ph.D., 1959; m. Helen Ethel Gilman, May 9, 1948; children—Sara Elizabeth, Barbara Michelle. Vis. prof. U. P.R., 1949-51; chief planning dept. P.R. Indsl. Devel. Co., San Juan, 1953-55; city planner U.S. Urban Renewal Adminstrn., San Juan, P.R., 1955-56; exec. dir. City Planning Commn., Syracuse, N.Y., 1957-59; prof. urban planning, dir. bur. community planning U. Ill. at Urbana, 1959-69; prof. pub. adminstrn. Grad. Sch. Pub. Affairs, State U. N.Y. at Albany, 1969—. Served with USAAF, 1942-46. Univ. fellow U. Chgo., 1952-53; Littauer fellow Harvard, 1956-57; Fulbright research fellow, Madrid, Spain, 1965-66. Mem. A.A.A.S., Am. Soc. Pub. Adminstrn., Am. Soc. Planning Ofcls. Contbr. profl. jours. and proc. Home: 1 Coronet Ct Schenectady NY 12309

HEIL, JOSEPH FRANK, mfr.; b. Milw., July 3, 1902; s. Julius Peter and Eliza (Conrad) H.; student Northwestern U.; m. Marjorie Nichols, May 31, 1924; children—Joseph F., Barbara Ann (Mrs. James G. Howard). With Heil Co., Milw., 1923—, pres., 1946-69, chmn., 1969—, also dir.; pres. Arnold Dryer Co.; dir. First Wis. Nat. Bank, Employers Mut., First Wis. Bankshares, First Wis. Trust, Sandusky Foundry & Machine Co. Trustee Carroll Coll. Home: 602 E Lake Terrace Milwaukee WI 53217 Office: 3000 Montana St Milwaukee WI 53215

HEILBRON, LOUIS HENRY, lawyer; b. Newark, May 12, 1907; s. Simon L. and Flora (Karp) H.; A.B., U. Cal. at Berkeley, 1928, LL.B., 1931, LL.D., 1961; LL.D., Golden Gate Coll., 1970; m. Delphine Rosenblatt, Oct. 30, 1929; children—John L., David M. Admitted to Cal. bar, 1931; with firm Heller, Ehrman, White & McAuliffe, 1934—, mem., 1948—; prin. atty. Bd. Econ. Warfare, 1942-43; asst. to dean of men U. Cal. at Berkeley, 1928-31; sec. Cal. Dept. Social Welfare, 1932; asst. relief adminstr. Cal., 1933; spl. cons. Cal. Relief Adminstrn., also Cal. Dept. Social Welfare, 1934-41. Mem. Cal. Bd. Edn., 1959-61, pres., 1960-61; mem. Cal. Coordinating Council Higher Edn., 1961-69; chmn. trustees Cal. State Colls., 1960-63, chmn. ednl. policy com. and faculty staff, 1963-69. Pres. San Francisco Jewish Community Center, 1949-52, San Francisco Pub. Edn. Soc., 1950-52. Trustee, exec. com. World Affairs Council No. Cal., 1951—, pres., 1965-67; v.p. Station KQED, 1966—; trustee Golden Gate Coll., 1969—, Newhouse Found., 1956—, U. Cal. Internat. House, 1953-60, 61—; mem. San Francisco Human Rights Commn., 1969—. Chmn. adv. San Francisco State Coll., 1970—. Served to maj. AUS, 1944-46; ETO. Decorated Bronze Star. Mem. Am. Bar Assn., Internat. Law Com., Phi Beta Kappa, Zeta Beta Tau. Jewish religion (pres. congregation 1954-57). Home: 2601 Lyon St San Francisco CA 94123 Office: 44 Montgomery St San Francisco CA 94104

HEILBRONER, ROBERT L., economist, author; B.A., Harvard; Ph.D., New Sch. Social Research; LL.D., LaSalle Coll. Lectr. Nat. War Coll., Coll. Air, also univ., bus. and labor groups. Chmn. bd. Town Sch., N.Y.C. Mem. Am. Econ. Assn. Club: Century Association (N.Y.C.). Author: Future as History, 1960; Great Ascent, 1963; Limits of American Capitalism, 1966; Between Capitalism and Socialism, 1970; The Making of Economic Society, 1962; The Economic Problem, rev. edit., 1971; The Worldly Philosophers, rev. edit., 1967; (with Peter L. Bernstein) A Primer of Government Spending; Between Capitalism and Socialism, 1970; also many articles and brochures in field. Address: care New Sch Social Research 66 W 12th St New York City NY 10011

HEILBRONNER, WALTER LEO, educator; b. Memmingen, Germany, May 10, 1924; s. Alfred M. and Helen (Liebschuetz) H.; came to U.S., 1940, naturalized, 1944; student Georgetown U., 1943-44; A.B., U. Mich., 1949, M.A., 1950, Ph.D., 1955, postgrad. (univ. fellow), Center for Study of Higher Edn., 1965-66; m. Florence Carolyn King, June 11, 1948; children—David Mark, Judith Ann. Instr. German, W.Va. U., 1953-56; asst. prof., U. Va., 1956-62, asso. prof., 1962-66, asst. dean arts, scis., dir. Echols scholars program, 1962-65; v.p. for acad. affairs, prof. German, State U. of N.Y. at Cortland, 1966-70, Montclair (N.J.) State Coll. 1970—. Cons. to commn. on pub. edn. Va. Gen. Assembly, 1959-60. Served with AUS, 1943-46, 50-52. Mem. Am. Assn. Higher Edn., Modern Lang. Assn., Am. Acad. Polit., Social Sci., Am. Assn. U. Profs., Am. Ednl. Research Assn., S. Atlantic Modern Lang. Assn. Mem. B'nai B'rith. Author: Printing and the Book in 15th Century England, 1967. Contbr. articles, revs. profl. jours. Home: 8 Skytop Terrace Upper Montclair NJ 07043

HEILIG, ALOIS B., corp. ofcl.; b. Mt. Joy, Pa., Aug. 20, 1908; s. William R. and Pauline A. (Bube) H.; B.S. cum laude, Franklin and Marshall Coll., 1931; m. Marguerite A. Wright, June 10, 1933; children—William W., Robert W. Accountant Lybrand, Ross Bros. & Montgomery, 1934-41; asst. to comptroller Campbell Soup Co., 1941-43, asst. comptroller, 1943, asst. treas., 1943-45, treas., 1945—; dir. Phila. Mfrs. Mut. Ins. Co. C.P.A., Pa. Mem. Delta Sigma Phi. Club: Rolling Green Golf. Mem. Delta Sigma Home: 10 Brookside Rd Wallingford PA 19086 Office Campbell Pl Camden NJ 08101

HEILING, FRANK JOSEPH, r.r. exec.; b. Robstown, Tex., Mar. 28, 1914; s. Martin and Anna (Heisenberger) H.; student Johnson Bible Coll., Kimberlin Heights, Tenn.; m. Margaret M. Magruder, Jan. 17, 1936. Spl. investigator Texas City disaster, 1947; with Texas City Terminal Ry. Co., 1947—, pres., gen. mgr., 1954-56, now dir.; v.p. indsl. development M.-K-T. R.R., 1956- 59, v.p. sales and service, 1959—, also supr. pub. relations and advt., 1971—; officer and/or dir. various affiliated railroads; dir. Texas City Terminal Ry. Co., Galveston, Houston & Henderson R.R. Co. Security rep., orgn. UN, San Francisco, 1945. Mem. Nat. Def. Transp. Assn., Nat. Freight Traffic Assn., Transp. Assn. Am., Am. Soc. Traffic and Transp., Asso. Traffic Clubs Am., Newcomen Soc. N.Am., Transp. Club Petroleum Industry. Clubs: St. Louis Traffic; Traffic, Press, Advertising City (Dallas); San Antonio Transp. Home: 4015 Santa Barbara Dr Dallas TX 75214 Office: 701 Commerce St Dallas TX 75202

HEILMAN, HORACE RICHARD, ins. co. exec.; b. Phila., Oct. 26, 1905; s. Eugene Augustus and Martha (Blair) H.; A.B., Haverford Coll., 1925; m. Eleanor Ford Jones, Sept. 6, 1944; children—Barbara La Fontaine, Richard. With Ins. Co. N.Am., Phila., 1925—, v.p., 1955-63, sr. v.p., 1963-66, pres., 1966- 68, vice chmn. bd., 1968-70, now dir.; dir. INA Corp., Life Ins. Co. N.Am., S. Jersey Industries. Vice pres. Com. of Seventy, Phila., 1958. Bd. mgrs. Haverford Coll., 1963; trustee Friends Central Sch., Phila. Republican. Presbyn. Clubs: Merion Cricket (Haverford, Pa.); Merion Golf (Ardmore, Pa.); Union League (Phila.). Home: 1534 Mount Pleasant Rd Villanova PA 19103

HEILMAN, ROBERT BECHTOLD, educator; b. Phila., July 18, 1906; s. Rev. Edgar James and Mary Alice (Bechtold) H.; A.B., Lafayette Coll., 1927; teaching fellow in English, Tufts Coll., 1927-28; A.M., Ohio State U., 1930; A.M., Harvard, 1931, Ph.D., 1935; Litt.D. (hon.), Lafayette Coll., 1967; LL.D., Grinnell Coll.; 1971; m. Ruth Delavan Champlin, July 31, 1935; 1 son, Champlin Bechtold. Instr. in English, Ohio U., 1928-30, Univ. of Me., 1931-33, 1934-35; instr. English La. State U., 1935-36, asst. prof., 1936-42, asso. prof., 1942-46, prof., 1946-48; prof. U. Wash., 1948—, chmn. dept. English, 1948-71. Recipient Ariz. Quar. essay prize, 1956; Longview Found. essay award, 1960. Huntington Library grantee, 1959; Guggenheim fellow, 1964- 65; Nat. Endowment for Humanities sr. fellow, 1971-72. Mem. Internat. Assn. Univ. Profs. English, Modern Lang. Assn. (mem. nat. exec. council 1966-69), Nat. Council Tchrs. English (Distinguished lectr. 1968), Philol. Assn. Pacific Coast (pres. 1959), Am. Assn. U. Profs. (mem. nat. council 1962- 65), Phi Beta Kappa (senator 1967—). Author: America in English Fiction, 1760-1800, 1937; This Great Stage: Image and Structure in King Lear, 1948; Magic in the Web: Action and Language in Othello, 1956 (recipient Explicator award $200, 1957); Tragedy and Melodrama: Versions of Experience, 1968. Editor Understanding Drama: Twelve Plays, 1948; Modern Short Stories: A Critical Anthology, 1950; Swift's Gulliver's Travels, 1950, rev. edit., 1969; An Anthology of Pre-Shakespearian Drama, 1952; Conrad's Lord Jim, 1957; Hardy's Mayor of Casterbridge, 1962; Eliot's Silas Marner, 1962; Shakespeare's Cymbeline, 1964; Euripides' Alcestis, 1965; Hardy's Jude the Obscure, 1966; Shakespeare's Taming of the Shrew, 1966; Hardy's Tess of the Dlurbervilles, 1971. Editorial adviser Coll. English 1951-53, 56- 61, Shakespeare Studies, 1965—. Home: 4554-45th Av NE Seattle WA 98105

HEILOMS, MAY, (Mrs. Samuel Helloms), painter; b. Russia; d. Mark A. and Eugenie (Mogilensky) Levinson; naturalized, 1932; student Hunter Coll., 1929, Art Students League; m. Samuel Heiloms, June 12, 1938. Exhibited paintings Pa. Acad., Bklyn. Mus., Cleve. Mus., Denver Mus., Silvermine Guild, Butler Inst. Am. Art, Nat. Acad., Nat. Arts Gallery, Mexico Mus. Fine Arts, Okla. City Mus., others; one man shows Monmouth Guild, 1960, Bennett Coll., 1961, Silvermine Guild Conn., Jeanette Nessler Gallery, N.Y.C., East Central State Mus. Okla., Cortland Art Center, N.Y., Paducah Art Guild, Ky., Warder Pub. Library, Springfield, O. Five Corners Library, Hudson Gallery, N.Y.C., Muhlemberg Library, N.Y., others, also univs. and colls.; traveling shows Cleve. Mus. Art, Allbright Art Gallery, Buffalo, Dallas Mus. Art, Corcoran Gallery, Rochester Meml. Art Gallery, Columbia Mus. Art, also Lisbon, Portugal, Naples, Italy, Athens, Greece, Brussels, Belgium, also Museo De Bellas Artes, Buenos Aires, Argentina; paintings permanent collections Phila. Mus. Art, Samuel S. Fleisher Meml. Art Found., Ludwig Bowman Collection, Collectors of American Art, Norfolk Mus. Art, Safed State Mus., Israel, Bat Yam Museum, Israel, Okla. City Mus., also pvt. collections. Adviser Ford Found. Program in Humanities, 1958, 59. Recipient prize for oil Jersey City Mus., 1950, 51, 59, 63, 1st prize, medal, 1956; prize Painters and Sculptors N.J., 1952, 55, Bocour prize, 1958, prize for oil, 1960, 62; prize Bklyn. Soc. Artists, 1957; Atwood Klinger prize for abstract oil Nat. Assn. Women Artists, 1954, Patricia Murphy prize, 1958, E. Morse Genius prize for watercolor, 1960, M. Grumbacher prize oil, 1961, Sarah E. Good prize oil, 1962, Bainbridge prize watercolor, 1963; prize watercolor Bklyn. Soc. Artists, 1958; Nat. Soc. Painters in Casein, prize casein, 1962, prize, 1967, 7O; prize for oil Painters and Sculptors N.J., 1964; prize for watercolor Nat. Assn. Women Artists, 1966; M.H. Steiglitz prize Nat. Soc. Painters in Casein, 1966; prize (oil) Am. Soc. Contemporary Artists, 1967, 68. Fellow Royal Acad. Arts (Eng.); mem. Am. Painters and Sculptors (dir.), Painters and Sculptors N.J. (hon. life pres.), Audubon Artists (v.p.), Painters in Casein (dir.), Artists Equity, Nat. Assn. Women Artists, Bklyn. Soc. Artists, Casein Soc., Allied Artists (officer exec. bd.), Watercolor Soc. Ala., Knickerbocker Artists, Silvermine Guild, N.Y. Soc. Women Artists (chmn. membership com.), Art Students League, Manhattan Gallery Group. Studio: 340 W 28th St New York City NY 10001

HEILPERIN, MICHAEL ANGELO, economist, author; b. Warsaw, Poland, May 6, 1909; s. Paul and Susanne (Aschkenasy) H.; Licentiate Commerce, U. Geneva, 1929, Ph.D., 1931; post grad. London Sch. Econs., 1929-30, Cambridge U., 1931; Rockefeller Found. fellow, 1933-35; m. Denise Arouh; 1 dau., Anne Claude. Came to U.S., 1939, naturalized, 1944. Lectr. econs. U. Geneva, 1932-33; asst. prof. internat. econ. relations Grad. Inst. Internat. Studies, Geneva, Switzerland, 1935-38, now prof. internat. econs.; lectr. econs. U. Cal. at Berkeley, 1939: prof. Acad. Internat. Law, The Hague, summer 1939; lectr. Canadian Inst. Internat. Affairs, 1939, 44; lectr. Inst. Internat. Edn., N.Y.C., 1939-40; lectr. econs. Bryn Mawr Coll., 1940-41; vis. asst. prof. Hamilton Coll., Clinton, N.Y., 1941-42, asso. prof. econs., 1942-45; econ. adv. Bristol-Myers Co., N.Y., 1943-53; research asso. Nat. Bur. Econ. Research, N.Y.C., 1943-44; econ. corr. Western Europe, Fortune and Time Inc., 1953—; asso. editor Fortune mag., 1959-64, bd. editors, 1964-66; dir., sec.-treas. The Dollar Fund, Geneva, 1966—; vis. prof. internat. finance U. So. Cal., 1967—. Expert monetary questions Internat. Studies Conf., Paris, 1937, Bergen, 1939. Fellow Royal Econ. Soc., Internat. Inst. Pub. Finance; mem. Am. Econ. Assn., Council Fgn. Relations N.Y.C., Council Internat. Faculty Comparative Econs., Internat. C. of C. (com. fgn. investments 1946-53, econ. adv. U.S. Council 1948-53), Soc. d'Econ. Politique (Paris), Royal Econ. Soc. Belgium (hon.). Author: Monetary Aspects of the Raw Materials Problems and the Revival of International Trade, 1938; International Monetary Economics, 1939; Economic Policy and Democracy, 1943; International Monetary Reconstruction: The Bretton Woods Agreement, 1945; The Trade of Nations, 1947-52; Studies in Economic Nationalism, 1960, 62; Aspects of the Pathology of Money, 1965: Contbg. author: Economics of Inflation, 1935; The World Crisis, 1938; A Forum on Finance, 1940; Science, Philosophy and Religion, 1943: Persistent International Issues, 1947; Aiding Underdeveloped Areas Abroad, 1950; European Integration, 1957; World Monetary Reform: Plans and Issues, 1963; Changing Patterns of Foreign Trade and Payments, 1964; Money, Financial Institutions, and the Economy, 1965. Home: 11 rue Michel Chauvet Geneva Switzerland Office: care Grad Sch Bus Adminstrn U So Cal Los Angeles CA 90007

HEILPRIN, LAURENCE BEDFORD, physicist, educator; b. N.Y.C., May 26, 1906; s. William Albert and Jessie Emma (Heine) H.; B.S. in Econs., U. Pa., 1928, M.A. in Physics, 1931; Ph.D. in Physics, Harvard, 1941; m. Marilyn Joyce Heyman, Sept. 3, 1953; children—Jean Frances, John Michael. Instr. physics and math. Northeastern U., 1935-40; asst. thermodynamics Harvard, 1941; with Nat. Bur. Standards, 1941-51; research ordnance electronics patents Diamond Ordnance Lab., 1945-51, tchr. in grad. sch., 1949-51; physicist Taub Engring. Co., 1952-54; analyst operations evaluation group, U.S. Navy, Mass. Inst. Tech., 1954-56; physicist information systems Documentation Inc., 1956-57; staff physicist Council Library Resources, Inc., 1958-67; prof. information sci. Library Sch. and Computer Center, U. Md., 1967—; professorial lectr. George Washington U. Grad. Sch. Engring., 1959-62, Am. U. Center Tech. and Adminstrn., 1965- 66. Founding mem., dir. Com. Investigate Copyright Problems Affecting Communican in Sci. and Edn., 1959—. Mem. Am. Soc. Information Sci. (chmn. com. orgn. information 1962-63; pres. 1965), Am. Phys. Soc., Optical Soc. Am., Am. Assn.

Physics Tchrs., Am. Math. Soc., I.E.E.E., Operations Research Soc Am., Philos. Soc. Washington, Washington Assn. Scientists (founding mem.), A.A.A.S., Am. Soc. Cybernetics, Sigma Xi. Club: Harvard (Washington). Author, co-editor: Proc. of Symposium on Education for Information Science. 1965. Home: 6402 Tone Dr Bethesda MD 20034 Office: Sch Library and Information Services U Md College Park MD 20740

HEIM, ALLAN R., sports exec.; b. Springfield, O., Sept. 12, 1929; s. Paul R. and Eleanor (Nafz) H.; student Wittenberg U., 1947-50; B.A. in Journalism, Ohio State U., 1956; m. Charlene McKenna, Dec. 30, 1950; children—Allan R., Julie Marie, Steve. Asst. bus. editor Cin. Enquirer, 1958-61, exec. sports editor, 1961-68; pub. relations dir. Cin. Bengals, 1968—. Sports expert Coca Cola Athletic Council, 1962—. Served with USAF, 1950- 54. Club: Cincinnati. Home: 4658 Rumpke Rd Cincinnati OH 45245 Office: 200 Riverfront Stadium Cincinnati OH 45202

HEIM, HAROLD CLIFFORD, univ. dean; b. Kewanee, Ill., Mar. 19, 1911; s. Martin E. and Mathilda (Wagner) H.; B.S., U. Colo., 1935, M.S., 1939, Ph.D., 1941; student U. Chgo., 1950; m. Eva N. Rocchio, Jan. 31, 1947; children—Philip M., Warren P. Tchr., Wheatridge (Colo.) schs., 1932-37, Frederick (Colo.) schs., 1937-38; mem. faculty U. Colo., Boulder, 1938-41, 47—, prof. pharmacy, 1947—, dean Sch. Pharmacy, 1964-; chemist FDA, San Francisco, 1941-47. Mem. Am. Pharm. Assn., Soc. Exptl. Biology and Medicine, Sigma Xi, Rho Chi, Phi Delta Chi, Phi Lambda Upsilon. Unitarian. Rotarian. Spl. research biochem. pharmacology. Home: 2927 11th St Boulder CO 80302

HEIM, JOHN RUSSELL, trading stamp co. exec.; b. Mpls., Apr. 16, 1914; s. Harry Russell and Ada (Michaelson) H.; B.A. cum laude, U. Minn., 1935, LL.B., 1937; m. Jeanne Kay Reiber, June 7, 1941; children—Joan H. (Mrs. Kenneth Jonson), Nancy E. Admitted to Minn. bar, 1937; atty. Employers Mut. of Wausau, Wis., 1937-42, 47-48; with FBI, 1942-47; mem. firm Stakler & Heim, Morris, Minn., 1948-52; with Dept. Army, 1952-54, FTC, 1954-61; with Premium Service Corp., Mpls., 1961—, v.p., sec., gen. counsel, 1963—; dir. Gold Bond Stamp Companies (U.S. and Can.), Premium Corp. Am., Inc., Performance Incentives Corp. Home: 3 Cooper Av Edina MN 55436 Office: 12715 B State Hwy 55 Minneapolis MN 55427

HEIMBERGER, ARTHUR ALBERT mfg. exec.; b. Lima, O., Apr. 1, 1932; B.S., U. San Francisco, 1954; M.S., Stanford University, 1956; m. Rosemarie Lois Brown, May 15, 1955; 1 son, Anthony Robinson. Sales rep. Ames-Brockton Fabricated Products, Akron, O., 1956-58, sales mgr. Coshocton, Ohio, 1959-61, gen. manager plant, 1961-68, v.p. sales, 1968--. Instr. bus. Cosyshocton Jr. College, 1968-69. Secretary Coshocton YMCA, 1960-61; active Boy Scouts of America. Trustee Coshocton Animal Welfare League, Curry Home for the Aged. Named Man of Year, Coshocton Junior Chamber of Commerce, 1968. Mem. Coshocton C. of C. (vice president 1967-68, pres. 1969-70), English Speaking Union, Coshocton Sertoma Club, Nat. Assn. Mfrs., Sales Executives Institute, Phi Beta Kappa, Sigma Chi, Phi Mu. Democrat. Mem. Christian Ch. (lay leader). Mason (32, Shriner). Clubs: Coshocton Country, Coshocton City, Running Deer Country. Home: 2d Av Coshocton OH Office: 3d Av Coshocton OH

HEIMBERGER, CHARLES J., banker; b. Erie, Pa., June 5, 1905; s. Charles J. and Elizabeth (Allen) H.; m. Kathryn Newkirk; 1 dau., Mary J. Cashier, Lawrence Park Nat. Bank, Erie, 1929-44; with First Nat. Bank Erie, 1944-69, exec. v.p., 1950-58, pres., 1958-69; merger First Nat. Bank of Erie and First Nat. Bank of Medville to form First Nat. Bank of Pa., chmn. bd., chief exec. officer, 1969-71, also dir.; dir. E. Erie Comml. R.R., Erie Casket Co., Gen. Telephone Co. Pa., Greater Erie Indsl. Devel. Corp., Parker White Metal. Co., Pa. Devel. Credit Corp. Bd. dirs. Erie United Fund, Hamot Hosp., Erie, Erie unit Shriners Hosps. Crippled Children. Home: 340 Indiana Dr Erie PA 16505

HEIMERICH, JOHN JAMES, educator, architect; b. Clay Center, Kan., Oct. 17, 1906; s. George and Mary Cecilia (White) H.; B.S. in Archtl. Engring., Kan. State U., 1933, M.S., 1945; student U. Okla., spring 1942, U. N.M., 1943-44; m. Audrey Argey Tedrow, Aug. 22, 1935; children—Denis Alton, Lynn Raymond. Tchr., Greenleaf (Kan.) High Sch., spring 1934, Scandia (Kan.) Jr. High Sch., 1934-36, Concordia (Kan.) Jr. and Sr. High Sch., 1936-41; mem. faculty U. Okla., 1941-42; mem. faculty U. N.M., 1942—, prof. architecture, 1951—, chmn. dept., 1948-66; part-time pvt. practice architecture, 195O—. Active local United Community Fund drives. Registered profl. engr. and arch., N.M. Mem. A.I.A. (treas. N.M. chpt. 1956-64, treas. Albuquerque 1965—). Mem. Christian Ch. (ofcl. bd.). Co-author: Workbook for Engineering Drawing, 1954. Home: 7020 Prospect Av NE Albuquerque NM 87110

HEIMERL, RAMON PAUL, educator; b. Winsted, Minn., June 22, 1916; s. Paul H. and Anna Irene (Keiser) H.; B.Ed., St. Cloud State Coll., 1938; B.S., 1946; M.A., U. Minn., 1949, Ph.D., 1952; m. Beatrice Bourelle, June 6, 1946. Tchr. pub. high schs., Hancock, Minn., 1938-41, Sauk Centre, Minn., 1946-49, Mpls., 1949-51; instr. U. Minn., 1951-52; with U. No. Colo., Greeley, 1952—, prof. bus., 1959—, dean Sch. Bus., 1965—. Served with USNR, 1942-45. Mem. N.E.A., Colo. Edn. Assn., Colo. Bus. Edn. Forum (pres. 1955, 56), Mountain Plains (pres. 1966-67), Colo. (pres. 1955), Nat. bus. edn. assns., Am. Marketing Assn., Am. Econs. Assn., Am. Council on Consumer Interests (exec. sec. 1956-66), Pi Omega Pi, Delta Pi Epsilon (nat. pres. 1966-67) Elk. Author textbook; also contbr. articles in bus. edn. to profl. mags. and yearbooks. Home: 2119 22d St Greeley CO 80631

HEIMERT, ALAN EDWARD, educator; b. Oak Park, Ill., Nov. 10, 1928; s. Ewald W. and Gertrude (Hilbert) H.; A.B., Harvard, 1949, Ph.D., 1960; M.A., Columbia, 1950; m. Arline Ireland Grimes, Oct. 20, 1962; 1 son, Andrew Jackson. Instr. English, history, lit. Harvard, 1959-60, asst. prof. English, 1960-65, asso. prof., 1965-69, Powell M. Cabot prof. Am. lit., 1969—, master Eliot House, 1968—. Mem. Inst. for Advanced Study, Princeton, 1960-61; vis. asso. prof. history U. Cal. at Berkeley, 1967. Served to sgt. AUS, 1952-55. Mem. Am. Studies Assn. Author: (with Reinhold Niebuhr) A Nation So Conceived, 1964; Religion and the American Mind: from the Great Awakening to the Revolution, 1966. Editor: (with Perry Miller) The Great Awakening, 1967. Home: 4 Robinson Circle Winchester MA 01890 Office: Eliot House Harvard U Cambridge MA 02138

HEIMONEN, HENRY S., educator; B.A., No. Mich. U.; Ph.D., U. Wis. Nov. prof., head dept. geography, earth and sci. and conservation No. Mich. U. Address: 315 E College St Marquette MI 49855*

HEIMSCH, CHARLES, educator; b. Dayton, O., May 4, 1914; s. Charles and Martha Louise (Sawesky) H.; A.B., Miami U., 1936; M.A., Harvard, 1939, Ph.D., 1941; m. Dorothy Hogue Johnson, Sept. 17, 1938; children—Richard Charles, Carolyn Marie, Alan. Teaching asst. biology Harvard, 1936-37, research asst. Wood Collection, 1939-40, Austin teaching fellow, 1940-41, Sheldon traveling fellow, 1941-42; teaching asst. biology Radcliffe Coll., 1937- 39; instr. botany Swarthmore Coll., 1942-46; asst. prof. biology Amherst Coll., 1946-47; asst. prof. botany U. Tex., 1947-50, asso. prof., 1950- 54, prof., 1954-59; prof. botany, chmn. dept. Miami U., 1959—. State exec. com. U. Interscholastic League, 1956-59. Tech. aide tropical deterioration OSRD-NDRC. Fellow A.A.A.S., Ohio Acad. Scis. (v.p. plant scis. sect. 1963-64); mem. Bot. Soc. Am. (chmn. membership com. 1952- 55, treas. 1962-63, v.p. 1971, pres. 1972), Internat. Assn. Wood Anatomists, Phi Beta Kappa, Sigma Xi, Omicron Delta Kappa, Phi Sigma, Phi Eta Sigma, Phi Delta Theta. Author: (with others) Principles of Biology, 1954, rev. 1964; (with A.E. Lee) Development and Structure of Plants, 1962. Author research papers on systematic and developmental plant anatomy. Editor Am. Jour. Botany, 1964-69. Address: Miami U Oxford OH 45056

HEIMSTRA, FRED ALBERT, air force officer; b. Chgo., Feb. 24, 1915; s. Fred and Helen (Bolt) H.; student Thornton Jr. Coll., Harvey, Ill., 1932-34; B.S., U. Ill., 1937, M.D., 1939; m. Thelma Pernette Gullickson, June 24, 1939; children—Frederick, Richard, Leslie (Mrs. James Miller), Linda. Intern Cal. Luth. Hosp., Los Angeles, 1939-40; resident W. Suburban Hosp., Oak Park, Ill., 1947-50; commd. 1st lt., M.C., U.S. Army, 1940, advanced through grades to lt. col., 1947; ret., 1947; commd. lt. col., M.C., USAF, 1949, advanced through grades to brig. gen., 1969; dir. plans and hospitalization Office Surgeon Gen., Hdqrs. USAF, 1968—. Decorated Army Commendation medal, Air Force Commendation medal, Legion of Merit. Diplomate Am. Bd. Obstetrics and Gynecology. Mem. Air Force Assn., Aerospace Med. Assn., Air Force Clin. Surgeons, Soc. Air Force Flight Surgeons, Preventive Medicine Assn., Assn. Mil. Surgeons U.S. (v.p.), Phi Chi. Home: 3916 Greshem Pl Alexandria VA 22305 Office: Forrestal Bldg Washington DC 20330

HEIN, JOHN WILLIAM, dentist, educator; b. Chester, Mass., Sept. 29, 1920; s. Rudolf Jacob and Mercedes Viola Hein; B.S., Am. Internat. Coll., 1941; D.M.D., Tufts U., 1944; Ph.D., U. Rochester, 1952; A.M. (hon.), Harvard, 1962; m. Jeanette Marie BeVier, Dec. 16, 1944. Student instr. oral pathology Tufts Coll. Dental Sch., 1943-44; head div. dental research U. Rochester, 1948-52, sr. fellow dental research, 1949-52, instr. pharmacology, 1951-53, asst. prof. dental research, 1952-55, asst. prof. pharmacology, 1954-55, chmn. dept. dentistry and dental research, 1952- 55; instr. anatomy and physiology Eastman Sch. Dental Hygiene, 1950-55, lectr. dental research, 1953-55; research specialist Bur. Biol. Research, Rutgers U., 1955-59; dental dir. Colgate Palmolive Co., 1955-59; prof. preventive dentistry, dean Sch. Dental Medicine, Tufts U., 1959- 62; dir. Forsyth Dental Center, 1962—; prof. dentistry Harvard Dental Sch., 1962-67. Trustee Am. Internat. Coll., 1960—. Served to capt. AUS, 1942-47. Fellow A.A.A.S., Internat. Coll. Dentists (dist. regent 1967—); mem. Am. Dental Assn., Mass. Dental Soc. (pres. 1964-65), Internat. Assn. Dental Research, Am. Acad. Dental Sci., Am. Acad. Periodontology, Am. Soc. Dentistry Children, Sigma Xi, Omicron Kappa Upsilon, Delta Sigma Delta. Club: Harvard (Boston). Home: Bridge St Medfield MA 02152 Office: 140 The Fenway Boston MA 02115

HEIN, LAWRENCE BERT, educator; b. Fairview, Okla., Feb. 27, 1914; s. William J. and Wilomina (Just) H.; B.S., Okla. State U., 1937, M.S., 1938; Ph.D., Mich. State U., 1946; m. Frances Denner, July 31, 1938; children—Cheryl (Mrs. William Donnithorne), Marilyn (Mrs. Stephen Keeling), Laura Sue. Sr. sect. chief TVA, Sheffield, Ala., 1947-55; asst. mgr. process div. Olin Mathieson Chem. Corp., N.Y.C., 1955-64; head dept. chemistry and chem. engring. Mich. Technol. U., Houghton, 1964—. Mem. Am. Chem. Soc., Am. Inst. Chem. Engrs., Fertilizer Soc. (London), Phi Lambda Upsilon, Alpha Chi Sigma, Sigma Tau. Bd. editors Jour. Agrl. and Food Chemistry, 1963- 65. Home: Sheridan Rd Houghton MI 49931

HEIN, RONALD JOSEPH, corp. exec.; b. Sheldon, N.D., Dec. 18, 1922; s. Edward Louis and Alice (Mielke) H.; student Loras Coll., 1946-48; B.S.C., State U. Ia., 1949; m. Hannah Jane Gustafson, Jan. 11, 1943; children—Katherine Ann, Ronald Joseph, Jeffrey Charles. Accountant, E.W. Bliss Co., Moline, Ill., 1949-55, asst. treas., 1955-61, corp. controller, Canton, O., 1961—, also treas. Served with AUS, 1943-46. Mem. Financial Execs. Inst. Roman Catholic. Home: 6201 Pickwick Circle NW North Canton OH 44720 Office: 217 2d St NW Canton OH 44702

HEINDEL, RICHARD HEATHCOTE, educator; b. Hanover, Pa., Aug. 24, 1912; s. Franklin E. and Lelia I. (Heathcote) H.; A.B., Harvard, 1933; M.A., U. Pa., 1934, Ph.D. (Penfield fellow), 1938; student Gettysburg Coll., 1929-31; Litt.D., Wagner Coll., 1957; m. Elizabeth Calvert, June 30, 1934 (dec. June 1962); children—Heath, Thomas, Bridget; m. second, Dorothy Pushaw, June 1963 (div. 1969); m. 3d, Ruth V. Noble, 1969. Tchr. Drexel Inst., 1934-36; Field fellow Social Sci. Research Council, 1936-37, exec. asso., 1949-50; instr., later asst. prof. modern European history U. Pa., 1938-46; dir. Am. Library, Am. Embassy, London, Eng., 1942-45; chief div. libraries and insts. State Dept., 1946-47; profl. staff asso. Senate Fgn. Relations Com., 1947-49; staff asso. Pub. Library Inquiry, 1947; consultant U.S. Nat. Commn. UNESCO, 1949-50, dep. dir. UNESCO relations staff State Dept. 1950- 54; cons.-lectr., inst. world affairs Pa. State College, summer 1952, 53, 54; dean Coll. Arts and Sci., 1954-56, prof. history and govt. U. Buffalo, 1954-58, vice chancellor, 1956-58; pres. Wagner Coll., S.I., N.Y., 1958-61; pres. Pratt Inst., Bklyn., 1961- 67; dean faculty, prof. internat. relations Capitol Campus, Pa. State Univ., Middletown, 1967—. Mem. U.S. nat. commn. for UNESCO, 1958-62; cons. Nat. Resources Planning Bd., 1942; dir., organizer War Documentation Service, 1939-42; field dir. Fgn. Policy Assn., 1939-40; regional di Survey Fed. Archives, 1936; dir. Phila. Survey Hist. Manuscripts, 1936; member U.S. delegation Gen. Conf., UNESCO, Paris, France, 1951; Am. observer Books and Periodicals Commission, Conf. Allied Minister Edn., London, 1943-45; secretary Com. Interchange Persons, Conf. Bd. Asso. Research Councils, 1949-50, 54; exec. sec Nat. Commn. Conservation Cultural Resources, 1941; overseas corr. sec Am. Council Learned Socs., 1943-45; mem. com. on lang. devel. U.S. Office Edn., 1958-63; mem. commn. internat. edn. Am. Council Edn. Hon. fellow Library Congress, 1941-55. Mem. Assn. Higher Edn., Am. Hist. Assn., Am. Polit. Sci. Assn., Phi Sigma Kappa, Phi Beta Kappa. Lutheran. Clubs: Harvard (N.Y.C.); Cosmos (Washington); Harrisburg (Pa.) Country. Author: The American Impact on Great Britain, 1940; War Check List, 1941; Integration of Federal and Non-Federal Research, 1942; The Present Position of Foreign Area Studies in the U.S., 1950; also numerous articles, reviews, govt. reports. Editor book reviews Social Studies, 1939-42; American Influence Abroad, 1950; editorial cons. Doubleday & Co., 1950. Address: Capitol Campus Pa State U Middletown PA 17057

HEINDL, WARREN ANTON, educator; b. Chgo., Dec. 2, 1922; s. Anton T. and Louise (Fiala) H.; student Morton Jr. Coll., 1941-43; LL.B., Chgo.-Kent Coll. Law, 1947, LL.M., 1948; B.S., Northwestern U., 1949; m. Margaret Carriger, July 11, 1958. Admitted to Ill. bar, 1947, practiced in Chgo., 1951-65; mem. faculty Chgo.-Kent Coll. Law, 1948-69, asst. prof., 1951-65, asso. prof., 1965-69; prof. law Ill. Inst. Tech., Chgo., 1969—. Fellow Chgo.-Kent Honor Council; mem. Am., Ill. bar assns., Soc. Kent Honor Men, Delta Mu Delta. Home: 508 Selborne Rd Riverside IL 60546 Office: Ill Inst Tech Sch Law Chicago IL 60616

HEINE, EDWARD JOSEPH, Jr., steamship co. exec.; b. Orange, N.J., Sept. 2, 1925; s. Edward Joseph and Jane E. (Regan) H.; B.S., U.S. Merchant Marine Acad., 1946; B.S., Seton Hall U., 1948; LL.B., Fordham U., 1953; student N.Y.U., 1956-58; m. Mary Jane Day, Apr. 11, 1953; children—Edward J., Timothy J., Christopher J., Kevin J., Brian J. Asst. mgr. dept. mem. firms N.Y. Stock Exchange, 1948-50, 52-53; admitted to N.Y. bar, 1954; atty., sr. partner firm Kirlin, Campbell & Keating, N.Y.C., 1953-67; exec. v.p. U.S. Lines Inc., N.Y.C., 1967-70, pres., 1970—, also dir.; dir. Atlantic Co. Ltd., U.S. Lines, Inc. Mem. Spring Lake First Aid Assn. Bd. dirs. U.K. Mut. Steamship Assn.; trustee United Seamen's Service. Served with U.S. Mcht. Marine, 1944-46, 50-51. Named Profl. Man of Year, U.S. Merchant Marine Acad., 1966. Mem. Nat. Cargo Bur., Inc., Propeller Club Port N.Y., Maritime Adminstrn. Bar Assn., Maritime Assos., Maritime Assn. Port N.Y., Maritime Law Assn. U.S., Nat. Def. Transp. Assn., Newcomen Soc. N. Am. Clubs: Downtown Athletic Assn., India House (N.Y.C.); Spring Lake (N.J.) Golf and Country; Union League. Home: 22 Tuttle Av Spring Lake NJ 07762 Office: 1 Broadway New York City NY 10004

HEINE, HAROLD WARREN, educator; b. Highland Park, N.J., Sept. 14, 1922; s. Charles Albert and Elizabeth (Gabriel) H.; B.S., Rutgers U., 1944, Ph.D., 1948; m. Marjorie Anne Boote, Aug. 1, 1953; children—Katharine E., Elizabeth J., Eric A. Asst. prof. chemistry Bucknell U., Lewisburg, Pa., 1948-51, asso. prof., 1951-54, prof. chemistry, 1954—, chmn. dept. chemistry, 1970—; vis. scientist Dow Chem. Co., Midland, Mich., 1957; vis. prof. U. Koln, 1961; cons. to surgeon gen., 1966-69; vis. prof. U. Heidelberg, 1969-70. Recipient Harbison prize Danforth Found., 1970. Nat. Sci. Sr. Faculty fellow, 1961-62. Mem. Am., Brit. chem. socs., Phi Beta Kappa, Sigma Xi, Phi Lambda Upsilon, Phi Eta Sigma. Contbr. chpt. to Mechanisms of Molecular Migrations, 1971. Contbr. articles profl. jours. Home: 944 Curtin Av Lewisburg PA 17837

HEINEKE, PAUL H. lawyer; b. Streatom, Ill., Aug. 29, 1895; s. William J. and Emma C. (Riel) H.; LL.B., U. Ill., 1917; m. Vivienne M. Kerr, Feb. 26, 1923. Admitted to Ill. bar, 1917, since practiced Chgo.; mem. Heineke Conklin & Schrader. Fellow Am. Coll. Trial Lawyers; mem. Soc. Trial Lawyers, Am., Ill., Chgo. bar assns., Phi Delta Phi, Sigma Nu. Home: 1500 Hinman Av Evanston IL 60201 Office: 135 S LaSalle St Chicago IL 60603

HEINEKEN, ALFRED HENRY, brewery exec.; b. Amsterdam, Netherlands, Nov. 4, 1923; s. H.P. and C. (Breitenstein) H.; ed. Kennemer lyceum; m. M.L. Cummins, 1948. Adviser to mgr. Heineken Breweries, Inc., U.S., 1945-48, now pres. bd. mng. dirs.; pres. Heineken Investment Trust; mem. supervisory bd. Gen. Bank Netherlands. Address: Heineken's Bierbrouwerij Maatschappij N V Amsterdam The Netherlands

HEINEMAN, BEN WALTER, corp. exec.; b. Wausau, Wis., Feb. 10, 1914; s. Walter Ben and Elsie Brunswick (Deutsch) H.; student U. Mich., 1930-33; LL.B., Northwestern, 1936; LL.D., Lawrence Coll., 1959, Lake Forest Coll., 1966, Northwestern U., 1967; m. Natalie Goldstein, Apr. 17, 1935; children—Martha Brunswick (Mrs. Henry F. Field), Ben Walter. Admitted to Ill. bar, 1936; pvt. practice law and govt. service, Chgo., Washington, Algiers, 1936-56; chmn. bd. dirs. Four Wheel Drive Auto Co., 1954-57; now pres. N.W. Industries, Inc.; chmn. C. & N.W. Ry. Co.; dir., mem. exec. com. 1st Nat. Bank, Chgo.; dir. Inmont Corp., Met. Life Ins. Co., Ill. Bell Telephone Co. Chmn. White House Conf. to Fulfill These Rights, 1966; chmn. Pres.'s Task Force on Govt. Orgn., 1966-67, Pres.'s' Commn. Income Maintenance Programs, 1967-69. Trustee, mem. investment com. U. Chgo.; chmn. Ill. Bd. Higher Edn., 1962-69; trustee, mem. investment com. Savs. and Profit Sharing Fund of Sears Roebuck Employees; vis. com. dept. econs. Harvard. Fellow Am. Bar Found. (life), Am. Bar Assn.; mem. Am. Law Inst., Ill., Chgo. bar assns., Order of Coif, Phi Delta Phi (hon.). Clubs: Ephraim (Wis.) Yacht; Mid-America, Chicago, Commonwealth, Wayfarers, Economic, Standard, Quadrangle, Executives, Commercial, Chicago Yacht (Chgo.); Nat. Press, Federal City (Washington). Home: 1126 E 48th St Chicago IL 60615 Office: 400 W Madison St Chicago IL 60603

HEINEMAN, WARNER, banker; b. Hannover, Germany, July 19, 1922; s. Hugo and Charlotte (Guthmann) H.; came to U.S., 1937, naturalized, 1945; B.A., U. Mich., 1943; M.B.A., U. So. Cal., 1952; m. Anne Fisher, Sept. 3, 1949; children—Lawrence Jeffrey, Carol Anne. With Union Bank, Los Angeles, 1943—, v.p., 1958-62, sr. v.p., 1962—, regional v.p. Beverly Hills, 1964—, exec. v.p., 1967-; chmn. bd. Union Internat. Bank; pres. Globa Lease, Inc.; dir. Unionamerica Capital Corp., Banque Occidentale, Paris, France, de Occidentale Bank, Amsterdam, The Netherlands; lectr. finance U. Cal. at Los Angeles. Treas. Music Guild; bd. dirs. Franz Alexander Psychosomatic Research Found. (both Los Angeles); bd. dirs. Music Center Opera Assn. Served with AUS, 1945- 46. Licensed pub. accountant, Cal. Mem. Bankers Assn. Fgn. Trade, Robert Morris Assos., Zeta Beta Tau. Clubs: Brentwood Country, University; Palm Canyon Country (Palm Springs, Cal.). Home: 457 St Pierre Rd Los Angeles CA 90024 Office: Union Bank PO Box 3100 Terminal Annex Los Angeles CA 90054

HEINEMAN, WILLIAM ARTHUR, chain store exec.; b. Bklyn., Jan. 8, 1924; s. William C. and Vera (Irwin) H.; B.S., N.Y. U. 1952, LL.B., 1956; m. Jean E. Bonvicino, June 25, 1950; children—Deborah Ann, Geoffrey W. Admitted to N.Y. bar, 1957, U.S. Supreme Ct. bar, 1964; with Mercantile Stores Co., Inc., N.Y.C., 1941—, treas. 1967—. Served with USNR, 1943-46. Mem. Beta Gamma Sigma. Home: 588 Madison Av Baldwin NY 11510 Office: Mercantile Stores Co Inc 128 W 31st St New York City NY 10001

HEINEMANN, EDWARD HENRY, corp. exec.; b. Saginaw, Mich., Mar. 14, 1908; s. Gustave Christian and Margaret (Schust) H.; student pub. schs., Mich. and Cal.; m. Zell Shewey, 1959; 1 dau. by previous marriage, Joan (Mrs. Allan Lamont). Engaged as designer and project engr., also asst. chief engr. Moreland Aircraft Corp., Internat. Aircraft Corp., Northrop Aircraft Corp., 1931-36; chief engr. El Segundo (Cal.) div. Douglas Aircraft Co., Inc., 1936-58, corporate v.p. in charqe combat aircraft engring. aircraft and Missiles, 1958-60; in charge design, devel. Navy BT, SB2D, TB2D, SBD Dauntless dive bombers, Navy R3D transport, A-20 Air Force Havoc attack bomber, DB-7 Boston attack bomber for Brit. and French, B-26 Air Force Invader attack bomber, Navy AD Skyraider attack bomber series, A2D Skyshark attack bomber, F3D Skyknight night fighter, F4D Skyray interceptor, D-558 Skystreak, D-558-2 Skyrocket research airplanes, A3D attack bomber, A4D Skyhawk attack bomber; v.p. European sales Douglas Aircraft Co., 1960; exec. v.p. Summers Gyroscope Co., 1960-62; v.p. engring. and Program devel. Gen. Dynamics Corp., N.Y.C., 1962—. Cons. to numerous govt. coms. Recipient Sylvanus Albert Reed award, 1952, Collier Trophy, 1953; So. Cal. Aviation Man of Yr. award, 1954; Paul Tissandier diploma Fedn. Aeronautique Internationale, 1955. Fellow Am. Inst. Aeros. and Astronautics, Soc. Aero. Weight Engrs. (hon.), Royal Aero. Soc., Am. Astronautic Soc.; mem. Soc. Naval Architects and Marine Engrs., Am. Soc. Naval Engrs., Nat. Acad. Engring., Soc. Automotive Engrs., Tau Beta Pi (hon.). Office: 1 Rockefeller Plaza New York City NY 10020

HEINEMANN, GUSTAV W., pres. West Germany; b. Schwelm/Westfalen, July 23, 1899; s. Otto and Johanna (Walter) H.; D. Polit. Sci., U. Marburg (Germany), 1921; D.Law, U. Münster

(Germany), 1929; m. Hilda Ordemann, Oct. 28, 1926; children—Uta Ranke-Heineman (Mrs. Edmund Ranke), Christa (Mrs. Eduard Delius), Barbara (Mrs. Manfred Wichelhaus), Peter. Aux. judge, Lünen/Westfalen; atty. at lawyer, Essen, Germany, 1926; lawyer, also legal counsel and confidential clk. Rheinische Stahlwerke, 1928-39; bd. mem. Rheinische Stahlwerke, Essen, 1936-39; lectr. mining, 1933-39, also econ. law U. Cologne; mayor of Essen, 1946-49; provincial del. in Düsseldorf, 1947; minister of justice Nordrhein-Westfalen, 1947-48; fed. minister of interior, 1949-50; lawyer, notary, Essen, 1951; resigned from Christian Dem. Union, 1952; co-founder Gesamtdeutsche Volkspartei, 1952; dissolution of Gesamtdeutsche Volkspartei, 1957; joined SPD, 1957; mem. German Parliament, 1957; mem. party bd. SPD, 1955—; fed. minister justice W. Germany, 1966; fed. pres. W. Germany, 1969—. Active Bekennenden Kirche, 1933—; chmn. CVJM, Essen, 1936; mem. council EKD, Treysa, 1945-67, wrote Stuttgart Declaration, 1945; mem. direction Evangel. Ch., Rheinland, 1945-62; mem. Commn. Internat. Affairs World Council Chs., 1948-61; pres. Constl. Ch. Assembly in Eisenach, 1948; pres. synod EKD, 1949-55; participant constl. found. German Evangel. Ch. Council, 1949. Home: 34 Schinkelstrasse 43 Essen West Germany Office: Villa Hammerschmidt 135 Adenauerallee 53 Bonn West Germany

HEINEN, ERWIN, accountant; b. Comfort, Tex., Mar. 17, 1906; s. Hubert and Else (Strohacker) H.; B.B.A., U. Tex., 1927; m. Emily Blanton Plummer, June 25, 1929; children—Nancy Blanton (Mrs. Arnold Earl Luetge), Hubert Plummer. With Ernst & Ernst, C.P.A.'s, Houston, 1927—, partner, 1948-69, cons., 1969—; former chmn. accounting faculty assos. U. Tex. Sch. Bus. Adminstrn. Vice pres. Houston Grand Opera Assn., 1958-69; treas. Music Guild, 1963-68. Bd. dirs. Houston Symphony Soc.; former treas. Houston Mus. Fine Arts. Mem. Am. Inst. C.P.A.'s, Tex. Soc. C.P.A.'s, So. States Conf. C.P.A.'s (past pres.), Nat. Accountants Assn. Episcopalian. Clubs: River Oaks Country, Houston, Houston Rotary (past pres.), Rotary (dist. gov. 1970-71), Harvard Business School (dir.). Home: 5406 Huckleberry St Houston TX 77027 Office: One Shell Plaza Houston TX 77002

HEINEN, PAUL A., automobile mfg. co. exec.; b. Teaneck, N.J., Jan. 9, 1930; s. Paul and Encarnacion (Maestu) H.; B.B.A., U. Mich., 1954, J.D., 1956, M.B.A., 1957; S.M. (Sloan fellow), Mass. Inst. Tech., 1963; m. Gloria Newman, Oct. 9, 1952; children—Heidi, Paul C. Admitted to Mich. bar; with Chrysler Corp., Detroit, 1957—, atty., 1957-62, 63-66, exec. asst. to v.p. legal affairs, 1966-68, asso. gen. counsel, 1968—, sec., 1969—. Served to 1st lt. AUS, 1950-53. Mem. Am., Mich., Detroit bar assns., Am. Soc. Corporate Secs., Order of Coif, Beta Gamma Sigma, Phi Alpha Delta, Sigma Alpha Epsilon. Clubs: Detroit; Oakland Hills Country. Home: 31925 Cross Bow Ct Birmingham MI 48010 Office: 341 Massachusetts Av Detroit MI 48231

HEINER, ROBERT GRAHAM, lawyer; b. West Point, N.Y., Aug. 19, 1900; s. Gordon Graham and Elizabeth Cloyd (Kent) H.; A.B., Johns Hopkins, 1921; B.A. in Jurisprudence, Oxford (Eng.) U., 1923; m. Frances Eliot Cassidy, July 31, 1926 (dec. July 1958); children—Clinton Graham, Frances Eliot; m. 2d, Nina King Colgate, Jan. 22, 1967. Admitted to N.Y. bar, 1929; asso., then partner firm Cotton & Franklin, N.Y.C., 1924-42; asst. gen. counsel office Lend-Lease Adminstrn., 1943; partner Cahill, Gordon, Reindel & Ohl, and predecessor, N.Y.C., 1943-61. Bd. dirs. Planned Parenthood of N.Y.C., Planned Parenthood Fedn. Am., 1963-68; trustee Knickerbocker Hosp., N.Y.C. Home: 201 E 62d St New York City NY 10021 Office: 80 Pine St New York City NY 10005

HEINER, ROBERT T., banker. Sr. v.p. First Security Bank Utah, Salt Lake City. Office: PO Box 478 Salt Lake City UT 84110*

HEINEY, JOHN WEITZEL, utility exec.; b. Lancaster, Pa., Nov. 9, 1913; s. George and Gertrude G. (Weitzel) H.; B.S. in Bus. Adminstrn., Lehigh U., 1935; m. Betty M. Horn, Apr. 12, 1941. With various subsidiaries Am. Water Works Co., 1935-41, 46-60; pres., chief exec. officer, dir. Indiana Gas Co., Inc., Indpls., 1960—; pres., dir. Ohio River Pipe Line Corp., 1964- -; dir. Mchts. Nat. Bank & Trust Co. Indpls. Served to lt. col., inf., AUS, 1941-46. Decorated Bronze Star medal. Mem. Am. (past chmn. spl. com. on consumer affairs, 1st v.p. 1968, pres. 1969, dir.), Ind. (past pres. and dir.) gas assns., Inst. Gas Tech. (trustee 1965, chmn. bd. trustees 1968), Newcomen Soc. N. Am., Independent Forum, Northwestern U. Law Sch. Alumni Assn. (bd. dirs. 1961—), Theta Pi. Clubs: Columbia, Meridian Hills Country. Home: 5933 Brendonridge Ct N Indianapolis IN 46226 Office: 1630 N Meridian St Indianapolis IN 46202

HEINFELDEN, CURT H.G., life ins. co. exec.; b. Haverhill, Mass., Aug. 30, 1909; s. Curt H.G. and Edith (Prentiss) H.; A.B., Rutgers U., 1932; student U. Chgo. Law Sch., 1934; grad. Advanced Mgmt. Program, Harvard, 1950; m. Lois Gantert, Nov. 30, 1935; 1 son, Curt H.G. III. Jud. Examiner U.S. Fidelity & Guaranty Co., 1934-38; sales mgr. Am. Mut. Liability Ins. Co., 1938-46; v.p. Employers Group Ins. Cos., 1946-58; chmn. bd., pres. Balt. Life Ins. Co., 1959—; dir. Md. Nat. Bank. Mem. exec. com. Gov.'s Operating Economy Survey Commn. Pres. Greater Balt. YMCA, 1967; v.p. Balt. Area council Boy Scouts Am., 1960. Bd. dirs. Balt. United Appeal, 1964, UN of Md., 1963, Jr. Achievement Balt., 1963, Greater Balt. Com., Goodwill Industries. Served with USNR, 1942-45; PTO. Mem. Am. Mgmt. Assn., C. of C. Met. Balt. (v.p.), Zeta Psi, Phi Delta Phi. Rotarian. Clubs: L'Hirondelle (Ruxton, Md.); Maryland, Country of Maryland, Center (Balt). Home: 910 Malvern Av Ruxton MD 21204 Office: Balt Life Ins Co Mt Royal Plaza Baltimore MD 21201

HEINISCH, DON, truck mfg. co. exec.; b. Chgo., Aug. 23, 1923; s. Gustav O. and Marie (Hausdorf) H.; B.S., Washington U., St. Louis, 1942; C.P.A., LaSalle Extension U., Chgo., 1948; m. Alyce N. Lovell, Jan. 23, 1946; 1 son, Kelby G. Gen. mgr. Darling Co., 1946-50; sec.-treas. Crescent Industries div. Sears-Roebuck, 1950-56; treas. AMI div. Automatic Canteen Corp., 1956-57; pres. Recordio Corp., 1957-63; pres. Diamond-Reo div. White Motors Corp., 1963-68; pres. FWD Corp., Clintonville, Wis., 1968—. Bd. dirs. Clintonville Community Hosp.; mem. exec. com. Valley council Boy Scouts Am Served with USAAF 1943-46; CBI Mason Rotarian Home: RR 2 Clintonville WI 54929 Office: E 12th St Clintonville WI 54929

HEINL, ROBERT DEGS, Jr., retired marine corps officer, writer; b. N.Y.C., Aug. 12, 1916; s. Robert Debs and Helen Margaret (Corbin) H.; B.A. with orations cum laude, Yale, 1937; m. Nancy Gordon Wright, Sept. 23, 1939; children—Pamela Gordon (Mrs. John R. Burdick), Michael Charles. Commd. 2nd lt. USMC, 1937, advanced through grades to col.; service Pearl Harbor, 1941; assigned relief expdn. Wake Is., 1941, S. Pacific, 1942, Iwo Jima, 1945, Japan, 1945, N. China, 1946; dir. Marine Corps history, 1946-49; with 1st Marine Div., also comdr. E. Coast Islands, Korea, 1952-53; comdr. U.S. Mil. Group and U.S. Naval Mission, Port-au-Prince, Haiti, 1958-63; retired, 1963; mil. corr. Detroit News, 1963—. Cons. long- range gun systems Navy Dept., 1967-68; guest lectr. Yale, Brown U., Naval War Coll., Fgn. Service Inst., InterAm. Def. Coll. Decorated Legion of Merit with combat V, Bronze Star with combat V; recipient award of merit U.S. Naval Inst., 1968. Mem. Inst. Strategic Studies, Am. Mil. Inst., Naval Inst., White House Corr. Assn. Episcopalian. Clubs: Army and Navy, Nat. Press (Washington); Army and Navy Country (Arlington, Va.); Yale (N.Y.C.); American (London, Eng.); Carabao. Author: The Defense of Wake, 1947; Marines at Midway, 1948; The Marshalls: Increasing the Tempo, 1954; The Marine Officer's Guide, 3d edit., 1967; Soldiers of the Sea, 1962; Dictionary of Military and Naval Quotations, 1966; Victory at High Tide (Aldfred Thayer Mahan award U.S. Navy League), 1968; Handbook for Marine NCOs, 1969; also articles. Home: 2400 California St NW Washington DC 20008 Office: Nat Press Bldg Washington DC 20004

HEINRICH, ROSS RAYMOND, geophysicist; b. St. Louis, Dec. 12, 1915; s. Edward Ernst and Mary R. (Busch) H.; A.B., U. Mo., 1936; M.S., St. Louis U., 1938, Ph.D., 1944; m. Marie Frances McKinnon, June 3, 1948; children—Rose Thaddeus, Christopher Edward, Anita Marie, Victoria Margaret. With St. Louis U., 1936—, successively grad. fellow geophysics, instr., asst. prof., asso. prof., 1936-51, prof., 1951—, dir. dept. geophysics and geophys. engring., 1956—, acting dean Inst. of Tech., 1968—; cons. ground vibration problems, 1938—. Exec. bd., trustee Univ. Corp. Atmospheric Research. Mem. Am. Inst. Mining and Metall. and Petroleum Engrs., Am. Meteorol. Soc., Am. Geophys. Union, A.A.A.S., Geol. Soc. Am., Am. Soc. Engring. Edn., Seismol. Soc. Am., Sigma Xi, Phi Beta Kappa. Home: 21 Larkin Lane St Louis MO 63128

HEINRICH, RUDOLF, stage designer; b. Halle, Germany, Feb. 10, 1926; s. Otto and Theresa (Foerster) H.; m. Joan Carroll, Oct. 5, 1960 (div. June 1966). Designer for Leipzig Opera, 1948-50, Halle Opera, 1950-54, Komische Opera, Berlin, Germany, 1954-61; prof. stage design and costumes Akademie der Bildenden Künste, Munich, Germany, 1964—; guest designer La Scala, Milan, Italy, Theatre de Nation, Paris, France, Stanislawsky Theatre, Moscow, USSR, Göteborg (Sweden) Theatre, Hamburgische (Germany) Staatsoper, Frankfurt (Germany) Opera, Cologne (Germany) Opera, Munich Opera, Residenz Theater, Munich, Kammerspiele, Munich, Vienna (Austria) Staatsoper, Burg Theater, Vienna, Zurich (Switzerland) Opera, Santa Fe Opera, Boston Opera, Met. Opera, Royal Nat. Theater, London, Eng., also Salzburg Festival, 1966. Home: Gabelsberger Strasse 26 Munich 2 West Germany Office: Akademie der Blindenden Künste Muncih West Gemany

HEINS, ALLISON EDWARD, newspaper editor; b. Marquette, Mich., May 4, 1931; s. Arthur Edward and Ululla (Prothero) H.; B.S., U. Wis., 1953; m. Audrey Louise Noring, Aug. 4, 1957; children—Alan, John, Susan. Weekly editor Crawford County Press, Prairie du Chien, Wis., 1953; legislative reporter, bur. mgr. U.P.I., Des Moines, 1956-60; weekly editor Waverly (Ia.) Newspapers, 1960-63; reporter, asst. mng. editor, mng. editor Des Moines Register & Tribune Co., 1963—. Served with AUS, 1954-56. Recipient Am. Polit. Soc. nat. award for distinguished govtl. reporting 1967. Mem. Am. Soc. Newspapers Editors, A.P. Mng. Editors. Methodist. Home: 3025 Aurora Av Des Moines IA 50310 Office: 715 Locust St Des Moines IA 50304

HEINS, ARTHUR JAMES, educator, economist; b. Tigerton, Wis., May 30, 1931; s. Rufus Carl and Emelyn (Murphy) H.; B.S., U. Wis., 1953, M.S., 1957, Ph.D., 1961; student U. Cal. at Los Angeles, 1957-58; m. Nancy Lee Woltman, Feb. 18, 1952; children-Michael James, Robert Todd, Barbara Lynn, Mary Margaret. Mem. faculty U. Ill. at Urbana, 1960—, prof. econs., 1969—; vis. staff mem. Inst. Research on Poverty, U. Wis., 1968-69; cons. to govt. Served with USN, 1953-56. Recipient award outstanding contbn. undergrad. edn. Zeta Beta Tau, 1965. Mem. Am., Midwest econs. assns. Author: Constitutional Restrictions Against State Debt, 1963; also articles. Home: 2507 S Cottage Grove Urbana IL 61801

HEINS, MAURICE HASKELL, educator; b. Boston, Nov. 19, 1915; s. Samuel and Rose (Golbert) H.; A.B. summa cum laude, Harvard, 1937, M.A. (Henry Russell Shaw travelling fellow 1937-38), 1939, Ph.D., 1940; m. Hadassah Wagman, Aug. 25, 1940; children—Sulamith Hannah, Samuel David. Asst., Inst. for Advanced Study, 1940-42; asst. prof. Ill. Inst. Tech., 1942- 44; mathematician Office Chief of Ordnance War Dept., 1944-45; asso. prof. Brown U., 1946-47, prof., 1947-58; prof. math., U. Ill., Urbana, 1958—; vis. prof. U. Cal. at Berkeley, 1963- 64; President's fellow, 1952-53; Fulbright Research scholar attached to the Faculté des Sciences, U. Paris, 1952-53; mem. Inst. for Advanced Study, 1956-57. Recipient Bowdoin prize, 1940. Fellow Am. Acad. Arts and Scis.; mem. Am. Math. Soc. (mem. council, editor Proc. 1962-68), Société Mathmatique de France, Phi Beta Kappa, Sigma Xi. Author: Complex Function Theory; Selected Topics in the Classical Theory of Functions of a Complex Variable; Hardy Classes on Riemann Surfaces. Asso. editor various math. jours. Home: 603 W Illinois St Urbana IL 61801

HEINSOHN, THOMAS WILLIAM, profl. basketball coach; b. Jersey City, Aug. 26, 1934; s. William B. and Bessie (Paul) H.; B.S. in Bus. Adminstrn., Holy Cross Coll., 1956; m. Diane Regenhard, Sept. 2, 1956; children—Donna Marie, Paul T., David. Life ins. underwriter, Boston, 1956; basketball player Boston Celtics, 1956-65, coach, 1969—. C.L.U. Home: 30 Indian Ridge Rd South Natick MA 01760 Office: 30 Federal St Boston MA 02110

HEINTGES, JOHN ARNOLD, army officer; b. Coblenz, Germany, Dec. 9, 1912; came to U.S., 1920, naturalized, 1920; ed. U.S. Forest Service, Alaska, 1929-30, Presbyn. Missionary, Alaska, 1930-31; B.S., U.S. Mil. Acad., 1936; postgrad. U. Heidelberg (Germany), 1946-47; LL.D., Kyung Hee U. Korea, 1970; m. Marianne Zichner, Aug. 17, 1946; children—Robert A., Karen A. Commd. 2d lt. U.S. Army, 1936, advanced through grades to lt. gen., 1965; various command assignments in U.S., P.I., Africa, Sicily, Europe, 1936-46; asst., then asso. prof. U.S. Mil. Acad., 1947-51; staff officer plans and operations field forces, Ft. Monroe, Va., 1952-54; planning operations, tng. new Germany Army, 1954- 57; chief army sect. U.S. Mil. Assistance Group, Germany, 1955-57; dep. comdg. gen., then comdg. gen. Inf. Tng. Center, Ft. Dix, N.J., 1957-58; with U.S. Army Element, Laos, 1958-61; dir. orgn. and tng. Office Dep. Chief Staff for mil. operations Army Dept., 1961-62; dep. dir. joint staff Joint Chiefs Staff, 1962-63; comdg. gen. 5th Inf. Div. and Ft. Carson (Colo.), 1963- 64, Inf. Center and Commandant Inf. Sch., Ft. Benning, Ga., 1964-65, I Corps (Group), 8th Army, Korea, 1965; dep. comdr. Mil. Assistance Command, Vietnam, 1965-67; dep. comdr.-in-chief U.S. Army, Europe, comdg. gen. 7th Army, 1967-69, dep. comdg. gen. 8th Army, Korea, 1969; U.S. permanent mil. dep. and chief U.S. Element, CENTO, Turkey, 1969—. Decorated D.S.M., Silver Star medal with oak leaf cluster, Legion of Merit with oak leaf cluster, Soldier's medal, Bronze Star medal with 5 oak leaf clusters and V device, Air medal with 12 oak leaf clusters, Purple Heart medal; Fourragere, Croix de Guerre with palm (France); Order of 10 Million Elephants (Laos); Ulchi Medal of Honor (Korea); Nat. Order Vietnam 3d Class; 2d Class Knight Comdrs. Cross (Germany). Mem. Trans.-Atlantic Council Boy Scouts Am. (pres.), German-Am. Club (pres.), Def. Transp. Assn., Nat. Rifle Assn., Assn. U.S. Army, Assn. Grads. West Point, Inf. Mus. Assn., Army Athletic Assn. Home: 24 Portales Rd Broadmoor Colorado Springs CO 80906 Office: US Permanent Mil Dep CENTO Ankara Turkey APO NY 09254

HEINTZ, JACK, corporate representative; b. Chenoa, Ill., Jan. 19, 1907; s. Michael Matthew and Ida Luella (Thayer) H.; student Ill. Wesleyan U.; m. Mary Louise Keller, June 4, 1927; 1 son, Michael. Dept. store mgr., 1928-33; dist. mgr. ins. firm, 1933-36; radio sales mgr., 1936-37; radio sta. mgr. WCBS, 1937-43; radio cons. The Copley Press, Inc., 1946-47, v.p., dir., 1958—, Hawaii resident mgr., officer, rep., 1964—; v.p., gen. mgr. KSDO radio sta., 1946-54, KCOP-TV, 1954-58, radio and TV gen. cons., 1957; pub. Ill. State Jour., Ill. State Register, 1958-64; pres. Radio Sta. KGU, Honolulu. Profl. marine and landscape artist, exhibited works in several one-man shows. Mem. exec. com. Aloha council Boy Scouts Am. Trustee, Lincoln Coll. Served as lt. USNR, 1943- 46. Mem. Navy League, Assn. Honolulu Artists, Tau Kappa Epsilon. Republican. Episcopalian. Mason (33, Shriner), Rotarian. Clubs: Nat. Press (Washington); Pacific Outrigger Canoe. Home: 1350 Ala Moana Blvd Honolulu HI 96814

HEINTZBERGER, HENRY JOHN, life ins. co. exec.; b. South Bend, Ind., Dec. 24, 1915; s. Henry John and Catherine (von Amersvoort) H.; A.B., DePauw U., 1938; M.S., U. Notre Dame, 1940; student U. Mich., 1945-46; m. Victoria S. Shelley, Aug. 6, 1943, children—Emily C., Edward H., Henry John, Victor C. Actuarial asst. Monumental Life Ins. Co., 1946-52; group actuary Am. United Life Ins. Co., 1952-59; with Phila. Life Ins. Co., 1959-69, exec. v.p., 1967-69, dir., 1971—; pres., dir. San Francisco Life Ins. Co., 1969—, v.p., dir. III Mgmt. Co., 1968-69; v.p., dir., prin. mem. III Distbg. Co. Served to lt. USNR, 1941-45. Mem. Asso. Soc. Actuaries. Home: 519 Alhambra Rd San Mateo CA 94402

HEINZ, HANS JOACHIM, educator; b. Vienna, Austria, Nov. 29, 1904; s. Julius and Camilla (Alt) H.; student Acad. Art, Berlin, Germany, masterclass F. Busoni in composition, voice studies with Fred Hussler, Berlin, also Vitorrio Moratti, Milan, Italy; m. Julia Schwarz, Mar. 4, 1928; 1 dau., Jenny (Mrs. Elias Rivera). Came to U.S., 1937, naturalized, 1944. With Municipal Opera, Dusseldorf Statt Opera, Berlin, 1929-33; appearances in Milan, Salzburg, Vienna, 1934-36; U.S. debut as tenor soloist in Das Lied von der Erde with Los Angeles Philharmonic Orch., 1937; tours with Salzburg Opera throughout U.S., 1937-38; appearances with maj. U.S. orchs., also concerts throughout U.S. and abroad, 1938-48; mem. faculty Peabody Conservatory Music, Balt., 1944-57, Juilliard Sch. Music, N.Y.C., 1956—, Summer Music Sch., Aspen, Colo., 1963—. Chmn adminstrv. bd. Music Assn. Aspen, 1964—. Mem. Nat. Assn. Tchrs. Singing, N.Y. Singing Tchrs. Assn. Home: 170 E 79th St New York City NY 10021

HEINZ, HENRY JOHN, Jr., food products mfr.; b. Sewickley, Pa., July 10, 1908; s. Howard and Elizabeth (Rust) H.; grad. Shadyside Acad., 1927; A.B., Yale, 1931; student Trinity Coll., Cambridge, 1931-32; LL.D., Bowling Green U., 1943, Allegheny Coll., 1944, U. Pitts., 1960; m. Joan Diehl, June 18, 1935 (div.); 1 son, Henry John III; m. 2d, Drue Maher, Aug. 22, 1953. Salesman H.J. Heinz Co., Ltd., Eng., 1932; salesman H.J. Heinz Co., U.S., 1933, worked in sales dept., 1934-37, asst. to pres., 1937-41, pres., 1941-59, chmn., 1959—; dir. Mellon Nat. Bank & Trust Co. Pres. Sarah Heinz House, Pitts.; mem. exec. com. Allegheny Conf. on Community Devel.; chmn. Agribus. Council, Inc., Yale Art Gallery; trustee U.S. council Internat. C. of C., Com. Econ. Devel.; v.p., dir. Pitts. Symphony Soc. Bd. dirs. Bus. Com. for Arts, Inc., Pitts. Regional Planning Assn.; trustee Carnegie Inst., Carnegie-Mellon U., Nutrition Found., World Affairs Council Pitts. Republican. Presbyn. Clubs: Duquesne, Pittsburgh Golf, Allegheny Country, Fox Chapel Golf (Pitts); Buck's and White's (London); Stanwich (Conn.); River, Fifth Avenue (N.Y.C.); Rolling Rock (Ligonier, Pa.); The Brook. Home: Goodwood Sewickley PA 15143 Office: 1062 Progress St Pittsburgh PA 15212

HEINZ, LUTHER CARL, ret. naval officer; b. Phila., June 15, 1912; s. C. Harry and Bertha L. (Asimos) H.; B.S., U.S. Naval Acad., 1933; grad. Naval War Coll., 1951; m. Dolores Cox Birkholm, Feb. 11, 1939; 1 dau., Lisa L. Commd. ensign USN, 1933, advanced through grades to vice adm., 1965; served in U.S.S. Santa Fe, PTO, World War II; assigned Bur. of Personnel, 1947- 50, 55-58; comdr. destroyer U.S.S. Norris, 1946-47, Destroyer Div. 601, 1951-52, attack transp. U.S.S. Menifee, 1954-55, guided missile cruiser U.S.S. Boston, 1958-59; dir. Far East region Office Asst. Sec. Def., 1960-63; comdr. cruiser-destroyer flotilla 12, 1964; staff CINPAC, 1965; dir. mil. assistance, 1965-68; comdr. amphibious forces Atlantic Fleet, 1968-71; ret., 1971. Decorated D.S.M., Bronze Star, Legion of Merit, PTO ribbon with 12 battle stars. Address: 1125 Isabella Av Coronado CA 92118

HEINZE, WALTER O., business exec.; b. Chgo., Nov. 11, 1903; s. August and Daisy P. (Tuchband) H.; grad. Lane Tech. High Sch., Chgo.; m. Louise Mendius, 1924; children—Don Richard, Carol Louise, Dorothy Ann. Founder W.O. Heinze mgmt. cons., Los Angeles, 1937; mem. Planning Bd., WPB, 1942; dir. operations Smaller War Plants, Inc., 1945; pres. Internat. Latex Corp., Dover, Del., 1943—; chmn. bd. STP Corp., 1968—, ILC Industries, Inc., 1968—; chmn. exec. com. Benrus Corp.; chmn. bd. Tamms Industries. Dir., pres. Child Welfare League Am., 1957-71. Home: Wildman Arms Yale and Harvard Avs Swarthmore PA 19081 Office: 350 Fifth Av New York City NY 10001

HEINZERLING, LYNN LOUIS, fgn. corr.; b. Birmingham, O., Oct. 23, 1906; s. Louis and Grace (Lawrence) H.; student Akron U., 1924-25, Ohio Wesleyan U., 1925-27; m. Agnes C. Dengate, July 21, 1934; 1 son, Larry. Reporter Cleve. Plain Dealer, 1928-33; editor Asso. Press, Cleve. and N.Y.C., 1934-38, fgn. corr. in Berlin, Danzig, Helsinki, 1938-41, N.Y.C., 1942, London and Cairo, Egypt, 1943, with British 8th Army and U.S. 5th Army, Italy and Austria, 1943-45, chief bur., Vienna, Austria, 1945-46, corr.,Berlin, 1947-48, chief bur., Geneva, Switzerland, 1948-57, chief bur., Johannesburg, S. Africa, 1957-61, asst. chief bur., London, Eng., 1961- 63, chief of bureau, Columbus, O., 1963-64, chief of Africa Operations, 1964—. Recipient Pulitzer prize internat. reporting; Overseas Press Club award for best reporting from abroad, 1961. Mem. UN Corr. Assn., fgn. corr. assns. Bern and S. Africa, Phi Delta Theta. Club: Overseas Press (N.Y.C.). Home: Town House 333 Washington Av Elyria OH 44035 Office: Asso Press 83 Farrington St London EC4 England

HEIRES, JOHN HOPKINS, fgn. service officer; b. Sept. 19, 1918; s. Arthur Francis and Frances (Hopkins) H.; B.A. magna cum laude, Yankton Coll., 1939; LL.B., Yale, 1946; B.Litt., Oxford (Eng.) U., 1948; m. Alice Rea Chamberlin, May 14, 1955; children—John Hopkins, David Chamberlin, Gregory Norris. Admitted to D.C. bar, 1950, also U.S. Supreme Ct.; with Dept. Justice, 1941; legal asst. firm Pillsbury, Madison & Sutro, San Francisco, 1949-50; asso. firm Covington & Burling, Washington, 1950-53; asst. to chief estimates staff and estimates officer Bd. Nat. Estimates, 1953-57; sec. intelligence adv. com. NSC, 1957-58; &exec. sec. U.S. Intelligence Bd., 1958-62; dep. legislative programs coordinator AID, 1962, officer charge Pakistan affairs, 1962-64, formerly regional legal counsel, attache embassy, missions to India, Nepal, Ceylon; moderator Naval Acad. Fgn. Affairs Conf., 1964. Served to lt. (s.g.) USNR, 1942- 46. Rhodes scholar, 1946-48. Mem. Am., D.C. bar assns., Am. Soc. Internat. Law., Assn. Am. Rhodes Scholars, Oxford Union, Yale Law Sch. Assn. Washington, English Speaking Union, Pi Kappa Delta, Phi

Delta Phi. Clubs: Yale (N.Y.C); Internat. (Washington); Delhi Gymkhana (New Delhi). Note editor Yale Law Jour., 1942, case editor, 1946. Home: (permanent) 5700 Broad Branch Rd NW Washington DC 20015

HEISENBERG, WERNER, physicist; b. Wurzburg, Germany, Dec. 5, 1901; s. August and Annie (Wecklein) H.; Dr. phil., U. Munich, 1923; Dr. phil. habil., U. Gottingen, 1924; m. Elisabeth Schumacher, Apr. 29, 1937; children—Wolfgang, Maria, Jochen, Martin, Barbara, Christine, Verena. Prof. theoretical physics U. Leipzig, 1927-41; dir. Kaiser-Wilhelm Inst. for Physics, prof. U. Berlin, 1941-45; dir. Max-Planck-Inst. for Physics, prof. U. Gottingen, 1946-58; dir. Max-Planck-Inst. for Physics and Astrophysics, prof. U. Munich, 1958-70. Pres. Alexander-von-Humboldt- Stiftung. Recipient Barnard medal Columbia, Matteucci medaille, Max- Planck medaille, Nobel prize for physics, 1932; Pour le mérite für Wissenschaften und Künste, 1957. Mem. Am. Philos. Soc. Home: Rhenilandstrasse Munich Germany Office: 6 Föhringer Ring 8 Munich Germany

HEISER, JOSEPH MILLER, Jr., army officer; b. Charleston, S.C., Jan. 22, 1914; s. Joseph Miller and Alma (Meitz) H.; student Providence Coll., 1932-34, The Citadel, 1939- 41. Command and Gen. Staff Coll., 1949; B.B.A., U. Chgo., 1956; postgrad. Nat. War Coll., Washington, 1960-61; m. Edith Cox, Sept. 24, 1937; children—Annette, Joel M., Joan (Mrs. William Weizel). Commd. 2d lt. U.S. Army, 1943, advanced through grades to lt. gen., 1969; asst. exec. officer Office Chief of Ordnance, 1946-49, exec. officer, 1956-60; ammunition supply officer, asst. ordnance officer Pusan Base Command, 1950; exec. officer, dir. tng. Ordnance Sch., CONUS, Aberdeen Proving Ground, Md., 1951-54; asst. chief of staff G-4, 4th Logistical Command, Verdun, France, 1961-62, chief of staff and dep. comdr., 1962- 63; chief of staff U.S. Army Communications Zone, Europe, Orleans, France, 1963-65, comdg. gen., 1965, spl. asst. CINCUSAREUR, 1965; asst. dep. chief of staff for logistics Dept. Army, Washington, 1966-68 dep. chief of staff, 1969—; comdg. gen. 1st Logistical Command, U.S. Army Vietnam, 1968-69. Dist. chmn. Fleur-de-Lis (France) council Boy Scouts Am., 1963-65; camp and athletic dir Boys Clubs Am., 1928-34. Decorated D.S.M. with oak leaf cluster, Legion of Merit with oak leaf cluster, Bronze Star medal, Air medal with three oak leaf clusters, Army Commendation medal. Mem. Am. Ordnance Assn., Assn. U.S. Army, Nat. Security Indsl. Assn., Am. Mgmt. Assn.; Roman Catholic. Club: Alumni U. Chicago. Home: Quarters 5 Fort Meyer Arlington VA 22211 Office: DCSLOG DA The Pentagon Washington DC 20310

HEISERMAN, ARTHUR RAY, educator; b. Evansville, Ind., Jan. 10, 1929; s. Arthur Ray and Anne (Weisman) H.; A.B., U. Chgo., 1948, A.M., 1951, Ph.D., 1959; m. Virginia Ruth Martin, Oct. 17, 1950; children—Regan, Lisa, Gina, Alison, Arthur Martin. Writer, Sta. KTAR, Phoenix, 1951-52; instr. English, U. Neb., 1952-54; instr. English, U. Ill., Chgo., 1954-56, dir. acad. programs Univ. Coll., 1956-59, dir. Summer Sch., 1959-61, asso. dean Univ. Coll., 1961-63, master Humanities Coll., 1965-67, prof. English, 1965—. Guggenheim Found. fellow, 1963-64. Mem. Medieval Acad. Am., Internat. Arthurian Soc., Modern Lang. Assn. Author: Skelton and Satire, 1961. Contbr. articles to profl. jours. Home: 5757 Blackstone Av Chicago IL 60637

HEISKELL, ANDREW, publishing exec.; b. Naples, Italy, Sept. 13, 1915; s. Morgan and Ann (Hubbard) H.; ed. in Switzerland, Germany, France; student Harvard Bus. Sch., 1935-36; m. Cornelia Scott, Nov. 12, 1937 (div.); children—Diane, Peter; m. 2d, Madeleine Carroll (div.); 1 dau., Anne M.; m. 3d, Marian Sulzberger Dryfoos, 1965. Reporter, N.Y. Herald-Tribune, 1936- 37; asso. editor Life mag., 1937-39, asst. gen. mgr., 1939-42, gen. mgr., 1942-46, pub., 1946-60; v.p. Time, Inc., 1949-60, chmn. bd., 1960-69, chmn. bd., chief exec. officer 1969—, also dir. Co-chmn. Urban Coalition. Mem. bd. Center Inter-Am. Relations, Internat. Exec. Service Corps, Inst. Internat. Edn. Trustee Bennington Coll. Mem. Inter-Am. Press Assn. (mem. bd.). Home: Darien CT Office: Time Inc Rockefeller Center New York City NY 10022

HEISKELL, AUGUSTUS LONGSTREET, lawyer; b. Memphis, Nov. 4, 1890; s. Frederick Hugh and Augusta (Lamar) H.; student U. Tenn., 1909-13, U. Va., 1913-14; m. Ardeane McNeil, June 15, 1918; children—Ann Longstreet (Mrs. Albert C. Rickey), Ardeane McNeil (Mrs. Warren Lee Smith). Admitted to Tenn. bar, 1914, since practiced in Memphis; sr. partner firm Heiskell, Donelson, Adams, Williams & Wall, 1964—; with legal dept. City Memphis, 1916-20, 29-41; gen. counsel Dixie Greyhound Lines, 1938-54; instr. med. jurisprudence U. Tenn., 1938-42. Commr., mem. council Chickasaw council Boy Scouts Am., 1921-26, del. nat. council, 1925. Trustee Gooch Found., 1943, 46, 69—. Served with U.S. Army, 1916. Fellow Am. Coll. Trial Lawyers; mem. Am., Tenn., Memphis and Shelby County (sec., treas. or bd. dirs. 1920-32) bar assns., Kappa Alpha. Democrat. Presbyn. (elder 1935—). Home: 2171 S Parkway E Memphis TN 38114 Office: First Nat Bank Bldg Memphis TN 38103

HEISKELL, JOHN NETHERLAND, editor; b. Rogersville, Tenn., Nov. 2, 1872; s. Carrick White and Eliza Ayre (Netherland) H.; A.B., U. Tenn., 1893; Litt.D., Little Rock Coll., 1929; LL.D., Ark. Coll., 1934, U. Ark., 1938, Colby Coll., 1958; m. Wilhelmina Mann, June 28, 1910; children-Mrs. George Whitfield Cook, Mrs. Hugh B. Patterson, Jr. In newspaper work; editor Ark. Gazette, 1902—; chmn. bd. Ark. Gazette Co. U.S. senator from Ark. by appointment of Gov. Donaghey, Jan. 6-Jan. 29, 1913. Pres. bd. trustees Little Rock Pub. Library. Former chmn. Little Rock City Planning Commn.; former mem. State Planning Bd. 2d v.p. A.P., 1926-27. Recipient citation A.L.A., 1957; medal and citation Syracuse U. Sch. Journalism, 1958; ann. award Columbia Sch. Journalism, 1958; Lovejoy award Colby Coll., 1958; U. Mo. Sch. of Journalism Distinguished Service medal, 1962; John Peter Zenger award dept. journalism U. Ariz.; citation and plaque Sigma Delta Chi, 1966. Fellow Sigma Delta Chi; mem. Sigma Alpha Epsilon. Democrat. Clubs: Country of Little Rock, Top of the Rock, Little Rock. Home: 6015 Greenwood Rd Little Rock AR 72207 Office: Ark Gazette Little Rock AR 72201

HEISKELL, MARIAN SULZBERGER (Mrs. Andrew Heiskell), newspaper exec., civic worker; b. N.Y.C., Dec. 31, 1918; d. Arthur Hays and Iphigene (Ochs) Sulzberger; grad. Frobeleague Kindergarten Tng. Sch., N.Y.C., 1941; m. Orvil Eugene Dryfoos, July 8, 1941 (dec. May 1963); children—Jacqueline Hays (Mrs. Stuart Price Greenspon), Robert Ochs, Susan Warms; m. 2d, Andrew Heiskell, Jan. 30, 1965. Dir. N.Y. Times Co., 1963—, Interstate Broadcasting Co., 1963—; dir. spl. activities N.Y. Times, 1963—. Council mem., adv. council Nat. Parks, Historic Sites, Bldgs. and Monuments; co-chmn. Mayor Lindsay's Council Environment. Bd. mgrs. N.Y. Bot. Gardens; trustee Consol. Edison, Rockefeller U.; bd. dirs., v.p. Community Service Soc. N.Y. Mem. Inter Am. Press Assn. (dir.). Jewish religion. Home: 870 UN Plaza New York City NY 10017 also Darien CT Office: Dept Special Activities NY Times 229 W 43d St New York City NY 10036

HEISLER, CLIFFORD BUDD, banker; b. Phila., Apr. 22, 1918; s. William Henry and Ethel (Budd) H.; grad. George Sch., 1936; B.S. in Bus. Adminstrn., Lehigh U., 1940; grad. in comml. banking Rutgers Grad. Sch. Banking, 1959; m. Mary-Elizabeth Boyer, Sept. 5, 1942; children—Clifford Budd, James Boyer. Bus. trainee Gen. Electric Co., Bridgeport, Conn., 1940-42; security analyst, asst. to sales mgr. Butcher & Sherrerd, Phila., 1946-48; v.p. charge portfolio and trust investments Central Penn Nat. Bank of Phila., 1948-66, sr. v.p., 1966-69, exec. v.p., 1969—; acting head trust dept., 1966; dir. Penn Berks Investors, Inc., Boyertown; instr. corp. finance and investments Am. Inst. Banking, Phila. Pres. Rosemont-Villanova Civic Assn., 1962-64; v.p. Reventhaler Meml. Home. Served with AUS, 1942-46; CBI; to capt. inf., Finance Corps, 1951-52. Decorated Legion of Merit, Bronze Star (U.S.), Chinese Medal of Valor. Mem. Financial Analysts Phila. (treas. 1955), Phila. Securities Assn. (bd. govs. 1963-65), Corporate Fiduciary Assn. Phila., Pa. Bankers Assn. (chmn. investment com. 1960, 61), George Sch. Alumni Assn. (pres. 1962-64). Clubs: Overbrook Golf, Union League (Phila.). Home: 311 Baintree Rd Rosemont PA 19010 Office: Broad and Walnut Sts Philadelphia PA 19101

HEISLER, JOHN COLUMBUS, mfg. co. exec.; b. Evanston, Ill., Mar. 19, 1926; s. John C. and Ruth (Ramsey) H.; student Purdue U., 1944-46; A.B., Harvard, 1948, M.B.A., 1950; m. Mary Anne Foley, Jan. 6, 1951; children—John Foley, Peter Ramsey, Tod Shelton, Anne Gilmore. With Eagle-Picher Industries, Inc., Cin., 1950—, treas., 1959-65, v.p., treas., 1965—, also dir.; dir. LeBlond, Inc., Cin. Trustee Cin. Community Chest; bd. govs. Cin. Country Day Sch. Served with USNR, 1944- 46. Republican. Presbyn. (elder). Club: Queen City (gov.). Home: 609 Miami Av Terrace Park OH 45174 Office: Am Bldg Cincinnati OH 45202

HEISLER, KENNETH GLENN, assn. exec.; b. Dufur, Ore., Oct. 31, 1905; s. Charles Monroe and Eva Lois (Powell) H.; A.B., U. Ore., 1927; LL.B., Harvard, 1930; m. Alice Baskerville Pollard, Dec. 24, 1930 (dec.); children-Kenneth Glenn, Alice (Mrs. Michael H. Hayes), Cynthia (Mrs. Richard C. Meininger), Elizabeth Powell; m. 2d, Lorna Salisbury; stepchildren—Stephanie Welsh, William Welsh. Law practice, Seattle, 1930- 34; atty. Fed. Home Loan Bank Bd., 1934-46, asso. gen. counsel, 1946-52, mem. Fed. Home Loan Bank Bd., 1952-53; gen. counsel Fed. Savs. and Loan Ins. Corp., Home Owners' Loan Corp., 1946-52; gen. counsel Nat. Savs. and Loan League, 1953-59; exec. dir. Nat. League Insured Savs. Assns., 1959—. Mem. Am., Washington, Fed. bar assns. Methodist. Mason. Home: 5019 Burke Dr Alexandria VA 22309 Office: 17th and M Sts NW Washington DC 20036

HEISLER, PHILIP SAMUEL, editor; b. Dallastown, Pa., Sept. 8, 1915; s. Chauncey Franklin and Anna (Flinchbaugh) H.; B.A., Penn State Coll., 1937; m. Helen Theresa Surratt, Sept. 8, 1945. Reporter McKeesport (Pa.) Daily News, 1937-39; Sunpapers war corr., 1944-45; editor Sunday Sun mag., Balt., 1945- 46; film dir. television sta. WMAR-TV, Balt., 1947-49; reporter Evening Sun, Balt., 1939-44, mng. editor, 1949—; partner Rabar Racing Stable. Mem. Nat. Press Club, Md. Press Assn. (pres.), Chesapeake Assoc. Press (pres.), Sigma Delta Chi. Lutheran. Club: Maryland. Home: 4406 Bedford Pl Baltimore MD 21218 Office: The Sunpapers Baltimore MD 21201

HEISS, CHARLES GORDON, hotel co. exec.; b. St. Louis, Jan. 12, 1925; s. Charles G. and Marie (Wagner) H.; m. Mary Aloyse Bick, June 17, 1947; children—Diane, Barbara, Carla. With Mayfair-Lennox Hotels, Inc., St. Louis, 1945—, pres., mng. dir., 1956-61, pres., chmn. bd., 1962—; dir. Clayton Bank (Mo.). Pres. Downtown St. Louis, Inc., 1965-66. Bd. dirs. St. Louis Municipal Theatre Assn., 1963—. Served to 2d lt., inf., AUS, World War II. Mem. Hotel Assn. St. Louis (pres. 1953-54), Am. Hotel Assn. (bd. dirs. 1965-66), Ark.-Mo.-Kan.-Okla. Hotel Assn. (pres. 1965-66), St. Louis C. of C. (bd. dirs. 1953-55, 60-61), St. Louis Ambassadors, Sigma Chi. Clubs: Racquet, Noonday, Old Warson Country (all St. Louis). Home: 323 Conway Hill Rd Creve Coeur MO 63141 Office: 806 St Charles St St Louis MO 63101

HEISS, RICHARD WALTER, banker; b. Monroe, Mich., July 8, 1930; s. Walter and Lillian (Harpst) H.; B.A., Mich. State U., 1952; LL.B., Detroit Coll. Law, 1963; LL.M., Wayne State U., 1969; m. Nancy J. Blum, June 21, 1952; children—Kurt Frederick, Karl Richard. Asst. trust officer Mfrs. Nat. Bank of Detroit, 1960-62, trust officer, 1962-66, v.p., trust officer, 1966-68, v.p., sr. trust officer, 1968—; lectr. Inst. Continuing Legal Edn., U. Detroit Bus. Sch. Served to 1st lt., Q.M.C., AUS, 1952-57. Mem. Am., Mich., Detroit bar assns., Delta Chi, Sigma Nu Phi. Republican. Lutheran. Clubs: Economic, Detroit, Detroit Golf. Home: 25537 Wessex St Farmington MI 48024 Office: 151 W Fort St Detroit MI 48226

HEIST, PAUL ADOLPH, psychologist educator; b. Waverly, Ia., Aug. 2, 1917; s. Ernst G. and Emma (Goppelt) H.; B.A., Luther Coll., Decorah, Ia., 1939; M.A., U. Ill., 1948; Ph.D., U. Minn., 1956; m. Mary Helen Unruh; children—Martin, Lauren, Jerome. Tchr., Carthage (Ill.) Coll., 1941-43; counselor U. Minn., 1946-47; tchr. Ore. State U., 1950-56; researcher, prof. U. Cal. at Berkeley, 1966—, chmn. div. higher edn., 1971—; adminstrv. staff, research dir. Center Study Higher Edn., 1956-70, dir. research project undergrad. edn., 1969—; cons. in field, 1961—. Served with AUS, 1943-45. Fellow Am. Psychol. Assn., A.A.A.S.; mem. Western Psychol. Assn., Soc. Psychol. Study Social Issues, Am. Assn. Higher Edn., Nat. Soc. Study Edn. Author book, articles, monographs, chpts. in books. Home: 2900 Forest Av Berkeley CA 94705

HEISTAD, GORDON THOMAS, educator; b. White Lake, Wis., Apr. 2, 1925; s. Ole Andrew and Bertha Caroline (Jensen) H.; B.A. summa cum laude, Concordia Coll., 1949; M.A., Johns Hopkins, 1950; Ph.D., U. Chgo., 1954; postdoctoral fellow U. Minn., 1954-56; m. Ruth Sylvia Gronhovd, Aug. 21, 1949; children—David, Carolyn, Mark, Marie, Kathryn. Research fellow U. Minn., 1954-56, asst. prof. psychology and psychiatry, 1956-60, asso. prof., 1960-65, prof., 1965—, dir. psychiatry research, 1963-70, program dir. psycho-pharmacology tng. program, 1964-70, dir. Drug Abuse Edn. Program, 1970—. Mem. Narcotics and Drug Abuse rev. com. USPHS, 1969-71; chmn. edn. and tng. adv. com. Spl. Action Office for Drug Abuse Prevention, Office of Pres., 1971—. Served with AUS, 1944-46; PTO. USPHS fellow, 1952-54; Commonwealth fellow 1963-64. Am. Psychol. Assn. Contbr. articles to profl. jours. Home: 5857 Fremont Av S Minneapolis MN 55419 Office: Box 392 Mayo Hosp Minneapolis MN 55455

HEITLER, EMMETT HENRY, mfg. co. exec.; b. Denver, July 12, 1909; s. Abram and Minnie (Goldsticker) H.; B.S., U. Colo., 1930; m. Dorothy Shwayder, Feb. 27, 1937; children—Dean J., Don A., Gail (Mrs. Jack A. Klapper), Bruce F., Lynn N. (Mrs. Jerry S. Goren). Factory mgmt. trainee Gen. Electric Co., Ft. Wayne, Ind., 1930-32; founder Fashion Bar Stores, Denver, 1933, partner, 1933-40; exec. v.p., chmn. exec. com. Samsonite Corp., Denver, 1940—; dir. Colo. Nat. Bank. Bd. dirs. Gen. Rose Meml. Hosp., Nat. Jewish Hosp. Denver; bd. dirs., com. chmn. Mile High United Fund; chmn. bd. trustees Jewish Community Centers Denver; mem. men's adv. bd. Childrens Hosp. Recipient Alumni of Year award U. Colo., 1958. Mem. Luggage and Leather Goods Mfrs. Am., Denver C. of C., Tau Beta Pi, Sigma Tau, Pi Tau Sigma, Beta Gamma Sigma. Jewish religion. Club: Green Gables Country (dir.) (Denver). Home: 170 S Dexter St Denver CO 80222 Office: 11200 E 45th Av Denver CO 80222

HEITLER, GEORGE, assn. exec., lawyer; b. N.Y.C., Sept. 3, 1915; s. John J. and Celia (Zeichner) H.; B.S., Columbia, 1936, J.D., 1938; m. Florence A. Posner, Apr. 21, 1940; children—James B., Richard S. Admitted to N.Y. bar, 1938, Ill. bar, 1962; asso. firm Cutler, Wilson & McMahon, N.Y.C., 1938-40; spl. asst. to David L. Podell, counsel to Hays, Podell & Schulman, N.Y.C., 1940; asso. atty. firm Coughlan & Russell, also mng. agt. and asst. sec. Central Manhattan Properties, Inc., N.Y.C., 1940-43; chief clk., legal adviser rents and claims bd., 4th Service Command, U.S. Army, 1943-45; engaged as bus. exec., also house counsel various comml. orgns., 1946-57; asst. sec., staff counsel Blue Cross Assn., N.Y.C., 1957-60, corporate sec., staff counsel, 1960-61, v.p., sec. gen. counsel, Chgo., 1961-71, v.p., corporate sec., gen. counsel, 1971—. Spl. adviser Dept. Labor, also speaker and panelist. Mem. Am., Chgo. bar assns., Assn. Bar City N.Y., Am. Ethical Union, Chgo. Ethical Soc. (trustee). Author articles. Home: 860 N Lake Shore Dr Chicago IL 60611 Office: 840 N Lake Shore Dr Chicago IL 60611

HEITMAN, CHARLES EDWIN, mfg. co. exec.; b. Bolton, Miss., Jan. 14, 1908; s. Charles Edwin and Daisy (Lusk) H.; B.S. in Elec. Engring., Ga. Sch. Tech., 1929; M.S. in Elec. Engring., Yale, 1931; m. Dorothy Jordan, Oct. 27, 1934; children—Susan (Mrs. A. Chalmers Omberg, Jr.), and Mary (Mrs. Donald L. Davis). Employed with the Budd Co., 1931-40, Pullman Standard Car Co., 1940, A. O. Smith Corp., 1940-56, Carter Carbureter div. A.C.F. Industries, 1956-60; with Bendix Corp., 1960—, now pres. N. Am. group, dir. Mem. Nat. Mgmt. Assn. (Gold Knight award 1962), Soc. Automotive Engrs. Clubs: Detroit Athletic, Recess; Bloomfield Hills Country. Home: 876 Covington Rd Birmingham MI 48010 Office: Bendix Center Civic Center Dr Southfield MI 48075

HEITMAN, HUBERT, Jr., educator; b. Berkeley, Cal., June 2, 1917; s. Hubert and Blanche (Peart) H.; B.S., U. Cal. at Davis, 1939; A.M., U. Mo., 1940, Ph.D., 1943; m. Helen Margaret McCaughna, Aug. 7, 1941; children—James Hubert, William Robert. Asst. instr. animal husbandry U. Mo., 1939-43; mem. faculty U. Cal. at Davis, 1946—, prof. animal sci., 1961—, chmn. dept., 1963- 68; livestock supt. Cal. State Fair, 1948-59. Pres. Yolo County Soc. Crippled Children, 1954-56. Bd. dirs. Cal. Soc. Crippled Children and Adults, 1954-56. Served to capt., San. Corps, AUS, 1943-46. Mem. Am. Soc. Animal Sci. (pres. Western sect. 1953), Animal Behavior Soc., A.A.A.S., Internat. Soc. Biometeorologists, Cal., N.Y. acads. scis., Sigma Xi, Alpha Zeta, Gamma Sigma Delta, Gamma Alpha, Sigma Chi. Home: 518 Miller Dr Davis CA 95616

HEITMAN, JOHN RUSSELL, free-lance writer; b. Sparta, Ill., June 24, 1904; s. Herman Dietrich and Martha Anna (McIntire) H.; B.J., U. of Mo., 1927; M.S., Northwestern, 1947; m. Mildred Reed Yates, June 11, 1932. Editor, co- publisher The Rantoul (Ill.) Press, 1927-31; instr. journalism U. of Ill., 1929-32; editor The Highland Park (Ill.) Press and The Lake Forester (Lake Forest, Ill.), 1932-36, publisher The Lake Forester, 1936- 47; dir. U. of Ala. News Bureau, and sec.-mgr. Ala. Press Assn., 1948- 50; prof., head dept. journalism Tex. Tech. Coll., dir. Tex. Tech. Press, Lubbock, 1950-54; chmn. dept. journalism University Denver, 1955- 66; Fulbright lectr. journalism Thammasat U., Bangkok, Thailand, 1963- 64; free-lance writer, 1966—. Mem. Kappa Tau Alpha, Sigma Delta Chi, Pi Alpha Mu, Delta Upsilon. Clubs: Lakeway Country (Austin); Antique Automobile Am. (hon.). A founder The Antique Automobile mag., 1943, pub., 1943-46. Home: 822 Sunfish Dr Austin TX 78746

HEITMANN, FRED WILLIAM Jr., banker; b. Chgo., Apr. 14, 1916; s. Fred William and Louise (Snyder) H.; B.S., Northwestern U., 1939; postgrad. U. Wis. Grad. Sch. Banking, 1950- 53; m. Peggy A. Smith, Sept. 6, 1941; children—Daryl J., Scott K. With N.W. Nat. Bank of Chgo., 1941—, pres., 1962—, also dir. mem. Faculty U. La. Sch. Banking, 1959—; U. Chgo. Sch. Banking, 1964. Chmn., Ill. Commn. Higher Edn., 1957-61; mem. Ill. Bd. Higher Edn., 1961—; chmn. bank div. Community Fund-A.R.C. Crusade of Mercy, 1962; vice chmn. Ill. Bd. Higher Edn., 1968—. Bd. dirs. Ill. Higher Edn. Assistance Corp. Recipient citation for community service Community Fund-A.R.C. Crusade of Mercy, 1962, Merit award Northwestern U., 1968, citation State Farm Ins. Cos., 1961, Silver Anniversary All Am., award Sports Illustrated, 1963. Mem. Ill. (pres. 1970-71), State Farm (pres.), Chgo. Dist. (pres.) bankers assns., Installment Bankers Assn. Chgo. (past pres.). Clubs: Mid- America, Banker, North Shore Country (Chgo.). Home: 734 Raleigh Rd Glenview IL 60025 Office: 3985 Milwaukee Av Chicago IL 60641

HEITMANN, WILFRED HENRY, banker; b. Chgo., Apr. 5, 1906; s. Henry Otto and Elizabeth (Young) H.; Ph.B., U. Chgo., 1928; LL.B., Chgo. Kent Coll. Law, 1934; m. Betty Ann Schmidt, Oct. 20, 1934; children-Caryl E. (Mrs. Gustave C. Aberle, Jr.), Susan E. (Mrs. John F. Daliere). Vice pres., dir. N.W. Nat. Bank of Chgo., 1941-45, pres., 1945-60, chmn. bd., 1960-69, chmn. exec. com., 1969—. Mem. Ill. Bankers Assn. (past pres.), Alpha Dlta Phi. Clubs: University (Chgo.); Skokie (Ill.) Country. Home: 1630 Sheridan Rd Wilmette IL 60091 Office: 3985 Milwaukee Av Chicago IL 60641

HEITNER, ROBERT RICHARD, educator; b. St. Louis, Feb. 1, 1920; s. Henry John and Anna (Waltke) H.; A.B., Washington U., St. Louis, 1941, M.A., 1942; Ph.D., Harvard, 1949; m. Pauline M. Spitz, Dec. 26, 1949; children—David H., Laura G. Asst. prof. German, Washington U., 1949-55; faculty U. Cal. at Los Angeles, 1955-64; prof. German, U. Tex., 1964-66; prof. German, head dept. U. Ill. at Chgo. Circle, 1966—. Served with AUS, 1942-45. Mem. Am. Assn. Tchrs. German, Modern Lang. Assn. Am., Am. Lessing Soc., Phi Beta Kappa, Phi Kappa Phi. Author: German Tragedy in the Age of Enlightenment, 1963. Editor, German Quar., 1967-70. Contbr. articles to profl. jours. Home: 7840 Greenfield St River Forest IL 60305 Office: Dept German Univ Ill at Chicago Circle Chicago IL 60680

HEITSCHMIDT, EARL T., architect; b. Portland, Ore., June 9, 1894; s. Theodore Frederick and Margaret (MacCormack) H.; student U. Ore., 1916-17, Mass. Inst. Tech., 1921-22; m. Mabel Cochran, Sept. 4, 1918; children—Margaret Louise, Earl. Draftsman U.S. Navy Yard, Bremerton, Wash., 1917-19; Pacific Coast mgr. Schultze & Weaver, architects, N.Y.C.; pvt. practice architecture, Los Angeles, 1929—; prin. works include pub. sch. bldgs., Los Angeles, Corona, Riverside; various pub. bldgs., office and indsl. bldgs., including C. of C. offices, Cal. Bank, Equitable Life Ins. bldg., U. Cal. library and organic chemistry bldgs., CBS, Hollywood, Pico Gardens Housing Project, Los Angeles Shipbuilding & Drydock Co., U.S. Naval Hosp. Expansion, Corona, Victor Orsatti Med. Bldg., Beverly Hills, Clayton Mfg. Co., White Meml. Hosp., Loma Linda U. Med. Center, phys. sci. bldgs. San Bernardino State Coll., Los Angeles Furniture Mart, variety of U.S. Naval Missile projects and others. Chmn. adv. com. Dept. of State for Internat. Brussels Expn. Mem. Cal. Bd. Archtl. Examiners (pres. 1952-53); adv. com. Los Angeles Bldg. Code, 1941-60; pres. Constrn. Industries Expn. and Home Show, 1948-50. Fellow A.I.A. (dir. Sierra Nev. dist. 1946-48, 1st v.p. 1954-55); mem. Cal. Council Architects (dir. 1945-48), C. of C. (dir. 1946-47, chmn. constrn. industries com. 1946-47, constrn. industries achievement award 1951), Phi Gamma Delta, Lambda Alpha. Republican.

Presbyn. Mason (32). Clubs: California, Jonathan. Home: 1345 Circle Dr San Marino CA 91108 Office: 3300 Temple St Los Angeles CA 90026

HEITZ, GLENN EDWARD, banker; b. Madison, Ind., Jan. 3, 1924; s. Edward Joseph and Dora (Wilkins) H.; student Davis and Elkins Coll., 1943-44; B.S., Purdue U., 1948, M.S., 1950; m. Lucille Poteete, Dec. 29, 1946; children—William Edward, Michael Glenn, Joseph Andrew. Teaching asst., research asst. agrl. econs. dept. Purdue U., 1948-50; asst. sec.-treas. Greenscastle (Ind.) Prodn. Credit Assn., 1950, asst. sec.-treas., then sec.-treas. LaFayette (Ind.) Prodn. Credit Assn., 1950-58; cons. FCA, Washington, 1958-70, dep. gov., dir. coop. bank service, 1959-68; pres. Fed. Land Bank St. Louis, 1970—. Bd. dirs. Roger Williams Found., Purdue. Served with USAAF, 1943-46. Recipient Ind. 4-H and Sears Agrl. scholarships, 1942-43. Mem. Ind. Fedn. Prodn. Credit Assns. (sec.- treas. 1955-58), Soc. Farm Mgrs. and Rural Appraisers (chmn. 1956-57), Am. Farm Econs. Assn., Ceres, Alpha Zeta. Baptist (deacon). Kiwanian, Rotarian. Home: 2405 Oak Springs Lane St Louis MO 63131 Office: Fed Land Bank St Louis MO 63103

HEITZMAN, HARRY JOHN, mfg. co. exec.; b. Emery, S.D., Apr. 9, 1932; s. Harry and Lena (Weeldreyer) H.; B.S., Sioux Fall Coll., 1954; M.B.A., Golden Gate Coll., 1963; m. Marilyn E. Nelson, Apr. 4, 1954; children—Jean Michelle, Debra A., John M. Accountant C & H Sugar Refining Corp., San Francisco, 1956-59, firm Ernst & Ernst, San Jose, Cal., 1959-62; auditor Lockheed Missile & Space Co., Sunnyvale, Cal., 1962-63; partner firm Berger, Lewis & Heitzman, C.P.A.'s, San Jose, 1963-67; tax mgr. Koehring Co., Milw., 1967-70, treas., 1970—. Served with USNR, 1954-56. C.P.A., Cal. Mem. Am. Inst. C.P.A.'s, Wis. Soc. C.P.A.'s, Financial Exec. Inst. Home: 645 Crystal Lane Elm Grove WI 53122 Office: 780 N Water St Milwaukee WI 53201

HEITZMANN, ALFRED OTTO, lawyer; b. St. Louis, Aug. 20, 1913; s. Alfred O. and Susanna (Herget) H.; A.B., Washington U., 1938; LL.B., Columbia, 1941; postgrad. Stanford U., 1943-44; m. Mary Jane Mattox, June 19, 1948; children—James A., Thomas W., Catherine Ann, John M. Admitted to N.Y. bar, 1941, Mo. bar, 1946; with Hines, Rearick Dorr & Hammond, N.Y.C., 1941-42; partner Lowenhaupt, Waite, Chaonoff & Stolar, St. Louis, 1946-56, Stolar, Heitzmann & Eder and predecessor firm, St. Louis, 1956—. Active St. Louis United Fund, 1969-70. Served as sgt., AUS, 1942-46. Mem. Phi Beta Kappa, Omicron Delta Gamma. Presbyn. (trustee). Home: 453 Yorkshire Pl Webster Groves MO 63119 Office: 515 Olive St St Louis MO 63101

HEIZER, ROBERT FLEMING, anthropologist; b. Denver, July 13, 1915; s. Ott Fleming and Martha (Madden) H.; A.B., U. Cal., 1936, Ph.D., 1941; D.Sc., U. Nev., 1965; m. Nancy Elizabeth Heizer, July 31, 1940; children—Stephen Rodney, Michael Madden, Sydney Alison. Instr., U. Ore., 1940-41; instr. U. Cal. at Los Angeles, 1945-46, asst. prof. at Berkeley, 1946-48, asso. prof., 1949- 52, prof., 1952—, dir. U. Cal. Archeol. Survey, Berkeley, 1948-60, dir. Archeol. Research Facility, dept. anthropology, curator N.Am. Archeology Lowie Mus. Anthropology, 1950—. Grantee Am. Philos. Soc., 1945-49, Wenner Gren Found. Anthrop., 1955-60, Nat. Geog. Soc., 1955, 57, 65, 68, 71, NSF, 1958-60, 63-64, 68-71; Guggenheim fellow, 1963. Fellow A.A.A.S.; mem. Soc. Am. Archeology (v.p. 1959-60), Am. Anthrop. Assn., Societé des Americanistes de Paris, Assos. Tropical Biogeography, Inst. Andean Research. Author: Francis Drake and the California Indians, 1947; (with John E. Mills) The Four Ages of Tsurai, 1952; A Guide to Archeological Field Methods, rev. edit., 1958; The Archeologist at Work, 1959; (with M.A. Baumhoff) Prehistoric Rock Art of Nevada and Eastern California, 1962; Man's Discovery of His Past, 1962; The California Indians, rev. edit., 1963; (with F. Hole) An Introduction to Prehistoric Archeology, 1965, rev. edit., 1969; (with T. Kroeber) Almost Ancestors, 1968; (with A. Almquist) The Other Californians, 1971; numerous articles in field. Home: 85 Menlo Pl Berkeley CA 94707

HEJDUK, JOHN QUENTIN, architect; b. N.Y.C., July 19, 1929; s. John Quentin and Mary (Henzler) H.; student Cooper Union Sch. Arch., 1950; B.S., U. Cin., 1952; M.A., Harvard Grad. Sch. Design, 1953; m. Gloria-Maria Fiorentino, Sept. 12, 1951; children—Rafael, Renata Lia. Archtl. designer I. M. Pei & Assos., N.Y.C., 1956-58; prof. arch. Cornell U., 1958-60; archtl. critic Yale Sch. Arch., 1961-64; chmn. dept. arch. Cooper Union Inst., 1964—; pvt. practice architecture, N.Y.C., 1966—. Mem. Am. Inst. Architects, Archtl. Assn. (London, Eng.), Archtl. League, Municipal Art Soc. Home: 5355 Henry Hudson Pkwy Riverdale NY 10471 Office: 200 E 37th St New York City NY 10016

HEJTMANCIK, MILTON RUDOLPH, medical educator; b. Caldwell, Tex., Sept. 27, 1919; s. Rudolph Joseph and Millie (Jurcak) H.; B.A., U. Tex., 1939, M.D., 1943; m. Myrtle Lou Erwin, Aug. 21, 1943; children—Kelly Erwin, Milton Rudolph, Peggy Lou. Resident internal medicine U. Tex., 1946-49, instr. internal medicine, 1949-51, asst. prof., 1951-54, asso. prof., 1954-65, prof. internal medicine, 1965—, dir. heart clinic, 1949—, dir. heart sta., 1965—; chief of staff John Sealy Hosp., 1957-58. Served from 1st lt. to capt., M.C., AUS, 1944-46; ETO. Diplomate in cardiovascular diseases Am. Bd. Internal Medicine. Fellow A.C.P., Am. Coll. Chest Physicians, Am. Coll. Cardiology; mem. Am. (fellow council clin. cardiology), Tex. (chmn. cardiac clinics com. 1956—, v.p. 1958), Galveston Dist. (pres. 1956) heart assns., A.M.A., Am. Fedn. Clin. Research A.A.A.S., Tex. Acad. Internal Medicine, Phi Beta Kappa, Sigma Xi, Alpha Omega Alpha, Mu Delta. Contbr. articles profl. jours. Home: 118 Marlin St Galveston TX 77550

HEKMAN, EDWARD JOHN, govt. ofcl.; b. Grand Rapids, Mich., July 5, 1914; s. John and Cornelia (Haan) H.; A.B., Calvin Coll., 1935; m. Florence Stuart, Sept. 25, 1937; children-Marilyn (Mrs. John Clark), Judy (Mrs. DuBois S. Thompson), John, Susan. With Hekman Biscuit Co., div. of United Biscuit Co. Am., 1935-60, v.p., 1946-50, pres., gen. mgr., 1951-60; dir. United Biscuit Co. Am. (co. name changed to Keebler Co. 1965), 1950-68, v.P., 1954-59, pres., 1960-67, vice chmn. bd. dirs., 1967-68; v.p. Valparaiso (Ind.) U., 1968-69; adminstr. Food and Nutrition Service U.S. Dept. Agr., 1969- -. Trustee Pine Rest Hosp., Grand Rapids, Nutrition Found. Served from ensign to lt. (j.g.) USNR, 1943-46. Lutheran. Clubs: Union League, Executives, Economic (Chgo.); River Forest (Ill.) Tennis; Capitol Hill, Kenwood Country (Washington). Address: 4201 Cathedral Av NW Washington DC 20016

HELBERT, CLIFFORD L., educator; b. Miles City, Mont., May 3, 1920; s. L. Roy and M. Mae (Stevenson) H.; Ph.B., Marquette U., 1948, A.M., 1955; m. Lorraine A. Herrell, June 15, 1944; children—Susan M., Thomas F., David P., Louise M., Anne R. Sugr., Marquette U. Press, 1947-51, asst. bus. mgr., 1951- 55, bus. mgr., 1955-61; mem. faculty Coll. Journalism, Marquette U., 1947—, prof., 1964—, dean coll., 1965-71; newspaper designer, 1951—; mag. designer, 1951—; book designer, 1947—; cons. in field, 1951—. Served to 1st lt. AUS, 1942-46. Named Internat. Craftsman of Year, 1961; recipient Andrew Hamilton award Marquette U., 1962; Benjamin Franklin award Graphic Arts Assn. Wis., 1966; fellow Internat. Newspaper Advt. Exec. Assn., 1963. Mem. Am. Acad. Advt., Am. Assn. U. Profs., Internat. Assn. Printing House Craftsman, Soc. Typographic Arts, Graphic Designer Can., Printing Hist. Soc. (London, Eng.), Internat. Center Typographic Arts, Alpha Sigma Nu, Kappa Tau Alpha, Sigma Delta Chi, Alpha Delta Sigma. Editor: Printing Progress a Mid-Century Report, 1959; also contbr. Harpers Ency. Sci. Home: PO Box 97 Milwaukee WI 53201 Office: 1135 W Kilbourn Av Milwaukee WI 53233

HELBLING, ROBERT EUGENE, educator; b. Lucerne, Switzerland, May 6, 1923; s. Emil and Senta (Lamm) H.; diplom, Handelsschule Lucerne, 1943; M.A., U. Utah, 1949; postgrad. Columbia, 1951; Ph.D., Stanford, 1958; postgrad. U. Cal., Berkeley, summer 1961; m. Suzanne Ottinger, June 9, 1956. Came to U.S., 1948, naturalized, 1954. Jr. exec. R.I. Geigy, Inc. Chem. Works, Basle, Switzerland, 1945-47; instr. dept. langs. U. Utah, Salt Lake City, 1950- 57, asst. prof. French, German and comparative lit., 1958-61, asso. prof., 1962-65, prof., 1966—, honors dir., 1964-66, coordinator humanities program, 1958—, chmn. dept. langs., 1965—; vis. asso. prof. L.I. U., summer 1962. Guest Fgn. Ministry German Fed. Republic, 1970. Served with Swiss Army, 1943-45. Named 1 of Outstanding Educators Am., 1971. Mem. Am. Assn. U. Profs. (past chpt. pres.), Modern Lang. Assn., Am. Assn. Tchrs. German, Am. Assn. French Tchrs., Phi Kappa Phi, Pi Delta Phi, Phi Sigma Iota, Sigma Delta Pi, Delta Phi Alpha. Author: (with Andrée M.L. Barnett) Le Langage de la France Moderne, 1961, L'Actualite Francaise, 1967. Author, editor Dürranmatt's Die Physiker, 1965; Kleist, Novellen und Aesthetische Schriften, 1968; Kleist, 1971. Editor: Les Carnets du Major Thompson, 1959; (with Donner and Eble) The Intellectual Tradition of the West, 1967, 68. Home: 3018 St Mary's Circle Salt Lake City UT 84108

HELCK, CLARENCE PETER, artist; b. N.Y.C., June 17, 1893; s. Henry Philip and Clara (Brand) H.; ed. public sch. and DeWitt Clinton High Sch., N.Y.C.; studied under George Bridgeman, 1915, Sir Frank Brangwyn, 1920-23, Harry Wickey, 1923- 28, Lewis Daniel, 1940-45; student Art Students League, 1912, 23; m. Priscilla Smith, Sept. 30, 1922; 1 son, Jerry Peter. Advt. artist for maj. indsl. and transp. corps., 1918—; illustrator leading publs., 1925-60; represented in permanent collections of Met. Mus. Art (N.Y.C.), Congl. Library (Washington), Mus. of Fine Arts (Phila.), Montagu Motor Mus., Beaulieu, Eng., Cunningham Automotive Mus., Costa Mesa, Cal., L.I. Auto Mus., Southampton, N.Y., Indpls. Speedway Mus., others, also pvt. collections; founding faculty mem. Famous Artists Schs., Westport, Conn., 1948—. Recipient Harvard award, 1929; Art Directors medal, 1931, 36, 41, 44, 51; Phila. Art Dirs. 1st awards, 1939, 40; Chgo. Art Dirs. medal, 1947; Detroit Art Dirs. 1st awards, 1950-52, medals, 1954, 56; Cleve. Art Dirs. medal, 1951; Distinguished Service citation Automotive Old Timers, 1966. Mem. N.A.D., Allied Artists, Am. Watercolor Soc., Audubon Artists, Phila. Watercolor Club, Soc. Illustrators, N.Y. Art Dirs. Club; hon. mem. Vet. Motor Car Club Am., Antique Automobile Club Am., Automobilists Upper Hudson Valley, Conn. Automobile Hist. Soc., H.H. Franklin Club. Presbyn. Author, illustrator The Checkered Flag, 1961 (winner gold medals Salmagundi Club 1961, Soc. Illustrators 1962, Thomas McKean Meml. trophy, 1962, Byron Hull cup, 1962). Editorial staff Bulb Horn, 1945—, Antique Automobile, 1946—, Automobile Quar., 1964—. Peter Helck Gallery founded, Costa Mesa, Cal., 1967. Home and studio: Boston Corners RD 2 Millerton NY 12546

HELD, AL, painter; b. N.Y.C.; student Art Students League. One-man shows Galerie 8, Paris, France, San Francisco Mus. Art; recipient Logan award of Art Inst. Chgo. for painting Genesis, 1964; other works include The Stranger, 7, 1962. Served with USNR, World War II. Address: 940 Broadway New York City NY 10010*

HELD, JULIUS SAMUEL, educator, lectr., writer; b. Mosbach, Germany, Apr. 15, 1905; s. Adolf and Nannette (Seligmann) H.; student U. Heidelberg, 1923, U. Berlin, 1923-24, 27-28, U. Vienna, 1925-26, 29; Ph.D., U. Freiburg, 1930; m. Ingrid-Märta Nordin-Pettersson, Oct. 31, 1936; children—Anna-Brita (Mrs. Louis G. Audette II), James Michael. Came to U.S., 1934, naturalized, 1940. Asst. Staatliche Museen, Berlin, 1931-33; lectr. N.Y. U., 1935-41; Carnegie lectr. Nat. Gallery, Ottawa, Can., 1936-37; lectr. art Barnard Coll., Columbia, 1937-44, asst. prof., 1944-50, asso. prof., 1950-54, prof., 1954-70, prof. emeritus, 1970—, chmn. dept. art history, 1967-70; vis. lectr. Bryn Mawr Coll., 1943-44; vis. prof. New Sch., N.Y.C., 1946-47, Yale, 1954, 58; Robert Sterling Clark prof. art Williams Coll., 1969; Carnegie fellow, 1935; spl. advanced fellow Belgian Am. Ednl. Found., 1947; Guggenheim fellow, 1952-53, 66-67; Fulbright fellow, 1952-53; lectr. Am. Coll. Council for Summer Study Abroad, 1957; cons. Mus. of Art, Ponce, P.R., 1959—; mem. Inst. for Advanced Study, Princeton, 1967. Pres. Am. Friends of Musée Plantin Moretus, Antwerp, 1969—. Mem. Coll. Art Assn. Am., Mediaeval Acad. Am., Renaissance Soc. Am., Société de l'Histoire de l'Art Francais, Deutscher Verein fur Kunstwissenschaft. Author: Dürer's Wirkung auf die Niederländische Kunst, 1931; (with Jan-Albert Goris) Rubens in America, Goris), 1947; Rubens, 1953; Flemish Painting, 1956; Rubens, Selected Drawings, 2 vols., London, 1959; Rembrandt and the Book of Tobit, 1969; Rembrandt's Aristotle and other Rembrandt Studies, 1969. Mem. editorial bd. The Art Bull., 1942—; Art Quar., 1959—. Contbr. articles art periodicals. Home: 21 Claremont Av New York City NY 10027

HELD, RICHARD MARX, educator, psychologist; b. N.Y.C., Oct. 10, 1922; s. Lawrence W. and Tessie (Klein) H.; B.A., Columbia, 1943, B.S., 1944; M.A., Swarthmore Coll., 1948; Ph.D., Harvard, 1952; m. Doris F. Bernays, June 29, 1951; children—Lucas D.B., Julia B., Andrew L.B. Research asst. Swarthmore Coll., 1946-48; research fellow Jackson Hole Wildlife Park, summer 1948; research asst. psycho-acoustic lab., Harvard, 1949-52; teaching fellow, 1950-51, NIH postdoctoral fellow, 1952-53; instr., then asst. prof. psychology Brandeis U., 1953-58, asso. prof., then prof., chmn. dept. psychology, 1958-62; mem. Inst. Advanced Study, Princeton, 1955-56; sr. research fellow NSF, 1962-63,; vis. prof. Mass. Inst. Tech., Cambridge , 1962-63; prof. psychology, 1963—. Mem. com. vision Armed Forces-NRC; mem. exptl. psychology study sect. NIH, 1964-66, chmn. 1966-68. Fellow Am. Acad. Arts and Scis., Am. Acad. Optometry, A.A.A.S., Am. Psychol. Assn.; mem. Eastern Psychol. Assn. (dir.), Internat. Brain Research Orgn., Soc. Neuroscis., Soc. Exptl. Psychologists, Psychonomic Soc., Sigma Xi. Co-editor Psychologische Forschung; cons. editor Jour. Exptl. Psychology; editorial bd. Perspectives in Biology and Medicine, Perception. Home: 102 Appleton St Cambridge MA 02138

HELD, WARREN HOWARD, Jr., educator; b. Allentown, Pa., Oct. 9, 1928; s. Warren H. and Evelyn (Muschlitz) H.; B.A., Princeton, 1950; M.A., Yale, 1952, Ph.D., 1955; m. Gerardina Vuyk, Sept. 1, 1951; children—Amy Ellen, Warren H. III. Instr. Fairleigh Dickinson U., 1956-58, asst. prof., 1958-61, asso. prof., 1961-67; asso. dean liberal arts, prof. classics U. N.H., 1967—. Served with AUS, 1954-56; comdr. Portsmouth Power Squadron, 1971—. Mem. Classical Assn. N.H. (hon.), Linguistic Soc. Am., Am. Oriental Soc., Classical Assn. New Eng., Am. Sch. Oriental Research. Home: 1 Woodridge Rd Durham NH 03824

HELDENFELS, FREDERICK WILLIAM, Jr., contractor; b. Beeville, Tex., Sept. 5, 1911; s. Frederick William and Alice (Cullen) H.; B.S. in Civil Engring., Tex. A. and M. Coll., 1933; m. Rae Orms, Mar. 4, 1934 (dec. Feb. 1967); children—Frederick William III, John Orms; m. 2d, Paula Jackson Gierhart, Sept. 20, 1969. Partner Heldenfels Bros., contractors, Corpus Christi, Tex., 1936—, Heldenfels Farms, 1951—; v.p. Harris Concrete Co., Inc., 1941-66, pres., 1966—; v.p. Counts Concrete Co.; sec. treas. Heldenfels Properties, Inc.; trustee, partner H.C. Heldenfels oil and gas operators, 1949—; dir. 1st Nat. Bank, Rockport, Tex. Corpus Christi State Nat. Bank; pres. Constructor Mag., 1958- 59. Mem. constrn. industry adv. com. OPA, 1951-53; dir. Inter-Am. Fedn. Constrn. Industry, 1960-66; del. Inter-Am. constrn. Congress, Mexico City, 1960, Rio de Janeiro, Brazil, 1962, Lima, Peru, 1964. Pres. bd. govs. United Community Services of Corpus Christi, 1963; chmn. bd. regents Del Mar Coll., 1963—; bd. Tex. Transp. Inst. of Tex. A. and M. Coll. System. Cited by Tex. Ho. of Reps. for outstanding service, 1957. Mem. Asso. Gen. Contractors Am. (pres. Tex. hwy.-heavy br. 1949-51; nat. chmn. hwy. div. 1952-53; nat. pres. 1958; co-chmn. joint coop. com. with Am. Assn. State Hwy. Ofcls. 2954-56), Cons. Constructors Council Am., U.S., Corpus Christi (dir.; Big Thinker award 1958; chmn. indsl. com. 1963-66) chambers commerce, Tex. Employers Ins. Assn. (dir.), Tau Beta Pi. Episcopalian (vestry). Home: 5015 Ocean Dr Corpus Christi TX 78412 Office: PO Box 4957 Corpus Christi TX 78408

HELDER, ROGER J., automobile co. exec. ; b. Grand Rapids, Mich., July 7, 1919; s. John L. and Dora (Scott) H.; A.B., Calvin Coll., 1941; M.B.A., U. Mich., 1947; m. Marian Vanderberg, Aug. 4, 1942; children-Roger J., Marga, Maelois. Sr. accountant Touche, Ross, Bailey & Smart, C.P.A.'s, Detroit, 1947-50; plant controller Ford Motor Co., 1951-57; corp. comptroller Chrysler Corp., 1957-69, v.p., corporate comptroller, 1969—. Served to lt. USNR, 1942-46. C.P.A., Mich. Mem. Financial Execs. Inst., Mich. Assn. C.P.A.'s. Home: 20240 Audette St Dearborn MI 48124 Office: 341 Massachusetts St Highland Park MI 48231

HELDMAN, ALAN WOHL, lawyer; b. Birmingham, Ala., Mar. 12, 1936; s. Max and Josephine (Wohl) H.; A.B. cum laude, Vanderbilt, 1957; J.D., Harvard, 1961; m. Ann Huntington, Jan. 28, 1961; children—Alan Wohl, Samuel H., Katherine Ann. Admitted to Ala. bar 1961, since practiced in Birmingham; asso. Deramus & Johnston, 1961-65; partner Deramus, Johnston, Barton, Proctor & Swedlaw, 1965—. Dir. at large Ala. Clean Air Com., 1970—. Served to capt. U.S. Army, 1958-65. Mem. Am., Ala., Birmingham bar assns. Democrat. Jewish religion. Club: Young Mens Business (past pres.) (Birmingham). Home: 3857 Cromwell Dr Birmingham AL 35243 Office: Bank for Savs Bldg Birmingham AL 35203

HELDRIDGE, RICHARD WALLACE, banker; b. Wessington Springs, S.D., Sept. 18, 1918; s. Alvin A. and Helen (De Maranville) H.; student U. Ia., 1936-40; m. Shirley Ann Van Decar, Jan. 5, 1943; children—Kathryn Helen (Mrs. Charles Tyson), Michael W., Dan Richard, Sarah Elizabeth. With Northwestern Nat. Bank, Mpls., 1946-47; v.p. N.W. Bancorp., 1957-59; exec. v.p., dir. 1st Nat. Bank Black Hills, Rapid City, S.D., 1960; v.p. Crocker Nat. Bank, Sacramento, 1961-64, v.p., mgr., Sacramento main office, 1964-67, sr. v.p., mgr., No. region, 1967-71, sr. v.p., regional mgr. Los Angeles met., 1971—; dir. Capital Fed. Savs. & Loan Assn., Sacramento. Vice pres. United Crusades Cal., 1970—; met. vice chmn., chmn. Nat. Alliance Businessmen, 1970—; pres. Sacramento Clearing House Assn., 1964; vice chmn. Sacramento Host Com., 1971—. Trustee Sutter Community Hosps.; bd. dirs., exec. com. Mercy Hosp. Served to capt. AUS, 1941-46, to lt. col., 1950-53; Korea. Decorated Bronze Star. Mem. Phi Gamma Delta. Republican. Conglist. Mason. Clubs: Sutter, Del Paso Country (Sacramento). Home: 6341 Rio Bonito Dr Carmichael CA 95608 Office: 400 Capitol Mall Sacramento CA 95814

HELDRING, FREDERICK, banker; b. Amsterdam, Netherlands, Mar. 25, 1924; s. Ernst and Marie (Bungener) H.; student Free U., Amsterdam, 2 years; grad. Wharton Sch., U. Pa., 1951; m. Colette Barr, June 12, 1954; children—Ernest Martin, James Alexander, Alicia Ann, Mary Carroll, Louise Marguerite, Claudia Colette, Theodore Barr. With internat. dir. Phila. Nat. Bank, 1951—, v.p., 1962-63, head internat. div., 1963-66, sr. v.p., now vice chmn. Pres., Pa.- Bahia Partners of Alliance, Phila. Center for Internat. Visitors, Netherland-Am. Found. Served with Royal Netherlands Marine Corps. Home: Health Rd Merion PA 19066 Office: Phila Nat Bank Broad and Chestnut Sts PA 19101

HELFAT, JERE NOEL, corp. exec.; b. N.Y.C., May 11, 1925; s. J. Nathan and Betty (Sloane) H.; B.Mgmt. Engring., 1944; children—Constance Eve, Daniel Lawrence. With Reliance Electric (Can.), Ltd., 1950-54, Reliance Electric Co., Cleve., 1954-57; mgmt. cons. Booz, Allen & Hamilton, Cleve., 1957-59; v.p. mfg. Bobbie Brooks, Inc., 1959-61; pres. Jeré Helfat Assos. Inc., mgmt. cons., Cleve.; pres., dir. Koracorp Industries Inc., San Francisco, 1966- -. Served with AUS, 1943-46. Office: 611 Mission St San Francisco CA Mailing Address:

HELFENSTEIN, LEONARD, lawyer, govt. ofcl.; b. Phila., Oct. 17, 1911; s. Charles and Kate (Gullish) H.; B.S. in Econs., U. Pa., 1932, LL.B., 1935, Gowen Meml. fellowship, 1935-37; m. Martha Sharp, Mar. 23, 1938; children-Carolyn Sybil (Mrs. Philip S. Hollman Myrna Claire, Admitted to Pa. bar, 1935, since practiced Phila.; div. dir. opinion writing SEC, 1951-66, dir. office opinions and review, 1966—. Mem. Fed., Pa., Phila. bar assns., Acad. Polit. Sci., Supreme Ct. Bar. Contbr. articles to legal jour. Home: 1371 Underwood St Washington DC 20012 Office: 400 N Capital St Washington DC 20025

HELFERICH, ELMER R., lawyer; b. Utica, Mich., 1894; B.S., U. Mich., 1932; LL.B., George Washington U., 1926. Admitted to D.C. bar, 1926, N.Y. State bar, 1928; mem. firm Watson, Leavenworth, Kelton and Taggard, N.Y.C. Mem. Assn. Bar City N.Y., Am. Bar Assn., N.Y., Am. patent law assns., Delta Theta Phi. Office: 100 Park Av New York City NY 10017*

HELFFERICH, DONALD LAWRENCE, coll. chancellor; b. Bath, Pa., Apr. 24, 1898; s. William Ursinus (D.D.) and Nora Helena (Shuler) H.; student Mercersburg Acad., 1914-17; A.B., Ursinus Coll., 1921, LL.D., 1952; LL.B., Yale, 1924; LL.D., Temple U., 1959; m. Anna Alverda Knauer, July 14, 1925; children—Ilse An (Mrs. Karl Heinz Munzinger), William Ursinus. Legal dept., asst. store mgr. Gimbel Bros., Inc., Phila., 1925-36; dir. Ursinus Coll. since 1927, exec. v.p., 1936-58, pres., 1958-71, chancellor, 1971—; dir. Upper Darby (Pa.) Nat. Bank, 1936-63, exec. v.p., 1936-58; sr. v.p. Girard Trust Corn Exchange Bank, Phila., 1958-63; chmn. bd. French Creek Granite Co., 1948-68; dir. Presbyn. Minister Fund for Life Ins. Mem. Pa. Council Edn., 1940-54, Bd. Vocational Rehab., 1944-54; co. chmn. citizens com. Hoover Report. Trustee Phila. Coll. Osteopathy, 1936-48; bd. regents Mercersburg (Pa.) Academy. Served as 2d lt. A.C., U.S. Army, 1917-19. Mem. Nat. Council Chs. of Christ in America (v.p.-at-large 1960-63), Pa. Soc. S.A.R., Pa. German Folklore Soc. (financial sec. 1956), Am. Legion, Am. Acad. Polit. Sci.,

Phi Delta Phi. Republican. United Ch. of Christ (elder; dir. bd. pensions and relief). Clubs: University (N.Y.C.); Yale (Phila). Home: Harmonyville Star Route Pottstown PA 19464

HELFFERICH, REGINALD HUMPHREY, church exec.; b. Bath, Pa., June 15, 1905; s. William Ursinus and Nora (Shuler) H.; student Wesleyan U., Middletown, Conn., 1924-27; B.A., Ursinus Coll., 1928; D.D., Chgo. Theol. Sem., 1949; m. Virginia Merritt, Oct. 19, 1932 (dec. Sept. 1957); m. 2d, Ruth Gulick Ernest, July 13, 1963; children—Merritt Randolph, Deborah Mary (Mrs. Sirreno Scranton), Alice Virginia (Mrs. Loren Orsini), Honora Hope (Mrs. Russell Seidler). Ordained to the ministry Ch. of Christ, 1932; pastor St. Paul's Reformed Ch., Butler, Pa., 1932-34, Christ Ch., Bath, 1934- 51; European dep. dir. Ch. World Service Nat. Council Chs. of Christ U.S.A., N.Y.C., 1949-51, also v.p., bd. dirs., vice chmn. bd. mgrs.; dir. U.S. Zone Germany, Dept. Reconstruction, World Council Chs., 1949- 51; exec. sec. Commn. World Service, St. Louis, 1951-62; gen. sec., bd. dirs. div. World Service United Ch. Bd. World Ministries, St. Louis, N.Y.C., Boston, 1962—; chmn. Africa div. Dept. of Missions, Nat. Council Chs. U.S.A.; v.p., bd. dirs. Meals for Millions Found.; treas., dir., mem. exec. com. Agrl. Missions, Inc.; v.p. Shelter for World, Inc.; exec. sec. congl. Christian Service Com., Inc., 1961—; chmn. bd. Technoserv.; exec. com., dir. Com. For Am. Relief Everywhere, Inc.; treas. U.S. Com. For Refugees, Inc.; dir., treas. Heifer Project, Inc.; bd. dirs. United Bd. For Christian Higher Edn. Asia. Chmn. Bd. Health, Bath, 1941-43; pres. Bd. Edn., Bath, 1943-45. Bd. dirs. Tb and Health Soc., Bethlehem, Pa., Childrens Aid Soc., Easton, Pa., Bethlehem council Boy Scouts Am., Crippled Childrens Soc., Blind Soc. Northampton County, Pa., Pusan (Korea) Childrens Charity Hosp., Internat. Vol. Services, Inc. Am. Immigration and Citizenship Conf., Internat. Devel. Consortium, Internat. ednl. Devel., inc. (v.p.), Tibetan Found., Tibet Soc., CODEL, Inc. Decorated Comdr's Cross Order Merit Pres. German Fed. Republic, 1961. Mem. Alpha Chi Rho. Democrat. Mason. Author: Doorways and Dormers, 1934; Footsteps of the Fathers, 1941. Editor The Home News, 1940-50. Home: RD No 1 Amston CT 06231 Office: 475 Riverside Dr New York City NY 10027

HELGESON, ARLAN CLAYTON, univ. dean; b. Holmen, Wis., Nov. 29, 1921; s. Alfred Carlton and Tillie Olava (Beito) H.; B.S., La Crosse (Wis.) State Coll., 1943; M.S., U. Wis., 1948, Ph.D., 1952; m. Candace Annette Stephenson, Jan. 28, 1944; children—Fleur L., J. Todd, Eric S. Mem. faculty Ill. State U., Normal, 1951, prof. history, 1961, dean Grad. Sch., 1962—, vis. lectr. U. Wis., summer 1958. Mem. Am. Hist. Assn., Orgn. Am. Historians, Ill. Hist. Soc., Assn. Higher Edn., Am. Assn. U. Profs. (asso.). Author: Farms in the Cutover 1962; co- author: The United States of America, A History for Young Citizens, 1963. Home: 714 N School St Normal IL 61761

HELIES, JOHN CLAUDE, mfg. co. exec.; b. Elizabeth, N.J., Jan. 16, 1917; s. Marian Pierre and Mary Elizabeth (Mead) H.; B.S., Holy Cross Coll., 1939; postgrad. N.Y. U., 1940; m. Sally Ann James, Feb. 17, 1941; children—John Claude, Pamela (Mrs. James Slater 3d), Sally Ann. With E.A. Labs., 1939- 40, 45-47, shipbldg. div. Bethlehem Steel Co., 1940-45; with Gen. Electric Co., 1947-54, gen. mgr. appliance control dept., 1951-54; with Dresser Industries, 1954-63, pres. security engring. div., 1959-63; with Scovill Mfg. Co., 1963—, v.p. corporate planning, group v.p., exec. v.p., 1966-69, pres., 1969—, also dir. Home: River Rd Roxbury CT 06783 Office: 99 Mill Rd Waterbury CT 06720

HELIKER, JOHN, artist; b. Yonkers, N.Y., Jan. 17, 1909; s. John Edward and Jane (MacLaughlin) H.; student Art Students League, N.Y.C.; studied with Kimon Nicolaides, Kenneth Hayes Miller, Boardman Robinson; A.F.D. (hon.), Colby Coll., 1966. Asso. prof. Columbia U. Paintings exhibited Whitney Mus., Corcoran Gallery Art, Toledo Mus. Art, Va. Mus. Fine Arts, Richmond, Art Inst. Chgo., Met. Mus. Art, Carnegie Inst., Pa. Acad. Fine Arts, Worcester (Mass.) Mus. Art, Cleve. Mus. Art, Fine Arts Club, Chgo., Mus. Modern Art, N.Y.C.; one man shows Maynard Walker Gallery, 1938, 41, Kraushaar Gallery, 1945, 51, 54, 68, 71; work represented Met. Mus., Phila. Mus., Pa. Acad., New Britain Mus., Telfair Acad., Walker Art Center, U. Neb., Fogg Mus. Art, Addison Gallery Am. Art, Andover, Mass., Corcoran Gallery, Whitney Mus., San Francisco Mus. of Art, in Brussels World Fair, 1958, Worlds Fair, Osaka, 1970; retrospective Whitney Mus. Am. Art, 1968. Recipient Nat. Inst. Arts and Letters award ($1000), 1957; Am. Acad. Arts and Letters award, 1967; Ford Found. purchase award, 1960; fellow in the Am. Acad., Rome, 1948; Guggenheim fellow. 1951. Mem. Nat. Inst. Arts and Letters. Office: Sch of Painting Columbia U New York City NY 10027

HELIN, FRANK EDWARD, retail mdse. corp. exec.; b. Lincoln, Neb., Jan. 9, 1922; s. George T. and Mable (Gradoville) H.; B.S. in Bus. Adminstrn., U. So. Cal., 1948, LL.B., 1951; m. Betty Marie Bailey, Jan. 23, 1943; children—Karen Jane (Mrs. Mark A. Curley), Patricia Ann (Mrs. Michael J. McMillin). Individual practice certified pub. accounting, Los Angeles, 1948-60; controller Fedco, Inc., Los Angeles, 1960-68, treas., 1968—. Served with USNR, 1942-45; PTO. C.P.A., Cal. Mem. Beta Alpha Psi, Beta Gamma Sigma. Home: 4615 Fairfield Dr Coronadel Mar CA 92625 Office: 1935 Tubeway Los Angeles CA 90022

HELION, JEAN, painter; b. Couterne, France, Apr. 21, 1904; s. Louis Bichier and Marguerite (Bernier) H.; self-educated; m. Jacqueline Ventadour, Aug. 7, 1963; children—Jean-Jacques Louis, Fabrice, David, Nicolas. Figurative painter until 1928; abstractive painter, 1928-39; mem. Groupe Art Concret, 1929; founder Abstraction Creation, 1931; ind. artist, 1934—; new figurative period, 1943-46; one-man exhbns. include Cahier d'Art, Paris, 1956, 58, 61, Retrospective Abstract, Paris, 1962, Retrospective, all periods, Gallery Modern Art, N.Y.C., 1964, Retrospective Drawings, Paris, 1964, Retrospective, London, 1965, Galerie du Dragon, Paris, 1966, 67, Galerie Arcanes, Brussels, 1967, Willard Gallery, N.Y.C., 1967, Galerie II Fante di Spade, Rome, 1968, Galeria Mutina, Modena, Italy, 1968, Galeria Eunomia, Milan, Italy, 1969, Mus. Rouen, Rennes, 1970, St. Omer, Beauvais, Brest, Nantes, others, retrospective, all periods Galeries Nationales, Grand Palais, Paris, 1970; Galerie Weiller, Paris, 1971, Galerie Henriotte Gomes, Paris, 1971. represented numerous group exhbns., pvt. and pub. collections. Served with French Army, 1940-42. Author: They Shall Not Have Me, 1943. Address: 4 rue Michelet Paris France

HELLAWELL, ROBERT, legal educator; b. Long Island, N.Y., Jan. 24, 1928; s. Edwin V. and Nora D. (Mahoney) H.; A.B., Williams Coll., 1950; LL.B., Columbia, 1953; m. Jane Buck, June 16, 1951; 1 dau., Kathleen Abbott. Admitted to N.Y. bar, 1954, Ohio bar, 1955; law clk. U.S. Circuit Ct. judge, 1953-54; with firm Jones, Day, Cockley & Reavis, Cleve., 1954-61, partner, 1961; atty., adviser formation Peace Corps, 1961, dir. projects in Tanganyika, 1961- 63, dep. asso. dir. corps, 1963-64; asso. prof. law Columbia Law Sch., N.Y.C., 1964-67, prof. law, 1967—, dir. African Law Center, 1971—; vis. prof. U. Ghana, 1969; cons. admiralty law UN Commn. Internat. Trade Law, 1971. Served with AUS, 1946-48; Korea. Mem. Delta Kappa Epsilon, Phi Delta Phi. Co-author: The Study of Federal Tax Law, 1971. Notes editor Columbia Law Rev., 1952-53. Home: Margaret Ct Demarest NJ 07627 Office: Columbia Law Sch New York City NY 10027

HELLEBRANDT, EDWIN THEODORE, educator; b. Chgo., June 3, 1904; s. Frank Joseph and Anna (Preucil) H.; B.S., U. Chgo., 1926; M.S., U. Wis., 1927, Ph.D., 1933; m. Melba Rowena White, Dec. 19, 1931; 1 dau., Mary Anna. Draftsman, Western Electric Co., Hawthorne, Ill., 1923; research fellow Inst. Land Econ. and Pub. Utilities, Chgo., 1928; instr. econs. U. N.D., 1928-29; asst. prof. econs. Ohio U., Athens, 1929-37, asso. prof., 1937-47, prof. econs. and mgmt., 1947—, formerly chmn. dept.; staff, mgmt. devel. inst. IMEDE, Switzerland, 1959-60; sr. partner Mgmt. Research Asso., Athens; mgmt. cons. to industry. Served from capt. to lt. col., Army Res., 1942-56 . Mem. Am. Econ. Assn., Inst. Mgmt. Soc., Acad. Mgmt., Innovation Group, Am. Soc. Quality Control, Am. Assn. U. Profs., Res. Officers Assn., Soc. Advancement Mgmt., Phi Mu Alpha, Delta Sigma Pi. Kiwanian. Author: (with John Stinson) General Business Management Simulation, 1965. Home: 4 Cable Lane Athens OH 45701

HELLENBRAND, SAMUEL HENRY, corp. ofcl.; b. N.Y.C., Nov. 11, 1916; s. Louis H. and Fannie (Cohen) H.; LL.B., Brooklyn Law Sch. St. Lawrence U., 1941, LL.M., 1942; m. Sheila Kurzrok, Dec. 5, 1948; children—Kathy Noreen, Linda Caryn. Admitted to N.Y. bar, 1942; with N.Y. Central R.R., 1942-68, atty., asst. to gen. atty., tax atty., 1942-52, gen. tax atty., 1952-56, dir. taxes finance dept., 1956-63, v.p. planning and devel., 1963-64, v.p. real estate, 1964-68; v.p. indsl. devel. and real estate Penn Central Co., 1968-70, v.p. real estate and taxes, 1970-71; pres. Pa. Co., 1970-71; v.p. exec. asst. to pres., dir. real estate affairs Internat. Tel. & Tel. Co., 1971—. Mem. Am., N.Y. State bar assns., Nat. Tax Assn., Assn. Bar City N.Y. Home: 177 E 75th St New York City NY 10021 Office: 466 Lexington Av New York City NY 10017

HELLENDALE, ROBERT, paper co. exec.; b. N.Y.C., Nov. 19, 1917; s. Sidney Louis and Madge (Zauner) H.; B.A., Wesleyan U., Middletown, Conn., 1939; LL.B., Harvard, 1942; m. Jill Hibben, Aug. 29, 1945; children—William C., Rufus P., Sheila. Admitted to N.Y. bar, 1946, Me. bar, 1954; practice in N.Y.C., 1946-54; engaged as atty. and pper co. exec., 1954—; v.p. Great No. Paper Co., 1964—; exec. v.p., sec. Great No. NeKoosa Corp., 1970—. Served with AUS, 1941-45. Home: 21 Shoal Point Lane Riverside CT Office: 75 Prospect St Stamford CT

HELLER, AUSTIN NORMAN, state govt. ofcl.; b. Elizabeth, N.J., Aug. 18, 1914; s. Samuel Sydney and Bessie (Rosenfield) H.; B.A., Johns Hopkins, 1938, postgrad., 1939; M.S., Ia. State U., 1941; m. Frances Sandler, Mar. 21, 1943; children—Richard D., Susan S. (Mrs. Jeffrey S. Zakem). Supr. indsl. waste devel. sect. Allied Chem. Corp., N.Y.C., 1948-60, coordinator long range planning, 1960-61; dep. chief, tech. asst. br. div. air pollution USPHS, Cin., 1961-66; commr. Dept. of Air Resources, N.Y.C., 1966-70; sec. Del. Dept. Natural Resources and Environmental Control, Dover, 1970—; research asso. civil engring. N.Y.U., 1946-48; adj. prof. environmental engring. Cooper Union, 1966-67; adj. asso. prof. environmental health Columbia, 1966-70; trustee Engring. Index, Inc. Served with USNR, 1942-46; PTO. Recipient award outstanding leadership Am. Soc. M.E., 1967, Humanitarian award Children's Asthma Research Inst. and Hosp., 1969; named engr. of distinction Engrs. Joint Council, 1970. Licensed profl. engr., N.Y. Diplomate Am. Acad. Environmental Engrs. Fellow Am. Pub. Health Assn., Am. Inst. Chemists; mem. Am. Inst. Chem. Engrs., Fedn. Water Pollution Control Assn., Air Pollution Control Assn. Republican. Jewish religion. Mason. Contbr. articles profl. jours. Home: 50 Greenway Sq M-23 Dover DE 19901 Office: Dept Natural Resources and Environmental Control D St and Legislative Av Dover DE 19901

HELLER, CHARLES KAYE, mfr., importer and exporter; b. Hostka, Czechoslovakia, Sept. 26, 1897; s. Theodor and Hermine (Kahn) H.; ed. high sch., Comml. Acad., Prague, Export Acad., Vienna; div.; children—Raymond A., Ruth A., Peter R., James A. Came to U.S., 1939, naturalized, 1944, Importer and exporter of fruit, offices in Usti, Czechoslovakia, Hamburg, Germany, Rotterdam, Holland, 1922-39; dir. shareholder Jaffa Citrus Co., Ltd., Jaffa-Tel Aviv, Palestine, growers, packers and exporters of citrus fruit, 1934-45; pres. Empire State Trading Co., Inc., N.Y.C., 1940—; pres. Helco Enterprises, Inc. and Helco Products, Inc., N.Y.C., mfrs., importers and exporter of food products, 1942—, 40 Hudson St. Corp., N.Y.C., real estate owners, 1944—, Empire Dehydrated Products, Inc., N.Y.C., Belmont Products Corp., 1948—, chmn. bd. Empire Dehydrated Products (Can.), Ltd., Montreal, 1951—. Home: 102-55 67th Dr Forest Hills NY 11375 Office: 60-05 37th Av Woodside NY 11377

HELLER, ELINOR RAAS, univ. regent; b. San Francisco, Oct. 3, 1904; d. Alfred E. and Ida B. (Fisher) Raas; B.A., Mills Coll., 1925, LL.D., 1952; m. Edward Hellman Heller, May 26, 1925 (dec. Dec. 1961); children—Clarence E., Alfred E., Elizabeth. Trustee Mills Coll., 1932-42, 46-56, 57-67; adv. com. San Francisco State Coll., 1950-61; bd. regents U. Cal., 1961—. Chmn. edn. sect. Cal. and Mass. war finance div. Treasury Dept., 1941-45; mem. council arthritis and metabolic diseases NIH, 1949-52. Dir. Stanford Bank; regional adv. bd. Union Bank. Mem. Democratic Nat. Com. from Cal., 1944-52, also past mem. exec. com.; del. Dem. Nat. Conv., 1944, 48, 56. Bd. dirs. Childrens Health Council Mid- Peninsula, Bay Area Ednl. TV Assn.; bd. trustees, exec. com. World Affairs Council No. Cal. Mem. League Women Voters (past bd. dirs. Cal., San Francisco and Palo Alto), Phi Beta Kappa. Author: (with David Magee) Bibliography of Grabhorn Press, 1915-1940, 1940. Address: 99 Faxon Rd Atherton CA 94025

HELLER, ERICH, educator, author; b. Komotau, Bohemia, Mar. 27, 1911; s. Alfred and Else (Hoenig) H.; Doctorate in Law and German Lit., Charles U., Prague, Czechoslovakia, 1935; Ph.D., Cambridge (Eng.) U., 1948; Litt.D. (hon.), Emory U., 1965. Came to the U.S., 1959. Asst. lectr. German, London Sch. Econs., 1943-45; lectr. German, dir. studies modern langs. Peterhouse Coll., Cambridge U., 1945-48; prof. German, U. Wales, 1948-60; vis. prof. U. Hamburg, 1947, U. Göttinger, 1948, U. Bonn, 1948, Harvard, 1953-54, Brandeis U., 1957-58; prof. German, Northwestern U., 1960-66, prof. humanities, 1966-68, Avalon prof. humanities, 1968—; vis. prof. German, U. Heidelberg, summer 1963; Carnegie vis. prof. humanities Mass. Inst. Tech., fall 1963. Recipient Kulturkreis lit. prize German industry, 1958; Johann-Heinnich-Merck prize for essay and lit. criticism German Acad. Lang. and Lit. , 1969. Mem. Am. Acad. Arts and Letters, Bayerische Akademie der Schönen KuEste, Deutsche Akademie Für Sprache und Dichtung; P.E.N. Club (Germany). Author: The Disinherited Mind, Essays in Modern German Literature and Thought, 1952; The Ironic German, a Study of Thomas Mann, 1958; The Artist's Journey into the Interior and Other Essays, 1965; Essays Über Goethe, 1970. Editor Studies in Modern European Lit. and Thought, 1950-68; editor: Kafka's Letter to his Fiancée, 1967. Contbr. profl. and lit. jours. Address: Dept German Northwestern U Evanston IL 60201

HELLER, FRANCIS HOWARD, educator; b. Vienna, Austria, Aug. 24, 1917; s. Charles A. and Lily (Grunwald) H.; came to U.S., 1938, naturalized, 1943; student U. Vienna, 1935-37; LL.B., U. Va., 1941, M.A., 1941, Ph.D., 1948; m. Donna De Munn, Sept. 3, 1949; 1 son, Denis Wayne. Asst. prof. govt. Coll. William and Mary, 1947; asst. prof. polit. sci. U. Kan., Lawrence, 1948-51, asso. prof., 1951- 56, prof., 1956—, asso. dean Coll. Liberal Arts and Scis., 1957-66, asso. dean of faculties, 1966-67, dean, 1967-70, vice chancellor for acad. affairs, 1970—; vis. prof. Inst. Advanced Studies, Vienna, 1965. Mem. Kan. Commn. on Constl. Revision, 1957-61; mem. Lawrence City Plan Commn., 1957-63; ednl. adv. commn. U.S. Army Command and Gen. Staff Coll., 1969—. Bd. dirs. Harry S. Truman Library Found. (vice chmn.), Inst. Community Studies. Served from pvt. to 1st lt., arty., AUS, 1942-47, to capt., 1951-52; maj. Res. ret. Decorated Silver Star, Bronze Star with cluster. Mem. Am. Polit. Sci. Assn. (exec. council 1958-60), Am. Assn. Univ. Profs., Midwest Conf. Polit. Sci., Phi Beta Kappa, Pi Sigma Alpha (mem. nat. council 1958-60). Author: Introduction to American Constitutional Law, 1952; The Presidency: A Modern Perspective, 1960. Home: 1648 Stratford Rd Lawrence KS 66044

HELLER, ISIDORE, educator; b. Safad, Turkey, Feb. 18, 1906; s. Samuel and Pearl (Binderly) H.; student U. Vienna, 1929-34; Sc.D., U. Geneva, 1950; m. Caroline Freudmann, Dec. 25, 1928; 1 dau., Gertrud. Came to U.S., 1950, naturalized, 1956. Research asso. George Washington U., 1951-56, professorial lectr., 1954-61; dir. mgmt. sci. staff U.S. Dept. Navy, 1956-61; research asso. Stanford U., 1961-63; prof. math. Catholic U., 1963—; cons. U.S. Arms Controls and Disarmament Agy., 1966-70, RAND Corp., 1961—. Mem. Am. Math. Soc., Econom. Soc., Soc. Ind. and Applied Math., Washington Acad. Sci., Sigma Xi. Home: 12115 Long Ridge Lane Bowie MD 20715 Office: Catholic U Washington DC 20017

HELLER, JACK ISAAC, govt. ofcl.; b. Passaic, N.J., July 12, 1932; s. Aaron and Ruth (Brown) H.; A.B., U. Chgo., 1952; LL.B., Columbia, 1958; m. Naomi Birnbaum, Mar. 8, 1959; children—Michael Adam, Daniel Noah, Rafael Gustav. Teaching fellow, research asst. internat. program in taxation Harvard Law Sch., 1958-61, sr. tax adviser OAS, Washington, 1961-62; tax economist Latin Am. bur. U.S. AID, 1962-65; with office of gen. counsel AID, 1965-66; legal adviser U.S. AID, Brazil, 1966-67, asst. dir., 1967-68; dir. Office of Devel. Programs, Latin Am. Bur. U.S. AID, 1969—. Served with AUS, 1953-55. Fellow Inst. Policy Studies, Washington, 1963-65. Author: Tax Incentives for Industry in Less Developed Countries, 1963. Home: 3431 Porter St NW Washington DC 20016 Office: State Dept Washington DC 20523

HELLER, JAMES, mfg. co. exec.; b. N.Y.C., Apr. 23, 1911; s. Isidore and Emma (Krinsky) H.; B.S. in Bus. Adminstrn., Lehigh U., 1931; LL.B., Columbia, 1934; m. Audrey Mancher, Sept. 22, 1940; children—Barbara (Mrs. Edgar Freitag), Steven Peter. Admitted to N.Y. bar, 1934; pres. Heller Bros. Packing Co., 1952—. Founder Albert Einstein Coll. Medicine. Home: 900 Fifth Av New York City NY 10021 Office: 600 Madison Av New York City NY 10022

HELLER, JAMES JOHN, coll. adminstr.; b. Utica, N.Y., May 5, 1921; s. John Frederick and Madeline (Forgy) H.; B.A. in Philosophy, Tex. Christian U., 1944; B.D., Princeton Theol Sem., 1947, Th.D. in New Testament Theology, 1955; m. Alice Mackey Wallace, Sept. 2, 1944; children—Janet Ann, Stephen James, Mark Jonathan, Elizabeth Grace. Ordained minister Moravian Ch., 1952; prof. bibl. theology Moravian Theol. Sem., Bethlehem, Pa., 1950-61, v.p. for academic affairs and dean of coll., 1961—; ednl. cons., evaluation team chmn. Middle States Assn. Secondary Schs. and Colls., 1968—. Mem. Blue Ribbon Search Com. for selection new supt. Bethlehem Area Sch. Dist., 1966. Trustee Moravian Preparatory Sch., Bethlehem. New Testament Theology fellow Princeton Theol. Sem., 1948-49. Mem. Am. Conf. Academic Deans, Eastern Assn. Academic Deans and Advisers of Students. Author: A Faith for Life, 1961. Contbr. profl. jours. Home: 1331 Bonnie Av Bethlehem PA 18017

HELLER, JEROME, dept. store exec., lawyer; b. N.Y.C., Feb. 3, 1938; s. Samuel and Ruth (Rosenberg) H.; B.A., U. Vt., 1959; LL.B., Cornell U., 1965; m. Phyllis C. Bromberg, Dec. 22, 1957; children—Stacie Lynn, Andrew Jordan. Admitted to N.Y. bar, 1965; mem. firm Leaf, Kurzman & Deull, N.Y.C., 1965-67; asst. corporate counsel Arlan's Dept. Stores, Inc., N.Y.C., 1967-70, sec., corporate counsel, 1970-71, sec., v.p., corp. counsel, 1971—. Served with USAF, 1960-63. Mem. Am. Bar Assn., Bar Assn. City of N.Y., Cornell Law Assn., Phi Sigma Delta. Club: Cornell of N.Y.C. Home: 150 E 84th St New York City NY 10028 Office: Arlan's Department Stores Inc 393 Seventh Av New York City NY 10001

HELLER, JOHN LEWIS, educator; b. Riegelsville, Pa., Oct. 2, 1906; s. Glenn Conley and Mary Belle (Stahr) H.; A.B., Haverford Coll., 1927; A.M., Princeton, 1928, Ph.D., 1933; m. Suzanne Wallace Finley, June 20, 1936; children—Susan Stahr (Mrs. Edwin J. Anderson), Mary Patterson (Mrs. David B. Rawcliffe). Instr. Greek and Latin, Wesleyan U., Middletown, Conn., 1928-29; instr. Latin, Haverford Coll., 1929-31; instr. classics Allegheny Coll., 1933-37; asst. prof. classical langs. U. Minn., 1937-45, asso. prof., 1945-47, prof., chmn. dept., 1947-49; prof. classics U. Ill., Urbana, 1949—, head dept., 1949-66, curator Classical Mus., 1949-61; Mellon vis. prof. classics U. Pitts., 1969-70. Mem. Am. Philol. Assn. (pres. 1966), Archaeol. Inst. Am., Soc. Biblphy. Nat. History, Phi Beta Kappa. Episcopalian. Contbr. profl. jours. Home: 702 W Indiana Av Urbana IL 61801

HELLER, JOHN RODERICK, Jr., cancer inst. exec.; b. Oconee County, S.C., Feb. 27, 1905; s. Dr. John R. and Elizabeth (Smith) H.; B.S., Clemson (S.C.) Coll., 1925; M.D., Emory U., 1929; m. Susie May Ayres, Dec. 27, 1934; children—John Roderick III, Hanes Ayres, Winder McGavock. Intern So. Pacific Gen. Hosp., San Francisco, 1929-30; resident Mills Meml. Hosp., San Mateo, Cal., 1930; clin. Ga. Dept. Health, Brunswick, 1931; acting asst. surgeon USPHS, 1931-34; with regular commd. corps, 1934-57, asst. surgeon gen. with grade brig. gen., 1957-60; med. dir., chief div. venereal disease, 1943; dir. Nat. Cancer Inst., 1948-60; pres., chief exec. officer Meml. Sloan-Kettering Cancer Center, 1960-65; spl. asst. in internat. med. and sci. activities Am. Cancer Soc., N.Y.C., 1965—; professorial lectr. George Washington U. Sch. Medicine, 1948-60. Mem. N.Y.C. Bd. Health, 1962-65; cancer coordinator regional med. program D.C. Med. Soc., 1967—. Served with Inf. Res. U. S. Army, 1926-34. Diplomate Am. Bd. Preventive Medicine Pub. Health. Mem. Am. Med. Assn., Am. Pub. Health Assn., Am. Venereal Disease Assn. (pres. 1948-49), Am. Cancer Soc. (dir. at large), Cancer Pub. Health Assn. (pres. 1957), N.Y. Acad. Medicine, Sigma Nu, Phi Chi. Presbyn. Mason. Clubs: Cosmos (Washington); University (N.Y.C.). Author: (with R.A. Vonderlehr) The Control of Venereal Disease. Editor Jour. Venereal Disease Information, 1943-48, Jour. Nat. Cancer Inst. Contbr. numerous articles to med. jours. Home: 5604 McLean Dr Bethesda MD 20014 Office: Nat Cancer Inst Bethesda MD 20014

HELLER, JOSEPH, writer; b. Bklyn., May 1, 1923; B.A., N.Y. U., 1948; M.A., Columbia, 1949; Fulbright scholar Oxford U., 1949-50; m. Shirley Held, Sept. 3, 1945; children—Erica Jill, Theodore Michael. Instr. Pa. State U., 1950- 52; advt. writer Time mag., 1952-56, Look mag., 1956-58; promotion mgr. McCall's, 1958-61. Nat. Inst. Arts and Letters grantee in lit., 1963. Served to lt. USAAF, World War II. Author: (novel) Catch-22, 1961; (play) We Bombed in New Haven, 1968. Address: care Alfred A Knopf Inc 501 Madison Av New York City NY 10022

HELLER, JULES, univ. dean; b. N.Y.C., Nov. 16, 1919; s. Jacob Kenneth and Goldie (Lassar) H.; A.B., Ariz. State Coll., 1939; A.M., Columbia, U 1940; Ph.D., U. So. Cal., 1948; m. Gloria Spiegel, June 11, 1947; children—Nancy Gale (Mrs. J. Bornstein), Jill Kay. Spl. art instr. 8th St. Sch., Tempe, Ariz., 1938-39; dir. art and music Union Neighborhood House, Auburn, N.Y., 1940- 41; prof. fine arts, head dept. U. So. Cal., 1946-61; vis. asso. prof. fine arts Pa. State U., summers 1955, 57, dir. Sch. Arts, 1961-62, dean Coll. Arts and Architecture, 1963-68; dean Faculty of Fine Arts, York U., Toronto, 1968—; lectr., art juror; group exhbns. include Santa Monica Art Gallery, Los Angeles County Mus., Phila. Print Club, Seattle Art Mus., Landau Gallery, Kennedy & Co. Gallery, Bklyn. Mus., Cin. Art Mus., Dallas Mus. Fine Arts, Butler Art Inst., Oakland Art Mus., Pa. Acad. Fine Arts; represented permanent collection Long Beach Mus. Art, Allan R. Hite Inst. of U. Louisville, Ariz. State U., also pvt. collections. Served with USAAF, 1941-45. Mem. Coll. Art Assn., Alpha Rho Chi. Author: Problems in Art Judgement, 1946; Printmaking Today, 1958. Contbg. artist: Prints by California Artists, 1954, Estampas de la Revolucion Mexicana, 1948. Illustrator: Canciones de Mexico, 1948. Author numerous articles. Home: 45 Spadina Rd Toronto 4 Ontario Canada

HELLER, LOUIS BENJAMIN, state supreme ct. justice; b. N.Y.C., Feb. 10, 1905; s. Max and Dora (Lazarowitz) H.; LL.B., Fordham U., 1926; m. Ruth S. Gulkis, Dec. 24, 1936; children—Robert Michael, Marcia Doris. Admitted to N.Y. bar, 1927; asso. justice Ct. Spl. Sessions, N.Y.C., 1954-58; justice Ct. City N.Y., 1959- 61, judge Civil Ct., 1962-65; justice N.Y. State Supreme Ct., 1966-; lectr. N.Y. Law Sch., 1960; guest lectr. Bklyn. Law Sch., St. John's Law Sch., Yale Sch. Law. Mem. N.Y. State Senate, 1943-44; leader, committeeman 6th Assembly Dist. Kings County Democratic Party, 1944-54; mem. 81st, 82d, 83d, congresses, 7th Dist. N.Y., chmn. Heller com., subcom. Interstate and Fgn. Com. Com. to Investigate SEC, 1951. Lay bd. advisers Cumberland St. Hosp., 1950—. Recipient merit citation Yeshiva U., 1955. Mem. Am., Bklyn. bar assns., Criminal Bar Assn. Kings County, Fedn. Jewish Philanthropies, Broadcast Music, Inc., Mem. B'nai B'rith. Author: Do You Solemnly Swear, 1968. Composer lyrics: Don't Take My Picture Take Me, 1954; Doggie Go to Sleep, 1954; It Never Rains Forever, 1954. Home: 435 Crown St Brooklyn NY 11225 Office: Supreme Ct State NY Civic Center Brooklyn NY 11201

HELLER, MAX, dept. store exec.; b. N.Y.C., Feb. 22, 1910; s. Nathan and Celia (Rubin) H.; B.C.S., N.Y. U., 1932; M.B.A., Harvard, 1935; m. Lydia Heller, Feb. 27, 1936; children-Linda Gay, Howard Nathan. Controllee, Pomeroy's, Inc., Pottsville, Pa., 1942-46, gen. mdse. mgr., Reading, Pa., 1953-55, mgr. dir., Reading, 1955-60, dir., 1955—; mng. dir. L. Samler, Inc., Lebanon, Pa., 1947-53; group supr. Allied Stores, Inc., 1957-58, gen. mgr. stores in Pa., 1958-63, v.p., group mgr. stores in Pa., 1963—; formerly v.p. Allied Stores Corp.; dir. Laubach's, Easton, Pa., Troutman's, Greensburg, Pa., New Castle Dry Goods Co. (Pa.). Club: Harvard Business School (Reading). Home: 750 Skylark Dr N North Miami Beach FL 33403 Office: Pomeroy's Inc 6th and Penn Sts Reading PA 19602 also 401 Fifth Av New York City NY 10016

HELLER, PAUL, medical educator; b. Komotau, Czechoslovakia Aug. 8, 1914; s. Alfred and Elsa (Hoenig) H.; M.D., Charles U., Prague, Czechoslovakia, 1938; m. Alice H. Florsheim, Aug. 3, 1946; children—Thomas Allen, Carol Elizabeth. Came to U.S., 1946, naturalized, 1948. Instr. biochemistry, Prague, 1935-37; imprisoned in German concentration camps, 1939-45; intern, then resident Beth Israel and Montefiore hosps., N.Y.C., 1946- 48; physician, Washington, 1948-51, VA Hosp., Omaha, 1952-54; dir. research West Side VA Hosp., Chgo., 1954-67, chief med. service, 1967-69; prof. medicine U. Ill. Coll. Medicine, 1963—, chief hematology sect., 1966—; sr. med. investigator VA, 1969—; cons. hematologist Presbyn.-St. Luke's Hosp., MacNeal Meml. Hosp. Mem. adv. bd. Cooleys Anemia Found., Chgo. Leukemia Found.; mem. hematology study sect. NIH. Fellow A.C.S.; mem. Central Soc. Clin. Research, Am. Assn. Immunologists, Assn. Am. Physicians, Am., Internat. socs. hematology. Author research papers, chpts. in books. Editorial bd. Jour. Clin. and Lab. Medicine, Yearbook of Medicine. Home: 1522 Dobson Evanston IL 60202 Office: 820 S Damen St Chicago IL 60612

HELLER, PETER JOACHIM, fgn. service officer; b. Nov. 27, 1916; m. Gisela Margaret Voss, July 31, 1947; children—Stefan D., Bruce E. Reporter, editor, 1947-54; exec. asst. to congressman, Washington, 1954-56; joined U.S. Fgn. Service, 1956; fgn. service officer, Reykjavik, Iceland, 1956-59, Copenhagen, Denmark, 1959-62, Rome, Italy, 1962-66, Saigon, Vietnam, 1966-68; fgn. policy information officer, Washington, 1968-70; consul, Hamburg, Germany, 1970—. Served to capt. AUS, 1943-46. Address: 27 Alsterufer 2 Hamburg 36 Federal Republic of Germany

HELLER, PHILIP, corp. exec.; b. 1910; B.S., City Coll., N.Y.; LL.B., Fordham U.; married. Admitted to N.Y. bar, 1934; engaged in pvt. law practice until 1956; with Fischbach and Moore, Inc., 1956—, exec. v.p. adminstrn., dir., 1969—. Address: 545 Madison Av New York City NY 10022

HELLER, PHILIP ALTER, assn. exec.; b. Austria, Aug. 6, 1911; s. Abram and Dina (Salat) H.; student Bklyn. Coll., 1930-34; B.A., N.Y.U., 1959; m. Evelyn Elkin, Sept. 27, 1941. Chief records and statistics employment div. City of N.Y., 1933-37; ednl. dir. Knitgoods Workers Union, N.Y.C., 1937-49; information officer ECA Mission to Austria and U.S. High Commn. to Germany, 1949-53; asst. to pres. Internat. Upholsterers Union, 1954-55; polit. officer Am. embassy, Conakry, Guinea, 1960-63; chief polit. sect., 1st sec. Am. embassy, Nairobi, Kenya, 1964-66; charge d'affairs, Bujumbuna, Burundi, 1966, State Dept., 1966; supervising polit. officer, Frankfurt, Germany, 1967-69; dir. internat. affairs Am. Fed. State, County and Municipal Employees, 1969—. Dir. Internat. Solidarity Com., 1945-49. Recipient Meritorious Service award Dept. State, 1963, Superior honor, 1967; Econs. Honor award, Founders Day Honor award N.Y.U. Mem. League Indsl. Democracy, Religion and Labor Council Am. Home: 6647 Western Av NW Washington DC 20015 Office: 1155 15th St NW Washington DC 20005

HELLER, RALPH, educator; b. Berlin, Germany, Feb. 28, 1914; s. Herman and Johanne C. (Altschul) H.; student U. Zürich (Switzerland), 1933-37; Ph.D., Yale 1940. Came to U.S., 1937, naturalized, 1944. Mem. faculty Worcester Poly. Inst., 1941—, prof. physics, 1953—. Fellow Phys. Soc. (London, Eng.); mem. Am. Phys. Soc., Sigma Xi, Tau Beta Pi. Address: Worcester Poly Inst Worcester MA 01609

HELLER, RICHARD H., editor; b. Yonkers, N.Y., Oct. 16, 1924; s. Otto and Mary (Cohen) H.; A.B. cum laude, Syracuse U., 1948; m. Sonja Mentikov, Mar. 28, 1953; 1 son, Matthew. Sr. writer Unicorn Press, 1949-50; editor Yearbooks Pub. Co., N.Y.C., 1951—; asso. editor men's mags. Mag. Mgmt., N.Y.C., 1952; editor men's detective mags. Hillman Periodicals, N.Y.C., 1952-53; editor, editorial dir. Sterling Group, N.Y.C., 1954-62; editor, Dell Pub. Co., also editorial dir. Dell Gearbooks, N.Y.C., 1962-68; editor in chief Pyramid Books, N.Y.C., 1968—, v.p., 1971—. Served with USMC, 1941-43. Mem. Am. Soc. Mag. Editors, Sigma Delta Chi, Sigma Alpha Mu, Orange Key. Jewish religion. Clubs: Westchester (pres, 1948) (Syracuse U.); Green Hills Country (bd. govs 1962-63) (Greenwich, Conn.); Dutch Treat. Author: The Helm, 1951; Who's Who in TV, 1967. Editor: The President Speaks, 1964; The Life and Death of Robert F. Kennedy, 1968. Photography editor: The Fall of Japan (William Craig), 1967. Home: 90 Daisy Farms Dr New Rochelle NY 10804

HELLER, ROBERT G., retired food co. exec.; b. Czechoslovakia, Jan. 12, 1890; s. Simon and Emma (Lobel) H.; widower; children—Muriel (Mrs. Howard Weinberger), Doris (Mrs. Ralph J. Tasch). Past vice chmn., treas. Vita Food Products, Inc., N.Y.C. Home: 15 W 81st St New York City NY 10024 Office: 644 Greenwich St New York City NY 10014

HELLER, WALTER WOLFGANG, educator; b. Buffalo, Aug. 27, 1915; s. Ernst and Gertrude (Warmburg) H.; A.B., Oberlin Coll., 1935, LL.D., 1964; M.A., U. Wis., 1938, Ph.D., 1941, LL.D., 1969; Litt. D., Kenyon Coll., 1965; LL.D., Ripon Coll., 1967; L.H.D., Coe Coll., 1967, Loyola U., 1970; m. Emily K. Johnson, Sept. 16, 1938; children—Walter P., Eric, Karen Louise. Fiscal economist U.S. Treasury, 1942-46, cons., 1946-53; asso. prof. econs. U. Minn., Mpls., 1946-50, prof., 1950-67, Regents prof. econs., 1967—, chmn. dept. econs., 1957-61; vis. lectr. U. Wis., 1947, U. Wash., 1950, Harvard, 1951; chmn. Council Econ. Advisers to the Pres., 1961-64. Dir. Northwestern Nat. Life Ins. Co., Internat. Multifoods, Inc., Comml. Credit Corp., Nat. City Bank, Mpls., Shelter Corp. Am., Mpls. Chief Internal finance U.S. Mil. Govt., Germany, 1947-48; cons. Com. Econ. Devel., 1948-49, 54-57, 65—; cons. UN, 1952-60, Minn. Dept. Taxation, 1955-60, N.E.A., 1958, Exec. Office of Pres., 1965-69; adv. com. Minn. Planning Bd.; tax adviser Gov. of Minn., 1955-60; mem. Treasury com. Internat. Monetary Arrangements, 1965-69; mem. OECD Group of Fiscal Experts, 1964—, chmn., 1966-68. Trustee Gen. Growth Properties, Oberlin Coll., Coll. Retirement Equities Fund. Mem. Am. Econ. Assn. (v.p. 1967-68), Nat. Tax Assn., Am. Finance Assn., Nat. Bur. Econ. Research (dir., chmn.), Am. Acad. Arts and Scis., Phi Beta Kappa, Beta Gamma Sigma, Alpha Kappa Psi. Club: Federal City (Washington). Author: (with Clara Penniman) State Income Tax Administration, 1959; New Dimensions of Political Economy, 1966; (with Richard Ruggles) Revenue Sharing and the City, 1968; (with Milton Friedman) Monetary vs. Fiscal Policy, A Dialogue. Editor: (with Francis M. Boddy, Carl L. Nelson) Savings in the Modern Economy, 1953; Perspectives on Economic Growth, 1968. Home: 2203 Folwell St St Paul MN 55108 Office: Dept Econs U Minneapolis MN 55455

HELLER, WILLIAM, business exec. Comptroller, Delco-Remy div. Gen. Motors Corp. Office: 2401 Columbus Av Anderson IN 46011*

HELLERICH, MAHLON HOWARD, ednl. adminstr.; b. Allentown, Pa., Jan. 20, 1919; s. Raymond John and Mabel (Conrad) H.; Ph.B., Muhlenberg Coll., 1940; M.A., Columbia, 1947; Ph.D., U. Pa., 1957; m. Frieda Cecelia Steiff, Dec. 26, 1942; children—Constance Maria, Conrad Mahlon. Asso. prof. history Elizabethtown Coll., 1946-51; prof. history State Tchrs. Coll. at Towson, 1951-59; dean, prof. history Albright Coll., Reading, Pa., 1959- 66; dean faculty, prof. history Wartburg Coll., 1966-69, v.p. acad. affairs, 1969-70; coordinator consortium Lehigh Valley Assn. Ind. Colls., 1970—. Trustee Gettysburg Theol. Sem., 1958-59. Ford Found. fellow Emory U., 1958; Carnegie fellow in coll. adminstrn. U. Mich., 1958-59. Served with AUS, 1944- 46. Mem. Am., Pa. hist. assns., Orgn. Am. Historians, Pa. German Soc., Am. Assn. Higher Edn., Am. Assn. U. Profs., Nat. Soc. Study Edn., History Edn. Soc., Phi Alpha Theta. Lutheran. Rotarian. Contbr. articles profl. jours. Home: 1112 Highland Av Bethlehem PA 18018

HELLERMAN, FRED, folksinger, composer; b. Bklyn., May 13, 1927; s. Harry and Clara (Robinson) H.; B.A., Bklyn. Coll., 1949; student N.Y.U., 1943, Columbia, 1950; m. Susan Lardner, Aug. 8, 1970; 1 son, Caleb H. Co-founder, 1948, mem. the Weavers, concert and recording artists, 1948-64; mus. dir. Elektra Records, 1954-58; mem. faculty Met. Sch. Music, N.Y.C., 1955-56; v.p. Sanga Music, Inc., 1957—, Fall River Music, Inc., 1961—, Appleseed Music, Inc., 1961—. Served with USCGR, 1944-45. Mem. A.S.C.A.P., Am. Guild Authors and Composers, Nat. Acad. Recording Arts and Scis. Author: (with others) Weavers Songbook, 1960, Kisses Sweeter Than Wine, 1951; (with M. Barer) I'm Just a Country Boy, 1954; (with F. Minkoff) Come Away Melinda, 1962, The Honey Wind Blows, 1964; Travelin' On With the Weavers, 1966; Quiet Room, 1966; others. Composer incidental music Broadway prodn. The Moon Besieged, 1962; contbr. Broadway prodn. New Faces of 1968; producer Alice's Restaurant. Home: 83 Goodhill Rd Weston CT 06880 Office: 200 W 57th St New York City NY 10019

HELLMAN, GEOFFREY THEODORE, writer; b. N.Y.C., Feb. 13, 1907; s. George S. and Hilda Emily (Josephthal) H.; grad. Taft Sch., Watertown, Conn., 1924; A.B. (columnist Yale Daily News 1927-28), Yale, 1928; m. 2d, Katherine Henry, Aug. 18, 1960; children—Daisy (by previous marriage), Katharine. Reporter, asso. editor New Yorker mag., 1929-31; asso. editor Fortune mag., 1931- 32; staff writer New Yorker mag., 1932-36; asso. editor Life mag., 1936-38; staff writer New Yorker mag., 1938—; on leave of absence as staff writer Office Coordinator Inter-Am. Affairs, 1942-44; spl. cons. Hdqrs. USAAF, 1944; mem. history sect. OSS, 1944-45. Mem. Chi Delta Theta. Clubs: Groiler, Coffee House, Century, Dutch Treat, Players (N.Y.C.); Graduates, Elizabethan (bd. govs. 1926-27) (New Haven); Cosmos (Washington). Author: How to Disappear for an Hour, 1947; Mrs. DePeyster's Parties, 1963; The Smithsonian, 1967; Bankers, Bones and Beetles: The First Century of the American Museum of Natural History, 1968. New Yorker "Profiles" and satirical articles have appeared in several anthologies. Office: care The New Yorker 25 W 43d St New York City NY 10036

HELLMAN, HAROLD, food products mfr.; b. Chgo., May 30, 1908; s. William and Tillie (Rosenthal) H.; E.E., U. Ill., 1931; m. Lotte Salomon, Feb. 26, 1942; children—Mary, Robert. Staff Argo plant, also N.Y.C. office Corn Products Refining Co., 1931-49, asst. to v.p. mfg., 1949-56, exec. asst. to pres., 1956-59, v.p. adminstrn., 1959-60, v.p., exec. asst. to pres., 1960-64, sr. v.p. tech., 1964-65, sr. v.p., exec. asst. to chief exec. officer, 1965—. Home: 375 Chestnut Dr Roslyn NY 11576 Office: 717 Fifth Av New York City NY 10022

HELLMAN, HENRY MARTIN, educator; b. Norrfors, Sweden, July 4, 1920; s. Karl Johan and Mathilda (Karlsson) H.; came to U.S., 1927, naturalized 1942; B.S., Ins. U., 1943; M.S., Purdue U., 1945, Ph.D., 1947; m. Isabel Julia Paul, Dec. 21, 1951. Instr., N.Y.U., 1947-50, asst. prof. chemistry, 1950-55, asso prof., 1955-69, prof. organic chemistry, 1969—, chmn. chemistry dept., 1964-70. Hon. fellow Am.-Scandinavian Found.; mem. Am. Chem. Soc., Chem. Soc. London, Sigma Xi, Phi Lambda Upsilon. Contbr. articles profl. jours. Home: 200 Cabrini St New York City NY 10033

HELLMAN, HUGO EDWARD, educator, parliamentarian; b. Muenste, Tex., Aug. 18 1908' s. August and Anna (Fette) H.; Ph.B., Marquette U., 1931, M.A., 1933, Ph.D., 1940; m. Margaret Shuengel, July 18, 1934; children—John, Robert. Tchr., Messmer High Sch., Milw., 1931-33; prof. Marquette U., 1936-40, dir. Sch. Speech, 1940-68, dean, 1968—, lectr. parliamentary law. Sch. Law, 1970—. Parliamentary cons. Am. Dental Hygiene Assn., others; parliamentarian Am. Bowling Congress. Mem. Speech Assn. Am., Forensic Assn., Am. Inst. Parliamentarians. Author ann. background books for high sch. debaters, 1949—; Parliamentary Procedure, 1965; Speaking in Groups, 1965. Home: 1530 Church St Wauwatosa WI 53213 Office: Marquette U Milwaukee WI 53203

HELLMAN, LILLIAN, playwright; b. New Orleans, La., June 20, 1907; d. Max B. and Julia (Newhouse) Hellman; ed. N.Y.U., Columbia U.; M.A., Tufts College, 1940; Litt.D., Wheaton Coll., 1961, Rutgers U., 1963, Brandeis U., 1965; m. Arthur Kober (div.). With Horace Liveright, Inc., pubs., N.Y. City, 1924-25; theatrical play-reader, 1927-30; book reviewer for Hearld Tribune, 1925-28; has been a writer, 1925—, scenario writer, 1935—. Recipient Gold medal for drama Nat. Inst. and Acad. of Arts and Letters 1964. Fellow Am. Acad. Arts and Sciences; mem. Am. Acad. Arts and Letters, Dramatists Guild. Author: The Children's Hour, 1934; Days to Come, 1936; The Little Foxes, 1939; Watch on the Rhine, 1941; The Searching Wind, 1944; Another Part of the Forest, 1946; Adapted Roble's Montserrat, 1949; The Autumn Garden, 1951. Dramatized for movies: The Dark Angel, 1935; These Three, 1935-36; Dead End, 1937; The Little Foxes, 1940; The North Star, 1943; The Searching Wind, 1945. Editor: The Letters of Anton Chekhov, Farrar, Straus, 1955; musical version of Voltaire's Candide, 1955; Adaptation of Anoulich's play. The Lark, 1955; Toys in the Attic, 1960; Adaptation My Mother, My Father and Me, from Burt Blechman's How Much, 1963. Author motion picture: The Chase. Editor: The Big Knockover (Dashiell Hammett), 1966; An Unfinished Woman (a memoir), 1969. Contbr. mags. Home: 630 Park Av New York City NY 10021

HELLMAN, LOUIS M., govt. ofcl., physician, educator; b. St. Louis, Mar. 22, 1908; s. Max and Helen (Schwab) H.; Ph.B., Yale, 1930; M.D., Johns Hopkins, 1934; m. Ernestine Crummel, Jan. 26, 1934; children—Michael Moore, Ann Harper. Instr., then asst. prof. Sch. Medicine, Johns Hopkins, 1938-42, asso. prof. obstetrics, 1945-51; asso. obstetrician Johns Hopkins Hosp.; prof., chmn. dept. obstetrics and gynecology State U. N.Y. Coll. Medicine, N.Y.C., and Kings County Hosp., 1950-70; dep. asst. sec. population affairs Dept. Health, Edn. and Welfare, 1970—. Chmn. adv. com. obstetrics and gynecology FDA, 1965-69. Served to lt. comdr., M.C., USNR, World War II. Mem. N.Y. Obstet. Soc. (pres. 1969), Assn. Profs. Gynecology and Obstet., Am. Assn. Obstetricians and Gynecologists, Am. Assn. Pathologists and Bacteriologists, Soc. Gynecologic Investigation (pres. A.C.S., N.Y. Acad. Medicine (trustee), Am. Gynec. Soc. (v.p. 1960), Phi Beta Kappa, Alpha Omega Alpha. Author: (with R.A. Hingson) Anesthesia for Obstetrics; (with J.A. Pritchard) Williams Obstetrics, 14th edit. Current devels. editor Am. Jour. Obstet.-Gynec. Contbr. med. jours. Home: 2475 Virginia Av NW Washington DC 20037 Office: 330 Independence Av SW Washington DC 20201

HELLMAN, WILLIAM, clothing store exec.; b. Chgo., Aug. 14, 1920; s. Nathan and Florence (Cohen) H.; m. Leanora Peltz, Nov. 14, 1948; children—Jeffrey N., Barbara N., David R. With Goldblatt's Dept. Stores, Chgo., 1936-59, div. mdse. mgr. mens and boys wear, 1952-59; pres., dir. Kennedy's Inc., apparel chain, Boston, 1959-68, chief exec. retail div., 1966-68; exec. v.p. Phillips-Van Heusen Corp., 1969—; dir. exec. council Boston Retail Trade Bd., Boston Better Bur. Home: 61 Clements Rd Newton Centre MA 02159 Office: Kennedy's Inc Summer and Hawley Sts Boston MA 02110

HELLMER, EDWARD JOHN, savs. and loan assn. exec.; b. Olpe, Kan., Feb. 20, 1922; s. George and Mary (Strutzell) H.; B.S., Kan. State U., 1943; m. Dorothy Mae Muetze, Mar. 10, 1944; children—Katherine Marie, Gary Evan, Ronald Paul, Kenneth James, Carl George, Michael John, Mark Edward. With Coast Fed. Savs. & Loan Assn., Los Angeles, 1946-54; mng. officer Empire Savs. & Loan Assn., Los Angeles, 1955-57; v.p. First Western Savs. & Loan Assn., Las Vegas, 1958-66, controller, 1958-59, pres., 1963-66; v.p. First Western Financial Corp., Las Vegas, 1958-66; v.p., dir. First Title Ins. Co., Corp., Las Vegas, 1962-66; sec., dir. S.W. Devel. Co., Las Vegas, 1959-62; formerly chmn. bd., pres. Home Savs. & Loan Assn., Albuquerque; pres. Desert State Financial Corp., Albuquerque, 1966—. Co-chmn. Century Club fund drive Boulder dam area council Boy Scouts Am., 1963-66. Bd. dirs. United Fund Clark County, Nev., 1965-66; trustee Neumeyer Found., 1962—. Served with AUS, 1943-46. Mem. U.S. Savs. and Loan League (bd. dirs. 1965-66), Nev. Econ. Devel. Assn. Republican. Roman Catholic. K.C. (4) Kiwanian. Home: 9024 Aspen Av NE Albuquerque NM 87112

HELLMUTH, GEORGE FRANCIS, architect; b. St. Louis, Oct. 5, 1907; s. George W. and Harriet M. (Fowler) H.; B.Arch., Washington U., 1928, M.Arch., 1930; Steedman traveling fellow, 1931; diploma Ecole des Beaux Arts, Fontainebleau, France; m. Mildred Lee Henning, May 24, 1941; children—George William, Nicholas Matthew, Mary Cleveland, Theodore Henning, Daniel Fox. With Hellmuth, Yamasaki & Leinweber, 1949-55; prin. Hellmuth, Obata & Kassabaum, 1955—, HOK Assos., 1968—; pres. Timber Farms-The Sinks, Gladden, Mo., Roaring Springs Corp. mfrs. charcoal; prin. archtl. works enclude: Nat. Air and Space Mus., Washington; Canadian Prison System; bldgs. at U. Mich., So. Ill. U.; Fed. Maximum Security Prison, Marion, Ill., McDonnell Planetarium, St. Louis, Neiman-Marcus Center, Houston, Am. embassy, El Salvador, IBM Advanced Systems Lab., Los Gatos, Cal., many others. Chmn., St. Louis Landmarks and Urban Design Commn., 1950-70. Recipient First Honor award A.I.A., 1956. Mem. A.I.A. Clubs: Racquet, Strathalbyn, Noonday. Home: 5 Conway Lane St Louis MO 63124 also 4464 Maryland Av St Louis MO 63108 Office: 315 N 9th St St Louis MO 63101

HELLMUTH, PAUL FRANCIS, lawyer; b. Springfield, O., Dec. 7, 1918; s. Andrew Alfred and Clara Elizabeth (Link) H.; A.B., U. Notre Dame, 1940; LL.B., Harvard, 1947; spl. courses Mass. Inst. Tech., Harvard Grad. Sch. Pub. Adminstrn. Admitted to Ohio bar, 1947, Mass. bar, 1952; mem. firm Hale & Dorr, Boston, 1947—, partner, 1952-56, sr. mng. partner, 1956—; v.p., trustee Cabot, Cabot & Forbes Co., Boston; pres. L & H Corp., Springfield, O.; treas., dir. Ritz Carlton Hotel; dir. Bessemer Securities Corp., Pioneer Fund, Inc., Fund Research & Mgmt., Inc., W.R. Grace & Co., Pioneer Western Corp. (Fla.), Western Res. Life Assurance Co. Ohio, Eastern Slope Hotel, Inc.; trustee Boston Five Cents Savs. Bank, Tech. Sq. Trust. Overseer, dir. Boys' Club of Boston, Inc. Pres., U. Hosp.; dir. Greater Boston Hosp. Assn; trustee Mus. of Science, Boston, Boston U. Med. Center, U. Notre Dame, Boston U., Cardinal Cushing Coll., pres., mem. bd. govs. New Eng. Aquarium; 1st v.p., trustee Children's Hosp., Med. Center; mem. law sch. council U. Notre Dame. Served from pvt. to 2d lt. AUS, 1941- 42, advanced to lt. col. USAAF, 1945. Decorated Legion of Merit, Bronze Star medal; French Croix de Guerre. Mem. Am. Bar Assn., Harvard Law Sch. Assn. (treas.). Clubs: Algonquin, Harvard, Union, Bay (Boston); Country (Springfield, O.); Executives. Home: 100 Memorial Dr Cambridge MA 02142 Office: 60 State St Boston MA 02109

HELLMUTH, WILLIAM FREDERICK, Jr., educator; b. Washington, Jan. 8, 1920; s. William Frederick and Sybel (Grant) H.; B.A., Yale, 1940, Ph.D., 1948; m. Jean A. Dieffenbach, Feb. 14, 1943; children—James (dec.), Suzanne, William L., Peter G. Instr. econs.

Yale, 1945-48; mem. faculty Oberlin Coll., 1948-68, prof. econs., 1958- 68, dean Coll. Arts and Scis., 1960-67; dep. asst. sec. treasury for tax policy, 1968-69; v.p. arts, prof. econs. McMaster U., Hamilton, 1969- -, also bd. govs.; econ. Fed. Res. Bd., 1954-56; prof. U. Wis., 1959, Univ. Coll., Dar es Salaam, Tanzania, 1965, 66. Mem. Oberlin City Council, 1957-63, 67- 68. Served to maj., F.A., AUS, World War II. Decorated Air medal, Bronze Star. Mem. Am. Econ. Assn., Nat. Tax Assn., Tax Inst., Am. Assn. U. Profs., Canadian Econs. Assn., Tax Found., Phi Beta Kappa. Club: Hamilton. Home: 177 Sterling St Hamilton Ontario Canada

HELLWEGE, HERBERT ELMORE, chemist, educator; b. Harsefeld, Germany, Mar. 3, 1921; s. Hans Andreas and Emma (Kroger) H.; Ph.D., U. Hamburg, 1953; m. Frieda Anna Tennert, Aug. 7, 1953; children—H. Steve, Roy N. Came to U.S., 1953, naturalized, 1958. Teaching asst. U. Hamburg, 1952-53; chemist Food Research Co., L.I. City, N.Y., 1953-54; mem. faculty dept. chemistry Rollins Coll., Winter Park, Fla., 1954—, now prof.; cons. Radiation, Inc., Melbourne, Fla., 1957-60; NSF sci. teaching fellow U. Gothenburg, Sweden, 1964-65. Mem. Am. Chem. Soc. (past chmn. Orlando subsect.) Patentee in field. Home: 1141 Banbury Trail Maitland FL 32751

HELLWIG, JUDITH, soprano. With Vienna State Opera; recorded Bartok's Bluebeard's Castle for Bartok Records. Address: care Vienna State Opera Vienna Austria ☆

HELLY, WALTER SIGMUND, educator; b. Vienna, Austria, Aug. 22, 1930; s. Edward and Elizabeth (Bloch) H.; came to U.S., 1938, naturalized, 1944; B.A., Cornell U., 1950; M.S., U. Ill., 1954; Ph.D., Mass. Inst. Tech., 1959; m. Dorothy Oxman, Mar. 4, 1956; 1 dau., Miranda. With Sylvania Electric Co., Waltham, Mass., 1954-56; sr. engr. Melpar Co., Boston, 1956-59; mem. tech. staff Bell Telephone Labs., N.Y.C., 1959-62; sr. engr. Port of New York Authority, 1962-65; prof. operations research Poly. Inst. Bklyn., 1966—; cons. on traffic flow. Mem. Operations Research Soc. Am. (past chmn. transp. sci. sect.). Book rev. editor Jour. Operations Research, 1970—. Contbr. articles profl. jours. Home: 91 Central Park West New York City NY 10023 Office: 333 Jay St Brooklyn NY 10023

HELLYER, CLEMENT DAVID, writer; b. Glendale, Cal., Aug. 15, 1914; s. Clement David and Frances Edna (Dodge) H.; A.B., Principia Coll., 1936; M.S., Columbia, 1938; Beaumont fellow U. Fla., 1950-52; m. Gertrude Gloria Phillips, Sept. 8, 1939; children—Gloria Penrose, David Phillips, John Christian. Newspaper reporter San Diego Union-Tribune, 1939-41; pub. relations dir. San Diego C. of C., 1941-43; civilian aerial navigator USN, 1943- 45; prof. journalism San Diego State Coll., 1947-49; dir. Centro Cultural Costarricense-Norteamericano, San Jose, Costa Rica, 1949-50; lectr. World Affairs Inst., San Diego, 1950; asst. dir. Sch. Inter-Am. Studies, U. Fla., 1950-52; vis. lectr. U.S. journalism, Dept. State program leaders and specialists exchange, Latin Am. countries, 1952; Latin-Am. editor San Diego Union, 1953-60; fellow Pan Am. Found., Sao Paulo, Brazil, 1960-62; writer, lectr. Latin Am. affairs, 1950—; U.S. del. Jose Toribio Medina Centenary, Santiago, Chile, 1952; editor, pub. South Pacific Mail, Santiago, 1964-66; editorial dir. radio-TV sta. KOGO, San Diego, 1966-69, U. Cal. at San Diego, 1969—. Recipient Maria Moors Cabot award Columbia, 1959; 1st prize radio editorial competition Radio and TV News Dirs. Assn., 1968. Mem. Sigma Delta Chi. Author: (with Charles Mattingly), American Air Navigator, 1946; Story of the U.S. Border Patrol, 1963. Contbr. articles prin. newspapers, periodicals U.S., 1939—. Home: Box 91 Rancho Santa Fe CA 92067 Office: Univ Cal La Jolla CA 92037

HELLYER, GEORGE MACLEAN, cons.; b. Riverside, Ill., Feb. 28, 1912; s. Harold J. and Dorothy A. (Maclean) H.; certificate U. Lausanne (Switzerland), 1935; m. Margaret H. Dawson, July 2, 1953; children by previous marriage—Marion M. (Mrs. Archibald E. King, Jr.), Harold J., Robert T., David R. Tea mfr. Hellyer and Co., Shizouka, Japan, 1932-34; lectr. Com. to Defend Am. by Aiding Allies, 1939; Western dir. Fed. Union, Inc., 1940-41; mgr. Robert Anderson and Co., tea mfrs., Hong Kong, 1946, Taipei, 1947-48, partner, 1949-52; with USIA and predecessors, 1952—, pub. affairs officer and attache, Saigon, Phnom Penh and Vientiane, 1952-54, dep. asst. dir., Washington, 1954-55, asst. dir. charge Far Eastern programs, 1955-58, counsellor for pub. affairs U.S. embassy, Tokyo, Japan, 1958-60, U.S. Mission to European Communities, Brussels, Belgium, 1961-67, Am. embassy, Kinshasa, Dem. Republic of Congo, 1967-69; U.S. delegation to NATO, Brussels, 1969-70; ret., 1970; cons., 1970—. Served from pvt. to capt., AUS, 1942-45. Decorated Bronze Star, Air medal; Mil. Cross (U.K.) Clubs: Hong Kong, Royal Hong Kong Yacht. Home: PO Box 192 Eastsound WA 98245

HELLYER, PAUL THEODORE, Canadian govt. ofcl.; b. Waterford, Ont., Can., Aug. 6, 1923; s. Audrey S. and Luila M. (Anderson) H.; diploma aero. engring., Curtiss- Wright Tech. Inst., 1941; B.A. U. Toronto, 1949; m. Ellen Jean Ralph, June 1, 1945; children—Mary Elizabeth, Peter Lawrence, David Ralph. With Fleet Aircraft Mfg. Co., Ft. Erie, Ont., until World War II; propr. Mari-Jane Fashions, Toronto, 1945-56; treas. Curran Hall Ltd., Toronto, 1950, pres., 1951-62; pres. Trepil Ltd., Toronto, 1951-62, Hendon Estates Ltd., Toronto, 1959-63; mem. House of Commons from Davenport Dist., 1949-57, from Trinity Dist., 1958-69; resigned 1969; parliamentary asst. to minister nat. def., 1956; mem. Privy Council, 1957-69; asso. minister def., 1957, minister nat. def., 1963-67; minister transport, 1967-69; minister responsible for housing, 1968-69; distinguished visitor environmental studies York U., 1969-71; founding chmn. Action Canada, 1971. Chmn. Task Force on Housing and Urban Devel., 1968-69. Served Royal Can. Air Force, Canadian Army, World War II. Mem. Toronto Bd. Trade. Independent Liberal. Home: 1982 Rideau River Dr Ottawa Ontario Canada Office: House of Commons Ottawa Ontario Canada

HELM, EVERETT, composer, musicologist; b. Mpls., July 17, 1913; s. Clyde and Alice (Stark) H.; B.A., Carleton Coll., 1934; M.A., Harvard, 1935, Ph.D., 1939; student mus. composition with F.G. Malipiero, also Ralph Vaughan Williams, 1936-38; student musicology with Alfred Einstein, 1937-38; m. Elisabeth Alber, Aug. 31, 1955. Tchr., Longy Sch. Music, Cambridge, Mass., 1938-42; prof. Music Western Coll., Oxford, O., 1942-44; chief theater and music br. U.S. Uil. Govt., Wiesbaden, Germany, 1948-50; editor-in-chief Musical Am. mag., N.Y.C., 1961-63; also composer numerous works including First Piano Concerto, 1950, Three Gospel Hymns for Orchestra, 1944, Concerto for Five Solo Instruments, 1953, Sinfonia da Camera, 1962, String Quartet, 1962, Woodwind Quintet, 1969, Concerto for Double Bass, 1969; composer, performer A Study In Communication, 1970, Franz Liszt, 1971. Mem. Am. Musicological Soc. Club: Harvard (N.Y.C.). Author book: Bela Bartók, 1966. Address: Casa Colmarion Asolo Treviso Italy

HELM, HAROLD HOLMES, banker; b. Auburn, Ky., Dec. 9, 1900; s. Thomas Oliver and Nellie (Blakey) H.; B.A., Princeton, 1920; LL.D., Hampden-Sydney Coll., Centre Coll., Ky., 1962, Bloomfield Coll., 1967; D.C.S. (hon.), N.Y.U., 1960; D.C.L., U. South, 1963; m. Mary Rodes, Feb. 14, 1925; children—Eleanor (Mrs. John C. Ketcham, Jr.), John. Clk., credit dept. Chem. Nat. Bank (later Chem. Bank & Trust Co.), N.Y.C., 1920-26, asst. cashier, 1926-28, asst. v.p., 1928-29, v.p., 1929-46, 1st v.p., 1946-47, pres., 1947-55, became dir., 1941; pres. chem. Corn Exchange Bank (merger Chem. Bank & Trust Co. and Corn Exchange Bank), 1955, bd. dirs., 1955-59; chmn. bd. dirs. Chem. Bank N. Y. Trust Co. (merger Chem. Corn Exchange Bank and N. Y. Trust Co.), 1959-66, chmn. exec. com., 1966—; dir. Colgate Palmolive Co., F.W. Woolworth Co., Cummins Engine Co., Inc., Equitable Life Assurance Soc. U.S., CPC Internat., Home Ins. Co., Western Electric Co., Asso. Dry Goods Corp., Lord and Taylor, The Home Indemnity Co., McDonnell-Douglas Corp., Uniroyal. Emeritus trustee Princeton U., mem. finance com., mem. exec com., hon. degrees, Ida Cason Callaway Found., Pine Mountain, Ga., Presbyn. Hosp.- Columbia Presbyn. Med. Center, N.Y.C.; chmn. exec. com. Fed. Hall Meml. Assos., Inc.; mem. adv. bd. Hoover Instn. Decorated Royal Order St. Olav (Norway). Mem. N.Y. So. Soc., Nat. Indsl. Conf. Bd., Pilgrims Soc. U.S., U.S. Srs. Golf Assn. Presbyn. (elder). Clubs: Nassau, Campus (Princeton); Economic, Filson (Louisville); Montclair Golf; Nat. Golf Links (trustee) (Southampton); University (past pres.), Links, Princeton, Bond (hon.), Kentuckians (N.Y.C.). Home: 49 Glenwood Rd Upper Montclair NJ 07043 also 563 Park Av New York City NY 10021 Office: 277 Park Av New York City NY 10017

HELM, ROBERT MEREDITH, educator; b. Winston-Salem, N.C., Feb. 19, 1917; s. Robert Meredith and Mary Alma (Jones) H.; B.A., Wake Forest Coll., 1939; M.A., Duke, 1940; Ph.D., 1950. Mem. faculty Wake Forest U., 1940—, prof. philosophy, 1962- -; asso. prof. Salem Coll., 1958-60; mem. faculty N.C. Sch. Arts, 1967- 69. Trustee, v.p. James W. Denmark Loan Fund. Served with AUS, 1941-46; ETO. Decorated Army Commendation medal. Mem. Am. Philos. Assn., Am. Acad. Religion, Am. Assn. U. Profs., N.C. Philos. Soc., Mil. Order World Wars, Phi Beta Kappa, Omicron Delta Kappa, Delta Sigma Rho, Tau Kappa Alpha, Sigma Pi. Democrat. Mem. Moravian Ch. Author: The Gloomy Alpha, Sigma Pi. Democrat. Mem. Moravian Ch. Author: The Gloomy Dean: The Thought of William Ralph Inge, 1962. Home: 2706 Tudor Rd Winston Salem NC 27106

HELM, W. STUART, state ofcl.; b. Cowansville, Pa., Apr. 8, 1908; s. Fred H. and Jennie L. (Clark) H.; student Pa. State U., Duquesne U.; m. Eraldine Rearick; 2 daus. Spl. asst. to gov. State of Pa., 1965, sec. state, 1965-67; exec. dir. Pa. Pub. Sch. Bldg. Authority, 1967-. Mem. Kittanning Borough Sch. Bd., 1937-55; pres. Nat. Legislative Conv., 1962-63; 2d v.p. Council State Govts., 1962. Mem. Pa. Ho., of Reps., 1940-65, speaker, 1957-58, 63-64, chmn, Republican policy com., 1959-62. Mason, Elk, Kiwanian. Office: Office of Sec of Commonwealth Harrisburg PA 17105

HELM, WILLIAM LLOYD, Jr., utilities exec.; b. N.Y.C., June 21, 1923; s. William Lloyd and May (Kelly) H.; grad. Hotchkiss Sch., 1942; B.S., Princeton, 1949; m. Eleanor Lloyd, Feb. 16, 1952; children—Pamela Kelly, Peter Lloyd, David Belknap, William Lloyd III. Test engr. Gen. Electric Co., 1949; tech. cadet Boston Gas Co., 1950-51; staff engr., 1952, asst. supt. electric dept., 1952-55, mgr. electric dept., 1955-64, v.p. marketing, 1967-69, dir., 1968-69; asst. to sr. v.p. Eastern Gas & Fuel Assos., Boston, 1964-65, exec. asst. to pres., 1965-67, controller, 1969—. Water commr., Weston, Mass., 1960-67; mem. Finance Com., Weston, 1968—. Pres., trustee Meadowbrook Sch., Weston; sec. Eastern Asso. Found. Served with USNR, 1943-46. Registered profl. engr., Mass. Mem. I.E.E.E., Sales and Marketing Execs. Assn. Greater Boston, Group to Advance Total Energy (past dir.). Home: 44 Hill Top Rd Weston MA 02193 Office: Prudential Tower Boston MA 02199

HELMAN, ALFRED BLAIR, coll. pres.; b. Windber, Pa., Dec. 25, 1920; s. Henry E. and Luie (Pritt) H.; A.B., McPherson Coll., 1946, D.D., 1956; M.A., U. Kan., 1947, postgrad. 1948-51; m. Patricia Ann Kennedy, June 22, 1947; 1946-54, children—Harriet Ann, Patricia Dawn. Ordained to ministry Ch. of Brethren, 1942; pastor, Newton, Kan., 1944-46, Ottawa, Kan., 1946-54, First Ch. of Brethren, Wichita, Kan., 1954-56; faculty Ottawa U., 1947- 48, 51-54, chmn. div. social scis., 1952-54; instr. extension div. U. Kan., 1951-54; instr. Friends U., 1955-56; pres. Manchester (Ind.) Coll., 1956- -. Chmn. com. higher edn. Ch. of Brethren, 1964-67. Trustee McPherson Coll., 1951-56, chmn., 1955-56; trustee Kan. Found. Pvt. Colls. and Univs., 1955-56; pres. Independent Colls. and Univs. of Ind., 1966-67; chmn. bd. dirs. Central States Coll. Assn., 1968; pres. Asso. Colls. of Ind., 1970—; mem. commn. on religion in higher edn. Assn. Am. Colls., 1968-71. Mem. Am. Hist. Assn., Soc. Advancement Edn; Inc., Soc. Historians of Am. Fgn. Relations, Comparative and Internat. Edn. Soc., Orgn. Am. Historians, Am. Assn. for Higher Edn., Council Protestant Colls. and Univs. (chmn. bd. 1967), Nat. Council Chs. of Christ Am. (policy bd. dept. of higher edn.), Ind. Council Chs. (dir., mem. exec. com. 1960-62), Ind. Conf. of Higher Edn. (pres. 1960-61), C. of C., Phi Beta Kappa, Phi Alpha Theta, Pi Sigma Alpha, Pi Kappa Delta. Republican. Kiwanian. Clubs: Columbia (Indpls.): University (Chgo.); University (N.Y.C.). Author articles religion and higher edn. Home: 1400 East St North Manchester IN 46992

HELMBOLD, F. WILBUR, librarian, clergyman; b. Fowlerville, Pa., May 13, 1917: s. Andrew K. and Emma L. (Hildebrand) H.; A.B. with honors, Sanford U., 1949; M.A., Duke, 1954; m. Neola E. Wood, June 10, 1942; children—Neola J. (Mrs. Robert N. Trapnell), Arthur J. (dec.), Martha W., Dale Marjorie. Newspaper reporter Wilkes- Barre (Pa.) Record, 1934-36; printer Dallas (Pa.) Post, also owner printing bus., 1936-42; ordained to ministry Baptist Ch., 1947; pastor, Selma, Ala., 1947-49, Springville, Ala., 1949-50, Durham, N.C., 1951-54; supply pastor, 1954—; librarian Barrington (R.I.) Coll., 1954- 57, Samford U., Birmingham, Ala., 1957—. Library cons., 1958—. Served with USAAF, 1942-46; ETO. Mem. Am., S.E., Ala. library assns., Ala. Hist. Assn., So. Bapt. (pres.), Ala. Bapt., Birmingham hist. socs., Nat. Geneal. Soc. Author: Born of the Needs of the People, 1967. Editor: (posthumous vol. by A.D. Zbinden) Studies in Hebrews, 1954; Classification of Religious Literature, 1957, Ala. Bapt. Historian, 1967—; gen. editor Banner Press (pubs.), 1961-66, pres., 1966—. Contbr. religious and hist. jours. Home: 2305 Harmony Lane Birmingham AL 35226

HELMER, FRANK VINCENT, retired coast guard officer; b. Lakewood, O., Jan. 16, 1913; s. Nicholas Arthur and Marie (Pigneguy) H.; B.S., U.S. Coast Guard Acad., 1935; m. Hilda Katherine Caldwell, Sept. 26, 1936; children—John Caldwell, Michael Francis, Hilda Mary. Commd. ensign USCG, 1935, advanced through grades to rear adm., 1965; duty in U.S.S. Leonard Wood, 1941-44; comdr. U.S.S. Vance, 1945; adminstr., comdr. various ships, 1946-61; asst. supt. USCG Acad., 1961-64; chief of staff 3d Coast Guard Dist., N.Y.C., 1964-65; comptroller Coast Guard Hdqrs., Washington,1965-66, chief office of operations, 1966-67; comdr. 13th Coast Guard Dist., 1967-70; retired, 1970. Home: 6570 NE Windermere Rd Seattle WA 98105

HELMER, GEORGE ALFRED, corp. exec., lawyer; b. Berkeley, Cal., Aug. 7, 1915; s. George A. and Nell (Hodnett) H.; A.B., U. San Francisco, 1936; LL.B., 1940; m. Nancy Noel Hoguet, Jan. 22, 1946. Admitted to Cal. bar, 1940; practice in San Francisco, 1940-61; dep. city atty., 1946-47; mem. firm Cooper, White & Cooper, 1947-61; sr. v.p., gen. counsel Engelhard Industries, Inc., Newark, 1961—; exec. v.p., gen. counsel Engelhard Hanovia, Inc. Served to lt. USNR, 1942-46. Mem. Am. Bar Assn., Assn. Bar City N.Y., State Bar Cal. Home: Old Army Rd Bernardsville NJ 07924 Office: 113 Astor Engelhard Industries Inc Newark NJ 07114

HELMER, HUGH JOSLIN, former banker; b. Pontiac, Mich., Dec. 10, 1909; s. Arthur J. and Genevieve (Weston) H.; B.A., U. Wis., 1932, grad. Grad. Sch. Banking, 1947; m. Jane E. L. Stratton, Nov. 23, 1932; children—Louise (Mrs. Karl H. Baumert), Frederick, James. Clk., First Nat. Bank & Trust Co., Pontiac, 1925-32; asst. examiner Wis. Banking Dept., 1932; examiner Fed. Deposit Ins. Corp., 1938; with Fed. Res. Bank Chgo., 1933-70, v.p., 1958-62, 1st v.p., 1962-70, ret., 1970. Mem. Chgo. Com. Mem. Newcomen Soc. N.Am., Alpha Kappa Psi, Phi Kappa Sigma. Clubs: Bankers, Executives, Union League (Chgo.). Home: 819 Redbud Lane Wilmette IL 60091

HELMERICH, WALTER HUGO, III, oil co. exec.; b. Tulsa, Jan. 12, 1923; s. Walter Hugo, Jr. and Cadijah (Colcord) H.; B.A., U. Okla., 1948; M.B.A., Harvard, 1950; m. Peggy Varnadow, Nov. 24, 1951; children—Walter Hogo IV, Dow Zachary, Matthew Galloway, Hans Christian, Jonathan David. With Helmerich & Payne, Inc., Tulsa, 1950—, pres., 1960—, also dir.; dir. White Eagle Overseas Oil Co., Inc., Lincoln Consolidated, Inc., Coca-Cola Bottling Co. Tulsa, Inc., Natural Gas Odorizing, Inc., Chromium Plating Co., Atwood Oceanics, Inc., 1st Nat. Bank & Trust Co. Chmn. Okla World's Fair Commn., 1964-65; bd. dirs. Okla. Academy for State Goals , Okla. Health Scis. Found., Okla. Med. Research Found., Holland Hall Sch. Mem. Ind. Petroleum Assn. Am. (dir.), Young Pres.'s Orgn., Sigma Nu. Methodist (bd. stewards). Home: 3003 S Rockford Rd Tulsa OK 74114 Office: Utica at 21st Tulsa OK 74114

HELMERICKS, CONSTANCE, author, explorer, lectr.; b. Binghamton, N.Y., Jan. 4, 1918; d. Arthur Smith and Winifred (Browning) Chittenden; student U. Ariz., 1937-40, B.A. in Sociology, 1954; m. Harmon Robert Helmericks, Apr. 27, 1941 (div. May 1956); children—Constance Jean, Carol Ann; m. 2d, Gilbert D.B.K. Barrett, July 2, 1969 (div. Feb. 1970). Comprehensive study (with Harmon Helmericks) Arctic populations and animals, Can. and Alaska, prin. studies including diet and ecology interpretation primitive life to civilized man; field researcher in sociology for U. Ariz., 1962-63; lectr. Mem. Arctic Inst. N. Am. Author: We Live in Alaska, 1944. Co-author nature books (with Harmon Helmericks): We Live in the Arctic, 1947; Our Summer With the Eskimos, 1948; Our Alaskan Winter. 1949; The Flight of the Arctic Tern, 1951. Author: Hunting in North America, 1957; Down the Wild River North, 1968; Australian Adventure (illus. Ann Helmericks), 1972; also articles. Producer films including: We Live in Alaska, We Live in the Arctic, Jeanie of Alaska, the Many Faces of Mexico. Lecture tour of U.S. on subject of Mexico, 1958. Home: 323 N 2d Av Tucson AZ 85705

HELMERICKS, HARMON, author, explorer; b. Gibson City, Ill., Jan. 18, 1917; s. Clarence James and Abbie (Cornelius) H.; student U. Ariz., 1940-41; m. Constance Chittenden, Apr. 27, 1941; children—Constance Jean, Carol Ann; m. 2d., Martha M. Paxton; children—James Woodrow, Mark Harmon, Jeffrey Todd. Sheet metal worker Army Engrs., Seaward, Alaska, 1941- 44; asso. with Constance Helmericks in study of Arctic, 1944-46; writer, lectr. on Arctic Am., 1946—; organizer expdn. by air north of Arctic Circle, Alaska and Can., 1947; founder Arctic Tern Fish-Freight Co., 1952; asst. curator Kansas City Mus.; cons. Arctic oil operation; films for Am. Motors Corp.; TV shows on Arctic research; Arctic cons. to Eastman Kodak Co.; master guide Alaskan Game Commn., active in conservation in Africa, India, Europe, Arctic Inst. N. Am., Airplane Owners and Pilots Assn. Clubs: Circumnavigators; Explorers. Author: Oolak's Brother, 1952; Arctic Hunters, 1955; (with Constance Helmericks) We Live in the Arctic, 1947, Our Summer With the Eskimos, 1948, Our Alaskan Winter, 1949, Flight of the Arctic Tern, 1952, Arctic Bush Pilot, The Last of the Bush Pilots, 1968, also mag. articles. Address: Colville River Delta Barrow AK 99723

HELMHOLZ, AUGUST CARL, physicist, educator; b. Evanston, Ill., May 24, 1915; s. Henry F. and Isabel G. (Lindsay) H.; A.B., Harvard, 1936; student Cambridge U., 1936- 37; Ph.D., U. Cal. at Berkeley, 1940; m. Elizabeth J. Little, July 30, 1938; children—Charlotte A., George L., Frederic V., Edith L. Instr. physics U. Cal. at Berkeley, 1940-43, asst. prof., 1943-48, asso. prof., 1948-51, prof., 1951—, chmn. dept., 1955-62, research physicist Radiation Lab., 1940—; Guggenheim fellow, 1962-63. Fellow Am. Phys. Soc.; mem. Am. Inst. Physics (governing bd. 1964-67), A.A.A.S., Am. Assn. Physics Tchrs., Am. Assn. U. Profs., Phi Beta Kappa, Sigma Xi. Home: 28 Crest Rd Lafayette CA 94549 Office: Dept Physics Univ California Berkeley CA 94720

HELMICK, LOUIS GASTON, Jr., engr., mfr. heavy equipment; b. Fairmont, W.Va., July 14, 1920; s. Louis G. and Harriet (Smith) H.; B.S. in Mech. Engring., Cornell U., 1943; m. Janice Priscilla Taylor, Oct. 2, 1943; children—Susan Taylor, Louis Gaston III, David Garner. Asst. v.p. prodn. Differential Steel Car Co., 1945-47; asst. works mgr. Joy Mfg. Co., Franklin, 1947-52, works mgr., Claremont, 1952-54, mgr. mfg., 1954-55, v.p. charge mfg. operations, 1955-56, v.p., gen. mgr. indsl. div., 1956-58, exec. v.p., Pitts., 1958- -, also dir.; dir. Helmick Foundry-Machine Co. Served to capt. AUS, 1943-46. Mem. Am. Mgmt. Assn., Am. Soc. Tool Engrs., Engrs. Soc. Western Pa., Tau Beta Pi. Club: Duquesne. Home: 675 Valleyview Rd Pittsburgh PA 15243 Office: Oliver Bldg Pittsburgh PA 15222

HELMIG, FRANCES, occupational therapist; b. Atlantic City, May 9, 1911; d. Charles and Minnie Hannah (Couse) Helmig; B.A., N.J. State Tchrs. Coll., Montclair, 1934; certificate Phila. Sch. Occupational Therapy, 1941; M.A., U. So. Cal., 1951. Family visitor N.J. Emergency Relief, 1934-35; tchr. Atlantic City pub. schs., 1935-39; asst. dir. curative workshop Phila. Sch. Occupational Therapy, 1941-42; dir. Rochester (N.Y.) Rehab. Center, 1946-49, 53-59; cons. occupational therapy Nat. Soc. Crippled Children and Adults, Chgo., 1949-50; rehab. cons. Phila. Health and Welfare Council, 1952-53; dir. occupational therapy E.P. Bissell Hosp., Wilmington, Del., 1959-61; chief occupation therapy N.Y. U. Med. Center, 1961-64; mem. Am. Occupational Therapy Assn., 1942-, speaker ho. of dels., 1955-58, exec. dir., 1964-68; chief occupational therapist Jefferson Med. Center Hosp., Phila., 1968-71; dir. occupational therapy Children's Seashore House, Atlantic City, N.J., 1971—. Mem. selection bd. USNR, 1964; occupational therapy adv. panel Vocational Rehab. Adminstrn., 1963-65. Served to lt. USNR, 1942-46. Mem. Nat. Rehab. Assn. (pres. region II, 1958), World Fedn. Occupational Therapists, Internat. Soc. Rehab. Disabled, Assn. Rehab. Centers, Kappa Delta Pi. Club: Soroptimist Internat. Contbr. articles profl. jours. Contbg. editor: Rehabilitation Medicine, 2d edit., 1964; Rehabilitation at U.S. Naval Hospital Philadelphia, 1946. Home: 35 E Ridgewood Av Pleasantville NJ 08232 Office: 4200 Atlantic Av Atlantic City NJ 08401

HELMKAMP, GEORGE KENNETH, educator; b. Eustis, Neb., Feb. 24, 1921; s. George Henry and Pauline (Moritz) H.; B.A., Wartburg Coll., 1942; M.A., Claremont Grad. Sch., 1950; Ph.D., Cal. Inst. Tech., 1953; m. Elizabeth Ann Fearing, Apr. 25, 1947; children—Ann Elizabeth (Mrs. Gary Kerchner), John Michael, Alice Louise, Amy Pauline. Chemist, Atmospheric Nitrogen Corp., South Point, O., 1942-43; analyst Wilshire Oil Co., Norwalk, Cal., 1943-45;

chemist Socal Oil Co., Huntington Beach, Cal., 1947-49; instr. Pomona Coll., Claremont, Cal., 1952-53; prof. U. Cal. at Riverside, 1953—, asso. dean Coll. Letters and Sci., 1966-70, chmn. dept. chemistry, 1970—. Served with USN, 1943-45. Mem. Am. Chem. Soc. Lutheran. Author: (with C. Hansch) Organic Chemistry, 1959; (with H.W. Johnson, Jr.) Selected Experiments in Organic Chemistry, 1964. Contbr. articles profl. jours. Home: 3627 Mt Vernon Av Riverside CA 92507

HELMKE, WALTER EDWARD lawyer; b. Ft. Wayne, Ind., Dec. 17, 1901; s. Herman and Mary (Engel) H.; LL.B., Ind. U., 1925; m. Wilma L. Wehrenberg, June 3, 1926; children—Walter Paul, Mary Ann (Mrs. Charles Scheele), Carolyn (Mrs. Charles R. Stultz). Admitted to Ind. bar, 1925, since practiced in Ft. Wayne; sr. mem. Helmke, Phillips & Beams; pros. atty. Allen Co., Ind., 1930-31; city atty. Ft. Wayne, 1935-47. Pres., dir. Jefferson Nat. Life Ins. Co., Indpls.; bd. dirs. Ready Mixed Concrete Corp., Jefferson Corp., Indpls. Republican candidate for 74th U.S. Congress, 4th Congl. Dist. Ind., 1934, for gov. Ind., 1948; Rep. County chmn. Allen County, 1940-50; ind. del. Rep. Nat. Conv., Phila., 1948. Trustee Ind. U., 1954-56; former mem. adv. bd. Valparaiso U. Mem. Allen County (past pres.), Am., Ind. bar assns., Tau Kappa Alpha, Phi Delta Phi, Phi Kappa Psi. Lutheran (pres. Internat. Walther League 1933-39). Home: 2412 Forest Park Blvd Fort Wayne IN 46805 Office: Standard Bldg Fort Wayne IN 46802

HELMREICH, ERNST CHRISTIAN, educator; b. Crescent City, Ill., Aug. 26, 1902; s. Christian and Augusta (Brueckner) H.; A.B., U. Ill., 1924, A.M., 1925; A.M., Harvard, 1927, Ph.D., 1932; m. Louise Bertha Roberts, 1932; children—Paul Christian, Jonathan Ernst. Instr. history, govt. Purdue U., 1924-26; asst. history Radcliffe Coll., 1927-29, 30-31; instr. history, govt. Bowdoin Coll., 1931-32, asst. prof., 1932-40, asso. prof. 1940- 46, prof., 1946—, Thomas Brackett Reed prof. history and polit. sci., 1959- -; prof. diplomatic history Fletcher Sch. Law and Diplomacy, 1943-44. Sheldon travelling fellow Harvard, 1929-30. Mem. Am. Hist. Assn., Am. Acad. Polit. and Social Sci., Phi Beta Kappa. Lutheran. Author: The Diplomacy of the Balkan Wars, 1912-13, reprinted, 1969; (with C.E. Black) Twentieth Century Europe: A History, 4th edit., 1971; Religious Education in German Schools; An Historical Approach, 1959, German edit., 1966; Religion and the Maine Schools: An Historical Approach, 1960. Editor: A Free Church in a Free State, The Catholic Church, Italy, Germany, France, 1864-1914, 1964; Hungary, 1957. Home: 6 Boody St Brunswick ME 04011

HELMS, E. ALLEN, educator; b. Veedessbury, Ind., Sept. 24, 1897; s. Allen Walker and Mary (Purdue) H.; A.B., U. Ill., 1922, M.A., 1923, Ph.D., 1927; m. Lois Light, July 26, 1924; 1 dau., Louise Marie (Mrs. Robert S. Smith). Mem. faculty Ohio State U., 1925—, prof. polit. sci., 1937-67, prof. emeritus, 1967—, chmn. dept., 1959-62; vis. prof. George Peabody Coll., summer 1927-37, U. Ill., 1941, Mich. State U., 1946, U. Oxford (Eng.), 1950-51, U. Wis., 1952. Mem. Am. Polit. Sci. Assn., Midwest Conference Polit. Scientists (pres. 1962-63, exec. council 1963-64. Author: Eighteenth Amendment, 1928. Co-author: Democracy in Transition, 1938; American Politics, 2d edit., 1947; The Presidency in Transition, 1949; Goals for Political Science, 1951; Nomination Politi, 1952. Home: 53 W Royal Forest Blvd Columbus OH 43214

HELMS, FRED BRYAN, lawyer; b. Union County, N.C., Apr. 12, 1896; s. Emanuel M. and Frances P. (Austin) H.; student U. Ga., 1919-20; LL.B., Wake Forest Coll., 1922; postgrad. Columbia, 1922; m. Margaret V. Harrelson, July 12, 1927; children—Margaret Harrelson (Mrs. Joseph B. Tyson) and Frances (Mrs. William C. Abernethy). Tchr. pub. schs., Union County, 1914-15; mgr. chain clothing stores, Athens, Ga., East Moline, Ill., Muscatine, Ia., 1919-22; admitted to N.C. bar, 1922, since practiced in Charlotte; pros. atty. City of Charlotte, 1925-27; county judge, Mecklenburg County, N.C., 1927-31; pvt. practice, specializing in civil law, 1931—; dir. gen. counsel R.S. Dickson & Co., Am. & Efird Mills, and subsidiaries. Organizer, 1st pres. Charlotte Community Chest, 1932-33; chmn. Citizens Com., 1941-45; mem. Commn. to Study and Revise Ins. Laws N.C., 1945-47, Commn. for Improvement Adminstrn. of Justice in N.C., 1947-49; mem. N.C. Jud. Council; mem. N.C. Gov.'s adv. commn. on segregation; mem. Nat. Commn. Reform Fed. Criminal Laws. Trustee Wingate Coll. Presdl. elector N.C., 1956. Organizer, atty., trustee Charlotte Meml. Hosp. Authority; mem., gen. counsel Dickson Found., Inc., Mt. Holly, N.C. Served as 2d lt., F.A., U.S. Army, 1918-19. Recipient Silver medallion Nat. Conf. Christians and Jews, 1958. Fellow Am. Coll. Trial Lawyers; mem. Am. Soc. Internat. Law, Am. Legion, Am., Mecklenburg County bar assns., N.C. State Bar, Inc. (v.p. 1944-46, pres. 1946-47), Am. Judicature Soc., Am. Law Inst. Democrat. Clubs: Kiwanis, City, Country (Charlotte). Home: 1571 Queens Rd W Charlotte NC 28202 Office: INC Nat Bank Bldg Charlotte NC 28202

HELMS, LLOYD ALVIN, economist, educator; b. Matthews, Ind., Jan. 12, 1902; s. Wilbert Alvin and Amy Augusta (Carter) H.; A.B. (Rector scholar), DePauw U., 1925; A.M. (Econs. Pub. Utilities scholar), U. Ill., 1926, Ph.D., 1931; m. Gladys Marie Leach, Aug. 14, 1927; children—Carl Wilbert, Carol Ann. Fellow U. Ill., 1926- 27, asst. in econs., 1927-30; prof. econs. and bus. adminstrn. Geneva Coll., 1930-38; mem. faculty Bowling Green (O.) State U., 1938-71, chmn. dept. econs. 1939- 55, prof. econs., 1945-71, ret., 1971, sec. faculty 1953-65, dean Grad. Sch., 1955-67. Mem. Am. Finance Assn., Am. Econ. Assn., Am. Arbitration Assn. (nat. panel arbitrators), Phi Kappa Phi, Sigma Alpha Epsilon, Omicron Delta Kappa (nat. treas., 1959-70), Beta Gamma Sigma. Methodist. Club: Town and Gown (past pres.). Author: The Contributions of Lord Overstone to the Theory of Currency and Banking, 1939. Home: 1416 Glendale Dr Marion IN 46952

HELMS, RICHARD MCGARRAH, govt. ofcl.; b. St. Davids, Pa., Mar. 30, 1913; s. Herman H. and Marion (McGarrah) H.; B.A., Williams Coll., 1935; m. Julia Bretzman Shields, Sept. 8, 1939 (div. 1968); 1 son, Dennis J.; m. 2d, Cynthia McKelvie, 1969. Staff correspondent in Europe, U.P., 1935-37; mem. staff Indpls. Times Pub. Co., 1937-42; with CIA, 1947—, dep. dir., 1965-66, dir. 1966- -. Served with OSS, USNR, 1942-46; ETO. Recipient Career Service award Nat. Civil Service League, 1965. Club: Chevy Chase (Md.). Office: Central Intelligence Agy Washington DC 20505

HELMSING, CHARLES HERMAN, bishop; b. Shrewsbury, Mo., Mar. 23, 1908; s. George and Louise (Boschert) H.; ed. St. Michael's Parochial Sch., 1914-22, St. Louis Prep. Sem., 1922-27, Kenrick Sem., 1927-33; ordained priest, 1933; parochial work in parishes of St. Liborius, Immaculate Conception, and St. Louis Cathedral, 1933-49; prof. Cathedral Latin Sch., religion, history, English, 1934-46; mem. Diocesan Tribunal, 1939; mem. high school bd., 1947, asst. supt. high schs. of St. Louis, 1936; dir. Soc. for Propagation of the Faith, 1947; personal sec. and master of ceremonies to Archbishop of St. Louis, 1946; apptd. titular bishop, 1949; consecrated auxiliary to Archbishop of St. Louis, 1949; bishop of diocese of Springfield-Cape Girardeau, Mo., 1956-62, Kansas City-St. Joseph, 1962—. Mem. Secretariate for Promotion of Christian Unity, 1963- -. Office: 300 E 36th St PO Box 1037 Kansas City MO 64141

HELMSWORTH, JAMES ALEXANDER, educator, physician; b. Jamestown, N.D., Mar. 13, 1915; s. Frederick William and Irma Belle (MacGillivray) H.; B.S., Jamestown Coll., 1935; M.D., U. Pa., 1939; m. Juliet Chase Muller, Feb. 6, 1971; children by previous marriage—Nancy, Thomas, Mary. Intern Univ. Hosp., Phila., 1939-41; resident surgery Cin Gen. Hosp., 1939-41; asst. clin. prof. surgery U. Cin., 1949-52, asst. prof. surgery, 1952-58, asso. prof., 1958-69, prof., 1969—, dir. cardiovascular and thoracic surgery div., 1970—; cons. thoracic surgery VA, Bethesda hosps., Shriners' Burns Inst.; mem. adv. bd. crippled children's program Ohio Dept. Pub. Welfare. Served to maj., M.C., AUS, World War II; PTO. Recipient research grantee USPHS, Am. Heart Assn., Southwestern Ohio Heart Assn. Fellow A.C.S.; mem. Am. Assn. Thoracic Surgery, Am. Coll. Cardiology, Am. Heart Assn., Am. Surg. Assn., A.M.A., Internat. Cardiovascular Soc., Soc. Univ. Surgeons, Soc. Vascular Surgery, Alpha Omega Alpha. Club: Queen City (Cin.). Contbr. articles profl. jours. Research heart-lung machine, treatment congenital cardiac malformities in children. Home: 1247 Cliff Laine Dr Cincinnati OH 45226

HELPERN, MILTON, physician, forensic pathologist; b. N.Y.C., Apr. 17, 1902; s. Moses and Bertha (Toplon) H.; B.S., Coll. City N.Y., 1922; M.D., Cornell U., 1926; LL.D., Ghent U., 1970; m. Ruth Vyner, July 10, 1927 (dec. Jan. 1953); children—Nancy (Mrs. Edward Moldover), Susan (Mrs. Paul Nettler), Alice; m. 2d, Beatrice L. Nightingale, Jan. 1, 1955; stepchildren—William and Stuart Nightingale. Intern 2d Med. Div., Bellevue Hosp., N.Y.C. 1927-29, resident pathologist, 1929-31, pathologist 2d Surg. Div., 1929-31; asst. med. examiner Office Chief Med. Examiner, City N.Y., 1931-43, dep. chief med. examiner, 1943-54, chief med. examiner, 1954; prof., chmn. dept. forensic medicine N.Y.U. Schs. Medicine, 1954—; asst. prof. clin. medicine, lectr. pathology Cornell U., 1940-66, vis. prof. pathology, 1966; dir. labs. Hosp. Spl. Surgery, 1941-58, cons. pathologist, 1958-68, chief pathology emeritus, 1968—; mem. med. adv. bd. N.Y. State Athletic Commn.; cons. pathologist Knickerbocker Hosp., Englewood Hosp., Bellevue Hosp., FAA, 1960-71; cons. U.S. Bur. Medicine, USPHS Hosp. S.I., Armed Forces Inst. Pathology, 1958-70; vis. prof. pathology S.C. Med. Coll., 1969. Spl. cons. War Dept., 1943-46. Decorated officer Order Leopold II (Belgium); recipient gold medal and citation Law Sci. Inst. and Found., U. Tex. Law Sch., 1958; Townsend Harris medal Alumni Assn. Coll. City N.Y., 1958; Distinguished Alumnus award Cornell U. Med Coll. Alumni Assn., 1964. Fellow N.Y. Acad. Scis., Am. Soc. Clin. Pathologists, Coll. Am. Pathologists, Am. Acad. Compensation Medicine (past pres.), N.Y. Acad Med., Internat. Coll. Surgeons (hon.); mem. Internat. Acad. Legal Medicine (past v.p.); hon. mem. fgn. med. socs.; mem. A.A.A.S., Soc. Med. Jurisprudence (trustee, past pres.), Nat. Assn. Med. Examiners (past pres.), N.Y. County Med. Soc. (past pres.), A.M.A. (del.), Internat. Acad. Traffic and Accident Medicine (past pres.), Am. Acad. Forensic Scis. (past pres.), Am. Assn. Pathologists and Bacteriologists, N.Y. Path. Soc. (past pres., sec.), Soc. Alumni Bellevue Hosp. (past pres.), Phi Beta Kappa (hon. and alumni Gamma chpt.), Alpha Omega Alpha. Jewish religion. Author: (with T.A. Gonzales, M. Vance, C.J. Umberger) Legal Medicine, Pathology and Toxicology, 2d edit., 1954; also articles in field. Editor Internat. Microform Jour. Legal Medicine; editorial bd. Zeitschrift fur Rechtsmedezin; asso. editorial bd. N.Y. State Jour. Medicine. Home: 303 N 57th St New York City NY 10022 Office: 520 1st Av New York City NY 10016

HELPHAND, BEN J., ins. co. exec.; b. Columbus, Neb., Feb. 2, 1915; s. David and Bessie (Krupinsky) H.; student U. Neb., 1932-35; B.A., U. Ia., 1936, M.A., 1937; m. Bessie H. Stine, Sept. 16, 1937; 1 dau., Cathy Dee. Actuarial asst. Pacific Mut. Life Ins. Co., Los Angeles, 1937-42, v.p. actuary, 1947—; actuary Dept. Ins. State S.C., Columbia, 1946-47. Served to maj. USAAF, 1942-46. Fellow Soc. Actuaries; mem. actuarial clubs States (past pres.), Los Angeles (past pres.). Am. Acad. Actuaries, Sigma Xi. Home: 12963 LaMaida St Sherman Oaks CA 91403 Office: 523 W 6th St Los Angeles CA 90054

HELPS, ROBERT, pianist, composer; student Juilliard Sch. Music; pupil of piano with Abby Whiteside, of composition with Roger Sessions. Appeared auspices Internat. Soc. Contemporary Music, also with chamber groups; joint recitals with Bethany Beardslee; soloist San Francisco Symphony; former tchr. piano San Francisco Conservatory Music, U. Cal. at Berkeley, Stanford, New Eng. Conservatory Music, Boston; now tchr. piano Manhattan Sch. Music Princeton; compositions performed throughout U.S. and abroad. Home: 156 Montague St Brooklyn NY 11201

HELRICH, MARTIN, educator, physician; b. N.Y.C., Mar. 31, 1922; s. Abraham and Anna (Kornblau) H.; B.S., Dickinson Coll., 1946; M.D., U. Pa., 1946; m. Ina Brunstein, Aug. 13, 1950; children—Carol Lisa, Karen Lee. Intern, Atlantic City Hosp., 1946-47; resident N.Y.U.-Bellevue Hosp., 1948-50; postdoctorate research fellow U. Pa. Med. Sch., 1953-54, asst. prof. anesthesiology, 1954-56; prof. anesthesiology, chmn. dept. U. Md. Sch. Medicine, 1956—; head dept. anesthesiology U. Med. Hosp., 1956—; cons. in field. Served to capt., M.C., AUS, 1947, 51-53. Diplomate Am. Bd. Anesthesiology. Fellow Am. Coll. Anesthesiologists; mem. Am. Soc. Pharmacology and Exptl. Therapeutics, Assn. U. Anesthetists, Am. Soc. Anesthesiologists (bd. dirs.), Internat. Anesthesia Research Soc., Md. Soc. Anesthesiologists (pres., sec.), Phi Beta Research Soc., Md. Soc. Anesthesiologists (pres., sec.), Phi Beta Kappa, Sigma Xi. Home: 3507 Old Post Dr Baltimore MD 21208

HELSABECK, FRED, coll. pres.; b. Rural Hall, N.C., Sept. 4, 1908; s. Edgar Numa and Nannie Ethel (Reynolds) H.; A.B., Lynchburg Coll., 1929; M.A., George Peabody Coll. Tchrs., 1932; Ph.D., Ohio State U., 1942; m. Emily Rae Ailsworth, Dec. 28, 1932; children—Emily Jane (Mrs. William R. Goode), Fred Robert Edgar, Henry Carter. Tchr., athletic dir. Holland (Va.) High Sch., 1928-30; asst. prin. West Point (Va.) High Sch., 1930-31; prin. Achilles (Va.) High Sch., 1931-34; elementary supr., Prince George, Va., 1934-37; instr. Ohio State U., 1937-39; high sch. curriculum counselor Radford Coll., 1939-42; prin. Lee Jr. High Sch., Roanoke, Va., 1942-45; dean Lynchburg Coll., 1945-51, asst. to pres., 1951-56; pres. Culver-Stockton Coll., 1956—. Past chmn. council agys., past pres. bd. higher edn. Christian Chs.; chmn. Christian Edn. Assembly, 1955-57; gen. bd. Christian Ch. (Disciples Christ); pres. Va. Conv. Christian Chs.; pres. Christian Ch. in Mo., 1969-71, pres. Mo. Coll. Joint Fund, 1966-68; chmn. Miss. Valley Coll. Assn., 1966-69. Vice mayor, mem. city council, Lynchburg, 1952-56. Mem. N.E.A., Canton Round Table, Canton C. of C., Phi Delta Kappa. Mem. Christian Ch. Mason (Shriner), Kiwanian (lt. gov.). Home: 800 College St Canton MO 63435

HELSON, HARRY, pyschologist; b. Chelsea, Mass., Nov. 9, 1898; s. William and Ida H.; A.B., Bowdoin Coll., 1921; A.M., Harvard, 1922, Ph.D., 1924; m. Lida Georgette Anderson, Sept. 3, 1926; children—Henry Berge, Martha Alice. Instr. in psychology Cornell U., 1924-25, U. Ill., 1925-26; asst. prof. psychology U. Kan. 1926-28; asso. prof psychology dir. lab., Bryn Mawr Coll., 1928-33, prof., 1933-49; prof. psychology, chmn. dept. Bklyn. Coll., 1949-51; prof. psychology U. Tex., 1951-61; John C. Peterson distinguished prof. Kan. State U., 1961-67; distinguished prof. psychology York U., 1967-68; prof. psychology U. Mass., 1968-71; acting prof., Thomas Welton Stanford fellow, Stanford, 1948-49; vis. prof. (summers) Cornell U., 1928, U. So. Cal., 1933, 47, Harvard, 1948, U. Cal. at Los Angeles, 1950, U. Cal. at Berkeley 1959, U. Colo., 1961; co-dir., anti-aircraft fire-control labs. Foxboro Co. (Mass.), 1942-44; dir. Radiobiol. Lab., U. Texas and USAF, 1952-54. Hogg Found. Research scholar, 1956-57. Recipient Howard Crosby Warren medal Soc. Exptl. Psychologists, 1959; Distinguished Sci. Contbn. award Am. Psychol. Assn., 1962; I.H. Godlove award Inter-Soc. Color Council, 1969. Fellow A.A.A.S. (council, 1941-42, 50-51, 70-72), Am. Psychol. Assn. (pres. div. 1, 1959, div. 10, 1954); mem. Soc. Exptl. Psychologists, Eastern Psychol. Assn. (sec.-treas. 1939-41, sec. 1941-42), Nat. Research Council, Phi Beta Kappa, Sigma Xi, Sigma Nu. Author: The Psychology of Cestalt, 1926; Adaptation-Level Theory, 1964. Contbr. articles profl. jours. Editor: Theoretical Foundations of Psychology, 1951; co- operating editor Am. Jour. Psychology, 1940-70; cons. editor, Jour. Exptl. Psychology, 1947-50; psychol. rev. editor Psychol. Bull., 1959-64. Co-editor: Contemporary Approaches to Psychology, 1967. Home: 15 The Crescent Berkeley CA 94708

HELSON, HENRY BERGE, educator; b. Lawrence, Kan., June 2, 1927; s. Harry and Lida G. (Anderson) H.; A.B., Harvard, 1947, Ph.D., 1950; Sheldon travelling fellow Warsaw and Wroclaw (Poland), 1947-48; m. Ravenna W. Mathews, June 12, 1954; children—David M., Ravenna A., Harold E. Lectr., U. Uppsala (Sweden), 1950-51; instr., then asst. prof. math. Yale, 1951-55; mem. faculty U. Cal. at Berkeley, 1955—, now prof. math.; vis. prof. Swedish univs., spring 1962, U. Paris (Orsay, France), 1966-67. Mem. Soc. Friends. Home: 15 The Crescent Berkeley CA 94708

HELSTEIN, RALPH L., labor union ofcl., lawyer; b. Duluth, Minn., Dec. 11, 1908; s. Henry and Lena (Litman) H; B.A., U. Minn., 1929, LL.B., 1934; m. Rachel Brin, Jan. 2, 1939; children—Nina, Toni. Admitted to Minn. bar, 1936, pvt. law practice, Mpls., 1936-43; labor compliance office for Minn. N.R.A., 1934-35; gen. counsel Minn. Council C.I.O., 1939-43; United Packinghouse Workers Am., 1942-46, internat. pres., 1946-68; spl. counsel, v.p. Amalgamated Meat Cutters and Butcher Workmen of North America, 1968—; v.p. indsl. union dept. AFL.-CIO, 1961-65, v.p., mem. exec. council, 1965-69, v.p. emenitus, 1969—. Dir. Hyde Park Fed. Savs. & Loan Assn. Mem. pension research council U. Pa., bd. Dirs. Chgo. Inst. Psychoanalysis. Home: 5806 S Blackstone Av Chicago IL 60637 Office: 2800 N Sheridan Rd Chicago IL 60657

HELSTOSKI, HENRY, congressman; b. Wallington, N.J., Mar. 21, 1925; s. Heronim and Margaret (Spiek) H.; B.A., Montclair (N.J.) State Coll., 1947, M.A. in Social Studies and Adminstrn., 1949; m. Victoria Ubaldo; children— Henry, Andrea. Tchr., East Rutherford (N.J.) High Sch., 1948-60; prin. Wallington High Sch., 1962-63; chmn. English dept. Cedar Grove (N.J.) High Sch., 1962-63; pres. Marpel Assos., advt., East Rutherford, 1963-65; mem. 89th to 92d Congresses from 9th Dist. N.J., mem. mcht. marine and fisheries com., govt. operations com., sci. and astronautics com., vets. affairs com. Chmn. Joint Sewer Meeting, Rutherford, East Rutherford, and Carlstadt, 1957-65; exec. com. Meadowland Regional Devel. Agy., 1959-65. Mem. N.J. Ho. of Reps. from 9th Dist., 1965; mem. city council, East Rutherford, 1956-57, mayor, 1957-65. Served with USAAF, 1943-45. Mem. N.J. Assn. Chiefs Police; Democratic Mayors Assn. Bergen County, N.J. Mayors Assn., Pulaski Assn., Columbian Assn., Middle State Council Social Studies, N.J. Tchrs. Assn., N.J. Tchr. Vets. Assn., N.J. Secondary Sch. Prins. Assn., Am. Legion, Holy Name Soc. Democrat. Roman Catholic. Elk. Club: Polish University (N.J.). Author articles. Home: 84 Cottage Pl East Rutherford NJ 07073 Office: Cannon Bldg Washington DC 20015 also 666 Paterson Av East Rutherford NJ 07073

HELTON, FLOYD FRANKLIN, educator; b. Council Bluffs, Ia., Sept. 6, 1912; s. Frank and Nancy (Davis) H.; A.B., Westminster Coll., Fulton, Mo., 1935; M.A., U. Mo., 1939; Ph.D., U. Ill., 1946; m. Marian Linnice Dufford, June 3, 1941; children—Philip Eugene, Barbara Ellen (Mrs. Robert H. Weaver). Tchr., Tebbetts (Mo.) High Sch., 1935-36, Koshkonong (Mo.) High Sch., 1936-38; from instr. to prof. math. Central Coll., Fayette, 1939-41, 44-59; prof. math. U. Pacific, 1959—. Mem. Math. Assn. Am., Am. Math. Soc., Nat. Council Tchrs. Math., Cal. Math. Council, Sigma Xi. Mason. Author: Introducing Mathematics, 1958. Home: 6916 N Pershing Av Stockton CA 95207

HELTON, PERCY, actor; b. N.Y.C., Jan. 31, 1894; s. Alfred and Ellen (Bosher) H.; student pvt. schs. and Peekskill Mil. Acad.; m. Edna Eustace, Oct. 24, 1931. Made debut (with father) in Tony Pastor's Theatre, N.Y.C., 1897; appeared on Broadway in Return of Peter Grimm, Young America, To the Ladies, Poor Nut. One Sunday Afternoon; appeared in approximately 200 movies, 1948—, including Miracle on 34th St., Hazard, Set Up, Crooked Way, Butch Cassidy; appeared on numerous television shows. Served with U.S. Army, World War I. Decorated D.S.C. Clubs: Lambs (N.Y.C.); Masquers (past 2d v.p.) (Hollywood, Cal.). Office: Masquers Club 1765 N Sycamore Hollywood CA 90028

HELTZER, HARRY, mfg. co. exec.; b. Cin., Aug. 22, 1911; s. Edward and Anna Heltzer; Metal. Engr., U. Minn., 1933; m. Bernice Mary Lejcher, June 15, 1933; children—James Robert, Mary Helen (Mrs. Robert Hanson). With Minn. Mining & Mfg. Co., 1933—, div. v.p. reflective products, 1959-61, v.p. corp., 1961-66, group v.p., 1963-66, pres., 1966-70, chmn. bd., 1970—, also dir.; dir. 1st Trust Co. St. Paul, Minn. Mut. Life Ins. Co., also several subsidiaries. Bd. dirs. U.S. C. of C. Mem. exec. bd. Indianhead Council Boy Scouts Am. Bd. dirs. Automotive Safety Found., Nat. Safety Council; chmn. Hwy. Users Found. Safety and Mobility, 1969-70. Mem. Internat. Road Fedn. (chmn., dir.). Minn. Alumni Assn. (dir.). Methodist. Mason (Shriner). Clubs: Minnesota; St. Paul Athletic. Inventor hwy. safety products. Office: 3M Center St Paul MN 55101

HELWIG, ELSON BOWMAN, physician; b. Pierceton, Ind., Mar. 5, 1907; s. Llewellyn and Grace (Bowman) H.; B.S., Ind. U., 1930, M.D., 1932; m. Mildred Stoelting, Apr. 20, 1933; children—Alan S., Warren B., Ann (Mrs. Thomas Gordon). Rotating intern Indpls. City Hosp., 1932-33, resident pathology, 1933- 34; asst. resident pathology Inst. Pathology, Western Res. U., 1934-35, resident pathology Cleve. City Hosp., 1935-36; asst. pathologist New Eng. Deaconess Hosp., Boston, 1936-39; mem. faculty Washington U. Sch. Medicine, St. Louis, 1939-46, asst. prof. pathology, 1946; sr. pathologist, chief skin and gastro-intestinal pathology br. Armed Forces Inst. Pathology, 1946—, chief dept. pathology, 1955—, asso. dir. for consultation, 1967—; profl. lectr. George Washington U. Sch. Medicine, 1947-64, clin. prof., 1964—; vis. profl. dermatol. pathology Temple U. Sch. Medicine, 1958—, cons. skin and cancer hosp. of univ., 1959—; cons. Walter Reed Army Hosp., 1953—, WHO, 1965—. Mem. Armed Forces Epidemiol. Bd., 1968—. Served to col., M.C., AUS, 1942-45; PTO. Recipient Meritorious Civilian Service award Dept. Army, Exceptional Civilian Service award, 1964; Distinguished Civilian Service award Dept. Def., 1965; President's award for Distinguished Fed. Civilian Service, 1966. Mem. Coll. Am. Pathologists, Am. Soc. Clin. Pathologists, Internat. Assn. Pathologists, Am. Assn. Pathologists and Bacteriologists, A.M.A., Mass. Med. Soc., Washington Pathology Soc., Washington Dermatol. Soc., Am. Acad.

Dermatology, Assn. Mil. Dermatologists, As. Soc. Dermatopathology (pres. 1964-65), Assn. Mil. Surgeons, Histochem. Soc., Stout-Pathology Soc., Pacific Dermatol. Assn., Soc. Columbiana de Patologica, French Soc. Dermatology and Syphiology (fgn. corr.). Author numerous articles in field. Identified and classified adnexal tumors of skin; established relationship between Bowen's disease and internal cancer; identified cloacagenic carcinoma of anus, anatomic and histochem. changes in skin after laser irradiation. Home: 14 W Maple St Alexandria VA 22301 Office: Armed Forces Inst Pathology Washington DC 20305

HEMBREE, HUGH LAWSON, III, diversified holding co. exec.; b. Fort Smith, Ark., Nov. 16, 1931; s. Raymond N. and Gladys (Newman) H., B.S. in Bus. Adminstrn., U. Ark., 1953, LL.B., 1958; m. Sara Janelle Young, Sept. 1, 1956; children—Hugh Lawson IV, Raymond Scott. In middle mgmt. Ark.-Best Freight pres., Inc., Fort Smith, 1958-61, dir. finance, 1961-65, v.p., 1965-67; pres., dir. Ark.-Best Corp., Fort Smith, 1966—; dir., chmn. exec. com. Nat. Bank of Commerce, Dallas; dir. Universal Variable e Annuity Ins. Co., Am. Found. Life Ins. Co., United Internat, Corp., Southwestern Die Casting Co.; chmn. 1st Bankers Real Estate Investment Trust. Sec. Fort Smith/Sebastin County Joint Planning Commn., 1959—; Ark. chmn. Radio Free Europe Program, 1968-69; mem. dean's adv. com. sch. bus. U. Ark.; mem. Democratic Central Com. Ark., 1968—; pres. Westark area council Boy Scouts Am., 1966-67, now mem. exrc. com. Region V. Trustee St. Edward Hosp. Served to capt. USAF, 1953-55. Recipient Silver Beaver award Boy Scouts Am., 1969. Mem. Nat. Assn. of Devel. Orgns. (chmn. adv. com.), Ark. (v.p.), Ft. Smith (pres.) chambers commerce, Nat. Young Presidents Orgn., U. Ark. Alumni Assn. (dir., mem. bldg. com.), Am. Trucking Assn. (mem. nat. accounting and finance council), Nat. Assn. Mfrs., Ark. Arts Center. Episcopalian (vestryman, co-chmn. ch. finance com.). Clubs: Chaparral, Lancers, Economics (Dallas); Fort Smith Hardscabble County and Town; New York Athletic. Home: 3220 Park Av Fort Smith AR 72901 Office: 301 S 11th St Fort Smith AR 72901

HEMELRIGHT, FRANK EDWARD, banker; b. Jermyn, Pa., Mar. 16, 1906; s. Frank H. and Edith (Voeste) H.; student Phillips Exeter Acad., 1928; Ph.B., Brown U., 1931; m. Ruth Helen Theobald, July 16, 1943; children—Ann, Andrew, Martha. With First Nat. Bank, Scranton, Pa., 1933-47, asst. v.p., 1941-47; exec. v.p. Scranton Lackawanna Trust Co., 1947-53, pres., 1953-54; pres. Northeastern Pa. Nat. Bank & Trust Co., and predecessor, Scranton, 1954—. now chmn. bd., chief exec. officer, also dir.; dir. U.S. Lumber Co., J.J. Newman Lumber Co., Commonwealth Telephone Co., Pa. Gas & Water Co., Lackawanna Indsl. Fund Enterprises, Scranton Lackawanna Indsl. Bldg. Co. Mem. Pa. Indsl. Devel. Authority, 1963—; v.p., dir. Pa. Devel. Corp., 1963—; mem. exec. com. 100,000 Pennsylvanians, 1964- -; bd. dirs. Econ. Devel. Council Northeastern Pa., 1964—. Chmn. Lackawanna United Fund, 1957. Bd. dirs. Geisinger Med. Center, Keystone Jr. Coll. Served to 1t. comdr. USNR, 1942-45. Recipient Americanism award B'nai B'rith, 1967. Mem. Pa. Bankers Assn. (2d v.p. 1967), U.S., Pa. (bd. dirs. 1947-), Greater Scranton (pres. 1966- -) chambers commerce. Republican. Presbyn. Clubs: Country of Scranton; Glen Oak Country (Waverly). Home: Carbondale Rd Waverly PA 18471 Office: Northeastern Pennsylvanian Nat Bank and Trust Co Spruce St and Wyoming Av Scranton PA 18501

HEMENWAY, CHARLES FRANCIS, investment banker; b. Auburn, N.Y., Apr. 10, 1890; s. Charles C. and Ida E. (Shackelford) H.; A.B., Hamilton Coll., 1910; m. Eleanor Lord, Apr. 17, 1922; children—Anne (Mrs. Merle E. Dowd), Charles C. Clk., salesman Patterson Sargent Co., Kansas City, Mo., 1910-12; salesman, mgr. Chgo. officer Smith & Hemenway Co., tool mfrs., 1912-26; mgr. Chgo. office Utica Drop Forge & Tool Co., 1926-28; salesman Ill. Mchts. Bank & Trust Co. (merger Continental Ill. Co.), Chgo., 1928-33; an organizer, v.p. Ill. Co., Inc., Chgo., 1933-62, chmn. bd., 1962—. Alderman 1st ward, Evanston, Ill., 1943-55. Bd. dirs., pres. Scholarship Fund Found., 1952-66, chmn. bd., 1966—; life trustee Hamilton Coll.; trustee Evanston Schs., 1956—. Served to ensign USNR, 1917-19. Mem. Psi Upsilon. Republican. Presbyn. Clubs: Union League, University, Bond, Municipal Bond (pres. 1949) (Chgo.); Westmoreland Country (Wilmette, Ill.). Home: 1625 Hinman Av Evanston IL 60201 Office: 135 S LaSalle St Chicago IL 60603

HEMENWAY, CURTIS LELAND, astrophysicist; b. Hope, Me., Sept. 11, 1920; s. Leland David and Clara (Hinckley) H.; A.B., Colby Coll, 1938; M.S., Rutgers U., 1946, Ph.D. in Physics, 1950; m. Vivian Bennett, July 29, 1948; children—Susan, David. Faculty Rutgers U., 1943-44, 47-49; asst. prof. physics Union Coll., Schenectady, 1949-54, asso. prof., 1954-59, prof., 1959-64, research prof. physics, 1964—; dir. Dudley Obs., Albany, N.Y., 1956—; prof., chmn. astronomy and space sci. dept. State U. N.Y., Albany, 1964-71, prof., 1971—. Mem. security bds., designee AEC, 1954—; chmn. cosmic dust panel COSPAR. Cons. Smithsonian Astrophys. Obs., 1957-58. Research fellow Harvard Coll. Obs., 1955-56. Fellow A.A.A.S., Am. Meteoritical Soc.; mem. Am. Phys. Soc., Am. Assn. Physics Tchrs., Am. Assn. U. Profs., Am. Astron. Soc., Internat. Astron. Union, Sigma Xi. Author: (with Richard W. Henry and Martin Caulton) Physical Electronics, 1962. Research and publs. on micrometeorites. Home: River Rd Route 144 Selkirk NY 12158 Office: 100 Fuller Rd Albany NY 12205

HEMENWAY, ROBERT, writer, editor; b. S. Haven, Mich., July 15, 1921; s. Earl Lee and Freda (Penoyar) H.; B.A., U. Chgo., 1946, M.A., 1951; m. Elizabeth Tingom, July 19, 1969. Mem. editorial staff New Yorker mag., 1959—. Recipient O'Henry Prize Story award, 1970. Author: The Girl who sang with the beatles, 1970. Home: 29 Perry St New York City NY 10014

HEMENWAY, WILLIAM GARTH, physician; b. Swift Current, Sask., Can., Aug. 13, 1921; s. William C. and Matilda (McKee) H.; B.A., U. Sask., 1942; M.D., U. Man., 1945. Came to U.S., 1950, naturalized, 1962. Intern Winnipeg (Can.) Gen. Hosp., 1944-45; gen. practice medicine, Broadview, Sask., 1948-50; resident ear, nose and throat Cook County Hosp., Chgo., 1950-51, U. Ill., Chgo., 1951-52, U. Chgo. Clinics, 1952-53; instr. to asso. prof. U. Chgo., 1953-62; asso. prof., head otolaryngology, asst. med. dir. U. Mo. Med. Center, Columbia, 1962-64; asso. prof. surgery, head otolaryngology U. Colo. Med. Center, Denver, 1964-68, also med. dir. outpatient services, 1964-66, prof. surgery, head div. otolarygoloy, 1968—. Served as pvt., M.C., Canadian Army, 1943-45, as flying officer, Royal Canadian Air Force, 1945-46. Decorated Boi Tinh Van-Hoa Giao-Duc, Y-TeBoi Tinh (Rep. of Vietnam). Fellow A.C.S.; mem. A.M.A., Am. Acad. Ophthalmology and Otolaryngology, Soc. Univ. Otolaryngologists, Trilogical Soc., Am. Soc. Head and Neck Surgery, Am. Sportsman's Club. Mason (Shriner, 32). Contbr. articles sci. jours. Research on human temporal bone pathology, pathology of salivary gland lesions, head and neck tumors. Home: 955 Eudora St Denver CO 80220

HEMINGWAY, ALLAN, physiologist, biophysicist; b. Leeds, Eng., Jan. 25, 1902; s. Arthur and Eleanor (Eastwood) H.; B.A., U. B.C., 1925; Ph.D., U. Minn., 1929; Sterling fellow, Yale, 1936-37; m. Gayle Shirey, Nov. 9, 1929, (dec.); 1 dau., Eleanor; m. 2d. Claire Conklin Carr, July 5, 1951. Instr., asst. prof. physiol. chemistry U. Minn., 1930-36, asst. prof., asso. prof. physiology, 1936-48, prof. physiology 1948-51; prof. physiology Med. Sch., U. Cal. at Los Angeles, 1951—; chief cardiopulmonary lab. San Fernando VA Hosp. (Cal.). Served as maj. USAAF, 1943-45; chief lab. biophysics Sch. Aviation Med., Randolph Field, Tex., 1942-45. Mem. Am. Physiol. Soc., Am. Phys. Soc., Am. Chem. Soc., Soc. Exptl. Biology and Medicine, Am. Assn. U. Profs., Sigma Xi, Gamma Alpha, Phi Beta Pi. Contbr. articles to physiol. and biochem. jours. Home: 123 S Bowling Green Way Los Angeles CA 90049

HEMINGWAY, RICHARD KEITH, banker; b. Salt Lake City, Oct. 18, 1920; s. Harold E. and Isabelle (Whitlam) H.; student U. Wash., 1938-42, Pacific Coast Sch. Banking-No. Western U., 1948, Sch. Financial Relations, 1955; m. Shirley V. Stranquist, Oct. 4, 1948; children—Harold, Ann, Henry, Helen, Jane. With Comml. Security Bank, Ogden, Utah, 1937—, v.p., 1950-60, exec. v.p., 1960-66, pres., 1966—, chmn. bd., 1966—; chmn. bd. Ida. Bank & Trust Co., Pocatello; dir. Box Elder County Bank, Brigham City, Utah. Chmn. local cancer drive, 1961-62, United Fund drive, 1966-67; mem. Utah Bldg. Bd., 1955-69; organizer Pro-Utah, 1964, v.p., 1965-66; co-chmn. drive to reactivate Weber County Indsl. Bur., 1954-55. Bd. dirs. St. Benedicts Hosp., Ogden. Mem. Ogden C. of C. (pres. 1970), Sigma Chi. Rotarian. Clubs: Ogden Golf and Country, Weber (Odgen); Alta (Salt Lake City). Home: 2815 Pierce St Ogden UT 84403 Office: 2491 Washington Blvd Ogden UT 84403

HEMLOW, JOYCE, educator, author; b. Liscomb, N.S., Can., July 30, 1906; d. William and Rosalinda (Redmond) Hemlow; B.A., Queen's Coll., Kingston, Can., 1941, M.A., 1942; A.M., Radcliffe Coll., 1944, Ph.D., 1948; LL.D., Queen's, 1967. Mem. faculty McGill U. 1945—, Greenshields prof. English lit. and lang., 1965—. Guggenheim fellow, 1951-52, 66-67; recipient James Tait Black Meml. book prize for best biography in U.K., The History of Fanny Burney, 1958, also Gov. Gen. Can. medal for academic non-fiction, 1958, Rose Mary Crashay prize Brit. Acad., 1960; Grad. Achievement medal Radcliffe Coll., 1969. Mem. Johnsonians, Phi Beta Kappa. Editor: Journals and Letters Fanny Burney (Madame d'Arblay). Home: 3555 Atwater Av Montreal 25 Quebec Canada also: Liscomb Nova Scotia Canada

HEMMERLING, CLIFFORD ARTHUR lawyer; b. Anaheim, Cal., Feb. 26, 1925; s. Arthur E. and Hulda (Meyer) H.; B.A., U. Cal. at Berkeley, 1947, LL.D., 1950; m. Geraldine Stein, Apr. 7, 1951; children—Keith, Karen. Admitted to Cal. bar, 1951; sr. partner firm Richards Watson & Hemmerling, Los Angeles, 1959-70; gen. counsel Western Center on Law and Poverty,Los Angeles, 1971—. Mem. Am., Cal., Los Angeles Country bar assns., Am. Judicature Soc., S. Cal. World Affairs Council. Democrat. Town Hall (Los Angeles). Home: 369 Homewood Rd Los Angeles CA 90047 Office: 1709 W 8th St Los Angeles CA 90017

HEMMINGS, DAVID, actor; b. Guilford, Eng.; began in opera; became motion picture actor, 1956; films include Some People, Two Left Feet, The System, The Eye of the Devil, Blow Up, Camelot, Only When I Larf, Barbarella, The Best House in London, Alfred the Great. Address: care William Morris Agy Inc 151 El Camino Beverly Hills CA 90212*

HEMMINGSEN, JOHN O., bus. exec.; b. 1913; B.A.Sc., U. B.C. (Can.), 1937; married. Successively with Port Renfrew, Bowarer Corp., Newfoundland, Cal.; with MacMillan, Bloedal Ltd., Vancouver, B.C., 1951—, v.p., gen. mgr. wood products group, dir., 1962—, now exec. v.p. Office: 1199 W Pender St Vancouver British Columbia Canada*

HEMPEL, CARL GUSTAV, educator; b. Oranienburg, Germany, Jan. 8, 1905; s. Carl Friedrich and Charlotte (Kessler) H.; student U. Goettingen, 1923-24, U. Heidelberg, 1924, U. Berlin, 1924-28, U. Vienna, 1929-30; Ph.D., U. Berlin, 1934; m. Eva Beate Ahrends, 1935 (dec. 1944); 1 son, Peter Andrew; m. 2d, Diane Perlow, 1947; 1 dau., Toby Anne. Came to U.S., 1937, naturalized, 1944. Pvt. research and writing, Brussels, Belgium, 1934-37; research asso. philosophy U. Chgo., 1937-38; mem. dept. philosophy Coll. City N.Y., 1939-40, Queens Coll., Flushing, N.Y., 1940-48, Yale, 1948-55; prof. philosophy Princeton, 1955, Stuart prof. philosophy, 1956—; vis. prof. philosophy Columbia, 1950; Hibben research fellow Princeton, 1952; Fulbright Sr. Research fellow, Oxford U., 1959-60; vis. lectr. Harvard, 1953-54. Guggenheim fellow, 1947-48; fellow Center Advanced Study Behavioral Scis., Stanford, 1963-64; hon. research fellow dept. philosophy U. Coll. London, 1971-72. Fellow Am. Acad. Arts and Scis.; mem. Am. Philos. Assn. (pres. Eastern div. 1961), Académie internationale de philosophie des sciences, Am. Philos. Soc., Assn. Symbolic Logic. Author: (with P. Oppenheim) Der Typusbegriff im Lichte der neuen Logik, 1936; Fundamentals of Concept Formation in Empirical Science, 1952; Aspects of Scientific Explanation and other Essays in the Philosophy of Science, 1965; Philosophy of Natural Science, 1966. Mem. editorial bd. Am. Philos. Quar.; cons. editor Jour. Symbolic Logic, 1940- 62. Contbr. profl. jours. Office: Dept Philosophy Princeton U Princeton NJ 08540

HEMPHILL, BERNICE MONAHAN, (Mrs. Charles D. Hemphill), assn. exec., civic leader; b. San Francisco; d. Thomas E. and Anne J. (McGinerty) Monahan; diploma bioanalyst U. Cal.; m. Charles D. Hemphill, June 30, 1939. Supervising technologist Honolulu Blood Plasma Bank, 1941- 43; mng. dir., sec. Irwin Meml. Blood Bank, San Francisco Med. Soc., 1944—; sec. Cal. Blood Bank System, 1951-57; charter mem., treas. Am. Assn. Blood Banks, 1949—, chmn. clearing house program, 1953—, mem. com. on govtl. liaison; cons. blood bank projects A.M.A., Am. Hosp. Assn., other nat. health orgns. Mem. adv. com. blood and blood derivatives Cal. Dept. Pub. Health, 1964- -; active San Francisco United Community Fund as mem. health council, mem. joint budget study com. program for hosps. and health agys., mem. casework services com. program for aging, 1961-62; mem. Cath. Social Service San Francisco; mem. Mayor San Francisco Citizens Com. Centennial Golden Gate Park, 1969-70; also mem. hosp. aux. U. Cal., aux. St. Francis Hosp., Cal., aux. Laguna (Cal.) Honda Home, aux. Little Children's Aid, St. Anthony's Dining Room, Guide Dogs for Blind. Name Distinguished Woman, San Francisco Examiner, 1960, U.S. Lady of Month U.S. Lady mag., 1963; recipient John Elliot award contbns. blood banking Am. Assn. Blood Banks, 1960, Award of Merit for Cath. charities services Archdiocese San Francisco, 1962, commendation exceptional services to patients Ft. Miley VA Hosp., San Francisco, 1961, citation for vol. community services Lane Bryant, 1965, 66, 67, 68. Mem. San Francisco Assn. Mental Health, Internat. Soc. Blood Transfusion. Republican. Clubs: Doctors' Wives; Francisca. Conceived, established 1st clearing house between blood banks, 1951. Home: 1070 Green St San Francisco CA 94133 Office: 270 Masonic Av San Francisco CA 94118

HEMPHILL, HERBERT AUGUSTUS, utilities exec.; b. Hattiesburg, Miss., Aug. 14, 1903; s. Herbert Augustus and Carrie (Favre) H.; student U. Tex., 1929; m. Helen Sellards, Feb. 6, 1927; children—Herbert Augustus, Susan (Mrs. William M. Bosworth), Nancy Carolyn. Asst. to Dr. H.P. Bybee, U. Tex., San Angelo, 1929-34; asst. dist. geologist Magnolia Petroleum Co., 1934-43, dist. geologist to 1952; pres., dir. Tex. Eastern Prodn. Corp. (merged to become Tex. Eastern Transmission Corp. 1955), 1952-55, v.p. charge exploration and prodn., 1955—. Mem. Am. Assn. Petroleum Geologists, West Tex. Geol. Soc., Ind. Natural Gas Assn., Am. Petroleum Inst. Presbyn. Clubs: Houston Petroleum, Houston; Lakeside Country. Home: 5 Westlane Houston TX 77019 Office: Texas Eastern Transmission Corp Box 2521 Texas Eastern Bldg Houston TX 77001

HEMPHILL, JAMES C., investment banker; b. Lancaster, Ky.; s. James C. and Sallie (Currey) H.; Ph.B., U. Chgo., 1920. Comml. paper bus. Hathaway & Co., Chgo., Until 1932; with Goldman Sachs and Co., investment bankers, Chgo., 1932—, gen. partner, 1942—; dir. Globe-Union, Inc., Wayne- Gossard Corp., Humboldt, Tenn., Mead Johnson & Co., Evansville, Ind. Treas. bd. trustees Chgo. Symphony; exec. v.p., dir. Lyric Opera of Chgo. Dir..Rehab. Inst. Chgo. Mem. Assn. Met. Opera, N.Y.C., Delta Kappa Epsilon. Clubs: Mid-American (dir.,) Attic, Saddle and Cycle, Casino (Chgo.); Shoreacres (Lake Bluff, Ill.); Knollwood (Lake Forest, Ill.); Biltmore (N.C.) Forest Country. Home: 1320 N State St Chicago IL 60610 Office: 135 S LaSalle St Chicage IL 60603

HEMPHILL, JAMES CALVIN, Jr., architect; b. Greenwood, S.C., July 25, 1920; s. James Calvin and Millwee (Davis) H.; B.S. in Architecture, Clemson U., 1942; m. Patricia Williams, May 30, 1943; children—James C., John A. Structural research engr. Glenn L. Martin Aircraft Co., 1942-44, NASA, 1944-45; draftsman firm Robert & Co., architects and engrs., Altanta, 1945-46; architect firm James C. Hemphill, Sr., architect, Greenwood, 1947-52; prin. asso. A.G. Odell, Jr. & Assos., Charlotte, N.C., 1952-70; practice as James C. Hemphill, Jr., architect, Charlotte and Greenwood, 1970—; vis. lectr. Clemson U., 1964—; mem. N.C. Bd. Architecture, 1970—; archtl. cons. Charlotte Redevel. Commn., 1971—. Fellow A.I.A. (pres. N.C. 1967, chmn. nat. specification com. 1963-65, chmn. nat. document rev. bd. 1966), Constrn. Specifications Inst. (past nat. bd. dirs.), Greenwood Jr. C. of C. (past pres.) Presbyn. Club: Civitan. Home: 954 Granville Rd Charlotte NC 28207 Office: 222 S Church St Charlotte NC 28202

HEMPHILL, ROBERT WITHERSPOON, dist. judge; b. Chester, S.C., May 10, 1915; s. John McLure and Helen (Witherspoon) H.; A.B., U. S.C., 1936, LL.B., 1938; m. Forrest Isabelle Anderson, June 29, 1942; children—Forrest Richardson, Harriet Witherspoon, Robert Witherspoon. Admitted to S.C. bar, 1938; asso. firm Hemphill & Hemphill, Chester, 1938-64; solicitor 6th S.C. Jud. Circuit, 1950-56; practice before VA, U.S. Civil Service Comm., ICC, 4th Circuit Ct. of Appeals U.S. Supreme Ct.; mem. S.C. Ho. of Reps., 1947-48; mem. 85th-88th Congresses, 5th S.C. Dist.; U.S. dist. judge Eastern, Western dists. S.C., 1964—. Served with USAAF, 1941-45; mem. USAF Res. Mem. Am. Judicature Soc., Am., S.C., Chester County bar assns., S.C. Employees Assn., S.C. Farm Bur., S.C. Wildlife Assn., Am. Legion, 40 and 8. Democrat. Presbyn. K.P. Home: Chester SC 29706 Office: US Courthouse Columbia SC 29201

HEMPHILL, WILLIAM EDWIN, historian, editor; b. Wake County, N.C., June 28, 1912; s. Rev. James Edwin and Nellie Stuckey (Jackson) H.; B.A. with first honors, Hampden- Sydney Coll., 1932; M.A., Emory U., 1933; Ph.D., U. Va., 1937; m. Susan Langhorne Moffett, June 6, 1939; children—Alice (Mrs. Thomas Bennett Clark), Susan (Mrs. James Francis Steadman). Tchr. history Hampden-Sydney Coll., 1934-35, Davidson Coll., 1937-38, U. Va., 1938-39, Emory U., 1940-41; mem. faculty history Mary Washington Coll., 1939-40, 41-44; acting archivist U. Va. Library, summers 1935-36, 38-39; acting dir. Hist. Records Survey, WPA in Va., summers 1936-37; asst. dir. Va. World War II History Agy., 1944-45, dir., 1946-50; editor Albemarle County (Va.) Hist. Soc., 1946-48; dir. history div. Va. State Library, 1950-59; editor Virginia Cavalcade, pictorial mag. Va. history, 1951-58; editor S.C. Archives Dept., editor Papers of John C. Calhoun at U. S.C., 1959—. Mem. gen. council of Presbyn. Ch. in U.S., 1967- 69. Trustee Presbyn. Coll., Clinton, S.C., 1967—. Fellow Soc. Am. Archivists; mem. Orgn. Am. Historians, Am., So., S.C. hist. assns., Am. Assn. State and Local History, Va., S.C., Albmarle County hist. socs., South Caroliniana Soc., history clubs U. Va., U. S.C., Phi Beta Kappa, Omicron Delta Kappa, Chi Phi. Presbyn. (ruling elder). Author: (with Schlegel and Engelberg) Cavalier Commonwealth: History and Government of Virginia, 1957. Co-author, editor: Pursuits of War: The People, 1948. Editor: Gold Star Honor Roll of Virginians, 1947; Aerial Gunner from Virginia. The Letters of Don Moody, 1950; Extracts from Journals of the Provincial Congresses of S.C., 1960; The Papers of John C. Calhoun, Vol. II, 1963, Vol. III, 1967, Vol. IV, 1969, Vol. V, 1971. Author hist. articles, revs. Home: 846 Camellia St Columbia SC 29205 Office: SC Dept Archives and History Columbia SC 29211

HEMPSTONE, SMITH, Jr., journalist; b. Washington, Feb. 1, 1929; s. Smith and Elizabeth (Noyes) H.; student George Washington U., 1946-47; B.A. with honors, U. of South, 1950, Litt.D. (hon.), 1969; Nieman fellow, Harvard, 1964-65; m. Kathaleen Fishback, Jan. 30, 1954. Rewrite man A.P., Charlotte, N.C., 1952; with Nat. Geog. mag., Washington, 1954; reporter Louisville Times, 1953, Eve. Star, Washington, 1955-56; fgn. corr. in Africa, Asia, Europe and Latin Am. for Chgo. Daily News, 1960-66; fgn. corr. Washington Eve. Star, 1966-69, asso. editor, 1970—. Fellow Inst. Current World Affairs, 1956-60; recipient Fgn. Corr. award Sigma Delta Chi. Episcopalian. Clubs: Chevy Chase (Md.); Metropolitan (Washington); Explorers (N.Y.C.). Author: Africa, Angry Young Giant, 1961; Rebels, Mercenaries and Dividends-The Katanga Story, 1962; A Tract of Time (novel), 1966; In the Midst of Lions (novel), 1968. Editorial bd. Nieman Reports, 1965-71. Address: care Washington Evening Star 225 Virginia Av SE Washington DC 20003

HEMRY, JEROME ELDON, lawyer; b. Kirksville, Mo., July 22, 1905; s. U.S.G. and Rose M. (Plumb) H.; A.B., Oklahoma City U., 1926; J.D., U. Okla., 1928; LL.M., Harvard, 1929; m. Martha L. Langston, Aug. 1, 1934; children— Jerome Louis, Kenneth Marshall. Admitted to Okla. bar, 1928; partner Hemry & Hemry, Oklahoma City, 1931—; prof. law Central Okla. Sch. Law, 1931- 41; dean, prof. law Langston U. 1948-49; dir., counsel Am. Gen. Life Ins. Co. Okla.; pres., gen. counsel Gen. Constrn. Corp., 1941-45; legislative counsel Okla. Chain Store Assn., 1941-44. Mem. Bd. Conf. Claimant's Okla. Ann. Conf., treas. Oklahoma City S. Dist. Bd. dirs. Family and Children's Service, 1939- 56. Mem. Okla. Assn. Municipal Attys. (pres. 1956-57), Am., Okla. bar assns., Order of Coif, Phi Delta Phi, Lambda Chi Alpha. Methodist (pres., counsel trustees). Clubs: Lions, Men's Dinner (Oklahoma City). Contbr. articles legal jours. Home: 2255 NW 55th St Oklahoma City OK 73112 Office: First Nat Bldg Oklahoma City OK 73102

HEMSING, ALBERT ERNST, fgn. service officer; b. Barmen, Germany, Feb. 27, 1921; s. Paul and Josephine (Ferder) H.; B.S.S., Coll. City N.Y., 1942; M.A., N.Y.U., 1947; m. Esther Davidson, Dec. 27, 1944; 1 dau., Josephine Claudia. With East and West Assn., 1942-43, OWI, 1943-46, State Dept., 1946-47; ind. documentary film producer, 1947-51; with ECA and USIA, Paris, France, 1951-55; chief overseas film operations div. USIA, Washington, 1955-58; press officer then pub. affairs officer U.S. mission, Berlin, Germany, 1958-64; counselor of embassy pub. affairs, Bonn, Germany, 1964-67, dep. asst. dir. USIA, 1968-69, asst. dir., in charge of Western Europe,

1969- -; mem. State Dept. Sr. Seminar Fgn. Policy, 1967—; mem. bd. examiners for Fgn. Service, 1970—; lectr. Coll. City N.Y., 1946-51, Am. U., 1956-58. Recipient Meritorious Honor award, 1966. Mem. Am. Fgn. Service Assn., Phi Beta Kappa. Home: 100 Cameron Mews Alexandria VA 22314 Office: US Information Agy Washington DC 20547

HENAHAN, DONAL JOSEPH, music critic; b. Cleve., Feb. 28, 1921; s. William Anthony and Mildred (Doyle) H.; student Kent U., 1939-40, Ohio U., 1940-42; B.A., Northwestern U., 1947; postgrad. U. Chgo., 1949; profl. study Chgo. Sch. Music, 1950-57; m. Margaret Pessin, May 17, 1951. With Chgo. Jour. Commerce, 1946; began with Chgo. Daily News, 1947, became music critic, 1957; now music staff N.Y. Times; writer on music Museum Quar., Holiday, Saturday Rev., Show, N.Y. Herald Tribune, Show Bus. Illus., Theatre Arts, Country Beautiful, Down Beat, HiFi-Stereo Rev., Clavier, others. Served to 1st lt. USAAF, 1942-45. Decorated Air medal with four oak leaf clusters; recipient Page One award, 1965, 66. Mem. Am. Newspaper Guild. Clubs: Arts, Press (Chgo.). Home: 1315 Elmwood St Wilmette IL 60091 Office NY Times NY 10036

HENCH, RALPH WOODS, Jr., publishing co. exec.; b. Bklyn., Mar. 28, 1911; s. Ralph Woods and Catharine Flora (Booth) H.; grad. Phillips Acad., Andover, Mass., 1930; A.B., Princeton, 1934; m. Helen Adelaide Forbush, Jan. 25, 1936; children—Helen Adelaide (Mrs. Richard P. Taft, Jr.), Brooke Elizabeth (Mrs. David Willett), Jean Stuart (Mrs. Edward Bourdon). With IBM, 1934-36; with marketing dept. Young & Rubicam, Inc., N.Y.C., 1936-41; with Curtis Pub. Co., 1946-64, N.Y.C. advt. mgr. Holiday mag., 1948-57, nat. advt. sales mgr., 1957-58, nat. advt. dir., 1958-64, v.p. co., 1958-64; v.p. Am. Heritage Pub. Co., Inc., N.Y.C., 1964; pub. Yorke Group, mag. div. Reuben H. Donnelly Corp., 1965-69; pres. Commonico, Inc., 1969—. Served to maj. AUS, 1941-46; ETO. Mem. Pharm. Mfrs. Assn., Am. Bus. Press, Pharm. Advt. Club. Presbyn. (mem. session bd. trustees). Clubs: Princeton (N.Y.C.); Rock Spring (West Orange, N.J.). Home: 383 Upper Mountain Av Upper Montclair NJ 07043 Office 466 Lexington Av New York City NY 10017

HENCKEL, GERALD C., Jr., city mgr.; b. San Antonio, May 24, 1924; s. Gerald C. and Cecilia (Heiligmann) H.; LL.B., St. Mary's U., San Antonio, 1949; m. Margaret E. Schneider, May 1, 1945; children—Karen (Mrs. John Taglieri), Gerald C. III, Kurt, John, Sherry, Kathy, Holly. Admitted to Tex. bar; sec.- treas., tax assessor-collector, Alamo Heights, Tex., 1952-58; city mgr., Terrell Hills, Tex., 1959-62; asst. city mgr., San Antonio, 1962-67, city mgr., 1967—. Trustee Tex. Municipal Retirement System. Mem. Internat., Tex. city mgrs. assns. Home: 1650 W Mistletoe St San Antonio TX 78201 Office Office City Mgr Military Plaza TX 78205

HENCKEN, HUGH O'NEILL, archaeologist; b. N.Y.C., Jan. 8, 1902; s. Albert Charles and Mary Creighton (O'Neill) H.; grad. Hill Sch., Pottstown, Pa., 1920; B.A., Princeton, 1924; B.A., Cambridge U., 1926, M.A., 1930, Ph.D., 1929; hon. D.Litt., Nat. U. Ireland, 1937; m. Mary Thalassa Alford Cruso of Pirbright, Surrey, Eng., Oct. 12, 1935; children—Ala Mary, Sophia, Thalassa. Carried out archaeol. excavations in Eng., 1928, 30, 31; dir. Harvard Achaeol. Expdn. in Ireland, 1932-36; curator European Archaeology, Peabody Mus., Harvard, since 1932; dir. Am. Sch. of Prehistoric Research since 1945 (directed excavations in Morocco 1947, Algeria 1949), chmn., 1959—; Monro lectr. Edinburgh U., 1959; lectr. Lowell Inst., 1942; spl. univ. lectr. London and Oxford univs., 1947; hon. fellow St. John's Coll., Cambridge, 1968. Fellow Soc. Antiquaries London, Soc. Antiquaries Scotland (hon.), Royal Soc. Antiquaries Ireland, Archaeol. Inst. Am. (hon. pres.), Am. Acad. Arts and Scis.; mem. Société des Antiquares de l'Quest, Instituto de Estudios Ibéricos (corr. mem.), Com. Honor Internat. Congress Prehistoric Scis., Royal Archaeol. Inst. Great Britian, German Archaeol. Inst., Internat. Inst. European Research and Edn. (corr.), Prehistoric Soc. Eng. (hon. corr.), Jutland Archaeol. Soc. (corr.) Royal Irish Acad. Recipient Erie Soc. Gold medal, 1951, Instituto di Studi Italici ed Etruschi (corr.), Instituto Italiano di Preistoria, Phi Beta Kappa (hon.). Democrat. Episcopalian. Clubs: United Universities (London, England); Somerset, Odd Volumes (Boston); Harvard Faculty (Cambridge, Mass.); University (N.Y.); Cloister Inn (Princeton, N.J.); Country (Brookline). Author: Archaeology of Cornwall, 1932; Cahercommaun, 1938; Lagore Crannog, 1950; Tarquinia, Villanovans and Early Etruscans, 1968; Tarquinia and Etruscan Origins, 1968. Contbr. Tech. articles. Home: 329 Hammond St Chestnut Hill MA 02167 Office Peabody Mus Cambridge MA 02101

HENCLEY, STEPHEN PAUL, coll. dean; b. June 8, 1924; B.Ed., U. Alta., 1946, M.Ed., 1958; Ph.D., U. Chgo., 1960; m. Hilda Gwendoline Miller, Sept. 20, 1945; children—Elaine Alvina, Bonnie Lorene. Came to U.S., 1960, naturalized, 1967. High sch. prin., Nordegg, Rocky Mountain House and Stettler, Alta., 1946-56; supt. schs., Warner County, Alta., 1956-58; instr. U. Chgo., 1958-60; asso. dir. Univ. Council for Ednl. Adminstrn., Columbus, O., 1960-62; prof. Sch. Adminstrn. U. Ill., Urbana, 1962-66; dean Grad. Sch. Edn., U. Utah, Salt Lake City, 1966—; adv. editor Rand McNally & Co. Bd. dirs. Far West Lab. Ednl. Research and Devel.; mem. Utah State Textbook Commn. Mem. Am. Assn. Sch. Adminstrs., Assn. Sch. Curriculum and Devel., N.E.A., Am. Ednl. Research Assn., Dept. Elementary Sch. Prins., Am. Assn. Coll. Tchrs. Edn.(com. internat. relations), Univ. Council Ednl. Adminstrn. Author, editor: Preparing Administrators, 1962; Educational Research, 1963; Politics of Education, 1964; Secondary School Administration, 1965; Elementary School Principalship, 1970. Home: 1505 Indian Hills Dr Salt Lake City UT 84108

HENDEE, CLARE WORDEN, forester; b. Pinckney, Mich., Aug. 17, 1908; s. Worden Churchill and Rose Caroline (Nash) H.; B.S., Mich. State U., 1930; M.A. in Pub. Adminstrn., Geo. Washington U., 1960; Myrtle Parker, Mar. 17, 1934; children—Myrtle Ann, John Clare. Forest guard Huron Nat. Forest, Mich., 1930, asst. ranger, 1931-32; forest guard Chippewa Nat. Forest, Min., 1930-31; ranger Ottawa Nat. Forest, Mich., 1932-35, asst. supr., 1935- 36, forest supr., 1936-39; forest supr. Superior Nat. Forest Minn., 1939- 44, Mt. Hood Nat. Forest, Ore., 1944-46; asst. regional forester, Denver, 1946-50, regional forester, San Francisco, 1951-55; dep. chief adminstrn., Washington, 1955-68. Recipient Distinguished Service award Dept. Agr., 1964. Mem. Am. Range Soc., Soil Conservation Soc., Soc. Am. Foresters, Am. Forestry Assn., Am. Soc. Pub. Adminstrn., Nat. Wildlife Fedn., Xi Sigma Pi. Home: 4812 Essex Av Chevy Chase MD 20015

HENDEL, CHARLES WILLIAM, prof. philosophy; b. Reading, Pa., Dec. 16, 1890; s. Charles William and Emma Leininger (Stolz) H.; B.Litt., Princeton, 1913; student Marburg U. (Germany), 1913-14, College de France, 1914; Ph.D., Princeton, 1917; M.A.(hons.), Yale, 1940; m. Elizabeth Phoebe Jones, Sept. 23, 1916; children—James Norman, Charles William. Tchr., Princeton Prep. Sch., 1919; instr. Williams Coll., 1919-20; asst. prof. Princeton, 1920-26, asso. prof., 1926-29; MacDonald prof. moral philosophy, chmn. dept. McGill U., 1929-40, dean faculty Arts and Scis., 1937-40; prof. moral philos. and metaphysics, chmn. dept. Yale, 1940-59, Clarke prof. moral philosophy and metaphysics emeritus, 1959—; Gifford lectr. natural theology U. Glasgow, 1962-63. Mem. Am. Philos. Assn. (pres. Eastern div.), Am. Soc. Polit. and Legal Philosophy (pres. 1959- 61), Institut Internationale de Philosophie. Democrat. Lutheran. Authur several books, the latest: Studies in the Philosophy of David Hume, Jean Jacques Rousseau, Moralist, 1963. Co-author; Philosophy 1963; Jean Jacques Rousseau, Moralist, 1963. Co-author; Philosophy in American Education, 1945; Preface to Philosophy, 1945; Goals for American Education, 1950; Freedom and Authority, 1953; The Philosophy of Kant and our Modern World, 1959; John Dewey and the Experimental Spirit in Philosophy, 1959. Home: The Brandon Inn Brandon VT 05733 ☆

HENDEL, SAMUEL, educator; b. N.Y.C., July 6, 1909; s. Jodah and Leah (Gerber) H.; LL.B. cum laude, Bklyn. Law Sch., 1930; B.S.S. cum laude, Coll. City N.Y., 1936; Ph.D., Columbia, 1948; m. Clara Hoch, May 14, 1932; children—Linda Susan, Steven. Admitted to N.Y. bar, 1931; practice in N.Y.C., 1931-41; legal cons., 1941—; mem. faculty Coll. City N.Y., 1941-70, prof. polit. sci., 1957-70, chmn. dept., 1957-62, chmn. Russian Areas Grad. Program, 1960-70, ombudsman, 1969-70; prof., chmn. dept. polit. sci. Trinity Coll., Hartford, Conn., 1970—; vis. prof. govt. grad. faculty Columbia, 1958-60, summer 1962; vis. prof. comparative govt. and internat. relations Claremont Grad. Sch., spring, 1962. Chmn. acad. freedom com. Am. Civil Liberties Union, 1959-60, 66—; chmn. commn. on internat. affairs Am. Jewish Congress, 1959-61. Ford Faculty fellow, 1953-54; grantee to visit USSR, Inter-University Com. Travel Grants, 1957. Mem. Am. Polit. Sci. Assn. (council 1965-67), Am. Assn. Advancement Slavic Studies, Am. Civil Liberties Union (dir. 1967—), Phi Beta Kappa (pres. Gamma chpt. 1960-61). Author: Charles Evans Hughes and The Supreme Court, 1951; co-author, co-editor The U.S.S.R. After 50 Years; Promise and Reality, 1967. Editor: The Soviet Crucible, 3d edit., 1967; The Politics of Confrontation, 1971; co-editor Basic Issues of American Democracy, 6th edit., 1970. Home: 125 Vernon St Hartford CT 06106

HENDERLITE, RACHEL, educator; b. Henderson, N.C., Dec. 30, 1905; d. James Henry and Nelle (Crow) Henderlite; student Mary Baldwin Coll., 1923-24; B.A., Agnes Scott Coll., 1928; postgrad. Bibl. Sem. N.Y., 1931-32, 36; M.A., N.Y.U., 1936; Ph.D., Yale Div. Sch., 1947; L.H.D., Queens Coll., 1956; student Mansfield Coll., Oxford (Eng.) U., 1965. English tchr. Belmont (N.C.) High Sch., 1928-29; dean, prof. Bible. edn. Miss. Synodical Coll., Holly Springs, 1936-38; prof. Bible, Montreat (N.C.) Coll., 1938-41; Bible tchr. Charlotte (N.C.) high schs., 1941-42; prof. applied Christianity and Christian nurture Presbyn. Sch. Christian Edn., 1944-60; dir. ednl. research Bd. Christian Edn., 1957-59, dir. curriculum devel., 1959-65; prof. Christian edn. Austin (Tex.) Presbyn. Theol. Sem., 1965—; ordained to ministry Presbyn. Ch., 1965; prof. Christian edn. Union Theol. Sem., N.Y. summer 1956. Mem. gen. assembly Nat. Council Chs., 1967-72. Recipient Emily Smith Medallion citation as distinguished alumnae Mary Baldwin Coll., 1967. Mem. N.A.A.C.P., Am. Acad. Religion, Religious Education Assn., Assn. Sem. Prof. in Practical Field, Grad. Profs. Christian Edn., Assn. Christian Educators Presbyn. Ch. U.S., Phi Beta Kappa. Author: Exploring the Old Testament, 1945; Exploring the New Testament, 1946; A Call to Faith, 1955; Paul, Christian and World Traveler, 1957; Forgiveness and Hope, 1960; The Holy Spirit in Christian Education, 1963. Mem. editorial council interpretation, Jour. Bible and Theology, 1947-63. Home: 108 Laurel Lane Austin TX 78705

HENDERSHOT, CLARENCE, educator; b. Bad Axe, Mich., Aug. 24, 1901; s. Horatio P. and Emma Jane (McGregor) H.; B.A., Alma Coll., 1923; M.A., U. Chgo., 1928, Ph.D., 1936; m. Elva O. Jenkins, 1928; children—Gladys Elaine (Mrs. John Christian Munson), James Brooks. Tchr. high sch., Midland, Mich., 1923- 24; prin. Cushing High Sch., Rangoon, Burma, 1924-27; tchr., prin. Branch High Sch., Escondido, Cal., 1928-29; asso. prof. edn. and history U. Ala., 1929-31; prof. history Judson Coll., Rangoon, 1932-35; lectr. Central YMCA Coll., Chgo., 1935-36; dir. Warren br. of Hiram Coll., 1936-37; asst. prof. Hiram Coll., 1937- 38; asso. prof. history U. Redlands, Cal., 1938-44, dean of men, 1942- 44; specialist S.E. Asia, OWI, Washington, 1944-45; pub. affairs officer U.S. Information Service, Rangoon, 1945-46; chief S.E. Asia br., pub. affairs area Dept. of State, 1946-48, mem. planning staff Office Pub, Affairs, 1949-52, UN affairs officer USIA, 1952-54; chief Far East-South Asia br., edn. div. ICA, Washington, 1954-57; chief edn. div. U.S. Operations Mission to Korea, 1957-61, to Iran, 1961-65; asst. dean internat. services div., lectr. S.E. Asia history So. Ill. U., 1965-71. Mem. adv. com. to dir. pub. instrn. in Burma, 1925-27; mem. U.S. delegation, conv. Internat. Red Cross, Toronto, 1952; mem. U.S. delegation to UN, 1953, to UNESCO World Lit. Conf., Teheran, 1965. Past mem. gen. council Am. Bapt. Conv.; past v.p. nat. council Am. Bapt. Men; past mem. brotherhood commn. So. Bapt. Conv. Mem. Nat. Assn. Fgn. Student Advisers, Phi Delta Kappa. Baptist. Contbr. articles, book reviews to profl. publs. Home: 110 S Rod Lane Carbondale IL 62901

HENDERSHOT, JAMES CALVIN, chem. co. exec.; b. Louisville, Dec. 30, 1917; s. Calvin Leroy and Ruth Vern (Kenady) H.; student U. Louisville, 1935-38; m. Elaine Dishion, Nov. 14, 1942; children—Kenady Lynne, James Calvin, Thomas Keith. With Reliance Universal, Inc., Louisville, 1938—, exec. v.p., 1962-63, pres., 1963—, also dir. Bd. overseers Louisville Country Day Sch., 1965- -; bd. dirs. Internat. Center, U. Louisville, Ky. Blue Cross, 1971—. Served with AUS, 1943- 45; ETO. Mem. Ky., Louisville (bd. dirs. 1971—) chambers of commerce, Am. Presidents Assn., Asso. Industries Ky., N.A.M., Conf. Bd., UN Assn. U.S.A., Nat. Kitchen Cabinet Mfg. Assn., Nat. Paint, Varnish and Lacquer Assn. (bd. dirs. 1971—). Republican. Mem. Christian Ch. (deacon, trustee). Clubs: Flight (dir.), Pendennis, Rotary, Louisville Country (Louisville); Lake Shore (Chgo.). Home: 1107 Red Fox Rd Louisville KY 40205 Office: 2100 Gardner Lane Louisville KY 40205

HENDERSHOT, LELAND C., dentist; b. Detroit, Aug. 11, 1924; s. Leland C. and Cecile (Haag) H.; student Wayne State U., 1942; B.S., U. Mich., 1948, D.D.S., 1953, Ph.D., 1956; m. Mary Clare Sullivan, June 14, 1947; children—Charles F., Joseph A., Mary Carol, Michael C., Peter J., Margaret M., Martha M., Timothy J., Therese M., Lisa M. Practice dentistry, Ann Arbor, Mich., 1953-55; pharmacologist Dow Chem. Co., Midland, Mich., 1955-59; asst. sec. Council Dental Therapeutics, Am. Dental Assn., Chgo., 1959-62, asst. editor, 1962-63, editor, 1963—; research asst. pharmacology U. Mich., 1949-53, research asso., 1953-55, lectr., 1955. Mem. com. health edn. and communications Bur. State Services, USPHS, Dept. Health, Edn. and Welfare, 1964; mem. Nat. Adv. Dental Research Council, 1966-70. City councilman, Auburn, Mich., 1958-59. Served with AUS, 1943-46. Fellow Am., Internat. colls. dentists, Acad. Gen. Dentistry; mem. Nat., Am. dental assns., Am. Soc. Pharmacology and Exptl. Therapeutics, Internat. Assn Dental Research, Am. Assn. Dental Editors, Fedn. Dentaire Internationale, Odontographic Soc. Chgo., Am. Acad. History Dentistry, Council Biol. Editors, Omicron Kappa Upsilon. Home: 2106 Orrington Av Evanston IL 60201 Office: Am Dental Assn 211 E Chicago Av Chicago IL 60611

HENDERSON, ALGO DONMYER, educator; b. Solomon, Kan., Apr. 26, 1897; s. Calvert Columbus and Ella Cora (Donmyer) H.; student Kan. Wesleyan Coll. Commerce, 1914-15, Georgetown U., 1917-18; J.D., U. Kan., 1921; C.P.A., Kan., 1922; postgrad. U. Chgo., 1923; M.B.A., Harvard, 1928; LL.D., Antioch Coll., 1948, Olivet Coll., 1959, Fenn Coll., 1963, Cleve. State U., 1968; L.H.D., Keuka Coll. 1950; m. Anne G. Cristy, 1923 (dec.); children—Joanne E. (Mrs. James Reece Pratt III), Philip C.; m. 2d, Jean C. Glidden, 1963; one dau., Carol (Mrs. Violé). Tchr. pub. schs., Kan., 1915-17, U. Kan., 1920-24; admitted to Kan. bar, 1922; mem. faculty Antioch Coll., Yellow Springs, O., 1925-48, asso. prof., prof., bus. mgr., dean, exec. v.p., acting pres. and pres., 1935-48; administered 21 colls. N.Y. State, 1948-49; asso. com. of edn. charge higher, profl. edn. U. State N.Y., 1948-50; prof. higher edn., sec. com. coll. relations U. Mich., 1950-67, emeritus prof., 1967—, dir. Center for Study of Higher Edn., 1957-66; research educator Center for Research and Devel. in Higher Edn., U. Cal. at Berkeley, 1966—. Mem. Mich. Commn. Coll. Accreditation, 1950- 64, President's Commn. Higher Edn., 1946-48, Exchange of Distinquished Persons with Japan, 1956; mem. commn. ednl. orgns. Nat. Conf. Christians and Jews; cons. U. Ala., 1967-68, U. N.M., 1968, 70, UNESCO, 1969, Ford Found. in Chile, 1970. Bd. dirs. Internat. Hospitality Center, San Francisco. Served to 2d lt. U.S. Army, 1917-19. Recipient Distinguished Alumnus award U. Kan., 1948; Sesquicentennial medal U. Mich., 1967; Honor award Colloquium on Higher Education, 1971. Mem. Am. Civil Liberties Union, Assn. Higher Edn., N.E.A., Am. Soc. Pub. Adminstrn., Alpha Kappa Lambda. Unitarian. Author books including: Policies and Practices in Higher Education, 1960; The Role of the Governing Board, 1967; The Innovative Spirit, 1970. Editor: Higher Education in Tomorrow's World, 1968. Contbr. to jours. Home: 239 Glorietta Blvd Orinda CA 94563 Office: Center for Research and Devel in Higher Edn U Cal Berkeley CA 94720

HENDERSON, ALLYN B., lawyer; b. Basin, Wyo., Jan. 2, 1922; s. Albert Bruce and Hazel (Blakesley) H.; J.D., U. Wyo., 1949; m. Betty Louise Shaffner, Aug. 27, 1946; 1 dau., Jeri Rae. Admitted to Wyo. bar, 1949, Cal. bar, 1954, also U.S. Supreme Ct.; acting regional adjudicator Dept. Interior, Billings, Mont., 1949-51; atty. Union Oil Co. Cal., 1951-62; v.p., sec. Santa Fe Internat. Corp., Orange, Cal., 1962—, dir. subsidiary cos., 1963- -. Served with USNR, 1942-45, 52-53. Mem. Am., Los Angeles County bar assns., Fgn. Law Assn., Am. Soc. Internat. Law, Am. Soc. Corporate Secs., Kappa Sigma. Editor Wyo. Law Rev., 1948-49. Contbr. articles to profl. jours. Home: 1300 Park Newport Newport Beach CA 92660 Office: South Tower Union Bank Square Orange CA 92668

HENDERSON, ARTHUR PEARCE, newspaperman; b. Portsmouth, Va., Sept. 3, 1909; s. Victor Lawson and Florine (Pearce) H.; A.B., Coll. William and Mary, 1929; seminar work Am. Press Inst., Columbia, 1956; m. Lorene Evelyn Cox, Oct. 8, 1938; children—Arthur Pearce, Richard Lawson. Reporter, Norfolk (Va.) Ledger- Dispatch, 1930-38, state editor, 1938-40, telegraph editor, 1940-56; Portsmouth editor Norfolk Ledger-Star, 1956-62, business-financial editor, 1962—; instr. Norfolk div. Coll. William and Mary, 1946- 49. Mem. Va. Methodist Conf. Commn. on Pub. Interests, 1964-68. Mem. Portsmouth City Council, 1946-50, Portsmouth-Norfolk County Ferry Bd., 1946-50. Trustee Va. Meth. Advocate, Richmond, 1964—. Mem. Sigma Delta Chi. Democrat. Mason, Elk, Kiwanian. Club: Portsmouth Executives (pres. 1969-70). Contbr. mags. Home: 3202 Dogwood Dr Portsmouth VA 23703 Office: 150 W Brambleton Av Norfolk VA 23510

HENDERSON, BRUCE DOOLIN, mgmt. exec.; b. Nashville, Apr. 30, 1915; s. John B. and Ceacy (Doolin) H.; B.S., Vanderbilt U., 1937; postgrad. Harvard Bus. Sch., 1940-41; m. Frances Fleming, Sept. 5, 1949; children—Asta, Bruce Balfour, Ceacy, Bruce Alexander. Trainee Frigidaire div. Gen. Motors Corp., 1937- 38; sales Leland Electric Co., 1938-39; buyer Westinghouse Electric Corp., 1941, asst. purchasing agt., Lima, O., 1942, purchasing agt., Newark, 1943-46, mgr. purchases, stores, Sharon, Pa., 1946-49; asst. to v.p. Westinghouse Electric Co., Pitts., 1950, gen. purchasing agt., 1951, gen. mgr. purchases and traffic, 1952, v.p., 1953-55, v.p., gen. mgr. air conditioning div., 1955-59; v.p. in charge mgmt. services div. Arthur D. Little, Inc., 1959-60, sr. v.p. charge mgmt. sci. div., 1960-63; sr. v.p. charge mgmt. cons. div. Boston Safe Deposit & Trust Co., 1963-68; pres. Boston Cons. Group, Inc., 1968—; sr. v.p., dir. The Boston Co., Inc. Trustee, mem. bldg. com., corp. mem. The Children's Hosp. Med. Center. Clubs: Farmington Country (Charlotteville, Va.); Duquesne (Pitts.); Union League (N.Y.): St. Croix Country (V.I.). Home: 163 Hampshire Rd Wellesley Hills MA 02181 Office: One Boston Pl Boston MA 02106

HENDERSON, C. A., corp. exec.; b. 1911; B.S., Okla. State U.; married. With City Products Corp., 1933—, v.p., 1964—; dir. Am. Nat. Bank, Midwest City, Okla., Liberty Nat. Bank, Oklahoma City, Great So. Life Ins. Co. Address: 1700 S Wolf Rd Des Plaines IL 60618

HENDERSON, CHARLES, Jr., educator; b. Lynchburg, Va., Aug. 22, 1923; s. Charles and Rosalie (Florance) H.; student Middlesex Sch., 1935-38; A.B., Davidson Coll., 1942; M.A., U. N.C., 1947, Ph.D., 1955; m. Ethel Ann Bolton, Aug. 16, 1944; children—Elizabeth Ann, Charles III, William Abbot, Rosalie Nathan, John Quintus. Teaching fellow U. N.C., 1942, 46-49; instr. classics N.Y. U., 1950-55; mem. faculty U. N.C. 1955-64; asso. prof. classics, 1958-64, dean student affairs, 1960-63; prof. classics Smith Coll., 1964—, chmn. dept., 1967—. Served to capt. USNR, 1942-46. Mem. Am. Philol. Assn. (sec.-treas. 1962-65), Classical Assn. New Eng., Phi Beta Kappa, Delta Phi Alpha, Sigma Delta Psi, Eta Sigma Phi, Phi Mu Alpha, Sigma Phi Epsilon. Democrat. Episcopalian. Author: (with B.L. Ullman) Latin for Americans, 2 vols., 1968; also articles: Editor: Studies in Honor of B.L. Ullman, 1963. Home: York Harbor ME 03911 Office: 603 W A Neilson Library Smith Coll Northampton MA 01060

HENDERSON, CHRISTOPHER LONGEST, govt. ofcl.; b. Jackson, Miss., Sept. 20, 1926; s. Chris Obadiah and Bertha (Fulgham) H.; student U. Md., 1944; B.S. Cornell U., 1948; m. Jo- Ann Reser, Aug. 27, 1949; children—John, Rebecca, Kathleen. With AEC, 1948—, spl. asst. to chmn., 1961-63, asst. dir. regulation for adminstrn., 1963—. Served with USAAF, 1945. Mem. Soc. Pub. Adminstrn., Am. Nuclear Soc., Sigma Alpha Epsilon. Home: 15104 Westbury Rd Rockville MD 20853 Office: 4915 St Elmo Av Bethesda MD 20014

HENDERSON, DAVID, found. dir.; b. Hamilton, Scotland, July 4, 1916; s. James Hamilton and Jean (McDougal) H.; brought to U.S., 1927, naturalized, 1934; A.B., Westminster Coll., 1938; M.A. (Grad. Council scholar 1939-41), U. Pitts., 1941, Ph.D., 1950; m. Isabelle Louise Patton, Apr. 24, 1943; children—Kaaren, Dona, Gail. Tchr. sociology high sch., Kittanning, Pa., 1939-41; instr. Westminster Coll., New Wilmington, Pa., 1941-42; fellow Fund Advancement Edn., 1955-56; asst. prof. Marietta (O.) Coll., 1946-48; prof. U. Pitts., 1949-61, chmn. dept. sociology com. 1956-58, asst. dean of coll., 1957-58, dir. ednl planning, 1958-61; exec. dean Chatham Coll., Pitts., 1961-68; dir. Buhl Found., 1968—. Mem. citizens' sponsoring com. Allegheny Conf. Community Devel. Served to staff sgt. USAAF, 1942-45. Mem. Am. Sociol. Soc. Author: (with H.A. Phelps) Contemporary Social Problems, 1952; Population in Its Human Aspects, 1958. Home: 303 Homer Dr Pittsburgh PA 15235 Office: 4 Gateway Center Pittsburgh PA 15222

HENDERSON, DAVID NEWTON, congressman; b. Hubert, N.C., Apr. 16, 1921; s. Isaac Newton and Virginia (Boney) H.; B.S., Davidson Coll., 1942; LL.B., U. N.C., 1949; m. Mary Wellons Knowles, Dec. 11, 1942; children—David Bruce, Wiley Bryant, Wimbric Boney. Admitted to N.C. bar, 1949, practiced in Wallace until 1960; asst. gen. counsel com. edn. and labor Ho. of reps., 1951-52; solicitor Duplin County Gen. Ct., 1953-57, judge, 1957-59; mem. 87th-92d Congresses 3d Dist. N.C. Served to maj. USAAF, 1942-46. Mem. Am. Legion, Vets. Fgn. Wars. Democrat. Presbyn. Lion, Mason (32). Home: 503 E Murphy St Wallace NC 28466 Office: House Office Bldg Washington DC 20515

HENDERSON, DAVID SIMUEL, army officer; b. Charleston, Miss., Jan. 16, 1921; s. David Simeon and Elizabeth (Harvey) H.; B.S., Miss. State Coll., 1942; M.B.A., Harvard, 1949; grad. Command and Gen. Staff Coll., 1956, Naval War Coll., 1961, Naval Post Grad. Sch., 1963; m. Mary Elizabeth Horton, Feb. 8, 1947; children—Barbara (Mrs. Richard Riordan), David S. Commd. 2d lt. U.S. Army, 1942, advanced through grades to brig. gen., 1967; mil. assistance advisor, Vietnam, 1956-57; staff and faculty Command and Gen. Staff Coll., 1957-60; operations staff officer, Germany, 1961-62; comdr. inf. battle group 3d Div., Germany, 1962-63; chief of staff 3d Div., 1963-64; chief program coordination and devel., dir. Army programs and force planning and analysis, Washington, 1964-67; dep. dir. operations DCSOPS, Washington, 1967; dep. comdt. Command and Gen. Staff Coll., 1967-69; asst. div. comdr. 25th Div., Vietnam, 1969-70; dep. ACS, CORDS, Vietnam, 1970; dep. comdg. gen. Inst. Land Combat, Combat Devels. Command, Carlisle Barracks, Pa., 1970—. Decorated D.S.M., Legion of Merit, D.F.C., Air medal, Bronze Star, Joint Services Commendation medal, Army Commendation medal, Purple Heart. Presbyn. Home: Quarters 28 Royal American Circle Carlisle Barracks PA 17013 Office: USACDCILC Carlisle Barracks PA 17013

HENDERSON, DOUGLAS, govt. cons.; b. Mass., Oct. 15, 1914; B.S., Boston U., 1940; M.A., Fletcher Sch. Law and Diplomacy, 1941. Instr., Tufts Coll., 1941- 42; entered diplomatic service, 1942; vice consul, Nogales, 1942, Arica, 1943, Cochabamba, 1943-47; assigned Dept. State, 1947, detached for assignment Dept. Commerce, 1947-50; 2d sec., consul, Bern, Switzerland, 1950-54, 1st sec., consul, 1954-56; asst. chief econ. def. div. Dept. State, 1956-59; sr. seminar fgn. policy Fgn. Service Inst., 1959-60; counsel econ. affairs, Lima, 1960-61, consul, counsellor, 1961-63; ambassador to Bolivia, 1963-68; former cons. policy planning staff Dept. State, Washington; now U.S. rep. to Inter Am. Com. Alliance for Progress, Dept. State, Washington. Home: 2329 Nebraska Av NW Washington DC 20016 Office: care Dept of State Washington DC 20525

HENDERSON, EDWARD, physician; b. Hendersonville, N.C., Dec. 16, 1896; s. Edward Everett and Muriel Lee (Bell) H.; M.B., B.Chir., M.D., Glasgow U., 1922; Ph.D., Oxford U., 1932; postgrad. Yale, 1937-38; diploma tropical medicine, Tulane U., 1944; m. Kathryn Silverthorne, 1944; children—Edward Bell, Susan Lee. Intern Royal Infirmary, 1922-23; med. officer sci. expdns. Malay archipelago, 1927, China, India, 1929, Central Africa, 1935, Amazon region, 1938-39; med. research div. Schering Corp., Bloomfield, N.J., 1939-62, sec., 1940-52, v.p., 1952-62, dir., 1940-43, dir. div. clin. research, 1945-62; cons. tropical medicine Med. Soc. N.J., 1945; research cons. Mound Park Hosp. Found., St. Petersburg, Fla., 1955—; pres. Ellis Bell & Co., Inc., N.Y.C., 1967—, Bansen, Inc., N.Y.C., 1967—, Henderson Safety Closure Co., Inc., N.Y.C., 1969—; chmn. bd. Elbesa Ltd., London, Eng., 1970—. Bd. dirs. Liberian Inst., Am. Found. Tropical Medicine, 1951—; trustee Aging Research Inst., Inc., 1953—, pres., 1953—; pres. Pneumonia Research Found., 1969—. Served as lt., inf., U.S. Army, 1917, capt. Intelligence Corps, 1918. Recipient Willard O. Thompson award, 1961; Malford W. Thewlis gold medal award, 1967. Mem. Internat. Soc. Tropical Dermatology, Pan Am. Med. Assn. (pres. sect. geriatrics and gerontology 1967—), A.A.A.S., Am. Soc. Tropical Medicine, Endocrine Soc., Gerontological Soc., Am. Geriatrics Soc. (dir. 1952—, pres. 1955, editor-in-chief jour. 1954—, exec. dir. 1962—), Am., N.J. rheumatism assns., Assn. Med. Dirs. (pres. 1949-50), N.Y. Acad. Scis. Clubs: New York Athletic; Graduates (New Haven); Columbia University (N.Y.C.). Author: Sixteenth Century Literature and Its Influence on Modern Civilization, 1932; Disorders of Calcium Metabolism, 1952; Section on Cholera, Clinical Tropical Medicine, Gradwohl, Benitex Soto, Felsenfeld, 1951. Contbr. articles sci. jours. patentee chemistry, sci. instruments, safety devices. Home: 220 Central Park S New York City NY 10019 Office: 10 Columbus Circle New York City NY 10019

HENDERSON, EDWIN HAROLD, clergyman; b. Pittsburgh, Tex., Sept. 17, 1927; s. Ether Chaney and Myrtle (Davis) H.; B.A. cum laude, Tex. Christian U., 1954; B.D., Southwestern Baptist Theol. Sem., 1957, Th.D., 1963; m. Velma Jean Smith, June 2, 1948; children—Steve Edwin, Cherilyn Cheree, Sharon Leigh. Ordained to ministry Baptist Ch., 1945; pastor First Bapt. Ch., Hydro, Okla., 1947-51, Parker St. Bapt. Ch., Mineral Wells, Tex., 1951- 53, First Bapt. Ch. Trinity Heights, Dallas, 1953-60; chmn. dept. Bible, Jacksonville, (Tex.) Bapt. Coll., 1960-61; pastor Central Bapt. Ch., Lubbock, Tex., 1961—; founder Inst. Bautista Biblico de Lubbock, 1971. Chmn. trustees Plains Bapt. Loan Assn. Am. Mem. Bapt. Missionary Assn. Tex. (mem. mission bd., pres.), Bapt. Missionary Assn. Am. (pres. 1966-68, writer Adult Sunday Sch. Quar. 1957—), Plains Bapt. Assn. (pres. 1965-70). Author: Now Abideth Faith, 1962; Roman Dogma and Bible Doctrine, 1964; Bible Doctrines Baptists Believe, 1964. Contbr. profl. jours. Home: 1615 57th St Lubbock TX 79412 Office: 1809 Av M Lubbock TX 79401

HENDERSON, ERNEST LEON chemist, educator; b. Chicago, 1928; B.S. in Physics, Yale, 1950; Ph.D. in Chemistry, Harvard, 1956; m. Sally Ann Jones, July 5, 1957; children--Kenneth J., Nancy A. Chemist, Acme Chem. Co., Blue Island, Ill., 1950-51; director of Reseach Lab., Indsl. Chemicals Corp., Cambridge, Mass., 1956-60; project coordinator environmental sect. Steinmetz Assos., Chgo., 1960-61; v.p. for reseach Bauer Bros. Chem. Co., Inc., Memphis, 1961-64; asst. prof. chemistry Washington U., St. Louis, 1964-66, asso. prof., 1966-70, prof., 1970--, head of chemistry dept., 1970-71. Vis. prof. So. Ill. U., summer 1967, U. of Ore., 1969. Scoutmaster, Boy Scouts America, University City, Mo., 1968-70. Bd. dirs. Rest Haven Home for Elderly, 1960-61; trustee of the Lutheran Hosp., 1965-71. Served from lt. to capt., AUS, 1951-53. Mem. Am. Chem. Soc., Sci. Research Soc. Am. (chpt. treas. 1967), Sigma Xi. Author: (with others) Basic Inorganic Chemistry, 1971. Contbr. articles to profl. jours., encys., also chpts. to books. Home: Fairfax Apts 7291 Windermere Dr University City MO 63105 Office: Dept Chemistry Washington University St Louis MO 63130

HENDERSON, FLORENCE, singer, actress; b. Dale, Ind., Feb. 14, 1934; d. Joseph W. and Elizabeth (Elder) Henderson; student Am. Acad. Dramatic Arts, 1951-52; m. Ira Bernstein, Jan. 9, 1956; children—Barbara Ellen, Joseph Carl, Robert Norman, Elizabeth Corrine. Broadway appearances include Fanny, 1954, The Girl Who Came to Supper, 1963; on tour in Oklahoma, Sound of Music, others; film appearance in Song of Norway, 1970; numerous TV appearance, including Brady Bunch.

HENDERSON, FORBES B., ry. co. exec.; b. Standish, Mich., Oct. 21, 1910; s. Ben J. and Marion (Reilich) H.; ed. Mich. State U., 1932; J.D., Detroit Law Coll., 1936; m. Josephine Mary Cavanagh, Sept. 25, 1937. With Grand Trunk Western R.R. Co., Detroit, 1934—, sec., gen. counsel, 1957—; pres., dir. Detroit & Toledo Shire Line R.R. Co., 1968—, Detroit Terminal R.R. Co., 1969—, Grand Trunk Milw. Car Ferry Co., 1967—. Mem. Mich. R.R.'s Assn. (exec. com.). Home: Lake Shore Rd Harbor Springs MI 49737 Office: 131 West Lafayette St Detroit MI 48226

HENDERSON, GEORGE EDWIN, agrl. engr.; b. Kenton, O., Sept. 10, 1906; s. James Scott and Ruth Anne (Armstrong) H.; B.S.A., Ohio State U., 1925-29; student Wittenberg Coll., U. Tenn.; m. Claribel Cary, June 17, 1933; children—Donald Edwin, Richard Lewis. Rural engr. Ohio Edison Power Co., Springfield, 1929-32; rural engr. Dayton Power & Light Co., Wilmington, O., 1932-37; rural electrification engr. in edn. TVA, Knoxville, 1937-39, head ednl. sect., 1939-41, asst. chief agrl. engring. div., 1941 45, chief div., 1945-47, chief agrl. engring. and food processing div., 1948; now exec. dir. Am. Assn. Vocational Instructional Materials; prof. agrl. engring. U. Ga., 1949—. Com. engring. in vocational agr. Recipient Distinguished Service award from Future Farmers Am., 1968. Mem. Am. Soc. Agrl. Engrs. (nat. councilor, sec., pres. S.E. sect.; recipient blue ribbon awards for best ednl. publs. 1952-57, 60), Tech. Soc. Knoxville, Engring. Club, Am. Soc. Engring. Edn., Gamma Sigma Delta, Delta Theta Sigma, Phi Kappa Phi. Presbyn. (elder). Kiwanian. Author: Planning Farm Water Systems, 1955; Planning a Machinery Storage Layout, 1956; Tractor Operation and Daily Care, 1959; Tractor Maintenance—Principles and Procedures, 1962; others. Home: 150 Valley Rd Athens GA 30601

HENDERSON, GEORGE MILLER, banker; b. Indpls., Aug. 19, 1915; s. Ben Wymond and Verlinda (Miller) H.; student Harvard, 1960; m. Janice Himmelwright, Sept. 2, 1952; children—Donna, Bonnie, Heather, Randall, Darcy. With S. H. Kress & Co., 1933-36; fire control supr. U.S. Forest Service, Zig Zag, Ore., 1936-42; asst. mgr. fgn. trade dept. Portland C. of C., 1946-47; with 1st Nat. Bank Ore., Portland, 1947—, v.p., 1953-62, sr. v.p., 1962—, Chmn. Portland Aviation Commn., 1950-51, Ore. Parks Commn., 1956—, Columbia Basin Export Import Conf., 1961-62. Pres. Family Counselling Service, 1959-60, Rose Festival Assn., 1953-54; chmn. world brotherhood banquet Nat. Conf. Christians and Jews, 1963; pres. Pacific Internat. Livestock Expn., 1965—. Mem. Ore. Bankers Assn. (pres. 1962), Assn. Res. City Bankers, Pacific Northwestern Ski Assn. (past pres.), Pacific N.W. Trade Assn. (pres. 1964-65). Clubs: Arlington, Waverley Country. Home: 5020 SW Humphrey Blvd Portland OR 97221 Office: Box 3131 Portland OR 97208

HENDERSON, GEORGE MORICE, oil co. exec.; b. Vancouver, B.C., Jan. 30, 1913; s. Henry Isaac and Alice (Wright) H.; B.Commerce, U. B.C., 1934; M.B.A., U. Chgo., 1937; m. Mary Elizabeth Nicholson, Sept. 20, 1942; children—Mary Virginia, Ian Douglas. with Imperial Oil Ltd., 1938—, gen. sec., 1962—. Served to capt. Canadian Army, 1941-46. Home: 58 Hillhurst Blvd Toronto 305 Ontario Canada Office: 111 St Clair Av W Toronto 195 Ontario Canada

HENDERSON, GIRARD BROWN, corp. exec.; b. Bklyn., Feb. 25, 1905; s. Alexander D. and Ella (Brown) H.; grad. Storn King Sch., Cornwall-on-Hudson, N.Y., 1923; m. Theodore Huntington, Jan. 28, 1927 (div. Aug. 1960); children—Theodora Ives, Dariel Firestone; m. 2d, Mary Hollingsworth, 1965. Comml. transp. pilot, 1931—; chmn. bd., pres. Alexander Dawson, Inc., 1946—; chmn. Blue Channel Corp., 1961—, White Wing Services, Inc., Harvey Assos., Inc., Hydrophonics, Inc.; pres., chmn. Dawson Corp., 1959—, chmn. Alarm Corp., 1952—; dir. Avon Products, Inc., Pan Am. Mines Ltd. Chmn. bd. trustees Alexander Dawson Found.; bd. dirs. Found. Nutrition and Stress Research. Las Vegas Country; Roundup Riders of the Rockies (Denver). Home: PO Box 2714 Las Vegas NV 89104 Office: PO Box 2956 Las Vegas NV 89104

HENDERSON, GORDON F., lawyer; b. Ottawa, Ont., Can., 1912; B.A., U. Toronto, 1934; LL.B., Osgoode Hall. Admitted to Ont. bar, 1937; partner firm Gowling, MacTavish, Osborne & Henderson; bencher Law Soc. Upper Can., 1966—. Mem. Canadian, Que. bar assns., Patent and Trademark Inst. (pres. 1953-55). Office: 116 Albert St Ottawa 4 Ontario Canada

HENDERSON, MRS. HAROLD G., see Benjamin; Mary Avezzna.

HENDERSON, HERBERT, retired utility exec.; b. Ia., 1897; grad. Ia. State Coll., 1925. Former exec. v.p. Ia. Electric Light & Power Co., now retired. Home: 209 25th St Cedar Rapids IA 52402 Office: Security Bldg Cedar Rapids IA 52401

HENDERSON, HERBERT BLAIR, educator; b. Madisonville, Tenn., Apr. 28, 1909; s. Oliver Cromwell and Kitty Mae (Ray) H.; B.S.A., U. Tenn., 1932; M.S.A., U. Vt., 1936; m. Mildred McPherson, Dec. 27, 1934; 1 dau., Louise Blair. Mem. Dairy dept. staff U. of Tenn., 1932-35, successively instr., research asso., asst. prof. 1936-41; research asst. U. Vt., 1935-36; prof., head dairy dept. U. Ga., Athens, 1941—, chmn. dairy div., 1951-56. Mem. adv. bd. Sealtest; U.S. del. Internat. Dairy Congress, Rome, Italy, 1956; mem. bd. Coll. Feed Conf. Mem. Am. Dairy Sci. Assn. (dir. 1948-51, pres. 1952-53; award of honor 1969), Alpha Gamma Rho, Alpha Zeta, Omicron Delta Kappa, Phi Kappa Phi, Gamma Sigma Delta. Democrat. Baptist. Kiwanian. Home: 135 Fortson Dr Athens GA 30601

HENDERSON, HORACE EDWARD, realtor; b. Henderson, N.C., July 30, 1917; s. T. Brantley and Maude (Duke) H.; student Coll. William and Mary, 1934-37, Yale, 1941-42; m. Vera S. Schubert; children by previous marriage—Terri P., Elizabeth L. Owner Henderson Real Estate & Ins., Williamsburg, Va., 1947-52; coordinator Nat. Automobile Dealers Assn., Washington, 1954-56; dir. gen. World Peace Through Law Center, Geneva, 1964-69; exec. dir. World Assn. Judges, 1968-69; now chmn. Community Methods, Inc.; chmn. bd. Henderson Real Estate Bd., McLean, Va., 1964-66. Adv. bd. Mut. Security Agy., 1952-53; mem. Pres.'s Conf. on Indsl. Safety, 1952-53; exec. com. U.S. Com for UN dir. Nat. Citizens Com. for Hoover Report; indsl. adv. com. Fed. Civil Def. Adminstrn., 1952-53; cons. to dir. ICA, 1956; dir. spl. liaison, spl. asst. dep. under sec. state, Washington, 1958; dep. asst. sec. state internat. orgn. affairs, 1959-60; dir. Exile Orgns. Free Europe Com., 1962; U.S. del. to ILO, UNESCO, FAO, WHO, UN. Mem. Republican Nat. Com., 1962-64; chmn. Va. Rep. party, 1962-64; chmn. Americans for Asian Security and Freedom, 1961; campaign dir. Am. Nationalities for Nixon- Lodge, 1960; Rep. candidate for Congress, 1956, later for lt. gov. Va.; 1957; permanent chmn. Va. Rep. Conv.; 1957; asst. nat. dir. Scranton for Pres. Campaign, 1964; mem. Williamsburg (Va.) City Council, 1948-50. chmn. Com. Against Recognition Red Hungary, 1963. World vice chmn. Operation Brotherhood, 1954-55; owner Powhattan Hist. Co., Williamsburg, Va., 1957. Trustee Valley Forge Found., 1952-55, Jr. C. of C. War Meml. Hdqrs. Served from pvt. to capt., C.E., AUS, 1942-46. Recipient spl. citizenship award Am. Heritage Found., 1953; named outstanding jaycee of World, 1954. Mem. Jr. C. of C. (internat. v.p. 1951, nat. pres. 1952-53), U.S. C. of C. (dir. 1954), Am. Soc. Internat. Law, Sigma Alpha Epsilon. Presbyn. Club: Yale. Visited 47 countries organizing young men's civic groups, 1953-54. Home: 1408 Berkshire Lane Virginia Beach VA 23451 Office: 1284 Laskin Rd Virginia Beach VA 23451

HENDERSON, HUBERT PLATT, educator; b. Milford, Conn., Aug. 24, 1918; s. Archibald Forbes and Harriet A. (Platt) H.; A.B., U. N.C., 1941, M.A., 1950, Ph.D., 1962; m. Georgia Bryan Logan, Aug. 30, 1947; children—Douglas Scott, Gordon Lyon, David Brooks. Instr. music U. N.C., 1946-51; dir. bands U. Mont., 1954- 55; asso. prof., dir. instrumental music U. Md., 1955-65; chmn. dept. music U. Ky., Lexington, 1965-66, dir. Sch. Fine Arts, 1966—; asso. dean. Coll. Arts and Scis., 1966—. Mem. Internat. Council Fine Arts Deans, 1966—; mem. adv. bd. Living Arts and Sci. Center, Lexington, 1967—; music cons. Ky. Arts commn., 1967—; dir. Am. Bandmasters Assn. Research Center, U. Md., 1964-65. Served with USAAF, 1941-46, USAF, 1951-53. Mem. Am. Bandmasters Assn. (dir. 1964-66), Am. Musical. Soc., Coll. Music Soc., Phi Mu Alpha, Kappa Kappa Psi. Episcopalian (vestryman 1966-69) Founding editor Jour. Band Research, 1964-66. Contbr. articles and revs. to periodicals, also material to music edn. source books. Home: 925 Albany Circle Lexington KY 40502

HENDERSON, IAN HAMILTON, educator, musician; b. Hamilton, Scotland, Jan. 28, 1925; s. John Hamilton and Agnes (Harris) H.; came to U.S., 1928, naturalized, 1938; student U. Pitts., 1941-43, Bucknell U., 1943-44; A.B., Oberlin Coll. and Conservatory, 1947, Ed.Mus. B., 1948, Ed.Mus. M., 1948; student Pa. State U., summer 1948; Ph.D. in Music and Edn., Syracuse U., 1953; m. Rita Hotz, Dec. 27, 1944; children—Ann, Ian, Mora. Instr., then asst. prof. State Tchrs. Coll., Brockport, N.Y., 1948-54; prof. State Tchrs. Coll., Indiana, Pa., 1954-57; asst. prof., then asso. prof. Syracuse U., 1957-65; prof. music, chmn. dept. State Univ. Coll., Brookport, 1965-70, dean fine arts, 1970—; moderator youth concerts Syracuse Symphony Orch., 1961-68. Served to lt. (j.g.) USNR, 1943-46. Mem. Music Educators Nat. Conf. (chmn. Eastern div. coll. sect. 1963-64), N.Y. State Sch. Music Assn. Author chpt. in book. Home: 4039 N Lake Rd Brockport NY 14420

HENDERSON, JAMES ALEXANDER, financial and banking exec.; b. N.Y.C., Feb 6, 1921; s. James A. and Charlotte (Fisher) H.; A.B., Hamilton Coll., 1941; postgrad. Columbia, 1946-47; m. Jean Conway, June 6, 1951; children—Elizabeth Jean, Hilary Anne, James Alexander, John Geoffrey. With Gen. Electric Co., 1941-42; with Am. Express Co., 1947—, asst. v.p., 1954-57, v.p., 1958-63, sr. v.p., 1964—, treas., 1966—, exec. v.p., 1968—; chmn. bd., pres., dir. U.S. Camera Pub. Corp.; dir. Nat. Surety Corp., Amex Holding Corp., Am. Express Internat., Inc. Trustee Hamilton Coll. Served with AUS, 1942-46; ETO. Decorated Bronze Star. Mem. Bankers Assn. Fgn. Trade. Democrat. Episcopalian. Clubs: River, University, Bankers (N.Y.C.); Hamilton, Nissequogue Golf. Home: Moriches Rd St James NY 11780 Office: 65 Broadway New York City NY 10006

HENDERSON, JAMES ARNOLD, educator; b. Cardale, Man., Can., Oct. 17, 1912; s. Robert and Fannie (Ritson) H.; D.V.M., U. Toronto, 1936; M.S., Cornell U., 1938; m. Valerie Underhill, May 18, 1946; children—James Rodney, Michael John. Came to U.S., 1963. Prof., Ont. Vet. Coll., U. Toronto, 1946-63; dean Coll. Vet. Medicine, Wash. State U., Pullman, 1963—; livestock cons. Central Romana Corp., Dominican Republic, 1959—. Served with RCAF, 1941- 45. Mem. Am. Vet. Med. Assn., Am. Soc. Animal Sci., British Soc. Animal Prodn. Author: (with D.C. Blood) Veterinary Medicine, 1963. Home: 1410 Upper Dr Pullman WA 99163

HENDERSON, JAMES B., gas pipeline co. ofcl.; b. Amarillo, Tex., June 13, 1909; s. James E. and Belle Vida (McBride) H.; LL.B., U. Okla., 1932; m. Laura Jane Brookins, Feb. 28, 1931; children—James B., Mary Jane. Admitted to Okla. bar, 1932; practiced in Okla., Kan., 1932-34; with Phillips, Tramme, Estes, Edwards & Orn, Ft. Worth, 1934-37; legal dept. Ark. Natural Gas Corp., 1937-49; v.p., gen. counsel Transcontinental Gas Pipe Line Corp., 1949-61, exec. v.p., 1961-67, pres., chief exec. officer, 1967—, also dir. Mem. Am., Tex., Okla., Houston bar assns., Am., So. gas assns., Independent Natural Gas Assn. Am. (dir.), Mid- Continent Oil and Gas Assn., Phi Delta Phi. Clubs: University, Petroleum, Ramada, River Oaks. Home: 303 Chapel Bell Lane Houston TX 77024 Office: 3100 Travis St Houston TX 77006

HENDERSON, JAMES HENRY MERIWETHER, educator; b. Falls Church, Va., Aug. 10, 1917; s. Edwin Bancroft and Mary (Meriwether) H.; B.S., Howard U., 1939; M.Ph., U. Wis., 1941, Ph.D., 1943; m. Betty Alice Francis, Mar. 28, 1948; children—Edith Ellen, Dena R., James F., Edwin B. II. Jr. chemist Badger Ordnance Works, Baraboo, Wis., 1942-43; research asst. U. Chgo., 1943-45; research asso. Carver Found., Tuskegee (Ala.) Inst., 1945-48, asst. prof., 1950-54, asso. prof., 1954-57, prof., 1957—, chmn. dept. biology, 1957-68, chmn. div. natural scis., 1968—, dir. Carver Research Found., 1968—; research fellow Cal. Inst. Tech., 1948-50; NSF fellow Le Phytotron-Gif-sur-Yvette, France, 1961-62; commnr. CUEBS, 1967-70. Trustee Montreat-Anderson Coll., Fellow A.A.A.S.; mem. Bot. Soc. Am., Am. Soc. Plant Physiologists (chmn. So. sect. 1970), Nat. Inst. Sci., N.Y. Acad. Sci., Soc. for Freedom in Sci., Soc. Devel. Biology, Tissue Culture Assn., Nat. Council Univ. Research Adminstrs., Phi Beta Kappa, Sigma Xi, Phi Sigma, Gamma Alpha, Beta Kappa Chi. Home: PO Box 247 Tuskegee AL 36088

HENDERSON, JAMES JACKSON, ins. co. exec.; b. Bristol, Tenn., Jan. 22, 1908; s. William Thomas and Sallie Ann (Richmond) H.; B.S. in Bus. Adminstrn., Hampton Inst., 1932; m. Julia Mildred Hicks, Mar. 27, 1937; children—C. Ann (Mrs. Charles T. Barrick), James Jackson. With Bankers Fire Ins. Co., Durham, N.C., 1932- -, asst. sec., 1937—, also dir.; with N.C. Mut. Life Ins. Co., Durham, 1937—, asst. treas., 1953-62, asst. v.p., 1962-64, treas., 1964—, v.p., 1970—; trustee Mechanics and Farmers Bank, Durham; dir. Mut. Savs. and Loan Assn., Durham. Mem. exec. com. Durham Com. Negro Affairs, 1940—; chmn. Durham Civic Com., 1950-58; vice chmn. Durham Housing Authority, 1958—; mem. Citizens Adv. Com., Durham, 1961- -; mem. Gov's Adv. Com. on Low-Income Housing. Trustee, vice chmn., mem. exec. com. Hampton Inst.; co-organizer Durham Bus. Sch., 1949, pres., 1949-52, bd. dirs., 1949—; bd. dirs. John Avery Boys Club; pres., chmn. bd. dirs. Daisy E. Scarborough Nursery Sch., Durham. Recipient Alumni-at-large award Hampton Inst., 1967, Centennial medallion, 1968. Mem. Nat. Bus. League (v.p., dir., exec. com.), Nat. Hampton Alumni Assn. (financial sec. 1945-48, past pres. Durham chpt., N.C. conf.; Hamptonian of Year award 1954), Kappa Alpha Psi (past grand keeper records, exchequer, past mem. grand bd. dirs., exec. com.; polemarch Durham Alumni chpt.; 4 honors awards). Mem. A.M.E. Ch. (vice chmn. sr. bd. trustees). Home: 202 Pekoe Av Durham NC 27707 Office: 411 W Chapel Hill St Durham NC 27702

HENDERSON, JAMES MARVIN, advt. exec.; b. Atlanta, Mar. 28, 1921; s. Isaac Harmon and Ruth (Ashley) H.; student Furman U., 1939-40, Clemson Coll., 1940-42, also night classes N.Y.U., 1943-44; B.S., U. Denver, 1946; grad. Advanced Mgmt. Program, Harvard, 1956; m. Donna Fern Baade, Apr. 28, 1945; children—Linda Dee, James Marvin, Deborah Fanchon. Sales supr. Gen. Foods Corp., N.Y.C., 1942-44; account exec. Curt Freiberger Advt. Agy., Denver, 1944-46; pres. Henderson Advt. Agy., Inc., Greenville, S.C., 1946—;

pres. Henderson, Ayer & Gillet Advt., Charlotte, N.C., 1962-69; Henderson-Saussy Advt., New Orleans, 1966-69; dir. Citizens & So. Nat. Bank. Spl. asst. to postmaster gen., 1969-70. Mem. Greenville Youth Commn., 1953-54. Chmn. Eisenhower campaign Greenville County, 1952; Republican candidate for lt. gov. S.C., 1970. Pres. Greenville Heart Assn.; pres., bd. dirs. Greenville Mental Hygiene Clinic, United Fund. Served with AUS, World War II. Named Young Man of Year, Greenville, 1954. Mem. S.C. (past dir.), Greenville (past pres.) jr. chambers commerce, Greater Greenville C. of C. (past pres.), Young President's Orgn. (chmn. S.E. chpt.), Greenville Advt. Council (past pres.), Am. Assn. Advt. Agys. (nat. dir.). Methodist. Kiwanian. Home: Route 7 Hickory Lane Greenville SC 29609 Office: 55 S Pleasantburg Dr Greenville SC 29607

HENDERSON, JAMES MCINNES, lawyer; b. Daingerfield, Tex., Sept. 16, 1911; s. John Morgan and Louella (Smith) H.; student U. Tex., 1929-1933; J.D., George Washington U., 1938; m. Mary Medora Jones, Feb. 4, 1935 (div. 1954); children—John McInnes, Mary Gainer; m. 2d, Marie B. York, Aug. 21, 1954; children—James Craig, William Morgan. Asst. to U.S. senator from Tex., 1933-38; gen. practice law, Washington, 1938; spl. asst. to atty. gen. of U.S., 1939-46; chief Mountain States office, anti-trust and war frauds div. U.S. Dept. Justice, 1940-42, chief West Coast offices, 1943-45; intelligence investigation for Army and Bd. Econ. Warfare, 1944-45; spl. mission to Japan for U.S. State, War and Navy Depts., 1945-46; chief of staff div. in gen. hdqrs., Tokyo, Japan, supervising operation and liquidation of 1200 zaibatsu corporate enterprises, legal advisor to Gen. Douglas MacArthur; Philippine alien property adminstr. supervising liquidation of Manila br. of Yokohama Specie Bank, Manila br. of Bank of Taiwan, and various other corporate supervisory postions; gen. counsel Economic Stblzn. Agy., 1951-52; apptd. dir. Office Rent Stblzn., 1952-53; practice law, Washington, 1953-58, 69—; gen. counsel FTC, until 1969; counsel subcom. on govt. activities U.S. Ho. of Reps.; adviser to Korean Govt. Patron and hon. del. from Philippine Bar Assn. to Internat. Bar Assn. meeting, The Hague, 1948. Served with USCGR, 1945. Mem. Fed. (nat. council, pres. 1967- 68), Am., D.C. bar assns., Nat. Lawyers (gov.), Delta Theta Phi Democrat. Episcopalian. Home: 6201 Stardust Lane Bethesda MD 20034; also Upper Horse Valley PA 27246 also Daingerfield TX Office: Davis Bldg 1629 K St NW Washington DC 20006

HENDERSON, JOHN BATTY, corp. exec.; b. Sydney, Australia, Apr. 6, 1925; s. Sydney Woodburn and Rosalind Louise (Funch) Batty; A.B., Brown U., 1946; J.D., Harvard, 1949; m. Virginia Bellows, May 3, 1945; children—Anita, Susan, Sophie. Admitted to R.I. bar, 1950; asso. firm Tillinghast, Collins & Tanner, Providence, 1949-50; with Office Gen. Counsel, Dept. Def., 1951-54; cons. sec. def., 1955; mem. legal dept. Aluminum Co. Am., 1956-62; with Textron Inc., 1962—, sec., 1966-67, v.p., gen. counsel, sec., 1968-70, sr. v.p., sec., 1971—. Served as ensign USNR, World War II. Mem. Phi Beta Kappa, Delta Phi. Clubs: Hope, Art (Providence); Harvard (N.Y.C.); Barrington (R.I.) Yacht; New Bedford (Mass.) Yacht. Home: 282 Benefit St Providence RI 02903 Office: 40 Westminster St Providence RI 02903

HENDERSON, JOHN BROWN, govt. ofcl., economist; b. Glasgow, Scotland, Jan. 3, 1918; s. John Brown and Mary (Kerr) H.; M.A., U. St. Andrews (Scotland), 1939; student King's Coll., Cambridge (Eng.) U., 1939-40; Ph.D., Harvard, 1956; m. Joanna Baxter, Sept. 10, 1954; children—Mary Joanna, Margaret Brown, Elizabeth Campbell, John Stalker Kerr. Came to U.S., 1950, naturalized, 1956. Lectr. polit. economy U. St. Andrews, 1946-52; vis. prof. Union Coll., Schenectady, 1950-51; tutor econs. Harvard, 1954-56; economist Fed. Res. Bank N.Y., 1956-60; Andrew Wells Robertson prof. econs. Allegheny Coll., Meadville, Pa., 1960-66; internat. economist Joint Econ. Com., U.S. Congress, 1966-68; dep. asst. sec. for econ. affairs Dept. Commerce, 1968-70; dir. econ. studies div. Bur. Labor Statistics, Dept. Labor, 1970—. Mem. Meadville Charter Commn., 1965. Served to flight lt. RAF, 1941-46. Mem. Am. Econ. Soc., Soc. Internat. Devel. Home: 4119 N 27th Rd Arlington VA 22207 Office: 441 G St NW Washington DC 20212

HENDERSON, JOHN O., judge; b. Buffalo, Nov. 13, 1909; LL.B., U. Buffalo, 1933. Admitted to N.Y. State Bar, 1934; mem. Cohen, Fleishman, Augspurger, Henderson & Campbell, Buffalo; clk. Surrogate Ct. of Erie County, 1947-48; apptd. U.S. atty., Western Dist. N.Y., 1953, now chief judge. Served as lt. col. AUS, 1942-46. Mem. adv. council Practicing Law Inst., 1949—. Mem. Erie County Bar Assn. (pres. 1949-50). Office: Federal Bldg Buffalo NY 14203

HENDERSON, JOHN WARREN, physician; b. Sidney, Neb., Sept. 11, 1912; s. Edgar Forrest and Lillian (Sending) H.; B.S., U. Neb., 1934, M.A., 1936, M.D., 1937; M.S., U. Minn., 1943; m. Nadine Evelyn Downing, June 25, 1933; children—Sally, Holly. Intern Cin. Gen. Hosp. 1937-38; fellow in ophthalmology Mayo Grad. Sch., U. Minn., 1938-41; 1st asst. dept. ophthalmology Mayo Clinic, Rochester, Minn., 1941-43, cons. dept. ophthalmology, 1946-61, chmn. dept., 1961—; prof. ophthalmology U. Minn. Grad. Sch., 1962—. Served with M.C., AUS, 1943-46. Mem. Am. Ophthal. Soc., Am. Acad. Ophthalmology and Otolaryngology, A.M.A., Phi Beta Kappa, Sigma Xi, Alpha Omega Alpha, Chi Phi. Contbr. numerous articles on ophthalmology and ophthalmic surgery to med. jours. Home: 932 SW 10th St Rochester MN 55901 Office: 200 1st St SW Rochester MN 55901

HENDERSON, JOHN WAYNE, univ. pres.; b. Windber, Pa., Aug. 21, 1922; s. John Elmer and Anna Belle (Johns) H.; B.S., Juniata Coll., 1949; M.A., Mich. State U., 1950, Ph.D., 1958; m. Myrtle Irene Wright, May 31, 1947; children—John Dirk, Abigail Jo. Instr. psychology and edn., athletic coach, also asst. dean students Manchester (Ind.) Coll., 1950-51; asst. placement officer Mich. State U., 1951-52; ednl. and evaluation cons. U.S. Army Provost Marshal Gen. Sch., Fort Gordon, Ga., 1952-55; conf. cons. in continuing edn., 1955-56; asst. to dean students Mich. State U., 1956-58; dean student personnel services Western Ill. U., 1959-62; pres. Ia. Wesleyan U., 1962- 65, Washburn U., 1965—. Dir. Security Ultra Fund, Security Bond Fund, Inc., Security Benefit Life Investment Fund. Mem. continuing bd. Office Econ. Opportunity, 1965—; chmn. Western sect. visitation and appraisal com. Nat. Council for Accreditation Tchr. Edn.; liaison rep. for Kan., Am. Assn. Colls. Tchr. Edn.; pres. Goals for Topeka; mem. Gov. Com. Criminal Adminstrn., Gov. Rural Planning Council; mem. pub. adv. bd. Upward Bound program; pres., mem. adv. council Kan. Council World Affairs. Bd. dirs. State Fair Employment Adv. Bd., Family Service and Guidance Center Topeka, Big Bros. of Topeka, Topeka United Fund and Community Concert Assn., Topeka YMCA, Mulvane Art Center, Topeka; exec. bd. Jayhawk council Boy Scouts Am., 1965- -; adv. bd. Salvation Army, 1966—. Served with USMC, 1942- 45. Mem. Marine Corps League, Internat. Assn. U. Profs., Internat. Platform Assn., Kan. Assn. Colls. and Univs. (treas.), Civic Symphony Soc. Topeka, S.A.R., Topeka C. of C. (dir.). Presbyn. Rotarian. Home: 3130 Shadow Lane Topeka KS 66604

HENDERSON, JOHN WILLIAM, Jr., mgmt. cons.; b. Culver, Ind., Dec. 30, 1924; s. John William and Norma (Wilson) H.; B.S. in Math., Denison U., 1949; M.B.A., Northwestern U., 1950; Ph.D. in Econs., U. Wis., 1960; m. Mary Josephine Works, Sept. 12, 1953; children—Harriet Anne, John William III, David Wilson, Mary Josephine. With Oscar Mayer & Co., 1950-52; sec., mfg. supt. Wooster (O.) div. Borg-Warner Corp., 1953-55; mgr. aircraft div. Bellanca Corp., 1955-56; asso. McKinsey & Co., mgmt. cons., 1957-62; exec. v.p. Buckeye Steel Castings Co., Columbus, O., 1963-64, pres., gen. mgr., dir., 1964- -; pres., chief exec. officer Buckeye Internat., Inc., 1967-70; pres. Henderson & Assos., 1970—. Home: 4740 Riverside Dr Columbus OH 43220

HENDERSON, JOHN WOODWORTH, ophthalmologist, educator; b. Clarinda, Ia., Mar. 8, 1916; s. Frank Arthur and Bertha (Woodworth) H.; A.B., Occidental Coll., 1937; M.S., M.D., Northwestern U., 1942; Ph.D., U. Mich., 1948; m. Joyce Hildebrandt, June 27, 1942; children—John H., Louise W. Intern U. Mich. Hosp., 1942, resident ophthalmology, 1943-48; mem. faculty U. Mich. Med. Sch., 1948—, prof. opthalmology, 1962—, chmn. of dept. ophthalmology, 1968—; cons. VA Hosp., USPHS Milan Prison, Mich. Eye Bank. Fellow A.C.S.; mem. Am. Ophthal. Soc. (mem. council), Am. Acad. Ophthalmology and Otolaryngology (mem. council), Assn. U. Profs. Ophthalmology, A.M.A., Assn. Research Ophthalmology. Home: 2113 Devonshire Rd. Ann Arbor MI 48104.

HENDERSON, JOSEPH WELLES, Jr., lawyer; b. Phila., Aug. 29, 1920; s. Joseph Welles and Anne K. (Dreisbach) H.; grad. St. George's Sch., 1939; A.B. cum laude, Princeton, 1943; LL.B., Harvard, 1949; m. Helen R. Lipscomb, 1943 (div. 1947); 1 son, Joseph Welles III; m. 2d, Hannah Lowell Bradley, Aug. 27, 1949; children—G.L. Cabot, David R., Elizabeth Mason, T. Handasyd Perkins. Admitted to Pa. bar, 1950, since practiced in Phila.; mem. firm Rawle & Henderson, 1956—. Past pres. Juristic Soc., Port of Phila. Maritime Soc.; trustee Reineman Wildlife Sanctuary; founder, pres. Phila. Maritime Mus. Served to 1st lt., F.A., AUS, World War II. Fellow Am. Bar Assn.; mem. Pa., Phila. bar assns., Jr. Bar Phila. (past exec. com.). Republican. Presbyn. Clubs: Racquet, Merion Cricket, Union League, Courts, Rittenhouse (Phila.). Author: (catalogue) Port of Philadelphia, 1957. Asso. editor: American Maritime Cases. Home: Maple Hill Rd Gladwyne PA 19035 Office: Packard Bldg Philadelphia PA 19102

HENDERSON, LAVELL MERL, educator, biochemist; b. Swan Lake, Ida., Sept. 9, 1917; s. George Merl and Nellie Marie (Gambles) H.; B.S. in Chemistry, Utah State U., 1939; M.S. in Biochemistry, U. Wis., 1941, Ph.D., 1947; m. Jennie Maurine Criddle, Aug. 16, 1939; children—Janet Louise, Jeanne, Linda Marie. Research asst. U. Wis., 1939-41, 46-47, instr., 1947-48; asst. prof. biochemistry U. Ill., 1948-57; prof. biochemistry, head dept. Okla. State U., 1957-63, U. Minn., 1963—. Collaborator Brookhaven Nat. Lab. and Lalor Found. award, summer 1955; mem. food and nutrition bd. NRC. Served AUS, 1941-46; lt. col. Res. Mem. Am. Soc. Biol. Chemists, Am. Inst. Nutrition, Am. Bd. Clin. Nutrition, Am. Chem. Soc., Am. Soc. Microbiologists, A.A.A.S., Sigma Xi, Phi Lambda Upsilon, Alpha Chi Sigma, Phi Kappa Phi. Mem. Ch. of Jesus Christ of Latter-day Saints. Author articles in field. Home: 2154 Folwell St St Paul MN 55108

HENDERSON, LAWRENCE JOSEPH, retired research exec.; b. Cambridge, Mass., June 11, 1911; s. Lawrence Joseph and Edith Lawrence (Thayer) H.; A.B., Harvard, 1932, LL.B., 1935, M.B.A., 1937; m. Mary Katherine Britton, June 25, 1939; 1 dau., Carolyn Nelson. Admitted to Mass. bar, 1935; with Chem. Bank & Trust Co., N.Y.C., 1937-42, Office of Exports, Bd. Econ. Warfare, 1942-43; staff mem. Radiation Lab., Mass. Inst. Tech., 1943-45; adviser on radar to comdr.- in-chief Mediterranean Allied Air Forces, 1944-45; cons. Office of Sec. of War, 1944-46; mil. research Douglas Aircraft Co., 1946-48, asso. dir., 1948-56; trustee Rand Corp., Washington, 1948-71, v.p., 1956-71; chmn. exec. com., 1958-71; trustee Analytic Services, Inc., 1958—. Decorated Bronze Star. Fellow A.A.A.S.; mem. Operations Research Soc. Am., Council Fgn. Relations. Home: Misgen PO Box 540 St Thomas VI 00801

HENDERSON, LEON, economist; b. Millville, N.J., May 26, 1895; s. Chester Bowen and Lida C. (Beebe) H.; A.B., Swarthmore Coll., 1920; postgrad. U. Pa., 1920-22; m. Myrlie Hamm, July 25, 1925; children—Myrlie Beebe, Lyn, Leon. Instr., Wharton Sch. U. Pa., 1919-22; asst. prof. econ., Carnegie Inst. of Tech., 1922-23; dep. sec. Commonwealth of Pa., 1924- 25; dir. consumer credit research Russell Sage Found., N.Y.C., 1925-34; econ. adviser, dir. research and planning div. NRA, 1934-35; mem. Nat. Indsl. Recovery Bd., 1934-35; econ. adviser U.S. Senate com. on mfrs., 1935; economist Dem. Nat. Campaign Com., 1936; cons. economist WPA, 1936-38; exec. sec. Temporary Nat. Econ. Com., 1938-39; commr. of SEC, 1939-41; commr. Adv. Com. to Council of Nat. Def. 1940; adminstr. Office of Price Administration and Civilian Supply, 1941; adminstr. OPA, also mem. Supply Priorities and Allocation Bd. and dir. Div. of Civilian Supply, O.P.M., 1941-42; apptd. dir. civilian supply div. War Prodn. Bd., 1942; cons. economist; pres. Am. Leduc Uranium Corp., 1956-57; pres. Doeskin Products Inc., 1957-58; cons. economist 1959—. Served from pvt. to capt. Ordnance Dept., U.S. Army, 1917-19. Mem. Am. Econ. Assn., Delta Upsilon. Democrat. Mason. Club: Nat. Press. Contbr. to mags. Address: 220 Madison Av New York City NY 10016

HENDERSON, LOWELL LAWRENCE, physician; b. Kokomo, Ind., Apr. 22, 1916; s. Lawrence Roy and Alzada Gladys (Baker) H.; A.B., Ind. U., 1938, M.D., 1941; M.S. in Medicine, U. Minn., 1948; m. Anna Margaret Shaffer, Oct. 28, 1939; children—Margaret Ann (Mrs. R.J. Smalling), Beverly Jean (Mrs. R.L. Nelson), Marilyn Kay (Mrs. T.M. Parker), Sue Ellen, Patricia Marie. Intern, Indpls. City Hosp., 1941-42; fellow internal medicine Mayo Clinic, 1942-44, 47-48; cons. internal medicine and allergy Carle Hosp. Clinic, Urbana, Ill., 1948-52, Mayo Clinic, 1953—; asst. prof. medicine Mayo Grad. Sch., U. Minn., 1962-67, asso. prof. clin. medicine, 1967-70, prof. clin. medicine, 1970—; mem. bd. med. dirs. Allergy Found. Am., 1965—; mem. bd. subcertification Allergy in Internal Medicine, 1961-66. Served to capt., M.C., AUS, 1944-46. Diplomate Am. Bd. Internal Medicine, 1948, in Allergy, 1957. Fellow Am. Coll. Allergists (pres. 1966); mem. A.M.A. (sec. sect. allergy 1965—), Am. Acad. Allergy, N. Central Allergy Soc. (pres. 1960-62), A.A.A.S., Internat. Soc. Allergology (treas. 1967-70), Midwest Forum on Allergy (exec. com. 1966-69), Phi Beta Kappa, Sigma Xi, Delta Upsilon, Nu Sigma Nu, Alpha Omega Alpha. Episcopalian (warden). Author articles in field. Home: 1102 10th St SW Rochester MN 55901 Office: 200 1st St SW Rochester MN 55901

HENDERSON, LOY WESLEY, ret. educator, fgn. service officer; b. Rogers, Ark., June 28, 1892; s. George Milton and Mary May (Davis) H.; A.B., Northwestern U., 1915, LL.D., 1953; student Denver U. Law Sch., 1917-18, D. Pub. Service, 1953; LL.D., U. Ark., Bates Coll., 1957, Wayne U., 1962; D. Pub. Adminstrn., Southwestern Coll., 1959; m. Elise Marie Heinrichson, Dec. 3, 1930. Mem. Inter-Allied Commn. to Germany for reparation of prisoners of war, 1919; mem. A.R.C. Commn. to Western Russia and Baltic States, 1919-20; in charge A.R.C. in Germany, 1920-21; vice consul, Dublin, 1922, Queenstown, 1923; with Div. of Eastern European Affairs, Dept. of State, 1925; 3d sec. of legation, Riga, Kovno and Tallinn, 1927, 2d sec., 1929; Div. of Eastern European Affairs, Dept. of State, 1930; 2d sec. of embassy, Moscow, 1934, 1st sec., 1935, 1st sec. and intermittently chargé d'affaires, 1935-38; asst. chief Div. of European Affairs, Dept. of State, 1938; insp. diplomatic missions and consulate offices, 1942-43; counselor of embassy and chargé d'affaires, Moscow and Kuibyshev, 1942; E.E. and M.P. to Iraq, 1943-45; dir. Near Eastern and African affairs Dept. of State, 1945-48; A.E. and P. to India, also E.E. and M.P. to Nepal, 1948; became A.E. and P. to Iran, 1951; dep. under sec. of state for adminstrn., 1955; bd. cons. Nat. War Coll., 1957-60; chief of mission to arrange for opening new diplomatic and consular establishments in newly emerging countries in Africa, 1960; ret.; prof. internat. relations, dir. Center for Diplomacy and Fgn. Policy, Am. U., 1961-68. Apptd. U.S. career ambassador, 1956. Del. 17th Internat. Geol. Congress, Moscow, 1937; del. Baghdad Pact Conf., Iran, 1956; Am. mem. Suez Com., Cairo; Suez Canal Conf., London and Cairo, 1956; mem. U.S. delegation 2d Suez Canal Conf., London, 1956; Am. observer Baghdad Pact Meeting, 1957. Bd. govs. Am. Nat. Red Cross, 1957. Recipient award of Merit, Northwestern Alumni Assn., 1952; Distinguished Service award Dept. State, 1954; Pres.'s award for Distinguished Fed. Civilian Service, 1958; decorated Insignia of Imperial Order Homayoun, 1st class (Iran); Grand Cross Royal Order George I (Greece); comdr. de l'Ordere de la Republic of Tunisia. Mem. Am. Fgn. Service Assn. (pres. 1956), Washington Inst. Fgn. Affairs (pres. 1961), Delta Tau Delta, Phi Delta Phi. Clubs: 1925 F St., Metropolitan, Internat. Home: 2727 29th St NW Washington, DC 20008.

HENDERSON, MARGARET MONROE, ret. marine corps officer; b. Cameron, Tex., Feb. 6, 1911; d. Dwight Monroe and Dora (Williamson) Henderson; B.B.A., U. Tex., 1932; student Denver U., 1948. Commd. 2d. lt. USMC, 1943, advanced through grades to col., 1959; instr. Women Marine Sch., 1943-44; officer-in-charge Bus. Sch., Marine Corps Inst., 1944-45; exec. officer Womans Bn., 1945-46; active duty, 1946-48; comdg. officer Womans Recruit Tng. Bn., 1949-50; staff officer Hdqrs. USMC, 1950-53; comdg. officer Womens Officer Tng. Detachment, 1953-54; asst. G-1, Camp Pendleton, 1955-56; staff officer Hdqrs. USMC, 1957-59; dir. Women Marines, 1959-64; asst. G-1 Marine Corps Depot, San Diego, 1964-66; ret., 1966. Decorated Legion of Merit. Home: 3709 66th St Lubbock TX 79401 Office: 2201 19th St Lubbock TX 79401

HENDERSON, MELVIN DUANE, bus. exec., ret. marine corps officer; b. Aug. 23, 1917; m. Winona Henderson; 5 children. Entered service U.S. Marine Corps, 1939, advanced through grades to brig. gen., 1964, ret., 1966; now mgr. indsl. devel. Port of Olympia (Wash.). Home: 2405 Vista Av Olympia WA 98501

HENDERSON, MILTON ARNOLD, assn. exec.; b. Chattanooga, June 22, 1922; s. Milton Arnold and Margaret (Rawlings) H.; B.S., Northwestern U., 1948; m. Joyce C. Henderson; children—George, Linda, Philip. Asst. sales mgr. Coca-Cola Bottling Co., Savannah and Macon, Ga., 1948-54; exec. dir. Gideons Internat., Nashville, 1954—. Served to capt. USAAF, 1942-46, USAF, 1951-52. Home: 2524 Stones River Ct Nashville TN 37214 Office: 2900 Lebanon Rd Nashville TN 37214

HENDERSON, OSCAR WARREN, bakery co. exec.; b. Balt., Mar. 19, 1917; s. Oscar Warren and Lucille (Minor) H.; A.B., Rutgers U., 1938; m. Ruth Buhl, Nov. 15, 1941; children—Richard Warren, Roger Buhl. Div. accountant Anaconda Am. Brass Co., Buffalo, 1949-55; adminstrv. mgr. Anaconda Aluminum Co., Terre Haute, Ind., 1955-60; adminstrv. mgr., controller Inland Container Corp., Indpls., 1960-63; asst. controller Air Products & Chems., Inc., Allentown, Pa., 1963-65, corporate controller, 1965-68; v.p., treas., dir. Tasty Baking Co., Phila., 1968—; v.p., dir. Phillips and Jacobs, Inc., Dixieplate, Inc., B. & B., Inc., Laramie Inc. Trustee Tasty Baking Found. Served to lt. col., Transp. Corps, AUS, 1942-46. Mem. Financial Execs. Inst., Nat. Assn. Accountants. Home: RD 1 Horseshoe Trail Malvern PA 19355 Office: 2801 Hunting Park Av Philadelphia PA 19129

HENDERSON, RALPH ERNEST, editor; b. Mongnai, Burma, June 4, 1899; s. Albert Haley and Cora May (Shinn) H.; student Anglo-Vernacular Sch., Burma, 1909-12; A.B., Harvard, 1921; m. Clifford West Sellers, May 30, 1927 (dec. Mar. 1971); children—Clifford Sellers, Lee West, Ralph Hale. Bus. mgr. The Reader's Digest, 1925-27, mng. editor, 1948—, v.p., editor Reader's Digest Book Club, 1950-65, editorial dir., 1965—. War corr. in India and Burma, 1944-45. Clubs: Coffee House, Harvard (N.Y.C.); Runaway Bay (Jamaica, W.I.) Golf; Sharon (Conn.) Country. Home: Green Meadow Rd Pleasantville NY 10570 Office: The Reader's Digest Pleasantville NY 10570

HENDERSON, ROBERT ARTHUR, educator; b. Oakland, Cal., Apr. 3, 1925; s. Harold Eugene and Charlotte (Peregrine) H.; A.B., U. Cal. at Berkeley, 1947; M.A., San Francisco State Coll., 1950; Ed.D., U. Ill., 1957; m. June Virginia Crawford, Sept. 15, 1945; children—Barbara Ann, Kerrie Lee, Lawrence A. High sch. tchr., elementary prin., Sonoma County, Cal., 1947-49; tchr. mentally retarded, Stockton, Cal., 1952-54; asst. prof. U. Conn., 1957-58; cons. bur. spl. edn. Cal. Dept. Edn., 1958-62; tchr., research asst. Inst. Research Exceptional Children, U. Ill., 1954-56; prof. Inst. Research Exceptional Children, chmn. dept. spl. edn. U. Ill., 1962—; mem. adj. faculty Marine Corps Command and Staff Coll., 1968—. Research fellow Nat. Inst. Mental Health, 1956-57; mem. adv. council div. tng. programs, bur. edn. handicapped. U.S. Office Edn., 1967-71. Active local Boy Scouts Am. Served to col. USMCR, World War II and Korea. Decorated Purple Heart. Fellow Am. Assn. Mental Deficiency; life mem. Council Exceptional Children, N.E.A.; mem. Nat. Soc. Study Edn., Phi Delta Kappa. Contbr. profl. jours. Cons. editor Jour. Edn. Research, 1964-67; asso. editor Exceptional Children, 1966—.

HENDERSON, ROBERT DEAN, educator, business cons.; b. Pitts., Sept. 22, 1916; s. William James and Margaret (Shaw) H.; B.B.A., Westminster Coll., 1938; M.B.A., Ohio State U., 1941; Ph.D., U. Pitts., 1949; m. Grace Waters, Sept. 3, 1941; children—Robert Dean, Carol Lynne. Prof. econs. Bucknell U., 1946-54; prof. mgmt. Bowling Green (O.) U., 1954—, chmn. dept. bus. adminstrn., 1954-66. Fellow Acad. Mgmt. (pres. Midwest div. 1964-65, nat. sec.-treas. 1965-68); mem. Nat. Assn. Purchasing Mgmt. (v.p. dist. six 1968-69), Purchasing Mgmt. Assn. Toledo (pres. 1967-68), Indsl. Relations Research Assn. (pres. N.W. Ohio chpt. 1960), Alpha Sigma Phi, Tau Kappa Alpha, Pi Gamma Mu, Pi Delta Upsilon, Beta Gamma Sigma. Clubs: Town and Gown, Rotary (Bowling Green). Asso. editor Jour. Purchasing, 1965—; bus. mgr. Acad. Mgmt. Jour., 1968—. Contbr. profl. jours. Home: 138 Williams St Bowling Green OH 43402

HENDERSON, SKITCH CEDRIC, pianist, condr.; b. Halstad, Minn., Jan. 27, 1918; studied piano with Malcolm Frost, Roger Aubert, conducting with Albert Coates, Fritz Reiner, harmony with Schoenberg. Performed with area bands, theater orchs., with film and radio studios, West Coast, 1939-40; piano soloist Crosby, Sinatra radio shows, 1946; on tour with own dance band, 1947-49; radio work, 1949-51; pianist, condr. NBC, N.Y.C., 1951—; leader, comedian Steve Allen TV Tonight Show, 1955-56; guest condr. N.Y. Philharmonic, Mpls. Symphony, others; frequent TV appearances. Served with USAAF, 1941-45. Address: care of Wilfred Van Wyck 80 Wigmore St London W1 England*

HENDERSON, VIVIAN WILSON, coll. pres.; b. Bristol, Tenn., Feb. 10, 1923; s. William Thomas and Sallie (Richmond) H.; B.S., N.C. Central U., 1947; M.A., U. Ia., 1948, Ph.D., 1952; m. Anna Powell, Sept. 8, 1949; children—Wyonella Marie, Dwight Cedric, David Wayne, Kimberly Ann. Instr. econs. Prairie View Coll. (Tex.), 1948-49; prof., chmn. dept. econs. Fisk U., Nashville, 1952-65; vis. prof. econs. N.C. State U., 1962-64; pres. Clark Coll., Atlanta, 1965—. Mem. U.S. Nat. Commn. to UNESCO, 1968-73, So. Regional Council, 1960—, Nat. Urban Coalition, 1969-71. Trustee Nat. Bur. Econ. Research, Ford Found. Served with AUS, 1943-46. Recipient Distinguished Service award Tchrs. Coll., Columbia, 1970. Mem. Am. Econ. Assn., Alpha Kappa Mu, Omicron Delta Epsilon, Kappa Alpha Psi. United Methodist. Author: The Economic Imbalance, 1961; Economic Dimensions in Race Relations, 1961; Economic Opportunity and Negro Education, 1962; The Economic Status of Negroes, 1963; The Advancing South, 1967; Employment, Race and Poverty, 1967. Home: 1125 Fountain Dr SW Atlanta GA 30314

HENDERSON, WARREN STANLEY PATRICK, army officer; b. Sask., Can., June 12, 1918; s. Harry W. and Evelyn H. (Northcott) H.; student U. B.C., 1936-39; B.S., U. Ore., 1941, M.D., 1943; M.S., Baylor U., 1955; m. Elaine Kelly McKinnon, June 26, 1943; children—Patrick M., Sharon E. (Mrs. George E. Washburn III), Henry M., James K., Kelly W. Came to U.S., 1923, naturalized, 1942. Commd. 2d lt. U.S. Army, 1942, advanced through grades to col., M.C., 1966; med. officer, Europe, 1946-48; chief of surgery 250th Sta. Hosp., Regensburg, 1948; chief of orthopedics, Ft. Lawton, Seattle, 1949; resident surgery Brooke Army Hosp., Tex., 1951-55; army hosp. comdr., Japan, 1956-59; chief gen. surgery Zama Hosp., Japan, 1959-60; chief of surgery, chief profl. services U.S. Army Hosp., Ft. Leonard Wood, Mo., 1960-65; comdr. Nobel Army Hosp., Ft. McClellan, Ala., 1965-66, 62d Med. Group, Bad Kreuznach, Germany, 1966-67, 7th Med. Brigade, Germany, 1967-68, Wurzburg Army Hosp., Germany, 1968-69; comdr. U.S. Army Hosp. Specialized Treatment Center, also dir. med. activities, Ft. Gordon, Ga., 1969—. Decorated Army Commendation Medal with 3 oak leaf clusters. Diplomate Am. Bd. Surgery. Mem. A.M.A., Assn. Mil Surgeons. Home: Quarters 5 Boardman Lake Ft Gordon GA 30905 Office: US Army Hosp Specialized Treatment Center Ft Gordon GA 30905

HENDERSON, WILLIAM E., state govt. ofcl.; m. Mary Brown Gattinger, Oct. 20, 1951; children—Mary Ann, Carol Eileen, Barbara Jean, Rebecca Jane. Exec. v.p. Little Rock C. of C., 1961-71. dir. Ark. Dept. Parks and Tourism, 1971—. Home: 1009 Fawnwood Rd Little Rock AR 72207 Office: State Capitol Little Rock AR 72201

HENDERSON, WILLIAM L., educator; B.S., A.M., Ph.D., Ohio State U. John E. Harris prof. econs., Denison U., 1960-63, 65—; asst. to pres., 1970—. Address: Doane Hall Denison U Granville OH 43023

HENDERSON, WILLON ALLEN, lawyer; b. San Francisco, Nov. 11, 1904; s. John Wesley and Irene (Allen) H.; LL.B., U. Cal. at Berkeley, 1930; m. Anne Townsend, Dec. 28, 1927; 1 son, Willon Allen. Admitted to Cal. bar, 1930; partner Henderson & Henderson, 1930-41; procedure adminstr. Mo. Ordnance Works, Bechtel-McCone-Parsons, 1941-42; asst. adminstrn. mgr. Canol Project, Can.-Bechtel-Price-Callahan, 1942-44; asst. sec., chief marketing atty. Gen. Petroleum Corp., 1944-55, asst. sec., asst. to gen. counsel, 1955-60; legislative counsel Mobil Oil Co., 1955-60; legal counsel, corporate sec. Ralph M. Parsons Co., Los Angeles, 1960-67; atty. for Tulare County Legal Service Assn., 1969-70; legal cons.; 1971—. Mem. Theta Chi, Phi Alpha Delta. Home: 386 S Burnside Av Los Angeles CA 90036

HENDERSON, ZACH SUDDATH, ret. educator; b. Gillsville, Ga., Jan. 24, 1902; s. Hollis and Onieda (Suddath) H.; B.S., Piedmont Coll., 1922, LL.D., 1948; A.M., Columbia Tchrs. Coll., 1928, postgrad., 1930-31; postgrad. U. Chgo., 1940-41; LL.D., LaGrange Coll., 1967; m. Marjorie Clark, July 2, 1927; children—Gene, Mary, Ann. Sci. tchr. Piedmont Coll. Demonstration Sch., 1922-23; sci. tchr., coach Plant City (Fla.) High Sch., 1923-24; prin., coach Eastman (Ga.) High Sch., 1924-26; supt. pub. schs., Eastman, 1926-27; dean Ga. So. Coll., 1927- 48, pres., 1948-68, pres. emeritus, also cons. tchr. edn. to univ. system chancellor, 1968—. Chmn. Ga. High Sch. Accrediting Commn., 1946-55; Meth. Conf. lay leader of South Ga. Conf., del. to gen. and jurisdictional confs., 1944, 48, 52, 56, 60, 64, 68; council, exec. com. Southeastern Jurisdiction. Trustee Piedmont Coll., 1928-30. Recipient Distinguished Alumni award Piedmont Coll., 1971. Mem. Boy Scouts Am. (Silver Beaver award), C. of C. (past pres. Stateboro), N.E.A. (dir. 1966—), Ga. Assn. Colls. (pres. 1966-67), Am. Assn. Sch. Adminstrs., Soc. Advancement Edn., Ga. Edn. Assn. (pres. 1965-66), Phi Delta Kappa, Kappa Delta Phi. Methodist. Club: Rotary (past pres., dist. gov. 1958-59). Contbg. editor Wesleyan Christian Advocate, 1942-45; contbr. articles to Ga. Edn. Assn. Jour., Meth. Laymen. Home: 518 Pitt-Moore Rd Statesboro GA 30458

HENDIN, HERBERT MARTIN, psychiatrist; b. Long Island, N.Y., Oct. 10, 1926; s. Louis and Pauline (Mass) H.; B.A., Columbia, 1945, degree psychoanalytic medicine, Pschoanalytic Clinic, 1958; M.D., N.Y. U., 1949; m. Josephine Gattuso, June 7, 1968. Intern U.S. Marine Hosp., Stapleton, N.Y., 1949-50; psychiat. resident Bellevue Pschiat. Hosp., 1950-52; studied suicide Bellevue Hosp., N.Y. Psychiat. Inst., also St. Luke's Hosp., N.Y.C., 1949-60, suicide and psychosocial problems in Norway, Sweden and Denmark, 1960-64, psychosocial problems Am. Negro at Harlem Hosp., N.Y.C., 1964—; tchr. course psychoanalytic study of soc. Columbia Psychoanalytic Clinic, 1963—; conducting project Culture, Character and Crisis in Coll. Students, Columbia, 1969—; pvt. practice, N.Y.C., 1952—; mem. staff Columbia-Presbyn., Harlem, Bellevue and St. Luke's hosps. Hon. fellow Am.-Scandinavian Found.; mem. Am. Psychiat. Assn., Am. Psychoanalytic Assn., Assn. Psychoanalytic Medicine (award original research 1964). Author: Suicide and Scandinavia, 1964; (with Gaylin and Carr) Psychoanalysis and Social Research; 1965; Black Suicide, 1969. Home: 1045 Park Av New York City NY 10028

HENDL, WALTER, conductor, composer; b. West New York, N.J., Jan. 12, 1917; s. William and Ella (Kittel) H.; grad. Curtis Inst. of Music; m. Edith Seaman Beich, Nov. 12, 1961. Mem. Faculty Sarah Lawrence Coll., Bronxville, N.Y., 1939-41; active as condr. and pianist Berkshire Music Center, 1941-42; asst. condr. N.Y. Philharmonic Symphony Orch., 1945-46, 46-47, 47-48; condr. Dallas Symphony 1949—, past mus. dir.; guest condr. and soloist Detroit Symphony, Nat. Symphony (Washington); Pitts. Symphony, Boston "Pops" Symphony, Balt. Symphony, N.Y. Philharmonic Symphony; condr. Chautauqua (N.Y.) Symphony Orch., 1933—; asso. condr. Chgo. Symphony Orch., from 1958, also mus. dir. Ravinia (Ill.) Festival; now. dir. Eastman Sch. Music, Rochester, N.Y. Composer Broadway prodn. Dark of the Moon, 1945. Recipient Alice M. Ditson award, Columbia, 1953. Office: Eastman Sch Music Rochester NY 14603

HENDLEY, COIT TAYLOR, Jr., newspaper editor; b. Charleston, S.C., July 17, 1920; s. Coit Taylor and Lois (Denaro) H.; A.B. in Journalism, U. S.C., 1940; m. Barbara Davidson, July 18, 1948; children—Dale, Coit Taylor III, Peter, Patricia. Copy boy, reporter, asst. city editor Washington Evening Star, 1940-65; exec. editor Elizabeth (N.J.) Daily Jour., 1965-67; editor Camden (N.J.) Courier-Post, 1967—. Served to lt. (s.g.) USCGR, 1942-45. Decorated Silver Star; Croix de Guerre (France). Mem. Am. Soc. Newspaper Editors, N.J. Press Assn. Home: 140 West End Av Haddonfield NJ 08033 Office: Courier Post Camden NJ 08101

HENDLEY, DAN LUNSFORD, banker; b. Nashville, Apr. 26, 1938; s. Frank E. and Mattie (Lunsford) H.; B.A., Vanderbilt U., 1960; grad. Stonier Grad. Sch. Banking, Rutgers U., 1969; m. Patricia Fariss, June 18, 1960; 1 son, Dan Lunsford. With N.Y. Life Ins. Co., 1960-62; with Fed. Res. Bank Atlanta, 1962—, v.p., officer in charge Birmingham br., 1969—. Mem. Tenn. Air N.G., 1961-67. Mem. Vanderbilt U. Alumni Assn., Phi Eta Sigma, Delta Phi Alpha, Kappa Sigma. Baptist. Kiwanian. Home: 2325 Garland Dr Birmingham AL 35216 Office: 1801 N 5th Av Birmingham AL 35203

HENDON, ROBERT CARAWAY, transp. and mfg. co. exec.; b. Shelbyville, Tenn., Jan. 13, 1912; s. William Oscar and Anna Bertha (Caraway) H.; B.A. in Journalism, U. Mont., 1931, LL.B., 1934; m. Ruth Perham, Apr. 23, 1936; children— Robert Caraway, Elizabeth Anne (Mrs. MacDonald Dunbar, Jr.). Admitted to Mont. and Tenn. bars, 1934; gen. practice law, Monterey, Tenn., 1934-35; spl. agt., spl. agt. in charge FBI, 1935-39, inspector, adminstrv. asst. to dir. FBI, 1939-47; exec. rep. to pres. Ry. Express Agy., N.Y.C., 1947, various exec. positions, 1947-50; asst. to pres., dir. personnel Mathieson Chem. Corp., 1950-52; v.p. personnel Ry. Express Agy., 1953-55, v.p. operations, 1955-64, v.p. exec. dept., 1964- 68; dir. REA Leasing Corp., 1961-68, pres., 1964-67, vice chmn. bd., 1967-68; pres., dir. TOFC Leasing Corp., 1965-68, REA Express-Seven Arts Transvision, Inc., 1965-68; dir., chmn. exec. com. Fast Service Shipping Terminals, Inc., 1961-68; v.p. Consol. Freightways Inc., 1968—; dir., mem. exec., nominating, auditing, exam. coms., mem. pres.'s adv. com. personnel and pub. relations Manhattan Life Ins. Co. Trustee, mem. exec. com., past pres. U. Mont. Found.; bd. dirs., chmn. awards com. Nat. Safety Council, 1963-68. Recipient Distinguished Service award U. Mont., 1967. Mem. Soc. Former Spl. Agts. FBI, Newcomen Soc. Phi Sigma Kappa, Sigma Delta Chi. Episcopalian (former vestryman, warden). Clubs: University (Larchmont, N.Y.); Union League (N.Y.C.); Grizzly Riders Internat. (Mont.). Author: Frontiers in Labor-Management Problems, 1956; Seniority. First In, Last Out, 1958; also articles. Home: 1128 Kensington Rd. McLean VA 22101. Office: World Center Bldg 918 16th St NW Washington DC 20006

HENDON, ROBERT RANDALL, lawyer; b. Earlsboro, Okla., Mar. 20, 1894; s. Robert Randall and Mary Belle (Neabors) H.; LL.B., U. Okla., 1916; grad. Command and Gen. Staff Sch., 1935, War Dept. Indsl. Coll., 1945; m. Kathlene Marie Grubaugh, Dec. 21, 1921 (dec. Oct. 6, 1956) children—Robert Randall, Owen William; m. 2d; Muriel Louise Mackenzie, Mar. 29, 1958. Admitted to Okla. bar, 1916, U.S. Supreme Ct. bar, 1920, D.C. bar, 1933, U.S. Ct. Hawaii, 1944, Md. bar, 1954, ICC bar, 1954, U.S. Ct. Claims, 1956; gen. law practice, Wewoka, Okla., 1916-17; mem. law firm, Shawnee, Okla., 1921-25; atty. Bd. Contract Adjustment, War Dept., 1919, asso. mem., 1920-21; atty., sr. atty. examiner Interstate Commerce Commn., 1925-50; asso. counsel U.S. Senate Com. Investigating R.R. Financing. 1934-36; dir. tax ammortization and def. loan div., Defence Transport Adminstrn.; 1950-54; gen. law practice, 1954—. Served as 1st lt., A.E.F., France, 1918-19; col. Arty., A.U.S., 1940-50, comdr. 98th Anti- Aircraft Regt. and Searchlight-Radar Groupment, P.T.O., 1942-45; chief contract termination div. Office Chief Engrs., Washington, 1945-46; spl. asst. to adminstr. War Assets Adminstrn., 1946-47, dir. property mgmt. div., Mar.-Dec. 1947, mem. gen. bd., Jan.-May 1948; chief spl. projects div. Munitions Bd., Office Sec. Def., 1948-49; pres. Army Phys. Review Council, Office Sec., Dept. Army, Jan.-Nov. 1950; dir. C. & G.S., Dept. Army, O.R.C. School, Washington, 1950-54. Decorated Purple Heart, Bronze Star citation, Legion of Merit, Commendation from Sec. of War, Nat. Mil. Establishment badge. Mem. ICC Practioner's Assn., Internat. Platform Assn.; Reserve Officer Assn. of U.S., Nat. Assn. Retired Civil Employees, Ret. Mil. Officers Assn.; Order of Lafayette. Democrat. Baptist. Mason (Shriner). Clubs: Army and Navy, Nat. Lawyers (founder, life mem.). Address: 4000 Massachusetts Av NW Washington DC 20016

HENDREN, JOHN HERBERT, lawyer; b. Polo, Mo., Aug. 16, 1907; s. John Herbert and Mary Agnes (Wilkison) H.; student U. Mo., 1926-31; m. Florence Wilmoth Mason, Apr. 12, 1941. Admitted to Mo. bar, 1931, since practiced in Jefferson City; sr. partner firm Hendren & Andrae, 1946—; mem. bd. law examiners Mo. Supreme Ct.; 1947-50. Vice pres., gen. counsel DeLong's, Inc., Jefferson City, Mo.; counsel Mississippi River Corp.; St. Louis. Chmn. of Mo. Democratic Com., 1948-50. Served to col. AUS, 1942-46 Fellow Am. Coll. Trial Lawyers; mem. Am. (council pub. utility sect. 1959-62), Mo. Fed. Power, Cole County bar assns., Judge Adv. Assn., Mo., Cole County hist. socs., Delta Theta Phi. Methodist. Clubs: Jefferson City Country, Rotary (past pres. Jefferson City); Army-Navy (Washington); Kansas City (Mo.); Old Warson Country, Racquet (St. Louis). Home: 1624 W Main St Jefferson City MO 65101 Office: Central Trust Bldg Jefferson City MO 65101

HENDRICK, GEORGE, ednl. adminstrn. Prof. English, asso. dean Grad. Coll. U. Ill. Address: 122 W Main St Urbana IL 61801*

HENDRICK, IVES, psychiatrist; b. New Haven, Mar. 10, 1898; s. Burton J. and Bertha Jane (Ives) H.; student Phillips Andover Acad., 1913-16, Williston Acad., 1916-17; A.B., Yale, 1921, M.D., 1925; postgrad. Psychoanalytical Inst., Berlin, 1928-30; m. Martha Marie Crawford McClung, Nov. 14, 1934 (div. 1945); children—Ives, Jr. (dec.), Jane (Mrs. James Rumsey), Martha (Mrs. Robert Rusnak). Intern. Lenox Hill Hosp. N.Y.C. 1925-26; asst. in dept. psychiatry Med. Sch., Harvard, 1930-34, instr., 1943-47, asso., 1947-48, asst. clin. prof., 1948-51, asso. clin. prof. 1951-54, clin. prof., 1954-65; emeritus, 1965—; clin. dir. emeritus Mass. Mental Health Center, 1968—; chief Harvard Teaching Unit, Southard Clinic, 1943-64; dir. med. edn. Boston Psychopathic Hosp., 1949-56; cons. McClean and Mass. Gen. Hosps., 1930-33; pvt. practice psychoanalysis and psychiatry; 1930—. Fellow Am. Psychiat. Assn. (life); mem. Am. Psychoanalytic Assn. (life; Pres.-elect, chmn. bd. prof. standards, 1951-53, pres. 1953-55) Boston Soc. Psychiatry and Neurology, Soc. Research in Psychosomatic Problems, Group for Advancement in Psychiatry, A.M.A., Mass. Psychiat. Soc., Mass. Med. Assn., Macy Found. Conf. on Infancy, Boston Psychoanalytic Soc. and Inst. (pres. 1944-45); Nu Sigma Nu. Clubs: Yale (N.Y.C.); Harvard, Yale, Harvard Music Assn. (Boston); Harvard Faculty (Cambridge, Mass.). Author: Facts and Theories of Pschoanalysis, 1934, 3d edit., 1958, rev. edit., 1967 (Spanish transl. 1951); Psychiatric Education Today, 1965. Author and editor: Birth of an Institute, 1961. Contbr. sci. publs. Contbg. editor Ency. Brit.; editorial bd. Jour. Am. Psychoanalytic Assn., 1952-56. Address: 84 Mount Vernon St Boston MA 02108 ☆

HENDRICK, JAMES POMEROY, former govt. ofcl.; b. Wainscott, N.Y., July 31, 1901; s. Ellwood and Josephine (Pomeroy) H.; B.A., Yale, 1923; student Corpus Christi Coll., Cambridge Eng., 1924; LL.B., Yale, 1927; m. Elnor Loomis Sullivan, Nov. 21, 1927; children—Arthur Pomeroy, Alice (Mrs. James Sutton Hardigg), Robert Ellwood Pomeroy. Admitted to N.Y. bar, 1929; atty. Winthrop, Stimson, Putnam & Roberts, N.Y.C., 1928-41; asst. to under sec. war, later sec. war, 1941-46; adviser to U.S. rep. UN Commn. on Human Rights, 1946-48; asst. to adminstr. ECA, 1948-53; asst. to sec. Treasury Dept., dep. asst. sec., 1953-67, spl. asst. to sec. (for enforcement), 1967-69. Vice pres. INTERPOL, 1968-69. Dir. Del. Fund, Inc., 1938-53. Treas., later 1st v.p. Opera Soc. Washington, 1959-69 also trustee; trustee St. Bernard's Sch., N.Y.C., 1937-41. Served to col., AUS, 1942- 46. Decorated Legion of Merit, 1945; Ordre Nationale de Viet Nam, 1953. Mem. Wolf's Head Soc., Alpha Delta Phi, Phi Delta Phi. Democrat. Episcopalian. Clubs: Century Assn., Dutch Treat, The Players, River, Metropolitan, Chevy Chase; Nat. Golf Links of Am. Contbr. articles to profl. publs. Home: PO Box 2931 Christiansted St Croix VI 00820

HENDRICK, MAX MORTON, chem. co. exec.; b. Portland, Ore., Apr. 28, 1910; s. Max William and Laura (Phillips) H.; B.A.Sc. in Mech. Engring., U. Toronto, 1932; Rockefeller scholar McGill U., 1934; m. Dorothy Somerville Stratton July 24, 1940. Commd. pilot officer RCAF, 1934, advanced through grades to air vice marshall, 1955; air mem. tech. service, 1955-58; chmn. Canadian Joint Staff, Washington, 1958-62; air officer comdg. Air Def. Command, 1962-64; ret., 1965; exec. v.p., dir. Allied Chem. Can. Ltd., Montreal, Que., 1965-68, pres., 1968—, also dir. Canadian mem. mil. com. permanent session NATO, 1958-62. Decorated officer Brit. Empire; Canadian Decoration. Mem. Engring. Inst. Can., Canadian Aero. and Space Inst. Clubs: University (Toronto); United Services, Mount Royal (Montreal); RAF (London); Canadian (N.Y.C.): Mt. Bruno Golf, St. Jame's (Montreal), Chevy Chase (Washington). Home: 1745 Cedar Av Montreal 25 Quebec Canada Office: 1155 Dorchester St W Montreal Quebec Canada

HENDRICKS, CHARLES DURRELL, Jr., educator, physicist; b. Lewiston, Utah, Dec. 5, 1926; s. Charles Durrell and Louise (McAlister) H.; B.S., Utah State U., 1949; M.S., U. Wis., 1951; Ph.D., U. Utah, 1955; m. Leah Funk, Mar. 4, 1948; children—Katherine, Martha Jane. Research asst. U. Utah, 1953-55; staff mem. Lincoln Lab., Mass. Inst. Tech., 1955-56; faculty U. Ill. at Urbana, 1956—, prof. dept. elec. engring., 1961—, prof. nuclear engring., 1965—, also dir. charged particle research lab.; v.p. prof. Mass. Inst. Tech., 1967-68; editor Blaisdell Pub. Co. Cons. indsl. firms. Fellow A.A.A.S.; mem. I.E.E.E., Am. Phys. Soc., Am. Assn. Physics Tchrs., Am. Inst. Aeros. and Astronautics, Electrostatics Soc. Am. (exec. council 1970—), Phi Beta Kappa, Sigma Xi, Tau Beta Pi, Phi Kappa Phi, Eta Kappa Nu. Home: 403 Sunnycrest Ct Urbana IL 61801

HENDRICKS, CHARLES HENNING, physician; b. Traverse City, Mich., Oct. 26, 1917; s. Henning Vitalis and Jennie (Burnett) H.; A.B., U. Mich., 1941, M.D., 1943; m. Geraldine Ruth Chisholm, Sept. 27, 1942; children—William Allen, Charles Henning, Mary Beth, Judith Ann, Cynthia Ruth. Intern Univ. Hosp., Ann Arbor, Mich., 1943-44, resident, 1944-46; resident Univ. Hosp., Columbus, O., 1948-49; practice medicine, specializing in obstetrics, and gynecology, Columbus, 1949-54, Cleve., 1954-68; instr. Coll. Medicine, Ohio State U., 1949-51, asst. prof., 1951-54; asso. prof. obstetrics and gynecology Sch. Medicine, Case Western Res. U., 1954-62, prof., 1962-68; prof. U. N.C. Sch. Medicine, Chapel Hill, 1968—, chmn. dept. obstetrics and gynecology, 1968—, Robert A. Ross distinguished prof., 1971—. Served to capt. AUS, 1946-48. Recipient Ann. Prize award Central Assn. Obstetricians and Gynecologists, 1955; Found. prize Am. Assn. Obstetricians and Gynecologists, 1956; Macy fellow U. Uruguay, 1957. Mem. A.M.A., Soc. Gynecol. Investigation (pres.), Am., Norman F. Miller, Allan C. Barnes gynecol. socs., Am., Central assns. obstetricians and gynecologists, Cleve. (past pres.), N.D. (hon.), Piedmont socs. obstetrics and gynecology, Am. Coll. Obstetricians and Gynecologists, A.A.A.S., Am. Assn. U. Profs., Edmonton Soc. Obstetricians and Gynecologists (hon.), Biol. Soc. Montevideo (hon.), Sociedad Ginecotologica del Uruguay (hon.), Am. Gynecol. Soc., Nat. Council Obstetrics-Gynecology, Durham-Orange County Med. Soc., Wash. Obstet. Assn. (hon.), N.C. Obstetric-Gynecologic Soc., Robert A. Ross Obstet. and Gynecol. Soc., Med. Soc. N.C., Sigma Xi. Club: Central Travel. Home: 1834 N Lakeshore Dr Chapel Hill NC 27514

HENDRICKS, DONALD DUANE, librarian; b. Flint, Mich., Nov. 3, 1931; s. Edgar F. and Grace L. (Roska) H.; A.B., U. Mich., A.M. in L.S., 1955; Ph.D, U. Ill., 1966; m. Mary Jean Elrich, Feb. 17, 1951; children—Philip, Scott, Randal. With Detroit Pub. Library, 1955-57; head librarian Owosso (Mich.) Pub. Library, 1957-60, Millikin U., 1960-63; dir. libraries Sam Houston State Univ., 1966-70; dir. S. Central Regional Med. Library Program, Dallas, 1970—; cons. in field. Grantee U.S. Office Edn., 1965. Mem. Am., Tex. library assns., Bibliog. Soc. (London, Eng.), Bibliog. Soc. Am. Author: Centralized Processing and Regional Library Development, 1970; also monographs, articles. Co-Author: Resources of Texas Libraries, 1968. Home: 13854 Rolling Hills Lane Dallas TX 75240

HENDRICKS, ERNEST L., civil engr.; b. St. Augustine, Fla., Oct. 8, 1909; s. Ernest Jackson and Alice (Carlton) H.; B.S. in Civil Engring., U. Fla., 1931; m. Idena Marguerite Bridges, June 14, 1934; children—E. LeRoy, Lauralee (Mrs. Ray Nelson Cooley, Jr.), Mary Hope (Mrs. James E. Bacon, Jr.). Tchr. math. various Fla. high schs., 1932-35; surface-water investigator and hydrologic researcher water resources div. U.S. Geol. Survey, Fla., Ga., La., 1935-52, staff engr., Ga., 1952-56, chief research sect. gen. hydrology br., Washington, 1956- 60, chief surface water br., 1960-63, asso. chief water resources div., 1963-66, chief hydrologist, 1966—. Recipient Distinguished Service award Dept. of Interior, 1963. Fellow Am. Soc. C.E.; mem. Am. Geophys. Union, A.A.A.S., Geol. Soc. Am. Club: Cosmos (Washington). Home: 2900 N Edison St Arlington VA 22207 Office: 18th and F Sts NW Washington DC 20242

HENDRICKS, GEORGE LINTON, educator; b. Bulloch County, Ga., Nov. 27, 1901; s. George Buford and Jincy (Nichols) H.; A.B., U. Ga., 1921, A.M., 1922; Ph.D. in History, Columbia, 1954; m. Elizabeth Whittelsey, Nov. 22, 1947; children— Elizabeth, Charles Marida, James Buford. Tchr. pub. schs., Union Springs, Ala., 1922-24; instr. Columbia, 1926-28, Knox Coll., 1928-30, Coll. City N.Y., 1931; tchr. Bklyn. Friends Sch., 1931-41; asst. prof. Ga. Tchrs. Coll., 1941-42; mem. faculty Ga. Inst. Tech., 1946—, prof. social scis., 1962-69, prof. emeritus, 1969—, head dept., 1956-69; spl. research occupational activities Union Army in S.C. Sea Islands. Served with AUS, 1942-45. Decorated Purple Heart. Mem. Am., So. hist. assns. Democrat. Mem. Soc. of Friends. Home: RFD 2 Powder Springs GA 30073

HENDRICKS, JOHN BURKE, lawyer; b. Farmersville, Ill., Aug. 7, 1916; s. Harry E. and Mabel Anna (Burke) H.; B.S., Bradley U., 1938; LL.B., Lincoln Coll. Law, Springfield, Ill., 1947; m.. Nancy Cudney, May 4, 1957; children—John C., Mary, Jennifer, Sheila, Lisa. With Hendricks Bros., Farmersville, 1938- 43; profl. baseball player, 1938-39; athletic dir., coach Cathedral Boys High Sch., Springfield,

1943-44, 44-45; gen. mgr. Citizens Tribune, Springfield, 1945-47; admitted to Ill. bar, 1947; partner firm Traymor & Hendricks, Springfield, 1948—. Pres., dir. JALDCO, Inc.; dir. State Bank of Virden (Ill.). Asst. supr. Capital Twp. (Springfield), 1951—; chmn. bd. suprs. Sangamon County, 1964-67. Sec.-treas. Ill. Bd. Law Examiners, 1953—; chmn. Nat. Conf. Bar Examiners, 1963-64. Named to Bradley U. Athletic Hall Fame, 1949. Mem. Am. (council sect. legal edn. 1965—), Ill., Sangamon County bar assns. Home: 96 Oakmont Dr Springfield IL 62704 Office: Ridgely Bldg Springfield IL 62701

HENDRICKS, JOHN CARL, songwriter, singer; b. Newark, O., Sept. 16, 1921; student U. Toledo. As a child sang at local banquets, also on radio in Toledo; sang with brother-in-law's band, Jessie Jones, Detroit; drummer with own group, Rochester, N.Y., after World War II; sang, played drums with own quartet, Toledo, until 1952; songwriter, 1957—; teamed with Dave Lambert to produce new version of Four Brothers for Decca, 1957; joined with Annie Ross to produce multi-tape recording of old Count Basie recordings; first album produced Sing a Song of Basie, 1958, 2d album Sing Along with Basie, 1958; trio played theatre dates with Basie, 1959; composer song: I Want You to be my Baby, 1957, also instrumental Minor Catastrophe. Recipient Down Beat Critics poll as new Vocal Star, 1959; trio won Down Beat Readers poll as number one Vocal group, 1959. Served with AUS, 1942-46; ETO. Address: care Willard Alexander 425 Park Ave New York City NY 10022 *

HENDRICKS, LOGAN BRAND, former govt. ofcl.; b. Pella, Ia., June 26, 1906; s. Udell L. and Byka (Brand) H.; B.S.C., U. Ia., 1930; student Kent Coll. Law, Chgo., 1934; m. Rose Ann Schobel, Aug. 13, 1937; children—Logan Brand II, Sandra Ann. Asst. sales mgr. Halsey Stuart & Co., Cleve. br., 1930-32; with RFC, 1932-52, chief warehousing div., war surplus liquidation, 1952; with Small Bus. Adminstrn., 1952-69, dep adminstr. financial assistance, 1964-69, ret., 1969. Served to lt. (j.g.) USNR, World War II; PTO. Recipient 30 year Govt. Service award; Distinguished Gold Medal award. Home: 5600 Ogden Rd Washington DC 20016

HENDRICKS, ROBERT, mining co. exec.; b. Kaslo, B.C., Can., May 17, 1908; s. Robert and Elizabeth Anne (Thatcher) H.; B.Sc. in Metallurgy, Wash. State U., 1929; m. Mildred Bernice Hayton, June 14, 1932; children—Robert Wayne, Judith Anne. With Cominco, Ltd. (formerly Consol. Mining and Smelting Co. Can., Ltd.), Montreal, Que., 1929— (loaned to Dept. Munitions and Supply as gen. supt. Alta. Nitrogen Products, Ltd., Calgary (Can.), 1941), mgr., 1943-45, in adminstrn., 1945-47, asst. to pres., 1947-56, v.p. sales, 1956-59, exec. v.p., 1959-66, pres., 1966—, chief exec. officer, 1969—, also dir., mem. exec. com.; chmn. bd., dir. West Kootenay Power & Light Co. Ltd., Trail, B.C.; dir. Cominco Am. Inc., Spokane, Cominco Binani Zinc Ltd., Kerala, India, Hawaiian Western Steel Ltd., Ewa, Pine Point Mines Ltd., Trail, Canadian Pacific Investments Ltd., Montreal. Mem. Mining Assn. Can., Zinc Inst. (bd. dirs.). Mem. United Ch. of Can. Clubs: Mount Royal, St. James (Montreal); Canadian (N.Y.C. and Montreal); University, Shaughnessy Golf and Country (Vancouver, B.C.). Home: 2002 Robson St Vancouver 5 British Columbia Canada Office: Cominco Ltd 1199 W Pender St Vancouver British Columbia Canada

HENDRICKS, STERLING B., scientist; b. Elysian Fields, Tex., Apr. 13, 1902; s. James G. and Daisy (Gamblin) H.; B. Ch.E., U. Ark., 1922; M.S., Kan. State Agrl. Coll., 1924; Ph.D., Cal. Inst. Tech., 1926; LL.D., U. Ark., 1946; D.Sc. (hon.), N.C. State Coll., 1962, Kan. State U., 1963; m. Edith Ochiltree, Feb. 21, 1931; 1 dau., Martha. Research asso. Rockefeller Inst. Med. Research, N.Y.C., 1927-28; scientist U.S. Dept. Agr., 1928—, prin. chemist U.S. Bur. Plant Industry 1945-48, chief chemist, 1948—. Recipient Hillebrand prize for work on crystal structure Am. Chem. Soc., 1938; sci. award for work on clays Washington Acad. Sci., 1940; Day medal Geol. Soc. Am., 1952; Pres.'s award for distinguished fed. service, 1958; Rockefeller Pub. Service award, 1961; Hoblitzelle Nat. award Texas Research Found., 1962. Fellow Am. Soc. Agronomy, Am. Soc. Arts and Scis., mem. Nat. Acad. Scis., Philos. Soc., Am. Chem. Soc., Am. Mineral. Soc. (pres. 1954). Clubs: Am. Alpine, Canadian Alpine. Contbr. about 125 articles sci. pubs. Made 3d ascent of Mount McKinley, Alaska, 1942. Home: 1118 Dale Dr Silver Spring MD 20910 Office: Plant Industry Station Beltsville MD 20705 ☆

HENDRICKS, WALTER, coll. pres., pub.; b. Chgo., July 24, 1892; s. Otto and Hilda (Johannesen) H.; student Northwestern U., 1912-14: B.A., Amherst, 1917; postgrad. U. Grenoble, France, 1927; M.A., U. Chgo., 1930; Ph.D., Northwestern U., m. Flora Bishop, Mar. 27, 1926; children—Hildamarie, Cynthia, Geoffrey, Nathaniel, Jon Sothern, Instr. English, Armour Inst. Tech., Chgo., 1922-23, asst. prof., 1923-26, asso. prof., 1926-32, prof., 1932-34, prof., chmn. dept., 1934-40; prof., chmn. dept. Ill. Inst. Tech., 1940-47; on leave as head dept. English, Biarritz Am. U., Biarritz, France, 1945-46; founder and pres. Marlboro (Vt.) Coll., 1946-51; founder and pres. Windham Coll., Putney, Vt., 1951-64, Mark Hopkins Coll., Brattleboro, Vt., 1964—; v.p., gen. editor Hendricks House-Farrar Straus, N.Y.; pres. Hendricks House, Inc., N.Y.; gen. editor Univ. Classics. Served as lt. Aviation Corps, U.S. Army, 1917; instr. in flying, 1918-19; col. U.S. Army, Information and Edn. Div., 1945-46. Mem. So. Vt. Assn. (past pres.), Greater Vt. Assn. (past dir.), N.E. Assn. Colls., Phi Delta Theta, Phi Beta Kappa. Mem. Soc. of Friends. Clubs: Amherst, Lions. Author: Double Dealer, 1931; Flames and Fireflies, 1926; Spires and Spears, 1928; Early Poems, 1967. Home: Putney VT 05346 Office: 103 Park Av New York City NY 10017

HENDRICKSON, FRANK ROGERS, physician; b. Springfield, Pa., Aug. 3, 1926; s. Frank Oscar and Pauline (Rogers) H.; B.A., Swarthmore Coll., 1947; M.D., Jefferson Med. Coll., 1950; m. Joan Scott, Dec. 10, 1955; children—David Scott, Cheryl Anne, Bruce, Brian. Intern Jefferson Med. Coll. and Hosp., Phila., 1950-51; resident radiology Jefferson Med. Coll. Hosp., 1951-52; fellow for European study Am. Cancer Soc., 1954-56; mem. staff Presbyn.-St. Luke's Hosp., 1956—, dir. radiation therapy, 1956—; asst. prof. radiology at U. Ill. Med. Sch., 1956-66, asso. prof., 1966-68, prof., 1968-71; prof. therapeutic radiology Rush Med. Coll., Chgo., 1971—. Served to lt. (s.g.) USNR, 1952-54. Mem. Radium Soc., Radiol. Soc. N.Am., A.M.A., Radiation Research Soc., Alpha Omega Alpha. Home: 304 N Scoville St Oak Park IL 60302 Office: 1753 W Congress St Chicago IL 60612

HENDRICKSON, JAMES BRIGGS, educator, chemist; b. Toledo, Jan. 3, 1928; s. Philip and Dorothy (Briggs) H.; B.S., Cal. Inst. Tech., 1950; M.A., Harvard, 1951, Ph.D., 1955; m. Sybil Pardee, May 30, 1953; children—Jared Jeffrey Raymond, Sonia Catherine Angell. NRC postdoctoral fellow U. London (Eng.), 1954-55; asst. prof. U. Cal. at Los Angeles, 1957-63; asso. prof. Brandeis U., 1963-66, prof. chemistry, 1966—; cons. Sandoz Pharms., Inc., Hanover, N.J. Served with AUS, 1946-48; Korea. Guggenheim fellow, 1964. Mem. Am. Chem. Soc., Chem. Soc. (London). Author: Biosynthesis of Steroids, Terpenes and Acetogenins, 1963; The Molecules of Nature, 1965; (with others) Organic Chemistry; also research papers. Home: 9 Acacia St Cambridge MA 02138 Office: Dept Chemistry Brandeis Univ Waltham MA 02154

HENDRICKSON, JOHN RAYMOND, educator; b. Kingston, N.Y., Nov. 22, 1908; s. Harvey and Mabel (Van Hise) H.; A.B., Temple U., 1936; A.M., 1938; Ph.D., U. Pa., 1947; m. Helen B. Kyler, Apr. 14, 1946. Mem. faculty Temple U., 1936—, prof. classics, 1967—. Mem. corp. Friends Hosp., Phila., 1970—. Served with AUS, 1944-46. Mem. Am. Assn. Univ. Profs., Am. Classical League, Baker St. Irregulars. Author: The Research Paper, 1957. Editor: (with H.W. Starr) The Complete Poems of Thomas Gray, 1966. Contbr. articles profl. jours. Office: Temple Univ Philadelphia PA 19122

HENDRICKSON, JOHN ROSCOE, zoologist, adminstr.; b. Tipton, Ia., Aug. 26, 1921; s. Louie Ole and Hattie (Dean) H.; B.S. with distinction, U. Ariz., 1944; M.A., U. Cal, 1949, Ph.D., 1951; m. Lupe Perez, June 8, 1946; children—Sharon Anne, Leslie Clare, Mark Allen, Carla Gail. Instr. zoology U. Cal., 1947-49; lectr. zoology U. Malay, 1951-59, prof., head dept. zoology Kuala Lumpur, 1959-63; vice chancellor Inst. Student Interchange, East-West Center, Honolulu, 1963-67; dir. Oceanic Inst., Waimanalo, Hawaii, 1967-69; prof. biology, dept. biol. scis. U. Ariz., 1969—; research asso. zoology Bishop Mus. Mem. marine turtle group Survival Service Commn., Internat. Union Conservation Nature and Natural Resources, Morges, Switzerland, 1968—; mem. giant tortoise com. Wild Animal Propagation Trust, 1969—; mem. standing com. Pacific botany Pacific Sci Assn., 1969—. Served with Hosp. Corps, USNR, 1945-46. Mem. A.A.A.S., Am. Inst. Biol. Scis., Am. Soc. Ichthyologists and Herpetologists, World Mariculture Soc., Zool. Soc. London, Malayan Nature Soc., Sea of Cortez Inst. Biol. Research, Sigma Xi. Contbr. articles profl. jours. Office: Dept of Biological Sciences Univ of Ariz Tucson AZ 85721

HENDRICKSON, MARSHALL DAVID, banker; b. Poplar Bluff, Mo., Apr. 19, 1935; s. Clyde Huston and Bula (Henson) H.; student Kan. U., 1953-56; A.B., Wichita State U., 1962; m. Ann Hoelscher, Aug. 10, 1958; children—Riley David, Melinda Ann. Programmer, Boeing Airplane Co., Wichita, Kan., 1956-62, Martin-Marietta Corp., Wichita, 1962-63; with City Nat. Bank & Trust Co., Kansas City, Mo., 1963-71, comptroller, 1969-71; comptroller Mo. Bankshares, Inc., Kansas City, 1971—. Mem. Bank Adminstrn. Inst. (v.p. Kansas City chpt.), Phi Kappa Tau. Methodist. Mason. Home: 9213 W 100th St Overland Park KS 66212 Office: PO Box 1771 10th and Grand Sts Kansas City MO 64141

HENDRICKSON, VIVIAN ECKERT, hosp. adminstr.; b. Kutztown, Pa., June 2, 1914; d. Walter S. and Jennie (Smith) Eckert; grad. Cooper Hosp. Nurses Tng. Sch., Camden, N.J., 1936; R.N., U. Pa., 1941; m. Mortimer Hendrickson, Oct. 4, 1941; children—Verna Zoe, Vincent Mort. With Camden County Psychiat. Hosp., Lakeland, NJ., 1936—, supt., 1951—; owner and pub. relation program for Radio Sta. WDVL, Vineland, N.J.; co-dir. Fed. sponsored program In-Services Tng. Hosp. Nursing Personnel; dir. Fed. sponsored program of Day Care. Mem. profl. adv. com. Camden County Mental Health Assn., 1956- 59; mem. Camden County Mental Health Planning Com., 1962-67; mem. Social Welfare Assn. Camden County, 1954—. Mem. Am. Coll. Hosp. Adminstrs., Am., N.J. hosp. assns., Am. Nurses Assn., Royal Soc. Health (Eng.). Address: Blackwood P O Lakeland NJ 08012

HENDRICKSON, WARREN EDWIN, electronics co. exec.; b. N.Y.C., Aug. 28, 1913; s. Burt Eaton and Mabel L. (Crowther) H.; B.S., N.Y. U., 1935, M.B.A., 1939; m. Mary E. Smyth, Sept. 4, 1937; children—Peter S., Jane A. With RCA, 1942—, staff v.p. banking and credit adminstrn., 1963—; pres., dir. RCA Credit Corp., 1957—; asst. treas. RCA Sales Corp., 1959—, RCA Internat. Devel. Corp., RCA de Puerto Rico. Club: University (N.Y.C.). Home: 46 Forrest Lane Bronxville NY 10708 Office: 30 Rockefeller Plaza New York City NY 10020

HENDRIE, JOSEPH MALLAM, physicist, nuclear engr.; b. Janesville, Wis., Mar. 18, 1925; s. Joseph Munier and Margaret Prudence (Hocking) H.; B.S., Case Inst. Tech., 1950; Ph.D., Columbia, 1957; m. Elaine Kostell, July 9, 1949; children—Susan Debra, Barbara Ellen. Asst. physicist Brookhaven Nat. Lab., Upton, N.Y., 1955-57, asso. physicist, 1957-60, physicist, 1960-71, sr. physicist, 1971—, chmn. steering com., project chief engr. high flux beam reactor design and constrn., 1958-65, acting head exptl. reactor physics div., 1965-66, project mgr. pulsed fast reactor project, 1967-70, asso. head engring. div., dept. applied sci., 1967-71, head, 1971—; lectr. nuclear power plant safety Mass. Inst. Tech., summers 1970—. Cons. radiation safety com. Columbia, 1964—; mem. adv. com. reactor safeguards AEC, 1966—, chmn., 1970. Served with AUS, 1943-45. Recipient E.O. Lawrence award, 1970. Registered profl. engr., N.Y. Fellow Am. Nuclear Soc.; mem. Am. Phys. Soc., Am. Soc. M.E., Am. Concrete Inst., I.E.E.E., Nat. Soc. Profl. Engrs., Sigma Xi, Tau Beta Pi. Co-inventor high flux beam reactor; research, publns. physics nuclear reactors, engring. design reactors, chem. physics nitrogen dissociation process, structure oxygen molecule. Home: 4 Eastgate Dr Sayville NY 11782 Office: Brookhaven Nat Lab Upton NY 11973

HENDRIX, ALGIE ALLEN, mfg. co. exec.; b. Lynville, Tenn., Aug. 17, 1912; s. Law Donald and Linnie Mae (Jolly) H.; student Rutgers U., 1938-45; m. Lottie Elaine Clark, Dec. 3, 1932; 1 son, Carver Edward. Insp., then chief insp. Fisher Body div. Gen. Motors Corp., 1933-38, safety dir., asst. personnel dir. Ternstedt div., Trenton, N.J., 1938-42, personnel dir. Eastern Aircraft div., Linden, N.J., 1942-45, Buick-Oldsmobile-Pontiac Assembly div., Wilmington, Del., 1945-48, corp. personnel staff Gen. Motors Corp., Detroit, 1948-58, asst. mgr., then mgr. AC Spark Plug div., Milw., 1958-62, dir. mgmt. devel. Gen. Motors Corp., Detroit, 1962- 63; v.p. Gen. Dynamics Corp., N.Y.C., 1963—; dir. Asbestos Corp., Montreal, Que., Can., Stromberg-Carlson Corp., Rochester, N.Y. With Dept. Labor, World War II; mem. manpower sub-com., bus. adv. com. Dept. Commerce. Trustee Foremanship Found; bd. dirs. Automation House, Inst. Collective Bargaining and Group Relations. Recipient Missile Man award USAF; name Tenn. squire. Mem. Am. Ordnance Assn. (life), Navy League U.S., Assn. U.S. Army, Air Force Assn., U.S. C. of C., Aerospace Industries Assn., Am. Mgmt. Assn., Indsl. Relations Soc., Machinery and Allied Products Inst., N.A.M. Clubs: Sky (N.Y.C.); Nat. Aviation (Washington). Home: 650 Park Av New York City NY 10021 Office: 1 Rockefeller Plaza New York City NY 10020

HENDRIX, CLYDE, Jr., banker; b. Decatur, Ala., Sept. 9, 1906; s. Clyde and Estelle (Yarbrough) H.; B.S., Auburn U., 1927; M.S., Columbia, 1929; m. Carolyn Fussell, June 4, 1934. Asst. nat. bank examiner, 1929-35; asst. supervising examiner FDIC, 1933-34; nat. bank examiner, 1936-42; with Hibernia Nat. Bank, New Orleans, 1946—, exec. v.p., 1965, pres., 1965- -, also chief exec. officer, dir. Bd. dirs. Better Bus. Bur. New Orleans, 1963-67. Trustee United Fund New Orleans, 1966-67; bd. dirs. New Orleans council Boy Scouts Am., 1964-66, Police Found. Greater New Orleans, 1962-67. Served to lt. comdr. USNR, 1942-45. Mem. C. of C. Greater New Orleans Area (bd. dirs. 1965-67, treas. 1966-67), Assn. Res. City Bankers, Pi Kappa Alpha, Alpha Kappa Psi, Blue Key, Scabbard and Blade, Clubs: Internat. House (bd. dirs. 1966-67), New Orleans Country, Metairie Country, Pickwick, Louisiana, Plimsoll (New Orleans). Home: 220 Sycamore Dr Metairie LA 70005 Office: Hibernia Nat Bank Carondelet and Gravier Sts New Orleans LA 70112

HENDRIX, EULA BELLE, marketing research co. exec.; b. Cullom, Ill., Dec. 10, 1907; d. Edward J. and Mildred (Kridner) Jensen; student Ill. State Normal U., 1925-27; m. E. Russell Hendrix, Oct. 25, 1930; 1 dau., Dona Joy (Mrs. J. Timothy Snyder). Tchr., Plattville (Ill.) Pub. Sch., 1927-28; bookkeeper Florsheim Shoe Co., Chgo., 1929-30; statist. typist A. C. Nielsen Co., Chgo., 1938-47, sec. to corp. sec, 1947-59, corp. sec., 1959—. Mem. United Ch. Christ. Home: 901 Sunset Ct Deerfield IL 60015 Office: 2101 Howard St Chicago IL 60645

HENDRIX, GEORGE K., hosp. adminstr. Adminstr. Meml. Hosp. Springfield (Ill.). Office: 1st and Miller Sts Springfield IL 62701*

HENDRIX, HAROLD VICTOR, (Hall), communications exec.; b. Kansas City, Mo., Feb. 14, 1922; s. Clarence Virgil and Grace Frances (Lee) H.; student Rockhurst Coll., 1941; m. Mary Frances Patricia Sheehan, May 25, 1944; 1 dau., Kathleen Ann. Mem. staff Kansas City Star, 1944-57; mem. staff Miami (Fla.) News, 1957-63, Latin Am. columnist-corr., 1947-63; with Scripps Howard Newspaper Alliance, 1963-67, Latin Am. corr., 1963-67; dir. inter-Am. relations Internat. Tel. & Tel. Corp., 1967-70, dir. pub. relations- Latin Am., 1970—. Organizer Kansas City Commn. Internat. Relations and Trade, 1956; pub. relations dir. Kansas City-Jackson County chpt. A.R.C., 1952-57. Recipient Pulitzer prize for internat. reporting, 1963. Mem. Inter-Am. Press Assn. (past bd. dirs., mem. Mergenthaler awards com.), White House, State Dept. corrs. assns., Sigma Delta Chi. Clubs: American San Isidro Country, Jockey (Buenos Aires); Kings Bay Yacht and Country (Coral Gables). Home: 1000 S Alhambra Circle Coral Gables FL 33146 also 320 Park Av New York City NY 10022 Office: 320 Park Av New York City NY 10022

HENDRIX, HERSCHEL J., univ. adminstr.; b. Paragould, Ark., Nov. 28, 1918; s. Louis Elmer and Laura (Langley) H.; A.B., Ark. State Coll., 1949; M.Ed., U. Miss., 1952, Ed.D., 1954; m. Frances Fiegler, Jan. 19, 1943; children—Dennis Herschel, Sylvia Pauline. Engaged in retail bus., 1945-46; prin. Bono (Ark.) High Sch., 1946-49; mem. faculty Upper Ia. U., Fayette, 1952—, acad. dean, 1957-61, v.p., dean univ., 1961—. Served with AUS, 1940-45. Mem. Nat., Ia. edn. assns., Am. Assn. Sch. Adminstrs., Phi Delta Kappa, Kappa Delta Pi, Sigma Pi. Clubs: Rotary (pres. Sumner, Ia. 1954); West Union (Ia.) Country (pres. 1960). Home: Hoot Owl Hill Fayette IA 52142

HENDRIX, THOMAS RUSSELL, educator; b. Fort Ancient, O., Oct. 17, 1920; A.B., U. Cal. at Los Angeles, 1947; M.D., Johns Hopkins, 1951; married; 3 children. Asst. in medicine Boston U., 1954-57; asst. in medicine Johns Hopkins, 1952-54, asst. prof., 1957-61, asso. prof., 1961-69, prof., 1969—, physician-in-charge Gastroenterological Clinic Hosp., 1957—; vis. physician, radioisotope unit VA Hosp., 1959—. Served with USNR, 1941-46. Diplomate Am. Bd. Internal Medicine. Mem. Am. Fedn. for Clin. Research. Office: Dept Medicine Johns Hopkins Sch Medicine Baltimore MD 21218*

HENDRY, GEORGE STUART, theologian; b. Aberdeen, Scotland, Mar. 20, 1904; s. William and Violet (Milne) H.; A.M., U. Aberdeen, 1924, D.D. (hon.), 1949; B.D., U. Edinburgh, 1927; student Univs. Tübingen and Berlin, 1928-29; m. Sheila Margaret Cowie, Apr. 6, 1932; children—Kenneth, Alan. Came to U.S., 1949, naturalized, 1956. Ordained to ministry Ch. of Scotland, 1930, served as pastor at Bridge of Allan, 1930-49; examiner in divinity U. Edinburgh, 1930-32, U. St. Andrews, 1931-34; Hastie Lectr. U. Glasgow, 1935; Charles Hodge prof. systematic theology Princeton Theol. Sem., 1949—; Croall lectr., U. Edinburgh, 1951. Sec. Joint Com. of Brit. Chs. on New Translation of Bible, 1946-49; pres. Scottish Ch. Theology Soc., 1947-49. Mem. Am. Theol. Soc. (pres. 1970-71). Presbyn. Author: God the Creator, 1937; The Holy Spirit in Christian Theology, 1956; The Gospel of the Incarnation, 1958; The Westminister Confession for Today, 1960. Contbr. articles to theol. jours., periodicals. Home: 23 Quaker Rd Princeton Junction NJ 08550

HENDRYSON, IRVIN EDWARD, orthopedic surgeon; b. Denver, June 20, 1912; s. Harry Edward and Zora (Beckwith) H.; B.A., U. Denver, 1932; M.S., M.D., U. Colo., 1936; m. Mary Short, July 17, 1942; children—Susan Jay, Robert Michael, John Galt, Jane Lacy, Mary Ann; m. 2d, Elizabeth Stayer Margulis, Sept. 25, 1965. Intern U. Colo. Med. Sch. and Hosps., 1936-37; resident U. Pa., 1939-40; pvt. practice orthopedic surgery, Denver, 1941-67; asso. clin. prof. surgery U. Coll. Sch. Medicine, 1949-67; asso. prof. surgery U. N.M. Sch. Medicine, 1967—, asst. dean Sch. Medicine, 1967-69, dir. Emergency Med. Services project, 1969—; med. adviser Nat. Ski Patrol System, 1948-64; asst. med. dir V111 Winter Olympics, 1960. Spl. Research soft tissue injury, disease of knee, elbow and foot. Trustee Nat. Council Alcoholism, 1960—, pres., 1971—; pres., chmn. bd. Denver Med. Soc., 1957-62. Trustee Denver United Fund, 1958-60, Denver Good Will Industries, 1958-66, Denver chpt. A.R.C., 1966, Colo. chpt. Am. Cancer Soc., 1960, Colo. chpt. Soc. Crippled Children and Adults. Served to lt. col., M.C., AUS, 1942-46. Decorated Purple Heart, Bronze Star; recipient Presdl. citation Nat. Found. Infantile Paralysis, 1960; award of merit Denver United Fund, 1958; named outstanding Ski Patrolman, Asociacion Sky Y Andinismo, 1958-59; Silberne Ehrenabzeichen, Österreichischer Skiverband, 1950. Diplomate Am. Bd. Orthopaedic Surgery. Mem. A.M.A. (trustee 1965-70, chmn. commn. on emergency med. services 1967—), Am. Trauma Soc. (dir. 1968—), A.A.A.S. (mem. council 1967-70), Am. Acad. Orthopaedic Surgery, A.C.S. Ednl. Council Fgn. Med. Grads. (bd.); hon. mem. Colo. Med. Soc. (chmn. bd. 1954-56; award merit 1968). Author numerous articles in field. Home: 6303 Indian School Rd NE Albuquerque NM 87110 Office: 920 Stanford NE Albuquerque NM 87106

HENDY, SIR PHILIP, mus. dir., art historian; b. Carlisle, Cumberland, Eng., Sept. 27, 1900; s. Frederick James Roberts and Caroline (Potts) H.; student Westminster Sch., 1914-19; M.A., Christ Ch., Oxford, 1919-22. Asst. keeper Wallace Collection, London, 1922-27; curator of paintings Mus. Pine Arts, Boston, 1930-33; dir. Nat. Gallery, London, Eng., 1946-67; adviser Israel Mus., Jerusalem, 1968-71. Specialist in Italian medieval and Renaissance painting particularly Venetian Renaissance. Mem. Internat. Council Museums (pres. Found.). Author: Piero della Francesca and the Early Italian Renaissance, 1968. Home: Whistlers Barn Great Haseley Oxford England

HENEBRY, JOHN PHILIP, bus. exec.; b. Plainfield, Ill., Feb. 14, 1918; s. Joseph Aloysius and Hanna (Blair) H.; grad. U. Notre Dame, 1940. A.A.C. Flying Sch., Kelly Field Tex., 1941; m. Mary Elizabeth McGuire, Aug. 7, 1944; children—Patricia Ann, John Philip, Walter McGuire, Mary Elizabeth, Jeanine F. Pres. Skymotive , Inc, O'Hare Field, 1946-59, chmn. bd., treasurer Lytle Corp., Chgo., 1959-60; vice pres. Fairbank-Morse, Chgo., 1961-62; dir. corporate devel. Mitchell Hotchins & Co., Chgo., mems. N.Y. Stock Exchange, 1962-66; pres. N.Am. Aluminum Corp., Kalamazoo, 1965-70. Served as col., USAAF, 1942-46, comdr. 3d attack group 5th Air Force; major gen. Res., 1958; comdr. Korean Airlift, 1951-52. Named one of ten outstanding young men Am., 1952. Mem. Air Force Assn. (past nat. pres., dir.). Home: 110 Abingdon Av Kenilworth IL 60043

HENEL, HEINRICH EDMUND KARL, educator; b. Saigon, Vietnam, Apr. 18, 1905; s. Edmund Julius and Helene Franziska Maria (Zinkand) H.; student U. Frankfurt (Germany), 1924-26, U. Munich (Germany), 1926-27; Ph.D., U. Frankfurt, 1927; M.A. (hon.), Yale, 1957; m. Ingeborg Charlotte Beithan, Mar. 18, 1932; children—Bettina Charlotte (Mrs. Donald W. Elliott), Rolf Heinrich Johannes. Came to U.S., 1947, naturalized, 1953. Asst. lectr. U. Aberdeen, Scotland, 1927-29; tchr. German, supr. Cambridge U., Eng., 1929-31; prof German, Queen's U., Can., 1932-47, U. Wis., 1947-57, Yale, 1957—, Sterling prof. German, 1963—, Fulbright vis. prof. Bonn U., 1962-63. Spl. Sterling research fellow, Yale, 1943-44, Guggenheim fellow, 1951-52, 54-55; Gold medal Goethe Inst., 1962. Mem. Conn. Acad. Arts and Sci., Am. Assn. of Tchrs. German, Internat. Assn. Germanic Studies (exec. com. 1966-70), Modern Lang. Assn. (2d v.p. 1958), Wis. Modern Lang. Tchrs. Assn. (pres. 1950); corr. mem. German Acad. Lang. and Lit. Author: The Poetry of Conrad Ferdinand Meyer, 1954; other. Contbr. articles learned jours. Home: 27 Marlborough Rd North Haven CT 06473 Office: Yale U New Haven CT 06520

HENEMAN, HARLOW JAMES, mgmt. cons.; b. Minn., Feb. 12, 1906; s. Herman and Alice (Burfield) H.; A.B., U. Minn., 1928; M.A., U. Cal., 1930; Ph.D., U. London; 1934; m. Avis Louise Dayton; children—Joyce, Burfield. Instr., later asso. prof. polit. sci. U. Mich., 1933-45; editorial adviser Oxford U. Press, 1939-57; mgmt. analyst U.S. Bur. Budget, 1944-45; U.S. Mil Govt., Berlin, 1945; mem. U.S. delegation negotiating merger, U.S. and U.K. zones, Germany, 1946; cons. U.S. rep. on U.N.A.E.C., 1947; cons. Dept. State and pvt. firms, 1947- 50; spl. asst. to asst. sec. for occupied areas, Dept. State, 1946-47, dir. mgmt. staff, 1950-52; formerly gen. partner firm Cresap, McCormick & Paget; pvt. cons.; adviser to Mayo Found. and Clinic. Served with M.I. Service, War Dept. Gen. Staff, 1942-44. Mem. Nat. Planning Assn. (trustee). Clubs: University (N.Y.C.); Mission Valley (Laurel, Fla.); Field (Sarasota, Fla.). Author: The Growth of Executive Power in Germany, 1934; (with others) Financing Higher Education, 1960-70, 1959, Professional Practices in Management Consulting, 1959, The Arts; A Central Element of a Good Society, 1965, The Arts: Planning for Change, 1966; Readings in Financial Analysis, 1970. Contbr. to profl. jours. Home: 8132 Sanderling Rd Siesta Key Sarasota FL 33581

HENEMAN, HERBERT GERHARD, Jr., educator; b. Lester Prairie, Minn., Dec. 2, 1916; s. Herbert Gerhard and Alta (Beise) H.; B.B.A., U. Minn., 1938, M.A., 1943, Ph.D., 1948; m. Jane Lloyd Roberts, Oct. 14, 1940; children—Alta (Mrs. John A. Fossum), Herbert Gerhard III, Robert Lloyd. Chief accountant Midland Coop. Wholesale, Mpls., 1938-40; faculty U. Minn., Mpls., 1948—, prof., 1954—, chmn. dept. indsl. relations, 1960—, asst. dir. Indsl. Relations Center, 1947-59, dir., 1959—, chmn. grad. faculty indsl. relations, 1959—. Vis. prof. Stanford, 1959, U. Richmond, 1952—, U.S. Naval Postgrad. Sch., 1962; cons. U.S. Civil Service Dept., U.S. Dept. Labor, U.S. Dept. Health, Edn. and Welfare, U.S. Postal Service; arbitrator, chmn. fact-finding commns. Chmn., Minn. Gov.'s Manpower Adv. Council, 1954—, St. Paul Fair Employment Practices Commn., 1956-61, Minn. Gov.'s Task Force Labor Relations, 1961-62, Minn. Gov.'s Task Force Unemployment Compensation-Workmen's Compensation, 1956. Served to lt. (j.g.) USNR, 1944-46. Fellow Social Sci. Research Council; mem. Am. Assn. U. Profs. (pres. Minn. 1960, mem. com. N 1969—), Indsl. Relations Research Assn., Am. Econ. Assn., Am. Soc. Personnel Adminstrn. (hon. life), Iota Rho Chi. Club: St. Paul Curling. Author: Labor Economics and Industrial Relations, 1959; Labor Economics, 1965; Employer Manpower Planning and Forecasting, 1971. Editor: Local Labor Market Research, 1948; Personnel Administration and Labor Relations, 1952; Employment Relations Research, 1960; Handbook of Personnel Management and Industrial Relations, 1958. Contbr. bulls., articles to profl. jours. Home: 1733 Blair Av St Paul MN 55104 Office: Indsl Relations Center 537 BA U Minn Minneapolis MN 55455

HENEY, THOMAS TRACY, sugar co. exec.; b. N.Y.C., Nov. 26, 1910; s. Thomas and Ellen (Farley) H.; B.A. Middlebury Coll. 1930; LL.B., Union U., Albany, N.Y., 1936; m. Helen Cronin, Apr. 15, 1939; children—Tracy (dec.), Marcia, Mary Ellen, William, John, Kevin, Timothy. Admitted to N.Y. bar, 1936, Fed. bar, 1936, U.S. Supreme Ct. bar, 1939; with firm Staley, Tobin & Manley, Albany, 1936-39, Blake, Voorhees & Stewart, N.Y.C., 1939-44; with Nat. Sugar Refining Co., N.Y.C., 1944—, exec. v.p., 1957-68, pres., 1968—, also dir.; lectr., adj. asst. prof. law N.Y.U. Sch. Law, 1951-66. Office: 2 Penn Plaza New York City NY 10001

HENGEN, WILLIAM LINCOLN, journalist; b. Mpls., Feb. 12, 1914; s. William Henry and Florence (Melchisedech) H.; B.A., St. Thomas Coll., St. Paul, 1935; m. Florence Eleanor Bott, Sept. 12, 1940; children—Patricia (Mrs. Larry Wayne Whittlef), Mary (Mrs. William Robert McCleary), William Michael, Catherine, Stephen, Elizabeth. Writer, Mpls. Jour., 1936-39; Sunday sports editor Mpls. Star-Jour. and Star Tribune, 1941-58, asst. sports editor Mpls. Star, 1958-67, sports editor, 1967-69, columnist, 1969—. Served with USMCR, 1944-46. Recipient Merit award Nat. Bowling Writers, 1959. Mem. Nat. Bowling Writers (past pres.). Home: 6844 Wentworth Av. S. Richfield MN 55423. Office: 425 Portland Av Minneapolis NY 55415

HENGST, RAYMOND GUTHRIE, lawyer; b. Columbus, O., Aug. 2, 1898; s. George C. and Myrta (Guthrie) H.; A.B., Oberlin Coll., 1920; LL.B., Harvard, 1925; m. Fanny S. Lister, Sept. 5, 1933; children—Barbara Snow (Mrs. Ernest L. Hartmann), William Guthrie. Admitted to Ohio bar, 1925; asso. with Hauxhurst, Inglis, Sharp & Cull, and predecessors, Cleve., 1925-35, partner, 1935-55; counsel, sec. Eaton Mfg. Co., Cleve., 1955-56, gen. counsel, sec., 1956-63; v.p., gen. counsel Eaton, Yale, & Towne, Inc., 1963-67; counsel Arter & Hadden, 1967—. Mem. Am., Ohio, Cleve. bar assns., Phi Beta Kappa, Phi Delta Theta. Conglist. Clubs: Union, Tavern, Court of Nisi Prius (Cleve.). Home: 13710 Shaker Blvd. Cleveland OH 44120. Office: Union Commerce Bldg Cleveland OH 44115

HENICAN, CASWELL ELLS, lawyer; b. New Orleans, Feb. 10, 1905; s. Joseph Patrick and Alice (Boning) H.; LL.B., Tulane U., 1926; m. Elizabeth Cleveland, June 18, 193O; children—Alice (Mrs. Claude V. Perrier, Jr.), Caswell Ellis, Margaret (Mrs. F. Gordon Wilson, Jr.), Dorothy (Mrs. Charles E. Heidingsfelder), Joseph Patrick III, Admitted to La. bar, 1926, since practiced in New Orleans; asso. Lemle, Moreno & Lemle, 1926-33; sr. partner Henican, Carriere & Cleveland, 1933-40, Henican, James & Cleveland 194O—. Chmn. La. State Bd. Pub. Welfare, 1940-47; pres. New Orleans Community Chest, 1940, Council Social Agencies, 1939, Asso. Cath. Charities New Orleans, 1938; chmn. bd. Mercy Hosp.; mem. exec. com., mem. Magnolia Sch. Bd. Named most outstanding young man in New Orleans, New Orleans Junior C. of C., 1940. Decorated Knight of St. Gregory. Mem. Am., Louisiana, New Orleans bar assns. Soc. of Hosp. Attys. of Am. Hosp. Assn. (charter mem.). Home: 1831 Octavia St New Orleans LA 7O115 Office: 225 Baronne St New Orleans LA 7O112

HENIGAN, GEORGE FRANCIS, educator; B.A., Kearney State Coll., 1936; Ph.M., U. Wis., 1940. Prof., chmn. dept. speech George Washington U. Office: Dept Speech George Washington U Washington DC 20006*

HENINGER, SIMEON KAHN, Jr., educator; b. Monroe, La., Oct. 27, 1922; s. Simeon Kahn and Elsye (Lieber) H.; B.S., Tulane U., 1944, B.A., 1947, M.A., 1949; B.Litt. (Fulbright scholar), Oxford, 1952; Ph.D., Johns Hopkins, 1955; m. Irene Callen, July 16, 1957; children—Dale Callen, Kathryn Leigh, Philip Ward, Polly Elizabeth, Simeon Kahn III; m. 2d, Dorothy Cooper Langston, May 30, 1971. Instr., Duke, 1955-57, asst. prof., 1957-62, asso. prof., 1962-65, prof., 1965-67; prof. English, U. Wis.-Madison, 1967—, chmn. dept. English, 1968-70. Exec. sec.-treas. Southeastern Renaissance Conf., 1958-67; mem. Nat. Shakespeare Anniversary Com., 1963-64. Served to capt. USAAF, 1943-46. Folger Library fellow, 1961; Guggenheim fellow, 1962-63; Southeastern Inst. Medieval and Renaissance Studies fellow, 1967; Huntington Library fellow, 1970-71. Mem. Modern Lang. Assn. Am., Renaissance Soc. Am. (mem. adv. council 1958-68), Mediaeval Acad. Am., Am. Civil Liberties Union, Phi Beta Kappa. Author: A Handbook of Renaissance Meteorology, 1960. Editor: Thomas Watson, The Hekatompathia, 1964; Edmund Spenser, Poetry, 1970. Asst. editor Modern Language Notes, 1953-55. Contbr. articles profl. jours. Home: Route 4 Box 449 Stoughton WI 53589 Office: Dept English U Wis Madison WI 53706

HENINGTON, DAVID MEAD, librarian; b. El Dorado, Ark., Aug. 16, 1929; s. Bud Henry and Lucile (Scranton) H.; B.A. in History, U. Houston, 1951; M.S. in L.S., Columbia, 1956; m. Barbara Gibson, June 2, 1956; children—Mark David, Gibson Mead, Paul Billins. Young adult librarian Bklyn. Pub. Library, 1956-58; head lit. and history dept. Dallas Pub. Library, 1958, asst. dir., 1962-67; dir. Waco (Tex.) Pub. Library, 1958-62, Houston Pub. Library, 1967—. Served with USAF, 1951-55. Rotarian. Home: 6225 San Felipe Rd Houston TX 77027 Office: 500 McKinney St Houston TX 77002

HENIZE, KARL GORDON, astronomer; b. Cin., Oct. 17, 1926; s. Fred R. and Mabel (Redmon) H.; student Dennison U., 1944-45; B.A., U. Va., 1947, M.A., 1948; Ph.D., U. Mich., 1954; m. Caroline Rose Weber, June 27, 1953; children— Kurt Gordon, Marcia Lynn, Skye Karen, Vance Karl. Observer, U. Mich. Lamont-Hussey Obs., Bloemfontein, Union S. Africa, 1948-51; Carnegie postdoctoral fellow Mt. Wilson Obs., Pasadena, Cal., 1954-56; sr. astronomer charge Photog. Satellite Tracking Stas., Smithsonian Astrophys. Obs., Cambridge, 1956- 59; asso. prof. dept. astronomy Northwestern U., 1959-64, prof., 1964- -; scientist-astronaut NASA, 1967—, mem. astronomy subcom. NASA Space Sci. Steering Com., 1965-68, AAS vis. prof., 1958-61; guest observer Mt. Stamlo Obs., Canberra, Australia, 1961-62. Served with USNR, 1944-46; lt. comdr. Res., ret. Recipient Robert Gordon Meml. award, 1968. Mem. Am., Royal Pacific astron. socs., Internat. Astron. Union, A.A.A.S., Phi Beta Kappa, Sigma Xi. Home: 18630 Point Lookout Dr Houston TX 77058 Office: Astronaut Office NASA Manned Spacecraft Center Houston TX 77058

HENKE, BURTON LEHMAN, educator, physicist; b. Cin., Aug. 27, 1922; s. Robert Christian and Laura E. (Partymueller) H.; A.B., Miami U., Oxford, O., 1944; Ph.D., (Research fellow 1953), Cal. Inst. Tech., 1953; m. Wilma E. Lange, Sept. 4, 1948; children—Raymond, Thomas. Faculty Pomona Coll., 1948-67, prof. physics, 1958-67; prof physics U. Hawaii, 1967—; spl. research ultrasoft X-ray physics, also cons. in field. Grantee USAF Office Sci. Research, 1954—; Guggenheim fellow, 1956; recipient Wig Distinguished Prof. award Pomona Coll., 1960. Mem. Am. Phys. Soc., Am. Assn. Physics Tchrs., Phi Beta Kappa, Sigma Xi. Unitarian. Home: 4620 Kahala Av Honolulu HI 96816

HENKE, HARRY, Jr., lawyer; b. Cin., Dec. 9, 1905; s. Harry and Josephine (Thornbury) H.; A.B., U. Wash., 1926, LL.B., 1928; m. Florence Vickers Fowlkes, Aug. 3, 1929; children—Harry III, Bradley F., Julia R. (Mrs. Donald C. Dahlgren), Joseph T. Admitted to Wash. State bar, 1928; asso. firm Skeel, McKelvy, Henke, Evenson & Betts, and predecessors, Seattle, 1928-35, partner firm, 1935—. Dir. Western Internat. Hotels Co. and affiliated corps., Scripps League Newspapers, Inc., Asso. Grocers, Inc., Calectron, Olympia Brewing Co., Olympic S.S. Co., Inc., also other indsl. and comml. corps. Trustee Thurston Charitable Found. Mem. Am., Wash. bar assns. Rotarian. Club: Rainier (Seattle). Home: The Highlands Seattle WA 98177. Office: Norton Bldg Seattle WA 981O4

HENKE, ROBERT HENRY, metals co. exec.; b. West View, Pa., Dec. 9, 1920; s. Henry J. and Edna (Janke) H.; B.S. in Metallurgy, Pa. State U., 1942; m. Frances Kurtz, June 24, 1945. With Am. Manganese steel div. Am. Brake Shoe Co., Chgo., 1943-44, U.S. Steel Corp., 1944-45; process metallurgist A.M. Byers Co., Ambridge, Pa., 1945-46; chief metallurgist Allegheny Ludlum Steel Co., Brackenridge, Pa., 1946-59; asst. dist. mgr., then dist. mgr. Republic Steel Corp., Massillon, O., 1959-64; v.p. Reynolds Metals Co., 1964-69; v.p. operations planning and engring. Allegheny Ludlum Industries, Inc., Pitts., 1969—, also pres. subsidiaries Internat. Powder Metallurgy Co., King Electronics, 1969—. Mem. Am. Iron and Steel Inst., Am. Soc. Metals, Am. Inst. Mining and Metall. Engrs., Am. Inst. Steel Engrs. Home: 4 Foxwood Dr Fox Chapel Pittsburgh PA 15238 Office: Oliver Bldg Pittsburgh PA 15222

HENKELMAN, WILLARD MAX, lawyer; b. Scranton, Pa., June 7, 1914; s. Max Frederick and Emilie (Neuls) H.; grad. Phillips Exeter Acad., Exeter, N.H., 1932; A.B., Princeton, 1936; J.D., Harvard, 1939; m. Elizabeth Tweedle, Feb. 21, 1943; children—Elizabeth L., Steven W. Admitted to Pa. bar, 1940; practiced in Scranton, 1940-41; asso. Warren, Hill, Henkelman & McMenamin, Scranton, 1946-52, partner, 1952—. Vice pres., dir. Citizens Savs. & Loan Assn. of Scranton. Mem. Exeter Grad. Council. Served from pvt. to maj. AUS, 1942-46; PTO. Decorated Bronze Star. Mem. Am., Pa., Lackawanna bar assns., Waynewood Assn. (pres. 1969-70), Lackawanna Hist. Soc. (v.p. 1969—), N.E. Pa. Princeton Alumni Assn. (pres. 1952-55, chmn. alumni schs. com. 1960-70), Northeast Pa. Exeter Assn. (pres. 1953-55). Presbyn. Kiwanian. Clubs: Princeton Tower, Nassau (Princeton N.J.). Home: 1741 N Washington Av Scranton PA 18509 Office: Scranton Electric Bldg Scranton PA 18503

HENKIN, DANIEL ZWIE, govt. ofcl.; b. Washington, May 10, 1923; s. Zalmen and Sadie (Wienberg) H.; B.A., U. Cal. at Berkeley, 1948; m. Hannah Ronen, May 19, 1957; children—Doron, Leora, Tamar. Asst. editor, then editor Jour. Armed Forces, 1948-65; dir. operations Office Asst. Sec. Def. Pub. Affairs, 1965-67; dep. asst. sec. def., 1967-69; asst. sec. def. for pub. affairs, 1969—; lectr. Nat. War Coll., Indsl. Coll. Armed Forces. Served with USCGR, 1942-45. Recipient Meritorious Civilian Service medal sec. def. Club: Nat. Press (Washington.). Home: 2306 Washington Av. Chevy Chase MD 20015. Office: The Pentagon Washington DC 20301

HENKIN, LEON ALBERT, educator, mathematician; b. Bklyn., Apr. 19, 1921; s. Ascher and Rose (Goldberg) H.; A.B., Columbia, 1941; M.A., Princeton, 1942, Ph.D., 1947; m. Ginette Potvin, Sept. 8, 1950; children—Paul Jacques, Julian David. Mathematician, Manhattan Dist. Project, 1942-46; Henry B. Fine instr., Frank Jewett postdoctoral fellow Princeton, 1947-49; from asst. prof. to asso. prof. math. U. So. Cal., 1949-53; faculty U. Cal. at Berkeley, 1953—, prof. math., 1958—, chmn. dept., 1966-68; vis. prof. Dartmouth, 1960-61, Fulbright research scholar, Amsterdam, Netherlands, 1954-55; Guggenheim fellow, mem. Inst. Advanced Study, Princeton, 1961-62; vis. fellow All Souls Coll., Oxford (Eng.) U., 1968-69. Fellow Nat. Council Tchrs. Math.; mem. Assn. Symbolic Logic (pres. 1962-64), Am. Math. Soc. (council 1962-64), Math. Assn. Am. (Chauvenet prize 1964), A.A.A.S., Am. Civil Liberties Union (bd. dirs. Berkeley 1964-66), Phi Beta Kappa, Sigma Xi. Author: La Structure Algebrique des theories Mathématique, 1955; (with others) Retracing Elementary Mathematics, 1962; Cylindric Algebras, 1971; also articles. Home: 9 Maybeck Twin Dr Berkeley CA 94708

HENKIN, LOUIS, educator, lawyer; b. Russia, Nov. 11, 1917; s. Yoseph Elia and Frieda Rebecca (Kreindel) H.; came to U.S., 1923, naturalized, 1930; A.B., Yeshiva Coll., 1937, L.H.D., 1963; LL.B., Harvard, 1940; m. Alice Barbara Hartman, June 19, 1960; children—Joshua, David Michel, Daniel Joseph. Admitted to N.Y. bar, 1941, also U.S. Supreme Ct.; law clk. to Judge Learned Hand, 1940-41, Justice Frankfurter, 1946-47; cons. legal dept. UN, 1947-48; with State Dept., 1945-46, 48-57; U.S. rep. UN Com. Refugees and Stateless Persons, 1950; adviser U.S. delegation UN Econ. and Social Council, 1950, UN Gen. Assembly, 1950-53, Geneva Conf. on Korea, 1954; asso. dir. Legislative Drafting Research Fund, lectr. law Columbia, 1956-57; vis. prof. law U. Pa., 1957-58, prof. law, 1958-62; prof. internat. law and diplomacy, prof. law Columbia, 1962, mem. Inst. War and Peace Studies, 1962—, Hamilton Fish prof. internat. law and diplomacy, 1963—; U.S. mem. Permanent Ct. Arbitration, 1963-69; Carnegie lectr. Hague Acad. Internat. Law, 1965; cons. to govt. Served with AUS, 1941-45. Decorated Silver Star. Mem. Council Fgn. Relations, Am. Soc. Internat. Law, Internat. Law Assn., Assn. Bar City N.Y., Am. Soc. Polit. and Legal Philosophy, Am. Polit. Sci. Assn. Author: Arms Control and Inspection in American law, 1958; The Berlin Crisis and the United Nations, 1959; Disarmament; The Lawyer's Interests, 1963; How Nations Behave: Law and Foreign Policy, 1968; Law for the Sea's Mineral Resources, 1968. Editor: Arms Control: Issues for the Public, 1961; bd. editors Am. Jour. Internat. Law, 1967—. Contbr. profl. jours. Home: 460 Riverside Dr New York City NY 10027

HENKLE, HERMAN HENRY, cons. librarian; b. Colorado Springs, Colo., Mar. 26, 1900; s. Horace Russell and Effa Hope (Phelps) H.; A.B., Whittier (Cal.) Coll., 1928, Litt.D., 1961; certificate in librarianship, U. of Cal., 1931, A.M., 1933; postgrad. Grad. Library Sch., U. Chgo., 1935-36; m. Genevieve Evelyn Moller, Nov. 19, 1928 (div. Dec. 1950), children—David Eldred, Douglas Herman; m. 2d, Ann Walker Davis, June 8, 1951. Farmer, 1919-23; asst., Berkeley and Oakland (Cal.) pub. libraries 1928-30; jr. librarian, biology library U. Cal., 1930-35, cataloger, 1935; asso. Library Sch., U. Ill., 1936-37; prof. library sci., dir. Sch. Library Sci., Simmons Coll., Boston, Mass., 1937-42; dir. processing dept. Library of Congress, 1942-47; librarian Crerar Library, Chgo., 1947- 65, exec. dir., 1963-69; dir. planning James Jerome Hill Reference Library, St. Paul, 1969-71; lectr. Grad. Library Sch., U. Chgo., 1959-66, Library Sch., U. Minn., 1970-71, Fla. State U., 1971. Sec.-treas. Jt. Com. Union List of Serials, Inc., 1958-68; cons. sci. libraries UNESCO, 1966; adv. council coll. library resources U.S. Office Edn., 1966-68; cons. to pub. adminstrn. service survey of Brookline, Mass., 1940, Detroit Pub. Library and Ford Motor Co. Library Survey, 1946; mem. spl. com. on tech. information Research and Devel. Bd., Nat. Mil. Establishment, 1948-50; dir. Center Research Libraries, 1950-69, exec. com., 1955-56, chmn. 1961; pres. Assn. Am. Library Sch., 1941-42. Fellow A.A.A.S.; mem. Spl. Libraries Assn. (mem. exec. bd. 1941-47; pres. 1945-46; named to Hall of Fame 1971). A.L.A. (bd. edn. librarianship 1942-44), Am. Documentation Inst. (pres. 1957-58), Am. Soc. Metals (metall. documentation com. 1958-61). Author: A Survey of the Indiana University Library (with Donald Coney and Flint Purdy), 1940; also articles. Editor: Catalog of the Clifford G. Grulee Collection on Pediatrics, 1959. Address: 325 3d St N Naples FL 33940

HENLE, GUY, mag. editor; b. N.Y.C., Dec. 22, 1920; s. James and Marjorie (Jacobson) H.; A.B., Swarthmore Coll., 1941; M.S. in Journalism, Columbia, 1942; m. Mary Ellen Bowlby, Jan. 5, 1947; children—Richard Flexner, Peter Bradley. With Vanguard Press, Inc., N.Y.C., 1946-53, asso. editor, 1949-51, sales mgr., 1951-53; workshop editor Woman's Home Companion mag., 1953-56; exec. editor House Beautiful mag., N.Y.C., 1957- -. Served to 1st lt. AUS, 1942-46; capt. Res. Author: How to Plan Your Attic and Basement, 1955. Home: 21 Round Hill Rd Scarsdale NY 10583 Office: 717 Fifth Av New York City NY 10022

HENLE, ROBERT JOHN, educator; b. Muscatine, Ia., Sept. 12, 1909; s. Edward M. and Mary Ann (Hauber) H.; student Creighton U., 1926-27, A.B., St. Louis U., 1931, A.M., 1932, Licentiate in Philosophy, 1935, S.T.L., 1941; Saint Stanislaus Novitiate, Cleve., 1941-42; student U. of Toronto, 1942-43, 44-45, Ph.D., 1954. Entered Soc. of Jesus, 1927; instr. classics St. Louis U. High Sch., 1935- 37; ordained priest, 1940; instr. Latin, Summer Sch., St. Louis U., 1938-41, asst. prof. philosophy, 1947-54, asso. prof., 1954-58, prof., 1958-69, dean Sch. of Philosophy and Sci.; 1943-51, dean Sch. Philosophy and Letters, 1951-52, dean Grad. Sch., 195O-64, mem. univ. council, 1947- 5l, trustee, 1949-69; pres. Georgetown U., Washington, 1969—. Mem. Am. Cath. Philos. Assn., Nat. Cath. Edn. Assn., A.A.A.S., Philosophy of Edn. Soc., Am. Philos. Soc., Midwest Conf. Grad. Study and Research. Author several Latin textbooks, latest publs.; Fourth Year Latin, 1941; Method in Metaphysics, 1950; Saint Thomas and Platonism, 1956. Editor: The Modern Schoolman, 1945-50. Address: Georgetown U Washington DC 20007

HENLEY, EARLE BURR, Jr., mfg. co. exec.; b. Oakland, Cal., Apr. 16, 1915; s. Earle Burr and Pauline (Matthews) H.; B.S., Cornell U., 1937, LL.B., 1940; m. Grace H. Jones 1940; children—Matthew O., Peter J. Admitted to N.Y. bar, 1940, also U.S. Supreme Ct. bar; with firm Mudge, Stern, Williams & Tucker, N.Y.C., 1940-43, Mudge, Stern, Baldwin & Todd, 1946-55; sec. Gen. Equipment Precision Corp., Tarrytown, N.Y., 1965-68; asst. sec. Singer Co., N.Y.C., 1968—. Mem. New Castle (N.Y.) Town Planning Bd., 1958—. Served to 1st lt. AUS, 1943-46. Republican. Club: Church (N.Y.C.). Home: 192 N. Bedford Rd. Chappaqua NY 10514. Office: 30 Rockefeller Plaza New York City NY 10021

HENLEY, ERNEST JUSTUS, educator; b. Frankfort am Main, Germany, Sept. 30, 1926; s. Clemens Isidore and Martha (Henle) H.; came to U.S., 1935, naturalized, 1939; S.B., U. Del., 1950; M.S., Columbia, 1951, D.Engring. Sci., 1953; M.E., Stevens Inst. Tech., 1963; m. Barbara Mayfield Miller, Jan. 17, 1957; children—Davis Clemens, Alan Miller. Asst. prof. chem. engring. Columbia, 1953-58; prof. chemistry, chem. engring. Stevens Inst. Tech., 1958-66; prof. chemistry, asso. dean engring. U. Houston, 1966—. Dir. RAI Research Inc., 1954—, Procedyne Corp., 1962—, Houston Glass Fabricating Co., 1968—. Trustee Tex. Tennis Found. Served to 1st lt. AUS, 1944-46; ETO. NSF, Am. Chem. Soc., AEC grantee. Fellow Am. Inst. Chemistry, N.Y. Acad. Sci.; mem. Sigma Xi, Tau Beta Pi, Phi Kappa Phi, Phi Lambda Upsilon. Club: Houston Racquet. Author: Chemical Engineering Calculations, 1959; Stagewise Process Calculations, 1963; Material and Energy Balance Computations,

1969; The Physics and Chemistry of High Energy Reaction, 1969. Co-editor Advances in Nuclear Science and Technology (6 vols.), 1961—. Contbr. articles to profl. jours. Home: 359 Westminster St Houston TX 77024

HENLEY, FRED LOUIS, state justice; b. Caruthersville, Mo., Oct. 25, 1911; s. Louis Moreau and Dottye Gray (Call) H.; LL.B., Cumberland U., 1934; m. Bernice Chilton, Aug. 3, 1939; children—Sally Kate (Mrs. Gerald W. Sisson). Lynda Wayne (Mrs. Lynda Wayne Masters), Karen Janet (Mrs. Karen Janet Hiesberger), Joseph Oliver Chilton. Admitted to Mo. bar, 1935, also U.S. Supreme Ct.; gen. practice, Caruthersville, 1936-64; judge 38th Jud. Circuit Mo., 1955-60, Supreme Ct. Mo., 1964—. Chmn. Mo. Hwy. Commn., 1961-64. Served with USAAF, 1942-46; mem. Res. Mem. Am. Bar Assn., Mo. Bar, Am. Judicature Soc. Mason (Shriner). Home: 1301 Dixon Dr Jefferson City MO 65101 Office: Supreme Ct Bldg Jefferson City MO 65101

HENLEY, HENRY HOWARD, Jr., mfg. co. exec.; b. Helena, Ark., Aug. 16, 1921; s. Henry Howard and Harriet Louise (Gibbs) H.; B.A., Hendrix Coll., 1943; m. Dorothy Ray Hutcheson, Aug. 23, 1943; children—Charles Ray, Philip Howard, Henry Howard III. With McKesson & Robbins, 1939-67, successively staff, Memphis, San Antonio, dist. operations mgr., dist. sales mgr., dist. v.p. S.W. dist., 1939-56, v.p. drug merchandising, 1956-59, exec. v.p. co., 1959-62, pres., 1962-67, mem. exec. com., 1962-67, now dir.; pres. Cluett-Peabody Co., N.Y.C., 1967—, chief exec. officer, 1970—, also dir.; dir. Home Life Ins. Co. Am-Express Co., Bristol-Myers Co., Clupak Co., Mfrs. Hanover Trust Co. Bd. govs. White Plains Hosp.; trustee Hendrix Coll. Served to lt. USNR, 1943-46. Mem. Am. Soc. Corporate Secs. Clubs: Economic, Madison Square Golf, Links (N.Y.C.); Blind Brook; Augusta (Ga.) Nat. Golf; Scarsdale; President's. Home: 89 Brookby Rd Scarsdale NY 10583 Office: 510 Fifth Av New York City NY 10036

HENLEY, JAMES WALTON, bishop; b. Cleveland, Tenn., July 14, 1901; s. Charles Walton and Teressa Dowthett (Johnston) H.; B.A., Emory U., 1923, D.D., 1946; B.D., Yale, 1926; postgrad. U. Edinburgh (Scotland), 1929-30; D.D., Fla. So. Coll.; L.H.D., Lycoming Coll., 1968; LL.D., Bethune-Cookman Coll., 1963; m. Huldah Jo Chapin, Dec. 31, 1931 (dec. Oct. 1968); children—James Walton, Chapin; m. 2d, Margaret Ward Hollis, June 20, 1970. Ordained to ministry Methodist Ch., 1926, consecrated bishop, 1960; pastor in Spring City, Tenn., 1926-27, Crossville, Tenn., 1927-28, Harriman, Tenn., 1928-29, Morristown, Tenn., 1930-31, Knoxville, Tenn., 1932-37, Chattanooga, 1937- 44, West Edn. Meth. Ch., Nashville, 1944-60; bishop of Jacksonville area, 1960-64; bishop of Fla. area, 1964—. Mem. gen. program council United Meth. Ch., 1968—. Meth. trustee Scarritt Coll. Christian Workers, Fla. So. Coll., Bethune Cookman Coll., Wesleyan Coll., Macon, Ga.; bd. govs. Wesley Theol. Sem. Mem. Meth. World Council (Am. sect.), Omicron Delta Kappa, Kappa Alpha. Author: Sermons on Our Lord's Prayer, 1952; His Twelve Apostles, 1958; Jesus Christ is Lord, 1961. Home: 127 Lake Hollingsworth Dr Lakeland FL 33801 Office: PO Box 1747 Lakeland FL 33802

HENLEY, JESSE SMITH, U.S. dist. judge; b. St. Joe, Ark., May 18, 1917; s. Ben H. and Jessie (Smith) H.; LL.B., U. Ark., 1941; m. Dorothy E. Ingram, Sept. 30, 1938; children—Jane Karen and Wordna Sharon (twins). Admitted to Ark. bar, 1941, practiced in Harrison, 1941-54; asso. gen. counsel FCC, Washington, 1954- 56; dir. Office Adminstrv. Procedure Dept. Justice, Washington, 1956-58; U.S. dist. judge Eastern Dist. Ark., 1958-59, Eastern and Western dists. Ark., 1959—. Mem. Am., Ark. bar assns. Presbyn. Home: 11780 Rivercrest St Little Rock AR 72207 Office: Federal Bldg Little Rock AR 72201

HENLEY, WILLIAM BALLENTINE, ch. ofcl., rancher, lawyer; b. Cin., Sept. 19, 1905; s. William Herbert and May G. (Richards) Ballentine (later assumed name of stepfather, Charles E. Henley); A.B., U. So. Cal., 1928, postgrad. Sch. Religion, 1928-29; postgrad. Yale, 1929-30; M.A., U. So. Cal., 1930, J.D., 1933, M.S. in P.A., 1935; LL.D., Willamette U., 1937; Sc.D., Kansas City Coll. Osteopathy and Surgery, 1949; R.Sc.D., Inst. Religious Sci. and Philosophy, 1949; L.H.D., Los Angeles Coll. Optometry 1958; Sc.D., Pepperdine Coll., 1966; m. Helen McTaggart, 1942. Lectr. pub. adminstrn., asst. to co-ordination officer U. So. Cal., 1928-29; dir. religious edn. First Methodist Ch., New Haven, 1929-30; lectr. in pub. adminstrn. U. So. Cal., 1930-33, exec. sec. Women's Civic Conf., same, 1930-40, acting dean Sch. of Govt. 1937-38, dir. 8th and 9th Inst. Govt., 1937-38, asst. to dean Sch. Govt., in charge "in-service" tng., Civic Center, 1934-36, asst. prof. pub. adminstrn., 1935-39, asso. prof., 1939-40, dir. co-ordination, 1938-40; pub. speaking instr. and debate coach Am. Inst. Banking, 1928-40; pres. Cal. Coll. Medicine, Los Angeles, 1940-66; provost U. Cal.-Cal. Coll. Medicine, 1966-69; pres., chmn. bd. trustees United Ch. Religious Sci., 1969—; exec., speakers' panel Gen. Motors Corp., 1956—. Dir. Glendale Community Hosp., Los Angeles County Health Assn.; bd. govs. Welfare Fedn. Los Angeles; adv. bd. Los Angeles YMCA. Mem. Bd. Water and Power Commrs., Los Angeles (pres. 1946, v.p. 57-58), 1944-62; mem. Employees' Pension and Retirement Bd. Mgmt, 1946; mem. adv. bd. Los Angeles County Gen. Hosp., 1940-65; mem. Los Angeles Def. Council, 1941-44, War Council, 1944-45, Cal. Civil Def. Com. Guest observer UN Conf., San Francisco, 1945. A.T. Still Meml. lectr., Washington, 1958. Mem. Am., Cal., Los Angeles bar assns., N.E.A., Am. Pub. Health Assn., Am. Mgmt. Assn., Am. Assn. History of Medicine, A.A.A.S., Am. Acad. Polit. and Social Scis., Am. Saddle Horse Breeding Futurity Assn. (dir.), Am. Aberdeen Angus Breeders Assn., Sigma Alpha Epsilon, Phi Delta Phi, Phi Kappa Phi, Phi Sigma Gamma, Sigma Sigma Phi, Delta Sigma Rho, Phi Delta Kappa, Pi Sigma Alpha, Alpha Delta Sigma, Phi Eta Sigma, Sigma Sigma, Skull and Dagger. Republican. Mason (32). Clubs: Los Angeles Rotary (pres. 1955-56; chmn. conf. dist. 160-A, gov. dist. 528, 1959-60; mem. internat. community service consultative group; chmn. host club exec. com. for 1962 internat. conv.; mem. world community service com.). Author: The History of the University of Southern California, 1940; also mag. articles. Home: 1224 Geneva St. Glendale CA 91207. Office: 1721 Griffin Av Los Angeles CA 90031 also Creston Circle Ranch Paso Robles CA 93446

HENLEY, WILLIAM SAUNDERS, lawyer; b. Prairie, Miss., June 11, 1896; B.S., Millsaps Coll., 1917, LL.B., 1918; postgrad. U. Mich. Admitted to Miss. bar, 1918; mem. firm Henley, Lotterhos & McDavid. Mem. Miss. Legislature, 1924-28. Fellow Am. Bar Found., Am. Coll. Trial Lawyers; mem. Am., Copiah County bar assns., Miss. State Bar (pres. 1957-58), Internat. Assn. Ins. Counsel, Am. Judicature Soc., Fedn. Ins. Counsel. Office: PO Box 326 Jackson MS 39205 also Henley Bldg Hazlehurst MS 39083

HENN, HARRY GEORGE, legal educator; b. New Rochhelle, N.Y., Oct. 8, 1919; s. Harry Christian and Mollie (Malsch) H.; B.A. summa cum laude, N.Y.U., 1941; LL.B. with distinction, Cornell U., 1943; J.S.D., N.Y.U., 1952. Admitted to N.Y. bar, 1944; asso. firm Whitmen, Ransom & Coulson, N.Y.C., 1943-53; mem. faculty Cornell U. Law Sch., 1953—, prof. law, 1957—, Edward Cornell prof. law, 1970—; spl. counsel Cornell Daily Sun, 1953-56, v.p., dir., 1966—; guest lectr. N.Y.U., 1953—; acting village justice, Cayuga Heights, Ithaca, N.Y., 1965—. Trustee Copyright Soc. U.S., 1953—, pres., 1961-63; mem. UNESCO panel internat. Copyright, also panel cons. gen. revision copyright law; cons. corp. law annotated project Am. Bar Found., 1959-60, 63-64, 68; research cons. N.Y. State Joint Legislative Com. to Study Revision Corp. Law; also Library of Congress. Pres. Ithaca Opera Assn.; trustee S. Central Research Library. Mem. Am. (past chmn. copyright div.), N.Y. State, Westchester County, Tompkins County bar assns., N.Y. County Lawyers Assn., Assn. Bar City N.Y., Fed. Bar Council (past v.p.), Am. Assn. U. Profs. (chpt. pres. 1968-70), N.Y. State Assn. Magistrates, Internat. Gesellschaft für Urheberrecht E.V., Phi Beta Kappa, Order of Coif, Delta Upsilon, Phi Kappa Phi (chpt. pres. 1964-65), Club: Ithaca Yacht. Author: Magazine Rights, 1951; Henn on Corporations and Other Business Enterprises, 2d edit., 1970; (with R.S. Stevens) Statutes, Cases and Materials on the Law of Corporations and Other Business Enterprises, 1965; also articles. Contbr. Ency. Britannica. Editor-in-chief Cornell Law Quar., 1943. Home: 130 Sunsey Dr Ithaca NY 14850

HENNE, FRANCES ELIZABETH, educator; b. Springfield, Ill., Oct. 11, 1906; d. J.Z. and Laura (Taylor) Henne; A.B., U. Ill., 1929, M.A., 1934; B.S., Columbia, 1935; Ph.D., U. Chgo., 1949. Mem. library staff Springfield (Ill.) Pub. Library, 1930-34, N.Y. Pub. Library, 1935, N.Y. State Tchrs. Coll., Albany, 1935-38; librarian U. High Sch., U. Chgo., 1939-42; instr. N.Y. State Coll. for Tchrs., 1937-38, 39, U. Chgo. Grad. Library Sch., 1939- 46; asst. prof. Grad. Library Sch., U. Chgo., 1946-49, asso. prof., 1949-54, asso. dean, dean of students, 1947-50, acting dean, 1951-52; asso. prof. Sch. Library Service, Columbia, N.Y.C., 1954, now prof.; vis. prof. U. Minn., summer 1950, Rutgers U., summer 1954. recipient Carnegie fellowship, 1938; Lippincott award, 1963. Mem. A.L.A., Am. Assn. U. Profs., Am. Assn. Sch. Librarians (nat. pres. 1948- 49). Author: Youth Communication and Libraries, 1949; Planning Guide for the High School Library Program, 1951; also numerous articles in field. Home: 345 E 50th St New York City NY 10022.

HENNE, FRANK REUBEN, hosp. adminstr.; b. Ontario Can., July 10, 1902; s. Oscar and Jennie (Norcross) H.; M.B., U. Toronto, 1926; m. Marguerite Phillips, Sept. 17, 1926 (dec. Jan. 1970); children—Barbara (Mrs. Frank D. Richart), Grant; m. 2d, Helen C. Fischer, June 15, 1967. Came to U.S., 1928, naturalized, 1935. Staff physician Marcy (N.Y.) State Hosp., 1936- 48; asst. dir. Harlem Valley State Hosp., Wingdale, N.Y., 1948-56; dir. Newark State Sch., 1956—. Served to capt., M.C., AUS, 1942-45. Diplomate Am. Bd. Psychiatry and Neurology. Mem. Am. Psychiat. Assn., Am. Assn. Mental Deficiency, A.M.A. Elk. Rotarian. Home: 522 Church St Newark NY 14513 Office: 529 Church St Newark NY 14513

HENNEBACH, RALPH L., non-ferrous metal co. exec.; b. Garfield, Utah, May 2, 1920; s. Leo and Consuelo (Herrerias) H.; Metall. Engr., Colo. Sch. Mines, 1941; M.S. in Indsl. Mgmt. (Sloan fellow), Mass. Inst. Tech., 1953; m. Mary Louise Johnston, Sept. 14, 1946; children—Mark Leo, Anne Louise, Margo Lynnne. With Am. Smelting & Refining Co., 1941—, asst. to v.p. smelting and refining, 1958-63, v.p. smelting and refining, 1963-66, exec. v.p., 1966-71, pres., 1971—, also dir.; dir. so. So. Peru Copper Sales Co., Asarco Mexicana, Capco, Ionics Internat. Bd. dirs. Zinc Inst. Served to lt. (j.g.) USNR, 1944-46. Mem. Am. Inst. Metall. Engrs., Mining and Metall. Soc., Colo. Sch. Mines Alumni Assn., Sigma Alpha Epsilon, Theta Tau. Clubs: Mining, Bankers, Pinnacle (N.Y.C.); Canoe Brook Country (Summit, N.J.); Economic. Home: 33 Tennyson Dr Short Hills NJ 07078 Office: 120 Broadway New York City NY 10005

HENNEKE, BEN GRAF, educator; b. St. Louis, May 20, 1914; s. Francis Joseph and Ruby (Graff) H.; A.B., U. Tulsa, 1935; A.M., U. Ia., 1941; Ph.D., U. Ill., 1956; m. Ellen Eaves, Dec. 26, 1940; children— Hilary, Ben Graf. Reporter, Tulsa Daily World, 1932-37; free lance corr., radio writer, 1935-37; dir. Tulsa U. Theater, 1937-52; staff dir. Cain Park Municipal Theater, Cleveland Heights, O., 1942-45; censor, day editor KVOO, 1942-45; dir. radio, also head speech dept. U. Tulsa, 1945-52, adminstrv. v.p., 1952-58, pres., 1958-67, Trustees' prof., 1967—. A founder U. Assn. for Profl. Radio Edn.; ednl. adviser to Nat. Assn. Broadcasters com. on edn.; speech cons. Pan Am. Petroleum Corp. Named to Okla. Hall of Fame, 1963. Mem. Tulsa C. of C. (dir.), Theta Alpha Phi, Pi Kappa Delta, Pi Kappa Alpha. Episcopalian. Author: Radio Announcer's Handbook, 1948; Reading Aloud Effectively, 1953; The Announcer's Handbook (with Edward Dumit), 1959. Home: 3826 S Birmingham Pl Tulsa OK 74105

HENNEMAN, ELWOOD, educator, neurophysiologist; b. Washington, Dec. 22, 1915; s. Harry Edwin and Rubina (Raihle) H.; A.B., Harvard, 1937; M.D., McGill U., 1943; m. Karel Van Syckel Toll, Dec. 30, 1950; children—Cyrena Van Syckel, Abby Hastings. Intern Royal Victoria Hosp., Montreal, 1943-44; house officer Montreal Neurol. Inst., 1944; fellow physiology Johns Hopkins Sch. Medicine, 1946-47; research asst. Ill. Neuropsychiat. Inst., Chgo., 1947-49; vis. investigator Rockefeller Inst. Med. Research, N.Y.C., 1949-51; asst. prof. physiology Johns Hopkins Sch. Medicine, 1951-55; mem. faculty Harvard Med. Sch., 1960—, prof. physiology, 1969—; neurophysiologist Mass. Gen. Hosp., Boston, 1960—. Served to lt. USNR, 1944-46. Guggenheim fellow, 1949-50. Mem. Am. Physiol. Soc., Internat. Brain Research Orgn., A.A.A.S., Sigma Xi. Clubs: Longwood Cricket (Chestnut Hill, Mass.); Badminton and Tennis (Boston). Mem. editorial bd. Am. Jour. Physiology, 1960-63, Jour. Neurophysiology, 1964-70, Physiol. Rev., 1965-66; sect. editor neurophysiology Am. Jour. Physiology, 1962-63. Home: 197 Coolidge Hill Cambridge MA 02138 Office: 25 Shattuck St Boston MA 02115

HENNEMEYER, ROBERT THOMAS, govt. ofcl.; b. Chgo., Dec. 1, 1925; s. Rudolph Johannes and Mary Matilda (Petersen) H.; student Chgo. Tchrs. Coll., 1950; Ph.B., U. Chgo., 1947, M.A.., 1950; postgrad., Oxford U., 1960-61, U. Md., 1965-66; m. Joan Therese Renaud, Dec. 28, 1954; children—Christian, Paul, Robin. Instr. high sch. and jr. coll., Chgo., 1948-52; fgn. service officer State Dept., 1952—; vice consul, Bremen, Germany, 1952-53; prin. officer, Bremerhaven, 1953-54; 2d sec. at Bonn, 1954-56; consul, Munich, 1956-57; with Office of Chief Protocol, State Dept., 1957-58, with Bur. African Afairs, 1958-60; consul, 1st sec. Dar-es-Salaam, 1961-64; with Office of Personnel, State Dept., 1966-68; 1st sec., Oslo, Norway, 1968-71; consul gen., Dusseldorf, Germany, 1971—; faculty adviser, instr. U.S. Naval Acad., 1964-66. Served with AUS, 1944-46. Mem. Am. Fgn. Service Assn., Am. Assn. U. Profs., U.S. Naval Inst., Royal African Soc. Alpha Delta Phi. Home: 8432 S Danee Av Chicago IL 60619

HENNEMUTH, ROBERT GEORGE, electronics co. exec.; b. Scranton, Pa., Oct. 25, 1921; s. George Henry and Kathryn (Conway) H.; A.B., Syracuse U., 1943; LL.B., Harvard, 1949; m. Mary Elizabeth Tonner, June 1, 1946; children—Anne Maureen, Susan Elizabeth, Robert George. Engaged in pub. relations Syracuse U., 1946- 47; instr. journalism Boston U., 1947-49, Northeastern U., 1949-61; admitted to Mass. bar, 1950, also U.S. Supreme Ct.; asso. atty. firm Nutter, McClenne & Fish, Boston, 1949-50; with Raytheon Co., 1950—, v.p. indsl. relations, 1964—. Chmn. Mass. Adv. Bd. Legislative Compensation; mem. Gov. Mass. Labor-Mgmt. Adv. Council Bd. dirs. Mass. Blue Cross, YMCA, Newton, Mass. Served to lt. (s.g.) USNR, 1943-46. Home: 22 Temple Rd Wellesley MA 02181 Office: Raytheon Co Lexington MA 02173

HENNES, ROBERT TAFT, advt. exec.; b. Jamestown, N.Y., Mar. 8, 1930; s. Theodore Preston and Lucille (Kane) H.; A.B., Harvard, 1951; M.B.A., Wharton Sch., U. Pa., 1952; m.. Frances Walker Pratt, May 9, 1953 (div. 1962); children—Robert Taft, Duncan Pratt, Margaret Nickerson, Theodore Preston II. With Lummus Co., N.Y.C., 1952-62; exec. v.p., dir. Conahay & Lyon, Inc., advt. N.Y.C., 1962-70; sr. v.p. Cole & Assos., Boston, 1970—, also dir.; dir. Oldwyck Industries, Inc., N.Y.C. Mem. Harvard Soc. Scientists and Engrs. Clubs: Harvard, Chemists (N.Y.C.). Home: 27 W 44th St New York City NY 10036 Office: 10 Post Office Sq Boston MA 02109

HENNESSEY, JOHN WILLIAM, Jr., coll. dean; b. Danville, Pa., Mar. 25, 1925; s. John William and Martha Scott (Braun) H.; A.B., Princeton, 1948; M.B.A., Harvard, 1950; D.Bus. Adminstrn., U. Wash., 1956; M.A. (hon.), Dartmouth, 1959; m. Jean Marie Lande, June 26, 1948; children—John William III, Martha Scott. From instr. to asso. prof. orgn. and adminstrn. Coll. Bus. Adminstrn., U. Washington, 1950-57; prof. Amos Tuck Sch. Bus. Adminstrn., Dartmouth, 1957—, asso. dean, 1962-68, dean, 1968—; prof. Institut pour l'Etude des Méthodes de Direction de l'Enterprise, Lausanne, Switzerland, 1959. Dir. Conn. Mut. Life Ins. Co.; trustee Dartmouth Savs. Bank. Mem. bd. visitors Grad. Sch. Bus., U. Pitts.; bd. dirs. N.H. Indsl. Devel. Authority, Am. Assn. Collegiate Schs. Bus.; trustee Mary Hitchcock Meml. Hosp., Hanover. Served to 1st lt. AUS, 1943-46. Mem. Phi Beta Kappa. Author: (with Austin Grimshaw) Organizational Behavior, 1960; (with others) Hospital Policy Decisions, 1966. Home: 4 Webster Terrace Hanover NH 03755

HENNESSEY, JOSEPH FRANCIS, govt. ofcl.; b. Springfield, Mass., June 14, 1910; s. Martin and Catherine (Stritch) H.; A.B., Holy Cross Coll., 1931; LL.B., Harvard, 1934; m. Elizabeth Lloyd, Oct. 28, 1945; 1 son, Kevin Lloyd. Admitted to Mass. bar, 1934; asso. firm King & Lyman, Springfield, 1934-38; atty. RFC, 1938-41; with AEC, 1947—, gen. counsel, 1962—. Served with AUS, 1941-47; legal adviser comdg. gen. Manhattan Project. Mem. Fed. Bar Assn. Home: 7506 Honeywell Lane Bethesda MD 20014 Office: Atomic Energy Commn Germantown MD 20767

HENNESSEY, THOMAS MICHAEL, business exec.; b. Lawrence, Mass., Nov. 12, 1901; s. James Francis and Margaret (Thornton) H.; A.B., Harvard, 1923; m. Esther G. Dwyer, June 30, 1931; children—James T., Ann, Thomas M. Asst. to operating ofcls. N.E. Tel. & Tel. Co., 1923-25, acting dist. mgr., dist. traffic mgr., 1925-26, local toll traffic supr., 1926-27, toll traffic supt., 1927-35, gen. traffic employment supr., 1935-40, div. traffic supt., Providence, 1940-44, Boston, 1944, asst. v.p., 1944- 45, dir. pub. relations, 1945-46, v. p., 1946—; dir. New Eng. Tel. & Tel. Co.; trustee Charlestown Savs. Bank, 1956—. Dir. N.E. Council 1946-53, 56-60, chmn. recreational devel., 1947-48; dir. YMCA, Boston, 1948-58; chmn. Greater Boston U.S.O. campaign, 1947; dir. Winchester Hosp., 1953-57, v.p., 1954-57; dir. Greater Boston C. of C., 1953— (chmn. bus. and indsl. com., 1954—); dir. United Fund Greater Boston, 1957—, v.p., 1957-60; dir. United Community Services Met. Boston, 1960—. Club: Harvard (Boston); Union; Down Town, Winchester Country. Home: 37 Cabot St Winchester MA 01890 Office: 185 Franklin St Boston MA 02110

HENNESSY, AUGUSTINE PAUL, clergyman; b. Phila., Mar. 11, 1914; s. John Parnell and Kathryn (Campbell) H.; S.T.B., Passionist Monastic Sem., 1941, S.T.L., 1943; S.T.D., Cath. U. Am., 1945. Joined Congregation of Passion, 1934, ordained priest Roman Catholic Ch., 1941; asso. editor Sign mag., Union City, N.J., 1945-48; tchr. theology Immaculate Conception Monastery, Jamaica, L.I., St. Michael's St., Union City; rector Holy Cross Sem., Dunkirk, N.Y., 1959-62; master novices St. Paul's, Pitts., 1962-65; dir. pastoral renewal Calvary Monastery, Shrewsbury, Mass., 1965-67; editor Sign mag., Union City, 1967—. Mem. Catholic Theol. Soc. (charter, sec. 1947-48, pres. 1955-56). Address: 1901 West St Union City NJ 07087

HENNESSY, CARROLL AMBROSE, mfg. co. exec.; b. Schenectady, Dec. 10, 1908; s. Frederick W. and Catherine (Carroll) H.; B.S. in Mech. Engring., Syracuse U., 1930; grad. Advanced Mgmt. Program, Harvard, 1958. With Lamson Corp., Syracuse, 1937- -, v.p. engineered sales, 1956-60, exec. v.p., 1960-64, pres., 1964—, also dir.; dir. Lamson Conveyors Can. Ltd., Lamson S.A. de C.V., Mexico, Lamson Mobillift Corp., Jampol Corp. Sr. mem. Citizens Found. Syracuse; mem. corp. adv. council Syracuse U. Mem. Syracuse C. of C., Mfrs. Assn. Syracuse, Am. Soc. M.E., Tau Beta Pi. Clubs: Harvard Business School (bd. govs.), Century (Syracuse); Wings (N.Y.C.). Home: 228 Standish Dr Syracuse NY 13224 Office: Lamson Corp Syracuse NY 13201

HENNESSY, DEAN MCDONALD, mfg. co. exec.; b. McPherson, Kan., June 13, 1923; s. Ernest Weston and Beulah A. (Dunn) H.; A.B. cum laude, Harvard, 1947, LL.B., 1950; M.B.A., U. Chgo., 1959; m. Marguerite Catherine Sundheim, Sept. 6, 1946; children—Joan Catherine, John Dean, Robert Dean, Scott Dean. Asso. firm Leibman, Bennett, Baird & Williams, Chgo., 1950-53; atty. Borg Warner Corp., Chgo., 1953-62; with Emhart Corp., 1962—, asst. sec., 1964-67, sec., gen. counsel, 1967—. Program chmn. trade and industries div. United Republican Fund Ill., 1961; chmn. citizens activities and sec. Ill. Citizens for Eisenhower, 1952; mem. town bd., also justice of peace Proviso Twp., Ill., 1953-57; mem. Hinsdale (Ill.) Town Caucus, 1962. Served to lt. (j.g.) USNR, 1943-46. Mem. Am. Bar Assn. Presbyn. Club: Wampanoag Country. Home: 148 Westmont St West Hartford CT 06117 Office: PO Box 1620 Hartford CT 06601

HENNESSY, EDWARD LAWRENCE, Jr., beverage co. exec.; b. Boston, Mar. 22, 1928; s. Edward Lawrence and Celina Mary (Doucette) H.; B.S., Fairleigh Dickinson U., 1951; student N.Y.U. Law Sch., 1951-54; m. Ruth Schilling, Aug. 18, 1951; children—Michael E., Elizabeth R. Controller Heublein, Inc., Hartford, Conn., 1964-71, v.p. finance, 1971—, sr. v.p. adminstrn., finance, 1971—; dir. Theodore Hamm Co., Ky. Fried Chicken, Madera Glass Co., Hartford Despatch Co., Conn. Bank and Trust Co. Served with USNR, 1948-55.. Mem. Financial Execs. Inst., Am. Mgmt. Assn., Nat. Assn. Accountants. Roman Catholic. Clubs: Indian Harbor Yacht (Greenwich, Conn.); St. Francis Yacht (San Francisco); Wampanoag Golf (West Hartford, Conn.). Home: 60 Sunset Farm Rd West Hartford CT 06107 Office: 330 New Park Av Hartford CT 06101*

HENNESSY, JAMES LAWRENCE, govt. ofcl.; b. Boston, Aug. 13, 1914; s. James A. and Mary (McCarthy) H.; A.B., Boston Coll., 1935; LL.B., Harvard, 1938; m. Mary Anderson, June 4, 1944; children—Ann Ellen, Jane, Lawrence N., John A. Admitted to Mass. bar, 1939; practiced in Boston, 1939-41; with Dept. Justice, 1941- -, exec. asst. to commr. Immigration and Naturalization Service, 1954—. Home: 3000 Russell Rd Alexandria VA 22305 Office: 119 D St NE Washington DC 20536

HENNESSY, JOHN FRANCIS, mech. engr.; b. N.Y.C. June 14, 1902; s. John J. and Nora (McCarthy) H.; B.S. in Mech. Engring., Mass. Inst. Tech., 1924; D.Eng., Manhattan Coll., 1956; LL.D., Iona

Coll., 1958; m. Dorothy A. O'Grady, Apr. 30, 1927; children—John Francis, Paul Kevin. Founder firm Syska, Hennessy, Inc., cons. engrs., N.Y.C., 1928, pres., 1938-67, chmn., chief exec. officer, 1967—; dir. Security Nat. Bank; trustee N.Y. Savs. Bank. Asst. to sec. navy, 1944-45. Mem. N.Y.C. Bd. Edn., 1961-63. Pres. Lincoln Hall, 1958—; mem. Manhattan Coll. Council, 1959—. Served with USAAF, 1942- 44. Decorated Legion of Merit; named knight of Malta, 1945, knight of Sepulchure, 1953. Registered profl. engr., N.Y. Mem. N.Y. Cons. Engrs. (pres. 1951-52), N.Y. Bldg. Congress (pres. 1955-58), Am. Inst. Cons. Engrs., Am. Inst. E.E., Nat. Soc. Profl. Engrs. Home: Remsenburg NY 11960 Office: 144 E 39th St New York City NY 10016

HENNESSY, JOHN WHITEmfg. exec.; b. Lima, O., Apr. 1, 1932; B.S., U. San Francisco, 1954; M.S., Stanford University, 1956; m. Rosemarie Lois Brown, May 15, 1955; 1 son, Anthony Robinson. Sales rep. Ames-Brockton Fabricated Products, Akron, O., 1956-58, sales mgr. Coshocton, Ohio, 1959-61, gen. manager plant, 1961-68, v.p. sales, 1968--. Instr. bus. Coshocton Jr. College, 1968-69. Secretary Coshocton YMCA, 1960-61; active Boy Scouts of America. Named Man of Year, Coshocton Junior Chamber of Commerce, 1968. Mem. Coshocton C. of C. (vice president 1967-68, pres. 1969-70), English Speaking Union, Coshocton Sertoma Club, Nat. Assn. Mfrs., Sales Executives Institute, Phi Beta Kappa, Sigma Chi, Phi Mu. Democrat. Mem. Christian Ch. (lay leader). Mason (32, Shriner). Clubs: Coshocton Country, Coshocton City, Running Deer Country. Home: 2d Av Coshocton OH Office: 3d Av Coshocton OH

HENNESSY, SIR PATRICK, mfg. exec.; b. Midleton, County Cork, Ireland, Apr. 18, 1898; s. Patrick and Mary (Benn) H.; student Christ Ch. Sch., Cork, Ireland, 1907-14; m. Dorothy Margaret Davis, 1923 (dec. Aug. 1949); children—Valerie Patricia (Mrs. Anthony Hough), Jerrold Anthony, Geoffrey Noel. Successively prodn. worker, road rep., service mgr., prodn. mgr. Henry Ford & Son, Ltd., Cork, 1920-31, now chmn.; purchase mgr. Ford Motor Co., Ltd., Dagenham, Essex, Eng., 1931-39, gen. mgr., 1939-45, gen. mgr., dir., 1945-49, mng. dir., 1948-57, dep. chmn., 1950-56, chmn., 1956- 68, chief exec. and exec. dir. until 1963; now chmn. Montego Freeport, Inc., Jamaica. Mem. adv. council Ministry Aircraft Prodn., 1940-41. Served with Royal Inniskilling Fusiliers, Brit. Army, World War I. Created Knight Bachelor, 1941. Home: Larkmead, Theydon Bois Essex England Office: 88 Regent St London W 1 England

HENNESSY, ROBERT EMMETT, distillery and chem. mfg. exec.; b. Louisville, Feb. 22, 1906; s. Daniel Joseph and Anna Marie (Sullivan) H.; student St. Xavier's Coll. High Sch., Louisville; m. Agnes Lyons Lindle, May 13, 1933; children— Robert Gaylord, Suzanne Lindle (Mrs. Henry J. Konzelmann, Jr.), Daniel Kraft, John Lamar. Mgr. and supr. Gt. Atlantic & Pacific Tea Co., 1924-27; sales and distbn. Harbison & Gathright, Inc., 1927-29; prodn., purchasing and ins. Am. Medicinal Spirits Co., 1929-34; asst. dir. purchases Nat. Distillers Products Corp., 1934-49, dir. purchases, 1949-57; v.p. purchasing Nat. Distillers & Chem. Corp., N.Y.C., 1957—. Mem. Nat. Assn. Purchasing Agts. K.C. Club: Union League (N.Y.C.); Canoe Brook Country (Summit). Home: 4 Manor Hill Rd Summit NJ 07901 Office: 99 Park Av New York City NY 10016

HENNESSY, WESLEY JOSEPH, coll. dean; b. Queens, N.Y., Aug. 17, 1914; s. Charles A. and Lydia (Schneider) H.; student Syracuse U., 1934-37; B.S. cum laude, Columbia, 1951; LL.D., Phila. Coll. Osteopathy, 1966; D.Sc., Bethany (W.Va.) Coll., 1966; m. Virginia Pershing MacArthur, June 20, 1942 (dec. Aug. 1955); children—Heather Michele, David Charles, Holly MacArthur; m. 2d, Virginia Ann Campbell, Apr. 4, 1959; children—Mark Campbell, Kevin, Karen, Anne. Pres., World's Fair Employees Assn., 1939; dir. tng. Grumman Aircraft Engring. Corp., Bethpage, L.I., 1940-44; asst. to dean 1944-48, asst. dean, 1948-53, asso. dean, 1953-64, exec. dean, 1964-69, dean Sch. Engring. and Applied Sci., Columbia U., N.Y.C., 1969—; resident dir. Summer Sch. Engring., Lakeside, Conn., 1946-64; spl. lectr. world econ. geography; condr. seminar on human relations ICA, Guatemala, 1959; cons. to Govt. South Korea on Indsl. Devel. Program, 1968—. Mgmt. cons. research and devel. div. Am. Machine & Foundry, Reflectone Electronics, Unidynamics div. Universal Match Corp., 1960-64; dir. refugee scientists program Nat. Acad. Scis., 1961-64; bd. dirs. Am. council for Emigres in the Professions, 1962—. Trustee St. Hilda's Sch., N.Y.C., 1952-55; bd. dirs. Armstrong Meml. Research Found., 1970—. Recipient Distinguished Pub. Service award Columbia U. Sch. Gen. Studies, 1967. Mem. Am. Soc. Engring. Edn., Columbia U. Engring. Sch. Alumni Assn. (asso.). Clubs: Litchfield (Conn.) Country; Men's Faculty, Columbia U. Home: 3 Crieff Lane New City NY 10956 Office: School of Engineering and Applied Science 520 W 120th St Columbia U New York City NY 10027

HENNEY, RICHARD BERNARD, found. exec.; b. Upper Montclair, N.J., June 21, 1918; s. David Simonds and Stella Caroline (Bruggeman) H.; B.A., U. Va., 1950; M.B.A., Hofstra Coll., 1957. With First Nat. City Bank N.Y., 1937-41, 50-53, ofcl. asst., 1950-53; with Duke Endowment, 1953—, treas., 1961-66, sec., 1966—, exec. dir., 1971—; treas. Doris Duke Trust, 1961-66, sec., 1966—, exec. dir., 1971—; sec. Angier B. Duke Meml., Inc., 1966—, v.p., 1970—; asst. treas. Duke Power Co., 1961- 67, dir., chmn. finance com., 1967—. Served to capt. AUS, 1941-47; PTO. Mem. Newcomen Soc. N. Am., Assn. Ex- Mems. Squadron A, Am. Legion, Phi Beta Kappa, Phi Eta Sigma, Phi Kappa Psi, Alpha Kappa Psi. Elk. Club: Rockefeller Center Luncheon (N.Y.C.). Home: 85 W Smith St Merrick NY 11566 Office: 30 Rockefeller Plaza New York City NY 10020

HENNIKER-HEATON, ROSE MORSE, C.S. practitioner; b. Lahore, Pakistan, Mar. 19, 1902; d. Amyas and Rose (Maddock) Morse; asso. Royal Coll. Music, London, Eng., 1925; m. Peter J. Henniker-Heaton, Sept. 10, 1934. Came to U.S., 1952. Mezzo-soprano in concert and radio appearances, Eng., 1925-49; C.S. practitioner, 1949—; 2d reader Mother Ch., Boston, 1965—. Recipient certificate Royal Humane Soc. Eng., 1917. Home: 100 Memorial Dr Cambridge MA 02142 Office: Statler Office Bldg Boston MA 02116

HENNING, PAUL WILLIAM, TV writer-producer; b. Independence, Mo., Sept. 16, 1911; s. William and Sophia (Albers) H.; student Kansas City Sch. Law, 1930-32; m. Ruth Margaret Barth, Jan. 14, 1939; children—Carol Alice, Linda Kay, Paul Anthony. Mem. staff radio sta. KMBC, Kansas City, 1933-37; co-writer radio program Fibber McGee and Molly, 1937-39; writer Joe E. Brown radio show, 1939, Rudy Vallee radio show, 1940-41; writer radio show, then TV show for Burns and Allen, 1942-52; writer Dennis Day TV show, 1952, Ray Bolger TV show, 1953; producer-writer Bob Cummings TV show, 1954-59; creator, producer, writer TV show Beverly Hillbillies, 1962—; creator, producer TV show Petticoat Junction, 1963—; exec. producer TV show Green Acres, 1965—; author feature films Lover Come Back, 1961, Bedtime Story, 1962. Democrat. Lutheran. Home: 4250 Navajo St North Hollywood CA 91602 Office: 1040 N Las Palmas Hollywood CA 90038

HENNING, VAL JOHN, elec. mfg. co. exec.; b. St. Charles, Mo., Oct. 31, 1918; s. William H. and Dorothy (Hollander) H.; student St. Louis U., 1940-42; m. Beverly Feiler, Feb. 14, 1942; children—Sharon (Mrs. John Ferguson), Karen (Mrs. Robert Gramm), David, Deborah. Asst. chief cost accountant Curtiss Wright Co., St. Louis, 1942-45; cost accountant Gen. Motors Corp., St. Louis, 1945-47; chief cost accountant Vickers Electric Div., St. Louis, 1947-51; comptroller, asst. sec. Emerson Electric Co., St. Louis, 1951-70; v.p. finance, 1970—. Mem. Nat. Assn. Accountants (past chpt. pres., nat. dir.). Home: 27 Prairie Haute Dr St Charles MO 63301 Office: 8100 W Florissant Av St Louis MO 63136

HENNINGER, G. ROSS, ret. educator, elec. engr.; b. Hamilton, O., May 22, 1898; s. George Henry Thomas and Harriet (Ross) H.; B.S. in Elec. Engring., U. So. Cal., 1922; m. Leah Katharine Craven, Nov. 16, 1923; children—Beverley Anne, Nancy Katharine. Power station operator So. Cal. Edison Co., Los Angeles, 1917-22, asst. elec. protection engr., 1923-24; engring. editor Elec. West mag., 1924-30; asso. editor Am. Inst. E.E., N.Y.C., 1930-33, editor, 1933-48; dir. publs. Illuminating Engring. Soc., 1948-50; prof., head engring. extension dept. Ia. State U., 1950-58, on leave as dir. Am. Soc. Engring. Edn. nat. survey tech. inst. edn., 1956-57; pres. Ohio Mechanics Inst. and Coll. Applied Sci. (now Ohio Coll. Applied Sci.), 1958-62; dir. instnl. research Ore. Tech. Inst., Klamath Falls, also asso. prof., 1962-67; cons. in engring. tech. edn., 1967—; NSF/U.S. AID spl. cons. to Indian Ministry Edn., New Delhi, 1970. Mem. bd. Midwest Power Conf., 1951-60; mem. information com. Engrs. Council for Profl. Devel., 1934-48, mem. nat. com. for accreditation of engring. tech. curricula, 1955-65, chmn., 1962-65; mem. publicity com. Am. Engring. Council, 1937-40. Mem. Haworth (N.J.) Bd. Edn., 1940-42, pres., 1942; mem. Haworth Borough Council, 1947-49. Trustee Haworth Municipal Library, 1936-42. Tech. cons. Office Sec. Navy, 1942; liaison officer on staff dir. gen. Army Specialist Corps, Washington, 1942; active duty to col. USAAF, 1942-45, Hdqrs. Air Tech. Command, Wright Field; chmn. A.A.F. printing control bd., Washington, 1944; col. USAF Active Res. 1945-56. Recipient Williston award Am. Soc. Engring. Edn., 1964. Registered profl. engr., N.Y. Fellow I.E.E.E. (life mem.); mem. Am. Soc. Engring. Edn. (life), Nat. Soc. Profl. Engrs. (life; chmn. com. on Am. Engr., 1958-61), Profl. Engrs., Ore. (life; chmn. state com. on certification of engring. technicians 1965-67), Eta Kappa Nu. Republican. Presbyn. Author: The Technical Institute in America, 1959. Contbr. trade and tech. publs. Home: 2432 Pine Knoll Dr Walnut Creek CA 94595

HENNINGER, JOHN GEORGE, banker; b. Cleve., Oct. 24, 1916; s. John and Antoinette (Heideman) H.; B.B.A., Fenn Coll., 1939; J.D., Cleve. Marshall Law Sch., 1947; m. Emily Stochmal, Nov. 29, 1941; children—Thomas P., Mary Ann, Rita M., Marcia A. With White Motor Co., 1939-40, Household Finance Corp., 1940-41, Gen. Motors Acceptance Corp., 1941-42, Thompson Products, 1942-45; asst. treas., br. mgr. Bank of Ohio, Cleve., 1945-54; admitted to Ohio bar, 1947; with Society Nat. Bank., Cleve., 1954—, sr. v.p., 1970—; also pres. Euclid Nat. Bank, Cleve.; dir. Kimsafe, Inc., Troy Mfg. Co., Process Industries Equipment Corp. Pres., bd., treas. Van Aken Center Assn.; councilman local United Appeal, Health Fund, A.R.C., Holy Name Soc. Trustee Fenn Coll., Cornelia Schnurmann Found., Fenn Ednl. Found., Madonna Hall; mem. nat. bd. Adrian Generalate. Named Man of Year, Fenn Coll., 1965. Mem. Cuyahoga Bar Assn., Delta Theta Phi. Roman Catholic (bd. dirs.). Clubs: Mid-Day, Skating (Cleve.). Home: 21900 Shelburne Rd Shaker Heights OH 44122 Office: 127 Public Sq Cleveland OH 44114

HENNINGER, PERN EMERSON, lawyer; b. Gowen City, Pa., July 30, 1907; s. Elmer and Alice M. (Wagner) H.; LL.B., Nat. U., 1932; m. Margaret Roller, Aug. 20, 1944; 1 son, Robert O.; m. 2d, Marlene M. Babarid Bell Oct. 18, 1969. Admitted to D.C. bar, 1933, N.Y. bar, 1950; practice in Washington, 1933-48, N.Y.C., 1948—; pvt. practice patent law, 1933-41; partner Miles D. Pillars, 1941-48; mem. firm Cooper, Byrne, Dunham, Keith & Dearborn, 1948-53; partner Cooper, Dunham, Henninger & Clark, 1953—. Mem. Am., N.Y., D.C. bar assns., Assn. Bar City N.Y., Am., N.Y. patent law assns., N.Y. County Lawyers Assn. Home: 91 Strawberry Hill Av Stamford CT 06902 Office: 330 Madison Av New York NY 10017

HENNINGS, ARTHUR GEORGE, hosp. adminstr.; b. Red Lake Falls, Minn., June 21, 1914; s. George Frederick and Pauline (Nieland) H.; B.B.A., U. Minn., 1946, M.H.A., 1948; m. Carmen Proehl, Dec. 26, 1941; children—Kathryn Hazen, Mary Nieland, Elizabeth Carsten, Stephen Arthur. Asst. prof. hosp. adminstrn. U. Minn., also hosp. cons., 1953-58; dir. hosps., prof. hosp. adminstrn. U. Tex., Galveston, 1958-59; exec. dir. St. Margaret Meml. Hosp., Pitts., 1960-67; coordinator Univ. Health Center of Pitts., 1967-69; exec. dir. McKeesport (Pa.) Hosp., 1970—; asso. adj. prof. hosp. and med. care adminstrn. U. Pitts., 1961—. Dir. Hosp. Utilization Project, Pitts., 1970—. Served to 2d lt., M.A.C., AUS, 1942-46. Fellow Am. Coll. Hosp. Adminstrs.; mem. Am. Hosp. Assn., Am. Pub. Health Assn., Am. Mgmt. Assn., Alpha Delta Phi. Episcopalian. Rotarian. Contbr. articles profl. jours. Home: 214 Hampton Rd Pittsburgh PA 15215 Office: 1500 5th Av McKeesport PA 15132

HENNINGSEN, PETER, Jr., mfg. co. exec.; b. Mpls., Oct. 6, 1926; s. Peter and Anna O. (Kjelstrup) H.; B.B.A., U. Minn., 1950; m. Donna J. Buresh, June 19, 1948; children—Deborah, Pamela, James. Packaging engr. govt. and aero. products div. Honeywell, Inc., Mpls., 1950—. Mem. Soc. Packaging and Handling Engrs., 1951—, fellow, 1970, pres., 1970-71, chmn. bd., 1972—, named Man of Year, 1968. Served with USNR, 1944-46. Mem. Am. Soc. Testing Materials, Nat. Inst. Packaging, Handling and Logiatics Engrs., Aerospace Industries Assn. (chmn. packaging com. 1967). Methodist (trustee). Mason (Shriner). Editorial cons. mags. in field. Home: 5717 Melody Lane Edina MN 55436 Office: 2600 Ridgeway Pky Minneapolis MN 55413

HENNINGSEN, VICTOR E., ins. exec.; b. Emmetsburg, Ia., May 5, 1908; s. Christian and Sena (Beck) H.; B.A. summa cum laude, U. Ia., 1930, M.S., 1931; m. Mary Roseman, June 27, 1936; children—Nancy, Philip, Paul, Ellen. Actuarial clk. Prudential Ins. Co., 1931-32; actuarial clk, Northwestern Mut. Life Ins. Co., Milw., 1932-33, asst. actuary, 1933-46, asso. actuary, 1946- 47, comptroller, 1947-53, actuary, 1953-68, v.p., 1963-68, sr. v.p. ins., 1968—. Recipient Distinguished Service award State U. Ia., 1964. Am. Mem. Am. Acad. Actuaries, Soc. Actuaries (past pres.), Phi Beta Kappa. Conglist. Home: 6019 N Berkeley Blvd Milwaukee WI 53217 Office: 720 E Wisconsin Av Milwaukee WI 53202

HENNINGTON, BURNETTE YARBROUGH, former mem. Dem. Nat. Com.; b. Hickory, Miss.; d. Lewis H. and Bertha (Everett) Yarbrough; student Baylor Coll., 1926-30; m. Carter Hennington, Feb. 12, 1939 (div. June 1949). Social Service work, Jackson, Miss., 1933-40; chief clk. SSS Bd., Jackson, 1940-46; owner Burnette Y. Hennington, realtor, Jackson, 1946—; sec.-treas. Jackson Real Estate Bd., 1956-57, parliamentarian, 1963—; dir. Multiple Listing Service, Jackson 1958-61, sec., treas., 1961-62. Dir. Miss. Women's Cabinet Pub. Affairs, 1954- -, pres., 1959-61, legislative chmn., 1965—, parliamentarian, 1968—; mem. Nat. Com. for Support Pub. Schs., 1964-67; del. White House Conf. on Natural Beauty, 1965; mem. U.S. delegation Internat. Congress Internat. Fedn. Bus. and Profl. Women's Clubs, 1965; co-chairman 1st Nat. Water Pollution Conf. for Women, 1961; pres., mem. Water Pollution Control Adv. Bd., 1964-67; Dem. Nat. Committeewoman for Miss., 1964-68. Dir. Hinds County Assn. Mental Health, 1953—. pres. 1959-61; dir. Cerebral Palsy Central Miss., 1954-60, Miss. Soc. Crippled Children and Adults, 1954-56, Jackson Music Assn., Hinds County unit Am. Cancer Soc., 1959-62; dir. Miss. Mental Health Assn., 1959—, pres., 1965-66, exec. dir., 1967—; mem. bd. dirs. United Givers Fund, 1959-, Community Services Assn. Hinds County, 1966- 68; active YWCA; trustee Bus. and Profl. Women's Found., 1964-65. Recipient citation Dept. Health Edn. and Welfare, USPHS for contbn. Div. Water Supply and Pollution Control, guidance Water Pollution Control Conf., 1963. Mem. C. of C., League Women Voters, Nat. (Miss. gov. women's council), Miss. assns. real estate bds. Nat. (nat. civilian participation chmn., nat. rec. sec. 1964-65), S.E. region (dir., past state pres., past state conv. chmn.), Miss. (parliamentarian 1966-67) fedns. bus. and profl. women's clubs, Jackson Bus. and Profl. Women's Club (past pres.; parliamentarian 1966-67, 68-69). Democrat. Baptist. Club: Zonta (dir. 1963—, pres. 1970—). Home: PO Box 9712 Northside Sta Jackson MS 39206 Office: 2300 Robinson St Jackson MS 39209

HENNION, GEORGE FELIX, prof. chemistry; b. South Bend, Ind., Aug. 23, 1910; s. Rene C. and Elodie (Van de Walle) H.; B.S. in Chem. Engring., U. Notre Dame, 1932, M.S., 1933, Ph.D., 1935; m. Alice C Braunsdorf, Aug. 23, 1933; children—Mary Claire, Alice, George Felix, Margaret. Grad. asst. in chemistry U. Notre Dame (Ind.), 1932-35, instr., 1935-38, asst. prof., 1938-41, asso. prof., 1941-45, dir. research in chemistry, 1942-45, Julius Arthur Nieuwland prof. chemistry, 1945—. Fellow Ind. Acad. Sci., A.A.A.S.; mem. Am. (chmn. St. Joseph Valley sect. 1938-39), Ind. chem. socs., Sigma Xi. Democrat. Roman Catholic. Home: 1441 E La Salle Av South Bend IN 46617 Office: Dept of Chemistry U Notre Dame Notre Dame IN 46556

HENNY, FRED ALFRED, oral surgeon; b. Saginaw, Mich., Oct. 17, 1912; s. Frank Andrew and Minnie (Fetting) H.; D.D.S., U. Mich., 1935; m. Jane Fauver, Oct. 29, 1938; children—Patricia Jane, Susan Margaret. Intern, resident Henry Ford Hosp., Detroit, 1935-38, asso. surgeon div. oral surgery, 1938-52, chief div. oral surgery and dentistry, 1952—; guest lectr. oral medicine U. Detroit; cons. VA, Surgeon Gen. USAF. Chmn. Internat. Conf. Oral Surgery, London, 1961; mem. Nat. Adv. Dental Research Council, 1967- -. Recipient Distinguished Alumnus award U. Mich. Diplomate Am. Bd. Oral Surgery. Fellow Am. Coll. Dentists, Royal Coll. Surgeons Eng. (hon.); mem. Am. Dental Assn., Acad. Oral Surgery Detroit, Am. (Pres. 1960), Mich. (past Pres.) dental assns., Nat. Insts. Dental Research (chmn. tng. grants com.), Brit. Assn. Oral Surgeons (hon.), Great Lakes Soc. Oral Surgeons, Chalmers J. Lyons Acad. Oral Surgeons, Internat. Assn. Oral Surgeons (hon.; pres. 1965-68), Am. Soc. Oral Surgeons (Distinguished Service award; chmn. bd. trustees of Ednl. Found.), Australian-New Zealand Assn. Oral Surgeons (hon.), Omicron Kappa Upsilon, Delta Sigma Delta. Rotarian. Editor Jour. Oral Surgery, 1951-64. Contbr. profl. jours. Home: 3218 Bradway Birmingham MI 48010 Office: 751 Chestnut St Birmingham MI

HENNY, GEORGE CHRISTIAN, educator, med. physicist; b. Alameda, Cal., Feb. 22, 1899; s. David Christian and Julia (Wetzel) H.; A.B., Reed Coll., 1920; M.S. in Physics, Cal. Inst. Tech., 1922; student Harvard Grad. Sch., 1922-23; M.D., U. Ore., 1930; m. Harriet Elizabeth Gore, Aug. 23, 1926; children—Jeanette, (Mrs. Thomas R. Conway), David Christian III. Transmission engr. Bell Telephone Labs., 1923-25; fellow radiology Temple U. Hosp., 1931-33; med. research physicist Sch. Medicine, Temple U., 1933-38, head dept. med. physics, 1936—, asso. prof. radiology, 1943-45, prof., head dept. med. physics Health Scis. Center, 1945-68, prof. emeritus, 1968—. Mem. com. on sci. and arts Franklin Inst., 1962—. Diplomate Am. Bd. Health Physics, Am. Bd. Radiology. Fellow Am. Coll. Radiology; mem. Radiol. Soc. N.Am. (Silver medal 1942), Phila. County Med. Soc., Am. Assn. Physicists In Medicine, A.M.A. (Silver medal 1946), Health Physics Soc., Am. Assn. Physicists Medicine, Delaware Valley Soc. Radiation Safety, Am. Roentgen Ray Soc., N.Y. Acad. Sci., Physics Club Phila. (pres. 1942-43), Sigma Xi, Alpha Omega Alpha, Theta Kappa Psi, Phi Beta Pi. Author: (with Dr. Mona Spiegel-Adolf) X-Ray Diffraction Studies in Biology and Medicine, 1947. Home: 6714 Wissahickon Av Philadelphia PA 19119

HENREID, PAUL (Paul Georg Julius von Hernried Ritter von Wasel-Waldingau), actor, director; b. Trieste, Austria; s. Carl Alphens and Maria Louise (Lendecke) von Henreid; grad. Academie Graphic Arts, Vienna, also Konservatorium Dramatic Arts, Vienna; m. Elizabeth Glueck, 1936; children—Mimi (Mrs. Russel J. Abbott), Monika (Mrs. Paul Veglia). Came to U.S., 1940. Mem. Max Reinhardt's Vienna Theatre, also appeared in Austrian films Hohe Schule, Nur Ein Komoediant; appeared in London plays Victoria Regina, The Jersey Lilly, also films Goodbye Mr. Chips, An Englishman's Home, Night Train (best fgn. actor in film N.Y.C. critics), 1935-40; N.Y.C. stage appearances in Flight to the West, 1941, Festival, 1955; motion pictures include Joan of Paris, Now Voyager, Casablanca, In Our Time, The Conspirators, Between Two Worlds, Of Human Bondage, The Spanish Main, Devotion, Deception, Song of Love, Hollow Triumph, Rope of Sand, For Men Only, Last of The Buccaneers, So Young So Bad, Man in Hiding, Stolen Face, Pirates of Tripoli, Battleshock (or Acapulco), Holiday for Lovers, Never So Few, The Four Horsemen of the Appocalypse, Madwoman of Chaillot, numerous others: producer film Hollow Triumph (The Scar); co-producer, costar Pardon My French, So Young So Bad; producer, dir., star For Men Only; dir. Battleshock, Take Five From Five, Seeds of Violence, Dead-Ringer (Dead Image) (outstanding award merit Motion Picture Council Cal.), Ballade in Blue; actor, director numerous TV films, 1957—. Mem. Screen Actors Guild, A.F.T.R.A., Directors Guild Am., Actors Equity, Acad. Motion Picture Arts and Scis. Club: Vereinigung Ehemaliger Theresianisten (Vienna). Home: Brentwood Park Los Angeles CA 90049 Office: care Paul Kohner Inc 9169 Sunset Blvd Los Angeles CA 90069

HENRICH, JOHN B., lawyer, business exec.; b. N.Y.C., June 14, 1912; s. John B. and Mary Anges (Roxbury) H.; A.B. summa cum laude, Fordham U., 1933, LL.B., 1936; spl. studies in patent law, Columbia, 1939-40; m. Marion E. Coleman, Jan. 28, 1938. Instr. Latin and philosophy Fordham U., 1933-35; admitted to N.Y. bar, 1937, since practiced in N.Y. C.; asst. sec. Nat. Lead Co., 1943-48, sec. and counsel, 1948-67, exec. v.p., gen. counsel, 1967-68, pres., 1968—, dir.; officer, dir. Baker Castor Oil Co., Canadian Titanium Pigments, Ltd., Nat. Lead Co. Ohio, Morris P. Kirk & Son, Inc.; dir. Titanium Metals Corp. Am. Mem. bar U.S. Supreme Ct., Fed. Bar; registered patent atty. in U.S., 1939, in Can., 1942. Mem. Am. Soc. Corporate Secs., Am., City N.Y. bar assns., Fordham U. Alumni Assn. Clubs: Lawyers (N.Y.C.); Wee Burn Country (Darien). Home: Georgian Lane Darien CT 06820 Office: 111 Broadway New York City NY 10006

HENRICKSON, EILER LEONARD, geologist; b. Crosby, Minn., Apr. 23, 1920; s. Eiler Clarence and Mabel (Bacon) H.; B.A., Carleton Coll., 1943; Ph.D., U. Minn., 1956; m. Anita Hazel Swanson, Dec. 17, 1949; children—Eiler Warren, Kristin Louise, Kurt Eric, Ann Elizabeth. Geologist, U.S. Geol. Survey, Cal., 1943-44; instr. Carleton

Coll., 1946-47, 48-51, asst. prof., 1951-53, 54-56, asso. prof., 1956-62, prof., 1962-70, Charles L. Denison prof. geology, chmn. dept., 1970—; wrestling coach, 1946-58; instr. U. Minn., 1947-48, 53-54. Cons. Jones & Laughlin Steel Corp., 1946-58, Fremont Mining Co., Alaska, 1958-61, G.T. Schieldahl Co., Minn., 1961- 62, Bear Creek Mining Co., Mich., 1965-66, U. Minn. Messenia Expdn., 1966—; cons. Argonne Nat. Lab., 1966—, research scientist, summers 1966-67; vis. lectr. numerous univs., Europe, 1962; field studies metamorphic areas, Norway and Scotland. Dir. Northfield Bd. Edn., 1960- 63; steering com. Northfield Community Devel. program, 1966-67. Served as 1st lt. USMCR, 1943, AUS, 1944-46 Fulbright research scholar, Greece, 1969-70. Mem. A.A.A.S., Mineral. Soc. Am., Am. Geogphys. Union, Nat. Assn. Geology Tchrs. (editor Central sect.), Minn. Acad. Sci. (vis. lectr.), Am. Geol. Inst., Geol. Soc. Am., Soc. Econ. Geologists, Nat. Wrestling Coaches and Ofcls. Assn., Sigma Xi. Author: Zones of Regional Metamorphism, 1957. Home: 205 E 2d St Northfield MN 55057

HENRIKSEN, MELVIN, educator, mathematician; b. N.Y.C., Feb. 23, 1927; s. Kaj and Helen (Kahn) H.; B.S., Coll. City N.Y., 1948; M.S., U. Wis., 1949, Ph.D. in Math., 1951; m. Lillian Viola Hill, July 23, 1946 (div. 1964); children—Susan, Richard, Thomas; m. 2d, Louise Levitas, June 12, 1964. Asst. math., then instr. extension div. U. Wis., 1948-51; asst. prof. U. Ala., 1951-52; from instr. to prof. math. Purdue U., 1952-65; prof. math., head dept. Case Inst. Tech., 1965-68; research asso. U. Cal. at Berkeley, 1968-69; prof., chmn. math. dept. Harvey Mudd Coll., 1969—; mem. Inst. Advanced Study, Princeton, 1956-57, 63-64; vis. prof. Wayne State U., 1960-61. Sloan Fellow, 1956-58. Mem. Am. Math. Soc., Math. Assn. Am. Author (with Milton Lees) Single Vanable Calculus, 1970. Contbr. articles profl. jours. on algebra, rings of functions, gen. topology. Home: 504 Bowling Green Dr Claremont CA 91711

HENRIOD, FREDERICK HENRI judge; b. American Fork, Utah, Jan. 26, 1905; s. Frederic Augustus and Selena (Greenwood) H.; A.B., U. Utah, 1929; LL.B., Harvard, 1932; m. Wilma Ellen Savage, Apr. 28, 1933; 1 son, Richard Henri. Admitted to Utah bar, 1933; practice law, Salt Lake City, 1933-51; justice Supreme Ct. Utah, 1951-65, 68—, chief justice, 1965-67. Served as capt. AUS, 1942-46, intelligence officer, judge adv., Africa, Sicily, Italy, Corsica. Mem. Utah Jr. (pres. 1938), Utah (commr. 1940, past v.p.) bar assns., Young Rep. League Utah (pres. 1938), Sigma Nu Phi. Republican (co. Com. chmn. 1942), Elk. Home: 235 E Capitol Salt Lake City UT 84110 Office State Capitol Salt Lake City UT 84110

HENRIQUEZ, M.F., banker. Mng. dir. Maduro and Curiel's Bank N.V., Curacao, Netherlands Antilles. Address: De Ruyterplein 2 Curacao Netherlands Antilles*

HENRY, ALLAN FRANCIS, physicist; b. Phila., Jan. 12, 1925; s. Edward James and Cecile Alice (Butler) H.; B.S., Yale, 1945, M.S., 1947, Ph.D., 1950. Vol. ambulance driver Am. Field Service, 1945-50; sr. scientist Bettis Atomic Power Lab., West Mifflin, Pa., 1950-52, mgr. reactor theory sect., 1952-69; vis. prof. Mass. Inst. Tech., 1968-69; prof., 1969—. Recipient E.O. Lawrence award, 1967. Fellow Am. Nuclear Soc. (dir.); mem. Am. Phys. Soc. Home: 8 Whittier Pl Boston MA 02114 Office: Mass Inst Tech Cambridge MA 02139

HENRY, ANTHONY RAY, community organizer; b. Houston, Aug. 14, 1938; s. Lawrence G. and Autry B. (Thomas) H.; B.A., U. Tex. at Austin, 1960; M.Ed., Springfield Coll., 1961. Community devel. vol. Am. Friends Service Com., Tanzania, East Africa, 1961-63; dir. preadolescent enrichment program Am. Friends Service Com., Chgo., 1963-66, dir. housing program, Chgo., 1966-69, dir. nationwide tenants rights program, Washington, 1969; dir. Nat. Tenants Orgn., Washington, 1969-71, Nat. Tenants Information Services, Washington, 1971—. Dir. Nat. Housing Conf., 1971, Rural Housing Coalition, 1971. Home: 1234 Massachusetts Av NW Washington DC 20005 Office: 425 13th St NW Washington DC 20004

HENRY, CARL FERDINAND HOWARD, clergyman, theologian; b. N.Y.C., Jan. 22, 1913; s. Karl F. and Johanna (Vaethroeder) H.; B.A., Wheaton (Ill.) Coll., 1938, M.A., 1940; B.D., No. Bapt. Theol. Sem., 1941, Th.D., 1942; Ph.D., Boston U., 1949; postgrad. Loyola U., 1941, Ind. U., 1944, New Coll., Edinburgh, 1953; Litt. D., Seattle-Pacific Coll., 1963, Wheaton Coll., 1968; m. Helga Bender, Aug. 17, 1940; children—Paul Brentwood, Carol Jennifer. Ordained to ministry Bapt. Ch., 1941; asst. prof. theology No. Bapt. Theol. Sem., 1940-42, prof., 1942-47; acting dean Fuller Theol. Sem., 1947, prof., 1947-56, Payton lectr., 1963; editor Christianity Today, 1956-68, editor at large, 1968-70; vis. prof. theology Wheaton Coll., Gordon Div. Sch.; vis. prof. summer sch., Eastern Bapt. Theol. Sem., 1969-70, prof.-at-large, 1970—; faculty mem. flying seminar to Europe and Nr. East, Winona Lake Sch. Theology, 1952; radio commentator daily program Let the Chips Fall, KOPL, Los Angeles, 1952-53; chmn. World Congress on Evangelism, Berlin, 1966, Consultation Scholars, Washington, 1967, Jerusalem Conf. Bibl. Prophecy, Israel, 1971. Mem. alumni council Boston U.; v.p. Inst. Advanced Christian Studies; co- chmn. com. Rose Bowl Easter Sunrise Service, 1950. Recipient Freedoms Found. award, 1954, 66. Mem. Soc. Sci. Study Religion, A.A.A.S., Am. Soc. Christian Ethics, Am. Acad. Religion, Am., Evang. (pres. 1969-70) theol. socs., Conf. Faith and History, Nat. Assn. Evangs. (bd. adminstrn.), Am. Philos. Assn., Am. Soc. Ch. History, Mind Assn., Soc. Oriental Research, Soc. Bibl. Lit. Club: Cosmos (Washington). Author: A Doorway to Heaven, 1941; Successful Church Publicity, 1942; Remaking the Modern Mind, 1948; The Uneasy Conscience of Modern Fundamentalism, 1948; Giving a Reason for Our Hope, 1949; The Protestant Dilemma, 1949; Notes on the Doctrine of God, 1949; Fifty Years of Protestant Theology, 1950; The Drift of Western Thought, 1951; Personal Idealism and Strong's Theology, 1951; Glimpses of a Sacred Land, 1953; Christian Personal Ethics, 1957; Contemporary Evangelical Thought (editor), 1957; Evangelical Responsibility in Contemporary Theology, 1957; Revelation and the Bible (editor), 1959; The Biblical Expositor (editor), 1960; Baker's Dictionary of Theology (editor), 1964; Aspects of Christian Social Ethics, 1964; Christian Faith and Modern Theology (editor), 1964; Frontiers in Modern Theology, 1966; The God Who Shows Himself, 1966; Jesus of Nazareth: Saviour and Lord (editor), 1966; Evangelicals at the Brink of Crisis, 1967; Faith at the Frontiers, 1969; Fundamentals of the Faith (editor), 1969; A Plea for Evangelical Demonstration, 1971. Home: 3824 N 37th St Arlington VA 22207

HENRY, CHAPIN, investment exec.; b. Seattle, Aug. 6, 1911; s. Langdon Chapin and Genevieve (Relfe) H.; student U. Wash., 1930-32; m. Elizabeth Calvert, July 27, 1933; children—Ann E. (Mrs. Milton H. Bohart), Barbara C. (Mrs. G. Philip Koon), Langdon Chapin III. With H.C. Henry Investment Co., 1932—, sec., 1946—, v.p., dir., 1937-62, pres., 1962—; dir. Safeco Ins. Cos., Simpson Timber Co., Greater Seattle, Inc., Seattle 1st Nat. Bank. Trustee N.W. Meml. Hosp. Served as lt. comdr. USNR, 1942-45. Mem. U. Wash. Alumni Assn., C. of C., Psi Upsilon. Elk. Clubs: Nat. Retriever Field Trial, Wash. Athletic, Seattle Golf, University (Seattle). Home: The Highlands Seattle WA 98177 Office 411 Seneca St Seattle WA 98101

HENRY, CHARLES JOSEPH, Jr., R.R. exec.; b. Phila., Apr. 11, 1919; s. Charles Joseph and Kathryn (McDevitt) H.; A.B., U. Pa., 1943, LL.B., 1949; m. Anna T. Stuart. Admitted to Md. bar, 1949; cost accountant Gen. Electric Co., 1940-42; atty. B. & O. R.R., Balt., 1949-52, asst. gen. atty., 1952-54, asst. gen. solicitor, 1954-56, asst. gen. counsel, 1956-60, gen. atty., 1960- 61, asst. v.p. traffic, 1961-62, v.p. marketing, 1962-66, v.p. comml. devel., 1966—; v.p. comml. devel. C. & O. Ry. Co., 1966—. Served to capt. USAAF, 1942-46, to maj. USAF, 1951-52. Mem. Nat. Freight Traffic Assn., Am. Bar Assn., Bar Assn. of Balt., Assn. ICC Practitioners. Clubs: Merchants, Center (Balt.). Home: 222 Worthmont Rd Baltimore MD 21228 Office: 2 N Charles St Baltimore MD 21201

HENRY, CHARLES R., fabricated metal products co. exec.; b. Morgantown, W.Va., May 29, 1925; s. C. Ray and Willa May (Furman) H.; B.S. in Mech. Engring., W.Va. U., 1950; m. Helen M. Sisler, June 4, 1948; children—Judy, Debbie. Design engr. Dravo Corp., 1951-53; sales mgr. Columbia Gas Systems, 1953-59; exec. v.p. The Coleman Co., Wichita, Kan., 1959—, also dir., mem. exec. com. Bd. dirs. Wichita YMCA; bd. dirs. Goodwill Industries; bd. dirs. Nat. Conf. Christians & Jews. Served with USNR, 1942-46. Mem. Mobile Home Mfg. Assn., Am. Soc. Heating and Air Conditioning Engrs., Wichita C. of C. Rotarian. Home: 1106 Gretchen Lane Wichita KS 67206 Office: 250 N St Francis St Wichita KS

HENRY, DAVID DODDS, educator; b. E. McKeesport, Pa., Oct. 21, 1905; s. Ferdinand William and Myrtle May (Byerly) H., A.B., Pa. State U., 1926, A.M., 1927, Ph.D., 1931; LL.D., U. Toledo, 1946, U. Louisville, 1951, U. Miami, 1957, Millikin U., 1957, U. R.I., 1958, Knox Coll., 1959, Butler U., 1962; H.H.D., Wayne State U., 1953; Litt. D., Albion Coll., 1954; D.Sc. in Ed., U. Akron, 1956; L.H.D., N.Y. U., 1955, Rockford Coll., 1957, So. Ill. U., 1969, Loyola U., 1970; Pd.D., Bradley U., 1957; Litt. D., U. Pitts., 1961, Monmouth Coll., 1962; LL.D., Roosevelt U., 1963, U. Notre Dame, 1964, Eastern Mich. U., 1966, Ind. Central, 1968, Shimer Coll., 1968, St. Louis U., 1969; Litt.D., DePaul U. Chgo., 1963, Lincoln Coll., 1963; D.C.L., U. Sierra Leone, 1969; m. Sara E. Koeper, May 6, 1927; 1 son, David Byerly. Instr. English, Pa. State Coll., 1925-26; supr. liberal arts extension, 1926-28, instr. English lit., 1928- 29; prof. English, head dept. Battle Creek (Mich.) Coll., 1929- 33, dean of men, 1930-31, dir. Sch. Liberal Arts, 1931-33; asst. supt. pub. instrn. Mich., 1933-35; prof. English, Wayne U., Detroit, 1935-52, asst. to exec. v.p., 1936-39, exec. v.p. 1939-45, pres., 1945- 52; exec. vice chancellor N.Y.U., 1952-55; pres. U. Ill., 1955-71, pres. emeritus, distinguished prof. higher edn., 1971—. Chmn. Am. Council Edn., 1960-61; mem. electoral coll. Hall Fame for Great Americans; pres. Nat. Assn. State Univs. and Land- Grant Colls., 1964-65, Assn. of Am. Univs., 1967-69, Nat. Commn. Accrediting, 1956-58; vice chmn. Pres's Com. Edn. Beyond High Sch., 1956-57; mem. Carnegie Commn. Ednl. TV; trustee Carnegie Found. Advancement Teaching, 1960-71, chmn., 1969-70; pres. Assn. Urban Univs., 1945-46. Mem. Phi Beta Kappa, Alpha Omega Alpha, Kappa Delta Pi, Alpha Kappa Psi, Scabbard and Blade, Omicron Delta Kappa, Delta Sigma Rho, Pi Delta Epsilon, Phi Kappa Phi, Phi Delta Kappa, Phi Kappa Psi. Clubs: University (N.Y.C. and Chicago); Mid-Am. (hon.) (Chgo.); Rotary. Contbr. to prof. jours. Home: 311 W University Av Champaign IL 61820

HENRY, DAVID HOWE II, polit. ofcl.; b. Geneva, N.Y., May 19, 1918; s. David Max and Dorothy (Buley) H.; student Hobart Coll., 1935-37, Sorbonne, 1937-38; A.B., Columbia, 1939, student Russian Inst., 1948-49; student Harvard, 1944- 45, Nat. War Coll., 1957-58; m. Margaret Beard, Nov. 16, 1946; children— David Beard, Peter York, Michael Max, Susan. Ins. agt., 1939-41; mem. fgn. service Dept. State, 1941-71, assigned Montreal, 1941-42, Beirut, 1942-44, Washington, 1944-45, 48-52, 57-66, 70, Moscow, 1945, 46-48, 52-54, Vladivostok, 1945-46, Berlin, 1955-57; acting dir. Office Research and Intelligence Sino-Soviet bloc, 1958-59; faculty Nat. War Coll., 1959-61; dep. dir. Office Soviet Affairs, 1961-64; dir. Office Soviet Union Affairs, 1964-65; mem. Policy Planning Council, 1965-66; dep. chief of mission Am. embassy, Reykjavik, Iceland, 1966-69; information systems specialist, 1970; polit. and security council affairs UN, N.Y.C., 1971—. Mem. Kappa Alpha. Presbyn. Rotarian. Home: 430 E 57th St New York City NY 10022 Office: UN New York City NY 10017

HENRY, DONALD LEE, banker; b. Evansville, Ind., Jan. 25, 1918; s. Robert D. and Mary A. (Swope) H.; B.S., Purdue U., 1939, M.S., 1941, Ph.D., 1947; postgrad. Chgo., 1946; m. Mary Lou Hess, Dec. 24, 1941; children—Judith Ann, Don Richard. Agrl. economist Fed. Res. Bank St. Louis, 1947-54, asst. cashier Louisville br., 1954-56, cashier, 1957, mgr., 1957—; v.p. Fed. Res. Bank St. Louis, 1957-68, sr. v.p., 1969—. Pres. Old Ky. Home council Boy Scouts Am., mem. Ky. Agrl. Council. Served to capt. AUS, 1942-46. Mem. Am. Farm Econ. Assn., Louisville C. of C., Sigma Xi, Alpha Zeta. Rotarian. Home: 212 Dorchester Rd Louisville KY 40223 Office: Box 899 Louisville KY 40201

HENRY, DONALD WALLACE, banker; b. Bklyn., Feb. 1, 1917; s. John R. and Louise (Tschetter) H.; grad. Phillips Andover Acad., 1935; B.A., Yale, 1939, LL.B., 1942; m. Jean Vansinderen, Mar. 19, 1944; children—John R., Paul W., Charles W., Anne L. Admitted to Conn. bar, 1946; ppartner firm Gager, Henry & Narkis, Waterbury, 1946—; chmn. bd. Colonial Bank and Trust Co., Waterbury, 1967—; dir. Eastern Co., Risden Mfg. Co., Lewis Engring. Co., Greenhouse Co. Pres. Waterbury Hosp., Waterbury Found.; v.p. Westover Sch. Served to lt. USNR, 1942-46. Decorated Bronze Star, Purple Heart. Mem. Am., Conn. bar assns., Delta Kappa Epsilon. Clubs: Elihu (New Haven); Yale (N.Y.C.); Highfield (Conn.). Home: South St Middlebury CT 06762 Office: 193 Grand St Waterbury CT 06702

HENRY, EDWARD J., educator; B.A., St. Peter's Coll.; M.A., Fordham U.; Ph.D., N.Y.U. Prof., chmn. dept. modern langs. Seton Hall U., South Orange, N.J. Office: Seton Hall U South Orange NJ 07079*

HENRY, EDWARD LOCKWOOD, supermarket exec.; b. Fresno, Cal., Oct. 12, 1922; s. Fred F. and Alice (Lockwood) H.; B.A., U. Cal. at Los Angeles, 1947; m. Jane Post, Sept. 26, 1946; children—William L., Marilyn L. Dept. mgr. Sears, Roebuck & Co., 1948-52; office and credit mgr. Firestone Stores, Los Angeles, 1952; salesman H.J. Heinz, Los Angeles, 1952-53; sales Touche, Niven, Bailey & Smart, Los Angeles, 1953-55; account Supr. U.S. Borax, Los Angeles, 1955-56; office mgr. Nat. Centrifugal Casting, Burbank, Cal., 1957; controller Lok Products, Los Angeles, 1957; supr. Scovell, Wellington & Co., Los Angeles, 1957-60; v.p. Arden-Mayfair, Los Angeles, 1960—. Served as capt. M.P., Aus, 1943-46. Mem. Am. Inst. C.P.A.'s, Cal. Soc. C.P.A.'s, U. Cal. at Los Angeles Alumni Assn., Chi Phi. Home: 531 Woodbury Rd Glendale CA 91206 Office: 2500 S Garfield Av Commerce CA 90022

HENRY, GEORGE DWIGHT, fgn. service officer; b. Reading, Pa., June 22, 1920; s. George Dwight and Emma Marie (Schrack) H.; A.B., Albright Coll., 1941; M.F.A., Yale, 1948; 1 dau. Carol Joyce; m. Constance Chaconas, Nov. 29, 1960. Joined U.S. fgn. service 1948; information specialist U.S. Govt., N.Y.C., 1948-50; fgn. service officer USIA, 1953-68, Yugoslavia, 1959-61, Israel, 1961-64, fgn. service information officer, New Delhi and Madras, India, 1968-71, Dacca, East Pakistan, 1971—. Served to inf., capt. AUS, 1942-46. Decorated Bronze Star, Purple Heart. Recipient Meritorious Service award USIA, 1959. Home: 809 Kenhorst Blvd Reading PA 19602 Office: Dacca Dept of State Washington DC 20521

HENRY, H. NEELY, utility exec.; b. Guntersville, Ala., Nov. 5, 1903; s. Jo L. and Ethyl (Neely) H.; B.S., Va. Mil. Inst., 1924; m. Virginia Dilworth, Dec. 21, 1925; children—Lois (Mrs. Franc P. White, Jr.), H. Neely, Margaret Ann. With Ala. Power Co., Birmingham, 1924—, successively office engr., dist. supt., dist. mgr., mgr. indsl. devel., v.p., asst. to gen. mgr., v.p. employee relations, sr. exec. v.p., dir., 1955—; dir. So. Electric Generating Co. Adv. bd. St. Vincents Hosp. Dir. Asso. Industries Ala. Gen. chmn. Second United Appeal Jefferson County, 1957; dir. Jr. Achievement Jefferson County; dir. Birmingham area chpt. A.R.C., chmn.; 1965-67. Served to lt. col., 7th Army Corps, AUS. Mem. Ala. Mining Inst. (gov.), Birmingham area C. of C. (past pres.), Am. Ordnance Assn., Ala. Hist. Assn., Newcomen Soc. in N.Am. Methodist. Mason (Shriner), Rotarian. Clubs: Birmingham Country, Downtown, The Club, Relay House. Home: 3266 E Briarcliff Rd Mountain Brook Birmingham AL 35223 Office 600 N 18th St Birmingham AL 35203

HENRY, HERMAN LUTHER, Jr., educator; b. Arcadia, La., Mar. 6, 1918; s. Herman Luther and Louannie (Rogers) H.; B.S. in Mech. and Elec. Engring., La. Poly. Inst., 1940; M.S. in Mech. Engring., Ill. Inst. Tech., 1946; m. Eva Grissom, Dec. 23, 1941; children—Krista Ann, David Michael. Instr. tech. drawing Ill. Inst. Tech., 1942-46; faculty La. Poly. Inst., 1946-51, 55—, prof., head indsl. engring. dept., 1964—; project engr. Dow Chem. Co., 1951-55. Registered profl engr., La. Mem. Am. Inst. Indsl. Engrs., Nat. Soc. Profl. Engrs. Home; 910 Dogwood St Ruston LA 71270

HENRY, HUGH FORT, physicist, educator; b. Emory, Va., Apr. 25, 1916; s. Howell Meadors and Addie Amanda (Fort) H.; B.A., B.S., Emory and Henry Coll., 1936; M.S. in Physics, U. Va., 1938, Ph.D., 1940; m. Emmaline Rust, Aug. 22, 1942; children—Hugh Littell, Margaret Fort, Howell George, Harold William. Head dept. physics and math. Coll. of Ozarks, Clarksville, Ark., 1940-41; asso. prof. physics U. Ga., 1941-49; head safety fire and radiation control dept. Oak Ridge gaseous diffusion plant Union Carbide Nuclear Co., 1949-61; prof. physics, chmn. dept. DePauw U., Green- castle; Ind.; 1961—. Pres. bd. dirs. Central States Univs., 1967. Vice chmn. com. N-13, radiation protection U.S.A. Standards Inst., 1956—, chmn. subcom. N-7.3, 1956—, mem. subcoms. N-7.2 and N-6.8, 1956—; organizer dirs. course nuclear safety fissionable materials user AEC, 1957, 59; U.S. del. tech. com. 85 Internat. Standards Orgn., 1958, 60, 65., Recipient Silver Beaver award Boy Scouts Am. Mem. Am. Phys. Soc. (treas. Southeastern sect. 1947-50), Am. Assn. Physics Tchrs., Am. Nuclear Soc., Health Physics Soc., Optical Soc. Am., A.A.A.S., Sigma Xi. Elk, Rotarian (pres. 1967-68). Author: Fundamentals of Radiation Protection, 1969; Author, editor tech. manuals. Home: 404 Linwood Dr Greencastle IN 46135

HENRY, JAMES BUCHANAN, lawyer; b. Balt., July 25, 1919; s. James B. and Mary (Mc Claughry) H.; B.S. summa cum laude, U. Ariz., 1939; LL.B. cum laude, Harvard, 1948; m. Eleanor C. Nixon, Dec. 22, 1945; children—James B., Mary C., Elizabeth E. Admitted to N.Y. bar, 1949; asso. Cahill, Gordon, Sonnett, Reindel & Ohl, N.Y.C., 1948-61; mem. firm Kaye, Scholer, Fierman, Hays & Handler, N.Y.C., 1962-67; v.p., gen. counsel, sec. Am. Electric Power Service Corp., N.Y.C., 1968—, also dir. and sec. affiliates. Spl. asst. atty. gen. N.Y., 1952-54. Served with C.E., AUS, 1941-46. Mem. Am. Bar Assn., Assn. Bar City N.Y., Harvard Law Sch. Assn., Phi Beta Kappa, Phi Kappa Phi, Phi Delta Phi, Phi Lambda Upsilon. Home: 86 Prospect Av Montclair NJ 07042 Office: 2 Broadway New York City NY 10004

HENRY, JAMES J., naval architect; grad. Webb Inst. Naval Architecture, 1935. Formerly with U.S. Bur. Marine Insp. and Navigation, U.S. Maritime Commn., Consol. Steel Corp.; pres. J.J. Henry Co., Inc., N.Y.C., 1946—. Mem. tech. coms. USCG, also Am. Bur. Shipping. Trustee Webb Inst. Naval Architecture. Mem. Soc. Naval Architects and Marine Engrs. (pres. 1968- 70; Capt. Joseph H. Linnard prize 1966, vice adm. Jerry Land medal 1967). Address: 21 West St New York City NY*

HENRY, JOHN A., ins. co. exec., lawyer; b. Devils Lake, N.D., Mar. 23, 1904; s. John F. and Martha (Jossman) H.; student Amherst Coll., Union U.; m. Elayne Jenni. Admitted to N.Y. bar, 1931, Ill. bar, 1945; with Utica Mut. Ins. Co., 1938-44; pres., dir. Continental Casualty Co., 1964-69, Transp. Ins. Co., Can. Health & Accident Ins. Co.; v.p., dir. CNA Financial Corp.; ins. operations officer, dir. Am. Casualty Co., Nat. Fire Ins. Co., Hartford, Transcontinental Ins. Co., Valley Forge Ins. Co.; dir. Continental Assurance Co., Ill. State Bank Chgo., CNA Investor Services, Inc. chmn., Gov.'s Ins. Adv. Bd., 1968-69. Bd. dirs. Ill. Ins. Information Service, pres. 1966-67; bd. dirs. Internat. Coll. Surgeons' Hall of Fame. Mem. Am., N.Y., Ill., Chgo. bar assns., Assn. Life Ins. Counsel, Internat. Assn. Ins. Counsel. Clubs: Chicago Athletic Assn., Chicago, Sunset Ridge Country, Bob O'Link Golf. Office: 301 S Michigan Av Chicago IL 60604

HENRY, JOHN BAILEY, Jr., air force officer; b. Christine, Tex., July 15, 1916; s. John Bailey and Esther Belle (Martin) H.; student S.W. Tex. State Coll., 1934-35, Southwestern U., Georgetown, Tex., 1936-37, N. Tex. Agrl. Coll., 1937-38; m. Maxine Harriet Schoeffler, Apr. 12, 1942; children—Elizabeth Anne, John Bailey III. Air cadet tng., 1938-39; commd. 2d lt. USAAF, 1939, advanced through grades to maj. gen. USAF, 1963; assigned C.Z., 1939-43; comdr. 339th Fighter Group, Cal. and ETO, 1943-45, several Air Transp. Command bases, 1945-47; assigned Armed Forces Staff Coll., 1947-48; comdr. 28th Bomb Group, SAC, 1948-49; successively dep. chief staff personnel, dep. chief staff operations 15th Air Force, March AFB, Cal., 1949-52; wing comdr. 22d Bomb Wing, SAC, 1952-54; assigned Air War Coll., 1954-55; successively chief promotions and separations div., dir. mil. personnel and exec., dep. chief staff personnel Hdqrs. USAF, 1955-59; successively dir. secretariat, asst. chief staff plans, asst. chief staff operations Hdqrs. Pacific Air Forces, Hickam AFB, Hawaii, 1959-63; dep. the insp. gen. USAF, Hdqrs. USAF, 1963-66, dir., sec. of air force personnel council, 1966-67; dir. Inter-Am. Def. Coll., Ft. McNair, 1967-70. Decorated Legion of Merit with 2 oak leaf clusters, D.F.C., Air medal with seven oak leaf clusters, numerous area and campaign ribbons; Croix de Guerre with palm (France). Mem. Air Force Assn. Methodist. Mason. Home: 5152 N 38th St Arlington VA 22207

HENRY, JOHN BERNARD, pathologist, educator; b. Elmira, N.Y., Apr. 26, 1928; A.B., Cornell U., 1951; M.D., U. Rochester, 1955; m. Georgette Boughton, June 10, 1953; children—Maureen Anne, Julie Patricia, William Bernard, Paul Bernard, John Bernard, Thomas David. Intern ward med. service Barnes Hosp., St. Louis, 1955-56; asst. resident pathology Presbyn. Hosp., N.Y.C., 1955-56; resident pathology New Eng. Deaconess Hosp., Boston, 1956-58; trainee Nat. Cancer Inst., NIH, 1958-60; clin. pathologist, chmn. clin. lab. com. Teaching Hosp. and Clinic, U. Fla., 1958-60; asst. medicine Washington U. Sch. Medicine, St. Louis, 1955-56; asst. pathology, then instr. pathology Columbia Coll. Phys. and Surg., 1955-58; teaching fellow pathology Harvard Med. Sch., 1959-60; asst. prof., then asso. prof. pathology U. Fla. Coll. Medicine, 1960-64; prof. pathology Coll. Medicine, State U. N.Y., Upstate, Syracuse, 1964—, dir. clin. pathology. Served with U.S. Navy, 1946-48, as lt. comdr. USNR, 1946-66. Diplomate Am. Bd. Pathology. Fellow Coll. Am. Pathologist, Am. Soc. Clin. Pathologists; mem. Am. Acad. Clin. Toxicology, A.A.A.S., Am. Assn. Blood Banks, Am. Assn. Clin. Chemists, Am. Assn. History Medicine, Am. Assn. Med. Writers, Am. Assn. Pathologists and Bacteriologists, Am. Chem. Soc., Am. Mgmt. Assn., A.M.A., Am. Soc. Exptl. Pathology, Assn. Am. Med. Colls., Blood Banks Assn. N.Y. State, Central N.Y. Soc. Pathologists, Internat. Acad. Pathology, Med. Soc. State N.Y., N.Y. Assn. Pub. Health Labs., N.Y. State Soc. Pathology, Onondaga County Med. Soc., Soc. Advanced Med. Systems, Am. Assn. Allied Health Professions, Alpha Omega Alpha. Author numerous articles in field. Address: 750 E Adams St Syracuse NY 13210

HENRY, JOHN CASE, retired journalist; b. Wickford, R.I., Nov. 4, 1905; s. William J. and Mariette (Porter) H.; Ph.D., Brown U., 1927; m. Elizabeth Baltz, Aug. 2, 1958; children—Alan Pemberton, Caroline Hazard. With Providence Jour., 1927- 34, Washington corr., 1933-34; with Evening Star, Washington, 1934 -71. Sunday editor, 1946-53, editorial writer, 1953-63, bus. news editor, 1963-71. Served from capt. to col., USAAF, 1942-46. Decorated Bronze Star. Mem. Overseas Writers, White House Corr. Assn. (past pres.), Soc. Am. Bus. Writers (past pres.). Clubs: Nat. Press, Nat. Aviation, Internat. (Washington); Columbia Country (Chevy Chase, Md.); City Tavern Assn. (Georgetown, D.C.). Home: 4000 Cathedral Av Rd NW Washington DC 20016

HENRY, JOHN F., banker; b. Seattle, 1908. Sr. v.p. comml. loan dept. Pacific Nat. Bank Wash. Home: 9312 Vineyard Crest Bellevue WA 98004 Office: PO Box 160 Seattle WA 98111*

HENRY, JOHN ROBERT, Jr., lawyer; b. Bklyn., Oct. 30, 1913; s. John Robertson and Louise Mildred (TSchetter) H.; student Andover; B.A., Yale, 1935, LL.B., 1938; m. Evelyn Earle, Mar. 29, 1947; children—Peter Robert, Susan Earle, Douglas Dyer. Admitted to N.Y. bar, 1939; asso. Sherman & Sterling & Wright, 1938-46; atty. Am. Can Co., N.Y.C., 1946-5O, gen. atty., 195O-55, sec., gen. counsel, 1955—, also v. p. Served as comdr. USNR, 1941-45. Decorated Bronze Star medal. Mem. Assn. Bar City N.Y., Alpha Delta Phi, Elihu. Republican. Methodist. Clubs: Apawamis, Manursing Island (Rye); Yale (N.Y.C.). Home: 51 Grace Church St Rye NY 10580 Office: 100 Park Av New York City NY 10017

HENRY, JOHN WILLIAM, govt. ofcl.; b. Douglas, Ariz., June 27, 1913; s. William Robert and Cora (Grey) H.; B.A., U. Ariz., 1936; m. Edith Nell Jones, May 7, 1940; children—Alice (Mrs. Herman Van Lunen), Helen (Mrs. Michael William Ueltzen). With State Dept., 1936—; clk., Managua, Nicaragua, 1936-39, Lisbon, Portugal, 1939-44; prin. officer, Mombasa, 1945-47; econ. officer, Toronto, Can., 1947-51, Bogota, Colombia, 1951-53; cons. officer, Athens, Greece, 1954-56; assigned Salzburg, Austria, 1956-57, Liverpool, Eng., 1957-59; dep. exchange program officer State Dept., 1959, supr. exchange program, 1959-61, supr. Edn.-Cultural Exchange Office, 1961-65; consul, Port-of-Spain, Trinidad, 1965-68; prin. officer, Vera Cruze, Mexico, 1968-71, with Bd. Examiners, 1971; 1st sec., consul, Djakarta, Indonesia, 1971—. Recipient Merit Service award State Dept., 1964. Home: 1060 Thomas Jefferson St NW Washington DC 20007 Office: American Embassy Djakarta Indonesia

HENRY, JOSEPH LOUIS, univ. dean; b. New Orleans, May 2, 1924; s. Varice S. and Mabel (Mansion) H.; D.D.S., Howard U., 1946; B.S., Xavier U., 1948; M.S., Ill. U., 1949, Ph.D., 1951; m. Dorothy L. Whittle, July 28, 1954; children—Joseph Louis, Ronald Maurice, Joan Alison, Leilani Cecile (Mrs. P. Smith), Peter Donald. Instr. oral medicine Coll. Dentistry, Howard U., Washington, 1946-48, asso. prof. oral medicine, 1951-53, supt. clinics, 1953-65, prof. oral medicine, 1958-66, dir. clinics, 1965-66, dean, 1966- -; research fellow U. Ill., extern U. Ill. Research and Ednl. Hosp., Chgo., 1948-51; cons. Freedmen's Hosp., 1951—, Tuskegee VA Hosp., 1951—, Crownsville (Md.) State Hosp., 1960—, Bakers Dozen Youth Center, Project Headstart, Peace Corps, Mt. Altoe Vets. Hosp.; cons. to bd. govs. D.C. Gen. Hosp., 197O—. Mem. White House Conf. Internat. Relations, 1965; cons. White House Conf. Employment Handicapped, 1967; sponsor Boys Town, 1955—; life mem. N.A.A.C.P.; sponsor Urban League, 1953—, program dir. YMCA, 1950-51; mem. St. Gabriel's P.T.A., 196O—. Trustee Washington sect. Am. Cancer Soc. Served to 2d lt. ASTP, 1942-43. Recipient Student Body and Student Council Faculty award, 1964; Chi Delta Mu Achievement award, 1967; Achievement award Howard U. Dental Coll., 1967; Wisdom award Honor, 197O; Inter-Alumni award United Negro Coll. Fund, 197O; Pub. Service award Urban League, 197O. Diplomate Am. Bd. Oral Medicine. Fellow A.A.A.S., Am. Coll. Dentists; mem. Nat. (Achievement award 1967), Am. dental assns., Robert T. Freeman, D.C., Maimonides dental socs., Internat. Assn. Dental Research, Washington Acad. Sci., N.Y. Acad. Scis.; Am. Assn. Tchrs. Practice Adminstrn. (pres., v.p., mem. exec. com.), Greater Washington Periodontal Soc. (pres. 197O), Am. Acad. Periodontology, Am. Assn. U. Profs., Am. Assn. Dental Schs., Acad. Practice Adminstrn., Acad. History of Dentistry, Am. Coll. Health Orgn., Howard U., U. Ill., Xavier U. alumni clubs, Sigma Xi, Alpha Eta Epsilon, Alpha Kappa Mu, Chi Delta Mu, Chi Lambda Kappa, Omicron Kappa Upsilon. Contbr. profl. jours. Home: 8900 Woodland Dr Silver Spring MD 20910 Office: 600 W St NW Washington DC 20001

HENRY, LAWRENCE MICHAEL, lawyer; b. Denver; Oct. 1, 1915; s. Michael J. and Rose (Werley) H.; student Regis Coll., Denver, 1933-36; LL.B., Denver U., 1939; m. Mary Jane Kelly, Oct. 27, 1945; children—Michael, Kevin, Christine, Kelly, Mary. Admitted to Colo. bar, 1939, since practiced in Denver; mem. firm Collins, Henry & Dolan; U.S. atty., Dist. Colo., 1961-69; mem. law firm Zall, Zall & Henry, 1969—. Pres. Denver Bd. of Adjustment Zoning. Rep. to Colo. Legislature, 1940-42, 46-48, senator, 1948-52; Democratic county chmn., Denver, 195O-6O; mem. Dem. Nat. Com. from Colo., 196O-61. Pres. Wozee Center for Unfortunates. Served from pvt. to maj., C.W.S., AUS, 1942-45. Decorated Order Brit. Empire. Mem. Am., Fed. (pres. Colo. 1964-65), Colo. bar assns., Denver Law Sch. Alumni Assn. (pres. 1964-65), Am, Judicature Soc. Home: 251 Magnolia St Denver CO 80220

HENRY, LEONARD DANIEL, corp. exec.; b. Topton, Pa., June 21, 1908; s. Jonas O. and Ida L. (Sefing) H.; B.S., U.S. Mil. Acad., 1931; grad. Command and Gen. Staff Sch., 1944, Air Force Officers Sch., 1945; m. Marjorie E. Martz, June 15, 1931 (dec. 1947); 1 son, Frank M.; m. 2d, Dorothy Clemens, Aug. 21, 1946 (dec. 1969); m. 3d, Elizabeth Gibson Bryan; June 25, 1970. Operator airline between Buffalo and Newark, 1931-33; asst. to pres. Martz Bus Lines & White Transit Co., Wilkes- Barre, Pa., 1933-36; supr. ICC, 1936-42, 46-51; founder Henry Assos., Inc., bus. mgmt. and sales cons., N.Y.C., 1951—; exec. asst. to pres. Avco Corp.; dir., mem. exec. com. Baldwin-Lima-Hamilton Corp., 1963-67; mem. tech. adv. bd. Aerojet-Gen. Corp., 1963-67 Trustee Seaman's Ch. Inst.; Pres. Marie Heye Clemens Fund. Served to lt. col. AUS, 1942-46; lt. col. USAF Res. Clubs: Links, Twenty Nine, Maidstone, Nat. Golf Links (N.Y.C.); Pine Valley Country (Clementon, N.J.) Burning Tree (Bethesda, Md.); Gulf Stream Golf, Country of Fla. (Delray Beach, Fla.). Home: 19E 72d St New York City NY 10017 10021 Office: 750 3d Av New York City NY 10017

HENRY, LESLIE, lawyer; b. Toledo, June 19, 1904; s. Herbert Leslie and Bertha (Yorkey) H.; A.B., U. Mich., 1926, J.D., 1928; m. Flora-Belle Bolin, Aug. 10, 1935; children—Herbert (dec.), Roberta (Mrs. James H. Raeder). Admitted to Ohio bar, 1928; asso. firm Fuller, Seney, Henry & Hodge, and predecessors, Toledo, 1928-37, partner, 1937—. Mem. Am. (council pub. utility sect. 1962-65), Ohio, Toledo bar assns. Club: Toledo. Home: 3317 W Bancroft St Toledo OH 43606 Office: 405 Madison Av Toledo OH 43604

HENRY, MARGUERITE, author; b. Milw.; d. Louis and Anna (Kaurup) Breithaupt; m. Sidney Crocker Henry. Author: Auno and Tauno, 1940; Dilly Dally Sally, 1940; Eight Pictured Geographies (Mexico, Canada, Alaska, Brazil, Argentina, Chile, West Indies, Panama), 1941; Geraldine Belinda, 1942; Birds at Home, 1942; Their First Igloo (with Barbara True), 1943; A Boy and A Dog, 1944; Justin Morgan Had a Horse, 1945, rev. edit., 1954; Robert Fulton, Boy Craftsman, 1945; The Little Fellow, 1945; Eight Pictured Geographies (Australia, New Zealand, Bahama Islands, Bermuda, Brit., Honduras, Dominican Republic, Hawaii, Virgin Islands), 1946; Benjamin West and His Cat Grimalkin, 1947; Always Reddy, 1947; Misty of Chincoteague, 1947; King of the Wind (John Newbery award), 1948; Little or Nothing from Nottingham, 1949; Sea Star: Orphan of Chincoteague, 1949; Born to Trot, 1950; Album of Horses, 1951; Portfolio of Horses, 1952; Brighty of the Grand Canyon, 1953 (William Allen White award 1956); Wagging Tails, 1955; Cinnabar, the One O'clock Fox, 1956; Black Gold, 1957 (Sequoyah Children's Book award 1959), Muley- Ears, Nobody's Dog, 1959; Gaudenzia, Pride of the Palio (Clara Ingram Judson award Soc. Midland Authors 1961), 1960; Misty (film), 1961; Five O'Clock Charlie, 1962; All About Horses, 1962, rev. edit., 1967; Stormy, Misty's Foal, 1963; White Stallion of Lipizza, 1964; Mustang, Wild Spirit of the West (Western Heritage award Nat. Cowboy Hall of Fame 1967) Sequoyah children's Book award 1970), 1966; Brighty (film), 1967; Dear Readers and Riders, 1969; Album of Dogs, 1970; (film) Justin Morgan Had a Horse, 1971. Home: Rancho Santa Fe CA 92067

HENRY, MATTHEW GEORGE, clergyman; b. Chapel Hill, N.C., Oct. 25, 1910; s. George Kenneth Grant and Mary Elizabeth (Harding) H.; A.B., U. N.C., 1931; B.D., Va. Theol. Sem., 1935, D.D., 1949; D.D., U. South, 1948; m. Cornelia Catharine Sprinkle, June 30, 1937; children—Anna Catharine, George K., Matthew G., Elizabeth H. Ordained to ministry Protestant Episcopal Ch., 1935; temporarily in charge St. Phillip's Ch., Durham, and St. Paul's Ch., Winston-Salem, N.C., 1935; in charge Christ Ch., Walnut Grove, St. Philip's Ch., Germanton, Messiah Ch., Mayodan, and Emmanual Ch., Stoneville, N.C., 1936; rector Calvary Prish, Tarboro, N. C., 1936-43, Christ Ch., Charlotte, N.C., 1943-48; bishop Diccese of Western N.C., Ashville, 1948—. Teaching fellow in chemistry U. N.C., 1931- 32. Trustee St. Augustine's Coll., Raleigh, N.C., Patterson Sch., U. South. Pres., N.C. Council Chs., 1965-67. Mem. Alpha Chi Sigma, Phi Beta Kappa, Delta Upsilon. Home: 9 Crowningway Dr Ashville NC 28804 Office: PO Box 368 Black Mountain NC 28711

HENRY, PHINEAS MCCRAY, lawyer; b. Des Moines, Apr. 9, 1889; s. George Farnum and Rose (Casady) H.; A.B., Harvard, 1909; LL.B., Drake U., 1911; m. Mildred Hippee, Jan. 14, 1914 (dec. 1944); children—Phineas McCray (dec.), Patrick; m. 2d, Caroline Keck Bridge, Aug. 24, 1945 (dec. 1949); m. 3d, Elizabeth R. O'Connor, Mar. 28, 1951. Admitted to Ia. bar, 1911, since practiced law in Des Moines. Served as 1st lt., F.A., AEF, 1918. Mem. Am., Ia., Polk County bar assns. (pres. 1949), Assn. Life Ins. Counsel (pres. 1943-45). Clubs: American Alpine (N.Y.C.); Des Moines. Home: 2337 Park Av Des Moines IA 50321 Office: Equitable Bldg Des Moines IA 50309

HENRY, RALPH SETH, investment co. exec.; b. East Palestine, O., Nov. 14, 1921; s. Cecil Charles and Mary Eleanor (Charlton) H.; A.B., Oberlin Coll., 1943; m. Hazel Marie Haddox, Dec. 17, 1944; children—Sandra Sue, Stephenie Jo, Jessica Ann, Ralph Seth. Salesman, Stone & Webster Securities Corp., Boston, 1945-54; v.p., dir. Wall St. Investing Corp., N.Y.C., 1955-57; partner John H.G. Pell, N.Y.C., also Wall St. Planning Corp., N.Y.C., 1956-57; chmn. bd. Trust Mgmt. Corp.; pres., dir. ITB Distbrs. Corp., Boston, 1957—, Devonshire St. Fund, Inc., Boston, 1960—, ITB Mgmt. Corp.; pres. Investment Trust Boston, Gov. Investment Co. Inst. Served with USNR, World War II; lt. comdr. Res. Mem. Newcomen Soc. N.Am. Clubs: Dedham Country and Polo; Laurel Brook. Home: Elm St Medfield MA 02052 Office: 104 Federal St Boston MA 02110

HENRY, RENE PAUL, oil co. exec.; b. Dallas, Mar. 9, 1917; s. R.P. and Grace (Cowden) H.; A.B., Baylor U., 1937; LL.B., U. Tex., 1940; Indsl. Adminstr. with distinction, Harvard, 1943; m. Ernestine Ryan, Sept. 1, 1939; children—Christine, Mary, Rene. Admitted to Tex. bar, 1940, Okla. bar, 1949; pvt. practice law, Dallas, 1940-42; atty. Office Chief Counsel, Bur. Internal Revenue, 1946-49; treas., tax counsel Mid-Continent Petroleum Corp., 1949-55; v.p finance DX Sunray Oil Co., 1955-64 also dir.; sr. v.p. finance and planning Sunray DX Oil Co., also dir., 1964- 69; v.p. financial planning and analysis Sun Oil Co., 1969—, also dir. Served to lt. USNR, 1943-46. Mem. Southwest Legal Found., Am., Okal., Tex. bar assns. Baptist. Home: 2401 Pennsylvania Av Philadelphia PA 19130 Office Sun Oil Co 1608 Walnut St Philadelphia PA 19103

HENRY, RICHARD WARFIELD, educator; b. N.Y.C., Nov. 23, 1932; s. Richard E. and Amanda (Sypret) H.; B.S., Union Coll., 1954; M.S., U. Ill., 1956, Ph.D., 1958; m. Marilynn Jean O'Connor, Sept. 4, 1954; children—Richard M., Jill L. Asst. prof. Union Coll., Schenectady, 1958-63, asso. prof., 1964-70; postdoctoral fellow Cal. Inst. Tech., 1963-64; vis. asso. prof. Mass. Inst. Tech., 1967-69; prof., chmn. dept. physics Bucknell U., Lewisburg, Pa., 1970—. NSF fellow, 1956-58, 63-64. Mem. Am. Phys. Soc. Author: Physical Electronics, 1962. Home: 135 S 15th St Lewisburg PA 17837

HENRY, RYDER, lawyer; b. East Quoque, N.Y., July 27, 1909; s. Clement S. and Adelaide R. (Jackson) H.; grad. cum laude Hotchkiss Sch., 1926; A.B., Princeton, 1930; J.D., Columbia, 1941; m. Frederica Poor, Oct. 18, 1955. With Bankers Trust Co., N.Y.C., 1930-37; admitted to N.Y. bar, 1941, since practiced in N.Y.C.; asso. White & Case, 1941-42, 46-52; partner Casey, Lane & Mittendorf, 1952—; partner Bache & Co., 1954-66. Pres., trustee Allen-Stevenson Sch. Served from 2d lt. to lt. col. USAAF, 1942- 46. Decorated Bronze Star. Mem. Am., N.Y. State, N.Y.C. bar assns., Huguenot Soc. (v.p.), Assn. Ex-Mems. Squadron A, Soc. Cin., St. Nicholas Soc., Phi Delta Phi. Episcopalian. Clubs: Union, Regency Whist, Harbor View (N.Y.C.); Piping Rock (Locust Valley, N.Y.); Dunes, Point Judith Country (Narragansett, R.I.). Home: 655 Park Av New York City NY 10021 Office: 26 Broadway New York City NY 10004

HENRY, THOMAS JACK, banker; b. Seaforth, Ont., Can., May 22, 1911; s. Clarence Norman and Hazel Jean (Roberts) H.; student McGill U., 1929-30; m. Frances Rae MacKinnon, Apr. 11, 1936; children—Carol (dec.), Thomas Jack. Came to U.S., 1941, naturalized, 1948. Account exec. N.W. Ayer & Son, Inc., 1935- 44, mgr. Detroit office, 1944-48, v.p., mgr. Detroit office, 1948-53; asst. gen. sales mgr. Mercury div. Ford Motor Co., 1953-57; v.p. McCann-Erickson, Inc., 1957-61, mgr. Detroit office, 1958-61, administrv. v.p., dir., mem. exec. policy com., N.Y.C., 1961-63; v.p. charge advt. and marketing services 1st Nat. City Bank, 1963—. Mem. Bank Marketing Assn., Phi Delta Theta. Club: Country (Detroit). Home: 333 E 46th St New York City NY 10017 Office: 399 Park Av New York City NY 10022

HENRY, WAIGHTS GIBBS, Jr., coll. pres., clergyman; b. Tuscaloosa, Ala., Feb. 13, 1910; s. Waights Gibbs and Mary Eliza (Davis) H.; student Emory U., 1927-28; A.B., Birmingham-So. Coll., 1930, D. D., 1947; B.D., Yale, 1934; m. Mamie Lark Brown, Feb. 16, 1935; children—George Madison, Waights Gibbs III, Mary Ann (Mrs. Ed P. Kirven). Asst. pastor Bunker Hill Congl. Ch., Waterbury, Conn., 1932-36; joined N. Ga. Conf. Meth. Ch., 1936; ordained to ministry Meth. Ch., 1938; pastor Hoschton, 1937-38, Clayton, 1939-42, Epworth Ch., Atlanta, 1943-44; exec. sec. Bd. Edn., No. Ga. Conf., 1945-48; pres. LaGrange (Ga.) Coll. 1948—; preacher Meth. Series of Protestant Hour (radio), 1960; Sunday columnist Columbus (Ga.) Ledger-Enquirer. Del. to Gen. Confs., 1948-56, Jurisdictional Confs., 1948-64. Chmn. bd. Protestant Radio and TV Center, 1970-71; chmn. Meth. Joint Radio Com., 1952-56, Gen. Bd. Edn., 1948-52; pres. Ga. Found. Ind. Colls., 1959-60, 70-71, Ga. Meth. Colls. Assn., 1950-62, Ga. Assn. Colls., 1959-60; mem. Ga. Higher Edn. Facilities Commn. Commr. Roosevelt Little White House. Dir. Pitts. Found. Meth. Found. Ret. Ministers; former bd. mgrs. Camp Glisson. Mem. Chattahoochee Valley Art Assn., Pi Kappa Alpha, Pi Gamma Mu. Mason, Rotarian. Club: Highland Country (LaGrange). Contbr. ch. publs.; Judge Miss America Pageant, 1952. Address: LaGrange Coll LaGrange GA 30240

HENRY, WALTER LESTER, Jr., educator, physician; b. Phila., Nov. 19, 1915; s. Walter Lester and Vera (Robinson) H.; A.B., Temple U., 1936; M.D., Howard U., 1941; student U. Pa. Grad. Sch. Medicine, 1948-49; m. Ada Clarice Palmer, Sept. 7, 1942. Intern Freedmen's Hosp., Washington, 1941-42, resident, 1949-51; fellow endocrinology Michael Reese Hosp., Chgo., 1951-53; mem. faculty Howard U., 1953—, prof. medicine, 1963—, chmn. dept., 1962—, William B. Allen prof. medicine, 1972—. Mem. Washington Med. Care and Hosp. Com. Faculty trustee Howard U., 1970—. Served to maj., M.C., AUS, 1942-46; Italy. Decorated Bronze Star with cluster; Markle scholar med. scis., 1953-58. Diplomate Am. Bd. Internal Medicine. Mem. Am., Nat. med. assns., A.C.P., Am. Fedn. Clin. Research, N.A.A.C.P., D.C. Med. Soc. (1st v.p.), Alpha Phi Alpha. Presbyn. (elder). Home: 1780 Redwood Terrace NW Washington DC 20012

HENRY, WILLIAM EARL, educator, psychologist; b. Holyoke, Mass., Nov. 14, 1917; s. Jesse Earl and Ellen (Elliott) H.; B.A., U. Utah, 1939; student U. Cal. at Berkeley, 1940; Ph.D., U. Chgo., 1944. Mem. faculty U. Chgo., 1944—, prof. psychology and human devel., 1958—, chmn. com. human devel., 1953- 58, 65-68; Ford distinguished vis. prof. Mich. State U., 1960-61, U. Wis., 1962; cons. Nat. Inst. Mental Health, 1964—; chmn. editorial com. Jossey-Bass Pubs., Inc., San Francisco, 1965—; editorial cons. Atherton Press, 1963-66. Fellow Am. Psychol. Assn., Gerontological Soc., Am. Sociol. Assn., Soc. Projective Techniques (pres. 1958-59); mem. Sigma Xi, Phi Kappa Phi. Author: The Analysis of Fantasy, 1956; (with E. Cumming) Growing Old, 1961; (with others) The Fifth Profession: Becoming a Psychotherapist, 1971. Cons. editor Excerpta Medica, 1962—, Bull. Suicidology, 1969—. Home: 1321 E 56th St Chicago IL 60637

HENRY, WILLIAM LAWRENCE, oil co. exec.; b. Worcester, Mass., Apr. 13, 1925; s. Lawrence William and Jane (O'Neil) H.; A.B., Harvard, 1950, M.B.A., 1952; part-time student U. Tulsa Law Sch., 1955-56; m. Mary Teresa Healy, Aug. 26, 1950; children—William Lawrence, Eileen Teresa, Michael Neil. With Gulf Oil Corp., 1952—, comptroller, 1964-66, v.p., 1966-69, sr. v.p., now exec. v.p. Bd. dirs. Allegheny Housing Rehab. Corp., 1968—; bd. dirs. Port Authority Allegheny County, 1968—, chmn., 1969. Trustee Assumption Coll., Worcester, 1967—, U. Pitts., 1966—. Served with USNR, 1943-46. Mem. Nat. Fgn. Trade Council (bd. dirs. 1966—), Pa. C. of C. (bd. dirs. 1962—), Am. Petroleum Inst., Mid-Continental Oil and Gas Assn. Clubs: Duquesne, South Hills Country, Harvard-Yale-Princeton (bd. dirs. 1967) (Pitts.); Pleasant Valley Country (Worcester); Harvard of Western Pa. (pres. 1962-63). Home: 140 Crestvue Manor Dr Pittsburgh PA 15228 Office: PO Box 1166 Pittsburgh PA 15230

HENRY, WILLIAM OSCAR EUGENE, lawyer; b. Ocala, Fla., Mar. 30, 1927; s. Jesse Dawson and Alice (Johnson) H.; B.S. in Journalism, U. Fla., 1950, J.D., 1952; m. Bobbie Jean Moorhead, May 9, 1952; children—Carol Ann, Robert Dawson, Jean Elizabeth. Newspaperman, Marion Pub. Co., Ocala, 1952-53; admitted to Fla. bar, 1952, since practiced in Bartow, Lakeland and Tampa; partner firm Holland & Knight, and predecessors, 1956—. Dir. Wellman-Power-Gas Inc., Moorhead Engring. Co., Rheinauers, Inc. Trustee Henry Found.; bd. dirs. U. Fla. Found. Served with USNR, 1945-46. Mem. Am., Internat. bar assns., Fla. Bar (chmn. tax sect. 1958-59), Am. Coll. Probate Counsel, U. Fla. Alumni Assn. (pres. 1968). Sigma Alpha Epsilon, Sigma Delta Chi, Phi Delta Phi, Blue Key. Methodist. Kiwanian. Clubs: Lakeland (Fla.) Yacht and Country; Peace River Country (Bartow). Home: 985 Helen Circle Bartow FL 33830 Office: 92 Lake Wire Dr Lakeland FL 33802 also 245 S Central Av Bartow FL 33830

HENRY, WILLIAM TAYLOR, food co. exec.; b. Imgram, Pa., Dec. 6, 1915; s. Eugene A. and Sarah (Azdell) H.; student Tex. Western Coll., 1936-40, Geneva Coll., Beaver Falls, Pa., 1957-58; m. Violet Smith, Nov. 25, 1937; children—William Taylor, Larry Smith, David Stewart. Traffic mgr. Curtiss-Wright Corp., Beaver, Pa., 1940-45; v.p., sec., dir. Treadwell Constrn. Co., Midland, Pa., 1945-64; sec., treas. Thorofare Markets, Inc., Pitts., 1964—. Sec.- treas. Brighton Twp. Municipal Authority, 1947-57. Mason (Shriner). Home: 25 Appennine Rd Pittsburgh PA 15239 Office: Meadowbrook Rd Murrysville PA 15668

HENRY, WYMAN L., aircraft mfg. co. exec.; b. 1906; student Okla. U.; married. With Commonwealth Utilities Corp., 1930-41; v.p. O.A. Sutton Corp., 1942-49; with White Motor Co., 1950-58; with Beech Aircraft Corp., Wichita, Kan., 1958—, v.p. marketing, dir., 1960—. Office: 9709 E Central Av Wichita KS 67206*

HENSARLING, PAUL REGINALD, educator; b. Madisonville, Tex., Oct. 21, 1910; s. James A. and Ollie (Runnels) H.; B.S., N. Tex. State U., Denton, 1933, M.S., 1940; Ed.D., U. Houston, 1957; postgrad. U. Mo., 1940, U. Colo., 1950, Columbia Tchrs. Coll., 1953; m. Mary Lou Spragins, Dec. 28, 1934; 1 dau., Paula (Mrs. J. Lee Hoffer). Prin., tchr., Cottonwood, Tex., 1930-31; prin. elementary and high sch. Mildred Consol. Sch., Corsicana, Tex., 1932-35; instr. phys. edn., coach, tchr. comml. subjects, also prin. elementary sch., dir. adminstrv. research and sch.-community relations Port Arthur (Tex.) Ind. Sch. Dist., 1935-55; supt. Aldine Ind. Sch. Dist., Houston, 1955-58; mem. faculty Tex. A. and M. U., 1958—, head dept. edn., 1961-68, prof. ednl. adminstrn., 1968—. Chmn. local March of Dimes, United Fund, Tb Assn., Camp Fire Council, Am. Cancer Soc.

Trustee Port Arthur Coll., 1950-55. Named Port Arthur Man of Month; honored Masonic Lodge and Tex. Sch. Bus. mag.; coach 2 championship football teams, 1942, 43; hon. life mem. Tex. Congress P.T.A.; recipient Tex. Golden Deeds for Edn. award, 1969. Mem. Am., Tex. assns. sch. admnstrs., Tex. Tchrs. Assn. (life), Nat. Sch. Pub. Relations Assn., Nat. Conf. Profs. Ednl. Adminstrn., Phi Delta Kappa, Pi Omega Pi. Methodist (chmn. bd., officer). Lion (pres., past officer), Mason. Author textbooks. Adv. publs. bd. Tex. Sch. Bus. Mag., 1962-65. Contbr. articles profl. jours. Home: 4104 Nagle St Bryan TX 77801

HENSCHELL, HERBERT RUSKIN mfg. exec.; b. Lima, O., Apr. 1, 1932; B.S., U. San Francisco, 1954; M.S., Stanford University, 1956; m. Rosemarie Lois Brown, May 15, 1955; 1 son, Anthony Robinson. Sales rep. Ames-Brockton Fabricated Products, Akron, O., 1956-58, sales mgr. Coshocton, Ohio, 1959-61, gen. manager plant, 1961-68, v.p. sales, 1968--. Instr. bus. Coshocton Jr. College, 1968-69. Named Man of Year, Coshocton Junior Chamber of Commerce, 1968. Mem. Coshocton C. of C. (vice president 1967-68, pres. 1969-70), English Speaking Union, Coshocton Sertoma Club, Nat. Assn. Mfrs., Sales Executives Institute, Phi Beta Kappa, Sigma Chi, Phi Mu. Democrat. Mem. Christian Ch. (lay leader). Mason (32, Shriner). Clubs: Coshocton Country, Coshocton City, Running Deer Country. Home: 2d Av Coshocton OH Office: 3d Av Coshocton OH

HENSEL, H. STRUVE, lawyer; b. Hoboken, N.J., Aug. 22, 1901; s. Herman D. and Eliza (Struve) H.; A.B., Princeton, 1922; LL.B., Columbia, 1925; m. Edith T. Wyckoff, Oct. 3, 1929 (div. 1948); m. 2d, Isabel S. Bower, June 9, 1948. Admitted to N.Y. State bar, 1925, D.C. bar, 1943; asso. Cravath, deGersdorff, Swaine & Wood, N.Y.C., 1925-33; mem. Milbank, Tweed & Hope, N.Y.C., 1933-41. Organizer, chief procurement legal div. USN Dept., 1941-44; gen. counsel Navy Dept., 1944-45; asst. sec. Navy, 1945-46; mem. Carter, Ledyard & Milburn, N.Y.C., 1946-53; cons., spl. adviser to Sec. Def., 1953, gen. counsel Dept. of Defense 1952-54; asst. sec. def. for internat. security affairs, 1954-55; returned to pvt. practice law, 1955; now partner Coudert Bros., N.Y.C., Washington, Dir. London EDO Corp., A.A.I. Corp.; chmn. United Nat. Corp. Cons. Nat. Security Resources Bd., Econ. Co- operation Adminstrn., Commn. on Orgn. Exec., 1948. Decorated D.S.M. Navy; Medal for Freedom, 1953. Republican. Clubs: City Tavern Assn., Chevy Chase, Metropolitan (Washington); University, Links, Fifth Avenue (N.Y.C.); Union Interalliee (Paris, France). Home: 322 E 57th St New York City NY 10017 Office: 200 Park Av New York City NY 10017

HENSEL, PHILIP HOWARD, educator, mgmt. cons.; b. Worcester, Mass., Aug. 2, 1899; s. Henry Walter and Pauline (Laib) H.; B.C.S. cum laude, Northeastern U., 1921; B.B.A. cum laude, Boston U., 1926; M.B.A., Harvard, 1928; student fgn. univs. Prof., head dept. bus. adminstrn. U. Western Ont., London, Can., 1928-39; prof., head. dept. mgmt. U. Toledo, 1939-59, prof. emeritus, 1959—, asst. dean Coll. Bus. Adminstrn., 1943—; mgmt. cons., 1928—; lectr. USAF Sch. Logistics, Air Force Inst. Tech. Sec.-treas. Hart Mfg. Co., Hartford, Conn., 1940-43; with Asso. Factory Mut. Fire Ins. Cos., Boston. Cons. Office Chief of Ordnance, Washington, 1951—; mem. bd. contract rev. Rossford Ordnance Depot, 1953, 54; hon. mem. faculty and staff Transp. Sch., Ft. Eustes (Va). Ordnance Sch.; Aberdeen Proving Ground, Md. Dir. nat. council Northeastern U., Boston. Mem. Soc. Advancement Mgmt., Beta Gamma Sigma, Delta Upsilon, Alpha Kappa Psi. Republican. Episcopalian. Mason. Clubs: Harvard (Worcester and Toledo); San Francisco (Boston). Author: Contract Pricing, Contract Adjustment; Contract Termination, others. Contbr. articles U.S. and fgn. trade mags. Home: 1010 Memorial Dr Cambridge MA 02138 Office: New York City San Francisco and Boston

HENSELMAN, FRANCES LORAINE WOOD (Mrs. Edward Roddy Henselman), librarian; b. Emmett, Ida., Sept. 2, 1916; d. Cartee and Dorothy Inger (Selby) Wood; student Boise Jr. Coll., 1936; B.A., U. Cal. at Los Angles, 1939, M.P.A., 1966; B.S. in L.S., U. So. Cal., 1943; postgrad. U. Chgo., 1946, Western Tng. Lab. in Human Relations, 1954; m. Edward Roddy Henselman, July 2, 1939. Mem. staff Long Beach (Cal.) Pub. Library, 1937—, head adminstrv. div., 1951-53, asst. librarian, 1953-69, city librarian, 1969—. Vis. lectr. U. So. Cal. Sch. Library Sci., 1968, mem. adv. council, 1969—. Sec., bd. dirs. Long Beach Regional Arts Council; bd. dirs. Long Beach Econ. Opportunities Commn. Mem. Fed. Adv. Council on U.S. Archives, Region IX. Mem. U. So. Cal. Sch. Library Sci. Alumni (life, pres. 1943-70), Am. (chmn. pub. relations sect. 1966, chmn. elect personnel adminstrn. sect.), So. Dist. Cal. (pres. 1970), Cal., Pub. (sec. 1969) library assns., Spl. Libraries Assn., Pub. Library Execs. Assn. So. Cal., Am. Soc. Pub. Adminstrn., Libraria Sodalitas, Long Beach Civic Light Opera Assn., Mus. Assn. Long Beach Mus. Art, Am. Assn. for UN, World Federalists-U.S.A., Long Beach Symphony Assn., Smithsonian Assn., Hist. Soc. Long Beach, Adult Edn. Assn. U.S., Freedom to Read Found., Long Beach C. of C., Long Beach Pub. Library Staff Assn. (pres. 1941), Long Beach City Employees Assn. (v.p. 1951-52), League Women Voters, Long Beach Civic League, Pi Simga Alpha. Club: Soroptimist. Contbr. articles to profl. jours. Home: 245 San Remo Dr Long Beach CA 90803 Office: Ocean at Pacific Av Long Beach CA 90802

HENSHAW, CLEMENT LONG, educator, physicist; b. Pittsfield, Mass., Dec. 18, 1906; s. Arthur Williston and Jessie (Darling) H.; B.S. in Physics, Union Coll., Schenectady, 1928; M.A., U. Mich., 1929; Ph.D. (univ. fellow 1933-34), Yale, 1936; m. Rosemary Forbes, June 25, 1938; children—Claire Mather (Mrs. Robert Kent McNeill), Arthur Clement, Philip Forbes. Instr. physics Lehigh U., 1929-31; instr. physics Yale, 1931-33, 35-36, asst., 1934-35; mem. faculty Colgate U., Hamilton, N.Y., 1936—, prof. physics, 1948—, chmn. dept. physics and astronomy, 1958-70; vis. prof. U. Chgo., 1956-57; cons. Ednl. Testing Service, Princeton; testing cons. Coll. Entrance Exam. Bd., 1949-61, 66—. Fellow fund Advancement Edn., 1952-53. Mem. Am. Phys. Soc.; Am. Assn. Physics Tchrs., Am. Assn. Higher Edn.; Assn. Gen. and Liberal Studies, Fedn. Am. Scientists, Am. Assn. U. Profs. (pres. Colgate chpt. 1958-59), Sigma Xi. Author: Problems in Physical Science, 2d edit., 1956; co-author: Atoms, Rocks and Galaxies, 2d edit., 1942. Editor: Science Reasoning and Understanding, 1954. Contbr. articles profl. jours. Home: 31 University Av Hamilton NY 13346

HENSHAW, FRANCIS HAROLD, retired librarian; b. New Castle, Ind., Feb. 8, 1903; s. Logan and Mary Knorr (Allen) H.; A.B., Occidental Coll., 1927; certificate Library Sch., Los Angeles Pub. Library, 1929; M.S., Columbia, 1932; m. Marie Hermine Holnar, May 27, 1932; children—Hermine, William, Logan, Kenneth (dec.). Asst. Los Angeles Pub. Library, 1929-31; asst. to dir. Queensborough (N.Y.) Pub. Library, 1932-34; librarian Berkshire Athenaeum, Pittsfield, Mass., 1934-46; state librarian Tex. State Library, Austin, 1946-51; instr. sch. library service Columbia, 1945-46, 47; asst. chief card div. Library of Congress, 1940-51, adminstrv. officer, processing dept. 1951, then chief, catalog maintenance div., chief, order div., 1953-71; cons. library adminstrn., 1971—. Chmn. ex-officio Tex. Bd. Library Examiners. Carnegie fellow 1931. Mem. com. Littlefield Fund for So. History. Mem. A.L.A., Mass. (pres. 1940- 42), Tex. library assns., Tex. Hist. Assn. (exec. com.), Phi Beta Kappa. Contbr. profl. publs. Home: 4204 Rail St Capitol Heights MD 20027

HENSHAW, MARSHALL B., lawyer; b. Downey, Cal., Nov. 24, 1889; A.B., Stanford, 1912. Admitted to Cal. bar, 1916, Hawaii bar, 1916; now mem. firm Henshaw, Conroy & Hamilton, Honolulu. Mem. Am. Bar Assn., Bar Assn. Hawaii. Office: 1st Hawaiian Bank Bldg Honolulu HI 96813*

HENSHAW, PAUL CARRINGTON, mining co. exec.; b. Rye, N.Y., Nov. 15, 1913; s. R. Townsend and Clara (Venable) H.; A.B. magna cum laude, Harvard, 1936, grad. Advanced Mgmt. Program, 1958; M.S., Cal. Inst. Tech., 1938, Ph.D., 1940; m. Helen Elizabeth Runals, May 25, 1939; children—Sydney Parker (Mrs. Paul W. Nordt III), Guy Runals, Paul Carrington. Head geologist Cerro Corp., Morococha, Peru, 1940-43; geologist Consorcio Minero del Peru, Mina Calpa, 1943-45, Compania Peruana de Cen ento Portland, Lima, 1945, Day Mines, Inc., Wallace, Ida., 1945-46; asso. prof., acting head dept. geology U. Ida., Moscow, 1946-47; chief geologist San Luis Mining Co., Tayoltita, Dgo, Mexico, 1947-53; chief geologist Homestake Mining Co., San Francisco, 1953-60, v.p., 1961-70, pres., 1970-71, pres., chief exec. officer, 1971—, also dir. Mem. Cal. Mining and Geology Bd. Adv. trustee Alta Bates Community Hosp., Berkeley, Cal. Mem. Prospectors and Developers Assn., Am. Inst. Mining and Metall. Engrs., Canadian Inst. Mining and Metallurgy, Geol. Soc. Am., Soc. Econ. Geologists (councilor), Geo-Chem. Soc., World Affairs Council No. Cal., Mining and Metall. Soc., Am. Geol. Inst., Societe de Geologie Appliquee, Phi Beta Kappa, Sigma Xi. Clubs: Commonwealth of Cal., Bankers, World Trade, Harvard, Le Conte Geological (San Francisco), Engineers (San Francisco); Mining (N.Y.C.); Harvard Varsity. Home: 875 Arlington Av Berkeley CA 94707 Office: 650 California St San Francisco CA 94108

HENSHEL, HARRY BULOVA, watch mfr.; b. N.Y.C., Feb. 5, 1919; s. Harry D. and Emily (Bulova) H.; A.B., Brown U., 1940; student U.S. Army Command and Gen. Staff Sch., 1945; M.B.A., Harvard, 1951; m. Joy Altman, Nov. 4, 1948; children—Dale, Patti, Diane, Judith. With Bulova Watch Co., Inc., Flushing, N.Y., 1938—, asst. sec., 1950, sec., 1951, v.p. finance, 1957, exec. v.p., 1958, pres., 1959—; dir. Bulova Watch Co., Ltd., Toronto, Can., 1953—; chmn., dir. Bulova Internat., Ltd., 1961—; chmn. Bulova, U.K., Eng., 1963—; chmn., dir. Universal-Geneve, Switzerland; chmn. Atlantic Time Products Corp., Bulova Citizen Co., Ltd. (Japan). trustee Adelphi U., Brown U. Fund. Mem. Amateur Athletic Union U.S. (timing com.), N.Y. C. of C. (dir.), Am. Ordnance Assn (life), Newcomen Soc. N.Am., Sigma Chi (recipient Significant Sis medal). Clubs: Harvard Business School, Sales Executives, New York (dir.), Brown Univ., Harmonie, Nat. Republican. (N.Y.C.); Army and Navy (Washington); Old Oaks Country (Purchase, N.Y.), Beach Point, Turf and Field; Town (Scarsdale). Home: 24 Murray Hill Rd Scarsdale NY 10583 Office: 630 5th Av New York City NY 10020

HENSHEL, WALTER MARCUS, pub. relations ofcl.; b. Chgo., May 12, 1904; s. Leo M. and Eva (Davidson) H.; B.S. in Econs., U. Ill., 1925; m. Beatrice Bach, Mar. 1, 1928; 1 son, Richard Lee; m. 2d, Pauline Goodman Steinberg, June 8, 1955; 1 stepson, Meredith. Publicity dir. Dallas-Interstate Circuit, Inc., 1931-43; publicity dir. Braniff Airways, Inc., Dallas, 1944-47, dir. pub. relations, 1947-54, v.p. pub. relations, 1954—. Former bd. dirs. Tex. Mental Health Assn., Dallas Mental Health Assn. Mem. Pub. Relations Soc. Am.; Air Transport Assn. (mem. pub. relations com.), Internat. Air Transport Assn. (pub. relations com.), Newcomen Soc. Home: 4822 Dorset Rd Dallas TX 75229 Office: Braniff Airways Bldg Exchange Park Dallas TX 75235

HENSILL, JOHN SAMUEL, univ. dean; b. San Jose, Cal., Aug. 22, 1908; A.B., San Jose State Coll., 1933; M.A., U. Cal., 1938; Ph.D. in Biology, Stanford, 1949; married; 2 children. Tchr. pub. schs., Cal., 1936-45; instr. biology Stanford, 1946, asst. prof. Hopkins Marine Sta., 1946, 50; asst. prof., San Francisco State Coll., 1947-50, asso. prof., 1950-56, prof., 1956—, chmn. dept., 1957—, dean Sch. Natural Scis., 1970—. Ford Found. Faculty fellow, 1952-53. Mem. A.A.A.S. Office: San Francisco State Coll San Francisco CA 94132*

HENSLEE, WILLIAM EDWARD, lawyer; b. Pine Bluff, Ark., Feb. 4, 1934; s. Joel Treadwell and Louise (Turner) H.; student Henderson State Coll., 1952-54; B.A., U. Ark., 1956, J.D., 1961. Admitted to Ark. bar, 1961; since practiced in Little Rock; law clk. to chief justice Ark. Supreme Ct., 1961-62; asso. Moses, McClellen, Arnold, Owen & McDermott, 1962-64; partner Henslee, Patty & Milwee, 1964-69; pvt. practice, 1969—. Pres., dir. Internat. Sponge Metal Corp.; dir. Fed. Funding Corp., New World Properties Internat., Inc. Mem. Pulaski County Democratic Com., 1968—. Bd. dirs. Office Econ. Opportunity of Consumer Action Com. Served with USNR, 1956-58. Mem. Am., Ark. (com. chmn., past mem. exec. com.), Pulaski County bar assns., Am. Judicature Soc., Phi Alpha Delta. Sigma Alpha Epsilon. Methodist. Lion. Home: 3700 Cantrell Rd Little Rock AR 72201 Office: Tower Bldg Little Rock AR 72201

HENSLEY, MARBLE JOHN, civil engr.; b. Ball Ground, Ga., Nov. 6, 1922; s. Paul and Ober (Penland) H.; B.C.E., Ga. Inst. Tech., 1949; m. Ruth Collins, Sept. 11, 1948; children—Carol and Sandra (twins), Kathlyn, Marble John. Loftsman, Bell Aircraft, 1942-44; field engr. Paul Hensley, 1946-48; design engr. Ga. Hwy. Dept., 1949; asst. traffic engr. City of Atlanta, 1950-54; dir. traffic and planning City of Chattanooga, 1954-58, city coordinator, 1958- 63; pres. Hensley-Schmidt, Inc., cons. engrs., Chattanooga, 1963-. Mem. Nat. Joint Com. on Uniform Traffic Control Devices, Chattanooga Safety Council. Served with USNR, 1944-46. Mem. Inst. Traffic Engrs. (treas., past pres. So. sect., nat. pres. 1969), Am. Soc. C.E., Nat. Soc. Profl. Engrs., Am. Soc. Planning Ofcls. Democrat. Presbyn. (elder). Kiwanian. Home: 1504 Dalewood Dr Chattanooga TN 37411 Office Am Nat Bank Bldg Chattanooga TN 37402

HENSLEY, STUART KNOX, mfg. co. exec.; b. Tampa, Fla., July 8, 1917; s. Robert Emmett and Edith (Boardman) H.; ed. pub. schs., Tampa; m. Montez Hart, Dec. 20, 1948; children—Juli, Gayla. With Toni Co., 1946-, exec. v.p., 1956-57, pres., 1957—; with parent co. Gillette Co., 1964—, exec. v.p., 1964-66, pres., 1966-67; also dir.; pres. Warner-Lambert Pharm. Co., 1967—, chmn., chief exec. officer, 1968—; dir. Jack Winter, Inc., First Nat. Bank Boston. Served with USNR, World War II. Home: 115 Common St Dedham MA 02026 Office: 201 Tabor Rd White Plains NJ 07950

HENSON, CHELSEA LUCERE, govt. ofcl.; b. Greenville, Mo., Aug. 5, 1915; s. Floyd Everett and Coza (Hughes) H.; student Flat River (Mo.) Jr. Coll., 1933-34; A.A. with distinction, George Washington U., 1952; m. Marion Anna Brockman, June 15, 1940; 1 dau., Patricia Ann. Mem. civil service staff Dept. Army, 1939—, beginning as clk. def. supply service, successively chief procurement div., asst. dir. def. supply service, dep. dir., 1939-57, dir., 1957—, mem. Army Bd. for Correction of Mil. Records, 1951—, mem. Army Loyalty- Security Rev. Bd., 1954—, Employment Policy and Grievance Rev. Bd., 1967—. Served with ground forces, AUS, 1945-46. Recipient meritorious civilian service award War Dept., 1943, Exceptional Civilian Service medal Dept. Army, 1970. Lutheran. Home: 3032 Cedar Lane Fairfax VA 22030 Office: Pentagon Washington DC 20310

HENSON, E. G., mng. editor Jacksonville (Fla.) Jour. Address: care Jacksonville Jour Jacksonville FL 32202*

HENSON, ELMER D., sem. dean; b. Colony, Okla., Aug. 7, 1901; s. Robert Alexander and Florence Belle (Bond) H.; B.A., Tex. Christian U., 1927, B.D., 1940, D.D., 1945; grad. study Union Theol. Sem., 1955; m. Eva May Kemp, Aug. 7, 1926; children—Edna Lucile (Mrs. Roy Tomlinson), Mary Lois (Mrs. Richard Wilkie). Ordained to ministry Christian Ch., 1927; pastor First Christian Ch., Van Alstyne, Tex., 1927-29, Garland, Tex., 1929-32, Commerce, Tex., 1932-37, San Angelo, Tex., 1937-45, Bethany Christian Ch., Houston, 1945-55; dean Brite Div. Sch., Tex. Christian U., Ft. Worth, 1955—. Pres. Tex. Conv., Disciples of Christ, 1947, dean Young Peoples Summer Conf., 1934-50, sec. com. on recommendations Internat. Conv., 1935-47; chmn. commn. on theol. edn., bd. higher edn. Christian Ch. (Disciples of Christ), 1968-69. Trustee Brite Coll., 1943-55, pres. trustees, 1944-55; trustee Tax. Christian U., 1948-55. Mem. Nat. (preachingteam to Armed Forces 1942-53), Tex. dir. 1946-49), Houston (v.p. 1955), councils chs., United Christian Missionary Soc. (bd. mgrs., trustee 1950-55), Ministerial Alliance San Angelo (pres. 1943-44), Council Southwestern Theol. Schs. (pres. 1960- 61, 68-69), Theta Phi, Phi Delta Kappa. Clubs: Lions (dep. dist. gov. Tex. 1934); Knife and Fork (dir. San Angelo 1943- 45). Home: 2606 Greene St Fort Worth TX 76109

HENSON, HOWARD I., union ofcl. Pres., Journeymen Stone Cutters Assn. N. Am. AFL-CIO. Office: 924 Peoples Bank Bldg Indianapolis IN 46204*

HENSON, PAUL HARRY, utility co. exec.; b. Bennet, Neb., July 22, 1925; s. Harry H. and Mae (Schoenthal) H.; B.E.E., U. Neb., 1947, M.S., 1950; m. Betty L. Roeder, Aug. 2, 1946; children—Susan Irene, Lizbeth Ann. Engr. Lincoln (Neb.) Tel. & Tel. Co., 1941-42, 45-48, div. mgr., 1948-54, chief engr., 1954- 59; v.p. United Utilities, Inc., Kansas City, Mo., 1959-60, exec. v.p., 1960-64, pres., 1964—, chmn., 1966—, also dir.; dir. BMA Corp., City Nat. Bank, Kansas City, Mo. Kansas City So. Industries, C.J. Patterson Co., Kansas City, Mo. Trustee Midwest Research Inst., U. Mo. at Kansas City. Served to capt. USAAF, 1942-45. Registered profl. engr., Neb. Mem. Nat. Soc. Profl. Engrs., I.E.E.E., Armed Forces Communications Electronics Assn., U.S. Ind. Telephone Assn. (dir. 1960—, pres. 1964-65), Sigma Xi, Eta Kappa Nu, Sigma Tau, Kappa Sigma. Mason (Shriner). Clubs: University, Kansas City, Mission Hills Country; River. Home: 3505 W 64th Shawnee Mission Kansas MO 62208 Office: 2330 Johnson Dr Kansas City MO 64112

HENTOFF, NATHAN IRVING, writer; b. Boston, June 10, 1925; s. Simon and Lena (Katzenberg) H.; B.A. with highest honors, Northeastern U., 1945; postgrad. Harvard, 1946; Fulbright fellow Sorbonne, Paris, 1950; m. Miriam Sargent, 1950 (div. 1950); m. 2d, Trudi Bernstein, Sept. 2, 1954 (div. Aug. 1959); children—Jessica, Miranda; m. 3d, Margot Goodman, Aug. 15, 1959; children—Nicholas, Thomas. Writer, producer, announcer radio sta. WMEX, 1944-53; originator programs Jazz Album, World in Folk Song, Bach to Bartok; announcer, writer WGBH-FM, Lowell Inst., ednl. sta., Boston, 1952-53; sometime lectr. jazz Harvard, Brandeis U., Boston U., Columbia, U. Conn.; asso. editor Down Beat mag., 1953-57; mus. adviser The Sound of Jazz, The Sound of Miles Davis, CBS-TV; co-founder, co-editor The Jazz Review, 1958-60; staff writer The New Yorker, N.Y.C., 1960—; faculty New Sch. Social Research; asso. prof. Grad. Sch. Edn. N.Y. U. mag. Bd. dirs. N.Y. Civil Liberties Union; mem. nat. bd. War Resisters League, Workers Def. League. Mem. Authors League Am., Am. Civil Liberties Union, N.Y. Civil Liberties Union (dir.), A.F.T.R.A. Editor: (with Nat Shapiro) Hear Me Talkin' to Ya, 1955, The Jazz Makers, 1957; (with Albert McCarthy) Jazz, 1959; The Collected Essays of A.T. Muste, 1966. Author: The Jazz Life, 1961; The Peace Agitator, 1963; The New Equality, 1964; Jazz Country, 1965; Call the Keeper, 1966; Our Children Are Dying, 1966; Onwards!, 1967; A Doctor Among the Addicts, 1967; I'm Really Dragged but Nothing Gets Me Down, 1967; Journey into Jazz, 1968; A Political Life: The Education of John V. Lindsay, 1969; In The Country of Ourselves, 1971. Contbr. Evergreen Rev., Playboy, N.Y. Times, others. Home: 25 Fifth Av New York City NY 10003 Office: The New Yorker 25 W 43d St New York City NY 10036

HENTSCHELL, CHARLES JOSEPH ret. newspaper exec.; b. Mpls., Feb. 14, 1899; s. George and Antonia (Richter) H.; grad. William Hood Dunwoody Inst., 1917; student U. Minn., 1922; m. Maxine Coon, Sept. 11, 1926; children—Robert, James. With Mpls. Tribune, 1917-35, St. Paul Dispatch Pioneer Press, 1935-41; with St. Louis Post-Dispatch, 1941-70, bus. mgr., 1949-60, gen. mgr., 1960-68, sr. v.p., chmn. exec. com., 1969-7O; sr. v.p., dir. KVOA TV, Inc., Tucson, KOAT TV, Inc., Albuquerque, unitl 1970, now dir. KOAT-TV; v.p. Pulitzer Pub. Co., until 1970, now dir.; trustee Newspaper Trust, 1954-57, Pulitzer Pub. Co. Voting Trust; v.p., dir. Ariz. Daily Star, Tucson, 1970-71. Dir. Am. Newspaper Pubs. Assn. Research Inst. Home: 11338 Mosley Lane St Louis MO 63141

HENZE, CALVIN RUDOLPH, utility exec.; b. Seguin, Tex., Jan. 28, 1924; s. Martin A. and Alice (Nolte) H.; A.A., Tex. Lutheran Coll., 1948; B.B.A., S.W. Tex. State Coll., 1949; m. Irene Daum, Feb. 14, 1947; children—Sandra (Mrs. Kimsey Cress), Patricia Ann. Internal auditor City Pub. Service Bd., San Antonio, 1949-56. comptroller City Water Bd., 1956-61; asst. controller Sweeney & Co., Inc., San Antonio, 1956-57; with Memphis Light, Gas & Water Div., 1961—, pres., 1969—. Bd. dirs. Jr. Achievement Club, Memphis. Served with USAAF, 1943-46. C.P.A., Tex. Mem. Nat. Assn. Accountants, Am. Pub. Power Assn. (chmn. accounting and finance com. 1966-67), Am. Gas Assn., Tex. Soc. C.P.A.'s, Memphis C. of C. (bd. dirs.). Rotarian. Home: 4325 Charleswood Rd Memphis TN 38117 Office: 220 S Main St Memphis TN 38101

HENZE, HANS WERNER, composer; b. Gutersloh, Westphalia, Germany, July 1, 1926; student of Wolfgang Fortner, Rene Leibowitz, also at Darmstadt (Germany) Holiday Acad. Served with German Army, World War II; prisoner of war in Eng. Composer in residence Dartmouth Coll., 1967. Composer: Chamber Concerto for piano, flute and strings, 1946; First Symphony, 1947; Concertino for piano and wind instruments, 1947; Violin Concerto, 1947; Theatre of Wonders (opera for actor and orch.), 1949; (ballet) Invocation to Apollo and Jack Pudding, 1949; Third Symphony (U.S. premiere by Chgo. Symphony Orch. 1963), 1949; Piano Concerto, 1950; (radio opera) Country Doctor (recipient Prix Italia) 1951; (opera) Boulevard Solitude, 1951; (radio opera) The End of a World, 195l; (ballet) The Idiot; (ballet) Maratoni di danza, 1956; (opera) King Stag, 1956; (opera) The Prince of Homburg, 1957; (ballet) Undine, 1959; (opera) Elegy for Young Lovers, 1961; Fifth Symphony (commnd. and performed by N.Y. Philharmonic), 1962; In Memoriam: Die Weisse Rose, 1967; also Five Neapolitan Songs. Address: 1 Via Bemondo Cavallino Naples Italy*

HENZE, HENRY RUDOLF chemist, educator; b. New Haven, Jan. 11, 1896; s. Henry Frederick and Wilhelmina Christina (Tamm) H.; Ph.B. magna cum laude, Sheffield Sci. Sch., Yale, 1918; Ph.D., Yale, 1921; m. Elizabeth Sledge, Aug. 24, 1933; 1 son, Henry Rudolf. Head dept. pharm. chemistry, med. br. U. Tex., 1921- 37, prof. pharm.

chemistry, 1929-49, grad. prof. chemsitry, 1949-70, chmn. dept. chemistry and chem. engring., 1929-39, Univ. research prof., 1945-46, also dir. premed. and predental program. Served as officer candidate Chem. Warfare Service, AUS, 1918; maj. Chem. Warfare Res. Recipient L. E. Scarbrough Found. award, 1956, Excellence in Teaching award U. of Texas, 1965. Fellow A.A.A.S., Tex. Acad. Sci.; mem. Am. Chem. Soc. (Southwestern Region award 1953), Am. Assn. U. Profs., Alpha Epsilon Delta, Phi Lambda Upsilon, Alpha Chi Sigma, Kappa Psi (nat. hon.), Sigma Xi. Episcopalian. Mason. Mem. bd. editors Jour. Organic Chemistry, 1948-55. Contbr. numerous articles in field to sci. jours. Home: 309 Moore Blvd Austin TX 78705

HENZE, PAUL BERNARD, fgn. service officer; b. Redwood Falls, Minn., Aug. 29, 1924; s. Paul Henry and Elizabeth Ann (Rush) H.; A.B., St. Olaf Coll., 1948; A.M., Harvard, 1950; postgrad. U. Neb., 1943-44, U. Me., 1947—, U. Minn., 1948—; m. Martha Elaine Heck, Sept. 15, 1950; children—John, Elizabeth, Martin, Mary, Alexander, Samuel. Fgn. affairs officer Dept. Def., 1950-51; policy adviser Radio Free Europe, Munich, West Germany, 1952-58; communications adviser, Turkey, 1958-59; mem. sr. research staff Operations Research Office, Johns Hopkins, 1960-61; exec. Dept. Def., 1961-68; 1st sec. Am. embassy, Addis Ababa, Ethiopia, 1969—. Served with AUS, World War II; ETO. Mem. Brit. Inst. Archeology at Ankara, Inst. Ethiopian Studies, Nat. Parks Assn., Ethiopian Wildlife and Natural History Soc., A.A.A.S., Appalachian Trail Conf., Sch. Am. Research Contbg. author The Middle East in Transition, 1958. Contbr. articles profl. jours. Home: 6014 Namakagan Rd Washington DC 20016 Office: Dept State Washington DC 20520

HENZIE, CHARLES A., music educator; b. Indpls., Sept. 10, 1913; s. Frank DeWitt and Caroline (Schlegel) H.; Mus.B., Butler U., 1936; M.Mus.Edn., Jordan Conservatory Music, Indpls., 1948; Ed.D., Ind. U., 1960; m. Ruth Charlotte Ruehrschneck, Aug. 14, 1938; children—Charles Leslie, Marilyn Jeanne (Mrs. David H. Cook). Teaching asst. Jordan Conservatory Music, 1934-37; music tchr. Manual Tng. High Sch., Indpls., 1937-46; mem. faculty Butler U., Indpls., 1946—, dir. grad. music programs, 1968—; ednl. cons. Smith-Walbridge Camps, Syracuse, Ind., 1951—; co-dir. Smith-Walbridge Drum Maj. Camps, 1951; dir. Smith-Walbridge Band Camps, 1952—. Mem. Young Audience Council, Indpls., 1967-69, Ind. Music Council, 1964-68, 500 Festival Com., 1963, 66, 69. Hon. mem. Canadian Bandmasters Assn.; mem. Nat. Assn. Coll. Wind and Percussion Instrs., Ind. Music Educators Assn. (pres. 1962-63), Ind. Bandmasters Assn. (pres. 1964-65), Am. Fedn. Musicians, Phi Mu Alpha (life), Phi Beta Mu (pres. 1961), Kappa Kappa Psi, Phi Delta Kappa, Kappa Delta Psi. Chmn. editorial com. Ind. Music Activities Guide, 1967-69, Smith-Walbridge Drum Major Manual, 1963, The Big Ten Drum Major, 1969. Home: 1022 Navajo Trail Indianapolis IN 46260

HEPBURN, AUDREY actress; b. Brussels, Belgium, May 4, 1929; d. Joseph Anthony and Baroness Ella (van Heemstra) H.; ed. Day Sch., Arnhem, Netherlands, Conservatory of Music, Arnhem; student ballet with Sonia Gaskel, Amsterdam, Marie Rambert, London: m. Melchor Gaston Ferrer, Sept. 25, 1954; 1 son, Sean; m. Andrea Dotti, 1969; 1 son, Luca. Mem. Corps de Ballet with Sauce Tartare, also Sauce Piquante, West End, London, also Cabaret on TV; small parts in motion pictures Laughter in Paradise, Lavender Hill Mob, Young Wives' Tale, Secret People, Nous irons a Monte Carlo; leading roles in Am. motion pictures Roman Holiday, 1953, Sabrina Fair, 1954, War and Peace, 1955, Funny Face, 1956; Love in the Afternoon, 1956; first legitimate play, Gigi, N.Y.C., 1951: appeared in Ondine, N.Y.C., 1954, Producers Showcase, TV, 1957; Green Mansions, 1958; The Nun's Story, 1959; The Unforgiven, Breakfast at Tiffany's, 1960; The Children's Hour, Charade, 1962, My Fair Lady, 1963, Paris When it Sizzles, 1964, How to Steal a Million, 1965, Two for the Road, 1966, Wait Until Dark, 1967. Recipient Acad. Award for Roman Holiday, 1953; Spl. Tony award, 1968. Office: care Kurt Frings 9025 Wilshire Blvd Beverly Hills CA 90210

HEPBURN, KATHARINE, actress; b. Hartford, Conn., 1909; m. Ogden Ludlow (div.). Awarded first honors, 1934, by vote of Acad. of Motion Picture Arts and Scis. for performance in Morning Glory, 1933; appeared in Little Women, Spitfire, The Lake (play), Alice Adams, Sylvia Scarlett, Mary of Scotland, Woman Rebels, Quality Street, Stage Door, Bringing Up Baby, Holiday, Break of Hearts, Christopher Strong, The Philadelphia Story (play), others; Woman of the Year, 1942; Without Love (play), 1942; Keeper of the Flame, 1943; Dragon Seed, 1944; Undercurrent, 1946; Sea of Grass, 1946; Song of Love, 1947; State of the Union, 1948; Adam's Rib, 1949; As You Like It (play) (Rosalind), 1950; African Queen, 1951 (award Acad. Motion Picture Arts and Scis. 1951); Pat & Mike, 1952; The Millionairess (play Eng. and U.S.A.), 1952; Summertime, 1955 (award Acad. Motion Picture Arts and Scis. 1955); Iron Petticoat, The Rainmaker, The Desk Set, 1957; (plays) Taming of the Shrew, Merchant of Venice, Measure for Measure (Eng. and Australia), 1955; Much Ado About Nothing, 1957 (play); Suddenly Last Summer, 1959 (film); Long Days Journey into Night (motion picture), 1962; Guess Who's Coming to Dinner (motion picture), 1967 (Acad. award for best performance by actress 1968); Lion in Winter (Acad. award best actress 1969); Mad Woman of Chaillot, 1969; Trojan Women, 1971; appeared on stage in CoCo (musical), N.Y., 1970, on tour 1971. Recipient gold medal as world's best motion picture actress, Internat. Motion Picture Expn., Venice, Italy, 1934; N.Y. Critic's award for performance in picture The Philadelphia Story, 1940; Annual award Shakespeare Club N.Y.C., 1950; Whistler Soc. award, 1957; Hasty Pudding Club's annual woman of yr. award, 1958. Home: 201 Bloomfield Av West Hartford CT 06117

HEPBURN, PHILIP ROMAN, lawyer; b. Cumberland, Md., Aug. 31, 1902; s. Arthur J. and Louisa (Roman) H.; grad. Lawrenceville Sch., 1921; A.B. Harvard, 1925; LL.B., U. Pa., 1928; m. Lucylle Austin, July 30, 1935; children—Lorraine Fleming, Philip Roman. Admitted to Pa. bar, 1929, mem. firm. Hart, Childs, Hepburn, Ross & Putnam, and predecessors, Phila., 1933—. Served from lt. to lt. comdr., USNR, 1943-45. Mem. Am., Pa., Phila. bar assns. Home: 238 W Chestnut Hill Av Philadelphia PA 19118 Office: 2 Penn Center Plaza Philadelphia PA 19102

HEPBURN, SAMUEL, Salvation Army exec.; b. Manchester, Eng., Apr. 21, 1901; s. James Marshall and Elizabeth (Cain) H.; brought to U.S., 1915, naturalized, 1932; student Salvation Army Coll., 1919; m. Rose Evangeline Hughes, Jan. 6, 1926; children—Samuel Brengle, Joseph and Elizabeth (Mrs. George Hansen) (twins), David, Rose (Mrs. Albert Hager). Commd. lt. Salvation Army, 1919; served in field, Toledo, Sandusky, O., Cleve., Cin., 1919- 36; divisional comdr., Buffalo, 1936-39, Phila., 1939-47; field sec. Eastern states, N.Y.C., 1947-52; chief exec. sec. western ty., Hawaii, Alaska, San Francisco, 1952-57, territorial comdr., 1957-62, comdr. central ty., 1962-65, nat. comdr., 1966—, sr. commr., 1970—. Recipient Award Merit for 50 yrs. unbroken service as Salvation Army officer, 1970; Holiness Proponent Yr. award Nat. Holiness Assn., 1971. Address: 120 W 14th St New York City NY 10011

HEPENSTAL, ROGER FREEMAN, orgn. exec.; b. Yonkers, N.Y., Mar. 28, 1903; s. George W. and Mary and Mary (Cotton) H.; M.E., Stevens Inst. Tech., 1925; postgrad. Harvard, 1948. 1948. With Am. Can Co., N.Y.C., 1925-68, v.p. charge mfg., 1951-55, treas., 1955-64, v.p., treas., 1964-68, ret., 1968; chmn. bd. Can Mfrs. Inst., 1968—. Dir. of cataloging, standardization and insp. Dept. of Def., Washington, 1954. Mem. Phi Sigma Kappa. Republican. Episcopalian. Mason. Clubs: Union League, Stevens Metropolitan (N.Y.C.). Home: 193 Dorchester Rd Scarsdale NY 10583 Office: 100 Park Av New York City NY 10017

HEPFER, FRANK FREDERICK, oil co. exec.; b. Upper Nyack, N.Y., Jan. 14, 1920; s. Frederick C. and Alice H. (Zwahlen) H.; B.S. in Accounting cum laude, N.Y. U., 1948, M.B.A., 1954; m. Jean M. Haesler, Oct. 5, 1945; children—Barbara, Marilyn. With Standard Oil Co. (N.J.), 1937-58; comptroller Esso Tankers, Inc., 1958-61; dep. comptroller Esso Petroleum Co. Ltd., London, Eng., 1961-63; controller Esso Internat. Inc., N.Y.C., 1963—. Served with USNR, 1942-44. Mem. Financial Execs. Inst., Beta Gamma Sigma. Conglist. (deacon 1957-61). Mason. Home: 110-41 84th Av Richmond Hill NY 11418 Office: 15 W 15th St New York City NY 10019

HEPLE, LOREN RAY engr., educator; b. Oakwood, Ill., Apr. 19, 1918; s. Eldridge Winfield and Mary Lucile (Oliphant) H.; B.C.E., Ia. State Coll., 1939, C.E., 1950; M.S., Harvard, 1940; Ph.D., Stanford, 1967; m. Bonnie E. Tillman, Apr. 20, 1944; children—Tim Alan, Lynne Alice. Service, devel. engr. Infilco, Chgo., 1940-41; jr. sanitary engr. Ia. Ordnance Plant, 1941; instr. civil engring. dept. Ia. State Coll., 1941-42, asst. prof., 1946-48; city engr., Boone, Ia., 1948-49; cons. engr. Pub. Adminstrn. Service, Chgo., 1949-50; prof., head civil engring. dept. U. Ark., Fayetteville, 1950-71, dean engring., 1971—. Served as capt. sanitary corps-U.S. Army, 1942-46; col. Res. Registered profl. engr., Ark., Ia. Diplomate Am. Acad. Sanitary Engrs. Mem. Am. Soc. C.E., Nat. Soc. Profl. Engrs., Am. Soc. Engring. Edn., Sigma Xi, Theta Tau, Tau Beta Pi. Presbyn. Rotarian. Home: 455 W Cleburn St Fayetteville AR 72701

HEPLER, JAMES WILLIAM, educator, psychologist; b. New Bethlehem, Pa., June 22, 1926; s. Clair Edward and Della (Shafer) H.; B.A., Allegheny Coll., 1949; M.A., Ohio U., 1950; Ph.D., Ohio State U., 1953; m. Dorothy LaRue Whittall, Dec. 12, 1948; children—James W., R. Neil, Douglas K. Faculty Butler U., 1953—, prof. psychology, 1964—, head dept., 1964—. Served with USAAF, 1944-47. Mem. Am. Psychol. Assn., Am. Assn. U. Profs., Sci. Research, Soc. Am., Midwestern, Ind. psychol. assns., Sigma Xi. Home: Box 217E R R 1 Noblesville IN 46060 Office: Psychology Dept Butler Univ Indianapolis IN 46208

HEPLER, JOHN CHISLETT, educator; b. Harrisburg, Pa., Nov. 1913; s. George W. and Emma (Chislett) H.; B.S., Shippensburg (Pa.) State Tchrs. Coll., 1935; M.S., Peabody Coll., 1937, Ph.D. in English, 1944; postgrad. Harvard, 1939; m. Ingrid Johnson, Dec. 27, 1942; children—Susan, John S., Darcy. Tchr. Boys High Sch., Atlanta, 1937-40; teaching fellow Peabody Coll., 1940- 42; instr. English, Dickinson Coll., 1942-46; prof. Central Mich. U., 1946—, chmn. dept. English, 1958-68. Mem. State Com. Lang. Arts, Com. Cultural Affairs. Active Boy Scouts Am. Research fellow U. Mich., summer 1957; Freedoms Found. citations, 1969. Mem. Mich. Coll. English Assn., Modern Lang. Assn., Delta Sigma Phi, Phi Delta Kappa, Kappa Delta Pi, Phi Sigma Phi. Republican. Presbyn. (trustee). Rotarian (dist. gov. 1963-64). Contbr. articles to mags. Address: 70 Cedar Dr Route 3 Mount Pleasant MI 48858

HEPNER, CHARLES K., corp. exec.; b. N.Y.C., 1923; ed. N.Y. U., 1949. Exec. v.p. Gulf American Corp. Home: 7125 SW 114th Terrance Miami FL 33156 Office: Gulf American Corp Biscayne and 79th St Miami FL 33138*

HEPP, EVERETT WARNE, judge; b. Milwaukee, Ore., Aug. 26, 1915; s. Louis O. and Louise (Pfaff) H.; student pub. schs., Ore. and Cal.; privately tutored in acad. and acad. and legal studies, Berkeley, Cal.; m. Dorothy L. Paulicheck, Nov. 10, 1945. 1945. Admitted to Cal. bar, 1941, Alaska bar, 1948, U.S. Supreme Ct. bar, 1951; bar, 1951; ins. adjuster, 1941-42; asst. U.S. dist. atty. 4th Jud. Div., Ty. Alaska, 1947-49, U.S. dist. atty., 1949-52; presiding judge Superior Ct., 1960—; engaged in private practice, 1952—. Served with AUS, G-2 Hdqrs., Pacific Ocean area, Honolulu, 1944-46. Mem. Armed Forces YMCA (chmn. local com. 1951). Clubs: Adventurers (N.Y.C.): Kiwanis. Home: 57 Michena Pump Rd Fairbanks AK 99701 Office: State Bldg Fairbanks AK 99701

HEPP, JOSEPH ANDREW, physician; b. Pitts., Mar. 10, 1900; s. Adolph and Clara Katherine (Snyder) H.; B.S., U. Pitts., 1923, M.D., 1925; m. Eleanor Keller, June 30, 1937; children—Joseph Andrew, Richard Stephen. Intern St. Francis Hosp., Pitts., 1925-26, asst. pathologist, 1926- 28, resident, 1929-31, now sr. gynecologist; resident Magee Womens Hosp., 1926-28, sr. gynecologist, 1942—; pvt. practice gynecology, Pitts., 1931—; mem. faculty dept. gynecology Med. Sch., U. Pitts., 1928—, prof. gynecology, chmn. dept., 1949-59, clin. prof. obstetrics and gynecology, 1959—; chief gynecologist St. Francis Hosp.; cons. gynecologist Tb League of Pitts., City Tb Hosp., USPHS; cons. gynecologist Allegheny Valley Hosp.; mem. Wainwright Tumor Clinic Assn. Served as pvt. U.S. Army, World War I. Diplomate Am. Bd. Obstetrics and Gynecology. Fellow A.C.S.; mem. Am. Cancer Soc., A.M.A., Am. Coll. Obstetricians and Gynecologists (founding mem.), World Med. Assn., Am. Com. Maternal Welfare, Pa., Allegheny Co. med. socs., Clin. Pathol. Soc. Pitts., Pitts. Obstet. and Gynecol. Soc., Pitts. Acad. Medicine, Internat. Corrs. Soc. Obstetricians and Gynecologists. Contbr. articles on splty. in med. jours. Home: 7417 Richland Manor Dr Pittsburgh PA 15208 Office: 121 University Pl Pittsburgh PA 15213

HEPP, K. KEVIN, glass co. exec.; b. Buffalo, Mar. 2, 1917; s. Harold H. and Frances W. (Keogh) H.; B.A., U. Mich., 1939; m. Betty A. Smith, June 2, 1943; children—K. Kevin, Christopher, Ryan, Constance. With Owens-Ill. Glass Co., 1939—, sales mgr. Central region, 1961-64, v.p., gen. mgr. Central region, glass container div., 1964—. Served to lt. USNR, 1942-45. Mem. Delta Upsilon. Club: Knollwood (Lake Forest). Home: 1700 N Waukegan Rd Lake Forest IL 60045 Office: 9933 Lawler Av Skokie IL 60076

HEPP, MAYLON HAROLD, philosopher, educator; b. Mpls., Aug. 30, 1913; s. Maylon H. and Helen (Fink) H.; A.B., Oberlin Coll., 1934, M.A., 1936; Ph.D. (Jubilee fellow 1938-39), Brown U., 1939; student Chinese, Stanford, summer, 1959, U. Hawaii, summer 1964, Ohio State U., summer 1966; m. Anne Woodbury, June 9, 1936; children—Barbara (Mrs. Michael K. Tandy), Susanna (Mrs. Thomas A. Bullard), David Maylon. Instr. philosophy Brown U., 1939-41; instr., then asst. prof. Haverford Coll., 1941-45, asst. dir. grad. reconstrn. and relief tng., 1943-45; asso. prof., chmn. dept. Park Coll., Parkville, Mo., 1945-46; faculty Denison U., 1946—, prof. philosophy, 1950—, chmn. dept., 1954- 57, 61-71, Maria Teresa Barney chair of philosophy, 1965—; vis. asso. prof. Kent State U., summer 1948; Fulbright participant Inst. Chinese Civilization, Tunghai U., Taiwan, summer 1962; participant 4th East-West Philosophers' Conf. U. Hawaii, summer 1964, 5th Conf., 1969; vice chmn. Western Conf. on Teaching Philosophy, 1964-66; Gt. Lakes Colls. Assn. faculty fellow in Chinese studies, 1966-67; research asso. U. Cal. at Berkeley, also vis. scholar San Francisco State Coll., 1966-67. Dir. Brasstown Vol. Work Camp, Am. Friends Service Com., 1945, adv. com. student work, 1945, regional com., 1951-56; pres. Granville Council Chs., 1958. Mem. Am., Ohio (sec.-treas. 1953-57) philos. assns., Assn. for Asian Studies, Am. Assn. Tchrs. of Chinese Lang. and Culture (editor Newsletter 1967—, 2d v.p. 1970-72), Phi Beta Kappa. Author: Thinking Things Through, 1956. Co-editor: The Range of Philosophy, 1964, 2d edit., 1970. Home: Cherry Ridge Route 2 Granville OH 43023

HEPPEL, LEON ALMA, biochemist; b. Granger, Utah, Oct. 20, 1912; s. Leon George and Rosa (Zimmer) H.; B.S. in Chemistry, U. Cal. at Berkeley, 1933, Ph.D. in Biochemistry, 1937; M.D., U. Rochester, 1941; m. Adelaide Keller, June 6, 1944; children—David E., Alan B. Intern Strong Meml. Hosp., Rochester, N.Y., 1941-42; officer USPHS, 1942—, med. dir., 1956; research indsl. toxicology, 1942-47, enzymology, 1948—, specializing in studies nucleic acids and related substances, 1952—; chief lab. biochemistry and metabolism Nat. Inst. Arthritis and Metabolic Diseases, NIH, 1958-67; prof. biochemistry Cornell U., Ithaca, N.Y., 1967—. Guggenheim fellow, Cambridge, Eng., 1953. Mem. Am. Soc. Biol. Chemists, Am. Chem. Soc. (Hillebrand award Washington sect. 1959). Editorial bd. Jour. Biol. Chemistry, 1959—. Home: 4511 Maple Av Bethesda MD 20014 Office: Cornell U Ithaca NY 14850

HEPTINSTALL, ROBERT HODGSON, physician; b. Keseick, Eng., July 22, 1920; s. James A. and Mabel (Sander) H.; M.B. B.S., London U., 1944, M.D., 1948; m. Ann Enraght Porter, Jan. 25, 1950; children—Bridget, Gillian, Jonathan, James, Caroline, Christopher. Intern, house surgeon Charing Cross Hosp., London, 1944; jr. lectr. pathology St. Mary's Hosp., London, 1947-50, sr. lectr. pathology, 1950-60; vis. prof. pathology Washington U., St. Louis, 1960-62; asso. prof. pathology Johns Hopkins Med. Sch., 1962-67, prof. pathology, 1967-69, Baxley prof. pathology, dir. dept. pathology, 1969—, pathologist-in-chief, Johns Hopkins Hosp., 1969—; pathology study sect. NIH, 1963-67, pathology tng. com., 1967-71; Sci. adv. bd. Nat. Kidney Found., 1970. Served with M.C., Royal Army, 1944-47. Mem. Am. Assn. Pathologists and Bacteriologists, Am. Soc. Exptl. Pathology, Internat. Acad. Pathology, Path. Soc. Gt. Britain and Ireland, Renal Assn., Am. Soc. Nephrology (council). Author: Pathology Of The Kidney, 1966. Editorial bd. Am. Jour. Pathology and Nephro., Medicine. Home: 104 Longwood Rd Baltimore MD 21210 Office: Johns Hopkins Hosp Dept Pathology Baltimore MD 21205

HEPWORTH, BARBARA, sculptor; b. Wakefield, Yorkshire, Eng., Jan. 10, 1903; d. Herbert Raikes and Gertrude Allison (Johnson) Hepworth; student Wakefield Girls High Sch., 1910-19, Leeds Sch. Art, 1919-20, Royal Coll. Art, London, 1920-23; traveling fellowship, Florence, Siena, Rome, 1923-25; D.Litt., U. Birmingham, 1960, U. Leeds, 1961, U. Exeter, 1966, U. Oxford, 1968, U. London, 1970; m. John Skeaping (div. 1931); 1 son, Paul (dec.); m. 2d, Ben Nicholson (div. 1951); children—Simon, Rachel and Sarah (triplets). Represented in permanent collections Mus. Modern Art (N.Y.C.), Smith Coll. Art, Detroit Mus. Art. Walker Art Center, Mpls., Tate Gallery, London, Yale U. Mus., Nat. Gallery of Victoria, Melbourne, Nat. Gallery of New South Wales, Sydney, Middelheimpark, Antwerp, Belgium, Museu de Arte Moderna de Sao Paulo, Brazil, Nat. Gallery to Can., Ottawa, Vancouver (B.C., Can.) Art Gallery, Victoria and Albert Mus., London, Rijksmuseum Kröller- Müller, Otterlo, Holland, museums of Leeds, Manchester, Birmingham, Bristol, Wakefield, Nat. Gallery of New Zealand, Washington U., St. Louis, Carlsberg Found., Copenhagen, Marie-Louise and Gunnar Didrichsen Art Found., Helsinki, Dag Hammarskjold Mus., Backakra, Sweden, UN, N.Y.C.; one-man exhbn. in Lefevre Gallery (London), 1933-52, Gimpel Fils, 1952-71, Marlborough Fine Art Ltd., 1966-70. Retrospective exhbn. XXV Venice Biennale, 1950, Whitechapel Art Gallery London, Eng., 1954, 62, Sao Paulo 5th Biennial, 1959, Tate Gallery, London, 1968; retrospective exhbn. touring Scandinavia 1964-65, HaKone Open-Air Mus., Japan, 1970. Exhibited outdoor sculpture in Battersea Park (London), Phila., Varese (Italy), Middleheim Park (Antwerp), Holland Park (London). Twentieth century sculpture exhbn. at Phila., Chgo., Mus. Modern Art (N.Y.C.), 1952-53. A 2d prize winner in Internat. Sculpture Competition for The Unknown Political Prisoner, 1953; Grandprize, Sao Paulo Biennal, 1959; Fgn. Minister's award at Mainichi Exhbn., 1963. Author monograph. Created dame comdr. Order British Empire; hon. freeman Borough St. Ives, 1968; bard of Cornwall, 1968. Address: Trewyn Studio St Ives Cornwall England

HERB, RAYMOND GEORGE, physicist; b. Navarino, Wis., Jan. 22, 1908; s. Joseph and Annie (Stadler) H.; Ph.B., U. Wis., 1931, Ph.D., 1935; hon. degrees U. Sao Paulo, 1959, U. Basel, 1960; m. Anne Williamson, Dec. 26, 1945; children—Stephen, Rebecca, Sara, Emily, William. Asst. prof. physics U. Wis., 1936-38, asso. prof. physics, 1938-45, prof. physics, 1945-60, Charles E. Mendenhall prof. physics, 1960—. Pres., chmn. bd. Nat. Electrostatics Corp., 1965—. Recipient Tom W. Bonner prize in nuclear physics, 1968. Mem. Nat. Acad. Scis., Am. Phys. Soc. Conducts research nuclear physics and develops electrostatic generators for work in nuclear physics. Home: RR 2 Madison WI 53711

HERBER, ELMER CHARLES, educator; b. New Tripoli, Pa., Jan. 26, 1900; s. Alfred James and Amanda (Sieger) H.; A.B., Ursinus Coll., 1925; M.A., U. Pa., 1929; Sc.D., Johns Hopkins, 1941; m. Verna Rosa Weiss, June 15, 1929; 1 son, Charles Joseph. Instr. to asso. prof. biology Dickinson Coll., 1929-50, prof. 1950—, head dept., 1955-65; parasitologist Stream Control Commn., Mich., 1940, 41; head biology dept. Evening Coll., Harrisburg, Pa., 1946- 47; mem. commn. Schistosome Dermatitis Investigation, El Salvador, 1960; vis. prof. biology Messiah Coll., 1968-70. Hon. collaborator Smithsonian Instn., 1957—. Recipient Darbaker prize in microbiology, 1954, 61. Fellow A.A.A.S.; mem. Pa. Acad. Sci. (pres. 1954), Am. Soc. Parasitology, Am. Soc. Tropical Medicine, Am. Soc. Biology Tchrs., Sigma Xi. Methodist. Rotarian. Author articles on parasites; Baird-Agassiz Letters. Home: 416 W South St Carlisle PA 17013

HERBERG, WILL, educator; b. N.Y.C., Aug. 4, 1909; s. Hyman Lewis and Sarah (Wolkov) H.; B.A., Columbia, 1928, M.A., 1930, Ph.D., 1932; L.H.D., Park Coll., 1956; Litt.D., Franklin and Marshall Coll., 1960; LL.D., Ohio Wesleyan U., 1963; widower. Research analyst, ednl. dir. Internat. Ladies Garment Workers Union, 1935-48; lectr., writer, 1948- 55; grad. prof. Judaic studies and social philosophy Drew U., 1955-63, grad. prof. philosophy and culture, 1963—. Mem. Am. Philos. Assn., Am. Hist. Assn., Metaphys. Soc. Am., Am. Sociol. Assn., Am. Studies Assn., Medieval Acad. of Am., Am. Theol. Soc., Am. Judicature Soc., Assn. Ch. History, Philosophy of Edn. Soc. Conservative. Jewish religion. Author: Judaism and Modern Man, 1951; Protestant-Catholic-Jew, 2d edit., 1960; The Writings of Martin Buber, 1956; Four Existentialist Theologians, 1958; Community, State and Church, 1960. Home: 17 Madison Av Madison NJ 07940

HERBERGER, G. ROBERT, bus. exec.; b. Osakis, Minn., Sept. 12, 1904; s. George and Emily (Curry) H.; student Hibbing Jr. Coll., U. Minn.; m. Katherine Kierland, Aug. 25, 1934; children—Gail Roberta, Gary Kierland, Judd Robert. Founder and pres. Herberger-Hart Co., St. Cloud, Minn., 1927; pres., gen. mgr. G.R. Herberger's Inc., 1942-47, chmn. bd., 1950—; pres. So. Land and

Cattle Co., 1937-47, dir., 1937-52; dir. St. Cloud Guaranty State Bank & Trust Co., 1947; v.p., dir. Keller Drug Co., Mpls., 1946-47; pres. Butler Bros., Chgo., 1947-49, dir. 1948-57, chmn. bd., 1949-50; chmn. bd. Tigrett Enterprises, Inc., 1950-51; pres., dir. Desert Springs Water Co., Scottsdale, Ariz, 1955- -, Paradise Valley Devel., Inc., 1956—, Bohmer-Herberger, 1967—; sec., dir. Herberger- Cruse Co., Osakis, Minn.; v.p., dir. Gainey Water Co., Scottsdale, 1956—; pres. Herberger Enterprises, Phoenix, 1952—, Chandler Heights Land Co., 1960—. Mem. Minn. State Vets. Service Building Commn., 1946-47; mem. UN Bd. State Minn., 1946-47; trustee Phoenix Fine Arts Assn., 1951-70; v.p., dir. Paradise Valley Improvement Assn., 1952-55; dir. Thunderbird Grad. Sch. Internat. Mgmt., 1952-70, exec. com., 1960-70; mem. pres's adv. com. for John F. Kennedy Center for Performing Arts, 197O—; mem. adv. council Small Bus. Adminstrn., 1970—; dir. Phoenix Symphony Assn. Mem. Republican Nat. Finance Com., 1959—. Trustee Ariz. Sunset Home, Phoenix; trustee, dir. numerous civic orgns. Del. Nat. Republican Conv., 1956, alternate del., 1968. Mem. Newcomen Soc. Presbyn. Elk. Clubs: Chicago (Chgo.); Phoenix Executives (pres. 1967-67, dir. 1961-68; Alexandria (Minn.) Country. Home: 7337 E Neale Dr Scottsdale AZ 85253 Office: 7045 E Camelback Rd Scottsdale AZ 85251

HERBERICK, BERNARD FELIX, assn. exec.; b. Marlborough-on-Hudson, N.Y., Jan. 1, 1910; s. Bernhardt and Crescentia (von Brückesteine) Zimmermann; A.B., Fordham U., 1931; postgrad. Sch. Fgn. Service, Georgetown U., 1932, N.Y. U. Sch. Commerce, 1934; m. Lucy Augusta Rosser, June 18, 1938; 1 son, James Bernard. Book rev. editor Prentice-Hall, Inc., N.Y.C., 1937-38, asso. editor, dir. pub. relations, 1938-42; with Nat. Indsl. Conf. Bd., N.Y.C., 1946-71, asst. v.p., 1963-65, exec. dir. operations services, 1965-71; dir. spl. projects Council Better Bus. Burs., Inc., 1971—; instr. pub. relations Baruch Sch. Bus. Adminstrn., Coll. City N.Y., 1948-57; lectr. Escuela de Periodismo, U. Chile, Santiago, Escuela de Caribineros, Santiago, U. Catolica, Valparaiso, 1957, Soc. Fomento Fabril, Santiago, Inst. Chileno de Administracion Rationale de Empresas, Santiago, U. Costa Rica, San Jose, 1963. U.S. Govt. assignments to Chile, 1957, Costa Rica, 1963. Pres. Cedar Gate Assn., 1954-55. Served with OSS, 1942-46; CBI. Decorated Purple Heart. Mem. Shanghai Tiffin, Vets. OSS, Newcomen Soc., Tokeneke Assn., MENSA, Inst. Chileno de Relaciones Publicas (hon.), Corps Arminia (U. Jeha). Author: Bitter Laughter, 1951; Management Guide for Competitive Marketing, 1954; (with Angel Sanhueza) Relacions Publicas: Una Introducion, 1958. Home: Scotts Cove Tokeneke Darien CT 06820 Office: 845 3d Av New York City NY 10022

HERBERT, SIR ALAN PATRICK, author; b. Eng., Sept. 24, 1890; s. P. H. and Beatrice (Selwyn) H.; student Winchester (Eng.) Sch.; grad. (lst Class Jurisprudence) New Coll., Oxford U.; m. Gwendolen Quilter, 1914; 4 children. Began writing for Punch (mag.), London, 1910, became staff mem., 1924; admitted to bar, 1918, but has never practiced; formerly pvt. sec. to Sir Leslie Scott. M.P. (Ind.) from Oxford U., 1935-50. Introduced into House of Commons a marriage bill, became Matrimonial Causes Act, 1938. Served with Brit. Royal Navy, 1914-17, and in Gallipoli and France. Rep. Punch at 3d Imperial Press Conference, Melbourne, Australia, 1925. With River Emergency Service, 1939—; with Naval Aux. Ptrol, 1940-45; Thames conservator, 1940. Trustee Nat. Maritime Mus., 1947. Knighted, 1945. Mem. Soc. Authors (pres. 1967). Clubs: Black Lion Skittles (pres.), Savage, Beefsteak, Pratt's. Author poems, revues, comic operas and novels; latest publs.: Big Ben, 1946; Point of Parliament, 1946; Topsy Turvy, 1947; Bless the Bride, 1947; Leave My Old Morale Alone (pub. U.S.) 1947; Mr. Gay's London, 1948; Southend Pier, 1948; Tough at the Top, 1949; The Topsy Omnibus, 1949; Independent Member, 1950; Number Nine, 1952; (with R. Arkell) Come to the Ball, 195l; Full Enjoyment, 1952; Codds Last Case, 1952; Why Waterloo?, 1952; Pools Pilot, 1953; Uncommon Law, 1953; The Right to Marry, 1954; No Fine on Fun, 1957; Made for Man, 1958; Look Back and Laugh, 1960; Silver Stream, 1961; Bardot M.P. and Other Modern Misleading Cases, 1964; Watch This Space, 1964; The Thames, 1966; Wigs At Work, 1966; Sundials Old and New, 1967; The Singing Swan, 1968. Address: 12 Hammersmith Terrace London 6 England ☆

HERBERT, DONALD JEFFRY, film and TV producer-performer; b. Wauconia, Minn., July 10, 1917; s. Herbert Geoffrey and Lydia (Peopple) Kemske; B.S., LaCrosse State Tchrs. Coll., 1940; m. Maraleita Dutton, Oct. 12, 1939; children—Jeffrey Dutton, Jay B., Jill A. Actor stage mgr. Minn. Stock Co., Mpls., 1940- 41, N.Y.C., 1941-42; radio actor, writer, Chgo., 1945-47; radio dir. Community Fund, Chgo., 1948-49; co-producer, interviewer radio show It's Your Life, Cong. Indsl. Health Assn., 1949-50; creator and star of Mr. Wizard TV show, 1951-65; television progress reporter Gen. Electric Co., 1954-62; pres. Prism Prodns., Inc., N.Y.C.; exec. producer Experiment: The Story of a Scientific Search, 1963-66, Science Close Up, ednl. film series, 1964—; Pres. Prism Enterprises, Inc., 1969—; producer Assignment: Science, video series for schools. Served from pvt. to capt. USAAF, 1942-45. Recipient D.F.C., Air Medal with 3 oak leaf clusters, Sch. Broadcast award, 1951, N.J. Sci. Tchrs. award, 1951, Chgo. Federated Advt. Club award, 1951, Peabody award, 1953, 1st award Inst. Radio and TV Broadcasting, Ohio State U., 1952-53; 1st award Inst. for Edn. by Radio-TV, Ohio State U., 1953, 54, 55, 57, Spl. award Mfg. Chemists Assn., 1957, 58, Thomas Alva Edison Found. Nat. Mass Media awards, 1955, 63. Mem. Nat. Acad. Television Arts and Scis. (gov. 1963-64). Author: Mr. Wizard's Science Secrets, 1952; Mr. Wizard's Experiments for Young Scientists, 1959; Beginning Science with Mr. Wizard, 1960; (with Fulvio Bardossi) Kilauea, Case History of a Volcano, 1968; Secret in the White Cell, 1969; Mr. Wizard's Experiments in Chemistry, 1970. Home: 9 Northway Bronxville NY 10708 Office: 220 E 23 New York City NY 10010

HERBERT, FRANCIS L., meat packing co. exec.; b. Lexington, Miss., June 19, 1921; s. John G. and Elouise (Watson) H.; B.S., Miss. State Coll., 1943; m. Martha Brandon, Jan. 4, 1944; children—Melissa V., Francis L., Lyon Brandon, Jame G., Daniel S., William Andrew. With Companhia Swift do Brasil, subsidiary Internat. Packers Ltd., 1949-67, pres., 1963-67; pres. Internat. Packers Ltd., 1967-69 (co.merged to form Deltec Internat. Ld. 1969), exec. v.p., dir. Deltec Internat. Ltd., 1969—. Served to capt. inf., Aus, 1943-46. Home: 337 Raleigh Rd Kenilworth IL 60043 Office: 401 N Michigan Av Chicago IL 60611

HERBERT, FREDERICK DAVIS, Jr., mech. engr.; b. Bklyn., Mar. 21, 1908; s. Frederick Davis and Jane (Mitchell) H.; B.S., Antioch Coll., 1932; m. Evelyn Makepeace Miles, 1934 (dec. 1966); children—Peter Miles, Evelyn Makepeace, Frederick Davis III, Thomas Newman; m. 2d, Marjorie Beaman Lawton, 1967. With Kearfott Co., Inc., Little Falls, N.J., 1932-62, v.p., 1935-50, exec. v.p., 1950-59, pres., 1959-62, also dir.; v.p. Gen. Precision Equipment Corp., N.Y.C., 1954-68, exec. com. of bd. dirs., 1962-68, also dir.; pres. aerospace group Gen. Precion, Inc., 1962-68; cons. to Singer Gen. Precision, Inc., 1970. Clubs: University (N.Y.C.); Upper Montclair Country, Montclair Golf. Home: 35 Glenwood Rd Upper Montclair NJ 07043

HERBERT, JAMES A., educator; B.S.C., Creighton U., 1947; A.M., U. Neb., 1956. Prof., chmn. dept. accounting Creighton U., Omaha. C.P.A., Neb. Office: Creighton U Omaha NB 68131*

HERBERT, JOHN KINGSTON, magazine exec.; b. Winthrop, Mass., Feb. 10, 1903; s. John William and Mary E. (Brickley) H.; m. Lucretia Reiner, Jan. 27, 1928; children—Sheila, John Kingston. Salesman, Standard Oil Co. of N.Y., Boston, 1921-28; cotton broker Cooper & Brush, New Bedford, Mass., 1928- 31, Jones, Gardner & Beal, 1931-32; salesman Esquire mag., N.Y.C., 1932-38; New Eng. Mgr. Good Housekeeping mag., Boston, 1938-43, eastern advt. mgr., N.Y., 1945-47; gen. advt. mgr., v.p. Hearst Mags., Inc., 1947-50; v.p. in charge radio network sales NBC, N.Y.C., 1950-52, v.p. charge radio and TV sales, 1952, v.p. charge radio and television, 1953-54; exec. pub. N.Y. Jour.-American, 1954-55; pub. The Am. Weekly and Puck, The Comic Weekly, 1955-61; pres. Mag. Pubs. Assn., N.Y.C., 1961-71; pres. Microfragrance Div. John B. Lanigan & Assos., Inc., N.Y.C., 1971—. Served as capt. aviation br. USMCR, 1943-45; lt. col. Res., ret. Clubs: Fifth Avenue (N.Y.C.); Everglades, Seminole (Palm Beach); Nat. Golf Links Am. Home: Southampton NY 11968 Office: 572 Madison Av New York City NY 10021

HERBERT, JOHN RUGGLES, editor; b. Boston, Nov. 30, 1908; s. Charles J. and Evelyn E. (Harvey) H.; B.S., Boston U., 1931, L.H.D., 1969; D. Journalism, Suffolk U., 1958; m. Elsa O. Johnson, Dec. 15, 1934; children—John A., Robert M. Mng. editor Patriot Ledger, 1936-52, editor, 1952—; editor Boston Herald, 1967- -; exec. editor Boston Herald Traveler, 1970—; dir., clk. Quincy Coop. Bank; editorial adv. bd. Am. Neptune mag. Chmn. Inter-Am. Press Assn. Tech. Center N.Y.; dir., mem. exec. com. Inter-Am. Press Assn. N.Y. Mem. Carribean Conservation Corp. Trustee Thayer Acad., New Eng. Aquarium; bd. dirs. Bostonian Soc., Internat. Center New Eng.; bd. visitors Boston U. Sch. Pub. Relations. Recipient Tom Wallace award for assistance to Latin Am. press Inter-Am. Press Assn., 1961; Maria Moors Cabot prize for promotion Inter-Am. relations Columbia, 1962; Yankee Quill award and citation Sigma Delta Chi, 1964; Order Merit Duarte, Sanchez and Mella, Grand Ofcl. Grade, Dominican Republic Latin Am., 1964. Mem. Am. Soc. Newspaper Editors, Internat. Press Inst., Brotherhood of Green Turtle, Acad. New Eng. Journalists, Pan Am. Soc. New Eng. (dir.), Sigma Delta Chi (mem. CBA Alumni Hall of Fame 1969). Clubs: Rotary (past pres.), Neighborhood (Quincy); Union (Boston); Overseas Press (N.Y.). Home: 181 Bellevue Rd Quincy MA 02171 Office: Boston Herald Traveler 300 Harrison Av Boston MA 02106

HERBERT, KEVIN BARRY JOHN, educator; b. Chgo., Nov. 18, 1921; s. William Patrick and Margaret (Lomasney) H.; B.A., Loyola U., Chgo., 1946; M.A., Harvard, 1949, Ph.D., 1954; m. Margaret Frances Lambin, Dec. 28, 1946; children—John Barry, Catherine Ann. Instr. classics Marquette U., Milw., 1948-52; instr. Ind. U., 1952-54; master St. Paul's Sch., Concord, N.H., 1954-55; asst. prof. Bowdoin Coll. (Me.), 1955-62; asso. prof., prof. Washington U., St. Louis, 1962—, reader Advanced Placement Latin, 1962-68, chief reader, 1969—, mem. Latin test com. Coll. Entrance Exam. Bd., 1968—. Served with USAAF, 1943-45. Decorated D.F.C., Air medal with two oak leaf clusters. Wilbour fellow Bklyn. Mus., 1967. Mem. Am. Philol. Assn., Archeol. Inst. Am., Am. Schs. Oriental Research, Classical Assn. Middle West and South Author: Hugh of St. Victor: Soliloquy on the Earnest Money of the Soul, 1956; Ancient Art in Bowdoin College, 1964; Greek and Latin Inscriptions in the Brooklyn Museum, 1971. Home: 1124 Basswood Lane St Louis MO 63132

HERBERT, PAUL ANTHONY, economist; b. Bklyn., Aug. 21, 1899; s. Paul George and Anna (Westner) H.; M.F., Cornell, B.S., 1922; student Mich. State Coll., 1924-26; Ph.D., U. Mich., 1940; m. Grace E. Smith, Aug. 3, 1923; 1 son, Paul Anthony; m. 2d, Dollie H. Nelson, Dec. 29, 1942 (dec.); children—Mary, Steven George; m. 3d, Maxine A. Garrett, Jan. 8, 1966. Asst. instr. Cornell, 1922-23; asst. prof., research asst. Mich. State Coll., 1923-26, prof. head dept. of forestry, 1930-50, dir. div. of conservation, 1950-56; dir. research Mich. Econ. Devel. Dept., 1956-66; conservation cons. Mich. United Conservation Clubs, 1967—; sr. forest economist U.S. Forest Service, 1926-30; editorial bd. Jour. Forest, 1930-35; editor Mich. Out-of-Doors, 1947-53, conservation cans., 1967—. Mem. Mich. State Planning Commn., 1935-38. Bd. dirs. Mich. Wildlife Found.; pres. Percy J. Hoffmaster Meml. Fund. Served as pvt. U.S. Army, 1918, capt. ordnance dept. ASF, 1942-45. Mem. Soc. Am. Foresters (chmn. Central states sect. 1936-37), Nat. Wildlife Fedn. (dir. 1941-42, 51-53, pres. 1961-63, dir.-at- large 1963-64), Am. Planning and Civic Assn. (chmn. Mich. chpt. 1937- 40), Nat. Tax Assn., Mich. Acad. Sci., Am. Forestry Assn., Wildlife Soc., Mich. United Conservation Clubs (pres. 1938-40, 45, dir 1936—), Nature Conservancy (gov. 1952-59), Soil Conservation Soc. Am., Phi Kappa Tau, Xi Sigma Phi (nat. sec. 1924-26), Sigma Lambda Chi. Unitarian. Contbr. articles profl. publs. Home: 1236 Blake St Lansing MI 48912

HERBERT, RALPH, singer, dir.; b. Vienna, Austria, Aug. 5, 1909; s. Maximilian and Irene (Munk) H.; LL.B., U. Vienna, 1935; grad. Neues Wiener Conservatorium, Vienna, 1936; m. Ada Amalia Mangold, July 19, 1937; children—Norman Gene, Carol Irene. Came to U.S., 1939, naturalized, 1945. Stage dir. Mannes Coll. Music, N.Y.C., 1941—; leading role musical Rosalinda, 1942- 44, Gypsy Lady, 1947; leading baritone N.Y.C. Center Opera, 1946—, San Francisco Opera Co., 1949—; leading baritone with NBC-TV Opera Theater, 1951—; stage dir. Manhattan Sch. Music, 1949-53, Henry St. Settlement, 1951-52; debut Met. Opera Co., 1954-55, now singer, stage dir.; appeared with N.Y. Philharmonic, Phila., Boston Pops, Dallas Symphony orchs., summer stock and European companies; dir. with opera cos., Balt., Ft. Worth, Flint, Mich., Cin., Saratoga; singer, dir., Milw., Cin., Ft. Worth. Prof. music U. Mich., Ann Arbor, 1961—. Home: 580 Riverview Dr Ann Arbor MI 48103

HERBERT, ROBERT LOUIS, educator; b. Worcester, Mass., Apr. 21, 1929; s. John Newman and Rose (Harr) H.; B.A., Wesleyan U., Middletown, Conn., 1951; student U. Paris (France), 1951-52; M.A., Yale, 1954, Ph.D., 1957; m. Eugenia Warren, June 6, 1953; children—Timothy, Rosemary, Catherine. Mem. faculty Yale, 1956—, prof. history of art, 1967—, chmn. dept., 1965-68; organized exhbns., author catalogues for Mus. Fine Arts, Boston, Barbizon Revisited, 1962-63, Neo-Impressionism, Guggenheim Mus., 1968. Author: Barbizon Revisited, 1962; Seurat's Drawings, 1962; The Art Criticism of John Ruskin, 1964; Modern Artists on Art, 1965; Neo-Impressionism, 1968; also articles. Home: Beacon Rd Bethany CT 06525 Office: 56 High St Yale New Haven CT 06520

HERBERT, THOMAS JEFFERSON, investment cons.; b. N.Y.C., Oct. 22, 1908; s. LeRoy Bedford and Blanche Luwella (Mollan) H.; B.B.A., Coll. City N.Y., 1929; diploma, Stonier Grad. Sch. Banking, Rutgers State U., 1940; m. Thelma E. Williams, June 13, 1931; 1 son, Thomas Jefferson III. With First Nat. City Bank (N.Y.), 1929-44; v.p. Am. Nat. Bank and Trust Co. of Chgo., 1944-51; v.p. Anchor Corp., 1951-54, pres., dir., 1959-62; exec. v.p. investors Mgmt. Co. Inc., 1954-59; exec. v.p., dir. Waddell and Reed, Inc., 1962; partner Arthur Wiesenberger and Co., 1963-65; pres., chief exec. officer, dir. Financial Programs, Inc., Financial Indsl. Fund, Inc., Financial Indsl. Income Fund, Inc., Financial Dynamics Fund, Inc., Financial Venture Fund, Inc., 1965-70, Financial Assurance, Inc., Financial Trust Co. Faculty mem. Stonier Grad. Sch. Banking, Rutgers U., 1943-59. Pres., Theta Delta Chi Ednl. Found., 1954-62. Mem. Soc. Colonial Wars, Theta Delta Chi. Republican. Episcopalian. Clubs: University (N.Y.C.); Barrington Hills Country (Barrington, Ill.); Denver, Denver Country, Mile High (Denver). Author: (textbook) Investments, 1951. Address: 3770 E Dartmouth Av Denver CO 80210

HERBERT, THOMAS OLIVER, patent lawyer; b. Washington, July 1, 1931; s. Earl Thomas and Lula (Clubb) H.; B.E.E., Cath. U. Am., 1953; J.D., George Washington U., 1959; m. Mary Ann Devlin, June 2, 1951; children—Terese Marie, Suzanne Elizabeth, Thomas Oliver. Admitted to Cal. bar, 1961; patent agt. Burroughs Corp., Washington, 1955-59; practice in San Francisco, 1959—; partner firm Flehr, Hohbach, Test, Albritton & Herbert, 1963—. Pres. San Carlos-Belmont (Cal.) Young Republicans, 1962-63. Served with AUS, 1953-55. Mem. Am. Bar Assn., Am., San Francisco (v.p. 1969-70) patent law assns., Barrister's Club San Francisco (chmn. patent, trademark, copyright sect. 1963), I.E.E.E. Home: 177 Mapache Portola Valley CA 94025 Office: 160 Sansome St San Francisco CA 94104

HERBERT, VICTOR JAMES, assn. exec.; b. Follansbee, W.Va., Aug. 6, 1917; s. Oliver James and Gertrude Mae (Lazear) H.; A.B., Bethany (W.Va.) Coll., 1940; m. Dorothy Clara Johnson, Sept. 2, 1942; children—Victor J., Dorothy Constance. Adminstr., negotiator, airline employee orgns.; a founder Air Line Stewards and Stewardesses Assn., Internat., 1946, acting pres., 1946-51, asst. to pres., 1951-59; in charge edn. and orgn. dept. Air Line Pilots Assn. A.F.L., 1946-62; pres. Airline Employees Assn. Pres. Cicero Indsl. Mission; bd. dirs. Bus. and Indsl. Ministry. Mem. Beta Theta Pi. Presbyn. Mason. Editor: Air Line Employee. Home: 5401 Central Av Western Springs IL 60558 Office: 5600 S Central Av Chicago IL 60638

HERBERT, WARD JAMES, state judge; b. East Liverpool, O., Dec. 6, 1902; s. Josiah Thompson and Elizabeth Jane (Hall) H.; B.A., Ohio State U., 1925; LL.B., Harvard, 1928; m. Isabelle F. Bragdon, June 27, 1931; children—Deborah P., Patia J. (Mrs. Denis H. Burns). Admitted to N.J. bar, 1929, practiced in Newark until 1961; mem. firm McCarter & English, 1942- 61; judge Superior Ct., N.J., 1961—. Dir. N.J. Mfrs. Ins. Cos., 1956-61. Gen. counsel N.J. Turnpike Authority, 1950-58. Pres. trustees Episcopal Fund and Diocesan Properties, Diocese of Newark; trustee N.J. Mfrs. Assn., 1958-61. Pres. Gertrude Butts Meml. Home Assn. Mem. Am., N.J., Essex County (pres. 1951-52) bar assns., Am. Law Inst., Harvard Law Sch. Assn. N.J. (pres. 1967-68). Episcopalian (sr. warden). Asso. editor N.J. Law Jour., 1947-61. Home: 488 Berkeley Av South Orange NJ 07079 Office: Essex County Hall Records Newark NJ 07102

HERBLOCK, see Block, Herbert Lawrence, cartoonist;

HERBRANDSON, HARRY FRED, educator, chemist; b. Watertown, S.D., July 25, 1921; s. Harry Oscar and Alice (Smith) H.; B.Chemistry, U. Minn., 1942; Ph.D., U. Ill., 1945; m. Doris Mae Hamilton, Oct. 27, 1946; children—Patricia J., Karen A., Carl H.R. Research chemist Nat. Aniline Co., 1945-46; research fellow Harvard, 1946-47; asst. prof. Union Coll., Schenectady, 1947-49; faculty Rensselaer Poly. Inst., 1949—, prof. chemistry, 1957—; cons. to industry, 1953—. Fellow Chem. Soc. London; mem. Am. Chem. Soc., A.A.A.S., N.Y. Acad. Scis. Phi Beta Kappa, Sigma Xi. Contbg. author: Determination of Organic Structures by Physical Methods, Vol. 1, 1955. Home: 214 Forts Ferry Rd Latham NY 12110 Office: Rensselaer Poly Inst Troy NY 12181

HERBST, EDWARD JOHN, educator; b. Jacksonport, Wis., Dec. 14, 1918; B.S., U. Wis., 1943, M.S., 1944, Ph.D. in Biochemistry (Williams-Waterman fellow), 1949; married; 3 children. Asst. prof. biochemistry Med. Sch., U. Md., 1949-51, asso. prof., 1951-62; prof., chmn. dept. biochemistry U. N.H., Durham, 1962—. Served with USNR, 1944-46. Mem. Soc. Microbiology, Am. Chem. Soc., Am. Soc. for Biol. Chemistry. Office: Dept Biochemistry U NH Durham NH 03824*

HERBSTER, BEN MOHR, ret. clergyman, ch. ofcl.; b. Prospect, O., Aug. 26, 1904; s. Richard W. and Mary E. (Mohr) H.; A.B., Heidelberg Coll., 1926, D.D.; B.D., Central Theol. Sem., 1929; D.D., Franklin Marshall Coll., 1962, Lakeland Coll., 1963; S.T.D., Talladega Coll., 1962; LL.D., Elmhurst Coll.; m. Elizabeth Beam, June 25, 1929; children—Jane (Mrs. Marcus Bueher), Anne (Mrs. Roger Liston). Ordained to ministry Reformed Ch. U.S., 1929; pastor Corinth Blvd. Reformed Ch., Dayton, O., 1929-31, Zion United Ch. of Christ, Norwood, O., 1931-61; pres. United Ch. of Christ, 1961-69, also mem. constn. commn., past co-chmn. exec. council; past pres. S.W. Ohio Synod, Evang. and Reformed Ch.; accredited visitor 1st assembly World Council Chs., 1948, del. 2d assembly, 1954, 3d assembly, 1961, 4th assembly, 1968; former mem. central com. World Council Chs., 1968, former vice chmn. U.S. Conf.; former mem. exec. com. Reformed World Alliance, also Internat. Congl. Council. Trustee Heidelberg Coll. Mem. Council Chs. Greater Cin. (past pres). Mason. Home: 855 Pondway Rd Dayton OH 45419

HERBUT, PETER ANDREW, pathologist, univ. pres.; b. Edson, Alta., Can., July 6, 1912; s. Andrew and Ahafia (Smetana) H.; student U. Alta., 1930-35; M.D., McGill U., 1937; m. Margaret Fetsko, Feb. 16, 1940; children—Linda, Paula. Came to U.S., 1937, naturalized, 1942. Intern Childrens Meml. Hosp., Montreal, 1936- 37, Gen. Hosp. Wilkes-Barre, Pa., 1937-38; resident pathologist Med. Coll. Va., 1938-38; faculty and staff Jefferson Med. Coll. and Thomas Jefferson Univ. Hosp., Phila., 1939—, prof. pathology, head dept., 1948-66, dir. clin. labs., 1952-66, pres. Thomas Jefferson U., 1966—; pathologist Meth. Hosp., Phila., 1954—; attending pathologist Thomas Jefferson U. Hosp. Recipient McCrae award Jefferson Med. Coll., 1947, Ward Burdick award Am. Soc. Clin. Pathologists, 1950. Fellow Coll. Am. Pathologists, A.C.P.: mem. Am. Soc. Exptl. Pathology, Am. Assn. Cancer Research, Am. Soc. Pathologists and Bacteriologists, Am. Soc. Clin. Pathologists, Soc. Am. Bacteriologists, Phila. Path. Soc., Coll. Physicians Phila., A.M.A., A.A.A.S., Am. Med. Writers Assn., Phila. County Med. Soc., Med. Soc. Pa., Jefferson Soc. Clin. Investigation, Pa. Assn. Clin. Pathologists, Pa. Trudeau Soc., World Med. Assn., Conf. State and Provincial Pub. Health Lab. Dirs., Internat. Acad. Pathology, Nat. Geog. Soc., Med. Club. Phila. Republican. Mem. Am. Orthodox Ch. Clubs: Union League (Phila.); Aronomink Golf (Newtown Square, Pa.). Author: Surgical Pathology, 2d edit., 1954; Urological Pathology, vol. 1 and 11, 1952, Spanish edit., 1959; Gynecological and Obstetrical Pathology, 1953; Pathology 2d edit., 1959; also numerous articles. Home: 1024 Great Springs Rd Rosemont PA 19010 Office: 1025 Walnut St Philadelphia PA 19107

HERD, CHARLES F., assn. exec. Exec. v.p. Louisville C. of C., 1966—. Address: Louisville Area C of C 300 W Liberty St Louisville KY 40202

HERD, JAMES RUSSELL, food co. exec.; b. Lawrence, Kan., June 29, 1907; s. Isaac Thomas and Lou Ella (Stewart) H.; ed. pub. schs.; m. Dorothy Mae Powell, Sept. 7, 1927; children—Shirley Mae (Mrs. Paul W. DeGood, Jr.), Connie Sue (Mrs. Michael Wooddell). Asso. with Armour and Co., 1930-60. gen. mgr. intro. Dial soap, 1950-56, gen. mgr. processed meats, 1956- 60; gen. mgr. Capital City Products Co., Columbus, O., 1962-64, pres., 1964-71, chmn. bd., 1971—, also dir.; v.p. Stokely Van Camp, Inc., 1964—. Recipient Outstanding Recognition award intro. and marketing Dial soap Fortune Mag., 1955. Mem. U.S., Columbus chambers commerce. Mason (32, Shriner). Clubs: Scioto Country, Brookside Country, Columbus Athletic (Columbus). Home: 1378 London Dr Columbus OH 43221 Office: Capital City Products Co 525 W 1st Av Columbus OH 43216

HERD, JOHN VICTOR, ins. exec.; b. Milw., Apr. 12, 1902; s. John and Laura (Prescott) H.; student pub. schs., Milw., Kansas City, Mo., St. Louis; m. Pauline May Hoffmann, Nov. 20, 1937; children—Pauline, Victoria. Chmn. investment com. Continental Ins. Cos., Firemen's Ins. Co. Newark. Comml. Ins. Co. Newark, Royal Gen. Ins. Co., Can., Continental Ins. Co., Niagara Fire Ins. Co. and Fidelity and Casualty Co. of N.Y., The Continental Corp.; dir., mem. exec. com. Am. Tel. & Tel. Co.; dir., chmn. bd. Diners Club, Inc.; dir. mem. exec. com. Union Carbide Corp., IBM World Trade Corp.; dir. Phoenix Assurance Co. Ltd., Phoenix Continental S.A., Am. Title Ins. Co., Dominick Fund, Inc., Franklin Life Ins. Co., Glen Falls Ins. Co., Niagara Ins. Co. (Bermuda), Ltd., Bklyn. Union Gas Co.; adv. com. Export-Import Bank Washington. Past pres. Assn. Casualty and Surety Cos., Nat. Bd. Fire Underwriters. Recipient Gold medal Gen. Ins. Brokers Assn., 1954. Bd. dirs. United Fund Greater N.Y., N.Y. Heart Assn.; trustee Bklyn. Hosp., Packer Collegiate Inst., Episcopal Found. for Edn. L.I. Diocese, Adelphi U., Nat. Safety Council, Bklyn. Inst. Arts and Scis.; dir., mem. governing com. Bklyn. Botanic Garden; mem. Salvation Army adv. bd. N.Y. Mem. Am. Arbitration Assn. (dir.), Downtown Bklyn. Assn. (dir.), Downtown-Lower Manhattan Assn. (dir., exec. com.), Bklyn. C. of C. (dir.), Nat. Indsl. Conf. Bd. (sr.), Am. Inst. for Property and Liability Underwriters (trustee). Mem. Grace Ch. (sr. warden) Clubs: Links: Downtown Assn., Union League; Arcola (N.J.) Country; Lawrence Beach (L.I.); Church (trustee) (N.Y.). Home: 2 Montague Terrace Brooklyn NY 11201 Office: 80 Maiden Lane New York City NY 10038

HERDER, JOHN HART, educator; b. Somerville, N.J., Dec. 8, 1924; s. John Hart and Marie (Armerding) H.; B.A., Rutgers U., 1947; M.A., Columbia, 1949; Ph.D., N.Y.U., 1954; m. Marilyn Burt, Sept. 8, 1951; children—Jan Burt, Paul Hill. Instr., Rutgers U., 1947-49; instr. N.Y.U., 1949-54; tng. specialist Union Carbide Co., N.Y.C., 1954-55; supr. edn., asst. v.p., asst. sec., asst. treas. So. New Eng. Telephone Co., New Haven, 1955-68; prof. Quinnipiac Coll., 1963—, pres., 1968-71; lectr. Fgn. Adminstrs. Tng. Program, U. Conn., 1964-68; cons. to Richard C. Lee, Mayor of New Haven, 1967. Dir. Hamden Nat. Bank. Mem. Citizens Adv. Com. on Welfare, State of Conn., 1969—; chmn. social scis. adv. com. Conn. Research Commn., 1969-70. Bd. dirs. Long Wharf Theater. Asso. fellow Calhoun Coll., Yale. Mem. Inst. Mgmt. Scis., Conn. Acad. Arts and Scis., Phi Beta Kappa, Phi Delta Kappa, Tau Kappa Alpha. Home: 2 Salem Rd North Haven CT 06517

HERDMAN, DONALD LAYTON, coll. dean; b. Bridgeport, Conn., May 14, 1921; s. Joseph E.L. and Elsie (Abbott) H.; A.B., Oberlin Coll., 1942; M.A., Yale, 1947, Ph.D., 1950; m. Elizabeth Fairchild Smith, Dec. 28, 1942; children—Stephen Whitney, Catherine Elizabeth (Mrs. Michael Headley), Deborah Leslie, Richard Allan, Marcia Anne. Tchr. math. and sci., pub. schs., Bridgeport, 1946- 49; tchr. psychology New Haven Jr. Coll., 1947-50; chmn. dept. edn. Trinity Coll., Hartford, Conn., 1950-61; dir. coll. curriculum for tchr. edn. N.J. Dept. Edn., 1961-65; dean Coll. Edn., Fairleigh Dickinson U., 1965—; spl. research comparative theories human devel., emotional components sch. learning, community based tchr. edn. Mem. Gov. N.J. Adv. Panel on Project Head Start, 1965-, N.J. Com. Rural Poverty, 1964-, Gov. N.J. Com. Adult Literacy, 1965—. Served with USAAF, 1942-46. Mem. Nat., N.J. edn. assns., Soc. Psychol. Study Social Issues, New Edn. Fellowship. Club: Torch of Central N.J. Home: 152 Pennington Av Passaic NJ 07055 Office: Coll Edn Fairleigh Dickinson Univ Rutherford NJ 07070

HEREFORD, FRANK LOUCKS, educator, physicist; b. Lake Charles, La., July 18, 1923; s. Frank L. and Marguerite (Roussel) H.; B.A., U. Va., 1943, Ph.D. in Physics, 1947; m. Ann Lane, Jan. 3, 1948; children—Frank, Frank, Sarah, Robert, Marguerite. Physicist, Bartol Research Found., Swarthmore, Pa., 1947-49; mem. faculty U. Va., 1949—, prof. physics, 1952—, dean Grad. Sch. Arts and Scis., 1962-66, Robert C. Taylor prof. physics, provost,1966—, v.p., 1970—. Fulbright scholar U. Birmingham (Eng.), 1957-58. Dir. Va. Nat. Bank, Charlottesville, 1966—. Bd. govs. Belfield Sch., Charlottesville, 1959-62, 63-65, chmn. bd., 1962; bd. dirs. St. Anne's Sch., Charlottesville, 1966—;trustee Woodberry Forest School, 1968—. Recipient Devel. award U.S. Navy Ordnance Dept., 1945; Horsley Research prize Va. Acad. Sci., 1953. Fellow Am. Phys. Soc. (chmn. Southeastern sect. 1961-62), Phi Beta Kappa, Sigma Xi, Omicron Delta Kappa, Alpha Tau Omega. Clubs: Farmington (Va.) Country, Farmington Hunt. Contbr. profl. jours. Home: Stillfield Barracks Rd Charlottesville VA 22901

HEREIL, GEORGES, automobile co. exec.; b. Paris, France, Aug. 28, 1909; s. Charles Elie and Henriette Antoinette (Hoidn) H.; D.Laws, Faculte de Droit de Paris, 1931; m. Fernande Gilot, Aug. 31, 1939. Ofcl. liquidator nr. Tribunal de Commerce de Paris, 1936-46, hon., 1949—; chmn. bd. Societe Sud- Aviation, 1946-62, Soc. Chrysler-France 1963-71; hon. chmn. Chrysler Internat.; v.p., dir. Chrysler Corp.; dir. Chrysler- Espana, Chrysler U.K. Hon. chmn. Union Syndicale des Industries Aeronautiques et Spatiales, 1952-56; mem. Conseil Economique Francais, 1951-59, Conseil Superieur du Plan, 1961—. Decorated comdr. Legion of Honor, others. Mem. Assn. Internationale des Constructeurs de Materiel Aérospatial (pres.-founder). Author articles on law and aviation. Home: 36 Chemin du Pommier Grand Saconnex GE Suisse France

HEREN, LOUIS, fgn. corr.; b. London, Eng., Feb. 6, 1919; s. William Frederick and Beatrice (Hannah) H.; m. Patricia Regan, June 2, 1948; children—Patrick, Katherine, Sarah, Elizabeth. Fgn. corr. for London Times, 1947—, war corr. Arab-Israeli war, 1948, Korea, 1950, Indo-China, 1951, former chief corr. Washington bur., asso. editor. Served with Brit. Army, 1939-46. Recipient Hannan-Swaffer Internat. Reporter of Year award, 1967; John F. Kennedy Meml. award, 1968. Author: The New American Commonwealth, 1967. Home: 4016 48th St NW Washington DC 20016

HERFURT, JACK ARNOLD, fgn. service officer; b. Cin., Aug. 14, 1914; s. Arthur and Evelyn (Arnold) H.; student U. Denver, 1937-38, U. Colo., 1938-40, Westminster Law Sch., Denver, 1940-42; m. Mildred Olson, Aug. 18, 1946; 1 dau., Lucinda Severin. Intelligence analyst S.E. Asia, 1947-49, staff Dept. State, Washington, 1949; asst. attache Am. embassy, Athens, Greece, 1949, Paris, France, 1950-51; attache Am. embassy, Cairo, Egypt, 1951-53, Bonn, Germany, 1953-54; 1st sec., consul Am. embassy, Baghdad, Iraq, 1954-56; exec. dir. bur. Inter-Am. affairs, Dept. of State, Washington, 1956-60; assigned Nat. War Coll. 1960-61; became counselor embassy, consul gen., Rome, Italy, 1961, Saigon, Viet Nam, now counselor embassy, consul gen. Am. embassy, London, Eng. Served as 1st lt., M.I., AUS, 1942. Mem. Fgn. Service Assn., Sigma Nu Phi. Rotarian. Home: PO Box 2667 Stateline NV 89449

HERGE, HENRY CURTIS, Sr., educator; b. Bklyn., June 29, 1905; s. Rev. Henry John and Theresa (Maaz) H.; B.S., N.Y.U., 1929, M.A., 1931, Ed.D., 1942; M.A. (hon.), Wesleyan, 1946; Ph.D., Yale, 1956; m. Josephine E. Breen, July 2, 1931; children—Joel Curtis, Henry Curtis. Instr. English, Sr. High Sch., Port Washington, N.Y. 1928- 38; supervising prin., Bayville, N.Y., 1938-41, Bellmore, N.Y. , 1941-45; asst. dir. study on Armed Services edn. programs Am. Council Edn., Washington. 1945-46; dir. higher edn., tchr. edn. certification Conn. Dept. Edn., 1948-53; dean, prof. edn. Rutgers U., 1953-64, prof. edn., 1964—, program asso. Center for Internat. Programs, 1968—; vis. prof. Hartford U., 1950-52, Fairfield U., 1950-53, U. So. Cal., summer 1964, N.Y. U. 1964-65. Del. White House Conf. Edn., 1957; edn. cons. USOM Asuncion and ICA dir. ednl. priorities study for ministry of edn. Paraguay, 1961; team leader Rutgers-U.S. AID field survey, Zambia and Malawi, 1961-62; chief human resource devel. officer U.S. AID, Jamaica, 1966-68. Past pres. troop com. Boy Scouts; v.p. Parents Assn. Rutgers Coll. Trustee Urban League, Greater New Brunswick, N.J., 1965-66. Served as officer USNR, 1942-45, lt. comdr. Res. ret. Recipient certificate of recognition, Nat. Conf. Christians and Jews, 1958. Mem. Nat. Assn. State Dirs. Tchr. Edn. and Certification (past pres.), Nat. Soc. for Study Edn., N.J. Congress Parents and Tchrs. (life), N.J. Secondary Sch. Tchrs. Assn. (trustee 1954-66, merit award 1966), Assn. Higher Edn., N.J. Council on Edn., N.J. Schoolmasters Club, Am. Assn. U. Profs., Phi Delta Kappa, Epsilon Pi Tau (trustee), Kappa Delta Pi. Author: Wartime College Training Programs of Armed Services, 1948; The College Teacher, 1966. Editor: Disarmament in the Western World, 1968. Contbr. articles to profl. publs. Home: 12 South Dr East Brunswick, NJ 08816

HERGENRATHER, EDMUND RICHARD, exec. recruiting cons.; b. Troy, O., Aug. 20, 1917; s. Harry F. and Mellie S. (Gillespie) H.; B.S. in Econs., Ia. State U., 1940; post grad. U. Chgo., 1940-42; m. Kathryn Monson, Dec. 7, 1941; children—John M., Jeffrey Y., Richard A., Holly Kay. Asst. mgr. Chgo. YMCA Hotel, 1940-42; cons. Booz, Allen & Hamilton, 1942-46; mfrs. rep. Leekley-Hergenrather, Los Angeles, 1946-49; asso. prof. alumni devel. Ia. State U., 1949-53; sales mgr. Miller Desk & Safe Co., Los Angeles, 1953-54; founder, pres. Hergenrather & Co., exec. recruiting cons. Los Angeles, 1954—; dir. Direction Sports. Mem. Republican Finance Com. Trustee San Francisco Theol. Sem.; bd. govs. Ia. State U. Found. Mem. Sigma Chi. Presbyn. (elder). Home: 340 Glen Summer Rd Pasadena CA 91105 Office: 3435 Wilshire Blvd Los Angeles CA 90010

HERGET, PAUL, astronomer, educator; b. Cin., Jan 30, 1908; s. Conrad Fred and Clara Louise (Brueckner) H.; A.B., U. Cin., 1931, M.A., 1933, Ph.D., 1935; D.Sc. (hon), Edgecliff Coll., 1969; m. Harriet Louise Smith, July 27, 1935; 1 dau., Marilyn Jean. Instr. astronomy U. Cin., 1931-40, asst. prof., 1940-43, prof., 1943—, Distinguished Service prof., 1965—; Morrison fellow Lick Obs., U. Cal., 1935-36; scientist Navy Dept., U.S. Naval Obs., 1942-46; dir. Cin. Obs., 1943—, Minor Planet Center of Internat. Astron. Union, 1947—; cons. Manhattan Project, Oak Ridge, AEC, Argonne Nat. Lab., Chgo., USAF Project Atlas, NRL Project Vanguard, Project Mercury; staff Watson Sci. Computing Lab., 1951-52. Recipient Engr. of Year award Tech and Sci. Socs. Council of Cin., 1957; Taft medal U. Cin. Alumni Assn., 1965. Mem. Nat. Acad. Scis. (recipient James Craig Watson gold medal 1965), Am. Astron. Soc. (council 1952-55), A.A.A.S., Engring. Soc. Cin. (hon.), Am. Assn. U. Profs., Internat. Astron. Union (pres. commn. 20 1961-67), Phi Beta Kappa, Sigma Xi. Author: The Computation of Orbits, 1948. Home: 1332 Ault View Cincinnati OH 45208 Office: Cincinnati Observatory Cincinnati OH 45208

HERING, CHRISTOPH ABRAHAM, educator; b. Glauchau, Saxony, Germany, Dec. 5, 1927; s. Karl Friedrich and Eleonore (Friederich) H.; student U. Marburg, 1948; Ph.D., U. Bonn, 1950; m. Dagmar Brands, June 19, 1951; 1 son, Detlev Michael. Came to U.S., 1953, naturalized, 1958. Tchr. German and English, Jacobi-Gynasium, Dusseldorf, Germany, 1952-53; instr. Greek and Latin, Midland Coll., Fremont, Neb., 1953-55; prof. German, Washington and Jefferson Coll., Washington, Pa., 1955-58; prof. German, U. Md., College Park, 1958—, also dept. chmn. Mem. Modern Lang. Assn., Am. Assn. Tchrs. German, Am. Assn. U. Profs., Soc. History of Germans in Md., Am. Goethe Soc. (v.p. Wash. chpt. 1961-64). Author: Friedrich Maximilian Klinger, 1966. Home: 6811 Darmouth Av College Park MD 20740

HERINGTON, GORDON ROSS, assn. exec.; b. Brandon, Man., Can., Aug. 8, 1914; s. Gordon and Frances Louise (Box) H.; student Victoria Coll., Toronto; B.A., U. Toronto, 1936; m. Marjory Lindsay Torrance, Apr. 9, 1949; children—Gordon Ross, Heather Louise. With Price Waterhouse & Co., chartered accountants, Toronto, Can., 1936-41, 45-46, Paris, France, 1946-48; v.p. Rootes Motors (Can.), Ltd., Rootes Motors, Inc., U.S., 1948-50; v.p. A.R. Williams Machinery Co., Ltd., Toronto, Can., 1950- 54, pres., dir. J.M. Douglas & Co., Ltd., Canadian Indsl. Alcohols & Chems., Ltd., Wiser's Distillery, Ltd. Lamb's Rum Co., Ltd.; v.p. dir. Consol. Alcohols, Ltd., West Indies Holdings, Ltd.; sec.- treas., later v.p. Corby Distilleries, Ltd., Montreal, Can., 1954-57, pres., 1958-69; pres. Assn. Canadian Distillers, Montreal, 1970—. Life gov. Montreal Gen. Hosp.; mem. Zeller Found. Served as lt. Royal Canadian Navy, on loan to Royal Navy, 1941-45. Mem. Montreal Amateur Athletic Assn., Canadian, Ont. assns. chartered accountants, U. Toronto Alumni Assn. (past pres.). Presbyn. Clubs: Town of Mt. Royal Curling, Town of Mt. Royal (Que., Can.); Kiwanis (pres. 1966), Royal Montreal Golf (Montreal); National, Royal Canadian Yacht, Granite (Toronto). Home: 16 Surrey Dr Montreal 304 Quebec Canada Office: Assn of Canadian Distillers 1080 Beaver Hall Hill Montreal 128 Quebec Canada

HERKNER, GEORGE W., corp. exec.; b. 1906; student Cornell U.; married. Formerly exec. v.p. Warner & Swasey Co. Address: 5701 Carnegie Av Cleveland OH 44103 *

HERLEMAN, WILLIAM NICHOLAS, mfr. mus. instruments; b. Quincy, Ill., Jan. 29, 1924; s. Russell D. and Ruth (Kiem) H.; B.S., U. Ill., 1948; m. Terry Fey, Aug. 20, 1950; children—Christine, Cynthia, Charles William. Asst. to gen. mgr. W.W. Kimball Co., 1948-52; sales mgr. electronics div. Central Comml. Co., 1952-56; with Wurlitzer Co., Chgo., 1956—, v.p., mgr. Dekalb div., 1960- 61, exec. v.p., 1961-67, pres., 1967—. Mem. Sigma Chi. Home: 116 W Lincoln St Sycamore IL 60178 Office: Wurlitzer Co Dekalb IL 60115

HERLIHY, DAVID JOSEPH, educator; b. San Francisco, May 8, 1930; s. Maurice Peter and Irene (O'Connor) H.; B.A., U. San Francisco, 1952; M.A., Cath. U. Am., 1953; Ph.D., Yale, 1956; m. Patricia McGahey, June 4, 1952; children—Maurice, Christopher, David, Felix, Gregory, Irene. Asst. prof., then asso. prof. history Bryn Mawr Coll., 1955-64; prof. history U. Wis., 1964—; lectr. other univs. Fulbright fellow, 1954-55; Guggenheim fellow, 1961-62; fellow Am. Council Learned Socs., 1966-67. Mem. Mediaeval Acad. Am., Am., Cath. hist. assns. Author: Medieval and Renaissance Pistoia, 1967; Pisa in the Early Renaissance, 1957; also articles. Home: 1102 Harrison St Madison WI 53711

HERLIHY, ERNEST HERBERT, lawyer; b. N.Y.C., Jan. 31, 1895; s. Theodore E. and Jenny M. (Schultz) H.; student Stanford; LL.B., U. Ariz., 1926; m. Elisabeth des Meloizes, July 3, 1922; children—Richard George, Patricia (Mrs. Troy E. Stone). Newspaper reporter Bklyn. Eagle, 1914-17; admitted to Cal. bar, 1926, since practiced in Los Angeles; sr. mem. firm Herlihy, Herlihy, Jones & Nelson, 1929—. Dir. Cal. Dept. Vets. and Mil. Affairs, 1941-43. Served as 1st lt. 28th Inf., 32d div., U.S. Army, 1917-19; 1t. col. Cal. N.G., World War 11. Mem. Am., Los Angeles bar assns., Cal. State Bar. Club: Lawyers of Los Angeles. Home: 501 N Wilcox Av Los Angeles CA 90004 Office: 727 W 7th St Los Angeles CA 90017

HERLIHY, FRANCIS BOND, indsl. exec.; b. Methuen, Mass., Nov. 20, 1921; s. Frank Joseph and Anne C. (Cronin) H.; B.S. in Metallurgy, Mass. Inst. Tech., 1942; children—David Michael, Patricia Anne, Mark Francis. Metallurgist, ABEX Corp., Mahwa, N.J., 1945-57, dir. research, 1957-65, v.p., N.Y.C., 1965- -; dir. Lloyds-Burton, Ltd., Lloyds-Abex Shoe, Ltd., Burton, Eng. Served to maj. AUS, 1942-46. Mem. Am., Brit. iron and steel insts., Inst. Metals (London), Indsl. Research Inst. Home: Horizon Tower S Fort Lee NJ 07024 Office: ABEX Corp 530 Fifth Av New York City NY 10036

HERLIHY, HORACE MURRAY, educator; b. Coleman, P.E.I., Can., Feb. 1, 1917; s. James Alexander and Minnie (MacPhee) H.; B.A., U. Alta., 1948; M.A. in Econs., U. Chgo., 1950, Ph.D., 1954; m. Doreen Alice Hosford, Aug. 5, 1942. Staff economist Joint Congl. Commn. on R.R. Retirement, Washington, 1952-53; lectr. St. Xavier Coll., 1953; asst. prof. Valparaiso U., 1954-55; asst. prof. Mich. State U., 1955-57; asso. prof. Lake Forest (Ill.) Coll., 1957-61, prof. 1961—, chmn. econs. dept., 1960—. Chmn., Gov.'s Commn. on Manpower Utilization, 1965-67; impartial chmn. pension commn. Fansteel Metall. Corp., 1958-61; ednl. TV lectr. Channels 11, 2, 7, Chgo., 1962-64. Mem. Internat. Relations Library, 1965- -; mem. pres.'s council Rosary Coll., River Forest, Ill., 1970—. Served with Royal Canadian Corps of Signals, 1940-45. Mem. Am. Econ. Assn., Indsl. Relations Research Assn., Am. Assn. U. Profs. (chpt. pres. 1962-63), Phi Delta Theta. Democrat. Club: Quadrangle (Chgo.). Contbg. author: Am. Educator Ency., 1963—. Home: 6007 Sheridan Rd Chicago IL 60626 Office: Econ Dept Lake Forest Coll Lake Forest IL 60045

HERLIHY, JAMES LEO, playwright, novelist; b. Detroit, Feb. 27, 1927; s. William Francis and Grace (Oberer) H.; student Black Mountain Coll., 1947-48, Pasadena Playhouse, 1948-50; RCA fellow Yale Drama Sch., 1956-57. Author: (play with William Noble) Blue Denim, 1957 (motion picture 1959); (play) Crazy October, 1958; The Sleep of Baby Filbertson and other stories, 1959; (novel) All Fall Down, 1960 (motion picture 1961); Midnight Cowboy, 1965 (motion picture 1969); A Story That Ends With a Scream, and Eight Others, 1967; (play) Stop, You're Killing Me, 1970; (novel) The Season of the Witch, 1971. Starred in prodn. of The Zoo Story, Paris, France, 1963. Served with USNR, 1945-46. Address: care Weissberger 120 E 56th St New York City NY 10022

HERLING, JOHN, newspaperman; b. N.Y.C., Apr. 14, 1907; s. Morris and Mollie (Konrad) H.; A.B., Harvard, 1928; m. Mary Fox, Sept. 16, 1937; 1 stepson, David Fox Stolberg. Publ. sec., also exec. sec. Emergency Com. Strikers Relief of League Indsl. Democracy, 1930-34; asst. editor United Features Syndicate, 1935; Washington corr. Milw. Leader, also other papers, 1936- 37; mem. Washington staff Time Inc., 1937; publicity dir. March of Time, 1937-38; dir. Childrens Crusade for Children, 1939-40; asst. sec. New Sch. Social Research, 1940-41; dir. labor and social relations div. Office Inter-Am. Affairs, 1941-46; spl. corr. in Europe for Newspapers, 1946; editor, pub. John Herling's Labor Letter, 1947—; syndicated columnist labor and gen. affairs Nat. Newspaper Syndicate, 1953—; lectr. abroad labor affairs for State Dept., 1956, 60, 63, 65. Recipient Journalist award Wash. Newspaper Guild, 1962, 64. Mem. Am. Polit. Sci. Assn., Authors Guild, Indsl. Relations Research Assn. (pres. Washington chpt. 1955), White House Corrs. Assn., Sigma Delta Chi. Clubs: Nat. Press, Overseas Writers, Federal City, Harvard (Washington); Silurians (N.Y.C.). Author: Great Price Conspiracy, 1962; Labor Unions in America, 1964; Right to Challenge, 1971. Contbr. magazines. Home: 6504 E Halbert Rd Bethesda MD 20034 Office: 1330 Massachusetts Av NW Washington DC 20005

HERMAN, ABE MITCHELL, lawyer; b. Ft. Worth, July 14, 1905; s. David Sam and Rose (Waxman) H.; J.D., U. Tex., Austin, 1927; m. Sarah Foreman, Oct. 29, 1933; children-Donald Sidney, Morton Lee. Admitted to Tex. bar, 1927, since practiced in Ft. Worth; sr. mem. firm Brown, Herman, Scott, Young & Dean, 1927—; participant Duolopy hearings FCC, 1940-45; lectr. Southwestern Legal Found., Bur. Nat. Affairs. Dir., v.p., gen. counsel Carter Publs., Inc; dir. First Nat. Bank Ft. Worth. Treas. Clear Channel Broadcasting Service, 1965—. Gen. counsel Amon G. Carter Found., Joseph R. White Lecture Found., Carter Blood Bank; bd. dirs. St. Joseph Hosp., Ft. Worth Childrens Hosp., Ft. Worth Osteo. Hosp., United Fund and Goodwill of Am.; trustee Janis and Phil North Found. Mem. Am. (chmn. radio sect.), FCC, Tex. (co-chmn. pub. relations com.), Ft. Worth- Tarrant County bar assns., Assn. Maximum Service Telecasters, Ft. Worth Squadron Assn., Tau Delta Phi. Mason (Shriner). Clubs: Fort Worth, Ridglea Country, Town, Admirals (Ft. Worth). Home: 3308 Tanglewood Trail Fort Worth TX 76109 Office: Ft Worth Club Bldg Fort Worth TX 76102

HERMAN, BEAUMONT ALEXANDER, coll. pres.; b. Lunenburg, N.S., Can., Mar. 24, 1909; s. Beaumont Gaetz and Mary May (Hebb) H.; A.B., Harvard, 1930, M.A., 1931; Ph.D., Boston Coll., 1937; postgrad. Tufts U., Boston U.; LL.D., Am. Internat. Coll., 1968; m. Winifred Elizabeth Small, Aug. 21, 1937; children—Natalie Winifred, Kenneth Beaumont. Tchr. pub. schs., Somerville, Mass., 1932-45; prin. Consol. Schs., Westminster, Mass., 1945-46, Westford (Mass.) Acad,, 1946-47; supt. schs., Westford, 1946- 48, Northbridge, Mass., 1948-55; pres. Western New Eng. Coll., Springfield, Mass., 1955— Trustee Springfield Five Cents Savs. Bank (Mass.). Vice pres. Joint Civic Agencies, Springfield. Police commr., Springfield. Treas. Council Advancement Small Colls.; dir. Assn. Ind. Colls. and Univs. in Mass. Mem. N.E.A., Am. Assn. Sch. Adminstrs., N.E. Conf. Bd. Edn. Meth. Ch., Boston Meth. Social Union (pres. 1945), Phi Beta Kappa. Mason, Kiwanian (pres. 1952, 62). Club: Colony. Home: 1366 S Branch Pkwy Springfield MA 01106

HERMAN, BERNARD, electronics co. exec.; b. Washington, Mar. 1O, 1927; s. Nathan Eli and Rose (Guberman) H.; B.E.E., Cornell U., 1950; postgrad. indsl. engring. Coll. City N.Y., 1950-51; m. Sylvia Kurtz, Apr. 15, 1951; children—Neil, Stephanie, Ann. With Loral Corp., Scarsdale, N.Y., 1950- -, pres. Loral electronic systems div., 1966-68, exec. v.p., dir. corp., 1968-69, pres., dir. corp., 1969—. Pres. Plainview (N.Y.) Ind. Voters Com., 1957-58. Served with AUS, 1944-47. Sr. mem. I.E.E.E.; mem. Air Force Assn., Am. Ordnance Soc. Home: 9 Princeton Dr Plainview NY 11803 Office: 688 White Plains Rd Scarsdale NY 10583

HERMAN, DAVID THEODORE, educator; b. Chgo., Apr. 1, 1916; s. William and Cecelia (Cohen) H.; B.A. with honors, Ind. U., 1940; M.A. in Speech Pathology, 1942, Ph.D. in Psychology, 1947; m. Evelyn A. Swartz, Jan. 29, 1967; 1 dau., by previous marriage,

Deborah Ann. Instr. psychology Ind. U., 1945-47; asst. prof. La. State U., 1947- 49; faculty Wichita State U., 1949—, prof. psychology, 1957—, chmn. dept., 1966—. Mem. Am. Psychol. Assn. Home: 2523 N Roosevelt Ct Wichita KS 67220

HERMAN, GEORGE EDWARD, fgn. corr.; b. N.Y. C., Jan. 14, 1920; s. Sydney H. and Tessie Samuels (Dryfoos) H.; A.B. cum laude, Dartmouth, 1941; M.S., Columbia, 1942; m. Patricia Kerwin, Feb. 19, 1955; children—Charles, Scott, Richard. Night news editor radio sta. WQXR, N.Y.C., 1942-44; joined CBS, 1944, bur. mgr., Tokyo, Japan, 1950-53; Washington corr., 1954—; also lectr. Mem. Overseas Writers Assn., Am. Automobile Assn., A.A.A.S. Clubs: Nat. Press (Washington); Overseas Press, Press (Tokyo). Author mag. articles. Address: 3115 O St NW Washington DC 20007

HERMAN, GRANT, printing co. exec.; b. Chgo., Feb. 11, 1913; s. Raymond Elmer and Carolyn (Weaver) H.; B.A., Dartmouth, 1935; M.B.A., Harvard, 1947; m. Marjorie Murray, Feb. 21, 1948; children—Mary Lynn, Laura, Grant Phelps, Barbara, Howell Sherer. With R.R. Donnelley Co., Chgo., Crawfordsville, Ind., 1936-52; pres. Kable Printing Co., Mt. Morris, Ill., 1952—, also dir. Pres., Mt. Morris P.T.A., 1961-63, Rock River Valley Craftsmen, 1960-61; dist. chmn. Blackhawk council Boy Scouts Am., 1963- 67, mem. exec. bd., 1963—. Bd. dirs. Gravure Research Inst., 1971—. Served with USNR, 1943-46. Mem. Printing Industries Am. (v.p. mag. printers sect. 1970—), Research and Engring. Council Graphic Arts (treas. 1971—), Delta Kappa Epsilon. Republican. Christian Scientist. Moose, Kiwanian. Home: RR 1 Mount Morris IL 61054 Office: 404 N Wesley Av Mount Morris IL 61054

HERMAN, HAMILTON, mfg. exec.; b. Chgo., Jan. 15, 1916; s. Raymond E. and Carolyn (Weaver) H.; A.B., Williams Coll., 1938; B.S. in Aero. Engring., Mass. Inst. Tech., M.S. in Aero. Engring., 1943; m. Martha Schueler, Mar. 11, 1944; 1 dau., Carolyn Herman. With Chgo. Daily News, 1938-40; flight test engr. Douglas Aircraft Co., 1943-46; mgr. Flight Engring., Inc., 1946- 48; mgr. Bedford flight facility Instrumentation Lab., Mass. Inst. Tech., 1948-53, spl. asst. to pres., 1953-55; v.p., dir. research and devel. Am. Machine & Foundry Co., 1955-67; pres. indsl. divs. Rockwell-Standard Corp., 1967-68; v.p. research and devel. Am. Can Co., N.Y.C., 1968-71, sr. v.p. devel., 1971—. Mem. Indsl. Research Inst., Delta Kappa Epsilon. Clubs: Woodway (Darien, Conn.); Williams, Union League (N.Y.C.). Home: 5 Canoe Hill Rd New Canaan CT 06840 Office: American Lane Greenwich CT 06830

HERMAN, HAROLD WILCOX, editor; b. Kodaikanal, India, May 22, 1913 (parents Am. citizens); s. Harold C. and Winifred (Wilcox) H.; A.B., Carleton Coll., 1935; m. Georga Fern Burk, July 6, 1939; 1 dau., Haleen Louise. Asst. membership sec. Dayton (O.) YMCA 1935, publicity dir., 1936-41; publs. sec. U.S. Jr. C. of C., 1941-44, exec. v.p., 1944-45; mng. editor Coll. and Univ. Bus., 1945-51, editor, 1952-68; v.p. Corco, Inc., Chgo., 1969—, The Vector Co., 1970—; sr. editor Field Enterprises Ednl. Corp., Chgo., 1971—. Faculty mem. coll. bus. mgmt. workshop U. Omaha, U. Cal. Mem. Family welfare review com. Community Fund Chgo.; v.p. Oak Park Community Lectures, 1968—. Trustee Village of Oak Park (Ill.), 1969—; bd. assos. Chgo. Theol. Sem.; bd. dirs. Med. Center YMCA. Served with USCGR, 1943-45. Recipient Jesse H. Neal editorial achievement award Am. Bus. Press, Inc., 1965. Fellow A.I.M.; mem. Irving Soc. (past pres.), Carleton Coll. Alumni Assn. Ill. (past pres.), Sigma Delta Chi. Conglist. (former chmn. Bd. World Service; chmn. bd. trustees). Clubs: Headline, Chicago Press (Chgo.). Contbr. coll. mags. Home: 641 N Grove Av Oak Park IL 60302 Office: Field Enterprises Ednl Corp Merchandise Mart Chicago IL 60654

HERMAN, HARRY A., assn. exec.; b. Providence, Feb. 7, 1905; s. Henry A. and Lula R. (Smith) H.; B.S., U. Mo., 1929, A.M., 1931, Ph.D., 1936; student Central Mo. State Coll., 1924-26, U. Wis., 1935; m. Lucille E. Land, June 9, 1932; children—Harry A., Donald Louis. Instr. dairy husbandry U. Mo., 1929-36, asst. prof., 1936-39, asso. prof., 1939-44, prof., 1944-53; exec. sec. Nat. Assn. Animal Breeders, Columbia, Mo., 1953—, also chmn. research com. Chmn., North Central tech. com. Regional Dairy Cattle Breeding Project; chmn. artificial insemination com., mem. nutrition com. Mo. Coll. Agr.; del. III Internat. Congress Reprodn., Cambridge, Eng., 1956; chmn. Purebred Dairy Cattle Research Com., 1958; 1st v.p. Performance Registry Internat., 1968—. Trustee Home for Aged Baptists, Ironton, Mo. Recipient Borden award for outstanding research in dairy prodn., 1956. Mem. Am. Dairy Sci. Assn. (dir., sec. Breed's relations com., chmn. prodn. sect., chmn. jour. mgmt. com. 1965—), Purebred Dairy Cattle Assn. (chmn. prodn. testing com., sec. dairy cattle breeding research council, chmn. research com.), Dairy Sci. Assn. (jour. mgmt. com.), Soc. Animal Prodn., Am. Guernsey Cattle Club (dir. 1967—, pres. 1967-71), Mo. Guernsey Breeders Assn. (pres.). Mo. Fedn. Artificial Breeding Orgns. (sec.), Dairy Shrine Club (pres.), Mo. Assn. Dairy Orgns. (pres. 1964—), Sigma Xi, Gamma Alpha, Gamma Sigma Delta (recipient distinguished service award 1966), Alpha Zeta. Democrat. Baptist. Rotarian. Co-author hand book and lab. manual Artificial Insemination of Dairy Cattle, 1948; also research bulls., manuals. Editor: A.I. Digest, 1953. Home: 1281 Sunset Dr Columbia MO 65201 Office: PO Box 1033 512 Cherry St Columbia MO 65201 ☆

HERMAN, HORTON, lawyer; b. Republic, Wash., Dec. 11, 1911; grad. U. Ida.; LL.B., Gonzaga U., 1938. Admitted to Wash. bar, 1938; partner firm Paine, Lowe, Coffin, Herman & O'Kelly, Spokane. Served as maj. AUS, 1941-45. Mem. Am., Wash. State, Spokane County bar assns. Office: Spokane & Eastern Bldg Spokane WA 99201*

HERMAN, JERRY, composer-lyricist; b. N.Y.C., July 10, 1932; s. Harry and Ruth (Sachs) H.; B.A., U. Miami, 1953. Composer-lyricist: I Feel Wonderful, 1955; Nightcap, 1958; Parade, 1960; Milk and Honey, 1961; Hello Dolly!, 1964 (also film 1970); Mame, 1966; Dear World, 1969; wrote President Lyndon B. Johnson's campaign song Hello, Lyndon!, 1964. Recipient Antoinette Perry award for Hello, Dolly!, 1965, Variety Poll award for best music and lyrics, 1965, Grammy award for best song, 1964, WPAT award for best song, Shalom, 1961, Radio-TV All Am. award best song of year, Hello, Dolly!, 1964; Variety poll award for best lyrics, Mame, 1966; Grammy award, 1967. Address: 50 W 10th St New York City NY 10011

HERMAN, MORRIS, physician; b. N.Y. C., Oct. 3, 1906; s. Jacob and Bertha (Faber) H.; B.S., Coll. City of N. Y. 1926; M.D., N.Y. U., 1930; m. June O'Brien, Apr. 19, 1932; children—Joan (Mrs. John Lepik), Henry. Interne, Bellevue Hosp., N.Y.C. 1930-32, psychiatrist, 1932- 40, asst. dir. psychiatry, 1941-48, vis. neurologist and psychiatrist, 1949—; instr. psychiatry N.Y. U., 1935-37; asst. clin. prof., 1938- 41, asst. prof., 1942-47, asso. prof., 1947-49, prof. clin. psychiatry, 1949-51, prof. psychiatry, 1951—, acting chmn. dept. psychiatry, 1969—; vis. psychiatrist U. Hosp., N.Y. U., 1950-69, asso. dir. psychiatry and neurology, 1969—, acting dir. psychiat. service, 1969—; chmn. adv. com. to divs. psychiatry, psychology and neurology VA, Washington. Mem. joint legislative com. to study narcotics problems N.Y. State; mem. adv. com. on alcoholism N.Y. State Interdepartmental Health Resources Bd. Diplomate Am. Bd. Psychiatry and Neurology. Fellow N.Y. Acad. Medicine; mem. N.Y. Soc. Clin. Psychiatry (pres.), Am. Psychiat. Assn., Am. Neurol. Assn. Contbr. to med. publs. Home: 3556 88th St Jackson Heights NY 11372 Office: 30 E 40th St New York City NY 10016

HERMAN, ROBERT S., state ofcl., educator; b. Newburgh, N.Y., Dec. 18, 1919; s. Bernard O. and Leona (Gottlieb) H.; A.B., Union Coll., 1941; M.A., U. Cin., 1942; Ph.D., N.Y. U., 1950; m. Beatrice Hirsch, June 20, 1942; children—Gerald W., Arthur P. Lectr., Syracuse U., 1947-60; vis. prof. Russell Sage Coll., 1948-57, State U. N.Y., 1960-62; vis. lectr. Econ. Devel. Inst., Washington, 1958-69; dir. research and fiscal policy div. budget N.Y. State Exec. Dept., Albany, 1950-63, dir. budget planning and devel. 1963, asst. budget dir., 1963-66; exec. dir. Commn. on Constl. Conv., 1966-67; exec. asst. to pres. N.Y. State Constl. Conv., 1967—; dir. N.Y. Senate Com. on Higher Edn., 1968—; prof. City U. N.Y., 1968, State U. N.Y., Albany, 1968-69; prof. econs. and pub. adminstrn., chmn. dept. Union Coll., Schenectady, 1969—. Cons. UN; former U.S. adviser to Venezuela, Peru, India, Greece, Ecuador, Nigeria, Turkey, Guatemala. Mem. adv. com. Nat. Planning Assn., Center for Econ. Projections, Rand Corp., Ford Found.; adviser Asso. Arts Councils, Inst. Man and Sci. Mem. Phi Beta Kappa. Contbr. articles to profl. jours. Home: 9 Southwood Dr Slingerlands NY 12159 Office: Union Coll Dept Econs Schenectady NY 12308

HERMAN, ROGER MYERS, educator; b. Torrington, Conn., Dec. 10, 1934; s. Donald W. and Katherine H. (Hood) H.; B.S., Lehigh U., 1957; M.S., Yale, 1959, Ph.D., 1963; m. Nicoletta M. Andrews, Sept. 7, 1958; children—Stephen A., Gregory R., Ellice K. Mem. tech. staff Space Tech. Labs., Inc., Redondo Beach, Cal., 1962-64; faculty Pa. State U., University Park, 1964—, prof. physics, 1968. Cons. Phys. Studies, Inc., Reno, 1965-70. Adviser, Gamma Nu chpt. Alpha Phi Alpha. Fellow Am. Phys. Soc. Elk. Contbr. articles to profl. jours. Home: 217 Homan Av State College PA 16801 Office: Osmond Lab Pa State Univ University Park PA 16802

HERMAN, RUSSEL HAROLD, Jr., petroleum co. exec.; b. Woodbury, N.J., Oct. 6, 1930; s. Russel Harold and Madelyn (Beck) H.; B.S. in Chem. Engring., Pa. State U., 1951; m. Linda Lou Brown Hillman, June 16, 1951; children—Mary Cynthia, Melissa Lou, Christina Lee, Russel Harold III, Tammy Ann. With Esso Research & Engring. Co., 1951-57; corporate planning and related activities in U.S. and London, Eng., Standard Oil Co. (N.J.), 1957-64; v.p. cargo sales Esso Internat., Inc., N.Y.C., 1967-70, exec. v.p., dir., 1970—. Mem. men's com. N.Y. Mus. Natural History. Mem. Am. Petroleum Inst. Republican. Presbyn. Club: New York Athletic.

HERMAN, STEPHEN MARK, lawyer; b. Evanston, Ill., Mar. 9, 1932; s. Edward Martin and Bernice Jane (Kitzelman) H.; B.A., Northwestern U., 1954; J.D., Harvard, 1957; m. Lail Lewis, Aug. 26, 1956; children—Ellen, William, Thomas, Jane. Admitted to Ill. bar, 1957, since practiced in Chgo. Sec. Wurlitzer Co., Chgo., 1969—. Home: 1051 Cherry St Winnetka IL 60093 Office: The Wurlitzer Company 105 W Adams St Chicago IL 60603

HERMAN, STEWART WINFIELD, clergyman, educator; b. Harrisburg, Pa., Aug. 4, 1909; s. Stewart Winfield and Mary (Benner) H.; A.B., Gettysburg Coll., 1930, Litt.D., 1945; B.D., Gettysburg Theol. Sem., 1934; B.Th., U. Strasbourg (France), 1935; postgrad. univs. Göttingen and Berlin, 1936-39; m. Ethelyn Frances Cantrell, Apr. 5, 1945; children—Nicholas Benner and Christopher Carr (twins), Stewart Winfield, Lynda Elizabeth. Ordained to ministry United Luth. Ch. Am., 1934; minister Am. Ch. Berlin, 1936-41; vis. prof. Hamma Div. Sch., Springfield, O., 1942; dep. dir. reconstrn. dept. World Council. Chs., Geneva, Switzerland, 1945-47, mem. dept. information, also spl. assistance to social projects, 1961-68; dir. refugee resettlement Luth. World Fedn., Geneva, 1948-52, dir. Latin Am. Com., 1952-63; exec. sec. div. Luth. World Fedn. affairs Nat. Luth. Council, N.Y.C., 1956-63; mem. dept. internat. affairs com. Nat. Council Chs. U.S., chmn. com. on cooperation Latin Am., also com. on program Latin Am. Ch. World Service, 1952-63, mem. dept. overseas union chs. com.; participant assemblies World Council Chs., Oxford, 1937, Amsterdam, 1948, Evanston, 1954, Uppsala, 1968, Luth. World Fedn., Lund, 1937, Hannover, 1952, Mpls., 1958, Helsinki, 1963, Evian, 1970; pres. Conf. Non-Govtl. Orgns. Chmn., Latin Am. com. Am. Council vol. Agencies, 1958-63; mem. U.S. Com. World Refugees, 1959-60, White House Conf. Food for Peace, 1960. Mem. bd. Faculdad Luterana de Teologia, Buenos Aires, 1958-63; pres. Luth. Sch. Theology, Luth. Ch. Am., Chgo., 1964-71. Served with OSS, 1943-45. Mem. Am. Bible Soc. (bd. mgrs.; life), Phi Beta Kappa, Phi Sigma Kappa. Clubs: Shelter Island (N.Y.) Yacht; University (Chgo.). Author: It's Your Souls We Want, 1942; The Rebirth of the German Church, 1947; Report from Christian Europe, 1953. Contbr. to Christianity Today (edited by H.S. Leiper), 1947; The Lutheran Churches of the World, 1957. Home: Shelter Island NY 11965

HERMAN, THEODORE, educator; b. Phila., Mar. 11, 1913; s. Carl Lehman and Mollie (Levy) H.; A.B., Swarthmore Coll., 1935; M.A., Columbia Tchrs. Coll., 1936; M.A., U. Wash., 1952, Ph.D., 1954; m. Ch'en Shih-ying, Apr. 28, 1941; 1 dau., Evelyn L. Asst. prof. geography Utah State Agrl. Coll., 1953-55; vis. asst. prof. U. Wash., 1955—; mem. faculty Colgate U., 1955—, prof. geography, 1966—; vis. lectr. U. Leeds (Eng.), 1965- 66. Mem. Assn. Am. Geographers, Am. Geog. Soc., Assn. Asian Studies, Am. Civil Liberties Union. Home: RD 2 Hamilton NY 13346

HERMAN, WOODROW CHARLES, (Woody Herman), orchestra leader; b. Milw., May 16, 1913; s. Otto C. and Myrtle (Barth) H.; grad. St. John's Cathedral Prep. Sch., Milw., 1930; student Marquette U., 1930-31; m. Charlotte Neste, Sept. 27, 1936; 1 dau., Ingrid. Appeared vaudeville as Boy Wonder of the Clarinet, 1919; with Tom Gerun Orch., 1931, Gus Arnheim, 1933, Harry Sesnick, 1933, Isham Jones, 1934-36; organized orch. Band that Plays the Blues, 1936, later named First Herd, also Third Herd; toured Europe, 1954; appeared Carnegie Hall, 1946; recorded for Decca, Columbia, Capitol, MGM, Mars and Verve Records; now known as Woody Herman, The Old Woodchopper and His Orch.; toured Europe for State Dept., 1960; appeared Waldorf Astoria, 1961. Composer songs including Apple Honey, Northwest Passage, Woodchoppers Ball, Blowin' Up a Storm, Blues on Parade, Goosey Gander. Winner popularity poll Down Beat mag., 1945, Metronome mag., 1946, 53; recipient Billboard award, 1946. Silver award Esquire mag., 1946-47. Mem. Am. Fedn. Musicians, A.S.C.A.P. Home: 8620 Hollywood Blvd Los Angeles CA 90069

HERMANIUK, MAXIME, bishop; b. Nowe Selo, Ukraine, Oct. 30, 1911, s. Mykyta and Anna (Monczuk) H.; student philosophy, Louvain, Belgium, 1933-35, student Maitre Agrege Theol., 1947, Orient. Philol. and History, 1943. Came to Can., 1948, naturalized, 1954. Joined Redemptorist Congregation, 1933, ordained priest, 1938; supr. vice provincial Can. and U.S., 1948- 51; aux. bishop Winnipeg, Man., Can., 1951, apostelic adminstr. 1956, archbishop met., 1956—. First editor Logos, Ukraine Theol. Rev., 1950-51; mem. Vatican II Council, 1962-65; mem. Secretariat for Promoting Christian Unity, Rome, 1963; prof. moral theology, sociology and Hebrew, Beauplateau, 1943-45; prof. moral theology and holy scripture Redemptor Sem. Waterford, Ont. Can., 1949-51. Co-founder, mem. Ukrainian Relief Com., Belgium, 1942-48; co-founder, 1st pres. Ukrainian Cultural Soc., Belgium, 1947; organizer Ukrainian univ. students orgn. Obnova, Belgium, 1946-48, Can., 1953; Mem. joint working group Cath. ch. and World Council Chs., 1969. Mem. World Congress Free Ukrainians, Taras Shevchenko Sci. Soc. Author: La Parabole Evangelique, 1957; Our Duty, 1960. Address: 235 Scotia St Winnipeg 17 Manitoba Canada

HERMANN, ARTHUR FRANCIS, newspaper corr.; b. Providence, Oct. 16, 1912; m. Mary Ann Calli, June 26, 1938; 1 son, Arthur Francis. With various financial news agys., N.Y.C., 1930-37; Washington corr. for financial news agys., 1937-41; Washington staff Internat. News Service, 1941-58, exec. editor, 1949-58; corr. for Gannett Newspapers, 1958-61, McGraw-Hill Mags., 1961- 65; dir. Office Pub. Affairs, Fed. Home Loan Bank Bd., 1965—. Recipient Nat. Headliners' award, 1946. Mem. Sigma Delta Chi. Roman Catholic. Club: Nat. Press (Washington). Home: 203 E Indian Spring Dr Silver Spring MD 20901 Office: Nat Press Bldg Washington DC 20004

HERMANN, ROBERT, educator; b. Bklyn., Apr. 28, 1931; s. Boris and Alice (Reich) H.; student U. Wis., 1948-50; B.A., Brown U., 1952; postgrad. U. Amsterdam, 1952-53; Ph.D., Princeton, 1955; m. Lana Herman, July 31, 1970. Instr. Harvard, 1956-59; staff mathematician Lincoln Labs. of Mass. Inst. Tech., 1959-61; lectr. U. Cal., 1961-62; prof. mathematics Northwestern U., 1962-65, U. Cal. at Santa Cruz, 1966-69; mem. Inst. Advanced Study, Princeton, 1969-70; prof. math. Rutgers U., 1970—. Fulbright fellow, 1952-53; NSF fellow, 1954-56. Author: Lie Groups for Physicists, 1966; Differential Geometry and the Calculus of Variation, 1968; Fourier Analyses on Groups, 1969; Lie Algebras and Quantum Mechanics, 1970; Vector Bundles in Mathematical Physics, vols. I-II, 1970; Lectures in Mathematical Physics, vols. I-II, 1970-71. Home: 10 Landing Lane New Brunswick NJ 08901

HERMANN, WILLIAM HENRY, hosp. adminstr.; b. Hillsboro, Ill., Apr. 6, 1924; s. Fred William and Mearle Hermann (Bunta) H.; B.A., U. Mo., 1951; M.S., Yale, 1953; m. Loretta Pfister, July 28, 1956; children—Karen Elise, Diane Ellen. With Arabian-Am. Oil Co., Dhahran, Saudi Arabia, 1953-58, adminstr. Dhahran Health Center, 1956-58; mem. staff Touro Infirmary, New Orleans, 1958-67, dir., 1962-64, exec. dir., 1965-66; coordinator program in hosp. adminstrn. Tulane U. Med. Sch., 1965-68; adminstr. Mary I. Bassett Hosp. and Clinics, Cooperstown, N.Y., 1968—; lectr. pub. health and adminstrv. medicine Columbia U. Sch. Medicine. Pres., Cooperstown P.T.A. Served with M.C., USNR, 1945-47. Mem. Am. Hosp. Assn., Am. Coll. Hosp. Adminstrs. Am. Pub. Health Assn., Cooperstown C. of C. (dir.), Pi Kappa Alpha (life). Lion. Club: Internat. House (New Orleans). Home: 67 Lake St Cooperstown NY 13326 Office: Atwell Rd Cooperstown NY 13326

HERMANOVSKI, EGILS P., designer, artist; b. Latvia; s. Theodor H.; ed. U. Latvia, Tech. U., Stuttgart, Germany. Came to the U.S., 1947, naturalized, 1952. Artist, designer; one man shows include Studio H Gallery; archtl. designs for residences, restaurants, offices, motels, clubs; designer furniture, built-ins, fabrics, lighting, also indsl. designs; owner Studio H Gallery, N.Y.C.; chmn. bd. Internat. Bus. Designs, N.Y.C. Imprisoned by Nazis, 1944-47. Recipient numerous awards including Nat. Award for best house of the year Am. Home mag.; Nat. Award for best design and use of materials U.S. Plywood Corp.; Design award for residences Today's Home mag.; 1st prize Bronze Plaque for excellence in design C. of C., Borough of Queens. Mem. A.I.D., Latvian Inst. Architects. Contbr. articles popular mags., trade papers, U.S. and Europe. Office: Studio H Gallery 130 E 61st St New York City NY 10021

HERMANSON, GORDON ELMER, coll. pres.; b. Chgo., Oct. 11, 1916; s. Elmer Carl and Hildur Christine (Bloomgren) H.; Ph.B., Wheaton (Ill.) Coll., 1940; S.T.B., Bibl. Sem., N.Y.C., 1944; S.T.M., Temple U., 1953; postgrad. in edn. Columbia, 1959- 61; D.D. (hon.), Buena Vista Coll., 1965; LL.D., Concord Coll., 1970; m. Mary Louise Arison, Aug. 9, 1940; children—Gordon Edward, Mary Elizabeth, Robert William, Carol Ann. Ordained to ministry Presbyn. Ch., 1943; dir. edn. Ft. Washington Collegiate Ch., N.Y.C., 1943-45; dir. youthwork, dir. Christian edn. Commn. on Ecumenical Mission and Relations, United Presbyn. Ch., French Camerouns, W. Africa, 1945-49; minister Christian edn. 1st Presbyn. Ch., Germantown, Phila., 1949-53; asso. field dir., Synod of Pa., 1953-55; field dir. Met. N.Y. area Bd. Christian Edn., United Presbyn. Ch. of U.S.A., 1955-62; v.p. devel. Buena Vista Coll., Storm Lake, Ia., 1962-64; pres. Davis and Elkins Coll., Elkins, W.Va., 1964—. Address: Davis and Elkins Coll Elkins WV 26241

HERMENS, FERDINAND ALOYS, polit. scientist, economist; b. Nieheim, Germany, Dec. 20, 1906; s. Joseph Adam and Theresa (Hoffmeister) H.; student univs. of Muenster, Freiburg, Bonn, and Berlin, 1925-30; Diploma in econs. U. Bonn, 1928, Ph.D., 1930; student Faculte de Droit, Paris, 1930-31, London Sch. Econ. and Polit. Sci., 1934-35; m. Mary Ruth Roberts, Aug. 28, 1937; 1 dau., Mary Theresa. Came to U.S. 1935, naturalized 1939. Research fellowships Notgemeinschaft der Deutschen Wissenschaft, 1930-33; research asst. Inst. World Econs., Kiel, 1931-32; asst. prof. econs. Cath. U. Am., Washington, 1935-38; asso. prof. politics U. Notre Dame, 1938-45, prof. polit. sci., 1945-59, mem. Notre Dame Com. Internat. Relations, 1963—; prof. polit. sci., dir. research, Inst. Polit. Sci., U. Cologne, Germany, 1959—. Recipient grant in aid Social Sci. Research Council for polit. studies in Ireland, Netherlands, Belgium, France, Switzerland and Austria, 1937; vis. prof. with grant by Rockefeller Found., univs. of Muenster and Bonn, summer 1948; cons. civil affairs div. U.S. High Commn., Germany, 1951; vis. U.S. specialist, Germany, 1953-54. Fellow Woodrow Wilson Internat. Center for Scholars, 1972. Mem. Am. Polit. Sci. Assn., Pi Gamma Mu. Roman Catholic. Author books in English and German, latest publs.: Democracy or Anarchy?: A Study of Proportional Representation, 1941, rev. edit., 1971; The Tyrants' War and the Peoples' Peace, 1944; Europe Between Democracy and Anarchy, 1951; The Representative Republic, 1958 (2d German edit. 1968, Italian edit. 1968, Hebrew edit. 1968); The Fifth Republic, 1960. Editor series of brochures and monographs. Address: Schallstrasse 6 Köln-Lindenthal Germany ☆

HERMES, THOMAS JOSEPH, publisher; b. Joliet, Ill., June 13, 1924; s. Jacob George and Matilda (Stupy) H.; student Loyola U. of Chgo., 1941-43, Bowling Green U., 1943; B.S.C., Loyola U. of Chgo., 1947, postgrad., 1947; m. Beryl Stevenson, Jan. 18, 1945; children—Jill Ann (Mrs. Richard C. Mahony, Jr.), Kathleen, Thomas S., Cindy, Amy, Daniel. With Rand McNally & Co., Skokie, Ill., 1947—, Eastern sales mgr., 1956-60, gen. mgr. comml. div., 1960-65, v.p., 1963, v.p. marketing, 1966-70, exec. v.p., dir., 1970—; dir. Rolph McNally Ltd. (Can.), Hubbard-McNally Co., Mondadori-Rand McNally GmbH (Germany), A. & T. Tower Corp. Mem. sr. marketing exec. panel Nat. Indsl. Conf. Bd. Mem. Chgo. Crime Commn. Served from pvt. to 2d lt., USMC, 1942-46, from 1st lt. to capt., 1951-52. Decorated Bronze Star. Mem. Newcomen Soc. Roman Catholic. Home: 236 Mortimer Rd Glencoe IL 60022 Office: 8255 N Central Park Av Skokie IL 60076

HERMSEN, EDWARD HERMAN, oil co. exec., lawyer; b. De Pere, Wis., Feb. 17, 1911; s. Chris and Emily (Herman) H.; LL.B., Marquette U., 1934; m. Janet L. McGaffey, July 13, 1940; children—Edward S., David C. Admitted to Wis. bar, 1934; practiced in Oconto, Wis., 1934-42; admitted to Cal. bar, 1944; with Tidewater Oil Co., Los Angeles, and successor Getty Oil Co., 1960—, sec., 1971—. Mem. Wis., Cal., Los Angeles County bar assns., Am. Soc. Corporate Secs. Home: 175 N Highland Av Los Angeles CA 90036 Office: 3810 Wilshire Blvd Los Angeles CA 90010

HERNANDEZ, AMALIA, choreographer, tchr., dancer; b. Mexico City; student ballet and modern dance; trained in Spanish dance by Argentinta. Now specialist study dances and folklore of Mexico; tchr. modern dance Nat. Inst. Fine Arts, Mexico; formed small group to present Mexican folklore programs on TV, 1952, now know as Ballet Folklorico of Mexico, Mexico's nat. company. Address: care Ballet Folklorico-Mexico Mexico City Mexico*

HERNANDEZ, ANDRES S., govt. ofcl.; b. Deming, N.M., Feb. 4, 1913; s. Norberto and Altagracia (Saldana) H.; m. Amelia Anelia Anaya, May 29, 1947; 1 son, Isidro Jr. Technician U.S. Forest Service, 1937-39; regional agrl. aide U.S. Soil Conservation Service, 1939-40; asst. dir. Taos County Project Adult Edn., U. N.M., 1940-42; tng. officer, contact officer VA, 1946-56; adviser community devel. agrarian resettlement and rural devel. in Guatemala, Internat. Devel. Services, Inc., 1956-61; dir. Peace Corps in Dominican Republic, 1962-64, in Guatemala, 1964-67; rural devel. adviser AID, Guatemala, 1967—. Served with AUS, World War II; ETO. Mem. Phi Sigma Iota. Democrat. Roman Catholic. Office: Am Embassy Guatemala City Guatemala

HERNANDEZ, BENIGNO CARLOS, U.S. ambassador; b. Sante Fe, N.M., July 7, 1917; s. Benigno Cardenas and Frances (Whitlock) H.; B.A., U. N.M., 1941; J.D., De Paul U., 1948; m. Evangeline C. DeBaca, Nov. 6, 1943; children—Andrea Laura, Daniel John, David Nicholas, Cristina Leah. Admitted to N.M. bar, 1949; practiced law, Albuquerque, 1949-51; spl. asst. U.S. atty., Albuquerque, 1951- 52; partner Hernandez, Atkinson & Kelsey, Albuquerque, 1962—; U.S. ambassador to Paraguay, 1967—. Chmn., Albuquerque Citizens Com., 1953- 58, 63-64; chmn. N.M. chpt. Nat. Conf. Christians and Jews, 1964-65; v.p. exec. com. N.M. Rehab. Center, Albuquerque, 1964-65; mem. N.M. Bd. Finance, 1963-67, N.M. Bd. Penitentiary Commrs., 1953-55; nat. citizens adv. com. vocational rehab. Dept. Health, Edn. and Welfare, 1963-67, nat. adv. council Upward Bound Program, Office Econ. Opportunity, 1965—. Served to lt. USNR, 1942-46. Mem. Am. Legion, Albuquerque, Am., N.M. bar assns., Albuquerque Lawyers Club. Democrat. Presbyn. Club: Albuquerque Country. Address: Dept State Washington DC 20521

HERNANDEZ, FIDEL SANCHEZ, pres. of El Salvador. Address: Office of President San Salvador El Salvador*

HERNANDEZ, JUAN ESTEBAN, banker. Mgr. Banco Central de la Republica Dominicana, Santo Domingo. Address: Avenida Dr Pedro Henriques Vrena Santo Domingo Dominican Republic*

HERNANDEZ-MATOS, RAFAEL, justice of Puerto Rico; b. Cabo Rojo, P.R., Oct. 24, 1902; s. Pablo Hernandez-Cartagena and Enriqueta Matos-Cardoza; LL.B., U. P.R., 1926; m. Dorinda B. Colon, Oct. 24, 1934; children—Rafael, Jose-Angel, Cesar- Ariel. Admitted to P.R. bar, 1926, practiced in Ponce until 1957; asso. justice Supreme Ct. P.R., 1957—. Home: 434 Llorens Torres St Hato Rey San Juan PR 00917

HERNDON, CHARLES HARBISON, orthopaedic surgeon; b. Dublin, Tex., Dec. 12, 1915; s. G. Perkins and May (Williams) H.; B.A., U. Tex., 1937; M.D., Harvard, 1940; m. Kathryn Blair, Apr. 14, 1944; children—Charles Laylin, David Newcomb. Rotating surg. intern Univ. Hosps., Cleve., 1940-41; jr. orthopaedic surgeon Am. Hosp., Oxford, Eng., 1942; Gerard Beekman fellow orthopaedic surgery Hosp. Spl. Surgery, N.Y.C., 1945-46, resident in orthopaedic surgery, 1946-47; mem. faculty Case-Western Res. U. Sch. Medicine, 1947—, Rainbow prof. orthopaedic surgery, 1961—; dir. div. orthopaedic surgery Univ. Hosps., Cleve., 1953—, Rainbow Hosp., Cleve., 1952—; sr. cons. orthopaedic surgery Crile VA Hosp., 1956—; asso. orthopaedic surgeon Highland View Hosp., 1953—. Mem. profl. adv. bd. Ohio Services Crippled Children, 1959—; skeletal system com. NRC-Nat. Acad. Scis., 1958-67, chmn., 1962-67. Trustee Jour. Bone and Joint Surgery, 1969—, treas., 1971—. Served to maj. M.C., AUS, 1942-45; ETO. Diplomate Am. Bd. Orthopaedic Surgery (rep. bd. Am. Orthopaedic Assn., 1960-66, chmn. exam. com. 1961-64, pres. 1964-66). Mem. A.M.A., Am. Surg. Assn., A.C.S., Am. Acad. Orthopaedic Surgeons (pres. 1968, exec. com. 1967—), Orthopaedic Research Soc. (pres. 1957, exec. com. 1954-60), Am. Orthopaedic Assn., Internat. Soc. Orthopaedic Surgery and Traumatology, Am. Rheumatism Soc., Cleve. (pres. 1963-64), Ohio (sec.-treas. 1956-57), Clin. orthopaedic socs. Contbr. numerous articles profl. jours., chpts. in books. Home: 2380 Edgehill Rd Cleveland Heights OH 44106 Office: 2065 Adelbert Rd Cleveland OH 44106

HERNDON, CLAUDE NASH, educator, physician; b. Greensboro, N.C., Feb. 23, 1916; s. Claude Nash and Annie Lee (Mann) H.; A.B., Duke U., 1935; M.D., Jefferson Med. Coll., 1939; postgrad. U. Mich., 1941-42; m. Margaret Forester Caldwell, Oct. 10, 1942; children—Anne Herndon (Mrs. Kent W. Wilcox), Claude Nash III. Intern Charity Hosp., New Orleans, 1939-40; Carnegie fellow med. genetics Bowman Gray Sch. Medicine, Winston-Salem, N.C., 1940-41; research asso. U. Mich., 1941-42; instr. Bowman Gray Sch. Med., 1942-45, asst. prof., 1945-51, asso. prof., 1951-54, prof. med. genetics, 1954—; chmn. dept. preventive med., genetics 1957-70, asso. dean research devel., 1966—. Mem. AEC genetics research adv. com., 1955-58; mem. NIH adv. coms. on research career awards and health research facilities, 1957-69; Mem. population com. Nat. Inst. Child Health and Human Devel., 1970—. Bd. dirs. Children's Home Soc. N.C. Mem. Am. Soc. Human Genetics (bd. dirs. 1951-58, pres. 1955), Am. Eugenics Soc. (pres. 1952-55). Editor Am. Jour. Human Genetics, 1961-64. Contbr. articles profl. jours. Home: 1600 Lynwood Av Winston-Salem NC 27104

HERNDON, EDWARD TARR, investment banker; b. Springfield, Mo., July 14, 1899; s. Edward Lillian and Bessie Alexandria (Tarr) H.; A.B., Princeton, 1921; M.B.A., Harvard, 1923; m. Ruth Holloway, Oct. 13, 1934; children—Edward Tarr, Barbara Whitcomb. Bur. bus. research Harvard, 1923-24; investment banker Hayden, Stone & Co., N.Y.C., 1924-26; pvt. banker J. Henry Schroder Banking Corp., N.Y.C., 1926-31; asst. sec. Petroleum Heat & Power Co., Stamford, Conn., 1931-33; asst. to v.p., treas. Valspar Corp., N.Y.C., 1933-35; investment banker, partner Eastman, Dillon & Co., N.Y.C., also successor firm Eastman Dillon, Union Securities & Co., 1935—; dir. Suburban Propane Gas Corp., Whippany, N.J. Bd. dirs. Manhattan Eye, Ear and Throat Hosp., N.Y.C. Mem. Phi Beta Kappa. Clubs: Union, Church (N.Y.C.); Country New Canaan, (Conn.); Tokeneke (Darien, Conn.); West Side Tennis (Forest Hills, L.I., N.Y.). Home: Gerrish Lane New Canaan CT 06840 Office: 1 Chase Manhattan Plaza New York City NY 10005

HERNDON, JAMES FRANCIS, educator; b. Indpls., Aug. 11, 1929; s. Francis Earl and Agnes (Demmer) H.; student John Herron Sch. Fine Arts, 1949; B.A., Ind. U., 1952; M.A., Wayne State U., 1956; Ph.D., U. Mich., 1963; m. Doris Arlene Beall, Dec. 24, 1952; 1 son, David Lyle. Instr., Drake U., Des Moines, 1959-60; asst. prof. U. N.D., 1960-63, asso. prof., 1963-67, coordinator Honors Program, 1965-66, asso. dean arts and scis., 1967; asso. prof. Va. Poly. Inst., Blacksburg, 1967-70, prof., chmn. dept. polit. sci., 1970—; dir. Summer Inst. in Math. Applications in Polit. Sci., 1969-71. Bd. dirs. Am. Civil Liberties Union of Va. Served with CIC, U.S. Army, 1952-54. Recipient Faculty-Student Teaching award U. N.D., 1965; Faculty lectr., 1966. Mem. Am., Midwest, So. polit. sci. assns., Soc. for Gen. Systems Research, Americans for Democratic Action. Unitarian. Co-editor: Selected Bibliography of Materials in State and Local Government, 1963; Mathematical Application in Political Science, Vols. V and VI, 1970, 71. Home: Kessler Park Blacksburg VA 24060

HERNDON, LYLE KERMIT, chem. engr.; b. Buckhannon, W.Va., June 25, 1905; s. James Edward and Wilna (Conn) H.; B.Sc., Ohio State U., 1929, M.Sc., 1931, Ph.D., 1938; Chem.E., W.Va. U., 1934; m. Ruth Elizabeth Weinman, July 3, 1939. City chemist, Charleston, W.Va., 1925-29; chem. engr. W.Va. water Commn., 1929-33, E.I. Dupont de Nemours, Belle, W.Va., 1933-36; with Ohio State U., 1936-60, beginning as instr. chem. engring., successively asst. and asso. prof., prof., 1946-60; cons. engr., 1944-49; dir. research Mathieson Chem. Corp., N.Y.C., 1949-53, v.p. chem. research, research and devel. div., 1953-54; tech. dir. Aviation div. Olin Mathieson Chem. Corp., 1954-56, v.p. energy div., N.Y.C., 1956-60, tech. adviser, 1960—; v.p., treas. Weinman Pump Mfg. Co., 1953-60, chmn. bd., 1960—, pres., 1962—. Mem. Sigma Xi, Tau Beta Pi, Phi Lambda Upsilon, Gamma Alpha. Republican. Methodist. Mason, Rotarian. Home: 2303 Onandaga Dr Columbus OH 43221 Office: 290 Spruce St Columbus OH 43215

HERNDON, VENABLE, author, (play) Until the Monkey Comes. Address: care Hill and Wang 141 5th Av New York City NY 10010 *

HERNDON, VERNON EDWARD, hotel exec.; b. Albuquerque, June 5, 1907; s. James Baird and Blanche (Dunkerley) H.; student U. Cal., 1927-30; m. Louise Carter, July 26, 1948; children—Peter V., Patricia, Michael, Sally. Various positions Hilton Hotel Corp., Tex., N.M., Cal., Ill., 1930-47; former gen. mgr. Palmer House, Chgo.; now sr. v.p. Hilton Hotels Corp. Served as lt. comdr. USNR, 1941-45. Mem. Internat. (exec. com.), Am. (chmn. Bd. 1960- 61), New Orleans (pres. 1933), West Tex. (pres. 1939), Chgo. (dir.) hotel assns., Beta Theta Pi. Home: 233 E Walton Pl Chicago IL 60611

HERNDON, WALTER ROGER, Jr., biologist, educator; b. Birmingham, Ala., Sept. 7, 1926; s. Walter Roger and Carrie (Moore) H.; B.S., U. Ala., 1947, M.S., 1948; Ph.D., Vanderbilt U., 1954; m. Sue Haynie, July 8, 1949; children—Martha, Susan, Stephen, Thomas. Mem. faculty U. Ala., 1947-48, 55-61, asso. prof. biology, 1959-61; grad. asst. teaching fellow Vanderbilt U., 1948- 50, 53-54; instr. Middle Tenn. State Coll., 1950-54, asst. prof., 1954- 55; prof. botany, U. Tenn., Knoxville, 1961—, asso. dean Coll. Liberal Arts, 1961-67, asst. v.p. acad. affairs, 1967-68, asso. vice chancellor for acad. affairs, 1968—. Mem. staff Mountain Lake Biol. Sta., summer 1958; mem. staff marine botany Marine Biol. Lab., 1959-63. Served to lt. comdr. USNR, 1943-46, 51-53. Mem. Tenn. Acad. Sci., So. Appalachian Bot. Club, Assn. Southeastern Biologists (exec. com. 1961-63), Internat. Phycological Soc., Phycological Soc. Am. (pres. 1965-66), Bot. Soc. Am. Home: 3833 Maloney Rd Knoxville TN 37920

HERNDON, WILLIAM CECIL, educator; b. El Paso, Tex., Aug. 12, 1932; s. Robert and Elizabeth (Masten) H.; B.S., Tex. Western Coll., 1954; Ph.D., Rice U., 1959; m. Nancy R. Fairbanks, Dec. 27, 1956; children—William Robert, Mathew Fairbanks. Research chemist Am. Cyanamid Co., 1957-61; asst. prof. U. Miss., 1961-64; asso. prof. Fla. Atlantic U., 1964-66; prof. chemistry Tex. Tech U., Lubbock, 1966—. Vis. prof. Bell Telephone Labs., 1966, 68. NSF fellow, 1954. Fellow A.A.A.S.; mem. N.Y. Acad. Sci., Am. Chem. Soc., Sigma Xi. Contbr. articles to profl. jours. Address: Chemistry Dept Tech Tech Univ Lubbock TX 79404

HERNTON, CALVIN C., author; b. Chattanooga, Apr. 28, 1932; s. Magnolia Jackson; B.A., Talladega Coll., 1954; M.A., Fisk U., 1956; postgrad. Columbia, 1961; married; 1 child, Antone. Instr. social sci. various colls. in South, 1957-61; child social worker, social investigator N.Y., 1956-57, 61-62. Author: (poetry) The Coming of Chronos to the House of Nightsong, 1963; Sex and Racism in America, 1965; also plays. Contbr. to anthologies and Negro Digest, Freedomways, others. Address: care Grove Press Inc 80 University Place New York City NY 10003 *

HERO, ALFRED OLIVIER, Jr., found. exec.; b. New Orleans, Feb. 7, 1924; s. Alfred Olivier and Effel Anita (Pearson) H.; student Va. Mil. Inst., 1941-42; B.S., U.S. Mil. Acad., 1945; M.A., Vanderbilt U., 1950; post grad. Georgetown U., 1950- 51; Ph.D., George Washington U., 1957; student Inf. Sch., 1952- 53; m. Barbara Ann Ferrell, May 22, 1954; children—Alfred Olivier III, Barbara Ann, Michelle, David. Commd. 2d lt. U.S. Army, 1945, advanced to capt., 1950; mem. occupation forces Office Mil. Govt. U.S., Germany, 1945- 48; staff Office Chief Personnel G-1, Dept. Army, 1950-52; faculty Inf. Sch., Fort Benning, Ga., 1953; exec. sec. World Peace Found., 1954-70, dir., sec., 1970—; mng. editor Internat. Orgn., 1954-70, dir., 1970—. Mem. Am. Polit. Sci. Assn. Author: The Southerner and World Affairs, 1965; The Reuther-Meany Foreign Policy Dispute, 1971; American Religious Groups View Foreign Policy; Trends in Rank-and-File Opinion, 1937-1969, 1971. Home: 67 Larch Rd Cambridge MA 02138 Office: 40 Mt Vernon St Boston MA 02108

HEROD, WILLIAM ROGERS, bus cons.; b. Indpls., Feb. 13, 1898; s. William P. and Mary Beaty (Applegate) H.; Ph.B. in Mech. Engring. magna cum laude, Sheffield Sci. Sch., Yale, 1918; m. Caroline K. Fries, Aug. 10, 1949. Student engr., test course Gen. Electric Co., Schenectady, 1919, spl. asst. constrn. engring. dept., 1919-29; asst. to pres. Internat. Gen. Electric Co., N.Y.C., 1929-34; asst. to mng. dir. Asso. Elec. Industries, Ltd., London, 1934-37; v.p. Internat. Gen. Electric Co., 1937-42, exec. v.p., July-Sept. 1945, pres., 1945-60, ret., 1960, dir. 1945-52; v.p. Gen. Electric Co., 1952-60, ret., 1960;. cons. on internat. bus., 1960—; dir. Transatlantic Fund, Inc., 580 Park Av., Inc., others. Apptd. coordinator def. prodn. NATO, 1951, with personal rank of minister. Mem. City Planning Commn., Schenectady, 1923. Served as pvt., 10th Regt., Conn. N.G., 1916; mem. R.O.T.C., Yale, 1917-18; from pvt. to 1st lt. U.S. Army, 1918; 1st lt. F.A., O.R.C., 1919-24; commd. lt. col. USAAF, 1942, col., 1943; inactive status, 1945. Mem. univ. council Yale and chmn. com. div. engring., 1948-51; ex-officio mem. Yale Alumni Bd., 1952—; asso. fellow Pierson Coll., Yale, 1948-51. Mem. Latin-Am. Subcom. Bus. Adv. Council, Washington, 1948-51, 56-58, chmn., 1950; dir. emeritus Internat. House, N.Y. C.; dir. Spanish Inst., Inc. Profl. engr., N.Y. Decorated Commenda dell' Ordine al Merito della Republica Italiana; Order of Sacred Treasure, 3d Class (Japan), 1957; Oficial, Ordem Nacional do Cruzeiro do Sul (Brazil), 1958; caballero Gran Cruz de la Ordendel Merita Civil (Spain), 1958; Capt. Robert Dollar Meml. Award for distinguished contbn. to advancement fgn. trade Nat. Fgn. Trade Council, 1958. Mem. Council Fgn. Relations; dir. Nat. Fgn. Trade Council, 1946-67, Philharmonic-Symphony Soc. N.Y.; mem. China Med. Bd., 1947-68. Mem. I.E.E.E. (life), Am. Soc. M.E. (life), Inst. Internat. Edn. (hon. trustee), Atlantic Council U.S. (dir.), Nat. Inst. Social Scis., Acad. Polit. Sci., Internat. C. of C. (U.S. council), Archaeol. Inst. Am., Sigma Xi. Republican. Clubs: Explorer, Pilgrims, University, Union, Yale, Metropolitan Opera (N.Y.C.); Graduates, Lawn (New Haven); American (London); Mohawk (Schenectady). Patentee elec. discharge due change humidity atmosphere. Home: 580 Park Av New York City NY 10021 Office: 53 E 66th St New York City NY 10021

HEROLD, CRESTON C., exec. dir. Am. Congress Phys. Medicine and Rehab., Chgo. Address: 30 N Michigan Av Chicago IL 60602*

HEROLD, PAUL GEORGE, educator; b. Mansfield, O., May 13, 1909; s. Jacob Samuel and Edith (Raab) H.; B. Ceramic Engring., Ohio State U., 1931, M.S., 1932, Ph.D., 1934; postdoctorate U. Ill., 1935; m. Grayce Leona Sutley, Aug. 31, 1934; children—Mary (Mrs. John L. Witwer), Margaret (Mrs. Rodney L. Kendig). Research engr. A.C. Spark Plug Co., Flint Mich., 1934-36; mem. faculty Mo. Sch. Mines, Rolla, 1936-65, asso. prof., 1938-41, prof., 1941-65, also head dept., 1938-65; prof. metallurgy Colo. Sch. Mines, Golden, 1963—, also head dept. metallurgy, 1969—. Dir. Mo. Clay Testing and Research Labs., Rolla, 1941-55; sr. engr. Radio Corp. Am., Lancaster, Pa., 1955-63; v.p. Information Systems Assos., Inc., Honolulu, 1970—, also dir. Fellow Am. Ceramic Soc. (chmn refractories div. 1953), mem. Am. Inst. Mining and Metall. Engrs., Inst. Ceramic Engrs., Am. Soc. Engring. Edn. (chmn. mineral industries div. 1970), Ceramic Edn. Council (past pres.), Sigma Xi, Sigma Pi, Alpha Chi Sigma, Tau Beta Pi, Keramos (grand pres. 1950), Kappa Kappa Psi. Presbyn. (elder). Patentee in field. Home: 1221 Illinois St Golden CO 80401

HERON, CHARLES L., utility co. exec.; b. McDonald, Pa., Oct. 30, 1918; s. Merle L. and Maude (Kunkle) H.; Bus. Adminstrn. degree, Robert Morris Coll., 1942, grad. student, 1949-50; m. LaVerne Pierson, Aug. 28, 1937; children—Joanne (Mrs. Joseph Delahaut), Janet (Mrs. R.S. Bakewell), James R. C.P.A. Price Waterhouse & Co., Pitts., 1942-53; supr. systems Peoples Natural Gas Co., Pitts., 1953-56, asst. treas., 1956-64, treas., dir., 1964—. Councilman McDonald, Pa., 1970—; Republican committeeman, 1963—; mem. adv. bd. Inst. for Mgmt. Robert Morris Coll., 1970—. Served with USMCR, 1944-45. Recipient Robert Morris Coll. Alumni Heritage award, 1965. Mem. Am. Gas Assn., Am. Inst. C.P.A.'s, Newcomen Soc., Financial Execs. Inst., Valley of Pitts. Consistory. Republican. Presbyn. Mason (32). Home: 317 4th St McDonald PA 15057 Office: 2 Gateway Center Pittsburgh PA 15222

HERON, DAVID WINSTON, librarian; b. Los Angeles, Mar. 29, 1920; s. Charles Morton and Elizabeth (Atsatt) H.; A.B., Pomona Coll., 1942; B.L.S., U. Cal. at Berkeley, 1948; M.A., U. Cal. at Los Angeles, 1951; m. Winifred Ann Wright, Aug. 24, 1946; children—Holly Winston, James, Charles. Reference asst. U. Cal. at Los Angeles Library, 1948-52; librarian Am. embassy, Tokyo, Japan, 1952-53; staff asst. to librarian, librarian Grad. Reading Room, U. Cal. at Los Angeles, 1953-55; asst. to dir. Stanford Libraries, 1955-57, asst. dir., 1959-61; asst. librarian Hoover Instn., Stanford, 1957-59; dir. libraries U. Nev., Reno, 1961-68, U. Kan., Lawrence, 1968- -. Library adviser U. Ryukyus, Naha, Okinawa, 1960-61. Served as 1st lt. AUS, 1942-46; ETO. Mem. Am. (exec. bd.), Kan. library assns., Am. Assn. U. Profs., Am. Civil Liberties Union, Internat. House Japan, Assn. Coll. and Research Libraries (editor monographs; chmn. U. libraries sect. 1970-71). Democrat. Editorial bd. Coll. and Research Libraries. Contbr. articles to gen. and profl. jours. Home: 802 Tennessee Av Lawrence KS 66044

HERPEL, GEORGE LLOYD, educator; b. St. Louis, Aug. 31, 1921; s. George Martin and Irene (Lloyd) H.; B.A., Vanderbilt U., 1943, M.A., 1943, M.B.A., 1955; Ph.D., St. Louis U., 1958; m. June L. Stamm, Nov. 22, 1944; children—John, Mark. Gen. sales mgr., dir. pub. relations C.V. Mosby Pub. Co., St. Louis, 1947-54; dir. mgmt. devel. Internat. Shoe Co., St. Louis, 1954- 62; prof. marketing, Temple U., 1962—, dean faculty, 1964- -; chmn. bd. trustees Grad. Sch. Sales and Marketing Mgmt., Syracuse U., 1962-64. Mem. Regional Export Expansion Com; chmn. Export Planning Com., Phila. Pres. Hedgerow Theatre Corp., 1971—; dir. W.A. Krueger Co., Milw., 1971—. Served with USNR, 1943-46. Mem. Sales Execs. Assn. St. Louis (pres. 1954-56), Am. Marketing Assn. (pres. St. Louis 1957-58, nat. v.p. 1963-65), Sales Marketing Execs. Internat. (bd. dirs., exec. com. 1954-64), Vanderbilt U. Alumni Assn. (pres. St. Louis 1950), Pi Sigma Epsilon (bd. dirs. 1960-69), Beta Theta Pi (pres. St. Louis 1949). Home: 9 Single Lane Wallingford PA 19086 Office: Temple Univ Philadelphis PA 19122

HERPICH, CHARLES RAYMOND, oil co. exec.; b. Wheeling, W.Va., Apr. 13, 1907; s. Charles R. and Lillie (Weiss) H.; student Carnegie Inst. Tech., 1927-28, 35-37, U. Pitts., 1928-29; m. Josephine Weaver, Sept. 8, 1943; children—Charles R., Lynn H., David S. With Plymouth Oil Co., Pitts., 1923-63, asst. treas., asst. sec., 1929-47, sec., asst. treas., 1947-50, sec., treas., 1950-56, dir., 1952-63, v.p., treas., exec. com., 1956-63; sec., treas., dir., mem. exec. com. The Permian Corp., Midland, Tex., 1963—. Served from 1st lt. to maj., AUS, 1942-45. Evangelical Lutheran. Mason, Rotarian. Home: 10622 Tupper Lake Dr Houston TX 77042 Office: Box 1183 Houston TX 77001

HERR, FREDERICK JOHN, Jr., electric utility exec.; b. Bklyn., Oct. 23, 1910; s. Frederick John and Meta (Hansen) H.; B.S., N.Y.U., 1936; m. Florence L. Farwell, Dec. 27, 1943; children—Roger Farwell, Evelyn. With Lehman Corp., 1936-41, Lehman Bros., 1946-53; asst. to pres. Central and South West Corp., 1953-58, v.p., 1958-68; financial v.p., 1968—; dir. Bank Del. Served to lt. comdr. USNR, 1941-45. Mem. Investment Analysts Soc. Club: University (Chgo.). Home: 2 Winding Way Greenville Wilmington DE 19807 Office: 300 Delaware Av Wilmington DE 19899

HERR, RICHARD, educator; b. Guanajuato, Mexico, Apr. 7, 1922 (parents Am. citizens); s. Irving and Luella (Winship) H.; A.B., Harvard, 1943; Ph.D., U. Chgo., 1954; m. Elene Fernandez Mel, Mar. 2, 1946 (div. 1967); children—Charles Fernandez, Winship Richard; m. 2d, Valerie J. Jackson, Aug. 29, 1968; 1 child, Sarah. Instr. Yale, 1952-57, asst. prof., 1957-59; asso. prof. U. Cal., Berkeley, 1960-63, prof. history, 1963—. Served with AUS, 1943-45. Social Sci. Research Council grantee, 1963-64; Guggenheim fellow, 1959-60; sr. fellow Nat. Endowment for Humanities, 1968-69. Mem. Am. Hist. Assn., Soc. For French Hist. Studies, Soc. for Spanish and Portuguese Hist. Studies, Real Academia de la Historia Madrid. Author: The Eighteenth Century Revolution in Spain, 1958; Tocqueville and the Old Regime, 1962; Spain, 1971. Co-editor, contbr. Ideas in History, 1964. Asst. editor: Jour. Modern History, 1949- 50. Mem. editorial bd. French Historical Studies, 1966-69.†

HERRERA, FELIPE, banker; b. Valparaiso, Chile, June 17, 1922; s. Joaquin and Ines (Lane) H.; student German and mil. schs.; Degree Licenciado in Law and Social Scis., U. Chile, 1946, law degree, 1947;

postgrad. London Sch. Econs.; Dr. Economy (hon.) U. San Marcos, Lima, Peru, 1964; Dr. (hon.), Nat. U. Asuncón (Paraguay), 1964; LL.D., Am. U., 1966, U. Pitts., Columbia U., U. Cal. Los Angeles, 1967, U. Miami, Hamilton Coll., 1970—; Dr. Social Scis. and Humanities, U. of Am., Bogota, Colombia, 1966; m. Rosa Alamos, June 28, 1947; children—Luis Felipe, Claudio; m. 2d, Ines Olmo, Sept. 2, 1961. Atty., legal dept. Central Bank of Chile, 1943-52; prof. econs. Sch. Law, Sch. Sociology, U. Chile, 1947-58; under-sec. economy and commerce, Chile, 1952, minister of finance, 1953; gen. mgr. Central Bank of Chile, 1953-58; 1953-58; gov. for Chile, Internat. Bank Reconstrn. and Devel., also IMF 1953-58; exec. dir. IMF, representing Argentina, Bolivia, Chile, Ecuador, Paraguay and Uruguay, 1958-59; pres. Inter-Am. Devel. Bank, 1960-71. Del. of Chile to Inter-Am. Econ. Conf., Rio de Janeiro, 1954, Buenos Aires, 1957. Decorated Great Cross for Distinguished Service (Germany); Cavalier Grand Cross Order of Merit (Italy); Civic medal Camilo Torress (Colombia); Great Cross Nat. Order for Ednl. Merit (Brazil); recipient Gormaz prize for outstanding scholarship U. Chile; Eugenio Maria de Hostos One America award Soc. Friends of P.R., 1965; Bronfman prize Am. Pub. Health Assn., 1969; others. Author numerous publs. on econs., 1945—. Home: 3041 Normanstone Terrace Washington DC 20008 Office: Inter-Am Develop Bank Washington DC 20577

HERRICK, ALLAN ADAIR, lawyer; b. Humboldt, Ia., Apr. 22, 1896; s. Fred Goodrich and Dora L. (Connor) H.; A.B., U. Ia., 1917, LL.B., 1920; m. Margie Pinkham, June 30, 1920; children—Robert Allan, Margie May (Mrs. Robert Henry), Jane Kathleen (Mrs. Martin J. Grothe). Admitted to Ia. bar, 1920; practiced law, Estherville, 1920-25; mem. Strock Sloan & Herrick, Des Moines, 1926-31, Herrick & Langdon, now mem. firm Herrick, Langdon, Belin and Harris. Judge, 9th Jud. Dist. Ia., 1931-35; spl. master chancery U.S. Dist., 1935-51; spl. asst. atty. gen. Ia. for prosecution conspiracy, manslaughter, assault and malicious mischief cases arising from labor dispute and packing house strike Rath Packing Plant, Waterloo, Ia., 1948-51. Chmn. Bd. Certified Ct. Reporters Examiners of Ia., 1936—, Bd. Examiners City Assessor and Deps., Des Moines, 1950—. Served from seaman to ensign USN, 1917-18, sr. lt. USNRF, 1933-39. Mem. Ia. (1st chmn. com. uniform jury instrn.), Polk County (chmn. jud. com.) bar assns., Am. Legion, Phi Delta Phi, Delta Sigma Rho. Omicron Delta Kappa, Acacia. Mason. Home: 3663 Grand Av Des Moines IA 50312 Office: Home Fed Bldg Des Moines IA 50309

HERRICK, ALLYN MARSH, forester, univ. dean; b. Syracuse, N.Y, July 15, 1912; s. Clinton S. and Olive (Andrews) H.; B.S., State U. N.Y., 1934, M.F., 1935; Ph.D., U. Mich., 1945; m. Nadine Van Patten, June 1, 1935 (div. Apr. 1968; children-Nadine Kay, Marsh Anne, Lucinda, Deverah; m. 2d, Jacqueline Dozier Moore, July 25, 1969. Asst. forester Tex. Forest Service, 1935; asst. prof. forestry U. Ga., 1936-37, dean Sch. Forestry, 1957—; instr., asst. prof., asso. prof., then prof. forestry Purdue U., 1937-56; collaborator U.S. Forest Service, 1942-43. Mem. Ga. Bd. Registration for Foresters. Mem. Soc. Am. Foresters, Forest Products Research Soc., Sigma Xi, Phi Kappa Phi, Xi Sigma Pi, Phi Gamma Delta. Episcopalian. Mason, Elk, Rotarian. Contbr. Research in the Economics of Forestry, 1953. Author: tech. papers. Home: 135 Danielsville Jefferson GA 30549

HERRICK, FRANCIS HERKOMER, educator, historian; b. Cleve., Aug. 24, 1900; s. Francis Hobart and Josephine (Herkomer) H.; B.A., Western Res. U., 1922; M.A., U. Wis., 1923; B.A., Oxford (Eng.) U., 1925; Ph.D., Yale, 1935; m. Mariam Arnold White, Nov. 23, 1930; children—Mariam Elizabeth (Mrs. D.F. Slater), Charles P. (dec.), Margaret Josephine (Mrs. Jay Ford). Faculty Mills Coll., 1926—, prof. history, 1942-66, prof. emeritus, 1966—; sec.-treas. Pacific Coast br. Am. Hist. Assn., 1934-40, mem. council, 1947, 56, v.p., 1959, pres., 1960; mem. exec. com. Western Coll. Assn., 1948-49, mem. commn. membership and standards, 1956-58, exec. sec.-treas., 1965-69. Rhodes scholar, 1923-26. Mem. Am. Hist. Assn., Assn. Am. Rhodes Scholars, Phi Beta Kappa. Mem. bd. editors Pacific Hist. Rev., 1944. Translator: Europe Under the Old Regime, 2d edit., 1964. Home: PO Box 5062 Carmel CA 93921

HERRICK, GEORGE Q., electronics exec.; b. Newburgh, N.Y., May 14, 1915; s. Henry F. and Clara B.(Quinette) H.; student N.Y. U., 1932-34; m. Lillian A. Campbell, July 22, 1938; children—Christopher, Gavin (dec.), George, Kathleen. Chief engr. Hearst Radio, Inc., 1935; now cons. engr. and design engr. UN, Mut. Broadcasting System and Capital Recording Co. Became chief engr. OWI, 1942; designer radio master control and recording system, 1943; rehab. Munich Short Wave installations, 1946; designer IBd-Clipper amplifiers, 1948; chief of facilities br. Internat. Broadcast Div. Dept. of State, 1948, responsibilities including design, constrn., installation, operations and maintenance of all radio broadcast facilities of the dept., both overseas and domestic; dir. U.S. anti-jam operations Dept. of State, 1949-53 (superior service medal 1951); asst. to v.p. engring. products Gen. Precision Lab. Inc., 1953-57; v.p., gen. mgr. research and devel. Prodn. Research Corp., Thornwood, N.Y., 1957-60; v.p., gen. mgr., research and devel. div., Radio Condenser Co., Camden, N.J., 1960-63; electronics product mgr. Singer Metrics div. The Singer Co., Bridgeport, Conn. 1963-67; dir. operations Radio Liberty, Munich, Germany, 1967—. Democrat. Home: Ludwig Thoma Str 9 8022 Grunwald Munich Germany Office: Radio Liberty Munich Germany

HERRICK, H.T., govt. ofcl.; b. N.Y.C., Apr. 24, 1920; s. Horace Terhune and Elinore (Morehouse) H.; B.S., Hamilton Coll., 1942; LL.B., Cornell U., 1948; m. Virginia Boardman Leigh, Oct. 6, 1945 (dec. 1964); children—Christine Terhune, David Morse; m. 2d, Allison Butler, May 1, 1965. Admitted to N.Y. bar, 1949; asso. firm Paul, Weiss, Wharton & Garrison, N.Y.C., 1948- 50; atty. NLRB, 1950-57; labor atty. Westinghouse Electric Corp., 1957- 61; asst. to asst. sec. labor, 1961-63; gen. counsel Fed. Mediation and Conciliation Service, 1963-65; dir. div. of labor relations AEC, 1966—; adj. prof. Georgetown U. Sch. Law, 1965. Served with USAAF, 1942- 45. Mem. Am., Fed. bar assns. Unitarian. Home: 2808 R St NW Washington DC 20007 Office: US AEC Germantown MD 20545

HERRICK, KENNETH G., corp. exec.; b. Jackson, Mich., Apr. 2, 1921; s. Ray W. and Hazel M. (Forney) H.; grad. mil. sch., 1940; m. Shirley J. Todd, Mar. 2, 1942; children—Todd W., Toni. With Tecumseh Products Co. (Mich.), 1940—, now pres., chief exec. officer; dir. Gen. Telephone Co. Mich., Nat. Bank Jackson, United Savs. Bank, Tecumseh Bd. dirs. Lenawee County YMCA, Howe Mil. Sch., Herrick Meml. Hosp., Herrick Found. Served with USAAF, 1942-45. Mem. Am. Legion. Mason, Elk. Home: 713 Red Mill Dr 49286 Office: Tecumseh Products Co Tecumseh MI 49286

HERRICK, MRS. MARGARET BUCK, librarian; b. Spokane, Sept. 27; d. Nathan Kimball and Adaline (Morie) Buck; A.B., U. Wash., 1927, B.S. in L.S., 1928. Children's librarian Yakima (Wash.) Pub. Library, 1928-29, city librarian, 1929-31; librarian Acad. of Motion Picture Arts and Scis., Hollywood, Cal., 1931-43, exec. dir., 1943-70. Mem. Am. Assn. U. Women, A.L.A. Republican. Episcopalian. Home: 165 S Bowling Green Way Los Angeles CA 90049

HERRICK, PAUL MURRAY, clergyman; b. Scandia, Kan., Apr. 3, 1898; s. Philo M. and Alice Mary (McKee) H.; A.B., Kansas City U., 1922; B.D., Union Theol. Sem., 1927; M.A., Phillips U., 1935; D.D., York Coll., 1937; LL.D., Otterbein Coll., 1960; m. Ruth Porter, June 7, 1922; children—Bruce O., Philip O., Laura Ruth. Ordained to ministry Evang. U.B. Ch., 1927; dist. supt., Mo., 1927- 29; pastor in Mo., Okla., Kan., 1929-41, 1st U.B. Ch., Dayton, O., 1941- 58; bishop Central Area, Evang. U.B. Ch., Dayton, 1958—. Served with U.S. Army, World War I. Mason (33), Kiwanian. Home: 2018 Harvard Blvd Dayton OH 45406 Office: 601 W Riverview Av Dayton OH 45406

HERRICK, SAMUEL, Jr., astronomer; b. Madison County, Va., May 29, 1911; s. Samuel and Fanny (Field) H.; A.B., Williams Coll., 1932, D.Sc., 1962; Ph.D., U. Cal., Berkeley, 1936; m. Betulia Toro, June 15, 1934; children—Henry Toro (killed in action in Vietnam, 1965), Nike Toro, Samuel Rufus. A.F. Morrison fellow Lick Obs., 1936-37; acting asst. prof. astronomy U. Wash., 1937; instr. U. Cal., Los Angeles, 1937-42, asst. prof., 1942-47, asso. prof., 1947-52, prof. astronomy, 1959-62, prof. astronomy and engring., 1962—, chmn. dept. astronomy, 1943-45, 46-51; Hunsaker prof. Mass. Inst. Tech., 1961-62. Mathematician Nat. Bur. Standards, 1948-49; orbit determination cons. govt., industry, 1947—. Guggenheim fellow, 1945- 46, 52-53. Fellow Brit. Inst. Nav. (hon. mem.), Royal Astron. Soc., Am. Astronautical Soc., Brit. Interplanetary Soc., Am. Inst. Aeros. and Astronautics (dir. 1963-65); hon. mem. Inst. Nav. (exec. sec. 1945-52, pres. 1952-53, chmn. space navigation com. 1957-60); mem. Internat. Astron. Union, Am. Astron. Soc., Internat. Acad. Astronautics, Astron. Soc., Pacific, Phi Beta Kappa. Author: Tables for Rocket and Comet Orbits, 1953; Astrodynamics, 1971. Home: 13500 Mulholland Dr Beverly Hills CA 90210 Office: Boelter Hall U California Los Angeles CA 90024

HERRIDGE, FRANCES, drama and film editor; b. Troy, N.Y.; d. Frederick and Elizabeth (Osgood) Herridge; B.A., Smith Coll., 1933; post grad. N.Y.U., New Sch. Social Research; m. John Tull Baker, 1947 (div.); 1 son, George Henry; m. 2d, Adna H. Karns. Asst. to Max Lerner, dance critic for PM, 1945-48; beauty and children's editor N.Y. Post, 1949-54, drama editor, dance critic, 1954-64, drama and movie editor, dance critic, 1964—. Home: 305 W 28th St New York City, NY 10001 Office: New York Post 210 South St New York City NY 10002

HERRIN, EUGENE THORNTON, educator, geologist; b. Dallas, Nov. 19, 1929; s. Eugene Thornton and Dorothy (Johnston) H.; B.S., So. Methodist U., 1951, M.S., 1953; Ph.D., Harvard, 1958; m. Barbara Bradshaw, Dec. 20, 1953; children—Kathleen, Laura. Mem. faculty So. Methodist U., Dallas, 1955—, prof. geology, 1964—, chmn. dept. geol. sci., 1971—, dir. Dallas Seismol. Obs., 1958—, cons. prof. S.W. Center for Advanced Studies, 1964—. Recipient Grove Karl Gilbert award, 1964. Carnegie Inst. Washington fellow, 1964. Fellow Am. Geophys. Union, Geol. Soc. Am.; mem. Dallas Geophys. Soc., Seismol. Soc. Am., Seismology of Am. Geophys. Union (v.p. 1964). Research and numerous publs. in seismology especially determination of seismic travel-times and location of earthquakes and explosion. Home: 5555 Winston Ct Dallas TX 75220

HERRIN, JOHN S., oil co. exec.; b. Charlie, Tex., 1907. Former pres., dir. Empire State Oil Co., Hamilton Pipeline Co.; v.p., sec., dir. Curtis, Inc; dir. First Nat. Bank Thermopolis (Wyo.). Mason (Shriner, K.T.), Elk. Home: P O Box 363 Thermopolis WY 82443 Office: 242 Amoretti St Thermopolis WY 82443*

HERRIN, MORELAND, educator, engring. cons.; b. Morris, Okla., Nov. 14, 1922; s. Birney D. and Lucille (Moreland) H.; B.S. in Civil Engring., Okla. State U., 1947, M.S., 1949; Ph.D., Purdue U., 1954; m. Nancy M. Jameson, Dec. 24, 1946; children—Jeannie N., Stanley M., Gwen M. Instr., Okla. State U., 1947- 49, asso. prof., 1954-58; prof. civil engring. U. Ill. at Urbana, 1958- -; design engr. Hudgins, Thompson & Ball, engrs., Oklahoma City, 1949- 50; materials engr. Garnett, Fleming, Cordray and Carpenter, Belvidere, Ill., 1957; asst. materials engr., road test Am. Assn. State Hwy. Ofcls., Ottawa, Ill., 1958; cons. hwy. materials, pavement design, 1955- -. Served to capt. USAAF, 1943-46. Recipient Epstein award U. Ill., 1962. Mem. Hwy. Research Bd., Assn. Asphalt Paving Technologists, Am. Soc. C.E., Am. Soc. Engring. Edn., Am. Soc. Testing Materials, Chi Epsilon, Tau Beta Pi. Mem. Disciples of Christ Ch. Contbr. profl. jours. Home: 1414 W William St Champaign IL 61820 Office: Talbot Lab Urbana IL 61801

HERRIN, RAYMOND CLYDE, educator; b. Marion County, Ind., July 9, 1900; s. Willard and May (Russell) H.; B.S., Purdue U., 1922; Ph.D., U. Wis., 1928; M.D., U. Chgo., 1933; m. M. Elizabeth Hooper, Sept. 5, 1934; children— Katherine, Patricia, Thomas, John, David. Mem. faculty U. Wis., 1928—, prof. physiology, 1946—. Mem. Am. Physiol. Soc., Sigma Xi. Home: R 1 De Forest WI 53532 Office: 426 N Charter St Madison WI 53706

HERRIN, W.V., hosp. adminstr. Adminstr. Meth. Hosp. Central Ill. Office: 211 NE Glen Oak Av Peoria IL 61603*

HERRING, CHARLES FERGUSON, lawyer, state senator; b. McGregor, Tex., June 1, 1914; s. Luther L. and Minnie (Townsend) H.; LL.B., U. Tex., 1938; LL.D., St. Edwards U., 1957; m. Doris Wallace, Sept. 4, 1935; children—Doris Carol, Cecelia Ann, Charles Ferguson, Antonia Minette. Farmer, McLennan County, Tex., 1931-33; admitted to Tex. bar, 1938; asso. Looney & Clark, Austin, 1938-41, 46-48; county atty., Travis County., Tex., 1941-42; area atty. OPA, 1942-43; sec. to Congressman Lyndon Johnson, Washington, 1943; parliamentarian Tex. State Senate, 1951; now partner law firm Herring & Werkenthin; U.S. atty., Western Dist. of Tex., 1951-55; chmn. bd. First Fed. Savs. & Loan Assn., Austin; state senator 14th Dist. Tex., 1956—. Served as lt. USNR, 1943-45; PTO. Mem. Tex. Bar Assn., Tex. Fine Arts Assn., Sigma Nu. K.C. (dep. grand knight, 4). Home: 3501 Bowman Rd Austin TX 78703 Office: Perry-Brooks Bldg Austin TX 78701

HERRING, CLYDE EDSEL, lawyer; b. Des Moines, Mar. 24, 1915; s. Clyde L. and E. Pearl (Spinney) H.; A.B., State U. Ia., 1937; LL.B., Drake U., 1940, J.D., 1968; m. Mary Lou Becker, Aug. 7, 1945; children—Victoria Louise, Mary Jane. Admitted to Ia. bar, 1940, D.C. bar, 1965; mem. firm Davis, Huebner, Johnson, Herring & Burt, Des Moines, 1955-60; asst. county atty., Polk County, Ia., 1947-48; county atty., 1951-52, 53-54; dist. dir. Bur. Census, 1949-50; commr. ICC, Washington, 1959-64; practice law, Washington, 1964—. Democratic candidate for gov. of Ia., 1954. Home: 5705 Mohican Pl Washington DC 20016 Office: 1111 E St NW Washington DC 20004

HERRING, EDWARD PENDLETON, assn. exec.; b. Balt., Oct. 27, 1903; A.B., Johns Hopkins, 1925, Ph.D., 1928, LL.D., 1968; A.M. (hon.), Harvard, 1944; LL.D., Princeton, 1958; m. Katherine Channing, June 21, 1933; children—H. James, Thomas S.; m. 2d, Virginia Staman Wood, May 16, 1971. Instr. to asso. prof. govt. Harvard, 1928-46, sec. Grad. Sch. Pub. Adminstrn., 1937-46; exec. asso. Carnegie Corp. of N.Y., 1946-48; dir. Atomic Energy Group of UN, 1946-47; pres. Social Sci. Research Council, 1948-68, pres. emeritus, 1969—; dir. Fgn. Area Fellowship Program, 1969—; con. personnel problems Central Statis. Bd., 1936; cons. War Dept., 1941-53, Bur. Budget, 1941-44, Navy Dept., 1945-51; mem. bd. advisers to Army Indsl. Coll., 1944-47; exec. sec. Com. on Records of War Adminstrn., Bur. Budget, 1942-45, chmn., 1945-46; mem. adv. council Human Resources Research Inst., 1949; vis. Ford Found. research prof. Princeton, 1963. Editor-in-chief Pub. Adminstrn. Rev., 1945-47, editorial bd., 1940-45; editorial bd. Am. Polit. Sci. Rev., 1943-45, also Pub. Opinion Quar., 1937-44. Exec. council Am. Polit. Sci. Assn., 1942-44, pres., 1952-53; vice chmn. com. on pub. adminstrn. Social Sci. Research Council, 1942-45, dir. council, 1946-68. Bd. dirs. Woodrow Wilson Found., 1950—, pres., 1962—; vis. coms. Harvard, 1947-71; adv. coms. Johns Hopkins, Mass. Inst. Tech., Princeton, Air U. Recipient Navy Citation and Distinguished Civilian Service award, 1946; Rosenberger medalist U. Chgo., 1970. Mem. Council Foreign Relations, Am. Philos. Soc., Am. Acad. Arts and Scis., A.A.A.S. (v.p. and chmn. Sect. K 1960), Am. Polit. Sci. Assn. (pres. 1952-53), Internat. Social Sci. Council (v.p. 1961-70), Phi Beta Kappa. Clubs: Cosmos (Washington); Century Assn., University (N.Y.C.). Author: Group Representation Before Congress, 1929; Federal Commissioners, Study of their Careers and Qualifications, 1936; Public Adminstration and the Public Interest, 1936; The Politics of Democracy, 1940; Presidential Leadership, 1940; The Impact of War, 1941. Home: Castle Howard Princeton NJ 08540 Office: 110 E 59th St New York City NY 10022

HERRING, JACK WILLIAM, educator; b. Waco, Tex., Aug. 28, 1925; s. Benjamin Oscar and Bertha (Shiplet) H.; B.A., Baylor U., 1947, M.A., 1948; Ph.D., U. Pa., 1958; m. Daphne L. Norred, June 10, 1944; children—Penny Elizabeth, Paul William. English instr. Howard Coll., Birmingham, Ala., 1948-50; asso. prof., acting chmn. dept. English, Grand Canyon Coll., Phoenix, 1951-55; asst. prof. English, Ariz. State U., Tempe, 1955-59; dir. Armstrong Browning Library, Baylor U., 1959—, asso. prof. English, 1959-62, prof. English, 1962—. Mem. Modern Lang. Assn., Nat. Council Tchrs. English, Tex. Library Assn., A.L.A., Am. Assn. U. Profs. Editor: Baylor Univ. Browning Interests. Home: 200 Guittard Av Waco TX 76706

HERRING, JAMES P., chain food store co. exec.; b. Greenville, N.C., June 29, 1914; s. Leslie Preston and Ruth Harrel (Woodward) H.; ed. pub. schs.; m.; 1 dau., Constance Lee (Mrs. Pieter Mayer); m. 2d, Jean Millicent, May 1, 1965. With Walgreen Co. as dir. self-service operations; founder Sav-On Drugs, Inc.; v.p. Kroger Co., 1960-70, pres., 1970—, also dir.; pres. SupeRx Drugs, Inc., 1961-70. Mason. Clubs: Cincinnati; Hyde Park Country. Home: 8445 Eustisfarm Lane Cincinnati OH 45243 Office: Kroger Bldg 1014 Vine St Cincinnati OH 45202

HERRING, JOHN HENRY, Jr., air force officer; b. Trenton, N.J., May 6, 1920; s. John H. and Anna (Poyer) H.; student Acad. Aeros., 1936-38, U. Md., 1955-56; grad. Air War Coll., 1958; m. Hannah B. Maas, Feb. 28, 1953; children—David James, Kathryn Ann. Commd. 2d lt. USAAF, 1942, advanced through grades to brig. gen. USAF, 1971; tactical airlift assignments, Europe and Africa, World War II, Japan, Korean War; comdr. all USAF airlift operations in Vietnam, 1969-71; assigned 839th Air Div., 1971—. Decorated D.S.M., D.F.C., Legion of Merit with 2 oak leaf clusters, Bronze Star, Air medal, Meritorious Service award. Mem. Air Force Assn., Nat. Def. Transp. Assn., Armed Forces Mgmt. Assn., Order Daedalians. Club: Saigon Golf. Home: 216 Maynard Dr Pope AFB NC 28308 Office: 839th Air Division Pope AFB NC 28308

HERRING, LEONARD GRAY, marketing co. exec.; b. nr. North Wilkesboro, N.C., June 18, 1927; s. Albert Lee and Josie (Sugg) H.; B.S., U. N.C., 1948; m. Rozelia Sullivan, June 18, 1950; children—Sandra Grey, Albert Lee II. With Dun & Bradstreet, Inc., Raleigh, N.C., 1948-49; with H. Weil & Co., Goldsboro, N.C., 1949-55; sr. v.p., sec.-treas. Lowe's Cos., Inc., North Wilkesboro, N.C., 1955—; dir. Northwestern Financial Corp. Trustee Lowe's Cos. Profit Sharing Plan and Trust. Mem. Chi Psi. Democrat. Methodist. Home: Finley Park North Wilkesboro NC 28659 Office: Lowe's Cos Inc Hwy 268 East North Wilkesboro NC 28659

HERRING, ROBERT RAY, utility co. exec.; b. Childress, Tex., Feb. 11, 1921; s. Lonnie Ray and Clara (Wolford) H.; B.A., Tex. A. and M. Coll., 1941; m. Sylvia Carmen Grant, Oct. 27, 1945; children—Sylvia Diane, Robert Ray, Randolph W. Vice pres. Fish Engring. Corp., 1950-52; pres. Fish Service Corp., 1952- 58; pres. Valley Gas Prodn., Inc., 1958-63; v.p., gen. mgr. Houston Pipe Line Co., 1963-65; sr. v.p. Houston Natural Gas Corp., 1965-67, pres., chief exec. officer, 1967—. Pres., Tex. Heart Inst.; mem. exec. com. Med. Research Found. Tex.; v.p. Houston Symphony Soc.; mem. U.S. Indsl. Payroll Savs. Com. Trustee U. Houston Found., Ray C. Fish Found., St. Luke's Episcopal Hosp., United Fund; bd. dirs. Salvation Army; bd. govs. Rice U. Mem. Houston C. of C. (pres.), Am. Gas Assn. (dir.), Inst. Gas Tech. (trustee), Ind. Petroleum Assn. Am. Home: 3195 Inwood St Houston TX 77019 Office: PO Box 1188 Houston TX 77001

HERRING, WILLIAM CONYERS, physicist; b. Scotia, N.Y., Nov. 15, 1914; s. William Conyers and Mary (Joy) H.; A.B., U. Kan., 1933; Ph.D., Princeton, 1937; m. Louise C. Preusch, Nov. 30, 1946; children—Lois Mary, Alan John, Brian Charles, Gordon Robert. NRC fellow Mass. Inst. Tech., 1937-39; instr. Princeton, 1939-40, U. Mo., 1940-41; mem. sci. staff Div. War Research, Columbia, 1941-45; prof. applied math. U. Tex., 1946; research physicist Bell Telephone Labs., Murray Hill, N.J., 1946—; mem. Inst. Advanced Study, 1952-53. Recipient Army-Navy Certificate Appreciation, 1947. Fellow Am. Phys. Soc. (Oliver E. Buckley solid state physics prize 1959), Am. Acad. Arts and Scis.; mem. A.A.A.S., Nat. Acad. Scis. Home: 3 Hawthorne Pl Summit NJ 07901 Office: Bell Telephone Labs Murray Hill NJ 07974

HERRINGTON, GEORGE SQUIRES, educator; b. Aurora, Ill., May 11, 1909; s. George Squires and Caroline Lucinda (Pratt) H.; Ed.B., No. Ill. State Tchrs. Coll., Dekalb, 1933; M.A., Columbia Tchrs. Coll., 1937; Ed.D., Stanford, 1947; m. Aubrey Nicely, June 1, 1936; 1 dau., Phyllis Jean. Tchr., Profl. Children's Sch., N.Y.C., 1934-37, City and Country Sch., N.Y.C., 1937- 40, Portola (Cal.) Jr.-Sr. High Sch., 1940-41; instr. Menlo (Cal.) Sch. and Jr. Coll., 1941-43; asso. prof. U. Denver, 1947-50; prof. sociology Sacramento State Coll., 1950—, also head dept. sociology. Served to lt. (s.g.) USNR, 1943-46. Mem. Am., Pacific sociol. socs., Am. Assn. U. Profs. Home: 320 Sandburg Dr Sacramento CA 95819

HERRIOTT, JAMES HOMER, educator; b. Lawrence, Kan., June 21, 1895; s. Walter Thomas Buchanan and Ada Evelyn (Oatman) H.; A.B., U. Kan., 1920, A.M., 1924; Ph.D., U. Wis., 1929; student U. Grenoble (France), 1919, U. Madrid, 1924; research fellow in Europe, Am. Council Learned Socs., 1931- 32; m. Bernadine Layman, June 5, 1924 (died 1924); m. 2d, Margot McLellan, Aug. 3, 1929; children—Andra James, Margot Bernadine. Grad. asst. in Spanish, U. Kan., 1923-24, instr., 1924-25; instr. U. Wis., 1925-29, asst. prof. Spanish, 1930-31, 1932-39, asso. prof., chmn. dept. Spanish and Portuguese, 1939-42, prof. Spanish, chmn. dept., 1942-45, prof., asso. dean Grad. Sch., 1945-63, asso. dean Coll. Letters and Sci., 1947-49; research asso. Princeton, 1929-30; Fulbright research prof., Spain, 1965-66; Distinguished lectr. U. Wis., Milw., 1966—. Served with

Norton-Harjes Ambulance Corps, France, 1917; cadet and 2d lt. (pilot). Signal Corps, AEF, France and Italy, 1917-19. Mem. Mediaeval Acad., Am. Folklore Soc., Modern Lang. Assn., Linguistic Soc. Am., Archaeol. Soc. Am., Wis. Hist. Soc., Delta Tau Delta. Conglist. Club: University. Author: Towards A Critical Edition of the Celestine, 1964. Contbr. articles. Home: 2974 N Frederick Av Milwaukee WI 53211 ☆

HERRIOTT, MAXWELL HAINES, lawyer; b. Des Moines, Apr. 21, 1899; s. Frank Irving and Mary (Haines) H.; A.B., Grinnell Coll., 1920; B.A. Juris., Oxford (Eng.) U., 1922, M.A., B.C.L., 1923; LL.B., U. Wis., 1924; m. Ruth G. Hewitt, Sept. 11, 1926; 1 dau., Mary Joan (Mrs. C.A. Wright). Admitted to Wis. bar, 1925; sec. to justice Supreme Ct. Wis., 1924-26; faculty U. Wis. Law Sch., 1924-27; asso. with firm Quarles, Herriott, Clemons, Teschner & Noelke, and predecessor, Milw., partner, 1934—; lectr. law suretyship Marquette U. Law Sch. Trustee Northwestern Mut. Life Ins. Co.; dir. Allis Chalmers Mfg. Co., Robertson, Inc., Milw. Pres. Whitefish Bay Library Bd., 1957—; vice chmn. met. problems com. Greater Milw. Com.; organizer Civil War Round Table Milw., 1946; speaker on life of Lincoln. Trustee Grinnell Coll., 1945—; bd. dirs. childrens Aid Soc., Wis., 1934-41, pres., 1938-41. Fellow Am. Bar Found., Am. Coll. Trial Lawyers; mem. Am., Milw. (pres. 1938- 39) bar assns., State Bar Wis. (bd. govs.), Am. Law Inst., Phi Alpha Delta. Clubs: Milwaukee, Milwaukee Country, Milwaukee Athletic, University (Milw.); Madison (Wis.). Home: 2020 E Glendale Av Milwaukee WI 53211 Office: 780 N Water St Milwaukee WI 53202

HERRIOTT, ROGER MOSS, research biochemist, educator; b. Des Moines, Mar. 13, 1908; s. Frank Irving and Mary (Haines) H.; A.B., Drake U., 1928; A.M., Columbia, 1929, Ph.D., 1932; m. Cynthia D. Walker, Oct. 22, 1932; children—Alison (Mrs. Donald R. Wilder), Jon Roger, Michael (dec.). Asst. gen. physiology Rockefeller Inst. Med. Research, 1932-37, asso., 1937-48; prof. biochemistry, chmn. dept. Johns Hopkins, 1948—. Mem. Soc. Biol. Chemists, Am. Chem. Soc., Biophys. Soc., Soc. Gen. Physiology, A.A.A.S., Soc. Am. Bacteriology, Am. Assn. U. Profs. Spl. research mechanism action pepsin and formation from pepsinogen, coli bacteriophage, mechanism bacterial genetic transformation, phys., chem. and genetic properties of DNA, photoreactivation, infectious viral nucleic acids. Home: 504 Highland Av Towson MD 21204 Office: 615 Wolfe St Baltimore MD 21205

HERRMAN, ARTHUR PHILIP, prof. architecture; b. Milw., Dec. 3, 1898, s. Otto F. and Theresa (Botzen) H.; B.Arch., Carnegie Inst. Tech., 1921; m. Isobel K. Riedl, July 9, 1920; children—Arthur John, Celia May. Became instr. architecture, U. Wash., 1923, prof. emeritus, former dean Coll. Architecture and Urban Planning; licensed architect in State of Wash., 1924, pvt. practice since 1924. Recipient Henry Adams Meml. fellowship, 1939. Fellow A.T.A.; mem. Tau Sigma Delta. Mason (33), Kiwanian. Home: 3635 76th St NE Bellevue WA 98004

HERRMANN, ARTHUR DOMINEY, banker; b. Louisville, Sept. 29, 1926; s. Arthur Chester and Mattie Belle (Dominey) H.; B.A., Ohio State U., 1947, J.D., 1949; postgrad. Rutgers U., 1956; m. Lucy Kindred, Apr. 7, 1951; children—Lucy Wharton, Anne Dominey, Martha Kindred. Admitted to Ohio bar, 1950; practice in Columbus, 1950; asst. trust officer Huntington Nat. Bank, Columbus, 1951- 56, trust officer, 1956-63, v.p., 1963-67, sr. v.p., 1967-69, exec. v.p., 1969—, dir., 1968—; sec. Huntington Bancshares, Inc., 1966-70, exec. v.p., dir., 1970—. Treas., bd. dirs. Columbus Retail Mchts. Assn.; bd. dirs. Columbus Conv. Bur. Mem. Ohio Bankers Assn., Columbus Bar Assn., Sigma Chi, Phi Delta Phi. Mason. Clubs: Columbus, Scioto Country, City (Columbus). Home: 2347 Abington Rd Columbus OH 43221 Office: 17 S High St Columbus OH 43215

HERRMANN, BERNARD, composer; b. N.Y.C., June 29, 1911; ed. N.Y. U., Juilliard Sch. Founder, condr. New Chamber Orch., 1931-32; conducting appearances with N.Y. Philharmonic, BBC Symphony; staff condr. CBS. Composer scores for films including Citizen Kane, Magnificient Ambersons, Jane Eyre, Anna and the King of Siam, Snows of Kilimanjaro, Beneath the 12-Mile Reef, King of the Khyber Rifles, Garden of Evil, The Egyptian, Prince of Players, The Trouble with Harry, The Kentuckian, Man in the Gray Flannel Suit, The Man Who Knew Too Much, The Devil and Daniel Webster, Fahrenheit 451; other works include Moby Dick, Welles Raises Kane (ballet), Wuthering Heights (opera); also composer works for orch., chorus, chamber music, theatre. Recipient Acad. award for best score All That Money Can Buy, 1941. Address: care Wilfred Van Wyck 80 Wigmore St London W1 England*

HERRMANN, CARL STRAUSS, pub. utility exec.; b. Worcester, Mass., July 11, 1890; s. Charles and Emma (Strauss) H.; ed. Worcester pub. schs., Becker Coll. Bus. Adminstrn. and Secretarial Sci.; m. Bertha Irene Bates, July 14, 1909; children—Marion Emma Hemeon, Carl Bates, Allen Milton, Richard, Barbara Davidson. Typist, clk. stenographer Am. Steel & Wire Co., 1906-12; with New Eng. Electric System, 1912—, pres., 1935-41, chmn. bd., 1941-55, ret.; dir. Liberty Mut. Ins. Co. Mem. Panel of Arbitrators of Arbitration Com. N.Y. Stock Exchange. Mem. chambers commerce of Boston and Worcester. Mason (32, Shriner), Elk. Club: Algonquin (Boston). Home: 6 Oakridge Rd Wellesley Hills MA 02181 also 216 Alora St St Petersburg FL 33704

HERRMANN, DANIEL LIONEL, justice; b. N.Y.C., June 10, 1913; s. Philip and Rose (Schendelman) H.; A.B., U. Del., 1935; LL.B., Georgetown U., 1939; m. Zelda W. Kluger, Apr. 14, 1940; children—Stephen Eric, Richard Kurt. Admitted to D.C. bar, 1938, Del. bar, 1940; practiced in Wilmington, 1940-51; asst. U.S. atty., 1948-51; asso. justice Del. Supreme Ct., 1951, 65—; asso. judge Superior Ct., Orphans Ct. Del., 1951-58; sr. partner Herrmann, Bayard, Brill & Russell, 1958-65. Dir., mem. exec. com. Del. Power & Light Co., 1962-65. Chmn. State Goals Commn., 1960-64; mem. Wilmington Bd. Pub. Edn., 1961-65; chmn. State Planning Commn., 1962-64. Pres. Legal Aid Soc. Del.; pres., chmn. bd. Jewish Fedn. Del., 1956-58; former mem. bd. dirs., exec. com. United Community Fund, Children's Bur. Del., Welfare Council Del., Del-Mar-Va council Boy Scouts Am., Jewish Community Center, Kutz Home for Aging; trustee, v.p. U. Del.; trustee Wilmington Med. Center; bd. mgrs. Wilmington Inst. Free Library. Served to maj. AUS, 1942-46. Fellow Inst. Jud. Adminstrn.; mem. Am., Del. bar assns., Am. Judicature Soc. (dir.). Rotarian. Home: 705 E Matson Run Pkwy Wilmington DE 19802 Office: Court House Wilmington DE 19801

HERRMANN, DONALD JOSEPH, coll. dean; b. Lee, Ill., Nov. 8, 1915; s. Fred and Agnes (O'Donnell) H.; B.Ed., No. Ill. U., 1941; M.A., Mich. State U., 1949, Ph.D., 1952; student U. Chgo., 1943, Northwestern U., 1946-47; m. Marcella Bastian, Aug. 27, 1955; children—Bernice Agnes, Mark Edward. Tchr. publ schs., La Grange, Ill., 1941-42; asst. personnel mgr. Ideal Industries, Inc., 1946- 47; counselor No. Ill. U., 1947-48, Mich. State U., 1948-51; mem. faculty Coll. William and Mary, 1951—, prof. edn., dir. summer session, coordinator branches, 1961-65, prof. edn., dir. summer session and extension, 1965-68, dean Sch. Continuing Studies, prof. edn., 1968—; cons. in field, 1952—. Served with USAAF, 1941-46. Mem. Am. Personnel and Guidance Assn., Nat. Soc. Study Edn., Assn. Higher Edn., Phi Delta Kappa, Kappa Delta Pi. Contbr. profl. jours. Home: 206 Matoaka Ct Williamsburg VA 23185.

HERRMANN, EDWARD J., bishop; b. Balt., Nov. 6, 1913; s. Walter E. and Jennie (Doyle) H.; A.B., Mt. St. Mary's Coll. and Sem., Emmitsburg, Md., 1947. Ordained priest Roman Catholic Ch., 1947; asst. Our Lady of Victory Parish, 1947-60; pastor, 1968—; pastor St. Mary's Ch., Washington, 1960-68; asst. chancellor Archdiocese of Washington, 1951-62, vice chancellor, 1962-64, counsultor, 1964—; aux. bishop Washington, titular bishop of Lamzella, 1966—. Home: 4835 Mac Arthur Blvd NW Washington DC 20036 Office: 1721 Rhode Island Av NW Washington DC 20036

HERRMANN, GEORGE, educator; b. Moscow, USSR, Apr. 19, 1921; C.E., Swiss Fed. Inst. Tech., 1945, D.Sc., 1949; m. Elizabeth Rütschi, Apr. 4, 1946; children—Anne Christine, Peter Michael. Came to U.S., 1950, naturalized, 1956. Asst. prof. Ecole Polytechnique, Montreal, Can., 1949-50; from asst. prof. to asso. prof. Columbia, 1950-62; prof. civil engrng. Northwestern U., 1962-70, Walter P. Murphy prof., 1968-70; prof. applied mechanics Stanford, 1970—. Fellow Am. Soc. M.E. (exec. com. applied mechanics div.), Am. Inst. Aero. and Astronautics (asso.). Founder, editor-in-chief Jour. Solids and Structures, 1965—. Contbr. articles profl. jours. Home: 451 Valencia Dr Los Altos CA 94022 Office: Dept Applied Mechanics Stanford U Stanford CA 94305

HERRMANN, GEORGE RUDOLPH, III, prof. medicine; b. Ft. Wayne, Ind., Nov. 20, 1894; s. George II and Sophia M. (Bechtoldt) H.; B.S. U. Mich., 1916, M.S., M.D., 1918, Ph.D., 1922; m. Anna Harriet Williams, June 30, 1921; children—Georgeanna Williams, Gretchen Sophia, George IV, Henry Christian. Mem. pathol. staff U. Mich., 1916-18; vis. physician Charity Hosp., New Orleans, 1925-31, dir. cardiographic lab., 1925- 31; prof. clin. medicine, U. Tex. Med. Sch., 1931-39, prof. medicine, 1939-65, 1st Distinguished Ashbel Smith prof. medicine, 1965—, dir. cardiovascular service and heart station, 1931-65. Dir. Latin-Am. relations in medicine U. Tex. Med. Sch., 1940; physician John Sealy Hosp., 1931—; cons. on vascular disorders Marine Hosp., 1934; cons. vascular diseases, cardiology and medicine to surgeon gens. of USPHS, U.S. Army, U.S. Air Force. Served with C.W.S., U.S. Army, 1918. Recipient medal for distinguished services Am. Heart Assn., 1960; Medal Homenagem Da Sociedade Interamericana de Cardiologia Rio de Janeiro, 1960; Distinguished Service award Tex. Med. Assn., 1964, Outstanding Civilian Service medal U.S. Army Med. Corps, 1968, Distinguished Service medal A.M.A., 1970; U.S. Army Surgeon Gen.'s medal for outstanding civilian service, 1968. Diplomate Nat. Bd. Med. Examiners, Am. Bd. Internal Medicine. Fellow A.C.P., Am. Coll. Chest Physicians (hon. fellow, gov. for Tex. 1955-57, regent for S.W. 1957-60); mem. A.A.A.S., Am. Coll. Cardiology (v.p. 1962, hon.), A.M.A., Am. Climatological and Clin. Assn., Am. Soc. Study Arteriosclerosis (charter), Inter-Am. Soc. Cardiology (founder, mem. honor council), Internat. Soc. Cardiology (charter), Internat. Soc. Internal Medicine, Am. Soc. Exptl. Pathology, Soc. for Exptl. Biology and Medicine, Soc. Academia Nacional de Medicina de Mexico, Sigma Xi, Alpha Omega Alpha, Beta Mu; hon. mem. St. Louis Med. Soc., Midwest Clin. Soc., Soc. Mex. de Med. Int., Soc. Mex. de Cardiol., Soc. Brazil de Cardiol., others. Author sci. publs., latest: Disease of the Heart and Arteries, 4th edit. 1952; Clinical Case Taking, 5th edit.; Methods in Medicine, 2d edit. Editor: Am. Jour. Syphilis, 1929-35; asso. editor Jour. Lab. and Clin. Medicine, 1927-47; mem. editorial com. Am. Jour. Clin. Investigation, 1934-48; editorial bd. Am. Heart Jour., 1938-49, Am. Jour. Cardiology. Contbr. over 385 articles to profl. jours. Home: 1409 Market St Galveston TX 77550 also Star Route La Coste TX also Gen Delivery Castroville TX Office: Univ Tex Medical School Galveston TX 77551 ☆

HERRMANN, OMER WESLEY, consultant; b. Boelus, Neb., July 28, 1897; s. John Martin and Katherine (Wieseman) H.; B.S. in Agr., U. Neb., 1922; postgrad. Columbia, summer 1923; Ph.D., U. Wis., 1938; m. Elizabeth Mickle, June 25, 1925; children—Robert Omer, John Martin. Instr. vocational agr., Tecumseh, Neb., 1922-25; asso. prof. agrl. marketing Okla. A. and M. Coll., 1928-31; sec. Okla. Agrl. Council, 1929-30; agrl. economist, marketing research FCA, U.S. Dept. Agr., 1931-42, asst. dir. fats and oils br., 1945-46, dir., 1946-47, asst. research adminstr. for program devel. and coordination, Agri. Research Adminstrn. Dept. Agr., 1947-51, dep. adminstr. for marketing research Agrl. Marketing Service, 1955-64, dep. adminstr. Agrl. Research Service, 1964-65; field research leader Consortium for Study of Nigerian Rural Devel., 1967, 68; cons. research, indsl. grants War on Hunger, AID, 1969—; agrl. attache Am. embassy, Paris, France, 1951-55. Mem. agrl. mission to Brazil, Argentina and Paraguay for Dept. Agr., 1939; U.S. mem. fats and oils com. Internat. Emergency Food Council, 1946-47; mem. U.S. Food Processing Mission to USSR, 1960. Served as pvt. U.S. Army, 1918; col. Gen. Staff Corps, AUS, MTO, ETO; chief food and agr. SHAEF, 1942-45. Decorated Bronze Star, various campaign medals and ribbons; Order of Orange Nassau with swords (Netherlands). Mem. A.A.A.S., Am. Farm Econ. Assn., Am. Econ. Assn., Am. Marketing Assn., Am. Statis. Assn., Mil. Order Fgn. Wars, Alpha Zeta, Gamma Sigma Delta, Alpha Kappa Delta, Farm House. Methodist. Club: Cosmos (Washington). Contbr. mags. and govt. publs. Home: 6817 Breezewood Terrace Rockville MD 20852 Office: US AID Washington DC 20523

HERRNSTEIN, RICHARD JULIUS, educator: b. N.Y.C., May 20, 1930; s. Rezso and Flora Irene (Friedmann) H.; B.A., Coll. City N.Y., 1952; Ph.D., Harvard, 1955; m. Barbara Brodo, May 28, 1951 (div. Feb. 1961); 1 dau., Julia; m. 2d, Susan Chalk Gouinlock, Nov. 11, 1961; children—Max Gouinlock, James Rezso. Research psychologist Walter Reed Army Med. Center, Washington, 1956-58; lectr. U. Md., 1957-58; faculty Harvard, 1958—, dir. psychol. labs., 1965- 67, prof., chmn. dept. psychology, 1967-71. Served to 1st lt. AUS, 1956-58. Mem. Am., Eastern psychol. assns., A.A.A.S., Phi Beta Kappa, Sigma Xi. Author: (with E.G. Boring) A Source Book in the History of Psychology, 1965; (with J.C. Stevens and G.S. Reynolds) Laboratory Experiments in Psychology, 1965. Contbr. articles to profl. jours. Home: 126 Brook St Wellesley MA 02181 Office: William James Hall Harvard Cambridge MA 02138

HERRO, NORMAN CHARLES, lawyer; b. Milw., Nov. 3, 1918; s. Charles A. and Sophia (Moutran) H.; B.A., U. Chgo., 1940; LL.B., U. Wis., 1949, J.D., 1966; m. Mary Stuart Smith, June 1, 1946; children-Stuart C., Mark A. Asst. sales mgr. Jewel Tea Co., Barrington, Ill., 1940-41; asst. erection engr. Babcock & Wilcox, Chgo., 1945-46; admitted to Wis. bar, 1949, since practiced in Madison; sr. mem. firm Herro, McAndrews & Porter and predecessor firms, 1949—; Wis. counsel N.Central Airlines, Inc. Dir. Glendale Devel., Inc. Mem. Edgewood Coll. Adv. Council, 1963-65, Edgewood High Sch. Bldg. Com., 1966-68. Served to capt. USAAF, 1941-45; ETO. Decorated Air medal with 3 oak leaf clusters. Mem. Am. Wis., Dane County bar assns., Am. Arbitration Assn., Phi Delta Phi. Clubs: Madison, Maple Bluff Country (Madison). Home: 3214 Bluff St Madison WI 53705 Office: 121 S Pinckney St Madison WI 53703

HERRON, FRANCIS WILLIAM, fgn. service officer; b. Boone, Ia., Aug. 9, 1913; s. John Richard and Mary (Jordan) H.; B.Journalism, U. Mo., 1934; student Cordoba U., Argentina, 1942; m. Ellen M. Doods, Aug. 26, 1944; children—Lillian, Margaret, Richard, Kathryn, Patricia, Philip. News editor Sibley (Ia.) Gazette-Tribune, 1935-41; asso. Inst. Current World Affairs, N.Y.C., 1941-42; joined U.S. Fgn. service, 1946; asst. press officer Am. embassy, Buenos Aires, 1946-47; pub. affairs officer Am. embassy, Quito, Ecuador, 1947-48, San Salvador, 1948-5O, Montevideo, 1950-51, Buenos Aires, 1954-58; assigned Bur. Inter-Am. Affairs, State Dept., 1942-44, 52-54, Bur. Pub. Affairs, 1959-64; Am. consul, Puerto La Cruz, Venezuela, 1964-65; counselor polit. affairs Am. embassy, Caracas, Venezuela, 1965-67, minister-councilor, dep. chief mission, 1967-69; charge d'affaires Am. embassy, Caracas, 1969-70; spl. adviser Office Interoceanic Canal Negotiations, Dept. State, Washington, 1970, ret.; writer current affairs, 1971—. Recipient Superior Honor award Dept. State, 1970. Roman Catholic. Author: Letters From The Argentine, 1943. Home: 1239 S Oakcrest Rd Arlington VA 22202

HERRON, HOWARD JAMES, Jr. educator, biologist; b. Ames, Ia.; B.A., Ia. State U., 1936, M.A., 1937, Ph.D. with honors, 1940; m. Ann Ross, Mar. 23, 1946; children--Edward, Thomas A., Mark. Instr., Ia. State U., 1946-47; asst. prof. biology Johns Hopkins, 1947-50, asso. prof., 1950-62, prof., 1962--, chmn. dept., 1963-69; vis. lectr. Stanford, 1970-71. Active Boy Scouts Am., 4-H Club. Served with AUS, 1940-46. Mem. Am. Soc. Biologists, Md. Soc. Cell Biologists, Am. Soc. Exptl. Biology, Internat. Union Biologists, A.A.A.S., Am. Acad. Arts and Scis., Phi Beta Kappa. Home: 48936 W Hancock Blvd Baltimore MD 20206

HERRON, JAMES JOHN, financial pub. co. exec.; b. Edge Hill Pa., Feb. 11, 1909; s. James and Mary Ann (Caul) H.; B.S., Ursinus Coll., Collegeville, Pa., 1932; m. Olivia Birdsong, June 27, 1936; children—James Birdsong, Constance Ann (Mrs. Joel Gravina). With Dun & Bradstreet, Inc., 1934-36, 38—, sr. v.p. adminstrn., 1966—, sec., 1967—, dir., 1967. Mem. Passaic Twp. Planning Bd., 1956-59. Served as lt. USNR, 1943-45. Mem. Comml. Law League Am., Am. Soc. Corporate Secs., Nat. Assn. Credit Mgmt. Home: 629 Long Hill Rd Gillette NJ 07933 Office: 99 Church St New York City NY 10007

HERRON, LOWELL WILLIAM, ednl. adminstr.; b. Salem, O., Feb. 2O, 1916; s. James and Susan (Sell) H.; B.S. in Bus Adminstrn. summa cum laude, Kent State U., 1938, LL.D., 1963; M.A., U. Ia., 1939; postgrad. study Ohio State U., 1939-4O; Sc.D., Clarkson Coll. Tech., 1963; D.H.L., Inter Am. U. of P.R., 1969; m. Mary Lucile Shriver, July 29, 1950; children—James Hoopes, Virginia Carolyn. With Clarkson Coll. Tech.. Potsdam, N.Y., 1940-66, prof. bus. adminstrn., 1944-66, chmn. dept., 1944-48, asst. to pres., 1948-50, dean Sch. of Arts, Scis. and Bus. Adminstr., 1950- 58, dean coll., 1958-63, v.p., 1963-66; v.p. acad. affairs Inter Am. U. of P.R., San German, 1966-69, prof. bus. adminstrn., 1966- 69; v.p. for financial affairs, prof. bus. adminstrn. Fairleigh Dickinson U., 1969—; indsl. cons. Aluminum Co. Am., Racquette River Paper Co., U.S. Hoffman Machinery Corp., Gen. Electric Co., Procter & Gamble Co., The Goodyear Tire and Rubber Co., others. Lectr. Canadian Mgmt. Confs., 1952-64. Mem. Middle States Assn. Colls. Bus. Adminstrn. (pres. 1954-55), Am. Soc. Engring Edn., Am. Mgmt. Assn., Sigma Tau Iota, Beta Gamma Sigma, Pi Delta Epsilon, Delta Upsilon, Order of Artus. Republican. Methodist. Contbr. to publs. Address: 1031 East Saddle River Rd Ho-Ho-Kus NJ 07423

HERRON, SAMUEL DAVIDSON, Jr., financial exec.; b. Bryn Mawr, Pa., Nov. 10, 1925; s. Samuel Davidson and Louise (Johnston) H.; grad. Phillips Andover Acad., 1943; B.S., Yale, 1946; m. Polly Presnell, Jan. 19, 1953; children—Cynthia D., Catherine L., A. Louise, Samuel Davidson III. Asst. v.p. Mellon Nat. Bank & Trust Co., Pitts., 1948-62; sr. v.p. Ins. Co. of N.Am., Phila., 1962- 70; financial v.p., treas. INA Corp., Phila., 1968—; dir. Del. & Bound Brook R.R. Co., N.P. R.R., Worldwide Spl. Fund N.V., INA Security Corp., Horace Mann Educators Corp., Am. Instl. Developers, Inc., Fideleo Growth Investors, Western Devel. Corp., INA Trading Corp., Ins. Co. N.Am., Life Ins. Co. N.Am. Trustee United Presbyn. Found.; bd. mgrs. Childrens Hosp. Phila. Served to ensign USNR, 1943-46, to lt. comdr., 1951-53. Mem. Nat. Investor Relations Inst., Phila. Com. on Fgn. Relations. Home: 214 Glenn Rd Ardmore PA 19003 Office: 1600 Arch St Philadelphia PA 19101

HERRON, TRUMAN ALDRICH, lawyer; b. Cin., Feb. 18, 1903; s. John W. and Georgie (Aldrich) H.; student Williams Coll., 1920-22; LL.B., U. Cin., 1925; m. Jean Scott Wilkinson, Apr. 20, 1929; children-Scott W., Jean (Mrs. Thomas M. Stanton), Patricia (Mrs. Richard Furman). Admitted to Ohio bar, 1925, since practice in Cin.; asso. Taft, Stettinius & Hollister, 1925-30; mem. firm Powers & Herron, 1930-34; mem. firm Wood, Herron & Evans, 1934- 37, partner, 1937—. Councilman, Indian Hill (O.) Village, 1946-50. Mem. Am., Cin. bar assns., Cin. Patent Law Assn. (pres. 1954). Republican. Presbyn. Home: 5250 Drake Rd Cincinnati OH 45243 Office: Carew Tower Cincinnati OH 45202

HERSBERGER, ARTHUR BUCHER, petroleum co. exec.; b. Milden, Sask., Can., Jan. 13, 1912; s. Arthur C. and Verlinda D. (Jones) H.; B.S., U. Md., 1932, Ph.D., 1936; m. Lucille Stinnett, July 2, 1938; children—Gaye C. (Mrs. John William Schwarz), Arthur Lee. Came to U.S., 1920, naturalized, 1928. With Atlantic Richfield Co., Phila., 1936-69, successively research chemist, sr. chemist, dir. div. research, sales mgr. chem. products, mgr. product sales div., mgr. hdqrs. sales, 1936-59, gen. mgr. fgn. marketing and mgr. spl. sales, 1959-61, gen. mgr. marketing, 1961, v.p., dir., 1961-66, sr. v.p., 1966-69; exec. v.p., dir. Husky Oil Co., 1969—. Mem. A.A.A.S., Am. Inst. Chemists, Am. Chem. Soc., Am. Petroleum Inst. Home: 2499 S Colorado Blvd Denver CO 80222 Office: 4040 E Louisiana Av Denver CO 80222

HERSCHBACH, DUDLEY ROBERT, educator, chemist; b. San Jose, Cal., June 18, 1932; s. Robert Dudley and Dorothy Edith (Beer) H.; B.S. in Math., Stanford, 1954, M.S. in Chemistry, 1955; A.M. in Physics, Harvard, 1956, Ph.D. in Chem. Physics, 1958; m. Georgene Botyos, Dec. 26, 1964; children—Lisa Marie and Brenda Michele. Jr. fellow Harvard 1957-59; faculty U. Cal. at Berkeley, 1959-63, asso. prof. chem., 1961-63; prof. chemistry Harvard, 1963—; cons. editor McGraw-Hill Book Co.; Phillips lectr. Haverford Coll., 1962; Falk-Plaut lectr. Columbia, 1963; vis. prof. Göttingen (Germany) U., summer 1963; Harvard lectr. Yale, 1964; Debye lectr. Cornell U. 1966; Rollefson lectr. U. Cal. at Berkeley, 1969; Guggenheim fellow U. Freiburg (Germany), 1968; vis. fellow Joint Inst. for Lab. Astrophysics U. Colo., 1969; Sloan fellow. 1959-63. Recipient pure chemistry award Am. Chem. Soc., 1965. Fellow Am. Phys. Soc., Am Acad. Arts and Scis; mem. Am. Chem. Soc., A.A.A.S., Nat. Acad. Scis., Phi Beta Kappa, Sigma Xi. Asso. editor Jour. Chem. Physics, Accounts Chem. Research, Am. Chem. Soc. Monograph Series. Office: 12 Oxford St Cambridge MA 02138

HERSCHEL, CARL ANDREW, ins. co. exec.; b. Phila., Nov. 16, 1909; s. Carl G. and Elizabeth (Shinkel) H.; B.A., U. Pa., 1931; m. Mary Louise Swain, Jan. 1935 (dec. 1969); children—Carol Ann (Mrs. Thomas P. Straus), James Andrew, Elisabeth Louise (Mrs. Leonard C. Gambler); m. 2d, Jean Stewart George, Aug. 1970. With

Colonial Life Ins. Co., Jersey City, 1931-45, asst. sec., 1943-45; with Nat. Life Ins. Co., Montpelier, Vt., 1945—, asst. sec., 1946-59, sec., 1959—, v.p., 1969—. Chmn. Vt. Gov.'s Com. on Children and Youth, 1965—. Pres. Montpelier City Council, 1955-56. Bd. dirs. Baird Children's Center. Methodist. Rotarian (gov. dist. 785, 1961-62). Home: 62 College St Montpelier VT 05602 Office: Nat Life Dr Montpelier VT 05602

HERSCHENSOHN, BRUCE, film dir., writer; b. Milw., Sept. 10, 1932; ed. Los Angeles. With art dept. RKO Pictures, 1953-55; dir., editor Gen. Dynamics Corp., 1955-56; dir., writer, editor Karma for Internat. Communications Found.; editor, co-dir. Friendship Seven for NASA; dir., editor Tall Man Five-Five for Gen. Dynamics Corp. and SAC; dir. motion picture and TV Service USIA, 1968—; directed and wrote films for USIA including Bridges of the Barrios, The Five Cities of June, The President, John F. Kennedy: Years of Lightning, Day of Drums, Eulogy to 5:02. Served with USAF, 1951-52. Recipient Arthur S. Flemming award as 1 of 10 outstanding young mem in fed. govt., 1969; Acad. award for Czechoslovakia 1968 as best documentary short, 1969. Address: USIA 1776 Pennsylvania Av NW Washington DC 20547

HERSCHER, IRENAEUS JOSEPH, librarian; b. Guebviller, Alsace, France, Mar. 11, 1902; s. Jean- Baptiste and Josephine (Hugendobler) H.; came to U.S., 1913, naturalized, 1921; B.A., St. Bonaventure U., 1929, M.A., 1930; S.T.B., Cath. U. Am., 1931; M.L.S., Columbia, 1934; Litt.D. (hon.), St. Bonaventure U., 1969. Joined Order of Friars Minor, 1920, ordained priest Roman Cath. Ch., 1931; master of clerics Croghan, N.Y., 1932-33, prof. philosophy, 1932-33; prof. ancient langs. St. Bonaventure U., 1934- 38, asst. librarian, 1934-37, librarian, 1937-71; librarian emeritus, 1971—; initiated Union Catalog of Franciscan Lit., 1952-58, Franciscan Bibliog., 1934—. Mem. Cath. Library Assn., U.S.-Cath. Hist. Soc., Cath. O-Pa-Hi Hist. Assn. Franciscan Ednl. Conf., Western N.Y. Cath. Library Conf., InterAm. Bibliog. and Library Assn. Spl. research history printing. Address: Friedsam Meml Library St Bonaventure U St Bonaventure NY 14778

HERSCHLER, ROBERT JOHN, biol. chemist; b. Portland, Ore., Mar. 10, 1923; s. William H. and Mildred (Haynes) H.; B.S., Washington U., St. Louis, 1948; m. Janet L. Kelly, Apr. 2, 1953; children—Rebecca Sue, Cynthia Lou, Jennifer Lee. With Crown Zellerbach Corp., 1948—, supr. applied research, 1962—. Served to lt. (j.g.) USNR, 1943-46. Recipient Gov. Ore. N.W. Scientist award, 1965. Patentee in field. Home: Route 2 Box 1592 Camas WA 98607 Office: Research Dept Crown Zellerbach Corp Camas WA 98607

HERSEY, JOHN, writer; b. Tientsin, China, June 17, 1914 (parents Am. citizens); s. Roscoe Monroe and Grace (Baird) H.; student Hotchkiss Sch., 1937-32, Clare Coll., Cambridge (Eng.) U., 1936-37; B.A., Yale, 1936; m. Frances Ann Cannon, Apr. 27, 1940 (div. Feb. 1958); children—Martin, John, Ann, Baird; m. 2d, Barbara Day Kaufman, June 2, 1958; 1 dau., Brook. Pvt. sec. to Sinclair Lewis, summer 1937; writer for Time mag., editor, 1937-44, sr. editor Life mag., 1944-45; also writer for New Yorker, other mags.; editor '47, '48 mag., 1947-48; master Pierson Coll., Yale, 1965-70; writer in residence Am. Acad. in Rome, 1970-71. Awarded Pulitzer prize for fiction, 1945. Author: Men on Bataan, 1942; Into the Valley, 1943; A Bell for Adano, 1944; Hiroshima, 1946; The Wall, 195O; The Marmot Drive, 1953; A Single Pebble, 1956; The War Lover, 1959; The Child Buyer, 1960; Here To Stay, 1963; White Lotus, 1965; Too Far To Walk, 1966; Under the Eve of the Storm, 1967; The Algiers Motel Incident, 1968; Letter to the Alumni, 1970; The Conspiracy, 1972. Trustee Nat. Com. Support Pub. Schs., 1962-68. Mem. Authors League Am. (v.p. 1948-54), Am. Acad. Arts Letters. Home: 420 Humphrey St New Haven CT 06511

HERSHBERGER, ARTHUR WAYNE, lawyer; b. Greensburg, Kan., Oct. 9, 1897; s. Anthony W. and Essie A. (Parcel) H.; LL.B., U. Kan., 1918, m. Nadyne Myers, June 11, 1919; children—Jean Ann (Mrs. McDowell), James W. Admitted to Kan. bar, 1918; practiced law, Greensburg, 1918-24, Wichita, 1924—; mem. Hershberger, Patterson, Jones & Thompson, 1937—. Mem. bd. regents State Kan., 1951-57, chmn., 1954, 57; asso. mem. Nat. Fund for Med. Edn. Mem. Am., Kan., Wichita bar assns., Inst. Jud. Adminstrn. Episcopalian. Home: 13 Lynnwood St Wichita KS 67207 Office: Union Center Bldg Wichita KS 67202

HERSHELMAN, CHARLES E., mfg. co. exec.; b. Meadville, Pa., 1910. Controller, Talon div. Textron; treas. Gibson Caribe, Inc.; pres., dir. Meadville Food Services, Inc. Home: 480 Sunnyside Av Meadville PA 16335 Office: 626 Arch St Meadville PA 16335*

HERSHENSON, DAVID BERT, educator; b. Boston, Aug. 30, 1933; s. Bert Barnet and Judith (Cohen) H.; A.B. magna cum laude, Harvard, 1955; A.M., Boston U., 1960, Ph.D., 1964; m. Marian Vogel, Aug. 18, 1957; children-Joseph Bert, Evan Stuart. Counseling psychology trainee VA, Brockton, Bedford and Boston, Mass., 1959-62; fellow USPHS, Boston, 1962-63; counseling psychologist State U. N.Y., Buffalo, 1963-65; asst. prof. to prof. psychology Ill. Inst. Tech., Chgo., 1965—; asst. prof. psychiatry Chgo. Coll. Osteopathy, 1969—; research asso. Chgo. Med. Sch., 1966—; cons. Chgo. Jewish Vocational Service, Chgo. Fedn. Settlement Houses, U.S. Social Security Adminstrn., 1968—. Mem. Ill. Com. on Service to Visually Handicapped, 1968—; mem. profl. adv. com. Ill. Mental Health Planning Bd., 1969—. Bd. dirs. Goodwill Industries Cook County. Mem. Am. Psychol. Assn., Am. Personnel and Guidance Assn. (past senate del.), Ill. (past dir.), Nat. rehab. assns., Ill. Rehab. Counseling Assn. (pres.), Council Rehab. Educators (past dir.). Jewish religion. Co-editor: The Psychology of Vocational Development, 1970; asso. editor Rehab. Counseling Bull., 1967- -; mem. editorial bd. Jour. of Vocational Behavior, 1970—. Home: 1195 Terrace Ct Glencoe IL 60022 Office: Dept Psychology and Edn Ill Inst Tech Chicago IL 60616

HERSHEY, ALFRED DAY, biologist; b. Owosso, Mich., Dec. 4, 1908; s. Robert Day and Alma (Wilber) H.; B.S., Mich. State Coll., 1930, Ph.D., 1934; m. Harriet Davidson, Nov. 15, 1945; 1 son, Peter Manning. Faculty Washington U., 1934-50; staff dept. genetics Carnegie Instn. of Washington, Cold Spring Harbor, N.Y., 1950—, dir., 1962-71. Recipient Lasker award Am. Pub. Health Assn., 1958; joint recipient Nobel prize for medicine, 1969. Mem. Am. Acad. Arts and Scis., Am. Soc. Microbiology, Nat. Acad. Scis. Home: Cold Spring Harbor NY 11724 Office: Carnegie Instn Cold Spring Harbor NY 11724

HERSHEY, BURNET, dramatist, newspaperman; b. Roumania, Dec. 13, 1896; s. Josef and Bertha (Bughici) H.; brought to U.S., 1899; ed. N.Y.C. pub. schs.; student Columbia Sch. Journalism, 1915, Sorbonne, Paris, 1917; m. Thyrza Putnam Sturges, June 1935. Gen. news staffs N.Y. Sun, N.Y. Tribune; Paris corr. N.Y. Sun, 1917-20; Corr. N.Y. Evening Post on Ford Peace Expedition, N.Y. Times with AEF and French Belgian G.H.Q.; covered Eastern Front, accredited to German Army with Field Marshal Von Mackensen; corr. Phila. Ledger Fgn. Service at London, Berlin, Geneva; Far East and Asia Minor assignments for Ledger and Times; attached to Am. Commn. to Negotiate Peace, Versailles Peace Conf,; press. rep. of Am. Commn. to French Expn. Indsl. Arts, 1925; fgn. news commentator Station WNCA, N.Y.C., accredited by War Dept., spl. corr. N.Y. Post, in Gr. Brit., North Africa, 1942-43; made air tour of U.S. bases in 1943; corr. Liberty Mag. covering S.H.A.E.F., 1944-45; U.S. Naval corr. in channel ports, 1955; corr. occupied Germany, 1945; N.Y. and Washington corr. Tribune de Geneve. Decorated Medaille Interallie, Palmes Academique, Officier de L'Instruction Publique, Legion of Honor (France). Mem. Authors League of Am., Dramatists Guild, Silurians. Clubs: Lambs (N.Y.C.); Overseas Press Club Am. (past pres.). Founder, Am. War Corr. Assn. Author: It's a Small World, 1934; World of Midgets, 1935; The Air Future, 1943; Skyways of Tomorrow, 1944; Bloody Record of Nazi Atrocities, 1945; Trial by Fire, 1964; From A reporters Little Black Book, 1966; You Cant Go To Heaven on A Roller Skate, 1969; The Pyromaniac (London film), 1969; Odyssey of Henry Ford and His Great Peace Ship, 1967. Plays: Scattered Seed, 1936; Dealers in Death, 1936; The Brown Danube, 1939, produced at Lyceum Theatre, N.Y.C. Compiled and edited A Documentary History of the Versailles Conference, 15 vols.; biography Dag Hammarskjold, 1963; From a Reporter's Little Black Book, 1967. Contbr. articles and fiction to newspapers, Look, Sat. Eve. Post, Liberty, Readers Digest, other nat. periodicals. Address: 91 Central Park W New York City NY 10023

HERSHEY, DANIEL, educator; b. N.Y.C., Feb. 12, 1931; s. Frank and Anna (Scharf) H.; B.S., Copper Union, 1953; M.S., U. Tenn., 1959, Ph.D., 1961; m. Barbara Fay Drury, Sept. 5, 1965; 1 son, Michael David. Chem. engr. Merck, Sharp & Dohme, 1961-62; faculty U. Cin., 1962—, prof. chem. engring., 1969—. Served with AUS, 1955-57. NIH grantee, 1964-69. Mem. Am. Assn. U. Profs. (pres. U. Cin. chpt. 1971-72), Sigma Xi (pres. U. Cin. chpt.). Club: International Torch. Author: My University, My God, 1970; Everday Science, 1971; Transport Analysis, 1971. Editor: Chemical Engineering in Medicine and Biology, 1967; Blood Oxygenation, 1970. Home: 726 Lafayette Av Cincinnati OH 45220

HERSHEY, FALLS BACON, educator, surgeon; b. Chgo., Aug. 16, 1918; s. Charles O. and Emma L. (Eby) H.; student Goshen (Ind.) Coll., 1935-37; B.S., U. Ill., 1939; M.D., Harvard, 1943; m. Julia K. Elder, Oct. 15, 1955; children—Charles O., Laura V., James E., Julian. Med. intern Peter Bent Brigham Hosp., Boston 1943; surg. intern, asst. resident surgery Mass. Gen. Hosp., 1946- 48, 1st asst. resident surgery, 1948-51; research asso. biology Mass. Inst. Tech., 1948-50; teaching fellow surgery Harvard Med. Sch., 1952; chief resident surgery Mass. Gen. Hosp., Boston, 1952; from instr. to asso. prof. surgery Washington U. Sch. Medicine, St. Louis, 1953-64, asso. prof. clin. surgery, 1966—; chief surgery VA Hosp., St. Louis, 1955-60; acting chief Hartford Burn Unit, Washington U., 1966-67; prof. surgery Chgo. Med. Schs., also chmn. dept. surgery Michael Reese Hosp. and Med. Center, Chgo., 1964-66. Bd. dirs. St. Louis Heart Assn.; councillor Mo. chpt. Am. Cancer Soc. Served as med. officer USPHS, 1944- 46. Diplomate Am. Bd. Surgery. Mem. Internat. Cardiovascular Soc., St. Louis County Med. Soc. (pres. 1971), Western Surg. Assn., Soc. for Cryobiology, Alpha Omega Alpha. Author: (with C.H. Calman) Atlas of Vascular Surgery, 1963; also articles. Home: 11 Wydown Terrace Clayton MO 63105 Office: 621 S New Ballas Rd St Louis MO 63141

HERSHEY, H. GARLAND, geologist, govt. ofcl.; b. Quarryville, Pa., Oct. 1, 1905; s. Howard Risser and Aretta Pearl (Reinhart) H.; A.B., Johns Hopkins, 1929, Ph.D., 1936; m. Erna Madelyn Eybs, Oct. 24, 1931; children—Howard Garland, Timothy Joseph. Geologist B. & O. R.R., Balt. 1930; asst. Md. Geol. Survey, 1931-36; geologist Ia. Geol. Survey, 1936-39, asst. state geologist, 1939-43, asso. state geologist, 1944-47, state geologist, dir., 1947-69, state geologist emeritus, 1970—; dir. office water resources research U.S. Dept. Interior, Washington, 1969—; dist. geologist U.S. Geol. Survey, 1944-55; lectr. State U. Ia., 1938-39, 43, adj. prof., 1968-69. Chmn. Ia. Gov. Spl. Flood Control Dam Com., Coralville, 1947, Chariton and Red Rock, 1948; mem. Govs. Spl. Com. Ionizing Radiation, 1959-61, Govs. Spl. Com. Coal Studies, 1960-61, dir. Interstate Conf. Water Problems, 1960-69, sec.-treas., 1961, chmn., 1963, state disaster coordinator, 1961-68, Ia. oil and gas adminstr., 1963-69; v.p. Rivers and Harbors Conf., 1960-68; mem. Ia. Interim Flood Control Com., 1948; Chmn. Ia. Natural Resources Council, 1949-69; cons. Presdl. Adv. Com. Water Resources Policy, 1954-55; mem. coop. forestry research adv. com. U.S. Dept. Agr., 1970—; mem. Miss. River Pkwy. Planning Commn., 1949-55, Midwestern States Flood Control Conf., 1947-69, chmn., 1951, 1961; mem. Iowa City Planning and Zoning Commn., 1950-55; Gov.'s Water Pollution Control Study Subcom., 1964-65; mem. U.S. Nat. Com. for Internat. Hydrological Decade, 1964—, now chmn.; mem. adv. com. water data for pub. use U.S. Dept. Interior, 1965-69; cons. to exec. dir. Water Resources Council, 1967; mem. Ia. Legislative Water Study Commn., 1955- 56; Gov.'s Commn. Social and Econ. Trends, 1958; Gov.'s alternate Mo.- Basin Inter-Agy. Com., 1957-69. Bd. dirs., v.p. Nat. Water Conservation Conf.; trustee Midwest Research Inst., Kansas City, Mo., 1947-55; bd. consultants Ia. Inst. Hydraulic Research, 1965-67. Fellow Geol. Soc. Am. (Councilor 1956-58, vice chmn. engring. geology div. 1969, chmn. 1970, mem. N. Central sect. mgmt. bd. 1966-68), Ia. Acad. Sci. (pres. 1954); mem. Am. Inst. Profl. Geologists (Ia. pres. 1965-66, sr. del. 1966-67), Geol. Soc. Ia. (hon.), Soc. Econ. Geologists, Soil Conservation Soc. Am., Assn. Am. State Geologists (hon.; historian 1955-57, v.p. 1957-58, pres. 1959), Am. Geophys. Union, A.A.A.S., Ia. Engring. Soc. (dir. 1949, v.p. 1951, pres. 1954), Am. Water Works Assn., Sigma Xi. Clubs: Triangle, Engineers (Iowa City). Author reports, maps, articles to tech., sci. jours. Home: 2400 Virginia Av NW Washington DC 20037 Office: Office of Water Resources Research 5410 Dept of Interior Washington DC 20240

HERSHEY, JACOB W., transp. co. exec.; b. Harrisburg, Pa., Dec. 13, 1912; s. Eli Nissley and Carrie (Mann) H,; grad. Phillips Acad., Andover, Mass., 1930; B.S., Yale, 1934; m. Olive Shelmire Duncan, June 10, 1940; children—Olive Shelmire (Mrs. Robert Spitzmiller, Jr.), John Michael, Susan Mann; m. 2d, Terese Tarlton Law, Dec. 19, 1958. Asst. v.p. Shell Oil Co., 1937- 39, mgr. crude oil purchasing dept., 1940-41; mgr. crude oil dept. Pan Am. Prodn. Co., 1941; mgr. Butcher-Arthur Co., Houston, 1941-45; v.p. Comml. Petroleum & Transp. Corp., also Comml. Transp. Corp., 1946-58; pres. Comml. Transp. Corp., 1957-58; pres. Am. Commercial Lines, Houston, 1959-60, chmn. bd., 1960—; v.p., dir. Tall Timbers Corp., 1960- -, Texas Gas Transmission Corporation; director of Gibraltar Savs. & Loan Assn., Hill & Hill Truck Line, Equity Annuity Insurance Co., 1st City National Bank, Houston, Tex. Mem. industry adv. council Petroleum Administrn. for War, 1941-44, transp. adv. com. to sec. commerce, 1954-61, Kennedy-Johnson Natural Resources Adv. Com. 1960-61; chmn. exchange delegation to observe Soviet Waterways, 1960; mem. Am. Nat. Commn. to Permanent Internat. Nav. Congress; 1960, mem. Nat. Defense Exec. Res., 1964—; mem. nat. council U. Houston, v.p. Houston Council World Affairs. Trustee Kinkaid Sch., Houston, 1955—, chmn., 1957-59; bd. dirs. Houston Symphony Soc., 1937, 57; chmn. adv. com. transp. Center at Northwestern U. Mem. Inland Waterway Common Carriers Assn. (pres.), Transp. Assn. Am. (dir. 1957-61), Am. Soc. Traffic and Transp. Assn. Clubs: Yale (N.Y.C.); N.Y. Yacht, Houston Country, Houston, Coronado Texas Corinthian Yacht (Houston). Home: 1 Longbow Lane Houston TX 77024 Office: 2919 Buffalo Dr Houston TX 77019

HERSHEY, LEWIS BLAINE, former army officer; b. Steuben County, Ind., Sept. 12, 1893; s. Latta Freleigh and Rosetta (Richardson) H.; B.S., Tri-State Coll., Angola, Ind., 1912, B. Pd., A.B., 1914; student Ind. U., 1917; attended Field Arty. Sch., Fort Sill, Okla., 1922-23; Command and Gen. Staff Sch., 1931-33, Army War Coll. 1933-34, U. Hawaii, 1935-36; LL.D. (hon.), Tri- State Coll., Ohio State Univ., Oglethorpe U., Norwich U., Albright Coll., LaFayette Coll., Columbia U., Ind. U.; m. Ellen Dygert, Nov. 29, 1917; children—Kathryn Elizabeth (Mrs. A. Alvis Layne, Jr.) Gilbert Richardson, George Frederick, Ellen Margaret (Mrs. Sam L. Barth). Began as country sch. tchr. Township School, Jamestown Tsp., Steuben, Ind., 1910; high sch. prin., Flint, Ind., 1914-16; successively pvt., corpl., sergt., 2d lt., 1st lt., Ind. Nat. Guard, 1911-16; commd. 1st lt. U.S. Army, 1916, and advanced through grades to gen., 1969; asst. prof. mil. science and tactics, Ohio State U., 1923-27; asst. G-4, Hawaiian Dept., 1934-36; mem. War Dept. Gen. Staff, 1936-40; sec. and exec. officer, Joint Army and Navy Selective Service Com., 1936-40; promoted to brig. gen. Oct. 1940, in recognition of work in preparing plans for Selective Service System; appointed dep. dir. Selective Service System. Dec. 19, 1940, dir. July 31, 1941; promoted to major gen., U.S. Army 1942; apptd. dir. Office of Selective Service Records, Mar. 31, 1947; appointed dir. of Selective Service, by President Truman, 1948; promoted to lt. gen., 1956; appointed spl. adviser to Pres. U.S. on Manpower Mobilization, 1970—. Chmn. of Montgomery County chpt. A.R.C., 1952-68; past pres. Nat. Capital area council Boy Scouts of America. Trustee Tri State Coll., Angola, Indiana. Awarded D.S.M. from Army and Navy; D.S.M. of Am. Legion, 1946 also N.G. Assn. of U.S., 1954; Distinguished Service award, Mil. Champlains Assn. U.S., 1957; George Washington medal Freedoms Found., 1958; Bernard Baruch award V.F.W., 1966; Silver Beaver award Boy Scouts, 1961, Silver Antelope award, 1963, Silver Buffalo award, 1966. Republican. Mason. Author: Selective Service in Peacetime; Selective Service in Wartime; Selective Service as the Tide of War Turns: Selective Service in Victory; also mag. articles. Home: 5500 Lambeth Rd Bethesda MD 20014 Office: The White House NEOB 8230 Washington DC 20500

HERSHEY, PAUL H., metal products co. exec.; b. 1889. Pres., treas. Hershey Metal Products, Inc., Ansonia, Conn., Penn Keystone Corp.; dir. Plastic Wire & Cable Co., Norwich, Conn., Birmingham Nat. Bank, Derby, Conn., Merritt-Chapman & Scott Corp., Dolly Madison Foods, Inc.; chmn. exec. com. Nautee Corp., N.Y.C. Home: Center Rd Orange CT 06477 Office: Hershey Metal Products Inc Division St Ansonia CT 06401*

HERSHEY, ROBERT DELP, clergyman; b. Reading, Pa., July 3, 1909; s. Harry C. and Ida May (Delp) H.; A.B., Gettysburg Coll., 1931; B.D., Lutheran Sem., Gettysburg, 1934, S.T.M., 1935; student U. Pa., 1935-36; S.T.D., Temple U., 1938, U. Berlin (Germany), 1939; student U. Madrid (Spain), 1959, U. Florence (Italy), 1962, Alliance Francaise, Paris, 1965, Dante Alighieri Sch., Rome, 1969, Knubley Sch., Athens, 1970; D.D., Muhlenberg Coll., 1949; L.H.D., Wagner Coll., 1968; postgrad. Centre Econ. and Polit. Studies, London, 1971; m. Mary Billman June 16, 1937; children—Robert Delp, Georgina Stuart. Instr., Gettysburg Coll., 1932-35; ordained to ministry Luth. Ch., 1934; pastor in Phoenixville, Pa., 1935-38, Berlin, 1938-39, Ambler, Pa., 1940- 42, Glenside, Pa., 1942-45, Phila., 1946-53, Holy Trinity Luth. Ch., N.Y.C., 1953—; radio and TV broadcaster. Pres. Phila. Council Chs., 1952-53, Manhattan div. N.Y.C. Council Chs., 1960-62. Bd. dirs. Lincoln Sq. Community Council. Mem. Soc. Bibl. Lit., Found. for Arts, Religion and Culture, Phi Beta Kappa, Alpha Kappa Alpha, Eta Sigma Phi, Phi Kappa Alpha, Lambda Chi Alpha. Author: The Secret of God, 1951; Letter to Lutherans, 1954; Think About These Things, 1958; also articles. Home: 340 Johnson Av Teaneck NJ 07666 Office: 3 W 65th St New York City NY 10023

HERSHKOVITZ, PHILIP, zoologist: b. Pitts., Oct. 12, 1909; s. Aba and Bertha (Halpern) H.; B.S., U. Mich., 1938. M.S., 1940; m. Anne Pierrette Dode, Sept. 15, 1945; children—Francine, Michael Dode, Mark Allen. Zool. expdn. Ecuador, also Upper Amazon region, 1933-37; grad. asst. mammal div. U. Mich. Mus. Zoology, 1939-41; zool. expdn., Columbia, 1941-43, Field Mus. Natural History, Colombian Zool. Expdn., 1948-52; Suriname Zool. Expdn., 1961-62. Walter Rathbone Bacon scholar Smithsonian Instn., 1941-43, 46-47; asst. curator div. mammals Field Mus. Natural History, Chgo., 1947-53, asso. curator, 1955-56, curator, 1956-62, research curator, 1962—. Served as pvt. AUS, 1943-46. Mem. Am. Soc. Mammalogists, Biol. Soc., Washington, Soc. Study Evolution, Soc. Systematic Zoology, Assn. Tropical Biology, Systematic Assn., Fauna Preservation Soc., Internat. Primatol. Soc. Contbr. tech. and science publs. Home: South Holland IL 60473 Office: Field Museum Natural History Roosevelt Rd and Lake Shore Dr Chicago IL 60605

HERSHMAN, JACOB EARL, govt. ofcl.; b. Mechanicsburg, Pa., Nov. 7, 1913; s. John R. and Fairy (Pfaltzgraff) H.; B.S., Elizabethtown (Pa.) Coll., 1936; M.Ed., U. Md., 1949, D.Ed., 1956; m. Alberta Garns, Jan. 2, 1942; children—Joan Elaine, John Garns, Lucie Ann. Regional display supr. Montgomery Ward Co., 1939- 42; high sch. tchr., Washington, Md., 1945-56; curriculum specialist South Hagerstown (Md.) High Sch., 1956-57; prin. Hancock (Md.) High Sch., 1957-61; dean Elizabethtown Coll., 1961-66; program specialist Bur. Higher Edn., Office of Edn. Dept. Health, Edn. and Welfare, Washington, 1966-67, higher edn. specialist, div. coll. facilities, 1967—. Active Boy Scouts, Community Chest, A.R.C. fund drives. Bd. dirs. Hancock Free Library. Served as sgt. AUS, 1942-45. Mem. N.E.A., Md., Washington County tchrs. assns., Nat., Md. assns. secondary sch. prins., Nat. Biology Tchrs. Assn., Md. History Tchrs. Assn., Eastern Assn. Coll. Deans, Pa. Assn. Acad. Deans, Phi Delta Kappa. Rotarian. Home: 6735 Tower Dr Alexandria VA 22306 Office: Div Coll Facilities US Office Edn GSA Bldg 7th and D Sts S W Washington DC 20024

HERSHMAN, MENDES, ins. co. exec.; b. Northampton, Pa., May 2, 1911; s. Joel and Rose (Grossman) H.; A.B., N.Y.U., 1929; LL.B., Harvard, 1932; m. Frances Sybil Stackell, June 2, 1935; children—Jane, Martha. Admitted to N.Y. bar, 1933; spl. counsel for housing N.Y. Life Ins. Co., N.Y.C., 1946-62, asst. gen. counsel, 1962-64, asso. gen. counsel, 1964-69, v.p., gen. counsel, 1969—; lectr. joint com. on continuing legal edn. Am. Law Inst.-Am. Bar Assn., Practising Law Inst. Mem. Mayor's Com. on Judiciary, 1966—. Vice pres., trustee Bronx-Lebanon Hosp. Center; v.p., bd. dirs. United Neighborhood Houses; bd. dirs. Community Action for Legal Services, N.Y. Pub. Devel. Corp.; mem. exec. com. Citizens Union. Recipient N.Y. State award, certificate of Outstanding Pub. Service, 1960. Fellow Am. Bar Found.; mem. Assn. Bar City N.Y. (com. chmn., past v.p., chmn. exec. com.), Am. Bar Assn. (com. chmn.), Harvard Law Sch. Assn. N.Y.C. (trustee), Phi Beta Kappa. Bd. editors: N.Y. Law Jour., 1969—. Contbr. articles profl. jours. Home: 200 E 66th St New York City NY 10021 Office: 51 Madison Av New York City NY 10010

HERSKIND, ELMER CHRISTEN, stock exchange exec.; b. Boston, Nov. 23, 1908; s. Soren B. and Bodil (Neilsen) H.; grad. Bentley Sch. Accounting, Boston, 1930; m. Esther L. Lawson, Oct. 20, 1934; children—Richard E., Carol (Mrs. Richard T. Ford), Ronald D., Ruth E. Accountant-auditor Robert, Finnegan & Lynah, C.P.A.'s, Boston, 1929-35; chief accountant Louis P. Mott & Co., Boston,

1935-38; self-employed as part-time pub. accountant, also mng. dir. Uncle Elmer's Song Circle, Inc., 1938-53; asst. treas. Blue Hill Cemetery, Braintree, Mass., 1953-57; auditor Boston Stock Exchange, 1957- -, exec. sec., 1964—, v.p. for finance, 1967—, v.p. dept. mem. firms, 1971—. Originator, prin. Uncle Elmer's Song Circle, religious and charitable broadcast, Boston, 1932-59. Conglist. Mason. Home: 177 Border Rd Needham MA 02192 Office: 53 State St Boston MA 02109

HERSON, LAWRENCE J. R., educator; b. Ill., 1923; s. Herman and Estelle (Reiss) H.; B.S., Northwestern U., 1948, M.A., 1949; M.A., Yale, 1952, Ph.D., 1955; m. Libuse Kormunda, 1951; children—Eric Sebastian, Victoria Sydney. Instr. Northwestern U., 1952-55; mem. faculty Ohio State U., 1955—, prof. polit. sci., 1962—, chmn. dept., 1962-69, dean for undergraduate programs Colleges of Arts and Sciences, Ohio State U., since 1969—; vis. prof. Northwestern, Ind. univs. Served with AUS, 1942-45. Mem. Am. Polit. Sci. Assn., Phi Beta Kappa. Co-author: Functions and Policies of American Government, 3d edit., 1967. Contbr. profl. jours. Home: 146 Glenmont Av Columbus OH 43214

HERSTAND, THEODORE, educator; b. N.Y.C., May 14, 1930; s. Max Arthur and Rose (Shyatt) H.; Certificate Advanced Studies, U. Birmingham, England, 1951; B.A., U. Ia., 1953, M.A., 1957; Ph.D., U. Ill., 1963; m. Jo Ellen Gillette, Aug. 23, 1957; children—Sarah Ellen, Michael Simpson. Instr. theatre Parsons Coll., Fairfield, Ia., 1953-54, Eastern Ill. U., Charleston, 1957-59; asst. prof. State U. N.Y. at Plattsburgh, 1960-64, asso. prof., 1963-64; asst. prof., U. Ill., 1964-66; asso. prof. U. Minn., Mpls., 1966-70; prof., chmn. dept. dramatic arts Case Western Res. U., 1970—; vis. prof. Mpls. Coll. Art and Design, 1969; vis. dir. Colo. Shakespeare Festival, Boulder, 1968; theatre bldg. cons. Eastern Ill. U., Charleston, Ill. State U., Bloomington, Jewsih Community Center Theater, Mpls. Bd. dirs. Theater-in-the-Round, Mpls., 1968, v.p. bd., 1969; bd. dirs. Great Lakes Shakespeare Festival, 1970—. Served to 1st lt. USAF, 1954-56. Mem. Omicron Delta Kappa. Author plays Sugar and Lemon, 1968, others. Asso. editor Drama Survey, 1967-70. Contbr. revs., articles profl. jours. Home: 3284 Braemar Rd Shaker Heights OH 44120 Office: Dept Dramatic Arts Case Western Res U Cleveland OH 44106

HERSTEIN, ISRAEL NATHAN, mathematician, educator; b. Lublin, Poland, Mar. 28, 1923; s. Jacob and Mary (Lichtenstein) H.; B.Sc. with honors, U. Man., 1945; M.A., U. Toronto, 1946; Ph.D., Ind. U., 1948; m. Marianne Deson, June 16, 1946. Came to U.S., 1946, naturalized, 1955. Instr., U. Kan., 1948-50; lectr. Ohio State U., 1951; asst. prof. math. U. Chgo., 1951-53, prof., 1962—; asst. prof. U. Pa., 1953-56, asso. prof., 1956-57; asso. prof. math. Cornell U., Ithaca, N.Y., 1957-58, prof., 1958-62; vis. prof. U. Rome, 1961-62, 63, 65, 66, 68, Stanford, 1960, 64; Fulbright lectr., Rio de Janeiro, Brazil, 1967; cons. Ramo Woodridge Co., 1956, Gen. Electric Co., 1958-6O, Lincoln Labs., 1958-59; editor Harper & Row, 1962—. Dir. Comitato Internat. Matematico Estivo, Varenna, Italy, 1965. Guggenheim fellow, 1961-62, 68-69. Mem. Am. Math. Soc., Math. Assn. Am. Author: Topics in Algebra, 1964; Non-Commutative Rings, 1967; Topics in Ring Theory, 1968. Contbr. numerous articles profl. jours. Home: 5000 Cornell Av Chicago IL 60615

HERTELENDY, PAUL, music critic, acoustician; b. Budapest, Hungary, June 10, 1932; s. Andor and Elizabeth (Hitt) H.; came to U.S., 1940, naturalized, 1953; grad. Phillips Exeter Acad., 1949; B.S.E., Princeton, 1953; M.S.E., Stanford, 1957; Ph.D. U. Cal. at Berkeley, 1965; m. Martha Margaret Sam, July 9, 1966. With U.S. Coast and Geodetic Survey, 1953-55; mech. engr. Nat. Bur. Standards, 1958-64; research engr. Physics Internat. Co., San Leandro, Cal. 1965-67; music critic Oakland (Cal.) Tribune, 1964—; partner Colgate Research and Development Co., Princeton, N.J., 1966—. Profl. journalism fellow Stanford, 1969. Mem. Phi Beta Kappa, Acoustical Soc. Am., Fair Play for Candenzas (founder 1968). Democrat. Roman Catholic. Club: Sierra (San Francisco). Composer opera libretto Tilman, 1967. Contbr. articles profl. jours. Translator Numerical Methods for Symmetric Matrices, 1970. Home: 60001 Rockwell St Oakland CA 94618 Office: Oakland Tribune 13th and Franklin Sts Oakland CA 94604

HERTER, CHRISTIAN ARCHIBALD, Jr., lawyer, corp. exec.; b. Bklyn., Jan 29, 1919; s. Christian A. and Mary Carolin (Pratt) H.; B.S. cum laude, Harvard, 1941, LL.B., 1948; m. Suzanne C. Clery, June 10, 1944 (div. 1963); children—Susan, Christian Archibald, III, Geoffrey; m. 2d, Susan C. Senior, Aug. 18, 1963. Admitted to Mass. bar, 1948; partner Bingham, Dana & Gould, Boston; adminstrv. asst. to Vice Pres. of U.S., 1953-54; mem. policy planning staff U.S. Dept. of State, 1954; gen. counsel FOA, 1954-56; elected to Gov.'s Council Mass., 1957; gen. mgr. govt. relations Socony Mobil Oil Co., Inc., 1961-67, now corporate v.p. for pub. affairs; dir. Berkshire Life Ins. Co., Inc., Pittsfield, Mass. Chmn., N.Y. Urban Coalition. Trustee Fisk U., Pratt Inst., bd. dirs. Nat. Fgn. Trade Council, Inc. Rep., Mass. Gen. Ct., 1951-53. Served as maj. AUS, 1941-46. Decorated Purple Heart, Bronze Star with oak leaf cluster (U.S.); Croix de Guerre with Silver Star. Mem. Am., Boston bar assns., Council on Fgn. Relations, Fgn. Policy Assn. (dir.). Home: 10 Mitchell Pl New York City NY 10017 Office: 870 United Nations Plaza New York City NY 10017

HERTER, FREDERIC P., surgeon; b. Bklyn., Nov. 12, 1920; s. Christian A. and Mary Caroline (Pratt) H.; A.B., Harvard, 1941, M.D., 1944; m. Harriet Ames Conel, Nov. 22, 1947; children—Frederic P., Caroline Ames, Brooke. Intern, then resident surgery. Presbyn. Hosp., N.Y.C., 1944-53; asst. to attending surgeon, 1954—; mem. faculty Columbia Coll. Phys. and Surg., 1953—, now prof. surgery, acting chmn. dept., 1969; dir. surgery, vis. surgeon Francis Delafield Hosp., N.Y.C., 1966-69; cons. surgery Harlem. Goldwater Meml. hosps. Trustee Mary Imogene Bassett Hosp. Served to capt., M.C., AUS, 1945-47. Contbr. med. jours. Home: 155 Sherman Av Dobbs Ferry NY 19522 Office: 161 Ft Washington Av New York City NY 10032

HERTIG, ARTHUR TREMAIN, physician; b. Mpls., May 12, 1904; s. Charles Marshall and Florence (Long) H.; B.S., U. Minn., 1928; M.D., Harvard, 1930; m. Linda Woodworth, Dec. 22, 1932; children—Helen (Mrs. T.G. Craig), Andrew. Entomol. asst. Kala Azar Field Studies, Rockefeller Found., Peking, China, 1925-26; pathol. tng. Peter Bent Brigham Hosp., Boston, Lying-in-Hosp. and Children's Hosp., 1930-33; Nat. Research fellow in embryology Carnegie Instn. of Washington, 1933-34; obstet. tng. Boston Lying Hosp., 1936-38; with Boston Lying-in Hosp., 1934—, asst. pathologist, 1934-39, pathologist, 1939-52, cons. pathology, 1952—; pathologist Free Hosp. for Women, Brookline, Mass., 1938- 52, cons. pathologist, 1952—; with Harvard Med. Sch., 1931—, prof. pathology, 1948-52, 70—, Shattuck prof. path. anatomy, 1952-70, chmn. dept. pathology, 1950-68; chief div. pathobiology New Eng. Regional Primate Research Center, Southboro, Mass., 1968—; cons. in pathology to Armed Forces Inst. of Pathology, Washington, 1948—, mem. sci. adv. bd. cons., 1970—; cons. in obstet. and gynecol. pathology USN, Chelsea, Mass., 1947-67; sr. cons. adminstrn., edn. pathology Lemuel Shattuck Hosp.; cons. pathologist Peter Bent Brigham, Beth Israel, Childrens hosps., all Boston. Trustee Boston Med. Library, 1945-48. Recipient Am. Gynecol. Soc. award (with John Rock) for fundamental research on human reproduction, 1949; Outstanding Achievement award Centennial Celebration U. Minn., 1951; Ward Burdick award Am. Soc. Clin. Pathologists, 1966. Diplomate Am. Bd. Obstetrics and Gynecology, Am. Bd. Pathology (trustee 1959-70, pres. 1969-70). Mem. Soc. Exptl. Pathologists, Coll. Am. Pathologists (gov. 1959-62), Am. Coll. Obstetricians and Gynecologists, Internat. Acad. Pathology, Am. Soc. Clin. Pathologists, Am. Assn. Pathology and Bacteriology, Am. Gynecology Soc., A.A.A.S., Am. Acad. Arts and Sci., Am. Assn. Anatomists, A.M.A., N.E. Obstet. and Gynecol. Soc. (pres. 1950-51), N.E. Pathol. Soc. (past pres.), Mass. and Middlesex East med. socs., Obstet. Soc. of Boston (past pres.), Sigma Xi, Alpha Omega Alpha, Nu Sigma Nu (past exec. councilor). Clubs: Harvard (Boston); Country (Winchester). Contbr. articles (with John Rock) on early development of normal and abnormal human embryos in Contribution to Embryology, 1941-58; (with Eleanor C. Adams) Ultrastructure of mammalian oocytes and human corpus luteum, 1960-68; physiology and pathology female reprodn. in subhuman primates, 1968—; also numerous articles in field. Home: 21 Everett Av Winchester MA 01890 Office: New Eng Regional Primate Research Center Southboro MA 01772

HERTZ, BARBARA VALENTINE (Mrs. David Bendel Hertz), ednl. adminstr.; b. N.Y.C., Mar. 1, 1921; d. Herbert I. and Helen (Lachman) Valentine; student Swarthmore Coll., 1939-40; B.A., Barnard Coll., 1943; m. David Bendel Hertz. Dec. 20, 1941; children—Barbara Bendel (Mrs. Winthrop A. Burr), Valentine (Mrs. Roger A. Pedersen). Comml. continuity radio sta. WQXR, 1945-46; free lance writing and publicity, 1947-51; asso. editor Parents mag., 1951-56, mng. editor, 1956-68; dir. devel. Barnard Coll., N.Y.C., 1968—. Pres. Class of 1943, Barnard Coll., 1953-58. Mem. Alumni Assn. Friends Sem. (pres. 1954-56), Woman's Conf. Group N.Y.C. (exec. com.) Home: 225 E 74th St New York City NY 10021 Office: 606 W 120th St New York City NY 10027

HERTZ, DAVID RALPH, lawyer; b. Cleve., July 21, 1898; s. Aaron Daniel and Bertha (Lichtman) H.; A.B., U. Mich., 1919; LL.B., Columbia, 1921; m. Marguerite Rosenberg, Aug. 27, 1922; children—Willard Joel, Harlan Stone. Admitted to Ohio bar, 1921; pvt. practice law, Cleve., 1922-29, 39—, counsel to Cuyahoga Co., 1929-32; city ry. commr., Cleve., 1932-33; judge Ct. of Common Pleas, Cuyahoga County, 1932-39; impartial umpire, labor disputes Cleve. Transit System, 1946-50. Mem. Bd. State Bar Examiners, Ohio, 1970—. Pub. panel mem. WLB, 1943-45; past instr. law agy. Cleve-Marshall Law Sch. Past. sec. Cleve. Center on Alcoholism; trustee Cleve. Jewish Center, 1923-39; pres. Cleve. Zionist Dist., 1920-30. Mem. panel arbitrators Fed. Mediation and Conciliation Service; mem. panel arbitrators, mem. pub. employment disputes settlement panel Am. Assn. Arbitrators. Mem. Am., Ohio, Cleve. bar assns., Am. Arbitration Assn., Cleve. Legal Aid Soc. (trustee 1960-66, treas. 1965-66), Nat. Legal Aid and Defender Assn., Columbia Law Sch. Alumni Assn., Cleve. Mental Hygiene Assn. (pres. 1946-48, 61-63). Democrat (mem. Cuyahoga county exec. com., 1928-70). Clubs: Commerce, City (v.p. 1963- 64). Home: 13800 Shaker Blvd Cleveland OH 44120 Office: Leader Bldg Cleveland OH 44114

HERTZ, RICHARD CORNELL, rabbi; b. St. Paul, Oct. 7, 1916; s. Abram J. and Nadine (Rosenberg) H.; A.B., U. Cin., 1938; M.H.L., Hebrew Union Coll., 1942, D.D., 1967; Ph.D., Northwestern U., 1948; m. Mary Louise Mann, Nov. 25, 1943; children—Nadine (Mrs. Michael Wertheimer), Ruth Mann. Ordained rabbi, 1942; asst. rabbi N. Shore Congregation Israel, Glencoe, Ill., 1942-47; asso. rabbi Chgo. Sinai Congregation, 1947-53; sr. rabbi Temple Beth El, Detriot, 1953—; adj. prof. Jewish thought U. Detroit, 1970—. Went on spl. mission for White House to investigate status Jews and Judaism in U.S.S.R., 1959; 1st Am. rabbi received in pvt. audience at Papal Palace by Pope Paul VI, 1963; del. to Internat. Conf. World Union for Progress in Judaism, London, 1959, 61. Lectr. Jewish Chautauqua Soc., Nat. Lecture Bur.; former mem. plan bd. Synagogue Council Am.; mem. chaplaincy commn. Nat. Jewish Welfare Bd.; exec. com., vice chmn. Citizen's Com. for Equal Opportunity; mem. Mich. Gov.'s Com. on Ethics and Morals, 1963-69; mem. nat. bd. dirs. Religious Edn. Assn., adv. bd. Joint Distbn. Com.; former mem. nat. rabbinical council United Jewish Appeal. Dir. Am. Jewish Com., mem. nat. exec. bd., former hon. vice-chmn. Detroit chpt.; past dir. Mich. Soc. Mental Health, Jewish Family and Children's Services, United Community Services, Jewish Welfare Fedn. Detroit, Jewish Community Council Detroit; dir. United Found., Boys Clubs, Jewish Community Council Detroit, Mich. region Anti-Defamation League, chmn. bd. overseers Hebrew Union Coll.-Jewish Inst. Religion, 1969—; bd. govs. Detroit Inst. Tech., 1955-70. Served as chaplain AUS, 1943-46. Fellow Am. Sociol. Soc.; mem. Detroit Hist. Soc., Central Conf. Am. Rabbis (former nat. chmn. com. on Jews in Soviet orbit), Am. Jewish Hist. Soc., Am. Legion (dept. chaplain 1956- 57), Jewish War Vets. (dept. chaplain 1958-59), Alumni Assn. Hebrew Union Coll.-Jewish Inst. Religion (past dir.). Clubs: Rotary, Economic (dir.) (Detroit); Wranglers (past pres.), Great Lakes, Standard, Franklin Hills, Knollwood, Tam O'Santer. Author: Rabbi Yesterday and Today, 1943; This I believe, 1952; Education of the Jewish Child, 1953; Our Religion Above All, 1953; Inner Peace for You, 1954; Positive Judaism, 1955; Wings of the Morning, 1956; Impressions of Israel, 1956; Prescription for Heartache, 1958; Faith in Jewish Survival, 1961; The American Jew in Search of Himself, 1962; What Counts Most in Life, 1963; What Can A Man Believe, 1967; also articles in sci., popular publs. Home: 15 E Kirby St Detroit MI 48202 Office: 8801 Woodward Av Detroit MI 48202

HERTZ, ROY, physician; b. Cleve., June 19, 1909; s. Aaron Daniel and Bertha (Lichtman) H.; A.B., U. Wis., 1930, Ph.D., 1933; M.D., 1939; M.P.H., Johns Hopkins, 1941, m. Pearl Ruby Fennell, June 23, 1934 (dec. Mar. 1962); children—Margaret Fennell, Jeremy Fennell; m. 2d, Dorothy Wright Oberdorfer, Nov. 9, 1965. Intern U. Wis. Hosp., 1939-40; bio. med. research specializing in endocrinology and cancer, 1940—; chief endocrinology br. Nat. Cancer Inst., NIH, Bethesda, Md., 1965, science director National Institute Child Health and Human Development, 1965-66; professor obstetrics and gynecology George Washington U. Med. Sch., Washington, 1966-69; chief reprodn. research br. Nat. Inst. Child Health and Human Development, NIH, Bethesda, Md., 1967-69; asso. dir. biomed. div. Population Council, 1969—; sr. physician Rockefeller U., N.Y.C. Recipient Superior Service award Dept. Health, Edn. and Welfare, 1957, award for cancer research A.A.A.S., 1958; awards cancer research Ewing Soc., 1966, Internat. Coll. of Surgeons, 1969. Fellow A.C.P., mem. Am. Physiol. Soc., Soc. Exptl. Biology and Medicine (mem. editorial bd), Am. Cancer Soc. (mem. Research Adv. Council), Endocrine Soc. (past v.p.), Fedn. Clin. Research, Phi Beta Kappa, Sigma Xi; hon. mem. Argentina, Santiago med. assns. Home: RFD 1 Box 102 Oscaleta Rd South Salem NY 10590 Office: Rockefeller U 66th and York Av New York City NY 10021

HERTZFELD, KURT MAXIMILIAN, univ. adminstr.; b. Austria, Oct. 9, 1918; s. Joseph Pierre and Elsa (Fishel) H.; came to U.S., 1935, naturalized, 1939; B.A., Harvard, 1941, M.B.A., 1942; m. Nora Elizabeth Alfs, July 4, 1942; children—Kurt Maximilian, Elizabeth Nora, Anne Morely, Susan Laurene. With Calvert Distilling Co., 1942-43, Ford Motor Co., 1946-47, Fasco Industries, 1947- 49; bus. mgr. U. Rochester, 1949-59; v.p. adminstrv. affairs Boston U., 1959-67, v.p., treas., 1967-68; treas. Amherst (Mass.) Coll., 1968—; chmn. bd. Permatach Diamond Tool Co., Milford, N.H.; dir. MBA, Inc., Cambridge, Mass., Exolon Co., Tonawanda, N.Y.; trustee Amherst Savs. Bank (Mass.). Mem. Mass. Ednl. Facilities Commn.; mem. Health and Ednl. Facilities Authority. Bd. dirs. Recreational Resources, Inc., N.Y., Amherst Community Chest; trustee Holy Cross Coll., Worcester, Mass., Coll. Entrance Exam. Bd., N.Y.C. Served with AUS, 1943-46. Mem. Nat. Fedn. Coll. and Univ. Bus. Officers (v.p. 1957-59, dir. 1955-65), Eastern Assn. Coll. and Univ. Bus. Officers (sec.-treas. 1955-65, pres. 1966). Author articles. Home: 74 College St Amherst MA 01002

HERTZKA, WAYNE SOLOMON, architect; b. Spokane, Wash., July 13, 1907; M. Arch., Mass. Inst. Tech., 1931. With Hertzka & Knowles, San Francisco, 1933—, Hertzka & Knowles, Inc., 1958—; prin. works include Anza Elementary Sch., San Francisco, 1953, Holiday Lodge, San Francisco, 1955, Am. Fore-Loyalty Group office bldg., San Francisco, 1957, Crown Zellerbach office bldg., San Francisco, 1959, State Bar of Cal. hdgrs. bldg., San Francisco, 1960, Pacific Tel. Co. hdgrs. bldg., Sacramento, 1961, Standard Oil Co. of Cal. bldg., 1964—. Served to lt. col. AUS, 1942-46. Decorated Legion of Merit. Recipient award of merit A.I.A. for Crown Zellerbach bldg., 1961. Fellow A.I.A. (pres. No. Cal. chpt. 1955-56, pres. Cal. council 1960; 2d v.p. 1964). Address: 32 Fremont St San Francisco CA 94105

HERTZLER, JOHN ROWE, bus. exec.; b. Lancaster, Pa., Oct. 2, 1905; s. Oliver Henry and Bessie Viola (Rowe) H.; M.E., Lehigh U., 1927; M.A. in Edn., U. Conn., 1962; m. Priscilla Bennett, May 6, 1944; children—Bennett, Timothy, Samuel, Daniel. Trainee York Corp., 1927-30; air conditioning sales engring., met. N.Y. Dist. office York Corp., 1930-35, work at hdqrs., Pa., 1935-42, mgr. air conditioning dept., 1935-37, gen. rep., 1937-40, gen. sales mgr., 1940-42, v.p., gen. sales mgr., 1945-54, dir., 1951-54; pres. Hertzler Enterprises, Inc., 1954—. Propr. Mt. Hope Rabbitry, Mansfield Center, 1959—. Dep. sec. of commerce of Pa., 1955. Chmn. utilities subcom. Mansfield (Conn.) Community Devel. Action Plan, 1969-70. Trustee Windham Community Meml. Hosp., Willimantic, Conn., 1967—. Served as liaison officer USNR active duty WPB, Washington, specializing gen. indsl. equipment, World War II. Mem. Am. Soc. Heating, Refrigerating and Air Conditioning Engrs., Lambda Chi Alpha, Tau Beta Pi, Pi Tau Sigma. Clubs: Engineers (N.Y.C.); Rotary (pres.) (Willamantic). Conglist. Author, editor: Hotel Guest Room Air Conditioning, 1940. Contbr. tech papers to engring. jours. Address: Route 1 Mansfield Center CT 06250

HERTZOG, AMBROSE JOHN, physician; b. Derry, La., Nov. 20, 1907; s. Ambrose J. and Sally (Junter) H.; B.S., Springhill Coll., Mobile, Ala., 1928; M.D., Tulane Tulane U., 1932; M.S., U. Minn., 1937, Ph.D., 1938; m. Irma Behrens, Oct. 11, 1940; children—Irma J., Ambrose J., Matthew. Intern Touro Infirmary, New Orleans, 1932-33; fellow in pathology Mayo Clinic, 1934-36; teaching fellow in path. and cancer research U. Minn., 1936-38; dir. labs. Luther Hosp., Eau Claire, Wis., 1938-42; asst. prof. path. U. Minn., 1942-48; dir. labs. St. Barnabas Hosp. and Mpls. Gen. Hosp., 1942-47, Northwestern Hosp., 1947-48, Touro Infirmary, New Orleans, 1948—; prof. med. tech. Loyola U., New Orleans, 1948—, clin. asso. prof. pathology La. State U., 1962—; lectr. in pathology Tulane U., 1950—. Mem. Am. Soc. Clin. Pathologists, Am. Med. Writers Assn., Internat. Acad. Pathology, Am. Assn. Pathol. and Bacteriol., Kappa Alpha, Nu Sigma Nu, Sigma Xi. Roman Catholic. Contbr. articles to sci. publs. Home: 4115 Vincennes Pl New Orleans LA 70125 Office: Touro Infirmary New Orleans LA 70115

HERVEY, DONALD FRANKLIN, educator; b. Longmont, Colo., Oct. 9, 1917; s. Edgar S. and Edna (Slee) H.; B.S., Colo. State U., 1939; M.S., U. Cal. at Berkeley, 1948; Ph.D., A. and M. Coll. Tex., 1955; m. Bettie E. Culbertson, Dec. 23, 1940; children—Vesta Dianne, Timothy Donald, Elizabeth Ellen. Range examiner U.S. Forest Service, 1939; staff Bur. Land Mgmt., formerly Dept. Interior Agencies, 1940-43; faculty Colo. State U. 1946—, successively instr., asst. prof., asso. prof., 1946-57, prof. range mgmt., head dept. range mgmt., 1957-63; chief forestry and range mgmt. sect. Colo. Agrl. Expt. Sta., 1952-63, asso. dir., 1963-69, dir., 1969—. Served from 1st lt. to capt., F.A., AUS, 1943-46. Mem. Am. Soc. Range Mgmt. (dir. 1955-58, pres. 1959), Sigma Xi, Phi Kappa Phi, Xi Sigma Pi, Beta Beta Beta. Mem. Christian Ch. (elder.) Home: 1608 Whedbee St Fort Collins CO 80521

HERVEY, FREDERICK TAYLOR, multiple co. exec.; b. El Paso, Tex., July 28, 1909; s. Taylor Master and Gertrude (Crossett) H.; children—Helen Shirleen (Mrs. John A. Gillett), Evelyn Diane, Frederick Taylor. Pres., OA Corp., 1930—, Fred Hervey Inc., 1948—, Circle K Corp., 1951—, Rio Grande Broadcasting Co., 1952—, Central Ariz. Broadcasting Co., 1969—; dir. Coaches Inc., Coaches Life Ins. Co. Met. chmn. Nat. Alliance of Businessmen, 1969-70. Republican candidate for U.S. Congress, 1950; mayor El Paso, 1951-54. Served with USNR, 1943-45. Mem. El Paso C. of C. (past pres.). Home: 4025 N Stanton St El Paso TX 79902 Office: 900 Magoffin Av El Paso TX 79901

HERWALD, SEYMOUR WILLIS, mfg. co. exec.; b. Cleve., Jan. 17, 1917; s. Robert and Sarah (Gidansky) H.; B.S., Case Inst. Tech., 1938; M.S., U. Pitts., 1940, Ph.D., 1944; m. Geraldine Greenberger, Dec. 21, 1941; children—Melvyn, Michelle, Bruce, Steven. With Westinghouse Electric Corp., 1939—, v.p. research, 1959- 62, v.p., group gen. mgr. components and splty. product div., 1962-68, v.p. engring. and devel., 1970—. Cons. Dept. Def., Nat. Acad. Engrs.; chmn. adv. com. communications, instrumentation and data processing NASA; chmn. guidance and control panel Air Force Sci. Adv. Bd.; chmn. Air Force Range Tech. Adv. Group. Registered profl. engr., Pa. Fellow I.E.E.E.; Am. Soc. M.E., Am. Inst. Physics, Am. Inst. Aeros. and Astronautics, Am. Ordnance Assn., Am. Soc. Naval Engrs. Home: 2282 Elmhill Rd Pittsburgh PA 15222

HERWEG, JOHN COURTRIGHT, univ. dean; b. Ft. Dodge, Ia., Mar. 19, 1922; s. James Ewald and Ouida (Courtright) H.; B.S. summa cum laude, Drury Coll., 1943; M.D. cum laude, Washington U., St. Louis, 1945; m. Janet Ruth Scovill, June 4, 1946 (dec. 1958); children—Judith Ann (dec.), Marjorie Lee, Mary Jo, James Scovill; m. 2d, Dorothy Marie Glahn, Jan. 17, 1959; 1 dau., Jan Marie. Intern St. Louis Children's Hosp., 1945-46, asst. resident, 1949, chief resident, 1949-50, asst. physician, 1951-60, 62-63; pvt. practice Monroe (Wis.) Clinic, 1950-51; faculty Washington U. Sch. Medicine, 1951- -, asso. prof. pediatrics, 1963- -, asso. dean, 1965—, chmn. com. admissions, 1965—; asst. dir. clin. research unit Barnes Hosp., also dir. clin. research unit St. Louis Children's Hosp., 1962-70; asso. pediatrician St. Louis Childrens, St. Louis Maternity, McMillan hosps., 1963—. Pediatric cons. Ft. Leonard Wood, Mo., 1952-60, 62—, U. Ill. Div. Crippled Children, 1952-60, child evaluation clinic Washington U. Sch. Medicine, 1956-60; chmn. med. adv. com. St. Louis Soc. Crippled Children, 1952-60; chmn. profl. adv. com. Spl. Dist. Edn. and Tng. Handicapped Children St. Louis, 1958-60. Served to capt., M.C., AUS, 1946-48. Diplomate Am. Bd. Pediatrics. Mem. St. Louis Pediatric Soc. (sec.-treas. 1953), Am. Acad. Pediatrics, N.Y. Acad. Sci., Am. Soc. Microbiology, Midwest Soc. Pediatric Research,

St. Louis Children's Hosp. Staff Soc. (pres. 1964), Alpha Omega Alpha. Contbr. med. jours. Home: 12134 Ridgelawn Dr St Louis MO 63131

HERWITZ, DAVID RICHARD, educator; b. Lynn, Mass., Dec. 8, 1925; s. Harry M. and Sarah (Shapiro) H.; student U. Wis., 1942-43; B.S., Mass. Inst. Tech., 1946; LL.B. magna cum laude, Harvard, 1949, m. Carla B. Cowett, Jan. 22, 1960; children—Andrew B., Juliet F. Admitted Mass. bar 1949; practiced in Boston, 1951-54; teaching fellow Harvard Law Sch., 1950-51, asst. prof. law, 1954-57, prof. law, 1957—; faculty supr. Harvard-Brandeis coop. research for Israel's legal devel., 1957-59; lectr. Northeastern Sch. Law, 1951-54. Cons., U.S. Treasury Dept., 1961-64. Author: (with Donald T. Trautman) Materials on Accounting, rev. edit., 1959; Cases and Materials on Business Planning, 1966. Home: Littles Point Swampscott MA 01907

HERWOOD, FRANCIS, banker; b. Natick, Mass., July 24, 1906; s. Michael Joseph and Elizabeth (Meskill) H.; ed. pub. schs., Los Angeles; m. Nell Chiappero, Sept. 27, 1934. With Bank Am. Nat. Trust & Savs. Assn., Los Angeles, 1923—, sr. v.p., 1965. Bd. dirs. Cal. Water Resources Assn.; trustee Southwestern U., Los Angeles. Served with USAAF, 1942-45. Clubs: Rancheros Visitadores (Santa Barbara, Cal.); Los Angeles Athletic, Stock Exchange (Los Angeles); Annandale Golf (Pasadena). Home: 218 La Mirada Pasadena CA 91105 Office: 650 S Spring St Los Angeles CA 90014

HERYFORD, FRED WISE, instl. adminstr.; b. Butte Falls, Ore., Aug. 19, 1923; s. Harry Lee and Bessie (Wise) H.; B.B.A., U. Ore., 1951; M.A., Western State Coll., 1956; Ed.D., Colo. State Coll., 1961; m. Beverly J. Pace, Nov. ll, 1951; children—Richard Willson, Annette Gale. Owner retail grocery, 1947-49; office mgr. Berg Constrn. Co., Juneau, Alaska, 1952-53; tchr. Lincoln Sch., Las Vegas, Nev., 1956-57; prin. State Home and Tng. Sch., Grand Junction, Colo., 1958-59; supt. Wyo. State Tng. Sch., Lander, 1961—. Mem. Am. Assn. on Mental Deficiency (regional pres. 1963-64), Council for Exceptional Children. Mason. Address: Wyo State Tng Sch Lander WY 82520

HERZ, GERHARD, educator; b. Duesseldorf, Germany, Sept. 24, 1911; s. Carl and Elizabeth (Aschaffenburg) H.; student U. Freiburg, 1930-31, U. Vienna, 1931, U. Berlin, 1932-33; Ph.D. magna cum laude, U. Zurich, 1934; m. Mary Jo Fink, June 2, 1943. Came to U.S., 1936, naturalized, 1943. Instr. music history U. Louisville, 1938, asst. prof., 1939-44, asso. prof., 1944, prof. music history, 1946-56, chmn. dept. music history, 1956—; acting asst. prof. musicology Ind. U., 1945-46; vis. prof. dept. music U. Chgo., summer 1965. Bd. dirs. Louisville Orch., 1947-67. Mem. Internat., Am. (chmn. S. Central chpt. 1965-66) musicol. socs., Coll. Music Soc., Louisville Chamber Music Soc. (trustee, pres. 1966-67, 68-71), Louisville Bach Soc. (dir.), Am. Assn. U. Profs., Gesellschaft fuer Musikforschung, Neue Bach Gesellschaft. Author: Bach-Cantata No. 4, 1967, Bach-Cantata No. 140, 1971 (both Norton Critical Scores). Contbr. articles to profl. jours. Home: 729 Midde Way Louisville KY 40206

HERZBERG, BEN, lawyer; b. Lincoln, Kan., Mar. 15, 1900; s. Gustav and Minnie (Neu) H.; B.S., U. Chgo., 1921, LL.B., 1923. Admitted to N.Y. bar, 1926; asst. U.S. atty., N.Y.C., 1925-27; mem. firm Cook, Nathan & Lehman, N.Y.C., 1935-47, Botein, Hays, Sklar & Herzberg, and predecessor firms, New York City. N.Y., since 1952—. Vice pres. Am. Jewish Com., 1952-55. Mem. Assn. Bar City N.Y. Home: 170 E 77th St New York City NY 10017 Office: 200 Park Av New York City NY 10017

HERZBERG, DONALD GABRIEL, educator, govt. ofcl., author; b. Orange, N.J., May 6, 1925; s. Max John and Edna (Newman) H.; B.A., Wesleyan U., 1946; postgrad. Maxwell Sch., Syracuse U., 1946-48; m. Marlene Grey, July 1, 1953 (div. Nov. 1967); children—John Max, Joan; m. 2d, Barbara Smith Schelling; stepchildren—Andrew Schelling, Melissa Schelling, Timothy Norton Schelling. Asst. to dean Maxwell Sch., Syracuse, N.Y., 1947-48; instr. govt. Wesleyan U., Middletown, Conn., 1948-49; spl. asst. to comptroller State of Conn., 1949-50; legislative asst. to Sen. William Benton, Conn., 1950-53; asst. to pres. Chatham Coll., Pitts., 1953-55; dep. dir. budget div. State of N.Y., 1955-56; dir. Eagleton Inst. Politics, Rutgers U., New Brunswick, N.J., 1956—, also prof. polit. sci., chmn. polit. sci. sect., 1963-65; Cons. elections and politics NBC News, 1962-64, ABC News, 1966—, pub. affairs dept. Ford Found., 1962-65; chief research cons. to pres. pro tem N.Y. Senate, 1965, minority leader N.Y. Assembly, 1969—; mem. bd. Operations and Policy Research, Washington, 1967—; chmn. Nat. Corp. for Policy Research and Operations, N.Y.C., 1968—, Election Law Revision Commn., N.J., 1966—; staff dir. Joint Legislative Commn. on Higher Edn., 1965, Pres.'s Commn. on Registration and Voter Participation, 1963-64, Select Commn. on Western Hemisphere Immigration, 1967-68; adviser Prime Minister Guyana, 1965—. Bd. dirs. United Fund of New Brunswick; bd. mgrs. Trenton State Hosp.; trustee Inst. for Am. Univs., Aix-en-Provence, France. Mem. Am. Polit. Sci. Assn., Am. Soc. for Pub. Adminstrn., A.A.A.S., A.F.T.R.A. Democrat. Author: (with Jack Peltason) A Student Guide to Campaign Politics, 1970; (with Jess Unruh) Essays on the Legislative Process, 1970; (with Gerald Pomper) American Party Politics, Essays and Readings, 1966; (with William Baumer) Politics is Your Business, 1960; (with Paul Tillett) The Politics of the Budget of New York, 1959; several chpts. in other vols. Home: The Great Rd Princeton NJ 08540 Office: The Eagleton Inst Politics Rutgers the State U New Brunswick NJ 08903

HERZBERG, FREDERICK, educator, psychologist; b. Lynn, Mass., Apr. 18, 1923l s. Lewis and Gertrude Ann (Copleman) H.; B.S.S., Coll. City N.Y., 1946; M.S., U. Pitts., 1949, Ph.D., 1950, M.P.H., 1951; m. Shirley Bedell, June 1, 1944; 1 son, Mark Allen. Lectr., U. Pitts., 1946-48, instr., 1949-51; prin. personnel adminstr. City Richmond, Va., 1948-49; research dir. Psychol. Service Pitts., 1953-57; prof. psychology, chmn. dept. Western Res. U., 1957—, now Douglas McGregor distinguished prof.; cons. VA, Am. Inst. Research, also govtl., social and indsl. orgns., 1951—; Fulbright research fellow, Finland, 1963-64. Served with AUS, 1943-46; res. scientist USPHS, 1953—. Mem. Am., Ohio psychol. assns., Am. Assn. U. Profs., Sigma Xi, Psi Chi. Author: Job Attitude: Research and Opinion, 1957; The Motivation to Work, 1959; Work and the Nature of Man, 1966. Home: 3729 Meadowbrook Blvd University Heights OH 44118 Office: Western Reserve Univ Cleveland OH 44106

HERZBERG, GERHARD, physicist; b. Hamburg, Germany, Dec. 25, 1904; s. Albin and Ella (Biber) H.; Dr. Ing., Darmstadt Inst. Tech., 1928; post-doctorate work, U. Goettingen, Germany and Bristol, England, 1928-30; LL.D., U. Saskatchewan, 1953, U. Toronto, 1958, Dalhousie U., 1960, U. Alta., 1961; D.Sc. hon. causa, Oxford U., 1960; D.Sc., McMaster U. 1954, Nat. U. Ireland, 1956, U. B.C., 1964, Queen's U., 1965, U. N.B., 1966, Carleton U., Ottawa, 1967, U. Chgo., 1967; Fil. Hed. Dr., U. Stockholm, 1966; Dr. rer. nat., U. Göttingen (Germany), 1968; D.Sc., Memorial U., Newfoundland, 1968, York U., 1969, U. Windsor, 1970, Royal Mil. Coll., Kingston, Ont., Cambridge U.; m. Luise H. Oettinger, Dec. 29, 1929 (dec.); children—Paul Albin, Agnes Margaret. Came to Canada, 1935, naturalized, 1945. Lectr. and chief asst., dept. physics, Darmstadt Inst. Tech., 1930-35; research prof. physics, U. Saskatchewan, Saskatoon, Can., 1935-45; prof. spectroscopy, Yerkes Observatory, U. Chgo., 1945-48; prin. research officer Nat. Research Council of Can., Ottawa, 1948, dir. div. of pure physics, 1949-69, distinguished research scientist, 1969—; Bakerian lectr., Royal Soc. London, 1960. Recipient Henry Marshall Tory medal Royal Soc. of Canada, Ottawa, 1953; award for achievement in physics Can. Assn. Physicists, 1957; Holder Francqui chair U. Liége, 1960; companion Order Can.; Willard Gibbs medal from Chgo. sect. of Am. Chem. Soc., 1969; Faraday medal, Chem. Soc. London, 1970. Academician of Pontifical Acad. of Scis. Fellow Royal Soc. London, Royal Soc. Can. (pres. 1966), Hungarian Acad. Sci. (hon.), Indian Acad. Scis. (hon.), Am. Phys. Soc.; mem. Internat. Union Pure and Applied Physics (v.p. 1957-63), Am. Acad. Arts and Scis. (hon. fgn. mem.), Am. Chem. Soc., Nat. Acad. of Sci. India, Indian Phys. Soc. (hon.), Nat. Acad. of Sci. fgn. asso., Faraday Soc., Am. Astron. Soc., Canadian Assn. Physicists (pres. 1956-57), Optical Soc. of Am. (hon. mem., Frederic Ives medal 1964). Author several books latest: Spectra of Diatomic Molecules, 1950; Electronic Spectra and Electronic Structure of Polyatomic Molecules, 1966; The Spectra and Structures of Simple Free Radicals: An Introduction to Molecular Spectroscopy, 1971. Home: 190 Lakeway Dr Rockcliffe Park Ottawa Ontario Canada Office: Nat Research Council Ottawa Ontario Canada

HERZBERG, JOSEPH GABRIEL, former editor-writer; b. N.Y.C., Jan. 1, 1907; s. Theodore and Sarah (Rosenthal) H.; student Townsend Harris Hall, Coll. City N.Y., 1921-25; m. Marion Burton Warendorff, Aug. 28, 1939; 1 son, Paul Burton. Paul Burton. Joined N.Y. Herald Tribune as copy boy, 1925; successively reporter, rewrite man, asst. night city editor, night city editor, city editor 1946-52, Sunday editor, 1952-56; joined N.Y. Times, 1956, asst. city editor, dir. cultural news, 1962-67, spl. writer on ednl., cultural subjects, 1967-70; instr. journalism N.Y. U., 1944-47, 56-57; adj. asst. adj. asst. prof. L.I. U., 1956-57; lectr. Grad. Inst. Book Pubs., 1960-62; Bd. dirs. James Gordon Bennett Found., 1960-70. Poynter fellow Yale, 1968. Editor: Late City Edition, 1947; editorial bd. Information Please Almanac, 1964-67. Home: 416 South Av New Canaan CT 06840

HERZBERGER, MAXIMILIAN JAKOB, optical research exec.; b. Charlottenburg, Germany, Mar. 7, 1899; s. Leopold and Sonja (Behrendt) H.; B.S., Schiller Real Gymnasium, 1917; M.S., Ph.D. in Math., Berlin U., 1922; student Jena U., 1923-24; m. Edith Kaufman, May 31, 1925; children—Ruth (Mrs. Roy A. Rosenberg), Ursula (Mrs. Ed Klima), Hans George. Came to U.S., 1935, naturalized, 1940. Lens designer, Emil Busch, Rathenow, Germany, 1923-25; charge lens computing dept. Leitz Co., Wetzlar, Germany, 1925-27; mathematician, personal asst. to dir. C. Zeiss Co., Jena, 1927-34; lectr. optics Delft U., 1934; lens designer Scophony TV Co., London, Eng., 1935; sr. research asso. charge geometrical optical research Eastman Kodak Co., Rochester, N.Y., 1935-65; mem. Inst. Advanced Study, Princeton, 1946; research on designing lenses, theory optical image, gen. field theory, theory of microscope, gen. math. problems; guest prof. Eidgenossische Technische Hochschule, Zurich, Switzerland, 1965-69; cons. prof. dept. physics La. State U., New Orleans, 1969—. Bd. dirs. Jewish Welfare, 1942, 53-57, 60-64. Recipient Cressy Morrison prize math. N.Y. Acad. Scis.,1945; Ives medal, Optical Soc. Am., 1962. Fellow Optical Soc. Am. (lectr. 1962-63), A.A.A.S.; mem. Am. Math. Soc., Deutsche Optische Gesellschaft (hon.), Am. Chess Assn. (life), N.Y. State Chess Assn. (pres. 1949, v.p. 1949—), Rochester Optical Soc. (program chmn.), German Math. Soc., Zuircher Schachgesellshaft, Sigma Xi (chpt. pres. 1964-65); corr. mem. Bavarian Acad. Scis.; hon. mem. Omicron Delta Kappa. Jewish religion (charge adult edn. 1963-64). Clubs: Swiss American, American. Author: Strahlenoptik, 1932; Modern Geometrical Optics, 1958. Contbr. Handbook of Physics, Condon and Odishaw, 1958; McGraw-Hill Ency. Science and Technology, 1960. Home: 6169 Paris Av New Orleans LA 70122

HERZENBERG, ARVID, physicist, educator; b. Vienna, Austria, Apr. 16, 1925; s. Harry and Wilhelmine (Pfeiffer) H.; B.S., U. Manchester, 1949, D.Sc., 1964; m. Marjorie Swift, Nov. 30, 1949; children—Catherine, Anne, Stehen. Mem. faculty U. Manchester (Eng.), 1952-69; prof. engring. and applied sci. Yale, 1969—. Mem. Brit., Am. phys. socs., Brit. Biophys. Soc. Contbr. articles profl. jours. Home: 6 Le Grand Rd North Haven CT 06473 Office: Mason Laboratory Yale University New Haven CT 06520

HERZENBERG, LEONARD ARTHUR, geneticist, educator; b. Bklyn., Nov. 5, 1931; s. William G. and Ann (Seidlitz) H.; A.B., Bklyn. Coll., 1952; Ph.D., Cal. Inst. Tech., 1955; m. Lenore A. Adlerstein, July 26, 1933; children-Barbara Janet, Michael, Eric. Am. Cancer Soc. postdoctoral fellow Pasteur Inst., Paris, 1955-57; officer NIH, USPHS, Bethesda, Md., 1957-59, mem. genetics study sect., 1970—; asst. prof. genetics Stanford Sch. Med., 1959-64, asso. prof., 1964-69, prof., 1969—. Mem. spl. grants com. Cal. div. Am. Cancer Soc., 1969—. Mem. Scientists and Engrs. for Social and Polit. Action; bd. dirs. Tech. and Soc. Com., 1969. Recipient Distinguished Alumnus award Bklyn. Coll., 1970. Mem. Genetics Soc. Am., Am. Assn. Immunologists, A.A.A.S., Fedn. Am. Scientists, Soc. Developmental Biology, Transplantation Soc., Phi Beta Kappa, Sigma Xi. Editorial bd. Transfusion, 1971—. Home: 876 Cedro Way Stanford CA 94305

HERZFELD, BERNARD H., lawyer; b. Balt., Oct. 7, 1907; s. Joseph and Lena (Long) H.; LL.B., U. Md.; m. Minna E. Hochberg, July 7, 1938; children—Harriet N., Jane Ellen. Practice in Balt., 1929—. Formerly chmn. bd., dir. Gulf American Corp.; chairman of the bd. Fenestra, Inc., 1966- 67. Active Jewish Big Brother League. Mem. Phi Alpha. Mason. Home: 3408 Janellen Dr Pikesville MD 21208

HERZFELD, CHARLES MARIA, physicist; b. Vienna, Austria, June 29, 1925; s. August Alfred and Frieda Auguste (Poehlman) H.; B.S. in Chem. Engring. cum laude, Cath. U. Am., 1945; Ph.D. (Carnegie Found. fellow), U. Chgo., 1951; m. Norma Ann Krause, May 15, 1954; children—Charles Christopher, Thomas Augustine, Paul Vincent. Came to U.S., 1942, naturalized, 1949. Lectr. chemistry Cath. U. Am., 1946; lectr. gen. sci. Coll. U. Chgo., 1946-47; lectr. physics DePaul U., Chgo., 1948-50; physicist Ballistic Research Lab., Aberdeen, Md., 1951-53, Naval Research Lab., Washington, 1953-55; lectr. physics U. Md., 1953-57, prof. physics, 1957-61; cons. chief heat and power div. Nat. Bur. Standards, 1955-56, acting asst. chief, 1956-57, chief heat div., 1957-61, asso. dir. bur., 1961; asst. dir. Advanced Research Project Agy., Dept. Def., 1961-63, dir. ballistic missile def., 1963, dep. dir. Advanced Research Projects Agy.; 1963- 65, dir., 1965-67; tech. dir. def. space group Internat. Tel.&Tel. Corp., Nutley, N.J., 1967—. Mem. Air Force Sci. Adv. Bd.; cons. USN; mem. Def. Sci. Bd.; fellow mem. Hudson Inst.; mem. Brookings Inst. Fifth Conf. for Career Execs. in Fed. Govt., 1958. Recipient Flemming award, 1963; Meritorious Civilian Service medal Dept. Def., 1967. Fellow Phys. Soc., Conf. on Sci., Philosophy and Religion; mem. Am. Ordnance Assn., Philos. Soc. Washington, N.Y. Acad. Scis., Inst. for Strategic Studies (London), Cath. Assn. Internat. Peace (pres. 1959-61), Sigma Xi. Club: Cosmos (Washington). Editor: Temperature, Its Control in Science and Industry, vol. III, 1962. Contbr. articles to profl. jours. Home: 534 Cherry Tree Terrace Kinnelon NJ 07405 Office: Internat Tel & Tel Corp Nutley NJ 02110

HERZFELD, KARL FERDINAND, physicist; b. Vienna, Austria, Feb. 24, 1892; s. Charles August (M.D.) and Camilla (Herzog) H.; student Schotten Gymnasium, Vienna, 1902-10, U. of Vienna, 1910-12, U. of Zurich, 1912-13, U. of Göttingen, 1913-14; Ph.D., U. of Vienna, 1914; D.Sc. honoris causa, Loyola Coll. (Baltimore), 1932, Marquette U., 1933; D.Sc., U. Md., 1956, Manhattan Coll., 1959; hon. degrees Fordham U., 1960, Inst. of Technology, Stuttgart, 1962, Cath. U. of Am., 1963, U. Notre Dame, 1965, Providence Coll., 1965; m. Regina Flannery, 1938. Privat- docent Univ. Munich, 1920, a. o. prof., 1923; Speyer guest prof., Johns Hopkins, 1926, prof. physics. 1926-36; head of dept. physics Cath. U. Am., 1936-61, prof., 1936-68, prof. emeritus, 1968—. Served as 1st lt., Austrian Army, 1914-18. Awarded Secchi medal, Georgetown U., 1938; USN Meritorious Pub. Service award, 1964; Papal Bene Merenli medal, 1965. Fellow Am. Phys. Soc., A.A.A.S., Acoustical Soc. Am.; mem. Washington Academy Science, Washington Philos. Soc., German Physical Soc., Am. Academy Arts and Scis., National Acad. Scis., Phi Beta Kappa, Sigma Xi, Gamma Alpha. Awarded Mendel medal, 1931. Received Certificate of Exceptional Service to Navy Ordnance Development, 1946. K.C. Author: Kinetische Theorie der Waerme, 1925; Absorption and Dispersion of Ultrasonic Waves (with T.A. Litovitz), 1959. Home: 3726 Connecticut Av NW Washington DC 20008 Address: Cath U Am Washington DC 20017 ☆

HERZIG, HENRY ALFRED, indsl. exec., b. Fulda, Germany, Aug. 16, 1906; s. Joseph and Katherine (Schneider) H.; M.E., Engring. Sch. Technicum Illmenau, Germany, 1926; m. Helen Schiebeck, Apr. 20, 1929. Came to U.S., 1928, naturalized, 1933. Design engr. Kaiser, Dolls & Co., 1926-28; designer German R.R. Co., 1927; cons. engr. O. Schram, 1928; asst. prodn. engr. Fokker Aircraft Corp. Am., 1928-29; design engr., asst. chief draftsman Varityper, Inc., 1929-3O; mech. engr. Mergenthaler Linotype Co., 1930- 37; design engr., mgr. mfg. Marine div. Sperry Gyroscope Co., Inc., 1937- 45; mgr. camera works Ansco div. Gen. Aniline & Film Corp., 1945-48; v.p. charge operations Simplicity Pattern Co., Inc., 1948-52; dir. mfg. Dresser Industries, Inc., Dallas, 1953-66, v.p., 1956-66; partner James G. Brown & Assos., petroleum producers, Dallas, Tex., 1966—; exec. Internat. Exec. Service Corps, N.Y.C. Profl. mech. engr., N.Y. Home: 4436 Laren La Dallas TX 75234 Office: IESC 720th Fifth Av New York City NY 10019

HERZOG, EDWIN H., investment banker; b. Albany, N.Y., Dec. 7, 1899; s. H. and Clara L. (Lehr) H.; B.A., Princeton, 1921; L.H.D., Hartwich Coll., 1964; m. Helen- Louise Heim, Aug. 12, 1950. Ltd. partner Lazard, Freres & Co. Served as col. USAAC, World War II. Decorated Chevalier of Legion of Honor (France). Republican. Lutheran. Clubs: Chevy Chase (Washington); Creek (Locust Valley, L.I., N.Y.); Meadowbrook (Westbury, L.I., N.Y.) Address: Lattingtown Rd Locust Valley NY 11560 also 37 Grosvenor Square London W1 England

HERZOG, FRITZ, educator; b. Posen, Germany, Dec. 6, 1902; s. Michael and Cecilia (Zuckermann) H.; student U. Berlin, Germany, 1928-33; Ph.D., Columbia, 1935; m. Helen Sarah Korngold, Sept. 21, 1937. Came to U.S., 1933, naturalized, 1938. Research asso. elec. engring. Cornell U., 1937-39, instr. math., 1938-43; asst. prof. math. Mich. State U., East Lansing, 1943-46, asso. prof., 1946-52, prof., 1952—; vis. asso. prof. Washington U., St. Louis, summer 1948; vis. asso. prof. U. Mich., 1949-50, vis. prof., summers 1956, 62. NSF research grantee, summers 1963, 64; recipient Distinguished Faculty award Mich. State U., 1969, Sigma Xi Sr. Research award Mich. State U. chpt., 1969. Mem. Am. Math. Soc., Math. Assn. Am., Am. Assn. U. Profs., Sigma Xi. Contbr. articles profl. jours. Home: 1532 Cahill Dr East Lansing MI 48823

HERZOG, GEORGE, anthropologist, ethnomusicologist, linguist, author; b. 1901; educated at the Hungarian Music Academy, Budapest, The High Sch. Music, Berlin, Germany, also U. Berlin, Columbia. Asst. phonogram archives Psychol. Inst., U. Berlin, 1922-24; research asso. dept. anthropology U. Chgo., 1930-32, charge dept. anthropology Expdn. to Liberia, 1937-31; research asso., asst. prof. anthropology Yale, 1932-35; G.S. Guggenheim Meml: fellow, 1935-36, 47; asst. prof. anthropology Columbia, 1936-48; cons. exptl. div. wartime communications research Library Congress, Washington, 1942-45; prof. anthropology Ind. U., 1948-64. In charge Archives Folk and Primitive Music, dept. anthropology Columbia, 1941-48, Ind. U., 1948-54. Fellow N.Y. Acad. Scis. (v.p. 1946-47). Author: (with Charles G. Blooah) Jabo Proverbs from Liberia, 1936; A Comparison of Pueblo and Pima Musical Styles, 1936; (with Harold Courlander) The Cow- Tail Switch and Other West African Stories, 1947.

HERZOG, GEORGE PETER, govt. ofcl.; b. Bklyn., Apr. 21, 1918; s. George Joseph and Mary (Wehle) H.; m. Kathryn Barbara Herzberg, Jan. 11, 1941; children—George Gary, Linda Anne. Chief budget and finance Nat. Agrl. Library, Washington, 1945-48; asst. budget dir. Rural Electrification Adminstrn., Washington, 1949-53, budget dir., 1954-69, asst. adminstr. for mgmt., 1969—. Chmn. awards com. Orgn. Profl. Employees, Dept. Agr., 1969-70, pres. REA chpt., 1966-67. Pres. Jefferson Village Park Corp., Falls Church, Va., 1948-49. Served with AUS, 1944-45. Fellow in congl. operations sponsored by Am. Polit. Sci. Assn. and U.S. Civil Service Commn., 1962-63. Lutheran. Home: 4008 Winfield Ct Bowie MD 20715 Office: South Agrl Bldg Independence and 12th Sts SW Washington DC 20250

HERZOG, JOSEPH JAMES ROBERTS chemist, educator; b. Chicago, 1928; B.S. in Physics, Yale, 1950; Ph.D. in Chemistry, Harvard, 1956; m. Sally Ann Jones, July 5, 1957; children--Kenneth J., Nancy A. Chemist, Acme Chem. Co., Blue Island, Ill., 1950-51; director of Research Lab., Indsl. Chemicals Corp., Cambridge, Mass., 1956-60; project coordinator environmental sect. Steinmetz Assos., Chgo., 1960-61; v.p. for research Bauer Bros. Chem. Co., Inc., Memphis, 1961-64; asst. prof. chemistry Washington U., St. Louis, 1964-66, asso. prof., 1966-70, prof., 1970--, head of chemistry dept., 1970-71. Vis. prof. So. Ill. U., summer 1967, U. of Ore., 1969. Scoutmaster, Boy Scouts America, University City, Mo., 1968-70. Bd. dirs. Rest Haven Home for Elderly, 1960-61; trustee of the Lutheran Hosp., 1965-71. Served from lt. to capt., AUS, 1951-53. Mem. Am. Chem. Soc., Sci. Research Soc. Am. (chpt. treas. 1967), Am. Assn. Chemistry Tchrs., Am. Assn. U. Profs., Wildlife Soc., American Institute Chemists, Ecological Soc. Am. (chpt. sec.), Sigma Xi. Author: (with others) Basic Inorganic Chemistry, 1971. Contbr. articles to profl. jours., encys., also chpts. to books. Home: Fairfax Apts 7291 Windermere Dr University City MO 63105 Office: Dept Chemistry Washington University St Louis MO 63130

HERZOG, LESTER WILLIAM, Jr., banker; b. Albany, N.Y., May 18, 1912; s. Lester W. and Ethel (Hawley) W.; grad. Albany Acad., 1929; A.B., Princeton U., 1933; grad. Sch. Mgmt., Northwestern U., 1956; m. Helen Van Orsdale, Oct. 12, 1935. With Nat. Commercial Bank (became Nat. Commercial Bank & Trust Co., 1920), Albany, 1933—, exec. v.p., 1958-63,dir., 1959—, pres., 1963—, also chief executive officer: director of W. M. Whitney & Company, also United Traction Co.; trustee Albany Savs. Bank. Dir., past pres. Albany Boys' Club. Bd. govs. Albany Med. Center Hosp.; trustee Albany Girls Acad., Parsons Coll. Served to capt. AUS, 1943-46. Mem. Am.

Bankers Assn. (chmn. orgn. com.), C.of C. (pres., bd. dirs), Clearing House Assn. Albany (past pres.). Presbyn. (bd. trustees). Mason (33; treas.). Clubs: Schuyler Meadows, Fort Orange (Albany); Cannon (Princeton); Princeton (N.Y.C.); Lake Placid (N.Y.). Home: 5 S Loudon Heights Loudonville NY 12211 Office: Nat Commercial Bank & Trust Co 60 State St Albany NY 12201

HERZOG, MAURICE, French govt. ofcl.; b. Lyon, Rhone, France, Jan. 15, 1919; s. Robert and Germaine (Beaume) H.; student Coll. Chaptal et Faculte des Droit de Paris, Faculte des Scis. de Lyon; M.S., LL.M.; degrees, Ecole des Hautes Etudes Commerciales; m. Countess Marie-Pierre de Cosse-Brissac, July 23, 1964; children—Laurent, Felicite. Dir. Kleber-Colombes Soc., 1945-48; Alpinist and explorer; chief French Himalayan Expdn., 1950; conqueror of Annapurna, 1950; dep. spl. projects in Andre Moynet cabinet, nat. sec. to pres. Council, 1954-55; high commr. Youth and Sports, 1960, 62, nat. sec., 1963-66; U.N.R. dep. Rhone Region, 4e circ. Lyon VII, VIII and XI, 1963-63; econ. and social councillor for determination of qualifications in Econ., Social, Sci. and Cultural domains, 1966-67; dep. Dept. of Haute-Savoie, 3d circ. Bonneville, Annemass, 1967—; adminstr. Silvafrance, 1966—. Vice pres. Union of Democrats for Republic; v.p. Prodn. and Exchange Commn. of Assemblee Nat., 1967-68; Com. chmn. for Sci. Research on Atomic and Space Questions. Mayor of Chamonix, 1968—. Decorated officer Legion of Honor, Croix de Guerre, comdr. Merite Sportif. Author: Annapurna; Looking at the Annapurna; The Annapurna Expedition; The Mountain. Address: 4 Rue Jean-Richepin Paris 16e France

HERZOG, PAUL M., lawyer, educator; b. N.Y.C., Aug. 21, 1906; s. Paul M. and Elsie (Lowenstein) H.; S.B. magna cum laude, Harvard, 1927; A.M., U. Wis., 1930; Harvard Law Sch., 1931-33; LL.B., Columbia, 1936; LL.D., Hobart and William Smith Colls., 1959, Washington U., St. Louis, 1971; m. Madeleine Schafer, Apr. 11, 1929 (div.), children—John Paul, Andrea Elsie (Mrs. George B. Chadwick); m. 2d, Julie Chamberlain d'Estournelles, 1959; stepchildren—Julie (Lady Wilson), Alexander B. Trowbridge, Jr. Instr., U. Wis., 1928-30, Harvard, 1930-31; asst. to sec. Nat. Labor Board, Washington, 1933-35; admitted to N.Y. bar and practiced, 1936-37; apptd. one of original mems. N.Y. State Labor Relations Bd., 1937, chmn., 1942-44; chmn. NLRB, 1945-53; asso. dean, grad. sch. pub. adminstrn. Harvard, 1953-57, acting dean, 1957—; exec. v.p. Am. Arbitration Assn., 1958-61, pres., 1961-63; pres. Salzburg Seminar in Am. Studies, 1965—; mem. council N.Y. State U. Colls. Medicine, 1959-65; mem. adv. council Labor and Mgmt. Practices Act, N.Y., 1959-67. Mem. com. of experts on application of convs. ILO, 1956-67. Trustee Colls. of Seneca (Hobart and Wm. Smith), 1946-56; Served as lt. USNR, 1944-45. Decorated Grand Medal Order Merit (Austria). Mem. Assn. Bar City N.Y., Am., N.Y. State bar assns., Am. Soc. Pub. Adminstrn., (v.p. 1956-57), Am. Law Inst., Council on Fgn. Relations, Harvard Alumni Assn. (v.p. 1951-52), Phi Beta Kappa. Democrat. Presbyn. (elder). Clubs: Harvard, Century (N.Y.), Metropolitan, Nat. Press (Washington); Harvard Faculty (Cambridge). Home: 14 E 75th St New York City NY

HERZOG, RAYMOND HARRY, mfg. co. exec.; b. Merricourt, N.D., Sept. 15, 1915; s. Harry George and Mollie (Klundt) H.; B.A., Lawrence U., 1938; m. Jane Cobb, Mar. 25, 1940; children—Mollie, Richard, Raymond Harry. Chemist, W.Va. Coal and Coke Co., 1937-38; coach, sci. tchr., St. Croix Falls, Wis., 1939-41; with Minn. Mining & Mfg. Co., 1941—, gen. mgr. duplicating products div., 1956-59, divisional v.p., 1959-61, corporate v.p., 1961-63, group v.p. graphic systems group, 1963-70, pres., 1970—, also dir.; dir. 1st Trust Co., St. Paul. Bd. dirs. BEMA, St. Paul Winter Carnival Assn.; trustee Lawrence U. Mem. St. Paul Area C. of C. (dir.). Clubs: Midland Hills Country, White Bear Yacht, Minnesota. Home: 23 Shady Woods Rd St Paul MN 55115 Office: 3M Center St Paul MN 55101

HERZOG, RICHARD FRANZ KARL, physicist: b. Vienna, Austria, Mar. 13, 1911; s. Karl and Luise (Hickel) H.; Ph.D., U. Vienna, 1933. Came to U.S., 1953, naturalized, 1958. Asst. U., Vienna, 1939-41, dozent, 1941-5O, asso. prof. physics, 1950-53; physicist Air Force Cambridge Research Center, 1953-58, also chief systems research sect. photochemistry lab.; mgr. ion physics dept., Geophysics Corp. Am., Bedford, Mass., 1958-62, scientific dep. dir. space sci. lab., 1962-66, chief scientist space sci. operations, 1966—. Home: 34 Whipple Rd Lexington MA 02173 Office: Bedford MA 01730

HERZOG, ROBERT, chem. co. exec.; b. N.Y.C., May 7, 1918; s. Jacob and Feige (Bedrick) H.; B.Chem. Engring., Cooper Union Inst. Tech., 1939; M.s., U. Mich., 1940; m. Justine Schmertz, Dec. 27, 1940; children—Helen Joan (Mrs. James B. Fadim), Richard Joseph, Charles Alan. With Ethyl Corp., Richmond, Va., 1940—, v.p. planning, 1964-69, exec. v.p., 1969—. Mem. Am. Chem. Soc., Phi Lambda Upsilon, Mu Alpha Omicron. Home: 1228 Meadow Lea Dr Baton Rouge LA 70808 Office: 451 Florida Av Baton Rouge LA 70801

HESBURGH, THEODORE MARTIN, clergyman, univ. pres.; b. Syracuse, N.Y., May 25, 1917; s. Theodore Bernard and Anne Marie (Murphy) H.; student U. Notre Dame, 1934-37; Ph.B., Gregorian U., 1939; Holy Cross Coll., Washington, 1940-43; S.T.D., Cath. U. Am., 1945; hon. degrees Bradley U., LeMoyne Coll., U. R.I., Cath. U. of Santiago, Chile, Dartmouth, Villanova U., St. Benedict's Coll., Columbia, Princeton, Ind. U., Brandeis U., Gonzaga U., U. Cal. at Los Angeles, Temple U., Northwestern U., U. Ill. at Urbana, Fordham U., Manchester Coll., Atlanta U., Wabash Coll., Valparaiso U., Providence Coll., U. So. Cal., Mich. State U., St. Louis U., Cath. U. Am., Loyola U., Chgo., Anderson Coll., State U. at N.Y., Utah State U., Lehigh U., Yale, LL.D., Lafayette Coll., Easton, Pa., 1963. Entered the Order of Congregation of Holy Cross, 1934; ordained priest U. Notre Dame, 1943; chaplain Nat. Tng. Sch. for Boys, Washington, 1943-44; vets. chaplain U. Notre Dame, 1945-47; asst. prof. religion, head dept. U. Notre Dame, 1948-49, exec. v.p., 1949-52, pres., 1952—. Dir. Woodrow Wilson Nat. Fellowship Corp.; mem. Civil Rights Commn., 1957—; mem. of Carnegie Commn. on Future of Higher Edn.; chmn. U.S. Commn. on Civil Rights, 1969; mem. Commn. on an All-Volunteer Armed Force, 1970. Bd. dirs. Am. Council Edn., Edn. Devel. Center, Freedoms Found. Valley Forge, Adlai Stevenson Inst. Internat. Affairs; trustee Rockefeller Found., Carnegie Found. for Advancement Teaching, Woodrow Wilson Nat. Fellowship Found., Inst. Internat. Edn., Nutrition Found., United Negro Coll. Fund, others; bd. visitors U.S. Naval Acad., Tulane U. Recipient U.S. Navy's Distinguished Pub. Service award, 1959; Presdl. Medal of Freedom, 1964; Gold medal Nat. Inst. Social Scis., 1969; Cardinal Gibbons medal Cath. U. Am., 1969; Bellarmine medal Bellarmine-Ursuline Coll., 1970; Meiklejohn award Am. Assn. U. Profs., 1970; Charles Evans Hughes award Nat. Conf. Christians and Jews, 1970; Merit award Nat. Cath. Ednl. Assn., 1971; Pres.' Cabinet award U. Detroit, 1971; Am. Liberties medallion Am. Jewish Com., 1971; Liberty Bell award Ind. State Bar Assn., 1971; others. Fellow Am. Acad. Arts and Scis.; mem. Internat. Fedn. Cath. Univs., Freedoms Found. (dir., mem. exec. com.), Nutrition Found., Commn. on Humanities, Inst. Internat. Edn. (pres., dir.), Cath. Theol. Soc. Author: Theology of Catholic Action, 1945; God and the World of Man, 1950; Patterns for Educational Growth, 1958; Thoughts for Our Times, 1962; More Thoughts for Our Times, 1965; Still More Thoughts for Our Times, 1966; Thoughts IV, 1968; Thoughts V, 1969. Home: Corby Hall Notre Dame IN 46556

HESCHEL, ABRAHAM JOSHUA, theologian, educator; b. Warsaw, Poland, 1907; s. Moshe Mordecai and Reisel (Perlow) H.; Ph.D., U. Berlin, 1933; grad. Hochschule fuer die Wissenschaft des Judentums, Berlin, 1934; LL.D., Notre Dame U.; L.H.D., St. Michael's Coll., Park Coll., Upsala Coll., Spartus Coll.; m. Sylvia Straus, Dec. 10, 1946; 1 dau., Hannah Susan. Came to U.S., 1940, naturalized, 1945. Instr., Talmud, Hochschule fuer die Wissenschaft des Judentums, Berlin, 1932-33; lectr. Mittelstelle fuer Juedische Erwachsenenbildung, Frankfurt, Germany, 1937- 38; docent philosophy Inst. Judaistic Studies, Warsaw, 1938-39; founder Inst. Jewish Learning, London, 1940; instr. Jewish philosophy and rabbinics Hebrew Union Coll., 1940-43, asst. prof., 1943-45; prof. Jewish ethics and mysticism Jewish Theol. Sem. Am., 1945-; Raymond Fred West lectr. Stanford U., 1963; vis. prof. theology U. Minn.; vis. prof. U. Ia., 1961; Henry Emerson Fosdick vis. prof. Union Theological Seminary, 1965-66. Co-chmn. Nat. Com. of Clergy Concerned About Viet- Nam. Fellow Am. Acad. Arts and Scis., Am. Acad. Jewish Research; mem. Am. Philos. Soc., Jewish Publ. Soc., Yivo (dir.), Inst. Non-Violent Social Change. Author: Poems, 1933; Maimondides, 1935; Die Prophetie, 1935; Abravanel, 1937; Ibn Gabirol, 1938; A Concise Dictionary of Hebrew Philosophical Terms, 1941; On the Essence of Prayer, 1941; An Analysis of Piety, 1942; The Holy Dimension, 1943; Faith, 1944; The Quest for Certainty in Saadia's Philosophy, 1944; The Earth is The Lord's, 1950; Man is Not Alone, 1951; Space, Time and Reality, 1952; The Sabbath, 1952; The Moment on Sinai, 1953; Symbolism and Jewish Faith, 1954; Man's Quest for God, 1954; God in Search of Man, 1956; Sacred Images of Man, 1958; The Prophets, 1962; Theology of Ancient Judaism Vol. 1, 1963, Vol. 2, 1965; Who Is Man?, 1965; The Insecurity of Freedom, 1966; Israel, An Echo of Eternity, 1969; God—Torah—Israel, 1970; others. Home: 425 Riverside Dr New York City NY 10025 Office: 3080 Broadway New York City NY 10027

HESKETT, JAMES LEE, educator; b. Cedar Falls, Ia., May 8, 1933; s. Gail Stewart and Leone (Stein) H.; A.B., Ia. State Tchrs. Coll., 1954; M.B.A., Stanford U., 1958, Ph.D., 1960; M.B.A. (hon.), Harvard, 1970; m. Marilyn Louise Taylor, July 13, 1955; children—Sarah Louise, Charles Taylor, Benjamin. Asst. prof. Ohio State U., 1960-63, asso. prof., 1963-65; asso. prof. Harvard Grad. Sch. Bus. Adminstrn., 1965-69, 1907 prof. bus. logistics, 1969—; pres. Logistics Systems, Inc., 1968-69, now dir.; dir. Distbn. Centers' Inc., Comsec Fund, Inc., Agribus. Mgmt. Corp., Comsec, Inc., The Window Shop, Inc.; mgmt. cons.; vis. lectr. York U., 1968. Dir. Transportation Research Found., 1965—. Served with AUS, 1954-56 ETO. Mem. Assn. Am. U. Profs., Am. Maketing Assn., Transportation Research Forum, Nat. Council Phys. Distbn. Mgmt., Am. Soc. Traffic and Transportation. Author: (with Ivie and Glaskowsky) Business Logistics, 1964; (with Germane and Glaskowsky) Highway Transportation Management, 1963. Bd. editors Jour. Marketing Research, 1962—. Home: 15 Shepard St Cambridge MA 02138

HESLIN, JAMES J., librarian, historian; b. Cambridge, Mass., June 15, 1916; s. James s. James Joseph and Helen (Burns) H.; B.S., Boston Coll., 1949; M.A., Boston U., 1949; Ph.D., 1952; M.S., Columbia, 1954; m. Phyllis Stacy Brissette, July 13, 1940. Fellow history Boston U., 1950-52; 1st asst. Am. history div. N.Y. Pub. Library, 1953-54; asst. dir. univ. libraries U. Buffalo, 1955-56; asst. dir., librarian N.Y. Hist. Soc., 1956-58, asso. dir.,1958- 60, dir., 1960—. Trustee Sleepy Hollow Restorations, Inc., Soc. for Preservation L.I. Antiquities. Served with AUS, 1943-46. Mem. Am. Hist. Assn., Am. Assn. State and Local History (mem. council), Mass. Hist. Soc. (corr. mem.), Am. Assn. Museums, Am. Antiquarian Soc ., Bibliog. Soc. of Am. (mem. council, 1st v.p.), Colonial Soc. Mass. Clubs: Century Assn., Grolier, Coffee Coffee House (N.Y.C.). Contbr. to books and periodicals. Home: 25 Central Park W New York City NY 10023 Office: 170 Central Park West New York City NY 10024

HESS, ARTHUR, anatomist; b. N.Y.C., Feb. 19, 1927; s. David and Anna (Kruger) H.; B.S., U. Ark., 1946, M.S., 1947; Ph.D., Univ. Coll. London, 1949; D.Sc., U. London, 1959; m. Gloria Joy Tomsen, Dec. 25, 1953; children—Douglas Thomas, Elisa Tilda. Faculty, Wash. U. Sch. Medicine, 1951-61, asst. prof. anatomy, 1954-61; asso. prof. physiology U. Utah Coll. Medicine, 1961-67; prof., chmn. dept. anatomy Rutgers Med. Sch., 1967—. Mem. Am. Assn. Anatomists. Research and publs. on fine structure of nerve and muscle-electron microscopy, histochemistry, histology. Home: 211 Lincoln Av Highland Park NJ 08904 Office: Dept Anatomy Rutgers Med Sch New Brunswick NJ 08903

HESS, ARTHUR E., govt. ofcl.; b. Reading, Pa.; grad. Princeton; LL.B., U. Md.; m. Ann McKeown Davis, Mar. 14, 1942; children—Jean, Ann, Elizabeth. With Social Security Adminstrn. (formerly Social Security Bd.), 1939—, organizer, 1st dir. social security disability operations, 1954, in charge advance planning for Medicare, 1965, dir. Bur. Health Ins., Dept. Health, Edn. and Welfare 1965-67, dep. commr. social security, 1967—. Mem. Adminstrv. Conf. U.S., 1968—. Recipient Nat. Civil Service League award, 1967; Pres.'s award for distinguished fed. civilian service, 1967; Arthur S. Flemming award for outstanding fed. service, 1955; Rockefeller Pub. Service award, 1969. Address: 4805 Woodside Rd Baltimore MD 21229

HESS, DONALD K., govt. ofcl.; b. Lititz, Pa, Nov. 18, 1930; s. Charles S. and Anna Mae (Kready) H.; B.A., Franklin and Marshall Coll., 1952; M.P.A., Syracuse U., 1953; m. Nancy Gordon, June 9, 1951; children—Jennifer, Lynn. Mgmt. officer AEC, Washington, 1953-58; asso. dir. Advanced Research Projects Agy., Washington, 1958-66, Office Econ. Opportunity, Washington, 1966-70; dir. Peace Corps, Korea, 1970—. Address: Peace Corps Am Embassy Seoul Korea

HESS, ECKHARD HEINRICH, educator, psychologist; b. Bochum, Germany, Sept. 27, 1916; s. Heinrich Peter and Wilhelmina (Salewski) H.; came to U.S., 1927, naturalized, 1943; A.B., Blue Ridge Coll., New Windsor, Md., 1941; M.A., Johns Hopkins, 1947, Ph.D., 1948; m. Dorothea Burghard-Nawiasky, Sept. 29, 1942. Jr. instr. Johns Hopkins, 1946-47; faculty U. Chgo., 1948—, prof. psychology, 1959—, chmn. dept., 1963-68, dir. W. C. Allee Lab. Animal Behavior, 1960—; spring vis. asso. prof. Swarthmore Coll., 1957, U. Cal. at Berkeley, 1958; vis. prof. Stanford, 1965. Cons.-dir. Perception Lab., Interpublic, Inc., N.Y.C., 1960-67. mem. com. comparative devel. Social Sci. Research Council, 1961-67. Served with AUS, 1943-44. Fellow Center Advanced Studies Behavioral Scis., 1955-56. Fellow A.A.A.S. (life), Am. Psychol. Assn.; mem. Internat. Brain Research Orgn., Soc. Exptl. Psychologists, Am. Mus. Natural History, Animal Behavior Soc., Nat. Geog. Sco., Psychonomic Soc., Soc. Neurosci., Sigma Xi. Club: Quadrangle (Chgo.). Author: Ethology: an approach toward the complete analysis of behavior; Imprinting. Co-editor: Psychologische Forschung; Brain, Behavior, and Evolution. Contbr. articles in field to sci. jours. Home: 1151 E 56th St Chicago IL 60637

HESS, EDWIN, L., cartoonist syndicated cartoon The Good Old Days. Address: care United Feature Syndicate 220 E 42d St New York City NY 10017 *

HESS, FARIS JAKE, rancher; b. McLean, Tex., Mar. 18, 1921; s. Jacob and Bessie E. (Sitter) H.; B.Animal Sci., Tex. A. and M. U., 1942; m. Leta Mae Phillips, Apr. 18, 1942; children—Nancy Jean (Mrs. James L. Hudson), Faris Jake II. Rancher hereford cattle, McLean, 1945—. Served with AUS, 1942-45; ETO. Decorated Purple Heart, Bronze Star. Mem. Top O'Texas (past pres.), Panhandle (past pres.), Tex. (past v.p.), Am. (pres. 1970—) hereford assns., Am. Hereford Ordnance (bd. dirs. 1968—). Address: Box 306 McLean TX 79057

HESS, GEORGE KELLOGG, Jr., engr.; b. Orange, N.J., Aug. 27, 1922; s. George Kellogg and Henrietta (Spruhan) H.; B.S. in Engring. Mechanics, B.S. in Math., U. Mich., 1945; m. Ruth Agnes Kelly, Nov. 3, 1945; children—Kathleen Janeth, James Douglas, Andrew Martin, Anne Elizabeth. Instr., U. Mich., 1946-49; mem. staff Los Alamos Sci. Lab., 1949-52; group leader, 1955- 59; project engr. A.D. Little & Co., Cambridge, Mass., 1952-54; project leader Bendix Corp., Detroit, 1954-55, asst. to gen. mgr., Southfield, Mich., 1959-62; chief scientist USAF, Patrick AFB, Fla., 1962-67; dep. for engring. to asst. sec. USAF, 1967-69; dir. Advanced Materiel Concepts Agy., U.S. Army, Alexandria, Va., 1970—; cons. Los Alamos Sci. Lab., 1959-60; spl. research ship vibration, nuclear rocket engine controls, missile range instrumentation. Mem. troop com. Central Brevard council Boy Scouts Am., 1963-65. Trustee Fla. Inst. Tech., Melbourne, 1962-1962- 68. Served as ensign USNR, 1945-46. Recipient Miller award in math. U. math. U. Mich., 1945; Outstanding Performance award USAF, 1964, 65, 66, 68. Exceptional Civilian Performance award, 1966. Mem. Am. Inst. Aeros. and Astronautics (dir. Canaveral chpt. 1963-64), Am. Rocket Soc., Am. Soc. M.E., I.E.E.E., Sigma Xi, Tau Beta Pi, Phi Eta Sigma. Episcopalian. Mailing address: Home: 1212 Pawnee Terrace Indian Harbour Beach FL 32937 Office: US Army Advanced Materiel Concepts Agy 2461 Eisenhower Av Alexandria VA 22314

HESS, HANS OBER, lawyer; b. Royersford, Pa., Nov. 8, 1912; s. Samuel Harley and Annamae (Wenger) H.; A.B., Ursinus Coll., 1933; LL.B., Harvard, 1936; LL.D., Muhlenberg Coll., 1965; m. Dolores Groke, May 18, 1940; children—Antonine (Mrs. Joseph J. Gal), Roberta (Mrs. Edward S. Trippe), Liese (Mrs. Arleigh P. Helfer, Jr.), Kristina. Admitted to Pa. bar, 1937; law sec. to Supreme Ct. Pa. Justice James B. Drew, 1936-38; gen. practice law, Norristown, Pa., 1938-40; asst. sec. Commonwealth Pa., also mem. Bd. Finance and Revenue, 1940-42; asso. firm Ballard, Spahr, Andrews & Ingersoll, Phila., 1942-47, partner, 1947—. Dir. U.S. Lumber Co., L. Frank Markel & Sons, Co., FML Growth Fund, Paper Mfrs. Co., Fleer Corp. Mem. exec. council Lutheran Ch. in Am., 1962-70; nat. chmn. Harvard Law Sch. Fund, 1967-69; mem. central com. World Council Chs.; mem. bd. overseers com. to visit Harvard Law Sch. Mem. Montgomery County Republican Finance Com., 1962—. Trustee Lankenau Hosp.; chmn. bd. Phila. Coll. Art; pres. Mary J. Drexel Home, Phila. Bar Found., Phila. Orch. Pension Found.; trustee Marie M. Barclay Endowment; bd. dirs. Phila. Orch. Assn. Mem. Am., Pa., Phila. (bd. govs., chmn. finance com.), Montgomery County bar assns. Clubs: Rittenhouse, Union League, Philadelphia Country (Phila.); Cotton Bay. Home: 1235 Conshohocken State Rd Gladwyne PA 19035 Office: Land Title Bldg Philadelphia PA 19110

HESS, HOWARD MARTIN, univ. ofcl., engr.; b. Akron, Mich., Sept. 11, 1908; S. Eugene Alva and Maggie Jeanette (Miller) H.; B.S., Wayne State U., 1934; M.S., U. Mich., 1937; postgrad. State U. Ia., 1940-41; m. Alice Margaret Baldwin, Aug. 21, 1937; children—Virginia Ann, Mary Jean, Nancy Ruth. With traffic div. Detroit Police Dept., 1926-27; installed dial office equipment Western Electric Co., Detroit, 1927-29, 30; mem. faculty Wayne State U., 1934—, instr. elec. engring. dept., asst. prof., asso. prof., 1935-50, prof., 1950—, head dept., 1945-57, asst. dean engring., 1956-57, asso. dean, 1957-67, 68-70, acting dean, 1967- 68, asso. dir. office univ. devel., 1970—. Sec.-treas. Wayne Engring. Research Inst., Inc., 1944-48, mem. bd., 1948-57. Vice pres. United Unitarian Appeal, 1959-62, chmn. budget com., 1957-6l; vice chmn. allocations com. Unitarian-Universalist Assn., 1962-63, chmn., 1963-65; v.p. Met. Detroit Sci. Fair, Inc., 1962- 65. Trustee Rackham Engring. Found., 1962-64. Fellow I.E.E.E. (chmn. orgn. dept. power group 1964-67, sec. Power Engring. Soc. 1970—); mem. Am. Soc. Engring. Edn. (chmn. Mich. 1949-50, rep. gen. council 1957-60), Engring. Soc. Detroit (dir. 1959-65, pres. 1962-63), A.A.A.S., Detroit Edn. Assn., Sigma Xi, Tau Beta Pi, Omicron Delta Kappa, Eta Kappa Nu, Sigma Pi Sigma. Home: 32355 Susanne Dr Franklin MI 48025

HESS, LESLIE MARION, metal working co. exec.; b. Waynesboro, Pa., Mar. 13, 1911; s. William T. and Ida M. (Benedict) H.; B.S. in Edn., Shippensburg (Pa.) State Coll., 1934; m. Margaret K. Schroyer, June 13, 1937; children—Jane, John, William. With Landis Machine Co., Waynesboro, 1934—, v.p., 1958- 62, pres., gen. mgr., 1962—, also dir.; dir. Canadian Landis Machine Co., First Nat. Bank & Trust Co. (both Waynesboro). Active Waynesboro Community Chest. Mem. Nat. Metal Trades Assn. (dir.), U.S., Pa., Waynesboro chambers commerce. Home: 143 W King St Waynesboro PA 17268 Office: Landis Machine Co Waynesboro PA 17268

HESS, LYNDLE WILLIAM, lawyer, food corp. exec.; b. Milton, Ill., Oct. 6, 1908; s. Lee R. and Sallye (Smith) H.; A.B., Ill. Coll., Jacksonville, 1930; J.D., Northwestern U., 1933; m. Mary Louise Martin, June 18, 1931; children—Anne Marie, Nancy Lee, William Byron. Admitted to Ill. bar, 1933; atty. Libby, McNeill & Libby, Chgo., 1933-48, gen. atty., 1948-56, v.p., 1956-62, dir., 1956—, sr. v.p., 1962-63, exec. v.p., 1963-67, pres., chief exec. officer, 1967-68, chmn., 1968-71. Trustee Ill. Coll. Mem. Am., Ill., N.Y., Chgo. bar assns. Home: 148 Maplewood Rd Riverside IL 60546 Office: 200 S Michigan Av Chicago IL 60604

HESS, OLEEN, govt. ofcl.; b. Plymouth, Utah, Oct. 25, 1923; s. George Albert and Elizabeth (Stokes) H.; B.S. in Agronomy, Utah State U., 1948; M.S. in Agrl. Edn., Ore. State U., 1958; Ed.D., U. Utah, 1964; m. Neva C. Moon, May 19, 1944; children—Kathryn, Jonathan Vaughan, Dwight, Marsha, Theresa, Jeffery. Tchr. vocational agr. Union High Sch., Molalla, Ore., 1949-56; agrl. edn. adviser AID, PI.I., 1956-59, agrl. tng. adviser, Liberia, 1960-62, tng. officer, Sudan, 1964-65, agrl. officer for East S.Africa, Washington, 1965-68, agrl. officer, Tanzania, 1968—. Served with USNR, 1942-44. Decorated Air Medal. Mem. Phi Delta Kappa. Republican. Mem. Ch. of Jesus Christ of Latter-day Saints (br. pres.). Author: History of Agriculture Education in Utah 1847-64; Approved Poultry Production Practice, 1957, 68; Vocational Guide in Coffee Production, 1958; Vocation Guide in Cacao Production, 1959; Agriculture Education and Agriculture Extension in Developing Nations, 1970. Home: 645 National St Henderson NV 89015 Office: Dar Es Salaam (ID) Dept State Washington DC 20251

HESS, OTIS RAYMOND, judge; b. Hillsboro, O., May 30, 1900; s. Anthony Daniel and Rose (Hibler) H.; LL.B., Xavier U., 1923; m. Lydia Mayer, June 16, 1927; children—Barbara Rose, Otis Raymond. Admitted to Ohio bar, 1922; gen. practice law, Cin., 1922-29; judge

Municipal Ct., Cin., 1930-47, Ct. Common Pleas, 1947-68, 1st Appellate Dist. Ohio, 1969—; instr. Salmon P. Chase Coll. Law, 1946—. Active various community drives. Served to maj. AUS, 1943-45; lt. col. Res. Mem. Am., Ohio, Cin. (past pres.) bar assns., Am. Bar Found., Res. Officers Assn., Mil. Order World Wars, Am. Legion, D.A.V., V.F.W., Cin. Lawyers Club, United Comml. Travelers, Mt. Lookout Civic Assn., Phi Alpha Delta. Mason (33, K.T., Shriner, Jester), Moose, K.P. Clubs: Cincinnati Automobile (chmn. safety dept., 1st v.p.), Cuvier Press, Hyde Park Country (Cin.). Home: 3759 Earl's Court View Cincinnati OH 45226 Office: Hamilton County Court House Cincinnati OH 45202

HESS, RAYMOND LEONARD, Jr., mfg. co. exec.; b. Indiana, Pa., Jan. 1, 1913; s. Raymond Leonard and Mary (Smith) H.; A.B., Princeton, 1935; LL.B., Duquesne U., 1940; m. Ruth Pealer, July 30, 1938; children—Judith P. (Mrs. Thomas B. O'Bryon), Deborah C., Raymond Leonard III. With Rust Engring. Co. div. Litton Industries, Pitts., 1937—, pres., 1968—. Pres., Health and Welfare Assn. Allegheny County. Bd. dirs. United Fund Allegheny County, Hosp. Planning Assn. Allegheny County; trustee Duquesne U. Mem. Pa., Allegheny County bar assns. Presbyn. (elder 1969-70). Clubs: Duquesne (Pitts.); Allegheny Country, Edgeworth (Sewickley); Princeton (N.Y.C.). Home: 1023 Davis Lane Sewickley PA 15143 Office: 930 Fort Duquesne Blvd Pittsburgh PA 15222

HESS, ROBERT DANIEL, educator; b. Shambaugh, Ia., Mar. 10, 1920; s. John Henry and Allilian (Weavers) H.; A.B. in Psychology, U. Cal. at Berkeley, 1947; Ph.D. in Human Devel., U. Chgo., 1950; m. Betsy N. Muelke, June 18, 1949; (div. June 1969); children—Jared A., Alyssa N., Devin A., Bradley B. Mem. faculty Com. on Human Devel., U. Chgo., 1949-59, chmn., 1959-64, dir. Urban Child Center, 1964-67; fellow Center Advanced Study Behavioral Scis., Stanford, Cal., 1966-67; Lee L. Jacks prof. child edn., prof. psychology Stanford, 1967—; edn. cons. Served with USMCR, 1942-46. Fellow A.A.A.S., Am. Psychol. Assn., Am. Sociol. Assn.; mem. Am. Ednl. Research Assn., Soc. Research Child Devel. Author: (with Gerald Handel) Family Worlds: A Psychosocial Approach to Family Life, 1959; (with Judith V. Torney) The Development of Political Attitudes in Children, 1967. Editor: (with Roberta M. Bear) Early Education: Current Theory, Research and Practice, 1968. Home: 3905A Middlefield Rd Palo Alto CA 94303 Office: Sch Edn Stanford U Stanford CA 94305

HESS, SIDNEY J., Jr., lawyer; b. Chgo., June 26, 1910; s. Sidney J. and Alma (Katz) H.; Ph.B., U. Chgo., 1930, J.D., 1932; m. Jacqueline Engelhardt, Aug. 28, 1948; children—Karen E., Lori Ann. Admitted to Ill. bar, 1932; practiced in Chgo., 1932—; mem. firm Aaron, Aaron Schimberg & Hess, Chgo., 1933—; dir., legal counsel Jewish Fedn. of Met. Chgo., 1968—, v.p., 1972—; dir., sec., legal counsel Jewish United Fund Met. Chgo., 1971—; legal counsel Jewish Welfare Fund Met. Chgo., 1969—. Dir. Dreis & Krump Mfg. Co., Silberman Fur Corp. Mem. exec. com. Anto-Defamation League, 1954-57. Bd. dirs. Schwab Rehab. Hosp., 1954—, pres., 1959-64. Mem. Am., Ill. State, Chgo. bar assns., Am. Judicature Soc., U. Chgo. Law Sch. Assn. (dir.), Phi Beta Kappa. Pi Lambda Phi. Clubs: Standard (past pres., dir.), Mid- Day (Chgo.); Northmoor Country (Highland Park, Ill.). Home: 1335 Astor St Chicago IL 60610 Office: One First Nat Plaza Chicago IL 60670

HESS, STEPHEN, govt. ofcl., author; b. N.Y.C., Apr. 20, 1933; s. Charles and Florence (Morse) H.; B.A., Johns Hopkins, 1953; student U. Chgo., 1950-52; m. Elena Shayne, Aug. 23, 1959; children—Charles P., James R. Jr. instr. polit. sci. Johns Hopkins, 1953-55; staff asst. to Pres., 1959-61; asst. to minority whip U.S. Senate, 1961; asso. fellow Inst. for Policy Studies, 1964-65; fellow Inst. Politics, J.F. Kennedy Sch. Govt., Harvard, 1967-68; dep. asst. to President Nixon for urban affairs, 1969; nat. chmn. White House Conf. on Children and Youth, 1969—. Served with AUS, 1956-58. Author: (with Malcolm Moos) Hats in the Ring: The Making of Presidential Candidates, 1960; America's Political Dynasties, 1966; (with David S. Broder) The Republican Establishment, 1968; (with Milton Kaplan) The Ungentlemanly Art; A History of American Political Cartoons, 1968; (with Earl Mazo) Nixon: A Political Portrait, rev. edit., 1969; also articles. Home: 3705 Porter St NW Washington DC 20016 Office: The White House Washington DC 20500

HESS, THOMAS BAER, writer, mag. editor; b. Rye, N.Y., July 14, 1920; s. Gabriel Lorié and Helen (Baer) H.; B.A., Yale, 1942; m. Audrey Stern, June 29, 1944; children—William, Helen, Philip. With Art News mag., N.Y.C., 1946—, exec. editor, 1949-65, editor, 1965—. Mem. of juries and award panels. Pres. Longview Found., 1958—. Served as pilot USAAF, 1942-45. Mem. Phi Beta Kappa. Author: Abstract Painting, Background and American Phase, 1951; William de Kooning, 1959, 1968, 1969; Barnett Newman, 1969, 71. Home: 19 Beckman Pl New York City NY 10022 Office: 444 Madison Av New York City NY 10022

HESS, W. JAKE, musician; b. Athen, Ala., Dec. 24, 1927; s. William Stovell and Lidia Rebecca Hess; grad. high sch.; m. Emily Joyce McWaters, Oct. 5, 1952; children—Rebecca, Chris, W. Jake. With Statesman Quartet, Imperial Quartet, Jake Hess and Sound of Youth, Nashville, 1970—. Recipient Grammy award for best sacred performance Everything is Beautiful, 1971. Home: 401 Williamsburg Rd Brentwood TN 37027 Office: James Robertson Pkwy Nashville TN 37201

HESS, WALTER C., coll. pres., biochemist; b. Phila., July 19, 1899; s. Edward and Theresa (Cohen) H.; B.S., U. Pa., 1920; Ph.D., George Washington U., 1930; m. Jeanette Samuel, June 11, 1922; 1 son, Walter C. Chemist USPHS, 1926-31; mem. faculty Georgetown U., 1931-68, prof. biochemistry, chmn. dept. Med. and Dental Sch., 1946-67, asso. dean, 1960-64, v.p. for grants and contracts, 1964-68, emeritus, 1968—; pres. Dumbarton Coll., Washington, 1968-70; ret. 1970. Adv. com. U.S. commr. edn., 1945-47. Exec. com. D.C. Community Chest, 1939-40. Served with U.S. Army, 1917-18. Mem. Am. Soc. Biol. Chemists, Soc. Exptl. Biology and Medicine (chmn. D.C. sect. 1945), Internat. Assn. Dental Research, Am. Chem. Soc., Washington Acad. Sci., D.A.V. (dep. comdr. 1939-41), Phi Beta Kappa, Sigma Xi. Home: 3607 Chesapeake St NW Washington DC 20008

HESS, WALTER J., banker; b. N.Y.C., Dec. 28, 1901; s. Jacob H. and Ida R. (Gute) H.; A.B., Columbia, 1922, LL.B., 1924; m. Anne C. Roeding, Nov. 10, 1927. Admitted to N.Y. bar, 1925; mem. firm Christman, McKeon & Hess, N.Y.C., 1926-48; pres. Ridgewood Savs. Bank, N.Y.C., 1948—; mem. Queens adv. council Chase Manhattan Bank; pres. Instl. Investors Mut. Fund, Inc., 1955-58, now dir. Chmn. trustees Fund for Savs. Banks, 1965-68. Trustee Wyckoff Heights Hosp. Mem. Savs. Banks Assn. N.Y. (group chmn., pres. 1953-54), Queens County Bar Assn. (pres. 1941). Mason, Elk. Club: Wheatley Hills Golf (East Williston, N.Y.). Home: 193-18 McLaughlin Av Holliswood NY 11423 Office: 1002 Forest Av Ridgewood Brooklyn NY 11227

HESS, WALTER RUDOLF, physiologist; b. Mar. 17, 1881; s. Dr. Clemenz and Gertrud (Fischer Saxon) H.; student medicine univs. Lausanne, Berne, Berlin, Kiel and Zurich, 1900-05; M.D., U. Zurich, 1906; Dr. honoris causa in philosophy, U. Berne, 1933, in medicine U. Geneva, 1944, in science, McGill U., Montreal, Can., 1953, in medicine, Freiburg, Germany, 1960; m. Luise Sandmeyer, 1909; children—Gertrud, Rudolf. Asst. Physician and ophthalmologist, 1905-08; oculist, 1906-12; asst. physiology, Zurich. Switzerland and Bonn, Germany, 1913-17; prof. physiology, dir. Physiol. Inst., U. Zurich, 1917-51, ret., 1951; prof. emeritus, med. faculty U. Zurich. Awarded Marcel Benoist prize (Swiss), 1933; Ludwig Medal, German Soc. for Circulation Research, 1938; Nobel prize for medicine and physiology (with Prof. Egas Moniz), 1949. Mem. or hon. mem. numerous Swiss and fgn. learned socs. Author Books, including: Die Regulierung von Blutkreislauf und Atmung, 1932; Beiträge zur Physiologie des Hirnstammes, I, II, 1932, 1938; Die funktionelle Organisation des vegetativen Nervensystemes, 1948; Das Zwichenhirn, 1949, 2d edit., 1953; Diencephalon, 1954; The Functional Organization of the Diencephalon Hypothalamus and Thalamus, 1956; The Biologie of Mind, 1964. Home: 6 Via Gabbio 6612 Ascona Switzerland

HESSE, ALFRED WILLIAM, Jr., railroad ofcl.; b. Fairmont, W.Va., May 19, 1912; s. Alfred William and Margaret (Dudley) H.; A.B., Pa. State U., 1933; LL.B., U. Pa., 1936; m. Leonore Schwarze, Mar. 6, 1937 (dec. May 1965); children—Janet E. (Mrs. Frederick W. Dreher 3d), Carolyn M. (Mrs. Kent B. Andrews), Virgina A.; m. 2d, Elizabeth Petsock, July 1966. Admitted Pa. bar, 1936; law sec. Pa. Supreme Ct., 1936-39; with Reading Co., 1939—, v.p. marketing, 1962- 67, vice pres., gen. counsel, 1967—. Pres. Bala-Cynwyd Civic Assn., 1955; mem. Eagle Bd. Rev., Valley Forge council Boy Scouts Am., 1963—. Mem. Alumni council Pa. State U., 1963—; trustee Merion Acad. Served with USNR, 1944-46. Mem. Phila. Bar Assn., Phi Kappa Psi. Presbyn. Club: Union League (Phila.). Home: 1026 Fairway La Gladwyne PA 19107

HESSE, DON, editorial cartoonist; b. Belleville, Ill., Feb. 20, 1918; s. Albert B. and Adele M. (Oexner) H.; student St. Louis Sch. Fine Arts, 1936-37; m. Ruth Jane Hexter, Oct. 12, 1940; 1 dau., Janice Lynn. Artist-photographer Belleville Daily News-Democrat, 1935-40; own photographic portrait studio, Belleville, 1940-42; joined art staff St. Louis Globe-Democrat, 1946, editorial cartoonist, 1951—, nat. syndicated McNaught Syndicate, Inc. of N.Y., 1956—. Served as sgt., photographer, artist with Air Force, 1942-45, Ground Force, PTO, 1945- 46. Recipient Freedoms Found. award, 1954; Christopher award, 1955. Mem. Nat. Cartoonist Soc., Assn. Am. Editorial Cartoonist, Sigma Delta Chi. Presbyn (elder). Home: 627 Garden Blvd Belleville IL 62221 Office: St Louis Globe-Democrat 12 Blvd at Delmar St Louis IL 63201

HESSE, ERNEST GEORGE, chem. co. exec.; b. Landsberg, Germany, Jan. 3, 1909; s. Felice and Frances (Luther) H.; came to U.S., 1909, naturalized, 1916; B.C.S., N.Y. U., 1933; m. Alice Walster, May 30, 1935. With Consol. Coal Co., N.Y.C., 1933-43, asst. to controller, 1940-43; with Am. Cyanamid Co., 1946—, mng. dir. internat. div., 1959-65, corporate v.p., 1965—, corporate dir., 1966—; pres. Cyanamid Internat. Corp., 1965—; dir. Formica Internat. Ltd., London, Eng. Served with USNR, 1943-45. Decorated Order of Merit (Italy), 1960. Mem. Internat. Econ. Policy Assn., Nat. Fgn. Trade Council, Fgn. Policy Assn., Council Fgn. Relations. Club: Hemisphere (N.Y.C.). Home: Nyack NY 10960 Office: Am Cyanamid Co Wayne NJ 07470

HESSE, EVERETT WESLEY, educator; b. Bklyn., Aug. 31, 1908; s. Fred William and Erna (Hertzberg) H.; B.A., N.Y.U., 1931, M.A., 1933, Ph.D., 1941. Prof. Spanish, U. Wis., 1941-59; prof., chmn. dept. Spanish, U. So. Cal., 1960-68; prof., chmn. dept. Spanish, U. Md., College Park, 1968—; dir. NDEA Inst. U. So. Cal., 1961-66. Mem. Hispanic Soc. Am. (corr.), Am. Assn. Tchrs. Spanish and Portuquese (pres. 1955), Modern Lang. Assn. So. Cal. (v.p. 1967), Sigma Delta Pi. Lutheran. Author: Calderon de la Barca, 1967; Analisis e Interpretacion de la Comedia, 1968. Home: 1771 Elton Rd Silver Spring MD 20903 Office: U Md College Park MD 20742

HESSE, HARRY RADER, lawyer; b. Wheeling, W.Va., July 27, 1908; s. Harry Louis and Elizabeth Lauretta (Rader) H.; A.B., W.Va. U., 1931, J.D., 1932; m. Mary Virginia Parker, Nov. 25, 1936. Admitted to W.Va. bar, 1932, practiced in Wheeling until 1934; with legal dept. Wheeling Steel Corp., 1934-58, sec., gen. counsel, 1958-64, past sec., gen. counsel subsidiaries; partner law firm Petroplus, Bailey, Byrum & Hesse, Wheeling, 1964—. Past pres. Ogelbay Inst., Ohio County Tb Assn.; past chmn. Ohio County Law Library, Ohio County Pub. Library. Mem. Am., W.Va., Ohio County (v.p. 1970—) bar assns., Phi Alpha Delta, Theta Chi. Lutheran. Mason (33). Home: 8 Lynwood Av Wheeling WV 26003 Office: Central Union Bldg Wheeling WV 26003

HESSE, RICHARD, hardware corp. exec.; b. Chgo., 1895. Pres. Ace Hardware Corp., Chgo.; dir. Mich. Av. Bank, Chgo. Trustee Henrotin Hosp., Chgo. Home: 1130 Lake Shore Dr Chicago IL 60611 Office: 6501 W 65th St Chicago IL 60638*

HESSE, STANLEY WILLIAM stock broker; b. Bklyn., Jan. 30, 1911; s. Maurice and Edith (Reiss) H.; grad. Browne's Bus. Coll., Bklyn., 1928; m. Elizabeth Gans Blass, Dec. 19, 1933; children—Barbara Leah (Mrs. Tedd Tabachnick), William Blass. With H. Hentz & Co., N.Y.C., 1928-70, partner, 1946-70, mem. exec. com., 1963-70. Mem. nominating com. N.Y. Stock Exchange, 1963-64, 69-70, floor ofcl., 1964-70. Active Fedn. Jewish Philanthropies, United Jewish Appeal, Nat. Brotherhood Christians and Jews. Jewish Guild for Blind, Am. Jewish Com. Served with AUS, 1942-43. Home: 1085 Park Av New York City NY 10028 Office: 72 Wall St New York City NY 10005 Died July 16 1970.

HESSE, WILLIAM R., advt. exec.; b. Dayton, O., Jan. 19, 1914; s. Julius R. and Margaret (Reid) H.; A.B., U. Cin., 1938; m. Anne E., Vandervort, July 3, 1941; children—William R., Carol Anne, Mark Vandervort. Supr. employment for men Procter & Gamble, Cin., then asst. to sales mgr., 1937-46: v.p. Batten, Barton, Durstine & Osborn, Inc., Pitts. and N.Y.C., 1946-56; sr. v.p. Benton & Bowles, Inc., N.Y.C., 1956-58, exec. v.p. 1958-61, pres. 1961-68, chief exec. officer 1965-68, dir.; pres., chief exec. officer William R. Hesse Assos., N.Y.C., 1968—. Mem. mgmt. com. YMCA; mem. adv. bd. Nat. Coffee Assn. Bd. dirs. Urban League of N.Y. Served as lt. col. Inf., AUS, 1941-45. Recipient Putnam award Nat. Indsl. Advertisers Assn., 1949. Mem. Am. Mgmt. Assn., Am. Assn. Advt. Agys. (dir.-at-large), Royal Soc. Arts. (hon. corr.). Clubs: Winged Foot Golf; N.Y. Athletic; Ardsley Country. Home: 131 Doubling Rd Greenwich CT 06830 Office: William R Hesse Assos 210 Central Park S New York City NY 10019

HESSELBERG, ARTHUR KENNETH, educator; b. Brockton, Mass., June 11, 1916; s. Arthur Francis and Gertrude Frances (Noonan) H.; A.B., St. Anselm's Coll., 1938; M.A., U. N.H., 1948; Ph.D., Cath. U. Am., 1952; m. Doris Boisvert, Apr. 1, 1942. Instr. Me. Central Inst., 1945-46; asst. prof. dept. polit. sci. Duquesne U., 1952-56, asso. prof., 1956-60, prof., 1960—, chmn. dept., 1956—. Served with USMC, 1938-45. Mem. Am. Assn. U. Profs., Am. Polit. Sci. Assn., Am. Acad. Polit. and Social Sci. Contbr. to profl. jours. Home: 82 Hall Av Pittsburgh PA 15205

HESSELBERTH, WILFRED MARION, educator; b. Minonk, Ill., May 6, 1907; s. Frederick William and Emma (Klesath) H.; B.S. in Elec. Engring., U. Ill., 1931, M.S. in Elec. Engring., 1932; m. Merno M. King. Dec. 27, 1933; children—Robert J., John F. Glassblower, Purdue U., 1933-36; research engr. Akay Electron Co., Chgo., 1936-37; engr. Am. Instrument Co., Silver Spring, Md., 1937- 38; research engr. CBS, 1944-45; mem. faculty Purdue U., 1945—, prof. elec. engring., 1958—. Mem. Am. Soc. Engring. Edn., I.E.E.E., Sigma Xi, Eta Kappa Nu. Author: (with G.E. Happell) Engineering Electronics, 1953. Devel. spl. vacuum tubes. Home: 1706 Ravinia Rd West Lafayette IN 47907 Office: Elec Engring Bldg Purdue U Lafayette IN 47907

HESSELDEN, LOUIS GILBERT, architect; b. Wendel, Okla., Feb. 5, 1895; s. Wallace and Annie (Peltier) H.; B.Arch., U. Pa., 1927, postgrad., 1927-29; postgrad. Pa. Acad. Fine Arts, Phila., 1929-30; m. Mary Lou Carney, June 10, 1943. Draftsman, Office of Paul Philippe Cret, Architect, Phila., 1928-31; practice architecture, Albuquerque, 1932—; prin. architect Albuquerque Bd. Edn., 1932-57. Chmn. N.M. Bd. Examiners for Architects, 1945-46. Bd. dirs. Albuquerque YMCA, 1948-50. Served to 1st lt., inf., U.S. Army, 1917-18; to lt. USNR, 1943-45. Mem. A.I.A. (pres. N.M. chpt. 1945-47), Pi Kappa Alpha. Republican. Roman Catholic. Rotarian, Elk. Clubs: Albuquerque Country, Albuquerque Petroleum. Important works include Town of Tyrone, N.M. for Phelps Dodge Corp., Albuquerque Main Exchange Bldg. for Mountain Bell Telephone Co., South Albuquerque Works, ACF Industries, Inc., Bernalillo County Court House, Highland High Sch. and Gymnasium, Albuquerque. Home: 1215 Las Lomas Rd Albuquerque NM 87106 Office: 314 4th St SW Albuquerque NM 87103

HESSELTINE, HENRY CLOSE, educator, researcher, physician; b. Promise City, Ia., May 10, 1901; s. Henry Elmer and Arminda Alice (Close) H.; B.S., U. Iowa, 1923, M.D., 1925, M.S., 1928; m. Grayce Chapman, Dec. 19, 1925; children—Glen Close, Marvin Henry. Intern U. Ia. Gen. Hosp., Iowa City, 1925-26; resident obstetrics and gynecology U. Ia., 1926-30, instr., 1927-30, asso., 1930-31; instr. obstetrics and gynecology U. Chgo., 1931-34, asst. prof., 1934-42, asso. prof., 1942-49, prof., sec. dept., 1949-58, Mary Campau Ryerson prof. obstetrics and gynecology, 1958-66, Mary Campau Ryerson prof. emeritus obstetrics and gynecology, 1966—; sr. staff Christ Community Hosp., Oak Lawn, Ill., 1969—; attending obstetrician, gynecologist Chgo. Lying-In Hosp., 1934-66, clin. asso. staff, 1966—; cons. Manpower Commn., 1952- 53, Trustee Ill. Med. Service (Blue Shield), 1947—, v.p., 1960-70, chmn., pres., 1970—. Mem. joint com. med.-legal edn. rev., 1957-61, A.M.A. speakers bur. 1961-65; chmn. Nat. Council Accreditation Nursing Homes, 1964-65; A.M.A. commr. for Joint Commn. Accreditation Hosps., 1962-70; chmn. Chgo. Maternal and Child Health Adv. Com., 1966-68, hon. chmn., 1968—. Recipient prize Central Assn. Obstetricians and Gynecologists, 1932-33. Diplomate Am. Bd. Obstetrics and Gynecology. Mem. A.M.A. (chmn. com. women in industry obstet. and gynecol. div. 1942-44; del. Ill.), Soc. Gynecology and Obstetrics El Salvador (Hon.), Am. Coll. Obstetricians and Gynecologists, Chgo. Gynecol. Soc., Ill. (chmn. council 1956-58, councillor 3d dist. 1952-59, pres. 1960-61), Chgo. med. socs., Am. Assn. Obstetricians and Gynecologists (life), Am. Gynecol. Soc. (Life), Ia. Med. Alumni Assn. (past sec.), U. Ia. Alumni, Sigma Xi (past sec., treas. Chgo. chpt.), Alpha Omego Alpha. Republican. Mason. Clubs: Quadrangle, South Shore Country (Chgo.). Contbr. articles med., sci. jours. Editor: Bull. Maternal Welfare, 1953-57. Inventor umbilical cord clamp; developed 1 stage operation for radical vulvectomy. Home: 5807 S Dorchester Av Chicago IL 60637 Office: 1836 W 87th St Chicago IL 60620

HESSER, LEON FRANCIS, govt. ofcl.; b. Winchester, Ind., July 27, 1925; s. George and Frances Madonna (Bolinger) H.; B.S., Purdue U., 1958, M.S., 1960, Ph.D., 1962; m. Florence Ellen Life, Aug. 11, 1946; children—Gwendolyn, George. Agr. economist U.S. Dept. Agr., Lafayette, Ind., 1958-62; agrl. economist Fed. Res. Bank of Kansas City (Mo.), 1962-66; asst. dir. for agrl. policy AID, State Dept., Islamabad, Pakistan, 1966—. Served with AUS, 1944-46. Vis. scholar Harvard, 1970-71. Mem. Internat. Assn. Agrl. Economists, Am. Econ. Assn., Am. Agrl. Econ. Assn. Methodist. Home: Islamabad (ID) State Department Washington DC 20521 Office: American Embassy Islamabad Pakistan

HESSEY, JOHN HAMILTON, lawyer; b. Worton, Md., Aug. 18, 1890; s. John Hamilton and Emma (Nicholson) H.; A.B., Washington Coll., Chestertown, Md., 1910, A.M., 1913; LL.B., U. Md., 1913; LL.D., Washington Coll., 1963; m. Gladys E. Messersmith, June 1, 1921; children—John Hamilton, Mahlon W. Admitted to Md. bar, 1912, since practiced in Balt.; lectr. U. Balt., 1928-59, asst. dean Sch. of Law, 1935-46, dean, 1946-69; lectr. corps., 1959-66. Chmn. appeal bd. SSS, 1940-67, Pub. Service Commn. Md., 1948-55; mem. 4th Regional Loyalty Bd., 1948-52; mem. loyalty review bd. U.S. Civil Service Commn., 1952-53; mem. Council Chs. and Christian Edn. Md., 1944- 63. Trustee U. Balt., Wesley Theol. Seminary; chmn. trustees South Baltimore Gen. Hosp.; bd. visitors and govs. Washington Coll., Chestertown, Md., 1943—, chmn., 1952-63; pres. George Washington Masonic Nat. Meml. Assn., Alexandria, Va. Served as 2d lt. A.S., U.S. Army, W.W. I; with A.S. Md. N.G., 1919-22. Mem. Assn. Ind. Colls. of Md. (treas.), Md. Bible Soc. (mem. bd. 1929—, pres. 1960), Am., Md. bar assns., Am. Judicature Soc., Am. Meth., Md. hist. socs. Methodist (trustee). Elk, Mason (past grand master). Club: Merchants (Balt.). Home: 6204 Pinehurst Rd Baltimore MD 21212 Office: Fidelity Bldg Baltimore MD 21201

HESSION, CHARLES HENRY, educator; b. Bklyn., May 1, 1911; s. Charles and Lillian (Carroll) H.; B.A., Coll. City N.Y., 1932; M.A., Columbia, 1933, Ph.D., 1948; m. Marie N. Struever, Jan. 26, 1946; children—William J., John C., Edwin A., Ann Marie. Mem. faculty Bklyn. Coll., 1932—, now prof. econs., chmn. social sci. program, 1967—; adviser U.S. Dept. Justice, 1963-64; sr. economist Econs. Inst., U. Colo., 1960. Pres. Vandever Park Civic Assn., 1950-52. Bd. dirs. N.Y. Met. Dist. Unitarian-Universalist Assn., 1968-69. Served with AUS, World War II; PTO. Decorated Bronze Star medal, Purple Heart. Mem. Am. Econ. Assn., Econ. History Assn., Assn. for Evolutionary Econs. Author: (with S.M. Miller and C. Stoddart) Dynamics of the American Economy, 1956; (with H. Sardy) Ascent to Affluence, 1969. Home: 1122 E 31st St Brooklyn NY 11210

HESSLER, ROBERT ROAMIE, diversified co. exec.; b. Toledo, O., Aug. 23, 1918; s. Roamie C. and Lily (Zenthoefer) H.; B.B.A., U. Toledo, 1940; m. Winifred J. Graves, Aug. 3, 1940; 1 son, Robert Roamie. Dir. taxes and ins. Willys Overland Motors, Inc., Toledo, 1946-54; gen. mgr. Buggie div. Burndy Corp., Toledo, 1955-60; v.p. finance Questor Corp., Toledo, 1961—; lectr. U. Toledo, 1946-48. Mem. adv. com. George C. Beinke Scholarship Trust, Goerlich Found. Served to 1st lt., Q.M.C., AUS, 1944-46. Mem. Am. Accounting Assn., Nat. Assn. Accountants (pres. Toledo chpt.

1953-54), Financial Execs. Inst. Mason (Shriner). Home: 2620 Pemberton Dr Toledo OH 43606 Office: Questor Corp Toledo OH 43601

HESSON, SAMUEL MOODIE, legal educator; b. Watervliet, N.Y., Oct. 2, 1906; s. Neil and Elizabeth (Moodie) H.; A.B., Union Coll., Schenectady, 1927, LL.D., 1965; LL.B., Albany Law Sch., 1931; LL.M., Columbia, 1939; m. Dorothy Miller Miller Betts, Jan. 25, 1933; 1 dau., Milda E. (Mrs. Nelson Enos). Admitted to N.Y. bar, 1931; practice in Schenectady, 1931-35; prof. law Albany Law Sch., 1935-64, dean, 1964—; cons. N.Y. State Jud. Council, 1940-55, N.Y. State Law Revision Commn., 1940—; v.p., dir. Schenedtady Savs. and Loan Assn. Del. N.Y. Constl. Conv., 1967. Mem. Phi Beta Kappa. Presbyn. (trustee). Home: 851 Lakewood Av., Schenectady NY 12309 Office: 80 New Scotland Av Albany NY 12208

HESTER, CLINTON MONROE, lawyer; b. Des Moines, Apr. 16, 1895; s. John Kenton and Sarah Hannah (Hamilton) H.; grad. Phillips Exeter Acad., 1916; A.B., George Washington U., 1920; LL.B., Georgetown U., 1922; m. Margaret Lee Bixby, July 30, 1965; children—Todd McCane, Jean Hamilton. Admitted to D.C. bar, 1922; atty. Dept. Interior, 1922; asst. counsel U.S. Shipping Bd., U.S. Shipping Bd. Emergency Fleet Corp., 1922-27; counsel Office U.S. Alien Property Custodian, spl. asst. to atty. gen. U.S., 1927; chief atty. U.S. Dept. Justice, 1927-34, U.S. Dept. Treasury, 1934- 35; asst. gen. counsel Dept. Treasury, 1935-38; adminstr. CAA, 1938- 40; pvt. practice law, 1940—. supr. constrn. Washington Nat. Airport; apptd. mem. NACA, 1938. Mem. James Madison Meml. Commn., 1960—; chmn. exec. com., 1961. Served with 301st Engrs., 76th Div., U.S. Army, 1918- 19. Mem. Am., D.C. bar assns., Phi Gamma Delta. Mason. Pioneer survey airplane flights for comml. passenger service across Atlantic, South Pacific. Home: 1371 Royal Palm Way Boca Raton FL 33432 Office: Shoreham Bldg 15th and H Sts NW Washington DC 20005

HESTER, E. ELIZABETH, educator; b. Cookeville, Tenn., Dec. 6, 1918; d. John S. and Ellen (Dunn) Hester; B.S., Memphis State U., 1939; M.S., Cornell U., 1947, Ph.D., 1952. Pub. sch. tchr., Memphis, 1939-42; instr., then asst. prof. food and nutrition N.Y. State Coll. Home Econs., 1947-50; asso. prof. food and nutrition Pa. State U., 1952-59; mem. faculty Cornell U., 1959- -, prof. food and nutrition, 1963—, chmn. dept., 1966—. Served to lt. (j.g.) USNR, 1943-45. Fellow A.A.A.S; mem. Am. Assn. Cereal Chemists, Inst. Food Tech., Am. Home Econs. Assn., Sigma Xi (chpt. pres. 1968-69), Phi Kappa Phi, Omicron Nu, Iota Sigma Pi, Sigma Delta Epsilon. Contbr. profl. jours. Home: 201 Taryton Dr Ithaca NY 14850

HESTER, JAMES DAVID, clergyman; b. Paducah, Ky., Mar. 18, 1931; s. Sam Terrell and Linda (Phillips) H.; B.A. cum laude, Bethel Coll., McKenzie, Tenn., 1953; B.D., Memphis Theol. Sem., 1957; M.A., Memphis State U., 1967; m. Barbara Anne Connor, July 6, 1952; children—Linda Dianne, Mark Stephen, Melanie Dawn, Timothy David. Ordained to ministry Cumberland Presbyn. Ch., 1951; pastor Cumberland Presbyn. Ch., Wingo, Ky., 1950-53, Waverly, Tenn., 1953- 58, Colonial Cumberland Presbyn. Ch., Memphis, 1958-70, First Cumberland Presbyn. Ch., Knoxville, Tenn., 1970—. Moderator, Gen. Assembly, Cumberland Presbyn. Ch., 1969. Recipient several local awards for community participation and work Boy Scouts Am. Democrat. Home: 7613 Sabre Dr Knoxville TN 37919 Office: 525 N Broadway Knoxville TN 37917

HESTER, JAMES LYNN, univ. dean; b. Vicksburg, Miss., Aug. 8, 1939; s. James Hosie and Rena (Maners) H.; B.S., Miss. State U., 1961, M.B.A., 1961; Ph.D., U. Ark., 1965; m. Ouida Blackmon, May 15, 1965; 1 dau., Jennifer Paige. Part-time instr. U. Ark., 1961-64; asst. prof. La. State U. at New Orleans, 1964-66; dir., div. bus. and econ. research La. Tech. U., Ruston, 1966-69, prof. mgmt., 1966—, dean Grad. Sch., dir. sponsored programs, 1969—; mgmt. cons. Bd. dirs. Sch. Bus. Adminstrn. Found. Mem. Acad. Mgmt., Nat. Council Research Adminstrs., Ozark Econ. Assn., Beta Gamma Sigma (pres. 1969), Phi Kappa Phi, Alpha Kappa Psi. Episcopalian (vestryman). Home: 315 Neal St Ruston LA 71270

HESTER, JAMES MCNAUGHTON, univ. pres.; b. Chester, Pa., Apr. 19, 1924; s. James Montgomery and Margaret (McNaughton) H.; B.A., Princeton, 1945, LL.D. (honoris causa), 1962; B.A. (Rhodes scholar 1947-50), Oxford (Eng.) U., 1950, D.Phil., 1955; LL.D., Lafayette Coll., 1964, Morehouse Coll., 1967; L.H.D., Hartwick Coll., 1964, Pace Coll., 1971, U. Pitts., 1971; D.C.L., Alfred U. 1965; LL.D., Hofstra U., 1967, Hahnemann Med. Coll., 1967, Fordham U., 1971; m. Janet Rodes, May 23, 1953; children—Janet McN., Margaret, Martha. Civil information officer Fukuoka Military Government Team, Japan, 1946-47; asst. to Am. secretary to Rhodes Trustees, 1950; asst. to pres. Handy Assos., Inc., mgmt. cons., N.Y.C., 1953-54; account supr. Gallup and Robinson, Inc., Princeton, N.J., 1954- 57; provost Bklyn. center L.I. U., 1957-60, v.p., 1958-60; prof. history, exec. dean arts and sci., dean Grad. Sch. Arts and Sci. N.Y.U., 1960-61, pres., 1962—. Chmn., Pres. Nixon's Task Force on Priorities in Higher Edn. Dir. Union Carbide Corp., Irving Trust Co., Charter N.Y. Corp., Lehman Corp. Trustee, Phelps-Stokes Fund, Met. Mus. Art, 1963—, Bklyn. Inst. Arts and Scis., 1960—, Inst. Internat. Edn. Served with USMCR, 1943-46, 51-52. Mem. Pilgrims U.S., Council Fgn. Relations, Japan Soc., Inc. (dir.), Assn. Am. Rhodes Scholars (dir.), Assn. Colls. and Univs. State of N.Y. (pres. 1970-71), Phi Beta Kappa. Clubs: Cosmos (Washington), Century Assn., University, N.Y. University, Prettybrook Tennis. Home: 37 Washington Square West New York City NY 10011 also 25 Cleveland La Princeton NJ 08540 Office: Washington Square South New York City NY 10003

HESTERBERG, GENE ARTHUR, educator; b. Cin., Aug. 30, 1918; s. Bert Julius and Bessie (Zentmeyer) H.; B.S., Purdue U., 1941; M.S., U. Mich., 1947, Ph.D., 1955; m. Margaret Grace Jones, June 8, 1941; children—William Gene, John Hugh. Biologist, Mich. Dept. Conservation, 1947-48; faculty Mich. Technol. U., Houghton, 1948—, now prof., head dept. forestry; cons. forester; mem. Council of Forestry Sch. Execs. Pres. Lake Linden-Hubbell Bd. Edn., 1969-70; mem. Mich. Bd. Registration for Foresters. Served to maj., F.A., AUS, 1941-46. Recipient citation of merit Mich. Acad. Sci., Arts and Letters, 1962. Mem. Soc. Am. Foresters, Am. Forestry Assn., Mich. Acad. Sci., Arts and Letters, Xi Sigma Pi, Alpha Zeta, Sigma Xi Phi, Kappa Phi. Home: 800 Calumet St Lake Linden MI 49945 Office: Mich Technol U Houghton MI 49931

HESTON, CHARLTON, actor; b. Evanston, Ill., Oct. 4, 1923; s. Russell Whitford and Lilla (Charlton) Carter; student Northwestern U., 1941-43; m. Lydia Marie Clarke, Mar. 17, 1944; children—Fraser Clarke, Holly Ann. Actor, with stage appearances in Antony and Cleopatra, 1947, Leaf and Bough, 1948, Design for a Stained Glass Window, 1949, The Tumbler, 1960; also TV performer, appearing in MacBeth, Taming of the Shrew, Of Human Bondage, Jane Eyre, Wuthering Heights, and others, 1949—; motion picture star, 1950—, appearing in Dark City, Greatest Show on Earth, Ruby Gentry, President's Lady, Naked Jungle, The Ten Commandments, The Big Country, Ben Hur, Wreck of the Mary Deare, El Cid, 55 Days at Peking, The Greatest Story Ever Told, Major Dundee, The Agony and the Ecstasy, Khartoum, Will Penny, Planet of the Apes, Pro, Julius Caesar, The Hawaiians, I Am Legend, others. Mem. Nat. Council on the Arts, 1967-71. Trustee, Los Angeles Center Theatre Group, Am. Film Inst., 1971—. Served in USAAF World War II. Recipient Acad. award for best actor in Ben-Hur, 1959. Mem. Screen Actors Guild (pres. 1966- 71). Office: 7750 Sunset Blvd Hollywood CA 90046

HESTON, JOHN EDGAR, oil co. exec.; b. Stillwater, Okla., May 24, 1910; s. John Adrian and Margaret Catherine (Shumate) H.; B.S., Okla. U., 1931; student Advanced Advanced Mgmt. Program, Harvard, 1950; m. Maudie C. Grinnell, Nov. 23, 1937; 1 1 dau., Marguerite (Mrs. John Meaders). Tchr., Westville (Okla.) High Sch., Sch., 1931-33; petroleum engr. Empire Oil & Refining Co., Seminole, Okla., 1933- 34; staff geologist, engr. Henry L. Doherty & Co., N.Y.C., 1934-36; dist. engr. Cities Service Oil Co., Hobbs, N.M., 1936-38, pres., dir., 1963-68, now dir.; petroleum geologist, engr. Cities Service Co., N.Y.C., 1938-41, asst. mgr. oil prodn. and oil pipe line, 1946-50, mgr. oil prodn., 1950-53, pres., chief operating officer, 1968—, also dir., mem. exec. com.; exec. v.p., dir. Cities Service Prodn. Co.; v.p., dir. Cities Service Gas Devel. Co., Can.- Cities Service Co., Bartlesville, Okla., 1953-56; pres., dir. Peruvian Pacific Petroleum Co., N.Y.C., 1953-56, Ark. Pipe Line Corp., Shreveport, Orange State Oil Co., Miami, Fla., 1956—. Asst. dir. prodn. Petroleum Adminstrn. for War, Washington, 1941-45; v.p. Internat. Petroleum Expn. Mem. Am. Assn. Petroleum Geologists, Am. Inst. Mining Metall. and Geol. Engrs., Am. Am. Petroleum Inst. (dir.), Newcomen Soc. Clubs: Shreveport; Bankers, Wall Street. Home: 400 E 56th St , New York City NY 10021 Office: 60 Wall Tower New York City NY 10005

HESTON, JOSEPH CARTER, psychologist, educator; b. Pataskala, O., Jan. 17, 1909; s. Joseph Z. and Luvadelle (Carter) H.; A.B., Muskingum Coll., 1931; M.A., Ohio State U., 1938, Ph.D., 1941; m. Martha Jane Allen, Aug. 25, 1934; children—Joseph Allen, Julie Lou. Tchr. high sch. West Jefferson, O., 1932-39; asst. psychology Ohio State U., 1939-41; prof. psychology DePauw U., 1941-52; guidance dir. Fresno State Coll., 1952-55; prof. psychology Albion (Mich.) Coll., 1955—, chmn. dept., 1961-63, dir. instnl. research and counseling, 1963—; vis. prof. Nat. Def. Act Guidance Inst., Ohio U., 1960-62; vis. prof. U. Ill., U. N.M., U. Neb., N.Y.U., Iliff Sch. Theology, Bay View Summer Coll. Cons. FSA, 1941- 42, Nat. Bd. Edn. Meth. Ch., 1946-52, Ministerial Tng. Bd. Mich. Conf. Meth. Ch., 1961—; mem. guidance com. Mich. Dept. Pub. Instrn., 1959—; vocational cons. Social Security Adminstrn., 1962—. Fulbright grant sr. lectr. psychology, Australian Nat. U. at Canberra, 1965. Diplomate guidance and cons. Am. Bd. Examiners Profl. Psychology. Fellow Am. Psychol. Assn; mem. Am. Personnel and Guidance Assn., Mich. Psychol. Assn., Am. Assn. Univ. Profs., Assn. Instl. Research (charter), Nat. Council Measurement Edn., Sigma Xi, Phi Delta Kappa, Phi Mu Alpha. Club: Alban (Muskingum Coll.). Author: Heston Personal Adjustment Inventory, 1949; How to Take a Test, 1953; Learning About Tests, 1955; Personal Traits Analysis, 1966; Counseling for the Liberal Arts Campus, 1968; About Tests, 1969; also articles. Home: 420 Elizabeth St Albion MI 49224

HESTON, WALTER ENOCH, geneticist; b. Lucas, Ia., Aug. 23, 1909; s. George Lewis and Roseanna Jane (Schnebly) H.; B.S., Ia. State Coll., 1932; M.S., Michigan State Coll., 1934, Ph.D., 1936; LL.D., Michigan State U., 1958; m. Vivian Mable Janney, June 5, 1937; children—David James, Donald Walter, Thomas Janney; m. 2d, Blanche Hyde Radhe, May 9, 1971. Teaching asst. Mich. State Coll., 1932-36; prof. biology, head dept. McMurray Coll., 1936-38; Nat. Cancer Inst. research fellow Jackson Meml. Lab., 1938-40; research fellow Nat. Cancer Inst., 1940-42, geneticist in cancer research, 1942-52, geneticist, head gen. biology sect. 1952-62, chief of laboratory of biology, 1962—; science editor Jour. Nat. Cancer Inst., 1953-55; coop. work AEC metall. lab., Chgo., 1942-46. U.S. ofcl. del. 8th Internat. Genetics Congress, Stockholm, 1948. Trustee Roscoe B. Jackson Meml. Lab., 1949-55. mem. bd. sci. dirs., 1955-69. Recipient Mich. State U. Centennial award, 1955; Alessandro Pascoli prize Perugia U., 1965. Mem. Jackson Lab. Assn. (dir.), Am. Cancer Soc. (panel on etiology 1955-58), NRC (panel mem. 1945-51, sect. chmn. 1946 committee on growth, Am. Genetics Assn. representative, 1954—), A.A.A.S., Am. Inst. Biol. Scis., Am. Assn. Cancer Research, Am. Genetic Assn. (mem. council 1951-70, sec. 1952-55, pres. 1956-58), Soc. for Exptl. Biology and Medicine, Am. Soc. Human Genetics (treas. 1955-57), Soc. Am. Naturalists, Japan Soc. Human Genetics, Società Italiana di Cancerolgia, Am. Soc. for Experiment Pathology, also mem. Sigma Xi. Presbyn. (elder). Contributor: Biology of the Laboratory Mouse, 1941; Monograph on Mammary Tumors in Mice, 1944; Advances in Genetics, 1948. Author articles in biol. jours. Home: 4501 Connecticut Av NW Washington DC 20008 Office: National Cancer Institute NIH Bethesda MD 20014

HESTON, WILLIAM MAY, ednl. adminstr.; b. Toledo, Nov. 2, 1922; s. William May and Helen Marie (Lippstreu) H.; B.Sc. with highest honors in Chemistry, Ohio State U., 1943; M.A., Princeton, 1948, Ph.D. in Chemistry (LeRoy Wiley McKay fellow 1949), 1949; m. Marian Cannon Watt, June 17, 1950; children—Mary, Elizabeth, Katherine, Richard. With E.I. duPont de Nemours & Co., Inc., 1949-59; dir. office research Western Res. U., 1959-63, asso. chemistry, 1959-67, v.p. research, 1963-64, v.p. student services, 1964- 66, vice provost, asso. dean Faculty Arts and Scis., 1966-67; v.p. plans and programs Case Western Res. U., 1967-69, exec. dir. Mental Devel. Center, cons. for spl. programs, 1969; v.p. Hofstra U., 1969—. Dir. Performed Line Products Co., Cleve., 1963-71. Chmn. Regional Com. Comprehensive Mental Health Planning Report, 1964- 66; cons. grad. chemistry research facilities br. NSF, 1965-68, cons. sci. devel. program br., 1968-70; tech. cons. chemistry AID, Govt. India, 1965; mem. program project com. Nat. Inst. Dental Research, NIH, 1964- 68, spl. cons. Dental Research Inst. program, 1968-70, mem. Dental Research Inst. and spl. program adv. com., 1970—; v.p. Cleve. chpt. UNICEF, 1968-69; mem. 12th grade sci. adv. com. Cleve. Bd. Edn., 1967-69; mem. adv. council Natural Sci. Mus., Cleve., 1967-69; mem. health goals com. Cleve. Welfare Fedn., mem. community planning and devel. com., 1965- 69, chmn. mental health planning co., 1966-69; mem. sci. adv. com. Nassau County Police Dept., 1969—. Sec. bd. trustees N.Y. Ocean Sci. Lab., 1969—; trustee Cleve. Center Alcoholism, 1961-64, Mental Health Rehab. and Research, 1963-69, Vocational Guidance and Rehab. Services, 1963-69, Laurel Sch., Cleve., 1967-69. Served with USNR, 1944-46. Fellow A.A.A.S., Am. Inst. Chemists; mem. Am. Chem. Soc., N.Y. Acad. Scis., Phi Beta Kappa, Sigma Xi, Phi Lambda Upsilon, Phi Eta Sigma. Unitarian (trustee 1963-66). Clubs: Cleveland Skating; Chapoquoit Yacht (sec. 1969) (West Falmouth, Mass.); Rowfant (Cleve.). Home: 47 Hilton Av Garden City NY 11530

HETENYI, MIKLOS, educator; b. Debrecen, Hungary, Nov. 5, 1906; s. Gèza and Etel J. (Jakab) H.; engring. diploma U. Tech. scis., Budapest, 1931; Ph.D., U. Mich., 1936; D.Tech. Scis., Budapest, 1965; LL.D., U. Glasgow, 1968; m. Jeanie G. Ritchie, Nov. 27, 1941; two children—Agnes Jeanie (Mrs. John L. Palmer), John Gilchrist. Came to U.S., 1934, naturalized, 1943. Staff mem. Office Danube Bridge Design, Budapest, 1930, 32-34, Hungarian State Rys., 1934; Jeremiah Smith fellow U. Ill., U. Mich., 1934-35; lectr. U. Mich. Grad. Sch., 1936, Horace H. Rackham postdoctorate fellow, 1936-37; research engr. Westinghouse Electric Corp., 1937-46; prof. theoretical and applied mechanics Tech. Inst., Northwestern, 1946-62, Walter P. Murphy prof., 1950-62; prof. engring. mechanics, structural engring. Stanford, Cal., 1962—. Mem. com. artificial limbs NRC, 1946-48; mem. adv. com. Q.M., 1949—; sci. adv. bd. Rock Island Arsenal; U.S. del. Internat. Union Theoretical and Applied Mechanics, 1957—; chmn. U.S. Nat. Com. Theoretical and Applied Mechanics, 1962—. Recipient Hollan prize Hungarian Soc. Engrs. and Architects, 1935. Registered professional engr., Ill. Fellow A.A.A.S., Am. Soc. C.E.; mem. Soc. Exptl. Stress Analysis (pres. 1944-45). A.S.M.E. (exec. com. applied mechanics div. 1952—, div. chmn. 1957), Am. Soc. Engring. Edn., Internat. Assn. Bridge and Structural Engring., Sigma Xi, Phi Kappa Phi, Pi Tau Sigma. Presbyn. Author: Beams on Elastic Foundation, 1946. Contbr. articles to tech. jours. Editor in-chief: Handbook of Experimental Stress Analysis, 1950. Office: Applied Mechanics Dept Stanford U Stanford CA 94305

HETH, DONALD G., ins. co. exec.; b. Park Ridge, Ill., Nov. 9, 1922; s. Donald D. and Harriet (Gerdis) H.; ed. Duke, 1945; m. Molly Christian McNutt, Jan. 16, 1942; children—Donald, Timothy, Mollie, Steven. Spl. agt. Ins. Co. N.Am., 1946-47; v.p. Continental Casualty Co., 1947-61; sr. v.p. INA-Life Ins. Co. N.Am. Phila., 1961—; dir. INA-Life Ins. Co., N.Y., INA-Life Ins. Co. Cal., INA Security Corp. Served with AUS, 1942-46. Mem. Phi Delta Theta. Home: 9 Farm Rd Wayne PA 19087 Office: 1600 Arch St Philadelphia PA 19101

HETHERINGTON, HECTOR ALASTAIR, editor; b. Llanishen, Glamorgan, Eng., Oct. 31, 1919; s. Hector and Alison (Reid) H.; M.A., Corpus Christi Coll., Oxford, 1940; m. Miranda Oliver, June 27, 1957; children—Thomas, Alexander, Lucy, Mary. Editorial staff The Glasgow Herald, 1946-50, The Guardian, London, England, 1950- -, editor, 1956—, director Guardian Newspapers, Ltd., Manchester Guardian and Evening Newspapers, Ltd. Served as maj., Royal Armored Corps, British Army, 1940-46. Clubs: Athenaeum, Nat. Liberal (London). Address: care The Guardian 192 Gray's Inn Rd London WCI England

HETHERINGTON, JAMES ALEXANDER, II, investment banker; b. Bound Brook, N.J., June 2, 1913; s. Arthur Fenton and Gladys (Sherin) H.; grad. Lawrenceville Sch., 1931; B.A., Yale, 1935; m. Mary W. Dallas, Jan. 13, 1961; children—Sherin H. (Mrs. James H. Knowles. Jr.), Fenton H., Dallas H. Asso. broker DeCoppet & Doremus, N.Y.C., 1935-41; partner Goodbody & Co., N.Y.C., 1945-70, asst. mng. partner, 1966-69, chmn. finance com., 1969-70; financial adminstr. Adams and Peck, 1971—. Mem. N.Y. Stock Exchange, 1935-59. Treas. Judson Health Center, 1956-60. Served to comdr. USNR, 1941-45. Mem. Assn. Stock Exchange Firms (past v.p., gov.). Home: PO Box 60 Gladstone NJ 07934 Office: 55 Broad St New York City NY 10004

HETHERINGTON, WILLIAM GREGORY, pub. relations counsel; b. Jersey City, Aug. 19, 1912; s. Bartholomew and Katherine P. (Bracken) H.; grad. Mercersburg (Pa.) Acad., 1930; m. Rosine Madeleine Snyder, Apr. 5, 1951; children—Jeffrey F., Robert W. With Newark News, 1936-62, fgn. corr., North Atlantic, Mediterranean theaters war, 1942-44, Europe, Middle East, 1948-53, UN corr., 1953-58, editorial writer, 1958-62; pub. relations counsel, 1962—; pres. William G. Hetherington & Co.; lectr. U.S. fgn. policy, UN affairs; news chief OWI, Cairo, 1944-46. Bd. dirs. Better Bus. Bur. Met. N.Y., A.R.C.-Essex County chpt., Drug Addiction Rehab. Enterprises, Salvation Army. Trustee Newark Acad. Recipient Columbian award, award for overseas radio reporting Billboard mag., 1948. Mem. UN Corrs. Assn., N.J. Press Assn., Silurians, Advt. Club N.J. (dir.), Essex Troop 102d Cavalry Assn., Greater Newark C. of C. (past dir.). Clubs: The Overseas Press (N.Y.C.); Nat. Press (Washington); Orange Lawn Tennis (past pres., gov.) (South Orange); Essex (Newark); Essex County Country (West Orange); Home: 149 Wyoming Av Maplewood NJ 07040 Office: 744 Broad St Newark NJ 07102

HETHERSTON, JOHN CUMMINGS, univ. adminstr.; b. Boston, Mar. 9, 1925; s. Victor M. and Ruth (Cummings) H.; student Yale, 1943-44; B.S. in Econs., U. Pa., 1946; m. Gene Hattersley, Dec. 20, 1952; children—John Cummings, Gordon B., Victor Montgomery II, Anne. Instr. insurance Wharton Sch., U. of Pennsylvania, 1946-47, asst. sec. Gen. Alumni Soc., 1947-48, asst. sec. univ., 1948-56, sec. of corp., 1956-62, asst. to pres., 1962-63, v.p. coordinated planning, 1963-71, v.p. facilities mgmt. and constrn., 1971—; sec. Asso. U. Pa. Clubs, 1947-48. Mem. adv. com. employee solicitation Phila. United Fund, 1951-56, chmn. com. year-round edn., 1953-54, vice chmn. edn. div., 1967, chmn. community services div., 1969-70, also mem. campaign planning bd.; mem. com. pre-induction edn. Greater Phila. YMCA, 1957—. Mem. Gen. Alumni Bd.; dir. University City Sci. Center, West Philadelphia Corp. Trustee Presbyn. U. Pa. Med. Center, Phila.; bd. dirs. Phila. Girl Scouts. Served as a lt. with USNR, 1946. Mem. Kappa Alpha (treas. Phila), Beta Gamma Sigma. Presbyn. Republican. Home: 250 Gypsy La Wynnewood PA 19096 Office: College Hall Univ of Pa Philadelphia PA 19104

HETKIN, ALFRED HENRY, lawyer; b. Bklyn., Jan. 26, 1907; s. Henry and Celia (Horwitz) H.; B.A., Columbia, 1927, LL.B., 1930; m. Berenice Berke, Feb. 22, 1953; children—Patricia Joan, Wendy Ann. Admitted to N.Y. bar and since practiced in N.Y.C.; with Henry Hetkin, 1930-34; partner Hetkin, Barshay & Tuchman, and predecessor firms, 1934—. Dir. New Yorker mag. Dir. Hebrew Tech. Inst. Mem. Real Estate Tax Rev. Bar Assn. (dir., past pres.), N.Y State Bar Assn., Assn. Bar City N.Y., N.Y. County Lawyers Assn. (past chmn. com. real property law). Home: 875 Fifth Av New York City NY 10021 Office: 9 E 40th St New York City NY 10016

HETLER, LOUIS, educator; b. Berestecsko, Poland, May 1, 1914; s. Morris and Nettie (Krusman) H.; B.F.A., U. Okla., 1946; M.A., Columbia Tchrs. Coll., 1947; Ph.D., U. Denver, 1957; m. Eliese Felsenthal, Apr. 9, 1941; children—Joel Herman, Robert Simon, Susan Betty. Instr. speech L.I. U., 1947, Hunter Coll., 1948-49; instr. speech and theatre State U. Coll. at Brockport, N.Y., 1949—, prof. theatre, chmn. dept., 1967—. Founder, dir. Brockport Summer Arts Festival, 1959-68; mem. Monroe County Cultural Council, 1968—. Served with AUS, 1941-45; PTO. Mem. Theatre Festival Assn. (founder, life mem. bd. dirs.), Monroe County Hist. Soc. (life), Eastern States Speech Assn., Am. Ednl. Theatre Assn., Am. Assn. U. Profs., Faculty Assn. State U. N.Y. State U. N.Y. Theatre Assn. (founder). Home: 29 Caroline Dr Brockport NY 14420

HETRICK, JACOB ADAM WERNER, coll. pres., otolaryngologist; b. Asbury Park, N.J., April 22, 1895; s. Jacob Adam Werner and Linnie S. (Evans) H.; M.D., N.Y. Med. Coll., 1918, D.Sc. (hon.); postgrad. in Vienna, Austria, 1927; m. Lilliam Morgan, Nov. 21, 1918; 1 dau. Lillian Janet. Interne Flower Hosp., N.Y.C., 1918- 20; prof. otolaryngology N.Y. Med. Coll., Flower and Fifth Av. Hosps., 1927—, registrar, 1925-27, asst. dean, 1927-29, asso. dean, 1939-40, dean, 1940—, pres., 1942—. Fellow A.C.S., Acad. of Opthalmology, N.Y. Acad. of Medicine; mem. A.M.A., N.Y. State Homeo. Soc. (pres. 1933-34), Acad. of Path. Sci. (pres. 1928), Harvey Soc., N.Y. Com. on Internships and Residencies, Nat. Inst. Social Scis., Acad. Polit. Sci., Alpha Sigma, Alpha Kappa Kappa, Alpha Omega Alpha. Mason. Club: Quill. Contbr. articles to med. jours. Home: Brielle NJ 08730

HETSKO, CYRIL FRANCIS, lawyer, corp. exec.; b. Scranton. Pa., Oct. 4, 1911; s. John Andrew and Anna (Lesco) H.; A.B., Dickinson Coll., 1933; J.D., U. Mich., 1936; m. Josephine G. Stein, Nov. 12, 1932; children—Jacqueline V. (Mrs. Charles F. Kaufer), Cyril M., Cynthia F. (Mrs. William J. Rainey). Jeffery F. Admitted to Pa. bar, 1937, N.Y. bar, 1938; U.S. Supreme Ct. bar, 1965; asso. firm Chadbourne, Parke, Whiteside & Wolff, 1936-55, partner, 1955-64; gen. counsel Am. Tobacco Co., (name changed Am. Brands, Inc.), 1964—, v.p., 1965-69, sr. v.p., 1969—, also dir.; dir. Acme Visible Records, Inc., Am. Tobacco Internat. Corp., James B. Beam Distilling Co., Duffy-Mott Co., Inc., Gallaher Ltd. (Gt. Britain), Master Lock Co., Swingline, Inc., Andrew Jergens Co. Mem. nat. devel. com. Dickinson Coll. Mem. Am., N.Y. State bar assns., Internat. C. of C., Assn. Bar City N.Y., U.S. Trademark Assn. (dir., pres. 1965-66, hon. bd. chmn. 1966-67), Order of Coif, Phi Beta Kappa, Phi Delta Theta, Delta Theta Phi. Rep. Presbyn. Clubs: Pinnacle (N.Y.C.); Nat. Lawyers (Washington); Ridgewood (N.J.) Country. Home: 714 Waverly Rd Ridgewood NJ 07450 Office: 245 Park Av New York City NY 10017

HETTICH, ARTHUR MATTHIAS editor; b. Bklyn., May 5, 1925; s. Arthur M. and Elsa (Shaeffer) H.; B.A., Amherst Coll., 1949; M.A., Columbia, 1950; m. Mary Elizabeth Fitz Randolph, Dec. 27, 1952; children—Michael, John, Elizabeth. Editor, Thos. Ashwell & Co., N.Y.C., 1950-52; asst. promotion dir. McCall Corp., N.Y.C., 1952-54; v.p., promotion dir. Family Circle, N.Y.C., 1954-66, v.p., editor, 1968—; v.p., dir. pub. relations Cowles Communications, N.Y.C., 1966-67. Served with USNR, 1943-46. Clubs: New York Athletic; Shore Acres Yacht (Mamaroneck). Editor, pub. The New York Suburbs, 1960. Home: 606 Shore Acres Dr Mamaroneck NY 10543 Office: 488 Madison Av New York City NY 10022

HETTINGER, ALBERT JOHN Jr., investment banker, economist; b. Strang, Neb., Sept. 16, 1891; s. Albert John and Florence Lillian (Walker) H.; A.B., Stanford, 1916, A.M., 1917; Ph.D., Harvard, 1920; m. Catherine Zirpoli, Nov. 11, 1929; 1 son, Albert John III. Asst. prof. Grad. Sch. Bus. Adminstrn., Harvard, 1920-26; pres. Investment Research Corp., Detroit, 1926-35; exec. sec. Durable Goods Industries Com., Washington, 1934-35; v.p., dir., mem. exec. com. Gen. Am. Investors Co., Inc., N.Y.C., 1935-43; partner Lazard Freres & Co., N.Y.C., 1944—; chmn. Providentia Ltd., Instoria, Inc.; dir. Gen. Reassurance Corp., Reins. Co. Australasia (Sydney), Gen. Reins. corp., Lincoln Nat. Life Ins. Co., Piedmont Adv. Corp., Gen. Reins. Life Corp., Harcourt Brace Jovanovich, Inc., Nat. Fire Ins. Co., Whitehall of Canada, Ltd., Olivetti Corp. Am. (mem. exec. com.), Lincoln Nat. Corp., Owens-Ill., Inc., Transcontinental Ins. Co., North Star Reins. Co., Moody's Capital Fund, Inc., Moody's Fund, Inc.; adviser trust investment com. Chem. Bank. Trustee Salzburg Seminar in Am. Studies, Brooks Sch., Nat. Bur. Econ. Research; ind. counsellor U.S. Steel and Carnegie Pension Fund. Mem. Phi Beta Kappa, Delta Kappa Epsilon. Presbyn. Clubs: Downtown Assn. (N.Y.C.); Cosmos (Washington); Quaker Hill Country (Pawling, N.Y.). Home: 40 Fifth Av New York City NY 10011 also Chapel Farm Pawling NY 12564 Office: 44 Wall St New York City NY 10005

HETTINGER, EDWARD C., bishop; b. Lancaster, O., Oct. 14, 1902; s. Edward and Clara (O'Brien) H.; ed. Holy Cross Coll. (Worcester, Mass.), St. Vincent's Sem. (Latrobe, Pa.). Ordained priest Roman Cath. Ch., 1928; Domestic Prelate, 1938; consecrated Titular Bishop of Teos, 1941, Auxiliary Bishop of Columbus, 1946. Chaplain St. Vincent's Orphange, Columbus, June-Sept. 1928; adminstr. St. Mary's Ch., Delaware, O., Sept.-Nov. 1928; chaplain St. Vincent's Orphanage, Nov. 1928-Mar. 1945; pastor Sacred Heart Ch. since 1945; diocesan consultor, Jan. 1946-Jan. 1949 and since Jan. 1950. Address: Sacred Heart Church 893 Hamlet St Columbus OH 43201

HETTLEMAN, PHILLIP, investment banker; b. Balt., June 17, 1899; s. Jacob H. and Lida (Hettleman) H.; B.C.S., U. N.C., 1921; M.S., Columbia, 1923; m. Evelyn Harris, June 26, 1926 (div.); m. 2d, Elizabeth Stern, Mar. 1933 (div.); m. 3d, Ruth McGregor Rea, Nov. 16, 1946; children—Thomas Philip, Nancy Elizabeth, Linda Ann, Phillip, Jane. Successively statistician, bond salesman, sales mgr. Ames, Emerich & Co., N.Y.C., 1922-28; mgr. bond dept. D.H. Silberberg & Co., 1928-32, gen. partner, 1933-37; sr. partner Hettleman & Co., mems. N.Y. Stock Exchange, 1937-53; propr. Hettleman & Co., N.Y.C., 1954—. Joint chmn. Wall St. div. Fedn. Jewish Philanthropies, 1948; mem. com. Wall St. div. Greater N.Y. area, Boy Scouts Am., 1947; chmn. student aid alumni fund Columbia Grad. Sch. Bus. 1956-58, chmn. alumni bldg. fund, 1964—. Trustee Rudolf Steiner Sch., N.Y.C., N.C. Soc. Served with SATC, 1918. Mem. Alumni Assn. Grad. Sch. Bus. Columbia (pres.), Alumni Fedn. Columbia U. Inc. (dir.), Nat. Assn. Security Dealers (vice chmn. dist. bus. conduct com., nat. gov.), U. N.C. Alumni Assn. (pres. N.Y. soc., dir. gen.). Clubs: Southampton (N.Y.) Golf; Harmonie, N.Y. Stock Exchange Luncheon, Bankers (N.Y.C.); Westhampton (L.I.) Yacht Squadron; Westhampton Country (L.I.); Turf and Field (N.Y.). Home: 1085 Park Av New York City NY 10028 Office: 61 Broadway New York City NY 10006

HETTRICK, JOHN LORD, banker; b. Lynchburg, Va., Apr. 24, 1934; s. Ames Bartlett and Frances (O'Brian) H.; B.A., Lehigh U., 1956; m. Marica Parkinson Allard, June 22, 1954; children—John Lord, James Parkinson. With Marine Midland Trust Co. Western N.Y. (changed name to Marine Midland Bank-Western 1970), Buffalo, 1957—, sr. v.p. comml. banking depts., 1968- 69, exec. v.p., 1969-70, pres., 1970—; dir. C.I.C. Leasing Corp. Pres. Jr. Achievement Niagara Frontier, 1967, chmn. bd., 1969; active Buffalo United Fund, 1962-65; exec. com. Nat. Jr. Achievement; met. chmn. Nat. Alliance Businessmen. Bd. dirs. Neighborhood House, Home of Good Shepherd, Children's Hosp., Buffalo Fine Arts Acad.; trustee U. Buffalo Found.; exec. bd. Nat. Conf. Christians and Jews; co-chmn. Buffalo area Nat. Jewish Hosp. at Denver; mem. Greater Buffalo Devel. Found. Served to capt. AUS. Named Businessman of Yr. Alumni Sch. Mgmt. State U. N.Y. at Buffalo, 1970. Mem. Greater Buffalo C. of C., Assn. Res. City Bankers (investment com.). Episcopalian (vestry 1965—). Clubs: Saturn, Tennis and Squash, Buffalo (Buffalo). Home: 53 Tudor Pl Buffalo NY 14222 Office: 241 Main St Buffalo NY 14203

HETZEL, FREDERICK ARMSTRONG, publisher, editor; b. Pitts., Sept. 6, 1930; s. Louis and Jean Bowman (Armstrong) H.; B.A., Washington and Jefferson Coll., 1952; M.A., U. Va., 1957; m. Nancy Miller, Dec. 14, 1957; children—Jean Armstrong, Jennifer Elizabeth, Frederick Armstrong, Emily Miller. Asso. editor Inst. Early Am. History and Culture, Williamsburg, Va., 1957-61; asso. editor U. Pitts. Press, 1961-64, dir., 1964—; sec.; dir. United Pocahontas Coal Co., 1960-68. Mem. adv. council Internat. Poetry Forum, 1966—. Bd. dirs., sec. U. Pitts. Center, 1969—; bd. dirs. Loaves and Fishes Coffee House; trustee Winchester- Thurston Sch., 1969—, mem. exec. com., 1970—. Served to 1st lt. AUS, 1952-54. Korea. Decorated Bronze Star. Mem. Assn. Am. U. Presses, Am. Hist. Assn., Pitts. History and Landmarks Found., Hist. Soc. Western Pa., Pitts. Bibliophiles (vice chmn. 1970—), Junta, Phi Kappa Sigma, Pi Delta Epsilon. Presbyn. (deacon 1969—). Clubs: Pittsburgh Press, University (Pitts.). Home: 1221 Wightman St Pittsburgh PA 15217 Office: 127 N Bellefield Av Pittsburgh PA 15213

HETZEL, FREDERICK JOSEPH, newspaper exec.; b. Staten Island, N.Y., Feb. 27, 1928; s. Frederick J. and Anna (Steers) H.; B.B.A., Pace Coll., 1959; m. Sue M. Casper, Sept. 2, 1950; children—Patricia Ann, Frederick John, Michael. With Dow Jones & Co., Inc., Princeton, N.J., 1953—, asst. treas., 1960-70, treas., 1970—. Sec. Parents Council, Rider Coll., Lawrence, N.J., 1970—. Served with AUS, 1948-50, 50-52. Mem. Tax Execs. Inst., Inc., Nat. Assn. Accountants, Tax Inst. Am., Inst. Newspapers Controllers and Finance Officers. Home: 310 Glenn Av Trenton NJ 08638 Office: PO Box 300 Princeton NJ 08540

HETZEL, RALPH DORN, Jr., economist, educator; b. Corvallis, Ore., Aug. 18, 1912; s. Ralph Dorn and Estelle (Heineman) H.; A.B. Pa. State Coll., 1933; postgrad. U. London, 1935-36; m. Marion Dubois, May 1, 1942; children—Otto Joseph, Ralph Dorn III. Pvt. sec. to Gov. Pinchot of Pa., 1933-35; engaged in study and spl. research, 1936- 37; exec. sec. Nat. Hdqrs., Congress of Indsl. Orgns., 1937-40, unemployment dir., 1938-40, econ. dir., 1940-42; assigned cons. on labor Nat. Selective Service Hdqrs., 1942; man power cons. WPB, 1942-43, dep. vice chmn. for manpower requirements, 1943-45, acting vice chmn., 1945; dir. Office of Labor Requirements, Civilian Prodn. Adminstrn., 1945- 46; asst. to sec. of commerce, U.S. Dept of Commerce, 1946-48, asst. to sec. and dir. Office of Program Planning, 1948-51; asst. adminstr. for operations Econ. Stablzn. Agy., 1941; v.p. Motion Picture Assn. Am., Inc., 1941-62, exec. v. p., 1962-63, 66-71, acting pres., 1963-66; exec. v.p. Motion Picture Export Assn., 1954-63, 66-71, acting pres., 1963-66; pres. Am. Motion Picture Export Co. (Africa), Inc., 1963-70, Internat. Fedn. Film Producers Assn., 1963- 67; prof. art Kent State U., 1971—, dean Coll. Fine and Profl. Arts, 1971—. Mem. adv. council Edward R. Morrow Center Pub. Diplomacy, 1967—; mem. adv. com. to dept. film Mus. Modern Art, 1966—. Trustee Cal. Inst. Arts, 1969—, Pa. State U., 1956—. Served from 1st lt. to maj., AUS, 1942-45. Mem. Phi Kappa Phi, Beta Theta Pi. Club: Century Assn. One-man exhbn. paintings Chase Gallery, N.Y.C., 1964. Home: 35 Cohasset Dr Hudson OH 44236 Office: Office Dean Coll Fine and Profl Arts Kent State U Kent OH 44240

HETZEL, ROGER H., glass co. exec.; b. Corvallis, Ore., Feb. 17, 1915; s. Ralph Dorn and Estelle (Heineman) H.; A.B., Pa. State U., 1935; m. Dorothy R. Macomber, Oct. 4, 1941; children—Darcy, Judith, Sarah. With Armstrong Cork Co., Lancaster, Pa., 1935-64, asst. gen. mgr. packaging materials, gen. sales mgr., 1957-59, v.p., gen. mgr. packaging materials operations, 1960-64; exec. v.p. Anchor Hocking Corp., Lancaster, O., 1964-71, pres., 1971—, also dir., mem. exec. com.; chmn. bd. Moldcraft, Inc., Plastics, Inc. Bd. dirs. Fairfield County Health Planning Com.; bd. govs. Lancaster-Fairfield County Hosp.; adv. bd. Lancaster br. Ohio U. Mem. Glass Container Mfrs. Inst. (past pres. trustee), U.S. Brewers Assn. (asso. dir. 1962-63). Home: Orchard Hill Lancaster OH 43130 Office: Anchor Hocking Glass Corp 109 N Broad St Lancaster OH 43130

HETZEL, THEODORE BRINTON, engring. educator; b. Phila., Sept. 28, 1906; s. Frederic Valerius and Grace (Brinton) H.; B.S., Haverford Coll., 1928; B.S. in Mech. Engring., U. Pa., 1929; student Tech. Hochschule, Munich, Germany, 1931-33; Ph.D., Pa. State U., 1936; m. Rebecca Wills, June 12, 1929; children—Frederic V., Helen (Mrs. Harry Bair), Janet (Mrs. Rolland Henderson), Stefanie (Mrs. Robert Johnston), Henry T., Jonathan K. Designer, Link-Belt Co., Phila., 1930-31; mem. faculty Haverford Coll., 1929-30, 36—, dir. grad. curriculum in social and tech. assistance, 1953-56, sec. faculty, 1965—, prof. engring., 1966—, prof. fine arts, 1970—; cons. in field. Bd. overseers William Penn Charter Sch., 1960; bd. dirs. Emlen Instn., 1956—; bd. dirs. Indian Rights Assn., 1955—, exec. dir., 1969—, gen. sec., 1971—, editor Indian Truth, 1969—; bd. dirs. Council Indian Affairs, 1957—. Mem. Soc. Automotive Engrs. (chmn. Phila. 1945-46), Am. Soc. M.E., Am. Soc. Engring. Edn., Franklin Inst., Soc. Social Responsibility Sci., A.A.A.S., Phi Beta Kappa, Sigma Xi. Author articles, and lectr. on contemporary Am. Indian affairs. Patentee in field. Hon. adoption by N.Y. Seneca Indians. Home: 768 College Av Haverford PA 19041

HEUER, JOHN HARLAND, paper co. exec.; b. Carthage, N.Y., Jan. 24, 1917; s. Harland Robert and Genevieve (Waters) H.; B.S. in Chem. Engring., U. Wash., 1939; D.Adminstrv. Scis., U. Moncton, 1970; m. Catherine M. Foley, Jan. 4, 1946; children—John Harland, Edward Frederick. Trainee, Oxford Paper Co., 1939-41; chemist Diamond Match Co., 1941-42; tech. dir. Newton Falls Paper Co., 1946-48, St. Regis Paper Co., 1948-51; with Great No. Paper Co., Bangor, Me., 1951—, mgr. mfg., 1957-59, v.p. mfg., 1959-62, v.p. operations 1962-68, also dir., mem. exec. com.; pres., chief exec. officer Fraser Cos., Ltd., 1968—, also dir., mem. exec. com.; pres., chief exec. officer Fraser Paper, Ltd., 1968—, also dir., mem. exec. com.; chmn. bd., chmn. exec. com., dir. exec. com., dir. Great So. Land and Paper Co., 1963. Sec., treas. Empire State Paper Research Assos. of State U. N.Y. Coll. Forestry, Syracuse, 1949-51, bd. dirs., 1965-71; chmn. exec. com. U. Me. Summer Inst., 1961-64; chmn. scholarship com. U. Me. Pulp and Paper Found., 1965—. Served to 1st lt., C.E., AUS, 1942-46. Named Man of Year, U. Me., 1969. Fellow T.A.P.P.I. (exec. com. 1959-61); mem. Canadian Pulp and Paper Industry (exec. bd. 1968), N.Y. Paper Trade Golf Assn. Elk, Kiwanian. Clubs: Canadian (N.Y.C.); Winged Foot Golf (Mamaroneck, N.Y.); St. James (Montreal, Que.); Edmundston (N.B.) Golf; Woodlands Country (Ft. Lauderdale, Fla.). Home: 5313 Bayberry Lane Tamarac FL 33313 Office: Fraser Paper Ltd 2 Greenwich Plaza Greenwich CT 06830

HEUMANN, KARL FREDRICH, chemist; b. Chgo., Mar. 3, 1921; s. Karl George and Anna Elise (Heiler) H.; B.S., Ia. State Coll., 1942, M.S., 1943; Ph.D., U. Ill., 1951; m. Doris B. Wilkinson, Mar. 24, 1947; children—David Wilkie, Elise Ann, Erika Jean. Chemist tech. information sect. Minn. Mining & Mfg., St. Paul, 1950-52; dir. chem.-biol. coordination center NRC, 1952-55; dir. research Chem. Abstracts Service, Ohio State U., Columbus, 1955-59; dir. office documentation Nat. Acad. Scis., 1959-66; asst. exec. editor Fedn. Proc. Fedn. Am. Socs. for Exptl. Biology, 1966- 67, exec. editor, 1967—; dir. editorial and information services, 1969—; pres. Am. Documentation Inst., 1959, v.p. Fedn. Internationale de Documentation, 1961-64. Sec. Council Biology Editors, 1969—. Served to lt. (j.g.) USNR, 1944-46. Mem. Am. Chem. Soc. (chmn. div. chem. lit. 1960), A.A.A.S., Spl. Libraries Assn. Home: 6410 Earlham Dr Bethesda MD 20034 Office: 9650 Rockville Pike Bethesda MD 20014

HEUMANN, RALPH LEWIS, utilities exec.; b. Chgo., Mar. 18, 1922; s. Adolf A. and Clara (Kempf) H.; C.P.A., Northwestern U., 1951; m. Mary H. Wagner, July 19, 1947; children—Gail, Joan. With Wilson & Co., 1941-42; cost accountant Am. Paper Goods Co., 1946-50; mgr. accounting Commonwealth Edison Co., Chgo., 1950-68, comptroller, 1968-. Served with AUS, 1942-46. Mem. Ill. Soc. C.P.A.'s. Home: 215 S Can-Dota St Mount Prospect IL 60056 Office: 1 First Nat Plaza PO Box 767 Chicago IL 60690

HEURTEMATTE, ROBERTO MANUEL, bus. exec.; b. Panama City, Panama, May 19, 1908; s. Robert Charles and Elisa Maria (Espinosa) H.; A.B., Yale, 1931; m. Elizabeth Dare Gibson, July 1, 1947; 1 son, Roberto Holbrook. Ambassador from Panama to U.S. Govt., 1951-54; negotiator Remon-Eisenhower Treaty between Panama and U.S., 1955; comptroller general of Panama, 1954-59; ambassador to Orgn. American States, 1951-54; gov. for Panama of IBRD and Internat. Monetary Fund; UN undersec. Commr. for Tech. Assistance, 1959-61; UN undersec., asso. mng. dir. UN Spl. Fund, from 1962, asso. adminstr. for UN devel. programs, until 1968; pres. and gen. mgr. of Panama Ins. Co.; now operator of San José de la Portada Cattle Ranch; pres. Heurtematte & Arias, S.A., and related cos., Isthmian Investment Corp., Pearl Islands Seafood Corp.; treas. Heurtematte & Co.; founder, dir. Cia. Panamea de Aviacion, Cemento Panama, S.A., Abattoir Nacional, S.A., Holeles Inter-americanos (El Panama). Nat. Brewery, Inc. Bd. dirs. Gorgas Meml. Inst. for Tropical Med. Research, Washington, Escuela Agricola Panamericana, Boston, Zamorano, Honduras; bd. regents U. Panama. Mem. Nat. Govt. Commn. for Adminstrv. Reforms. Mem. Savs. and Loan Assn. for Housing (chmn. bd.). Clubs: New York Farmers, Brook, Racquet and Tennis (N.Y.C.); Union (Panama City); Metropolitan (Washington), Panama Golf. Home: Box 6982 Panama City 5 Republic of Panama Office: Box 293 Panama City 1 Republic of Panama

HEUSER, GUSTAVE A., machine co. exec.; b. Louisville, Dec. 23, 1879; s. William Henry and Fredericka (Ackerman) H.; student U. Ky.; m. Anna Margaret Vogt, Jan. 14, 1904; children—Evelyn Vogt, Henry Vogt. With Henry Vogt Machine Co., Inc., Louisville, 1904—, beginning as clk., successively asst. sec., sec.-treas., 1904-37, pres., 1937-57, chmn. bd., 1957—; pres. Nat. Realty Co., 1937—. Pres. Masonic Widows and Orphans Home; past pres. Louisville Safety Council. Mem. N.A.M. (past dir.), Nat. Safety Council (past dir.). Republican. Presbyn. Mason (33). Clubs: Rotary, Pendennis, Audubon Country. Home: 2101 Eastern Pkway Louisville KY 40204 Office: 1002 W Ormsby Av Louisville KY 40210

HEUSON, WILLIAM GEORGES, educator; b. St Louis, Sept. 6, 1921; s. Georges H. and Lee (Miesenbach) H.; B.A., St. Louis U., 1942, M.S., 1947, Ph.D., 1954; m. Jane E. Spiegelhalter, June 30, 1954; 1 dau., Andrea. Instr. finance St. Louis U., 1947-48; mem. faculty U. Miami, 1948—, prof. finance, 1954—; mem. faculty Sch. Banking of South, La. State U., 1961—, Mortgage Banking Sch., NorthWestern U., 1963—, Sch. Mortgage Banking U. Miami, 1969—; cons. to industry, 1952—. Mem. Local Govt. Study Commn., 1970—; treas. Zool. Soc. Fla. Faculty adviser Young Republicans, 1964—. Served to lt. USNR, 1941-46. Mem. Am., So. econs. assns., Am., So. finance assns., Am. Acad. Polit. and Social Scis., Econ. Soc. S. Fla., Soc. Financial Analysts Miami, Order Artus, Alpha Kappa Psi, Omicron Delta Gamma, Beta Gamma Sigma, Lambda Chi Alpha (Order of Merit 1962). Author: Public Finance, 1962; Investing in Mortgages, 1961. Home: 5978 Miller Rd South Miami FL 33155 Office: Box 8094 Coral Gables FL 33124

HEUSSLER, ROBERT WILLIAM, social scientist; b. Buffalo, Aug. 11, 1924; s. Herman K. and Carlotta (Morgan) H.; B.A., Dartmouth, 1948; student Coll. Chinese Studies, Peking, 1948, Woodrow Wilson Sch. Pub. and Internat. Affairs, Princeton, 1950-52; Fulbright scholar St. Antony's Coll., Oxford (Eng.) U., 1959- 61; Ph.D. in Politics, Princeton, 1961; m. Ten Broeck Jackson, Jan. 12, 1957; children—Morgan Ten Broeck, Lowry Elizabeth, Sarah Stuyvesant, Ann Bayard. Aviation exec. Standard Oil Co., Far East, 1948-50; overseas rep. Lowell Thomas, 1952-55; dir. Africa-Asia program U.S. univs. Syracuse U., 1961-62; Ford Found. exec. Latin Am. program, 1962-64; research appointments Ahmadu Bello U., Nigeria, 1965, Univ. Coll., Tanzania, 1968; pres. Trenton (N.J.) State Coll., 1968-70; with Center Internat. Studies, Princeton U., 1970-71; Nat. fellow Hoover Instn. Stanford U., 1971—. Served to 1st lt. USAAF, World War II; ETO. Decorated D.F.C., Air medal (4). Fellow Royal Commonwealth Soc. (London). Author: Yesterday's Rulers: The Making of the British Colonial Service, 1963; The British in Northern Nigeria, 1968; British Tanganyika, 1971. Address: Moscow VT 05662

HEUSTON, DUSTIN HULL, headmaster; b. N.Y.C., Apr. 24, 1932; s. Harold Zell and Patricia (McGushon) H.; A.B., Hamilton Coll., 1954; A.M., Stanford, 1959; Ph.D., N.Y. U., 1968; m. Nancy Moebus, Sept. 12, 1959; children—Kimberley, Kary, Kelley, Heather, Hilary. With Hanover Bank, 1954; mem. faculty Brigham Young U., 1959-64; instr. Vassar Coll., 1964-65; chmn. English dept. Pine Manor Jr. Coll., 1966-69; headmaster Spence Sch., N.Y.C., 1970—. Served with AC, USNR, 1955-58. Home: 1088 Park Av New York City NY 10028

HEWARD, BRIAN, stock broker; b. Brockville, Ont., Can., July 15, 1900; s. Arthur Richard Graves and Sara Efa (Jones) H.; grad. Lower Can. Coll., 1915; M.A., St. John's Coll., Cambridge (Eng.) U., 1921; m. Anna Barbara Lauderdale Logie, Dec. 28, 1925; children—Barbara, Chilion F.G., Efa (Mrs. Donald Greenwood), Faith (Mrs. William Berghuis). Accountant, P.S. Ross & Sons, 1921-22, Oswald & Drinkwater, 1922-25; partner Jones Heward & Co., 1925-64, sr. partner, 1945-64, co. inc., 1965, pres. Jones Heward & Co., Ltd., 1965, chmn. bd., 1966— (all Montreal, Que., Can.); chmn. bd. Consumers Glass Co., Ltd., Montreal, Toronto, Ont., 1960—; pres., dir. MPG Investment Corp., Ltd.; Served as midshipman Royal Canadian Navy, 1918. Home: 11 Anwoth Rd Westmount 217 Quebec Canada Office: 249 St James St Montreal 126 Quebec Canada

HEWATT, WILLIS GILLILAND, educator; b. Gainesville, Tex., July 10, 1904; s. John Walter and Susie Irma (Gilliland) H.; B.S., Tex. Christian U., 1927, M.S., 1929; Ph.D., Stanford, 1934; m. Elizabeth Georgine Harris, Dec. 19, 1931; children—Elizabeth (Mrs. Jay Milner), Joan (Mrs. Johnny Ray Swaim). Mem. faculty Tex. Christian U., 1933—, prof. biology, 1942—, chmn. depts. biology, 1952-69, geology, 1952-64; vis. prof. Woods Hole Marine Biol. Lab., summer 1942, La. State U., 1944-45, U. P.R., 1945-46; marine biology cons. Tex. A. and M. Research Found., 1947-51; research cons. Socony Mobil Oil Co., Inc., 1954-61; marine biology cons. Va. Inst. Marine Sci., 1950—. Bd. dirs. Council Sci. Socs. Ft. Worth- Dallas (chmn. bd. 1966—), Ft. Worth Regional Sci. Fair, 1952-71, Ft. Worth Mus. Sci. and History (pres. bd. dirs. 1969—). Recipient Distinguished Alumnus award Tex. Christian U., 1961; Piper award as prof. of 1968. Mem. A.A.A.S., Ecol. Soc. Am., Nat. Shellfish Soc., Soc. Am. Limnologists and Oceanographers, Am. Soc. Systemmatists, Phi Beta Kappa (founding mem. Delta Chpt. 1971—). Mem. Christian Ch. Author articles to profl. jours. Home: 3813 Glenmont Dr Fort Worth TX 76133

HEWELL, MARION MCJUNKIN, savs. and loan assn. exec.; b. Greenville, S.C., June 10, 1898; s. Dr. John Witherspoon and Annie Almeta (McJunkin) H.; B.A., Furman U., 1918; m. Mary Clara Burdine, Sept. 4, 1923; 1 son, Harold Marion. Prin. Bennettsville (S.C.) High Sch., 1919-1920; asst. cashier Peoples Nat. Bank, Bennettsville, 1920-25; sec. Am. Bldg. & Loan Assn. (now Fidelity Fed. Savs. & Loan Assn.), Greenville, S.C., 1925-44, pres., 1944—, also dir.; dir. Fed. Home Loan Bank of Greensboro, 1946-62; pres. Southeastern Group U.S. Savs. & Loan League, 1951-52. Tchr. John Holmes men's bible class, 1956—; mem. Greenville County Planning Commn., 1963-67; city sch. trustee, 1933-38. Bd. dirs. Greenville YMCA, prs., 1957-58; mem. adv. council trustees Furman U. Recipient Bell Tower award trustees Furman U., 1969. Mem. Greenville County Hist. Soc. (first pres. 1962-64). Methodist (former chmn. ofcl. bd.). Rotarian (pres. 1944-45). Club: Poinsett (Greenville). Contbr. hist. articles to Names in South Carolina. Home: Route 9 Altamount Rd Greenville SC 29609 Office: E Washington St at Spring St Greenville SC

HEWES, HENRY, drama critic; b. Boston, Apr. 9, 1917; s. Henry Fox and Margaret (Warman) H.; B.S., Columbia, 1949; m. Jane Fowle, Aug. 21, 1945; children—Henry Fox, Tucker Fowle, Havelock. Staff writer N.Y. Times, 1949-52; drama editor Saturday Review, 1953-, drama critic, 1954-; lectr. Sarah Lawrence Coll., 1955-56. Columbia, 1956-57. Adapter of play La Belle Aventure (produced as Accounting for Love), London, 1954; dir. Tennessee Williams' Three Players of a Summer Game, Westport, Conn., 1955; (with Siobhan McKenna) Exptl. Hamlet, N.Y.C., 1957. Exec. sec. Bd. Standards and Planning for Living Theatre, 1956-66, Am. Theatre Planning Bd., 1966—; mem. Pulitzer Prize Jury for Drama 1968; chmn. Margo Jones Award Com., 1967—, Joseph Maharam Award Com., 1965—. Served as tech. sgt. USAAF, 1941-45. Mem. Theatre Research Council Am., N.Y. Drama Critics Circle (v.p. 1969-71), Drama Desk (pres. 1967—), ANTA (exec. dir. Greater N.Y. chpt. 1953-58), Internat. Assn. Theatre Critics, The Critics Circle, London. Editor Famous American Plays of the 1940s; The Best Plays of 1961-62; The Best Plays of 1962-63; The Best Plays of 1963-64; adaptor (with Ossia Trilling) My Love is a Rose. Address: 1326 Madison Av New York City NY 10028

HEWES, LAURENCE IPSLEY, Jr., natural resources economist; b. Kingston, R.I., Apr. 17, 1902; s. Laurence Isley and Agnes Bancroft (Danforth) H.; B.Sc., Dartmouth, 1924; Ph.D., George Washington U., 1945; M.P.A., Harvard, 1956; m. Patricia Esther Jackson, Jan. 29, 1932; 1 son, Laurence Ilsley III. Engaged in investment banking, San Francisco, 1925-33; asst. to undersec. agr., 1935; asst. to adminstr. Farm Security Adminstrn., 1935-39, regional dir., San Francisco, 1939-44; West Coast dir. Am. Council Race Relations, San Francisco, 1944-47; land reform adviser Hdqrs. SCAP, Tokyo, Japan, 1947-49; chief land settlement and agrl. economist Bur. Reclamation, Denver, 1950-59; chief forecasts and econs. U.S. Outdoor Recreation Resources Rev. Commn., 1959-62; asst. to adminstr. Office Rural Areas Devel., Dept. Agr., 1962-63; rural devel. adviser AID mission to India, New Delhi, 1963-65; chief natural resources conservation Rural Community Devel. Service, U.S. Dept. Agr., Washington, 1965-68; now v.p. for rural devel. of an overseas planning and devel. firm. Sr. cons. UN Devel. Program with assignment Ethiopia, Panama, India, Ceylon, S. Vietnam, Mexico, 1968—. Mem. Gov. Colo. Com. Resources Devel., 1952, U.S. Inter Agy. Com. Post Def. Planning, 1939-41, Dept. Agr., War Bd. Cal. and Ariz., 1941-43; U.S. rep. Mexican Labor Transp. Negotiations, 1942-43; exec. sec. land and water policy com. Dept. Agr. Bd. dirs. Mile High Housing Assn., Denver, 1952-53, Mem. Soil Conservation Soc. Am., Am. Econs. Assn., A.A.A.S., Artus, Sigma Nu. Unitarian. Clubs: Cosmos (Washington); Harvard (N.Y.). Author: Japanese Land Reform Program, 1950; Japan-Land and Men, 1955; Boxcar in the Sand, 1957. Home: 3001 Veazgy Terrace NW Washington DC 20008

HEWES, LESLIE, geographer; b. nr. Guthrie, Okla., Feb. 25, 1906; s. Willis and Pearl Edna (Gifford) H.; A.B., U. Okla., 1928; Ph.D., U. Cal., 1940; m. Elma Graham Beary, June 14, 1933; children—Carolyn (Toft), Robert Willis. Student asst. and grad. asst. in geography U. Okla., 1926- 29; teaching fellow U. Cal., 1929-32; field asst. in geography (Mexico) autumn, 1931; tchr. geography Western Ky. State Tchrs. Coll., 1928-29 and summers 1928-31; instr. in geography U. Okla., 1932-39, asst. prof., 1939-43, asso. prof. 1943-45; prof. geography U. Neb., Lincoln, 1945—, chmn. dept., 1946-68; Fulbright lectr. U. Vienna, 1958-59. Fellow Okla. Acad. Sci. (chmn. geography sect. 1941); mem. Assn. Am. Geographers (chmn. Gt. Plains div. 1949-50; mem. council 1954-57, 1968-, citation for meritorious contbn. 1965), Internat. Geog. Union, Nat. Council Geography Tchrs., Am. Geog. Soc., Neb. Acad. Sci., Phi Beta Kappa (pres. Okla. 1945, pres. Neb. 1959-60), Sigma Xi (Neb. Pres. 1952-53), Phi Eta Sigma. Presbyn. Contbr. articles on Gt. Plains and hist. geography of interior U.S. to various publs. Home: 3022 S 27th St Lincoln NB 68502 ☆

HEWETT, JOHN BRAND, sch. adminstr.; b. Boston, Nov. 27, 1931; s. Merritt Alfred and Gaynor (Brand) H.; grad. Milton Acad. Boys' Sch., 1949; B.A., Williams Coll., 1953; M.A. L.S., Wesleyan U., 1963; m. Lisa Landon, Apr. 3, 1954; children—John Brand, Sabrina. Tchr., adminstr. Gilman Sch., Balt., 1957-66; headmaster Bordentown (N.J.) Mil. Inst., 1966—. Mem. Burlington Council exec. com. Boy Scouts of Am., 1969—. Chmn. bd. dirs. Greensboro Free Library, 1966—. Served to comdr. USNR, 1953-57. Mem. Boarding Sch. Headmasters' Assn. Middle Atlantic States (exec. bd. 1970-71, v.p. 71-72), Assn. Mil. Colls. and Schs. (exec. bd. 1971-72). Presbyn. (chmn. bd. trustees 1969—). Club: American Alpine (N.Y.C.). Home: 54 Park St Bordentown NJ 08505

HEWINS, KENNETH FITZGERALD, journalist, educator; b. Evansville, Ind., Nov. 16, 1902; s. Dan and Etta (Gardner) H.; B.A., Ind. U., 1925, M.A., 1926; postgrad. U. Miss., 1952; m. Lillian Louise Loge, July 3, 1927 (dec.); children— Marilyn June (Mrs. Leary Leo Wright), Eleanor Joyce (Mrs. Charles F. Robinson). Reporter, Evansville Press, summer 1922; editor-in-chief Ind. U. Daily Student, 1924; city editor Bloomington (Ind.) Star, 1924; asst. editor Ind. U. Alumnus, 1924-26; alumni editor, mgr. Press Bur. U. Ark., 1926-29; asst. prof. to prof., head journalism dept., dir. publicity La. Tech. U., Ruston, 1929-68; cons. in journalistic field, 1968—. Mem. Acacia, Sigma Delta Chi, Sigma Tau Delta. Author: Mississippi Press Laws, 1952. Home: 306 E Arizona Av Ruston LA 71270

HEWINS, RALPH ANTHONY, author; b. Broadway, Worcestershire, Eng., Feb. 16, 1909; s. Harold Preece and Margaret Elizabeth (Britton) H.; M.A., Christ Ch., Oxford (Eng.) U., 1930; m. Margrethe Wahgensteen, July 2, 1966. Copywriter advt. agy. S.H. Benson's Ltd., London, Eng., 1930-35; sports correspondent London Observer, 1935-38; reporter London Daily Mail, 1932-38, correspondent in Scandinavia, Middle E., 1940-47; press attache to Finland, Baltic States, Brit. Fgn. Office, London, 1939; fgn. corr. Christian Sci. Monitor, London, News of the World, Daily Express, Kemsley Newspapers, 1948-55; author, 1949—. Mem. Inst. Inc. Practicioners in Advt. Church of Eng. Clubs: Press (London, England); Achilles, Ski of Great Britian. Author: Count Folke Bernadotte, pub. 1949; Mr. Five Per Cent (C.S. Gulbenkian), 1957; The Richest American (J. Paul Getty), 1960; A Golden Dream: The Miracle of Kuwait, 1963; Quisling- Prophet Without Honor, 1965; The Japanese Miracle Men, 1967. Compiler album, Vey Royal and Holy Island, 1964. Address: Sentral Sykehuset Nordbyhagen Akershus Norway

HEWITT, ALFRED WOLCOTT, banker; b. Grand Rapids, Mich., Jan. 14, 1915; s. A.F. and Mabel (Wolcott) H.; A.B., Calvin Coll., 1939; LL.B., U. Mich., 1941; m. Virginia E. Wyatt, Feb. 2, 1943; children—James R., Stephen W., Roger F., Nancy V. Admitted to Mich. bar, 1941; practice in Grand Rapids, 1941-42, 45-54; with Mich. Nat. Bank, Grand Rapids, 1954-71, sr. v.p., Flint, 1967-71; v.p. finance Rapistan, Inc., Grand Rapids, 1971—; also dir.; dir. McInerney Spring and Wire Co. Pres. Flint Inst. Arts, 1969—, E. Grand Rapids Bd. Edn., 1958-61, Grand Rapids Arts and Museum Commn., 1962-66. Trustee C.S. Mott Children's Health Center, 1969—; bd. dirs. Grand Rapids Found., Flint YMCA, Musical Performing Arts Assn. Served to capt. AUS, 1942-45. Recipient Distinguished Service award Grand Rapids Jr. C. of C., 1950. Mem. Am., Grand Rapids (pres. 1964-65) bar assns., State Bar Mich., Flint Area C. of C. (pres. 1970—). Home: 5447 Provincial Rd Grand Blanc MI 48439 Office: 507 Plymouth St NE Grand Rapids MI 49502

HEWITT, ANDERSON FOWLER, advt. exec.; b. N.Y.C., May 8, 1908; s. Edward Shepard and Mary Elenor (Fowler) H.; Phillips Exeter Acad., 1928; A.B., Princeton U., 1932; m. Mollie Page, July 15, 1938 (div. Mar. 1964); children—Mollie Cary (Mrs. Kari Vitikainen), Hannah Brewster (Mrs. Donald E. Leveille), Emily Page (Mrs. Thomas Wallace Bryant III), Penelope Hall and Victoria Arthur (Mrs. Terry Lynn Swanton) (twins), Constance Durell; m. 2d, Ellen Fales Lomasney, Apr. 28, 1964; stepchildren—David Lomasney, Lynne (Mrs. Wallace Pyle Woodruff), Lauren Lomasney. Creative copywriter McCann-Erickson, 1932-35; copywriter, account exec. J. Stirling Getchell, N.Y.C., 1935-38; account exec. J. Walter Thompson, N.Y.C., San Francisco, Chgo., 1938-48; pres. Hewitt, Ogilvy, Benson & Mather, Inc., 1948-52, chmn. bd., 1952-53; v.p., dir. Kenyon & Eckhardt, Inc., 1953-56, sr. v.p. charge account mgmt., dir., 1956-59, exec. com., 1957-59; sr. v.p., dir. mem. exec. com. Compton Advt., Inc., 1959-64; sr. v.p. Geyer, Morey, Ballard, Inc., 1967—; chmn. bd., mem. exec. com. Teltronic Systems, Inc., 1968-69; affiliated with Piping Rock Assos., real estate; partner Ellen Fales Lamasney, Antiques. Trustee Barnard Coll., 1951-58; bd. dirs. Huntington Hosp., 1950-68. Served as lt. comdr. USNR, 1941-45, exec. officer Patrol Squadron 12 Black Cats, Guadalcanal; asst. naval air officer, Salerno, naval air officer, Anzio. Mem. English Speaking Union (N.Y. bd. dirs.), Newcomen Soc. N. Am. Clubs: Century Assn., Racquet and Tennis (N.Y.C.); Piping Rock. Home: West Shore Rd Oyster Bay NY 11771 Office: 200 Park Av New York City NY 10017

HEWITT, ARTHUR WENTWORTH, clergyman; b. West Berlin, Vt., June 22, 1883; s. Arthur Lee and Florence Elnora (Eddy) H.; grad. Montpelier (Vt.) Sem., 1904; D.D., Middlebury Coll., 1923; Litt. D., Norwich U., 1956; L.H.D., U. Vt., 1968; m. Nina A. Battles, Sept. 18, 1907; 1 dau., Hilda (dec.). Ordained M.E. ministry, 1904; pastor, Glover, Vt., 1904-08, Plainfield, 1908-33, Moretown and South Duxbury, 1933-35, Northfield, 1939-56; pastor Riverton (Vt.) Ch., 1956—. Supt. schs., Glover, 1905-06, Plainfield, 1910-11; lectr., U.S., Can.; Slover lectr. on preaching Southwestern U., 1952; preacher Middlebury Coll., 1927-37; headmaster Montpelier Sem., pres. Vt. Jr. Coll., 1935- 38. Mem. Vt. Ho. of Reps., 1912-17; mem. Vt. State Bd. Edn., 1915-35, chmn., 1923-35; Vt. rep. Nat. Conf. on Vocational Edn., Indpls., 1917, Nat. Conf. on Rural Edn., Washington, 1918. Mem. Gen. Conf. M.E. Ch., 1920, 28, 32, 36; pres. Vt. Council Religious Edn., 1933-36; mem. Fed. Council Chs., 1932-39; rep. Vt. Conf. M.E. Ch., Boston Area Council, 1933-37; mem. U. Senate M.E. Ch., 1936-38. Pres. trustees Montpelier Sem., 1921-36; chaplain Vt. State Grange 6 years. Recipient Quadrennial award honor Nat. Meth. Town and Country Conf., 1959. Mem. Vt. State Tchrs. Assn., Poetry Soc. Vt. (pres. 1959-67). Democrat. Mason (32). Author: Harp of the North, 1916; Bubbles, 1920; Songs of the Sea, 1923; Steeples Among the Hills, 1926; The City of Joy, 1926; Highland Shepherds, 1939; God's Back Pasture, 1941; The Shepherdess, 1943; Jerusalem the Golden, 1944; The Bridge, 1948; The Mountain Troubadour, 1962; The Old Brick Manse, 1966. Contbr. articles to theol. mags. Home: Highland Manse Riverton VT 05668

HEWITT, BARNARD, educator; b. North Tonawanda, N.Y., Dec. 23, 1906; s. Charles Edward and Ruth (Barnard) H.; B.A., Cornell U., 1928, M.A., 1929, Ph.D., 1934; m. Rose Schaff Lancaster, Aug. 2, 1932; 1 dau., Diana (Mrs. Alan F. Neidle). Instr. English, dramatics U. Colo., 1930-31; instr. Mont. State U., Missoula, 1932-35, asst. prof., 1935-36; instr. Bklyn. Coll., 1936- 41, asst. prof., 1941-47; prof. speech and theatre U. Ill., Urbana, 1948- 67, prof., chmn. dept. theatre, 1967—. Guggenheim fellow, 1962-63. Fellow Am. Ednl. Theatre Assn. (pres. 1953, editor Books of Theatre 1959- 61, Sr. award 1962); mem. Am., Brit. socs. for theatre research, ANTA, ANTA, Phi Beta Kappa, Phi Kappa Phi. Unitarian. Author: Art and Craft of Play Production, 1940; (with J.F. Foster and M.S. Wolle) Play Production: Theory and Practice, 1949; Theatre U.S.A., 1959; History of the Theatre from 1800 to the Present, 1970. Editor: Ednl. Theatre Jour., 1949-51. Home: 2205 Brett Dr, Champaign IL 61820

HEWITT, CHRISTIAN B., educator; A.B., Columbia; A.M., Ph.D., Boston U. Prof., chmn. dept. English, Florham-Madison campus Fairleigh Dickinson U. Office: Grad Sch Dept English Fairleigh Dickinson U Rutherford NJ 07070*

HEWITT, DAVID COLEY, banker; b. Griswold, Conn., Dec. 2, 1910; s. Harold Dwight and Blanche (Keen) H.; student Wesleyan U., Middletown, Conn., 1932; m. Elizabeth Lichtwald, June 9, 1945; children—Susan (Mrs. Richard Hodge), William David, Peter Chadwick. With Hartford Nat. Bank & Trust Co. (Conn.), 1933-, pres., 1964-67, chmn., chief exec. officer, 1967-, also dir.; dir. Travelers Ins. Co., Charter Oak Fire Ins. Co., Travelers Indemnity Co., Travelers Life Ins. Co., Phoenix Ins. Co., United Aircraft Corp., Travelers Corp., N. Am. Philips Corp. Treas. Conn. Pub. Expenditure Council. Trustee Hartford Found. for Pub. Giving; bd. dirs. Hartford Hosps., Hartford Legal Aid Soc.; chmn. regional bd. dirs. Nat. Conf. Christians and Jews, Conn. Council Equal Employment Opportunity; trustee Kingswood Sch., W. Hartford, Conn.; corporator Mt. Sinai Hosp., Hartford, St. Francis Hosp. Served to capt. USAAF, 1942-45. Mem. Am. (mem. exec. council), Conn. (pres. 1967- 68) bankers assns., Greater Hartford C. of C. (chmn., dir.), Am. Inst. Banking (past pres. Hartford chpt.). Episcopalian. Home: 80 E Weatogue St Simsbury CT 06070 Office: Hartford Nat Bank & Trust Co 777 Main St Hartford CT 06115

HEWITT, DON S., TV news producer; b. N.Y.C., Dec. 14, 1922; s. Ely S. and Frieda (Pike) H.; student N.Y.U., 1941; m. Frankie Lee Teague, June 8, 1963; children—Jeffrey, Steven, Jill, Lisa. Corr.-spl. assignment War Shipping Adminstrn., World War II; producer 1st Kennedy-Nixon TV debate, 1960; producer-dir. A Conversation with President Kennedy, 1962, A Conversation with President Johnson, 1964; exec. producer CBS Eve. News with Walter Cronkite, 1961-64; producer-dir. CBS News coverage Eisenhower in Europe and India, 1960-61, President Kennedy in Europe, 1962-63, also polit. convs. and inaugurations; CBS News producer Cape Canaveral, 1960-65; exec. producer CBS News, 60 Minutes, 1968-. Home: 510 E 86th St New York City NY 10019

HEWITT, EDWIN, educator, mathematician; b. Everett, Wash., Jan. 20, 1920; s. Irenaeus Prime and Margaret (Guthrie) H.; A.B., Harvard, 1940, M.A., 1941, Ph.D., 1942; m. Carol Blanchard, Mar. 4, 1944 (div. Apr. 1962); children—Margaret, Elizabeth; m. 2d, Pamela Jones Meyer, May 28, 1964. Operations analyst with USAAF, 1943-45; Guggenheim fellow, mem. Inst. Advanced Study, 1945-46, 55-56; asst. prof. math. Bryn Mawr Coll., 1946- 47; lctr. U. Chgo., 1947-48; mem. faculty U. Wash., 1948—, prof. math., 1954—; vis. prof. U. Uppsala (Sweden), 1951-52, Australian Nat. U., Canberra, 1963, 70, Math. Inst. of Acad. Scis., USSR, 1969-70. Mem. div. math. NRC, 1957—, exec. com,, 1960-62, 67-. Mem. Am. Math. Soc. (council 1955-), Math. Assn. Am., Phi Beta Kappa, Sigma Xi. Author: Theory of Functions of a Real Variable, 1961; (with Kenneth A. Ross) Abstract Harmonic Analysis I, 1963, Vol. II, 1970; (with Karl R. Stromberg) Real and Abstract Analysis, 1965; also research papers. Home: 5125 Kenilworth Pl NE Seattle WA 98105

HEWITT, HARLAN DOUGLAS, assn. exec.; b. Locke, N.Y., Nov. 21, 1910; s. O. Dewitt and Bertha (Sellen) H.; A.B., Colgate U., 1934; M.A. in Comparative Lit., Cornell, 1935; m. Kathleen Avent, May 26, 1934; children—Marcella (Mrs. Daniel C. Rauscher), John, Guy (dec.). Tchr., 1935-42; engaged in bus. and pub. relations, Ithaca, N.Y., 1946-51; organizer in N.Y. State for Taft campaign, 1952; with Asso. Industries N.Y. State, 1953-56, Minn. Employers Assn., 1956-58; exec. sec. and treas., Farm and Indsl. Equipment Inst., 1958-. Served with AUS, 1942-46. Decorated Order White Cloud (Republic China). Author articles, bulls. Patentee safety design for automobiles and aux. units for tractors. Home: 1210 Astor St Chicago IL 60610 Office: 410 N Michigan Av Chicago IL 60611

HEWITT, HAROLD GEORGE, ret., coll. dean; b. Milw., Oct. 14, 1901; s. Bert Edwin and Ada (Collins) H.; B.S., U. Wis., 1923, M.S., 1925, Ph.D., 1926; m. Martha C. Alexander, Aug. 18, 1926. Dept. chemistry U. Buffalo, 1926-47, prof. chemistry, 1940-47; prof. chemistry, dean coll. pharmacy U. Conn., 1947-70, emeritus, 1970, also dir. Pharmacy Research Inst. Chmn. program com. 4th Pan-Am. Congress Pharmacy and Biochemistry. Mem. Am. Assn. Colls. Pharmacy (pres. 1956-57, chmn. exec. com. 1958-62), Am. Council on Pharm. Edn., A.A.A.S., Am. Chem. Soc., Am. Assn. U. Profs., Am. Pharm. Assn., Conn. Acad. Arts and Scis., Sigma Xi, Tau Kappa Epsilon, Phi Sigma, Gamma Alpha, Kappa Psi, Rho Chi, Phi Lambda Upsilon. Republican. Contbr. articles jours. and mags. Home: Hanks Hill Rd Storrs CT 06268

HEWITT, HARRY REYNOLDS, ret. judge; b. Hartford, Mich., Apr. 5, 1893; s. George and Nina (Reynolds) H.; A.B., U. Mich., 1915, J.D., 1917; Sorbonne, Paris, 1919; m. Esther Carol Tully, Oct. 10, 1925 (div.). Admitted to Hawaii bar, 1920; law clk. with Peters & Smith, Honolulu, 1920-21; dep. city atty., 1921; dep. atty. gen. of Hawaii, 1922-28, atty. gen., 1928-34; judge 5th Div., 1st Circuit Ct., Honolulu, 1953-63, adminstrv. judge, 1953-54, 58-62; first judge of Land Ct., 1953-63. Enlisted in U.S. Army, 1917, advanced to 1st lt.; regtl. supply officer with A.E.F. Mem. Bar Assn. Hawaii (past pres.), Theta Chi, Phi Alpha Delta. Republican. Club: Pacific. Home: 999 Wilder Av Honolulu HI 96822

HEWITT, HELEN MARGARET, ret. educator; b. Granville, N.Y., May 2, 1900; d. Fred William and Jennie Mae (Powell) Hewitt; B.A., Vassar Coll., 1921; Mus.B. (Juilliard fellow), Eastman Sch. Music, 1925; postgrad. Conservatoire Americain, Americain, Fontainebleau, France, summer 1926, Curtis Inst. Music, 1928-30; postgrad. (Mary Alice Longfellow fellow 1936-37, Boston Alumnae fellow 1937-38) Heidelberg U., 1936-38; pvt. study (Victor Baier fellow fellow in ch. music) Brit. Mus., 1933-34; M. Sacred Music, Union Theol. Sem., 1932; M.A., Columbia U., 1933; Ph.D., Radcliffe Coll., 1938; Litt.D., Smith Coll., Northampton, Mass., 1968. Tchr. math., physics Warwick (N.Y.) High Sch., 1921-22; organist, tchr. organ, theoretical subjects Crane Dept. Music, State Normal Sch., Potsdam, N.Y., 1925-28; organist, choirmaster Market Sq. Presbyn. Ch., Harrisburg, Pa., 1930-31; organist, tchr. history music, organ Fla. State Coll. Women, Tallahassee, 1938-39; instr. Hunter Coll., N.Y.C., 1942; asst. prof. Sch. Music, N.Tex. State State U., Denton, 1942-43, asso. prof., 1944-47, prof., 1948-69. Conducted 1st Conducted 1st organ forum Fla. Music Tchrs. Assn., 1938. Sterling fellow Yale, 1943- 44, John Simon Guggenheim Meml. Found. fellow, Paris, 1947-48; named Minnie Stevens Piper Prof., 1965. Mem. Am. Musicological Soc. (past (past v.p., mem. exec. bd. 1969-71), Am. Assn. U. Women, Am. Assn. U. Profs. U. Profs. (local past pres.), Am. Guild Organists, Phi Beta Kappa, Mu Phi Epsilon. Editor: Harmonice Musices Odhecaton, 2d edit., 1946; Canti B numero numero cinquanta, 1967. Translator: (Herman Keller), The Organ Works of Bach, 1967. Compiler: Doctoral Dissertations in Musicology, 4th edit., 1965. 1965. Mem. editorial bd. Jour. Am. Musicological Soc., 1958-69. Contbr. articles profl. jours. Home: 1903 Whippoorwill Lane Denton TX 76201

HEWITT, JOHN G., banker; b. Phila., Dec. 1, 1918; s. Carroll B. and Helen (Goorley) H.; B.A., Rutgers U., 1946; m. Loretta Giering, Aug. 15, 1948; children—John P., Joanne G., Frank G., Jane L. Exec. v.p. First Nat. Bank, Jersey City, 1949-63; pres. First Merchants Nat. Bank, Asbury Park, N.J., 1963- -, also dir. Bd. dirs. Monmouth County United Fund; bd. dirs., pres. Jersey Shore Med. Center. Mem. N.J. Bankers Assn. (exec. com.). Home: 2 Sydney Av Deal NJ 07723 Office: 601 Mattison Av Asbury Park NJ 07712

HEWITT, KENNETH CHADBOURNE, investment exec.; b. Pitts., Aug. 8, 1912; s. Frank Anson and Electa (Stuck) H.; A.B., Princeton, 1935; M.B.A., Harvard, 1937; m. Mary Seaver, June 21, 1937; 1 son, Frank Seaver. Security analyst Union Trust Co., Pitts., 1937-46; investment officer Mellon Nat. Bank & Trust Co. (merger Union Trust Co. and Mellon Bank, 1946), 1947-49, asst. v.p., 1949-51, v.p., 1951-65, sr. v.p., 1965—. Bd. dirs., Allegheny Gen. Hosp. Served to lt. USNR, 1943-46. Home: 801 Hulton Rd Oakmont PA 15139 Office: Mellon Nat Bank & Trust Co Mellon Sq Pittsburgh PA 15230

HEWITT, LAWRENCE PURSER, editor; b. Columbus, Miss., May 21, 1905; s. William Allen and Olive (Haley) H.; B.A. cum laude, Miss. Coll., 1925; m. Julia Toy Johnson, Nov. 28, 1928; children-Julia Toy (Mrs. Powell Hall), Jacqueline (Mrs. Judson Allen), Olive (Mrs. R. Thomas Hudson). Reporter, Clarion-Ledger, Jackson, Miss., 1926-29, sports editor, 1930-32, city editor, 1933-37, news editor, 1938-40, mng. editor, 1941-58, exec. editor, 1959—; pres. Ch. Bldg. & Savs. Assn., Jackson. Bd. dirs. Miss. Devel. Bd., 1957-60, Miss. Hosp. and Med. Service, Jackson; trustee William Carey Coll., Golden Gate Theol. Sem., Mill Valley, Cal. Served to lt. col. AUS, 1942- 46. Mem. Jackson C. of C. (v.p. 1961), Sigma Delta Chi (pres. Miss. 1956). Baptist (pres. Miss. conv. 1947-48; mem. exec. com. 1948-55). Home: 949 Morningside St Jackson MS 39202 Office: 311 E Pearl St Jackson MS 39205

HEWITT, PHILIP COOPER, educator, geologist; b. Boston, Sept. 28, 1925; s. Morris M. and Jennie (Cooper) H.; A.B., Harvard, 1949; M.S. U. Tenn., 1953; Ph.D., Cornell U., 1958; m. Molly Muriel Weinstein, Sept. 14, 1952; children—Susan Tobie, Martin Alan, David James, Natalie Ann. Mem. faculty Union Coll., Schenectady, 1956-67; prof. geology, chmn. dept. 1960-67; chmn. dept. geology State U. N.Y., Brockport, 1967—, coordinator of Faculty of Sciences, 1968-70; field geologist Vt. Geol. Survey, summers 1957-59; vis. lectr. Syracuse U., summer 1962; vis. asso. prof. Rensselaer Poly. Inst., 1963-64. Mem. Schenectady Water Resources Com., 1960-67; cons. on ground water geology, environmental landfills. Chmn., Commn. for Conservation of Environment, Greece, N.Y., 1971. Served with USAAF, 1943-45; MTO. Fellow Geol. Soc. Am.; mem. Paleontol. Soc. Am., A.A.A.S., Am. Assn. U. Profs., Nat. Assn. Geology Tchrs. (pres. Eastern sect. 1963-64, nat. pres. 1965-66), N.Y. State Geol. Assn. (pres. 1964- 65, permanent sec. 1967—), Sigma Xi (pres. Union Coll. chpt. 1962-64, Brockport club 1968-69). Author: Guidebook to

Field Trips in the Capital District of New York State, 1961-65; also numerous articles. Home: 7 Bridgewood Dr Rochester NY 14612 Office: State U NY Coll Brockport NY 14420

HEWITT, RICHARD MINER, medical editor; b. New London, Conn., Aug. 20, 1892; s. Richard Wheeler and Carie (Miner) H.; A.B., Wesleyan U. (Conn.), 1914; M.A., Princeton U., 1917; M.D., George Washington U., 1924; m. Dr. Edith Lillian Swartwout, Aug. 19, 1925. Teacher English, Sanford Sch., Redding Ridge, Conn., 1914-16; interne, Gorgas Hosp. Canal Zone, 1924-25; asst. editor, Jour. A.M.A., Chgo., 1925-28; asso. editor div. of publs., Mayo Clinic, Rochester, Minn., 1928-33, head of div., 1933-49, sr. cons., 1949-57, mem. emeritus staff, 1957—; instr., medical lit. Mayo Found. Grad. Sch., U. Minn., 1934, asst. prof., 1935-55, asso. prof. 1955-57, emeritus, 1957—; Alfred P. Sloan visiting prof. Menninger Sch. Psychiatry, Topeka, Kan., 1958. Served in U.S. Army, 1917-19, engaged in clin. pathology and writing Med. Dept., Surgeon Gen.'s Office. Fellow Am. Med. Writers Assn. (chmn. ednl. com., 1951-54; distinguished service award, 1943, pres. 1955-56; mem. A.M.A. (asso.), Coffman Memorial Union (life), Alumni Assn. of the Mayo Found. Mem. com. on information, Div. of Med. Scis., Nat. Research Council, 1940-44; mem. sub-com. on information, procurement and assignment service for physicians, dentists and veterinarians, Office Def. Health and Welfare, Fed. Security Agency (later under War Manpower Commn.), 1941-44; expert cons. to Preventive Med. Div., Surgeon General's Office, U.S. Army, 1943-44; Minn. State Med. Assn., Delta Tau Delta, Phi Chi, Phi Beta Kappa, and Phi Beta Kappa Assos., Sigma Xi, Am. Legion. Republican. Baptist. Recipient Alumni Achievement Award. George Washington U., 1944, also from Wesleyan U., (Conn.), 1963. Author: The Physician- Writer's Book, pub. 1957. Joint editor; Collected Papers of the Mayo Clinic and the Mayo Foundation (annual vols.), 1928-57; gen. manuscript editor Nat. Research Council series of 12 Military Surgical Manuals, 6 vols., 1942-43; mem. editorial bd. War Medicine, 1941-42, and its sponsoring com., 1942-44, The Am. Illustrated Med. Dictionary, 22d, 23d edts. Contbr. med. jours. Home: Yacht Basin Apts Clearwater Beach FL 33515 Died June 4 1970

HEWITT, ROBERT RUSSELL, univ. dean; b. Los Angeles, Oct. 28, 1923; s. Claude Nathan and Lillie Christina (Anderson) H.; B.A. in Physics, U. Cal. at Berkeley, 1951, Ph.D., 1956; m. Carol La Verne Heins, Sept. 9, 1951; children—Robin Lee, Catherine Anne, Tammy Lynne. Instr. U. Cal. at Berkeley, 1956-57; asst. prof. U. Cal. at Riverside, 1957-62, asso. prof., 1962-68, prof. physics, 1968—, asso. dean research, 1966-68, dean Grad. Div., 1968—. Cons. Gen. Atomic, San Diego, Union Oil Research, Brea, Cal., Aerospace Research Assos., West Covina, Cal. Served with USNR, 1944-46. A.P. Sloan postdoctoral fellow U. Cal. at Berkeley, 1958-59. Mem. Am. Phys. Soc., Am. Physics Tchrs. Assn., A.A.A.S., Phi Beta Kappa, Sigma Xi. Contbr. articles physics jours. Home: 533 Massachusetts Av Riverside CA 92507

HEWITT, VIVIAN ANN DAVIDSON, (Mrs. John Hamilton Hewitt), librarian; b. New Castle, Pa., Feb. 17, 1925; d. Arthur Robert and Lela Luvada (Mauney) Davidson; A.B., Geneva Coll., 1943; B.S. in Library Sci., Carnegie Library Sch., Carnegie Inst. Tech., 1944; postgrad. U. Pitts., 1947-48; m. John Hamilton Hewitt, Dec. 26, 1949; 1 son, John Hamilton III. Sr. asst. librarian Carnegie Library, Pitts., 1944-49; instr., librarian Sch. Library Sci., Atlanta U., 1949-52; with Readers Reference Service, Crowell-Collier Pub. Co., N.Y.C., 1953-55; librarian Rockefeller Found., N.Y.C., 1955-63; librarian Carnegie Endowment for Internat. Peace, N.Y.C., 1963—; librarian Rockefeller Found., Mexican Agrl. Program, summer 1958. Conducted profl. seminars for Am. Mgmt. Assn., 1968-69, Spl. Libraries Assn., 1969; Spl. Libraries Assn. rep. to Pacem In Terres Convocation, 1965, White House Conf. Internat. Cooperation Year, 1965; Spl. Libraries Assn. non-govtl. observer UN, 1964—. Bd. dirs. Windham Childrens Service and Child Care Center, N.Y. Recipient Outstanding Community Service awards United Fund of N.Y., 1965, 67, 69. Mem. Spl. Libraries Assn. (pres. N.Y. chpt. 1970-71), A.L.A., Jack and Jill of Am., Inc. (Eastern regional dir. 1967-69), Alpha Kappa Alpha. Mem. P.E. Ch. Contbr. chpt. to The Black Librarian in America, 1970. Home: 862 West End Av New York City NY 10025 Office: UN Plaza at 46th St New York City NY 10017

HEWITT, WARREN EDGAR, govt. ofcl.; b. Watertown, N.Y., July 18, 1922; s. William E. and Jane (Rahn) H.; A.B., Ursinus Coll., Collegeville, Pa., 1943; LL.B., M. Internat. Affairs, Columbia, 1950; m. Gertrude M. Graedel, Sept. 4, Sept. 4, 1948; 1 dau., Jacqueline N. Admitted to N.Y. bar, 1951; joined State Dept., 1951, asst. legal adviser, 1961-64, legal officer U.S. Mission, Geneva, Switzerland, 1964-68; asst. legal adviser, counsel internat, law, 1968—. Served with AUS, 1943-46; ETO, 1944-46. Home: 45 Chemin de Valauran Genthod Switzerland Office: US Mission 80 Rue de Lausanne Geneva Switzerland

HEWITT, WILLIAM ALEXANDER, mfg. exec.; b. San Francisco, Aug. 9, 1914; s. Edward Thomas and Jeannette (Brun) H.; A.B., U. Cal., 1937; LL.D., Augustana Coll., 1963, St. Ambrose Coll., 1964, Knox Coll., 1965; m. Patricia Deere Wiman, Jan. 3, 1948; children—Anna, Adrienne, Alexander. With the John Deere Plow Co., San Francisco, 1948-54, v.p., 1950-54; bd. dirs. Deere & Co., Moline, Ill., 1951—, exec. v.p., 1954-55, pres., 1955-64, chmn., chief exec., 1964—; dir. Continental Ill. Nat. Bank & Trust Co. of Chgo., Am. Tel. & Tel., Continental Oil Co.; internat. adv. com. Chase Manhattan Bank; dir. Conill Corp. Bd. dirs. Internat. Exec. Service Corps; mem. Bus. Council; founding mem. Bus. Com. for Arts, Emergency Com. for Am. Trade; an incorporator Nat. Corp. for Housing Partnerships, 1968-70. Trustee St. Katharine's-St. Mark's Sch., Davenport, Ia., Cal. Inst. Tech.; vis. com. Harvard Grad. Sch. Design and the Visual Arts, 1967—; bd. govs. Am. Nat. Red Cross, 1967-70, trustee Carnegie Endowment for Internat. Peace, Nat. Safety Council, Council Americas; bd. dirs. UN Assn.; governing mem. Ill. Council on Econ. Edn.; Smithsonian Nat. Assos. Bd. Served as lt. comdr. USNR, 1942-46. Mem. Advt. Council, Inc., Am. Soc. Agrl. Engrs., Soc. Automotive Engrs., Farm and Indsl. Equipment Inst., Conf. Bd., Internat. C. of C. (trustee U.S. council), Com. for Econ. Devel. (trustee), Pilgrims of U.S., A.I.A. (hon.), Council on Fgn. Relations, Alpha Delta Phi. Clubs: Pacific-Union, Bohemian (San Francisco); Burlingame (Cal.) Country; Chicago. Home: 38th St and Blackhawk Rd Rock Island IL 61201 Office: John Deere Rd Moline IL 61265

HEWITT, WILLIAM CASE, oil co. exec.; b. Bartlesville, Okla., July 19, 1912; s. Harry E. and Myrtle (Case) H.; B.S., Okla. U., 1935; m. Carrol Stobaugh, Feb. 6, 1937; children—Marcia, Michael. Laborer Phillips Petroleum Co., 1935, mgr. butadiene plant Phillips Chem. Co., 1949, mgr. synthetic rubber plant, 1950, supt. operations, 1951-55, asst. mgr., 1955-57, vice chmn. operating com., 1957, chmn. operating com., 1963, v.p. internat., 1964, exec. v.p., 1965, chmn. exec. com., 1968—, also dir. Mem. Nat. Safety Council; mem. Washington County dist. com. Boy Scouts Am. Mem. Phi Delta Theta, Sigma Tau. Presbyn. (pres. trustees 1957). Clubs: Bartlesville Rotary (pres. 1959), Hillcrest Country. Home: 1845 Moonlight Dr Bartlesville OK 74003 Office: Phillips Petroleum Co Bartlesville OK 74003

HEWITT, WILLIAM LANE, educator, physician; b. Hebron, Neb., Nov. 25, 1916; s. William Thomas and Iva Lee (Lane) H.; B.A., U. Cal. at Berkeley, 1938, M.D., 1942. Intern, San Francisco City and County Hosp., 1942-43; resident Evans Meml. Hosp., Mass. Meml. Hosp., 1943-45, mem. staff div. infectious diseases NIH, 1945-48; instr. medicine Boston U. Sch. Medicine, 1948-51; faculty U. Cal. at Los Angeles Med. Sch., 1951—, prof. medicine and infectious diseases, 1958—, chief div., 1953—; acting chief medicine Harbor Hosp., Torrance, Cal., 1965-66. Mem. A.C.P., Western Assn. Physicians, Western Soc. Clin. Investigation, Alpha Omega Alpha. Home: 20109 Big Rock Dr Malibu CA 90265

HEWITT, WILLIAM PAXTON, mining geologist; b. Manila, Philippines, Feb. 9, 1909; s. James Henry and Euphemia Sinclair (Paxton) H.; B.A., Columbia, 1930, B.S., 1931, Mining Engr., 1932, Ph.D., 1943; m. Louise Pettigrew Zwick, June 28, 1936; children—Harry Paxton, Anne Brownlee. With Mexican mining dept. Am. Smelting & Refining Co., 1933-54, Western mining dept., 1954-61; cons. geologist, 1961; dir. Utah Geol. and Mineral. Survey, also prof. econ. geology U. Utah, 1961-; dir. United Park City Mines Co., 1958-63; mem. Utah Map Com., 1961-63, chmn., 1964. Fellow Geol. Soc. Am.; asso. mem. Am. Assn. Petroleum Geologists; mem. Am. Inst. Mining and Metall. Engrs., Soc. Econ. Geologists, Am. Orchid Soc., Utah Geol. Assn. (pres. predecessor Utah Geol. Soc. 1964), Sigma Xi, Tau Beta Pi, Delta Upsilon. Home: 462 9th Av Salt Lake City UT 84112

HEWLETT, FRANK WEST, newspaperman; b. Pocatello, Ida., Dec. 30, 1910; s. Albert J. and Annie (Neaf) H.; student Ida. State U.; Nieman fellow Harvard; m. Virginia Bryant, June 23, 1939; 1 dau., Norma Jean Petty. Reporter, editor newspapers Ida., Cal., Hawaii, Japan; fgn. corr. United Press, 1941, mgr., Manila, 1941, war corr., World War II, covering fall and recapture of P.I., Merrill's Marauders in Burma, Papuan and New Georgia campaigns in So. Pacific; Washington corr. Salt Lake Tribune, Honolulu Star Bulletin, Pacific Daily News, Agana, Guam. Mem. Corregidor-Bataan Meml. Commn., 1958, 62, 66; mem. standing com. corrs. covering U.S. Congress, 1970-71, chmn. com., 1971. Recipient Nat. Headliners award for series of articles on Fall of Bataan, Corregidor, 1942. Mem. Sigma Delta Chi. Roman Catholic. Club: Nat. Press (Washington). Home: 3412 N Thomas St Arlington VA 22207 Office: Nat Press Bldg Washington DC 20004

HEWLETT, GREGORY, editor; b. Interlaken, N.Y., Sept. 18, 1907; s. Benjamin Reed and Calvina (Willers) H.; A.B., Rutgers U., 1929; m. Betty Cole, Aug. 26, 1933; children—Gregory Cole, Susan (Mrs. Piero Resta). With Perth Amboy (N.J.) Eve. News, 1929-31, A.P. in Newark and N.Y.C., 1931- 41; asst. regional dir. Farm Security Adminstrn., 1941-43; div. chief enemy intelligence Bd. Econ. Warfare, also mem. com. operations analysts USAAF, 1943-45; intelligence work in India and China, 1944-45; asso. chief Far East div. Mil. Intelligence Service, 1945; dir. alumni and pub. relations Rutgers U., 1945-46; editor-pub. News-Record S. Orange-Maplewood (N.J.), 1946-68, cons. editor, 1968—; editor-pub. The Dispatch, New Providence-Berkeley Heights (N.J.), 1958-61; pres. Hewlett Pub. Co., 1946—, Hewlett Printing Co., 1949—. Chmn. Eleanor Roosevelt Internat. Workshop Human Relations, 1964-65, N.J. Vols. for McCarthy, 1968; mem. Gov.'s Task Force on Pub. Welfare, 1969-71. Public trustee Rutgers-The State U. N.J., 1960-70; trustee So. Ocean County Hosp. Assn., 1970—. Recipient Americanism award South Mountain lodge B'nai B'rith, 1959, Distinguished Service award Essex County Ednl. Assn., 1959. Mem. N.J. Press Assn. (bd. dirs. 1948-59, pres. 1958-59), Nat. Editorial Assn., U.S. C.G. Aux., Sigma Delta Chi, Delta Upsilon. Home: Loveladies Long Beach Island NJ 08008 Office: 463 Valley St Maplewood NJ 07040

HEWLETT, HORACE WILSON, ednl. adminstr., assn. exec.; b. Derby, Conn., July 27, 1915; s. Horace Barnes and Barbara Atwater (Lewis) H.; B.A., Amherst Coll., 1936; M.A., Yale, 1941; m. Mary Estelle Lazear, June 24, 1939; children—William Tuthill, Elisabeth Bane. Asst. to producer March of Time (cinema), 1936- 37; tchr. Curtis Sch., 1937-39, Hill Sch., 1941-43; asst. dir. pub. relations, univ. editor U. Denver, 1946-47; dir. pub. relations Amherst Coll., 1947-58, sec. coll., 1958—; dir. Western Mass. Broadcasting Council, Inc., 1952—, pres., 1957—; dir. Mass. Exec. Com. Ednl. TV, 1962-71. Chmn., Amherst Bicentennial Com., 1959; trustee Jones Library, Amherst, Mass., 1969—, chmn., 1970—; bd. overseers Williston Acad., 1955-59, pres., 1958-59. Served to lt. (s.g.) USNR, 1943-46. Mem. Amherst Community Assn. (pres. 1958), Am. Coll. Pub. Relations Assn. (sec.-treas. 1959-60, pres. 1963-64), Chi Phi. Mem. Congregational Ch. Clubs: Rotary (pres. 1958); Yale (N.Y.C.). Editor Amherst Alumni News, 1947—, New Eng. Assn. Rev., 1963-71; In Other Words, 1964. Home: Middle St Amherst MA 01002

HEWLETT, RICHARD GREENING, govt. ofcl.; b. Toledo, Feb. 12, 1923; s. Timothy Younglove and Gertrude Josephine (Greening) H.; student Dartmouth, 1941-43, Bowdoin Coll., 1943-44; M.A., U. Chgo., 1948, Ph.D., 1952; m. Marilyn Eloise Nesper, Sept. 6, 1946. Intelligence specialist USAF Hdqrs., Washington, 1951-52; reports analyst AEC, Washington, 1952-57, chief historian, 1957—. Mem. U.S. delegation 2d UN Internat. Conf. Peaceful Uses Atomic Energy, 1958. Served with USAAF, 1943-46. Recipient David D. Lloyd prize, 1970. Mem. Am. Hist. Assn., Orgn. Am. Historians, Soc. History Tech., Am. Nuclear Soc. Episcopalian. Author: The New World, 1939-46, 1962; Atomic Shield, 1947-52, 1969. Home: 7909 Deepwell Dr Bethesda MD 20034 Office: AEC Washington DC 20545

HEWLETT, WILLIAM REDINGTON, engr.; b. Ann Arbor, Mich., May 20, 1913; s. Albion Walter and Louise (Redington) H.; A.B., Stanford, 1934, E.E., 1939; M.S., Mass. Inst. Tech., 1936; LL.D., U. Cal. at Berkeley, 1966; m. Flora Lamson, Aug. 10, 1939; children—Eleanor (Gimon), Walter B., James S., William A., Mary J. Electromed. research, 1936-39; co-founder Hewlett-Packard Co., Palo Alto, 1939, partner, 1939-46, exec. v.p., dir., 1947-64, pres., dir., 1964—, also chief exec. officer, 1969—; dir. Chase Manhattan Bank, Overseas Devel. Corp., Chrysler Corp., FMC Corp.; trustee Rand Corp. Mem. Pres.'s Gen. Adv. Com. on Fgn. Assistance, 1965-68, Pres.'s Sci. Adv. Com., 1966-69; mem. vis. com. Harvard Grad. Sch. Bus.; mem. Inst. Medicine Nat. Acad. Scis., 1971—. Trustee Stanford U., San Francisco Bay Area Council, Carnegie Instn. Washington. Served lt. col. AUS, 1942-45. Fellow I.E.E.E.; mem. Nat. Acad. Engring., Cal. Acad. Sci. (hon. trustee 1969—), Am. Acad. Arts and Scis. Patentee electronic devices. Clubs: Bohemian, Pacific Union (San Francisco). Office: 1501 Page Mill Rd Palo Alto CA 94304

HEWSON, EDGAR WENDELL, educator, meteorologist; b. Amherst, N.S., Can., July 12, 1910; s. Edgar Ellis and Helen (Bell) H.; B.A., Mt. Allison U., 1932; M.A., Dalhousie U., 1933; M.A., U. Toronto, 1935; D.I.C., Imperial Coll. Sci. and Tech., London, 1937; Ph.D., U. London, 1937; m. Julia Elizabeth O'Brien, Aug. 17, 1935; children—David Garnet, Barbara Elizabeth (Mrs. Douglas M. Foley). Came to U.S., 1948, naturalized, 1956. With Meteorol. Service of Can., Toronto, 1938-48; dir. diffusion project Mass. Inst. Tech., Round Hill Field Sta., South Dartmouth, Mass., 1948-53; prof. meteorology U. Mich., Ann Arbor, 1953-68; prof., chmn. dept. atmospheric scis. Ore. State U., 1969—. Cons. to industry, govt. agys. Fellow Royal (Buchan prize 1939), Am. (award 1969) meteorol. socs., Royal Soc. Can.; mem. Am. Geophys. Union, Am. Phys. Soc. Author: (with R.W. Longley) Meteorology, Theoretical and Applied, 1944; also articles. Research in application of meteorology to solution of air pollution problems, research on aeroallergens. Home: 3363 NW Crest Dr Corvallis OR 97330

HEWSON, WALTER NORMAN, British diplomat; b. Surrey, Eng., May 20, 1911; s. Walter and Florence (Dove) H.; student Imperial Coll. Sci. and Tech., 1928-32; B.Sc., London U., 1932; m. Magdalene Jeanette Houlder, June 24, 1939; children—Andrew Walter John, Penelope Jane (Mrs. Arthur Kaiserlian), Anthea Jill (Mrs. Paul McLintic). Research chemist, Morgan Crucible Co., London, 1932-37; insp. chemist War Dept., 1937-39; chem. insp. dept. staff Ministry Supply, 1939-44; with Brit. Ministry Def., 1948-64; dep. dir. U.K. Sci. Mission, Washington, 1964—. Served with Ordnance Corps, Indian Army, 1944-47. Fellow Royal Inst. Chemistry. Clubs: Cosmos, International (Washington). Patentee solid propellants. Home: 4940 Cathedral Av NW Washington DC 20016 Office: 3100 Massachusetts Av NW Washington DC 20008

HEXTER, DAVID BENJAMIN, lawyer, govt. ofcl.; b. N.Y.C., Feb. 24, 1908; s. Joseph Goldsmith and Rachel (Katz) H.; A.B., W.Va. U., 1930; LL.B. magna cum laude, Harvard, 1933; m. Louise Lantz, 1940 (div. 1959); children—Joseph Andrew, Rachel Ann; m. 2d, Sybil Rom Goldberg, Sept. 13, 1959. Admitted to N.Y. bar, 1935; also Supreme Ct. U.S.; law clk. Judge Augustus N. Hand U.S. Ct. Appeals, 1933-34; atty. A.A.A., 1934-35; atty. Securities and Exchange Commn., 1935-39; atty., asso. chief counsel Treasury Dept., 1939-53; asst. gen. counsel, bd. govs. Fed. Res. System, 1953-65, asso. gen. counsel, bd. govs., 1965-67, gen. counsel, bd. govs., 1968-70, asst. to bd. govs., 1970—; asst. gen. counsel Fed. Open Market Com., 1960—. Recipient Sears prize Harvard, 1931. Mem. Phi Beta Kappa, Pi Lambda Phi, Eta Sigma Phi. Club: Harvard (Washington). Editor: Harvard Law Rev., 1931-33. Home: 3900 Watson Pl Washington DC 20016 Office: Fed Res Bldg 20th St and Constitution Av NW Washington DC 20551

HEXTER, JACK H., educator, historian; b. Memphis, May 25, 1910; s. Milton J. and Alma (Marks) H.; B.A., U. Cin., 1931; M.A., Harvard, 1933, Ph.D., 1937; Litt.D., Brown U., 1964; m. Ruth Mullin, Mar. 29, 1942; children—Christopher, Eleanor, Anne, Richard. Tchr., U. Cin., 1936, Harvard, summer 1937, Mass. Inst. Tech., 1938, Queens Coll., 1939- 57; mem. faculty Washington U., St. Louis, 1957-64, prof. history, 1957- 64, chmn. dept., 1957-60; prof. history Yale, 1964—, Charles L. Stillé prof., 1967—; dir. Yale Parliamentary Diary Project, 1965—; asso. seminars Columbia U., 1948—. Served with AUS, 1942-46. Guggenheim fellow, 1942, 47; Social Sci. Research Council grantee, 1947, 71; Yaddo fellow, summer 1949; Fulbright Research fellow, 1950, 59-60; Ford fellow, 1954; fellow Center Advanced Study in Behaviorial Scis., 1966-67. Mem. Am., New Eng. (pres. 1970-71) hist. assns., Econ. History Assn., Econ. History Soc. (Gt. Britain), Renaissance Soc. Am., Conf. Brit. Studies, Am. Acad. Arts and Scis. Author: The Reign of King Pym, 1941; More's Utopia: The Biography of an Idea, 1952; Reappraisals in History, 1961; The History Primer, 1971; Doing History, 1971; The Vision of Politics on the Eve of the Reformation, 1971; also articles; co-author: Western Civilization, 1968. Asso. editor Jour. Brit. Studies, 1961—, Jour. History of Ideas, 1964—; co-editor Utopia, Complete Works of Thomas More, 1965; gen. editor The Traditions of the Western World, 1967. Home: 455 Orange St New Haven CT 06511

HEXTER, ROBERT MAURICE, educator; b. Atlanta, Oct. 15, 1925; s. Leo Solomon and Rachel Belle (Schwartz) H.; B.A., U. Minn., 1948; M.S., Columbia, 1950, Ph.D., 1952; m. Norma Goldberg, Aug. 29, 1948; children—Claudia Sue, Nancy Joy, Daniel Jonathan. Research asst. U. Minn., 1948; teaching asst. Columbia, 1948-50, DuPont fellow, 1950-51, lectr., 1951-52; instr. Cornell U., 1952-54, asst. prof., 1954-57; lectr. U. Pitts., 1964-65; adj. prof. Carnegie Inst. Tech., 1965-67; prof. Carnegie-Mellon U., 1967-69; prof., chmn. dept. chemistry U. Minn., Mpls., 1969—. Cons. in field. Served with AUS, 1944-46; PTO. Sr. fellow Mellon Inst., 1957-69; Guggenheim fellow, 1961-62; Fulbright scholar, 1961-62. Mem. Am. Chem. Soc., Am. Phys. Soc., Sigma Xi, Phi Lambda Upsilon, Phi Epsilon Pi. Contbr. articles to profl. jours. Home: 5117 James Av S Minneapolis MN 55419

HEY, RICHARD NOBLE, educator, counselor; b. Okeene, Okla., Jan. 12, 1919; s. Louis and Gertrude (Scholz) H.; A.B., Berea (Ky.) Coll., 1948; B.D. cum laude, Andover Newton Theol. Sch., Newton Centre, Mass., 1952; Ph.D., Columbia, 1963; m. Miriam Jennings, Aug. 23, 1943; children—Richard Nobel, Philip Colwell, Janet Ellen. Minister edn. Calvary Bapt. Ch., Washington, 1953- 55; asso. family study in psychiatry Sch. Medicine U. Pa., 1955-64; asst. dir. Marriage Council Phila., 1963-64; lectr., counselor Centenary Coll. for Women, Hackettstown, N.J., 1960-63; asso. prof. family study and sociology, asst. dir. Marriage Counseling Tng. Program, U. Minn., 1964-70, prof., chmn. div. family social sci., St. Paul, 1970- -; spl. cons. Air Forces Chaplains in Europe and N.Africa, 1954; tchr. marriage courses Bryn Mawr Coll. Swarthmore and Beaver Colls., Phila. Div. Sch., 1955-64. Mem. tech. adv. com. White House Conf. on Children and Youth, 1970. Bd. dirs. Planned Parenthood Phila.; mem. adv. bd. Single Parents Soc. Served with USAAF, 1941-45. Recipient Osborne award for excellence in teaching Nat. Council on Family Relations, 1969. Fellow Am. Assn. Marriage Counselors, Am. Sociol. Assn.; mem. Nat. Council on Family Relations (pres.). Home: 1882 W Shryer Av Roseville MN 55113 Office: Div Family Social Sci U Minn St Paul MN 55101

HEYBORNE, ROBERT LINFORD, educator; b. McCornick, Utah, Apr. 17, 1923; s. Robert Leigh and Junetta (Nielsen) H.; B.S. in Elec. Engring., Utah State U., 1949, M.S., 1960; Ph.D. in Elec. Engring., Stanford, 1967; m. Denese Theobald, Aug. 21, 1942; children—Linford, Brenda. Chief engr. So. Utah Broadcasting Co., 1949-51, asst. mgr., dir. news, 1953-57; prof. elec. engring. Utah State U., 1957-69; dean U. Pacific Sch. Engring., Stockton, Cal., 1969—; cons. elec. engring. to industry; lectr. NSF Vis. Scientist Program, 1966-67. Mem. San Francisco Bay Area Relations With Industry Com., 1969—. Served with USNR, 1942-46, 51-52. Recipient Prof. of the Year award Utah State U., 1962; named Outstanding Engring. Prof., Sigma Tau Logan, 1967; NSF sci. faculty fellow, 1963-65. Mem. I.E.E.E., Am. Soc. Engring. Edn. (chmn. Rocky Mountain sect. 1969; nat. developing colls. com. 1969—; vice chmn. Pacific S.W. sect. 1970), Am. Geophys. Union, Internat. Sci. Radio Union, Sigma Xi. Kiwanian (lt. gov. Utah-Ida. dist. 1957). Contbr. articles profl. jours. Home: 7523 Park Woods Dr Stockton CA 95207

HEYDEN, FRANCIS J., clergyman, astronomer; b. Buffalo, May 3, 1907; s. Frederick John and Clara Elizabeth (Drescher) H.; A.B., Woodstock Coll., Md., 1930, A.M., 1931, S.T.L., 1938; A.M., Harvard, 1942, Ph.D., 1944. Ordained priest Roman Catholic Ch., 1937, mem. Jesuit Order; chief astronomer Manila Obs., 1931-34, dir. solar optical research, 1972—; tchr. nav. and astronomy, Harvard, 1942-44; assigned to Georgetown Obs., Washington, 1945, dir., 1948-72, emeritus prof. astronomy Georgetown U., 1972—; mem. Nat. Geog. Eclipse Expdn. to Brazil, 1947, China, 1948; sci. adviser USAF Eclipse expdn., 1952, 54, 55, 58, 63. Mem. Washington Acad.

Scis. (chmn. com. encouragement sci. talent). Contbr. articles on astron. subjects to Astrophys. Jour. Address: Manila Observatory care Am Embassy San Francisco CA 96528

HEYDENBURG, NORMAN PAULSON, educator; b. Big Rapids, Mich., June 8, 1908; s. Hiram Jay and Sophia (Paulson) H.; B.A., Olivet Coll., 1930; M.S., State U. Ia., 1931, Ph.D., 1933; m. Mary Katherine Fisher, Aug. 6, 1935; children-Helen Jean (Mrs. Thomas Carmichael), Richard Jay, Janet Louise (Mrs. John Oldham). Nat. Research fellow N.Y.U. 1933-34; Nat. Research fellow U. Wis., 1934-35; staff physicist dept. terrestrial magnetism Carnegie Inst., Washington, 1935-60; research physicist Applied Physics Lab., Silver Spring, Md., 1943-46; prof. physics dept. Fla. State U., Tallahassee, 1960-66, chmn. physics dept., 1967—; sr. research asso. Rice U., 1966-67. Fellow Am. Phys. Soc. Democrat. Presbyn. Contbr. articles profl. jours. Home: 2202 Killarney Way Tallahassee FL 32303

HEYDT, RICHARD GORDON, banker; b. N.Y.C., May 4, 1903; s. Charles Otto and Ellen (Hunter) H.; B.S., Dartmouth, 1925, M.C.S., 1926; m. Anita Mueller, Oct. 18, 1930; children—Don M., Charles Read, Robert G. With Cleve. Trust Co., 1926-44, Bank of Manhattan Co., 1944-47; with 1st Nat. Bank of Toledo, 1947—, pres., 1962-68, chmn., chief exec. officer, 1968—; dir. Seaway Food Town Co., Lamson Bros. Co. Trustee Toledo Hosp.; chmn. resolutions com., bd. govs. A.R.C., 1971. Mem. Toledo Area C. of C. (pres. 1968). Clubs: Toledo, Inverness, Belmont (Toledo). Office: First Nat Bank Madison and Huron Sts Toledo OH 43603

HEYER, GEORGETTE, author; b. London, Eng., Aug. 16, 1902; d. George and Sylvia (Watkins) Heyer; ed. privately; m. G.R. Rougier, Aug. 18, 1925; 1 son, Richard George. Author hist. and detective novels, 1921—, including The Black Moth, 1921, An Infamous Army, 1937, The Spanish Bride, 1940, The Corinthian, 1941, Friday's Child, 1944, Cotillion, 1953, Sylvester, 1957, A Civil Contract, 1961, The Nonesuch, 1962, False Colours, 1964; Frederica, 1965; Black Sheep, 1966; Cousin Kate, 1968; Charity Girl, 1970. Address: care Mrs Owen 78 Narrow St London E14 England

HEYER, MILDRED JOHNSON, ret. librarian; b. Sawyer, N.D., Jan. 2, 1908; d. Perry William and Margaret Elsie (Russell) Johnson; B.A., State Tchrs. Coll., Minot, N.D., 1932; summer student U. N.D., 1927, U. Minn., 1928; M.A. in L.S., U. Denver, 1959; m. James Q. Hall, Sept. 19, 1942 (dec. Mar. 1945); m. 2d, George Heyer, June 21, 1946 (div. 1954); 1 dau., Mary Kathleen. Tchr. pub. schs., N.D., 1925-42, Nev., 1942-57; librarian Rancho High Sch., Las Vegas, 1957-59; sch. library supr. Clark County, Nev., 1960-61; librarian Nev. State Library, Carson City, 1962-70. Chmn. Nev. Sch. Library Devel. Project, 1961-62. Bd. dirs. Clark County Tchrs. Fed. Credit Union, 1950—. Mem. Am., Nev. (pres. 1959-60) library assns., Delta Kappa Gamma. Club: Soroptomist. Home: 205 Corbett St Carson City NV 89701

HEYERDAHL, THOR, anthropologist, author, explorer; b. Larvik, Norway, Oct. 6, 1914; s. Thor and Alison (Lyng) H.; Realartium, Larvik Coll., 1933; postgrad. U. Oslo; Ph.D. (hon.), Oslo, 1961; m. Liv Coucheron Torp, Dec. 24, 1936; children—Thor, Bjorn; m. 2d, Yvonne Dedekam-Simonsen, Mar. 7, 1949; children—Anette, Marian, Elisabeth. Ethnol. collection and research primitive man, his habits, Polynesia and Brit. Columbia, 1937-40; sci. expdns. Pacific Islands to test theory that inhabitants of these islands, partly originated in prehistoric S.A.; to conduct expt., replica of prehistoric Inca balsa-wood raft was fashioned, crew 6 Norwegian scientists, tech. experts, went on-board off Callao, Peru, drifted westward until safely landed on Polynesian Atoll Raroia, Tuamotu Archipelago (direct oversea drift of 4300 miles), 1947; prod. authentic film, Kon-Tiki, 1951; leader, organizer Norwegian archaeol. expedition Galapagos, 1953; research Andes region, 1954; prod. film, Galapagos, 1955; leader, organizer Norwegian archaeol. expdn. Easter Island and East Pacific, 1955-56; field expdns. and research, Bolivia, Peru, Mexico, Chad, Ethiopia, Egypt, 1966-69; Ra I Expdn. with 7 men from 7 nations, 2700 miles by papyrus boat across the Atlantic from Safi, in Morocco to a point 600 miles short of Barbados Island, in the Lesser Antilles, 1969; Ra II Expdn. with 8 men from 8 nations crossing Atlantic from Safi to Barbados (3270 miles), 1970; produced film Papyrusboat Voyages, 1970. Mem., lectr. Internat. Congress Americanists, Cambridge, 1952, Sao Paulo, 1954, San Jose, 1958, Vienna 1960, Barcelona, Madrid, Sevilla, 1964, Mar del Plata, 1966, Internat. Congress Anthropology and Ethnology, Paris, 1960, Moscow, 1964, Internat. Pacific Sci. Congress, Honolulu, 1961, Tokyo, Japan, 1966. Founder, mem. bd. Kon-Tiki Mus. Oslo. Served as lt. Norwegian Army, 1942-45. Awarded Retzius medal Royal Swedish Anthrop. and Geog. Soc., 1950, Vega medal, 1962, Mungo Park medal Royal Scottish Geog. Soc., 1951, U.S. Camera achievement award, 1951; comdr. Order St. Olav (Norway), Comdr. with star; Oscar documentary award Acad. Motion Picture Arts and Scis., 1951; officer Order Al Merito Por Servicios Distinguidos (Peru), 1952; Prix Bonaparte-Wyse, Société de Geographie Paris, 1951; Elish Kane gold Medal Geog. Soc. Phila., 1952, Lomonosov medal Moscow U., 1962, Royal Gold medal Royal Geog. Soc., 1964; grande ufficiale Order Al Merito della Republica Italianan; comdr. Sovereign Order St. John, Knights Malta; comdr. Knights of Malta (U.S. br.), Order of Merit 1st class (Egypt), grand officer Royal Alaouites Order (Morocco). Fellow Am. Anthrop. Assn., N.Y. Acad. Scis., mem. Belgian, Brazilian, Peruvian, Russian, Swedish Geog. Soc. (hon.), Norwegian Acad. Sci., Norwegian Geog. Soc. (hon.). Club: Explorers'. Author: Paa Jakt Efter Paradiset (Oslo), 1938; Kon-Tiki, Am. edit., 1950; American Indians in the Pacific: The Theory Behind the Kon-Tiki Expedition, 1952; Archaeological Evidence of pre-Spanish Visits to the Galapagos Islands, 1956; Aku-Aku, The Secret of Easter Island, Am. edit., 1958; Reports of the Norwegian Archaeological Expedition to Easter Island: Archaeology of Easter Island, Vol. I, 1961, Miscellaneous Papers, Vol. II, 1965; Indianer und Alt-Asiaten im Pazifik, 1966; Sea Routes to Polynesia, Am. edit., 1968; Expedition Ra, Am. edit., 1971; also articles sci. and popular mags. Biography, Seior Kon-Tiki (by Arnold Jacoby) pub. in Am., 1969. Address: Laiguegia Italy

HEYKE, JOHN ERICSON, Jr., corp. exec.; b. New Haven, Sept. 29, 1910; s. John Ericson and Marie C. (Miller) H.; B.S., Yale, 1933; m. Gertrude B. Mack, Dec. 11, 1936; 1 son, John Ericson. Began as cadet engr. Bklyn. Union Gas Co., 1933, now chmn., dir.; dir. Bklyn. Savs. Bank, Mfrs. Hanover Trust Co. Bd. dirs. Bklyn. Inst. Arts and Sci. Served as lt. comdr. USN, 1942-45. Mem. Am. Gas Assn. (past pres.; dir.), Soc. Gas Lighting. Clubs: Brooklyn, Yale. Home: Laurel Lane Locust Valley NY 11560 Office: 195 Montague St Brooklyn NY 11201

HEYL, HENRY LIVINGSTON, surgeon; b. Chgo, Oct. 2, 1906; s. Ernst Oscar and Charlotte (Taylor) H.; A.B., Hamilton Coll., 1928; M.D., Harvard, 1933; m. Katharine Agate Grove, 1944; children—Nicholas, Michael. Intern, Johns Hopkins, Boston Children's hosps., 1933-35; asst. resident surgery and neurosurgery New Haven Hosp., Lahey Clinic, Boston, 1935- 38; resident neurosurgery Children's, Mass. Gen. hosps., Boston, 1938-40; asst. surgery Harvard Med. Sch., 1940; registered cons. neurosurgery Brit. Emergency Med. Service, Midland Area, Birmingham, Eng., 1940-41; neurosurgeon Am. Hosp. in Britain, 1940- 41, Hitchcock Clinic, Hanover, N.H., 1942—; asst. prof. surgery Dartmouth Med. Sch., 1946—, asst. dir. med. scis., 1957- 60, asso. dean, 1960-65, asso. prof. anatomy, 1962—, sr. cons. neurosurgery VA Hosp., White River Junction, Vt., 1942-52. Exec. dir. Hithcock Found., 1953-63. Served as neurosurgeon, capt. AUS, 1942-43. Diplomate Am. Bd. Neurol. Surgery. Mem. Am. Acad. Neurol. Surgery, Soc. Neurol. Surgeons, Assn. Research Nervous and Mental Diseases, Boston Soc. Neurology and Psychiatry, Harvey Cushing Soc., Phi Beta Kappa, Alpha Delta Phi. Conglist. Editor: Jour. Neuro-surgery, 1965—. Contbr. articles to med. jours. Home: Norwich VT 05055 Office: Dartmouth Med Sch Hanover NH 03755

HEYMAN, DAVID JOHN, found. exec.; b. N.Y.C., Sept. 4, 1922; s. David Melville and Ruth (Stein) H.; B.A., Columbia, 1947; m. Geraldine Lederer, July 4, 1945; children—Stephen, Linda, Janet. Investment analyst Marine Midland Trust Co., 1947-49; asst. to sales mgr. Miami Copper Co., 1949-52; owner Whistle Stop, Inc., Mt. Kisco, N.Y., 1952-55; asso. dir. Home Adv. Council, Inc., N.Y.C., 1955-57; dir. N.Y.C. chpt. WAIF-ISS, 1957-58; project adminstr. research facility Rockland State Hosp., Orangeburg, N.Y., 1958-60; dir. operations Neighborhood Conservation Program, N.Y.C., 1960-62; exec. officer N.Y.C. Rent and Rehab. Adminstrn., 1962- 64; engaged in pvt. investment, 1965—. Sec., N.Y. Found., 1955- 67, pres., 1967—; mem. exec. Com. Am. Korean Found., 1960—; v.p. Heyman Family Fund; past pres. Internat. Psychiat. Research Fund; v.p. Internat. Com. Against Mental Illness, 1962—; chmn. bd. Nat. Com. Against Discrimination in Housing; past pres. Career Center for Social Service, N.Y.C., 1965—; v.p. State Communities Aid Assn; mem. N.Y.C. Bd. Correction, 1957—; vice chmn. Nat. Scholarship Service and Fund for Negro Students; pres. Barnard Coll. Parents Assn., Bd. dirs. Tougaloo Coll., Zeta Beta Tau Found., N.Y. U. Med. Center. Served with AUS, 1942-45. Decorated comdr. Order Toussaint-Louberture (Haiti); Mil. Order of Santa Maria Gloriosa (Italy). Mem. Zeta Beta Tau. Club: Columbia University. Home: 169 King St Armonk NY 10504 Office: 4 W 58th St New York City NY 10019

HEYMAN, IRA MICHAEL, educator; b. N.Y.C., May 30, 1930; s. Harold Albert and Judith (Sobel) H.; A.B., Dartmouth, 1951; LL.B., Yale, 1956; m. Therese Helene Thau, Dec. 17, 1950; children—Stephen Thomas, James Nathaniel. Legislative asst. to U.S. Senator Ives, 1950-51; admitted to N.Y. bar, 1956, Cal. bar, 1961; with firm Carter, Ledyard & Milburn, N.Y.C., 1956-57; law clk. to U.S. Circuit Judge Charles Clark, 1957-58, to Supreme Ct. Justice Earl Warren, 1958-59; prof. law U. Cal. at Berkeley, 1959—, also prof. city and regional planning, 1968—. Vis. prof. Yale Law Sch., 1962-63, Stanford Law Sch., 1971-72. Mem. City of Berkeley Human Relations Commn., 1965—, Cal. adv. com. U.S. Commn. Civil Rights, 1961—. Served to 1st lt. USMCR, 1951-53. Mem. Am. Law Inst. (asst. reporter). Democrat. Contbr. profl. jours. Home: 785 San Luis Rd Berkeley CA 94707

HEYMAN, JOSEPH KOHN, banker; b. Atlanta, Oct. 9, 1908; s. Arthur and Minna (Simon) H.; A.B., U. Ga., 1928; M.B.A., Harvard, 1930; m. Bertha Schwabacher, July 16, 1935; children—Leslie (Mrs. David Zinman), Barbara Jo (Mrs. Julian Yudelson), Margaret (Mrs. George M. Cohen). Investment and econ. analyst Tri-Continental Corp., N.Y.C., 1930-42; regional exec. officer W.P.B., Atlanta, 1942-45; owner Joseph K. Heyman Co., Atlanta, 1945-51; v.p. Trust Co. of Ga., Atlanta, 1951-56, sr. v.p., economist, 1959—; v.p. Rich's, Inc., Atlanta, 1957-58; also dir. Pres. Met. Atlanta Community Services, Inc. 1960. Chmn. bd. trustees Atlanta United Appeal, 1961; trustee Rich Found.; trustee, treas. Atlanta Arts Alliance, Inc. Home: 3860 Vermont Rd NE Atlanta GA 30319 Office: Trust Co of Ga 25 Pryor St Atlanta GA 30302

HEYMAN, KEN, photo-journalist; b. N.Y.C., Oct. 6, 1930; s. David M. and Ruth (Stein) H.; B.A., Columbia, 1953; m. Wendy Drew, Sept. 11, 1960; children—Jennifer C., Timothy E., Christopher D., Jason D., Amanda K. Photographer, Life mag., 1956-62; exhibited at Smithsonian Mus., Washington, 1965, Hallmark Gallery, N.Y.C., 1966. Pres. Meridian Photographics. Served with AUS, 1952-54. Author: Willie, 1963; Clyde of Africa, 1963; Pop Art, 1965; Family, 1965; This America, 1966; Where There's A Woman, 1967; The Color of Man, 1968; The Private World of Leonard Bernstein, 1968; City Duck, 1969; They Became What They Beheld, 1970. Address: 64 E 55th St New York City NY 10022

HEYMAN, RALPH EDMOND, lawyer; b. Cin., Mar. 14, 1931; s. Ralph and Florence (Kahn) H.; A.B. magna cum laude (Rufus Choat scholar), Dartmouth, 1953; LL.B. cum laude, Harvard, 1956; LL.M., U. Cin., 1957; m. Mary Lou Levy, Apr. 10, 1957; children—Michael Cary, Cynthia Ann, Ginger Florence. Admitted to Ohio bar, 1956; practice in Cin., 1956-58, Dayton, 1958—; asso. Freider & Wolf, 1956-58; asso. Smith & Schnacke and predecessor firm, 1958-61, partner, 1961—. Lectr. estate planning U. Cin., 1958-61; lectr., participant Southwestern Ohio Tax Inst., 1957—; dir. Towne Properties, Inc., Progressive Industries Corp., Rookwood Constrn. Co., Automated Data Service, Inc., Mega Systems Design, Ltd., Care Centers, Inc. Commr., Bd. Rural Zoning Commn. Montgomery County, 1969—. Mem. Am., Ohio, Dayton bar assns., Phi Beta Kappa. Jewish religion (treas., v.p. temple). Mem. B'nai B'rith. Home; 3659 Wales Dr Dayton OH 45405 Office: Talbott Tower Dayton OH 45402

HEYMANN, PHILIP BENJAMIN, lawyer; b. Pitts., Oct. 30, 1932; s. Sidney Philip and Bessie (Kann) H.; B.A. summa cum laude, Yale, 1954; postgrad. U. Paris, 1954- 55; LL.B. magna cum laude, Harvard, 1960; m. Ann Ross, June 16, 1954; children—Stephen, Sally Jo. Admitted to D.C. bar, 1960; law clk. to Justice Harlan, 1960; asst. to solicitor gen. Dept. Justice, 1961-65; dep. adminstr. Bur. Security and Counsular Affairs, Dept. State, 1965, acting adminstr., 1966-67; dep. asst. sec. state Bur. Internat. Orgns., 1967; exec. asst. to under sec. of state, 1967-69; with Legal Aid Agy. D.C., 1969; prof. law Harvard Law Sch., Cambridge, Mass., 1969—. Served with USAF, 1955-57. Fulbright scholar, 1954-55. Mem. D.C. Bar Assn., Torch Honor Soc., Phi Beta Kappa. Case editor: Harvard Law Rev. 1959-60. Home: 275 Marsh St Belmont MA 02178 Office: Harvard Law School Cambridge MA 02138

HEYMANN, ROBERT L., banker; b. Chgo., May 26, 1921; s. Walter M. and Gladys (Leopold) H.; B.S., U. N.C., 1943; m. Idrienne Levy, Nov. 18, 1946; children—Caryl, Robert L., Thomas, Jeffrey. With First Nat. Bank Chgo., 1946—, v.p. charge B div., 1963—; dir. Phillips-Van Heusen Corp., Abercrombie & Fitch Co., H.C. Prange Co. Trustee Chgo. Med. Sch., bd. dirs. Chgo. Better Bus. Bur. Served with USNR, 1942-46. Home: 2248 Linden Av Highland Park IL 60035 Office: 38 S Dearborn St Chicago IL 60690

HEYMANN, WALTER, physician, educator; b. Brussels, Belgium, Nov. 22, 1901; s. Gustave and Selma (Kaufmann) H.; M.D., U. Kiel (Germany), 1923; m. Marion Oberdorfer, Aug. 28, 1939; 1 son, Peter Walter. Came to U.S., 1933, naturalized, 1939. Privat dozent pediatrics U. Freiburg (Germany) Med. Sch., 1931-33; mem. faculty Sch. Medicine, Case Western Res. U., 1936—, prof. pediatrics, 1962—, dir. Renal Services Pediatrics, 1964—. Charter mem. Kidney Found. Ohio, 1952, chmn. med. adv. bd., 1952-67. Co- founder Cleve. Chamber Music Soc., 1950, pres., 1952, mem. exec. com., 1952—. Fellow A.M.A., Am. Acad. Pediatrics; mem. Am. Pediatric Soc., Soc. Exptl. Biology and Medicine, Am. Soc. Exptl. Pathology, A.A.A.S., Am. Soc. for Pediatric Nephrology (pres. 1968-69), Sigma Xi. Home: 3060 Woodbury Rd Cleveland OH 44120

HEYMANN, WALTER M., banker; b. N.Y. City, Aug. 1, 1892; s. Louis H. and Celia (Shroder) H.; A.B., U. Wis., 1914; m. Gladys Leopold, Nov. 14, 1916. Pres. Liberty Nat. Bank, Chgo., later chmn. bd. Liberty Nat. Bank, Sears-Community State Bank; hon. dir., past vice chmn. 1st Nat. Bank Chgo.; dir. Federated Dept. Stores, Inc., N.Y., The Brunswick Corp., C., R.I.&P. R.R., Music Corp. of Am., Hilton Hotels Corp., Hart Schaffner & Marx. Mem. Beta Gamma Sigma. Clubs: Standard (Chgo.); Lake Shore Country, Mid-Day, U. of Wisconsin (Chgo.); Commercial; Tamarisk Country (Palm Springs); O'Donnell Golf (Palm Springs). Home: 60 Ravinoaks Highland Park IL 60035 Office: 38 S Dearborn St Chicago IL 60603

HEYN, ARNO HARRY ALBERT, educator; b. Breslau, Germany, Oct. 6, 1918 (father U.S. citizen); s. Myron and Margarete M.E.C. (Cierpinski) H.; B.S., U. Mich., 1940, M.S., 1941, Ph.D., 1944; m. Helen A. Pielemeier, Mar. 14, 1942; children—Evan A., Margaret L., Robert E. Exptl. chemist Sun Oil Co., Norwood, Pa., 1944-47; from instr. to prof. chemistry Boston U., 1947—; vis. scientist Brookhaven Nat. Lab., summers 1954-56; acad. guest Eidg. Techn. Hochschule, Zurich, 1965; sci. advisor Boston Dist. of U.S. Food and Drug Adminstrn. Fellow A.A.A.S.; mem. Am. Chem. Soc. (councilor, chmn. Northeastern sect. 1968), Sigma Xi, Phi Lambda Upsilon. Club: Sub Sig Outing (Boston). Contbr. articles profl. jours. Home: 21 Alexander Rd Newton Highlands MA 02161 Office: Boston Univ Boston MA 02215

HEYN, ERNEST V., former editor; b. N.Y.C., Oct. 30, 1904; s. Herbert Alexander and Frieda (Senner) H.; ed. Trinity Sch., Horace Mann Sch.; grad. magna cum laude, Princeton, 1925; postgrad., U. Berlin, Germany; m. Ethel Kenyon, May 1, 1942; children—Susan (Mrs. Willard F. Lochridge III), Dalma. Founder, editor Modern Screen mag., 1931; editor Radio Mirror, 1935, Photoplay, 1938; editor-in-chief Liberty mag., 1942; founder, editor Sport mag.; editor-in-chief True Story mag., editor-in-chief, all Macfadden publs., 1948-51; editor Am. Weekly, 1951-59, editor-in- chief Family Weekly, Suburbia Today, 1959-64; asso. pub., editor-in- chief Popular Sci. Monthly, 1964-70, ret., 1970. Served with AUS, 1942-45. Mem. Sigma Delta Chi. Presbyn. Clubs: Dutch Treat, Shorehaven, Overseas Press; Princeton (N.Y.C.). Author: 100 Years of Popular Science. Editor: The Book of True Stories; Twelve Sport Immortals; My Favorite True Mystery; My Most Inspiring Moment. Home: 240 Hillspoint Av Westport CT 06880

HEYNS, ROGER WILLIAM, univ. ofcl.; b. Grand Rapids, Mich., Jan. 27, 1918; s. Garrett and Rosa (Klooster) H.; student Hope Coll., 1936-37; A.B., Calvin Coll., 1940; M. Clin. Psychology, U. Mich., 1942, Ph.D., 1948, LL.D., 1967; LL.D., U. San Francisco, 1968; m. Esther Gezon, Sept. 20, 1941; children—Michael, John, Dan. Instr. psychology U. Mich., 1947-48, asst. prof., 1948-55, asso. prof., 1955-57, prof., 1957-65, v.p. acad. affairs, until 1965, prof. psychology and edn., 1971—; chancellor U. Cal. at Berkeley, 1965-71. Dir. Norton Simon, Inc. Vice chmn. Nat. Sci. Bd. Trustee Am. Council on Edn. Served from pvt. to capt. USAAF, 1942-46. Recipient outstanding tchr. award U. Mich., 1952, faculty distinguished service award, 1958. Fellow Am. Psychol. Assn.; mem. Phi Beta Kappa, Sigma Xi, Phi Kappa Phi. Office: U Mich Dept Psychology Ann Arbor MI 48104

HEYSE, MARGARET FARR, educator; b. Colorado Springs, Colo., Nov. 4, 1911; d. Rudolph W. and Mary A. (Farr) Heyse; B.A., Colo. Coll., 1933; M.S., U. Rochester (N.Y.), 1934; diploma Mass. Gen. Hosp. Sch. Nursing, Boston, 1937. Instr. nursing U. Colo. Sch. Nursing, Denver, 1937-40; instr. clin.-med. nursing Yale Sch. Nursing, 1940-41; instr., asst. prof. nursing U. Minn. Sch. Nursing, 1941-46; asst., asso. prof. nursing Wayne State U. Coll. Nursing, Detroit, 1946-54; cons. nursing edn., prof. nursing U. Ark. Sch. Nursing, Little Rock, 1954-57; dean, prof. nursing U. N.D. Coll. Nursing, Grand Forks, 1958—; cons. nursing VA Hosp., Fargo, N.D.; mem. rev. com. for constrn. nurse tng. facilities Dept. Health, Edn. and Welfare. Mem. N.D. Health Council, 1962—, N.D. State Health Planning Council, 1967—. Adv. bd. N. Central States Planning Project for Continuing Edn. in Nursing. Mem. Am. Assn. U. Women, Am. Nurses Assn., Nat., N.D. (pres. 1963-67) leagues nursing, Am. Assn. Higher Edn., Am. Assn. Deans Colls. and Schs. Nursing, Mortar Bd. (hon.), Phi Beta Kappa, Delta Kappa Gamma, Sigma Theta Tau. Conglist. Club: Quota (pres. 1968-69) (Grand Forks, N.D.). Home: 2106 2d Av N Grand Forks ND 58201

HEYSINGER, JACK DEAN, univ. dean; b. Clinton, Ia., Sept. 3, 1922; s. Charles C. and Ada M. (Hall) H.; B.A., State U. Ia., 1947, J.D., 1949; LL.M. (Cook fellow), U. Mich., 1957; m. Marilyn J. Nelson, June 11, 1949; children—Sheryl Lynn, Sandra Lee. Instr. U. Kan. Sch. Bus., 1949-52, asst. prof., 1952-57, asst., acting dean, 1953-57, dir. Bus. Placement Bur., 1952-57; dean, prof. Coll. Bus. Adminstrn. and Industry, U. Wichita, 1957-64; dean, prof. Sch. Adminstrn., U. Mo. at Kansas City, 1964-. Mem. bd. dirs. Mid-Continent Nat. Bank. MEm. Kansas City Regional Export Expansion Council. Bd. dirs. Alpha Kappa Psi Found. Edn. and Research; bd. dirs. Mid- Continent council Girl Scouts U.S.A. Served to 1st lt., judge adv. gen. dept., AUS, 1943-45; lt. col. Res. Mem. Am. Midwest (pres. 1959-60) business law assns., Am., Midwest econ. assns., Mo., Ia. bar assns., Kansas City C. of C. (exec. planning bd. of research council), Alpha Kappa Psi, Delta Theta Phi. Author legal, bus. publs. Home: 10206 Cedar St Overland Park KS 66207 Office: Sch of Adminstrn U Mo 51st and Rockhill Rd Kansas City MO 64110

HEYWARD, ALEXANDER SALLEY, Jr., naval officer; b. Columbia, S.C., Mar. 22, 1908; s. Alexander Salley and Lucretia Douglas (Shannon) H.; B.S., U.S. Naval Acad., 1930; grad. Army-Navy Staff Coll., 1944, Naval War Coll., 1949; m. Virginia Nicholson, Aug. 2, 1930; children—Alexandra (Mrs. Henry D. Boykin), Shannon Douglas, McCartney Nicholson. Commd. ensign U.S. Navy, 1930, advanced through grades to vice adm., 1964; comdr. Patrol Squadron 73, 1942-43, Drone Control Squadron 2, 1949-50, seaplan tender U.S.S. Timblaier, 1951- 52, aircraft carrier U.S.S. Lexington, 1955-56, Carrier Div. 5, 1960-61; asst. chief Bur. Naval Personnel, dep. chief naval personnel, 1961-64; chief naval air tng., 1964—. Decorated Legion of Merit with gold star and combat V, numerous area and campaign ribbons. Episcopalian. Home: Quarters A US Naval Air Station Pensacola FL 32508 Office: Chief Naval Air Tng U S Naval Air Sta Pensacola FL 32508

HEYWOOD, ANNE, actress; b. Birmingham, Eng., Dec. 11, 1937; d. Harold James and Edna Elizabeth (Heywood) Pretty; ed. schs. in Eng.; m. Raymond Stross, Feb. 11, 1960; 1 son, Mark. Came to U.S., 1965. Films include The Fox, 1967; The Midas Run, 1968; The Chairman, 1968; Lady of Monza, 1968; Novice, 1969; I Want What I Want, 1969. Recipient Baxendale award for art, 1957; United Critics award Berlin Film Festival 1966. ‡

HEYWOOD, EDWIN WESTON, adjutant gen. Maine; b. Bingham, Me., Mar. 12, 1917; s. Roy Edwin and Barbara (Weston) H.; grad. Stanton Acad., Cornwall, N.Y., 1937, West Point Prep. Sch., Ft. Williams, Me., 1938; m. Virginia Elizabeth Llewellyn, June 7, 1940; children—Dianne Lorraine, Suzanne, Joanne. Enlisted as pvt. C.A., 1934, advanced through grades to lt. col., 1940; joined Me. N.G., aided during reorgn. in recruiting, comdr. 240th AAA Group; asst. adj. gen. Me., 1951-58, acting adjutant gen., 1958, adj. gen. Me., 1958—. Maine chmn. United Services Orgn., 1962-65; mem. Dept. Def. Res. Forces Policy Bd., 1968-71. Decorated Asiatic Pacific ribbon with three stars, Philippine Liberation ribbon. Mem. Adj. Gen. Assn. U.S. (pres. 1963-67), 5th U.S. Infantry Assn. Rotarian. Home: 59 Greenwood Av Winthrop ME 04364 Office: Adjutant General's Dept Camp Keyes Augusta ME 04330

HEYWOOD, GEORGE HENRY, Jr., furniture co. exec.; b. Boston, Oct. 11, 1920; s. George Henry and Alice (Sawyer) H.; grad. Phillips Acad., Andover, Mass., 1939; B.S., Bowdoin Coll., 1943; m. Mary Alberta Greenwood Dellenbaugh, Feb. 3, 1950 (dec. June 1961); children—Geoffrey G. Dellenbaugh (stepson), George Henry III, Martha, Janet; m. 2d, Nancy Dutton Pinkham, Aug. 3, 1963; stepchildren—Pamela, Anne C., Catherine W., Polly. With Heywood-Wakefield Co., Gardner, Mass., 1944—, v.p., asst. to pres., 1959-66, pres., 1966—, also dir., mem. exec. com.; dir., mem. exec. com. First Safety Fund Nat. Bank, Gardner; trustee Gardner Savs. Bank. Mem. corp. Henry Heywood Meml. Hosp., 1947—; trustee Levi Heywood Meml. Library Assn., 1954—. Served with inf. AUS, 1942-44. Mem. Greater Gardner C. of C. Republican. Conglist. Club: Fay (Fitchburg, Mass.). Home: 85 Elm St Gardner MA 01440 Office: 206 Central St Gardner MA 01440

HEYWOOD, STANLEY JOHN, coll. pres.; b. Vancouver, B.C., Can., Mar. 18, 1925; s. John Albert and Lillian (Burton) H.; B.A., U. B.C., 1949, B.Ed., 1949; A.M., U. Chgo., 1952, Ph.D., 1954; m. Joan Olive Murton, Aug. 18, 1950; children—John Spencer, Philip Arthur. Came to U.S., 1950, naturalized, 1959. Faculty pub. schs., B.C., 1945-47; lectr. adminstrn. RCAF, Royal Mil. Coll., Kingston, Ont., 1951, 52; instr. adminstrn. U. B.C., 1953; research asso. Midwest Adminstrn. Center, U. Chgo., 1954; registrar, chmn. dept. tchr. edn., dir. summer session Coe Coll., 1954- 56, adminstrv. asst. to pres., registrar, dir. summer session, 1957-58; dean Coll. Edn., Ida. State U., 1958-66; pres. Eastern Mont. Coll., Billings, 1966—. Mem. Carnegie Commn. on Future of Higher Edn., 1969—; bd. dirs. Am. Assn. State Colls. and Univs. Served to flying officer RCAF, 1943-45, 51, 52. Mem. N.E.A., Am. Assn. U. Profs., Phi Delta Kappa. Episcopalian. Rotarian. Home: 432 Silver Lane Billings MT 59102

HEYWORTH, 1ST BARON OF OXTON, (Geoffrey Heyworth), business exec.; b. Birkenhead, Eng., Oct. 18, 1894; s. Thomas Blackwell and Florence (Myers) H.; student Dollar Acad.; LL.D., St. Andrews and Manchester, 1950, London U., 1962, Bristol U., 1966, Sussex U., 1966, Southampton U., 1970; D.C.L. (hon.) Oxford U., 1957; D.Litt., Warwick U., 1967; m. Lois Dunlop, 1924. Joined Lever Brothers Ltd., Liverpool, 1912, filled various positions, Can. and Eng., until 1931, dir. parent co., London, 1931—; chmn. Unilever Ltd. (formerly Lever Bros. and Unilever Ltd.), 1942-60. Pres. Nat. Council of Social Service, 1959-70; chmn. ct. of govs. London (Eng.) Sch. Hygiene and Tropical Medicine, 1964-69; hon. fellow Nuffield Coll. Created Knight, 1948, 1st Baron, 1955. Decorated grand officer Order Orange Nassau (Netherlands). Club: Athenaeum. Address: 29 Sussex Sq London W 2 England

HIAASEN, CARL ANDREAS, lawyer; b. Benson County, N.D., May 26, 1894; s. K.O. and Mary Mary (Flaagen) H.; student State Tchrs. Coll., Valley City, N.D., 1914-17, 1914-17, U. Ill., 1919-20; J.D., U. N.D., 1922; m. Clara Landmark, June 3, 1924 1924 (dec. Oct. 1930); 1 son, Kermit Odel. Admitted to Fla. bar, 1923, U.S. Supreme Ct. bar, 1926; practice law, Ft. Lauderdale, 1923—; mem. firm McCune, Hiaasen, Crum, Ferris & Gardner P.A., 1923—. Served with with A.U.S., World War I. Life fellow Am. Bar Found.; mem. Am. Bar Assn., Bar Assn. City N.Y., Order Coif, Phi Delta Phi, Delta Sigma Rho. Republican. Lutheran. Contbr. articles to legal jours. Home: 2417 N E 27th Av Fort Lauderdale FL 33305 Office: Broward Nat Bank Bldg Fort Lauderdale FL 33302

HIATT, HOWARD H., educator, physician; b. Patchogue, N.Y., July 22, 1925; s. Alexander and Dorothy (Askinas) H.; M.D., Harvard, 1948; m. Doris Bieringer, Nov. 29, 1947; children—Jonathan, Deborah, Frederick. Intern, then resident medicine Beth Israel Hosp., Boston, 1948-50; research fellow Cornell Med. Coll., 1950-53; clin. investigator USPHS, 1953-55; mem. faculty Harvard Med. Sch., 1955—, H.L. Blumgart prof. medicine, 1963—; physician-in-chief Beth Israel Hosp., 1963—. Mem. Am. Soc. Clin. Investigation, Assn. Am. Physicians, Am. Acad. Arts and Scis., Alpha Omega Alpha. Home: 22 Hyslop Rd Brookline MA 02146 Office: 330 Brookline Av Boston MA 02215

HIATT, ROBERT WORTH, fgn. service officer; b. San Jose, Cal., Dec. 23, 1913; s. Elwood B. and Bernice (Bane) H.; B.A., San Jose State Coll., 1936; Ph.D., U. Cal. at Berkeley, 1941; m. Elizabeth A. Matthews, July 18, 1938; children—Judith L., Gerald A., William R. Instr., asst. prof. zoology Mont. State Coll., 1941-43; asst. prof. zoology U. Hawaii, 1943-45, asso. prof., prof., sr. prof., chmn. dept., 1946-55, dean Grad. Sch., dir. research, 1955-63, v.p. acad. affairs, 1963-68, acting pres., 1968-69; exec. dir. U. Hawaii Research Corp., 1969; scientific counselor U.S. embassy, Tokyo, 1970—; sci. liaison officer Am. embassy, London, Eng., 1957-58; dir. Hawaii Marine Lab., 1943-55, Eniwetok Marine Biol. Lab., 1952-69. Chmn. adv. com. hydrobiology Office Naval Research, 1951-65, mem. adv. com. on biology, 1951-56; mem. com. on internat. relations Am. Inst. Biol. Sci., 1959-63; mem. Office Instnl. Programs Council, NSF, 1960-66; mem. FAO panel of experts on marine fisheries, 1962-69; cons. div. biology and medicine NSF, 1968-69; chmn., editor Proc. Internat. Conf. on Marine Labs., Rome, 1955. Fellow A.A.A.S.; mem. Pacific Sci. Assn., Nat. Acad. Sci. (Pacific sci. bd.), Am. Ornithol. Union, Am. Fisheries Soc., Am. Soc. Zoologists, Am. Soc. Ichthyologists and Herpetologists, Soc. Systematic Zoologists, Ecol. Soc. Am., Am. Soc. Limnology and Oceanography. Editor: Directory of Hydrobiological Laboratories and Personnel in North America, 1954; World Directory to Hydrobiologic Institutions, 1963. Contbr. articles to sci. jours. Home: Am Embassy APO San Francisco CA 96503

HIATT, VERGIL EMERY, educator; b. Portland, Ind., Oct. 7, 1902; s. Luther Ervin and Elnora (Shultz) H.; A.B., Ind. U., 1926; A.M., 1929; student U. Mich., 1934; Ph.D., U. Chgo., 1946; m. Marie Rowls, Aug. 13, 1927; children—Ricard R., Margaret M. Tchr., Hardinsburg (Ind.) High Sch., 1926-27; instr. Latin, Ind. U., 1927-29; asst. prof. Latin, Coll. Wooster, 1929-47; prof. Latin, head dept. classical langs. and archaeology Butler U., 1947- -. Mem. Classical Assn. Middle West and South, Am. Classical League, Am. Phil. Assn., Am. Inst. Archaeology, Am. Assn. U. Profs. Presbyn. Home: 207 Blue Ridge Rd Indianapolis IN 46208

HIBBARD, ALDRO THOMPSON, artist; b. Falmouth, Mass., Aug. 25, 1886; s. James Thompson and Katherine D. (Swift) H.; grad. high sch., Dorchester, Mass., 1906, Mass. Normal Art Sch., 1909, Museum Sch. of Fine Arts Boston, 1913; awarded Paige traveling scholarship, 1913-15; m. Winifred D. Jackman, May 31, 1925; children—Elaine W. and Malcolm J. Instr. Boston U. Art Dept., founder of Rockport Summer Sch. of Drawing and Painting, Rockport, Mass., 1921-48; academic artist Springfield Famous Art Sch., 1964, Has exhibited throughout U.S. Recipient numerous prizes including First prize for The City Beyond, Duxbury, Mass., 1920; hon. mention Art Inst. Chgo., 1921; 1st Hallgarten prize N.A.D., 1921; Jennie Sesnan gold medal Pa. Acad. Fine Arts, 1922; William Stotesbury prize Pa. Acad. Fine Arts, 1927; 2d Altman prize N.A.D., 1927, 1st Altman prize N.A.D., 1931; Albert M. Davis landscape prize Esther M. Groom prize and Mr. and Mrs. Horace Bean prize, North Shore Art Assn., 1931; Best landscape prize Springfield Art League, 1931; New Haven paint and clay prize, 1933; landscape prize Palm Beach Art Center, 1936; Charles Noel Flagg prize Conn. Acad. of Fine Arts, 1937; landscape prize Jordan Marsh Exhbn., Boston, 1938; 1st prize popular vote Internat. Business Machines Corp., San Francisco World's Fair, 1940; Downes Landscape prize New Haven Paint and Clay Club, 1941; layman's prize Salmagundi Club, 1942; Tonsberg prize Rockport Art Assn., 1942; John Henry Hammond prize Allied Artists of Am., Inc., 1943; The Moate Range purchased by Nat. Acad. Design (Ranger fund), and donated to Portland Art Museum, 1928; Ice Harvest, Addison Gallery prize best landscape Rockport Art Assn., 1933, 48, 54, 57, 60, 66, 68, gold medal of honor, 1965, 70; prize best landscape N. Shore Art Assn., 1954, 60, 64, meml., 1969, best picture, 1963; prize best landscape Academic Artists, Springfield, Mass., 1958, meml. award, 1962, Morton Donald Catak meml. award, 1966, 67; award Dr. M.J. Ritchie Meml., 1970; gold medal of honor Hudson Valley Art Assn., 1965. Retrospective exhbn. Hibbard Collection, Ledgendsea Gallery, 1970. Represented Met. Mus. Fine Arts, N.Y., Boston Museum Fine Arts, Addison Gallery, Andover, Mass., New Britian Mus., Conn., Currier Gallery (Manchester, N.H.), Portland Art Mus., Me., Rochester Athenaeum, Chandler Sch. Women, Boston, Avery Meml. Mus., Hartford, Conn., others. National Academician. Mem. Nat. Acad. of Design, Allied Artists of Am., North Shore (v.p.), Hudson Valley art assns., Guild of Boston Artists (pres), Rockport Art Assn. (pres. 1926, 40, 42), Conn. Acad. Fine Art, Vermont Artists Guild, Inc. Republican. Clubs: Salmagundi (N.Y.C.); New Haven Paint and Clay. Home: 38 Granite St Rockport MA 01966 Studio: Ledgendsea Gallery Rockport MA 01966

HIBBARD, EDWIN DAVIS, dental educator; b. Wasta, S.D., Dec. 16, 1924; s. Edwin Bolles and Bright (Tisdale) H.; student S.D. Sch. Mines and Tech., 1942-43, U. S.D., 1943; D.D.S., U. Neb., 1947, B.S., 1951, M.S.D., 1951; m. Patricia Luella Weidler, Sept. 1, 1951; children-Laurence Russell, Edwin Mark, Patricia Ann. Pvt. practice dentistry, Los Alamos, 1951-52, York, Neb., 1952-57; prof. pedodontics, chmn. dept. Emory U. Sch. Dentistry, 1957—; dental dir. Scottish Rite, Elk chmn. dept. Emory U. Sch. Dentistry, 1957- -; dental dir. Scottish Rite, Elk Aimdore hosps.; cons. U.S. Army. Served to lt., Dental Corps, USNR, 1947-49. Diplomate Am. Bd. Pendodontics. Mem. Am. Acad. Pedodontics, Am. Soc. Dentistry Children, Ga. Soc. Dentistry Children (pres. 1967), Assn. Pedodontic Diplomates (v.p. 1970), Sigma Xi, Omicron Kappa Upsilon, Delta Tau Delta, Delta Sigma Delta. Author articles. Home: Tau Delta, Delta Sigma Delta. Author articles. Home: 2681 Cosmos Dr Atlanta GA 30345 Atlanta GA 30345

HIBBARD, WALTER ROLLO, Jr., glass co. exec.; b. Bridgeport, Conn., Jan. 20, 1918; s. Walter Rollo and Helen S. (Kenworthy) H.; A.B., Wesleyan U., Middletown, Conn., 1939; D.Eng., Yale, 1942; LL.D. (hon.), Mich. Technol. U.; D.Eng. (hon.), Mont. Coll. Mineral Sci. and Tech., 1968; m. Charlotte Tracy, Mar. 21, 1942 (dec. 1970); children—Douglas, Lawrence, Diana. From asst. to asso. prof. metallurgy Yale, 1945-51; with research lab. Gen. Electric Co., 1951-65, mgr. alloy studies, 1953-60, mgr. metallurgy and ceramics research, 1960-65; adj. prof. metall. engring. Rensselaer Poly. Inst., 1952-65; dir. Bur. of Mines, Dept. of Interior, 1965-68; v.p. tech. services Owens Corning Fiberglas Corp., Toledo, O., 1968—. Chmn. materials adv. bd. Nat. Acad. Scis.-NRC, 1965-66; mem. adv. com., engring. div. NSF, 1965-69; mem. at large NRC. Mem. vis. com. Stanford U.; asso. fellow Davenport Coll., Yale. Served to lt. USNR, 1942-45. Recipient Yale Engring. Assn. award advancement basic and applied sci., 1959. Registered profl. engr., Conn., Ohio. Fellow Am. Acad. Arts and Scis., Metall. Soc. of Am., Am. Inst. M.E. (pres. 1958), A.A.A.S., Am. Ceramic Soc., Am. Soc. Metals; mem. Am. Inst. Metall. Engrs. (Rossiter W. Raymond award 1950), Ohio Acad. Sci., N.Y. Acad. Scis., Am. Inst. Mining, Metall. and Petroleum Engrs. (pres. 1967, recipient James Douglas gold medal), Mining and Metall. Soc. Am., Nat. Acad. Engring., Phi Beta Kappa, Sigma Xi, Alpha Chi Sigma, Delta Tau Delta, Gamma Alpha. Contbr. profl. jours. Editor: (with F.P. Bundy and H.M. Strong) Progress in Very High Pressure Research, 1961. Home: 1920 Collingswood Av Toledo OH 43624 Office: Owens Corning Fiberglas Corp Tech Center Toledo OH

HIBBEN, FRANK CUMMINGS, educator, anthropologist; b. Lakewood, O., Dec. 5, 1910; s. Fred M. and Lucy (West) H.; A.B., Princeton, 1933; M.S., U. N.M., 1934; Ph.D., Harvard, 1940; m. Eleanor Brown, June 6, 1936; children—Nora (Mrs. William Liddell), Margaret (Mrs. Tom Bahti), Patrick (dec.). Archaeologist, Ohio State Mus., 1928-29; asst. archaeology and sociology Cleve. Mus., 1930-33; faculty U. N.M., Albuquerque, 1934—, prof. anthropology, 1952—, dir. Maxwell Mus. Anthropology, 1959—; lectr. Archeol. Inst., 1961—; del. Geneva Conf., Dept. State, 1957; chmn. Albuquerque Zoo Bd., 1960—, N.M. Dept. Game and Fish Commn., 1961—. Served to lt. comdr. USNR, 1942-45. Decorated Legion of Merit. Ford Found. grantee, 1956, NSF grantee, 1961. Author: The Lost Americans, 1946; Prehistoric Man in Europe, 1958; Digging Up America, 1960; also articles. Contbns. include excavations Sandia cave, delineation of Paleo Indian cultures of Am. S.W.; compilation of N.Am. archaeology translated into major langs. of world; outline of Paleolithic sequences in Africa. Home: 3005 Campus NE Albuquerque NM 87106

HIBBERT, DONALD RAYMOND, mfg. co. exec.; b. Ironwood, Mich., Jan. 30, 1926; s. Raymond Henry and Emma (Braunel) H.; B.A., Mich. State U., 1950; m. Marilyn Joyce Vickers, Sept. 8, 1951; children—Mary Jo, John Vickers. Supr., Touche, Ross, Bailey & Smart, Detroit, 1950-58; v.p., treas., dir. Wyandotte Chems. Corp. and prin. domestic and fgn. subsidiaries, 1958-69; treas. the Bendix Corp., Southfield, Mich., 1969-70; v.p finance, treas. Kimberly-Clark Corp., Neenah, Wis., 1970—; dir. Detroit, Toledo & Ironton R.R., Spruce Falls Pulp & Paper Co., Toronto, Ont., Can. Served with USNR, 1943-46. C.P.A., Mich. Mem. Am. Inst. C.P.A.'s, Financial Execs. Inst., Beta Alpha Psi, Beta Theta Pl. Republican. Episcopalian. Clubs: Detroit Athletic; Union League (N.Y.C.). Home: 3 Westfield Ridge Neenah WI 54956 Office: N Lake St Neenah WI 54956

HIBBERT, WILLIAM A., utilities co. exec.; b. Wilmington, Del., 1909; married. Credit mgr. B.F. Goodrich Co., 1932-38; with Delmarva Power and Light Co., Wilmington, 1938—, asst. treas., 1949-55, treas., asst. sec., 1955-60, treas., sec., 1960—. Home: 40 Pashcall Rd Wilmington DE 19803 Office: 500 Market St Wilmington DE 19899*

HIBBETT, HOWARD SCOTT, educator; b. Akron, O., July 27, 1920; s. Howard Scott and Florence (Line) H.; A.B. summa cum laude, Harvard, 1947, Ph.D., 1950; m. Tomi Kuwayama, Feb. 16, 1946 (div. 1958); children—Mariko, Reiko; m. 2d, Akiko Yamagawa, Jan. 20, 1960; 1 son, David. Jr. fellow Harvard Soc. Fellows, 1949-52; from instr. to asst. prof. Oriental langs. U. Cal. at Los Angeles, 1952-58; mem. faculty Harvard, 1958—, prof. Japanese lit., 1963—, chmn. dept. Far Eastern langs., 1965-70. Fulbright research scholar, Japan, 1956-57, 64-65; Guggenheim fellow, 1964-65. Served to 1st lt. AUS, 1942-46. Mem. Assn. Asian Studies, Am. Acad. Arts and Scis., Phi Beta Kappa. Author: The Floating World in Japanese Fiction, 1959; (with Gen. Itasaka) Modern Japanese: A Basic Reader, 1965. Translator: (J. Tanizaki) The Key, 1961; Seven Japanese Tales, 1963; Diary of A Mad Old Man, 1965. Home: 220 Pleasant St Arlington MA 02174 Office: 2 Divinity Av Cambridge MA 02138

HIBBS, BEN, editor, writer; b. Fontana, Kan., July 23, 1901; s. Russell and Elizabeth (Smith) H.; A.B., U. Kan., 1923; D.Litt., Northwestern U., 1947, Temple U., 1948, Southwestern Coll., Winfield, Kan., 1964; m. Edith Kathleen Doty, June 3, 1930; 1 son, Stephen Doty. News editor Fort Morgan (Colo.) Times, 1923, Pratt (Kan.) Tribune, 1924; prof. journalism Hays (Kan.) State Coll., 1924-26; editor, mgr. Goodland (Kan.) News-Republic, 1926-27; mng. editor Arkansas City (Kan.) Traveler, 1927-29; asso. editor Country Gentleman, Phila., 1929-40; editor, 1940-42; editor Sat. Eve. Post, 1942-61, sr. editor, 1962; sr. editor The Reader's Digest, 1963—; mem. exec. com. Curtis Pub. Co., 1940-61. Mem. U.S. Adv. Commn. on Information, 1951-54. Recipient U. Pa. Journalism award, 1947; U. Kan. Distinguished Alumni citation, 1942; nat. award journalistic merit William Allen White Found., 1959; Freedoms Found. George Washington medal award, 1963; School Bell award N.E.A., 1964. Mem. Phi Beta Kappa, Sigma Delta Chi, Sigma Phi Epsilon. Republican. Methodist. Club: Merion Cricket. Contbr. articles Country Gentleman, Saturday Evening Post, Readers Digest. Address: 737 Braeburn Lane Penn Valley Narberth PA 19072

HIBBS, LEON, coll. pres.; b. Balko, Okla., Oct. 15, 1930; s. Paschal Otho and Luella (Smith) H.; B.S., Northwestern Okla. State Coll., 1952; Ed.M., U. Okla., 1956; M.S., Okla. State U., 1957, Ed.D., 1959; m. Maxine Parker, Sept. 6, 1950; children—Max, Gaye, Craig, LeAn. Successively tchr., prin., supt. Greenough schs., Beaver County, Okla., 1952-56; dir. instructional TV, Okla. Dept. Edn., 1957-60; dir. course devel., coordinator spl. projects Purdue Research Found., 1960-62; dean edn. Oklahoma City U., 1962-67; pres. Southeastern Okla. State Coll., 1967—; cons. in field, 1960—. Chmn. Goals for Durant, 1969—. Chmn. bd. dirs. Southeastern State Coll. Research Found., 1967—. Recipient Favorite Faculty award Oklahoma City U., 1965; Student Edn. Assn. award, 1966; fellow NSF, 1956. Mem. Nat., Okla. edn. assns., Durant C. of C. (dir. 1967—). Mason, Rotarian (dir. Durant, 1967—). Author: Using the Stereomicroscope, 1964; A Programmed Textbook in Mathematics for Elementary School Teachers, 1966; Living Science, 1966. Home: 1401 N 6th St Durant OK 74701

HIBBS, RICHARD GUYTHAL, educator; b. Winner, S.D., Feb. 17, 1922; s. George G. and Verna (Smith) H.; student Loyola U., Chgo., 1947-49; B.A., U. S.D., 1950; Ph.D., U. Minn., 1955; m. Dorothy H. Taggart, Aug. 19, 1946; children—Richard Gene, Linda Marie, Mary Jo. Instr. anatomy U. Minn. Med. Sch., 1954-55; mem. faculty Tulane U. Medical Sch., New Orleans, 1955—, asso. prof. anatomy, 1963-66, prof. anatomy, 1966—, spl. research electron microscopy of skin and appendages, electron microscopy and histochemistry cardiovascular system. Served with USMC, 1940-46. Recipient gold award original research Am. Acad. Dermatology and Syphology, 1958, Career Devel. award USPHS, 1960-65, 65-70. Mem. Am. Assn. Anatomists, Am. Physiol. Soc., La. Soc. Electron Micriscopy, So. Soc. Anatomists, Sigma Xi. Home: 344 Audubon St New Orleans LA 70118

HIBEL, BERNARD, apparel co. exec.; b. N.Y.C., Dec. 22, 1916; s. Jacob and Leah (Singer) H.; B.B.A., St. Johns U.; m. Forence Browser, Jan. 30, 1941; children—Laurel, Karen Ruth, Miriam. Mgr., B.M. Joffe & Co., 1946-48; mgr. Aronson & Oresman, 1948-55; v.p., controller, asst. treas. Kayser Roth Corp., N.Y.C., 1955—; tchr. Bklyn. Coll., 1955. Dir. Miss Universe Beauty Pageant, 1964. Served with AUS, 1945-46; ETO. C.P.A., N.Y. Mem. Financial Execs. Inst., Am. Mgmt. Assn., N.Y. Soc. C.P.A.'s, Am. Inst. C.P.A.'s, Nat. Assn. Accountants. Home: 70 Shrubhollow Rd Roslyn NY 11576 Office: 640 Fifth Av New York City NY 10019

HIBEL, EDNA (Mrs. Theodore Plotkin), artist; b. Boston, Jan. 13, 1917; d. Abraham B. and Lena (Rubin) Hibel; student Boston Mus. Sch. Fine Arts, 1934-39; Ruth Sturtevant traveling fellow to Mexico, 1939; m. Theodore Plotkin, Jan. 7, 1940; children—Jon, Andrew, Richard. Exhibited Robert C. Vose Gallery, Boston, DeCordova Mus., Lincoln, Mass., Boston Mus. Fine Arts, Miami Beach Library Art Gallery, Mass. Sch. Art, Art Inst. Chgo., Boston Inst. Modern Arts, Am. Fedn. Art traveling exhbn., Pa. Acad. Art, Boston Mus. Modern Art, Logan Internat. Airport, Hall Art, N.Y.C., N.A.D.; works in permanent collections Boston Mus. Fine Arts, Norton Gallery Mus., West Palm Beach, Fla., Harvard, Boston U., U. N.H., Fleichman Coll., Cin., Detroit Art Inst., Milw. Mus. Art, Phoenix Art Mus., Flint Inst. of Art, numerous pvt. collections; one man shows Tanglewood, Lenox, Mass., 1962, Wenham (Mass.) Mus., 1962, Sally Maren Gallery, Marblehead, Mass., 1962, Hall of Art, N.Y.C., 1962, 66, 68, 69, 70, Constn. Gallery, Hartford, Conn., 1962, Marble Arch Gallery, Miami Beach, Fla., 1963, St. Armands Key, Sarasota, Fla., 1963, Oehlschlaeger Gallery, 1969, 70, 71, Sarasota, 1965, 66, Chgo., 1965, 67, 68, Galerie de Tours, Carmel, Cal., 1968, 69, 70, 71, Helen Winter Gallery, Farmington, Conn., 1969, 70, Guggenheim Gallery, London, Eng., 1971, Hammer Gallery, N.Y.C., 1971, De Saisset Mus., Santa Clara, Cal., 1970, Harmon Gallery, Naples, Fla., 1969, 70, 71. Home: 2923 Lake Dr Riviera Beach FL 33404

HIBINO, TSUNEJI, advt. exec.; b. Gifu Prefecture, Japan, July 11, 1903; s. Hidejiro and Kama (Yasuda) H.; grad. Tokyo U.; m. Mineko Kotanaka, Aug. 10, 1931; children—Takeshi, Hisako Hatano, Susumu. With Dentsu Advt. Ltd., Tokyo, 1928—, exec. v.p., 1960-63, pres., 1963—; dir. Tokyo Broadcasting Co., Ltd. Named grand officer of merit Italian Republic. Mem. Internat. C. of C. (advt. dept. com.), Japan Fedn. Econ. Orgn. (councilor). Home: 2-21-14 Kakinokizaka Meguroku Tokyo Japan Office: 1-11 Tsukiji Chuo-ku Tokyo Japan

HICHEW, JOHN O., lawyer; b. Washington, July 2, 1903; LL.B., Nat. U., 1929. Admitted to D.C. bar, 1929, Mo. bar, 1934; mem. firm Thompson, Mitchell, Douglas, Neill & Guerri, St. Louis. Mem. Bar Assn. Met. St. Louis, Mo. Bar, Am. Bar Assn. Office: 705 Olive St St Louis MO 63101*

HICK, JOHN HARWOOD, philosopher, educator; b. Scarborough, Eng., Jan. 20, 1922; s. Mark Day and Mary Aileen (Hirst) H.; M.A. with 1st class honours, Edinburgh U., 1948; D.Phil., Oxford U., 1950; student Westminster Theol. Coll., Cambridge, Eng., 1950-53; m. Joan Hazel Bowers, Aug. 29, 1953; children—Eleanor, Mark, Peter, Michael. Came to U.S., 1956. Ordained to ministry Presbyn. Ch., 1953; minister in Northumberland, Eng., 1953-56; asst. prof. philosophy Cornell U., 1956-59, Stuart prof. Christian philosophy Princeton Theol. Sem., 1959-69; lectr. philosophy of religion Cambridge U., 1965—. Mem. Am. Philos. Assn., Am. Theol. Soc., Mind Assn., Royal Inst. Philosophy, Soc. Psychical Research. Author: Faith and Knowledge, 1957; Philosophy of Religion, 1963; Classical and Contemporary Readings in the Philosophy of Religion, 1964; Faith and the Philosophers, 1964; The Existence of God, 1964; Evil and the Love of God, 1965. Mem. editorial bd. Theology Today, Ency. Philosophy. Home: 277 Hawthorne Av Princeton NJ 08540

HICKAM, HUBERT, lawyer; b. Spencer, Ind., Apr. 19, 1892; s. Willis and Sallie (Meek) H.; LL.B., Indiana U., 1913; m. Ruth Moffett, Oct. 28, 1915 (dec. Jan. 22, 1935); 1 dau., Barbara (Mrs. Audley Wasson); m. 2d, Mary Elizabeth Randolph Woods, Sept. 9, 1939; children—James P. Woods, Mrs. Elizabeth W. Adams. Associated with law firm Hickam & Hickam, Spencer, Ind., 1913- 19; removed to Indianapolis, 1919; mem. firm Noel, Hickam & Boyd, 1923- 26, Noel, Hickam, Boyd & Armstrong, 1926-40, Barnes, Hickam, Pantzer & Boyd since 1940. Mem. Ind. General Assembly, 1915. Member alumni board of visitors of School of law, at Indiana U., 1964—, recipient Distinguished Alumni award, 1967. Served as 1st lt. QMC, U.S. Army, 1918-19. Chairman Alien Enemy Hearing Bd., Southern Dist. of Ind., 1941; selective service appeal agent, World War II. Fellow Am. Coll. of Trial Lawyers; mem. Am. Law Inst. (joint com. on continuing edn. legal edn.), Am. chmn. antitrust section 1958-59, joint com. on continuing edn. legal edn.), Fed., 7th Fed. Circuit, Ind., Indpls. (ex-pres.) bar assns., and also mem. National Assn. R.R. Trial Lawyers, Mil. Order Loyal Legion, Phi Kappa Psi. Presbyn. Mason. Clubs: Woodstock, University, Athletic Traders Point Hunt, Contemporary (past pres.), Lawyers (past pres.) (Indpls.); Tavern (Chgo.). Author: A Civil Action: From Pleadings to Trial; co- author Preparation for Trial. Home: 7649 Washington Blvd Indianapolis IN 46204 Office: Merchants Bank Bldg Indianapolis IN 46204

HICKAM, WILLIS, lawyer; b. Spencer, Ind., May 3, 1894; s. Willis and Sallie (Meek) H.; LL.B., Indiana University, Bloomington, 1918, Doctor of Laws, 1967; m. Ruth Elliott, Feb. 4, 1919; children—Elliott, Jane Gay (Mrs. Joel E. Grizzell). Admitted to Ind. bar, 1918, since practiced in Spencer; part- time prof. law Ind. U., 1949—. Vice pres., dir. Owen County State Bank, 1952—; dir. Owen County Savs. & Loan Assn. Mem. commn. on state tax and financing policy Ind., 1953-57. Trustee Ind. U., 1953-65, pres. trustees, 1959-65; bd. dirs. Ind. U. Found. Served with U.S. Army, 1918. Fellow Am. Coll. Trial Lawyers, Am. Bar Found.; mem. Am. Judicature Soc., Am., 7th Fed. Circuit, Ind. (bd. mgrs. 1938-40), Owen County bar assns., Am. Legion. Phi Kappa Psi, Phi Delta Phi. Democrat. Presbyn. Mason, Elk. Club: Columbia (Indpls.). Home: 187 W Hillside Av Spencer IN 47460 Office: 10 S Main St Spencer IN 47460

HICKCOX, CURTISS BRONSON, anesthesiologist; b. Watertown, Conn., July 14, 1913; s. Frank Bronson and Elizabeth May (Atwood) H.; S.B., Middlebury (Vt.) Coll., 1934; M.D., Tufts Coll., Boston, 1938; m. Helen Theresa Burke, June 7, 1941; children—Maryann Elizabeth, Patricia Katherine, Curtiss Bronson, Edward Frank. Intern Waterbury (Conn.) Hosp., 1938-39, cons. staff, 1955; resident in anesthesiology Hartford (Conn.) Hosp., 1939-41, clin. asst., 1942-43, acting chief, 1942-45, asst., 1943-44, asso., 1944-45, acting dir., 1963-64, dir. dept., 1964—, sr. anesthesiologist, 1959—; prof., head dept. anesthesiology Temple U. Med. Sch. and Hosp., 1946-49; cons. Conn. Vets. Home and Hosp.; cons., Mount Sinai, Manchester Meml., Day Kimball, Waterbury hosps., Newington Childrens Hosp. Mem. Adv. Bd. Med. Specialists, 1948-59, exec. com., 1958-59. Diplomate Am. Bd. Anesthesiology (dir.; sec.-treas. 1948-58, pres. 1959). Mem. Am. Soc. Anesthesiologists (bd. dirs. 1943-49, sec. 1946-49), A.M.A., Conn., Hartford County, Hartford med. socs., New Eng., Conn. socs. anesthesiologists, Kappa Delta Rho. Methodist. Home: 30 Rosedale Rd West Hartford CT 06107 Office: 85 Jefferson St Hartford CT 06106

HICKEL, WALTER JOSEPH, constrn. co. exec.; b. Ellinwood, Kan., Aug. 18, 1919; s. Robert A. and Emma (Zecha) H.; student pub. schs., Claflin, Kan.; D.Eng., Stevens Inst. Tech., 1970; LL.D., St. Mary of Plains Coll., St. Martin's Coll., U. Md., Adelphi U.; D.Pub. Adminstrn., Willamette U.; m. Janice Cannon, Sept. 22, 1941 (dec. Aug. 1943); 1 son, Theodore; m. 2d, Ermalee Strutz, Nov. 22, 1945; children—Robert, Walter, Jack, Joseph, Karl. Builder-owner Traveler's Inn, Anchorage, Alaska, 1953—, Traveler's Inn, Fairbanks, Alaska, 1955—, Hickel Constrn. Co., Anchorage, 1947—, Hotel Captain Cook, Anchorage, No. Lights Shopping Center, Anchorage; former chmn. bd. Anchorage Natural Gas Co.; gov. State of Alaska, 1966- 69; U.S. sec. of interior, 1969-70. Mem. Republican Nat. Com., 1954- 64. Bd. regents Gonzaga U. Named Alaskan of Year, 1969; recipient DeSmet medal Gonzaga U., 1969; named Man of Year, Ripon Soc., 1970. Mem. Pioneers of Alaska, Alaska C. of C. (chmn. econ. devel. com.), Equestrian Order Holy Sepulchre, Knights Malta. Elk, K.C. Clubs: Capitol Hill, Washington Athletic, Arctic (Washington). Home: 1905 Loussac Dr Anchorage AK 99503 Office: 935 3d Av Anchorage AK 99501

HICKEN, PHILIP BURNHAM, artist; b. Lynn, Mass., June 27, 1910; s. Willis and Lena (Burnham) H.; student Mass. Sch. Art, 1928-32; m. Evangeline Chase, June 5, 1937; children—Tana Val, Theo Jo. Nat., internat exhibits 1936—; lectr. Sch. of Mus. Fine Arts, Boston, Sch. Practical Arts, Boston, and Butera Sch. Fine Arts, Boston, 1947; instr. Grad. Sch. Design, Harvard, 1954; instr. drawing Boston U. Sch. Fine and Applied Arts, 1955-56; chmn. dept. design Sch. Practical Art, Boston, 1956—; chmn. dept. fine arts Art Inst. Boston, 1969- -; represented in permanent collections Met. Mus. Art, N.Y.C., Library of Congress, Phila. Mus. Fine Art, Nat. Bezalel Mus., Jerusalem, many others; mural Boston Five Cents Savs. Bank. Served as artist, AUS, 1942-45. Recipient prizes Black Mountain (N.C.) Art Club, 1943; Springfield (Mass.) Soldier Art, 1944; New Eng. Soldier Art, 1944; Mint Mus., Charlotte, N.C., 1946, 1st Cambridge (Mass.) Art Assn. Ann., 1953; purchase award Bklyn. Museum Print Ann., 1958; 1st award Nantucket Art Assn. Annual, 1958, 68; Directors award Nat. Soc. Casein Painters, 1963; 1st award Natick (Mass.) Art Festival, 1971. Fellow Royal Soc. Arts, London; mem. Nat. Serigraph Soc., Boston Printmakers, Boston Soc. Water Color Painters, Nantucket Artists Assn. Easel and mural painter, Fed. Art Project. Address: 108 Morse St Watertown MA 02172 ☆

HICKEN, VICTOR, historian, educator; b. Witt, Ill., Sept. 28, 1921; s. Thomas and Ann (Atherton) H.; B.Ed., So. Ill. U., 1943; M.A., U. Ill., 1947, Ph.D., 1955; m. Mary Patricia O'Connell, Dec. 28, 1943; children—Jeffrey Price, Brian Thomas, Elizabeth Ann, Daniel Joseph. Asst., U. Ill., 1950-51; instr. Western Ill. U., Macomb, 1947-50, prof., 1951—, chmn. dept. history, 1967-69; vis. prof. U. Salzburg (Austria), 1971. Mem. faculty com. Higher Edn. Planning Commn. Ill. Served to lt. USNR, 1943-46. Mem. Ill. Hist. Soc. (v.p.), Pi Alpha Theta, Pi Gamma Mu. Episcopalian. Club: Macomb Country. Author: Illinois in the Civil War, 1966; The Settlement of Western Illinois, 1966; Western Illinois Factbook, 1968; Illinois at War, 1968; The American Fighting Man, 1969; The Purple and the Gold, 1970. Home: 615 Lincoln Dr Macomb IL 61455

HICKERSON, GLENN LINDSEY, airlines exec..; b. Burbank, Cal., Aug. 22, 1937; s. Ralph M. and Sarah Lawson (Linsey) H.; B.A. in Bus. Adminstrn., Claremont Men's Coll., 1959; M.B.A., N.Y. U., 1960. Exec. asst. Douglas Aircraft Co., Santa Monica, Cal., 1963; sec., treas. Douglas Finance Corp., Long Beach, Cal., 1964-67, regional mgr. customer financing, 1967; exec. asst. to pres. Universal Airlines, Inc., Detroit, 1967-68, v.p., treas., asst. sec., 1968-69, pres., 1969—; v.p., treas., asst. sec. Universal Aircraft Service, Inc., Detroit, 1968—; v.p., treas. Universal Airlines Co., Detroit, 1968-69, pres., 1969—; dir. Nat. Air Carrier Assn. (NACA), NACA Facilities and Service Corp., Washington, mem. exec. coms., 1971—. Served to lt. (j.g.) USCGR, 1960-62. H.B. Earhart Found. fellow, 1962. Mem. Internat. Assn. Charter Airlines (exec. com. 1971—). Home: 128 Culebra Terrace San Francisco CA 94109 Office: Oakland Internat Airport Oakland CA 94614

HICKERSON, MARCUS REA, investment co. exec.; b. Waco, Tex., Sept. 10, 1926; s. Marcus Carroll and Emily Pope (Sparks) H.; B.B.A. with honors, N. Tex. State U., 1950; m. Renda Louise Morgan, July 6, 1951; children—Marcus Neale, Lisa Annette, Stephen Rea. Dept. mgr. Dallas br. Ely-Walker Drygoods Co., 1950-51; gen. partner Hickerson's Food Store, Ltd., Waxahachie, Tex., 1951-61; pres. Holly Corp., Dallas, from 1961, now dir.; pres., treas. Rapid Transit Equipment Co., 1962—; dir. Mt. Vernon Co., also subsidiaries Holly Corp. Mem. Democratic Adv. Council Tex. Served with U.S. Merchant Marine, World War II; with USAF, Korea; capt. Res. Mem. Pi Omega Pi, Alpha Chi. Mason (Shriner). Home: 677 W 12th St Claremont CA 91711 Office: 1111 W Foothill Blvd Azusa CA 91702

HICKEY, CHARLES JOHN, photog. equipment co. exec.; b. New Britain, Conn., June 12, 1923; s. Charles J. and Betty F. (McNiff) H.; B.A., Yale, 1947, LL.B., 1950; m. Mary Nebbia, Aug. 27, 1960; 1 son, Stephen. Admitted to Conn. bar, 1950; atty. Office Chief Counsel, Treasury Dept. 1951-53; engaged in business, 1953-60; with W.Va. Pulp and Paper Co., N.Y.C., 1960-70, comptroller, 1961-70; v.p. finance Bell & Howell, Chgo., 1970—. C.P.A., Ill. Mem. Am. Bar Assn., Am. Inst. C.P.A.'s. Club: Yale (N.Y.C.). Home: 207 Maple Ct Lake Forest IL 60045 Office: 7100 McCormick Rd Chicago IL 60645

HICKEY, DENNIS W., bishop. Ordained priest Roman Cath. Ch.; titular bishop of Rusuccuru and aux. bishop Rochester, N.Y., 1968—. Address: 168 Spencerport Rd Rochester NY 14606*

HICKEY, EDWARD HUTCHINS, lawyer; b. Boston, July 22, 1912; s. James M. and Mary (Simpson) H.; A.B. cum laude. Harvard, 1933, LL.B., 1936; m. Ragnhild Tait, Feb. 25, 1941; children—Shelagh (Mrs. George M. Covington), Karen, John. Admitted to Mass. bar, 1936, D.C. bar, 1946, Ill. bar, 1957; practice in Boston, 1936-38, Washington, 1938-57, Chgo., 1957—; with Dept. Justice, 1938- 42; spl. asst. Atty. Gen., chief gen. litigation sect., 1945-57; partner Bell, Boyd, Lloyd, Haddad & Burns, 1957—. Dir. First Nat. Bank of Winnetka, Watson & Boaler, Inc. Pres., Winnetka Community Chest; bd. dirs. Scholarship and Guidance Bd., United Charities of Chgo. Served to lt. USNR, World War II. mem. Am., Ill., Chgo. (chmn. legal aid, 1969, chmn. urban affairs, 1970), 7th Fed. Circuit (sec.) bar assns., Nat. Legal Aid and Defender Assn. (dir.), Am. Law Ist., Am. Judicature Soc., Law Club Chgo. Clubs: Attic, Harvard, University (Chgo.), Indian Hill (Winnetka). Home: 823 Humboldt Av Winnetka IL 60093 Office: 135 S LaSalle St Chicago IL 60603

HICKEY, EDWARD JOSEPH, Jr., lawyer; b. Washington, Mar. 30, 1912; s. Edward Joseph, Sr., and Margaret Josephine (dec.) H.; Ph.B., Brown U., 1934; J.D., Georgetown U., 1938, LL.M., 1947; graduate U.S. Naval War Coll., 1943; m. Edith Lenora Sappenfield, June 7, 1941; children—Edward Joseph, Sharon Dee, Susan. Admitted D.C. bar, 1937; practiced in Washington since 1948; now partner Mulholland, Hickey & Lyman, offices Washington and Toledo; trial atty. U.S. Dept. Justice, 1937-42, spl. asst. to atty. gen., 1946- 48; prof. law Georgetown U. Law Sch. (part time), 1949-63; general counsel, Ry. Labor Executives Assn. Mem. adv. com. Civil Aeronautics Board, 1950. Served in U.S. Navy, 1942-46, overseas, 1943-45; lt. comdr. Res., 1946. Decorated Bronze Star. Mem. Internat. Soc. Barristers, Am. Trial Lawyers Assn., Am., D.C. bar assns., I.C.C., Practitioners Assn., Maryland State Golf Assn. (pres. 1963), Am. Legion, Barristers, Pi Gamma Mu (hon.), Phi Kappa Psi. Gamma Eta Gamma Clubs: Columbia Country (pres. 1965-67) (Chevy Chase, Md.); University (Washington). Home: 4803 Broad Brook Ct Locust Hills MD 20014 Office: Tower Bldg Washington DC 20005

HICKEY, JAMES ALOYSIUS, clergyman; b. Midland, Mich., Oct. 11, 1920; s. James P. and Agnes (Ryan) H.; Juris Canonici Doctor, Latern U. (Italy), 1950; S.T.D., Angelicum U. (Italy), 1951; M.A., Mich. State U., 1962. Ordained priest Roman Catholic Ch., 1946; sec. to Bishop of Saginaw, 1951-60; rector St. Paul Sem., Saginaw, Mich., 1960-68; aux. bishop Saginaw, 1967-69; chmn. bishops' com. on Priestly Formation, 1968-69; rector N.Am. Coll., Rome, Italy, 1969-. Address: N Am Coll 00120 Vatican Rome Italy

HICKEY, JOHN THOMAS, electronics co. exec.; b. Chgo., Oct. 28, 1925; s. Matthew J., Jr. and Naomi (Pope) H.; B.S. in Commerce, Loyola U., Chgo., 1948; M.B.A., U. Chgo., 1952; m. Joanne R. Keating, Sept. 17, 1949; children—Kathleen, John, Michael, James, Roger. With Motorola Inc., and Subsidiaries, 1948- -, gen. mgr. semiconductor div., 1955-58, asst. to pres., 1958-62, dir. long range planning, 1962-65, v.p. planning, 1965-70, v.p. finance and sec., 1970—; dir. Hickey & Co., Chgo. Bd. dirs. St. Francis Hosp., Evanston, Ill. Served with AUS, 1944- 46. Club: Skokie Country (Glencoe). Home: 324 Vernon Av Glencoe IL 60022 Office: 9401 W Grand Av Franklin Park IL 60131

HICKEY, JOSEPH JAMES, biologist; b. N.Y.C., Apr. 16, 1907; s. James B. and Sarah (Mooney) H.; B.S., N.Y. U., 1930; M.S., U. Wis., 1943; postgrad. U. Chgo., 1943-44, U. Mich., 1944-46; Ph.D., 1949; m. Margaret Brooks, June 20, 1942; 1 dau., Susan. Asst. track coach N.Y. U., 1930-33; power salesman Consol. Edison Co. N.Y., 1933-41; research asst. Wis. Soil Conservation Com., Madison, 1941-43, Toxicity Lab., U. Chgo., 1943-44; asst. curator mus. zoology U. Mich., 1944-46; asst. prof. U. Wis., 1948-49, asso. prof., 1949-58, prof. dept. wildlife ecology, 1958-. Vis. scientist Vogelschutzwarte für Hessen, Rheinland-Pflaz und Saarland, 1964; prof. zoology Lake Itasca Biol. Sta., 1952, 59, 62. Guggenheim fellow, 1946-47. Fellow Am. Ornithol. Union (Council 1945-48, 63-66, v.p. 1970-72); mem. Ecol. Soc. Am., Linnean Soc. N.Y. (v.p. 1935-37, pres. 1937-39, editor proc. 1940-41), Wis. Soc. Ornithology (pres. 1954-55), Nature Conservancy (treas. 1950- 56, council 1963-70), Wildlife Soc., Wilderness Soc., Wilson, Cooper ornithol. socs., Am. Inst. Biol. Scis., A.A.A.S., Wis. Acad. Arts, Scis. and Letters. Author: A Guide to Bird Watching, 1943; Survival Studies of Banded Birds, 1952; Peregrine Falcon Populations: Their Biology and Decline, 1969. Editor Jour. Wildlife Mgmt., 1956-59; asso. editor Proc. 13th Internat. Ornithol. Congress, 1962-63. Home: 5517 Dorsett Dr Madison WI 53711 Office: Russell Labs U Wis Madison WI 53706

HICKEY, LAWRENCE THOMAS, mfg. co. exec.; b. Reedsburg, Wis., Nov. 12, 1916; s. John E. and Helen (Brennan) H.; A.B., U. Wis., 1938; M.B.A., Harvard, 1941; m. Margaret Miller, Aug. 30, 1947; children—Lawrence T., Ann, Peter, John, Joseph. Mgr. welding products div. A.O. Smith Corp., Milw., 1946-53, v.p., gen. mgr. Glascote Products subsidiary, Cleve., 1953-64; group exec. Textron, Inc., Providence, 1964-66, v.p. operations, 1966-68, pres. Burkart Randall div., St. Louis, 1968—. Republican precinct committeeman, asst. dist. leader, Cleve., 1954-64. Served to lt. comdr. USNR, 1941-46. Decorated Bronze Star medal. Mem. Harvard Bus. Sch. Assn., Phi Delta Theta. Clubs: Mo. Athletic, Martin Matthew-Dickey Boys (mem. adv. bd. 1968—) (St. Louis). Home: 1856 Nettlecreek Rd St Louis MO 63131 Office: 4900 N 2d St St Louis MO 63147

HICKEY, MARGARET A., editor; b. Kansas City, Mar. 14, 1902; d. Charles L. and Elizabeth (Wynne) Hickey; J.D., U. Mo., 1928; LL.D., Cedar Crest Coll., 1952; LL.D., MacMurray Coll., 1957; L.H.D., Wilson Coll., 1962; Litt.D., St. Mary's Coll. Notre Dame, 1964; D.Ed., Culver-Stockton Coll., 1966; m. Joseph T. Strubinger, Oct. 20, 1935. Pvt. practice of law, 1928-33; founder, and dir. Miss Hickey's Sch. for Secretaries, St. Louis, 1933-69; editor Ladies Home Jour., N.Y.C. Apptd. chmn. nat. women's adv. com. and observer Labor-Mgmt. Com., War Manpower Commn., 1942-45; adv. com. citizens participation Community Chests and Councils; sec. nat. citizens com. U.S. Office Edn.; mem. exec. com. Nat. Social Welfare Assembly, v.p.; mem. adv. bd. Point Four Program, 1950-52; mem. President's adv. com. Vol. Fgn. Aid, AID, 1952—, vice-chmn., 1962—; com. White House Conf. Edn.; bd. govs. A.R.C., 1947-53, 55-60, vice chmn. bd., 1947-53, 59-61, dep. to chmn., 1960—; vice chmn. med. and social adv. com. League Red Cross Socs.; mem. Nat. Manpower Council; mem. bd. Nat. Health Council, 1948-56; mem. President's Nat. Com. White House Conf. Children and Youth, 1960; pres. Nat. Conf. Social Work, 1956-57; chmn. organizing com. Internat. Conf. Social Work, 1966—; chmn. Nat. Citizens Council Status Women, 1964—; mem. commn. social scis. NSF, 1968-69. Mem. bd. overseers Brandeis U.; mem. vis. com. Grad. School Edn., Harvard; trustee Tuskegee Inst., Am. Youth Found. Recipient Benjamin Franklin award for distinguished pub. service journalism, 1953; St. Louis Woman of Achievement award, 1957. Mem. Internat. (chmn. UN com., v.p.), Nat. (hon. pres.) fedns. bus. and profl. women, Am. Assn. Sch. Adminstrs., Am. Council of Guidance and Personnel (bd. reps.), Mo. Bar, Women's Bar Assn., Kappa Beta Pi. Pub. affairs editor Ladies Home Jour. Home: 3940 E Timrod Tucson AZ 85711 Office: Ladies Home Jour 641 Lexington New York City NY 10022

HICKEY, MATTHEW JOSEPH, III, investment banker; b. Chgo., Oct. 26, 1929; s. Matthew Joseph and Naomi (Pope) H.; student Holy Cross Coll., 1947-48; B. Sc., Loyola, U., Chgo., 1950. With Hickey & Co., Chgo., 1950—, v.p., 1954-69, pres., 1969—, dir., 1969—. Mem. Midwest Stock Exchange, 1950—; dir. Van C. Argiris & Co., Chgo. Mem. citizens bd. Loyola U., 1959—, Mundellein Coll., 1959- -, De Paul U., 1960—; finance chmn. Chgo. Red Cross, 1955-57. Trustee St. Joseph's Coll., Rensselear, Ind., Sch. St. Maur, Atchinson, Kan. Served with AUS, 1951-54. Mem. Chgo. Assn. Stock Exchange Firms (gov. 1955-61, treas. 1958-59, vice chmn. 1960-61), Am. Inst. Mgmt., U.S. Naval Inst., (dir.), Chgo. Athletic Assn. (dir.), Bond Club Chgo. Roman Catholic. Mem. Sovereign Mil. Order Knights of Malta. Clubs: Chicago Athletic, Tavern, MidAmerica, Attic, Chicago Yacht (Chgo); Palm Bay (Miami, Fla.). Home: 1340 N Astor St Chicago IL 60610 Office: 135 S LaSalle St Chicago IL 60603

HICKEY, MAURICE JOHN, dentist and physician; b. Solvay, N.Y., Aug. 27, 1907; s. Daniel Coveny and Eleanor (Cole) H.; student Syracuse Univ., 1926-28; D.M.D., Harvard, 1932; M.D., Columbia, 1937; m. Doris Harrison, July 3, 1933; children—Jean Karen, Dean Harrison. Interne, surgery, Strong Meml. Hosp., Rochester, N.Y., 1937-38; fellow Nat. Cancer Inst., Presbyn. Hosp., N.Y., 1938-41; instr. in surgery, Columbia, 1940-45, prof. oral surgery, 1945, faculty of medicine, 1946-56, exec. officer dept. dentistry, 1949-56; asso. dean, faculty medicine Columbia Sch. Dental and Oral Surgery, 1949-56; head, div. oral surgery, 1945-56; asst. attending surgeon, Presbyn. Hosp., 1945-56; dean sch. dentistry U. Wash., 1956—; cons. oral surgery, Kingsbridge Vets. Hosp. Entered Dental Corp., U.S. Army, 1942, commd. maj., 1942, and advanced to lt. col., 1943. Diplomate Am. Bd. Oral Surgery, 1947, N.Y. State Bd. Oral Surgery, 1947 (dir. 1947—). Fellow N.Y. Acad. Dentistry; mem. A.M.A., Am. Dental Assn., Am. Soc. of Plastic and Reconstruction Surgery, Am. Soc. Maxillo-Facial Surgeons, N.Y. State and County Med. Soc., N.Y. State Dental Soc., First Dist. Dental Soc., Omicron Kappa Upsilon. Republican. Home: 4536 Stanford Av Seattle WA 98105 Office: Sch Dentistry U Wash Seattle WA 98105

HICKEY, ROBERT, journalist. Motion picture and theatrical editor San Jose Mercury and Mercury News. Office: 750 Ridder Park Dr San Jose CA 95131*

HICKEY, ROBERT CORNELIUS, surgeon, educator; b. Hallstead, Pa., Dec. 9, 1915; s. Cornelius E. and Jennie (Murphy) H.; B.S., Cornell U., 1938, M.D., 1942; postgrad. State U. Ia., U.S. Naval Hosp., San Diego, Meml. Hosp. Cancer and Allied Diseases, N.Y.C.; m. Rose Van Vranken, June 11, 1942; children—Kathryn Ann, Robert C., Stephen, Dennis V., Sarah E. Staff U. Hosp. and State U. Ia., 1951-62, successively asso. surgery, clin. asst. prof., asso. prof., 1951-57, prof. surgery, 1957-62, asso. dean research in medicine, 1955-62; asso. dir. U. Tex. M.D. Anderson Hosp. and Tumor Inst., 1962- 63, exec. v.p., dir., 1969—; prof. surgery U. Tex. Postgrad. Sch. Medicine, 1962-63, 68—; prof., chmn. dept. surgery U. Wis. Med. Sch., Madison, 1963-68; cons. surgeon gen. USPHS, 1959-68. Dir., research chmn. Ia. div. Am. Cancer Soc., 1954—, pres. Ia. div., 1959-60, dir.-at-large Tex. div., 1968-. Served to lt. (s.g.), M.C., USNR, 1943-46. Diplomate Am. Bd. Surgery. Fellow A.C.S. (gov. 1968—); mem. Houston Surg. Soc., Am. Soc. Clin. Oncology, A.A.A.S., Am. Assn. U. Profs., Am. Radium Soc. (v.p. 1964-65). Central Surg. Assn., A.M.A., Wis. Med. Soc., N.Y. Acad. Scis., Soc. Exptl. Biology and Medicine, James Ewing Soc. (v.p. 1964- 65), Western Surg. Assn., Soc. Head and Neck Surgeons, Ia. Acad. Surgery, Am. Surg. Assn., Soc. Surgery Alimentary Tract, Tex. Surg. Soc., Sigma Xi. Home: 435 Tallowood Dr Houston TX 77024

HICKEY, SISTER RUTH CECELIA, hosp. cons.; b. Erie, Pa., July 28, 1914; d. Sherman Sylvester and Nell (McKinney) Hickey; grad. St. Vincent's Sch. Nursing, Toledo, 1936; B.S., d'Youville Coll., U. Montreal, 1949; postgrad. Cath. U., 1950, U. B.C.; M.A., Columbia, 1954. Head nurse medicine-surgery St. Vincent Hosp. and Med. Center, Toledo, 1936-38, nursing service and asst. adminstr., 1956-62, adminstr., 1962-69; nursing cons., 1969—; nursing instr. St. Mary's Hosp., Montreal, 1940-42; supr. obstetrics, surgery St. Peter's Gen. Hosp., New Brunswick, 1942-47, dir. sch. nursing and nursing service Regina Grey Nuns Hosp., Regina, Sask., Can., 1955-56. Mem. Pres.'s Commn. on Employment Handicapped. Named Toledo Woman of Year, 1969. Trustee Hosp. Planning Assn. Greater Toledo. Fellow Am. Coll. Hosp. Adminstrs.; mem. Am. Acad. Med. Adminstrs., Am., Ohio hosp. nurses assns., Am. Cath. Psychol. Assn., Am., Ohio nurses assns., Nat. Council Cath. Nurses, Nat. Assembly Women Religious Edn. Address: 6364 N Sheridan Rd Chicago IL 60626

HICKEY, WALTER B. D., men's clothing co. exec.; b. Rochester, N.Y., Mar. 29, 1906; s. Jeremiah G. and Constance (Duffy) H.; B.A., Georgetown U., 1927; m. Elizabeth Flint, July 7, 1934; children—Margaret G. (Sister Mary Walter), Walter B. D., Jeremiah F., Elizabeth (Mrs. Connell Macken). Associated with the Hickey-Freeman Co., Rochester, 1927—, pres., 1963—; dir. Hart-Schaffner- Marx. Bd. dirs. Highland Hosp., Rochester, St. John Fisher Coll., Rochester. Mem. Men's Clothing Mfrs. Assn. (bd.). Home: 3 Dunbridge Circle Rochester NY 14618 Office: 1155 Clinton Av N Rochester NY 14621

HICKEY, WILLIAM MACE, bus. exec.; b. Boston, July 2, 1906; s. William Fred and Frances (Mace) H.; B.S. in E.E., Harvard Engr. Sch., 1927; m. Lucy Murphy, June 18, 1929; children—Frances (Mrs. T.W. Ashton), William Mace (dec.). Pres., dir. The United Corp., 1943-, Monterey Ry. Light & Power Co.; chmn. Internat. Power Co., Canadian Internat. Power Co., Ltd.; dir. Barbades Light & Power Co., Bolivian Power Co., Energia Eléctrica de Venezuela, En. El. de Barquisimeto, Fiveca, S.A., D.H. Baldwin Co., Financiera Venezolana de Creditos, Empresas El. de Ven., Cia Industrial de Novedades y Plasticcs. Home: 15 Dogwood Lane Larchmont NY 10538 Office: 250 Park Av New York City NY 10017

HICKEY, WINSTON EDWARD, engring. co. exec.; b. Alma, N.B., Can., June 6, 1912; s. Frederick John and Annie Ermina (Connely) H.; B.Sc., Mt. Allison U., 1933, LL.D., 1966; M.C.E., N.S. Tech. Coll., 1938; m. Louise Gladys Murray, Jan. 4, 1941; children—David William, Linda Louise. With Strayhorne & Hickey Lumber Co., 1933-36, N.B. Dept. Hwys., 1936-39; field engr. Hydro-Electric Power Commn. Ont., 1939-40, design engr. hydraulic dept., 1940-42, 45- 46; with Canadian Found. Co., 1946-68, v.p., dir. engring., 1958-62, exec. v.p., dir. engring., 1962-65, chmn. bd., dir. engring., 1965-66, vice chmn. bd., director of engring., 1966-68; chmn. bd., dir. engring Found. Co. Can. Ltd., 1965-68; owner W.E. Hickey Assos., engring., 1968—; pres. Tantramar Contractors, Ltd., 1968—, McNamara Engring. Ltd.; chmn. Found. Can. Engring. Corp. Ltd., Frontier Constrn. Co., Inc.; v.p., dir. Found. Maritime Ltd.; v.p. Geocon Ltd.; dir. Found. Co. Ont. Ltd., Found. Overseas Ltd., La Compagnie Found. Limitee, Eastern Salvors Ltd., Coneco Acceptance Ltd., Constructora Diminico-Canadiense C. por A. A. D. Ross & Co. Ltd., Constrn. Equip. Co. Ltd., Atlantic Tug & Equipment Co. Served to lt. Royal Canadian Engrs., 1942-45; ETO. Mem. Assn. Profl. Engrs. Ont., Engring. Inst. Can., Canadian Inst. Mining and Metallurgy, Am. Cocrete Inst., Assn. Iron and Steel Engrs., Prospectors and Developers Assn., Canadian C. of C. Toronto Bd. Trades. Clubs: National (Toronto); Moles, Empire, Canadian, Toronto Railway. Home: 11 Edenbrooke Hill Toronto 18 Ontario Canada

HICKLIN, ROBERT MCLEAN, textile co. exec.; b. Richburg, S.C., May 10, 1925; s. Ira Kell and Helen (McRae) H.; B.S. in Textile Engring., Clemson U., 1948; m. Jean Ellen Horton, Oct. 2, 1948; children—Robert, David Mark, Ann Ivy, Ira Kell. Trainee, Springs Mills, Lancaster, S.C., 1948-49; various mgmt. positions Reeves Bros. Inc., Spartanburg, S.C., 1949—, exec. v.p., dir., 1968—. Served with USNR, 1943-46. Presbyn. Home: 420 E Park Dr Spartanburg SC 29302 Office: PO Box 892 Spartanburg SC 29301

HICKLIN, WAYNE, cosmetic co. exec.; b. Missouri City, Mo., Dec. 29, 1911; s. James Benton and Clara Belle (Munkres) H.; student Central Bus. Coll., Kansas City, Mo., 1931-32, Kansas City (Mo.) Bus. Coll., 1933-35; m. Hallie Bernice Hulsey, Mar. 18, 1933; dau., Linda van Gerbig. With Avon Products, Inc., 1928—, sr. v.p., 1960-62, exec. v.p., 1962, pres., 1962- 67, chmn. bd., chief exec. officer, 1967—, also dir.; pres. Avon Products Can. Ltd., 1962-67, chmn. bd., chief exec. officer, 1967—, also dir.; dir. Irving Trust Co., Prudential Ins. Co. Am. Trustee Stamford (Conn.) Hospital. Mem. Cosmetic, Toiletry and Fragrance Assn. (v.p., dir. 1969-71, chmn. 1971—). Mason. Clubs: Wee Burn Country (Darien); Norwalk (Conn.) Yacht; Union League (N.Y.C.). Home: 30 Crooked Mile Rd Darien CT 06820 Office: 30 Rockfeller Plaza New York City NY 10020

HICKMAN, BERT GEORGE, Jr., economist; b. Los Angeles, Oct. 6, 1924; s. Bert George and Caroline E. (Douglass) H.; B.S., U. Cal. at Berkeley, 1947, Ph.D., 1951; m. Edythe Anne Warshauer, Feb. 9, 1947; children—Wendy Elizabeth, Paul Lawrence, Alison Diane. Instr., Stanford, 1949-51; research asso. Nat. Bur. Econ. Research, 1951-52; asst. prof. Northwestern, 1952-54; mem. sr. staff Council Econ. Advisers, 1954-56; research asso. Brookings Instn., 1956- 58, mem. sr. staff, 1958-66; prof. Stanford U., 1966—; vis. prof. U. Cal. at Berkeley, 1960; NSF fellow, Netherlands Econometric Inst., Rotterdam, 1964-65; Ford Found. Faculty research fellow, 1968-69; mem. com. econ. stability Social Sci. Research Council, 1959-61, chmn., 1962—. Served with USNR, 1943-46. Mem. Econometric Soc., Am. Econ. Assn. (chmn. census adv. com. 1968—, tech. subcom. to rev. bus. cycle devels. 1962- -), Phi Beta Kappa, Phi Eta Sigma. Author: Growth and Stability of the Postwar Economy, 1960; Investment Demand and U.S. Economic Growth, 1965. Editor: Quantitative Planning of Economic Policy, 1965. Contbr. articles profl. jours. Home: 904 Lathrop Dr Stanford CA 94305

HICKMAN, CLEVELAND PENDLETON, Jr., educator; b. Greencastle, Ind., Oct. 29, 1928; A.B., DePauw U., 1950; M.S., U. N.H., 1953; Ph.D. in Zoology (B.C. Elec. scholar), U. B.C., 1958; married; 2 children. Demonstrator zoology DePauw U., Greencastle, 1948-50; asst. in biology U. N.H., 1950-52; fishery researcher U. Wash., Seattle, 1954-55; asst. in zoology U. B.C., 1955-58; asst. prof. U. Alta., 1958-63, asso. prof., 1963-67; asso. prof. zoology Washington and Lee U., Lexington, Va., 1967-70, prof., 1970—. Office: Dept Zoology Washington and Lee U Lexington VA 24450*

HICKMAN, DON RUE, army officer; b. Torrey, Utah, Feb. 16, 1918; s. Don F. and Julia (Mott) H.; B.A. in Edn., Ariz. State Coll., 1941; grad. Army War Coll., 1960; postgrad. advanced mgmt. program Harvard, 1966; m. LoRee Terry, Oct. 6, 1942; children—De Ann (Mrs. Reid Giles), Mary (Mrs. Glen Higbee), Pamela, Judy. Joined U.S. Army, 1941, commd. 2d lt. inf., 1942, advanced through grades to brig. gen., 1967; assigned 25th Div., Korea, 1949-51; chief plans div. Hdqrs. III Corps., Ft. MacArthur, Cal., 1952-53; plans officer Hdqrs. Caribbean Command, C.Z., 1953-56; chief assignment sect. Office Adjutant Gen., 1956-59; sr. adviser to Imperial Iranian Army Infantry Center and Sch., 1961-62; comdr. 1st bn., 10th Inf., 5th Inf. Div., Ft. Carson, Colo., 1962, 3d brig. 5th Inf. Div., 1963-64; chief mobilization plans br. plans div. Office Asst. Chief Staff, Washington, 1964-65, chief inf. br. Office Personnel Operations, 1965-67; asst. comdr. 4th Inf. Div., Vietnam, 1967-68; dep. chief staff for personnel and adminstrn., Vietnam, 1968-69; dep. chief staff for personnel Hdqrs. Continental Army Command, Ft. Monroe, Va., 1969—. Decorated D.S.M., Silver Star with oak leaf cluster, Legion Merit, Bronze Star with 4 oak leaf clusters and combat V, Army Commendation medal, Purple Heart, Air medal with 5 oak leaf clusters; Presdl. Citation (Korea); Gallantry Cross with Gold Star, Army Distinguished Service Order 1st class, Armed Forces Honor medal 1st class Republic Vietnam). Home: 101 Bernard Rd Fort Monroe VA 23351 Office: Hdqrs Continental Army Command Fort Monroe VA 23351

HICKMAN, J. KENNETH, accountant; b. Bklyn., July 8, 1928; s. Walter E. and Mildred C. (Ehrhardt) H.; B.S. cum laude, Fordham U., 1951; m. Irene A. Davis, May 12, 1956; children—Patricia, Carolyn. Salesman, Charles W. Sommer & Bro., Inc., N.Y.C., 1946- 51; with Arthur Anderson & Co., C.P.A.'s 1953—, mng. partner Newark office, 1963—. Pres. Community Chest, Leonia, N.J., 1966-68; mem. council Fordham U.; bus. adv. council Seton Hall U. Served as 1st lt. AUS, 1951-53. Named Fordham Businessman of Yr., 1966. Mem. N.J., Greater Newark chambers commerce, Fordham Coll. Bus. Alumni Assn. (pres. 1967-69), Am. Inst. C.P.A.'s, N.J. Soc. C.P.A.'s (pres. Bergen chpt. 1970-71, trustee 1971—), Nat. Assn. Accountants, Am. Accounting Assn., Beta Alpha Psi, Beta Gamma Sigma. Clubs: Essex, Downtown (trustee) (Newark); Beacon Hill (Summit). Home: 45 Templar Way Summit NJ 07901 Office: 765 Broad St Newark NJ 07102

HICKMAN, LEON EDWARD, lawyer, business exec.; b. Sioux City, Ia., July 27, 1907; s. Charles Addison and Edith Winifred (Fogg) H.; A.B., Morningside Coll., 1922, LL.D., 1944; LL.B., Harvard, 1925; LL.D., Western Md. Coll., 1958, W.Va. Wesleyan Coll., 1960; L.H.D., S.D. Sch. Mines and Tech., 1956; D.B.A. Tenn. Wesleyan Coll., 1965; m. Mayme Hoyt. Aug. 12, 1926; children—Hoyt Leon, Herbert Wilbur. Admitted to Pa. bar, 1926; partner Smith, Buchanan & Ingersoll and predecessor firms, Pitts., 1930-51; counsel law firm Eckert, Seamans & Cherin, Pitts.; vice pres., gen. counsel Aluminum Co. Am., 1951-60, exec. v.p., 1959-69, exec. com., 1951-69, finance com., 1953-70, also dir.; dir. Liggett Spring & Axel Company, Payless Cashways, Inc. Chmn., Action Housing, Inc., Pa. Housing Agy., Gov's Commn. to Revise Pub. Employee Laws Pa., 1968; vice chmn. jud. council United Meth. Ch. Trustee St. Paul Sch. Theology Meth.; pres. bd. trustees Morningside Coll. Mem. Am., Pa., N.Y., Allegheny County bar assns., Assn. Bar City N.Y. Republican. Methodist. Mason. Clubs: Union League (N.Y.C.); Duquesne, University (Pitts.); Harvard (N.Y.C., Pitts.); Harvard-Yale- Princeton Western Pa., St. Clair Country; Rolling Rock Country. Home: 829 Osage R Pittsburgh PA 15243 Office: Porter Bldg Pittsburgh PA 15219

HICKMAN, MARCUS TOBIAS, lawyer; b. Hudson, N.C., Oct. 2, 1922; s. Marcus Tobias and Claudia (Cline) H.; A.B., Duke, 1943, LL.B., 1948; m. Debra Dee Harner, May 23, 1970; children-Mary Stuart, William Davidson, Marcus Tobias. Admitted to N.C. bar, 1948, since practiced in Charlotte; mem. firm Kennedy, Covington, Lobdell & Hickman. Mem. Mecklenburg County Republican Exec. Com., 1952—; mem. N.C. Rep. Exec. Com., 1953—; mem. exec. com. Young Rep. Nat. Fedn., 1953-57; chmn. N.C. Fedn. Young Rep. Clubs, 1954-55; chmn. Rep. Exec. Com. Mecklenburg County, 1955-68; del. Rep. Nat. Conv., 1956, 64; alternate-at-large Rep. Nat. Conv., 1960. Bd. dirs. Kidney Found. Mecklenburg County. Served from ensign to lt., USNR, 1943-46. Mem. Am., N.C., 26th Judicial Dist. bar assns., Charlotte C. of C., Order of Coif, Phi Beta Kappa, Kappa Alpha, Tau Kappa Alpha, Phi Delta Phi. Epsicopalian. Clubs: Executives, City, Myers Parks Country (Charlotte); Hound Ears Golf and Ski (Blowing Rock, N.C.); Phinhurst (N.C.), Home: 3500 B Colony Rd Charlotte NC 28211 Office: N C Nat Bank Bldg Charlotte NC 28202

HICKMAN, ROBERT ZACHARIAH, lawyer; b. Benton, Ill., June 10, 1907; s. Robert Edward and Delia (Whittington) H.; B.A., U. Ill., 1929; B.A., U. Oxford, 1931, B.C.L., 1932; m. Margery D. Gunn, Oct. 5, 1940; children—Judith Ann, Robert Gunn. Admitted to Ill. bar, 1932; with Hickman & Hickman, Benton, Ill., 1932-35; asso. Poppenhusen, Johnston, Thompson & Raymond, Chgo., 1935- 42; member of the firm Gunn, Hickman, Kesler & Jenkins, Danville, Ill., 1945—. Served with AUS, 1942-45. Mem. Phi Beta Kappa, Phi Delta Theta, Phi Delta Phi. Democrat. Baptist. Mason (32, Shriner). Home: 1212 Sherman St Danville IL 61832 Office: 4 N Vermilion St Danville IL 61832

HICKMAN, WILLIAM HERBERT, economist, educator; b. Kirwin, Kan., Feb. 1, 1920; s. Isaac Herbert and Anna Myrtle (Powell) H.; B.S., Kan. State U., 1941; M.A., Stanford, 1949, Ph.D., 1952; m. Louise Weaver, Sept. 4, 1942. Instr., Stanford, 1946-49; asst. prof. Humboldt State Coll., 1949-51, Ford Found. faculty fellow, 1951-52; asso. research technician State Cal., 1952-53; asst. prof., asso. prof. Sacramento State Coll., 1953-61, prof., 1961—, head dept. econs., 1961-70; vis. asso. prof. U. So. Cal., Pakistan, 1960-62; cons. AID, Brazil, 1959. Served to 1st lt. USAAF, 1942-46. Mem. Am., Western econ. assns., Am. Assn. U. Profs. Home: 4201 Loazell Ct Sacramento CA 95825

HICKOK, ALAN OSCAR, mfg. exec.; b. Rochester, N.Y., 1920. Executive v.p., dir. Hickok Mfg. Co., Rochester, N.Y. Home: 1076 Fairport Rd Fairport NY 14450 Office: 850 St Paul St Rochester NY 14601

HICKOK, JAMES PARKER, banker; b. Farmington, Mo., Sept. 28, 1902; Chauncery Chaucery E. and Margaret (Parker) H.; A.B., U. Mo., 1926; m. Florence Brooks, Apr. 26, 1938; two children. Nat. bank examiner, 1928-30; cashier Clayton (Mo.) Nat. Bank, 1930-33; exec. v.p. Manchester Bank, St. Louis, 1933-35, pres., 1935-43; pres. Mfrs. Bank & Trust Co., St. Louis, 1943-50; with First Nat. Bank St. Louis, 1950—, chmn. bd., 1962—, chmn. exec. com., 1970—, also dir.; dir. St. Louis Union Trust Co., Transit Casualty Co., Gulf, Mobile & Ohio R.R., St. Louis Nat. Baseball Clubs, Inc. Pres. Civic Center Redevl. Corp., St. Louis. Trustee Westminster Coll.; bd. dirs. YMCA, United Fund, Municipal Theatre Assn., St. Louis C. of C. Clubs: Racquet, Noonday, Bogey, Missouri Athletic, Old Warson Country (St. Louis). Home: 42 Fair Oaks St St Louis MO 63124 Office: 510 Locust St St Louis MO 63101

HICKOK, RAY T., mfg. exec.; b. Rochester, N.Y., Mar. 13, 1918; s. S. Rae and H. Justine (Tiffany) H.; student Choate Sch., Wallingford, Conn., 1934-37, Rollins Coll., Winter Park, Fla., 1937-41; m. Sally Street, May 25, 1948; children—Holly, Thomas Alan, Kimberly R. Vice pres. Hickok Mfg. Co., 1940-45, became pres., dir., 1945, chmn. bd., 1948; chmn. bd., chief exec. officer Challenger Corp.; chmn. bd. KARE Franchises, Minit Car Wash. Mem. Monroe County chpt. Nat. Found.; dir. Rochester Rehab. Center; exec. com., past nat. chmn. U.S. Com. for UN; hon. chmn., mem. exec. com., bd. dirs. World Bus. Council; hon. mem., bd. mem. Chief Execs. Council; bd. dirs. Project HOPE; citizen chmn. Brighton Police Dept., trustee Young Pres.' Found. Mem. Young Pres. Orgn. (founding pres., since hon. pres., mem. exec. com., dir.), Am. Inst. Men's and Boys' Wear, Inc. (dir.), A.I.M. (pres.'s council). Boxing Writers' Assn. (hon.), Police Athletic League (v.p.), Com. of Council of Youth, C. of C. (trustee 3 terms), Phi Delta Theta. Clubs: Rochester, Trap and Skeet, Country; Genesee Valley, Oak Hill Country; Rolling Rock Country (Ligonier, Pa.), Palm Bay (bd. govs.). Donor S. Rae Hickok $10,000 Award Belt to profl. athlete of the year. Home: 40 Sandringham Rd Rochester NY 14610 Office: 850 St Paul St Rochester NY 14605

HICKOK, ROBERT BLAIR, musician, conductor; b. Slaton, Tex., Feb. 2, 1927; s. George B. and Minnie (Paul) H.; Mus.B., pupil of Paul Hindemith, Yale, 1949; m. Roanne Newman, June 23, 1953; children—Paul, Laura. Conductor chorus Albertus Magnus Coll., New Haven, 1949-50, Bklyn. Coll. chorus, 1952—, Bklyn. Coll. chorale, 1952—, annual festival Baroque Choral Music, Bklyn. Coll., 1954—, New Haven Chorale, 1959-61, Washington Sq. Chamber Orch. concerts, 1963-64, Manhattan Sch. Music chorus, 1967—, Cantata Singers N.Y.C., 1967—; vis. lectr., conductor Union Theol. Sem., summer 1958; asso. conductor N.Y.C. Pro Musica vocal study group, 1959-60; chmn. dept. music Bklyn. Coll., 1962-68; Sidore lectre. U. N.H., 1966, 68; conductor 1st performances numerous composers. Mem. com. Sch. Music, Yale U. Council, 1966-68. Served with AUS, 1950-52. Gen. editor Bklyn. Coll. Choral Series, 1954—. Specialist performance Renaissance and Baroque music.‡

HICKS, ALLAN CHARLES, corp. exec.; b. Batavia, Ill., Mar. 6, 1921; s. Frank and Bessie (Hunt) H.; B.S. in Accountancy, U. Ill., 1943, C.P.A., 1947; m. Dorothy Stephens, Nov. 11, 1947; children—Randall, Brian, Susan. Sr. auditor Price, Waterhouse & Co., C.P.A.'s, Chgo., 1946-50; with R.R. Donnelley & Sons Co., Chgo., 1950—, controller, 1957—. Served to 1st lt. AUS, 1943- 46. Mem. Financial Execs. Inst., Am. Inst. Accountants. Methodist. Home: 6004 Washington St Downers Grove IL 60515 Office: 2223 S King Dr Chicago IL 60616

HICKS, ALLEN MORLEY, hosp. adminstr.; b. Toronto, Ia., May 11, 1928; s. Perle and Grace (Mowry) H.; student Long Beach City Coll., 1949-50; B.S., U. Ia., 1952, M.S., 1954; m. Delores Freese, May 15, 1948; children—David, Dennis, Wendy, Patricia. Adminstrv. resident St. Lukes Hosp., Davenport, Ia., 1953-54; adminstr. Schmitt Meml. Hosp., Beardstown, Ill., 1954-57, Pekin (Ill.) Meml. Hosp., 1957-63, Ill. Masonic Hosp. and Med. Center, Chgo., 1963—. Preceptor, Masters degree program in Health and Hosp. Adminstrn. U. Ia.; chmn. com. extended care Council on Assn. Service, 1963; pres. Chgo. Hosp. Council, 1970-71. Campaign chmn., bd. dirs., chmn. indsl. div. United Fund, Pekin, Ill., 1959-64; pres. Tazwell County United Cerebral Palsy, 1960-61; chmn. Cancer Crusade, Pekin, 1960-61, service chmn. Tazewell County, 1958-60; chmn. bd. Tomahawk dist. Creve Coeur council Boy Scouts Am., 1963-64. Bd. dirs. Cancer Soc. Served with USNR, 1945- 49, 51-52. Recipient Outstanding Young Man of Year award State Ill., 1960: Distinguished Service award Pekin Jr. C. of C., 1960; Boss of Year award Marquette chpt. Nat. Secs. Assn., 1962. Mem. Am. (del. 1971—, chmn. com. community relations), Ill. (trustee, chmn. com. personnel relations) hosp. assns., Am. Coll. Hosp. Adminstrs., Am. Assn. Maternal and Infant Health, Ill. Welfare Assn., Ill. C. of C., Am. Legion, Am. Vets., Beta Gamma Sigma. Presbyn. (elder, trustee). Mason, Elk, Kiwanian. Home: 901 S Cumberland St Park Ridge IL 60068 Office: 836 Wellington Av Chicago IL 60657

HICKS, ARCHIE RAY, Jr., lawyer; b. Levanna, O., Oct. 13, 1915; s. Archie Ray and Nellie (Pangburn) H.; LL.B., Ohio State U., 1937; m. Monica Brown, Nov. 17, 1937; children-Carol J. (Mrs. John L. Cooper), Linda Kay. Admitted to Ohio bar, 1937, since practiced in Ripley; mem. firm Hicks and Stapleton, 1968—; solicitor villages of Ripley, Aberdeen, Russellville and Higginsport, O., 1939—; pros. atty. Brown County, O., 1941-49. dir. Citizens Nat. Bank, Ripley. Pres. Ripley Pub. Library. Mayor Ripley, 1940; alternate del. Republican Nat. Conv., 1948, 52, 60; sic., mem. Brown County Rep. Cntral Com. Trustee Brown County Gen. Hosp., 1961-70. Mem. Am., Ohio, Brown County bar assns., Ohio bar Assn. Found. Kiwanian (past pres.). Home: 417 Main St Ripley OH 45167 Office: 104 1/2 Main St Ripley OH

HICKS, BEATRICE ALICE, engring. exec.; b. Orange, N.J., Jan. 2, 1919; d. William Lux and Florence Benedict (Neben) Hicks; B.S. in Chem. Engring., Newark Coll. Engring., 1939; M.S. in Physics, Stevens Inst. Tech., 1949; grad. study Columbia; Sc.D., Hobart and William Smith Colleges, 1958; D.Eng., Rensselaer Poly. Inst., 1965; m. Rodney D. Chipp, Aug. 12, 1948 (dec. Dec. 1966). Research asst. Newark Coll. Engring., 1939-42; research, design, mfg. quartz crystal oscillators Western Electric Co., Kearny, N.J., 1942-45; chief engr. Newark Controls Co., Bloomfield, N.J., 1945- 46, v.p., chief engr., 1946-55, pres., 1955-67; head Rodney D. Chipp & Assos., 1967—; lectr., cons. U.S. del. Internat. Mgmt. Congress, Sao Paulo, Brazil, 1954, Paris, 1957, Australia, 1960, N.Y., 1963, Netherlands, 1966, Japan, 1969. Mem. Def. Adv. Com. on Women in Services, from 1960-63; vis. com. Margaret Morrison Carnegie Coll., 1963—; dir. 1st Internat. Conf. on Women Engrs. And Scientists, N.Y.C., 1964; U.S. del. 2d Conf., Cambridge, Eng., 1967. Trustee Newark Coll. Engring. Alumni Assn., pres., 1958-59. Recipient Newark Coll. Engring. Alumna award, 1961. Registered profl. engr., Pa., D.C., N.J., N.Y. Mem. Soc. Women Engrs. (pres. 1950-52, chmn. bd. trustees scholarship fund also hdqrs. fund), I.E.E.E. (radio communications com. 1967—), Am. Soc. M.E., Am. Soc. Heating, Refrigerating and Air Conditioning Engrs., Nat. Soc. Profl. Engrs., Women's Engring. Soc. Gt. Britain, Newark Coll. Engring. Alumni Assn., Eta Kappa Nu. Address: RD 1 Dover NJ 07801

HICKS, CHARLES ROBERT, educator; b. Syracuse, N.Y., Apr. 7, 1920; s. Seward Bliss and Abbie (Teeple) H.; A.B., Syracuse U., 1942, M.A., 1944, Ph.D., 1953; m. Ruth Frances Muller, June 13, 1942; children—William Seward, Robert Peter, John Charles. Grad. instr. Syracuse U., 1942-44, instr. math. and edn., 1946-53; quality control engr. Eastman Kodak Co., 1944-46; mem. faculty Purdue U., Lafayette, Ind., 1953—, prof. edn., head dept., 1964—, dir. tchr. edn., 1970—; cons. in field, 1946—. Trustee Judson Coll., Elgin, Ill., 1970—. Fellow Am. Soc. Quality Control (Brumbaugh award 1957, nat. v.p. 1969-71); mem. Am. Statis. Assn., Comparative and Internat. Edn. Soc., Am. Assn. Sch. Adminstrs., Biometric Soc., Phi Beta Kappa, Phi Delta Kappa. Baptist. Kiwanian (past pres. Harrison club Lafayette). Home: 1016 S 22d St Lafayette IN 47905

HICKS, CLIFFORD BYRON, mag. editor; b. Marshalltown, Ia., Aug. 10, 1920; s. Nathan LeRoy and Kathryn Marie (Carson) H.; B.S. cum laude, Northwestern U., 1942; m. Rachel G. Reimer, May 12, 1945; children—David P., Douglas L., Gary R. With Popular Mechanics mag., Chgo., 1945—, editor, 1960- 63, spl. projects editor, 1963—. Served to maj. USMCR, 1942-45. Decorated Silver Star medal. Mem. Soc. Midland Authors, Sigma Delta Chi. Club: Chgo. Press. Author: Do-It-Yourself Materials Guide, 1955; First Boy on the Moon, 1958; The Marvelous Inventions of Alvin Fernald, 1960; Alvin's Secret Code, 1963; The World Above, 1965; Alvin Fernald, Foreign Trader, 1966; Alvin Fernald, Mayor for a Day, 1969; also author fiction and non-fiction in mags. Editor: Popular Mechanics Do-It-Yourself Ency. Home: 226 Highland Av Elmhurst IL 60126 Office: 520 N Michigan Av Chicago IL 60611

HICKS, CLIFFORD MILTON, educator; b. Lincoln, Neb., Feb. 8, 1903; s. Charles Edwin and Gertrude Ethel (Wheeler) H.; A.B., U. Neb., 1924, J.D., 1925, M.A., 1927; m. Clarice Greene, June 12, 1928; children—Miriam Jane (Mrs. Charles Stewart), Marolyn Grace (Mrs. Lloyd Reed). Instr., Coll. Bus. Administrn., U. Neb., Lincoln, 1925-30, asst. prof., 1930-38, asso. prof., 1938- 50, prof., chmn. dept. bus. orgn. and mgmt., 1950—. Cons. custom pension designs Dean's Custom Pensions, Inc., Lincoln, 1968—. Chmn. finance com. Camp Fire Girls, 1946-56, chmn. nat. bd. dirs., 1956-60; bd. dirs. Family Welfare Assn., Lincoln: trustee Lincoln Symphony Orch. Found., 1959—. Mem. nat. budget com. United Community Funds and Councils. Recipient distinguished teaching award Bd. Regents U. Neb., 1955. Mem. Am. Interprofl. Inst. (pres. Lincoln chpt. 1949), Lincoln C. of C. (dir. 1939), Nat. Assembly for Social Policy and Devel., Am., Midwest econ. assns., Am. Finance Assn., Omaha-Lincoln Financial Analysts, Neb. Bar Assn., Phi Beta Kappa (sec. Neb. chpt. 1927- 57), Beta Gamma Sigma, Alpha Kappa Psi, Phi Alpha Delta. Presbyn. (deacon, trustee, elder). Clubs: Lincoln Country, Lincoln University (dir. 1956-59, 65-68, treas. 1966). Author: Introduction to Business, latest rev. edit., 1960; Corporation Finance, rev. edit., 1964; Business Law, 1958, 3d rev. edit., 1968. Home: 3210 S 27th St Lincoln NB 68502

HICKS, DENYS THEODORE, lawyer; b. Bristol, Eng., May 2, 1908; s. Cuthbert Crowden and Alice Mabel (Hodder) H.; m. Irene Elizabeth Mansell Leach, Apr. 19, 1941; children—Sarah, Charlotte, Louise, Emma. Admitted as solicitor Supreme Ct., Eng., 1931; partner firm Stanley, Wasbrough & Co., Bristol, 1931-39, 45—. Dep. chmn. Horserace Betting Levy Bd., 1961—; dir. various pub., pvt. cos. U.K. Mem. Royal Commn. on Assizes and Quarter Sessions, 1966-69. Served to lt. col. Royal Arty., 1939-45. Decorated Officer Most Excellent Order Brit. Empire. Knight Bachelor. Dep. lt. counties Gloucester and Bristol. Mem. Law Soc. (pres. 1960-61), Internat. Bar Assn. (chmn. 1966-70, pres. 1970—); hon. mem. Am., Va. bar assns., Collegie de Abagados de Mexico. Home: 39 Durdham Park Bristol BS6 6XF England Office: 12/13 Berkeley Sq Bristol BSS 1HD England

HICKS, E. WYATTE, advt. agy. exec. Sr. v.p. J. Walter Thompson Co. N.Y.C. Office: 420 Lexington Av New York City NY 10017*

HICKS, EDWIN HUGH, accountant; b. Detroit, Jan. 15, 1932; s. Willis and Anna (Dunlop) H.; B.B.A., U. Mich., 1953, M.B.A., 1956; m. Joan Marie Mayer, July 26, 1958; children—Scott Mayer, Sharon Anne, Douglas Edwin. Supr. Touche, Ross, Bailey & Smart, Detroit, 1956-63; mgr. tax dept. Am. Motors Corp., Detroit, 1963-67; gen. tax mgr. Massey Ferguson, Inc., Des Moines, 1967-69, treas., 1969-70; mgr. Touche Ross & Co., Cleve., 1970, partner, 1971—. Served with U.S. Army, 1953-55. C.P.A., Mich., Ohio. Mem. Am. Inst. C.P.A.'s, Mich. Assn. C.P.A.'s, Ohio Soc. C.P.A.'s, Financial Execs. Inst., Nat. Assn. Accountants, Delta Sigma Pi, Phi Kappa Phi, Beta Alpha Psi. Lutheran. Home: 20950 Fairmount Blvd Shaker Heights OH 44118 Office: Hanna Bldg Cleveland OH 44115

HICKS, EVERETT MILTON, business exec.; b. Lynn, Mass., July 5, 1909; s. Percy Clayton and Abbie J. (Halliday) H.; A.B., Amherst (Mass.) Coll., 1929; M.B.A., Harvard, 1931; m. Eleanor McCue, June 25, 1932; children—James E., David M., Donald J., Robert F., Peter C. Asst. to treas. Hamilton Woolen Co., Southbridge, Mass., 1932-36; v.p. Noanet Mfg. Co., Waltham, 1936-37; controller's staff Norton Co., Worcester, 1937, chief cost acct., 1939- 41, asst. controller, 1942-47, asst. mgr. grinding machine div., 1947-50, mgr. grinding machine div., 1950-68, v.p., 1952-68, also dir.; v.p. Norton Internat., Inc., 1958-68; chmn. bd. dirs. Norton- Asquith Ltd., Shrewsbury, England, 1962-68; v.p. finance Dennison Mfg. Co., 1968—, also dir.; dir. Dennison Mfg. Co. Can. Ltd.; Dunn Paper Co., Guaranty Bank and Trust Co.; trustee Worcester Five Cents Savs. Bank. Asst. gen. chmn. Community Chest Campaign, pres., 1955-56, gen. chmn., 1957; pres. Community Services, Worcester, 1966-67; sec., dir. Worcester chpt. A.R.C., 1958-62. Trustee Amherst Coll., 1965-70, mem. endowment com. Mem. Nat. Machine Tool Builders Assn. (dir. 1954-56, 58- 61, pres. 1960-61), Nat. Assn. Accountants (past pres. Worcester chpt.), U.S. Lawn Tennis Assn., Amherst Alumni Assn. Unitarian (moderator). Mason. Clubs: Worcester, Worcester Country; Coral Beach (Bermuda). Home: 45 Westwood Dr Worcester MA 01609 Office: 300 Howard St Framingham MA 01701

HICKS, FLOYD V., congressman; b. Prosser, Wash., May 29, 1915; s. J. Otis and Ruth I. (Crofutt) H.; B.Edn., Central Wash. Coll., 1938; LL.B., U. Wash., 1948; m. Norma Jeanne Zintheo, June 20, 1942; children—Tracie, Betsie. Sch. tchr., athletic coach, 1935-42; admitted to Wash. bar, 1948; practice in Tacoma, 1948-61, 63—; judge Pierce County Superior Ct., 1961-63; mem. 89th-92d Congress from 6th Dist. Wash. Served to capt. USAAG, 1942-46. Mem. Am. Bar Assn. Democrat. Kiwanian (past pres. Parkland, Wash.). Home: 118 S 116th St Tacoma WA 98444 Office: Longworth House Office Bldg Washington DC 20515

HICKS, GRANVILLE, author; b. Exeter, N.H., Sept. 9, 1901; s. Frank Stevens and Carrie Weston (Horne) H.; A.B., Harvard, 1923, A.M., 1929; L.H.D., Skidmore Coll., 1968, Ohio U., 1969; Litt.D., Siena Coll., 1971; m. Dorothy Dyer, June 27, 1925; 1 dau., Stephanie. Instr. Smith Coll., 1925-28; asst. prof. English, Rensselaer Poly. Inst., 1929-35; counsellor Am. civilization Harvard, 1938-39; editorial staff New Masses Mag., 1934-39; chmn. radio program Speaking of Books, 1941-43; dir. Corp. of Yaddo, 1942—. Lectr. Pacific Northwest Writers' Conf., 1948; lit. cons. New Leader mag., 1951-58; instr. novel writing New School, N.Y.C., 1955-58; McGuffey prof. Am. lit. Ohio U., 1967-68; contbg. editor Saturday Rev., 1958-69. Recipient Clarence Day award A.L.A., 1968. Author: The Great Tradition-An Interpretation of American Literature since the Civil War, 1933, rev. edit., 1935; (with Lynd Ward) Cne of Us, 1935; John Reed-The Making of a Revolutionary, 1936; I Like America, 1938; Figures of Transition, 1939; The First to Awaken, 1940; Only One Storm, 1942; Behold Trouble, 1944; Small Town, 1946; There Was a Man in Our Town, 1952; Where We Came Out, 1954; Part of the Truth: An Autobiography, 1965; James Gould Cozzens, 1967; Literary Horizons, 1970. Co-editor: Proletarian Literature in the United States, 1935; The Letters of Lincoln Steffens (with Ella Winter), 1938. Editor: The Living Novel, 1957. Home: Grafton NY 12082

HICKS, HARRY LESLIE, advt. exec.; b. Mineola, N.Y., June 30, 1920; s. H. Leslie and Louise (Van Nostrand) H.; A.B., Colby Coll., 1942; m. Mary Louise Yoder, Sept. 15, 1961; children—Andrea L., Lisa L., Thomas H., Yonathan Y. With Hicks & Greist, Inc., N.Y.C., 1946—, pres., 1964—. Served with USAAF, 1942- 46. Home: 28 Whistler Rd Manhasset NY 10030 Office: 850 3d Av New York City NY 10022

HICKS, HENRY DAVIES, univ. ofcl.; b. Bridgetown, N.S., Can., Mar. 5, 1915; s. Henry Brandon and Annie May (Kinney) H.; B.A. With honours in Chemistry, Mt. Allison U., 1936; B.Sc., Dalhousie U., 1937; B.C.L., Oxford, 1940, M.A. (Rhodes scholar), 1944; D.Ed., St. Anne's; LL.D., Mt. Allison U.; D.C.L., King's Coll., U. N.B.; m. Paulene Banks, Dec. 28, 1945 (dec. Feb. 1964); m. 2d, Margaret Gene Morison, Apr. 15, 1965; children—Catherine Kinney, Henry Randolph Harlow, John George Herbert, Paulene Jane Francess. Admitted to bar, 1941; with Orlando & Hicks, Bridgetown, N.S., Can., 1946-50; dean arts and sci. Dalhousie U., Halifax, N.S., 1960- 61, v.p. 1961-63, pres., vice chancellor, 1963—. Apptd. Queen's counsel, 1957. Mem. Canada Council, 1963-69; bd. dirs. Assn. Univs. and Colls. Can., 1966-69, 70—, rep. on bd. govs. U. Guyana, 1970—; pres. Assn. Atlantic Univs., 1968—. Mem. Nova Scotia Legislature, 1945-60, minister edn., 1949-54, provincial sec., 1954, premier, 1954-56; leader Liberal Party in N.S., 1954; leader Her Majesty's loyal opposition, 1956-60. Served as capt. Royal Canadian Arty., 1941-45. Invested companion Order Can. Fellow Royal Philatelic Soc. London, Royal Philafelio Soc. Can. Clubs: Saraguay, Halifax, Waegwolfic. Home: 6446 Coburg Rd Halifax Nova Scotia Canada

HICKS, J. HOWARD, union ofcl. Sec.-treas. Office and Profl. Employees Internat. Union. Office: 265 W 14th St New York City NY 10011*

HICKS, JAMES JOHNSTON, physician, educator; b. Washington, Apr. 19, 1920; s. Julius Washington and Thelma (Norton) H.; A.B., Emory U., 1940; M.D., Tulane, 1944; m. Joan Ludington, Sept. 21, 1948; children—Kathryn, Jane, Leslie. Intern, So. Pacific Hosp., San Francisco, 1945; resident U. Ala. Med. Coll., Birmingham, 1946-48; pvt. practice medicine, Birmingham, 1948—; mem. faculty U. Ala. Med. Coll., 1963—, clin. prof. otolaryngology dept. surgery, head dept., 1965—, head dept. otolaryngology, 1971—; mem. staff Hillcrest, Baptist, St. Vincents and S. Highlands, Children's hosps. Chmn. health affairs Ala. Partners of Alliance project; mem. cabinet campaign Lurleen Wallace Courage Crusade, 1968; hon. consul Guatemala in Ala. Bd. govs. Tulane U.; bd. dirs. Portmann Internat. Found., Mercy Hosp., Ala. Council Arts, Gallaudet Coll., Ala. Boy's Ranch. Served with USAF, 1945, 55-56. Recipient regional and nat. awards Sertoma Internat., 1968; award Future Farmers Am. Fellow A.C.S.; mem. Am. Acad. Otolaryngology dir.), Am. Assn. U. Profs., Ala. Med. Assn., Tulane Internat. Alumni Assn. (pres. 1967-68), Birmingham Surg. Soc., Ala. Eye, Ear, Nose and Throat Soc., Birmingham Acad. Medicine. Contbr. profl. jours. Home: 2732 Abingdon Rd Mountain Brook AL 35243 Office: 924 S 18th St Birmingham AL 35205

HICKS, JOHN, educator; b. Port Arthur, Tex., Aug. 11, 1909; s. John H. and Maud (Doran) H.; B.A., U. Louisville, 1929, M.A., 1931; Ph.D., U. Ia., 1939; m. Martha Alice Brown, July 15, 1939; children—Melissa (Mrs. Peter J. Nassiff), Lynette (Mrs. Frank Marlin). Instr. English, Miss. State U., 1934-37, Purdue U., 1937-40; asst. prof. Miami U. (Ohio), 1940-46; asso. prof. Lawrence Coll., 1946-49; prof. English, Stetson U., 1949-60, dir. English studies, 1956-60; prof. humanities U.S. Fla., 1960-63, also chmn. humanities programs; prof. English, dean Univ. Coll., So. Methodist U., 1963-67, prof. lit. and arts, chmn. comparative arts, 1967- -. Carnegie-Stetson Research grantee, 1951, 52; research fellow So. Regional Edn. Bd., 1959-60. Mem. Coll. English Assn. (exec. dir. 1960- 63), Modern Lang. Assn., Nat. Collegiate Honors Council, Am. Assn. U. Profs., Assn. Gen. and Liberal Studies (pres. 1967-68), Assn. for Higher Edn., Am. Conf. Acad. Deans. Author: The Stoicism of Matthew Arnold, 1942; Writing in Freshman Studies, 1947; (with C.R. Thompson) Thought and Experience in Prose, 2d edit., 1956; Guide to the Humanities, 1963. Home: 6964 Walling Lane Dallas TX 75231

HICKS, JOHN DARWIN, lawyer, utility co. exec.; b. Charlotte, N.C., Aug. 20, 1923; s. Ernest Lee and Susan (Bible) H.; B.S., U.S. Naval Acad., 1944; LL.B., Yale, 1953; m. Maurine Marie Gracy, Apr. 6, 1946; children—James Stephen, John Gracy, Maurine Clark. Admitted to N.C. bar, 1953; asso. law firm Helms and Mulliss, Charlotte, 1953-57; asst. gen. counsel Duke Power Co., Charlotte, 1957—, sec., 1961—, also dir., 1966—. Served from ensign to lt. USN, 1944-50. Mem. Am., N.C. bar assns., Phi Delta Phi. Home: 1540 Queens Rd Charlotte NC 28207 Office: 422 S Church St Charlotte NC 28201

HICKS, JOHN DONALD, ret. educator; b. Pickering, Mo., Jan. 25, 1890; s. Rev. John Kossuth and Harriett Gertrude (Wing) H.; B.A., Northwestern, 1931, M.A., 1914, LL.D., 1956; Ph.D., U. Wis., 1916; M.A., U. Cambridge (Eng.), 1950; LL.D., U. San Francisco, 1957, U. Cal., 1960; m. Lucile Harriet Curtis, June 15, 1921; children—Jane (Mrs. F.N. West), Carolyn (Mrs. John A. Pierce), Marjorie (Mrs. Louis K. Krall). Asst. prof. and prof. history Hamline U., 1916-22; prof. history N.C. Coll. for Women, Greensboro, 1922-23; prof. Am. history U. Neb., 1923-32, chmn. dept. history, 1925-29, dean Coll. Arts and Scis., 1929-32; prof. history U. Wis., 1932-42, chmn. dept., 1938-42; A.F. and May T. Morrison prof. history U. Cal., 1942-57, emeritus, 1957—, dean grad. div., 1945-47, chmn. dept. history, 1947-50; Phi Beta Kappa vis. scholar, 1958-59. Lectr. history Harvard, 1st half year, 1931-32; Walker-Ames lectr. U. Washington, 1944; vis. prof. Am. history and instns. U. Cambridge (fellow Trinity Hall), 1950-51; tchr. summers, Northwestern U., Syracuse U., U. Minn., George Washington U., W Va. U., U. So. Cal., Columbia, U. Cal. at Los Angeles, U. Hawaii. Mem. Am. Hist. Assn. (exec. council 1932-36, pres. Pacific coast br. 1955) Miss. Valley Hist. Assn. (pres. 1932-33), Agrl. Hist. Soc. (pres. 1948-49), Cal. Hist. Soc., Delta Upsilon and Phi Beta Kappa (hon.). Author: The Constitutions of the Northwest States, 1923; The Populist Revolt, 1931; The Federal Union, 1937; The American Nation, 1941; A Short History of American Demoracy, 1943; (with T. Saloutos) Agricultural Discontent in the Middle West, 1900-1939, 1951; The American Tradition, 1955; Republican Ascendancy, 1921-1933, 1960; Rehearsal for Disaster, 1961; My Life With History, 1968. Contbr. hist. publs. Home: 66 Southampton Av Berkeley CA 94707

HICKS, JOSEPH ROBERT, rubber co. exec.; b. Bloomsburg, Pa., Aug. 27, 1922; s. Joseph Arch and Ada (Correll), H.; B.A. in Commerce and Finance, Pa. State U., 1943; m. Mary Rita Schlitzer, Dec. 12, 1946; children—Robert William, Nancy Jane, Jeffrey Alan, Thomas Joseph, Joanne Elizabeth. With Gen. Electric Co., 1946-62, dist. mgr. finance and service operation, Cleve., 1957-62; asst. comptroller Goodyear Tire & Rubber Co., Akron, O., 1962-64, comptroller, 1964-68, v.p., comproller, 1968—. Trustee Akron Art Inst.; lay bd. St. Thomas Hosp. Served with AUS, 1943-46. Mem. Financial Execs. Inst. (bd. dirs. Cleve. 1967-70), Nat. Assn. Accountants, Pa. State U. Alumni Council (exec. com. 1967—), Delta Chi. Club: Portage Country (Akron). Home: 2390 Stockbridge Rd Akron OH 44313 Office: 1144 E Market St Akron OH 44316

HICKS, LOUISE DAY, congresswoman; b. Boston, 1923; d. William J. Day; grad. Wheelock Coll., 1938; B.S. in Edn., Boston U., 1952; J.D., Boston U., 1955; m. John Hicks; 2 sons. Tchr. primary grades, Brooklin, Mass., 1938-40; mem. Boston Sch. Com., 1961-67, chmn., 1963-65; candidate for mayor, Boston, 1967; mem. Boston City Council, 1970; mem. 92d Congress from 9th Mass. dist. Home: 1780 Columbia Rd South Boston MA 02127 Office: 11 Beacon St Boston MA 02108

HICKS, ORTON HAVERGAL, coll. adminstr.; b. Mpls., Nov. 6, 1900; s. Eliphalet G. and Mabel (Pease) H.; grad. Shattuck Sch., 1917; A.B., Dartmouth, 1921, M.B.A., Tuck Sch., 1922; m. Lois Paddock, Jan. 19, 1924; children—Orton H., Caryl Ann (Mrs. James H. Smith, Jr.), Wendy Joan (Mrs. Milo G. Coerper). Salesman, Eastman Kodak Co., 1922-26; pres. Films, Inc., 1927-38, Seven Seas Film Corp., 1938-45; dir. Loew's Internat. Corp., 1945-58, Barnett Internat. Corp., Ency. Britannica Films, Inc.; v.p. Dartmouth, 1958—. Cons. WPB, 1941-42. Trustee Shattuck Sch. Served to lt. col., Signal Corps, AUS, 1942-45. Clubs: University, Military Naval, Dartmouth (N.Y.C.); Creek (Locust Valley, N.Y.); Hanover Country. Home: 6 Rope Ferry Rd Hanover NH 03755

HICKS, ROBERT GEORGE, physician; b. N.Y.C., Apr. 1, 1923; s. Walter C. and Catherine (Kennedy) H.; student N.Y.U., 1940-43; M.D., Cornell U., 1946; m. Mary Jane Rooney, Apr. 27, 1946; children—Robert F., Stephen G., Thomas W., Mary Pat, Kathryn A., Francis E., Laurence M. Intern Orange (N.J.) Meml. Hosp., 1946-47; resident anesthesiology St. Vincent's Hosp. and Med. Center, N.Y.C., 1949-50, mem. attending staff 1950—, dir. anesthesiology, 1957—, program chmn. residency tng. anesthesiology, 1957—; asso. clin. prof. anesthesiology N.Y.U. Sch. Medicine, 1961-62; cons. County of Richmond, St. Joseph's Hosp., Columbus Hosp., U.S. VA Hosp., Castle Point, N.Y. Served with AUS, 1943-46, 47-49. Mem. Am. Soc. Anesthesiologists (pres. 1970-71). Home: 35 Iroquois Rd Yonkers NY 10710 Office: 153 W 11th St New York City NY 10011

HICKS, ROBERT T., business exec.; b. 1918; B.B.A., Western Res. U., 1948; J.D., Cleve. Marshall Law Sch., 1953; married. Asst. treas. Cleve. Pneumatic Tool Co., 1948—; asst. treas. Pneumo Dynamics Corp., Cleve., 1960-69, treas., 1969—. Served with USAAC, 1942-45. Office: 3781 E 77th St Cleveland OH 44105

HICKS, WELMER K., coll. pres.; b. Topeka, Kan., May 9, 1909; s. Ira Evans and Margaret Cleo (Wolfe) H.; grad. Peddie Sch., 1928; A.B., Princeton, 1932; A.M., Cornell U., 1935; LL.D. (hon.), Ripon Coll., 1949, Western Mich. U., 1962, U. Mich., 1964; m. Jean D. Johnstone, July 1, 1934; children—Weimer K., Susan Jean. Master of English, The Peddie Sch., Hightstown, N.J., 1932-43, alumni sec., 1933-36, dir. guidance, 1937-43; pres. Wayland Acad. and Jr. Coll., Beaver Dam, Wis., 1943-54; pres. Kalamazoo Coll., 1954—. Mem. Sponsoring com. Wis. Centennial Arts Collection, 1948; past pres. Gt. Lakes Colls. Assn.; past vice chmn. Ind. Coll. Funds Am. Edn. Mem. Assn. Am. Bapt. Ednl. Instns. (past pres.), Midwest Coll. Council (past chmn.), Assn. Ind. Colls. and Univs. of Mich. (past pres.), Cum Laude, Phi Beta Kappa, Pi Kappa Delta. Bapt. Mason. Kiwanian (past pres. Beaver Dam; past lt. gov. Wis.). Clubs: Cannon (Princeton); Outlook, Kalamazoo Country. Home: 1327 Academy St Kalamazoo MI 49003

HICKS, WILLIAM NORWOOD, educator; b. Durham, N.C., June 18, 1901; s. James Thomas and Ora (Holloway) H.; B.Mech. Engring., N.C. State Coll., 1922, M.S., 1929; A.B., Duke, 1924; M.A., Oberlin Coll., 1928; m. Ann Pitts, June 30, 1930; m. 2d, Mabel Lewis, Sept. 9, 1941; children—William Norwood III, Brona Frances. Mem. faculty N.C. State U., Raleigh, 1924-66, head dept. philosophy and religion, 1935-66, prof. philosophy and religion, 1949-66, prof. emeritus, 1966—, mem. adminstrv. bd. Sch. Liberal Arts, 1961-66. Active Inter-Racial Commn. South, local United Fund, Travelers Aid Soc., Family Service Soc., Danforth Asso., 1938-43, hon. Danforth asso., 1943- 63. Mem. Am. Soc. Engring. Edn., Am. Metaphys. Soc., Nat. Council Family Relations, So. Soc. Philosophy and Psychology, N.C. Philos. Soc., Blue Key, Golden Chain, Phi Kappa Phi, Tau Beta Pi, Sigma Chi. Home: 2505 Vanderbilt Av Raleigh NC 27607

HICKS, R. V., lawyer; b. 1917; B.A., U. Western Ont., 1939; postgrad. in law Osgoode Hall. Admitted to Ont. bar, 1942; partner firm Miller, Thomson, Hicks, Sedgewick, Lewis & Healy. Mem. Canadian Bar Assn. Office: 21 King St E Toronto 1 Ontario Canada*

HICKSON, DANIEL CORNWALL, banker; b. Iloilo, Island of Panay, P.I., May 14, 1906; s. Joseph Howard and Elizabeth (Bates) H.; B.S., Yale, 1927; m. Helen Davis Sterling, Dec. 31, 1949; stepchildren—Graham Lee Sterling III, Mrs. Craig Norton. Served various positions Western Electric Co. and subsidiaries, including pres. Gen. Service Studios, Inc., Hollywood, Cal., Washington rep., 1927-44; v.p., gen. mgr. Empire Prodns., Inc., 1945-47; v.p. Bankers Trust Co., N.Y.C., 1947-71. Mem. Chi Phi, Tau Beta Pi. Club: Hartwood (N.Y.C.). Home: 32322 Crete Rd Laguna Niguel CA 92677

HICKSON, JOHN LEFEVER, mgmt. cons.; b. Milford, N.H., June 17, 1916; s. George A. and Blanche L. (LeFever) H.; B.A., Ohio Wesleyan U., 1937; postgrad. U. Ill., 1937-38; M.S., Purdue U., 1952, Ph.D., 1953; m. Elizabeth Caldwell, Aug. 14, 1938 (dec. 1969); children—Carolyn (Mrs. J.J. Brehm, Jr.), Janet Sue (Mrs. J.W. Mueller), Linda Dianne; m. 2d, Doris McFadden, Feb. 21, 1971; stepchildren—David G. McFadden, Dennis L. McFadden. Research chemist Nat. Aniline div. Allied Chem. and Dye Corp., Buffalo, 1938-46; asst. prof. Kan. Wesleyan U., 1946-48; asst. chemist State Chemist of Ind., Lafayette, 1948-50; research fellow Purdue U., Lafayette, 1950-53; asst. to pres. Sugar Research Found., Inc., N.Y.C., 1953-60, v.p. dir. research, 1960-68, v.p., dir. research Internat. Sugar Research Found., 1968-71; mgmt. cons., Bethesda, Md., 1971—. Mem. Am. Chem. Soc. (chmn. carbohydrate div. 1959-60), Chemists Club (trustee 1967-69), Am. Inst. Chemists (pres. 1966-67), A.A.A.S., Assn. Research Dirs. (pres. 1964- 65), Sigma Xi, Phi Lambda Upsilon, Alpha Chi Sigma, Sigma Pi Sigma, Pi Mu Epsilon. Home: 7517 Westfield Dr Bethesda MD 20034

HIDALGO-QUEHL, GUILLERME, banker, lawyer; b. San Salvador, El Salvador, Dec. 22, 1923; s. Jose Alberto and Albina (Qüehl) Hidalgo; LL.D., U. El Salvador, 1952; postgrad. London Sch. Econs. and Polit. Sci., 1956-58; m. Isebelle Widmer, July 17, 1958; children—Cristina, Beatrice. Prof. law U. El Salvador, 1954-55, 59-60; judge, Sonsonate, 1953, San Salvador, 1953-56; legal adviser Ministry Justice, 1959-60; under sec. finance, 1961; v.p. Central Res. Bank El Salvador, 1961—, alternate gov. for El Salvador Inter Am. Devel. Bank, 1962—. Mem. Assn. Abogados El Salvador. Address: 15 Calle Poniente 4340 San Salvador El Salvador Central America

HIDY, RALPH WILLARD, historian, educator; b. Portland, Ind., Apr. 21, 1905; s. Urban Wilson and Helen Varella (Willard) H.; A.B., Miami U., 1926; M.A., Clark U., 1928; Ph.D., Harvard, 1935; m. Muriel Emmie Wagenhauser, June 12, 1928; 1 dau., Ann Helen. Tchr. history, high sch., Portsmouth, O., 1926-27; instr. Norwich U., 1928-30, Wheaton Coll., 1932-36, asst. prof., 1936- 41, asso. prof., 1941-46, prof., 1946-47; prof. history Grad. Sch. Arts and Sci., N.Y. U., 1950-57; Isidor Straus prof. bus. history Grad. Sch. Bus. Adminstrn., Harvard, 1957-71. Served as comdr. USNR, 1941-46. Mem. Econ. History Assn. (sec. 1950-62, pres. 1970-71), Am. Hist. Assn., Orgn. Am. Historians, Econ. History Soc. (Eng.), Phi Beta Kappa. Author: The House of Baring in American Trade and Finance, 1949; (with Muriel E. Hidy) Pioneering in Big Business, 1882-1911, 1955; (with Edward C. Bursk, Donald T. Clark) The World of Business, 1962; (with F.E. Hill and Allan Nevins) Timber and Men, The Weyerhaeuser Story, 1963; also articles in profl. jours. Editor: Harvard Studies in Bus. History, 1962- -; editor-in-chief Bus. History Review, 1962-65. Home: 108 Radcliffe Rd Belmont MA 02178

HIEBERT, ERWIN NICHOLAS, educator, historian; b. Waldheim, Sask., Can., May 26, 1919; s. Cornelius Nicholas and Tina (Harms) H.; B.A., Bethel Coll., 1941; M.A., U. Kan., 1943; M.S., U. Chgo., 1949; Ph.D. in Phys. Chemistry and History Sci., U. Wis., 1954; m. Elfrieda Franz, June 3, 1943; children—Catherine, Margaret, Thomas. Research chemist Standard Oil Co. (Ind.), also Manhattan Project, 1943-46, Inst. Study Metals, U. Chgo., 1947-50; mem. faculty U. Wis., 1957-70, prof. history of sci., 1963-70; prof. history of sci. Harvard U., 1970—; Fulbright lectr. Max Planck Inst. Physics, Göttingen, Germany, 1954-55; Am. specialist U. Kabul (Afghanistan), summer 1961; vis. prof. Inst. Advanced Studies, Princeton, 1961-62, 68-69, U. Tübingen (Germany), 1964- 65, Harvard, 1965-66. Mem. adv. com. history and philosophy of sci. Am. Inst. Physics, 1963—. Fellow A.A.A.S.; mem. Am. Chem. Soc., Am. Assn. Physics Tchr., History Sci. Soc., Sigma Xi. Mennonite. Author: The Impact of Atomic Energy, 1961; Historical Roots of the Principle of Conservation of Energy, 1962; also numerous articles. Asso. editor for chemistry Dictionary of Scientific Biography. Home: 40 Payson Rd Belmont MA 02178

HIEBERT, JOHN MARK, drug co. exec; b. Hillsboro, Kan., Feb. 21, 1904; s. J. K. and Sarah (Eitzen) H.; B.A., Tabor Coll., Hillsboro, Kan.; postgrad. U. Kan.; M.D., Boston U., 1932; Pharm.D. (hon.), New Eng. Coll. Pharmacy, 1952; m. Dorothy Prior, Sept. 22, 1933; 1 son, John

Mark. Asst. in pharmacology Sch. Medicine, Boston U., 1929-31; med. house officer Mass. Meml. Hosp., 1931-33, Mass. Gen. Hosp., 1933-34; pres. Sterling Drug, Inc., 1955-63, chmn. bd., 1960—, chief exec. officer, 1963—, dir., 1949—, asso. Sterling subsidiaries and affiliates, 1934—, chmn. research bd.; dir. W.R. Grace & Co. Trustee, Boston U., Columbia U. Coll. Pharm. Scis., Am. Child Guidance Found. Recipient Gold medal N.Y. Bd. Trade, 1961. Mem. A.M.A., Internat. C. of C. (trustee U.S. council), N.Y., New York County med. socs., N.Y. Acad. Scis., N.Y. Acad. Medicine, Commerce and Industry Assn. N.Y. (past pres., dir.), Newcomen Soc. N.Am., Phi Chi. Baptist. Mason. Clubs: Kansas, Union League (N.Y.C.); Schuyler Meadows (Loudonville, N.Y.); Delray Dunes Golf and Country, Ocean of Fla.; La Coquille (Palm Beach). Home: 898 Park Av New York City NY 10021 also 83 Island Dr S Harbour Island Delray Beach FL 33444 Office: 90 Park Av New York City NY 10016

HIEBERT, RAY ELDON, educator, author; b. Freeman, S.D., May 21, 1932; s. Peter Nicholas and Helen (Kunkel) H.; B.A., Stanford, 1954; M.S., Columbia, 1957; M.A., U. Md., 1961, Ph.D., 1962; m. Roselyn Lucille Peyser, Jan. 30, 1955; children—David, Steven, Emily, Douglas. Editorial work Los Angeles, Examiner, Washington Times-Hearald, L.I. Press, Am. Banker, 1950-57; instr. U. Minn., Duluth, 1957-58; faculty Am. U., 1958- 67, prof. journalism, chmn. dept. journalism and pub. relations and broadcasting, 1962-67; head dept. journalism U. Md., College Park, 1967—; dir. Washington Journalism Center, 1965-67. Editorial cons., speech writer Dept. Commerce, 1961-63; cons. Labor Dept. 1969, HUD, 1970-71. Trustee Found. for Pub. Relations Edn. and Research. Served with AUS, 1954-56. Mem. Am. Studies Assn., Am. Soc. Journalism Sch. Adminstrs., Assn. Edn. in Journalism, Am. Assn. U. Profs., Pub. Relations Soc. Am., Authors Guild, Sigma Delta Chi, Kappa Tau Alpha. Club: National Press (Washington). Author: Books in Human Development, 1965; The Press in Washington, 1966; Courtier to the Crowd, 1966; also monographs, articles, chpts. in books. Co-author: Franklin Delano Roosevelt, 1968; The Voice of Government, 1968; Thomas Edison, 1969; The Stock Market Crash, 1970; Atomic Pioneers, 1970. Editor: (series) Government and Communication, 1966—; Radio TV New Dirs. Assn. Communicator, 1971—; contbg. editor Pub. Relations Jour., 1964-70. Home: 10615 Harper Av Silver Spring MD 20901 Office: U Md College Park MD 20742

HIERONYMUS, CLARA BOOTH WIGGINS, journalist; b. Drew, Miss., July 25, 1913; d. Bruce Charles and Maude (Watson) Wiggins; B.A. cum laude, U. Tulsa, 1932; M.S.W., U. Okla., 1936; m. Senator Cleo Hieronymus, Apr. 24, 1937; children—Bruce Lee, Jane (Mrs. David Piller). Employment sec. and counselor YWCA, Tulsa, 1936-38; labor market analyst Okla. Employment Service, also instr. sociology U. Tulsa, 1938-50; free-lance writer Nashville Tennessean, 1951-56, art and drama critic, home furnishings editor, 1956—; book review radio sta. KFMJ, Tulsa, 1938- 45; speaker before groups, 1950—. Mem. panel jurors for selection Am. children's theaters to perform at Internat. Conf. U.S.A., 1972. Bd. dirs. Samaritans, Inc., 1967—, pres., 1967-69; bd. dirs. Middle Tenn. chpt. Nat. Arthritis Found., 1967- -; charter mem. bd. Middle Tenn. Historic Sites Fedn., 1968—; mem. Tenn. Fine Arts Center and Bot. Gardens, 1959—. Recipient Dorothy Dawe award Am. Furniture Mart, 1960, 63, 66, 69; Dallas Market Center award, 1965; named Woman of Year in Communications, Bus. and Profl. Women's Club, Nashville, 1966. Mem. Am. Inst. Interior Designers, Nashville Children's Theatre, Assn. Internationale du Theatre pour L'Entance et Jeunesse, Theta Sigma Phi. Democrat. Episcopalian. Clubs: Centennial, Le Petit Salon (Nashville). Author: (with Barbara Izard) Requiem for a Nun, On Stage and Off. Home: 2200 Hemingway Dr Nashville TN 37215 Office: 1100 Broad St Nashville TN 37202

HIETT, EDWARD EMERSON, glass co. exec.; b. Toledo, Nov. 24, 1922; s. Stanley J. and Clara I. (Jones) H.; B.B.A., U. Mich., 1946, M.B.A., LL.B., 1949; m. Margaret J. Winter, July 1, 1944; 1 dau., Katherine L. Admitted to Ohio bar, 1949; practice in Toledo, 1949-52; mem. legal dept. Libbey-Owens-Ford Co., Toledo, 1952—, sec., asst. gen. counsel, 1963—; lectr. econs., bus. law U. Toledo, 1949-69. Served with USNR, 1942-46. Mem. Am., Ohio, Toledo bar assns. Clubs: Tennis, Inverness, Toledo (Toledo). Home: 3723 Brookside Rd Toledo OH 43606 Office: 811 Madison Av Toledo OH 42624

HIGBEE, ARTHUR LLOYD, Jr., fgn. corr.; b. Chgo., June 26, 1925; s. Dr. Arthur Lloyd and Harriet Pleasant (Fawcett) H.; A.B. in History, U. Mich., 1949; m. Eda Sherwin Michel, Oct. 21, 1961 (div. 1964). Reporter Port Huron (Mich.) Times Herald, 1949-50; reporter United Press bur., Detroit, 1950-53, London, 1953-55, Paris, 1955-60, Cairo, 1960-62, Tokyo, 1962-65, Asia div. news editor, 1962-65, Middle East mgr., 1960-62, bur. mgr., Paris, 1957-60; asso. editor Newsweek, 1964-65, Mideast corr., 1965-67, Periscope editor, from 1967. Served with USNR, 1944-46. Mem. Delta Tau Delta, Sigma Delta Chi. Presbyn. Club: Overseas Press. Home: care Higbee 20 Silver Brook Rd Westport CT 06880

HIGBEE, DALLAS CLAY, newspaper exec.; b. Durham, N.C., Dec. 6, 1916; s. Charles L. and Lena M. (Ralls) H.; student Tex. A. and M. Coll., 1935-36; B.A., Marshall Coll., 1939; m. Mary I. McClung, Dec. 8, 1941; children—Carolyn, Judith, Charles, Mary, Marcia. Copy reader Huntington (W.Va.) Herald- Advertiser, 1939; sports editor Logan (W.Va.) Banner, 1939; reporter Huntington Herald-Dispatch, 1939; with Charleston (W.Va.) Gazette, 1940- -, news editor, 1948-56, exec. news editor, 1956-62, exec. editor, 1962—. Served as pilot U.S. Army Air Force, 1943-45; mem. W.Va. Air N.G., 1949-50. Mem. W.Va. Asso. Press Assn. (pres. 1955, 68-69), A.P. Mng. Editors Assn. (dir.), Charleston C. of C. (div.), W.Va. Press Assn., Pi Kappa Alpha. Methodist (steward). Club: Charleston Press (pres. 1954). Home: 2018 Carson St Charleston WV 25302 Office: 1001 Virginia St E Charleston WV 25330

HIGBEE, EDWARD, geographer, educator; b. N.Y.C., Dec. 29, 1910; s. Roscoe B. and Celia (Walker) H.; B.A., U. Wis., 1932, M.A., 1939; Ph.D., Johns Hopkins U., 1949; m. Olive E. Bellere; 1 dau., Heather Lynn. Soil conservationist, sr. agronomist Dept. Agr., 1940-48; fellow, asst. prof. Johns Hopkins, 1948-50; prof. Grad. Sch. Geography, Clark U., 1950-57, U. Del., 1957-62, U. R.I., 1962—; vis. prof. Yale U., 1950, U. B.C., 1967; dir. research Study Agrl. Revolution, 20th Century Fund, 1961-63, dir. research study Am.'s pub. environment, 1964-66; spl. research and cons. land utilization; cons. urban policy Brookings Inst. Mem. tech. adv. group to U.S. Congress Com. on Environmental Quality, 1969—. Mem. A.A.A.S., Am. Geog. Soc., Soil Sci. Soc. Am., Am. Soc. Agronomy, Soc. Sigma Xi, Phi Kappa Phi. Author: American Oasis-The Land and Its Uses, 1957; American Agriculture-Geography, Resources, Conservation, 1958; The Squeeze- Cities without Space, 1960; Farms and Farmers in an Urban Age, 1963; A Question of Priorities, 1970. Home: Mooresfield Farm Mooresfield Rd Kingston RI 02881

HIGBEE, FLOYD F., govt. ofcl.; b. Carlton, Colo., May 20, 1903; s. Samuel J. and Emily (Swords) H.; B.S.A., Kan. State U., 1924; m. Vivian Mae Hobbs, Dec. 29, 1926; children—Floyd Farrell, Michael K. Tchr. vocational agr., coach, schs. Kan. and Colo.; farm mgmt. adviser regional office Farm Security Adminstrn., predecessor agy., 1937-39, agrl. economist, liaison officer agrl. lending instns., developed nat. tenure improvement program for Farm Security Adminstrn. borrowers, 1937-43, regional dir., successor agy. Farmers Home Adminstrn., 1943-54; farmer, rancher, 1954-58; with ICA, Washington, 1958-59, agrl. credit adviser, hdqrs., Amman, Jordan, 1959-61; dep. adminstr. FHA, Washington, 1961—. Mem. Great Plains council adv. com., water policy com. U.S. Dept. Agr. Mem. Farm House Frat. Mason. Elk. Home: Town Center Plaza 1001 3d St Washington DC 20001

HIGDON, ARCHIE, educator; b. Saline, Mo., Oct. 22, 1905; s. James Cleveland and Angie (Robb) H.; B.S., S.D. State U., 1928; M.S., Ia. State U., 1930, Ph.D., 1936; m. Alice Mae Cole, Sept. 7, 1931; children—Mary Jane, Sarah Ann, Martha Jean. Instr. math. N.D. State U., 1930-34, Ia. State U., 1934-36, instr. dept. theoretical and applied mechanics, 1936-38, asst. prof., 1938-42, asso. prof., 1946-49, prof., 1949-51; commd. officer USAF, and advanced through ranks to brig. gen., 1967; lt. col. tng. command USAAF, 1942-46; with 15th Air Force, 1951-52, col., 1953-67; instr. mechanics U.S. Mil. Acad., 1952-53, asso. prof., 1953-54; prof., head dept. math. USAF Acad., Colo., 1954-56, 66-67, prof., head dept. mechanics, 1956-65, prof., head dept. physics, 1959-61, chmn. engrng. sci. div., 1956-58, 61-63, 64-66, asso. dean for engrng. and basic scis., 1965-66, chmn. basic sci. div., 1966- 67, permanent prof., 1958-67; dean engrng. Cal. State Poly. Coll., San Luis Obispo, 1967—. Asst. dir. undergrad. study, goals of engrng. edn. Am. Soc. Engrng. Edn., 1963-64, mem. bd. analysts, goals engrng. edn., 1963-67. Decorated Legion of Merit with oak leaf cluster. Registered profl. engr., Colo. Mem. Am. Soc. Engrng. Edn., Math. Assn. Am., Sigma Xi, Phi Kappa Phi, Pi Mu Epsilon. Co-author: Engineering Mechanics, 1948, 3d edit., 1968, vector edit., 1962; Mechanics of Materials, 1960, 2d edit., 1967. Home: 654 Rancho Dr San Luis Obispo CA 93401

HIGDON, EARNEST D., union ofcl. Pres., sec.-treas. Cooper's Internat. Union N. Am. AFL-CIO. Office: 429 W Walnut St Louisville KY 40202*

HIGDON, EMERSON GRANVILLE, mfg. co. exec.; b. Marshall, Mo., Jan. 6, 1909; s. Herbert Lovell and Sarah (Martin) H.; B.S. in Bus., U. Kan., 1930; grad. Advanced Mgmt. Program, Harvard, 1958; D.B.A. (hon.), Missouri Valley Coll., 1968; m. Alice Luverne Watt, June 8, 1930; children—Emerson Granville, Sherry Alice. Pub. accountant, Ernst & Ernst, C.P.A.'s, Chgo., 1930-33; with Maytag Co., 1933—, comptroller, 1941-60, v.p., 1956-60, exec. v.p., treas., dir. 1960-62, pres., treas., dir., 1962—, chief exec. officer, 1966—; chmn., dir. Fed. Res. Bank Chgo. Mem. Financial Execs. Inst., Newton C. of C., Alpha Kappa Psi. Republican. Presbyn. Elk. Home: 923 S 12th Av W Newton IA 50208 Office: Maytag Co Newton IA 50208

HIGDON, JOHN CLINE, ins. exec.; b. Indpls. Mar. 20, 1897; s. John E. and Lillie Dale (Cline) H.; A.B., U. Tex., 1917; m. Aimée Vanneman, Aug. 17, 1918; children—William Eugene, Robert Vanneman, Ruth Irene (Mrs. K.P. Knudtson), John Kenneth, Donald Thayer. Survey Near East Relief, 1919; mil., consular service, Tabriz, 1920-21; cons. actuary, 1922; mgr. life dept. Bus. Men's Assurance Co., 1923-26, sec., actuary, 1926-31, v.p., 1931-44, dir., 1934—, exec. v.p., 1944-45, pres., 1945-60, chmn., 1960-68, hon. chmn., 1968—; dir. City Nat. Bank & Trust Co. Past chmn. Kansas City Crime Commn. Pres. Am. Life Conv., 1959. Past chmn. bd. United Funds of Kansas City; hon. dir., past chmn. Kansas City and Jackson chpt. A.R.C.; trustee Starlight Theatre Assn., Liberty Meml. Assn.; bd. dirs. Am. Royal Assn. Served as 2d lt. USAAF, 1918. Recipient Catholic Community Service citation, 1960; Silver Beaver award Boy Scouts Am., 1963; named Unico Citizen of Year, 1959; Mr. Kansas City, Kansas City C. of C., 1963; Alumnus of Year, Manual High Sch., Indpls., 1967. Mem. Inst. Life Ins., Sales and Advt. Execs. Club, Health Ins. Assn. Am. (pres. 1963), Am. Legion, Kansas City C. of C. (pres. 1953), 40 and 8. Presbyn. Clubs: Mercury, Kansas City, Mission Hills Country, Saddle and Sirloin, River. Home: 3610 Wyncote Lane Shawnee Mission KS 66205 Office: BMA Tower Kansas City MO 64141

HIGDON, WILLIAM CLARENCE, engr., steel co. exec.; b. Rogers, Ark., Jan. 14, 1912; s. Agustus D. and Madeline (Corfield) H.; B.S. in Mech. Engrng., Kan. State Coll., 1934; m. Margaret Miller, June 6, 1937; children—William D., Robert L., Suellyn Elayne. Engr., Sheffield Steel Corp., Kansas City, 1934-42; chief engr. Sheffield Steel of Tex., Houston, 1942-52; asst. works mgr. Sheffield div. Armco Steel Corp., Houston, 1952-57, work mgr., 1957-58, v.p. planning and devel., 1958-61, v.p. mfg., 1961-65, v.p. engrng. and planning, 1965-66, v.p. engring. services, 1966-69, v.p. facilities planning, 1967-69, v.p. spl. ventures, Middletown, O., 1969—. Mem. Am. Inst. Mining, Metall. and Petroleum Engrs., Assn. Iron and Steel Engrs., Am. Iron and Steel. Inst., Sigma Nu, Sigma Tau. Methodist. Home: 4209 Rosedale Rd Middletown OH 45042 Office: Armco Steel Corp Middletown OH 45042

HIGGINBOTHAM, ALOYSIUS LEON, Jr., judge; b. Trenton, N.J., Feb. 25, 1928; s. Aloysius Leon and Emma Lee (Douglass) H.; student Purdue U., 1944-45; B.A., Antioch Coll., 1949; LL.B., Yale, 1952; LL.D., N.C. Coll., Durham, 1964; LL.D., Wilberforce (O.) U., 1968; J.S.D., Villanova (Pa.) U., 1969; LL.D., Haverford (Pa.) Coll., 1969; LL.D., LaSalle Coll. (Pa.), 1969; LL.D., Rutgers U., 1969; LL.D., Atlanta U., 1970; m. Jeanne Louise Foster, Aug. 21, 1948; children—Stephen Lee, Karen Lee, Kenneth Lee. Field examiner-trainee NLRB, Chgo. and Phila., 1951-52; admitted to Pa. bar, 1953; asst. dist. atty. Philadelphia County, 1952-54; partner Norris, Green, Harris & Higginbotham, Phila., 1954-62; spl. dep. atty. gen. Commonwealth of Pa., 1956-62; spl. hearing officer for conscientious objectors U.S. Dept. Justice, 1960-62; commr. Pa. Human Relations Commn., 1961-62; commr. FTC, 1962-64; U.S. dist. judge Eastern Dist. Pa., Phila., 1964—; judge U.S. Dist. Ct., V.I., 1969. Dir. Phila. Sav. Fund Soc.; vice chmn. Nat. Commn. on Causes and Prevention of Violence; vis. prof. sociology Wharton Sch., U. Pa. Trustee Yale, U. Pa., Thomas Jefferson U., N.A.A.C.P. Legal Def. and Ednl. Fund, Nat. Council YMCAs of U.S.A. Recipient Nat. Human Relations award Nat. Conf. Christians and Jews, 1968, William C. Menninger Meml. medallion, 1969, Samuel S. Fels award Sch. Dist. Phila., 1969, Russwurm award Nat. Newspaper Pubs. Assn., 1969; named One of Ten Most Outstanding Young Men in Am., 1964, Most Outstanding Young Man in Govt., 1964, Most Outstanding Young Man Phila., 1964. Home: 44 W Upsal St Philadelphia PA 19119 Office: US Court House 9th and Market Sts Philadelphia PA 19107

HIGGINBOTHAM, FRED CASWELL, Jr., oil co. exec.; b. Dallas, Oct. 19, 1919; s. Fred Caswell and Etta R. (Anderson) H.; B.B.A., So. Methodist U., 1942; student Northwestern U., 1942-43, advanced mgmt. program Harvard, 1970; m. Jean McLachlan, Mar. 23, 1945; children—Virginia Ann, Gary Jon. Agt., Internal Revenue Service, 1946-51; with Gen. Am. Oil Co. of Tex., Dallas, 1951—, asst. treas., controller, 1954-59, v.p., controller, 1959-66, v.p., treas., 1966-70, sr. v.p., treas., 1970—, also dir., mem. exec. com.; v.p., asst. sec., dir. Gen. Am. Oils, Ltd., Gen. Am. Pipe Line Co.; v.p., mem. exec. com., dir. Premier Petrochem. Co.; exec. v.p., dir. Meadows Bldg. Corp., Meadows Bldg. Services, Inc.; v.p., dir. Gen. Pipelines, Inc.; dir., mem. exec. com. Stockton, Whatley, Davin & Co. C.P.A., Tex. Mem. Financial Execs. Inst., Petroleum Accountants Soc. Dallas (pres. 1959-60), Ind. Petroleum Assn. Am. (chmn. tax com.), Mid-Continent Oil and Gas Assn. (mem. exec. com), Tax Execs. Inst. (past pres. Dallas chpt.), Tex., Dallas chpts. C.P.A.'s, Am. Petroleum Inst., Dallas-Ft. Worth Harvard Advanced Mgmt. Assn., Phi Delta Theta (pres. So. Meth. U. chpt. 1941), Beta Gamma Sigma. Clubs: Texas (dir.), Dallas Athletic, Dallas Petroleum (Dallas). Home: 6533 Greenwich Lane Dallas TX 75230 Office: Meadows Bldg Dallas TX 75206

HIGGINBOTHAM, JAY CEE, musician; b. Atlanta, May 11, 1906; s. Charlie and Tenpie (Lewis) H.; student Morris Brown Coll., Cin. Indsl. Sch. for Tailoring; m. Margaret Stratton, Dec. 27, 1957. Played with Chick Webb, Fletcher Henderson, Lucky Millinder, 1931-32; with Louis Armstrong, 1932-40, Red Allen sextet, 1940-49; composer Give Me Your Telephone Number, Higginbotham Blues, Swing Out. Recipient gold award Esquire mag., Metronome award winner poll Down Beat. Elk. Home: 152 W 118th St New York City NY 10030

HIGGINBOTHAM, SANFORD WILSON, educator; b. Fordyce, Ark., Apr. 19, 1913; s. Sanford Wilson and Amanda Alice (March) H.; B.A., Rice U., 1934; M.A., La. State U., 1941; Ph.D., U. Pa., 1949; m. Evangeline Marrin, May 29, 1942; children—John McCants, Bruce Marrin, Susan. With United Gas Pipe Line Co., Tex. and La., 1934- 38; teaching fellow La. State U., 1938-39, 40-41, U. Pa., 1939-40, 41- 42; lectr. Atlantic City Center, Rutgers U., 1946-47; from asst. prof. to prof. history U. Miss., 1947-56, univ. editor, 1955-56; dir. bur. research, publs. and records Pa. Hist. and Museum Commn., 1956-61, also asso. editor Pa. History Jour.; dean students, asst. to pres. Rice U., Houston, 1961-65, prof. history, 1961—. Served to maj. USMCR, 1942-46, 50-52. Mem. Orgn. Am. Historians, Am., So. hist. assns., Phi Beta Kappa, Phi Kappa Phi, Sigma Chi. Episcopalian. Author: The Keystone in the Democratic Arch: Pennsylvania Politics, 1800-1816, 1952; also articles. Editor Jour. Miss. History, 1953-56, Jour. So. History, 1965—. Home: 2415 Dryden Rd Houston TX 77025

HIGGINBOTTOM, SAMUEL LOGAN, airline exec.; b. North Lawrence, O., Oct. 5, 1921; s. Samuel Bradlaugh and Vera Abbie (Gutchess) H.; B.S. in Civil Engring., Columbia, 1943; grad. Advanced Mgmt. Program, Harvard; m. Fair Steinschneider, Aug. 30, 1947; children—Samuel Logan, Marie Fair, Michele Rowan. Design engr. Parsons, Brinckerhoff, Hogan & McDonald, N.Y.C., 1945-46; v.p. engring., flight, test and inspection Trans World Airlines, Inc., 1946-64; v.p. engrng. and maintenance Eastern Air Lines, Inc., 1964-67, v.p. operations group, 1967-69, sr. v.p., 1969, exec. v.p., 1969-70, pres., chief operating officer, 1970—; dir. First Nat. Bank of Miami. Charter founder mem. bd. govs. Greater Miami Philharmonic Soc.; trustee United Fund, U. Miami; bd. dirs. U.S.O. of N.Y.C., S. Fla. council Boy Scouts Am. Served to capt. USAAF, World War II; ETO. Fellow Am. Inst. Aeros. and Astronautics (asso.); mem. Soc. Automotive Engrs., Miami-Dade County C. of C. (bd. govs.), Newcomen Soc. N.Am., Fla. Council 100, Conquistadores del Cielo, Theta Tau, Tau Beta Pi, Psi Upsilon. Roman Catholic. Clubs: Columbia University, Hemisphere (N.Y.C.); Bath (Miami Beach, Fla.); Am. Yacht; Riverside Yacht; Ocean Reef Yacht (Key Largo, Fla.). Home: 32 Twin Lakes Lane Riverside CT 06878 Office: 10 Rockefeller Plaza New York City NY 10020 also Miami Internat Airport Miami FL 33148

HIGGINS, CARLISLE WALLACE, justice; b. Ennice, N.C., Oct. 17, 1889; s. Martin Alexander and Jennie (Bledsoe) H.; A.B., U. N.C., 1912, LL.D., 1914; m. Myrtle Bryant, Nov. 26, 1916; children—Carlisle W., Mary Cecile. Admitted to N.C. bar, 1914; mem. N.C. Ho. of Rep., 1924-26, State Senate of N.C., 1928-30; solicitor 11th Jud. Dist. of N.C., 1931-34; U.S. atty. Middle Dist. of N.C., 1934- 47; now asso. justice Supreme Ct. N.C. Asst. and acting chief of counsel Internat. Prosecution Sect., S.C.A.P. Hdqrs., Tokyo, Japan, 1945-47. Served in U.S. Army, World War I. Mem. Am., N.C. bar assns., Am. Legion. Democrat. Mason. Address: Supreme Court Bldg Raleigh NC 27601

HIGGINS, DICK, author, publisher; b. Cambridge, Eng., Mar. 15, 1938; s. Carter Chapin and Katharine (Bigelow) H.; student Yale, 1957; B.S., Columbia, 1960; postgrad. Manhattan Sch. Printing, 1960-61; m. Alison Knowles, May 31, 1960 (div. 1970); children—Hannah and Jessica (twins). Author with Richard Maxfield first electronic opera Stacked Deck, 1958-59; active in Happenings (Theater) movement, 1958-60; co-founder Fluxus movement, 1961- -; U.S. editor De-Collage Mag., Germany, 1962; founder Something Else Press, N.Y.C., 1964, pub., 1964—; prof. publishing Cal. Inst. Arts, 1970—; dir. Worcester Pressed Steel Co. Mem. N.Y. Audiovisual Soc. (v.p.), N.Y. Mycol. Soc., Am. Mongolian Soc. Author: What Are Legends, 1960; Jefferson's Birthday/Postface, 1964; A Book About Love and War and Death, Canto One, 1965; Act. Ed 912, 1968; FOEW & OMBWHNW, 1968; Die Fabelhafte Geträume von Taifun-Willi, 1969. Editor: (with Wolf Vostell) Pop Architektur, 1969, Fantastic Architecture, 1971. Author: numerous plays, movies. Home: PO Box 26 West Glover VT 05875

HIGGINS, EDGAR JAMES, beverage co. exec.; b. East Chicago, Ind., Mar. 14, 1906; s. Edgar T. and Harriet (Spencer) H.; B.S., Ill. Inst. Tech., 1928; m. Ellen Day, June 26, 1929. Engaged as architect, 1928-32, as real estate mgr., 1932-39; treas. Pepsi Cola Bottling Co., East Chicago, 1939-46, pres., 1946-61; chmn. bd., Pepsi Cola Gen. Bottlers, Inc., Chgo., 1961—; chmn. Chgo. Bulls (Nat. Basketball Assn.); dir. First Nat. Bank of East Chicago (Ind.), IC Industries, Chgo. Bd. dirs. Calumet Council Boy Scouts Am. Served with AUS, 1944-45. Mem. Ind. Bottlers Assn. (past pres.), Nat. Soft Drink Assn. (dir.), Pepsi Cola Bottlers Assn. U.S. (past pres.), East Chicago C. of C. (past dir.), Chgo. Conv. Bur. (dir.). Mason (Shriner), Kiwanian. Home: 7332 Forest Av Hammond IN 46324 Office: 1745 N Kolmar Av Chicago IL 60639

HIGGINS, EDWARD ALOYSIUS, Jr., journalist; b. St. Louis, Aug. 22, 1931; s. Edward Aloysius and Elsie (Gummersbach) H.; A.B. St. Louis U., 1953; Stanford Journalism fellow, Stanford, 1968-69; m. Mary Suzanne Vallar, May 15, 1954; children—Nancy Elizabeth, David Francis, Carol Marie. Gen. assignment reporter St. Louis Post-Disptch, 1953-62, 63-67, asst. city editor, 1962-63, editorial writer, 1967—. Home: 7103 Waterman Av University City MO 63130 Office: 1133 Franklin Av St Louis MO 63101

HIGGINS, FRANCIS J. lawyer; b. Chgo., Dec. 31, 1936; s. Frank James and Lois (Lundell) H.; A.B. magna cum laude, Holy Cross Coll., 1958; LL.B. cum laude, Harvard, 1961; m. Patricia C. Maloney, Dec. 26, 1959; children—Brian, Maura, Colin. Admitted to Ill. bar, 1961, since practiced in Chgo.; asso. Bell, Boyd, Lloyd, Haddad & Burns, 1961-68, partner, 1969—. Bd. dirs. Arlington Heights (Ill.) Meml. Library. Mem. Ill., Chgo. bar assns. Club: Union League (Chgo.) Home: 921 Cambridge Lane Wilmette IL 60091 Office: 135 S LaSalle St Chicago IL 60603

HIGGINS, FRED J., air force officer; b. Glendive, Mont., Dec. 15, 1915; s. Robert J. and Julia (Ford) H.; B.A., U. Mont., 1937, LL.B., 1941; m. Virginia Rimel, Oct. 2, 1944; children—Kathleen, Susan, Nora. Commd. 2d lt. USAAF, 1941, advanced through grades to brig. gen. USAF, 1963; staff judge adv. Hdqrs. Air Force Logistics Command, 1963—. Decorated Bronze Star, Sir Force Commendation medal. Home: 438 C St Wright Patterson AFB OH 45433 Office: Hdqrs Air Force Logistics Command Wright Patterson AFB OH 45433

HIGGINS, GEORGE EDWARD, sculptor; b. Gaffney, S.C., Nov. 13, 1930; B.A., U. N.C. Instr. sculpture Parsons Sch. Design, N.Y.C., 1961-62; one man show Leo Castelli Gallery, N.Y.C., 1960; exhbns. Art; USA, 1959, Detroit Inst. Art, 1959-60, Carnegie Inst., 1961, Mus. Modern Art, 1961, Martha Jackson Gallery, N.Y.C., 1960, Andrew Dickson White Gallery, 1960, Bernard Gallery, Paris, France, 1960; works rep. Mus. Modern Art, Albright Art Gallery, Chase Manhattan Bank, N.Y.C. Address: RFD 4 Easton PA 18042*

HIGGINS, HOWARD DAVID, bishop; b. N.Y.C., Aug. 23, 1903; s. Peter David and Emma (Howard) H.; A.B., Columbia, 1927, A.M., 1938; B.D., Ref. Episcopal Theol. Sem. Phila., 1924, D.D., 1939; Th.M., Princeton Theol. Sem., 1928; m. Ethel Louise Scott, Sept. 23, 1944. Ordained presbyter of Ref. Episcopal Ch., 1925; rector of First Ref. Episcopal Ch., New York, 1928-54; became asst. bishop, N.Y. and Phila. Synod, Jan. 19, 1937, bishop co-adjutor, Oct. 18, 1939; bishop of the Synod since Aug. 1, 1942; lectr. theology, Ref. Episcopal Theol. Sem., 1930-37, lectr. practical theology, 1933-37, prof. church hist. and apologetics, 1937—; presiding bishop Reformed Episcopal Church, 1957—. Trustee Ref. Episcopal Theol. Sem., Bd. Fgn. Missions (past v.p.), N.Y. and Phila. Synod (pres.), Bd. Home Missions, Lord's Day Alliance U.S. (past dir.), Gen. Council R.E. Ch. (gen. com.). Editor: Episcopal Recorder Home: 109 Glenwood Rd Merion Station PA 19066

HIGGINS, JAMES HENRY, banker; b. Kansas City, Mo., Feb. 28, 1916; s. Henry Bertram and Helen (Agnew) H.; grad. Groton (Mass.) Sch., 1935; B.A., Yale, 1939; m. Elysabeth C. Barbour, Feb. 3, 1945; children—Elysabeth Cochran, James Henry III, Hilary Barbour. With Bank of Manhattan Co., N.Y.C., 1939-41, 46-50, 51-54, asst. treas., 1947-50, 46-51; asst. v.p. Mellon Nat. Bank, v.p., 1951-54, v.p., 1954-65, sr. v.p., 1965-68, exec. v.p., 1968—; dir. Gulf Oil Corp., Joy Mfg. Co., White Consol. Industries, Inc. Mem. citizens sponsoring com. Allegheny Conf. Community Devel. Bd. trustees Pitts. Regional Planning Assn., Presbyn.-U. Hosp. Served with USNR, 1941-45. Mem. Assn. Res. City Bankers. Republican. Presbyn. Clubs: Allegheny Country, Edgeworth (Sewickley); Duquesne (Pitts.); Rolling Rock, Laurel Valley (Ligonier, Pa.); Yale (N.Y.C.). Home: 608 Maple Lane Sewickley PA 15143 Office: Mellon Nat Bank & Trust Co Mellon Sq Pittsburgh PA 15230

HIGGINS, JAMES HENRY, Jr., lawyer; b. Pawtucket, R.I., Feb. 11, 1910; s. James Henry and Ellen Frances (Maguire) H.; student Phillips Exeter Acad., 1927-28; A.B., Brown U., 1932; LL.B., Harvard, 1935; m. Betty Hall, May 26, 1939; children—James Henry III, Barbara Hall (Mrs. Thomas M. Rhine), Louis Hall. Admitted to R.I. bar, 1937; practiced in Pawtucket, 1937-43, Providence, 1943—; asso. Greenough, Lyman & Cross, 1943-45, James L. Taft, 1945-52; partner Higgins, Kingsley & Williamson, 1952-55, Higgins, Cavanagh & Cooney, 1955—; dir. Leonard Valve Co., Cranston, R.I., Livermore & Knight Co., Providence, Mays Mfg. Co., Warwick, R.I. Mem. devel. com. Gov. Dummer Acad., South Byfield, Mass.; trustee U. R.I. Found.; life mem. scholarship com. Harvard Law Sch. Fellow Am. Bar Found.; mem. Am. (ho. of dels.), R.I. (pres., past sec.) bar assns., Am. Judicature Soc. (dir.), Delta Upsilon. Clubs: Turks Head (pres.), Hope (Providence); Agawan Hunt (East Providence); Union League (N.Y.C.); Mid-Ocean (Bermuda); Lake Placid (N.Y.). Home: 1034 Smithfield Rd North Smithfield RI 02895 Office: Turks Head Bldg Providence RI 02903

HIGGINS, JAMES JOSEPH, lawyer; b. Jersey City, Dec. 20, 1917; s. James J. and Mary V. (Slack) H.; grad. St. Benedict's Prep. Sch.; B.A., Manhattan Coll., 1940; J.D., Fordham U., New York City, 1946; m. Patricia M. de la Pena, June 19, 1954. Admitted to N.Y. bar, 1947; staff Kirlin, Campbell & Keating, N.Y.C., 1948—, mem. firm, 1960—. Speaker, panelist Prac. Law Inst., N.Y.C. Mem. N.Y. County Democratic Com., 1961-64. Served with USAAF, 1943-45; capt. N.J. N.G. Res. Mem. Am. Bar Assn. (ho. of dels. 1968—), Maritime Law Assn. U.S. (pres. 1968), Assn. Average Adjusters U.S., Assn. Average Adjusters London, Soc. Am. Wars (sr. vice comdr. 1960-61), Am. Legion. Club: India House. Home: 174 E 74th St New York City NY 10021 Office: 120 Broadway New York City NY 10005

HIGGINS, JOHN SEVILLE, bishop; b. London, Eng., Apr. 14, 1904; s. Herbert and Alice Caroline (Browne) H.; A.B., Oberlin Coll., 1928, A.M., 1929; B.D., Seabury- Western Theol. Sem., 1931, D.D., 1947; LL.D., Brown U., 1955; D.D., U. R.I., 1964; m. Florence Marion Laird, Sept. 11, 1933; children—John Laird, Anne Gore-Browne (Mrs. Joseph M. Self). Ordained to ministry Episcopal Ch., 1931; rector Ch. Advent, Chgo., 1932-38, Gethsemane Ch., Mpls., 1938-48, St. Martin's Ch., Providence, 1948-53; bishop co-adjutor of R.I., 1953-55, bishop, 1955—. Mem. Joint Commn. Ecumenical Relations Episcopal Ch. Pres. bd. trustees St. George's Sch., Middletown, R.I., St. Michael's Sch., Newport, R.I., St. Andrew's Sch., Barrington, R.I., St. Mary's Home, North Providence, St. Elizabeth Home, St. Dunstan's Sch., Providence; trustee Barrington (R.I.) Coll. Mem. Nat. Council Chs. Christ U.S. (gen. bd. 1950-58), Ch. Hist. Soc. Mason. Author: The Expansion of the Anglican Communion, 1942; This Means of Grace, 1944; The Anglican Communion Today, 1947; The Hope of Glory, 1952; One Faith and Fellowship, 1958; Home: 10 Brown St Providence RI 02906 Office: 275 N Main St Providence RI 02906

HIGGINS, JOHN THOMAS, mfg. co. exec.; b. N.Y.C., Mar. 17, 1919; s. John Thomas and Nettie Viola (Stein) H.; B.S. in Econs., U. Pa., 1941; LL.B., Fordham U., 1946; m. Mary Louise Drebinger, Jan. 17, 1943; children—Susan Doris (Mrs. Allen Crews McSween), John Thomas. With firm Haskins & Sells, C.P.A.'s, N.Y.C., 1941-43, Deering Milliken & Co., Inc., 1943-49; admitted to N.Y. bar, 1947, N.C. bar, 1954; with Burlington Industries, Inc., Greensboro, N.C., 1949—, v.p., 1961—, tax counsel, 1964—. C.P.A., N.Y., N.C. Mem. N.C. Bar, N.C. Assn. C.P.A.'s, Beta Gamma Sigma. Presbyn. Home: 108 Kemp Rd W Greensboro NC 27410 Office: 3330 Friendly Av Greensboro NC 27420

HIGGINS, MILTON P., mfg. exec.; b. Worcester, Mass., 1903; s. Aldus C. Higgins; grad. Harvard, 1928; D. Engring., Worcester Polytech. Inst., 1955; Dr. Indsl. Sci., Assumption Coll., 1957; D.C.S., Holy Cross U., 1959; LL.D., Clark U., 1962; m. Alice Lord Coonley; 3 sons, 2 daus. With research lab., sales tng., sales engring. depts. Norton Co., Worcester, Mass., 1928-35, sales research mgr., 1935-38, resident mgr. Chippawa (Ont.) plant, 1938-40, asst. mgr. abrasive prodn. and research, Worcester, 1940, treas., 1941-45, exec. v.p., treas., 1945-46, pres., 1946-61, chmn., 1961-70, chmn. finance com., 1971—; dir. Worcester County Nat. Bank, New Eng. Tel. & Tel. Co., Mut. Boiler & Machinery Ins. Co., Liberty Mut. Ins. Co., Arkwright Boston Mfrs. Mut. Fire Ins. Co. Dir. Community Services of Greater Worcester, Inc., Boy's Club Worcester; treas. Worcester Redevel. Authority; mem. Bus. Council, Wash. Pres. Worcester Art Mus.; trustee Bancroft Sch., Meml. Hosp., Worcester Poly. Inst. Clubs: Harvard, Worcester, Tennis (Worcester); Hochgebirge Ski, Midas, Owl (Harvard); Tatnuck Country. Home: 757 Salisbury St Worcester MA 01609 Office: New Bond St Worcester MA 01606

HIGGINS, ROBERT LOUIS, trade assn. exec.; b. Youngstown, O., Apr. 30, 1919; s. John F. and Rosella (Johnson) H.; B.S. in Elec. Engring., Ohio U., 1949; m. Carol Geary, Jan. 18, 1946; children—Robert Louis, Melinda Jane, Geary Michael, Mark Stuart. With Nat. Elec. Contractors Assn., 1949—, exec. v.p., 1960. Mem. Pres. Nixon's Commn. on Constrn. Industry Collective Bargaining; mem. Council Constrn. Employers, Council Mech. Splty. Contracting Industries; mem. council indsl. relations Elec. Contracting Industry; mem. exec. com. Electrification Council. Co-trustee Nat. Elec. Benefit Fund. Served with AUS, 1941-46. Mem. Acad. Elec. Contracting (dir.). Home: 7713 Glennon Dr Bethesda MD 20034 Office: 1730 Rhode Island Av NW Washington DC 20036

HIGGINS, RUTH LOVING, educator; b. Columbus, O., June 21, 1895; d. Charles and Jessie Hoover (Schatzman) Higgins; B.A., B.S. in Edn., Ohio State U., 1917, M.A. (scholarship), 1921, Ph.D. (2 fellowships), 1926; postgrad. U. Wis., summer 1922, Cambridge (Eng.) U., summer 1929; LL.D. (hon.), Beaver Coll., 1953. Tchr. history, civics Ohio high schs., 1917-20, instr. history, polit. sci. Elmira (N.Y.) Coll., 1924-25; asst. prof. Earlham Coll., Richmond, Ind., 1925-26; prof., head dept. Huntingdon Coll. (formerly Woman's Coll. of Ala.), Montgomery, 1926-34; mem. history faculty U. Ala., summers 1930-31; dean, prof. history Beaver Coll., Glenside, Pa., 1934-60, chmn. dept. history and govt., 1949-60, emeritus, 1960—. Trustee Cheltenham (Pa.) Adult Sch., 1940-48, pres. 1943-45. Mem. Am. Conf. Acad. Deans (sec., treas. 1945-47, editor 1946-48), Japan Internat. Christian U. Found. (mem. women's planning com.), Am. Acad. Polit. and Social Scis., Am. Hist. Assn., Orgn. Am. Historians, Nat. (editorial staff 1935-37), Pa. (chmn. publs. 1938-41) assns. women deans and counselors, Assn. for Higher Edn., Ohio State U. Assn., Am. Assn. U. Women, Ohioana Library Assn., Ohio Hist. Soc., D.A.R., World Affairs Council Phila., Delta Kappa Gamma (state founder Ala. and Pa.). Presbyn. Author: Expansion in New York; with Especial Reference to Eighteenth Century, 1931; American Conference of Academic Deans—Developments and Abstracts, 1945-1969, 1969; also articles, hist. revs. Home: 5155 N High St Columbus OH 43214

HIGGINS, STANLEY CARMEN, Jr., lawyer; b. Logan County, W.Va., Oct. 26, 1913; s. Stanley Carmen and Virginia Meridan (Perkins) H.; LL.B., Washington and Lee U., 1937; m. Jean Annette Kent, Dec. 20, 1938; children—Stanley Kent, David Kent. Admitted to W.Va. bar, 1937, since practiced in Fayetteville; senior mem. firm Higgins, Thrift & Mahan, 1946—; mem. Jud. Council W.Va., 1962-70. Served to lt. (s.g.) USNR, 1942-45. Mem. Am., W.Va. (pres. 1960-61) bar assns., Am. Judicature Soc., W.Va. State Bar, S.A.R., Phi Gamma Delta, Phi Delta Phi. Episcopalian. Home: 203 W Maple Av Fayetteville WV 25840 Office: 108 E Maple Av Fayetteville WV 25840

HIGGINS, THOMAS W., banker; b. Worcester, Mass., 1908; grad. Georgetown U., 1931. Pres., chief exec. officer Merchants Nat. Bank & Trust Co. Syracuse; dir. Charter N.Y. Corp. Bd. dirs. Bishop Foery Found., St. Joseph's Hosp., Better Bus. Bur. Syracuse, Met. Devel. Assn.; bd. dirs., treas. Syracuse Govtl. Research Bur.; trustee Syracuse Pub. Library. Home: 444 Brattle Rd Syracuse NY 13203 Office: 216-220 S Warren St Syracuse NY 13201*

HIGGINS, WALTER MARTIN, Jr., army officer; b. Mobile May 22, 1914; s. Walter Martin and Mary (Hagan) H.; B.S., U.S. Mil. Acad., 1939; student Army Commd. and Gen. Staff Coll., 1949; Armed Forces Staff Coll., 1952, Army War Coll., 1955; m. Ann Hart Curtin, Aug. 24, 1939; 1 son, Robert Walter. Commd. 2d lt. U.S. Army, 1939, advanced through grades to maj. gen., comdg. officer 9th Infantry, 2d Infantry div., Korea, 1954; mem. faculty Army War Coll., 1956-59; chief staff I Corps, Korea, 1967, 8th Army, Korea, 1967-69; comdg. gen. Fort Hamilton Commd., Bklyn., 1969—. Mem. exec. bd. Greater N.Y. councils Boy Scouts Am., 1969—. Bd. dirs. USO N.Y.C. Decorated D.S.C., D.S.M., Silver Star, Bronze Star with 2 oak leaf clusters, Purple Heart; Croix Guerre (Luxembourg). Mem. Assn. U.S. Army, 2d Div. Assn., West Point Soc. N.Y. Roman Catholic. Club: Army-Navy Country Club. Home: Qtrs #1 Fort Hamilton Brooklyn NY 11209 Office: Hdqrs Fort Hamilton Brooklyn NY 11252

HIGGINSON, JAMES JACKSON, lawyer; b. N.Y.C., Dec. 10, 1921; s. James J. and Virginia (Mitchell) H.; grad. Groton (Mass.) Sch., 1940; B.A., Harvard, 1943, LL.B., 1949. Admitted to N.Y. bar, 1949, since practiced in N.Y.C.; partner firm Appleton, Rice & Perrin, 1969—. Dir. F.H. Prince & Co., Inc. Served to capt. AUS, 1943-46, 50-52. Mem. Am., N.Y. State bar assns., Assn. Bar City N.Y., Am. Judicature Soc. Home: Old Westbury Rd Old Westbury NY 11568 Office: 63 Wall St New York City NY 10005

HIGGINSON, THOMAS LEE, lawyer; b. N.Y.C., Jan. 2, 1920; s. James Jackson and Lucy Virginia (Mitchell) H.; student Groton Sch.; A.B., Harvard, 1942, LL.B., 1949; m. Theodora Winthrop, Sept. 11, 1948; children—Thomas Lee, Elizabeth, Robert Winthrop. Admitted to N.Y. bar, 1950, since practiced in N.Y.C.; mem. firm Shearman & Sterling, 1957—; pres., dir. Natural Minerals, Inc.; v.p., dir. Hamiltonian Corp.; dir. Fiduciary Trust Co. of N.Y. Bd. dirs. Nassau Hosp. Assn.; trustee Groton Sch., Am. Mus. Natural History, Frick Collection. Served from 2d lt. to maj. AUS, 1942-46. Decorated Bronze Star medal. Mem. Am., N.Y. State bar assns., Assn. Bar City N.Y. Republican. Episcopalian. Clubs: Brook, Links, Downtown Assn., Church (N.Y.C.); Links Golf, Piping Rock (L.I.). Home: Upper Brookville NY 12123 Office: 53 Wall St New York City NY 10005

HIGGS, DEWITT A., lawyer; b. Soldier, Ida., Dec. 13, 1907; s. DeWitt P. and Vina (Reedy) H.; LL.B., Cal. Western U., 1934; m. Florence J. Fuller, Dec. 25, 1929; children—Barbara Lee, Craig DeWitt. Admitted to Cal. bar, 1934, U.S. Supreme Ct., 1939; practice of law, specializing trial work, municipal and water law, San Diego; now sr. partner Higgs, Jennings, Fletcher & Mack; city atty., Chula Vista, 1940-42, 46-47; mem. Jud. Council Cal., 1961-64. Mem. bd. regents U. Cal., 1966—, chmn., 1968-70, vice chmn., 1970—. Served lt. comdr. USNR, 1942-45. Fellow Am. Coll. Trial Lawyers, Am. Bar Found.; mem. Am., San Diego County (dir. 1938-40, pres. 1940) bar assns., State Bar of Cal. (bd. govs. 1952-55, pres. 1955), Am. Legion (post comdr. 1947). Clubs: San Diego Country (Chula Vista); Cuyamaca (San Diego). Home: 12 Toyon Lane Chula Vista CA 92010 Office: 707 Broadway San Diego CA 92101

HIGGS, HORACE WILLIS, nonferrous metal mining exec.; b. Salt Lake City, Mar. 27, 1918; s. Horace H. and Myrtle (Perkins) H.; B.S., U. Utah, 1940, M.S. in Metall. Engring., 1941; m. Leah Baxter, Sept. 15, 1940; children—Valerie R., Jeffrey B. Metallurgist, Am. Smelting & Refining Co., East Helena, Mont., 1941-49; with Cerro de Pasco Corp. S.A., La Orova, Peru, 1950-55, asst. mgr. operations, 1955-57, mgr. operations, 1957-64, v.p., 1964-67; exec. v.p. Cerro de Pasco, N.Y.C., 1967-68; v.p. mining operations Cerro Corp., 1968-69, vice chmn., 1969—. Mem. Am. Inst. Metall. Engrs., Mining and Metall. Soc. Am. Home: 22 Wyngate Rd Greenwich CT 06830 Office: Cerro Corp 300 Park Av New York City NY 10022

HIGH, HERMON AGEE, consultant; b. Greensboro, N.C., Apr. 28, 1907; s. Alfred B. and Margaret (Patterson) H.; grad. U. N.C., 1928; m. Lois Schoonover, Dec. 7, 1933 (dec. 1957); children—Margaret, Susan; m. 2d, Cathryne S. Minahan, 1961. With Vick Chemical Co. (name changed to Richardson- Merrell, Inc.), 1929, became general sales mgr., 1940, v.p., 1948-57, sr. v.p., 1957-71; cons., 1971—. Mem. Proprietary Drug Assn., Am. (pres. 1967-69). Clubs: University (N.Y.C.); Boca Raton (Fla.) Hotel and Country. Home: 600 S Ocean Blvd Boca Raton FL 33432 Office: 122 E 42d St New York City NY 10017

HIGH, MARATHON EBY, physicist, educator; b. Chgo., Oct. 13, 1904; s. Samuel W. and Ethel (Eby) H.; A.B., McPherson Coll., 1925; M.A., Ohio State U., 1928, Ph.D., 1931; m. Edith M. Early, Aug. 16, 1927; children—Norma Jean (Mrs. Jack E. Sigler), Janice (Mrs. Winston D. Bowman), Marilyn (Mrs. Richard G. Gilbert). Instr., asst. prof. physics N.D. State Coll., 1931-38; prof. physics Minn. State Coll., Bemidji, 1938-45; vis. prof. physics Princeton, 1943-44; vis. prof. physics U. Rangoon, Burma, 1952-53; prof., chmn. dept. physics U. Mo., Kansas City, 1945—. Mem. Am. Assn. Physics Tchrs. (past pres. Mo. sect.), Am. Assn. U. Profs., Mo. Acad. Sci., Sigma Xi, Sigma Pi Sigma. Presbyn. Home: 400 E 54th St Kansas City MO 64110

HIGHET, GILBERT, educator; b. Glasgow, Scotland, June 22, 1906; s. Gilbert and Elizabeth Gertrude (Boyle) H.; ed. Hillhead High Sch., Glasgow, 1912-24; M.A., Glasgow U., 1929, D. Litt., 1951; M.A., OXford U., 1936 (Craven Scholar and Chancellor's Prizeman), D. Litt., 1956; L.H.D., Case Inst. Tech., 1952; Dr. Litt., Syracuse U., 1960; L.H.D. Adelphi U., 1964; m. Helen Clark McInnes, Sept. 22, 1932; 1 son, Gilbert Keith MacInnes. Came to U.S., 1937, naturalized, 1951. Fellow and tutor in classics St. John's Coll., Oxford, Eng., 1932-38; vis. asso. in classics Columbia, 1937-38, prof. Greek and Latin, 1938-50, Anthon prof. Latin lang. and lit., 1950—, chmn. dept. Greek and Latin, 1965-68. Guggenheim fellow, 1951. Served Brit. mission, U.S. and Can., 1941-43; Brit. Army, 1943-46; lt. col. mil. govt. Germany, 1945-46. Fellow Royal Soc. Lit.; hon. mem. Phi Beta Kappa. Clubs: Maidstone (East Hampton); Century (N.Y.C.). Author: The Classical Tradition, 1949; The Art of Teaching, 1950; People, Places and Books, 1953; Man's Unconquerable Mind 1954; The Migration of Ideas, 1954; A Clerk of Oxenford, 1954; Juvenal the Satirist, 1954; Poets in a Landscape, 1957; Talents and Geniuses, 1957; The Powers of Poetry, 1960; The Anatomy of Satire, 1962 (award of merit Am. Philol. Assn. 1963); Explorations, 1971. Translated Werner Jaeger's Paideia, 1939-44; poems in The Oxford Book of Greek Verse. Chmn. editorial adv. bd. Horizon, 1959—. Mem. bd. judges Book of the Month Club. Home: 15 Jefferys Lane East Hampton NY 11937 ☆

HIGHET, MRS. GILBERT, (see MacInnes, Helen),

HIGHFILL, JESTER VIRGIL, ednl. adminstr.; b. Hartman, Ark., June 30, 1904; s. John D. and Nancy (Roberds) H.; A.S., Ark. Poly. Coll., 1928; B.S., U. Ark., 1930; m. Dorothy Almedia Greene, June 24, 1931; 1 son, John Virgil. Asst. county agt. Conway, Ark. and county agt., Ozark, Ark., 1930-33; asst. agrl. editor, agrl. statistician, asst. to dean, dir. Coll. Agrl. U. Ark., 1934-40; state dir. Farmers Home Adminstrn. for Ark., 1940-54; asst. regional dir. Region 6, asst. adminstr. Farmers Home Adminstrn., Washington, 1954-69; registrar Columbia Tech. Inst., Arlington, Va., 1970—. Home: 3937 36th St N Arlington VA 22207 Office: Columbia Tech Inst Arlington VA

HIGHLAND, CECIL BLAINE, Jr., newspaper pub., lawyer, banker; b. New Martinsville, W.Va., Nov. 23, 1918; s. Cecil Blaine and Ella C. (Clark) H.; A.B., W.Va. U., 1939; J.D., Harvard, 1949; m. Barbara Brennan, June 4, 1955; 1 dau., Ellen Brennan. Admitted to W.Va. bar, 1949; pvt. practice, Clarksburg, 1949—; now partner McWhorter, McNeer and Highland. Pres. Empire Nat. Bank, Clarksburg 1957—, also dir.; dir. Clarksburg Pub. Co., 1949—, pres., gen. mgr., treas., 1957—; pub. Clarksburg Exponent, Clarksburg Telegram & Sunday Exponent-Telegram, 1957—. Served with AUS, 1940-46; lt. col. Res. Mem. Am., W.Va., Harrison County bar assns., Am. Legion, Harvard, W.Va. law sch. assns., Phi Beta Kappa, Phi Kappa Psi. Republican. Episcopalian. Mason (32, Shriner), Elk, Lion. Office: Empire Nat Bank Clarksburg WV 26301

HIGHLAND, JOHN NORBERT, Jr., architect; b. Buffalo, May 4, 1916; s. John Norbert and Maybelle (Schiedemantel) H.; student George Washington U., 1934-36, U. Mich., 1936-38, Cornell U., 1942-44; m. Alfietta Thompson, June 11, 1938; children—Valerie Sandra, John Norbert III. Engaged in practice architecture, 1938—; owner Highland & Highland, Buffalo, 1947—. Mem. Buffalo-Erie County Planning Assn.; chmn. profl. jury Plastics Indsutry Archtl. Competition; chmn. Housing Task Force Buffalo Waterfront Development Project, 1960-61; mem. A.I.A. adv. task force to Dept. Housing and Urban Devel. Operation Breakthrough. Registered architect, N.Y. State, 1947; certificate Nat. Council Archtl. Registration Bds., 1952. Fellow A.I.A. (chmn. home bldg. industry com. 1951-52; mem. gov. adv. com. housing research, pres. Buffalo-Western N.Y. chpt. 1964-66, nat. com. housing 1965-71, chmn. single family housing 1966- 67); mem. N.Y. State Assn. Architects (pres. Buffalo-Western N.Y., chmn., profl. adviser spl. com. concrete masonry competition), Nat. (chmn. design and constrn. com.), Nat. Guild for Religious Architecture, Niagara Frontier (dir.), Rochester home builders assns., Buffalo C. of C., Greater Buffalo Advt. Club, U. Mich. Alumni Conf. (dist. chmn.). Royal Archtl. Inst. Can. (adviser com. inquiry residential environment). Clubs: Niagara, Aeor, Univ. of Mich., Buffalo Athletic, Ellicott, Niagara Falls Country. Home: 832 Hillside Dr Lewiston NY 14092 Office: 522 Franklin St Buffalo NY 14202

HIGHSAW, JAMES LEONARD, Jr., lawyer; b. Memphis, Jan. 6, 1914; s. James Leonard and May (Baker) H.; A.B., Princeton, 1935, J.D., Harvard, 1941; m. Jane Fillmore Dunlap, June 20, 1945; children-Rhoda Jane (Mrs. Alan P. Agle), James Leonard III, Carol Ann. Admitted to Tenn. bar, 1940, D.C. bar, 1954; staff atty. Nat. Home Loan Bd., 1941-44, CAB, 1944-48; chief intercarrier relationship CAB, 1948-51, chief litigation, 1951-55; partner firm Mulholland, Hickey & Lyman, Washington, 1955-69; sr. partner Highsaw & Mahoney, Washington, 1970—; lectr. aviation law Am. U. Law Sch. Chmn. Drummond (Md.) Citizens Com., 1966—. Mem. Am., Fed., D.C. bar assns., Phi Beta Kappa. Democrat. Presbyn. Author articles in field. Home: 4601 Drummond Av Chevy Chase MD 20015 Office: 1015 18th St N W Washington DC 20036

HIGHSAW, ROBERT BAKER, educator; b. Memphis, Dec. 20, 1917; s. James Leonard and May (Baker) H.; A.B., Princeton, 1939; A.M., Harvard, 1942, Ph.D., 1945; m. Mary Church Wagner, Mar. 3, 1945; children—Mary Winfrey, Robert Baker. Instr. polit. sci. Vanderbilt U., 1942-44; asst. prof. govt. La. State U., 1944-45; dir. Miss. Bur. Pub. Adminstrn., asso. prof. polit. sci. U. Miss., 1945-47, chmn. dept. research bus. and pub. adminstrn., prof. pub. adminstrn., 1947-55; prof. polit. sci., ednl. dir. so. regional tng. program pub. adminstrn. U. Ala., 1955-56, dir. bur. pub. adminstrn., 1956—, head dept. polit. sci., 1957—. Vis. prof. Duke U., 1952; cons. adminstrn. and mgmt. bus. enterprises, govt. units; adminstrv. adv. state agys.; dir. tech. staff legislative fact finding com. Reorgn. Miss. State Govt., 1950-51; mem. of com. research pub. adminstrn. in South; mem. exec. council Conf. Deans and Dirs. Grad. Programs Pub. Adminstrn., 1959-62; chmn. So. Regional Tng. Program in Pub. Adminstrn., 1957—. Mem. Am., So. (exec. council 1949-51, v.p. 1957-58) polit.

sci. assns., Am. Soc. Pub. Adminstrn. (council 1961-64), Phi Beta Kappa, Beta Gamma Sigma. Club: Court. Author: Missisippi's Wealth, 1947; Aids for Governing: An Analysis of Technical Assistance in Mississippi, 1948 (with E. McK. Johnson, Jr.); A Guidebook of the County Sheriff, 1948 (with C. D. Mullican, Jr.); A Guidebook of the County Superintendent of Education, 1951 (with H. S. Thames); The Government and Administration of Mississippi (with C. N. Fotenberry), 1954; Conflict and Change in Local Govermnent (with John A. Dyer), 1966; also handbooks, monographs. Editor: The Deep South in Transformation: A Symposium, 1964. Adv. bd. editors Jour. Politics, 1953. Contbr. profl. publs. Address: 33 Woodland Hills Tuscaloosa AL 35401 Office: U Ala University AL 35427 ☆

HIGHSMITH, RICHARD MORGAN, Jr., educator, geographer; b. Portland, Ore., Aug. 29, 1920; s. Richard Morgan and Laura (Jones) H.; B.A., Central Wash. State Coll., 1941, M.A., 1946; Ph.D., U. Wash., 1950 m. Marijane Harkema, June 1942 (div. 1967); children—Jill (Mrs. James N. Kelley), Brooke, Richard Morgan III, Nan, April. Mem. faculty Ore. State U., 1947—, prof. geography, 1955—, chmn. dept., 1964—. Served as officer USMCR, 1942-46; PTO. Decorated Silver Star. Mem. Assn. Am. Geographers, Assn. Pacific Coast Geographers (pres. 1964-65), A.A.A.S., Sigma Xi, Gamma Theta Upsilon. Acacia. Mason. Presbyn. Author: (with O.H. Heintzelman) World Regional Geography, 3d edit., 1967; author (with others), edtor: Case Studies in World Geography, 1961, (with J. G. Jensen) Geography of Commodity Production, 2d edit., 1963, (with others) Conservation in the United States, 1962, 2d edit., 1969; (with Ray M. Northam) World Economic Activities, 1968. Editor: Atlas of the Pacific Northwest, Resources and Development, 4th edit., 1968. Home: 3024 Firwood Way Corvallis OR 97330

HIGHSMITH, WILLIAM EDWARD, univ. ofcl.; b. Eastland, Tex., Mar. 21, 1920; s. Robert A. and Dollie (Marshall) H.; A.B., Southeastern Coll., 1942; M.A., La. State U., 1947, Ph.D., 1953; m. Allene Sugg, Aug. 15, 1953; children—William Edward, John Marshall. Julius Rosenwald research fellow, 1948-49; instr. history U. Ark., 1949-50, La. State U., 1950-51; dir. Caribbean program La. State U., 1951-54; dir. Gadsden Center U. Ala., 1954-57; prof. Jacksonville U., 1957, dean, 1957-62; pres. Asheville-Biltmore Coll., 1962-69; chancellor U. N.C., Asheville, 1969—. Dir. Duval Safety Council, Jacksonville; chmn. Opportunity Corp. Asheville-Buncombe County. Mem. bd. advisers St. Luke's Hosp. Sch. Nursing. Chmn. bd. dirs. Greater Asheville Council, United Fund, Asheville Symphony Soc., Asheville Community Concert Assn.; trustee St. Mary's Jr. Coll.; dir. Art Mus., Meml. Mission Hosp. Sch. Nursing. Served to cpl. USAAF, 1942- 46. Mem. So., Miss. Valley hist. assns., Asheville C. of C. (dir.), N.C. Assn. Colls. and Univs. (dir.), Conf. Acad. Deans So. States (sec.- treas. 1961-62), Blue Key, Phi Kappa Phi, Theta Xi (nat. pub. relations com.). Democrat. Episcopalian (vestryman). Rotarian (dir.). Author articles, reviews. Home: 62 Macon Av Asheville NC 28801

HIGHTOWER, JAMES ROBERT, educator; b. Sulphur, Okla., May 7, 1915; s. L. Denzil and Bertha (McKedy) H.; A.B., U. Colo., 1936; M.A., Harvard, 1940, Ph.D., 1946; m. Florence Cole, June 1, 1940; children—James, Samuel, Josephine, Thomas. Asst. dir. Harvard-Yenching Inst., dir. Am. Inst. for Asiatic Studies, Peking, China, 1946-48; asst. prof. Far Eastern langs. Harvard, 1948-52, asso. prof., 1952-58, prof., 1958—, now also prof. Chinese literature, chmn. dept. Far Eastern languages, 1961-65; dir. Harvard Language and Area Center for Eastern Asian Studies, 1960-64; vis. prof. Hamburg U., 1959, 61, 62: visiting lectr. at Oxford U., 1958-59. Served to capt., M.I., AUS, 1944-46. Guggenheim fellow, 1958. Fellow Am. Acad. Arts and Scis.; mem. Assn. Asian Studies (dir. 1960-63). Home: 321 Central St Auburndale MA 02166 Office: 2 Divinity Av Cambridge MA 02138

HIGHTOWER, JOHN BRANTLEY, museum dir.; b. Atlanta, May 23, 1933; s. Edward A. and Margaret (Kimzey) H.; B.A. in English, Yale, 1955; m. Caroline H. Warner, Nov. 2, 1962; Amanda, Matthew. Asst. to pub. Am. Heritage Pub. Co., Inc., N.Y.C., 1961-63; exec. asst. N.Y. State Council Arts, N.Y.C., 1963-64, exec. dirs., 1964-70; dir. Mus. Modern Art, N.Y.C., 1970—. Cultural adviser Rockefeller Mission to Latin Am. for Pres. Nixon, 1969; Am. rep. UNESCO Conf. on Performing Arts, Canberra, Australia, 1969; chmn. Planning Corp. for Arts. Bd. dirs. Urban Arts Corps, MacDowell Colony. Served with USMCR, 1955-57. Recipient N.Y. State award, 1970. Mem. N.Y. State Council Arts. Club: Century Assn. (N.Y.C.) Home: 333 Central Park W New York City NY 10025 Office: 11 W 53d St New York City NY 10019

HIGHTOWER, JOHN MILTON, army officer; b. Coleman, Tex., July 29, 1916; s. John Milton and Mamie Laura (Jarrell) H.; B.A., N.M. A. and M. Coll., 1940; grad. Command and Gen. Staff Coll., 1946, Army War Coll., 1955, State Dept. Sr. Seminar Fgn. Policy, 1962; m. Lois Ellen Dunkel, May 20, 1941; children—Helen Ann (Mrs. Harvey M. Pickel), Jane Ellen (Mrs. Anthony J. Ficara), Christopher John. Commd. 2d lt. U.S. Army, 1940, advanced through grades to maj. gen., 1966; successively platoon leader Battalion S-1, company comdr., battalion exec. officer, battalion comdr., 1st Battalion, 23d Inf. Regt., U.S. and ETO, 1940-45; patient William Beaumont Gen. Hosp., El Paso, Tex., 1945-46; tactical officer U.S. Mil. Acad., 1946-48; operations and tng. officer, asst. sec. gen. staff Hdqrs. Far East Command, 1948-51; comdg. officer 32d Inf. Regt., Korea, 1951-52; dir. instrn. Inf. Sch., Ft. Benning, Ga., 1952-54; chief orgn. and equipment br. G-3, Allied Land Forces Central Europe, 1955-58; sec. joint strategic survey council Joint Chiefs Staff, 1958-61; chief staff MAAG, Republic China, Taiwan, 1962-63; dep. dir. net evaluation subcom. Nat. Security Council, 1963-65; dep. dir. Spl. State-Def. Study Group, 1965; mem. holding detachment Office Chief Staff, Dept. Army; 1965-66; comdg. gen. Ft. Dix, N.J., 1966-67; dep. chief Office Res. Components, Dept. Army, 1968-70; chief JUSMAGG, 1970—. Decorated D.S.C., Silver Star with two oak leaf clusters, Legion of Merit with two oak leaf clusters, Bronze Star with oak leaf cluster, Army Commendation medal with oak leaf cluster, Purple Heart, Croix de Guerre with palm (France); Star of Ethiopia; Belgian Fourragere. Mem. Assn. U.S. Army. Episcopalian.

HIGHTOWER, JOHN MURMANN, educator; b. Coal Creek, Tenn., Sept. 17, 1909; s. James Edward and Mary Elizabeth (Murmann) H.; student U. Tenn., 1927-28; m. Martha Nadine Joiner, Nov. 19, 1938; children—John Murmann, Leslie, James Edward. Asso. editor Drug Topics mag., 1929-30; reporter Knoxville (Tenn.) News- Sentinel, 1931-33; reporter, editor Asso. Press, Nashville, 1933-36, assigned Washington Bur., 1936-71, gen. reporting, news editing 1936- 40, Navy Dept. coverage, 1940-42, Dept. State and internat. affairs coverage, 1943-71, spl. corr., 1964-71; covered UN orgn., San Francisco, 1945, opening session UN, London, Eng., 1946, N.Y.C., 1946, European peace treaty sessions, Council Fgn. Ministers, London, Moscow, U.S.S.R., N.Y.C., 1946-48, orgn. Marshall Plan, North Atlantic Treaty, Japanese Peace Conf., San Francisco, 1951, Bermuda Conf., 1953, Berlin Fgn. Ministers Conf., 1954, Big-Four Summit Conf., Four Power Fgn. Ministers Conf., Geneva, 1955, 2d Bermuda Conf., 1957, NATO Summit Conf., 1957, Berlin, Disarmament Negotiations, Paris Summit, 1960, Kennedy-Khrushchev Meeting, 1961, Manila Summit Conf. on Vietnam, 1967, Paris Peace Talks, 1968; asso. prof. journalism U. N.M., 1971—. Recipient Pulitzer prize internat. reporting, 1961; Raymond Clapper Meml. award, 1951; Sigma Delta Chi award for nat. reporting, 1951; citation Overseas Press Club Am., 1955; Am. Acad. Achievement award for Washington correspondence, 1970. Club: Gridiron (Washington). Home: 916 Old Santa Fe Trail Santa Fe NM 87501 Office: Journalism Bldg U NM Albuquerque NM 87106

HIGHTOWER, WILLIAM HARRISON, Jr., textile co. exec.; b. Lagrange, Ga., Mar. 3, 1912; s. William Harrison and Annie (Turner) H.; B.B.A., Emory U., 1934; m. Elinor Hamilton, June 29, 1935; children—William Harrison III, Neil Hamilton. With Thomaston Mills (Ga.), 1934—, v.p., 1954-61, sec., 1954—, exec. v.p., 1961-65, pres., treas., 1965—, also dir., mem. exec. com.; pres., dir. Thomaston Broadcasting Co.; dir. C & S Nat. Bank Atlanta, Interfinancial Inc., Atlanta; adv. bd. Citizens & So. Nat. Bank, Atlanta. Chmn. Thomaston Bd. Edn., 1950-51. Trustee, v.p. Community Enterprises, Thomaston. Mem. Am. Camellia Soc. (life), Alpha Kappa Psi, Sigma Chi. Methodist (past chmn. trustees). Kiwanian. Clubs: Capital City (Atlanta); Thomaston Country. Home: 1 Poplar Dr Thomaston GA 30286 Office: Thomaston Mills Thomaston GA 30286

HIGINBOTHAM, NOE, educator; b. Sullivan Co., Ind., Sept. 6, 1913; s. Charles Francis and Cora (Tarrh) H.; A.B., Butler U., 1935; student Johns Hopkins, 1935-37; Ph.D., Columbia, 1940; m. Betty Louise Wilson, Apr. 3, 1937. Instr. algae Chesapeake Biol. Lab., 1941; Theresa Seessel research fellow Yale, 1941- 42; plant physiologist Tex. Agrl. Expt. Sta., Beaumont, 1942-45; asst. prof. U. Notre Dame, 1945-47; sr. scientist Argonne Nat. Lab., 1947-48; asso. prof. Wash. State U., 1948-53; chmn. botany dept., 1949-55, prof., 1953—. Fulbright research scholar, Australia, 1963. Fellow A.A.A.S.; member The Biophysical Society, Botanical Soc. of Am., Bot. Soc. Am., Am. Soc. of Plant Physiologists (chmn. Western sect. 1957-58), Am. Bryological Soc., Am. Assn. U. Profs., N.W. Sci. Assn. (councillor 1952-55), Sigma Xi. Home: S 105 Spring St Pullman WA 99163

HIGINBOTHAM, WILLIAM ALFRED, physicist; b. Bridgeport, Conn., Oct. 25, 1910; A.B., Williams Coll., 1932, D.Sa., 1963; postgrad. Cornell U., 1932-40; m. Julie Ann Burritt, July 9, 1949; children—Julie Eileen, Robin Ann, William Burritt. Radar research, Radiation Lab., Mass. Inst. Tech., 1941-43; Manhattan Project, Los Alamos, N.M., 1943-45, head electronics group, 1944-45; chmn. Fedn. of Am. Scientists, Washington, 1946, 59, 63, exec. sec., 1947, vice-chmn., 1948, 51; asso. head, electronics div., Brookhaven Nat. Lab., 1947-51, head instrumentation div., 1951-68, sr. physicist Tech. Support Group, 1968—. Fellow Am. Phys. Soc., I.E.E.E., Am. Nuclear Soc., A.A.A.S.; mem. Sigma Xi. Invented Higinbotham scaler circuit. Home: 11 N Howell's Pt Road Bellport NY 11713 Office: Brookhaven Nat Lab Upton NY 11973

HIGLEY, CYRUS MARTIN, banker; b. Norwich, N.Y., Mar. 9, 1894; s. Homer Harvey and Cornelia (Martin) H.; grad. Phillips Andover Acad.; Ph.B., Yale, 1915; m. Dorothy Lindley; 1 dau., Alice (Mrs. Philip L. Gilbert). With Chenango County Nat. Bank & Trust Co., Norwich, N.Y., 1915—, cashier, 1929-39, pres., 1939—, also dir.; mem. bd. directors Chenango & Unadilla Telephone Corp., Victory Chain, Inc., W. H. Dunne Co. Pres. Norwich bd. edn. Trustee Harper Coll. Mem. Nat. Sch. Bds. Assn. Inc. Episcopalian (treas.). Home: 8 Cortland St Norwich NY 13815 Office: 33 N Broad St Norwich NY 13815

HIGMAN, HENRY B., physician, educator; b. Millington, Md., 1927; M.D., U. Md., 1955. Intern, Del. Hosp., Wilmington, 1955-56; resident in neurology Charity Hosp., New Orleans, 1956-59; NIH spl. tng. fellow in neurochemistry Columbia, 1959-62; practice medicine, specializing in neurology, 1962—; vis. physician Charity Hosp., 1962-64; cons. in neurology Central La. State Hosp., Alexandria, 1962-64, VA Hosp., Tuskegee, Ala., 1964, Great Lakes Naval Hosp. (Ill.), 1966-67, VA Hosp., Pitts., 1968—; asst. attending physician Presbyn.-St. Luke's Hosp., Chgo., 1964-66, asso. attending physician, 1966-67; attending physician Presbyn. U. Hosp., Pitts., 1968—; sr. attending staff Children's Hosp., Pitts.; from asst. prof. to asso. prof. neurology U. Ill. Med. Sch., 1964-67; prof., chmn. dept. neurology U. Pitts. Sch. Medicine, 1968—. Served with AUS, 1945-47. Diplomate in neurology Am. Bd. Psychiatry and Neurology. Mem. A.M.A., Am. Acad. Neurology, Am. Neurol. Assn., Internat. Soc. Neurochemistry. Office: Dept Neurology Sch of Medicine U Pitts Pittsburgh PA 15213*

HIGUCHI, TAKERU, educator; b. Los Altos, Cal., Jan. 1, 1918; s. Iekichi and Chiye (Shiki) H.; A.B., U. Cal. at Berkeley, 1939; Ph.D., U. Wis., 1943; D.Sc., U. Mich., 1967; m. Aya Toki, Jan. 1, 1944; children—Kenji W., Junji H., Chie S., Peter T. Research asso. U. Wis., 1943-44; research chemist Office Rubber Res., U. Akron, 1944-47; mem. faculty U. Wis., 1947-67, prof. pharm. chemistry, 1954-64, pharm. U. Kan., Lawrence, 1967—. Revision com. U.S. recipient Ebert prize Am. Pharm. Assn., 1951, 52, winner, 1954; recipient Sturmer Lectr. award PCPS chpt. Rho Chi, 1956; Research Achievement award phys. pharmacy Am. Pharm. Assn. Found., 1962, Justin Power award pharm. analysis, 1964; research achievement award in stimulation of research, 1967; hon. citation U. Wis., 1969; Scheele lectr. award Pharm. Soc. Sweden, 1970. Fellow Acad. Pharm. Scis.; mem. Am. Chem. Soc., Am. Pharm. Assn., (life mem.; past chmn. sci. sect.), Am. Oil Chemists Soc., Internat. Assn. Dental Research, Chem. Soc. (London, Eng.), Acad. Pharm. Scis. (pres. 1965-67), Japanese Pharm. Soc. (hon.), Sigma Xi, Rho Chi. Author numerous papers in field. Home: 2811 Schwarz Rd Lawrence KS 66044

HILALY, AGHA, diplomat of Pakistan; b. 1911; B.A. with honors, U. Cambridge (Eng.); M.A., U. Madras (India); m. Malek Taj Begum; three children. Joined Indian Civil Service, 1936; magistrate, Bengal, 1938-39; undersec. Ministry Finance, Govt. Bengal, 1939-41; undersec. Ministries Agr., Food, Commerce and Edn., Govt. India, 1941-43; dep. sec. Ministry Finance, Govt. Bengal, 1943-47; dep. sec. Ministry Commerce, Govt. India, 1947; dep. sec. Ministry Fgn. Affairs and Commonwealth Relations, Govt. Pakistan, 1947-51, joint sec., 1951-54, acting sec., 1954-55; assigned Imperial Def. Coll., London, Eng., 1955-56; ambassador of Pakistan to Sweden, also minister to Norway, Denmark and Finland, 1956- 59; mem. Pakistan delegation to 12th session UN Gen. Assembly, 1958-59; ambassador of Pakistan to USSR, 1959-61; high commnr. to India, 1961-63, to U.K., 1963-67; ambassador of Pakistan to U.S., 1967-71, also accredited to Mexico, Venezuela, Jamaica; now ret.; Clubs: Travellers' (London); Internat. (Washington); SIND (Karachi).

HILARY, JENNIFER MARY, actress; b. Frimley, Surrey, Eng., Dec. 14, 1942; d. Richard Mouteney and Rosemary Lillian (Reynolds) Hilary; student Elmhurst Ballet Sch., 1950-58, Royal Acad. Dramatic Art, 1959-61. Appeared at Liverpool (Eng.) Playhouse in The Seagull, The Enchanted, School for Scandal, 1961-62; at Birmingham Repertory Theatre in The Tempest, Look Back in Anger, Troilus and Cressida, 1962-63; on Broadway in The Rehearsal, 1963, Ivanov, 1966, Avanti, 1968; in London in The Wings of the Dove, 1964, A Scent of Flowers, 1964, Relatively Speaking, 1967; motion picture appearance in Becket, 1964, Heroes of Telemark, 1965, The Idol, 1966; One Brief Summer, 1969; also numerous TV appearances; dir. Anthony Mann, 1965; Recipient Bancroft Gold medal Royal Acad. Dramatic Art, 1961, Tree prize, 1961. Home: 8 Embankment Gardens London SW3 England Office: 8 Upper Brook St London W1 England

HILBE, ALFRED JOHANN, govt. ofcl. Liechtenstein; b. Gmunden, Austria, July 22, 1928; s. Franz Xaver and Elizabeth (Glatz) H.; Dipl. Polit. Sci. U. Paris, 1950; Ph.D., Innsbruck U., 1951; m. Virginia Joseph, Oct. 27, 1951; 1 dau., Katrin. Fgn. service counselor legation, Bern, 1954-65; dep. head govt. The Liechtenstein Govt., 1965-70, head govt., 1970—. Decorated Grand Cross of the Liechtenstein Order of Merit. Home: FL 9494 Schaan Liechtenstein Office: Government's Palace Vaduz Liechtenstein

HILBERG, RAUL, educator; b. Vienna, Austria, June 2, 1926; s. Michael and Gisela (Schachter) H.; came to U.S., 1939, naturalized, 1944; B.A., Bklyn. Coll., 1948; M.A., Columbia, 1950, Ph.D., 1955; m. Christine Katherine Hemenway, Mar. 14, 1964; children—David, Deborah. Research specialist War Documentation Project, Washington, 1951-52; temporary lectr. Hunter Coll., 1954; lectr. U. P.R., 1954-55; mem. faculty U. Vt., 1956—, prof. polit. sci., 1967—. Served with AUS, 1944-46. Mem. Am. Polit. Sci. Assn., Am. Soc. Internat. Law. Author: The Destruction of the European Jews, 1961; Documents of Destruction, 1971. Home: 236 Prospect Pky Burlington VT 05401

HILBERRY, NORMAN, educator, cons.; b. Cleve., Mar. 11, 1899; s. Howard King and Bertha (Sabin) H.; A.B. in Physics, Oberlin Coll., 1921; Ph.D. in Physics, U. Chgo., 1941; LL.D., Elmhurst Coll., 1961, Marquette U., 1962; D.Sc., Monmouth Coll. (Ill.), 1962; m. Ann Hepburn, May 21, 1927; 1 dau., Joan Pryde. Asst. physics U. Chgo., 1922-25; instr. Physics Washington Sq. Coll., N.Y.U., 1925-28, asst. prof. Coll. Arts and Scis., 1928-42; asso. project dir. Metall. Lab., U. Chgo., 1942-46 asso. dir. Argonne Nat Lab, Argonne, Ill., 1946-49, dep. dir., 1949-57, dir. lab., 1957-61, sr. scientist, 1961-64, dir. Sch. Nuclear Sci. and Engring., 1954-56; prof. nuclear engring. U. Ariz., 1964—; participated in U. Chgo.-Dept. of State cosmic ray expdn. to S.A., 1941, in constrn. and operation first chain reacting pile, 1942; head IAEA to Latin Am., 1958; commr. Ariz. AEC; mem. Nat. Acad. Scis.- NRC adv. panel to U.S. Office Emergency Preparedness; cons. Argonne Nat. Lab.; Recipient Arthur Holly Compton award Am. Nuclear Sci., 1967; citation for meritorious service U.S. AEC, 1969. Fellow Am. Phys. Soc., A.A.A.S., N.Y. Acad. Scis., Am. Nuclear Soc. (pres. 1965-66, dir. 1958-61, 65-68); mem. Nuclear Medicine Soc. (hon. life), Am. Soc. Engring. Edn. (dir. atomic indsl. forum 1961-68), Am. Mgmt. Assn., Research Soc. Am. (gov. 1956-59), Sigma Xi. Home: 6434 E Santa Aurelia Tucson AZ 85715

HILBORNE, TOM GEORGE, banker; b. Racine, Wis., Aug. 26, 1914; s. Thomas P. and Elsie C. (Wood) H.; B.A., Oklahoma City U., 1946; student, Inst. Investment Banking, 1956, Wharton Sch. of U. Pa., 1958; m. Bula L. Buercklin, Mar. 12, 1942; 1 son, Tom George. With First Nat. Bank & Trust Co., Oklahoma City, 1935-54, H.I. Josey & Co., Oklahoma City, 1954- 56; with Liberty Nat. Bank & Trust Co., Oklahoma City, 1956—, now v.p. Mem. Investment Bankers Assn. (past chmn. Southwestern group, nat. bd. dirs. 1962-64), Oklahoma Bond Club (past pres.), Oklahoma City C. of C., Lambda Chi Alpha. Methodist. Lion. Clubs: Petroleum (Oklahoma City); Economic. Home: 2012 NW 56th Terrace Oklahoma City OK 73118 Office: Box 25848 Oklahoma City OK 73125

HILBURN, EARL DRAYTON, communications co. exec.; b. Mpls., Minn., April 16, 1920; s. Earl D. and Jess U. (Neutson) H.; student U. Wis., 1938-40, Indpls. extension br., Purdue U., 1943-44; m. Charlotte B. Johnson, Sept. 16, 1940; children—Scott L., Bruce J. Communications dept. United Air Lines, 1940-42; sr. engr. test equipment dept. RCA, Indpls., 1942- 44, field engr., Camden, N.J., 1944-46; project engr. Melpar, Inc., Alexandria, Va., 1946-47, cons., 1947-50, asst. to exec. v.p., 1950-53; Melpar, Inc. became subsidiary Westinghouse Air Brake Co., 1953; v.p. govt. contracts Westinghouse Air Brake Co., 1953-56; v.p. Link Aviation Inc., Binghamton, N.Y., 1956-60; pres., dir. Burtek, Inc., Tulsa, 1960- 62; v.p., gen. mgr. Electronics Dir. of Curtiss-Wright Corp., 1962-63; dep. to the asso. adminstr. and gen. mgr. NASA, 1963-66; v.p., asst. to pres. Western Union Telegraph Co., N.Y.C., 1966-69, exec. v.p., 1969-70, pres., 1970—; chmn. bd. Western Union of Hawaii; chmn., pres. Numex, Mexico D.F., Mexico; dir. Western Union Data Services Co., N.Y.C., Gold and Stock Telegraph Co. of N.Y., Western Union Telegraph Co., Western Union Realty Co. Chmn. joint mil. industry com. flight simulation Nat. Security Indsl. Assn., 1956. Mem. I.E.E.E., Am. Ordnance Assn., Armed Forces Communications and Electronics Assn., U.S. C. of C. (transp. and communications com., postal adv. panel; dir.), N.Y. Bd. Trade, U.S. Power Squadron. Clubs: Internat., Nat. Aviation (Washington); Merchants (N.Y.C.); Tarrytown (N.Y.) Boat; Jockey (Miami). Home: PO Box 258 Short Hills NJ 07078 Office: Western Union Telegraph Co 60 Hudson St New York City NY 10013

HILD, WALTHER JOHANNES, anatomist; b. Wesel, Germany, Nov. 3, 1919; s. Peter and Sophie (Kirchner) H.; student U. Freiburg, Germany, 1941-43; M.D., U. Kiel, 1949; m. Ursula Marianne Schuster, Feb. 12, 1955; children—Susanne Barbara, Peter George. Came to U.S., 1954, naturalized, 1959. Asst. dept. anatomy U. Kiel, 1949-54; Rockefeller Found. fellow U.S., 1952-53; with U. Tex. Med. br., 1954—, prof. anatomy, 1966—, chmn. dept., 1968- -. Mem. Neurology B Study Sect., 1968-72. Mem. Am. Assn. Anatomists, Tex. Acad. Sci., Anatomische Gesellschaft, Endocrinologische Gesellschaft. Author: Das Neuron, 1959. Co-editor Ergebnisse der Anatomie und Entwicklungsgeschichte, 1965—. Research and numerous publs. on neurosecretion leading to recognition of physiol. significance of hypothalamic neurosecretion in mammals, in vitro cultivation of central nervous tissue in connection with electrophysiol. expts. involving single neurons and neuroglia cells, discovery of specific electro-physiol. properties of neuroglia cells. Home: 126 Tuna Av Galveston TX 77550

HILDEBRAND, FRANCIS BEGNAUD, educator; b. Washington, Pa., Sept. 1, 1915; s. Frank Alonzo and Inez (Patin) H.; B.S., Washington and Jefferson Coll., 1936, M.A., 1938, Sc.D. (hon.), 1969; Ph.D., Mass. Inst. Tech., 1940; m. Eleanor Maclaren Jenkins, Sept. 18, 1943; children—Susan Lee (Mrs. John Gardner Hartley), Robert Craig, Jean Ellen. Mem. faculty Mass. Inst. Tech., Cambridge, 1938—, asso. prof. math., 1950-67, prof., 1967—. Mem. Am. Math. Soc., Math. Assn. Am., Sigma Xi, Phi Beta Kappa, Phi Delta Theta. Author: Advanced Calculus for Applications, 1949, 62; Methods of Applied Mathematics, 1952, 65; Introduction to Numerical Analysis, 1956; Finite-Difference Equations and Simulations, 1968. Home: 7 Bucknell Rd Wellesley MA 02181 Office: 77 Massachusetts Av Cambridge MA 02138

HILDEBRAND, FRANK CHILDS, food mfr.; b. Hinsdale, Ill., Oct. 6, 1909; s. Clement A. and Helen (Childs) H.; B.S., Beloit Coll., 1931; M.S., U. Wis., 1933; Ph.D., Columbia, 1935; m. Joyce Wadmond, Aug. 3, 1935; children—Nancy E. (Mrs. F. N. Jones III), David K., Marcia J. (Mrs. Paul M. Ginsburg). Chemist, research dept. Gen. Mills, Inc., 1935-43, products control dept., 1943-52, asst. to pres., 1952-55, dir. products control dept., 1956—, v.p., 1956—, v.p. quality control, 1966-68; v.p., exec. dir. Gen. Mills Found., 1968—. Trustee

Beloit Coll., 1967-70, chmn., 1971—. Mem. Am. Assn. Cereal Chemists (pres. 1949-50), Am. Chem. Soc. Home: 4722 Forest Circle Minnetonka MN 55343 Office: 9200 Wayzata Blvd Minneapolis MN 55440

HILDEBRAND, GEORGE HERBERT, economist; b. Oakland, Cal., July 7, 1913; s. George Herbert and Irene (Colegrove) H.; B.A., U. Cal. at Berkeley, 1935; M.A., Harvard, 1941; Ph.D., Cornell U., Ithaca, N.Y., 1942; m. Margaret Boardman, Aug. 28, 1937; children—George Colegrove, Stephen Boardman, Richard Whitney. Asst. prof. econs. U. Tex., Austin, 1941-43; prin. economist NWLF, 1943-45; asst. prof. social instns. U. Cal. at Berkeley, 1945-47, vis. prof., 1959-60; from asst. to prof. econs. U. Cal. at Los Angeles, 1947-60, dir. Inst. Indsl. Relations, 1956-60; prof. econs. and indsl. and labor relations Cornell U., Ithaca, N.Y., 1960-70, Maxwell M. Upson prof. econs. and indsl. relations, 1970—; indsl. relations, 1970—; on leave as dep. undersec. labor for internat. affairs U.S. Dept. Labor, 1969—; mem. bd. fgn. service, U.S. Dept. State, 1969—. Vis. prof. econs. Mass. Inst. Tech., 1964-65; cons. OSS, 1942; labor arbitrator, 1951—; cons. Dept. Labor, also mem. also mem. com. to guide sec. labor study basic steel industry, 1959-60; pub. mem. minimum wage bd. Restaurant Industry N.Y. State, 1961-62; chief U.S. delegation Internat. Labor Orgn., 1969—; also mem. governing body, U.S. govt.; bd. fgn. service U.S. Dept. State; cons. Dept. Health, Edn. and Welfare, 1961-62; chmn. adv. com. on research Social Security Adminstrn., 1965-67; tech. adviser President's Cost of Living Com., 1966; bd. dirs. Social Sci. Research Council, 1961-67. Guggenheim fellow, 1952-53, 57-58; Fulbright fellow, 1952-53. Mem. Am. Econ. Assn., Indsl. Relations Research Assn. (exec. bd. 1964-67, pres. 1971), Nat. Acad. Arbitrators, Phi Beta Kappa. Mem. Congl. Church. Clubs: Cornell (N.Y.C.); Sierra. Author: Growth and Structure in the Economy of Modern Italy, 1965; (with TaChung Liu) Manufacturing Production Functions in the United States: 1957, 1965. Co-author: Pacific Coast Maritime Shipping Industry, 1930-48, 2 vols., 1952, 54. Editor: The Idea of Progress, 1949. Bd. editors Am. Econ. Rev., 1954-57. Home: 3215 Scott Pl NW Washington DC 20007

HILDEBRAND, JOEL HENRY, ret. chemist; b. Camden, N.J., Nov. 16, 1881; s. Howard Ovid and Sarah Regina (Swartz) H.; B.S., U. Pa., 1903, Ph.D., 1906, hon. D.Sc., 1939; student U. Berlin, 1906-07; LL.D., U. Cal., 1954; m. Emily J. Alexander, Dec. 17, 1908; children—Louise, Alexander, Milton, Roger Henry. Instr. chemistry U. Pa., 1907; asst. prof. chemistry, 1913, asso. prof., 1917, prof., 1918-52, prof. emeritus, 1952, dean of men, 1923-26, faculty research lectr., 1936, dean Coll. Letters and Sci., 1939-43, chmn. dept. chemistry U. Cal., 1941-43, dean Coll. Chemistry, 1949-51. Cons. chemist U.S. Bur. Mines, 1924-26; liaison for OSRD, Am. embassy, London, 1943-44. Mem. citizen's adv. commn. to Joint Com. on Edn. of Cal. Legislature, 1958-60; mem. adv. com. to Cal. Bd. Edn., 1966. Commd. capt. O.R.C., 1917; maj. Chem. Warfare Service, 1918; lt. col., 1919; dir. C.W.S. lab. nr. Paris, later comdt. Hanlon Field, nr. Chaumont, which included exptl. field and A.E.F. Gas Def. Sch. Mem. chem. referee bd. War Prodn. Bd., 1942-43; expert cons. mil. planning div. Q.M.C., 1942-45. Decorated D.S.M. (World War I); King's Medal (Brit.), 1948; Citation by Army and Navy for OSRD service, World War II; Nichols medal, 1939; Guthrie lectr. Phys. Soc., London, 1944; Walker Meml. lectr., 1944, Romanes lectr., 1953 (both U. Edinburgh); Remsen Meml. lecture and award, 1949; Am. Chem. Soc. award in chemistry edn., 1952, Priestley medal, 1962, James Norris Flack award New Eng. sect., 1961; Spiers Meml. Lecture, Faraday Soc., 1953; Bampton lectr. Columbia U., 1956; Willard Gibbs medal Chgo. sect. Am. Chem. Soc., 1953; William Proctor prize Sci. Research Soc. Am., 1962. Fellow A.A.A.S. (v.p. Pacific div. 1924-27, pres. mem. 1933-34; mem. exec. com. 1929-35), Am. Phys. Soc.; hon. fellow Royal Soc. Edinburgh, Cal. Acad. Sci.; mem. Am. Philos. Soc., Am. Chem. Soc. (pres. 1955), Nat. Acad. Scis., Faraday Soc. (hon. life), Am. Inst. Chemists (hon.), Phi Beta Kappa, Sigma Xi. Clubs: Faculty, Sierra (pres. 1937-40). Author: Principles of Chemistry, 1918, 7th edit., 1964; Solubility of Non-electrolytes, 1924, 36, (with R.L. Scott) 1950; Reference Book of Inorganic Chemistry (with W. M. Latimer), 1929, 40; Camp Catering (with Louise Hildebrand), 1938, 41; Science in the Making, 1956; An Introduction to Molecular Kinetic Theory, 1963; Is Intelligence Important?, 1963; Regular and Related Solutions (with J.M. Prausnitz and R.L. Scott), 1970; also numerous papers on chemistry, edn., skiing. Mgr. U.S. Olympic Ski Team, 1936; Joel Henry Hildebrand Hall dedicated by U. Cal., 1966. Home: 500 Coventry Rd Berkeley CA 94702

HILDEBRAND, KENNETH NORMAN, clergyman; b. Los Angeles, Oct. 29, 1906; s. John Augustine 3d and Grace Wadleigh (Clemons) H.; B.A., Coll. of Emporia, 1930, D.D., 1945; diploma, McCormick Theol. Sem., 1933, M.A., 1938; postgrad. Northwestern U., 1948-50; m. Nell Benson, Aug. 10, 1926; children—Grace (Mrs. Bernard E. Welch), Ruth (Mrs. Vernon L. Welge, Jr.). Ordained to ministry Presbyn. Ch. U.S.A., 1933; pastor Brighton Park Ch., Chgo., 1933-36, Chgo. Lawn Ch., 1936-42; asso. pastor 4th Ch., Chgo., 1942-48; pastor Central Ch. of Chgo. (nondenominational), 1948—. Radio and TV personality appearing on various Chgo. programs, WGN-TV. Bd. dirs. Nat. Safety Council, Wabash YMCA Hotel, McCormick Theol. Sem., Chgo. Council on Community Nursing. Named 1 of 100 Outstanding Citizens, 1971. Mem. Broadcast Pioneers, Nat. Acad. Religion and Mental Health, Newcomen Soc. N.Am. (Chgo. Com.), Chgo. Bible Soc. (dir.). Clubs: Lake Shore, Saddle and Cycle (Chgo.); Evanston (Ill.) Golf; Ill. Athletic. Author: Achieving Real Happiness, 1955. Home: 164 Eugenie St Chicago IL 60614 Office: 8 S Michigan Av Chicago IL 60603

HILDEBRAND, ROGER HENRY, physicist; b. Berkeley, Cal., May 1, 1922; s. Joel Henry and Emily (Alexander) H.; A.B. in Chemistry, U. Cal. at Berkeley, 1947, Ph.D. in Physics, 1951; m. Jane Roby Beedle, May 28, 1944; children—Peter Henry, Alice Louise, Kathryn Jane, Daniel Milton. Physicist, Radiation Lab., U. Cal. at Berkeley, 1942-51, Tenn. Eastman Corp., Oak Ridge Nat. Lab., 1945; asst. prof. physics Enrico Fermi Inst., U. Chgo., 1952-55, asso. prof., 1955-60, prof., 1960—, dir. Enrico Fermi Inst., 1965-68, dean coll., 1969—; asso. lab. dir. for high energy physics Argonne (Ill.) Nat. Lab., 1958-64, acting dir. div., 1959-64. Chmn. sci. policy com. Stanford Linear Accelerator Center (Cal.), 1962-66; mem. physics adv. com. Nat. Accelerator Lab., 1967-69. Guggenheim fellow, 1968-69. Fellow Am. Phys. Soc.; mem. Midwestern Univs. Research Assn. (dir. 1956-58, 62-68), Sierra Club, Phi Beta Kappa, Sigma Xi. Office: 5630 S Ellis Av Chicago IL 60637

HILDEBRAND, RUTH MOORHEAD, (Mrs. Francis E. Hildebrand), civic worker; b. Kittanning, Pa.; d. Robert West and Elizabeth (Findley) Moorhead; B.S., Simmons Coll., 1922; postgrad. George Washington U., 1926-29; m. Francis Edwin Hildebrand, Apr. 20, 1935; children—Melissa Ann (Mrs. Robert D. Crawford). Bd. trustees Young Women's Christian Home, Washington 1940—, pres. bd. trustees, 1950-52; mem. Gray Lady service D.C. chpt. A.R.C., 1943-50, chmn., 1950-56, chmn. vols., 1956-64, nat. vice chmn. vols., 1964-68, nat. chmn. vols., 1968—. Mem. Am. Newspaper Women's Club, Phi Delta Delta. Republican. Methodist. Home: 4501 Cathedral Av NW Washington DC 20016

HILDEBRANDT, F. DEAN, chem. co. exec.; b. S.I., N.Y., Aug. 19, 1902; s. Frederick and Mary Leona (Dean) H.; ed. Staten Island Acad., Am. Inst. Banking, night classes Columbia, N.Y.U.; m. Ruth Taylor Barry, May 27, 1932; children—Frederick Dean, Barry Taylor. With Mechanics & Metals Nat. Bank, 1921-26; advt. mgr. Chase Nat. Bank, 1926-29; pres., dir. Retail Council, Inc., Phila., 1929-33; mgr. Chgo. br. J. T. Baker Chem. Co., 1933-38, Prior Chem. Co., 1938-42; pres., dir. Hildebrandt & Co., 1942- 45; v.p. charge chem. dept. McKesson & Robbins, Inc., N.Y.C., 1945-55, sr. v.p., 1955-59, exec. v.p., 1959-67; exec. v.p., Foremost-McKesson Inc., 1967-71, dir., 1967—. Home: Lakeville CT 06039 Office: 155 E 44th St New York City NY 10017

HILDEGARDE, (Hildegarde Loretta Sell), singer and pianist; b. Adell, Wis., Feb. 1, 1906; d. Charles Frederick and Ida (Jermain) Sell; student St. John's Cathedral High Sch., Milwaukee, 1921-24, Marquette U., 1925. Radio singer and supper club entertainer, Continental Europe, 1933-38, appearing in London, Paris, Cannes, Brussels, etc.; supper club entertainer, U.S., since 1938, appearing in hotels and clubs of N.Y. City, Chicago, San Francisco, Washington, Detroit, Boston, St. Louis, etc., as singer, pianist and comedienne; first Am. singer to obtain Brit. Broadcasting Co. contract, 1934; radio singer on "99 Men and a Girl," Columbia Broadcasting System, 1939, "Beat the Band," Nat. Broadcasting Co., 1943; created supper club of the air, "Raleigh Room," Nat. Broadcasting Co., 1943-46, "Campbell Room," CBS; star theater revue, Chgo., Detroit, N.Y.C., 1946; many TV nat. shows as singer and comedienne, 1936—; Am. debut as mus. comedy star in Can-Can, Dallas, 1956; appeared in Can-Can, Dallas and Kansas City, 1957; TV religious series Zero, 1960, 1957, 59; Introduced hit songs, "The Last Time I Saw Paris, Darling, Je Vous Aime Beaucoup, My Heart Sings, I'll Be Seeing You, I'll Be Yours, Hi Lili Hi Lo, Lilli Marlene, Wunderbar; concert tour of One-Woman Show, U.S., Paris, London, 1951-53. Vice pres. Mountain Valley Water. Founding dir. Young Women's Towne House, v.p. Muscular Dystrophy Assn. Am. Mem. Delta Omicron. Roman Catholic. Selected one of ten best dressed women in U.S., 1940-46. Author: Over 50, So What, 1962. Address: care Hotel Plaza New York City NY 10019

HILDEN, GEORGE THOMAS, chain store executive; b. Starkweather, N.D., May 22, 1911; s. Afton and Grace (Stong) H.; ed. pub. schs., N.D.; m. Martha Haugen, 1933 (dec.); m. 2d, Marjorie Hensley, Dec. 25, 1946; children—George Thomas, Mary Marjorie. With Quality Food Stores, Inc., Mpls., 1929-36; with Osco Drug., Inc., and predecessors, 1937—, v.p. mdsg., 1942-65, pres., 1965- 67, chmn. bd., 1967—, dir. marketing, 1969-71; v.p. gen. mdse. Jewel Companies, Inc., 1963-70. Mem. Chgo. Assn. Commerce and Industry Econ. Mission to Japan. Mem. Nat. Assn. Chain Drug Stores (v.p. 1969, pres. 1971, dir.). Methodist (trustee). Clubs: Skokie Country (Glencoe); Chicago Curling (Northbrook, Ill.). Home: 743 Bluff St Glencoe IL 60022 Office 3030 Cullerton Dr Franklin Park IL 60131

HILDING, ANDERSON CORNELIUS, physician; b. Tacoma, June 29, 1892; s. Gustav Adolph and Anna Lavinia (Tilderquist) Anderson; student U. Wash., 1910-13; B.S., U. Minn., 1915, M.B., 1918, M.D., 1919, M.A., 1922, Ph.D., 1929; postgrad U. Vienna, 1925-26, Mayo Clinic, 1930-32, Eye Clinic of Sir Henry Holland, India, 1934; Sc.D., Gustavus Adolphus Coll., 1957; m. Inez Marie Melander, Jan. 1, 1929; children—David, Cecile, Wendell, Stephen, Jean. Intern, Mpls. Gen. Hosp., 1917-19; practice medicine, specializing in ophthalmology and otolaryngology, Duluth, 1921-54; research St. Luke's Hosp., Duluth, 1954—; clin. prof. otolaryngology U. Minn., 1944- 60, emeritus, 1960—. Vis. prof. research otolaryngology Columbia Coll. of Phys. and Surgs., N.Y.C., 1951-52; research in kidney disease, hypertension, retinitis, cataract surgery, exptl. nasal and sinus surgery, anatomy of bronchial tree, common cold; studies in anatomy and physiology of internal ear, theory of hearing, anatomy and physiology of eye, epithelial transplants in the eye; physiology and anatomy of respiratory tract; cons. and surg. practice in fields of ophthalmology and otology, 1954-64. Recipient Research award Minn. Society Internal Medicine, 1930; first prize for sci. exhibits Am. Acad. Opthalmology and Otolaryngology, 1934, 38, Honor Key, 1951; Casselberry award Am. Laryngol. Assn., 1934; Shambaugh prize Collegium Oto-Rhino- Laryngologicum Amicitiae Sacrum, 1963; Chevalier Jackson award Am. Broncho-Esophagological Assn., 1970. Fellow A.C.S.; mem. Am. Med. Assn., Am. Broncho-Esophagological Assn., Minn., St. Louis County med. socs., Am. (1st v.p. 1963-64), Minn. acads. opthalmology and otolaryngol., Am. Triological Soc., Collegium Oto-Rhinolaryngologicum, Am. Otol. Soc. (recipient award merit 1965), Otosclerosis Study Group, Royal Physiograph. Soc. Lund, Alumni Assn. Mayo Foundation for Medical Education and Research, A.A.A.S., N.Y. Acad. of Sci. Am. Laryngological Assn. (president 1963-64, chmn. DeRoaldes award, Casselberry award coms. 1969-70, chmn. research com. 1970—), Sigma Xi. Lutheran. Author articles in field. Home: 421 36th Av E Duluth MN 55804 Office: Research Lab St Lukes Hosp Duluth MN 55805

HILDRETH, CLIFFORD, educator; b. McPherson, Kan., Dec. 8, 1917; s. George W. and Lillian Belle (Huenergardt) H.; A.B., U. Kan., 1939; M.S., Ia. State U., 1941, Ph.D., 1947; m. Mary Louise McGee, Jan. 1, 1942; children—Richard, Robert, Susan, Mary. Asst. prof., then asso. prof. econs. Ia. State U., 1946-48; asst. prof., then asso. prof. econs. and mem. Cowles Commn., U. Chgo., 1949-52; prof. agrl. econs. N.C. State U., 1953-55; prof. agrl. econs. Mich. State U., 1955-58, prof. econs., head dept., 1958-60, prof. econs. and agrl. econs., 1960-64; prof. econs., statistics and agrl. econs. U. Minn., 1964—; Fulbright lectr. U. Tokyo, Hitotsubashi U., Keio U., Tokyo, Japan, 1970. Fellow Center Advanced Study Behavioral Scis., Stanford, Cal., 1961-62. Served to lt. (s.g.) USNR, 1943-46. Fellow Econometrics Soc., Am. Statis. Assn. (editor jour. 1960-65, v.p. 1968-69, pres.-elect 1972), Inst. Math. Statistics; mem. Am. Econ. Assn., Am. Farm Econ. Assn. Author: (with Frank Jarrett) A Statistical Study of Livestock Production and Marketing, 1955. Home: 4809 Knox Av S Minneapolis MN 55409

HILDRETH, EUGENE A., physician; b. St. Paul, Mar. 11, 1924; s. Eugene A. IV and Lila K. (Clator) H.; B.S., Washington Jefferson Coll., 1943; M.D., U. Va., 1947; m. Dorothy Anne Myers, Mar. 23, 1946; children—Jeffrey Reed, William Myers, Anne Sarver, Katherine Clator. Intern, Johns Hopkins, 1947-48; resident in medicine Hosp. U. Pa., 1948-49, USPHS Postdoctoral Research fellow in cardio-vascular disease, 1949-51, chief resident in medicine, 1953-54, fellow in allergy and immunology, 1954-58, faculty, 1954-69, 71—; instr. medicine U. Pa., Phila., 1953-54, asso. medicine, 1954-55, asst. prof. medicine, 1955-60, asso. prof., 1960-69, asso. dean Sch. Medicine, 1964-69, prof. clin. medicine, 1971—, acting chmn. dept. research medicine, 1960-64. Cons. project site visits USPHS, 1965-70, rev. devel. new methods research in chronic pulmonary disease, 1967-69; cons. VA Hosp. Phila., 1955—; nat. adv. com. Medic Alert Found. Internat., 1964—; cons. Citizens' Com. to Study Grad. Med. Edn., 1966. Served with USNR, 1943-45, 51-53. John and Mary R. Markle scholar in acad. medicine, 1958-63; USPHS Research grantee. Diplomate Am. Bi. Internal Medicine, also diplomate and co-chmn. allergy and immunology subsplty. bd. Fellow Am. Clin and Climatologic Assn., A.C.P.; mem. Peripatetic Soc., A.A.A.S., Fedn. Am. Socs. for Exptl. Biology, N.Y. Acad. Scis., Am. Art Assn., Pa. Thoracic Soc., Phila. Art Mus., Phila. Allergy Soc., A.M.A., Am. Acad. Allergy, Physiol. Soc. Phila. Republican. Editorial bd. Annals Internal Medicine, 1960-68, Postgrad. Medicine, 1969—, Jour. Berks County Med. Soc., 1969—, Internal Medicine Digest, 1971—. Co-author: Low Fat Diet, 1953; also research articles, chpt. in book. Office: Reading Hosp 6th and Spruce Sts Reading PA 19602 Home: Box 1181 RD 2 Mohnton PA 19540

HILDRETH, JAMES BERTRAM, naval officer; b. Ukiah, Cal., July 19, 1920; s. Louis Murry and Jessie Norma (Standley) H.; B.S., U. Cal. at Berkeley, 1941; student Naval War Coll., 1960-61, Armed Forces Staff Coll., 1956-67; m. Kathryn Halliday, Sept. 20, 1941; children—James, Bruce, Kevin. Commd. ensign U.S. Navy, 1941, advanced through grades to rear adm., 1968; comdg. officer U.S.S. George, 1947-48, U.S.S. Hopewell, 1952-54, U.S.S. Springfield, 1964-65; naval aide to under sec. Navy, 1962-64; comdr. Naval Base, Guantanamo Bay, Cuba, 1968-70; comdr. Crudesflot Four, 1970—. Decorated Legion of Merit with gold star, Bronze Star with gold star. Mem. U.S. Naval Inst., Sigma Nu. Home: Quarters SP-21 Naval Air Sta Norfolk VA 23511 Office: Comdr-Crusier Destroyer Flotilla Four Norfolk VA 23511

HILDYARD, DAVID HENRY THOROTON, internat. govt. ofcl.; b. May 4, 1916; s. G.M.T. and Sybil (Hoare) H.; ed. Oxford U. (Eng.).; m. Millicent Baron Longmore, 1947; 1 son, 1 dau. Entered Brit. Fgn. Service, 1948; now minister, alternate rep to UN. Served with RAF, 1940-46. Office: Permanent Mission of UK to UN 845 3d Av New York City NY 10002*

HILE, E. T., mfg. exec.; b. Curwensville, Pa., Mar. 28, 1907; s. C. Thornton and Pearl M. (Henry) H.; B.S., U. Mich., 1929; m. Martha E. Byers, Oct. 28, 1933; children—Ellen, Jane, Mary. With Harbison-Walker Refractories Co. (now div. Dresser Industries), 1925—, supt. Hays Works, Pitts., 1935-40, asst. v.p., Pitts. office, 1940-50, v.p. charge mfg., 1950-67, pres., 1967-70, group pres., 1970—, also dir.; pres. N.W. Magnesite Co., 1968. Mem. Phi Kappa Tau. Presbyn. Home: 1185 Prospect Rd Pittsburgh PA 15227 Office: 2 Gateway Center Pittsburgh PA 15222

HILEMAN, DONALD GOODMAN, coll. dean; b. Anna, Ill., Sept. 8, 1925; s. Turner Clifford and Mary (Goodman) H.; student Carthage Coll., 196-48; B.S. in Journalism, U. Ill., 1949, M.S. in Journalism, 1951, Ph.D. in Mass Communications, 1955; m. Shirley Ann Rau, Aug. 28, 1948; children-David, Mark, Mike, Kathryn. Instr. U. Ill., 1949-52; asst. prof. bus. adminstrn. Wash. State U., Pullman, 1952-55; asso prof. journalism So. Ill., U., 1955-69; chmn. dept. advt. U. Tenn., 1969-70, dean Coll. communications, 1970—. Mem. synod ethics com. Tenn., 1969-70, dean Coll. communications, 1970- -. Mem. synod ethics com. Presbyn Ch. Ill., 1960-62; mem. Council pub. relations Boy Scouts Am., 1958-68. Bd. dirs., asso. Danforth Found. Served with USNR, 1943-46. Recipient spl. awards U. Ill., 1967, Tex. A. and M. Coll., 1969; distinguished service award Am. Motel Assn. Ill. Fellow Am. Assn. Advt. Agys., Direct Mail Advt. Assn., Splty. Advt. Assn., Advt. Age Creative Workshop; mem. Assn. Edn. in Journalism, Am. Marketing Assn., Am. Assn. U. Profs., Am. Acad. Edn. in Journalism, Am. Marketing Assn., Am. Assn. U. Profs., Am. Acad. Advt. Alpha Delta Sigma (exec. dir. 1961-70; recipient 6th Key, spl. awards). Author: (with Billy I. Ross) Towards Professional in Advertising, 1969. Editor Linage, 1963-70. Contbr. articles profl. jours. Home: 5109 Angeles Dr Knoxville TN 37918

HILEMAN, RONALD LYLE, chain food store exec.; b. Hubbard, Neb., Aug. 18, 1914; s. Meryl Montgomery, and Jenny (Demaray) H.; B.S., Morningside Coll., 1937; student Northwestern U., 1937-38; m. Mary Ann Gray, Feb. 13, 1945; children—Gregory, Jane, Monica, Cary. With Jewel Cos., Inc., 1937—, grocery mdse. mgr., 1961-63, v.p. grocery mdsg., 1963-66, v.p. perishable operations, 1966—. Served to 1st lt., Q.M.C., AUS, 1941-45. Mem. Mdsg. Exec. Club Chgo. (past v.p., dir.). Home: 684 Grand Av Glen Ellyn IL 60137 Office: 666 Industrial Dr Elmhurst IL 60126

HILGARD, ERNEST ROPIEQUET, psychologist; b. Belleville, Ill., July 25, 1904: s. George Engelmann and Laura (Ropiequet) H.; B.S., U. of Ill., 1924; Ph.D., Yale, 1930; D.Sc., Kenyon Coll., 1964; m. Josephine Rohrs, Sept. 19, 1931; children—Henry Rohrs, Elizabeth Ann. Asst. instr. in psychology, Yale, 1928-29, instr., 1929-33; successively asst. prof., asso. prof., prof. psychology, Stanford U., 1933-69, emeritus prof., 1969—, exec. head dept. 1942-50, dean grad. div., 1951-55. Bd. dirs. (pres.) Ann. Reviews, Inc. With Dept. Agr., Washington, 1942, OWI 1942-43, Office Civilian Requirements, WPB, 1943-44. Collaborator, div. child devel. and tchr. personnel Am. Council Edn., 1940-41; nat. adv. mental health council USPHS, 1952-56; fellow Center Advanced Study Behavioral Scis., 1956-57. Bd. curators Stephens Coll., Mo. 1953-68. Recipient Warren medal in exptl. psychology, 1940; Wilbur Cross medal, Yale, 1971. Mem. U.S. Edn. Mission to Japan, Mar., 1946. Hon. fellow British Psychol. Assn.; mem. Am. Psychol. Assn. (pres. 1948-49), American Acad. Arts and Scis., Nat. Acad. Edn., Soc. Psychol. Study of Social Issues (chmn. 1944-45), A.A.A.S., Nat. Acad. Scis., Am. Philos. Soc., Sigma Xi. Author several books latest: Theories of Learning, 1948, rev. 1966; Introduction to Psychology, 1953, rev. 1971; Hypnotic Susceptibility, 1965. Home: 1129 Hamilton Av Palo Alto CA 94301

HILGER, JEROME ANDREW, physician; b. St. Paul, 1912; M.D., U. Minn., 1937, M.Sc. in Otolarynology, 1939. Intern Ancker Hosp., St. Paul, 1936-37; teaching fellow otolarngology Minn. Gen. Hosp., Mpls., 1937-39; now mem. staff Charles T. Miller Hosp., Children's Hosp., St. Joseph's Hosp., Univ. Hosp. Mpls.; clin. prof. otolaryngology U. Minn. Med. Sch. Served to lt. col., M.C., AUS. Diplomate Am. Bd. Otolaryngology. Fellow A.C.S.: mem. Am. Acad. Ophthalomology and Otolaryngology (pres. elect 1969). Am. Otol. Soc., Am. Laryngol. Assn. Address: Lowry Med Arts Bldg St Paul MN *

HILKER, WALTER ROBERT, Jr., lawyer; b. Los Angeles, Apr. 18, 1921; s. Walter Robert and Alice (Cox) H.; B.S., U. So. Cal., 1942, LL.B., 1948; m. Ruth Margaret Hibbard, Sept. 7, 1943; children—Anne Katherine, Walter Robert III. Admitted to Cal. bar, 1949, since practiced in Los Angeles; partner firm Parker, Milliken, Kohlmeier, Clark & O'Hara, 1955—. Dir. H. & J. Mabury Co. Bd. dirs. Earl B. Gilmore Found., Houchin Found. Served to lt. USNR, 1942-45. Decorated Bronze Star, Navy Unit Commendation ribbon. Mem. Am., Cal., Los Angeles bar assns. Republican. Club: Beach (Santa Monica, Cal.). Home: 17217 Weddington St Encino CA 91316 Office: 606 S Olive St Los Angeles CA 90014

HILKERT, ROBERT NEWTON, educator; b. N.Y.C., Feb. 10, 1905; s. Guy Elihu and Sarah Etta (Roberts) H.; Ph.B., Yale, 1926; M.A., Columbia Tchrs. Coll.; 1932; LL.D., Ursinus Coll.; m. Alice Isabelle Greene, Aug. 26, 1927; children—Anne Harvey, John Roberts. Tchr. social sci. Hill Sch., Pottstown, Pa., 1926-41; asso. dir. Ednl. Records Bur., N.Y.C., 1941; with Fed. Res. Bank of Phila., 1942-70, 1st v.p., 1958-70; faculty Stonier Grad. Sch. Banking, Rutgers U., 1956-66; vis. prof. Carroll Coll., Waukesha, Wis., 1970-71. Chmn. bd. Central Rehab. Service Phila., 1956-63; v.p. United Cerebral Palsy Assn. Phila., 1958- 63. Bd. dirs., pres. Health and

Welfare Council Phila., 1962; bd. dirs. Community Services Pa.; chmn. adv. bd. Sch. Social Work, U. Pa. Mem. Soc. Advancement Mgmt. (dir.), Indsl. Relations Assn. Phila. (pres.), Am. Inst. Banking, Bank Officers Club Phila. (pres.), Nat. Social Welfare Assembly (dir.). Presbyn. (elder; trustee Phila. Presbytery; mem. bd. nat. missions). Home: 409 Strath Haven Av Swarthmore PA 19081

HILL, ALBERT GORDON, physicist; b. St. Louis, Jan. 11, 1910; s. Glenn C. and Alberta (Boogher) H.; B.S., Washington Univ., 1930, M.S., 1934; Ph.D., U. Rochester, 1937; m. Ruth Harriet Parker. Served in engring. with Bell Telephone Labs., 1930-32; fellow in physics, U. Rochester, 1934-37; instr. physics Mass. Inst. Tech., 1937-41; physicist Research Corp., 1941; staff mem. Radiation Lab., M.I.T., 1942- 46; asso. prof. physics, 1946-47, prof. physics, 1947—, lectr. in polit. sci., 1965—, dir. Research Lab. Electronics, 1949-52, dir. Lincoln lab., 1952-55, chmn. physics council, 1967-70, v.p. for research, 1970—, chmn. bd. dirs. C. Stark Draper Lab., 1970—. Adviser SHAPE Air Defense Center, 1955-63; dir. research Weapons Systems Evaluations Group, 1955-58; v.p. Inst. Def. Analyses, Washington, 1956-59, trustee, 1956-61. Dir. P.R. Mallory & Co. Trustee, Asso. Univs., Inc., 1970—. Recipient Presdl. Certificate of Honor, 1948; Distinguished Civilian Service award USAF, 1955, Am. Ordnance Assn., 1956; Meritorious Civilian Service award Office of Sec. of Def. Fellow Am. Phys. Soc., I.E.E.E., Am. Acad. Arts and Sci.; mem. Am. Acad. Polit. and Social Scis., Acad. Polit. Sci. Author (with L. N. Ridenour and Ralph Shaw) Bibliography in an Age of Science, 1951. Home: 987 Memorial Dr Cambridge MA 02138 Office 77 Massachusetts Av Cambridge MA 02139

HILL, ALFRED R., investment banker; b. Cin., Sept. 6, 1901; s. A. and Madge M. Hill; ed. Ohio State U., Cin. U.; m. Marie J. Hill May 12, 1928; children—Marjorie Sayers (Mrs. Sarran), Barbara Irwin. Partner Hill & Co., Cin. Mem. Cin. Stock Exchange. Mason (Shriner). Club: Cin. Country. Home: 6720 Drake Rd Cincinnati OH 45243 Office Provident Tower Cincinnati OH 45202

HILL, ALFRED TUXBURY, assn. exec.; b. Montclair, N.J., May 17, 1908; s. Charles and Edith E. (Tuxbury) H.; student Haverford (Pa.) Coll., 1926-28; A.B., Brown U., 1933; Ed.M., Harvard, 1936-37; Ph.D., Columbia, 1949; H.H.D., Nasson Coll., Springvale, Me., 1957; D.C.L., New England Coll., 1959; Ph.D., Salem Coll., W.Va.; 1960; LL.D. Los Angeles Pacific Coll., 1961; Litt.D., Coll. St. Joseph on Rio Grande, 1962; m. Eunice Garland, June 23, 1934; children—Geraldine, Kate. Instr. English, Cushing Acad., Ashburnham, Mass., 1933-36, Culver (Ind.) Mil. Acad., 1937-43; exec. asst., personnel counselor Office Chief Ordnance, War Dept., Detroit, 1943; radio div. Western Electric Co., 1944-45, govt. contract service specialist, coordinator and spl. studies asst., chief employment and placement sect. personnel div., 1945; securities analyst Herrick, Waddell & Co., 1945-51; v.p., acting pres. Lake Erie Coll., 1951; dir. Dana Hall Schs., 1951-56; pres. Pine Manor Jr. Coll., 1952-56; exec. sec. Council for Advancement of Small Colleges, Washington, 1956-67; v.p. Heald, Hobson & Assos., edn. cons., 1968; asso. in higher edn. Conn. Commn. for Higher Edn., Hartford, 1969—. Mem. New Eng. Jr. Coll. Council (chmn. research com., mem. exec. com.), Am. Assn. Jr. Colls. (adminstrn. com., chmn. sub-com. pub. relations), Am. Council on Edn., Am. Assn. Higher Edn., Phi Delta Theta, Phi Delta Kappa. Republican. Episcopalian. Kiwanian. Clubs: Harvard (Boston, N.Y.C.); Woods Hole Golf; Quissett Yacht. Author: Campus and Classroom, 1942; The Small College Meets the Challenge, 1959; also articles. Home: 26 Gloucester Lane West Hartford CT 06107 also Box 724 Falmouth MA 02541 Office: 340 Capitol Av Hartford CT 06115

HILL, ALLAN CAMERON ERSKINE, railroad ofcl.; b. N.Y.C., May 10, 1921; s. Ebenezer Erskine and Margaret (Eadie) H.; grad. transp. mgmt. program, Stanford, 1968; m. Marie Krumacker, July 10, 1954; 1 son, Andrew Erskine. With S.P. Co., 1955—, sec., 1970—. Trustee E.C. Hill Trust. Served with Army U.K. World War II. Mem. Am. Soc. Corp. Secretaries, Nat. Trust for Scotland. Clubs: Commonwealth, Commercial (San Francisco). Home: 810 Gonzalez Dr San Francisco CA 94132 Office: 1 Market St San Francisco CA 94105

HILL, ALWYN SPENCER, educator; b. Logan, Utah, June 4, 1925; s. Reuben Lorenzo and Theresa (Snow) H.; B.S., Utah State U., 1949; postgrad. U. Utah, 1951-52, 55; M.S., U. Wis., 1951, Ph.D., 1960; m. Beth Elaine Powell, July 17, 1946; children—Gregory Spencer, Michael Bleak, Theresa Jeanine, Marybeth, Rebecca Ann, Donald Reuben. Tchr. Latter-day Saints Sem., Malad, Ida., Salt Lake City, 1951-56; teaching asst. U. Utah, U. Wis., 1956-59; asst. prof. polit. sci. Drury Coll., Springfield, Mo., 1959-61; chmn. dept. social sci. Eastern N.M. U., 1961-65, chmn. dept. social sci., 1967-69; asso. prof. polit. sci. U. Nev., 1965-67; head dept. social scis., prof. polit. sci. Mich. Technol. U., Houghton, 1969—. Govt. intern dir., N.M., 1962; mem. staff Commn. for Study Statewide Problems Higher Edn., N.M., 1963-64; project dir. State-wide Survey Libraries, Nev., 1966-67. Served with AUS, 1944-46. Named Tchr. of Year, Eastern N.M. U., 1964. Mem. Am. Polit. Sci. Assn. Contbr. articles profl. jours. Home: 205 Isle Royale Houghton MI 49931

HILL, ANDREW WILLIAM, pianist, composer; b. Port au Prince, Haiti, June 30, 1937; s. William R. and Hattie (Matthews) Hille; came to U.S., 1941, naturalized, 1941; m. Laverne Gabille, Jan. 8, 1963. Jazz pianist, composer, 1949—; accompanist Dinah Washington, 1954; pianist Lighthouse Group, Los Angeles, 1962, Roland Kirk Quartet, 1962; recorded with Blue Note Records, N.Y.C., 1963—; records include Black Fire, 1963, Judgement, 1964, Point of Departure, 1964. Bd. dirs. Andrew Hill & Assos., Inc. Founder Andrew Hill Found., 1966—. Nat. Endowment Art grantee, 1971. Compositions include: Symetry, Black Monday, le Groits, Duplicity, Alfred, Reconciliation (all 1964), Legacy, Premonition, Moon Childe, Heritage, Image of Time Ghetto Lights (all 1965), Violence, Hope, Illusion, Pain, Desire (all 1966), Awake, Prevue, Now, Yomo (all 1967); Golden Spook (opera), 1970; String Quartet No. 1, 1970; Ectasy (brass quartet), 1970, numerous others. Address: Route 1 Smyrna NY 13464

HILL, ARCHIBALD ANDERSON, educator; b. N.Y.C., July 5, 1902; s. Archibald Alexander and Mary Dorsey (Anderson) H.; A.B., Pomona Coll., Claremont, Cal., 1923; M.A., Stanford, 1924; Ph.D., Yale, 1927; m. Muriel L. Byard, Aug. 27, 1928. Instr. English, U. of Mich., 1926-29, asst. prof., 1929-30; asso. prof. English Philology, U. of Va., 1930-39, prof. English Philology, 1939-50, prof. English lang., 1950-53; vice dir. Inst. Langs. and Linguistics, Georgetown U., 1953-55; prof. English and linguistics U. Tex., 1955—. Fellow gen. edn. bd. for study Linguistic Atlas, U.S. and Can., Brown U., 1934. Lt. comdr. USNR, 1944-45. Decorated Commendation Ribbon with citation on completion of mil. service. Mem. adv. com. Linguistic Atlas of U.S. and Can. Mem. Modern Lang. Assn. of Am., Linguistic Soc. of Am. (sec. 1951-68; pres. 1969), Mediaeval Acad., Am. Dialect Soc., Phi Beta Kappa, Raven. Clubs: Austin, Headliners (Austin, Tex.). Author: Introduction to Linguistic Structures, 1958; Oral Approach to English, 2 vols., 1965. Editor: Linguistics Today, 1969. Home: 3403 Mt Bonnell Dr Austin TX 78731

HILL, ARCHIBALD VIVIAN, physiologist; b. Bristol, England Sept. 26, 1886; s. Jonathan and Ada Priscilla (Rumney) H.; attended Blundell's Sch., Tiverton; M.A., Sc.D., Cambridge (Trinity), Hon. D.Sc., Oxford, Manchester, Pa., Bristol, Algiers Columbia, Liege, Johns Hopkins, U. Brazil, also Rockefeller U., U. of Rochester; LL.D., Edinburgh, Belfast; M.D. (hon.), Louvain, Brussels, Toulouse; m. Margaret Neville Keynes, June 18, 1913 (dec. 1970); children—Mary Eglantyne (Mrs. Humphreys), David Keynes, Janet Rumney (Mrs. Humphrey), Maurice N. (dec.). Prof., physiology, Manchester U., 1920-23; prof. physiology Univ. Coll., London, 1923-25; Foulerton research prof., Royal Soc., 1926-51, ret. (sec., 1935-45, fgn. sec., 1946). chmn. exec. com., Nat. Physical Lab., 1940-45; com. of award, Commonwealth Fund Fellowships. 1934-39; pres. Soc. Protection of Sci. and Learning. Mem. of Parliament, 1940-45. Served as captain, brevet major, World War I; dir. anti-aircraft exptl. sect., Ministry of Munitions. Supernumerary airattaché, British Embassy, Washington, 1940; sci. adviser, govt. of India, 1943-44. Decorated Companion of Honour (England). Received Nobel Prize for Physiology; Medal of Freedom with Silver Palm (U.S.) for sci. research, World War II; decorated Chevalier French Legion of Honor. Fellow Royal Soc.; mem. Marine Biol. Assn. United Kingdom (pres. 1955-60), Nat. Acad. Scis., Am. Philos Soc., Am. Acad. of Arts and Scis., and others, Author: The Ethical Dilemma of Science, 1960; Trails and Trials in Physiology, 1965; First and Last Experiments in Muscle Merchanics, 1970. Contbr. sci. pub. Home: 11 A Chaucer Rd Cambridge England

HILL, ARMIN JOHN, coll. dean; b. Riverdale, Ida., June 7, 1912; s. John Ensign and Ivy Hooper (Blood) H.; B.S. in Elec. Engring., Mont. State Coll., 1932, M.S., 1938; M.S., Cal. Inst. Tech., 1949, Ph.D., 1950; m. Virginia Adeline Nelson, Aug. 25, 1933; children—Ivy Josephine (Mrs. Bruce Gilchrist), Walter E., Doris (Mrs. W. Boyd Giles), David N., Carolyn V. (Mrs. J. Daniel Blakeslee), A. Kent. Asst. prof. N.D. Sch. Forestry, 1932-37; rural elec. engr. Mont. State Coll. Extension Service, 1938-41, asst. prof. physics, 1941-48; staff physicist Motion Picture Research Council, Hollywood, Cal., 1950-57; dean Coll. Phys. and Engring. Scis., Brigham Young U., 1957—, mem. bd. dirs. Engring. Coll. Adminstrv. Council, 1967—, vice chmn., 1969-71, chmn., 1971—. Adv. council Utah Indsl. Services Agy., 1967-70, pres., 1969-70. Fellow Soc. Motion Picture and TV Engrs. (Best Paper award 1953); mem. Utah Conf. on Higher Edn. (pres. 1968-69), A.A.A.S., Am. Soc. Engring. Edn. (nat. chmn. engring. coll. council 1971—), Sigma Xi, Phi Kappa Phi. Tau Beta Pi. Mem. Ch. of Jesus Christ of Latter-Day Saints. Home: 1793 Pine Lane Provo UT 84601

HILL, ARTHUR, actor; b. Can.; studied law U. B.C.; m. Peggy Hassard; children—Douglas, Jennifer. Performed in plays in London, including Home of the Brave, The Male Animal, Man and the Superman, The Country Girl, Matchmaker; in U.S. on Broadway; Matchmaker, Look Homeward Angel, All the Way Home, The Gang's All Here, Who's Afraid of Virginia Woolf? 1962-63; TV actor in Born Yesterday, The Defenders, A Clearing in the Woods, Ethan Frome, Slattery's People, Vanished, Owen Marshall, Counselor at Law; appeared motion picture Ugly American, Moment to Moment, The Moving Target, Harper, The Chairman, The Andromeda Strain. Served with RCAF, 1942-45. Recipient Tony award as best actor, 1962-63. Address: 1515 Club View Dr Los Angeles CA 90024

HILL, AUSTIN BRADFORD, educator; b. London, Eng., July 8, 1897; s. Leonard Erskine and Janet (Alexander) H.; student Chigwell Sch., Essex. Eng., 1908-16; B.Sc., London U., 1922. Ph.D., 1926. D. Sc., 1929; D.Sc. (honoris causa), Oxford U. 1963; M.D. (honoris causa), Edinburgh Univ., 1968; m. F. M. Salmon, July 31, 1923; children—Rosemary, David, Peter. Staff Brit. Med. Research Council, 1923-33. hon. dir. statis. research unit, 1945-61; reader epidemiology, vital statistics London U., 1933-45, prof. med. statistics, sch. hygiene and tropical medicine, 1945-61; dean London Sch. Hygiene, Tropical Med., 1955-57; Cutter lectr. Harvard, 1953. Mem. Brit. Med Research Council. 1954-58; consultant on medical statistics Royal Air Force and the Royal Navy. Decorated Commander Order Brit. Empire, Knight, 1961. Recipient Galen medal Soc. Apothecaries; Harben medal, Royal Inst. Public Health and Hygiene; Jennet medal Royal Society of Medicine; also the Heberden medal, Heberden Society. Fellow Royal Society, Royal Coll. of Physicians (hon.), also the U. Coll. London. Am. Pub. Health Assn. (hon.), Soc. Medical Officers of Health (hon.); mem. Gold Medallist Soc. (past pres.). Royal Statis Soc., Inst. of Actuaries (hon.) . Soc. of Occupational Medicine (hon.), Internat. Statis. Inst., Royal Soc. Medicine (hon. fellow: past pres. sect. epidemiology and preventive medicine and section on occupational medicine). Author: Principles of Medical Statistics pub. 1937, rev. edit. 1966: Statistical Methods in Clinical and Preventive Medicine, 1963. Comtbr. articles sci. jours Home: Green Acres Little Kingshill Great Missenden Buckinghamshire England

HILL, B. HARVEY, banker; b. 1908; grad. U. Ga., also Emory U. Law Sch.; married. Engaged in practice law, 1933-48; with Citizens & So. Nat. Bank, from 1948, exec. v.p. trust, from 1966. Address: Box 4899 Atlanta GA 30302

HILL, CARL MCCLELLAN, coll. pres.; b. Norfolk, Va., July 27, 1907; s. William F. and Sarah A. (Rowe) H.; B.S., Hampton Inst., 1931; M.S., Cornell U., 1935, Ph.D., 1941; postgrad. U. Pa., summers 1938-40; LL.D., U. Ky., 1966; m. Mary E. Elliott, Sept. 21, 1927 (dec.); 1 dau., Doris E. McGhee. Asst. prof. chemistry Hampton Inst., 1931-41; asso. prof. chemistry Greensboro (N.C.) Agr. and Tech. U., 1941-44; prof. chemistry Tenn. State U., 1944-62, head dept. chemistry, 1944-51, chmn. Sch. Arts and Scis., 1951-58, dean sch., dean faculty, 1958-62; pres. Ky. State Coll., Frankfort, 1962—. Supt. chem. research projects TVA. 1948-52, Research Coop., 1948-52, USAF Research and Devel. Command, 1951-52, NSF 1951-52. Mem. bd. commrs. Nat. Commn. Accrediting; mem. Ky. Med. Scholarship Bd., mem. U.S. Bd. World Missions, Ky. Sci. and Tech. Adv. Council, 1966, Ky. Authority Ednl. TV, 1965, Ky. Council on Pub. Higher Edn. Bd. dirs. Frankfort chpt. Am. Heart Frankfort chpt. Am. Heart Assn., Blue Cross Hosp. Plan, Presbyn. Westminster Found.; trustee Stillman Coll. Recipient Mfg. Chemists Assn. chem. tchrs. award, 1962. Fellow A.A.A.S., Am. Inst. Chemists, Tenn. Acad. Sci.; mem. Am. Chem. Soc., N.E.A., N.Y., Ky. acads. sci., Sigma Xi, Omega Psi Phi. Presbyn. (elder). Mason (33). Author: General College Chemistry. Chemistry. 1954: Laboratory Experiments in Organic Chemistry 1955. Contbr. articles to profl. jours. Home: Ky State Coll Frankfort KY 40601

HILL, CHARLES FRANCIS, Jr., paper co. exec.; b. Marietta. O. June 4, 1923; s. Charles Francis and Laura Caroline (Close) H.; student N.M. A. and M. Coll., 1943; B.S., Ohio State U. 1948; postgrad. U. Cin., 1949, Xavier U., 1955-56; m. Rita Rose Deger, May 10, 1958; children—Charles Francis III, Mark Alan, Cheryl Lynn. Chemist, asst. tech. dir. Sorg Paper Co., Middletown, O., 1948-57; mill mgr. Deerfield Glassine Co., Monroe Bridge, Mass., 1957- 61; asst. to pres Paterson Parchment Paper Co., Bristol, Pa., 1962-63, exec. v.p., 1963-65, pres., 1965—, chairman board, 1969—, also chief executive officer, dir.; pres., dir. Paterson Carbon & Ribbon Co.; dir. Paterson Pacific Co. Kee Lox Mfg. Co. Served with AUS, 1943-46. Mem. T.A.P.P.I., Am. Pulp and Paper Assn. (bd. govs.), Newcomen Soc. Home: 10 Stafford Pl Yardley PA 19067 Office: Paterson Parchment Paper Co Bristol PA 19007

HILL, CHARLES GERARD, ins. co. exec.; b. Welland, Can., Nov. 18, 1915; s. Malcom Gordon and Lillian Marie (Weiss) H.; B.A. with honors. Queen's U., Kingston. Ont., 1938; m. Marjorie Helen McQuitty, June 10, 1937; children—Gary William. Judity Ann. Came to U.S., 1942. naturalized. 1948. Actuarial dept. Sun Life Assurance Co. of Can., Montreal, 1938-42; with Mass. Mutual Life Ins. Co., 1942—, v.p. charge group ins., 1954—. Mem. Soc. Actuaries, Health Ins. Assn. Am. (chmn. group ins. commn.). Clubs: Actuaries (Hartford and Boston). Home: Wilbraham Rd Hampden MA 01036 Office: 1295 State St Springfield MA 01109

HILL, CHARLES STRUNK, r.r. exec.; b. Balt., July 14, 1919; s. Charles Strunk, Jr. and Ruth (Graeber) H.; student Am. U., 1937-38, Boston U., 1939-42; B.C.S., Benjamin Franklin U., 1951; m. Virginia Arnette Beohm, May 10, 1947; children—Dierdra Carlen, Cheryl Ann. Field supr., chief corp. accounting sect., group leader tech. staff, mem. accounting policy com. CCC, Washington, 1946-53; dir. accounting div., regional comptroller Northwestern region U.S. Post Office Dept., Portland, Ore., 1953-55; methods engr., auditor of expenditures, mgr. internal auditing, mgr. regional accounting, mgr. gen. accounting Pa. R.R., Phila., 1955-68; asst. v.p. accounting, comptroller, v.p., controller Penn Central Transp. Co., Phila., 1968; comptroller, v.p.-controller Penn Central Co., Phila., 1969-70; pres., dir. Richmond-Washington Co.; dir. Niagara River Bridge Co., Nicholas, Fayette & Greenbrier R.R. Co., Owasco River Ry., Penn Towers, Inc., St. Lawrence & Adirondack R.R. Co.; trustee Penn Central Mut. Assos. Bd. dirs. Better Bus. Bur. Phila. Served with AUS, 1943-46. Mem. Am., Pa. insts. C.P.A.'s, Am. Accounting Assn., Nat. Assn. Accountants. Home: 484 Hilltop Rd Paoli PA 19301 Office: 6 Penn Center Plaza Philadelphia PA 19104

HILL, CHARLES THOMAS, bus. and financial cons.; b. Phila., Aug. 10, 1906; s. Francis J. and Anne E. (McCullough) H.; B.S. in Econs., Wharton Sch., U. Pa., 1927; m. Mary D. Fagan, Nov. 22, 1928; children—Charles Thomas, Nicholas Biddle, Mary Dorothea. Mgr. Francis I. duPont & Co., Phila., 1931-43, W. E. Hutton & Co. Phila., 1943-57; partner Dixon & Co., Phila., 1958-64; dir., mem. finance com. Pittston Co., 1956—; chmn. Metal Diffusion, Inc., Phila., 1956—: dir. Alleghany Corp., Gen. Refractories Co, W. H. Newbold's Son & Co.; author. lectr. bus. and finance; cons. to corps., family holding cos., charitable founds. Mem. Research Socs. N.Y.C. and Phila., Am. Rowing Assn., Friars Soc. U. Pa., Sigma Alpha Epsilon (trustee). Mem. Christian Ch. Clubs: Varsity (U. Pa.) ; Cricket, College Boat, Undine Barge (Phila.). Home 7350 Rural Lane Philadelphia PA 19119 Office: W H Newbold's Son & Co 1517 Locust St Philadelphia PA 19102

HILL, CLYDE CECIL, Jr., mfr.; b. Ashtabula, O., Nov. 25, 1914; s. Clyde Cecil and Nancy Elizabeth (Humphrey) H.; A.B., Ohio Wesleyan U., 1937; m. Ruth Helen Westfall, May 10, 1941; children—Nancy (Mrs. Jay MacDonald Davis), Thomas, Susan, Barbara. With Ernst & Ernst, Cleve. and Pitts., 1937-42; controller Clark div. Dresser Industries, Inc., Olean, N.Y., 1942-53, treas., 1953-57, asst. treas. parent company, Dallas, 1957-70, treas., 1970—; officer affiliated cos. Pres., dir. YMCA, Olean, 1950-53, Community Chest, 1948-51; mem. adv. bd. Salvation Army, 1950-53; officer dir. council Boy Scouts Am., 1948-51. C.P.A., Pa. Mem. Dallas Mfrs. and Wholesalers Assn. (dir. 1970-71), Financial Execs. Inst. (v.p. Dallas chpt. 1971), Olean C. of C. (past officer, dir.), Phi Gamma Delta, Omicron Delta Kappa. Republican. Methodist. Clubs: Rotary, Brookhaven Country (Dallas). Home: 4431 Alta Vista Lane Dallas TX 75229 Office: PO Box 718 Dallas TX 75221

HILL, DAVID GARRETT, industrialist; b. Pitts., June 6, 1902; s. William Fulton and Eleanor Patton (Garrett) H.; M.E., Cornell, 1924; m. Eleanor Campbell Musser, Oct. 6, 1928; children—William Fulton, John Howard. Began as indsl. engr. Pitts. Plate Glass Co. (name changed to PPG Industries, Inc. 1968), 1924, asst. to v.p., 1929-40, gen. supt. plate glass factories, 1940-52, v.p., 1952-55, dir., 1954—, pres., 1955-66, chmn. bd., chief exec. officer, 1966-67, chmn. exec. com., 1962-67, dir. cons., 1967—, mem. exec. com., 1967—; dir. Pitts. Corning Corp., Bell Telephone Co. Pa., Brockway Glass Co., Inc. Bd. dirs. Pitts. Symphony Soc.; trustee Presbyterian-U. Hosp. Mem. Sigma Alpha Epsilon. Republican. Presbyn. Mason. Clubs: Duquesne, Fox Chapel Golf (Pitts.); Rolling Rock (Ligonier, Pa.). Home: 21 Edgewood Rd Pittsburgh PA 15222

HILL, DELMAS CARL, judge; b. Wamego, Kan., Oct. 9, 1906; s. Ray G. and Elfie E. (Smith) H.; LL.B., Washburn Coll., 1929, LL.D., 1958; m. Katherine V. Hooven, July 29, 1933. Admitted to Kan. bar, 1929 and practiced in Wamego, 1929- 43, 46-49; county atty. Pottawatomie County, Kan., 1931-34; asst. U.S. atty., Dist. of Kan., 1934-36; gen. counsel, Kan. State Tax Commn., 1937-39; chmn. Democratic State Com., 1946-48; U.S. dist. judge, 1949-61, U.S. circuit judge, 10th circuit, 1961—. Served with AUS, 1943-46; prosecution staff in trial of Gen. Yamashita, Manila. P.I., 1945. Episcopalian. Home: 341 N Crestway St Wichita KS 67208 Office: Federal Bldg Wichita KS 67202

HILL, DONALD WALTER, coll. dean; b. Hazleton, Pa., Jan. 13, 1922; s. Richard Joseph and Anna Martha (Lohrke) H.; student Wilkes Coll., 1947-48, 49-50; B.S., Bucknell U., 1953; M.S., Cornell U., 1955; Ph.D., Am. U., 1964; m. Elsa Louise Schiel, May 14, 1949; children—Douglas Warren, Randall Richard, Jane Louise, Christine Lois. Lab. analyst Pa. Power and Light Co., 1940-42; flight radio engr. TWA, 1944; transmission engr. Am. Tel. & Tel. 1944-50; comml. engineer, marketing research, 1954-58; instr. Bucknell U., 1952- 53; grad. asst. Cornell U., 1953-54; asst. prof. Rollins Coll., Winter Park, Fla., 1958-59; vis. lectr. Am. U., 1959-61; asst. prof. Lehigh U., 1961-62; mem. faculty Rollins Coll., 1962—, dean adminstrv. affairs, 1965-66, dean of coll., 1966—. Chmn. planning council Assn. Mid Fla. Coll., 1966—; rep. to Am. Council Edn., Am. Assn. Coll., 1966—; rep. So. Assn. Colls. and Sch., 1966—. Served with USCGR, 1942-44. Gen. Electric fellow U. Chgo., 1963; Republic Steel fellow Case Inst. Tech., 1965; Ford fellow, Duke, 1964. Mem. Am., So. econs. assns., Tau Kappa Epsilon, Omicron Delta Kappa, Psi Chi, Delta Mu Delta. Republican. Methodist. Home: 1085 Park Av N Winter Park FL 32789

HILL, DOUGLAS GREEN, musician; b. Tulsa, Oct. 7, 1930; s. Israel Phillip and Mabel (Turner) H.; B.Music Edn., U. Tulsa, 1951, M.M., 1957; postgrad. U. N.M.; m. Kathryn Thomas, Oct. 21, 1951; children—Cynthia Ann, Barbara Diane, Lawrence Thomas. Mem. string bass sect. Tulsa Symphony Orch., 1945-52, 54-57, New Orleans Symphony, 1949-50, ElPaso Symphony, 1950, Albuquerque Symphony, 1961—; string bassist Fred Waring Orch., 1950-51; tuba mem. N.M. Brass Ensemble, 1961-68, Albuquerque Brass Ensemble, 1968—; mem. string bass sect. Santa Fe Opera, 1962—. Elementary band specialist Albuquerque Pub. Schs., 1960—; instr. low brass and strings U. Albuquerque, 1967-70. Del. conf. on art in Ams., UNESCO, 1959. Served with AUS, 1952-54. Mem. Am. Fedn. Musicians, Music Educators Nat. Conf., N.M. Music Educators

Assn., Phi Mu Alpha, Kappa Kappa Psi. Home: 7113 Seminole Rd NE Albuquerque NM 87110 Office: PO Box 1927 Music Dept Albuquerque Pub Schs Albuquerque NM 87103

HILL, DOUGLAS WAINWRIGHT, stock broker; b. Cin., Jan. 21, 1898; s. Alfred and Madge (Martin) H.; graduate Yale University New Haven. Connecticut, 1918; m. Elizabeth Donaldson, 1955 (dec.); children—Douglas W., Donald P. Partner, Hill & Co., mem. N.Y. Stock Exchange, Cin., 1919—. Clubs: Cincinnati Country, Coldstream Country (Cin.). Home: 7552 Ayres Rd Cincinnati OH 45230 Office: Provident Tower Cincinnati OH 45202

HILL, EDGAR STEWART, co. exec.; b. Canada, Sept. 1, 1914; s. Charles S. and Susan (Warner) H.; came to U.S., 1927, naturalized, 1941; B.S.C., Ohio U., 1938; m. Sara M. Mansfield, Sept. 7, 1940; 1 son, Andrew S. Asst. div. controller Firestone Tire & Rubber Co., 1938-44; div. controller gen. auditor Freeport Sulphur Co., 1944-47; chief accountant Deering Milliken & Co., 1947-56; v.p. comptroller Fairchild Camera & Instrument Corp., from 1956, also dir.; now mem. adv. bd. Nat. City Bank of New Nassau County; dir. Fairchild Credit Corp., Winston Research Corp., Electro-Metrics Corp., World Magnetics, Inc., Semikor, Ltd. (Korea), Fairchild Camera & Instruments Can., Ltd., Fairchild Instrumentation (U.K.) Ltd., Semiconductor Ltd. (Hong Kong). Mem. Financial Execs. Inst., Am. Assn. Accountants. Home: 96 McCouns Lane Glen Head NY 11545

HILL, EDWARD LEE, educator, physicist; b. Hartford, Ark., Nov. 3, 1904; s. Robert Lee and Louise (McKnight) H.; B.S. in Elec. Engring., U. Minn., 1925, Ph.D., 1928; m. Irene Ellison, June 8, 1928. Fellow NRC, Harvard, 1928-30; mem. faculty physics U. Minn., Mpls., 1930-37, asso. prof., 1937-46, prof., 1946-62, prof. physics and math., 1962-70, emeritus, 1970—; research physicist Physics-Tech. Inst. Leningrad, USSR, 1934-35. Mem. Am. Phys. Soc., Am. Math. Soc., Am. Geophys. Union, I.E.E.E., A.A.A.S., Math. Assn. Am., Minn., N.Y. acads. scis., Sigma Xi, Tau Beta Pi. Editor: Phys. Rev., 1950. Research on quantum mechanics, theory of relativity, atmospheric physics. Address: Sch Physics and Astronomy Univ Minn Minneapolis MN 55455

HILL, EUGENE, newspaper exec. Mng. editor Sacramento Bee. Office: 21st and Q St Sacramento CA 95813*

HILL, EVERETT WENTWORTH, writer; b. Russell, Kan., Jan. 10, 1884; s. John Harris and Frances Emily (Wentworth) H.; student Cascadilla Prep. Sch., Ithaca, N.Y., 1903; B.S. in Econs., Wharton Sch. of Finance and Commerce U. Pa., 1907; m. Ethel Laing, June 3, 1908 (dec.) ; 1 dau., Ethel Frances; m. 2d Cleo Shaffer Riley. With Standard Oil Co., 1907-08; settled at Shawnee, Okla., in ice mfg., 1908; settled at Oklahoma City, 1922; moved to Indian Bluff Farm, located on James River in Ozarks, nr. Springfield, Mo., 1941; moved to Lakeshore Gardens, nr. Polson, Mont., 1945; moved to Springfield, Mo., 1963, Oklahoma City, 1969; owner extensive farm lands. Mem. internat. bd. dirs. Waterton-Glacier Internat. Peace Park. Mem. Nat. Boys and Girls Week com. Mem. Kansas Ind. Oil and Gas Assn., Am. Acad. Polit. and Social Sci., Nat. Econ. League, Phi Kappa Sigma, Rotary Internat. (1st v.p. 1923-24; pres. 1924-25). Democrat. Episcopalian. Mason (32, Shriner). Clubs: Oklahoma City; Polson (hon. mem.) . Author: Toward the Sun; Light Across the Valley; He Who Seeks Gold; also writer of verse, essays, philoso; articles and short stories. Mem. Sunshine Magazine Adv. Staff. Speaker before Rotary clubs in North America and other countries. Address: 2525 N West 62d St Oklahoma City OK 73112

HILL, FRANCIS FREDERICK, gas co. exec.; b. Portland, Ore., Dec. 13, 1908; s. James F. and Bertha M. (McIntire) H.; LL.B., U. Ore., 1933; m. Barbara Jean Campbell, Dec. 25, 1941; children—Cinda, Jeffrey. Admitted to Ore. bar, 1933; with firm Laing, Gray & Smith and predecessors, Portland, 1933-55; partner firm Smith, Gray, Hill & Rodgers, 1955-61; v.p., gen. counsel Northwest Natural Gas Co., Portland, 1961, pres., dir., 1962—; dir. First Nat. Bank of Ore. Mem. emergency adv. com. for natural gas Dept. Interior. Mem. econ. stblzn. group Ore. Office Emergency Planning; mem. Portland Citizens Com. Bd. dirs. Portland Rose Festival Assn., 1950-56; Portland Civil Service Bd. Trustee N.W. Hosp. Service-Blue Cross; bd. dirs. Good Samaritan Found. Served to lt. comdr. USNR, 1942-46. Mem. Am., Ore., Multnomah bar assns., Assn. Wash. Gas Utilities (trustee) , Portland C. of C., Am. (dir.) , Pacific Coast (pres. 1969, dir.) gas assns. Presbyn. Clubs: Kiwanis, Arlington, Waverley (Portland). Home: 127 SW Kingston Av Portland OR 97201 Office: 735 SW Morrison St Portland OR 97205

HILL, FRANCIS WILLIAM, lawyer; b. Upper Marlboro, Md., May 2, 1895; s. Francis William and Grace (Clagett) H.; J.D., Georgetown U., 1917, LL.M., 1922; m. Daviette Corbell Ficklen, June 23, 1923; children—Daviette (Mrs. Philip R. Stansbury), Frances (Mrs. Ellis J. Parker III). Admitted to D.C. bar, 1917; asst. corp. counsel for D.C., 1918-22; mem. com. on admissions and grievances U.S. Dist. Ct. for D.C., 1943-70. Dir. Columbia Mortgage Co., Prudential Bldg. Pres., dir. Suburban Hosp. Assn., 1954-57; bd. dirs. D.C. Soc. for Prevention Blindness, 195O-52, Am. Hearing Soc., 1957-62. Served to lt. USCG, World War I. Mem. Am. Bar Assn. (bd. govs. 1963-66), Bar Assn. D.C. (past pres.) , Soc. of Cincinnati of Md. (past pres.) , Lords of Md. Manors. Clubs: Chevy Chase (Md.) ; Metropolitan (Washington). Home: 5826 Highland Dr Kenwood Chevy Chase MD 20015 Office: Tower Bldg Washington DC 20005

HILL, FRANK WHITNEY, Jr., ins. co. exec,; b. Topeka, Aug. 4, 1914; s. Frank Whitney and Blanche (Scott) H.; student Kan. U., Kansas City Sch. Law; m. Mary Louise Booth, May 18, 1940; children—Frank Whitney III, Marilyn Louise, Barbara Jane. With Equitable Life Assurance Soc. U.S., 1946—, beginning as field asst., Peoria, Ill., successively asst. agy. mgr., dist. mgr. Bloomington, Ill., agy. mgr., Albany, N.Y., 1946-58, field v.p., N.Y.C., 1958-61, v.p. of agy. affairs N.Y. Met. dept., 1961-61, agy. mgr., 1962—. Mem. nat. bd. Gen. Agts. and Mgrs. Conf. Chmn. life div. Greater Alegehny United Fund; gen. chmn. Greater Albany Community Chest Fund, 1957-8, Mem. Albany (past pres.) , Pitts. (pres.) gen. agts. and mgrs. assns., Pitts. Life Underwriters Assn. Club: Duquesne. Home: 15 Woodland Dr Mt Lebanon PA 15228 Office: 717 Gateway Pittsburgh PA 15207

HILL, FREDRIC WILLIAM, educator, nutritionist, b. Erie, Pa., Sept. 2, 1918; s. Vaino Alexander and Mary Elvira (Holmstrom) H.; B.S., Pa. State U., 1939, M.S., 1940; Ph.D., Cornell U., 1944; m. Charlotte Henrietta Gummoe, Apr. 1, 1944; children—Linda Charlotte, James Fredric, Dana Edwin. Research asst. Pa. State U., 1939-40, Cornell U., 1940-44; head nutrition div. research labs. Western Condensing Co., Appleton, Wis., 1944-48; asso. prof., then prof. animal nutrition Cornell U., 1948-59; prof. poultry husbandry, chmn. dept. U. Cal. at Davis, 1959-65, prof., chmn. dept. nutrition, 1965—, asso. dean Coll. Agr., 1965-66. Research adv. com. Nat. Cottonseed Products Assn., Soybean Council Am.; subcom. hormonal relationships and applications NRC, 1953, subcom. poultry nutrition, 1953—; commr. Cal. Poultry Improvement Commn., 1959-65; participant 8th Easter Sch. Agrl. Scis., U. Nottingham (Eng.), 1961, World Conf. Animal Prodn., Rome, Italy, 1963, U.S. AID-Nat. Acad. Sci. Seminar on Protein Foods, Bangkok, 1970. Fellow Danforth Found., 1938; recipient Nutrition Research award Am. Feed Mfrs. Assn., 1958, Newman Internat. Research award British Poultry Assn., 1959; Guggenheim Found. fellow, 1966-67. Fellow A.A.A.S.; mem. Soc. Exptl. Biology and Medicine, Nutrition Soc. (Gt. Britain), Poultry Sci. Assn. (Research prize 1957, Borden award 1961), World's Poultry Sci. Assn., Am. Inst. Nutrition, Am. Inst. Biol. Scis., Am. Soc. Animal Sci., Am. Chem. Soc., Sigma Xi, Phi Eta Sigma, Gamma Sigma Delta, Phi Kappa Phi, Delta Theta Sigma, Gamma Alpha. Contbr. articles profl. jours. Editorial bd. Poultry Sci. Jour., 1960- 64; editorial bd. Jour. of Nutrition, 1964-68, editor, 1969—. Home: 643 Miller Dr Davis CA 95616

HILL, GEORGE E., judge; b. 1919; B.S., J. D., U. Ill. Admitted to bar, 1951; former U.S. atty. Western Dist. Mich.; atty., bd. control No. Mich. U., Marquette, from 1967; now dist. judge. Home: 527 E Michigan St Marquette MI 49855 Office: Marquette County Court House Marquette MI 49855

HILL, GEORGE H., Jr., lawyer, corp. exec.; b. Tupelo, Miss., Mar. 7, 1909; s. George H. and Myrtle (Motley) H.; LL.B., U. Miss., 1939; m. Matt Adelaide Smith, June 28, 1931; children—George Henry, III, Leonard Allen, Marjorie Ann. Dorothy Jean. Admitted to Miss. bar, 1928, and practiced in Tupelo, 1928- 32; became atty. R.F.C., Washington, D.C., August 1932, and served successively as atty., counsel, gen. counsel for R.F.C. Mortgage Co. then gen. counsel for Defense Supplies Corp., 1942-45; sr. v.p., dir. Cities Service Co., 1959-63, gen. counsel, 1963-64, exec. v.p., gen. counsel, 1964-70, mem. exec. com., 1966-70; pres., dir. Peruvian Pacific Petroleum Co., Cities Service Internat., Inc.; v.p., dir. or other officer numerous subsidiary of affiliated cos. Decorated Officer de l'Ordre de Leopold II Bruxelles (Belgium). Mem. Sigma Nu, Phi Delta Phi. Club: Royal Palm Yacht and Country (Boca Raton, Fla.). Home: 2134 Silver Palm Rd W Boca Raton FL

HILL, GEORGE MAURICE, corp. exec.; b. Rutherford County, N.C., Oct. 28, 1905; s. Robert Martin and Lucy Lorena (Callahan) H.; student U. N.C., 1921-25, U. N.C. Law Sch., 1941-42, U. N.C. Sch. Bus. Adminstrn., 1954-55; Dr. Humanities, N.C. State U., Raleigh, 1968; m. Elva Dare Andrews, June 24, 1925; 1 son, George Maurice. Mem. staff U. N.C., 1926-43, asst. to pres., 1938-40; with Drexel Furniture Co. (N.C.), 1944-65, v.p., dir. mfg., 1954-59, pres., 1960-65, also dir.; v.p., dir., mem. exec. com. Drexel Enterprises, Inc. (N.C.), 1960-65, pres., 1965-70; sr. v.p., dir. U.S. Plywood-Champion Papers, Inc., 1968—; dir. N.C. Nat. Bank, N.C. Nat. Bancorp., Charlotte; mem. adv. bd. Liberty Mut. Ins. Co., Charlotte, N.C., 1965-70 Mem. Gov. N.C. Adv. Council Employment Security Commn., Gov. N.C. Com. Employment Hamdicapped, Gov. N.C. Com. Occupational Health and Environmental Hazards Com. Bd. dirs. N.C. Indsl. Council, N.C. CItizens Assn., N.C. Engring. Found., Outward Bound Sch., Furniture Found.; trustee Wake Forest U., 1959—, pres. bd. trustees, 1965-67; trustee Western Piedmont Community Coll., Morganton, N.C.; South Mountain Inst., Nebo, N.C., Grace Hosp., 1945-69, trustee emeritus, 1970; trustee Drexel Found. So. Bapt. Theol. Sem., Louisville; mem. adv. com. Appalachian State U., Boone, N.C. Mem. N.A.M. (past dir.), So. Furniture Mfrs. Assn. (dir., past pres.), Morganton C. of C., Newcomen Soc. N.A. Mason, Elk, Kiwanian. Home: 112 Terrace Pl Morganton NC 28655 Office: Drexel Enterprises Inc Drexel NC 28619

HILL, GEORGE RICHARD, coll. dean; b. Ogden, Utah, Nov. 24, 1921; s. George Richard and Elizabeth (McKay) H.; A.B. in Chemistry, Brigham Young U., 1942; Ph.D. in Phys. and Inorganic Chemistry, Cornell U., 1946; m. Melba Parker, Aug. 25, 1941; children-George Richard IV, Margaret (Mrs. Paul Nielson), Robert Parker, Carolyn, Susan, Nancy, David Parker. Chemist, Am. Smelting & Refining Co., 1937-42; asst., part-time instr. Cornell U., 1942-46; project dir. Air Force Combustion Research, 1952-57; project dir. Dept. Interior, Office Coal Research, 1962—; mem. faculty U. Utah, 1946—, prof. chemistry, 1950—, chmn. fuels engring., 1951-65, dean. Coll. Mines and mineral industries, 1966—. Project dir. Air Force Office Sci. Research, 1956-61, Equity Oil Shale Research 1961. Mem. exec. bd. region XII Boy Scouts Am., 1961—, chmn. Explorer activities sect. 6, 1959-61, mem. Explorer com., nat. exec. bd., 1965—. Bd. dirs. Deseret Gymnasium, 1967—. Recipient Distinguished Service award, Utah Petroleum Council, 1968, Outstanding Profl. Engr. award Utah Engring. Council, 1970. Fellow Am. Inst. Chemists; mem. Am. Chem. Soc. (Utah award Salt Lake sect., 1969), Salt Lake City C. of C., Sigma Xi, Phi Kappa Phi. Sigma Pi Sigma, Alpha Phi Omega. Mem. Ch. of Jesus Christ of Latter-day Saints (asst. gen. supt. Y.M.M.I.A.). Contbr. papers on kinetics of coal conversion, oil shale, corrosion, catalysis. Home: 1430 Yale Ave Salt Lake City UT 84105

HILL, GEORGE WATTS, Jr., ins. co. exec., educator; b. Balt., Aug. 3, 1926; s. George Watts and Anne (McCulloch) H.; A.B. in Econs., U. N.C., 1947; LL.B., N.C. Central U., 1968; m. Mary Drake Lamberton, July 22, 1946; children—George Watts, Deborah Lamberton. With Bankers Trust Co., N.Y.C., 1947-50; v.p. Central Carolina Bank, Durham, N.C., 1950-58; with Home Security Life Ins. Co., Durham, 1958—, pres., 1961-67, chmn. bd., 1967—; edn. cons. Edn. Commn. of States, Coll. Entrance Exam. Bd., Edn. Testing Service, So. Regional Edn. Bd., others. Chmn. N.C. Bd. High Edn., 1965-69. Mem. Durham City Council, 1955-56, N.C. Ho. of Reps., 1957-61. Trustee Oldfields Sch., Glencoe, Md., Johnson C. Smith U., Charlotte, N.C. Served as ensign USNR, 1944-46. Mem. Cap and Gown, Order Golden Fleece, Beta Gamma Sigma. Democrat. Presbyn. Home: 610 Greenwood Rd Chapel Hill NC 27514 Office: 505 W Chapel Hill St Durham NC 27701

HILL, GILBERT ROBERT, banker; b. Delaware, O., June 13, 1918; s. Percy Herriott and Edith (Smith) H.; Grad. Ohio Sch. Banking, Ohio U., 1964, Am. Inst. Banking, 1959; m. Mabel Halbert, Nov. 3, 1951. With VA, 1946-51; with Huntington Nat. Bank, Columbus, O., 1951—, auditor, 1961—, asst. v.p., 1970—. Served with AUS, 1941-45. Mem. Bank Adminstrn. Inst. (pres. Central Ohio 1963-64), Am. Inst. Banking (pres. Columbus 1963-64). Home: 974 Birchmont Rd Columbus OH 43221 Office: 17 S High St Columbus OH 43215

HILL, GORDON MANDEL, accountant; b. Atlanta, Aug. 27, 1893; s. Malvern and Nannie C. (McCollum) H.; student Ga. Inst. Tech., 1911-12. With J.B. McCrary Engring. Corp., Atlanta, 1912-16; with Haskins & Sells, C.P.A.'s 1918-, mem. firm, 1935—, located in Atlanta, 1919-20, New Orleans, 1920-25, Jacksonville, Fla., 1926-31, N.Y.C., 1932—. C.P.A., N.Y. State, La., Tex., Fla., S.C. Mem. N.Y. State (dir., exec. com. 1953-54) , La., Tex., Fla. (v.p. 1928), S.C. socs. C.P.A.'s, Am. Accounting Assn., Am. Inst. Accountants (council 1955-57, exec. com. 1956-57, trial bd. 1955-57; chmn. coms.) , Am. Sr., Long Island Sr., N.Y. State Sr., Met. (exec. com. 1955-57), U.S. Sr. golf assns., Sigma Mu. Mason. Clubs: Union League; Metropolitan Opera (gov. 1952-53), Bankers (N.Y.C.); Garden City (N.Y.) Golf. Home; 41 Park Av New York City NY 10016 Office: 2 Broadway New York City NY 10004

HILL, HARRY GERALD, lawyer; b. Bklyn., Dec. 26, 1900; s. Henry Charles and Mary Loretta (Fitzgerald) H.; B.S., N.Y. U., 1923; LL.B., St. John's U., 1928, LL.M., 1929, LL.D., 1943; m. Grace Marie Byrne, Oct. 17, 1931; children—Harry Gerald, Peter David, Elizabeth Anne. Planning engr. Western Electric Co., 1923-26, sect. head charge planning engrs., 1926-28; admitted to N.Y. bar, 1930; asso. firm Cullen & Dykman, 1929-40, mem., 1941—; gen. counsel Todd Shipyards Corp., 1946—, v.p., 1953, dir., 1952—, exec. v.p., 1958- -; dir. Lester Engring. Co.; chmn. retirement bd. Todd Shipyards Corp. Retirement System. Mem. Am. Soc. of Naval Engrs., Am., N.Y. State, Bklyn. bar assns., Soc. Naval Architects and Marine Engrs., Bklyn.-Manhattan Trial Counsel Assn., Cath. Lawyers' Guild Diocese of Bklyn., Pi Kappa Alpha, Phi Delta Phi. Clubs: Brooklyn, Lawyers (Bklyn.); New York Athletic; National Lawyers; Propeller of U.S. Home: 175 Kensington Rd Garden City NY 11530 Office: 177 Montague St Brooklyn NY 11201 also One State St Plaza New York City NY 10004

HILL, HENRY ALLEN, educator, physicist; b. Port Arthur, Tex., Nov. 25, 1933; s. Douglas and Florence (Kilgore) H.; B.S., U. Houston, 1953; M.S., U. Minn., 1956, Ph.D., 1957; m. Ethel Louise Eplin, Aug. 23, 1954; children—Henry Allen, Pamela Lynne, Kimberly Renee. Research asst. U. Houston, 1952-53; teaching asst. U. Minn., 1953-54, research asst., 1954-57; research asso. Princeton, 1957- 58, instr., then asst. prof., 1958-64; asso. prof. Wesleyan U., Middletown, Conn., 1964-66, prof. physics, 1966—; prof. physics U. Ariz., 1966—. Sloan fellow, 1966-68. Mem. Am. Phys. Soc. Contbr. profl. jours. Research nuclear physics, relativity. Mailing address: ‡

HILL, HENDRICKSON HARVARD mfg. exec.; b. Lima, O., Apr. 1, 1932; B.S., U. San Francisco, 1954; M.S., Stanford University, 1956; m. Rosemarie Lois Brown, May 15, 1955; 1 son, Anthony Robinson. Sales rep. Ames-Brockton Fabricated Products, Akron, O., 1956-58, sales mgr. Coshocton, Ohio, 1959-61, gen. manager plant, 1961-68, v.p. sales, 1968--. Instr. bus. Coshocton Jr. College, 1968-69. Mem. Coshocton C. of C. (vice president 1967-68, pres. 1969-70), Sales Executives Institute, Phi Beta Kappa, Sigma Chi, Phi Mu. Democrat. Mem. Christian Ch. (lay leader). Mason (32, Shriner). Clubs: Coshocton Country, Coshocton City, Running Deer Country. Home: 2d Av Coshocton OH Office: 3d Av Coshocton OH

HILL, HEYWARD GIBBES, ret. fgn. service officer; b. Hammond, La., Jan. 16, 1900; s. Samuel Lindsay and Kate Turpin (McKnight) H.; ed. La. State U., 1916-20, also private tutors in France and Switzerland. Apptd. fgn. service officer, vice consul and sec. in the diplomatic service, 1930, fgn. service Sch. Dept. State, 1930; vice consul, Kobe, Japan, 1930, Taihoku (temporary), 1931, Kobe, 1931, Yokahama, 1931, Buenos Aires, 1933; Asst. Sec. Am. delegation, 7th Internat. Conf. of Am. States Montevideo, 1933; sec. Am. delegation, Pan Am. Conml. Conf., Buenos Aires, 1935; sec. Am. delegation, Chaco Peace Conf., Buenos Aires, 1935-36; vice consul Geneva, Switzerland, 1936, consul, 1937; Sec. Am. delegation meeting of Intergovernmental Com. on Polit. Refugees, Evian, France and London, England, 1938; sec. Am. delegation, Eighth Internat. Conf. Am. States, Lima, Peru, 1938; consul, Basel, Switzerland, 1939; second sec. embassy Panama 1939, 2d sec. embassy for duty with U.S. rep. to Politico- Mil. Commn., Algiers, 1943; temporarily detailed Dept. of State, Washington, European Div., 5 mos. in 1944; 1st sec. embassy, Ankara, Turkey, June, 1945; counselor of embassy, Jidda, Saudi Arabia, 1949-50; consul gen., Marseilles, France, 1951-54; counselor of embassy, consul gen., Manila, P.I., 1954-56, consul gen., Alexandria, Egypt, U.A.R., 1957-61. Clubs: University (Washington); Athens Lawn Tennis. Address: Hilton Hotel Athens Greece

HILL, HOMER SPURGEON, marine corps officer; b. Winnsboro, Tex., July 21, 1918; s. Gary Lewis and Ivy Juanita (Connelly) H.; B.S., Tex. A. and M. Coll., 1940; m. Fauna Ruth Long, June 12, 1942; 1 dau., Diane Elisabeth. Commd. 2d lt. USMC, 1942, advanced through grades to maj. gen., 1970; served with 1st Marine Aircraft Wing, World War II; pilot exec. officer Air Sta., Hawaii, 1945-47; asst. operations officer, asst. flight safety officer, 1947-49; asst. coordinator detail br. personnel dept., 1949-51; comdg. officer VMF-314, MAG-31 3d Marine Aircraft Wing, 1951-53; comdg. officer, Japan, Korea, Korean conflict; comdg. officer Aircraft Engring. Squadron 12, Quantico, 1955-57; group S-3 officer, 1957-58; comdg. officer marine detachment and air officer U.S.S. Princeton, 1959-61; head officer plans br. G-1 div., 1961-65; staff hdqrs. Fleet Marine Force, 1965-66; asst. wing comdr. 2d Marine Aircraft Wing, Cherry Point, N.C., 1967; asst. wing comdr., Vietnam, 1968-69; asst. dept. chief staff (air), 1969-70; dir. marine corps aviation, 1970—. Decorated D.S.M., Legion of Merit, D.F.C. with gold cross, Air medal with one silver and one gold star, Navy Commendation medal. Mason. Home: 907 Dalebrook Dr Alexandria VA 22308 Office: Hdqrs Marine Corps Washington DC

HILL, IRVING, judge; b. Lincoln, Neb., Feb. 6, 1915; s. Nathan and Ida (Ferder) H.; A.B., U. Neb., 1936; LL.B., Harvard, 1939; m. Maydee Taylor, June 23, 1939; children—Lawrence N., Steven C., Richard F. Admitted to Neb. bar, 1939, D.C. bar, 1942, Cal. bar, 1946; spl. asst. to U.S. atty. gens. Biddle and Clark, Dept. Justice, Washington, 1942-46; legal adviser U.S. Delegation to UN Econ. and Social Council, 1946; pvt. practice, Beverly Hills Col.; 1946-61; judge Cal. Superior Ct., 1961-65; U.S. dist. judge, Los Angeles, 1965—. Pres. Jewish Fedn.-Council Greater Los Angeles, 1960-63; v.p. Council Jewish Fedns. and Welfare Fund, 1962-65; dir. gen. bd. United Way, Los Angeles County, 1963—. Served to lt. (j.g.) USNR, 1944-46. Mem. Phi Beta Kappa. Office: US Court House 312 N Spring St Los Angeles CA 90012

HILL, ISAAC WILLIAM, newspaper editor; b. Opelika, Ala., Aug. 8, 1908; s. Isaac W. and Laura (Jones) H.; A.B., Washington and Lee U., 1929; m. Catherine H. Dawson, June 25, 1932; children—Catherine R., Joyce E. Reporter-editor Mobile Press, 1929-30; deskman Washington Evening Star, 1930-37, city editor, 1937-49, news editor, 1949-54, asst. mng. editor, 1954-62, mng. editor, 1962-68, asso. editor, 1968—; lectr. newspaper personnel Am. Press Inst., Columbia, 1955—. Dir. Md. Media, Inc. Mem. Am. Soc. Newspaper Editors, A.P. Mng. Editors Assn. (pres. 1967, chmn. new tech. com. 1969—); Newspaper Comics Council, Inc., Lambda Chi Alpha, Pi Delta Epsilon, Sigma Delta Chi. Clubs: International, National Press, Chevy Chase (Washington). Co-author: Mirror of War, 1961; author short stories and articles popular mags. Home: 3203 Leland St Chevy Chase MD 20015 Office: 225 Virginia Av SE Washington DC 20003

HILL, JACK A., educator; Ph.D., U. Tex. Prof., head dept. mgmt. U. Neb., Omaha. Office: U Neb Omaha NB 68132*

HILL, JAMES JEROME, motion picture producer; b. St. Paul, Mar. 2, 1905; s. Louis Warren and Maud Van Cortlandt (Taylor) H.; grad. St. Paul Acad. Country Day Sch., 1922; B.A., Yale, 1927; student Brit. Acad. Painting, Rome, 1927-28, Scandinavian Acad. Art, Paris, 1928-32. Painted frescoes, Chem. Lab. of St. Paul Acad., 1921-22, Stations of the Cross, Chapel Our Lady of Mercy, Boca Grande, Fla.; one man shows Carstairs Babcock galleries; exhibited Salons des Tuileries, Salons d'Automne, Paris, 1929-37, Galleria 88, Rome; dir. motion pictures, including Skiflight, 1937, Albert Schweitzer (Academy award winner), 1938; The Seeing Eye, 1940; Grandma Moses (nominated for the Academy award), 1953; The Sand Castle, 1961; Winter City Haiku, 1962; Open The Door, 1964; Schweitzer and Bach, 1965; Merry Christmas, 1968, Anti Corrida, 1968, The Artist's Friend, 1969, also The Canaries, 1969. Served with Signal Corps, AUS, World War II. Decorated Medaille de la Liberation, 1945. Author: Trip to Greece, 1937. Home: Sugar Bowl Norden CA 95724 Office: 1860 Broadway New York City NY 10023

HILL, JAMES L., oil co. exec.; b. Farwell, Tex., Aug. 30, 1924; s. Fred Warren and Estelle (Sossman) H.; B.B.A., Tex. Tech. Coll., 1949; m. Peggy Jean Gibson, Dec. 20, 1945; children—James Keith, Jeannie Kay. Asst. treas. Shamrock Oil & Gas Corp., 1959-62, treas., 1962-67; sec.-treas. Emerald Corp., 1962—; sec.-treas. West Emerald Pipeline Corp., 1962—, Emerald Pipeline Corp., 1962—; treas. Shamrock Pipeline Corp.; unit treas. Diamond Shamrock Oil & Gas Co. unit Diamond Shamrock Corp.; treas. AGM Corp., 1970. Vice pres., mem. bd. Amarillo (Tex.) YMCA. Served with USNR, 1943-46. Baptist (deacon). Home: 6213 Adirondack St Amarillo TX 79106 Office: Box 631 Amarillo TX 79105

HILL, JAMES LEVAN, educator; b. Altoona, Pa., May 29, 1907; s. James H. and Lillie (Mullin) H.; B.S., State Tchrs. Coll., California, Pa., 1943; M.Ed., Pa. State U., 1945, D.Ed., 1953; m. Marion V. Truax, Jan. 23, 1942. Apprentice, journeyman, machinist Pa. R.R., McLanahan & Stone Machine Co., Hollidaysburg, Pa., also Westinghouse Mfg. Co. Lester, Pa., 1923-39; faculty State Tchrs. Coll., California, Pa., 1941-43; tchr. pub. schs., Progress, Pa., also Altoona, Pa., 1943-48; vis. instr. Pa. State U., summers 1947-52; prof., chmn. dept. indsl. arts and engring. drawing Bowling Green State U., 1954-66, prof. indsl. edn., 1966- -. Exhibited works at Exhbn. Craftsmen Central States Mus. Contemporary Crafts, N.Y.C., Herron Mus. Art, Indpls.; one man show of silver at the Toledo Mus. Art. also at Massillon Museum, 1965. Recipient art ambassadors popularity award, Toledo Area Artists Exhibition at Toledo Mus. Art, 1957, 1st award, 1963, 64, 65; purchase award, 1964; best in show prize Ohio Artists' and Craftsmen's Show, Massilon Museum, 1966. Mem. Nat. Assn. Indsl. Tchr. Educators, Ohio Indsl. Arts Assn., Am. Vocational Assn., Epsilon Pi Tau, Iota Lambda Sigma, Phi Delta Kappa. Methodist. Mason (Shriner). Home: 124 S College Dr Bowling Green OH 43402

HILL, JAMES SCOTT, chem. co. exec.; b. Boston, Mar. 21, 1924; s. Benjamin B. and Dorothy (Scott) H.; grad. Deerfield (Mass.) Acad., 1941; B.A., Williams Coll., 1947; LL.B., Columbia, 1949; m. Sally C. Foss, June 28, 1945; children—Richard B., Chessye F., Cynthia C., Michael O. Admitted to N.Y. bar, 1949, N.J. bar, 1958; asso. firm Baldwin, Todd & Lefferts, N.Y.C., 1949-50; sec., atty. Johnson & Johnson, 1950-66; gen. counsel Celanese Corp., N.Y.C., 1966—, v.p., sec.,1967—. Judge Princeton (N.J.) Twp., 1959-65. Treas. N.J. Republican Finance Com., 1965-70. Trustee, v.p. Princeton Hosp., 1962-68. Served to 1st lt. USAAF, 1943-46. Mem. Chi Psi. Republican. Episcopalian (Warden 1969-71). Clubs: Metropolitan (Washington); Pinnacle, Princeton (N.Y.C.); Mid-Ocean (Bermuda). Home: 152 Galbreath Dr Princeton NJ 08540 Office: 522 Fifth Av New York City NY 10036

HILL, JAMES STANLEY, life ins. co. exec.; b. Merrickville, Ont., Can., July 24, 1914; m. Doris C. Haelster, 1938; children—George, Janice, Mary, Beverly, Richard. With Minn. Mut. Life Ins. Co., 1930-69, sr. v.p., 1966-69; pres. Digiplan, Inc., Mahtomedi, Minn., 1969—. Treas. Minn. High Sch. Math. Contest Com.; mem. adv. com. Minn. Nat. Lab. Improvement Secondary Sch. Math. Curriculum; mem. Minn. Industry Edn. Bd. Bd. mem. Charles T. Miller Hosp. Mem. Soc. Actuaries (bd. govs., v.p.) Internat. Congress Actuaries. Home: 70 Spruce St Mahtomedi, MN 55115. Office: Digiplan Inc 70 Spruce St Mahtomedi MN 55115

HILL, JAMES TOMILSON, Jr., corp. dir.; b. Salt Lake City, Mar. 2, 1916; s. James T. and Clara Frances (Quirk) H.; A.B. with great distinction, Stanford, 1937; LL.B. cum laude, Harvard, 1940 m. Dorothy Helen Kutcher, July 6, 1941; children—Susan Tomilson, James Tomilson III. Admitted to Wyo. bar, 1940, N.Y. bar, 1941, U.S. Supreme Ct., 1945; lawyer Sullivan & Cromwell, N.Y. C., 1940-42, 47-50; spl. asst. to Under Sec. of Navy, 1942-43; counsel Bur. Aeronautics, Navy Dept., also asst. gen. counsel, gen. counsel Navy Dept., 1946-47; gen. counsel, later asst. sec., Dept. Air Force, 1950-53; with Wm. A.M. Burden & Co. (pvt. capital investments), N.Y.C., 1953-65, gen. partner, 1954-65; exec. v.p. Inmont Corp., 1965, pres., 1966-70, chief exec. officer, 1969-70, dir., 1960-70, mem. exec. com., 1961-70; dir. Alcan Aluminum, Ltd., ITEK Corp. Trustee Wellesley Coll. Com. Econ. Devel.; mem. Stanford Assos.; trustee mem. exec. comm. Nightingale-Bamford Sch., 1963-69. Served from ensign to lt. comdr., USNR, 1943-46. Mem. Am. Bar Assn., Council Fgn. Relations, Phi Beta Kappa. Clubs: Century Assn., Harvard, Economic, Knickerbocker (N.Y.C.); Ekwanok (Manchester, Vt.); Wianno (gov.; mem. exec. com.; chmn. finance com.) (Mass.); Meadow Brook (Jericho, N.Y.); National Golf Links of America (Southampton, N.Y.); Country of Florida, Ocean of Florida (Delray Beach). Home: 870 United Nations Plaza New York City NY 10017 also Ocean View Av Cotuit MA 02635

HILL, JOHN, ins. exec.; b. Colfax, Wis., Mar. 13, 1907; s. Elmer B. and Mary (Burch) H.; A.B., U. Minn., 1929; M.B.A., Harvard, 1933; m. Audrey Booth, Jan. 1, 1938; 1 son, Jonathan B. Accountant, St. Paul Fire & Marine Ins. Co., 1929-31; editor New Eng. Mut. Life Ins. Co., Boston, 1933, asst. to pres., 1940-41, v.p., 1948-64, sr. v.p., 1964—. Mem. exec. bd. Boston council Boy Scouts Am. Mem. corp. Mus. of Sci. Served as lt. comdr. USNR, 1942-46. Mem. Boston Life Underwriters Assn., Health Ins. Assn. Am. (adminstrv. Com.), Chartered Life Underwriters; Boston C. of C. Episcopalian (warden). Club: St. Botolph Country (Boston). Home: 388 Beacon St Boston MA 02116 Office: 501 Boylston St Boston MA 02116

HILL, JOHN ALEXANDER, hosp. corp. exec.; b. Shawnee, Okla., Feb. 24, 1907; s. John E. and Mary B. (Cheek) H.; A.B., U. Denver, 1928, LL. D., 1965; m. Margaret M. Mikesell, June 14, 1929; children—Mary (Mrs. Lowell R. King), John, Jane (Mrs. John Georgiades). With Aetna Life Ins. Co. as group rep., Denver, 1928-30, mgr. group and pension depts., Detroit, 1930-33, dist. supr., 1933-36, gen. agt. John A. Hill & Assos., Toledo, 1936-58, sr. v.p., Hartford, Conn., 1958-62; pres. Aetna Life & Casualty, 1962-70; pres., dir. Hosp. Corp. Am., Nashville, 1970—; dir., mem. exec. com. Owens-Ill. Glass Co.; dir. Arrow-Hart, Inc., Wells Fargo Mortgage Investors, Genesco, Sherwin-Williams Co. Trustee Am. Coll. Life Underwriters; pres. Toledo Community Chest, 1952; chmn. Toledo chpt. A. R.C., 1946-49. Bd. dirs. Greater Hartford Community Chest, Conn. Hosp. Planning Commn. Corporator Hartford Hosp., Mt. Sinai Hosp., Hartford Pub. Library; dir. Am. Sch. for the Deaf. Mem. Pilgrims U.S., Million Dollar Round Table, Toledo C. of C. (pres. 1953), Am. Soc. Corp. Exec., Assn. Episcopal Colls. (mem. nat. com.), Inst. Living (dir.), Beta Theta Pi. Republican. Episcopalian. Clubs: Toledo, University (N.Y.C.); University (Hartford, Conn.); Hartford, Hartford Golf; Country (Farmington); Links (N.Y.C.); Belle Meade Country (Nashville). Home: High St Farmington CT 06032 Office: 250 Constitution Plaza Hartford CT 06103

HILL, JOHN ANTHONY, lawyer, business exec.; b. Washington, May 6, 1904; s. Moxley Anthony and Marie (Cowen) H.; A.B., Amherst Coll., 1925; LL.B., Columbia Law Sch., 1928; m. Helen Mahan; 1 dau., Judith. Lawyer with firm Shearman and Sterling, 1928-39; with Air Reduction Co., Inc., 1939—, dir., 1947—, pres., 1948, chmn. board, 1964-69, chmn. exec. com., 1969—; dir. Marine Midland Bank-N.Y., N.Y.C., Marine Midland Banks, Inc.; trustee Harlem Savs. Bank. Trustee Presbyn. Hosp. N.Y., Amherst Coll. Mem. N.Y., Mass. bar assns., Phi Kappa Psi, Phi Delta Phi. Clubs: Union League, Pinnacle, Links, Amherst of N.Y.; Whippoorwill Country. Home: 200 E 66th St New York City NY 10021 Office: Air Reduction Co Inc 150 E 42d St New York City NY 10017

HILL, JOHN CALVIN, fgn. service officer; Ft. Smith, Ark., Aug. 1, 1921; s. John Calvin and Isabel P. (Hill) H.; A.B., Princeton U.; 1943; M.A., George Washington U., 1967; m. McCoy Youmans Metts, Apr. 19, 1947; children—Katharine W., John Calvin, Isabel M. With Dept. State, 1946—, fgn. service officer, 1947—; 3d sec. Am. legation, Bucharest, 1947-50; asst. U.S. polit. adviser, Trieste, 1950-52; 2d sec. Am. embassy, Guatemala City, 1952-55; 2d sec. Am. embassy, Bangkok, 1955, 1st. sec., 1956-58; alt. U.S. council rep. S.E. Asia Treaty Orgn., 1956-58; spl. asst. to asst. sec. state for inter-Am. affairs, 1958-60; Nat. War Coll., 1960-61; consul gen. Dominican Republic, 1961, Charge d'Affaires, 1962; minister-counselor, Am. Embassy, Caracas, 1962-65; dir. Office of North Coast Affairs, Bur. Inter-Am. Affairs, Dept. State, 1965-69; fgn. service inspr.; 1969—. Served as captain, F.A., AUS, 1943-46. Decorated Silver Star. Mem. Am. Fgn. Service Assn. Home: 1601 Forest Lane McLean VA Office: Dept of State Washington DC 20525

HILL, JOHN CORNELL, lawyer, corp. exec.; b. Pitts., Dec. 9, 1916; s. William Fulton and Eleanor (Garrett) H.; B.A., Cornell U., 1938; LL.B., U. Pitts., 1941; m. Mary Louise Goetz, Dec. 1, 1945; children—Nancy H., Linda G., Mary Ellen, John Cornell. Admitted to Pa. bar, 1942; pvt. practice law, Pitts., 1947-63; atty. U.S. Dept. State, 1942, Ordnance Dept., U.S. Army, 1942-44; gen. atty. H.H. Robertson Co., bldg. products, Pitts., 1944-63, v.p., sec., 1963-, gen. counsel, 1968—, also dir. Mem. Am., Pa., Allegheny County bar assns., Am. Soc. Corp. Secs., Newcomen Soc., Sigma Alpha Epsilon, Phi Delta Phi. Presbyn. Home: W Waldheim Rd Pittsburgh PA 15215 Office: 2 Gateway Center Pittsburgh PA 15222

HILL, JOHN DEKOVEN, mag. editor, architect; b. Cleve., May 19, 1920; s. John deKoven and Helen Elizabeth (Muckley) H.; Taliesin fellow Frank Lloyd Wright Sch. Architecture, 1938-42; m. Heloise Fichter, 1957; 1 son, Christopher deKoven. Asso. of Frank Lloyd Wright, 1942-59; editorial dir. House Beautiful mag., 1953-63; dir. Joel Design Projects, N.Y.C., 1956-63; mem. Taliesin Asso. Architects, 1959—, sec. 1963—; sec. Frank Lloyd Wright Sch. Architecture, 1963—; designer domestic and comml. bldgs. and interiors. Bd. dirs. Frank Lloyd Wright Found. Writer, critic architecture and aesthetics. Address: Taliesin West Scottsdale AZ 85252 also Taliesin Spring Green WI 53588

HILL, JOHN HUB, industrialist; b. Paris, Tex., Nov. 8, 1905; s. Joe Wilson and Tommie (Roberts) H.; student Paris Bus. Coll., 1923-25; m. Alstachia Walker, June 6, 1953. Classer-buyer McFadden Cotton Co., Paris, 1925-26; salesman House Jewelry Co., Paris, 1926-27, Dallas Paper and Box Co., 1927-28; salesman Acme Brick Co., Dallas, 1928-32, div. mgr. sales, 1932- 51; propr. Hub Transp. Co., Dallas, 1933-40; pres. Houston-Harris Co., 1944-48, Hub Devel. Corp., 1944-48, Hub Improvement Corp., 1944-48, Denton Housing Corp., 1944-48, Sherman Housing Corp., 1944-48, Clearview Bldg. Corp., 1947-55, Clearview Park, Inc., 1948-55, Dodd Corp., 1950- 60, Hill-Elliott, Inc., Dallas, 1950—, Lakewood Terrace, Inc., Dallas, 1950—, Bergstrom Corp., 1951-58, Sill Corp., 1951-60, Hub Hill, Inc., Dallas, 1960—, Hill-Elliott Investment Co., Dallas, 1960—, Tex-Ariz. Motor Freight, Inc., 1964-65; partner Sherman Bldg. and Supply Co., 1945-58, Jenkins Wholesale Lumber Co., 1946-50, Cavalier Lodge Motor Hotel, 1947-61, Hub Investment Co., 1948-65, Goodhue Bldg. Co., 1950-52, Lufkin Pine Lumber Co., 1950-54, Don Elliott Gen. Contractor, Dallas and Sherman, Tex., 1955—, Rio Grande Valley farming interests, McAllen and Edinburg, Tex., 1961—; pres., dir. Builders Loan Co., 1955—; dir. Dallas Title and Guaranty Co., 1955—, Mercantile Security Life Ins. Co., Dallas, 1956—, Mercantile Nat. Bank, Dallas, 1962—; pres. Wherry Mil. Housing Assn., 1958-61; chmn. bd., chmn. exec. com. Acme Brick Co., 1959—; an organizer, mem. exec. com., dir. Park Cities Bank & Trust Co., 1959-62; developer, chmn. bd. Penn Towers, Inc., 1960-61; v.p., dir. L.M.S. Corp., 1961-65. Mem. nat. adv. council Small Bus. Adminstrn., 1966—, chmn. Tex. adv. council, 1963—. Bd. dirs. Dallas Civic Opera, 1961—, Children's Med. Center, Dallas, 1961—; bd. visitors Tex. U.-M.D. Anderson Hosp. and Tumor Inst., Houston; mem. citizens council Scott and White Hosp., Temple, Tex., 1962-65. Mem. Dallas Council World Affairs, Dallas, North Dallas, Dallas East, Oak Cliff, East Tex., Lamar County (hon. life mem.), U.S. Chambers commerce, Tex. Research League, Newcomen Soc. N.Am., Internat. Platform Assn., Trinity Improvement Assn., Navy League U.S., Am. Trucking Assn. (bd. govs. common carrier conf.), Ind. Producers Assn. Am., Nat. Structural Clay Producers Assn., Mid-Continent Oil and Gas Assn., Tex. Ind. Producers and Royalty Assn., Southwest Clay Products Assn., Dallas Real Estate Bd., Tex. Real Estate Assn., Nat. Assn. Real Estate Bds., Dallas Execs. Club, Dallas Petroleum Club, Ins. Club Dallas. Methodist (past steward). Club: National Capital Democratic (Washington). Home: 4209 Bordeaux St Dallas TX 75205 Office: Mercantile Bank Bldg Dallas TX 75201

HILL, JOHN HUGH, educator; b. McKinney, Tex., July 4, 1905; s. John High nd Carrie (Bristow) H.; B.A., Austin Coll., 1925, M.A., 1926; M.A., U. Cal. at Berkeley, 1948; Ph.D., U. Tex., 1946; m. Laurita Addison Lyttleton, May 27, 1931. Prof. history Coll. of Marshall, 1926-40; instr. U. Tex., 1943- 46; asst. prof. Tex. A. and M. Coll., 1946-49, asso. prof. 1949-54, prof., 1954-59; vis. prof. U. Tex., 1959-60; prof. U. Houston, 1960—. Recipient Fulbright award, 1962-65; grantee Am. Philos. Soc., Am. Council Learned Socs.; recipient Albert Marfan Prix for Prose L'académie des jeux floraux; vis. mem. Inst. Advanced Study, Princeton, 1971. Mem. Mediaeval Acad. Am.; corr. mem. etranger L'Academie des Scis., Inscriptions at Belles Lettres de Touloure. Author: (with Laurita Hill) Raymond V de Saint-Giles, 1959; Raymond IV, County of Toulouse, 1962; Raymond d'Aguilers, Historia Francorum Qui Ceperunt Iherusalem, 1968; Le Liber de Raymond d'Aguilers, 1969. Contbr. articles prof. jours. Home: 1617 Fannin Houston TX 77001

HILL, JOHN JEPTHA, lawyer; b. Mobile, Ala., Oct. 30, 1927; s. Edward Ashton and Ella (Blacksher) H.; B.A., Vanderbilt U., 1949; LL.B., U. Ala., 1951; LL.M., N.Y.U., 1956; m. Mary Frances Deer, Aug. 18, 1949; children—John Jeptha, Edward Ashton, Mary Debra, David Knight. Admitted to Ala. bar, 1951; practice in Mobile, 1956—; asso. firm McCorvey, Turner, Rogers, Johnstone & Adams, 1956-61, partner, 1961-67; partner Johnstone, Adams, May, Howard & Hill, 1968—. Pres., dir. Shomo Land Co., Inc., 1958-68; dir. Landel, Inc., 1964—. Pres. Estate Planning Council Mobile, 1968-69; chmn. Bd. Adjustment City of Mobile, 1970-71; mem. Christian Businessmens Com., Mobile, 1969—. Mem. Mobile County Republican Exec. Com., 1964-70, Ala. Rep. Exec. Com., 1966-70. Served to lt. (j.g.) USNR, 1951-55. Mem. Am., Ala. (past chmn. sect. on taxation). Mobile County bar assns., Phi Delta Phi, Sigma Chi. Baptist. Kiwanian. Club: Mobile Country. Home: 5809 Fairfax Rd S Mobile AL 36608 Office: PO Box 1988 Mobile AL 36601

HILL, JOHN RUTLEDGE, Jr., constrn. materials co. exec.; b. Dallas, Oct. 13, 1922; s. John Rutledge and Catharine (Scarborough) H.; B.S. in Civil Engring., Tex. A. and M. U., 1947; m. Peggy Sloan, May 5, 1962; children—John Rutledge III, Nancy, Cynthia, Sara. With Gifford-Hill & Co., Inc., Dallas, 1946—, 1st v.p., 1958-68, exec. v.p., 1968-69, pres., chief exec. officer, 1969—; dir. Tex. Bank & Trust Co., Dallas. Pres. Timberlawn Found., 1968-70. Bd. dirs. Dallas Day Nursery Assn. Served with 13th Airborne Div., AUS, 1943-46. Mem. Tex. Soc. Profl. Engrs., Chi Epsilon. Methodist. Clubs: Dallas Country, City (pres. 1966—). Home: 4209 Edmondson St Dallas TX 75205 Office: 2949 Stemmons Freeway Dallas TX 75247

HILL, JOHN WALKER, banker; b. Bridgeport Conn., 1893; ed. Cornell U. Chmn. trust com. Conn. Nat. Bank, Bridgeport. Pres., bd. dirs. Bridgeport Hosp. Home: 201 Old Academy Rd Fairfield CT 06431 Office: 888 Main St Bridgeport CT 06603

HILL, JOHN WILEY, pub. relations counsel; b. Shelbyville, Ind., Nov. 26, 1890; s. T. Wiley and Katherine (Jameson) H.; student Ind. U., 1911-12 LL. D.; 1971; L.H.D., Boston U., 1950; m. Elena K. Hill. Began career as reporter for Cleve. News, 1915-17; financial editor Iron Trade Rev., 1917-27; instituted Monthly Bus. Bull. of Cleve. Trust Co., 1920i contbr. syndicated newspaper column and author many bus., econ. articles and studies; entered field of pub. relations as counsel Union Trust Co., other large firms, 1927; became pub. relations counsel Am. Iron and Steel Inst., 1933; formed firm Hill & Knowlton, 1933, chmn. policy com. Hill & Knowlton, Inc.; formed H & K, Internat., 1952; pub. relations counsel indsl. corps. and assns. Clubs: Sleepy Hollow; Pinnacle (N.Y.C). Author: Corporate Public Relations, 1957; The Making of a Public Relations Man, 1963 Contbr. articles on pub. relations. Home: 800 Park Av New York City NY 10021 also Towners New York City NY Office: 150 E 42d St New York City NY 10017 also One McPherson Sq Washington DC 20005 and Wardour St London England

HILL, JOSEPH KNOERLE, univ. adminstr.; b. Springfield, Mo., Nov 6, 1918; s. Clyde Milton and Doris (Knoerle) H.; A.B., Dartmouth, 1941; M.S., Yale, 1942, Ph.D., 1949; D.Sc. (hon.), L.I.U., 1967; m. Jean Lee Lichty, Sept. 12, 1942; children—Laurinda Lee, Joseph Knoerle. Instr. pub. health Yale Sch. Medicine, 1949-51; lectr. edn. and pub. health Yale, 1951-53; asso. prof. So. Conn. State Coll., 1951-52; asst. to dean, asst. prof. pub. health and preventive medicine Coll. Medicine in Syracuse, State U. N.Y., 1953- 56; exec. asst. to pres., exec. sec. Downstate Med. Center, State U. N.Y., 1956-63, v.p. adminstrn., asso. prof. adminstrn., 1963-66, pres., dean Coll. Medicine, 1966—. Served with AUS, 1942-46; PTO. Clubs: Morys Assn. (Yale); Dartmouth, Yale (N.Y.C.); Pine Orchard (Brantford, Conn.). Devel. total computer information system for hosps., computer assisted admission program for med. schs. Home: 310 Lenox Rd Brooklyn NY 11226

HILL, JOSEPH MACGLASHAN, pathologist and hematologist; b. Buffalo, Mar. 26, 1905; s. William and Cassie (Groh) H.; B.S., U. Buffalo, 1928, M.D., 1928; Dr. Honoris Causa, U. Guadalajar, 1944; D.Sc., Baylor U., 1945; m. Isobel Pogue, Aug. 30, 1932; children—Robert William, Norwood Oakley, Joseph M., Patricia Louise and Barbara Ann (twins). Intern Fitzsimons Gen. Hosp., Denver, 1928-29; resident pathology Buffalo City Hosp., 1929- 31, asso. pathologist, 1931-32; instr. pathology U. Buffalo, 1929-32; asst. prof. pathology U. Okla., 1932-33, asst. prof. anatomy, 1933; asst. prof. pathology Sch Medicine, Baylor U., 1934-37, asso. prof. pathology, 1937-43, prof. pathology Sch. Dentistry, 1945-70, prof., dean Grad. Research Inst., 1948-68, dir. labs. U. Hosp., 1934-59; dir. Wadley Research Inst. and Blood Bank, Dallas, 1942- 68; exec. dir. Wadley Insts. Molecular Medicine, 1968—; cons. clin. pathology Brooke Gen. Hosp., 1947—; clin prof. pathology Southwestern Med. Sch. U. Tex., 1957—; research cons. Baylor U. Med. Center, 1959—; sr. cons. pathology M.D. Anderson Hosp. and Tumor Inst., 1964—. Recipient 1st award for sci. exhibit Tex. Med. Assn., 1938, 40; certificate of merit A.M.A., 1941; award of merit Tex. Soc. Pathologists, 1946; Marchman award Dallas So. Clin. Soc., 1947; citation for outstanding ability and distinguished service medicine U. Buffalo, 1951; 1st award sci. exhibit So. Med. Assn., 1955, Research medal, 1957. Diplomate Nat. Bd. Med. Examiners, Am. Bd. Pathology. Fellow A.C.P., Coll. Am. Pathologists; mem. Am. Soc. Clin. Pathologists, Am. Soc. Pathologists and Bacteriologists, A.M.A., Tex. Soc. Pathologists, Tex., So. med. assns., Dallas So. Clin. Soc., Internat. Soc. Hematology (past pres.), Tex. State, Dallas (past pres. acads. internat. medicine, Dallas County Med. Soc., A.A.A.S., Am. Soc. Hematology (founding mem.), Sigma Xi. Editor: (with Dr. William Damashek) The Rh Factor in the Clinic and in the Laboratory, 1948; mem. editorial staff Transfusion, 1961-68. Home: 4339 Shady Hill Dr Dallas TX 75229 Office: 9000 Harry Hines Blvd Dallas TX 75235

HILL, KARL ALLEN, educator; b. Littleton, N.H., Feb. 22, 1915; s. Allen F. and Lyle K. (Morse) H.; student Worcester Acad., 1932-34; A.B. cum laude, Dartmouth, 1938; M.C.S. with distinction, Amos Tuck Sch., 1939; LL.D., Drury Coll., 1968; m. Phyllis A. Mann, Oct. 16, 1937; children—Allen C., George F. Instr. bus. adminstrn. Nichols Jr. Coll., 1940-43; dir. purchases Holtzer-Cabot div. of First Indsl. Corp., 1943-46; prof. indsl. mgmt. Amos Tuck Sch., Dartmouth Coll., 1946-68, asso. dean Amos Tuck Sch., 1953-57, dean, 1957-68; dean Sch. Bus., Washington U., St. Louis, 1968—. Dir. Moody's Fund, Inc., Moody's Capital Fund, Inc., Permaneer Corp., Wehr Corp., Milw. Bd. dirs. St. Louis Interracial Council for Bus. Opportunity. Mem. Delta Kappa Epsilon, Sphinx. Republican. Home; 529 Purdue Av St Louis MO 63130

HILL, KATHLEEN LOUISE, author; b. Halifax, N.S., Can., Apr. 7, 1917; d. Henry and Margaret Elizabeth (Ross) Hill; grad. high sch. Steno-sec. various comml. firms, 1935-57; free lance writer for radio, TV, juvenile books and stage, 1957—. Can. Council grantee for research on biography of Cabot, 1965; recipient Vickey Metcalf award. Author: Glooscap and His Magic, 1963; Badger The Mischief Maker, 1965; And Tomorrow the Stars, 1968; More Glooscap Stories, 1970. Address: Ketch Harbour Nova Scotia Canada

HILL, KENNETH EVAN, banker; b. Oakland, Cal., Dec. 5, 1915; s. G. Leslie and Ollie (Moreland) H.; B.S., U. Cal. at Berkeley, 1938, M.S., 1941; m. Dorothy Vogeley, Oct. 10, 1946; children—Meredity Jane, Jonathan Andrew. Engr. Texas Co., Los Angeles, 1938, Depthograph Co., San Marino. Cal., 1938- 39; mem. conservation com. Cal. Oil Producers, Los Angeles, 1941-42; with Chase Manhattan Bank (merger Chase Nat. Bank, Bank of Manhattan Co.), N.Y.C., from 1946, v.p., 1952-58; partner Eastman Dillon, Union Securities & Co., 1958—; dir. Skelly Oil Co., Tidewater Marine Service, Inc., Intex Oil Co. Monterey Oil Co., United Carbon Co. Served with USNR, 1942-45. Mem. Am. Inst. Mining and Metall. Engrs., Am. Assn. Petroleum Geologists, Ind. Petroleum Assn. Am. Republican. Conglist. Clubs: Baltusrol Golf: Echo Lake Country. Home: 109 Golf Edge Westfield NJ 14787 Office: 1 Chase Manhattan Plaza New York City NY 10005

HILL, KENNETH MARTIN, advt. exec.; b. Lebanon, Tenn., Jan. 29, 1913; s. Homer Allen and Lois (Ayers) H.; ed. Huron (S.D.) Coll.; m. Josephine Lucas, Apr. 4, 1938; 1 dau., Margaret Diane. With Internat. Harvester, 1935-42, Montgomery Ward, 1942-49, Aubrey, Finlay, Marley & Hodgson, Inc., Chgo., 1950-63; exec. v.p., dir., mem. mgmt. com. The Griswold-Eshleman Co., 1963-69; cons. corp. communications J. Walter Thompson Co., Chgo., 1970—. Episcopalian. Clubs: Sunset Ridge Country (Winnetka, Ill.); Chicago. Home: 601 Longboat Club Rd Sarasota FL 33577 Office: 1255 N State St Chicago IL 60610

HILL, KENNETH WILLIAM, pub. co. exec.; b. Sac City, Ia., Oct. 24, 1910; s. Henry J. and Annie (Manly) H.; B.C.S., Drake U., 1932; grad. Internat. Accountants Soc., 1933; LL.B., LaSalle Extension U., 1949; m. Marie E. Mitchell, Oct. 11, 1936; 1 son, J. Scott. With auditing dept. Des Moines Register & Tribune, 1934-37; with Meredith Corp., Des Moines, 1937-71, controller, 1956-71. Bd. dirs. Polk-Des Moines Taxpayers Assn., Ia. Mental Health Assn., Polk County Mental Health Assn. Served with USAAF, 1942-45. Mem. Financial Execs. Inst., Nat. Assn. Accountants, Am. Accounting Assn., Delta Sigma Pi. Methodist. Mason. Home: 1530 41st St Des Moines IA 50311

HILL, KNOX CALVIN, educator; b. Oak Park, Ill., Dec. 15, 1910; s. Howard Copeland and Hermione (Ireland) H.; B.S., U. Chgo., 1930, M.A., 1936, Ph.D., 1954; m. Pauline Willis, June 19, 1939; childrenVirginia, Joan, Thomas, Susan. Mem. faculty U. Chgo., 1939—, prof. philosophy, 1962—, chmn. coll. staff, 1961—, also dir. undergrad. programs in philosophy, Sec. faculties, 1969—; vis. prof. U. P.R., 1957. Served to lt. col. AUS, 1942-46; col. Res. Decorated Bronze Star; recipient Quantrell Teaching prize U. Chgo., 1952; Ford Found. fellow, 1952-53. Mem. Am. Philos. Assn., Am. Soc. Aesthetics, Sigma Alpha Epsilon. Club: Quandrangle (U. Chgo.). Author: Interpreting Literature, 1966. Mng. editor Jour. Gen. Edn., 1956-60 Contbr. profl. jours. Home: 5834 S Stony Island Av Chicago IL 60637

HILL, LEE FORREST, physician; b. W. Runmey, N.H., Feb. 8, 1894; s. Clarence and Nellie (Morrow) H.; B.S., Dartmouth, 1917; M.D., Harvard, 1920; married Marian Robbins, November 8, 1919; children—Charlotte (Mrs. Robert Stickler), Elizabeth (Mrs. John C. Carson). Interne Boston City Hosp;, 1919-20, resident in pediatrics, Infants Hospital and South Department and Boston City Hosp;, 1920-21, pvt. practice of medicine, Des Moines, Ia., since 1921, splist, in pediatrics; dir. of pediatric edn. Raymond Blank Memorial Hosp. for Children; clin. prof. pediatrics U. Ia. Medical School. Served as hosp. apprentice 1/c, U.S.N.R.C.,1918. Diplomate Am. Bd. Pediatrics (past pres. Mem. Am. Medical Assn., Am. Pediatric Soc., Am. Acad. Pediatrics (pres. 1947), Northwest Pediatric Soc., Ia. State Med. Soc., Alpha Omega Alpha (hn. mem. 1948). Republican. Unitarian. Clubs: Des Moines, Wakonda. Mem. adv. com. U.S. Children's Bur., 1945-48. Author: Yoru Baby (with Gladys Denny Shultz), 1948. Home: 3232 John Lynde Rd Des Moines IA 50312 Office: 1200 Pleasant St Des Moines IA 50309

HILL, LEE H., mgmt. cons.; b. Toms River, N.J., Mar. 8, 1899; s. David and Anna (Applegate) H.; E.E., Cornell U., 1921; m. Helen Wolfram, Dec. 25, 1922; 1 son, Lee. Instr. elec. engring., Cornell U., 1920-22, design and devel. engr. Westinghouse Electric & Mfg. Co., 1922-28; mgr. transformer div. Am. Brown Boveri Co., 1928-30; mgr. transformer div. Allis-Chalmers Mfg. Co., 1931-40, asst. mgr. elec. dept., 1940-41, v.p. in charge indsl. relations, 1941-45, pub. and gen. mgr. Elec. World, Elec. Constn. and Maintenance, Elec. Wholesaling, McGraw-Hill Pub. Co., 1945-47; partner Rogers, Slade & Hill, mgmt. cons., 1947-62, chmn. bd., 1962-65; pres. Burdett Mfg., 1959-66, Lee H. Hill Cons.'s, 1965—, Hill-Donnelly Corp., Inc., 1965—, also Pan Am. Devel. Corp., 1965—, Fla. Airlines, Inc., 1969—, Hill- Leasing Corp., 1969—. Industry mem. Nat. War Labor Bd., World War II; del. Pres's Labor Mgmt. Conf., 1945. Fellow I.E.E.E. Republican. Methodist. Mason. Author: Transformers, 1940. Co-author: Management at the Bargaining Table, 1942; Pattern for Good Labor Relations, 1944; Business Management for More Profits, 1951; Business Management Handbook, 1952; Handbook of Business Administration, 1968; Upward in the Black, 1969. Contbr. to tech. mags. Home: 225 Plymouth Rd West Palm Beach FL 33405 also Box 604 Lake George NY 12845 Office: 225 Plymouth Rd West Palm Beach FL 33405 also 2507 S MacDill Av Tampa FL 33609

HILL, LEON WALTER, govt. ofcl.; b. Winters, Tex., Apr. 21, 1910; s. Walter and Annie Lee (Cook) H.; B.A., N.M. A. and M. Coll., 1934; M.A. in Econs. U. Tex., 1941; m. Jackie Bell, Jan. 31, 1942; children—Linda Beth, Gary Lee, Jackie Gail. Instr., Las Cruces (N.M.) Union High Sch., 1934-36; jr. economist Resettlement Adminstrn., Amarillo, Tex., 1936-38; asst. agrl. economist Dept. Agr., 1938-41, agrl. economist, 1941-42; agrl. economist region 5, Bur. Reclamation, 1946-48, chief div. allocation and repayment, 1948-50, asst. regional operation and maintenance supr., 1950- 52, regional supr. irrigation, 1952-59, regional dir., 1959—. Mem. Internat. Commn. Irrigation and Drainage, U.S. Com. Large Dams. Served to lt. col. C.E., AUS, 1942-46; col. Res. Home: 4502 W 3d St Amarillo TX 79106 Office: PO Box 1609 Amarillo TX 79105

HILL, LEWIS WARREN, city ofcl.; b. Ft. Worth, Feb. 25, 1926; s. Alvin Carnes and Constance (Lewis) H.; B.S. in Design, Inst. Design, Ill. Inst. Tech., 1951; B.A. in Math., U. Minn., 1946; m. Dorothy Mae Hey, Sept. 11, 1954; children—Mary Lew, Martha, Katherine, Thomas David, Sara. Various positions Chgo. Land Clearance Commn., U. Ill. Med. Center, Community Conservation Bd. Chgo., 1951-54; supervising project planner PHA, Chgo., 1956-57; asst. commr. Dept. Urban Renewal (merged with Community Conservation Bd.), 1957-63, dep. commr., 1963-65, chmn., also commr., 1965-67; commr. dept. devel. and planning, also chmn. and commr. of dept., 1967—. Lectr. urban studies Loyola U., Chgo., 1964—. Mem. Ill. Mental Health Planning Bd., Northeastern Illinois Planning Commn.; mem. exec. com. Chgo. Com. Urban Opportunity; sec. Chgo. Plan Commn., Pub Bldg. Commn. Chgo. Mem. Chgo. Com. on Hist. and Archtl. Landmarks, Chgo. Com. on Criminal Justice; asst. sec., bd. dirs. Chgo. Boys Clubs. Served to lt. comdr. USNR, 1944-46. Mem. Am. Inst. Planners (vice chmn. Chgo. sect. 1959-60), Internat. Fedn. Housing and Planning, Nat. Assn. Housing, Redevel. Ofcls. (chmn. Chgo. chpt. 1959-62), Western Soc. Engrs., Chgo. Assn. Commerce and Industry, Lambda Alpha. Roman Catholic. K.C. Mem. Holy Name Soc. Clubs: Economic, Lake Shore (Chgo.). Mem. editorial adv. bd. Urban Affairs Reporter. Home: 5858 N Kenton Av Chicago IL 60646 Office: City Hall 121 N LaSalle St Chicago IL 60602

HILL, LISTER, former senator; b. Montgomery, Ala., Dec. 29. 1894; s. Luther L. (M.D.) and Lilly (Lyons) H.; grad. Stark Univ. Sch., Montgomery, 1911; A.B., U. Ala., 1914, LL.B., 1915; LL.B., Columbia, 1916; spl. course, U. Mich.; LL.D., U. Ala., Ala. Polytech. Inst., Nat. Univ., Woman's Med. Coll., Columbia U., Washington U., St. Louis, U. Pa., Phila., 1965; Sc.D., Hahemann Med. Coll., N.Y. Med. Coll. Gallaudet Coll., also Jefferson Medical Coll.; m. Henrietta Fontaine McCormick, Feb. 20, 1928; children—Mrs. Charles Hubbard, Luther Lister. Began practice at Montgomery, 1916; mem. 68th Congress from 2d Ala. Dist. (to fill unexpired term of dec. Hon. John R. Tyson), mem. 69th to 75th Congresses; elected U.S. senator to fill unexpired term of Hugo L. Black, 1938, reelected 1939-45, 45-51, 51- 57, 57-63, 63-69; majority Whip Senate, 77th, 78th and 79th Congresses. Served with U.S. Army, 1917-19. Recipient Albert Lasker award med. research, 1959, 68; award of honor Am. Hosp. Assn., 1966; award Nat. Acad. Scis.; Alumnus of Year, Univ. of Ala. Hon. fellow Am. Coll. Hosp. Adminstrs., Am. Coll. Dentists, Am. Psychiat. Assn., Internat. Coll. Surgeons, A.C.P., A.C.S.; mem. Nat. Ophthalmology Assn. (honorary), Internat. Med. Club (hon.), Am. Dental Assn. (hon.), Phi Beta Kappa. Democrat. Mem. M.E. Ch. Mason. Home: 1618 Gilmer Av Montgomery AL 36104

HILL, LUTHER LYONS, army officer, publisher; b. Montgomery, Ala., Dec. 9, 1896; s. Luther Leonidas and Lily (Lyons) H.; A.B., U. of Ala., 1916; B.S., U.S. Military Acad., 1919; LL.D. (hon.) Yankton Coll., 1951; m. Mary Hippee, Oct. 26, 1921; children—Luther L., Mildred. Pres. McMurray Hill & Co., Des Moines, Ia., 1929-35; dir. Viking Pump Co. and Knapp- Monarch Co., St. Louis, Mo., 1928-33; financial advisor to Reconstruction Finance Corp., 1933; vice pres. and dir., Ia. Broadcasting Co., Des Moines, 1933-42, Register and Tribune Co., 1946—; v.p. Cowless Broadcasting Co., 1946-60; pres. broadcasting div., dir. corp. Cowles Magazines and Broadcasting, Inc., 1960—; chmn. bd. Universal Cable Vision of Florida; director of Gen. Devel. Corp.; pub. Des Moines Register and Tribune, 1950-60. Adv. bd. Mercy Hosp.; trustee Ia. 4-H Club Found. Trustee Drake Univ.; bd. consultants Nat. War Coll.; pres. and dir. Greater Des Moines Comm., 1952; mem. bd. dirs. Y.M.C.A. Mem. bd. trustees Naples (Fla.) Community Hosp. Commd. 2d lt., U.S. Army, 1919; resigned, 1923; recalled to active service, 1942, and advanced through grades to brig. gen., 1945; dir. bur. pub. relations, War Dept., May-Oct. 1945. Awarded Legion of Merit. Mem. Phi Beta Kappa, Delta Kappa Epsilon. Clubs: Des Moines, Pow Wow; Naples Yacht, Port Royal Beach (pres.) (Naples, Fla.); Wellington (London, Eng.). Home: 3490 Ft Charles Dr Naples FL 33940

HILL, LUTHER LYONS, Jr., ins. co. exec.; b. Des Moines, Aug. 21, 1922; s. Luther Lyons and Mary (Hippee) H.; B.A., Williams Coll., 1947; LL.B., Harvard, 1950; m. Sara S. Carpenter, Aug. 12, 1950; children-Luther Lyons III, Mark L. Admitted to Ia. bar, 1951, since practiced in Des Moines; law clk. Justice Hugo L. Black, 1950-51; asso., partner Henry & Henry, 1951-69; mem. legal staff Equitable Life Ins. Co. of Ia., 1952—, exec. v.p., 1969—, gen. counsel, 1970—. Pres. United Community Services Greater Des Moines; trustee, vice chmn. Simpson Coll., Indianola, Ia. Served with AUS, World War II. Home: 2801 Park Av Des Moines IA 50321 Office: 604 Locust St Des Moines IA 50306

HILL, MARTHA, educator; b. East Palestine, O.; d. Grant and Grace (Todd) Hill; B.S., Columbia, 1929; M.A., N.Y., 1941; L.H.D., Adelphi U. 1965; D.F.A.; Mt. Holyoke Coll., 1966; D.Litt.; Bennington Coll.; 1969i m. Thurston Davies, Oct. 3, 1952. Charge dance Kellogg Sch. Phys. Edn., Battle Creek, Mich., 1920-23; charge dance, Kan. State Tchrs. Coll., 1923-26; charge dance, asst. prof. U. Ore., 1927-29; tchr. dance Lincoln Sch. Tchrs. Coll., 1929- 3O; mem. Martha Graham Co., 1929-31; chmn. dance Bennington Coll., 1923-51; summer dir. Bennington Sch. Dance, dir. dance Bennington Sch. Arts, 1934-42; charge dance, sch. edn. N.Y.U., 1930-51, founder, co-dir. N.Y.U.-Conn. Coll. Sch. Dance; cons. U.S. Office Edn., 1943; tchr. dance U. So. Cal., summer 1946; dir. dance div. Juilliard Sch.; 1951—. Chmn. dance adv. com. on performing arts Sch. Performing Arts, N.Y.C.; mem. dance panel cultural presentations program Dept. of State. Fellow Am. Acad. Phys. Edn. Home: 210 Columbia Heights Brooklyn NY 11201 Office: Juilliard Sch Lincoln Center Plaza New York City NY 10023

HILL, MARTIN, U.N. official; b. Cork, Ireland, Apr. 8, 1905; s. William Henry and Stella Amelia (Harris) H.; B.A., Oriel Coll., Oxford, 1926, M.A., 1931; student London Sch. Economics, 1926-27, Univ. Vienna (Rockefeller fellowship), 1932-33; m. Diana Grove-Annesley, Dec. 3, 1932; 1 son, Colin Patrick Martin. Entered League of Nations Secretariat Oct. 1927, staff economic and financial sect., 1927-34, political sect., 1934-39, economic, financial and transit dept., 1939-45; sec. to the "Brice Com.", 1939, to Economic and Financial coms., 1942-45; asst. to sec.-gen., 1945- 46; spl. adviser to exec. sec., San Francisco Conf., 1945; chief, adminstrv. and budgeting sect., Preparatory Commn. of U.N., 1945; joined permanent Secretariat of U.N., 1946, spl. adviser sec.-gen., 1946-48, deputy exec. asst. to sec.-gen. and dir. of co-ordination of specialized agencies and econ. and social matters, 1948-55, dep. under-sec. and later asst., secretary general for interagency affairs, since 1967—. Member of Anglican Church. Club: Athenaeum (London, England). Author: The Economic and Financial Organization of the League of Nations, published 1945; Immunities and Privileges of International Officials, 1947. Contbr. articles on economic theory, trade, finance and internat. orgn. Home: 260 Snowden Lane Princeton NJ 08540 Office: UN New York City NY 10017

HILL, MATTHEW WILLIAM, govt. ofcl.; b. Bozeman, Mont., June 26, 1894; s. Saxton D. and Mary Elma (Noe) H.; LL.B., U. of Wash., 1917; LL.D., Seattle Pacific Coll., 1947; m. Irma Verne Young, May 17, 1924; children—Irma Lane (Mrs. Don Clausen), Mary Bea (Mrs. Edward Sakraida), Matthew Hale. Admitted to Wash. State Bar, May 3, 1918, and practiced in Seattle, 1919-45; asst. U.S. dist. atty., Seattle, 1923-24; apptd. judge, King County Superior Ct., 1945-46; judge, Wash. Supreme Court, 1947- 69, chief justice, 1957-59; chmn. Wash. State Pollution Control Hearings Bd. Hon. mem. bd. Linfield Coll.; mem. bd. curators Wash. State Hist. Soc., 1st v.p. Am. Bapt. Conv., 1955-56, mem. gen. council, 1957-63, now mem. of finance com. 1964- -; mem.-at-large nat. council, mem. adv. com. regions XI Boy Scouts Am. Mem. Am. Judicature Soc., Am., Wash. bar assns., World Peace Through Law Assn., Internat. Order Good Templars, Am. Legion, Knights Round Table, Delta Upsilon, Phi Alpha Delta, Tau Kappa Alpha. Republican. Baptist. Mason (33; past grand master Wash. 1940-41), Kiwanian. Home: 2303 S Otis St Olympia WA 98501 Office: Capitol Center Bldg Olympia WA 98501

HILL, MERRITT DUNSTON, corporation exec., b. Pontiac, Mich., Aug. 27, 1902; s. Charles B. and Elizabeth (Dunston) H.; student U. Detroit, 1924-27, LL.D. (hon.), 1955; m. Charlotte Louise Strickland, May 8, 1925; children—Charles C., Richard B. With United Motors Service, 1929-41, gen. mdsg. mgr., 1941; regional mgr., then v.p., dir. Harry Ferguson, Inc., 1942-46; mgr. Western Implement Merchandisers, 1946; gen. sales mgr., then v.p. Dearborn Motors Corp., 1947-53; asst. gen. mgr. Ford Motor Co., 1953-57, v.p., gen. mgr., 1957-62, v.p. of company 1959-62; pres. J.I. Case Co., Racine, Wis., 1962-66, chmn. bd., 1966-68, now dir.; chairman board Hill Assos. Bloomfield Hills, Mich., 1968—; mem. board directors Dundee Cement Co. (Mich.), The Ann Arbor R.R. Co., Dearborn, Mich., Consol Papers, Inc., 1st Nat. Bank, Racine, Pres. Farm Equipment Inst., 1963-64; mem. Nat. 4-H Service Com., 1960—. Lay trustee U. Detroit; bd. dirs. Epilepsy Found., Lincoln Lutheran Home. Mem. Pi Sigma Epsilon. Episcopalian. Clubs: Mid-Am. (Chgo.); Thunderbird Country (Palm Springs, Cal.); Bloomfield Hills (Mich.) Country; Olympic (San Francisco). Home: 1735 Tiverton Rd Bloomfield Hills MI 48013 Office: 74 W Long Lake Rd Bloomfield Hills MI 48013

HILL, NORMAN STEWART, investment banker; b. Cin., Aug. 14, 1889; s. Alfred and Madge (Martin) H.; student Miami U., Oxford, O., 1909-10; m. Elizabeth Alexander, Dec. 1, 1921; 1 son, Dr. Norman A. Mem. Hill & Co., investment bankers, Cin. Clubs: Cincinnati Country, Bankers, Coldstream Country (Cin.). Home: 1340 Observatory Dr Cincinnati OH 45208 Office: Provident Towers Cincinnati OH 45202

HILL, ORION ALVAH, Jr., banker; b. Sweetwater, Tex., May 6, 1920; s. Orion Alvah and Lillian (Reynolds) H.; A.B. in Econs., U. Cal. at Berkeley, 1943; grad. Bank Adminstrn. Inst. Sch., U. Wis., 1961; m. Portia Joy Myhre, June 14 , 1941; children—Gretchen Annette (Mrs. Phillip John Peterson), Orion Ellsworth, John Adrian, Brian Adair. With Wells Fargo Bank, N.A., and predecessor, 1941—, gen. auditor, 1968—; gen. auditor Wells Fargo & Co., 1970—; on leave with Bank Am. Samoa, mgr., cashier, 1954-56, dir. budget and finance, treas. Govt. Am. Samoa and dir. Bank Am. Samoa, 1956-58; speaker in field, 1947—. Served with USNR, 1944-46. Chartered bank auditor, 1969. Mem. Inst. Internal Auditors (pres. San Francisco chpt. 1968-69), Bank Adminstrn. Inst. (pres. San Francisco chpt. 1969-70). Republican. Methodist. Author articles in field. Home: 1040 Bella Dr Napa CA 94558 Office: 464 California St San Francisco CA 94120

HILL, OWEN L., oil co. exec.; b. 1917; grad. U. Okla.; m. Oil auditor Peat, Marwick, Mitchell & Co., before 1950; sec.-treas. Seaboard Oil Co., 1950-58; asst. controller Tex Co., 1958-59; with Clark Oil and Refining Corp., 1959 v.p. finance, 1966-70, pres., 1970—, dir., 1966—. Served to lt. AUS, World War II. C.P.A. Address: 8530 W National Av Milwaukee WI 53227

HILL, PHILIP SHERIDAN, mfg. co. exec.; b. Boise, Ida., Dec. 24, 1909; s. Henry Jacob and Elizabeth Bell (Wilson) H.; student Benson Tech. Sch., 1922-26; m. Evelyn May Emrich, Nov. 28, 1928; children—Carolyn (Mrs. James W Kenney), Philip Sheridan. With Hyster Co., Portland, Ore., 1933—, exec. v.p., 1956-61, pres, 1961-66, chief exec. officer, 1966—, chmn. bd. 1971—, dir. Consol. Freightways, Inc., Bank of Cal. N.A. Mem. Indsl. Truck Assn. (pres. 1960- 61). Home: 1333 S Skyland Dr Lake Oswego OR 97034 Office: PO Box 2902 Portland OR 97208

HILL, RALPH H., business exec.; b. Miller, Mo., 1914. Pres., dir. Alfred M. Lewis, Inc., Orange Stamp, Inc. Home: 1891 Fairview Riverside CA 92506 Office: 2727 Kansas Riverside CA 92507*

HILL, REUBEN LORENZO, Jr., sociologist, educator; b. Logan, Utah, July 4, 1912; s. Reuben Lorenzo and Mary Theresa (Snow) H.; B.S., Utah State U., 1935; Ph.M., U. Wis., 1936, Ph.D., 1938; postdoctoral study U. Chgo., 1941; Dr. honoris causa U. Louvain (Belgium), 1970; m. Marion Ensign, Sept. 9, 1935; children—Judith Ann (Mrs. Gordon P. Wright), David Reuben, Susan (Mrs. Sven Oppegaard), Gladys Paulena (Mrs. Alan Cassell), George Richard. From instr. to asst. prof. social edn. U. Wis., 1938-42; prof. sociology, head dept. U. S.D., 1942-44; asso. prof. sociology Ia. State U., 1944-49; research prof. sociology U. N.C., 1949-53, 54-57; dir. Minn. Family Study Center, prof. sociology and child devel. U. Minn., 1957-61, 62-64, 66-68, research program dir. Minn. Family Study Center, also prof. sociology, 1968-70; fellow Center for Advanced Study in Behavioral Scis., 1970-71. Program cons. population Ford Found., 1964, 65-66, Fulbright sr. lectr. in family sociology Catholic U. Louvain (Belgium), 1961-62; dir. family research, vis. prof. sociology U. P.R., 1953-54; dir. Groves' Conf. Marriage, 1950-57; cons. nat. orgns.; bd. dirs. Sex Information and Edn. Council U.S., 1964-66, Family Service Assn. Am. Fellow Soc. Research Child Devel., Am. Sociol. Assn. (chmn. com. on internat. cooperation); mem. Nat. Council Family Relations (dir.), Sociol. Research Assn., Internat. Sociol. Assn. (chmn. family research 1959-70, pres. 1970—). Mem. Ch. of Jesus Christ of Latter-Day Saints. Author: (with H. Becker) Marriage and Family, 1942; (with E.M. Duvall) When You Marry, 1945, rev. edit., 1967; Families Under Stress, 1949; (with W. Waller) The Family: A Dynamic Interpretation, 1951; (with J. Moss, C. Wirths) Eddyville's Families, 1953; (with Howard Becker) Family; Marriage and Parenthood, rev. edit., 1955; (with J.M. Stycos, K. Back) The Family and Population Control: A Puerto Rican Experiment in Social Change, 1959; (with E.M. Duvall) Being Married, 1960; (with Rene Konig) Families in East and West: Socialization Process and Kinship Ties, 1970; Family Development in Three Generations, 1970. Home: 4650 Fremont Av S Minneapolis MN 55409

HILL, RICHARD DEVEREUX, banker; b. Salem, Mass., Nov. 6, 1919; s. Robert W. and Grace (Dennis) H.; grad. Phillips Exeter Acad., 1937; A.B., Dartmouth, 1941; M.C.S., Amos Tuck Sch. Adminstrn. and Finance, 1942; student Rutgers U. Grad. Sch. Banking, 1951; m. Polly Bergstedt, Sept. 13, 1947; children—Steven D., Johanna E., Richard Devereux. With First Nat. Bank of Boston, 1946- -, loan officer, 1948-51, asst. v.p., 1951-55, v.p., 1955-65, exec. v.p., 1965-66, pres., 1966—; also dir.; dir. Polaroid Corp., John Hancock Mut. Life Ins. Co., United Brands, Inc., Boston Overseas Financial Corp., 1st Captial Corp. Boston, Bank of Boston Internat., Firstbank Financial Corp., Bank of Boston Trust Co., (Bahamas) Ltd. Former chmn. transp. com. New Eng. Council; mem. Met. area Planning Council, Boston. Mem. vis. com. Sloan Sch. Mgmt., Mass. Inst. Tech., 1967-70; mem. Greater Boston adv. bd. Salvation Army; mem.-at-large Dartmouth Alumni Council, 1967-70; trustee North Shore Childrens Hosp.; bd. dirs. Northeastern region Nat. Conf. Christians and Jews. Served to lt. comdr. USNR, 1942-46; PTO. Mem. Transp. Assn. Am. (dir., past chmn. investor panel), Mass. Bankers Assn. (past mem. exec. council), Assn. Res. City Bankers, Greater Boston C. of C. (dir., past mem. exec. com.), Dartmouth Alumni Assn. Boston (past v.p.), New Eng. Exeter Alumni Assn. (past pres.), Sigma Nu. Republican. Conglist. Mason. Clubs: Algonquin, Commercial, Downtown, Somerset (Boston); Corinthian Yacht (past commodore), Eastern Yacht (Marblehead). Home: Sargent Rd Marblehead MA 01945 Office: 67 Milk St Boston MA 02110

HILL, RICHARD J., railroad ofcl.; b. 1932; B.S., Ia. State U., 1953; married. With Chgo. and Northwestern Ry. Co., 1955—, sec., 1968—; with Northwest Industries Inc., 1967—, sec., 1970—. Served as officer USAF, 1953-55. Address: 400 W Madison St Chicago IL 60606

HILL, RICHARD KEITH, educator; b. Erie, Pa., June, 1, 1928; s. Ranald Keith and Lois Rebecca (Bingham) H.; B.S. in Chemistry, Pa. State U., 1949; M.A., Harvard, 1950, Ph.D., 1954; m. Joan Ethel Caine, Aug. 7, 1954; children—Julie Bingham, Sybil Anne, Holly Caine, Ellen McBride. Instr. chemistry Princeton, 1953-56, asst. prof., 1956-62, asso. prof., 1962-68; prof. chemistry U. Ga. at Athens, 1968—, acting chmn. dept., 1969-71. Mem. Medicinal Chemistry Study Sect. A, NIH, 1968-72, Fulbright fellowship chemistry panel, 1970-72. Mem. Bd. Edn., Rocky Hill, N.J., 1968. Alfred P. Sloan Found. research fellow, 1961-65; N.S.F. sr. postdoctoral fellow, 1965-66. Mem. Am. Chem. Soc., A.A.A.S., Chem. Soc. London. Home: 115 Broomsedge Trail Athens GA 30601

HILL, ROBERT CAREY, investment banker; b. Los Angeles, Oct. 10, 1920; s. Carey S. and Lilla (Lovell) H.; B.A., U. Cal. at Berkeley, 1943; m. Elizabeth Fennimore, Feb. 6, 1943; children—Lindalee, Robert F. Account exec., v.p. Hill Richards & Co., 1946-63, pres.,

1963-66; pres., dir. Bateman Eichler, Hill Richards, Inc., Los Angeles, 1966—; dir. Tri Data Corp., Mountain View, Cal., Collins Foods Internat., Inc., Culber City, Cal. Served with USNR, 1943-46. Mem. Nat. Assn. Securities Dealers (bd. govs. 1964-66), Investment Bankers Assn. Am. (chmn. Cal. 1968, nat. bd. govs. 1969). Home: 464 N June St Los Angeles CA 90004 Office: 460 S Spring St Los Angeles CA 90013

HILL, ROBERT CHARLES, ambassador; b. Littleton, N.H., Sept. 30, 1917; s. Allen and Catherine Lyle (Morse) H.; grad. Taft Sch., Watertown, Conn., 1938; student Dartmouth, 1942; LL. D., New Eng. Coll., Henniker, N.H. 1957; LL. D., St. Mary's U., 1960, Dartmouth, 1960; L.H.D., U. Dallas, 1960; hon. degree Mexican Acad. Internat. Law; m. Cecelia Gordon Bowdoin, Dec. 1, 1945; children—William Graham Bowdoin, James Bowdoin. Vice Consul Fgn. Service of Am., 1943-45; clk. Senate Com. on Banking and Currency, 1947; asst. v.p. W.R. Grace & Co., N.Y.C., 1949-53; ambassador to Costa Rica, 1953-54, to El Salvador, 1954-55; spl. asst. to under sec. of state for Mut. Security Affairs, 1955-56; asst. sec. of state for congressional relations, 1956- 57; ambassador to Mexico, 1957-61; mem. N.H. Ho. of Reps., 1961-62; ambassador to Spain, 1969—; dir. Canadian Internat. Power Co., Internat. Power Co. of Can., Monterey Ry. Light and Power Co., N.E. Airlines, Boston, Todd Shipyards Corp., N.Y.C. Spl. ambassador to innauguration, El Salvador, 1956, Costa Rica, 1958-61, Mexico, 1958, Mexico's 150th Anniversary Independence Ceremonies, 1960. Chmn. Republican Nat. Com. Fgn. Policy Task Force, 1965-68; mem. Rep. Coordinating Committee's Task Force on Nat. Security, 1967-68. Decorated Defensores de la Republica Mexicana y Sus Descendientes (Mex.), Aztec Eagle (Mexico); Grand Cross of Merit (Peru); La Orden Mexicana del Derecho y La Cultura (Mexico); recipient 1st annual fraternities award Mexico City College, Mexico; Americas award Rollins Coll., Winter Park, Fla. Mem. Pan Am. Soc. New Eng., Pan Am. Soc. U.S., N.H. Hist. Soc., Newcomen Soc., Mayflower Soc. N.H., World Affairs Council, Boston, Alpha Delta Phi. Republican. Conglist. Clubs: Metropolitan, Chevy Chase (Chevy Chase, Md.); University (Washington); Elkridge (Balt.); Metropolitan (N.Y.C.). Contbr. Orbis, Readers Digest, Washington Report. Home: The Boulders Littleton NH 03561

HILL, ROBERT EUGENE, corp. exec.; b. Kincaid, Ill., Dec. 9, 1925; s. Glenn William and Lucille (Payne) H.; B.A. in Econs., Ill. Wesleyan U., 1954; M.B.A., Ind. U., 1955; Ph.D. in Commerce and Bus. Adminstrn., U. Ala., 1957; m. Mary Therese Williams, Oct. 28, 1950; 1 son, David Ellis. Comptroller, Ill. Wesleyan Jr. Coll., 1947-51; bus. mgr. Springfield (Ill.) Municipal Opera Assn., 1949-51; asst. prof. finance U. Ill., 1957-60, chmn. 1st year programs Grad. Sch. Bus., 1959-60; prof. econs., dean Coll. Bus. Adminstrn., Kent State U., 1960-65; dean Coll. of Bus., So. Ill. U., Carbondale, 1965-66; pres. Chico (Cal.) State Coll., 1966-70; exec. asst. W. Clement Stone Enterprises, Chgo., 1970—. Participant seminar Am. and Duth Ednl. Values and Engring. Africa, The Hague, 1962. Trustee Va. Union U., Richmond; bd. dirs. W. Clement and Jessie V. Stone Found. Found. for Econ. Edn. fellow, 1957, Econ.-in-Action fellow, 1958. Served with AUS, 1951-54; Korea. Mem. Am., So. econ. assns., Am. Finance Assn., Am. Assn. U. Profs., Nat. Planning Assn., Am. Soc. Personnel Adminstrs., Ohio Council Econ. Edn. (bd. dirs. 1962-65), Ins.-Econs. Soc., Omicron Delta Epsilon (nat. pres. 1963-65), Alpha Kappa Psi (nat. expansion com. 1959—; Distinguished Service award 1960), Theta Chi, Pi Gamma Mu, Beta Gamma Sigma, Beta Alpha Psi, Phi Eta Sigma. Clubs: Akron City; Commonwealth (San Francisco). Contbr. articles profl. jours. Home: 8 Milburn Park Evanston IL 60201 Office: 5050 Broadway Chicago IL 60604

HILL, ROBERT LELAND, educator; b. Coffeyville, Kan., July 12, 1922; s. Earl Winfred and Mary Greenshields (Latta) H.; B.A. in Econs., U. Mo. at Kansas City, 1949, M.A., 1951; Ph.D., Georgetown U., 1958. Economist, Fed. Res. Bd., 1955-59; sr. asso. Cresap, McCormick and Paget, N.Y.C., 1959-61; economist deptl. planning staff Dept. Commerce, 1961, dir. Office Emergency Readiness, 1962-65; prof. econs., chmn. econs. dept. Lynchburg (Va.) Coll., 1965—, dir. program plans and research, 1965-68, William R. Perkins Jr. prof. econs., 1969—. Served with AUS, 1942-45. Mem. Am. Econ. Assn., Order DeMolay, Gold Key Soc., Delta Xi. Mason. Author articles, reports. Home: 3908 Faculty Dr Lynchburg VA 24501

HILL, ROBERT MASON, trust co. exec.; b. Elizabeth, N.J., Aug. 18, 1922; s. Roger W. and Margaret (Himmelberger) H.; A.B., Princeton, 1947; m. Evelyn Cronn, May 13, 1949; 1 son, Robert Mason II. With Guaranty Trust Co., N.Y.C., 1947-58; 2d v.p., 1958; asst. v.p. Morgan Guaranty Trust Co. (merger Guaranty Trust Co. and J.P. Morgan & Co.), N.Y.C., 1959-61, v.p., 1961-70, sr. v.p., 1970—; dir. Morgan Guaranty Internat. Finance Corp. Adv. bd. Internat. Bus. Inst., Sch. Bus. Adminstrn., Rutgers U., 1968—. Served with AUS, 1943-46. Clubs: Campus (Princeton, N.J.); Morris County Golf (Convent Station, N.J.). Home: 8 West Dr Convent Station NJ 07961 Office: 23 Wall St New York City NY 10015

HILL, SAMUEL RICHARDSON, Jr., educator; b. Greensboro, N.C., May 19, 1923; s. Samuel Richardson and Nona (Sink) H.; B.A., Duke, 1943; M.D., Bowman Gray Sch. Medicine, 1946; m. Janet Redman, Oct. 28, 1950; children—Susan Dustin, Samuel Richardson III, Elizabeth, Margaret. Intern medicine Peter Bent Brigham Hosp., Boston, 1947-48, asst. resident medicine, 1948-49, asst. medicine, 1949- 50; teaching fellow medicine Harvard Med. Sch., 1948-49, research fellow medicine, also Dazian Med. Found. research fellow, 1949-50; chief resident medicine N.C. Bapt. Hosp., also instr. medicine Bowman Gray Sch. Medicine, 1950-51; asst. medicine Harvard Med. Sch., also Peter Bent Brigham Hosp., 1953-54; asst. prof. medicine, dir. metabolic and endocrine div. Med. Coll. Ala., also chief metabolic div. VA Hosp., Birmingham, 1954-57; asso. prof. medicine, dir. metabolic and endocrine div. U. Ala. Med. Center and VA Hosp., Birmingham, 1957-62; prof. medicine, dean U. Ala. Med. Coll., 1962-68, prof. medicine, 1968—, v.p. for health affairs, dir. Med. Center, 1968—. Served to maj. M.C., USAF, 1951-53. Fellow A.C.P. (Willard O. Thompson Meml. traveling scholar 1960), A.A.A.S.; mem. Soc. Exptl. Biology and Medicine, Am. Fedn. Clin. Research (pres. 1961-62), Endocrine Soc., Am., Ala. diabetes socs., N.Y. Acad. Scis., Mass., Jefferson County med. socs., Am. Thyroid Soc., A.M.A., So. Soc. Clin. Research (councillor), Med. Assn. State Ala., Assn. Am. Med. Colls., Sigma Xi, Alpha Omega Alpha. Episcopalian. Contbr. articles med. jours. Home: 3337 Briarcliff Rd Birmingham AL 35223

HILL, SARAH JEANNETTE, educator; b. Concord, N.H., May 19, 1909; d. George Vernon and Mary Genevieve (Gannon) Hill; A.B., Smith Coll., 1929; Ph.D. in Astronomy, Columbia, 1942. Tech. staff Bell Telephone Labs., 1929-34; sec., research asst. dept. astronomy Columbia, 1934-41, sci. staff div. war research, 1942-45, research asso. astronomy, 1946-50; instr. physics and astronomy Hunter Coll., 1941-42, 47-49; asst. prof. math. and astronomy Wheaton Coll., 1950-52; faculty Wellesley Coll., 1952—, prof. astronomy, 1960—, dir. Whitin Obs., Wellesley, Mass., 1952—. Mem. Am. Assn. Variable Star Observers, Am. Astron. Soc., Phi Beta Kappa, Sigma Xi. Home: Observatory House Wellesley Coll Wellesley MA 02181

HILL, STEPHEN VAN, mfg. co. exec.; b. Springfield, Ill., June 28, 1933; s. Roy G. and Daisy (Richards) H.; B.S. in Bus. Adminstrn., U. Ill., 1955; LL.B., 1957; C.P.A., 1962, m. Jane W. Thiem, Aug. 20, 1955; children-Stephen G., Susan Jane, Peter Becker, Michael Van. Admitted to Ill. bar, 1957; tax and audit staffman Arthur Andersen & Co., C.P.A.'s, Chgo., 1958-61; investment mgr. Prudential Ins. o. Am., 1961-69; treas. Nat. Can Corp., Chgo., 1969—; dir. Opelika Mfg. Co. Served with AUS, 1955-61. Mem. Am. Inst. C.P.S.'s, Ill. Soc. C.P.A.'s. Presbyn. Home: 919 S Spring Av LaGrange IL 60525 Office: 5959 S Cicero Av Chicago IL 60638

HILL, TERRELL LESLIE, chemist, biophysicist; b. Oakland, Cal., Dec. 19, 1917; s. George Leslie and Ollie (Moreland) H.; A.B., U. Cal. at Berkeley, 1939, Ph.D., 1942; postgrad. Harvard, 1940; m. Laura Etta Gano, Sept. 23, 1942; children—Julie Lisbeth (Mrs. Yaakov Eden), Carolyn Jo, Ernest Evan. Instr. chemistry Western Res. U., 1942-44; research asso. radiation lab. U. Cal. at Berkeley, 1944-45; research asso. chemistry, then asst. prof. chemistry U. Rochester, 1945-49; chemist U.S. Naval Med. Research Inst., 1949-57; prof. chemistry U. Ore., 1957-67; prof. chemistry U. Cal. at Santa Cruz, 1967-71, vice chancellor for scis., div. natural scis., 1968- 69. Mem. biophysics study sect. USPHS, 1954-57; chemistry panel NSF, 1961-64; research chemist NIH, 1971—. Guggenheim fellow Yale, 1952-53; recipient Arthur S. Flemming award U.S. Govt., 1954; Distinguished Civilian Service award U.S. Navy, 1955; award Washington Acad. Scis., 1956; Sloan Found. fellow, 1958-62; Kendall award Am. Chem. Soc., 1969. Mem Nat. Acad. Scis., Am. Chem. Soc., Biophys. Soc., A.A.A.S., N.A.A.C.P., Am. Civil Liberties Union, Phi Beta Kappa. Author: Statistical Mechanics, 1956; Statistical Thermodynamics, 1960; Thermodynamics of Small Systems, Vol. I, 1963, Vol. II, 1964; Matter and Equilibrium, 1965; Thermodynamics for Chemists and Biologists, 1968; also research papers. Asso. editor Jour. Chem. Physics, 1948-51. Home: 9626 Kensington Pkwy Kensington MD 20795

HILL, THEODORE ALBERT, psychiatrist; b. Denver, June 12, 1908; s. Albert Lyon and Helen (Brown) H.; B.A., U. Cal., at Los Angeles, 1930; M.A., Stanford, 1931; M.D., Loma Linda U., 1947; m. Eva Grace Harris, June 30, 1934; children—Helen Julia Felicia, Marvin Dice, Grace Lorraine, Chandler McPherson, Theodora Susan, Roy Landstrom. Adminstrv. analyst Div. Research, County of Los Angeles, 1937-40; adminstrv. analyst personnel div. Treasury Dept., Washington, 1940, adminstrv. analyst procurement div., 1940-41; adminstrv. inspector Bur. Reclamation, Dept. Interior, Washington, 1941-42; resident psychiatry Los Angeles County Gen. Hosp., 1947-50; dir. St. Joseph County Adult and Child Guidance Clinic, South Bend, Ind., 1952-56; pvt. practice medicine, specializing in psychiatry, South Bend, 1956-58; supt. Dr. Norman M. Beatty Meml. Hosp., Michigan City, Ind., 1968—; instr. psychiatry Sch. Medicine, Ind. U., 1967—. Psychiat. cons. Peace Corps, 1962—, also Memmonite Ch. Bd. Missions, Diocese of No. Ind. Episcopal Chs., Nat. Missionary Bd. Methodist Chs. Served to maj., M.C., U.S. Army, 1950-52. Diplomate Am. Bd. Psychiatry and Neurology. Fellow Am. Psychiat. Assn. (alternate del. Assembly of Dist. Brs.), Am. Orthopsychiatric Assn.; mem. Am. Group Psychotherapy Assn., No. Ind. Psychiat. Soc. (past pres.). Address: 1606 Lake Shore Dr Long Beach Michigan City IN 46360

HILL, THOMAS BOWEN III, lawyer; b. Montgomery, Ala., Oct. 21, 1929; s. Thomas Bowen, Jr. and Mildred (Abrams) H.; B.S., U. Ala., 1951, LL.B., 1953; m. Maria Paschall, Dec. 29, 1955; children—Thomas Bowen IV, Mason P., William IV, Chappell H. Admitted to Ala. bar, 1953, since practiced in Montgomery; mem. firm Hill, Hill, Stovall & Carter, 1953—, partner, 1957—; dir., gen. counsel So. United Life Ins. Co. Mem. Gov.'s staff, 1963-71. Pres., bd. dirs. Childrens Center Montgomery; mem. adv. bd. St. Margarets Hosp. Recipient Algernon Sydney Sullivan medallion as outstanding male grad. U. Ala., 1953. Mem. Am., Ala. (com. chmn.), Montgomery County (past pres.) bar assns., U. Ala. Nat. Alumni Assn. (past v.p.), Ala. Assn. Canterbury Clubs, Druids, Jasons, Quadrangle, Tau Kappa Alpha, Phi Delta Phi, Alpha Tau Omega, Omicron Delta Kappa. Presbyn. (deacon). Kiwanian. (past pres.). Home: Route 4 Box 30 Montgomery AL 36101 Office: PO Box 116 Montgomery AL 36101

HILL, THOMAS BOWEN, Jr., lawyer; b. Montgomery, Ala., Nov. 11, 1903; s. Thomas Bowden and Lida Tunstall (Inge) H.; A.B., U. Ala., 1922, LL.B., 1924; m. Mildred Ellen Abrams, Sept. 22, 1925; children—Thomas Bowen, III, Mildred Inge, Luther Abrams, William Inge, II. Asso. prof. German, U. Ala., 1923-24; admitted to Ala. bar, 1924, since practiced in Montgomery; sr. mem. firm Hill, Hill, Stovall, Carter & Franco, 1947—; spl. chief justice Supreme Ct. Ala., 1966, 67, 68. Chmn. bd., dir. Union Bank & Trust Co., Montgomery. Former mem. bd. dirs. Montgomery YMCA, Children's Protective Home; vice chmn. U. of Ala. Found., Inc., dir. U. Ala. Law Sch. Found. Recipient George Washington Honor mmedal Freedoms Found., 1970. Fellow Am. Coll. of Trial Lawyers, Internat. Acad. Trial Lawyers, Am. Bar Found.; mem. Am., (mem. ho. of dels.), Ala. State (v.p. 1951-52, pres. 1952-53, mem. bd. commrs., 1953—), Montgomery County (past pres.) bar assns., Farrah Law Soc. (charter), Ala. Bible Soc. (dir.), Ala. C. of C. (dir.), Am. Judicature Soc., Ala. Motorists Assn. (dir.), Phi Beta Kappa, Phi Alpha Delta. Episcopalian (vestryman, sr. warden). Mason (Shriner), Kiwanian (past pres. Montgomery). Home: 1831 Hillwood Dr Montgomery AL 36106 Office: Hill Bldg Montgomery AL 36104

HILL, THOMAS ENGLISH, educator; b. Gadsden, Ala., Feb. 12, 1909; s. William Edwin and Zaida Dumond (English) H.; A.B., Davidson Coll., 1929; B.D., Union Theol. Sem., Richmond, Va., 1932; M.A., U. Richmond, 1939; Ph.D., U. Edinburgh (Scotland) 1937; postgrad. Tubingen (Germany) U., 1933, Harvard, 1944- 46, 52-53, Oxford (Eng.) U., 1959; m. Sara Prather Armfield, Aug. 14, 1933; children—Sara Prather, Thomas English, Mary Armfield (Mrs. David Lewis Porter). Ordained to ministry Presbyn. Ch., 1934; pastor College Park (Ga.) Presbyn. Ch.; 1934-38; instr. Greek U. Ga., Atlanta, 1935-37; prof. Bible and philosophy King Coll., Bristol, Tenn., 1938-40, Southwestern Coll., Memphis, 1940-46; mem. faculty philosophy Macalester Coll., St. Paul, 1946-, asso. prof., 1946- 47, prof., 1947—, Bloedel prof., 1962—, chmn. dept., 1964-68. Recipient Thomas Jefferson award Macalester Coll., 1968; Ford fellow, 1952-53; Harvard Corp. research fellow, 1944-46, 52-53. Mem. Am., Minn. (pres. 1963) philos. assns., Phi Beta Kappa. Author: Contemporary Ethical Theories, 1940; Ethics in Theory and Practice, 1956; Contemporary Theories of Knowledge, 1961; The Concept of Mening, 1971. Home: 1681 Princeton Av St Paul MN 55105

HILL, THOMAS MASON, educator; b. Bucksport, Me., Dec. 5, 1914; s. Widber Trane and Bernice (Mason) H.; A.B., U. Me., 1936; M.B.A., Harvard, 1938; postgrad. Stanford, 1940-41; m. Hildreth Montgomery, Sept. 5, 1936; children—Thomas Mason, Joanna C. Instr., Yale, 1938-40; fellow Stanford U., 1940-41; mem. faculty Mass. Inst. Tech., from 1946, former prof.; vis. prof. U. Leeds (Eng.), 1956; fellow Inst. Basic Math., Harvard, 1959-60; project dir. Indian Inst. Mgmt., Calcutta, 1961-63; dir. Internat. Studies Center, Cambridge. Dir. Gen. Electronics Labs., 1965—. Bd. dirs. Boston Council Internat. Visitors. Served to lt. col. AUS, 1941-46. Mem. Am. Econ. Assn., Am. Accounting Assn., Inst. Mgmt. Scis., Phi Beta Kappa. Co-author: Accounting: A Management Approach, 1959. Home: 5 Agawam Rd Winchester MA 01890

HILL, THOMAS RUSSELL, bus. exec., lectr., writer; b. Williamstown, Ky., Dec. 15, 1894; s. George William and Mary Elizabeth (Hayden) H.; A.B., Georgetown Coll., 1915, LL.D., 1940; Dr. Humanities, Lincoln Meml. U., 1949; m. Iris Francis, Nov. 19, 1921 (dec.). Coach football, high sch. prin. and supt. schs., 1915-18; lectr. Redpath Chautauqua, summers 1915-18; pres. Hill-Lawson Co., Corbin, Harlan and Middlesboro, Ky., 1920-29; with RKO Lyceum Bur., 1927-31; state mgr. advancing to v.p. and dir. Air-Way Electric Appliance Corp., Toledo, 1929-35; chmn. Rexair, Inc., Detroit; former pres. Martin-Parry Corp., Martin-Parry, Ltd., Ward Industries Corp., Ward Industries, Ltd. Former trustee Lincoln Meml. U., Harrogate, Tenn., Kalamazoo Coll. Past pres. Middleboro (Ky.) C. of C.; past nat. councillor, U.S. C. of C. chmn. Mem. Nat. Soc. Marine Architects, Kappa Alpha. Baptist (chmn. trustees). Mason (Shriner), Rotarian (hon.), Elk, Kiwanian (past pres.). Author: Press On; Out Front; How Big; Producers; Gimme; 16 to 1; Dig, Ships, Bata. Home: Park Shelton 15 E Kirby St Detroit MI 48202 Office: Buhl Bldg Detroit MI 48226

HILL, THOMAS WILLIAM Jr., lawyer; b. N.Y.C., Dec. 25, 1924; s. Thomas William and Marion (Bond) H.; B.S., U. Pa., 1948; M.B.A., N.Y.U., 1950; J.D., Columbia, 1953; m. Elizabeth Rowe, June 18, 1949; children—Gretchen P., Catherine B., Thomas William III. Sr. tax accountant Hurdman & Cranstoun, C.P.A.'s, 1949-50; admitted to N.Y. bar, 1953; asst. U.S. atty. So. Dist. N.Y., 1953-54; asso. Cahill, Gordon, Reindel & Ohl, 1954-58; sr. partner Spear & Hill, 1958—. Pres. Belco Petroleum Co., N.Y.C., 1962-63. Served as 1st lt. AUS, 1943-46. C.P.A., N.Y. Mem. Am. Bar Assn., Assn. Bar City of N.Y., Am. Inst. C.P.A.'s, N.Y. State Soc. C.P.A.'s, Phi Delta Phi, Kappa Sigma. Clubs: Lunch, Pinnacle (N.Y.C.); Winged Foot. Contbr. articles legal pubs. Home: 10 Briar Del Circle Larchmont NY 10538 Office: 63 Wall St New York City NY 10005

HILL, TOBY A., spark plug mfg. co. exec.; b. 1903; student U. Toledo; married. With Champion Spark Plug Co., Toledo, 1936—, asst. sec., 1938-50, sec., 1950—; sec. Magnaflux Corp., Baron Drawn Steel Corp. Office: 900 Upton Av Toledo OH 43607*

HILL, WARREN GARDINER, state edn. ofcl.; b. Brooklyn, N.S., Can., Oct. 19, 1918; s. Andrew William and Hannah (Walker) H.; brought to U.S., 1922, naturalized, 1942; B.S., Gorham State Tchrs. Coll., 1939; Ed. M., Boston U., 1941; Ed.D., Columbia, 1947; L.H.D., Bowdoin Coll., 1961; D.Sc., U. Me., 1964; m. Catherine Lewis, Aug. 26, 1942; children—Senetta Louise, Charles Douglas. Prin. Islesford (Me.) Elementary Sch., 1939-40; instr. maths., sci. Gorham State Tchrs. Coll., 1941-42; asst. to pres., acting pres. New Haven State Tchrs. Coll., 1947-55; chief bur. fed.- state-local relations Conn. Dept. Edn., 1955-56; commr. edn., Me., 1956- 63; pres. Trenton (N.J.) State Coll., 1963-66; chancellor Higher Edn., State Conn., 1966—. Past chmn. Nat. Commn. Tchr. Edn. and Profl. Standards; chmn. Catalyst in Edn.; mem. Leadership Tng. Inst., tng. of tchrs. program EPDA; mem. bd. dirs. tchr. edn. program. New Eng. Regional Commn.; commr. Edn. Commn. States. Served as lt. USCGR, 1942-46. Mem. Am. Assn. Sch. Adminstrs., Conn. Edn. Assn., N.E.A., Horace Mann League. Conglist. Mason. Home: 89 Sunset Dr Glastonbury CT 06033 Office: Commn Higher Edn Box 1320 Hartford CT 06101

HILL, WILLIAM EDWIN, mgmt. cons.; b. N.Y.C., Nov. 5, 1910; s. William Edwin and Alice I. (Haggerty) H.; B.S., Sheffield Sci. Sch., Yale, 1932; m. Jane E. Herrmann, June 4, 1938; children—Alice Susan (Mrs. John S. McLaughlin), Sarah Knipe. Indsl. cons. engr., instr. Ruston Acad., Havana, Cuba, 1932-36; mgr. comml. dept. Am. Radiator & Standard San. Corp., N.Y.C., 1936-38; founder, 1938, Turck, Hill & Co., Inc., indsl. engrs., N.Y.C.; founder, pres. William E. Hill Internat., Inc., N.Y.C., 1953—; v.p., dir. 125 E. 74th St. Corp.; v.p. Dun & Bradstreet, Inc., 1971—; trustee Emigrant Savs. Bank; dir. Bangor & Aroostook R.R. Corp., Bangor Punta Corp., Peninsular Life Ins. Co. Pres. Catholic Youth Orgn., 1946- 49; exec. com., dir. Boys Clubs Am.; mem. Educators Adv. Council Coll. and Univ. Profs.; trustee Children's Aid Soc., Wells Coll., Aurora, N.Y. Mem. Am. Soc. M.E. (v.p., dir.), Nat. Inst. Social Scis., (v.p.), Yale Engring. Assn. (chmn. indsl. adv. council). Clubs: University (N.Y.C., Milw.); Yale, Sky (N.Y.C.). Contbr. articles tech., trade publs. Home: 125 E 74th St New York City NY 10021 also Old Black Point CT 06357 Office: 640 Fifth Av New York City NY 10019 also Rue de la Loi-64 Brussels 4 Belgium also Castle Lane Buckingham Gate London SW 1 England

HILL, WILLIAM LINCOLN, banker; b. Newark, July 4, 1901; s. Harry and Rose (White) H.; grad. Rutgers U. Grad. Sch. Banking, 1946; m. Susan D. Bryant, Oct. 22, 1925; children—Ann, Charles, William. Asst. treas. Colonial Trust Co. N.J., 1928-30; gen. bookkeeper Asbury Park Nat. Bank (N.J.), 1930-42; br. mgr. Maplewood Bank & Trust Co. (N.J.), 1942-46; sec. Bank of Sussex County (merged with Nat. Community Bank of Rutherford, 1970), Franklin, N.J., 1946-58, pres., 1958-70; sr. v.p. Nat. Community Bank, Rutherford, 1970—, also dir. Mem. adv. council Small Bus. Adminstrn., 1969—, also mem. active execs. corps; bd. govs. Morris-Sussex chpt. Am. Inst. Banking. Mem. Sussex County (N.J.) Planning Bd., chmn., 1966-69. Trustee, Franklin Hosp., N.J. chpt. Multiple Sclerosis, 1965-68. Elected to Half-Century Club, N.J. Bankers Assn., 1970. Mem. Am. (adv. council savs. div. 1965-68), N.J. (exec. com. 1963-68), Sussex County (pres. 1965) bankers assns. Presbyn. (elder). Mason. Rotarian (pres., organizer Vernon Twp. club 1969). Home: RD 1 Sussex NJ 07461 Office: 46 Main St Franklin NJ 07416

HILL, WILLIAM RYLAND, coll. dean; b. Seattle, Feb. 1, 1911; s. William Ryland and Ottie (Armstrong) H.; B.S. in Elec. Engring., U. Wash., 1934; M.S. in Elec. Engring., U. Cal. at Berkeley, 1938, E.E., 1940; m. Francel Tozer Wilt, June 21, 1940; children—Sinclair Garton, Ann Stirling, Judy Francel. Radio engr. No. Radio Co., Seattle, 1934-36; engr. Standard Oil Co. Cal., 1938-41: mem. faculty U. Wash., 1941—, prof. elec. engring., 1953- -, cons. applied physics lab., 1953-60, asso. dean Coll. Engring., 1959- -, acting dir. Applied Physics Lab., 1969-71; acting head faculty electronics Madras (India) Inst. Tech., 1957-58; on leave dept. application sci. UNESCO, 1966-68. Sr. mem. I.E.E.E.; mem. Am. Soc. Engring. Edn., Sigma Xi, Tau Beta Pi. Club: American Alpine (N.Y.C.). Author: Electronics in Engineering, 2d edit., 1961; also articles. Home: 20345 8th Av NW Seattle WA 98177

HILLAM, KENNETH LOREN, educator; b. Salt Lake City, July 15, 1927; s. Loren Abram and Ruth (Olsen) H.; B.S., U. Utah, 1949, M.S., 1956; Ph.D., U. Colo., 1962; m. Beverly Mae Myers, Mar. 16, 1950; children—Bradford K., Karen B., Brent K. Instr. math. U. Colo., 1956-57; instr. Brigham Young U., Provo, Utah, 1957-62, asst. prof., 1962-64, asso. prof., 1964-67, prof., 1967—, chmn. dept. math., 1963—; mem. com. examiners math. Advanced Placement Program in Math., Coll. Entrance Exam. Bd. Served with USNR, 1945-46. Mem. Am. Math. Soc., Math. Assn. Am., Sigma Xi. Home: 528 E 3950 N Provo UT 84601

HILLARD, JAMES MILTON, librarian; b. Nortonville, Ky., Sept. 27, 1920; s. Cornelius and Leona L. (Hicks) H.; B.A. with high honors, Ohio U., 1947; M.S. in L.S. with honors, U. Ill., 1948; m. Ella Louise Winzenried, Dec. 23, 1944; children—James Randolph, Jerrold Manley. Asst. librarian Free Pub. Library, Summit, N.J., 1948-50; city librarian Carnegie City Library, Ft. Smith, Ark., 1950-52; dir. Curtis Meml. Library, Meriden, Conn., 1952-55; asso. librarian U.S. Mil. Acad., West Point, N.Y., 1955-57; librarian The Citadel, Charleston, S.C., 1957-. Served with AUS, 1942- 46. Mem. Am., Southeastern, S.C. (sec. 1960; treas. 1965—) library assns., Am. Assn. U. Profs. Methodist. Optimist. Contbr. profl. jours. Address: The Citadel Charleston SC 29409

HILLARY, EDMUND PERCIVAL, explorer, author, lectr.; b. Auckland, New Zealand, July 20, 1919; s. Percival Augustus and Gertrude (Clark) H.; student Auckland U., 1936-37; m. Louise Mary Rose, Sept. 3, 1953; children—Peter Edmund, Sarah Louise, Belinda Mary. Expdns. include New Zealand Garwhat Expdn., 1951, Brit. Everest Reconnaissance, 1951, Brit. Cho Oyu Expdn., 1952, Brit. Everest Expdn. (reached summit with Tenzing), 1953, New Zealand Alpine Club Himalayan Expdn., 1954, New Zealand Antartic expdns. (leader), 1956- 58; reached S. Pole overland with tractors, 1958; leader Himalayan expdns., 1960-61, 63, 64-66; constructed 7 schs., hosp., airfield, 3 bridges for Sherpa people with funds raised in U.S., New Zealand, Great Britain; cons. in field; dir. Australasian Dirs. Field Enterprises, 1964—. Pres. New Zealand Vol. Service Abroad, 1963—. Served as navigator Royal New Zealand Air Force, World War II; PTO. Created knight, 1953; recipient Gurkha Right Hand (Nepal), 1953, Hubbard medal Nat. Geog. Soc., 1953, Founders medal Royal Geog. Soc., 1958. Hon. mem. New Zealand Alpine Club, Explorers Club, N.Y.C. Author: High Adventure, 1955; No Latitude for Error, 1961; (with Desmond Doig) High in the Thin Cold Air, 1963; Schoolhouse in the Clouds, 1965. Address: 278A Remuera Rd Auckland New Zealand

HILLCOURT, WILLIAM, (Bjerregaard-Jensen, Vilhelm Hans), author, editor; b. Aarhus, Denmark, Aug. 6, 1900; s. Johannes Hans and Andrea Kristina (Pedersen) Bjerregaard-Jensen; prep. edn. Aarhus Latinskole; M.Sc., Pharm. Coll., Copenhagen, Denmark, 1924; m. Grace Constance Brown, June 3, 1933. Came to U.S., 1926, naturalized, 1939. While studying pharmacy became editor ofcl. Danish Scout mag. and started to write boy's fiction; journalist, asst. editor Ferslew Newspapers, Copenhagen, 1924, corr. on tour of Europe and Am., arriving in U.S., 1926; mem. nat. staff Boy Scouts Am., 1926-65, asst. to dir. publs., 1927-44, mng. editor Scouting mag., 1927-31; feature writer, asst. editor, contbg. editor Boys' Life mag., 1932—; nat. dir. Scoutcraft, 1944-54, asst. to dir. program, 1954-56, nat. dir. program resources, 1956-65. Spl. instr. U.S. Army 2d Service Command Tactical Sch., 1941-45. Attended World Scout Jamborees, 1920, 24, 29, 33, 37, 47, 51, 55, 63, 67, Nat. Jamborees, 1937, 50, 53, 57, 60, 64, 69. Recipient Medal Merit, Danish Boy Scout Assn.; Certificate of Merit award Freedoms Found., 1951, Honor medal awards, 1953-57, Badge of Honor, Norwegian Boy Scout Assn.; Medal of Honor, Dutch Boy Scout Assn.; Silver Horse, Venezuelan Boy Scout Assn.; Silver Wolf, Brit. Boy Scouts Assn.; Silver Hawk, Boy Scouts of Japan; also other Scout decorations. Mem. Authors League Am., Nat. Audubon Soc. Author: Handbook for Patrol Leaders. 1929: (with James E. West) The Scout Jamboree, 1933; Handbook for Scoutmasters, 1936; Scout Field Book, 1944; Field Book of Nature Activities, 1950; Boy Scout Handbook, 1959, 65; Field Book of Nature Activities and Conservation, 1961; (with Olave, Lady Baden- Powell) Baden-Powell—The Two Lives of a Hero, 1964; Physical Fitness for Boys, Physical Fitness for Girls, 1967; Fun with Nature Hobbies, 1970; Field Book of Nature Activities and Hobbies, 1970; Golden Book of Camping, 1971; also other publs., pamphlets, mag. articles. Editor: The 1929 World Jamboree Book, 1929: World Brotherhood Editions of Baden-Powell's Aids to Scoutmastership, 1944; Scouting for Boys, 1946. Home: 43 Pardun Rd North Brunswick NJ 08902

HILLEBOE, HERMAN ERTRESVAAG, physician; b. Westhope, N.D., Jan. 8, 1906; s. Peter S. and Inga (Jacobson) H.; B.S., U. Minn., 1927, M.B., 1929, M.D., 1931; grad. tng. pediatrics, U. Minn. Hosp., Mpls. 1932-34; M.P.H., Johns Hopkins Sch. of Hygiene and Pub. Health, 1935; D.Sc. (hon.), U. Rochester, 1954; m. Alida Claire Champeau, Sept. 28, 1929; children—Joyce (Mrs. Torben Kiaer), Theresa (Mrs. Richard McUmber), Herman Ertesvaag. Began career in rural gen. practice of medicine, Swanville, Minn., 1929-31. Commd. officer USPHS, sr. asst. surgeon, June 1939; in charge Tb control activities Pub. Health Service, Washington, 1942-46; Tb control officer, USCG, 1942-45; apptd. chief of Tb control div. with rank of med. dir., 1944; apptd. asso. chief Bur. of State Services with rank of asst. surgeon gen., 1946; N.Y. State commr. of health, 1947-63; prof. pub. health and preventive medicine Albany Med. Sch., 1948-62; DeLamar prof. pub. health practice Columbia Sch. Pub. Health and Adminstrv. Medicine, 1963-70, prof. emeritus, 1970; med. sch. rep. Fla. Regional Med. Program, Tampa, 1971—. Panel experts WHO, 1948—. Diplomate Am. Bd. Preventive Med. and Pub. Health. Mem. Am. Coll. Chest Physicians, Am. Epidemiological Soc., Am. Pub. Health Assn. (pres. 1954-55), Assn. Tchrs. of Preventive Medicine, Assn. State and Terr. Health Officers (past pres.). Lutheran. Author: (with Dr. R.H. Morgan) Mass Radiography of the Chest, 1944: (with Dr. G.W. Larimore) Preventive Medicine, 1965. Home: 2401 Bayshore Blvd Tampa FL 33609 Office: 1 Davis Blvd Tampa FL 33606

HILLEBOE, JOHN STRAND, newspaper publisher; b. Warren, Minn., Jan. 11, 1911; s. John and Clara (Strand) H.; student Coll. Puget Sound, 1928-30; B.A. in Journalism, U. Minn., 1932; m. Edith Nina Nelson, Aug. 20, 1938; children—John William, James Strand, Susan Claire. Advt. mgr. Polk County Leader, Crookston, Minn., 1932-33; advt. salesman Yankton (S.D.) Press and Dakotan, 1934, advt. mgr., 1935-39; advt. salesman Sioux City Tribune, 1939-41; with Billings (Mont.) Gazette, 1941—, formerly salesman, advt. mgr., gen. mgr., now publisher; operations mgr. also bd. dirs. Western divs. Lee Enterprises, Inc. Organizer Billings United Fund, 1961, pres., 1964; chmn. adv. bd. St. Vincent Hosp., 1967. Served to lt. USNR, 1943-46. Mem. Pacific Northwest Newspaperr Assn. (bd. dirs.), Billings C. of C. (v.p. dir.), Mont. Press Assn. (pres. 1969), Billings Sales and Advt. Club (charter pres. 1957). Republican. Lutheran. Rotarian. Home: 524 Av D Billings MT 59102 Office: 401 Broadway Billings MT 59013

HILLENBRAND, HAROLD, dentist; b. Chgo., July 19, 1906; s. George Henry and Eleanor (Schmitt) H.; student Loyola Acad., 1920-24; student Sch. of Arts and Scis., Loyola U., Chgo., 1924-26; D.D.S., B.S.D., Loyola, 1930; D. Sc., 1958; MDS, Nat. U. Ireland, 1952; D.Sc., U. Pa., 1953, Coll. Holy Cross, 1970, U. P.R., 1969, U. Md., Balt., 1970, Boston U., 1969; LL.D., Temple U., 1963; Dr. Pub. Service, U. Pacific, 1967; m. Marie Rose, April 26, 1934; children—Keith Harold (dec. 1945), Gerald Bruce. Pvt. practice of dentistry, Chgo., 1930-45; asso. prof. of ethics and social relations. Sch. of Dentistry, Loyola U., 1938-51. Recipient of gold medal R.I. State Dental Society, 1952; Fones Medal Conn. State Dental Assn., 1954; Henry Spenadel award First Dist. Dental Soc., N.Y., 1954; Comdr. Order Duarte, Sanchez and Mella, Dominican Republic, 1956; Hon. Prof., Universidad de Santo Domingo, 1956; Chevalier de l'Ordre de la Sante' Publique (France); Knight of Order of Leopold II (Belgium); Officers Cross Order of Merit (German Fed. Republic); gold medal Pierre Fauchard Acad., 1967. Fellow Royal Coll. Surgeons Eng. (dental surgery), Am. Coll. Dentists; hon. mem. Internat. Assn. Dental Research, Internat. Coll. Dentists, Swedish, Greek, Danish, Belgian, British, Finnish, Mexican, Dutch, Indian, Norwegian, Canadian, Philippine and French, German, Chilean, Argentinean, Italian, Peruvian, Swiss, Australian dental assns.; mem. Am. Dental Assn. (sec. 1946-70), A.A.A.S., Am. Pub. Health Assn., Ill. Chgo. dental socs., Odontographic Soc. of Chgo., Am. Hosp. Assn. (hon. mem.), Delta Sigma Delta, Omicron Kappa Upsilon. Roman Catholic. Club: Tavern. Editor: Fortnightly Review of Chgo. Dental Soc., 1936-40; Ill. Dental Jour., 1940-42; asst. editor Jour. Am. Dental Assn., 1942- 45, editor, 1945-47. Contbr. numerous articles on various topics of dental practice to various jours. Home: 540 Aldine Av Chicago IL 60657 Office: 211 E Chicago Av Chicago IL 60611

HILLENBRAND, MARTIN JOSEPH, fgn. service officer; b. Youngstown, O., Aug. 1, 1915; s. Joseph John and Mary Magdalene (Walter) H.; A.B., U. Dayton, 1937, Litt.D., (honoris causa), 1963; M.A., Columbia, 1938, Ph.D., 1948; postgrad. Harvard, 1949-50; m. Faith Stewart, June 27, 1941; children—Ruth Marie, David Martin, John Steven. Apptd. fgn. service officer career, 1939; vice consul, Zurich, Switzerland, 1939, Rangoon, Burma, 1940, Calcutta, India, 1942, Lourenco Marques, S.E. Africa, 1944; fgn. service officer, Bremen, Germany, 1945, consul, 1946, officer in charge div. govt. and adminstrn., Bur. German Affairs, Dept. State 1950-52, 1st sec., Paris, 1952-56, U.S. polit. adviser, Berlin, Germany, 1956-58, dir. Office of German Affairs, 1958-62; dir. of Berlin Task Force, 1962-63; minister, dep. chief of mission, Bonn, Germany, 1963-67; ambassador to Hungary, 1967-69; asst. sec. of state for European affairs, 1969—; chmn. Fulbright Commn. for Germany, 1963-67. Mem. Am. Polit. Sci. Assn., Am. Fgn. Service Assn. Roman Catholic. Author: Power and Morals, 1949; co-author Zwischen Politik und Ethik, 1968. Office: Dept of State Washington DC 20525

HILLENKOETTER, ROSCOE HENRY, bus. exec.; b. St. Louis, May 8, 1897; s. Alexander and Olinda (Deuker) H.; B.S., U.S. Naval Acad., 1920; m. Jane E. Clark, Nov. 21, 1933; 1 dau., Jane G. Commd. ensign U.S. Navy, June 1919, and advanced through grades to vice admiral, 1956, ret., 1957. Dir. Central Intelligence Agy., 1947-50; comdt. Third Naval Dist., 1952. Vice chmn., v.p., treas. Hegeman-Harris Co., Inc., 1962—; dir. Electronics & Missile Facilities, Inc. Decorated Comdr. Legion of Honor (France). Mem. U.S. Naval Inst. Home: 3 Kingswood Rd Weehawken NJ 07087 Office: 30 Rockefeller Plaza New York City NY 10020

HILLER, ARTHUR, motion picture dir.; b. Edmonton, Alta., Can., Nov. 22, 1923; ed. univs. Alta., Toronto and B.C. TV prodns. include Matinee Theatre, Playhouse 90, Alfred Hitchcock Presents, Gunsmoke, Ben Casey, Route 66, Naked City; films include Americanization of Emily, 1965, Tobruk, 1966, The Tiger Makes Out, 1967, Popi, 1968, Out of Towners, 1969, Love Story, 1970, Plaza Suite. Address: care Phil Gersh Agy Canon Dr Beverly Hills CA 90210

HILLER, CHARLES FRANCIS, coll. adminstr.; b. Washington, May 24, 1903; s. Alexander Hamilton and Anna Laura (Sprague) H.; B.A., Lehigh U., 1924; A.M., Harvard, 1930, Ph.D., 1935; Leverett B. Saltonstall Scholar, Paris U., 1934-35; m. Marion Beatrice Haynes, Aug. 31, 1935; children—Jane Gibson (Mrs. Donald Charles Lamm), Elizabeth (Mrs. Stanley Alton Starrett, Jr.). Mgr. Buchanan (Mich.) Lumber & Coal Co., 1924-29; instr. French, tutor in modern langs., Harvard, 1932-34, instr. modern langs., Houston U., 1935-40, asso. prof., 1940-47, prof. 1947—, bursar, 1936-41, registrar, 1937-39, since 1944, v.p. univ. devel. and pub. relations, 1950—, dean of the Jr. Coll. div., 1955-63; head Coll. Community Service, dir. extension, dir. head Navy Tng. Sch.; dir. Sch. of Arts and Scis., U. Houston. Recipient Wilbur Scholarship Prize, Lehigh U., 1922. Mem. Phi Beta Kappa. Methodist. Democrat. Clubs: Torch, Engineers (Houston). Address: 5335 Carew St Houston TX 77035

HILLER, LEJAREN ARTHUR, Jr., composer, educator; b. N.Y.C., Feb. 23, 1924; s. Lejaren and Sara Anita (Plummer) H.; B.A., Princeton, 1944, M.A., 1946, Ph.D., 1947; M.Mus., U. Ill., 1958; m. Elizabeth Halsey, Apr. 18, 1945; children—Amanda, David. Research chemist E.I. duPont de Nemours & Co., Waynesboro, Va., 1947-52; research asso., asst. prof. dept. chemistry U. Ill., Urbana, 1953-58, asst. prof., 1958-61, asso. prof. music, 1961-65, prof. music, 1965-68, also dir. exptl. music studio; Slee prof. music, co-dir. Center for Creative and Performing Arts, State U. N.Y. at Buffalo, 1968—; lectr. Darmstadt Ferienkurse für Neue Musik, 1963, 65, 68. Mem. Am. Soc. U. Composers, A.S.C.A.P., Am. Assn. U. Profs. Author: (with L.M. Isaacson) Experimental Music, 1959; (with R.H. Herber) Principles of Chemistry, 1960; Informationstheorie und Computermusik, 1964. Composer: Fifth Piano Sonata, 1960; Music for Time of the Heathen, 1961; Fourth String Quartet, 1962; Amplification for the Tape Recorder and Band, 1962; Music for Man With the Oboe, 1962; Music for Spoon River Anthology, 1962; Seven Electronic Music Studies, 1963; (with R.A. Baker) Computer Cantata, 1963; Machine Music for Piano, Percussion and Tape, 1964; A Triptych for Hieronymus, 1965; Suite for Two Pianos and Tape, 1966; Algorithms I for Nine Instruments and Tape, 1968; (with Frank Parman) An Avalanche for Pitchman, Prima Donna, Player Piano, Percussionist and Prerecorded Playback, 1968; (with John Cage) HPSCHD, 1968; (with G. Allan O'Connor) Computer Music for Percussion and Tape, 1968; Three Rituals For Percussion And Lights, 1969; Third Violin Sonata, 1970. Contbr. articles profl. jours. Home: 359 Berryman Dr Snyder NY 14226 Office: Dept of Music State Univ of NY at Buffalo Buffalo NY 14214

HILLER, STANLEY Jr., investment co. exec.; b. San Francisco, Nov. 15, 1924; s. Stanley and Opal (Perkins) H.; ed. Atuzed Prep. Sch.; U. Cal., 1943; m. Carolyn Balsdon, May 25, 1946; children—Jeffery, Stephen. Designed, built and flew world's first co-axial helicopter, 1944; dir. Helicopter div. Kaiser Cargo, Inc., Berkeley, Calif., 1944-45; organized Hiller Aircraft Corp. (formerly United Helicopters, Inc.), Palo Alto, Cal., 1945, became pres. and gen. mgr., pres., 1950-64 (co. bought by Fairchild Stratos 1964), became pres. of five operating divs.; resigned as exec. v.p., dir., mem. exec. com. Fairchild Hiller Corp., 1965; partner Hiller Investment Co., Palo Alto, Lathrop Co., Palo Alto, Cal.; dir. Benicia Industries, ELTRA Corp. Recipient Fawcett award, 1944; Grand Trophy, World Inventors Congress, Los Angeles, 1947; Distinguished Service award Nat. Def. Transp. Soc., 1958; named 1 of 10 Outstanding Young Men U.S., 1952. Hon. fellow Am. Helicopter Soc.; mem. Am. Inst. Aeronautics and Astronautics, Am. Soc. of Pioneers, Phi Kappa Sigma. Home: 150 Elena Av Atherton CA 94025 Office: 770 Welch Rd Palo Alto CA 94304

HILLER, WENDY, actress; b. Stockport, Eng., Aug. 15, 1912; d. Frank and Marie (Stone) Hiller; ed. Winceby Sch.; m. Ronald Gow, Feb. 25, 1937; children—Ann, Anthony. Broadway debut in Love on the Dole, 1936; stage appearances include The Heiress, 1947, Moon for the Misbegotten, 1957, Flowering Cherry, 1959, Aspern Papers, 1961-62, Wings of the Dove, 1963-64, Sacred Flame, 1967, When We Dead Awaken, 1968, The Battle of Shrivings, 1970; motion pictures include Pygmalion, 1939, Major Barbara, 1941, I Know Where I'm Going, 1945, Separate Tables (Acad. award for best supporting actress 1958), 1958, Sons and Lovers, 1960, Toys in the Attic, 1963, Man for All Seasons, 1966, David Copperfield, 1969. Decorated Order Brit. Empire. Home: Spindles Beaconsfield England

HILLES, FREDERICK WHILEY, educator; b. Lancaster, O., June 1, 1900; s. Charles Dewey and Sarah Bell (Whiley) H.; student Taft Sch., 1915-18; Cambridge, Eng., 1922-23; A.B., Yale, 1922, Ph.D., 1926; L.H.D., St. Lawrence, U., 1959; m. Susan Toy Morse, June 14, 1930; children—Susan E. (Mrs. Geoffrey Bush), Frederick W. Instr. English, Yale, 1926-30, asst. prof., 1931-40, asso. 1940-48, prof., 1948-65, Bodman prof. emeritus, 1965—, also dir. humanities, 1956-59; v.p. Yale University Press. Served U.S. Army as capt. advancing through the grades to lt. col., 1942-46. Awarded Hon. Order of the Brit. Empire, 1947; Legion of Merit (U.S.). 1946. Mem. Modern Lang. Assn. (N.Y.C.), Alpha Delta Phi. Republican. Presbyn. Clubs: The Century Assn., Grolier (N.Y.C.). Author: Literary Career of Sir Joshua Reynolds, 1936. Editor: Portraits by Sir Joshua Reynolds, 1952; The Age of Johnson, 1949; New Light on Dr. Johnson, 1959; mem. editorial bd. Yale edits. Private Papers of James Boswell; co-editor From Sensibility to Romanticism, 1965. Home: PO Box 553 Old Lyme CT 06371 Office: Yale U Library New Haven CT 06520

HILLIARD, HARRIET, actress; b. Des Moines, Ia.; d. Roy E. and Hazel Dell (McNutt) Hilliard; student St. Agnes Acad.; m. Ozzie Nelson, Oct. 8, 1935; children—David Ozzie, Eric Hilliard. Began as vocalist with Ozzie Nelson's orch.; on radio programs with Joe Penner, Bob Ripley, Feg Murray, Red Skelton; began radio program, Adventures of Ozzie and Harriet, Oct. 1944, later Ozzie and Harriet television program; has appeared in motion pictures including, Follow the Fleet, Life of the Party, Cocoanut Grove, Sweethearts of the Campus, The Falcon; recorded for Brunswick, Vocalian, Victor, Blue Bird. Awarded Nat. Family Week Radio citation by Internat. Council on Christian Family Life, 1947; 7th consecutive yr. Ozzie and Harriet voted Best Husband-Wife Team in television by readers TV-Radio Mirror, 1960: Woman of Yr. in entertainment field, Los Angeles Times; Genii award, Radio and TV Women So. Cal., 1960‡

HILLIARD, PAULINE, educator; b. Clinton, Ky., Feb. 1909; d. Ernest A. and Gena (Finch) Hilliard; A.B., Murray State U., 1931; M.A., Duke, 1937; Ed.D., Columbia, 1950. Rural sch. tchr., Hickman County, Ky., 1928-30; tchr. English, Central High Sch., Clinton, 1932-37; critic tchr. Memphis State Coll., 1937-42; supervising tchr. U. Ky., 1946-47, dir. Workshop, summer 1947, editorial asso., instr., 1948-49; instr. Tchrs. Coll., Columbia, summers 1947, 49, 50, 54; asso. prof. U. Fla., Gainesville, 1950-52, prof., 1952—, chmn. dept. elementary edn., 1960-68; cons. pub. schs. and profl. groups in Ala., Ky., Tenn., La., Tex., Ark., S.C., Va. Mem. N.E.A. (life), Fla. Edn. Assn., Assn. for Supervision and Curriculum Devel., Assn. for Childhood Edn. Internat. (past chmn. bd. editors) (life), Assn. for Tchr. Edn., Delta Kappa Gamma, Pi Lambda Theta, Kappa Delta Pi. Author: Improving Social Learnings in the Elementary School, 1954; (with Marion Nesbitt) David Writes a Letter, 1954; Greater Than Man, 1957. Contbr. articles profl. jours. Home: 515 NE 9th Av Gainesville FL 32601

HILLIARD, ROBERT JOHN, corp. exec.; b. Chgo., Nov. 10, 1924; s. Robert John and Agenes (Keleher) H.; B.S., Northwestern U., 1948, LL.B., 1951; postgrad. U. Chgo., 1956, Harvard Bus. Sch., 1959; m. Janet Newell, Apr. 27, 1946; children—Janet, Jo Ann, Robert, Richard. Admitted to Ill. bar, 1952; atty., indsl. relations asst. Am. Bakeries Co., 1953-57, asst. dir. indsl. relations, 1957-60, dir. indsl. relations, 1960-63, v.p. indsl. relations and law, 1963-68, pres., 1968-70, sr. v.p. indsl. relations, 1970—, corp. dir., 1966; dir. United of Am. Bank. Bd. dirs. Econs. of Distbn. Found.; bd. dirs., sec. Wheat and Wheat Foods Found. Served with AUS, 1943-46. Mem. Am. Bakers Assn. (chmn. indsl. relations com.), Pvt. Truck Council Am. (bd. dirs.), Am. Inst. Baking (vice chmn. bd.), Bakers Ambassador Assn. (bd. dirs.), Ill., Chgo. bar assns., Newcomen Soc. North Am. Home: 671 Timber Lane Lake Forest IL 60045 Office: 10 S Riverside Plaza Chicago IL 60606

HILLIER, JAMES, research exec., b. Brantford, Can., Aug. 22, 1915; s. James and Ethel Anne (Cooke) H.; B.A., U. Toronto, 1937, M.A., 1938, Ph.D., 1941; m. Florence Marjory Bell, Oct. 24, 1936; children—James Robert, William Wynship. Came to U.S., 1940, naturalized, 1945. Staff labs. Radio Corp. Am., research physicist for fundamental electron microscope research, 1940-53; dir. research dept. Melpar, Inc. (subsidiary of Westinghouse Air Brake Co.), 1953-54; adminstrv. engr. RCA, 1954-55, chief engr. comml. electronics products, 1955-57; gen. mgr. RCA Labs., 1957-58, v.p., 1958-68; v.p. research and engring., RCA Corp., 1968- 69, exec. v.p. research and engring., 1969—; pres. Indsl. Reactor Labs., 1964-65; vis. lectr., dept. biology Princeton, 1950-53, chmn. adv. council dept. elec. engring., 1965-69; chmn. clean air and water scholarship selection com. N.J. Dept. Health, 1968—; mem. N.J. Higher Edn. Study Com., 1963-64; mem. indsl. adv. com. NASA, 1962- 64; mem. tech. adv. bd. U.S. Dept. of Commerce, 1964-70. Mem. governing bd. Am. Inst. Physics, 1962-65. Recipient Lasker award design, constrn., perfection electron microscope, 1960. Fellow Soc., A.A.A.S., Am. Physical Soc., I.E.E.E.; mem. Am. Mgmt. Assn., Indsl. Research Inst. (past pres.), N.A.M., (mem. research com.), Electron Microscope Soc. Am. (past pres.), Nat. Acad. Engrs. (council 1971—), Sigma Xi, Eta Kappa Nu. Author: (with others) Electron Optics and the Electron Microscope, 1945. Author approximately 150 tech. articles. Holds 40 patents, including improvements related fields of electron diffraction, ultra-thin sectioning, viral and bacteriological techniques; designer, builder (with Albert Prebus) 1st successful high- resolution electron microscope in western hemisphere, 1939-40. Home: 22 Arreton Rd Princeton NJ 08540 Office: RCA Labs Princeton NJ 08540

HILLIKER, GRANT GILBERT, fgn. service officer; b. Tomah, Wis., June 26, 1921; s. Vernon Gilbert and Celeste (Reich) H.; B.A., U. Wis., 1942; student Northwest Technol. Inst., 1943; student George Washington U., 1946-47, 50-55; m. Miriam Lucile Chrisler, Apr. 3, 1943; children—Janet Lee, Laurie Ann. Information, editorial specialist Dept. State, Washington, 1946, fgn. affairs analyst No. European affairs, 1950-55; fgn. service officer, 1947-50, 55—; vice consul Am. consulate gen., Naples, Italy, 1947-49; 3d sec., Am. embassy, Stockholm, Sweden, 1949-50; 2d sec., polit. officer Am. embassy, Helsinki, Finland, 1955-59, 1st sec., 1959-60; coll. prof., head dept. univ. tng. and area studies Fgn. Service Inst., Dept. State, 1960-62, asst. dean for area studies, 1962-63; dep. exec. sec. Dept. State, 1963-65; fed. exec. fellow Brookings Instn., 1965-66; Am. consul gen., Recife, Brazil, 1967-68; spl. asst. to the under sec. of state, 1968-70; information systems coordinator Bur. Intelligence and Research, 1970—. Mem. city Council of Falls Church, Va., 1953-55. Served to 1st lt. AUS, 1943-46. Recipient Sterling Day and Sigma Delta Chi awards U. Wis., 1942. Mem. Am. Fgn. Service Assn., Am. Polit. Sci. Assn., Phi Beta Kappa, Phi Eta Sigma, Phi Kappa Phi, Alpha Delta Sigma. Methodist. Home: 604 Abbott Lane Falls Church VA 22046 Office: Dept of State Washington DC 20520

HILLILA, BERNHARD HUGO PAUL, educator; b. Gwinn, Mich., May 21, 1919; s. Hugo Mathias and Hannah Maria (Mattonen) H.; grad. Suomi Coll., Hancock, Mich., 1938, Suomi Theol. Sem.,

Hancock, 1941; B.A., Boston U., 1943; M.A., Western Res. U., 1945, postgrad., 1945-46; Ed.D., Columbia, 1955; m. Esther Pauline Halttunen, June 28, 1944; children—Esther Pauline, Sarah Christine, Martin Bernhard. Ordained to ministry Lutheran Ch., 1941; pastor, Maynard, Mass., 1941-43, Fairport Harbor, O., 1943-46, Bklyn., 1946-49, 52-57; instr. Wagner Coll., S.I., 1948-49; pres. Suomi Coll. and Theol. Sem., 1949-52; pastor, Warren, O., 1957-60; dean, prof. practical theology Hamma Div. Sch., Wittenberg U., 1960-64, dir. grad. div., 1961-63; dean Cal. Luth. Coll., Thousand Oaks, Cal., 1964-68, prof. of edn. Valparaiso (Ind). U., 1968—; lectr. Purdue U., 1969—. Vice pres. Finnish Evang. Luth. Ch., 1955- 60; mem. Joint Commn. Luth. Unity, 1956-62; mem. Inter-Luth. Consultation Commn., 1962-66; councillor Nat. Luth. Council, 1962- 66; del. Luth. World Fedn. Assembly, 1957. Dir. Fair Havens, Inc., Middleboro, Mass. Mem. Mich. Tb Sanatorium Commn., 1950-52. Bd. dirs. Suomi Coll., 1949-52, 57-60, Suomi Theol. Sem., 1957-60. Mem. N.E.A., Am. Psychol. Assn., Kappa Delta Pi, Phi Delta Kappa. Editor: The Luth. Counselor, 1942-44. Home: 703 Hastings Terrace Valparaiso IN 46383

HILLINGER, RAYMOND PETER, clergyman; b. Chgo., May 2, 1904; s. Peter Leonard and Mary (Neuses) H.; grad. Quigley Prep. Sem., Chgo.; St. Mary of the Lake Sem., Mundelein, Ill. Ordained to priesthood Roman Catholic Ch., 1932; asst., St. Aloysius Parish, Chgo., 1932-35; missionary Chgo. Archiocesan Mission Band, 1935-50; rector Angel Guardian Orphanage, 1950-53; bishop of Rockford, 1953- 56; aux. bishop to Cardinal Stritch, 1956, Cardinal Meyer, now Cardinal Cody. Home: Maryville Haven-West 1700 E Lake St Glenview IL 60025 Office: Washington Blvd & Kildare Av Chicago IL 60624

HILLIS, ELWOOD HAYNES, congressman; b. Kokomo, Ind., Mar. 6, 1926; s. Glen R. and Bernice (Haynes) H.; B.S. in Bus., Ind. U., 1949, J.D., 1952; m. Carol Hoyne, June 12, 1949; children—Jeffrey H., Gary L., Bradley R. Admitted to Ind. bar, 1952; mem. firm Marshall, Hillis, Hillis & Button, Kokomo 1952—; mem. U.S. Ho. of Reps, from Ind., 1970—. dir. (hon.) Union Bank & Trust Co., Kokomo. Served with AUS, 1944-46. Mem. Am. Ind., Howard County bar assns., Am. Legion, V.F.W., AMUETS, Republican. Presbyn. (elder). Elk, Mason. Home: 2331 S Wabash St Kokomo IN 46901 Office: Longworth House Office Bldg Washington DC 20515

HILLIS, MARGARET, musician; b. Kokomo, Ind., Oct. 1, 1921; d. Glen R. and Bernice (Haynes) Hillis; B.A., Ind. U., 1947; grad. student choral conducting, Juilliard Sch. Music, 1947-49; D.Mus., Temple U., 1967. Dir. Met. Youth Chorale, Bklyn., 1948-51; asst. condr. Collegiate Choral, N.Y.C., 1952-53; mus. dir., condr. Am. Concert Choir, N.Y.C., 1950-, Am. Concert Orch., 1950—; condr., instr. Union Theol. Sem., 1950- 60, Juilliard Sch. Music, 1951-53; dir. choral dept. Third St. Music Sch. Settlement, 1953-54; founder, music dir. Am. Choral Found., Inc., 1954—; choral dir. N.Y.C. Opera Co., 1955-56, Chgo. Musical Coll. of Roosevelt U., 1961-62; condr., choral dir. Santa Fe Opera Co., 1958-59, Chgo. Symphony Orch. Chorus, 1957—; music dir. N.Y. Chamber Soloists, 1956-60; chorale condr. Am. Opera Soc., N.Y.C., 1952-68; mus. asst. to music dir. Chgo. Symphony Orch., 1966-68; music dir., condr. Kenosha Symphony Orch., 1961-68; condr., choral dir. Cleve. Orch. Chorus, 1969-71; chmn. dept. choral activities Sch. Music, Northwestern U., 1971—; resident condr. Chgo. Civic Orch., 1967—; music dir. Choral Inst., 1968, 69, 70; artists' adviser Nat. Fedn. Music Clubs Youth Auditions, 1966—. Recipient Golden Plate award Am. Acad. Achievement, 1967, Alumnus of Year award Ind. U. Sch. Music Alumni, 1969, Steinway award, 1969. Civilian flight instr., USN CAA, WTS, World War II. Mem. Nat. Fedn. Music Clubs (hon.), Am. Choral Dirs. Assn., Assn. Choral Conductors, Am. Music Center, Inc., P.E.O., Sigma Alpha Iota (hon.), Alpha chpt. Pi Kappa Lambda (hon.), Kappa Kappa Gamma. Club: Musicians of Women (hon.). Office: Am Choral Found Inc 130 W 56th St New York City NY 10019 also 220 S Michigan Av Chicago IL 60604

HILLIS, MARY OLIVE, educator; b. Beardstown, Ill., Dec. 11, 1919; d. Arthur Burl and Maude (Schaefer) Hillis; A.B., MacMurray Coll. Women, 1941; M.S., U. Ill., 1942, Ph.D., 1944. Mem. faculty Vassar Coll., 1944—, prof. chemistry, 1962—, chmn. dept., 1961-63, 67-69, 71—, sr. adviser office dean studies, 1967. Vassar Faculty fellow, 1961, 69-70. Mem. Am. Chem. Soc., A.A.A.S., Phi Beta Kappa, Sigma Xi, Iota Sigma Pi. Conglist. Home: 20 Williams House Vassar Coll Poughkeepsie NY 12601

HILLIX, ALBERT FICKLIN, lawyer; b. Weston, Mo., Oct. 3, 1896; s. Albert Sidney and Kathleen (Ficklin) H.; A.B., U. Mo., 1920; LL.B., George Washington U., 1924; m. Dorothy Swaney, June 4, 1923; children—Hazel Kathleen (Mrs. Clarence D. Barton), Dorothy Alice (Mrs. Charles F. McCord). Auditor income tax U.S. Treasury Dept., 1925; admitted to Mo. bar, 1925, since practiced in Kansas City; sr. partner in firm of Hillix, Brewer and Myers, and predecessors, 1937—; lectr. taxation Kansas City Sch. Law, 1937-39. Mem. Mo. Supreme Ct. Bar Com., 1935-40, chmn., 1938-40. Pres. Roby Realty Co.; gen. counsel, Hallmark Cards, Inc., The Vendo Co.; dir. Woolf Brothers, Inc. Pres. Kansas City Bd. Police Commnrs., 1952-55; diocesan standing com., past sr. warden Episcopal Ch. Bd. dirs. Mo. Scholarship Found., Pierson Found., Battenfield Found., Kansas City Gen. Hosp. and Med. Center; hon. life dir. St. Luke's Hosp. Served to 2d lt., aviation sect., U.S. Army, 1917-19; to col. USAAF, 1942-45. Recipient Bishop's medal, Diocese of West Mo.; Episcopal. Mem. Am., Mo., Kansas City bar assns., Mo. State, Kansas City (pres. 1947-48) chambers commerce. Rotarian (past 1st v.p.). Clubs: Kansas City Country (past pres.), University (past pres.) (Kansas City, Mo.). Home: 450 W 51st St Kansas City MO 64112 Office: Commerce Towers Kansas City MO 64199

HILLMAN, ABRAHAM P., educator; b. Bklyn., Dec. 18, 1918; s. Joseph Elias and Lena (Backinoff) H.; student Coll. City N.Y., 1935-37; B.A., Bklyn. Coll., 1939, M.A., 1940; postgrad. Columbia, 1940-42; Ph.D., Princeton, 1950; m. Josephine Gottesman, May 28, 1955. Mathmatician Nat. Bur. Standards, Commerce Dept., N.Y.C., 1941-43, 45-48; instr. Princeton, 1944-45, Columbia, 1950-56; asst. prof. Wash. State Coll., Pullman, 1956-57; asst. prof. U. Santa Clara (Cal.), 1957-59, asso. prof., 1959-65; asso. prof. U. N.M., Albuquerque, 1965-67, prof., 1967—; adminstr. 8 insts. for secondary sch. tchrs. NSF, 1959—; dir. various undergrad. honors programs, 1956—; organizer math. contests for secondary students U. Santa Clara, 1958—, U. N.M., 1966—. Del. N.M. Democratic Conv., 1968. Individual winner, also mem. 1st place team W.L. Putnam Intercollegiate Math. Competition, 1939. Mem. Am. Math. Soc., Math. Assn. Am. (gov. 1967-70), Fibonacci Assn. (asso. editor Fibonacci Quar. 1964—), Albuquerque Council Tchrs. Math. Author: (with G.L. Alexanderson) Functional Trigonometry, 2d rev. edit., 1971, Algebra and Trigonometry, 1963, Algebra Through Problem Solving, 1966. Contbr. profl. jours. Home: 707 Solano Dr SE Albuquerque NM 87108

HILLMAN, ARTHUR, educator; b. Nevada City, Cal., June 26, 1909; s. Adolph and Mary (Forsman) H.; A.B., U. Wash., 1931, A.M., 1934; Ph.D., U. Chgo., 1940; m. Stina Eklund, Aug. 17, 1936 (dec. Feb. 1956); m. 2d, Maire Salomaa, August 30, 1958. Tchr. high sch., Elma, Wash., 1931-32; teaching asst. and grad. student, U. of Wash., 1932-35; grad. study and research asst., U. Chgo., 1935-38, C.R. Henderson fellow sociology, 1937-38; asst. prof. sociology, Bucknell U., 1936; instr; asst. prof. Central YMCA Coll., Chgo., 1938-45; asso. prof. Roosevelt U., 1945-48, prof., 1948—, chmn. dept. sociology, 1946-55, 62-64, dean coll. of arts and scis., 1955-60, chmn. urban studies program, 1969—. With office community war services Fed. Security Agency, 1943-45, asst. regional dir., 1944-45; dir. social work-labor project Council Social Agys. of Chgo., 1945-46. Fulbright research scholar in sociology, U. of Oslo, Norway, 1950; participated in 1st World Congress of Sociology and Polit. Sci., Zurich, 1950; dir. survey neighborhood goals project Nat. Fedn. Settlements and Neighborhood Centers, 1958-59; dir. Tng. Center, 1960—. Mem. bd. trustees Roosevelt Coll., 1947-50; mem. bd. civic and social agys. Pres. Hyde Park Co-op. Soc., 1941-43. Mem. Am. Sociol. Soc., Nat. Assn. Social Workers, Am. Scandinavian Found., Am. Assn. U. Profs. Lutheran. Author: Unemployed Citizens League of Seattle, 1934; Community Organization and Planning, 1950, Italian edit., 1953; Tomorrow's Chicago (with R.J. Casey), 1953; Sociology and Social Work, 1956; (with W. Kloetzli) Urban Church Planning, 1958; (with T.D. Eliot) Norway's Families, 1960. Home: 5901 N Sheridan Rd Chicago IL 60626

HILLMAN, CHRISTINE HUFF, (Mrs. Howard S. Hillman), educator, assn. exec.; b. Danville, Ky., Aug. 30, 1908; d. Philip T. and Margaret (Hungate) Huff; B.S., Flora Stone Mather Coll., 1940; M.S., Western Res. U., 1942, Ph.D., 1951; m. Howard S. Hillman, Jan. 31, 1940; 1 son, Colby. Dist. home mgmt. supr. Farm Security Adminstrn., 1940-42; prof. Western Res. U., 1942-45; prof. Ohio State U. and Ohio Agrl. Expt. Sta., 1952-58, Nat. Agrl. Extension Center Advanced Study, U. Wis., 1958-59, Sch. Home Econs. Ohio State U., 1959; then sec. Nat. Council on Family Relations, Mpls.; now prof., asst. dean U. Mass. Active Cub Scouts, YWCA. Mem. Am. Home Econs. Assn., Am. Assn. U. Profs., Am. Sociol. Soc., Soc. Research Child Devel., Phi Upsilon Omicron. Author articles and bulls. Home: 57 Frost St Framingham MA 01701

HILLMAN, DONALD JOHN, information scientist, educator; b. London, Eng., Nov. 21, 1931; s. Robert and Gladys (Tweedy) H.; B.A., Cambridge U., Eng., 1955, M.A., 1959, M. Litt., 1962; m. Susan Ruth Erisman, Nov. 15, 1958; children—Stephanie Kim, Lisa Beth, Jennifer Lynn. Came to U.S., 1956, naturalized, 1964. Research asso. U. Pa., 1958-60; instr. Lehigh U., Bethlehem, Pa., 1960-62, asst. prof., 1962-63, asso. prof., 1963-64, prof., 1964—, chmn. dept. philosophy, 1963-, dir. Center for Information Sci., 1967—; cons. Arthur D. Little, Cambridge, Mass., sci. and tech. communications com. Nat. Acad. Scis.; mem. biomedical communications study sect. NIH. Served to 2d lt. Brit. Army, 1950-52. Recipient Robinson award Lehigh U., 1963. Mem. Am. Soc. Information Sci. Assn. for Symbolic Logic, Am. Philos. Assn., Assn. Computing Machinery. Republican. Home: 1557 Lois Lane Bethlehem PA 18018

HILLMAN, HENRY L., bus. exec.; b. Pitts., Dec. 25, 1918; s. J.H. (Jr.) and Juliet Cummins (Lea) H.; A.B., Princeton, 1941; m. Elsie Mead Hilliard, May 12, 1945; children—Lea, Audrey, Henry, William. With Pitts. Coke & Chem. Co., 1941—, v.p., 1950-52, exec. v.p., 1952-55, pres., 1955—, chmn. bd., 1961- -, dir., 1946—; pres. Hillman Co.; chmn. Hillman Coal & Coke Co.; dir. Chem. Bank N.Y. Trust Co. (N.Y.), Tex. Gas Transmission Corp., Nat. Steel Corp., Global Marine, Inc., Nichols- Homeshield Industries, Inc., Pitts. Nat. Bank, Cummins Engine Co., Inc., Marion Power Shovel Co., Inc. Copeland Refrigeration Corp., Shakespeare Co. Chmn., Allegheny Conf. on Community Devel.; mem. exec. com. Pitts. Regional Planning Assn.; dir. Regional Indsl. Devel. Corp. Southwestern Pa. Pres. Hillman Found., Inc.; trustee, mem. exec. com. U. Pitts.; trustee Carnegie Hero Fund Commn., Children's Hosp. of Pitts. Served from ensign to lt., naval aviator, USNR, 1942-45. Clubs: Duquesne, Pitts. Golf, (Pitts.), Fox Chapel Golf, Rolling Rock (gov.), Laurel Valley Golf (Ligionier, Pa.); Links (N.Y.C.); Princeton (N.Y.); Union (Cleve.). Home: Morewood Heights Pittsburgh PA 15213 Office: Grant Bldg Pittsburgh PA 15219

HILLMAN, HERMAN DAVID, lawyer, corp. exec.; b. N.Y.C., Aug. 8, 1911; s. Max and Rae (Brown) H.; grad. Townsend Harris Hall, 1925-28; A.B., Coll. City N.Y., 1932; J.D., N.Y. U., 1936; m. Edith N. Geilich, April 2, 1939; children—Richard, Robert, Alan. Admitted to N.Y. bar, 1936; asst. mgr. Bur. Legal Research, N.Y. U. Sch. Law, 1936-38, mem. grad. faculty Grad. Sch. Pub. Adminstrn., also faculty law, 1946—, adj. prof. pub. adminstrn., 1962—, adj. prof. law, 1963—; atty. for the U.S. Housing Authority, 1939-42, Fed. Pub. Housing Adminstrn., 1942-43; atty. PHA, 1946-49, regional atty., 1949-53, acting dir. N.Y. regional office, 1953-54, dir., 1954-66, adminstr. housing assistance N.Y. regional office Dept. Housing and Urban Devel., 1966-70; v.p., asso. gen. counsel Stirling Homex Corp., 1970—; adj. prof. of housing N.Y. U., 1957. Mem. nat. council Boy Scouts Am., 1967—. Served lt. USNR, 1943-46. Mem. Am. Bar Assn., Nat. Assn. Housing and Redevelopment Ofcls., Citizens Housing and Planning Council. Jewish religion. Contbr. articles legal periodicals. Home: 1335 Surrey Lane Rockville Centre NY 11570 Office: 437 Madison Av New York City NY 10022

HILLMAN, IVAN LESLIE, financial exec.; b. Sewickley, Pa., Aug. 4, 1905; s. John Henry and Margaret (Mehrlich) H.; B.S., Duquesne U., 1931; LL.B., LaSalle U., 1949; m. Dorothy May Hammett, June 27, 1933 (dec. July 1966); 1 son, James D.; m. 2d, Josie Oellig, Mar. 15, 1968. With Doubleday Hill Elec. Co., Pitts., 1920-27; with Dravo Corp., Neville Island, Pa., 1927-70, asst. sec.-asst. treas., 1935-60, treas., 1960-70; treas., dir. Dravco Can., Ltd., Dravco Constrn., Ltd.; treas. Dravco-Doyle Co., Union Barge Line Corp., Potomac Sand & Gravel Co., Seni-McKinney-Williams Co., Cardinal Carriers, Inc., So. Transfer Co.; instr. accounting, credit mgmt. Duquesne U., 1940-48. C.P.A., Pa. Fellow Nat. Inst. Credit; mem. Credit Assn. Western Pa. (past pres.), Nat. Assn. Credit Mgmt. (past dir., chmn. legislative com.), Pa., Pitts. chambers commerce, Am. Inst. C.P.A.'s, Pa. Soc. C.P.A.'s, Indsl. Credit Club, Delta Phi Sigma. Mason (32). Club: Duquesne (Pitts.). Home: 208 Tech Rd Pittsburgh PA 15205

HILLMAN, JAMES FRAZER, bus. exec.; b. Pitts., Oct. 10, 1888; s. John Hartwell and Sallie Murfree (Frazer) H.; B.S., Yale, 1912; LL.D., U. Pitts., 1965; m. Marguerite Cabell Wright, Nov. 25, 1914; children—Constance Cabell (Mrs. John Oliver, Jr.), Marguerite (Mrs. Richard Purnell), Audrey (Mrs. Thomas Hilliard, Jr.), Sally Frazer (Mrs. J. Mabon Childs). Pres., dir. Harmon Creek Coal Corp. and affiliates, 1934—; trustee Dollar Savs. Bank, Pitts., dir. Pitts. Chmn. Allegheny Conf. Community Devel., 1950-52; pres. Pitts. Park and Playground Soc.; trustee Carnegie Inst.; dir. Civic Light Opera Assn., v.p. Carnegie Library; mem. fine arts com. Carnegie Mus.; mem. adv. com. Home Crippled Children. Served as capt. inf., 82d Div., U.S. Army, 1918-19. Mem. Pitts. C. of C., Chi Phi. Episcopalian (trustee Pitts. diocese). Clubs: Duquesne, Pittsburgh Golf, Rolling Rock, Fox Chapel Golf, Elizabethan. Home: Parish Lane Morewood Heights Pittsburgh PA 15213 Office: First National Bank Bldg Pittsburgh PA 15222

HILLMAN, JIMMYE STANDARD, educator; b. McLain, Miss., Mar. 1, 1923; s. Joseph Levi and Agnes (Butler) H.; B.S., Miss. State U., 1942; M.S., Tex. A. and M. U., 1946; Ph.D., U. Cal. at Berkeley, 1954; student U. Guadalajara, Mexico, 1947; m. Helen Frances Smith, Aug. 22, 1947; children—Brent B., Brenda L., Bradley I. Asst. prof. agrl. econs. Miss. State U., 1946-50; agrl. economist U.S. Operations Mission to Brazil, 1955-57; mem. faculty U. Ariz., 1950—, head dept. agrl. econs., 1961—; exec. dir. President's Nat. Adv. Commn. Food and Fiber, 1966-67; cons. in field, 1956—. Mem. Gov. Ariz. Migratory Labor com., 1965-66; mem. Western States manpower adv. com. to secretaries labor and health, edn. and welfare, 1967-69. Mem. sch. bd. Dist. 1, Tucson, 1966-67. Served to 1st lt. AUS, 1942-45. Rockefeller fellow, 1948-50. Mem. Am. Agrl. Econs. Assn. (pres. 1970-71, bd. dirs. 1967-68), Western Farm Econs. Assn. (pres. 1966-67), A.A.A.S., U.S. Chess Fedn., Gamma Sigma Delta, Omicron Delta Epsilon. Democrat. Baptist. Author articles in field. Home: 730 N Alamo St Tucson AZ 85711

HILLMAN, JOHN WESLEY, found. exec.; b. Cleve., Mar. 21, 1904; s. John Linnaeus and Lizzie (Howes) H.; A.B., Simpson Coll., 1925, Litt.D., 1948; A.M., Northwestern, 1926; m. Esther Gentry, Mar. 31, 1929; m. 2d, Helen Ritchel Frohbieter, Oct. 2, 1954; children—Sharon (Mrs. J. Edwin Cole), Scott Frohbieter. Asso. dir. journalism, instr. English, DePauw U., 1926- 28; dir. journalism Albion Coll., 1928-29; head journalism dept. Baker U., 1931-33; copy editor, makeup editor Indpls. Star, 1929-31, telegraph editor, dept. editor, 1933-43; editorial writer, columnist Indpls. Times, 1943-45; asso. editor Indpls. News, 1945, editorial dir., 1947-52; exec. editor Evansville Courier, 1952- 53, editor, 1954-57; dir. communications Mead Johnson & Co., 1957-60, community relations mgr., 1960-62; program dir. Mead Johnson & Co. Found., Inc., 1961-62; asso. sec. Riley Meml. Assn., 1962, exec. sec., 1962—. Bd. dirs. Community Council, 1958; exec. com. Vanderburgh County Tb Assn., 1958, 61-; trustee Fund for Advancement of Camping, 1965—; v.p. Vanderburgh County Community Chest, 1958; pres. of Evansville and Vanderburgh County United Fund, 1959; chmn. Bradford Woods adv. com. Ind. U. Recipient of the Blue Ribbon award Wallaces' Farm Editorial Contest, 1946, Sigma Delta Chi Distinguished Service award for editorial writing, 1946; Freedoms Found. George Washington Gold Medal, 1953. Mem. Ind. Soc. Assn. Execs., West Highland White Terrier Club of Am., Alpha Tau Omega, Sigma Delta Chi, Sigma Tau Delta, Pi Kappa Delta. Clubs: Rotary (pres. 1959), Indianapolis Literary (pres. 1967- 68), Indianapolis Press (pres. 1945), Columbia. Home: 6902 Mohawk Lane Indianapolis IN 46260 Office: Bd of Trade Bldg Indianapolis IN 46204

HILLMAN, JORDAN JAY, lawyer, educator; b. Waukegan, Ill., July 8, 1924; s. Louis and Della (Miller) H.; M.A. in Polit. Sci., U. Chgo., 1947, J.D., 1950; Dr. of Juridical Sci., Northwestern U., 1966; m. Jean Goodsitt, Mar. 3, 1947 (div. Feb. 1953); children—Deborah Jay, Amy Elizabeth; m. 2d, Karen Farnbacher, Nov. 20, 1955. Admitted to Ill. bar, 1950; mem. legal staff Ill. Commerce Commn., 1950-53; asst state's atty., appelate div. Cook County, Ill., 1953; with C. & N.-W. Ry., 1954-67, gen. counsel, 1963-67, v.p. law, 1966-67; prof. law Northwestern U., 1967—. Mem. Constn. Study Commn., State of Ill.; mem. zoning amendment com., Evanston, Ill., 1963-68; mem. Bd. Edn., Dist. 202, Evanston Twp. High Sch., 1968- -. Served to 1st lt. USAAF, 1943-45. Mem. Am., Ill., Chgo. (past chmn. com. constl. revision, past chmn. com. on civil rights bd. mgrs. 1970—) bar assns., Phi Beta Kappa. Jewish religion. Author: Competition and Railway Price Discrimination: Legal Precedent and Economic Policy, 1968. Home: 1024 Lake Shore Blvd Evanston IL 60202 Office: 357 E Chicago Av Chicago IL 60611

HILLMAN, MURRAY, bus. cons.; b. N.Y.C., Nov. 23, 1922; s. Abraham and Fannie (Worton) H.; B.B.A., Coll. City N.Y., 1942; M.B.A., Columbia, 1947; m. Harriet Chefetz, Sept. 14, 1946; children—Linda Ellen, Stephen Allan. Instr. statistics Coll. City N.Y., 1942-43, lectr., 1946; v.p. charge research Am. Mgmt. Counsel, Inc., 1946-49; mgr. mfrs. counsel div. Amos Parrish & Co., 1949—; pres. Adam Hat Stores, Inc., N.Y.C., 1953—; exec. v.p., dir. McCann Erickson, N.Y.C., 1967—; mng. dir. Strategy Workshop, 1969—. Served as 1st lt. USAAF, 1943-46. Mem. Am. Marketing Assn., Am. Econ. Assn., A.I.M. Contbr. articles tax jours. Home: 18 Carthage Rd Scarsdale NY 10583 Office: 485 Lexington Av New York City NY 10017

HILLMAN, RICHARD MCLEOD, steel co. exec.; b. Pitts., Sept. 20, 1914; s. Ernst and Clara (Gregg) H.; student Shadyside Acad., Pitts.; grad. Hotchkiss Sch., Lakeville, Conn., 1933; A.B., Williams Coll., 1937; m. Joan Walther, Nov. 6, 1943; children—Madeleine Clark, Richard Gregg, David McLeod. With Pitts. Steel Co., 1937—, beginning as mill employee, successively sales dept. trainee, staff treasury dept., asst. treas., 1937-52, treas., 1952-56, v.p., treas., 1956-58, v.p., sec., treas., 1958—, dir., adminstrv. vice pres., sec., treas., 1967-68 (Co. merged with Wheeling Steel Corp. 1968), exec. v.p., corporate treas., dir. Wheeling-Pitts. Steel Corp., 1968-70, exec. v.p. corp. and finance, 1970—; dir. of Dollar Savs. Bank, Schaefer Equipment Co., PBI Industries. Bd. dirs. Port Authority of Allegheny County; trustee Shadyside Hosp., Shadyside Acad., Chatham Coll. Served from ensign to lt. comdr. USNR, 1941-46. Clubs: Duquesne, Pittsburgh Golf, Fox Chapel Golf (Pitts.); Rolling Rock, Laurel Valley Golf (Ligonier, Pa.); Sky (N.Y.C.). Home: W Woodland Rd Pittsburgh PA 15232 Office: 1933 Gateway Center 4 Pittsburgh PA 15230

HILLMAN, STANLEY ERIC GORDON, mfg. co. exec.; b. London, Eng., Oct. 13, 1911; s. Percy Thomas and Margaret Eleanor Fanny (Lee) H.; ed. Holyrood Sch., also Tonbridge Sch., Eng.; m. May Irene Noon, May 2, 1947; children—Susan, Deborah, Katherine. Came to U.S., 1951, naturalized, 1957. With British-Am. Tobacco Co., Ltd., in London and Shanghai, 1933-47; dir. Hillman & Co., Ltd., Cosmos Trading Co., FED Inc., U.S.A., Airmotive Supplies Co. Ltd., Hong Kong, 1947-52; v.p. Gen. Dynamics Corp., 1953-61; v.p., group exec. Am. Machine & Foundry Co., N.Y.C., 1962-65; v.p. Gen. Am. Transp. Corp. 1965-67; exec. v.p. Ill. Central Industries, 1968—, also dir.; dir. United Life and Accident Ins. Co. of N.H., Abex Corp., N.Y.C., Pepsi Cola Gen. Bottlers. Mem. Soc. Automotive Engrs., Am. Mgmt. Assn., Air Force Assn., Am. Ordnance Assn., Navy League, Newcomen Soc. Clubs: Chicago, Executive (Chgo.); Onwentsia. Home: 1001 Hawthorne Pl Lake Forest IL 60045 Office: 135 E 11th Pl Chicago IL 60605

HILLS, GEORGE BURKHART, b. Chgo., May 5, 1890; s. George Adelbert and Louise (Burkhart) H.; B.S., Armour Inst. of Tech., Chgo., 1911, C.E., 1918; m. Anna Donna McEnery, 1912 (dec. Jan. 1941); children—Mace Banta (Mrs. Philip M. Travis), Mary Ann, George Burkhart, John Robert, Thomas Marion; m. 2d, Beatrix M. Riley, Dec. 1942. Member Reynolds Smith and Hills, architects and engrs., cons., 1969—. Mem. Newcomen Soc. N.A., Am. Soc. C.E., Am. Inst. Cons. Engrs., Nat. Soc. Profl. Engrs., Tau Beta Pi. Presbyn. Home: 8023 Philips Hwy Jacksonville FL 32216 Office: PO Box 4850 Jacksonville FL 32201

HILLS, GEORGE STROUGH, lawyer; b. Winter Park, Fla., Nov. 1, 1900; s. Elijah Clarence and Metta V. (Strough) H.; A.B., Ind. U., 1922; LL.B., Harvard, 1925; m. Alice G. Shaw, Sept. 14, 1926; children—Joan Lee, Alice Ann. Admitted to N.Y. bar, 1926, admitted U.S. Supreme Ct. 1936; mem. law firm Rogers, Hoge & Hills; sec., gen. counsel Sterling Drug, Inc.; dir. and sec. Bacardi Corp.; dir. Am. Machine & Foundry Co.; dir. Raymond Internat., Inc. Mem. Assn.

Bar City N.Y., Am. Bar Assn., Am. Law Inst., Beta Theta Pi. Clubs: Union League (N.Y.C.); Larchmont (N.Y.) Yacht; University (Washington). Author: The Law of Accounting and Financial Statements, 1957. Contbr. numerous articles on corp. law in various pubs. Home: 396 Forest Av New Rochelle NY 10804 Office: 90 Park Av New York City NY 10016

HILLS, LEE, publisher; b. Granville, N.D., May 28, 1906; s. Louis Amos and Lulu Mae (Loomis) H.; student Brigham Young U., 1924-25, U. Mo., 1927-29; grad., Oklahoma City U. Sch. Law, 1934; Sc.D. in Bus. Adminstrn., Cleary Coll., 1958; L.H.D. (hon.), U. Utah, 1969; LL.D., Eastern Mich. U., 1969; m. Eileen Whitman, June 4, 1948 (dec. 1961); 1 son (by previous marriage), Ronald Lee, 1 stepdau., Toni Terry (Mrs. Carl Griffith); m. 2d, Tina S. Ramos, Oct. 31, 1963. News reporter News-Advocate, Price, Utah, 1924-25, editor, 1926; reporter Oklahoma City Times, 1929-32; polit. writer Okla. News, 1932-35, editor, 1938-39; reporter, copyreader Cleve. Press, 1935-36; chief editorial writer, asso. editor Indpls. Times, 1936-37; asso. editor Memphis Press- Scimitar, 1939-40; news editor Cleve. Press, 1940-42; mng. editor, Miami (Fla.) Herald, 1942-51, exec. editor, 1951-66, asso. pub., 1966-69, pub., 1970—; exec. editor Detroit Free Press, 1951-69; leave as war corr., Europe, 1945; pub. Detroit Free Press, 1963—, pres., 1967—; exec. editor Knight Newspapers, Inc., 1959- 66, exec. v.p., 1966-67, pres., 1967—, chmn. exec. com., 1969—. Admitted Okla. bar, 1935. Pres. Detroit Arts Commn.; trustee Founders Soc., Detroit Inst. of Arts; trustee Washington Journalism Center. Awarded Maria Moors Cabot Gold medal for distinguished contbn. Inter- Am. Relations, Columbia, 1946; Pulitzer prize in journalism, 1956. Mem. Internat. Press Inst., Inter-Am. (dir., pres. 1967-68), Mich. press assns., Am. Soc. Newspaper Editors (pres. 1962-63), Am. Newspaper Pubs. Assn., AP Mng. Editors Assn. (past pres.), Fla. AP Assn. (past pres.), United Found. (dir.), Sigma Delta Chi (past pres.). Clubs: National Press; Detroit Athletic, Detroit, Hundred, Grosse Pointe (Detroit); Miami, Bath and Surf (Miami, Fla.). Home: 4450 Banyan Lane Miami FL 33137 also 321 W Lafayette Blvd Detroit MI 48226 Office: Miami Herald Miami FL 33101 also Detroit Free Press Detroit MI 48231

HILLS, REUBEN WILMARTH, III, coffee mfr.; b. Oakland, Cal., Aug. 4, 1923; s. Reuben Wilmarth, Jr., and Everard (Hunt) H.; B.S., Stanford U., 1944; m. Marilyn Mattke, June 27, 1966; children—Heidi, Mart, Vaughn. Asst. to pres. Hills Bros. Coffee, Inc., San Francisco, 1946-54, v.p., 1954-60, pres., chmn.bd., 1960—; dir. Cal. Canadian Bank. Advisor to U.S. Dept. of State, 1960-65, to U.S. delegation to UN Econ. and Social Council on Internat. Coffee Agreement, 1962. Active San Francsico Opera Assn., Cal. Acad. Sci., Cal. Hist. Soc., Nat. Audubon Soc., Conferie des Chevaliers due Tastevin, DeYoung Mus. Soc. Trustee San Francisco Children's Hosp. and Adult Med. Center; pres., chmn. bd. trustees Edward E. Hills Fund. Served to 1st lt., AUS, World War II; PTO. Mem. Nat. (dir.), Pacific Coast (past pres.) coffee assns., Indsl. Conf. Bd., Grocery Mfrs. Assn., Stanford Affiliates, Phi Delta Theta. Clubs: Pacific Union, Burlingame Country, San Francisco Golf (San Francisco). Office: 2 Harrison St San Francisco CA 94119

HILLS, ROBERT CHADWICK, metallurgist; b. New Orleans, Jan. 3, 1909; s. Thomas Chadwick and Sophie (Hoehn) H.; B.S., Tulane U., 1932; M.S., Cornell, 1934; m. Dorothy Fleury, Nov. 25, 1936; children—Anne, John Fleury, Thomas Chadwick. Chief metallurgist Nicaro Nickel Co., 1942-44, metall. mgr., 1944-46, v.p., 1950-55, exec. v.p. and dir., 1955-61; chemist Freeport Sulphur Co., 1934-37, supt. lab., 1937-42, asst. to pres., 1946-50, dir. devel. v.p., 1950-55, exec. v.p., dir., 1955-61, pres., dir., 1961-69, former chmn. exec. com., chief exec. officer, dir. subsidiaries. Gov. Tulane Med. Center; trustee Lenox Hill Hosp., N.Y.C. Mem. Soc. of Chem. Industry, Am. Inst. of Mining and Metall. Engrs., Am. Chem. Soc., Mining and Metall. Soc. Am., Council Fgn. Relations, Sigma Xi, Sigma Gamma Epsilon, Kappa Sigma. Democrat. Clubs: Univeristy (N.Y.C.); Pickwick, Round Table (New Orleans). Home: 579 Woodvine Av Metairie LA 70005 Office: Commerce Bldg New Orleans LA 70160

HILLS, RODERICK M., lawyer; b. Seattle, Mar. 9, 1931; A.B., Stanford, 1952, LL.B., 1955. Admitted to Cal. bar, 1957, U.S. Supreme Ct. bar, 1960; law clk. to justice U.S. Supreme Ct., 1955-57; now mem. firm Munger, Tolles, Hills & Richerhauser. Vis. prof. law Harvard, 1969-70; lectr. law Stanford, 1960—. Mem. Am., Los Angeles County bar assns., State Bar Cal.; Order of Coif, Phi Delta Phi. Club: Chancery. Mem. bd. editors, comment editor Stanford Law Rev., 1953-55. Office: Western Fed Bldg 606 S Hill St Los Angeles CA 90014*

HILLWAY, TYRUS, educator, author; b. Mpls., Jan. 5, 1912; s. William H. and Martha (Milbrett) H.; A.B., Willamette U., 1934; M.A., U. Cal., 1939; Ph.D., Yale, 1944; post-grad. U. Ore., 1934, Harvard, 1942; m. Hazel Andrews, Aug. 28, 1937; children—Holly Ann, Richard Andrews. Tchr., Ore. State Sch. for Blind, Salem, 1934-38; bus. experience, Berkeley, Cal., 1938- 40; dean evening div. Hillyer Coll., Hartford, Conn., 1940-44; dir. ednl. counseling and planning Bridgeport (Conn.) Program Postwar Readjustment, 1944-46; pres. Mitchell Coll., New London, Conn., 1946-51; asso. prof. edn. U. No. Colo., Greeley, 1951-54, prof. edn., 1954-66, asst. to pres., 1966-69, prof. higher edn., 1966—, dir. of acad. devel., 1969—; Fulbright guest prof. U. Vienna (Austria), 1964-65, 70-71; guest prof. U. Salzburg, Austria, 1970-71. Mem. U.S. Mil. Manpower Com. Former pres. Conn. Conf. Jr. Colls.; mem. com. standards Conn. Council Higher Edn., 1946-51; mem. com. accreditation New Eng. Jr. Coll. Council, 1948-51; mem. adv. com. Conn. Gov's Commn. Edn., 1949-50; Conn. state chmn. Am. Youth Hostels, 1947. Trustee Estes Park Center for Edn. and Research, Austro-America Inst. of Edn. Am. Philos. Soc. research grantee, 1959, 61, 64. Mem. Soc. Advancement Edn., Modern Lang. Assn. Am., Melville Soc. (co-founder, sec. 1945-59, pres. 1960), Citizens Com. Hoover Report, Yale Library Assos., Sigma Chi. Author: Melville and the Whale, 1950; (play) Captain Ahab; Introduction to Research, 1956, rev., 1964; American Two-Year College, 1958; Education in American Society, 1961; Herman Melville, 1963; Handbook of Educational Research, 1969. Editor: (with Luther S. Manfield) Moby Dick Centennial Essays, 1953; American Education, 1964. Contbr. to lit. anthologies, periodicals, and Ency. Americana (articles on Herman Melville); Collier's Ency. Authority on life and work of Herman Melville. Home: 1127 16th St Greeley CO 80631

HILLY, JOHN CHRYSOSTOM, lawyer, r.r. exec.; b. N.Y.C., Jan. 11, 1914; s. Arthur Joseph and Ismay (Neary) H.; LL.B., Fordham U., 1939; m. Eileen T. Campbell, Oct. 8, 1934; children—Joseph C., Sean P. Auditor, Dept. Internal Revenue, 1935- 41; admitted to N.Y. bar, 1939; asst. U.S. atty. criminal div., So. Dist. N.Y., 1941-50; exec. v.p. Security Bur., Inc., N.Y.C., 1950-53, now dir.; now traffic mgr., pres., dir., Bush Terminal Co., N.Y.C.; v.p., dir. Bush Terminal R.R. Co., Hamilton Watch Co. Mgmt. rep. curriculum Inst. Commerce and Law Enforcement, Grad. Sch. N.Y.U., 1950—. Mem. Nat. Def. Transp. Assn., Warehousemen's Assn. Port of N.Y. (dir.), Bar Assn. City N.Y., N.Y. State Dist. Attys. Assn., Cath. Lawyers Guild, Maritime Assn. Port of N.Y., Sons of Xavier. Roman Catholic. K.C. Clubs: Clements; Whitehall; Propeller. Home: 245 W 107th St New York City NY 10025 Office 100 Broad St New York City NY 10004

HILLYER, RAPHAEL, violist; b. Ithaca, N.Y.; student Curtis Inst. Music; B.A., Dartmouth; M.A., Harvard. Formerly mem. Boston Symphony and NBC Symphony, also Stradivarius and NBC string quartets; mem. Symphony of the Air; violist Juilliard String Quartet, 1946—; mem. chamber music and viola faculty Juilliard Sch. Music, from 1946.*

HILPERT, ELMER ERNEST, educator; b. Bertha, Minn., Dec. 30, 1905; s. Theodore and Emma (Paschke) H.; A.B., U. Minn., 1929, A.M., 1931; LL.B., Western Res. U., 1936; J.S.D., Yale (Sterling fellow, grad. sch. of law, 1936- 37), 1939; m. Brunette Powers, Aug. 1, 1938; childrenMargaret Ray, Elmer Ernest. Teacher, elementary schs., Verndale, Minn., 1922-23, Elk River, Minn., 1923-24, Hewitt, Minn., 1924-25; principal, Vergas, Minn., 1925-26; teaching fellow in polit. sci. U. Minn., 1930; instr. in polit. sci. Western Res. U., 1930-37, asst. prof. law, 1938-39; asst. prof. law La. State U., 1937-38; asso. prof. law Washington U., St. Louis, 1939-41, prof. law since 1941; admitted to Ohio bar 1936, Mo. bar, 1944; practiced law in St. Louis, 1944-46 (part- time) with Thomas F. McDonald and McDonald, Bartlett & Muldoon arbitrator in various indsl. disputes, 1941—; panel mem. Am. Arbitration Assn., Fed. Mediation and Consiliation Service; Nat. Acad. Arbitrators; compliance commr. Wage Stabilization Bd., 1951-52; staff mem. of Bur. for Research in Govt. U. of Minn., part time, 1928-30; staff mem. Nat. Inst. of Pub. Adminstrn., N.Y.C., summer, fall, 1929; dir. of research Regional Govt. Com. of Greater Cleve., summer, fall, 1934. Participator in civic campaigns. Specialist in adminstrv. and constl. law, labor law, labor relations; impartial referee Allis-Chalmers Mfg. Co.-UAW, AFL-CIO, 1953-58, 60-64. Mem. Am., Mo. (various coms.), St. Louis (various com.) bar assns., Indsl. Relations Research Assn., Am. Assn. U. Profs., Mo. Welfare League (mem. bd.), Order of the Coif, Phi Beta Kappa. Club: University. Co-author: Missouri Practice Methods, 1953, rev. edit., 2 vols., 1969. Opinions as arbitrator in American Labor Arbitration Awards and Labor Arbitration Reports; contbr. articles in law jours. Home: 6321 Pershing Av St Louis MO 63130

HILSMAN, ROGER, educator; b. Waco, Tex., Nov. 23, 1919; s. Roger and Emma (Prendergast) H.; B.S., U.S. Mil. Acad., 1943; M.A., Yale, 1950, Ph.D., 1951; m. Eleanor Willis Hoyt, June 22, 1946; children—Hoyt R., Amy, Ashby, Sarah. Commd. 2d lt. U.S. Army, 1943, advanced through grades to maj., 1951; with Merrill's Marauders, Burma, 1944; comdg. officer OSS guerrilla group in Burma, 1944-45; asst. chief Far East intelligence operations, Hdqrs. OSS, Washington, 1945-46; spl. asst. to exec. officer CIA, 1946-47; planning officer NATO affairs, Joint Am. Mil. Adv. Group, London, Eng., 1950-52, internat. politics br. Hdqrs. U.S. European Command, 1952-53; resigned, 1953; research fellow Center Internat. Studies, Princeton, 1953-54, research asst., 1954-55, research asso., also lectr. Woodrow Wilson Sch., lectr. internat. relations Columbia, 1958; research asso. Washington Center Fgn. Policy Research, also lectr. internat. affaris Sch. Advanced Internat. Studies, Johns Hopkins, 1957-61; prof. govt. Columbia, 1964—; chief fgn. affairs div., legislative reference service Library Congress, 1956-58, dep. dir. for research, 1958-61; dir. bur. intelligence and research State Dept., 1961-63; asst. sec. state Far Eastern affairs, 1963-64; lectr. Nat. War Coll., Army War Coll., Indsl. Coll. Armed Forces. Recipient Rockefeller fellowship, 1958. Mem. Am. Polit. Sci. Assn. (pres. D.C.). Author: Strategic Intelligence and National Decisions, 1956; To Move a Nation, 1967. Co-author: Military Policy and National Security, 1956; Alliance Policy in the Cold War, 1959; NATO and American Security, 1959; Foreign Policy in the Sixties, 1965; The Politics of Policy Making in Defense and Foreign Affairs, 1971. Home: 448 Riverside Dr New York City NY 10027

HILSTON, NEAL WILLIAM, coll. dean; born Warren, O., Apr. 25, 1913; s. Charles William and Wilhelmina (Lundy) H.; B.S., W.Va. U., 1934; M.S., Pa. State U., 1935, Ph.D., 1937; m. Gertrude Herrick Cullinan, Aug. 14, 1935; children—Suzanne Ila, Neal William. Mem. faculty U. Wyo. since 1945, head dept. animal prodn., 1949-58, dean Coll. Agr., dir. Wyo. Agrl. Expt. Sta., 1958—, dir. agrl. extension service, 1964—. Mem. Newcomen Soc. Am., Sigma Xi, Phi Kappa Phi, Gamma Sigma Delta, Alpha Zeta, Delta Tau Delta. Lutheran. Elk, Moose. Author articles. Home: 716 University Av Laramie WY 82070

HILTNER, SEWARD, clergyman; b. Tyrone, Pa., Nov. 26, 1909; s. Clement S. and Charlotte (Porter) H.; A.B., Lafayette Coll., 1931; Div. Sch., U. Chgo., 1931-35; Ph.D., U. Chgo.; D.D., Lafayette Coll.; m. Helen Margaret Johansen, May 29, 1936; children—James Seward (dec.), Anne Porter. Sec. Westminster Found., U. Chgo., 1933-35; exec. sec., Council for Clin. Tng. of Theol. Students, 1935-38; exec. sec. Dept. of Pastoral Services, Fed. Council of Chs. of Christ in Am., 1938-50; asso. prof. pastoral theology U. Chgo., 1950, then prof.; prof. theology and personality Princeton (N.J.) Theol. Sem., 1961—; Alfred P. Sloan vis. prof. Menninger Sch. Psychiatry, 1957, hon. alumnus, 1970; Fulbright research scholar, New Zealand, 1958-59; vis. prof. U. Utrecht (Holland), 1970. Cons. The Menninger Found. 1957—. Recipient Ann. award Acad. Religion and Mental Health, 1966. Fellow Nat. Council Religion in Higher Edn.; mem. Phi Beta Kappa, Phi Gamma Delta. Presbyn. Author: Religion and Health, 1943; Pastoral Counseling, 1949; Self-Understanding, 1951; The Counselor in Couseling,1952; Sex Ethics and the Kinsey Reports, 1953; Sex and the Christian Life, 1957; Preface to Pastoral Theology, 1958; The Christian Shepherd, 1959; (with Lowell G. Colston) The Context of Pastoral Counseling, 1961; (with Karl Menninger) Constructive Aspects of Anxiety, 1963; Ferment in the Ministry, 1969; (with James L. Adams) Pastoral Care in the Liberal Churches, 1970. Editor: Christianity and Mental Hygiene, 1939; Clinical Pastoral Training, 1945. Mem. editorial bd. Jour. Religion and Health, Theology Today, Am. Image, Quar. Jour. Studies on Alcohol, Medical Aspects of Human Sexuality, Scholars Choice, Pastoral Psychology mag., Sexual Behavior, Life Threatening Behavior. Office: Princeton Theol Sem Princeton NJ 08540

HILTNER, WILLIAM ALBERT, astronomer; b. Continental, O., Aug. 27, 1914; s. John Nicholas and Ida Lavina (Schafer) H.; B.S., U. Toledo, 1937; M.S., U. Mich., 1938, Ph.D., 1942; m. Ruth Moyer Kreider, Aug. 12, 1939; children—Phyllis Anne, Kathryn Jo, William Albert, Stephen Kreider. Mem. faculty U. Chgo., 1943- 70, prof. astronomy, 1955-70, dir. Yerkes Obs., 1963-66, acting dir. Cerro Tololo Inter-Am. Obs., 1966-67; prof., chmn. dept. astronomy U. Mich., Ann Arbor, 1970—. Bd. dirs. Assn. Univs. for Research Astronomy, 1959-71, pres. bd., 1968-71. NRC fellow, 1942-43. Mem. Astron. Soc. Pacific, Am. Astron. Soc. (councilor 1962-65), A.A.A.S. Co-author: Photometric Atlas of Stellar Spectra, 1946. Editor: Astronomical Techniques, 1962. Home: 801 Berkshire Ann Arbor MI 48104

HILTON, ANDREW CARSON, mfg. co. exec.; b. D'Lo, Miss., Nov. 20, 1928; s. A.C. and Pearl (Walters) H.; B.A., U. Md., 1952; M.A., George Washington U., 1953; Ph.D., Western Res. U. Formerly research asso. Personnel Research Inst., Western Res. U.; cons. Psychol. Corp., N.Y.C.; dir. personnel relations Raytheon Co.; then dir. personnel Internat. Tel. & Tel. Corp.; v.p. Colt Industries Inc., N.Y.C., 1963-68, v.p. adminstrn., 1968—. Corporate trustee Colt Industries Found.; bd. overseers Case Western Res. U. Served with USAF, 1946-49. Mem. Am. Psychol. Assn., N.Y. Acad. Scis. Club: University (N.Y.C.). Author articles in field. Office: 430 Park Av New York City NY 10022

HILTON, BARRON, hotel exec.; b. 1927; s. Conrad Hilton. Founder, pres. San Diego Chargers, Am. Football League, until 1966; v.p., Hilton Hotels Corp., 1954, pres., chief exec. officer, 1966—, also dir.; mem. gen. adminstrv. bd. Mfrs. Hanover Trust Co., N.Y.C.; dir. Eversharp, Inc., M S L Industries, Inc., Metro-Goldwyn-Mayer, Inc., Los Angeles. Office: 720 S Michigan Av Chicago IL 60605*

HILTON, CONRAD N., hotel exec.; b. San Antonio, N.M., Dec. 25, 1887; s. August H. and Mary (Laufersweiler) H.; ed., N.M. Mil. Inst., 1900-01, 02-04; St. Michael's Coll., Santa Fe, N.M. 1901-02; N.M. Sch. of Mines Socorro, 1907-09; LL.D., U. Detroit, 1953, Adelphi Coll., 1957, N.M. Coll. Archtl. and Mech. Arts, 1957; Litt.D., DePaul U., 1954, Sophia U., Tokyo, 1963; L.H.D., Barat Coll. Sacred Heart, 1955; m. Mary Barron, 1925; children—Conrad Nicholson (dec.), William Barron, Eric Michael; m. 2d, Sari Gabor. Partner of father in mercantile bus.; organizer, cashier, later pres., 1922, N.M. State Bank, San Antonio; rep. in 1st State Legislature, N.M., 1912-13; built Hilton Hotel, Dallas, 1925, and Hilton Hotels in Waco, Longview, Plainview, Lubbock, El Paso and Marlin, Tex., 1926-31; chmn. Hilton Hotels Corp.; chmn. Hilton Internat. Co.; chmn. bd. Hilton-Burns Hotels Co., Inc., 1965—; chmn. of Hotel Waldorf Astoria Corp., owners, operators hotels major U.S. and fgn. cities. Served 1st R.O.T.C., Presidio, Cal., 1917; served A.E.F. as lt., Q.M. Corps. Recipient Brotherhood award Nat. Conf. Christians and Jews; decorated Chevalier de la Legion d'Honneur (France); Order Ruben Dario (Nicaragua), Knight Comdr. in the Order of Merit (Italy); Knight Sovereign Mil. Order of Malta. Elk. Author: Be My Guest, 1957. Home: 10644 Bellagio Rd Bel-Air Los Angeles CA 90024 Office: 9990 Santa Monica Blvd Beverly Hills CA 90212

HILTON, HOWARD JUDD, univ. educator; b. Albuquerque, Mar. 15 1919; s. Howard Judd and Zella (Thurman) H.; B.A., U. Wash., 1942; M.A., Am. U., 1947; Ph.D., George Washington U., 1967; m. Mary L. Nelson, Apr. 22, 1943; children—Howard Nelson, Mary Alice, Richard Judd. Asst. liaison officer Office Lend Lease Adminstrn., also Fgn. Econ. Adminstrn., 1942-44; div. asst. State Dept., 1944-45, country specialist, 1945-47; asst. attache Am. embassy, Budapest, 1947-49; assigned State Dept., 1949, div. asst., 1949-52, internat. economist, 1952-53, internat. relations officer, 1953-55, cons. sec., 1955; 1st sec., consul, Am. embassy, Bonn, 1955-60; asst. chief div. Devel. Assistance Com., AID, 1960-63; chief IBRD div. Internat. Devel. Orgns., AID, 1963-67; prof. social sci. and econs. Pa. State U., Capitol campus, Middletown, 1967—. Dir., cons. Disc, Inc., 1967-69; chmn. bd. Internat. Information Utility, Inc., Hilmac United Corp.; dir. Internat. Scientific Labs. Inc. Exec. sec. Devel. Assistance Group, 1960, mem. U.S. delegations, 1961-67; chmn. Ad Hoc Task Group Legal Aspect Involved in Nat. Information Systems COSATI; Fed. Council for Sci. and Tech., 1967, chmn. copyright Subpanel COSATI panel 7. Mem. Am. Soc. for Information Sci. (chmn. copyright com. 1968). Club: Kenwood Golf and Country, International. Author: Unique Code for Identification of Recorded Knowledge and Information; also articles on internat. devels. Home: 281 W Main St Middletown PA 17057 also Hilmac Farms Landisburg PA 17040 and 5022 Reno Rd Washington DC 20015

HILTON, MARY NELSON, govt. ofcl.; b. Junction City, Ore., Nov. 22, 1914; d. Charles R. and Della (Myhre) Nelson; student Willamette U., 1932-34; B.A., U. Ore., 1936, M.A., 1941; m. Howard J. Hilton, Apr. 22, 1943; children—Howard Nelson, Mary Alice, Richard Judd. Grad. asst. econs. U. Ore., 1936-38, research asst. Bur. Municipal Research, 1938-39; jr. economist Maritime Labor Bd., 1939-40; asst. economist wage and hour div. Dept. Labor, 1940- 41; div. chief NWLB, 1941-46; chief research div., Women's Bur., Dept. Labor, 1949-55, chief sect. area unemployment and labor force surveys Bur. Labor Statistics, 1955, br. chief div. fgn. labor conditions, 1960- 62; spl. asst. Pres.'s Commn. on Status of Women, 1962-63; dep. dir. Women's Bur., Dept. Labor, 1965—. Chmn. Am. Women's Group, Bonn, Germany, 1958-60. Recipient Pres.'s Commn. on Status Women Distinguished Service award, 1963. Mem. Am. Econ. Assn., Phi Beta Kappa. Home: 5022 Reno Rd NW Washington DC 20008 Office: Dept of Labor Washington DC 20210

HILTON, PETER, advt. exec.; b. N.Y.C., Mar. 22, 1913; s. Augustine J. and Dorothy (Connolly) H.; student Columbia, 1931-32; m. Rita Williamson, Feb. 22, 1936; children—Nancy, Pamela. With Lord & Thomas, 1930-34; advt. mgr. Nat. Hotel Mgmt. Co., 1934-38; v.p. Maxon, Inc., 1938-47; with Peter Hilton, Inc., 1947-50; pres. Hilton & Riggio, Inc., N.Y.C., 1950- 58, Kastor, Hilton, Chesley, Clifford & Atherton, Inc., 1958-66; chmn., dir. Kastor, Hilton, Chesley, Clifford & Atherton, Ltd., 1957-66; pres. Corporate Diversification, Ltd., 1966—. Founder, pres. New Products Inst. Cons. Small Bus. Adminstrn., Washington. Bd. regents St. Peter's Coll., Jersey City. Decorated Knight of Malta. Mem. Assn. for Corporate Growth (founder, pres.), Young Pres.'s Orgn. (sec.), Chief Execs. Forum (pres.). Clubs: Metropolitan (N.Y.C.); Dorset (Vt.) Field; Ekwanok Golf (Manchester, Vt.). Author: New Product Guide Book, 1947; Handbook for New Product Development, 1961; Keeping Old Products New, 1967; Planning Corporate Growth and Diversification, 1969. Contbr. periodicals. Home: Hudson House Ardsley-on-Hudson NY 10503 also Dorset VT 05251 Office: 405 Lexington Av New York City NY 10017

HILTON, PETER JOHN, mathematician, educator; b. London, Eng., Apr. 7, 1923; s. Mortimer and Elizabeth (Freedman) H.; M.A., Oxford (Eng.) U., 1948; D.Phil., 1950; Ph.D., Cambridge (Eng.) U., 1952; m. Margaret Mostyn, Sept. 14, 1949; children—Nicholas, Timothy. Lectr., Manchester (Eng.) U., 1948-52, sr. lectr., 1956-58; lectr. Cambridge U., 1952-55; Mason prof. pure math. Birmingham (Eng.) U., 1958-62; prof. math. Cornell U., 1962—; guest prof. Eidgenössiche Technische Hochschule, Zurich, Switzerland, 1966-67, Courant Inst. Math. Scis., N.Y.U., 1967-68; vis. fellow Battelle Seattle Research Center, 1970-71. Co-chmn., Cambridge Conf. on Sch. Math., 1965. Mem. Am. Math. Soc., Math. Assn. Am. Math. Soc. Belgium (hon.), London Math. Soc., Cambridge Philos. Soc. Author: Homotopy Theory, 1953; (with S. Wylie) Homology Theory, 1960; Homotopy Theory and Duality, 1966; (with H.B. Griffiths) Classical Mathematics, 1970; General Cohomology Theory and K. Theory, 1971; Editor: Ergenbnisse der Mathematik, 1964—, Ill. Jour. Math., 1962-68, Jour. Pure and Applied Algebra, 1970—, Topics in Modern Topology, 1968. Contbr. articles profl. jours. Home: 132 N Sunset Dr Ithaca NY 14850

HILTON, RONALD, educator; b. Torquay, Eng., July 31, 1911; s. Robert and Elizabeth Alice (Taylor) H.; B.A., Oxford U., Eng., 1933, M.A., 1936; student Sorbonne, Paris, 1933-34, U. Madrid, 1934-35, U. of Perugia, Italy, 1935-36, U. Calif. (Commonwealth Fund fellow), 1937-39; m. Mary Bowie, May 1, 1939; 1 dau., Mary Alice Taylor. Came to U.S., 1937; naturalized, 1946. Dir. Comité Hispano Ingleés Library, Madrid, 1936; asst. prof. modern langs. U. of B.C., 1939-41; asso. prof. Romanic langs. Stanford, 1942-49, prof., 1949—, dir. Inst. Hispanic Am. and Luso-Brazilian studies; hon. prof. U. de San Marcos, Lima, Peru; vis. prof. U. of Brazil, 1949; cultural dir. U. of the

Air, KGEI, San Francisco. Founder exec. dir. Cal. Inst. Internat. Studies. Officer, Cruzeiro do Sul (Brazil). Author: Campoamor, Spain and the World, 1940; Handbook of Hispanic Source Materials in the U.S., 1942, 2d edit., 1956; Four Studies in Franco-Spanish Relations, 1943; La Amèrica Latina de Ayer y de Hoy, 1970; The Scientific Institutions of Latin America, 1970. Asso. editor for Southern Republics, Who's Who in America. Editor Who's Who in Latin America. Editor, Hispanic Am. Report, The Life of Joaquim Nabuco, 1950; The Movement Toward Latin American Unity, 1969. Mem. Am. Assn. Tchrs. Spanish, Hispanic Soc. of Am., Am. Acad. of Franciscan History. Home: 766 Santa Ynez St Stanford CA 94305

HILTZ, JOHN PHILIP, Jr., r.r. exec.; b. Balt., Sept. 8, 1911; s. John P. and Nora D. (Copper) H.; student Balt. Poly. Inst., 1929, Harvard, 1952; B.S., Carnegie Inst. Tech., 1934; m. Beatrice B. Farmer, Apr. 13, 1940; 1 son, John Philip III; m. 2d, Dorothy E. O'Donnell, Aug. 12, 1967; stepchildren—Gretchen, Cecilia, John, Thomas Freund. Structural engr., designer Fireproof Products Co., Charleston, W.Va., 1929-31; asst. in engring. corps Pa. R.R., 1934-45, Jamaica, L.I., 1945; engr. track D., L.&W. R.R., Scranton, Pa., 1945-48, engr. maintenance of way, 1948-53; chief engr. maintenance of way N.Y.C.R.R., N.Y.C., 1953-55: v.p., dir. N.J. Rwy., 1959; gen. mgr. D.& H. R.R., 1955-56, v.p. operations and maintenance, 1956-62, pres., gen. mgr., 1962-67, pres., chief exec. officer, 1967, also dir.; bd. mgrs. D. & H. Co.; v.p., dir. Napierville Junction Ry. Co., 1959-62, pres., gen. mgr., 1962-67; chmn. Nat. Ry. Labor Conf., 1967—, dir. Blue Cross Hosp. Service, Albany, N.Y., Nat. Comml. Bank and Trust Co. Mem. Assn. Am. R.R. (dir.), Am. R.R. Engrs. Assn., Sigma Nu, Tau Beta Pi, Phi Kappa Phi. Mason. Clubs: Fort Orange (Albany); Traffic, Canadian (N.Y.C.); Mount Stephen (Montreal, Can.); Union League (Chgo.); Metropolitan, University (Washington); Seigniory (Montebello, Que., Can.). Home: 1306 Bishop Lane Alexandria VA 22302 Office: 1225 Connecticut Av NW Washington DC 20036

HIMES, CHESTER BOMAR, author; b. Jefferson City, Mo., July 29, 1909; s. Joseph Sandy and Estelle (Bomar) H.; student Ohio State U., 1926-27; m. Jean Lucinda Johnson, Aug. 13, 1937. Rosenwald fellow creative writing, 1944-45. Author: If He Hollers Let Him Go, 1945; Lonely Crusade U.S.A., 1947; Cast The First Stone, U.S.A., 1952; The Third Generation, U.S.A., 1954; The Primitive, U.S.A., 1956; Pinktoes, 1965; Cotton Comes to Harlem, 1968; The Heat's On, 1968; Run Man Run, 1968; Blind Man With a Pistol, 1969; Hot Day, Hot Night; also numerous articles. Address: Casa Groit Pla Del Mar Moraira Alicante Spain

HIMMELFARB, GERTRUDE, (Mrs. Irving Kristol), author, educator; b. N.Y.C., Aug. 8, 1922; d. Max and Bertha (Lerner) Himmelfarb; B.A., Bklyn. Coll., 1942; M.A., U. Chgo., 1944, Ph.D., 1950; m. Irving Kristol, Jan. 18, 1942; children—William, Elizabeth. Prof. history dept. Bklyn. Coll., also City U. N.Y., 1965-. Recipient Rockefeller Found. award, 1962-63; Guggenheim fellow, 1955-56, 57-58; sr. fellowship Nat. Endowment for Humanities, 1968-69. Mem. Am. Hist. Assn., Conf. on Brit. Studies. Author: Lord Acton: A Study in Conscience and Politics, 1952; Darwin and the Darwinian Revolution, 1959; Victorian Minds, 1961. Office: City Univ 33 W 42d St New York City NY 10036

HIMMELMAN, L.P., hotel chain exec.; b. Mankato, Minn., 1912; grad. Cornell U., 1933. Pres., dir. Western Internat. Hotels Co., Western Internat. Hotels, Ltd., Hotel Benson; dir. Farmers New World Life Ins. Co. Mem. Am. Hotel & Motel Assn. (dir.), Societe d'Etudes (dir.). Home: 1919 Shenandoah Dr Seattle WA 98102 Office: Olympic Hotel Seattle WA 98111*

HIMMELSBACH, CLIFTON KECK, univ. dean; b. Phila., Mar. 17, 1907; s. Adam Jones and Blanche Gertrude (Keck) H.; M.D., U. Va., 1931; fellow pharmacology, Western Res. U., 1933; m. Virginia Thurmond Martin, Nov. 28, 1928 (dec. 1959); 1 son, Robert Peale; m. 2d, Kathryn Kilgour Kilian, June 15, 1961; 1 stepdau., Nina Louise Kilian. Intern USPHS Hosp., New Orleans, 1931-32; commd. USPHS, 1932, med. dir., 1949; clin. research drug addiction Ft. Leavenworth, Kan., Pondville, Mass., Lexington, Ky., 1933-44; clin. dir. USPHS Hosp., Lexington, 1938-39, dir. research, 1940-44; with NIH, Bethesda, Md., 1944-45; regional med. cons. Office Vocational Rehab., Kansas City, Mo., and Chgo., 1945-47; med. officer charge USPHS outpatient clinic, Washington, 1948-53; asst. chief, then chief div. hosps., USPHS, 1953-57; dir. spl. programs, div. research grants NIH, 1957-59, asso. dir. clin. center, 1959-65; asso. dean (research) Georgetown U. Sch.'s of Medicine and Dentistry, Washington, 1965—, prof. community medicine and internat. health, 1966—, adminstr. sponsored programs, 1970—. Chmn. com. infections hosps. Am. Hosp. Assn., 1961-70, mem. council on planning, 1969—. Recipient USPHS Meritorious Service award. Fellow A.C.P.; mem. Council Med. Adminstrs. (pres. 1961), S.A.R., Sigma Xi, Phi Beta Pi. Author articles pharmacology, drug addiction, hosp. infections. Home: 3731 Harrison St NW Washington DC 20015

HINCHLIFF, JAMES DONOHUE, banker; b. New Haven, July 4, 1915; s. William and Florence (Donohue) H.; B.A., Yale, 1938; M.B.A., Harvard, 1940; m. Mae Bliss, 1945; 1 son, William Bliss. With No. Trust Co., Chgo., 1940—, v.p., 1955-68, sr. v.p., 1968—. Bd. dirs. Chgo. Tennis Patrons. Served to maj., F.A., AUS, 1941-45. Mem. Chgo. Assn. Commerce and Industry (dir.). Clubs: Chicago, University, Yale (Chgo.); Indian Hill (Winnetka). Home: 616 Ridge Rd Winnetka IL 60093 Office: 50 S LaSalle St Chicago IL 60690

HINCHLIFFE, STEPHEN FREEMAN, Jr., mfg. co. exec.; b. Los Angeless, July 18, 1933; s. Stephen Freeman and Katherine Morris (Gruettner) H.; B.A., Occidental Coll., 1955; M.B.A. with distinction, Harvard, 1957; m. Ann Louise Hoffmann, June 7, 1956; children—Lisa, Stephen, John. Asso., McKinsey & Co., Inc, Los Angeles, 1960-64; chief exec. officer The Leisure Group, Inc., Los Angeles, 1964—. Bd. dirs. Met. YMCA, Los Angeles. Alumni trustee Occidental Coll. Served to lt. AUS, 1957-60. Mem. Mchts. and Mfrs. Assn. Los Angeles (dir.). Home: 3825 Paseo Del Campo Palos Verdes Estates CA 90274 Office: 445 S Figueroa St Los Angeles CA 90017

HINCKLE, WARREN JAMES III, mag. editor; b. San Francisco, Oct. 12, 1938; s. Warren James and Angela (Devere) H.; B.S., U. San Francisco, 1960; m. Denise Libarle, Oct. 27, 1962; children—Pia Jeanne, Hilary Devere. Pub. relations dir. Blackfriars of West, San Francisco, 1959-59; asso. dir. news bur. Stanford Med. Center, 1959; asst. news features dir. VIII Winter Olympic Games, 1960; v.p. Barth, Hughes & Hinckle, pub. relations, San Francisco, 1960-62; reporter San Francisco Chronicle, 1962-64; editor Ramparts mag., 1964-69, pres., 1967-69; v.p., dir. Scanlan's Lit. House, Inc., San Francisco, 1969—, editor Scanian's Monthly, 1969—. Adviser, San Francisco Youth Assn.; v.p. Citizens Planning Com. San Francisco. Recipient Tom Paine award Emergency Civil Liberties Com., 1967. Author: Guerrilla War in the U.S.A., 1971. Contbr. to anthologies. Home: 263 Castro St San Francisco CA 94133 Office: 451 Pacific Av San Francisco CA 94133

HINCKLEY, ELMER DUMOND, psychologist; b. Margaretville, N.Y., Jan. 11, 1903; s. Elmer Lewis and Mary Louise (Sears) H.; A.B., U. Fla., 1924; Ph.D., U. Chgo., 1929; m. Martha Brown, Jan. 1, 1927. Statistician Merrill-Palmer Sch., Detroit, 1925-26; asst. prof., U. Fla., 1926-29, asso. prof., 1929-30, prof., head psychology dept., 1930-57, prof. psychology, 1957- 63, now emeritus; dir. Bur. Vocational Guidance and Mental Hygiene, 1931- 50, asso. since 1950; dir. (part-time) Fla. Merit Systems, 1936-44, cons., 1944-46, cons. Fla. Parole Commn., VA. Diplomate clin. psychology Am. Bd. Examiners in Profl. Psychology. Fellow A.A.A.S., Am. Psychol. Assn.; mem. Psychometric Soc., Psychol. Corp., Fla. Acad. Scis., Nat. Vocational Guidance Assn. (profl. mem.), Am. Assn. U. Profs., So. Soc. of Philosophy and Psychology, Fla. Edn. Assn., Southeastern, Fla. (pres. 1948-49) psychol. assns., S.A.R., Phi Beta Kappa, Sigma Xi, Phi Kappa Phi, Pi Gamma Mu, Delta Tau Delta, Blue Key. Democrat. Methodist. Mason, Rotarian. Contbr. Jour. Soc. Psychology and Jour. Psychology, Jour. Gen. Psychology, U. Fla. Press, U. Chgo. Press, others. Home: Box 12007 University Station Gainesville FL 32601

HINCKLEY, GORDON BITNER, ch. ofcl.; b. Salt Lake City, June 23, 1910; s. Bryant S. and Ada (Bitner) H.; A.B., U. Utah, Salt Lake City, 1932; m. Marjorie Pay, Apr. 29, 1937; children—Kathleen (Mrs. N. Alan Barnes), Richard G., Virginia (Mrs. James R. Pearce), Clark B., Cynthia Jane. Missionary, Ch. of Jesus Christ of Latter-Day Saints in Britain, 1933-35, mem. Sunday sch. gen. bd., 1937-46, tchr. ch. sem. system, 1935-36, exec. sec. ch. radio publicity and mission lit. com., 1935-50, counselor East Mill Creek stake, 1946-56, pres. stake, 1956-58, asst. to Council Twelve Apostles, 1958-61, mem. council, 1961—, also exec. sec. missionary com., mem. exec. com. ch. bd. edn. Dir. KSL, Inc., KIRO, Inc., Deseret Mgmt. Corp., Bonneville Internat. Corp., also dir. Zion's First Nat. Bank, Salt Lake City, Deseret News Pub. Co., Beneficial Life Ins. Co.; v.p. Recording Arts, Inc. Trustee Brigham Young U. Mem. Soc. Mayflower Descendants. Author books, articles. Home: 3703 South 2700 East Salt Lake City UT 84109 Office: 47 East South Temple Salt Lake City UT 84111

HINCKLEY, RICHARD AINSWORTH, lawyer, oil co. exec.; b. New Orleans, Apr. 8, 1923; s. Norbert B. and Inez (Reynaud) H.;J.D., Loyola U., New Orleans, 1948; m. Gloria Ann Lehmann, May 31, 1948; children—Adele, Richard, Leila. Admitted to La. bar, 1948; practiced law, New Orleans, 1948-52, 53-54; v.p. Marquette Casualty Co., 1952-53; asst. sec. N.Y. Shipbldg. Corp., Camden, N.J., 1955-61, sec., 1961-69; exec. asst. Kewanee Oil Co., Bryn Mawr, Pa., 1969—; dir. Shen Mfg. Co., Inc., Phila. Served with AUS, 1943- 46. Mem. Fed. Bar Assn., Soc. Naval Architects and Marine Engrs., Am. Mgmt. Assn., Delta Theta Phi. Republican. Roman Catholic. Home: 720 Clarendon Rd Penn Valley Narberth PA 19072 Office: 40 Morris Av Bryn Mawr PA 19010

HIND, JOSEPH EDWARD, Jr., educator; b. Chgo., Apr. 2, 1923; s. Joseph Edward and Dorothy Elsie (Burmester) H.; B.S. in Elec. Engring., Ill. Inst. Tech., 1944; Ph.D. in Psychology, U. Chgo., 1952; m. Ruth Anita Lueders, Sept. 12, 1947; children—David, Thomas, Susan. Asst. mfg. engr. Western Elec. Co., Chgo., 1944-45; radar engr. Naval Research Lab., Washington, 1945; research asst. in otolaryngology U. Chgo., 1947-53; research asso. Central Inst. for Deaf, St. Louis, 1953-54; mem. faculty U. Wis. Med. Sch., Madison, 1954—, prof. neurophysiology, 1964—. Cons., communicative scis. study sect. NIH, 1962-66, computer and biomath. scis. study sect., 1969—. Trustee Beltone Inst. for Hearing Research, Chgo. Served with USNR, 1945. Fellow Acoustical Soc. Am.; mem. Am. Physiol. Soc., A.A.A.S., Sigma Xi, Tau Beta Pi, Eta Kappa Nu. Lutheran. Research in auditory neurophysiology, emphasizing electrophysiol. studies; application of digital computers to biomed. research; contbr. articles to profl. jours. Home: 5410 S Hill Dr Madison WI 53705

HINDEN, STANLEY JAY, newspaper editor; b. N.Y.C., Jan. 27, 1927; s. Edward I. and Rose (Kroshinsky) H.; B.A., Syracuse U., 1950; m. Sara Leopold, May 24, 1953; children—Alan, Lawrence, Pamela. With Newsday, Garden City, N.Y., 1952- -, seccessively reporter, polit. editor, editor editorial pages, now nat. corr., Washington. Served with AUS, 1945-46. Contbr. polit. column. Inside Politics, Newsday, 1955-65. Home: 10 Kirkwall Ct Potomac MD 20854 Office: 550 Stewart Av Garden City NY 11530 also 621 Nat Press Bldg Washington DC 20004

HINDERAKER, IVAN, educator; b. Hendricks, Minn., Apr. 29, 1916; s. Theodore and Clara (Hanson) H.; B.A., St. Olaf Coll., 1938; M.A., U. Minn. 1942, Ph.D., 1949; m. Evelyn Birkholz, June 7, 1941; 1 son, Mark. Research asst. Minn. League Municipalities, 1939-40; asso. budget examiner U.S. Bur. Budget, 1942-43; mem. faculty U. Cal. at Los Angeles, 1948—, prof. polit. sci., 1959-, chmn. dept. 1960—; vice chancellor acad. affairs U. Cal. at Irvine, 1962-64; chancellor U. Cal. at Riverside, 1964—; asso. dir. Citizenship Clearing House, Law Center, N.Y.U., 1956-57; asst. to sec. Dept. Interior, 1959-60. Cons. interim com. elections and reapportionment Cal. Assembly, 1951, Cal. Study Commn. Senate Apportionment, 1961. Mem. Minn. Ho. of Reps. from Lincoln County, 1941- 43; chmn. Lincoln County Republican Com., 1946-48. Served to 1st lt., pilot, USAAF, 1943-46. Mem. Am., Western (pres. 1962-63) polit. sci. assns. Author: Administrative Districts and Field Offices of the Minnesota State Government, 1942; Party Politics, 1956. Co-editor: The Politics of California, 1951. Home: 4171 Watkins Dr Riverside CA 92507 Office: U Cal Riverside CA 92502

HINDIN, MAURICE JACOB, lawyer; b. Los Angeles, Oct. 10, 1910;Fs. Theodore J. and Ida (Fisch) H.; B.S. in Bus. Adminstrn., U. So. Cal., 1933, LL.B., 1935; m. Dorothy Sweet, Aug. 11, 1938; children-Arthur T., Carol. Admitted to Cal. bar, 1935 also U.S. Supreme Ct.; practice in Los Angeles, 1935-61, Beverly Hills, Cal., 1961; sr. partner firm Hindin and Hindin. Mem. Am. Bar Assn., Am. Trial Lawyers Assn., I.E.E.E. Home: 10471 LeConte Av Los Angeles CA 90024 Office: 8920 Wilshire Blvd Beverly Hills CA 90211

HINDLE, BROOKE, historian, educator; b. Drexel Hill, Pa., Sept. 28, 1918; s. Howard Brooke and Marion (Manchester) H.; student Mass. Inst. Tech., 1936-38; A.B., Brown U., 1940; A.M., U. Pa., 1942, Ph.D., 1949; m. Helen Elizabeth Morris, Aug. 21, 1943; children—Margaret Joan (Mrs. Robert Miller Hazen), Donald Morris. Asst. in history U. Pa., 1941-42, 45-48; research asso. Inst. Early Am. History and Culture, 1948-50; asso. prof. history N.Y.U., 1950-61, prof., 1961—, chmn. dept. history Univ. Coll., 1965-67, dean, 1967-69, head univ. dept. history, 1970—; sr. resident scholar Eleutherian Mills-Hagley Found., 1969-70. Mem. fellowship com. Macy Found., 1970—. Served to lt. USNR, 1942-45; PTO. Guggenheim fellow, 1964-65. Mem. History of Sci. Soc. (past sec., council mem.), Soc. for History Tech. (exec. council, past adv. council mem.), Phi Beta Kappa. Author: The Pursuit of Science in Revolutionary America, 1956; David Rittenhouse, 1964; Technology in Early America, 1966. Contbr. articles profl. jours. Home: 62 N Monroe St Ridgewood NJ 07450 Office: Dept History NY U New York City NY 10003

HINDS, JACKSON CEIVERS, utility co. exec.; b. Brownsville, Tex., Aug. 28, 1921; s. Jackson Ceivers and Tallulah G. (Raffo) H.; B.B.A., U. Tex., 1942, LL.B., 1948; postgrad. indsl. adminstrn. Harvard, 1943, M.B.A., 1947; m. Artie Lee Page, June 18, 1946; children—Stephen Randolph, Page Aline, Denise Jacqueline. Admitted to Tex. bar, 1948, since practiced in Houston; with firm Fulbright, Crooker, Freeman, Bates & Jaworski, 1948-56; gen. counsel Houston Natural Gas Corp. and subsidiaries, 1956-69, sr. v.p., dir., 1962-67, exec. v.p., dir., 1967-69; pres. United Gas Distbn. Co., Houston, 1969—; dir. Med. Center Bank, Houston, Main Bank Houston, Univ. Savs. & Loan Assn, Houston. Pres. Houston Housing Devel. Corp., 1968—; chmn. Mayor Houston Adv. Com. on Housing, 1967—. Served to lt. USNR, 1942-46. Decorated Bronze Star medal. Mem. Am., Tex., Houston, Fed. Power Communications bar assns., Am., So. gas assns. Home: 2437 Brentwood Dr Houston TX 77019 Office: PO Box 2628 Houston TX 77001

HINDUS, MILTON, educator; b. N.Y.C., Aug. 26, 1916; s. Meyer and Minnie (Slutsky) H.; B.A., Coll. City N.Y., 1936, M.S., 1938; postgrad. Columbia, 1938-39, U. Chgo., 1947-48; m. Eva Tenenbaum, Aug. 30, 1942; 1 dau., Myra Gladys. Lectr. lit. Hunter Coll. and New Sch., 1943-46; asst. prof. humanities Coll. U. Chgo., 1946-48; asst. prof. English, Brandeis U., Waltham, Mass., 1948-54, asso. prof., 1954-62, prof., 1962—; summer faculty N.Y. U., U. Cal. at Los Angeles, City U. N.Y. Recipient Walt Whitman prize Poetry Soc. Am., 1959. Mem. Am. Assn. U. Profs. (chpt. pres.), Modern Lang. Assn., Jewish Publns. Soc. Am., Jewish Faculty Group Greater Boston (chmn.). Author: The Crippled Giant, 1950; The Proustian Vision, 1954; Leaves of Grass: One Hundred Years After, 1955; A Reader's Guide to Marcel Proust, 1962; F. Scott Fitzgerald: An Introduction and Interpretation, 1968; The Old East Side, 1969. Contbr. book reviews to newspapers and mags. Editor sect. Am. lit. Ency. Judaica, 1968—. Home: 24 Stiles Terrace Newton Centre MA 02159 Office: Dept English Brandeis U Waltham MA 02154

HINE, DARYL, poet; b. Burnaby, B.C., Can., 1936; s. Robert Fraser and Elsie (James) H.; student McGill U., 1954-57; M.A., U. Chgo., 1965, Ph.D., 1967. Came to U.S., 1965. Asst. prof. U. Chgo., 1967-69; editor Poetry Mag., 1968—. Author: (poems) Five Poems, 1954; The Carnal and the Crane, 1957; The Devil's Picture Book, 1960; The Wooden Horse, 1965; Minutes, 1968; (novel) The Prince of Darkness and Company, 1961; (travel book) Polish Subtitles, 1962; (play) The Death of Seneca, 1970. Office: 1228 N State St Chicago IL 60610

HINE, GILBERT CLARENDON, banker; b. Lancaster, Pa., July 27, 1917; s. Cecil C. and Frances (Julian) H.; A.B., Gettysburg Coll., 1939; J.D., U. N.C., 1941; m. Evelyn Messenger, June 16, 1945; children—Gilbert Clarendon, Sarah, Cecily, Isabel, Julian. Admitted to N.C. bar, 1941; practice in Charlotte, 1941-42; mem. firm Tillett & Campbell, 1941; fed. tax service editor Prentice Hall, Inc., N.Y.C., 1946; mgr. tax dept. H.J. Heinz Co., Pitts., 1947-50; asst. trust officer Security Trust Co., Miami, Fla., 1951; trust officer Wachovia Bank & Trust Co., Winston-Salem, N.C., 1951- 60; v.p., sr. trust officer Nat. Bank Westchester, 1960-61; sr. v.p., sr. trust officer Nat. Bank of Commerce, San Antonio, 1961—. Chmn. bd. dirs. Winston-Salem chpt. A.R.C., 1951-56; exec. sec. Winston-Salem Found.; pres. Town North YMCA; sec., bd. dirs. Boysville, Inc. Served to capt. USAAF, 1941-46; ETO. Decorated Air medal, Bronze Star. Mem. Am., Tex. (exec. com.) bankers assns. Episcopalian. Kiwanian. Contbr. articles trade publs. Home: 3215 Northridge St San Antonio TX 78209 Office: Nat Bank Commerce Soledad and Martin Sts San Antonio TX 78205

HINE, JACK, educator; b. Coronado, Cal., July 2, 1923; s. Virgil Sylvester and Mildred Virgina (Wing) H.; B.S., U. Ark., 1944; Ph.D., U. Ill., 1948; LL.D., Lewis Coll., 1965; m. Mildred Halacek, May 24, 1946; 1 dau, Katherine (Mrs. Gary W. Good). Asst. research chemist Cities Service Oil Co., Okmulgee, Okla., 1943-45; research asso. Mass. Inst. Tech., 1947-48; postdoctoral fellow Harvard, 1948-49; asst. prof. chemistry Ga. Inst. Tech., 1949-51, asso. prof., 1951-54, prof., 1954-58, Regent's prof., 1958-65; prof. chemistry Ohio State U., 1965—, cons. Medicinal and Organic Chemistry Fellowship Rev. Com. NIH, 1964-68. Alfred P. Sloan Research Fellow, 1956-60. Recipient Fla. award Am. Chem. Soc., 1962, Herty Medal, 1963. Mem. Am. Chem. Soc. (mem. exec. com. div. organic chemistry 1963-65), Chem. Soc. London. Am. Phys. Soc., Societe Chemique de France, A.A.A.S., Faraday Soc., Phi Beta Kappa, Sigma Xi, Phi Kappa Phi, Alpha Chi Sigma, Phi Lambda Upsilon, Omicron Delta Kappa, Pi Mu Epsilon. Author: Physical Organic Chemistry, 1956, 62; Divalent Carbon, 1964. Editorial adv. bd. Jour. Organic Chemistry, 1965-70. Home: 2730 Crafton Park Columbus OH 43221

HINE, MAYNARD KIPLINGER, educator; b. Waterloo, Ind., Aug. 25, 1907; s. Clyde Lucius and Delia (Kiplinger) H.; D.D.S., U. Ill., 1930, M.S., 1932; Rockefeller fellow U. Rochester Sch. of Medicine, 1934-35, Carnegie fellow, 1935-36; D.Sc., Case Western Res. U., 1967, U. Ill., 1969, Boston U., 1969, Ohio State U., 1970; m. Harriett A. Foulke, Apr. 30, 1932; children—Maynard K., Judith Foulke, William C. Mem. faculty U. Ill. Coll. of Dentistry, Chgo., 1936-44, asst. prof. and head dept. oral pathology, 1944; prof. and head dept. of histopathology and periodontia, Ind. U. Sch. Dentistry, Indpls., 1944-45, dean, 1945—; chancellor Ind. U.-Purdue U. at Indpls., 1968—. Cons. Dental Corps, USAF. Regent Nat. Library of Medicine, 1959-63. Mem. Am. Assn. Endodontists (pres. 1947), Ind. Cancer Soc., Inc. (dir.), Am. Assn. Dental Editors (dir. and editor, 1941-47, pres. 1948), Internat. Assn. for Dental Research (pres. 1952), Am. Coll. Dentists (chmn. of the research com. 1959), Am. Dental Assn. (mem. research commn. since 1943, chmn. 1952, council on dental edn. 1956-58, 68-71, mem. trustees 1958, pres. 1966), Ind. Bd. Health, Ind. State Dental Assn. (pres. 1957), Am. Assn. Dental Schs. (pres. 1953), Indpls. Dental Soc. (pres. 1952), Internat. Coll. Dentists, Ind. Acad. of Sci., Am. Acad. Oral Pathology, Am. Acad. Periodontology (former editor; pres. 1964), Sigma Xi, Omicron Kappa Upsilon, Delta Sigma Delta, Phi Eta Sigma. Republican. Presbyn. Contbr. to profl. and sci. jours. Home: 4580 N Meridian St Indianapolis IN 46208

HINER, ARTHUR WILBUR III, banker; b. Denver, Apr. 29, 1929; s. Arthur Wilbur and Kathryn L. (Farnsworth) H.; B.S., U. Colo., 1950; postgrad. U. Denver, Ind. U.; grad. diploma Am. Savs. and Loan Inst.; m. Joan Marie Vonier, May 15, 1954; children—Cynthia Kay, Gary Arthur, Ronald Wilbur. With Capitol Fed. Savs., Denver, 1950—, treas., 1954-59, now pres., vice chmn., also dir.; dir. Capitol Guaranty Corp., Capitol Ins. Agy., Inc., Center State Bank Denver, Fed. Home Loan Bank of Topeka, also Center State Bldg. Corp.; former instr. Denver U. Bd. dirs. Denver Better Bus. Bur. Bd. dirs. Denver Central YMCA, chmn. YMCA Health Club; maj. United Fund Drive; dir. Southeast area Boy Scouts Am., 1966. Republican committeeman. State membership chmn. Savs. and Loan Found., Washington. Served with USAAF, 1950. Mem. Am. Legion, Denver Realty Bd., Am. Savs. and Loan Inst. (pres. Denver chpt. 4, 1962-63, nat. edn. com.) Soc. Residential Appraisers (asso.), Council Mut. Savs. Instns. N.Y.C. (exec. com.), Savs. and Loan League Colo. (dir. Denver area), Nat. League Insured Savs. Assns. (bd. govs., Washington), U.S. Savs. and Loan League (mem. legislative com., dir.), Savs. League Colo. (past pres.), U.S. Ski Assn., Beta Theta Pi. Presbyn. Mason (Shriner, Jester). Clubs: Colorado Mountain, Cherry Hills Country, Mount Vernon Country, University of Colorado Alumni, Indiana University Alumni, Denver, Denver Athletic (Denver); Garden of the Gods (Colorado Springs). Home: 3209 S Detroit St Denver CO 80210 also Royal Buffalo Dr PO Box 156 Dillon CO 80435 Office: 2625 S Colorado Blvd Denver CO 80222

HINER, L. DAVID, dean pharmacy; b. Platte, S.D., May 6, 1905; s. William D. and Anna (Momsen) H.; Ph.C., S.D. State Coll., 1929, B.S., 1929; M.S., U. Fla., 1931, Ph.D., 1938; m. Janet E. Carter, Sept.

1, 1929; children—Shirley, Anne. Instr. pharmacy, U. Fla., 1931-33, S.D. State Coll., 1933-35; asst. prof. pharmacy S.D. State Coll., 1935-37, prof. pharmacy, head dept. pharmacognosy, pharmacology, 1938-39; prof. pharmacy Ohio State U., 1940-47; prof. pharmacognosy U. Utah, 1947—, dean coll. pharmacy, 1947-70. Chmn., faculty rep. U. Utah Athletic Bd. Fellow Am. Coll. Apothecaries; mem. Am. (life), S.D. State, Utah State (hon.) pharm. assns., Sigma Xi, Phi Delta Chi, Phi Sigma, Rho Chi. Clubs: Aztec, Bonneville Knife and Fork. Contbr. articles in profl. jours. Home: 2548 Skyline Dr Salt Lake City UT 84108

HINERFELD, NORMAN MARTIN, mfg. co. exec.; b. N.Y.C., May 17, 1929; s. Benjamin B. and Anne (Blitz) H.; A.B., Harvard, 1951, M.B.A., 1953; m. Ruth Jean Gordon, Dec. 25, 1952; children—Lee Ann, Thomas Benjamin, Joshua Gordon. Security underwriter, underwriting dept. Goldman Sachs & Co., 1953; asst. to pres. Julius Kayser & Co., 1955-56, Catalina, Inc., 1956-57, v.p. mfg., 1957- 64, sr. v.p., 1964—, dir., 1956—; v.p. Kayser-Roth Corp., 1964-67, now exec. v.p., also dir. Chmn. Center Council Center for Study Democratic Instns. Served from 2d lt. to 1st lt., AUS, 1953-55. Mem. Am. Arbitration Assn. (mem. arbitration panel), Am. Apparel Mfrs. Assn. (dir., past pres.), Nat. Knitted Outerwear Assn. (exec. com.). Author: (with D. Moross) Automation-Challange to Management, 1953. Home: 11 Oak Lane Larchmont NY 10538 Office: 640 Fifth Av New York City NY 10019

HINES, ANDREW HAMPTON, Jr., utilities exec.; b. Lake City, Fla., Jan. 28, 1923; s. Andrew Hampton and Louise (Howland) H.; B.S. in Mech. Engring. with high honors, U. Fla., 1947; m. Ann Groover, June 28, 1947; children—Hampton, Elizabeth, Brad, Daniel. Research and devel. Gen. Electric Corp., 1947-51; with Fla. Power Corp., St. Petersburg, 1951—, now exec. v.p., dir; dir. Union Trust Nat. Bank. Campaign chmn. Pinellas United Fund, 1965, pres., 1968. Past mem. exec. bd. Com. of 100, Bd. dirs. St. Petersburg Meth. Home, 1962-65; trustee Al Childrens Hosp. 1968-71. Served to 2d lt. USAAF, 1944-45. Decorated Air medal. Mem. Am. Soc. Mech. Engrs., St Petersburg C. of C. (bd. govs. 1966), Sigma Tau, Phi Kappa Phi, Tau Beta Pi. Methodist (Sunday sch. tchr.). Clubs: St. Petersburg Yacht, Commerce, Lakewood Country (St. Petersburg, Fla.). Home: 249 Colony Point Rd S St Petersburg FL 33705 Office: 101 5th St S St Petersburg FL 33733

HINES, CHARLES ANDERSON, lawyer; b. Guilford County, N.C., Feb. 14, 1886; s. E. DeVault and Belle (Wright) H.; ed. Jefferson Acad., McLeansville, N.C., 1900-02, Elon (N.C) Coll., 1902-04, U. of N.C. Law Sch., 1907-08; m. Ida Edwards Winstead, Nov. 12, 1912 (dec.); children—Dorothy Byrd, Charles Anderson, Winstead (dec.); m. 2d, Annie McNairy. Tchr. in Guilford County, 1903-04; reporter Greensboro Telegram, 1904-05; editor Lumberton Robesonian, 1905-06; city editor Greensboro Daily News, 1906- 07; admitted to N.C. bar, 1908, since practiced in Greensboro; admitted to U.S. Supreme Ct., 1928; city atty. Greensboro, 1917-22; spl. judge Superior Ct., 1925; chmn. emeritus Gate City Bldg. and Loan Assn.; hon. chmn. bd. Woodmen of World Life Ins. Soc., Omaha; hon. chmn. bd. E.F. Craven Co., Greensboro. Served as N.C. state senator, 1927-29; chmn. State Bd. of Elections, 1928-30. Past mem. bd. trustees Moses H. Cone Meml. Hosp.; also former N.C. Fraternal Congress. Awarded 1929 Civitan Citizenship Trophy for "unselfish vol. civic service" to city of Greensboro. Mem. Am., N.C., Greensboro bar assns. Democrat. Methodist (mem. official bd., and former chmn.) Mason, Woodman of World. Club: Civitan. Home: 2303 N Elm Greensboro NC 27408

HINES, CHARLES MOODY, lumber exec.; b. Chgo., Sept. 19, 1901; s. Edward and Loretta (O'Dowd) H.; prep. edn., Chgo. Latin Sch.; student Yale, 1921-23; m. Florence Notz, Feb. 9, 1929; children—Barbara Notz, Edward. Identified since beginning of active career with lumber bus. established by father; former chmn. bd. now dir. Edward Hines Lumber Co. Republican. Roman Catholic. Clubs: Chicago, Mid- day, Indian Hill. Home: 11 Indian Hill Rd Winnetka IL 60093 Office: 200 S Michigan Av Chicago IL 60604

HINES, COLIN OSWALD, educator; b. Toronto, Ont., Can., June 4, 1927; s. Oswald Otis and Winnifred (Mills) H.; B.A., U. Toronto, 1949, M.A., 1950; Ph.D., Cambridge (Eng.) U., 1953; m. Bernice Eleanor Bishop, May 29, 1948; children—David Bruce, Michael Andrew, Margot Lynn, Karen Louise. With Def. Research Bd. Can., 1950-51, 53-62, supt. radio physics lab., 1958-60, head theoretical studies group, 1960-62; prof. aeronomy U. Chgo., 1962-67; prof. physics (aeronomy) U. Toronto (Ont.), 1967—; cons. in field; spl. research radio-wave propagation, ionospheric motions, sun-earth relations, upper atmospheric dynamics. Recipient Napier Shaw Meml. prize Royal Meteorol. Soc., 1962. Mem. Am. Geophys. Union, Canadian Assn. Physics, Am. Meteor. Soc., Inter-Union Commn. on Solar-Terrestrial Physics (past chmn. upper atmospher dynamics sect.). Office Physics Dept U Toronto Toronto 5 Ontario Canada

HINES, EARL KENNETH FATHA, pianist, jazz band leader; b. Duquesne, Pa., Dec. 28, 1905; studied piano with Pitts. area tchrs. Leader trio performing in clubs while in high sch., Pitts.; pianist with band leader-singer Lois B. Deppe, Chgo., 1922; toured, played with Carroll Dickerson, Sammy Stewart, Jimmie Noone, Louis Armstrong; band leader, 1924-48, mainly at Grand Terrace, Chgo., 1928-40; mem. Armstrong's All Stars, 1948-51; moved to San Francisco, played with small bands on West Coast; performed with Jack Teagarden in Europe, 1957; at Little Theatre, N.Y.C., 1964, Village Vanguard, N.Y.C., 1965; in Europe, 1965. Featured in weekly broadcasts from U.S. Treasury Dept.; artist on Capitol, Columbia, RCA Victor, Focus, Fantasy records Recipient Esquire Silver award, 1944. Leading influence in devel. large swing band and jazz piano styles; helped establish (through his band) musicians including Dizzy Gillespie, Charlie Parker, Billy Eckstine, Sarah Vaughan. Home: 815 Trestle Glen Rd Oakland CA 94604*

HINES, EMMETT WOMACK, bus. exec.; b. Milledgeville, Ga., Aug. 25, 1899; s. Edward Roberts and Nelle (Womack) H.; B.S. in mech. engring., Ga. Inst. Tech., 1922, B.S. in elec. engring., Harvard Bus. Sch., 1948; m. Frederica Boatwright, May 28, 1924; children—Emmett Womack, Martha, Frederica. Mgr. Otis Elevator Co., Tampa, Fla., 1926-28, Balt., 1928-30, Washington, 1930-34, Buffalo, 1935-46, N.Y.C., 1946-50, gen. service mgr., N.Y.C., 1950-51, v.p., gen. zone mgr., 1952-60, sr. vice pres., dir., 1960-64, ret., 1964. Trustee Found. Ga. Coll. Served as 2d lt. U.S. Army, 1918. Mem Harvard Advanced Mgmt. Assn. (pres. 1951), Phi Delta Theta. Club: Milledgeville (Ga.) Country. Home: 601 N Tattnall St Milledgeville GA 31061

HINES, GERALD DOUGLAS, investment builder; b. Gary, Ind., Aug. 15, 1925; s. Robert Gordon and Myrtle Lillian (McConnell) H.; B.S., Purdue U., 1948; m. Dorothy Schwarz, Mar. 8, 1952; children—Jeffrey, Jennifer. Organizer, 1957, since owner Gerald D. Hines Interests, Houston; prin. works include One Shell Plaza, Galleria Post Oak, 2000 Smith Office Park Bldg., One Shell Square, New Orleans, Galleria West, Trans World Airlines, Inc. Adminstrn. Bldg. Kansas City, Mo. Participant Developers Conf. Joint Center Urban Studies, Mass. Inst. Tech. and Harvard; dir. South Main Bank, Galleria Bank. Bd. dirs. devel. bd. YMCA, Houston Symphony Soc.; bd. dirs. United Fund; bd. dirs. Nat. Space Hall Fame; mem. devel. council Houston Mus. Natural Sci.; mem. adv. com. U. Houston's Sch. Bus.; trustee St. John's Sch. Served with C.E., U.S. Army, 1943-45. Named Key Houstonian, Houston Bd. Realtors, 1967; Marketing Man of Yr., Am. Marketing Assn. Houston, 1968. Mem. Urban Land Inst. (exec. com.), Houston C. of C. (dir.-at- large). Home: 146 Radney Rd Houston TX Office: 2100 Post Oak Tower 5051 Westheimer Houston TX 77027

HINES, HAROLD H., Jr., ins. co. exec.; b. Chgo., Nov. 21, 1924; s. Harold H. and Babette (Schnadig) H.; B.A., Yale, 1948; m. Mary Pick, Jan. 23, 1954; children—William H., Anne, David F. Sr. v.p. Marsh and McLennan, ins. brokers, Chgo. Lectr. profl. ins. groups and assns., 1957—. Chmn. Ill. Health Edn. Commn. Bd. dirs. North Shore Country Day Sch., Great Books Found.; trustee Michael Reese Hosp. and Med. Center, Chgo. Hosp. Planning Council. Served with AUS, 1943-46. Mem. Am. Soc. Property and Casualty Underwriters. Clubs: Standard, Mid-Am. (Chgo.); Lake Shore Country (Glencoe, Ill.). Contbr. articles ins. jours. Home: 1350 Hackberry Lane Winnetka IL 60093 Office: 231 S LaSalle St Chicago IL 60604

HINES, HERBERT WALDO, educator; b. Boston; Aug. 14, 1887; s. John Henry and Jennie Henderson (Gwinn) H.; A.B., Harvard, 1909, A.M., 1910; B.D., U. Chgo., 1911, Ph.D., 1922; studied U. Berlin, Germany, 1912-13, Marburg, 1913-14; LL.D. (hon.), Westminster Coll., 1954; m. Helen Gartside, June 21, 1910; children—Herbert Waldo Bedell, Paul Henry, Harold Cheney, Wallis Gartside, Marion Louise, Mildred Elizabeth, Marshall, Burton Abbott, Donald Alan. Ordained Bapt. ministry, 1912; pastor, El Paso, Ill., 1915-21, 1st Ch., Kankakee, 1921- 25, Central Ch., Springfield, 1925-35; sabbatical year of travel and writing, 1935-36; dir. Inst. of Internat. Understanding for Rotary Internat., 1936-51; pres. Rocky Mountain Coll., 1951-58, now emeritus; prof. Russian lang. Morningside Coll., 1958-63, Hope Coll., Holland, Mich., 1963-65. Young People's Com. Bapt. World Alliance, 1928-33; dir. of the Ill. Baptist State Conv., 1916-26; mem. and sec. exec. com. Ill. Bapt. State Conv., 1931-34; moderator Bloomington (Ill.) Bapt. Assn., 1919-21; moderator Springfield (Ill.) Bapt. Assn., 1926-27; recording sec. Bapt. Young People's Union of Am., 1921-22, mem. exec. com., 1923-25; spl. lectr. in humanities Chgo. Jr. Colls., 1938-51. Mem. Modern Lang. Assn. Republican. Mason (32, Shriner). Clubs: Harvard (Chgo.), Rotary (mem. of dist. conf. com., gov. of Rotary Dist. 167, 1952- 53). Author: Missionary Education in the Local Church, 1925; Clough, Kingdom Builder in South India, 1929. Contbr. numerous articles on young people's problems, fgn. travel and internat. relations made several cultural and research trips to Europe, 4 to Latin Am. countries, and one around-the-world tour since 1923. Home: 67 E 10th St Holland MI 49423

HINES, HOWARD HARRY, social scientist; b. Iowa City, June 30, 1922; s. Harry Matlock and Leona (Fisher) H.; B.A., U. Ia., 1942; A.M., Harvard, 1948, Ph.D., 1950. Tchr. econs. U. Ia., 1947, Bowdoin Coll., 1948, Harvard, 1948-50, U. Minn., 1957; from asst. prof. to prof. econs. Ia. State U., 1950-62; program dir. for econs. NSF, 1962-64, div. dir. for social scis., 1964—; acting asst. prof. bus. adminstrn. U. Cal. at Berkeley, 1955-56. Served with AUS, 1943-46. Mem. Am., Midwest (1st v.p. 1957-58) econ. assns., Royal Econ. Soc., Econometric Soc., Phi Beta Kappa, Delta Sigma Rho. Office: Nat Science Found Washington DC 20550

HINES, J. HERMAN, chmn. exec. com. Deposit Guaranty Nat. Bank, Jackson, Miss. Chmn. exec. com. Jackson Symphony Orch. Assn.; 1971 campaign chmn. Miss.-Radio Free Europe; mem. Vice Pres.' cabinet com. Miss. for Support Pub. Sch. Edn.; chmn. Fed. Ct. Bi-racial Com. Jackson (Miss.) Separate Sch. Dist. Address: 200 E Capitol St Jackson MS 39201

HINES, JEROME, opera singer; b. Hollywood, Calif., Nov. 8, 1921; s. Russell Ray and Florence Mildred (Link) Heinz; B.A., U. Cal. in Los Angeles; m. Lucia Evangelista, July 23, 1952; children—David Jerome, Andrew, John. Began as singer with the Civic Light Opera Co. of Los Angeles, 1940, San Francisco Opera Co., 1941, Hollywood Bowl soloist, 1942, 47; Opera Assn. of the Golden West, 1943; chemist, Union Oil Co. of Los Angeles, 1944-45; with New Orleans Opera Co., 1945, 46, Met. Opera Co., 1946, 47; leading basso of Met. Opera, Teatro Colon, Buenos Aires. Performed in Glyndebourne, Edinburgh festivals, 1953, Munich Opera Festival, 1953, Wagner Opera Festival, Bayreuth, Germany 1958. Recording artist London, Victor recording cos. Recipient Caruso Scholarship, Cornelia Bliss Scholarship.

HINES, JOHN ELBRIDGE, bishop; b. Seneca, S.C., Oct. 3, 1910; s. Edgar Alphonso and Mary Woodbury (Moore) H.; A.B., U. of South, 1930, D.D., 1946; B.D., Va. Theol. Sem., 1933, D.D., 1946; D.D. (hon.), Princeton, 1968; m. Helen Louise Orwig, Apr. 22, 1935; children—Michael John, Nancy, John Christoph, John Moore, John Stephen. Ordained to ministry P.E. Church, 1933; curate, Ch. of St. Michael and St. George, St. Louis, 1933- 35; rector, Trinity Episcopal Ch., Hannibal, Mo., 1935-37, St. Paul's Episcopal Ch., Augusta, Ga., 1937-41, Christ Episcopal Ch., Houston, Tex., 1941-45; consecrated bishop, coadjutor of diocese of Tex., Oct. 18, 1945; became bishop of Tex., Oct., 1955; presiding bishop P.E. Ch., 1965—. Mem. Tex. Bd. for Hosps. and Spl. Schs. Bd. regents Va. Theol. Sem. Mem. Phi Beta Kappa, Omicron Delta Kappa, Sigma Nu. Democrat. Home: 338 Round Hill Rd Greenwich CT 06830 Office: 815 2d Av New York City NY 10017

HINES, LAWRENCE GREGORY, educator; b. Leavenworth, Kan., Oct. 31, 1915; s. Michael Joseph and Louise Ann (Rokoski) H.; A.B., U. Kan., 1938; A.M., U. Minn., 1942, Ph.D., 1947; A.M., Dartmouth, 1953; m. Ann Williston Philips, Nov. 27, 1937; 1 son, Terence Michael. Teaching asst. U. Minn., 1940-41, research asst. Employment Stablzn. Research Inst., 1941-42, instr. econs., 1942-46, asst. prof. econs., summer 1947; asst. prof. econs. Dartmouth, 1947-53, prof., 1953—, chmn. div. social scis., 1959-62, chmn. dept. econs., 1963-65; cons. Fed. Res. Bank of Boston; also econ. cons., water control div. USPHS: vis. prof. econs. U. Mich. summer 1948; lectr. econs. George Washington U., summer 1949. Mem. Fed. Interagy. Com. Evaluation Standards; vice-chmn. subcom. evaluation standards Northeastern Resources Com. Served air intelligence specialist Office Naval Intelligence, Washington, 1946-47. Recipient Ford Found. essay prize award, 1958; NSF grantee, 1965-66. Fellow Royal Econ. Soc., mem. Regional Sci. Assn., Am. Econ. Assn., Am. Assn. U. Profs. (nat. council mem.), Soil Conservation Soc. Am., Quetico- Superior Found. Author: The Size, Shape, and Distribution of Economic Income, 1952. Contbr. articles profl. publs. Home: 5 Kingsford Rd Hanover NH 03755

HINES, MERRILL ODOM, surgeon, med. adminstr.; b. Jackson, Miss., Nov. 17, 1909; s. Hulon Hunter and Ava Ione (Odom) H.; B.S., Millsaps Coll., 1931; M.D., Tulane U., 1936; m. Margaret McLaurin Davis, Aug. 24, 1937; children—Margaret Anne, Merrill Odom. Intern Baroness Erlanger Hosp., Chattanooga, 1936- 37, resident, 1937-38, chief resident surgery, 1938-39; staff surgeon Tylertown (Miss.) Hosp., 1939-42; mem. staff Alton Ochsner Med. Found., New Orleans, 1944—, head dept. proctology, 1946-61; head dept. proctology Ochsner Found. Hosp., 1947-62, pres. staff, 1946-47; asst. med. dir. Ochsner Clinic, 1954-60, mem. bd. mgmt., 1960—, med. dir., 1960—; sr. vis. surgeon Charity Hosp., New Orleans, 1956—; courtesy staff Sara Mayo Hosp., New Orleans, 1954—; sr. asso. surgery Touro Infirmary, New Orleans, 1954-64; courtesy staff Flint-Goodrige Hosp., New Orleans, 1949—; asst. prof. clin. surgery Tulane Med. Sch., 1949-62, asso. prof. clin. surgery, 1962-64, prof. clin. surgery, 1964—; cons. Ill. Central Hosp., New Orleans, 1958-70, Ill. Central R.R., 1958—; cons. group practice of medicine Dept. Health, Edn. and Welfare, 1966-70; mem. Govt. Health Ins. Benefits Adv. Council, 1968—. Bd. dirs. Am. Cancer Soc. Greater New Orleans, 1957—, sec., 1957-58, v.p., 1959-60, pres., 1961-62, mem. exec. com., 1962—; mem. La. State Bd. Nurse Examiners, 1962-66; co-chmn. health com. New Orleans C. of C., 1959-65; mem. Adv. Bd. Med. Specialties, 1962- -, mem. exec. com., 1968-70. Trustee Alton Ochsner Med. Found., sec.- treas. 1966-70, pres., 1970—. Served to capt. M.C., AUS, 1942-44. Commonwealth fellow from Miss., 1932-36. Diplomate Am. Bd. Proctology (mem. bd. 1956—), Am. Bd. Colon and Rectal Surgery (v.p. 1960-61; pres. 1961-63). Fellow Am. Coll. Surgeons (mem. bd. govrs. 1967—); mem. Am. (chmn. sec. proctology 1963), So. (treas. 1954—) med. assns., Orleans Parish, La. med. socs., Am. (pres. 1961-62), Mid West, Southeastern (pres. 1954) proctologic socs., New Orleans (treas. 1945), Southeastern, La., Alton Ochsner surg. socs., Alumni Alton Ochsner Med. Found. Fellows Assn. (1st pres. 1954-56), New Orleans Grad. Med. Assembly. Democrat. Methodist (chmn. ofcl. bd. 1957-59). Clubs: Louisiana, Round Table, International House (New Orleans). Mem. editorial bd. Jour. Diseases Colon and Rectum, 1957—. Home: 1634 Robert St New Orleans LA 70115 Office: 1514 Jefferson St New Orleans LA 70121

HINES, RODERICK LUDLOW, educator, physicist; b. Cleve., Nov. 20, 1925; s. Paul Randolph and Winifred (Pellett) H.; B.A., Oberlin Coll., 1947; Ph.D., U. Mich., 1954; m. Jean Vivian Olson, Apr. 2, 1949; children—Theodore, Pamela, Terrence, Victoria, Jennifer. Physicist Ford Motor Co., Dearborn, Mich., 1953-57; asst. prof. physics Northwestern U., 1957-62, asso. prof., 1962-67, prof., 1967—; patent cons. Served with AUS, 1945-46. Nat. Insts. Health fellow, 1968-69. Mem. Am. Phys. Soc., Electron Microscope Soc. Am. Research on electrostatic spraying, radiation effects of ion bombardment, high resolution electron microscopy. Home: 2252 Orrington Av Evanston IL 60201 Office: Northwestern Univ Evanston IL 60201

HINES, VINCENT JOSEPH, clergyman; b. New Haven, Sept. 14, 1912; ed. St. Thomas Sem., Conn., 1930-32, St. Sulpice Sem., Paris, France, 1932-37; J.C.D., Lateran U., Rome, Italy, 1949. Ordained priest Roman Catholic Ch., 1937; curate, Manchester, Conn., 1937-43; chancellor Hartford (Conn.) Diocese, 1959; bishop Diocese Norwich, Conn., 1959—. Served as chaplain AUS, 1943-46. Address; 274 Broadway Norwich CT 06360

HINES, WILLIAM EUGENE, banker, orgn. ofcl.; b. N.Y.C., July 5, 1914; s. William J. and Alice M. (Callahan) H.; student Columbia; grad. Rutgers U. Grad. Sch. Banking, 1948; m. Dorothy H. Moore, June 4, 1949; children—Alice M., Dorothy H., Margaret M., William J., Elizabeth A., Robert J. With Bankers Trust Co., N.Y.C., 1950—, asst. v.p., 1958-63, v.p., 1963—; instr. Am. Inst. Banking, 1948-64, Am. Youth Hostels, 1954-65, former chmn., now dir. Mem. N.Y. Soc. Security Analysts, Accountants Club N.Y.C., Nat. Assn. Mental Health (nat. treas., dir. 1966; nat. trustee). Home: 6 Edgewood Rd Scarsdale NY 10583 Office: 280 Park Av New York City NY 10022

HINES, WILLIAM MEREDITH, Jr., journalist; b. San Jose, Cal., Sept. 11, 1916; s. William Meredith and Ethel (Sain) H.; student Guilford (N.C.) Coll., 1936-37; Editorial positions with Boston Transcript, 1936-37, U.P.A., 1937-40, Chattanooga Times, 1940-41; mem. staff Washington Eve. Star, 1950-68, sci. editor, 1957-68; with Field Enterpises, Inc., 1968—, sci. editor Chgo. Sun-Times, 1969—; sci. corr. Westinghouse Broadcasting Co., 1968—; sci. corr. Die Welt, Hamburg, W. Germany, 1969—. Served to 1st lt. AUS, 1941- 46. Recipient Sci. Writing award A.A.A.S.-Westinghouse Found., 1959, 60, 61, 65; Atomic Indsl. Forum award, 1965; Robert S. Ball award Aviation-Space Writers Assn., 1966. Mem. Nat. Assn. Sci. Writers, Am. Inst. Aero. and Astronautics. Clubs: Nat. Space, Nat. Press, (Washington). Author: Conquest of the Moon, 1964. Home: 152 G St SW Washington DC 20024 Office: 1366 Nat Press Bldg Washington DC 20004

HINGLE, PAT, actor; b. Denver, July 19, 1924; s. Clarence M. and Marvin (Patterson) H.; B.F.A., U. Tex., 1949; m. Alyce Dorsey, June 3, 1947; children—Jody, Billy, Molly. Numerous acting roles, among latest being End as a Man, 1953, Festival, 1954, Cat on a Hot Tin Roof, 1955, Girls of Summer, 1956, Dark at the Top of the Stairs, 1957, J.B., 1958, The Deadly Game, 1960, Macbeth, 1961, Troilus and Cressida, 1961, Strange Interlude, 1963, Blues for Mr. Charlie, 1964, A Girl Could Get Lucky, 1964, The Glass Menagerie, 1965, The Odd Couple, 1966, Johnny No-Trump, 1967, The Price, 1968, Childs Play, 1970. Served with USN, 1942-46, 51-52. Home: 41 Viola Rd Suffern NY 10901

HINGSON, ROBERT ANDREW, physician; b. Anniston, Ala., Apr. 13, 1913; s. Robert A. and Elloree Elizabeth (Haynes) H.; A.B. U. of Ala., 1935; student of medicine, U. of Ala. Med. Sch., 1933-35; M.D., Emory U., 1938; fellow in anesthesia, Mayo Clinic 1940-41; H.H.D., Monrovia Coll., Liberia, 1962; LL.D., Wm. Jewell Coll., 1963, E. Pa. Bapt. Coll., 1963, Litt.D., Hardin- Simmons Univ., 1965; m. Gussie Dickson, Mar. 2, 1940; children—Dickson James, Andrew T., Roberta, Ralph W., Luke L. Became chief of dept. of anethesia, U.S. Marine Hosp., S. I., 1941; commd. passed asst. surgeon, USPHS, July 1, 1942; surgeon USPHS, 1943, sr. surgeon 1950, med. dir. USPHS (Res.), 1965; dir. post-grad. course in Technic Continuous Caudal Analgesia for relief of pain in childbirth, Phila. Lying-In Hosp., Jefferson Med. Coll., 1943-45; dir. postgrad. course in anesthesiology, first prof. anesthesiology U. Tenn., 1945-48; asso. prof. and anesthesiologist, dept. obstetrics, Johns Hopkins U., 1948-51; faculty of Anesthesiology Royal Coll. of Surgeons (Eng., First prof. of anesthesia Western Res. U., 1951-68; also dir. anesthesiology U. Hosps.; prof. anesthesiology, dir. Magee Womens Hosp., U. Pitts. Sch. Medicine, 1968—, prof. pub. health pracitce Grad. Med. Sch.; cons. U.S. Veterans, Sunny Acres, Highland View, Met. and St. Anne's hosps.; sr. cons. Amigos de Honduras Med. Service Mission; vis. prof. Columbia, 1953, Venezuela, 1956, U. New Zealand, Australia, S.Am., 1963-64. Dir. Baptist World Alliance Interdenominational, Inter-Racial Med. Mission Survey of Asia-Africa, 1958; dir. Operation Brother's Brother to Liberia in mass vaccination program, 1962; dir. medical survey of C. Am. republics, 1967; service missions Bolivia, Peru, Ecuador, Panama, El Salvador, 1968-70; pres. Brother's Brother Found., Ednl. and Relief Found., World Fedn. Socs. Anesthesiology, 1963—. Recipient award as one of America's outstanding young mem, U.S. Jr. C. of C., 1947; decorated knight Grand Comdr. Humane Order African Redemption, 1962 (Liberia); Maximum Hero's Order of Gen. Francisco Morizan (Honduras), 1968; Order Ruben Dario (Nicargua), 1968; Service citations (Costa Rica), 1967, El Salvador, 1968; Hadassah service award and med. survey Israel, 1968; Lane Bryant Internat. Service award, 1969. Trustee Religious Heritage Found., Service award, 1968. Fellow of Internat. Coll. of Anesthesia, William Crawford Gorgas Med. Soc.,

Am. Soc. Anesthetists, Internat. Coll. Surgeons, Am. Coll. of Anesthesiology; mem. Coll. Physicians & Surgeons Republic Costa Rica (hon.), Internat. Research Soc. (v.p.), Am. Soc. Anesthesiologists (dir.), Pi Kappa Alpha, Sigma Xi. Baptist (deacon). Kiwanian, Rotarian. Author: Control of Pain in Childbirth. Co-author: Anesthesia for Obstetrics. Co-editor: Pitkin's Conduction Anesthesia. Contbr. papers, chpts. in field. Developed clin. use of hypospray, dermojet, also continuous caudal and peridural analgesia; inventor. Home: 334 S Lexington Av Pittsburgh PA 15208 Office: Magee Womens Hospital Forbes and Halket Sts Pittsburgh PA 15213

HINICH, MELVIN JAY, educator; b. Pitts., Apr. 29, 1939; s. Joseph and Sara (Rubinstein) H.; B.S. in Math., Carnegie Inst. Tech., 1959, M.S. in Math., 1960; Ph.D. in Statistics, Stanford, 1964; m. Sonje Gregg, Sept. 14, 1966; 1 dau., Amy Sara. Asst. prof. indsl. adminstrn. Carnegie Inst. Tech., 1963-68; asso. prof. indls. adminstrn. and statistics, 1968-70; prof. statistics and polit. economy Carnegie Mellon U., 1970—; cons. Teledyne-Isotopes, Inc., 1968—, Internat. Research and Tech., Inc. Mem. Inst. Math. Statistics, Am. Statis. Assn., Sigma Xi. Author: Introduction to Continuous Probability, 1969; also articles. Asso. editor Jour. Math. Soc., 1969—. Home: 528 A Guyasnta Rd Aspinwall PA 15215 Office: Carnegie Mellon U Pittsburgh PA 15213

HINKE, KARL, retired banker; b. Phila., Jan. 11, 1906; s. William John and Bertha Agnes (Berleman) H.; grad. Mercersburg (Pa.) Acad., 1923; B.A., Hamilton Coll., Clinton, N.Y., 1927; m. E. Donne Zick, Dec. 27, 1947; 1 son, Frederick W. II. With Marshall, Meadows & Stewart, Inc., Auburn, N.Y., 1927-30; with Marine Trust Co., 1930-71, sr. v.p., 1961-71; v.p. Marine Midland Banks, Inc., 1961-62, exec., v.p., 1962-71, also dir.; v.p. Marine Midland Trust Co. Western N.Y., 1961-71; formerly chmn., dir. Interbank Card, Inc., now chmn. emeritus; dir. Marine Midland Internat. Corp., Auburn Plastics, Inc., Auburn Publishing Co. Bd. dirs. Auburn Theol. Sem. Served to capt. USMCR, 1942-45. Mem. Assn. Res. City Bankers, Am. Bankers Assn., A.I.M. (asso.), Buffalo C. of C. Club: Buffalo. Home: Girdle Rd East Aurora NY 14052 Office: 241 Main St Buffalo NY 14240

HINKLE, JAMES R. utility exec.; b. Salisbury, N.C., Jan. 29, 1930; s. Hollis Leo and Emma (Leonard) H.; B.S., N.C. State U., 1951; M.B.A., U. N.C., 1954. Dir. Commerce and Industry div. NC., 1961-64; mgr. area devel. Carolina Power & Light, Raleigh, N.C., 1964-68, group v.p. adminstrn., 1968—; dir. N.C. Bus. Devel. Corp. Vice-chmn. N.C. Research Triangle Found. Mem. So. Assn. State Planning Agys. (pres. 1962). Home: 2470 Wade Av Raleigh NC 27607 Office: Box 1551 Raleigh NC 27602

HINKLE, PAUL, banker; b. Rockford, O., Aug. 19, 1909; s. T.W. and Nellie (Snyder) H.; B.S., Miami U., Oxford, O., 1931; m. Myfanwy Williams, Mar. 16, 1946. Instr., football coach Rockford High Sch., 1933-36; clk. ct. Common Pleas, Mercer County, O., 1937-44; dir. pub. relations First Nat. Bank of Celina, O., 1954-55; supt. banks State Ohio, 1955-58; pres. Charleston Nat. Bank (W.Va.), 1958-68, chmn. bd., chief exec. officer, 1968—; dir. Celina Nat. Life Ins. Co., Celina Financial Corp. Treas., W.Va. Indsl. Devel. Authority. Mem. Ohio Legislature, 1947-55; alternate del. Democratic Nat. Conv., 1956. Trustee Morris Harvey Coll., Charleston Meml. Hosp. Served as lt. comdr. USNR, 1942-46. Recipient Bishop medal Miami U., 1954; Silver Beaver award Boy Scouts Am., 1968. Mem. Am. Bankers Assn. (pres. nat. bank div. 1965-66), Am. Legion, Sigma Chi. Methodist. Mason, Rotarian (past pres. Charleston). Home: 1 Comstock Pl Charleston WV 25314 Office: 201 Capitol St Charleston WV 25301

HINKLEY, DON RAYMOND, chem. co. exec.; b. Buffalo, June 3, 1922; s. Don R. and Marion (Clark) H.; B.A., Dartmouth, 1943; M.B.A., Harvard, 1947; m. Lela Emery, Apr. 1950 (div.); children—Don Howett, Phyllis Emery, Elizabeth Gibson. Pres., Emery Industries, Inc., Cin., 1966—; v.p. Pepsi Cola Internat., Europe, 1963—; chief exec. officer Procter & Gamble Co., Germany, 1960—. Served to 2d lt. USAAF, World War II. Home: 10 Grandin Lane Cincinnati OH 45208 Office: Carew Tower Cincinnati OH 45202

HINKLEY, LEO THOMAS, Jr., mfg. co. exec.; b. Springfield, Mass., Mar. 23, 1926; s. Leo Thomas and Alice (McMahon) H.; B.S., Holy Cross Coll., 1950; postgrad. Stanford Bus. Sch., 1969; m. Anna Marie Cantalini, June 30, 1951; children—Maureen, Leo, Margaret, Mary, Michael, James, Martha Ann. Accountant, Scovell, Wellington & Co., C.P.A.'s, Springfield, 1950-60; treas. Savage Arms Co., Westfield, Mass., 1960-63; asst. treas. Am. Hardware Corp., New Britain, Conn., 1963-64; asst. controller Emhart Corp., Bloomfield, Conn., 1964-67, controller, 1967-69, v.p., controller, 1969—. Served with AUS, 1944-45. Decorated Purple Heart. C.P.A., Mass. Mem. Am. Inst. C.P.A.'s, Nat. Assn. Accountants, Financial Execs. Inst. Clubs: Springfield Ski; Wilbraham Country. Home: 7 Scenic Dr Wilbraham MA 01095 Office: 950 Cottage Grove Rd Bloomfield CT 06002

HINKS, KENNETT WEBB, govt. cons.; b. Mpls., Sept. 3, 1897; s. William Herbert and Florence Mary (Webb) H.; A.B., U. Minn., 1920; m. Elizabeth Porter Dial, Nov. 2, 1946 (dec.); step-children—Nathaniel Victor, Diana. With J. Walter Thompson Co., N.Y.C., 1921-64, Pacific Coast mgr., 1925-28, Central European mgr., 1929-32, v.p., 1936-61, sr. v.p., 1961-63, dir., 1949-64; dir. Caribbean and Canadian subsidiaries of J. Walter Thompson Co. until 1964; cons. U.S. Fgn. Agrl. Service 1963—. Council Assn. for Aid of Crippled Children, 1948; dir. The Advt. Council, N.Y.C., 1958-70. Served to 2d lt., inf., U.S. Army, World War I; to lt. comdr. USNR, World War II; mem. planning group, chief of planning staff, OSS, 1942-45. Mem. Nat. Planning Assn. (trustee), Phi Beta Kappa, Chi Psi, Phi Delta Phi. Episcopalian. Clubs: University (N.Y.C.); Army and Navy Metropolitan (Washington); Farmington Hunt, Farmington Country (Charlottesville, Va.). Home: Ivy VA 22945

HINKSON, J.H. WARD, lawyer; b. Ridley Park, Pa., Oct. 17, 1895; s. Joseph H. and Bessie (Ward) H.; B.S., U. Pa., 1917, LL.B., 1922; m. Edith Haines, Mar. 12, 1936 (dec. Oct. 1957); m. 2d, Eileen Hart McMichael, Aug. 12, 1961; 3 sons. Admitted to Pa. bar, 1922, since in gen. practice; mem. firm Hinkson & Cantlin; dir. Oliver B. Cannon & Son, Inc., Gash-Stull Co., Indsl. & Farm Equipment Corp., Murphy Ford Co., G.M. Stull Co. Mem. Am., Pa. bar assns. Club: Union League (Phila.). Home: Holly Hill Media PA 19063 Office: 19 W 5th St Chester PA 19013

HINMAN, CARROLL STEWARD, ret. govt. ofcl.; b. Yakima, Wash., May 16, 1913; s. Charles Henry and Caroline (Steward) H.; student Yakima Valley Jr. Coll., 1929-31, Central Wash. Coll. Edn., 1932; A.B., Syracuse U., 1936, M.S. in Pub. Adminstrn., 1938; m. Andrea Jean Surratt, June 26, 1943; children—John C., Andrea J., Donald L., Keith R. Budget examiner N.Y. State Budget Div., 1938-41; budget examiner, adminstr. analyst, fiscal economist U.S. Budget Bur., 1946-49; fgn. economist NSRB, 1950; mgmt. adviser State Dept., 1951-53; chief evaluation staff fgn. aid programs FOA, ICA, Washington, 1953-55, spl. asst. to dep. dir. mgmt., 1955-57; chief program and econ. div. U.S. Operations Mission to Spain, 1957-62; dir. Office Mediterranean Affairs, AID, 1962- 64, dir. office devel. planning African Bur., 1964-67; dir. AID Mission to Kenya, 1967-68; dir. AID East Africa Office regional activities, 1968-69, spl. asst. Africa Bur., 1969-70. Served from pvt. to capt., AUS, 1941-46. Recipient Meritorious Service award ICA, 1956. Mem. Am. Soc. Pub. Adminstrn., Am. Fgn. Service Assn. Presbyn. Home: 1405 Namassin Rd Alexandria VA 22308

HINMAN, CHARLTON JOSEPH KADIO, educator; b. Ft. Collins, Colo., Feb. 10, 1911; s. Claude Harrison and Ethel (Charlton) H.; B.A., Cornell U., 1933; B.A. (Rhodes scholar 1933- 36), Oxford (Eng.) U., 1936, M.A., 1939; Ph.D. (Du Pont Research fellow), U. Va., 1941; m. Jane van Meter, Nov. 8, 1936 (div. Sept. 1966); 1 dau., Barbara; m. 2d, Myra Mahlow, Feb. 22, 1968. Instr. U. Mo., 1937-39; research fellow Folger Shakespeare Library, Washington, 1941-42, hon. fellow, 1952-58; asst. prof. Johns Hopkins, 1946-50; prof. English, U. Kan., 1960-63, Univ. Distinguished prof., 1963—. Guggenheim fellow, 1954-55; Bollingen Research fellow, 1956-58. Served to comdr. USNR, 1942-46, 50-52. Mem. Bibliog. Soc. London, Malone Soc. Oxford, Modern Lang. Assn. Am., Shakespeare Assn. Am., Phi Beta Kappa. Author: The Printing and Proof-reading of the First Folio of Shakespeare, 2 vols., 1963; also articles. Editor: Shakespeare Quarto Facsimiles, 1960- -; The Norton Facsimile of the First Folio of Shakespeare, 1968. Inventor Hinman collating machine. Home: 1020 Crestline Dr., Lawrence, KS 66044

HINMAN, EDWARD BARRETT, paper co. exec.; b. N. Straford, N.H., Dec. 10, 1913; s. John H. and Jenny Crawford (Drew) H.; B.A., Dartmouth, 1935; postgrad. Harvard Sch. Bus. Adminstrn., 1935-36; m. Helen Simpson, June 29, 1941; children—John Amos, George B., Hugh H. With Canadian Internat. Paper Co., 1936-66, pres., 1961-66, dir., 1956—; with Internat. Paper Co., 1966—, pres., chief exec. officer, from 1966, now dir.; dir. Toronto-Dominion Bank (Can.). Served with AUS, 1943-46; PTO. Home: 120 E 55th St New York City NY 10022 Office: 220 E 42d St New York City NY 10017

HINMAN, GEORGE LYON, lawyer; b. Binghamton, N.Y., Sept. 25, 1905; s. Harvey D. and Phebe (Brown) H.; A.B., Princeton, 1927; LL.B., Harvard, 1930; LL.D., Union Coll., 1962; L.H.D., Elmira Coll., 1950; D.C.L., Colgate U., 1967; m. Barbara Davidge, Sept. 12, 1929; children—Constance, Martha, Virginia, Harvey II. Admitted to N.Y. State bar, 1930, and since practiced law in Binghamton; asso. Hinman, Howard & Kattell, 1930—, partner, 1937; spl. counsel Rockefeller Bros.; dir. IBM Corp., N.Y. Telephone Co., First City Nat. Bank of Binghamton, also Arlington Hotel, Security Mutual Life Ins. Co., Binghamton, N.Y., Lincoln 1st Banks, Inc., Russell Reynolds Assos., Inc.; counsel N.Y. State Temporary Commn. on Constl. Conv. and Spl. Legislative Com. on Constl. Revision and Simplification 1956-58; exec. asst. to gov. of N.Y., 1958-59. Mem. Lt. Gov.'s Com. on Tchrs. Salaries, 1951; mem. N.Y. Atty.-Gen.'s Com. on ethical standards in govt. Mem. N.Y. State Adv. Conf. Salvation Army. Republican Nat. Committeeman for N.Y.; del.-at-large Rep. Nat. Conv., 1960, 64; mem. exec. com. Rep. Nat. Com. Mem. adv. council Cornell U. Law Sch. Trustee, Elmira Coll., 1950-63, State U. N.Y., Colgate U.; bd. regents U. State N.Y., 1948-50. Mem. Am., N.Y. State (chmn. banking law sect. 1954), N.Y.C. bar assns. Presbyn. Clubs: Capitol Hill (Washington); Harvard, Century Association, Links, Pilgrims, University (N.Y.C.); Binghamton City, Edgartown Yacht; Cypress Point (Pebble Beach, Cal.); Country of Florida; Edgartown Golf. Home: Hawleyton Rd Binghamton NY 13901 Office: Rockefeller Plaza New York City NY 10020 also Security Mutual Bldg Binghamton NY 13901

HINMAN, JOHN GILBERT, food co. exec.; b. West Norfolk, Va., June 8, 1904; s. G. and Lilla (Vaughn) H.; B.S. in Commerce, U. Va., 1926; postgrad. Harvard Advanced Mgmt. Program, 1954; m. Katherine Adams Mayers, Feb. 5, 1947. With treas. dept. E.I. du Pont Nemours & Co., Wilmington, Del., 1926-37; asst. to pres. Rumford Chem. Works (R.I.), 1938; with Thomas J. Lipton, Inc., Englewood Cliffs, N.J., 1944—, asst. controller, 1949-59, treas., from 1959; mem. adv. bd. 1st Nat. Bank Jersey City, 1960—. Treas., Thomas J. Lipton Found., Inc., Englewood Cliffs, 1959—. Served with CIC, AUS, 1942-43. Mem. Newcomen Soc., English Speaking Union, Delta Sigma Pi. Clubs: Cornell (N.Y.C.); Skytop (Pa.). Home: 14 Sutton Pl New York City NY 10022

HINMON, DONALD LEROY, mfr. constrn. materials; b. Nashua, Ia., Nov. 14, 1910; s. Ray R. and Carrie M. (Funk) H.; B.S., in Civil Engring., Ia. State U., 1934; grad. student nuclear physics, U. Cal. at Los Angeles, 1947; student Am. Mgmt. Assn., 1954; m. Beatrice Loretta Bernick, July 7, 1935; children—Donald LeRoy, John Sanford, Mary Beatrice. With Johns-Manville Corp., 1936—, beginning as staff sales dept., Los Angeles, successively mgr. transite pipe dept., Los Angeles, mgr. aviation products, div. hdqrs. N.Y.C., asst. mgr. transite pipe dept., asst. to gen. mgr. indsl. products div., v.p. and gen. mgr. indsl. insulations div., 1936-60, sr. operating v.p. indsl. divs. group, 1960—; dir. Johns-Manville Products Corp. of Del., Johns-Manville Products Corp. of Mass., Johns-Manville Products Corp. of Pa., Johns-Manville Sales Corp.; dir. Johns-Manville Fiber Glass, Inc.; speaker growth and profit planning Am. Mgmt. Assn. course. Bd. govs. Ia. State U. Found. Served to capt., F.A., AUS, 1941-46. Decorated Bronze Star. Mem. Nat. Insulations Mfrs. Assn., Am. Ordnance Assn., Am. Rocket Soc., Ia. State U. Alumni Assn. (pres. N.Y.C. 1957). Clubs: Union League, Wings, Canadian (N.Y.C.); Blind Brook (Purchase, N.Y.). Home: 55 Hathaway Lane White Plains NY 10605 Office: 22 E 40th St New York City NY 10016

HINN, HAROLD JOSEPH, grain co. exec.; b. Plainview, Tex., Sept. 11, 1910; s. Albert George and Annie Lochie (Mayhugh) H.; student U. Wis., 1927-30, U. Tex., 1930- 31; m. Evelyn Caughron, Sept. 8, 1951; children—Albert George, Carol Robert. With Harvest Queen Mill & Elevator Co., 1933-, chmn. bd., 1940- 50, pres., chief exec. officer, 1950—; pres. Gibraltar Minerals Co., 1955—, Metall. Resources, Inc., 1960—, Internat. Metal Processing Corp., Ltd., 1965—; dir. Citizens Nat. Bank (Lubbock, Tex.), Continental Nat. Bank (Ft. Worth), Preston State Bank. Bd. dirs. Tex. Tech. Coll., Lubbock, 1957—; a founder, chmn. trustee High Plains Research Found., Plainview, Tex., 1956—; trustee Tex. 4-H Youth Devel. Found., 1964—. Home: 5915 Desco Dr Dallas TX 75225 Office: Republic Nat Bank Tower Dallas TX 75201

HINNER, ELMER FRANCIS, retired mfg. co. exec.; b. Reading, Pa., May 12, 1905; s. Elmer Francis and Lulu (Kerling) H.; B.S. in Chem. Engring., Pa. State U., 1927; m. Mae Thelma Yost, June 14, 1927; children—Nancy Ellen (Mrs. J. Statler Miller), Virginia (Mrs. Virginia H. Schoen), Susan (Mrs. Richard S. Brown). With Hercules Powder Co. (name changed to Hercules, Inc. 1966), 1927-70, gen. mgr. cellulose products dept., 1954-60, v.p., mem. exec. com., 1960-68, chmn. bd., 1968-70, also dir., vice chmn. exec. com.; past chmn. Hystron Fibers, Inc.; dir., mem. exec. com. Bank of Del. Trustee Wilmington Med. Center. Mem. Am. Chem. Soc., Soc. Plastics Industry, Sigma Tau, Phi Lambda Upsilon, Phi Kappa Psi. Clubs: N.Y. Athletic (N.Y.C.); Wilmington Country, Hercules Country, Hercules Mens, Wilmington (Wilmington); Pine Valley (N.J.) Golf; Bidermann Golf (Greenville, Del.). Home: PO Box 58 Hillendale Rd Mendenhall PA 19357 Office: Hercules Towers 910 Market St Wilmington DE 19899

HINRICHSEN, JOHN JAMES LUETT, coll. dean; b. Davenport, Ia., July 21, 1903; s. Bernhardt and Maria Louise (Luett) H.; B.S., Ia. State U., 1925; A.M., Harvard, 1927, Ph.D., 1929; student U. Munich, 1934; m. Helen Barnard, June 29, 1929 (dec. Apr. 1936); 1 dau., Helen Louise (Mrs. Richard Hamilton Jones); m. 2d, Margaret Looft, Sept. 3, 1938; children—Sara Margaret (Mrs. Arthur Putnam Roy), John James, MaryAnn (Mrs. Peter Reed Pavan). Instr. math. Ia. State U., 1929-30, asst. prof., 1930-40, asst. to dean Grad. Coll., 1934-38, asso. prof., 1940-54, prof., head math., 1954-60, prof. math., asso. dean Coll. Scis. and Humanities, 1960-61, acting dean, 1961-62, asso. dean and prof. maths., 1962-69, prof. math. and budget and personnel coordinator, 1969—, acting head sociology and anthropology, 1967-69. Mem. Am. Soc. Engring. Edn. (chmn. math. sect. 1961-62), A.A.A.S., Am. Math. Soc., Math Assn. Am. (gov.), Soc. Indsl. and Applied Math., Ia. Acad. Sci. (pres. 1957-58), Sigma Xi, Phi Kappa Phi, Tau Beta Pi, Pi Mu Epsilon, Pi Tau Sigma, Alpha Kappa Delta. Rotarian. Contbr. articles math. jours. Home: 321 Pearson Av Ames IA 50010

HINSDALE, KENNETH PRESTON, actuary; b. Hendersonville, N.C., Oct. 30, 1923; s. William Clinton and Ida (Wood) H.; A.B., U. N.C., 1945; M.A., U. Mich., 1948; m. Marion Mills Herbin, Nov. 16, 1958; children—Catherine Preston, Marjorie Ann. With Jefferson Standard Life Ins. Co., Greensboro, N.C., 1948—, 2d v.p., asso. actuary, 1959-64, v.p., asso. actuary, 1964-67, v.p., actuary, 1967-69, sr. v.p., actuary, 1969—. dir.; 1970—. Served to lt. USNR, 1943- 46, 51-53. Fellow Soc. Actuaries; mem. Acad. Actuaries, Middle Atlantic Actuarial Club (past pres.), Southeastern Actuaries Club. Home: 402 Rockford Rd Greensboro NC 27408 Office: Jefferson Sq Greensboro NC 27420

HINSEY, JOSEPH CLARENCE, med. educator, former med. coll. dean; b. Ottumwa, Ia., Apr. 29, 1901; s. Joseph Edgar and Sarah Belle (Majors) H.; student Ia. Wesleyan Coll., 1918-20; B.S., Northwestern U., 1922, M.S., 1923, D.Sc., 1951; Ph.D., Washington U. Sch. of Medicine, St. Louis, 1927; D.SC. (hon.). Union Coll., 1955, Ia. Wesleyan Coll., 1958; D.H.L., N.J. Coll. of Medicine, 1965; m. Sarah Lillian Callen, June 18, 1926; children—Elaine (Mrs. Donald P. Reynolds), Joseph. Asst. in zoology Northwestern U., 1921-23; instr. biology Western Res. U., 1923-24; asst. in neuro-anatomy, Washington U., 1924- 27, asst. prof., 1927-28; asst. prof. in neuro-anatomy, Northwestern U. Med. Sch., 1928-29, asso. prof., 1929-30; prof. of anatomy Stanford, 1930-36; prof. of physiology and head dept. Cornell U. Med. Sch., New York, 1936-39, prof. of anatomy and head dept., 1939-53, dean, 1942-53; dir. N.Y. Hosp.-Cornell Med. Center, 1953-66, cons., 1966-69; prof. neuroanatomy Cornell U. Med. Coll., 1956-67, prof. neuroanatomy emeritus, 1967—; dir. Am. Hosp. Supply Corp. Chmn. China Med. Bd. N.Y., 1956-70. Mem. Pres.'s Commn. on Med. Needs of Nation, 1952. Mem. bd. mgrs. Meml. Hosp. N.Y.C. Trustee Sloan-Kettering Inst., China Med. Bd.; chmn. NRC commn. acad. radiology, 1966-68. Faculty rep., bd. trustees Cornell U., 1942-53. Recipient Merit award Nu Sigma Nu, 1956; Abraham Flexner award for service to med. edn. Assn. Am. Med. Colls., 1958; Medal award N.Y. Med. Coll., 1960; distinguished service award N.C. Coll. Medicine, 1964, Alumni Merit award Northwestern U., Washington U., Ia. Wesleyan Coll. Fellow A.A.A.S. (v.p. 1950), N.Y. Acad. Scis. (v.p. 1949), Assn. Am. Med. Colls. (pres. 1949; chmn. exec. council 1946-54), Cal. Acad. Sci., Am. Neurol. Soc. (hon.); mem. Am. Assn. Anatomists, Am. Physiol. Soc., Soc. Exptl. Biology and Medicine, Harvey Soc., N.Y. Acad. Medicine, Calif. Acad. Medicine, S.A.R., Pilgrims U.S., Newcomen Soc., St. Andrews Soc., Phi Beta Kappa, Sigma Xi, Phi Delta Theta, Nu Sigma Nu, Alpha Omega Alpha. Republican. Presbyn. Mason (K.T., Shriner). Clubs: Century Assn. (N.Y.C.). Contbr. to med. jours. Home: Apt 5-M Chateau Lorraine Scarsdale NY 10583

HINSHAW, DAVID BURDG, univ. dean; b. Whittier, Cal., Nov. 24, 1923; s. Lindsey and Hazel Grace (Burdg) H.; student La S'erra Coll., Riverside, Cal., 1940-43; M.D., Loma Linda U., 1946; m. Mildred Helen Benjamin, Dec. 23, 1943; children—David Burdg, Kathleen Marie, Daniel Benjamin. Intern, White Meml. Hosp., Los Angeles, 1946-47; fellow Loma Linda U., 1947-48; resident surgery VA Hosp., Portland, Ore., 1950-54; mem. faculty Loma Linda U. Sch. Medicine, 1954—, prof. surgery, chmn. dept., 1961—, dean Sch. Medicine, 1962—. Served with M.C., AUS, 1948-50. Mem. A.C.S., Soc. Univ. Surgeons, Pacific Coast Surg. Assn., Soc. Internat. Surgery, Soc. Surgery Alimentary Tract, Am., Cal. med. assns., San Bernardino County Med. Soc. Contbr. med. jours. Home: 25039 Crestview Dr. Loma Linda CA 92354

HINSHAW, HORTON CORWIN, physician; b. Iowa Falls, Ia., 1902; s. Milas Clark and Ida (Bushong) H.; A.B., Coll. Ida., 1923, D.Sc., 1947; A.M. U. Cal., 1926, Ph.D., 1927; M.D., U. Pa., 1933; m. Dorothy Youmans, Aug. 6, 1924; children—Horton Corwin, Barbara (Mrs. Barbara Baird), William, Dorothy (Mrs. Gregory Patent). Asst. prof. zoology U. Cal., 1927-28; adj. prof. parasitology and bacteriology Am. U., Beirut, Lebanon, 1928-31; instr. bacteriology U. Pa. Sch. Medicine, 1931-33; fellow, 1st asst. medicine. Mayo Found., U. Minn., 1933-35, asst. prof., 1937-46, asso. prof., 1946-49; cons. medicine Mayo clinic, 1935- 49, head sec. medicine, 1947-49; clin. prof. medicine, head div. chest diseases Stanford Med. Sch., 1949-59; clin. prof. medicine U. Cal. Med. Sch., 1959—; chief thoracic disease service So. Pacific Meml. Hosp., 1958-69; dir. med. services Harkness Community Hosp. and Med. Center, San Francisco, 1968—. Mem. Cal. Com. Regional Med. Programs, 1969—. Diplomate Am. Bd. Internal Medicine, Nat. Bd. Med. Examiners. Fellow A.C.P., Am. Coll. Chest Physicians; hon. mem. Miss. Valley Med. Assn.; mem. Nat. Tb Assn. (bd. dirs., chmn. com. therapy, v.p., 1946- 47, 67-68, research com.), Am. Thoracic Soc. (pres. 1948-49), Am. Clin. and Climatol. Soc., Minn. Med. Assn., Am. Bronchoesophalogical Assn., A.M.A., Am. Soc. Clin. Investigation, Central Soc. Clin. Research, Soc. Exptl. Biology and Medicine, Aero-Med. Assn., Minn. Soc. Internal Medicine, Sigma Xi, Phi Sigma, Gamma Alpha. Mem. Soc. of Friends. Del. various internat. confs., 1928-59. Author: Diseases of the Chest, rev. edit., 1969; co-author: Streptomycin in Tuberculosis, 1949. Contbr. over 200 articles to med. publs. Co- discoverer anti-Tb chemotherapy, exptl. and clin., with several drugs. Home: 63 W Shore Rd Belvedere CA 94920 Office: 450 Sutter St San Francisco CA 94108

HINSHAW, RANDALL WESTON, economist; b. La Grange, Ill., May 9, 1915; s. Virgil Goodman and Evelyn (Piltz) H.; A.B., Occidental Coll., 1937, M.A., 1939; Ph.D., Princeton, 1944; m. Pearl Electa Stevens, June 19, 1949; children—Frederic Randall, Robert Louis, Elisabeth Mary. Teaching fellow Harvard, 1942-43; asst. prof. Amherst Coll., 1946-47; vis. prof. Yale, 1957-58, Oberlin Coll., 1958-59, U. So. Cal., 1963-64, Bologna Center, Johns Hopkins, 1965-67; prof. econs. Claremont Grad. Sch., 1960—, chmn. dept., 1967-69; economist div. internat. finance Fed. Res. Bd., 1943-46, 47-52. Spl. adviser and/or U.S. rep. various internat. confs. and coms. South East Club fellow Princeton, 1940-41. Mem. Am. Econ. Assn., Econometric Soc., Council Fgn. Relations, Phi Beta Kappa. Author: The European Community and American Trade, 1964; Monetary Reform and the Price of Gold, 1967; The Economics of International Adjustment, 1970, Contbr. articles to various jours. Home: 755 W 8th St Claremont CA 91711

HINSHAW, VIRGIL GOODMAN, Jr., educator; b. LaGrange, Ill., Nov. 3, 1919; s. Virgil Goodman and Eva (Piltz) H.; B.A., Stanford, 1941; M.A., State U. Ia., 1942; M.A., Princeton, 1943, Ph.D., 1945; m. Alene Kinsey Pryor, June 12, 1950; children—Stephen, Sally. Asst., State U. Ia., Iowa City, 1941-42; instr. philosophy Ohio State U., Columbus, 1946-47, asst. prof., 1947-53, asso. prof., 1953-60, prof., 1960—, dir. grad. studies, 1968—; cons. Army Research Office, 1963, Congress Neurol. Surgeons, 1964. Mem. Am. Philos. Assn., Assn. for Symbolic Logic, A.A.A.S., Am. Assn. U. Profs., Philosophy of Sci. Assn., Ohio Coll. Assn. (sect. pres. 1955-58), Phi Beta Kappa. Democrat. Methodist. Contbr. articles profl. jours. Home: 1573 Kirkley Rd Columbus OH 43221

HINSON, EVERETTE CHAUNCEY, utility co. exec.; b. Monroe, N.C., Nov. 25, 1929; s. Chauncey D. and Carrie (Griffin) H.; student N.C. State U., m. Patsy Jean Wiles, July 18, 1948; 1 son, Everette Chauncey. With Piedmont Natural Gas Co., Inc., Charlotte, N.C., 1953—, asst. treas. 1965-70, treas., 1970—. Trustee Charlotte Nature Museum. Named Outstanding Young Man of Year, Charlotte Jr. C. of C., 1964. Mason (32, Shriner). Home: 6300 Old Providence Rd Charlotte NC 28211 Office: 4301 Yancey Rd Charlotte NC 28201

HINSON, ROBIN LEDBETTER, lawyer; b. Rockingham, N.C., May 26, 1931; s. Minor T. and Emma (Gray) L.; B.S., Davidson Coll., 1953; J.D., U. N.C., 1958; m. Frances Reid Garrett, Mar. 21, 1953; children—Robin L., Reid G., Minor T. Admitted to N.C. bar, 1958; asst. prof. Sch. Law, U. N.C., Chapel Hill, 1958-61, asst. dean, 1959-61; partner firm Leath, Bynum, Blount & Hinson, Rockingham, N.C., 1961-69; asso. gen. counsel Carolina Power & Light Co., Raleigh, N.C., 1969-70; v.p., gen. counsel, sec. Hanes Corp., Winston-Salem, N.C., 1970—; Tchr. N.C. bar rev. course, 1960-70. Mem. N.C. Gen. Statutes Commn., 1961-65, Constn. Study Commn. N.C., 1967-68. Democrat. Methodist. Home: 822 N Pine Valley Rd Winston-Salem NC 27102 Office: PO Box 1413 Winston-Salem NC 27102

HINSVARK, INEZ GENIEVE, univ. dean; b. Brandt, S.D., May 3, 1918; d. Jacob Adolph and Clara Idianna (Moan) Hinsvark; R.N., Luther Hosp. Sch. Nursing, Watertown, S.D., 1939; A.B. San Francisco State Coll., 1951; M.A., Stanford, 1952; Ed.D., U. Cal. at Los Angeles, 1965. Supr. obstetrics Luther Hosp., 1939-40; staff nurse Community Hosp., Montevideo, Minn., 1940-42; staff, then head nurse Phys. and Surg. Hosp., Glendale, Cal., 1942-44, Herrick Meml. Hosp., Berkeley, Cal., 1947-52; coordinator, head clin. dept., also dean S.D. State U., 1952-67; dean Sch. Nursing, U. Wis., Milw., 1967—. Cons. USPHS, 1967—, Purdue U. Sch. Nursing, A & T U. Sch. Nursing, S.D. State U. Sch. nursing. Past pres. S.D. Bd. Nursing. Co-chmn. regional planning com. Gov. S.D. Conf. Aging, 1960; mem. Nat. Com. Edn. Sch. Health Nurses, 1960-61; mem. council Maternal and Child Health, 1953-68; chmn. membership services com. Southeastern Wis. Comprehensive Health Planning Agy., nursing chmn. Red Cross Disaster Com., 1969-70; adv. com. Milwaukee County Hosp. Sch. Nursing; coordinating council Continuing Edn. for Nurses-Milw.; mem. joint com. on revision Wis. Nurse Practice Act; Nat. Adv. Panel on Constrn. Grants to Schs. Nursing; Am. Hosp. Assn. adv. com. to study report Nat. Commn. on Nursing Edn. Mem. bd. Brookings Hosp., Brookings Area Guidance Center. Served with Army Nurses Corps, 1944-47. Mem. Nat. League Nursing, Am., Wis. nurses assns., Am. Legion, Urban League, Am. Public Health Assn., Am. Assn. U. Women, Nat. Soc. Programmed Instrn., Sigma Theta Tau, Phi Kappa Phi, Alpha Lambda Delta (hon.), Pi Gamma Mu, (pres. Gamma chpt. 1959-60), Pi Lambda Theta. Club: Zonta. Office: Sch Nursing U Wis at Milw Milwaukee WI 53211

HINTIKKA, KAARLO JAAKKO, philosopher, research scientist; b. Helsingin pitäjä, Finland, Jan. 12, 1929; s. Toivo Juho and Lempi J. (Salmi) H.; Cand. Phil. Lic. Phil., U. Helsinki (Finland), 1952, Dr.Phil., 1956; exchange student Williams Coll., 1948-49; post-doctoral scholar Harvard, 1954; m. Soili Mirja Iremli Suhonen, June 3, 1956. Jr. fellow Soc. Fellows, Harvard, 1956-59; prof. philosophy U. Helsinki, 1959-70; research prof. Acad. Finland, 1970—; vis. prof. Brown U., 1962, U. Cal. at Berkeley, 1963; prof. philosophy Stanford, winter and spring, 1964—; John Locke lectr. Oxford (Eng.) U., 1964; asst. dean faculty social sci. U. Helsinki, 1963-66. Fellow Center for Advanced Study in Behavioral Scis., 1970-71; fgn. mem. and mem. Forschungsrat of Internationales Forschungszentrum, Salzburg, Austria, 1966—. Decorated comdr. Order of Lion (Finland). Mem. Assn. Symbolic Logic (council 1961-63, European exec. com. 1966—, v.p. 1968-70), Internat. Inst. Philosophy, Internat. Union History and Philosophy Sci. (mem. council div. logic methodology and philosophy of sci. 1968-71, v.p. 1971—), Finnish Acad. Sci. and Letters, Philosophy of Sci. Assn. (governing bd. 1970-72), Societas Scientiarum Fennica. Author: Knowledge and Belief, 1962; Models for Modalities, 1969; Tieto on Valtaa, 1969; Logic, Language-Games and Information, 1972; also articles. Editor-in-chief Internat. Jour. Synthese, 1965—; editor Synthese Library, 1965—; adv. editor Studies in Logic, 1965—; editor Philosophy of Mathematics, 1969, (with Patrick Suppes) Aspects of Inductive Logic, 1966; (with Donald Davidson) Words and Objections, 1969; (with Patrick Suppes) Information and Inference, 1970; cons. editor Metaphilosophy, 1968-, Archiv fuer die Geschichte der Philosophie, 1968—. Home: Mäntypaadentie 13 as 3 00830 Helsinki 83 Finland Office: Dept Philosophy Stanford Univ Stanford CA 94305

HINTON, CLAUDE WILLEY, educator; b. Gatesville, N.C., Aug. 1, 1928; s. Claude W. and Addie (Hudgins) H.; A.B., U. N.C., 1948, M.A., 1950; Ph.D., Cal. Inst. Tech., 1954; m. Jean Marie Belmont, Dec. 26, 1952; children—Rebecca, Claire. Research asso. biology Oak Ridge Nat. Lab., 1954-55; asst. prof. to prof. zoology U. Ga., 1955-68; Mateer prof. biology Coll. Wooster (O.), 1968—; summer vis. prof. U. Wash., 1962, U. Ore., 1965; cons. in field, 1949—. Predoctoral fellow AEC, 1950-52, USPHS, 1952-54. Fellow A.A.A.S.; mem. Genetics Soc. Am., Soc. Am. Naturalists, Sigma Xi. Research behavior chromosomes and its genetic control in Drosophila. Home: 510 Beechwood Av Wooster OH 44691

HINTON, DEANE ROESCH, fgn. service officer; b. Fort Missola Mont., Mar. 12, 1923; s. Joe A. and Doris (Roesch) H.; grad. Elgin (Ill.) Acad., 1940; B.A., U. Chgo., 1943, grad. study, 1946; student Fletcher Sch. Law and Diplomacy, 1951- 52; m. Angela E. Peyraud, May 10, 1946; children—Deborah, Christopher, Jeffrey, Joanna, Veronica. Apptd. fgn. service officer, 1946; with Dept. State, Washington, 1946, 51-52, 55-58; 3d sec., vice consul, Damascus, 1947-48, 2d sec., vice consul, 1948-49; vice consul, Mombasa, Kenya, 1949, consul, 1949-51; 2d sec., consul, Paris, France, 1952-55; attache U.S. Mission to European Communities, Brussels, Belgium, 1958-59, 1st sec., 1959-61; grad. Nat. War Coll., 1962; chief commodity programming div. Dept. of State, 1962-63, dir. Office Atlantic Polit. Econ. Affairs, 1963-67; former dir. European community and Atlantic polit.-econ. affairs; dir. AID mission to Guatemala, 1967-69; dir. AID mission to Chile, econ. counselor, Santiago, 1969-71; asst. dir. Council Econ. Policy, Washington, 1971—; professorial lectr. Am. U., Washington. Served to 2d lt. AUS, 1943-45. Mem. Middle East Inst., Fgn. Service Assn., Royal Central Asian Soc. Home: 6025 Dellwood Pl Bethesda MD 20014 Office: The White House Washington DC

HINTON, JAMES WILLIAM, surgeon; b. Reedville, Va., Mar. 12, 1894; s. John Braxton and Anne Augusta (Crosswell) H.; student Cluster Springs Acad., Va., 1910-13; M.D., U. Va., 1919; LL.D., Hampden Sydney Coll., 1961; m. Jannett Lord, May 19, 1951. Intern surg. service Boston City Hosp., 1917. U. Va. Hosp., 1918-19, N.Y. Post-Grad. Hosp., 1919-21, Sloane's Hosp. for Women, 1921-22; former dir. fourth surg. service, dir. children's surg. service Bellevue Hosp., N.Y.C.; prof., chmn. dept. surgery Post Grad. Med. Sch., N.Y.U., 1949-60; former dir. surg. service Univ. Hosp.; attending surgeon Beekman Downtown Hosp., N.Y.C., Gouverneur Hosp.; cons. surgery N.Y. Women's Infirmary, Jersey City Med. Center, Norwalk (Conn.) Gen. Hosp., Southampton (N.Y.) Hosp., Jamaica (N.Y.) Hosp., St. Agnes Hosp., White Plains, N.Y., Good Samaritan Hosp., Suffern, N.Y., United Hosp., Portchester, N.Y., Nassau Hosp., Mineola, N.Y., Central Suffolk Hosp., Riverhead, N.Y., Elizabeth A. Horton Meml. Hosp., Middletown, N.Y., Wyckoff Height Hosp., Bklyn., Bellevue Hosp., University Hosp., Manhattan VA Hosp., Sherbrooke Hosp.; cons. Columbus Hosp., Manhattan State Hosp. Pres., trustee Royal Coll. Surgeons Found., 1967—. Diplomate, founders group Am. Bd. Surgery. Fellow Royal Coll. Surgeons Eng. (hon.), Royal Coll. Edinburgh (hon.), A.C.S. (chmn. credentials com.), Am. Surg. Assn., Royal Coll. Surgeons in Ireland (hon.), Internat. Surg. Soc., N.Y. Acad. Medicine (v.p. 1944-46); mem. N.Y. (past pres.), Eastern surg. socs., Am. Gastroenterological Soc., Pan Pacific, So. surg. assns., N.Y. Cardiovascular Surgery, James IV Assn. Surgeons (foundeer, sec. 1957-67), Hon. Company Edinburgh Golfers, Alpha Omega Alpha. Club: Links (N.Y.C.). Home: 222 E 80th St New York City NY 10021

HINTON, LONGSTREET, banker; b. Memphis, Apr. 11, 1902; s. Charles Wheat and Linda Branham (West) H.; B.A., Williams Coll., 1923; m. Penna Tew, May 28, 1931 (div. 1949); children—Dirck Longstreet, Christopher Scott, Gail; m. 2d, Odette O'Higgins, Oct. 31, 1952; children—Odette, Charles. Clk., dept. head, mgr. J.P. Morgan Co., N.Y.C., 1923-40; v.p., trust officer J.P. Morgan Co., Inc., 1940-55; sr. v.p., 1955-59, dir., 1957-59; sr. v.p. Morgan Guaranty Trust Co., 1959-62, exec. v.p., 1962—, dir., chmn. trust com., 1963--; dir. Am. Research & Devel. Corp., Transatlantic Reins. Co. Treas., trustee Nassau Hosp.; mem. Abu Dhabi Investment Bd.; mem. com. on trust funds Domestic and Fgn. Missionary Soc. Protestant Episcopal Ch. U.S.A. Clubs: University (N.Y.C.); Creek (gov.), Piping Rock (Locust Valley, N.Y.). Home: Linden Farms Rd Locust Valley Long Island NY 11560 Office: 23 Wall St New York City NY 10008

HINTON, WILLIAM MILLER, psychologist, educator; b. Paris, Ky., Mar. 19, 1907; s. William Miller and Eddie Chiles (Spears) H.; A.B., Washington and Lee U., 1929, M.A., 1930; Ph.D., Ohio State U., 1937; m. Mary Moore Harper, Dec. 22, 1934; 1 son, William Miller. Instr. Washington and Lee U., 1931-36, asst. prof., 1937-42, asso. prof., 1946-51, prof., 1951—, head dept. psychology, 1959—; dir. Washington and Lee U. Counseling Service, 1946-52; personnel cons. U.S. Army, 1942-44, chief counseling br. Separation Center, Ft. Meade, Md., 1944-46; vis. prof. U. Va., 1947—; field psychologist George Fry & Assos., 1953—; cons. counseling psychology VA Central Office, 1955—. Served from 1st lt. to maj., AUS, 1942-46; lt. col. Res., 1950—. Fellow Am. Psychol. Assn., A.A.A.S.; mem. Va. Acad. Sci. (pres. 1959-60), Va. Psychol. Assn. (pres. 1956-57), So. Soc. Philosophy and Psychology (council 1957-60; pres. 1961-62). Democrat. Episcopalian. Home: 15 Jordan St Lexington VA 24450

HINTZ, AUGUST MCCURDY, clergyman; b. Syracuse, Mo., Apr. 14, 1914; s. Fredrick Jacob and Alice (McCurdy) H.; B.A., William Jewell Coll., 1936, D.D., 1948; B.D., Colgate Rochester Div. Sch., 1939; D.H.L. (hon.) Sioux Empire Coll., 1966; postgrad. Am. Bapt. Sem., 1969; m. Dorothy Storm, June 22, 1939; children—John McCurdy, Judith Leigh, Robert August and William August (twins). Ordained to ministry Baptist Ch., 1939; pastor, Buckner, Mo., 1934-36, Pittsford, N.Y., 1937-39; asso. pastor, Dayton, O., 1939-41; pastor, Sioux Falls, S.D., 1941-53, N. Shore Bapt. Ch., Chgo., 1953-63; now minister First Bapt. Ch. Seattle; lectr. Redpath Bur.; condr. radio counseling series The Pastor's Study, WGN, Chgo., 1956-58, devotional programs Power for Living, WMAQ, 1958-59, Outline for Living, 1962; speaker The Layman's Hour, radio program, 1965-66, Good Things Happening series KIRO Radio, 1971—; program planning com. ABC. Bd. mgrs. Am. Bapt. Fgn. Mission Soc., 1946-56, pres., 1956-57; bd. dirs. Council Chs. Greater Seattle; mem. program com. Am. Bapt. Conv., 1968- 69. Mem. bd. Alcohol Problem Assn. Mem. Newcomen Soc. Eng. Mason (32, Shriner). Club: Washington Athletic. Co-author: One Blood. Address: 1111 Harvard Av Seattle WA 98122

HINTZ, CARL WILLIAM EDMUND, librarian; b. London, Eng., Oct. 14, 1907; s. Max Emil and Edith Helen (Newstead) H.; came to U.S., 1924, naturalized, 1937; A.B., DePauw U., Greencastle, Ind., 1932; A.B., U. Mich., 1933, A.M. in Library Sci., 1935; Ph.D., U. Chgo., 1952; m. Frances Julia Bryant, June 5, 1939; children—Stephen Edmund Carl, Peter Bryant. Jr. clk. Brit. Passport Control Office, Berlin, Germany, 1922-24; clk. Studebaker Corp., S. Bend, Ind., 1924-27; asst. charge circulation DePauw U. Library, 1933-35, asst. librarian, 1935- 37; librarian, asso. prof. library sci. U. Md., 1937-43, dir. libraries, prof., 1943-46; librarian Chgo. Natural History Museum, 1946-48; librarian U. Ore., 1948—; dir. libraries of Ore. State System Higher Edn., 1965—; lectr. library sci. Cath. U. Am., 1941-45; Fulbright lectr., India, 1961. Mem. state-wide library survey com. Md. Planning Commn., 1941-45; pres. Md. Library Assn., 1941-43; v.p. Middle Eastern Library Assn., 1938-39. Mem. A.L.A. (council 1954-58; pres. edn. div. 1962-63; chmn. commn. on nat. plan for library edn. 1965-67), Ore. Library Assn. (pres. 1955-56), Pacific N.W. Library Assn. (pres. 1957-58), Assn. Coll. and Research Libraries (sec. univ. libraries sect. 1943-46, chmn. 1958-59), Am. Assn. U. Profs., Delta Upsilon, Delta Sigma Rho, Pi Sigma Alpha, Phi Eta Sigma, Beta Phi Mu. Presbyn. Home: 2460 Pioneer Pike Eugene OR 97401

HINTZ, PHILIP CHANDLER, mfg. exec.; b. Cleve., 1912; grad. Colgate U., 1934; m., 2 children. Vice pres., gen. mgr. Standard Tube Co., subsidiary Mich. Seamless Tube Co., Detroit. Mem. Delta Upsilon. Clubs: Detroit Golf, Detroit Athletic. Home: 1748 Timson Lane Bloomfield Hills MI 48013 Office: 24400 Plymouth Rd Detroit MI 48239

HINTZ, ROBERT LOUIS, r.r. exec.; b. Chgo., May 25, 1930; s. Louis A. and Gertrude V. (Herman) H.; B.S. magna cum laude, Northwestern U., 1960, M.B.A., 1965; m. Gloria M. Safbom, Nov. 12, 1955; children—Cary, Leslie, David, Erin. With C.& O./B.& O. R.R., Balt., 1963—, asst. to v.p., 1968-69, dir. accounting, 1969-70, comptroller, 1970—. Served with USAF, 1950-54. Mem. Cleve. Soc. Security Analysts. Home: 5184 Eliot's Oak Rd Columbia MD 21043 Office: B & O Central Bldg Baltimore MD 21201

HINTZE, GUENTHER, missile scientist; b. Breslau, Germany, July 8, 1906; s. Erwin and Elisabeth (Tottman) H.; B.S. in Elec. Engring., Tech. Coll., Breslau, Germany, 1927, M.Sc., 1929; Ph.D. (hon.), N.M. State U., 1962; m. Else Martinec, June 30, 1939; children—Dagmar Ingrid, Klaus Juergen, Peter Jochen. Came to U.S., 1945, naturalized 1954. Electronic engr. Gen. Electric Co., Breslau, 1929-35; operating mgr. Osram Philips, Berlin, 1935-40; research engr., guidance and control German Rocket Research Center, Peenemuende, 1942, chief design sect. for system evaluation, adviser prodn. and test firings, 1943-45; staff U.S. Army Ordnance, 1945—, head missile evaluation, Ordnance Research and Devel. div., Sub. Office Rocket, Ft. Bliss, Tex., 1946-49, chief system analysis br., Redstone Arsenal, 1949-52, asst. to chief tech. staff White Sands Proving Ground, N.M., 1952-53, chief dynamic systems br., 1953-55; chief flight simulation lab., 1955-64, dir. computer directorate, 1965-66; dir. analysis and computation directorate, 1966 -68, sci. program chmn. first flight simulation symposium, 1956; research prof. dept. elec. engring. Sch. Engring. and Applied Sci., George Washington U., 1968—. Served with German Army, 1940-41. Mem. A.A.A.S., Soc. for Gen. Systems Research. Presbyn. Author: Fundamentals of Digital Machine Computing, 1966; papers on flight simulation. Home: 1733 34th St NW Washington, DC 20007

HINTZE, LEHI FERDINAND, educator, geologist; b. Denver, Apr. 14, 1921; s. Ferdinand F. and Henrietta (Jones) H.; A.B. in Geology, U. Utah, 1941; M.A., Columbia, 1949, Ph.D., 1951; m. Ione Nelson, Nov. 20, 1942; children—Sharon, David N., Paul F., Wayne J. Instr., then asst. prof. Ore. State U., 1949-55; mem. faculty Brigham Young U., 1955—, prof. geology, 1959—, chmn. dept., 1961—. Fellow Geol. Soc. Am.; mem. Am. Assn. Petroleum Geologists, Utah Geol. Soc. (past pres.), Phi Beta Kappa, Phi Kappa Phi. Mem. Ch. of Jesus Christ of Latter Day Saints (high councilman Brigham Young U. stake). Author: Geological Map of Oregon, 1956; Geological Map of Utah, 1963. Home: 1835 North 1450 East St Provo UT 84601

HINZ, CARL FREDERICK, Jr., physician, educator; b. Cleve., Apr. 9, 1927; s. Carl Frederick and Marie (Jones) H.; B.S., Western Res. U., 1948, M.D., 1951; m. Joan Herndon, June 5, 1953; children-Elizabeth, Richard, Catherine, Gretchen. Faculty dept. medicine Western Res. U. Sch. Medicine, Cleve., 1953-67, asst. prof., 1961-67, research asso. div. research in med. edn., 1964- 67; prof., asso. dean U. Conn. Sch. Medicine, 1967—. Markle scholar, 1959-64. Mem. Am. Soc. Clin. Investigation, Am. Assn. Immunologists, Am. Soc. Hematology, Central Soc. Clin. Research, Am. Fedn. Clin. Research, Hartford, Conn. med. socs., Hartford County med. Assn. Home: 11 Highwood Dr Avon CT 06001 Office: U Conn Sch Medicine Hartford CT 06105

HIPP, FRANCIS MOFFETT, ins. exec.; b. Newberry, S.C., Mar. 3, 1911; s. William Frank and Eunice Jane (Halfacre) H.; student The Citadel, 1929-31; A.B., Furman U., 1933, LL.D., 1968; LL.D U. S.C., 1964, The Citadel, 1968; m. Mary M. Looper, Nov. 10, 1935 (dec. 1962); children—Mary Elizabeth (dec.), William, John, Mary Jane; m. 2d. Shirley A. Mattoon, May 11, 1964. With Liberty Life Ins. Co., 1933—, asst. treas., 1936-41, v.p., 1942, pres., chmn. bd., 1943—; pres., chmn. bd. Liberty Corp., Greenville, S.C., 1967—; v.p., dir. Cosmos Broadcasting Corp., Greenville; dir. S.C. Nat. Bank, Columbia, Carolina Pipeline Co., Columbia. Mem. S.C. Devel. Bd., 1955—, chmn., 1959- 63; state v.p. Am. Life Conv., 1947-57, mem. exec. com., 1957-63; mem. exec. com. Life Insurors Conf., 1961-64. Trustee S.C. Found. Ind. Colls., Benedict Coll. (S.C.), Coll. (N.C.), Winchendon Sch. (Mass.); bd. overseers Sweet Briar (Va.) Coll.; adv. council Furman U., U.S.C. Mem. Newcomen Soc., Kappa Alpha, Beta Gamma Sigma. Presbyn. Clubs: Greenville Country, Poinsett, Green Valley Country (Greenville, S.C.); Biltmore (N.C.) Forest Country; Plantation (Hilton Head Island, S.C.); Augusta (Ga.) National Golf. Home: 33 W Avondale Dr Greenville SC 29609 Office: Wade Hampton Blvd Greenville SC 29602

HIPP, SHIRLEY RICHARD, Jr., lawyer; b. Monette, Ark., June 26, 1937; s. Shirley Richard and Dorothy (Jones) H.; student Ark. State U., 1955-56; B.S., U. Ark., 1959, J.D., 1962; m. Myrna Louise Williams, Sept. 15, 1962; children—Richard Allen, Lisa Diane. Admitted to Ark. bar, 1963, since practiced in Fayetteville; asso. firm Wade & McAllister, 1963-65; trust officer, asst. v.p. McIlroy Bank, 1965-67; mem. firm Niblock, Hipp & Gibson, 1967—. Lectr. in law U. Ark., 1964-65; Juvenile Ct. judge Washington County, 1966-69, pres. adv. bd. Founder, pres. N.W. Ark. Estate Planning Council, 1965; dist. dir. Boy Scouts Am., 1966-68; v.p. Abilities Unlimited, Inc. Legal counsel Ark. Young Democrats, 1967. Vice pres., bd. dirs. Boyland of Ark; bd. dirs. Arthritis Found. Recipient Distinguished Service award Fayetteville C. of C., 1965, Kiwanis, 1967; named Ark. Outstanding Young Man, 1968. Mem. Am., Ark., Washington County bar assns., Am. Judicature Soc., Fayetteville Jr. C. of C. (v.p., dir. 1964-67, Distinguished Service award 1967), Delta Theta Phi (dist. chancellor 1968—), Sigma Pi. Episcopalian (vestryman). Kiwanian. Home: 2103 Old Wire Rd Fayetteville AR 72701 Office: 20 E Mountain St Fayetteville AR 72701

HIPPEL, JOHN F. E., lawyer; b. Phila., June 17, 1901; s. John H. and Anna B. (Frey) H.; A.B., U. Pa., 1923, LL.B., 1926; m. Myrabel E. Port, Oct. 29, 1927; children—Barbara P. (Mrs. Andrej Kodjak), Judith P. (Mrs. James T. Lile). Admitted to Pa. bar, 1926, since practiced in Phila.; partner firm Obermayer, Rebmann, Maxwell & Hippel, 1931—. Dir. Bryn Mawr Trust Co. (Pa.). Past pres. bd. dirs. Lower Merion Twp. (Pa.) Sch. Bd. Treas., trustee Hahnemann Med. Coll. and Hosp., Phila.; sec., treas., bd. mgrs. Edwin Forrest Home, Phila. Served with USCGR, 1941-45. Mem. Am., Pa., Phila. (past chmn. com. censors, past bd. govs.) bar assns., Juristic Soc., C. of C. Greater Phila. (past chmn. labor legislation com.), Am. Bible Soc. (hon. life), Phi Delta Phi, Pi Kappa Alpha (nat. pres. 1953- 56; pres. Meml. Found. 1964-66). Presbyn. Mason. Clubs: Union League, Philadelphia Country, Bachelors Barge, Caveat (Phila.). Home: Harriton Rd Bryn Mawr PA 19010 Office: Packard Bldg Philadelphia PA 19102

HIPPLE, ROBERT B., publisher; b. Pierre, S.D., Apr. 23, 1900; s. John Elmer and Ruth (Bowman) H.; student S.D. State Coll., 1917-18; Ph.B., Yale, 1923; m. Lois Henry, Dec. 10, 1926; children—George Robert, John Henry. Mng. editor Capital Jour., Pierre, 1923-39, editor, pub., 1940—. Pres. Hipple Printing Co. Dir. Oabe Conservancy Sub-Dist. Del. Republican Nat. Conv., 1952—. Served as 1st sgt., inf., U.S. Army, 1918-19. Conglist. Home: 331 N Evans St Pierre SD 57501 Office: Capital Jour Pierre SD 57501

HIPPLE, WALTER JOHN, Jr., educator; b. Chgo., Mar. 14, 1921; s. Walter John and Emilie (Scheu) H.; B.A., U. Chgo., 1947, M.A., 1948, Ph.D., 1954; postdoctoral Courtauld Inst., U. London, 1957, Cambridge (Eng.) U., 1961-62; m. Anne Ruth Poier, Nov. 27, 1962. Lectr. Roosevelt U., 1948; instr. U. Chgo., 1948-50, U. Ark., 1951-52; asst. prof. U. Fla., 1952-56; asso. prof. Cornell Coll., 1957-61; prof. U. Pacific, 1962, Ida. State U., 1963, U. So. Cal., summer 1963; chmn. dept. humanities, prof. Ind. State U., Terre Haute, 1963—. Chmn. Com. on Humanities in Secondary Schs. Ind., 1965-69. Served with Signal Corps attached to Air Corps, AUS, 1943-45. Guggenheim fellow, 1961-62. Mem. Modern Lang. Assn., Am. Philos. Assn., Am. Soc. Aesthetics. Author: The Beautiful, The Sublime, and the Picturesque in Eighteenth-Century British Aesthetic Theory, 1957. Editor: An Essay on Taste (1759) by Alexander Gerard with an Introduction by Walter J. Hipple, Jr., 1963. Contbr. articles profl. jours. Home: 1000 S Center St Terre Haute IN 47807

HIPPS, WILLIAM GROVER, corp. exec.; b. Lumber City, Pa., June 8, 1912; s. Gary Peterman and Martha H. Hipps; B.S., U.S. Mil. Acad., 1937; grad. Air War Coll., 1949; m. Juanita Redmond, June 14, 1946; 1 son, William Grover. Comnd. 2d lt. USAAF, 1937, advanced through grades to brig. gen. USAF, 1953; instr. Air War Coll., 1949-51; exec. asst. to sec. air force, 1951, 55; comdr. 313th Air Div., Okinawa, 1955-58; dir. readiness, insp. gen. Hdqrs. USAF U., 1958-62; dep. material Tactical Air Command, 1962-65; dir. operations Air Force Logistics Command, 1965-67, ret., 1967; exec. Philco Ford Corp., Washington, 1967—. Home: 4033 N 27th St Arlington VA 22207 Office: 815 Connecticut Av Washington DC 20006

HIRATA, SHIGEO, architect; b. Tokyo, Japan, Sept. 9, 1906; s. Tokujiro and Narae (Kitagawa) H.; B.Arch., Cornell U., 1931; m. Yasuko Uenoyama, Apr. 16, 1933; children—Tokusuke, Hatsuko (Mrs. Kazuhira Kato). With Delano & Aldrich, N.Y.C., 1930; principal Matsuda & Hirata, architects and engrs., Inc., Tokyo, 1931-66, Matsuda, Hirata & Sakamoto, architects and engrs., Inc., 1966—; archtl. cons. Mitsui & Co., Ltd., Tokyo, 1969—. Fellow A.I.A. (hon.); mem. Archtl. Inst. Japan, Japan Architects Assn. Rotarian. Club: Tokyo. Prin. works include Bank of Japan head office, Tokyo, 1970; Mitsui Bank head office, Tokyo, 1960; Tokyo Internat. Airport Terminal bldgs., 1955—. Home: 2-10-6 Mita Meguro-ku Tokyo Japan Office: Matsuda Hirata & Sakamoto 1-5-17 Motoakasaka Minato-Ku Tokyo Japan

HIROHITO, EMPEROR OF JAPAN; b. Tokyo, Apr. 29, 1901; s. Emperor Yoshihito and Empress Sadako; ed. spl. tutors and The Peers' Sch., m. Princess Nagako Kuni, Jan. 26, 1924; children—Shigeko (dec.), Kazuko, Atsuko, Akihito (Crown Prince), Masahito, Takako. Became regent because of father's illness, 1921; became emperor, 1926; formally enthroned, 1928. Address: Imperial Palace Tokyo Japan

HIRSCH, ARTHUR HENRY, educator, research specialist, writer: b. LeMars, Ia., s. John Leonard and Louise (Kluckhohn) H.; A.B., Cornell Coll., Mt. Vernon, Ia., 1901, A.M., 1907; Ph.D., U. Chgo., 1915. Asst. prof. history and polit. sci. Earlham Coll., 1911-13; prof. history and polit. sci., Ursinus Coll., 1913-16; prof. history Morningside Coll., 1916-19; prof. Am. history on James S. Britton Found., head of dept. Ohio Wesleyan U., 1919-33; vis. prof. Am. history, U. Mich., 1928-30, Roosevelt Coll., 1946-47; lectr. Am. history, Duke U., summers, 1924-27; prof. Am. history, U. of Colo, summer, 1925; research, Library of Congress, summers, 1922-23, 25, New Eng. libraries, 1927; investigator, Ill. Commn. Occupational Diseases, 1912; editor, publs., United Educators, Inc., 1942-44; picture editor publs., Amalgamated Book Prodn. Syndicate, Inc., since 1946; nation wide research projects; exec. dir. Human Relations Research Found. Mem. Netherlands-Walloon-Huguenot Commn., 1924, White House Conf. on marriage and the family; Ohio Hist. Commn. Fellow, stipend scholar, U. Chgo., 1910-12. Fellow Royal Hist. Soc. (Brit.), Soc. for Sci. Study of Sex.; mem. Am. Hist. Assn., Miss. Valley Hist. Soc., Huguenot Soc. of S.C. (life), Am. Assn. U. Profs., Ohio Acad. Social Scis., Nat. Council for Social Studies, Ohio Hist. Soc. (pres. 1919-20), Authors League Am., Phi Beta Kappa. Methodist. Mason, Kiwanian. Club: University (Ann Arbor, Del., Ohio). Author: The Huguenots of Colonial South Carolina, 1925; Sexual Misbehavior of the Upper Cultured, in the U.S., 1930—, 1955; The Love Elite, 196 numerous articles for ednl., profl. publs., including Dictionary Am. Biography. Address: 220 Bagley St Detroit MI 48226

HIRSCH, CHARLES BRONISLAW, educator; b. Bklyn., Jan. 23, 1919; s. Hugo G. and Mary (Romanitch) H.; B.A. in History, Atlantic Union Coll., S. Lancaster, Mass., 1948; M.A. in History and Polit. Sci., Ind. U., 1949, Ph.D., 1954; m. Patricia Parsons, June 1, 1941; children—Judith Rae, Susan Kathryn, Cynthia Jean. Instr. State Tchrs. Coll., New Britain, Conn., 1950-51; asso. prof., chmn. dept. social scis., dir. pub. relations La Sierra Coll., Arlington, Cal., 1951-57; prof. history, chmn. dept. Columbia Union Coll., Washington, 1957-59, pres., prof. history, 1959-65; v.p., prof. history Andrews U., Berrien Springs, Mich., 1965-66; sec. dept. edn. Gen. Conf. Seventh Day Adventists, Washington, 1966—. Bd. trustees Loma Linda U., Andrews U. Served with AUS, 1941-45; ETO. Decorated Bronze Star. Mem. Am. Hist. Assn., Orgn. Am. Historians, Am. Assn. Sch. Adminstrs., Am. Polit. Sci. Assn., Phi Alpha Theta. Rotarian. Home: 4605 Barbara Dr Beltsville MD 20705

HIRSCH, EDWIN WALTER, urologist; b. Chgo., Nov. 23, 1892; s. Samuel and Rosa (Rosenbaum) H.; B.S., U. Chgo., 1914; M.D., Rush Med. Coll., 1916; m. Elsa Newman, June 10, 1928; children—Edwin Joel, Joy Carol. Practice of medicine since 1917, specializing urology; asso. urology, coll. medicine U. Ill., 1923- 36; mem. urological staff Mich. Av. Hosp., Chgo. Served as 1st lt. M.C., AEF, 1917-19. Mem. Am. Assn. Advancement of Sci., A.M.A., Am. Urol. Assn., Chgo. Med. Soc., Chgo. Urol. Soc., Michael Reese Internes Alumni Assn. (past pres.). Author: The Power To Love, 1948; Modern Sex Life, 1948; Sexual Fear, 1950; Prostate Gland Disorder, 1951; How To Improve Your Sexual Relations, 1951; also articles profl. jours. Contbg. author: Sex, Society, and the Individual, 1952; The Sex Life of the American Woman and the Kinsey Report, 1953. Home: 1755 E 55th St Chicago IL 60615 Office: 185 N Wabash Av Chicago IL 60601

HIRSCH, ERIC DONALD, cotton mcht.; b. Marvell, Ark., June 11, 1898; s. Adolph and Getty (Weil) H.; B.A., Cornell U., 1921; m. Lean Aschaffenburg, Apr. 28, 1926; children—Eric Donald, Eleanor (Mrs. Ben K. Baer), Eugene Aschaffenburg. With Allenberg Cotton Co., Memphis, 1921—, pres., 1945-65, chmn. bd., 1965—. Bd. dirs. Memphis Cotton Exchange, 1934-35, 50-51, 52-53, 53-54, 62-63, pres., 1963-64; bd. dirs. N.Y. Cotton Exchange, 1963-64, New Orleans Cotton Exchange, 1948-53; mem. Bremen (Germany) Cotton Exchange, 1958—, Liverpool (Eng.) Cotton Exchange, 1951—; mem. Nat. Export Expansion Council, 1965-66. Served with U.S. Army, World War I; with USNR, World War II. Home: 232 S Highland St Memphis TN 38111 Office: 104 S Front St Memphis TN 38103

HIRSCH, ERIC DONALD, Jr., educator; b. Memphis, Mar. 22, 1928; s. Eric Donald and Leah (Aschaffenburg) H.; B.A., Cornell U., 1950; M.A., Yale, 1955, Ph.D., 1957; m. Mary Monteith Pope, June 15, 1958; children—John, Frederick, Elizabeth. Instr. Yale, 1956-61, asst. prof. English, 1961-64, asso. prof., 1964-66; prof. U. Va., 1966—, chmn. dept. English, 1968—; lectr. in field. Served with USNR, 1950-52. Fulbright fellow, 1955-56; Morse fellow, 1961-62; Guggenheim fellow, 1964-65; sr. fellow Nat. Endowment for Humanities, 1971. Mem. Modern Lang. Assn. Author: Wordsworth and Schelling, A Typological Study of Romanticism, 1960; Innocence and Experience, an Introduction to Blake, 1964; Validity in Interpretation, 1967. Contbr. articles profl. jours. Home: 2006 Pine Top Rd Charlottesville VA 22903

HIRSCH, FELIX EDWARD, historian, librarian; b. Berlin, Germany, Feb. 7, 1902; s. Felix and Stephanie (Szamatolski) H.; Ph.D., U. Heidelberg, 1923; B.S. in L.S., Columbia, 1940; m. Elisabeth Feist, Nov. 6, 1938; children—Roland Felix, Thomas Feist. Came to U.S., 1935, naturalized, 1941. Polit. editor German newspapers, 1924-34; librarian Bard Coll., Annandale-on-Hudson, 1936-54, asso. in German, 1937-42, asst. prof. history, 1942-45, asso. prof., 1945-46, prof., 1946-54, chmn. area tng. program A.S.T.P., 1943- 44; librarian, prof. history Trenton State Coll., 1955—; lecture tour Western Germany, sponsored Am. Mil. Govt., univs. Göttingen, Heidelberg and Munich, summer, 1949; lecture tour Can., sponsored Canadian Inst. Internat. Affairs, 1951; vis. lectr. history Technische U., Karlsruhe, Germany, 1954-55, vis. prof. of history, 1962; vis. prof. history Heidelberg, 1965. Mem. N.Y. bd. regents commission to study integration coll. and univ. library resources, N.Y. State, 1952-54. Research fellow Am. Philos. Soc., 1954-55. Recipient Bard medal for distinguished service, Bard Coll., 1961. Mem. Assn. Coll. and Research Libraries (chmn. com. on standards 1957- 63), A.L.A. (council 1953-57; chmn. history section 1967-68), N.J. Council State Coll. and U. Librarians (chmn. 1968-69), N.J. Library Assn. (exec. bd. 1958-61, 2nd v.p. 1962-63, pres. coll. and univ. sec. 1959-60), Am. Assn. U. Profs., Am. Council on Germany (bd. dirs. 1952-56), Am. Hist. Assn. Mem. Soc. Friends. Author: Germany Ten Years After Defeat, 1955; Biography of Gustav Stresemann, 1964; Twentieth Century America, 1971. Editor: Lassalle Biography (Hermann Oncken), fifth edition, 1966. Contbr. to Studies in Diplomatic History and Historiography in Honor of G.P. Gooch, 1961; Bibliotheca Docet, 1963; Memorial to Federal President Theodor Heuss, 1964; Gegenwart in Rueckblick, 1970. Contbr. articles to profl., gen. publs. Home: 14 Pershing Av Trenton NJ 08618

HIRSCH, GEORGE AARON, publisher; b. N.Y.C., June 21, 1934; s. George J. and Sylvia (Epstein) H.; A.B. magna cum laude, Princeton, 1956; M.B.A., Harvard, 1962; m. Brenda Baldwin Walker; 1 son, David Aaron. With Time-Life Internat., 1962—; pres., treas., dir. New York Mag. Co., 1967- -; dir. Aeneid Equities, Inc. Mem. exec. com. Princeton Alumni Council; mem. council Princeton U. Community. Bd. dirs. Union Settlement Assn. Served as officer USNR, 1957-60. Home: 246 E 32d St New York City NY 10016 Office: New York Mag 207 E 32d St New York City NY 10016

HIRSCH, HAROLD SELLER, mfg. exec.; b. Portland, Ore., Sept. 3, 1907; s. Max S. and Clementine (Seller) H.; A.B., Dartmouth, 1929; m. Barbara Honeyman, May 25, 1934 (div.); children—Frederic S., Janet H.; m. 2d, Elizabeth Blair, Nov. 5, 1949. With White Stag Mfg. Co., Portland, Ore., 1929—, beginning as factory apprentice and stockroom clk., successively salesman, designer, advt. and sales mgr., planning mgr. womens div., v.p., exec. v.p., 1929- 54, pres., 1954-64, chmn. bd., 1964-70, chmn. exec. com., 1970—; dir. Warnaco, Inc. Commr. Port of Portland, 1961-69, treas., 1962, sec., 1963, v.p., 1966, pres., 1967; mem. nat. adv. council Nature Conservancy; Portland Met. chmn. Nat. Alliance Businessman, 1970—. Pres., trustee Gabel Country Day Sch., Portland; pres. Ore. Mental Health Assn.; treas. Boys and Girls Aid Soc. Ore.; mem. Dartmouth Coll. Alumni Council, 1960-61; v.p. Dartmouth Alumni Assn., 1969—; bd. Ore. Ceramic Studio, Portland Art Mus. Sch., Portland Civic Theatre, Council Social Agys. Mem. SSS Bd., Portland 1942-43; spl. cons. O.Q.G., Research and Devel. Div., Washington, 1943-44. Trustee Reed Coll., Portland; bd. dirs. Isam and Rose White Found., 1966—, pres., 1971; bd. dirs. Neskowin Coast Found., 1970—, treas., 1970—. Mem. Ore. Mens' Apparel Assn. (pres.), Pacific N.W. Apparel Mfrs. Assn. (pres.), United World Federalists (nat. adv. bd.), Ski Industries Am. (pres. 1963- 65, hon. chmn. 1965-69, hon. dir. 1969—), Nat. Ski Patrol (hon.), U.S. Ski Writers Assn. (hon.). Clubs: Portland Hunt, Highlands Racquet, Multnomah Athletic, Columbia Hounds (Portland); University, Dartmouth (N.Y.C.). Home: 255 SW Harrison St Portland OR 97201 Office: 5200 SE Harney Dr Portland OR 97226

HIRSCH, HENRY, appliance and furniture co. exec.; b. Bklyn. June 9, 1903; s. Louis and Esther (Reyer) H.; student Textile Sch., 1920; m. Myrtle Getelson, June 22, 1937; children—Carole (Mrs. Michael Friedman), Richard, David. Pres. Welbilt Corp., Maspeth, N.Y., 1955-70, chmn., 1970—; chmn. Unagusta Mfg. Corp., Waynesville, N.C., 1969—; dir. Gen. Instrument Corp., N.Y.C. Home: 910 Fifth Av New York City NY 10021 Office: Welbilt Corp Maspeth NY 11378

HIRSCH, HOWARD CARLYLE, investment banker and broker; b. N.Y.C., Sept. 10, 1896; s. Charles Sidney and Ida (Hesslein) H.; student Columbia, 1916-17; LL.D. (hon.), Syracuse U. 1961; m. Suzanne Madeleine Couton, Feb. 18, 1937, With Hirsch & Co., N.Y.C., 1920—, sr. partner, 1938—. Pres. Solomon and Blanche de Jonge Found.; trustee Montefiore Hosp.; hon. gov. Am. Hosp., Paris. Served with USNRF, 1918-20. Mem. Chgo. Bd. Trade, N.Y. Commodity Exchange, Liverpool Cotton Exchange. Mem. N.A.M. Clubs: Travellers (Paris); Motor Yacht de la Cote d'Azur (Cannes, France). Home: 440 Park Av New York City NY 10022 Office: 191 W Route 59 Nanuet NY 10954

HIRSCH, IRA JEAN, coll. dean; b. N.Y.C., Feb. 22, 1922; s. Ellis Victor and Ida (Bernstein) H.; A.B., N.Y. Coll. for Tchrs., 1942; A.M., Northwestern U., 1943; M.A., Harvard, 1947, Ph.D., 1948; m. Shirley Helene Kyle, Mar. 21, 1943; children—Eloise, Richard, Elizabeth, Donald. Research asst. psycho-acoustic lab. Harvard, Cambridge, Mass., 1946-47, research fellow, 1947-51; with Central Inst. for Deaf, St. Louis, 1951—, asst dir. research, 1958-65, dir., 1965—; mem. faculty or adminstrn. Washington U., St. Louis, 1951—, prof. psychology, 1961—, dean faculty arts and scis., 1969—; vis. prof. U. Paris, France, 1962-63. Chmn. standards Am. Nat. Standards Ins., also U.S. del Internat. Standards Orgn., 1962—. Bd. dirs. St. Louis Coalition for the Environment. Served with USAAF, 1943-45, AUS, 1945-46. Recipient Biennial award Acoustical Soc. Am., 1956, Assn. Honors, Am. Speech and Hearing Assn., 1968. Fellow Acoustical Soc. Am. (pres. 1967-68), Am. Psychol. Assn., Am. Speech and Hearing Assn. (exec. council 1958-61, 65-68). Author: The Measurement of Hearing, 1952. Contbr. profl. jours. Home: 6629 Waterman St St Louis MO 63130

HIRSCH, JACQUES MAURICE GEORGES, advt. agy. exec.; b. Liege, Belgium, May 27, 1907; s. Henry H.; ed. Institute Polytechnique de Glons (Belgium); m. Marie-Magdeleine Lucy, Mar. 15, 1950. Pres., mgmt. dir. Dorland & Gray S.A., Paris, France. Office: 65167 Av des Champs Elysees Paris 8e France*

HIRSCH, JAMES GERALD, physician, scientist; b. St. Louis, Oct. 31, 1922; s. Mack J. and Henrietta B. (Schiffman) H.; B.S., Yale, 1942; M.D., Columbia, 1946; m. Marjorie Manne, June 6, 1943; children—Ann I., Henry J. Intern, then asst. resident physician Barnes Hosp., St. Louis, 1946-48; NRC fellow Rockefeller U., N.Y.C. 1950-52, asst. prof. medicine and microbiology, 1952-56, asso. prof., 1956-60, prof., mem. inst., 1960 —. Served to capt. USAF, 1948-50. Mem. Harvey Soc., Am. Assn. Immunologists, Soc. Am. Bacteriologists, Am. Acad. Microbiology, Soc. Exptl. Biology and Medicine, A.A.A.S., Am. Soc. Clin. Investigation, Assn. Am. Physicians, Alpha Omega Alpha. Home: 201 E 62d St New York City NY 10021

HIRSCH, JERRY, educator, biologist, psychologist; b. N.Y.C., Sept. 20, 1922; s. Samuel M. and Mollie (Barnett) H.; student Johns Hopkins, 1938-40; B.A., U. Cal. at Berkeley, 1952, Ph.D., 1955; m. Marjorie J. Barrie, July 29, 1950; 1 son, Wesley M. NSF fellow U. Cal. at Berkeley, 1955-57; asst prof. psychology Columbia, 1956-60; NJH fellow Center For Advanced Study in Behavioral Scis., Stanford, Cal., 1960-61; asso. prof. U. Ill., Urbana, 1960-63, prof. psychology and zoology, 1963—. Mem. com genetics and behavior Social Sci. Research Council, 1962-65; mem. behavioral scis. tng. com. Nat. Inst. Gen. Med. Scis., NJH, 1966-70. Recipient Aux. Research award Social Sci. Research Council, 1962. Mem. A.A.A.S., Am. Assn. U. Profs., Animal Behavior Soc., Am. Genetics Assn., Am. Inst. Biol. Scis., Am. Psychol. Assn. Am. Soc. Naturalists, Ecol. Soc., Genetics Soc. Am., Psychonomic Soc., Soc. Study Evolution. Contbr. to Roots of Behavior, 1962; Expanding Goals of Genetics in Psychiatry, 1962. Contbr. articles profl. jours. Home: 2012 Zuppke Circle Urbana IL 61801

HIRSCH, JOHN, theatre dir.; b. Siofok, Hungary, Jan. 5, 1930; s. Joseph and Ilona (Horjath) H.; student Gymanasium, Budapest; B.A., U. Man. (Can.), 1952, D.Litt. (hon.), 1966; LL.D. (hon.), U. Toronto, 1967. Arrived in Can., 1947; founder Theatre 77, also Man. Theatre Concert; work at Vancouver Internat. Festival, Crest Theatre, Toronto, Canadian Broadcasting Corp.; asso. artistic dir. Stratford Festival, Can.; dir. prodn. Lincoln Centre Repertory, also New Haven prodn.; exec. Theatre Communication Group, Canadian Theatres Centre, also Royal Winnipeg Ballet. Recipient Order of Can. Service medal, 1967, Centennial medal; hon. fellow Univ. Coll., U. Man.; recipient Nat. Council Jewish Women award, 1958; Leonard Meml. scholar, 1952, Poetry Soc. award, 1952. Author: (play for children) Box of Smiles; also articles, poems, drawings.

HIRSCH, JOSEPH, artist; b. Phila., Apr. 25, 1910; s. Charles S. (M.D.) and Fannie (Wittenberg) H.; B.A., Central High Sch., Phila., 1927; student Phila. Coll. of Art, 1927-31; m. Ruth L. Schindler, Oct. 30, 1938; children—Charles, Paul; m. 2d Genevieve Baucheron, July 19, 1955; 1 son, Frederic Henri-Joseph. Paintings exhibited in prin. museums and galleries of U.S., 1934—; one-man shows, N.Y.C., Paris, Phila., Chgo., Beverly Hills, 1934—; also represented permanent collections. Instr. painting Art Students League, 1959-67; vis. artist at Dartmouth Coll., 1966. War artist corr. AUS, USNR, 1943-44. Awarded Woolley fellowship to Paris, Inst. Internat. Edn., 1935; Guggenheim fellowship 1942, 43; awarded grant Nat. Inst. Arts and Letters, 1947; Fulbright research fellowship to France, 1949. Recipient 4th prize Met. Mus. Art, 1951; $000 Altman prize, figure painting, N.A.D., 1959, 66; purchase prize Butler Inst., 1965; Carnegie prize N.A.D., 1968. Mem. Artists Equity Assn. (founder; 1st treas.), N.A.D., Phila. Water Color Club, Nat. Inst. Arts and Letters (life). Home: 90 Riverside Dr New York City NY 10024 Studio: 2231 Broadway New York City NY 10024

HIRSCH, JULES, physician; b. N.Y.C., Apr. 6, 1927; s. Benjamin and Eva (Rand) H.; student Rutgers U., 1943-45; M.D., Southwestern Med. Sch. U. Tex., 1948; m. Constance Pendergast, Aug. 15, 1957 (div. 1970); children—David Raphael, Joshua Michael. Intern Duke Hosp., 1948-50; asst. resident medicine N.Y. State Coll. Medicine, Syracuse, 1950-51, resident, 1951-52, instr. medicine, 1952; research and teaching medicine and lipid metabolism, N.Y.C., 1954- -; asst. physician Rockefeller Inst. Med. Research and Hosp., 1954-55, asst., sr. asst. physician, 1955-56, asst. prof., asso. physician, 1956-60, asso. prof., physician to hosp., 1960-67, prof., sr. physician to hosp., 1967—. Chmn. Scientists Com. Pub. Information, 1957-61, bd. dirs., 1962-68; chmn. Gordon Conf. Lipid Metabolism, 1961; vice chmn. Scientists Inst. Pub. Information, 1963-69; lectr. New Sch. for Social Research, 1967; mem. adv. bd. N.Y.C. Dept. Mental Health. Bd. dirs. Assn. Mentally Ill Children of Manhattan; mem. adv. bd. Young Adult Inst. Served with USCGR and USPHS, 1952-54. Recipient Distinquished Alumnus award Southwestern Med. Sch., U. Tex., 1968. Diplomate Am. Bd. Internal Medicine, Am. Bd. Nutrition. Mem. A.A.A.S., Am. Fedn. Clin. Research, Am. Inst. Nutrition, Am. Oil Chemists Soc., Am. Psychosomatic Soc., Am. Soc. Clin. Investigation, Am. Soc. Clin. Nutrition, Am. Heart Assn., Harvey Soc., Soc. Exptl. Biology and Medicine, Assn. Am. Physicians, Sigma Xi, Alpha Omega Alpha. Editorial bd. Jour. Nutrition, 1962-67. Asso. editor Jour. Lipid Research, 1959-69, adv. bd., 1969—; editorial bd. Archives Internal Medicine, 1967- -, Psychosomatic Medicine, 1968—. Contbr. articles profl. jours. Home: 1680 York Av New York City NY 10028

HIRSCH, MAURICE, lawyer; b. Houston, Jan. 13, 1890; s. Jules and Theresa (Meyer) H.; B.A., MA., U. Va., 1910; J.D., Harvard, 1913; LL.M., U. Tex., 1914; m. Winifred Busby, Jan. 25, 1947. Practiced in Houston, 1914-17, 18-42, 47—, sr. partner firm Hirsch, Westheimer & Block. Chmn. Civil Service Commn., City of Houston, 1915-17; sec. priorities com. War Industries Bd., 1917-18. Expert cons. War Dept. Price Adjustment Bd., 1942, chief, settlements div. of War Dept. Price Adjustment Bd., 1942; mem. and vice chmn. Price Adjustment Bd., and dep. dir. renegotiation div., Hdgrs. A.S.F., 1943; dir. renegotiation div. and chmn. War Dept. Price Adjustment Bd., 1944-1947; mem. and chmn. Joint Price Adjustment Bd. (War, Navy and Treasury Depts., R.F.C., Maritime Commn. and War Shipping Adminstrn.), 1944-47; mem. War Contracts Price Adjustment Bd. (War, Navy and Treasury Depts., etc.), 1945-47, chmn. Feb. 1945-47. Chmn. bd. Wald Transfer and Storage Co., Wald Terminal Warehouse Co., Falstaff Distbg. Co.; dir. Houston Nat. Bank. Hon. lipe mem. exec. bd. Sam Houston Area council Boy Scouts Am. Served as col., AUS, 1944; detailed in Judge Adv. Gen.'s Dept., 1944; Gen. Staff Corps 1944-47; brig. gen., AUS, 1946- 50; brig. gen. USAR., 1950-58. Decorated D.S.M. (U.S.); Stella Della Solidariata Italiana. Life mem. bd. trustees Salesmanship Club Camp for Children; mem. internat. council Mus. Modern Art (N.Y.C.); bd. dirs. Houston Grand Opera Assn.; past chmn., hon. life mem. U.S.O. Council Houston and Harris County; bd. govs. Shrine Hosps. Crippled Children; mem. Met. Opera Nat. Council of New York. Recipient Distinguished Service medal Texas Heritage Found. Mem. Jr. C. of C. (hon. life), Am., Tex., Harris Co. bar assns., Houston Symphony Soc. (pres. 1956-70, dir.), Com. Fgn. Relations, Confrerie des Chevaliers du Tastevin, Confrerie de la Chaine Des Rotisseurs, Rice U. Assos., Japan-Am. Soc. of Houston (pres.), Am. Legion, Res. Officers Assn., Raven Soc. U. Va., Phi Beta Kappa, Delta Sigma Rho, Mason (32 Shriner), Kiwanian, Elk (hon. life); mem. B'nai B'rith (past pres. dist. 7). Clubs: Houston, Salesmanship (hon. life), Houston Press (hon. life), Petroleum, Town, Coronado, Allegro, Criterion, Ramada, Lakewood Yacht, River Oaks Country, Bolero, University (Houston); Army and Navy; Nat. Aviation (Washington); Mt. Kenya Safari (Africa); Southern Cross (Little Cayman). Home: 3308 Chevy Chase Dr Houston TX 77019 Office: Niels Esperson Bldg Houston TX 77002

HIRSCH, MORRIS WILLIAM, mathematician, educator; b. Chgo., June 28, 1933; s. David Edelstadt and Valia (Porwancher) H.; student St. Lawrence U., 1950-52; M.A., U. Chgo., 1954, Ph.D., 1958; m. Charity Burns, May 18, 1957; children—Jennifer, Michael. Postdoctoral fellow Inst. Advanced Study, Princeton, 1958-59; prof. math. U. Cal. at Berkeley, 1960—, vice chmn. dept., 1966; vis. scholar, Cambridge (Eng.) U., 1963, U. Geneva (Switzerland), 1968. Organizer, co-chmn. Vietnam Day Com. Berkeley 1965. Mem. Am. Math. Soc., U. Chgo., Folklore Soc. (founder). Sigma Xi. Asso. editor Annals of Mathematics. Home: 841 Coventry Rd Kensington CA 94707 Office: Math Dept U Cal at Berkeley Berkeley CA 94720

HIRSCH, NATHAN OVERMEYER, diversified mfg. co. exec.; b. Cin., May 21, 1910; grad. Phillips Acad., Andover, Mass., 1927; B.S., Princeton, 1931; postgrad. Mass. Inst. Tech., 1931-33; m. Jean R. Holland, June 16, 1935; children--Lois A., Andrew M., James. Salesman, Brown Mfg. Co., Boston, 1932-33; jr. engr. Ball Metals Co., Carson City, Nev., 1933-36, engr., 1936-37, sr. engr., 1937-40; project engr. Kingston Engrng. Co., Los Angeles, 1940-43; with dept. engrng. City of Denver, 1946-50, dep. head, 1950-52; 2d v.p. Johnson Mfg. Co., Kansas City, Kansas, 1952-54, v.p. for engrng., 1954-57; v.p. research Consol. Industries, Inc., South Bend, Ind., 1957-60, exec. v.p., 1960-65, pres., 1965-70, chmn. bd., chief exec. officer, 1970--, also dir.; dir. ABC Chem. Co., 2d Nat. Bank, Country Food Storage Co., Providence Indsl. Corp. (Ind.), Wilson Investment Co., Inc., Hammond Life Ins. Co., Inc. (Ind.), Prudential Ins. Co., Haverford Mfg. Co., Leader Pub. Co. Pres., Dewey High Sch., Kansas City, Mo., 1953-54; fund chmn. local div. Salvation Army, 1959-60. Mem. South Bend Republican Com., 1964-68. Bd. dirs. Ind. council Boy Scouts Am., 1969-71; trustee Lovell Found. Served to lt., Corps Engrs., AUS, 1943-45. Decorated Bronze Star medal. Member N.A.M., South Bend C. of C. (v.p. 1963-65, dir. 1965-70), Am. Mgmt. Assn., Ind. Engrs. Soc. (program com. 1961-62), Princeton Alumni Assn. Episcopalian. Rotarian, Optimist. Clubs: South Bend Golf; Links (N.Y.C.). Home: 6823 Broad Terrace Av South Bend IN 46505 Office: PO Box 1019 Los Angeles CA 90054

HIRSCH, R.F., bank exec. Auditor, Bank of Can. Office: Bank Canada Ottawa Ontario Canada*

HIRSCH, RICHARD LEWIS, industrialist; b. Bklyn., May 4, 1941; s. Henry and Myrtle (Getelson) H.; student Brown U., 1959-63; m. Joyce Finker, Mar. 15, 1964; children—Lawrence Allen, Daniel Paul. With Welbilt Corp., Maspeth, N.Y., 1963—, pres, 1970—; v.p. Padar Realty, Inc. Sec., bd. dirs. Fifth Av. Synagogue; bd. dirs. Yeshiva Torah Vodaath. Home; 630 Park Av New York City NY 10021 Office: Welbilt Sq Maspeth NY 11378

HIRSCH, ROBERT WILLIAM, lawyer; b. Tripp, S.D., Oct. 12, 1925; s. Raymond and Linda (Schmiedt) H.; B.A. in Math., U. S.C., 1946; J.D., U. S.D., 1949; m. Lyla Voorhees, Feb. 14, 1968; children—John, James, Jayne, Sarah. Admitted to S.D. bar, 1949—; atty., Tripp, 1950-68; state's atty. Hutchinson County, 1953-57. Scoutmaster Sioux council Boy Scouts Am., 1949-65; past chmn., mem. exec. bd. Legislative Research Council. Chmn. Young Republicans, Hutchinson County (S.D.), 1949-52; mem. S.D. Senate, 1956-69. Served with USNR, 1943-47. Mem. Luth. Laymen's League (internat. pres. 1964-68), S.D., Am. bar assns., Am. Trial Lawyers Assn., Jud. Council S.D., Phi Kappa Delta, Phi Delta Phi, Phi Mu. Home: 2110 Mulberry St Yankton SD 57078 Office: 311 W 3d St Yanktown SD 57078

HIRSCH, WERNER ZVI, educator; b. Linz, Germany, June 10, 1920; s. Waldemar and Toni (Morgenstern) H.; came to U.S., 1946, naturalized, 1955; B.S. with highest honors, U. Cal., 1947, Ph.D., 1949; m. Hilde E. Zwirn, Oct. 30, 1945; children—Daniel, Joel, Ilona. Instr. econs. U. Cal., 1949- 51; econ. affairs officer UN, 1951-52; economist Brookings Instn., Washington, 1952-53; asst. research dir. St. Louis Met. Survey, 1956-57; prof. econs. Washington U., St. Louis, 1953-63; economist Resources for Future, Inc., Washington, 1958-59; dir. Inst. Govt. and Pub. Affairs, U. Cal. at Los Angeles, also prof. econs., 1963—; cons. Internat. Inst. Ednl. Planning, Paris, 1969—, Rand Corp., 1958—, VA, 1970—. Trustee Midwest Research Inst., 1966—; bd. dirs. Grunwald Graphic Arts Found., 1970—. Mem. Nat. Acad. Scis. (com. research recreation and leisure 1968), Am. Econ. Assn., Am. Farm Econ. Assn., Regional Sci. Assn., Am. Statis. Assn., Phi Beta Kappa, Sigma Xi. Author: Introduction to Modern Statistics, 1957; Analysis of the Rising Costs of Education, 1959; Urban Life and Form, 1963; Elements of Regional Accounts, 1964; Regional Accounts for Public Decisions, 1966; Inventing Education for the Future, 1967; The Economics of State and Local Government, 1970; Regional Information for Government Planning, 1971; Fiscal Crisis of America's Central Cities, 1971. Home: 11601 Bellagio Rd Los Angeles CA 90049

HIRSCHBACH, FRANK DONALD, educator; b. Berlin, Germany, May 13, 1921; s. Martin and Rose (Borchard) H.; came to U.S., 1939, naturalized, 1943; B.S., S. Conn. State Coll., 1946; M.A., Yale, 1949, Ph.D., 1952. Asst. prof. German, Clark U., 1957-58; faculty U. Minn., Mpls., 1958—, prof. German, 1966—, dir. honors div., 1971—. Dir. Classrooms Abroad, Inc., 1956-70. Served with AUS, 1943-45. Morse fellow Yale, 1954-55. Mem. Modern Lang. Assn., Midwest Modern Lang. Assn. (v.p. 1962-64), Am. Assn. Tchrs. German (pres. Minn. 1964-66), Am. Assn. U. Profs. Author: The Arrow and the Lyre: The Role of Love in the Works of Thomas Mann, 1955. Contbr. articles to profl. jours. Home: 1913 Penn Av S Minneapolis MN 55405

HIRSCHBERG, JOSEPH GUSTAV, educator, physicist; b. Chgo., Apr. 13, 1921; s. Joseph Gustav and Lillian (Kahn) H.; A.B., Dartmouth, 1943; M.S., U. Wis., 1951, Ph.D., 1952; m. Ginette Henriette Tetard, Apr. 26, 1947; children—Dorothy Jean, Joseph Gerald, Anne Marie, Lynn Susan. Research asso. U. Wis., 1953-57; head optical group, also research physicist Plasma Physics Lab., Princeton, 1958-65, now cons.; professeur d'Echange U. Paris (France), 1963; prof. physics, chmn. dept. U. Miami (Fla.), 1965—; contractor Langley Research Center, NASA, 1966—. Served to capt. USAAF, 1943-47. Fellow Am. Phys. Soc., Optical Soc. Am.; mem. A.A.A.S., Fla. Acad. Scis., Phi Beta Kappa, Sigma Xi, Sigma Pi Sigma. Co-discoverer telluric sodium absorption in solar radiation; inventor optical spectroscopic devices. Home: 1046 Alfonso Av Coral Gables FL 33146

HIRSCHBOECK, HERBERT C., lawyer; b. Milw., June 5, 1898; s. Stephen H. and Katherine (Heiser) H.; LL.B., Marquette U., 1921; m. Myrtle J. Dundon, Sept. 29, 1934; children—Nancy E., Cathy M. Admitted to Wis. bar, 1921, since practiced in Milw. Chmn. Whyte, Hirschboeck, Minahan, Harding & Harland, S.C.; dir. Cudahy & Sons, Inc., Yahr-Lange Inc. Pres. Milw. Bar Assn. Found., 1958-65. Mem. Am., Wis., Milw. (pres. 1945-46) bar assns., Am. Judicature Soc., Nat. Tax Assn., Am. Law Inst. Clubs: Milwaukee Athletic, Town. Roman Catholic. K.C. Home: 405 E Montclaire Av Milwaukee WI 53217 Office: 2100 Marine Plaza Milwaukee WI 53202

HIRSCHBOECK, JOHN STEPHEN, physician, educator; b. Milw., Mar. 25, 1910; s. Stephen H. and Katherine (Heiser) H.; B.S., Marquette U., Milw., 1931, M.D., 1937, M.S., 1941; m. Rosemary Louise Bach. May 22, 1943; children—Paula, John Karl, Lisbeth, Katherine, Laura Marie. Research erythrocyte physiology and blood coagulation, 1938-42; instr. physiology Marquette U. Sch. Medicine, 1938-42, instr. medicine, 1945- 47, dean sch. medicine, 1947-65, v.p. sch. of medicine, 1965-66, regional program coordinator, 1966—; cons. hematology Milwaukee County Hosp. and VA Hosp., Wood, Wis. Served as lt. comdr., M.C., USNR, 1941-45; Guam, 1944-45. Diplomate Am. Bd. Internal Medicine. Mem. Internat. Soc. Hematology, A.M.A., Am. Coll. Physicians, A.A.A.S., Soc. for Exptl. Biology and Medicine, Central Soc. for Clin. Research, Milw. Acad. Medicine, Alpha Omega Alpha, Phi Beta Pi. Roman Catholic. Club: University (Milw.). Home: 3948 N Harcourt Pl Milwaukee WI 53211 Office: 110 E Wisconsin Av Milwaukee WI 53202

HIRSCHFELD, ALBERT, artist; b. St. Louis, June 21, 1903; s. Isaac and Rebecca (Rothberg) H.; student Nat. Acad., Art Students Leaque, County Council, London, Julienne's, Paris; m. Florence Ruth Hobby, July 13, 1927; m. 2d, Dorothy Dolly Haas, May 8, 1943; 1 dau., Nina. Sculptor; one- man exhbns. include Newhouse Gallery, 1928, Waldorf Astoria, 1932, Morgan Gallery, 1936, Guy Mayer Gallery, 1942, John Heller Gallery, 1959, Hammer Gallery, 1967; theatr corr. in Moscow for N.Y. Herald Trib., 1927; theater caricaturist for N.Y. Times, 1925—; rep. permanent collections St. Louis Art Mus., Butler Inst. Am. Art, Whitney Mus. Am. Art, Cleve. Art Mus., N.Y.C. Mus., N.Y. Pub. Library, Fogg Mus., Bklyn. Mus., Met. Mus. Art, Mus. Modern Art, Davenport Municipal Art Gallery, Mus. U. Wis., Lincoln Center Mus. Performing Arts, N.Y.C.; murals in Fifth Av. Playhouse, Manhattan Playbill Room, N.Y.C., Am. Pavilion, World's Fair, 1958. Recipient Am. Specialist grant U. S. State Dept., 1960. Author: Manhattan Oases, 1932; Harlem, 1942 (musical comedy) Sweet Bye and Bye, 1946; The American Theatre, 1961; (with S. J. Perlman) Westward Ha 1949, Show Business is No Business, 1951; Hirschfeld Folio, 1964; The World of Hirschfeld, 1970; Rhythm (folio 10 lithographs) 1970. Home: 122 E 95th St New York City NY 10028

HIRSCHFELD, RUDOLF ARNO, educator, mathematician; b. Rotterdam, The Netherlands, Feb. 17, 1928; s. Hirsch and Clasina (Tollig) H.; M.Sc., U. Amsterdam, 1952; Ph.D., U. Utrecht, 1960; m. Francisca Cammelot, July 11, 1951; children—Anja, Frank. Came to U.S., 1969. Tchr., Dutch high schs., 1951-60; asst. prof. U. Utrech, 1960-63; asso. prof. U. Nijmegen, 1963-69; prof. math. U. Hawaii, 1969—. Mem. Am. Math. Soc., Wiskundig Genootschap. Editor: New Archive for Math, 1969. Home: 1007 Maniniholo St Honolulu HI 96821

HIRSCHFELDER, JOSEPH OAKLAND, educator, chemist, physicist; b. Balt., May 27, 1911; s. Arthur Douglass and May Rosalie (Straus) H.; student U. Minn., 1927-29; B.S., Yale, 1931; Ph.D., Princeton, 1936, postgrad. 1936- 37; m. Elizabeth Stafford Sokolnikoff, Mar. 7, 1953. Research asso. Wis. Alumni Research Found., 1937-40; instr. chemistry and physics U. Wis., 1940-41, asst. prof. chemistry, 1941-42, prof., 1946—, dir. U. Wis. Naval Research Lab., 1946-59, dir. Theoretical Chemistry Lab., 1959-62, Homer Adkins prof., dir. Theoretical Chemistry Inst., 1962—; cons. Nat. Def. Research com. interior ballistics guns and rockets and group leader of geophys. lab., 1942-43, group leader theoretical physics and ordnance Los Alamos Atomic Bomb Lab., 1943-46; head theoretical physics div. Naval Ordnance Test Sta., Inyokern and Pasadena, 1945-46; chief phenomenologist Bikini Atomic Bomb Test, 1946; cons. Army and Navy ordnance AEC. Mem. bd. advisers Argonne Nat. Lab., 1962-66, Nat. Bur. Standards, 1962-67; NSF computing panel mem., 1962-65; chmn. phys. chemistry com. NRC, 1958-63. Recipient Debye award Am. Chem. Soc., 1966; Egerton Gold medal Combustion Inst., 1966. Fellow Am. Phys. Soc., Am. Acad. Arts and Sci., Phys. Soc. (London); mem. Am. Chem. Soc. (chmn. div. phys. chemistry 1959-61), Nat. Acad. Sci., Norwegian Royal Soc., Am. Soc. M.E. (hon.), Internat. Acad. Quantum Molecular Sci., A.A.A.S., Sigma, Xi, Alpha Chi Sigma, Gamma Alpha, Phi Lambda Upsilon. Clubs: Madison (Wis.); Cosmos (Washington). Author: Molecular Theory of Gases and Liquids; Intermolecular Forces; also articles tech. jours. Chmn. bd. editors The Effects of Atomic Weapons. Home: Thorstrand Rd Madison WI 53705

HIRSCHFIELD, ROBERT SIDNEY, educator; b. St. Louis, Sept. 1, 1928; s. Charles and Rose (Susman) H.; A.B., Harvard, 1950; LL.B., 1953, M.A., 1954; Ph.D., N.Y.U., 1958. Teaching asst. Harvard, 1953-54; instr. N.Y.U., 1955-57; instr. Hunter Coll., City U. N.Y., 1958-60, asst. prof., 1961-63, asso. prof., 1964-66, prof., 1967—, also chmn. polit. sci. dept., chmn. Univ. Senate, dir. Center for Edn. in Politics. Staff dir. N.Y. State Joint Legislative Com. on Higher Edn., 1965-66. Mem. Am. Polit. Sci. Assn., Am. Assn. U. Profs., Pi Sigma Alpha. Author : The Constitution and the Court, 1962; The Power of the Presidency, 1968. Home: 67 Riverside Dr New York City NY 10024

HIRSCHMAN, ALBERT OTTO, economist; b. Berlin, Germany, Apr. 7, 1915; s. Carl and Hedwig (Marcuse) H.; student Sorbonne, H.E.C., London Sch. Econs., 1933-36; Dr. Econ. Sc., U. Trieste, 1938; Rockefeller fellow U. Cal. at Berkeley, 1941-43; m. Sarah Chapiro, June 22, 1941; children—Catherine Jane, Elisabeth Nicole. Economist, Fed. Res. Bd., Washington, 1946-52; financial adviser Nat. Planning Bd., Bogotá, Colombia, 1952-54; pvt. econ. cons., Bogotá, 1954-56; research prof. econs. Yale, 1956-58; prof. internat. econ. relations Columbia, 1958-64; prof. polit. economy Harvard, 1964—, Littauer prof. polit. economy, 1967- -. Fellow Center Advanced Study Behavorial Scis., 1968-69. Served with AUS, 1943-45. Mem. Am. Econ. Assn., Council Fgn. Relations, Royal Econ. Soc. Author: National Power and the Structure of Foreign Trade, 1945; The Strategy of Economic Development, 1958; Journeys Toward Progress: Studies of Economic Policy-Making in Latin America, 1963; Development Projects Observed, 1967; Exit, Voice, and Loyalty: Responses to Decline in Firms, Organizations and States, 1970; A Bias for Hope: Essays on Development and Latin America, 1971; also articles in field. Editor: Latin American Issues-Essays and Comments, 1961. Home: 45 Holden St Cambridge MA 02138

HIRSCHMAN, FRANK FREDERICK, container co. exec.; b. Indpls., Apr. 9, 1936; s. Russell Robert and Gertrude (Burr) H.; B.A., DePauw U., 1958; M.B.A., Northwestern U., 1960; m. Carol Sue Strickland, June 25, 1960; children—Ann Katherine, Susan Elizabeth, John Frank. Mgmt. trainee, staff accountant adminstrn. div. Inland Container Corp., Indpls., 1960-62, supr. accounting dept., 1963-65, mem. corporate ownership staff, 1965, asst. sec., asst. treas., 1966- 68, sec., asst. treas., 1968—. Coordinator Jr. Achievement, 1961-69; mem. Washington Twp. Sch. Planning Com.; mem. allocations com. United Fund. Mem. Am. Soc. Corporate Secs. Methodist. Home: 7234 Merriam Rd Indianapolis IN 46240 Office: 120 E Market St Indianapolis IN 46204

HIRSCHMANN, HANS, educator, biochemist; b. Fuerth, Germany, July 1, 1909; s. Carl and Alice (Buechenbacher) H.; M.D., U. Basel (Switzerland), 1934; Ph.D., Columbia, 1938; m. Frieda S. Berliner, Aug. 5, 1938; 1 son, John Frederick. Came to U.S., 1934, naturalized, 1941. Research fellow U. Pa. Med. Sch., 1938- 42; mem. faculty Case Western Res. U., Cleveland, 1942—, prof. biochemistry, 1962—, prof. chemistry, 1968—. Mem. Am. Soc. Biological Chemists, Am. Chem. Soc., Chem. Soc. (London, Eng.). Home: 14018 Becket Rd Shaker Heights OH 44120 Office: Univ Hosps Cleveland OH 44106

HIRSCHMANN, IRA, business exec.; b. Balt., July 7, 1906; s. Adolph and Jennie (Potts) H.; student Balt. City Coll., 1914-18, student Johns Hopkins, 1918-20. Office boy Bamberger's Newark, 1921; dir. sales and advt. L. Bamberger & Co., 1921-31; v.p. Lord & Taylor, 1932-35, Saks Fifth Av., 1935-38, Bloomingdale Bros., Inc., 1936-46; past chmn. com. Colonial Trust Co.; pres. TV Systems Am., Inc., Ira Hirshmann Co., Inc.; past chmn. bd. Gotham Bank, N.Y.C.; instr. N.Y.U., 1930-32, New Sch. Social Research, 1971; lectr. Brandeis U., 1964. Spl. asst. to William H. Davis, Nat. War Labor Bd., 1942; spl. rep. War Refugee Bd., U.S. envoy at Ankara, Turkey, 1944; spl. insp. gen. UNRRA, 1946. Founder, pres. New Friends of Music; pres. Civic Found. N.Y. State; bd. govs. Hebrew U.; trustee Bd. Higher Edn. N.Y.C., New School Social Research. Winner 1949 One-World award. Author: Lifeline to a Promised Land; The Embers Still Burn, 1949; Caution to the Winds, 1962; Red Star Over Bethlehem, 1971; co-author: Reflection on Music (with Artur Schnabel), 1937. Contbr. to Nazism, An Assault on Civilization, 1934. Home: 1075 Park Av New York City NY 10028

HIRSCHOWITZ, BASIL ISAAC, physician; b. Bethal, S. Africa, May 29, 1925; s. Morris and Dorothy (Drieband) H.; B.S., Witwaters U., Johannesburg, 1943, M.B.B.Ch., 1947, M.D., 1954; m. Barbara L. Burns, July 6, 1958; children—David E., Karen, Edward A., Vanessa. Came to U.S., 1953, naturalized, 1961. Intern, resident Johannesburg Gen. Hosp., 1948-50; house physician Postgrad. Med. Sch., London, Eng., 1950; registrar Central Middlesex Hosp., London, 1951-53; instr., asst. prof. U. Mich., 1953-56; asst. prof. Temple U., 1957-59; asso. prof. medicine, dir. div. gastroenterology U. Ala. Med. Center, Birmingham, 1959-64, prof. medicine, asso. prof. physiology, 1964—; dir. gastroenterology dept. medicine U. Ala. Hosp. and Clinics, 1959—. Bd. dirs. Digestive Disease Found. Fellow A.A.A.S., A.C.P., Royal Coll. Physicians (Edinburgh); mem. Royal Coll. Physicians (London), S. African, Brit., Ala. med. assns., Med. Research Soc. Gt. Britain, Am. Fedn. Clin. Research, So. Soc. Clin. Investigation, Am. Physiol. Soc., Am. Gastroenterol. Assn., Ala. Acad. Sci., Am. Soc. Gastro-Intestinal Endoscopy, Soc. Exptl. Biology and Medicine, Sigma Xi, Alpha Omega Alpha. Office: U Ala Med Center Birmingham AL 35233

HIRSCHTRITT, RALPH, govt. ofcl.; b. N.Y., Nov. 28, 1918; s. Samuel L. and Ray (Bremmer) H.; B.S. in Social Sci., Coll. City N.Y., 1939; M.A., Columbia, 1940; postgrad. Am. U., 1949-53; m. Anita Gloria Filler, Dec. 1, 1940; children—Kay Terry (Mrs. Arthur Tuch), Steven Lewis. Economist with USES, Albany, N.Y., 1941-42, WPB, 1942, State Dept., 1946-47; with Office Internat. Finance, Treasury Dept., 1948—, dep. to asst. sec. internat., 1964—, insp. gen. for internat. finance, 1970—; temp. alternate U.S. exec. dir. World Bank, Internat. Devel. Assn., also Internat. Finance Corp., 1964-65; instr. econs. Coll. City N.Y., 1939-41, Howard U., eves. 1946-49; economist Brookings Instn., 1939. Mem. numerous U.S. delegations internat. confs.; mem. spl. Presdl. Econ. Mission to Korea, 1952. Vice pres., then pres. Glen Haven P.T.A., Silver Springs, Md., 1955-57; trustee Montgomery County (Md.) Bd. Edn., 1957. Served to lt. USNR, 1943-46. Recipient Exceptional Service award Treasury Dept., 1966, Alexander Hamilton award, 1968. Mem. Am. Econ. Assn., Phi Beta Kappa. Home: 1712 Republic Rd Silver Spring MD 20902 Office: Treasury Dept 15th St Washington DC 20220

HIRSHEN, SANFORD, architect; s. Harry and Mildred (Zaidman) H.; A.B., Columbia, 1955, B.Arch., 1959; m. Vivian Greenberg, June 2, 1957; children—Richard, Julie. Architect on projects Wurster, Bernardi & Emmons, San Francisco, 1964-65; prin. Hirshen & Partners, Berkeley, Cal., 1964—; dir. Tech. Consortium, Inc., Berkeley; lectr. U. Cal. at Berkeley, 1966—, co-ordinator Center for Tech., 1970—. Served with AUS, 1959-60. Recipient Nat. Honor award A.I.A., 1968, 1st Gov.'s Design award, 1966, Archtl. Record award, 1969, award of merit, 1969; Brunner scholar, 1970. Mem. A.I.A. (chmn. nat. sub-com. on continuing edn. on housing 1970—). Writer monographs on housing design for migrants and other subjects. Home: 2832 Benevenue St Berkeley CA 94705 Office: 731 Virginia St Berkeley CA 94710

HIRSHFIELD, JAMES ALBERT, ret. shipping assn. exec. and ret. coast guard officer; b. Cin., July 30, 1902; s. E.A. and Katherine (Devine) H.; student Tex. U., 1921-22; B.S., USCG Acad., 1924; LL.B., George Washington U., 1939; m. Marjorie Mulford Prentis, May 29, 1935; children—Katherine (Mrs. Thomas M. Wallace), James Albert, Mary (Mrs. Frank Alan Jones). Commd. ensign USCG, 1924, advanced through grades to vice adm., 1960; mem. bd. control U.S. Naval Inst., 1951-62; asst. comdt. USCG, 1954-62; pres. Lake Carriers Assn., 1962-70; ret., 1970. Admitted to D.C. bar, 1939. Decorated Navy Cross, D.S.M. Mem. Newcomen Soc., Kappa Alpha. Clubs: Propeller of United States; Army and Navy (Washington); Columbia Country (Chevy Chase, Md.). Home: 1036 Wilbert Rd Lakewood OH 44107

HIRSHHORN, JOSEPH H., mining co. exec.; b. 1900. A financier program that uncovered large uranium deposit in Blind River area Can., 1953; major stockholder Galena Silver and Lead Mine in Ida., also Pinnacle Explorations, Inc. and Bunker Hill Co.; dir. Callahan Mining Corp., 1955—, chmn. bd., 1963—. Address: 277 Park Av New York City NY 10019

HIRSHLER, ERIC ERNEST, educator; b. Ludwigshafen on Rhine, Germany, May 8, 1924; s. Max and Helen (Riess) H.; B.A., Bowdoin Coll., 1946, M.A., Yale, 1946, Ph.D., 1951; m. Marilyn Lois Nair, May 3, 1953; 1 dau., Erica Eve. Instr. history Rutgers U., Newark, 1951-52; adminstrv. asst. United Restitution Orgn., N.Y.C., 1953-55; asst. dir. Leo Baeck Inst., N.Y.C., 1955-57; instr. Bklyn. Coll., 1957-59; asst. prof. modern langs. Denison U., Granville, O., 1959-64, asso. prof., 1964-68, prof. art history, chmn. dept. art, 1968—; asst. editor UNESCO History of Mankind, 1957-59; dir., prin. investigator archeol. excavation in Sremska Mitrovica (Sirmium) Yugoslavia, Smithsonian Instn., 1969-71. James Bowdoin fellow, 1944; O'Brien fellow, 1946-47; Samuel H. Kress fellow, 1966-67; Smithsonian fellow, 1968-69. Mem. Columbus Gallery Fine Arts, Am. Assn. U. Profs., Modern Lang. Assn., Am. Coll. Art Assn., Am. Hist. Assn. Author: Jews from Germany in the U.S., 1955. Contbr. profl. jours Home: 328 E Elm St Granville OH 42023

HIRSHMAN, GEORGE WHITE, banker; b. St. Louis, Mar. 21, 1913; s. George Jerome and Celeste (White) H.; A.S., in Commerce, St. Louis U., 1948, B.S., 1951; m. Catherine Ann Fahrenhorst, Nov. 22, 1951; 1 dau., Karen Marie. With Cosmopolitan State Bank, Chgo., 1929-33, Gunther Salt Co., St. Louis, 1934-35, Am. Bur. Credit, St. Louis, 1935-36; with Fed. Res. Bank St. Louis, 1936—, gen. auditor, 1951—. Chmn. Conf. Gen. Auditors of Fed. Res. System, 1961. Served with USAAF, 1942-46. Mem. Bank Adminstrn. Inst. (pres. St. Louis 1964-65). Roman Cath. Home: 12108 Ridgelawn Dr Des Peres MO 63131 Office: 411 Locust St St Louis MO 63166

HIRSON, MAX M., lawyer; b. N.Y.C., July 5, 1891; LL.B., N.Y. U., 1910. Admitted to N.Y. State bar, 1912; mem. firm Putney, Twombley, Hall and Hirson, N.Y.C. Mem. N.Y. County Lawyers Assn. Office: 250 Park Av New York City NY 10017*

HIRST, WILLIAM, Jr., bag mfg. co. exec.; b. Phila, Sept, 5, 1920; s. William and Mary (Davie) H.; B.S., U. Pa., 1947; m. Mary E. Bortz, Apr. 12, 1952; children—Leslie, W. Bradley, Donald L., James C. Jonathan D. Travelling auditor Chase Bag Co., Greenwich, Conn., 1947-52, chief accountant, 1952-57, controller, 1957-61, treas., 1961-68, v.p., 1968-71, dir., 1967—, sr. v.p., treas., 1971—; sec.-treas., dir. Arkell Safety Bag Co.; sec.-treas., dir. Strawberry Hill Press (both

Greenwich, Conn.). Served with USNR, 1942-46. Mem. Nat. Assn. Accountants, Financial Exec. Inst., Sigma Alpha Epsilon. Home: 58 Fallow Field Rd Fairfield CT Office: 2 Greenwich Plaza Greenwich CT 06830

HIRT, AL, musician; b. New Orleans, Nov. 7, 1922; s. Alois and Linda (Guepet) H.; student Loyola U., New Orleans; hon. doctorate Cin. Conservatory Music; m. Mary Patureau, Aug. 13, 1942; children—Mary Lee, Gretchen, Rebecca, Bridgid, Rachel, Stephen, Jennifer, Jefferson Davis. Profl. trumpet player, 1940- -; owner Al Hirt Club, New Orleans, 1961—; owner New Orleans Saints football team; appeared Basin St. East, New York City, Eden Roc Hotel, Miami, Fla., Creek Theatre, Los Angeles, Carter Barron Theatre, Washington, President Kennedy's Inaugural Ball, Starlight Theatre, Kansas City, Mo., Riviera Hotel, Las Vegas, Nugget Sparks, Nev., Carnegie Hall, N.Y.C.; TV appearances on Dinah Shore, Ed Sullivan, Andy Williams, Dean Martin shows, Kraft Music Hall, Al Hirt Fanfare series. Served with AUS, 1942- 46. Home: 7540 Canal Blvd New Orleans LA 70124 Office: 801 National American Bank Bldg New Orleans LA 70140

HIRT, GERALD E., corp. exec.; b. 1918; B.S. in Mech. Engring., U. Ia., 1941; married. Dep. dir. research and devel. Frankford Arsenal, Phila., 1951-54; with Talco Engring. Co., 1954-59; v.p., sec., dir. Talley Industries Inc., 1959—; pres., chief exec. officer, dir. Gen. Time Corp., 1969—. Address: General Time Corp 2300 N Central Av Phoenix AZ 85004

HISCOCK, IRA VAUGHAN, educator; b. Farmington, Me., May 7, 1892; s. Eugene and S. Angie (Corbett) H.; B.A., Wesleyan U., Conn., 1914; M.A., 1916; Sc.D., 1939; M.P.H., Yale, 1921; M.A., 1931; m. Margaret McConway Scoville, Feb. 26, 1921; children—William McConway, Margaret Brooks (Weatherly). Started his career as a bacteriologist Conn. State Dept. Health, 1914-17, A.R.C., 1917-18; served as 1st lt., A.E.F., 1918-19; col., U.S. Army, 1942—, chief of pub. health, Civil Affairs Div., War Dept., 1943- 45. Mem. faculty Yale, 1920-60, prof. pub. health emeritus, 1960—; sometime lectr. pub. health several univs. Mem. New Haven Bd. of Health, 1928—, pres. 1942; pres. Conn. State Pub. Health League, 1951-52; mem. Conn. State Public Health Council, 1952—; health research cons. N.J. Health Dept., 1961-62; mem. Conn. State Pub. Welfare Adv. Com., 1962-69, Nat. Com. Community Health Action Studies, 1962—. Pres. Nat. Health Council, 1938-40; exec. com. med. adv. bd. A.R.C., 1945-51; cons. pub. health Conn. Commn. on Reorganization of State Dept.; mem. Conn. Commn. on Care and Prevention of Sickness, 1939-40; v.p. Nat. Social Welfare Assembly; active in direction of state and local health agys. sometime officer several nat. health affiliated agys. including: pres. Nat. Soc. Prevention Blindness, 1958—. Mem. health adminstrn. com., WHO, 1951-66; cons. to surgeon gen. AUS, 1957—. Decorated Legion of Merit; recipient Sedgwick medal Am. Pub. Health Assn., 1962; Samuel Shattuck medal Mass. Pub. Health Assn.; medal Am. Cancer Society, C.E.A. Wilslow medal, Nat. Mental Health Bell. Fellow Am. Pub. Health Assn. (pres. 1955-56); mem. and sometime pres. several state health orgns., including Conn. Diabetes Assn., Assn. for Mental Health, mem. several profl. assns., Sigma Xi, Delta Omega, Sigma Chi. Episcopalian (vestryman). Mason. Clubs: Cosmos, Army-Navy (Washington); Graduate; Nat. Travel, Yale Club of N.Y.; Randolph Mountain. Author: Health and Welfare in Honolulu, Hawaii, 1929; Community Health Organization, 1929; Public Health in Hawaii, 1935; District Health Administration, 1936; Ways to Community Health Education, 1939. Contbr. reports of health surveys, articles in scientific mags. Home: 215 Highland St New Haven CT 06511

HISE, A.W., tufted carpet co. exec.; b. Trion, Ga., Nov. 28, 1940; s. Albin and Irene (Emmons) H.; student Emory U., 1958-61. With E.T. Barwick Industries, Inc., Chamblee, Ga., 1961—, sec., treas., 1968-70, group v.p., dir., 1970—. Home: 1476 Peachtree Battle Av NW Atlanta GA 30327 Office: 5025 New Peachtree Rd Chamblee GA 30341

HISE, HARLEY, business exec.; b. Houston, Ind., Jan. 26, 1890; s. James Martin and Sarah Ann (Brown) H.; ed. high sch., bus. coll., spl. work in accounting and law; m. Grace Greenlaw, July 24, 1915. Clk in auditing div., Dept. Justice, Washington, 1913-18; land bank examiner, then chief examiner bd., Fed. Farm Loan Bd., 1919-22; v.p., mgr. Pacific Coast Joint Stock Land Bank of San Francisco (later merged with Pacific Coast Joint Stock Land Bank of Los Angeles), 1922-38; v.p., mgr. Merc. Mortgage Co., v.p., mem. exec. com. real estate loan dept. Am. Trust Co., San Francisco, 1927-29; v.p., dir. Pacific Coast Mortgage Co., Bankamerica Co., Golden Gate Ferry Co.; pres., dir. Western Lands Securities Co., No. Cal. Mortgage Co.; dir. Gen. Metals Corp., San Francisco; v.p., dir. Reclaimed Island Lands Co., Sears Point Toll Road Co., Vallejo and Marin Cos.; trustee, Reclamation Dists. 2058 and 2062, San Joaquin Co., Cal., 1925-40; apptd. custodian in receivership of Pacific States Savings & Loan Co., State Bldg. and Loan Commr. of Cal., 1940-43; apptd. mem. bd. dirs. Reconstrn. Finance Corp., 1947, chmn. 1949, term expired 1950. Del. at large Dem. Nat. Conv., 1948, 52. Mason (32, Shriner). Presbyn. Home: 1880 Jackson St San Francisco CA 94109 Retired

HISE, HENRY WILLIAM, marine corps officer; b. Shamrock, Tex., July 7, 1920; s. Henry Luther and Stella Marie (Williams) H.; student North Tex. State Coll., 1938-40, U. Tex., 1940-41; B.A. in Edn., Jackson Coll., 1964; M.A., George Washington U., 1966; m. Mary Frances Halcum, Sept. 28, 1949; children—Lewis T., Barbara (Mrs. Trent Sheppard), Nancy, Martha, Joseph, Mary. Commd. 2d lt. USMC, 1942, advanced through grades to brig. gen., 1967; squadron comdr., World War II, Korea, 1952, Vietnam, 1968; staff assignments, 1952, asst. tng. officer Naval Air Basic Tng. Command, Pensacola, Fla., 1956-58; comdr. All-Weather Fighter Squadron, 1958-60; operations officer Office Joint Chiefs of Staff Operations Directorate, J-3, Pacific Div., 1966-67; asst. wing comdr. 3d Marine Aircraft Wing, 1967-68; comdr. Marine Corps Air Bases West, 1969—. Mem. exec. bd. Boy Scouts Am., Orange County, Cal., 1969; bd. dirs. Santa Ana (Cal.) Boys Club, 1969—, A.R.C., El Toro, Cal., 1969—, U.S.O. Los Angeles, 1969—; pres. Navy Relief Soc., El Toro, 1969—. Decorated Legion of Merit with gold star, D.F.C., Air medal, Navy Commendation medal. Rotarian. Home: Quarters B MCA El Toro (Santa Ana) CA 92709 Office: Marine Corps Air Sta El Toro (Santa Ana) CA 92709

HISE, JOHN ANDREW, Jr., advt. agy. exec.; b. St. Joseph, Mo., Aug. 24, 1910; s. John Andrew and Dorothy (Foster) H.; student Coe Coll., 1928-29, U. Va., 1929-30; m. Elizabeth Browne, July 9, 1933; children—Nancy Lou (Mrs. Peter S. Krieger), Sandra, John Andrew III. With Western Grocer Co., Mpls., 1930- 39, Lever Bros. Co., Mpls. and Kansas City, Mo., 1939-46; sales promotion mgr. Lehn & Fink Corp., N.Y.C., 1946-47; sales mgr. Am. Home Foods, 1947-49; with Compton Advt., Inc., N.Y.C., 1949—, account supr., 1955-58, then sr. v.p., asst. to pres., later exec. v.p., now vice chmn. bd. and dir. chmn. of scholarship fund com. of Pleasantville, N.Y., 1954, chmn. sch. adv. bd., 1959. Mem. Am. Assn. Advt. Agys. Club: Campfire (Chappaqua, N.Y.). Home: 61 Grandview Av Pleasantville NY 10570 Office: 625 Madison Av New York City NY 10022

HISKEY, GEORGE REUBEN, hosp. dir.; b. Bellevue, O., Sept. 2, 1910; s. Edward L. and Blanche (Rubert) H.; B.A., Ohio State U., 1932, M.A., 1933; m. Doris Farrow, June 10, 1949; children—Karen, Robert, Kathy. Dir. VA Hosp., Cleve., 1955-59, VA Center, Bay Pines, Fla., 1959-67, VA Center, Johnson City, Tenn., 1967-71, VA Hosp., Tampa, Fla., 1971—. Vice pres. Appalachian Regional Center Healing Arts. Bd. dirs. Johnson City United Fund, Appalachian Preaching Mission. Served to lt. comdr. USNR, 1942-45. Recipient citations A.R.C., Disabled Am. Vets., Am. Legion, Cleve. City Council, St. Petersburg Com. 100. Fellow Am. Coll. Hosp. Adminstrs.; mem. E. Tenn. Hosp. Council, Alpha Tau Omega, Pi Sigma Alpha. Methodist. Kiwanian. Address: VA Center Tampa FL 33612

HISKEY, MARSHALL S., educator; b. Highland, Kan., 1908; s. Fred C. and Olive M. (White) H.; B.S., Kan. State Tchrs. Coll., 1932; M.S., Ohio State U., 1938; Ph.D., U. Neb., 1940; m. Olga Marie Lauber, June 1, 1933; children—Mary Sue, Robert Marshall. Derby (Kan.) High Sch., 1932-35, supt. schs., 1935-38; instr. ednl. psychology and measurement U. Neb., 1938-41; dean men and dir. psychol. ednl. clinic Pa. State Tchrs. Coll., 1941-46; acting dean coll. edn. So. Ill. U., Carbondale, 1948, dean men and dir. testing 1946- 49, chmn. dept. guidance spl. edn., 1949-54; prof. ednl. psychology and measurements, dir. Ednl. Psychol. Clinic, U. Neb., 1954—; vis. prof. guidance and personnel adminstrn., N.Y.U., summer 1949. Mem. C. of C. Served in USNR Aviation, 1943-45. Mem. Am., Mid-Western psychol. assns., N.E.A., Nat. Council on Measurement in Edn., Am. Coll. Personnel Assn., Council Exceptional Children, Am. Assn. U. Profs., Phi Delta Kappa, Kappa Delta Pi. Mason, Lion. Author: Nebraska Test of Learning Aptitude, 1941, rev., 1955; How to Get Help for Exceptional Children, 1941; Handbook of Ill. Guidance and Personnel Assn., 1953; Planning for Mentally Retarded Children, 1957; also articles. Home: 5640 Baldwin Lincoln NB 68540

HITCH, CHARLES JOHNSTON, univ. pres.; b. Boonville, Mo., Jan. 9, 1910; s. Arthur Martin and Bertha (Johnston) H.; A.A., Kemper Mil. Sch., 1929; B.A. with highest distinction, U. of Arizona, 1931, LL.D. (honorary), 1962; student Harvard, 1931-32; B.A. with first class honors (Rhodes scholar), Oxford U., 1934, M.A., 1938; D.Sc. in Commerce, Drexel U., 1963; LL.D., U. Pitts., 1968, U. Mo., 1968; m. Nancy Winslow Squire, Mar. 20, 1942; one daughter, Caroline Winslow. Began as fellow, praelector, tutor Queen's Coll., Oxford U., 1935-48, gen. editor Oxford Econ. Papers, 1941-48; vis. prof. U. Sao Paulo, Brazil, 1947; chief econs. div. Rand Corp., 1948-61, dir. research program; asst. Sec. Def. (Comptroller), Washington, 1961-65; v.p. bus. and finance U. Cal., 1965-66, v.p. of adminstrn., 1966-67, pres. U., 1968—; prof. econs. U. Cal. at Berkeley, 1965—; vis. professor U. Cal. at Los Angeles, 1949-50; Irving Fisher research prof. Yale, 1957. Staff economist Mission for Econ. Affairs, U.S. Embassy, London, 1941-42; staff economist planning com. WPB, 1942-43; chief stblzn. controls div. Office War Moblzn. and Reconversion, 1945-46; Trustee Kemper Mil. Sch.; hon. fellow Queen's Coll., Oxford, Worcester Coll., Oxford. Trustee Asia Found., Resources for Future. Served as 1st lt., OSS, U.S. Army, 1943-45. Recipient Pub. Service award U.S. Navy, 1965. Fellow A.A.A.S., Am. Acad. Arts and Scis.; mem. Am. Econ. Assn. (v.p. 1965), Royal Econ. Soc., Econometric Soc., Operations Research Soc. Am. (council 1955-58, pres., 1959-60), Council Fgn. Relations, Nat. Acad. Pub. Adminstrn., Phi Beta Kappa. Democrat. Presbyn. Clubs: Bohemian (San Francisco); Cosmos (Washington). Author: America's Economic Strength, 1941; The Economics of Defense in the Nuclear Age, 1960; Decision Making for Defense, 1965. Editor: Introduction to Economic Analysis and Policy, 1938. Home: 70 Rincon Rd Kensington CA 94707 Office: U Cal 2200 University Av Berkeley CA 94720

HITCH, JOSEPH DELANO, Jr., engr., business exec.; b. South Orange, N.J., Jan. 31, 1904; s. Joseph Delano and Adeline V. N. (Dorr) H.; student Colo. Coll., 1923, Harvard Engring. Sch., 1927; m. Katherine Dalton, June 6, 1928; children—Joseph Delano III, Henry H., Joan V. N., Katherine D., Philip D. With Dorr Co., Stamford, Conn., 1927-61, beginning as field and sales engr., successively engring. rep. in Far East, mgr. fgn. sales. dir., 1952-61, v.p. sales, exec. v.p., pres., 1953-54; pres., dir. Dorr-Oliver, Inc., 1955-59, chmn. bd. 1959-60, cons. internat. operations, 1960-61; v.p. internat. sales Babcock & Wilcox Co., N.Y.C., 1961-67; N.Y. dir. Multi-Nat. Bus. Assos., internat. cons. group, N.Y.C., 1967—. Engring. adviser OSS, China, 1945. Rep. town mem., Westport, Conn. Registered profl. engr., Conn., N.Y. Mem. Am. Inst. Mining and Metall. Engrs., Mining and Metall. Soc. Am., Council Tech. Advancement, Harvard Engring. Soc. Clubs: Harvard, Squadron A (N.Y.C.); Owl (Cambridge Mass.); Aspetuck Valley (Conn.) Country; Royal Bermuda Yacht, Mid Ocean (Bermuda). Home: Dogwood Lane Weston CT 06880

HITCH, ROBERT MARK, lawyer; b. Savannah, Ga., May 24, 1908; s. Robert Mark Sr. and Virginia Epps (Walker) H.; grad. Lawrenceville Sch., 1926; A.B., Yale, 1930, LL.B., 1932; m. Margery Fulenwider, Dec. 23, 1929; children—Margery Lane, Virginia Walker, Robert Mark III, Harry Fulenwidern. Admitted to Ga. bar, 1932, since practiced in Savannah; mem. firm of Hitch, Miler, Beckmann, & Simpson, Savannah, 1956—. Bd. dirs. Savannah Sugar Refining Corp., Savannah & Atlanta Ry. Co., Citizens & So. Nat. Bank of Savannah, Leopold Adler Co., Savannah. Mem. Savannah Bar Assn. (pres. 1957), Psi Upsilon, Corbey Court. Clubs: Oglethorp, Savannah Golf, Savannah yacht (Savannah); Yale (N.Y.C.). Home: 649 Victory Dr Savannah GA 31406 Office: Georgia State Bldg Savannah GA 31401

HITCH, THOMAS KEMPER, economist; b. Boonville, Mo., Sept. 16, 1912; s. Arthur Martin and Bertha (Johnston) H.; A.B., Stanford, 1934; A.M., Columbia, 1946; Ph.D., U. London, 1937; student Nat. U. Mexico, 1932; m. Margaret Barnhart, June 27, 1940; children—Hilary Marshall, Leslie, Caroline, Thomas Kemper. Mem. faculty Stephens Coll., Columbia, Mo., 1937-42; spl. study commodity markets Commodity Exchange Adminstrn., Dept. Agr., 1940; acting head current bus. research sect. Dept. Commerce, 1942-43; labor adviser Vets. Emergency Housing Program, 1946- 47; economist labor econs. Pres.'s Council Econ. Advisers, 1947-50; dir. research Hawaii Employers Council, Honolulu, 1950-59; sr. v.p., chmn. research div. First Hawaiian Bank, 1959—; dir. Hawaiian Telephone Co. Chmn. Hawaii Gov.'s Adv. Com. on Financing, 1959-64; chmn. research com. Hawaii Vistors Bur., 1962-69; chmn. Mayor's Financial Adv. Com., 1960-69; trustee Tax Found. of Hawaii, Leahi Found. Trustee, Hawaii Joint Council Econ. Edn.; state dir. Econ. Stblzn.; chmn. taxation and finance com. Constl. Conv. Hawaii, 1968. Served as lt. O.R.C., 1933-38; as lt. (s.g.) USNR, 1943-46. Mem. Nat. Planning Assn., C. of C. of Hawaii (chmn. bd. 1971), Nat. Assn. Bus. Economists, Am., Western, Hawaii econs. assns., Indsl. Relations Research Assn., Am. Statis. Assn., Phi Beta Kappa, Pi Sigma Alpha, Alpha Sigma Phi. Clubs: Waialae Country, Pacific. Contbr. articles profl. jours. Home: 257 Portlock Rd Honolulu HI 96821 Office: First Hawaiian Bank Honolulu HI 96801

HITCHCOCK, ALFRED JOSEPH, motion pictures dir.; b. England, Aug. 13, 1899; s. William and Emma H.; student St. Ignatius Coll., London; D.F.A. (hon.), Univ. Cal. at Santa Cruz, 1968; m. Alma Reville; 1 dau. Began as jr. technician, Famous Players Lasky Brit. Studios, 1920; scenario writer, prodn. mgr., art dir., Gainsborough Studios, Islington, Eng., 1923; became motion picture dir., 1925. Has directed: The Lodger; Downhill; Easy Virtue; The Farmer's Wife; The Ring; Blackmail; Pleasure Garden, 1925; Juno and the Paycock, 1932; Murder; The Skin Game, 1932; Waltzes from Vienna, 1933; The Man Who Knew Too Much, 1934; The 39 Steps, 1935; Secret Agent, 1937; Sabotage; A Woman Alone, 1937; The Girl Was Young, 1937; The Lady Vanishes, 1938; Young and Innocent; Jamaica Inn, 1939; Rebecca, 1940; Foreign Correspondent, 1940; Mr. and Mrs. Smith, 1941; Suspicion, 1941; Saboteur, 1942; Shadow of a Doubt, 1942; Lifeboat, 1943; Spellbound, 1944; Notorious, 1945; The Paradine Case, 1947; Rope, 1948; Under Capricorn, 1949; Stage Fright, 1950; Strangers on a Train, 1951; I Confess; Dial M. for Murder; Rear Window; To Catch a Thief; The Trouble with Harry; The Man Who Knew Too Much; The Wrong Man; Vertigo; North By Northwest; Psycho; The Birds; Marnie; Torn Curtain; Topaz; Frenzy; presented the television series of Alfred Hitchcock Presents, 1955-61; Alfred Hitchcock Hour, 1961-65. Decorated Chevalier French Nat. Order Legion of Honor; recipient Irving G. Thalberg Memorial award Academy Motion Picture Arts and Sciences, 1968. Author: My Favorite In Suspense, 1959; Alfred Hitchcock's Ghostly Gallery, 1962; Stories My Mother Never Told Me, 1963. Address: Universal City Studios Universal City CA 91608

HITCHCOCK, ARTHUR ALLEN, educator; b. Albany, N.Y., Nov. 6, 1910; s. George Royal and Helen (Page) H.; A.B., Wesleyan U., Middletown, Conn., 1932; Ed. M., Harvard, 1934; Ph.D., Yale, 1948; m. Charlotte Winifred Murray, June 28, 1941; children—Arthur Allen III, Charles Christopher. Counselor-tchr. high schs., Greenfield, Mass., 1936-38; dir. guidance pub. schs., Bristol, Conn., 1938-43; asst. dir. guidance center, also lectr. guidance, Harvard, 1946-49; dir. jr. div. and counseling service, also prof. ednl. psychology and measurements, U. Neb., 1949-55; exec. dir. Am. Personnel and Guidance Assn., 1955-66; prof. edn. State U. N.Y. at Albany, 1966—, dir. Two Year Coll. Student Devel. Center, 1968—. Cons. U.S. Office of Edn., 1966—; mem. fed. adv. council employment security Dept. of Labor, 1958-65, adv. com. young workers, 1959-62; mem. commn. coll. student Am. Council Edn., 1959-62; exec. com. Council Nat. Orgns. Children and Youth, 1960; mem. Montgomery County (Md.) Curriculum Planning Com., 1960-62; mem. edn. com. Pres.'s Com. on Employment Physically Handicapped, 1966—; rehab. counseling adv. panel Dept. Health, Edn., Welfare; dir. Project on the Puerto Rican Child, Coll. Entrance Exam. Bd., 1970—. Served to 1st lt. AUS, 1943 -46. Recipient ed. award Nat. Assn. Colored Womens Clubs, 1964. Fellow counseling psychology, also diplomate counseling psychology Am. Bd. Exam. Profl. Psychology. Fellow A.A.A.S.; mem. N.E.A. (coun. ednl. policies commn. 1955-62), Am. Ednl. Research Assn., Nat. Assn. Trade and Tech. Schs. (accrediting commn.), Am. Personnel and Guidance Assn. (life), Nat. Vocational Guidance Assn., Am. Psychol. Assn., P.T.A. (pres. high sch. 1959-60). Methodist (ofcl. bd., chmn. ch. guidance com. ednl. commn.). Author articles profl. publs. Home: 393 Highland Dr Schenectady NY 12303 Office: State U of NY at Albany Edn Bldg 1400 Washington Av NY 12203

HITCHCOCK, BILLY, baseball exec.; b. Inverness, Ala., July 31, 1916; s. James Franklin and Sally (Davis) H.; student Staunton (Va.) Mil. Acad., 1934; B.S., Auburn U., 1938; m. Alice Rebecca Rice, Mar. 8, 1941; 1 adopted son, John Franklin. Coach, tchr. Opelika (Ala.) High Sch., 1939-41; profl. baseball player Kansas City Blues, 1939-41, Detroit Tigers, 1942, 53, Washington Senators, 1946, St. Louis Browns, 1947, Boston Red Sox, 1948- 49, Phila. Athletics, 1950-52; mgr. Buffalo Bisons, 1954; coach Detroit Tigers, 1955-60; mgr. Vancouver, 1961; mgr. Balt. Orioles, 1962-63; scout Atlanta Braves, 1964-65, coach, 1966, mgr., 1966-68; spl. accounts mgr. Diversifield Products Corp., 1968-69; Southeast scout supr. Montreal Expos, 1969-70, field dir., 1970-71; pres. So. League Profl. Baseball, Opelika, 1971—. Served to maj. USAAF, 1943-45. Decorated Bronze Star medal. Presbyn. (deacon). Mason, Kiwanian. Home: 1117 W Collinwood Circle Opelika AL 36805 Office: 605 2d Av Opelika AL 36805

HITCHCOCK, CHARLES LEO, educator; b. Newhall, Cal., Apr. 23, 1902; s. Francis William and Margaret Estella (Duncan) H.; A.B., Pomona Coll., 1927; M.A., Claremont Coll., 1929; Ph.D., Washington U., St. Louis, 1931; m. Evelyn Harvey, July 29, 1931; children—Susan Abigail, Nancy Anne. Instr., Pomona Coll., 1931-32; asst. prof. U. Mont., 1932-34, asso. prof., 1934-37; asst. prof. U. Wash., 1937-39, asso. prof., 1939-41, prof., exec. officer dept. botany, 1941-62, prof. and curator of the Herbarium, 1962—. Men. Bot. Soc. Am., Am. Soc. Taxonomists, Cal. Bot. Soc., Sigma Xi, Phi Sigma. Author articles on grasses, flowering plants. Home: 9239 Matthews Av N E Seattle WA 98115

HITCHCOCK, CLAUDE RAYMOND, surgeon, educator; b. Mpls., Oct. 14, 1917; s. Ralph C. and Lucy (Morris) H.; B.A., U. Minn., 1940, B.S., 1943, M.B., 1944, M.D., 1945, Ph.D., 1954; m. Wilma Ruth Baker, Apr. 23, 1949; children—Jeffry, Claudia. Intern, St. Lukes Hosp., Duluth, Minn., 1944-45; surg. resident Med. Sch. U. Minn., 1947-52, asst. prof., 1954-56, asso. prof. surgery, 1956-62, prof., 1962—, dir. Cancer Detection Research Center, 1952-55; chief surgery Hennepin County Gen. Hosp., 1955—; pres. Mpls. Med. Research Found., Inc., 1957—. Mem. State Cancer Com., 1957—; mem. State Dialysis Com., 1966—; mem. sci. review com. health research facilities NIH. Served with M.C., AUS, 1945-47. Recipient Sci. Achievement award So. Minn. Med. Assn., 1964; Francis E. Harrington Meml. award, 1968. Diplomate Pan Am. Med. Assn. Mem. A.M.A., Minn., Hennepin County med. socs., Central Surg. Assn., Minn. (pres.), Mpls. surg. socs., Am. Surg. Assn., Transplantation Soc., Minn. (dir.), Hennepin County (dir.) cancer socs., Sigma Xi. Contbr. articles profl. jours. Home: 6616 W Shore Dr Edina MN 55424 Office: Hennepin County Gen Hosp 5th and Portland Sts Minneapolis MN 55415

HITCHCOCK, ETHAN ALLEN, lawyer; b. Milton, Mass., July 12, 1909; s. George Collier and Elizabeth (Fiske) H.; grad. St. Louis Country Day Sch., 1927; A.B., Yale, 1931; LL.B., Harvard, 1934; m. Elizabeth French, Apr. 2, 1937; children—Constance, Mary Elizabeth. Admitted to N.Y. bar, 1935, practiced in N.Y.C., 1934-41, 46—; partner firm Webster, Sheffield, Fleischmann, Hitchcock & Brookfield, 1961—; chmn. bd. dir. Olivetti Corp. Am. Pres. bd. Lenox Hill Neighborhood House, 1938-40, Brearley Sch., 1954-60; mem. council Yale; trustee Lenox Hill Hosp., 1950-70; chmn. bd. trustees Channel 13 Ednl. Broadcasting Corp.; bd. dirs. N.Y. Philharmonic; chmn. bd. dirs. MFY Legal Services, 1968-70. Served from lt. to lt. comdr., USNR, 1941-46. Mem. Chi Psi. Presbyn. Home: 25 E 93d St New York City NY 10028 Office: One Rockefeller Plaza New York City NY 10020

HITCHCOCK, H. WILEY, musicologist, educator; A.B., Dartmouth; M.Mus., Ph.D., U. Mich. Now prof. music, chmn. dept. Hunter Coll., N.Y.C.; vis. prof. music N.Y.U. Mem. Music Library Assn. (pres. 1966-67). Address: 52 E 83d New York City NY 10021

HITCHCOCK, HENRY PERRY, dentist, educator; b. Sanford, Me., Apr. 8, 1921; s. Henry Sylvester and Cassilena (Perry) H.; student Am. Internat. Coll., 1940-42; D.M.D., Tufts Coll., 1946; M.S.D., U.

Ala., 1958; m. Anna Ruth Gant, Dec. 19, 1948; children—Henry Malcolm, Edgar Perry, George Samuel, Amy Ruth. Pvt. dental practice, Belchertown, Mass., 1946; instr., asst. prof., asso. prof., prof. dentistry U. Ala. Sch. Dentistry, Birmingham, 1948—, chmn. dept. orthodontics, 1964—; pvt. practice orthodontics, Birmingham, 1951-58; vis. prof. Zahnarztliches Institut, U. Zurich, Switzerland, 1969-70; cons. cleft palate team State of Ala., VA Hosp., Birmingham. Served to capt. AUS, 1946-48. Diplomate Am. Bd. Orthodontics. Mem. Am. Dental Assn., Am. Assn. Orthodontists, Sociedad Colombiana de Ortodontia (hon.), Omicron Kappa Upsilon. Contbr. chpt. to Clinical Pedodontics, 1967. Office: 1919 7th Av S Birmingham AL 35233

HITCHCOCK, HENRY RUSSELL, educator, archtl. historian; b. Boston, Mass., June 3, 1903; s. Henry Russell and Alice Whitworth (Davis) H.; student Middlesex Sch., 1917-20; A.B., Harvard, 1924, A.M., 1927; student Harvard Sch. of Architecture, 1923-24. Asst. prof. art Vassar Coll., 1927-28; asst. prof. art Wesleyan U., Middletown, Conn., 1929-41, asso. prof., 1941-47, prof., 1947-48; prof. art Smith Coll., 1948-61, Sophia Smith prof. art, 1961-68; prof. art U. Mass., Amherst, 1968; adj. prof. Inst. Fine Arts, N.Y.U., 1969—; dir. Smith Coll. Museum Art, 1949-55; lectr. architecture Mass. Inst. Tech., 1946-48; vis. lectr. architecture Yale, 1952-53, 59-60, 69, Cambridge (Eng.) U., 1962, Harvard, 1965; teacher Conn. Coll., 1934-42; prepared architectural exhbns, Mus. Modern Art, N.Y.C., Springfield, Mass., Hartford, Conn., Worcester, Buffalo and Providence Mus.; circulated archtl. exhbns. from Wesleyan; lectr. Inst. Fine Arts, N.Y.U., 1940, vis. lectr., 1951, 57; vis. lectr. Columbia, 1971. Civilian employe, Navy Dept., 1942; tech. author Pratt & Whitney Aircraft, 1943-45. Guggenheim fellow, 1945-46; recipient Am. Council Learned Socs. award, 1961. Hon. corr. mem. Royal Inst. Brit. Architects, London; mem. Coll. Art Assn., Soc. Archtl. Historians (dir., pres. N.Y. chpt. 1970—), Royal Soc. Arts (London; Franklin fellow), Pilgrim Soc. (trustee), Victorian Soc. (London), Victorian Soc. Am. (pres. 1970—), Am. Assn. U. Profs., Mass. Soc. Mayflower Descs., Soc. Preservation N.E. Antiquities. Democrat. Unitarian. Author: Frank Lloyd Wright, 1928; Modern Architecture, 1929; J.J.P. Oud, 1931; Modern Architects (with others), 1932; The International Style (with Philip Johnson), 1932; The Architecture of H. H. Richardson, 1936; Modern Architecture in England (with others), 1937; Rhode Island Architecture, 1939; In the Nature of Materials, the Buildings of Frank Lloyd Wright, 1942; American Architectural Books, 1946; Painting Toward Architecture, 1948; Early Victorian Architecture in Britain, 1954; Latin-American Architecture since 1945, 1955; Architecture: 19th and 20th Centuries, 1958; German Rococo: The Zimmermann Brothers, 1968; Rococo Architecture in Southern Germany, 1968; also articles U.S., foreign mags. Home: 152 E 62d St New York City NY 10021

HITCHCOCK, JOHN THAYER, educator, anthropologist; b. Springfield, Mass., June 29, 1917; s. Arthur Cornwall and Ruth Harriet (Thayer) H.; B.A., Amherst Coll., 1939; M.A., U. Chgo., 1941; Ph.D., Cornell U., 1956; m. Patricia Jennings, Nov. 27, 1947; children—Emily Robertson, Marion Thayer, Benjamin Jennings. Instr. Amherst Coll., 1946-48; acting asst. prof. anthropology U. Cal. at Los Angeles, 1958-63; asst. prof. anthropology U. Cal. at Berkeley, 1957-58, asso. prof., 1963-66; prof. anthropology and Indian studies U. Wis., Madison, 1966—. Bd. dirs. Anthropol. Film Research Inst. Served to lt. USNR, 1941-45. Decorated D.F.C.; Henry P. Field fellow, 1940-41; Ford Found. fellow, 1953-55; NSF grantee, 1960-62; Nat. Inst. Mental Health grantee, 1966-68; Wenner-Gren Found. grantee, 1965. Mem. Nepal Studies Assn. (exec. com. 1971—), Royal Anthropol. Inst., Am. Anthropol. Assn., Himalayan Club, Am. Assn. for Advancement Sci., Assn. for Asian Studies, Alpha Delta Phi, Phi Beta Kappa. Author: The Rajputs of Khalapur, 1966; The Magars of Banyan Hill, 1966; Sickle and Khukri, 1971. Producer ethnographic films: North Indian Village, 1956; Gurkha Country, 1966; Himalayan Farmer, 1966; Himalayan Shaman, 1966. Research Ute Indians, 1952, India, 1953-55, Nepal, 1960-62, 66-68. Home: RD 1 Mt Horeb WI 53572 Office: Dept Anthropology U Wis Madison WI 53706

HITCHCOCK, LAUREN BLAKELY, cons. chem. engr., educator; b. Paris, France (parents U.S. citizens), Mar. 18, 1900; s. Frank Lauren and Margaret Johnson (Blakely) H.; S.B. in Chem. Enging., Mass. Inst. Tech. 1920, S.M., 1927, Sc. D., 1933; m. Eleanor M. Mulhern, Sept. 22, 1920 (dec. Aug. 1963); children—Eleanor M. (Mrs. John R. Higgins) (dec.), Patricia (Mrs. Peter Malof), Jacquelyn I. (Mrs. K. E. Aamodt), Hope M. (Mrs. J. A. Maurice Cantin), John; m. 2d, Lusyd Wright Smith, Mar. 1, 1966 (dec. Feb. 1971). Chemist, H. P. Hood & Sons, Boston, 1920; prof. chem. enging. U. Va., 1928-35; cons. chem. engr., research exec., mgr. sales devel. Hooker Electro-Chem. Co., Niagara Falls, 1935-44; mgr. chems. dept. Quaker Oats Co., Chgo., 1944-46, v.p. charge, 1946-49; dir. research and devel. Nat. Dairy Prpducts Corp., also pres. Nat. Dairy Research Labs., Inc., N.Y.C., 1949-53; mgmt. cons., N.Y.C., 1953; pres., mng. dir. Air Pollution Found., Los Angeles, 1954-56; cons. chem. engr. Lauren B. Hitchcock Assos., 1957-63; prof. enging. State U. N.Y. at Buffalo, 1963—; dir. grad. enging. Mgmt. TV Network, 1969—. Served with U.S. Naval Aviation Corps, 1918; officer U.S. Army, 1921-28. Registered profl. engr., Cal., N.Y., Va. Mem. Am. Soc. Enging. Edn., Am. Inst. Chem. Engrs. (Profl. Achievement award Western N.Y. sect. 1971), Am. Chem. Soc., Soc. Chem. Industry (chmn. Am. sect. 1953-54), Air Pollution Control Assn., Comml. Chem. Devel. Assn. (pres. 1947-49), Niagara Frontier Assn. Research and Devel. Dirs. (pres. 1970-71), Sigma Xi, Alpha Chi Sigma. Clubs: Cosmos (Washington); M.I.T., Chemists (N.Y.C.); Saturn (Buffalo). Author numerous sci. articles field chem. technology and research mgmt. Home: 800 W Ferry St Buffalo NY 14222

HITCHCOCK, RICHARD ELONZO, lawyer; b. Bakersfield, Cal., Apr. 16, 1925; s. Arthur Ralph and Erma (Davis H.; student Bakersfield Coll., 1946; B.A., U. Cal. at Berkeley, 1948; J.D., Hastings Coll. Law, 1951; m. Wilma Ann Tieck, Feb. 24, 1945; children—Richard Scott, Carol Ann (Mrs. Brian W. Aherne), Sara Tieck. Claims rep. Cal-Farm Ins. Co., 1951-53; admitted to Cal. bar, 1952; practiced in Bakersfield, 1953—; pvt. practice, 1953-58; dep. dist. atty. 1958-65; asso. Borton, Petrini, Conron & Brown, 1965-69; partner Borton, Petrini, Conron, Wetteroth & Hitchcock, 1969—. Served to 2d lt. USAAF, 1943-45. Mem. Def. Research Inst., Am., Kern County (past pres.) bar assns., Cal. State Bar, Kern County Peace Officers Assn. (past pres.), Assn. Def. Counsel (2d v.p., dir.). Presbyn. (elder, trustee). Home: 3800 Pontiac Bakersfield CA 93304 Office: 1712 19th St Bakersfield CA 93301

HITCHCOCK, ROBERT M., lawyer; b. French Creek, N.Y., June 19, 1904; s. James Emmett and Florence (Morrison) H.; A.B., Georgetown U., 1925; LL.B., Fordham U., 1928; m. Winifred Woodruff McCord, Feb. 19, 1931; children—Barbara McCord (Mrs. David R. Hershey), Patricia Jane (Mrs. Rober R. Hayes II), Sally Norris (Mrs. Francis P. Brady). Admitted to N.Y. State bar, also U.S. Supreme Ct.; practiced in N.Y.C., Dunkirk, N.Y., 1929-35; asst. U.S. atty. Western Dist. N.Y., 1935-43; spl. asst. to U.S. atty. gen., 1943-47; mem. firm Phillips, Lytle, Hitchcock, Blaine & Huber, and predecesor firms, Buffalo, 1947, now sr. partner firm. Vice chmn. Buffalo Bd. Redevel., 1933-57; mem. Niagara Frontier Port Authority, 1959-67, chmn., 1964-67. Mayor, Dunkirk, 1947. Fellow Am. Coll. Trial Lawyers; mem. Am., N.Y. State, Erie County bar assns. K.C., Elk (past exalted ruler Dunkirk). Clubs: Saturn (Buffalo); Cherry Hill Country (Ont., Can.). Author: Digest of Lectures in Sociology, 1930. Home: 6 Cleveland Av Buffalo NY 14222 Office: Marine Trust Bldg Buffalo NY 14203

HITCHCOCK, WILLIAM KENNETH, fgn. service officer; b. Wray, Colo., Feb. 21, 1919; s. William Henry and Lucy Laura (Thompson) H.; A.B., U. Colo., 1941; student Nat. Inst. Pub. Affairs, 1941-42; m. Maxine Elizabeth Miller, Apr. 3, 1945; 1 dau., Victress Marion. With U.S. Dept. Agr., Civil Service Commn., 1941-43; with Dept. of State, 1946—, Washington, 1946-52, 1st sec., London, 1952-56, NATO Def. Coll., Paris, France, 1956, 1st sec., Madrid, 1956-60, with U.S. Disarmament Adminstrn., 1960-62, State Dept., 1962-64; counsul gen. Calcutta, India, 1964-71; polit. officer Am. embassy, Saigon, Vietnam, 1971—. Served to capt. (pilot), USAAF, 1943-46; economist bombing survey, Eng. and Continent. Decorated D.F.C., Bronze Star. Address: Am Embassy APO San Francisco CA 96253

HITCHENS, WILLIAM REESE, lawyer; b. Sussex County, Del., Aug. 9, 1906; s. William R. and Mary E. (Issacs) H.; A.B., Dickinson Coll., 1928, LL.B., 1931; m. Alice M. Cohee, Nov. 28, 1935; childrenWilliam Reese, Carol (Mrs. James F. Jorden), Patricia (Mrs. J. Daniel Shaver, Jr.). Admitted to Del. bar, 1931; tchr. Dickinson Sch. Law, 1931-32; with firm Morris, James., Hitchens & Williams, Wilmington, Del., 1932—, partner, 1937—; dir., gen. counsel Bank of Del.; v.p. Title Guarantee Co. Dept. atty. gen. Del. charge taxes, 1935-36; chmn.. Del. Tax Bd., 1945-49. Pres. bd. Wilmington Y's Mens Club, 1944, Mt. Pleasant P.T.A., 1945. Bd. dirs., trustee New Castle (Pa.) Presbytery, 1965-; bd. dirs., pres. Homes New Castle Presbytery. Mem. Corpus Juris Soc., Del. Savs. Loans League (chmn. legislative com. 1956-), Phi Beta Kappa, Phi Kappa Psi, Omega Delta Kappa. DeMolay Legion of Honor. Presbyn. (past pres. trustees, elder) Home: 1506 Brandywine Blvd Wilmington, DE 19809. Office: Bank of Delaware Bldg Wilmington DE 19801

HITCHING, HARRY JAMES, lawyer; b. N.Y.C., Nov. 20, 1909; s. Harry and Sara (James) H.; A.B., Columbia, 1929, LL.B. (Kent scholar), 1931, J.D., 1969; m. Virginia Wyber, June 22, 1933; children-Virginia B. (Mrs. John Dodson), James F. Admitted to N.Y. State bar, 1932, Tenn. bar, 1938, Ga. bar, 1969; pvt. practice, N.Y.C., 1931-37; prin. atty. TVA, 1937-40, asst., gen. counsel, 1940-44; mem. Firm Miller, Martin and Hitching, Chattanooga, 1944-46 partner, 1946—, firm name now Miller, Martin, Hitching, Tipton, Lenihan & Waterhouse; asst. atty. Lookout Mountain, Ga. Gen. counsel Coca Cola Bottling Co. (Thomas), Inc., Benwood Found.; dir. Krystal Co., W.L. Jackson Mfg. Co. Pres. Tonya Meml. Found., Estate Planning Council Chattanooga; bd. dirs. Community Found. Greater Chattanooga; chmn. Adv. bd. Chattanooga Salvation Army. Served to ensign USCGR, 1943-45. Mem. Am., Tenn., Ga., Chattanooga (v.p.) bar assns., Chattanooga C. of C. (dir.). Democrat. Episcopalian. Clubs: Lookout Mountain Fairyland; Mountain City Geology. (Chattanooga). Home 1701 Wood Nymph Trial Lookout Mountain GA 37350 Office: Volunteer State Life Bldg Chattanooga TN 37402

HITCHMAN, ROBERT BRUCE, ins. co. exec.; b. Denver, Oct. 28, 1908; s. Herbert Samuel and Hazel (Chamberlin) H.; B.A., U. Wash., 1929; m. Helen Marie Evens, Oct. 1, 1967. With Unigard Mut. Ins. Co., (formerly Northwestern Mut. Ins. Co.), Seattle, 1928—, sr. v.p., 1968-69, pres., 1969—, also dir.; pres., dir. Unigard Ins. Co., 1969—, Unigard Security Ins. Co., 1970—, Olympic Nat. Life Ins. Co., 1970—, Jamestown Mut. Ins. Co., 1971—. Adv. bd. King Co. Council on Alcoholism, Seattle, 1959—; bd. curators Wash. Hist. Soc., 1952—; editorial bd. The American West, 1968—; regional adv. bd. Nat. Archives, 1969—; bd. councillors Am. Antiquarian Soc., 1970—. Trustee Seattle Found. Served to col. AUS, 1942-46; ETO. Decorated Bronze Star medal. Mem. Champlain Soc. Rotarian. Clubs: Rainier, Washington Athletic, The Monday (Seattle), Explorers (N.Y.C.). Pub. Sighted From The Crow's Nest, (booklist) 1953—. Home: 2820 W Dravus St Seattle WA 98199 Office: 217 Pine St Seattle WA 98101

HITCHNER, STEPHEN BALLINGER, educator, veterinarian; b. Daretown, N.J., Feb. 4, 1916; s. Herbert and Sarah (Ballinger) H.; B.S., Rutgers U., 1939; V.M.D., U. Pa., 1943; m. Mariana T. White, Mar. 27, 1943; children-Stephen Ballinger, Roger Elliott, Sarabelle Irma, Thomas Reeves, Robert Terhune. Asso. prof. Poly. Tech. Va., 1947-49; prof. U. Mass., 1949-53; research veterinarian Am. Sci. Labs., Madison, Wis., 1953-60; dir. research L & M Labs., Berlin, Md., 1960-64; group leader Abbott Labs., N. Chgo., 1965-66; prof. avian diseases, chmn. dept. N.Y. State Vet. Coll., Ithaca, 1966—. Served to capt., Vet. Corps, AUS, 1943-46. Mem. Am. Vet. Med. Assn., N.Y. Acad. Scis., Poultry Sci. Assn., Am. Assn. Avian Pathologists (pres. 1960-61), Am. Poultry Sci. Assn., Am. Assn. Avian Pathologists (pres. 1960-61), Am. Coll. Vet. Microbiologists, Sigma Xi. Lion (sec. Berlin club 1964-65). Discovered, developed B strain of Newcastle virus for vaccination. Home: 156 Cascadilla Park Ithaca NY 14850

HITCHOCK, PHILIP STANLEY, orgn. exec.; b. Pomeroy, Wash., Sept. 28, 1904; s. Cecil Glenn and Ethel (Gammon) H.; A.B., Wash. State U., 1926; grad. student U. Ore., 1954-55; LL.D., Whitworth Coll., Spokane, 1962, Storm Lake (Ia.) Coll., 1966; m. Sally Wyatt, July 22, 1939; children—Martha (Mrs. John Garofalo), Philip, Steven. Owner, Hitchcock Delivery Service, Lewiston, Ida., 1930-34; partner Hitchcock & Crawford Lumber Co., Sisters, Ore., 1934-43; pres. W. Hitchock Corp., Klamath Falls, Ore., 1943-54; dir. ch. and pub. relations Lewis and Clark Coll., Portland Ore., 1954-58; v.p., logging supt. White Swan Lumber Co., White Swan, Ore., 1958-64; exec. sec. United Presbyn. Men, 1964—. Moderator Presbyn. Synod Ore., 1948; pres. Ore. Council Chs., 1948-49; mem. gen. council United Presbyn. Ch. U.S.A., 1962-64; commr. to 4th World Conf. Faith and Order, Montreal, 1963. Mem. Ore. Senate from Klamath County, 1948-54; Republican candidate for nomination U.S. Senate, 1956. Bd. dirs. Whitworth Coll., Tarkio (Mo.) Coll. Recipient Brotherhood citation Ore. chpt. Nat. Conf. Christians and Jews, 1955. Kiwanian (gov. Pacific N.W. div. 1943). Address: Box 491 Sisters OR 97759

HITE, GARTH E., publisher; m. Gretchen Hite; children—Hollis, Kristin. With Holiday mag., 1950-66, advt. dir., 1963-66, v.p. Curtis Pub. Co., 1964-66, also pub. Holiday mag., until 1966; pub. New Republic, 1966-68, Atlantic Monthly, 1968—. Home: 191 Commonwealth Av Boston MA 02116 Office: 8 Arlington St Boston MA 02116

HITE, ROBERT ERNEST, Jr., (The Bear), musician; b. Torrance, Cal., Feb. 26, 1943; s. Robert Ernest and Anne (Carson) H.; ed. pub. schs., Denver; m. Verlie Bea Marrow, Mar. 21, 1969; 1 son, Daniel Allen Loss; children by previous marriage—Eddie Ray Marrow, Paula Jean Marrow. Musician, 1960—; trumpeter, 1952—; formed Canned Heat, 1966; recording of neglected blues artists, 1967-; producer blues artists, 1967-; co-compiler Liberty Records Legendary Masters Series, 1968—; co-editor, pub. R and B mag., Northridge, Cal. Active local Cub Scouts Little League Baseball. Mem. Soc. Early Recorded Music, A.F.T.R.A. Home: 701 Topanga Canyon Blvd Topanga CA 92090 Office: 9118 Sunset Blvd Hollywood CA 90069

HITE, SAMUEL CHARLES, enging. educator; b. Ft. Wayne, Ind., Aug. 20, 1922; s. Willis DeFord and Edith (Stecher) H.; B.S. in Chem. Enging., Purdue U., 1943; Ph. D., 1951; m. Harriet Ann Thompson, Dec. 20, 1953; 1 son, Samuel Charles. From instr. to asso. prof. chem. enging. Purdue U., 1943-57, research asso., 1948-51; prof. chem. enging., chmn. dept. U. Ky., 1957-66, Rose Poly. Inst., 1966—. Cons. Comml. Solvents Corp., Eli Lilly & Co. Pres. Lexington (Ky.) Rotary Club Scholarship Fund, 1965. Mem. Am. Inst. Chem. Engrs., Am. Soc. Enging. Edn., Am. Chem. Soc., Sigma Zi, Tau Beta Pi, Omega Chi Epsilon, Phi Lambda Upsilon, Alpha Chi Sigma, Sigma Pi, Lamp and Cross, Catalyst. Spl. research venting and home humidity control. Home: 116 Canter Dr Terre Haute IN 47802

HITESHEW, FRANK MELTON, pub. co. exec.; b. Carlisle, Pa., Feb. 6, 1911; s. John Charles and Sara Maola (Shetron) H.; B.A. in Fine Arts, Carnegie Inst. Tech., 1934; m. Elizabeth Prince Miller, Dec. 18, 1953; children—Elizabeth Prince, Sara Shetron. Mural painter, N.Y.C., 1938-41; mag. illustrator, 1946-50; advt. cons. NBC-TV, Columbia Motion Pictures, N.Y.C., 1950-59; editor, pub. Carte Blanche Mag., Los Angeles, 1959-71, Western's World Mag., 1970—; pub. Destinations Mag., Easy Going Mag., 1971—. Served with AUS, 1943-46; PTO. Mem.. Internat. Platform Assn. Club: Los Angeles. Home: 1014 Amherst Av Los Angeles CA 90049 Office: 3345 Wilshire Blvd Los Angeles CA 90010

HITESMAN, WALTER WOOD, publishing co. exec.; b. Baton Rouge, Aug. 9, 1918; s. Walter Wood and Anna (Allen) H.; B.A., La. State U., 1939; m. Betty Parker, Oct. 8, 1948; 1 son, Jonathon. News editor Baton Rouge Advocate, 1939-40; bus. mgr. comml. printing div. McCall Corp., 1946-48; mng. dir. Reader's Digest (Can.), 1948-60; v.p. Reader's Digest Assn., Inc., Pleasantville, N.Y., 1960-69, sr. v.p., 1969-70, exec. v.p., 1970-71, 1st v.p., 1971—, also dir. Bd. dirs. Readers Digest Found., Patent Trader News, Boscobel Restoration, Inc. Served to col. USMCR, 1940-46. Mem. Sigma Pi, Sigma Delta Chi. Republican. Episcopalian. Clubs: Union League, Sky (N.Y.C.); Bedford Golf and Tennis; Chappaquiddick Beach, Edgartown (Mass.) Yacht, Edgartown Golf; Mill Reef (Antigua); Blind Brook Golf (Purchase, N.Y.). Home: PO Box 338 Bedford NY 10506 Office: Reader's Digest Assn Inc Pleasantville NY 10570

HITNER, CHARLES GRANT, food exec.; b. Nashville, Mar. 31, 1920; s. Charles Grant and Mary Alice (Hayes) H.; student Tenn. Poly. Inst., 1938-39; m. Evelyn Ragan Greer, Nov. 2, 1942; children—Charles Vernon, Robin Grant. Staff accountant Ernst & Ernst, Nashville, 1943-63; controller Donlon Constrn. Co., Nashville, 1963-64; treas. Ky. Fried Chicken Corp., Louisville, 1964—; dir. Nat. Automated Petroleum Services Corp., K-Lake Theatre Workshop, Inc. Trustee Belmont Coll., Nashville. Home: 4716 Chalmers Dr Nashville TN 37215 Office: PO Box 3693 Nashville TN 37217

HITT, HOMER LEE, ednl. chancellor; b. Comanche, Tex., Apr. 22, 1916; s. Allen and Sammie (Daniel) H.; student Edinburg Jr. Coll., 1932-33; B.S., La. State U., 1935, M.A., 1937; Ph.D., Harvard, 1941; m. Douglas Grace Callari, Aug. 2, 1939; children-Dian (Mrs. James O. Sanders, III), Louvin (Mrs. Robert J. Skinner). Social scientist for Bur. Agrl. Econs., U.S. Dept. Agr., 1939-41; asst. prof. sociology, asst. rural sociologist La. State U., 1941-44, asso. prof., asso. rural sociologist, 1945-47, prof. sociology, rural sociologist, head depts. sociology and rural sociology, 1947—, acting dean of the grad. sch., July-Dec. 1952, clin. prof. preventive medicine Sch. Medicine, La. State U., 1953-54, asso. dean grad. sch., 1954-57; dean La. State U. in New Orleans, 1957-59; v.p. in charge La. State U. in New Orleans, 1959-63, chancellor, 1963—; lectr. founds. social sci. Atlanta U., 1950. Chmn. Gov.'s Council on Mental Health Tng. and Research, 1957-. Dir. La. Health Council; chmn. budget com. Baton Rouge Community Chest. Bd. dirs. New Orleans Philharmonic Symphony Soc.; pres. bd. of trustees WYES-TV Ednl. TV Found.; council trustees Gulf South Research Inst. Served as ensign, U.S.N.R., 1944-45. Decorated Certificate Commendation, (Navy), 1945. Awarded Robert Treat Paine Meml. award by Harvard, 1937-38; Headliner of Year award New Orleans Press Club, Community Service award Greater New Orleans AFL-CIO, Grant-in-Aid, Social Sci. Research Council, 1942. Mem. Am., Rural So. (pres. 1956-57) sociol. socs., Assn. So. Agrl. Workers (chmn. agrl. econs. and rural sociol. sect. 1953-54), Union Internat. pour L'Etude Sci. de la Population, Sociol. Research Assn., Population Assn. Am., Am. Acad. Polit. and Social Sci., La. State U. New Orleans Alumni Assn. (hon. life), Lambda Chi Alpha, Omicron Delta Kappa, Phi Kappa Phi, Pi Gamma Mu. Episcopalian. Rotarian (past pres.). Club: Plimsoll. Author: Social Aspects of Hospital Planning in Louisiana (with A. L. Bertrand), 1947; People of Louisiana (with T. Lynn Smith), 1952; also articles sci. jours. Editor: Rural Sociology 1952-53. Home: 6301 Paris Av New Orleans LA 70122

HITT, JAMES, business exec.; b. 1924; B.S., U. Cal. at Los Angeles, 1951. With U.S. Maritime Adminstrn., 1957-65, chief of audits, 1962-65; asst. to treas. Pacific Far East Line Inc., San Francisco, 1965-68, asst. treas., 1968-70, treas., asst. sec., 1970—. Served with AUS, 1943-46. Office: 141 Battery St San Francisco CA 94111*

HITT, JOE STEPHEN, enging. educator; b. McGregor, Tex., June 13, 1934; s. A.N. and Faye (Mitchell) H.; B.S., Carnegie Inst. Tech., 1962, M.S., 1962, Ph.D., 1964; m. Laurene Ann Lally, Dec. 27, 1954; children—Leo Newton, Frank Joseph, William James, Jolene Ann, Irene Evelyn, Maurene Clare. Instr., Allegheny Tech. Inst., Pitts., 1959-62; dir. Pameco, Pitts., 1958-62; instr. Carnegie Inst. Tech., 1962-64; lab. mgr. Philco Corp., 1963-64; chief engr. Hamner Electronics Co., Princeton, N.J., 1964-65; asst. prof. bioengring. Carnegie Mellon U., 1965-66; prof. elec. enging., chmn. dept. U. Detroit, 1966—; cons. to industry, 1958—. Mem. SSS Bd. local 187, Wayne County, 1968—. Served to capt. USMCR, 1952-58. Mem. I.E.E.E., Armed Forces Command Electronics Assn., Am. Phys. Soc., Optical Soc. Am., Enging. Soc. Detroit, A.A.A.S., Sigma Xi, Eta Kappa Nu, Tau Beta Pi. Home: 19314 Canterbury St Detroit MI 48221

HITT, PATRICIA REILLY, (Mrs. Robert James Hitt) businesswoman, govt. ofcl., former mem. Republican Nat. Com.; b. Taft. Cal., Jan 24, 1918; d. John Bernard and Vera (Hearle) Reilly; B.S., B.A. in Edn., U. So. Cal., 1939; hon. Dr's Degree, Chapman Coll., 1969; children by previous marriage—John William Hamilton, Patrick Terrence Hamilton; m. 2d, Robert James Hitt, Sept. 26, 1947. Partner, Miller-Hitt Co., 1952—; now asst. sec. Dept. Health, Edn. and Welfare, Washington. Organizer, charter mem. Newport Harbor (Cal.) Women's Civic Club, 1949-51; pres. Villa Park P.T.A., 1954-56; mem. Orange (Cal.) Citizens Com. Better Schs., 1954-58; mem. U.S.-Mexico Commn. Border Devel., 1969—; mem. women's adv. council Internat. Marketing Inst., 1969—; chmn. Fed. Woman's Award Bd., 1969—. Pres. Orange County Fedn. Rep. Women, 1956-60; bd. dirs. So. div. Cal. Fedn. Rep. Women, 1955-60, mem. Cal. bd., 1960-64; Orange County committeewoman Rep. Central Com., 1955-62, vice-chmn., 1959-62, served on exec. com., 1960—; Cal. mem. Rep. Nat. Com., 1960-64; co-chmn. nat. Nixon-Agnew campaign, 1968. Bd. dirs. Reilly Found., Assistance League Orange, Nat. Assistance League; bd. govs. Chapman Coll., 1959—. vice-chmn. centennial com., 1960-61. Named Woman of Year Los Angeles Times, 1968. Mem. Orange C. of C., U. So. Cal. Alumnae Assn., P.E.O., Delta Gamma. Methodist. Home: 18102 S Mesa Dr Orange CA 92667 Office: Dept Health Edn and Welfare North Bldg 330 Independence Av SW Washington DC 20003

HITTI, PHILIP KHUR, Orientalist; b. Shimlan, Mt. Lebanon (Lebanon), June 24, 1886; s. Iskandar and Sacda (Nawfal) H.; B.A. with first honors, Am. U. of Beirut, 1908, L.H.D., 1969; Ph.D., Columbia, 1915; Litt. D. (hon.), Princeton, 1966; m. Mary George, May 22, 1918: 1 dau., Viola. Came to U.S., 1913, naturalized, 1920. Tchr., Am. High Sch., Lebanon, 1903-06, Am. U. of Beirut, 1908-13; lectr. Oriental dept. Columbia, 1915-19; prof. history Am. U. Beirut, 1919-26; mem. faculty Princeton, 1926-54, ret. as prof. Semitic lit. and chmn. dept. Oriental langs., 1954. Founder, pres. Syrian Edn. Soc. 1916; trustee École Nationale, Beirut, 1921-24; asso. mem. Corp. Am. Schs. Oriental Research 1934-54 hon. prof., 1946; mem. cultural com. East and West Assn., 1942-54, v.p. 1954; trustee of donations for edn. in Near East 1942- 54; bd. trustees Am. U. Beirut, 1945—; hon. trustee Lebanon Coll., Su al-Gharb, 1947—; has been active in numerous items related to study of Nr. East langs. and history; promotion of internat. cultural orgns.; del. to various internat. confs. Decorated Lebanese Republic La Médaille d'Honneur du Mérite Libanais en Vermeil; officer de l'Ordre du Cèdre, 1946, and several others, including Order of Merit, First Degree, Syrian Govt., 1953, commandant de l'ordre national du Cedre, Lebanon, 1956. Hon. fellow Indo-Arab Cultural Assn. of Bombay, 1947—. Mem., past officer several profl. assns. Author many works on Oriental subjects, 1916—; later ones include: Lebanon in History, 1957; Ta'rikh Sūrilya wa-Lubnan wa-Falastin, 1958; Syria: A Short History, 1959; Lubnan fi al-Ta'rikh, 1959; The Near East in History, 1961; A Short History of Lebanon, 1965; Short History of the Near East, 1966; The History of the Arabs, 1964; A Short History of the Near East, 1966; Makers of Arab History, 1968; Islam: A Way of Life, 1970; Gen. editor of Princeton Oriental Texts (now Studies), 15 vol., 1930-54; contbg. editor to numerous works including both Ency. Americana, Ency. Britannica. Home: 144 Prospect Av Princeton NJ 08540 ☆

HITTINGER, WILLIAM CHARLES, electronics co. exec.; b. Bethlehem, Pa., Nov. 10, 1922; s. John Tilghman and Pearl (Heimbach) H.; B.S. in Metall. Engring., Lehigh U., 1944; m. Elizabeth Herman, July 9, 1944; children—Patricia, William, David, Nancy. Engr., Western Electric Co., 1946-52; prodn. mgr. Nat. Union Electric Co., 1952-54; exec. dir. Bell Telephone Labs., 1954-66; pres. Bell Commn. Inc., Washington, 1966-68, Gen. Instrument Corp., N.Y.C., 1968-70; v.p., gen. mgr. RCA Corp., Somerville, NJ., 1970—. Bd. dirs. Bethlehem (Pa.) Fgn. Policy Assn., 1960-62. Served to capt. AUS, 1943-46. Named hon. citizen, Bethlehem, 1966. Fellow I.E.E.E.; mem. Inst. Mining, Metall. and Petroleum Engrs., Omicron Delta Kappa, Phi Gamma Delta. Home: 149 Bellevue Av Summit NJ 07901 Office: Route 202 Somerville NJ 08876

HITTLE, JAMES D., govt. ofcl.; b. Bear Lake, Mich., June 10, 1915; s. Harry F. and Margaret Jane (McArthur) H.; B.A., Mich. State U., 1937; M.A. in Oriental History and Geography, U., Utah, 1952; m. Edna Jane Smith, Dec. 9, 1939 (dec. 1969); children—Harry McArthur, James R.; m. 2d, Patricia Ann Herring, Sept. 5, 1970. Commd. 2d lt. USMC, 1937, advanced through grades to brig. gen., 1960; legislative asst. to comdt. USMC, 1952-58; asst. to sec. def. legislative affairs, 1959-60; retired, 1960; dir. nat. security and fgn. affairs V.F.W., 1960- 67; syndicated columnist Copley News Service, 1964-69; mil. commentator MBS, 1964-69; dir. DISC, Inc., 1960-67; spl. counsel Senate Armed Services Com., 1968-69; cons. House Armed Services Com., 1968-69; dir. D.C. Nat. Bank, 1965-69; asst. sec. navy for manpower and res. affairs, 1969—. Mem. adv. bd. Blinded Vets. Assn. Decorated Legion of Merit, Purple Heart; Medal of Combat Merit (France); recipient Alfred Thayer Mahan award Navy League U.S., 1960; George Washington award Freedom Found., 1968. Mem. V.F.W., Am. Legion, Mil. Order World Wars, Navy League, Battleship Assn. U.S., Phi Kappa Phi, Phi Kappa Delta. Author: History of the Military Staff, 1949; also articles. Editor: Jomini's Art of War, 1945. Home: 3137 S 14th St Arlington VA 22204 Office: The Pentagon Washington DC 20350

HITZIG, WILLIAM MAXWELL, physician; b. Austria, Dec. 15, 1904; s. Maier and Jeannette (Kreisberg) H.; brought to U.S., 1914, naturalized, 1926; A.B., Columbia U., 1926; M.D., Cornell U., 1929; children—Candis, Rupert, Saartje, Pietr, William Maxwell, Myron S. Hall and Elizabeth Topping (twins). Intern Mount Sinai Hosp., N.Y. City, 1929-32, asso. physician in medicine, 1946—; practice of medicine, N.Y. C., 1934—, specializing in internal medicine and cardiovascular diseases, 1936—; instr. medicine Columbia, 1938-50, asst. clin. prof. medicine, 1959—; prof. clin. medicine Mt. Sinai Sch. Medicine, N.Y. Med. cons. Ravensbrueck Lapins Project, 1958. Med. officer N.Y.C. Fire Dept., 1942-43, physician Police Dept., 1943—; med. observer, atomic bomb tests at Bikini, 1946. Citation and Alumni medal for conspicuous service to Columbia U., 1951; Dean's award Columbia Coll. 1968; hon. mem. Honor Legion, Police Dept. N.Y. City. Diplomate Am. Bd. Internal Medicine. Fellow A.C.P., Acad. of Medicine N.Y.; mem. Am. Fedn. for Clin. Research, Pilgrims U.S., Phi Beta Kappa, Mu Sigma, Phi Sigma Delta, Phi Delta Epsilon, Alpha Omega Alpha. Club: City Athletic (N.Y. City). Author sci. articles. Book reviewer Sat. Rev. Lit., 1946-50. Sponsor (with Norman Cousins) of Hiroshima Maidens Project which brought 25 Japanese girls disfigured by atom bomb to U.S. for plastic surgery and reconstructive surgery. Home: 15 Central Park W New York City NY 10023 Office: 787 Park Av New York City NY 10021

HIXON, ERNEST HOWARD, educator; b. Karlsruhe, Germany, Dec. 20, 1922; (parents U.S. citizens); s. Ralph Malcomb and Stella (Saddler) H.; student Ia. State Coll., 1940- 42; D.D.S., U. Ia., 1945, M.S., 1949; student Hogskolan, Stockholm, 1949-50; m. Margaret Stroud, Oct. 23, 1945 (div. 1964); children— Katherine, Douglas. Cleft palate research cons. U. Toronto, 1950-51; asso. prof. U. Ia., 1951-54, prof., head dept. orthodontics, 1954- 60; prof., head dept. orthodontics U. Mexico, 1960-61, U. Ore., 1961—. Served as lt. (j.g.) USNR, 1945-47. Mem. Am. Dental Assn., Am. Assn. Orthodontists, Am. Assn. Cleft Palate Rehab., Soc. Research Child Devel., Sigma Xi. Address: U Ore Dental Sch Portland OR 97201

HIXON, LAWRENCE BETTS, educator; b. Chesterton, Ind., May 10, 1910; s. Warren Hosmer and Mabel (Betts) H.; A.B., Colgate U.; M.S., Syracuse U., 1933, Ed.D., 1947; m. Clara Pauline Simons, June 30, 1941; children-Virginia Carol (Mrs. Richard W. Torpey), David Lawrence. Tchr. math. Altmar (N.Y.) Union Sch., 1933-36; dir. guidance Millbrook (N.Y.) Meml. Sch., 1941-42; asso. prof. edn. St. Lawrence U., 1947-52; prof. (N.Y.) Meml. Sch., 1941-42; asso. prof. edn. St. Lawrence U., 1947-52; prof. ednl. adminstrn. Cornell U., 1952—, dir. Ford Inter Univ. Project 1, 1962-65. Served to lt. comdr. USNR, 1942-46. Mem. Assn. Sch., Coll. and Univ. Staffing, Middle Atlantic Assn. Sch., Coll. and Univ. Staffing, Collegiate Assn. Devel. Ednl. Adminstrn., Council Adminstrv. Leadership, Nat. Orgn. Legal Problems of Edn., Univ. Council Ednl. Adminstrn., Mu Pi Delta, Kappa Phi Kappa, Phi Delta Kappa. Episcopalian. Mason. Author: Study Guide for New York State School Law, 1965. Home: 62 Woodcrest Av Ithaca NY 14850

HIXSON, EPHRIAM, ret. govt. ofcl.; b. Vernon, Tex., Jan. 21, 1902; s. Byron Ephriam and Martha May (Stone) H.; B.S., Okla. State U., 1929, M.S., 1930; Ph.D., Ia. State U., 1940; m. Veallon Grimes, Nov. 12, 1928; 1 son, Ephriam. Grad. fellow Okla. State U., 1929-30, instr., 1930-32, asst. prof. entomology, 1932-40, asso. prof., 1940-46; prof., head entomology U. Neb., 1946-50; asso. dir. resident instrn. agr. and home econs., 1949-54; dean, dir. coll. agr. S.D. State U., 1954-57; with Tech. Coop. Mission-AID univ. devel., New Delhi, 1957-62, br. chief, Nigeria, 1962-65, U. Alexandria (Egypt), 1965-67, agronomist, Turkey, 1967-70, br. chief univ. devel. India, 1970-71, ret., 1971. Mem. bd. mgmt. Utter Pradesh Agrl. U., India, 1949. Served with U.S. Army, 1918-19. Recipient AID citation agr., 1969. Mem. Entomol. Soc. Am., Nat. Geog. Soc., Farmhouse (nat. dir. 1950-52), Sigma Xi, Alpha Zeta, Phi Kappa Phi. Contbr. articles profl. jours. Home: 10759 Saratoga Circle Sun City AZ 85351

HIXSON, HAROLD HARRY, univ. adminstr.; b. Meadow Grove, Neb., Nov. 8, 1909; s. Harve Millard and Chloe Inez (Pugh) H.; student Neb. State Tchrs. Coll., Chadron., 1940; m. Lora Callaway, Mar. 21, 1952; 1 dau., Linda Jean. Bursar, Neb. State Tchrs. Coll., 1938-41; asst. bus. mgr. U. Omaha, 1941-42; prodn. supr. Glenn L. Martin-Neb. Co., 1942-43; asst. bus. mgr. U. Cal. at Berkeley, 1947-49, also adminstr. Cowell Hosp., Berkeley, 1947-49; bus. mgr., asst. hosp. adminstr. U. Cal. Med. Center, San Francisco, 1950-53; asso. adminstr. U. Cal. Hosps., San Francisco, 1953-56, adminstr., 1956- 70; asst. vice chancellor Cal. at Cal., San Francisco, 1970—; lectr. hosp. adminstr. U. Cal. Sch. Pub. Health, Berkeley, 1960—. Founding pres. Hosp. Council No. Cal., 1961-63, bd. dirs., 1963-67; bd. dirs. Bay area Health Facilities Planning Assn., 1965-70, Bay Area Comprehensive Health Planning Council, 1970—, San Francisco Comprehensive Health Planning Council, 1970—; mem. 1965 White House Conf. on Health. Served to lt. comdr. USNR, 1944-46; comdr. Res. Fellow Am. Coll. Hosp. Adminstrs.; mem. Assn. Western Hosps. (treas. 1961- 63, pres. 1965-66, founding pres. edn. and research found., 1961-63, pres. 1965-66), Am. Assn. Med. Colls. (chmn. teaching hosp. sect. 1964-65, exec. com. 1961-67), Am. Pub. Health Assn., Am., Cal. (Ritz Heerman Meml. award 1962, trustee 1966-69) hosp. assns., San Francisco Hosp. Conf. (treas. 1960-61, pres. 1961-63), Nat. League Nursing. Rotarian. Home: 40 Halkin Lane Berkeley CA 94708 Office: U Cal 3d and Parnassus Sts San Francisco CA 94122

HIXSON, WILLIAM AASE, educator; b. Gettysburg, S.D., Oct. 21; 1922; s. Harry and Lisa (Aase) H.; B.S., Ia. State Coll., 1945; Ph.D., Stanford, 1949; m. Phyllis Jane Mauritson, Aug. 15, 1946; children—Donald, Susan, Steven, Cynthia. Research engr. Gen. Electric Co., 1949-52; mem. faculty S.D. Sch. Mines and Tech., Rapid City, 1952—, prof. elec. engring., head dept., 1955—; examiner, cons. N. Central Assn. Colls. and Univs., 1963—. Clk., Dist. 85 Sch. Bd., 1966-68. Served with USNR, 1943-46. Registered profl. engr., S.D. Mem. I.E.E.E. (pres. Black Hills sub-sect. 1957, 66), Am. Soc. Engring. Edn., Sigma Xi, Eta Kappa Nu, Phi Kappa Phi, Sigma Tau. Elk. Home: Route 4 Box 599 Rapid City SD 57701

HJEJLE, BERNT RUBEN HANSEN, lawyer; b. Copenhagen, Denmark, Sept. 25, 1901; s. Hans Nicolaj Hansen and Ella (Ruben) H.; grad. in law, U. Copenhagen, 1927, LL.D., 1941; m. Ulla Cold, Nov. 26, 1927; children—Marianne, Benedicte. Advocate High Ct. Copenhagen, 1931, Supreme Ct. Denmark, 1942; asst. pub. prosecutor high treason cases, 1946-50; pvt. practice, Copenhagen, 1931—. Chmn. Copenhagen Savs. Bank, Nordisk BAT A/S, Carlsberg Bryggerierne og Tuborgs Bryggerier, De Forenede Bryggerier A/S; dir. De Danske Spritfabrikker/A/S. A.P. Möller Shipping Co. Chmn. Copenhagen Bar Assn., 1950-55; pres. Danish Bar Assn., 1955-61; chmn. Internat. Bar Assn., 1964-66; chmn. Danish bd. Scandinavian Lawyers Meetings, 1957—. Mem. council Fedn. Danish Industries; chmn. Childrens Ring, 1950-71; pres. Danish Students Assn., 1950-51; mem. Danish nat. com. World Vet. Found. Decorated grand comdr. Order of Dannebrog. Author: Commercial Arbitration, vol. 1, 1937, vol. 11, 1941. Danish editor Scandinavian Law Rev. 1943—. Home: Valeursvej 52900 Copenhagen-Hellerup Denmark Office: 24 Amagertorv 1160 Copenhagen K Denmark

HJELLE, JOHN ORIO editor; b. Mercer, N.D., Nov. 15, 1913; s. Ole S. and Ella T. (Myrah) H.; A.B., Luther Coll., 1936; m. Alice Marie Driver, Dec. 19, 1943; children—Ann Marie, Kathryn Lynn, Barbara, Kristin. Reporter, sports editor, telegraph editor Bismarck Tribune, 1936-41, city editor, 1941-45, editor, 1948—; exec. sec., adminstrv. asst. U.S. Senator M.R. Young, Washington, 1945-48. Mem. Am. Soc. Newspaper Editors, Izaak Walton League, N.D. Press Assn. (pres. 1969-70). Lutheran. Elk. Mason (Shriner), Rotarian. Contbr. to profl. publs. Home: 106 W Sioux Av Bismarck ND 58501 Office: 224 4th St Bismarck ND 58501

HJELLUM, JOHN, lawyer; b. Aurland, Sogn, Norway, Mar. 29, 1910 (parents U.S. citizens); s. Olav Iversen and Belle (Ohnstad) H.; LL.B., U. N.D., 1934; m. Helen Jeanette Fodness, May 12, 1935; children—Janice Ann, Joan Mae, John II. Admitted to N.D. bar, 1934, since practiced in Jamestown; mem. firm Hjellum, Weiss, Nerison, Jukkala & Vinje; investigator fed. violations Dept. Justice, 1934; asst. states atty. Stutsman County, N.D., 1943-47, states atty., 1948-50. Sec. N.D. Broadcasting Co., 1950-62; sec., dir. North Am. Uranium Inc., Jamestown, N.D., 1954-69; dir. Soo Line R.R. Co., Jamestown Nat. Bank. Active community drives. Chmn. N.D. Eisenhower for President group, also N.D. Citizens for Eisenhower-Nixon; vice chmn. Stutsman County Republican Orgn., 1955-58; mem. Stutsman County Central Com., 1958-62; del. Rep. Nat. Conv., 1952. Trustee Jamestown Coll.; chmn. trustee N.D. Independent Coll. Fund, 1957-68. Served as sgt 465th CIC, AUS, 1944-45. Fellow Internat. Acad. Trial Lawyers; mem. Am., Internat., N.D. (pres. 1957-58), 4th Jud. Dist. (pres. 1949-50), Stutsman County (pres. 1940-41, 49-50) bar assns., Am. Legion, V.F.W., Law-Sci. Acad. Am., Order of Coif (hon.), Lambda Chi Alpha. Phi Delta Phi, Kappa Kappa Psi. Methodist (chmn. bd.). Mason. Home: 916 2d Av NW Jamestown ND 58401 Office: PO Box 1560 Jamestown ND 58401

HLADKY, JOSEPH F., Jr., newspaper exec.; b. Cedar Rapids, Ia., Aug. 25, 1910; s. Joseph Frank and Laura (Krchmar) H.; student Coe Coll., 1928-29, Ia. U., 1930-31; m. Jane Miller, Sept. 15, 1935; children—John Miller, Joseph F., III. Mfr. mdse. vending machines, 1931-35; newspaper exec., 1935—, radio exec., 1947—, T.V. exec., 1953—, pres., gen. mgr., pub. Gazette Co., Cedar Rapids; pres. Cedar Rapids TV Co., also dir.; dir. Mchts. Nat. Bank, Cedar Rapids, Ia. Nat. Mut. Ins. Co., Cedar Rapids. Mem. Ia. Gov.'s Econ. Adv. Council Com.; mem. Cedar Rapids Hosp. Council. Bd. dirs., mem. exec. com. St. Luke's Methodist Hosp., Cedar Rapids; bd. dirs. YMCA, Cedar Rapids; trustee, mem. exec. com. Coe Coll., Cedar Rapids. Mem. Ia. Daily Press Assn. (dir. 1938—, pres. 1953—, chmn. ABC-TV affiliates com. 1958—), Inland Daily Press Assn. (dir., sec.), C. of C. (dir., v.p. 1964-65, pres. 1966), Beta Theta Pi. Mason (Shriner), Moose, Elk. Clubs: Nat. Press (Washington); Chicago Press. Home: 263 E Post Rd SE Cedar Rapids IA 52403 Office: Gazette Co Cedar Rapids IA 52406

HLA MAUNG, U., Burmese diplomat; b. Meiktila, Burma, Sept. 20, 1911; s. U San and Daw Ma Ma; B.A., U. Rangoon, 1939; m. Saw Than Yin, Apr. 4, 1942; children—Pyle, Phyo, Sann, Htoo. Dept. sec. Ministry Fgn. Affairs, 1942- 45; parliamentary sec. forest and agr., 1947; minister for home and jud. affairs, 1947; mem. Parliament, and predecessor, from Magwe Constituency, 1948—; ambassador to Thailand, 1949-51, to Indonesia, 1950-51, to People's Republic of China, 1951-58, to People's Republic of Mongolia, 1957-58, to Israel, 1958-61, to Court of St. James, 1961-68, to Norway, Sweden and Denmark, 1963-69, to U.S., from 1968. Rep. Burma at Havana Conf. Trade and Tariffs, 1947; rep. minister of trade at GATT Conf., Geneva, 1963. A leader, original founder Anti-Fascist Peoples' Freedom League, World War II; founder, mem. Burma Socialist Party. Decorated 2d class of 1st order Thado Thiri Thudamma.

HO, CHINN, investment banker; b. Waikiki, Honolulu, Feb. 26, 1904; s. Ti Yuen and Lan (Kam) H.; student U. Hawaii Extension, 1925-26; m. Betty Ching, Oct. 13, 1934; children—Stuart, Dean, Karen, John, Robin, Heather. Various positions Bishop Bank, Duisenberg Wichman & Co., Swan Culbertson & Fitz (Philippines) and Dean Witter & Co., Honolulu, 1924-43; pres., dir. Capital Investment Hawaii, Inc., 1944—; chmn. bd. Honolulu Star-Bull., Inc.; pres., dir. Ilikai, Inc., Makaha Valley, Inc., Hawaii Islanders, Inc.; dir. Host Internat., Inc., Victoria Ward, Ltd., Theo. H. Davies & Co., Pacific Ins. Co.; mng. trustee Mark A. Robinson Trust, Mark A. Robinson Estates. Civilian aide to sec. of army, Hawaii, 1965-71. Named Optimist of Year, Hawaii, 1956, Father of Year, 1961, Sportsman of Year 1964, Salesman of Year, Hawaii, 1966; recipient Golden Plate award Am. Acad. Achievement, 1968; Golden Eagle award, 1971. Mem. Bishop Mus. Assn. (past pres.), Honolulu Stock Exchange (past pres.), Hawaii Visitor's Bur. (past pres.), Honoluly Realty Bd. Clubs: Waialae Country, Rotary. Home: 1777 Ala Moana Honolulu HI 96815 Office: 239 Merchant St Honolulu HI 96813

HO, DAVID T.C., banker. Dep. gen. Hang Seng Bank Ltd., Victoria, Hong Kong. Office: 77 Des Voeux Rd Victoria Hong Kong*

HO, DON, entertainer; b. Kakaako, Oahu, Hawaii, Aug. 13, 1930; s. James A. Y. and Emily (Silva) H.; grad. Kamehameha Sch., 1949; student Springfield (Mass.) Coll., 1950; B.A., U. Hawaii, 1952; m. Melvamay Wong, Nov. 22, 1951; children—Donald Tai Loy, Donalei, Dayna, Dondi, Dorianne, Dwight. Propr., entertainer Honey's, Honolulu, Kanehoe, 1958-60, Hale Ho, Honolulu, 1960—; player Duke Kahanamoku's, 1960-70; nightclub entertainer in Hawaii and U.S; radio program on sta. KHVH, Honolulu, 1961—; star own show Cinerama Reef Tower Hotel, Honolulu; star network TV series, TV spls.; rec. artist for Reprise Records. Hon. chmn. Hemophilia Found. of Hawaii. Served with USAF, 1952-58. Recipient Civilian Service award U.S. Army. Address: 2003 Kalia Rd Honolulu HI 96815

HO, PING-TI, educator, historian; b. Tientsin, Hopei, China, Sept. 1, 1917; s. Shou- ch'üan and Yung-Lan (Chang) H.; B.A., Nat. Tsing-Hua U., Peiping, China, 1938; Ph.D., Columbia, 1952; m. Ching-lo Shao, July 3, 1940; childrenSidney K'o-yüeh, Bartlet K'o-chün. Naturalized Canadian citizen, 1958. Instr. history Tsing-hua U., 1939-45; from instr. to prof. history and Asian studies U. B.C., 1948-63; prof. Chinese history and instns., U. Chgo., 1963-65, James Westfall Thompson prof. history, 1965—. Mem. Academia Sinica; mem. Council of Sino-Am. Coop. in Humanities and Social Studies, 1966—. Sino-Am. Boxer Fund Scholar, 1945-48; recipient Gold medal for scholarship Ministry Edn. Republic China, 1962. Mem. Assn. Asian Studies (dir. 1968—). Author: Studies on the Population of China, 1368-1953, 1959; The Ladder of Success in Imperial China, 1368-1911, 1962; (in Chinese) Landsmannschaften in China, 1966; The Loess and the Origin of Chinese Agriculture, 1969; also numerous articles. Mem. editorial Tsing-Hua Jour. Chinese Studies, 1964—. Home: 4741 S Woodlawn Av Chicago IL 60615

HO, YU-CHI, educator; b. China, Mar. 1, 1934; s. Chin-Woo and Ching-Yi (Pan) H.; S.B., Mass. Inst. Tech., 1953, S.M., 1955; Ph.D., Harvard, 1961; m. Sophia Hu, Oct. 10, 1959; children—Adrian, Christine. Sr. engr. Bendix Corp., 1955-58; asst. prof. elec. engring. Harvard, 1961-65, asso. prof., 1965-69, Gordon McKay prof., 1969—. Mem. Army Sci. Adv. Panel, 1968—. Guggenheim fellow, 1970. Sr. mem. I.E.E.E. Office: Pierce Hall Harvard Univ Cambridge MA 02138

HOAD, JOHN G., cons. engr.; b. Lawrence, Kan., Sept. 20, 1909; s. William C. and Louise (Green) H.; B.S., U. Mich., 1932, postgrad., 1932-33, 39-40; m. Grace Hamilton, Nov. 24, 1937. Engr., accountant Pub. Adminstrn. Service, Chgo., 1933; asst. civil engr. Mich. State Ferries, 1933-34; with Mich. Hwy. Dept., 1934-37; engr. Detroit Edison Co., 1937-42. power sales engr., 1946-50; engr. Cummins & Barnard, Inc., Ann Arbor, Mich., 1950-53; pres., dir. Lincoln Mining Co., Wallace, Ida., 1949-53; pres., dir. John G. Hoad & Assos., Inc., Ypsilanti, Mich., 1953—; pres., dir. Hoad Corp., Ypsilanti, 1956—. Served from capt. to lt. col., USAAF, 1942-45. Registered profl. engr., Mich., other states. Fellow Am. Soc. C.E., Am. Soc. M.E.; mem. Nat., Mich. socs. profl. engrs., Mich. Engring. Soc., T.A.P.P.I., Am. Inst. Cons. Engrs. (pres. 1966—), Engring Soc. Detroit, Delta Upsilon. Clubs: Detroit Athletic; Dearborn Country; Engineers (N.Y.C.). Home: 40 Shady Hollow St Dearborn MI 48124 Office: 1159 E Michigan Av Ypsilanti MI 48197

HOADLEY, GEORGE BURNHAM, educator; b. Swarthmore, Pa., June 24, 1909; s. George Arthur and Fannie Burnham (Kilgore) H.; B.Sc. in Elec. Engring. with highest honors, Swarthmore Coll., 1930; M.S., Mass. Inst. Tech., 1932, D.Sc., 1937; m. Mary Elizabeth Betts, Feb. 17, 1934; children—Peter George, Robert Alan, Arthur Bruce. Instr. Mass. Inst. Tech., 1931-40; asst. prof. Poly. Inst. Bklyn., 1940-45, asso. prof., 1945-48; prof. elec. engring. N.C. State Univ., Raleigh, 1948-53, head dept. elec. engring., 1953—. Mem. bd. edn., Sea Cliff, N.Y., 1945-48. Fellow I.E.E.E.; mem. Am. Soc. Engring. Edn., N.Y. Acad. Scis., Sigma Xi, Tau Beta Pi, Sigma Tau, Eta Kappa Nu. Author: Principles of Electrical Engineering, rev. edit., 1951. Editor I.E.E.E. Trans. on Instrumentation and Measurement, 1954—. Home: 3213 Leonard St Raleigh NC 27607

HOADLEY, WALTER EVANS, economist, financial exec.; b. San Francisco, Aug. 16, 1916; s. Walter Evans and Marie Howland (Preece) H.; A.B., U. Cal., 1938, M.A., 1940, Ph.D., 1946; Dr. C. S.; Franklin and Marshall Coll., 1963; LL.D., Golden Gate Coll. 1968; m. Virginia Alm, May 20, 1939; children—Richard Alm, Jean Elizabeth (Mrs. Richard A. Price, Jr.). Collaborator U.S. Bur. Agrl. Econs., 1938-39; research economist Cal. Gov.'s Reemployment Commn., 1939, Planning Bd., 1941; research economist, teaching fellow U. Cal., 1938-41, supr. indsl. mgmt. war tng. office, 1941-42; econ. adviser U. Chgo. Civil Affairs Tng. Sch., 1945; sr. economist Fed. Res. Bank Chgo., 1942-49; economist Armstrong Cork Co., Lancaster, Pa., 1949-54, treas. 1954- 60, v.p., treas., 1960-66, dir., 1962—; sr. v.p., chief economist, mem. mng. com. Bank of Am. NT & SA, San Francisco, 1966-68, exec. v.p., chief economist, mem. mng. Com., mem. adv. council bd. dirs., 1968—; dep. chmn. Fed. Res. Bank, Phila., 1960-61, chmn., 1962-66; faculty Sch. Banking U. Wis., 1945-49, 55, 58-66. Adviser various U.S. Govt. agys.; mem. pub. adv. bd. U.S. Dept. Commerce, 1970—; mem. White House Rev. Com. for Balance Payments Statistics, 1963- 65; mem. Presdl. Task Force on Growth, 1969-70. Mem. Meth. Ch. Commn. on World Service and Finance. Phila. Conf., 1957-64, chmn. investment com., 1964-66. Mem. board trustees Pacific Sch. Religion; adviser Nat. Commn. to Study Nursing and Nursing Edn.; trustee Duke U.; mem. bd. overseers U.S. com. Harvard Coll. Econs.; chmn. investment com. Cal.- New Meth. Found. Fellow Am. Statis. Assn. (v.p. dir. 1952-54, pres. 1958) Nat. Assn. of Bus. Economists; mem. Am. Finance Assn. (dir. 1955-56, pres. 1969), Conf. Bus. Economists (chmn. 1962), C of C.

of U.S., Am., Western Econ. Assns., Am. Marketing Assn., Financial Analysts San Francisco, Conf. Bd. (econ. forum), Bus. Council Tech. Cons. (chmn. 1962-66). Comptrollers Cons. Com. Bank Econ., Nat. Bur. Econ. Research (dir.), Western Finance Assn. (dir.), Internat. Conf. Comml. Bank Economists, Phi Beta Kappa, Kappa Alpha. Methodist. Clubs: Lancaster (Pa.) Country; St. Francis Yacht, Commonwealth Bankers (San Francisco). Home: 999 Green St San Francisco CA 94133

HOAG, ARTHUR HOWARD, Jr., architect; b. Lakewood, O., May 19, 1923; s. Arthur Howard and Ada Rose (Keyse) H.; student U. Tex., 1942-43, 47-48, Wooster Coll., 1943, Fenn Coll., 1949, Whitman Coll., 1944, St. Mary's Coll., 1944, U.S. Mcht. Marine Acad., 1945, Western Res. U., 1948-49; m. Nancy Louise Elliott, May 26, 1949; children—Patricia, Victoria, Lawrence, Daniel, Leslie, Jeffery. Field engr., asso. architect McGeorge-Hargett & Assos., 1949-59; architect, partner McGeorge-Hargett & Hoag, 1959-62, Hargett-Hoag Assos., 1962-65; sr. partner Hoag-Wismar-Henderson Assos., Cleve., 1965—; chmn. bd. dirs., treas. HWH Assos., Inc.; dir. Citizens Fed. Savs. & Loan of Cleve. Active Welfare Fedn., United Appeal. Mem. Rocky River Bd. Zoning and Bldg. Appeals, 1956-66; chmn. Rocky River Design and Constrn. Review Bd., 1966-68. Trustee Rocky River Pub. Library, Architects Soc. Ohio Found. Served with USNR, 1942-45. Recipient award of merit, Architects Soc. Ohio, 1965, Top Ten Plant award, 1963, 68. Mem. A.I.A., Architects Soc. Ohio (pres. 1970), Consulting Engrs. Council, Greater Cleve. Growth Bd., Cleve. Builders Exchange, Phi Gamma Delta. Clubs: Cleveland City, Cleveland Yachting, Cleveland Rotary. Home: 55 Kensington Oval Rocky River OH 44116 Office: 1150 W 3d St Cleveland OH 44113

HOAG, CHARLES LEONARD, educator; b. Albion, Mich., Nov. 15, 1907; s. John Charles and Sarah (Huggins) H.; A.B. summa cum laude, Albion Coll., 1929; M.A. (State fellow), U. Mich., 1930; Ph.D. (fellow 1934-36), Clark U., 1938; m. Mary Graham Croom, June 28, 1941; children—Mary Moore, Charles Leonard. Instr. Ill. Wesleyan U., 1930-34; instr., then asso. prof. Springfield (Mass.) Coll., 1936-42; regional analyst div. program surveys Bur. Agrl. Econs., Dept. Agr., 1942; regional analyst OWL, 1942-43; analyst Opinion Research Corp., Princeton, N.J., 1943-44; asso. market research Stewart, Dougall & Assos., N.Y.C., 1943-47; field research Am. Inst. Pub. Opinion, Elmo Roper & Assos., 1947; mem. faculty Middlebury Coll., 1947—, prof. polit. sci., 1962-68, Alumni prof. polit. sci., 1968—, chmn. dept. contemporary civilization, 1955-62; vis. prof. polit. sci. U. Conn., summer 1948; fgn. affairs specialist State Dept., 1950-52; Fulbright lectr. Law and Polit. Coll., Kyungpook U., Taegu Coll., also Chungu Coll., Taegu, Korea, 1961-62; asso. mil. history Dept. Army, 1965-70. Participant, Atlantic Coast Migratory Labor Survey, summer 1940; adv. council dept. employment security Vt., 1965-71. Chmn. Ind. Sch. Bd. 4, 1956-61. Bd. dirs. Vt. Council World Affairs, 1961-67, pres., 1967-71; v.p. Vt. Council Arts and Scis., 1966-67. Mem. Middlebury Town Democratic Com., 1952—; del. Vt. Dem. Conv., 1956, 64, alternate del., 1968; justice peace Addison County, 1960—; town moderator, 1964-69; chmn. Dem. Town Com., Middlebury, 1968-69. Recipient Am. Philos. Soc. grant, 1967-68. Mem. Am. Polit. Sci. Assn., Assn. Asian Studies, Phi Gamma, Delta Sigma Rho. Sigma Nu. Conglist. Author: American Opinion on the Navy, 1919-22, 1941; also articles. Home: Box 468 Middlebury VT 05753

HOAG, DONALD, clergyman; b. Phila., Aug. 15, 1900; s. John and Anna (Cavanaugh) H.; B.A., St. Bonaventure U., 1926. Joined Franciscan Order, 1923, ordained priest Roman Cath. Ch., 1929; asst. pastor in N.Y.C., Wilkes-Barre, Pa., 1930-32; asst. pastor, then pastor, Allegany, N.Y., 1932-42; pastor, Rutherford, N.J., 1946-49, 52; councilor to provincial Franciscan Order, N.Y.C., 1952-55, asst. to provincial, 1955-61, provincial, 1961—. Pres. bd. trustees St. Bonaventure U., Siena Coll. Served as chaplain AUS, 1942-46. Address: 112 Erskine Rd Ringwood NJ 07456

HOAG, FRANK STEPHEN Jr., publisher; b. Pueblo, Colo., June 11, 1908; s. Frank S. and Louise (Allebrand) H.; B.A., Princeton, 1931; Litt.D (hon.), So. Colo. State Coll., 1965, m. LeVert Wiess, June 15, 1935. Pub., Pueblo Star-Jour. and Chieftain, 1943—. Mem. audit com. Asso. Press. Dir. Minnequa Bank. Dir., v.p. Colo. Public Expenditures Council; mem. Colo. Commn. Higher Edn. Trustee Colo. Coll., Colorado Springs; bd. dirs. USAF Acad. Found., Colorado Springs; trustee Parkview Episcopal Hosp., Pueblo Devel. Found.; pres. So. Colo. State Coll. Found. DeMolay Legion of Honor. Mem. Pueblo C. of C. (past pres.), Am. Soc. Newspaper Editors, Colo. Press Assn. (past pres.), Am. Newspaper Pubs. Assn., Sigma Delta Chi. Presbyn. Mason (32), Rotarian (past pres.), Elk. Home: 305 Argyle St Pueblo, CO 81005. Office: 825 W 6th St Pueblo CO 81002

HOAG, GARRETT SCATTERGOOD, lawyer; b. Phila., Apr. 15, 1901; s. Clarence G. and Anna (Scattergood) H.; student Westtown Sch., 1912-19; B.S., Haverford Coll., 1923; LL.B., Yale, 1930; m. Margaret Ewing, Sept. 13, 1924; children—Nancy Blanchet, Margaret Myer, Alice Bator. Mgr. Pocono Manor (Pa.) Inn., 1923-27; admitted to Mass bar, 1931; asso. Ropes, Gray, Best, Coolidge & Rugg, Boston, 1930-43; partner Foley, Hoag & Eliot, Boston, 1943—; dir. liquidations Mass. trust cos., 1939-43; clk. and dir. Windram Mfg. Co., S. Boston; pres., dir. Eliot St. Garage Co., Boston; dir. Robert Abel & Co., Inc. Selectman, Town of Wellesley, Mass., 1940-46; mem. Loyalty Rev. Bd., Washington, 1947-53. Trustee Convalescent Home for Children, Wellesley; mem. bd. mgrs. Haverford Coll. Home: 131 Glen Rd Wellesley Hills MA 02181 Office: 10 Post Office Sq Boston MA 02109

HOAG, LEVERETT PADDOCK, educator; b. Moorhead, Minn., Nov. 17, 1916; s. Stephen H. and Ethel I. (Hull) H.; B.Ed., Moorhead State Coll., 1937; M.A., U. Minn., 1953, Ph.D., 1958; m. Helga G. Guttormsson, June 12, 1940; children—Elin E. (Mrs. Donald D. Cadmus), Stephen G., David L., Donald R. Asst. prof. No. State Tchrs. Coll., Aberdeen, S.D., 1955-56, Kan. State U., 1956-58; faculty U. Minn., Duluth, 1958—, prof. geography, 1966—, head dept., 1970—. Served with USNR, 1945-46. Mem. Assn. Am. Geographers, Am. Geog. Soc., Nat. Council Geog. Edn., Minn. Council Geog. Edn., Minn. Acad. Sci. Home: 610 Arrowhead Rd Duluth MN 55811

HOAG, MERRITT ELDRED, coll. pres.; b. New Castle, Pa., May 25, 1909; s. Walter Scott and Edna Pearl (Zimmerman) H.; B.S., Edinboro Coll., 1931; Ed.M., Duke, 1936; LL.D., Norwich U., 1960; m. Ruth Ann Lowry, June 24, 1933; 1 son, John Randall. Prin., tchr. pub. schs., Franklin, Pa., 1932-35; dean Masonic Sch., Ft. Worth, 1938-42; asst. to pres., comdt. North Ga. Coll., 1946- 49, pres., 1949-70, pres. emeritus, 1970—. Served as lt. comdr. USNR, 1942-46; lt. col. Army Res. Decorated D.S.M. Democrat. Methodist. Mason (32). Home: Dahlonega GA 30533

HOAGLAND, DONALD WRIGHT, lawyer; b. N.Y.C., Aug. 16, 1921; s. Webster Comley and Irene (Wright) H.; B.A., Yale, 1942; LL.B., Columbia, 1948; m. Mary Tiedeman, May 14, 1949; children—Peter M., Mary C., Sara H., Ann W. Admitted to N.Y. bar, 1948, Colo. bar, 1951; asso. firm Winthrop, Stimson, Putnam & Roberts, N.Y.C., 1948-51; asso., then partner firm Lewis, Grant & Davis, Denver, 1953-63; with AID, 1964-66, asst. adminstr. devel. finance and pvt. enterprise, 1965-66; partner Davis, Graham & Stubbs, Denver, 1966- -. Chmn. bd. Bi-Nat. Devel. Corp., 1968—; dir. Centennial Fund, Inc., 2d Centennial Fund, Inc., Gryphon Fund, Inc., 1959-63. Mem. Denver Planning Bd., 1955-61, 67-70 chmn., 1959-61. Bd. dirs., vice chmn. Denver Art Mus., 1959-63; bd. dirs. Colo. Urban League, 1960-63, chmn. bd., 1968—; bd. dirs. Vols. Internat. Tech. Assistance, 1970—; trustee Phillips Exeter Acad., 1960-67; bd. dirs., vice chmn. bd. Denver chpt. A.R.C., 1959-61. Served as dive bomber pilot USNR, 1943-45. Decorated Air medal (2). Mem. Am., Colo., Denver bar assns., Am. Judicature Soc., Am. Soc. Internat. Law, Soc. Internat. Devel. Home: 2250 S Columbine St Denver CO 80210 Office: Am Nat Bank Bldg Denver CO 80202

HOAGLAND, HUDSON, physiologist; b. Rockaway, N.J., Dec. 5, 1899; s. Mahlon Lounsbury and Ella (Baylis) H.; student Morris Acad., Morristown, N.J., 1913-17; A.B., Columbia, 1921; M.S., Mass, Inst. Tech., 1924; Ph.D., Harvard, 1927; D.Sc., Colby Coll., 1945, Wesleyan U., 1959, Clark U., 1962, Bates Coll., 1965, Boston U., 1966, Worcester Poly. Inst., 1966; m. Anna Plummer, June 9, 1920; children—Mahlon Bush, Ann Holland, Peter, Joan. Fellow NRC at Harvard, 1927-28, instr. physiology, tutor biology, 1928-30; Parker fellow, spl. lectr. Cambridge (Eng.) U., 1930-31; prof. gen. physiology, dir. physiology labs. Clark U., Worcester, Mass., 1931-44; co-founder, exec. dir. Worcester Found. for Exptl. Biology, 1944-67, pres., 1967-68, pres. emeritus, 1969—; Research asso. physiology, Harvard Medical School, tutor biochemical sciences, Harvard College, 1940-41; cons. physiologist, Worcester State Hospital, 1945-57, vis. lectr. physiol. psychology Harvard, 1945-46; research prol. physiology, Tufts Med. Sch., 1946- 50, Boston U., 1950-68 cons. M.C., U.S. Army, 1948-54; dir. Guarantee Bank & Trust Co.; Chmn. Macy Found. Conf. on Neuropharmocology, 1954-59; v.p. Conf. Sci., Philosphy and Religion, Inc., 1954. Trustee George Washington Carver Found., 1960-68, Worcester Meml. Hosp., 1956-68, Woods Hole Oceanographic Instn., 1959-68; vis. com. Harvard Med. Sch. and Sch. Dental Medicine, 1959-54, vis. com. dept. biology, 1965—, dept. psychology and social relations, 1965-70. Recipient Humanist of Year award, 1965; Modern Medicine award, 1965. Guggenheim fellow, 1944-45. Served in 29th Div., U.S. Army 1917-18. Fellow A.A.A.S. (dir. 1966-70), Am. Acad. Arts and Scis. (pres. 1961-64); mem. Soc. Biol. Psychiatry (pres. 1967-68), Am. Physiol. Soc., Sigma Xi. Clubs: Harvard Faculty, Worcester; St. Botolph (Boston, Mass.); Century Association (N.Y.C.); Author: Pacemakers in Relation to Aspects of Behavior, 1935. Editor: Hormones, Brain Function and Behavior, 1957. Co-editor Explt. Biology Monographs; mem. editorial bd. Ann. Rev. of Physiology; co-editor Evolution of Man's Progess, Contbr. profl. articles. Home: Deerfood Rd Southboro MA 01772 Office: 222 Maple Av Shrewsbury MA 01545

HOAGLAND, LAURANCE REDINGTON, newspaper exec.; b. Omaha, Sept. 26, 1913; s. Paul Ingalls and Edith Mary (Jackson) H.: A.B., Stanford, 1935, M.B.A., 1937; m. Naomi Ann Carpenter, Feb. 22, 1936; children—Laurance, Peter Jackson, Jayne Summers. With Carpenter Paper Co. (became corporate div. Champion Papers, Inc. 1961), 1937-61, successively credit mgr., operations mgr., sec., v.p., dir. operations, 1937-54, exec. v.p., dir., 1954-62, pres., 1962-64; sr. v.p., dir. Nationwide Papers, Inc., subsidiary Champion Papers, Inc., 1963-64; sr. v.p., dir. World Pub. Co. (pubs. Omaha World-Herald), 1965—. Bd. dirs. Big Bros. Assn.; trustee Forest Lawn Cemetery Assn., Joslyn Art Mus. Mem. Delta Chi. Episcopalian. Mason (32, Shriner, Jester). Clubs: Omaha Country, Omaha. Home: 8721 Capitol Av Omaha NB 68114 Office: World-Herald Sq Omaha NB 68102

HOAGLAND, MAHLON BUSH, educator, biochemist; b. Boston, Oct. 5, 1921; s. Hudson and Anna (Plummer) H.; student Williams Coll., 1940-41, Harvard, 1941-43, M.D., 1948; m. Olley Virginia Jones, Jan. 10, 1961; children by previous marriage—Judith, Susan, Mahlon Bush, Robin. From research fellow to asst. prof. medicine Harvard Med. Sch. at Mass. Gen. Hosp., 1948-60; asso. prof. bacteriology and immunology Med. Sch., 1960-67; prof. biochemistry, chmn. dept. Dartmouth Med. Sch., 1967-70; research prof. U. Mass. Med. Sch., 1970—; dir. Worcester Found. for Exptl. Biology, Shrewsbury, Mass., 1970—; research asso. Carlsberg Labs., Copenhagen, Denmark, 1951-52, Cavendish Labs., Cambridge, Eng., 1957-58. Exec. sec. com. research Mass. Gen. Hosp., 1954-57; cons. NIH, 1961-64, Am. Cancer Soc., 1965-68. Trustee Worcester Meml. Hosp. Scholar cancer research Am. Cancer Soc., 1953-58. Fellow Am. Acad. Arts and Scis.; mem. Am. Soc. Biol. Chemists. Contbr. profl. jours. Research on mechanism of carcinogenic action of beryllium, mechanism of synthesis of coenzyme A; discovery mechanism of amino acid activation and role of transfer ribonucleic acid in protein synthesis. Home: 398 Walnut St Shrewsbury MA 01545 Office: Worchester Found 222 Maple Av Shrewsbury MA 01545

HOARD, JAMES LYNN, educator, research chemist; b. Beckham Co., Okla., Dec. 28, 1905; s. Charles Ellsworth and Bertha Arminnie (Terpening) H.; B.S., U. Wash., 1927, M.S., 1929; Ph.D., Cal. Inst. Tech., 1932; m. Florence Marion Fahey, Sept. 28, 1935; children—David, Thomas Daniel, Laurence Graham. Instr. chemistry Stanford, 1932-35, Ohio State U., 1935-36; instr. chemistry Cornell, 1936-38, asst. prof., 1938-42, asso. prof., 1942-46, prof. chemistry, 1946-71, prof. emeritus, 1971—; dir. work OSRD contract with Cornell U., 1942-45, subcontract Columbia with Cornell (Manhattan Project), 1943-44; co-dir. research under contracts between Cornell U. and Office Naval Research 1946-50, Army Ordnance, 1946-55. Guggenheim fellow, 1947, 60, 66; NSF grantee, 1956- 58; AEC grantee, 1950-55; NIH grantee, 1961—. Mem. Am. Chem. Soc., Am. Phys. Soc., Am. Crystallographic Assn., Phi Beta Kappa, Sigma Xi. Author articles sci. jours. Home: 42 Cornell St Ithaca NY 14850

HOBAN, GEORGE SAVRE, lawyer; b. Faribault, Minn., Nov. 20, 1914; s. George W. and Margaret (Savre) H.; B.A., Ripon Coll., 1935; LL.B., Northwestern U., 1938; m. June Tullar, Feb. 4, 1939; children—William J., Robert G. Admitted to Ill. bar, 1938, since practiced in Chgo.; partner firm Hinshaw, Culbertson, Moelmann, Hoban & Fuller, 1949—. Trustee Ripon Coll., 1965—, Northwest Community Hosp., Arlington Heights, Ill., 1963-70, Ravenswood Hosp. Med. Center, 1970—. Served to capt. AUS, 1942-46. Mem. Am., Ill., Chgo. bar assns., Ill. C. of C. (chmn. legislative com. 1963-64), Phi Delta Phi. Club: Medinah (Ill.) Country (pres. 1965-67). Home: 3 Old Saybrook on Auburn Rolling Meadows IL 60008 Office: 1 N LaSalle St Chicago IL 60602

HOBAN, RICHARD MATTHEW, Jr., air force officer; b. St. Louis, Mar. 29, 1922; s. Richard Matthew and Virginia (Haney) H.; student U. Omaha, 1959-61; m. Alenen T. Thompson, Nov. 10, 1944; children—Virginia A., Deborah E., Richard M. Commd. 2d lt. U.S. Air Force, 1943, advanced through grades to maj. gen., 1943; operations staff officer Offutt AFB, Neb., 1959-62, div. dir. operations Walker AFB, N.M., 1962-64; comdr. Strat. Aerospace Wing, Walker AFB, 1964-65; inspector gen. 15th Air Force, 1965-66; comdr. various bomb wings, 1966-69; vice comdr. air material area, San Antonio, Tex., 1969-70; comdr. air material area, Ogden, Hill AFB, Utah, 1970—. Decorated D.S.M., Legion Merit, Air Medal with 6 oak leaf clusters, Air Force Commendation medal with oak leaf cluster. Home: Quarters 1110 Area A Hill AFB UT 84401 Office: Bldg 1102 Ogden Air Material Area Hill AFB UT 84401

HOBART, ANDREW WALTER, ins. co. exec.; b. Mpls., Aug. 17, 1913; s. Mell Walter and Lydia (Schroedel) H.; B.A., Macalester Coll., 1935; m. Catherine Mary Carey, Sept. 1, 1937; 1 dau., Sara (Mrs. Charles Homeyer). With Ministers Life and Casualty Union, Mpls., 1935—, v.p., 1954-59, pres., 1959—. Treas. Minn. Council Chs., 1965—; mem. exec. bd. Dept. Ministry, Nat. Council Chs., 1967—. Mem. Health Ins. Assn. Am. (sec. 1962-64). Presbyn. Home: 4327 Brook Lane Minneapolis MN 55416 Office: 3100 W Lake St Minneapolis MN 55416

HOBART, DONALD MARCENE, bus. cons.; b. Pemberville, O., Sept. 15, 1897; s. Clayton S. and Marguerite E. (Heisler) H.; student Wooster Coll., 1915-17; B.S. in Econs., U. Pa., 1919; D.B.A., Bowling Green State U., 1957; m. Elizabeth Ostrom Cross, Jan. 17, 1931; children—Elizabeth Joan (Mrs. Juan del Valle), Rachel Laramy (Mrs. Philip R. Thornton). Instr. merchandising Wharton Sch. Finance and Commerce, 1919-20; mgr. sales sch. Dunlop Tire & Rubber Co., 1920-21; dist. rep. Syracuse Rubber Co., 1921-22; mem. research staff Curtis Pub. Co., 1923-28, dir. research, v.p., 1951-56, sr. v.p., dir. research, 1956-62; rep. Sat.Eve.Post, 1928-38, mgr. div. comml. research, 1938-43, mgr. research, 1943-47; cons. Fgn. Agrl. Service, U.S. Dept. Agr., 1963—; cons., dir. Sea Pines Co., 1964—. Served with U.S. Army, World War I. Parlin Meml. lectr., 1954; elected to Hall of Fame in Distbn., 1954. Mem. Am. Marketing Assn. (pres. 1945), Beta Gamma Sigma, Alpha Tau Omega. Republican. Presbyn. Mason (32). Club: Plantation. Author: (with James P. Wood) Selling Forces, 1953. Editor: Marketing Research Practice, 1950. Contbr. articles to mags., pamphlets. Home: 16 Cedar Waxwing Rd Hilton Head Island SC 29928

HOBART, EDWARD A., mfg. exec.; b. Middletown, O., Dec. 25, 1888; s. Charles Clarence and Lou E. (Jones) H.; E.E., Ohio State U., 1912; D.Sc. (hon.), 1969; m. Martha L. Lantis, Oct. 12, 1921. With Hobart Bros. Co., Troy, 1917—, beginning as engr., pres., 1932—; v.p. Welded Products Co.; v.p., dir. First Troy Nat. Bank; dir. Fla. Minerals Co., Continental Minerals Co. Mem. Miami Valley Conservancy Bd. Fellow I.E.E.E.; mem. Newcomen Soc., Am. Welding Soc., American Inst. Elec. Engrs., Engrs. Club, Ordnance Assn., Eta Kappa Nu. Presbyn. Clubs: Moraine Country, Engineers (Dayton, O.); Troy Country; Queen City, Cincinnati; Rio Mar Yacht (Vero Beach, Fla.). Home: Troy OH 45373 Office: Hobart Sq Troy OH 45373

HOBART, GEORGE MAXWELL, former paper mfr.; b. Kingston, Ont., Can., Nov. 11, 1894; s. Samuel Walters and Mary (Peplow) H.; B.Sc., McGill U., 1920; LL.D., Sir George Williams U., 1970; m. Marguerite Tuckey, Apr. 28, 1924; children—George Maxwell, Mary Elizabeth (Mrs. Fuller), Richard Renfrew, David Gordon. Chem. engr. Somerville, Ltd., London, Ont., 1921-26, pres., 1943-45; exec. v.p. Consol. Paper Corp., Ltd. (name changed to Consol. Bathurst, Ltd. 1967), Montreal, 1945-47, pres. 1947-64, chmn. bd., pres., chief exec. 1964-67, chmn. 1967-70; ret., 1970; dir. Boston Common Stock Fund, Belgium Standard Ltd. Served as lt., arty., Canadian Army, 1914-19, Mem. Assn. Profl. Engrs. Ont. Mem. United Ch. Clubs: University, St. James's, Forest and Stream Mount Royal (Montreal). Home: 3940 Cote des Neiges Rd Montreal 15 Quebec Canada Office: 800 Dorchester Blvd W Montreal Quebec Canada

HOBBES, ALAN BUXTON, optical corp. exec. lawyer; b. N.Y.C., June 30, 1917; s. Stephen Bertram and Laural Albertine (Buxton) H.; A.B., Washington and Lee U., 1939; J.D., George Washington U., 1947, LL.M., 1950; m. Ann Marie Katalinich, June 6, 1946; children—Thomas Buxton, Laurence Parsons, Martha Felicity Ann, Elizabeth Marie. Admitted to D.C. bar, 1946, also U.S. Supreme Ct.; with accessions div. Library of Congress, Washington, 1939-42; dean Marine Corps Inst., Washington, 1946-48; atty. FTC, Washington, 1948-55, legal asst. to Fed. Trade Commr. W.C. Kern, 1955-59, asst. gen. counsel, FTC, 1959-61; asst. to gen. counsel Am. Optical Corp., Southbridge, Mass., 1961-67, gen. counsel, 1967-69, sec., gen. counsel, 1969—. Mem. finance com., Sturbridge, Mass., 1969-71. Served to capt. USMCR, 1942-46. Decorated Purple Heart. Mem. Mensa, Buxton Family Assn. (pres.), Am., Boston bar assns., S.A.R. (pres. D.C. Soc., 1957-58, nat. trustee, 1958-59). Democrat. Episcopalian (warden, 1971—). Contbr. articles to law jours., Everyman's Ency. Home: Fiske Hill Rd Sturbridge MA 01566 Office: 14 Mechanic St Southbridge MA 01550

HOBBIE, JANET ELIZABETH HAMILTON, librarian; b. Bklyn., May 18, 1914; d. Samuel Lourie and Jeannett Valerie (Eckert) Hamilton; A.A., Stephens Coll., Columbia, Mo., 1933; A.B., Smith Coll. 1935; B.S. in L.S., Columbia, 1940; M.A., N.Y.U., 1952; m. John Remington Hobbie, Oct. 29, 1955. Library asst. Newark Pub. Library, 1936-39, librarian Quantico Post Sch., Marine Barracks, Quantico, Va., 1940-41, McKinley Jr. High Sch., Newark, 1941-43, Franklin High Sch., Hasbrook Heights, N.J., 1943-45, Monmouth Coll., W. Long Branch, N.J., 1945—. Mem. Am., N.J. library assns., N.E.A., Am. Assn. U. Profs., Forest Hill Lit. Soc. (Newark), League Women Voters, Am. Assn. U. Women. Home: 34 Hendrickson Pl West Long Branch NJ 07740

HOBBS, CHARLES SERIGHT, educator; b. Inman, Kan., Feb. 2, 1909; s. Charles S. and Ella Mae (Olson) H.; B.S., Okla. A. & M. Coll., 1938; M.S., Ph.D., Cornell, 1938- 41; m. Corinne K. Clay, Jan. 6, 1931; children—Charles Seright, Patricia Corinne, Frank Barron, William Clay, Robert Carlton. Prof. animal husbandry, vet. sci. head agrl. research and teaching U. Tenn. 1947—. Mem. Am. Soc. Animal Sci. (president; distinguished service award 1966), A.A.A.S. (president), Alpha Zeta, Sigma Xi, Block and Bridle, Phi Eta Sigma, Omicron Delta Kappa, Beta Theta Pi, Phi Kappa Phi. Rotarian. Co-author: The Livestock Book. Author articles profl. jours. Home: RFD 2 Louisville TN 37777 Office: U Tenn Knoxville TN 37916

HOBBS, EDWARD HENRY, educator; b. Selma, Ala., Jan. 14, 1921; s. Edward Henry and Mary Olivia (Dannelly) H.; A.B. in Am. History, U. N.C., 1943; M.A. in Polit. Sci., Assn. U. Profs. Forest Hill Lit. Soc. (Newark), League Women Voters, Adminstrn. advanced scholar 1947-48, 48-49), Harvard, 1949, Ph.D., 1951; m. Marleah Marguerite Kaufman, Dec. 23, 1943; children—Milton Milton Dannelly, Miriam, Edward Henry, Vivian. Instr., U. Ala., 1946-47; faculty U. Miss., 1949-67, acting chmn. dept. research in bus. and pub. adminstrn., prof. polit. sci., 1957-59, chmn. dept., prof., 1959-61, chmn. dept. research in bus. and govt., prof. polit. science, 1961-67; dean Sch. Sci. and Lit., Auburn U., 1967-69, dean Sch. Arts and Scis., 1969—. Corr. So. Regional Tng. Program in Pub. Adminstrn., 1955—; sec. Univ. House Assn. Chmn. Oxford (Miss.) Planning Commn., 1959-67; chmn. Oxford Council Aging, 1959; cons. Miss. Council Aging, 1957; pres. Miss. Research Clearing House, 1957-58; bd. dirs. Miss. Planning Conf., 1959—; chmn. campaign dist. II, Miss. Mental Health Assn., 1960; corr. Nat. Municipal League, 1955—, Conf. Met. Area Problems, 1958—. Bd. dirs. Miss. Heart Assn. Served to lt. (s.g.) USNR, World War II; capt. in Res. Nat. fellow to 2d Summer Inst. in Social Gerontology, U. Cal. at Berkeley, 1959. Mem. So. Polit. Sci. Assn., So. Pub. Adminstrn. Research Council, Am. Soc. Pub. Adminstrn. (nat. adv. com. 1957—), Am. Assn. U. Profs., Am. Polit. Sci. Assn., Oxford-Lafayette County C. of C., Pi Sigma Alpha, (nat. exec. com. 1958- -), Delta Kappa Epsilon, Omicron Delta Kappa (honoris causa 1955), Phi Kappa Phi. Presbyn. (elder). Rotarian. Club:

Rex Investment. Author: Behind the President: A Study of Executive Office Agencies, 1954; Yesterday's Constitution Today: An Analysis of the Mississippi Constitution of 1890, 1960; Legislative Apportionment in Mississippi, 1956; Executive Reorganization in the National Government, 1953; A Manual of Mississippi Municipal Government, 1962; (with others) Mississippi in Maps-Industry, Resources and Agriculture, 1959; A Directory of Mississippi Municipalities, 3d edit., 1962; also articles. Co-author: A Compendium of Selected Information on Mississippi Municipalities 1966, 1966. Co-compiler: Annotated Bibliography on Mississippi Economy, Business, Industry and Government, 1950-1963, 1964; co-author Power in State Legislatures, 1967. Editor: Mississippi's Workmen's Compensation: Selected Cases, 1964; U.S.A. and the World's Three Biggest Economic Myths, 1965. Contbr. numerous articles in acad. and profl. jours. Home: 926 Terrace Acres Auburn AL 36830

HOBBS, GEORGE WARD, airline exec.; b. Balt., Aug. 6, 1908; s. Stewart Seymour and Lida (Hopkins) H.; student Balt. Poly., 1925-29, U. Richmond, 1952, Cornell U., 1954; m. Barbara E. Vallis, Oct. 21, 1935; children—John Weldon, Joan Snowden, Kathy Haskell. With Clarence Chamberlain, 1930, Maine Air Transport, 1931-32, Pitcairn-Eastern Air Transport, 1933-34; dispatcher Am. Airlines, 1934-36, sta. mgr., Huntington, W.Va., Phila., Newark, Buffalo, Richmond, Va., 1936-42, regional mgr. flight operations, 1955- 57, asst. v.p. operations services, 1957-59; v.p. customer services Capital Airlines, Washington, 1959-60; dir. Bur. Nat. Capital Airports, FAA, 1960-66; v.p. customer service Northeast Airlines, Boston, 1966-69, v.p. pub. affairs, 1969—. Served from 1st lt. to col., AUS, World War II. Clubs: Nat. Aviation (Washington); Wings (N.Y.C.). Home: 56 Deep Run Cohasset MA 02025 Office: Northeast Airlines Logan Internat Airport Boston MA 02128

HOBBS, GRIMSLEY TAYLOR, coll. pres.; b. Greensboro, N.C., June 14, 1923; s. Richard J. M. and Gretchen (Taylor) H.; B.A., Guilford (N.C.) Coll., 1947; M.A., Haverford Coll., 1948; Ph.D. in Philosophy, Duke, 1955; m. Lois Ann Hunkele, Nov. 1, 1943; children—Grimsley Taylor, Louise B. Ruffin M., Herbert J., Richard M., Elise M. Mem. faculty Earlham (Ind.) Coll., 1951-65, prof. philosophy, 1958-65; pres. Guilford Coll., 1965—. Exec. com. Piedmont Univ. Center, N.C. Found Ch. Related Colls.; chmn. Assn. Friends Colls. Served USAAF, 1943-46. Ford Found. Postdoctoral fellow, 1955; recipient Doan Distinguished Prof. award Earlham Coll., 1960. Mem. Am., Ind. (past pres.) philos. assns. Democrat. Mem. Soc. of Friends. Rotarian. Contbr. profl. jours. Home: Nathan Hunt Rd Greensboro NC 27410

HOBBS, HERMAN HEDBERG, educator; b. Dallas, June 25, 1927; s. Morris F. and Edla (Hedberg) H.; B.S., George Washington U., 1953, M.S., 1955; Ph.D., U. Va., 1958; m. Joyce Gray Pritchett, Aug. 18, 1948. Physicist Nat. Bur. Standards, Washington, 1953; instr. physics U. Va., 1955-58, post-doctoral fellow, 1958-59; prof. physics George Washington U., 1960—, chmn. dept. physics, 1963-68. Served with USAAF, 1945-46. Sanders fellow George Washington U., 1954-55; Virginia fellow U. Va., 1958-59. Mem. Am. Phys. Soc., Am. Assn. Physics Tchrs., Am. Assn. U. Profs, Washington Philosoph. Soc., Sigma Xi, Sigma Pi Sigma. Home: 301 S Jefferson St Arlington VA 22204 Office: Physics Dept George Washington U Washington DC

HOBBS, HERSCHEL HAROLD, clergyman; b. Talladega Springs, Ala., Oct. 24, 1907; s. Elbert Oscar and Emma (Whatley) H.; B.A., Howard Coll., 1932, D.D., 1941; Th.M., So. Bapt. Theol. Sem., Louisville, 1935, Ph.D., 1938; Litt.D., William Jewell Coll., Liberty, Mo. 1962; L.H.D., Oklahoma City U., 1968; LL.D., John Brown U., 1970; m. Frances Jackson, Apr. 10, 1927; children—Jerry Marlin, Harold Elbert. Ordained to ministry Baptist Ch., 1929; pastor Emmanuel Bapt. Ch., Alexandria, La., 1941-44, Dauphin Way Bapt. Ch., Mobile, Ala., 1945-49, First Bapt. Ch., Oklahoma City, 1949- -; permanent preacher Internat. Bapt. Hour (radio), 1958—. Mem. fgn. mission bd. So. Bapt. Conv., Richmond, Va., 1942-44, exec. com., Nashville, 1951-63; pres. So. Bapt. Pastor's Conf., 1949-51, Bapt. Gen. Conv. of Okla., 1959, So. Bapt. Conv., 1961-63; v.p. Bapt. World Alliance, 1965-70. Trustee Okla. Bapt. U., 1955-58, 70—, pres. bd. trustees, 1958—, now chmn.; trustee New Orleans Bapt. Theol. Sem., 1945-49; mem. Bapt. Found. of Okla. Recipient E. Y. Mullins Denominational service award, 1964, Samford U. citation of achievement, 1970. Mem. Okla. City C. of C., Okla. Hall Fame. Mason, Kiwanian. Author: Cowards or Conquerors, 1951; The Gospel of Giving, 1954; The Crucial Words From Calvary, 1958; Moses' Mighty Men, 1958; Messages on the Resurrection, 1959; Fundamentals of Our Faith, 1960; The Epistles to the Corinthians, 1960; New Testament Evangelism, 1960; The Gospel of Matthew, 1961; Christ in You, 1961; Preaching Values from the Papyri, 1964; An Exposition of the Gospel of Matthew, 1965; The Life And Times of Jesus, 1966; An Exposition of the Gospel of Luke, 1966; The Holy Spirit, 1967; Welcome Speeches, 1967; The Cosmic Drama-An Exposition of Revelation, 1971; The Thessolonian Epistles, 1971; and others, also numerous booklets. Contbr. religious publs. Home: 2608 Country Club Dr W Oklahoma City OK 73116 Office: 1201 N Robinson Oklahoma City OK 73103

HOBBS, HORTON HOLCOMBE, Jr., educator; b. Alachua, Fla., Mar. 29, 1914; s. Horton Holcombe and Johnnie (Strickland) H.; B.S., U. Fla., 1935, M.S., 1936, Ph.D., 1940; m. Georgia Cates Blount, June 29, 1939; children—Nina Thompson, Horton Holcombe III. Instr. biology U. Fla., 1937-41, asst. prof., 1941-44, asso. prof., 1944-46; asso. prof. U. Va., 1946-55, prof., 1955-62; dir. Mountain Lake Biol. Sta., 1956-60; chmn. dept. zoology U.S. Nat. Mus., Smithsonian Instn., 1962-64, sr. scientist, 1964—. Mem. A.A.A.S., Am. Inst. Biol. Scis., Soc. Systematic Zoology, Biol. Soc. Washington, Am. Micros. Soc. (pres. 1963-64), Assn. Southeastern Biologists (pres. 1959-60), Va. (pres. 1961-62), Fla., Tenn. acads. sci., Phi Beta Kappa, Phi Kappa Phi, Phi Sigma, Sigma Xi, Alpha Epsilon Delta, Raven Soc. Kiwanian. Author: The Crayfishes of Florida, 1942. Home: 3438 Mansfield Rd Falls Church VA Office: U S Nat Mus Smithsonian Instn Washington DC 20560

HOBBS, JOHN SALMON, lawyer; b. San Diego, Feb. 11, 1928; s. John C. and Mary K. (Salmon) H.; B.A., U. Ariz., 1951, LL.B., 1958; postgrad. U. Cal. at Los Angeles, 1953- 54; m. Suann Walton, June 16, 1951; children—John C. II, David W., Nancy H. Owner, Aetna Container Corp., Culver City, Cal., 1954-56; admitted to Ariz. bar, 1958; since practiced in Phoenix; partner Jennings, Strauss & Salmon, 1958—. Served to 1st lt. USMCR, 1946-47, 51- 53. Mem. Am., Ariz., Maricopa County bar assns., Am. Bd. Trial Advs., Phi Delta Phi. Home: 508 E Kaler Dr Phoenix AZ 85020 Office: 111 W Monroe St Phoenix AZ 85003

HOBBS, MARCUS EDWIN, educator; b. Chadbourn, N.C. Aug. 11, 1909; s. Julius Charles and Maude Elizabeth (Player) H.; A.B., Duke, 1932, M.A., 1934, Ph.D., 1936; m. Sarah Ferguson Blanchard, July 3, 1937; children—Sarah Lillian, Joan Elizabeth. Indsl. research fellow tobacco Duke, 1931-33, instr. chemistry, 1936, asst. prof., 1942, asso. prof., 1945, prof., 1950—, chmn. dept. chemistry, 1951-54, dean Grad. Sch. Arts and Scis., 1954-58, dean of univ., 1958-64, vice provost, 1960-64, provost, 1969-71, charge spl. sources of chemistry of explosives, 1941-42; research asso. NDRC, George Washington U., 1942-45, civilian cons. div. 2, 1942-44, div. 3, 1943-45; adviser Office Ordnance Research, 1951-61, chief scientist, acting, June 1951—Mar. 52. Mem. adv. council Army Research Office, 1960—; mem. NSF adv. panel U.S.-Japan Coop. Service Program, 1963-65; adv. com. utility research and devel. U.S. Dept. Agr., 1964-70; mem. N.C. Bd. Sci. and Tech., 1963—. Bd. dirs. N.C. Blue Cross and Blue Shield, Inc., 1967—; chmn. exec. com. Research Triangle Inst., 1965-70, mem. exec. com., 1965—. Recipient Army-Navy Certificate of Merit for sci. work with OSRD during World War II, 1957; Outstanding Civilian Service medal Dept. Army, 1959; Cigar Industry Research award, 1959. Fellow A.A.A.S.; mem. Am. Chem. Soc. (chmn. N.C. sect. 1946), Am. Assn. U. Profs., Phi Beta Kappa, Sigma Xi, Phi Lambda Upsilon, Sigma Pi Sigma, Sigma Chi. Contbr. profl. jours. Home: 115 Pinecrest Rd Durham NC 27705

HOBBS, MARY MONTEUESE, newspaper editor; b. Eskridge, Kan., Feb. 5, 1917; d. Galen Elwood and Elma Ellen (Rehrig) Hobbs; student Washburn Coll., Topeka, 1934-35, U. Kan., 1935-37. With Kansas City Power & Light Co., Overland Park, Kan., 1937-41, N.Am. Aviation Co., Fairfax, Kansas City, Kan., 1942-43; asst. city editor Ft. Scott (Kan.) Tribune, 1944; reporter-columnist Ottawa (Kan.) Herald, 1945; wire editor, reporter Royal Oak (Mich.) Daily Tribune, 1946; ch. editor Kansas City Star, 1946-71, garden editor, 1959—; corr. Religious News Service. Bd. dirs. Cerebral Palsy Assn. Recipient citation for human relations contbns. of ch. editorship Mo. Dist. Missionary Soc. Christian Meth. Episcopal Ch., 1965. Fellow Nat. Religious Pub. Relations Council, 1966. Mem. Religious Newswriters Assn. (v.p., past chmn.), Garden Writers Am., Nat., Mo. press women, Theta Sigma Phi. Methodist. Clubs: Kansas City Athletic, Kansas City Garden, Kansas City Hemerocallis, Kansas City Color Slide. Office: 1729 Grand Av Kansas City MO 64108

HOBBS, NICHOLAS, univ. provost, psychologist; b. Greenville, S.C., Mar. 13, 1915; s. Caswell Owen and Alberta Judson (Jones) H.; A.B., The Citadel, 1936; M.A., Ohio State U., 1938, Ph.D., 1946; m. Mary Madeline Thompson, May 21, 1949; 1 son, Nicholas Thompson. Tchr., Riverside Mil. Acad., 1936-37, Spartanburg (S.C.) High Sch., 1937-38; asso. prof., dir. tng. clin. psychology Columbia Tchrs. Coll., 1946-50; chmn. dept. psychology La. State U., 1950-51; chmn. div. human devel. Peabody Coll., 1951-65; dir. Kennedy Center Research on Edn. and Human Devel., 1965-70; provost Vanderbilt U., 1967—; dir. selection, research Peace Corps., 1961-62; lectr. Inst. Humanistic Studies for Execs., U. Pa., 1956-60. Dir. So. Regional Edn. Bd. Mental Health Tng. and Research Project, 1954-55; vice chmn. So. Regional Council Mental Health Tng. and Research; vice chmn., trustee Joint Commn. on Mental Illness and Health; mem. President's Panel on Mental Retardation; mem. Nat. Adv. Council Child Health and Human Devel., Nat. Adv. Mental Health Council; v.p. Joint Commn. Mental Health Children; mem. U.S. Nat. Commn. UNESCO. Fellow Center Advanced Study Behavioral Scis., 1966-67. Served with USAAF, 1941-46. Mem. Am. (dir. 1952-55, pres. 1965-66; pres. div. clin. psychology), Southeastern (pres. 1956-57) psych. assns., Am. Assn. Gifted Children, A.A.A.S., So. Soc. Philosophy and Psychology (treas. 1954-55), Sigma Xi. Club: Cosmos. Home: 1054 Lynwood Blvd Nashville TN 37215

HOBBS, RANALD PURCELL, publisher; b. Bartlett, N.H., Sept. 14, 1909; s. Don P. and Blanche (Stevens) H.; A.B., Dartmouth, 1930; m. Vera Ingeborg Andren, June 27, 1936; children—Ronald D., Linda A. With The Macmillan Co., 1935-43; with Rinehart & Co., Inc., 1943-60, exec. v.p., 1955-60; exec. v.p. Hobbs- Merrill Co., Inc., 1960-61; pres. Hobbs Internat., Inc., 1962-63; pres. Hobbs, Dorman & Co., Inc., 1964—, Cowles Book Co., Inc., 1968-69. Mem. Bd. Edn., Darien, Conn., 1948-55, chmn., 1950-52; chmn. coll. sect. Am. Textbook Pubs. Inst., 1954-55, bd. dirs., 1956-59, sec., 1957, treas., 1958. Clubs: Union League, Dutch Treat. Home: Shagbark Rd Wilson Point South Norwalk CT 06854 Office: 441 Lexington Av New York City NY 10017

HOBBS, RICHARD LEWIS, shoe machinery co. exec.; b. Medford, Mass., June 8, 1918; s. Don P. and Blanche (Stevens) H.; B.A., Dartmouth, 1939; J.D., Harvard, 1942; m. Dorothy Dunham, June 27, 1942; children—Steven, Lee, Jane. Admitted to Mass. bar, 1942, N.H. bar, 1946; patent atty. research div. USM Corp. (formerly United Shoe Machinery Corp.), Boston, 1947-55, atty. law dept., 1955-65, asst. gen. counsel, 1965-68, v.p., gen. counsel, 1968—. Mem. Planning Bd., Lynnfield, Mass., 1954-58, chmn. Bd. Selectmen, 1959-62, chmn. Sch. Com., 1967-68. Served with Signal Corps, AUS, 1942-46. Mem. Am., Boston bar assns., Boston Patent Law Assn. Home: 8 Tapley Rd Lynnfield MA 01940 Office: 140 Federal St Boston MA 02107

HOBBS, SAMUEL EARLE GREENE, lawyer; b. Selma, Ala., Apr. 23, 1917; s. Samuel Francis and Sarah Ellen (Greene) H.; A.B., U. N.C., 1939; A.M., George Washington U., 1940; LL.B., U. Ala., 1948; LL.M., Yale, 1949; m. Emily Huntington Nicolson, June 10, 1941; children—Ralph Nicolson, Samuel Francis II, Ellen Earle. Spl. agt. FBI, 1940-44; instr. polit. sci. U. Ala., 1946-48, asst. prof. law, 1949-52; admitted to Ala. bar, 1948; practice in Selma, 1952—; partner Hobbs & Hain, 1959—; judge Dallas County Ct., 1957-58; mem. Bd. Bar Examiners Ala., 1967-69. Chmn. bd., dir. Citizens Bank & Trust Co.; v.p., dir. New Vaughan Meml. Hosp., Inc. Mem. Selma Sch. Bd., 1952-63, chmn., 1961-63. Pres. United Community Services, Selma, Sturdivant Mus. Assn.; bd. dirs. Selma YMCA; trustee U. Ala. Served from ensign to lt. (j.g.), USNR, 1944-46. Mem. Am. Judicature Soc., Am., Ala. (past sect. chmn.), Dallas County, Selma bar assns., U. Ala. Law Sch. Alumni Assn. (past pres.), Episcopal Churchmen Ala. (past pres.), Order Golden Fleece, Farrah Order Jurisprudence, Farrah Law Soc., Delta Kappa Epsilon, Phi Delta Phi. Democrat. Home: 34 Berkeley Rd Selma AL 36701 Office: 100 Church St Selma AL 36701

HOBBS, TRUMAN MCGILL, lawyer; b. Selma, Ala., Feb. 8, 1921; s. Sam F. and Sarah Ellen (Greene) H.; A.B., U. N.C., 1942; LL.B., Yale, 1948; m. Joyce Cummings, July 9, 1949; children—Emilie C., Frances John, Dexter Cummings, Truman McGill. Admitted to Ala. bar, 1948; practiced in Montgomery, 1951—; law clk. U.S. Supreme Ct., 1948-49; partner Hobbs, Copeland, Franco, Gill & Screws, 1951—. Chmn., Ala. Unemployment Appeal Bd., 1952-58; pres. United Appeal Montgomery, Montgomery County Tb Assn.; v.p. Ala. Com. for Better Schs. Chmn., Montgomery County Exec. Democratic Com., 1970. Served to lt. USNR, 1942-46; ETO, PTO. Decorated Bronze Star medal. Fellow Am. Coll. Trial Lawyers; mem. Internat. Acad. Trial Lawyers, Ala. Plaintiffs Lawyers Assn. (past pres.), Ala. (pres. 1970-71), Montgomery County (past pres.) bar assns. Home: 3310 Fernway Dr Montgomery AL 36111 Office: 444 S Perry St Montgomery AL 36101

HOBBS, WILLIAM, aluminum co. exec.; b. Warren, Ark., 1924; s. Houston and Irma (Blankenship) H.; B.S., LL.B., U. Colo., 1950; m. Joan Cummings, Sept. 1, 1948; children—Stephen, Donald. With Kaiser Aluminum & Chem. Corp., Oakland, Cal., 1950—, treas., 1961—. Home: 3730 Meadow Lane Lafayette CA 94549 Office: 300 Lakeside Dr Oakland CA 94612

HOBBS, WILLIAM CALVIN, corp. exec.; b. Elwood, Ind., Oct. 7, 1915; s. Alfred Arch and Hazel (Stiegelman) H.; B.A., Ind. U., 1937; student U. So. Cal., 1943- 44, U. Cal. at Los Angeles, 1944, Pacific Coast Sch. Law, 1946; m. Lorraine Chase, Nov. 8, 1966; children (by previous marriage)— William, Patricia, Michael. With U.S. Steel Corp., 1937-41; with No. Am. Aviation, Inc., 1943-68, v.p. facilities, asst. to sr. v.p. adminstrn., 1956-61, v.p., 1961-63, sr. v.p., 1963-68; Con Am. Services, engring. and constrn., Modular Systems Corp., engrng. and mfg.; pres. Homico Inc., investment and devel. Mason (Shriner). Address: 73651 A Golf Course Lane Palm Desert CA 92260

HOBBSON, WARNER GLESSNER educator, biologist; b. Ames, Ia.; B.A., Ia. State U., 1936, M.A., 1937, Ph.D. with honors, 1940. Instr., Ia. State U., 1946-47; asst. prof. biology Johns Hopkins, 1947-50, asso. prof., 1950-62, prof., 1962--, chmn. dept., 1963-69; vis. lectr. Stanford, 1970-71. Active Boy Scouts Am., 4-H Club. Served with AUS, 1940-46. Mem. Am. Soc. Biologists, Md. Biologists, A.A.A.S., Am. Acad. Arts and Scis., Phi Beta Kappa.

HOBBY, OVETA CULP, (Mrs. William P. Hobby), ex-govt. ofcl., newspaper pub.; b. Killeen, Tex., Jan. 19, 1905; d. I. W. and Emma (Hoover) Culp; student Mary Hardin Baylor College, L.H.D., 1956; L.H.D., Bard Coll., 1950, Lafayette Coll., 1954; LL.D., Baylor U., Sam Houston State Tchrs. Coll., U. Chattanooga, 1943, Bryant Coll., Ohio Wesleyan U., 1953, Columbia, Smith Coll., Middlebury Coll., 1954, U. Pa., Colby Coll., 1955, Farleigh Dickinson, Western Coll.; D.Litt., Colo. Women's Coll., 1947, C. W. Post Coll., 1962; m. William P. Hobby, Feb. 23, 1931 (dec. 1964); children—Wm., Jessica (Mrs. Henry Catto, Jr.). Parliamentarian Tex. Ho. of Reps., 1926-31, incomplete terms 1939, 41; joined Houston Post as research editor, 1931, successively lit. editor, asst. editor, v.p., exec v.p., exec. v.p., editor. 1931-53, editor, pub., 1952-53, pres., editor, 1955-65, chmn. bd., editor, 1965—; dir. sta. KPRC AM-TV, 1945-53, 55-69; chmn. bd., dir. Channel Two TV Co., 1970—; chief women's interest sect. War Dept. Bur. Pub. Relations, 1941-42; apptd. dir. WAAC, 1942, commd. co. AUS, dir. WAC, 1943-45; fed. security adminstr., 1953; sec. Dept. Health, Edn. and Welfare, 1953-55; dir. Gen. Foods Corp., Corp. Pub. Broadcasting; trustee Mut. Ins. Co. N.Y.; dir. Corp. for Pub. Broadcasting. Gov. A.R.C.; nat. vice chmn. Am. Cancer Soc. campaign, 1949; pres. So. Newspaper Pubs. Assn., 1949; mem. Am. Design Awards com., mem. nat. com. Am. Mus. Immigration, 1956. Mem. nat. adv. com. Citizens for Eisenhower, 1956; sponsor Clark Sch. for Deaf; mem. Coll. Commn. Diocese of Tex., 1956; trustee Eisenhower Birthplace Meml. Park; mem. President's coms. on Employment Physically Handicapped, Civilian Nat. Honors; trustee Am. Assembly, 1957-66, Eisenhower Exchange fellowship; dir. Houston Symphony Soc.; mem. S.W. adv. bd. Inst. Internat. Edn.; mem. Com. of 75, U. Tex., 1958—; mem. So. regional com. Marshall Scholarships, 1957—; mem. Rockefeller Bros. Fund Spl. Studies project. Dir. Com. for Econ. Devel; mem. nat. bd. devel. Sam Rayburn Found.; mem. Crusade for Freedom, Inc.; nat. council Eleanor Roosevelt Meml. Found.; trustee Rice U., also Soc. Rehab. Facially Disfigured. Recipient Distinguished Service medal, 1944; Philippine Military Merit medal, 1947; Pub. of Yr. award, 1960; Living History award, Research Inst. Am., 1960; Honor award National Jewish Hosp., 1962. Mem. Acad. Tex. (charter), Gamma Alpha Chi (hon. vice chmn.). Episcopalian. Clubs: Houston Country, Bayou, Ramada, Junior League (Houston). Author: Mr. Chairman (parliamentary law textbook), also syndicated column same title. Home: Houston TX Office: Houston Post Houston TX 77001

HOBBY, WILLIAM PETTUS, Jr., newspaper editor; b. Houston, Jan. 19, 1932; s. William Pettus and Oveta (Culp) H.; B.A., Rice U., 1953; m. Diana Poteat Stallings, Sept. 11, 1954; children—Laura Poteat, Paul William, Andrew, Katherine. Asst. sec.- treas. Houston Post, 1957-59, asso. editor, 1959-60, mng. editor, 1960- 63, exec. editor, 1963—; pres. Houston Post Co. Parliamentarian, Tex. Senate, 1959. Served to lt. (j.g.) USNR, 1953-57. Mem. Am. Soc. of Newspaper Editors, Texas State Hunter and Jumper Assn. (dir. 1953—, pres. 1959-61), U.S. Equestrian Team Inc. (v.p. 1959-60), Houston C. of C. (dir.). Home: 1506 South Blvd Houston TX 77006 Office: 4747 Southwest Freeway Houston TX 77003

HOBEN, WILLIAM JOSEPH, univ. dean; b. Hardinsburg, Ky., May 19, 1927; s. William Joseph and Maud (Smith) H.; B.S., U. Dayton, 1950; M.B.A., Xavier U., 1960. Sr. accountant David E. Flagel & Co., Dayton, O., 1952-57; assistant prof. U. Dayton, 1957-59, asso. prof., asst. dean, 1959-62, acting dean, 1962-63, dean, 1963—. Pres., chmn. bd. dirs. Teach Fund, Inc.; bd. dirs. Malachi, Inc. Served with USNR, World War II and Korean War. C.P.A., Ohio. Mem. Am. Inst. C.P.A.'s, Ohio Soc. C.P.A.'s (dir., com. chmn. Dayton chpt.), Nat. Assn. Accountants, Nat., Ohio bus. tchrs. assns., Inst. Internat. Auditors, Am. Mgmt. Assn., Dayton C. of C., Alpha Kappa Psi. Clubs: Bicycle, Torch (Dayton). Home: 114 Yale Av Dayton OH 45406 Office: 300 College Park Dayton OH 45409

HOBERECHT, EARNEST newspaper exec.; b. Watonga, Okla., Jan. 1, 1918; s. Earnest Trevar, Sr. and Grace (Woolman) H.; B.A., U. Okla., 1941; m. Laurette Heger, May 6, 1959 (div. June 1969); children—Antonia, Earnest Trevar III, Nathalie, and Shelley; m. 2d, Mary Ann Shaklee Karns, Apr. 26, 1970. Reporter with Watonga Republican, 1935; pub. Reflector mag. Watonga, 1936; free-lance writer, also part-time staff Oklahoma City News, Daily Oklahoman, Oklahoma City, 1937-41; reporter Memphis Press-Scimitar, 1941-42; laborer Navy Yard, Pearl Harbor, T. H., 1942-43; editor Pearl Harbor Bull., 1944-45; war corr. Pacific, United Press, 1945, staff Tokyo Bur., 1945-48, chief corr., mgr. for Japan, 1948-51, gen. mgr. for Asia, 1951-66; v.p. U.P.I., 1953-66; chief United Press War Corrs. in Korea, 1950-53; pres. Am. Suppliers, Inc., 1966—; pres. Okla. Land Trust, Blaine County Abstract Co., S.E. Asia Corp.; owner Earnest Hoberecht Ins. Mem. Fgn. Corrs. Club, Sigma Delta Chi. Presbyn. Clubs: Koganei Country (Tokyo); Karuizawa (Japan) Country. Author: Tokyo Romance English and Japanese, 1947; (pub. in Japanese); Tokyo Diary, 1947; Democratic Etiquette, 1948; Fifty Famous Americans, 1949; Shears of Destiny, 1949; Asia In My Beat, 1961. Home: 1317 N Noble Av Watonga OK 73772 Office: Am Suppliers Inc 3715 Poplar St Erie PA 16508

HOBERG, RICHARD PAUL, electronics co. exec.; b. Lakeport, Cal., Dec. 21, 1934; s. Paul Frank and Mildred (Koehler) H.; B.A., Stanford, 1956, M.B.A., 1958; m. Maureen Garry, Sept. 15, 1956; children—Kristen E., Lynn K. Asst. controller Thermatest Labs. Inc., Sunnyvale, Cal., 1962-63; financial analyst Ampex Corp., Redwood City, Cal., 1963-68; controller audio-visual-communications div. Ampex Corp., 1968-69, corporate controller, 1969—. Served to 1st lt. Finance Corps, AUS, 1958-61. Mem. Stanford Alumni Assn., Stanford Bus. Sch. Assn. Home: 836 Driftwood Dr Palo Alto CA 94303 Office: 401 Broadway St Redwood City CA 94063

HOBERMAN, MORTON, physician, b. N.Y.C., Dec. 7, 1910; s. Isaac and Sarah (Lipschutz) H.; B.S., N.Y.U., 1931; M.B., Wayne State U., 1935, M.D., 1936; post-grad. student, Mayo Found., 1943, Inst. Crippled and Disabled, 1946, Elizabeth Dicke Inst., Uberlingen, Germany, 1956; m. Shirley Ethel Gall, June 12, 1938; children—Peter Ian, Judith Marcia. Intern Lebanon Hosp., N.Y.C., 1935-36, house surgeon, 1936-37; with U.S. Indian Service, 1938-40; attending rehab.

medicine Columbia-Presbyn. Med. Center; chief rehab. services and research N.Y. State Rehab. Hosp., W. Haverstraw, N.Y., 1947—; asst. attending physician Delafield Hosp., N.Y.C., 1952-58; clin. prof. rehab. medicine Columbia Coll. Phys. and Surg.; cons. Nat. Found. Infantile Paralysis, 1948-49; jr. cons. N.Y. regional office VA. 1947-53; cons. Bulova Sch. Watchmaking, 1947—; attending and dir. phys. medicine and rehab. Yonkers Gen. Hosp., N.Y.; pvt. practice physical medicine and rehab., N.Y.C., 1947—. Mem. orthopaedic adv. com. N.Y.C. Bur. Handicapped Children, 1956-58; chmn. sub-com. standards recreation Coordinating Council Cerebral Palsy, 1956-57; mem. President's Com. Employment Handicapped, 1960—; med. cons. Am. Paraplegic Olympic Tean, 1960—; cons. phys. medicine and rehab. Nyack Hosp. Diplomate Am. Bd. Phys. Medicine and Rehab. Mem. N.Y. Soc. Phys. Medicine and Rehab. (pres. 1953-55), Am. Congress Phys. Medicine and Rehab., Am. Acad. Phys. Medicine and Rehab. (bd. govs. 1957-62, pres. 1963-64), A.M.A., N.Y. State, N.Y. County med. socs., A.A.A.S., N.Y. Acad. Sci., Nat. Soc. Crippled Children and Adults, World Fedn. Welfare Disabled. Author numerous articles in field. Home: 912 N Broadway Yonkers NY 10701 Office: 127 Ashburton Av Yonkers NY 10701

HOBGOOD, BURNET MCLEAN, educator; b. Lotumbe, DCCM, Congo Belge, Africa, June 23, 1922 (parents U.S. citizens); s. Henry Clay and Tabitha Lou (Alderson) H.; Transylvania Coll., 1947; M.A., Western Res. U., 1949, M.F.A., 1950; Ph.D., Cornell U., 1964; m. Mary Jane Bishop, June 1, 1957; children—Laurence Bishop, Cathleen Stuart, Brent McLean. With Lexington (Ky.) Herald-Leader, 1947-49; prof. drama and speech Catawba Coll., 1950-61; prof. drama and theatre, chmn. div. dramatic arts So. Meth. U., Dallas, 1964—; dir. summer theatre prodns. The Lost Colony, 1957, Stars in My Crown, 1962, The Liberty Tree, 1969. Served with AUS, 1943-46. Fellow Am. Ednl. Theatre Assn. (adminstrv. v.p. 1960-61, pres. 1970); mem. S.W. Theatre Conf. (pres. 1965-66), Southeastern Theatre Conf. (exec. sec.-treas. 1956-58), Am. Assn. U. Profs., Am. Soc. Aesthetics, Speech Communication Assn., Phi Kappa Tau, Phi Kappa Phi. Unitarian. Founding editor So. Theatre Quar., 1956-58; gen. editor Directory of Am. Coll. Theatre, 1st edit., 1960, cons. editor, 2d edit., 1967; book rev. editor Ednl. Theatre Jour., 1966-68. Contbr. articles profl. jours. Home: 6810 Ellsworth Av Dallas TX 75214

HOBGOOD, CHARLES GOYNE, educator; b. Jackson, La., Sept. 7, 1911; s. James B. and Mary (Hubbs) H.; B.S., La. State U., 1936, M.S., 1938; m. Norma Benton Holden, July 14, 1937; 1 dau., Elizabeth Joy. Soil scientist Soil Conservation Service Flood Control Surveys, Ft. Worth, 1938-41; prof., head dept. agronomy and hort. La. Poly, Inst., Ruston, 1941—; cons. Humble Oil Refining Co., summer 1963. Judge La. Flower Show, 1952-54, 57, 60, 65; judge N. La. State Fair, 1950-53, 58, 61, 63. Served with AUS, 1942-46. Recipient Community Service award La. Garden Club Fedn., 1952. Hon. state farmer, 1959. Mem. La. Assn. Agronomists (pres.), La. Turf and Grass Assn., Farm Bur., Am. Legion, Am. Soc. Agronomy, La. Coll. Conf., Nat. Assn. Colls. and Tchrs. Agr., Omicron Delta Kappa, Phi Kappa Phi, Lambda Chi Alpha. Contbr. articles profl. jours. Home: 1212 Hodges Av Ruston LA 71270

HOBGOOD, PRICE, educator; b. Iredell, Tex., Apr. 5, 1911; s. Willim Henry and Tella (Alexander) H.; B. S., Tex. A. and M. U., 1938, M.S., 1940; grad. student Ia. State U., 1940; m. Merle Plummer, June 10, 1941; 1 dau., Patricia Gail. Math. tchr., pub. sch. prin., 1932-33, part-time, 1933- 37; drainage engr. Dept. Agr., 1938-39; mem. faculty Tex. A. and M. U., 1939-42, 46—, prof. agrl. engring., 1948—, head dept., 1958—; research dir. Tex. Farm Electrification Com., 1956-58; co-owner H&A Constrn., Co., 1952—; cons. engr., 1947—; v.p. Lynndales, Inc. 1955- -. Chmn. equipment and structures research adv. com. Dept. Agr., 1958- 63. Served with USAAF, 1942-46. Registred profl. engr., Tex. Fellow Am. Soc. Agrl. Engrs. (pres. elect 1963-64); mem. Nat., Tex. socs. profl. engrs., Am. Soc. Engring. Edn., Sigma Xi, Tau Beta Pi, Phi Kappa Phi. Presbyn. Contbr. articles profl. jours. Patentee electronic control systems for materials handling. Home: 509 Moran St Bryan TX 77801 Office: Agrl Engring Dept Tex A and M Univ College Station TX 77840

HOBGOOD, WILLIAM GORDON, Jr., banker; b. New Orleans, Aug. 23, 1932; s. William Gordon and Barbara (Hautz) H.; Asso. Sci., Arlington State Coll., 1951; B.B.A., So. Meth. U., 1953, J.D., 1959; postgrad. Stonier Grad. Sch. Banking, 1966; m. Martha Carol Goodwin, July 3, 1957; children—Amy Sue, William Gordon III. Admitted to Tex. bar, 1960; with First Nat. Bank, Dallas, 1959—, sr. v.p., trust officer, 1970—. Trustee So. Bapt. Annuity Bd. Served with USAF, 1953-55. Mem. Am. Inst. Banking, Tex., Dallas bar assns., Lambda Chi Alpha, Delta Theta Phi. Home: 1824 Sedona Lane Dallas TX 75232 Office: PO Box 6031 Dallas TX 75222

HOBLITZELLE, GEORGE KNAPP, steel co. exec. b. St. Louis, Sept. 28, 1921; s. Harrison and Mary D. (Jones) H.; A.B., Princeton, 1943; m. Katharine L. Wells, Nov. 18, 1950; children—Katharine, Laura Trimble, Lucy. With Gen. Steel Industries, Inc., 1946—, successively spl. apprentice, asst. to v.p., treas., 1946- 53, sec., asst. to pres., 1953-60, v.p., 1960-65, v.p., sec., 1965—, Dir. Arts and Edn. Council Greater St. Louis; bd. dirs. St. Luke's Hosp. Served to capt., F.A., AUS, 1943-46; ETO. Decorated Bronze Star. Mem. Nat. Def. Transp. Assn. Episcopalian. Home: 42 Glen Eagles Dr St Louis MO 63124 Office: 1 Memorial Dr St Louis MO 63102

HOBSON, CHARLES, TV producer; b. Bklyn., June 23, 1936; s. Charles Samuel and Cordelia (Spencer) H.; student Bklyn. Coll., 1955-60, New Sch. Social Research, 1967-68. Free lance writer, lectr., 1965—; prodn. dir. WBAI-FM, 1965-68; producer-writer ABC-TV program Like It Is, N.Y.C., 1968—; faculty Vassar Coll., 1970—; cons. Ford Found., 1970-71. Mem. Mayor Lindsey's Com. on Adoption, 1968—. Bd. dirs. Pacificia Found.; trustee Studio Mus. in Harlem. Served with N.Y. N.G., 1962-64. Recipient Emmy award N.Y. Acad. TV Arts and Scis., 1969. Mem. Screen Writers Guild Am., Omega Psi Phi. Contbr. articles mags. Home: 312 W 89th St New York City NY 10024 Office: 77 W 66th St New York City NY 10023

HOBSON, HENRY WISE, Jr., lawyer; b. Worcester, Mass., Nov. 17, 1921; s. Henry Wise and Edmonia (Bryan) H.; grad. Phillips Acad., Andover, Mass., 1939; B.A., Yale, 1943; LL.B., U. Cin., 1948; m. Elizabeth Balch, Apr. 17, 1944; children—Henry Wise III, Elizabeth Loretto, Susan Bryan, Sarah Knight, Anthony Woodford. Admitted to Ohio bar, 1948, since practiced in Cin.; partner firm Frost & Jacobs, 1955—. Dir. Cin. Enquirer, Inc., Ohio Nat. Life Ins. Co., LeBiond Inc., J.H. Day Co., Cin. Terminal Warehouses, Inc., Potter Shoe Co. Mem. exec. com. region 4 Boy Scouts Am., 1963—; v.p., bd. mem. Children's Home Cin., 1967; past chpt. chmn., mem. exec. com. Cin. Area A.R.C., nat. bd. govs., 1966—; pres. Cin. Community Chest and Council; chmn. adv. council Boys Clubs Cin. Trustee United Appeal, Cin. Inst. Fine Arts; pres. trustees Thomas J. Emery Meml. Served to 1st lt. USAAF, 1943-45. Decorated D.F.C., Air medal; named Outstanding Young Man of Year, Cin. Jr. C. of C., 1954. Mem. Am., Ohio, Cin. bar assns. Clubs: Queen City, Camargo, Commercial, Commonwealth (Cin.). Home: 8650 Hopewell Rd Cincinnati OH 45242 Office: DuBois Tower 511 Walnut St Cincinnati OH 45202

HOBSON, JOHN W., advt. agy. exec. Chmn., Bates Internat. Europe group Ted Bates and Co., Inc., N.Y.C. Office: 666 Fifth Av New York City NY 10019*

HOBSON, MRS. LAURA ZAMETKIN, author; b. N.Y.C., d. Michael and Adella (Kean) Zametkin; A.B., Cornell; m. Thayer Hobson, July 23, 1930 (div. 1935); children—Michael and Christopher (adopted). Advt. writer, until 1934, except for year as reporter N.Y. Eve. Post; promotion writer Time, Life, Fortune mags., 1934-40, becoming copy chief of all Time, Inc. mag. promotion, then dir. promotion for Time mag.; wrote first short story, 1935, continued spare- time writing short stories, 1935-41; devoted full time to writing, including fiction, daily newspaper columns, etc., 1941-56; cons. Time, Fortune, Sports Illustrated mags., 1956-62, Saturday Review mag., 1960—. Overseer Coll. of Virgin Islands. Mem. Authors League Am., P.E.N., Americans for Democratic Action, Am. Civil Liberties Union. Club: Regency Whist. Author: A Dog of His Own (juvenile), 1941; The Trespassers, 1943; Gentleman's Agreement, 1947 (made into motion picture, winning Acad. Award as best picture of 1947); The Other Father, 1950; The Celebrity, 1951; First Papers (Lit. Guild selection), 1964; "I'm Going to Have a Baby" (juvenile), 1967; The Tenth Month, 1971. Office: Simon & Schuster 630 Fifth Av New York City NY 10020

HOBSON, MERK, educator; b. N.Y.C., Apr. 9, 1921; s. Asher and Thea D. (Dahle) H.; B.Sc., U. Wis., 1943; M.Sc., Northwestern U., 1948, Ph D., 1951; m. Jane C. Green, Jan 17, 1948; children—Kent, Kim. Process engr. Esso Standard Oil Co. of La., 1943-46; lectr. chem. engring. Northwestern U., 1949- 50; asst. prof. chem. engring. U. Neb., 1950-54, asso. prof., 1954-57, asst. dean. Coll. Engring. and Architecture, 1956, prof. chem. engring., dean Coll. Engring. and Architecture, 1957-65, vice chancellor research, dean Grad. Sch., 1965-66, vice chancellor, dean faculties, 1966-68, vice chancellor for acad. affairs, acting chancellor, corp. sec., mem. bd. regents, from 1968. Bd. dirs. Bryan Meml. Hosp.; sci. adv. com. State Selective Service. Served from 2d lt. to 1st lt., Q.M.C., AUS, 1946-49. Registered profl. engr., Neb. Mem. Am. Inst. Chem. Engrs., Am. Chem. Soc., Am. Soc. Engring. Edn., Nat. Soc. Profl. Engrs., Neb. Engring. Soc., Lincoln C. of C. (dir.), Sigma Xi, Tau Beta Pi, Sigma Tau, Phi Lambda Upsilon, Pi Tau Sigma, Phi Kappa Phi. Contbr. tech. articles to profl. jours. Home: 2223 Van Dorn St Lincoln NB 68502

HOBSON, ROBERT COCHRAN, lawyer; b. Louisville, Aug. 16, 1918; s. Robert Pusey and Catherine (Cochran) H.; A.B., Washington and Lee U., 1940, LL.B., 1942; m. Elizabeth Crews, Aug. 4, 1942; children—Elizabeth Crews, Ann Peyton, Robert Cochran, Jane Bower. Admitted to Ky. bar, 1942; practice in Louisville, 1945—; sr. partner firm Woodward, Hobson & Fulton, 1966—. Served to lt. USNR, 1942-45. Mem. Am., Ky., Louisville bar assns., Am. Coll. Trial Lawyers, Pi Kappa Alpha, Omicron Delta Kappa. Home: 411 Mayfair Lane Louisville KY 40207 Office: Ky Home Life Bldg 5th St Louisville KY 40202

HOBSON, ROBERT LOUIS, indsl. psychologist; b. Blountstown, Fla., Aug. 15, 1918; s. Claude C. and Lenna S. (Van Gundy) H.; A.B., Grinnell Coll., 1940; M.S., Purdue U., 1943, Ph.D., 1948; m. Elizabeth A. Maxwell, Aug. 15, 1941; childrenBarbara L., James A., Caroline A., Henry C., Linda S., William T. Lab. instr. Grinnell Coll., 1940-41; pvt. practice indsl. psychology cons., 1941—; purchasing and materials control Nat. Homes Corps., 1942-44; vocational appraiser Purdue U., 1946-47, test editor div. edn. reference, 1947-48; tng. cons., maintenance Am. Airlines, 1955-57; with psychology dept. U. Tulsa, 1948- -, head dept., 1956-70; personnel cons. Skelly Oil Co., 1965—. Dir. research Nat. Tng. Dirs. Joint Elec. Apprentice Programs. Served with USAAF, 1944-45. Mem. Am., Midwest, S.W. psychol. assns., Grinnell Friars, Tulsa Personnel Group, Tulsa Tng. Group, Sigma Xi, Psi Chi. Mason. Contbr. articles to profl. publs. Inventor flexible gunnery trainer. Home: 6415 S Hudson Tulsa OK 74135

HOCH, FRANK WILLIAM, banker; b. White Plains, N.Y., May 14, 1921; s. Herman and Hanny (von Salis) H.; student Kantonales Gymnasium, Zurich, Switzerland; LL.D., U. Geneva, Zurich U., Switzerland Law Sch., 1947; m. Lisina de Schultess, Aug. 14, 1951; children—Steven George, Alix Monica, Daphne Lisina, Roland Eric. With Brown Bros. Harriman & Co., N.Y.C., 1947—, partner, 1960—; dir. Christiana Gen. Ins. Co. Treas., dir. Internat. Social Service, Geneva, Switzerland, also dir. Am. br., N.Y.C. Home: Matthiessen Park Irvington-on-Hudson NY 10533 Office: 59 Wall St New York City NY 10005

HOCH, LAMBERT ANTHONY, bishop; b. Elkton, S.D., Feb. 6, 1903; s. George Edward and Philomena (Kniest) H.; A.B., Creighton U., 1924; grad. St. Paul Sem., 1928. Ordained priest, Roman Cath. Ch., 1928; named Papal Chamberlain by Pope Pius XI, Jan. 1935, Domestic Prelate by Pope Pius XII, May 1943; prof. philosophy Columbus Coll., Sioux Falls, S.D., 1928-29; asst. pastor Immaculate Conception Ch., Watertown, S.D., 1929-32; chancellor Diocese of Sioux Falls, 1933-52; apptd. bishop of Bismark (N.D.) with deg. of D.D., 1952; former bishop of Sioux Falls, S.D. K.C. Address: 423 N Duluth Av Sioux Falls SD 57104

HOCHBERGER, SIMON, educator; b. York, Pa., Aug. 29, 1912; s. Charles Michael and Lena (Freireich) H.; B.Journalism, U. Mo., 1933, M.A., 1935; m. Bella Hirschfield, Dec. 26, 1937; 1 son, Charles Michael. Engaged in publicity and pub. relations, 1933-34, 35-37; mem. faculty U. Miami (Fla.), 1937- -, prof. journalism, chmn. dept., 1947-66, prof. mass. communications, chmn. dept., 1966—. Vis. prof. U. Nev., 1962, 69, 71-72; asso. editor Fla. Tchr. mag., 1937-42; book reviewer Miami News, 1939-40, 48-51; editorial adviser, manuscript editor Glade House Book Pubs., Miami, 1942-45; copy editor, Sunday mag. writer, editorial writer Nashville Tennessean, 1946-47, 53; asso. editor, drama reviewer Playtime mag., Miami, 1957, Beachcomber mag., 1957-59, v.p. Beachcomber Pub. Co., Inc., Miami, 1957- 59; mem. editorial bd. Journalism Educator, 1958-65; editorial cons., 1940—. Mem. pub. information com. Heart Assn. Greater Miami, 1967—; editorial cons. Dade County (Fla.) Bd. Pub. Instrn., 1970-71. Recipient Gold Key award Columbia Scholastic Press Assn., 1949. Mem. Am. Soc. Journalism Sch. Adminstrs. (sec.-treas. 1962-65), Assn. Edn. Journalism (nat. dep. sec.-treas. 1962-65), Mo. Hist. Soc. (life), Am. Assn. U. Profs., Inter-Am. Press Assn. (asso.), Am. Acad. Polit. and Social Sci., Phi Kappa Phi (pres. U. Miami chpt. 1961-62), Iron Arrow, Omicron Delta Kappa, Kappa Tau Alpha (mem. nat. council 1958—, nat. sec. 1968-70), Sigma Delta Chi (life). Club: Univ. Miami Faculty (v.p. 1959-61, bd. dirs. 1959-63). Author articles and revs., editor and or editorial cons. Home: 5329 Granada Blvd Coral Gables FL 33146

HOCHE, PHILIP ANTHONY, life ins. co. exec.; b. Cape Girardeau, Mo., Jan. 29, 1906; s. Philip Aloysius and Mary Edith (Meyers) H.; B.A., Southeast Mo. State Coll., 1926; m. Angela Genevieve Hayes, Jan. 2, 1941; children—A. Henry, John Philip. Sales rep. Sherwin-Williams Co., Chgo., 1926-31; agt., ednl. dir. New Eng. Mut. Life Ins. Co., Chgo., 1932-39; gen. agt. Kansas City Life Ins. Co., Bloomington, Ill., 1940-43, Orlando, Fla., 1946—. Mem. ins. bd., Winter Park, Fla., 1965—; trustee Life Underwriters Tng. Council, 1956-59; trustee Nat. Assn. Life Underwriters, 1961-63, sec., 1962, v.p., 1965, pres., 1966. Pres. Orange County (Fla.) Heart Assn., 1963-64; chmn. fund raising adv. com. So. region Am. Heart Assn., 1969, 71; gov.'s ambassador good will for Fla., 1965- 66; pres. Central Fla. Estate Planning Council, 1968-69. Bd. dirs. Fla. Heart Assn., 1965. Served to lt. comdr. USNR, 1943-45. Recipient C.G. Snead Meml. award Fla. Assn. Life Underwriters, 1961. Mem. Am. Soc. C.L.U., Internat. Platform Assn., Guild Former Pipe Organ Pumpers, Navy League. Clubs: University, Rotary (pres. 1958- 59) (Winter Park). Home: 1431 Temple Dr Winter Park FL 32789 Office: 1320 Lang St PO Box 6606 Orlando FL 32803

HOCHFELD, HYMEN MEYER, financial cons.; b. Phila., June 11, 1915; s. Samuel and Jennie (Kramer) H.; B.S., Temple U., 1937; grad. student Columbia; m. Evelyn Rose, Mar. 23, 1947; children—Kurt, Paul. With Commonwealth of Pa., 1937- 40; with Panama Canal R.R., 1940; staff Fed. Works Agy., 1940-42, Fed. Maritime Bd., 1942-57; v.p. Matson Navigation Co., San Francisco, 1957- 66; v.p. Alexander & Baldwin, Inc., San Francisco, 1966-70; financial cons. Harper Group, 197O—. Home: 2001 Barbara Dr Palo Alto CA 94303 Office: 545 Sansome St San Francisco CA 94111

HOCHHUTH, ROLF, author; b. Eschwege, Germany, Jan. 4, 1931; s. Walter and Ilse (Holzapfel) H.; student univs. Munich and Heidelberg, 1952-55; m. Marianne Heinemann, June 29, 1957; 1 son, Martin. Reader, editor pub. house C. Bertelsmann-Lesering, Gütersloh, Germany, 1955—. Author: (play) The Deputy, 1964 (Frederic Melcher book award 1965); Soldiers, 1968. Editor: Essays by Thomas Mann, 1963; Essays by Otto Flake, 1962; German Stories of 20th Century, 2 vols., 1964; Complete Works by Wilhelm Busch, 1959; Choice of Works by Theodor Storm, 1960; Choice of Works by Erich Kästner, 1961; Contemporary German Love Stores, 2 vols., 1960; Deutsche Erzlähler von Grimmelshausen bis Fontane, 1965; Anatomy of Revolution, 1969; The Guerillas, 1970. Address: care Stadtstheater Basel Switzerland

HOCHMAN, ROBERT FRANCIS, educator; b. Chgo., May 1, 1928; s. Francis and Anna (Holak) H.; B.S. in Metallurgy, U. Notre Dame, 1950, M.S., 1954, Ph.D., 1959; m. Carolyn Bennett, June 22, 1960; 1 son, Robert Francis. Instr., U. Notre Dame, 1957-58; instr. Mich. State Extension Service, Benton Harbor, 1957-58; asst. prof. Ga. Inst. Tech., Atlanta, 1959-62, asso. prof. metallurgy Sch. Chem. Engring., 1962-68, prof. metallurgy, 1968—, asso. dir. for metallurgy, 1971—, dir. research stress corrosion Advanced Research Project Agy., Dept. Def., 1966—, Advanced Research Project Agy., Dept. Agy. Tng. grantee in dental materials, 1963—; cons. Zimmer Mfg. Co., Warsaw, Ind., 1957—, Lockheed-Ga. Co., Marietta, Ga., 1964—; dir. Fulton Engring. Co., Atlanta. Pres., Confraternity Christian Doctrine program Holy Spirit Parish, Atlanta, 1967-68. Served with U.S. Army, 1951-52; Korea, 1967-68. Decorated D.S.M. NSF grantee to attend Internat. Conf. Metallic Corrosion, Moscow, USSR, 1966. Mem. Nat. Assn. Corrosion Engrs. (chmn. nat. edn. com., 1963-67, dir. 1963-67), Am. Soc. Metals (chmn. So. Metal Conf. 1961-69), Am. Soc. Testing Materials, Soc. for Non-Destructive Testing, Nat. Inst. Dental Research, Sigma Xi. Club: Atlanta Notre Dame (pres. 1961-63, dir. 1963—). Contbr. articles profl. jours. Editor: Field Ion Microscopy in Physical Metallurgy and Corrosion. Patentee in field. Home: 3186 River Heights Dr Smyrna GA 30080 Office: Dept Chem Engring Ga Inst Tech Atlanta GA 30332

HOCHOY, SOLOMON, gov. gen. of Trinidad and Tobaco; b. Jamaica, Apr. 20, 1905; s. David and Kuiyin (Lue) H.; student St. Mary's Coll., Port-of-Spain, Trinidad; m. Thelma Edna Huggins, Feb. 3, 1935. Mem. Civil Service Trinidad and Tobgo, 1927-49, commr. labour, 1949-55, chief sec., 1956-60, gov., 1960-62, gov. gen. 1962—, also comdr. in chief. Chief scout Trinidad and Tobago; hon. patron World Scouting, Trinidad and Tobago br. RAF Assn.; chmn, Nat. Scout Council; patron St. John Council, all ambulance and nursing divs. St. John Ambulance Brigade, Trinidad and Tobago Red Cross Soc., Trinidad Soc. Prevention Cruelty to Animals, Trinidad Philatelic Soc., Trinidad Football Assn., Trinidad Automobile Assn., Rifle Assn., Mariners Club, Trinidad and Tobago Soc. Architects, Trinidad and Tobago Hockey Control Bd. Decorated Trinity Cross (Trinidad and Tobago Order of Trinity), knight grand cross Royal Victorian Order; knight grand cross Order St. Michael and St. George; knight comdr. Order St. Michael and St. George; comdr. Order St. Michael and St. George; officer Order Brit. Empire; knight Venerable Order St. John Jerusalem; recipient Queen's Coronation medal, 1953. Fellow Royal Commonwealth Soc.; life mem. Chinese Assn. Trinidad and Tobago; hon. mem. North Trinidad Lions Club, Port-Of-Spain Rotary Culb, Queen's Park Cricket Club, St. Andrew's Golf Club, Union Club. Clubs: Corona (Eng.); Clipper. Address: Governor-General's House St Ann's Trinidad Trinidad and Tobago

HOCHSCHILD, GERHARD P., educator. Prof. math. U. Cal. at Berkeley. Office: 301 Campbell Hall U Cal Berkeley CA 94720*

HOCHSCHILD, HAROLD K., mining co. exec.; b. N.Y.C., May 20, 1892; s. Berthold and Mathilde (Blumenthal) H.; student Yale, 1908-12, M.A. (hon.), 1962; LL.D., St. Lawrence U., 1963; L.H.D., Hamilton Coll., 1968; Litt.D., Princeton, 1968; m. Mary Marquand, Nov. 1941; 1 son, Adam. With Am. Metal Co., Ltd., N.Y.C., 1913—, chmn., 1947-57, hon. chmn., 1957—. Chmn. N.Y. State Adirondack Study Commn., 1969-71. Hon. chmn. bd. African- Am. Inst.; trustee African-Am. Inst., Valeria Home, Correctional Assn. N.Y., Inst. Advanced Study, Princeton. Served to lt. col. AUS, World War II. Mem. Adirondack (pres.), N.Y. (trustee, mem. bd.) hist. assns. Clubs: Yale, Century (N.Y.C.). Author: Township 34. Office: 1270 Av of Americas New York City NY 10020

HOCHSCHILD, WALTER, business exec.; b. N.Y.C. Sept. 27, 1900; s. Berthold and Matilde (Blumenthal) H.; student Phillips Andover Acad., 1915-16; A.B., Yale, 1920; m. Kathrin Samstag, May 16, 1923; children—Ann (Mrs. Richard G. Poole), Patricia (Mrs. George Labalme, Jr.), Lynn (Mrs. Claude E. Boillot). Employee Am. Metal Co. Ltd., N.Y.C., 1920, dir., 1928—, pres., 1950-57, chmn. bd., 1957; chmn. exec. com., dir. Am. Metal Climax, Inc., 1966—. Trustee Expt. in Internat. Living, Valeria Home. Served with AUS, 1942-45; ETO. Mem. Am. Inst. Mining and Metall. Engrs., Council Fgn. Relations, Mining and Metall. Soc. Am., Internat. C. of C. (exec. com. U.S. Council) Clubs: Mining, Creek; Regency Whist. Home: Blue Mountain Lake NY 12812 Office: 1270 Av of Americas New York City NY 10020

HOCHSTADT, HARRY, educator, mathematician; b. Vienna, Austria, Sept. 7, 1925; s. Samuel and Amalie (Dorn) H.; B. Chem. Engring., Cooper Union, 1949; M.S., N.Y.U., 1950, Ph.D., 1956; m. Pearl Schwartzberg, Mar. 29, 1953; children—Julia Phyllis, Jesse Frederick. Research engr. W. L. Maxson Corp., N.Y.C., 1951-57; mem. faculty Poly. Inst. Bklyn., 1957—, prof. math., 1961—, head dept., 1963—. Served with inf. AUS, 1943-45. Decorated Bronze Star, Combat Inf. badge. Mem. Am., London, Indian math. socs., Math. Assn. Am., Soc. Indsl. and Applied Math., Sigma Xi, Tau Beta Pi. Author: Special Functions of Mathematical Physics, 1961; Differential Equations, A Modern Approach, 1964; The Functions of Mathematical Physics, 1971. Translation editor Linear Equations of Mathematical Physics (Mikhlin), 1967. Home: 126 Joralemon St Brooklyn NY 11201

HOCHSTIM, ADOLF RUDOLF, educator, physicist; b. Poland, Nov. 13, 1928; s. Tadeusz and Lucia (Dürer) H.; came to U.S., 1949, naturalized, 1955; student Goethe U., Frankfurt, W. Germany, 1946-49; B.S., U. Miami (Fla.), 1951; M.S., Fla. State U., 1953; Ph.D., U. Fla., 1967; m. Gloria G. Clayman, Dec. 16, 1955; children—Sylvia, Diana. Staff scientist Convair, 1956-62; mem. tech. staff, sci. and tech. div. Inst. Def. Analysis, 1962-68; prof. engring. scis., dir. Research Inst. Engring. Sci., Wayne State U., Detroit, 1968—. Cons. in field. Mem. Am. Phys. Soc., Am. Inst. Aeros. and Astronautics, Philos. Soc. Washington, A.A.A.S., Detroit Engring. Soc., N.Y. Acad. Scis., Sigma Xi. Home: 19245 Parkside Rd Detroit MI 48221

HOCHSTRASSER, ROBIN M., educator. Blanchard prof. chemistry U. Pa., Phila. Office: Dept Chemistry U Pa Philadelphia PA 19104*

HOCHULI, PAUL RICHARD, banker; b. Newark, July 3, 1928; s. Henry W. and Elsie (Kreisel) H.; A.B. in Econs., Union Coll., Schenectady, 1949; m. Audrey K. Walker, Aug. 26, 1950; children—Joan Carol, Carolyn Ann, Richard Paul. With Gen. Electric Co., 1949-67; treas. Popular Mdse. Co., Inc., Passaic, N.J., 1967-69; auditor Seamen's Bank for Savs., N.Y.C., 1969—. Presbyn. (trustee 1967-69, treas. 1968, 69, elder 1970—). Home: 230 Mulberry Pl Ridgewood NJ 07450 Office: 30 Wall St New York City NY 10005

HOCHWALD, WERNER, educator, economist; b. Berlin, Germany, Jan. 21, 1910; s. Moritz and Elsa (Stahl) H.; student U. Freiburg, 1928-29; LL.B., U. Berlin, 1933; B.S., Washington U., St. Louis, 1940, A.M., 1942, Ph.D., 1944; m. Hilde Landenberger, Jan. 28, 1938 (dec. June 1958); children—Miriam Ruth, Eve Fay. Counsel, Com. on Aid and Reconstrn., 1933-38; instr. ASTP, 1942-44; instr. to asso. prof. Washington U., St. Louis, 1944-49, prof., 1950—, chmn. dept. econs., 1955-63, Tileston prof. polit. economy, 1958—; Cons., Fed. Res Bank of St. Louis, 1947-58; mem. citizens budget com., St. Louis. Mem. Am., So. (pres. 1966-67), Midwest econ. assns., Nat. Bur. Econ. Research, Am. Statis. Assn. (nat. council 1950- 52), Econometric Soc., Econ. History Assn., Indsl. Relations Research Assn., Phi Beta Kappa (chapt. pres.). Author: Local Impact of Foreign Trade, 1960; An Economist's Image of History, 1968; The Rationality Concept in Economic Analysis, 1971. Contbg. author: Twentieth Century Economic Thought, 1950; Studies in Income and Wealth, 1957; Local Economic Activity and Foreign Trade, 1958; Design of Regional Accounts, 1962; Southern Economic Development, 1964. Home: 6910 Cornell Av. University City MO 63130 Office: Washington U St Louis MO 63130

HOCHWALT, CARROLL ALONZO, research chemist; b. Dayton, O., Apr. 29, 1899; s. Albert Frederick and Adele (Butz) H.; B.Ch.E., U. Dayton, 1920, D.Sc., 1935; D.Sc., Washington U., 1962, St. Louis U., 1964; m. Pauline Burkhardt, Sept. 27, 1922; children—Carroll A., Richard, Paula (Mrs. Robert E. Morie). Research chemist Gen. Motors Corp., Dayton, O., 1920-24; prodn. mgr. Ethyl Gasoline Corp., Dayton, 1924-25; v.p., Thomas & Hochwalt Labs., Dayton, 1926-36; asso. dir. central research dept. Monsanto Chem. Co., St. Louis, 1936-45, dir., 1945-48, coordinator research, devel. and engring., v.p., 1947-64, dir., 1949-64; pres. Chemstrand Corp., 1949-50, dir., 1949-64; vice chmn. St. Louis Research Council, 1964—; chmn. mgmt. com. Argus Chem. Corp. subsidiary Witco Chem. Co., Inc., N.Y.C.; dir. Boatmen's Nat. Bank, Carboline Co. St. Louis, Nat. Computer Service, Inc., Petrolite Corp. (both St. Louis); mem. cons. to policy com. Mallinckrodt Chem. Works, St. Louis. Mem. Manhattan Project on atomic bomb research, also mem. Div. 8., Nat. Def. Research Com., World War II; mem. ordnance adv. com. research and devel. div. Dept. Army; ofcl. witness Operation Crossroads, Bikini Atoll, 1946; mem. Gov.'s adv. com. Mo. State Tech. Services Program, 1966-70; mem. Greater St. Louis Arts and Edn. Council, 1963-69. Mem. lay bd. trustees St. Louis U., chmn. 1963-66, mem. pres.'s council 1957—); trustee Cath. U. Am., chmn. bd. trustees 1968-70, U. Dayton, Charles F. Kettering Found., Air Force Mus. Found.; Am. sponsors com. Am. Coll. in Paris, France; adv. bd. Internat. Inst. Recipient Midwest award Am. Chem. Soc., 1956; Brotherhood citation Nat. Conf Christians and Jews, 1969; Cardinal Gibbons award Cath. U. Am., 1970. Mem. Am. Chem. Soc., Soc. Chem. Industry, Electrochem. Soc., Am. Inst. Chemists, Am. Inst. Chem. Engrs., A.A.A.S., Am. Phys. Soc., Am. Ordnance Assn., Cath. Commn. Intellectual and Cultural Affairs, Sigma Xi, Tau Beta Pi. Clubs: St. Louis, Bogey, Stadium. Home: 7 Upper Ladue Rd Clayton MO 63124 Office: 7701 Forsyth Blvd St Louis MO 63105

HOCKEIMER, HENRY ERIC, mfg. co. exec.; b. Winzig, Germany, Apr. 3, 1920; s. Erich and Gertrude (Masur) H.; came to U.S., 1946, naturalized, 1951; student RCA Insts., 1946-47, electronics and bus. mgmt. N.Y.U., 1948-51; m. Margaret Feeny, May 26, 1956; children—Ellen Patricia, Henry Eric. With Philco Corp., Phila., 1947—, gen. mgr. communications and tech. services div., 1962-63, v.p., 1963—. Mem. Franklin Inst., I.E.E.E., Am. Ordnance Assn., Armed Forces Communications and Electronics Assn. Home: 1249 Cox Rd Rydal PA 19046 Office: 3900 Welsh Rd Willow Grove PA 19090

HOCKENSMITH, ROY DOUGLAS, soil conservationist, b. Gallatin, Mo., Feb. 27, 1905; s. Edward and Myrtle (Royston) H.; B.S., U. Mo., 1927, M.S., 1928; m. Edith McKenzie, Aug. 4, 1930; 1 son, Duane A. Asst. soils U. Mo., 1927-29; asso. prof. agronomy Colo. State Coll., 1929-34; asso. land bank appraiser Fed. Land Bank, Wichita, Kan., 1934-37; head conservation survey sect., soil conservation service Dept. Agr., Amarillo, Tex., 1937-39, asst. chief, Washington, 1939-46, chief, 1946-52, dir. soil survey operations, 1952- -. Mem. A.A.A.S., Internat. Soc. Soil Sci., Soil Conservation Soc. Am. (pres.), Soil Sci. Soc. Am., Am. Soc. Agronomy. Contbr. articles to bulls., jours. Home: 2832 McKinley Pl NW Washington DC 20015 Office: Soil Conservation Service Dept Agr Washington DC 20250

HOCKER, LON, lawyer; b. St. Louis, May 20, 1910; s. Lon O. and Mary (Berry) H.; A.B., Princeton, 1931; J.D., Washington U., 1934; m. Esther Wilson Sands, Oct. 19, 1937; children— Priscilla Sands (Mrs. V.N. Claman), Lon O. Admitted to Mo. bar, 1934, Fed. Cts., 1934, U.S. Supreme Ct. bar, 1949, Mass. bar, 1969; mem. Hocker, Goodwin, Koenig, Gibbons & Fehlig (and predecessor firms), 1934—; dir. Ozark Air Lines, Bayless Bldg. Materials Co.; gen. counsel St. Louis Globe-Democrat Pub. Co. Mem. St. Louis City Plan Commn., 1941-45, chmn., 1943. Chief hearings counsel U.S. Senate Subcom. on Constl. Rights, 1955. Republican candidate for gov. of Mo., 1956 and U.S. senator, 1960. Served as lt. USNR, 1944-45, comdg. officer LST 889. Fellow Am. Coll. of Trial Lawyers (pres. 1960-61); mem. Bar Assn. of St. Louis (pres. 1953), Am. Bar Assn. Episcopalian. Author articles, legal subjects. Mem. U.S. Internat. Fencing Team, Eng. 1930; Midwest sabre fencing champion, 1935-38. Home: 7637 Shirley Dr Clayton MO 63105 Office: 411 N 7th St St Louis MO 63101 also 1 Fay Rd Woods Hole MA 02543

HOCKERSMITH, FORREST DAVITTE, retired govt. ofcl.; b. Nashville, Sept. 19, 1906; s. Thomas Milton and Melissa (Davitte) H.; B.S. in Civil Engring., Ga. Inst. Tech., 1932; m. Bessie Florence Sisk, Feb. 9, 1935; children—Thomas Edward, Joseph Davitte, Teresa Ann. With W. Horace Williams Co., Inc., Tavares, Fla., 1926-27, Ga. Hwy. Bd., 1928-32, Spur Distbg. Co., 1932-34; asst. sci. aide U.S. Coast and Geodetic Survey, 1934-35; sr. constrn. engr. WPA, 1935-43; asst. dir. indsl. projects div. FEA, 1943-46; asst. dir. material div. Office Housing Expediter, 1946-47; cons. engr., Washington, 1947-48; with Dept. Commerce, 1948-69, acting and dep. adminstr. Bus. and Def. Services Adminstrn., 1965-66, dep. adminstrn., 1966-69; ret., 1969. Mem. com. mgmt. Fairfax County (Va.) YMCA, 1958-61, mem. fund drive com., 1960-61. Recipient Silver medal Dept. Commerce, 1961, Gold medal, 1967. Methodist (chmn. ofcl. bd. 1958-61). Home: 4209 Penner Lane Fairfax VA 22030

HOCKETT, CHARLES FRANCIS, educator, anthropologist; b. Columbis, O., Jan. 17, 1916; s. Homer Carey and Amy (Francisco) H.; B.A., M.A. in Ancient History, Ohio State U., 1936; Ph.D. in Anthropology, Yale, 1939; m. Shirley Orlinoff, Apr. 25, 1942; children—Alpha, Asher Orlinoff, Amy Roberta, Rachel, Carey Beth. Mem. faculty Cornell U., 1946—, prof. linguistics and anthropology, 1957—, Goldwin Smith prof. linguistics and anthropology, 1970—. Fellow Center Advanced Study Behavioral Scis., 1955-56. Mem. Linguistic Soc. Am. (pres. 1964), A.A.A.S., American Anthrop. Assn., Ithaca Composers Club, Phi Beta Kappa, Sigma Xi. Author: A Manual of Phonology, 1955; A Course in Modern Linguistics, 1958. Composer: (opera) The Loves of Dona Rosita, 1962; also instrumental works, songs. Home: 145 N Sunset Dr Ithaca NY 14850

HOCKETT, HARRY GOLDEN, former hosp. adminstr.; b. Anderson, Ind., Sept. 11, 1903; s. George Hodson and Edna (Curtis) H.; premed. student, Ind. U., 1922-25; M.D., Hahnemann Med. Coll., 1929; m. Evelyn E. Snyder, May 6, 1931; children—George Charles (dec.), Harry Donald. Intern Miami Valley Hosp., Dayton, O., 1929-30; pvt. practice, Anderson, Ind. and St. Thomas, V.I., 1930-40; staff physician Ft. Wayne (Ind.) State Sch., 1940-42; psychiatrist VA Hosp., Marion, Ind., 1942-61, hosp. adminstr., 1956-61; psychiatrist VA Hosp., Salisbury, N.C., 1961-69, adminstr., 1961-69, ret., 1969. Served to maj. M.C., AUS, 1944-46. Diplomate Am. Bd. Psychiatry and Neurology. Fellow Am. Psychiat. Assn.; mem. A.M.A. Rotarian. Home: 5043 SW 91st Terrace Cooper City Fort Lauderdale FL 33314

HOCKING, ELTON, educator; b. Benton, Wis., Sept. 8, 1901; s. Henry and Martha (Whitman) H.; A.B., U. Wis., 1925, A.M., 1926, Ph. D., 1930; m. Clara Ruedebusch, Aug. 7, 1926; 1 son, Norman James. Instr. Romance langs. U. Wis., 1926-30; Markhamm traveling fellow (France, Germany, Italy, England), 1930-31; instr. Northwestern U., 1931-36, asst. prof., 1936-41, asso. prof. Romance langs, 1941-47; prof., head dept. modern langs. Purdue U., 1947-62, prof. modern lang. edn., 1962-70, prof. emeritus, 1970—; tchr. U. Wyo., 1940, Middlebury Coll., 1947; lectr., cons. dept. audio-visual instrn. N.E.A. Fulbright research scholar, France, 1952-53; recipient Nat. Distinguished Fgn. Lang. Leadership award N.Y. State Fedn. Fgn. Lang. Tchrs.; decorated chevalier l'Ordre des Palmes Academiques. Mem. Am. Assn. Tchrs. Italian (sec.-treas. 1940-45, pres. 1946), Modern Lang. Assn. Am. (initiated survey lang. teaching in Army, 1944; co-author report with F.B. Agard, et. al.: A Survey of Language Classes in the A.S.T.P., 1944), Nat. Fedn. Modern Lang. Tchrs. Assns. (v.p. 1949), Central States Modern Lang. Tchrs. Assn. (pres. 1946), Am. Assn. Tchrs. French. Author: Language Laboratory and Language Learning; author, co-author several books. Home: 1201 Sunset Lane West Lafayette IN 47906 ☆

HOCKING, FRED GIRVIN, milling co. exec; b. Lancaster, Pa., Sept. 5, 1915; s. John Doble and Maude (Girvin) H.; B.A., Franklin and Marshall Coll., 1937; m. Doris Arlene Eaby, Feb. 19, 1938 (dec. June 1950); children—Fred, Guy Eaby, Ann (Mrs. Daniel Costello); m. 2d, Eugenia Ione Boynton, Aug. 12, 1951; 1 son, John Doble. Accountant, Gen. Electric Co., 1937-46; with Grain Processing Corp., Muscatine, Ia., 1946—, exec v.p. planning and growth, dir., 1966—; pres., dir. Muscatine Corp.; exec. v.p. planning and growth, dir. Kent Feeds, Inc., Muscatine; v.p., dir. Roth Lumber Co., Muscatine; treas., dir. No. Gravel Co., Muscatine. Past pres. bd. dirs. Muscatine YMCA; mem. adv. bd. Illowa council Boy Scouts Am.; trustee Kent-Stein Found. Mem. Muscatine C. of C. (past bd. dirs.), Phi Beta Kappa. Presbyn. Mason, Elk. Home: 3 Wilson Dr Muscatine IA 52761 Office: 1600 Oregon St Muscatine IA 52761

HOCKING, JOHN GILBERT, educator; b. Caspian, Mich., Sept. 26, 1920; s. John Pearce and Ethel (Faragher) H.; B.S. with distinction, U. Mich., 1946, M.S., 1948, Ph.D., 1953; m. Virginia Marilyn Yinger, Mar. 6, 1944; children—Claudia Megan (Mrs. James Hunter Thrall), John Chadwick, Judith Wendell, Nancy Reid. Mem. faculty dept. math. Mich. State U., East Lansing, 1951—, prof., 1964—; vis. lectr. U. B.C., Vancouver, Can., 1956; Fulbright guest lectr. U. Tubingen, Germany, 1962-63; vis. prof. Westfield Coll., U. London, Eng., 1970-71. Served with USAAF, World War II; CBI. Mem. Am. Math. Soc., Math. Assn. Am., Sports Car Club Am., Phi Beta Kappa, Sigma Xi. Author: (with G.S. Young) Topology, 1961; Calculus, 1970. Editor conf. proc. Topology of Manifolds, 1969. Home: 4205 Meridian Rd Okemos MI 48864 Office: Math Dept Mich State U East Lansing MI 48823

HOCKING, RICHARD BOYLE O'REILLY, educator; b. Berkeley, Cal., Aug. 26, 1906; s. William Ernest and Agnes Boyle (O'Reilly) H.; B.S. cum laude, Harvard, 1928, M.A., 1930; lab. asst. Cal. Inst. Tech., 1930-31, U. Berlin 1933-34; Ph.D., Yale, 1935; m. Katherine Everts Ewing, Aug. 12, 1939; children—Lillian Everts (Mrs. Calvin Farwell), Jennifer Maeve (Mrs. George Wiley), Penelope Boyle O'Reilly. Instr. philosophy U. Minn., 1935-37; asst. prof. Williams Coll., 1937-40, U. Cal. at Los Angeles, 1940-46, U. Chgo., 1946-49; exchange prof. U. Frankfurt (Germany), 1949; prof. philosophy Emory U., 1949-70, prof. emeritus, 1970—, chmn. dept., 1962-66. Mem. Ga. Council Human Relations; chmn. Madison (N.H.) Conservation Commn., 1971. Del. N.H. Republican Conv., 1968. Trustee Ella Lyman Cabot Trust. Mem. Acad. Polit. Sci., Am. Philos. Assn., Am. Soc. Internat. Law, Aristotelian Soc. (Eng.), Canadian Philos. Assn., Guild Scholars in Episcopal Ch. (pres. 1951, 66), Hegel Soc. Am., Metaphys. Soc. Am. (treas. 1954, pres. 1969), Soc. Asian and Comparative Philosophy, Soc. Phenomenology and Existential Philosophy, So. Soc. Philosophy Religion (pres. 1954), Council Religion Higher Edn., Nat. Grange. Episcopalian. Contbr. profl. jours. Home: Madison NH 03849

HOCKNEY, DAVID, artist; b. Bradford, Eng., July 9, 1937; s. Kenneth and Laura (Thompson) H.; student Royal Coll. Art. One-man shows include Kasmin Ltd., London, Eng., 1963, 65, 66, 68, 69, Editions Alecto, London, 1964, Alan Gallery, N.Y.C., 1964, 66, Sledligile Mus., Amsterdam, Holland, 1966, Whitworth Gallery, Manchester, Eng., 1969, Whitechapel Art Gallery, 1970. Recipient Gold medal Royal Coll. Art, 1962. Address: care Kasmin Ltd 118 New Bond St London W 1 England

HOCTOR, THOMAS FRANCIS, educator; b. N.Y.C., Nov. 22, 1918; s. Frank M. and Catherine E. (Quirk) H.; B.S., City Coll. N.Y., 1939; M.B.A., N.Y.U., 1949; postgrad. U. Mich., 1953; m. Ruth Meyers, Mar. 4, 1950; 1 son, Ralph. Joined U.S. Fgn. Service, 1949; resident officer, Frankfurt, Germany, 1950-52; assigned State Dept., also Fgn. Service Inst., 1950- 53; 2d sec., vice consul, Bucharest, Roumania, 1953-56; internat. relations officer State Dept., 1956-60; consul, Calcutta, India, 1960- 64; officer in charge Greek affairs, 1964-67; chmn. fgn. service econ. studies Fgn. Service Inst.; chief office of programs and research Export- Import Bank of U.S., Washington, 1968-70; cons. Dept. State, 1970-71; prof. econs. U. Balt., 1971—. Served with AUS, 1941-45. Mem. Am. Econs. Assn. Home: 7129 Fairfax Rd Bethesda MD 20014 Office: Dept of Economics University of Balt Baltimore MD 21201

HODARI, ABRAHAM ALBERTO, physician; b. Paris, France, Sept. 12, 1934; s. Adolfo and Esther (Berco) H.; student Ward Coll., Buenos Aires, Argentina, 1948-53; B.A., U. Buenos Aires, 1953, M.D., 1959; m. Rosa Bezverg, May 25, 1959; children—Claudia, Patricia, Adolfo. Instr. dept. anatomy U. Buenos Aires, 1957-59; intern Mt. Sinai Hosp., Mpls., 1959-60; resident surgery U. Minn., 1960-61; resident obstetrics Fernandez Hosp., Buenos Aires, 1961-62; resident obstetrics and gynecology Henry Ford Hosp., Detroit, 1962-65, asso. obstetrics, gynecology, 1967—; fellow research div. Cleve. Clinic, 1966-67; practice medicine, specializing in obstetrics and gynecology, Detroit, 1967—; dir. med. edn. and research Crittenton Hosp., 1968—; asst. clin. prof. Wayne U., 1968—; dir. residency program in obstetrics and gynecology Detroit Meml. Hosp.; pres. Downtown Obstetrics and Gynecology Center. Recipient Ephraim McDowell Meml. awards, 1964, 68, 69, 70, First prizes, 1966, 67, Purde Frederick award, 1967, President's award, 1968 all from Am. Coll. Obstetricians and Gynecologists; certificate of merit A.C.S., 1965; First prize Am. Assn. Obstetrics and Gynecology, 1966; William E. Lower Fellowship Thesis prize Cleve. Clinic Found., 1966; First prize Central Assn. Obstetricians and Gynecologists, 1967, 68; Sama-Mead Johson hon. mention, 1967; Hektoen Gold medal A.M.A., 1969, Bronze medal Natl. Med. Assn., 1969. Fellow A.C.S., N.Y. Acad. Sci., Am. Coll. Obstetricians and Gynecologists, Am. Fertility Soc.; mem. Argentina Med. Soc. Contbr. articles profl. jours., books. Home: 25625 Catalina St Southfield MI 48075 Office: Crittenton Hosp 1554 Tuxedo St Detroit MI 48206

HODDER, EDWIN JAMES, investment banker; b. Cambridge, Mass., June 25, 1908; s. Edwin and Mary J. (Johnston) H.; B.A., Harvard, 1928; m. Rora Melville, Feb. 25, 1930; children—Edwin Edwin James, Melville T. With Hayden, Stone & Co., Inc., N.Y.C., 1928—, now sr. v.p. Mem. Boston Stock Exchange. Trustee Tabor Acad., Marion, Mass. Mem. Phi Beta Kappa. Home: 154 Goden St Belmont MA 02178 Office: 10 Post Office Sq Boston MA 02109

HODDY, GEORGE WARREN, industrialist; b. Columbus, O., Mar. 7, 1905; s. Arthur H. and Mary E. (Lutz) H.; B.E.E., Ohio State U., 1926, E.E., 1932; m. Lois L. Mitchell, May 30, 1947; children—John, Peter, Matthew, Elizabeth, Rebekah, Melissa. Engr., Day-Fan Electric Co., Dayton, O., 1926-29, Robbins & Myers, Inc., Springfield, O., 1929-31; chief engr. Pioneer div. Master Electric Co., Dayton, 1932-34; v.p., gen. mgr. Redmond Co., Inc., Owosso, Mich., 1934-43; pres., gen. mgr., dir. Universal Electric Co., Owosso, 1942—, also chief exec. officer; vice chmn., dir. State Savs. Bank, Owosso, 1946—; chmn., dir. Am. Universal Electric (India), Ltd., New Delhi, 1962—; pres., dir. Fiji Marina, Inc., Los Angeles, 1968—; dir. Ventrola Mfg. Co. Mem. Mfr.'s Council. Mem. Nat. council Boy Scouts Am., 1961—. Mem. Owosso Bd. Edn., 1957—. Bd. dirs. Shiawassee County United Fund, Mich. United Fund; trustee Meml. Hosp., Flint Osteo. Hosp. Mem. Owosso Area C. of C. (adv. bd.), Newcomen Soc., Sigma Xi, Tau Beta Pi, Pi Mu Epsilon, Eta Kappa Nu, Lambda Chi Alpha. Methodist. Mason. Home: 508 W William St Owosso MI 48867 also Lakeside Rd Cedarville MI 49719 Office: 300 E Main St Owosso MI 48867

HODEIR, ANDRE, composer; b. Paris, France, Jan. 22, 1921; s. Oidih and Angèle (Guionnet) H.; ed. Conservatoire national supérieur de musique; m. Renée Collet, Mar. 23, 1948; 1 dau., Catherine. Editor-in-chief Jazz Hot, 1947- 50; pres. Academie du jazz, 1954-60; mus. dir. Jazz Groupe of Paris, 1954-60; mem. jury Conservatoire national supérieur de musique. Author: Hommes et problémes du jazz, 1954; la Musique Depuis Debussy, 1960; Toward Jazz, 1962; Les Mondes du Jazz, 1970. Composer: Paradoxe II, The Alphabet, Around the Blues, Jazz cantata, Transplantation, Flautando; (music for films) Une Parisienne, Histoire d'un poisson rouge (with Henri Crolla), le Palais Idéal, De l'Amour, L'Ecume des jours; Anna Livia Plurabelle (opera), 1966. Address: 66 rue du Colonel de Rochebrune 92 Garches France

HODEL, DONALD PAUL, govt. ofcl.; b. Portland, Ore., May 23, 1935; s. Philip E. and Theresia Rose (Brodt) H.; B.A., Harvard, 1957; J.D., U. Ore., 1960; m. Barbara Beecher Stockman, Dec. 10, 1956; children—Philip S., David B. Admitted to Ore. bar, 1960; practice in Portland, 1960-63; lawyer Ga.-Pacific Corp., Portland, 1963-69; dep. adminstr. Bonneville Power Adminstrn., Portland, 1969—. Chmn. Ore. Republican Com., mem. for Ore., Rep. Nat. Com., 1966-67; chmn. Clackamas County (Ore.) Rep. Party, 1965-66; alternate del. Rep. Nat. Conv., 1968. Bd. dirs. Easter Seal Soc. Ore., Delauney Inst. Mental Health, 1968-70; bd. dirs., mem. exec. com. United Fund. Club: Harvard of Oregon. Home: 2825 Dellwood Dr Lake Oswego OR 97034 Office: PO Box 3621 Portland OR 97208

HODES, ARTHUR WILLIAM, musician; b. Nikoliev, Russia, Nov. 14, 1904; s. William and Dora Hodes; came to U.S., 1906, naturalized, 1916; student pub. schs., Chgo.; m. Thelma Johnson, Feb. 14, 1938; children—Janet (Mrs. Bruce Gordley), Bob, Karen, Dan, Margaret. Recorded for Vocalion Records, 1929, Mercury Records, 1958-60, Delmar, Liberty; with Benny Goodman in jam sessions, N.Y.C., 1938-50; concerts at Carnegie Hall, 1946-47, Yale, Harvard, Pa. State U., 1947- 49; pub. Jazz Record mag., 1943-47; writer Downbeat mag., 1960—; appearances at Bourbon Street Club, Jazz, Ltd., Chgo., 1956—; tchr. art Park Forest (Ill.) Conservatory, 1958—; lectr. concerts to high schs., Parons Coll., U. Minn., Ohio Wesleyan U., 1962-63; active Chgo. Jazz Inst.; writer Park Forest Reporter, 1962—; band leader, 1940—. Mem. A.S.C.A.P. Address: 232 Berry St Park Forest IL 60466

HODES, BARNET lawyer; b. La Salle, Ill., May 13, 1900; s. Simon and Ruth (Mansfield) H.; J.D., Northwestern U., 1921; m. Eleanor Cramer, Apr. 23, 1936; children—Scott, Kay Lynn. Began legal practice in Chgo., 1921; asst. corp. counsel City Chgo., 1923-37; pvt. practice, 1927-33; alderman 7th Ward, 1931-33; mem. Ill. Tax Commn., 1933-35; corp. counsel of Chgo., 1935-47. Pres. Nat. Inst. Municipal Law Officers, 1944; chmn. Chgo.'s Redevel. Commn., 1942-45; vice chmn. Chgo. Archtl. Landmarks Comm.; mem. U.S. Civilian Def. Vol. Participation Com.; sec.-treas. Triopian Found., Cassandra Found.; pres. Patriotic Found. Chgo.; impartial arbitrator Ladies Dress Industry. Active participant in numerous Chgo. city activities such as memls., fund drives, Christmas benefits, civilian def., planning commns.; also at state level on interfaith coms., and other civic activities Mem. bd. govs. Louis A. Weiss Meml. Hosp., Mus. Contemporary Art, Chgo. Served to lt. comdr. USNR, 1944-47. Decorated cross chevalier Legion of Honor (France); recipient Civic Merit award Jr. Assn. Commerce, Chgo., 1934; Chgo. Civil Liberties Com. award for distinguished service in def. of democracy, 1939; Decalogue Soc. of Lawyers award of merit for distinguished services, 1941. Mem. Am., Ill., Chgo. bar assns., Delta Sigma Rho, Nu Beta Epsilon (founder), and other assns. and orgns. Democrat. Mason, Elk.

Clubs: Standard, Quadrangle, Arts (Chgo.). Author three books. Home: 5555 Everett Av Chicago IL 60637 Office: One N La Salle St Chicago IL 60602 ☆

HODES, HORACE LOUIS, physician, educator; b. Phila., Dec. 21, 1907; s. Morris and Anna (Jacobson) H.; A.B., U. Pa., 1927, M.D., 1931; m. Anne E. Reber, June 10, 1931; children—Ruth Anne, David Samuel. Intern, asst. resident Children's Hosp., Phila., 1931-33, chief resident, 1934-35; asst. resident pediatrics Johns Hopkins Hosp., 1933-34, dir. pediatric dispensary, 1935-36; asst. pathology and bacteriology Rockefeller Inst. Med. Research, 1936-38; lectr. epedemiology, sch. hygiene Johns Hopkins, 1938-49, asst. prof. pediatrics, 1938-45, asso. prof., 1945-49; dir. Sydenham Hosp., Balt., 1938-49; dir. med. research Balt. Health Dept., 1938-49; dir. pediatrics dept. Mt. Sinai Hosp., N.Y.C., 1949—; clin. prof. pediatrics, Columbia, 1949—; prof., chmn. dept. pediatrics Mt. Sinai Med. Sch., 1964—. Adv. council N.Y. Pub. Health Research Inst.; med. adv. bd. Hebrew U. Mem. commn. control measles and mumps, U.S. Army, 1940-42; cons. sec. of war. Served as lt. comdr. USNR, 1942-46; officer charge virus lab., Guam. Mem. Am. Pediatric Soc., Soc. Pediatric Research (pres. 1951-52), Am. Acad. Pediatrics (Mead-Johnson award 1946), Soc. Explt. Biology and Medicine, N.Y. Acad. Scis., N.Y. Acad. Medicine, Pediatric Travel Club. Co-author: Common Contagious Diseases, 1956. Editorial bd. Pediatrics. Contbr. profl. jours. Home: 41 Sutton Crest Manhasset NY 11030 Office: Mount Sinai Hosp 11 E 100th St New York City NY 10029

HODES, MARION EDWARD, physician, educator; b. N.Y.C., Aug. 6, 1925; s. Louis and Esterre (Berman) H.; student Cornell U., 1941-43, U. Rochester, 1943-44; M.D., U. Buffalo, 1947; Ph.D., Columbia, 1955; m. Halina Zora Markowicz, Nov. 23, 1949; children—Marquis Z., Zachary I., Jonathan E., Abigail J. Intern, Jewish Hosp., Bklyn., 1947-48; officer-in-charge dept. physiol. chemistry U.S. Naval Med. Sch., 1951-52; resident Goldwater Meml. Hosp., N.Y.C., 1955-56; faculty Ind. U. Sch. Medicine, Indpls., 1956—, prof. medicine and biochemistry, 1966—. Cons. Eli Lily & Co., 1958-62; med. cons. City of Hope Med. Center. Served with USNR, 1943-45, 50-52. Eleanor Roosevelt fellow, 1962-63; Guggenheim fellow, 1969-70; Leukemia Soc. scholar, 1961-66. Mem. A.A.A.S., Am. Assn. Cancer Research, Am. Soc. Biol. Chemists, Am. Assm. Clin. Chemists, Am. Chem. Soc., Am. Fedn. Clin. Research, Sigma Xi. Home: 648 Edgemere Dr Indianapolis IN 46260 Office: 1100 W Michigan St Indianapolis IN 46202

HODES, PHILIP JACOB, physician, educator; b. N.Y.C., Apr. 15, 1906; s. Jacob and Rose (Cohen) H.; B.S., U. Pa., 1928, M.D., 1931, D. Sc. in Radiology, 1940; children— Barton Lyle, Maisie. Research asst. Pa. Hosp., 1929-31; intern, then fellow radiology Hosp. U. Pa., 1931-35; mem. faculty U. Pa. Grad. Sch. Medicine, 1935-59, prof. radiology, 1949-59; mem. faculty U. Pa. Med. Sch., 1935-59, prof. radiology, 1949-59; prof. radiology, head dept. Jefferson Med. Coll., Phila., 1958—; attending radiologist Jefferson Med. Coll. Hosp., 1958—; cons., lectr. Armed Forces Inst. Pathology, 1949-62, Walter Reed Army Hosp., 1949-62, U.S. Naval Hosp., Phila., 1949—; chief cons. VA area III, 1949-62; cons. VA Hosp., Phila., 1949—, VA Hosp., Wilmington, Del., 1949—, VA Hosp., E. Orange, N.J., 1949—, Jeanes Hosp., Phila., 1952-58; vis. guest lectr. U. Minn., 1954; Russell Carmen hon. lectr. Minn. Med. Soc., 1954; vis. prof. U. P.R., 1955; Marmal lectr. Caracas, Venezuela, 1955; Russell Carmen hon. lectr. Med. Soc. St. Louis, 1956; Riley lectr. Pa. Radiol. Soc., 1956; vis. guest lectr. Kan. U., 1957; vis. prof. Louisville Coll. Medicine, 1960, U. Cal. at San Francisco, 1962, Western Res. U., 1966; Leo Rigler lectr., Israel, 1963. Disaster chmn. Phila. A.R.C., 1952-55; sec. 5th Inter-Am. Congress Radiology, 1955, chmn. Am. delegation, Lima, Peru, 1958; chmn. editorial commn. Acta Radiologica Inter-Am., 1961—; mem. adv. bd. history radiology World War II, Hist. Unit, U.S. Army Med. Service, 1961. Trustee Phila. B'nai B'rith, 1952-60, Hillel Found. at U. Pa., 1952-60; trustee, Am. Cancer Soc., 1959—, pres. Phila. div., 1969- 70; trustee Main Line Reform Temple, Phila., 1960- 62, Phila. Chamber Orch., 1962—, Long Beach Is. Found. Arts and Scis., 1962—. Served to col., M.C., AUS, 1941-46; CBI. Recipient gold medal Inter-Am. Coll. Radiology, 1968, Gold medal Am. Coll. Radiology, 1969. Diplomate Am. Bd. Radiology. Fellow Am. Coll. Radiology (chancellor 1957-61, v.p. 1961—), Phila. Coll. Physicians; mem. N.Am. Radiol. Soc. (v.p. 1959), Am. (v.p. 1955), Phila. (pres. 1948; Meml. lectr.) Roentgen ray socs., A.M.A., Pa., Phila. County med. socs., Pa. Radiol. Soc. Sect. editor Ency. Medicine, 1939; asso. editor Penrose Cancer Seminar, 1953; guest editor Radiol. Clinics N. Am. 1st vol., 1964; contbg. editor: (with Dr. Harry Bockus) Gastroenterology, Vol. III, 1964; (with Dr. E. P. Pendergas) Head and Neck in Roentgen Diagnosis, vols. I and II, 1956; (with Dr. Jack Edeiken) The Roentgen Diagnosis of Diseases of the Bone, 1966. Editor-in- chief Atlas of Tumor Radiology, 1966. Home: Penn Towers Apt Philadelphia PA 19103 Office: Jefferson Med Coll Hosp Philadelphia PA 19107

HODES, SCOTT, lawyer; b. Chgo., Aug. 14, 1937; s. Barnet and Eleanor (Cramer) H.; A.B., U. Chgo., 1956; J.D., U. Mich., 1959; LL.M., Northwestern U., 1962; m. Barbara P. Zisook, Dec. 19, 1961; children—Brian Kenneth, Valery Jane. Admitted to Ill. bar, 1959, D.C. bar, 1962; partner firm Arvey, Hodes & Mantynband, Chgo., 1961—. Dir. First Investors Life Ins. Co. N.Y., Chicken Unlimited Enterprises, Inc. All Am. Bank Chgo., Birmingham TV Corp. Chmn. Philippine Exchange Nurses award com., 1966; nat. chmn. Lawbooks U.S.A., 1962—; co-chmn. Chgo. World Friendship Day, 1967. Sec. Citizens for Re-election of Sen. Paul H. Douglas, 1966; Dem. state central committeeman, 1970—. Bd. dirs. Tourism Council Greater Chgo., Michael Reese Hosp. Research Inst., Found. of Fed. Bar Assn. Served to capt. AUS, 1962-64. Decorated Army Commendation medal; named one of Chicago's ten outstanding young men Jr. Assn. Commerce and Industry, 1968. Mem. Am., Fed. (chmn. council financing 1966—, chmn. younger lawyers div. 1963-64, nat. council 1965—), Ill., Chgo. bar assns., Chgo. Art Inst. (life), Chgo. Hist. Soc. (life), Judge Adv. Gen.'s Assn. (life) Zeta Beta Tau, Tau Epsilon Rho. Jewish religion (dir. temple). Clubs: Standard, Economic, Union League (Chgo.). Author: The Law of Art and Antiques, 1966. Asso. news editor Fed. Bar News; co-editor Conf. Mut. Funds., 1966. Contbr. articles profl. jours. Home: 1242 Lake Shore Dr Chicago IL 60610 Office: 1 N LaSalle St Chicago IL 60602

HODGDON, ALBION REED, educator, botanist; b. Boothbay, Me., Nov. 1, 1909; s. Lewis Percival and Laura (Hodgdon) H.; B.S., U. N.H., 1930, M.S., 1932; Ph.D., Harvard, 1936; m. Audrey MacKown, Aug. 11, 1940; children—Alan Lewis, Anthony Jason, Ariel Josephine. Plant collecting trips for Harvard, Cuba, Va., Fla., Ky., 1936-40, ind. collecting, Mexico, 1938; head bot. dept. N.H. Agrl. Expt. Sta., 1941-67; curator U. N.H. Herbarium, 1941—; head bot. dept. U. N.H., 1941-67, asso. prof., 1941-49, prof., 1949—; ecol. work for Boston U. in N. Alaska, 1952. Fellow A.A.A.S.; mem. N.H. Acad. Sci. (sec. 1942-46, pres. 1952-53), New Eng. Bot. Club, Soc. Plant taxonomists, Soc. Study Evolution, Sigma Xi. Author: Taxonomic Study of the Genus Lechea, 1938; (with Frederic Steele) Woody Plants of New Hampshire, 1958, Trees and Shrubs of Northern New England, 1968; (with R. Pike) Flora of Wolf Islands, N.B., 1963, Flora of Bird Islands on the Gulf of Maine, 1969; Rubus Subgenus Eubatus (blackberries) in New England, 1966. Editor Taxonomic Jour. Rhodora, 1962—. Home: RD Box 97 East Barrington NH 03825

HODGDON, FREDERICK, architect; b. Boston, Jan. 20, 1894; s. Charles and Emaline (Mendum) H.; student Chgo. Art Inst., 1911-15; European scholarhip in architecture, Eng., France, Italy, 1920-22; student archtl. design with Howard Van Doren Shaw, 1915-17, Shepley, Rutan & Coolidge, 1917-26; m. Violet M. Harvey, Nov. 2, 1914; children—Frederick, Raymond A. Pvt. practice, Chgo., 1926-43, Los Angeles and Newport Beach, Cal., 1943—; partner Coolidge & Hodgdon, Chgo., 1926-30; asso. architect Jane Adams and Trumbull Park Housing Projects, Chgo.; works include: Highland Park (Ill.) City Hall, Temple Sholem (Chgo.), 1938, 1st Presbyn. Ch. (Clinton, Ia.; 2d prize prize Nat. Ch. Competition), 1930, U. Chgo. Med. Sch., 1932, Wilshire Presbyn. Ch. (Santa Ana, Cal.; commn. by competition), 1954, Collins Island (Newport Harbor), 1955, 1st Evang. Brethren Ch. (Santa Ana; 1st prize Ch. Archtl. Guild and Nat. Council Chs.), 1956, Newport Heights Elementary Sch., 1956, Episcipal Ch. St. John the Divine (Costa Mesa, Cal.), 1957, 1st Presbyn. Ch. (Orange, Cal.), 1957, First Ch. of God (Fresno, Cal.), 1959, Mariners Sch., 1959, Abraham Lincoln Jr. High Sch., 1961 (both at Newport Beach, Cal.), Calvary Ch., Santa Ana, Cal., Magnolia Bapt. Ch., Anaheim, Cal., South Bay Christian Ch., Redondo Beach, Cal., Good Shepherd Presbyn. Ch., Los Alamitos, Cal., Wilshire Presbyn. Ch., Santa Ana, Northminster Presbyn. Ch., Diamond Bar, Cal. Mem. A.I.A., Cal. Council of Architects, Ch. Archtl. Guild Am., Chgo. Art Inst. (life), Newport Harbor C. of C. Clubs: Balboa Yacht (Newport Beach); Architectural (pres. 1923) (Chgo.). Home: 234 A Calle Aragon Laguna Hills CA 92653 Office: 400 West Coast Hwy Newport Beach CA 92663

HODGDON, HERBERT JAMES, savs. and loan assn. exec.; b. New Bedford, Mass., Mar. 6, 1924; s. Herbert James and Edna M. (Niles) H.; student Occidental Coll., 1946, U. Cin., 1943-44, Ind. U., 1943; m. Carol Jane Murphy, Feb. 12, 1944; 1 dau., Janis Elizabeth. With Security First Nat. Bank Los Angeles, 1946, Bank of Ceres (Cal.), 1946-51; with Stanislaus-Merced (Cal.) Savs. and Loan Assn., 1951-63, exec. v.p., 1962-63, merged with State Savs. & Loan Assn., Stockton, Cal., 1963, pres., 1964—; pres. First Channel Corp., Stockton, 1962—, Norco Service Co., Los Angeles, 1966; pres. Budget Industries, Inc., Budget Finance Plan; dir. Century Bank, Los Angeles, Padre Island Investment Corp., Corpus Christi, Tex. Past mem. citizens adv. com. city Merced; past chmn. Merced County March of Dimes; active local chpts. Am. Cancer Soc., United Givers; pres. Stockton Jr. Achievement, 1966, bd. dirs. Western region, 1966—, also nat. bd. dirs.; Past chmn. Merced County Republican Central Com. Served with inf. AUS, 1942- 45. ETO Mem. U.S., Cal. (bd. dirs., vice chmn. govtl. relations com.) savs. and loan leagues, Cal. (exec. com. San Joaquin Valley council), Stockton chambers commerce, Am. Mgmt. Assn., President's Assn., Merced Pilots Assn. (past pres.), Am. Legion. Clubs: Commonwealth (San Francisco); Commercial Exchange, Yosemite, Delta Yacht (sec.-treas. 1966, vice commodore 1967) (Stockton). Home: 24921 Kit Carson Rd Hidden Hills CA 91302 Office: 6434 Wilshire Blvd Los Angeles CA 90048

HODGE, BLANCHE MOORE, church woman; b. Arkansas City, Kan.; d. William S. and Susan Isabelle (Northern) Moore; student Va. Intermost Jr. Coll., Bristol, Va., 1922- 23, Western Bapt. Theol. Sem., Portland, Ore., 1929-31, Reed Coll., Portland, 1947; L.H.D., Linfield Coll., 1958; m. Maurice B. Hodge, Feb. 17, 1923. Pres., Ore. Bapt. Conv., 1947-48; state dir. Baptist Girls Work, 1931-42; dir. Woman's Am. Bapt. Fgn. Mission Soc., 1941-51; pres. Nat. Council Am. Bapt. Women, 1951-55; exec com. Bapt. World Alliance, 1955-70, sec. women's dept., 1960-65; pres. N.A. Bapt. Women's Union, 1955- 61; pres. Am. Bapt. Conv., 1958-59, mem. gen. council, 1960-63; chmn. editorial com. Crusader, 1955-63; exec. com. United Ch. Women, 1951-55; bd. Nat. Council Chs., 1955-58, 63-66, exec. com., 1965; bd. mgrs. Ore. Bapt. Conv., 1963—, exec. com., 1966—; study com. Berkeley Bapt. Div. Sch.; officer United Ch. Women Ore.; pres. Portland Council Chs.; del. World Council Chs. TRustee Linfield Coll.; bd. regents Berkeley Bapt. Div. Sch.; chmn. Urban Tng. and Research Center. Named woman of achievement Portland chpt. Theta Sigma Phi, 1958; woman of accomplishment, Ore. Jour., 1969. Home: 5605 SW Edgemont Pl Portland OR 97201

HODGE, CHARLES JOSEPH, investment banker; b. Washington, Aug. 30, 1907; s. Howard Bailey and Elizabeth (Skelley) H.; student Fgn. Service Sch., Georgetown U., 1928- 29, N.Y.U., 1939; m. Marie Louise Renton, Nov. 18, 1937; children— Charles Joseph, Marie Louise, Patricia Renton, James Howard. Chmn. exec. com. Glore Forgan, William R. Staats, Inc., N.Y.C.; v.p., dir. Tropical Gas Co., Inc.; mem. bd. dirs. Hudson Leasing Co., Del. & Bound Brook R. R. Co., Inc., Gt. S.W. Corp. Chmn. bd. trustees New St. Barnabas Med. Center, Short Hills, N.J. Mem. N.J. N.G., 1940-41, 45-55; served to brig. gen., cav., AUS, 1941-45. Decorated Bronze Star, Croix de Guerre (twice) with gold star, Medaille Militaire Volontaire (France). Mem. Investment Bankers Assn. (chmn. membership com.). Republican. Clubs: Down Town Assn., Links (N.Y.C.); Short Hills; Gulf Stream Golf (Fla.); Baltusrol Golf (Springfield, N.J.). Home: 18 Madison Terrace Short Hills NJ 07078 Office: Glore Forgan William R Staats Inc 45 Wall St New York City NY 10005

HODGE, EDWIN, Jr., mfg. exec.; b. Henderson, Ky., Aug. 26, 1890; s. Edwin and Frances A. (Ditto) H.; B.S., Va. Mil. Inst., Lexington, 1910; LL.D., Thiel Coll., 1951, Washington and Jefferson Coll., 1962; m. Emma L. Clyde, June 10, 1915; children—Mrs. Margaret Dauler, Mrs. Frances Gordon, Mrs. Emma Sarosday. Chmn. bd., pres. Pitts. Forgings Co., Greenveille Steel Car Co.; dir., mem. exec. com. P. & L. E. R. R.; chmn., dir. Neville Chem. Co.; dir. Neville Cindu Chemie N.V., Uithoorn, Holland. Mem., chmn. Greater Pitts. Airport Adv. Com. Bd. dirs., mem. exec. com. Children's Hosp. Pitts.; trustee, mem. exec. com. Thiel Coll.; trustee Found. Ind. Colls., Episcopal Diocese of Pitts. Pres. Am. Ry. Car Int., 1943-45, Drop Forging Assn., 1942-44. Episcopalian. Mason. Clubs: Pittsburgh, Pittsburgh Athletic Assn., Duquesne Fox Chapel Golf (Pitts.); Laurel Valley Golf Rolling Rock (Ligonier, Pa.); Hole-in-the-Wall Golf (Naples, Fla.); Sky (N.Y.C.); Detroit. Home: R D 2 Ligonier PA 15658 Office: 401 Liberty Av Pittsburgh PA 15222

HODGE, HAROLD CARPENTER, educator; b. Chgo., Dec. 19, 1904; s. James Alexander and Angie (Carpenter) H.; B.S., Ill. Wesleyan U., 1925, D. Sc., 1949; M.S., State U. Ia., 1927, Ph. D., 1930; D. Sc. (hon.), Case Western Res. U., 1967; m. Katherine Talbot, Nov. 9, 1928; children—Archibald T., Margaret. Asst. prof. chemistry Coll. of Pacific, 1929-30; prof. chemistry Ottawa (Kan.) U., 1930-31; Rockefeller fellow dentistry U. Rochester Sch. Medicine and Dentistry, 1931-33, sr. fellow, 1933-36, asst. prof. dentistry, 1936-37, asst. prof. biochemistry and pharmacology, 1937-40, asso. prof., 1940-46, prof. pharmacology and toxicology, 1946-58, cons. dental research, 1940-67, prof. pharmacology, chmn., 1958-70, prof. radiation biology, 1958-68, prof. dental research, 1967-70, chief pharmacologist Atomic Energy Project, 1943-58, Bikini Tests, 1946; prof. pharmacology U. Cal. at San Francisco, 1970—. Cons. USPHS, 1942-44, mem. dental research study sect. grants-in-aid, 1946-47, mem. pharmacology tng. com. 1961-65; chmn. tech. adv. com. fluoridation water supplies N.Y. State Dept. Health, 1944-57; mem. com. to visit Harvard Med. Sch., Sch. Dental Medicine, 1944-57; adv. council Army Chem. Corps, 1947-52; mem. Nat. Adv. Dental Research Council, 1948-52, 57-58; dept. medicine and surgery VA, 1948-52; mem. NRC, 1949-58, chmn. subcom. biochemistry, com. of dentistry, 1951-54, chmn. com. on toxicology, div. chemistry and chem. tech., 1951-58, exec. com. Chem. Biol. Coord. Center, 1951-52; civilian panel med. scis. Dept. Def., 1954-62; mem. U.S. nat. com. Internat. Union Pure and Applied Chemistry, 1954-57; expert adv. panel on dental health WHO, 1956—, Dept. Health, Edn. and Welfare Environmental Protection Agy., Nat. Air Pollution Control Adv. Council, 1970—. Trustee Ill. Wesleyan U., 1960—; vis. prof. St. Mary's Hosp. Med. Sch., London, 1962, U. Cal. at San Francisco, 1963. Fellow Am. Coll. Dentists, Am. Dental Assn. (hon.), Royal Soc. Med. (London); mem. Soc. Toxicology (pres. 1961-62, council 1962—), Am. Chem. Soc. (vice chmn. Rochester sect. 1940, chmn. 1941, councillor 1944-49), Am. Soc. Biol. Chemists, Soc. Explt. Biology and Medicine (sec. Western N.Y. sect. 1939-42, membership com. 1945-48, chmn. 1947-48), Am. Soc. Pharmacology and Exptl. Therapeutics (pres. 1966-67), N.Y., Kan., Rochester (editorial bd. 1949-70), acads. scis., Internat. Assn. Dental Research (pres. 1947, trustee 1949-57), A.A.A.S., Am. Indsl. Hygiene Assn., Am. Assn. U. Profs., N.Y. State Soc. Med. Research (pres. 1960-61), Am. Assn. Med. Colls., Assn. Med. Sch. Pharmacologists (pres. 1968-70), Western Pharm. Soc., Sigma Xi, Alpha Chi Sigma, Pi Kappa Delta, Alpha Omega Alpha. Republican. Unitarian. Author: (with Marion Gleason, B.E. Gosselin and Roger P. Smith) Clinical Toxicology of Commercial Products; (with Frank A. Smith and Philip S. Chen) Biological Effects of Organic Fluorides; (with Frank A. Smith) Biological Effects of Inorganic Fluorides. Editor (with Carl Voegtlin) Pharmacology and Toxicology of Uranium Compounds. Mem. editorial bd. Jour. Pharm. Exptl. Therapeutics, 1957-65, Jour. Dental Research, 1957-60, Annals of Occupational Hygiene, 1958-60; Jour. Toxicology Applied Pharmacology, 1960-65, Archives Internationales de Pharmacodynamics 1962—, Ann. Rev. Pharmacology, 1965-69. Author articles. Home: Box 5812 Carmel CA 93921 Office: University of Cal at San Francisco San Francisco CA 94122

HODGE, HARRY, canning co. exec.; b. Jersey City, June 11, 1905; s. Charles and Augusta (Ackerman) H.; B.C.S., N.Y.U., 1932; m. Dolores Joan Luther, Dec. 17, 1959; children—Beryl Jean (Mrs. Donald Zipoy), Kenneth Brownlee, James David, Starr Allison, Stacey Lynne. Practice as pub. accountant N.Y. and N.J., 1923-39; auditor Talon, Inc., 1939-40; controller U.S. Steel Corp., subsidiary, 1940-45, Sealed Power Corp., 1945-48; asst. to pres., dir. Allen B. Wrisley Co., 1948-52; controller Am. Woolen Co., 1952-54; v.p., dir. Pocono Co., 1952-54; controller Pillsbury Co., 1954-60; controller Green Giant Co., Le Sueur, Minn., from 1960, v.p., 1962-68; dir. Com-Share, Inc., Asso. Wild Rice Co., Brick Ch. Bldg. & Loan Assn., Lackawanna Bldg. & Loan Assn., Rainy Day Bldg. & Loan Assn., Elmwood Bldg. & Loan Assn., Montclair Bldg. & Loan Assn., Fed. Home Loan Bank N.Y., Hinsdale Fed. Savs. & Loan Assn., Dawn Fresh Mushroom Co., Green Giant Co., Wettergren Dairy Co., Dulany Foods, Inc., Erickson Industries, Inc. C.P. A., Ill., Mich., N.J., Minn. Mem. A.I.M., Am. Inst. C.P.A.'s, Financial Execs. Inst., Mich. Soc. C.P.A.'s. Home: 3431 E Surrey Dr Saline MI 48176 Office: Com-Share Inc P O Box 1588 Ann Arbor MI 48106

HODGE, JAMES, Jr., lawyer; b. Toledo, Feb. 8, 1906; s. James and Grace (Hallaran) H.; A.B., Williams Coll., 1928; LL.B., Harvard, 1931; m. Elizabeth Kountz, Feb. 11, 1950. Admitted to Ohio bar, 1931, since practiced in Toledo; partner firm Fuller, Seney, Henry & Hodge, and predecessors, 1941—. Served with USAAF, 1943-45. Mem. Am., Ohio, Toledo bar assns., Phi Beta Kappa, Delta Phi. Conglist. (chmn. trustees 1963-64). Clubs: Toledo Country, Toldeo. Home: 3843 Brookside Rd Ottawa Hills Toledo OH 43606 Office: 300 Madison Av Toledo OH 43604

HODGE, JAMES CAMPBELL, engring., mfg. exec.; b. Falkirk, Scotland, Sept. 3, 1902; s. James and Anne (Campbell) H.; came to U.S., 1916, naturalized, 1941; B.S., Case Sch. Applied Sci., 1923; D.Sc., Harvard, 1933; D.Eng., Fenn coll., 1965; D. Eng., Cleve. State U., 1968; m. Emma C. Meinke, June 12, 1926; children—Jean Elizabeth (Mrs. Harold C. Colley), Carol Anne (Mrs. Donald L. Poe), Emily Jane (Mrs. Philip H. Brasfield). A cons. metallurgist Bennett & Christensen, Cleve., 1923-27; metallurgist Babcock & Wilcox Co., Barberton, O., 1927-32, chief metallurgist, 1932-40; v.p., dir. Wellman Engring. Co., Cleve., 1940-44, exec. v.p., dir., 1944-54, pres., dir., 1954-55; v.p. Warner & Swasey Co., Cleve., 1956, exec. v.p., dir., 1956-62, pres., dir., 1962-69, chmn. bd., dir., 1969—; dir. Brown Industries; dir. Sterling Foundry Co.; v.p., dir. Wyandot Castings Co.; dir. Lake Shore, Inc., Midwest Machine & Tool Co., Union Commerce Bank, Union Commerce Corp., Warner Swasey Asquith, Ltd., Halifax, Eng., Wang Lab., Inc., Warner & Swasey Financial Corp., Cooper Industries, Inc.; chmn. bd., dir. Digital Gen. Corp. Trustee Case Inst. Tech., 1964-67, of Case Western Res. U., Fenn Coll., 1952-65, Cleve. Community Fund, 1964-68, Univ. Circle Research Center Corp.; vice chmn. bd. trustees Fenn Ednl. Found.; mem. bd. govs. Asso. Industries Cleve. 1965-71, v.p., 1967-68, pres., 1970-71; bd. govs. Western Res. U., 1965-67; chmn. Greater Cleve. adv. bd. Salvation Army, 1955-57; mem. exec. bd. Greater Cleve. council Boy Scouts Am.; vice chmn. bd. trustees John Carroll U. Corp. mem. bd. dirs. Greater Cleveland Growth Assn., 1968—; mem. adv. bd. lay trustees John Carroll U., 1968-69. Recipient Hon. Alumnus Membership award Cleve. State U., 1966, Pres.'s Achievement award Case Inst. Tech., 1966, Silver Knight award as Mgmt. Man of Year, Mgmt. Club of Greater Cleve., 1967, Alumni citation Case Western Res. U., 1968, Gold Medal award Case Alumni Assn., 1968, Distinguished Service award Cleve. Tech. Socs. Council, 1970. Mem. Am. Inst. Mining and Metall. Engrs., Am. Soc. Naval Engrs., Eastern States Blast Furnace and Coke Oven Assn., N.A.M. state dir. 1966-68), Machinery and Allied Products Inst. (exec. com.), Am. Soc. Metals (Sauveur Meml. lectr. Cambridge 1954), Am. Soc. Testing Materials, Am. Welding Soc., Assn. Iron and Steel Engrs., Profl. Engrs. Soc., Cleve. Engring. Soc. (past bd. govs.), Cleve. Astron. Soc., Am. Ordnance Assn. (pres. dir.), U.S. C. of C. (mem. policy com. 1966-67), Newcomen Soc., Sigma Alpha Epsilon, Tau Beta Pi. Clubs: Akron City; Pepper Pike, Skating, Union, Hillbrook (Cleve.). Home: 2004 S Belvoir Blvd South Euclid Cleveland OH 44121 Office: 11000 Cedar Av Cleveland OH 44106

HODGE, JOHN DENNIS, govt. ofcl.; b. Leigh-On-Sea, Essex, Eng., Feb. 10, 1929; s. John Charles Henry and Emily (Corbett) H.; B.S. in Engring. with 1st class honours, U. London (Eng.), 1949; D.Sc., City U., London, 1966; m. Audrey Cox, Apr. 5, 1952; children— Robert John, Janice Margaret, Nicola Ann, Jonathan Andrew. Came to U.S., 1959, naturalized, 1964. Aerodynamicist, Vickers-Armstrongs Ltd., Waybridge, Eng., 1949-52; part-time lectr. Twickenham Tech. Coll., Middlesex, Eng., 1949-52; tech design coordinator AVRO Aircraft, Ltd., Toronto, Can., 1952-58, project engr., 1958-59; chief flight control div. NASA, Manned Space Craft, Langley Field, Va. and Houston, 1959-68, mgr. Advanced Missions Program Office, Houston, 1968-70; dir. transp. systems concepts Transp. Systems Center, Cambridge, Mass., 1970—; devel. flight control operations documentation for tng. flight controllers and real time fight control projects Gemini and Apollo. Recipient Quality award NASA, 1963, Sustained Superior Performance award, 1964, NASA Group Achievement award Mercury Program, 1962, Gemini Program, 1967, Apollo Program, 1969, Arthur S. Fleming award,

1968, NASA medal for exceptional service, 1967, 69. Home: 34 Revere St Lexington MA 02173 Office: Transp System Center 55 Broadway Cambridge MA 02142

HODGE, WILLIAM VALLANCE DOUGLAS, mathematician; b. Edinburgh, June 17, 1903; s. Archibald James and Janet (Vallance) H.; student George Watson's Coll., Edinburgh, 1909-20; M.A., Edinburgh U., 1923, LL.D., 1958; B.A., St. John's Coll., Cambridge, 1925, M.A., 1930, Sc.D., 1950; D.SC., Bristol U., 1956, Leicester U., 1959, Sheffield U., 1960, Exeter U., Liverpool U., U. Wales, 1961; m. Kathleen Cameron, 1929; children—Michael Robert, Gillian Janet. Lectr. U. Bristol, 1926-31; univ. lectr. Cambridge U., 1933-36, Lowndean prof. astronomy and geometry Cambridge, 1936-70; fellow St. John's Coll., Cambridge, 1930-33, Pembroke Coll., Cambridge, 1935-58, master Pembroke Coll., 1958-70. Knighted, 1959. Recipient of the Berwick prize, de Morgan medal London Math. Soc., Royal medal Royal Soc., 1957. Fellow Royal Soc. (sec. 1957-65), Royal Soc. Edinburgh (Gunning Victoria Jubilee medal 1968); mem. Royal Danish Acad., Am. Philos. Soc. (fgn. mem.), Am. Acad. Arts and Scis., U.S. Acad. Scis. Author: Harmonic Integrals, 1941. Co-author: Methods of Algebraic Geometry, 1947-56. Home: 13 Amhurst Ct Grange Rd Cambridge England

HODGELL, MURLIN RAY, univ. dean; b. Mankato, Kan., Jan. 6, 1924; s. Ray Darius and Lora Henrietta (Overman) H.; B.S., Kan. State U., 1949; M.S., U. Ill., 1952; M.R.P., Cornell U., 1956, Ph.D., 1959; m. Billie RoJean Seward, July 20, 1947; children—Janet, Kristen, Kevin. Prof. U. Ill., 1950-54, Kan. State U., 1957-63; chmn. dept. city and regional planning Rutgers U., 1963-64; dir. Sch. of Architecture of U. Neb., 1964-69; dean Coll. Environmental Design of U. Okla., 1969—; prin. Hodgell Assos. in Architecture, Engring. and Planning. City planning dir., Manhattan, Kan., 1957-58, planning commr., 1959-63; dir. Kan. State U. Center Community Devel., 1959-63. Trustee Weigal Found., Leonard Bailey Found. Served to lt. (j.g.) USNR, 1943-45. Named Kan. Outstanding Young Man of Year, Kan. Jr. C. of C., 1959, Man of Year, Manhattan, Kan., 1960; recipient citation distinguished community service Lane-Bryant Found., 1960. Fellow Am. Soc. C.E.; mem. Am. Inst. Planners, A.I.A., Am. Soc. Planning Ofcls., Assn. Collegiate Schs. Architecture, Asso. Schs. Constrn. Licensed architect, engr. and planner. Author: Contemporary Farmhouses, 1956; Forgotten Millions, 1959; Zoning, 1957. Home: 712 W Linsday St Norman OK 73069

HODGERS, ROBERT WILLIAM, Jr., bus. devel. corp. exec.; b. W. Terre Haute, Ind., Sept. 25, 1921; s. Robert William and Ethel (Clare) H.; B.S. in Elec. Engring. (Hemingway Gold medal), Rose Poly. Inst., 1943; m. Ellen Louise Roush, Nov. 8, 1942; children—Linda, Darla, Richard, Carole. With Gen. Electric Co., 1943-64, mgr. engring., Milw., 1960-64; v.p. planning and engring. operation Western Union, 1964-70; pres., chief exec. officer, dir. Nat. Bus. Corp., Franklin Lakes, N.J., 1970—. Mem. I.E.E.E., Tau Beta Pi. Home: 879 Scioto Dr Franklin Lakes NJ 07417 Office: 808 High Mountain Rd Franklin Lakes NJ 07417

HODGES, CHARLES EDWARD, ins. exec.; b. Brookline, Mass., Nov. 20, 1897; s. Charles E. and Mary E. (O'Neil) H.; student Harvard, 1919; m. Gladys Fox, Mar 3, 1923; children—Charles Charles Edward, Russell Fox, Pres. Am. Mut. Liability Ins. Co., 1935-64, chmn. bd., 1964-69, hon. chmn. and dir., 1969—; pres. Am. Mut. Ins. Co. of Boston, 1937-65, chmn., 1965-69, hon. chmn. and dir., 1969—; pres. Am. Policyholders Ins. Co., 1937-65, chmn., 1965-69, hon. chmn. and dir., 1969—; chmn., dir. A M Life Ins. Co., 1964-69, hon. chmn. and dir., 1969—; adv dir. State Street Bank & Trust Co. Club: Somerset. Office: Wakefield MA 10466

HODGES, CLARENCE VERNARD, surgeon; b. Terry, S.D., Nov. 11, 1914; B.S., Ia. State Coll., 1937; M.D., U. Chgo., 1940. Research fellow in surgery U. Chgo. Clinics, 1940- 41, intern, 1941-42, resident in urol. surgery, 1945-46; instr. Hopkins Hosp., 1947-48; asso. prof. urology U. Ore. Med. Sch., 1948-58, prof. surgery, 1958—, head div. urology, 1948—. Research on prostatic and bladder carcinoma, lower nephron nephrosis; used stibestrol in treatment of metastatic carcinoma of prostate (with C. Huggins), 1941. Office: U Ore Med Sch Portland OR 97201

HODGES, DONALD CLARK, educator; b. Fort Worth, Oct. 22, 1923; s. Count Hal and Elinor (Clark) H.; B.A. summa cum laude, N.Y. U., 1947; M.A., Columbia, 1948, Ph.D., 1954; m. Margaret Helen Deutsch, Jan. 31, 1963; children—MacIntyre Hardy, John Oliver, Ernest Van Every. Instr. philosophy Hobart and William Smith Colls., Geneva, N.Y., 1949-52; instr. U. Mo. at Columbia, 1952-54, asst. prof., 1954-57, asso. prof., 1957-63; prof. philosophy U. So. Fla., 1963-64; prof., chmn. philosophy dept. Fla. State U., 1964-69, prof., 1969—; dir. Fla. Center for Social Philosophy, 1967—. Vis. prof. U. Neb., 1963. U. Hawaii, 1965. Research fellow U. Mo., 1955, 58-59, 63, Fla. State U., 1967; research grantee U. Mo., 1958, 61, 62, Fla. State U., 1968, 70, 71. Mem. Mo. State Philos. Assn. (sec.-treas. 1954-61, pres. 1962- 63), Soc. Philos. Study Dialectical Materialism (sec.-treas. 1963-69, 69- 73). Author: Socialist Humanism: The Outcome of Classical European Morality, 1971; (with K.T. Fann) Readings in U.S. Imperialism, 1971; (with Abu Shanab) National Liberation Fronts: Documents, Interviews, Essays, 1971. Mem. editorial bd. Philosophy and Phenomenological Research, 1969—; asso. editor Social Theory and Practice, 1969—; cons. editor Indian Sociol. Bull., 1964—. Contbr. articles to anthologies and profl. jours. Home: 707 Lothian Dr Tallahassee FL 32303

HODGES, ELMER BURKETT, lawyer; b. College View, Neb., July 11, 1903; s. Charles Huntley and Mabel Gerturde (Blocher) H.; student Jr. Coll. of Kansas City, Mo., 1921-23; LL.B., Kansas City Sch. of Law, 1927; m. Maebelle Parsons, May 28, 1948; children—Deborah, Richard. Admitted to Mo. bar, 1927; U.S. Supreme Ct.; asst. county counselor, Jackson County, Mo., 1929-35; mem. firm Gage, Hodges, Park & Kreamer, 1960-69; partner Gage, Tucker, Hodges, Kreamer, Kelly & Varner, Kansas City, 1970—; lectr. on fed. taxation and econ. theories, 1939—. Sec., dir Parmelee Industries, Inc., U.S. Safety Service Co. Ray Printing Co., Country side Fund, Inc.; dir. Ellfeldt Machinery & Supply Co., Kirk-Wiklund & Co., Midland Steel & Aluminum Co. Mem. Am., Mo., Kansas City bar assns., Lawyer's Assn. of Kansas City. Republican. Mem. Christian Ch. Mason. Clubs: Kansas City, Mission Hills Country, Owl Creek Kansas City, Mo. Home: 5512 Central St Kansas City MO 64113 Office: Bryant Bldg Kansas City MO 64106

HODGES, FLETCHER, Jr., curator; b. Indpls., Aug. 6, 1906; s. Fletcher and Rebecca T. (Andrews) H.; A.B., Harvard, 1928; Litt.D., Lincoln Meml. U., Harrogate, Tenn., 1945; m. Sarah Margaret Moore, Sept. 10, 1932; children—Fletcher III, Arthur Carlisle, John Andrews. Engaged in bus., Indpls. and Chgo., 1928- 31; curator Foster Hall Collection, Indpls., 1931-36, Foster Hall Collection, U. Pitts. 1937—; mgr. Stephen Foster Meml., 1943—. Pres. U. Pitts. Fed. Credit Union, 1968—. Treas. Pitts. Bibliophiles, 1966—. Mem. bd. mgmt. U. Pitts, YMCA, 1952—; trustee Calvin Fletcher Sch., Indlps., 1965—. Named Ky. col., 1945. Episcopalian (former mem. vestry, jr. and sr. warden.). Club: Indpls. Literary; Junta (Pitts.). Author: A Biographical Sketch of Stephen C. Foster, 1958. Editor: The Foster Hall Reproductions of the Songs, Compositions and Arrangements by Stephen C. Foster, 1933. Home: 5812 Kentucky Av Pittsburgh PA 15232

HODGES, GILBERT, manager N.Y. Mets Profl. Baseball Team, Oct. 1967—. Address: Shea Stadium Roosevelt Av at 126th Av Flushing NY 11368*

HODGES, GUS MACEY, educator; b. Hoyt, Tex, Feb. 12, 1908; s. Gus M. and Carrie (Burns) H.; B.B.A., U. Tex., 1930, LL.B., 1932; m. Elizabeth Julia Brown, June 17, 1938; children—Richard H., Macey (Mrs. Harry M. Reasoner). Admitted to Tex. bar, 1932; practice in Dallas, 1932-40; mem. faculty U. Tex., 1940—, prof. law, 1940—. Commr., Uniform State Laws, 1955-57. Served with USNR, World War II. Mem. Tex. Bar Assn., Order of Coif, Phi Delta Phi. Episcopalian. Author: Special Issue Submission, 1959; Trial and Appellate Procedure, 1963; Judicial process Prior to Trial, 1966. Home: 3714 Meredith St Austin TX 78703

HODGES, JOHN HENDRICKS, physician, educator; b. Harpers Ferry, W.Va., Aug. 1, 1914; s. Joseph Howard and Edna (Hendricks) H.; B.S., Cath. U. Am., 1935; M.D., Jefferson Med. Coll., Phila., 1939; m. Elizabeth May Wallace, Jan. 27, 1940; 1 son, John Hendricks. Intern Phila. Gen. Hosp., 1939-41; gen. practice, Martinsburg, W. Va., 1941-42; resident medicine Jefferson Med. Coll. Hosp., 1942-46; mem. faculty Jefferson Med Coll., 1944— , Ludwig A. Kind prof. medicine, 1964—, dir. div. gen. medicine, 1944—; cons. hematology Lankenau Hosp., Phila., 1963—; pres. Henry K. Mohler Physicians Office, Phila., 1955—. Bd. dirs. Mercy Catholic Med. Center. Mary Markle Found. fellow tropical medicine, 1944; recipient Christian R. and Mary F. Lindback Found. award excellence teaching, 1966. Diplomate Am. Bd. Internal Medicine. Fellow A.C.P.; mem. A.M.A., Am. Heart Assn., Am. Thoracic Soc., Pa., Phila., Montgomery County med. socs., Am. Soc. Tropical Medicine and Hygiene, Internat., Am., Phila. socs. hematology, Internat. Soc. Internal Medicine, Alumni Assn. Jefferson Med. Coll. (pres.-elect), Alpha Omega Alpha. Editor: Manual for Laboratory Medicine, 11th edit., 1966. Contbr. articles to med. jours. Home: 436 Sabine Av Wynnewood PA 19096 Office: 1025 Walnut St Philadelphia PA 19107

HODGES, JOSEPH C., corp. exec.; b. 1911; B.A., in Bus. Adminstrn., Northwestern U.; C.P.A., Ill.; married. With Chemetron Corp., 1942—, treas., 1968—. Address: 840 N Michigan Av Chicago IL 60611*

HODGES, JOSEPH GILLULY, lawyer; b. Denver, Apr. 30, 1909; s. William Vanderveer and Mabel (Gilluly) H.; grad. Hotchkiss Sch., 1926; A.B., Yale, 1930; LL.B., Harvard, 1933; m. Elaine Chanute, Mar. 31, 1939; children—Elaine M. (Mrs. Duval Edward Harvey), Joseph Gilluly, Ann V. Admitted to Colo. bar, 1933, since practiced in Denver; dep. dist. atty. Denver County, 1933-34; mem. firm Hodges, Wilson & Vidal, 1934-36; partner Hodges, Wilson & Vidal and Hodges, Vidal & Goree, 1936-53; partner Hodges, Silverstein, Hodges & Harrington and Hodges, Silverstein & Harrington, 1953-69, Hodges, Harrington, Kerwin and Otten, 1970—. Dir. Colo. Nat. Bank Denver. Pres. Denver Water Bd., 1963-64. Bd. dirs. Childrens Hosp. Assn., Denver, 1969—; trustee Denver Mus. Natural History, Colo. Hosp. Service. Served to maj. USAAF, 1942-45. Fellow Am. Bar Found., Am. Law Inst.; mem. Am. (past del.), Colo. (past pres.), Denver bar assns., Denver C. of C. (past dir.), Alpha Delta Phi. Episcopalian. Rotarian. Home: 150 Vine St Denver CO 80206 Office: 1360 Denver Club Bldg Denver CO 80202

HODGES, JOSEPH HOWARD, bishop; b. Harpers Ferry, W. Va., Oct. 8, 1911; s. Joseph Howard and Edna Belle (Hendricks) H.; student St. Charles Coll., Catonsville, Md., 1928-30; student North Am. Coll., Rome, Italy, 1930-36, D.D. (hon.), 1952. Ordained priest Roman Cath. Ch., Rome, 1935; asst. Sacred Heart Ch., Danville, Va., 1936-39, St. Andrew's Ch., Roanoke, Va., 1939-45; adminstr. St. Mary's Ch., Richmond, Va., also dir, Diocesan Missionary Fathers, 1945-55; pastor St. Peter's Ch., Richmond, 1955-61; consecrated Titular Bishop of Rusadus, and Aux. Bishop of the Cath. Diocese of Richmond, 1952; vicar gen. Diocese of Richmond, 1958-61, coadjutor bishop and vicar gen. Diocese of Wheeling, W. Va., 1961, bishop, Wheeling, 1962—. Office: 1300 Byron St PO Box 230 Wheeling WV 26003

HODGES, LOUIS WENDELL, educator; b. Eupora, Miss., Jan. 24, 1933; s. John C. and Lorene (Phillips) H.; B.A., Millsaps Coll., 1954; B.D, Duke U., 1957, Ph.D., 1960; m. Helen Elizabeth Davis, June 6, 1954; children—John David, George Kenneth. Asst. prof. Washington and Lee U., 1960-64, asso. prof., 1964-68, prof., 1968—. Mem. Va. adv. com. U.S. Commn. Civil Rights, 1970—; pres. Rockbridge Area Housing Corp., 1968—. Mem. Am. Soc. Christian Ethics. Author: The Christian and His Decisions: An Introduction to Christian Ethics, 1969. Home: RFD 5 Lexington VA 24450

HODGES, LUTHER HARTWELL, former sec. commerce; b. Pittsylvania County, Va., Mar. 9, 1898; s. John J. and Lovicia (Gammon) H.; A.B., U. N.C., 1919; recipient several hon. degrees from other univs.; children—Betsy, Nancy, Luther. Sec. to gen. mgr. of eight mills, Spray, N.C., 1919, mgr., 1933; prodn. mng. all mills of Marshall Field & Co., 1936, gen. mgr., 1938, v.p. charge of mills and sales, 1943-50, ret. officer, dir. local corps.; head textile div. OPA, 1944; cons. to sec. of agr., 1945; head industry div. ECA, W. Germany, 1950; lt. gov. N.C., 1952-54, gov., 1954-60; sec. of commerce, 1961-65; chmn. bd. Research Triangle Found. N.C., Raleigh. Dir. Servomation Corp., Gulf & Western Industries. Former dir. So. Regional Edn. Bd. Democrat. Methodist. Clubs: University, Rotary (pres. 1967-68). Author: Businessman in the State House; The Business Conscience. Home: 3061 Wycliff Rd Raleigh NC 27607 Office: Box H Research Triangle Park NC 27405

HODGES, MARY DORIS, hosp. adminstr.; b. Peoria, Ill, Sept. 30, 1912; d. Samuel G. and Edna G. (Wright) Hodges; B.S., Ind. U., 1968. Med. record librarian trainee St. Elizabeth Hosp., Lafayette, Ind., 1930-33; chief med. record librarian St. Alexis Hosp., Cleve., 1933-38, St. Joseph Hosp., Memphis, 1938-43; chief med. record librarian St. Margaret Hosp., Hammond, Ind.,, 1943-68, hosp. adminstr., 1968—, dir. Sch. Med. Record Technicians, 1962-67. Pres. N.W. Ind. Hosp. Council, 1970-71 Registered record librarian. Mem. Am. Med. Record Assn. Address: 25 Douglas St Hammond IN 46320

HODGES, THOMPSON GENE, librarian; b. Clinton, Okla., Jan. 30, 1913; s. Kiah and Allie Lee (Thompson) H.; B.S., U. Okla., 1934, M.L.S., 1955; B.D., McCormick Theol. Sem., Chgo., 1939; m. Claire Surbeck, June 19, 1935; 1 son, Thompson Gene. Ordained to ministry Presbyn. Ch., 1939; pastor, Pawhuska and Lawton, Okla., 1939-47; aquisitions librarian U. Okla., 1955-58; dir. library Central State Coll., Edmond, Okla., 1958—. Mem. Am., Southwestern, Okla. (pres. 1965-66) library assns., Okla. Ednl. Assn., Kappa Sigma, Beta Phi Mu, Kappa Kappa Psi. Home: 415 Macy St Norman OK 73069 Office: Central State Coll Edmond OK 73034

HODGES, WALTER PAUL, oil co. exec.; b. Ft. Smith, Ark., Feb. 24, 1921; s. Walter H. and Mae (Williams) H.; B.S., U. Ark., 1942; m. Arline J. Kreuzberger, Apr. 29, 1945; children—Jeffery Paul, David Steven. With Haskins & Sells, C.P.A.'s Tulsa, 1945-49; with Deep Rock Oil Corp., Tulsa, 1949-54; asst. controller Forest Oil Corp., Bradford, Pa., 1954-58; sr. v.p. finance, dir. Quaker State Oil Refining Corp., Oil City, Pa., 1958—. Served to 1st lt. USAAF, 1942-45. C.P.A., Okla. Mem. Am. Inst. C.P.A.'s Okla. Soc. C.P.A.'s Am. Petroleum Inst., Inst. Internal Auditors Financial Exec. Inst. Home: 301 W 3d St Oil City PA 16301 Office: PO Box 989 Oil City PA 16301

HODGINS, HUGH JOHN, forest engr.; b. Arcola, Sask., Can., Oct. 28, 1904; s. Thomas George and Minnie A. (Winters) H.; B.A. Sc., U. B.C., 1928; m. Hedvig Hillas, Mar. 31, 1934; 1 dau., Jane (Mrs. Charles Tucker Battle). With Forest Service, B.C., 1928-44; with Crown Zellerbach Canada, Ltd., Vancouver, B.C., 1944-50, 57—, v.p., 1958-69 also dir.; forest cons. H.J. Hodgins, Ltd., 1950-57, 69—. Mem. Canadian Forestry Assn. (past pres.), British Columbia Loggers Assn. (past chmn.), Canadian Inst. Forestry (past pres.), Western Forestry and Conservation Assn. (past pres.), Phi Delta Theta. Home: 2075 Nelson St Vancouver 5 British Columbia Canada Office: Crown Zellerbach Canada Ltd 1030 W Georgia St Vancouver 5 British Columbia Canada

HODGKIN, ALAN LLOYD, physiologist, educator; b. Feb. 5, 1914; s. G.L. and M.F. (Wilson) H.; student Trinity Coll., Cambridge, fellow 1936—; M.D. (hon.), univs. Berne, Louvain; D.Sc., U. Sheffield, 1963; U. Newcastle, 1965 U. East Anglia, 1966, U. Manchester, 1971, U. Leicester, 1971; m. Marion de Kav Rous, 1944; 1 son, 3 daus. Sci. officer radar Air Ministry, also Ministry Aircraft Prodn., 1939-45; lectr., then asst. dir. research Cambridge, 1947-52; Foulerton research prof. Royal Soc., 1952-69, Plummer prof. biophysics, 1970—; chancellor U. Leicester, 1971. Mem. Med. Research Council, 1959-63. Recipient Baly medal, 1955, Royal medal Royal Soc., 1958; Copley medal Royal Soc., 1965; co-recipient of the Nobel prize for medicine, 1963. Fellow Royal Soc. (pres. 1970); mem. Physiol. Soc. (fgn. sec. 1960-67), Marine Biol. Assn. (pres. 1966—, Am. Acad. Arts and Scis. (fgn. hon.), Royal Danish Acad. Scis., Leopoldina Acad., Am. Philos. Soc., Pontifical Acad. Sci. Author sci. papers on nature of nervous conduction. Home: 25 Newton Rd Cambridge England

HODGKIN, DOROTHY CROWFOOT, chemist, educator; b. 1910; d. J.W. Crowfoot; ed. Somerville Coll., Oxford U.; D.Sc. (hon.), Leeds U., also Manchester U.; Sc.D. (hon.), Cambridge U., others; m. Thomas Hodgkin; two sons, one dau. Fellow Somerville Coll.; Wolfson research prof. Royal Soc., 1960—. Recipient Nobel prize for chemistry, 1964. Fellow Royal Soc. (Medallist 1956); fgn. mem. Royal Netherlands Acad. Scis. and Letters, Am. Acad. Arts and Scis., others. Author articles on chemistry and crystallography. Address: 20C Bradmore Rd Oxford England

HODGKIN, JOHN PEASE, financial co. exec.; b. Chentu, Szechuan, China, Jan. 12, 1909 (parents Brit. subjects); s. Henry Theodore and Elizabeth Joy (Montgomery) H.; B.A. in Econs. with honors, Kings Coll., Cambridge (Eng.) U., 1931; C.P.A., Pa., 1947; m. Ruth Sherlock Walenta, July 2, 1934 (dec. Dec. 1961); children—Margaret, Christopher; m. 2d, Elizabeth Davis, Jan. 12, 1963. Came to U.S., 1931, naturalized, 1946. Tchr. math., Hudson, O., 1931-32; tchr. math. and French, Newton Sq., Pa., 1932-34; activities sec. Internat. House, N.Y.C., 1935; accountant Price Waterhouse & Co., C.P.A.'s, Phila., 1936-60; with Office Messrs. Rockefeller, N.Y.C., 1960- 67; treas. Rockefeller Brothers Fund, Inc., 1961-67, Rockefeller Brothers Inc., 1961-67, Martha Baird Rockefeller Fund Music, Inc., 1962- 67; financial asst. office of Stewart R. Mott, 1967—; v.p. Spectemur Agendo, Inc., 1967—; dir. Minerals and Industries, Inc., 1968—; author, lectr. on taxes. Founding mem., past pres. Bryn Gweled Homesteads, Southampton, Pa.; treas. Country Dance Soc., N.Y.C.; dir., treas. N.Y. Pro Musica Antiqua, 1970—. Mem. Financial Execs. Inst., Am., Pa. insts. C.P.A.'s. Mem. Soc. Friends (elder). Home: 124 E 24th St New York City NY 10010 Office: 515 Madison Av New York City NY 10022

HODGKINS, EARL WARNER, assn. exec.; b. Woodsville, N.H., June 30, 1919; s. Earl Warner and Elizabeth (Mitchell) H.; B.S. in Civil Engring., U. N.H., 1950; m. Ruth Abbie Davison, Sept. 23, 1939; children—Earl Warner III, Linda Ruth (Mrs. William R. Jacobs), Lorraine Dawn. With Railway Express Agy., Woodsville, N.H., 1936-50; structural designer B. & M. R.R., 1950-52, student supr., Greenfield, Mass., 1952; asst. supr. bridges and bldgs. Me. Central R.R., Portland, 1953-54, asst. engr. structures, 1954-58; asso. editor Ry. Track and Structures mag., Chgo., 1958-64; asso. engring. editor Ry. Age Weekly, 1958-64; exec. sec. Am. Railway Engring. Assn., Chgo., 1964-68, exec. mgr. 1968—; exec. vice chmn., engring. div. Assn. Am. Railroads, Chgo., 1964-71, exec. dir. engring, div., 1971—. Active local Boy Scouts Am., 1954-60. Served to lst lt., C.A.C. and Transp. Corps, AUS, 1942-45; ETO. Mem. Am. Ry. Engring. Assn., Am. Ry. Bridge and Bldg. Assn., Roadmasters and Maintenance of Way Assn. Am., Maintenance of Way Club Chgo., Am. Soc. Engring. Edn., Am. Soc. C.E., Council Engring. and Sci. Soc. Secretaries, Nat. Geog. Soc. Mem. Ch. of Jesus Christ of Latter- day Saints. Office: 59 E Van Buren St Chicago IL 60605

HODGKINS, EDWARD RUGGLES, ins. exec.; b. Andover, Mass., June 27, 1910; s. Willis Bradlee and Helen Osgood (Ruggles) H.; B.S., U.S. Naval Acad., 1932; m. Ruth Gulliver Hodgkins, Mar. 24, 1933. With Mass. Protective Assn., Inc. and Paul Revere Life Ins. Co. (both Worcester, Mass.), 1932—, asst. sec., 1935, field supr., 1946, supt. agys., 1949, dir., v.p., 1949, v.p., supt. agys., 1955—; v.p., dir. Paul Revere Variable Annuity Ins. Co; dir. Avco Corp. Trustee of Garland Junior Coll., Boston. Served from 1t. (j.g.) to 1t. comdr., USNR, 1942-45. Mem. U.S. Naval Acad. Alunni Assn. Mason (32, Shriner). Clubs: Dedham Country and Polo, Webhannet, Worcester, Royal and Ancient Golf, Mid Ocean, Tatnuck. Home: 5 Whitman Rd Worcester MA 01609 Office: 18 Chestnut St Worcester MA 01608

HODGKINS, HENRY FOLLETT, business exec.; b. Syracuse, N.Y., Feb. 2, 1892; s. Henry Clarence and Mary Ida (Follett) H.; M.E., Cornell, 1915; m. Ruth Simmons, Oct. 6, 1917; 1 son, Henry Follett. Prodn. engr. Savage Arms Corp., Utica, N.Y., 1916-19; prodn. mgr. Peters Mfg. Co., Ithaca, 1919-21; dist. sales mgr. Wales Adding Machine, Syracuse, 1921-23; gen. mgr. Jule Motors, 1923-26, Lipe-Rollway Corp., 1926-29, gen. mgr., 1929-42, pres., 1929-58, chmn., 1958-68; pres. Rollway Bearing Co., 1936-58, chmn. bd., 1958-68; dir. 1st Trust & Deposit Co. Mem. Bd. councillors Syracuse Meml. Hosp. hon. chmn. Met. Devel. Corp., 1959—. Bd. Govs. Syracuse U. Research Inst. Profl. engr., N.Y. Mem. Anti-Friction Bearing Mfrs. Assn. (past chmn., dir.), Soc. Automotive Engrs., Nat. Mfrs. Assn. (past v.p., dir.), Mfrs. Assn. Syracuse (past pres., chmn. bd.); Citizens Found., Am. Ordnance Assn. (dir.), Navy Indsl. Assn., Inc., Syracuse Home Assn. (dir.). Mason (32). Clubs: Onandage Golf and Country, Technology, Century, Rotary, University, Great Lakes Cruising, Cornell (Syracuse); Coral Harbour Yacht. Home: 989 James St Syracuse NY 13203 Office: 806 Emerson Av Syracuse NY 13204

HODGKINSON, CHARLES PAUL, physician; b. New Castle, Pa., Apr. 13, 1907; s. William Henry and O'Rilla Laura (Lambert) H.; student U. Pitts. Sch. Pharmacy, 1925-28, U. Pitts. Pre-Med. Sch., 1929-32, U. Buffalo Med. Sch., 1932-33; M.D. (W. Wayne Babcock Gold medal, Temple U. Faculty prize 1936), Temple U., 1936; M.S. in Obstetrics and Gynecology, U. Mich., 1940; m. Amy Virginia Walker, Jan. 22, 1929; children—Charles Paul II, Grace Ann. Intern, Henry Ford Hosp., Detroit, 1936-37, resident gen. surgery, 1937-39, resident gynecology and obstetrics, 1939-42, chmn. dept. gynecology and obstetrics, 1952—, sec. adv. bd., 1952-68; clin. prof. dept., obstetrics and gynecology Wayne State U. Sch. Medicine, Detroit. Sec.-treas. Am. Assn. Obstetricians and Gynecologists Found., Inc., 1965—. Served to capt., M.C., AUS, 1942-46. Recipient Cum Laude award Radiol. Soc. N.A., 1952; Hektoen medal A.M.A., 1967. Diplomate Am. Bd. Obstetrics and Gynecology. Fellow Am. Gynecol. Soc., Am. Assn. Obstetricians and Gynecologists; mem. Am. Acad. Obstetricians and Gynecologists (sec. 1953-55; 1st award for sci. display 1953), Am. Coll. Obstetricians and Gynecologists (sec. 1955-57, pres. 1960-61), Mich. Soc. Obstetricians and Gynecologists (pres. 1959- 60), Central Assn. Obstetricians and Gynecologists (Annual Prize award 1952, pres. 1966-67), A.C.S. (gov., 1958- 61, 63-66; certificate of merit 1957), A.M.A. (certificate of merit 1953), Central Travel Club Obstetricians and Gynecologists (council 1959-62), A.A.A.S., hon. mem. Kansas City Gynecol. Soc., Ky. Obstet. and Gynecol. Soc., Pitts. Soc. Obstetricians and Gynecologists. Author numerous articles in field. Home: 17546 Meadowood St Lathrup Village MI 48075 Office: 2799 W Grand Blvd Detroit MI 48202

HODGSON, CHARLES ARTHUR, advt. exec.; b. E. St. Louis, Ill., Jan. 7, 1920; s. Edward Stith and Gertrude (Niebling) H.; B.S., Washington U., St. Louis, 1941; m. Mary E. Greene, Apr. 22, 1944 (dec. 1958); children—Cynthia Ann, Marilyn Elizabeth, Kathryn Ellen; m. 2d, Jean E. Buettner, Sept. 17, 1960; 1 son, Jeffrey Charles. Partner Eggers-Ranking Advt., St. Louis, 1947-49; v.p. Batz-Hodgson-Neuwoehner Advt., St. Louis, 1950—. Mem. exec. com. St. Louis Heart Assn., St. Louis Play Goers. Served with USNR, 1943-46. Mem. Advt. Club St. Louis, Assn. Indsl. Advertisers, Media Club. Presbyn. (deacon). Club: Algonquin Golf (St. Louis). Home: 332 McDonald Pl Webster Groves MO 63119 Office: 411 N 10th St St Louis MO 63101

HODGSON, CHARLES CLARK, lawyer; b. Kane, Pa., Oct. 24, 1906; s. J. Keene and Honora (Clark) H.; A.B., Holy Cross Coll., 1927; LL.B., Temple U., 1939; m. Helen G. Day, Jan. 6, 1937; children—Charles Clark, Helen (Mrs. Kerry L. Overlan), Stephen J., Richard J. Admitted to Pa. bar, 1931, since practiced in Phila.; partner firm Stradley, Ronon, Stevens & Young, 1945—; instr. bus. law U. Pa., 1940-52. Chmn. Phila. Parking Authority, 1953-55. Bd. dirs. Big Brother Assn., 1955—. Mem. Am., Pa., Phila. (bd. govs. 1954-55, com. censors 1960-62, chmn. com. specialization 1968-69) bar assns. Democrat. Roman Cath. Club: Phila. Cricket. Home: 814 E Phil Ellena St Philadelphia PA 19119 Office: Girard Trust Bldg Philadelphia PA 19119

HODGSON, CORRIN HALEY, physician; b. Fergus Falls, Minn., June 7, 1908; s. Fred E. and Anastasia (Haley) H.; student U. Notre Dame, 1925-27; B.S., M.B., U. Minn., 1931, M.D., 1932, M.S., 1945; m. Florence Mary Pitman, Aug. 6, 1932; children—Corrin John, Stephen Fredric, Clague Pitman. Intern Cin. Gen. Hosp., 1932; resident Hamilton County (O.) Tb Sanatorium, 1933; practice medicine, Fergus Falls Clinic, 1934-37; resident internal medicine Mayo Grad. Sch. Medicine, 1937-39, now prof. emeritus clin. medicine; practice medicine, specializing in internal medicine Brit. Am. Hosp., Lima, Peru, 1939-44, Mayo Clinic, Rochester, Minn., 1944-66; cons. internal medicine Mayo Clinic, 1944-66; med. dir. Minn. Mining & Mfg. Co., 1966—. Past pres., trustee Minn. Med. Found. Hon. prof. U. San Marcos, Lima, 1965; hon. Peruvian consul, Rochester, St. Paul, 1961—. Diplomate Am. Bd. Internal Medicine. Mem. Am. Acad. Occupational Medicine, Minn. Thoracic Soc., A.M.A., Minn. Med. Assn., Zumbro Valley (past pres.), Ramsey County med. socs., A.C.P., Am. Coll. Chest Physicians, Minn. Soc. Internal Medicine, Indsl. Med. Assn., Sigma Xi. Home: 49 E Pleasant Lake Rd North Oaks Farm St Paul MN 55110 Office: 3M Co-3M Center St Paul MN 55101

HODGSON, JAMES, advt. exec.; b. Batley, Eng., Oct. 21, 1907; s. James Herbert and Edith (Meyers) H.; came to U.S., 1917, naturalized, 1928; B.S., U. Utah, 1930; m. Margaret Anna Berg, Nov. 12, 1930; children—Bonnie Wakefield), Robert James, Richard Alex. Sports editor Salt Lake Tribune, 1935-38; with David W. Evans and Assos., Salt Lake City, 1948—. pres., 1967—, also chief exec. officer; dir., treas. Evans Supply Co.; chmn. bd. Evans-Williams & Assos., San Francisco. Mem. Mut. Improvement Assn. Gen. bd. Ch. Jesus Christ Latter Day Saints. Bd. dirs. Utah Kayo Polio campaign, 1964, Utah Measles Eradication campaign, 1967. Mem. Salt Lake City Advt. Club (pres. 1953-54), Advt. Assn. West (award 1956), Am. Fedn. Advt. Kiwanian (dir. Salt Lake City 1958-59). Home: 4870 3 Fountains Dr Murray UT 84107 Office: 110 Social Hall Av Salt Lake City UT 84111

HODGSON, JAMES DAY, sec. of labor; b. Dawson, Minn., Dec. 3, 1915; s. Fred Arthur and Casaraha (Day) H.; A.B., U. Minn., 1938, grad. student, 1940; grad. student, U. at Los Angeles, 1947-48; m. Maria Denend, Aug. 24, 1943; children—Nancy (Mrs. Richard J. Nachman), Frederic. Supr. youth employment Minn. Dept. Employment, 1940-41; with Lockheed Aircraft Corp., 1941-69, corp. v.p. indsl. relations, 1968-69; under sec. labor, 1969-70; sec. of labor Dept. Labor, Washington, 1970—. Mem. exec. com. Mayor Los Angeles Labor-Mgmt. Com., 1962- 69; cons. Cal. Com. Automation and Manpower, 1965-67. Served to lt. USNR, 1943-46. Author articles. Home: 2801 New Mexico Av NW Washington DC 20007 Office: Dept of Labor 14th and Constitution Av Washington DC 20210

HODGSON, JOSEPH VERNON, lawyer; b. Boyne Falls, Mich., Jan. 2, 1899; s. Joseph V. and Ada Delphine (Adams) H.; A.B., U. Michigan, 1921, LL.B. (Law Sch.), 1925; J.D., 1968. Admitted to Cal. bar, 1925, Hawaii bar, 1926, U.S. Supreme Ct. bar; 1944; in pvt. practice, Honolulu, T.H. 1926-34; dep. atty. gen. of Hawaii, 1934-37, asst. atty. gen., 1937-38, atty. gen., 1938-42. Served as lt. inf., U.S. Army during World War I; col. J.A.G.C., A.U.S., World War II; U.S. dep. commr. United Nations War Crimes Commn. in London, 1944, the U.S. rep. U.N. War Crimes Commn., 1945-46; practiced in Honolulu, 1946—. Mem. Hawaii Aero. Commn., 1955-60; chmn. Hawaii adv. com. U.S. Civil Rights Comm., 1959-62; Hawaii adviser Young Ams. for Freedom. Decorated D.S.M. (U.S.), others. Mem. Nat. Conf. Commrs. on Uniform State Law, 1940-42; mem. Bar Examiners of Hawaii, 1938-42, 48. Procedural Rules Com., Supreme Ct., Hawaii, 1938- 42, and 1952-54. Fellow Am. Coll. Trial Lawyers; mem Am. Bar Assn., Bar Assn. Hawaii, State Bar Cal., Sigma Phi Epsilon, Phi Alpha Delta. Presbyn. Mason, Elk (hon. life). Club: Pacific. Home: 1617 S Beretania St Honolulu HI 96814 Office: 612 Pioneer Tower 1136 Union Mall Honolulu HI 96813

HODGSON, PATRICK, H., lawyer; b. Doncaster, Eng., Mar. 17, 1906; s. William Egerton and Florence Anne (Glasier) H.; ed. Malvern Coll., Leeds U. Law Sch., Eng.; m. Wilhelmina Schoellkopf, Feb. 8, 1930; children—Nina (Mrs. Robert Spier), Patrick William Egerton; m. 2d, Martha Ann Keeling, Dec. 24, 1962. Came to U. S., 1930, naturalized, 1935. Admitted Solicitor Supreme Ct. of Judicature in Eng., 1929; practiced in London, 1929-30; admitted to N.Y. bar, 1935; practiced in Buffalo, 1935-62; sr. partner Hodgson, Russ, Andrews, Woods & Goodyear, 1946-62; Pvt. Practice of law, London, Eng., 1964—; dir. devel. (U.K.) Pan Am. World Airways, 1967-71. Spl. asst. to under sec. of navy and counsel Bur. Ships, Navy Dept., Washington, 1941-44; asst. gen. counsel Navy Dept. and mem. Bd. Contract Appeals, 1944; gen. counsel Navy Dept., 1945; spl. asst. to secs. of army, navy and air, 1950, to atty. gen. U.S., 1953-56. Trustee, past chmn. bd. Buffalo and Erie County Pub. Library; past trustee Buffalo Philharmonic Orch. Soc., Buffalo chpt. A.R.C., Travelers Aid Soc. (pres.), Grosvenor Library (pres.), Hamburg (U.F.) Sch. Dist. (chmn. bd.), Buffalo Mus. Natural Sci. Decorated Presdl. Medal for Merit for outstanding services in war effort. Fellow Am. Bar Found.; mem. Internat., Am., N.Y. State, Erie County (pres. 1961-62) bar assns., Buffalo Fine Arts Acad. (life), The Law Soc. (London). Clubs: Metropolitan (Washington); University, India House (N.Y.C.); St. Moritz Toboggan (Cresta Run); Garrick, St. James' (London). Home: 51 Onslow Sq London SW 7 England

HODGSON, RALPH E., govt. ofcl.; b. Arena, Wis., July 20, 1906; s. Edgar James and Rose (Ralph) H.; B.S., U. Wis., 1929, Ph.D., 1941; M.S., Kan. State Coll., 1930; m. Eleanor Fay Wilson, Sept. 18, 1931; children—Eleanor Ruth, Fleur Louise. Agt. bur. dairy industry Dept. Agr., asst. dairy husbandman Wash. Agrl. Expt. Sta., 1930-39, asso. dairy husbandman, Puyallup, Wash., 1940-41, dairy husbandman bur. dairy industry, Beltsville, Md., 1941-42, survey dairy instr. Latin Am., Dept. Agr., coordinator inter-Am. affairs, 1942-43, prin . dairy husbandman, bur. dairy industry, 1943-46, asst. chief bur. dairy industry, Washington, 1946-53, chief Dairy Husbandry Research Br., Beltsville, Md., 1953-56, dir. animal husbandry research div., agrl. research service, Dept. Agr., 1957—. Chmn. ofcl. U.S. delegation to 13th Internat. Dairy Congress, The Hague, Netherlands, 1953, 14th Internat. Dairy Congress, Rome, Italy, 1956, 15th Internat. Dairy Congress, London, Eng., 1959, 16th Internat. Dairy Congress, Copenhagen, 1962; del. 17th Internat. Dairy Congress, Munich, W. Germany, 1966, 18th Internat. Dairy Congress, Sidney, Australia, 1970; chmn. World Conf. Animal Prodn., U.S.A., 1968, 2d FAO Internat. Conf. Dairy Edn., Copenhagen, 1969. Recipient Borden award for research dairy prodn. Am. Dairy Sci. Assn., 1939, award of honor, 1966, Distinguished Service award, 1971; Superior Service award Dept. Agr., 1947. Fellow Am. Soc. Animal Sci.; mem. World Assn. Animal Prodn. (pres. 1966-68), Am. Dairy Sci. Assn. (pres. 1960), A.A.A.S. (v.p. sect. agr. 1961), Poultry Sci. Assn., Am. Soc. Animal Prodn., Sigma Xi, Delta Theta Sigma, Alpha Zeta, Phi Kappa Phi. Clubs: Cosmos, Rotary. Author: Handbook for Dairying in Latin America, Spanish, 1953, Portugese, 1969; also articles on dairy prodn. Editor: Germ Plasm Resources, 1961. Home: 7006 Wake Forest Dr College Park MD 20740 Office: Animal Husbandry Research Div Agrl Research Service Dept Agr Beltsville MD 20705

HODGSON, RAYMOND J., banker; b. Stewartville, Minn., March 14, 1904; s. Frank L. and Jennie R. (Marshall) H.; U. of Mich., 1929; m. Elizabeth Chisholm, Jan. 18, 1930; 1 son, Richard. Examiner Mich. State Banking Dept., 1928-29; in auditing dept. Detroit Trust Co., 1930-32; asso. with Detroit Loan Agy., R.F.C., 1933-41, mgr., 1938-41; pres. Graham-Paige Motors Corp., 1942-45; v.p. Nat. Bank Detroit, 1945-62, sr. v.p. 1962-69, ret., 1969; chmn. bd. govs. Detroit Automobile Inter-Ins. Exchange, Motor State Ins. Co.; dir. Detroit Met. Indsl. Devel. Corp., Cin. Garage Co., Detroit Marine Terminals, Am. Automobile Assn., Penobscot Bldg., Inc., Detroit, Automobile Club Mich., St. Raymond Paper Co., Que., Can. Mem. Newcomen Soc. N. Am., Lambda Chi Alpha. Methodist. Mason. Clubs: Detroit Athletic, Detroit Golf, Detroit, University, Country, Economic (Detroit). Home: 570 Renaud Rd Grosse Pointe MI 48236 Office: Penbscot Bldg Detroit MI 48226

HODGSON, RICHARD, communications company exec.; b. Anyox, B.C., Jan. 7, 1917; s. Arthur R. and Mabel (Malmstrom) H.; A.B. in Engring., Stanford, 1937; M.B.A., Harvard, 1939; m. Geraldine Reed, Nov. 26, 1945; children—Philip, Morgan, Brooke, Peter. With Radiation Lab., Mass. Inst. Tech., 1942-45; head engr. mgmt. div. Brookhaven Nat. Lab., AEC, 1946; dir. TV, Paramount Pictures, 1947-50; pres., dir. Chromatic TV Labs., 1950-56; exec. v.p. Fairchild Camera & Instrument Corp., Syosset, L.I., 1955-62, pres., dir., 1962-68; dir. Research-Cottrell Corp., Beecham, Inc.; v.p., group mgr. Internat. Telephone & Telegraph Corp., 1969—. Expert cons. Sec. War, 1943-45. Mem. I.E.E.E. (sr.), Tau Beta Pi. Home: Ponus Ridge Rd New Canaan CT 06840

HODGSON, ROBERT JAMES, lawyer; b. Glens Falls, N.Y., Apr. 2, 1919; s. Henry W. and Inez (Thornton) H.; A.B., Colgate U., 1940; student Albany Law Sch., 1943; J.D., U. Mich., 1947; m. Shirley MacMillan, May 27, 1950; children— Angus, Martha, Susan T. Admitted to N.Y. bar, 1947, since practiced in Buffalo; partner firm Ohlin, Damon, Morey, Sawyer & Moot, and predecessor, 1955—. Mem. bd. dirs. Jeffrey-Fell Co., Inc., Buffalo Clin. Lab., Inc., Ethylox Products, Inc., Bd. dirs. Erie County chpt. N.Y. State Assn. Retarded Children, 1961—, pres., 1964-66; bd. govs. N.Y. State Assn. Retarded Children, 1961-63, 66—, pres., 1969—; chmn. guardianship com. Nat. Assn. Retarded Children, 1966—, dir. 1968—; mem. adv. council N.Y. State Joint Legislative Com. Mental and Phys. Handicap, 1965—; mem. N.Y. State Health Planning Adv. Council, 1968—; mem. Regional N.Y. State Planning Com. Mental Disorders, 1964-65; del. White House Conf. on Children, 1970. Served to lt. comdr. USNR, 1943-46, 52-53; PTO. Mem. Am., N.Y. State, Erie County bar assns., Navy League, Am. Assn. Mental Deficiency, Colgate Alumni Assn. (pres. Western N.Y. 1961), Lambda Chi Alpha, Phi Alpha Delta. Clubs: Mid- Day, Marshall, Lawyers, Park Country (Buffalo). Home: 128 Doncaster Rd Kenmore NY 14217 Office: 1800 Liberty Bank Bdlg Buffalo NY 14202

HODGSON, VOIGT RALPH, educator; b. Turtle Creek, Pa., June 7, 1923; s. Henry Herman and Amy (Olsson) H.; B.S. in Aero. Engring., Wayne State U., 1955, M.S. in Engring Mechanics, 1961, Ph.D., 1968; m. Judith Lorraine Ramsey, Sept. 15, 1956; children—Matthew Charles, Loraine Susan, Edward Alan, Albert Paul, Jane Louise. Test engr. Ford Motor Co., 1955-56, missile div. Chrysler Corp., 1956-59; mem. faculty Wayne State U., 1959—, research asso. engring. mechanics, dept. neurosurgery Coll. Engring., 1960—, part-time instr. phys. therapy, 1967—; indsl. research cons., 1960—. Served with USNR, 1943-46. Mem. Creation Research Soc., Am. Soc. Testing Materials (chmn. F8.13 subcom. on head and neck of F-8 com. for protective equipment for sports), Soc. Automotive Engring., Am. Coll. Sports Medicine. Lutheran (steward). Author articles on biomechanics, especially head injury. Home: 15540 Deerfield St East Detroit MI 48021 Office: 550 E Canfield St Detroit MI 48201

HODGSON, WALTER HUTCHINSON, music educator; b. Spokane, Wash., Feb. 20, 1904; s. Dr. John Edward and Effie (Hutchinson) H.; B.S., U. of Minn., 1925; A.M., U. of Ia., 1934, Ph.D., 1936; postgrad. U. of Berlin, 1928-29; m. Elaine Virginia Bavard, July 5, 1928; children—Richard Corrin, David Walter. Supr. of music Austin, Minn., 1925-26; tchr. West High Sch., Mpls., 1926-31; instr. of music Cornell Coll., 1931-36; dir. Conservatory of Music, Mt. Union Coll., Alliance, O., 1936-41; prof. music N. Tex. State Coll., 1941-47, dean of music, 1947-58; prof., past head dept. music Mich. State U., 1958—; conductor operas and oratorios, 1947—. Eastern examiner Nat. Assn. Schs. of Music, 1941-43; pres. Tex. Assn. Schs. of Music, 1949-51, examiner, 1949-57. Mem. Music Tchrs. Nat. Assn., Am. Musicol. Assn., Music Educators Nat. Conf., Tex. Music Educators Assn. (coll. chmn. 1955- 58), Tex. Assn. of Music Schs. (pres. 1950-51, v.p. 1949-50), Am. Assn. U. Profs., Nat. Assn. Am. Composers, Conductors (Henry Hadley Award 1952), Phi Mu Alpha, Pi Kappa Lambda. Methodist. Kiwanian. Adjudicator in band and orch. contests and festivals. Composer: Symphony in D major, 1936; chamber music, songs, etc. Speaker at commencements, etc. Address: 413 Clarendon Rd East Lansing MI 48823

HODIN, JOSEF PAUL, author, art historian and critic; b. Prague, Czechoslovakia, Aug. 17, 1905; s. Eduard David and Rosa (Klug) H.; Dr. jur, Charles U., Prague, 1929; Ph.D. honoris causa, Uppsala U., 1969; student Courtauld Inst., London U., art acads. Dresden and Berlin; m. Doris Pamela Simms, May 22, 1945; children—Michael, Annabelle. Press attaché to Norwegian govt., London, 1944-45; dir. studies, librarian Inst. Contemporary Arts, London, 1949-54; hon. mem. editorial council Jour. Aesthetics and Art Criticism, Cleve., 1955—; editor Prisme des Arts, Paris 1956-59, Quadrum, Brussels, 1956-66; dir. fgn. editorial com. Studio Internat., London, 1966—. Decorated Distinguished Service medal 1st class (Czechoslovakia); Order Merit, Commendatore (Italy); grand cross Order of Merit (Austria), Order of Merit 1st class (Germany), St. Olaf medal (Norway); 1st prize for art criticism, Biennale, Venice, 1954. Mem. Brit. Soc. Aesthetics (exec. com.), Assn. Internationale des Critiques d'Art. Author monographs: Henry Moore, 1958; The Dilemma of Being Modern, 1959; Barbara Hepworth, 1961, Lynn Chadwick, 1961; Alan Reynolds, 1962; Oskar Kokoschka, 1963, 66, 68, 71, Edvard Munch, 1963, 69, 71; Ruszkowski, 1966; Walter Kern, 1966; Bernard Leach, 1967; Kafka and Goethe, 1968; Emilio Greco, 1969; Giacomo Manzu, 1969; Modern Art and the Modern Mind, 1971; The Painter Alfred Manessier, 1971. Contbr. to lit. and art internat. periodicals. Home: 12 Eton Av London NW 3 England

HODNETT, EDWARD, writer; b. Sag Harbor, L.I., N.Y., Oct. 15, 1901; s. John and Mary (Radigan) H.; A.B., Columbia, 1922, Ph.D., Columbia, 1935; m. Jessie Patrick, 1923; 1 child, Grey. Tchr. English, Columbia, 1922 40; adv. editor Columbia U. Press, 1936-42; editor Columbia U. Quar., 1940-41; prof. English, dean Coll. Arts and Scis., U. Newark, 1940-42; editor Houghton Mifflin Co., 1945-46; v.p. U. Mass., 1946- 48; pres. Fenn Coll., 1948-51; prof. English, Ohio U., 1951-57; head pub. relations Dow Corning Corp., 1957-67. Served to lt. comdr., USNR, World War II. Mem. Beta Theta Pi. Author: Plain English, 1931; English Woodcuts: 1480-1535, 1935; Problem Solving, 1955; Industry-College Relations, 1955; Poems to Read Aloud, 1957; Working with People, 1959; Which College for You?, 1960; So You Want to Go into Industry, 1960; The Cultivated Mind, 1963; Effective Presentations, 1967; Marcus Gheeraerts the Elder, 1971; Addenda et Corrigenda, English Woodcuts, 1480-1535, 1971. Editor: A Tale of a Tub (Swift), 1930. Address: Trust Dept Chemical Bank Midland MI 48640

HODSON, ALEXANDER CARLTON, educator; b. Reading, Mass., June 17, 1906; s. Alexander William and Delia (Converse) H.; B.S., U. Mass., 1928; M.A., U. Minn., 1931, Ph.D., 1935; m. Audrey Jane Kennedy, June 12, 1932; children—Nancy Jane (Mrs. Frank Pince), Robert C. Research asst. bur. entomology Dept. Agr., summers 1927-29; mem. faculty U. Minn., 1928-, prof. entomology, fisheries and wildlife, 1947—, head dept., 1960—; spl. reseach insect ecology, forest entomology. Mem. Entomol. Soc. Am. (sec. 1951, v.p. 1952, chmn. N. Central br. 1968-69), Entomol. Soc. Can., Ecol. Soc. Am. (treas. 1953-55), A.A.A.S., Am. Inst. Biol. Sci., Sigma Xi (pres. Minn. 1953), Gamma Sigma Delta, Gamma Alpha. Home: 1236 Roselawn Av St Paul MN 35113

HODSON, ARTHUR LESLIE, lawyer; b. Burslem, Eng., 1902; s. Joseph William and Emily (Garnett) H.; A.B., Washington and Jefferson Coll., 1925; LL.B., Harvard, 1929; m. Olive Lee Langfried, May 31, 1930; 1 dau., Marja Lee (Mrs. George Durfee Newton, Jr.). Came to U.S., 1919, naturalized. Admitted to Ill. bar, 1930; asso. firm Kirkland, Fleming, Green & Martin, 1929-42, partner, 1942— (firm became Kirkland, Ellis, Hodson, Chaffetz & Masters 1958). Mem. bd. Tb Inst. Chgo. and Cook County. Mem. Am., Ill., Chgo. bar assns., Am. Coll. Trial Lawyers, Selden Soc. Clubs: Chicago, Mid-Day (Chgo.); Indian Hill (Winnetka). Home: 1630 Sheridan Rd Wilmette IL 60091 Office 130 E Randolph Dr Chicago IL 60601

HODSON, KENNETH JOE, lawyer, army officer; b. Crestline, Kan., Apr. 27, 1913; s. Charles Asa and Lillian (Raymer) H.; A.B., U. Kan., 1935, LL.B., 1937; student Judge Adv. Gen. Sch., 1944; grad. Army Command and Gen. Staff Coll., 1954, Army War Coll., 1958; m. Helen J. Butterfield, Nov. 29, 1935 (dec. 1965); children—Terria Loua, Kenneth Joe, Kay Altia, David Michael; m. 2d, Marjorie Bell, Sept. 8, 1968. Admitted to Wyo. bar, 1938; practiced in Jackson, 1938-41; commd. 2d lt. arty., U.S. Army, 1934, advanced through grades to maj. gen., 1967; arty. officer, 1941- 42; judge adv. Dept. Army, Trinidad, Europe and Japan, 1942-62, faculty Judge Adv. Gen. Sch., 1951-53; U.S. chmn. U.S.-Japan Criminal Juris Com., 1955-57; asst. judge adv. gen. for mil. justice U.S. Army, 1962- 67, judge adv. gen. U.S. Army, 1967-71; chief judge U.S. Army Ct. Mil. Rev., 1971—. Decorated Legion of Merit. Mem. Am. (spl. com. standards for adminstrn. criminal justice 1964—, chmn. criminal law sect. 1964-65; sec. 1965—), Fed. (past pres. Pentagon chpt.; nat. council) bar assns., Internat. Acad. Trial Lawyers, Inst. Jud. Adminstrn., Judge Advs. Assn. (dir. 1960—). Episcopalian (sr. warden 1964-65). Author procedural sects. U.S. Manual for Courts-Martial, 1951. Co-editor: Am. Criminal Law Quar., 1963-67. Home: 2931 Garfield St NW Washington DC 20008 Office: US Army Judiciary Falls Church VA 22041

HOEBEL, BARTLEY GORE, educator; b. N.Y.C., May 29, 1935; s. Edward Adamson and Frances (Gore) H.; A.B., Harvard, 1957; postgrad. Rockefeller Inst., 1957-60; Ph.D., U. Pa., 1962; m. Cynthia A. Eney, June 22, 1963; children—Valerie, Carolyn, Brett. Mem. faculty psychology dept. Princeton, 1962—, prof, 1970—. Mem. Am. Psychol. Assn., Am. Physiol. Assn. Unitarian. Author articles in field. Home: 207 Hartley Av Princeton NJ 08540

HOEBEL, EDWARD ADAMSON, educator; b. Madison, Wis., Nov. 16, 1906; s. Edward Charles and Kathryn (Arnold) H.; A.B., U. Wis., 1928; student, Cologne, Germany, 1928-29; A.M., N.Y.U., 1931; Ph.D., Columbia, 1934; m. Frances Elizabeth Gore, June 20, 1930 (dec. July 1962); 1 son, Bartley Gore; m. 2d, Irene Holth, Aug. 26, 1963; 1 dau., Sue Dunbar. Instr. sociology N.Y.U., 1929-35, asst. prof. sociology and anthropology, 1935- 41, assoc. prof., 1941-48, lectr. anthropology, dept. psychiatry Sch. Medicine, 1946-48; vis. prof. various schs.; prof., head dept. anthropology U. Utah, 1948-54, dean Univ. Coll., 1953-54; prof. anthropology, chmn. dept. U. Minn., 1954-66, Regent's prof., 1966—, chmn. dept., 1966-69; Fulbright prof., Oxford (Eng.) U., 1956-57, Cath. U., The Netherlands, 1970. Research fellow Lab. Anthropol., Santa Fe; dir. Social Science Research Council; adv. panel social sci. research NSF, 1958-60; sr.

specialist Inst. Advanced Study, East-West Center Cultural and Tech. Interchange, Honolulu, 1964-65; mem. Gov.'s Commn. Human Relations, 1955-64; behavioral scis. panel Nat. Inst. Gen. Med. Sci., 1962-66; cons. Dept. State, U.S. Arms Control and Disarmament Agy., 1969—. Trustee St. Paul Sci. Mus. Recipient research fellowship Columbia U. Council Research in Social Scis., Am. Council Learned Socs.; fellow Center Advanced Studies Behavioral Scis., 1960-61. Fellow A.A.A.S.; mem. Am. Philos. Soc., Am. Ethnol. Soc. (pres. 1947), Am. Anthropol. Assn. (pres. 1956-57), Assn. Am. Indian Affairs (dir. 1945-56), Alpha Kappa Lambda. Alpha Kappa Delta, Phi Kappa Phi. Club: Skylight. Author several books, latest being: Social Meaning of Legal Concepts; Inheritance (with others), 1948, Man in the Primitive World; An Introduction to Anthropology, 1949; The Commanches (with E. Wallace), 1952; The Law of Primitve Man; A Study in Comparative Legal Dynamics, 1954; The Cheyenne Indians, 1961; Anthropology: The Study of Man, 1966; also articles, revs. in legal, hist. and anthropol. jours. Asso. editor Law and Soc. Rev., 1969—. Home: 2273 Folwell St Paul MN 55108 Office: Ford Hall U Minn Minneapolis MN 55455 ☆

HOEBEL, LOUIS FREDERIC, ins. co. exec.; b. Madison, Wis., Mar. 5, 1912; s. Edward C. and Kathryn (Arnold) H.; B.A., U. Wis., 1934, M.A., 1935; m. Virginia Lee Vollmer, Aug. 29, 1936; 1 dau., Jeris Ann (Mrs. Richard Rovsek). With Halsey Stuart & Co., Chgo., 1935-40; with No. Trust Co., Chgo., 1942-50; exec. v.p., treas. Mut. of Omaha, 1950-69, exec. v.p., 1969—; dir. Campanion Life Ins. Co., Mut. of Omaha Fund Mgmt. Co., Omaha Indemnity Co. Mem. Neb. Investment Bd. Bd. dirs. Goodwill Industries, Childrens Meml. Hosp., Jr. Achievement. Mem. Financial Analysts Fedn. Home: 10333 Broadmoor Ct Omaha NB 68144 Office: 3316 Farnam St Omaha NB 68131

HOEBER, PAUL B., pub.; b. N.Y. City, Oct. 11, 1914; s. Paul B. and Catherine (Putzel) H.; student Antioch Coll., 1931-34, Am. U. Sch. Pub. Affairs, 1934-37; m. Elizabeth Price, June 20, 1940; children—Paul Richard, Thomas Edward. With Paul B. Hoeber, Inc., med. book dept. Harper & Bros., 1937—, pres., 1945-69, exec. v.p. Am. Elsevier Pub. Co., 1970—. Served with USNR, 1942-45; South Atlantic Fleet, 1942-43; inactive Res. since 1945. Democrat. Clubs: Players, Overseas Press (N.Y.C). Home: 350 Central Park W New York City NY 10025 Office: 52 Vanderbilt Av New York City NY 10017

HOECKER, FRANK EDWARD, educator, radiol. physicist; b. St. Joseph, Mo., July 2, 1903; s. Frank Joseph and Lula Mae (Newkirk) H.; A.B., Coll. Emporia, 1930; M.A., U. Kan., 1932, Ph.D., 1935; m. Margaret Hildreth Sturges, June 13, 1935; 1 dau., Margaret Hildreth (Mrs. David Weddington). Asst. prof. physics, chmn. dept. physics U. Kansas City (Mo.), 1934-42; mem. magnetic mine sect. Naval Ordnance Lab., 1942; sr. physicist USPHS, 1942-43; research asso. Manhattan Dist. project Columbia, 1943-45; faculty U. Kan., 1945—, prof. physics, 1950—, prof. radiation biophysics, 1952—, chmn. dept., 1952-68. Mem. task force I, Operation Crossroads, 1946; cons. to hosps., govt. and industry, 1945—; mem. Kan. Civil Def. Council, 1950- 60, chief radiol. def. div., 1950-60; adviser Am. del. 1st Internat. Conf. Peaceful Uses Atomic Energy, Geneva, Switzerland, 1955. Diplomate Am. Bd. Radiology, Am. Bd. Health Physics. Asso. fellow Physics Am. Coll. Radiology; mem. Am. Phys. Soc., Radiol. Soc. N.Am., Health Physics Soc., Radiation Research Soc., Kan. Radiol. Soc., Kan. Acad. Sci. Spl. research dielectric constants dilute solutions, alpha particle autoradiology, radio deposition in bone, radiation polymerization of monomers. Patentee cardioscope, bone sectioning device, irradiated volumn dose, radiation polymerization dosimeter. Home: 1503 Haskell St Lawrence KS 66044

HOEFER, JOHN HENRY, advt. exec.; b. St. Cloud, Minn., Nov. 12, 1915; s. John James and Marie E. (De Longchamps) H.; A.B., U. Cal. at Berkeley, 1938; M.B.A., Stanford, 1940; m. Katharine Adele Foster, Sept. 9, 1939; children—Carolyn (Mrs. John Pelkan), Susan (Mrs. Peter Witter), John Foster, William Edward, Mary Ann. Pres., Hoefer, Dieterich & Brown, Inc., San Francisco, 1967—, chmn. bd., 1967—; chmn. bd. John H. Hoefer Co., 1965—. Advt. Graphic Arts, Inc., 1965—. Served to rear adm. USNR, 1940. Mem. Advt. Assn. of West (past pres.), San Francisco Advt. Club (past pres.), Am. Assn. Advt. Agys. (past sec.-treas., dir.), San Francisco C. of C. (v.p. 1968—), San Francisco Better Bus. Bur. (past pres.). Episcopalian. Home: 32 Peninsula Rd Belvedere CA 94920 Office: 414 Jackson Sq San Francisco CA 94111

HOEFER, PAUL FREDERICK ADAM, physician; b. Munich, Germany, Nov. 21, 1903; s. Paul Adam and Sophie (Gutkin) H.; Ph.D., U. Berlin (Germany), 1927; M.D., U. Wuerzburg (Germany), 1928; m. Maria Kuehl, Sept. 27, 1932. Came to U.S. 1934, naturalized, 1939. Asst. physiology U. Berlin, 1929-32; asst. neurology U. Heidelberg (Germany), 1932-33; instr. Tufts U., 1934-36; research fellow, asst. neurology Harvard, 1936-39; faculty Columbia Coll. Phys and Surg., 1939—, prof. neurology, 1962—; exchange prof. Free U. Berlin, 1953-54; cons. Walter Reed Hosp., Washington, 1946-50; chief neurology VA Clinc, Bklyn., 1969—. Mem. A.M.A., Am. Neurology Assn., Am. Physiol. Soc., Am. Electroencephalograph Soc., Royal Soc. Medicine Eng., Am. Psychiat. Assn., Am. Acad. Neurology, Assn. Research Nervous and Mental Disease. Research, numerous publs. on electrophysiology, nerve, muscle and brain, modern research instrumentation, motor disorders central nervous system, neurol. disorders, studies Myasthenia Gravis. Home: 355 E 72d St New York City NY 10021

HOEFER, RICHARD A., former pub.; b. Chgo., 902. Pub. House Beautiful mag.; v.p. Hearst Mag., Inc.; v.p. Hearst Corp. Home: 28 Valley Rd Bronxville NY 10708 Office: 572 Madison Av New York City NY 10022

HOEFFEL, MARTIN EDWARD, lawyer; b. Paulding County, O., Oct. 2, 1903; s. John Albert and Magdalena (Rusch) H.; LL.B., Ohio State U., 1934; m. Catherine M. Hahn, Nov. 6, 1937; children-Anthony, John, Susan. Asst. in County Auditor's Office, Napoleon, O., 1923-27; admitted to Ohio bar, 1934, since practiced in Napoleon; sr. mem. firm Hoeffel, Funkhouser & Short, 1970- -; prosecuting atty. Henry County, 1935-41. Mem. Ohio Supreme Ct. Grievance Bd. Sec. bd. dirs. S.M. Heller Hosp. Mem. Am., Ohio, Northwestern Ohio, Henry County bar assns. Democrat. K.C., Elk, Kiwanian. Home: 403 W Main St Napoleon OH 43545 Office: Corner Perry and Shelby Sts Napoleon OH 43545

HOEFLIN, RUTH MERLE, univ. dean; b. Ft. Dodge, Ia., Jan. 4, 1918; d. Herbert and Edna (Mathias) Hoeflin; B.S., Ia. State U., 1940; M.A., U. Mich., 1945; Ph.D., Ohio State U., 1950. Nursery sch. tchr., Detroit, 1940-42, 43-44; recreation dir. Home for Delinquents, Detroit, 1942-43; instr. Merrill- Palmer Sch., Detroit, 1944-46; asst. prof. home life dept. Okla. State U., 1946-47; asso. prof. child devel. Ohio State U., 1945-57; prof. family and child devel., head dept. Kan. State U., 1957-60, asso. dean Coll. Home Econs., 1960—; speaker, condr. family life insts. Sec. Nat. Council Family Relations, 1962-63; Kan. chmn. middle state project for familty life edn. Am. Social Health Assn. Recipient Diamond Anniversary award for distinguished service in home econs. Ohio State U., Alumni award in home econs. Ia. State U. Mem. Am. Assn. U. Profs., Soc. Research Child Devel., Am., North Central (chmn.) home econs. assns., Am. Assn. Adult Edn., Nat. Assn. Nursery Edn., Kan. Home Econs. Assn. (mem. bd.), Kan. Farm Life Assn. (mem. bd.), Assn. Adminstrs. Home Econs. (chmn.), Mortar Bd., Phi Upsilon Omicron, Omicron Nu, Phi Kappa Phi, Pi Lambda Theta. Author: Essentials of Family Living, 1960; Careers in Home Economics, 1970; also research bulletins, articles. Co-author; (monograph) Society for Research in Child Development, 1959. Home: 814 Wildcat Ridge Manhattan KS 66502

HOEGH, LEO ARTHUR, lawyer, corp. exec.; b. Audubon County, Ia., Mar. 30, 1908; s. William and Annie K. (Johnson) H.; B.A., U. Ia., 1929, J.D., 1932; m. Mary Louise Foster, June 29, 1936; children—Kristin, Janis. Admitted to Ia. bar, 1932, Ill. bar, 1962, Colo. bar, 1964; with firm Hoegh & Meyer, Chariton, Ia., 1942-57; city atty., Chariton, 1941; atty. gen. Ia., 1953-54; gov. Ia., 1954-57; civil def. adminstr., 1957-58; dir. Office Civil and Def. Mblzn., 1958-61; gen. counsel, dir. Soypro. Internat.; dir. Ia. Fund, Inc., Bank of Man., Total Pole, Inc. Mem. Nat. Sec. Council; mem. President's Com. Edn. Beyond High Sch. Mem. Ia. Ho. Reps., 1937-42. Served to lt. col. AUS, 1942-46. Decorated 3 battlefield decorations. Mem. AMVETS, Am. Legion (post comdr.), Am., Colo., Ia. bar assns., Pi Kappa Alpha, Delta Theta Phi. Republican (co-chmn.). Methodist. Clubs: Rotary; Garden of Gods (Colorado Springs, Colo.); Kenwood Country (Bethesda, Md.). Author: Timberwolf Tracks, 1946. Home: Timpa Rd Chipita Park CO 80811

HOEHN, ELMER L., lawyer, govt. ofcl.; b. Memphis, Ind., Dec. 19, 1915; s. Louis and Agnes (Goss) H.; B.S., Canterbury Coll., 1936, Northwestern U., 1937; J.D., U. Louisville, 1940; m. Frances Cory, June 10, 1943; children—Kathleen Cory, G. Patrick. Admitted to Ky. bar, 1940, D.C. bar, 1969, U.S. Supreme Ct. bar, 1969, U.S. ct. Appeals bar, 1970; prof. bus. and law Jeffersonville (Ind.) High Sch., 1946-50, Ind. U., 1940-41; with legal and personnel div. Am. Barge Lines, 1942-44; apptd. dir. by gov., Ind. Oil and Gas, 1949-53; apptd. adminstr. by Pres., U.S. Oil Import Adminstrn., 1965-69; sec.-treas. Am. Assn. Oil Well Drilling Contractors, 1956-60; exec. sec. Ind. Oil Producers and Land Owners Assn., 1953-64; counsel firm Batzell-Nunn, Washington, 1969—; pvt. practice law, Washington, 1969—; relator, 1949-70; cons. petroleum, natural resources, energy and environment. Mem. Ind. Gen. Assembly, 1945- 49, minority floor leader, 1947, chief clk., 1949; Democratic chmn. Clark County, Ind., 1945-52; Ind. del. Dem. Nat. Conv., 1964, 8th Congl. Dist. 1952-58; mem. Ind. Dem. Exec. Com., 1952-58; Ind. and Mid-west campaign mgr. LBJ campaign for president, 1960. Named hon. citizen, Ind., Tex., Ky., Neb., S.D., La., Okla. Mem. Am., Fed., Ky., D.C. bar assns., Am. Petroleum Inst., Sigma Delta Kappa. Roman Catholic. Clubs: Lawyers (Washington); Indiana Legislators (Indpls.); Elks Country (Jeffersonville). Home: 4317 9th St S Arlington VA 22204 also 18 Blanchel Terrace Jeffersonville IN 47130 Office: 1523 L St NW Washington DC 20005 101 Sparks Av Jeffersonville IN 47130 also Ohio Valley Bank Bldg Henderson KY 42420

HOEHN, KENNETH WILLIAM, broadcasting co. exec.; b. N.Y.C., Mar. 30, 1918; s. William August and Catherine (Hefner) H.; B.A., U. Wis., 1941; LL.B., Harvard, 1948; m. Jean Meredith, Nov. 15, 1943; children—W. Michael, Carol Jean. Admitted to N.Y. bar, 1949; with law dept. RCA, 1948-51; with CBS, 1951—, tax dir., 1956-64, treas., 1964—, v.p., 1971—. Served to lt., aviator, USNR, 1941-45. Home: 40 Stonehenge Rd Manhasset NY 11030 Office: 51 W 52d St New York City NY 10019

HOEKENDIJK, JOHANNES CHRISTIAAN, theologian; b. Garut, Indonesia, May 3, 1912; s. Cornelis Johannes and Suzanne (van der Kris) H.; Th.D., U. Utrecht, 1948; m. 2d, Letty Mandeville Russell, Jan. 3, 1970. Sec., Student Christian Movement Netherlands, 1939-42; missions consul, Indonesia, 1945- 47; sec. Netherlands Missionary Council, 1947-49; sec. Evangelism World Council Chs., Geneva, 1949-52; prof. theology Utrecht U., Netherlands, 1953-65; prof. missions Union Theol. Sem., N.Y.C., 1965—. Served as maj. Dutch Army, 1945-47. Mem. German Soc. Missiology, Utrecht Acad. Scis. Author: Evangelism in France, 1950; The Church Inside Out, 1966; Bibliography: Kirche und Volk in der deutschen Missionswissenschaft, 1967; Horizons of Hope, 1970. Contbr. profl. jours. Address: 99 Claremont Av New York City NY 10027

HOEKSTRA, RAYMOND, educator. Prof. philosophy Wayne State U, Detroit. Office: Dept Philosophy Wayne State U Detroit MI 48202*

HOEL, PAUL, (Gerhard), statistician, educator; b. Iola, Wis., Mar. 23, 1905; s. Carl S. and Inga (Loken) H.; A.B., Luther Coll., 1926; postgrad. U. Pitts., 1926-27; M.A., U. Minn., 1929, Ph.D., 1933; m. Hazel Bessie Helvig, Sept. 7, 1932; children—David, Carlton, Marie, Instr., Rose Poly. Inst., 1933-36; instr. Ore. State U., 1936-39; from instr. to prof. U. Cal. at Los Angeles, 1939—. Am.-Scandinavian Found. fellow, Norway, 1936-37; Fulbright research fellow, Norway, 1953-54. Author: Introduction to Mathematical Statistics, 4 edits., 1947-70; Elementary Statistics, 3 edits., 1960-70; (with R. Jessen) Basic Statistics for Business and Economics, 1970; (with C. Stone and S. Port) Probability, Statistics, Stochastic Processes, 3 vols., 1970. Home: 1726 Westridge Rd Los Angeles CA 90049

HOELDTKE, CATHRYN GRAY, church woman; b. Little Rock, Sept. 4, 1911; d. Daniel Lewis and Nancy (Miller) Gray; student Agnes Scott Coll., 1929-30, Wheaton (Ill.) Coll., 1930-32; B.S. in L.S., Goerge Peabody Coll., 1933; m. Ernest H. Hoeldtke, Dec. 23, 1935; children—Ernest Frederick, Robert Daniel. Pres. Buffalo-Niagara Presbyterial Soc., 1955-58, United Presbyn. Women, 1958- 61; treas. United Ch. Women, 1961-64; mem. bd. nat. missions United Presbyn. Ch., 1962-71, v.p., 1967-71, mem. gen. council Synod N.Y., 1962- 64; bd. dirs. Bible So. Western N.Y., 1958-62. Address: 188 Smallwood Dr Buffalo NY 14224

HOELKER, RUDOLF FRANZ, space flight scientist; b. Halle, Westphalia, Germany, Mar. 16, 1912; s. Cornelius and Christina (Ochsenfarth) H.; Abitur Friedrich-Wilhelm Gymnasium, Trier, Germany, 1930; Dr.Sc., U. Muenster, 1942; m. Anneliese Wibben, Apr. 27, 1948; 1 dau., Melanie Cornelia. Came to U.S., 1945, naturalized, 1955. Chief guidance simulation lab. Heeresversuchsanstalt, Peenemuende, Germany, 1940-45; research scientist Dept. Army, Ft. Bliss, Tex. and Huntsville, Ala., 1945-51; chief flight mechs. sect. Army Ballistic Missile Agy., Huntsville, 1951-58, dep. dir. aeroballistics div., 1958-60; dept. dir. aeroballistics div., chief future projects br. NASA, Marshall Space Flight Center, Huntsville, 1960- 63, chief astrodynamics and guidance theory div., 1963-65; sr. scientist guidance lab. Electronics Research Center, NASA, Cambridge, Mass., 1965—. Served with German Army, 1943. Recipient Achievement award for contbns. to Pioneer IV Lunar Probe, 1959. Fellow Am. Inst. Astronautics and Aeros. (asso.); mem. Soc. Indsl. and Applied Math., Hermann Oberth Soc. (hon.). Contbr. articles profl. jours. Patentee dual measuring principle for stabilizing flight of large space vehicles; discovered bi-elliptical transfer between orbits; instrumental in trajectory design, control concepts, stablizn. and path guidance methods of missiles and space vehicles as Redstone, Jupiter, Saturn, including boosters for early Am. spaceshots as Explorers and Pioneers. Home: 29 Brook St Wellesley MA 02181 Office: 575 Technology Sq Cambridge MA 02139

HOELLE, WILLIAM JOHN, food co. exec.; b. San Francisco, Jan. 21, 1915; s. Emil and Minnie M. (Rippe) H.; A.B., Stanford, 1935; m. Edith K. Feuille, May 22, 1942; children—Carole Ann, Mary Christine, Thornton Emil, Karen Louise. Founder, dir., v.p. sales Cal. Eastern Airways Air Freight, 1946- 49; dist. mgr. No. Cal., Bing Crosby Minute Maid Corp., 1950- 54; asst. gen. mgr. Hi-C div., Minute Maid Corp., 1955-57, gen. mgr., 1959-62, sales mgr. corp., 1957-58; v.p. sales United Fruit Co., 1962-64, v.p. marketing, 1964—, pres. Sovereign Fruit Co. subsidary, 1967—; chmn. bd. United Fruit Sales Corp., 1966—. Served to maj. USAAF, World War II. Decorated D.F.C. with 3 oak leaf clusters, Air medal with 5 oak leaf clusters, Purple Heart. Mem. Theta Chi. Clubs: Eastern Yacht; University (Boston); Tedesco Golf (Marblehead, Mass.). Home: 615 Ocean Dr Key Biscayne FL 33149 Office: 801 S Bayshore Dr Miami FL 33131

HOELSCHER, HAROLD EWALD, educator; b. St. Louis, Sept. 28, 1922; s. Emil H. and Lillian (Merifield) H.; B.S., Princeton, 1944; M.S., Washington U., St. Louis, 1947, Ph.D., 1949; m. Anna Hunter Stockton, Dec. 28, 1946; children—David Hunter, Lillian Anna. Instr. Washington U., 1946-49; asst. prof. U. Cin., 1949- 52; asst. prof. Johns Hopkins, 1952-54, asso. prof., 1954-56, prof., chmn. dept. chem. engring., 1956-65; prof. chem. engring., dean School Engring., U. Pitts., 1965—, dir. Space Research Coordination Center, 1968-70; cons. chem. industry. Sr. Fulbright lectr. U. Madras, India, 1963-64. Served with USAFF, 1944-46. Mem. Am. Inst. Chem. Engrs., Am. Chem. Soc., Am. Soc. Engring. Edn., Soc. Applied Anthropology, Sigma Xi, Tau Beta Pi. Contbr. tech. papers sci. jours. Home: 724 S Negley Av Pittsburgh PA 15232

HOELSCHER, LEONARD WILLIAM, cons.; b. Wilton, Mo., Jan. 5, 1900; s. Louis F. and Mary (Fahrendorf) H.; m. Edna King, Oct. 17, 1925; 1 son, Kenneth King. Draftsman, engr. C. E. Smith & Co., St. Louis, 1918-25; resident engr. Harland Bartholomew & Assos., 1925-31; successively city planning engr., asst. city mgr., city mgr., Fort Worth, 1931-37; staff mem., gen. field supr. Pub. Adminstrn. Service, Chgo., Oakland, Cal. and Seattle, 1937- 40; successively cons., staff mem., br. chief Bur. of Budget, 1940-50; spl. asst. Dept. Army, 1950-52, dep. comptroller, 1952-68; now cons.; dir. study basis to comp. reorgn. Dept. Army, 1962; cons. Pub. Adminstrn. Service, 1968-70. Served with U.S. Army, 1918. Recipient Exceptional Civilian Service award War Dept., 1945; Meritorious Civilan Service award Dept. Army, 1952, Exceptional Civilian Service award, 1962; Distinguished Civilian Service award Dept. Def., 1963. Mem. Am. Soc. Pub. Adminstrn. (pres. Nat. Capital Area chpt. 1955-56), Am. Polit. Sci. Assn., Am. Soc. Mil. Comptrollers (pres. Washington chpt. 1964-65). Home: 2300 Kilkenny W Tallahassee FL 32303

HOELSCHER, WILFRED FREDERICK, steel co. exec.; b. Granite City, Ill., Feb. 5, 1910; s. Fred H. and Wilhelmina (Holtgrewe) H.; B.S., U. Ill., 1935; m. Barbara Jane Black, Aug. 23, 1938; children—Fred, John, Ellen. Accountant, Price Waterhouse & Co., C.P.A.'s, 1935-41; with Granite City Steel Co. (Ill.), 1947—, sec.-treas., 1957—, v.p., 1965—; dir. Central States Steel, Inc., Granite Intake Corp., Granco Products Co., Granite Office Bldg. Corp. Trustee, Deaconess Hosp., St. Louis. Served to maj. USAAF, 1941-47. Mem. Am. Iron and Steel Inst., Financial Execs. Inst., Am. Mgmt. Assn., Tax Execs., Am. Soc. Corp. Secretaries, Granite City C. of C. (bd. dirs.), Phi Sigma Kappa. Mem. United Ch. Christ (elder). Clubs: Glen Echo Country (Normandy, Mo.); Missouri Athletic (St. Louis). Home: 60 Berkshire St St Louis MO 63117 Office: Granite City Steel Co 20th and State St Granite City IL 62040

HOEN, THOMAS IRVING, neurosurgeon; b. Balt., Feb. 11, 1903; s. Albert B. and Mary (Lyons) H.; A.B., Catholic U., 1924, M.D., John Hopkins, 1928; m. Annie Townsend Stocking, Sept. 9, 1933; children—Thomas Townsend, Robert Martin, Jonathan Stocking. Halstead research fellow under Walter Dandy, 1929; asst. under Harvey Cushing, 1930-31, under Wilder Penfield, 1931-32; prof. neurology, neurosurgery, N.Y. Med. Coll., 1939-51; prof. neurosurgery N.U.U. Sch. Medicine, 1951—, chmn. dept. neurosurgery, 1951-61; dir. neurosurgery service Bellevue Hosp., N.Y.U., 1951-61, Univ. Hosp., 1951-61; cons. neurosurgery Hosp for Spl. Surgery, N.Y.C., 1951—; sr. cons. U.S. Naval Hosp., St. Albans, N.Y., 1951—, Manhattan VA Hosp., N.Y.C., 1951—. Served with M.C., USNR, 1943-46, chief neurosurg. center U.S. Naval Hosp., St. Albans, disch. capt. Fellow A.C.S.; mem. Assn. Research in Nervous and Mental Diseases, A.A.A.S., N.Y. Surg. Soc., Harvey Cushing Soc., N.Y. Neurosurg. Soc., N.Y. Acad. Medicine. Clubs: River (N.Y.C.); Rockaway Hunting (Cedarhurst, N.Y.C.). Home: 181 Briarwood Crossing Cedarhurst NY 11516 Office: Milbank Research Lab 340 E 24th St New York City NY 10010 also 1550 1st Av New York City NY 10022

HOENACK, AUGUST FREDERICK, architect; b. N.Y.C., Apr. 1, 1908; s. Hugo H. and Hulda (Kilian) H.; B.Arch., Pratt Inst., 1938; student Columbia, 1930-31; postgrad. George Washington U., 1940-41; m. Mary Margery Course, June 14, 1939; children—Stephen A., Judith (Mrs. Paul Schultz), Francis A., August Jeremy. Architect PBA, Washington, 1938-41; asso. architect hospital facilities USPHS, Washington, 1942-46, asst. chief, 1946-55, chief architecture, engring. equipment br., 1955-68; v.p. firm Jensen & Halstead, Architects, Egrs. & Consultants, Chgo., 1968—. Recipient Superior Service award HEW, 1967, Outstanding Alumnus award Pratt Inst., 1968. Fellow A.I.A. (mem. health environment com. 1960-67), Am. Assn. Hosp. Planning (Distinguished Service to Hosp. Design award 1967), Am. Hosp. Assn., Internat. Hosp. Fedn., Am. Pub. Health Assn. Contbr. profl. jours. Home: 8409 Seven Locks Rd Bethesda MD 20034 Office: 600 S Michigan Av Chicago IL 60605

HOENEMEYER, FRANK JOSEPH, ins. co. exec.; b. Cin., Nov. 1, 1919; s. Frank Joseph and Irene (Perry) H.; B.S., Xavier U., Cin., 1941; M.B.A., Wharton Sch. of U. Pa., 1947; m. Lucille F. De Jaco, Nov. 14, 1942; children—Frank Joseph, Cheryl Ann, Mary Lynn, David. With Prudential Ins. Co., Newark, 1947—, v.p., 1958- 64, sr. v.p., 1964-65, exec. v.p. investments, 1965—; dir. Cin. Inc., N.J. Bus. Devel. Corp., Newark. Served with USAAF, 1941- 46. Home: 10 Midwood Terrace Madison NJ 07940 Office: Prudential Plaza Newark NJ 07101

HOENGEN, ELISABETH, mezzosoprano; b. Gevelsberg, Westphalia, Germany, Dec. 7, 1906; d. Theodor and Elisabeth (Peters) Hoengen; ed. U. Berlin, 1928-30, Acad. Music, Berlin, 1930-33. Appeared at Municipal Theater, Wuppertal, 1933- 35, Municipal Theater, Duesseldorf, 1935-40; mem. State Opera, Dresden, 1940-43, State Opera, Vienna, 1943-71; appearances festival plays at Salzburg, 1948-50, 54, 57, 59, Berlin, 1939, Munich, 1939, 52, 59, Bayreuth, 1951, also Maggio Musical, Florence, Italy, 1942, 47, 48, Empire State Festivals, Ellensville, N.Y., 1957; guest performances Milano Scala, London Covent Garden, Paris Grand Opera, N.Y.C. Met. Opera, also Barcelona, Zurich, Naples, Buenos Aires, Oslo, Copenhagen; lieder recitals and oratories in Vienna, Salzburg, Berlin, Muenchen, Zurich, London, Rome, Venedig, others; condr. operatic classes Vienna Acad. Music, 1957-60; prof. Vienna, 1964; condr. course dramatic art, Austrian pavilion, Brussels World Exposition, Brussels, Belgium, 1958; television appearances in Austria, also Germany; recording artist for Columbia, Gramophon,

Decca, Telefunken, Amadeo, Electrola. Named Kammersaengerin, Vienna State Opera, 1947; recipient Mozart medal, and title prof., 1964. Home: Zuckerkandlgasse 28 1190 Vienna Austria

HOENIG, SIDNEY B., educator; b. N.Y.C., Apr. 6, 1907; s. Joseph and Lena (Goldfarb) H.; B.S.S., City Coll. N.Y., 1927; rabbi, Yeshiva U., 1931; Ph.D., Dropsie Coll., 1934; m. Ann Whitehorn, Mar. 28, 1939; children—Hava, Joseph (dec.), Herschel, Fredda, Jacob. Ednl. dir. Young Israel Movement, 1939- 41; prin. Hebrew Tchrs, Tng. Sch. Girls, 1941-45; Jewish chaplain Bklyn. House Detention, 1947—; prof. Jewish history, dir. adult edn. Yeshiva U., 1955—, also dean Bernard Revel Grad. Sch. Author: Passover Haggadah, 1949; The Great Sanhedrin, 1953; A Guide to the Prophets, 1957; Jewish Identity, 1965; Dr. Revel: Rabbinics and Research, 1968; Solomon Zeitlen Bibliography, 1971; also articles. Contbr. Ency. Brit., Interpreters Dictionary of the Bible. Home: 215 Beach 126th St Rockaway Park NY 11694 Office: Yeshiva U 186th St at Amsterdam Av New York City NY 10033

HOENIGER, BERTHOLD HEINRICH, lawyer; b. Freiburg Br., Germany, Oct. 4, 1928; s. Heinrich and Josephine (Reck) H.; came to U.S., 1938, naturalized, 1945; B.A., Columbia, 1948, LL.B., 1950; m. Doris E. Sanders, Dec. 6, 1958; children-Felicia Sanders, Matthew Sanders. Admitted to N.Y. bar, 1950, since practiced in N.Y.C.; law sec. U.S. Dist. Judge William Bondy, 1950- 51; asso. firm Milbank, Tweed, Hope & Hadley, then Spiro, Felstiner and Prager, 1951-58; mem. firm Shapiro & Hoeniger, 1958-61, Hoeniger & Rozen, 1961-64; partner firm Carrow, Bernson, Hoeniger, Freitag & Abbey, and predecessor, 1964—. Dir., sec., gen. counsel Ecologic Resources Corp. Sec., gen. counsel Ridgebury Found., Inc. Mem. Conn., N.Y. State bar assns., Bar Assn. City N.Y. Author: (with Henry P. DeVries) The Post- Liberation Nationalizations in France, 1950. Home: RD 2 Chestnut Hill Rd Ridgefield CT 06877; also Castle Rd Truro MA 02666Office: 1 E 44th St New York NY 10017

HOERNER, WILLIAM F., food processing exec.; b. New Orleans, Sept. 4, 1910; s. William and Anna (Cooney) H.; LL.B., Loyola U., 1945; m. Mary Connell, June 21, 1939; children—William F., Mary Ann, Jane Ellen, Gregory John. With Wesson Oil & Snowdrift Co., Inc., 1925-68, accountant, 1932-40, cost accountant, 1940-48, co. merged with Hunt Foods & Industries, Inc., 1960, v.p., 1960-68; admitted to La. bar, 1945; practice law, New Orleans, 1945-48; pub. accountant, 1937-48; v.p. So. Cotton Oil Co., Inc., Southport Paint Co., Inc., So. Shell Fish Co., Inc. C.P.A., La. Mem. Am. Inst. C.P.A.'s Nat. Assn. Accountants, La., New Orleans bar assns., Soc. La. C.P.A.'s. Roman Catholic. Author articles on accounting. Home: 8121 San Lucas Dr Whittier CA 90605 Office: 14501 E Artesia Blvd La Mirada CA 90638

HOERR, STANLEY OBERMANN, surgeon; b. Chgo., Sept. 29, 1909; s. Charles Ferdinand and Lillie Sophia (Obermann) H; A.B., Antioch Coll., 1932; M.D., Harvard, 1936; m. Janet Urie, July 9, 1932; children—Mary (Mrs. Roger L. Meyer), Joan (Mrs. W.A. Hayden Schilling), Stanley O., Charles M., Mark R. Intern, resident Peter Bent Brigham Hosp., Boston, 1936-42; pathology resident Huntington Meml. Hosp., Boston, 1938-39; asso. in surgery Peter Bent Brigham Hosp., 1945-47; asso. prof. surgery Ohio State U. Sch. Medicine, 1947-50; surg. staff Cleve. Clinic Found., 1950—, chmn. div. surgery, 1956—. Served from capt. to maj., AUS, 1942-45; ETO. Diplomate Am. Bd. Surgery. Fellow A.C.S. (gov. 1963—, 2d v.p. 1970-71, pres. Ohio chpt. 1963); mem. A.M.A. (sec. sect. gen. surgery 1965-68), Am., Central (pres. 1970-71) surg. assns., Internat., Eastern surg. socs., Soc. Surgery Alimentary Tract (pres. 1971-72), Soc. Univ. Surgeons, Whipple Surg. Soc., Am. Gastroent. Assn., Cleve. Surg. Soc. (pres. 1958). Clubs: Pasteur, Harvard (Cleve.). Contbr. articles profl. jours., textbooks. Home: 997 Richmond Rd Lyndhurst OH 44124 Office: 2020 E 93d St Cleveland OH 44106

HOESEL, WALTER RICHARD, educator; b. Staunton, Va., Dec. 25, 1938; s. Walter Oskar and Gerturde (Voitel) H.; B.S, Princeton, 1960; M.S., Temple U., 1966; postgrad. U. Pa., 1965-66; m. Katherine Keating Desmond, Sept. 2, 1961; children—Lisa Margaret, Christopher Walter. Engr., Gen. Electric Co., 1959-60; asst. headmaster Germantown Acad., Fort Washington, Pa., 1966-69; headmaster Lake Forest (Ill.) Acad., 1969—. Mem. Human Relations Commn., Lake Forest, Lake Bluff, 1970-71. Mem. Newcomen Soc., Black Hawks Internat. Club: University (Chgo). Address: 1500 W Kennedy St Lake Forest IL 60045

HOEY, JOSEPH PATRICK, lawyer; b. Bklyn., Oct. 21, 1912; s. Patrick J. and Margaret (Kelly) H.; A.B., Fordham U., 1934; LL.B., St. Johns U.; m. Kathryn Daly, Sept. 18, 1943; children—Anne Marie, Joseph Patrick, Patrick Thomas, Kathryn Marie. Admitted to N.Y. bar, 1938; with James E. Turner, lawyer, Bklyn., 1937-39; dep. asst. dist. atty. Kings County, 1940-42, asst. dist. atty., 1945-61; U.S. atty. Eastern Dist. N.Y., 1961-69; lectr. Practicing Law Inst., 1954—. Served to lt. USNR, 1942-45. Mem. Bklyn. (trustee), N.Y. State bar assns., Lawyers Club Bklyn., Catholic Lawyers Guild, Am. Legion, Emerald Assn. L.I. (pres. 1959-60), St. Patricks Soc. Bklyn. (pres. 1947), Friendly Sons St. Patrick Bklyn. K.C. Club: Catherdral (Bklyn.) Home: 2121 Albemarle Terrace Brooklyn NY 11226 Office: 17 E 63d St New York City NY 10021

HOFACRE, WILLIAM MARION, constrn. co. exec.; b. Axtell, Kan., July 29, 1933; s. Michael Howard and Nellie Marie (Wilson) H.; B.S. in Bus. Adminstrn., U. Neb., 1957; M.B.A., Mich. State U., 1967; m. Janet Elizabeth Hemmer, June 12, 1959; children—Michael Lane, Tracey Elizabeth. Internal auditor Bendix Corp., South Bend, Ind., 1957-63, controller indsl. controls div., Detroit, 1963-67; controller Itek Corp. bus. products div., Rochester, N.Y., 1967-69; corporate controller Am. Air Filter, Louisville, 1969-70; corporate controller Daniel Internat. Corp., Greenville, S.C., 1970—. Served with AUS, 1953-55. Mem. Financial Execs. Inst., Delta Sigma Pi. Democrat. Mem. Ch. of Christ. Club: Green Valley Country (Greenville). Home: 8 Hunting Hollow Rd Greenville SC 29607 Office: Daniel Bldg Greenville SC 29602

HOFER, PHILLIP, librarian, trustee; b. Cin., Mar. 14, 1898; s. Charles Frederick and Jane (Arms) H.; A.B. cum laude, Harvard, 1921, A.M., 1929, D.H.L., 1967; D.Arts, Bates Coll., 1962; m. Frances L. Hecksher, Nov. 1, 1930; 1 son, Myron Arms. Asso. with coal-mining firm W. H. Warner Co., Cleve., 1922-27, asst. to pres., 1922-26; partner financial firm Philip Hofer & Co., Cleve., 1924-27; apptd. adviser to Spencer collection N.Y. Pub. Library, 1929-34; asst. dir. Pierpont Morgan Library, 1934-37; founder and curator dept. printing and graphic arts emeritus Harvard Library, asst. dean Harvard Bus. Sch., 1942-44, trustee Bishop Rhinelander Meml. for Student Work, sec. Fogg Art Mus., Harvard, 1952-64. Lyell lectr. in bibliography Oxford U., 1962; resident scholar Am. Acad. in Rome, 1958. Trustee Corning Glass Mus., Mass. Hist. Soc., Mus. of Fine Arts, Inst. Modern Art (Boston), Boys Club of Boston, Boston Athenaeum, Am. Sch. Classical Studies, North Bennett St. Indsl. Sch. Mem. Soc. Antiquaries, Council Fgn. Relations, English-Speaking Union (trustee Boston br., v.p. 1965—). Clubs: Athenaeum (London, Eng.); Century Association; Brook (N.Y.C.). Home: 88 Appleton St Cambridge MA 02138

HOFF, EBBE CURTIS, educator; b. Rexford, Kan., Aug. 12, 1906; s. Hans Jacob and May (Knudson) H.; B.S. summa cum laude, U. Wash., 1928; B.A. with honors in Physiology, Oxford (Eng.) U., 1930, Ph.D., 1932, B.M., B.Ch., 1941, M.D., 1953; m. Phebe Margaret Flather, June 2, 1934; children—Phebe May (Mrs. Leigh Van Valen), David Christiansen. Sterling research fellow Yale, 1932-33, Coxe research fellow, 1933-34, instr. physiology, 1934- 36, resarch fellow, 1940-43; prof. psychiatry, chmn. psychiat. research Med. Coll. Va., 1962—, dean Sch. Grad. Studies, 1956-66, med. dir. Bur. Alcohol Studies and Rehab., 1948—, also mem. adminstrv. council; cons. to surgeon gen. U.S. Army, Nat. Inst. Mental Health. Served from lt. comdr. to comdr., M.C., USNR, 1943-46. Fellow N.Y. Acad. Scis., Royal Soc. Medicine; mem. A.M.A., Am. Physiol. Soc., Am. Psychiat. Assn. (asso.), Am. Acad. Neurology (asso.), A.A.A.S., Brit. Med. Assn., History Sci. Soc., Soc. Exptl. Biology and Medicine, Phi Beta Kappa, Sigma Xi, Alpha Omega Alpha. Contbr. articles profl. jours. Home: 117 Gaymont Rd Richmond VA 23229

HOFF, EDMOND VICTOR, ins. co. exec.; b. Starbuck, Minn., Apr. 6, 1908; s. Edward L. and Vilborg (Anondson) H.; B.E., State U., Superior, Wis., 1930; M.S., U. Ia., 1932; m. Naomi Mulligan, Feb. 14, 1931; children—Edward Gary, Dennis Ray, Richard Bradley. High sch. sci. tchr., Black Earth, Wis., 1930-31; asst. actuary, actuary Union Mut. Life Co. Ia., Des Moines, 1932-36; actuarial asst. Occidental Life Ins. Co. Cal., Los Angeles, 1936-39, statistician, 1939-42, asst. controller, 1942-46, asso. treas., 1956-58, treas., 1958—, v.p., 1968—; treas. Transamerica Life Ins. & Annuity Co., Los Angeles, 1966—. Cubmaster, vice chmn. dist. council Boy Scouts Am., 1945-60. Recipient Vets. award Boy Scouts Am., 1960. Mem. Ins. Accounting and Statis. Assn. (past pres. Los Angeles chpt.), Actuarial Club Pacific States (past sec.), Am. Acad. Actuaries, Sigma Xi. Home: 6250 N Willard St San Gabriel CA 91775 Office: 1149 S Hill St Los Angeles CA 90054

HOFF, HEBBEL EDWARD, coll. dean, physiologist, educator; b. Urbana, Ill., Dec. 2, 1907; s. Hans Jacob and May (Knudson) H.; B.Sc., U. Wash., 1928; B.A., D. Phil. (Rhodes scholar), Oxford (Eng.) U., 1932; M.D. (Ware fellow), Harvard, 1936; m. Helen Curtis Sullivan, Aug. 21, 1936; children—Johanna, Victoria. Instr. Yale Coll. Medicine, 1932-34, asst., asso. prof., 1936-42; Joseph Morley Drake prof. physiology, chmn. dept. McGill U., 1942-48; James Hambleton prof. physiology, chmn. dept. Baylor Coll. Medicine, 1948-68, Distinguished Service prof., asso. dean acad. and clin. affairs, 1968—; cons. physiology Hermann, Meth., VA hosps., Houston. Mem. Med. Mission to Japan, 1950. Mem. Am. Physiol. Soc., Soc. Exptl. Biology and Medicine, Phi Beta Kappa, Sigma Xi. Home: 78 Patti Lynn Lane Houston TX 77024

HOFF, MARGO, artist; b. Tulsa, June 12, 1912; d. C. W. and A. A. (Hayes) H.; m. George F. Buehr; 1 dau., Mia. Group exhbns., Saidenberg Gallery, N.Y.C., Barone Gallery, Banfer Gallery, Fairweather Hardin Gallery, Chgo., Bklyn. Mus., Dallas Mus. Fine Arts, Downtown Gallery, N.Y.C., Wildenstein Gallery, Paris, Honolulu Acad. Arts; Ball State U.; San Francisco Mus., others; represented in collections Art Inst. Chgo., Bklyn. Mus., Carnegie Inst., Libarary Congress, Rosenwald Found., U. Ill., U. Minn., U. Chgo., Bibliotheque Nationale, Paris, Victoria and Albert Mus., London, Whitney Mus., N.Y.C., Smithsonian Instn., U. Notre Dame; Design opera costumes, stage set Soc. Contemporary Music, 1954; vis. artist Am. U., Beirut, Lebanon, 1955-56, St. Maria Goretti Sch., Ft. Portal, Uganda, 1971; artist in residence So. Ill. U., 1968, St. Mary Coll., Notre Dame, Ind., 1969-70; mural executed Mayo Clin., Rochester, Minn.; commn. for woodcut I.G.A.S., 1956; rug design, executed in Parkistan, Design Research, Inc., 1957; Illustrator 3 books. Home: 218 E 12th St New York City NY 10003 Office: care Fairweather-Hardin Gallery 101 E Ontario St Chicago IL 60611

HOFF, NICHOLAS JOHN, educator; b. Magyarovar, Hungary, Jan. 3, 1906; s. Miklos and Lenke (Meller) H.; diploma Poly. Inst. Zurich (Switzerland), 1928; Ph.D., Stanford, 1942; m. Vivian Church, July 20, 1940 (dec. Apr. 1969). Airplane designer, stress analyst Manfred Weiss Aeroplane & Motor Works Ltd., Budapest, Hungary, 1928-38; research asst. Vibration and Earthquake Lab., Stanford, 1939-40; instr. aeronautical engring. Poly. Inst. Bklyn., 1940, successively asst. prof., asso. prof., prof., also head dept. aero. engring. and applied mechanics, 1950-56; prof., head dept. aero. and astronautics Stanford, 1957-71, emeritus, 1971—; William Murray lectr. Soc. Exptl. Stress Analysis, 1958. Past chmn. U.S. Nat. Com. for Applied Mechanics; mem. research and technology adv. council NASA, 1967-70. Recipient medal U. Liege (Belgium), 1956; medal Swedish Soc. Engrs., 1949; Worcester Reed Warner medal Am. Soc. M.E., 1967; G. Edward Pendray award Am. Inst. Aeros. and Astronautics, 1971, Structures, Structural Dynamics and Materials award, 1971. Fellow Am. Inst. Aeros. and Astronautics, Royal Aero. Soc. (Wilbur Wright Meml. lectr. 1954), Am. Soc. M.E. (past chmn. applied mechanics div.); mem. Soc. Exptl. Stress Analysis, Nat. Acad. Engring., Am. Soc. C.E., Am. Soc. Engring. Edn., Internat. Union Theoretical and Applied Mechanics, Aero. Soc. India (hon.), Sigma Xi, Tau Beta Pi. Author: The Analysis of Structures, 1956. Editor: High Temperature Effects in Aircraft Structures, 1958; Creep in Structures, 1962; co-editor: Structural Mechanics, 1960; Aeronautics and Astronautics, 1960. Contbr. engring. jours. Home: 782 Esplanada Way Stanford CA 94305

HOFF, PHILIP HENDERSON, former gov. Vt.; b. Greenfield, Mass., June 29, 1924; s. Olaf Jr. and Agnes E. (Henderson) H.; A.B., Williams Coll., 1948; LL.B., Cornell U., 1951; m. Joan P. Brower, Aug. 28, 1948; children—Susan, Dagny, Andrea, Gretchen. Admitted to Vt. bar, 1952; asso. firm Black & Wilson, Burlington, 1950-56; partner firm Black, Wilson & Hoff, 1956-60; gov. State of Vt., 1963-69; practiced in Burlington, 1969—. Clk., E.B. & A.C. Whiting Co., 1969. Former chmn. States Urban Action Center (Urban America); teaching fellow Inst. Politics, John Fitzgerald Kennedy Sch. Govt., Harvard. Rep. of Burlington to Vt. Gen. Assembly, 1961-63. Dir. Vt. Children's Aid Soc., Greater Burlington Indsl. Corp.; trustee Vt. Rehab. Center, Williams Coll.; asso. trustee St. Michaels Coll. Served with USNR, 1943-46. Mem. Am., Vt., Chittenden County bar assns., Am. Legion, Lake Champlain C. of C. Democrat. Rotarian. Home: 214 Prospect Pkwy Burlington VT 05401 Office: 192 College St Burlington VT 05401

HOFF, SYD cartoonist, author; b. N.Y.C., Sept. 4, 1912; s. Benjamin and Mary (Barnow) H.; ed. pub. schs., N.Y.C.; m. Dora Berman, 1937; children—Susan, L., Bonnie J. Cartoonist, 1939—; daily cartoon feature, Laugh it Off, King Features Syndicate, 1957—; contbr. cartoons to New Yorker, Esquire, other mags. Author: (childrens books) Danny and the Dinosaur, 1958, Sammy the Seal, 1959, Julius, 1959; (cartoons) Muscles and Brains, 1943; (adult books) Feeling No Pain, 1945, Oops! Wrong Party!, 1950, Oops! Wrong Stateroom!, 1954, Okay, You Can Look Now!, 1955, It's Fun Learning Cartooning, 1956; Lengthy, 1963, Grizzold, 1963. Author, illustrator: Ogluk The Eskimo, 1960; Where's Prancer?, 1960; Who Will Be My Friends?, 1960; Oliver Children's Books, 1961; Albert the Albatross, Chester Little Chief, 1961; Upstream, Downstream and Out of My Mind, 1961; The Better Hoff, 1961; Little Chief, 1961; Letters From Camp, 1961; Twixt the Cup and the Lipton, 1962; So This is Matrimony, 1963; From Bed to Nurse, 1963; Stanley, 1962; Hunting, Anyone?, 1963; How to Run a Country, 1963; Mrs. Switch, 1967; The Witch, The Cat and a Baseball Bat, 1967; Irving and Me, 1968; Roberto and The Bull, 1969; Jeffrey At Camp, 1969; Baseball Mouse, 1969; Mahatma, 1969; Slithers, 1969; Siegfried, Dog of the Alps, 1970; Palace Bug, 1970; Wilfred the Lion, 1970; The Horse in Harry's Room, 1970; Herschel the Hero, 1970; Litter Bug, 1970; Thunderhoof, 1971. Illustrator: Hello Mudder, Hello, Fadder, 1964; I Can't Dance, 1964; I Shoud Have Stayed in Bed, 1965; The Rooftop Mystery, 1968; Chanukah Fable for Christmas, 1969; Henri Goes to the Mardi Gras; Wilfred the Lion, 1970; Herschel the Hero, 1970; The Mule Who Struck It Rich, 1971. Address: 4335 Post Av Miami Beach FL 33140

HOFF, WILLIAM JAY, lawyer; b. N.Y.C. June 28, 1907; s. Samuel H. and Amanda L. H.; A.B., Yale, 1928; LL.B., Columbia, 1931; m. Pauline Stockton Parker, Sept. 20, 1935; children—John Seabury, Paul Stockton. Law clerk with Peaslee & Brigham, N.Y.C., 1931-32, partner, 1935-38; asst. U.S. atty., So. dist. N.Y., 1932-33; asst. counsel N.R.A., 1933-35, asst. corp. counsel, N.Y.C., 1938-40; counsel O.P.M., 1940-42; asst. gen. counsel WPB, 1943-45; counsel Nat. Dairy Products Corp., N.Y.C., 1945-47; gen. counsel fgn. liquidation commn. Dept. State, Paris and Washington, 1947- 48; asso. gen. counsel, dir. tech. assistance div. and legislative counsel ECA, 1948-51; spl. asst. to adminstr., asst. adminstr. for post attack prodn. Def. Prodn. Adminstrn., 1951-53; gen. counsel NSF, 1953—. Chmn. D.C. Health and Welfare Council, 1963-64; trustee Planned Parenthood, Washington met. area, 1965-71. Recipient Merit citation, Nat. Civil Service League, 1956. Mem. Fed. Bar Assn., Bar Assn. D.C. Home: 2402 Wyoming Av NW Washington DC 20008 Office: NSF 1800 G St NW Washington DC 20006

HOFF, P. J., see Hoffstrom, Piercy J.

HOFFA, HARLAN EDWARD, educator; b. Kalamazoo, June 23, 1925; s. Leolan William and Pearl (Foster) H.; B.S., Wayne U., 1948; M.Ed., 1949; Ed.D., Pa. State U., 1959; m. Marian Perko, Aug. 10, 1946 (div. 1971); children—Kathryn Jane, Thomas Scott; m. 2d, Suzanne Dudley, Sept. 9, 1971. Tchr. Evanston (Ill.) pub. schs., 1949-51; Instr. art edn. Ohio State U., 1951-53; asst. prof. art State U. Coll. at Buffalo, 1953-59; asso. prof. fine arts and edn. head dept. Boston U., 1959-65; art edn. specialist U.S. Office Edn., 1964-67; prof. edn. and fine arts, chmn. art edn. program Ind. U., 1967-70; prof., head dept. edn. Pa., State U., 1970—. Served with AUS, 1943-45. Mem. Nat. Art Edn. Assn. (pres. 1971-73). Home: 341 Toftrees Av State College PA 16801 Office: Chambers Bldg Pa State U University Park PA 16802

HOFFA, J. MILTON, retired banker; b. Hatfield, Pa., Dec. 18, 1908; s. David and Bertha (Mertin) H.; m. Nellie E. Wink, Oct. 2, 1935. With Columbia Av. Trust Co., 1926- 29, Integrity Trust Co., 1929-40; with Girard Trust Bank, Phila., 1940- 70, asst. v.p., 1950-51, comptroller, 1952-70; past v.p., treas. Girard Internat. Investment Corp., Girard Internat. Bank; past treas. The Girard Co.; past treas., dir. Finance Bldg. Corp. Mem. Financial Execs. Inst., Bank Adminstrn. Inst., Am. Inst. Banking, Acad. Natural Scis. Lutheran. Home: 2918 Concord St Sarasota FL 33581

HOFFA, JAMES RIDDLE, labor union exec.; b. Brazil, Ind., Feb. 14, 1913; s. John and Viola (Riddle) H.; m. Josephine Poszywak, Sept. 25, 1937; children—Barbara Ann, James Phillip. Mem. Internat. Brotherhood of Teamsters, from 1932, pres. local 299, from 1935, chmn. central conf. teamsters, from 1953, v.p. union, 1952-57, former gen. pres. Home: 16154 Robson St Detroit MI 48235

HOFFACKER, LEWIS, fgn. service officer; b. Glenville, Pa., Feb. 11, 1923; s. Roscoe Edward and Beulah Viola (Barbehenn) H.; student Gettysburg (Pa.) Coll., 1941- 42, B.A. in Fgn. Affairs (Joshua Evans III Meml. prize 1948, Alexander Wilbourne Weddell prize 1948), George Washington U, 1948; M.A. in Internat. Affairs, Fletcher Sch. Law and Diplomacy, 1949; student African studies, Oxford (Eng.) U., 1960-61; m. Constance Harrison Alling, Jan. 27, 1951; children—Anne Alling, Rebecca Wood. Desk officer Greek affairs State Dept., 1949-51; 3d sec. embassy, Tehran, Iran, 1951- 53; vice consul, Istanbul, Turkey, 1953-55; desk officer Egyptian, Sudanese and Ceylonese affairs State Dept., 1955-58; 2d sec. embassy, Paris, France, 1958-60; consul, Elisabethville, Congo, 1961-62; 1st sec. embassy Leopoldville, Congo, 1962-63; assigned to Nat. War Coll. 1963-64; dir. Operations Center, Dept. of State, 1964-65; counselor of embassy Am. embassy, Algiers, from 1965, now ambassador to Yaounde, Cameroon and Santa Isabel, Equatorial Guinea. Served to 1st lt., inf., AUS, 1943-46; PTO. Decorated Purple Heart, Combat Inf. award. Mem. African Studies Assn., Phi Beta Kappa, Phi Sigma Kappa, Delta Phi Epsilon. Home: 2836 Albermarle St NW Washington DC 20008 Office: Dept of State Washington DC 20525

HOFFBERGER, JEROLD CHARLES, brewer; b. Balt., Apr. 7, 1919; s. Samuel H. and Gertrude (Miller) H.; grad. Tome Sch., 1937, U. Va., 1940; m. Alice Berney, June 10, 1946; children—David B., Richard J., Carol S., Charles P. Pres., dir. Nat. Brewing Co., Balt., 1947—; chmn., pres. Divex, Inc.; dir., mem. exec. com. Fairchild Hiller Corp.; dir. Mchts. Mortgage Co., Real Estate Holding Co., Md. Nat. Bank, Howardale Industries, Terminal Refrigeration & Warehousing Corp.; v.p., dir. Jerval Enterprises, Inc.; chmn. bd. Baltimore Orioles. Mem. nat. cabinet United Jewish Appeal; mem. Vol. Council Equal Opportunity; chmn., mem. nat. bd. Am. Israel Pub. Affairs Com., Balt.; v.p. Jewish Welfare Fund Balt.; mem. exec. com. Greater Balt. Com. Dir. Mercy Hosp., Harford County Fair Assn., Hoffberger Found., Asso. Jewish Charities and Welfare Fund, United Fund Central Md., Sinai Hosp.; trustee Johns Hopkins Hosp., Balt., Goucher Coll. Served to capt. AUS, World War II. Mem. Balt. Assn. Commerce, U. Va. Alumni Assn., Young Presidents' Orgn., Md. (pres. 1950-51), Balt. (v.p. 1949-50, dir. 1949-51) jr. chambers commerce, U.S. Brewers Assn. (exec. com.), Phi Epsilon Pi. Jewish religion. Club: Suburban Country. Home: Sunset Hill Riderwood MD Office: 225 N Calvert St Baltimore MD 21202

HOFFBERGER, STANLEY ALAN, food co. exec.; b. Balt., Aug. 7, 1929; s. Jack H. and Mildred (Rosenstien) H.; A.B. cum laude, Princeton, 1951; m. Judith Rosenberg, Feb. 12, 1955; children—Jeffrey Alan, Russell Jay. Vice pres. Merchants Terminal Corp., Balt., 1954-58, dir., 1962-; pres. Pompeian, Inc., Balt., 1964-68, chmn. bd., 1969—, also dir.; pres. The Solarine Co., Laco Corp., Laco Products, Inc., C.W. Abbott, Inc.; v.p., dir. Nat. Brewing Co.; dir. Divex, Inc. Bd. dirs. v.p. Balt. Symphony Orch.; pres. Md. Com. Day Care for Children. Served with AUS, 1951-54. Jewish religion. Home: 6529 Bradley Blvd Bethesda MD 20034 Office: 4201 Pulaski Hwy Baltimore MD 21224

HOFFER, ERIC, author; b. N.Y.C., July 25, 1902; s. Knut and Elsa (Goebel) H. Migratory worker, Cal., 1920-43; longshoreman, 1943—. Author: The True Believer, 1951; The Passionate State of Mind, 1955; The Ordeal of Change, 1963; Temper of Our Time, 1967; Working and Thinking on the Waterfront, 1969. Address: 1547 Clay St San Francisco CA 94109

HOFFER, JOE RALPH, social worker; b. N.Y. City, Mar. 22, 1907; s. Andrew and Mary Lottie (Hoffer) H.; B.S., Ohio State U., 1932, Ph.D., 1942; m. Mary B. Rusnak, Nov. 28, 1936. Activities dir. (Xenia) Ohio Soldiers and Sailors Orphan Home, 1933-35; dir. community orgn., N.Y.A. in Ohio, 1935-37; sec. community div. Council Social Agencies Phila., 1937-42; exec. officer U.S. Joint Com. on Evacuation, Washington, 1942-43; dir. capitol liaison office U.N.R.R.A., Nanking, China, 1945-46; exec. dir. Social Work Vocational Bur., N.Y. City and cons. Am. Assn. Social Workers, 1946-48; exec. sec. Nat. Conf. Social Welfare, sec. gen. Internat. Conf. Social Work, 1948-66. Served as seaman first class USN, 1943-45. Distinguished Centennial awardee Sch. Adminstrv. Sci. Ohio State U.; 1970; Distinguished Centennial awardee Ohio State U.; 1970. Fellow Assn. Sociol. Assn.; mem. Nat. and Internat. confs. social work; Nat. Assn. Social Workers (treas. 1969-71); Am. Pub. Welfare Assn., Am. Soc. Information Sci. (chmn. Central Ohio chpt.), Delta Tau Delta, Sphinx, Bucket and Dipper, Varsity "0" Association. Author: An Activity analysis of the Duties of Recreation and Informal Education Leaders and Supervisors, 1942; Outline for Agency Self-Evaluation of Personnel Practices, 1947; A Community Plan for Youth, 1947. Mng. editor Social Welfare Forum, annual; Social Work Practice ann.; A Manual for a Hand-Sort Punch Card System for Indexing Social Welfare Publs. Home: 276 Mayfair Blvd Columbus OH 43213 Office: 22 W Gay St Columbus OH 43215

HOFFER, ROBERT M., utility exec.; b. Muncie, Ind., Feb. 28, 1921; s. Vern Howard and Howard and Charlene (Ingersol) H.; B.S., Ball State Univ., Muncie, 1948; M.B.A., U. Mich., 1949; m. Martha C. Quirk, June 7, 1946; 1 dau., Elizabeth Jane. Partner, Arthur Andersen & Co., C.P.A.'s, Chgo. and Detroit, 1949-57; financial v.p., controller, dir. Am. Natural Gas Service Co., 1957-64, now dir.; financial v.p., controller, dir. Mich. Wis. Pipe Line Co., 1957-64, now dir.; exec. v.p. Wis. Gas Co., 1964-69, pres., 1969—, also dir.; dir. Am. Natural Gas Prodn. Co., Central Ind. Gas Co., Marshall and Ilsley Bank, Milw., Badger Meter Mfg. Co., Am. Natural Gas Co., Krause Milling Co., Marshall & Ilsley Bank Stock Corp. Served with USNR, World War II. C.P.A., Mich. Mem. Am. Inst. C.P.A.'s, Mich. Assn. C.P.A.'s, Midwest Gas Assn., Wis. Utilities Assn. Clubs: Milwaukee Country, University (Milw.). Home: 4600 N Lake Dr Whitefish Bay WI 53211 Office: 626 E Wisconsin Av Milwaukee WI 53201

HOFFMAN, ANNA ROSENBERG, pub. and indsl. relations cons.; b. Budapest, Hungary, July 19, 1902; d. Albert and Charlotte (Bacskai) Lederer; brought to U.S., 1912, naturalized, 1919; hon. Master of Humane Letters, Russell Sage Coll., 1943; LL.D., Tufts Coll., 1951; L.H.D., Columbia, 1952: 1 son, Thomas J.; m. 2d, Paul G. Hoffman, July 19, 1963. With N.R.A., 1934-39, regional dir., 1935; regional dir. Social Security Adminstrn., 1936-43, also Office of Def. Health and Welfare Services, 1941-42; regional director War Manpower Commn., 1942-45; cons. Retraining and Reemployment Adminstrn., 1941-45; asst. sec. Dept.Def., 1950-53; sr. partner Anna M. Rosenberg Assos., pub. and indsl. relations cons.; dir. Hoffman Specialty Mfg. Corp. Served personal rep. of Pres. Roosevelt (1944) and Pres. Truman (1945) to European Theater of War to report on problems of returning soldiers. Mem. N.Y.C. Indsl. Relations Bd., 1937; mem. commn. apptd. by Pres. Roosevelt to study indsl. relations in Great Britain and Sweden, 1938; mem. Gov. Harriman's Conf. on Problems of Aging; mem. Mayor's Transit Adv. Bd. Organizer and hon. chmn. exec. com. N.Y.C. Def. Recreation Com., 1941-46. Cons. on manpower problems to chmn. Nat. Secrutiy Resources Bd.; mem. Fed. Adv. Council, Bur. Employment Security; mem. Tch. Adv. Council, Nat. Planning Assn.; mem. War Moblzn. and Reconversion Adv. Bd.; lay dir. Am. Cancer Soc.; mem. Am. Commn. for UNESCO 1946-50; mem. adv. com. on Compulsory Mil. Tng.; apptd. spl. cons. to W. Stuart Symington, 1950. Dir. Franklin D. Roosevelt Found., Albert and Mary Lasker Found.; trustee John Hay Whitney Found., Nat. Fund for Med. Edn., Franklin Delano Roosevelt Meml. Commn., Eleanor Roosevelt Meml. Found.; mem. bd. Hosps. N.Y.C.: co-chmn. Nat. Heart Com., mem. Nat. Commn. Automation, Tech. and Econ. Progress. 1964-66. Temporary Commn. City Financers, N.Y.C., 1963-66; mem. bd. edn., N.Y.C., 1961-63; mem. nat. adv. commn. SSS, 1966-67; mem. Pres.'s Commn. on Income Maintenance Programs; mem. States Urban Action Center, Inc., N.Y. Urban Coalition, Inc., N.Y. Mayor's Com. on Rent Control. Bd. dirs. UN Assn. U.S.A. Recipient Medal of Freedom. 1945: Medal for Merit. 1947. Author of Chpt. Social Security and the National Purpose in Family in a World at War, 1942. Mem. adv. bd. Ency. Brit. Films, Inc. Home: 8 Sutton Sq New York City NY Office: 444 Madison Av New York City NY

HOFFMAN, ARTHUR SAMUEL, govt. ofcl.; b. Camden, N.J., June 22, 1926; s. Louis and Rose (Wessel) H.; A.B., Oberlin Coll., 1947; student U. Minn., 1945; M.A., Johns Hopkins, 1948; Docteur es scis. politiques, U. Geneva, Switzerland, 1951; m. Roberte Anne Piot de Cesse, Nov. 13, 1950; children—Richard, Alan, Sidney, Elizabeth. Corr., Camden-Phila. newspapers, Western Europe, 1949; econ. and polit. officer Dept. State, Germany, 1950-51, Czechoslovakia, 1957-59; information and cultural officer Dept. State and USIA, Germany, 1951-54, Japan, 1954-56, Washington, 1956, 62-65, 70—, France, 1959-62, Turkey, 1966-68, Vietnam, 1969-70; acting dir. Edward R. Murrow Center Pub. Diplomacy, Fletcher Sch., Tufts U., 1965-66; producer television program on communications satellites WGBH, Boston, 1966; chief planning and operational policy USIA, Washington, 1970—; lectr. univs., 1965-66. Served with AUS, 1944-46. Author: Speech, American Legion Oratory Anthology, 1944. Co-editor: Communications Satellites Seminar papers, 1967; editor: International Communication and the New Diplomacy, 1968. Contbr. articles U.S. newspapers and KYKLOS Mag., Zurich, 1949. Home: 400 Kings Point Dr Miami Beach FL 33160 Office: 1750 Pennsylvania Av NW Washington DC 20547

HOFFMAN, BRIAN FRANCIS, educator; b. N.Y.C., Mar. 26, 1925; A.A., Princeton, 1943; M.D., L.I. Coll. Medicine, 1947. Intern, Lenox Hill Hosp., 1947-48, asst. resident medicine, 1948-49; instr. psysiology and pharmacology L.I. Coll. Medicine, 1949-52; asst. prof. physiology Coll. Medicine, State U. N.Y., 1952-55, asso. prof., 1955; now chmn. dept. pharmacology Columbia. Mem. Am. Physiol. Soc., Harvey Soc. Home: 269 Lakeview Av Brightwaters NY 11718

HOFFMAN, CHARLES HIRAM, accountant; b. Boonsboro, Md., Nov. 26, 1918; s. Lewis E. and Edna (Beachley) H.; B. Comml. Sci., Strayer Coll. Accountancy, Washington, 1938, M. Comml. Sci., 1940; m. Roberta Leonore Haynes, Jan. 14, 1946; 1 son, Kent Charles. With Ernst & Ernst, C.P.A.'s, 1946—, partner charge Balt. office, 1960—. Served with USNR, 1942-46. C.P.A., Md., Va., La., R.I., N.C. Mem. Am. Inst. C.P.A.'s, Md. Assn. C.P.A.'s (pres. 1964), Nat. Assn. Accountants, Am. Accounting Assn., Soc. Advancement Mgmt., Advt. Club Balt., Beta Alpha Psi. Lutheran. Clubs: Center, Merchants, Balt. Country, Hunt Valley (Balt.). Office: 1 N Charles St Baltimore MD 21201

HOFFMAN, CLYDE HARRIS, educator; b. Jamestown, N.D., Mar. 24, 1925; s. Clarence William and Ada (Gensrich) H.; B.S. in Elec. Engring., U. N.D., 1950; M.S. in Elec. Engring., U. Notre Dame, 1952, Ph.D., 1962; postgrad. U. Wis., summer 1955; m. Betty Myra Ledingham, May 29, 1950. Instr. elec. engring. U. Notre Dame, 1951-52; project engr. Jack & Heintz, Inc., Cleve., 1952- 53; asst. prof. elec. engring. U. Notre Dame, 1953-62; asso. prof. elec. engring. Ill. Inst. Tech., Chgo., 1962—, head elec. engring. dept. Kabul (Afghanistan) U., 1966-68. Mem. evaluation panels for undergraduate sci. instructional equipment program, NSF, 1963-65; mem. Nat. Acad. Scis. adv. com. to electronics instrumentation div. Nat. Bur. Standards, 1965-68. Trustee Nat. Electronics Conf., Inc. Served with inf. AUS, 1943-46. Registered profl. engr., Ind., Ill. Sr. mem. I.R.E. (chmn. S. Bend sect. 1960-61, region V edn. com. 1959-60, 60-61), I.E.E.E. (exec. com. Chgo. 1964-65, chmn. student activities Chgo. 1963, chmn. group automatic control com. Chgo. 1964-65), Instrument Soc. Am. (gov. bd. Chgo. 1964-65, chmn. tech. div. prodn. processes 1964, 1st vice chmn. Chgo. 1965); mem. Am. Ordnance Assn., A.A.A.S., L'Assn. Internat. pour le Calcul Analogique, Simulations Councils, Am. Soc. M.E., Marine Tech. Soc., Assn. Computing Machinery, Am. Soc. Engring. Edn., Nat. Electronics Conf. (bd. dirs. 1957-64, asso. chmn. proc. com. 1958, chmn. 1959, chmn. trust adv. com. 1963, chmn. fellowship award com. 1964, spl. events com. 1965). Author numerous articles in field Address: 6701 S Crandon Chicago IL 60649

HOFFMAN, DANIEL, educator, poet; b. N.Y.C. Apr. 3, 1923; s. Daniel and Frances (Beck) H.; B.A., Columbia, 1947, M.A., 1949, Ph.D., 1956; m. Elizabeth McFarland, May 22, 1948; children—Kate, Macfarlane. Instr. English, Columbia, 1952-56; vis. prof. Am. lit. Faculté des Lettres, Dijon, France, 1956-57; asst. prof. English, Swarthmore Coll., 1957-61, asso. prof., 1961-65, prof., 1965-66; prof. English, U. Pa., 1966—; fellow Ind. U. Sch. Letters, 1959; George Elliston lectr. poetry U. Cin., 1964; lectr. 6th Internat. Sch. Yeats Studies, Sligo, Ireland, 1965. Served to 1st lt. USAAF, 1943-46. Decorated Legion of Merit; recipient Poetry Center Introductions prize, 1951; Yale Series of Younger Poets award, 1954; Ainsley prize, 1957; Lit. award Athenaeum of Phila., 1963; medal for excellence Columbia, 1964; Nat. Inst. Arts and Letters award in poetry, 1967; poetry grant Ingram Merrill Found., 1971-72; fellow Am. Council Learned Socs., 1961- 62, 66-67. Mem. Modern Lang. Assn., Phila. Art Alliance (dir. 1968-70, English Inst. Club: Franklin Inn (Phila.). Author: (poetry) An Armada of Thirty Whales, 1954; A Little Geste and Other Poems, 1960; The City of Satisfactions, 1963; Striking the Stones, 1968; Broken Laws, 1970; (criticism) Paul Bunyan: Last of the Frontier Demigods, 1952; The Poetry of Stephen Crane, 1957; Form and Fable in American Fiction, 1961; Barbarous Knowledge, 1967; Poe, Poe, Poe, Poe, Poe, Poe, Poe, 1972. Editor: The Red Badge of Courage, 1957; American Poetry and Poetics, 1962. Office: Dept English U Pa Philadelphia PA 19104

HOFFMAN, DORETTA SCHLAPHOFF, univ. dean; b. Wabash, Neb., Dec. 16, 1912; d. Carl and Emma (Luetchens) Schlaphoff; B.S., U. Neb., 1941, D.Sc., 1966; M.S. Mich. State Coll., 1943; Ph.D., Cornell U., 1949; D.SC. (hon.) U. of Neb., 1966; m. Wendell Hoffman, Feb. 6, 1956; children—Reo Lowell, Roger Lester. Instr. home econs. U. Ariz., 1943-44; instr. home econs. U. Neb., 1944- 49, asso. prof., 1949-50, prof., chmn. dept., 1950-54; prof., dean Coll. Home Econs., Kan. State U., 1954—. Recipient Distinguished Alumni award Mich. State U., 1964. Fellow A.A.A.S., mem. Am. Home Econs. Assn. (past. chmn. research dept.), Am. Dietetics Assn. (past pres. Neb.), Assn. Land Grant Colls. and Univs. (past chmn., sec. resident instrn. home econs. div.) Mortar Bd., Sigma Xi, Omicron Nu, Sigma Delta Epsilon. Phi Kappa Phi, Alpha Lambda Delta, Delta Kappa Gamma, Iota Sigma Pi, Phi Upsilon Omicron (nat. pres. 1970-72). Contbr. articles to profl. jours. Home: 500 Oakdale Dr Manhattan KS 66502

HOFFMAN, DUSTIN, actor; b. Los Angeles, Aug. 8, 1937; s. Harry Hoffman; ed. Santa Monica City Coll., Pasadena Playhouse; m. Anne Byrne, May 4, 1969. Stage debut in Sarah Lawrence Coll. prodn. of Yes Is For a Very Young Man; Broadway debut in A Cook for Mr. General, 1961; appeared in Harry, Noon and Night at Am. Place Theatre, N.Y.C., 1964-65, also the Journey of the Fifth Horse, 1966, Star Wagon, 1966, Fragments at Berkshie Theatre Festival, Stockbridge, Mass., 1966, Eh?, 1966-67, Broadway play Jimmy Shine, 1968-69; recorded Death of a Salesman for Caedman Records; appeared in motion pictures The Graduate, 1967, Midnight Cowboy, 1969, John and Mary, 1969, Little Big Man. Recipient Obie award as best off-Broadway actor of 1965-66, Oscar award nominee, 1967. Address: c/o Dir Pub Relations 20th Century Fox 444 W 56th St New York City NY 10019*

HOFFMAN, EDGAR PETER, banker; b. Oklahoma City, Mar. 8, 1920; s. Roy and Estelle (Conklin) H.; grad. Hotchkiss Sch., 1939; B.A., Yale, 1943; m. Marion Briscoe, Mar. 18, 1942 (div. Mar. 1967); children—Susan (Mrs. Arthur Wheelock), Edgar Peter, Marion (Mrs. Thomas White), Kent Briscoe; m. 2d, Jane Van Cleef Corbyn, Jan. 17, 1968. Exec. v.p. First Nat. Bank, Oklahoma City, 1946—. City councilman, Nichols Hills, 1959-64, mayor, 1962-64; chmn. Okla. Indsl. Finance Authority, 1965—. Treas., mem. exec. com. United Fund; chmn. bd. dirs. Oklahoma County chpt. A.R.C.; bd. dirs. Community Council Oklahoma City; mem. exec. com. Okla. Med. Research Found.; v.p. bd. trustees Casady Sch. Served to capt., F.A., AUS, 1943- 46; PTO. Decorated Bronze Star medal. Home: 5505 N Brookline St Oklahoma City OK 73112 Office: 120 N Robinson St Oklahoma City OK 73125

HOFFMAN, EDWIN KARL, retail co. exec.; b. Chgo., June 29, 1922; s. Joseph M. amd Mildred (Page) H.; B.S., Northwestern U., 1947; m. Gladys Steigerwaldt, Nov. 6, 1943; children—Mark Joseph, Kimberly Anne. Trainee Carson Pirie Scott & Co., Chgo., 1948-52, div. merchandise mgr. ready-to-wear, 1951-52; gen. mdse. mgr. De Pinna, N.Y.C., 1952-55; div. mdse. mge. women's ready-to-wear The Higbee Co., Cleve., 1955-58, gen. mdse. mgr. 1958, v.p., 1958-62. pres., 1962-67; pres. John Wanamaker, Phila., 1967-68; exec. v.p., gen. mgr. Woodward & Lothrop, Washington, 1968, pres., 1969—; dir., mem. exec. com. Asso. Merchandising Corp.; dir. Am. Security & Trust Co. Mem. Metropolitan Washington Bd. Trade. Bd. dirs. Nat. Symphony Orchestra Assn.; trustee Meridian House Found., Federal City Council. Served with AUS, 1942-45. Clubs: Union League (N.Y.C.); Columbia Country, University (Washington). Home: 11021 Stanmore Dr Potomac MD 20854 Office: Woodward & Lothrop 11th and F Sts NW Washington DC 20013

HOFFMAN, FRANCIS BURRALL, architect; b. New Orleans, Mar. 6, 1882; s. Francis Burall and Lucy (Shattuck) H.; A.B., Harvard, 1903; diploma Ecole Beaux Arts, Paris, 1970; m. Mary Virginia Kimball, May 19, 1927. Draftsman, Carrers & Hastings, N.Y.C., 1903-08; pvt. practice, N.Y., N.J., Mass., Washington, Ky., Cal., Fla., France, 1909—; asso. Harry Ingals, 191O- 18; prin. works include Deering residence, Miami, Fla., 1912-17, Little Theatre, N.Y.C., 1910, apt. house, N.Y.C., 1928, World Bank, Paris, 1958. Recipient Gold medal San Francisco World's Fair. Mem. Archtl. League, Soc. Architects de Govt. Republican. Catholic. Club: Knickerbocker (N.Y.C.). Address: P O Box 1211 Hobe Sound FL 33455

HOFFMAN, FRED STANLEY, govt. ofcl.; b. N.Y.C., June 30, 1924; s. Aaron and Sarah (Falk) H.; B.A., U. Cal. at Los Angeles, 1947, M.A. in Econs., 1948; grad. student econs. U. Cal. at Berkeley, 1951; m. Ellen Sigman, June 15, 1947; children—Andrea Rachel, Jonathan Daniel, Jennifer Anne. Research asst. Inst. Indsl. Relations, U. Cal. at Los Angeles, 1947-49; with RAND Corp., 1951-65; dep. asst. sec. def. strategic programs Dept. Def., 1965- 67; asst. dir. budget U.S. Bur. Budget, from 1967. Mem., later acting dir. force planning group U.S. delegation NATO, Paris, France, 1963-64. Served to 1st lt. USAAF, 1943-46; CBI. Mem. Am. Econ. Assn., Am. Statis. Assn., Inst. Strategic Studies, Operations Research Soc. Am.

HOFFMAN, GRACE, contralto. Recordings for London Records in Strauss' Salome, by Vox in Mahler's Das Lied von der Erde. Address: care Vox Prodns Inc 236 W 55th St New York City NY 10019 *

HOFFMAN, HALLOCK BROWN, ednl. adminstr.; b. Columbia, S.C., Jan. 15, 1919; s. Paul G. and Dorothy (Brown) H.; A.B., Kenyon Coll., 1941; m. Elinor Gene Knudsen, July 18, 1949; children—Nikolas Knudsen, Valley Via, Paul Craig, Erik Thorkild, Kristian Robert, Nina Kiriki, Kai Lathrop. Mem. staff Am. Friend's Service Com., 1952-54; mem. staff Center Study Democratic Institutions, Santa Barbara, Cal., 1954-69, sr. fellow, 1967, coordinator studies, 1967-69; sec. Communications. Assos., Santa Barbara, 1969-70; asst. to provost Cal. Inst. Arts, 1970—, dean critical studies, 1971—; sec. treas. Fund for Republic, 1959-67; pres. Pacifica Found., part-time 1964-66, chmn. bd., 1966—. Served with USAAF, 1942-46. Home: 1387 School House Rd Santa Barbara CA 93108 Office: 24700 McBean Pky Valencia CA 91355

HOFFMAN, HARRY, lawyer; b. Ottawa, Can., Sept. 14, 1892; s. Edward Hoffman and Sarah (Rosen) H.; LL.B., N.Y.U., 1913; m. Ethyle Miller, Mar. 26, 1917; children—Edward Norman, Helen Grace (Mrs. Arthur Cranman), Ruth Paula (Mrs. Lee J. Sisisky), Flora Jean (Mrs. Fred F. A. Jacobsen). Admitted to N.Y. bar, 1915; pvt. sec. Samuel Untermyer, 1908-16; pvt. practice law, 1917-18; sec. to police commr. of N.Y.C., 1917; asso. Sutro Bros. & Co., 1920-22; sec.-treas. Fabrics Factors Corp., 1923-30; with Guggenheimer & Untermyer, N.Y.C., 1932—, partner, 1944—; partner Guggenheimer, Untermyer, Goodrich & Amram, Washington, 1944-60, Guggenheimer, Untermyer & Goodrich, 1960-64. Asst. sec. Democratic Nat. Conv., 1916; spl. asst. atty. gen. for elections, 1934-37. Dir., pres., Andrew Freedman Home. Served as pvt. and A.F.C., U.S. Army, 1918-19. Mem. Am., N.Y. bar assns., Bar Assn. City N.Y., N.Y. County Lawyers Assn., Am. Soc. Internat. Law, Am. Judicature Soc., Am. Legion, Acad. Polit. Sci. Mason. Clubs: Bankers Am., Nat. Democratic, City Athletic (N.Y.C.); Woodmere Country (past gov.). Home: 338 Westwood Rd Woodmere NY 11598 Office: 80 Pine St New York City NY 10005

HOFFMAN, HOWARD STANLEY, exptl. psychologist, educator; b. N.Y.C., May 23, 1925; s. Melvin Leo and Henrietta (Rosenthal) H.; B.A., New Sch. for Social Research, N.Y.C., 1952; M.A., Bklyn. Coll., 1953; Ph.D., U. Conn., 1957; m. Alice Marie Cruikshank, June 7, 1961; children— Randall, Gwendolyn, Russell, Franklin, Daniel, Martha. Research fellow in auditory perception U. Conn., 1953-56, instr. dept. statistics, 1956-57; asst. to prof. psychology Pa. State U., 1957-70; prof. psychology Bryn Mawr Coll., 1970—. Mem. exptl. psychology research rev. com. Nat. Inst. Mental Health, 1968-72. Served with AUS, 1943-45. Fellow Am. Psychol. Assn., A.A.A.S.; mem. Eastern Psychol. Assn., Am. Assn. U. Profs., Sigma Xi, Phi Kappa Phi, Psi Chi. Bd. editors Jour. Exptl. Analysis Behavior, 1966-69. Reviewer Behavior, Sci., Psychol. Rev., Jour Comparative and Physiol. Psychology. Home: 265 Hathaway Lane Wynnewood PA 19096 Office: Dept Psychology Bryn Mawr Coll Bryn Mawr PA 19010

HOFFMAN, INGFRIED, organist; b. Stettin, Germany, Jan. 30, 1935; student piano as a child. Sideman with Klaus Doldinger, 1963—; toured S. Am., N. Africa; played concert in New Orleans; recording artist for Philharmonic, Deutsche Gramaphone, Emarcy records. Address: Severinstrasse 92-96 Cologne West Germany *

HOFFMAN, IRWIN, orch. conductor; b. N.Y.C., Nov. 26, 1924; s. Harry and Augusta (Cohen) H.; student Juilliard Sch. Music, 1942-43, 45-48; m. Esther Glazer, Feb. 21, 1946; children—Joel H., Gary, Toby, Deborah. Condr. Phila. Orch. at Robin Hood Dell, summer 1942; teaching fellow Juilliard Sch. Music, 1948; condr. Bronx (N.Y.) Symphony, 1948-52, Yonkers (N.Y.) Philharmonic, 1950-52, Westchester (N.Y.) Chamber Orch., 1950-52, for Martha Graham Dance Co., 1949-50; condr., mus. dir. Vancouver (B.C., Can.) Symphony Orch., 1952-64; asso. condr. Chgo. Symphony Orch., 1964-68, acting music dir., 1968- 69, condr., 1969-70; prin. condr. Grant Park, Chgo., 1965-70; music dir. Fla. Gulf Coast Symphony Orch., 1968—; condr. St. Louis Little Symphony, summers, 1959-64; lectr., condr. U. B.C., State Coll. Wash., 1958; guest condr., Toronto, Vancouver, Chgo., Israel Philharmonic, 1960, Dallas Symphony, 1962, Brazil, 1962, St. Louis Symphony Orch., 1963, Miami and Tampa symphonies, 1967; protege Serge Koussevitzky, Tanglewood, 1948-50; guest condr. BBC Symphony, Manchester, Eng., 1968, Brussels (Belgium) Radio Orch., 1968, Strassbourg (France) Radio Orch., 1968, BBC Welsh, 1969-71, BBC Scottish, 1971, Orch. Nat. (France), 1970, Orch. Philharmonique (France), 1970, Orch. Nat. (Peru) 1970, Philharmonia Orch. (Eng.), 1971, Chgo. and Vancouver symphonies, 1971. Served with AUS, 1943-45. Composer two string quartets, violin sonata, others. Collector autography music manuscripts, mus. memorablia. Home: 1901 Brightwaters Blvd St Petersburg FL 33704 Office: 26 2d St N St Petersburg FL 33701

HOFFMAN, IRWIN D., artist; b. Boston, Mar. 8, 1901; s. Jacob Hillel and Minna (Aronson) H.; ed. Boston pub. schs.; student Boston Mus. Fine Arts Sch., 1917-24; studied in Paris, Madrid, Rome, Florence, Vienna, Amsterdam on Page Traveling Fellowship, 1924-26; m. Dorothea Gabriel Geyer, 1930. Painter and etcher, N.Y.C., 1927—; best known for paintings and etchings of mining scenes. Prin. work: Murals for History of Mining (6 panels) for Mining Exhibit, Golden Gate Internat. Expn., San Francisco. Five one-man shows in N.Y.C.; painted portrait Pres. Hector Triyillo of Dominican Republic, 1956, Cardinal Spellman, Justice Frankfurter, Dr. Samuel Belkin, Mischa Elman, Dr. Bela Schick, David Ben Gurion, 1964. Recipient Henry F. Noyes prize for etching, ann. exhibit Soc. Am. Etchers, 1937. Mem. Soc. Am. Etchers. Studio: 54 W 74th St New York City NY 10023

HOFFMAN, JACK LEROY, lawyer; b. Portland, Ore., Aug. 30, 1922; s. Daniel William and Lillian (Huget) H.; A.B., Linfield Coll. 1946; LL.B., U. Ore., 1949; m. Louise S. Montag, Oct. 7, 1951; children—Kenneth J., William S. Admitted to Ore. bar, 1949; asst. statute reviser Ore., 1949-50; practice in Portland, 1950—; mem. firm Bullivant, Wright, Johnson, Pendergrass & Hoffman, 1950—. Mem. dist. com. local Boy Scouts Am., 1965-67, troop com., 1966-69, instl. rep., 1967-69. Bd. dirs. Ore. Tb and Respiratory Disease Assn., 1957—, mem. exec. com., 1961—, pres., 1969—; bd. dirs. Nat. Tb and Respiratory Disease Assn., 1963—. Served to 1st lt. USAAF, World War II, to capt. USAF, Korea. Mem. Am., Ore. (chmn. legal ethics com. 1968-69), Multnomah County bar assns., Am. Judicature Soc., Phi Alpha Delta. Clubs: City, Multnomah Athletic (Portland). Home: 2160 SW Sunset Dr Portland OR 97201 Office: Pacific Bldg Portland OR 97204

HOFFMAN, JAMES HARVEY, lawyer; b. Mansfield, O., Aug. 29, 1911; s. Charles and Sarah Estelle (Phillips) H.; grad. Culver Mil. Acad., 1929; B.S., Lafayette Coll., 1933; LL.B., Western Res. U.,

1936; m. Virginia Stookey, Aug. 29, 1942; children—James Harvey, Philip Newton, Virginia Ann. Admitted Ohio bar, 1936, practice in Mansfield; asst. sec., gen. counsel Mansfield TireRubber Co., 1938-40, sec., gen. counsel, 1940-45, v.p., gen. counsel, 1945-51, exec. v.p., gen. counsel, 1951-52, pres., 1952—; pres., dir. Chas. Hoffman Co., 1951—, Pa. Tire Co., Inland Rubber Corp.; dir. Copolymer Rubber & Chem. Co.; sec., dir. Denman Rubber Mfg. Co. Bd. advisors Mansfield Friendly House: exec. bd. Ohio-W. Va. YMCA; v.p. Ohio-W. Va. area council. YMCA; nat. bd., internat. com. YMCA. Served from 2d lt. to capt. AUS, 1942-45. Mem. Mansfield C. of C., Rubber Mfrs. Assn. (dir.), Am. Legion, Alpha Chi Rho, Phi Delta Phi. Mason (32, Shriner), Elk, Moose. Club: Westbrook Country. Home: 550 Edgewood Rd Mansfield OH 44907 Office: Mansfield Tire & Rubber Co PO Box 428 Mansfield OH 44902

HOFFMAN, JAMES WILLIAMS, writer; b. Phila., May 25, 1919; s. William and Charlotte (Dinter) H.; B.A., U. Wis., 1945; M.A., N.Y.U., 1959; m. Jae Lyle, May 26, 1955; children—Paul William, Tony James. Free-lance writer, 1940-65; editor Pageant mag., 1965-68; tchr. English, U. Wis., 1945, N.Y.U., 1958-61; faculty New Sch. Social Research, 1962—; free-lance writer; cons. editor Lithopinion. Mem. Modern Lang. Assn., English Grad. Assn. N.Y.U., Summerhill Soc. (pres.). Address: 44 Rayfield Rd Westport CT 06880

HOFFMAN, JOHAN HENRIK, Norwegian govt. ofcl.; b. Kristiansand, Norway, Aug. 9, 1909; s. Fritz Wilhelm and Hanna (Christie) H.; grad. faculty law, U. Oslo, 1932; m. Marta Kvadsheim, Jan. 25, 1936; children—Fivind, Jorgen. Dep. judge, 1932; sec. Ministry Law, 1935; dept. head Price Control Office, 1940; sec. Prime Minister's Office, 1945; mng. dir. State Housing Bank Norway, since 1946—. UN expert on financing housing in Iceland, 1962. Co-author: Norwegian Dictionary of Law, 1948. Home: 28 Almenueg Oslo 8 Norway Office: 11 Nedre Vollgt Oslo 1 Norway

HOFFMAN, JOSEPH FREDERICK, educator; b. Oklahoma City, Mar. 7, 1925; s. Henry Raymond and Rena Virginia (Crossman) H.; B.S., U. Okla., 1947, M.S., 1948; M.A., Princeton, 1951, Ph.D., 1952; M.A. (hon.), Yale, 1965. Lectr., research asso. Princeton, 1953-56; head sect. membrane physiology, lab. kidney and electrolyte metabolism Nat. Heart Inst., NIH, 1957-65; prof. physiology Yale, 1965—. Home: 226 Fountain St New Haven CT 06515

HOFFMAN, JOSEPH GILBERT, ecuator; b. Buffalo, Aug. 19, 1909; s. Joseph and Helene (Seyler) H.; A.B. with honors, Cornell U., 1935, Ph.D., 1939; m. Ruth A. Buckland, Aug. 17, 1940; children—Joseph H., Paul G. Research asst. physics Cornell U., 1935-39; staff Roswell Park Meml. Inst., 1939-46, dir. cancer research, 1946-54, now cons. cancer research; physicist Carnegie Inst. Washington, 1940-42, Nat. Bur. Standards, 1942-44; sci. staff Los Alamos Sci. Labs., 1944-46, cons., 1946—; research prof. U. Buffalo Sch. Medicine, 1947—, prof. biophysics, 1954- -, prof. physics, 1957—. Recipient awards Naval Ordnance, 1943, Manhattan Dist., 1945, OSRD, 1945. Fellow Am. Phys. Soc.; mem. Am. Assn. Cancer Research, A.A.A.S., Soc. Exptl. Biology and Medicine, Soc. Exptl. Biology and Medicine Western N.Y., Austin Flint Soc. Med. Research, N.Y. Acad. Scis., Sigma Xi, Phi Kappa Phi. Unitarian. Author: Size and Growth of Tissue Cells, 1953; Life and Death of Cells, 1957. Contbg. author Acute Radiation Syndrome, Ann. Internal Medicine, vol. 36, 1952. Home: 195 Crescent Av Buffalo NY 14214

HOFFMAN, JULIUS J., judge; b. Chgo.; July 7, 1895; s. Aaron and Bertha Hoffman; student Lewis Inst., Chgo.; Ph.B., Northwestern U., 1912, LL.B., 1915, LL.D., 1955; m. Eleanor H. Greenebaum, Sept. 20, 1928. Admitted to Ill. bar, 1915; practiced in Chgo., 1915-47; served as v.p. gen, counsel, Brunswick-Balke-Collender Co.; mem. faculty Northwestern U. Law Sch.; asso. editor Am. Jour. of Criminal Law and Police Sci.; judge Superior Ct. of Ill. (Cook County), 1947-53, U.S. Dist. Ct. for No. Dist. of Ill., 1953—. Former mem. Ill. State Housing Bd. Fellow Am. Bar Found.; mem. Northwestern U. Alumni Assn. (pres.; award of merit, 1954, service award 1962), Am. law Inst., Fed., Am., Ill., Chgo. bar assns., Am. Judicature Soc., Northwestern U. Assos. Republican. Clubs: Standard, Tavern, Union League, Mid-Day, Law (Chgo.); Lake Shore Country (Glencoe, Ill.); Post and Paddock (Arlington Heights, Ill.). Home: 179 East Lake Shore Drive Chicago IL 60611 Office: 219 Dearborn St Chicago IL 60604

HOFFMAN, KENNETH MYRON, mathematician, educator; b. Long Beach, Cal., Nov. 30, 1930; s. Myron Grant and Madge (Harrison) H.; A.A., John Muir Coll., 1950; A.B. Occidental Coll. 1952; M.A., U. Cal. at Los Angeles, 1954, Ph.D., 1956; m. Patti L. Braden, Aug. 30, 1952; children—Donna, Laura, Robert. Instr. math. Mass. Inst. Tech., Cambridge, 1956-59, asst. prof., 1959-61, asso. prof., 1961-63, prof., 1963—, chmn. pure math., 1968-69, chmn. Commn. on Edn., 1969-71. Cons. editor math. Prentice-Hall, Inc., Englewood Cliffs, N.J. Fellow Alfred P. Sloan Found., 1964-66. Mem. Am. Math. Soc. (past mem. council), Phi Beta Kappa. Author: (with Ray Kunze) Linear Algebra, 1961; Fundamentals of Banach Algebras, 1962; Banach Spaces of Analytic Functions, 1962. Contbr. articles to profl. jours. Mailing Address: Office: Mass Inst Tech Cambridge MA 02139

HOFFMAN, LEON-FRANCOIS, educator; b. Paris, France, Apr. 11, 1932; s. Jean and Nadja (Bloch) H.; came to U.S., 1948, naturalized, 1954; B.A., Yale, 1953; M.A., Princeton, 1955, Ph.D., 1959; m. Anne Schmidt, Feb. 1, 1960; children—Jacques-Henry, Philippe-Edgard. Instr. Princeton, 1957-60, asst. prof., 1960-65, asso. prof., 1965-68, prof. French, 1968—. Served with AUS, 1956-57. Mem. Am. Civil Liberties Union, Am. Assn. U. Profs., Modern Lang. Assn., Soc. Profs. of French in Am. Author: Romantique Espagne, 1961; La Peste à Barcelone, 1964; L'Essentiel de la grammaire francaise, 1964; Repertoire geographique de La Comedie humaine, 2 vols., 1965, 68. Contbr. articles books, revs. ‡

HOFFMAN, LESLIE ARTHUR, banker; b. Phila., Dec. 7, 1909; s. William Albert and Mary Ellen (McKenna) H.; B.S.C., Temple U., 1931; hon. grad. Am. Inst. Banking, 1940, Stonier Grad. Sch. Banking, Rutgers U., 1945; m. Ruth Kathryn Cruikshank, June 7, 1933; 1 dau., Carolyn A. (Mrs. Carroll B. Ripley, Jr.). With Girard Trust Bank, Phila., 1931—, v.p., 1955—, sec., 1963- -; v.p., sec. Girard Internat. Bank, Girard Internat. Investment Corp.; sec. Girard Co., 1969—, Girard Financial Corp., 1970—, Studely, Shupert & Co., Inc. Phila., 1970—, Girard Trust Bank Found. Pres., trustee Westminster Found., 1968—; pres. Presbyn. Social Union Phila., 1970—; vice chmn. Phila. Commn. for United Ministries in Higher Edn., 1968—; chmn. ann. fund, mem. exec. com. devel. council Temple U., 1965—. Mem. Am. Soc. Corp. Secs. (adv. com. middle Atlantic group), Am. Inst. Banking (past pres. Phila.), Temple U. Sch. Bus. Adminstrn. Alumni Assn. (mgr., pres.), Stonier Grad. Sch. Banking at Rutgers U. Alumni Assn. (past pres. Delaware Valley), U. Pa. Banking Club (past pres.), Phila. Bank Officers Club, Delta Sigma Pi. Clubs: Temple U. Downtown (pres.); Wyncote Men's (past pres.). Home: 123 Hewett Rd Wyncote PA 19095 Office: Girard Trust Bank Philadelphia PA 19101

HOFFMAN, LIONEL RICHARD, educator, psychologist; b. Taunton, Mass., June 6, 1930; s. Harry and Leah (Stampel) H.; B.S., Queens Coll., 1952; M.A., U. Mich., 1953, Ph.D., 1957; m. Roslyn Braverman, June 21, 1953; children—Cynthia Anne, Karen Elaine, Elizabeth Diane, Valerie Joan. Instr. psychology U. Mich., 1958-60, asst. prof., 1960-62, asso. prof., 1962-65, asst. study dir. Survey Research Center, 1954-56, study dir., 1957-59, research asso. Engrng. Research Inst., 1957-59; prof. psychology Grad. Sch. Bus., U. Chgo., 1965—; cons. psychol. problems of orgns., 1957—. Fellow Am. Psychol. Assn.; mem. Eastern, Midwestern psychol. assns., A.A.A.S., Soc. Applied Anthropology, Sigma Xi. Author: Automation and the Worker, 1960; (with F.C. Mann) Superior-Subordinate Communication in Management, 1961; also numerous articles on automation, orgn., problem-solving and tng. Home: 3731 Aspen St Flossmoor IL 60422 Office: Grad Sch Bus U Chgo Chicago IL 60637

HOFFMAN, MARK, musician, educator; b. Merrill, Wis., Jan. 24, 1904; s. Martin George and Margaretha (Fritsch) H.; Sr. Diploma (gold medalist) Chgo. Mus. Coll., 1921; B.M. cum laude, Eastman Sch. Music, 1929, Ph.D., 1953; (Hutcheson scholar) Juilliard Grad. Sch. Music, 1929-31; A.M., N.Y.U., 1934; study and concertizing in Germany, 1932; m. Elaine Marie Faulkner, May 31, 1925; children—Margaret Elaine, Mark. Head piano dept. Kan. State Coll., Hays, 1924-26, James Millikin U., Decatur, Ill., 1926-28; dean music Greensboro (N.C.) Coll. Music, 1934-47; chmn. dept. music U. Miss., 1947-69, prof. piano and theory, 1966-69, prof. emeritus, 1969—. Concert appearances Town Hall, N.Y.C., Kimball Hall, Chgo.; with Rochester Philharmonic, N.Y. Civic, N.C. Symphony, Brandenburg (German) Orch.; staff pianist radio sta. WINS, N.Y.C., also WOR, 1930-34; appearances Duke U., U. N.C., French Embassy, Washington; accompanist Isaac Stern (violinist), 1948, and others. Fellow Internat. Inst. Arts and Letters; mem. Music Tchrs. Nat. Assn., Music Educators Nat. Assn., N.C. Music Tchrs. Assn. (past pres.), Nat. Assn. Schs. Music (v.p. Region 8), Miss. Music Tchrs. Assn. (pres. 1954-56), Phi Mu Alpha. Home: 621 N Pine St Little Rock AR 72205

HOFFMAN, MICHAEL LINDSAY, economist; b. Salisbury, N.C., June 13, 1915; s. Edwin Michael and Mary (Lindsay) H.; student Berea Coll. Acad., 1928-31; A.B. summa cum laude, Oberlin Coll., 1935; Ph.D. (fellow Social Sci. Research Council), U. Chgo., 1942; m. Catherine Legal Hughes, Sept. 3, 1936; 1 son, Peter Lindsay. Instr. econs. Trinity Coll., Hartford, Conn., 1938-40, Oberlin (O.) Coll., 1940-42; staff Fgn. Funds Control, U.S. Treasury, 1942-45, also U.S. Treasury rep. Allied Force Hdqrs., Algiers, London, Paris; European econ. corr. N.Y. Times, 1945-56; dir. Econ Devel. Inst., Internat. Bank Reconstrn. and Devel., 1957-62, dir. devel. adv. service, 1962-63; exec. v.p., dir. Lambert Internat. Corp., 1963-65; asso. dir. devel. services dept. Internat. Bank for Reconstrn. and Devel., 1965—. Decorated chevalier de l'Ordre de la Couronne (Belgium). Mem. Royal Econ. Soc., Am. Econ. Assn., Geneva Assn. UN Corrs., Council Fgn. Relations, Phi Beta Kappa. Clubs: Cosmos (Washington); Reform (London). Home: 2601 36th St NW Washington DC 20007 Office: 1818 H St NW Washington DC 20433

HOFFMAN, PAUL GRAY, corp. exec.; b. Chgo., Apr. 26, 1891; s. George Delos and Eleanor (Lott) H.; student U. Chgo., 1908-09; hon. degrees from numerous univs., including U. Cal., Columbia, Harvard, Yale; m. Dorothy Brown, Dec. 18, 1915 (dec.); children- -Hallock Brown, Peter Brown, Donald Gray, Robert Chesboro, Lathrop Gray, Barbara, Kiriki; m. 2d, Anna M. Rosenberg, July 19, 1962. Began as auto salesman Studebaker Corp., Los Angeles, 1911, sales mgr. Los Angeles br., 1915, dist. br. mgr., 1917, purchased Los Angeles retail br., 1919, v.p., 1925-33, pres., 1935-48, chmn. bd., 1953; chmn. bd. Studebaker-Packard Corp., 1954-56; adminstr. ECA, 1948-50; pres. trustee Ford Found., 1951-53. Mem. U.S. Delegation to UN, 1956-57; mng. dir. UN Spl. Fund, 1959-66; adminstr. of UN Devel. Programme, 1966—, UN Vols., 1970—. Trustee Com. Econ. Devel., chmn., 1942-48; chmn. pub. policy com. Advt. Council; mem. bus. adv. council Dept. Commerce. Trustee U. Chgo., 1937- 50; Kenyon Coll., trustee Automotive Safety Found., pres., 1937-41, chmn., 1941-48; dir. N.Y. Life Ins. Co., Time, Inc., Ency. Brit. Inc., Ency. Brit. Films, Inc. Hon. chmn. Fund for Republic; dir. Inst. for Internat. Order; mem. exec. com. UN Assn. U.S.A. Served with U.S. Army, 1917-19. Recipient Freedom House award, 1951, numerous other awards. Mem. Am. Soc. French Legion Honor, Delta Tau Delta. Republican. Mason. Clubs: Stanwich (Greenwich, Conn.); Metropolitan (Washington); Century (N.Y.C.); Thunderbird, California. Author: Seven Roads to Safety, 1939; Peace Can Be Won, 1951; World Without Want, 1962. Home: 8 Sutton Sq New York City NY 10022 Office: 866 UN Plaza New York City NY 10017

HOFFMAN, PHILIP EISINGER, lawyer, real estate co. exec.; b. N.Y.C., Oct. 2, 1908; s. David S. and Hildegarde (Eisinger) H.; A.B. cum laude, Dartmouth, 1929; LL.B., Yale, 1932; m. Florence L. Lehman, Sept. 9, 1933; children—David L., Lynne B. (Mrs. Roger L. Manshel). Admitted to N.Y. bar, 1933, since practiced in N.Y.C.; corp. law practice, 1933-42, 45—; partner Goodell, Hoffman & Spark, 1937-42, Hoffman & Tuck, 1962—; chmn. exec. com. U.S. Realty & Investment Co., Newark, 1962—, also dir.; dir. Comml. Mortgage Co., Ray Miller, Inc., Realty Capital Corp., Ltd., Toronto, Ont., Can. Mem. N.J. Commn. on Civil Rights, 1969—, Bipartisan Conf. on Civil Rights, 1960—, N.J. adv. com. U.S. Commn. on Civil Rights, 1964-69; chmn. Community Relations Council Essex County (N.J.), 1960-63; co-chmn. housing com. Com. of Concern Newark, 1967-69; asst. gen. counsel WPB, Washington, 1942- 45; hearing commr. Nat. Prodn. Authority, 1950-53; mem. liaison com. Friends of Alliance Israelite Universelle; adult sponsor Youth Com. for Peace and Democracy in Middle East; chmn. coodinating com. Retail Jewelry Industry, 1954-60. Chmn. bd. govs. Am. Jewish Com., 1963-67, pres., 1969—, chmn. nat. exec. bd., 1967-68; hon. chmn. Appeal for Human Relations, 1962—; mem. exec. com. Nat. Community Relations Adv. Council, 1966—, Am. Israel Pub. Affairs Com., 1969—; mem. liaison com. Friends of Alliance Israelite Universelle; adult sponsor Youth Com. for Peace and Democracy in Middle East. Trustee Leonard M. Sperry Research Center, East Orange Gen. Hosp., Jewish Community Council Essex County. Recipient numerous awards in human relations field. Mem. Am. Bar Assn., Assn. Bar City N.Y., N.Y. County Lawyers Assn., Phi Beta Kappa. Jewish religion. Clubs: Essex, Down Town (Newark); Mountain Ridge Country (Caldwell, N.J.). Home: 218 N Woods Dr South Orange NJ 07079 Office: 972 Broad St Newark NJ 07102

HOFFMAN, PHILIP GUTHRIE, univ. pres. and adminstr.; b. Kobe, Japan, Aug. 6, 1915 (parents U.S. citizens); s. Benjamin Philip and Florence (Guthrie) H.; student George Washington U., 1936-37; A.B., Pacific Union Coll., 1938; M.A., U. So. Cal., 1942; Ph.D., Ohio State U., 1948; H.H.D., Jacksonville U.; LL.D., U. Ams., U. Akron; L.H.D., Pikeville Coll.; m. Mary Elizabeth Harding, Aug. 31, 1939; children—Philip Guthrie, Mary Victoria (Mrs. Stephen F. Forsyth), Ruth Ann, Jeanne. Engaged as credit mgr. Harding Sanitarium, Worthington, O., 1938-40; instr. history Ohio State U., 1946-49; asst. prof. history U. Ala., 1949-51, asso. prof., 1951-53, dir. arts and scis. extension services, 1949-53; vice dean, asso. prof. history gen. extension div. Ore. System Higher Edn., 1953-55, dean and prof., 1955- 56; dean faculty, prof. history Portland State Coll., 1956-57; v.p., dean faculties, prof. history U. Houston, 1957-61, pres., 1961—. Dir., Fed. Res. Bank of Dallas. Mem. bd. Am. Council on Edn., 1966-68, Nat. Commn. on Accrediting, 1970—. Served from ensign to lt. (j.g.), USNR, 1943-45. Recipient Centennial Achievement award Ohio State U. Mem. Tex. Gulf, Am. hist. assns., Assn. Tex. Coll. and Univs. (pres.), Assn. Urban Univs. (pres. 1965-66), Nat. Assn. State Univs. and Land-Grant Colls. (dir. 1970—), So. Assn. Colls. and Schs. (dir. 1967-69), Am. Assn. U. Profs., Phi Kappa Phi, Phi Alpha Theta (nat. pres. 1952-54), Omicron Delta Kappa. Clubs: University, Rotary, Petroleum, Torch, Houston, River Oaks (Houston). Contbr. articles to profl. jours. Home: 427 Brown Saddle St Houston TX 77027

HOFFMAN, RICHARD WAGNER, physicist, educator; b. Cleve., Apr. 9, 1927; s. Clifford Robert A. and Ada (Wagner) H.; B.S., Case Inst. Tech., 1947, M.S., 1949, Ph.D., 1952; m. Yvette Anne Herot, July 1, 1950; children—Emily Jo, Karen Sue, Richard Wagner. Instr., Case Inst. Tech., 1952-55, asst. prof., 1956-59, asso. prof. physics, 1959-64; Prof. physics Case Western Res. U., Cleve., 1964—; with Bell Telephone Labs., 1955-56; mem. faculty U. Oxford Eng., 1962-63. Mem. Am. Phys. Soc., Am. Vacuum Soc. (dir. 1969—), Sigma Xi, Tau Beta Pi. Home: 34660 Sherwood Dr Solon OH 44139 Office: University Circle Cleveland OH 44106

HOFFMAN, RICHARD WILLIAM, banker; b. Rice Lake, Wis., Feb. 8, 1918; s. William A. and Anna (Amundson) H.; B.A., U. Wis., 1939, M.B.A., 1954; postgrad. Grad. Sch. Banking, U. Wis., 1952, BAI Sch. for Bank Auditors and Comptrollers, 1957; grad. certificate, Am. Inst. Banking, 1960; m. June M. Weink, June 27, 1948; children—William H., Stephen C. With First Wis. Nat. Bank Milw., 1939—, asst. v.p., asst. comptroller, 1959-63, v.p., comptroller, 1963-70, 1st v.p., 1970—; v.p. First Wis. Bankshares Corp.; dir. L.I.C. Corp., Schroeder- Manatee, Inc.; instr. Duke, 1943-45, Army Finance Sch., Ft. Benjamin Harrison, 1945, Am. Inst. Banking, 1946-62, U. Wis., 1946-62, BAI Sch. Bank Adminstrn., 1956-69. Mem. Polit. Edn. and Action League, 1962-68; adv. com. Pub. Expenditure Survey Wis., 1963—; asso. div. chmn. Milw. County United Fund, 1960-63. Served to maj., Finance Corps, AUS, 1941-46. Mem. Am. Inst. Banking, Am. Inst. C.P.A.'s, Assn. Registered Bank Holding Cos., Army Finance Assn., Am. Legion, Financial Execs. Inst. (dir. Milw.), Bank Adminstrn. Inst., Nat. Alumni Assn. BAI Sch., Res. Officers Assn., Wis. Bankers Assn., Wis. Soc. C.P.A.'s, Met. Milw. Assn. Commerce, Beta Alpha Psi, Beta Gamma Sigma. Clubs: Badger Bankers; Milwaukee Athletic; Wisconsin Alumni. Home: 7103 N Crossway Rd Fox Point WI 53217 Office: 743 N Water St Milwaukee WI 53201

HOFFMAN, SAMUEL KURTZ, aviation cons.; b. Williamsport, Pa. Apr. 15, 1902; s. George and Louise (Bruner) H.; B.S., Pa. State U., 1925, M.E., 1945; m. Genevieve Wieland, June 18, 1932; children—Jean (Mrs. Edward Harker), Susan (Mrs. Robert Laughlin), Louise (Mrs. Ronald Rosequist), John. Sales engr. Reliance Elec. & Engrng. Co., 1925-27; design engr. Fairchild, Farmingdale, L.I., 1927-28, Lycoming Mfg. Co., 1928-29, Allison div. Gen. Motors Corp., 1929-30; engr. Gen. Motors Research Lab., 1930-32; project engr. Lycoming div. Aviation Corp., 1932-34, asst. chief engr., 1934-36, chief engr., 1936-45; prof. aero. engrng. Pa. State U., 1945-49; chief propulsion sect. aerophysics N. Am. Aviation, Inc. (now N.Am. Rockwell Corp.), 1949-54, mgr. propulsion center, 1954-55, v.p., 1957- 68, v.p. aerospace and systems group, 1968-70, gen. mgr. Rocketdyne div. Canoga Park, 1955-57, v.p., gen. mgr., 1957-59, div. pres., 1960-70; aerospace cons., 1970—; dir. Missile, Space and Range Pioneers, Inc. Bd. dirs. Presbyn. Hosp., San Fernando Valley; adv. bd. San Fernando State Coll. Recipient Goddard Meml. Trophy, Missiles and Rockets mag., 1959; ARS Godard award, 1959; co-recipient Louis W. Hill Transp. award Inst. Aero. Scis., 1960; recipient Spirit of St. Louis award Am. Soc. M.E., 1962, Distinguished Alumnus award Pa. State U., 1963. Fellow Am. Inst. Aero. and Astronautics, Royal Aero. Soc.; mem. Am. Soc. M.E., Soc. Automotive Engineers (v.p. 1943), Internat. Astronautical Fedn., Nat. Space Club (bd. govs.), Sigma Tau, Theta Xi. Address: 5432 Wilbur Av Tarzana CA 91356

HOFFMAN, STEPHEN PETER, Jr., mathematician, educator; b. Norwich, Conn., Apr. 10, 1926; s. Stephen Peter and Janina (Midouszewski) H.; B.A., Yale, 1949; M.A., 1951, Ph.D., 1957. Asst. prof. Poly. Inst. Bklyn., 1951-57; asst. prof., asso. prof. Trinity Coll. (Conn.), 1957-66; prof., chmn. dept. math. State U. N.Y. Coll. at Cortland, 1966-68; prof., chmn. dept. math. Bates Coll., Lewiston, Me., 1968—. Served with USNR, 1943-46. Mem. Am. Math. Soc., Math. Assn. Am., Soc. for Indsl. and Applied Math., Am. Assn. U. Profs. Author: Basic Analysis, 1960; (with M.F. Willerding) Modern Intermediate Algebra; 1969; Advanced Calculus, 1970. Home: 438 Webster St Lewiston ME 04240

HOFFMAN, WALTER EDWARD, U.S. dist. judge; b. Jersey City, July 18, 1907; s. Walter and Ella Adele (Sharp) H.; B.S. in Econs., U. Pa., 1928; grad. student Coll. William and Mary, 1928-29; LL.B., Washington and Lee U., 1931, LL.D., 1970; m. Evelyn Virginia Watkins, Apr. 6, 1939 (dec. Feb. 1971); children—Carole Lee, Walter Edward. Admitted Va. bar, 1931; pvt. practice, Norfolk, 1931-35; partner firm Breeden & Hoffman, 1935-54; instr., then asst. prof. Coll. William and Mary, 1933-42; referee in bankruptcy Eastern Dist. Va., Norfolk div., 1942-44; U.S. dist. judge Eastern Dist. Va., 1954-62, chief U.S. judge Eastern dist., 1962—. Mem. jud. Conf. U.S., 1964-70, chmn. com. adminstrn. probation system, 1966-71; mem. Supreme Ct. adv. com. criminal rules, 1960—; mem. state-fed. relations com. Fed. Jud. Center, 1968—. Del. Republican Nat. Conv. 1952. Trustee Randolph-Macon Coll. Mem. Am., Va. (v.p. 1948-49), Norfolk and Portsmouth (pres. 1948-49) bar assns. Methodist (dist. lay leader 1949-53). Mason (Shriner) Club: Cosmopolitan (pres. 1953). Home: 1489 Emory Pl Norfolk VA 23509 Office: Federal Bldg Norfolk VA 23510

HOFFMAN, WARREN EUGENE, educator; b. Buffalo, Apr. 5, 1923; s. Franklin David and Selma Mildred (Johnson) H.; B.S. in Chemistry, Union Coll., Schenectady, 1951; Ph.D., U. Buffalo, 1955; m. Jeanne Torrisi, July 3, 1948; children-Linda Jeanne, Becky Anne, Warren Eugene II. With Western Electric Co., 1960- 61, E.I. duPont de Nemours & Co., Inc., 1963, Nat. Aniline div. Allied Chem. Corp., 1954-60; mem. faculty Ind. Inst. Tech., 1960—, prof. chemistry, chmn. dept., 1965—; cons. to industry. Mem. Ft. Wayne com. Citizens for Humphrey, 1968. Served with AUS, 1942-46. Named Citizen Engr. of Year, 12 Professional Societies making up the Engineers' Week committee, 1969. Mem. Am. Chem. Soc. (chmn. Northeastern Ind. sect. 1963, nat. councillor 1965-68; named Chemist of Year, Northeastern Ind. sect. 1967), Am. Inst. Chemists, Am. Sci. Affiliation, A.A.A.S., Soc. Applied Spectroscopy, Ft. Wayne Engrs. Club, Am. Inst. Chem. Engrs., Ft. Wayne Acad. Sci., Ind. Acad. Sci., Am. Assn. U. Profs., Am. Soc. Engrng. Edn., Am. Oil Chemists Soc., Am. Soc. Microbiology, Sigma Xi. Author articles in field. Home: 1006 Hollyhill Dr Fort Wayne IN 46809

HOFFMAN, WAYNE MELVIN, airline ofcl.; b. Chgo., Mar. 9, 1923; s. Carl A. and Martha (Tamillo) H.; B.A. with high honours, U. Ill., 1946, J.D. with high honors, 1947; m. Laura Majewski, Jan. 26, 1946; children—Philip, Karen, Kristin. Admitted to Ill. bar, 1947, N.Y. bar, 1958; atty. I.C. R.R., 1948-52; with N.Y.C. R.R. Co., 1952-67, exec. asst. to pres. 1958-60, v.p. freight sales, 1960-61, v.p. sales, 1961-62, exec. v.p., 1962-67; chmn. N.Y. Central Trans. Co., 1960-67, Flying Tiger Line, Inc., 1967—, Flying Tiger Corp., 1970—;

dir. N. Am. Car Corp. Mem. Pres. Nixon's Adv. Council on Mgmt. Improvement, 1970—. Served to capt., inf., AUS, World War II. Decorated Silver Star, Purple Heart with oak leaf cluster. Mem. Am. Bar Assn., Phi Beta Kappa. Clubs: Chicago; Bel Air Country (Los Angeles); Eldorado Country (Indian Wells, Cal.). Home: 425 N Barrington Av Los Angeles CA 90049 Office: 7401 World Way W Los Angeles CA 90009

HOFFMAN, WILLIAM LOWRY, aircraft co. exec.; b. Seattle, Dec. 18, 1916; s. Arthur William and Frances (Lowry) H.; student Santa Monica City Coll., 1934-37; m. Helen Marie MacPherson, Nov. 24, 1942; children—Robert James, Sue (Mrs. Ronald Hebb). Foreman prodn. control Northrop Aircraft Corp., 1936-38; supr. material control N. Am. Aviation, 1938-42; mgr. material and prodn. control Avco, Nashville, Tenn., 1942-50; mgr. materials Chance-Vought Aircraft Co., Dallas, 1950-60; v.p. adminstrn., material Hughes Aircraft Co., Culver City, Cal., 1960—. Vice pres. Jr. Achievement, Los Angeles, Co., 1965—, also bd. dirs.; mem. adv. bd. Daniel Freeman Hosp., Inglewood, Cal., 1964—, dir. devel. com., 1965—. Bd. dirs. United Crusade Los Angeles Co. (also gen. campaign chmn., 1963). Recipient Pub. Service award Small Bus. Adminstrn., 1965. Mem. Los Angeles C. of C., Am. Mgmt. Assn., Am. Ordnance Assn. Clubs: Cal. Yacht (Los Angeles); San Juan Hills Golf and Country (San Juan Capistrano, Cal.). Home: 8203 Zitola Terrace Playa del Rey CA 90291 Office: Centinela and Teale Sts Culver City CA 90230

HOFFMANN, DONALD, art critic; b. Springfield, Ill., June 24, 1933; s. George C. and Ines (Catron) H.; student U. Chgo., 1949-53; student U. Kansas City (Mo.), 1958; m. Theresa Cecelia McGrath, Apr. 12, 1958; children—George, Alan, Eric, Michael, Valerie. Mem. staff Kansas City (Mo.) Star, 1956—, art critic and editor, 1965—. Mem. journalism adv. com. Fulbright Scholarship Program, 1968-70. Younger Humanist fellow Nat. Endowment Humanities, 1970-71. Mem. Soc. Archtl. Historians (bd. dirs. 1968-70), Coll. Art Assn. Am., Art Inst. Chgo. (life). Editor: The Meanings of Architecture- Buildings and Writings by John Wellborn Root, 1967. Asst. editor Jour. Soc. Archtl. Historians, 1970—. Contbr. jours. in field. Home: 6441 Holmes St Kansas City MO 64131 Office: 1729 Grand Av Kansas City MO 64108

HOFFMANN, EDWARD C., banker. Sr. v.p., also cashier Central Bank and Trust Co. Office: 15th and Arapahoe Sts Denver CO 80217*

HOFFMANN, FELIX, artist; b. Aarau, Switzerland, Apr. 18, 1911; s. Emil Adolf and Mina (Fröhlich) H.; student Akademie Karlsruhe (Germany), 1931-33, Akademie Berlin (Germany), 1933-35; m. Gretel Kienschof, Jan. 18, 1936; children—Sabine, Christine, Susan, Dieter. Illustrator books for young people and children, 1932—; illustrator biliophile books for German and Am. pubs., 1951—; executed stained glass windows in Bern, also numerous chs., town halls and colls.; mural paintings in Thun, Aarau, Küttigen, Deusbüren. Recipient Schweizer-Jugendbuchpreis, 1957; honours list Hans Christian Andersen award, 1960, 62; Children's Spring Book Festival award, 1963. Mem. Gesellschaft Schweizer Maler. Bildhauer Architekten, Internat. Vereingung der Holzschneider, Verband deutsche Buchkünstler. Address: Rütliweg 2 Aarau Switzerland

HOFFMANN, JOHN PETER, banker; b. Chgo., May 21, 1910: s. Peter Joseph and Mary (Freis) H.; student Northwestern U., 1934; m. Hazel Ellen Bishop, July 6, 1935. With Continental Ill. Nat. Bank & Trust Co., Chgo., 1924—, v.p., 1950-65, sr. v.p. comml. banking dept., 1965-69, sr. v.p. met. div., from 1969; dir. Kellwood Co., Maremont Corp., Mich. Chem. Corp., Opelike Mfg. Corp., Standard Kollsman Industries, Inc. Mem. Robert Morris Assos. Clubs: Chicago, Chicago Athletic Assn., Economic, Executives, Bankers (Chgo.). Home: 1105 Delles Rd Wheaton IL 60187 Office: 231 S LaSalle St Chicago IL 60690

HOFFMANN, MALCOLM ARTHUR, lawyer; b. N.Y.C., Nov. 26, 1912; s. Abraham A. and Minna (Newmark) H.; A.B. magna cum laude, Harvard, 1934, LL.B., 1937; m. Anna Frances Luciano, Apr. 13, 1939; children—Gertrude Nina (Mrs. William Bolter), Jessica Ann (Mrs. William Merritt Davis). Admitted to N.Y. bar, 1938, also U.S. Supreme Ct.; practice in N.Y.C., 1944—; successively atty., asso. atty., sr. atty. NLRB, 1939-43; spl atty. appellate sect. criminal div. Dept. Justice, 1943, spl. asst. to atty. gen. U.S. antitrust div., 1944-55; asso. Rosenman, Colin, Kaye, Petschek, Freund & Emil, 1955-59; counsel Greenbaum, Wolff & Ernst, 1959-60; pvt. practice, 1960—; lectr. Practicing Law Inst., 1957—; mem. faculty Joint Com. on Continuing Legal Edn., Am. Law Inst., Am. Bar Assn., 1966; lectr. trade problems Am. Mgmt. Assn., 1967-71; lectr. antitrust sect. meeting Am. Bar Assn., Honolulu, 1967. Mem. adv. com. Day Care Children N.Y.C. Dept. Health, 1952-56; v.p., sec. Hoffman Sch., Inc. Mem. Am. Judicature Soc., Am. (com. vice chmn.), Fed., N.Y. State (past com. chmn., mem. exec. com.) bar assns., Bar Assn. City N.Y. (past chmn. subcom.), Fed. Bar Assn. N.Y., N.J. and Conn. (past sec. trade regulation com.). Club: Harvard (N.Y.C.). Author: Government Lawyer, 1955; (with Morris L. Ernst) Back and Forth, 1966. Contbr. chpt. to A Tip of the Hat to Mr. B, The Teacher, 1967. Editor: Hoffmann's Antitrust Law and Techniques, 1963. Home: 5440 Independence Av Riverdale NY 10471 Office: 12 E 41st St New York City NY 10017

HOFFMANN, OSWALD CARL JULIUS, clergyman; b. Snyder, Neb., Dec. 6, 1913; s. Carl John and Bertha (Seidel) H.: student Luther Inst., Chgo., Concordia Coll., Milw. and St. Paul; M.A., U. Minn., 1935; B.D., Concordia Sem., St. Louis, 1936, D.D., 1952; LL.D., Valparaiso U., 1952; m. Marcia Rosalind Linnell, June 23, 1940; children—Peter, Paul, John, Katharine Ann. Instr. Bethany Luth. Coll., Mankato, Minn., 1936-40, also dean of men, dir. music, head English dept.; chmn. Minn. Jr. Coll. Conf. Forensic Festival; ordained to ministry Luth. Ch., 1939; pastor English Luth. Ch., Cottonwood, Minn., 1939-40; instr. U. Minn., 1940-41; prof. Concordia Collegiate Inst., Bronxville, N.Y., 1941-48; dir. pub. relations dept. Lutheran Ch., Mo. Synod, 1948-63; asst. pastor St. Matthew Luth. Ch., Manhattan, 1948-63; bd. dirs. Aid Assn. for Luths., Lutherland, Inc., 1963—. pres. Luth. Council in U.S.A., 1970—; speaker Internat. Luth. Hour, 1955—; sec. Luth. Church Prodns., supervised prodn. of films Question Seven and Martin Luther; editorial asso. American Lutheran mag.; mem. bd. This is the Life, nat. TV program. Mem. nat. religious adv. com. Fed. Civil Def. Adminstrn.; pres. Nat. Religious Publicity Council, 1953-55. Dir. Wheat Ridge Found. (care and prevention Tb), Found. Reformation Research. Mem. Am. Philol. Assn., Am. Bible Soc. (life; bd. mgrs.). Author: The Passion Journey, 1956; The Joyful Way, 1958; Life Crucified, 1959; God Is No Island, 1969; Hurry Home Where You Belong, 1970. Home: 586 Oak Valley Dr St Louis MO 63131 Office: 2185 Hampton Av St Louis MO 63139

HOFFMANN, PAUL OTTO, educator; b. Germany, May 6, 1909; s. Paul A. J. and Emma (Janz) H.; B.S., Newark Coll. Engring., 1933; A.M. Columbia, 1938; Ph.D., N.Y.U., 1950; m. Dorothy J. Thiele, July 21, 1933; children—Paul R., James E., Dorothy L. Came to U.S., 1925, naturalized, 1933. Mem. faculty Newark Coll. Engring., 1933—, successively instr., asst. and asso. prof., prof. physics, chmn. physics dept. and tech. group, 1947-66, chmn. dept. physics, 1966—, dist. prof. physics, 1968—; cons. U.S. Munitions Command, Dover, N.J. Mem. Am. Soc. Engring. Edn., Am. Soc. Physics Tchrs., A.A.A.S., Sigma Xi, Tau Beta Pi, Phi Eta Sigma, Sigma Pi Sigma, Pi Tau Sigma. Home: 6 Park Av Maplewood NJ 07040 Office: Newark Coll Engring High St Newark NJ 07102

HOFFMANN, ROALD, chemist, educator; b. Zloczow, Poland, July 18, 1937; s. Paul and Clara (Rosen) H.; came to U.S., 1949, naturalized, 1955; B.A., Columbia, 1958; M.A., Harvard, 1960, Ph.D., 1962; m. Eva Börjesson, Apr. 30, 1960; children—Hillel Jan, Ingrid Helena. Jr. fellow Soc. Fellows, Harvard, 1962-65; asso. prof. Cornell U., Ithaca, N.Y., 1965-68, prof., 1968—. Recipient Am. Chem. Soc. award in pure chemistry, 1969; Fresenius award Phi Lambda Upsilon, 1969; Harrison Howe award Rochester sect. Am. Chem. Soc., 1970; ann. award Internat. Acad. Quantum Molecular Scis., 1970. Author: (with R.B. Woodward) Conservation of Orbital Symmetry, 1970. Home: 4 Sugarbush Lane Ithaca NY 14850

HOFFMANN, ROBERT FREDERICK, hosp. adminstr.; b. Brainerd, Minn., Apr. 6, 1921; s. Henry David and Ellen (Gedosch) H.; A.S., Brainerd Jr. Coll., 1941; student Gustavus Adolphus Coll., 1944, Harvard, 1945; B.A., U. Minn., 1948, M.H.A., 1950; m. Delores L. Frees, June 9, 1951; children—Bruce, Scott, Susan, Mark. Adminstr., Wright Meml. Hosp., Fergus Falls, Minn., 1950-51, Meeker County Hosp., Litchfield, Minn., 1951-52; asst. supt. Fergus Falls State Hosp., 1952-62, adminstr., 1962—. Chmn. Minn. Med. Records Com., 1964- 70. Chmn. Fergus Falls United Fund, 1953-57. Served with USNR, 1942-46. Mem. Am. Legion. Elk. Home: 1315 N Park St Fergus Falls MN 56537 Office: Box 157 Fergus Falls MN 56537

HOFFMANN, SAL B., labor ofcl.; b. Aversa, Italy, Apr. 5, 1899; s. Leopoldo and Anna (Tornicaso) H.; ed. at high sch.; m. Frances Zeichner, June 2, 1920; children—Mrs. Jackie Toll, Benjamin, Richard. With Bell Telephone Co. and Western Electric Co., 1917-18; joined Phila. Wholesale Upholsters' Union, 1919; formed Upholsterers' Internat. Union regional dist. council, 1935, exec. sec., 1935-37, elected Internat. pres. at Cleve. conv., 1937, 39, 40, 43, 44, 46, 48, 50, 53, 56, 59, 62-66, 70. Mem. Community Services Com. AFL-CIO, 1956—; del. White House Conf. on Aging, 1961. Chmn. bd. trustees Health and Welfare Fund, 1944-71, Retirement Plan, 1950—, chmn. bd. govs. Nat. Pension Plan, 1953-71; chmn. bd. mgrs. Salhaven Found., 1957-71, Gerontol. Retirement Village, Jupiter, Fla. Mem. Furniture Labor Adv. Bd. of the WPB; panel mem. Nat. War Labor Bd.; adv. mem. Furniture Industry Com. in drafting of Wage and Hour Law, 1941. Author: Trade Unions under War Conditions (pamphlet), 1943; Work Of A Business Agent(pamphlet), 1942. Contbr. articles to various periodicals. Home: Rittenhouse Plaza Apts Philadelphia PA 19103 Office: Upholsterers' International Union 25 N 4th St Philadelphia PA 19106 ☆

HOFFMANN, STANLEY, educator, polit. scientist; b. Vienna, Austria, Nov. 27, 1928; grad. Inst. d'Etudes Politiques, Paris, France, 1948; doctrate Paris Law Sch., 1953; M.A. in Govt., Harvard, 1952. Came to U.S., 1955, naturalized, 1960. Research, Fond. Nationale des Sciences Politiques, Paris, 1952-53, 55; mem. faculty Harvard, 1955—, prof. govt., 1963—, research asso. Center Internat. Affairs, 1961-62, 63—. Fellow Center Advanced Study Behavioral Scis., Stanford, Cal., 1965-66. Mem. Council Fgn. Relations, Am. Acad. Arts and Scis., Am. Polit. Sci. Assn., Am. Soc. Internat. Law. Author: Organisations Internationales et Pouvoirs Politiques des Etats, 1954; Le Mouvement Poujade, 1956; The State of War, 1965; Gulliver's Troubles, 1968; co-author: In Search of France, 1963; The Relevance of International Law, 1968. Editor: Contemporary Theory in International Relations, 1960; Conditions of World Order, 1968. Home: 91 Washington Av Cambridge MA 02140

HOFFMANN, WILLIAM LEHNER, banker; b. Buffalo, Oct. 20, 1914; s. Samuel R. and Maverette (Eaton) H.; A.B., Dartmouth, 1936; M.C.S., Amos Tuck Sch., 1937; m. Catharine Baldwin, June 17, 1939; children—John Baldwin, Anne Elizabeth, James Stuart, Ellen Hayes. With Guaranty Trust Co., 1937-42; sr. v.p. Fidelity Union Trust Co., Newark, 1942—; dir. Faber, Coe & Gregg Co. Co-chmn. Bus. and Indsl. Coordinating Council, Newark, 1966—. Treas., trustee Hosp. Center Orange; trustee Beard Sch., Orange. Home: Fox Hunt Rd New Vernon NJ 07969 Office: Fidelity Union Trust 765 Broad St Newark NJ 07102

HOFFMEISTER, BERTRAM MERYL, orgn. exec.; b. Vancouver, B.C., Can., May 15, 1907; s. Louis George and Flora Elizabeth (Rodway) H.; student pub. schs., Vancouver; m. Amber Donalda Strauss, Sept. 8, 1936; children—Margot Aldyne, John Rodway. With Rat Portage Lumber Co., 1924-30; various positions Canadian White Pine Co., 1930-39, gen. mgr., 1945-49; gen. mgr. Macmillan Industries, Ltd., 1945-49; v.p. H.R. MacMillan Export Co., Ltd., 1949, pres., 1949- 51; pres., dir. MacMillan & Bloedel, Ltd., Vancouver, 1951-56, chmn. bd., dir., 1956-57; agt.-gen. for B. C., London, Eng., 1958-60; pres. Council of Forest industries of B.C., 1961—. Decorated Companion of Bath, Comdr. Order Brit. Empire, Dist. Service Order (Eng.); Legion Merit (U.S.); Order of Orange Nassau (Holland). Clubs: Vancouver, Capilano Golf and Country. Address: 1477 W Pender St Vancouver 5 British Columbia Canada

HOFFMEISTER, DONALD FREDERICK, educator, biologist; b. San Bernardino, Cal., Mar. 21, 1916; s. Percival George and Julia Bell (Hillgartner) H.; A.B., U. Cal. at Berkeley, 1938, M.A., 1940, Ph.D., 1944; m. Helen E. Kaatz, Aug. 11, 1938; children—James Ronald, Robert George. Research, curatorial asst. Museum Vertebrate Zoology, U. Cal. at Berkeley, 1941-44, teaching asst. zoology at univ., 1943-44; asso. curator modern vertebrates Mus. Natural History, U. Kan., 1944-46, asst. prof. zoology at univ., 1944-46; dir. Mus. Natural History, U. Ill., 1946—, mem. faculty univ., 1946—, prof. zoology, 1959—. Fellow A.A.A.S.; mem. Am. Soc. Mammalogists (sec. 1946-52, v.p. 1961-64, pres. 1964-66), Midwest Museum's Conf. (exec. v.p. 1962-63, pres. 1963-64), Am. Assn. Museums, Australian Mammal Soc., Southwestern Naturalists, Soc. Vertebrate Paleontology, I11. Acad. Scis. Author: Mammals, 1955; Mammals, 1963; Fieldbook of Illinois Mammals, 1957; Zoo Animals, 1967; Mammals of Grand Canyon, 1971; also articles reports. Home: 1505 W Charles St Champaign IL 61820 Office: Museum Natural History Univ Illinois Urbana IL 61801

HOFFMEISTER, HAROLD MAXWELL, r.r. exec.; b. Palestine, Tex., Aug. 18, 1910; s. Carroll King and Marion (Graham) H.; B.S. in Chem. Engring., Tex. A. and M. Coll., 1932; m. Ruth C. Busick, Sept. 12, 1936; children—Harold M., Sara. With M.P. R.R., 1932—, successively asst. chemist, Houston, positions in mech. dept., asst. to chief mech. officer, gen. purchasing agt., 1958-61, v.p., 1961—. Dist. commr. St. Louis area council Boy Scouts Am., 1961-65, dist. chmn., 1965- 67; mem. Federal Com. Apprenticeship, 1968—. Past dir. Webster Groves Sch. Bd.; councilman, Webster Groves, 1960-68. Bd. dirs. Jr. Achievement Mississippi Valley, 1960-65. Served from 1st lt. to maj., AUS, 1942-45. Decorated Bronze Star. Mem. Am. Ry. Engring. Assn., Assn. Am. Railroads (chmn. purchases and materials mgmt. div. 1967-68), Nat. Transp. Apprenticeship Conf. (past chmn.). Club: Civitan (past pres. St. Louis). Home: 412 Sunningwell Dr Webster Groves MO 63119 Office: Missouri Pacific Bldg St Louis MO 63103

HOFFMEISTER, JOHN EDWARD, prof. geology; b. Balt., Feb. 1, 1899; s. Edward and Katherine (Spring) H.; grad. Baltimore City Coll. (high sch.), 1916; A.B., Johns Hopkins, 1920, Ph.D., 1923; m. Ruth Tuthill, June 24, 1924; children—John Tuthill, Robert Edward. Prof. biology, Balt. Coll. Dental Surgery, 1921-23; instr. geology, U. of Rochester, 1923, asst. prof. geology, 1924-28, prof., 1928-65, chmn. geology dept., 1946-65, acting dean, Coll. for Men, 1941-42, dean, 1942- 43, dean of faculty Coll. of Arts and Sci., 1943-44, dean of Coll. of Arts and Sci., 1944-56; prof. marine geology Inst. of Marine Sci., U. Miami, 1965—. Mem. bd. dirs. Rochester YMCA; mem. Local Draft Bd. 76; mem. Citizens Adv. Com., 1st Army. Cons. Army Map Service, 1942-44, Bikini Bomb Test, 1946; chmn. Rochester Armed Forces Adv. Com., 1956—; vis. prof. Marine Lab., U. Miami (Fla.), 1963- 64. Pres. Rochester Mus. Assn., 1944-48, now dir.; dir. YMCA. Trustee Colgate-Rochester Div. Sch.; dir. Wards Natural Sci. Establishment. Fellow Geol. Soc. Can., Geol. Soc. Am. (councilor, treas.), Paleontol. Soc. Am.; mem. Phi Beta Kappa, Sigma Xi, Delta Upsilon, Gamma Alpha. Methodist. Author and co-author books on S. Pacific. Contbr. to Biological Abstracts; also papers in Nat. Geog. Mag., Am. Jour. Sci., Jour. Geology, Bull. Geol. Soc. Am. Research on Fla. reef tract, geology of Keys and Everglades. Home: 4254 Lennox Dr Coconut Grove Miami FL 33133

HOFFMEYER, ERIK, banker; b. Rärup, Denmark, Dec. 25, 1924; s. Skat and Aase (Thejll) H.; M.Sc. in Econs., U. Copenhagen, 1951, D.Sc., 1958; m. Eva Keop, Jan. 6, 1949; 1 son, Torsten. With Danmarks Nationalbank, 1951-59, econ. counsellor, 1959-62, gov. Bikuben Savs. Bank, 1962-64, chmn. bd., 1964—, gov., chmn. bd. Danmarks Nationalbank, 1965—, gov. for Denmark to Internat. Monetary Fund, 1965—. Lectr. econs. U. Copenhagen, 1956, prof., 1959-64. Mem. presidency Econ. Council, 1962-65, Danish Sci. Adv. Council, 1963, C.L. David Collection, 1960-66, Housing Mortgage Fund, 1969. Rockefeller fellow, 1954-55. Mem. Assn. Polit. Economy (pres. 1951-53), Econ. Soc. (bd. mgmt.). Contbr. books, articles to nat., internat. econ. jours. Home: 22 Hegefsvej Charlottenlund 2920 Denmark Office: Danmarks Nationalbank 17 Holmens Kanal Copenhagen K Denmark

HOFFSOMMER, HAROLD CHARLES, educator, sociologist; b. Roxbury, Kan., Dec. 8, 1898; s. John Adam and Rose Ida (Manshardt) H.; grad. Bethany Acad., Lindsborg, Kan., 1914-16; student Bethany College, 1917-19; B.S., Northwestern U., 1921, A.M., 1923; student U. Chicago, summer 1923; Ph.D., Cornell U., 1929; m. Ruth Andrews, May 28, 1930; children—John Charles, Elizabeth Andrews. Acting prof. sociology Rockford (Ill.) Coll., 1921-22; prof. sociology Ala. Polytech. Inst., 1929-35; dir. cotton area rural research, also Ala. supr. rural research, 1934-35; sr. research supr. WPA, Washington, 1935-36; rural sociologist La. State U., 1936-42; leader area VI div. farm population and rural welfare Dept. Agr., 1939-40; dir. regional land tenure research project, Fayetteville, Ark., 1942-45; prof. chmn. div. social scis. U. Md., 1945-66, head dept. sociology, 1945-66, now emeritus prof.; cons. Ford Found. community devel., India, 1961. Mem. Am., D.C. (pres.) Rural (past pres.) sociol. socs., Alpha Kappa Delta, Phi Delta Kappa, Phi Mu Alpha-Sinfonia. Presbyn. (elder). Author: Regional Research Cooperation: The Sociology of American Life, 1958. Co- author, editor and project dir.: The Social and Economic Significance of Land Tenure in the Southwestern States; also agr. expt. sta. bulls. Editor-in-chief Rural Sociology. Contbr. articles sociol. jours. Home: 6900 Darmouth Av College Park MD 20740

HOFFSTOT, WILLIAM HENRY, Jr., lawyer, banker; b. Kansas City, Mo., May 27, 1908; s. William Henry and Eva (Fellows) H.; A.B., Washburn Coll., 1931; LL.B., Washburn Law Sch., 1934; postgrad. Harvard Law Sch., 1931-33; m. Susan Snyder, Feb. 22, 1935; children—George William. Admitted to Mo. bar, Kan. bar, 1934, Supreme Ct. bar, 1960, Hawaii bar, 1962; asso. law firm Langworthy, Spencer & Terrell, Kansas City, Mo., 1934-39, Langworthy & Matz, Kansas City, 1939-42; partner Morrison, Hecker, Buck, Cozad & Rogers, Kansas City, 1942-60; asst. sec. Bank of Hawaii, Honolulu, 1961-65, sec., 1965- 66, v.p., sec., 1966—. Pres., mem. bd. Hawaii council Camp Fire Girls, 1960-65. Dir. Honolulu Symphony, Vol. Service Bur., Freedoms Found. at Valley Forge. Served to lt. USNR, 1944-45. Mem. Am., Mo., Kan., Hawaii bar assns., Lawyers Assn. Kansas City, Internat. Assn. Ins. Counsel, Honolulu C. of C., Navy League (dir.); Assn. of Army, Am. Judicature Soc., Am. Soc. Corp. Secs., Honolulu Acad. Arts, Bishop Museum, Honolulu Community Theatre, Phi Delta Theta. Clubs: Oahu Country (Honolulu), Harvard Hawaii. Home: 48 Niuiki Circle Honolulu HI 96821 Office: Bank of Hawaii PO box 2900 Honolulu HI 96802

HOFFSTROM, PIERCY J. (P. J. Hoff), cartoonist, weatherman; b. Mounds, Oklahoma. January 11, 1896; s. of Frank Henry and Emma Jane (Marshall) H.; student U. Washington, Seattle, 1915-16; m. Sue Virginia Miller, Jan. 11, 1917; 1 dau., Virginia. Engr., Pacific Telephone & Telegraph Co., Seattle, Wash., 1917-23; with St. Paul Dispatch, 1923-54, as political, topical cartoonist, also daily column under signature as "Hoff"; teacher of cartooning, St. Paul Inst., 1923-24, Y.M.C.A., 1938; conducted two daily TV programs over sta. KSTP-TV, using cartoons; weatherman for WBBM- TV radio, Chgo. as P.J. Hoff, 1954-68; lectr., freelance writer on weather and photomicrography. Served with Co. F, 2d Inf., Mexican Border, 1916. Mem. Am. Meteorol. Soc., Am. Soc. Cartoonists, Chgo. Exec. Club, Delta Phi Lambda, Sigma Delta Chi. Clubs: Headline: Brusnwick (Ga.) Press. Home: 326 Peachtree St St Simons Island GA 31522

HOFGREN, AXEL AUGUST, lawyer; b. Chgo., Sept. 19, 1896; s. Herman A. and Hanna C. (Peterson) H.; B.S., Armour Inst. Tech., 1918; LL.B., Chgo. Kent Coll. Law, 1926; m. Mabel Waterman, June 25, 1929; 1 son, Robert Axel. Elec. engr. Gen. Electric Co., Schenectady, also Chgo., 1918-24; admitted to Ill. bar, 1926; asso. Chindahl, Parker & Carlson, 1925-30; pvt. practice patent law, 1931-44; partner firm Hofgren, Wegner, Allen, Stellman & McCord and predecessors, Chgo., 1944—. Mem. com. dels. Ill. Commn. Higher Edn., 1959-61; mem. Winnetka Zoning Commn., Trustee Ill. Inst. Tech. (v.p. acad. affairs), IIT Research Institute. Mem. Am., Chgo. bar assns., Am. Patent Law Assn., Internat. Patent and Trademark Assn., Patent Law Assn. Chgo. (pres. 1961), Phi Delta Phi, Tau Beta Pi, Theta Xi, Eta Kappa Nu. Republican. Conglist. Clubs: Kenilworth. University (Chgo.); Skokie Country. Home: 555 Ash St Winnetka IL 60093 Office: 20 N Wacker Dr Chicago IL 60606

HOFHEIMER, HENRY CLAY, II, bldg. materials exec.; b. Norfolk, Va., Dec. 28, 1906; s. Julius Caesar and Bessie (Hirschler) H.; B.S., U. Va., 1928; m. Elise Nusbaum, Sept. 25, 1931; children—Elise Bessie (Mrs. Wesley Wright, Jr.), Linda (Mrs. George M. Kaufman), Clay (Mrs. J.D.A. Barr). Pres. So. Materials Co., Inc., Norfolk; pres., dir. So. Shopping Center, Inc., Tidewater Shopping Center, Inc.; chmn. bd. Southern Block & Pipe Corp., Va. Real Estate Investment Trust; dir. First Colony Life Ins. Co., dir., mem. exec. com. Lone Star Cement Corp.; dir. Virginia Nat. Bank, Norfolk. Bd. trustees Va. Found. Independent Colls. Nat. Trust for Historic Preservation, Va. Mus. Fine Arts, Norfolk Acad. for Boys, Coll. William and Mary Endowment Assn., James River Basin Assn., Jamestown Corp.; trustee Tidewater, Va. Devel. Council; chmn. bd. Va. Real Estate Investment Trust. Home: 828 Graydon Av Norfolk VA 23507 Office: 977 Norfolk Sq Norfolk VA 23502

HOFHEINZ, ROY MARK, profl. baseball exec.; b. Beaumont, Tex., Apr. 10, 1912; s. Frederick Joseph and Nonie (Planchard) H.; student Rice Inst., 1928-29, U. Houston, 1929-30; LL.B., Houston Law Sch., 1933; m. Irene Cafcalas, July 19, 1933; children—Roy Mark, James Frederick, Dene. Admitted to Tex. bar, 1932; mem. Tex. Legislature, 1934-36; judge, Harris County, 1936-44; chmn. bd. Tex. Radio Corp., sta. KTHT, Houston, Pilot Broadcasting Corp., sta. WILD, Birmingham, 1951—; partner Houston Slag Materials Co., 1946—; v.p. Houston Consol. Television Co.; pres., chmn. bd. Houston Astros Baseball Club. Past mayor of Houston. Mem. Am. Bar Assn., Am. Arbitration Assn., Sons of Hermann. Elk, Eagle. Clubs: Optimists, Pine Forest Country, Lakeside; Houston, Yacht, Briar (Houston). Home: 2400 Yorktown Dr Houston TX 77027 Office: Houston Baseball Club The Astrodome Houston TX 77025

HOFMANN, HANS, educator, author; b. Basel, Switzerland, Aug. 12, 1923; s. Oscar and Henriette (Burbiel) H.; A.B., Thurg. Kantonsschule 1943; B.D., U. Basel, 1948; Th.D., U. Zurich, 1953; m. Emilie Scott Welles, Oct. 15, 1955; children—Elizabeth Scott, Mark Lawrence, David Hans, Scott Cluett. Came to U.S., 1951, naturalized, 1956. Mem. faculty Princeton Theol. Sem., 1953-57, asso. prof., 1956-57; mem. faculty Harvard Div. Sch., 1957-62, prof. theology, 1961-62, Ingersoll lectr. at univ., 1956-57, leader Danforth seminar religion and bus. ethics Grad. Sch. Bus. Adminstrn., 1958, dir. project religion and mental health at univ., 1957-61; inaugural Thorp lectr. Cornell U., 1955-56; exec. dir. Center Study Personality and Culture, Inc., Cambridge, Mass., 1964- 66; pres. Inst. for Human Devel., Cambridge, 1966—; ordained to ministry United Ch. Christ, 1957; cons. dept. internat. affairs Nat. Council Chs. Mem. bd. overseers Shady Hill Sch., Cambridge. Mem. Internat. Platform Assn., Nat. Cum Laude Soc. (hon. mem.), Nat. Inst. Arts and Letters, English-Speaking Union, Soc. Sci. Study Religion, Am. Soc. Christian Social Ethics, Fedn. Am. Scientists, Am. Assn. U. Profs., Signet Soc. Author: The Theology of Reinhold Niebuhr, 1955; Religion and Mental Health, 1961; Incorporating Sex, 1967; Breakthrough to Life, 1969; Discovering Freedom, 1969. Editor: Making the Ministry Relevant, 1960; The Ministry and Mental Health, 1960; Sex Incorporated, 1967. Home: 21 Bates St Cambridge MA 02140 Office: 345 Harvard St Cambridge MA 02138

HOFMANN, HERBERT ANDREW, corp. exec.; b. Queens County, N.Y., Feb. 24, 1917; s. John and Agnes (Brutschin) H.; B.B.A., St. John's U., 1937; m. Erna Kast, Apr. 13, 1941; children—Herbert Charles, Erna Margaret, Gregory, Marilyn Agnes, Mary Edna. With Price, Waterhouse & Co., C.P.A.'s, N.Y.C., 1939-40, Harris, Kerr, Forster & Co., C.P.A.'s N.Y.C., 1940-50; with Tisch Hotels, Inc., N.Y.C., 1951—, treas., 1951—, exec. v.p., from 1958, also dir.; exec. v.p., treas., dir. Americana Hotel, Inc., 1956—; sr. v.p. Loew's Theatres, Inc., 1960—, also dir.; pres., dir. Loew's Hotels, Inc. Served with USNR, 1943-46. C.P.A., N.Y. Mem. Am. Inst. C.P.A.'s, N.Y. State Soc. C.P.A.'s Home: 70 Greenhaven Rd Rye NY 10580 Office: 1540 Broadway New York City NY 10018

HOFMANN, KLAUS, educator, biochemist; b. Karlsruhe, Germany, Feb. 21, 1911; s. Fritz and Marianne (Bally) H.; diploma chem. engring., Fed. Inst. Tech., Zurich, Switzerland, 1933, Ph.D., 1936; m. Paula Blum, Sept. 5, 1911 (div. 1964); 1 dau., Suzanne Elizabeth; m. 2d, Frances Finn, 1965. Came to U.S., 1938, naturalized, 1952. Postdoctorate fellow Fed. Inst. Tech., 1936-38, Rockefeller Found., Rockefeller Inst. Med. Research, N.Y.C., 1938-40; research asso. biochemistry Cornell U. Med. sch., 1940-42; sci. guest research labs. Ciba Pharm. Products, Inc., Summit, N.J., 1942-44; successively asst., asso., research prof. chemistry U. Pitts., 1944-52, prof. biochemistry, chmn. dept., 1953-64 Commonwealth prof., dir. protein research lab., 1964—. Mem. Nat. Acad. Scis. Author sci. publs. Home: 1467 Mohican Dr Pittsburgh PA 15228

HOFMANN, PHILLIP B., pharm. exec.; b. Ottumwa, Ia., May 25, 1909; s. Frank P. and Isabel (Matson) H.; student Wharton Sch. Finance and Commerce, U. Pa., 1930; m. Mary E. Kain, July 29, 1934; children—Judith, Carol I. With Johnson & Johnson, New Brunswick, N.J., 1931—, div. mgr., Boston, 1939, mgr. Ortho-Gynol. div., 1940, dir., 1945—, vice chmn. bd., 1949-63, chmn. exec. com., 1957-63, chmn. bd., 1963—; pres. Ortho Pharm. Corp., 1941, chmn. bd., dir., 1948—; chmn. bd., pres. Ethicon, Inc., Ortho Pharm. (Can.), Ltd., Ortho Pharm., Ltd., 1941-57; chmn. Johnson & Johnson-Ethicon G.M.H., Germany, Chicopee Mfg. Corp., Chicopee Mills, LePage's Inc. (Mass.), Permacel Tape Corp., Johnson & Johnson- Ethicon, A.B., chmn. bd. Johnson & Johnson Internat., 1962—, also chief exec. officer; v.p. Johnson & Johnson Research Found.; dir. LePage's, Inc. (N.J.). Vice pres. U.S. Equestrian Team, Inc. Mem. Sch. Bd. of Branchburg Twp., 1944—; mem. drug, chem. and allied trades sect. N.Y. Bd. Trade. Trustee and chmn. Joint Conf. com. Somerset Hosp. Mem. Am. Cancer Soc. (pres. Somerset County chpt., N.J., div., Inc., 1946-49), Somerset County Community Forum (pres. 1948-49), Pharm. Mfrs. Assn. (dir. 1961—). Clubs: Capitol Hill: Essex Fox Hounds (Peapack, N.J.); Raritan (N.J.) Valley Country. Home: Burnt Mills Rd North Branch NJ 08876 Office: 501 George St New Brunswick NJ 08901

HOFREITER, CHARLES G., corp. exec.; b. N.Y.C., Oct. 12, 1915; student Pace Coll., N.Y.C. Chief accountant Hauck Mfg. Co., Bklyn., 1938-41; plant controller A.T.F., Inc., Elizabeth, N.J., 1945-47; treas. Nat. Starch Products, Inc., N.Y.C., 1947-54; v.p., treas. Mack Trucks, Inc., Plainfield, N.J., 1956- 69; past v.p., treas., dir. Mack Trucks Can.; past v.p.finance Mack Financial Corp.; now treas. Gulf Am. Corp. Address: 7880 Biscayne Blvd Miami, FL 33138.

HOFSESS, RUSSELL WALTER, natural gas co. exec.; b. Ness City, Kan., Nov. 2, 1907; s. E.A. and Mima (Dawson) H.; B.S. in Civil Engring., Kan. State U., 1929; m. Effie G. Rasher, Apr. 30. 1932; 1 dau., Barbara Janet (Mrs. Robert T. Clift). Constrn. engr. Bateman Contracting Co., Ark. and Tenn., 1931-32; athletic instr., engr. Kan. State Prison, 1932-33; with Cities Service Gas Co., 1933—, sr. v.p., 1966—, also dir., Served to col. AUS, 1941-45. Decorated Croix de Guerre (France). Mem. Am. Gas Assn., Ind. Natural Gas Assn., Am., Mid-Continent Oil and Gas Assn., Kan. (bd. dirs. 1968-72), Oklahoma City chambers commerce. Democrat. Methodist. Clubs: Oklahoma City Golf and Country, Beacon, Petroleum (Oklahoma City). Home: 1125 Huntington Av Oklahoma City OK 73116 Office: First Nat Bldg Oklahoma City OK 73101

HOFSTADTER, ALBERT, educator; b. N.Y.C., Mar. 28, 1910; s. Louis and Henrietta Hofstadter; B.S. Coll. City N.Y., 1929; M.A., Columbia, 1934, Ph.D. 1935; m. Manya Huber, Feb. 12, 1936; 1 son, Marc. Successively instr., asst. prof., asso. prof. N.Y.U.; asso. prof. Columbia, 1950-52, prof. philosophy, 1952-67, chmn. dept. fine arts and archaeology, 1955-57; prof. philosophy Coll. Five, U. Cal. at Santa Cruz, Cal., 1967—, chmn. bd. studies in philosophy, 1971—. Fellow Conf. on Sci., Philosophy and Religion in Relation to Democratic Way of Life. Guggenheim fellow, 1945; fellow Center Advanced Study Behavioral Scis. Stanford, Cal. 1966-67. Mem. Am. Philos. Assn. (v.p. Eastern div. 1968-69), N.Y. Philosophy Club (sec. 1950-64). Author: Locke and Scepticism, 1946; (with Richard Kuhns) Philosophies of Art and Beauty, 1964; Truth and Art, 1965; Agony And Epitaph, 1970; also articles profl. jours. Home: 114 Spring St Santa Cruz CA 95060

HOFSTADTER, ROBERT, physicist, educator; b. N.Y.C., Feb. 5, 1915; s. Louis and Henrietta (Koenigsberg) H.; B.S. magna cum laude (Kenyon prize), Coll. City N.Y., 1935; M.A. (Procter fellow), Princeton, 1938, Ph.D., 1938; LL.D., City U. N.Y., 1961; D.Sc., Gustavus Adolphus Coll.; Laurea Honoris Causa, U. Padua, 1965; D.Sc., Carleton U., Ottawa, Can., 1967; m. Nancy Givan, May 9, 1942; children—Douglas Richard, Laura James, Mary Hinda Coffin fellow Gen. Electric Co., 1935-36; Harrison fellow U.Pa., 1939; instr. physics Coll. City N.Y., 1941; physicist Norden Lab. Corp., 1943-46; asst. prof. physics Princeton, 1946-50; asso. prof. physics Stanford, 1950-54, prof., 1954- -, dir. high energy physics lab., 1967—. Guggenheim fellow, Ford Found., Geneva, Switzerland, 1958-59; Cal. Sci. of Year, 1959; co- recipient of Nobel prize in physics, 1961; Townsend Harris medal Coll. City N.Y. 1961. Fellow Am. Phys. Soc., Phys. Soc. London; mem. Italian Phys. Soc., Nat. Acad. Scis., Am. Assn. U. Profs., Phi Beta Kappa, Sigma Xi. Author: (with Robert Herman) High-Energy Electron Scattering Tables, 1960. Editor: Investigations in Physics, 1952; Electron Scattering and Nucleon Structure, 1963. Co- editor: Nucleon Structure, 1964. Asso. editor Phys. Review, 1951-53; mem. editorial bd. Review Sci. Instruments, 1953-55; Reviews of Modern Physics, 1958-61. Home: 639 Mirada Av Stanford CA 94305

HOFSTATTER, LEOPOLD, hosp. adminstr., physician; b. Vienna, Austria, Mar. 11, 1902; s. Leopold H. and Josefine (Eibuschuetz) H.; M.D., U. Vienna, 1926; m. Lilli Schwarz, Apr. 16, 1930; m. 2d, Theresa Adams Mayer, Sept. 4, 1971. Came to U.S., 1938, naturalized, 1944. Intern Allgemeines Krankenhaus Wien, Vienna, 1927-28; resident Maria Theresian Schzessel, 1930-33, St. Louis State Hosp., 1941-42; mem. staff St. Vincent's Hosp., 1948—; asst. supt. St. Louis State Hosp., 1942-62, chief gen. med., surg. div., 1960-62; supt. St. Louis State Sch. and Hosp., 1962-67; sr. cons. resident tng. program Mo. Inst. Psychiatry, 1967-69, med. dir., 1968—; supt. St. Louis State Hosp. Complex, 1970—; mem. staff Deaconess Hosp., Christian Hosp., Faith Hosp. Fellow Am. Psychiat. Assn.; mem. Mo. Hosp. Physicians Assn. (past pres.), Sci. Research Assn. Am., Eastern Mo. Psychiat. Soc., Sigma Xi. Home: 768 Glenvista Glendale MO 63122 Office: 5400 Arsenal St St Louis MO 63139

HOFSTETTER, HENRY W., optometrist, educator; b. Windsor, O., Sept. 10, 1914; s. Kaspar and Augusta (Kresin) H.; student Western Res. U., 1931-33, Kent State U., 1933; B.S., Ohio State U., 1939, M.S., 1940, Ph.D., 1942; D. Optometric Sci., Los Angeles Coll. Optometry, 1954, Mass. Coll. Optometry, 1968; Sc.D., Pa. Coll. Optometry, 1969; m. Frances Jane Elder, July 5, 1941; children—Ann Kresin, Susan Claire. Elementary sch. tchr. Middlefield (O.) Pub. Sch., 1933-36; faculty Ohio State U., 1942-48, asso. prof., 1947-48; dean Los Angeles Coll. Optometry, 1948-52; prof. optometry Ind. U., Bloomington, 1952—, dir. div. optometry, 1952-70. Mem. Nat. Adv. Council on Edn. for Health Professions, 1964-67; mem. com. on vision Armed Forces NRC, 1961—. Mem. Optical Soc. Am., Am. Optometric Assn. (past pres.), Am. Acad. Optometry, Assn. Schs. and Colls. (past pres.). Author: Optometry, 1948; Industrial Vision, 1956; (with M. Schapero, David Cline) Dictionary of Visual Science, 1960, 2d edit., 1968; also numerous articles. Research on graphical analysis of relationship between accomodation and convergence of eyes and application to clin. techniques, accommodation fatigue and age-amplitude relationships, heredity in astigmatism, role of stereopsis in vehicle control. Home: 1107 Southdowns Dr Bloomington IN 47401

HOGADONE, EDWINA BELLE, retired coll. dean; b. Grand Rapids, Mich., Mar. 19, 1907; d. Charles Edwin and Lotta (Buck) Hogadone; B.A., U. Mich., 1928; A.M., U. Pitts., 1929. Personnel supr. Kaufmann's Dept. Store, Pitts, 1929-31; instr. retailing dept. Rochester Inst. Tech., 1934-36; personnel supr. Ed. Schuster Co., Milw., 1934-36; head retailing dept. Rochester Inst. Tech., 1936-59, chmn. div. bus., 1952-59, dean Coll. Bus., dir. Sch. Retailing, 1959-71. Mem New York Woman's Council, 1958—. Mem. Am. Collegiate Retailing Assn. (nat. pres. 1959—), Eta Mu Pi (hon.), Pi Beta Phi. Baptist. Clubs: Rochester City (dir. 1956); Zonta (pres. internat. 1952-54, chmn. internat. pub. relations com. 1958-60). Author: (with Donald K.Beckley) Merchandising Techniques, 1942; Careers in Retailing, 1963. Home: 1939 Middle Rd Rush NY 14543

HOGAN, BARTHOLOMEW WILLIAM, physician, orgn. exec.; b. Quincy, Mass., 1901; M.D., Tufts Coll., 1925, D.Sc.; LL.D., St. Mary's Coll., Emmitsburg, Md., Vilanova U.; D.Sc., Boston Coll., Marquette U., Tufts U.; m.; children—Bartholomew William, Thomas F. III, Mary Ledie. Rear adm. M.C., USN; Surgeon General of U.S. Navy, 1955-61; chief of medicine and chief of psychiatry various naval hosps.; asso. prof. psychiatry Georgetown U. Sch. Medicine; deputy med. dir. Am. Psychiat. Assn. Mem. Pres.'s Com. on Employment of Handicapped. Decorated Silver Star, Purple Heart, Navy and Marine Corps medal, D.S.M., six battle stars on ribbons. Diplomate and examiner Am. Bd. Psychiatry and Neurology. Fellow A.C.P., Am. Psychiat. Assn.; mem. A.M.A. (ex.-mem. ho. of dels), Am. Hosp. Assn. (ex.-mem. bd. trustees), Am. Psychiat. Assn., John Carroll Soc. (pres.). Home: 5512 Grove St Chevy Chase MD 20015 Office: 1700 18th St NW Washington DC 20009

HOGAN, CLARENCE LESTER, co. exec.; b. Great Falls, Mont., Feb. 8, 1920; s. Clarence Lester and Bessie (Young) H.; B.S. in Chem. Engring., Mont. State Coll., 1942; M.S. in Physics, Lehigh U., 1947, Ph.D., 1950; A.M. (hon)., Harvard, 1954; D.Eng., Montana State U., 1967; D.Sc. (hon.), Worcester Polytech. Inst., 1969; m. Audrey Biery Peters, Oct. 13, 1946; 1 dau., Cheryl Lea. Research chem. engr. Anaconda Copper Mining Co., 1942-43; instr. physics Lehigh U., 1946-50; tech. staff Bell Telephone Labs., 1950-52, sub. dept. head, 1952-53; asso. prof. Harvard, 1953-57, Gordon McKay prof. applied physics, 1957-58; gen. mgr. semi- conductor products div. Motorola, Inc., Phoenix, 1958-60, v.p., 1960-68; pres., chief exec. officer Fairchild Camera & Instrument Corp., Mountain View, Cal., 1968—; dir. United Cal. Bank. Gen. Chmn. Internat. Conf. on Magnetism and Magnetic Materials, 1959, 60; materials advisory bd. Dept. Def., 1955-57; adv. council dept. elec. engring. Princeton, 1962-68; vis. com. Lehigh U., 1966, trustee, 1971—; trustee Western Electronic Edn. Fund; governing bd. Maricopa County Jr. Coll. Served from ensign to lt. (j.g.), USNR, 1943- 46. Fellow I.E.E.E.; mem. Am. Phys. Soc., Inst. Elec. Engrs., Sigma Xi, Tau Beta Phi, Phi Kappa Phi, Kappa Sigma. Home: 36 Barry Lane Atherton CA 94025 Office: 464 Ellis St Mountain View CA 94040

HOGAN, COLEMAN FRANCIS, mfg. co. exec.; b. Boston, Apr. 1, 1917; s. Patrick J. and Annie M. (McKeone) H.; B.B.A., Northeastern U., 1952; m. Margaret M. Lawrence, Feb. 27, 1943. Works accountant, comptroller Walworth Co., N.Y.C., 1946-59; treas. Sucrest Co., N.Y.C., 1960-61; pres. Davidson Rubber Co., Dover, N.H., 1961-65; chmn. bd. McCord Corp., Detroit, 1965—. Served to capt. USAAF, 1942-46. Mem. Financial Execs. Inst., Nat. Assn. Accountants, Engring. Soc. Detroit. Clubs: Algonquin, Detroit Athletic. Home: 72 High St Exeter NH 03833 Office: McCord Corp Riopelle and E Grand Sts Detroit MI 48211

HOGAN, DANIEL WISE, banker; b. Modesto, Ill., Oct. 24, 1867; s. Daniel Wise and Arminda Jane (Turner) H.; grad. Northwestern Normal Sch., and Bus. Inst., Stanberry, Mo., 1889; m. Anna S. Harvey, Dec. 25, 1891 (died Oct. 14, 1939); children—Clark Harvey, Daniel Wise; m. 2d, Faye B. Locker, Apr. 20, 1946. Bank clk., 1890-92, organized First Nat. Bank of Yukon, Yukon, Okla., 1892; organized City Nat. Bank, Muskogee, Okla., 1904; cashier Am. Nat. Bank, Oklahoma City, 1907-11; pres. City Nat. Bank & Trust Co., Oklahoma City, from 1911, now chmn. bd.; v.p., dir. City Nat. Bank, Sayre, Okla.; past pres. Oklahoma City Clearing House Assn. Chmn. nat. bd. field advisers for Okla., of Small Bus. Adminstrn., Washington. Mem. Taxpayers Research Inst. (past pres.), C. of C. (life dir.), Okla. Bankers Assn. (charter mem., past pres., 1st treas.), Okla. State Fair Assn. (exec. council), Motion Picture Panel of Arbitrators, Okla. Future Farmers of Am. and 4-H Club (hon.), Collegiate Engrs., Knights of St. Patrick Assn., Newcomen Soc. Eng., Beta Gamma Sigma (hon. mem.). Methodist. Clubs: Capitol City Gun (pres.), Men's Dinner (charter mem.); Sirloin, Lotus (Oklahoma City); Beacon of Okla., City Golf and Country. Home: 300 NW 16th St Oklahoma City OK 73103 Office: Oklahoma City OK 73101

HOGAN, ERNEST LYNN, Jr., ins. co. exec.; b. Davy, W.Va., Apr. 10, 1913; s. Ernest Lynn and Edna (Harris) H.; student W.Va., Bus Sch., 1932-33, Oxford Bus. Sch., 1933-34; m. Mildred Shepard, Jan. 18, 1936; 1 dau., Dorothy (Mrs. James D, Sheker). With Peoples Life Ins. Co., Washington, 1935—, agt., 1935-37, asst. mgr., 1937-41, dist. mgr., 1941-47, div. supt. agts., 1947-54, supt. agts., 1954-57, asst. v.p., 1957-59, 2nd v.p., 1959-63, v.p. agy., 1963- 68, exec. v.p., 1968-70, pres., 1970—, also dir., mem. exec., finance coms.; dir., mem. exec. com. Capital Holding Corp., dir. Plicom. Investments, Inc., Mem. Life Ins. Agy. Mgmt. Assn. (bd. dirs. 1969-72), Nat. Assn. Life Underwriters, Gideons. Baptist. Elk, Kiwanian. Club: Loudoun Golf and Country (Purcellville). Home; Route 1 Box 134 Purcellville VA 22132 Office: 601 New Hampshire Av NW Washington DC 20037

HOGAN, FRANK SMITHWICK, lawyer; b. Waterbury, Conn., Jan. 17, 1902; s. Michael F. and Anne (Smithwick) H., B.A., Columbia, 1924, LL.B., 1928, LL.D, 1952; LL.D., Suffolk Law School, 1955; m. Mary Egan, Nov. 11, 1936. Admitted to N.Y. bar, 1929; with Gleason, McLanahan, Merritt & Ingraham, 1928-30; partner ins. and real estate law Anthony J. Liebler, 1930-35; asst. to spl. pros. N.Y. County, 1935-37; adminstrv. asst. N.Y. Co. Dist. Atty., 1937-41, dist. atty. N.Y. Co., 1942—. Trustee Columbia U., 1959—, Knickerbocker Hospital, 1961—, St. Luke's Hospital, 1967—. Democratic candidate for U.S. Sen., 1958. Awarded Columbia U. medal for exceptional pub. serv., 1942, Columbia Alumni medal for conspicuous alumni serv., 1946, Medal of Merit, N.Y. Co. Grand Jury Assn., 1947, gold medal Am. Irish Hist. Soc., 1952, Medal of Merit of St. Nicholas Soc., 1951, Alexander Hamilton Medal of Alumni of Columbia Coll., 1954; Futherance of Justice award Nat. Dist. Attys. Assn., 1959. Mem. Columbia Coll. Council (chmn. 1961-62), Assn. Alumni Columbia Coll. (pres. 1946-49), Alumni Fedn. Columbia U. (pres. 1949-51), Dist. Attys. Assn. State N.Y. (pres. 1947), N.Y. State Bar Assn., Assn. Bar City N.Y. (mem. exec. com. 1959-63), Friendly Sons St. Patrick. Democrat. Roman Catholic. Club: Columbia University (N.Y.C.). Home: 404 Riverside Dr New York City NY 10025 Office: 155 Leonard St New York City NY 10013

HOGAN, HENRY LEON, III, air force officer; b. Cin., Feb. 7, 1920; s. H. Leon and Helen (Bolan) H.; B.S., U.S. Mil. Acad., 1943; grad. Nat. War Coll., 1960; m. Anne Surkamp, June 1, 1943; children—Robin (Mrs. Jon H. Brosseau), Christine, James A., Patricia, Elizabeth. Commd. 2d lt. USAAF, 1943, advanced through grades to maj. gen. USAF, 1970; pilot 483d Bombardment Group, Italy, World War II; mil. aide to secs. of USAF, 1953-55; dep. comdt. cadets U.S. Air Force Acad., Colo., 1955-59; dep. comdr. maintenance, vice comdr. 68th Bombardment Wing, Lake Charles, La., 1960-62; wing comdr. 384th Bombardment Wing, 1962-63; comdr. 810th Air div. SAC, 1965- 68; dep. dir., then dir. information office sec. USAF, Washington, 1968- -. Decorated Legion Merit with oak leaf cluster, D.F.C., Air medal with four oak leaf clusters. Home: Quarters 32 Bolling AFB Washington DC 20332 Office: SAFOI Pentagon Washington DC 20330

HOGAN, JAMES JOHN, bishop; b. Phila Oct. 17, 1911; s. James F. and Mary E. (Molloy) H.; B.A., St. Mary's Sem., Balt., 1934; S.T.L., Gregorian U., Rome, Italy, 1938; J.C.D., Cath. U. Am., 1941. Ordained priest Roman Cath. Ch., 1937; diocesan ofcl. and consultor Diocese of Trenton, N.J., chancellor of diocese, auxiliary bishop of Trenton; pastor St. Catharine's Ch., Spring Lake, N.J.; now bishop Diocese of Altoona, Johnston, Pa. Home: Logan Blvd and Sylvan Hills Dr Hollidaysburg PA 16648 Office: 1406 12th Av Altoona PA 16601

HOGAN, JOHN ARTHUR, educator, arbitrator; b. Boise, Ida., Aug. 11, 1909; s. Michael and Olive (McConnell) H.; A.B., U. Wash., 1932, A.M., 1934; law student, Denver U., 1938; Ph.D., Harvard, 1952; m. Rhoda Doyle, 1936. Economist, Bur. Labor Statistics, 1935; asst. prof. econs. U. Denver 1935-39; teaching fellow Harvard, 1940-41; instr. Tufts Coll., 1942; disputes dir. Nat. War Labor Bd., New Eng. region, 1945-46; pub. mem. Nat. Wage Stblzn. Bd., 1946-47; part-time lectr. mgmt. tng. program Radcliffe Coll., 1946-53; asso. prof., prof. econs. bus. U. N.H., 1947-63, Carter prof. econs. Whittemore Sch. Bus. and Econs., 1963—; vice chmn. pub. mem. Wage Stblzn. Bd., New Eng., 1951-53. Impartial umpire collective bargaining agreements. Mem. New Eng. Gov.'s Textile Commn., 1957—. Mem. Am. Arbitration Assn. (label arbitration panel), Nat. Acad. Arbitrators, Am. Econ. Assn., Indsl. Relations Research Assn., Sigma Alpha Epsilon. Author: (with others) The New England Economy, 1952. Contbr. articles profl. jours. Home: Winding Creek Farm Box H Durham NH 03824

HOGAN, JOHN FRANCIS, Jr., fgn. service officer; b. Lewiston, Me., July 28, 1917; s. John Francis and Della Maud (Martin) H.; A.B. in Journalism, Mercer U., 1940; m. Jeanne Marie East, Nov. 6, 1956; children—Kathleen, Martin. Radio news editor, writer and producer, Macon, Ga., 1940-43; pub. relations specialists U.S. Maritime Service, 1943-45; news dir. Me. Network News Service, Portland, 1945-49; dir. Washington program cneter, chief world-wide spl. events, Voice of Am., 1949-56, dir. Middle East program center, Cairo, UAR, 1956-60; pub. affairs officer USIS, Dar es Salaam, Tanganyika, 1961-62, Nairobi, Kenya, 1963; supervisory information specialist USIA, 1963-70; chief psychol. operations region I, CORDS/JUSPAO, Vietnam, 1970—. Mem. Radio-TV News Dirs. Assn. (founding pres. 1946-48), Am. Fgn. Service Assn. Club: Nat. Press (Washington). Home: 7501 Democracy Blvd Bethesda MD 20034 Office: USIA Washington DC 20547

HOGAN, JOSEPH CHARLES, univ. dean; b. St. Louis, May 26, 1922; s. Joseph D. and Anna (Lange) H.; B.S. in Elec. Engring., Washington U., 1943; M.S. U. Mo., 1949; Ph.D. (univ. fellow 1951-53), U. Wis., 1953; m. Mary Elizabeth Carrere, June 21, 1944; children—Joseph Charles (dec.), Mary E., Susan L., Thomas C., Stephen J., Michael C., Martha A., William G., Daniel C. Instr., U. N.D., 1947; mem. faculty U. Mo., Columbia, 1947-67, prof., 1958-67, dean engring., 1961-67; prof., dean engring. U. Notre Dame, 1967—; engr. Commonwealth Assos., Inc., summers 1953-54; cons. Columbia Water & Light Dept., 1954-56, Central Electric Power Corp., 1959-60. Chmn. water and light adv. bd. City of Columbia 1957-61. Served as ensign USNR, 1943-45. Registered profl. engr., Mo., Ind. Mem. I.E.E.E. (sr.), Nat., Mo., Ind. socs. profl. engrs., Am. Soc. Engring. Edn. (chmn. Mo. Ark. sect. 1959-60), Sigma Xi, Tau Beta

Pi, Eta Kappa Nu. Theta Xi. Contbr. research articles profl. jours. Home: 2516 S Twyckenham Dr South Bend IN 46614 Office: Coll Engring U Notre Dame Notre Dame IN 46556

HOGAN, JOSEPH EDWARD, clergyman, educator; b. Troy, N.Y., Nov. 21, 1914; s. John J. and Elizabeth (Ryan) H.; student Niagara U., 1932-34; A.B., St. Joseph's Coll., Princeton, N.J., 1936; M.A., Catholic U. Am., 1942, Ph.D., 1951. Ordained priest Roman Cath. Ch., 1941; tchr. philosophy coll. and sem., Niagara U., 1942-49; asst. rector Sem. of Our Lady of the Angels, Niagara, N.Y., 1947-49; prof. philosophy, dir. scholastics Mary Immaculate Sem., Northampton, Pa., 1951-54; dean Grad. Sch., St. John's U., N.Y., form 1954, exec. v.p., from 1957, now prof., also trustee. Mem. exec. com. on Cath. grad. study. Mem. Am. Assn. U. Profs., Nat. Cath. Ednl. Assn., Am. Cath. Philos. Assn. Author: The Virtue of Prudence in the Social Philosophy of St. Thomas Aquinas, 1951; also articles. Home: 75 Lewis Av Brooklyn NY 11206 Office: St John's University Grand Central and Utopia Parkways Jamaica NY 11432

HOGAN, JOSEPH F., banker; b. Kansas City, Mo., Feb. 22, 1905, s. William E. and May (Burke) H.; LL.B., Kansas City (Mo.) Sch. Law, 1927; m. Rose Hughes, June 27, 1934; children—William, Patricia, Paul, Martha, Mary Jo, Joseph F. With legal dept. Dierks Forest Products Co., Kansas City, Mo., 1927-32, asso. firm. Watson, Ess, Marshall & Enggas, Kansas City, Mo., 1932-40; asst. mgr. real estate loan dept., also asst. v.p. Anglo-Cal. Nat. Bank, San Francisco, 1940-44 asso. firm Brobeck, Phleger & Harrison, San Francisco, 1944-46; with Crocker-Citizens Nat. Bank, and predecessors, San Francisco, 1946—, now pres., dir., mem. exec. com.; chmn., chief exec. officer, dir. Crocker-Citizens Internat. Bank: pres., dir. Crocker-Citizens Internat. Corp., Crocker Nat. Corp. Mem. Am. Bar Assn., State Bar Cal., Bar Assn. San Francisco, Assn. Res. City Bankers. Clubs: San Francisco Golf, Pacific Union (San Francisco); Jonathan, Rotary (Los Angeles). Home: 10787 Wilshire Blvd Los Angeles CA 90024 Office: 611 W 6th St Los Angeles CA 90054

HOGAN, JOSEPH LLOYD, bishop; b. Lima, N.Y., Mar. 11, 1916; s. MIchael C. and Mary (Shaw) H.; student St. Andrew's Sem., Rochester, N.Y., 1934-36, St. Bernard's Sem., Rochester, 1936-42; M.A., Canisius Coll., Buffalo, 1949; D.S.T., Pontifical U. Angelicum, Rome, Italy, 1951. Ordained priest Roman Catholic Ch., 1942; asst. St. Marys Ch., Elmira, N.Y., 1942-45; prof. Latin and social studies St. Andrew's Sem., 1945-49, 51-53; prin. DeSales High Sch., Geneva, N.Y., 1953-55; prof. fundamental dogma, dean studies, prof. catechetics St. Bernard's Sem., also prof. theology St. John Fisher Coll. and prof. ascetical theology Sisters of St. Joseph Novitiate, 1955-65; 1st rector Becket Hall, diocesan prep. sem. 1965-67; pastor St. Margaret Mary Ch., Irondequoit, 1968; bishop of Rochester, 1969—. Raised by Pope Paul VI to rank of Domestic Prelate, 1966; named Diocesan Consultor by Bishop Fulton J. Sheen, 1968. Address: 50 Chestnut St Rochester NY 14604

HOGAN, KENNETH EDGAR, educator; b. Plains, Kan., Sept. 26, 1925; s. Edgar B. and Minnie (Angell) H.; B.A., Ottawa U., 1950; M.A., U. No. Colo., 1953, Ed.D., 1962; m. Betty Ruth Ashley, Dec. 21, 1948; children—Marla, Delaine, Cindy. Dist. credit mgr. Sherwin Williams Co., Greeley, Colo., 1950; tchr. Estes Park (Colo.) elementary schs., 1950-52; prin. Lamar (Colo.) elementary schs., 1952-54; chmn. dept. edn. and psychology Pueblo Coll., 1954-57; guest prof. Western State Coll., summers 1955-57; mem. faculty U. No. Colo., 1957—, prof., 1969—, dir. spl. services, 1957-60, dir. continuing edn., 1960-64, asst. dir. pub. relations, 1960-64, dir. placement, 1964-66, chmn. higher edn., 1966-71. Mem. adv. bd. Center Research and Continuing Edn., Estes Park, Colo., 1960-67; chmn. leadership tng. Pueblo Council Chs., 1955-57. Bd. dirs. Colo. Baptists Homes Assn., Roger Williams Found. Served with AUS, 1944-46. Mem. N.E.A., Colo. Edn. Assn. (chmn. student edn. assn. adv. bd. 1955-58, chmn. profl. relations com. 1967-69). Baptist (chmn. bd. deacons 1969-70, sec. bd. trustees 1963-64). Home: 2176 Buena Vista Dr Greeley CO 80631

HOGAN, LAWRENCE J., congressman; b. Boston, Sept. 30, 1928; B.A., Georgetown U., 1949, J.D., 1954; M.A., Am. U., 1965; grad. student San Francisco State Coll., 1956- 57, U. Md., 1966-67; m. Nora Maguire; children—Mary Theresa (Mrs. William Robert Lazarus), Lawrence J. Admitted to D.C. bar, also U.S. Supreme Ct.; practicing atty. and bus. exec.; with FBI, 1948-58; tchr. U. Md., 1960-68; mem. 91st-92d Congresses 5th Dist. Md. Mem. Gov. Md. Commn. Law Enforcement and Adminstrn. Justice 1967-68. Trustee Cath. Youth Orgn.; bd. dirs. Prince Georges County chpt. Am. Cancer Soc. Mem. D.C. Bar Assn., Pub. Relations Soc. Am., Am. Soc. Assn. Execs., Prince Georges County C. of C., Am. Assn. U. Profs., Nat. Acad. TV Arts and Scis., Am. Studies Assn., Soc. Former Spl. Agts. FBI. Club: Nat. Press (Washington). Address: 6504 Osborne Rd Hyattsville MD 20784

HOGAN, MARK, former lt. gov. Colo.; b. Chgo., Jan. 27, 1931; s. Mark Anthony and Alice (Glavin) H.; A.B., Georgetown U., 1952; m. Nancy Lucile Stevenson, Feb. 6, 1954; children—Cary Lucille, Mark, Lisa, Matthew, Michael. Vice pres. Koelbel & Co., Denver, 1954-64; pres. Hogan/Stevenson Realtors, 1964- -. Mem. Colo. Ho. of Reps., 1962-66, majority whip, 1964-66; lt. gov. of Colo., 1966-70. Bd. dirs. Cath. Charities; bd. dirs. Met. Denver YMCA; mem. Nat. Democratic Policy Council. Bd. trustees Loretto Hts. Coll. 1964-68. Served to lt. (j.g.) USNR, 1952-54. Named Colo. Young Man of Year, 1957- 58. Democrat. Club: University (Denver). Home: 1861 S Niagara Way Denver CO 80206 Office: 1429 Larimer Sq Denver CO 80203

HOGAN, MICHAEL JOHN, ophthalmologist, educator; b. Kemmerer, Wyo., Aug. 26, 1907; s. Arthur John and Vilate (Douglas) H.; A.B., U. Utah, 1930; M.D., Cornell U., 1932; m. Vera Merrill, 1937; children—Judith Ann, Michael Timothy, Shelley. Intern Paterson (N.J.) Gen. Hosp., 1932-33; resident surgeon Bellevue Hosp., N.Y.C., 1933-35; pvt. practice medicine, San Diego, Cal., 1935-38; resident ophthalmology U. Cal. at San Francisco, 1938-40, instr. dept. ophthalmology, 1941-43, asst. clin. prof., 1946-48, asso. clin. prof., 1948-51, clin. prof., 1951-57, prof., 1957—, vice chmn. dept., 1951-59, chmn. dept. ophthalmology, 1959—. Dir. U. Cal. Eye Bank; dir. Francis I. Proctor Found., 1947-59; bd. trustees Nat. Med. Found. for Eye Care, Nat. Com. for Research in Ophthalmology and Blindness, Joint Com. on Eye Banks; mem. sci. adv. com. Nat. Council to Combat Blindness; v.p. Nat. Soc. for Prevention of Blindness; pres. No. Cal. Soc. for Prevention of Blindness. Diplomate, asso. examiner Am. Bd. Ophthalmology. Fellow A.C.S.; mem. Cal. Med. Assn., A.M.A., Assn. U. Profs. Ophthalmology (chmn.), Am. Ophthalmol. Soc., Assn. Research Ophthalmology, Pacific Coast Oto-Ophthalmology Soc., Nat. Soc. Prevention Blindness, Am. Acad. Ophthalmology. Home: 500 Lovell Av Mill Valley CA Office: 95 Kirkham St San Francisco CA 94122

HOGAN, THOMAS BERNARD, accountant; b. Bklyn., Aug. 10, 1917; s. Thomas Joseph and Elizabeth (Moore) H.; B.S.C., U. Notre Dame, 1939; m. Grace McCabe, June 14, 1941; children—Nancy, Kathleen, Thomas, John, Joseph. With Haskins & Sells, C.P.A.'s 1939—, partner, 1951—, charge N.Y.C. office, 1960—, exec. office, 1967—. Bd. dirs. N.Y. Heart Assn.; trustee Pace Coll. Home: 319 Brooklyn Blvd Sea Girt NJ 08750 Office: 2 Broadway New York City NY 10004

HOGAN, TIMOTHY S., judge; b. Wellston, O., Sept. 23, 1909; s. Timothy S. and Mary Adele (Deasey) H.; A.B., Xavier U., 1930; LL.B., U. Cin., 1931; m. Evalon Roberts, Dec. 27, 1934; children—Nanci Ann (Mrs. Fred Dutton), Margaret M. (Mrs. J.K. Nelson), Timothy S. III. Admitted to Ohio bar, 1931; pvt. practice with firm Cohen, Baron, Todd & Hogan, Cin., 1931-66; spl. counsel, atty. gen. Ohio, 1937-41, 48- 50; U.S. dist. judge So. Dist. Ohio, Cin., 1966—; lectr. trial practice U. Cin. Law Sch., 1950-62. Mem. Clermont (O.) County Planning Commn., 1958-62. Del.-at-large Ohio Democratic Nat. Conv., 1952; mem. Hamilton County (O.) Dem. Policy Com., 1958-66. Served to lt. col. USAAF, 1942-46. Mem. Fed., Ohio, Cin., Clermont County bar assns., Order of Coif. Roman Catholic. Home: 2136 Madison Rd Cincinnati OH 45208 also 5939 Cook Rd Milford OH 45150 Office: US Post Office and Court House Cincinnati OH 45202

HOGAN, WILLARD NEWTON, educator; b. Dry Ridge, Ky., Mar. 26, 1909; s. Ellie B. and Mary (Jones) H.; A.B., Transylvania Coll., 1930; M.A., U. Ky., 1934; Ph.D., U. Chgo., 1939; m. Hildur J. Canter, Apr. 3, 1937; children—Carolyn (Mrs. Dean W. Rounds), Jeannette (Mrs. Michael C. Tighe), Edward. Various research and adminstrv. positions U.S. Govt., 1937-45; asso. prof. history and polit. sci. Berea Coll., 1945-49; prof. polit. sci. State U. Coll., New Paltz, N.Y., 1949-63; prof. polit. sci. U. Neb., Lincoln, 1963—; staff mem., cons. Brookings Instn., 1952-53. Chmn. Zoning Commn., New Paltz, 1956, 59-63. Mem. Am., Internat. polit. sci. assns., Am. Assn. U. Profs., Commn. to Study Orgn. of Peace. Author: International Conflict and Collective Security, 1955; Representative Government and European Integration, 1967; (with Amry Vandenbosch) The United Nations, 1952, Toward World Order, 1963. Contbr. articles profl. jours. Home: 1115 Idylwild Dr Lincoln NB 68503

HOGAN, WILLIAM, journalist; b. Oakland, Cal., Aug. 15, 1914; s. Will R. and Mildred May (Foster) H.; m. Phyllis M. Barnett, Aug. 3, 1948; children—William Dennis, Mary Ann. Drama editor San Francisco Chronicle, 1952-55, book editor, 1956—. Editor: (with William German) The San Francisco Chronicle Reader, 1962. Home: 14 Circle Way Mill Valley CA 94901 Office: San Francisco Chronicle 5th and Mission Sts San Francisco CA 94103

HOGAN, WILLIAM JOSEPH, advt. exec.; b. St. Louis, Aug. 2, 1902; s. Joseph and Josephine (Grainey) H.; student St. Louis U., 1920-24; m. Verna L. Coultas, July 12, 1925 (dec.); 1 son, William J.; m. 2d, Jean Miller, Aug. 27, 1955; 1 dau., Mary Elizabeth. Mem. controller's staff Firestone Tire & Rubber Co., Akron, O., 1929-43; treas., controller, dir. H.J. Heinz Co., Pitts., 1943-47; v.p., treas. Am. Airlines, Inc., N.Y.C., 1947-54, sr. v.p. finance, 1954-58, exec. v.p. charge finance, dir., 1958-67; chmn. finance com., treas., dir. Interpublic Group Cos., 1968—; pres., dir. Victory Carriers, Inc.; dir. Raytheon Co., Franklin Nat. Bank, Menasco Mfg. Co., Page Airways Corp., Cherry-Burrel Corp. Knight of Malta. Mem. Financial Execs. Inst. Clubs: Union League (N.Y.C.); Union (Boston); Fifth Avenue (N.Y.C.); Clove Valley Rod and Gun; Rolling Rock; Winged Foot Golf. Home: 34 Greenfield Av Bronxville NY 10708 Office: 1271 Av of Americas New York City NY 10020

HOGAN, WILLIAM RANSOM, educator; b. Toledo, Nov. 23, 1908; s. Lemuel Ransom and Irene (Logan) H.; A.B., Trinity U., 1929; A.M., U. Tex., 1932; Ph.D., 1942; m. Mrs. Jane Carpenter Ogg, June 20, 1949; stepchildren—Mary (Mrs. Randolph Farenthold), Thomas, Jon. Tchr. Ranger (Tex.) Jr. Coll. and High Sch., 1929-31; regional historian Southwestern Nat. Park Service, Dept. Interior, 1935-38; asst. archivist La. State U., 1938-41, asso. archivist, 1941-42, head dept, archives, 1946; asso. prof. history U. Okla., 1946-47; asso. prof. history Tulane U., New Orleans, 1947-49, prof., 1949—, chmn. dept., 1953-68, faculty adminstrv. chmn. Archive New Orleans Jazz, 1958-65. Served from pvt. to capt. M.I., AUS, 1942-45. Recipient Guggenheim fellowship, 1962-63. Fellow Tex. Hist. Assn.; mem. Am., Miss. Valley, So. hist. assns., Louisiana Historical Assn., Philos. Soc. Tex., Phi Beta Kappa (hon.). Author: The Texas Republic, 1946; The Barber of Natchez (with E. A. Davis), 1954. Editor: Guide to Manuscript Collections in the Department of Archives, Louisiana State University, 1940; William Johnson's Natchez: The Ante-Bellum Diary of a Free Negro (with E.A. Davis), 1951; (with Jane Hogan) Tales from the Manchaca Hills, 1960. Contbr. to hist. and lit. jours. Home: 1328 State St New Orleans LA 70118

HOGAN, WILLIAM ROBERT, bldg. material mfg. co. exec.; b. Jersey City, N.J., June 19, 1927; s. William and Agnes (Murtha) H.; B.B.A., Coll. Holy Cross, 1948; m. Clare P. Young, Oct. 12, 1950; children—William Robert II, Mary Eileen, Barbara, Patricia, Ellen, Michael, Cathleen, Paul. Analyst, Chase Manahattan Bank, N.Y.C., 1948; with U.S. Gypsum Co., 1949—, treas., 1968—. Served with USNR, 1945-46. Mem. Finance Mgrs. Assn., Economic Club Chgo. Republican. Roman Catholic. Home: 1294 Scott St Winnetka IL 60093 Office: 101 S Wacker Dr Chicago IL 60606

HOGARD, EARL L., Jr., chem. co. exec.; b. 1926; B.S., U. Tulsa, 1948; married. With Witco Chem. Corp., N.Y.C., 1953—, controller, 1966—. Office: 277 Park Av New York City NY 10017*

HOGARD, EARL LEWIS, accountant; b. Gainesville, Mo., Oct. 7, 1900; s. John S. and Lorena (Chevalley) H.; grad. Internat. Accountants Soc., 1925; student Draughon's Business Univ., Springfield, Md., 1918-19, Okla. State U., 1966; m. Lora Elisabeth McKinney, Dec. 22, 1921 (dec. Sept. 1968); children—Earl Lewis, John William, Joseph Alan; m. 2d, Juanita Mae Williamson, Apr. 2, 1970. Tchr. pub. schs., Mo. and Okla., 1917-18; staff account C.P.A. firms W. O. Ligon & Co., also Willson & Garnett, Tulsa, 1925-37; partner Robert E. Garnett & Co., C.P.A.'s, Tulsa, 1938-54, Earl L. Hogard & Co., C.P.A.'s, Tulsa, 1955-68; part-time accounting supr. Daniel, Hurst, Thomas & Co. C.P.A.'s, 1968-70; cons. J.E. and L.E. Mabee Found., Tulsa, 1949-70, Hardman and Cranston, Penney & Co., 1970—. Cons. estates and trusts, 1955-70. Mem. Okla. Bd. Accountancy, 1943- 48. Auditor investigating com. 14th Okla. Legislature, 1933. Mem. Am. Inst. C.P.A.'s, Okla. Soc. C.P.A.'s (pres. Tulsa 1941-42), Tulsa Geneal. Soc. (pres. 1971—). Methodist (bd. stewards). Home: 1403 S Knoxville Av Tulsa OK 74112 Office: Nat Bank Tulsa Bldg Tulsa OK 74103

HOGARTH, CHARLES PINCKNEY, coll. pres.; b. Brunson, S.C., Nov. 14, 1911; s. Charles Pinckney and Maude (Griner) H.; B.S., Clemson Coll., 1932; B.D., Yale, 1935, M.A., 1941; Ph.D., Peabody Coll., 1947; m. Nancy Harris, Dec. 14, 1940; children—Nancy, Charles. Sec., Christian Assn., student counselor Pa. State Coll., 1935-37; asst. to pres., dir. pub. relations Lander Coll., Greenwood, S.C., 1939-41; dir. pub. relations, bus. mgr., tchr. Detroit Country Day Sch., 1941-42; dean Ward-Belmont Coll., Nashville, 1942-47; registrar Fla. State U., 1947-49; v.p., prof. psychology Gulf Park Coll., Gulfport, Miss., 1949-50, pres., 1950-52; pres. Miss. State Coll. for Women, Columbus, 1952—. Lectr., Europe, summer 1934; research asso. Am. Council Edn., Harvard, 1938. Chmn., Pres.'s Council State Instns. Higher Learning. Bd. dirs. area council Boy Scouts Am., Columbus Community Chest. Mem. Columbus C. of C., N.E.A., Miss. Assn. Sch. Adminstrs., So. Assn. Colls. for Women (past pres.), Miss. Assn. Colls. (past pres.), Jr.-Sr. Coll. Conf. Miss. (past pres.), So. U. Conf. (sec.-treas.), Internat. Platform Assn., Newcomen Soc. N.Am., Miss. Edn. Assn., Pres.'s Council State Instns. Higher Learning in Miss. (past pres.), Am. Assn. Sch. Adminstrs., A.I.M. (past mem. pres.'s council), Pub. Instns. Higher Learning So. States (pres.), Phi Theta Kappa, Pi Tau Chi, Pi Kappa Delta, Phi Kappa Phi, Phi Delta Kappa, Pi Gamma Mu, Kappa Pi, Chi Psi. Methodist. Mason, Rotarian. Club: Columbus Country. Author: Policy Making in College Related to the Methodist Church, 1949; Crisis in Higher Education, 1957. Contbr. articles to ednl. pubs. Home: 1217 Second Av S Columbus MS 39701

HOGBEN, CHARLES ADRIAN MICHAEL, physiologist, educator; b. Buckinghamshire, Eng., Nov. 12, 1921; s. Lancelot T. and Enid (Charles) H.; B.S., U. Wis., 1941, M.D., 1943; Ph.D., U. Minn., 1950; m. Anne A. Stanbery, Nov. 1, 1948; children—Carol Leslie, Virginia Lynn. Intern Phila. Gen. Hosp.; 1944; fellow medicine Mayo Clinic, Rochester, Minn., 1946-50; NRC fellow med. sci., Zoophysiology Lab., Copenhagen, Denmark, 1950-51; med. officer, sect. on kidney and electrolyte metabolism Nat. Heart Inst., Bethesda, Md., 1951- 57; research asso. medicine George Washington U., 1952-57, prof., exec. officer dept. physiology, 1957-61; prof., head dept. physiology U. Ia., 1961. . Research career award com., medical student research tng., physiology study section of Nat. Insts. Health; mem. post doctoral fellowship com. Nat. Sci. Found. Chmn. Gt. Plains adv. com. Am. Heart Assn. 1968-69. 8d. dirs. Gastroenterology Research Group, Incorporated; trustee Mount Desert Island Biology Lab. Served to captain M.C., AUS, 1944-46. Mem. Am. Physiol. Soc., Am. Soc. Pharm. and Exptl. Therapeutics, Biophysical Soc., Am. Gastroenterological Assn., Phi Beta Kappa, Sigma Xi, Alpha Omega Alpha. Editorial bds. Am. Jour. Physiol., Jour. Applied Physiology, Am. Jour. Digestive Diseases, Handbook of Physiol. Pharmacology. Home: 910 Rider St Iowa City IA 52240

HOGBEN, LANCELOT, author, univ. prof.; b. Southsea, Hampshire, Eng., Dec. 9, 1895; s. Thomas and Margaret (Prescott) H.; ed. Trinity Coll. (Senior scholar, Frank Smart prizeman); M.A., Cambridge U., Eng., D.Sc., London U.; LL.D. (hon.) Birmingham U.; Fellow Royal Soc.; m. Enid Charles, 1918 (div. 1957); children—Ennyd Syvia, Charles Adrian Michael, Clare Estelle, David Julian Lancelot; m. 2d, Sarah Jane Evans, 1957. Prof. emeritus med. statistics U. Birmingham, hon. sr. fellow linguistics, 1961; vice chancellor U. Guyana, 1963—. Awarded Keith prize and gold medal by Royal Soc. of Edinburgh, 1936. Croonian Lecture, Royal Soc., 1943. Author: Comparative Physiology of Internal Secretions, 1927; Genetic Principles in Medicine, 1931; Nature and Nurture, 1933; Mathematics for the Million, 1936; Science for the Citizen, 1938; Chance and Choice, 1950; Statistical Theory, 1957; Mathematics in the Making, 1960; The Mother Tongue, 1964; The Vocabulary of Science, 1970; also sci. articles in Proc. Royal Soc. Jour. of Genetics, others. Address: Glyn-Ceiriog Llangollen Wales

HOGBERG, CARL GUSTAV, steel co. exec.; b. Escanaba, Mich., July 19, 1913; s. Claus E. and Anna C. (Franson) H.; B.S. in Metall. Engring., Mich. Coll. Mining and Tech., 1935; D. Engring., Mich. Technol. U., 1967; m. June L. Evans, June 10, 1935; children—David K., Janet H. Blast-furnace apprentice South Chicago works, Carnegie-Ill. Steel Corp., 1935, various operating positions blast-furnace dept., 1935-39, sec. blast-furnace and coke-oven com., Pitts., 1939-41; asst. chmn. blast furnace com. U.S. Steel Corp., Pitts. 1942-54, asst. to v.p. Mich. Limestone div., Detroit, 1955, asst. v.p., 1956, v.p., 1957-60, pres., 1960, pres., 1960-64, v.p. raw materials services, 1964-65, pres. Orinoco Mining Co., from 1965. Mem. Am. Inst. Mining, Metall. and Petroleum Engrs. (J.E. Johnson, Jr. award 1945), Assn. Iron and Steel Engrs. (Kelly award 1950), Am. Iron and Steel Inst., blast furnace and coke assns. Eastern States, Western States, Pa. Soc., Phi Kappa Phi. Republican. Presbyn. Clubs: Caracas Country (Caracas, Venezuela); Caronoca (Puerto Ordaz, Venezuela). Contbr. tech. articles trade publs. Home: Casa C-13 Puerto Ordaz Estado Bolivar Venezuela Office: Ed La Estancia Cdad Comercial Tamanaco La Mercedes Venezuela

HOGE, HENRY WILLIAM, educator; b. Island, Ky., Feb. 15, 1919; s. Henry Herman and Elizabeth (Kest) H.; B.A., Ind. U., 1941; M.A., U. Wis., 1942, Ph.D., 1948; postdoctoral studies Columbia, 1952; m. Doris Eleanor McIntosh, July 26, 1939; children—Henry William, Jane Anne, John Douglas, Nancy Elizabeth. Instr. Spanish and Portuguese, Ind. U., 1947-52, asst. prof., 1952-58; Fulbright lectr. in Spanish, Instituto Caro y Cuervo, Colombia, 1958; asso. prof., chmn. dept. Spanish and Portuguese, U. Wis., Milw., 1959-64, prof., 1964-68, dir. Center for Latin Am. Studies, 1964-68, dir. linguistics program Peace Corps Center, 1962-64; prof., chmn. dept. modern langs. Fla. State U., Tallahassee, 1968—; AID/Consortium of Midwest Univs. binational cons. on higher edn. to Brazil, 1967-68. Served to lt. col. USAAF, 1942-45. Ford Found. sr. fellow, 1952-53. Mem. Modern Lang. Assn., Am. Assn. Tchrs. Spanish and Portuguese, Am. Assn. Tchrs. Fgn. Langs. (exec. council), Latin Am. Studies Assn., Programa Interamericano de Linguistica y Ensenanza de Idiomas. Author: Lope de Vega: El principe despenado, 1955; (with others) Oral Brazilian Portuguese, 1964, rev. edit., 1968; (with others) Modern Portuguese, 1970; Brazilian Portuguese Syntax, 4 parts, 1966-70. Contbr. articles profl. jours. Home: 2329 Killarney Way Tallahassee FL 32303

HOGE, JAMES FULTON, lawyer; b. Concord, N.C., Aug. 2, 1901; s. Beverly Lacy and Nettie (Hatcher) H.; LL.B., Wake Forest (N.C.) Coll., 1922, LL.D. (hon.), 1954; m. Virginia McClamroch, Mar. 26, 1932; children—Barbara (Mrs. Robert A. Daine), James Fulton, Warren McClamroch, Virginia Howe. Admitted to N.C. bar, 1922, N.Y. bar, 1931; in practice of law, Greensboro, N.C., 1922-23; with legal dept. Vick Chem. Co., Greensboro, 1923-27, gen. counsel, 1927-35; mem. firm Rogers, Hoge & Hills (formerly Rogers, Ramsay & Hoge), N.Y.C., specializing in law of trademarks, unfair competition and trade regulation, 1933—; past gen. counsel U.S. Trademark Assn. Hon. mem., gen. counsel Am. Found. Pharm. Edn.; mem. Internat. Patent and Trade-Mark Assn., Am. Patent Law Assn., Acad. Polit. Sci., N.C. Bar Assn., Am. Bar Assn. (mem. trademark div., section of patent, trademark, copyright law, anti-trust sect., sect. on adminstrv. law, corp., banking and mercantile law sect.), N.Y. State Bar Assn. (mem. drug com. sect. on food, drug and cosmetic law, sect. on anti-trust law), Assn. Bar City N.Y., N.C. Soc. N.Y. (past pres.), Commerce and Industry Assn. of N.Y. (dir. chmn. com. on FTC and anti-trust laws), N.Y. So. Soc., Am. Mus. Natural History, Nat. Geog. Soc., Met. Mus. Art, Met. Opera Gui'd, S.A.R. (N.C. Soc.), Mus. City of New York, Point O'Woods Assn (dir.), Omicron Delta Kappa (hon. mem.), Kappa Alpha (formerly pres. N.Y. alumni chpt.), Phi Delta Phi (hon.). Mem. bd. trustees, exec. com. Riverside Ch. Mason. Clubs: Pinnacle (N.Y.C.), University (N.Y.); Nat. Lawyers (Washington). Mem. editorial adv. com. Food, Drug, Cosmetic Law Jour. Editor and pub. The Family of Hoge, 1927. Home: 960 Park Av New York City NY 10028 Office: 90 Park Av New York City NY 10016

HOGE, JAMES FULTON, Jr., newspaper editor; b. N.Y.C., Dec. 25, 1935; s. James Fulton and Virginia (McClamroch) H.; grad. Phillips Exeter Acad., 1954; B.A. in Polit. Sci., Yale, 1958; M.A. in Modern Am. and European History, U. Chgo., 1961; m. Alice Patterson Albright, June 2, 1962; children—Alicia McClamroch, James Patrick, Robert Warren. Financial writer Chgo. Sun Times, 1958-62 Am. Polit. Sci. Assn. Congl. fellow, 1962-63; Washington corr. Chgo. Sun Times, 1963-64, city editor, 1965-67, mng. editor, 1967-68, exec. editor, 1968, editor, 1968—. Mem. council Yale. Vice chmn. bd. dirs. Central YMCA Community Coll.; chmn. Adlai Stevenson Inst. Internat. Affairs. Clubs: Tavern (Chgo.); Federal City (Washington). Home: 63 E Bellevue Pl Chicago IL 60611 Office: 401 N Wabash Av Chicago IL 60611

HOGE, JOHN HAMPTON, lawyer; b. Washington, Sept. 24, 1889; s. Emory Eaton and Georgie (Rust) H.; student U. Va., 1909, Balt. Law Sch., 1912; m. Mary Estelle McIntosh, Dec. 10, 1910; 1 son, J. Hampton. Admitted to Md. bar, 1914, Cal. bar, 1919; practice in Md., 1914-19, San Francisco, 1919-51, Monterey and San Jose, Cal., 1951—; mem. firm Hoge, Fenton, Jones & Appel, 1951—. Mem. Am. Coll. Trial Lawyers, Delta Phi, Phi Alpha Delta. Episcopalian (past vestry mem. bldg. com). Club: Pebble Beach. Home: PO Box 432 Pebble Beach CA 93953 Office: PO Box 791 Monterey CA 93940

HOGEMAN, GEORGE L., ins. co. exec.; b. Chatham, N.J., Dec. 14, 1916; s. George H. and Gladys (Moore) H.; A.B., Princeton, 1938; m. Mary Danter. With Aetna Life & Casualty Co., Hartford, 1940-69, asso. actuary, 1956-57, asst. v.p., 1957-58, v.p., 1958-69; pres. Paul Revere Life Ins. Co., Worcester, Mass., 1969—. Home: 29 Westwood Dr Worcester MA 01609 Office: 18 Chestnut St Worcester MA 01608

HOGG, ASTOR, state ofcl.; b. Roxana, Ky., Nov. 13, 1901; s. George and Mahala (Combs) H.; LL.B., U. Ky., 1924; m. Gertrude Lewis, June 29, 1927; children—Stanley, Janelle Pope (Mrs. William Grable). Admitted to Ky. bar, 1924; practice in Whitesburg, 1924-35, Harlan, 1941-51; county atty. Letcher County, Ky., 1930-34; trial atty. FTC, Washington, 1935-37; spl. asst. to atty. gen. U.S., Washington, 1937-39; commonwealth's atty. 26th Jud. Dist. Ky., 1942-45, circuit judge, 1951-55; judge Ct. Appeals of Ky., Frankfort, 1955-57; chief asst. atty. gen. Dept. Hwys., Frankfort, 1957-60; adminstrv. dir. Cts. of Ky., 1960—. Mayor of Whitesburg, 1927-28; del. Dem. Nat. Conv., 1928. Mem. Am., Ky. bar assns., Am. Judicature Soc., Ky. Hist. Soc., Phi Alpha Delta. Baptist. Clubs: Whitesburg Rotary (pres.); Kiwanis (Harlan); Filson (Louisville). Home: 200 Paul Sawyier Frankfort KY 40601 Office: State Capital Frankfort KY 40601

HOGG, JAMES FELTER, educator; b. Denison, Tex., Dec. 11, 1918; s. James Franklin and Edith (Felter) H.; B.A., Rice U., 1941; M.A., U. Tex., 1942, Ph.D., 1947; m. Lucy Joan Winternitz, Sept. 8, 1945; children—Nancy Ann, Susan Elise. Research chemist Charles Pfizer & Co., Bklyn., 1944-45; mem. faculty U. Mich., Ann Arbor, 1947-64, asst. prof. biochemistry, 1952-64; prof. chemistry Queens Coll., City U. N.Y., Flushing, 1964—, exec. officer biochemistry, 1966-70, chmn. dept. chemistry, 1968—; vis. scientist Oxford (Eng.) U., 1961; plenary lectr. 2d Internat. Conf. Protozoology, London, 1965. Mem. Am. Chem. Soc., Am. Soc. Biol. Chemistry, Biochem. Soc., Am. Soc. Microbiology, Soc. Proptzoologists, Am. Assn. U. Profs., Sigma Xi, Phi Lambda Upsilon, Editorial bd. Jour. Protozoology, 1962—. Home: 168 Elm Av Glen Cove NY 11542 Office: Queens Coll Flushing NY 11367

HOGG, ROBERT LYNN, lawyer; b. Point Pleasant, W. Va., Dec. 30, 1893; s. Charles Edgar and Nancy Berden (Hawkins) H.; A.B., W.Va. U., 1914, LL.B., 1916; LL.D., Morris Harvey Coll., 1956; m. Mary Louise Holliday, June 24, 1926; children—Mary Lynn (Mrs. John E. Shackelford), Charles Edgar II. Began practice at Point Pleasant, 1916; mem. Hogg & Hogg; pros. atty. Mason County, W.Va., 1920-24; mem. W.Va. Senate, 1924-28 (chmn. com. on taxation and finance); mem. 71st and 72d Congresses (unexpired term 1930-31, 31-33), 4th W.Va. Dist.; asst. gen. counsel Life Ins. Assn. Am., 1935-43, asso. gen. counsel, 1943-45; mgr., gen. counsel Am. Life Conv., Chgo., 1944-46, exec. v.p., gen. counsel, 1946-54; sr. v.p., adv. counsel Equitable Life Assurance Soc. U.S., 1954-56, dir., 1955, vice chmn. bd., 1956- 59, mem. bd., 1959—; counsel Jackson, Kelley, Holt and O'Farrell, Charleston, W.Va., 1960—. Served with U.S. Army, 1917-19; AEF. Mem. Am., W.Va. bar assns., Assn. Life Ins. Counsel. Republican. Presbyn. Mason. Clubs: Congressional Country, Burning Tree, Nat. Press (Washington); Metropolitan (N.Y.C.); Kenwood Golf and Country (Bethesda, Md.). Co-author: Hogg's Pleadings and Forms. Home: Lewisburg WV 24901 Office: Kanawha Valley Bldg Charleston WV 25301

HOGG, TONY JEFFERSON, editor; b. London, Eng., Jan. 27, 1925; s. Richard Jefferson and Lilian (Currie) H.; ed. Brit. pvt. schs.; m. Elizabeth Moroney Maxon, Aug. 25, 1957; 1 son, John Jefferson. Came to U.S., 1953. Automotive editor Esquire mag., 1970—; editor Sci. and Mechs., N.Y.C., 1969—; contbg. editor Road and Track 1961—, tech. editor, 1963-65; writer and photographer; contbr. articles, numerous mags. Mem. Am. Soc. Mag. Editors. Home: 60 Iselin Terrace Larchmont NY 10538 Office: Science and Mechanics 229 Park Av S New York City NY 10003

HOGG, WILLIAM RICHEY, educator; b. Vandergrift, Pa., June 3, 1921; s. William LeRoy and Mildred (Richey) H.; B.A., Duke, 1943; B.D., Yale, 1946, Ph.D., 1951; m. Wilma Ruth Eaton, M.D., Dec. 19, 1949; children—Ruth Ellen, Mary, Sarah. Ordained to ministry Meth. Ch., 1946; sec., Interseminary Movement, 1946- 47; adminstrv. asst. Internat. Missionary Council, 1950-52; instr. Leonard Theol Coll., Jabalpur, India, 1952-55; asst. prof. world christianity Perkins Sch. Theology, So. Meth. U., 1955-57, asso. prof., 1957-60, prof., 1960—, Fondren lectr., 1967. Mem. Phi Beta Kappa, Pi Gamma Mu. Author: (with K.S. Latourette) Tomorrow Is Here, 1948, World Christian Community in Action, 1949; Ecumenical Foundations, 1952; New Day Dawning, 1957; One World-One Mission, 1960. Mem. editorial bd., contbr. The History of American Methodism, 3 vols., 1964. Home: 3617 Haynie Av Dallas TX 75205

HOGGART, RICHARD, educator, author; b. Leeds, Eng., Sept. 24, 1918; s. Tom Longfellow and Adeline Emma (Long) H.; B.A. with 1st class honours in English, Leeds U., 1939, M.A. in English, 1940; m. Mary Holt France, July 18, 1942; children—Simon David, Frances Nicola, Paul Richard. Staff tutor lit., dept. adult edn. U. Hull (Eng.), 1946-56, sr. staff tutor, 1957-59; vis. prof. English, U. Rochester (N.Y.), 1956-57; sr. lectr. English, U. Leicester (Eng.), 1959-62; prof. English, U. Birmingham, 1962—, dir. Centre for Contemporary Cultural Studies, 1964—; asst. dir. gen. social scis., human scis. and culture UNESCO (on leave of absence from U Birmingham), 1970—. Mem. Brit. books overseas com. Brit. Council, 1959-64; gen. adv. council BBC, 1959-60, 64- -; gov. Royal Shakespeare Theatre, 1966—; mem. culture adv. com. U.K. Nat. Commn. to UNESCO, 1966-70; mem. Com. Inquiry Into Youth Service, 1958-60; mem. Youth Service Devel. Council, 1960-62; mem. Pilkington Com. Inquiry Into Broadcasting Services, 1960-62. Dir. Birmingham Repertory Theatre, 1963-70. Served with Royal Arty., 1940-46. Author: Auden, 1951; The Uses of Literacy, 1957; W.H. Auden, 1957; W. H. Auden-A selection, 1961; Teaching Literature, 1963; Speaking To Each Other, 1970; also chpts. in books, introductions, essays, reviews. Address: UNESCO Place de Fontenoy 75 Paris 7e France

HOGIN, PHILIP EDWARD, mfg. co. exec.; b. Oak Park, Ill., May 4, 1920; s. Ralph M. and Loretta (Murphy) H.; B.S. in Engring., Cornell U., 1942; M.S. in Indsl. Mgmt. (Alfred P. Sloan fellow), Mass. Inst. Tech., 1954; m. Betty Jane Harrison, Nov. 5, 1949; children—Harrison David, Christen Evangeline, Lauretta Joann, Sarah Elizabeth. With Western Electric Co., 1942-48, 50—, gen. mgr. service div., central region, 1963-64, v.p. staff, mfg. div., 1964-65, v.p. pub. relations, 1965-66, v.p. mfg., 1966-67, exec. v.p., dir., 1967- -; mem. tech. staff Bell Telephone Labs., 1948-50; dir. Teletype Corp., Belcomm, Inc., Sandia Corp., Phoenix Mut. Life Ins. Co. Served to lt. (j.g.) USNR, 1944-46. Registered profl. engr., N.Y., N.J., Ill., Conn. Mem. Soc. Sloan Fellows, Phi Kappa Sigma, Kappa Tau Chi. Home: Cos Cob CT 06807 Office: 195 Broadway New York City NY 10007

HOGLE, GEORGE HOLLISTER, psychiatrist; b. Salt Lake City, Apr. 10, 1915; s. James Albert and Mary Cecelia (Copley) H.; grad. St. Paul's Sch., Concord, N.H., 1932; B.S. in Engring., Yale, 1936; M.D. Columbia, 1954; m. Lois Clare Crozier, Dec. 9, 1949 (div. Aug. 1966); children—Allan Crozier, Stephen Copley, Frances; m. 2d, Ann Meilstrup Raymond, Aug. 1966. Metall. engr. Consol. Eureka Mining Co., Eureka, Nev., 1936-37; gen. partner J.A. Hogle & Co., Salt Lake City, Utah., 1936-63; intern Presbyn. Hosp., N.Y.C., 1954-55; psychiat. tng. Inst. Psychiatry, also Soc. Analytical Psychology, London, 1955-59. Stanford, 1959-61; psychiatrist San Mateo Mental Health Services, 1961-64; relief worker in Germany, Am. Friends Service Com., 1946-48; clinical asst. prof. psychiatry Stanford and U. Cal., 1968—. Mem. Royal Soc. Medicine, Analytical Psychology Club, Soc. Jungian Analysts, San Francisco, Am. Psychiat Assn., Am. Group Psychotherapy Assn., Sigma Xi, Tau Beta Pi, Alpha Omega Alpha. Mem. Soc. of Friends. Clubs: Sierra, St. Elmo, University. Home: 45 Meadow Rd Woodside CA 94062 Office: 800 Welch Rd Palo Alto CA 94304

HOGLUND, ELIS S., corp. exec.; b. Chgo., July 29, 1898; s. Gustave E. and Ida (Sterner) H.; Ph.B., U. Chgo., 1921; m. Helen Klinger, June 21, 1924; children—Peter Klinger, Charlotte (dec.), Margaret Jane, William Elis. Asst. gen. mgr. Square D Co., 1922-27; various exec. positions Gen. Motors Overseas Operations, G.M. Internat., Copenhagen, Denmark, 1927- 28; mng. dir. G.M. Nordiska, Stockholm, Sweden, 1928-37; with Adam Opel, A.G., Russelsheim, Germany, 1937-41, regional mgr., 1945-47, asst. gen. mgr., 1947-59; v.p. Gen. Motors Corp., 1949-63, gen. mgr. overseas operations div., 1959-60, group exec. in charge Canadian and overseas operations, dir., also mem. exec. com., 1961-63; chmn. Nat. Fgn. Trade Council, N.Y.C., 1963—; mem. bd. dirs. Internat. Bank of Detroit Spl. consultant USN Dept., 1942-43, Office Mil. Govt. Germany, 1945. Mem. Council Fgn. Relations, Sigma Nu. Clubs: Economic (Detroit and N.Y.C.); Recess (Detroit): Bloomfield Hills (Mich.) Country: University. Home: 45 Sutton Pl S New York City NY 10022 Office: 10 Rockefeller Plaza New York City NY 10020 Rockefeller Plaza New York City NY 10020

HOGLUND, JOHN H., lawyer; b. Wymore, Neb. Aug. 9, 1920; s. Harold J. and Hazel M. (Hultman) H.; A.B., U. Mich., 1942, J.D., 1943; m. Patricia Price, June 17, 1944; children—J. Steven, Anne L., Mark W. Admitted to Ill. bar, 1944, since practiced in Chgo.; mem. firm Chadwell, Keck, Kayser and Ruggles, Chicago. Mem. at large West Suburban council Boy Scouts Am., 1958—. Chmn. Fire and Police Commn. Riverside, Ill. Bd. dirs. MacNeal Meml. Hosp., Berwyn, Ill. Mem. Am., Ill., Chgo. bar assns., Legal Club Chgo., Law Club Chgo., Am. Judicature Soc., Am. Coll. Probate Counsel. Clubs: University, Mid-Day (Chgo.); Riverside Golf. Home: 322 Northwood Rd Riverside IL 60546 Office: 135 S LaSalle St Chicago IL 60603

HOGLUND, RUNE ERIK ANDERS, dept. store exec.; b. Hanebo, Sweden, Mar. 16, 1920; s. Per and Emma (Skogberg) H.; M.A., Uppsala U., 1944; Ph.D. Stockholm Sch. Econs., 1947; m. Anne Marie Selander, June 14, 1947; children—Mans, Ola. Sec. Study Group Adminstriv. Questions, 1947-52; leader sci. work, 1953-54; prof. Stockholm Sch. Econs., 1953; cons. Svenska Handelsbanken, 1954-55; mem. mgmt. staff Ahlen & Holm AB, Stockholm, 1955-60, pres., 1966-70, chief gen. mgr., 1970—; chmn. AGA AB; dir. Almedahl-Alingas AB, Försäkrings AB Hansa. Decorated comdr. Order Vasa; comdr. Order Al Merito della Republica Italiana. Mem. Mus. Modern Art, Royal Coin Cabinet. Home: 38 Sturegatan Stockholm Sweden Office: 100 Ringvägen Stockholm Sweden

HOGNESS, DAVID SWENSON, biochemist, educator; b. Oakland, Cal., Nov. 17, 1925; s. Thorfin R. and Phoebe (Swenson) H.; B.S., Cal. Inst. Tech., 1949, Ph.D., 1952; m. Judith Gore, Sept. 18, 1948; children—Peter Swenson, Christopher Gore. NRC fellow with Jacques Monod, Pasteur Inst., Paris, 1952-54; Nat. Found. fellow N.Y. U. Med. Sch., 1954-55; instr. microbiology Washington U., St. Louis, 1955-57, asst. prof., 1957-59; asst. prof. biochemistry Stanford, 1959-61, asso. prof., 1961-66, prof., 1966—. Adviser molecular biology panel NSF, 1962-65. Served with UNSR, 1944-46. Mem. A.A.A.S. (Newcomb Cleveland prize, 1966), Am. Soc. Biol. Chemists, Genetics Soc. Am., Am. Assn. U. Profs. Office: Dept Biochemistry Stanford U Sch Med Stanford CA 94305

HOGNESS, JOHN RUSTEN, sci. assn. exec.; b. Oakland, Cal., June 27, 1922; s. Thorfin R. and Phoebe (Swenson) H.; student Haverford Coll., 1939-42; B.S., U. Chgo., 1943, M.D., 1946; m. Katharine Ruenauver, Dec. 19, 1944; children—Erik, Susan, Karen, David, Jody. Intern medicine Presbyn. Hosp., N.Y.C., 1946- 47, asst. resident, 1949-50; chief resident King County Hosp., Seattle, 1950-51; asst. U. Wash. Sch. Medicine, 1950-52, Am. Heart Assn. research fellow, 1951-52, mem. faculty, 1954—, prof. medicine, 1964—, med. dir. univ. hosp., 1958-63, dean Med. Sch., chmn. bd. health scis., 1964-69, exec. v.p. of the univ., 1969-70, dir. Health Scis. Center, 1970-71; pres. Inst. Medicine, Nat. Acad. Scis., 1971—. Mem. commr.'s adv. com. on exempt orgns. Internal Revenue Service, 1969-71, adv. com. for environmental scis. NSF, 1970-71, adv. com. to dir. NIH, 1970-71. Trustee China Med. Bd. Served with AUS, 1943-46, 47-49. Recipient Distinguished Service award Med. Alumni Assn. U. Chgo., 1966. Diplomate Am. Bd. Internal Medicine. Fellow A.C.P.; mem. Assn. Am. Med. Colls. (exec. council, chmn.-elect council of deans 1968-69), A.M.A., Alpha Omega Alpha. Contbr. profl. jours. Home: 6820 51st Av NE Seattle WA 98115

HOGNESS, THORFIN RUSTEN, educator; b. Mpls., Dec. 9, 1894; s. Peter Gunerius and Amanda (Rusten) H.; B.S., U. Minn., 1918, Chem. E., 1919; Ph.D., U. Cal., 1921; postgrad. (research fellow) U. Göttingen (Germany), 1926-27; m. Phoebe Dorothy Swenson, July 31, 1920; children—John Rusten, David Swenson. Instr. chemistry U. Cal., 1921, asst. prof., 1925-28, asso. prof., 1928-30; asso. prof. chemistry U. Chgo., 1930-38, prof., 1938—, dir. phys. sci. devel., 1947-48, dir. Inst. Radiobiology and Biophysics, 1948-51, Labs. Applied Scis., 1962—, Chgo. Midway Labs., 1951. Mem. OSRD, 1941; sci. liason officer Am. embassy, London, Eng., 1942-43; dir. Md. Research Lab., OSS,1943; dir.chem. div. on atomic energy work U. Chgo., 1943-45, cons. War Dept. and OSRD with E.T.O.U.S.A., 1945. Served with U.S. Army, 1918. Recipient Outstanding Achievement award U. Minn., 1950. Mem. A.A.A.S., Am. Chem. Soc., Sigma Xi, Phi Lambda Upsilon, Alpha Chi Sigma. Clubs: Quadrangle. Home: 5805 S Dorchester Av Chicago IL 60637

HOGREFE, PEARL, educator; b. Holt County, Mo., Sept. 17; d. John Henry and Rosanna (Van Gundy) Hogrefe; B.A., Southwestern Coll., Winifield, Kan., 1910; M.A., U. Kan., 1913; Ph.D., U. Chgo., 1927. Instr. English, Ia. State Tchrs. Coll., Cedar Falls, 1921-25, prof. 1925-28; prof., head dept. English, La. Polytech. Inst., 1928-31; asso. prof. English, Ia. State U., 1931- 44, prof., 1944—. Fellow Folger Shakespeare Library, Washington, 1951, 61. Mem. Modern Lang. Assn., Shakespeare Assn., Am. Assn. U. Profs., Am. Assn. U. Women (Founders fellow 1952-53; chmn. fellowship Ia. 1941-46, pres. Ia. 1946-48., mem. nat. com. higher edn. 1954-60), Phi Kappa Phi, Delta Kappa Gamma. Author: (poems) Renewal, 1940; The Process of Creative Writing, rev. edit., 1963; The Sir Thomas More circle, 1959; The Life and Times of Sir Thomas Elyot, Englishman, 1967; also articles. Co-editor: Interpreting Experience, 1935. Home: 512 Stanton Av Ames IA 50010

HOGROGIAN, NONNY, children's book illustrator; b. N.Y.C., May 7, 1932; d. Mgrditch and Rachel (Ansoorian) Hogrogian; B.A., Hunter Coll., 1953; student New Sch. Social Research, 1957; m. David Kherdian, 1971. Illustrator: Arbor Day, 1965; The Kitchen Knight, 1965; Hand in Hand We'll Go, 1965; Always Room for One More (Caldecott medal 1966), 1965; Once There Was and Was Not, 1966; Bears Are Sleeping, 1967; The Renowned History of Little Red Riding Hood, 1967; The Fearsome Inn, 1967; The Thirteen Days of Yule, 1968; The Story of Prince Ivan, The Gray Wolf, and The Firebird, 1968; Sir Ribbeck of Ribbeck of Havelland, 1969; In School, 1969; Favorite Tales Told in Greece, 1970; Vasilisa The Beautiful, 1970; Paz, 1971; Three Apples Fell From Heaven, 1971; The Armenian Cookbook, 1971; author-illustrator: One Fine Day, 1971; About Wise Men and Simpletons, 1971. Home: Lyme Center NH 03769

HOGUE, ALEXANDRE, artist, univ. prof.; b. Memphis, Mo., Feb. 22, 1898; s. Rev. Charles Lehman and Mattie (Hoover) H.; m. Maggie Joe Watson, July 16, 1938; 1 dau., Olivia. Mem. summer faculty Tex. State Coll. for Women, 1931-42; head of art dept. Hockaday Jr. Coll.; 1936-42; tech. illustrator N. Am. Aviation, 1942-45; head dept. of art U. Tulsa, 1945-63, former prof. art, emeritus prof. art, 1968—. Has exhibited art works both internationally and U.S. including Mus. of Modern Art, Carnegie Internats., Pitts., Art Inst., Chgo., Whitney and Corcoran biennials, Met Museum Art, Asso. Am. Artists, also in 21 Latin American countries, Canada, England, France, Italy and Scotland. Works reproduced in various art journals and books. Represented in colls. Encyclopedia Britannica, Museé National D'Art Moderne (Paris), Internat. Bus. Machines, Library Congress, Phila. Mus. Art, Carl Milles, Dallas Mus. Fine Arts, Philbrook Art Center (Tulsa), Gilcrease Mus. (Tulsa), Santa Barbara Mus. Art, Springfield (Mo.) Art Mus. Democrat. Presbyn. Home: 4052 23d St Tulsa OK 74114 also Cologah OK 74053

HOGUE, LILLIAN GENEVIEVE, ins. underwriter; b. Detroit, Sept. 29, 1899; d. George Wilson and Lillie M. (Glenning) Hogue; C.L.U., Am. Coll. Life Underwriters, 1946. Estate analyst Am. Life Ins. Co., Detroit, 1926-33, N.Y. Life Ins. Co., Detroit, 1934-44; life ins. underwriter, 1944—. Mem. Inter-Group Council Women as Pub. Policy Makers; mem. Mich. League Crippled Children; sec. office safety div. Mich. Safety Council, 1954-55. Dir. Rep. Bus. and Profl. Women, 1957-58. Pres. bd. trustees Elliott Gen. Hosp. and its divs., The Allan Dee Nursing Centers; trustee Marygrove Coll., Detroit, mem. finance com., 1969, 70. Mem. Am. Soc. C.L.U. (pres. Detroit 1952-53, chmn. chpt. activities com. 1955-56, dir. Middle Western region, 1955-57, sec., chmn. membership com. 1957- 58, mem. planning commn. 1956-57, exec. com. 1957-62, chmn. joint com. candidates 1958-60, pres. soc. 1960-61), Am. Coll. Life Underwriters (bd. trustees 1959-62, bd. overseers nat. devel. council, vice chmn. nat. devel. fund), Nat. Assn. Life Underwriters (life mem. women leaders round table, vice chmn. tng. and edn. com.) Detroit Assn. Life Underwriters, Detroit Life Ins. and Trust Council (dir. 1958-60, treas. 1960-61, v.p. 1962-63, pres. 1963-64), Detroit Bus. Woman's Club (pres. 1953-55), Bus. and Profl. Women's Club (chmn. Detroit Inter-Club council 1957). Home: 1110 Yorkshire Rd Grosse Point Park MI 48230 Office: Ford Bldg Detroit MI 48226

HOGUET, LAWRENCE, business exec.; b. N.Y.C., May 30, 1915; s. J. Peter and Helen (Gourd) H.; grad. Middlesex Sch., Concord, Mass.; m. Katherine Dudley, May 10, 1944; 1 son, Lawrence Dudley. With Mfrs. Trust, N.Y.C., Bunge y Born, Ltda., Buenos Aires, Argentina, Am. Embassy, Buenos Aires, Guaranty Trust Co., N.Y.C.; now sr. v.p., treas., dir. Engelhard Minerals & Chems. Corp., Murray Hill, N.J.; pres. N.J. Bus. Devel. corp.; v.p., treas., dir. Am.- South African Investment Co. Ltd.; dir. 1st Nat. State Bank, Newark, 1st Nat. State Bancorp., Newark. Trustee, Charles Engelhard Found. Served to 1st lt. AUS; ETO. Mem. Greater Newark C. of C. (dir.). Home: 125 E 63d St New York City NY 10021 Office: 430 Mountain Av Murray Hill NJ 07974

HOGUET, ROBERT LOUIS, Jr., investment banker; b. N.Y.C., Dec. 23, 1908; s. Robert Louis and Louise Robbins (Lynch) H.; A.B., Harvard, 1931, M.B.A., 1933; m. Constance M. Roberts, Aug. 3, 1940; children—Robert Louis III, Constance Middleton, George Roberts. With office of sec. U.S. Treasury Dept., Washington, 1933-35; with First Nat. City Bank, 1935-69, v.p., 1947-58, sr. v.p., 1958-62, exec. v.p., vice chmn. bd., 1962-69; dir. Internat. Banking Corp., N.Y.C., 1954-70, 1st Nat. City Trust Co. Can., 1964-70, N.Y. London Trustee Co., Ltd., 1964-70, Ananaconda Co., 1964-67, Consumers Power Co., 1950-55, 60-65; partner Tucker, Anthony & R.L. Day, 1970—; dir. London Guarantee and Accident Co., N.Y.C., Phoenix Assurance Co., N.Y.C. Mem. bd. mgrs. Hosp. Spl. Surgery, N.Y.C.; bd. dirs. Lincoln Center Performing Arts, chmn., bd. dirs. Repertory Theatre; bd. dirs. French Inst., Fedn. French Alliances; vice chmn. bd., trustee Barnard Coll., N.Y.C.; bd. overseers Harvard Coll. Served from lt. to comdr., USNR, 1942-45. Knight of Malta. Mem. Council Fgn. Relations, Soc. Friendly Sons St. Patrick. Clubs: Links, Century, Downtown Assn., Recess, River (N.Y.C.); Piping Rock; Maidstone. Home: 1 E 66th St New York City NY 10021 Office: 120 Broadway New York City NY 10005

HOHBACH, HAROLD CARL, lawyer; b. Plankinton, S.D., Dec. 3, 1921; s. Charles C. and Rose (Miller) H.; B.S. in Elec. Engring., S.D. State U., 1943; B.S. in Bus. Adminstrn., U. Cal., Berkeley, 1947, LL.B., 1952; m. Marilyn Alice Krouser, July 30, 1955; children—Douglas, Ann, Janet, Ellen. Sales engr. Westinghouse Electric Corp., 1947-49; admitted to Cal. bar, 1953; patent lawyer Flehr, Hohbach, Test, Albritton & Herbert, San Francisco, 1952—, partner, 1958—. Dir. Sutter Hill Capital Co. Guardsmen of San Francisco, 1954—. Chmn. Menlo Atherton Young Republicans, 1957. Served to 1st lt., Signal Corps, AUS, 1943-46. Mem. Am., San Francisco, San Mateo County bar assns., State Bar Cal., Am. Patent Law Assn., Blue Key, Sigma Tau, Phi Alpha Delta. Republican. Lutheran. Clubs: Commonwealth (San Francisco); University (Palo Alto). Home: 29 Lowery Dr Atherton CA 94025 Office: 160 Sansome St San Francisco CA 94104

HOHENBERG, JOHN, writer, educator; b. N.Y.C., Feb. 17, 1906; s. Louis and Jettchen (Scheuermann) H.; student U. Wash., 1922-24; Litt.B., Columbia, 1927; postgrad. U. Vienna, 1928. Reporter, Seattle Star, 1923-24; writer N.Y. World, 1925; fgn. corr. N.Y. Evening Post, Vienna, Paris, U.P.I., Vienna, 1927-28, asst. city editor, 1928-33; reporter, writer nat. politics N.Y. Jour.-Am., 1933-42; UN, Washington and fgn. corr. N.Y. Post, 1946-50; lectr. English, Columbia, 1948, asso. in journalism, 1949-50, prof. journalism, 1950—. Adminstr., Pulitzer prizes, sec. adv. bd., 1954—; spl. cons. to USAF, 1953-63; Am. specialist lectr. State Dept. Asian countries, 1963-64; discussion leader Internat. Press Inst., New Delhi, 1966; sr. specialist East-West Center, Honolulu, 1967; mem. Japanese-Am. Assembly, Shimoda, Japan, 1967. Served with AUS, 1943-45. Pulitzer traveling scholar Europe 1927-28; research fellow Council Fgn. Relations, 1964; Ford travel study grantee Asia, 1970. Mem. Council Fgn. Relations, Am. Assn. Edn. Journalism, Internat. Press Inst., Columbia Journalism Alumni Assn. (pres. 1954), Sigma Delta Chi (Distinguished Service award to journalism 1965, 68). Author: The Pulitzer Prize Story 1959; The Professional Journalist, 1960, rev. edit., 1968; Foreign Correspondence—The Great Reporters and Their Times, 1964; The New Front Page, 1965; Between Two Worlds. Policy, Press and Public Opinion in Asian-American Relations, 1967; The News Media: A Journalist Looks at His Profession, 1968; Free Press/Free People, The Best Cause, 1961. Home: 90 Morningside Dr New York City NY 10027 also Aguebogue NY 11931

HOHENSTEIN, PAUL CECIL, mfg. co. exec.; b. nr. Elbow Lake, Minn., Oct. 15, 1914; s. Paul G. and Selma (Anderson) H.; student U. Ill., 1934-38; m. Louise E. Rainey, Sept. 24, 1940; children—David, Jean (Mrs. James Elliott), Susan, Gail, Laurie. With Haskins & Sells, C.P.A's, N.Y.C. and Chgo., 1938-41; auditor USN, 1941-43; gen. auditor Hudson Motor Car Co., Detroit, 1943- 52; comptroller Copco Steel Co., Detroit, 1953-54; treas., dir. Tecumseh Products Co. (Mich.), 1954—; dir. Sharon Mfg. Co. Trustee Herrick Meml. Hosp. Mem. Beta Gamma Sigma, Phi Kappa Phi. Home: 915 Red Mill Dr Tecumseh MI 49286 Office: Tecumseh Products Co Tecumseh MI 49286

HOHL, ELIZABETH MASON, physician and surgeon; b. Beaver City, Neb., Aug. 8, 1890; d. William Henry and Nellie Lavina (Booth) Mason; B.Sc., U. Neb. 1913, M.D., 1915; m. Harrison L. Hohl, 1916 (div. 1934); 1 son, Mason. Intern Neb. Methodist Hosp., Omaha, 1915- 16; general practice, McCook, Neb., 1916-24. Hollywood, Cal., 1924—; cons. surgeon Los Angeles City Receiving Hosp.; chief Sunset Boulevard and Hollywood West hosps.; mem. staff Hollywood Presbyn., Los Angeles County Gen. hosps.; chief staff Good Shepherd Convent Sch.; formerly staff Plaza Community Center; co-founder, chief staff Cancer Prevention Soc. and Detection Clinic 1944—, also adminstr. Founder, pres. Los Angeles Physicians Aid Assn., Career Women and Pan Am. Med. Women's Alliance. Mem. bd. Clark House for Girls, YWCA. Named Woman Physician of Year, 1954, 55; Los Angeles Times Woman of Yr., 1956. Mem. Am. Med. Woman's Assn. (historian past pres.), Am., Cal., Los Angeles County (council) med. assns., Internat., Los Angeles med. woman's assns., Hollywood Acad. Medicine, Pub. Health League, Am. Geriatrics Soc., Barlow Soc. History Medicine (past pres.), Nu Republican. Translator: Diseases of Women (Tortula of Salerno), 1940. Contbr. Ency. Brit., 1944. Home: 1850 N Whitley Hollywood CA 90028 Office: 303 Loma Dr Los Angeles CA 90017

HOHLER, GEORGE ROBERT, sch. adminstr.; b. Boston, Sept. 24, 1932; s. Robert Anthony and Eileen (Dutcher) H.; B.A. magna cum laude, Northeastern U., 1960; m. Barbara Ann Abbott, Jan. 23, 1951; children—Robert Tillman, Cynthia Ann, Julie Barbara. Asst. to dep. comptroller Harvard, 1956-60; dir. office information Unitarian Universalist Assn., Boston, 1960-63, exec. dir. Laymen's League, 1963-69, Fellowship for Renewal, 1969; dir. devel. Putney (Vt.) Sch., 1970—. Pres., Liberty Tree Assoc., cons. vol. orgns., 1966—; editor Respond mag., 1966-70, Challenge mag., 1964-65, Putney Post, 1970—. Hon. distinguished minister congregation Arlington St. Ch., 1967. Founding mem. Citizens Boston Schs., 1961; founder Bostonian of Year award, 1960; founder, mem. bd. Boston Center for Arts, 1970—. Mem. Am. Alumni Council, Adult Edn. Assn. Am. Author: You Can't Jail Us All, 1964. Home: 28 Atherton Rd Brookline, MA 02146. Office: Putney Sch Putney VT 05346

HOHNSTEDT, LEO FRANK, chemist, educator; b. Alton, Ill., June 12, 1924; s. Leo Thomas and Esther (Paris) H.; B.S. in chemisty, St. Louis U., 1949; Ph.D., U. Chgo., 1955; m. Margaret Mary Gorman, Aug. 13, 1960. Instr. chemistry St. Louis U., 1954-55, asst. prof., 1955-60, asso prof., 1963-69, prof., 1969—, chmn. chemistry dept., 1966—; asso. prof. Poly. Inst. Bklyn., 1960-61; weapon systems analyst Weapon Systems Evaluation Div. Inst. for Def. Analysis, Washington, 1961-63. Bd. dirs. Inst. for Theol. Encounter with Sci. and Tech. Served with AUS, 1943-46. Recipient Chemist of Year award St. Louis U. Alumni Chemists, 1970. Fellow A.A.A.S., Am. Inst. Chemists; mem. Am. Chem. Soc., St. Louis Soc. Analysts, St. Louis U. Alumni Chemists, Sigma Xi, Pi Lambda Upsilon, Phi Mu Epsilon, Alpha Chi Sigma. Roman Catholic. Home: 621 E 15th St Alton IL 62002 Office: 221 N Grand St St Louis MO 63103

HOHSTADT, THOMAS DOWD, condr., musical dir.; b. Ryan, Okla., Sept. 5, 1933; s. Leslie Melvin and Maye (Waid) H.; B. Music, Eastman Sch. Music, 1955, M. Music, 1956, D. Mus. Arts, 1962; grad. Vienna (Austria) Akademie Musik, 1960; m. Muriel Virginia Colvin, July 21, 1957; children—Lowell Lynn, Leslie Lynn. Conducting staff Eastman Sch. Music, Rochester, N.Y., 1960-62; asst. condr. Honolulu Symphony, 1962-63; mus. dir. Amarillo (Tex.) Symphony, 1963—; works performed Rochester, Houston, Amarillo symphonies. Active Amarillo Citizens' Assn., Amarillo Council Progress, Greater S.W. Music Festival. Served with U.S. Army Band, 1956-59. Fulbright scholar, 1959-60; named one Five Outstanding Young Texans, Tex. Jr. C. of C., 1968 . Mem. Am. Symphony Orch. League, Amarillo C. of C., Phi Mu Alpha, Lambda Chi Alpha. Presbyn. (elder). Club: Am. Business. Author: Modern Concepts in Music for Brass, 1967; Solo Literature for the Trumpet, 1960; Composer Impetus Lineaus, 1962. Home: 3706 Kingston St Amarillo TX 79109 Office: Box 2552 Amarillo TX 79105

HOIJER, HARRY, anthropologist; b. Chgo., Sept. 6, 1904; s. John Oscar and Agnes Sophia (Peterson) H.; A.B., U. Chgo., 1927, A. M., 1929, Ph.D., 1931; m. Dorothy Jared, June 7, 1927; children—Charlotte, Peter, Susan. Instr. anthropology U. Chgo., 1931-40; mem. faculty U. Cal. at Los Angeles, 1940—, prof. anthropology, 1940-70, prof. emeritus, 1970—, chmn. dept. anthropology and sociology, 1948-51. Fellow Center Advanced Study in Behavioral Scis., 1959-60. Mem. Am. Anthropol. Assn. (v.p. 1949, Memoirs editor 1948-52, pres. Western states br., 1950, nat. pres. 1958), Linguistic Soc. Am. (pres. 1959), Sigma Xi. Author monographs. Contbr. articles. Home: 191 Beloit Av Los Angeles CA 90049

HOILAND, ANDREW CALVIN, architect; b. Great Falls, Mont., Aug. 3, 1926; s. Andrew C. and Ida (Mohundro) H.; B.S. in Architecture, Mont. State Coll., 1949; m. Patricia Ruth Willits, Aug. 13, 1950; children—William H., Richard C., Diana Ruth. Draftsman, A.V. McIver, architect, Great Falls, 1949-52; prin. A. Calvin Hoiland, architect Great Falls, 1952-54; partner Hoiland & Lund, architects, Great Falls, 1953-63, Hoiland-Zucconi, architects, Great Falls, 1964—. Pres. Mont. Bd. Archtl. Examiners, 1968. Chmn. charity ball for Great Falls Rehab. Center, 1961-62, master plan com. Great Falls Swimming Pool, 1962-65. Bd. dirs. Great Falls Camp Fire Girls. Served with USAAF, World War II. Named to Legion of Honor, Order DeMolay, 1956. Mem. A.I.A. (pres. Mont. 1961-62, editor Mont. publn. 1965—), Great Falls Soc. Architecture (charter; pres. 1953), Mont. Tech. Council (charter; pres. 1960-61), Sigma Chi. Methodist dist. (chmn. bd. trustees; mem. Mont. bd. missions). Mason (Shriner), Kiwanian (pres. Great Falls 1964). Prin. projects include master plan prison facilities Mont. State Prison, 1968, Mountain View Sch., Great Falls, 1968-69, fire stas., Great Falls, 1969-71. Asso. editor Am. Architects Directory, 1969-70; editorial adv. bd. Symposia mag., 1968—. Home: 2826 3d Av S Great Falls MT 59405 Office: PO Box 1552 Strain Bldg Great Falls MT 59401

HOISINGTON, ELIZABETH PASCHEL, retired army officer; b. Newton, Kan., Nov. 3, 1918; d. Gregory and Josephine (Suing) Hoisington: B.A., Coll. Notre Dame of Md., 1940, LL.D., 1967. With Women's Army Aux. Corps., 1942-43, WAC, U.S. Army, 1943-71; advanced to brig. gen.; assigned WAC Detachment ETO, 1944-46, Gen. Hdqrs., Far East Command, 1948-50, Office Dir. U.S. Women's Army Corps, 1951-54, Hdqrs. 6th U.S. Army, Presidio of San Francisco, 1954-57, Office Dept. Chief of Staff for Personnel, Dept. of Army, Washington, 1957-61, Hdqrs. U.S. European Command, Paris, 1961-64; dir. WAC, 1966-71; retired, 1971. Decorated Bronze Star, Army Commendation medal, D.S.M., Legion of Merit with oak leaf cluster; Croix de Guerre with silver star (France). Mem. Soc. Daus. U.S. Army, Delta Epsilon Sigma. Home: 1800 Las Tunas Rd Santa Barbara CA 93103

HOISINGTON, ROBERT MORRIS, govt. ofcl.; b. Claflin, Kan., July 10, 1907; s. Morris Earl and Bess (Henderson) H.; B.A. in Bus., U. Colo., 1931; M.S. in Pub. Adminstrn., Syracuse U., 1931; m. Hazel Harriet Carton, Aug. 28, 1937; 1 dau., Donna Lee. Exec. sec. Cin. Regional Crime Commn., 1931-35; property mgr. TVA, 1936-44; mgmt. adviser FPHA, 1944-45; city mgr., Ashtabula, O., 1945-49, Springfield, O., 1950-54, Sioux City, Ia., 1954-58, Huntington, W.Va., 1958-63; pub. adminstrn. adviser AID, Vietnam, 1964—. Address: USOM/PAD APO San Francisco, CA 96243 (Vietnam)

HOKANSON, RUSSELL VINCENT, lawyer; b. Bellingham, Wash., June 18, 1913; s. Erick H. and Bina (Johnson) H.; B.A., U. Wash., 1937, LL.B., 1939; m. Mildred F. Kolb, Feb. 11, 1945; children—Constance, Erika, Alicia, Sarah, Russell V., Johanna. Admitted to Wash. bar, 1939, since practiced in Seattle; mem. firm Helsell, Paul, Fetterman, Todd & Hokanson, 1952—; spl. counsel, legislative adviser to gov. of Wash., 1949, 55; lectr. U. Wash. Law Sch., 1953-55. Mem. Seattle Found.; pres. bd. trustees Seattle Pub. Library. Dir., Seattle-King County chpt. A.R.C., 1950-62, 63—, chmn. 1962-63; bd. govs. Am. Nat. Red Cross, 1957-63, vice chmn. bd., 1961-63, chmn. program com., 1961-63, mem. exec. com., 1960-63, vice chmn. nat. conv., 1967; dir., exec. com. United Good Neighbor Fund, Seattle, 1953-56, 57—, v.p., 1960-61, pres., 1965. Served as lt. USNR, 1942-46. Mem. Am., Wash. State, Seattle (trustee 1949-52) Seattle-King County (pres. 1964-65) bar assns., U. Wash. Law Sch. Alumni Assn. (pres. 1950), Am. Judicature Soc., Nat. Council Christians and Jews (Seattle adv. council), Phi Delta Phi. Bd. editors U. Wash. Law Rev., 1937-39. Home: 333 W Kinnear Pl Seattle WA 98119 Office: Washington Bldg Seattle WA 98101

HOKE, RUSSELL ALLEN, former publisher, writer; b. Harrisburg, Pa., June 17 1896; s. Howard Markle and Bertha Nims (Keet) H.; E.E., U. Pa., 1920; m. Anna Gertrude Stokell, June 6, 1925. Editorial staff Youth's Companion, Boston, 1920-21, Little, Brown & Co., 1921-26; free lance writer, 1926-28; owner, pub. Town Crier (weekly newspaper), Newton Centre, Mass., 1928-36, Lexington (Mass.) Times—Minute Man, 1931-32; pres., Bellman Pub. Co., Inc., 1932-48; treas. Bur. Student Guidance, Inc.; pres. Research Pub. Co., Inc., pubs. ednl., guidance and occupational information materials. Served with CAC, 1918. Republican. Lutheran. Contbr. serials, short stories to nat. mags. Home: 1197 Beacon St Brookline MA 02146

HOKIN, LOWELL EDWARD, educator, biochemist; b. Chgo., Sept. 20, 1924; s. Oscar E. and Helen (Manfield) H.; student U. Chgo., 1942-43, Dartmouth, 1943-44, U. Ill. Sch. Medicine, 1946-47; M.D., U. Louisville, 1948; Ph.D., U. Sheffield (Eng.), 1952; m. Mabel Neaverson, Dec. 1, 1952; children—Linda Ann, Catherine Esther, Samuel Arthur. Postdoctoral fellow dept. biochemistry McGill U., 1952-54, faculty, 1954-57, asst. prof., 1955-57; mem. faculty U. Wis.-Madison, 1957—, prof. physiol. chemistry, 1961-68, prof., chmn. dept. pharmacology, 1968—. Mem. Am. Soc. Biol. Chemists, Biochem. Soc. (U.K.), A.A.A.S., Am. Chem. Soc. Contbr. numerous articles to tech. jours., chpts. to numerous books on phospholipids, biol. transport, pancreas. Home: 1234 Sherman Av Madison WI 53703

HOLADAY, ALLAN GIBSON, educator; b. Grand Ledge, Mich., Jan. 16, 1916; s. Robert Clayton and Effie (Hooks) H.; B.A., Miami U., 1938; M.A. (Grad. fellow), Cornell U., 1939; Ph.D. (Grad. Council fellow), George Washington U., 1943; m. Ruby Roxane Lees, Sept. 30, 1945; children-Allan Scott, Bruce Lees. Instr. English, U. Ill. at Urbana, 1942-47, asst. prof., 1947-53, asso. prof., 1953-57, prof., 1957—. Mem. Modern Lang. Assn., Modern Humanities Research Assn., Cambridge Bibliog. Soc., Am. Assn. U. Profs., Phi Beta Kappa, Phi Eta Sigma, Delta Phi Alpa. Author, editor: Thomas Heywood's The Rape of Lucrece, 1950; The Plays of George Chapman, 1970. Co-editor: The Life ofLazarillo de Tormes, 1955. Contbr. articles profl. jours. Home: 308 E Colorado Av Urbana IL 61801

HOLADAY, BEVERLEY ELI, educator, psychologist; b. Newcastle, Ind., Feb. 4, 1910; s. John F. and Carrie (Tackett) H.; student Earlham Coll., 1925-26; A.B., Wittenberg U., 1929; Ph.D., U. Vienna (Austria), 1933, Ohio State U., 1937; m. Alta L. Waldron, June 4, 1941; children—Julie Peake (dec.), John Waldron, Delaney Butler (Mrs. Mack D. Hixon). Asso. prof. psychology Fredonia (N.Y.) State Coll., 1937- 47; personnel cons. 2d Service Command, U.S. Army, 1942-46; prof., chmn. dept. ednl. psychology U. Tenn., 1947-58; Fulbright prof. ednl. psychology U. Marburg (Germany), 1955-56; prof. ednl. psychology, chmn. dept. U. Ala., 1958—; cons. in field, 1947—; mem. guest faculty Squadron Officers Sch., Air U., Maxfield Field, Ala. Mem. Sigma Xi, Kappa Phi Kappa, Phi Delta Kappa, Phi Mu Delta. Episcopalian. Author: Grösenkonstanz der Sehdinge, 1933; Educational Psychology in the Third Reich, 1937. Home: 138 The Highlands Tuscaloosa AL 35401 Office: Box 2424 University AL 35486

HOLADAY, DUNCAN ASA, physician; b. Denver, July 22, 1916; s. Horace Asa and Julia M. (Beaver) H.; B.S., U. Chgo., 1940, M.D., 1943; m. Anita M. Christ, Jan. 3, 1941; children—Phyllis, Susan (Mrs. Peter Paul Karasz), Duncan, Linda, Thomas. Intern, St. Luke's Hospital. N.Y.C., 1943, resident, 1944- 45; practice medicine, specializing in anesthesiology, N.Y.C., 1950-59, Chgo., 1959-68, Miami, Florida 1968—; Sharp & Dohme fellow in pharmacology Johns Hopkins U., Balt., 1947-50; asst. prof. anesthesiology Columbia Coll. Phys. and Surgs., 1950-58, asso. prof., 1958-59; asst. attending anesthesiologist Presbyn. Hosp., N.Y.C., 1950- 56, asso. attending anesthesiologist, 1956-59; prof. surgery, head sect. anesthesiology Sch. Medicine U. Chgo., 1959-68; prof. anesthesiology, dir. research in anesthesiology U. Miami (Fla.) Sch. Medicine 1968—; med. dir. inhalation therapy Jackson Memorial Hospital, Miami. Med. advisor Mid-Am. Med. Chpt. A.R.C., 1961-68. Served to capt., M.C., AUS, 1945-47. Diplomate Am. Bd. Anesthesiology. Fellow Am. Coll. Chest Physicians, N.Y. Acad. Scis.; mem. Am. Registry Inhalation Therapists (v.p.), Am. Soc. Pharmacology and Exptl. Therapeutics, Am. Physiol. Soc., Am., Fla. socs. anesthesiologists, A.A.A.S., Sigma Xi. Home: 6660 S W Montgomery Dr Miami FL 33156 Office: PO Box 875 Biscayne Annex Miami FL 33152

HOLAHAN, JOHN FRANK, banker; b. Galesburg, Ill., Nov. 16, 1913; s. John and Lucille (Boutin) H.; B.S. magna cum laude Notre Dame U., 1935; m. Louise Goeckel, Sept. 28, 1940; children—John Frank, Jr., William L., Rita. Asst. nat. bank examiner 3d Fed. Reserve Dist., Phila., 1935-45; nat. bank examiner, 1945-54; rev. examiner, Fed. Res. Bd., 1954-59; v.p. Nat. Bank of Westchester, White Plains, N.Y., 1959-69, sr. v.p., 1969—. Bd. govs. Robert Morris Assos. Trustee Good Counsel Coll.; chmn. nominating com., bd. dirs. Westchester County United Fund. Mem. N.Y. State Devel. Regional Com., Am. Inst. Banking, Am. Mgmt. Assn., Westchester County Assn. Clubs: Notre Dame Club N.Y., Windmill Club, Tamarack Country Club. Home: 4 Long Pond Ct Windmill Farm Armonk NY 10504 Office: 31 Mamaroneck Av White Plains NY 10601

HOLAHAN, RICHARD VINCENT, mag. and book publisher; b. Darien, Conn., Dec. 4, 1909; s. Michael Joseph and Margaret (Callery) H.; grad Hotchkiss Sch., 1929; B.S., Yale, 1933; m. Pamela Crawford Mar. 4, 1938; children—Michael N., Thomas R., Richard J., Stephen C., David W. With Time, Inc., 1936-50, bus. mgr. Fortune mag., 1943-50; prodn. dir. Street & Smith Publs., 1950-53; plant mgr. O.E. McIntyre, Inc., Westbury, N.Y., 1953-56; with Scholastic Mags., Inc., N.Y.C., 1956—, v.p., 1960—. Sec. Stamford Planning Bd., 1949-51; chmn. Stamford Bd. Finance, 1951-54, Huntington Planning Bd., 1961-67; town councilman, Huntington, 1970—. Trustee Performing Arts Found., Huntington; chmn. Yale Alumni Bd., 1952-54. Mem. Vernon Hall, Phi Gamma Delta. Clubs: Yale (N.Y.C.); Huntington Country. Home: 162 Bay Av Huntington NY 11743 Office: 50 W 44th St New York City NY 10036

HOLBEL, SYLVESTER J., clergyman; b. Buffalo, Apr. 23, 1903; s. Benjamin and Mary (Haeti) H.; B.A., Canisius Coll., 1924; A.M., Niagara U., 1926; student Cath. U. Am.; LL.D. (hon.), St. Michaels Coll., Vt., 1963. Ordained priest Roman Cath. Ch., 1928; supt. Cath. schs. Diocese of Buffalo, 1941-62, sec. of edn., 1962—; pastor Nativity Ch., Orchard Park, N.Y. Named papal chamberlain to Pope Pius XII with title very rev. msgr., 1946; named domestic prelate title rt. rev. msgr., 1953. Mem. Nat. Cath. Edn. Assn., Nat. Cath. Music Educators Assn. (pres.). K.C. Home: 26 Thorn Av Orchard Park NY 14127 Office: 100 S Elmwood Av Buffalo NY 14202

HOLBERG, RALPH GANS, Jr., lawyer; b. Mobile, Nov. 5, 1908; s. Ralph G. and Lilliam (Frohlichstein) H.; LL.B., U. Ala., 1932; m. Amelia Schwarz, Feb. 16, 1938; children—Ralph G., Robert S. Admitted to Ala. bar, 1932, since practiced in Mobile; partner firm Holberg, Tully and Hodnette, 1962—. Pres. Mobile County chpt. A.R.C., 1954-55, chmn. Southeastern area council, 1957-58, bd. mem. emeritus Mobile County chpt., Ala. nat. v.p., 1960-61, mem. nat. bd. govs., 1965-68, 68-71; chmn. bd. Mobile County Bd. Pensions and Security, Mobile Gen. Hosp., 1963-67; mem. Ala. Docks Adv. Bd., 1962—, 3d Army Area Adv. Com., Gov. Ala. Com. Adult Edn. Negroes, 1949; chmn. Mobile Pub. Library Bd., 1954-55; appeal agt. local selective service bd. Served to lt. USNR, 1944-46. Recipient Distinguished Service Key, Mobile Jr. C. of C., 1938; named Mobilian of Year, 1963. Fellow Am. Coll. Probate Counsel; mem. Am., Ala., Mobile (pres. 1942) bar assns., V.F.W., Ala. Hist. Assn., Sons Confederate Vets., Am. Legion (post comdr. 1947-48), Mobile C. of C. (past bd. dirs.), Am. Judicature Soc., Am. Arbitration Assn., Mobile Hist. Preservation Soc. (past bd. mem.), P.T.A. (pres. 1954-55), Mobile's Azalea Trail (past pres.), Navy League, Am. Council Judaism (nat. adv. bd. 1955), Spring Hill Av. Temple (past pres., mem. bd.), Zeta Beta Tau. Clubs: Exchange (charter, past pres.), Touchdown (past mem. bd.), Mobile Country. Home: 1723 Springhill Av Mobile AL 36604 Office: Commerce Bldg Mobile AL 36601

HOLBERT, ALLAN BROWN, music critic; b. Weston, W.VA., Nov. 17, 1934; s. Robert Fletcher and Lois (Brown) H.; B.Mus.Edn., U. Neb., 1956; M.S. in Journalism with honors, Columbia, 1960; m. Sue Elisabeth Ramey, Dec. 17, 1955; children—Virginia Sue, Roger Frederick. Reporter, Lincoln (Neb.) Star, 1957-58; editor Neb. Ednl. News, Lincoln, 1958-59; former mem. staff Mpls. Tribune, from 1960, music critic, from 1964. Home: 4041 Vincent Av S Minneapolis MN 55410

HOLBERT, THEODORE FRANK, banker; b. Sussex, N.J., July 15, 1921; s. Theodore M. and Charlotte (Lawrence) H.; B.A., Denison U., Granville, O., 1947; postgrad. Rutgers U., 1954; m. Florence M. Conrad, June 8, 1948 (dec., Feb. 1970); children-Amy Amanda, Philip. Vice pres., dir. Farmers Nat. Bank, Sussex, 1947-63; exec. v.p., dir. Bank of Sussex County, Franklin, N.J., 1963- 69; sr. v.p., dir., mem. exec. com. Nat. Community Bank, Rutherford, N.J., 1970—. Pres. Sussex County Bd. Realtors, 1958. Councilman, Boro of Sussex, 1949-59. Pres. High Point Regional Bd. Edn.; trustee, treas. Alexander Linn Hosp., Sussex. Served with USAAF, 1943-46; ETO. Mem. Am., N.J. bankers assns., N.J. Agr. Soc., Kappa Sigma. Republican. Episcopalian. Mason, Rotarian. Home: 39 Bank St Sussex 07461 Office: Route 206 Newton NJ 07860

HOLBROOK, CLYDE AMOS, educator; b. Greenfield, Mass., Mar. 20, 1911; s. Fred Earl and Adella (Caswell) H.; A.B., Bates Coll., 1934; B.D., Colgate-Rochester Div. Sch., 1937; Ph.D., Yale University, New Haven, 1945; studies at univs. St. Andrews and Basel 1956; S.T.D., Denison U., 1969; m. Dorothy Bush Wheeler, Dec. 27, 1937; children—Richard Clyde, Arthur Wheeler, Deborah. Ordained to ministry Baptist Church, 1937; pastor, Weston, Conn., 1937-42, New Haven, 1942-45; dean of chapel, asso. prof. religion Colo. Coll., 1945-49; asso. prof. religion Denison U., 1949-51; prof. religion, chmn. dept. Oberlin Coll., 1951—, prof. Christian ethics Graduate School of Theology, 1951-56; Danforth chair of religion, 1957. Colgate-Rochester fellow, Yale, 1937-40: sr. fellow Council of Humanities, Princeton, 1961-62. Mem. commn. on higher edn. Nat. Council of Chs. of Christ. Trustee Oberlin Shansi Memorial Assn., 1956—, v.p., 1960-68, pres., 1968—. Recipient E. Harris Harbison award; 1966- 67. Mem. Am. Assn. U. Profs., Am. Acad. Religion (pres. 1963), Soc. Religion in Higher Education, Am. Theol. Soc., Phi Beta Kappa. Conglist. Author: Faith and Community, 1959; Religion a Humanistic Field, 1963; Jonathan Edwards: Original Sin, 1970. Co-author; The Humanities at Oberlin, 1958; A Handbook of Christian Theologians, 1965; A Heritage of Christian Thought, 1965. Editorial bd. Jour. Bible and Religion, 1969. Home: 21 Hawthorne Dr Oberlin OH 44074

HOLBROOK, DAVID STEARNS, steel exec.; b. St. Louis, July 17, 1912; s. Harold L. and Lucy (Styring) H.; B.S., U. Pitts., 1932; LL.D. (hon.), Laurentian U.; m. Marguerite Somers, Nov. 14, 1931;

children—Diane (Mrs. Hugh H. Hansard), David Stearns, Richard Lyman. Employed as steam engineer with Carnegie Steel Co., Youngstown, O., 1933-35; project engr. Carnegie-Ill. Steel Corp., 1935-40; asst. chief engr. Homestead works Carnegie-Ill. Steel Corp., 1940-44; asst. gen. mgr. Algoma Steel Corp., Ltd., Sault Ste. Marie, Ont., Can., 1944-45, exec. asst. to pres., 1945-46, v.p. 1946- 49, exec. v.p., 1949-56, pres., 1956—, chmn., 1962—; co-dir. Du Pont of Can., Royal Bank of Can., Can. S.S. Lines, Ltd.; dir. Dominion Bridge Co., Ltd. Prof. engr., Ont., Pa. Mem. Am. (dir.), Internat. (dir.) iron and steel insts., Assn. Iron and Steel Engrs., Conf. Bd., Sigma Alpha Epsilon. Presbyn. Clubs: York (Toronto); Mount Royal (Montreal); Rideau (Ottawa); Cosmos (Washington). Home: 6 Summit E Sault Ste Marie Ontario Canada Office: Algoma Steel Corp Ltd Sault Ste Marie Ontario Canada

HOLBROOK, DONALD, financial cons.; b. Newton, Mass., May 27, 1897; s. Walter and Katharine (Thayer) H.; ed. Harvard, 1920; D.Sc., New Eng. College, Henniker, N.H., 1964; m. Barbara Root Hollister, Apr. 25, 1942; children by previous marriage—Katherine (Mrs. James H. Patteson 3d), Jane (Mrs. Robert A. Deevey), Donald. With Coffin & Burr, Inc., investment bankers, Boston, 1919-28; v.p., gen. mgr. Franklin Mgmt. Corp., Boston, 1928-30; founder The Holbrook Co., 1930; pres. Fire Protection Research Internat., Inc.; chmn., trustee Gen. Investors Trust, mut. fund open-end, Boston, 1956-66. Volunteer fire chief Meadowood County Area Fire Dept., Fitzwilliam, N.H., 1953-68. Trustee New Eng. Coll., Henniker, N.H. Served to lt. (j.g.) with USNRF, World War I; to maj. USAAF, World War II. Mem. Internat. Assn. Fire Chiefs, Nat. Fire Protection Assn. Clubs: Country (Brookline, Mass.); Union (Boston); Harvard (N.Y.C.); Royal Bermuda Yacht (Hamilton). Author: The Boston Trustee, 1937; Civilian Mission, 1947; Up the Ladder, 1957; An Unlikely Firemaster, 1968. Home: 21 Charles River Sq Boston MA 02114 also Meadowood Fitzwilliam NH 03447 Office: 31 Milk St Boston MA 02109

HOLBROOK, DONALD BENSON, lawyer; b. Salt Lake City, Jan. 5, 1925; s. Robert Sweeten and Kinnie (Benson) H.; student Colo. Coll., 1943; LL.B., U. Utah, 1952, J.D., 1965; m. Betty J. Gilchrist, Apr. 23, 1949; children—Mark, Thomas, Gregory, Mary. Admitted to Utah bar, 1953; clk. Chief Justice James A. Wolfe Utah Supreme Ct., 1953-55; asst. city atty., Salt Lake City, 1955- 57; partner firm Jones, Waldo, Holbrook and McDonough, Salt Lake City 1958—. Vice chmn., then chmn. finance com. bd. regents U. Utah, 1965- 67, chmn. bd. regents, 1967-68; chmn. Utah Bd. Higher Edn., 1969—. Mem. exec. com. Democratic Party, Utah, 1955-65; chmn. antitrust and monopoly sub-com. Western States Dem. Conf., 1962-66; campaign mgr. Gov. Calvin L. Rampton, 1964-68; chmn. resolutions com. Utah Dem. Convention, 1968. Served to 1st lt. USMC, 1943-45. Mem. Utah (chmn. com. World Peace through Law 1964, mem. com. jud. retirement 1968), Am. (gen. chmn. Rocky Mountain meeting 1962, mem. com. banking and bus. law 1962—), Salt Lake County (pres. 1964-65) bar assns., Order of Coif, Beta Theta Phi, Phi Kappa Phi. Club: University (Salt Lake City). Home: 1752 Laurelhurst Dr Salt Lake City UT 84108 Office: 800 Walker Bank Bldg Salt Lake City UT 84111

HOLBROOK, GEORGE EDWARD, chem. co. exec.; b. St. Louis, Mar. 4, 1909; s. Edward M. and Doretta C. (Krentler) H.; B.S., U. Mich., 1931, M.S., 1932, Ph.D., 1933; m. Dorothy H. Williams, June 12, 1933; children—James E., Thomas E. With E.I. duPont de Nemours & Co., Inc., Wilmington, Del., 1933—, asst. gen. mgr. organic chems. dept., gen. mgr. elastomer chems. dept. 1955-57, v.p., dir., mem. exec. com., 1958-69, dir., finance com., 1970—. Bd. dirs. Del. Research Found., Devel. Council U. Mich.; bd. visitors Washington Coll.; mem. adv. bd. residencies in engring. Ford Found.; mem. chem. engring. adv. bd. U. Rochester, U. Del. Mem. Engrs. Joint Council (v.p., dir., mem. exec. com. 1960-61), Mfg. Chemists Assn. (dir., mem. exec. com. 1960-61), Am. Inst. Chem. Engrs. (pres. 1958), Am. Chem. Soc., Soc. Chem Industries, Am. Phys. Soc., A.A.A.S., N.Y. Acad. Sci., Franklin Inst., Instn. Chem. Engrs. London (hon.), Sigma Xi, Tau Beta Pi, Phi Lambda Upsilon, Phi Kappa Phi, Phi Eta Sigma. Contbr. articles to profl. jours. Home: 409 Milton Dr Wilmington DE 19802 Office: E I duPont de Nemours & Co Wilmington DE 19802

HOLBROOK, HAL, actor; b. Cleve., Feb. 17, 1925; s. Harold Rowe and Aileen (Davenport) H.; student Suffield Acad., 1933-37, Culver Mil. Acad., 1938-42; B.A. with honors, Denison U., 1948; m. Ruby Elaine Johnston, Sept. 22, 1945; children—Victoria, David. Played summer stock cos., 1947-53; organized two-person stage prodn. with wife, touring high schs., clubs, univs., 1948-53, repertoire included scenes from Shakespeare, Moliere, Victoria Regina, Elizabeth the Queen, and a sketch based on Mark Twain's short story An Encounter with an Interviewer; appeared TV as Abraham Lincoln, 1953; assembled solo show Mark Twain Tonight, 1953, night club performances, 1953-55, on tour U.S., TV appearances, 1956-59, in N.Y.C., 1959; recording theatre presentation Mark Twain Tonight, 1959, 61; concert engagements U.S., Can., Vancouver Festival, Edinburgh Festival, Saudi Arabia, European tour auspices Dept. State with ANTA, 1959-60; performed two-character play Do You Know the Milky Way, Vancouver, also N.Y.C., 1961, Am. Shakespeare Festival, Stratford, Conn., 1962; toured Mark Twain Tonight, 1962; Abe Lincoln in Illinois, 1963; appeared in Incident at Vichy, After the Fall, Tartuffe; appeared in play I Never Sang for My Father, 1968; appeared in motion picture Wild in the Streets, 1968. Mem. com. on internat. cultural exchange Nat. Council on Arts and Govt. Served with C.E., AUS 1943-46. Recipient Vernon Rice Meml. award, 1959, Outer Circle award, 1959; spl. citation for Mark Twain Tonight, N.Y. Drama Critics Circle, 1966. Mem. Mark Twain Meml. Assn. Clubs: Players, Lambs (N.Y.C.). Author: Mark Twain Tonight, 1959. Address: care CMA 8899 Beverly Blvd Los Angeles CA 90048

HOLBROOK, HOLLIS HOWARD, prof. art; b. Natick, Mass., Feb. 7, 1909; s. Goldwin P. and Jessie (Underwood) H.; student Boston U. Evening Sch., 1928-30, Mass. Sch. of Art, 1930-34; B.F.A., Yale Sch. of Fine Art, 1936; m. Vivian Alma Nicholas, June 26, 1937; children—Ferris, Nicholas (dec.), Peter W. Designer Dennison Mfg. Co., Framingham, Mass., 1929-30; illustrator A.P., N.Y.C., 1943; designer Warren Telechron Co., 1943; tchr. art U. Fla., 1938, successively instr., asst. and asso. prof., prof., 1947-48, and 1951—, head prof., 1948-51, U. Fla. Grad. Sch. grant for creative work, 1965. Represented in collections including Sheldon Swope Art Gallery, U. Ga. Mus., Richmond (Va.) Library, Norfolk (Va.) Mus. Arts & Scis., U. Fla., Coll. William and Mary, Walter Chrysler Jr., So. Coll. at Lakeland, Fla.; frescoes in Biblioteca Michoacan, Mexico; murals Fountain of Youth Mus., St. Augustine, Fla., Library of U. Fla.; murals (awarded by govt. in competitions) in post offices, Natick, Mass., Haleyville Ala., Jeanerette, La., New York and Md.; mural series, adminstrn. bldg. R.I. Coll. Edn., Providence, 18 panels in Post Office, Ocala, Fla., 1963. Served USN, 1944-45. Mem. Fla. Edn. Assn. (art. sect. sec. 1943), So. States Art League (dir. 1946-48), Fla. Fedn. Art (pres. 1947), Fla. Artists Group (pres. 1948-51), Nat. Soc. Mural Painters, Am. Assn. U. Profs. Home: 1710 SW 35th Pl Gainesville FL 32601

HOLBROOK, JOHN BROOKFIELD, co. exec.; b. Halifax, N.S., Can., Apr. 12, 1913 (parents Am. citizens); s. Elmer Allen and Edith Laura (Brookfield) H.; B.S. in Indsl. Engring., U. Pitts., 1934; grad. Advanced Mgmt. Course, Am. Mgmt. Assn., 1958; m. Maxine Lucille Christensen, Apr. 16, 1938; children— Linda Ward, Richard Brookfield. Mem. sales and credit staff Firestone Tire & Rubber Co., 1934-35; service scheduler, analyst Pitts. Ry. Co., 1935-40; successively indsl. engr., prodn. planning supr., asst. to supt., asst. to dir. prodn. planning, prodn. engr. U.S. Steel Co., 1940- 52; sr. cons. Booz Allen & Hamilton, 1952-54; mfg. asst. to v.p. Am. Machine & Foundry Co., 1954-60; asso. dir. mfg. and engring. Gen. Foods Corp., 1960-63; v.p. capital improvements Consol. Foods Corp., Chgo., 1963-68; pres. John B. Holbrook and Assos., Inc., Lake Forest, Ill., 1968-71; dir. planning and devel. Sea Pak div. W.R. Grace Co., 1971—. Dir. Mt. Lebanon (Pa.) Civic League, 1950-52. Registered profl. engr., 1947. Mem. Am. Mgmt. Assn., U. Pitts. Alumni Assn., Scabbard and Blade, Phi Gamma Delta, Omicron Delta Kappa, Sigma Tau. Presbyn. (elder, chmn. bd. trustees, chmn. bldg. com.). Clubs: Chicago Athletic; Milbrook Country (past sec., dir.) (Greenwich, Conn.); Exmoor Country (Highland Park, Ill.); Sea Palms Golf and Country (St. Simons Island, Ga.). Address: Black Banks Dr St Simons Island GA 31522

HOLBROOK, LUTHER GARDNER, bus. exec.; b. Walpole, Mass., Aug. 25, 1912; s. Henry G. and Marian S. (Higgins) H.; B.S., Bowdoin Coll., 1934; M.B.A., Harvard, 1936; m. Ruth Price, Dec. 5, 1936; children—Deborah (Mrs. John Winthrop), Penelope (Mrs. Watson D. Reid), Sarah, Henry G. II. Employed comml. banking dept. Worcester County Trust Co. (Mass.), 1936-40; asst. dean Harvard Bus. Sch., 1940-48, asst. prof., 1944-48; asst. v.p. T. Mellon & Sons, Pitts., 1949-56, v.p. and gov., 1957-58, v.p., treas., gov., 1958-70; v.p. Richard K. Mellon & Sons, Pitts., 1971—; dir. First Boston Corp., Gen. Reinsurance Corp., North Star Reinsurance Corp., Gen. Reassurance Corp., Inter-Reins. Corp. (Switzerland). Trustee Richard King Mellon Found., Richard King Mellon Charitable Trusts, Pitts., Brookings Instn., Washington, Wheaton Coll., Norton, Mass., Eisenhower Exchange Fellowships, Phila., Blue Hill (Me.) Meml. Hosp., Inc., Blue Hill Pub. Library. Clubs: Duquesne (Pitts.); Allegheny Country, (Sewickley, Pa.); Rolling Rock (Ligonier, Pa.); Links, Harvard (N.Y.C.); Kollegewidgwok Yacht, Blue Hill Country (Blue Hill). Home: 601 Poia Rd Sewickley PA 15143 also Windswept East Blue Hill ME 04629 Office: Mellon Sq Pittsburgh PA 15230

HOLBROOK, WILLIAM DOUGLAS, psychiatrist; b. Canon, Ga., July 23, 1923; s. Ralph Mitchell and Ethel (Martin) H.; M.D., Bowman Gray Sch. Medicine, 1946; m. Betty K. Brimhall, June 18, 1947; children—Douglas Mitchell, Pamela Gayle, Cindy Kay. Rotating intern Jersey City Med. Center; resident psychiatry Bowman Gray Sch. Medicine; pvt. practice, Charlotte, N.C., 1953—. Served with M.C., USMCR, 1950-52. Diplomate Am. Bd. Psychiatry and Neurology. Mem. Am., Charlotte psychiat. assns., N.C., Mecklenburg County med. soc., A.M.A., Charlotte Mental Health Assn. Home: 4141 Arbor Way Charlotte NC 28207. Office: 1928 Randolph Rd Charlotte NC 28207

HOLBURY, ROBERT JAMES, air force officer; b. Avon Lake, O., Feb. 10, 1920; s. George J. and Rose (Thompson) H.; student U. Omaha, 1961; grad. advanced Mgmt. Program, Harvard, 1965; m. Dorthoy G. Becker, Oct. 10, 1942; children—Nancy Lee (Mrs. Louis Holscher), Rollin G., Robert James. Commd. 2d lt. USAAF, 1943, advanced through grades to brig. gen., 1969; flyer in ETO, Wold War II; operations officer 363th Tactical Reconnaissance Wing, Langley AFB, Va., 1947- 48; assigned U.S. Armed Forces Inst. Tech. tng. program, 1948-50; with operations staff Hdqrs. USAF, 1950-54; chief combardment reconnaissance and trans. br., directorate of operations Hdqrs. USAFE, 1954-56; student NATO Def. Coll., Paris, France, 1956-57; dep. comdr. operations 55th Strategic Reconnaissance brig. Forbes AFB, Kan., 1957-59; chief reconnaissance br., directorate operations Hdqrs. SAC, Offutt AFB, Neb., 1959-61; comdr. Detachment 1, 1129th Spl Activity Squadron, Las Vegas, 1961-66; comdr. 66th Tactical Reconnaissance Wing, 1966-67, 460th Tactical Reconnaissance Wing, Tan Son Nhut AB, Vietnamm, 1967-68; dir. combat operations 7th Air Force, Vietnam, 1968-69; comdr. Tactical Air Reconnaissance Center, Shaw AFB, S.C. 1969-70; dep. chief staff plans Hdqrs. Tactical Air Command, Langley AFB, 1970—. Decorated D.S.C., D.S.M., Legion of Merit with 2 oak leaf clusters, D.F.C. with 2 oak leaf clusters, Air medal with 20 oak leaf clusters, Air Force Commendation medal, Commendation ribbon, numerous area and campaign ribbons. Home: 2512 Pontiac Dr Pontiac MI 48053 Office: 152 Benedict Av Landley AFB CA 23365

HOLCK, FREDERICK HORST, educator; b. Neuenburg, Germany, June 6, 1927; s. Edward W. and Elizabeth (Luger) H.; student U. Heidelberg, 1947-49, U. Tuebingen, 1949-52; Lic. Phil. in Philosophy, U. Salzburg, 1953, Ph.D. in Comparative Religion, 1954; m. Miriam I. Ahlgren, Jan. 23, 1954; children—Mark, Christopher, Thomas, David, Timothy. Came to U.S., 1963, naturalized in 1968. Tutor, Helsinki, 1954-56; parish minister Lutheran State Ch., Germany, 1956-57; sr. lectr. Peshawar U., Pakistan, 1957-59; parish minister in Can. 1960-62; prof. theology and history of religions Luth. Theol. Sem., Saskatoon, Sask., Can., 1962-63; asst. prof. religion Lake Erie Coll., Painesville, O., 1963-66; asst. prof. religion and Oriental philosophy Cleve. State U., 1966-68, asso. prof., acting chmn. dept. philosophy and religion, 1968-70, prof., chmn. dept. religion, 1970—, chmn. assembly and speakers com., 1968-70, faculty adviser Council of Religious Orgns., 1967—, dir. Asian Studies Program, 1969—. Mem. Archtl. and Zoning Bds., Kirtland Hills, O., 1970—. Mem. Am. Acad. Religion, Am. Philos. Assn. Contbr. articles profl. jours. Home: 9087 Boyer Lane Kirtland Hills Mentor OH 44060 Office: Cleve State U Cleveland OH 44115

HOLCOMB, DONALD FRANK, physicist; b. Chesterton, Ind., Nov. 8, 1925; s. Roger L. and Ethel (Frank) H.; A.B., DePauw U., 1949; M.S., U. Ill., 1950, Ph.D., 1954; m. Barbara Page, Aug. 26, 1950; children—Douglas Page, Jane D., Nancy M. Instr., U. Ill., 1954; mem. faculty Cornell U., 1954—, prof. physics, 1962—, dir. lab. atomic and solid state physics, 1964-68, chmn. dept. physics, 1969—; cons. Corning Glass Research Lab., 1959-64, Central Inst. Indsl. Research, Oslo, Norway, 1962; spl. research solid state physics, chem. physics. Served with USNR, 1944-46. Senior visiting fellow NATO, 1962; Guggenheim fellow, 1968-69. Mem. Am. Phys. Soc., Am. Assn. Physics Tchrs., Sigma Xi. Presbyn. Contbr. profl. jours. Home: 141 Northview Rd Ithaca, NY 14850.

HOLCOMB, DYSART EDGAR, chemist; b. Wellington, Tex., May 1, 1917; s. Henry Alvin and Jennie (Dysart) H.; B.S., Texas Tech. Coll., 1937; M.S., U. Mich., 1938, Ph.D., 1941; m. Margaret Appleman, Aug. 6, 1938, Ph.D., children— Dysart Edgar, Margaret Ann, Mary, John. Research chem. engr. Universal Oil Products Co., Chgo., 1941-46; asso. prof. chem. engring. Purdue, 1946- 49; sr. projects technologist Research and Development Labs., Sinclair Refining Co., Harvey, Ill., 1949-50; prof. chem. engring., dean engring. Texas Tech. Coll., Lubbock, Texas, 1950-55; pres. Texas Western Coll. 1955- 58; dir. research El Paso Natural Gas Co., 1958-65; dir. research Pennzoil United, Inc., Shreveport, La., 1965-68, v.p. research, engring. and devel., 1969—; dir. El Paso br. Fed. Res. Dallas. Pres. El Paso County Hosp. dist. bd. mgrs., 1959-65. Mem. Am. Inst. Chem. Engrs., Am. Chem. Soc., Tau Beta Pi, Phi Kappa Phi, Phi Lambda Upsilon, Omega Chi Epsilon. Author science and tech. articles. Home: 731 Oneonta St Shreveport LA 71106 Office: Pennzoil United Inc P O Box 1407 Shreveport LA 71102

HOLCOMB, GEORGE RUHLE, univ. dean; b. Kankakee, Ill., Oct. 25, 1927; s. William Irving and Rosa (Ruhle) H.; B.A., U. Wis., 1950, M.A., 1952, Ph.D., 1956; m. Ellen Jean Kaia Jacobsen, Aug. 3, 1952; children—Kaia Christine, Ellen Elizabeth, Carolyn Jean. Teaching asst. U. Wis., 1951-53, research asst., 1953-54; instr. anatomy Sch. Medicine Creighton U., 1954-57; asst. prof. anatomy Sch. Medicine, U. of N.C., Chapel Hill, 1957-68, prof. anthropology, 1968—, asso. dean of Grad. Sch., 1962-65, dean research adminstrn., 1965—; mem. council Oak Ridge Asso. Universities. Bd. dirs. Chapel Hill Concert Series. Served with AUS, 1946-47. Fellow A.A.A.S., Am. Anthropol. Assn.; mem. Nat. Council U. Research Adminstrs. (past pres.), Am. Assn. Phys. Anthropologists, Am. Assn. Anatomists, Am. Assn. U. Profs. Clubs: U. North Carolina Faculty; Chapel Hill Tennis. Contbr. articles sci. jours. Home: 302 Burlage Circle Chapel Hill NC 27514.

HOLCOMBE, ARTHUR NORMAN, educator; b. Winchester, Mass., Nov. 3, 1884; s. Franklin Gibbons and Inez Norman (Maynard) H.; A.B., Harvard, 1906, Ph.D., 1909; postgrad. U. Berlin, 1907-08, London Sch. Econs., 1909; L.H.D., Columbia, 1954. Faculty, Harvard, 1909-55; chmn. Commn. to Study Orgn. of Peace, 1955-64. With U.S. Bur. of Efficiency, 1917-18, U.S. Tel.&Tel. Adminstrn., 1919; chmn. appeals bd. WPB, 1942-45. Trustee, Estate of Edwin Ginn (World Peace Found.), 1917—. Home: Cotchpinicut Rd North Chatham MA 02650

HOLCOMBE, EDWARD JOSEPH, utility exec.; b. Lambertville, N.J., Sept. 13, 1927; s. Richard Andrew and Margaret (Curtin) H.; B.S. in Bus., Lehigh U., 1949; m. Frances B. Lyons, May 12, 1951; children—Daniel, Mark, Keith, Michael, Richard, Christopher, Mary Frances, Craig, Kathleen. With Pub. Service Electric & Gas Co., Newark, 1949-66; comptroller Gen. Pub. Utilities Corp., N.Y.C. Served with USNR, 1944-46. Home: Clarksville Rd Princeton, NJ 08540. Office: 80 Pine St New York City NY 10005

HOLCOMBE, WILLIAM JONES, mfg. co. exec.; b. Piedmont, S.C., Sept. 7, 1925; s. Hovey W. and Hattie (Jones) H.; B.S., Rutgers U., 1952, grad. student, 1953-54; m. Judith Boyce, June 7, 1945; children—Judith M., Cheryl L. Controller Robins engrs. div. Hewitt-Robins, Inc., N.Y.C., 1946-56; v.p., gen. mgr., dir. Adsco Industries, Inc., Buffalo, 1956-58; v.p., chief financial officer, dir. Yuba Consol. Industries, Inc., San Francisco, 1958-60; v.p. chief financial officer Gen. Metals Corp., 1961-62, group v.p., operating gen. mgr., 1963-65; pres., chief exec. officer, dir. De Laval Turbine Inc., Princeton, N.J., 1966—; chief exec. officer, dir. De Laval Turbine Can. Ltd., Toronto, 1966—; dir. N.J. Nat. Bank, Trenton. Mem. adv. council Rider Coll., 1967—. Served with USNR, 1943-46. Mem. Newcomen Soc. N.Am., Trenton- Mercer C. of C. (bd. dirs. 1967—). Clubs: Trenton Country, Engineers (Trenton); Nassau (Princeton); Canadian (N.Y.C.). Home: 71 Independence Dr Princeton NJ 08540 Office: PO Box 2072 Princeton NJ 08540

HOLDAM, JAMES VANCE, Jr., mfg. co. exec.; b. Chattanooga, Sept. 20, 1917; s. James Vance and Anna (Forstner) H.; B.S., U. Chattanooga, 1938; M.S., U. Mich., 1939; m. Claire Warner, May 28, 1938; children—Nancy (Mrs. Donald Jacobson), James Vance III, Margaret, Gwendolyn Ann. Staff mem. Mass. Inst. Tech., 1941-46; v.p. Lab. for Electronics. Inc., Boston, 1946-53, 57-61, dir., 1948-61; v.p. Tracerlab, Inc., Waltham, Mass., 1953-57, Dresser Industries, Inc., Dallas, 1961-64; exec. v.p., dir. Scantlin Electronics, Inc., Los Angeles, 1964-65, pres., dir., 1965-70; chmn., pres. Brentwood Computer, Inc., Los Angeles, 1971—; dir. Ovivo, Santa Barbara, Cal. Recipient Certificate Merit, Dept. Def., 1948. Mem. Am. Inst. Aeros. and Astronautics, I.E.E.E. (sr.), Am. Phys. Soc. Home: 2155 Westridge Rd Los Angeles CA 90049 Office: 1720 Pontius Av Los Angeles CA 90025

HOLDEN, ARTHUR CORT, architect; b. N.Y. City, Nov. 29, 1890; s. Edwin B. and Alice (Cort) H.; Litt.B., Princeton U., 1912; B. of Architecture and A.M. in Economics, Columbia, 1915; m. Miriam Young, Feb. 10, 1917; children—Edwin Arthur, Jame (Mrs. Clay) (dec.), Richmond Young. Began practice of architecture, 1920; mem. Arthur C. Holden & Assos., 1920-30, Holden, McLaughlin & Assos., 1930-54; mem. Holden, Egan, Wilson & Corser, 1954-68; mem. Holden, Yang, Raemsch & Corser, 1968—; cons. architect to N.Y. State Bd. Housing, 1926; spl. cons. to Temporary Commn. to Examine and Revise Tenement House Law, 1927; dir. Architect's Small House Service Bur. to 1931; mem. bd. architects exec. com., N.Y.C. Housing Authority, 1934; spl. advisor Div. of Economic Research and Planning NRA. Mem. President's Conf. on Home Building and Home Ownership, 1931; Mayor's Com. on City Planning, 1934-38, 20th Century Fund Housing Com., 1940-41. Fellow A.I.A. (dir., chmn. N.Y. com. on apartment house awards; v.-chmn. com. on postwar reconstrn.; medal honor N.Y. chpt. 1957); pres. N.Y. Chapter, 1944-45; exec. com. 1945-47; Medal of Honor, awarded by N.Y. chpt., 1957; mem. N.Y. Bldg. Congress, v.p., 1936-43; chmn. land utilization com., 1933-38), N.Y. Urban League (pres. 1922-31, mem. exec. bd. to 1943); Com. on Economic Recovery; exec. board Citizens Housing Council, 1936; chmn. Conference Planning Man's Physical Environment, Princeton Bicentennial, 1947; trustee Lenox Hill Hosp., N.Y. Author: Brick Architecture of the Colonial Period in Md. and Va. 1919; Settlement Idea, 1922; Primer of Housing, 1927; Money in Motion, 1940; Sonnets for My City-An Essay on the Kinship of Art and Finance, 1965; At the Roots of the Urban Crisis, 1970; also articles dealing with homebuilding and housing. Contbr. to leading mags., Britannica and Nat. encys. Designer of Garden Plan Apts., 5 projects; architect of Queensborough Community Coll., housing projects in Jacksonville, Fla., Balt., Charleston., S.C., Dragerton, Utah, N.Y. City (4 projects), Princeton, N.J. (3 projects), 1946; reconstructed Minetta Lane "Slum", 1924. Clubs: University, Architectural League; Cosmos (Washington); Grolier, Players, Coffee House (N.Y.C.). Home: 57 E 78th St New York City NY 10021 and Quogue NY 11959 Office: 251 Park Av S New York City NY 10010

HOLDEN, CREIGHTON DAVIDSON, hotel exec.; b. Detroit, Jan. 19, 1917; s. Creighton and Belinda (Davidson) H.; B.A., Dartmouth, 1940; m. Jean Harshbarger, Mar. 24, 1941; children—Holly, Creighton Davidson, Belinda, Becky, Heather. Pres. St. Clair (Mich.) Inn & Country Club, 1946—, St. Clair North Inc. Mem. Clair Sch. Bd., 1951- 60; mem. St. Clair Planning Commn.; mem. Gov. Mich. Com. Higher Edn.; bd. dirs. Citizens for Mich., Mich. Ambassadors. Bd. overseers Hanover Inn, Dartmouth. Served with AUS, 1943-46. Decorated Purple Heart. Mem. Am. Hotel and Motel Assn. (sec., dir., chmn. resort com., pres., chmn. bd.), Michigan Tourist Council (chairman), Mich. C. of C. (chmn., dir.), Phi Gamma Delta. Clubs: Detroit Athletic; St. Clair River Country. Home: 710 Brown St St Clair MI 48079 Office: St Clair Inn St Clair MI 48079

HOLDEN, DAVID JUSTIN, educator; b. White Plains, N.Y., Dec. 16, 1911; s. Charles Emerson and Edna (Morgenroth) H.; student Haverford Coll., 1930-32; S.B., Harvard, 1935, postgrad., 1938-41; postgrad. fellow, Julliard Sch. Music, 1935-37; m. Margaret Cordelia

Harold, June 27, 1939; children— Lawrence, Jill. Instr. Boston Conservatory Music, 1938-43; mem. faculty Mt. Holyoke Coll., 1943—, prof. music, 1963—; critic, annotator Chautauguan (N.Y.) Daily, 1949- 68; instr. Syracuse U., summers 1960-67; judge Epstein Found. Music awards, 1956—. Trustee Lincoln Sch., Providence, 1959-69. Recipient NBC Music Guild Chamber Music award 1936, Knight prize Harvard, 1939, Cleve. Orch. award, 1942. Mem. Music Tchrs. Nat. Assn., Coll. Music Soc. Mem. Soc. Friends. Composer: Symphony in G, 1950; String Quartet in E, 1936; String Quartet in D, 1951; Cantata on Appalachian Christmas Carols, 1950; Passacaglia, 1952; Toccata for Orchestra, 1952; Choral Symphony for Chorus and Orchestra, 1971. Home: 61 Silver St South Hadley MA 01075

HOLDEN, DONALD ARCHER, ret. shipbldg. co. exec.; b. Reading, Mass., Apr. 7, 1910; s. Archer Harvey and Alice Edith (Wickens) H.; B.S., Mass. Inst. Tech., 1931, M.S., 1932; m. Eleanor Watson Holden, Sept. 4, 1937; 1 son, Hugh Warren. With Newport News Shipbldg. and Dry Dock Co. (Va.), 1934-70, prodn. mgr., 1957- 59, v.p., prodn. mgr., 1959-60, exec. v.p., 1960-64, pres., 1964-69, chmn. bd., 1965-70. Exec. dir. Council Ind. Colls. in Va., 1971—; mem. Va. Commn. Higher Edn. Facilities. Mem. council U. Va. Tayloe Murphy Inst.; alumni mem. corp. Mass. Inst. Tech.; mem. corp. devel. com. Mass. Inst. Tech.; v.p., trustee Mariners' Mus., Newport News, Va.; trustee Va. Found. for Ind. Colls. Fellow Am. Soc. M.E.; mem. Am. Soc. Naval Engrs., Nat. Security Indsl. Assn. (past exec. com., trustee), Navy League, Soc. Naval Architects and Marine Engrs. (pres. 1967, 68), Propeller Club U.S. (past pres. Port of Newport News, nat. v.p. Middle Atlantic region 1960), Newcomen Soc., Chi Epsilon, Pi Tau Sigma. Clubs: Farmington Country (Charlottesville, Va.); James River Country (dir.) (Newport News). Home: 201 Montvue Dr Charlottesville VA 22901 Office: 1022 W Main St Charlottesville VA 22903

HOLDEN, HERBERT F., business exec. Controller Friden Inc., San Leandro, Cal. Office: 2350 Washington Av San Leandro CA 94577*

HOLDEN, J. MICHAEL C., physician; b. Liverpool, Eng., June 20, 1928; s. John Almond and Doris (Heaton) H.; M.R.C.S., L.R.C.P., U. Liverpool, 1951, D.P.M., 1956; M.R.C.P., U. Glasgow, 1964; M.D., N.Y.U., 1967; m. Una Philomena O'Neill, Apr. 3, 1956; children—Cormac, Caitriona, Niall, Niamh. Cons. psychol. medicine Liverpool Regulatory Hosp. Bd., also teaching cons. U. Liverpool, 1961-64; clin. dir. Mo. Inst. Psychiatry, St. Louis, 1968-69; physician supt. St. Louis State Hosp. Complex, 1969—; asso. prof. psychiatry U. Mo. Med. Sch. Served to maj. Royal Army Med. Corps. Mem. Royal Soc. Medicine, Royal Medico-Psychol. Assn., A.A.A.S., Soc. Biol. Psychiatry, Assn. Am. Profs., St. Louis Med. Soc. Mem. Ch. of Eng. Mason. Home: Nesfield Hall Nesfield Ilkley Yorkshire England Office: 5400 Arsensal St St Louis MO 63139

HOLDEN, JAMES STUART, U.S. dist. judge; b. Bennington, Vt., Jan. 29, 1914; s. Edward Henry and Mary Anstiss (Thayer) H.; A.B., Dartmouth, 1935; LL.B., Union U., 1938; m. Helen Elizabeth Vetal, Mar. 3, 1941; children—Susan Spaeth, Peter Vetal, James Stuart. Admitted to Vt. bar, 1938; practice in Bennington, 1938-41, 46-48; state's atty., Bennington County, 1946-48; chmn. Vt. Pub. Service Commn., 1948-49; superior judge State 1949-56, asso. justice Supreme Ct. Vt., 1956-63, chief justice, 1963-72; U.S. dist. judge for Dist. fof Vt., 1972—. Chmn. Vt. Statutory Revision Commn., 1957-62; chmn. provisional con. to establish Nat. Center for State Cts., 1971. Trustee Vt. State Library, 1959—. Served to maj., 43d Inf. Div., AUS, 1941- 46. Mem. 43d Inf. Div. Vets. Assn. (past comdr.), Am., Vt. bar assns., Conf. Chief Justices (vice chmn. 1969-70, chmn., 1971—), Am. Judicature Soc., Inst. Jud. Adminstrn. Protestant Episcopalian. Home: North Bennington VT 05257

HOLDEN, JOHN BERNARD, educator; b. DeCliff, O., Sept. 18, 1910; s. William Edward and Elsie Mae (Kohn) H.; B.S., Ohio U., 1932; M.A., Ohio State U., 1936, Ph.D., 1955; m. A. Alberta Stegemiller, Feb. 2, 1941; children—John Bernard, Peggy Ann, Charles Eugene. Prin., tchr. Ohio schs., 1932-37; head history and speech dept. Wyoming (O.) schs., 1937-41; dir. adult edn., tchr. speech and history, Hamilton, O., 1941-50; cons. continuing edn. Mich. State U., 1950-56; specialist gen. adult edn. U.S. Office Edn., 1956-58; dir. Grad. Sch., U.S. Dept. of Agr., 1958—. Pres. World Federalist Ednl. Fund, 1968—. Served with AUS, 1944-46. Recipient Spl. Merit award Nat. Assn. Pub. Sch. Adult educators, 1955; Meritorious award Adult Edn. Assn. Mich., 1956; Distinguished Alumni award Ohio U., 1964; Delbert Clark adult edn. award, 1966. Mem. Ohio Tchrs. Speech Assn. (past pres.), Ohio Adult Edn. Assn. (past pres.), Adult Edn. Assn. Mich. (past pres.), Adult Edn. Assn. U.S. (exec. bd., past chmn. nat. pub. relations and membership, pres. 1964-65), United World Federalists (chmn. Washington chpt. 1958-60), Phi Delta Kappa, Kappa Kappa Tau, Tau Kappa Alpha. Clubs: Cosmos, Internat. (Washington). Author: Score Card for Community Adult Education Program, 1951. Contbr. chpt. to Handbook on Adult Education. Contbr. articles edn. publs. Home: 510 N St S W Washington DC 20024

HOLDEN, RAYMOND THOMAS, physician; b. Washington, Apr. 11, 1904; s. Raymond Thomas and Celeste Selma (Moritz) H.; student U. Notre Dame, 1922-24; M.D., Georgetown U., 1928; m. Mary Lightle, Oct. 9, 1958; 1 dau., Mary Elliott. Intern, Providence Hosp., Washington, 1928-29, asso., then attending obstetrician and gynecologist, 1932-56, cons., 1956—; resident Columbia Hosp. for Women, Washington, 1929-30, asst., asso., attending staff, 1933, chief med. staff, 1952-54, 62-64, acting adminstr., 1958-59; preceptorship Dr. R.Y. Sullivan, Georgetown U. Sch. Medicine, 1930-32; asso., attending obstetrics and gynecology D.C. Gen Hosp., 1932-47; asst., asso., also attending obstetrics and gynecology Georgetown U. Hosp., 1933—; from clin. instr. to clin. prof. obstetrics and gynecology Georgetown U. Sch. Medicine, 1933—; cons. obstetrics and gynecology U.S. Naval Hosp., Bethesda, Md., 1948—. Bd. dirs., exec. com. Tb Assn. D.C., 1947- 49; bd. dirs., exec. com. D.C. div. Am. Cancer Soc., 1950-56; mem. Health Facilities Planning Council, Washington, 1964—, bd. dirs. D.C. chpt. A.R.C. Trustee Columbia Hosp. for Women. Served to capt., M.C., USNR, 1942-46; rear adm. Res. Diplomate Am. Bd. Obstetrics and Gynecology. Fellow A.C.S., Am. Coll. Obstetrics and Gynecologists; mem. A.M.A. (D.C. mem. Ho. Dels., 1952-68, chmn. com. on human reporduction 1964-68, trustee 1968—), D.C. Med. Soc. (chmn. exec. bd. 1951-52, pres. 1946-47), Washington Gynecology Soc. (sec. 1950-54, pres. 1956), Am. Legion, Alpha Omega Alpha. Club: Chevy Chase. Home: 5120 Watson St N W Washington DC 20016 Office: 1835 I St N W Washington DC 20006

HOLDEN, REUBEN ANDRUS, coll. pres.; b. Louisville, Sept. 2, 1918; s. Reuben Andrus and Grace (Morgan) H.; grad. Asheville Sch., 1936, B.A., Yale, 1940, M.A., 1948, Ph.D., 1951; m. Elizabeth C. Walker, June 23, 1951; children—Grace Morgan, Reuben Andrus, 5th, George, Mary. Asst. to dean of coll. Yale, 1946-47, asst. to pres., 1947-52, sec. of univ., 1953-71; pres. Warren Wilson Coll., Swannanea, N.C., 1971—. Trustee Conn. Savings Bank, 1955-71. Civilian aide to sec. army, 1962-68. Bd. dirs. New Haven YMCA (v.p. 1960-71), Community Progress, Inc., 1962-65 (pres. 1965-68). Trustee Asheville Sch., 1948—, Hopkins Grammar Sch., 1952-71, Edward W. Hazen Found. (chmn.), Jane Coffin Child Fund Med. Research, Charles A. Coffin Fund, Foote Sch., 1964-71 (pres. 1968-71). Served with AUS, 1941-46; CBI. Decorated Bronze Star (U.S.); Spl. Breast of Yun Hwei (China); Distinguished Civilian award. Mem. Culinary Inst. Am. (chmn. 1968-70), Yale-in-China Assn. (pres.), Mory's Assn., Phi Beta Kappa, Zeta Psi, Skull and Bones. Mem. Ch. of Christ. Clubs: Yale (N.Y.C.); Graduates (New Haven). Home: Warren Wilson Coll Swannanea NC 28778

HOLDEN, WILLIAM DOUGLAS, surgeon; b. Pittsfield, Mass., Aug. 25, 1912; s. Harry and Katherine C. (MacInnis) H.; A.B., Cornell U., 1934, M.D., 1937; m. Janet Cobb, Dec. 28, 1936; children—John, Frank, Katherine. Instr. surgery Case-Western Res. U. Med. Sch., 1946-47, sr. instr. surgery, 1947-48, asst. prof., 1948- 49, asso. prof., 1948-49, Oliver H. Payne prof. surgery 1950—, dir. surgery Univ. Hosps., Cleve., 1950—. Mem. Am., Central surg. assns., Soc. U. Surgeons, Soc. Vascular Surgery, Soc. Exptl. Biology and Medicine. Contbr. profl. jours. Home: 2195 Demington Dr Cleveland Heights OH 44106 Office: Lakeside Hospital Cleveland OH 44106

HOLDEN, WILLIAM FRANKLIN, motion picture actor; b. O'Fallon, Ill., Apr. 17, 1918; s. William Franklin and Mary (Ball) Beedle; student Pasadena Jr. Coll., 1937-38; m. Ardis Ankerson (Brenda Marshall), July 13, 1941; children—Peter Westfield, Scott Porter. Actor, starring in pictures: Golden Boy, 1939, Our Tour, 1939, Arizona, I Wanted Wings, 1940, Dear Ruth, 1946, Apartment for Peggy, 1947, Sunset Boulevard, 1949, Born Yesterday, 1950, Stalag 17, 1952, The Moon is Blue, 1953, Executive Suite, 1953, Bridge at Toko-ri, 1954, Country Girl, 1954, Love is A Many Splendored Thing, 1955, Picnic, 1956, Proud and Profane, 1956, Toward Unknown, 1956, Bridge On The River Kwai, 1957, The Key, 1957, Horse Soldiers, 1958, Counterfeit Traitor, 1962, World of Suzy Wong, Satan Never Sleeps, The Lion, also The Longest Day, Alvarez Kelly, Casino Royal, 1967, The Devil's Brigade, 1968, The Wild Bunch, The Christmas Tree; v.p. George W. Gooch Labs., Los Angeles; pres. Toluca Prodns. Corp. Commr. Parks and Recreation, City of Los Angeles. Recipient Look Mag. award, best actor, 1953, Internat. Film. Exhibitors' award, 1954. Mem. Motion Picture Acad. Arts and Scis. (bd.; named best actor 1953), Motion Industry Council; Star of the Year award, Theatre Owners of Am., 1956. Advisor to Hollywood Coordinating Com. Office: Gordean-Friedman Agency Inc 9229 Sunset Blvd Los Angeles CA 90069

HOLDEN, WILLIS SPRAGUE, coll. prof., journalist; b. Grand Rapids, Mich., Jan. 3, 1909; s. Charles Wayne and Marie (Sprague) H.; grad. Grand Rapids Jr. Coll., 1927; A.B., U. of Mich., 1930; A.M., Columbia, 1932; m. Sheila (Edna) Richart, May 24, 1934. Sports space writer Grand Rapids Herald, 1926; coll. corr. for newspapers, 1926-29; staff writer Time, news mag., N.Y.C. 1930; theater and motion picture editor San Francisco Argonaut, 1932-36, asso. editor, 1933-34, mng. editor, 1934-36; editorial writer Akron (O.) Beacon Jour., 1936-40; editorial writer. Detroit Free Press, 1940-46, columnist, 1942-46; prof. journalism Wayne State U., 1946—, chmn. dept. journalism, 1949—; on sabbatical leave in Australia, 1956-57, 66; 29th Arthur Norman Smith lectr. in journalism U. Melbourne, 1966. Awarded Fulbright Grant, U.S. State Department, to make study Australian daily met. newspapers, 1956-57, to study indsl. arbitration-conciliation systems in Australia, 1966. Ford Found grant, 1966. Recipient sr. class Rhetoric medaal, U. Mich., 1930. Mem. Assn. for Edn. in Journalism, Internat. Press Inst., Nat. Conf. Editorial Writers, also Am. Assn. U. Pros., Am. Soc. Journalism Sch. Adminstrs., Mich. acad. Sci., Arts and Letters, Australian Polit. Sci. Assn., Friends Detroit Pub. Library, Detroit Hist. Assn., Am. Civil P.E.N., Sigma Delta Chi. Clubs: Torch. Schoolmen's, Press (Detroit); Wayne State University Press (Detroit). Author: Australia Goes To Press, 1961; also articles mags. and newspapers. Address: Journalism Dept. Wayne State U Detroit MI 48202.

HOLDER, CALE JAMES, judge U.S. Dist. Ct.; b. Lawrenceville, Ill., Apr. 5, 1912; s. John Wesley and Martha (Glaser) H.; LL.B., Benjamin Harrison Law Sch., 1934; J.D., Ind. Law Sch., 1938; m. Martha Mae Stanton, Apr. 16, 1942; 1 dau., Martha Sue. Admitted to Ind. bar, 1934, practiced in Indpls., 1934-54; judge U.S. Dist. Ct. So. Dist. Ind., 1954—; dep. prosecutor 19th jud. circuit Marion Co. (Ind.) Criminal Ct., 1940-42; spl. counsel Ind. State Personnel Bd., 1946-49; dep. atty. gen., Ind., 1953. Chmn. Rep. State Central Com., Ind., 1949-52, mem. Rep. Nat. Com., 1952. Served as lt. USNR, 1942-46, comdg. officer naval base, island comdr. Wallis Islands, also legal officer, judge adv., gen. ct. martial bd., New Hebrides Islands. Mem. Marion Co. Rep. Vets. World War II (pres. 1946- 47, dir. 1947-54), Lawyers Assn., Indpls. Legal Soc., Am. Legion, VFW, Am., Ind., Indpls. (sec., 1948-52, exec. com. 1953-54) bar assns., Sigma Delta Kappa. Home: 1816 Remington Pl Indianapolis IN 46227 Office: Federal Bldg Indianapolis IN 46204

HOLDER, GEOFFREY, dancer; b. Port-of-Spain, Trinidad, 1930; student native dances in W. Indies; m. Carmen de Lavallade. Tchr., Katherine Dunham Sch., N.Y.C.; appeared in House of Flowers, N.Y.C., then Met. Opera Ballet, 1955; formed own company, choreographing works based on ethnic sources. Guggenheim fellow, 1957. Address: 164 W 88th St New York City NY*

HOLDER, HAROLD DOUGLAS, communications co. exec.; b. Anniston, Ala., June 25, 1931; s. William Chester and Lucile (Kadle) H.; student Anniston Bus. Coll., 1949, Jacksonville State U., 1954-57, Druitt Sch. Speech, 1962; m. Shirlee Stine, Apr. 5, 1971; children—Debra Marie, Harold Douglas, Robert Leonard. Dept. mgr. Sears, Roebuck & Co., Anniston, 1954-57, merchandising mgr., Atlanta, 1957-59, dir. coll. recruiting, 1959-61, dir. exec. devel. program, 1961, asst. personnel dir., 1962-63, store mgr., Cocoa, Fla., 1965-67, Ocala, Fla., 1963-65, asst. zone mgr., Atlanta, 1967-68, asst. gen. mgr. mdse., 1968- 69, sales promotion mgr. Sears in South, 1968; pres. Cunningham Drug Stores, Inc., Detroit, 1969-70, also dir.; v.p. Interstate Stores, 1971; pres. Rahall Communications Corp., 1971- -, also dir.; dir. Miracle Inc. of Bevard Co., Tara Groves, Inc., 2001, Inc., E.R. Miller and Assos. Chmn. United Appeal, Ocala, Fla., 1964, Cocoa, Fla., 1966, Heart Fund Drive, Ocala, 1964, Marion (Fla.) Com. of 100. Bd. dirs. So. Coll. Placement Assn., Marion A.R.C., Opera Arts Assn. Served with USMC, 1950- 53. Recipient Distinguished Service award Marion County 4-H Club, 1965; named among The Outstanding Young Men of Am., U.S. Jr. C. of C., 1966, Outstanding Personality of the South, 1967. Mem. C. of C. (chmn. beautification com., retail bus. com.), St. Petersburg Commerce Club. Episcopalian. Club: Detroit Athletic. Home: 5050 62d Av S St Petersburg FL 33715 Office: PO Box 14000 St Petersburg FL 33733

HOLDERNESS, HAYWOOD DAIL, telephone co. exec.; b. Tarboro, N.C., July 30, 1909; s. George Allan and Harriet (Howard) H.; A.B., U. N.C., 1931; M.B.A., U. Pa., 1933; m. Nancy Burton Braswell, Mar. 19, 1938; children—Haywood Dail, Jr., James Braswell, Zelle H. Jester (Mrs. John Carlton III), Nancy DuVal, Russell Braswell. With Carolina Tel. & Tel. Co., Tarboro, 1933—, sec., treas., 1937-41, v.p., sec., treas., 1941-57, pres., 1957—; dir. Federal Res. Bank Richmond, Va., United Utilities, Inc., Rocky Mount Investment Co., Sero Corp. Chmn. United Fund, Tarboro, 1962-63; mem. Tarboro City Sch. Bd., 1963-69. Trustee St. Andrews Presbyn. Coll., Laurinburg, N.C.; bd. trustees Union Theol. Sem. Mem. U.S. (pres. 1966-67), N.C.; (past. pres.) ind. telephone assns., U.N.C. Alumni Assn. (past pres.). Presbyn. (elder). Rotarian. Home: 805 S Howard Circle Tarboro NC 27886 Office: 122 E St James St Tarboro NC 27886

HOLDERNESS, HOWARD, ins. exec.; b. Tarboro, N.C., Nov. 2, 1902; s. George Allen and Harriet (Howard) H.; A.B., U. N.C., 1923; M.B.A., Harvard, 1925; LL.D., U. N.C. at Chapel Hill., U. N.C. at Greensboro, 1969; m. Adelaide Fortune, Apr. 4, 1936; children—Adelaide Lucinda, Howard, Alexandra Fortune, Richard Thurston, Pamela Louisa. Chmn. bd. Jefferson Standard Life Ins. Co., Greenboro, N.C., also Jefferson-Pilot Corp.; dir. Duke Power Co., Burlington Industries, Carolina Tel. & Tel. Co., Pilot Life Ins. Co.; trustee Wachovia Realty Investments. Civilian aide to sec. of army for N.C., 1958-62. Recipient citation for distinguished citizenship N.C. Citizens Assn., 1970. Mem. Inst. Life Ins. (dir.; mem. exec. com. 1957-60, chmn. 1959), Life Ins. Assn. Am. (dir. 1957-60). Home: 2000 Granville Rd Greensboro NC 27408 Office: PO Box 21008 Greensboro NC 27420

HOLDERNESS, RICHARD C., wholesale grocery exec.; b. Denver, Nov. 12, 1907; s. Chauncey and Grace (Bowman) H.; B.A., U. Colo., 1929; m. Darlene Alberta Lemke, Oct. 11, 1940; children—Richard A., Ann D., Deborah D. Reporter, drama editor Denver Post, 1929-36; with Certified Grocers of Cal., Ltd., 1936—, now sr. v.p., sec.; sec., dir. Grocers Equipment Co.; sec. Grocers & Merchants Ins. Service, Sparton Grocers, Inc. Bd. dirs., past pres. Los Angeles Food Employers Council, Indsl. Council City Commerce, Cal. Bd. dirs., past pres. Rio Hondo Boys Club. Served to maj. USAAF, 1942-46. Mem. Newcomen Soc., Sigma Delta Chi, Sigma Chi. Republican. Conglist. Rotarian. Club: Los Angeles Press. Home: 14046 Mar Vista St Whittier CA 90602 Office: 2601 S Eastern Dr Los Angeles CA 90040

HOLDHEIM, WILLIAM WOLFGANG, educator; b. Berlin, Germany, Aug. 4, 1926; s. Hugo and Margarete (Lehmann) H.; came to U.S., 1947, naturalized, 1953; B.A. summa cum laude, U. Cal. at Los Angeles, 1949, M.A., 1951; Ph.D., Yale, 1956; m. Evelyn M. Stanislawski, Sept. 6, 1954; children—Sylvia, Robert. Instr., Ohio State U., 1955-57; instr. Brandeis U., 1957-58, asst. prof., 1958- 61, asso. prof., 1961-64; prof. Washington U., 1964-69; prof., chmn. comparative lit. Cornell U., Ithaca, N.Y., 1969—. Mem. Phi Beta Kappa, Pi Delta Phi. Author: Benjamin Constant, 1961; Theory and Practice of the Novel, 1968; Der Justizirrtum als literarische Problematik, 1969. Home: 15 Uptown Village Ithaca NY 14850

HOLDING, LEWIS ROYALL, banker; b. Smithfield, N.C., Sept. 29, 1927; s. Robert Powell and Maggie Louise (Brown) H.; B.S., U. N.C., 1950; M.S., Harvard Graduate School of Business Administration, 1952; m. Carolyn Ann Short, 1959; children—Carolyn Royall, Carmen Price. Pres. First-Citizens Bank & Trust Co., Smithfield, N.C. Served as 2d lt. USAAF, 1952-53. Home: Raleigh NC Office: 20 E Martin St Raleigh NC

HOLDT, ROY HOWARD, mfg. co. exec.; b. Edgewood, Md., Nov. 27, 1920; s. Jacob S. and Francis (Hansen) H.; student Dyke Bus. Coll., 1941, Cleve. State U., 1947; m. Marilyn S. Schaffer, Sept. 29, 1945; children—Linda D., Douglas M. With Lake Erie Chem. Co., Cleve., 1938-40; with Apex Elec. Mfg. Co., 1941-56; div. controller White Consol. Industries, Inc., Cleve., 1956-58, corporate controller, 1958-61, v.p., controller, 1961-64, v.p. finance, 1964-67, sr. v.p., 1967-69, exec. v.p., dir., 1969—. Served with AUS, 1942-45. Mem. Nat. Assn. Accountants. Club: Treasurers (Cleve.). Home: 12700 Lake Av Lakewood OH 44107 Office: 11770 Berea Rd Cleveland OH 44111

HOLE, FRANK, educator; b. Oak Park, Ill, Nov. 13, 1931; s. Andrew Frank and Leta (Arnold) H.; B.A., Cornell Coll. of Ia., 1953; postgrad. Harvard, fall 1957-58; M.A., U. Chgo., 1958; Ph.D., 1961; m. Barbara Adkins, Aug. 20, 1954 (div. Sept. 1970); children—Steven, Robert. Asst. prof. anthropology Rice U., Houston, 1961-65, asso. prof., 1965-68, prof., 1968—; dir. archeol. projects, Iran, 1961, 63, 65, 68-69; archeologist Smithsonian Instn. project, Oaxaca, Mexico, summer 1966, research asso. U. Md. archeol. project, summer 1967. NSF fellow, 1959-60, U. Tehran (Iran), post-doctoral fellow, 1961-62, grantee, 1963-64, 65-66, 66, 68-70. Served with AUS, 1953-55. Fellow Am. Anthrop. Assn.; mem. Soc. Am. Archaeology, A.A.A.S., Prehistoric Soc. (Eng.), Sigma Xi. Author: (with Robert F. Heizer) An Introduction to Prehistoric Archeology, 1965, 69, Spanish edit., 1969. Contbr profl. jours. Office: Dept Anthropology Rice U Houston TX 77001

HOLE, JOHN WESLEY, church exec.; b. Burns, Kan., Aug. 19, 1903; s. David B. and Lucretia E. (Storer) H.; LL.D. (hon.), Samuel Huston Coll., Austin, Tex., 1947; m. Velma E. Edwards, Sept. 20, 1924; children—John Wesley, Marilyn (Mrs. William F. Peer). Purchasing agt. Hawthorne Furniture Shops, Los Angeles, 1925-28; office mgr. L.C. Phenix Co., Los Angeles, 1928-34; exec. sec.-treas. So. Cal.-Ariz. Conf., United Methodist Ch., 1934—; sec. Gen. Conf., United Meth. Ch., 1964-68, 70—, mem. bd. pensions, 1948—, v.p. div. nat. missions, 1960-64, mem. Western Jurisdictional Conf., 1939-68. Bd. dirs. Meth. Hosp., Arcadia, Cal., 1955-65. Home: 3890 Valleylights Dr Pasadena CA 91107 Office: 5250 Santa Monica Blvd Los Angeles CA 90029

HOLE, WILLIAM EDWARD, Sr., exec.; born Versailles, O., Aug. 25, 1899; s. Harrison B. and Ottillie (Engelken) H.; student Mercersburg Acad., 1917-18; A.B., Princeton, 1922; student Harvard Law Sch., 1924-25; m. Dorothy Coppock, June 25, 1925; children—Jean Louise (Mrs. W.I. Thieme), William Edward, Susan Jane (Mrs. R. L. Brewer), Barbara Kell (Mrs. W.D. Brewer). Joined the Am. Aggregates Corp., 1927, successively sec., sec.-treas., exec. v.p., 1932-51, dir., 1945- -, pres., 1951-64, chmn. bd., 1964-69, chmn. exec. com., 1969—, mem. exec. com., 1950—; pres. Greenville Nat. Bank, 1957—. Past trustee Wayne Hosp. Member Nat. Sand and Gravel Assn. (past pres. and dir.), Am., Ohio, Darke County bar assns. Ohio C. of C. (dir. 1959—, exec. com. 1964). Home: 403 N Broadway Greenville OH 45331 Office: Corner of Garst Av and Av B Greenville OH 45331

HOLE, WILLIAM EDWARD, Jr., mfg. co. exec.; b. Greenville, O., July 2, 1927; s. William Edward and Dorothy (Coppock) H.; B.S. in Mech. Engring., U. Mich., 1951; m. Gloria Beth Shiverdecker, June 24, 1951; children—William Jeffrey, Julie Ann. With Am. Aggregates Corp., Greenville, 1951—, v.p., 1957-64, exec. v.p., 1964-69, pres., 1969—, also dir., mem. exec. com.; dir. Greenville Nat. Bank. Bd. dirs. Greenville Community Chest, 1955-57. Served with USAAF, 1945-46. Mem. Nat. (bd. dirs. 1964—, exec. com. 1965—, v.p. 1970-71), Ohio (bd. dirs. 1956—, pres. 1958-59), sand and gravel assns., Ohio (bd. dirs. 1971—), Greenville (bd. dirs. 1962-69, pres. 1967) chambers commerce. Republican. Conglist. Home: Box 122 Greenville OH 45331 Office: Drawer 160 Greenville OH 45331

HOLE, WILLIAM GEORGE, air filter co. exec.; b. Edmonton, Alta., Can., Dec. 20, 1910; s. Harry and Ann (King) H.; B.Sc. Civil Engring., U. Alta., 1933; m. Jean Morrison, May 30, 1939; children—Katherine Ann (Mrs. J. Barrie Gilbert), James D., Margaret

J. (Mrs. B. Luttmer). Cons. engr. T. Pringle & Son, Montreal, Que., Can., 1941-43; product mgr. Darling Bros., Ltd., Montreal, 1943-51; gen. mgr. Am. Air Filter of Can., Ltd., Montreal, 1951-69, chmn., 1969—. Mem. Am. Soc. Heating, Refrigerating and Air Conditioning Engrs. (pres. 1969-70, Distinguished Service award 1965), Engring. Inst. Can., Profl. Engrs. Que. Club: Town of Mount Royal Curling (pres.). Home: 76 Balfour Av Montreal 304 Quebec Canada Office: 400 Stinson Blvd Montreal 379 Quebec Canada

HOLFORD, FRANCIS DELBERT, meat packing co. exec.; b. El Dorado, Kan., Oct. 8, 1913; s. Orville and Minnie (Clark) H.; A.B., Washburn Coll., Topeka, 1935; M.B.A., Stanford, 1940; m. Mary Ellen Goodwin, June 23, 1936; children—Ann (Mrs. Roger G. Mayer), Margaret (Mrs. Thomas B. Cummins), Thomas. Mgr., Swanson & Holford, Topeka, 1935-38; audit mgt. Price Waterhouse & Co., Los Angeles, 1940-53; controller Oscar Mayer & Co., Madison, Wis., 1953—, v.p. 1964—. Past pres., bd. dirs. United Community Chest; past mem. exec. bd. Four Lakes council Boy Scouts Am.; bd. dirs. A.R.C. Served to lt. USNR, 1942-45. C.P.A., Cal., Wis. Mem. Am. Inst. C.P.A.'s, Wis. Soc. C.P.A.'s, Am. Accounting Assn., Financial Execs. Inst. (past dir. Milw.), Am. Meat Inst. (past chmn. accounting com.). Clubs: Maple Bluff Country (past pres., treas., dir.); Rotary (past v.p., dir.).

HOLGATE, RONALD CLARE, actor, baritone; b. Aberdeen, S.D., May 26, 1937; s. Clare Hartley and Helen (Fishbeck) H.; student Northwestern U., 1955-58; student drama New Eng. Conservatory Music, 1958; studied under Lotte Lehman, Boris Goldovsky, Hermanus Baer, Alvina Krause, John Berggren; m. Dorothy Collins, Dec. 21, 1966; children—Deborah, Elizabeth, Melissa. Operatic debut in La Traviata, New Eng. Opera; mem. touring co. Rigoletto, 1960, Don Giovanni, 1961, La Boheme, 1965, Don Pasquale, 1966; stage appearance include Hobo (off Broadway), 1961, Milk and Honey, 1962, Sweet Charity, 1966 (both Broadway); also performed in Sweet Charity, Las Vegas, 1968, 1967, Broadway; gave 2 concerts, Town Hall, N.Y.C., 1969. Weyerhauser scholar Met. Opera; recipient Tony award 1967. Mem. Muscular Dystrophy Assn. Am. Club: Lambs (N.Y.C.). Home: 35 Hering Rd Montvale, NJ 07645.

HOLGUIN, ALFONSO HUDSON, physician; b. El Paso, Tex., Apr. 3, 1931; s. Alfonso and Effie (Hudson) H.; B.A., Tex. Western Coll., 1953; M.D., U. Tex., 1957; M.P.H., Harvard, 1964; m. Irby Hanna Spring, Sept. 12, 1954; children— Laura Marie, Mark Hudson, Theresa Lynn, Carol, Paul, Stephen. Intern, USPHS Hosp., Seattle, 1957-58; respiratory virus research, lab. br. USPHS, Berkeley, Cal., 1958-59, polio virus research 1959-62, asst. to chief lab. br., 1962-63, asst. chief Tb br., 1964-65; chief Tb br., Communicable Disease Center, USPHS, Atlanta, 1965-69, dir. state and community service div., 1969—. Mem. A.M.A., Assn. Mil. Surgeons, U.S., Am. Pub. Health Assn., USPHS Commd. Officers Assn., Tau Kappa Epsilon, Phi Rho Sigma, Alpha Omega Alpha. Author papers in field. Home: 2408 Henderson Mill Ct NE Atlanta, GA 30329. Office: 1600 Clifton Rd NE Atlanta GA 30333

HOLIDAY, HARRY, steel co. exec.; b. Pitts., July 2, 1923; s. Harry and Charlotte (Rutherford) H.; B.S. in Metall. Engring., U. Mich., 1949; m. Kathlyn Collins Watson, Sept. 6, 1947; children—Edith, Harry III, Albert. Metallurgist, Armco Steel Corp., Middletown, O., 1949-52, spl. assignment, 1952-55, asst. to supt., 1955-57, blast furnace supt., 1957- 59, asst. gen. supt., 1959-64, gen. supt., 1964-66, dir. raw materials, 1966-67, v.p. operatons, 1967-68, v.p. steel group, 1968—. Active YMCA, Boy Scouts Am.; mem. Civic Assn. Served with AUS, 1943-46. Mem. Am. Inst. M.E. (Blast Furance award 1959), Assn. Iron and Steel Engrs., Am. Iron and Steel Inst. Home: 1616 Schirm Dr Middletown OH Office: 703 Curtis St Middletown OH 45042

HOLIFIELD, CHET, congressman; b. Mayfield, Ky., Dec. 3, 1903; s. Ercie Vira and Bessie Lee (O'Brady) H.; ed. in pub. schs. of Ark.; A.A. (hon.), East Los Angeles Coll., 1962; LL.D., Lynchburg Coll., 1964, Whittier Coll., 1966; m. Vernice Caneer, Sept. 14, 1922; children—Louis Anita (Mrs. William Mulholland), Betty Lee (Mrs. Robert Feldman), Willa Mae (Mrs. Donald Douglas), JoAnn (Mrs. Robert Ward). Began as retailer, 1920; sec. Caneer Co., Inc., 1936—; chmn. Los Angeles County Dem. Central Com. 51st Dist., 1934-38; chmn. Cal. State Central Com., 12th Congl. Dist., 1938-40; mem. 78th to 92d Congresses, 19th Cal. Congl. Dist., mem. joint com. on atomic energy, 1946—, chmn., 1961-62, 65-66, 69-70, vice chmn., 1963-64, 67-68, chmn. govt. operations com., also house mil. operations subcom.; mem. com. standards of ofcl. conduct; vice chmn. Commn. on Govt. Procurement, 1970-71; congl. adviser delegations to numerous Confs. atomic energy, disarmament. Mem. Pres.'s Spl. Evaluation Commn. on Atomic Bomb Tests at Bikini Atoll, 1946; mem. Commn. on Orgn. Exec. Br. Govt.; del. Democratic Nat. Convs. 1940, 1944, 48, 52, 56, 60, 64. Mem. Christian Ch. Moose. Home: 2001 Lincoln Av Montebello CA 90640 Office: Pico Rivera CA 90660 also Rayburn Bldg Washington DC 20510

HOLL, JOHN S., bus. exec.; b. St. Paul, 1905. Dir., former chmn. bd. Dayton Rogers Mfg. Co.; dir. Whirlpool Corp., Gould Nat. Battery, St. Paul First Nat. Bank. Home: 100 Imperial Dr W St Paul MN 55118 Office: 850 Arcade St St Paul MN 55106

HOLLADAY, HARLAN, educator, artist; b. Greenville, Mo., Dec. 10, 1925; s. Franklin and Mae (Croy) H.; B.S. in Edn., S.E. Mo. State Coll., 1949; student Washington U., St. Louis, 1947- 49; M.A., U. Ia., 1951; Ph.D., Cornell U., 1966; m. Elsie Ruffena Calbert, Jan. 27, 1950; children—Joan Adrian, Carol Lisa, Jeffrey Carl. Tchr. art, dir. art Polar Bluff (Mo) pub. schs., 1951-53; tchr. art Des Moines High Sch., 1953-55; instr., then asst. prof. art U. Nev., 1955-58; teaching asso. Cornell U., 1958-59; asst. prof. drawing Cornell U. State Coll. Agr., 1959-60; mem. faculty St. Lawrence U., Canton, N.Y., 1961—, prof. fine arts, 1966—, head dept. fine arts, 1966, Flint prof., 1967; painting rep. numerous regional and nat. museums; tchr., artist-in-residence Am. Coll. Switzerland, Leysin, 1968-69. Served with AUS, 1944-46. Recipient prizes in nat. and regional exhbns. Mem. Am. Assn. U. Profs., Coll. Art Assn. Soc Archtl. Historians. Unitarian-Universalist Ch. Home: 23 Judson St Canton NY 13617

HOLLADAY, WENDELL GENE, coll. dean; b. Huntingdon, Tenn., Aug. 23, 1925; s. Carlie Bertran and Josie (Crider) H.; B.A., Vanderbilt U., 1949, M.A., 1950; Ph.D., U. Wis., 1954; m. Virginia Beatrice Mershon, Mar. 17, 1949; children—Frank Warren, Mark Wendell, Jane Mershon, Mary Joyce. Alumni Research Found. fellow U. Wis., 1950-52, NSF fellow, 1952-54; vis. research asst. Brookhaven Nat. Lab., summer 1953; mem. faculty Vanderbilt U., 1954—, prof. physics. 1962—, chmn. dept. physics and astronomy, 1965-69, dean Coll. Arts and Sci., 1969—; vis. project asso. U. Wis., summer, 1955, vis. asso. prof., 1959-60; vis. research physicist U. Cal. Radiation Lab., summer 1956. Mem. exec. com. Vanderbilt U. Employees Credit Union, 1963-66. Served with USNR, 1943-46. Fellow Am. Phys. Soc. (council S.E. sect. 1964-66, v.p. sec. 1966-67, vis. scientist 1967, pres. Southeastern Section 1967-68), A.A.A.S., Tenn. Acad. Sci. (treas. 1957-59, vis. scientist 1966-67); mem. Am. Assn. U. Profs. (pres. Vanderbilt U. chpt. 1963), Phi Beta Kappa, Sigma Xi. Unitarian (chmn. bd. dirs. 1963). Club: University (Nashville). Author: (with O. Oldenberg) Introduction to Atomic and Nuclear Physics, 4th edit., 1967; also articles. Home: 1305 Hildreth Dr Nashville TN 37215

HOLLAENDER, ALEXANDER, biophysicist; b. Samter, Germany, Dec. 19, 1898; s. Heymann and Doris (Rotholz) H.; came to U.S., 1921, naturalized, 1927; A.B., U. Wis., 1929, M.A., 1930, Ph.D., 1931, D.Sc., 1969; D.Sc., U. Vt., 1959, U. Leeds (Eng.), 1962, Marquette U., 1967; M.D., U. Chile Med. Sch., 1970; m. Henrietta Wahlert, Oct. 10, 1925. Asst. phys. chemistry U. Wis., 1929-31; NRC fellow in biol. scis., 1931-33; investigator Rockefeller Found., 1934; investigator charge radiation work NRC project Wis., 1934-37; asso. biophysicist Washington Biophysics Inst., NIH, USPHS, 1937-38, biophysicist, 1938- 41, sr. biophysicist, 1941-45, prin. biophysicist, 1945-46, head biophysicist, 1946-50; dir. biol. div. Oak Ridge Nat. Lab., 1946-66, sr. research adviser, 1967—; prof. radiation biology, U. Tenn., 1957-66; prof. biomed. scis. U. Tenn.-Oak Ridge Grad. Sch. Biomed. Scis., 1966—; dir. Archives Radiation Biology, U. Tenn., 1966—. Civilian with AEC, OSRD, Office Surgeon Gen., USN: mem. com. radiation biology, mem. com. photobiology, div. biol. and agr., chmn. and mem. subcom. radiobiology, div. phys. scis. NRC. Recipient AEC citation for outstanding service to atomic energy program, 1966, Finsen medal 5th Internat. Congress on Photobiology, 1968. Fellow Tenn. Acad. Sci., A.A.A.S., Am. Acad. Arts and Sci.; mem. Radiation Research Soc. (pres. 1954-55), Am. Soc. Cell Biology, Internat. Assn. Radiation Research, Nat. de Photobiologie (pres. 1954-60, hon. pres. 1964, exec. com. 1960-66), Genetics Soc. Am., Am. Soc. Naturalists (v.p. 1952-53), Soc. Gen. Physiologists, Nat. Acad. Sci., Genetic Assn., Soc. Gen. Physiologists, Soc. Exptl. Biology, Am. Soc. Microbiology, Am. Physiol. Soc., Environmental Mutagen Soc. (pres. 1969—). Editor: Radiation Biology (3 vols.), Vol. III, 1956; Radiation Protection and Recovery, 1960; Chemical Mutagens: Principles and Methods for their Detection, 1971. Home: 48 Outer Dr Oak Ridge TN 37830

HOLLAND, ARTHUR JOHN, mayor; b. Trenton, N.J., Oct. 24, 1918; s. Joseph F. and Helen (Groh) H.; grad. St. Francis Coll., S.I., 1954; A.B. in Social Studies, Rutgers U., M.A. in Pub. Adminstrn., 1959; m. Elizabeth Anne Jackson, July 28, 1962; children—Cynthia, Elise, Christopher, Timothy, Matthew. Research analyst Opinion Research Corp., Princeton, N.J., 1945-49; asso. dir. Princeton Research Service, 1949-51; dep. dir. Dept. Pub. Affairs, Trenton, 1951-52, Dept. Parks and Pub. Property, Trenton, 1952-55; dir. Dept. Pub. Affairs, Trenton, 1955-62; acting city mgr., Passaic, N.J., 1967; mayor, Trenton, N.J., 1959-66, 70—; past cons. Dept. Housing and Urban Devel.; cons. Nat. Inst. Pub. Affairs; adj. research prof. Urban Studies Center, Rutgers U., 1966-70, lectr. polit. sci., 1967—. Pres. Mercer County League Municipalities, 1956-57; bd. govs. Del. Valley United Fund, 1962-63, pub. div. chmn. 1954, 55, 63, 70, 71; bd. mem. Del.-Raritan Tb Respiratory Disease Assn., also Social Service Council Greater Trenton, 1960-66, local chpt. A.R.C., 1953-68, Trenton Social Service Exchange, 1951—, chmn., 1959-62; hon. bd. mem. Mercer County Soc. Prevention Cruelty to Animals, 1950-62, publicity dir., 1952; bd. dirs., 1957-58, hon. bd. dirs., 1958-62; hon. mem. Trenton Assn. of Blind, 1957—; bd. dirs., Mercer County Assn. Mental Health, 1960-66; del. White House conf. To Fulfill These Rights, 1966; N.J. v.p. and bd. mem. Del. Valley Citizens Council for Clean Air; mem. bd. Del. Valley Citizens Transp. Com. (chmn. 1969-70), Human Relations Council Serving Greater Trenton Area. Bd. dirs. Urban League Met. Trenton, Social Welfare Research Found. N.J., Inc., N.J. Social Welfare Council. Recipient Young Man of Year, Jr. C. of C., 1954; award for Interracial Justice Cath. Interracial Council New York, 1964, N.J. Americanization Conf. Citizenship award, 1964, Commendation for Meritorious Achievement Town Affiliation program Pres.'s People-to-People program. Mem. Nat. League of Cities (chmn. municipal facilities com., mem. exec. com., adv. council), N.J. League Municipalities (3d v.p.), Trenton Hist. Soc., Navy League U.S., N.A.A.C.P., Am.-Hungarian Civic Assn., Trenton Cath. Alumni Assn. (pres. 1938-39), Ancient Order Hibernians, 1st Cath. Slovak Union, Regional Conf. Elected ofcls. (past pres., mem. exec. com. 1961-66). K.C. Clubs: Rutgers of Mercer County (N.J.) (v.p. 1955-56); Mercer County Social Welfare (treas. 1956-57); Torch (Trenton); Polish-American of Central New Jersey (Trenton). Home: 138 Mercer St Trenton NJ 08611 Office: City Hall Trenton NJ 08608

HOLLAND, BEVERLY DIXON, physician; b. Cumby, Tex., June 17, 1910; s. George Washington and Ethel (Dixon) H.; B.S., U. Tex., 1932, M.D., 1934; M. Pub. Health, Johns Hopkins, 1947; m. Minnie M. Keis, 1933 (dec. Sept. 1953); children— Dorothy E., Carolyn E.; m. 2d, Eleanor M. Nicholson, June 1, 1955; children—Elizabeth A., Richard D., William George. Rotating intern Tacoma (Wash) Gen. Hosp., 1934-35; army med. officer Civilian Conservation Corps, 1935-36; health officer City of Olympia, also County of Thurston, Wash., 1936; commd. 1st lt., M.C., U.S. Army, 1937, advanced through grades to col., 1950; ret., 1956; various med. assignments U.S., Jamaica, B.W.I., 1937-42; med. officer, Puerto Rico, 1942-44; chief med. officer Wurzburg Mil. Post, 1949-50, Munich (Germany) Mil. Post, 1950-53, So. Area Command, Munich, 1953; chief occupational health br. Office Surgeon Gen., 1953-55; sec. Council on Occupational Health, A.M.A., 1956-62; dir. dept. occupational Health A.M.A., 1960-62; dir. div. profl. practice Am. Hosp. Assn., 1962-63; asso. dir. dept. clin. research Abbott Labs., 1964—; cons. in accident prevention to Surgeon Gen., Pub. Health Service, 1960-62. Sternberg medal for work in preventive medicine Army Med. Sch., 1937. Diplomate pub. health and occupational medicine Am. Bd. Preventive Medicine. Fellow Am. Pub. Health Assn.; mem. Am. Coll. Preventive Medicine, Am. Acad. Occupational Medicine. Home: 631 Forest Av Evanston IL 60202 Office: Abbott Labs North Chicago IL 60064

HOLLAND, CECELIA ANASTASIA, author; b. Henderson, Nev., Dec. 31, 1943; d. William D. and Katharine A. (Schenck) Holland; B.A., Conn. Coll., 1965; m. Robert Rood, Dec. 1969; 1 dau., Julie Ruth. Judge, Irving Stone prize, 1970. Mem. Authors Guild, Writers Guild West. Author: The Firedrake, 1966; Rakossy, 1967; Kings in Winter, 1968; Until the Sun Falls, 1969; Antichrist, 1970; The Earl, 1971; (juveniles) Ghost on the Steppe, 1969, The King's Road, 1970; (as Robert Stone Pryor) Cold Iron, 1970. Address: 2065 N Marengo Av Pasadena CA 91103

HOLLAND, CHARLES DONALD, engring. educator; b. Irdell County, N.C., Oct. 9, 1921; s. Charles Cyrus and Texie (Bess) H.; B.S. in Chem. Engring., N.C. State Coll., 1943; M.S., Tex. A. and M. U., 1949, Ph.D., 1953; m. Eleanore Marie Williams, Aug. 22, 1945; children—Thomas P. Fowler, Nancy Lee, Charlotte Claire. Jr. engr. Burlington Mills Corp., 1947-48; mem. faculty Tex. A. and M. U., 1952—, prof. chem. engring., head dept., 1964—; cons. in field, 1960—. Served to lt. USNR, 1943-46. Recipient award Former Students Assn., Tex. A. and M. U., 1955, Outstanding Prof. Coll. Engring. award, 1962. Registered profl. engr., Tex. Mem. Am. Soc. Engring Edn., Am. Chem. Soc., Am. Inst. Chem. Engrs. (Publn award S. Tex. sect. 1960, 65, 67), Am. Inst. Chemists, Tex. Soc. Profl. Engrs., Sigma Xi, Phi Kappa Phi, Phi Lambda Upsilon, Tau Beta Pi. Author: Multicomponent Distillation, 1963; Unsteady State Processes with Applications in Multicomponent Distillation, 1966; also articles. Home: 1019 Harrington Av College Station TX 77840

HOLLAND, CHARLES EDWARD, retired newspaper editor; b. Boston, July 7, 1904; s. John Henry and Mary Katherine (Murray) H.; D. Journalism (hon.), Suffolk U., Boston, 1964; m. Dorothea Agnes Marsh, Oct. 5, 1929; children—Robert Edward, David John. With Boston Daily Record, 1929-61, asst. mng. editor, 1958-61; mng. editor Boston Record Am., 1961-71; mem. TV news analysis panel Starring the Editors, sta. WBZ-TV, Boston, 1952-68; incorporator Belmont Savs. Bank (Mass). Mem. President's Task Force Mental Retardation, 1963- 64; mem. Mass. Spl. Legislative Recess Commn. Needs Retarded Children, 1962. Bd. dirs. Boston chapter A.R.C.; mem. corp. Walter E. Fernald State Sch., Waltham, Mass. Recipient (with others) Amasa Howe award best news story of year under pressure deadline Boston Press Club, 1960. Home: 24 Carleton Rd Belmont MA 02178

HOLLAND, CHARLES THOMAS, coll. dean, mining engineer; b. Winona, W.Va., Mar. 3, 1905; s. William Henry and Catherine Dickinson (Lowry) H.; B.S. in Mining Engring., W.Va. U., 1928, M.S. in Mining Engring. (research fellow 1930-34), 1932; m. Helen Miller Rose, Apr. 18, 1946. Mining engr. H. E. Willson Engring. Co., Thurmond, W.Va., 1928-30; supr. mines, mining engr. Lookout Smokeless Coal Co. (W.Va.), 1934-39; faculty W.Va. U., 1939-48, prof. mining engring., acting dir. Sch. Mines, 1946-48; spl. lectr. Sheffield U. (Eng.), 1945; prof., head dept. mining engring. Va. Poly. Inst., 1948-61; dean Sch. Mines, W.Va. U., 1961-71, prof. mining engring., 1961—. Cons. U.S. Bur. Mines, also mining corps. Chm. Mine Inspectors Examining Bd. W.Va., 1961-70; chmn. Mine Safety Bd. Rev. W.Va., 1961-70; mem. State Water Resources Bd., 1964—. Recipient Percy Nicholls award for 1966. Registered profl. engr., W.Va. Fellow Geol. Soc. Am.; mem. Am. Inst. Mining, Metall. and Petroleum Engrs. (chmn. coal div. 1957-58, sec.-treas. Central Appalachian sect. 1946—), Am. Soc. Engring. Edn., Nat., Va., W.Va. socs. profl. engrs., Coal Mining Inst. Am., W.Va. Coal Mining Inst., Ky., Rocky Mountain mining insts., Appalachian Geol. Soc., Midland Inst. Mining Engrs. (Eng.), S. Wales Inst. Engrs., Instn. Mining Engrs. (London), Sigma Xi, Tau Beta Pi, Sigma Gamma Epsilon. Kiwanian. Author articles in field. Home: 109 McLane Av Morgantown WV 26505

HOLLAND, DANIEL E., editorial cartoonist; b. Guthrie, Ky., Feb. 2, 1918; s. Oscar Carson and Mable (Beasley) H.; student, David Lipscomb Coll., 1936-38, Chgo. Acad. of Fine Arts, 1938-39; m. Allene Hyden, Sept. 5, 1942; 1 son, Daniel. Directorial cartoonist, Nashville Banner, 1939-41, Chgo. Tribune, 1945-50, 54—; cartoonist Washington Times-Herald, Washington 1950-54; instr. editorial cartooning Chicago Acad. Fine Arts since Jan. 1, 1946. Served with U.S.A.A.F., 1941-45; received wings Aug. 5, 1942, dive-bomber, pursuit pilot, European Theatre, 1943; instr. combat tactics, 1944-45. Awarded Air medal with 4 oak leaf clusters; recipient Freedom Found. certificate of merit, 1949, also medals, 1950, 51, 68. Mem. Am. Legion. Republican. Home: 412 Laurel Av Libertyville IL 60048

HOLLAND, DANIEL MARK, educator; b. N.Y.C., July 7, 1920; s. Abraham and Anna (Nydorf) H.; B.A., Columbia, 1941, postgrad., 1946-51; m. Jeanne A. Ormont, June 3, 1942; children—Laura, Jonathan, Andrew. Instr., Columbia, 1946-51; staff mem. Nat. Bur. Econ. Research, 1951—; asso. prof. N.Y. U., 1947- 58; asso. prof. Sloan Sch., Mass. Inst. Tech., Cambridge, 1958-62, prof., 1962—. Served with USNR, 1943-46. Mem. Am. Econ. Assn., Royal Econ. Soc., Nat. Tax Assn., Am. Finance Assn. Author: Income Tax Burden on Stockholders, 1958; Dividends Under the Income Tax, 1962; Private Pension Funds; Projected Growth, 1966. Editor: Nat. Tax Jour., 1966—. Contbr. articles profl. jours. Home: 41 Turning Mill Rd Lexington MA 02173 Office: Sloan Sch Mass Inst Tech 50 Memorial Dr Cambridge MA 02139

HOLLAND, EUGENE, Jr., banker; b. Lincoln, Neb., Dec. 13, 1922; s. Eugene and Louise (Bedwell) H.; A.B., Princeton, 1944; m. Martha Randall, May 15, 1948; children-Diane, Randall, Mary Susan, Jean, Robert. Sr. v.p. Continental Ill. Nat. Bank & Trust Co., Chgo., 1969—; v.p., dir. Holland Lumber Co. Bd. dirs. Evanston Hosp. Served with USNR, 1943-46. Mem. Am. Petroleum Inst., Ind. Petroleum Assn. Am., Ind., Am. gas assns. Clubs: Chicago, Economic, Bankers (Chgo.); Glen View. Home: 416 Sheridan Rd Kenilworth IL 60043 Office: 231 S LaSalle St Chicago IL 60690

HOLLAND, GEORGE KENNETH, ednl. adminstr.; b. Los Angeles, May 10, 1907; s. Charles Alfred and Cora Effie (Spring) H.; A.B., Occidental Coll., 1929, LL.D., 1946; M.A., Princeton, 1931; student U. Grenoble, summer 1931; Faculty of Law (Am. Field Service fellow), U. Paris, 1931-32; LL.D., Middlebury Coll., 1951; D.H.L., Dickinson Coll., Carlisle, Pa., 1958; LL.D., U. Notre Dame, 1960, Fairleigh Dickinson U., 1963, Brandeis U., 1968; m. Mary Frances Kimball, July 11, 1966; children—Kenneth Kimball, Susan Sawyer, Marcia Spring, Wendell Allen. Sec. Internat. Student Service, 1932-33; dir. edn. Civilian Conservation Corps Camps, New Eng. area, 1933-35; asso. dir. Am. Youth Commn. Am. Council Edn., 1935-41; chief edn. sect. Office Inter-Am. Edn. Affairs, 1941-42, dir. div. edn., 1942-45, pres. Inter-Am. Ednl. Found., 1945-46; asst. dir. Office Internat. Information and Cultural Affairs, Dept. State, 1946-48, dir. Office Ednl. Exchange, 1949; pres. Inst. Internat. Edn., 1950—. Tech. cons. U.S. delegation UNESCO Conf., London, 1945; mem. U.S. delegation UNESCO Conf., Paris, 1946, 49, Mexico, 1947, Beirut, 1948; permanent U.S. rep. UNESCO, Paris, 1948-50. Dir. Corning Mus. Glass. Decorated Officer French Legion of Honor; officer Brazilian Order of the So. Cross: Comdr. Cross Order of Merit (Fed. German Republican); recipient Medal Honor, Georgetown U., 1964. Mem. Council on Fgn. Relations, Iran Found. Japan Soc., Nat. Planning Assn., Pan Am. Soc., Am. Soc. for Friendship with Switzerland (dir.), French Inst. (dir.) Germanistic Soc. (dir.), Fedn. French Alliances in U.S. (chmn.), Phi Beta Kappa. Clubs: Century Association, Fifth Avenue Luncheon (N.Y.C.); Cosmos (Washington); Bronxville (N.Y.) Field. Home: 28 Avon Rd Bronxville NY 10708 Office: 809 UN Plaza New York City NY 10017

HOLLAND, HEINRICH DIETER, educator, geochemist; b. Mannheim, Germany, May 27, 1927; s. Otto and Jeannette (Liebrecht) H.; came to U.S., 1940, naturalized, 1948; B.A., Princeton, 1946; M.S., Columbia, 1948, Ph.D., 1952; m. Alice Tilghman Pusey, June 20, 1953; children—Henry Lawrence, Anne Liebrecht, John Pusey, Matthew Tilghman. Mem. faculty Princeton, 1950—, prof. geology, 1966—; Fulbright lectr. Durham (Eng.) U., 1956-57; NSF postdoctoral fellow Oxford (Eng.) U., 1963-64; vis. prof. U. Hawaii, 1968-69. Pres. sch. bd., Rocky Hill, N.J. 1961-63, 67-68. Chmn. No. N.J. chpt. Scientists and Engrs. for Johnson, 1964. Served with AUS, 1946-47. Fellow Geol. Soc. Am.; mem. Mineral. Soc. Am., Geochem. Soc. (v.p. 1969-70, pres. 1970-71), Am. Geophys. Union, Am. Assn. U. Profs. Author articles in geochemistry, ore forming fluids, ocean atmosphere evolution. Home: 118 Washington St Rocky Hill NJ 08553 Office: Dept Geology and Geophys Scis Princeton Univ Princeton NJ 08540

HOLLAND, HUBERT BRIAN, lawyer; b. London, Eng., Mar. 28, 1904; s. Charles Hubert and Lois Amy (Barber) H.; student Taft Sch., 1918-21; Ph.B., Yale, 1925; LL.B., Harvard, 1928; m. Gertrude Bancroft, Aug. 4, 1931; children—Alice Katharine, Charles Howard. Came to U.S., 1915; naturalized, 1929. Admitted to Pa. bar, 1929, Mass. bar, 1935; asso. Williams, Brittain & Sinclair, Phila., 1928-30;

atty. Dept. Justice, Washington, 1930-35, asst. atty. gen. U.S., 1953-56; asso. firm Roper & Gray., Boston, 1935-42, partner, 1942-53, 56—; lectr. Fed. Tax Inst. N.E., Inst. Fed. Taxation N.Y.U., 1950-51. Mem. corp. Walter E. Fernald State Sch., Waverly, Mass. Fellow Am. Bar Found.; mem. Assn. Bar City N.Y., Am. Law Inst., Am., Mass., Boston bar assns., Fed Tax Inst. N.E. Episcopalian. Home: 22 Skyline Dr Wellesley MA 02181 Office: 225 Franklin St Boston MA 02110

HOLLAND, JACK, ednl. adminstr.; b. Mansfield, Tex., Sept. 9, 1911; s. Fred Darwin and Martha Mae (Harris) H.; B.B.A., U. Tex., 1936, M.B.A., 1952; m. Angela Beatrice King, June 18, 1938; children—Barbara, Darwin, Jeffrey. Employment supr. Consol. Vultee Aircraft Corp., 1943-46; asst. dean of men U. Tex., 1946-48, dean of men, 1948-60, asst. prof. mgmt., 1958-60, dir. univ. personnel office, 1960-64, dean of students, 1964-68, system adviser for student affairs, 1968-69, asst. vice chancellor student affairs, 1969-71, asso. dir. Office Instl. Studies, 1971—. Dir. Tex. Soc. Crippled Children, 1954-57, 63-66, pres. Travis County, 1951-53; dir., treas. Tex. Assn. Retarded Children, 1967-69; dir. exec. com. United Cerebral Palsy Tex. 1952-57, v.p. 1953-58; exec. v.p. 1957-58; dir. United Cerebral Palsy Travis County, 1953-58, United Cerebral Palsy Regional Conv. Com., 1956; pres. Austin Council Retarded Children, 1949- 50, 59-60, exec. com., 1950-56, mem. bd. dirs., 1958-60; active Boy Scouts Am. Mem. Am. Personnel and Guidance Assn., Tex. Personnel and Mgmt. Assn. (state adv. bd.), Austin Personnel Assn. (pres. 1964-65), Tex. (pres. 1954) Southwest (pres. 1968-69) assns. student personnel adminstrs., Am. Soc. Pub. Adminstrs. (pres. Austin chpt. 1965-66), Sigma Iota Epsilon, Alpha Phi Omega (life), Omicron Delta Kappa. Mason, Rotarian. Home: 6703 N Park Dr Austin TX 78757

HOLLAND, JAMES FREDERICK, educator, physician; b. Morristown, N.J., May 16, 1925; s. Albert H. and Mary (Layer) H.; A.B., Princeton, 1944; M.D., Columbia, 1947; m. Jimmie Coker, July 7, 1956; children—Diane, Steven, Mary, Sally, Peter, David. Intern, asst. resident Presbyn. Hosp., N.Y.C., 1947-49; resident Francis Delafield Hosp., N.Y.C., 1951-52; investigative medicine, specializing in cancer, Buffalo, 1954—; staff Nt. Cancer Inst., Bethesda, Md., 1953-54; chief medicine A, Roswell Park Meml. Inst., Buffalo, 1956—. dir. Cancer Clin. Research Center, 1963—; asso. research prof. medicine State U. N.Y., Buffalo, 1962-70 research prof. medicine, 1970—. Mem Acute Leukemia Group B, 1955—; chmn. Acute Leukemia Coop. Group B, 1963—, Internat. Union Against Cancer Trophohlastic Neoplasia Group 1967—; mem. clin. panel cancer chemotherapy Nat. Service Center, 1955-58, Nat. panel Cons. of Conquest of Cancer. Mem. Am. Assn. Cancer Research, (pres. 1970-71), A.A.A.S., Am. Fedn. for Clin. Research, Am. Soc. Hematology, Am. Soc. Clin. Investigation. Editor: (with Hreshchyshyn) Choriocarcinoma, 1967; (with Micscher and Jaffe) Leukemia and Lymphoma, 1970. Contbr. articles profl. jours. Home: 137 Depew Av Buffalo NY 14214 Office: Roswell Park Meml Inst 666 Elm St Buffalo NY 14203

HOLLAND, JAMES JOHN, banker; b. Cleve., Mar. 31, 1907; s. James John and Anna Maude (Briggs) H.; student Albion Coll., 1925-27; m. Thelma Elizabeth Long, Jan. 8, 1927; 1 dau., Mary Lou. Office mgr. White Sewing Machine Co., Cleve., 1927-34; mgr. Universal Credit Co., Cleve. and Akron, O., 1934-42; with Central Nat. Bank, Cleve., 1942—, sr. v.p., 1963—. Vice pres., treas. Greater Cleve. Safety Council, 1964—. Mem. Am. Bankers Assn. (award contbn. constructive growth consumer credit in comml. banks 1960), Delta Tau Delta. Clubs: Midday, Playhouse (Cleve.); Canterbury Golf (Shaker Heights). Home: 2560 N Moreland Blvd Shaker Heights OH 44120 Office: 123 W Prospect St Cleveland OH 44115

HOLLAND, JAMES RONALD, advt. exec.; b. Watch Hill, R.I., Dec. 22, 1931; s. Charles Brayton and Alice Elizabeth (Sullivan) H.; student U. Conn., 1951-55. Creative dir. Papert, Koenig, Lois, Inc., 1961-67; exec. v.p. Lois Holland Callaway Inc., N.Y.C., 1967—. Served with AUS, 1955-57. Office: 745 Fifth Av New York City NY 10022

HOLLAND, JEROME HEARTWELL, ambassador; b. Auburn, N.Y., Jan. 9, 1916; s. Robert Howard and Viola (Bagby) H.; B.S., Cornell U., 1939, M.S., 1941; Ph.D., U. Pa., 1950; D.H.L. Northeastern U., 1965; D. Litt., Union Coll., 1966; LL.D., U. Cin., 1966, Colgate U., 1969, Washington U., 1970, Del. State Coll., 1970; D.H.L., Hobart and William Smith Colls., 1965; D. H. L., Hamilton Coll., 1967; m. Laura Mitchell, Aug. 22, 1948; children—Lucy, Joseph. Instr. sociology, phys. edn., also asst. coach Lincoln (Pa.) U., 1939-42; dir. personnel yard 4, Sun Shipbldg. and Dry Dock Co., 1942-46; dir. div. polit. and social scis., also edn. coach football Tenn. A. and I. State U., 1947-51; social research cons. Pew Meml. Found., Phila., 1951-53; pres. Del. State Coll., Dover, 1953-60, Hampton (Va.) Inst., 1960-70, ambassador to Sweden, Stockholm, 1970—. Dir. Firemen's Ins. Co. Newark. Mem. 2d citizens adv. com. FDA, 1961-62; com. sponsors William Howard Taft Meml. Assn., 1961; mem. Nat. Conf. Christians and Jews, Conf. Equality of Employment Opportunity, 1961; mem. Nat. Adv. Council on Health Research Facilities; exec. bd. Peninsula council Boy Scouts Am.; mem. Nat. Adv. Com. on TV; council Cornell U. Bd. dirs. Expt. Internat. Living. Putney, Vt., Nat. Med. Fellowships, Planned Parenthood Assn.; bd. govs. A.R.C.; bd. dirs. Eberstadt Fund; bd. overseers Coll. of V.I.; adv. com. Norfolk Area Med. Center Authority; trustee Nat. Commn. Co-op. Edn., Cornell U., Freedoms Found. Valley Forge; bd. advisers Nat. Art Mus. Sport; bd. visitors U. W.I. Recipient Freedom citation Chapel of Four Chaplains Temple U., 1958, Young Man of Year award Christian St. Y Mens Club, Phila., 1958, Human Relations award Cheyney State Tchrs. Coll., 1959, Masonic award M. W. Prince Hall Grand Lodge, 1959, award Mens Club Community Presbyn. Ch., Wilmington, Del., 1960; Am. award Salvation Army, 1968. Mem. N.A.A.C.P. (life), Am. Mgmt. Assn. (dir.), Assn. Higher Edn. (exec. com.), So. Assn. Colls. and Schs. (commn. on colls. class of 1967), Internat. Inst. of Arts and Letters. Author: A Sociological Analysis of the Problems of Public School Desegregation and Integration in Delaware, 1955; Status of Negro Employment in Delaware, 1956; Patterns of Negro Residency in Delaware, 1957; Health of Negro in Delaware, 1958; Black Opportunity, 1969. Address: Am Embassy Stockholm Sweden

HOLLAND, JOHN JOSEPH, microbiologist; b. Pitts., Nov. 16, 1929; s. George Joseph and Valetta (Coyne) H.; B.S., Loyola U., Los Angeles, 1953; Ph.D., U. Cal. at Los Angeles, 1957; m. Dorothy Lee Delaney, July 30, 1960; children—Mark John, Lynn Maureen. Instr., asst. prof. U. Minn., 1957-60; asst. prof., asso. prof. dept. microbiology U. Wash., 1960-64; prof. microbiology U. Cal., Irvine, 1964-68; prof. biology U. of Cal. at San Diego, 1968—. Vis. scientist Inst. Molecular Biology, Geneva, Switzerland. Recipient Eli Lilly award in microbiology, 1963. Mem. Am. Soc. Microbiology, Soc. Exptl. Biology and Medicine, Am. Soc. Immunologists, Sigma Xi. Home: 14202 Pinewood Dr Del Mar CA 92014 Office: Dept Biology U Cal at San Diego La Jolla CA 92037

HOLLAND, JOSIAH GILBERT, lawyer; b. Denver, Nov. 16, 1900; s. Theodore and Florence (Ward) H.; student U. Colo., 1918-20, Yale, 1920-22; LL.B. cum laude, Denver U., 1925; m. Elizabeth Welborn, Aug 10, 1927 (div. 1961); children— Diana, Lorna, Penelope; m. 2d, Meriwether Lewis Montgomery, Nov. 2, 1961. Admitted Colo. bar, 1925, since practice in Denver; asso. firm Grant, Ellis, Shafroth and Toll, 1928-34; partner firm Lewis, Bond and Holland, 1934- 42, White and Holland, 1945-47, Holland & Hart, 1947—. Dir. Joy Mfg. Co., 1968-71. Mem. Colo. Legislature, 1931. Mem. Am., Colo., Denver bar assns. Republican. Episcopalian. Clubs: Denver, Denver Country, Arapahoe Hunt. Home: 1510 E 10th Av Denver CO 80218 Office: Equitable Bldg Denver CO 80202

HOLLAND, KENNETH GEORGE, ednl. adminstr.; b. Los Angeles, May 10, 1907; s. Charles Alfred and Cora Effie (Spring) H.; A.B., Occidental Coll., 1929, LL.D., 1946; M.A., Princeton, 1930; postgrad. U. Grenoble, summer 1931; Am. Field Service fellow, U. Paris, 1931-32; LL.D. (hon.), Middlebury Coll., 1951, Notre Dame U., 1960, Fairleigh Dickinson Coll., 1961, Brandeis U., 1968; D.H.L. (hon.), Dickinson Coll., Carlisle, Pa., 1958; m. Mary Frances Kimball, July 11, 1936; children—Kenneth Kimball, Susan Sawyer, Marcia Spring, Wendell Allen. Sec., Internat. Student Service, 1932-33; dir. edn. Civilian Conservation Corps, New Eng. area, 1933-35; asso. dir. Am. Youth Commn. Am. Council Edn., Washington, 1935-41; chief edn. sect. Office Inter-Am. Affairs, Washington, 1941-42, dir. div. edn., 1942-45; pres. Inter-Am. Edn. Found., Washington, 1945-46; asst. dir. Office Internat. Information and Cultural Affairs Dept. State, Washington, 1946-48, dir. office ednl. exchange, 1949; pres. Inst. Internat. Edn., N.Y.C., 1950—. Tech. cons. U.S. delegation UNESCO Conf., London, 1945, mem. delegation, Paris, 1946, 49, Mexico, 1947, Beirut, 1948, Florence, 1950; permanent U.S. rep. UNESCO, Paris, 1948-50; mem. Presdl. Com. on Latin Am. Affairs; mem. task force Pan Am. Union for Alliance for Progress; sec. gen. Council Higher Edn. in Am. Republics, 1958—. Chmn. Fedn. French Alliances in U.S. Bd. dirs. Am. Soc. for Friendship with Switzerland, Corning Glass Mus. Decorated officer French Legion of Honor, Brazilian Nat. Order Cruzeiro de Sul, comdr. Order of Merit, Fed. Republic Germany; recipient Carnegie Corp. plaque, 1958, Georgetown U. Medal of Honor, 1964, Thomas F. Cunningham Inter-Am. award, 1968, U. Paris award, 1970. Mem. Council Fgn. Relations, Nat. Planning Assn., Century Assn., Am. Swiss Assn. (dir.), Germanistic Soc. (dir.), French Inst. (dir.), Fedn. French Alliances in U.S., Phi Beta Kappa. Clubs: Cosmos (Washington); Bronxville Field, Century, Fifth Avenue, Princeton (N.Y.C.). Author: Youth in European Labor Camps, 1938; Youth in the CCC, 1940. Contbr. articles to profl. jours., chpts. to books. Home: 28 Avon Rd Bronxville NY 10708 Office: 809 United Nations Plaza New York City NY 10017

HOLLAND, LEONARD, state govt. ofcl., army officer; b. Providence, Apr. 9, 1916; s. Charles and Ida (Levine) H.; ed. pub. schs., Providence; m. Bernice Berry, Mar. 3, 1946; children—Richard G., Glenn A., Ronald L. Enlisted inf., AUS, 1941, commd. 2d lt., 1942, advanced through grades to maj. gen., 1968; served with 43d Inf. Div., Guadalcanal, other Solomon Islands, New Guinea, 1942-46; mem. Officers Res. Corps, 1946—; maj. gen. N.G. U.S., 1961; adj. gen. R.I., 1961—. Pres. Shipyards Sports Center, Providence, 1958—, Dryden Corp.; mem. corp. Peoples Sav. Bank. Chmn. United Jewish Appeal, Pawtucket, R.I., 1959-60; committeeman Pawtucket council Boy Scouts Am., mem. Nat. council; active R.I. Cancer Soc. Mem. corp. Miriam Hosp. Decorated Bronze Star, Legion of Merit, Purple Heart, Combat Inf. badge; named to Hall Fame, Inf. Officers Sch., Ft. Benning, Ga.; named Man Yr., B'nai B'rith, R.I. Jewish Congress. Mem. Assn. U.S. Army (chmn. bd. dirs.), Res. Officer Assn., Toura Frat. Orgn. Mason. Home: 34 Wilcox Av Pawtucket RI 02860 Office: 1051 N Main St Providence RI 02904

HOLLAND, LYMAN FAITH, Jr., lawyer; b. Mobile, June 17, 1931; s. Lyman Faith and Louise (Wisdom) H.; B.S. in Bus. Adminstratn., U. Ala., 1953. LL.B., 1957; m. Leanna Louise Platt, Mar. 6, 1954; children—Lyman Faith III, Laura. Admitted to Ala. bar, 1957; asso. firm Hand, Ardendall & Bedsole, Mobile, 1957-62; partner firm Hand, Ardendall, Bedsole, Greaves and Johnston, 1963—. Mem. Mobile Historic Devel. Com., 1965-69, v.p., 1967-68, Bd. dirs. Mobile Azalea Trail, Inc., 1963-68, chmn. bd., 1963-65; bd. dirs. Mobile Mental Health Center, Mobile chpt. A.R.C. Served to 1st lt. USAF, 1953- 55; maj. Res. Mem. Am., Mobile County bar assns., Ala. State Bar, Pi Kappa Alpha, Phi Delta Phi. Baptist (deacon). Clubs: Athleston, Skyline Country (Mobile). Home: 1155 E Skyland Circle Mobile AL 36609 Office: Box 123 Mobile AL 36601

HOLLAND, LYNWOOD M., educator; b. Bronwood, Ga., Mar. 31, 1905; s. John Christie and Mary Ann (Martin) H.; A.B., Emory U., 1932, A.M., 1933; Ph.D., U. Ill., 1945; m. Wilma Martin, Aug. 18, 1946. High sch. supt., Ga., 1932-37; asst. prof. U. Ga., 1937-39; grad asst. polit. sci. U. Ill., 1940-42; asst. prof. U. Ariz., 1945-46; from asst. prof. to prof. Emory U., 1946-67; prof. pub. adminstrn. Tex. Technol. U., 1967—; cons. in field. Precinct chmn. DeKalb County Democratic Party. Served with USAAF, 1942-45. Mem. Am., So., Western polit. scis. assns., Nat. Assn. Pub. Adminstrn., Southwest Social Sci. Assn., Phi Beta Kappa, Omicron Delta Kappa, Pi Sigma Alpha, Kappa Phi Kappa. Author: The Direct Primary in Georgia, 1949; Administrative Agencies of Georgia, 1950; State and Local Government in United States, 1951; P.M.B. Young, The Warwick of South, 1963; Georgia Government, 1966. Home: 4021 21st St Apt 17 Lubbock TX 79410

HOLLAND, NORMAN NORWOOD, lawyer; b. Princess Anne, Md., Feb. 19, 1896; s. John A. and Elizabeth (Powell) H.; B.E., Johns Hopkins, 1920; LL.B., Fordham U., 1923; postgrad. Columbia, 1923; m. Harriette Breder, Oct. 22, 1924; 1 son, Norman Norwood. Admitted to N.Y. bar, 1924; sr. partner Holland, Armstrong, Carlson & Wilkie and predecessor firms, 1926-67, Holland, Armstrong, Wilkie & Previto, N.Y.C., 1967—. Lectr., cons. Practising Law Inst. on Patent and Trademark Law, 1956-67. Mem. Am. Bar Assn. (chmn. sect. patent trademark copyright law 1951, mem. council 1946-49, 51-54), Bar City N.Y. (chmn. patent com. 1959-61), Am. (bd. mgrs. 1955-58), N.Y. (pres. 1954-55) patent law assns., Internat. Patent and Trademark Assn. (sec. 1949-52, exec. com. 1960-68), Johns Hopkins Alumni Assn. N.Y., N.J.and Conn. (pres. 1951-53), Scabbard and Blade, Tau Beta Phi, Omicron Delta Kappa. Republican. Clubs: N.Y. Athletic, Downtown Athletic, Johns Hopkins (pres. 1942-46 N.Y.C.). Home: 880 Fifth Av New York City NY 10021

HOLLAND, PARK, Jr., oil co. exec.; b. San Antonio, Tex., July 31, 1919; s. Park and Helen (Hotaling) H.; student U. Md., 1938-39, Auburn U., 1939-41, George Washington U., 1941-42; LL.B. cum laude, Albany Law Sch. of Union U., 1944, J.D. cum laude, 1968; m. Carolyn Letetia Lively, Oct. 13, 1945; 1 son, Park III. Admitted to N.Y. bar, 1944; asso. atty. firm Woollard & Morris, Albany, 1944-45, Cravath, Swaine & Moore, N.Y.C., 1945-47; prin. atty. N.Y. State Banking Dept., 1947-50; atty. Cities Service Co., N.Y.C., 1950-63, asst. gen. counsel, 1963-67, sec., asst. gen. counsel, 1967—, also dir. and/or officer various subsidiaries. Mem. Am., N.Y. State bar assns., Assn. ICC Practitioners, Assn. Bar City N.Y., Justinian Soc., Am. Petroleum Inst., Am. Horse Shows Assn., lawyers clubs N.Y.C., D.C. Home: 162 Merlin Av North Tarrytown NY 10591 Office: 70 Pine St New York City NY 10005

HOLLAND, PAUL DELEVAL, lawyer; b. Los Angeles. Feb. 1, 1910; s. Christopher Franklin and Louise (Deleval) H.; student U. Cal., Los Angeles, 1928-31; A.B., U. So. Cal., 1933, LL.B., 1934; m. Claudine Florence Atkins, Apr. 28, 1962. Admitted to Cal. bar, 1934; pvt. practice in Los Angeles, 1934-42, Beverly Hills, 1945-70, Los Angeles, 1970—. Mem. Conf. Bd. Pensions, United Methodist Ch., 1968—. Pres. Cal. Epilepsy Soc.; v.p., bd. dirs. Epilepsy Found. Am.; bd. dirs. Epi Hab, Los Angeles. Mem. Am. Judicature Soc., Am., Los Angeles. County bar assns., Phi Gamma Delta, Delta Theta Phi. Democrat. Home: 12023 Monogram Av Granada Hills CA 91344 Office: 1880 Century Park East Los Angeles CA 90067

HOLLAND, RAY LAURIMORE, financial cons.; b. Rich Hill, Mo., Sept. 10, 1916; s. Ralph Lee and Florence Grace (Horton) H.; A.B., U. Mo. at Kansas City, 1937; m. Thasia Gladys Tidd, Jan. 21, 1939 (div. May 1966); children—Dennis Lee, Laurel Marie, Ray Charles; m. 2d, Aina Piladzis, July 23, 1966. With Arthur Andersen & Co., C.P.A.'s, Kansas City, Mo., Seattle, Milw., and Chgo., 1940-57; controller Union Tank Car Co., Chgo., 1957-65; financial cons., Cleve., 1966—. C.P.A., Kan., Wash., Wis., Ill. Mem. Am. Inst. C.P.A.'s, Financial Execs. Inst. Home: 24911 S Woodland Rd Beachwood OH 44224

HOLLAND, REGINALD VALENTINE, educator; b. Cadillac, Mich., June 4, 1916; s. Valentine V. and Amelia C. (Schmelling) H.; B.S., Northwestern U., 1939; M.A. (fellow 1939-40), Mich. State U., 1948; Ph.D. (fellow 1948-51), Cornell U., 1951; m. Beryl F. Cleveland, June 14, 1941; children—Patricia Ellen, Holly Jean. Teacher at the Muskegon (Mich.) Sr. High Sch., 1940-41; teaching fellow Cornell U., 1948-51; mem. faculty N. Tex. State U., Denton, 1951—, prof., dir. speech and drama dept., 1951—. Served with USNR, 1941-46. Named an outstanding prof. N. Tex. State U., 1960. Mem. Tex. (pres. 1966-67), So. (exec. council 1959-61) speech assns., Am. Ednl. Theatre Assn., Speech Assn. Am., Am. Assn. U. Profs., Southwest Theatre Conf., Alpha Delta Phi. Home: 1421 Kendolph St Denton TX 76201

HOLLAND, ROBERT CARL, govt. ofcl.; b. Tekamah, Neb., Apr. 7, 1925; s. Carl Luther and Gretchen (Thompson) H.; student U. Neb., 1942-43, 46, U. Wis., 1943-44; B.S. in Finance, U. Pa., 1948, M.A. in Econs., 1949, Ph.D. in Econs., 1959; m. DeEtte Harriet Hedlund, Sept. 7, 1947; children—Joan DeEtte, Nancy Gretchen, Timothy Robert. Instr. money and banking U. Pa., 1948-49; with Fed. Res. Bank Chgo., 1949-61, v.p., 1959-61; with bd. govs. Fed. Res. System, 1961—, asso. economist, fed. open market com., 1962-66, adviser to bd., 1965-67, sec. of bd., 1968-71, exec. dir., 1971—, sec. to fed. open market com., 1966—. Served with AUS, 1943-45. Mem. Am. Econ. Assn., Am. Finance Assn., Beta Theta Pi. Clubs: Cosmos (Washington); Kenwood Country (Bethesda, Md.). Home: 5508 Cromwell Dr Washington DC 20016 Office: Fed Reserve Bd 20th and Constitution Av NW Washington DC 20551

HOLLAND, ROBERT DEBNAM, investment co. exec.; b. Norfolk, Va., Mar. 5, 1922; s. Ralph Frederick and Erma (Debnam) H.; grad. U.S. Merchant Marine Acad., 1943; B.A., Centre Coll. of Ky., 1949; grad. student U. Va., 1951: m. Frances Lee Hodges, Dec. 26, 1943; children—Robert Debnam, Elizabeth Lee, William Peyton. Salesman, IBM Corp., 1952-56, Burroughs Corp., 1956-61; mgr. indsl. marketing RCA, 1961-65; v.p. finance CEIR, Inc., Washington, 1965, exec. v.p., 1965-66, pres., 1966-67; pres., chmn. bd. Computer Leasing Co., 1967-70; chmn. bd. Alcorn Combustion Co., Transnat. Electronic & Funding Corp.; dir. Bell Equipment Corp. Served to lt. comdr. USNR. 1941-46, 50-52. Mem. Inst. Automation Research, Am. Mgmt. Assn., A.I.M., Sigma Chi, Omicron Delta Kappa, Pi Kappa Delta. Episcopalian. Home: 7219 Honeywell Lane Bethesda MD 20014 Office: 1625 I St NW Washington MD 20006

HOLLAND, ROBERT FRANCIS, educator; b. Holley, N.Y., Sept. 21, 1908; s. Robert B. and Mary (Parker) H.; B.S., Cornell U., 1936, M.S., 1938, Ph.D., 1940; m. Ruth McCargo, Aug. 10, 1930; children—Robert G., Daniel M., Deborah R., James S. Asso. research N.Y. State Agr. Expt. Sta., Geneva, 1939-41; dir. chem. research Coop. Grange League Fedn., Soil Bldg. Service, Ithaca, N.Y., 1941-45; prof. dairy industry Cornell U., 1945-55, head dept. dairy and food sci., 1955-65, also head dept. bacteriology and div. food sci., head dept. food sci.; with FAO, Kenya, Africa, 1964. Mem. Inst. Food Technologists, Am. Dairy Sci. Assn., Soc. Am. Bacteriologists, Internat. Assn. Milk and Food Sanitarians, Sigma Xi, Phi Kappa Phi. Home: 71 Old Main St Trumansburg NY 14886 Office: Cornell Univ Ithaca NY 14850

HOLLAND, ROBERT WELLER, lawyer; b. Tulsa, Aug. 15, 1934; s. Thomas W. and Helen (McCormick) H.; B.A., U. Tulsa, 1956; J.D., So. Methodist U., 1959; m. Mary Ann Ball, July 10, 1959. Admitted to Okla. bar, 1959, Tex. bar, 1959, Ariz. bar, 1963; practice in Tulsa, 1959-60. Phoenix, 1962—; mem. firm Connor, Winters, Randolph & Ballaine, 1959-60; atty. Office of Solicitor, Dept. Interior, 1960-62; mem. firm Carson, Messinger, Elliott, Laughlin & Ragon, 1963—, partner, 1966—; instr. comml. law W. Tex. State Coll., Canyon, 1962. Chmn. bd. dirs. Wesley Found. Ariz. State U.; bd. dirs. Ariz. Inst. Marital Relations. Mem. Am., Ariz., Okla., Tex. bar assns., Phi Alpha Delta, Lambda Chi Alpha. Republican. Methodist. Kiwanian. Club: Arizona (Phoenix). Home: 3630 E Colter St Phoenix AZ 85018 Office: 3550 N Central Av Phoenix AZ 85012

HOLLAND, SESSARD LINDSEY, former senator, lawyer; b. Bartow, Fla., July 10, 1892; s. Benjamin and Fannie Virginia (Spessard) H.; Ph.B., Emory U., 1912, LL.D., 1943; LL.B., U. Fla., 1916, D.C.L., 1953; LL.D., Rollins Coll., Fla. So. Coll., 1941, Fla. State U., 1956, U. Miami, 1962, Stetson U., 1970; H.H.D., U. Tampa, 1956; m. Mary Agnes Groover, Feb. 8, 1919; children—Spessard Lindsey, Mary Groover, William Benjamin, Ivanhoe. High sch. tchr., Warrenton, Ga., 1912-14; tchr. sub- freshman dept. U. Fla., 1914-16; admitted to Fla., bar, 1916, since practiced in Bartow; pros. atty. Polk County, 1919-20, county judge, 1921-29; mem. Fla. State Senate, 1932-40; gov. Fla., 1941-45; U.S. senator from Fla., 1946-71, mem. coms. on agr. and forestry, appropriations, aero. and space scis. Trustee Fla. Presbyn. Coll., Fla. So. Coll., Emory U.; bd. visitors Naval Acad., USAF Force Acad., Mil. Acad. Served to capt. CAC, U.S. Army, World War I; 24th Squadron AC in France. Decorated D.S.C. Mem. S.A.R., U. Fla. Alumni Assn. (exec. council 1922—, pres. 1931), Am. Legion, V.F.W., Phi Beta Kappa, Phi Kappa Phi, Alpha Tau Omega, Phi Delta Phi. Democrat. Methodist. Mason (33, Shriner). Elk, Kiwanian. Home: 1005 S Broadway Bartow FL 33830

HOLLAND, STANLEY LEO, bus. exec.; b. Athol, Mass., May 17, 1908; s. George Franklin and Annie Mildred (Hoyt) H.; grad. Derby (Vt.) Acad., 1925; student Worcester Poly. Inst., 1926-27; m. Dorothy Annette Smith, Aug. 17, 1929; children—Frederick G., Richard E., Linda J., James S. With Union Twist Drill Co., Athol, 1927—, gen. mgr. Butterfield div., Derby Line, Vt., 1947-55, pres., dir., Athol 1955-71 (co. name now UTD Corp.); chmn. Cutting Tools Group of Litton Industries, Inc., 1971—. Mason. Home: Rindge NH 03461 Office: UTD Corp Athol MA 01331

HOLLAND, THOMAS WILLARD, economist; b. Woodville, Mich., Dec. 21, 1900; s. Martin and Ann (Drew) A.B., U. Mich., 1923; LL.B., Columbia, 1934; Ph.D., U. Wis., 1939; m. Marion Hall, Jan. 29, 1937; children—Barbara, Nicholas, Judith, Rebecca, Andrew. Asst. labor mgr. Hart, Shaffner & Marx, Chgo., 1923-25; prof. U. N.C., 1926-29, Rutgers U., 1929-34; with NRA, 1934-35; chmn. pub.

contracts bd. Dept. of Labor, 1936-40, adminstr. Wage and Hour Div., 1942; employment chief War Relocation Authority, 1943; chmn. appeals com., War Labor Bd., 1944-45; chief, div. internat. labor, social and health affairs, Dept. of State, 1946-48; vis. prof. U. Miami, 1948-50; prof. George Washington U., until 1966, prof. emeritus, 1966—. Admitted to D.C. bar. Chmn. appeals com. WSB, 1951-53; vice chmn. Atomic Energy Labor Mgmt. Relations Panel, 1953-59; chmn. bd. of inquiry longshoremen's strike, 1956-57. Home: 4100 Rosemary St Chevy Chase MD 20015

HOLLAND, WILLIAM CANNON, educator, physician; b. Barton, Ala., Sept. 26, 1921; s. William C. and Willie (Abbey) H.; B.A., Vanderbilt U., 1944, M.D., 1948; m. Jane Elizabeth Medearis, June 1, 1946; children—Sue Franklin, Betty Adele, William C., Robert, Carol. SUccessively instr., asst. prof., asso. prof., prof. pharmacology Sch. Medicine, Vanderbilt U., 1948-58; prof. pharmacology Sch. Medicine, U. Miss., 1959—, chmn. dept. pharmacology, 1959—. Mem. Am. Soc. Pharmacology, So. Soc. Clin. Investigation, Am. Coll. Clin. Pharmacology, Am. Chem. Soc., Sigma Xi. Author: The Chemistry of Heart Failure, 1960; Introduction to Molecular Pharmacology, 1964. Contbr. articles sci. jours. Home: 5328 Runnymeade Rd Jackson MS 39211

HOLLAND, WILLIAM LANCELOT, educator; b. South Malvern, N.Z., Dec. 18, 1907; s. Frederick G. and Ada Elizabeth (Jewell) H.; came to U.S., 1929; B.A., Canterbury Coll., U. New Zealand, Christchurch, 1928, M.A., 1930; research student Caius Coll., Cambridge (Eng.) U., 1932; m. Doreen Patricia McGarry, Mar. 15, 1932, (div. Apr. 1960, remarried Nov. 1968); 1 dau., Patricia Grace. Research asst. Inst. Pacific Relations, Honolulu, 1928-32, research sec., N.Y.C., Tokyo, Shanghai, and Berkeley, Cal., 1933-43, sec. gen., rsearch dir., 1946-60; prof. dept Asian studies U. B.C., 1961—; lectr. USN Sch. of Mil. Govt., Columbia, 1944; editor Pacific Affairs, N.Y.C., 1943, 53-60, Vancouver, B.C., 1961—; co-editor Far Eastern Survey, 1953-60. Attended Inst. Pacific Relations confs., Kyoto, Japan, 1929, Shanghai, 1931, Banff, Can., 1933, Yosemite, Cal., 1936, Virginia Beach, Va., 1939, Mont Tremblant, Que., 1942, Hot Springs, Va., 1945, Stratford-on-Avon, 1947, Lucknow, 1950, Kyoto, Japan, 1954, Lahore, Pakistan, 1958; Internat. Studies Conf. at London, 1933, Internat. Congress Orientalists, New Delhi, 1964. Dir. U.S. OWI, China div., Chungking, 1945-46. Mem. Asia Soc., Japan Soc., Assn. Asian Studies, Canadian Soc. Asian Studies (pres. 1970-71). Author: China's Economic Development, 1931; Migration in the Pacific, 1931. Co-author: Next Step in Asia, 1949. Editor: Commodity Control in the Pacific, 1935; Problems of Economic Reconstruction in the Far East, 1949; Asian Nationalism and the West, 1953; co-editor: Problems of the Pacific; War and Peace in the Pacific, 1943. Contbr. articles to Nation, Va. Quar., Pacific Affairs, Far Eastern Survey, Internat. Affairs. Home: 4655 Langara Av Vancouver 8 British Columbia 26 Canada

HOLLANDER, HANS SEBALD, distillery co. exec.; b. Berlin, Germany, Apr. 20, 1904; s. Eugen and Emmy (Boehm) H.; B.A., U. Berlin, 1926; m. Ruth von Richtofen, Nov. 22, 1957; 1 dau., Barbara Marie (Mrs. Don Estes). European export mgr. Caterpillar Tractor Co., 1929-33; with Nat. Distillers Products Co., 1951-66, internat. v.p. export and import supervision, 1965-66. Named Kentucky col., 1965; Officer Commanderie de Champagne, 1967. Home: 1945 Linda Flora West Los Angeles CA 90024 Office: 99 Park Av New York City NY 10016 also 292 S La Cienega Blvd Beverly Hills CA 90212

HOLLANDER, JOHN, educator, author; b. N.Y.C., Oct. 28, 1929; s. Franklin and Muriel (Kornfeld) H.; A.B., Columbia, 1950, A.M., 1952; Ph.D., Ind. U., 1959; m. Anne Helen Loesser, June 15, 1953; children—Martha, Elizabeth. Jr. fellow Soc. Fellows, Harvard, 1954-57; lectr. English, Conn. Coll., New London, 1957-59; instr. English, Yale, 1959-61, asst. prof. English, fellow Ezra Stiles Coll., 1961-64, asso. prof., 1964-66; prof. Hunter Coll., Coll. City N.Y., 1966—; vis. prof. Linguistic Inst., Ind. U., 1964; Christian Gauss seminarian Princeton, 1962; Editorial asso. for poetry Partisan Rev., 1959- 65; mem. poetry bd. Wesleyan U. Press, 1959-62. Recipient Yale Younger Poets award, 1958, Poetry Chap Book award, 1962; grantee Nat. Inst. Arts and Letters, 1963; Overseas fellow Churchill Coll., Cambridge (Eng.) U., 1967-68. Mem. English Inst., Phi Beta Kappa. Author: A Crackling of Thorns, 1958; The Untuning of the Sky, 1961; Movie-Going and Other Poems, 1962; Various Owls, 1963; Visions from the Ramble, 1965; The Quest of the Gole, 1966; Types of Shape, 1968; Images of Voice, 1970; The Night Mirror, 1971. Editor: Poems of Ben Jonson, 1961; (with Harold Bloom) The Wind and the Rain, 1961: (with Anthony Hecht) Jiggery-Pokery, 1966; Poems of Our Moment, 1968; Modern Poetry: Essays in Criticism, 1968; American Short Stories since 1945. Contbg. editor Harper's mag., 1969-71. Contbr. poems, articles various jours. Home: 88 Central Park W New York City NY 10023

HOLLANDER, LORIN, pianist; b. N.Y.C., July 19, 1944; s. Max and Mary Louis (Yarbro) H.; student Profl. Children's Sch., N.Y.C., 1960, Juilliard Coll. Music, 1964—, also C. W. Post Coll., Brookville, N.Y. Debut, Carnegie Hall, N.Y.C., 1956; concerts on Bell Telephone Hour, at Carnegie Hall, also on NBC radio and TV, 1957; youngest artist on Great Artist Series, 1956; concert tours U.S., 1959—, Europe, 1965—; recording artist for RCA Victor. Home: West Shore Rd Oyster Bay NY 11771 Office: care Columbia Artists Mgmt 165 W 57th St New York City NY 10019

HOLLANDER, RICHARD ISAAC, editor; b. N.Y.C., Apr. 6, 1912; s. Herman and Bertha (Gichner) H.; student Georgetown U., Washington, 1928-30, George Washington U., 1931; m. Helen Cornelia Eskesen, Mar. 7, 1953. Editorial staff Wash. Daily news, 1929—, editor, 1966—; engaged as lectr., inst. langs. and linguistics Sch. Fgn. Service, Georgetown U., also George Washington U. Decorated Order Brit. Empire, 1945. Compiler: History of the Psychological Warfare Division, Supreme Headquarters Allied Expeditionary Forces, 1945. Home: 3502 Macomb St NW Washington DC 20016 Office: 1013 13th St NW Washington DC 20005

HOLLANDER, SIDNEY, pharm. mfr. retired; b. Balt., Dec. 29, 1881; s. Edward and Fanny (Koshland) H.; Pharm D., U. of Md., 1902; H.H.D., Morgan Coll., 1961; m. Clara D. Lauer, June 3, 1908; children—Edward D., Edith L. (Mrs. Frank Furstenberg), Sidney, Emily D. (Mrs. Frederick Kunreuther). Began as mfg. druggist, 1900; pres. Md. Pharm. Co., The REM Co., 1900-56, ret. Trustee, Md. Dept. of Welfare, 1920-53; pres. Nat. Council Jewish Fedns. and Welfare Funds, 1938-46: v.p. Family Service Assn. of Am., 1938—, Nat. Budget Com., 1940—, Nat. Conf. of Social Work, 1938-54, Nat. Community Relations Adv. Council, 1945-50; exec. com. Community Chests and Councils, Inc., 1940—, Am. Jewish Com. 1940—, United Service for New Americans, 1940—, U.S.O., Am. Jewish Congress (past pres. Balt.), United Community Def. Services, Nat. Conf. Christians and Jews, Council Jewish Fedns. and Welfare Funds; exec. com. Nat. Social Welfare Assembly, 1945—, pres., 1955-56; exec. bd. Nat. Travelers Aid Assn., 1960-61; v.p. Council on Social Work Edn., 1954—; mem. bd. Nat. Urban League, 1945—, Asso. Jewish Charities, 1930—, Nat. Publicity Council, Nat. Legal Aid Bur., Am. Council on Race Relations, Nat. Health and Welfare Retirement Assn., Fair Employment Practices Com., Child Welfare League Am., United Def. Fund; trustee Nat. War Fund. Recipient Spl. award Phila. Fellowship Commn., 1956; founder Sidney Hollander award; spl. award Md. Civil Liberties Union, 1957; Stephen Wise award Balt. Jewish Congress, 1960; awards Family Service Assn. Am., Balt. Urban League, Council Jewish Fedns. and Welfare Funds, Nat. Community Relations Adv. Council. Mem. Trail Tiders Canadian Rockies (pres.), Trail Hikers Canadian Rockies (pres.). Club: Alpine (Switzerland). Home: 2513 Talbot Rd Baltimore MD 21216

HOLLE, HENRY AUGUST, former pub. health physician; b. Brenham, Tex., Aug. 21, 1904; s. Henry William and Mary (Fischer) H.; grad. Blinn Meml. Coll., 1921; student Tex. A. and M. Coll., 1921-23; M.D., U. Tex., 1927; m. Bernice Knolle, July 3, 1926; 1 son, Henry Bernard. Intern Hermann Hosp., Houston, 1927; pvt. practice medicine, Brenham, 1928-34; med. officer USPHS, 1934-62; med. adviser U.S. Employees Compensation Commn., Washington, 1934-36; mem. staff hdqrs. Fed.-State Pub. Health Program, 1936, USPHS Hosp., S.I., N.Y., 1937; Litthauer research fellow spl. study pneumonia Harlem Hosp., N.Y.C., 1937-38; dir. pneumonia control Pa. Dept. Health, 1938; cons. state depts. health NIH, Bethesda, Md., 1939-40; regional pub. health cons., Chgo., 1940-42; chief quarantine officer Panama Canal, Balboa Heights, C.Z., 1942-44; med. div. European office UNRRA, London, 1944-45; chief med. officer UNRRA Mission Poland, Warsaw, 1945-46; assigned Office Surgeon Gen., Washington, 1947-48; regional med. dir. USPHS, N.Y.C., 1948-54; commnr. health Texas, 1954-59; spl. adviser U.S. delegation com. on information, non- self governing ters., 1952; adv. com. Nat. Assn. Prevention Blindness, 1953; USPHS med. officer charge U.S. Quarantine Sta., Rosebank, S.I., N.Y., 1959-62; dir. health projects State Charities Assn. N.Y., 1962- 63; exec. dir. Nat. Council Accreditation Nursing Homes, 1963-65; med. dir. Ill. Dept. Pub. Aid, Chgo., 1965-71. Decorated Order of Polonia Restituta (Poland), 1946. Diplomate Am. Bd. Preventive Med. and Pub. Health. Mem. Assn. Mil. Surgeons U.S. (past pres. N.Y. chpt.), Soc. Asso. Sanitarian Tex., A.M.A. (ho. dels.), Royal Soc. Health London, Am. Pub. Health Assn., Am. Assn. Pub. Health Physicians (past pres.; Distinguished Service award 1970), U.S.-Mexico Border Pub. Health Assn. (past pres.), Tex. Dental Assn. (hon.), Am. Coll. Preventive Medicine. Mason (32, Shriner), Rotarian. Home: 10019 Pine Forest Houston TX 77042

HOLLEB, ARTHUR IRVING, surgeon; b. N.Y.C., Apr. 1, 1921; s. Simon and Kate (Liss) H.; A.B., Brown U., 1941; M.D., N.Y.U., 1944; m. Carolyn R. Oglesby, June 16, 1951; children—Susan Jane and David Gene (twins). Intern Queens Gen. Hosp., Jamaica, N.Y., 1944-45; resident tumor surgery and pathology Meadowbrook Hosp., Hempstead, N.Y., 1945-46, chief resident gen. surgery, 1948-50, asst. dir. tumor service, 1954-56; mem. staff Meml. Hosp., N.Y.C., 1950—, asso. chief med. officer, 1966-67, cons. breast service, surgery dept., 1968—; asso. vis. surg. James Ewing Hosp., 1966-67; mem. staff M.D. Anderson Hosp. and Tumor Inst., Houston, 1967-68, mem. research staff, 1967-68, cons. breast cancer study sect., 1968—; sr. v.p. med. affairs and research, chief med. officer Am. Cancer Soc., N.Y.C., 1968—; from instr. to clin. asso. prof. surgery Cornell U. Med. Coll., 1965-67; asso. clinician Sloan-Kettering Inst., 1961-67; asso. prof. surgery U. Tex. M.D. Anderson Hosp. and Tumor Inst., 1967-68, asso. dir. edn., 1967-68. Mem. evaluation panel, sr. clin. traineeships in surgery, cancer control br., USPHS, 1965-68. Served with USNR, 1946-48. Diplomate Am. Bd. Surgery. Mem. Am. Assn. Cancer Edn., Am. Assn. Cancer Research, A.M.A., Am. Cancer Soc. (bd. dirs. N.Y.C. 1964-67), A.C.S., Am. Radium Soc. (v.p. 1969-70), Assn. Am. Med. Colls., Assn. Hosp. Dirs. Med. Edn. (chmn. surg. edn. com. 1965-67), Harris County Med. Soc., Am. Soc. Clin. Oncology, James Ewing Soc. (pres.-elect 1970-71), N.Y. Acad. Medicine, N.Y. County Med. Soc., N.Y. Acad. Scis., N.Y. Cancer Soc. (pres. 1971), N.Y. Surg. Soc. Clubs: Brown, Marco Polo (N.Y.C.). Editor in chief Jour. CA; editorial adv. bd. Jour. Cancer. Home: 215 E 68th St New York City NY 10021 Office: 219 E 42d St New York City NY 10017

HOLLEIN, HANS, architect; b. Vienna, Austria, Mar. 30, 1934; s. Leo and Gertrud (Czermak) H.; diploma Acad. Fine Arts, Sch. Architecture, Vienna, 1956; student Grad. Sch. Architecture and Planning, Ill. Inst. Tech., 1958-59; M.Arch., U. Cal. at Berkeley, 1960; m. Helen Marie-Therese Jenewein, June 20, 1966. Came to U.S., 1958. Architect with Ahlgren-Olsson-Silow, Stockholm, Sweden, 1956-58; pvt. practice architecture, Vienna, 1958, 64- -; architect with F. Kiener, Vienna, 1960-63; vis. prof. Washington U., St. Louis, 1963-64, 66; cons., 1964—; editor Austrian archtl. and planning mag. BAU, 1964—; rep. exhbn. Architektur, Vienna, 1963, Mus. Modern Art, 1964, 67, Stockholm, 1965, Selection 66, Vienna, 1966, Feigen Gallery, N.Y.C., 1967, Toronto Art Gallery, 1967, Bienale Brno, Czechoslovakia, 1968, Triennale Milano, 1968, Richard Feigen Gallery, Chgo., 1969, Mönchengladbach, Germany, 1970; prof. architecture Düsseldorf (Germany) Acad. Fine Arts. Mem. Aspen (Colo.) Design Conf., 1968. Recipient Reynolds Meml. award A.I.A., 1966, 67, Mem. Austrian Chamber Architects, Austrian Architects Assn. (mem. bd.). Home: Prinz Eugenstrasse 80 1040 Vienna 4 Austria

HOLLEMAN, FRANK L., gas co. exec.; b. Little Rock, Jan. 30, 1912; s. Frank G. and Alma (Thornton) H.; student U. Ark., 1929-33; m. Thelma Ruth Simpson, Aug. 25, 1935; children—F. Larry, Helen Anne. Clk., Ark. Natural Gas Corp., Shreveport, La., 1934-42, chief clk. accounting, 1942- 50; asst. sec., chief statistician Ark. La. Gas Co., Shreveport, 1950-55, sec., treas., 1955—; sec., treas. Ark. Cement Corp., Arkla Industries Inc., Arkla Chem. Corp., Ark. La. Finance Corp., Arkla Exploration Co.; dir. Luxury Lodges, Inc. Bd. dirs. Shreveport chpt. A.R.C., 1944-46. Mem. Am., So. gas assns., Nat. Assn. Accountants, Financial Execs. Inst., Am. Soc. Corporate Secs., Mid-Continent Oil and Gas Assn., Red River Valley Assn., Shreveport C. of C., Petroleum Club Shreveport. Methodist. Club: Highland. Home: 902 Audubon Pl Shreveport LA 71105 Office: Slattery Bldg Shreveport LA 71102

HOLLENBACH, JOHN WILLIAM, educator; b. Allentown, Pa., Feb. 10, 1913; s. Frederick John and Escie Judith (Reichard) H.; B.A., Muhlenberg Coll., 1934; M.A., Columbia, 1935; Ph.D., U. Wis., 1941; m. Winifred Lohman, Aug. 23, 1941; children—David John, John Frederick. Instr. English, High Bridge (N.J.) High Sch.; asst. prof. English, Northeast Mo. State Tchrs. Coll., 1941- 45; prof. English, Hope Coll., 1945-47, dean of coll. 1947-55, v.p. 1957- 66, chmn. English dept., 1966—; dean faculty Am. U., Cairo, Egypt, 1955-57; vis. prof. Am. U. of Beirut, Lebanon, 1965-66. Mem. Nat. Council Tchrs. English, Modern Lang. Assn., Middle East Studies Assn., Phi Kappa Tau, Omicron Delta Kappa, Kappa Phi Kappa. Mem. Reformed Ch. Clubs: Century, Professional. Contbr. articles scholarly jours. Home: 107 W 11th St Holland MI 49423

HOLLENBECK, WALTER EMIL, retired life ins. co. exec.; b. N.Y.C., Nov. 29, 1906; s. Walter E. and Catherine L. (Curley) H.; ed. pub. schs.; m. Florence D. Bruthanz, June 2, 1929; children—Barbara Ann (Mrs. Howard R. Forbes), Peter. With Met. Life Ins. Co., N.Y.C., 1925-71, asst. sec., 1945-58, asst. v.p., sec. to bd., 1958-60, sec., 1960-71. Chmn. Econ. Corp. Giving, Alberton, N.Y. Bd. govs. Human Resources Center. Home: 120 Country Club Dr Port Washington NY 11050

HOLLENBERG, RICHARD HENRY, lawyer; b. Phila., Mar. 6, 1909; s. Harry George and Katherine (Leippe) H.; A.B., U. Pa., 1929, LL.B., 1932; m. Ruth S. Kalberer, Sept. 29, 1934; 1 dau., Gwen (Mrs. Howard Hecht). Admitted to Pa. bar, 1932; gen. law practice, Phila., 1932-35; legal asst. Fidelity Mut. Life Ins. Co., Phila., 1935-44, asst. counsel, 1944-48, asso. gen. 1948-61, 2d v.p., asso. gen. counsel, 1961-68, counsel, 1968-69, v.p., 1968—, gen. counsel, 1969—; sec., dir. Fidelity Mut. Devel. Corp., Joppatowne Utilities Corp. Mem. Abington Twp. Zoning Bd. Adjustment, 1950—. Mem. Am., Pa., Phila. bar assns., Assn. Life Ins. Counsel. Presbyn. (trustee). Home: 805 Glen Rd Jenkintown PA 19046 Office: Parkway at Fairmount Av Philadelphia PA 19101

HOLLENDER, ALFRED LEO, mfg. co. exec.; b. Chgo., Sept. 29, 1912; s. Leo and Beatrice (Halper) H.; B.S., U. Ill., 1934; m. Lucille Marsh, Nov. 5, 1952; children—Jeffrey, Peter. Mgr. radio sta. WIND, WJJD, Chgo., 1934-43; overseas br. chief outpost div. OWI, 1943; co-founder Louis G. Cowan, Inc., 1945- 52; v.p., dir. Grey Advertising Agy., N.Y.C., 1952-58, exec. v.p., 1959- 64; pres. Grey Internat., N.Y.C., 1965-68; exec. v.p. Chris Craft Industries, Inc., 1968—. Mem. exec. com. U.S. Com. for UN, 1957—. Bd. mgrs. N.Y. Inst. Blind; trustee Baldwin Sch., N.Y.C. Served with psychol. warfare div., SHAEF, 1943-45. Mem. Internat. Advt. Assn. (v.p., treas., exec. com. 1967). Home: 911 Park Av New York City NY 10021 Office: 600 Madison Av New York City NY 10022

HOLLENDER, MARC HALE, educator; b. Chgo., Dec. 19, 1916; s. Abraham Risel and Anna (Winsberg) H.; student Loyola U., Chgo., 1934-35, Northwestern U., 1935-37; B.S., U. Ill., 1939, M.D., 1941; m. Betty Jane Schultz, July 7, 1943; children—Mary Jo, David Albert. Intern, Cook County Hosp., Chgo., 1941-42; resident Neuropsychiat. Inst. U. Ill., Chgo., 1946-48; clin. asst. to asso. prof. dept. psychiatry U. Ill., 1946-56; prof., chmn. dept. psychiatry State U. N.Y. Upstate Med. Center, 1956-64, prof., 1964-66; prof. psychiatry U. Pa., 1966-70; prof., chmn. dept. psychiatry Vanderbilt U., Nashville, 1970—; mem. staff Inst. Psychoanalysis Chgo., 1953-56, dir. Syracuse Psychat. Hosp., 1957-64. Served from 1st lt. to maj. M.C., USAAF, 1942-46. Fellow Am. Psychiat. Assn., Am. Coll. Psychiatrists, Coll. Physicians Phila.; mem. Am. Psychoanalytic Assn., Am. Psychosomatic Soc., A.M.A., Sigma Xi, Alpha Omega Alpha. Author: The Psychology of Medical Practice, 1958; The Practice of Psychoanalytic Psychotherapy, 1965. Home: 4200 Harding Rd Nashville TN 37205

HOLLENDER, SAMUEL SYLVAN, optometrist, business exec.; b. Chgo., Dec. 8, 1900; s. Joseph and Mary (Koss) H.; Dr. Optometry, No. Ill. Coll. Ophthalmology and Otology, 1923; L.H.D. (hon.), Hebrew Union Coll., 1956, Jewish Inst. Religion; m. Sylvia Vivian Jacobson, July 26, 1922; children—Elaine Ann Kaplan, Caryl Rose Susman. Gen. merchandise mgr. dept. store, Chgo., 1930-32; organizer, pres. S. S. Hollender, Inc., 1933—; gen. mgr., partner Merryweather Optical Co., Chgo. and N.Y.C; chmn. bd. Almer Coe Optical Co., Chgo., 1955—. Dir. Mt. Sinai Hosp., 1934-39; mem. bd. govs. Chgo. Opera Co., 1935—; bd. dirs. Jewish Fedn. Chgo., 1941—, treas., 1947- 50, v.p., 1951, pres. 1956, gen. chmn. bldg. campaign, 1963; a founder Roosevelt U.; mem. bd. Jewish Braille Inst.; bd. dirs. Jewish Vocational Service and Employment Service, 1938-40; chmn. Met. Chgo. war records com. Nat. Jewish Welfare Bd., 1954-55, mem. nat. council; pres. Chgo. Fedn. Union Am. Hebrew Congregations, 1944-45, mem. nat. exec. bd., 1944—, v. chmn. exec. bd., 1946-51, chmn., 1951—, pres. 42d Biennial Assembly, 1953; mem. bd. World Union for Progressive Judaism; nat. chmn. Combined Appeal Union of Am. Hebrew Congregations, Hebrew Union Coll., and Jewish Inst. Religion, 1948-54; bd. dirs. Nat. Joint Distbn. Com., 1947—; gen. chmn. Combined Jewish Appeal, Chgo., 1951, pres., 1952; bd. dirs. United Jewish Bldg. Fund, 1946—; bd. trustees Hebrew Union Sch. of Edn. and Sacred Music; bd. govs. Hebrew Union Coll., Cin.; mem. nat. bd. Chgo. Med. Sch. Recipient award of merit Chgo. Fedn. Reform Synagogues, 1948, Man of Valor award Union of Am. Hebrew Congregations, 1955, Julius Rosenwald Meml. award Jewish Fedn. Met., Chgo., Bibl. Breastplate award, 1963; named to Golden Age Hall of Fame, Jewish Community Center of Chgo., 1967. Mem. Art Inst. Chgo. (life), Ill. Inst. Tech. (life; mem. bd. 1955-56), Alumnus Lewis Inst. (life), Zeta Beta Tau. Jewish religion. Mason (32, Shriner), B'nai B'rith. Clubs: Bryn Mawr (pres. 1950-51), Convenant (pres. 1935-37), Standard (bd. mgrs., 1950- 56), Chgo. Executives (Chgo.); Harmonie (N.Y.C.). Home: 247 E Chestnut St Chicago IL 60611 Office: 6 N Michigan Av Chicago IL 60602

HOLLENGREEN, MILBURN ALFRED, mfg. exec.; b. Renovo, Pa., Mar. 2, 1903; s. A.B. and Alfreda (Ostrom) H.; grad. Cornell, 1926; m. Leah Fisher, Oct. 4, 1930; children—Jon, M. A. (dec.). Asst. chief engr. Landis Machine Co., Waynesboro, 1926-36; asst. gen. mgr. Landis Tool Co., 1936-42, gen. mgr., 1942—, pres., 1948—; pres. Gardner Machine Co., Beloit, Wis., 1951—; chmn. Landis- Lund, Ltd., Eng., 1958—; pres. Landis-Grendron, S.A., France, 1960—; dir. 1st Nat. Bank & TrusT Co., Waynesboro. Bd. dirs. Waynesboro Hosp. Mem. Nat. Machine Tool Builders Assn. (chmn. govt. relations com., 1st v.p., pres. 1955, dir. 1965—). Home: 205 Clayton Av Waynesboro PA 19096 Office: Landis Tool Co Waynesboro PA 19096

HOLLENHORST, GEORGE DONALD, educator; b. St. Cloud, Minn., Sept. 6, 1918; s. John F. and Josephine (Meinz) H.; A.B. magna cum laude, St. John's U. (Minn.), 1940; M.A. maxima cum laude, U. Notre Dame, 1942, Ph.D., 1955; m. Ann Margaret Lynch, June 2, 1951; children—John, Sarah, Martha, Kate. Teaching fellow U. Notre Dame, 1946-47; mem. editorial staff The Great Ideas, 1947-48; lectr. Univ. Coll., U. Chgo. 1947-48; instr. philosophy Loyola U., Chgo., 1949-51; prof. philosophy Barat Coll., Lake Forest, Ill., 1952—, chmn. dept. philosophy, 1954—, also trustee; lectr. Sheil Sch. Social Studies, Chgo., 1947-51; cons. Our Wonderful World Ency. Served with AUS, 1942-46. Decorated Bronze Star medal. O'Hare fellow U. Notre Dame. Mem. Am., Am. Catholic philos. assns., Metaphys. Soc. Am., Am. Assn. U. Profs. (past chpt. pres.). Translator: (with others) The Material Logic of John of St. Thomas, 1955. Contbr. to The New Scholasticism. Mem. editorial staff The Great Ideas, Great Books of the Western World, 1952. Home: 2606 Elizabeth Av Zion IL 60099 Office: Barat Coll Lake Forest IL 60045

HOLLENHORST, ROBERT WILLIAM, educator, ophthalmologist; b. St. Cloud, Minn., Aug. 12, 1913; s. John and Josephine (Meinz) H.; student St. Cloud State Coll., 1931-33, St. John's U., 1933-35; B.S. cum laude, U. Minn., 1938, M.B., 1940, M.D., 1941, M.S. in Ophthalmology, 1948; m. Alice Cecilia Nolan, June 17, 1939; children—Robert W., Michael J., Mary E., John T., Mark T., James N., Kathleen E., Thomas M., Stephen E. Intern Abbott Hosp., Mpls., 1940, Ancker Hosp., St. Paul, 1940-41; resident ophthalmology Mayo Grad. Sch. Medicine, 1946-48, mem. faculty, 1948—, prof., 1965—; cons. ophthalmology Mayo Clinic, 1948—. Chmn. bd. Pre-sch. Survey Vision and Hearing, 1964-67; sr. cons. sect. perimetry and neuro- ophthalmology, home study course Am. Acad. Ophthalmology and Otolaryngology, 1960-68; cons. Minn. Services for Blind, 1961—. Served with M.C., AUS, 1941-46; PTO. Decorated Bronze Star. Diplomate Am. Bd. Ophthalmology (dir. 1968—). Mem. Am. Ophthalmol. Soc., Am., Minn. (pres. 1961-62) acads. ophthalmology, Assn. Research Ophthalmology, Am. Assn. History Medicine, Am., Minn. med. assns., Sigma Xi. Republican.

Roman Catholic. Author articles, chpts. in books. Editorial bd. Am. Jour. Ophthalmology, 1968—. Home: 420 5th Av SW Rochester MN 55901 Office: Mayo Clinic Rochester MN 55902

HOLLENSHEAD, CLYDE WILLYS, gas co. exec.; b. Ruple, La., Apr. 2, 1914; s. Thomas Frank and Kathryn (Miller) H.; B.S., La. Poly. Inst., 1935; student Mid South Exec. Devel. Program, 1960-63, advanced mgmt. program Harvard, 1967; m. Armenta Scott, Aug. 19, 1963; children—Thomas C., Richard D. With United Gas Pipe Line Co., Houston, 1935—, sr. v.p. engring. and operations, dir., 1969—; dir. Pennzoil Pipeline Co., United Offshore Co. (Shreveport, La.), also sr. v.p. Mem. exec. bd. Boy Scouts Am., Citizens Action Program of Houston. Mem. Shreveport Met. Planning Commn., 1963-69. Mem. Am. (vice chmn.), So. gas assns., Am. Petroleum Inst., Ind. Natural Gas Assn. Am., La. Engring. Soc., La. Bd. Profl. Engrs., Nat. Soc. Profl. Engrs., Natural Gas Mem. Houston. Mid Continent Oil and Gas Assn., Clubs: Petroleum Houston, and Shreveport; Shreveport. Home: 221 Blue Willow Dr Houston TX 77042 Office: Southwest Tower Houston TX 77002

HOLLENSHEAD, DAVID SMITH, banker; b. Needmore, Pa., Apr. 1, 1926; s. David and Blanche C. (Smith) H.; B.S.S., Hagerstown (Md.) Bus. Coll., 1943; B.A., Dickinson Coll., 1948; student Wharton Sch., 1948-50, Northwestern U., 1956-57; m. Raymeta L. Chaffee, Dec. 22, 1945; children—Karen Lee, Kathy Lynn. With Fed. Res. Bank Phila., 1948-50; with York Bank & Trust Co. (Pa.), 1950- -, exec. v.p., 1958—, also dir.; dir. York County Indsl. Devel. Corp., El- Ge Potato Chip Co., Inc. Bd. dirs. York Symphony Assn., Credit Bur. York (past pres.), York County Cancer Soc.; trustee Sheltered Workshop of York County, Inc. Served with AUS, 1944-46; ETO. Mem. York Area C. of C., Sigma Chi. Clubs: Country of York, Lafayette (dir.), Sertoma (past pres. York). Home: 49 Jolo Way York PA 17403 Office: 107 W Market St York PA 17404

HOLLERAN, ALOYSIUS JOSEPH, ins. co. exec.; b. Pitts., May 14, 1913; s. Anthony A. and Katherine (Moore) H.; B.A. in Bus. Adminstrn., Duquesne U., 1935; m. Ruth Wilkenson, Aug. 22, 1961; 1 son, Patrick A. Salesman, IBM Corp., 1937- 40, Standard Register Co., 1940; with Am. States Ins. Co., 1946—, sr. v.p. finance, 1967—, also dir.; dir. Am. States Ins. Group. Served to lt. (j.g.) USNR, 1943-46. Mem. Ins. Accounting and Statis. Assn. Club: Indianapolis Athletic. Home: 5354 Channing Rd Indianapolis IN 46226 Office: 542 N Meridian St Indianapolis IN 46206

HOLLERAN, EUGENE MARTIN, educator; b. Kingston, Pa., June 25, 1922; s. Michael John and Mary (Zipfel) H.; B.S., U. Scranton, 1943; Ph.D., Catholic U., 1949; m. Mary Margaret Walter, Aug. 13, 1947; children—Michael, Stephen, Mary, Mark Peter, Ann, Eileen, Margaret. Instr. Regis Coll. 1948-50; mem. faculty St. John's U., 1950—, prof. chemistry, 1955—, chmn. dept., 1961-65, 70—, dir. sci., 1965-67. Served to lt. (j.g.) USNR, 1944-46. Mem. Am. Chem. Soc., Holy Name Soc. (pres. parish 1961-62), A.A.A.S., Am. Phys. Soc., Sigma Xi. Roman Catholic. K.C. Home: 57 S Corona Av Valley Stream NY 11580 Office: St John's U Jamaica NY 11432

HOLLETT, BYRON PIERCE, lawyer; b. Indpls., Sept. 28, 1914; s. John Everett and Katherine (Sullivan) H.; A.B., Wabash Coll., 1936; J.D., Harvard Law Sch., 1939; m. Joan Piel Metzger, Sept. 11, 1940; children—Joan K. (Mrs. Thomas E. Brady), Byron Pierce II. Admitted to Ind. bar, 1939; partner firm Baker & Daniels, Indpls., 1939—, Dir. Am. Fletcher Nat. Bank, Lilly Endowment, Inc. Trustee Wabash Coll., Crown Hill Cemetery; gov. James Whitcomb Riley Hosp. Children. Served with USNR, 1942-45. Decorated Bronze Star. Mem. Sigma Chi. Episcopalian (chancellor Diocese Indpls. 1964—). Clubs: Woodstock, Columbia. Home: 5797 Sunset Lane Indianapolis IN 46208 Office: Fletcher Trust Bldg Indianapolis IN 46204

HOLLEY, CLYDE EUGENE, lawyer; b. nr. Hillsdale, Mich., Mar. 17, 1891; s. Ephriam Eugene and Ella Francelia (Kies) H.; A.B., Pomona Coll., 1913; student Wharton Sch. Finance, U. Pa., 1919-20; LL.B., Harvard, 1923; m. Elizabeth Ford Martin, Sept. 10, 1924; children—Nancy Elizabeth (Mrs. Edward McKenzie Hitchcock), Jeanne Louise (Mrs. Harold George Koos, Jr.), Patricia Ann (Mrs. John Alan Karsten), Geraldine Frances (Mrs. John Ludwig Christiansen). Promoter, organizer athletics in S.W. for A.G. Spalding & Bros., 1913-16; auditor Bur. of Supplies and Accounts, USN, 1919-21; admitted to Cal. bar, 1923; asso. Newin & Ashburn, Los Angeles, 1923-28, mem. firm, mng. partner, 1928-45; mng. partner Newlin, Holley, Sandmeyer & Coleman, 1945-48, Newlin, Holley, Sandmeyer & Tackabury, 1948-50, Newlin, Holley, Tackabury & Johnston, 1950-56; partner Baird, Holley, Baird & Galen, and predecessor firm, 1956—. Chmn. San Marino Citizens Com. of 100, 1944-48; mem. San Marino Community Council, 1936- -, pres., 1944-46, 64-65; mem. San Marino Planning Commn., chmn., 1955- -; hon. life mem. Cal. P.T.A; alumni council Pomona Coll, 1933- 40, 44-48, bd. overseers, 1926-33, sec., 1928-33. Served from chief yeoman to lt. USNRF, World War I. Recipient Citizenship award for meritorious accomplishment for community, San Marino Rotary, 1948. Mem. Am. Judicature Soc., Am. (Cal. mem. adv. com. on ethics and grievances 1953-58), Cal., Los Angeles (del. to ann. conv. Cal., 1956-69, chmn. membership com. 1962-68, mem. ethics com. 1935-45, 57-59) bar assns., Am. Legion. Republican. Conglist. (chmn. bldg. com.). Mason (Shriner). Clubs: Town Hall, Chancery, Kiwanis (Los Angeles); Harvard of Southern Cal.; Nat. Lawyers. Home: 1015 Roxbury Rd San Marino CA 91108 Office: 612 W 6th St Los Angeles CA 90017

HOLLEY, DONALD LEAGUE, educator; b. Normal, Ill., Oct. 1, 1916; s. Robert Earl and Minnie (League) H.; B.Ed., Ill. State Normal Coll., 1938; M.A., U. Ill., 1942; Ed.D., Colo. State Coll. (U. No. Colo.) 1961; m. Charlotte Woodworth, Aug. 2, 1938; children—Michael James, Jane Lee (Mrs. Richard Sullivan), Peggy Sue (Mrs. Don Wagner). Tchr., John Greer High Sch. Hoopeston, Ill., 1938-42, Geneseo (Ill.) High Sch., 1942-57; prof., chmn. dept. speech communication U. No. Colo., Greeley, 1957—. Mem. tean-faculty Frontiers of Sci. Inst., 1959-63; coordinator Pakistan Project U. No. Colo., 1965-66. Precinct committeeman Democratic Party, Greeley, 1969-70. Honored alumni Ill. State U., 1966. Mem. Colo. Speech and Drama Tchrs. Assn., Colo. Speech Assn. (pres.), U. Profs. for Acad. Order, Speech Communication Assn., N.E.A., Nat. Thespian Soc. (hon.), Phi Delta Kappa. Kiwanian. Author: Extempore Speaking: A Handbook, 1947. Home: 2043 22d Av Greeley CO 80631

HOLLEY, EDWARD GAILON, univ. dean; b. Pulaski, Tenn., Nov. 26, 1927; s. Abe Brown and Maxie Elizabeth (Bass) H.; B.A. magna cum laude, David Lipscomb Coll., Nashville, 1949; M.A., George Peabody Coll., 1951; Ph.D., U. Ill., 1961; m. Robbie Lee Gault, June 19, 1954; children—Gailon Boyd, Edward Jens, Amy Lin, Beth Alison, Holley. Asst. librarian David Lipscomb Coll., 1949- 51; mem. staff U. Ill., 1951-62, librarian edn., philosophy and psychology library, 1957-62; dir. libraries U. Houston, 1962-72; dean Sch. Library Sci., U. N.C. at Chapel Hill, 1972—; vis. lectr. U. Wis., Madison, summer, 1968; vis. prof. N. Tex. State U., summer, 1970. Mem. adv. council library resources U.S. Office Edn., 1968-71. Served to lt. (s.g.) USNR, 1953-56. Mem. Am. (Scarecrow Press award 1964), Tex. (pres. 1971) library assns., Assn. College and Research Librarians (editor Monographs 1969—), Phi Kappa Phi, Kappa Delta Pi, Beta Phi Mu. Democrat. Mem. Ch. of Christ. Author: Charles Evans, American Bibliographer, 1963; Raking the Historical Coals, 1967; (with Don Hendricks) Resources of Texas Libraries, 1968; also articles. Address: Sch Library Sci Univ NC Chapel Hill NC

HOLLEY, FRANK EDWARD, banker, b. Urbana, Ill., Nov. 24, 1919; s. Charles Elmer and Viola Esther (Wolfe) H.; B.S. with high honors, U. Ill., 1940; m. Florence Esther Blekking, June 7, 1941; children—Douglas Edwin, Esther Annette (Mrs. Georgette L. Greene), David Russell. With Eastman Kodak Co., 1940-53, asst. credit mgr., 1951- 53; with Union Trust Co., Rochester, N.Y., 1953-55, comptroller, 1954- 55, bank merged with Marine Midland Bank-Rochester (formerly Genesee Valley Union Trust Co.), 1955, exec. v.p., 1962-68, dir., chmn. exec. com., 1968—; dir. Midland Marine Services Corp., Marine Midland Municipals Co. Faculty, Grad. Sch. Credit and Financial, Mgmt., Dartmouth, summers 1955, 57-59, 65-69. Vice pres., trustee Credit Research Found.; bd. dirs. Rochester Civic Music Assn., 1961-70, pres., 1965-67, chmn. bd., 1967-69; bd. dirs. Rochester Credit Bur., Rochester Area Ednl. TV Assn., Rochester Assn. for UN; pres. Gates Chili Central Sch. Bd., 1956-58; bd. dirs., chmn. finance com. Rochester Gen. Hosp., 1963—. Served to lt. (j.g.) USNR, 1943-46. Mem. Financial Execs. Inst. (past pres. Rochester), Rochester Credit and Financial Mgmt. Assn. (past pres.), Rochester Credit Mens Service Corp. (past pres.). Presbyn. (pres. trustees). Clubs: Genesee Valley, University (Rochester). Contbr. chpts. to books. Home: 5 S Pittsford Hill Lane Pittsford NY 14534 Office: 1 Marine Midland Plaza Rochester NY 14604

HOLLEY, HOWARD LAMAR, physician, educator; b. Marion, Ala., July 14, 1914; s. Warren Alton and Lula (Fretwell) H.; B.S., U. S.C., 1935; M.D., Med. Coll. S.C., 1941; m. Martha Holcomb, Sept. 7, 1946; children—Dan, Nancy, Warren, Howard, Jane. Mem. faculty U. Ala. Med. Sch., 1947—, prof. internal medicine, 1959—, dir. div. rheumatology, 1955-70, distinguished faculty lectr., 1969, Anna Lois Waters prof. medicine in rheumatology, 1970—. Chmn. arthritis tng. grants com. Nat. Inst. Arthritis, 1964-65. Recipient Seale Harris Research award, 1962; Distinguished Service award Ala. chpt. Arthritis Found., 1968. Fellow A.C.P. (gov. Ala.); mem. So. Soc. Clin. Investigation, Am. Rheumatism Assn., Am., So. med. assns., Am. Fedn. Clin. Research, Med. Assn. Ala., Sigma Xi. Author: (with Allen E. Hussar) Antibiotics and Antibiotic Therapy, A Clinical Manual, 1954; (with others) Potassium Metabolism in Health and Disease, 1955; A Continual Remembrance: Letters From Sir William Osler to his Friend, Ned Milburn, 1865-1919, 1968. Contbr. articles profl. jours. Home: 4016 Old Leeds Circle Birmingham AL 35213

HOLLEY, JACK KARL, newspaperman; b. Denver, Jan. 2, 1937; s. W. Jack and Grace (Hood) J.; B.A., U. Colo., 1960; m. Ann M. Dewitz, July 23, 1960; children—Richard T., Michael D., Laura A. With Omaha World-Herald, 1961- -, entertainment editor, 1965-66, city govt. reporter, 1966-67, municipal affairs writer, 1967-69, asst. city editor, 1969—. Mem. bd. Omaha Regional Ballet Acad., 1964-65. Mem. Army N.H., 1960- 65. Recipient Ak-Sar-Ben Outstanding Nat. Guardsman award, 1963. Mem. Phi Kappa Tau, Sigma Delta Chi. Conglist. Club: Omaha Press. Home: 1537 Skylark Dr Omaha NB 68144 Office: World-Herald 14th and Dodge Sts Omaha NB 68102

HOLLEY, ROBERT WILLIAM, scientist; b. Urbana, Ill., Jan. 28, 1922; s. Charles E. and Viola (Wolfe) H.; A.B., U. Ill., 1942; Ph.D., Cornell U., 1947; m. Ann Dworkin, Mar. 3, 1945; 1 son, Frederick. Am. Chem. Soc. fellow State Coll. Wash., 1947-48; asst. prof., asso. prof. organic chemistry N.Y. State Agr. Expt. Sta., Cornell U., 1948-57; Guggenheim fellow Cal. Inst. Tech., 1955-56; research chemist plant, soil and nutrition lab. U.S. Dept. Agr., Cornell U., Ithaca, N.Y., 1957-64, prof. biochemistry Cornell U., 1964- 69, chmn. dept. biochemistry 1965-66; resident fellow Salk Inst. Biol. Studies, La Jolla, Cal., 1968—; mem. biochemistry study sect. NIH, 1962-66; vis. fellow Salk Inst. Biol. Studies; vis. prof. Scripps Clinic and Research Found., La Jolla, Cal., 1966-67. Recipient Distinguished Service award U.S. Dept. Agr., 1965, Albert Lasker award Basic Med. Research, 1965; U.S. Steel Found. award in molecular biology, Nat. Acad. Scis., 1967; Nobel prize for medicine and physiology, 1968. Fellow A.A.A.S.; mem. Am. Acad. Arts and Scis., Am. Soc. Biol. Chemists, Am. Chem. Soc., Nat. Acad. Scis., Phi Beta Kappa, Sigma Xi. Home: 7381 Rue Michael La Jolla CA 92037 Office: PO Box 1809 San Diego CA 92112

HOLLEY, RUDOLPH EUGENE, lawyer, state senator; b. Aiken, S.C., Feb. 15, 1926; s. Norton Hansford and Harriett (Holley) H.; B.B.A., U. Ga., 1949, LL.B. magna cum laude, 1958; m. Louise Herman Brittingham, Sept. 19, 1953; children-Robert Eugene, Phillip Gerard, Stephen Thomas, Anna Louise, Eugene Norton. Admitted to Ga. bar, 1957; practice in Augusta, 1958—; mem. firm Congdon & Leonard, 1958, Congdon & Holley, 1959-66, Sanders, Hester & Holley, 1967-68; partner Sanders, Hester, Holley, Ashmore & Boozer, Augusta 1968—; mem. Ga. State Senate, 1965—; dep. asst. atty. gen., Ga., 1964-65. Dir. West Lake Devel. Co., Medi-Center of Augusta, Met. Land & Investment Co. (all Augusta). Trustee Hillcrest Meml. Park Perpetual Care Trust. Served with USAAF, 1943-45; to capt. USAF, 1949- 55. Decorated D.F.C. Mem. Augusta C. of C., Phi Beta Kappa, Chi Psi, Phi Kappa Phi. Democrat. Baptist. Club: Sertoma (Augusta). Editor Ga. Bar Jour., 1957-58. Home: 2715 Walton Way Augusta GA 30904 Office: Commerce Bldg Broad at 7th St Augusta GA 30902

HOLLEY, THOMAS WALTERS, tobacco co. exec.; b. Buhl, Minn., Oct. 12, 1908; s. Albert Bernard and Kate (Walters) H.; m. Mabel De Campo, Feb. 7, 1963; children by previous marriage—Carol (Mrs. John K. Kelley), Elizabeth (Mrs. Gordon Armstrong). With U.S. Tobacco Co., 1931—, dept. mgr., 1954-64, v.p., 1960-67, exec. v.p., dir,, 1967—; v.p., dir. J.C. Winter & Co., Red Lion, Pa., 1965—, House of Windsor, Inc. (Pa.), 1965—; dir. Nat. Tobacco Co. Ltd., Montreal, Can., Tuckersharp Pen Co., Richmond, Va. Mason. Home: 109 Westover Rd Stamford CT 06902 Office: 100 W Putnam Av Greenwich CT 06830

HOLLIDAY, ALAN SMITH, printing co. exec., assn. ofcl.; b. Stockton-on-Trees, Thornby, Eng., Dec. 23, 1920; s. William Smith and Sara Edna (Brach) H.; came to U.S., 1924, naturalized, 1943; student Millersville (Pa.) State Tchrs. Coll., 1939-41; m. Adeline Curnow, July 26, 1945; children—William Smith, Barbara Lynn. Compositor, Montrose Pub. Co. (Pa.), 1945-48; with Craftsmen, Inc., subsidiary Hughes Corp., 1940-60, pres., 1954-60; pres. Science Press, subsidiary Printing Corp. Am., 1960—; dir. research Hughes Corp., 1950-62; pres. Trade Press, 1958—. Pres. Pa. YMCA, 1966-67. Bd. dirs. Hughes Found., 1959—. Mem. Internat. Assn. Printing House Craftsmen (pres. Lehigh Valley club 1956, internat. bd. govs. 1960-62, internat. v.p. 1961-62, internat. pres. 1963-64), Tech. Assn. Graphic Arts, Printing Technologist Great Britain, Susquehanna Lith Club (Lancaster, Pa.). Mason (K.T.). Club: Hamilton (Lancaster). Home: 225 Murray Hill Dr Lancaster PA 17601 Office: 300 W Chestnut St Ephrata PA 17522

HOLLIDAY, RAYMOND MIDDLETON, tool co. exec.; b. Winfield, Tex., Aug. 14, 1914; s. Charles Calvin and Carrie Roan (Middleton) H.; B.S., E. Tex. State Coll., 1935; grad. student Tex. A. and M. Coll., 1937-38; LL.B., S. Tex. Coll. Law, 1949; m. Mary Frances McCulloch, Oct. 1, 1938. With Hughes Tool Co., Houston, 1938—, v.p., sec., 1955-63, exec. v.p., 1963—, also dir.; admitted to Tex. bar, 1949; asst. dist. atty. Harris County. 1949; v.p., sec., dir. Hughes Tool Co. of Australia, Ltd.; v.p., dir. Hughes Tool Co. S.A.C.I.F.I., Hughes de Mexico, S.A. de C.V., Hughes Tool Co. de Mex., S.A. de C.V., HTC de Mexico, S.A. de C.V.; sec., dir. Hughes Tool Co. Ltd.; dir. Tex. Commerce Bank, Houston; dir., mem. exec. com. Hughes Air Corp. Sec., treas., exec. com. Howard Hughes Med. Inst. Bd. regents East Tex. State U. Served to lt. USNR. 1943-45. C.P.A. Tex. Mem. Am. Inst. C.P.A.'s, Tex. Soc. C.P.A.'s, Am. Mgmt. Assn., Houston, C. of C. Methodist. Mason (Shriner). Clubs: Lakeside Country, Petroleum, Internat., Houston. Home: 450 Westminster St Houston TX 77024 Office: Humble Bldg Houston TX 77002

HOLLIDAY, THOMAS WENDELL, banker; b. Chattanooga, July 20, 1929; s. Thomas J. and Thelma (Burk) H.; B.S., U. Chattanooga, 1961; grad. Stonier Sch. Banking, Rutgers U., 1965; m. Starlena Land, Sept. 20, 1950; children—Michael Stephen, Thomas Warren. With Hamilton Nat. BAnk, Chattanooga, 1947—, v.p., 1963—, comptroller, 1964—; sec.-treas. Hamilton Nat. Assoc., Inc., 1963—, also dir.; dir. First Nat. Bank, Lenoir City, Tenn., 1966—. Served with USNR, 1952-53. Mem. Greater Chattanooga C. of C., Inst. Internal Auditors (pres. Chattanooga 1965, bd. dirs. 1966-67), Financial Execs. Inst. (pres. Chattanooga 1967), Am. Inst. Banking. Baptist. Club: Rivermont Golf and Country (Chattanooga). Home: 1005 Roselawn Dr Chattanooga TN 37421 Office: 701 Market St Chattanooga TN 37401

HOLLIDAY, VIVIAN LOYREA, educator; b. Manning, S.C., Feb. 25, 1935; s. Louis Arlo and Ellen Loyrea (Brewer) H.; B.A., Winthrop Coll., 1957; M.A., U. Mo., 1959; Ph.D., U. N.C., 1961. Mem. faculty Coll. Wooster (O.), 1961—, Aylesworth prof. Latin, 1970—. Fulbright fellow, Italy, summer 1965; grantee Nat. Endowment for Humanities, 1970. Mem. Am. Philogical Assn., Classical Assn. Middle W. and S., Modern Greek Studies Assn. Author: Pompey in Cicero's Letters and Lucan's Civil War, 1969; also articles. Home: 236 Spring St Wooster OH 44691

HOLLIFIELD, GUY FOSTER, physician; b. Courtland, Va., June 15, 1922; s. June Foster and Nell (Graham) H.; B.S., Va. Mil. Inst., 1943; M.D., U. Va., 1950; m. Katherine Crompton Elmer, Dec. 28, 1946 (div.); children—Guy Foster, William Hart, James Evans. Fellow in medicine U. Minn., 1951-53; B. Armistead Shepherd Meml. fellow med. research U. Va. Med. Sch., 1953-54, instr. medicine, 1954-58, asst. prof. medicine, 1958-60, asso. prof. medicine, 1960-66; prof. medicine Northwestern U. Med. Sch., 1966—; chmn. dept. medicine Chgo. Wesley Meml. Hosp., Northwestern U. Med. Center, 1966—; sr. attending physician Chgo. Wesley Meml. Hosp., 1966—. Served with USAAF, 1943-45. Recipient John Horsley Meml. prize for research, 1962. Fellow Am. Coll. Physicians, Am. Pub. Health Assn.; mem. Am., So. socs. clin. investigation, Central Soc. Clin. Research, Inst. Medicine Chgo., Am. Fedn. Clin. Research, Endocrine Soc., Sigma Xi. Contbr. publs. in endocrinology and metabolic disorders. Office: 250 E Superior St Chicago IL 60611

HOLLIMAN, JOE MILTON, lawyer; b. Bartlesville, Okla., Oct. 13, 1921; s. John M. and Prudie (Smith) H.; B.A., Okla. State U., 1943; LL.B., Okla. U., 1946; m. Jean Felt, July 29, 1944; children—Janice (Mrs. Rowland D. Stanfield, Jr.), John Howard, Joanna. Admitted to Okla. bar, 1946, since practiced in Tulsa; mem. firm Holliman, Langholz, Runnels & Dorwart. Pres., dir. Holarud, Inc.; sec., dir. Falcon Seaboard, Inc.; dir. Nat. Galvanizing Co., Utica Sq. Nat. Bank. Vice pres., sec. Howard E. Felt Found.; bd. advisers Tulsa Salvation Army. Mem. Am., Okla., Tulsa County bar assns. Methodist. Clubs: Tulsa (pres.), Southern Hills Country (sec., dir.) (Tulsa). Home: 2716 S Birmingham Pl Tulsa OK 74114 Office: Fourth Nat Bank Bldg Tulsa OK 74119

HOLLINGER, PAUL HENRY, physician; b. Chgo., Mar. 13, 1906; s. Jacques and Cora (Lange) H.; B.S., U. Chgo., 1928; M.S., Northwestern U., 1930, M.D., 1933; m. Julia Drake, June 26, 1940; children—Lauren Drake, William Jacques, Paul Campbell, Richard Lange. Asst. to Dr. Chevalier Jackson, Bronchoscopic Clinic, Temple U. Hosp., Phila., 1934-35 mem. faculty U. Ill. Coll. Medicine, 1936—, successively instr. laryngology, asso. laryngology, asst. prof. otolaryngology, asso. prof. laryngology, rhinology, otology, 1936-50, prof. bronchoesophagology, 1950—; attending bronchoesophagologist Presbyn.-St. Luke's Hosp., Children's Meml. Hosp., Chgo., 1936—; cons. Armed Forces Inst. Pathology, 1956—; Samuel Cowe prof. otolaryngology Johns Hopkins Hosp., Balt., 1959; cons. U.S. Naval Hosp., Great Lakes, Ill.; pres. med. staff St. Luke's Hosp., 1953-55; Sir Felix Semon lectr. U. London, 1960; vis. prof. otolaryngology U. Cal., Los Angeles, 1961. Gen. sec. 6th Internat. Congress Otolaryngology, 1957. Bd. trustees Chgo. Med. Sch. Recipient Casselberry award in otolaryngology, 1946; 1st prize for sci. film on bronchial tumors Brussels Film Festival, 1947; Louis Schmidt award Biol. Photog. Assn., 1959; 1st prize for film on endoscopic photography 1st Internat. Congress Med. Photography, 1961; Chevalier Jackson award Am. Bronchoesophagological Assn., 1962; Newcomb award Am. Laryngol. Assn., 1962, deRoaldes award, 1966; Rudolf Schindler award Am. Soc. Gastrointestinal Endoscopy, 1968. Fellow Biol. Photog. Assn., A.M.A. (chmn. sect. laryngology, rhinology, otology 1959- 60, ho. of dels. 1963-67, chmn. interspecialty com. 1966—), Am. Coll. Chest Physicians, A.C.S. (gov., bd. regents), Am. Assn. Thoracic Surgeons, Am. Laryngol. Assn. (pres. 1965-66); mem. Am Broncho- esophagol. Assn. (pres. 1948-49), Internat. Bronchoesophagolog. Soc. (pres. 1962-65), Inst. Medicine Chgo. (chmn. bd. govs. 1961-66), Am. Soc. Gastrointestinal Endoscopy (pres. 1963-64), Sigma Xi. Home: 3500 Lake Shore Dr Chicago, IL 60610. Office: 700 N Michigan Av Chicago IL 60611

HOLLINGER, WILBUR D., utility exec.; b. 1911; married. With Met. Edison Co., Reading, Pa., 1929—, asst. sec., asst. treas., 1959-68, sec., treas., 1968—. Office: Met Edison Co PO Box 542 Reading PA 19603

HOLLINGS, ERNEST FREDERICK, U.S. senator; b. Charleston, S.C., Jan. 1, 1922; s. Adolph G. and Wilhelmine D. (Meyer) H.; B.A., The Citadel, 1942; LL.B., U. S.C., 1947; m. Martha Patricia Salley, Mar. 30, 1946; children—Michael Milhous, Helen Hayne, Patricia Salley., Ernest Frederick III. Admitted to S.C. bar, 1947; mem. S.C. Ho. of Reps., 1948-54, speaker pro tem, 1950-54; lt. gov. of S.C., 1955-59; gov. of S.C., 1959-63; practiced in Charleston, 1963—; U.S. senator State of S.C., 1966—. Mem. Hoover Comm. on Intelligence Activities, 1954-55; mem. President's Adv. Comm. on Intergovernmental Relations, 1959-63; mem. exec. council Lutheran Ch. Am. Trustee Newberry Coll. Named one of Ten Outstanding Young Men, U.S. Junior C. of C., 1954. Mem. Assn. Citadel Men, Hibernian Soc., Phi Delta Phi. Democrat. Lutheran. Club: Sertoma (Charleston). Home: 120 S Battery Charleston SC 29401 Office: Senate Office Bldg Washington DC 20510

HOLLINGSHEAD, AUGUST DE BELMONT, educator; b. Lyman, Wyo., Apr. 15, 1907; s. William Thomas and Daisy E. (Rollins) H.; A.B., U. Cal., 1931, M.A., 1933; Ph.D., U. Neb., 1935; m. Carol E. Dempsey, Nov. 4, 1931; children—Anne Marie, Ellen May. Instr. sociology U. Ia., 1935, U. Ala., 1935-36; instr. sociology

Ind. U., 1936- 39, asst. prof., 1939-41, asso. prof., 1946-47; Social Sci. Research Council postdoctoral fellow U. Chgo., 1941-42, vis. prof., 1948; vis. prof. U. So. Cal., 1946, 51; asso. prof. sociology Yale, 1947-52, prof. 1952—, chmn. dept. sociology, 1959-65, William Graham Summer prof., 1963—; vis. prof. Psychiat. Inst., U. London, 1957- 58; senior Fulbright scholar U.K., 1957-58; cons. surgeon gen. USPHS, 1960-69; temporary adviser WHO, Geneva, Switzerland, 1968; mental health cons. U. P.R., 1956-64; research cons. Planned Parenthood, 1956; tech. cons. Nat. Assn. Mental Health, 1969—. Mem. bd. Nat. Assn. Retarded Children; mem. Midwestern region Nat. Resources Planning Bd., 1937-41. Served to 1st lt. USAAF, 1943-45. Mem. Am. Assn. U. Profs. (pres. Yale 1955-57), Am. (chmn. publs. com. 1953-55, mem. exec. council 1963-66, v.p. 1957), Eastern (exec. com. 1952-55, v.p. 1957, pres. 1961) sociol. socs., Internat. Inst. Sociology, Am. Psychopathol. Assn. Sigma Xi, Alpha Kappa Delta (pres. 1947-50). Republican. Episcopalian. Author: Principles of Human Ecology, 1938; Elmtown's Youth, 1949; sr. author: Social Class and Mental Illness, 1958; Principles of Sociology, 1969. Co-author: Trapped: Families and Schizophrenia, 1965; Sickness and Society, 1968. Contbr. sci. jours. Home: Enoch Dr Woodbridge CT 06525 Office: Yale U New Haven CT 06520

HOLLINGSWORTH, ALAN MERRILL, educator; b. Westwood, Cal., Aug. 3, 1920; s. Merrill Windsor and Amy Marie (Weldt) H.; A.B., U. Cal. at Berkeley, 1948, M.A., 1949, Ph.D., 1956; m. Jeanne Marie Heimann, June 9, 1958; children—Jeffrey Alan, Amy Marie. Prof. English, Ind. U., 1954-67; chmn. English dept. Mich. State U., East Lansing, 1967—; Cons. U.S. Office Edn., Health, Edn. and Welfare, Assn. Depts. of English. Served with AUS, 1942-45. Recipient Ulysses G. Weatherly Distinguished Teaching award, 1960. Mem. Midwest Modern Lang. Assn. (pres. 1969). Home: 330 Kensington Rd East Lansing MI 48823

HOLLINGSWORTH, AMOR, former paper co. exec.; b. Milton, Mass., Aug. 12, 1909; s. Amor and Evelyn Knapp (Parsons) H.; grad. St. Mark's Sch., Southboro, Mass., 1927; A.B., Harvard, 1931, M.B.A., 1933; m. Eleanor Gibson, June 6, 1936; children—Eleanor (Mrs. Stokley P. Towles), Evelyn (Mrs. Robert W. Doran), Nancy (Mrs. Charles F. Taplin). Vice Chmn. Penobscot Co. (formerly Penobscot Chem. Fibre Co.), Great Works, Me., 1960-68, also dir.; pres., dir. Whiting & Co., 1962-65, chmn., 1965-66, also dir.; pres., dir. Tileston & Hollingsworth Co., Boston, 1942-70; dir. Arkwright-Boston Mfrs. Mut. Ins. Co., Hollingsworth & Vose Co., Old Colony Trust Co., Penobscot Devel. Co., Mut. Boiler & Machinery Ins. Co., Hersey-Sparling Meter Co.; trustee Dedham Instn. Savs., Middlesex Mut. Bldg. Trust Bd. overseers Boys Club Boston; bd. mgrs. Adams Nervine Hosp.; corporator Childrens Hosp., Boston; trustee Faulkner Hosp., West Chop Trust. Clubs: Somerset (Boston); Country (Brookline, Mass.), West Chop. Home: 59 Church St Dedham MA 02026 also Boca Grande FL 33921

HOLLINGSWORTH, CAREY FERGUSON, Jr., banker; b. Bessemer, Ala., Sept. 28, 1929; s. Carey Ferguson and Elizabeth (Lipscomb) H.; B.S. in Chemistry, U. Ala., 1952, LL.B., 1956; postgrad. Nat. Trust Sch., Northwestern U., 1960, Stonier Grad. Sch. Banking, Rutgers U., 1964; m. Joan Alene Wall, June 8, 1956; children—Carey Ferguson III, David Wall, Jay Lipscomb, James Matthews. Admitted to Ala. bar, 1956; law clk. Supreme Ct. Ala., 1956; with Birmingham Trust Nat. Bank (Ala.), 1957-60, 65—, trust officer, 1965—, v.p., 1967—; trust officer City Nat. Bank Tuscaloosa, 1960-65. Served with AUS, 1952-54. Mem. Ala. Bankers Assn. (mem. probate study com. trust div.), Ala., Birmingham bar assns., S.A.R. (treas. Birmingham chpt. 1970), Phi Delta Phi, Omicron Delta Kappa, Phi Gamma Delta. Presbyn. Kiwanian. Club: Birmingham Country. Co- editor: How to Administer Estates in Alabama, 1968. Home: 4009 Old Leeds Ridge Birmingham AL 35213 Office: 112 N 20th St Birmingham AL 35203

HOLLINGSWORTH, JACK WARING, educator; b. S. Haven, Kan., Mar. 3, 1924; s. Virgil Braxton and Ethel (Waring) H.; B.S. in Engring. Physics, U. Kan., 1948, B.A., 1949; M.S., U. Wis., 1951, Ph.D., 1954; m. Nancy Lee Harris, Sept. 14, 1950; children—Joel, Priscilla, Seth. Teaching asst. U. Kan., 1947-49, U. Wis., 1949-50, computing asst., 1950-54; gen. sci. aide U.S. Naval Ordnance Lab., 1950; mathematician Gen. Electric Co., 1954-57; mem. faculty Rensselaer Poly. Inst., 1957—, prof. math., 1961—, supr. computer lab., 1957-70, chmn. interdisciplinary com. computer sci., 1967- -. Served to 1st lt. USAAF, 1943-45. Decorated D.F.C., Air medal with 4 oak leaf clusters, Purple Heart. Mem. Assn. Computing Machinery (treas. spl. interest group of univ. computing centers 1964—), Am. Math. Soc., Soc. Indsl. and Applied Math., Math. Assn. Am., Sigma Xi, Tau Beta Pi, Omicron Delta Kappa, Kappa Eta Kappa. Mem. Reformed Ch. (elder). Mason. Home: 36 Terrace Ct Country Knolls Ballston Lake NY 12019 Office: Dept of Math Rensselear Poly Inst Troy NY 12181

HOLLINGSWORTH, JAMES FRANCIS, army officer; b. Sanger, Tex., Mar. 24, 1918; s. James Newton and Mamie Ella (Browning) H.; B.S., Tex. A. and M. U., 1940; M.A., George Washington U., 1963; grad. Command and Gen. Staff Coll., 1952, Army War Coll., 1957; m. Katherine Elizabeth Nicholson, Mar. 19, 1940; 1 son, James Francis II (dec. 1960). Commd. 2d lt. U.S. Army, 1940, advanced through grades to maj. gen., 1965; comdr. armored forces, 1940-45; instr. Army schs., also U.S. Mil. Acad., 1945-53; gen. staff officer Office Sec. Army, 1953-56; comdr. army brigade, 1956-61; dep. asst. sec. def., 1961-65; comdg. gen. combat troops, 1966-67, U.S. Inf. Tng. Center, 1968-70, U.S. Army Alaska, 1970—. Trustee Youth Service Am.; v.p., Scholarship Found. 1st Div. Decorated D.S.C. with 2 oak leaf clusters, D.S.M. with oak leaf cluster. Mason (32 , Shriner). Home: 65 Greyling St APO Seattle WA 98749 Office: Comdg Gen US Army Alaska Seattle WA 98749

HOLLINGSWORTH, ROBERT EDGAR, govt. ofcl.; b. Dawson, Ga., Sept. 23, 1918; s. John Cullen and Lillie (Christie) H.; A.B., Columbia, 1939, grad. student, 1938-40, Rosenwald fellow, 1946-47; m. Florence Beatrice Krieg, May 13, 1945; children—John Krieg, Joni Louise; m. 2d, Margaret Camille Jacob, July 14, 1960; children—Robert Edgar, Barbara Camille, William Lee, Bradford Damion. Mem. staff AEC, 1947—, asst. gen. mgr. for adminstrn., 1956-59, dep. gen. mgr., 1959-64, gen. mgr., 1964—. Served as lt. col., AUS, 1942-46. Recipient Arthur S. Flemming award, 1957; Distinguished Fed. Civilian Service award, 1966; Distinguished Service award AEC, 1969. Club: Bethesda Country. Home: 11316 Rouen Dr Potomac MD 20854 Office: AEC Washington DC 20545

HOLLINGSWORTH, ROBERT EDMUND, newspaper exec.; b. Montoe, La., June 30, 1926; s. Oswald Murray and Ora (Redfearn) H.; student U. Tex., Austin, 1946-49; m. Ann Elizabeth Prather, July 9, 1949; 1 dau., Lynn. Reporter, Dallas Times Herald, 1949- 55, polit. editor, 1955-61, city editor, 1961-63, chief Washington Bur., 1963-65, mng. editor, 1965-70, corp. adminstrv. asst., 1970—. Mem. adv. bd. journalism edn. U. Tex. System; mem. scholarship selection com. St. Johns Coll., Santa Fe. Served with USNR, 1944-46. Mem. S.W. Journalism Forum, Am. Polit. Sci. Assn., Headliners, Sigma Delta Chi. Home: 4920 Mill Creek Rd. Dallas TX 75234. Office: Herald Sq Dallas TX 75202

HOLLINGSWORTH, WILLIAM THOMAS, univ. dean; b. Newton, Miss., Dec. 7, 1917; s. John E. and Virginia (Prince) H.; B.S., Miss. State U., 1948; M.A., Columbia, 1948, Ed. D., 1959; m. Jane Elizabeth Majure, Oct. 30, 1943; children—Elizabeth Jane, David Majure. Dir. student activities Miss. State U., 1949-57; dean students Berry Schs., Mt. Berry, Ga., 1957-60; dean men Miami U., Oxford, O., 1960—. Served to maj. USAAF, World War II Decorated D.F.C., theatre medal with 2 bronze stars, Air medal with three oak leaf clusters. Mem. Am. Personnel and Guidance Assn., Am. Coll. Personnel Assn., Assn. Higher Edn., Nat., Ohio assns. student personnel adminsters., Miami Area Guidance Assn., Omicron Delta Kappa, Phi Delta Kappa, Kappa Sigma, Blue Key. Presbyn. (elder). Clubs: Oxford Country, Oxford Men's. Home: 11 Panda Lane Oxford OH 45056

HOLLINGTON, RICHARD RINGS, lawyer; b. West Unity, O., Apr. 7, 1907; s. William A. and Lucy (Rings) H.; A.B., Ohio State U., 1929; LL.B., Western Res. U., 1932; m. Annett Kirk, Oct. 24, 1931; children—Richard Rings, Mary E. (Mrs. George N. Chandler, III). Marcia K. (Mrs. James Kehres), David W., Annett E. Admitted to Ohio bar, 1932, also U.S. Supreme Ct.; practice in Cleve., 1936—; partner firm McDonald, Hopkins, Hardy, & Hollington, Cleve.; pres., dir. Ohio Bank & Savs. Co., Findlay. 1953—; dir. Fed. Res. Bank, Cleve., also numerous other corps.; asst. atty. gen., spl. counsel to supt. banks Ohio, 1933-36. Mem. Am., Ohio, Cleve. bar assns., Am., Ohio bankers assns., Cleve., Findlay chambers commerce, Newcomen Soc., Phi Kappa Psi. Episcopalian (past clk., warden, vestryman). Clubs: Findlay Country; Country (sec.), Cleveland Athletic, Skating, Midday. Union (Cleve.); Gulf Stream Golf (Delray Beach, Fla.) Home: 2761 Sherbrooke Rd Shaker Heights OH 44122 Office: East Ohio Bldg Cleveland OH 44114

HOLLINS, GERALD V., investment exec.; b. East Islip, N.Y., Sept. 17, 1912; s. Gerald V. and Virginia (Kobbe) H.; student Harvard, 1932-34; m. Elizabeth Armour, June 3, 1939; children—Peter, Danforth, Michael. With U.S. Lines, N.Y.C., also Chgo., 1934-38, mgr. freight dept., Cleve., 1938-39; asst. to pres. Rathborne, Hair & Ridgway Co., Chgo., 1939-42; with Harris, Upham & Co., Chgo., 1945—, now first v.p. Dir. Infant Welfare Soc., Chgo. Served as lt. comdr. USNR, 1942-45. Clubs: Chicago, Attic; Old Elm (Fort Sheridan, Ill.); Shoreacres (Lake Bluff, Ill.); Onwentsia (Lake Forest). Home: Old School Rd Libertyville IL 60048 Office: 135 S LaSalle St Chicago IL 60603

HOLLINSHEAD, BYRON S., Jr., pub. co. exec.; b. Danville, Pa., May 14, 1929; s. Byron S. and Clara (Stevens) H.; A.B. cum laude, Princeton, 1951; m. Judith Brown, June 25, 1955; children—Elinore, Ralph. Editor, Oxford U. Press, N.Y.C., 1956-64, v.p., 1964-68, exec. v.p., editor-in-chief, 1968—. Served to capt. USMCR, 1951-53. Decorated D.F.C., Air medal with four oak leaf clusters, Navy Commendation medal with combat V. Clubs: Princeton (bd. govs., N.Y.C.), Englewood Field. Home: 99 Glenwood Rd Englewood NJ 07631 Office: 200 Madison Av New York City NY 10016

HOLLINSHEAD, WILLIAM HENRY, educator; b. Winchester, Tenn., June 17, 1906; s. Warren Henry and Margaret Buckingham (Roberson) H.; A.B. magna cum laude, Vanderbilt U., 1926, M.S., 1927. Ph.D., 1932: m. Isobel Barker, Sept. 20, 1928. (dec. 1970); children—Betty Layne, Warren Henry; m. 2d, Dolores Pierucci, Feb. 28, 1971. Instr. biology Vanderbilt U., 1927- 30; instr. anatomy Duke Sch. Medicine, 1930-35, asso., 1935-39, asst. prof., 1939-44, asso. prof., 1944-46, prof. anatomy, 1946-47; vis. asso. prof. anatomy U. Tenn. Sch. Medicine, 1945; prof. anatomy Mayo Grad. Sch. Medicine, also head dept. of anatomy, Mayo Clinic and Mayo Found., 1947-71); vis. prof. U. Wash. Sch. Medicine, 1963; vis. prof. anatomy U. N.C. Sch. Medicine, 1971—. Mem. Am. Assn. Anatomists, (2d v.p. 1966-68), Am. Physiol. Soc., A.A.A.S., Nat. bd. of Med. Examiners, Phi Beta Kappa, Sigma Xi, Phi Beta Pi. Presbyn. Author: Functional Anatomy of the Limbs and Back, 1951; Anatomy for Surgeons: Vol. I, Head and Neck, 1954, Vol. II, Thorax, Abdomen and Pelvis, 1956, Vol. III. Back and Limbs, 1958; Textbook of Anatomy, 1962. Contbr. articles anat. and allied jours. Office: Dept Anatomy Univ NC Med Sch Chapel Hill NC 27514

HOLLIS, CHARLES CARROLL, educator; b. Needham, Mass., Oct. 27, 1911; s. Stanley Meredith and Agnes (Carroll) H.; Ph.B., Marquette U., 1935; M.A., U. Wis., 1937; Ph.D., U. Mich., 1954; m. Alice Willard, Sept. 19, 1936; children—Charles C., Joseph W., Michael S. Grad. fellow English. St. Louis U., 1937-38; faculty U. Detroit, 1938-61; prof. English, 1957-61, chmn. dept., 1959-61; manuscript specialist in Am. cultural history Library Congress, Washington, 1961-63; prof. Am. lit. U. N.C., Chapel Hill, 1963—, chmn. dept. English, 1966—. Supr. Dept. Parks and Recreation, City Detroit, summers 1945-55. Precinct del. Dem. Party, 1955-61; exec. bd. 15th Dist. Ofcl. Dem. Orgn., 1957-61. Mem. Founders Soc. Detroit Inst. Arts. Mem. Cath. Renascence Soc. (bd. dirs. 1960); Am. Studies Assn. (pres. Mich. 1957). Mich. Acad. Arts. Scis. and Letters (chmn. lang. and lit. 1955), Am. Assn. U. profs . (pres. local chpt. 1969-70), Coll. English Assn.; English Inst., S. Atlantic Modern Language Assn.; Modern Humanities Research Assn., also Modern Lang. Assn., Nat. Council Tchrs. English, Manuscript Soc., S. Atlantic Assn. Depts. English (exec. bd. 1968-70), S. Atlantic Grad. English (pres. 1970). Author: Literary Criticism of Orestes Brownson, 1954; also sects. in books. Editorial bd. Fresco, 1957-61, U. Detroit Press, 1959-61 Home: 104 Glendale Dr Chapel Hill NC 27514

HOLLIS, EVERETT LOFTUS, lawyer; b. Wilkes-Barre, Pa., Dec. 6, 1914; s. Frank E. and Mary C. (Loftus) H.; B.S., U. Ill., 1936; LL.B., Harvard, 1939; m. Marion Jennings, June 21, 1941; children—Nicholas, Mary, Benjamin. Admitted to Mass. bar, 1939, N.Y. bar, 1954, Ill. bar, 1966, D. C. bar, 1970; law clk. to Justice H. T. Lummus, Mass. Supreme Jud. Ct., 1940; pvt. law practice, Boston, 1941; atty. OPA, 1941- 43; with AEC, 1947-52, gen. counsel, 1951-52; formerly gen. corp. counsel Gen. Electric Co., N.Y.C. now partner firm Mayer, Brown and Platt, attys., Chicago and Washington; exec. dir. Commn. on Founds. and Pvt. Philanthropy. Mem. pres. Com. Contract Compliance, 1952. Served as lt., USNR, 1943-46. Mem. Internat., Fed., Am., Ill., Chgo., N. Y. C. bar assns., Am. Law Inst., Am. Acad. Polit. and Social Sci., Chgo. Council Fgn. Relations, English-Speaking Union, Beta Gamma Sigma. Clubs: University (Chgo.): Harvard (N.Y.C.). Co-author: Federal Conflict of Interest Laws, 1960. Home: 3400 N Lake Shore Dr Chicago IL 60657 Office: 231 S LaSalle St Chicago IL 60604 also 1101 17th St N W Washington DC 20036

HOLLIS, FLORENCE, educator, social worker; b. Phila., Jan. 11, 1907; d. Louis Herbert and Bertha (Hoerig) Hollis; B.A., Wellesley Coll., 1928; M. Social Sci. Smith Coll., 1931, L.H.D., 1967; Ph.D., Bryn Mawr Coll., 1947. Caseworker, dist. dir. family service agys. Phila., Cleve., 1928-37; asst. prof. Western Res. U.; editor, dir. publs. Social Casework Family Service Assn. Am., N.Y.C., 1942-47; asso. prof. social work Columbia Sch. Social Work, 1947-50, prof. 1950—; seminar leader UN Seminar for Social Workers, Leicester, Eng., 1954. Mem. Nat. Assn. Social Workers, Family Service Assn. Am., Am. Assn. Marriage Counselors, Am. Assn. U. Profs., internat. Conf. Social Work, Council Social Work Edn. Author: Social Casework in Practice: Six Case Studies, 1939; Women in Marital Conflict, 1949; Casework: A Psychosocial Therapy, 1964, rev. edit., 1972; A Typology of Casework Treatment, 1968; also articles. Home: 235 E 22d St New York City NY 10010 Office: 422 W 113th St New York City NY 10025

HOLLIS, FRANKLIN, lawyer; b. Concord, N.H., Mar. 26, 1904; s. Allen and Amoret (Nichoson) H.; grad. Phillips Exeter Acad., 1923; B.A., Harvard, 1927, student Law Sch., 1927-29; m. Eleanor A. Slaker, June 22, 1929; children—Allen, Eleanor. Admitted to N.H. bar, 1930, since practiced in Concord; partner firm Sulloway, Hollis, Godfrey & Soden, and predecessors, 1930—. Pres., dir. Concord Electric Co., Exeter & Hampton Electric Co.; counsel, dir. Pub. Service Co. N.H., Rumford Printing Co.; trustee Concord Savs. Bank. Past pres., dir. Concord Regional Devel. Corp., 1959—; mem. Concord Sch. Bd., 1937-49, chmn., 1941-49; mem. N.H. Bd. Edn., 1950—, chmn., 1959-66; chmn. Concord Civilian Def., World War II. Trustee Concord Hosp., Spaulding Council Nurse Edn. Mem. Am., N.H. bar assns., N.H. Sch. Bds. Assn. (past pres.). Home: 5 Hillside Rd Concord NH 03301 Office: 9 Capital St. Concord NH 03301

HOLLIS, HARRIS WHITTON, army officer; b. Richburg, S.C., June 25, 1919; s. William Gill and Gertha (Henderson) H.; B.S., Clemson U., 1942; grad. The Armed Forces Staff Coll., 1958; grad. U.S. Naval War Coll., 1962; m. Anna Airheart, June 25, 1946, children—Harris Whitton Jr., William Alexander. Commd. 2d. lt. U.S. Army, 1942, advanced through grades to maj. gen.; comdr. U.S. 9th and 25th Infantry divs., Vietnam, 1969-70; dep. chief staff personnel U.S. Army, Europe, 1970—. Mem. exec. bd. dirs. Transatlantic council Boy Scouts Am., 1970—. Decorated D.S.M. with oak leaf cluster, D.F.C., Bronze Star, Air medal with 12 oak leaf cluster. Mem. Assn. U.S. Army (pres. European dept. 1970—). Episcopalian (pres. Protestant Men of the Chapel U.S. Mil. in Europe 1970-71, layman 1946-71).‡

HOLLIS, HOWELL, lawyer; b. Columbus, Ga., Dec. 8, 1919; s. Howell and Aylmer (Illges) H.; B.S. Commerce, U. Ga., 1940, student Law Sch., 1941; m. Janet Bowers, Dec. 6, 1941; children—Howell III, Mary Jane. Admitted to Ga. bar, 1941; mem. firms Young & Hollis, Columbus, 1945-60, Foley, Chappell, Hollis & Schloth, 1960-69, Hatcher, Stubbs, Land, Hollis & Rothschild, 1969—; chmn. bd. dirs. Fourth Nat. Bank Columbus; dir. various indsl., financial corps. Pres. St. Francis Hosp., 1950—. Chmn. jud. coms. Ga. Senate and House Reps., 1948-60. Served to lt. col. USAF, 1941-45. Mem. Ga. Bar Assn. (pres. 1956-57). Home: 844 Overlook Av Columbus GA 31906 Office: PO Box 2707 Columbus GA 31902

HOLLIS, MARK D., pub. health service officer; b. Buena Vista, Ga., Sept. 24, 1908; s. Mark Dexter and Ann (Tharpe) H.; B.S. in C.E., U. Ga., 1931, C.E., 1938; D.Sc., U. Fla., 1956; m. Virginia Dare Houchens, Aug. 10, 1927; children—Mark Dexter, Virginia Ann. Typhus fever research and investigations, Ala., Va., Washington, asso. with USPHS and Rockefeller Found., 1931-34; state engr. of N.D., 1934-39; research and investigations in stream pollution, 1939-41; commd. capt., regular corps, USPHS, 1941; officer charge. Pub. Health Service Communicable Disease Center, Atlanta, 1942-47; exec. officer Office of Surgeon Gen., 1947; asst. surgeon gen. with rank of maj. gen., 1951-61; dep. chief Bur. State Services, 1952-54; chief san. engring. officer, 1954-61; chief engr., dir. environmental health program, WHO, Geneva, Switzerland, 1961- 63; chief engr. PAHO/WHO, Washington, 1963—. Mem. Am. Water Works Assn., Water Pollution Control Fedn. (pres. 1960), Nat. Malaria Soc. (pres. 1946-47), Am. Pub. Health Assn., Am. Soc. C.E., Conf. State San. Engrs., Nat. Acad. Engring. Episcopalian. Club: Cosmos. Home: 867 Island Way Clearwater FL 33515 Office: PAHO/WHO Washington DC 20203

HOLLIS, ORLANDO JOHN, educator; b. Eugene, Ore., Aug. 20, 1904; s. Moody M. and Amelia (Benner) H.; B.S., U. Ore., 1926, J.D., 1928; m. Marian Herbert, Sept. 5, 1937. Asst. trust officer First Nat. Bank, Eugene, 1928- 31; prof. law. U. Ore. Law Sch., 1931—, acting dean, 1942- 45, dean, 1945-67, Distinguished prof. law, 1967—, acting pres. of univ., 1944-45. Mem. Eugene Water Bd., 1931-41; mem. local S.S.S. Bd., 1940-47. Mem. Ore. State Bar, Am. Bar Assn., Am. Judicature Soc., Phi Beta Kappa, Order of Coif, Phi Delta Phi. Elk. Kiwanian. Home: 1908 Hilyard St Eugene OR 97405

HOLLISTER, BARRETT, ch. exec.; b. Omaha, Feb. 24, 1914; s. Robert Russell and Susan (Holdrege) H.; A.B., Antioch Coll., 1936; postgrad. Syracuse U., 1936-39; LL.D. (hon.), Wilmington Coll., 1966; m. Katharine Senseney Maxwell, Dec. 27, 1941; children—Robert Maxwell, Virginia, Joan, Donald Holdrege. Mem. faculty Antioch Coll., 1937-69, prof. polit. sci., 1946-69, asso. personnel dir., 1939-44, dean students, 1946-50, asso. to pres., 1950-54, dir. internat. edn., 1966-69; Am. Friends Service Com. Quaker rep. to UN, N.Y.C., 1969—. Dir. conf. for diplomats Am. Friends Service Com., Geneva, Switzerland, 1954-56, sec. internat. affairs, 1961-63, mem. exec. bd., 1950-54, 63—, chmn. regional exec. com., 1951-54, 57-61; chmn. central com. Friends Gen. Conf., 1959-68; mem. U.S. Nat. Commn. for UNESCO, 1962-68; mem. World Council Chs., Uppsala Assembly, 1968—. Mem. Yellow Springs Home Rule Charter Commn., 1949-50; mem. Yellow Springs Sch. Bd., 1957-61, pres., 1959-61. Kent fellow Soc. Religion in Higher Edn., 1946. Mem. Am. Polit. Sci. Assn., Soc. Internat. Devel., Assn. Asian Studies. Home: 247 E 48th St New York City NY 10017

HOLLISTER, CHARLES WARREN, educator, author; b. Los Angeles, Nov. 2, 1930; s. Nathan and Carrie (Cushman) H.; A.B., Harvard, 1951; M.A., U. Cal. at Los Angeles, 1957, Ph.D., 1958; m. Edith Elizabeth Müller, Apr. 12, 1952; children—Charles Warren, Lawrence Gregory, Robert Cushman. Teaching asst. U. Cal. at Los Angeles, 1955-57; lectr. Griffith Planetarium, Los Angeles, 1957-58; mem. faculty U. Cal. at Santa Barbara, 1958—, prof. history, 1964—, chmn. dept., 1967-70; vis. asst. prof. Stanford, 1962-63; vis. research fellow Merton Coll., Oxford (Eng.) U., 1965-66; lectr. Oxford U., 1965, Cambridge (Eng.) U., 1966, U. Ghent (Netherlands), 1966, U. Leyden (Netherlands), 1966, U. Utrecht (Netherlands), 1966, U. Bologna (Italy), 1967. Served to 2d lt. USAF, 1951-53. Recipient Triennial Book prize Conf. Brit. Studies, 1963; E. Harris Harbison award for distinguished teaching Princeton, 1966. Mem. Pacific Coast Conf. Brit. Studies (pres. 1968-70), Conf. Brit. Studies (exec. council 1968-70), Am. Hist. Assn. (exec. council Pacific Coast br. 1968—), Medieval Assn. Pacific (exec. council 1971—). Author: Anglo-Saxon Military Institutions, 1962; Medieval Europe, 2d edit., 1968; The Military Organization of Norman England, 1965; The Making of England, 2d edit., 1971; Roots of the Western Tradition, 1966; The Impact of the Norman Conquest, 1969; The Twelfth-Century Renaissance, 1969; The Moons of Meer (with Judith Pike), 1969. Home: 4592 Via Clarice Santa Barbara CA 93111

HOLLISTER, JOHN BAKER, ex-congressman, lawyer; b. Cin., Nov. 7, 1890; s. Howard Clark and Alice (Keys) H.; A.B., Yale. 1911: studies U. Munich, 1911-12; LL.B., Harvard, 1915: m. Ellen West Rollins, Aug. 15, 1917 (dec. Mar. 1960); children—Anne (Mrs. Anne H. Stevenson), Alice (Mrs. Daniel Scott), John Baker; m. 2d, Florence B. Wigglesworth. Partner Taft, Stettinius & Hollister, 1925-55, 57-67, sr. partner 1941- 67, counsel, 1967—; dir. several corps.; mem. U.S. Congress, 1931-36; exec. dir. Hoover Commn., 1953; cons. Secretary

State 1954-55; dir. Internat. Coop. Administrn. 1955-57; pres. Little Miami R. R. Gov. nat. A.R.C., 1947-51; chmn. Mission to Netherlands, UNNRA. 1945. Del. to Rep. Nat. Convention, 1940; 44; 48; 52. Served as capt. 46th Arty., C.A.C., 1917-19; with Am. Relief in Poland, 1919, and in charge relief in Lithuania. Mem. Cin. Bd. Edn. 1921-29. Trustee Cin. Art Mus. Spring Grove. Cemetery; mem. exec. Com. Cin. Boy Scouts; Cin. Summer Opera. Mem. Am. Ohio and Cin. bar assns., Psi Upsilon. Republican. Presbyterian. Clubs: Queen City (Cincinnati), Camargo (Cincinnati); Metropolitan (Washington); Yale, Links (N. Y.C.). Home: 1831 Keys Crescent Cincinnati OH 45206 Office: Dixie Terminal Bldg Cincinnati OH 45202

HOLLMANN, E. W., mfg. co. exec.; b. 1908; married. with Outboard Marine Corp., 1930—, treas., asst. sec., 1955—; sec., treas. Outboard Marine Internat. Fgn. Sales. Address: 100 Pershing Rd Waukegan, IL 60085.*

HOLLOMAN, DELMAR WINSTON, lawyer; b. Frederick, Okla., June 28, 1913; s. Andrew Harvey and Dora (Prophit) H.: A.B., U. Okla., 1935; LL.B., Harvard, 1941; m. Marjorie Louise Clas, Oct. 11, 1941; children—Douglas Winston, Marcia Carin. Admitted to D.C. bar, 1942, Md. bar, 1950; asso. Davies, Richberg, Tydings, Beebe & Landa, 1946-50; mem. firm, 1950—. Dir. Baruch Foster Co., Steel Rolling Mills, Inc. Union Tex. Oil Co. Legal cons. Task Force on Water Resources and Power of Hoover Commn., 1953-55. Bd. dirs. Washington Heart Fund; trustee Joseph E. Davies Found., Marquis Library Soc., Inc. Eberhard Sch. Served to col., M.I. Corps, U.S. Army, 1941-46. Mem. Am. Bar Assn., Bar Assn. D.C., Am. Legion, Sigma Nu. Methodist. Mason (Shriner). Clubs: University, Congressional Country, Harvard (Washington); Denver; Hiwan Country. Home: 5321 Kenwood Av Chevy Chase MD 20015 Office: 1000 Vermont Av Washington DC 20005

HOLLOMON, JOHN HERBERT, educator; b. Norfolk Va., Mar. 12, 1919; s. John Herbert and Pearl (Twiford); grad. Augusta Mil. Acad., Ft. Defiance, Va., 1936; B.S., Mass. Inst. Tech., 1940, Sc. D., 1946; hon. doctorates Worcester Polytechnic Inst., 1964, Michigan Technological U., 1965, Rensselaer Polytech. Inst., 1966, Carnegie-Mellon U., 1967, Northwestern U., U. Akron, 1967; m. to Margaret Knox Wheeler, August 12th, 1941 (dec.); children—Jonathan Bradford, James Martin, Duncan Twiford, Elizabeth Wheeler; m. 2d, Nancy Elizabeth Gade, Dec. 27, 1970. Instr. Harvard U. Grad. Sch. Engring., 1941-42; research asso. Gen. Electric Research Lab., Gen. Electric Co., 1946-49, asst. to mgr. metallurgy research dept., 1949-51, mgr. metallurgy and ceramics research dept., 1952-60, general manager Gen. Engring. Lab., 1960-62; asst. sec. for sci. and tech. Dept. Commerce 1962-67 also acting under sec.; pres. U. Okla., 1967-70; cons. to pres. Mass Inst. Tech.; adj. prof. Rensselaer Poly. Inst. Cons. President's Sci. Advisory Com., chmn. Interdept. Com. Atmospheric Scis., 1963-67. Mem. Nat. Adv. Heart Council, 1968—. Served as major AUS, 1952-46, chief phys. metallurgy sect. Watertown (Mass.) Arsenal. Decorated Legion of Merit; received Rossiter W. Raymond award Am. Inst. Mining, Metall. and Petroleum Engrs., 1946, Alfred Noble prize, Combined Engring. Socs., 1947; Rosenhain medal Brit. Inst. of Metals, 1958. Fellow Am. Acad. of Arts and Scis; Am. Physical Soc.; Am. Inst. Mining and Metall. Engrs. (dir. metall. soc., 1958), Am. Soc. Metals (trustee, 1957); mem. A.A.A.S., Mid-Am. State Univs. (pres. 1969-70), Acta Metallurgica (Sec.-treasurer), N.Y. Acad. Scis.; Fed. Council Sci. and Tech., Nat. Acad. Engring. (a founder), Cornell U. Engring. Coll. Council, Sigma Xi, Kappa Sigma. Clubs: Harvard (Boston); The Mohawk (Schenectady); Cosmos (Washington). Author: Ferrous Metallurgical Design (with Leonard Jaffe), 1947. Adv. editor: Series on the Science and Technology of Materials. Contbr. articles to profl. jours. Address: 121 Carleton St Brookline MA 02146

HOLLON, WILLIAM EUGENE, author, historian; b. Commerce, Tex., May 28, 1913; s. Samuel Horace and Myrtle (Payne) H.; B.A., E. Tex. State Coll. Commerce, 1934; M.A., U. Tex., 1937, Ph.D., 1942; m. Francis Elizabeth Cross, May 10, 1941: 1 dau., Susan Jean. Tchr. pub. schs., Tex., 1934-40; prof. history, instr. Ground Sch., Schreiner Inst., Kerrville, Tex., 1942-45; mem. faculty U. Okla., 1945-67, prof. history, 1956-67; curator history Stovall Mus. Natural History and Scis., 1947-67; research prof. history U. Toledo, 1967-68, Ohio regents prof. Am. history, 1968—; vis. prof. U. N.M., summer 1959, Cath. U., Lima, Peru, 1958, U. Mont., summer 1965. Fellow Newberry. Library, 1953, Am. Philos. Soc., 1947, 50, 64, Huntington Library, 1969; Fulbright and Smith-Mundt fellow to Peru, 1958, to Spain, 1966-67; recipient Distinguished Alumni award E. Tex. State U., 1971. Mem. Orgn. Am. Historians, Southwestern Ariz., (editorial bd.), Western (mem. exec. com., pres. 1966-67), Great Plains (editorial bd.), Ohio hist. assns. Democrat. Presbyn. (elder). Author: The Lost Pathfinder: Zebulon Montgomery Pike, 1949; History of Pre-Flight Training in the USAF, 1917- 52, 1953; Beyond the Cross Timbers: The Travels of Randolph B. Marcy, 1955; William Bollaert's Texas, 1956; Outline History of the United States (with Berthrong and Owings), 2 vols., 1957; The Southwest Old and New (Merit award Assn. State and Local Hist. Societies 1961, Theta Sigma Phi 1961), 1961; The Great American Desert, 1966; (with LeRoy Hafen), Western America, 1970; also articles, book revs. Home: 3644 Kenwood Blvd Toledo OH 43606

HOLLOS, PAUL EDMOND, banker, economist; b. Budapest, Hungary, Apr. 24, 1900; s. Edmond and Aurelie (Neustadt) H.; student U. Lausanne, Switzerland, 1919, London (Eng.) Sch. Econs., 1920; D.Polit.Sci., U. Budapest, 1922; m. Innes Kane Drury, Mar. 26, 1953; children—Paul Andrew, Delancey Kane. Came to U.S., 1947, naturalized, 1953. With Hungarian Comml. Bank, Budapest, 1922-46; U.S. rep. Comml. Bank, Zurich, Switzerland, 1948-66; pres., chief exec. officer, dir. Am. Swiss Credit Co., Ltd., N.Y.C., 1958—; sr. v.p., dir. Franklin Internat. Corp., N.Y.C., 1967—; dir., U.S. rep. Banque Vernes Et Commerciale De Paris, France. Bd. dirs. Presbyn. Sr. Services, Presbyn. Progress Found. (exec. com.); chmn. Am. Hungarian Found. Mem. Inst. Fgn. Bankers (pres. N.Y. 1971—), Fgn. Policy Assn. Council. Clubs: Metropolitan, Bankers of America (N.Y.C.); Misquamicut (Watch Hill, R.I.). Contbr. articles profl. jours. Home: 1185 Park Av New York City NY 10028 Office: Franklin Nat Bank 10 Pine St New York City NY 10005

HOLLOWAY, BRUCE KEENER, air force officer; b. Knoxville, Tenn., Sept. 1, 1912; s. Frank P. and Elizabeth (Keener) H.; student U. Tenn., 1930-31; B.S., U.S. Mil. Acad., 1937; student Cal. Inst. Tech., 1941; grad. Nat. War Coll., 1951; m. Frances Purdy, Oct. 14, 1944; children—Candace, Taylor, Amy. Commd. 2d lt. USAF, 1937, advanced through grades to gen., 1965; comdr. fighter aviation 14th Air Force, China Theater, 1942-43, 1st Fighter Group, March AFB, Cal., 1946; various staff assignments Air Def. Command, 1947-50; dep. dir. requirements Hdqrs. USAF, 1951-55; dep. comdr. 9th Air Force, Shaw AFB, S.C., 1955-57, 12th Air Force, Waco, Tex., 1957-59; dir. requirements USAF, also dir. mil. liaison com. AEC, 1959-61; dep. comdr. in chief U.S. Strike Command, MacDill AFB, Fla., 1961-65; comdr. in chief U.S. Air Forces in Europe, 1965-66; vice chief of staff Dept. Air Force, 1966-68; comdr. in chief SAC Offutt AFB, Neb., 1968—. Decorated D.S.M. Silver Star D.F.C., Legion of Merit, Air medal (U.S.); Order Sacred Tripod (China); also other fgn. decorations. Mem. Am. Ordnance Assn., Am. Fighter Aces Assn., 14th Air Force Assn., Order Daedalians, Phi Gamma Delta. Presbyn. Home: Quarters 16 Offutt AFB NB 68113 Office: Strategic Air Command Offutt AFB NB 68113

HOLLOWAY, CLARKE LEE, educator; b. Atmore, Ala., May 2, 1926; s. Albert Lee and Estelle Maude (Petty) H.; D.V.M., Auburn U., 1949, M.S., 1962; Ph.D. (NIH spl. fellow 1965-67), Ia. State U., 1969; m. Peggy Hartley, Sept. 18, 1948; children—Laura Elizabeth, Richard Lee, Keith Andrew. Practice vet. medicine, Mobile Ala., 1949-60; asst. prof. Auburn (Ala.) U., 1960-65, prof., head dept. anatomy and histology, 1968—; asso. prof. U. Ga., Athens, 1967-68. Served with USNR, 1944-45. Spl. fellow Nat. Inst. Neurol. Diseases and Blindness, 1965-67. Mem. Am. Vet. Med. Assn., Am. Assn. Vet. Anatomists, World Assn. Vet. Anatomists. Lion. Research gerontology fo the eye. Home: 426 Blake St Auburn AL 36830

HOLLOWAY, EDGAR AUSTIN, food co. exec.; b. Anguilla, Miss., Mar. 29, 1925; s. Tom W. and Lillie (Martin) H.; B.S., U. Louisville, 1947; m. Bettye Jo Marmor, Oct. 3, 1947; 1 dau., Janis Lynn. Accountant, Haskins & Sells, Louisville, 1947- 49-Cin., 1957-59; C.P.A. Lybrand, Ross Bros. & Montgomery, Louisville, 1949-51; asst. treas. Diamond Crystal Salt. Co., St. Clair, Mich., 1951-57; controller Diamond Internat. Corp., 1959-66; corp. controller Cudahy Co., Phoenix. 1966-68, v.p. controller, 1968—. - City treas. Jeffersontown, Ky., 1943-47 Served to lt. (j.g.) USNR, 1954-57. Ohio, Miss., Ky. Mem. Am. Arbitration Assn., Financial Execs., Inst., Am. Inst. C.P.A.'s. Rotarian. Home: 5302 Calle Del Medio Phoenix AZ 85018. Office: 100 W Clarendon St Phoenix AZ 85013

HOLLOWAY, FRED GARRIGUS, bishop; b. Newark, Mar. 28, 1898; s. Frank Demott and Alice (Garrigus) H.; A.B., Western Md. Coll., Westminster, 1918, D.D., 1932; student Westminster Theol. Sem., 1918-19; B.D., Drew Theol. Sem., Madison, N.J., 1921, fellow, 1921-23; LL.D., Dickinson Coll., Carlisle, Pa., 1936; L.H.D., Baldwin-Wallace Coll., 1947; Litt.D., Kan. Wesleyan U., 1957; LL D., Rider Coll., 1959; D.D., Adrian Coll., 1959; LL.D., Western Md. Coll., 1963; m. Winifred Maxwell Jackson, Apr. 12, 1923; children—Fred Garrigus, William. Ordained to ministry Meth. Protestant Ch., 1921; pastor First Ch., Wilmington, Del., 1921-23, Wilton Heights Ch., Balt., 1923-26, Cherrydale, Va., 1926-29; prof. Bibl. langs., Balt., Westminster Theol. Sem., 1927-35, pres., 1932-35; pres. Western Md. Coll., 1935-47; dean Drew Theol. Sem., 1947-48; pres. Drew U., 1948-60; bishop Meth. Ch., Charleston, W.Va., 1960—; Marshall Evans prof. Norris Harvey Coll., 1968-71. Del. Gen. Conf. Meth. Protestant Ch., 1936, Uniting Conf. of Methodism, 1939, Gen. Conf. Meth. Ch., 1940—, Jurisdictional confs, 1940—; ministerial del. of Meth. Ch. 2d ann. assembly World Council Chs. Evanston, Ill., 1954; past pres. Nat. Assn. Schs. and Colls. Meth. Ch., Assn. Meth. Theol. Schs. Mem. nat. council Chs. of Christ in Am.; past pres. Council Protestant Colls. and Univs.; pres. Meth. Ch. Bd. Hosps. and Homes. Trustee Wesley Theol. Sem., Washington, Morris Harvey Coll., Charleston, W.Va., W.Va. Wesleyan Coll., Buckhannon. Rotarian. Author articles on religion and edn. Home: 1301 N Harrison St Wilmington DE 19806

HOLLOWAY, FREDERIC ANCRUM LORD, oil co. exec.; b. Lumberton, N.C., Nov. 8, 1914; s. Elisha Lambert and Cammie Amderson (Lord) H.; B.S. in Chem. Engring., Ga. Inst. Tech., 1935; Sc.D. in Chem. Engring., Mass. Inst. Tech., 1939; grad. Advanced Mgmt. Program Harvard, 1962; m. May Bolling Cross, Oct. 18, 1941; children—Nell Cross (Mrs. W.J. Belin), Frederic Lord, Mary Bolling (Mrs. J.B. McEntire III), Ann Howard. Research asst. Mass. Inst. Tech., 1937-38, instr., 1938-39; with Esso Standard Oil Co., 1939-60, asst. gen. mgr. mfg. div., 1957-60; v.p. mfg. Humble Oil and Refining Co., 1960-62; dep. refining coordinator Standard Oil Co. (N.J.), 1962-64; pres. Esso Research & Engring. Co., Linden, N.J., 1964-68; coordinator corporate planning and econs. Standard Oil Co. (N.J.), 1968-70, v.p. corporate planning, 1970—. Trustee Stevens Inst. Tech. Mem. A.A.A.S., Dirs. Indsl. Research, Soc. Chem. Industry, London (v.p. 1971—), Am. Inst. Chem. Engrs., Am. Chem. Soc., Am. Petroleum Inst., Nat. Acad. Engring. (exec. com. 1971—), Sigma Xi, Tau Beta Pi, Beta Theta Pi. Clubs: University (N.Y.C); Baton Rouge Country; Boston (New Orleans); Canoe Brook (Summit, N.J.); Baltusrol Golf (Springfield, N.J.); Statton Mountain (Vt.) Country. Home: 43 Greenbriar Dr Summit NJ 07901 Office: 30 Rockefeller Plaza New York City NY 10020

HOLLOWAY, JAMES LEMUEL, III, naval officer; b. Charleston, S.C., Feb. 23, 1922; s. James Lemuel, Jr. and Jean (Hagood) H.; B.S. in Elec. Engring., U.S. Naval Acad., 1942; grad. Nat. War Coll., 1962; m. Dabney Hix Rawlings, Dec. 14, 1942; children—James Lemuel IV (dec.), Lucy Dabney, Jane Meredith. Commd. ensign U.S. Navy, 1942, designated naval aviator, 1946, advanced through grades to vice adm., 1971; served in destroyers, World War II; addigned various carrier-based squadrons, 1946-51; flew jet fighters, Korean War; comdr. jet squadron, Lebanon landings, 1958; assigned The Pentagon, 1959, AEC, 1963; comdr. U.S.S. Enterprise, 1965-67; dir. Navy Strike Warfare, 1968-70; comdr. Carrier Div. 6, 1970-71; dep. comdr. in chief Atlantic and U.S. Atlantic Fleet, Norfolk, Va., 1971—. Trustee St. James Sch., Washington County, Md. Decorated D.S.M. with gold star, Legion of Merit with oak leaf cluster, D.F.C., Bronze Star, Air medal with two oak leaf clusters, Navy Commendation medal with oak leaf cluster, Nat. Order Vietnam, Gallantry cross (Vietnam). Home: 439 Dillingham Blvd Norfolk VA 23511 Office: Deputy Comdr in Chief Atlantic and US Atlantic Fleet Norfolk VA 23511

HOLLOWAY, JEROME KNIGHT, fgn. service officer; b. Phila., May 8, 1923; s. Jerome Knight and Emily Margaret (Ennis) H.; A.B., Cath. U., 1947; M.A., U. Mich., 1959; lang. student, Tokyo, Japan, 1958-60; fellow Harvard, 1968-69; m. Gertrude Harms, Apr. 16, 1953; children—Jerome Knight III, Karen M., Nicholas H. Joined U.S. Fgn. Service, 1947; 3d sec., Rangoon, Burma, 1947-49; vice-consul, Shanghai, China, 1949-50, Bremen, Germany, 1950-52; consul, Hong Kong, 1952-57; 2d sec., Tokyo, 1960-61; assigned State Dept., Washington, 1961-64, 69- 70; 1st sec., Stockholm, Sweden, 1964-65; counselor, 1965-68; consul gen., Osaka-Kobe, Japan, 1970—. Served to lt. (j.g.) USNR, 1942-46. Mem. U.S. Naval Inst., Assn. Asian Studies. Home: 13-13 Natsugi-cho Nishinomiya-shi Hyogo Japan Office: Am Consulate Gen Osaka Japan

HOLLOWAY, LEONARD LEVEINE, found. exec.; b. Ada, Okla., Mar. 23, 1923; s. Leonard L. and Mamie (Burroughs) H.; B.A., Okla. Bapt. U., 1948; M.A., U. Okla., 1949, M.S., 1950, D.D. (hon.), 1958; m. Betty Gould, May 29, 1944; children—Shalia Kay, Jamie Lynn. Mem. faculty Tex. Women's U., 1950-51, Wayland Coll., 1951-52; dir. pub. relations Tex. Bapt. Gen. Conv., 1953-59; v.p. H.E. Butt Found., Corpus Christi, Tex., 1959-61, mem. exec. staff, 1970—; v.p., prof. New Orleans Bapt. Theol. Sem., also So. Bapt. Theol. Sem., 1961-66; pres. Mary Hardin- Baylor Coll., 1966-68, U. Corpus Christi, 1968-69; part-time pub. relations and mgmt. cons., 1958-66. Bd. dirs., past pres. Bapt. Pub. Relations Assn.; program coordinator Nat. Layman's Leadership Inst.; edn. tng. dir. local Civil Def.; community relations adviser Peace Corps; mem. President's Com. Refugee Placement. Bd. dirs. local A.R.C., Christian Men, Inc., Conf. S.w. Founds., Gulf Coast council Boy Scouts Am. Served with USAAF, 1941- 45, 52-53. Decorated D.F.C., Air medal with clusters. Author booklets, articles. Home: 33 Townhouse Lane Corpus Christi TX 78412

HOLLOWAY, MARSHALL GLECKLER, physicist; b. Lincoln County, Okla., Nov. 23, 1912; s. Charles and Lucinda (Gleckler) H.; B.S. in Edn., U. Fla., 1933, M.S., 1935; Ph.D. in Physics, Cornell U., Ithaca, N.Y., 1938; m. Harriet P. Fish, Dec. 4, 1941; 1 son, Jerry M. Teaching asst. physics U. Fla., 1933-35, Cornell U., Ithaca, N.Y., 1935-36, research asst. nuclear physics, 1936-38, research asso., 1938-42; research asso. nuclear physics Manhattan dist. Purdue U., 1942-43; staff mem. Los Alamos Sci. Lab., 1943-55, asso. group leader water boiler group, 1943-44, asso. group leader critical assemblies group, 1944-45, charge design nuclear components atomic bombs, 1945-46, asso. div. head weapons div., 1945-48, div. head Los Alamos Tech. div. at Bikini, 1946, head weapons div., 1948-51, spl. assignment hydrogen bomb constrn., 1951-55; dir. Lincoln Lab., Mass. Mass. Inst. Tech., 1955-57; pres. Nuclear Products-Erco div. ACF Industries, Inc., Riverdale, Md., 1957-59; v.p. research The Budd Co., Phila., 1959- 69, ret. Mem. sci. adv. bd. USAF, 1955-60; mem. tech. adv. panel atomic energy Dept. Def., 1955-61. Fellow Am. Phys. Soc.; mem. Nat. Acad. Engring., Sigma Xi. Club: Cosmos (Washington). Home: 217 Pirates Pl Jupiter Inlet Colony FL 33458

HOLLOWAY, ROBERT J., educator; b. Walker, Ia., Sept. 13, 1921; s. John Theron and Mabel Marie (Condon) H.; B.S.C., U. Ia., 1943; M.B.A., Stanford, 1948, Ph.D., 1952; m. Lois Anita Ita, Jan. 13, 1945; children—Steven Robert, Anne Louise, Bruce Ita. Prof. bus. environment and marketing U. Minn., Mpls., 1950—, chmn. dept. bus. adminstrn., 1957-59. Mem. Am. Marketing Assn. (pres. 1967-68). Co- author: Marketing in a Changing Environment. Co-editor: The Environment of Marketing Behavior. Home: 1576 Vincent St St Paul MN 55108

HOLLOWAY, STANLEY, actor; b. London, Eng., Oct. 1, 1890; s. George and Florence (Bell) H.; grad. Worshipful Company of Carpenter's Sch., London, 1905; m. Violet Marion Lane, Jan. 2, 1939. Boy choirister, 1903-06; student singing, Milan, Italy, 1914; appeared musical comedies London including Hit the Deck, 1927; an original mem. Co-Optimists (concert party), 1921-27; motion pictures include Hamlet, 1947, Lavender Hill Mob, 1950, Brief Encounter, 1945, This Happy Breed, 1943, The Way Ahead, 1943; appeared Met. Opera Co. prodn. Midsummer Nights Dream, 1954; originated role of Mr. Doolittle in My Fair Lady, 1956, same role in film version; TV series Blandings Castle, 1967; films Mrs. Brown You Have a Lovely Daughter; Run A Crooked Mile, 1969, The Private Life of Sherlock Holmes, 1969, The Flight of the Doves, 1970; played in Bernard Show Festival, Canada, 1970; played Burgess in Candida. Decorated Order Brit. Empire. Author: Wiv A Little Bit of Luck, 1967. Home: Pyefleet Tamarisk Way East Preston Sussex England Office: 42 Welbeck St London W1 England

HOLLOWAY, WILLIAM, J., U.S. Judge 10th Circuit Ct. Appeals. Address: US Ct Appeals Denver CO 80202

HOLLOWAY, WILLIAM LAWSON, lawyer; b. Helena, Mont., Mar. 16, 1903; s. William Lawson and Lalia (Holmes) H.; A.B., U. Mich., 1924, J.D., 1926; m. Esther Kavaney, July 20, 1929. Admitted to Cal. bar, 1926, since practiced in San Francisco; mem. firm Morrison, Foerster, Holloway, Clinton & Clark; admitted to bar U.S. Supreme Ct., 1938. Mem. Order of Coif, Phi Delta Phi. Clubs: Pacific Union, Bohemian (San Francisco). Home: 528 Edgewood Rd San Mateo CA 94402 Office: Crocker Bldg San Francisco CA 94104

HOLLOWAY, WILLIAM VERNON, former educator; b. Weimer, Tex., Oct. 18, 1903; s. John William and Ethel (Carlton) H.; B.A., Southwestern U., 1925; M.A., U. Wis., 1928; Ph.D., U. Wash., 1932; m. Mary Catherine Bowen, Oct. 31, 1925 (dec. 1965); children—William Bowen, Catherine Carlton; m. 2d, Pauline Poundstone Jackson, July 5, 1969. Asst., then asso. prof. polit. sci. U. Ala., 1928-36; asso. prof. polit. sci. Tulane U., 1936- 46; asso. prof., then prof. polit. sci. U. Tulsa, 1946-56, dean Grad. Sch., 1958-69, v.p. univ., 1959-69; prof. pub. adminstrn. Fla. State U., 1956-58. Chief classification div. New Orleans Civil Service Commn., 1943-46; cons. Stanolind Oil and Gas Co., Tulsa, summers 1952- 54; mem. Tulsa County Excise Bd. and Bd. Equalization, 1961-65. Mem. Am. Polit. Sci. Assn., Southwestern Social Sci. Assn., Pi Kappa Alpha, Pi Gamma Mu, Phi Eta Sigma. Author: State and Local Government in the U.S., 1951; (with others) American Government, 1959; (with other) Study Guide in American Government, 1959. Home: 5518 E 46th St Tulsa OK 74135

HOLLOWOOD, ALBERT BERNARD, journalist; b. Staffordshire, Eng., June 3, 1910; s. Albert and Sarah Elizabeth (Robinson) H.; diploma edn., St. Paul's Coll., Cheltenham, 1931; B.Sc. in Econs., London, U., 1935, M.Sc. in Econs., 1940; M.A. (hon.), Keel, 1968; m. Marjorie Duncan Lawrie, July 22, 1938; children—Jane (Mrs. Jeremy Barlow), Susan (Mrs. Angus Swanson), Duncan. Lectr. econs. Sch. Commerce, Stoke on Trent, also Loughborough Coll., 1932-43; lectr. to His Majesty's forces, 1939- 44; mem. staff The Economist, 1944-45; research officer Council Indsl. Design, 1946-47; editor Pottery and Glass, 1944-50; pocket cartoonist Sunday Times, 1957-60, Sunday Telegraph, 1961-68, Times, 1970—; mem. Punch Table, 1945- -; editor Punch, 1957-68, broadcaster, 1939—. Mem. ct. govs. London Sch. Econs. Author: Direct Economics, 1943; Money is No Expense, 1946; An Innocent at Large, 1947; Britain Inside Out, 1948; Scowle and Other Papers, 1948; Poor Little Rich World, 1948; Pottery and Glass, 1949; The Hawksmoor Scandals, 1949: Cornish Engineers, 1951; The Story of Morro Velho, 1954; Tory Story, 1964; Pont, 1969; Cricket on the Brain, 1970; Tales of Tommy Barr, 1970. Author numerous papers on econs. Home: Blackmoor Paddock Haldish Lane Shamley Green Surry England

HOLLSTEIN, MILTON CLIFFORD, educator; b. Salt Lake City, Sept. 6, 1926; s. Erick O.H. and Elizabeth (Kalt) H.; B.A., U. Utah, 1948; M.S., Columbia, 1949; Ph.D., State U. Ia., 1955; m. Shirley Waller, Sept. 1, 1948; children—Helynne, John, Mark. Reporter Salt Lake Tribune, 1946-52; instr. State U. Ia., 1952-54; asst. prof. to asso. prof., dir. journalism Humboldt State Coll., 1954-60; Fulbright lectr. U. Rangoon, Burma, 1960-61; asso. prof. to prof., chmn. dept. journalism U. Utah, 1961—. Served with USNR, 1944-46. Mem. Sigma Delta Chi (pres. Utah chpt. 1968). Home: 1072 Bonneville Dr Salt Lake City UT 84108

HOLLWEG, WILLIAM H., utility co. exec.; B.S., Northwestern U. With Peoples Gas Light & Coke Co., 1946—, treas., 1961-66, v.p. finance and pub. relations, treas., 1966-67; treas., asst. sec., 1967-71, v.p., 1971—. Address: 122 S Michigan Av Chicago IL 60603*

HOLLY, JAMES FRANCIS, librarian; b. Pitts., June 9, 1915; s. Glenn Wendell and Jennie Luella (Welsh) H.; B.A., Pa. State Coll., 1939, M.A., 1951; B.S. in L.S., Carnegie Inst. Tech., 1941; m. Margaret Elizabeth Beckwith, June 28, 1940; children—Robert Glenn, James Michael. Circulatiion staff librarian Carnegie Library, Pitts., 1941-42; asso. librarian, asst. prof. library sci. Gene Eppley Library, U. Omaha, 1957-59; librarian Weyerhaeuser Library, asso. prof. Macalester Coll., St. Paul, 1959-69; dean library services

Evergreen State Coll., Olympia, Wash., 1969—; vis. prof. State U. Coll., Geneseo, N.Y., summer 1965, U. Ia., 1969. Served to maj. AUS, 1942-57; cartographic editor, historian Office Mil. History, Dept. Army, 1953-57; col. Res. Mem. Am., Minn. library assns., Assn. Coll. and Research Libraries (chmn. midwest acad. librarians conf. 1963-65), Am. Assn. U. Profs., Am. Civil Liberties Union, Twin Cities Manuscript Soc., Res. Officers Assn. Democrat, Presbyn. Clubs: St. Paul University, St. Paul Torch. Home: 3004 Cloverfield Dr Olympia WA 98501

HOLLY, JOHN FRED, educator and arbitrator; b. Elizabethton, Tenn., Dec. 29, 1915; s. Earl H. and Rada C. (Jordan) H.; A.B., Milligan Coll., 1937; A.M., U. Tenn., 1938; Ph.D., Clark U., 1949; m. Sarah Wilma Dickenson, June 2, 1941; children—William Frederick (dec.), John Fred. Prof. bus. adminstrn. Milligan Coll., 1940-45; insp., wage-hour and pub. contracts div. Dept. Labor, 1943; indsl. cons., 1945-47; prof. labor relations U. Tenn., 1947-51, prof. econs., 1951—, head econs. 1951-68; exec. dir. Tenn. Council Edn., 1965-68. Mem. nat. panel arbitrators Fed. Mediation and Conciliation Service; cons. Tenn. Dept. of Labor, 1954-55; mem. Exec. Res. U.S. Dept. Labor, 1968—. Trustee Joint Council on Econ. Edn., 1954-56. Mem. Nat. Acad. Arbitrators (mem. bd. govs. 1960-63), Am. Arbitration Assn. (nat. panel arbitrators), Tenn. Council on Econ. Edn. (treas.), Am., So. (v.p.) econ. assns., Indsl. Relations Research Assn., Phi Kappa Sigma, Phi Kappa Phi, Omicron Delta Kappa, Beta Gamma Sigma. Author: The Economy of Greeneville, Tenn., 1950; Protective Labor Legislation and its Administration in Tennessee, 1955; Economics, Principles, Problems, and Perspectives, 1957. Home: 1029 Cherokee Blvd Knoxville TN 37919

HOLLY, ROY G., educator; b. Waupaca, Wis., Sept. 29, 1919; s. Roy and Mabel (Groves) H.; B.S., U. Minn., 1942, M.D., 1944, Ph.D., 1952; m. Cynthia R. Phillips, Dec. 19, 1942; children—Phillip Carol, Hugh. Intern, U. Minn. Hosp., 1944, resident, 1944-46; instr. obstetrics and gynecology U. Minn, 1948-54; prof. obstetrics and gynecology, chmn. dept. U. Neb. Sch. Medicine, 1954-61, dean Grad. Coll., 1961-62, vice chancellor, dean Grad. Sch., 1962-65; prof. obstetrics and gynecology, chmn. dept. Jefferson Med. Coll., Phila., 1965—. Chmn. program project com. NIH, 1964—; editor-in-chief Commerce Clearing House Med. Publs., Chgo., 1962— ; chmn. obstetrics and gynecology test com. Nat. Bd. Med. Examiners, 1964-65. Served to capt., M.C., AUS, 1946-48. Diplomate Am. Bd. Obstetrics and Gynecology. Mem. Assn. Profs. Obstetrics and Gynecology (pres. 1963-64), Am. Coll. Obstetricians and Gynecologists (vice chmn. correlated seminars 1966—; chmn. com. edn. obstetrics and gynecology 1966—), Am. Assn. Obstetricians and Gynecologists, Soc. Gynecol. Investigation, Am. Hematologic Soc., N.Y. Acad. Medicine, Am. Gynecol. Soc., Am. Assn. Maternal and Infant Hygiene, Sigma Xi. Author: Anemia in Pregnancy, 1958; also chpt. in book. Home: 228 Locust St Philadelphia PA 19106

HOLM, CELESTE, actress; b. N.Y.C., Apr. 29, 1919; d. Theodor and Jean (Parke) Holm; ed. Univ. Sch. for Girls (Chgo.), Lycée Victor Durui (Paris), Francis Parker Sch. (Chgo.). Appeared on Broadway in role of Mary L. in the Pulitzer prize play, The Time of Your Life, 1939; opposite George M. Cohan in The Return of the Vagabond, 1940; in Eight O'Clock Tuesday, also My Fair Ladies, 1941; Broadway and on tour in Papa Is All, 1941-42; in The Damask Cheek, 1942-43; first musical comedy role Ado Annie, in Oklahoma, 1943-44; then starred in Bloomer Girl, 1944; made supper club appearance in La Vie Parisienne, 1943, Persian Rm., Plaza Hotel (N.Y.C.), 1944, 45, 53, 54, 55; U.S.O. entertainer, ETO, Aug.-Nov. 1945; appeared in film Three Little Girls in Blue, 1946; starred in films: Gentlemen's Agreement, Snake Pit, Road House, Chicken Every Sunday, Come to the Stable, 1948; Everybody Does It, 1949; Champagne for Caesar, All About Eve, 1950; The Tender Trap, 1955; High Society, 1956; made 21,000 mile tour U.S. Army Air Bases entertaining mil. personnel, 1949; starred on stage in Broadway comedy hit, Affairs of State, Sept. 1950-June 1951; for Dept. State recreated original role in Oklahoma, Berlin Arts Festival (Germany), 1951; starred in revival of Anna Christie (Eugene O'Neill), N.Y.C. Center Theatre, January 1952; appeared on Broadway in The King and I, 1952; Third Best Sport, 1958; Invitation to a March, 1960-61, off Broadway in A Month in the Country, 1963; condr. radio program People at the UN, WNBC radio sta., N.Y.C., 3 yrs.; toured U.S. in program Theatre-in-Concert, 1963, 64; appeared as fairy godmother in color TV spl. Cinderella, 1965, 66, 67; starred TV presentations, 1966; star, dir. Affairs of State, Pasadena Playhouse, 1967; starred as Mame in Nat. Co., 1967, 68. Mem. governing bd. U.S. Com. Refugees; mem. bd. Nat. Assn. Mental Health Bd. Coll. and Career Cons. Received Motion Picture Academy award for best performance by an actress in a supporting role for 1947 for picture, Gentlemen's Agreement; nominated for Acad. Award for work in Come to the Stable, 1950, and again for work in All About Eve; Performer of Year, Variety Clubs Am., 1966; Woman of Year award Alliance Francaise; Sarah Siddens award for role in Mame. Office: care Lloyd V Amirall 1 Chase Manhattan Plaza New York City NY 10005 also Internat Famous Agency 1301 Av of Americas New York City NY 10019

HOLM, GEORGE PHILIP, army officer; b. N. Branch, Minn., July 11, 1918; s. William and Josephine (Hawkinson) H.; student N.Y. U., 1948-49; grad. Officer Candidate Sch., 1942, Command and Gen. Staff Sch., 1946, Army War Coll., 1959; m. Marjorie Jean Craig, Aug. 11, 1948; children—William, John, Kathrin. Commd. 2d lt. U.S. Army, 1970, advanced through grades to maj. gen., 1970; comdg. officer 536th Ordnance Co., U.S. and Europe, 1943-45, 32d and 335th ordnance battalions, Korea, 1951-52; exec. officer to chief field service div. Office Chief Ordnance, 1954-55; chief orgn. and doctrine div. Ordnance Combat Devel. Agy., Aberdeen Proving Grounds, Md., 1962-63; comdg. officer U.S. Army Depot, Tooele, Utah, 1964-66; dir. maintenance lst Logistic Command, Vietnam, 1966-67; asst. dep. chief staff logistics Hdqrs. U.S. Continental Army Command, Ft. Monroe, Va., 1967-68; comdg. gen. 8th Field Army Support Command, Korea, 1968-70, Korea Support Command, 1970-71; ret. 1971. Chmn. Korea Chpt. Boy Scouts Am., 1968-70. Decorated Legion of Merit with 2 oak leaf clusters, D.S.M. recipient mgmt. improvement certificate President U.S., 1971. Home: 1859 E Arlington St St Paul MN 55119

HOLM, GLENN CARLOS, coll. dean; b. Shelley, Ida., Dec. 17, 1909; s. Alma and Emma (Neilson) H.; B.S.A., U. Ida., 1932, M.S., 1933; D.V.M., Ia. State Coll., 1936; m. Jewell Leighton, Sept. 5, 1933. Asst. bacteriology dept. U. Ida., 1931- 33, asst. prof. bacteriology and pathology, 1938-40, prof., veterinarian, 1940-47; asst. vet. hygiene Ia. State Coll., 1933-36; gen. practice vet. medicine, Rexburg, Ida., 1936-38; asso. dir. Ida. Agrl. Expt. Sta., 1947- 49; prof. bacteriology, vet. sci. N.D. Agrl. Coll., 1949-53; dean sch. agr., dir. N.D. Agrl. Expt. Sta., 1953-56; dean coll. vet. medicine Okla. State U., 1956-67; chief univ. devel. U.S. AID Mission to India, 1967-71, U.S. AID Mission to El Salvador, San Salvador, 1971—. Chmn. Gt. Plains Agrl. Council, 1964-65. Mem. of So. Vet. Med. Assn. (dir. 1963—, v.p. 1966), So. Animal Disease Research Workers (chmn.), Am. Assn. Land Grant Colls. and Univs. (past dir., chmn. vet. div.), Am. Vet. Med. Assn., U.S. Livestock San. Assn., Okla. Vet. Medicine Assn., Sigma Xi, Alpha Zeta, Gamma Sigma Delta, Phi Zeta, Phi Kappa Phi, Alpha Epsilon Delta, Sigma Alpha Epsilon, Alpha Psi. Episconalian. Elk, Rotarian (past pres. Moscow, Ida.). Office: AID Mission Am Embassy San Salvador El Salvador U S AID U D Am Embassy Chanakya Pur New Delhi India

HOLM, HANYA, choreographer, dancer, dance educator; b. Worms-am-Rhine, Germany; d. Valentin and Marie (Moerschel) Eckert; ed. in pvt. schs. in Germany; student of music Hoch Conservatory and Dalcroze Inst., Frankfurt-am- Main; grad. Dalcroze Inst., Hellerau; dance diploma Mary Wigman Central Inst., Dresden, Germany; Dr. of Fine Arts (hon.), Colo. Coll., 1960; married and divorced; 1 son, Klaus Holm. Came to U.S., 1931, naturalized, 1939. Chief instr., dir. Wigman Inst., Dresden, 10 yrs.; mem. original Wigman Co.; performer, dance dir., choreographer, Europe, until 1931; founder, dir. of New York Wigman Sch. of Dance, which later became Hanya Holm Sch. of Dance, 1931; began Am. concert career, 1936; major prodns.: Trend, 1937 (received N.Y. Times award from John Martin as best dance composition of year, 1937-38); Metropolitan Daily, 1938; Tragic Exodus, 1939 (Dance Mag. award for best group choreography in modern dance, 1938-39); in work with theatre, choreographer: Ballet Ballads, 1948; Kiss Me, Kate (Cole Porter), 1948 (best choreographer N.Y. Drama Critics award, 1948-49), Eng. prodn., 1951; Out of this World (C. Porter), 1950. Choreographer, dir. The Golden Apple, 1954; staged dances for film Vagabond King, 1954-55; choreography for musical Reuben- Reuben, 1955-56, choreography and mus. numbers My Fair Lady, 1955-56 (Israeli prodn. 1964), Where's Charley, My Fair Lady (English prodns.), 1958, Christine, and Camelot, 1960-61, Anya, 1965; choreographer television show Pinocchio, 1957; dir. opera The Ballad of Baby Doe, Central City, Colo. opera house, 1956; dir. dance dept. Mus. Theatre Acad., N.Y.C., 1962—. Secured copyright for first time on a choreographic composition, My Darlin' Aida, 1952; dir. summer sessions in dance Colo. Coll., 1941—; appeared on Am. Cancer Soc. series, Tactic (NBC), 1959; dir., choreographer opera, Orpheus and Euridice (Gluck), Vancouver Internat. Festival, 1959. Mem. Am. Arbitration Assn. (nat. panel arbitrators), Soc. Stage Dirs. and Choreographers (v.p.). Address: 1233 6th Av. New York City NY 10019.

HOLM, IAN, actor; b. Ilford, Essex, Eng., Sept. 12, 1931; s. James Harvey and Jean (Wilson) Cuthbert; student Tyttenhanger Prep. Sch., 1942-44, Chigwell Grammer Sch., 1946-48; m. Lynn Mary Shaw, Oct. 5, 1955 (div. Apr. 1965); children—Jessica Lynn, Sarah Jane. Trainee, Royal Acad. Dramatic Art, 1952-53; with Stratford-on-Avon Co., 1954-55, 58-68, repertory co. in Sussex, summer 1956; appearances include Romeo and Juliet, Richard III, Henry V, King Lear, Midsummer Night's Dream; Broadway prodns. include Homecoming (Tony award 1966); appeared in A Bequest to the Nation (Terence Rattigan), 1970-71; films include The Fixer, O What a Lovely War, The Bofors Gun, 1968, A Severed Head, 1969, Mary Queen of Scots, 1971, Nicholas and Alexandra, 1971. Served with British Army, 1950- 51. ‡

HOLM, JEANNE MARJORIE, air force officer; b. Portland, Ore., June 23, 1921; d. John E. and Marjorie (Hammond) Holm; B.A., Lewis and Clark Coll., 1956. Commd. 2d lt. USAF, 1943, advanced through grades to brig. gen., 1971; chief manpower and mgmt. Hdqrs. Allied Air Forces So. Europe, Naples, Italy, 1957-61; congl. liaison officer, directorate manpower and orgn. Hdqrs USAF, Washington, 1961-65, dir. Women in the Air Force, 1965—. Trustee Air Force Hist. Found. Decorated Legion of Merit, medal for Human Action (Berlin Airlift), Nat. Def. Service medal with Bronze Star. Club: Prince Georges Yacht (Fort Washington, Md.). Home: 807 S Fairfax St Alexandria VA 22314 Office: Dir WAF Hdqrs USAF (DPW) Washington DC 20330

HOLM, MELVIN CARL, corp. exec.; b. Iron River, Mich., Nov. 9, 1916; s. Charles F. and Edith (Nyquist) Aspholm; student Mich. State Coll., N.Y. U., Syracuse U.; m. Beatrice A. Fritcher, Sept. 28, 1940; children—Melvin E., Joyce Ann. With Carrier Corp., Syracuse, N.Y., 1937—, comptroller, 1950-57, v.p., treas., 1957-60, exec. v.p., dir., 1960-65, pres., dir., 1965-68, chmn. bd., chief exec. officer, dir., 1968—; dir. Lincoln 1st Banks, Inc., Home Capital Funds, Inc., Lincoln Nat. Bank & Trust Co. Central N.Y.; trustee Mut. of N.Y., Warner & Swasey Co. Mem. Nat. Export Expansion Council, Com. for Econ. Devel., Emergency Com. for Am. Trade, Nat. 4-H Adv. Council. Trustee Syracuse U. Mem. Am. Mgmt. Assn., N.A.M. (dir.), Nat. Indsl. Conf. Bd. Newcomen Soc., Machinery and Allied Products Inst. (exec. com.). Mason (past-master). Clubs: California; Century, Onondaga Golf and Country, India House; Economic (N.Y.C.). Home: 100 Marvelle Rd Fayetteville NY 13066 Office: Carrier Pkwy Syracuse NY 13201

HOLM, RICHARD WILLIAM, educator, biologist; b. Dallas, June 2, 1925: s. Clyde William and Beryle (Joyce) H.; A.B., Washington U., St. Louis, 1946, A.M., 1948, Ph.D., 1950. Instr. botany Washington U., St. Louis, 1948; herbarium botanist U. Cal. at Berkeley, 1948-49; mem. faculty Stanford, 1949—, prof. biol. scis., 1965—, dir. div. systematic biology, 1961-71. Cons., Behavioral Research Labs., Palo Alto, Cal., 1963—; cons. editor McGraw Hill Book Co. Fellow A.A.A.S.; mem. Phi Beta Kappa, Sigma Xi. Contbr. articles to profl. jours., books on evolution and population biology. Editor: Evolution, 1964-66. Home: 834 Cedro Way Stanford CA 94305

HOLM, TRYGGVE OTTO ANDREAS, confedn. exec.; b. Kristinehamn, Sweden, Feb. 5, 1905; s. Hans Th. and Augusta (Mathiesen) H.; Mining and Metall. Engr., Royal Inst. Tech., 1929; postgrad. Carnegie Inst. Tech., 1931; m. Gunvor Berta Bruu, Oct. 19, 1929; children—Inger-Marie (Mrs. Eric Zetterqvist), Gunvor Margareta (Mrs. John G. Berg). Engr., AB Bofors, Bofors, Sweden, 1929-30, engr. in steel works, 1932-36, chief engr., mgr., 1936-39; engr. Hess Bright Mfg. Co., Phila., 1930-31; pres. AB Svenska Jarnvagsverkstaderna, Linkoping, 1940-50, mem. bd., 1940—; pres. SAAB Aktiebolag, Linkoping, 1950-67, mem. bd., 1943—; chmn. bd. Gusums Bruk AB, 1964—, Hexagon AB, 1965—, Vegete Ins. Co., 1968—, Alfa-Laval AB, 1969—; mem. bd. Skandinaviska Traimport AB, 1940—, chmn. bd., 1967—; Danish consul, 1949—; mem. bd. Holmens Bruks AB, 1955—, Allmanna Pensionfonden, 1959—, SILA, 1950—, ABA, 1957—, AB Bofors, 1968—, Stockholms Enskilda Bank, 1969—; mem. assembly of reps. Scandinavian Airlines System, 1957—. Chmn. Swedish Employers' Fedn., 1967—, vice chmn., 1957-67; chmn. Swedish Metal Trades Assn., 1955-67; bd. dirs. Fedn. Swedish Industries, 1967—. Decorated comdr. Order of Dannebrog 1st class, comdr. Swedish Vasa Orden 1st class. Home: 13 Vasavagen Linkoping Sweden Office: 54 Nygatan Linkoping Sweden

HOLMAN, BENJAMIN F., govt. ofcl.; b. Columbia, S.C., Dec. 18, 1930; s. Benjamin F. and Joanna (Hardy) H.; student Lincoln U. (Pa.), 1948-50; B.S., U. Kan., 1952; postgrad. U. Chgo., 1954-57. Reporter, Chgo. Daily News, 1952-62; commentator WBBM-TV, Chgo., 1962-63; reporter, assignment editor CBS News, N.Y.C., 1963-65; asst. dir. for media relations Community Relations Service, U.S. Dept. Justice, Washington, 1965-68, dir., 1969- -; producer NBC News, 1968-69. Bd. dirs., local affairs chmn. for chgo., Independent Voters Ill., 1961. Bd. dirs. Ill. Council for Freedom of Residence. Friendship House, Chgo., Beatrice Caffrey Youth Service, Ada S. McKinley House, Chgo. Served with U.S. Army, 1952-54. Home: 2922 W St SE Washington DC 20020 Office: Dept Justice Washington DC 20530

HOLMAN, CHARLES NIXON, educator, hosp. adminstr.; b. Molalla, Ore., Mar. 7, 1909; s. Ralph L. and Luella (Blair) H.; M.D., U. Ore., 1936; m. Dorothy M. Everhart, Dec. 12, 1933; children—Blair A., Jeanne L., David C. Resident radiology U. Ore. Med. Sch. Hosp. and Clinics, Portland 1936-37, internal medicine, 1937-39, faculty Med. Sch., 1940-, successively instr., asst. prof., asso. prof. medicine, 1940-55, prof., 1955—, asso. dean, 1955-68, dean, 1968—; asst. med. dir. Multnomah Hosp., 1940-42, med. dir. hosps. and clinics, 1943, adminstr., 1946; adminstr. U. Ore. Med. Sch. Hosp., 1955—. Diplomate Am. Bd. Internal Medicine. Fellow A.C.P.; mem. Am. Coll. Hosp. Adminstrs., Ore., Multnomah County med. socs., North Pacific Soc. Internal Medicine. A.M.A. Home: 3504 N E U S Grant Pl Portland OR 97212 Office: U Ore Med Sch 3181 S W Sam Jackson Park Rd Portland OR 97201

HOLMAN, CHARLES RICHARDSON, chem. co. exec.; b. Norwood, Mass., Aug. 5, 1915; s. Charles F. and Emma (Richardson) H.; B.S., Mass. Inst. Tech., 1936, M.S., 1937; m. Priscilla Denison, June 24, 1939; children—Charles Richardson, Donald B. and David W. (twins). Chem. engr. exptl. sta. E. I. duPont Co., Wilmington, Del., 1937-38; research engr. Columbia-So. Corp., subsidiary Pitts. Plate Glass Co., Barberton, O., 1938-41; with Pitts. Plate Glass Co., 1945-68, successively devel. engr., Milw., mgr. plastics prodn., Springdale, Pa., asst. gen. mgr., Newark, gen. mgr., East Point, Ga., 1945-58, chief process engr., Pitts., 1958-59, gen. mgr., Springdale, 1959-61, v.p. mfg. coatings and resins div., 1961-68; v.p., tech. asst. to chmn. bd. Reichhold Chems., Inc., White Plains, N.Y., 1969-71, v.p. corporate operations, dir., mem. exec. com., 1971—. Bd. dirs. Fulton County unit Am. Cancer Soc. Served from 2d lt. to maj., AUS, 1941-45; lt. col. Ga. Gov.'s staff. Fellow Am. Inst. Chemists; mem. East Point C. of C. (v.p., dir. 1956-58), Am. Chem. Soc., Am. Inst. Chem. Engrs., Pitts. Soc. Paint Tech., Paint, Varnish and Lacquer Assn. Presbyn. Kiwanian. Home: 55 Weeburn Dr New Canaan CT 06840 Office: 525 N Broadway White Plains NY 10602

HOLMAN, CLARENCE HUGH, educator, writer; b. Cross Anchor, S.C., Feb. 24, 1914; s. David Marion and Jessie Pearl (Davis) H.; B S., Presbyn. Coll., 1936, A.B., 1938, Litt.D., 1963; Ph.D., U. N.C., 1949; L.H.D., Clemson U., 1969; m. Verna Virginia McLeod, Sept. 1, 1938; children—Margaret McLeod, David Marion. Dir. pub. relations Presbyn. Coll., 1936-39, dir. radio, 1939- 41, instr. English, 1941-45, acad. dean, 1945-46: instr. English. U. N.C., 1946-49, asst. prof., 1949-51, asso. prof., 1951-56, prof., 1956- 59, Kenan prof. English, 1959—, chmn. div. humanities, 1959-62, chmn. dept. English, 1958-62, chmn. Coll. Arts and Scis., 1954-55, dean Grad. Sch., 1963-66, provost, 1966-68. State publicity dir. S.C. Council Nat. Def., 1942-44. Acad. coordinator 2199th BU. USAAF, 1943-45. Guggenheim fellow, 1967-68. Mem. N.C. Univ. Press (chmn. bd. govs.), Coll. English Assn., S. Atlantic Modern Lang. Assn., Modern Lang. Assn. Am., Am. Studies Assn., Nat. Council Tchrs. English, Phi Beta Kappa, Alpha Sigma Phi. Democrat. Presbyn. Author 5 detective novels, 1942-47; (with others) The Development of American Criticism, 1955; (with W. F. Thrall and A. Hibbard) A Handbook to Literature, rev. edit., 1960; (with others) The Southerner as American, 1960, Southern Writers Appraisals in Our Time, 1964, Seven Modern American Novelists, 1964; Thomas Wolfe, 1960: John P. Marquand, 1965: The Am. Novel Through Henry James, A Bibliography, 1966; Three Modes of Modern Southern Fiction, 1966; Southern Fiction Today, 1969; articles in field. Editor: Short Novels of Thomas Wolfe, 1961; The Yemassee, 1961; The World of Thomas Wolfe, 1962; The Thomas Wolfe Reader, 1962; Simms's View and Reviews, 1962; Garretson Chronicle (G.W. Brace), 1964; Of Time and the River (Thomas Wolfe), 1965; Tucker's Partisan Leader, 1971; co-editor: The Letters of Thomas Wolfe to His Mother, 1968; Southern Literary Jour., 1968—; Southern Writing 1585-1920, 1970. Collaborator: Annual Rev. Am. Lit. Scholarship, 1963-65. Home: PO Box 2056 109 Pine Lane Chapel Hill NC 27514

HOLMAN, CRANSTON WILLIAM, surgeon; b. Pasadena, Cal., Jan. 5, 1907; s. Frank Henry and Carolyn (Fieth) H.; A.B., Stanford, 1927, M.D., 1931; m. Marion Nicholas, Sept. 17, 1928; children—Eric Williamson, Martha. Asst. resident surgeon Cin. Gen. Hosp., 1931-32, N.Y. Hosp., N.Y.C., 1932-35, resident surgeon, 1935-36, attending surgeon, 1953- -: research fellow surgery Cornell U. Med. Coll., 1937, asso. surgery, 1938, asst. prof. surgery, 1938-48, asso. prof. clin. surgery, 1946-58, prof. clin. surgery, 1958—; cons. Hosp. for Spl. Surgery, 1955—. Vis. surgeon Bellevue Hospital, 1949—, dir. 2d surg. div., 1951-62, cons., 1962—; cons. surgeon VA Hosp., Montrose, N.Y., 1950—, North Shore Hosp., Manhasset, N.Y., 1954—. Served as col., M.C., AUS, 1942-46. Decorated Bronze Star medal Diplomate Am. Bd. Surgery, Am. Bd. Thoracic Surgery. Mem. Soc. U. Surgeons, A.C.S., A.M.A., N.Y. Acad. Medicine, Am. Assn. Thoracic Surgery, N.Y. Surg. Soc. (pres. 1960), N.Y. Med. and Surg. Soc., Royal Soc. Medicine London (affiliate), Am. Surg. Assn.,. Soc. Clin. Surgery, Internat. Soc. Surgery. Century Assn., A.A.A.S, Am. Thoracic Soc., N.Y. Heart Assn., Societa Triveneta di Chirurgia (hon., Padova, Italy), Inter-Soc. Cytology Council, N.Y. Soc. for Thoracic Surgery (pres. 1964), N.Y. Gastroent. Assn., N.Y. Cancer Soc., Southwestern Ont. Surg. Assn. (hon.). Author: (with Drs. George J. Heuer, William Cooper) Treatment of Peptic Ulcer, 1944. Contbr. profl. jours. Home: 435 E 52d St New York City NY 10022 Office: 862 Fifth Av New York City NY 10021

HOLMAN, CURRIER J., meat co. exec.; b. Sioux City, Ia., 1911; ed. U. Notre Dame, 1933. Chmn. bd. Ia. Beef Processors, Inc. Home: 3909 Sylvian Way Sioux City IA 51104 Office: Ia Beef Processors Inc Dakota City NB 68731

HOLMAN, EDWARD LEE, educator; b. Liverpool, Pa., Aug. 13, 1894; s. Adam Truman and Ida (Long) H.; B.A., Gettysburg (Pa.) Coll., 1921, M.A., 1922; LL.B., Am. Extension U. (corr.), Los Angeles, 1929; m. Anna Helen Bower, Aug. 22, 1917; children—Ida Helen Partridge, Clark Lee (dec.), Elizabeth Anne Reynolds, Carson Edward Richard. Country school tchr., 1912; asst. prin. Carson Long Inst. Mil. Sch., 1921-22, headmaster, 1922-49, prof. mil. sci. and tactics, 1926-42, 46-63, pres., 1944- -, trustee inst., dir. Camp Carson, 1922-41. Past chmn. Perry Co. Selective Service Bd.; past chmn. bd. Perry County Citizens Mil. Tng. Corps. Bd. dirs. Dept. Pub. Assistance. Served to officer, World War I; officer in World War II. Mem. The Pennsylvanians (1st pres. Perry County chpt.), Am. Legion Res Officers Assn., Perry County Hist. Assn. (pres.), Tau Kappa Alpha. Democrat. Lutheran. Lion Club.: Pike's Peak Summit Motor. Author: The Color of Life Is Red, or This Way Up, 1930; We'll Win, 1942; Warriors All, 1969. Home: New Bloomfield PA 17068

HOLMAN, FRANCIS EDWARDS, lawyer; b. Salt Lake City, Sept. 13, 1915; s. Frank E. and Carrol (Edwards) H.; A.B., Stanford, 1936; B.A. in Jurisprudence, Oxford (Eng.) U., 1938, M.A., 1943; J.D., Harvard, 1940; m. Eloise Dorothy Ferguson, July 5, 1941; children—Virginia Carrol, Frank Wyatt, Wendy. Law clk. U.S. Ct. Appeals, Washington, 1940-41; admitted to Wash. bar, 1941, since practiced in Seattle. Mayor City of Lake Forest Park, Wash., 1961-67; mem. Wash. Ho. of Reps., 1st Dist., 1967-69; mem. Wash. Senate, 1969—. Mem. Council Municipality Met. Seattle, 1965-67; mem. Wash. Uniform Law Commn., 1967—, Wash. Jud. Council, 1967—. Bd. dirs. Shoreline Sch. Dist., 1956- 65, pres., 1958-59, 63-64; trustee Northwest Hosp., Seattle. Served to capt. AUS, 1941-46, 51-52.

Mem. Am., Wash., Seattle, King County bar assns., Am. Judicature Soc., King County Sch. Dirs. Assn. (past pres.), Theta Delta Chi. Republican. Presbyn. Elk. Home: 5050 NE 178th St Seattle WA 98155 Office: Denny Bldg Seattle WA 98121

HOLMAN, HALSTED REID, physician, educator; b. Cleve., Jan. 17, 1925; s. Emile Frederick and Ann Peril (Purdy) H.; student Stanford, 1942-43, U. Cal. at Los Angeles, 1943-44; M.D., Yale, 1949; m. Barbara Lucas, June 26, 1949; children—Michael, Andrea, Alison. Intern, Montefiore Hosp., Bronx, N.Y., 1952-53, resident, 1953-55; asst. physician, asst. prof. Rockefeller Inst., N.Y.C., 1955-60; prof. medicine, exec. head dept. Stanford Sch. Medicine, 1960—, Guggenheim prof., 1960—. Mem. Am. Soc. Clin. Investigation, Assn. Am. Physicians, Alpha Omega Alpha. Home: 747 Dolores St Stanford CA 94305 Office: 300 Pasteur Dr Stanford CA 94305

HOLMAN, HARLAND EUGENE, mfg. co. exec.; b. Waupaca, Wis., Oct. 4, 1914; s. Clair R. and Elizabeth (Anderson) H.; B.A., U. Wis., 1936; C.P.A., Wis., Cal.; m. Evelyn June Hooper, Dec. 24, 1940; children—John H., June Elizabeth (Mrs. Jon D. Huss), Catherine Ellen. Auditor, ,Gen. Mills, Inc., 1936-42; v.p. finance Aviation Maintence Corp., Van Nuys, Cal., 1946-48; studio mgr. Warner Bros. Pictures, Inc., 1948-70; v.p. finance, treas. A.J. Industries, Inc., Los Angeles, 1970—; dir. Western Costume Corp., Warner Bros. Cosmetics Inc., Warner Bros. Records, Inc., Central Casting Corp. Treas. Burbank (Cal.) Citizens Crime Prevention Com., 1960—. Served to lt. comdr. USNR, 1942-46; rear adm. Res. Decorated commendation USMC; recipient Civilian commendation Vice Pres. U.S., 1967; Minuteman award Treasury Dept., 1967. Mem. Assn. Motion Picture and TV Producers (bd. dirs.), Am. Inst. C.P.A.'s, Cal. Soc. C.P.A.'s Navy League, Phi Beta Kappa. Presbyn (elder). Home: 5011 Hayvenhurst Av Encino CA 91316 Office: 10889 Wilshire Blvd Los Angeles CA 90024

HOLMAN, JACK PHILIP, educator; b. Dallas, July 11, 1934; s. John Henry and Bessie Marie (Blew) H.; B.S. in Mech. Engring., So. Meth. U., 1955, M.S., 1956; Ph.D., Okla. State U., 1958; m. Katherine Karin Knowles, June 4, 1964; children—Blake Knowles, Bevin Winters. Asso. prof. mech. engring. So. Meth. U., Dallas, 1960-66, prof., dir. thermal and Fluid Scis. Center, 1966—. Dir. Delta P, Inc. Served with USAF, 1958-60. Recipient Excellence in Engring. Teaching award Gen. Dynamics Corp., 1970; named Outstanding Faculty mem. So. Meth. U., 1961, 65, 69, 71. Mem. Am. Soc. M.E., Am. Soc. for Engring. Edn. (chmn. mech. engring. div. 1970). Methodist. Author: Heat Transfer, 1963; Experimental Methods for Engineers, 1966; Thermodynamics, 1969. Research and publs. on acoustic effects on heat transfer, fluidization, droplets, boiling, vortex flow and radiation. Home: 11407 Crest Brook St Dallas TX 75230

HOLMAN, JOHN FRANCIS, banker; b. San Mateo, Cal., Jan. 19, 1911; s. Franklin H. and Fannie (McNulty) H.; ed. pub. schs., Cal.; m. Yolanda M. Follini, Nov. 18, 1942; children—John Francis, Susan, Jeffrey H. With Wells Fargo Bank (merger of Am. Trust Co. and Wells Fargo Bank), San Francisco 1928—, sr. v.p. loan adminstrn., 1966-67, sr. v.p., 1967-70, exec. v.p., 1970—, chmn. loan com., 1967—; dir. Dymo Industries, Inc., Emeryville, Cal., Grand Auto, Inc., Oakland, Cal., Dental Service Plans Ins. Co., Chgo. Bd. regents John F. Kennedy U., Martinez, Cal., 1971—. Served with USNR, 1941-46. Mem. Robert Morris Assos. Club: Merchants Exchange (San Francisco). Home: 3154 Lucas Dr Lafayette CA 94549 Office: 464 California St San Francisco CA 94120

HOLMAN, LAWRENCE, state justice; b. Huntsville, Mo., June 12, 1906; s. William Waldo and Ollie Nadine (Stamper) H.; student Central Coll., Fayette, Mo., 1924-26; LL.B., U. Mo., 1929; m. Amy Ogle, May 30, 1930; children—Joseph Lawrence, Elisabeth (Mrs. James M. Luetjen). Admitted to Mo. bar, 1928; gen. practice law, Moberly, 1929-48; pros. atty. Randolph County, 1931-35; judge 9th Circuit Ct. Mo., 1948-55; commnr. Mo. Supreme Ct., Jefferson City, 1955-63, judge, 1963—, chief justice, 1967-69. Mem. Mo. Ho. of Reps. from Randolph County, 1939-40. Trustee U. Mo. Law Sch. Found., 1957-63. Recipient Distinguished Alumni plaque Central Coll., 1955. Mem. Am. Bar Assn., Am. Judicature Soc., Mo. Bar, Order of Coif, Delta Theta Phi. Democrat. Baptist. Home: 1320 Moreau Dr Jefferson City MO 65101 Office: Supreme Court Bldg Jefferson City MO 65101

HOLMAN, RALPH THEODORE, educator, biochemist; b. Mpls., Mar. 4, 1918; s. Alfred Theodore and May (Nilson) H.; A.A., Bethel Jr. Coll., 1937; B.S., U. Minn., 1939; M.S., Rutgers U., 1941; Ph.D., U. Minn., 1944; m. Karla Calais, Mar. 26, 1943; 1 son, Nils Teodor Calais. Instr., U. Minn., 1944-46, asso. prof. phys. chemistry, 1951-56, prof. at Hormel Inst., 1956—; asso. prof. Tex. A. and M. U., 1948-51. NRC fellow Med. Nobel Inst., Stockholm, Sweden, 1946-47; Am. Scandinavian Found. fellow U. Uppsala (Sweden), 1947; spl. fellow NIH, U. Gothenburg (Sweden), 1962. Mem. Am. Che. Soc., Am. Soc. Biol. Chemists, Am. Inst. Nutrition (Borden award 1966), Am. Oil Chemistry Soc. (gov. bd. 1968-70), Soc. Exptl. Biology and Medicine, Sigma Xi. Editor (with W. O. Lundberg and T. Malkin) Progress in the Chemistry of Fats and Other Lipids, vols. 1-6, 1951-63, sole editor, vols. 7-11, 1963—; asso. editor Lipids, 1966—; editorial bd. Jour. Lipid Research, 1959-61, Jour. Nutrition, 1962-66. Research, numerous publs. on spectrophotometric studies fat oxidation, isolation and characterization lipoxidase, displacement chromatography lipids, biochem. characterization fatty acid deficiency; established nutritional requirements essential fatty acids; research on metabolism polyunsaturated fatty acids, near-infrared spectra lipids, mass spectrometry lipids; developed methods for lipid analysis. Home: 1403 2d Av SW Austin MN 55912 Office: Hormel Inst Austin MN 55912

HOLMAN, RICHARD H., hospital cons., educator; b. Chgo., Aug. 5, 1927; s. Ake and Grace (Tuinstra) H.; A.B., Hope Coll., 1951; postgrad. State U. Ia., 1957-58; M.A., Mich. State U., 1964; postgrad. U. Mich., 1962-66; m. Sylvia Lolkema, Jan. 30, 1953. Sales rep., 1951; ins. investigator, 1952; mem. faculty Coll. Bus., Mich. State U., 1959-65, asso. prof., 1969-70; adminstr. Mich. State U. Hosp., 1958-66; research asso. Bur. Hosp. Adminstrn., Sch. Bus. Adminstrn., U. Mich., 1966-67; with R.H. Holman & Assos., Lansing, Mich., 1967—. Mem. Am. Coll. Hosp. Adminstrs., Am., Mich. hosp. assns. Home: 1655 Boynton Dr Lansing MI 48917 Office: 809 Center St Lansing MI 48906

HOLMAN, ROBERT WILLIAM, steel co. exec.; b. Chgo., July 24, 1911; s. William G. and Olga (Kalies) H.; B.S., Purdue U., 1935; m. R. Janice Harlan, Oct. 30, 1938; children—Linda (Mrs. Phillip K. Hargesheimer), Gerald R. With U.S. Steel Corp., 1929—, asst. gen. mgr. engring. services, 1966-67, asst. gen. mgr. design and engring. services, Pitts., 1967-69, gen. mgr., 1969—. Instl. officer Explorer Post 944 Boy Scouts Am., 1970-71. Registered profl. engr., Ind., Ala. Mem. Assn. Iron and Steel Engrs. (pres. 1970), Am. Iron and Steel Inst., I.E.E.E., S.A.R. Presbyn. (elder). Mason (Shriner). Club: University (Pitts.). Patentee in field. Home: 191 Devonwood Dr Pittsburgh PA 15241 Office: 600 Grant St Pittsburgh PA 15230

HOLMAN, WAYNE JAMES, Jr., corp. exec.; b. Huntingdon, Tenn., Nov. 12, 1907; s. Wayne J. and Louise (Grizzard) H.; B.S., Ga. Inst. Tech., 1928; M.S., Yale, 1930; M.S., Mass. Inst. Tech., 1939; Ph.D., N.Y. U., 1949; m. Elsa Ezell, Sept. 1, 1934; 1 son, Wayne James III. Asst. dist. mgr. Newburgh dist. Central Hudson Gas & Elec. Corp., 1931-40; with Chicopee Mfg. Co., 1940—, gen. mgr. lumite div., 1940-48, v.p., 1946-48, pres., 1954-58, chmn., 1958-63, dir., 1946—; chmn. bd. Personal Products Corp., 1959- 63; v.p., gen. mgr. Chicopee Mills, Inc., 1948-50, pres., 1950-58; dir. Johnson & Johnson, 1950—, mem. exec. com., 1958—, treas., 1963-67; chmn. bd. Jelco Labs. and Devro, Inc., 1967—. Trustee Ga. Tech. Found., N.Y. U., Found. for Econ. Edn., Converse Coll. Recipient Distinguished Alumnus award Ga. Inst. Tech., 1953; Man of Year achievement award, Grad. Sch. Bus. Adminstrn., N.Y. U., 1957. Licensed profl. engr. N.Y. Alfred P. Sloan Found. fellow, 1938- 39. Mem. Am. Textile Mfrs. Inst., Mgmt. Execs. Soc., Yale Engring. Assn., I.E.E.E., Am. Econ. Assn., Am. Mgmt. Assn., Tenn. Soc. N.Y. (pres. 1961-63), N.Y. So. Soc. (pres. 1963-64), Mont Pelerin Soc., Econ. Club N.Y., Sigma Xi, Tau Beta Pi, Beta Gamma Sigma, Sigma Chi, Omicron Delta Kappa. Republican. Episcopalian. Clubs: University, Merchants, Yale, Plainfield Country. Home: 1039 Rahway Rd Plainfield NJ 07060 Office: 501 George St New Brunswick NJ 08903

HOLMAN, WILLIAM ROGER, librarian; b. Oklahoma City, Sept. 7, 1927; B.A., U. Okla., 1949; M.S. in Library Sci., U. Ill., 1950; m. Barbara Louise Switzer, Sept. 1, 1945; children—David, Roger, Gregory. With circulation dept. U. Kan. Library, 1950-51; head librarian Pan Am. Coll., 1951-55, Rosenberg Library, Galveston, Tex., 1955-57; dir. San Antonio Pub. Library, 1957-60; city librarian San Francisco Pub. Library, 1960-67; dir. acad. programs Humanities Research Center, U. Tex., Austin, 1967—. Mem. Am. (chmn. friends of libraries com. 1957-59, mem., council 1966—), Tex. (chmn. legislative 1951-52, pub. libraries sect. 1957-58), Southwestern (chmn. pub. libraries div.) library assns. Author: Library Publications, 1965. Home: 3412 Foothill Terrace Austin TX 78731. Office: Box 8254 U Tex Austin TX 78712

HOLMBERG, ALBERT WILLIAM, Jr., publishing co. exec.; b. Orange, N.J., Sept. 18, 1923; s. Albert William and Margaret (Flanagan) H.; B.S. in Bus. Adminstrn., Lehigh U., 1947; m. Dorothy McCollum, Oct. 27, 1945; children—Jeanne (Mrs. Fletcher J. Johnson, Jr.), Margaret D. (Mrs. Roy D. Duckworth III), Ellen T. With N.Y. Times, 1947-70, circulation mgr., 1964-70; pres., gen. mgr. Chattanooga Times, 1970—; pres., dir. Times Pub. Co. Mem. No. Valley Regional High Sch. Bd., Demarest, N.J., 1958-62. Trustee Huguonot Meml. Ch., Pelham, N.Y., 1967-70. Served to 1st lt. USAAF, World War II. Clubs: Rotary, Mountain City (Chattanooga). Home: 611 E Brow Rd Lookout Mountain TN 37350 Office: 117 E 10th St Chattanooga TN 37401

HOLMBERG, ARTHUR LLEWELLYN, life ins. co. exec.; b. Kansas City, Kan., Nov. 21, 1911; s. Albert T. and Kate G. (Baker) H.; m. Olive A. Atkinson, June 2, 1933; children—Donna G. (Mrs. Edgar Lee Walden), Dale E. With Kansas City Life Ins. Co. (Mo.), 1930—, treas., 1967—. Home: 3921 W. 98th St. Terrace Overland Park KS 66207. Office: 3520 Broadway Kansas City MO 64141

HOLMBERG, KARL V., banker. Sr. v.p. Nat. Bank of Alaska. Office: PO Box 600 4th Av and E St Anchorage AK 99501*

HOLMBERG, LAWRENCE OSCAR, advt. exec.; b. Sac City, Ia., July 29, 1908; s. Bror Frichoff and Ruth Sophia (Greenwall) H.; B.C.S., Drake U., 1929; m. Lura Phillips Schreiner, Apr. 26, 1941; 1 son, Lawrence Oscar. Traffic mgr. Yellow Cab Airways, Des Moines, Ia., 1929; field service Campbell-Ewald Co., Detroit, 1929-30; asst. advt. mgr. Vacuum Oil Co., Chgo., 1930-32; owner L. O. Holmberg Advt., 1932-36; Chgo. mgr. J. Stirling Getchell, Inc., 1936-43; Chgo. mgr. Compton Advt., Inc., 1943-59, v.p., 1948-59; propr. Lawrence O. Holmberg Co., Chgo., 1959-62, pres., 1962—. Bd. dirs. Union League Found., Boys Clubs, Central YMCA Coll. Trustee Shimer Coll. Mem. Nat Outdoor Advt. Bur. (dir. 1951-60), Traffic Audit Bur. (dir., v.p. 1958-59), Am. Assn. Advt. Agys. (dir. 1955-56). Clubs: Chicago, Indian Hill. Home: 1410 Sheridan Rd Wilmette IL 60091 Office: 332 S Michigan Av Chicago IL 60604

HOLMBERG, PAUL ALGODTE, ret. naval officer; b. Stanberry, Mo., Apr. 18, 1915; s. John Peter and Hilma (Johnson) H.; student U. Mo., 1935; B.S. in Elec. Engring., U.S Naval Acad., 1939; M.S. in Aero. Engring., Mass. Inst. Tech., 1947; student Harvard Bus. Sch., 1964; m. Louise Gallagher, Feb. 7, 1942; children—Louise (Mrs. William Keppel), Mary Patricia, Carl Christopher, Kathleen Mildred, Martha Ellen. Commd. ensign U.S. Navy, 1939, designated naval aviator, 1941, advanced through grades to rear adm., 1965; participated Midway Battle and Guadalcanal Campaign, World War II; specializing in aero. engring., 1947—; active in pioneering missile weapons systems; now asst. comdr. research and tech. group Naval Air Systems Command. Decorated Navy Cross with oak leaf cluster, Naval Commendation medal. Home: 3760 N Upland St Arlington VA 22207

HOLMBOE, JORGEN, educator; b. Hammerfest, Norway, Nov. 8, 1902; s. Leonhard and Louise (Shetelig) H.; M.Sc., Oslo U., 1930; m. Kirsten Bendixen, Apr. 4, 1935; 1 dau., Anna. Came to U.S., 1936, naturalized, 1944. Meterologist, Norwegian Weather Service, 1930-36; mem. Lincoln Ellsworth Antaractic Expdn., 1933-35; asst. prof. meterology Mass. Inst. Tech., 1936-40; prof. meterology U. Cal. at Los Angeles, 1943—; cons. USAAF, 1945, 1950. Fellow Am. Geophys. Union; mem. Am. Meteorol. Soc., Norwegian Geophys. Soc. (fgn. mem.), Norwegion Acad. Sci. (fgn.), Sigma Xi. Author: Dynamic Meteorology (with George Forsythe, W. Gustin), 1945; also articles. Home: 449 Levering Av Los Angeles CA 90024

HOLMBOE, VAGN, composer; b. Horsens, Jutland, Dec. 20, 1909; s. Christian and Marie (Dreyer) H.; diploma Royal Danish Music Conservatory, 1927-29; m. Meta May Graf, Nov. 6, 1933; children—Ileana (Mrs. Damian Noguera), Thor. Tchr., Royal Inst. Blind, 1940-49; music critic daily Politiken, 1947— 55; prof. composition and theory Royal Danish Conservatory, Copenhagen, 1955-65. Decorated knight of Danebrog. Mem. Svenska musikaliska Acad. Composer 9 symphonies, 10 quartets, 12 chamber concertos, 3 chamber symphones, 14 motets, 1 ballet, also orchestral works, chamber music in different constellations, songs, operas. Address: RamLöse 3200 Helsinge Denmark

HOLME, PETER HAGNER, Jr., lawyer; b. Denver, June 5, 1918; s. Peter Hagner and Jamie (Sexton) H.; A.B., Yale, 1939; postgrad. Harvard, 1939-41; LL.B., U. Colo., 1942; m. Lena Phillips, Aug. 20, 1940; children—Richard Phillips, Howard Kelley, Peter Hagner. Admitted to Colo. bar, 1942; asso. firm Dines, Dines & Holme, Denver, 1942, 46-48, partner, 1948—, firm now Holme, Roberts & Owen; dep. dist. atty., Denver, 1944-46. Vice chmn. Legal Aid Soc., 1960—, pres., 1963-65. Bd. dirs. U. Colo. Alumni Fund; trustee U. Denver. Served with USAAF, 1942-44. Fellow Am. Coll. Trial Lawyers (bd. regents 1962- 65, sec. 1964), Am. Bar Found.; mem. Am. Judicature Soc., Nat. Legal Aid and Defender Soc., Am. Law Inst. (mem. council 1968—), Am. (ho. of dels. 1957-60, chmn. legal edn. and admissions to bar sect., chmn. mng. com. fund for legal edn. 1964-68), Colo. (gov. 1952, 66-70, pres. 1968-69), Denver (award of merit 1966, trustee) bar assns., Law Club Denver (pres. 1952), Phi Delta Phi. Clubs: Cactus, University, Mile High, Denver Country. Home: 5833 Montview Blvd Denver CO 80207 Office: 1700 Broadway Denver CO 80202

HOLME, THOMAS TIMINGS, educator, engr.; b. Frankford, Pa., Mar. 12, 1913; s. Justus Rockwell and Margaret (Mitchell) H.; B.S., Lehigh U., 1935, M.S., 1940, I.E. (profl.), 1948; M.A. (hon.), Yale, 1950; Dr. Engring., Lehigh U., 1970; m. Marjory Evans Walton, July 7, 1936; children—Judith Walton (Mrs. L. Bradley Clough), Thomas Timings, Penelope Walton. Began career as an industrial engineer E. I. duPont de Nemours & Co., Wilmington, Del. and Fairfield, Conn., 1935-37; asst. prof. mech. engring., Lehigh U., Bethlehem, Pa., 1937-41, asso. prof. indsl. engring., 1946-49, prof. indsl. engring., head dept. and dir. curriculum, July 1949-June 1950; prof. of indsl. engring., dept. adminstrv. sci., Yale, 1950—, chmn. dept., dir. grad. studies 1954-63, fellow Trumbull Coll.; cons. U.S. Army Ordnance Corps, 1952-53, 56-57, Hughes Aircraft, 1959, 61-62, Hamilton Standard div. United Aircraft, 1963; nat. exec. sec. Sigma Xi, 1953-69, nat. exec. dir., 1969—. Dir. Henry G. Thompson Co. Bd. dirs. Jr. Achievement, New Haven, Yale Coop. (exec. com.), New Haven; mem. of Yale-Industry Com. of New Haven. With Ordnance Dept., U.S. Army, 1941-46; asst. works mgr., Springfield Armory, 1941-42, E.T.O., July 1942-Mar. 1944; officer in charge engring., Springfield Armory, 1944-46; disch. rank of lt. col.; lt. col. Ordnance Res., 1946-53. Recipient U.S. Army Citation medal, Ordnance Certificate of Commendation, Legion of Merit. Registered profl. engr., Pa., Conn. Fellow A.A.A.S.; mem. Am. Inst. Ind. Engrs., Am. Meteorol. Soc. (asso.), Am. Soc. Engring. Edn., New Haven C. of C. (mem. indsl. devel. com.), Newcomen Soc., Sigma Xi, Tau Beta Pi, Pi Tau Sigma, Pi Gamma Mu. Club: Yale (N.Y.C. and New Haven). Home: Pine Orchard Rd Pine Orchard Branford CT 06405 Office: Dept Adminstrv Sci Yale U also 155 Whitney Av New Haven CT 06510

HOLMEN, GEORGE, formerly vice chmn., then co-chmn. Electrolux Corp., N.Y.C.; ret., 1967. Address. 235 E 42d St New York City NY 20036*

HOLMER, PAUL LEROY, educator; b. Mpls., Nov. 14, 1916; s. Paul Emmanuel and Elsie (Johnson) H.; B.A., U. Minn., 1940, M.A., 1941; student U. Chgo., 1940; PhD., Yale, 1945; L.H.D., U. N.D., 1960; LL.D., Norwich U., 1964, also from St. Olaf Coll., 1969; LL.D., North Park Coll., 1966; m. Phyllis June Schulberg, Oct. 18, 1944; children—Paul L., Linnea K., Jonathan. Instr. philosophy Gustavus Adolphus Coll., 1944, Yale, 1944- 46; mem. faculty U. Minn., 1946-60, prof., 1955-60; prof. theology Yale, 1960—; vis. prof. Northwestern U., summer 1952, Chgo. Lutheran Sem., 1953, Dartmouth, 1958, Sacramento State Coll., summer 1959, Moorhead State Coll., 1963, Macalester Coll., 1967, U. Cal., 1969-70; lectr. Oxford U., 1967; vis. lectr. Frankfurt-am-Main U. (Germany), summer 1954. Treas. bd. Christian higher edn. Agustana Luth. Ch., 1954-60; mem. bd. coll. edn. Luth. Ch. Am., 1964—. Mem. adv. bd. Danforth Found., 1956—. Fulbright research prof. Denmark, 1953-54; Guggenheim fellow Oxford U., 1964-65. Mem. Am. Philos. Assn., Am. Theol. Soc., Am. Metaphys. Soc., Mind Assn. Editor: Kierkegaard's Edifying Discourses, 2d edit., 1958; Philosophy and the Common Life, 1960; Theology and the Scientific Study of Religion, Vol. 1, 1961; Faith, Doubt and Certainty, 1964. Mem. editorial bd. Christian Scholar, 1955- 61, Dialogue, 1960—. Home: 43 Swarthmore St Hamden CT 06514 Office: Yale Univ New Haven CT 06504

HOLMES, ALAN ROBERT, banker; b. Danbury, Conn., July 16, 1920; s. Robert H. and Margaret (Griffin) H.; B.A., Millsaps Coll., 1942; postgrad. Columbia, 1946-48; m. Isolde Ruhmer, Nov. 18, 1950; 1 son, Robert R. With Fed. Res. Bank of N.Y., 1948—, mgr. Fed. Res. System open market account, 1965—, sr. v.p., 1969—; adviser Fgn. Operations Mission to Vietnam, 1955; mem. Fed. Res. Mission to Sudan, 1956; adviser U.S. Treasury on fgn. exchange operations, 1962. Trustee Millsaps Coll., Jackson, Miss. Served with AUS, 1943-45. Mem. Council on Fgn. Relations, Am. Finance Assn., Am. Econ. Assn. Author: The New York Foreign Exchange Market, 1959. Home: 380 Hillside Pl South Orange NJ 07079 Office: 33 Liberty St New York City NY 10045

HOLMES, ANN HITCHCOCK, journalist; b. El Paso, Tex., Apr. 25, 1922: d. Frederick E. and Joy (Crutchfield) Holmes; student Whitworth Coll., 1940; Mus. D., So. Coll. Fine Arts, 1954. With Houston Chronicle, 1942—, fine arts editor, 1948- -. Recipient Ogden Reid Found. award for study of arts in Europe, 1953; Guggenheim fellow, 1960-61; recipient Ford Found. award, 1965. Home: 10807 Beinhorn Rd Houston TX 77024 Office: Houston Chronicle 512-20 Travis St Houston TX 77002

HOLMES, BERT OTIS E., Jr., newspaperman; b. Milan, Tenn., Sept. 20, 1921; s. Otis E. and Mary (Lassiter) H.; A.A., Magnolia A. and M. Jr. Coll., 1940; B.S., So. Meth. U., 1942; m. Marian Bush, June 10, 1942 (dec. Nov. 1964); children—Bert Otis E., Richard Bush; m. 2d, Helen Hankins, July 24, 1965; children—Chris, David. Employed with Dallas Times Herald, 1946—, successively copy reader, makeup editor, state editor, city staff reporter, city editor, 1946-56, news editor, 1956-60, asst. mng. editor, 1960-64, exec. editor, 1964-65, asso. editor, 1965—. Pres. Family Service Agy., 1963-68, Tex. United Community Services, 1970—. Bd. dirs. Dallas United Fund, Dallas Community Council. Served with AUS, 1942-46; PTO. Mem: Dallas ASsembly, Sigma Delta Chi. Methodist. Club: Dallas Press (pres. 1957). Home: 12618 Croydon Circle Dallas TX 75230 Office: Herald Square Dallas TX 75201

HOLMES, BROOX GARRETT, lawyer; b. Mobile, Ala., Nov. 15, 1932; s. Williams Coghlan and Philomene (Boogaerts) H.; B.A., U. Ala., 1954, J.D., 1960; m. Laura Claire Hays, Feb. 21, 1955; children—Broox Garrett, Dupree Hays, Williams Coghlan II. Admitted to Ala. bar, 1960, since practiced in Mobile; mem. firm Armbrecht, Jackson & DeMouy, 1960—. Trustee St. Paul's Episcopal Day Sch. Served to capt. USMCR, 1954-58. Mem. Am., Ala., Mobile bar assns., Nat. Assn. R.R. Trial Counsel, Internat. Assn. Ins. Counsel, Delta Kappa Epsilon, Phi Delta Phi. Episcopalian (vestryman). Clubs: Mobile Country, Athelstan (Mobile). Home: 609 Fairfax Rd E Mobile AL 36608 Office: Mchts Bank Bldg Mobile AL 36601

HOLMES, BURTON HARLEY, editor; b. Lima, O., Sept. 15, 1914; s. Branson H. and Helen Hope (Burton) H.; B.S., Oberlin Coll., 1936; B. Arch., Yale, 1949; m. Frances Eleanor Lelasher, Aug. 30, 1947; children—Burton Harley, Alexandra Jean. Archtl. and structural designer Lockwood Greene Engrs., Inc., N.Y.C., 1947-49; tech. editor Progressive Architecture mag., Stamford, Conn., 1949- 65, sr. editor, 1965, mng. editor, 1965-69, exec. editor, 1969—. Served to maj., F.A., AUS, 1941-46. Decorated Bronze Star medal. Mem. A.I.A. Author: Materials and Methods in Architecture, 1954. Home: 25 Lancer Lane Stamford CT 06905 Office: 600 Summer St Stamford CT 06901

HOLMES, CHARLES HARVEY, ins. co. exec.; b. Rochester, N.Y., Apr. 5, 1918; s. William Harvey and Lillian L. (Popp) H.; B.A., U. Toronto, 1940, M.A., 1946; m. Mary Celestine Phelan, Nov. 3, 1943; children—Jane Elizabeth (Mrs. David Traber), Mary Ann (Mrs. Charles Delissio, Jr.), Peter Charles, William Harvey. With Phoenix

Mut. Life Ins. Co., Hartford, Conn., 1947—, controller, 1966—; treas. Phoenix Equity Planning Corp., 1968—, Phoenix Fund, Inc., 1970—, Phoenix Capital Fund, Inc., 1970—. Treas. Phoenix Fed. Credit Union, 1957-66, St. Mary's Fed. Credit Union, Simsbury, Conn., 1956—. Served to capt. USAAF, 1941-46, now lt. col. USAF Res. ret. Fellow Life Mgmt. Inst. K.C. Home: 21 Northfield Rd Simsbury CT 06070 Office: 1 American Row Hartford CT 06115

HOLMES, CHARLES SHIVELEY, educator; b. Oberlin, O., Jan. 13, 1916; s. Harry N. and Mary V. (Shiveley) H.; grad. Deerfield Acad., 1933; A.B., Oberlin Coll., 1938; Ph.D., Princeton, 1941; m. Marian T. Crain, Aug. 6, 1937. Mem. faculty Pomona Coll. (Cal.), 1941—, prof. English, 1957—. Fulbright prof. U. Graz (Austria), 1955-56, U. Vienna (Austria), 1962-63. Served to lt. USNR, 1943-46. Mem. Modern Lang. Assn. Am., Philol. Assn. Pacific Coast, Am. Studies Assn. Contbr. articles to profl. jours. Editor: (with E. Fussell and R. Frazer) The Major Critics, 1957. Home: 1010 Berkeley Av Claremont CA 91711

HOLMES, DARRELL, univ. pres.; b. Angola, Ind., May 28, 1921; s. G.W. and Catharine (Conrad) H.; B.A., Ohio State U., 1941, M.A., 1948, Ph.D., 1950; m. Eleonore Hohmann, Nov. 20, 1943; children—Kip Lee, Jefferey, Lynn Ellen, Mary Ann. Research asst. bur. ednl. research Ohio State U., 1949-50; asst. prof. Muskigum Coll., New Concord, O., 1950-52; asst. prof. San Diego State Coll., 1952-54, asso. prof., 1955-58, exec. dean, 1958-64; pres. U. No. Colo., Greeley, 1964-71. Pres. Southwestern Research Assos., Inc., 1957-64; dir. First Nat. Bank, Greeley, Colo. Mem. Commn. Internat. Edn., 1969—; mem. nat. adv. com. Air Force ROTC, to Sec. Air Force, 1965-69. Served from pvt. to 2d lt., C.E., AUS, 1942- 45. Mem. Am. Council Edn. (dir. 1967- -), A.A.A.S., Am. Statis. Assn., Am. Edn. Research Assn., Am. Assn. State Colls. and Univs. (dir. 1967—, pres. 1971-72). Rotarian (dir.). Contbr. articles profl. jours. Home: Pres Residence U No Colo Greeley CO 80631

HOLMES, DONALD ADAM, lawyer; b. St. Paul, Nov. 1, 1904; s. Adam J. and Georgina (Woodland) H.; A.B. cum laude, Harvard, 1927; J.D. (note editor Law Rev.), U. Minn., 1930; m. Harriette A. Hatcher, June 11, 1932. Admitted to Minn. bar, 1930, since practiced in Mpls.; partner firm Mackall, Crounse, Moore, Helmey & Holmes, 1947-70, counsel, 1970—. Chmn. bd. ch. extension Presbytery Mpls., 1952-57; v.p. Mpls. Good Govt. Group, 1946-57; mem. planning and zone com. Citizens League Mpls., 1952-54; mem. Mpls. Citizens Charter Com., 1947-50. Mem. Hennepin County Republican Com., 1950-54, Minn. Rep. Central Com., 1950-54, 5th Dist. Rep. Com., Mpls., 1950-54, Vets. Rep. League, Mpls., 1946-48; chmn. 13th Ward Rep. Com., Mpls., 1950-54. Guarantor Minn. Symphony Orch. Assn., 1960—; mem. Mpls. Inst. Fine Arts, 1957—. Served to lt. col. USMCR, 1942-46. Mem. Am., Minn. (chmn. spl. com. nonprofit corp. laws 1947-65, spl. planning com. 1965-66), Hennepin County bar assns., Marine Corps Res. Officers Assn., Minn. Law Alumni Assn., Am. Legion (past comdt.), Lincoln Meml. Soc., St. Paul Acad. Alumni Assn., Mpls. C. of C. (chmn. armed forces service com. 1947-53), Phi Alpha Delta (chief justice Mitchell chpt.). Presbyn. (deacon, trustee, elder). Mason. Clubs: Harvard, Mpls. Athletic, Social Squares, Noname (Mpls.); Interlachen Country (Edina, Minn.); Falcon (pres. 1925- 27) (Harvard). Home: 74 Woodland Circle Minneapolis MN 55424 Office: First Nat Bank Bldg Minneapolis MN 55402

HOLMES, DYER BRAINERD, corp. exec.; b. Bklyn., May 24, 1921; s. Marcellus B. and Theodora (Pomeroy) H.; B.S. in Elec. Engring. (McMullen scholar 1939-43), Cornell U., 1943; postgrad. Bowdoin Coll., also Mass. Inst. Tech. 1943- 44; m. Dorothy Ann Bonnet, May 22, 1943; children—Dorothy, Katherine. Design engr. Western Electric Co., also mem. tech. staff Bell Labs., 1945- 53; initiated, developed first precision recording transmission measuring set, other test equipment; participated devel. long distance coaxial telephone and TV systems, RCA, 1953-61, gen. mgr. maj. def. systems div., 1961; project mgr. Navy Talos land based missile system devel., 1954-57, Air Force Atlas launch control and checkout equipment devel., 1957, USAF ballistic missile early warning system, 1958-61; dep. asso. adminstr. manned space flight NASA, 1961-63; sr. v.p., dir. Raytheon Co., Lexington, Mass., 1963-69, exec. v.p., dir., 1969—. Mem. Cornell U. Council. Served with USNR, 1942-45. Registered profl. engr., N.J. Fellow I.E.E.E.; mem. Am. Inst. Aeros. and Astronautics (sr.), Am. Ordnance Assn., Navy League, Red Key, Sphinx Head, Chi Psi, Tau Beta Pi, Eta Kappa Nu. Clubs: Metropolitan, Algonquin, Gibson Island, New Bedford Yacht, Nat. Space. Author articles, papers in field. Home: 72 White Oak Rd Wellesley Hills MA 02181 Office: Raytheon Co Lexington MA 02173

HOLMES, EDWARD H., ret. hwy. engr.; b. Kingston, Mass., Oct. 29, 1906; s. Horace and Carrie W. (Dunbar) H.; B.S., Mass. Inst. Tech., 1928; M.S., Harvard, 1930; m. Elizabeth Boynton, May 25, 1936; children—Joseph B., David D. Hwy. engr. Bur. Pub. Rds., Washington, chief div. hwy. transport research, 1945-55, asst. commr. for research, 1955-62, dir. planning, 1962-67; dir. policy planning Fed. Hwy. Adminstrn., Washington 1967-70, asso. adminstr. for planning, 1970-71. Mem. Inst. Traffic Engrs., Chi Epsilon. Home: 4 Elm St Kingston MA 02360

HOLMES, EPHRAIN PAUL, ret. naval officer; b. Downsville, N.Y., May 14, 1908; s. Edward Augustus and Dolly May (Hathaway) H.; B.S., U.S. Naval Acad., 1930; grad. communications, U.S. Naval Postgrad, Sch., 1938; m. Nancy Jane Sellers, Oct. 11, 1933; children—Diane Hathaway (Mrs. L. G. Walker), Ephraim Paul. Commd. ensign U.S. Navy, 1930, advanced through grades to adm., 1967; served in ships of Scouting Force and Atlantic Fleet, 1930-36, in U.S.S. Maryland, 1938-41; aide to and flag lt. to comdr. battleships, Pacific, 1941-43; duty at sea during World War II; comdr. U.S.S. Stockham, 1943-45; instr. U.S. Naval Postgrad. Sch. 1945-47; mem. staff Adm. Blandy, 1947-50; assigned Naval War Coll., 1950-51, Armed Forces Staff Coll., 1951-52; comdr. U.S.S. Sanborn, 1952-53, U.S.S. Northampton, 1955-56; staff Comdr. Amphibious Force, Atlantic Fleet, 1953-55; assigned Office Chief Naval Operations, 1956-59; comdr. Cruiser Div. 4, Atlantic and Mediterranean, 1959-60; asst. chief naval operations for gen. planning Navy Dept., 1960-63; command amphibious force Pacific Fleet, 1963-64, command U.S. 1st Fleet, 1964; dir. Navy program planning Office Chief Naval Operations, 1964-67; comdr. in chief Atlantic and Atlantic Fleet and supreme allied comdr. Atlantic (NATO), 1967-70; ret., 1970; exec. dir. Va. Port Authority, Norfolk, 1970—. Decorated Silver Star medal, D.S.M. with oak leaf cluster, Bronze Star medal with oak leaf cluster. Episcopalian. Home: 4329 Alfriends Trail Virginia Beach VA 23455 Office: 1600 Maritime Tower Norfolk VA 23510

HOLMES, EUGENE CLAY, educator; b. Paterson, N.J., Oct. 12, 1905; s. Samuel Eugene and Arabelle (Clay) H.; A.B., N.Y.U., 1931; M.A., Columbia 1936, Ph.D., 1942; m. Margaret Cardozo, Jan. 2, 1939. Mem. faculty Howard U., Washington, 1932—, prof. philosophy, 1961—, head dept., 1952—; vis. prof. City Coll. N.Y., 1946. Mem. Washington Philos. Soc. (pres. 1962- 63), Am. Philos. Assn., Washington Philosophy Club, Humanist Soc., Peirce Soc., John Dewey Soc., Santayana Soc., A.A.A.S., Am. Assn. Sci. Workers, Alpha Phi Alpha. Author: The Social Philosophy and the Social Mind, A Study of the Genetic Methods of J.M. Baldwin, G. H. Mead and J.E. Boodin, 1942; also articles. Editor: Dictionary of Philosophy, 1940. Home: 1721 T St NW Washington DC 20009

HOLMES, FRANCIS A., banker; b. Yonkers, N.Y., 1913; grad. N.Y.U., 1932. Pres. Peoples Savs. Bank of Yonkers (N.Y.). Home: 26 Homewood Av Yonkers NY 10701 Office: 12 S Broadway Yonkers NY 10701

HOLMES, FRED GILLESPIE, sugar co. exec.; b. Grand Junction, Colo., Aug. 29, 1913; s. Fred G. and Agnes Arnett (Whitley) H.; B.S. in Bus., U. Colo., 1939; m. Alma Jeanne Sager, Nov. 11, 1946; chilren—Charles F., Winifred F. With Garden City Co. (Kan.), 1932-39, Great Western Sugar Co., Denver, 1939—, labor commr., 1948-61, v.p. agrl. adminstrn., 1961—. Mem. Am. Soc. Sugar Beet Technologists, Delta Tau Delta. Home: 3435 E Virginia Av Denver CO 80209 Office: Great Western Sugar Co Sugar Bldg Denver CO 80217

HOLMES, GEORGE LEWELLYN, ins. co. exec.; b. Toronto, Can., June 1, 1898; s. George W. and Gertrude M. (Thomas) H.; student Jarvis Collegiate, U. Toronto; m. Ada H. Harrop, July 4, 1924; children—Marion, Sylvia, Gwendolyn. With Mfrs. Life Ins. Co., Toronto, Ont., Can., 1919—, successively asst. actuary, actuary, asst. gen. mgr. and actuary, v.p and actuary, v.p., 1919-55, pres., 1956, chmn. bd., 1964—. Served with 6th Battery, F.A., Canadian Army, 1916- 19. Fellow Soc. Actuaries; mem. Canadian Life Ins. Assn. (pres. 1953- 54). Clubs: University (Toronto); Royal Canadian Yacht, Granite. Home: 29 Hedgewood Rd Willowdale Ontario Canada Office: 200 Bloor St Toronto 285 Ontario Canada

HOLMES, GEORGE WASHINGTON III, educator; b. Alamance County, N.C., Feb. 22, 1919; s. George Washington and Fannie (Thompson) H.; A.B., High Point (N.C.) Coll., 1939; M.A., U. N.C., 1947, Ph.D., 1951; postgrad. Columbia Tchrs. Coll., 1951-52; m. Mary Maxine Templeton, July 9, 1949; children—Leonard George, Mary Elizabeth. High sch. tchr., Mayodan, N.C., 1939-42; high sch. prin., Asheboro, N.C., 1947-49; dir. research Am. Sch. Pub. Corp., N.Y.C., 1951-52; ednl. asso. Jay C. Van Nuys Architects, Sommerville, N.J., 1952-54; asst. supt. schs., Roanoke, Va., 1954-58; faculty U. Va., Charlottesville, 1958—, prof. edn., 1962—, chmn. dept. adminstrn. and supervision, 1967—. Cons. sch. plant planning. Exec. sec. Va. Sch. Bds. Assn., 1958—; mem. com. edn. Va. C. of C. Served with USMCR, 1942-45. Mem. Council Ednl. Facility Planners, Am., Va. assns. sch. adminstrs., Nat., Va. edn. assns., Phi Delta Kappa (Distinguished Service award 1969). Methodist. Contbr. articles to ednl. jours. Home: 238 Stribling Av Charlottesville VA 22903

HOLMES, HARRY EDWARD, hotel exec.; b. Abilene, Tex., Dec. 5, 1925; s. Harry and Rita (Simmons) H.; A.B., U. Cal. at Berkeley, 1950; m. Gayle Walter, Sept. 1, 1957; children—Marshall Walter, Hillary, Gay. Mgr., San Ysidro Ranch, Santa Barbara, Cal., 1953-57, Santa Barbara Biltmore, 1957-59, Clift Hotel, San Francisco, 1959-60; v.p. Allied Properties, San Francisco, 1960-62; pres. Am. Convalescent Hosps., San Francisco, 1963-65; v.p., dir. Janss Corp., Thousand Oaks, Cal., 1965-67; pres., gen. mgr. Snow Valley Co., Sun Valley, Ida., 1967—. Served with USAAF, 1944-45. Decorated Air medal with 4 oak leaf clusters, Purple Heart. Mem. Am. Hotel/Motel Assn. (resort com.), Ida. C. of C. (dir.). Address: Sun Valley Co Inc Sun Valley ID 83353

HOLMES, J. LISTER, architect; b. Seattle, July 6, 1891; s. Samuel Judd and Alice (Lennox) H.; student engring. U. Wash., 1913, architecture U. Pa., 1915, Beaux Inst. Design, 1915-17; m. Jane Lambuth, Dec. 15, 1917; 1 son, Joseph L. Various archtl. positions, Phila., N.Y.C., 1917- 22; practice architecture, Seattle, 1922—, with J. Lister Holmes & Assos., 1939—. Developed comprehensive plan for Ft. Lewis, 1950- 55; mem. Wash. State Architects Licensing Bd., 1944-47, Seattle Planning Commn., 1947-56. Bd. dirs. Seattle Art Mus., 1929. Fellow A.I.A.; mem. Am. Soc. Planning Ofcls. (nat. bd. 1951-53), Pacific N.W. Acad. Arts. Club: University. Works include large scale group housing, Seattle, Vancouver, 1940-45; architect adminstrn. bldg. for pub. schs., other large structures, 1945-50. Home: 615 36th Av E Seattle WA 98102 Office: 215 8th Av N Seattle WA 98109

HOLMES, JAMES, mining co. exec.; b. Eng., Oct. 24, 1919; s. David T. and Emily (Hill) H.; B.Sc. in Econs., U. London, 1949; m. Mildred Alice Deans, July 14, 1943; children—David Caird, Barbara Mary. With Canadian Pacific Ry. Co., Montreal, Que., Can., 1949-70, sr. research economist, 1960-61, spl. asst. finance dept., 1961-63, asst. treas., 1963, treas., 1964-69, dir. financial planning, 1969-70; dir. finance Falconbridge Nickel Mines Ltd., Toronto, Ont., Can., 1970-70, v.p. finance, treas., 1971—; dir. Kilembe Copper Cobalt Ltd., Western Platinum Ltd. Served with RAF, 1940-46. Mem. Am. Mgmt. Assn. (financial planning council), Financial Execs. Inst. Home: 363 Balsam Dr Oakville Ontario Canada Office: 7 King St E Toronto Ontario Canada

HOLMES, JAMES CLIFFORD, coll. dean; b. Brockton, Mass., June 2, 1919; s. James and Ruby Alice (Renshw) H.; A.B., U. Redlands, 1941; M.A., U. Denver, 1948, Ph.D., 1951, Danforth seminar in counseling, 1960; student Inst. for Deans of Students, Inst. for Acad. Deans, Harvard Grad. Sch. Bus., 1957, 60; m. Patricia Nancy Poling, June 5, 1943; children—Katherine Elaine, Carolyn Sue, Richard James. Tchr. pub. schs., 1946-47; grad. asst., counseling fellow U. Denver, 1947-49, asst. to dean of students, 1949-51; asst. prof. ednl. psychology, guidance cons., asst. dir. jr. div. and counseling service, U. Neb., 1951-54; dean men, then dean students U. Redlands, 1954-58; dean of coll., prof. psychology Morningside Coll., 1958-62; dean Coll., George Williams Coll., Chgo., 1962—. Mem. bd. review, also mem. profl. edn. com. Nat. Council on YMCA's; del. Am. Council on Edn.; del. Gen. Assembly of Am. Personnel and Guidance Assn.; mem. accreditation team Western Coll. Assn.; chmn. Asso. Colls. Chgo. Area; adv. com. undergrad. edn. Argonne Nat. Lab.; mem. Ill. Bd. Higher Edn. Com. Preparation Undergrad. Tchrs. Served AUS, 1942-46. Mem. Am. Coll. Personnel Assn. (editor jour. 1957-58), Am. Assn. Acad. Deans, Assn. Higher Edn. of N.E.A., Neb. Personnel Assn. (founder mem.), Neb. Personnel Guidance Assn., Neb. Com. on Tng. Social Workers, N. Central Assn. Dirs. Summer Schs., A.A.A.S., Am. Psychol. Assn., Assn. Higher Edn., Pi Kappa Delta, Psi Chi, Omicron Delta Kappa. United Ch. Christ. Home: 628 36th St Downers Grove IL 60515

HOLMES, JOHN CLELLON, author; b. Holyoke, Mass., Mar. 12, 1926; s. John McClellan and Elizabeth (Emmons) H.; student Columbia, 1943, 45-46, New Sch. Social Research, 1949-50; m. Shirley Anise Allen, Sept. 9, 1953. Lectr., Yale, 1959; vis. lectr. writers workshop State U. Ia., 1963-64; writer in residence U. Ark., 1966; vis. prof. Bowling Green State U., 1968, Brown U., 1971-72. Served with Hosp. Corps, USNR, 1944-45. Recipient Playboy Mag. award for best article, 1964; John Clellon Holmes Collection award Boston U., 1966. Author: Go, 1952; The Horn, 1958; Get Home Free, 1964; Nothing More To Declare, 1967. Contbr. to popular mags. Home: Box 75 Old Saybrook CT 06475

HOLMES, JOHN RICHARD, physicist, educator; b. Chula Vista, Cal., Sept. 24, 1917; s. Robert and Mary Elizabeth (Burns) H.; A.B. in Physics, U. Cal., Berkeley, 1938, M.A., 1941, Ph.D., 1942; m. Louise Murphy, 1951; children—Susan Diana, Ronald John, Sandra Kathleen. With radiation lab. U. Cal., Berkeley, 1942-45; faculty physics U. So. Cal., Los Angeles, 1945-63, prof., 1954-63, chmn. dept. physics, 1956-62; prof., chmn. physics dept. U. Hawaii, Honolulu, 1963—; Fulbright lectr. U. Madrid, Spain, 1962-63. Cons. Autonetics Corp., Anaheim, Cal., Douglas Aircraft, Santa Monica, Cal., Electro-Optical Systems, Pasadena, Cal.; lectr. Edwards AFB, Loyola U., Los Angeles. UNESCO cons., Argentina, 1970. Fellow Am. Phys. Soc., Optical Soc. Am.; mem. A.A.A.S. Home: 41-543 Kalanianole Hwy Waimanalo HI 96795 Office: Dept Physics U Hawaii Honolulu HI 96822

HOLMES, JOSEPH HENRY, educator, physician; b. Champaign, Ill., May 2, 1909; s. Willis Bolt and Ethel (Dimmitt) H.; A.B., Amherst Coll., 1930; M.D., Western Res. U., 1934; D.M.S., Columbia, 1941; m. Mary Carlisle Hearon, Aug. 22, 1938; children—Robert Henry, Joseph McKenzie, John Carlisle. Intern, Emory U., Atlanta, 1934-35; resident internal medicine U. Md., Balt., 1935-37; staff dept. physiology Columbia Coll. Phys. and Surg., 1937-46; mem. faculty U. Colo., Denver, 1947—, prof. internal medicine, 1951—, head div. renal disease, 1960- -, dir. Sch. Med. Tech. and Allied Health Professions, Sch. Medicine, 1953-68. Cons., Denver VA, Fitzsimons Army, Denver Gen., Grand Junction VA hosps. Active Kidney Found. Colo., Colo. Health Careers Council, community pesticide study programs. Served to capt. USAAF, 1943-46. Diplomate Am. Bd. Internal Medicine, Am. Bd. Clin. Pathology. Fellow A.C.P., Am. Soc. Clin. Pathology; mem. Am. Physiol. Soc., Central Soc. for Clin. Investigation, Am. Clin. and Climatol. Assn., Am. Soc. Nephrology, Am. Inst. Ultrasonics (pres 1968-70). Contbr. articles profl. jours. Home: 434 Dexter St Denver CO 80220

HOLMES, LARRY, educator; b. Kalamazoo, Mich., July 17, 1919; s. Carl Benton and Ruth (Miller) H.; B.A., U. Ia., 1940, M.A., 1941; M.A., Harvard U., 1949, Ph.D., 1962; m. Genevieve Lechevalier, June 14, 1951; children—Christopher, Sarah Louise, Peter. Instr. philosophy Conn. Wesleyan U., 1949-51; fgn. affairs officer U.S. Arms Control and Disarmament Agy., 1961-63; asso. prof. philosophy State Univ. Coll., New Paltz, N.Y., 1963-64, prof., 1965—, chmn. dept. philosophy, 1969—, dir. philosophy program in Paris, 1971—. Mem., chmn. Planning and Zoning Commn., Vienna, Va., 1959-63. Served with AUS, 1943-46. Am. Council Learned Socs. fellow, 1942-43. Mem. Am. Philosoph. Assn., Am. Assn. U. Profs., Charles S. Peirce Soc. Episcopalian. Club: Harvard of Mid-Hudson. Home: 18 Hummel Rd New Paltz NY 12561 also 55 Bank St Harwich Port MA 02646

HOLMES, MARGUERITE C., coll. dean; Sc.B., A.M., Ed.D., N.Y.U. Prof., dean nursing edn. Hunter Coll., N.Y.C. Office: Sch Nursing Hunter Coll 695 Park Av New York City NY 10021*

HOLMES, OLIVER WENDELL, historian, archivist; b. St. Paul, Feb. 2, 1902; s. Henry Anderson and Charlotte (Benson) H.; B.A., Carleton Coll., 1922; Ph.D., Columbia, 1956; m. Dorothy Behner, Sept. 14, 1927; children—Benson Venables, Helena Victoria (Mrs. Charles E. Morrison). Asst. in history Mont. State U., 1923-24; staff asst. reference br. N.Y. Pub. Library, 1926-28; editorial asst. Ency. Brit., 1928-29, Columbia U. Press, 1929-30, 32-35; research specialist Inst. Social and Religious Research, 1930-31; asso. archivist, chief div. archives, Interior Dept. dir. research and record description, program adviser, chief archivist Nat. Resources Records div., chief archivist social and econ. records div. Nat. Archives, Washington, 1936-61, exec. dir. Nat. Hist. Pubs. Commn., 1961—. Rep. on Interdeptl. Com. on Sci. and Cultural Coop., 1944-49, to Nat. Council Historic Sites and Bldgs., 1948-52. Adj. prof. archives adminstrn. Am. U., Washington, 1957-64. Mem. Soc. Am. Archivists (council mem. 1948-50, del to 1st Internat. Congress Archivists, Paris, 1950, pres. 1958-59), Inst. Early Am. History and Culture (council 1963-66), Am., Western hist. assns., Orgn. Am. Historians, Agrl. History Soc., Columbia History Soc., Am. Assn. State and Local History, Am. Antiquarian Soc., Md., Minn., Mass., Va. hist. socs., The Westerners (sheriff Potomac Corral 1959-60). Club: Cosmos (Washington). Editor: Handbook of Federal World War Agencies and Their Records 1917- 1921, 1943; Records of the Columbia Historical Society, 1951-54, 55, 59. Contbr. articles to profl. jours. Home: 3422 Fulton St NW Washington DC 20007 Office: Nat Archives Washington DC 20408

HOLMES, ROBERT WILLIAM, educator; b. Somerville, Mass., Jan. 9. 1929; s. Theodore Ewen and Marie (Kilduff) H.; Mus. B., Boston U., 1953, A.M., 1955, Ph.D., 1960; m. Grace Feener, Oct. 11, 1951; children—Robert William, Elizabeth Grayce. Asst. librarian music ref. div. Boston Pub. Library, 1956-58; chief librarian, instr. music history and theory Boston U. Sch. Fine and Applied Arts, 1958-60; asst. prof. music history Oakland U., Rochester, Mich., 1960-62, asst. prof., asst. dean, 1962-63; asst. dir. Univ. Center Adult Edn., Detroit, 1963-64, dir., 1964-66; prof. music history, head music dept. Western Mich. U., Kalamazoo, 1966—. Pianist; program annotator Gardner Museum, Boston, 1957-62, Detroit Symphony Orch., 1965—. Mem. Adult Edn. Assn. Mich. (chmn. coll.-univ. sect.), Mich. Acad. Sci., Arts and Letters (vice chmn. fine arts sect. 1969—), Nat. Symposium on Music Adult Edn., Mich. State Council on Arts (chmn. music com. 1967-70), Am. Musicol. Soc., Sinfonia (life alumni mem.), Pi Kappa Lambda. Home: 2609 Werner St Richland MI 49083. Office: Western Michigan University Kalamazoo MI 49001

HOLMES, ROGER ARNOLD, educator; b. Peekskill, N.Y., Aug. 31, 1931; s. Robert Hancock and Louise (Velte) H.; B.Sc., U.S. Coast Guard Acad., 1953; M.Sc., Mass. Inst. Tech., 1958; Ph.D., Purdue U., 1962; m. Esther Georgia Bender, Apr. 30, 1955; children—Carol, Susan, Ruth Melissa. Teaching asst. elec. engring. Mass. Inst. Tech., 1956-58; instr. elec. engring. Purdue U., 1958-61, asst. prof., 1961-63, asso. prof. elec. engring., 1964-70; dean Coll of Engring., U. S.C. at Columbia, 1970—; dir. research Radiation Dynamics, Inc., Westbury N.Y., 1963-64; cons. Allison div. Gen Motors Corp., Western Electric Corp., RCA. Served with USCG, 1949-56. Mem. I.E.E.E., Sigma Xi, Tau Beta Pi, Eta Kappa Nu. Author: Physical Principles of Solid State Devices, 1970. Research in earth resources remote sensing, solid state devices. Home: 254 Tram Rd Columbia SC 29210

HOLMES, ROGER WELLINGTON, educator; b. Boston, Sept. 2, 1905; s. John Haynes and Madeleine Hosmer (Baker) H.; B.S., Harvard, 1926, Ed.M., 1927, Sheldon Travelling Fellow, 1928-29, M.A., 1931, Ph D., 1933; m. Louise Taylor, June 30, 1933; children—Adria, Janice. Assistant, Harvard Grad. Sch. Edn., 1929-30, instr. edn., 1930-31, Mount Holyoke Coll., South Hadley, Mass., 1933-36, asst. prof. philosophy, 1936-39, asso. prof., 1939-45, prof. 1945—, chmn. dept., 1944-69. Vis. prof. Amherst Coll., 1951-55, Golden Gate Coll., 1960-61, Mills Coll., 1960-61, Smith Coll., 1965—; vis. lectr. Am. Internat. Coll., 1950-51, Smith Coll., 1948-50, 58-59; cons. Hampshire Coll., 1966-68; mem. grad. faculty U. Mass., 1964—; mem. Western Mass. Broadcasting Council, 1959—, v.p., 1959-65, treas., 1965-67. Engaged in tng. officers for U.S. Army Signal Corps, in communications for USN, during World War II. Recipient Bowdoin prize Harvard, 1933; Atlantic Monthly prize,

1940; Founders award Hampshire Coll., 1970. Mem. Assn. for Symbolic Logic, Am. Philos. Assn. (sec.-treas. Eastern Div., mem. nat. bd. 1945-47), Am. Assn. Univ. Profs., Photog. Soc. Am. Author: The Idealism of Giovanni Gentile, 1937; The Rhyme of Reason, 1939; Exercises in Reasoning, 1940; also articles in Atlantic Monthly, Am. Mercury and profl. jours. Designer, builder electronic machine for solution of symbolic logic problems, 1955. Home: 9 Jewett Lane South Hadley MA 01075 ☆

HOLMES, SAMUEL L., lawyer; b. Salt Lake City, May 16, 1918; A.B., U. Utah, 1938, LL.B., 1942. Admitted to Utah bar, 1943, Cal. bar, 1945; now mem. firm Angell, Adams & Holmes, San Francisco. Mem. Am., Bar Assn., State Bar Cal., Utah State Bar, Bar Assn. San Francisco (chmn. labor law com. 1963, dir. 1964-65). Office: 200 Bush St San Francisco CA 94104*

HOLMES, THOMAS A., machinery mfg. co. exec.; b. Wilmington, Mass., Sept. 12, 1923; s. John Thomas and Marion (Burtt) H.; B.S.M.E., Mo. Sch. Mines, 1950; postgrad. Harvard Bus. Sch., 1969; m. Joan Merritt, March 15, 1952; children-Nanne, Susan, John, Bruce. With Ingersoll-Rand Co., N.Y.C., 1950—, now exec. v.p., Dir. N.Y. Bd. Trade, Bituminous Coal Research, Inc. Served with USNR, 1943-46. Mem. Am. Inst. Mining Engrs., Mining and Metall. Soc. Am., Club: Mining. Home: 8 Haomatong Way Bedminster NJ 07921 Office: 11 Broadway New York NY 10004

HOLMES, URBAN TIGNER, educator; b. Washington, July 13, 1900; s. Urban Tigner and Florence Fielding (Lawson) H.; student U.S. Naval Acad., 1916-17; A.B., U. Pa., 1920; A.M., Harvard, 1921, Ph.D., 1923; postgrad. U. Paris, 1922-23; Litt.D., Washington and Lee U., 1948, Western Mich. U., 1965; m. Margaret Gemmell, June 22, 1922; children—Mary (Mrs. L.L. Bernard), Florence Anne (Mrs. H. Hubbard), Urban Tigner. Asst. prof. Romance langs. U. Mo., Rolla, 1923-25; asso. prof. U. N.C., 1925-27, prof. Romance philology, 1927-45, Kenan prof. 1945-71, prof. emeritus, 1971—. Vis. prof. U. Chgo., spring 1929, U. So. Cal., summer 1939, La. State U., fall 1950; Distinguished vis. prof. Mich. State, 1959, cons. prof., 1960-62; Fulbright prof. U. Melbourne, Australia, 1960; lectr. Mediaeval Inst. (Notre Dame), 1948, 56; sr. fellow Southeastern Mediaeval and Renaissance Inst., 1966. With OSS, Washington, 1943-44. Del., Gen. Conv. P.E. Ch., 1946, 49, exec. council Diocese, 1946-49; adv. com. So. Fellowship Fund, 1960-63. Served with USNRF, 1918. Decorated chevalier Legion of Honor (France); recipient John Keble award Am. Ch. Union, 1968. Fellow Mediaeval Acad. Am. (clk. 1954-57, 2d v.p. 1964-67, pres. Fellows 1969-72), Am. Numis. Soc., Soc. Antiquaries (London). Linguistic Soc. Am., (dir. Linguistic Inst. 1941-42), Royal Archaeol. Inst., Modern Lang. Assn. Am. (exec. council 1940-43), S. Atlantic Modern Lang. Assn. (pres. 1941), Société de linguistique Paris, Phi Beta Kappa, Delta Phi. Democrat. Co-editor: Works of Du Bartas, 1938-40; Mediaeval Studies, 1948; Franch and Provencal Lexicography, 1964. Author: A French Composition, 1925; Guillaume de Salluste, Sieur du Bartas, 1935; (with H. Giduz) Sept. Contes de la Vieille France, 1930; Contes des Sept Sage, 1936 (with A.H. Schutz) A History of the French Lang., 1933; Source Book for French lang., 1939; History of Old French Lit., 1937, 1962; New Interpretation of Conte del Graal, 1948; Daily Living in Twelfth Century, 1952-66; Samuel Pepys in Paris and other Essays, 1954; (with Sister M. Amelia Klenke) Chrétien, Troyes and the Grail, 1959; (with K. Scholberg) French and Provencal Lexicography, 1964; Mediaeval Studies in Memory of E.B. Ham, 1967; (with Raymond J. Cormier) Essays in Honor of Louis Francis Solano, 1970; Chretian de Troyes, 1971. Editor: vol. I, Cirtical Bibliography of French Lit. (Middle Ages), 1947, 52; Berte aus, grans pies, 1946; North Carolina Studies in Romance, 1940—, Romance Notes, 1960—; asso. editor studies in Philology. Contbr. articles to mags., encys. Home: 102 Pine Lane Chapel Hill NC 27514

HOLMES, VERNER SMITH, physician; b. Tylertown, Miss., July 10, 1909; s. Byron Berkley and Dixie (Smith) H.; B.A., Miss. Coll., 1931; med. certificate, U. Miss., 1934; M.D., Tulane U., 1936; m. Emma Dunbar Bauer, Oct. 31, 1945; children—Mary Melissa, Verner Smith. Intern, West Balt. Gen. Hosp., 1936- 37, Balt. City Hosp., 1937-38; resident otolaryngology Eye, Ear, Nose & Throat Hosp., New Orleans, 1945-47; practice medicine, specializing in otolaryngology, McComb, Miss., 1947—; chief staff S.W. Miss. Gen. Hosp.; mem. staff McComb City Hosp., mem. planning com. U. Med. Center, Dir. Consol. Am. Life Ins. Co., Jackson, Miss., Mechanics State Bank, McComb. Chief staff Gov. Coleman's Hon. Cols., 1956-60. Served to maj. AUS, 1942-45. Mem. A.M.A., Miss., Pike County med. assns., Flying Physicians Assn., McComb C. of C. (dir.), Newcomen Soc. N.Am., Am. Legion, V.F.W., Pi Kappa Alpha, Phi Chi, Omicron Delta Kappa. Presbyn. Mason (Shriner), Rotarian. Home: 1611 Lissa Dr McComb MS 39648 Office: 210 N Front St McComb MS 39648

HOLMES, WALTER STEPHEN, Jr., corporate exec.; b. South River, N.J., May 23, 1919; s. Walter Stephen and Frances Evans (Heckman) H.; B.S., Lehigh U., 1941; M.B.A., N.Y.U., 1947; m. Elizabeth Jean Pringle, Aug. 20, 1941; children—Walter Stephen III, Richard Alan. With Haskins & Sells, C.P.A.'s, Phila., 1941-42, Franke, Hannon & Withey, N.Y.C., 1946-47; asst. tax dir. RCA, 1947-51, asst. controller, 1951-53, controller, 1954-59; controller CIT Financial Corp., 1959-62, v.p., 1961-64, exec. v.p., 1965-68, pres., chief adminstrv. officer, 1968-70, pres., chief exec. officer, 1970—; dir. CIT Corp., CIT Financial Services, Inc., All-Steel Equipment, Inc., N. Am. Co., Life, & Health Ins., Wm. Iselin & Co., Inc., CIT Financial Corp., Picker Corp., Tuition Plan, Inc., Canadian Acceptance Co., Ltd., Holt Renfrew, Ltd., Meinhard Comml. Corp., Nat. Bank North Am., Service Fire Ins. Co., Service Casualty Ins. Co., Gibson Greeting Cards, Inc. Mem. Presdl. Commn. Financial Structure and Regulations, 1970—. Served as lt., supply corps, USNR, 1942-45. Mem. Financial Execs. Inst., Am. Inst. C.P.A.'s. Methodist. Clubs: Upper Montclair Country, Seaview Country. Home: 507 Ridgewood Av Glen Ridge NJ 07028 Office: 650 Madison Av New York City NY 10022

HOLMES, WILFRED JAY, (pseudonym, Alec Hudson), naval officer, educator; b. Stockport, N.Y., Apr. 4, 1900; s. John Eric and Esther (Moett) H.; B.S., U.S. Naval Acad., 1922; M.S., Columbia, 1929; m. Isabelle M. West, June 17, 1922; 1 son, John Eric II. Commd. officer U.S. Navy, 1922, advanced through ranks to lt., 1936; comdg. officer U.S.S. S-30, 1934-35; asst. prof. engring., math. U. Hawaii, Honolulu, 1936-41, prof., 1946—, dean Coll. Applied Sci., 1951-54, dean emeritus Coll. of Engring., 1954—. Served as capt. USN 1941-46. Decorated D.S.M., Legion of Merit. Mem. U.S. Naval Inst., Am. Soc. Engring. Edn., Hawaiian Acad. Sci., Phi Kappa Phi, Epsilon Chi. Author: Battle Stations, 1940; Enemy Sighted, 1941; Open Fire, 1942; Undersea Victory: The Influence of Submarines on the War in the Pacific, 1966. Contbr. articles popular mags. Home: 4009 Black Point Rd Honolulu HI 96816

HOLMES, WILLIAM HEWITT, dentist; b. Hiawatha, Kan., Dec. 5, 1907; s. Joseph A. and Mary (Hewitt) H.; student U. Kan., 1926-27; B.S.D., Northwestern U., 1931, D.D.S., 1931, M.S.D., 1933; m. Dorothy Eliza Dawson, May 10, 1934; children—Richard, Mary. Staff St. Luke's Hosp. (merged with Presbyn. Hosp., now called Presbyn-St. Luke's Hosp. 1958), Chgo., 1934—, chmn. dental surgery, 1946-68. Mem. Omicron Kappa Upsilon. Home: Route 1 Box 210 Barrington, IL 60010. Office: 25 E Washington St Chicago IL 60602

HOLMES, WILLIAM J., Jr., coll. pres.; b. Cedar Rapids, Ia., June 30, 1927; s. William J. and Libbie (Stodold) H.; B.A., State U. Ia., 1951, Ph.D., 1962; m. Joanne Prokop, Sept. 8, 1951; children—Mary, Ann, Sara. Mem. faculty dept. English, Ohio U., Athens, 1951-70, asst. to pres., 1968-70; pres. Simmons Coll., Boston, 1970—. Trustee WGBH radio-TV Ednl. Found. Served to capt. USAAF, 1945-49. Fellow Am. Council Edn.; mem. Modern Lang. Assn. Author: Nineteenth Century American Short Fiction, 1970. Home: 245 Lee St Brookline MA 02146 Office: 300 The Fenway Boston MA 02115

HOLMES, WILLIAM P., sporting goods co. exec.; b. Chgo., 1911. Pres., dir. Wilson Sporting Goods Co., River Grove, Ill., now chmn. bd.; exec. v.p. Wilson & Co. Home: 1312 Somerset Dr Glenview IL 60025 Office: 2233 West St River Grove IL 60171

HOLMESLY, EDWARD STERLIN, editor; b. Haskell, Tex., May 21, 1932; s. James Edward and Ida Pearl (Kreger) H.; B.S., W. Tex. State Coll., Canyon, 1953, postgrad., 1956-57; m. Doris Melle Chapman, June 22, 1954; 1 dau., Anne. Corr., Amarillo (Tex.) Globe-News, also A.P., 1950-53; mem. staff Amarillo Globe-News, 1953-57, news editor, 1956-57; reporter- photographer Hereford (Tex.) Brand, 1957-58; copy editor, asst. news editor Corpus Christi (Tex.) Caller, 1958-61; staff San Antonio Express, 1961—, mng. editor, 1963-66, editor Sunday Express-News, 1966-69, mem. editorial bd., asso. editor, mem. editorial bd. Express and News, 1970—. Served with AUS, 1953-55. Book reviewer. Home: 431 Maplewood St San Antonio TX 78216 Office: Express-News Av E 3d St San Antonio TX 78206

HOLMGREN, HARRY D., educator, physicist; b. Mpls., Apr. 21, 1928; s. Harry W. and Myrtle (Dahl) H.; B.Physics, U. Minn., 1949, M.S., 1950, Ph.D., 1954; children—Diane, Bruce, Cheryl, Cynthia. Physicist, U.S. Naval Research Lab., Washington, 1954-61; mem. faculty U. Md., College Park, 1961—, prof. physics, astronomy, dir. Cyclotron Lab., 1965—. Recipient Edward O. Hulburt award U.S. Naval Research Lab., 1960, Arthur S. Flemming award Jr. C. of C. Washington, 1961. Mem. Am. Phys. Soc., Phi Beta Kappa, Sigma Psi. Research, numerous publs. on exptl. nuclear physics, basic structure of nucleus of atoms and processes by which nuclear particles interact with atomic nucleus, theoretical studies related to prodn. of stellar energy, nuclear instrumentation, accelerators for nuclear research, effects of nuclear weapons. Home: PO Box 391 College Park MD 20740

HOLMGREN, LATON EARLE, clergyman; b. Mpls., Feb. 20, 1915; s. Frank Albert and Freda Ida (Lindahl) H.; student U. Minn., 1934-35; A.B. cum laude, Asbury Coll., 1936; M. Divinity, summa cum laude, Drew U., 1941; postgrad. Edinburgh (Scotland) U., 1947; D.D., Ill. Wesleyan U., 1956. Ordained to ministry Methodist Ch., 1942; asso. minister Calvary Meth. Ch., East Orange, N.J., 1940-42, Christ Ch. Meth., N.Y.C., 1943-48; minister Tokyo (Japan) Union Ch., 1949-52; lectr. internat. dept. Tokyo U. Commerce, 1950-52; adviser Japanese Fgn. Office, Tokyo, 1951; sec. for Asia Am. Bible Soc., N.Y.C., 1952-54, exec. sec., 1954-62, gen. sec., 1963—; chmn. exec. com. United Bible Socs., London, Eng., 1963—. Mem. Japan Soc., Asia Soc., English- Speaking Union. Clubs: Union League, University, Quill. Home: 128 Central Park S New York City NY 10019 Office: 1865 Broadway New York City NY 10023

HOLMGREN, MARVIN EDWARD, educator; b. Plainview, Tex., Mar. 20, 1918; s. Albin Edward and Mabel Christina (Landholm) H.; B.S., St. Cloud (Minn.) State Tchrs. Coll., 1940; M.A., U. Minn., 1946, Ph.D., 1949; m. Joyce Lorraine Lachelt, Oct. 25, 1940; children—Charles Allan, Susan Jane, Lindsay Ann. Tchr., Ogilvie (Minn.) High Sch., 1940-41, Rush City (Minn.) High Sch., 1941-43; research asst. U. Minn., 1947, teaching asst., 1948-49, lectr., 1950; asso. prof. edn. St. Cloud State Coll., 1949-56, dir. Bur. Research, 1950-63, dean Sch. of Grad. Studies, 1953-65, prof. edn., 1956- -, dean of acad. adminstrn., 1965-67, v.p. for acad. affairs, 1967—. Participant, recorder Midwest Invitational Conf. Coop. Research, 1955-61; mem. Minn. Sch. Financial Accounting Com., 1949- 52; treas. bd. edn. Sartell (Minn.) Pub. Sch., 1961-64; mem. Minn. Adv. Com. on Tchr. Edn., 1965-68. Mem. inservice tng. com. synod Minn., United Presbyn. Ch., 1955-61; comr. 170th Gen. Assembly United Presbyn. Ch., 1958; chmn. com. ch. extension Presbytery St. Cloud, 1961- 67, vice moderator, 1966-67. Bd. dirs. Westminster Found. Minn. Served with USNR, 1943-46. Mem. Nat. (life), Minn. edn. assns., Am. Ednl. Research Assn., Nat. Council on Measurment in Edn., Nat. Soc. Study Edn., Kappa Delta Pi (pres. St. Cloud 1939-40), Phi Delta Kappa (pres. Epsilon Theta chpt. 1961). Club: St. Cloud Sertoma (v.p. 1960). Author (with others) Religious Activies in Public Colleges, 1959; Preparatory Programs for Elementary School Teachers, 1961. Home: Route 2 St Cloud MN 56301

HOLMQUEST, DONALD LEE, astronaut; b. Dallas, Apr. 7, 1939; s. Sidney Browder and Lillie Mae (Waite) H.; B.S. in Elec. Engring., So. Meth. U., 1962; M.D., Baylor U., 1967, Ph.D. in Physiology, 1968; m. Charlotte Ann Blaha, July 15, 1961. Student engr. Ling-Temco-Vought, Dallas, 1958-61; electronics engr. Tex. Instruments, Inc., Dallas, 1962; intern Meth. Hosp., Houston, 1967-68; pilot tng. USAF, Williams AFB, Ariz., 1968-69; scientist-astronaut NASA, Houston, 1967—; research asso. Mass. Inst. Tech., 1968-70; asst. prof. radiology and physiology Baylor Coll. Medicine, 1970—. Mem. I.E.E.E., Aerospace Med. Assn., Assn. Advancement Med. Instrumentation, Am. Fighter Pilots Assns., Sigma Xi, Alpha Omega Alpha, Sigma Tau. Contbr. med. jours. Home: 4019 Elderwood Seabrook TX 77586 Office: Manned Spacecraft Center Houston TX 77058

HOLMQUEST, P.S., glass co. exec.; b. 1914; B.S., U. Ind., 1937. Mgr. glass container div. Armstrong Cork Co., 1937-55; v.p. sales Thatcher Glass Mfg. Co., 1955- 59; with Brockway Glass Co. Inc., 1959—, exec. v.p., from 1965, now pres.; dir. Du Bois Deposit Nat. Bank. Address: Brockway Glass Co Inc Wood St Brockway PA 15824*

HOLMQUIST, EMILY, dean nursing sch.; b. Sommerville, Mass., Oct. 16, 1909; d. Charles and Alma (Swanbeck) Holmquist; diploma Mt. Auburn Hosp. Sch. Nursing, Cambridge, Mass., 1931; B.S. in Nursing Edn., U. Pitts., 1941, M.A., 1944; postgrad. U. Chgo., 1952-53, 55; H.H.D. (hon.), Evansville (Ind.) Coll., 1966. Head surg. nursing Vanderbilt U. Hosp., 1931-35; adminstr. supr. med.-surg. nursing Norfolk (Va.) Gen. Hosp., 1935-38; jr. staff nurse Bedford (Mass.) VA Hosp., 1938; part-time staff Elizabeth Steel Magee Hosp., Pitts., 1938-41; instr., then asst. prof. founds. of nursing and med.-surg. nursing U. Pitts., 1941-45, chmn. dept., asso. prof. nursing dept. of med.-surg. nursing, 1945-50, dir. Kellogg Research project, 1950-52, chmn. dept. nursing edn., asso. prof. nursing, 1955, 55-57; cons. planning non-profl. staff edn. VA Hosp., Aspinwall, Pa., 1948; cons. work conf., curriculum-selecting learning experience U. Ia. Coll. Nursing, 1954; research asso. curriculum project basic nursing edn. U. Wash. Sch. Nursing, 1954-55; prof. nursing, dean Sch. Nursing, Ind. U., Indpls., 1957—, dean Unified and Ind. Sch. Nursing including grad. and undergrad. edn., 1965—; cons., speaker Cal. Bd. Nurse Examiners, also Cal. League for Nursing, 1956, Wash. Heart Assn., also Wash. League Nursing, 1956. Chmn. steering com. dept. baccalaureate and higher degree programs Nat. League Nursing, 1959-63, mem. interim adv. com. accreditation policies and procedures, 1960—; mem. nursing research study sect. NIH, 1957-61. Mem. Am. (mem. com. on edn. 1963- -), Ind. (pres. 1969-71, 71-73) nurses assns., Assn. Supervision and Curriculum Devel., Nat. Soc. Study Edn., Am. Assn. Deans Coll. and Univ. Schs. Nursing, Adult Edn. Assn., Sigma Theta Tau (research com.), Pi Lambda Theta, Alpha Tau Delta. Author articles in field. Home: 1508 Collingwood Dr Indianapolis IN 46208

HOLMQUIST, WILLIAM AXEL, lawyer; b. Waukegan, Ill., Apr. 15, 1923; s. Axel H. and Maybelle (Olsen) H.; student Eureka Coll., 1942; B.A., Northwestern U., 1947, J.D., 1950. Admitted to Ill. bar, 1950; asso. George G. McGaughey, Waukegan, 1950-52, Snyder, Clarke & Dalziel, Waukegan, 1952-54; partner Snyder, Clarke, Dalziel, Holmquist & Johnson, Waukegan, 1954—; city atty., Zion, Ill., 1954-59; spl. asst. atty. gen. Ill., 1963-64. Pub. mem. Jud. Adv. Council Ill., 1961—. Vice chmn. Elk Service Cneter, Waukegan, 1952—. Served as 2d lt. USAAF, 1942-45. Mem. Am., Ill., Lake County bar assns., Internat. Soc. Barristers, Am. Judicature Assn., Soc. Trial Lawyers, Lambda Chi Alpha, Phi Alpha Delta. Episcopalian. Elk. Clubs: Glen Flora Country, Swedish Glee (Waukegan). Home: 428 Lorraine St Waukegan IL 60085 Office: 301 Washington St Waukegan IL 60085

HOLOSKI, JOSEPH WALTER, pharm. co. exec.; b. Newark, Mar. 1, 1916; s. Casmir Chocholowski and Stella (Zebloski) H.; B.S. cum laude, U. Rutgers, 1941, M.B.A., 1956; m. Marie K. Czupryk, July 1, 1939; children—Joanne Marie (Mrs. Park), Joseph Richard, Rita Margaret. Retail tire sales mgr. Muellers Automotive Service, Jersey City, 1935-37; jr. accountant Am. Home Products Corp., 1937-39, chief accountant, 1940-41; asst. gen. mgr. Whitehall Pharmacal Co., N.Y.C., 1941-42; asst. gen. auditor Irvington Varnish & Insulator Co. (N.J.), 1942-44, asst. controller, 1944-47; asst. to treas. Ortho Pharm. Corp., Raritan, N.J., 1947-48, treas., 1948-63, dir., 1951-63; asst. to controller Schering Corp., Bloomfield, N.J., 1963—; lectr. accounting Rugers U. Sch. Bus. Adminstrn., 1943-47. Mem. Millburn Bd. Edn., 1951-54. Mem. Nat. Assn. Accountants (past dir. Newark chpt.), Nat. Office Mgmt. Assn. (past dir. Newark chpt., v.p.), Alumni Assn. Rutgers Sch. Bus. Adminstrn. (past pres.), Rutgers U. Alumni Fedn. (past bd. govs.), Delta Sigma Pi, Beta Gamma Sigma. Roman Catholic. Elk. Home: 47 Dedar St Millburn NJ 07041 Office: Schering Corp 60 Orange St Bloomfield NJ 17003

HOLOVAK, MIKE, football coach; b. Lansford, Pa., Sept. 19, 1919; s. Peter and Helen (Homcha) H.; B.S. in History, Boston Coll., 1943; m. Edith Casavant, June 11, 1943; children—Michele, Terrie.Football player Los Angeles Rams, 1 year, Chgo. Bears, 2 years; freshman tutor Boston Coll., 1 year, varsity football coach, 9 years; dir. player personnel Boston Patriots, 1959-61, head coach, 1961-68. Served with USNR, World War II; lt. comdr. Res. Named AFL Coach of Year, 1966. Home: Claybrook Rd Dover MA 02030 Office: 78 Lansdowne St Boston MA 02215

HOLROYD, HARRY JAMES, architect; b. Steubenville, O., Dec. 12, 1920; s. Harry E. and E. Gilberta (Carter) H.; m. Helen Marie Hammond, Sept. 17, 1939; children—Connie Lee (Mrs. Larry K. Fairchild), Patricia Anne (Mrs. Geoffrey R. Louis), Vicki Lynn. Draftsman F & R Lazarus & Co., 1939-41, Larcomb Constrn. Co., 1941-42, F. J. Pichler-Architect, 1945- 48; engr. Curtis-Wright Corp., 1942-45, Dennison Engring. Co., 1945; architect Tully, Hobbs & Hansen, 1948-50, Tuttle & Holroyd, 1950-53, H. Jas. Holroyd, 1953-57, Holroyd & Myers, Columbus, O., 1957—. Mem. Ohio Bd. Examiners Architects, 1966—, pres., 1970. Vice chmn. Columbus Met. Airport and Aviation Commn., 1957-58, Columbus Planning Commn., 1958-61; exec. com. Regional Planning Commn., 1959-61; chmn. Mayor's Adv. Com. Community Improvements, 1964-69. Served with C.E., AUS, 1943. Recipient Golden award Mut. of Omaha, 1959. Fellow A.I.A. (pres. Columbus 1957); mem. Architects Soc. Ohio (treas. 1959-60). Mason (Shriner). Prin. works include officed and factory Nippert Co., Delware, O., 1968, Mill St. Married Students Apts., Ohio U., 1970, Sch. Allied Med. Professions, Ohio State U., 1971. Home: 620 Yaronia Dr N Columbus OH 43214 Office: 1881 E Dublin Granville Rd Columbus OH 43229

HOLROYD, LOUIS VINCENT, educator; b. Vancouver, B.C., Can., Jan. 22, 1925; s. Ernest George and Lalita Ann (Eva) H.; B.A., U. B.C., 1945, M.A., 1947; Ph.D., U. Notre Dame, 1950; m. Helene Marie Laberge, May 20, 1950; children—Barbara Jane, John Edward, George Walter, Suzanne Marie. Came to U.S., 1950. Mem. faculty U. Mo., 1950—, prof. physics, chmn. dept., 1956—. Mem. Parish Sch. Bd., 1966-68; commr. Great Rivers council Boy Scouts Am., 1967—; pres. Parish Council, 1969—; v.p. Columbia Cath. Sch. Bd., 1970—. Served to 2d lt., Signal Corps, Canadian Army, 1944-45. Recipient Centennial of Sci. award U. Notre Dame, 1966. Mem. Am. Inst. Physics, Am. Assn. Physics Tchrs., Sigma Xi. Author: Physics Laboratory Manual 1965. Home: 400 Blair Ct Columbia MO 65201

HOLROYDE, E. B., sugar refining co. exec.; b. Winnipeg, Man., Can., July 15, 1912; s. and Eva (Carveth) H.; came to U.S., 1922, naturalized, 1934; student U. Hawaii; grad. Advanced Mgmt. Program, Harvard, 1959; m. Eugenie Muench Speckart, May 6, 1939; children—E. Alan, Paula E. Mgr., dir. Kahuku Plantation Co., 1952-59, McBryde Sugar Co., 1959-60, Hawaii Comml. Sugar Co., 1961- 62; v.p. Alexander & Baldwin, Inc., Honolulu, 1962—; dir. Cal.-Hawaiian Sugar Refining Corp.; pres., dir. Kahuku Plantation Co., McBryde Sugar Co. Mem. Hawaii Constl. Conv., 1953. Clubs: Oahu Country, Pacific, Outrigger Canoe (Honolulu). Home: Rural Route 1 Box 382 Kula Maui HI 96790 Office: 822 Bishop St Honolulu HI 96813

HOLSCHUH, CARL G., mfg. exec.; b. N.Y.C., Apr. 23, 1909; s. Jacob W. and Elizabeth (Kopp) H.; B.S., Rutgers U., 1931, D. Eng. (hon.), 1950; m. Mary A. Hobbs, June 15, 1935; children—Frederick, Ann, John. Research engr. Sperry Gyroscope Co., 1933-42, dir. fire control dept., 1942-43, asst. chief research dir., 1943-46, chief engr., 1946, v.p., works mgr., 1946-49, v.p. mfg., 1949-51, v.p., asst. gen. mgr., 1951-55, exec. v.p., gen. mgr., 1955-56, pres., gen. mgr. Sperry Gyroscope div. Sperry Rand Corp., 1957-58, exec. v.p., dir. of corp., 1958-65; v.p. Gen. Dynamics Corp., N.Y.C., 1965-66, group v.p. marine systems, from 1966. Mem. Soc. Naval Architects and Marine Engrs., Tau Beta Pi. Clubs: Crescent (Huntington, N.Y.); University (N.Y.C.); Burning Tree (Washington). Home: Cove Rd Huntington NY 11743

HOLSCHUH, JOHN DAVID, lawyer; b. Ironton, O., Oct. 12, 1926; s. Edward A. and Helen (Ebert) H.; B.A., Miami U., 1948; J.D., U. Cin., 1951; m. Carol Stouder, Aug. 13, 1927; 1 son, John David. Admitted to Ohio bar, 1951; law clk. U.S. Dist. Ct. judge, 1952-54; mem. firm Alexander, Ebinger, Holschuh, Fisher & McAlister, Columbus, O., 1954—; adj. prof. law Coll. Law, Ohio State U., 1970. Pres. bd. dirs. Neighborhood House, 1969-70. Fellow Am. Coll. Trial

Lawyers; mem. Nat. Assn. R.R. Trial Counsel (exec. com.), Order of Coif, Phi Beta Kappa, Omicron Delta Kappa. Home: 2028 Wyandotte Rd Columbus OH 43212 Office: 17 S High St Columbus OH 43215

HOLSEN, ROBERT CHARLES, accountant; b. Manitowoc, Wis., Nov. 10, 1913; s. Herman J. and Lilly (Krumm) H.; Ph.B., U. Wis., 1938; m. Constance Weber, Nov. 18, 1938; children—Robert Charles, Catherine Jane. Staff accountant Ernst & Ernst, Chgo., 1938-56, partner Nashville office, 1956-62, partner Cleve. office, 1962—. Served to lt. comdr. USNR, 1944-46. C.P.A., Wis. Mem. Am. Inst. C.P.A.'s, Ohio, Tenn., Ill. socs. C.P.A.'s, Nat. Assn. Accountants, Am. Inst. Mgmt. Mason. Clubs: Country (Pepper Pike, O.), Clevelander, Cleveland Athletic. Home: 19600 Shelbourne Rd Shaker Heights OH 44118 Office: Union Commerce Bldg Cleveland OH 44115

HOLSHOUSER, DON FRANKLIN, educator; b. Dwight, Kan., Mar. 23, 1920; s. John Frederick and Lillian (Nordeen) H.; B.S., Kan. State Coll., 1942; M.S., U. Ill., 1950, Ph.D., 1958; m. Marion Delores Stankus, May 19, 1943; children—Judy (Mrs. Herman Tison), Donna, Eric. Devel. engr. RCA, Lancaster, Pa., 1942-46; research asso. elec. engring. dept. U. Ill., Urbana, 1946-51, asst. prof., 1951-58, research dir., 1958—, prof., 1965—; cons. Hallicrafters Co., 1961-66. Recipient Air Force research grants, 1959-71. Fellow A.A.A.S.; mem. I.E.E.E., Sigma Xi, Eta Kappa Nu, Sigma Tau. Home: 2030 Burlison Dr Urbana IL 61801

HOLSINGER, GEORGE ROBERT, Jr., univ. adminstr.; b. Youngstown, O., May 1, 1925; s. George R. and Saidee (Gibson) H.; B.S., Ohio State U., 1947, M.A., 1948, Ph.D., 1952; m. Yvonne Lamoreaux, Feb. 3, 1945; children—Sarah Anne, Stephen, Paul, Sue, Lise, Jonathan. News dir. sta. WOSU Radio, Ohio State U., 1951-52, asst. program supr., 1952-56; program dir. WOSU-TV, 1956-58; asst. dean Coll. Arts and Scis., Ohio State U., 1958-61, dean part-time and continuing edn., 1961—66, exec. asst. to the pres. 1966-68 asst. v.p. acad. affairs, from 1968, sec. univ. faculty and faculty council, from 1961. Mem. bd. edn., Worthington O., 1960—; chmn. citizens adv. com. on adult edn. Ohio Bd. Edn. Trustee Blue Cross of Central Ohio. Mem. Am. Philol. Assn., Adult Edn. Assn. U.S., Ohio Assn. Adult Edn., Assn. U. Evening Colls., Sigma Delta Chi, Sigma Phi Epsilon. Episcopalian. Home: 204 Chaucer Ct Worthington OH 43085

HOLSTEIN, EDWIN JOSEPH, educator, economist; b. Utica, N.Y., Apr. 17, 1921; s. Clarence E. and Elizabeth (Linfoot) H.; B.A., State U. N.Y. at Albany, 1942, M.A., 1947; Ph.D., N.Y.U., 1957; m. Katherin Jean Hansen, Jan. 31, 1948; children—John Joseph, Lynn Marie, Ann Judith. Instr. history and sociology State U. N.Y. at Cortland, 1946-47; mem. faculty Rensselaer Poly. Inst., 1947—, prof. econs., 1963—, chmn. dept., 1968- -, prof. Gen. Electric Co. Edn. Found. Fellowship program, 1959—; vis. prof. State U. N.Y. at Albany, Russell Sage Coll., Union Coll., Schenectady; cons. in field, 1958—. Mem. study com. Eastern Mohawk Valley Devel. Council, 1961; mem. study group Charles Kettering Found., 1964—. Served to lt. USNR, 1942-46. Recipient Founder's Day award N.Y.U., 1957. Mem. Am. N.Y. State (pres. 1970-71) econs. assns., Am. Assn. U. Profs., Pi Gamma Mu, Kappa Phi Kappa, Kappa Delta Rho. Author: (with E. J. McGrath) Liberal Education and Engineering, 1960; also articles. Home: 76 S Lake Av Troy NY 12180

HOLT, ANDREW DAVID, educator; b. Milan, Tenn., Dec. 4, 1904; s. Andrew David and Mary E. (Brown) H.; A.B., Emory U., 1927; M.S., Columbia, 1929, Ph.D., 1933; LL.D., Union U., 1950; student West Tenn. State Coll., 1923, George Peabody Coll., 1928; Litt. D., Tusculum Coll., 1962; D.SC. (hon.). U. Chattanooga, 1965; m. Martha Chase, Nov. 25, 1938; children—Ann Elizabeth, Martha Frances, Andrew David. Prin., Bluff Springs Elem. Sch., Milan., 1926; tchr., athletic coach Humboldt (Tenn.) High Sch., 1927-28; prin. tng. sch. West Tenn. State Coll., Memphis, 1929-30, prof. edn., 1930-37; high sch. supr. for West Tenn., 1930-37; exec. sec. Tenn. Edn. Assn., 1937-50; adminstrv. asst. to pres. U. Tenn., 1950-53, v.p., 1953-59, pres., 1959-70. Dir., South Central Bell Tel. & Tel. Co., Birmingham, Ala., Hamilton Internat. Corp., Farmington, Mich., Provident Life & Accident Ins. Co., Chattanooga, Hamilton Nat. Bank, Knoxville; ednl. cons. Holiday Inns of Am., Am. Sch., Chgo. Mem. at large nat. council, Boy Scouts Am. Exec. com. So. Regional Edn. Bd.; former pres. So. Assn. Colls. and Schs.; chmn. White House Conf. Edn.; mem. Nat. Commn. To Promote Eradication of Adult Illiteracy; nat. chmn. sch. savs. com. U.S. Treasury Dept.; chmn. Am. del. World Orgn. Teaching Profession, Berne, Switzerland. mem. council advisers U.S. Commn. on Edn., N.A.M., Air Transport Assn.; adviser to Ednl. Policies Commn. Mem. Bd. trustees Am. Fund for Dental Edn. Served as maj. AUS, 1943-45; chief pre-induction tng. sect. Army Service Forces in War Dept. Life mem. Nat. Congress Parents and Tchrs.; mem. N.E.A. (pres. 1949-50, dir.), Am. Legion, Amateur Chefs of Am., So. Assn. Land-Grant Colls. and State Univs., Am. Council Edn. (com. taxation and fiscal reporting federal govt., Nat. Adv. Dental Research Council, Internat. Assn. of U. Presidents, Nat. Assn. State Univs. and Land-Grant Colls. (chmn. com. traffic safety research and edn.), Alpha Kappa Psi, Delta Tau Delta, Phi Kappa Phi, Iota Lambda Sigma, Phi Sigma Sigma, Phi Delta Kappa, Omicron Delta Kappa. Methodist (steward). Mason (32, Shriner), Rotarian (dir). Author: Struggle for a State Sys. of Pub. Schs. in Tennessee. 1937. Editor The Tenn. Tchr., 1937-50. Contbr. articles to various ednl. publs. Home: 5331 Lyons View Pike Knoxville TN 37919

HOLT, BRYCE ROSWELL, lawyer; b. nr. Winston-Salem, N.C., Nov. 7, 1901; s. William T. and Rachel L. (Spease) H.; A.B., Duke, 1923, A.M., 1924, LL.B., 1926; m. Marion Knaur, Dec. 28, 1926; children—Holt, Bryce R., Jr., Helen Catherine. Admitted to N.C. bar, 1926, since practiced in Greensboro; mem. firm Holt, McNairy & Harris; asst. U.S. atty. Middle Dist. N.C., 1934-45, acting U.S. atty., 1945-46, U.S. atty., 1947-54. Mem. N.C. Com. Improved Cts. Mem. Am., N.C., Greensboro (pres. 1952-53) bar assns., Duke Law Alumni (pres. 1952-53). Democrat. Methodist. Club: Civitan (pres. 1945). Author: The Supreme Court of North Carolina and Slavery, (pub. in Historical Papers by Duke Univ. Press), 1924. Home: 2131 Wright Av Greensboro NC 27460 Office: 205 Ashe St Greensboro NC 27401

HOLT, CHARLES HENRY, mcht.; b. San Francisco, May 6, 1913; s. C. Parker and Ruth (Norton) H.; A.B., Stanford, 1936. With Theo. H. Davies & Co., Ltd., Honolulu, 1938—, sec., 1948—; also officer, dir. subsidiaries. Trustee Davies Found. Served to capt. AUS, 1941-46. Mem. Beta Theta Pi. Clubs: Pacific, Outrigger Canoe (Honolulu). Home: 2549-B Tantalus Dr Honolulu HI 96813 Office: PO Box 3020 Honolulu HI 96802

HOLT, DAVID EARL, librarian; b. Magna, Utah, May, 17, 1928; s. William Renold and Jenny (Kerr) H.; student U. Utah, 1946-47, 52-54, 58-59; B.A., Brigham Young U., 1957, M.A., 1958; M.S., Emory U., 1963; m. Mary Elizabeth Black Apr. 30, 1955; children—Helen Lorraine, Jane Elizabeth, David Renold, Steven Earl. Trombonist, Sonny Dunham Orch., Tony Pastor Orch., Glenn Gray Orch., Gene Krupa Orch., Tex. Beneke Orch., 1947-52; trombonist, arranger Tommy Dorsey Orch., 1954-55; library dir. Hayner Pub. Library, Alton, Ill., 1963-65; dir. libraries Waco-McLennan County Library, Waco, Tex., 1965-67; dir. Austin (Tex.) Pub. Library, 1967—; book editor Austin Am.-Statesman, 1967-69; staff Library/U.S.A. Exhibit, Fed. Pavilion, New York Worlds Fair, 1965; tchr. library adminstrn. Baylor U., 1966; columnist Waco Herald-Tribune, 1967. Mem. Am., Tex., S.W. library assns. Mem. Ch. of Jesus Christ of Latter-day Saints. Rotarian. Editor: Waco Rotary Club Bull., 1966-67. Contbr. articles profl. jours. Address: 1802 Forest Trail Austin TX 78703

HOLT, DOCTOR DILLON, coll. pres.; b. Albermarle, N.C. July 20, 1899; s. David Alexander and Elizabeth Sophronia (Rummage) H.; A.B., Duke, 1927, B.D., 1933; D.D., Wesley Coll., 1960, U. N.D., 1960; m. Grace Elizabeth Sanders, Jan. 4, 1936; children—David Dillon, John Sanders. Instr. Bible and psychology Rutherford (N.C.) Coll., 1927-30; ordained to ministry Methodist Ch., 1930; minister in Charlottesville, Va., 1936-40, Lynchburg, Va., 1940- 44, Portsmouth, Va., 1944-45, Durham, N.C., 1945-53; exec. dir. Meth. Coll. Found, N.C., 1953-56; dir. financial promotion quadrennium Commn. Christian Higher Edn., Meth. Ch., 1956-60; pres. Scarritt Coll. for Christian Workers, Nashville, 1970; acting pres. Pfeiffer Coll., Misenheimer, N.C., 1971—. Lectr. ecumenical movements, before assemblies, commencements, others; active Council of Chs.; counselor family life and vocational guidance, higher edn., fund raising. Mem. Nashville C. of C. Mason, Rotarian. Contbr. articles religious periodicals. Home: Route 2 West Jefferson NC 28694

HOLT, DON S., textile mfg. co. exec.; b. Graham, N.C., Mar. 7, 1908, s. Seymour S. and Glenna (Shaw) H.; A.B., U. NC., 1929; m. Margaret McConnell, 1932. Exec. v.p. Travora Mfg. Co., 1938-49; dir. Nat. Bank of Alamance, 1939-50; v.p. Cannon Mills Co., 1951-58, exec. v.p., 1959-61, pres. 1962—, chmn. bd., 1971—, also mem. bd. dirs.; dir. Cabarrus Bank & Trust Co. Mem. U.S. bd. Anglo-Am. Textile Mission to Japan, 1950; dir. N.C. Textile Mfrs. Assn., Inc., 1952. Served to lt. comdr. USNr, 1942-45. Mem. Am. Textile Mfrs. Inst. (dir.). Methodist. Office: Cannon Mills Co Kannapolis NC 28081

HOLT, EDWARD ERMEN, educator; b. Adams County, O., Nov. 12, 1901; s. O. V. and Emma K. (Moore) H.; A.B., Wilmington Coll., 1926; A.M., Miami U., 1936, LL.D., 1957; LL.D., Wittenberg Coll., 1954, Ashland Coll., 1960, Wilmington Coll., 1961; m. Nelle Shumaker, Apr. 7, 1923; children—Jack E., Jane (Mrs. Paul Hersey). Tchr., Brown County, O., 1921; supt. schs., Higginsport, O., 1922-25. Georgetown, 1925-32, Hillsboro, 1932-40, Marion, 1940-48, Springfield, 1948-57; supt. pub. instrn. Ohio Dept. Edn., 1957-66; cons., program for research and devel. in vocational- tech. edn. Sch. Edn., U. Cal., Berkeley, 1966-67; research prof. Ore. State System Higher Edn., Monmouth, 1967-70, ednl. cons. on pub. sch. adminstrn., Worthington, O., 1970—. mem. N.E.A., Ohio Edn. Assn., Am., Ohio (past pres.) assns. sch. adminstrs., Phi Delta Kappa. Presbyn. Mason, Rotarian. Club: University. Contbr. articles profl. jours. Home: 482 Oxford Ct Worthington OH 43085

HOLT, EDWIN GRAVES, mill co. exec.; b. Greensboro, N.C., Aug. 28, 1914; s. James Ernest and Edna Broughton (Graves) H.; B.B.A., Davidson Coll., 1935; M. Dorothy S. Creech, Mar. 12, 1938; 1 son, Edwin Creech. With Cone Mills, Inc., 1935—, 1935, southwestern rep., 1938-50, asst. v.p., 1950-52, v.p., 1952—. Served as lt. col. Inf., Aus, 1942-46. Mem. N.Y. So. Soc., Am. Arbitration Assn., N.Y. Sales Execs., S.A.R. Clubs: Engineers (N.Y.C.); Canoe Brook Country (Summit, N.J.), Weavers. Home: 9 Colt Rd Summit NJ 07901 Office: 1440 Broadway New York City NY 10018

HOLT, ERNEST HOWARD, research physicist; b. Eng., Mar. 26, 1927; B.Sc. in Engring., U. London, 1948, Ph.D., 1952; m. Lois Anne Chorlian, Sept. 8, 1956; children—Elizabeth Anne, Timothy Howard, James Edward. Came to U.S., 1954, naturalized, 1965. Engr. trainee Met. Vickers Elec. Co., Manchester, Eng., 1952-53; research engn., research lab. Asso. Elec. Industries, Aldermaston, Eng., 1953-54; mem. research staff. instr. Mass. Inst. Tech., 1954-56; asst. prof. elec. engring. U. Ill. at Urbana, 1956-58; prof. elec. engring. Rensselaer Poly. Inst., 1958-68, dir. plasma dynamics lab., 1960-68, asso. chmn. elec. engring. curriculum, 1967-68; sr. physicist, chief remote atmospheric sensing tech. area, atmospheric scis. lab. U.S. Army Electronics Command, 1968—; adj. prof. physics and elec. engring. U. Tex., 1969—; adj. prof. physics N.M. State U., 1970—. Chmn. ethics com. Engrs. Council Profl. Devel., 1967—69 Registered profl. engr., N.Y. Mem. I.E.E.E. (chmn. Schenectady sect. 1962—63), Am. Inst. Aero. and Astonautics, Am. Phys. Soc., A.A.A.S., Am. Meteorol. Soc., Optical Soc. Am., Sigma Xi, Eta Kappa Nu. Author: (with R. E. Haskell) Foundations of Plasma Dynamics. 1965. Home: 9141 McFall El Paso TX 79925 Office: ASL US Army ECOM White Sands Missile Range NM 88002

HOLT, EVERETT WILLIAM, coll. dean; b. Attleboro, Mass., Nov. 12, 1907; s. Charles Henry and Annie M. (Walker) H.; A.B., Colgate U., 1929; S.M., U. Chgo., 1941; m. Segrid E.F. Lindbeck, July 15, 1937 (dec. May 1968); 1 dau., Ellen (Mrs. Richard B. Arnold). Math. instr. Lawrence Acad., Groton, Mass., 1937-42, Muhlenberg Coll., 1946-51; chmn. math. dept. dept. Bethlehem (Pa.) Area Coll., 1946-47; engr. Western Electric Co., 1951- 58; from asst. prof. to asso. prof. math. Monmouth Coll., W. Long Branch, N.J., 1958-62, dean faculty, 1962—. Served to lt. comdr. USNR, 1942-46. Mem. Res. Officers Assn., Math. Assn. Am., Soc. Indsl. and Applied Math., U.S. Naval Inst., N.J. Assn. Colls. and Univs., N.J. Jr. Coll. Assn., Am. Council Acad. Deans, A.A.A.S., Navy League of U.S., Delta Sigma Pi. Home: 200 Castle Wall Av Elberon NJ 07740 Office: Monmouth Coll West Long Branch NJ 07764

HOLT, HAMILTON TATUM, Jr., co. exec.; b. Tampa, Fla., Apr. 20, 1925; s. Hamilton Tatum and Melva (Clark) H.; student Emory U., 1943-44; A.B., U. Ga., 1947; M.B.A., Stanford, 1949; m. Susan Marie Phister, Sept. 20, 1948; children—Susan Winther, Hamilton Tatum III, Lisa Clark m. 2d, Jackie Jean Crouch, Jan. 24, 1970. Controller, Clark Memls., Inc., Macon, Ga., 1949-52 chmn. bd, 1963—; v.p. marketing, dir. Kickernick, Inc., Mpls., 1953-57; asso. Mckinsey & Co., San Francisco, 1958-60; partner, founder Strong, Wishart & Holt, San Francisco, 1960-62; ind. mgmt. cons., San Francisco, 1963-64; v.p., dir. Hitco, Los Angeles, 1965-67, pres., 1967-70; pres. dir. All-Tech Industries, Miami, Fla., 1970—, Ga. Marietta Co., 1971—, Holt Co., Inc., 1971—. Vice chmn. Macon chpt. A.R.C., 1950. Bd. govs. Marin County (Cal.) Republican Alliance, 1961-62. Asso. U. So. Cal., 1969-70. Served to lt. USNR, 1943-47, 52-53. Mem. Am. Mgnt. Assn., Am. Ordnance Assn., Phi Beta Kappa, Phi Eta Sigma, Phi Delta Theta. Mem. Religious Sci. Ch. Clubs: San Francisco Yacht; Idle Hour Country (Macon, Ga.); Commerce (Atlanta). Home: 2412 Laguna Dr Fort Lauderdale FL 33316 Office: 1400 NW 57th Ct Miami Lakes FL 33014

HOLT, HARRY HOWARD, Jr. lawyer; b. Hampton, Va., Oct. 28, 1904; s. Harry Howard and Mary Whiting (Chisman) H.; B.S., Va. Mil. Inst., Lexington, 1925; LL.B., U. of Va., 1928; m. Charlotte Meade Burrage, Nov. 12, 1930 (div.): children —Charlotte Meade, Harry Howard III, Diana; m. 2d, Jean M. Eckley, Dec. 7, 1956. Admitted to Va. bar, 1928; mem. firm Montague & Holt, 1928-44; formed partnership Montague, Ferguson & Holt, 1944; apptd. asst. U.s. atty., Eastern Dist. of Va., 1933, spl. asst. to U.S. atty. gen., 1940; U.S. atty, Eastern Dist. of Va., 1944-47; dir. United Va. Bank/Citizens & Marine, Peninsula Broadcasting Corp.; v.p., dir. Newport News Distilled Ice Co.; dir. Peninsula Radio Corp. sec., dir. Nuclear Service and Constrn. Co., Inc.; sec.; dir., gen. counsel Newport News Ship bldg. & Dry Dock Co. Sec., bd dirs. Newport News Shipbldg. Co. Found. Mem. Jud. Council of Va.; mem. bd. commrs. Va. State Ports Auth. Mem. Am., Va., Newport News bar assns., Newcomen Soc. N. Am. Kappa Alpha. Mason (Shriner). Clubs: Hampton Yacht: The Anglers, N.Y.; University (Washington); Propeller, James River Country; Engineers (N.Y.C.). Home: 136 Meredith Av Hampton Va 23369 Office: care Newport News Shipbldg and Dry Dock Co Newport News VA 23607

HOLT, HOMER ADAMS, former gov., lawyer; b. Lewisburg, W.Va., Mar. 1, 1898; s. Robert Byrne and Emma (McWhorter) H.; A.B., Washington and Lee U., 1918, LL.B., 1923; LL.D., W.Va. U., 1937, Bethany Coll., W.Va., 1940; m. Isabel Hedges Wood, Mar. 22, 1924; children—Julia Kinsley (Mrs. Coyle), Isabel Drury (Mrs. Dannenberg), Robert Byrne. Instr. math. Washington and Lee U. 1920-23, asst. prof. law, 1923-24, asso. prof., 1924- 25; in practice law; mem. firm Hubard, Bacon & Holt, 1925-26, Dillon, Mahan & Holt, Fayetteville, W.Va., 1927-33; atty. gen. W.Va.,1933- 37; gov. W.Va., 1937-41; mem. law firm Brown, Jackson & Knight, Charleston, W.Va., 1941-46; dir. Union Carbide&Carbon Corp., N.Y., 1944-55, gen. counsel, 1947-53, v.p., 1949- 53, exec. com., 1950-53; mem. Jackson, Kelly, Holt & O'Farrell, 1953—; dir. Kanawha Valley Bank Charleston, Slab Fork Coal Co. Mem.-at-large Nat. council Boy Scouts Am., 1959—; chmn. W.Va. Commn. Constle Revision, 1957-63. Trustee Meml. Hosp. Assn. Charleston, 1958—, pres., 1961-63; trustee, mem. exec. com. Wash. and Lee U., 1940-69, now emeritus. Served to 2d lt. C.A., U.S. Army, 1918-19. Mem. Am., W.Va. (past pres.), Fayette County, Kanawha County bar assns., Bar Assn. N.Y.C., Am. Counsel Assn., Assn. Gen. Counsel (emeritus), Am. Law Inst., Am. Judicature Soc., W.Va. C. of C. (pres. 1945-46), Am. Legion, N.Y. So. Soc., Order of Coif, Phi Beta Kappa, Phi Kappa Psi, Phi Delta Phi. Omicron Delta Kappa. Democrat. Presbyn., Mason, Elk, Rotarian. Home: 1521 Bridge Rd Charleston, WV 25314. Office: Kanawha Valley Bldg Charleston WV 25322

HOLT, IVAN LEE, Jr., judge; b. Marshall, Mo., May 4, 1913; s. Ivan Lee and Leland (Burks) H.; student Princeton, 1931-34; A.B., U. Chgo., 1935, J.D., 1937; LL.D., McKendree Coll., 1962; m. Mary Edward Depping, Dec. 26, 1945; children—Mary Diana (Mrs. John W. Hoxie), Janet Mildred Depping (Mrs. Michael D. Resnik), Ivan Lee III. Admitted to Mo. bar, 1937; asso. Marion C. Early, St. Louis, 1937-40; asst. circuit atty. City of St. Louis, 1940-42; asst. prof. law Washington U. Law Sch., 1947-48; asso. Jones, Hocker, Gladney & Grand, St. Louis, 1948-49; judge 22d Circuit Mo., 1949- -; mem. faculty Nat. Coll. State Trial Judges, 1967-70. Mem. exec. com. adv. council judges Nat. Council on Crime and Delinquency, 1970—; nat. adv. council Practicing Law Inst. Mem. bd. Goodwill Industries, Mo. Hist. Soc., Methodist Children's Home of Mo.; bd. trustees Barnes Hosp.; mem. adv. council St. Louis U. Sch. Law. Served from lt. (j.g.) to comdr., USNR, 1942-46. Fellow Inst. Jud. Adminstrn., 1966-70. Mem. Nat. Conf. State Trial Judges (Mo. del. 1957-64, 67-70), Am. (council sect. jud. adminstrn. 1955-62, chmn. jud. adminstrn. 1962-63, ho. of dels. 1963-66, mem. spl. coms. standards criminal justice and standards jud. conduct), St. Louis bar assns., Mo. Bar, Am. Judicature Soc. (dir. 1962-64), Lawyers Assn. St. Louis, Mo. Council Juvenile Ct. Judges, Am. Law Inst., Law Library Assn. (mem. bd.), S.R., Sigma Alpha Epsilon, Phi Delta Phi. Democrat. Methodist (jud. council 1956-60). Clubs: University; Pike County Country. Contbr. articles profl. publs. Home: 56 Kingsbury Pl St Louis MO 63112 Office: Civil Courts Bldg 10 N 12th St St Louis MO 63101

HOLT, L. EMMETT, Jr., physician; b. N.Y.C., Mar. 20, 1895; s. L. Emmett and Linda F. (Mairs) H.; A.B., Harvard, 1916; M.D., Johns Hopkins, 1920; Sc.D., New York Med. Coll., 1967; m. Olivia Cauldwell, June 17, 1921; children—Niel MacL., Arnold R., Linda H. Holz. Intern, Presbyn. Hosp., 1920-21, Babies Hosp., 1921-22 (both N.Y.C.); teaching, med. research dept. pediatrics Johns Hopkins, 1922-44; prof. pediatrics N.Y.U. Coll. Medicine, N.Y.C., 1944—, chmn. dept. pediatrics, 1944-60, med. missions to Czechoslovakia, 1947; sec. Internat. Congress Pediatrics, N.Y.C.; cons. nutrition WHO. Decorated Order White Lion, medal of Charles U. (Czechoslovakia); Mannerheim medal (Finland), Al-Istiglal of Second Order (Jordan); recipient Borden Nutrition award, Am. Acad. Pediatrics, 1955; Harlow Brooks medal, New York Acad. Medicine, 1957, Modern Medicine award, 1960; McCollum award, 1960, Osborne Mendel award Am. Inst. Nutrition, 1964, Howland award Am. Pediatric Soc. 1966, Goldberger award A.M.A., 1969. Mem. Am. Middle East Rehab. (pres. 1950-60), Nutrition Soc. Gt. Britain, Assn. Am. Physicians, Am. Soc. Clin. Nutrition, Am. Soc. Clin. Investigation, Am. Pediatric Soc., Soc. Pediatric Research, Am. Acad. Pediatrics. Soc. Exptl. Biology and Medicine, Am. Inst. Nutrition, Am. Soc. Biol. Chemists, A.A.A.S., Practitioners Soc., Interurban Clin. Club, Harvey Soc.; also mem. numerous fgn. pediatric socs. Club: Century assn. (N.Y.C.). Author: Holt's Pediatrics (with R. McIntosh and H. L. Barnett); Pioneer of a Children's Century, 1939, (with R. L. Duffus) Good Housekeeping Book of Infant and Child Care, 1958; pediatrics, nutrition, biochemistry articles med. jours. Home: 330 E 33d St New York City NY 10022 Office: Bellevue Hosp New York City NY 10016

HOLT, LEON CONRAD, Jr., business exec., lawyer; b. Reading, Pa., June 19, 1925; s. Leon Conrad and Elizabeth (Bright) H.; B.S. cum laude in Metall. Engring., Lehigh U., 1948; LL.B., U. Pa., 1951; m. June M. Weidner, June 30, 1947; children—Deborah L., Richard W. Admitted to N.Y. bar, 1952; with firm Mudge, Stern Williams & Tucker, attys., N.Y.C., 1951-53; atty. Am. Oil Co. and predecessor co., N.Y.C., 1953-57; gen. atty. Air Products & Chems., Inc., Allentown, Pa., 1957-61, v.p., gen. counsel, 1961—, also dir., mem. exec., finance coms.; dir. Catalytic Constrn. Co.; v.p., dir. Escambia Chem. Corp. Vice chmn. Lehigh Centennial Fund, 1964-65; chmn. Allentown Bd. Ethics, 1970—; campaign chmn. Lehigh County United Fund, 1972. Bd. dirs. Allentown YMCA 1965-69. Served to lt. (j.g.) USNR, 1943-46. Mem. Allentown C. of C. (gov. 1965-68), Am., N.Y. State bar assns., Assn. Bar N.Y.C., Pa. Soc., Alpha Tau Omega. Republican. Episcopalian. Club: Lehigh Country (bd. govs. 1970—) (Allentown). Home: 3003 Parkway Blvd Allentown PA 18104 Office: PO Box 538 Allentown PA 18105

HOLT, MARMADUKE BURRELL, Jr., lawyer; b. Silverton, Colo., Sept. 21, 1905; s. Marmaduke Burrell and Mabel (Brown) H.; grad. Phillips Exeter Acad., 1923; A.B., Williams Coll., 1927; LL.B. cum laude, U. Denver, 1931: m. Jessica Matlock, Feb. 7, 1931 (dec. 1940); children—Marmaduke Burrell II, Robert W., Alan M.; m. 2d, Mary S. Barkalow, Oct. 3, 1942; children—John S., Peter B., Katherine B. Admitted to Colo. bar, 1931, since practice in Denver; mem. firm Martin and Holt, 1943-64. Gen. atty. Gt. Western Sugar Co., 1944-55, gen. counsel, 1955-70. Recipient Mayor Denver award pub. service, 1965. Mem. Am., Colo. (v.p. 1952-53, bd. govs. 1961-67), Denver (pres. 1964-65) bar assns., Colo. Bar Found. (chmn.), Order St. Ives, Phi Delta Phi, Delta Psi. Episcopalian (clk., vestryman, sr. warden). Clubs: Law, University, Cactus, Mile High (Denver). Home: 300 Race Denver CO 80206 Office: 100 Fillmore St Denver CO 80206

HOLT, MATTHEW LESLIE, educator; b. Ellsworth, Ia., June 19, 1904; s. Peter and Olive Margaret (Lyders) H.; B.S., St. Olaf Coll., 1926; M.S., U. Wis., 1928, Ph.D., 1930; m. Gretchen Mueller, Aug. 29, 1952. Instr. chemistry U. Wis., 1930-37, asst. prof., 1937-43, asso. prof., 1943-46, prof., 1946—, asso. chmn. dept., 1952-69. Mem. Am. Chem. Soc., Electrochem. Soc., Alpha Chi Sigma. Republican. Conglist. Home: 3502 Blackhawk Dr Madison WI 53705

HOLT, MAURICE, educator, mathematician; b. Wildboarclough, Eng., May 16, 1918; s. Percy Grimshaw and Elizabeth (Higgins) H.; B.Sc., Manchester (Eng.) U., 1940, M.Sc., 1944, Ph.D., 1948; m. Eileen Campbell, June 20, 1942; children—Nicholas Campbell, Christopher, Valerie, Helen Clare, Caroline Jean. Came to U.S., 1956, naturalized, 1964. Aircraft engr. Blackburn Aircraft Co., Brough, Eng., 1940-45; asst. lectr. applied math. U. Liverpool (Eng.), 1948-49; lectr. applied math. U. Sheffield (Eng.), 1949-51; prin. sci. officer Brit. Ministry Supply, 1952-55; vis. lectr. math. Harvard, 1955; from asst. to asso. prof. applied math. Brown U., 1956-60; prof. aero. scis. U. Cal. at Berkeley, 1960—; cons. to govt. and industry, 1956—. Mem. Am. Math. Soc., Am. Phys. Soc., Sigma Xi. Author papers high speed aerodynamics. Home: 547 Spruce St Berkeley CA 97407

HOLT, RALPH MANNING, Jr., hosiery mill exec.; b. Burlington, N.C., Sept. 7, 1931; s. Ralph Manning and Margaret (McElwee) H.; B.S., Davidson Coll., 1953; student Harvard Bus. Sch., 1956-57; m. Eda Luciana Contiguglia, June 3, 1957: children—Ralph Manning III, Margaret Berrena, John Anthony, Michael McElwee. With Holt Hosiery Mills, Inc., Burlington, 1957—, v.p., 1958- 66, treas., 1959-66, exec. v.p., 1966-67, pres., 1967—; v.p., treas. Holt Hosiery Corp., N.Y.C., 1959-69; dir. Bush Universal, Inc., N.Y.C., Hamilton Watch Co. Lancaster, Pa. Div. leader Burlington United Fund, 1960-61. Chmn. bd. trustees Meml. Hosp., Burlington; bd. visitors Davidson Coll. Served to lt. (j.g.) USNR, 1953-55. Mem. Beta Theta Pi. Club: N.Y. Athletic. Home: Mays Lake Burlington NC 27216 Office: Box 219 Burlington NC 27215

HOLT, ROBERT HAROLD, lawyer; b. Gardiner, Me., Sept. 25, 1889; s. John Franklin and Mary G. (Robinson) H.; A.B., Harvard, 1911, LL.B., 1914; m. Lilian S. Clapp, Oct. 28, 1916 (dec. Feb. 1959); children—Richard P., Rosamund (Mrs. Wallace F. Haley), Deborah (Mrs. James R. McIntosh); m. 2d, Margaret Bartlett Wells, Mar. 26, 1960. Admitted to Mass. bar, 1914; asso. firm Gaston, Snow, Motley & Holt, and predecessors, Boston, 1914—, partner, 1920-40, sr. partner, 1940—. Moderator, Lexington Town Meeting, 1924-49. Served to 2d lt. U.S. Army, World War I. Mem. Am., Boston bar assns. Clubs: Union, Harvard (Boston); Duxbury (Mass.) Yacht. Home: 184 Marshall St Duxbury MA 02332 Office: Devonshire St Boston MA 02109

HOLT, ROBERT LEROI univ. adminstr.; b. Dixie, Ga., Jan. 1, 1920; s. John Gordon and Willie (Grimes) H.; A.A., Mars Hill (N.C.) Jr. Coll., 1941; A.B., Wake Forest Coll., 1943, M.A., 1946; Ph.D., Duke, 1951; m. Claire Rebecca Hardin, June 3, 1943; children—James Lawrence, Claire Rebecca, Susan Elaine. Ordained to ministry Bapt. Ch., 1942; minister various chs., 1941-50; dir. religious activities E. Carolina U., Greenville, N.C., 1950-53, registrar, dir. admissions, 1958-60, dean, 1960-64, v.p., dean of univ., 1964—; v.p. Mars Hill Jr. Coll., 1953-58. Exec. com. N.C. Coll. Conf., 1961; mem. com. on coll. So. Assn., 1964-69, chmn. com. on standards and reports, 1965-69; mem. N.C. Adv. Council Civil Rights, 1966-71; chmn. com. standards and membership N.C. Assn. Colls and Univs., 1966-67, mem. adminstrv. com., 1967-70; mem. N.C. Adv. Council on Tchr. Edn. and Profl. Standards, 1961-69, N.C. Evaluation Com. on Tchr. Edn., 1970—, Nat. Com. on Emeriti, 1971—. Pres. United Fund, Madison County, 1957-58. Trustee Wake Forest U., 1965-68; adv. council N.C. Community Coll., 1963—. Named Man of Year, Civitan Club, Madison County, 1958. Mem. Assn. Acad. Deans N.C. Colls., N.C. Edn. Assn., N.E.A., Phi Delta Kappa, Pi Omega Pi (hon.). Baptist (deacon). Clubs: Mars Hill Civitan (dir. 1957); Greenville Rotary (dir. 1960). Home: 1711 Knollwood Dr Greenville NC 27834

HOLT, ROBERT RUTHERFORD, educator, psychologist; b. Jacksonville, Fla., Dec. 17, 1917; s. Walter John and Grace Lloyd (Hilditch) Watson; B.A., Princeton, 1939; M.A., Harvard, 1941, Ph.D., 1944; m. Louisa C. Pinkham, Feb. 1944 (div. Feb. 1953); children—Dorothy Catherine; m. 2d, Crusa Adelman, Dec. 1957 (dec. 1959); m. 3d, Joan Esterowitz, Aug. 2, 1963; children—Daniel, Michael. Research asst. Harvard Psychol. Clinic, 1941- 44; study dir. div. program surveys Bur. Agrl. Econs., USDA, Washington, 1944-46; clin. psychologist Winter VA Hosp., Topeka, 1946-49; asso. psychologist, sr. psychologist research dept. Menninger Found., 1947-53, dir. psychol. staff, 1951-53, cons. research dept., 1953-60; asso. prof., prof. psychology Grad. Sch. Arts and Sci., N.Y.U., 1953—, dir. Research Center Mental Health, 1953-63, co- dir., 1963-69; vis. prof. clin. psychology Harvard, 1967-68. Cons. psychology panel Armed Forces-NRC Com. on Bio-Astronautics, 1959-60; tng. cons. N.Y. area VA, 1953-60; cons. Milledgeville (Ga.) State Hosp., 1962—; chmn. com. of cons. Mental Health Book Rev. Index, 1958—. Mem. fellowship com. Found. Fund for Research Psychiatry, 1956-61; mem. mental health rev. panel CDRB, NIH, 1963-66; mem. adv. com. on extramural research Nat. Inst. Mental Health, 1968-69. Director Dessoff Choirs, 1953-56; pres. Council for Research in Bibliography, 1965—; Spl. Research fellow Nat. Inst. Mental Health, 1960-61; fellow Center Advanced Study Behavioral Scis., 1960-61; recipient Research Career award Nat. Inst. Mental Health, 1962—. Diplomate clin. psychology Am. Bd. Exam. Profl. Psychology. Mem. Am. Assn. U. Profs., Am. (pres. div. clin. psychology 1961-62), N.Y. psychol. assns., Am. Civil Liberties Union, A.A.A.S., Common Cause, Village Ind. Democrats N.Y., Fedn. Am. Scis., Phi Beta Kappa, Sigma Xi. Author: (with B. Klopfer, Mary Ainsworth, W. Flopfer) Developments in the Rorschach Technique, Vol. 1, 1954; (with Lester Luborsky) Personality Patterns of Psychiatrists, 2 vols., 1958; (with I. Janis, G. Mahl, J. Kagan) Personality: Dynamics, Development and Assessment, 1969; Assessing Personality, 1971. Editor: Motives and Thought, 1966; Diagnostic Psychological Testing (Rapaport), 1968; New Horizon for Psychotherapy 1971. Editor TAT Newsletter, 1946-52; editorial bd. Jour. Nervous and Mental Disease, 1957—, Psychol. Issues, 1958—, Jour. Psychol. Researches, 1956—, Psychoanalysis and Contemporary Sci., 1969—. Bd. consultants Am. Imago, A Psychoanalytic Jour. Culture, Sci. and Arts, 1963—. Home: 20 E 8th St New York City NY 10003

HOLT, THAD, mgmt. cons.; b. Sumterville, Ala., Sept. 23, 1898; s. LeRoy and Elizabeth Cunningham (Burwell) H.; A.B., Colo. Coll., 1920; m. Sarah Ames Oliver, Feb. 4, 1928; children—Thad, Samuel Clark Oliver. In advt. and sales work 24 yrs.; advt. and sales mgr. Wofford Oil Co., 1921-27; 27; served as state dir. F.E.R.A., W.P.A., C.W.A., N.Y.A., Mongomery, 1932- 36; asst. nat. adminstr. W.P.A., Washington, 1936-37; v.p. (half-owner) owner) Famous Features Syndicate, N.Y.C., 1921-22; pres. and treas. The TV Corp., stas. WAPI, WAFM and WAFM-TV, 1937; cons. New Orleans Times- Picayune, Voice of Am. (TV), Ampex Corp., CBS, Inc., Royal Crown Cola Cola Corp.; chmn. Metaplate & Coating, Inc. State chmn. U.S. Savs. Bond Com.; Com.; communications officer Civil Def.; vice chmn. local bd. SSS, 1943-45. Dir. Birmingham Art Mus. Served in O.T.C., Camp Presidio, San Francisco, 1918. Mem. Ala. Hist. Assn. (exec. com. 1955—), Newcomen Soc., C. of C. of C. (past v.p.), Com. Fgn. Relations, Am. Legion, Phi Beta Kappa, Phi Gamma Delta. Democrat. Episcopalian. Clubs: Kiwanis (pres. Birmingham 1950), Birmingham Country, Mountain Brook, Dowtown, Redstone. Home: 28 Ridge Dr Birmingham AL 35213 Office: First Nat Bank Bldg Birmingham AL 35203

HOLT, VICTOR, Jr., rubber co. exec.; b. Heavener, Okla., Mav 8, 1908; s. Victor and Ethel (Morrisson) H.; B.S., U. Okla., 1928; m. Rowena Turner, Feb. 17, 1934; children—Hanna Lu, Victoria Sue, Judith Carol. Pres., Goodyear Tire & Rubber Co., Akron, O. Mem. Rubber Mfrs. Assn. (dir.), Alpha Tau Omega. Club: Portage Country (Akron). Home: 630 Delaware Av Akron OH 44303 Office: 1144 E Market St Akron OH 44304

HOLT, VICTORIA, author. Publs. include: Bride of Pendorric; Mistress of Mellyn, 1960; Kirkland Revels, 1962; Legend of the Seventh Virgin, 1965; Menfreya In the Morning, 1966; The King of the Castle, 1967; The Queen's Confession, 1968. Address: care Doubleday & Co Garden City NY 11530

HOLT, WALTER A., mfg. co. exec.; b. Buffalo, Wyo., Apr. 1, 1911; s. Wilbur R. and Mary (Given) H.; A.B., U. Mich., 1932; M.B.A., Harvard, 1934; m. Eleanor Horton, Sept. 21, 1935; children—Walter V., Carolyn G., Eleanor B. Research asst. Harvard, 1935; asst. sec. Sunbeam Electric Mfg. Co., Evansville, Ind., 1935-45; asst. sec.-treas. successor co. Seeger Refrigerator Co., Evansville, 1945-55; with Whirlpool Corp., St. Joseph, Mich., 1955—, treas., 1960-62, v.p. finance, chief financial officer, 1962—; chmn. bd. Appliance Buyers Credit Corp.; treas. Warwick Electronics, Inc., 1966—. Trustee, treas. Mercy Hosp., Benton Harbor, Mich., 1970—. Clubs: Point O'Woods Golf and Country (dir.) (Benton Harbor); Union League (Chgo.). Home: Marquette Woods Rd Stevensville MI 49127 Office: Whirpool Corp Adminstrv Center Benton Harbor MI 49022

HOLTER, EDWARD FRANKLIN, agronimist; b. Jefferson, Md., June 6, 1900; s. Melvin Franklin and Annie Catherine (Kefauver) H.; B.S., U. Md., 1921; m. Naomi Grace Keplar. Oct. 16, 1924; 1 dau., Esther Grace (Mrs. John Wesley Bossard). Farm owner, operator, 1932-52, owner, 1952—; vocational agr. instr., Frederick County, Md., 1937-45. Sec., Md. State Grange, 1933-45, master, 1945-53, lectr. Nat. Grange, 1947-61; pres. Farmer's Coop. Assn., 1953-57; mem. Md. Bd. Agr., 1947—; pres. Farmer's and World Affairs, Inc., 1956-62; state dir. Farmers Home Adminstrn. for Md. and Del., 1961—. Bd. dirs. Md. State Fair, 1947-53, dir. State Fair, 1949-53; mem. U.S. Commn. for UNESCO, 1957-60, Citizen's Adv. Com. Youth Fitness, 1957. Commr., County of Frederick (Md.), 1954-56. Vice chmn. bd. regents U. Md. Mem. Am. Country Life Assn. (dir.), Frederick Co. of C. (dir.), Alpha Zeta. Mason. Home: 300 N College Parkway Frederick, MD 21701. Office: Hartwick Bldg 4321 Hartwick Rd College Park MD 20740

HOLTER, NORMAN JEFFERIS, biophysicist; b. Helena, Mont., Feb. 1, 1914; s. Norman B. and Florence (Jefferis) H.; A.B., U. Cal. at Los Angeles, 1937, M.A., 1940; M.S., U. So. Cal., 1939; postgrad. U. Heidelberg, 1937, U. Chgo., 1939, Oak Ridge Inst. Nuclear Studies, 1949, Med. Sch., U. Ore., 1956; D.Sc., Mont. State U., 1965; m. Eleanor Wheeler, Sept. 1941 (div. Jan. 7, 1952); children—Troy Jefferis, Marian; m. 2d, Joan Treacy, July 18, 1952; children—John Treacy, Anton Jeffery. Chemist, Cal. Consummers Corp., Los Angeles, 1937-38; teaching asst. U. Cal., 1940-41, sr. scientist U. Cal.-Navy Dept. Capricorn Expdn., 1952; asst. physicist Nat. Def. Research Com., San Diego, 1941; asst. physicist Navy Dept., 1941-42, asso. physicist, 1942-44, physicist, 1944-45, sr. physicist, 1946-47; mem. tech. staff Bikini Atomic Bomb Expdn., 1946-47; participant Eniwetok Hydrogen Bomb Tests, 1952; specialist in physics Inst. Geophysics and Planetary Plysics U. Cal., San Diego, La Jolla, 1964-65, asst. to the chancellor, 1965-66. Pres. Holter Research Found. Inc., Helena and La Jolla, 1947—; past pres. Bozeman State Coll. Research Found.; adviser med. physics Western Found. Clinic Research. Past pres. Rancho Cal. Corp.; pres. Holter Realty Co.; past pres. A. M. Holter Hardware Co.; past v.p. N Bar Ranch Co., Park Av. Apts. Corp., Helena, Angus Sales Co.; past dir., mem. exec. com. Ind. Coal & Coke Co. (Salt Lake City); past dir. First Nat. Bank & Trust Co. (Helena). Recipient US PHS grant. Past adv. council Sch. Bus., Mont. State U.; past trustee, v.p., pres. St. Peter's Hosp.; mem. adv. bd. Mont. Crippled Children's Home and Hosp.; past cons. biophysics VA Hosp., Ft. Harrison, Mont. Past editorial bd., Jour. Nuclear Medicine. Mem. adv. com. sci. activities SSS. Trustee La Jolla Country Day Sch., La Jolla Mus. Art. Fellow A.A.A.S.; mem. Am. Phys. Soc., Soc. Nuclear Medicine (past pres.), Am. Acoustical Soc., Am. Assn. Physics Tchrs., Mont. Med. Assn. (hon.), Biophysical Soc., N.Y. and Mont. acads. scis., A.M.A. (asso.), Sigma Xi, Phi Kappa Sigma. Clubs: Montana; University, Alta (Salt Lake City); La Jolla Country, La Jolla Beach and Tennis (Cal.); Cosmos (Washington). Contbr. to profl. and govtl. jours. Home: 531 Monroe Av Helena MT 59601 also 8252 El Paseo Grande La Jolla CA 92037 Office: 100 Neill Av Helena MT 59601 also 2610 Torrey Pines Rd La Jolla CA 92037

HOLTFRETER, JOHANNES FRIEDRICH KARL, zoologist; b. Richtenberg, Germany, Jan. 9, 1901; s. Johannes K. and Sabine (Peters) H.; student U. Rostock, 1918-19, U. Leipzig, 1919-20 Ph.D., U. Freiburg, 1924. Came to U.S., 1946, naturalized, 1951. Asst., Kaiser Wilhelm Inst. Biology, Berlin-Dahlem, Germany, 1928-33; asst. prof. Zool. Inst. U. Munich, 1933-38; research staff Zool. Inst. U. Cambridge (Eng.), 1939-40, zool. dept. McGill U., Montreal, Can., 1942-46; prof. dept. biology U. Rochester (N.Y.), 1946-66, Tracy H. Harris prof. zoology, 1966-69, prof. emeritus, 1969—. Fellow A.A.A.S., Am. Acad. Arts and Scis.; mem. Deutsche Akad. Leopoldina, Nat. Acad. Scis., Zool. Soc. India (hon.), Asociacion Venezolanaa para la avance de la Ciencia, Soc. for Study Development and Growth, Inst. Internat. d'Embryology, Am. Genetic Assn., Am. Assn. Anatomists, Am. Soc. Zoologists, Royal Acad. Scis. (Uppsala). Home: 29 Knolltop Dr Rochester NY 14610

HOLT-HARRIS, JOHN EVAN, Jr., lawyer, judge; b. Stapleton, S.I., N.Y., Feb. 10, 1917; s. John Evan and Edith (Screen) H.-H.; A.B., Cornell U., 1937, LL.B., 1939; m. Susan Elizabeth Schenck, Aug. 10, 1941; children—John Evan III, Susan Elizabeth. Admitted to N.Y. bar, 1939, since practiced in Albany; mem. firm Brown & Gallagher, 1939-42, DeGraff & Foy, 1946-52, DeGraff, Foy, Conway & Holt-Harris, 1952—; lectr. Albany Law Sch.; judge Recorders Ct., Albany, 1952—. Mem. Nat. Conf. Bar Exmaniners, N.Y. State Bd. Law Examiners. Mem. Bd. Edn., Albany, 1952—. Bd. dirs. Mid Hudson Library Assn., Albany Pub. Library, YMCA; bd. govs. Albany Med. Center Hosp.; trustee Albany Acad.; v.p. bd. govs. St. Agnes Sch. Served from ensign to lt. comdr., USNR, 1942-46. Recipient Page One award Newspaper Guild, 1959, Wisdom Hall of Fame award, 1970. Mem. Albany County (past pres.), Am., N.Y. State bar assns., Fedn. Bar Third Jud. Dist. (past pres.), Am. Judicature Soc., Nat. Conf. State Trial Judges, Internat. Platform Assn. Clubs: Bourbonnais- Kiamika Hunting and Fishing (Que., Can.); Ft. Orange; Albany Country; Lake George. Home: Waverly Pl Albany NY 12203 Office: 90 State St Albany NY 12207

HOLTHUSEN, HANS E., educator; b. Rendsburg, Germany, Apr. 15, 1913; s. Johannes and Alma (Hagelstein) H.; Ph.D., U. Munich (Germany), 1937; m. Inge Havemeier, Oct. 28, 1952; chilren—Henriette, Stefan. Pvt. tchr., lectr., Munich, 1937-39; free lance writer, poet, novelist, essayist, 1945—; dir. Goethe House, N.Y.C., 1961-64; prof. German Northwestern U., 1968—. Served with German Army, 1939-45. Mem. Berlin Acad. Arts, Bavarian Acd. Fine Arts (pres. 1968). Author: Hier in der Zeit, 1949; Der Unbehauste Mensch, 1951; Das Schone Und das Wahre, 1958; Kritisches Verstehen, 1961; Indiana Campus, 1969; Edward Mörke, 1971. Home: 1725 Orrington Av Evanston IL 60201

HOLTHUSEN, HENRY FRANK, lawyer; b. N.Y.C., Aug. 3, 1894; s. Henry and Barbara (Schindler) H.; A.B., Columbia, 1915, LL.B., 1917; m. Lenore Adeline Sutter, Oct. 10, 1953. Asso. Cadwalader, Wickersham & Taft, 1917; practiced law, N.Y.C., and Norfolk, Va., 1920- 24; spl. asst. U.S. atty. gen., Washington, 1924-26; partner House, Holthusen & McCloskey, N.Y.C., 1927-34; apptd. E.E. and M.P. to Czechoslovakia, 1931; partner House, Holthusen & Pinkham, N.Y.C., 1934-37, Holthusen & Pinkham, 1937-51; staff Bur. Municipal Research Condr. negotiations with Mexican Govt. for Econ. Survey of Mexico joint U.S.-Mexican Econ. Commn., 1944; cons. fgn. relations sub-com. U.S. Senate, 1947; chief Telecommunications Mission to Japan, Turkey, other countries, 1951- 52; counsel, cons. fgn. relations subcom. on overseas information progrmas, 1953; chief Communications Mission for Egypt, 1953; gen. counsel com. on banking and currency U.S. Senate Study Internat. Bank & Export-Import Bank U.S., 1954; cons. fgn. relations com. Tech. Cooperation Program, 1955; cons. spl. com. U.S. Senate to study fgn. aid program, 1956; cons. fgn. relations com. U.S. Senate, Latin Am. study, 1958; Am. specialist U.S. State Dept., 1959; cons. fgn. relations com. U.S. Senate, 1962, 63; pub. mem. insp. U.S. Fgn. Service, 1968; insp. Fgn. Service (France), 1969, West Africa, 1970. Del., Jud. Conv., N.Y. State, 1926. Counsel, Protestant Unity League, 1932-34. Served as maj. U.S. Army, World War I. Mem. Phi Kappa Psi. Republican. P.E. Ch. (past vestryman) Author: James W. Wadsworth, Jr., 1926; Turning the Hour Glass, 1928. Home: 128 Central Park S New York City NY 10019

HOLTHUSEN, H. H., savs. and loan assn. exec. Pres., mgr. Southland Savs. and Loan Assn. Office: 8347 La Mesa Blvd La Mesa CA 92041*

HOLTMAN, DARLINGTON FRANK, educator, bacteriologist; b. Randolph, Kan., Oct. 12, 1903; s. Frank Oscar and Adelia (Hall) H.; A.B., U. Kan., 1927; M.A, U. Tenn., 1930; Ph.D., Ohio State U., 1937; m. Harriet Hithcock, Sept. 4, 1937: children—Virginia Ann, Mary Jean. Instr. bacteriology U. Tenn., 1927-32, prof. bacteriology, head dept., 1943-69, research prof., 1969—; asst., then instr. bacteriology Ohio State U., 1932-42; asst. prof. bacteriology and hygiene Western Res. U. Sch. Medicine, 1942-43; chief microbiology br. Chem. Corps Biol. Labs., Ft. Detrick, Md., 1949-50; cons. TVA, 1944-47, Oak Ridge Nat. Labs., 1952- 57, tng. grants com. NIH 1959-60; spl. research host-parasite relationships, factors influencing susceptibility to poliomyelitis; co- discoverer antifungal antibiotic, Tennecetin. Dir. Tenn. Biol. Warfare Def., 1950—. Lt. col. USAFR, 1950-58. Diplomate Am. Bd. Med. Microbiology. Fellow Am. Acad. Microbiology, A.A.A.S.; mem. Am. Soc. Microbiology (councilor 1952-56, pres. Ky.-Tenn. br. 1947-48), Soc. Exptl. Biology and Medicine, Radiation Soc. Am., Knoxville Sci. Club (pres. 1948-49), Execs. Club, Sigma Xi (pres. Tenn. 1960-61). Club: Deane Hill Country (Knoxville). Home: 309 West End Lane Knoxville TN 37919

HOLTON, A. LINWOOD, gov. Va.; b. Big Stone Gap, Va., Sept. 21, 1923; s. Abner Linwood and Edith (Van Gorder) H.; B.A., Washington and Lee U., 1944; LL.B., Harvard, 1949; m. Virginia Harrison Rogers, Jan. 10, 1953; children—Virginia Tayloe, Anne Bright, A. Linwood III, Dwight Carter. Founding partner firm Eggleston, Holton, Butler and Glenn, Roanoke, Va. Gov. Va., 1970—. Past chmn. Roanoke City Republican Com.; vice chmn. Va. Rep. Central Com., 1960—; mem. exec. com. Nat. Gov's Conf.; del. Rep. Nat. Conv., 1960, 68; Rep. candidate for Va. Ho. of Dels., 1955, 57; Va. campaign mgr. for H. Clyde Pearson, candidate for gov., 1961; Rep. candidate for gov., 1965; one of six original members Nat. Nixon for Pres. Com., 1967; regional coordinator Nixon for Pres. Com. Bd. dirs. Roanoke Fine Arts Center. Served with USNR, World War II. Mem. Am., Va. (past v.p.), Roanoke (past bd. dirs.) bar assns., Va. State Bar, Washington and Lee Alumni Assn. (pres. Roanoke chpt. 1964), Backbone Club of Roanoke C. of C., Omicron Delta Kappa. Presbyn. (elder. Sunday sch. tchr.). Home: 3125 Avenham Av SW Roanoke VA 24014 Office: Governor's Office State Capitol VA 23219

HOLTON, GERALD, physicist, educator; b. Berlin, Germany, May 23, 1922; s. Emanuel John and Regina (Rossman) H.; nat. certificate elec. engring. Sch. Tech., Oxford, 1940; B.A., Wesleyan U., 1941, M.A., 1942, Harvard, 1946, Ph.D., 1948; D.Sc., Grinnell Coll., 1967; m. Nina Rossfort. Sept. 12, 1947; children—Thomas, Stephan. Research asst., then instr. Wesleyan U., 1940-42, Brown U., 1942-43; staff, officers radar course OSRD, Harvard, 1943-45, various faculty positions, 1945-59, prof. physics, 1959—, mem. history sci. dept., co-dir. Harvard Project Physics, Faculty Council, 1970. Mem. Inst. for Advanced Study, Princeton, 1964; mem. com. on scholarly communications with People's Republic of China, Nat. Acad. Scis.; exchange prof. Harvard-Leningrad U., 1962. NSF faculty fellow, 1959-60. Trustee Boston Mus. Sci., Van Leer Found. Recipient Distinguished Service citation Am. Assn. Physics Tchrs., 1962; Robert A. Millikan medal, 1967. Fellow A.A.A.S. (dir. 1965-71, George Sarton meml. lectr. 1962), Am. Acad. Arts and Sci. (editor 1957-62, mem. exec. bd. 1970—), Am. Phys. Soc. (chmn. N.E. sect. 1962-63), Académie Internationale d'Histoire des Scis.; mem. Am. Inst. Physics (governing bd. 1968—), Acoustical Soc. Am., Am. Assn. Physics Tchrs. (commn. coll. physics 1960-64), History Sci. Soc. (council 1959-63, 63-65), Fedn. Am. Scientists, Philosophy of Sci. Assn., Phi Beta Kappa, Sigma Xi. Author: Introduction to Concepts and Theories in Physical Sci., 1952; (with D.H.D. Roller) Foundations of Modern Physical Science, 1958; Science and the Modern Mind, 1958; Science and Culture, 1965; (with others) The Project Physics Course, 1970; The 20th Century Sciences: Studies in Intellectural Biography, 1971. Editor-in-chief Daedalus, 1958-61; gen. editor Classics of Sci. series, 1960—. Contbr. papers profl. jours. Home: 14 Trotting Horse Dr Lexington MA 02173 Office: Jefferson Phys Lab Harvard U Cambridge MA 02138

HOLTON, IRA JAMES, meat co. exec.; b. Cedar Rapids, Ia., Aug. 16, 1919; s. Ed Bacon and Mabel (Donnan) H.; B.A. in Econs., U. Ia., 1941, J.D., 1947; m. Adelaide Elizabeth Roeder, June 23, 1941; children—Janet, Brooks, Ann. Admitted to Ia. bar, 1947, Minn. bar, 1947; with Geo. A. Hormel & Co., Austin, Minn., 1947—, sec., 1956—, exec. v.p., 1968—, dir., 1961—; pres. Hormel Co., 1969—; dir. First Nat. Bank of Austin (Minn.). Pres. Austin Community Scholarship Com., 1963—. Bd. dirs. Austin YMCA, 1964—, Hormel Found., U. Ia. Found. Served to maj., inf., AUS, 1941-45. Decorated Croix de Guerre (France). Mem. Phi Beta Kappa. Republican. Unitarian. Home: 403 21st St SW Austin MN 55912 Office: Box 800 Austin MN 55912

HOLTON, JOHN PRESLEY, paper co. exec.; b. Hartford City, Ind., June 6, 1914; s. John P. and Martha (Decker) H.; A.B., De Pauw U., 1936; m. Lois Lamont, May 14, 1938; children—John Presley,

William Lamont, James Decker. With Anderson Box Co., div. Inland Container Corp., 1936—, pres., 1956—, v.p. parent corp., 1963-65, group v.p., 1965—, also dir. Mem. bd. dirs., exec. and allied industry coms. Poultry and Egg Nat. Bd.; mem. allied industry com. Nat. Turkey Fedn. Mem. Inland Container Corp. Found.; trustee De Pauw U. Mem. Beta Theta Pi (pres. De Pauw chpt. 1935-36). Republican. Kiwanian. Clubs: Indpls. Athletic, Meridian Hills Country (bd. dirs.) (Indpls.). Home: 155 Forest Blvd Indianapolis IN 46240 Office: 7601 W Washington St Indianapolis IN 46241

HOLTON, JOSEPH WALTON, former steel co. exec.; b. Cin., June 21, 1905; s. Malcom Walton and Gertrude Annie (Woolery) H.; student U. Ky., 1925-28; m. Helen Elizabeth Fagaly, Jan. 5, 1929; children—Joseph Fagaly, Jerry Thomas. With Armco Steel Corp., Middletown, O., 1928-70, dir. finance, 1962-65, v.p. mng. dir. internat. div., 1965-70, ret. Mem. Nat. Indsl. Conf. Bd. Chmn. A.R.C. fund drive, 1945-46; chmn. YMCA fund drive, 1948-49; chmn. troop com., scoutmaster Pokey Griffith council Boy Scouts Am., 1935-45. Bd. dirs. Nat. Fgn. Trade Council, Far East-American Council. Mem. Internat. C. of C. (trustee bd. U.S. council 1965- -), Am. Iron and Steel Inst., U.S. C. of C., Phi Kappa Tau, Delta Sigma Pi. Episcopalian. Club: American (Paris). Home: 402 The Alameda Middletown OH 45042

HOLTON, PHILLIP FORBES, mill and container mfg. exec.; b. Pitts., May 10, 1909; s. John P. and Martha (Decker) H.; student DePauw U., 1927; B.S. in Indsl. Engring and Commerce cum laude, U. Ill., 1929; m. Ruth Clark, Sept. 23, 1930; 1 dau., Jane. With Inland Container Corp., Indpls., 1925—, successively planning mgr., supt., plant mgr., sales mgr., nat. accounts sales mgr., gen. plants prodn. mgr., 1925-49, v.p., 1949-63, dir., 1950—, sec., 1951-63, pres., 1963—; with Ga. Draft Co., 1947- -, v.p., 1959-65, pres., 1965-67, chmn. bd., 1967—. Chief technical sect. paperboard div. forest products bur. WPB, World War II. Bd. dirs. Inland Container Corp. Found., Herman Charles & Ellnora D. Krannert Found., Fourdrinier Draft Board Inst., Inst. Paper Chemistry. Mem. Nat., Ind. mfrs. assns., Nat. Paperboard Assn., Fibre Box Assn., Ind., Indpls. chambers commerce, Beta Theta Pi. Episcopalian. Clubs: Indianapolis Athletic, University, Meridian Hills Country (Indpls.); Coosa Country (Rome, Ga.); Mid-America, Chicago (Chgo.); Union League (N.Y.C.); Columbus (Ga.) Golf. Home: 5880 Sunset Lane Indianapolis IN 46208 Office: 120 E Market St Indianapolis IN 46204

HOLTON, RAYMOND WILLIAM, educator; b. Riverside, Cal., Apr. 30, 1929; s. Homer Hopkins and H. Charlotte (Hall) H.; B.A., Pomona Coll., 1951; M.S., U. Mich., 1954, Ph.D., 1958; m. Suzanne Lee Kork, June 15, 1952; children—Betsey Diane, Nancy Joann, William Louis, Thomas Raymond. Instr. botany U. Mich.-Flint Coll., 1957-59, asst. prof., 1959-61; research asso. U. Tex., 1961-62, USPHS trainee, 1962-63; asst. prof. botany U. Tenn., 1963-64, asso. prof., acting head botany, 1964-65, prof., head botany, 1965—. Mem. Botan. Soc. Am., Am. Soc. Plant Physiologists, Am. Chem. Soc., Phycol. Soc. Am., Am. Assn. U. Profs., A.A.A.S. Physiol. and biochem. research on plants, particularly blue-green algae. Home: 3000 Ticonderoga St Knoxville TN 37920

HOLTON, RICHARD HENRY, univ. dean; b. Columbus, O., Mar. 17, 1926; s. Caryl Ames and Celia (Cathcart) H.; B.S. in Bus. Adminstrn., Miami U., Oxford, O., 1947; M.A. in Econs., Ohio State U., 1948; Ph.D., Harvard, 1952; m. Constance Elizabeth Minzey, June 7, 1947; children—Melissa Louise, Jane Margaret, Timothy Hammond. Field research dir. Social Sci. Research Center, U. P.R., 1951-52; asst. prof. econs. Ohio State U., 1953, Harvard, 1953-57; asso. prof. bus. adminstrn. U. Cal. at Berkeley, 1957-61, prof., 1961—, dean Schs. Bus. Adminstrn., 1967—; dir. Inst. Bus. and Econ. Research, 1959-61, on leave, 1961-65. Fulbright research grantee U. Naples (Italy), 1961-62; spl. asst. for econ. affairs to sec. commerce, 1962-63; asst. sec. commerce for econ. affairs, 1963-65; chmn. Pres.'s Consumer Adv. Council, 1965-66. Mem. Am. Econ. Assn., Phi Beta Kappa, Omicron Delta Kappa, Beta Theta Pi. Democrat. Unitarian. Author: (with J.K. Galbraith) Marketing Efficiency in Puerto Rico, 1955; (with R.E. Caves) The Canadian Economy, 1959. Home: 436 Boynton Av Berkeley CA 94707

HOLTONER, JOSEPH STANLEY, electronic co. exec., former air force officer; b. N.Y.C., Aug. 4, 1911; s. Joseph and Madeline (Kompass) H.; B.S., N.Y.U., 1932; grad. Advanced Flying Sch., 1934, Command and Gen. Staff Sch., 1945; m. Mary Jane Thomas, Nov. 15, 1941 (dec. 1967); children—Joseph Stanley, Mary Jane. Commd. 2d lt. USAAF, 1932, advanced through grades to maj. gen. USAF, 1959; comdr. fighter aviation, Iceland, 1942-43, 85th, 54th fighter groups, 1944-45, 82d Fighter Group, Italy, 1945-46; assigned research and engring. Hdqrs. USAF, 1946-50; asst. dep. devel. Hdqrs. Air Research and Devel. Command, 1950-52; comdr. USAF Flight Test Center, Edwards, Cal., 1952-57; dep. comdr. 3d Air Force, U.K., 1957-58; comdr. 832d Air Div., 1958-59; mil adviser to dir. def. research and engring. Office Sec. Def., 1959-61; USAF mem. Joint Strategic Survey Council, 1961-63; commdt. Armed Forces Staff Coll., Norfolk, Va., 1963-65; vice comdr. CONAC, Robins AFB, Ga., 1965-67; pres. G.S.E. Corp., N.Y.C., 1970—. Decorated D.S.M., Legion Merit, D.F.C. with cluster, Commendation ribbon with cluster; Comte de la Vaux, Medaille d l'Aeronautique (France); recipient Thompson trophy, 1953 (world closed course jet aircraft speed record 690.118 miles per hour). Mem. Daedalians, Air Force Assn. Episcopalian. Club: Caterpillar (Lexington, Ky.). Contbr. article test flying Ency. Americana. Home: 280 River Rd Piscataway NJ 08854 Office: 425 E 63d St New York City NY 10021

HOLTUM, WILLIS MELVILLE, diversified bus. exec.; b. San Jose, Cal., Dec. 9, 1900; s. Gary Lorraine and Willie (Scott) H.; A.B., U. Cal. at Berkeley, 1924; grad. law U. Santa Clara (Cal.), 1926; m. Treva Foust, Feb. 25, 1938; 1 son, Gary Foust. With Cal. Pacific Title & Ins. Co., San Francisco, 1926-30; partner Holtum- Tissot Co., mortgage loan brokers, San Rafael, Cal., 1930-35; field supr. Fed. Home Loan Bank, 1935-39; mgr. mortgage loans Coldwell-Bankers Assos., Los Angeles, 1939-46; with Equitable Life Assurance Soc. U.S., 1946-66, regional v.p. 1961, v.p. charge city mortgage dept., 1962-64, v.p. mortgages, 1964-66; pres. Brooks, Harvey Co. of Cal., San Francisco, 1966—; dir. Continental Capital Corp., San Francisco, Crocker Land Co., Crocker Estate Co., Merced Water Co., Simon Stores, Inc., Parr Indsl. Corp., Universal Land Co., Eureka Fed. Savs. & Loan Assn. Mem. Am. Inst. Real Estate Appraisers (pres. No. Cal. 1952), No. Cal. Mortgage Bankers Assn. (pres. 1952), San Francisco C. of C. (pres. 1962), Navy League. Clubs: Bankers, Bohemian (San Francisco). Home: 199 Heather Dr Atherton CA 94025 Office: 44 Montgomery St San Francisco CA

HOLTZCLAW, BENJAMIN CLARK, former educator; b. Perry, Ga., July 28, 1894; s. Benjamin Clark and Cornelia Goode (Smith) H.; A.B., Mercer U., 1914, (Rhodes Scholar) Oxford U., Eng., 1917, A.M., 1920; Ph.D., Cornell U., 1923; m. Merle Marie Wood, Sept. 12, 1922; 1 dau., Alnita (Dyall). Faculty modern langs. Mercer U., Macon Ga., 1919-21, prof. philosophy, 1926-29, dean Grad. Sch., 1927-29, dean Coll., 1928-29; instr. Greek, Cornell U., 1921-23, asst. prof., 1923-25; asst. prof. philosophy N.Y. U., 1925-26; prof. philosophy U. Richmond (Va.), 1929-65, chmn. Faculty Personnel Com., 1932-42, dean Grad. Sch., 1939-65, dean, 1942-45. Served as 2d lt., 317th F.A., 81st Div., U.S. Army, 1917-19; A.E.F., 1918-19. Mem. Am. Philol. Assn., Am. Philos. Assn., So. Soc. for Philosophy and Psychology, Phi Beta Kappa, Phi Kappa Phi, Psi Upsilon, Omicron Delta Kappa, Kappa Alpha. Baptist. Contbr. articles to profl. jours. Home: 11 Ampthill Rd Richmond VA 23226

HOLTZER, ALFRED MELVIN, educator; b. Bklyn., Feb. 22, 1929; s. Abraham and Miriam (Brecher) H.; A.B., Wash. U., 1950; Ph.D., Harvard U., 1954; m. Joanne Rappaport, Feb. 6, 1954; (dec. Nov. 16, 1967); children—Esther Rachel, Dan Robert; m. 2d, Marilyn Frances Emerson, June 24, 1969. Instr. chemistry Yale, 1954-57; asst. prof. chemistry Washington U., St. Louis, 1957-59, asso. prof., 1959-65, prof., 1965—. Mem. Am. Chem. Soc., Am. Soc. Biol. Chemists. Home: 6636 Pershing Av St Louis MO 63130

HOLTZMAN, KEN, pitcher with Chicago Cubs Profl. Baseball Team. Address: care Wrigley Field Chicago IL 60613*

HOLTZMAN, RICHARD EDWARD, hotel exec.; b. Millersburg, Pa., Oct. 18, 1919; s. Lester Gilbert and Esther Zinn (Hess) H.; B.S. in Hotel Adminstrn., Cornell U., 1941; m. Janet Akin, Jan. 2, 1943; children—Sonda, Richard A., Cynthia. Dir. sales Pick Hotels Corp., Chgo., 1950-55; mgr. Greenbrier Hotel, White Sulphur Springs, W. Va., 1955-60; pres., gen. mgr. Sheraton Hawaii Corp., mgrs. Royal Hawaiian, Moana, Surfrider, Princess Kaiuloni and Maui hotels, 1960-66; pres. Rock-resorts, Inc., N.Y.C., 1966—; dir. hotel operation L.S. Rockefeller Resorts, 1966—. Vice pres. Hawaii Visitors Bur., 1961-66; mem. Hawaii Bd. Planning and Econ. Devel., 1964—. Bd. dirs. Hawaii Chpt. A.R.C., 1963-66. Served with USAAF, World War II. Decorated Air medal, D.F.C. Mem. Hawaii Hotel Assn. (past pres.), Cornell Soc. Hotelmen (pres. 1967), Honolulu C. of C. (dir.). Home: 128 Wellesley Dr New Canaan CT 06840 Office: 30 Rockefeller Plaza New York City NY 10019

HOLTZMAN, WAYNE HAROLD, educator, psychologist; b. Chgo., Jan. 16, 1923; s. Harold Hoover and Lillian (Manny) H.; B.S., Northwestern U., 1944, M.S., 1947; Ph.D., Stanford, 1950; m. Joan King, Aug. 23, 1947; children—Wayne Harold, James K., Scott E., Karl H. Asst. prof. psychology U. Tex., Austin, 1949-53, asso. prof., 1953-59, prof., 1959—, dean Coll. Edn., 1964-70, prof. psychology and edn., 1965—; asso. dir. Hogg Found. Mental Health, 1955-64, pres., 1970—. Dir. Social Sci. Research Council, 1957-63, Centro de Investigationes Sociales, Mexico, 1960—; cons. USAF, mem. sci. adv. bd., 1969-71; mem. com. on basic research com. NRC, 1968-71; mem. behavioral sci. study sect. USPHS, 1957-59, mental health study sect., 1960, chmn. personality and cognition research rev. com., 1968-72; research adv. panel Social Secutiry Adminstrn., 1961-62; mem. adv. com. computing activities, 1970—; mem. computer sci. and engring. bd. Nat. Acad. Scis., 1971—. Served from ensign to lt. (j.g.), USNR, 1944- 46. Faculty Research fellow Social Sci. Research Council 1953-54, Center Advanced Study Behavioral Scis., 1962-63. Fellow Am. Psychol. Assn.; mem. Tex. (pres. 1957), S.W. (pres. 1958) psychol. assns., Am. Statis. Assn., A.A.A.S., Interam. Soc. Psychology (pres. 1966-67), Am. Ednl. Research Assn., Am. Assn. U. Profs., Sigma Xi. Methodist (steward). Author: (with B. M. Moore) Tomorrow's Parents, 1964; Computer Assisted Instruction Testing and Guidance, 1971. Editor Jour. Ednl. Psychology, 1966—. Home: 3300 Foothill Dr Austin TX 78731

HOLTZMANN, HOWARD MARSHALL, lawyer; b. Bklyn., Dec. 10, 1921; s. Jacob L. and Lillian (Plotz) H.; A.B., Yale, 1942, LL:B., 1947; Litt.D. (hon.), St. Bonaventure U., 1952; m. Anne Fisher, Jan. 14, 1945; children—Susan, Betsey. Labor relations dept. Colo. Fuel & Iron Corp., 1947-49, now sec. gen. pension bd.; admitted to N.Y. bar, 1949; with firm Holtzmann, Wise & Shepard, N.Y.C., 1949—, partner, 1953—; vis. lectr. law and labor relations. Sec. ACF-Wrigley Stores, Inc., Case Mfg. Co.; dir. Ogden Corp., Luria Bros. & Co., Inc., Teleregister Corp., Syntex Corp., Am. Steriods, Inc. Bd. overseers Jewish Theol. Sem. Am., 195O—; mem. bd. Jewish Mus., N.Y.C., 1952—; bd. govs. Bklyn. Jewish Center, 1951—. Served with USAAF, 1942-46. Decorated Commendation medal. Mem. Am. Arbitration Assn. (dir. 1953—, exec. com. 1955—), Am. Bar Assn., N.Y. County Lawyers Assn. (chmn. com. fed. legislation 1957- -), Indsl. Relations Research Assn. Republican. Jewish religion. Clubs: Yale, Bankers (N.Y.C.). Home: 519 Alda Rd Mamaroneck NY 10543 Office: 30 Broad St New York City NY 10004

HOLWAY, DARWIN AUSTIN, banker; b. Deadwood, S.D., Apr. 9, 1912; s. Austin Parsons and Alma (Oberg) H.; B.S., Northwestern U., 1934; m. Irene Clark, Sept. 12, 1935; 1 dau., Barbara. Asst. cashier Continental Ill. Nat. Bank & Trust Co., Chgo., 1934-48: asst. v.p. Cal. Bank, Los Angeles, 1948-50, v.p., 1950- 59, sr. v.p., 1959; exec. v.p. First Western Bank & Trust Co., San Francisco, 1959-61, pres., dir. 1961-64; pres., dir. Santa Barbara Products Corp. (Cal.), 1964-67, Pacific Coast Pub. Co., 1966-67; v.p. Glore Forgan, Wm. R. Staats, Inc., 1968-69; investment banker, 1969—; sr. v.p. United Cal. Bank, Tokyo, Japan, 1972—. State park commr. Cal., 1964-68, chmn., 1967. Served from capt. to maj., M.A.C., AUS, 1942-45. Mem. Beta Alpha Psi. Republican. Episcopalian. Address: CPO Box 1833 Tokyo 100 Japan

HOLY, THOMAS CELESTINE, ednl. cons.; b. Vandalia, Ia., Oct. 21, 1887; s. John and Mary Theresa (Gulling) H.; A.B., Des Moines U., 1919; A.M., Ia. State U., 1922, Ph.D., 1924; m. Gladyce Grayce Webb, Aug. 14, 1913 (dec. Sept. 1958). Rural sch. tchr., Ia., 1909-10; supt. schs., Runnells, Ia., 1912- 15, Lynnville, Ia., 1915-17, 19-21; instr. Columbia Tchrs. Coll., 1924; dir. div. housing and equipment St. Louis pub. schs., 1925-27; head survey div. Bur. Ednl. Research, Ohio State U., 1927-42, dir. Bur. Ednl. Research, 1942-51; spl. cons. in higher edn. U. Cal., 1952-61; chief cons. Bd. Higher Edn., N.Y.C., 1961-62; spl. cons. Coordinating Council for Higher Edn. in Cal., 1962-64, Ore. Dept. Edn., 1965-66, Ia. Bd. Regents, 1966-69. Chmn. Ohio commn. to erect state schs. for blind and deaf, 1944-51; cons. states bldg. programs. Served with U.S. Army, World War I. Mem. N.E.A., Am. Assn. Sch. Adminstrs., Am. Ednl. Research Assn. (pres. 1934), Ohio Edn. Assn., Nat. Council Schoolhouse Constrn. (pres. 1937), Phi Delta Kappa, Kappa Phi Kappa. Democrat. Methodist. Mason (32, Shriner). Club: Faculty (U. Cal.). Author, contbr. reports on surveys of schs., equipment, salaries, health and other related topics of ednl. systems throughout U.S., 1929—; latest reports include: The Need for Additional Centers of Public Education in California (with others), 1957; Faculty Demand and Supply in California 1957-1970 (with others), 1958; (with others) A Master Plan for Higher Education in California 1960-75; A Long-Range Plan for The City University of New York, 1961-1975 (with others) Education in the States, Nationwide Development Since 1900, 1969. Contbr. ednl. publs. Address: 407 North St E Prairie City IA 50228 ☆

HOLYOAKE, KEITH JACKA, prime minister New Zealand; b. Pahiatua, New Zealand, Feb. 11, 1904; s. H.V. and Esther (Eves) H.; ed. Hastings, Omokoroa and Brooklyn (Motueka) schs.; m. Norma Ingram, Jan. 11, 1935; children—Roger, Peter, Diane, Lynley, Keitha. Engaged in dairy farming, fruit, hops and tobacco growing, Riwaka, Motueka Dist., 1917-41, hillcountry sheep farming, Waitahora, Dannevirke Dist., 1941—. Mem. New Zealand Parliament for Motueka electorate, 1932-38, Pahiatua electorate, 1943—; dep. leader Nat. Party (opposition), 1947; minister of agr. and dep. prime minister, 1949-57; prime minister, 1957; leader of opposition, 1957-60; prime minister and minister fgn. affairs, 1960—; privy councillor, 1954; Companion of Honor, 1963, Companion Order St. Michael and St. George, 1970. Rep. of the New Zealand farmers at 1st World Conf. Farmers, London, Eng., 1946; pres. FAO Conf., Rome, Italy 1955. Mem. Farmers Fedn. (past dominion v.p.). Motueka Fruit Growers Assn. (past exec. mem.), New Zealand Tobacco Growers Fedn., New Zealand Hop Marketing Com., Motueka Progress League, Nelson Progress League. Clubs: Ruahnine (Dannevirke); Pahiatua; Wellington, National (Wellington). Home: 41 Pipitea St Wellington New Zealand Office: Parliament House Wellington New Zealand

HOLYOKE, THOMAS CAMPBELL, educator; b. Milw., June 9, 1922; s. Sydney Archibald and Mary (Gibbs) H.; B.S. in Mech. Engring. magna cum laude, Harvard, 1943; Ph.D. in Math., Ohio State U., 1950; postgrad. in physics, U. Cal. at Berkeley, 1957-58; m. Leona Evadene Garber, Sept. 7, 1947; children—Linda (Mrs. John Odell), Kitty, Andrew Carter. Engr. Curtiss-Wright Co., 1943-44; instr. Ohio State U., Columbus, 1949-50; asst. prof. Northwestern U., 1950-55; asst. prof. Miami U., Oxford, O., 1955-58; prof. Antioch Coll., Yellow Springs, O., 1958—, dir. Sci. Inst., 1969—; vis. mathematician Wright-Patterson AFB, Ohio, 1956; mem. faculty, adminstrn. various NSF Insts., 1957-62; Fulbright-Hayes lectr. Mindanao State U., Philippines, 1964-65, Ford Found. cons., project leader, 1967-69. Chmn. Yellow Springs Community Council, 1963. Bd. dirs. Am. Civil Liberties Union Yellow Springs, 1963, 71-72, Ohio, 1963, 71-72, Yellow Springs Credit Union, 1963. Served with USNR, 1944-46. Northwestern faculty fellow, 1952, NSF sci. faculty fellow, 1957-58. Fellow Ohio Acad. Sci. (v.p. 1963); mem. Am. Assn. U. Profs. (chmn. Chgo. area council 1963), Am. Math. Soc., Math. Assn. Am., Nat. Council Tchrs. Math., Sigma Xi, Phi Beta Kappa, Pi Mu Epsilon. Author: (with others) Foundations of College Mathematics, 1971. Editor (with others) Foundations of Mathematics, 1969. Home: 608 S High St Yellow Springs OH 45387

HOLZ, LEFFERT, lawyer; b. Austria, Aug. 28, 1896; s. Jacob L. and Rose (Manne) H.; student N.Y.U. Law Sch.; m. Alice Englander, Nov. 8. 1921; 1 dau., Ruth (Mrs. Raphal Dubrowin). Admitted to N.Y. bar, 1921; asst. corp. counsel, N.Y.C., 1923-25; supt. ins. State N.Y., 1955-58; now counsel law firm Carb, Luria, Glassner & Cook, N.Y.C.; lectr. Practicing Law Inst. Pres. chmn. bd. Mortgage Facilities Corp., 1956-66. Chmn. Local Bd., N.Y. Selective Service; chmn. com. state and regional orgn. Bur. War Records, Nat. Jewish Welfare Bd., World War II. Served with U.S. Army, World War I. Mem. Real Estate Bd. N.Y. (past v.p., gov.), Assn. Bar City N.Y., N.Y. County Lawyers Assn., Am., N.Y. bar assns., Am. Legion, N.Y.U. Law Alumni Assn., Pi Lambda Phi. Mason; mem. B'nai B'rith. Club: Players (N.Y.C.). Home: 2600 N Flagler Dr West Palm Beach FL 33407 Office: 529 Fifth Av New York City NY 10017

HOLZAPEL, F., chem. co. exec. Sec. Am. Hoechst Corp. Office: Am Hoechst Corp PO Box 2500 Somerville NJ 08876*

HOLZAPPLE, JOSEPH RANDALL, ret. air force officer; b. Peoria, Ill., Sept. 7, 1914; s. Nathaniel A. and Annetta (Ritchie) H.; B.S., Bradley U., 1938, LL.D., 1958; grad. Armed Forces Staff Coll., 1950, Nat. War Coll., 1955; m. Lois M. Miller, Mar. 1, 1945; children—Lynn, Nancy. Commd. 2d lt. USAAF, 1941, advanced through grades to gen. USAF, 1969; pilot 38th Bomb Group, 1941-42; group operations officer 319th Bomb Group, 1942-43, comdr., 1943-45; staff Hdqrs. USAF requirements div., 1946-49; chief devel. div. Armed Forces Spl. Weapons Project, 1950-51; staff Hdqrs. Air Research and Devel. Command, 1951-54; comdr. 47th Bomb Wing, Eng., 1955-56; dep. chief staff operations, chief staff Hdqrs. USAF Europe, comdr. AIRSPECCOME, 1956-58; dep. dir. operational forces, Hdqrs. USAF, 1958- 59; asst. dep. comdr. systems Air Research and Devel. Command, Wright Field, O., 1959; dir. systems mgmt. ARDC, 1960; Wright Air Devel. Div., Wright-Patterson AFB, O., 1960-61; asst. dep. chief staff Systems and Logistics Hdqrs. USAF, 1961-64, dir. weapons systems evaluation group Office of Sec. of Def., 1964-66, dep. chief staff, research and devel. Hdgrs. USAF, 1966-69; comdr. in chief USAF, Europe, 1969-71; sr. Air Force mem. mil. staff com. UN, 1968-69. Decorated Legion of Merit, D.F.C. with cluster, Silver Star, Air medal with clusters, Distinguished Unit Citation with cluster; D.F.C. (Britain); Croix de Guerre with palm, Croix de Guerre with Etoile d'argent (France): D.S.M with two oak leaf clusters, grande ufficiale Order of Merit (Italy), Grosse Verdienstkreuz with stern and schutterband (Germany). Home: 2712 S Ives St Arlington VA 22202

HOLZBERG, JULES DONALD, educator; b. N.Y.C., Mar. 5, 1915; s. Samuel and Mary (Lurie) H.; B.S., Coll. City N.Y., 1937, M.S., 1938; Ph.D., N.Y. U., 1949; m. Betty Abrams, Jan. 25, 1942; children—Carol Ruth, Mark Allen, Robert Lincoln. Dir. psychol. labs. Conn. Valley Hosp., 1946-64; dir. research, 1964-68; asst. clin. prof., then asso. clin. prof. psychiatry (psychology) Yale, 1948-68; asst. prof., then asso. prof. psychology U. Conn., 1949-68; cons. Wesleyan U., Middletown, Conn., 1949-53, lectr., 1953-63, prof. psychology, 1963—. Mem. psychol. com. Com. Internat. Exchange Persons, 1968—. Served with AUS, 1943-46. Fellow Am. Psychol. Assn., Am. Orthopsychiat. Assn. (v.p. 1954-55), Soc. Projective Techniques (pres. 1955-56); mem. Conn. Psychol. Assn. (pres. 1955-56), Sigma Xi. Editor Jour. Consulting and Clin. Psychology, 1965—. Contbr. profl. jours. Home: 55 Clover St Middletown CT 06457

HOLZER, HANS, author; b. Vienna, Austria, Jan. 26, 1920; s. Leo and Martha (Stransky) H.; student U. Vienna, also Columbia; m. Catherine de Buxhoeveden, Sept. 29, 1962; 1 dau., Nandine Joan de Buxhoeveden. Author and parapsychologist known as The Ghost Hunter: numerous appearances on radio and TV; documentary films and radio series on ESP, 1964-65; editor- in-chief EPS News Syndicate, N.Y.C., 1948-53, also columnist Psychic News; writer, producer off-Broadway muscial revues; composer, lyricist recorded songs. Grantee Parapsychology Found., 1960-61. Mem. Dramatists Guild, Autors Guild of Authors League Am., A.S.C.A.P. Club: Kit Kat (v.p.). Author: Ghost Hunter, 1962; Ghosts I've Met, 1965; Coins. Revues and stage prodns. include Hotel Excelsior, 1956; A La Carte, 1958; Adam and Evenings, 1963. Drama and music critic Sporting Rev., 1949-60; theatre columnist Dance, 1952-55. Contbr. magazines, anthologies. Address: 140 Riverside Dr New York City NY 10024*

HOLZER, JANE, art film dir. Address: 313 E 53d St New York City NY 10022*

HOLZER, PETER DAMIAN, coll. adminstr.; b. Holton, Ind., Apr. 22, 1922; s. Anthony Peter and Christina (McNew) H.; A.B., Our Lady of Angels Sem., Cleve., 1945; M.A., Fordham U., 1951, Ph.D., 1953. Asst. prof. Quincy (Ill.) Coll., 1953-59, asso. prof., 1959-64, prof., 1964—, head polit. sci. dept., 1953-63, v.p., acad. dean, 1963—, trustee, 1963—; ordained priest Roman Catholic Ch., 1948. Mem. Am. Polit. Sci. Assn., Am. Acad. Polit. and Social Scis. Am. Soc. Internat. Law, N-Central Assn. Acad. Deans, Delta Epsilon Sigma. Address: 1831 College Av Quincy IL 62301

HOLZER, ROBERT EDWARD, educator; b. Portland, Ore., Nov. 21, 1906; s. Charles Emil and Emma (Schlegel) H.; A.B., Reed Coll., 1926; M.A., U. Cal., 1928, Ph.D., 1930; m. Wilma Edith Botts, Aug. 6, 1931; children—Roberta, William, Thomas. Instr. physics U. Cal., 1930-31, 34-35; NRC fellow physics U. Chgo., 1931-33; asst. prof. Fenn. Coll., 1933-34; instr. physics U. N.M., 1935-37, asst. prof., 1937-39, asso. prof., 1939-43, prof., 1943-46; prof. physics, head dept. Pomona Coll., 1946-47; prof. geophysics U. Cal. at Los Angeles, 1947—, chmn. dept. planetary and space scis., 1966-68. Coordinator N.M. Council Nat. Def., 1941; asso. sci. dir. Office Naval Research, London, Eng., 1959-60; mem. sci. adv. bd. USAF, 1956-62. Fellow Am. Phys. Soc.; mem. A.A.A.S., Am. Meterol. Soc., Am. Geophys. Union, Am. Assn. U. Profs., Sigma Xi. Contbr. articles profl. jours. Home: 1514 Veteran Av Los Angeles CA 90024

HOLZMAN, ALAN STEWART, mfg. co. exec.; b. Los Angeles, July 9, 1932; s. Joseph J. and Virginia (Stewart) H.; A.B. in Econs., Stanford, 1954, M.B.A., 1958; m. Nancy Dunn, June 14, 1958; children—Gregory, Mark, Laura Virginia, Patrick, Peter. Sr. accountant Webb & Webb, C.P.A.'s, San Francisco, 1954-58; asst. to controller Nat. Cash Register Co., Dayton, 1958-60, dir. pricing, 1960-64, controller, 1964-68; v.p. finance MSL Industries, Inc., Los Angeles, 1969—. Pres. asso. bd. Dayton Art Inst., 1964-65 C.P.A., Cal. Mem. Am. Inst. C.P. A.'s, Cal. Soc. C.P.A.'s Financial Execs. Inst. Home: 2818 Victoria Pl Palos Verdes Estates CA 90274 Office: 8600 Melrose Av Los Angeles CA 90069

HOLZMAN, BENJAMIN GRAD, retired govt. ofcl.; b. Los Angeles, Jan. 25, 1910; s. Zeke and Esther (Holzman) H.; B.S., Cal. Inst. Tech., 1931, M.S., 1933; m. Katherine Margaret Holzman, June 12, 1941; 1 dau., Katherine Margaret. Meteorologist, Eastern Airlines, Inc., Washington, 1934; chief meterologist Am. Airlines, N.Y.C., 1935; research meteorologist Dept. Agr., Washington, 1936; teaching fellow Cal. Inst. Tech., 1937, 38; supervising meteorologist U.S. Weather Bur., Washington, 1939-42; commd. officer USAF, 1942, advanced through grades to brig. gen., 1958; staff weather officer, adviser, cons. atomic bomb tests, 1945, 51; dep., research and devel. hdqrs. Air Force Spl. Weapons Center 1952-55; dir. air weapons Hdqrs. Air Research and Devel. Command, Balt., 1955-57, dir. research, 1957- 59, comdr., 1960; comdr. Air Force Cambridge Research Labs., Bedford, Mass., 1960-64; spl. adviser Hdqrs. NASA, Washington, 1964-67; dep. dir. environmental data service Environmental Sci. Service Adminstrn., Dept. Commerce, Silver Springs, Md., 1967-71. Fellow Meteorol. Soc.; mem. Geophys. Union. Home: 11305 Maryvale Rd Upper Marlboro MD 20870

HOLZMAN, FRANKLYN DUNN, educator; b. Bklyn., Dec. 31, 1918; s. Abraham and Mollie (Mandel) H.; B.A., U. N.C., 1940; M.A., Harvard, 1948, Ph.D., 1952; m. Mathilda Sara Wiesman, Dec. 14, 1946; children—Thomas Ludwig, David Carl, Miriam Alexandra. Economist Dept. Treasury, 1947-48, cons., 1949-52; research fellow Russian Research Center, Harvard, 1949-52, research asso., 1961—; prof. econs. U. Wash., 1952-61; prof. econs. Tufts U., mem. faculty Fletcher Sch. Law and Diplomacy, 1961—; vis. prof. U. Cal. at Los Angeles, 1956, Stanford, 1957, Columbia, 1962, Mass. Inst. Tech., 1963. Cons. UN, 1963-64, U.S. Arms Control and Disarmament Agy., 1964-71. Served to staff sgt. USAAF, 1942-45. Mem. Am. Econ. Assn., Am. Assn. Advancement of Slavic Studies (exec. com., 1964-65), Am. Assn. Study of Soviet-Type Economies (exec. com., 1966-67), Econometric Soc. Author: Soviet Taxation: The Fiscal and Monetary Problems of a Planned Economy, 1955. Home: 33 Peacock Farm Rd Lexington MA 02173

HOLZMAN, JAC EASTON, record co. exec.; b. N.Y.C., Sept. 15, 1931; s. Jacob Easton and Minette (Sternberger) H.; student St. Johns Coll., 1948-50; m. Nina Merrick, Dec. 24, 1955; children—Adam Jonathan, Jaclyn Estelle. Founder, Elektra Records, 1950, Nonesuch Records, 1964, Checkmate Records, 1967; pres. Elektra Corp., N.Y.C., 1950—; pres. Paradox Music Group, Elektra Broadcasting Co.; chmn. Elektra Records (U.K.), Ltd. Mem. Record Industry Assn. Am. (dir.), Audio Engring. Soc. Home: 37 W 12th St New York City NY 10011 Office: 47 E 67th St New York City NY 10023

HOLZMAN, PHILIP SEIDMAN, psychologist, educator; b. N.Y.C., May 2, 1922; s. Barnet and Natalie (Seidman) H.; B.A., Coll. City N.Y., 1943; Ph.D., U. Kan., 1952; postgrad. Topeka Inst. for Psychoanalysis, 1949-54; m. Hannah Abarbanell, Sept. 18, 1946; children—Natalie Kay, Carl David, Paul Benjamin. Psychology intern Topeka VA Hosp., 1946-49; psychologist Topeka State Hosp., 1949-50, cons., 1956-58; psychologist Menninger Found., Topeka, 1949-68, dir. research tng., 1963-68; tng. and supervising psychoanalyst Topeka Inst. for Psychoanalysis, 1964-68; prof. psychiatry and psychology U. Chgo., 1968—; tng. and supervising psychoanalyst Chgo. Inst. for Psychoanalysis, 1968—. Mem. small grants com. Nat. Inst. Mental Health, 1960-64, clin. projects research rev.-com., 1964-68; clin. program projects research rev. com., 1970—; vis. prof. U. Minn., 1965, U. Kan., 1966; cons. Ill. State Psychiat. Inst. Mem. Topeka Mayor's Com. on Human Relations, 1963-68. Served with AUS, 1943-46 Diplomate Am. Bd. Examiners Profl. Psychology. Fellow Am. Psychol. Assn.; mem. A.A.A.S., Chgo. Psychoanalytic Assn., Am. Psychopath. Assn., Sigma Xi. Author: (with others) Cognitive Control, 1959; Psychoanalysis and Psychopathology, 1970. Bd. editors Psychol. Issues, 1968—, Contemporary Psychology, 1969—, Bull. of Menninger Clinic, 1961—. Home: 1228 E 57th St Chicago IL 60637 Office: 950 E 59th St Chicago IL 60637

HOLZMAN, ROBERT STUART, educator, tax cons.; b. Paterson, N.J., Nov. 18, 1907; s. Samuel and Lillian (Hamburger) H.; B.S., U. Pa., 1929; A.M. N.Y. U., 1947, Ph.D., 1953; m. Eleanore Grushlaw, May 27, 1938. Tax cons., lectr. finance N.Y. U. Grad. Sch. Bus. Adminstrn., 1946-53, prof. taxation, 1953- -, dir. univ. budget, 1958-63. Past pres. Fed. Tax Forum, Civil War Round Table N.Y.C. Mem. Am. Hist. Assn., Commerce and Industry Assn. N.Y. (tax com.), Financial Execs. Inst., Soc. Am. Historians, Estate Planners Council N.Y.C., Beta Alpha Psi, Beta Gamma Sigma. Clubs: Lawyers, New York University, New York Numismatic. Author: Corporate Reorganizations: Their Federal Tax Status, 1948; Guide to Pension and Profit-sharing Plans, 1953, rev., 1969; Stormy Ben Butler, 1954; General Baseball, Doubleday, 1955; The Romance of Fire Fighting, 1956; The Tax on Accumulated Earnings, 1956; Arm's Length Transactions, 1958; Sound Business Purpose, 1958; Federal Income Taxation, 1960; The Taxpayer's Problem of Proof, 1962; Tax Basis for Managerial Decisions, 1965; Tax-Free Reorganizations, 1967; Holzman on Estate Planning, 1967; Federal Taxation of Capital Assets, 1969; Tax Free Reorganizations After the Tax Reform Act of 1969, 1970. Editor: Tax Practitioners Library, 15 vols., 1956-62; co-editor: Big Business Methods for the Small Business, 1952. Editorial bd. Taxation for Accountants. Contbr. articles to profl. publs. Home: 1199 Park Av New York City NY 10028

HOLZNER, BURKART, educator; b. Tilsit, Germany, Apr. 28, 1931; s. Hans Otto and Brigitte (Prenzel) H.; student U. Munich, 1949-52, 53-54, U. Wis., 1952-53, postgrad., 1957-59; Diplom Psychologe, U. Bonn, 1957, Ph.D., 1958; m. Anne Sagel, Feb. 6, 1955; children—Steven, Daniel, Claire. Came to U.S., 1957, naturalized, 1965. Grad. asst., acting instr. U. Wis., 1958-60; asst. prof. U. Pitts., 1960-63, asso. prof., 1963-65, prof., chmn. sociology dept., 1966—, dir. bd. visitors field staff Learning Research and Devel. Center, 1964-66, also mem. policy planning com. U. Center for Internat. Studies. Asso. sociologist, asso. dir. Social Sci. Research Inst., U. Hawaii, 1965-66; vis. prof. sociology, dir. Social Research Centre, Chinese U., Hong Kong, 1969-70; field reader U.S. Office Edn. Bd. dirs. Pitts. Chamber Music Soc. Mem. Am., Ohio Valley, Pa., Hong Kong sociol. assns., Sozialwissenschaftlicher Studienkreis für Internationale Probleme. Author: Amerikanische und deutsche Psychologie, 1958; Völkerpsychologie, 1960; Reality Construction in Society, 1968. Home: 947 La Clair Av Pittsburgh PA 15218

HOMANS, GEORGE CASPAR, educator; b. Boston, Aug. 11, 1910; s. Robert and Abigail (Adams) H.; student St. Paul's Sch., Concord, N.H.; A.B., Harvard, 1932; M.A., Cambridge (Eng.) U., 1955; m. Nancy Parshall Cooper, June 27, 1941; children—Elizabeth C., Susan W., Peter B. Jr. fellow Harvard, 1934- 39, instr., 1939-41, asso. prof. sociology, 1946-53, prof., 1953—, Ford Found. vis. prof. Grad. Sch. Bus. Adminstrn., 1961; Simon vis. prof. U. Manchester (Eng), 1953; prof. social theory Cambridge U., 1955-56; fellow Center Advanced Studies Behavioral Scis., 1958-59; vis. prof. U. Kent (Eng.), 1967. Served from ensign to lt. comdr., USNR, 1941-45. Mem. Am. Acad. Arts and Scis., Mass. Hist. Soc., Mass. Soc. Cin., Colonial Soc. Mass., Am. Sociol. Assn. (pres. 1963-64), Am. Philos. Soc. Club: Tavern (Boston). Home: 11 Francis Av Cambridge MA 02138

HOMAYOUN, ASSAD, Iranian diplomat; b. Saveh, Iran, Oct. 9, 1932; s. Ali and Fatema (Shaker) H.; B.A., Tehran U., 1960; M. Philosophy Internat. Relations, Karachi U., 1967; m. Nahid Maleky, Apr. 16, 1968. 3d sec. Ministry Fgn. Affairs, Tehran, 1961; 3d, then 2d sec. Iranian embassy, Karachi and Rawalpindi, Pakistan, 1963-67; 1st sec. Ministry Fgn. Affairs, Tehran, 1967-68; 1st sec. Iranian embassy, Washington, 1968—, counselor polit. affairs, 1971—. Decorated Order Homayoun 4th class. Home: 4201 Cathedral Av NW Washington DC 20016 Office: 3005 Massachusetts Av NW Washington DC 20008

HOMBURGER, FREDDY, physician, scientist, artist; b. St. Gall, Switzerland, Feb. 8, 1916; s. Ludwig and Cécile (Gaille) H.; student U. Vienna (Austria), 1936-37; M.D., U. Geneva (Switzerland), 1941; m. Regina Thürlimann, Nov. 8, 1939. Came to U.S., 1941, naturalized 1952. Research fellow, intern pathology Yale Med. Sch. and New Haven Hosps., 1941-43; intern, research fellow in medicine Harvard Med. Sch., Thorndike Meml. Lab., also Boston City Hosp., 1943-45; fellow in medicine Meml. Hosp., N.Y.C., 1946-48; chief clin. investigation Sloan-Kettering Inst. Cancer Research, N.Y.C., 1945-48, instr. medicine Cornell U. Med. Coll., 1946-48, research prof. medicine, 1948-57; dir. cancer research and control unit Tufts U. Sch. Medicine, Boston, 1948-57; mem. courtesy staff Mt. Desert Island Hosp., Bar Harbor, Me., 1955- -, Eastern Meml. Hosp., Ellsworth, Me., 1957-60; sci. asso. Roscoe B. Jackson Meml. Lab., Bar Harbor, 1951-60. Mem. corp. Gesell Inst. Child Devel.; chmn. adv. com. Am. Students, U. Geneva; b. dir. cancer control unit, vice chmn. com. on planning and devel. Childrens Cancer Research Found., Boston, 1957; pres., dir. Bio-Research Inst., Inc.; pres., treas. Bio-Research Cons., Inc.; pres. Trenton Exptl. Lab. Animal Co., Bar Harbor; hon. consul of Switzerland in Boston; neutral member mixed med. commn. War Dept., 1944-46. Mem. overseers com. to visit Harvard, 1965-71; trustee Cambridge Soc. Early Music, 1970, Opera Compnay Boston, 1967-69; bd. dirs. Boston Playhouse, 1964-69; mem. adv. bd. Lachaise Found. Diplomate Nat. Bd. Med. Examiners. Fellow A.A.A.S., N.Y. Acad. Scis. (ednl. adv. com. 1967); mem. Am. Gerontol. Soc., Am. Geriatrics Soc., A.M.A., Endocrine Soc., Am. Assn. Cancer Research, Fedn. Clin. Research, N.Y. Acad. Medicine, Soc. Exptl. Biology and Medicine, Am. Writers Assn., Am. Soc. Exptl. Pathology, Soc. Toxicology, Teratology Soc., Am. Soc. Pharmacology and Exptl. Therapeutics, Soc. Study Reproduction, Cambridge C. of C. (dir.), Sigma Xi. Clubs: Harvard (Boston); Yale (N.Y.C.); Cosmos (Washington). Author: The Medical Care of the Aged and Chronically Ill, 1955, 2d edit., 1964; The Biological Basis of Cancer Management, 1957; also numerous sci. papers. Editor: The Physiopathology of Cancer, 3d edit., 1972; Progress in Experimental Tumor Research, vols. I-XVIII, 1960—; sr. editor Symposia on Research Advances Applied to Medical Practice. Exhibited paintings one-man shows N.Y.C., Paris, Zurich, Geneva, Boston, 1953-58. Home: 759 High St Dedham MA 02026 also Trenton ME Office: 9 Commercial Av Cambridge MA 02141

HOME, ALEXANDER FREDERICK DOUGLAS, Brit. govt. ofcl.; b. London, Eng., July 2, 1903; s. K. T., 13th Earl and Lady Lilian (Lambton) H.; grad. Eton Coll., Christ Ch., Oxford U.; m. Elizabeth H. Alington, Oct. 3, 1936; children—Caroline, Meriel, Diana, David. Mem. Parliament for South Lanark, 1931-45, Lanark div. of Lanarkshire, 1950-51; parliamentary pvt. sec. to Prime Minister, 1937- 40; joint parliamentary under-sec. Fgn. Office, 1945; minister of state, Scottish office, 1951-55; sec. of state for commonwealth relations, London, Eng., 1955-60, also lord pres. of council, leader House of Lords, 1957-60, sec. of state for fgn. affairs, 1960-63; prime minister of Gt. Britian, 1963-64; mem. Parliament, 1963—; leader of the opposition, 1964-65. Decorated Knight of Thistle. Clubs: Travellers; New (Edinburgh); Carlton. Home: The Hirsel Coldstream Berwickshire Scotland also Castlemains Douglas Lanarkshire England also Carleton Gardens London SW 1 England

HOMER, PORTER WYMAN, non-profit ednl. corp. exec.; b. Oxford, N.Y., Apr 7, 1923; s. Willis Heald and Grace Katherine (Wyman) H.; B.A., U. Conn., 1948; postgrad. Syracuse U., 1948- 49; m. Laura Magdalen McHale, Nov. 10, 1949; children—Katherine, Peter, Gregory, Andrew, Pierce. Dir. research, budget, Kansas City, Mo., 1949- 55; city mgr., Tucson, 1955-62; city mgr., Rochester N.Y., 1962-65; county mgr., Dade County, Miami, Fla., 1965-70; pres. Tech. Application Program, Inc., 1970—. Adv. com. urban devel. Dept. Health, Edn. and Welfare. Served with inf., AUS, 1943-46; ETO. Mem. Internat. City Mgrs. Assn. (v.p., chmn. goals com.), Am. Soc. Pub. Adminstrn., Nat. Assn. County Ofcls., Am. Soc. Planning Ofcls. (dir.), Municipal Finance Officers Assn., Nat. League Cities, L.P. Cookingham Alumni Assn. (past pres.). Home: 401 N Lee St Alexandria VA 22314 Office: 1140 Connecticut Av Washington DC 20036

HOMER, SIDNEY, investment banker; b. West Chester, Pa., Oct. 20, 1902; s. Sidney and Louise (Beatty) H.; A.B., Harvard, 1923; m. Marion Symmes, July 5, 1924; children—Louise (Mrs. John James Connolly), Marion (Mrs. William Hall Painter), Georgina Susan (Mrs. Nicholas Holt). With Equitable Trust Co., 1923-25; mgr. statis., sales and trading dept. Gilbert Eliott & Co., mems. N.Y. Stock Exchange, 1925-31; pres., dir. Homer & Co., Inc., instl. bond dealers, 1931-43; chief enforcement sect., blockade div. Fgn. Econ. Adminstrn., 1943-45; mgr. instl. dept. Scudder Stevens & Clark, investment counsel, N.Y.C., 1945-61; gen. partner Salomon Bros., N.Y.C., 1961—; past dir. Scudder Fund Can.; lectr. in field. Past bd. dirs. Union Settlement Assn. N.Y.; nat. chmn. League for Declared War, 1941. Mem. Council on Fgn. Relations, N.Y. Soc. Security Analysts, A.S.C.A.P. Clubs: Adirondack League; Marshall Chess; Nat. Arts. Author: A History of Interest Rates, 2000 B.S. to 1963; Bond Buyers Primer; The Price of Money; also articles. Home: 36 Gramercy Park New York City NY 10003 Office: 1 New York Plaza New York City NY 10005

HOMER, WILLIAM INNES, educator, author: b. Merion, Pa., Nov. 8, 1929; s. Austin and Evelyn (Innes) H.; A.B., Princeton, 1951; postgrad. N.Y.U., 1952-53; M.A., Harvard, 1954; Ph.D. (Sachs Traveling Research fellow 1957-58), 1961; m. Virginia D. Keller, Aug. 14, 1954; 1 son, Stacy Innes. Instr. dept. art and archeology Princeton, 1955-59, lectr., 1959-61, asst. prof., 1961-64; asso. prof. history of art Cornell U., 1964-66; prof., chmn. dept. art history U. Del. at Newark, 1966—, prof. Winterthur Program Early Am. Culture, 1966—. Mem. Del. Arts Council, 1969-70, New Castle County Beautification Bd., 1967—. Mem. adv. com. Am. Studies Inst., Lincoln U., 1967—; mem. corp. Mus. Art, Ogunquit, Me., 1958—. Fellow Royal Soc. Arts (London), Council of Humanities, Am. Council Learned Socs.; mem. Coll. Art Assn. Am., Soc. Archtl. Historians, Am. Studies Assn., Wilmington Soc. Fine Arts. Clubs: Princeton, Nat. Arts (N.Y.C.). Author: Seurat and the Science of Painting, 1964; Robert Henri and His Circle, 1969. Contbr. articles profl. jours. Home: 15 Dickinson Lane Wilmington DE 19807 Office: Dept Art History U Del Newark DE 19711

HOMEWOOD, HARRY, journalist. Editorial writer Chgo. Sun-Times. Office: 401 N Wabash Chicago IL 60611*

HOMEYER, FRED J., state justice; b. Eureka, S.D., Apr. 10, 1913; s. Fred W. and Sophia (Wruck) M.; student Eureka Jr. Coll., 1930-32; LL.B. cum laude, U. S.D., 1935; grad. Appellate Judges Seminar, N.Y.U., 1963; m. Zella Ann Myers, Sept. 16, 1939; children—Ann, Mary E. Admitted to S.D. bar, 1935; pvt. practice in Eureka, 1935-43, Selby, 1946-62; states atty. McPherson County, 1941-45; city atty. Eureka, 1936-43, Selby, 1946-55; asso. justice Supreme Ct. S.D., 1962—. Served with AUS, 1944-45. Mem. Am. Bar Assn., S.D. State Bar. Home: 1418 E Cabot St Pierre SD 57501 Office: Supreme Court State Capitol Pierre SD 57501

HOMOLKA, OSCAR, actor; b. Vienna, Austria, 1903; s. Heinrich and Anna (Handl) H.; student Royal Acad., Vienna; m. Grete Morsheim; m. 2d, Baroness Vally Hatvany (dec.); m. 3d, Florence Meyer; m. 4th, Joan Tetzel. Stage debut, Komoedienhaus, Vienna, 1918, later appeared at Graz, Munich, Berlin, Vienna; appeared leading roles in The Ringer, The Squeaker, Juarez and Maximilian; producer Pygmalion, Berlin, also Ten Minute Alibi in Vienna; 1st appearance in Great Britain, King's Theatre, 1935, later in Close Quarters, The Embassy, London, 1935; actor Grey Farm, Hudson Theatre, N.Y.C., 1940; other Plays include The Innocent Voyage, 1943, I Remember Mama, 1944, The Last Dance, 1948, Bravo, 1948, The Master Builder, 1955, Rashoman, 1959, Tempest, 1959, and numerous motion pictures including The Wonderful World of The Brothers Grimm, 1962. War and Peace, The Long Ships, Funeral in Berlin, The Assignment, The Executioner, 1969, Song of Norway, 1970. Recipient Look award as best supporting actor, 1956. Address: 72 Roebuck House London SW1E 5BD England

HOMPE, ROBERT WILBUR, former pharm. and chem. mfg., exec.; b. Auburn, N.Y., Sept. 10, 1898; s. Henry A. and Isabelle (Downing) H.; student Western Res. U., 1917-21; m. Beatrice Pfanner, Jan. 10, 1928; children—Patricia (Mrs. Jacob A. Gibson, Jr.), Robert Downing. With Strong Cobb & Co., Inc., Cleve., 1922- 38, v.p., 1933-38, dir., 1935-38; with Smith, Kline & French Labs., Phila., 1938-62, dir., 1944-63, v.p., 1945-62. Mem. planning commn. Radnor Twp., 1953-58. Bd. visitors, govs. Washington Coll., Chestertown, Md. Served with USMC, 1918. Mem. Delta Tau Delta. Presbyn. Clubs: Merion Cricket, Union League (Phila.); Union (Cleve.); Merion Country. Home: Church Rd Villanova PA 19085 Office: 1700 Market St PA 19103

HOMRIGHAUSEN, ELMER GEORGE, sem. dean, author; b. Wheatland, Ia., Apr. 11, 1900; s. Henry George (Keller) and Sophia Julia (Mordhorst Kuehl Ballien) H.; A.B., Lakeland Coll., 1921, D.D. (hon.); Th.B., Princeton Theol. Sem., 1924; Th.M., U. Dubuque, 1927, Th.D., 1930; A.M., Butler U., 1931; D.D., Union Theology Sem., Tokyo, 1958; student U. Chgo., Ia. U., U. Geneva, Rutgers U.; L.H.D., Bucknell U., 1963; m. Ruth Willa Strassburger, Sept. 17, 1923; children—Richard James, Ruth Karolyn (Mrs. Taylor), Elmer Paul, David Karl, Mary Elizabeth (Mrs. Candland), John Frederick. Pastor, 1st English Ref. Ch., Freeport, Ill., 1924-29, Carrollton Av. Evang. and Ref. Ch., Indpls., 1929-38; Thomas Synnott prof. Christian edn. Princeton Sem., 1938-54, Charles R. Erdman chair pastoral theology, 1954—, dean sem., 1955- 65; lectr. univs. and colls.; travel lectr., Asia, 1948, 55, 58, 64, 66, Africa, 1958, 66, 68, Latin Am., 1960, 65, 71; Del. Pan Presbyn. Conf., Belfast, Ireland, 1933, Universal Council, Denmark, 1934, World Council, Oxford and Edinburgh 1937, World Council Christian Edn., Mexico City, 1941, Tokyo, 1958, Belfast 1962, Lima, 1971; cons. World Council Chs. Assembly, Amsterdam, 1948; mem. N.Am. com. World Council Christian Edn.; mem. div. overseas ministries and ministry to nat. parks Nat. Council Churches; mem. Acad. Religion and Mental Health; vice moderator United Presbyn. Ch., 1951-52, 70-71. Mem. bd. edn. Princeton Boro, 22 yrs. Trustee Hood Coll., Fredericks, Md., mem. bd. founders Internat. Christian U., Tokyo; mem. Internat. com. Nat. YMCA. Named Hon. Citizen of Seoul, Korea. Mem. N.E.A., Religious Edn. Assn., Hugenot Soc., Phi Kappa Phi. Mason. Club: Nassau. Author books and articles including: Choose Ye This Day; I Believe in the Church; Christianity in America—A Crisis; Let the Church Be the Church; Current Theological Trends; Rethinking the Great Commission; Christian Education (in Indonesian). Co-translator: God in Action; Come Holy Spirit; God's Search for Man. Contbg. editor Theology Today, 1946—. Contbr. Ency. Americana, Twentieth Century Ency. Religious Knowledge, Interpreters Bible, Dictionary Christian Edn., Interseminary Series, Colliers Ency., Handbook World Christianity; also religious jours. Home: 150 Leabrook Lane Princeton NJ 08540 ☆

HOMSEY, SAMUEL, architect, artist; b. Boston, Aug. 29, 1904; s. Elias Samuel and Margaret (Sabbag) H.; B.S., M.S., Mass. Inst. Tech., 1926; m. Victorine duPont, Apr. 27, 1929; children—Coleman duPont, Eldon duPont. Practicing architect, 1926—, archtl. projects include U.S. embassy, Tehran, Iran. Bd. dirs. Wilmington Acad. Art, 1941-42. Served as comdr., Office Research and Inventions, USNR; lt. comdr. Bur. Aeros. Recipient prize for instl. bldgs., Pitts. Glass Inst., 1938; diploma of merit for design of Cambridge Yacht Club, Md. Soc. of Architects, 1940; 1st prize Del. Ann. 1st Oil Show, Wilmington Soc. Fine Arts; two 1st prizes Del. Ann. Water Color Show. Fellow A.I.A. (v.p.); mem. Am., Phila. watercolor socs., N.A.D. (asso.), Confrerie Des Chevaliers du Tastevin. Republican. Club: Century Assn. Contbr. articles to Archtl. Forum. Home: 1800 Wawaset St Wilmington DE 19806 Office: 2003 N Scott St Wilmington DE 19804

HOMSEY, VICTORINE (Mrs. Samuel E. Homsey), architect; b. Grosse Pointe Farms, Mich., Nov. 27, 1900; d. Antoin Bidermann and Ethel (Clark) duPont; A.B., Wellesley Coll., 1923; M.Arch., Cambridge (Mass.) Sch. Architecture, 1925; m. Samuel E. Homsey, Apr. 27, 1929; children—Coleman duPont, Eldon duPont. Practice as architect, 1926—; mem. archtl. firm Victorine and Samuel Homsey; major works include U.S. embassy, Tehran, Iran. Recipient 1st prize instl. architecture for Children's Beach House, Lewes, Del Pitts. Glass Inst.; regional, state awards for Cambridge Yacht Club, Md. Soc. of Architects; hon. mention award for design Stubbs Elementary School,

Wilmington, Del. Sch. Exec. Mag. Fellow Am. Inst. Architects; mem. Colonial Dames. Episcopalian. Club: Wilmington Garden (Del.). Contbr. to Archtl. Forum, Guide to Modern Architecture. Home: 1800 Wawaset St Wilmington DE 19806 Office: 2003 N Scott St Wilmington DE 19806

HONAMAN, EARL M., retired bishop; b. Lancaster, Pa., Apr. 13, 1904; s. Walter Hugh and Ada (Miller) H.; B.A., Franklin and Marshall Coll., 1925, D.D., 1959; D.D., Phila. Div. Sch., 1953; postgrad. U. Pa., 1926-28; m. Mary Priscilla Shenk, Sept. 1, 1928; children—William Frederick, Walter Hugh (dec.). Ordained to ministry Episcopal Ch., 1928; pastor various parishes Diocese Harrisburg (Pa.), 1928-56; consecrated bishop, 1956; suffragan bishop Diocese Harrisburg, 1956-69; ret., 1969. Pres. Anglican Soc., Episcopal Ch., 1962-64. Served to lt. col., inf., AUS, 1941-45, 50-51. Decorated Bronze Star Mem. Phi Beta Kappa, Sigma Pi. Home: 12 Westminster Briarcrest Gardens Hershey PA 17033

HONAMAN, RICHARD KARL, bus. cons.; b. Lancaster, Pa., Sept. 17, 1895; s. Walter H. and Ada. R. (Miller) H.; B.S., Franklin and Marshall Coll., 1916, M.S., 1917; m. Alice M. Garman, Dec. 1, 1917; children—Richard Karl, Ruth Dorothy (Mrs. John T. Burgess). Devel. studies aeros. program, 1917-19; asst. prof. elec. engring. George Washington U., 1918- 19; with Am. Tel. & Tel. Co., Bell Telephone Labs., N.Y.C., 1919-60, dir. sch. for war tng., 1942-45, dir. publ., 1945-60, ret., 1960; on leave for govt. service, 1954-55; bus. cons., 1960—; chmn. bd. Visual Internat., Inc., N.Y.C. Cons. to sec. commerce, dir. Office Strategic Information, 1954-55; dept. asst. sec. def. for pub. affairs, Washington, 1955; cons. U.S. Army Mgmt. Engring. Tng. Agy., Rock Island, Ill., Found. Econ. Edn. Clergy, Joint Commn. N.J. Legislature Water Mgmt. Policy, 1968-70. Mayor, Borough of Glen Ridge, N.J., 1948-52; mem. Glen Ridge Municipal Planning Bd.; mem. nat. council, nat. personnel com. Boy Scouts Am., 1942—. Bd. dirs. N.J. Council on Econ. Edn., Burgess Adv. Reports; trustee Mountainside (N.J.) Hosp., 1952-58, v.p., 1954. Recipient Alumni citation Franklin and Marshall Coll., 1956; Seton Hall U. Centennial medal, 1958. Registered profl. engr., N.Y. Fellow I.E.E.E., A.A.A.S.; mem. Am. Mgmt. Assn., N.Y. Elec. Soc. (pres. 1952-54), Soc. for Advancement Mgmt., Nat. Acad. Sci. (exec. com., nat. com. fedn. internationale de documentation 1961-65), Engrs. Joint Council (chmn. com. engring. information 1956-63), N.Y. Pub. Relations Soc. Republican. Episcopalian. Club: University (N.Y.C.). Address: 2 Cambridge Rd Glen Ridge NJ 07028

HONCHELL, FLOYD C., financial exec.; b. Denver, May 26, 1912; s. Montgomery and Catherine (Goins) H.; student Bennett Coll., London, Ky., 1928-30, also LaSalle Extension U.; m. Dorothy D. Perry, July 21, 1962; 1 dau. by previous marriage, Catherine Lou (Mrs. Charles C. Carpenter). With Pond Creek Pocahontas Co., 1930-39, Marianna Smokeless Coal Co., 1939-45; with Island Creek Coal Co., Huntington, W.Va., 1945-67, controller, 1955-61, v.p., finance, 1961-62, v.p. finance, treas., 1962-67; v.p. finance, treas. Island Creek Fuel & Trans. Co., 1962-67, Island Creek Coal Sales Co., 1962—; sec., treas. Beatrice Pocahontas Co., 1962-67; v.p., treas. Cleve. Builders Supply Co., Cleve., 1967—. Chmn. ration bd. Wyoming County, W.Va., World War II. Mem. N.A.M., Financial Execs. Inst., Nat. Assn. Accountants. Episcopalian. Mason. Club: Chardon Lalses Country. Home: 3015 E Belvoir Oval Shaker Heights OH 44122 Office: 2100 W 3d St Cleveland OH 44113

HONDA, SOICHIRO, mfg. co. exec.; b. Komyo, Japan, 1906; ed. tech. sch. Owner automobile repair co., Hammamatsu, Japan, 1927—; auto racer, until 1935; owner piston ring prodn. factory, 1939—; mfr. motorcycles, Hamamatsu, 1947- -; now pres. Honda Motor Co., Tokyo, Japan. Office: Honda Motor Co 5-5 Yaesu Chuo-ku Tokyo Japan*

HONDERICH, BELAND, publisher; b. 1918. With Toronto Daily Star, Ltd. (Ont., Can.), 1943—, editor in chief Daily Star and Star Weekly, 1955-66, pres., pub., 1967—. Address: 80 King St Toronto 1 Ontario Canada

HONEY, DAVID CHARLES, corp. dir.; b. Portland, Ore., June 3, 1925; s. John Kohnen and Margaret Fargo (Larrison) H.; B.S., Yale, 1945; M.B.A., Harvard, 1950; m. Joan Lansinger, Dec. 26, 1950; children—Tamisie, Stanley Kohnen. With McKinsey & Co., mgmt. cons., 1950-54; with Riverside Cement Co., div. Am. Cement Corp., 1954-62, exec. v.p., 1959-62, v.p. operation parent co., 1962-64; exec. v.p. Pacific Western Industries, Inc., 1966-68; dir. Enterprise Fund, Harbor Fund, Fletcher Fund, Fletcher Capital Fund, Pace Fund, Comstock Fund, SMC Investment Corp., Inc., Solid State Radiation, Inc., Sterigard Corp., Railtec Corp., Lewis Brothers Battery Co., Inc., Morgan Industries, Inc., Buttes Gas & Oil Co., On Line Computer Systems, Inc. Vice chmn. United Republican Party finance com. Los Angeles County, 1963. Bd. dirs., pres. Mental Health Assn. Los Angeles County; bd. dirs. Cal. Assn. Mental Health, Nat. Assn. Mental Health. Mem. Tau Beta Pi. Club: Los Angeles Yacht (dir.). Home: 1906 E California St San Marino CA 91108 Office: 606 S Olive Los Angeles CA 90014

HONEY, JAMES KUHN, assn. exec., lawyer; b. Edmore, N.D., July 31, 1907; s. Charles C. and Rose (Kuhn) H.; B.A., U. Minn., 1926, LL.B., 1928; m. Phyllis Fleuchaus, Oct. 26, 1957; 1 son, John A. Admitted to Minn. bar, 1928, N.Y. bar, 1953; atty. Travelers Ins. Co., N.W. Nat. Life Ins. Co., Fidelity Mut. Life Ins. Co., Provident Life and Accident Ins. Co., Life Ins. Asso. Am., also ins. dept. Standard Oil Co., (N.J.); dep. supt. N.Y. State Ins. Dept., 1964-69; counsel Health Ins. Assn. Am., 1970—. Mem. Am. (chmn. social security com., health ins. law com., nonoccupational disability com.; mem. council ins. sect., chmn. ins. sect.), N.Y. bar assns., Am. Arbitration Assn. (nat panel arbitrators), Am. Judicature Soc. Home: 281 Av C New York City NY 10009 Office: Health Ins Assn Am 750 3d Av New York City NY 10017

HONEYCUTT, JOHN THOMAS, ret. army officer; b. Rochester, N.Y., Oct. 11, 1911; s. Francis Webster and Margaret (Harmon) H.; B.S., U.S. Mil. Acad., 1933; m. Ann Parker, May 19, 1945; children—John Parker, Mary Middleton. Commd. 2d lt. U.S. Army, 1933, advanced through grades to maj. gen., 1961; asst. G-3 II Corps, MTO, 1942-44; with operations div. War Dept. G.S., 1944-46; Korean Mil. Assistance Group, Korea, 1957-58; comdg. gen. 47th Arty. Brigade, Ft. MacArthur, Cal., 1958-61; comdg. gen. 5th Region, Army Air Def. Command, Ft. Sheridan, Ill., 1961-63; dir. program div. SHAPE, Paris, 1963-66; comdr. Field Command Def. Atomic Support Agy., Sandia Base, N.M., 1966—. Decorated Legion of Merit with oak leaf cluster, Bronze Star medal. Home: 2100 E Sandia Dr Sandia Base NM 87115

HONG, CHOI SIEW, banker. Dep. gov. Bank Negara Malaysia, Kuala Lumpur. Office: 4 Leboh Pasar Besar Kuala Lumpur Malaysia*

HONG, HOWARD VINCENT, educator; b. Wolford, N.D., Oct. 19, 1912; s. Peter B. and Ada (Cooper) H.; B.A., St. Olaf Coll., Northfield, Minn., 1934; postgrad. Wash. State U., 1934-35, U. Copenhagen (Denmark), 1938-39; Ph.D., U. Minn., 1938; m. Edna Hatlestad, June 8, 1938; children—Irena (Mrs. Roy Elveton), Erik, Peder, Rolf, Mary (Mrs. Thomas Loe), Judith (Mrs. Patrick O'Sullivan), Theodore, Nathaniel. Mem. faculty St. Olaf Coll., 1938—, prof. philosophy, 1950—, sec. faculty Christian fellowship, 1953-56; vis. lectr. U. Minn., 1954. Field sec. war prisoners aid World's YMCAs, U.S. and Europe, 1943-46; sr. rep. service to refugees Luth. World Fedn., Europe, 1947-49; sr. field officer refugee div. World Council Chs., Germany, 1947-48. Bd. dirs. Minn. Luth. Welfare Bd., 1954-58. Recipient J.A.O. Preus award, 1951, Nat. Book award, 1967; grantee Am. Scandinavian Found., Am. Council Learned Socs., Rockefeller Found., Hill Family Found., Fulbright Com., Nat. Humanities Found. Mem. Am., Minn. (v.p. 1958) philos. assns., P.E.N., Kierkegaard Selskabet. Lutheran. Author: This World and the Church, 1955. Editor, contbr.: Integration and the Christian Liberal Arts College, 1956; Christian Faith and the Liberal Arts, 1960. Translator, editor: (with Edna H. Hong) S. Kierkegaard, For Self-Examination, 1940, Works of Love, 1962, Journals and Papers, I, 1967, II, 1970, Armed Neutrality and An Open Letter, 1968, G. Malantschuk, Kierkegaard's Thought, 1971. Home: RFD 1 Northfield MN 55057

HONG, RICHARD, educator; b. Danville, Ill., Jan. 10, 1929; s. William and Louise (See) H.; B.S., U. Ill., 1949, M.D., 1953; m. Marion Shaw Taylor, May 31, 1952; children—Susan, Steven, Andrew, Laura. Intern Cook County Hosp., Chgo., 1953-54; resident Children's Hosp., Cin., 1957-60; research asso. immunology dept. pediatrics Coll. Medicine U. Cin., 1957-65; asst. prof. pedidatrics U. Minn., 1965-67, prof., 1967-69; prof. pediatrics U. Wis. Med. Sch., Madison, 1969—. Served with USAF, 1954-57. Mem. Soc. Pediatric Research, Am. Assn. Immunologists, Am. Soc. Clin. Investigation, Phi Beta Kappa, Phi Kappa Phi. Home: 201 Saratoga Circle Madison WI 53705

HONG, SUNG WOOK, Korean diplomat; b. Kyongnam, Korea, Dec. 27, 1919; s. Du Young and In Jae (Kim) H.; B.A. in Econs., U. Japan, 1940; m. Chung Ja Nam, Aug. 23, 1939; children—Myung Hai (Mrs. Chong Tsun Yun), Myung Ran. Politico-econ. counselor Korean embassy, Rome, Italy, 1959-61; chief protocol Ministry Fgn. Affairs, Seoul, 1961-62; charge d'affaires Korean embassy, Turkey, 1962-63; consul gen. of Korea, Phnom Penh, Cambodia, 1963-66; consul gen. of Korea, Cairo, U.A.R., 1966-69, N.Y.C., 1969—. Recipient Blue and Red Star, Fgn. Ser. of Korea, 1963. Home: 1385 York Av New York City NY 10021 Office 9 E 80th St New York City NY 10021

HONIG, EDWIN, educator, poet; b. N.Y.C., Sept. 3, 1919; s. Abraham David and Jane (Freundlich) H.; A.B., U. Wis., 1941, A.M., 1947; M.A. (hon.), Brown U., 1958; m. Margot S. Dennes, Dec. 15, 1963; children—Daniel D., Jeremy D. Instr. English, Purdue U., 1942-43, N.Y.U. and Ill. Inst. Tech., 1946-47, U. N.M., 1947-48, Claremont Coll., summer 1949; instr. English, Harvard, 1949-52, Briggs-Copeland asst. prof. English, 1952-57; mem. faculty Brown U., 1957—, prof. English, 1960—, chmn. dept., 1967, prof. comparative lit., 1962—; vis. prof. U. Cal. at Davis, 1964-65. Recipient Golden Rose award New Eng. Poetry Club, 1961; grantee Nat. Acad. Arts and Letters, 1966; Poetry prize Sat. Rev., 1956; Phi Beta Kappa poet Brown U., 1961; Guggenheim fellow, 1948, 62; Amy Lowell traveling poetry fellow, 1968. Author: Garcia Lorca, rev. edit., 1963; (poems) The Moral Circus, 1955, Dark Conceit: The Making of Allegory, 1959, The Gazabos: 41 Poems, 1960, Survivals, 1964, Spring Journal: Poems, 1968; (translations) Calderon: 4 Plays, 1961, Cervantes' Interludes, 1964, Calderon's Life Is A Dream, 1970; Fernando Pessoa's Selected Poems, 1971; (anthologies) (with Oscar Williams) The Mentor Book of Major American Poets, 1961, The Major Metaphysical Poets, 1968; Spenser, 1968. Produced plays: (Cambridge, Mass.) The Widow, 1953; (N.Y.C., Washington and Denver) The Phantom Lady, 1964; (Stanford Summer Festival) Calisto and Melibea, 1966; (BBC Radio, London) Life Is A Dream, 1970. Office: Brown Univ Providence RI 02912

HONIGMAN, JASON LESTER, lawyer; b. Russia, Oct. 25, 1904; s. Louis and Sarah (Hoffman) H.; A.B., U. Mich., 1924, J.D., 1926; m. Edith Horwitz, Mar. 26, 1931; children—Daniel M., Julie R. (Mrs. Edward C. Levy, Jr.). Came to U.S., 1911, naturalized, 1922. Admitted to Mich. bar, 1926; with firm Groesbeck, Sempliner, Kelly & Baille, then Sempliner, Dewey, Stanton & Honigman, 1929-48; sr. partner Honigman, Miller, Schwartz & Cohn, Detroit, 1948—. Chmn. Allied Supermarkets, Inc., 1960-68, now dir.; dir. Dayco Corp., Detroit Bank & Trust Co., Federal's Inc. Past chmn. civil proc. com. Jud. Conf. Mich. and State Bar Mich.; chmn. Mich. Law Revision Commn.; mem. Mich. Jud. Tenure Commn. Republican nominee for atty. gen., 1958. Trustee Shiffman Found. Mem. Am., Mich., Detroit bar assns., Tau Epsilon Rho. Jewish religion. Clubs: Franklin Hills Country, Standard-City (Detroit). Author: Michigan Court Rules Annotated. Home: 333 Covington Dr Detroit MI 48203 Office: First Nat Bldg Detroit MI 48226

HONKALA, FRED SAUL, educator, geologist; b. Concord, N.H., Nov. 30, 1919; s. Walter and Anna Louise (Tolvanen) H.; B.S., U. N.H., 1940; M.A., U. Mo., 1942; Ph.D. (Rackham fellow 1947-48), U. Mich., 1949; m. Rose Marie Fraher, Mar. 15, 1951; children—Eric Ethan, Lisa Louise, Karl Frederick. Geologist, U.S Geol. Survey, summers 1948-52; mem. faculty geology dept. U. Ont., 1948- 50, asst. prof., 1950-55, asso. prof., 1955-57, prof. geology, 1957-68, chmn. dept., 1956-64, dean Grad. Sch., dir. Research Found., 1964-68; pres. Yankton Coll., 1970—; dir. Adv. Sci. Edn. Program NSF 1968-70; with Shell Oil Co., summers 1954-57; mem. staff NSF Insts., Univ. of Mont., summers 1958-59; dir. NSF gen. sci. program Mont. secondary sch. sci. and math. tchrs., 1959-60; vis. prof. geologic field sta. and NSF Insts., Ind. U., 1960-63. Mem. gen. tech. adv. com. Office Coal Research, Dept. Interior, 1966-70; chmn. exec. com. Rocky Mountain Sci. Council 1967-68. Served to capt., C.E., AUS, 1942-46. Fellow Geol. Soc. Am. (sec. Rocky Mountain sect. 1958-59), Sigma Xi; mem. Am. Assn. Petroleum Geologists, A.A.A.S., Mont. Geol. Soc., Pi Kappa Alpha. Conglist. Home: 1201 Douglas Av Yankton SD 57078

HONNOLD, JOHN OTIS, Jr., educator, lawyer, UN ofcl.; b. Kansas, Ill., Dec. 5, 1915; s. John Otis and Louretta (Wright) H.; B.A., U. Ill., 1936; J.D., Harvard, 1939; m. Annamarie Kunz, June 26, 1939; children—Carol (Mrs. Vinton Deming), Heidi (Mrs. David Spencer), Edward. Admitted to N.Y. bar, 1940, Pa. bar, 1953, also U.S. Supreme Ct.; atty. firm Wright, Gordon, Zachry & Parlin, N.Y.C., 1939-41, SEC, 1941; chief ct. rev. br. OPA, 1942-46; mem. faculty U. Pa. Law Sch., 1946-71, prof. law, 1952-71; chief internat. trade law br. UN, sec. UN Commn. on Internat. Trade Law, 1969—; mem. faculty law sessions Salzburg (Austria) Seminar Am. Studies, 1960, chmn., 1963, 66; chief consel Miss. Office, Lawyer's Com. for Civil Rights under Law, 1965; U.S. rep. internat. practices com. Internat. C. of C. 1964-70, del., mem. drafting com. diplomatic conf. preparing uniform law for internat. sales of goods, The Hague, Holland, 1964; U.S. del UN Commn. Internat. Trade Law, 1969. Del. Dem. Nat. Conv. 1968. Bd. dirs., mem. exec. com. Am. Friends Service Com., 1968-70. Guggenheim fellow, 1958; Fulbright sr. research scholar U. Paris, 1958. Mem. Am., Phila. bar assns., Soc. de Legislation Comparée, Phi Beta Kappa, Phi Kappa Phi. Democrat. Mem. Soc. of Friends. Author: Sales and Sales Financing, 3d edit., 1968; The Life of the Law, 1964; (with E.L. Barrett, Jr. and P.W. Bruton) Cases and Materials on Constitutional Law, 3d edit., 1968; (with E. Allen Farnsworth) Commercial Law, 2d edit., 1968; Unification of the Law Governing International Sales of Goods, 1966; also articles. Bd. editors Am. Jour. Comparative Law, 1959-70. Home: Braxmar Dr S Harrison NY 10528 Office: Secretariat 3464A UN New York City NY 10017

HOOBLER, SIBLEY WORTH, physician; b. N.Y.C., Apr. 30, 1911; s. Bert Raymond and Madge (Sibley) H.; A.B., Princeton, 1933; Sc.D., Johns Hopkins, 1937, Ph.D., 1938; m. Katherine Taylor, Mar. 16, 1940 (div.) children—Raymond, Patricia. m. 2d Janet DeGelleke Woods, 1969. Mem. faculty U. Mich. Med. Sch., 1945—, prof. internal medicine, 1959—. Served to capt., M.C., AUS, 1942-46. Mem. Am. Heart Assn. (chmn. high blood pressure council 1963-64), Soc. Exptl. Biology and Medicine, Am. Physiol. Soc., Central Soc. Clin. Research, Am. Soc. Clin Investigation, Am. Coll. Cardiology. Author: Hypertensive Diseases, 1959; also articles. Home: 1198 Warrington Dr Ann Arbor MI 48103 Office: Kresge Bldg U Mich Med Center Ann Arbor MI 48103

HOOD, HARVEY PERLEY, dairy exec.; b. Sommerville, Mass., Apr. 12, 1897; s. Charles Harvey and Katherine Wyman (Eastman) H.; B.S., Dartmouth, 1918, LL.D. (hon.); postgrad. Harvard, 1919-20; m. Barbara Ellen Churchill, Apr. 18, 1928; children—Charles Harvey, II, Helen Olivia, Barbara Ellen Churchill, Olivia Churchill. Treas. H.P. Hood & Sons, dairy experts, Boston, 1922-39, pres., 1936-62, chmn. bd., chief exec. officer, 1962-66, chmn. bd., 1966-69, dir., 1922—; dir. Fed. Res. Bank Boston, 1951-58, dep. chmn., 1958; mem. exec. com., adv. bd. State St. Bank & Trust Co. Life trustee, chmn. exec. com. Dartmouth Coll., 1951- 67; trustee Children's Hosp.; mem. corp., bd. dirs. Boston Mus. Sci.; bd. overseers Boys' Club of Boston; mem. corp. Northeastern U., Cardigan Moutain Sch., Canaan, N.H., Mass. Gen. Hosp. Clubs: Harvard, Union, University, Brookline Country, Essex Country, Manchester Yacht (Boston); Dartmouth (N.Y.C.). Home: Masconomo St Manchester MA 01944 Office: 500 Rutherford Av Manchester MA ☆ ☆27

HOOD, RICHARD BYRNES, r.r. ofcl.; b. Newcomer, Pa., Aug. 28, 1908; A.B., Dartmouth, 1930; postgrad. Harvard, 1931; LL.B., U. Pitts., 1934; m. Hilda L. Forsberg, Dec. 7, 1935. Spl. agt. F.B.I., 1934-53; asst. to pres. B. & L.E. & U.R.R., 1953-56; sec.-treas. B. & L.E., Union, Y.&N., J.&S., and C.&M. R.R.s., 1956-62, L.T., N. & S.S., McK. Con., N. & B., 1962-65; sec. D.M. & I.R., also E., J. & E. Ry. Cos., 1965—, treas., 1970—; dir. Am. Short Line R.R. Assn. Mem. Traffic Club Pitts. (pres. 1970-71), Ry. Club Pitts. (pres. 1959). Republican. Presbyn. Clubs: Pitts. Athletic Assn., Pittsburgh, Duquesne, Rotary (pres. 1961) (Pitts.). Home: 298 Shadowlawn Av Pittsburgh PA 15216 Office: PO Box 536 Pittsburgh PA 15230

HOOD, ROBERT CHAMBERS, chem. mgf. exec.; b. Marinette, Wis., Apr. 3, 1917; s. Francis G. and Katharine (Chambers) H.; student U. Wis., 1935-39; m. Marjorie Woodward, June 22, 1940; children—Sarah, Cynthia, Deborah. With Ansul Co., Marinette, 1939—, successively accountant, sales corr., founder and editor employee's publ., advt. mgr., sec., v.p., 1940-49. pres., 1949—, also dir.; Mem. spl. tng. mission to Austria, FOA, 1954; mem. U.S. delegation Internat. Human Relations Conf., Rome, Italy, 1956, nat. bd. Nat. Tng. Labs. in Group Devel., mem. bus. adv. council U. Wis., Green Bay. Trustee Midwest Research Inst.; mem. research adv. council Am. Found. Mgmt. Research. Served to lt. gunnery officer, USCGR, World War II. Recipient citation for best co-ordinated design program Am. Industry Package Designers Council, 1954. Mem. Wis. Safety Council (trustee). Am. Mgmt. Assn., Wis. Mfrs. Assn. (dir.) Nat. Indsl. Conf. Bd., Def. Orientation Conf. Assn., U.S. (mem. bus. relations com.), Marinette (past pres., dir.) C.'s of C. Chief Execs. Forum (bd. dirs.), Mfg. Chemists Assn. Clubs: Metropolitan (N.Y.C.); Chicago Yacht; Marinette and Menominee' Yacht (past commodore). Home: Box 406 River Rd Marinette WI 54143 Office: 1 Stanton St Marinette WI 54143

HOOD, ROBERT ERIC, mag. editor, writer; b. Mildred, Pa., Apr. 15, 1926; s. Charles Dunbar and Alice Victoria (Johnson) H.; B.A., Harpur coll., 1951; student (grad. fellow), N.Y.U. 1951-53; m. Ann Margaret King, Oct. 15, 1955; children—Carol Ann, Eric Charles. Grad. asst. English dept. Sch. Commerce, N.Y.U., 1951-53; with Boys' Life mag., 1953—, editor, 1964—; spl. cons. community Relations Service, 1964-66; editorial cons. G.P. Putnam's 1960—; book series editor Coward-McCann, 1964-66; free-lance childrens' book critic N.Y. Times, 1958—. Vol. pamphlet and speech writer John F. Kennedy presdl. campaign, 1960; speech writer Senator Harrison Williams, 1964; cons., speech writer Gov. LeRoy Collins, 1964- 66. Served with USNR, 1944-46; PTO Mem. Am. Soc. Mag. Editors. Author: Find a Career in Photography, 1959; 12 at War, 1967; also articles. Home: 12 Berwick Rd Kendall Park NJ 08824 Office: Boys' Life New Brunswick NJ 08903

HOOF, WAYNE, coll. dean; b. What Cheer, Ia., Aug. 29, 1917; s. Oscar William and Maude (Tilton) H.; student U.Ia., 1935-37; B.S., U.S. Naval Acad., 1941; postgrad. U.S. Naval Postgrad. Sch., 1942; M.S. in Naval Architecture and Marine Engring., Mass. Inst. Tech. 1948; m. Mary Elinor English, Feb. 8. 1941; children—Allen W., David L., J. Bruce. Commd. ensign U.S. Navy, 1942, advanced through grades to capt., 1961; with Bur. Ships, U.S. Navy, 1942-46, design officer, 1957-61; served in U.S.S. Helena, 1948- 50; with Mare Island Navy Shipyard, 1950-53, U.S. Navy Pacific Fleet, 1953-57; tech. liaison officer Royal Navy Admiralty, Bath, Eng., also asst. naval attache, London, Eng., 1961-63; head engring. dept. U.S. Naval Acad., Annapolis, Md., 1963-65, head English, history and govt. depts., 1965-67; ret. 1967; chmn. math., sci. and engring. div. Montgomery Coll., 1967-70, acad. dean, 1970—. Mem. Am. Soc. Engring. Edn., Soc. Naval Architects and Marine Engrs. Home: 15443 Carrolton Rd Rockville MD 20853

HOOFNAGLE, JAMES EDWARD, govt. ofcl.; b. Atkins, Va., Jan. 6, 1912; s. Edgar B. and Martha (Purdy) H.; B.S., U.Va., 1937, M.A., 1938; student Marion Jr. Coll.; m. Evelyn F. Houston, 1939; children—John E., James H., Van R. Tchr., 1933- 36; with U.S. Dept. Agr., 1938-44, budget officer, 1946-50, dep. dir. food distbn., 1950-52; gen. mgr., dep. dir. USIS, Germany, 1952-56; asst. dir. for adminstrn. USIA, 1956- 60; counselor of embassy Am. Embassy, Bonn, Germany, 1960-64; dep. dir. gen. Fgn. Service, Washington, 1965-68; dep. asst. sec. orgn. and mgmt. State Dept., 1968-69; dep. chief of mission, Dublin, Ireland, 1969—. Served to lt. USNR, 1944-46. Home: 6502 Smoot Dr McLean VA 22101

HOOG, ARMAND MARC FRANCOIS MARIE, educator; b. Paris, France, Dec. 17, 1912; s. Georges and Madeleine (Coquelin) H.; student Collège Stanislas, Lycée Henry IV and Ecole Normale Supérieure, Paris, Agrégé de l'Université, 1937; m. Marie- Jacques Debrix, Aug. 30, 1943; children—Isabelle, Guillaume, Marjorie. Maitre de conférences, Cairo U., Egypt, 1938-39, Strasbourg U., France, 1945-51; lit. critic Carrefour, Paris weekly paper, 1941-51 and La Neuf, Paris monthly, 1944-49; vis. lectr. French lit. Harvard, 1951-53; vis. prof. Smith Coll., 1953-54; vis. prof. Princeton, 1954-55, Meredith Howland Pyne prof. of French literature, 1955—; Guggenheim fellow, 1958- 59. Decorated Chevalier de la Légion d'Honneur, Croix de Guerre. Recipient Prix Max Barthou, Académie Francaise, 1946. Prix Sainte- Beuve, 1948. Prix Au Service de la Pensée Francaise, 1950. Author: Littérature en Silésie, 1944; La Rochefoucauld, Maximes, Réflexions diverses, 1945; La Poésie et la

Grace humaine, 1946; Mythologie francaise due coeur, 1946; Laclos. Les Liaisons dangereuses, 1946; L' Accident, 1948; Le Roman du Graal, 1949; Retz, Histoire de la Conjuration de Fiesque, 1949; La Fayette, La Princesse de Clèves, 1949; Emily Brontë, Le Mont des Temptes, 1949; Balzac, La Femme Abandonnée, Un début dans la vie, 1949; La Révolte métaphysique des Petits Romantiques, 1949; Le Dernier Tonnerre, 1959; Fromentin, Domnique, 1959. Home: RD 4 Box 921 Brunswick Pike NJ 08401 Office: Princeton University Princeton NJ 08540

HOOGENBOOM, ARI ARTHUR, historian, educator; b. Richmond Hill, N.Y., Nov. 28, 1927; s. Ari and Clara (Behn) H.; B.A., Atlantic Union Coll., 1949; M.A., Columbia, 1951, Ph.D., 1958; m. Olive Gwendoline Youngberg, Aug. 28, 1949; children—Lynn Cordelia, Ari Arthur, Jan Margaret. Lectr., Columbia, 1955-56; from instr. to asst. prof. U. Tex., El Paso, 1956-58; faculty Pa. State U., 1958-68, prof., 1966-68; prof., chmn. history dept. Bklyn. Coll., 1968—; vis. lectr. U. Wis., Milw., summer 1960; vis. asso. prof. U. Ore., summer 1965. Pres. Central Pa. chpt. Am. Assn. UN, 1963-64. Guggenheim fellow, 1965-66. Mem. Am., Pa. (past sec.) hist. assns., N.Y.. Hist. Soc., Orgn. Am. Historians. Democrat. Unitarian. Author: Outawing the Spoils: A History of the Civil Service Reform Movement, 1865-1883, 1961; (with William S. Sachs) The Enterprising Colonials: Society on the Eve of the Revolution, 1965. Editor: Spoilsmen and Reformers, 1964;; (with Olive Hoogenboom) The Gilded Age, 1967. Home: 1451 E 21st St Brooklyn NY 11210

HOOK, AUGUST F., retail drug chain exec.; b. Indpls., July 6, 1907; s. John A. and Florence B. (Weiss) H.; Ph.C., B.S. in Pharmacy, Purdue U., 1929; m. Marguerte A. Bowers, Feb. 14, 1931; 1 dau., Ann (Mrs. David Caperton). With Hook Drugs, Inc., Indpls., 1930—, pres., 1956—; pres. Senate Realty Co., Salt Creek Realty Corp.; dir. Ind. Nat. Bank Corp. Mem. Ind. Bd. Pharmacy; past mem. Lederle Pharmacy Cons. Bd. Bd.dirs, Central Ind. council Boy Scouts Am., 1938—, pres., 1960-61, chmn. camp devel. fund drive, 1963-64, chmn. pub. relations com., chmn. exec. com. Region 7, 1967-68, exec. com., 1961—, mem. nat. bd., 1967—, chmn. region VII Boypower '76 program; campaign chmn. United Fund Greater Indpls., 1965, vice chmn. advance corp. div., 1962, chmn., 1963; finance chmn. Mental Health Assn. Ind., 1969; bd. govs. Indpls. Jr. Achievement; mem. One Hundred Club Indpls.; chmn. Ind. Rose Bowl Fund, 1963; mem. Gov. Ind. Economy Program, Indpls. Civic progress Assn. Recipient St. George award Boy Scouts Am., 1965, Silver Beaver award, 1947, Silver Antelope award 1964, Distinguished Eagle Scout award, 1969, Silver Buffalo award, 1971; Distinguished Citizens award Am. Legion, 1963; 30 Year Vet. award Indpls. Kiwanis Club, 1966. Mem. Nat. Assn. Chain Drug Stores (past pres.), Asso. Chain Drug Stores (past pres.), Indiana Soc. Chgo., Phi Kappa Psi. Kappa Psi. Clubs: P Men's Gimlet (Purdue U.); Athenaeum Turners, Century, Wildwood Valley Hunting (Ogleville, Ind.). Home: 5220 N Illinois St Indianapolis IN 46208 Office: PO Box 26285 Indianapolis IN 46226

HOOK, EDWARD WATSON, physician; b. Sumter, S.C., Aug. 10, 1924; s. Edward and Theola (Brogdon) H.; B.S., Wofford Coll., Spartanburg, S.C., 1943; student Yale, 1943-44; M.D., Emory U., 1949; m. Jessie Dale Thurecht, June 14, 1949; children—Edward Watson III, Susan Dale, Margaret Jane, Robert Randall. Intern. Univ. Hosps., Mpls., 1949-50; jr. asst. resident in medicine Grady Meml. Hosp., Atlanta, 1950-51, sr. asst. resident, 1953- 54, chief resident, 1954-55, fellow dept. medicine Emory U. Sch. Medicine, Grady Meml. Hosp., 1955-56; practice medicine, specializing in internal medicine and infectious diseases, Charlottesville, 1969—; instr. medicine Johns Hopkins Sch. Medicine, Balt., 1956-58, asst. prof., 1958-59; asso. prof. medicine Cornell U. Med. Coll., N.Y.C., 1959-64, prof., 1964-69, vice chmn. dept. medicine, 1969; asso. attending physician N.Y. Hosp., 1959-64, attending physician, 1964-69, mem. med. bd., 1967-69; prof. honorario U. Bahia Sch. Medicine, Salvadore, Brazil, 1966; prof., chmn. dept. medicine U. Va. Sch. Medicine, Charlottesville, 1969—; physician-in-chief U. Va. Hosp., 1969—. Served with M.C., AUS, 1943-46, 51-53. Diplomate Am. Bd. Internal Medicine. Mem. A.C.P., Am. Fedn. Clin. Research, Am. Thoracic Soc., A.M.A., N.Y. State N.Y. County, Albemarle County med. socs., Soc. for Exptl. Biology and Medicine, N.Y. Acad. Medicine, Am. Soc. Clin. Investigation, Johns Hopkins Med. and Surg. Assn., Grady Clin. Soc., Royal Soc. Tropical Medicine and Hygiene, Am. Assn. Immunologists, Am. Clin. and Climatology Assn., N.Y. Med. and Surg. Assn., N.Y. Acad. Scis., Harvey Soc., Infectious Disease Soc. Am., Assn. Am. Physicians, Internat. Coll. Tropical Medicine, Sigma Xi, Alpha Omega Alpha. Contbr. articles profl. jours. Home: 1203 Hilltop Rd Charlottesville VA 22901 Office: Sch of Medicine U Va Charlottesville VA 22901

HOOK, EMMETT ROBINSON, banker; b. Mansfield, La., Oct. 26, 1921; s. Roy Calvin and Sallie (Robinson) H.; B.A., U. Kan., 1942; m. Jean Jackson, Nov. 25, 1948; 1 son, Emmett Robinson. With Comml. Nat. Bank, Shreveport, La., 1949—, v.p., 1955-61, sr. v.p., 1961-63, exec. v.p., 1963-64, pres., 1964—, dir., 1952—; dir Fairfield Investment Co., Shreveport, Frost Whited Co., Inc., Shreveport, Gt. So. Life Ins. Co., Houston. Trustee Centenary Coll., Shreveport. Served to capt. AUS, 1942-46. Mem. Shreveport C. of C. Clubs: Shreveport, Shreveport Petroleum, Shreveport Country. Pierremont Oaks Tennis. Home: 611 Monrovia St Shreveport LA 71102 Office: 329 Texas St Shreveport LA 71102

HOOK, HENRY BERNARD, newspaper pub.; b. Aplington, Ia., Dec. 23, 1909; s. Barney H. and Johanna (DeBuhr) H.; B.A., U. Ia., 1933; m. Ruth Sanders, May 7, 1938; children—Sanders H.B., Steven Paul. Editor, mgr. weekly newspaper, 1933- 37; news editor, promotion mgr. radio sta. KGLO, Mason City, Ia., 1937- 48, mgr. 1948-51; pub. Times-Democrat, Davenport, Ia., 1952—. Commr., sec. Davenport Municipal Airport Comm. Trustee Davenport Indsl. Devel. Corp.; v.p. Ia.-Ill. Indsl. Devel. Group; regional dir. Nat. Conf. Christians and Jews. Campaign mgr. gov. of Ia., 1938. Trustee Beloit Coll. Served as maj. AUS, World War II. Decorated Bronze Star medal. Mem. Am. Cancer Soc. (past pres. Ia. div.), Ia. Motor Club AAA (state dir.), Davenport C. of C. (past pres.), Am. Legion (past comdr.), Res. Officers Assn., Sigma Delta Chi. Delta Upsilon. Democrat. Conglist. Mason (Shriner), Elk. Club: Davenport Town. Home: 217 Hillcrest St Davenport IA 52803 Office: 124 E 2d St Davenport IA 52808

HOOK, HOWARD ARTHUR, aero. engineer; b. Balt., Sept. 7, 1901; s. Sebastian Henry and Edith (Thompson) H.; grad., Balt. Polytech. Inst., 1919; engring. student, Cornell U., 1920-21; m. Ruth De Motte, Feb. 23, 1924 (div. 1939); 1 son, William Arthur; m. 2d Olive Charlotte Winslow, May 26, 1939; children—Patrick Arthur, Kathleen Charlotte and Charleen Marjorie (twins). Civil engr. Interstate Commerce Commn. and War Dept., 1923-28; with airways div. Bur. of Air Commerce (now FAA), Washington, 1928-41; adminstr., region 6, CAA, 1942-46; asst. adminstr. for airports, Washington, 1946-48; supt. of airports, region 6 (Calif. Ariz., Nev., Utah), CAA, 1948-53; dir. master planning Architects and Engrs., Spanish Bases, 1953-55; adminstr. civil airport installations for asso. firms of Orr, Strange & Inslee, architects and Koebig & Koebig, engrs., 1955—; supervising structural engr. Office Fed. Airways, CAA, Washington, 1956; indsl. engr. for facilities planning Northrup Aircraft, Inc., Hawthorne, Cal., 1956-57, chief aviation div. County Engr. Dept., County of Los Angeles, 1958-62; supervisory airway engr. Western region FAA, 1962-67. Mem. Soc. Am. Mil Engrs., Am. Assn. Airport Execs. Mason. Home: 1323 14th St Santa Monica CA Retired.

HOOK, RALPH CLIFFORD, Jr., educator; b. Kansas City, Mo., May 2, 1923; s. Ralph Clifford and Ruby (Swanson) H.B.A., U. Mo., 1947, children—Ralph Clifford III, John Gregory. Instr. U. Mo., 1947-48; lectr. U. Tex., 1951- 52; co-owner, mgr. Hook Buick Co., also Hook Truck & Tractor Co., Lee's Summit, Mo., 1952-58; asso. prof. U. Kansas City, 1953-58; dir. Bur. Bus. Research and Services, Ariz. State U., 1958-66, prof. marketing, 1960-68; dean Coll. Bus. Adminstrn., U. Hawaii, 1968- -. Dir. Am. Pacific Group Ltd., Hilo Coast Processing Co. Ltd., First Southwest Small Bus. Investment Corp., Saguaro Bancorp. Ariz. Vice chmn. regional export expansion council Dept. Commerce; bd. dirs. Consumer Credit Counseling Service Hawaii. Bd. dirs. Jr. Achievement Hawaii. Served to 1st lt., F.A., AUS, 1943-46; lt. col. Res. Recipient alumni citation of merit U. Mo. Coll. Bus. and Pub. Adminstrn., 1969. Mem. Hawaii World Trade Assn. (exec. com.), Am. Marketing Assn. (v.p. 1965-67, pres. Central Ariz. chpt. 1960-61), Nat. Council Small Bus. Mgmt. Devel. (pres. 1963), Sales and Marketing Execs. Internat., Assn. Edn. Internat. Bus., Newcomen Soc. N. Am. Beta Gamma Sigma, Omicron Delta Kappa, Beta Theta Pi, Delta Sigma Pi (gold council). Methodist. Rotarian. Author: (with others) The Economy of Arizona, 1964. Contbr. monograph series Western Bus. Roundup. Founder, moderator Western Bus. Roundup radio series, 1958-68. Home: 452 Dune Circle Kailua HI 96734 Office: Coll Bus Adminstrn U Hawaii Honolulu HI 96822

HOOK, SIDNEY, educator; b. N.Y.C., Dec. 20, 1902; s. Isaac and Jennie (Halpern) H.; B.S., Coll. City N.Y., 1923; M.A., Columbia, 1926, Ph.D., 1927, L.H.D., 1960, LL.D.; m Carrie Katz, Mar. 31, 1924; 1 son, John Bertrand; m. 2d, Ann Zinken, May 25, 1935; children—Ernest Benjamin, Susan Ann. Teacher N.Y.C. pub. schs., 1923- 28; lectr. Columbia summer session, 1927, 1930; instr. philosophy Washington Square Coll., N.Y. U., 1927-32, asst. prof., 1932-34, asso. prof. and chmn. dept. philosophy, 1934-39, prof., 1939 —, head all-univ. dept. philosophy N.Y.U., 1948-69, chmn. Washington Sq. Coll. Arts and Scis., until 1969. Vis. prof. Harvard, summer 1961; regents prof. U. Cal. at Santa Barbara, spring 1966. Organizer Conf. on Methods in Philosophy and Sci., Conf. on Sci. Spirit and Dem. Faith, Am. Com. for Cultural Freedom, and Congress for Cultural Freedom, N.Y. U. Inst. for Philosophy. Guggenheim Am. Acad. Arts and Cal., 1961-62. Fellow Scis.; mem. Am. Philos. Assn. (pres. eastern div. 1959), Internat. Com. for Acad. Freedom, John Dewey Soc. Author books including most recent: Education for Modern Man, 1946; Heresy, Yes-Conspiracy, No, 1953; The Ambiguous Legacy: Marx and the Marxists, 1955; Common Sense and the Fifth Amendment, 1957; Political Power and Personal Freedom, 1959; The Quest for Being, 1961; The Paradoxes of Freedom, 1962; The Place of Religion in A Free Society, 1968; Academic Freedom and Academic Anarchy, 1970. Contbr. articles philos. jours. Editor: American Philosophers at Work: The Current Philosophic Scene, 1956; Determinism and Freedom in An Age of Modern Science; others. Address: Dept Philosophy New York University New York City NY 10003 ☆

HOOKER, CHARLES WRIGHT, educator; b. Fries, Va., Sept. 15, 1910; s. Robert Ruffin and Ella Madge (Cornett) H.; A.B., Duke 1930, A.M., 1932, Ph.D., 1933; m. Elma Black, Sept. 2, 1937; children—Elizabeth Kinard, Robert Wright. NRC fellow U. Rochester, 1933-34; NRC fellow in medicine Duke 1934-36; instr. anatomy Tulane U., 1936- 37; instr. anatomy Yale, 1937-42, asst. prof., 1942-46, asso. prof., 1946-48; prof. cytology Emory U. Sch. Medicine, 1948-49; prof. anatomy U.N.C. Med. Sch., 1949—. Mem. A.A.A.S., Am. Assn. Anatomists, Am. Soc. Zoölogists, Endocrine Soc., Am. Assn. Cancer Research (sec.-treas. 1945-51), Soc. Exptl. Biology and Medicine, N.Y. Acad. Sci., Phi Beta Kappa, Sigma Xi. Presbyn. Home: 508 Pittsboro St Chapel Hill NC 27514

HOOKER, CLIFFORD PAUL, educator; b. McClure, Ill., Aug. 8, 1920; s. Everett Lee and Francis Virginia (Phillips) H.; B.S., So. Ill. U., 1941, M.A., 1949; Ed.D., Ind. U., 1954; postgrad. Columbia, 1954; m. Avelyn Hardin, June 7, 1941; children—Sherrill, Donald. Tchr., sch. adminstr., Ill., 1941-52; asso. prof., asst. dean Sch. Edn., U. Pitts., 1954-58; prof. edn., asso. dir. Bur. Field Studies and Surveys, U. Minn., Mpls., 1958-64, prof. and chmn. dept. ednl. adminstrn., 1964—. Served to lt. USNR, 1943- 46; PTO. Mem. Am. Ednl. Research Assn., Nat. (life), Minn. edn. assns., Am. Assn. Sch. Administrs., Am. Assn. U. Profs. Phi Delta Kappa. Mason. Contbr. to textbook, author numerous articles. Home: 1756 St Mary's Av St Paul MN 55113 Office: Univ of Minnesota Minneapolis MN 55455

HOOKER, JOHN LEE, singer, guitarist; b. Clarkdale, Miss., 1917. Sang in spiritual groups at age of 14, then studied guitar under Will Moore; recording artist for Riverside, Vee-Jay, Modern records. Address: care Chess Record Corp 320 E 21st St Chicago IL 60616*

HOOKER, RICHARD JAMES, historian; b. Mil., Sept. 6, 1912; s. Harry A. and Edith (O'Donnell) H.; A.B., U. Chgo., 1934, Ph.D., 1943; m. Nancy Harvison, Jan. 5, 1952. Research asst. U. Chgo., 1936-40; instr. Central Y.M.C.A. Coll. Chgo., 1941- 44, asst. prof., acting chmn. dept. history, 1944-45; asso. prof. Roosevelt U., Chgo., 1945-49, chmn. dept. history, 1945-49, 50-62. prof. Am. history, 1949-69, prof. emeritus, 1969—, Trustee 1952-55, 64-67. Mem. Am., Miss. Valley hist. assns., Japan Am. Soc. (trustee 1961-68, v.p. 1964-68), Am. Assn. U. Profs., Alpha Delta Phi. Author: The Carolina Backcountry on the Eve of the Revolution: The Journal and Other Writings of Charles Woodmason, Anglican Itinerant; The American Revolution: The Search for Meaning. Contbr. articles to profl. jours. Home: Route 1 Box 457H Englewood FL 33533 summer Box 555 Lyndonville VT 05851

HOOKER, THOMAS, banker; b. Boston, 1916; ed. Yale, 1938. Exec. v.p., dir. First New Haven Nat. Bank; dir. Linsley Lake Corp. Home: 94 E Rock Rd New Haven CT 06511 Office: 1 Church St New Haven CT 06510*

HOOKS, ROBERT, actor, producer, dir.; b. Washington, Apr. 18, 1937; s. Edward and Bertha (Ward) H.; student Temple U.; m. Yvonne Hooks, Oct. 6, 1957; children—Kevin, Eric. Plays include A Raisin In the Sun, 1959, A Taste of Honey, 1961, Ballad for Bimshire, 1962, Dutchman, 1965, The Milktrain Doesn't Stop Here Anymore, 1965, Where's Daddy, 1966, Happy Ending, 1967, Day of Absence, 1967, Hallelujah Baby, 1968; films include Sweet Love Bitter, 1966, Hurry Sundown, 1967; TV prodns. include N.Y. Police Dept.; producer Happy Ending, A Day of Absense, Walk Together Children; founder, since exec. dir. Negro Ensemble Co. Club: Players (N.Y.C.). Home: 160 West End Av New York City NY 10023 Office: care Chartwell Artists Ltd 1345 Av of Americas New York City NY 10019

HOOKS, WILLIAM GARY, educator, geologist; b. Asheville, N.C., Oct. 4, 1927; s. John Brantley and Virginia Evelyn (Fortune) H.; B.S., U. N.C., 1950, M.S., 1953, Ph.D., 1961; m. Peggy Raye Lucas, Dec. 27, 1951; children—William Gary, Deborah, Judson David, Stephen Borden. Asst. prof. dept. geology and geography U. Ala., 1954-61, asso. prof., 1961-67, prof., 1968—, chmn. dept., 1969—; geol. cons., 1955—. Mem. Geol. Soc. Am. (vice chmn. Southeastern sect.), Soc. Econ. Paleontologists and Mineralogists, Ala. Geol. Soc. (pres. 1966), Phi Beta Kappa, Sigma Xi, Sigma Gamma Epsilon. Home: 8 Riverside Circle Tuscaloosa AL 35401 Office: Box 1945 Dept Geology and Geography U Ala University AL 35486

HOOLE, WILLIAM STANLEY, librarian; b. Darlington, S.C., May 16, 1903; s. William Brunson and Minnie Eva (Powers) H.; A.B., Wofford Coll., 1924, A.M., 1931, Litt.D., 1954; Ph.D., Duke U., 1934; B.S. in Library Sci., North Tex. U., 1943; student Columbia, 1927, U.S.C., 1929, U. Chgo. Grad. Library Sch., summers 1935, 36, 38, 39; m. Martha Anne Sanders, Aug. 7, 1931 (dec. May 1960); children—Martha DuBose, Elizabeth Stanley; m. Addie Shirley Coleman, May 31, 1970. Tchr. Spartanburg (S.C.) High Sch., 1924-25, Darlington (S.C.) High Sch., 1927-31; teaching fellow Duke U., Durham, N.C., 1931-34; asst. prof. English, Birmingham (Ala.)-Sou. Coll., 1934-35, librarian, 1935-37. Baylor U., Waco, Tex., 1937-39; dir. libraries North Tex. State Univ., 1939- 44; dean libraries U. Ala., Tuscaloosa, 1944-71, prof. librarianship, 1971—. Library cons. So. Assn. Schs. and Colls., 1942-60, mem. commn. instns. higher learning, 1948-50; Fulbright research fellow U.K., 1956-57; research cons. U.S. Ho. of Reps. subcom. on spl. edn., 1957-58; cons. U.S. Office Edn., 1959-60, Pres.'s Nat. Commn. on Libraries, 1967, U.S. Dept. Commerce, 1968, also various govt. agys., coms. Recipient Lit. award Ala. Library Assn., 1958. Mem. Am., S.E. Ala. library assns., Newcomen Soc. N. Am., Sou., Ala. hist. assns., S. Atlantic Modern Lang. Assn., Phi Alpha Theta, Pi Tau Chi, Phi Beta Kappa Phi Kappa, Pi Kappa Phi. Methodist. Editor: North Texas Regional Union List of Serials, 1943; Classified List of Reference Books and Periodicals for the College Library, 1957, rev., 1955; Seven Months in the Rebel States, 1863, 1958; Reconstruction in West Alabama, 1959; A Visit to the Confederate States of America in 1863, 1962; And Still We Conquer, 1968. Author: Charleston Periodicals, 1936: Sam Slick in Texas, 1945; The Ante-Bellum Charleston Theatre, 1946; Let the People Read, 1946; A Library for Lauderdale; Alias Simon Suggs: The Life and Times of Johnson Jones Hooper, 1952; The James Boys Rode South, 1955; Vizetelly Covers the Confederacy, 1957; The Alabama Tories, 1862- 65, 1960; Four Years in the Confederate Navy, 1964; Lawley Covers the Confederacy, 1964; And Still We Conquer, 1968. Co-Author: Mississippi Study of Higher Education, 1945; Studies of Higher Education in the South, 1947; A Study of Stillman Institute, 1947. Editor The Alabama Rev., 1948-67, The Southeastern Librarian, 1951- 52; asso. editor South Atlantic Modern Lang. Assn. Bull., 1947-52; Confederate Centennial Studies, 1956-65. Contbr. to Tex. Hist. Handbook, Ency. Brit., Grolier Ency.; also articles to scholarly profl. and popular publs. Home: 39 University Circle Tuscaloosa AL 35401

HOOLEY, HARRY E., optical equipment mfg. co. exec.; b. 1925; B.S., Rutgers U.; married. Supr., Chicopee Mfg. Co., 1950-55; asst. controller Permacel Tape Corp., 1959-60; mfg. financial accountant Johnson & Johnson, 1960-61; asst. controller Bausch & Lomb Inc., Rochester, N.Y., 1961-65, controller, 1965—. Office: 6355 St Paul St Rochester NY 15602*

HOOLEY, NEALE FRANCIS, machinery mfg. co. exec., atty.; b. Larchmont, N.Y., Oct. 21, 1931; s. John W. and Agnes (Burger) H.; A.B., St. Francis Coll., 1953; J.D. (scholar), Villanova U., 1956; m. Margaret P. McLaughlin, Nov. 3, 1962. Admitted to N.Y. bar, 1958, N.J. bar, 1969; asso. Keegan & Clarke, N.Y.C., 1958-61; counsel Tchrs. Ins. & Annuity Assn., also Coll. Retirement Equity Fund, N.Y.C., 1961-67; asso. Shea, Gallop, Climenko & Gould, 1967-69; partner Hooley, Perselay, Butler & Kelly, Westfield, N.J., 1969—; sec. Triangle Industries, Inc., Newark, and subsidiaries, 1969—, Reserve Fund, Inc., N.Y.C., 1970—. Served with USMC, 1956-58. Mem. Assn. Bar City N.Y. (ins. com. 1964-67), N.J., Union County bar assns. Home: 550 Sherwood Pkwy Westfield NJ 07090 Office: 190 Elm St Westfield NJ 07091

HOON, PAUL WAITMAN, theologian; b. Chgo., Feb. 11, 1910; s. Clarence Earl and Fannie Ruth (Waitman) H.; student U. Cin., 1926-28; A.B., Yale, 1931; B.D., Union Theol. Sem., N.Y.C., 1934; postgrad. U.Marburg, Germany, 1934, Cambridge U. (Eng.), 1935; Ph.D., U. Edinburgh, 1936; S.T.D. (hon.), Ursinus Coll., 1948; m. Grace Nichols, Nov. 23, 1938 (dec. 1943); children—Peter Waitman, David Nichols; m. 2d, Alice Emerson Blodgett, Oct. 15, 1950. Student asst. minister Madison Av. Presbyn. Ch., N.Y.C., 1931-32; asst. minister Chester Hill Meth. Ch., Mt. Vernon, N.Y., 1932-34; ordained to ministry Meth. Ch., 1933; minister, New Milford Conn., 1936-38, Summerfield Ch., Bridgeport, Conn., 1938-41, First Ch., New Rochelle, N.Y., 1941-43, First Ch., Germantown, Phila., 1943-53; lectr. Drew Theol. Sem., 1949-50; Henry Sloane Coffin prof. pastoral theology Union Theol. Sem., 1953—; Zimmerman lectr. Gettysburg Theol. Sem., 1955; Greene lectr. Andover Newton Theol. Sem., 1970; also lectr., preacher colls., univs., sems. Mem. Am. Assn. Sem. Profs. Practical Theology (v.p. 1956-58, pres. 1958-60), Ch. Soc. and Fedns., Phila. Council Chs. (pres. 1947-48), Beta Theta Pi, Tau Kappa Alpha, Delta Sigma Rho. Author: Exposition of the Epistles of St. John, The Interpreter's Bible; The Integrity of Worship: Studies In Liturgical Theology, 1971. Contbr. Companion to the Book of Worship, 1970; also religious, theol. jours. Home: 527 Riverside Dr New York City NY 10027 Office: Union Theol Sem Broadway at 120th St New York City NY 10027

HOOPER, BILLY ERNEST, vet. pathologist, educator; b. Pawnee City, Neb., June 22, 1931; s. James Ernest and Beulah (Thieman) H.; B.S. in Agr., U. Mo., 1961, D.V.M., 1961; M.S., Purdue H., 1963, Ph.D., 1965; m. Janice Jewell Kerr, Apr. 17, 1954; children—Roger William, Robin Suzanne. Asst. prof. Purdue U., 1965-67, asso. prof., 1967-68; asso. prof. U. Mo., Columbia, 1968- 69, chmn. dept. vet. pathology, 1969—. Served with USMCR, 1949-53. Mem. Am. Coll. Vet. Pathologists, Am. Vet. Med. Assn., Am. Soc. Vet. Clin. Pathologists. Home: 908 Shepard Ct Columbia MO 65201

HOOPER, BLAKE HOWARD, pharm. and chem. exec.; b. Chgo., Oct. 20, 1922; s. William Dane and Helen (McLernon) H.; B.S. in Chem. Engring., Ill. Inst. Tech., 1944; m. Frances Eleanor Barnes, Aug. 17, 1944; children—Kathy Ellen (Mrs. Volkert Hans Goebel), David Blake. Chem. engr. Darling & Co., Chgo., 1950-55; gen. mgr. Wilson Martin div. Wilson & Co., Phila., 1955-67, v.p., 1967-68; pres., chief exec. officer, dir. Wilson Pharm. & Chem. Corp., Chgo., 1968—. Mem. Cherry Hill Twp. (N.J.) Zoning Bd., 1965. Served to lt. comdr. USNR, 1943-46. Mem. Am. Oil Chemists Soc., Fatty Acid Producers Council, Delta Tau Delta. Clubs: Flossmoor (Ill.) Country, Mid America (Chgo.). Home: 2238 Flossmoor Rd Flossmoor IL 60422 Office: Prudential Bldg Chicago IL 60601

HOOPER, EDWIN BICKFORD, naval officer; b. Winthrop, Mass., Feb. 26, 1909; s. Fred Albra and Jenny Flora (Foster) H.; B.S., U.S. Naval Acad., 1931; M.S., Mass. Inst. Tech., 1940; grad. Nat. War Coll., 1953; m. Elizabeth Withers Patrick, June 26, 1934; children—Edwin Bickford, Robert C., James E., William P. Commd. ensign U.S. Navy, 1931, advanced through grades to vice adm., 1969; assigned destroyers, cruisers, battleships, amphibious ships and auxiliaries; with div. mil. application AEC, 1947-49; asst. nuclear applications Bur. Naval Ordnance, 1950-52, asst. chief bur. for research, 1955-58; comdr. Destroyer Squadron 26, 1958-59; dir. naval long range studies project, also Inst. Naval Studies, 1959-61; comdr. Amphibious Force, Western Pacific, 1961-62; dir. anti-submarine warfare research and devel. programs, 1962-64; asst. chief naval operations for devel., 1964; dep. chief naval operations for devel., 1965; comdr. service force Pacific Fleet, 1965-68; asst. dep. chief naval operations (logistics), 1968-69; Joint Logistics Rev. Bd., 1969-70; dir. naval history, curator Dept. Navy, 1970—. Decorated D.S.M. with gold star, Legion Merit, Bronze Star with combat V. Mem. Am. Hist. Assn., Sigma Xi. Home: 7005 Hillcrest Pl Chevy Chase MD 20015 Office: Navy Dept Washington DC 20025

HOOPER, EMMET THURMAN, Jr., educator, biologist; b. Phoenix, Aug. 19, 1911; s. Emmet Thurman and Frances Jewell (McDonald) H.; student San Diego State Coll., 1929-32; A.B., U. Cal. at Berkeley, 1933, A.M., 1936, Ph.D., 1939; m. Helen Winifred Bacon, Feb. 19, 1936; children—Alan Bacon, Nicholas Kim. Research asst. Mus. Vertebrate Zoology, U. Cal. at Berkeley, 1934-36, teaching asst. zoology, 1936-38; asst. prof. zoology U. Mich., 1946-52, asso. prof., 1952-58, prof., 1958—, curator mammals, 1956—; program dir. NSF Washington, 1964-65; chmn. biology faculty Orgn. Tropical Studies, 1967-70. Served to capt. USAAF, 1943-46. Mem. Biol. Soc. Washington, Soc. Study Evolution, Am. Soc. Mammalogists (corr. sec. 1941- 46, v.p. 1958-62, pres. 1962-64), Am. Inst. Biol. Scis., Wildlife Soc., Assn. Tropical Biology, Australian Mammal Soc., A.A.A.S., Sci. Research Club (U. Mich.), Sigma Xi. Author tech. reports on evolution, ecology, systematics vertebrate animals; sci. expdns. N. Am. Home: 1210 Bydding Rd Ann Arbor MI 48103

HOOPER, FRANK ARTHUR, judge; b. Americus, Ga., Apr. 21, 1895; s. Frank Arthur and Helena (Callaway) H.; student Ga. Inst. Tech.; LL.B., LL.M, LL.D., Atlanta Law Sch.; LL.D., Mercer U.; m. Carolyn Newton, June 20, 1926; children—Frank A. III, Charles N., Ellis C. Admitted to Ga. bar, 1916; sec. to judge Ga. Ct. Appeals, 1917, judge, 1932; practiced in Atlanta, 1919-43; instr., Atlanta Law Sch., 1934-43; asst. city atty., Atlanta, 1940-43; judge Superior Ct., Atlanta Judical Circuit, 1943-49; U.S. dist. judge, No. dist. Ga., 1949-67, U.S. sr. dist. judge, 1967—. Rep. Ga. Legislature, 1925-28. Served as lt. (s.g.) U.S.N.R.F., 1919. Mem. Am., Ga., Atlanta bar assns., Am. Legion, Ga. Tech. Nat. Alumni Assn. (pres. 1945-47), Sigma Alpha Epsilon. Democrat. Baptist. Mason (32, Shriner), Kiwanian. Club: Atlanta Lawyers. Home: 3303 Habersham Rd NW Atlanta GA 30305 Office: PO Box 1476 Atlanta GA 30301

HOOPER, FREDERICK RICHARD, headmaster; b. San Francisco, July 31, 1908; s. John Franklin and May (Frisbee) H.; A.B., Pomona Coll., 1933; postgrad Claremont Grad. Sch., 1933-34; m. Grace Fletcher Read, June 24, 1937; 1 son, Robert Moore. Master, Webb Sch. of Cal., Claremont, 1933-62, head math. dept., 1939-1962, dir. studies, 1955-62, mem. faculty exec. com., 1957-62 headmaster, 1962—. Troop committee- man Old Baldy council Boy Scouts Am., 1953-56. Mem. Cal. Assn. Ind. Schs. (head math. sect. 1958-62, treas. 1964-70), Am. Philatelic Soc., S.A.R., John More Assn., Headmasters Assn., First Century Families Cal., Cum Laude Soc., Phi Delta Kappa. Conglist. Rotarian. Clubs: Newport Beach Tennis; Bear Valley Gang; Pomona Valley; Los Angeles. Home: 1175 W Base Line Rd Claremont CA 91711

HOOPER, GILMAN STANLEY, textile corp. exec.; b. Danvers, Mass., Mar. 18, 1909; s. George D. and Mary P. (Elliott) H.; B.S., Colby Coll., 1929; M.S., Brown U., 1930, Ph.D., 1933; m. Virginia L. Keyes, May 17, 1935; 1 son, George Gilman. Successively research chemist, research supr., asst. research dir., tech. supt., mgr. tech. service E.I. du Pont de Nemours & Co., 1934-49; with Indsl. Rayon Corp., Cleve., 1949-60. research mgr., 1951-57, dir. research, 1957, v.p. charge research, 1958-60; dir. research and devel., fiber devel. dept. Hercules Powder Co., 1960-63; v.p. Deering Milliken Research Corp., Spartanburg, S.C., 1963—. Past pres., bd. dirs. United Cerebral Palsy Assn. Cuyahoga County (O.); bd. dirs. Spartanburg United Fund, Spartanburg County United Cerebral Palsy Assn., Spartanburg County Retarded Children's Assn., Council for Spartanburg County; chmn. bd. Charles Lea Center Handicapped Children. Mem. Am. Chem. Soc., Am. Assn. Textile Tech., Phi Beta Kappa, Sigma Xi, Kappa Delta Rho. Home: 1075 Partridge Rd Spartanburg SC 29302 Office: P O Box 1927 Spartanburg SC 29301

HOOPER, JOHN WILLIAM, educator; b. Laona, Wis., Nov. 6, 1926; s. Frank Arnold and Myldred (Barlement) H.; B.A. in Econs., Stanford, 1950, Ph.D., 1961; Postgrad, U.Wash., 1950-51; m. Elva Salmang, Aug. 14, 1959; children—Ellen Myldred, Carol Ann, Joan Claire. Research economist Rand Corp., 1958-59; asso. prof. econs. Yale, 1955-66; prof. econs. U. Cal. at San Diego, 1966—, chmn. dept., 1967—; asst. dir. Cowles Found. Research Econs., 1961-64. Served with USNR, 1944-46. Fulbright scholar, 1957-58; sr. fellow Social Sci. Research Council, 1964-65; Ford Found. faculty research fellow, 1971-72. Mem. Am. Econ. Assn., Econometric Soc., Royal Econ. Soc. Home: 5878 Soledad Rd La Jolla CA 92037

HOOPER, LESLIE JAMES, hydraulic engr.; b. Essex, Mass., Feb. 15, 1903; s. William John and Ethel (Cruze) H.; B.S., Worcester Poly. Inst., 1924, M.E., 1928; m. Edith Carolyn Stockwell, May 24, 1930; children—Donald Leslie, William Robert, Lee Monroe, Neal Cruze. Hydraulic test engr. Canadian Gen. Finance Co., Brazil, 1924-27; asst. to Prof. Allen, Alden Hydraulic Lab., Worcester Poly Inst., 1928-32, asst., part time tchr., 1932-38, asst. prof., 1938-45, prof. hydraulic engring., dir. lab., 1950-68, prof. emeritus cons. lab., 1968—; pvt. cons. practice on flow measurements. Internat. pres. tech. com. 4 Internat. Electrotech. Commn. Mem. Holden Sch. Com., 1940-49, several coms. on sch. bldg. and water supply, 1947-53. Recipient John R. Freeman scholarship, 1934-36, Charles T. Main, Jr. award, 1937. Fellow Am. Soc. Mech. Engrs., Am. Soc. C.E.; mem. A.A.A.S., Am. Soc. Engring. Edn., Boston Soc. Civil Engrs. (past pres.), Sigma Xi, Tau Beta Pi. Contbr. profl. jours. Home: 31 Highland Av Holden MA 01520 Office: Alden Research Lab Worchester Poly Inst Worchester MA 01609

HOOPER, LUCIEN OBED, investment analyst; b. Biddeford, Me., July 9, 1896; s. William Howard and Jennie Wait (McIntire) H.; student Boston U., Harvard, 1918; m. Vivian Lois Cole, Sept. 6, 1919 (dec. Oct. 1969); children—Lois (Mrs. Harry S. Gould, Jr.), David (dec.); m. 2d, Bernadine Oefner, May 6, 1970. Asso. editor Boston Comml. 1919-23; investment analyst E.A. Pierce & Co., 1923-27; head research dept. Frazier Jekle & Co., 1927-38; market letter writer Shearson, Hammill & Co., 1928-41; dir. research W.E. Hutton & Co., 1941-63, sr. analyst, sr. v.p., 1963—. Mayor, Westwood, N.J., 1934-37, mem. planning bd., 1945-48, chmn., 1945- 48. Trustee Cushing Acad. Served with USN, World War I. Mem. N.Y. Soc. Security Analysts (chmn. forum com. 1942-43, pres. 1943-44), Analyst's Club (chmn. 1944-45), Financial Analysts Fedn. (v.p. 1947, pres. 1948), Sigma Alpha Epsilon. Democrat. Methodist (trustee). Contbr. articles financial, econ. jours.; signed column in Forbes mag. Home: 1 Stratton Av Westwood NJ 07675 Office: 14 Wall St New York City NY 10005

HOOPER, PETER, Jr., fgn. service officer; b. Boston, June 9, 1920; s. Peter and Emily Mabel (Mullen) H.; B.A. in Govt., Yale, 1942; student internat. relations, Am. U., 1947; grad. U.S. Army War Coll., 1961; divorced; children—Peter III, Diana Ray, Eleanor Carol; m. 2d, Pamela Sheila Doutre, Dec. 22, 1960; 1 dau., Tanya Elizabeth. Dir. planning div. Office Fgn. Liquidation Commn., Washington, 1946-47; chief vets. affairs sect. Dept. of State, 1947; jointed U.S. Fgn. Service, 1947; vice consul, 3d sec. Am. mission, Berlin, Germany, 1947-48; assigned Am. missions in Baden-Baden, Frankfurt, Bonn (all Germany), 1948-52; 2d sec., polit. and mil. affairs officer Am. embassy, Taipei, Formosa, 1953; with Bur. German Affairs, State Dept., 1954-57; opened 1st U.S. fgn. service mission, Uganda, 1957; consul, prin. officer at Kampala to 1960; spl. asst. to dir. personnel Dept. of State, 1961-62, officer-in-charge Algerian affairs, 1962-63, dep. dir. So. African affairs, 1963-65; counselor, dep. chief of mission Am. embassy, Pretoria, South Africa, 1965-70; personnel officer for sr. assignments and career counseling Dept. State, Washington, 1971—. Mem. U.S. delegation Conf. Fgn. Ministers, Geneva, Switzerland, 1955. Served to lt. comdr. USNR, 1942-46. Recipient Superior Honor award Dept. State, 1971. Mem. Am. Fgn. Service Assn. Episcopalian. Contbr. articles. Home: 3544 Halfmoon Circle Falls Church VA 22044 Office: O/DG/PER Dept of State Washington DC 20520

HOOPER, VIRGINIA FITE, mem. Republican Nat. Com.; b. Byhalia, Miss., Sept. 23, 1917; d. Pleasant LaFayette and Nell Estelle (Brooks) Fite; B.S. in Econs., U. Ala., 1940; m. James Fullerton Hooper III, Jan. 29, 1943; children—Cynthia (Mrs. Rood), James Fullerton IV, Pleasant Fite. Vice chmn. Miss. Rep. Party, 1960-62; mem. Rep. Nat. Com. for Miss., 1962—; mem. Nat. Rep. Executive Com., 1969—. Mem. adv. bd. So. Debutante Assn.; past pres. Lowndes County Garden Council; mem. membership com. Miss. Heart Assn.; mem. Columbus City Beautification Com.; chmn. meml. gifts Lowndes County Heart Assn.; Mem. Lowndes County Kidney Found.; del. trustee Miss. Kidney Found. Named Outstanding Alumna of Chi Omega 1968; Outstanding G.O.P. Woman of Yr. for Miss., 1969. Mem. Nat. Assn. Jr. Auxs. (pres. 1949-50), Columbus C. of C. (chmn. merit awards 1960-62), D.A.R. (past regent), U.D.C., (past pres.), Nat. Assn. Parliamentarians, Lowndes County Soc. Preservation Antiquities, Columbus and Lowndes County Hist. Soc., Am. Legion Aux., Delta Beta Sigma (v.p. 1937), Chi Omega (pres. Nu Beta chpt. 1940, founder, past pres. N.E. Miss. alumna chpt.). Presby. (1st v.p. Women of Ch. 1969-70, circle leader, 1970-72). Mem. Order Eastern Star. Clubs: Columbus Country, Lowndes County Chowder and Marching Soc. (Columbus); Magowa Gun (Lowndes County, Miss.); Cherokee Garden (past pres.). Address: 800 8th St N Columbus MS 39701

HOOPES, DARLINGTON, Socialist party hon. chmn., lawyer; b. Vale, Md., Sept. 11, 1896; s. Price and Elizabeth L. (Tucker) H.; student U. Wis., 1914-15; studied law in office G. Herbert Jenkins, Norristown, Pa., 1917-21; m. Hannah L. Foulke, Oct. 21, 1921 (dec. Jan. 1923). m. 2d, Hazelette Miller, Oct. 16, 1925; children—Darlington, Rae, Delite. Admitted to Pa. bar, 1921; practiced in Norristown, 1921-27, Reading, 1927—; asst. city solicitor, Reading, 1928-32, city solicitor, 1936-40; dir. Eastern Coops., Inc., 1947-51. Mem. Socialist Party, 1914—, mem. nat. exec. com,, 1932-36, 44-68, nat. chmn., 1946-57, 60-68, hon. nat. chmn., 1968—; mem. Pa. Ho. of Reps., 1930-36; candidate for v.p. U.S., 1944, for pres. U.S. 1952, 56. Mem. exec. com. Pa. Council for Fair Employment Practices Com., 1948-58, vice chmn., 1954-58. Active YMCA, Boy Scouts Am.; v.p. Pa. Equal Rights Council, Reading Berks Human Relations Council; pres. Fellowship House of Reading, 1962-67. Bd. dirs. Equal Opportunity Council Reading and Berks County, 1964—. Mem. Am., Pa., Berks County bar assns., Comml. Law League Am., Am. Fedn. Tchrs., N.A.A.C.P. Mem. Society of Friends. Home: 1521 Greenview Av Reading PA 19601 Office: 212 N 6th St Reading PA 19601

HOOPES, DONELSON FARQUHAR, museum curator; b. Phila., Dec. 3, 1932; s. Donelson W. and Esther T. (Dechert) H.; student Pa. Acad. Fine Arts, 1950-53; B.A., U. Pa., 1960. Student asst. U. Mus. U. Pa., 1956-60; dir. Portland (Me.) Mus. Art, 1960-62; curator exhibits Corcoran Gallery Art, Washington, 1962-63, curator, 1963-64; curator paintings and sculpture Bklyn, Mus., 1965-69; research asso. 1969—; state adviser for Me., Am. Fedn. Arts, 1961-62; cons. N.Y. State Council on Arts, 1965—. Served with U.S. Army, 1953-55. Mem. Am. Assn. Museums, Coll. Art Assn.; Delta Phi. Author: (with others) Maine And Its Role in American Art, 1963; The Art of George L.K. Morris, 1965; The Private World of John S. Sargent, 1964; William Zorach; Paintings, Watercolors and Drawings, 1911-1922, 1968; Winslow Homer Watercolors, 1969; John S. Sargent Watercolors, 1970; Eakins Watercolors, 1971. Home: Glenrock Glendale Rd Ossining NY 10562

HOOPES, JOHN EUGENE, educator, plastic surgeon; b. Boone, Ia., Aug. 8, 1931; s. John Wilton and Olga (Peterson) H.; B.A., Rice U., 1953; M.D., John Hopkins, 1957; m. Nancy Phyllis Martin, May 27, 1967; children by previous marriage—John Wilton II, Molly Ozella, Duncan Rainey. Surg. intern Johns Hopkins Hosp., 1957-58; resident, 1958-59; resident plastic surgery U. Miss. Med. Center, 1959-62; U. Va. Med. Center, 1962-64; mem faculty Johns Hopkins Sch. Medicine, 1964-68; asso. prof. plastic surgery, plastic surgeon-in-chief Washington U. Sch. Medicine and Barnes and Allied Hosps., St. Louis, 1968-70; prof. plastic surgery, plastic surgeon-in-chief Johns Hopkins Sch. Medicine and Johns Hopkins Hosp., 1970—; cons. Children's Hosp., VA Hosp., USPHS Hosp., Baltimore City Hosps. Mem. Am. Soc. Plastic and Reconstructive Surgeons, Plastic Surgery Research Council, A.C.S., Am. Cleft Palate Assn., Am. Burn Assn., Soc. Head and Neck Surgeons, Phi Beta Kappa, Sigma Xi, Alpha Omega Alpha. Contbr. articles med. jours. Home: 1005 Poplar Hill Rd Baltimore MD 21210

HOOPES, LORENZO NEVILLE, retailing exec.; b. Brigham City, Utah, Nov. 5, 1913; s. Jesse W. and Matilda (Eastman) H.; student Weber Coll., 1931-33, U. Utah, 1934-35; grad. Harvard Sch. Bus. Administrn., 1952; m. Stella Sorenson, Apr. 9, 1938; children—David Craig, Janet. Engaged in coop. marketing agrl. commodities, 1935-40; operator egg shell processing plants, Ida., Cal., 1941-46; installed, supervised 25 egg processing plants in U.S., 1946-49, 15 fluid milk plants, 1949-53; exec asst. to sec. of agr., 1953- 54; exec. asst. to county mgr. and plant operations mgr. Lucerne Milk Co. div. Safeway Stores, Inc, 1949-59, mgr. dairy and egg div., 1959- 67; v.p., mgr., supply operations Safeway Stores, Inc., Oakland, Cal., 1963—, also dir. Pres. Oakland Bd. Edn. Bd. dirs. United Bay Area Crusade, Oakland Symphony Assn. Mem. Nat. Dairy Council (chm., sec., dir.). Mem. Ch. of Jesus Christ of Latter-day Saints (bishop). Rotarian (pres. 1945- 46). Home: 45 Mott Pl Oakland CA 94619 Office: 4th and Jackson Oakland CA 94607

HOOPES, THOMAS TEMPLE, mus. curator; b. Boston, Mar. 31 1898; s. Wilford Lawrence and Lillie Edith (Merrill) H.; A.B., Harvard, 1919; A.M., N.Y. U., 1926, Ph. D., 1931; m. Edith Kende, Aug. 7, 1936 (dec. Dec. 1954); m. 2d, Catherine Filsinger, June 8, 1964. Asst., asst. curator Met. Mus. Art, N.Y.C., 1920-27; pvt. study Orient, Europe, 1927-29; resident research fellow fine arts N.Y. U., 1929-30; lectr. art U. Chgo., 1931; Guggenheim fellow, research in Europe, 1932; spl. research fellow history fire arms Carnegie Found., 1934-36, on loan to Austrian govt, for reinstallation Austrian nat. collection firearms, 1935-36; curator City Art. Mus., St. Louis, 1963-64, curator emeritus, 1964—. Cons. museology, arms, armor, others; dir. Mus. Research Bur. Hyderabad, India. Served from ensign to lt. AC; USN, 1917-19. Recipient Verdienst Orden, Ritterkreutz (Austria), 1936. Hon. mem. Am. Soc. Arms Collectors. Clubs: Union (Boston); Harvard, Armor and Arms (past sec.) (N.Y.C.); University, St. Louis Arms Collectors (hon., past pres.) (St. Louis). Author: Armor and Arms. Contbr. articles to profl. publs. Home: 48 Washington Terrace St Louis MO 63112

HOOPLE, GORDON DOUGLASS educator, physician; b. Bklyn., Feb. 19, 1895; s. William Howard and Victoria Irene (Cranford) H.; B.S. Syracuse U., 1915, M.D., 1919, LL.D. (honoris causa), 1967; postgrad. in otolaryngology Mass. Eye and Ear Infirmary, Boston, 1925-26; m. Dorothea Brokaw, 1922. Intern, Bklyn Hosp., 1919-21, U. Hosp. Syracuse, N.Y. 1924; missionary hosp. work West China, 1922-23; prof. otolaryngology Syracuse U. Coll. Medicine, 1946-53, emeritus, 1953—, also dir. Hearing and Speech Center Former otolaryngology cons. N.Y. State VA; chmn. Onondaga County Hosp. Conf. Com., 1968, Onondaga Pastoral Counseling Center, 1968—. Trustee Syracuse U. chmn. emeritus; mem. bd. corporators Clarke Sch. for Deaf, Northampton, Mass., 1952-57; mem. specialist med. adv. group VA, 1958- 60; med. adviser Deafness Research Found., 1960—. Served as maj., AUS, 1942-45; Diplomate Am. Bd. Otolaryngology (pres. 1958-60). Mem. Am. Laryngological Rhinol. and Otol. Soc. (pres. 1958-59), Am. Acoustical Soc., Am. Phys. Soc., Central N.Y. Eye, Ear, Nose and Throat Soc., A.M.A. Onondaga County Med. Soc., Syracuse Acad. Medicine. Am. Otol. Soc., Inc. (pres. 1952), Am. Laryngol. Assn., Am. Acad. Ophthalmology and Otolaryngology, Syracuse U. Alumni Assn. (p.p.), Phi Beta Kappa, Sigma Phi Epsilon, Nu Sigma Nu, Sigma Xi, Alpha Omega Alpha. Republican. Methodist. Home: 801 Westmoreland Av Syracuse NY 13210 Office: 1100 E Genesse St Syracuse NY 13210

HOORNSTRA, EDWARD HANSEL, foods and services co. exec.; b. Sault Ste. Marie, Mich., Oct. 10, 1921; s. William John and Gertrude Helen (Brock) H.; grad. high sch.; m. Mildred Marguerite Smith, Dec. 20, 1941; children—Sharon Lynn (Mrs. John Snyder), Edward Hansel. Pres., C.E.O.-Food Services, Inc., Fla. and La., 1950-63; regional v.p. Li'l Gen. Stores, Inc., Tampa, Fla., 1963-64, v.p. operations, 1964-65, pres., chief exec. officer, 1966-69; v.p. operations Gen. Host Corp., N.Y.C., 1969-70, pres., 1970—, also dir.; dir. Tropicana Pools, Inc., Comml. Bank Tampa. Served with AUS, 1940-45. Mason (Shriner). Club: University (Tampa). Home: 1761 Long Bow Lane Clearwater FL 33516 Office: 245 Park Av New York City NY 10017

HOOS, SIDNEY SAMUELS, educator, economist; b. Buffalo, May 10, 1911; s. Jacob and Rose (Gerrish) H.; student U. Me., 1929-31; A.B., U. Mich., 1934, A.M., 1935; Ph.D., Stanford, 1939; fellow Inst. Freedon and Competitive Enterprise, Claremont Coll., 1954; m. Ida Russakoff, June 13, 1942; children—Phyllis Ellen (Mrs. Deleon), Judith Marjorie. Research fellow Food Research Inst., Stanford, 1936-38; instr. U. Cal. at Berkeley, 1938-41, asso. prof. agrl. econs., asso. economist expt. sta., asso. economist Giannini Found. Agrl. Econs. 1946-49, prof. agrl. econs., also prof. econs. and bus. adminstrn., economist expt. sta., Giannini Found, Agrl. Econs., 1950--, univ. dean acad. personnel, 1964-67; sr. economist, asst to pres. CCC, Dept. Agr., 1941-42; chief economist, dep. chief requirements br. Office Q.M. Gen., War Dept., 1942-45; cons. Falk Project Econ. Research, Israel, 1960-61, cons. Agrl. Settlement Dept., Jewish Agy., Israel, 1960-61; econ. cons. various agrl. products, agencies fed. and state govts. Recipient Commendation for Meritorious Service, War Dept., Citation of Merit, Am. Marketing Assn. Mem. Am., Pacific Coast econ. assns., Am. Statis. Assn., Econometric Soc., Am. (exec. com. 1951, editorial council 1954-57, exec. com. v.p. 1962-63), Western (exec. com. 1950-52, pres. 1951) farm econs. assns., Inst. Mgmt. Scis., Internat. Soc. Hort. Scis. Author monographs and articles on prices, prodn., marketing and agrl. policy. Home: 868 The Arlington Berkeley CA 97407

HOOT, WILLIAM JOHN, brewery exec.; b. Rochester, N.Y., Oct. 19, 1916; s. William Irving and Jenny Elizabeth (Raab) H.; A.B., U. Rochester, 1940; postgrad. Siebels Inst. Tech., 1946; m. Doris Allan Erskine, May 14, 1942; children—Jeanne Landreth, William Erskine. Asst. brewmaster Genesee Brewing Co., Rochester, 1946-50, purchasing agt., 1950-55, asst. to pres., 1955-58, v.p. sales, 1958-60, v.p. marketing, dir., 1960-69, pres., 1969—; mem. adv. com. Lincoln-Rochester Bank, 1970—. Treas., Upstate Beverage Inst., 1962—; mem. adv. com. Inst. Food Scis. and Marketing, Cornell U., 1971—. Trustee Genesee Hosp. Sch. Nursing. Served to lt. comdr. USNR, 1942-46. Mem. Psi Upsilon. Presbyn. (chmn. trustees). Club: Monroe Golf. Home: 371 Allens Creek Rd Rochester NY 14618 Office: 445 St Paul St Rochester NY 14605

HOOTEN, WILLIAM JARVIS, former newspaper editor; b. Chocowinty, N.C., Sept. 5, 1900; s. William Thomas and Martha (Jarvis) H.; student St. Paul's Sch., Beaufort, N.C., 1906- 10, Belhaven (N.C.) Sch. 1911-15; m. Grace Bull, June 17, 1922; children—William Pearce, Grace, Charles Carlton. Comml. and r.r. telegrapher, 1916-18; with A.P., 1918-27; reporter El Paso (Tex.) Herald, 1927-29, city editor, 1929-31; city editor El Paso Times, 1931, mng. editor, 1931-40, editor, 1940-56, v.p., editor, 1956- 70. Bd. dirs. Roderick Found. Mason (33, Shriner), Rotarian. Home: 3611 Clifton Av El Paso TX 79903

HOOVER, ALTA NEWKIRK (Mrs. Wayne Hoover), corp. exec;.; b. Joplin, Mo., Jan. 3, 1911; d. Jefferson and Izora (Pertuch) Newkirk; student U. Tex., Austin, 1959-60, U.S. Army Intelligence Sch., Dallas, 1961, Am. Mgmt. Assn., N.Y.C., 1965; m. Wayne Hoover, Dec. 25, 1947; 1 son, Francis Allen Collins. Sec. to chief engr. Caterpillar Mil. Engine Co., Decatur, Ill., 1942-45; sec. to pres. Decatur Brass Works, 1945-52; adminstrv. sec. acoustics div. Def. Research Lab., U. Tex., Austin, 1952-58; adminstrv. asst. Tex. Research Assos. Corp., Austin, 1958-61; corporate sec., chmn. bd. TRACOR, Inc., Austin, 1961—; asst. sec. Rudmose Assos., Richardson, Tex., 1963; corporate sec. Sulzer Labs., Rockville, Md., 1964-65; corporate sec. Allison Labs., Inc., LaHabra, Cal., 1965-67; corporate sec. Gen. Tech. Corp., Los Angeles, 1966- 70; corporate sec. No. Sci., Inc., Middleton, Wis., 1970—; asst. sec. TRACOR Indsl. Land Co., 1966—; sec. to chmn. bd. Tracor Computing Corp., Tracor Data Systems. Mem. adminstrv. com. TRACOR and affiliates retirement plans and savs. and thrift plan. Club: Balcones Country (Austin). Home: 4913 Strass Dr Austin TX 78731 Office: 6500 Tracor Lane Austin TX 78721

HOOVER, ARTHUR MCCALL, mfr.; b. Columbus, O., Mar. 27, 1901; s. Jacob B. and Alice R. (McCall) H.; m. Josephine E. Blacksten, Sept. 11, 1932; 1 dau., Ruth Ann (Mrs. Lynn H. Graves). With Ranco, Inc., Columbus, 1920—, beginning as engr., successively chief engr., factory mgr., and v.p., pres., now chmn., dir. Home: Route 1 Powell OH 43065 Office: 601 W 5th Av Columbus OH 43201

HOOVER, BENJAMIN B., educator. Prof. English Brandeis U. Office: Dept English Brandeis U Waltham MA 02154*

HOOVER, CALVIN BRYCE educator, economist, B. Berwick, Ill., Apr. 14, 1897; s. John Calvin and Margaret Delilah (Roadcap) H.; A.B., (Ill.) (ILL.) Coll., 1922, L.H.D., 1935; postgrad. U. Minn., 1923-25; Ph. D., U. Wis., 1922-23,25 Litt. D., Columbia, 1934; 1935;

LL. D., Case Western Res. U., 1968, Duke, 1970; m. Faith Miriam Sprole, July 5, 1919; children—Carol Faith, Sylvia Joan, Instr., Sch. Bus. U. Minn., 1923-25; asst. prof. econs. Duke U., Durham, N.C., 1925-27, prof., 1927—, dean Grad. Sch., 1937-47, now James B. Duke prof. econs. Cons. Nat. Resources Comm., 1937; cons. adv. comm. to Council of Nat. Def., 1940; dir. Research, Com. of the South, 1947; mem. Research and Analysis Div., O.S.S., 1941-44; chief economic intelligence and economic adviser U.S. group Control Council for Germany, 1945; mem. President's Com on Fgn. Aid, 1947: spl. adviser to U.S. rep. in Europe, E.C.A., 1948. Served as pvt. inf., U.S. Army, later in F.A., 1917-19; in battles of St. Mihiel and Meuse-Argonne. Recipient Medal of Freedom. Mem. Am. (pres. 1953), So. (pres. 1936) econ. assns., Assn. for Comparative Econs. (pres. 1964), Phi Beta Kappa. Clubs: Cosmos, Century Association. Author: Memoirs of Capitalism, Communism and Nazism (autobiography), 1965; also books on econs. Home: 1702 Duke University Rd Durham NC 27706 ☆

HOOVER, CHARLES M., appliance corp. exec., b. Okla., 1920; ed. Okla. State U., 1942. Gen. sales mgr. Marquette Corp. 1942-60; with Roper Corp., Kankakee, Ill., 1960—,chmn. bd., pres., chief exec. officer, 1967—, also dir.; chmn. bd., pres., chief exec. officer Roper Sales Corp.; pres. Eastern Products Corp. Home: 1255 S Poplar St Kankakee, IL 60901. Office: 1906 W Court St Kankakee IL 60901*

HOOVER, CLIFFORD DALE, educator, agronomist; b. nr. Alden, Kan., Feb. 16, 1907; s. John Mahlon and Clara Belle (Stewart) H.; student Sterling (Kan.) Coll., 1925-27; A.B., Kan. State Coll., Pittsburg, 1934, M.S. 1935; Ph.D., Ia. State U., 1939; m. Myrtle Louise McMullin, Aug. 16, 1931; children—Jack Clifford, Donald Gene, Darrel Dean. Prin., tchr. Oxford (Kan.) Grade Sch., 1927-32; prin. Gypsum (Kan.) Grade Sch., 1932- 33; teaching fellow Kan. State Coll., 1935; research asst. Ia. Agrl. Expt. Sta., 1935-39; asso. prof., agronomist Miss. State U. Exptl. Sta., College, 1939-46, head dept., 1946—. Fellow Am. Soc. Agronomy (sec- treas. Miss. sect.); mem. Soil Sci. Soc. Am., Crop Sci. Soc. Am., State Farm Bur. Fedn., Sigma Xi, Omicron Delta Kappa, Gamma Sigma Delta. Democrat. Baptist. Contbr. articles. profl. jours. Address: Box 5248 State College MS 39762 ☆

HOOVER, DWIGHT WESLEY, educator; b. Oskaloosa, Ia., Sept. 15, 1926; s. Homer Samuel and Ruth (Hull) H.; A.B., William Penn Coll., 1948; M.A. (T. Wistar Brown fellow), Haverford Coll., 1949; Ph.D., State U. Ia., 1953; m. Nannie Elizabeth Crosby, Aug. 14, 1954; children—Polly Ruth, Sara Adeline, Elizabeth Ann. Prof., head social sci. dept. Bethune-Cookman Coll., Daytona Beach, Fla., 1953-55, 58; asst. prof. gen. studies dept. Kan. State U., 1958- 59; mem. faculty Ball State U., Muncie, Ind., 1959—, asso. prof. history, 1963-67, prof., 1967—. Served to lt. USNR, 1955-58; Japan. Mem. Am. Assn. U. Profs., Am. Hist. Assn., Orgn. Am. Historians, Pi Gamma Mu, Phi Alpha Theta. Republican. Mem. Soc. Friends. Author: Understanding Negro History, 1968; Henry James Sr., and the Religion of Community, 1969. Home: 301 Wheeling Av Muncie IN 47303

HOOVER, FRANCIS LOUIS, educator, editor; b. Sherman, Tex., Mar. 12, 1913; s. Guy F. and Marie Louise Elizabeth (Louis) H.; B.S. (scholarship 1930-33), N. Tex. State U., 1933; M.A (scholarship 1934-35), Columbia, 1935; Ed. D., N.Y.U., 1942; student Art Students League, Sch. Social Research; m. Lucille Eddlemen, Sept. 1, 1935; 1 son, Jon Julien. Co-dir. LaSalle Art Gallery, N.Y.C., 1934-36; art dir. Carden Pvt. Sch., N.Y.C., 1934-36; free lance package designer, N.Y.C., 1934-36; asst. prof. art N. Tex. State Coll., 1936-40, Eastern Ill. U., 1941-44; prof. art, head dept. Ill. State U., Normal, 1944—, dir. Internat. Collection Child Art, Research Center Ewing Mus. of Nations, 1970—. editor Arts and Activities mag., 1951-66 editor Davis Publs., Inc., Worcester, Mass., 1966-70; publs. editor Art Resource Publs., Normal, 1964-66; dir. Fairway Gallery Art, Bloomington, Ill., 1962-67; rep. exhbns. in N.Y. Ill., Tex., 1935—; sponsor diennial exhbns. Am. Child Art, 1955, 57, 59, 61. Bd. dirs. Art Edn. Found., 1956-66. Recipient Merit award editorial excellence, 6th ann. editorial competition Indsl. Marketing. Assn., 1954. Mem. Nat. (exec. council 1959- 61). Ill. (pres. 1951) art edn. assns., Western Arts Assn. (pres. 1949). Nat. Ill. edn. assns ., Am. Assn. U. Profs., Am. Appraisers Assn., Delta Phi Delta, Phi Delta Kappa. Author: Guide for Teaching Art Activities in the Classroom, 1956; Art Activities for the Very Young, 1961; (filmstrip) Art and Activities in the Classroom, 1955; also numerous articles. Editor: Young Printmakers; Young Sculptors; Young Printmakers II. Travel in Middle and S. Am. to study archaeol. sites; research on Cuna Indians. Home: 305 N University A Normal IL 61761

HOOVER, FRED W., mfg. co. exec.; b. Tacoma, Mar. 1, 1918; s. Fred W. and Edith (Reid) H.; student U. Wash., 1937-38, U. Cal. at Berkeley, 1939-40, Harvard Grad. Sch. Bus., 1954; m. Genevive M. Fernan, July 9, 1942; children—Michael D., Merilyn A. (Mrs. James T. Bunch), F. Gary. With Carnation Co., 1938-59, pres. subsidiary Albers Miling Co., also dir. parent co.; sr. v.p. Langendorf Bakeries, San Francisco, 1960-61; now exec. v.p., gen mgr. metal div. Continental Can Co., Inc.; dir. U.S. Life. Served to maj. AUS, 1941-45. Home: 25 Sutton Pl S New York City NY 10022 Office: 633 3d Av New York City NY 10017

HOOVER, H. EARL, appliance mfg. co. exec.; b. Kansas City, Dec. 12, 1890; s. Frank Kryder and Effie Laura (Phelps) H.; B.S. in Engring., U. Mich., 1912; m. Miriam F. Ulvinen, Oct. 2, 1951; children—Gorden, Robert, John, H. Earl II. Engr. phosphate mines, Mt. Pleasant, Tenn., 1912-13; engring. asst. Hoover-Mason Phosphate Co., Chgo., 1913-18, pres., treas., 1935-52; v.p. Hoover Co., Chgo., 1915-53, vice chmn., 1953-54, chmn., 1954-56; v.p., dir. Hoover Co., Ltd., Hamilton, Ont., Can., 1915- 56; chmn. Ruhm Phosphate & Chem. Co., 1946-53. Pres. bd. edn., Glencoe, Ill., 1924-25. Trustee, v.p. Highland Park (Ill.) Hosp. Assn., 1935-43; founder, dir., fellow Palm Springs (Cal.) Desert Museum; founder, trustee The (H. Earl) Hoover Found.; adv. exec. bd. Chgo. council Boy Scouts Am.; voting trustee Chgo. YMCA: v.p., bd. dirs. Bishop McLaren Center, Sycamore, Ill. Hon. Colley fellow U. Mich., 1953; recipient Silver Beaver award Boy Scouts Am. Mem. Am. Soc. M.E., A.A.A.S., Indsl. Research Inst. (pres. 1940-41), Phi Delta Theta. Episcopalian (vestryman, treas.). Clubs: University, Farmers (Chgo.). Address: 1801 Green Bay Rd Glencoe IL 60022

HOOVER, HELEN D., author; b. Greenfield, O., Jan. 20, 1910; d. Thomas Franklin and Hannah (Gomersall) Blackburn; student Ohio U., 1927-29. DePaul U., U. Chgo., 1943-49; m. Adrian Everett Hoover, Feb. 13, 1937. Addressograph operator H. Paulsen Co., 1930; proofreader Audit Bur. Circulations, 1931-43; chemist Pitts. Testing Lab., 1943-45; prodn. metallurgist Ahlberg Bearing Co., 1945-48; free-lance writer, Minn. and N.M., 1954—. Recipient Annual Achievement award Metal Treating Inst., 1959. Mem. Authors Guild, Am. Platform Soc., Mystery Writers Am., Sierra Club, Nat. Audubon Soc., Wilderness Soc., Defenders of Wildlife, Nat. Wildlife Fedn., Nature Conservancy, Friends of the Sea Otter, Com. Preservation of Tule Elk, Humane Soc. U.S., Minn. Ornithologists Union, Mpls. Audubon Soc., Jersey Wildlife Preservation Trust, Internat. Council Bird Preservation, Internat. Union for Conservation of Nature, Fauna Preservation Soc., Save the Redwoods League, World Wildlife Fund, Nat. Cath. Soc. for Animal Welfare. Author: The Long-Shadowed Forest, 1963; The Gift of the Dear, 1966; Animals at My Doorstep, 1966; Great Wolf and the Good Woodsman, 1967; A Place in the Woods, 1969; Animals Near and Far, 1970. Patentee agrl. implement disks. Office: Brandt and Brandt 101 Park Av New York City NY 10017

HOOVER, JOHN EDGAR, dir. F.B.I.; b. Washington, Jan. 1, 1895; s. Dickerson N. and Annie M. (Scheitlin) H.; LL.B., George Washington U., 1916, LL.M., 1917, LL.D., 1935; LL.D., Pa. Mil. Coll., N.Y. U., 1936, Westminster Coll., 1937, Okla. Bapt. U., 1938, Georgetown U., 1939, Drake U., 1940, Notre Dame U., 1942, St. John's U., 1942, Rutgers U., 1943, U. Ark., 1943, Seton Hall Coll., 1944, Holy Cross Coll., 1944, Marquette U., 1950, Pace Coll., 1954, Morris Harvey Coll., 1959, Cath. U. Am., 1964; D.Sc., Kalamazoo Coll., 1937; D.C.L., U. of South, 1941. Mem. bars of Dist. Ct. U.S. for D.C., U.S. Ct. of Claims, U.S. Supreme Ct.; entered Dept. of Justice, 1917; spl. asst. to atty. gen. of U.S., 1919-21; asst. dir. Bur. of Investigation, 1921-24; dir. F.B.I., U.S. Dept. of Justice, 1924—. Hon. trustee George Washington U.; elected mem. nat. bd. Boys' Clubs of Am., 1943; mem. Nat. Ct. of Honor; hon. mem. nat. council Boy Scouts Am.; mem. nat. adv. council Girl Scouts Am. Recipient President's award for Distinguished Fed. Civilian Service, 1958; Great Living Americans award U.S. C. of C., 1958; Am. Citizenship award Jr. Order United Am. Mechanics, 1959; U.S. Senate resolution of commendation for distinguished service to U.S., 1961; Criss award Mut. Omaha, 1961; George Washington Honor Medal and other awards Freedoms Found.; Gold Medal Merit, Jewish War Vets, U.S., 1962; Pro Deo et Juventute award Nat. Cath. Youth Orgn., 1963; Americanization Gold Medal award and citation V.F.W., 1963. Hon. fellow Am. Bar Found.; life mem. Internat. Assn. Chiefs of Police; hon. mem. many police, sheriff and other law enforcement assns.; mem. Kappa Alpha, Omicron Delta Kappa, Delta Theta Phi, Alpha Phi Omega, Zeta Sigma Pi; hon. life mem. Internat. Assn. for Identification, Chief Constables Assn. Can. Presbyn. Mason (33, grand cross honour; K.T., Shriner), Order of De Molay (active mem. grand council). Author: Persons in Hiding, 1936; Masters of Deceit, 1958; A Study in Communism, 1962; J. Edgar Hoover on Communism, 1969; articles in numerous mags., law revs. and police jours. Club: Columbia Country. Office: FBI Dept of Justice Bldg Washington DC 20535

HOOVER, JOHN PAGE, educator, govt. adviser; b. Burlingame, Cal., Nov.7, 1910; s. Howard Lynn and Cora (Page) H.; student San Mateo Jr.Coll., 1927-29, Yale, 1933-34; A.B., Stanford University, 1931, A.M., 1932; Ph.D., Am. U., 1967; m. Virginia Lee Froman, Oct. 31, 1942; children—John Page, James, Virginia, Beverly. Regional tariffs expert Bur. Fgn. and Domestic Commerce, 1934-35; clk. to comml. attache Am. Legation, Guatemala City, 1936; asst. trade commr. Am. embassy, Havana, Cuba, 1936-39, vice consul, 1939-42; asst. comml. attache Am. embassy, Caracas, Venezuela, 1942-48; 1st sec. Am. embassy, Montevideo, Uruguay, 1948-50; asst. chief div. fgn. reporting services Dept. State, Washington, 1950-51; in charge econ. devel. affairs Bur. Inter-Am. Affairs, 1951-52, with bur., 1960-62; consul gen. Fedn. of Rhodesia and Nyasaland, 1952-54, Havana, Cuba, 1954-56; dir. U.S. operations mission to Haiti and counselor of embassy for econ. affairs, Port-au-Prince, Haiti, 1956-58; prof. sr. seminar fgn. policy Fgn. Service Inst., Dept. State, 1958-59; with OAS, 1962—, spl. adviser, 1964—; adj. asso. prof. Cath. U. Am., Washington, 1964—; professorial lectr. Am. U., Washington, 1967—. Home: 6622 Braeburn Pkwy Bethesda, MD 20034. Office: Pan Am Union Washington DC

HOOVER, JOSEPH SAMUEL, govt. ofcl.; b. Washington, Apr. 17, 1909; s. Ulysses Simpson Grant and Rose B. (West) H.; B.C.S., Benjamin Franklin U., 1932, M.C.S., 1933; LL.B., Georgetown U., 1937; passed C.P.A., D.C., 1933; m. Miriam Esther Zimmerman, Aug. 16, 1958; children—Joseph Samuel, Marie Elaine. Admitted to D.C. bar, 1938, since practiced in Washington; asso. dir. budget Dept. Air Force, 1949-57, chief asst. to dep. chief of staff materiel, 1958-60; dir. mgmt. evaluation, comptroller Dept. Def., 1960-61, dep. asst. sec. def. comptroller, 1961-66, prin. dep. asst. sec. of def. (comptroller), 1966—. Served from 2d lt. to col., USAAF, 1942-49; brig. gen. Res. Decorated Legion of Merit; recipient Exceptional Civilan Service award USAF, 1952, Nat. Civil Service League Merit citation 1955, Distinguished Civilan Service award Dept. Def., 1966. Mem. Am. Numismatic Assn., Gamma Eta Gamma. Club: Rod and Gun. Home: 3221 Military Rd NW Washington DC 20015 Office; Pentagon Washington DC 20301

HOOVER, JOSEPH SCHILTZ, vacuum cleaner mfr.; b. North Canton, O., Dec. 18, 1916; s. Daniel P. and Clarice (Schitz) H.; grad. Culver Mil. Acad., 1935; A.B., Dartmouth, 1939; student Babson Inst., 1940-41; m. Carol Jones, Oct. 7, 1948; children—Catherine, Elizabeth, Michael, Ann, Jane. With Hoover Vacuum Cleaner Co. (became Hoover Co. 1922), North Canton, O.,1940—, successively salesman, sales supr., sales research mgr. dealer relations, dir. pub. relations, 1940-55, v.p., sec., 1956-62, vice chmn., sec., 1962—, dir., 1950—. Active United Fund, Boy Scouts Am., YMCA; trustee Aultman Hosp. Served from pvt. to capt., AUS, 1941- 45. Mem. Canton (past pres.), Ohio (bd. dirs.) chambers commerce. Republican. Home: 286 Rose Lane Canton OH 44720 Office: 101 E Maple St North Canton OH 44720

HOOVER, LINN, geologist; b. Balt., Apr. 13, 1923; s. Z. Linn and Harriet (Beall) H.; A.B., U.N.C., 1948; M.A., U.Mich., 1951; Ph.D., U. Cal. at Berkeley, 1959; m. Joan Patricia Williams, Jan. 31, 1953; children—Peter Linn, Hilary Joan. Geologist U.S.Geol. Survey, 1948-60; exec. sec. div. earth scis. Nat. Acad. Sci., Washington, 1960-63; exec. dir. Am. Geol. Inst., Washington, 1963—. Served with AUS, 1943-45. Fellow Geol. Soc. Am.; mem. Am. Assn. Petroleum Geologists, Am. Geophys. Union. Republican. Episcopalian. Club: Cosmos (Washington). Home: 6902 Oakridge Av Chevy Chase MD 20015 Office: 2201 M St N W Washington DC 20037

HOOVER, RICHARD ANDREW, performing arts adminstr.; b. Indpls., July 4, 1914; s. Andrew and Mary Jane (Falk) H.; m. Barbara Ruth Henderson, Mar. 1, 1952; children—Meredith (Mrs. Armin E. Wille), Margery (Mrs. Charles H. Stull), Richard E., Michael A., Deborah M. Actor, stage mgr., asst. dir. Civic Theatre Indpls., 1931-38, dir., 1940-42; pres. agt. Pitts. Playhouse, 1938-40, gen. mgr., 1945-67; mng. dir. Milw. Performing Arts Center, 1967—; co- owner S. Shore Players, Cohasset, Mas., 1938-48; sr. lectr. Carnegie Inst. Tech., 1950-67; lectr. theatre mgmt. U. Wis., summers 1960-68. Served with inf. AUS, 1942-45. Decorated Bronze Star with cluster. Mem. ANTA (v.p. 1953-60). Home: 2233 N Summit Av Milwaukee WI 53202 Office: 929 N Water St Milwaukee WI 53202

HOOVER, ROBERT W., constrn. co. exec.; b. Huntington, Ind., Oct. 16, 1921; s. John S. and Hattie (Smethurst) H.; m. Marjorie A. DaPore, Sept. 17, 1949; children—Robert D., Barbara A., John S. Controller, Utah Radio Products Co., Inc., Huntington, 1946-55; asst. sec.-treas. Newport Steel Corp. (Ky.), 1956-57; with Merritt, Chapman & Scott Corp., from 1957, v.p. adminstrn., 1965-66, v.p., sec., from 1966; sec. Revday Industries, Indsl. Finance Corp. Served with USAAF, 1943-46, U.S. Army, 1950-52. Mem. Advt. Club N.Y.C. Presbyn. Home: 1916 Graymill Dr Scotch Plains NJ 07090

HOOVER, SAMUEL RANDOLPH, chemist; b. Elkins, W.Va., Nov. 13, 1910; s. Benjamin Milton and Sallie Wellford (Scott) H.; B.S., Davis and Elkins Coll., 1930; M.A., George Washington U., 1933; Ph.D., Georgetown U., 1940; m. Katherine Lacy, June 24, 1933; children—Benjamin Neff, Katherine Lacy (Mrs. J.C. Schwab). Staff, Am. Petroleum Inst., Nat. Bur. Standards, 1930-31; staff Dept. Agr., 1931—, successively research asst., chemist metabolism of nitrogen-fixing organisms, enzyme research, milk proteins, Emergency Rubber Project, treatment dairy wastes, chief of hide, leather and tanning materials sect., 1931-55, asst. dir. Eastern Utilization Research and Devel. div., 1955-60, asst. to adminstr. Agrl. Research Service, 1960-64, staff scientist Research Program Devel. and Evaluation Staff, Washington, 1964-65, asst. dep. adminstr. Agr. Research Service, 1965-70, asst. to asso. adminstr., 1970—, asst. research dir. Pres.' Commn. on Increased Indsl. Use of Agrl. Products, 1956-57; spl. study Rubber Devel. Corp., Haiti, 1943. U.S. rep. to India, Internat. Mission on Milk, 1955; adviser U.S. delegation 15th Dairy Congress, 1959. Trustee Davis and Elkins Coll. Recipient Borden award in chemistry of milk, 1956. Mem. Am. Chem. Soc., Am. Soc. Biol. Chemists, Am. Diary Sci. Assn., NRC, Soc. International Devel., Am. Inst. Chemists, A.A.A.S., Sigma Xi, Sigma Chi. Clubs: Cosmos (Washington). Contbr. articles to profl. publs. Home: 2017 Hillyer Pl Washington DC 20009 Office: Adminstrn Bldg US Dept Agr Washington DC 20250

HOOVER, THERESSA, Religious exec.; b. Fayetteville, Ark., Sept. 7, 1925; s. James Cortez and Rissie (Vaughn) H.; B.A., Philander Smith Coll., 1946; M.A., N.Y.U., 1962; Asso. dir. Little Rock Meth. Council, 1946-48; field worker womens' div. Meth. Ch., N.Y.U., 1948-58, Christian social relations worker, 1958-65, head sect. program and edn., 1965-68, head staff womens' div., 1968—. Mem. nat. bd. YWCA, 1963—; trustee Paine Coll., Augusta, Ga., Office: 475 Riverside Dr New York NY 10027

HOOVER, WILLIAM JAY, educator; b. Champaign, Ill., Mar. 26, 1928; s. Walter Scott and Dorothy Edwina (Green) H.; B.S., U. Ill., 1950, M.A., 1954, Ph.D., 1963; m. Ellen Louise Kesler, June 18, 1950; children—Michael, Jane, Laura. Food technologist QM Food and Container Inst., Chgo., 1950-51; asst. to dir. Refrigeration Research Found., Colorado Springs, Colo., 1953-56; adminstrv. v.p. Corn Industries Research Found., Washington, 1956-66; head dept. grain sci. and industry, Kan. State U., Manhattan, 1966—, also dir. Food and Feed Grain Inst. Cons. in field. Mem. Inst. Food Technologists, Assn. Am. Cereal Chemists, Am. Chem. Soc., Sigma Xi, Alpha Zeta, Gamma Sigma Delta, Phi Tau Sigma. Contbr. articles to profl. jours. Patentee in field. Home: 920 Fairway St Manhattan KS 66502

HOPE, ASHLEY GUY, educator; b. Norfolk, Va., Sept. 8, 1914; s. William Frank and Anne Elizabeth (Guy) H.; LL.B., U. Va., 1936, J.D., 1970; postgrad. Worcester Coll., 1936, Columbia, 1936-37, Princeton, 1944-45, Stanford, 1945, Nat. War Coll., 1955-56; M.A. in Internat. Affairs, George Washington U., 1964; Ph.D., Syracuse U., 1967; m. Janet Barker, June 1, 1949; children—Anne and Jean (Mrs. Robert N. Nye) (twins). Admitted to Va. bar, 1935; practice in Richmond, 1937-39; atty., later clk. spl. congl. com. for investigation NLRB, 1939-40; atty. D.C. Unemployment Compensation Bd., 1940-41; asst. dir. securities div. Va. Corp. Commn., 1941; fgn. service officer, 1946-64, assigned successively Shanghai, Dairen, Brussels, Tel Aviv, 1946-49, staff Office Chinese affairs, 1950-55; consul, Istanbul, 1956-58; officer-in-charge Turkish affairs, 1958-60; dep. dir. Office Near Eastern and So. Asian Regional Affairs, 1960-61, dir., 1961-62; dep. chief of mission Am. embassy, Abidjan, Ivory Coast, 1962-63; dir. multilateral policy planning staff Bur. Ednl. and Cultural Affairs, 1963-64; acting dir. South Asia program Syracuse U., 1964-65, lectr. polit. sci. Maxwell Grad. Sch., 1965-67; prof. govt. Western Ky. U., 1967-69; prof. politics, dir. social and behavioral scis. program St. Andrews Presbyn. Coll., 1969-71; lectr. polit. sci. Va. Commonwealth U., 1971—; Cons. State Dept. Fgn. Service Inst., Washington, 1966-67; adviser U.S. Delegation UN Gen. Assembly, 1960- 61. Served from ensign to comdr., USNR, 1941-45. Mem. Internat. Studies Assn., Am. Fgn. Service Assn., Am. Polit. Sci. Assn., Am. Acad. Polit. and Social Sci., Am. Assn. Asian Studies, Phi Alpha Delta. Episcopalian. Clubs: Internat., Dacor (Washington). Author: America and Swaraj, 1968. Contbr. articles profl. jours. Home: 2011 Monument Av Richmond VA 23220

HOPE, BOB, radio, film, tv comedian; b. London, Eng., D.F.A. (hon.), Brown U., 1968. Began in vaudeville and has also appeared on stage; now in motion pictures, TV, radio. Has appeared in (stage); "Roberta"; Ziegfeld Follies; Red Hot and Blue, 1936; (motion pictures) Big Broadcast of 1938; College Swing, 1938; Give Me a Sailor, 1938; Thanks for the Memory, 1938; Never Say Die, 1938; Some Like It Hot, 1939; Cat and the Canary, 1939; The Road to Singapore, 1940; The Ghost Breakers, 1941; Caught in the Draft, 1941; Nothing But the Truth, 1941; Road to Zanzibar, 1941; Louisiana Purchase, 1942; Road to Morocco, 1942; My Favorite Blonde, 1942; They Got Me Covered, 1943; Let's Face It, 1943; The Road to Utopia, The Princess and the Pirate, Road to Rio, Where There's Life, My Favorite Brunette, 1946; Variety Girl, 1947; Road to Rio, 1947; Paleface, 1947; Sorrowful Jones, 1948; Fancy Pants, 1949; Lemon Drop Kid, 1950; My Favorite Spy, 1951; Son of Paleface, 1951; Military Policemen, 1952; Road to Bali, 1952; 7 Little Foys, 1955; Off Limits, 1953; Here Come the Girls, 1953; Casanova, 1953; That Certain Feeling, 1956; Iron Peticoat, 1957; Beau James, 1957; The Facts of Life, 1961. Dir., Cleve. Indians Baseball Club, 1963—. Recipient radio- television citation, 1951; Variety Clubs Internat. Humanitarian award, 1968; spl. citation for newspaper columns from Vietnam at Christmas Overseas Press Club, 1968; Peabody award in recognition of three decades in broadcasting, 1968, Pub. Service award Dept. Navy, 1971. Author: I Never Left Home, 1944; They Got Me Covered, 1941; So This is Peace, 1946; Have Tux, Will Travel; Alias Jesse James, 1959; I Owe Russia $1200, 1963. Entertained Service Forces, overseas, 1945. Home: 10346 Moorpark North Hollywood CA Address: care Paramount Studios Hollywood CA 90028

HOPE, CLARENCE CALDWELL, Jr., banker; b. Charlotte, N.C., Feb. 5, 1920; s. Clarence Caldwell and Margaret Boyd (Kidd) H.; diploma Mars Hill Coll., 1941; B.S., Wake Forest Coll., 1943; diploma Harvard Grad. Sch. Bus. Adminstrn., 1944, Rutgers U. Grad. Sch. Banking, 1953, 56; m. Mae D. Duckworth, Feb. 5, 1944; children—Stephen Douglas, Clarence Caldwell III, Joan Jennings. With Esso Standard Oil Co., 1946-47; with First Union Nat. Bank N.C., Charlotte, 1947—, successively br. mgr., Dilworth, mgr. credit dept., asst. cashier, asst. v.p., v.p., 1949-56, sr. v.p., 1956-60, exec. v.p., 1960—, also dir., sec. bd.; dir. First Union Nat. Bancorp, Inc. Bd. dirs., past pres. Mecklenburg County chpt. A.R.C., also mem. southeastern area adv. council, fund vice chmn. for N.C.; mem. social planning council United Appeal; pres. Central Charlotte Assn.; pres. N.C. Symphony Soc., Inc. Trustee Wake Forest U. (v.p. bd.); trustee Pub. Library Charlotte and Mecklenburg Counties, N.C. Bapt. Hosp. Served to lt. USNR, World War II. Mem. N.C. Bankers Assn., Charlotte Mchts. Assn. (treas., dir., chmn. finance com.), Assn. Res. City Bankers, Charlotte, C. of C., Robert Morris Assos. (past pres. Carolina-Virginias chpt.), Newcomen Soc., Wake Forest Coll. Central Charlotte Assn. (past pres.), Omicron Delta Kappa, Sigma Phi Epsilon. Baptist. Clubs: Charlotte Country, Executives, Harvard,

Myers Park County, City (Charlotte, N.C.); Army-Navy (Washington). Home: 3807 Pomfret Lane Charlotte NC 28211 Office: 301 S Tryon St Charlotte NC 28201

HOPE, CLAUDE ALLISON, lawyer; b. Airmount, Ala., Nov. 5, 1893; s. Robert Milton and Lucy (Crawford) H.; A.B., U. Ala., 1914; LL.B., Columbia, 1917; m. Florence Legg, Feb. 23, 1918; children—Robert M., Leighton A. Admitted to N.Y. bar, 1920; law clk., Hughes, Schurman & Dwight, N.Y.C., 1917; spl. atty. Bur. Internal Revenue, Washington, 1921-22; mem. Delafield, Thorne & Burleigh (now Delafield, Hope, Linker & Blane), 1923—; law practice specializing in taxation, estates and trusts; dir. Upland Meadows, Inc. Served to maj. judge adv. U.S. Army, World War I; mem. Bd. Contract Adjustment, 1919. Mem. Am. Bar Assn., Assn. Bar City N.Y., Ala. Alumni Assn. (pres. N.Y. chpt. 1961-63), Kappa Alpha. Republican. Methodist. Clubs: University (N.Y.C.); Gipsy Trail (Carmel, N.Y.); Columbia University Home: 40 E 66th St New York City NY 10021 Office: 342 Madison Av New York City NY 10017

HOPE, HENRY RADFORD, editor, art historian; b. Chelsea, Mass., Dec. 15, 1905; s. Frank Radford and Blanche (Lovett) H.; student, Columbia, 1931; certificate Sorbonne, 1937; M.A., Harvard, 1941, Ph.D., 1942; m. Dorothy Weil, Apr. 11, 1927 (div. Apr. 1944); m. 2d, Sarahanne Adams, June 3, 1944; children—Adams McClennen, James McClennen, Helen McClennen, Sarah Jane, Roy, Ray. Grad. asst. dept. fine arts Harvard, 1939-40; chmn. fine arts dept. Ind. U., 1941-67, dir. Art Museum, 1961-70; editor Coll. Art Jour., 1942-49, 52-60, editor of Art Jour., 1960—; chmn. editorial bd. Mag. Art, 1958-61. Mem. U.S. Nat. Commn. for UNESCO, 1951-63. Trustee Ft. Lauderdale (Fla.) Mus. of Arts. Ben- jamin Franklin fellow Royal Soc. Arts; mem. Coll. Art Assn. (pres. 1949-51, trustee), Am. Fedn. Art (trustee). Author: Catalogue of Exhibition of work of Georges Braque, 1949; Catalogue of Exhibition of Sculpture of Jacques Linchitz, 1954. Home: 1 Las Olas Circle Fort Lauderdale FL 33316

HOPE, LESLIE TOWNE, see Hope, Bob.

HOPE, NORMAN VICTOR, educator; b. Edinburgh, Scotland, Apr. 7, 1908; s. Alexander and Margaret Duff (Symons) H.; grad. George Heriot's Sch., Edinburgh, 1925; M.A. with double 1st class honors in History and Econ. Sci., U. Edinburgh, 1930, B.D. summa cum laude, 1933, Ph.D., 1944; student U. Berlin (Germany), 1933-34; m. Isabella Logan, Aug. 24, 1935 (dec.); m. 2d, Wanda Swoll Christiff, 1967. Came to U.S., 1938, naturalized, 1954. Ordained to ministry Ch. of Scotland, 1935; minister, Glasgow, Scotland, 1935-38; lector systematic theology New Brunswick (N.J.) Sem., 1938-39, James Suydam prof. systematic theology, 1939-46; Archibald Alexander prof. ch. history Princeton Theol. Sem., 1946—, chmn. dept. history, 1946-59, 71—. Mem. Scottish Ch. History Soc., Phi Beta Kappa. Author: One Christ, One World, One Church, 1953. Home: 98 Mercer St Princeton NJ 08540

HOPE, QUENTIN MANNING, educator; b. Stamford, Conn., Jan. 25, 1923; s. Frank Radford and Blanche (Lovett) H.; B.A., Harvard, 1942, M.A., 1946; Ph.D., Columbia, 1956; m. Nathalie Weaver, May 22, 1944; children-Kenneth, Geoffrey, Persis. Tchr. French, Los Alamos Ranch Sch., 1942; tchr. Elisabeth Irwin High Sch., 1946-51; Cutting traveling fellow, Paris, 1952-53; instr. Wesleyan U., Middletown, Conn., 1953-56; asst. prof. Ind. U., Bloomington, 1956-61, asso. prof., 1961-66, prof., 1966—, chmn. dept. French and Italian, 1965—; postdoctoral Fulbright fellow, Paris, 1962- 63; mem. grad. student fgn. lang. test com. Ednl. Testing Service, 1968- -, grad. record exam. com., 1969—. Served with Am. Field Service, 1943- 45. Mem. Modern Lang. Assn., Am. Assn. Tchrs. French, Phi Beta Kappa. Author: Saint-Evremond, the honnte homme as Critic, 1962; Spoken French in Review, 1963; Reading French for Comprehension, 1965. Contbr. articles profl. jours. Home: 800 Sheridan Rd Bloomington IN 47401

HOPF, HANS, tenor; b. Nuremberg, Germany, Aug. 2, 1916; s. Johann H. and Anna (Müller) H.; studied with Kammersänger Paul Bender, Munich, also Ragnwald Bjärne, Oslo, Norway; m. Ilse Löschner. Performed opera houses of Munich, Augsburg, Oslo, Dresden, Berlin and Vienna; participated Bayreuth and Salzburg festivals; performed La Scala, Milan, Rome Opera, festivals in Florence, Dublin, Monte Carlo, Rio de Janeiro, Barcelona, Covent Garden Opera in London; mem. Metropolitan Opera, N.Y.C., 3 seasons. Recipient title of Kammersänger. Address: Steinebach Wörthsee Bayern West Germany

HOPFIELD, JOHN JOSEPH, educator; b. Chgo., July 15, 1933; s. John Joseph and Helen (Staff) H.; A.B., Swarthmore Coll., 1954; Ph.D., Cornell U., 1958; m. Cornelia Fuller, June 30, 1954; children—Alison, Jessica, Natalie. Mem. tech. staff Bell Telephone Labs., 1958-60; vis. research physicist Ecole Normale Superieure, Paris, France, 1960-61; asst. prof., then asso. prof. physics U. Cal. at Berkeley, 1961-64; prof. physics Princeton, 1964—. Guggenheim fellow, 1969. Fellow Am. Phys. Soc. (Oliver E. Buckley prize 1968); mem. Phi Beta Kappa, Sigma Xi. Home: 183 Hartley Av Princeton NJ 08540

HOPKIN, MARY ELIZABETH BLODWEN, entertainer; b. Ystradgynlais, Breconshire, South Wales, May 3, 1950; d. David Howel and Marie Elizabeth Jane (Morgan) Hopkin; grad. Pontardawe Grammar Sch., Pontardawe, Swansea, Glamorganshire, Wales, 1968. First appearance on talent show Opportunity Knocks, 1968; recording artist for Apple Records. Mem. hon. bd. of Gorsedd of Royal Nat. Eisteddfod of Wales, 1970—. Recipient 3 Golden Discs. Home: 29 Brynawel Rd Pontardawe Swansea Glamorganshire Wales Office: AMA 24/25 New Bond St London W 1 England

HOPKINS, ALBERT LAFAYETTE, lawyer; b. Hickory, Miss., Apr. 27, 1886; s. Oliver and Helen V. (Tucker) H.; student Millsaps Coll., 1900-01, U. Miss., 1901-02; A.B., U. Chgo., 1905, J.D., 1908; LL.B., Harvard, 1909; m. Florence Odil, Apr. 19, 1922; children—Nancy H. Gerson, Catharine H. Ruml, Albert Lafayette. Admitted to Ill. bar, 1908; asst. U.S. atty. No. dist. Ill., 1913-17; asst. counsel ICC, Washington, 1917-19; spl. atty. Internal Revenue Bur., 1919; mem. firm Hopkins, Sutter, Owen, Mulroy & Davis, Chgo., Democrat. Methodist. Clubs: Chicago, Legal, Law, Mid-Day, Flossmoor Country, Mid-America. Author: Autobiography of a Lawyer; Save Our Country. Home: 1308 E 58th St Chicago IL 60637 Office: 1 First National Plaza Chicago IL 60670

HOPKINS, BERT EARL, lawyer, educator; b. Bowdon, N.D., Nov. 16, 1902; s. William H. and Marie (Larson) H.; Ph.B., U. Wis., 1924; LL.B., Yale, 1927; LL.M., Columbia, 1939, J.S.D., 1944; m. Marie Hayes, Aug. 22, 1931; 1 son, William Hayes. Admitted to Minn. bar, 1927; practiced law, St. Paul, 1927-29; state investigator and examiner Travelers Ins. Co., 1927-29; prof. law U. Ida., 1929-45, Ind. U., 1945-46; dean, prof. law U. Conn., 1946-66, Univ. prof. law, 1966—. Mem. Am. Conn. bar assns. Author: Monograph on Conflict of Laws in Administration of Decedents' Estates, 1944; also contbr. articles to profl. jours. Home: 37 Middlefield Dr West Hartford CT 06107

HOPKINS, CHARLES HOWARD, educator; b. Ukiah, Cal., Apr. 14, 1905; s. Charles Blodgett and Lucia (Cleveland) H.; A.B., U. Redlands, 1931; B.D., Yale, 1934, Ph.D., 1937; m. E. Winifred Hawes, June 28, 1941; children—Peter, Anne. Ordained minister United Ch. of Christ; instr. history Mt. Hermon (Mass.) Sch., 1937-39; chmn. div. social scis. Stockton (Cal.) Coll., 1939-44; asso. prof. ch. history Bangor (Me.) Theol. Sem., 1944-47; vis. asso. prof. Bible, Scripps Coll., Claremont, Cal., 1947-48; asso. prof. religion Coll. of Pacific, Stockton, Cal., 1941-44; historian Nat. Council YMCA, N.Y.C., 1948-50; dean, prof. history Stetson U., 1950-58; dean Westminister Choir Coll., Princeton, N.J., 1958-65, prof., 1965-68; prof. history, dir. interim study program Rider Coll., Trenton, N.J., 1968—: prof. history Rutgers-The State U., part-time 1965- 66; vis. lectr. Am. ch. history Pacific Sch. Religion, spring 1941; lectr. religion U. So. Cal., summer 1947; Gay lectr. So. Bapt. Theol. Sem., 1954. Pres. Fla. Assn. Colls. and Univs., 1954-55; biographer John R. Mott Biography project Nat. Council YMCA and Nat. Council Chs. Christ U.S.A., 1966—. Fellow Soc. for Religion Higher Edn.; mem. Am. Assn. U. Profs., Am. Hist. Assn., Orgn. Am. Historians, Am. Soc. Ch. History, Am. Studies Assn., Omicron Delta Kappa, Pi Kappa Delta, Alpha Phi Gamma, Pi Gamma Mu. Author: The Rise of the Social Gospel in American Protestantism, 1865-1915, 1940; History of the YMCA in North America, 1951; also articles. Home: 3 Windsor Dr Princeton Junction NJ 08550 Office: Rider Coll Trenton NJ 08602

HOPKINS, DAN WALTON, banker; b. Macon, Ga., Apr. 22, 1937; s. McDaniel and Bernice (Walton) H.; B.B. A. with distinction, Emory U., 1959; M.B.A., Harvard, 1961; m. Cecelia Ann Hearn, 1958 (dec. 1966); children-Suzanne, Valerie; m. 2d, Evelyn Irene Cartee, June 21, 1967; 1 dau., Melanie. Mem. mgmt. tng. program First Nat. Bank, Atlanta, 1961-63, asst. cashier, 1964-66, asst. v.p., 1967-68, v.p., 1969; v.p. Commerce Union Bank, Nashville, 1969, sr. v.p. charge credit standards group, 1970—; dir. Pepsi-Cola Bottling Co., Valdosta, Ga., Pepsi-Cola Bottling Co. of Crisp, Inc., Cordele, Ga. Mem. Omicron Delta Kappa, Chi Phi, Beta Gamma Sigma. Lion. Clubs: Harvard Business School, Cherokee Town and Country (Atlanta); Nashville City, Hillwood Country (Nashville). Home: 213 Robin Hill Rd Nashville TN 37205 Office: 400 Union St Nashville TN 37219

HOPKINS, DAVID LUKE, former banker; b. Balt., Dec. 29, 1898; s. Robert Dixon and Isabel (Luke) H.; A.B., Princeton, 1921; LL.D., Goucher Coll. 1952; m. Katherine Disston Porter, Feb. 12, 1927; children—David Luke, Charles A.P., Florence D. (Mrs. Charles A. Borda III), Katherine P. (Mrs. Charles H. Mellon III). With Drovers & Mechanics Nat. Bank, Balt., 1921-30, v.p., 1925-30; exec. v.p., dir. Mercantile-Safe Deposit & Trust Co., 1946-54; v.p., dir. Md. Trust Co., Balt., 1930-45; ret. chmn. Md. Nat. Bank, Balt., now dir.; dir., exec. com. Chespeake & Potomac Tel. Co. Md., Fidelity & Deposit Co. Md., Savs. Bank Balt.; dir. Balt. Equitable Soc. Chmn. Balt. Emergency Relief Commn., 1933-35, Balt. Civil Works Adminstrn., 1933; mem. AEC security survey panel AEC, 1950-52; past commr. Md. Port Authority; asst. sec. gen. NATO, 1952-53. Former mem. bd. mgrs. Family Welfare Assn., Balt. Council Social Agys., Henry Watson Children's Aid Soc., pres. (1930- 34); trustee Johns Hopkins, Johns Hopkins Hosp.; chmn. Johns Hopkins Fund, 1958-61; pres. Evergreen House Found., 1963-64; chmn. bd. trustees Walters Art Gallery; trustee Chpt. of Protestant Episcopal Found. D.C. (Washington Cathedral), Greater Balt. Med. Center; bd. mgrs. Harriet Lane Home for Invalid Children; bd. dirs. Loudon Park and Druid Ridge Cemeteries, 1931-70; authorized rep. Applied Physics Lab., Johns Hopkins, 1942-46. Served with USN, World War I. Recipient medal of Merit, 1946. Mem. Internat. Assn. Nav. Congresses (internat. commn. U.S. nat. commn. 1959-64), Council Fgn. Relations. Episcopalian. Clubs: Maryland, Elkridge, Metropolitan (Washington); Brook (N.Y.C.) Home: Tyrconnell 120 Woodbrook Lane Baltimore MD 21212 Office: PO Box 987 Baltimore MD 21203

HOPKINS, ELLIE, editor, writer; b. Meridian, Miss., May 26, 1909; s. Jack W. and Elizabeth (Swanner) H.; student E. Tex. Bapt. Coll., 1927-29; m. Nina Hall, Apr. 8, 1933; children—Mary Beth (Mrs. James Quillen), Jack Hall. Proofreader, reporter Marshall (Tex.) News Messenger, 1928- 29; news editor Jefferson (Tex.) Jour., 1930; with Longview (Tex.) Daily News and Longview Morning Jour., 1930—, editor-in-chief, 1945—, v.p., 1967—; editor Texas Oil Jour., 1945—; dir. Lone Star Steel Co., Dallas. Mem. bd. lectrs. Freedoms Found., Valley Forge, Pa., 1963-65; mem. pub. relations adv. bd. Bapt. Gen. Conv. Tex., 1958-60. A founding sponsor, mem. first bd. dirs. Longview (Tex.) YMCA, 1954- 55; bd. dirs. LeTourneau Coll., Longview, 1959-65, Recipient George Washington Honor medal for editorials Freedoms Found., 1952, 53, 54, 55, 56, 62, 63, 69; Press award for religious news writing Tex. Bapt. Conv., 1957; Sam C. Holloway Meml. award N. and E. Tex. Press Assn., 1969. Mem. Tex. Press Assn. (pres. 1970-71), Assn. Petroleum Writers (past dir.), N. and E. Tex. Press Assn. (pres. 1966-67). Baptist (deacon.). Rotarian (pres. Longview 1953-54). Home: 1603 Hillmont Av Longview TX 75601 Office: 314 E Methvin St Longview TX 75601

HOPKINS, EVERETT HAROLD, educator; b. Linville, O., Oct. 24, 1912; s. John F. and Clara May (Dillon) H.; B.S., Wittenberg U., 1934, LL.D., 1958; M.A., U. Pa., 1935; student U. Minn., summers, 1939, 41, 48; m. Bernice Brubaker, June 15, 1939; children—Jay Everett, David Harold, Richard Alan. Asst. dir. personnel and instr. psychology Wittenberg U., Springfield, O., 1935-37; freshman adviser, instr. psychology Miami U., Oxford, O., 1937-40; asst. prof. psychology, dir. asso. in arts program, 1940-42; asst. to pres. Wash. State Coll., 1946, dean students, 1947, v.p., 1947-51; asso. dean faculties Washington U., St. Louis, 1951-52, asst. to chancellor, 1952-54, vice chancellor, 1954-61; v.p. instnl. advancement, asst. provost, prof. edn. Duke, 1961-63, v.p. planning and instl. studies, prof. edn. 1963- 66, v.p. regional programs, asst. provost, prof. edn., 1966-70, prof. edn., 1970—; pres. Regional Edn. Lab. for Carolinas and Va., 1967-71, Nat. Lab. Higher Edn., 1971—. Cons. higher edn. U.S. Office Edn. and to individual colls. and univs., also mem. tech. adv. com. on regional higher edn. to 11 western govs., 1949-51; chmn. Wash. state survey com. on higher edn., 1949-51; mem. exec. com. Nat. Conf. Mblzn. Edn., 1950-51; mem. council advisers to U.S. commr. edn., 1950-52. Trustee Learning Inst.; bd. dirs. Council Ednl. Devel. and Research, 1971—. Served to lt. comdr. USNR, 1942-46; dir. personnel U.S. Naval Tng. Center, Farragut, Ida., 1942-45; officer in charge West Coast Naval Classification Centers, 1945-46. Recipient Outstanding Achievement award in pub. relations for higher edn. Am. Coll. Pub. Relations Assn., 1958. Mem. Am. Coll. Pub. Relations Assn. (trustee 1961-64, chmn. devel. sect. 1958- 59), Nat. Soc. Study Edn., N.E.A., Am. Psychol. Assn., Assn. Higher Edn., A.A.A.S., Am. Acad. Polit. and Social Sci., Assn. Instl. Research, Am. Edn. Research Assn., Soc. Research Higher Edn., Crimson Circle, Kappa Phi Kappa, Phi Delta Kappa, Psi Chi, Alpha Tau Omega, Phi Kappa Phi, Phi Eta Sigma, Kappa Delta Pi, Omicron Delta Kappa. Methodist. Contbr. ednl. jours. Home: 1520 Pinecrest Rd Durham NC 27705

HOPKINS, FRANK SNOWDEN, assn. exec.; b. Gloucester County, Va., Mar. 8, 1908; s. Nicholas Snowden and Selina Lloyd (Hepburn) H.; A.B., Coll. William and Mary, 1927; A.M., Columbia, 1928; postgrad. Johns Hopkins, 1936-38, (Nieman fellow) Harvard, 1938-39; m. Ruth Hazen, Oct. 20, 1934; children— Nicholas Snowden, Martha Hazen, Richard Snowden. Editorial asst. D. Appleton & Co., pubs., 1929; reporter, feature writer Mpls. Star, 1930-31, Richmond (Va.) Times-Dispatch, 1933-36, Balt. Sun, 1936-41; dir. tng. Md. Drydock Co., Balt., 1941-45; with Dept. State, 1945-68, asst. chief div. tng. services, 1945-47, asst. dir. Fgn. Service Inst., 1947-51, State Dept. mem. faculty Army War Coll., 1951; consul, sec. Diplomatic Service, pub. affairs officer, Stuttgart, Germany, 1952; dep. dir. UNESCO Relations Staff, 1956-58; consul, Martinique, 1958-60; consul gen., Melbourne, 1960-64; dir. Office U.S. Programs, Bur. Edn. and Cultural Affairs, Dept. State, 1964-68; spl. asst. long range planning Policy Planning Council, 1967-68; Washington chmn. World Future Soc., 1968—. Mem. Phi Beta Kappa, Sigma Nu. Episcopalian. Clubs: Cosmos, Kenwood Golf (Washington); 14 West Hamilton St. (Balt.). Contbr. articles to popular, profl mags., chpts. to book on fgn. affairs and futuristic topics. Home: 5108 Lawton Dr Washington DC 20016 Office: Box 19285 20th St Sta Washington DC 20036

HOPKINS, FREDERICK MERCER, Jr., former air force officer; b. N.Y.C., June 8, 1895; s. Frederick Mercer and Cora Belle (Collins) H.; student Columbia, 1914-17; B.S., N. Y. U., 1926; grad. Air Corps Engring. Sch., 1932, AC Tactical Sch., 1937, Command and Gen. Staff Sch., 1938; m. Henrietta Marsh, Sept. 9, 1920; children—Henrietta Marsh (Mrs. Rupert W. Jernigan, Jr.), Frederick Mercer III. Commd. 2d lt., C.A. Res., 1918, and advanced through grades to maj. gen. USAF, 1947; Command pilot, combat observer, aircraft observer; dir. Observation Flying, AC Advanced Flying Sch., 1924-25; asst. prof. mil. sci. and tactics N.Y.U., 1926-30; comdt. AC Engring. Sch., 1932-36; instr. AC Tactical Sch., Maxwell Field, Ala., 1938- 40; chief, resources div., material and service Hdqrs. U.S. Army Air Corps, 1940-45; comdg. gen. Army and Navy Forces, Iwo Jima, 1945-46, 20th Air Force, Guam, 1946, Pacific Air Service Command and Far East Air Materiel Command, Manila, P.I., and Fuchu, Japan, 1946-1947; dep. comdg. gen. operations Air Materiel Command, Dayton, O., 1947-51; ret. 1951. Gen. campaign chmn., v.p. Cleve. chpt. Arthritis and Rheumatism Found., 1954-55, pres., gen. campaign chmn., 1956; vice chmn. commerce and industry div. Cleve. Community Chest, 1953-56; mem. Mayor's Traffic Safety Com., aviation sub- com. Dept. Port Control, Cleve., cadet selection bd. Civil Air Patrol. Decorated D.S.M., Legion of Merit with oak leaf cluster. Fellow Inst. Aero. Scis. (vice chmn. Cleve.-Akron sect. 1954-55), Ohio C. of C. (dir.), Scabbard and Blade, Arnold Air Soc., Tau Beta Pi, Iota Alpha, Sigma Nu. Clubs: Union (Cleve.) ; Mid-Day, Quiet Birdmen; Shaker Heights Country. Home: 16120 Parkland Dr Shaker Heights OH 44120

HOPKINS, GARLAND EVANS, clergyman, cons. internat. affairs; b. Saluda, Va., Dec. 28, 1913; s. Edward Henry and Zipporah (Evans) H.; A.B., Randolph-Macon Coll., 1933; student William and Mary Coll., summer 1930, T.C. Williams Sch. of Law, U. Richmond, 1933-34, Union Theol. Sem., 1934-36, Chaplain Sch., Harvard, 1942; A.M. in Internat. Relations, Am. U., 1950; Dr. Internat. Law (hon.), Lafayette Coll., 1956; m. Margaret Lail, Dec. 23, 1935; children—Nancy Lail (Mrs. William K. Phillips), Edward Christopher David, Peter Evans. Mem. faculty Randolph-Macon Coll., 1932-33; licensed minister Meth. Ch., 1934, ordained deacon, 1936, elder, 1938; minister Richmond, Norfolk and Winchester, Va., 1934-42; sr. minister Walker Chapel, Arlington, Va., 1960- 62; sec.-gen. World Fellowship Muslims and Christians; asso. sec. div. fgn. missions Bd. Missions and Ch. Extension of Meth. Ch., N.Y.C., Washington, 1946-50; organized 1st Muslim-Christian Convocation, Lebanon, 1954, confs. Egypt, 1955, Lebanon, 1956, Iran, 1957, Wash., 1958. Vis. observer serveral Near East confs., 1947-52; accredited non-govtl. rep. to U.N., 1947-50. Surveyed cultural, hist. and religious background Okinawa for mil. govt., 1945; chmn. exec. com. Citizens Com. Am. Policy Near East; chmn. Joseph Ferris Meml. Fund, 1964- -; del. 2d Internat. Islamic Colloquium, Lahore, Pakistan, 1958. Sec., Am. com. Mehr Found. Served in chaplain corps, AUS, 1942-45. Recipient Cross of Hiroshima for dist. service to atom bomb victims, 1951; Medal of Merit first class (Syria), 1952; Asiatic-Pacific medal, Philippine Liberation medal with bronze star. Fellow Inst. Am. Genealogy; mem. Sons Confederate Vets. (asst. chaplain-in-chief), Va. Soc., S.A.R., Sigma Nu Phi, Tau Kappa Alpha, Beta Pi Theta. Democrat. Author books, monographs, mag. articles on internat. affairs, religion and So. history. Former editor several ch. mags. Chmn. editorial bd. U.S.A. and the Arab World, 1964-. Home: 300 Bright Av McLean VA 22101 Office: Dupont Circle Bldg Washington DC 20036

HOPKINS, GENE, electronics co. exec.; b. Gotebo, Okla., July 13, 1925; s. Don and Bertie (Ashlock) H.; B.S. in Civil Engring., Okla. State U., 1950; m. Sharon Hulsey, Sept. 27, 1963; children—Jill D., Cheryl Lynn, Lisa Ann. Midwestern mgr. Martin Co., Dayton, O., 1958-59; exec. v.p. Electrada, Inc., Beverly Hills, Cal., 1960; v.p., gen. mgr. Avien, Inc., Woodside, N.Y., 1961; pres., chmn. bd. Dorsett Electronics, Inc., Tulsa, 1962-68; pres., dir. LaBarge, Inc., Tulsa, 1968—; pres., chmn. Triple H Rodeo, Maverick Rodeo, Maverick de Mexico, Texoma Rodeo cos.; exec. dir. Merc. Bank & Trust Co. Mem. sci. adv. bd. U. Tulsa; trustee Childrens Med. Center, Tulsa. Served to lt. col. USAF, 1947-59. Decorated Silver Star with oak leaf cluster, Purple Heart with 2 oak leaf clusters, D.F.C. with 4 oak leaf clusters, Air medal with 9 oak leaf clusters, Bronze Star. Mem. Internat. Rodeo Assn. Championship in steer roping. Home: 3433 E 62d St Tulsa OK 74135 Office: 5200 S Yale Penthouse W Tulsa OK 74135

HOPKINS, HARRY MILLER, machinery mfg. co. exec.; b. Springfield, O., Aug. 28, 1915; s. Glenn Charles and Isabel (Miller) H.; B.Indsl. Engring., Ohio State U., 1938; m. Mary Knepper, July 23, 1938 (dec. Oct. 1968); children—Bruce A., Martha S.; m. 2d, Barbara Freedman, Oct. 30, 1969. Indsl. engr. Cin. Planer Co., 1938-41; with Tool Steel Gear & Pinion Co., Cin., 1941—, v.p. charge operations, 1952-61, v.p. operations, sec., dir., 1961-69, exec. v.p., 1969—; dir. Badall Co., Inc., Hammond, Ind. Sec. Council Internat. Progress in Mgmt., 1960-63, pres., 1963-66, chmn., 1966-68. Pres. Cin. Bd. Edn., 1966-69. Home: 1046 Hatch St Cincinnati OH 45202 Office: Tool Steel Gear & Pinion Co Cincinnati OH 45216

HOPKINS, HENRY POWELL, architect; b. Annapolis, Md., Feb. 12, 1891; s. Harry Jump and Frances Elizabeth (Chattle) H.; B.Arch., Columbia, 1914; postgrad. Cornell, Ithaca, N.Y., 1909-10, Eng., France, Italy, Spain, 1914-15; M.A. (hon.), St. Johns Coll., 1917; A.F.D., Washington Coll., Chestertown, Md., 1960; m. Constance Medea Hummel, Jan. 12, 1915; 1 son, Henry Powell. Instr. architecture Tex. A. and M. Coll., 1916; lectr. history architecture Columbia, 1919; practicing architect, Baltimore, 1919—; adviser Md. State Code Commn., 1949; supervising architect for restoration of Md. State House; architect for devel. of Colonial Annapolis. Fellow A.I.A. (pres. 1948-49); mem. S.A.R. (v.p. 1951), Soc. Colonial Wars (gov.), Eastern Shore Soc. (pres. Baltimore chapter), Sons Revolution, Soc. of War of 1812. Clubs: Maryland, Rotary (past pres.), Wine and Food Soc., Chester River Yacht and Country (Balt.). Prin. works include: library U. Md., Balt. Jr. Coll., Woodlawn Sr. High Sch., Balt. County, Md., sci. bldg. Washington Coll., Chestertown, Md.; Jr. Coll., Catonsville, Md.; Lansdowne and Dulaney Sr. High Schs., Balt. County; Fine Arts Bldg., U. Md.; library U. Balt.; dormitory and fine arts bldg. Hood Coll.; sr. and 2 jr. high schs., Frederick County, Md. Home: 106 Elmwood Rd. Baltimore MD 21210. Office: 10 E Mulberry St Baltimore MD 21202

HOPKINS, HOMER BENJAMIN, fgn. service officer; b. Portsmouth, O., Aug. 12, 1917; s. Owen and Margaret May (Warnock) H.; student Ohio State U., 1940, Johns Hopkins, 1961-62; m. Elaine McPeak, Feb. 14, 1944; 1 dau., Elaine Margaret. With Calumite Co., Hamilton, O., 1947-48, A.G. Dudley Co., San Mateo, Cal., 1948-51, Henningsen & Co. Ltd., Hong Kong, 1951-55; with AID, and predecessors, 1956—; assigned Vietnam, 1956-61, Indonesia, 1961; dep. dir. Office Mgmt. Operations, Bur. Far East, 1962-67; dir. Office Mgmt. Operations, Bur. East Asia, 1967-68; asst. dir. for mgmt. USOM, Thailand, 1968—. Served with USAAF, 1941-45, 46- 47. Mem. Delta Sigma Phi. Address: USOM APO San Francisco CA 96346

HOPKINS, HOWARD, educator; b. Brownsburg, Ind., Dec. 12, 1910; s. Harry Harding and India McKee (Catterson) H.; student Evansville (Ind.) Coll., 1930-31, Butler U., 1932, Ind. U. extension, 1932-35; B.S. in Pharmacy (Harry Coleman Meml. scholar 1938), Purdue U., 1938, postgrad. 1940-41; M.S., U. Neb., 1940, Ph.D. (Am. Found. Pharm. Edn. fellow 1957-59), 1959; m. Elizabeth Frances Leachman, June 4, 1939. Grad. asst. U. Neb., 1938- 40; dean Coll. of Pharmacy, Ferris State Inst., Big Rapids, Mich., 1941-44; research pharmacist Smith-Dorsey div. Wander Co., 1944-52, plant mgr., 1952-54, asso. dir. pharm. devel., 1954-57; head dept. pharmacy U. Ky. Coll. Pharmacy, Lexington, 1959-67, asst. dean for instrn., 1967—. Fellow A.A.A.S.; mem. Am., Ky., Ind. pharm. assns., Ky. Acad. Sci., Am. Chem. Soc., Sigma Xi, Phi Lambda Upsilon, Rho Chi, Phi Delta Chi, Phi Delta Kappa. Methodist. Home: 1020 Celia La Lexington KY 40504

HOPKINS, JAMES THEODORE, advt. and pub. relations exec.; b. Eau Claire, Wis., June 19, 1921; s. Rosswell R. and Alice (Govin) H.; student U.S. Armed Forces Inst. U. Ala., 1948-50; m. Vivian Maureen Stokes, Dec. 5, 1942; children—Leslie Lynn, Mark James. Editor, West Fla. Daily Globe, Crestview also Okaloosa News Jour., Crestview, 1952-54; pub. relations dir. Fla. Citrus Commn., Lakeland 1954-58; indsl. relations dir. Fla. Citrus Exchange, Tampa, 1958-62; dir. advt. and publicity Fla. Citrus Commn., 1962-66; v.p. Rumrill-Hoyt, Inc., Rochester, N.Y., 1966-68, v.p., gen. mgr., 1968—, also dir. Bd. dirs. Met. Rochester Found. Served with AUS, 1941-45, USAF, 1945-52. Decorated Bronze Star. Mem. Pub. Relations Soc. Am. (pres. 1969-70, bd. dirs.). Author: Fifty Years of Citrus, 1960. Home: 104 Kirklees Rd Pittsford NY 14534 Office: 1895 Mt Hope Av Rochester NY 14620

HOPKINS, JOHN ISAAC, educator, physicist; b. Nokesville, Va., Dec. 25, 1912; s. Narcissus W. and Sabina (Bender) H.; B.S., Duke, 1934, M.A., 1936, Ph.D., 1938; m. Genevie Matheny, Dec. 26, 1938; children—J. Thomas, Mary C., Linda J., Gail A. Prof. physics and math. W. Ga. Coll., Carrollton, 1938-39; asst. prof. N.C. State Coll., Raleigh, 1940-46; asst. prof. physics, then asso. prof. Vanderbilt U., 1946-49, 50-58, chmn. radiation safety com., 1957-58; sr. physicist Oak Ridge Nat. Lab., 1949-50, cons., 1950—; asso. prof. physics Davidson (N.C.) Coll., 1958-60, prof., 1960-61, James Buchanan Duke prof., chmn. dept. physics, 1961—; cons. Charlotte (N.C.) Meml. Hosp., 1958—. Project leader div. biology and medicine AEC, 1953- 58; mem. Gov. N.C. Adv. Com. Atomic Energy, 1959—. Fellow A.A.A.S.; mem. Am. Assn. Physics Tchrs., Am. Phys. Soc., Health Physics Soc., Sigma Xi, Sigma Pi Sigma (exec. council 1962-65). Presbyn. (elder). Lion (pres. 1966-67). Contbr. articles profl. jours. Home: Lynbrook Dr Davidson NC 28036

HOPKINS, JOHN J., business exec.; b. 1933; B.S., Fordham U., 1955; married. Auditor, Arthur Young & Co., 1955-61; with Collins & Aikman Corp., N.Y.C., 1961—, dir. budget, 1965-66, controller, 1966-70, sec., 1970—. Office: 210 Madison Av New York City NY 10016*

HOPKINS, LINDSEY, investment; b. Greensboro, N.C., Mar. 10, 1908; s. Lindsey and Leonora (Balsley) H.; student U. of Ga., 1927-29; m. Dorothy Smith, Apr. 2, 1932; children—Lindsey, Carter Wayne. Mem. advt. dept., sales and service The Coca-Cola Co., Atlanta, 1929-31; mem. investment dept., Courts & Co., mems. New York Stock Exchange, Atlanta, 1933-34, mgr. Miami Beach (Fla.) br. Abbott, Proctor & Paine, mems. N.Y. Stock Exchange, 1935; asst. mgr. Lindsey Hopkins Properties, Miami, Fla., 1931- 33; chmn. bd. dir. Security Trust Co., Miami; pres. Montauk (N.Y.) Beach Co., Inc., 1945-59; dir. Carl G. Fisher Corp., Cocoa Cola Co. Trustee Good Samaritan Clinic, Atlanta. Clubs: Surf, La- Gorce Country (Miami Beach); Piedmont Driving (Atlanta). Home: 1821 W 27 St Sunset Island 2 Miami Beach FL 33139 Office: 119 E Flagir St Miami FL 33131

HOPKINS, MALCOLM TOWNSEND, airline exec.; b. Sayville, N.Y., Mar. 13, 1928; s. Wilbur Daniel and Dorothy (Townsend) H.; A.B., Union Coll., 1949; LL.B., Albany Law Sch., 1953; m. Dorothy Elaine Clark, Aug. 27, 1949; children—Susan Susan Elaine, Nancy Anne. Admitted to N.Y. bar, 1953; asst. to treas., asst. treas. Electric Bond & Share Co., N.Y.C., 1955-66; treas. Eastern Air Lines, Inc., N.Y.C., 1966, v.p., treas., 1967-68; v.p., treas. Trans-World Airlines, 1968—; dir. Bank of Commerce. Served with AUS, 1953- 55. Mem. U.S. C. of C., Chi Psi. Home: 125 Beekman Rd Summit NJ 07901

HOPKINS, RAYMOND C., clergyman; b. Danbury, Conn., July 29, 1919; s. Clarence W. and Mary (Halstead) H.; A.B. magna cum laude, Tufts U., 1947, S.T.B., 1949; S.T.D., Starr King Sch. Ministery, 1964; m. Barbara G. Blethen, Apr. 3, 1943; children—Patricia Rae, Linda Sue, Janet Louise. Ordained to ministry Universalist Ch., 1949; minister in Brockton, Mass., 1941-61; adminstr. Council Liberal Chs., 1958-59; exec. v.p. Unitarian Universalist Assn., 1961—. Sec. to joint merger commn. UCA-AUA, 1959- 61, chmn. coordinating com. consol., 1960-61. Trustee Clarence Darrow Community Center, Friends of Albert Schweitzer Coll. Served with USAAF, 1940-41. Mem. Unitarian Universalist Ministers Assn., Universalist Hist. Soc., Tufts Alumni Assn. Home: RFD 4 Georgetown MA 01833 Office: 25 Beacon St Boston MA 02108

HOPKINS, SAM (Lightnin'), singer; b. Centerville Tex., Mar. 15, 1912. Farm worker, began playing guitar and singing on full-time basis, 1946; remained an itinerant singer, mainly in Tex. until rediscovered by folklorist Mack McCormick; went to N.Y.C., 1960, playing clubs including the Village Gate; appeared in TV workshop A Pattern of Words and Music. Address: care Verve Records 1540 Broadway New York City NY 10019*

HOPKINS, SAMUEL, investment banker; b. Highland, Md., Oct. 18, 1913; s. Samuel Harold and Roberta (Smith) H.; B.S., Johns Hopkins, 1934; LL.B., U. Md., 1938; m. Winifred Holt Bloodgood, Oct. 15, 1938 (dec. Oct. 1954); children—Samuel, Henry; m. 2d, Anne E. Dankmeyer, Oct. 21, 1955; children—Robert Frederick. With Fidelity & Deposit Co. of Md., 1934-69, asst. to treas., 1934-50, asst. treas., 1950-54, sec., 1954- 67, v.p., sec., dir., 1967-69; dir., mem. trust com. Equitable Trust Co., Balt.; sec., dir., Md. Life Ins. Co., 1963-69; gen. partner Alex, Brown & Sons, investment bankers, Balt., 1970—. Mem. adv. com. housing for elderly U.S. Housing and Finance Agy., 1956-60; mem. Balt. Bd. Recreation and Parks, 1965—, pres., 1965-67, v.p., 1968—; Republican candidate for Congress, 1952; mem. Md. Ho. of Dels., 1950-54; Rep. candidate for mayor, Balt., 1955. Trustee Balt. Mus. Art, Peale Mus.; trustee, v.p. State Colls. Md., 1963-70. Served from ensign to lt., USNR, 1942-45. Mem. Am. Bar Assn., Am. Soc. Corporate Secs., Balt. Security Analysts Soc., Md. Hist. Soc. (treas. 1956-69, pres. 1970), Inst. Chartered Security Analysts. Episcopalian. Home: 4302 Wendover Rd Baltimore MD 21218 Office: Alex Brown & Sons 135 E Baltimore St Baltimore MD 21202

HOPKINS, STANLEY MARSHALL, can mfr.; b. Portsmouth, O., Nov. 22, 1896; s. Stanley G. and Nona (Dunn) H.; student Franklin and Marshall Coll., 1916-17; m. 2d, Genevieve Lifson, Nov. 21, 1947; 1 step dau., Patricia (Mrs. Richard Sobel). With Wheeling Steel Corp., 1919-43, West coast sales mgr., 1940- 43; v.p. Pacific Can Corp., 1943-55; co. purchased by Nat. Can Corp., Chgo., 1955, pres., 1960-63, vice chmn. bd., 1963-. Served with USNRF, World War I. Home: 2200 Pacific Av San Francisco CA 94115 Office: Nat Can Corp 290 Division St San Francisco CA 94103

HOPKINS, W. DEAN, lawyer; b. nr. Savannah, O., Nov. 10, 1909; s. Clayton J. and Ethel (Patterson) H.; B.S. magna cum laude Coll. Wooster, 1930; LL.B., Harvard Law Sch., 1933; m. Harriet Angene Painter, May 30, 1936; children—Angene (Mrs. Jack A. Wilson), Frances (Mrs. William A. Irwin), Walter P., Lewis D., Giles P. Admitted to Ohio bar, 1933; asso. firm Fackler & Dye (name changed to Fackler, Dye & Hopkins), Cleve., 1933-46; mem. firm McDonald, Hopkins & Hardy Co., L.P.A., Cleve., 1946—. Sec., dir. The Taylor Chair Co., Bedford, O. Mem. Lakewood (Ohio) Bd. Edn., 1957-70. Trustee Coll. Wooster. Mem. Cleve., Ohio, Am. bar assns. Presbyn. (elder, trustee). Home: 18144 Clifton Rd Lakewood OH 44107 Office: East Ohio Bldg Cleveland OH 44114

HOPKINS, WELLY KENNON, lawyer; b. Gonzales, Tex., Sept. 3, 1898; s. Sam Houston and Frances (Rainbolt) H.; student Univ. of Tex., 1920-23; m. Alice Isaacs, Apr. 27, 1935; 1 dau., Kennon Lee. Admitted to Tex. bar, 1923, U.S. Court of Appeals for Dist. of Columbia, Supreme Court of U.S. Gen. practice of law, Gonzales, Tex., 1923-36; mem. Tex. House of Reps., 1929-30; mem. Tex. Senate, 1930-36; spl. asst. to Atty. Gen. of U.S., Washington, D.C., Mar. 1936-May 1940; gen. counsel United Mine Workers Am., 1940-66; counsel trustees United Mine Workers Am. Welfare and Retirement Fund, 1966—; dir. Nat. Bank Washington. Del. from Texas Dem. Nat. Convs., 1928, 32, 36. Served with U.S. Army (S.A.T.C.), Sept.-Dec. 1917. Mem. Am. Bar Assn., Fed. Power Bar Assn., Newcomen Soc., Nat. Lawyers Club (Wash.), Sons of Republic of Tex., Sigma Alpha Epsilon. Dem. Episcopalian. Mason. K.P. Club: University (Washington). Home: 207 S Fairfax St Alexandria VA 22314 Office: 907 15th St Washington DC 20005

HOPKINS, WILLIAM J., ret. govt. ofcl.; b. Netawaka, Kan., May 13, 1910; s. John and Lillie (Spurgin) H.; student Chillicothe (Mo.) Bus. Coll., 1927-28, George Washington U.; LL.B., Southeastern U., 1938; m. Marie C. Frech, 1934; children—Anne Marie, John Edward, Gail Evelyn. Clk., Chgo., Burlington and Quincy R.R., Centerville, Ia., 1928-29; under clk.-typist Bur. Naturalization, Dept. Labor, Washington, 1929-31; with White House, 1931—, exec. clk., 1943-49, sr. exec. clk., 1949-66, exec. asst. to Pres., 1966-71; ret., 1971. Recipient President's award for distinguished fed. civilian service, 1960, Spl. Presdl. citation, 1966, Presdl. Medal of Freedom, 1971. Home: 814 Rowen Rd Silver Spring MD 20910

HOPKINS, WILLIAM STEPHEN, educator; b. Portland, Ore., May 24, 1902; s. Fred H. and Enola (Woodward) H.; B.S., U. Ore., 1925, A.M., 1928; Ph.D., Stanford, 1932; m. Ann Chapman, Sept. 3, 1925 (dec. 1952); children—William S., John C., Sally Ann (Mrs. Gerald C. Wilson); m. 2d, Ruth Latourette, May 28, 1954. Mem. staff Social Sci. Research Council, 1939-40; pub. mem. Regional War Labor Bd., San Francisco, 1942-46; instr. Stanford, 1930-35, asst. prof., 1935- 40, asso. prof., 1940-45, prof., 1945-46; prof. econ., dir. Bur. Labor Econ., U. Wash., 1946-69, prof. emeritus, 1969—; serves as arbitrator in labor-mgmt. disputes. Mem. Gov. Wash. Council on Aging, 1959-66; pres. Seattle Council Aging, 1962-64. Fellow Gerontological Soc.; mem. Am., Western (pres. 1947) econ. assns., Royal Econ. Soc. Author: Seasonal Unemployment, 1936; Labor in the American Economy, 1948; Aging in the State of Washington, 1960. Contbr. articles profl. econs. publs. Home: 13249 15th St NE Seattle WA 98125

HOPLA, CLUFF EARL, med. zoologist; b. Mapleton, Utah, Dec. 28, 1917; s. David S. and Lilly (Erickson) H.; student Brigham Young U., 1936-41, 46-47; B.S., U. Utah, 1942; M.S., Tulane U., 1947, Ph.D., U. Kan., 1950; m. Moyra Ullock, Dec. 12, 1941; children—Richard E., Dan M., Anna Kristine. Med. entomologist USPHS, 1950; postdoctorate fellow U. Kan., 1950-51; asst. prof. zoology and pub. health U. Okla., 1951-56, asso. prof. zoology, 1956-63, prof., 1963-69, chmn. dept. zoology, 1963-69, George Lynn Cross research prof., 1969—. Cons. Okla. Dept. Health, 1956—, NIH, 1967—. Mem. Council on Research Oklahoma City Zoo; explorer adviser Last Frontier council Boy Scouts Am. Served to lt. comdr. USNR, 1942-46. Fellow Okla. Acad. Scis.; mem. Entomol. Soc. Am. (vice-chmn. sect., chmn. 1960-62, program chmn. 1968- -). Contbr. articles in field. Home: 1123 Berry Circle Norman OK 73069

HOPP, WILLIAM BEECHER, educator; b. Terre Haute, Ind., Sept. 4, 1917; s. William Henry and Kathryn Elsie (Beecher) H.; B.S., Ind. State Tchrs. Coll., 1939; M.S., Purdue U., 1941, Ph.D., 1953; m. Eva Helen Cook, June 3, 1949; 1 son, William Beecher. Instr. biology Purdue U., 1946-47; asst. prof. zoology Eastern Ky. State Coll., Richmond, 1947-55; faculty Ind. State U., 1955- -, prof. zoology, 1961—, chmn. sci. div., 1961-68; weekly radio program, 1957—, TV program, 1959—. Bd. dirs. Terre Haute Humane Soc., 1964-67. Mem. Wabash Valley Audubon Soc. (pres. 1962-63), Am. Soc. Parasitologists, Am. Soc. Ichthyologists and Herpetologists, Ind. Acad. Sci., A.A.A.S., Am. Inst. Biol. Scis., Am. Assn. U. Profs., Sigma Xi, Kappa Delta Pi. Contbr. profl. jours. Home: 335 S Brown Av Terre Haute IN 47803

HOPPE, ARTHUR WATTERSON, journalist; b. Honolulu, Apr. 23, 1925; s. Arthur S. and Margaret (Watterson) H.; B.A. cum laude, Harvard, 1949; m. Gloria Nichols, Apr. 28, 1946; children—Leslie, Andrea, Arthur N., Prentiss. Mem. staff San Francisco Chronicle, 1949—, reporter, 1950-60, columnist, 1960—. Served with USNR, 1942-46. Author: Love Everybody Crusade, 1962; Dreamboat, 1964; The Perfect Solution to Absolutely Everything, 1968; Mr. Nixon and My Other Problems, 1971. Office: San Francisco Chronicles San Francisco CA 94119

HOPPER, BRUCE CAMPBELL, educator; b. Litchfield, Ill., Aug. 24, 1892; s. Joseph and Katherine (Turnbull) H.; student U. Mont., 1913-16, B.S., Harvard, 1918, A.M., 1925, Ph.D., 1930; student Sorbonne, 1919, 20, Oxford U., 1919-20; m. Effie Toyé, Aug. 26, 1924. Editorial writer China Press, Shanghai, 1921-22; asst. in history Harvard, 1925-26, asst. prof. govt., 1930-37, asso. prof. govt., 1937-61, asso. prof. emeritus, 1961—; lectr. Naval War Coll., Army War Coll., Armed Forces Staff Coll.; lectr. Europe, 1954, Inst. Aero. Scis., 1956; mem. group Am. profs. vis. univs. and govtl. insts. Fed. Republic of Germany, summer 1958; observer for Inst. Current World Affairs in USSR, 1926-29. Trustee World Peace Found.; mem. Air Force Acad. Site Selection Bd., Air Force Hist. Found., Ednl. Exchange Program, Dept. State. Served with Am. Field Service, French Army, 1917, Am. A.S., 96th Sq., 1917-19, hist. sect. G.H.Q. Chaumont, 1919, Sorbonne Detachment, 1919; attached Am. legation, Stockholm, 1942-43; chief hist. sect. 8th Air Force and USSTAF, 1943-45; cons. to Comdg. Gen., Air Force, 1945-47. Decorated Silver Star, Air Force Exceptional Civilian Service award, Croix de Guerre, Aero. medal (France); officier Ouissan (Alacuite (Moroccan); chevalier Legion d'Honneur (France). Mem. Fgn. Service Assn. Episcopalian. Club: Army and Navy (Washington). Author: Pan-Sovietism, 1931; Siberia's Population Capacity, 1937; The Second World War: Why?, 1940; also series of articles in Fgn. Affairs. Editor: Let's Talk About (monthly discussion brochures), 1952-53. Home: 3 Craigie Circle Cambridge MA 02138 also 131 E Arrallaga St Santa Barbara CA 93104

HOPPER, CLARENCE HELLER, corp. ofcl.; b. Berwick, Pa., Feb. 11, 1915; s. Harry Burton and Margaret (Hosler) H.; student pub. and tech. schs., West Philadelphia, Pa.; m. Elizabeth Auner Humes, Sept. 1, 1934; children—C. Douglas, Bruce D. Machine operator, plant engr. A.C.F. Brill Motors Co., Phila., 1933- 41, mgr. prodn. engring. and planning, 1941-44, gen. supt. 1944-45, prodn. mgr., 1945-47, 49-51, works mgr. operations, 1951-54; factory mgr. Oneida Products Corp., Canastota, N.Y., 1947-49; works mgr., v.p. mfg. Am. Bosch Arma Corp., Garden City, N.Y., 1954-56; v.p. prodn. services CBS, N.Y.C., 1956-59, v.p. facilities, 1959—, pres. CBS Electronics div., Lowell, Mass., 1960-61, v.p. facilities CBS, Inc., 1961-64, v.p. facilities and personnel, 1965—; pres. Riverfront Redevel. Corp. Bd. dirs. Av. Americas Assn. Mem. Am. Mgmt. Assn. Episcopalian. Mason. Home: 39 Hilton Av Garden City NY 11530 Office: 51 W 52d St New York City NY 10019

HOPPER, CLIFTON CHARLES, wholesale drug co. exec.; b. Rosebud, Tex., Jan. 30, 1921; s. Charles Jones and Clara (Hinsley) H.; ed. pub. schs., Houston; m. Rosemary Catherine Sullivan, Nov. 17, 1946; children—Roseanne, Clifton Charles. With Southwestern Drug Corp., Houston, 1940—, regional v.p., 1964-67, exec. v.p., 1967-68, pres., 1968—, chmn. bd., 1970—, also dir. Served to maj. AUS, 1941-46; CBI. Mem. Nat. Wholesale Druggists Assn. (bd. control), Service Wholesale Druggists Assn. Tex. (pres. 1967-68), Drug Travelers Tex. (bd. dirs.). Baptist. Mailing Address:

HOPPER, DENNIS, actor; b. Dodge City. Kan., May 17, 1936; ed. San Diego pub. schs. TV appearances include Medic, Loretta Young show; films include Jagged Edge; Rebel Without a Cause; Giant; Easy Rider. Address: care Robert Raison Agency 9000 Sunset Blvd Los Angeles CA 90069*

HOPPER, GRACE BREWSTER MURRAY, mathematician; b. N.Y.C., Dec. 9, 1906; d. Walter Fletcher and Mary Campbell (Van Horne) Murray; B.A., Vassar Coll., 1928; M.A. (Vassar fellow, Sterling scholar), Yale, 1930, Ph.D., 1934; postgrad. (Vassar Faculty fellow) N.Y.U., 1941-42; m. Vincent Foster Hopper, June 15, 1930 (div. 1945). Instr. to asso. prof. math. Vassar Coll., 1931-44; asst. prof. math. Barnard Coll., summer 1943; research fellow engring. scis., applied physics Computation Lab. Harvard, 1946-49; sr. mathematician Eckert-Mauchly Computer Corp., Phila., 1949-50, sr. programmer Eckert-Mauchly div. Remington Rand, 1950-59; systems engr., dir. automatic programming devel. UNIVAC div. Sperry Rand Corp., Phila., 1959-61, staff scientist systems programming, 1964-71; ret., 1971. Vis. lectr. Moore Sch. Elec. Engring., U. Pa., 1959-63, vis. asso. prof. elec. engring., 1963—; lectr. George Washington U., 1971—. Served to comdr. WAVES, 1944-46, 67—, presently serving active duty in the Pentagon. Recipient Naval Ordnance Devel. award, 1946, Connelly Meml. award, 1968. Fellow I.E.E.E., A.A.A.S.; mem. Assn. Computing Machinery (editorial bd. 1957-58), Franklin Inst., Soc. Indsl. and Applied Math. (v.p. 1952-53, trustee 1957-59), Soc. Women Engrs. (Achievement award 1964, sci. achievement award Am. Motors com. 1970), U.S. Naval Inst., Internat. Oceanographic Found., D.A.R., Dames Loyal Legion, Hist. Soc. Pa., Geneal. Soc. Pa., Valley Forge Hist. Assn., Retired Officers Assn. Huguenot Soc. Pa., Pechin Soc., Asso. Alumnae Vassar Coll., Phila. Vassar Club, Phi Beta Kappa, Sigma Xi. Contbr. articles to profl. jours. Home: 1400 S Joyce St Arlington VA 22202 Office: Dept Navy Pentagon Washington DC 20350

HOPPER, HENRY GEORGE, banker; b. West Long Branch, N.J., Jan. 3, 1912; s. George K. and Elisabeth (Schaper) H.; student Am. Inst. Banking, also N.Y. U.; m. Wilma Rose, Dec. 1, 1934; children—Lynn (Mrs. Dale Martin) and Gail (Mrs. Tilman E. Wheeler, Jr.). With S.G. Adams and Co., brokerage, N.Y.C., 1928-32; with U.S. Trust, N.Y.C., 1932—, in charge real estate and mortgage div., 1952—, exec. v.p., 1966—; dir., mem. real estate com. Chgo. Dock and Canal Trust Co. Home: 40 Tulip Lane Colts Neck NJ 07722. Office: 45 Wall St New York City NY 10005

HOPPER, STANLEY ROMAINE, educator; b. Fresno, Cal., Mar. 22, 1907; s. Samuel Duff and Emma Evaline (Foster) H.; A.B., U. So. Cal., 1928; S.T.B., Boston U., 1931; Ph.D., Drew U., 1936; student Harvard, U. Zurich (Switzerland), Mansfield Coll. (Eng.); D.D., Allegheny Coll., 1963; m. Eva Helen Bagby, Mar. 3, 1928; children—Stanley Duff, Arthur Jeffrey, David Romaine, John Alan. Ordained minister Methodist Episcopal Ch., 1931; pastor in San Joaquin, Cal., 1927-28, Dinuba, Cal., 1928, Farmington, N.H., 1928-31, Clifford, Pa., 1932-33, New Haven, 1933- 35; lectr., instr. English bibl. lit. Brothers Coll., Drew U., Madison, N.J., 1932-35, instr., asst. prof., asso. prof. homiletics and Christian criticism of life Theol. Sem., 1935-44, asst. to dean sem., 1935-44, prof. Christian ethics univ., 1944-52, prof. philosophy and letters univ., 1952-68, dean Grad. Sch., 1954-68; Bishop W. Earl Ledden prof. religion Syracuse (N.Y.) U., 1968—. Spl. lectr. Inst. Religious and Social Studies, Jewish Theol. Sem. Am., 1949-52; Am. del. First Conf. Christianity and Art, Switzerland, 1950; lectr. Christian ethics Garrett Bib. Inst., summer 1951; chmn. com. lit., dept. worship and the arts, Nat. Council Churches of Christ in U.S.A., 1953-61; mem. adv. council dept. religion Princeton; A.J. Jarrell lectr. Emory U. Chandler Sch. Theology, 1959; James Sprunt aux. lectr. Union Theol. Sem., Richmond, Va., 1961; Arlo Ayres Brown lectr. Drew U., 1962; Shumate lectr. Lynchburg (Va.) Coll., 1965; del. 1st Meth. Conf. on Theology, Oxford, Eng., 1960, Eranos Conf., Ascona, Switzerland, 1960, 63, 65; vis. prof. theology Aoyama Gakuin U., Tokyo, also lectr. religion and lit. Tokyo Union Theol. Sch., 1967-68; vis. prof. philosophy religion Kyoto (Japan) U., 1968; Chmn. Madison Sports Commn., 1962. Pres., dir. Found. for Arts, Religion and Contemporary Culture Inc.; trustee, pres. St. John's on Lake Assn. Recipient book award Abingdon-Cokesbury Press, 1943. Mem. Am. Homiletic Assn. (sec.), Duodecim Soc., N.Y. Browning Soc. (hon.), Am. Theol. Soc., Phi Sigma Tau, Sigma Phi Epsilon, Delta Sigma Rho, Pi Sigma Alpha, Alpha Phi Epsilon, Pi Delta Kappa. Mason, Kiwanian. Author: The Crisis of Faith, 1944; Exposition of Book of Jeremiah (in Interpreter's Bible), 1956. Editor: Spiritual Problems in Contemporary Literature, 1953; co-editor: Interpretation: The Poetry of Meaning, 1967. Mem. editorial bd. Religion in Life, 1953—.

Contbr. profl. jours., chpts. in books. Home: 120 Paddock Dr. DeWitt NY 13214. Office: Crouse Hall Dept Religion Syracuse U Syracuse NY 13210

HOPPER, THOMAS WASHBURN, cons. engr.; b. Suffern, N.Y., Dec. 25, 1908; s. Thomas M. and Mary (Washburn) H.; M.E., Cornell U., 1929; m. Helene White Miner, Sept. 12, 1930; children—Thomas Miner, Maryellen White (Mrs. John Priedeman), Helene Washburn (Mrs. James A. Wade). Jr. engr. Stone & Webster Engring. Corp., Boston, Hopewell, Va. and Pottsville, Pa., 1929-31, mech. engr., Boston, 1936-41; indsl. engr., prodn. supr. Avon Products Corp., Suffern, N.Y., 1932-36; with Day & Zimmermann, Inc., Phila., 1942-71, engring. mgr., 1942-56, pres., 1957-61, dir., 1955-61, 65-71, v.p., 1961-71; participated in survey Rep. of Korea 1944; pres. Day & Zimmermann Cons. Services, 1967-71, cons. engr., 1971—. Pres. Cornell Soc. Engrs., 1954. Mem. Swarthmore (Pa.) Borough Council, 1949-57, pres., 1953-57. Mem. Nat. Soc. Profl. Engrs., Nat. Constructors Assn. (exec. com. 1957-60), Am. Soc. Mech. Engrs., Franklin Inst., Holland Soc. Clubs: Engineers, Union League, Racquet (Phila.); Rolling Green Golf (Springfield, Pa.). Home: 10 Dogwood Lane Swarthmore PA 19081 Office: 1700 Sansom St Philadelphia PA 19103

HOPPER, VINCENT FOSTER, educator; b. West New York, N.J., Apr. 19, 1906; s. Abram Whittaker and Isabel Jayne (Timmons) H.; student Blair Acad., 1922-23; A.B., Princeton, 1927, A.M., 1928; Ph.D., Columbia, 1938; m. Grace Brewster Murray, June 12, 1930; m. 2d, Mabel Sterling Lewis, May 6, 1945; 1 son, David Whittaker. Instr., N.Y. U. Sch. Commerce, Accounts, and Finance, 1928-32, asst. prof., 1932-41, asso. prof., 1941-48, prof. gen. lit., 1948-64; asst. to head English dept., prof. English, Washington Sq. Coll., N.Y. U., 1964—. Mem. Modern Lang. Assn., Coll. English Assn., Nat. Council Tchrs. English, Phi Beta Kappa. Author: Medieval Number Symbolism, 1938; Chaucer's Canterbury Tales (selected), An Interlinear Translation, 1948, 2d edit., 1970; Backgrounds of European Literature (with Rod W. Horton), 1948; (with Bernard D.N. Grebanier) Essentials of European Literature, 1952, Bibliography of European Literature, 1954; (with Cedric Gale) Essentials of Effective Writing, 1960, Practice for Effective Writing, 1960. Contbg. editor Ency. of Religion, 1945. Co-editor: The School for Scandal; The Rivals; The Way of the World; She Stoops to Conquer; Volpone; The Importance of Being Ernest; Lady Windermere's Fan, 1959; The Duchess of Malfi, 1960; Medieval Mysteries, Moralities, and Interludes, 1962; The Beaux' Strategem, 1963. Editor: Classic American Short Stories, 1964; 1001 Pitfalls in English Grammar, 1969, 2d edit., 1970. Home: 203 River Edge Rd Tenafly NJ 07670 Office: NY U Washington Sq Coll New York City NY 10003

HOPPER, WALTER EVERETT, lawyer; b. Houghton, Mich., Oct. 29, 1915; s. Walter E. and Maude (Crum) H.; A.B., Cornell U., 1937, J.D., 1939; m. Diana Kerensky, Sept. 24, 1958; 1 dau., Nancy Cameron; 1 stepdau., Nicole Sudrow. Admitted to N.Y. bar, 1939, D.C. bar, 1958, also U.S. Supreme Ct.; practice in Ithaca, 1939-42, N.Y.C., 1946—; v.p., dir. Davis Brake Beam Co. Chmn. trustees Loyal Legion Found.; trustee Inst. on Man and Science. Served to lt. col. inf., AUS, World War II; ETO; col. Res. Decorated Army Commendation medal with oak leaf cluster; N.Y. State Conspicious Service Cross; Order Ruben Dario (Nicaragua); Comdr. Order Orange-Nassau (Netherlands). Mem. Internat. Assn. Protection Indsl. Property (exec. com. Am. group 1958-71), Nat. Fgn. Trade Council, Internat. C. of C. (U.S. council 1949—), Inst. Trademark Agts. (London, Eng.), Inst. Patent Agts. (London), U.S. Trademark Assn. (past v.p., dir., chmn. internat. com.), N.Y. State Trial Lawyers Assn., Holland Soc. (pres. 1966-71), Loyal Legion (comdr.-in-chief 1964-67), Am. Bar Assn., Assn. Bar City N.Y., Res. Officers Assn. (pres. N.Y. State 1949), Confrerie des Chevaliers du Tastevin, Pilgrims, Mayflower Descendants, Soc. Colonial Wars, St. Nicholas Soc., S.R., Huguenot Soc., Mil. Order Fgn. Wars. Clubs: Economic, Explorers, University (N.Y.C.); Metropolitan, Army-Navy (Washington); Union Interalliee (Paris, France). Home: 27 E 65th St New York City NY 10021 Office: 685 3d Av New York City NY 10017

HOPPING, LOUIS MELBERT, lawyer; b. Havana, Ill., May 31, 1900; s. Oliver Perry and Nannie Elizabeth (Yates) H.; pre-med. and pre-law student, U. Ill., 1919-23; A.B., George Washington U., 1925, LL.B. 1927; m. Helen Irene Boutwell, Nov. 27, 1924; children—Eleanor Jean (Mrs. Lawrence J. MacDonald), Helen Irene (Mrs. Chalmer P. Emigh, Jr.), George Boutwell, William Yates. With various companies, Ill., also Washington, to 1924; sec. to mng. editor Washington Herald, 1924-26; sec. Congressman Clarence McLeod, 1926-31; asst. U.S. atty., 1931-45; admitted to Mich. bar 1932, also U.S. Supreme Ct.; with firm Fitsgerald, Walker, Conley & Hopping, Detroit, 1945—. Pres. Identity Registry, Inc. Mem. Detroit council Boy Scouts Am.; dir. Detroit Amateur Baseball Fedn.; pres. Mackenzie Meml. Assn.; founder, pres. Fed. Grand Jurors Assn.; mem. nat. awards jury Freedoms Found., Valley Forge, 1963. Served with USNRF, 1918-21. Named Distinguished Alumnus, George Washington U. Mem. Inter-Am. (del. cons. 1949—), Am., Fed., Detroit bar assns., Detroit Bd. Commerce, State Bar Mich., George Washington Law Assn., Am. Soc. Internat. Law, Am. Judicature Soc., Mich. Hort. Soc. (trustee). Christian Scientist. Club: Civitan (pres. Detroit 1946-47, lt. gov. Great Lakes dist. 1949-50, gov. 1950-51, internat. sgt.-at-arms 1950-51, internat. judge adv. 1951-52, trustee internat. found., internat. pres. 1963-64, exec. bd. 1964-65). Home: 18165 Jamestown Circle Northville MI 48167 Office: Penobscot Bldg Detroit MI 48226

HOPPOCK, DAVID WILLARD, mfg. co. exec.; b. Balt., July 5, 1914; s. Clarence A. and Rae (Willard) H.; B.S., Lehigh U., 1936; m. Ruth Cora Farr, Dec. 14, 1940; children—Susan Rae (Mrs. John Howard Avery), David Farr. With Gen. Electric Co., 1936-40; with Carrier Corp., Syracuse, N.Y., 1945-57; v.p. marketing, Bryant (Ind.) d.v., 1957-70, pres., 1970—, v.p. parent corp., 1970—; with Def. Prodn. Adminstrn., Washington, 1950-51. Dir. Central Ind. Council Boy Scouts Am., 1970-71. Served from 1st lt. to lt. col., Ordnance Dept., AUS, 1940-45. Decorated Legion of Merit. Mem. Air Conditioning Inst. (dir.), Gas Appliance Mfrs. Assn. (dir.), Tau Beta Pi, Phi Beta Kappa. Episcopalian. Home: 5710 Walden Lane Indianapolis IN 46208 Office: 7310 W Morris St Indianapolis IN 46231

HOPPS, HOWARD CARL, pathologist, educator; b. Schenectady, Aug. 14, 1914; s. Carl Walter and Alice Clara (Janzer) H.; B.S., U. Okla., 1935, M.D. with honors, 1937; Ph.D., U. Chgo., 1970; m. Ellen Clare Connellee, June 3, 1937; children—Christopher, David C., Susan L.; m. 2d, Hilda M. Pinkelman, Apr. 20, 1968. Intern, Evanston Hosp., 1937-39; asst. pathology U. Chgo., 1940, instr., 1941-43, asst. prof., 1943-44; prof., chmn. dept. U. Okla., 1944-56, U. Tex. Med. Br., Galveston, 1957-63; chief div. geog. pathology Armed Forces Inst. Pathology, Washington, 1964-70; Curators' prof. pathology U. Mo., Columbia, 1970—. Cons. NIH, 1954-64, NSF, 1960-61, Am. Cancer Soc., 1958, Nat. Acad. Scis., 1970—; clin. prof. pathology U. Md., 1964-70; mem. pathology test com. Nat. Bd. Med. Examiners, 1956-59; Fulbright vis. prof. Otago U., Dunedin, New Zealand, 1955-56; vis. prof. Temple U. Sch. Medicine, 1967-70; Cons. geog. pathology NASA, 1969—; mem. subcom. geochem. environment related to health and disease Nat. Acad. Sci., 1970—; registrar Am. Registry Geog. Pathology, 1964-70. Recipient Howard Taylor Ricketts prize for research, 1942; Distinguished Service award Med. Alumni Assn. U. Chgo., 1970; certificate Distinguished Service, AFIP, 1971. Diplomate pathologic anatomy and forensic pathology Am. Bd. Pathology; certified Am. Bd. Legal Medicine. Mem. Am. Soc. Clin. Pathology, Am. Assn. Pathologists and Bacteriologists, Am. Assn. Cancer Research, Am. Soc. Exptl. Pathology, Am. Assn. Immunology, Coll. Am. Pathologists, Internat. Acad. Pathology, Soc. Exptl. Biology and Medicine (chmn. southwestern sect. 1955-56), Am. Acad. Forensic Sci., Am. Soc. Tropical Med. and Hygiene, Internat. Coll. Tropical Medicine, Reticuloendothelial Soc., Sigma Xi, Alpha Omega Alpha. Author: Principles of Pathology, 1959, 2d edit., 1964. Editor Internat. Pathology, 1965- 70. Contbr. articles med. jours., sci. publs.; also chpts. in books. Home: 606 Longfellow Lane Columbia MO 65201

HOPSON, CLIFFORD ANDRAE, educator, geologist; b. Portland, Ore., Feb. 2, 1928; s. Eric Ernest and Gertrude (Andrae) H.; B.S., Stanford, 1951; postgrad. U. Wash., 1951-52; Ph.D., Johns Hopkins, 1955; m. Mary Dickson Arrowood, Sept. 10, 1955; children—Robert Forrest, Erin Kathryn, Eric Roger. Geologist, U.S. Geol. Survey, 1952-54, 57; asst. prof., then asso. prof. Johns Hopkins, 1955- 64; faculty U. Cal. at Santa Barbara, 1964—, prof., 1966—; guest investigator Geophys. Lab., Carnegie Instn., 1953-55. Served with AUS, 1946-47. NSF fellow, 1953-55, Fellow Geol. Soc. Am.; mem. Geochem. Soc., Am. Geophys. Union, A.A.A.S., Phi Beta Kappa, Sigma Xi. Research igneous and metamorphic petrology. Home: 6597 Camino Venturoso Goleta, CA 93017. Office: Dept Geology University California Santa Barbara CA 93106

HOPTON, LESTER CHARLES, mfg. exec.; b. Cin., June 17, 1902; s. Walter E. and Anna B. (Chew) H.; B.S. in Engring. Adminstrn., Mass. Inst. Tech., 1926; m. Phylis M. Pack, July 10, 1928; children—Lester Charles, Elsie F. With Ingersoll-Rand Co., N.Y.C., 1926—, successively gen. factory controller, comptroller, sec. and comptroller, v.p. and comptroller, 1st v.p., dir., pres. and dir., now dir. and mem. exec. com.; dir. Canadian Ingersoll- Rand Co. Mem. Phi Beta Epsilon. Presbyn. Clubs: Plainfield Country, Whitehall, M.I.T.; Mid-Ocean (Bermuda). Home: 1215 Martine Av Plainfield NJ 07060 Office: 55 Broad St New York City NY 10004

HOPWOOD, KATHRYN LOUISE, coll. dean, educator; b. Lenox, O., Aug. 25, 1908; d. Burton Clifford and Cassie (Mills) Hopwood; A.B., Oberlin Coll., 1930, M.A., 1940, L.H.D., 1970; Ph.D., Ohio State U., 1953. English tchr. Shelby (O.) High Sch., 1930- 1930- 38; tchr., girls' counselor Elyria (O.) High Sch., 1938-43; asst. dean women Ohio State U., 1943-48, asso. dean women, 1948-55, instr. psychology, 1944-54, asst. prof., 1954-55; lectr. N.Y. U., 1954; dean dean students, prof. psychology Hunter Coll., 1955-67, dean of students, prof. counseling and student devel., 1967—. Trustee Oberlin Coll., 1956-67. Mem. Am. Psychol. Assn., Am. Coll. Personnel Assn., Nat. Assn., Nat. Vocational Guidance Assn., Nat. Assn. Women Deans and Counselors, Am. Assn. U. Women, Mortar Bd., Pi Lambda Theta, Phi Beta Kappa (hon.). Contbr. articles profl. jours. Home: 440 E 79th St New York City NY 10021

HOPWOOD, WILLIAM W., corp. exec.; b. Wheeling, W.Va., 1915; ed. N.Y. U., 1939. Pres., dir. Calgon Corp., Pitts., Calgon Corp. (Can.) Ltd.; dir. Bruner Corp. Home: 58 Hoodridge Dr Pittsburgh PA 15228 Office: PO Box 136 Pittsburgh PA 15230*

HORACK, BENJAMIN S., lawyer; b. Iowa City, Ia., Oct. 3, 1917; A.B., Duke, 1939, LL.B., 1941. Admitted to N.C. bar, 1941; now mem. firm Ervin, Horack & McCartha, Charlotte, N.C. Mem. Charlotte Sch. Bd. Mem. Am., N.C., 26th Jud. Dist. (pres. 1967-68) bar assns., N.C. State Bar, Phi Beta Kappa, Phi Delta Phi, Order of Coif. Office: 806 E Trade St Charlotte NC 28202*

HORADAM, WEYMAN WILSON, banker; b. Yoakum, Tex., May 25, 1916; s. Frank A. and Verna (Willemin) H.; B.B.A., U. Tex., 1941; m. Lucile Simonton, July 12, 1952; children—Diana Louise, William Warren. With RFC, Houston, 1946-52; with Bank of Southwest, N.A., Houston, 1952—. sr. v.p., mgr. loan and investment div., 1966—. Served to capt. USAAF, 1942-46. Mem. Robert Morris Assos. (nat. bd. dirs.), Houston C. of C., Beta Gamma Sigma, Beta Alpha Psi. Home: 5642 Sylmar St Houston TX 77036 Office: 900 Main St Houston TX 77001

HORAN, FRANCIS HARDING, lawyer; b. Saxtons River, Vt., May 18, 1900; s. John Harding and Mary (Flynn) H.; A.B. Dartmouth, 1922; LL.B., Harvard, 1926; m. Elizabeth S. Rogers, Feb. 9, 1935; children—John, Elizabeth, Anthony, Honora. Admitted to N.Y. bar, 1927; with Dept. of Justice, 1931-34; chief civil asst. U.S. atty. So. Dist. N.Y., 1934-37; counsel Commn. Adminstrv. Law, 1939- 42; partner Webster, Sheffield & Horan, 1942-51; gen. counsel Liggett & Myers Tobacco Co., 1951-65, v.p., 1956-65; with firm Webster, Sheffield, Fleischman, Hitchcock & Chrystie, 1965—. Trustee Vt. Acad. Mem. Am., N.Y. State bar assns., Assn. Bar City N.Y., Am Arbitration Assn. (exec. com.). Club: Century Assn. (N.Y.C.). Home: R D Falls Village CT 06031 Office: 1 Rockefeller Plaza New York City NY 10020

HORAN, HUBERT JOSEPH, Jr., lawyer; b. Phila., June 30, 1889; s. Hubert Joseph and Elizabeth Cecelia (Gartland) H.; LL.B. cum laude, U. Pa., 1911; LL.D., LaSalle U., 1953; LL.D., St. Joseph's Coll., 1963; m. Agnes R. Mack, Sept. 27, 1916; 7 daus., 2 sons. With Continental Bank & Trust Co. (formerly Broad Street Trust Co.), Phila., 1921-69, pres., 1938-59, chmn. bd., chief exec. officer, 1959-65, chmn. exec. com., 1965-66, dir., now dir. emeritus; dir. Warner Co., Union Paving Co., Day and Zimmerman Rep. U.S. Govt. on Intergovt. Com. for European Migration Geneva, 1955. Chmn. A.R.C., Southeastern Dist. of Pa., 1946; mem. Mayor's Com. to Reorganize Finances of Phila., 1947-48; dir. City Trusts, 1946-49; chmn. Phila. Parking Authority Board. Dir. Misericordia Hosp.; trustee, 1st v.p. Estate of Stephen Girarb; dir. United Fund. Decorated Cross of Comdr. Order of Phoenix (Greece), 1951; Papal Knight Malta: Knight Comdr. Equestrian Order Gregory Gt., Pope Paul VI. Republican. Roman Catholic. Clubs: Union League (Phila.). Home: The Barclay Philadelphia PA 19103 Office: Continental Bank & Trust Co Philadelphia PA 19101

HORAN, JAMES D., author; b. N.Y.C., July 27, 1914; s. Eugene and Elizabeth (Schaub) H.; student Drake Coll., Jersey City, also Writing Center, N.Y. U.; m. Gertrude Dorrity, Sept. 4, 1938; children—Patricia, Brian, Gary, James C. Newspaper editor, novelist, historian; ret. asst. mng. editor, Sunday editor, spl. events editor N.Y. Jour. Am., N.Y.C. Recipient award Mystery Writers of Am., 1957, Westerners Buffalo award, 1960, Gold Typewriter award N.Y. Reporters Assn., 1960, hon. mention, 1962; award N.J. Tchrs. English, 1962, Page One citation Am. Newspaper Guild, 1961. Mem. Westerners (co-founder N.Y. Corral), N.Y. Civil War Round Table (past pres.), N.Y. Reporters Assn., Writers Guild Am., Am. Newspaper Guild. Author: (with Gerold Frank) Out In the Boondocks, 1943, U.S. Seawolf, 1945; Action Tonight, 1945; Desperate Men, 1949; (with Howard Swiggett) The Pinkerton Story, 1951; Desperate Women, 1952; (novel) King's Rebel, 1953; Confederate Agent, 1954; (with Paul Sann) Pictorial History of the Wild West, 1954; Mathew Brady, Historian with a Camera, 1955; Across the Cimarron, 1956; The DA's Man, 1957; (novel) Seek Out and Destroy, 1958; The Mob's Man, 1959; The Great American West, 1959; (novel) Teh Shadow Catcher, 1961; The Desperate Years, 1962; The Seat of Power, 1965 (novel of year N.J. Assn. Tchrs. English); America's Forgotten Photographer: Timothy O'Sullivan, 1966; (novel) The Right Image, 1967; The Pinkertons: The Detective Dynasty That Made History, 1968; The Life and Art of Charles Schreyvogel: Painter-Historian of the Indian Fighting Army of the American West, 1969 (Westerners Buffalo award 1970; N.J. Tchrs. English award 1970). Home: 2302 Palisade Av Weehawken NJ 07087

HORAN, JENNINGS FISHWORTH mfg. exec.; b. Lima, O., Apr. 1, 1932; B.S., U. San Francisco, 1954; M.S., Stanford University, 1956; m. Rosemarie Lois Brown, May 15, 1955; 1 son, Anthony Robinson. Sales rep. Ames-Brockton Fabricated Products, Akron, O., 1956-58, sales mgr. Coshocton, Ohio, 1959-61, gen. manager plant, 1961-68, v.p. sales, 1968--. Instr. bus. Coshocton Jr. College, 1968-69. Named Man of Year, Coshocton Junior Chamber of Commerce, 1968. Mem. Coshocton C. of C. (vice president 1967-68, pres. 1969-70), English Speaking Union, Coshocton Sertoma Club, Nat. Assn. Mfrs., Sales Executives Institute, Phi Beta Kappa, Sigma Chi, Phi Mu. Democrat. Mem. Christian Ch. (lay leader). Mason (32, Shriner). Clubs: Coshocton Country, Coshocton City, Running Deer Country. Home: 2d Av Coshocton OH Office: 3d Av Coshocton OH

HORAN, JOHN J., pharm. co. exec.; b. S.I., N.Y., July 9, 1920; s. Michael T. and Alice (Kelly) H.; A.B., Manhattan Coll., 1940; LL.B., Columbia, 1946; m. Julie Fitzgerald, Jan. 2, 1945; children—Mary Alice, Thomas, Jack, David. Admitted to N.Y. bar, 1946; with firm Nimes, Verdi & Martin, N.Y.C., 1946-52; atty., trademark counsel Merck & Co., Inc., 1952-55, counsel Merck Sharp & Dohme div., 1955-57; dir. pub. relations Merck & Co., 1957- 61, exec. dir. research adminstrn., research labs., 1961-62, dir. corp. planning, 1962-63; exec. v.p. marketing Merck Sharp & Dohme, 1962-67; exec. v.p., gen. mgr., 1967-69, pres., 1969—. Bd. dirs. Mgmt. Sci. Center of Wharton Sch. of U. Pa., Am. Found. Pharm. Edn., Acad. Natural Scis. Phila., Manhattan Coll. Council Planning and Devel. Served to lt. USNR, 1942-46. Clubs: Columbia Univ. (N.Y.C.); Whitemarsy Valle Country. Home: Morris Rd Ambler PA 19002 Office: Merck Sharp & Dohme West Point PA 19486

HORD, STEPHEN Y., banking and investment adv. service; b. Indpls., Nov. 7, 1897; s. Francis T. and Eleanor (Young) H.; ed. Phillips Acad., Andover, Mass., 1913-17; B.A., Yale, 1921; m. Catharine Norcross, Oct. 29, 1926; children—Stephen Y., Frederic N., Catharine Brent. With No. Trust Co., Chgo., 1921-27; asso. Lee, Higginson & Co., Chgo., 1927-32; with Brown Bros., Harriman & Co., 1932—, gen. partner, 1945—; dir., exec. com. Ill. Central Industries, Inc., I.C.R.R. Co.; dir. Abex Corp. Trustee Cowles Commn. Bd. dirs. Passavant Meml. Hosp.; trustee emeritus Phillips Acad. Mem. Sr. Soc. (Yale), Skull and Bones, Delta Kappa Epsilon. Clubs: Onwentsia (Lake Forest); Chicago, Commercial, Attic (Chgo.); Old Elm (Ft. Sheridan); River (N.Y.C.). Home: 450 W Deerpath Rd Lake Forest IL 60045 Office: 135 S LaSalle St Chicago IL 60603 ☆

HORDER, MARGARET L'ANSON, (Mrs. Arthur Roland Freeman), book illustrator; b. Sydney, Australia; d. Thomas and Elsie I'Anson (Bloomfield) Horder; student Redlands, Sydney, Sydney Art Sch., St. Martin's Art Sch., London, Westminster Art Sch., London, London Central Sch. Arts and Crafts; m. Arthur Roland Freeman, 1939. Free lance illustrator children's books Oxford U. Press, William Collins, Frederick Muller, London, 1938-49; illustrator for pubs. Angus & Robertson (Sydney), Constable Young Books (London), Hutchinson (London), Harcourt, Brace & World (N.Y.C.), 1949—. Recipient Children's Spring Book Festival award for The Family Conspiracy, 1964. Mem. Children's Book Council Australia. Home: 22 Taylor St Woy Woy Bay New South Wales 2256 Australia Office: Harcourt Brace & World 757 3d Av New York City NY 10017

HORDERN, WILLIAM EDWARD, theologian; b. Dundurn, Sask., Can., Sept. 8, 1920; s. Paul Sylvester and Ethyl (Davis) H.; B.A. with great distinction, U. Sask., 1941; B.D., St. Andrews Coll., Saskatoon, Can., 1945; S.T.M. magna cum laude, Union Theol. Sem., N.Y.C., 1946, Th.D., 1951: m. Marjorie Joyce, Jan. 28, 1944; children—Richard, Joyce, Davis. Ordained to ministry United Ch. Can., 1943: minister Marsden- Neilberg United Ch., 1943-45; asst. minister St. John's Luth. Ch, Richmond Hill, N.Y., 1945-49; tchr. philosophy and religion Swarthmore Coll., 1949-57; prof theology Garrett Theol. Inst., 1957-66, Henry Pfeiffer prof., 1960-66; pres. Luth. Theol. Sem., Saskatoon, Sask., Can., from 1966; asst. minister Trinity Luth. Ch., Skokie, Ill., 1960-66. Mem. Am. Theol. Assn., Am. Acad. Religion (pres. 1966). Author: Christianity, Communism and History, 1954; A Layman's Guide to Protestant Theology, 1955; The Case for a New Reformation Theology, 1959; Speaking of God, 1964; world of Learning, 1971. Author, editor: New Directions in Theology Today, 1966. Home: 2 Morton Pl Saskatoon Saskatchewan Canada

HORECKER, BERNARD LEONARD, biochemist; b. Chgo., Oct. 31, 1914; s. Paul and Bessie (Bornstein) H.; B.S., U. Chgo., 1936, Ph.D., 1939; m. Frances Goldstein, July 12, 1936; children—Doris, Marilyn, Linda. Research asso. chemistry U. Chgo., 1939-40; examiner U.S. Civil Service, 1940-41: biochemist USPHS, NIH, Bethesda, Md., 1941-59, with biochemistry study sect., 1956-59, chief lab. of biochemistry and metabolism Nat. Inst. Arthritis and Metabolic Disease, 1956-59; professorial lectr. enzyme chemical George Washington U., 1950-57; guest research-worker Pasteur Inst., Paris, France, 1957-58; prof. microbiology, chmn. dept., N.Y. U. Coll. Medicine, 1959- 63: prof. molecular biology, chmn. dept. Albert Einstein Coll. Medicine, 1963-71, asso. dean for sci. affairs, 1972—; research respiratory enzymes and intermediary metabolism; vis. prof. biochemistry U. Cal., 1954; vis. lectr. U. Ill., 1956; Ciba lectr. Rutgers U., 1962; Phillips lectr. Haverford Coll., 1965; vis. prof. biochemistry and molecular biology Cornell U., 1965; Reilly lectr. Notre Dame U., 1969—; vis. lectr. U. Rotterdam, 1970; chmn. sci. adv. bd. Roche Inst., 1970—. Bd. dirs. Academic Press, Inc. Mem. Research Career Award com. Nat. Inst. Gen. Med. Scis., 1966-70; mem. personnel com. Am. Cancer Soc., 1968—. Recipient Paul Lewis Labs. award in enzyme chemistry, 1952; Rockefeller Pub. Service award, 1957; Hillebrand prize Am. Chem. Soc., 1954; award in biol. scis. Washington Acad. Sci., 1954; Fulbright Travel award, 1963; Commonwealth Fund fellow, 1967. Fellow A.A.A.S., Am. Acad. Arts and Scis.; mem. Japanese Biochem Soc. (hon. mem.), Am. Chem. Soc., Biochem. Soc. (Eng.), Swiss Biochem. Soc. (hon.), Am. Soc. Biol. Chemists (pres. 1967-68), Nat. Acad. Scis., Harvey Soc. (v. p. 1969-70, pres. 1970-71), PanAm. Assn. Biochem. Socs. (vice chmn. 1971, chmn. 1972), Phi Beta Kappa, Sigma Xi. Author: Pentose Metabolism in Bacteria, 1961; articles sci. publs. Editor Biochem. and Biophys. Communications, 1959—, Current Topics in Cellular Regulation, chmn. editorial bd. Archives of Biochemistry and Biophysics, 1967. Home: 340 E 64th St New York City NY 10021 Office: Albert Einstein College of Medicine 1300 Morris Park Av Bronx NY 10461

HORENSTEIN, JASCHA, conductor, composer; b. Kiev, Russia, May 6, 1899; s. Abraham and Marie (Jekels) H.; student U. Vienna; grad. Acad. music, Vienna; Ernestina Diaz Saenz Valiente, Jan. 30,

1958; 1 son by previous marriage, Peter. Made debut with Vienna Symphony Orch.; conductor Berlin Symphony, 1925-28; mus. dir. Dusseldorf Municipal Opera, also guest condr. with many leading European orchestras, 1929-33; filled regular engagement as condr. in Russia, France, Belgium and Poland, 1933- 37, appearing with Moscow and Leningrad Philharmonic orchs., Orchestre Symphoniquede Paris, Lamoureux Orch. of Paris, Brussels Philharmonic, Warsaw Philharmonic and Warsaw State Opera, also appearing as guest condr. in Stockholm, Helsingfors, Riga and Vienna; toured Australia and New Zealand, 1938; one of four condrs. (with Arturo Toscanini) Palestine Symphony Orch., 1939; made U.S. debut, 1941; appeared as condr. N.Y. Philharmonic Symphony Soc., Montreal, Havana and Brazilian Symphony (Rio de Janeiro), Teatro Colon Orch. (Buenos Aires), 1946-49; made Mexican debut, 1944; condr. for all major European Orchs., also Opera House of West Berlin, Royal Opera House Covent Garden, London, La Scala, Milano, San Francisco Opera House, festivals of Edinburgh, Florence, Vienna; tours of S.Am., S.Africa, Australia; debut Am. Symphony Orch., 1969; recs. with Vienna Symphony Orch., London Symphony Orch., New Philharmonic Orch. London. Recipient Grand Prix du Disque (3). Address: 12 Chemin du Coteau Lausanne-Pully Switzerland

HORGAN, JAMES DONALD, biomed. engr.; b. Grand Rapids, Mich., May 21, 1922; s. James T. and Nona M. (Van Camp) H.; B.Elec. Engring., Marquette U., 1946, M.S., 1951; Ph.D., U. Wis., 1957; m. Rose Marie Rhora, Sept. 6, 1945; children—Kathleen, Daniel. Mem. staff Radiation Lab., Mass. Inst. Tech., 1942-45; mem. faculty Marquette U., 1946—, prof. elec. engring., 1958- -, chmn. dept., 1956-61, bio-med. engring. research, 1961-, prof. engring. in medicine, 1968; spl. research computer simulation of human physiol. systems. Fellow I.E.E.E.; mem. N.Y. Acad. Scis., Am. Soc. Engring. Edn., Sigma Xi, Eta Kappa Nu, Tau Beta Pi, Triangle. Roman Catholic. Home: 1530 Longwood St Elm Grove WI 53122 Office: Marguette U Milwaukee WI 53233

HORGAN, JOHN JOSEPH, Jr., banker; b. Worcester, Mass., July 26, 1925; s. John Joseph and Catherine M. (Burke) H.; A.B., Harvard, 1949; M.B.A., Columbia, 1950; m. Catherine E. O'Neil, Sept. 11, 1948; children—Kathleen, Patricia, Jean, Daniel, Mary, Peter, Christine, Timothy, Tara. Asst. treas. Chase Manhattan Bank, N.Y.C., 1950-55; v.p. Peoples Trust Co., Hackensack, N.J., 1955- 59; exec. v.p., cashier N.J. Nat. Bank, 1959—; lectr. Fairleigh Dickinson U. Chmn. Renewal Adv. Commn., Trenton, 1965-69; vice chmn., treas. Mercer County Improvement Authority. Pres., bd. dirs. Trenton Community Found., 1969—; pres. Delaware Valley United Fund, 1971—; asst. treas., bd. dirs. Mercer Hosp. Served with AUS, 1943-46. Mem. N.J. (exec. com.), Mercer County (dir., past pres.) bankers assns. Clubs: Rotary, Serra, Trenton (past pres., trustee), Harvard of New Jersey (dir.). Home: 38 Burning Tree Lane Trenton NJ 08638 Office: 1 W State St Trenton NJ 08638

HORGAN, PAUL, author; b. Buffalo, Aug. 1, 1903; s. Edward Daniel and Rose Marie (Rohr) H.; student N.M. Mil. Inst., 1920-23; Litt. D., Wesleyan U., 1956, So. Meth. U., 1957, Notre Dame U., 1958, Boston Coll., 1958, N.M. State U., 1962, Coll. Holy Cross, 1963, U. N.M., 1963, Fairfield U., 1964; D.H.L., Canisius Coll., 1960, Georgetown U., 1962, Litt.D., D'Youville Coll., 1965, Pace Coll., 1968, Loyola Coll., Balt., 1968, Lincoln Coll., 1968, St. Bonaventure U., 1970; L.H.D., LaSalle U., 1971. Prodn. staff Eastman Theatre, Rochester, N.Y., 1923-26; librarian N. M. Mil. Inst., Roswell, 1926- 42, asst. to pres., 1947-49; Guggenheim fellow, 1947-48, 58; sr. fellow Center Advanced Studies, Wesleyan U., Middletown, Conn., 1959-61, dir., 1962-67, sr. fellow in letters, 1967-68, adj. prof. English, 1967-71, prof. emeritus, 1971—, author in residence, 1969—. Lectr., Grad. Sch. Letters, U. Ia., Feb.-June 1946; lectr. English, Yale U., 1969; scholar in residence Aspen Inst. Humanistic Studies, 1968, 71. Chmn. bd. Santa Fe Opera, 1958-69, mem., 1969—; mem. adv. bd. John Simon Guggenheim Found., 1963-69; pres. bd. dirs. Roswell Mus., 1948-55, mem. bd. Roswell Pub. Library, 1958-62, hon. mem., 1962—; bd. mgrs. Sch. Am. Research, 1959—; bd. judges Book of Month Club, 1969—. Served from capt. to lt. col. AUS, 1942-46; through active dutv Dept Armv, Washington, 1952. Hoyt fellow Saybrook Coll., Yale, 1965; asso. fellow Saybrook Coll., 1966—. Decorated Legion of Merit; recipient Campion award of Catholic Book Club, 1957; Cath. Book award Cath. Press Assn., 1965, 68; Roswell Mus. addition named after him, N.M. Mil. Inst. library named after him. Mem. Nat. Council Humanities, Nat. Inst. Arts and Letters, Am. Catholic Hist. Assn. (pres. 1960). Roman Catholic. Clubs: Graduate (New Haven, Conn.); Century, University (N.Y.C.); Cosmos, Army- Navy (Washington), Athenaeum (London, Eng.). Author: Men of Arms, 1931; The Fault of Angels (Harper prize 1933), 1933; No Quarter Given, 1935; Main Line West, 1936; From the Royal City, 1936; The Return of the Weed, 1936; A Lamp on the Plains, 1937; New Mexico's Own Chronicle (with Maurice Garland Fulton), 1937; Far from Cibola, 1938; Figures in a Landscape, 1940; The Habit of Empire, 1941; biog. intro. to Diary and Letters of Josiah Gregg, Vol. 1, 1941; A Tree on the Plains, an Am. Opera (music by Ernst Bacon), 1942; Yours, A. Lincoln (drama), 1942; The Common Heart, 1942; The Devil in the Desert, 1952; One Red Rose for Christmas, 1952; Great River: The Rio Grande in North American History (Pulitzer prize, Bancroft prize 1955), 1954; Humble Powers, 1954; The Saintmaker's Christmas Eve, 1955; The Centuries of Santa Fe, 1956; Give Me Possession, 1957; biog. intro. Diary and Letters of Josiah Gregg, Vol. 2, 1943; Rome Eternal, 1959; A Distant Trumpet, 1960; Citizen of New Salem, 1961; Mountain Standard Time, 1962; Conquistadors in North American History, 1963: Toby and the Nighttime, 1962; Things as They Are, 1964; Songs after Lincoln, 1965; Peter Hurd: A Portrait Sketch from Life, 1965; Memories of the Future, 1966; The Peach Stone, 1967; Everything To Live For, 1968; The Heroic Triad, 1970; Whitewater, 1970; Maurice Baring Restored, 1970; Encounters with Stravinsky, 1972. Contbr. articles, fiction to mags. Created Knight of St. Gregory, 1957. Address: Wesleyan U Middletown CT 06457

HORKAN, VINCENT JOSEPH, clergyman; b. Lancashire, Eng., Dec. 12, 1915; s. Patrick and Catherine (Harlow) H.; B.A., Sacred Heart Sem., Detroit, 1937; M.A., Cath. U., 1947, Ph.D., 1953. Ordained priest Roman Cath. Ch., 1941; asst. pastor St. Paul's Ch., Grosse Pointe, Mich., 1941-45; asst. supt. Cath. schs., Detroit Archdiocese, 1950-57, supt., 1957-65; pastor St. Norbert Ch., Inkster, Mich., 1965-70, Martha Ch., Dearborn, Mich., 1970—; elevated to papal chamberlain with title Very Reverend Monsignor, 1959. Author: (with L. Lamont Okey) A Guide to High School Speech, 1959. Contbr. articles to profl. and religious jours. Home: 18307 Oakwood Blvd Dearborn MI 48124

HORKEY, WILLIAM RICHARD, diversified oil co. exec.; b. Tulsa, Apr. 22, 1925; s. William Edward and Clara Doris (Rice) H.; B.A., State U. Ia., 1947; LL.B., U. Okla., 1950; grad. Advanced Mgmt. Program, Harvard, 1962; m. Barbara Jeanne Williamson, Oct. 18, 1952; children—Elaine Gail, Edward Richard, Ellen Beth. Admitted to Okla. bar, 1950; with Gulf Oil Corp., 1950-51, Skelly Oil Co., 1951-55; with Helmerich & Payne, Inc., Tulsa, 1955—, sec., legal counsel, 1957-64, v.p., 1960-64, exec. v.p., 1964—, also dir.; v.p., treas., dir. Helmerich & Payne, C.A., Venezuelan drilling contractor; v.p., dir. White Eagle Overseas Oil Co., Inc., Philippines, Helmerich & Payne Internat. Drilling Co.; pres., dir. Tulsa Engineered Products Corp., Helminerals, Inc., Taiwan Mining Co.; dir. Utica Sq. Nat. Bank, Tulsa. Vice chmn. of oil div. of Tulsa Community Chest, 1964-69. Mem. bd. of mgmt. S.E. Tulsa YMCA, 1963—, vice chmn. 1969—. Served to 2d lt. USAAF, 1943-45. Mem. Am., Okla., Tulsa County bar assns., Am. Judicature Soc., Order of Coif, Phi Delta Phi, Phi Delta Theta. Presbyn. (chmn. bd. deacons). Clubs: Tulsa, Empire (bd. dirs.), Mid-Continent Harvard AMP (pres.) (Tulsa). Home: 5686 Evanston Evanston Tulsa OK 74105 Tulsa OK 74105 Office: 1579 E 21st St Tulsa OK 74114

HORLACHER, JOHN PERRY, educator; b. Phila., July 5, 1901; s. John Perry and Gertrude Irene (Misselwitz) H.; A.B., Ashland Coll., 1922; A.M., U. Pa., 1928, Ph.D., 1935; m. Alma B. Schultz, Oct. 23, 1924; 1 dau., Nancy Gaye (Mrs. Samuel R. Roberts). Exec. sec. Labor Relations Council, Wharton Sch. U. Pa., 1946-59, chmn. dept. polit. sci., 1953-71, mem. adminstrv. bd. Inst. Local and State Govt., 1953—, prof. polit. sci., 1954—, chmn. univ. senate, 1957-58; polit. sci. editor J. B. Lippincott Co., 1956—. State compensation officer WPA of Pa., 1935; research dir. Gov.'s Com. to Investigate Affairs of Phila. Registration Commn., 1941; exec. dir. wage stblzn. div. Phila. Regional War Labor Bd., 1945; chmn. Phila. WSB, 1946, 51-53; chmn. Fair Labor Standards Act Industry Com. P.R. Dir. Pa. Mental Health, Inc. Mem. Am. Arbitration Assn. (labor arbitration panel), Fed. Mediation and Conciliation Service (labor arbitration panel), Am. Assn. U. Profs., Am. Acad. Polit. and Social Sci., Indsl. Relations Research Assn., Nat. Acad. Arbitrators (Phila. regional chmn. 1955; mem. bd. govs., v.p.), Am. Polit. Sci. Assn., Nat. Assembly Mental Health Edn. (chmn. 1958), Pi Gamma Mu, Pi Sigma Alpha. Presbyn. Author: Results of Workmen's Compensation in Pennsylvania, 1934. Co-author monographs. Editor: Administrative Regulation of Private Enterprise, 1942. Contbr. articles to profl. jours. Home: 3608 Darby Rd Bryn Mawr PA 19010

HORN, ANDRE RAPHAEL, mfg. co. exec.; b. Paris, France, May 8, 1928; s. Edouard E. and Helen Horn; B.S.C. in Math., U. Paris, 1946; grad. Ecole des Hautes Etudes Commerciales, 1950; C.P.A., France, 1952; m. Dolores Horn. Came to U.S., 1966. With Arthur Young & Co., C.P.A.'s, Paris, 1950-55; controller Joy France, Paris, 1955-58; v.p. finance and adminstrn. Joy Internat., Brussels, Belgium, 1953-66; chief financial officer, dir. Joy Mfg. Co., Pitts., 1967—. Mem. Financial Execs. Inst. Office: Oliver Bldg Pittsburgh PA 15222

HORN, ANDREW HARLIS, educator, librarian; b. Ogden, Utah, July 22, 1914; s. Edward Cooper and Cora (Harlis) H.; student Santa Monica City Coll., 1932-35, Am. U., 1951; A.B., U. Cal. at Los Angeles, 1937, M.A., 1940, Ph.D., 1943, B.L.S., U. Cal. at Berkeley, 1948; m. Mary Amelia Baier, Jan. 4, 1948. Lab. asst. Santa Monica City Coll., 1933-35; teaching asst. U. Cal. at Los Angeles, 1937-40, 42-43, research asst., 1940-41, Hattie Hellar scholar history, 1941, lectr. European history, extension div., 1941-42; tech. writer Douglas Aircraft Co., 1942-43; asst. prof. history Johns Hopkins, 1946- 47; asst. head dept. spl. collections U. Cal. at Los Angeles Library, 1948-49, univ. archivist, 1950-54, head dept. spl. collections, 1950-51, asst. librarian, 1951-52, asso. librarian, 1952-54; univ. librarian, prof. librarianship U. N.C., 1954-57; librarian Occidental Coll., Los Angeles, 1957-59, asst. dean Sch. Library Service, U. Cal. at Los Angeles, 1959-66, dean, 1966—, asso. prof., 1959-63, prof., 1963—. Served as sgt. AUS, 1943-46. Mem. Am., Cal. library assns. Am. Assn. U. Profs., Soc. Am. Archivists, Bibliog. Soc. (London), Printing Hist. Soc. (London), Medieval Acad. Am., Bibliog. Soc. Am., Phi Beta Kappa, Phi Delta Kappa, Pi Gamma Mu, Phi Eta Sigma, Blue Key, Kappa Alpha. Club: Rounce and Coffin (Los Angeles). Home: 1919 Alpha Rd Glendale CA 91208 Office: U Cal Los Angeles CA 90024

HORN, BURR ALLEN, Jr., steel co. exec., lawyer; b. Chgo., Mar. 31, 1916; s. Burr Allen and Dorothy W. (Emery) H.; student U. Mo., 1933-35; B.A. magna cum laude, Colgate U., 1937; LL.B., Harvard, 1940; spl. student, U. Liverpool (Eng.), 1945; m. Florence Rick, June 3, 1950. Spl. agt. FBI, 1940-42; admitted to Mich. bar, 1942, Pa. bar, 1943, W.Va. bar, 1965, also U.S. Supreme Ct.; asst. counsel Koppers Co., Inc., Pitts., 1942-63; v.p., gen. counsel Peabody Coal Co., St. Louis, 1964; gen. counsel Wheeling Steel Corp., 1964—. Mem. exec. council Huroquois council Boy Scouts Am., 1964—; pres. Inter-Club Bridge League, Pitts., 1957-61. Served with AUS, 1944-46; ETO. Decorated Bronze Star, Purple Heart, Combat Inf. badge; award of Colmar (France). Mem. Am., Fed., Pa., Allegheny County (Pa.), W.Va., Ohio County (W.Va.) bar assns., Colgate Alumni Assn. (past pres. Pitts.), Phi Beta Kappa, Phi Eta Sigma. Home: Clover Fields Wheeling WV 26002 Office: Wheeling Steel Corp Bldg Wheeling WV 26004

HORN, CARL, Jr., utility exec.; b. Rutherfordton, N.C., Oct. 21, 1921; s. Carl and Freda Wagner (Warden) H.; A.B., Duke, 1942, LL.B., 1947; m. Frances Alice Emmet, Feb. 7, 1948 (dec. 1966); children—Carl III, Claire, Katherine, Thomas E.; m. 2d, Virginia Grey Johnston, Oct. 27, 1967. Admitted to N.C. bar, 1947, practiced in Charlotte until 1953; asst. gen. counsel Duke Power Co., Charlotte, 1954-59, gen. counsel, 1959-63, v.p., gen. counsel, 1963-66, v.p. finance, gen. counsel, 1966-69, exec. v.p., gen. counsel, 1970-71, pres., 1971—. Bd. dirs. Charlotte Meml. Hosp. Served to capt. AUS, 1942-46; PTO; mem. N.C. N.G., 1953-54. Mem. Am., N.C. bar assns., Edison Electric Inst. (chmn. legal com. 1967—), Duke Univ. Law Alumni Assn. (pres. 1961), Newcomen Soc. N. Am., Order of Coif. Presbyn. (elder). Home: 2111 Wendover Rd Charlotte NC 28211 Office: 422 S Church St Charlotte NC 28202

HORN, CHARLES LILLEY, explosives mfr.; b. Mt. Vernon, Ia., Mar. 5, 1888; s. George Lilley Horn and Anna May (Cooper) H.; B.L. U. Minn., 1912; Sc.D., Clemson Agrl. Coll., 1953, Cornell (Ia.) Coll., 1954, Worcester (Mass.) Poly. Inst., 1960; L.D., Bucknell U., 1955, U. So. Cal., 1962; Litt.D., Lafayette U., 1956; Sc.D. (hon.), Colo. Coll., Colorado Springs, 1962; LL.D., Macalester Coll., St. Paul, 1964, Case Inst. Tech., Cleve., 1966, Colgate U., 1970; m. Louise Brace, Nov. 20, 1924 (dec.); children—Charles Lilley, William Brace; m. 2d, Alice Robertson, May 1, 1951. Pres. Fed. Cartridge Corp., Mpls., 1921—; operated Twin Cities Ordnance Plant, 1941-46, Twin Cities Arsenal, 1950; pres. Hoffman Engring. Corp., Olin Found., Inc. Chmn. commrs. Mpls. Housing and Redevel. Authority, 1960—. Recipient citation medal for conservation edn. and outstanding leadership Dept. Agr., 1956; Distinguished Grad. award Law Alumni Assn. U. Minn., 1961. Mem. Pilgrims of U.S., Phi Delta Phi, Sigma Alpha Epsilon. Mason. Clubs: Minneapolis, Minikahda (Mpls.). Home: 3807 Zenith Av S Minneapolis MN 55410 Office: Foshay Tower Minneapolis MN 55402

HORN, CLAYTON G., editor; b. Bellevue, O., Mar. 11, 1906; s. Gustav G. and Clara Louise (Miller) H.; A.B., Western Res. U., 1928; m. Juanita K. Schwenn, July 21, 1928; children—Phyllis Diane (Mrs. James T. Harrington), Wendell Gene. Sports writer Canton (O.) Repository, 1928-31, asst. city editor, 1931-32, asst. telegraph editor, 1932-33, news editor, 1933-34, mng. editor, 1939-46, became editor-in-chief, 1946; mng. editor East Liverpool (O.) Rev., 1935-39; exec. editor Brush-Moore Newspapers, Inc. (now Thomson-Brush-Moore Newspapers, Inc.), 1957—, dir., 1959-68. Trustee Kent (O.) State U., 1964-71, Profl. Football Hall of Fame, Canton; adv. com. Malone Coll., Canton, Canton YMCA, Walsh Coll., Canton. Am. Soc. Newspaper Editors, Sigma Delta Chi. Republican. Lutheran. Clubs: Brookside Country, Canton, Rotary. Home: 2815 W Dale Rd Canton OH 44708 Office: 500 Market Av S Canton OH 44702

HORN, DANIEL, research dir.; b. Rochester, N.Y., May 28, 1916; s. Samuel Joseph and Ethel Esther (Finkle) H.; S.B., Northeastern U., 1938; A.M., Harvard, 1942, Ph.D., 1943; m. Janet Dayton Patterson, Jan. 2, 1937; children—Elizabeth, Nathaniel Brewster, Marguerite, Roger Ludlow. Statistician child growth study Harvard, 1938-40, Gen. Edn. Bd. tng. fellow child psychology, 1940-41, research asst. psychol. clinic, 1941-43, teaching fellow, 1942-43, instr. psychology, 1943-44; instr. psychology Northeastern U., 1942-43; asst. dir. statis. research Am. Cancer Soc., 1947-57, dir. program evaluation, 1957-62; asst. chief research Cancer Control Program, USPHS, 1962-64, chief spl. projects sect. cancer control program, div. chronic diseases, 1964-65; now dir. Nat. Clearinghouse for Smoking and Health, U.S. Dept. Health, Edn. and Welfare; lectr. psychology Princeton, 1949; lectr. pub. health Yale, 1953-56. Served as aviation psychologist USNR, 1944-46; chief pilot error study br., med. safety div., flying safety service USAAF, 1946-47. Fellow A.A.A.S., Am. Pub. Health Assn.; mem. Pub. Health Cancer Assn. (pres. 1966-67), Am. Statis. Assn., Am. Psychol. Assn., Sigma Xi. Home: 18400 New Hampshire Av Ashton MD 20702 Office: 5600 Fishers Lane Rockville MD 20852

HORN, FRANCIS HENRY, coll. pres.; b. Toledo, Nov. 18, 1908; s. Henry Frederick and Orpha Ford (Bennett) H.; A.B., Dartmouth, 1930; M.A., U. Va., 1934; M.A., Yale, 1942, Ph.D. (Sterling fellow 1946-47), 1949; LL.D. (hon.), U. Hartford, 1955, Providence Coll., 1959, Dickinson Coll., 1961; D.H.L., So. Ill. U., 1958, Ricker Coll., 1963, U. Nev., 1969, Molloy Coll., 1971; D.C.L., Pace Coll., 1961; Litt.D., Ohio No. U., 1961; D.Sc. Edn., Bryant Coll., 1961; Pd.D., R.I. Coll., 1962; LL.D., Brown U., 1963, U. N.H., 1964, Defiance Coll., 1966, U. Me., 1967, D'Youville Coll., 1968, Wagner Coll., 1969, U.R.I., 1969; Ed.D., Western New Eng. Coll., 1966; H.H.D., Windham Coll., 1965; m. Xenia Beliavsky, June 8, 1935; children—Michael Serge, Barbara Ann (Mrs. Helmut Schaefer), Elizabeth Marie. Instr. English and history Am. U. at Cairo (Egypt), 1930-33; asst. dean Jr. Coll. of Commerce (now Quinnipiac Coll.), New Haven, 1936-37, acting dean, 1937-38, dean, 1938-42; asst. dean Biarritz Am. U., France, 1945-46; editor reports coop. study Lincoln (Neb.) schs., 1946-47; dean eve. div., dir. summer session, asso. prof. edn., Johns Hopkins, 1947-51, acting chmn. dept. edn., 1951, vis. prof. edn., 1952-53; exec. sec. Am. Assn. Higher Edn., 1951-53; pres. Pratt Inst., Bklyn., 1953-57; vis. distinguished prof. higher edn. So. Ill. U., 1957-58; pres. U. R.I., 1958-67; pres. Commn. on Ind. Colls. and Univ., State of N.Y., 1967-71; pres. Albertus Magnus Coll., New Haven, 1971—. Nat. adv. bd. United World Federalists; nat. council Boy Scouts Am.; exec. com. Yale Grad. Sch. Assn., vice chmn. Theta Delta Chi Ednl. Found. Bd. dirs. Near East Found., Futures for Children; chmn. trustees United Bd. Christian Higher Edn. Asia; trustee U. R.I. Found., Harvard-Yenching Inst.; hon. trustee Windham Coll. Served from 1st lt. to lt. col., AUS, 1942-46. Decorated Legion of Merit, Army Commendation medal with cluster; recipient medal for distinguished pub. service U.S. Navy, 1967, outstanding civilian service award U.S. Army, 1967. Mem. Am. Assn. U. Profs., N.E.A., Phi Beta Kappa, Pi Sigma Alpha, Phi Delta Kappa, Omicron Delta Kappa, Theta Delta Chi, Delta Sigma Pi, Alpha Delta Sigma. Conglist. Author: Challenge and Perspective on Higher Education, 1971. Editor: College and University Bull., 1951-53; Current Issues in Higher Edn., 1952, 53; Literary Masterpieces of the Western World, 1953; Twenty Five Years in the Wide, Wide World, 1955. Contbr. ednl. Jours., N.Y. Times Book Rev. Home: 850 Prospect St New Haven CT 06511

HORN, FRIEDRICH JOSEF MARIA, educator, chem. engr.; b. Vienna, Austria, Oct. 9, 1927; s. Friedrich and Olga (Zitterbart) H.; Abitur, Bundeslehr-und Versuchsansalt für Chemische Industrie, Vienna, 1947; Dipl.Ing., Tech. U., Vienna, 1954, Dr.Techn., 1958; m. Elisabeth Nowak, Oct. 11, 1954; children—Andreas, Corinna. Came to U.S., 1964. Physicist, Farbwerke Hoechst, Frankfurt am Main, W. Germany, 1954-62; lectr. chem. engring. Imperial Coll., U. London (Eng.), 1962-64; prof. chem. engring. Rice U., 1964-70, U. Rochester (N.Y.), 1970—; vis. Inst. Theoretical Physics, U. Giessen (W. Germany), 1959; vis. prof. U. Minn., 1964, Stanford, summer 1965, Abt. Techn. Chemie, Tech. U., Munich (W. Germany), 1967, U. Natal (S. Africa), 1969, Carnegie Mellon U., 1970, U. Waterloo, 1970. Recipient Max Buchner prize of Dechema, W. Germany, 1963. Mem. Am. Inst. Chem. Engrs., Deutsche Bunsengesellschaft für Physikalische Chemie, Tau Beta Pi. Research periodic processes in tech. chemistry, chem. reactor theory, chem. kinetics. Home: 630 Claybourne St Rochester NY 14618

HORN, JAMES P., transp. co. exec.; b. 1928; B.S., Lehigh U., 1951; married. With Koppers Co. Inc., 1951-53, Haskins & Sells, C.P.A.'s, 1953-62; formerly with Am. Export Isbrandtsen Lines Inc., from 1962, sr. v.p., treas., from 1967, also dir. Address: 26 Broadway New York City NY 10004 *

HORN, JOHN STEPHEN, Jr., univ. pres.; b. Gilroy, Cal., May 31, 1931; s. John Stephen and Isabelle (McCaffrey) H.; A.B. with great distinction, Stanford, 1953, postgrad., 1953-54, 55-56, Ph.D. in Polit. Sci., 1958; M.Pub. Adminstrn., Harvard, 1955; m. Nini Moore, Sept. 4, 1954; children—Marcia Karen, John Stephen. Congl. fellow, 1958-59; adminstrv. asst. to sec. labor, Washington, 1959-60; legislative asst. to U.S. Senator Thomas H. Kuchel, 1960-66; sr. fellow The Brookings Instn., 1966-69; dean grad. studies and research Am. U., 1969-70; pres. Cal. State Coll., Long Beach, 1970—; sr. cons., host The Govt. Story on TV, The Election Game, radio series, 1967-69. Mem. urban studies fellowship adv. bd. Dept. Housing and Urban Devel., 1969-70, chmn. 1969; vice-chmn. U.S. Commn. Civil Rights, 1969—; mem. Pres.-elect Nixon's Task Force on Orgn. Exec. Br., 1968; mem. law enforcement edn. program, adv. commn. law enforcement assistance adminstrn. Dept. Justice, 1969—. Co-founder Western U.S. Com. Arts and Scis. for Eisenhower, 1956. Fellow John F. Kennedy Inst. Politics, Harvard, 1966-67. Mem. Stanford Assos., Phi Beta Kappa, Pi Sigma Alpha. Republican. Club: El Capitan Eating (Stanford). Author: The Cabinet and Congress, 1960; Unused Power: The Work of the Senate Committee on Appropriations, 1970. Home: 3944 Pine Av Long Beach CA 90807

HORN, MARTIN LOUIS, Jr., restaurateur; b. N.Y.C., Mar. 12, 1927; s. Martin Louis and Kathryn (Albert) H.; student Seton Hall U., 1946-47; B.S., Cornell U., 1950; m. Leone L. Behrendt, June 18, 1949; 1 dau., Leone Susan. Vice pres. Pals Cabin Restaurant, West Orange, N.J., 1951—; v.p. Mayfair Farms Restaurant, 1951—; pres. Pals Pancake Houses, 1961—, Longhorn Restaurants, 1968—, Horn Family Restaurants, 1971—. Served with USNR, 1945-46. Named to Hall of Fame, Hospitality mag., 1968. Mem. Nat. (pres.), N.J. (past pres.) restaurant assns., Am. Hotel-Motel Assn. (dir.), Cornell Soc. Hotelmen, Sigma Nu. Clubs: New York Athletic; Essex County Country (W. Orange, N.J.). Home: 25 Saratoga Way Short Hills NJ 07078 Office: 265 Prospect Av West Orange NJ 07052

HORN, PAUL JOSEPH, musician; b. N.Y.C., Mar. 17, 1930; s. Jack L. and Frances (Sper) H.; Mus.B., Oberlin Conservatory Music, 1952; Mus.M. (fellow), Manhattan Sch. Music, 1952; children—Marlen L., Robin F. Mem. Sauter-Finigan Band, 1956-57, Chico Hamilton Quintet, 1957-58, NBC Staff Orch., Hollywood, Cal., 1960; free-lance studio work, 1960-66; formed Paul Horn Quintet, 1959; recording artist for Dot, World Pacific, HiFi, Columbia, RCA Victor records; concerts throughout U.S. and Europe, 1957—; appeared jazz festival, Bologna, Italy, 1967; guest speaker, performer jazz clinics at numerous univs., 1961—; tchr. system transcendental meditation U. Cal. at Los Angeles, also at Berkeley and adult centers; student Acad. Meditation, Himalayas, India, 1967, 68; motion picture appearances; guest TV performer; producer, artist Epic Records. Bd. dirs. Victoria Symphony Orch. Served with AUS, 1953-56. Recipient 5 Grammy nominations, 1966, 2 Grammy awards, 1966; also awards from Jazz Polls, Downbeat mag., Playboy mag. Home: 2066 Paul's Terrace Victoria British Columbia Canada

HORN, ROBERT CHISHOLM, Jr., pathologist; b. Allentown, Pa., July 7, 1913; s. Robert Chisholm and Zelie (Soleliac) H.; B.S., Muhlenberg Coll., 1933; M.D., Yale, 1937; m. Dorothy Louise App, Jan. 1, 1940; children—Robert Chisholm III, Thomas Landes, Ethel Marion. Intern Geisinger Mem. Hosp., Danville, Pa., 1937- 38; spl. tng. pathology and surg. pathology Columbia-Presbyn. Med. Center, N.Y.C., 1938-42; from asso. to prof. surg. pathology U. Pa. Sch. Medicine, also surg. pathologist and dir. tumor clinic U. Pa. Hosp., 1942-55; chmn. dept. pathology Henry Ford Hosp., Detroit, 1955—; cons. Armed Forces Inst. Pathology, 1948—, Phila. VA Hosp., 1948-55, Phila. Naval Hosp., 1944-55. Mem. adv. com. to surgeon gen., 1960-64; mem. study sect. NIH, 1966-70; trustee, exec. com. Mich. Cancer Found., 1965—; bd. dirs. Phila. div. Am. Cancer Soc., 1948-55, Southeastern Mich. div., 1956-65, mem. nat. adv. com. clin. investigation, 1969—; chmn. Nat. Com. Careers in Med. Tech., 1961-66. Recipient Distinguished Alumnus awards Muhlenberg Coll., 1965, Geisinger Meml. Hosp., 1965. Mem. A.M.A. (sect. chmn. 1962), Coll. Am. Pathologists (speaker assembly, 1964-68, bd. govs. 1968—, sec.-treas. 1970—), Mich., County med. socs., Internat. Acad. Pathologists (council 1965-68), Mich. Soc. Pathologists (pres. 1965), Am. Soc. Clin. Pathologists (chmn. council pathology 1967-70), Am. Assn. Pathologists and Bacteriologists, Am. Thyroid Assn., Sigma Xi, Alpha Omega Alpha. Author articles in field, chpts. in books. Home: 90 N Edgewood Dr Grosse Pointe MI 48236 Office: 2799 W Grand Blvd Detroit MI 48202

HORN, STANLEY FITZGERALD, editor, publisher; b. nr. Nashville, May 27, 1889; s. Williamson Williams and Sadie Ashby (Graves) H.; grad. Fogg High Sch., Nashville, 1906; Litt. D. (hon.), U. Chattanooga; m. Alice Beryl Williams, June 12, 1913; children—Stanley Fitzgerald, Ruth. With J.H. Baird pub. Co., pubs. So. Lumberman, Nashville, 1908—, (except short period on Phila. Eve. Ledger 1914); editor, part owner So. Lumberman, 1917—; pres. J. H. Baird Pub. Co. Chmn. Tenn. Civil War Centennial Commn.; mem. Tenn. Hist. Commn. Mem. Tenn. Hist. Soc., Phi Beta Kappa. Democrat. Episcopalian. Clubs: Coffee House, Cumberland, Belle Meade Country, Round Table. Author: Boy's Life of Robert E. Lee, 1935; The Hermitage: Home of Andrew Jackson, 1938; Invisible Empire, 1939; The Army of Tennessee, 1941; This Fascinating Lumber Business, 1943; Gallant Rebel, 1947; Robert E. Lee Reader, 1949; The Decisive Battle of Nashville, 1957. Editor, compiler: Tennessee's War, 1965. Home: Golf Club Lane Nashville TN 37215 Office: 2916 Sidco Dr Nashville TN 37204

HORN, STEFAN FERDINAND, educator; b. Vienna, Austria, Jan. 4, 1900; s. Paul and Therese (Strisower) H.; D. rerum politicarum, U. Vienna, 1922; diploma parliamentary interpreter, U. Geneva (Switzerland), 1946; m. Nancy Christensen, July 3, 1951; children—Nikolaus, Lise Mrs. Thomas F. Florey). Came to U.S., 1948, naturalized, 1954. Engaged in banking, Austria, 1923, in food industry, Austria, 1923-36, in real estate, Austria, 1936-38; internee camps in France and Switzerland, World War II; interpreter Nuremberg War Crimes Trials, 1946-48; instr. German, French and govt. Merrimac Coll., Andover, Mass., 1948-49; with Sch. Langs. and Linguistics, Georgetown U., 1949—, prof. interpretation and translation and interpretation, 1966-68, emeritus, 1968—, head div. interpretation and translation, 1956—; interpreter numerous internat. congresses and confs.; translator for govt. and industry; personal interpreter internat. statesmen; lectr. U.S. and Europe. Decorated Golden Cross of Honor for meritorious services to Republic of Austria, 1st class, 1958; recipient 175th Anniversary Medal of Honor, Georgetown U., 1964; Distinguished Service citation Am. Austrian Soc., 1964: Outstanding Service award Sch. Langs. and Linguistics, Georgetown U., 1968-69; Vicennial medal Georgetown U., 1949-69. Mem. Am. Translators Assn., Am. Assn. Lang. Specialists, Am. Austrian Soc. (pres. Washington 1962). Club: Cosmos (Washington). Author: Glossary of Financial Terms, 1965. Home: 7109 Central Av Takoma Park MD 20012 Office: Sch Langs and Linguistics Georgetown Univ Washington DC 20007

HORN, WALTER WILLIAM, educator; b. Waldangelloch, Germany, Jan. 18 1908; s. Karl and Matilde (Peters) H.; student univs. Heidelberg, Berlin; Ph.D., U. Hamburg, 1933; m. Dr. Alberta West Parker, Apr. 14, 1949; children—Michael P., Peter M., Rebecca A. Came to U.S., 1938, naturalized, 1943. Research asso. German Inst. Art, Florence, Italy, 1934-37; faculty U. Cal. at Berkeley, 1938—, successively vis. lectr. art, asst. prof., asso. prof., 1938-48, prof., 1948—, chmn. dept. art, 1957-60, chmn. faculty Coll. Letters and Sci., 1961-64, humanities research prof., 1964-65. Served to capt., inf., AUS, 1943-46. Guggenheim fellow, 1960-61. Mem. Coll. Art Assn. (dir. 1950-54, 58-60, 64—), Soc. Archtl. Historians (dir. 1965). Club: Faculty. Author: The Facade of St. Gilles, 1937; (with Ernest Born) The Barns of the Abbey of Beaulieu, 1965; also articles in field. Home: 339 Western Dr Richmond CA 94801 Office: U Cal Berkeley CA 94720

HORN, WOODROW SCHLEY, osteo. physician, surgeon; b. Wharton, W.Va., Mar. 13, 1913; s. William F. and Minora (White) H.; student W.Va. U., Morgantown, 1932-35; grad. Kirksville Coll. Osteopathy and Surgery, 1939; m. Cora Mae Critz, Dec. 23, 1938. Practice osteo. medicine, Charleston, W.Va., 1939-43; intern N.W. Hosp., Miami, Fla., 1943-45; county health officer, Bushnell, Fla., 1945-46; practice osteo. medicine and surgery, Palmetto, Fla., 1946—. Mem. Fla. State Bd. Health, 1959-67. Treas., bd. dirs. Fla. Osteo. Found. Recipient Distinguished Service award Fla. Osteo. Med. Assn., 1960. Mem. Am. Osteo. Assn. (past pres.), Fla. Osteo. Med. Assn. (past pres., exec. dir., recipient Physician of Year award 1971), Palmetto C. of C. (past pres.). Mem. Ch. of Jesus Christ of Latter-day Saints (bishop). Mason. Home: 150 Bayshore Dr Terra Ceia FL 33591 Office: 1500 8th Av Palmetto FL 33561

HORNADAY, FRED EUGENE, assn. exec; b. Indpls., June 28, 1900; s. James Parks and Mary Gertrude (Willis) H.; student George Washington U., 1921; B.S. in Journalism, Wharton Sch. Finance and Commerce, U. Pa., 1924; m. Annie Claire Mayfield, July 6, 1927; children—Fred Eugene, Richard Mayfield. Field sec. C. of C. of U.S., Washington, 1924-26; field sec. U. S. Daily, Washington, 1926- 28; with Am. Forestry Assn., Washington, 1928-68, exec. v.p., 1956-68, hon. v.p., 1971—. Mem. nat. council Boy Scouts Am. Mem. Soc. Am. Foresters, Phi Sigma Kappa. Presbyn. (elder). Clubs: Rotary, Cosmos (pres. 1971). Home: 3508 Runnymede Pl Washington DC 20015 Office: 919 17th St Washington DC 20006

HORNBACK, JOSEPH HOPE, educator; b. Nevada, Mo., Apr. 20, 1910; s. Joseph Thomas and Georgia (Munn) H.; A.B., Central Coll., 1932; M.A., Harvard, 1933; Ph.D., U. Ill., 1952; postgrad. U. Chgo., 1933-34, 41-42, 46-49. Tchr. math. Calumet City (Ill.) High Sch., 1934-37, U. Chgo. Lab Sch., 1937-42; asst. prof. math. U. Ala., 1952-57, asso. prof., 1957-63, prof., 1963—; vis. scientist to high schs. for Ala. Acad. Sci. Served as lt. USNR, 1942-46. Mem. Am. Math. Soc., Math. Assn. Am., Sigma Xi, Phi Kappa Phi. Mem. Disciples of Christ Ch. Mason. Home: 3A Read St Apts Tuscaloosa AL 35401 Office: U Ala Dept Math University AL 35486

HORNBAKE, RALPH LEE, univ. ofcl.; b. Coal Center, Pa., Dec. 18, 1912; s. Ralph and Sudie (Frantz) H.; M.A., Ohio State U., 1936, Ph.D., 1942; LL.D., Eastern Mich. U., 1963; m. Evelyn Young, Sept. 12, 1939; 1 dau., Barbara Ann. Instr. California (Pa.) State Coll., 1937-39; asso. prof. indsl. arts State U. N.Y. Coll. at Oswego, 1940-43; dir. prodn. tng., airplane div. Curtiss-Wright Corp., Columbus, O., 1943-45; asso. prof. indsl. edn. U. Md., 1945-47, prof., 1947—, head dept., 1954-57, faculty dean, 1957-60, v.p. acad. affairs, 1960—; lectr. Ohio State U., summers 1939, 40. Pres. Am. Council Indsl. Arts Tchr. Edn., 1957-58; mem., vice chmn. commn. on higher edn. Middle States Assn. Colls. and Secondary Schs. Recipient fellowship in edn. Harvard Grad. Sch., 1949-50. Mem. Nat. Assn. State Univs. and Land-Grant Colls. (chmn. council acad. affairs), Phi Kappa Phi, Phi Delta Kappa, Phi Sigma Pi (nat. sec. 1946 -48), Epsilon Pi Tau (hon.), Omicron Delta Kappa, Iota Lambda Sigma. Methodist. Author: (with Donald Maley) Superior Practices in Industrial Arts Teacher Education. Home: 7001 Wells Pkwy College Heights West Hyattsville MD 20782 Office: University of Maryland College Park MD 20740

HORNBAKER, GAYLE STORY, mfg. co. exec.; b. Van Buren County, Ia., Oct. 23, 1924; s. Roger Bernard and Nona (Story) H.; B.S. in Commerce, State U. Ia., 1947; M.B.A., Harvard, 1948; m. Rosalind Alice Hoover, Nov. 25, 1948; children— Susan Kay, Gordon Lee, Beth Ann, Kerry Sue. Formerly with Studebaker Corp., from 1948, asst. treas., 1959-64, treas. from 1964, asst. treas., Studebakers Worthington Inc., 1967-68, treas., from 1968. Served to lt. (j.g.) USNR, 1943-46. Home: 18711 Norwich Ct South Bend IN 46614

HORNBEAK, MACK HAYNES, banker; b. Hornbeak, Tenn., June 23, 1906; s. Pleas and Ada (Haynes) H.; B.S. in Commerce, U. Tenn., 1929; M.A., La. State U., 1933, Ph.D., 1937; m. Barbara Thomas, June 5, 1958; 1 dau., Anne Haynes. Mem. faculty La. State U., 1932-41; with City Nat. Bank, Baton Rouge, 1949—, pres., 1957- -, also dir.; dir. Crawford Corp. Served to lt. col., inf., AUS, 1942- 45; ETO. Decorated Legion of Merit, Bronze Star with 1 oak leaf cluster; Croix de Guerre with palm (France and Belgium); Croix de Guerre (Luxembourg). Mem. La. (treas. 1959—), Baton Rouge (pres. 1958-59) chambers commerce, Sigma Nu, Phi Kappa Phi. Clubs: Boston (New Orleans); Baton Rouge Country (pres. 1953-54), City, Rotary (Baton Rouge). Home: 165 Nelson Dr Baton Rouge LA 70808 Office: 124 N 3d St Baton Rouge LA 70821

HORNBECK, LYLE WESTBROOK, lawyer; b. Preston Center, Pa., Dec. 16, 1903; s. Frank E. and Irene (Moore) H.; A.B., Amherst Coll., 1925; LL.B., Harvard, 1928; m. Olga Anderson, Sept. 30, 1942; children—John W., Richard. Admitted to N.Y. bar, 1928; partner firm Bond, Schoeneck & King, Syracuse, N.Y., 1950—; corp. counsel, Syracuse, 1946-50. Dir. Unity Mut. Life Ins. Co. N.Y. Mem. Atty. Gen. Adv. Commn. Ethics, 1954-59; vice chmn. N.Y. State Temporary Commn. Ednl. Finance, 1953-54; chmn. Syracuse Charter Revision Commn., 1958-60; mem. Ohio River Valley Sanitation Commn., 1962—, chmn., 1970—; mem. State Atomic and Space Devel. Authority, 1964—. Sec. N.Y. Republican State Com., 1959-65. Bd. dirs. Pratt- Northam Found. Home: 1812 Euclid Av Syracuse NY 13224 Office: State Tower Bldg Syracuse NY 13202

HORNBEIN, VICTOR, architect; b. Denver, Oct. 26, 1913; s. Samuel and Rose (Frumess) H.; student Atelier Denver, Beaux-Arts Inst. Design, 1930-35; m. Ruth Kriesler, Mar. 20, 1947; children—Victoria Ann, Peter. Practice as Victor Hornbein, architect, 1940-60; with firm Victor Hornbein and Edward D. White, Jr., Denver, 1940—, partner, 1960—; vis. lectr. U. Denver, 1949-52, U. Colo., 1958-59, 68. Mem. design rev. bd. U. Colo., 1969-71; design adv. panel region 8 Gen. Services Adminstrn., 1967-70. Pres. Met. Council Community Services, 1957. Served with AUS, 1942-45. Decorated Bronze Star medal. Fellow A.I.A. (pres. Colo. Central chpt. 1971); mem. Constrn. Specification Inst. Major works include conservatory and edn. bldg. Denver Bot. Gardens, 1966-71; Porter Library, Temple Buell Coll., Denver, 1962; Bethesda Hosp., Denver, 1970, René Spitz Children's div. Ft. Logan Mental Health Center, Denver, 1965. Home: 714 Pontiac St Denver CO 80220 Office: 5909 E 38th Av Denver CO 80220

HORNBERGER, THEODORE, educator; b. Northville, Mich., Jan. 13, 1906; s. John Jacob and Katharine (Watson) H.; B.S., U. Mich., 1927, M.A., 1929, Ph.D. 1934; student King's Coll., London, Eng., 1927-28; m. Marian Louise Welles, Feb. 7, 1929; children—Jean Alice (Mrs. Roland Cleveland), Katharine Watson (Mrs. Allan Denenberg). Instr. English, U. Mich., 1928- 36, asst. prof., 1936-37; research fellow Huntington Library, 1936-37; prof. English, U. Tex., 1937-46; vis. summer lectr. Harvard, 1938, Northwestern U., 1940, Duke, 1941, 42, 50, Ohio State U., 1945, U. Colo., 1966; prof. English, U. Minn., 1946-60, chmn, dept. 1950-58; prof. English, U. Pa., 1960—, John Welsh Centennial prof. history and English lit., 1968—, acting chmn. dept., 1968-69, chmn. grad. group English, 1965-67; vis. prof. N. Am. lit. U. Brazil, 1952. Guggenheim fellow, 1967-68. Mem. Modern Lang. Assn. Am. (chmn. Am. lit. group 1956, chmn. Am. Lit. I 1970), History Sci. Soc. (council 1947- 50), Nat, Council Tchrs. English (chmn. coll. sect. 1951-52), Coll. English Assn., Am. Dialect Soc., Colonial Soc. Mass., Phi Beta Kappa, Phi Gamma Delta. Author: Scientific Thought in the American Colleges, 1638-1800, 1945; Os Estados Unidos através de sua literatura, 1953; Benjamin Franklin, 1961. Editor; Compendium Physicae (Charles Morton), 1940; Mark Twain's Letters to Will Bowen, 1941; Literature of the United States (with Walter Blair, Randall Stewart, James E. Miller), 6th edit., 1966; William Cullen Bryant and Isaac Henderson, 1950; others. Home: 23 Univeity Mews 45th and Spruce Sts Philadelphia PA 19104

HORNBLOW, ARTHUR, Jr., motion picture producer; b. N.Y., City, March 15, 1893; s. Arthur and Natalie (Lambert) H.; student Dartmouth. D.H.L.; N.Y. Law Sch.; m. Leonora Schinasi, Nov. 4, 1945; son, Michael; one son by prev. marriage, John Terry. Admitted to N.Y. bar, 1917; wrote and produced plays in N.Y.C., 1920-27; writer for Samuel Goldwyn, Hollywood, 1927; chief prodn. exec., 1923-33; film producer, Paramount, 1933-42; producer Metro-Goldwyn-Mayer, 1942-52; pictures produced: Ruggles of Red Gap, 1939; Gaslight, 1947; The Hucksters, 1947; Cass Timberlane, 1948; The Asphalt Jungle, 1950; produced film Oklahoma for Rodgers and Hammerstein; pres. Arthur Hornblow Prodns.; producer Witness for the Prosecution; The War Lover; translator plays from French for Broadway, among them, Pasteur by Sacha Guitry, 1925, The Captive by Edouard Bourdet, 1926. Chmn. theatre adv. board Dartmouth Coll. Served as 1st. lt. U.S. Army attached to counter-espionage section of Intelligence Corps, 1918-19. Decorated: Etoile Noire de la Legion d'Honneur (France); U.S. Presdl. Citation. Clubs: Dartmouth (N.Y.C.); Bucks (London). Author juvenile books: (with Leonora Hornlow) Animals Do the Strangest Things, Insects Are the Strangest Things, Birds Do the Strangest Things, Fish Do the Strangest Things, Reptiles Do the Strangest Things. Home: 45 Sutton Pl S New York City NY 10022

HORNBLOWER, HENRY, II, investment broker; b. Boston, Nov. 5, 1917; s. Ralph and Eleanor (Greenwood) H.; B.S., Harvard, 1941; m. Dorothy Shapard, June 6, 1942; children—Henry, Harriet, Augusta, Eleanor. Cranberry grower Cape Cod Co., 1945-46; with Hornblower & Weeks-Hemphill, Noyes, 1946—, partner, 1950—; pres., dir. Cape Cod Co., H & W. Agy., Inc.; pres. Plimoth Plantation, Inc. Mem. Pilgrim Soc. (trustee), Mass. Bible Soc. (trustee), Mass. Hist. Soc. Clubs: The Country (Brookline); Union, Somerset, Bond, Odd Volumes (Boston). Home: 109 Chestnut St Boston MA 02110 Office: 160 Franklin St Boston MA 02110

HORNBLOWER, RALPH, Jr., investment banker, b. Boston, Feb. 1, 1919; s. Ralph and Eleanor (Greenwood) H.; student Milton Acad., 1934-37; B.S., Harvard, 1941; m. Priscilla Alder Blumer, Feb. 9, 1944 (dec. Feb. 1960); children—Rosalie, Ralph III, Paul Skinner, Priscilla; m. 2d, Phoebe Mary Blumer, Oct. 12, 1960; children—John Greenwood, David Maitland, James Wainwright. With firm Hornblower & Weeks, 1946—, gen. partner, 1950- -; dir. Cape Cod Co. Bd. dirs. Greenwich Boys Club Assn. Clubs: Owl (Cambridge, Mass.); Harvard (N.Y.C.); Round Hill, Greenwich Skating (Greenwich); Squibnocket Associates (Chilmark, Mass.). Home: Fairfield Rd Greenwich CT 06830 Office: 8 Hanover St New York City NY 10004

HORNBOSTEL, VICTOR OTTO, coll. dean; b. Canten, Kan., Sept. 17, 1919; s. Otto Henry and Hulda Sophia (Luehrmann) H.; A.A., St. John's Coll., Winfield, Kan., 1936; B.S., Kan. State Tchrs. Coll., 1942; M.S., U. Wis., 1947, Ph.D., 1954; m. Rubye Florence Laprarie, June 8, 1946; children—V. Patrick, Charles Thomas, William James, Gary Bruce. Dir. research Wis. Edn. Assn., Madison, 1948-52; asst. dir. research N.E.A., Washington, 1952-64; prof. Okla. State U., 1964-67; postgrad. edn. Bowling Green State U., 1967-70; dean U. Tulsa Coll. Edn., 1970—. Instr. sch. finance Johns Hopkins, 1960, 62. Served with USNR, 1943-46. Mem. Am. Ednl. Research Assn., A.A.A.S., Am. Assn. Sch. Adminstrs., N.E.A. Editor Yearbooks Dept. Elementary Sch. Prins., 1954-58, Reports Nat. Conf. Sch. Finance N.E.A., 1959-64. Home: 3622 E 56th St Tulsa OK 74135

HORNBRUCH, FREDERICK WILLIAM, Jr. mgmt. cons.; b. Roselle, N.J., July 14, 1913; s. Frederick William and Elsa M. (Becker) H.; M.E., Stevens Inst. Tech., 1934; m. Helen Novak, Apr. 10, 1936; children—Frederick William III, Harlan Richard. Engr., Weston Elec. Instrument Corp., Newark, 1934-40, Falstrom Co., Passaic, N.J., 1940-41; indsl. engr. Bendix Aviation Corp., Phila., 1941-43; prodn. mgr. Columbia Machine Works, Bklyn., 1943-44; chief engr., dir. Rath & Strong, Inc., Boston, 1944-57; v.p. Landers, Frary & Clark, Inc., New Britain, Conn., 1957-59; v.p. Atlas Corp., N.Y.C., 1959-64; pres., dir. Titeflex, Inc., Springfield, Mass., 1960-64, Internat. Air, Inc., N.Y.C., 1962; chmn. bd. Metronics Corp., Santa Monica, Cal. 1960-64; v.p. Calumet & Hecla, Inc., Chgo., gen. mgr. Flexonics div., 1964-68; v.p. Aero-Chatillon Corp., N.Y.C., 1968-69; v.p. adminstrn. Macrodyne- Chatillon Corp., N.Y.C., 1969; organizer cons. bus.; Barrington Hills, Ill; 1970—. Mem. Am. Soc. M.E., Soc. Advancement Mgmt., Am. Mgmt. Assn., Newcomen Soc., Tau Beta Pi. Pi Delta Epsilon, Phi Sigma Kappa. Presbyn. Clubs: Engineers (N.Y.C.); Barrington Hills Country. Author: (with Bruce, Chadruc) Practical Planning and Scheduling, 1950. Contbr. to Handbook Bus. Administrn., 1967; contbr., mem. adv. bd. Handbook Modern Manufacturing Management, 1967-68. Patentee instrument synchronizing aircraft engines. Home: Rural Route 2 Three Lakes Rd Barrington Hills IL 60010

HORNBY, HERBERT, brewing co. exec.; b. Clifton, N.J., Jan. 5, 1913; s. Richard and Martha (Cohn) H.; student N.Y.U., 1930-32; m. Roma Eugena Elizabeth Berry, Nov. 9, 1935; children—Richard, David. Staff accountant Price Waterhouse & Co., N.Y.C., 1930-43; tax mgr. Joseph E. Seagram & Sons, N.Y.C., 1943-45; treas. Waldrich Co., Clifton, 1945-57; v.p. finance Okonite Co., Passaic, N.J., 1957-61; v.p. finance F. & M. Schaefer Brewing Co., Bklyn., 1961—, dir., 1968—; treas. F. & M. Schaefer Corp., N.Y.C., 1968—; instr. accounting Rutgers U., 1949-51. Patron Valley Hosp., Ridgewood, N.J. C.P.A., N.Y. Mem. Nat. Assn. Accountants, Newcomen Soc. N.Am. Home: 1 Bridle Way Ho-Ho-Kus NJ 07423 Office: 430 Kent Av Brooklyn NY 11211

HORNBY, LESLEY, (Twiggy), photog. model; b. London, Eng., Sept. 19, 1949; d. William Norman and Helen (Reeman) Hornby; student Brondesbury and Kilburn Grammar Sch., 1960-66. Model, 1966—; dir., mgr. Twiggy Enterprises Ltd., 1966—; starred in movie The Boy Friend, 1971. Address: 14 Charlotte Mews London W 1 England

HORNBY, ROBERT ALFRED, corp. exec.; b. Topeka, 1900; s. Alfred Joseph and Louise E. (McJilton) H.; C.E., U. Cal.; m. Mary Louise Duffy, Jan. 16, 1925; 1 dau., Janis Hornby French. Dir., mem. exec. com. Pacific Lighting Corp., Los Angeles, 1945—, pres., 1956-68; hon. dir. Broadway-Hale Stores, Inc.; dir. Barclays Bank Cal.; cons. prof. U. So. Cal. Sch. Bus. Administrn. Mem. Gov. Cal. Com. Creative Soc. Trustee U. So. Cal., also mem. campus plan, acad. affairs and devel. coms., mem. adv. council Sch. Bus. Administrn.; trustee Cal. State 4-Yr. Coll., also mem. finance, ednl. policy, pub. affairs coms.; trustee Cal. Council Econ. Edn. Served in USMC, World War I; served to lt. col USAAF, 1942-45. Decorated Legion of Merit. Registered civil engr., Cal. Mem. Am. Enterprise Inst. (past trustee), Am. (dir. 1952-60, chmn. com. execs. taxation, com. execs. pub. affairs, com. promotion, advt., research), Pacific Coast (past pres.) gas assns., Inst. Gas Tech. (past trustee), Chevaliers de Tastevi n. Republican. Conglist. Clubs: Family (San Francisco); Los Angeles, Los Angeles Country. Home: 435 S Curson Av Los Angeles CA 90036 Office: 810 S Flower St Los Angeles CA 90017

HORNBY, WILLIAM HARRY, newspaperman; b. Kalispell, Mont., July 14, 1923; s. Lloyd G. and Margaret E. (Miller) H.; A.B. in Humanities, Stanford, 1944, M.A. in Journalism, 1947; postgrad. U. London (Eng.), 1949-50; m. Rosemary Cross, 1947; children—Margaret (dec.), Megan, Melinda; m. 2d, Helen Schnitzler Sullivan, 1957; children—John, Mary Catherine. Reporter, copyreader San Francisco News, 1947-48; reporter A.P., San Francisco, 1949; research asst. Hoover Library, Stanford, 1949-50; information officer ECA, Paris and The Hague, 1950-52; asst. gen. mgr. Kalispell Lumber Co., 1953-56, partner, 1955-62; reporter Great Falls (Mont.) Tribune, 1957; copy-desk chief, editorial writer Denver Post, 1957-60, mng. editor, 1960-70, exec. editor, 1970—; v.p. Eastern Mont. Pub. Co., Miles City, Mont.; dir. Schnitzler Corp., Froid, Mont., 1st State Bank, Newcastle, Wyo. Trustee, Kent Sch. Mem. Sigma Delta Chi, Sigma Nu. Republican. Episcopalian. Elk.

Clubs: Cactus, Denver Press, Denver Athletic, University. Home: 5300 E Mansfield St Denver CO 80237 Office: Denver Post 650 15th St Denver CO 80202

HORNE, CHARLES FREDERICK, electronic exec.; b. N.Y.C., Jan. 3, 1906; s. Charles F. and Sarah (Durham) H.; B.S., U.S. Naval Acad., 1926, postgrad. 1933-34; M.S., Harvard, 1935; m. Evelyn Tuttle, May 16, 1930; children—Charles F., Anne (Mrs. Frederick B. Warder, Jr.). Commd. ensign USN, 1926, advanced through grades to rear adm., 1951; gen. line, communication, electronic devel. duties, 1926-39; comdg. officer U.S.S. Long, 1940-41; radar, communications officer, staff comdr. battleships, 1941; communications officer South Pacific area, 1942-43; communications, radar officer Amphibious Forces Pacific, 1944-45; dep. chief Naval Communications, 1946-48; dir. Fed. Airways, 1949-50; adminstr. CAA, 1951-52; mgr. Convair, Gen. Dynamics Corp., Pomona, Cal., 1953-56, v.p., 1957-61, pres. Gen. Dynamics Pomona, and v.p. Gen. Dynamics Corp., 1961-70, v.p. corp., 1970—. West Coast adviser Radio Tech. Commn. for Aeros. Mem. bd. councilors sch. engring. U. So. Cal.; bd. fellows Claremont Grad. Sch. and U. Center. Mem. Nat. Commn. on Indsl. Arts Edn. Twice decorated Combat Legion of Merit; recip. internat. regional medal CAA; medal of honor award Electronic Industries Assn. Fellow Inst. Elect and Electronic Engrs.; mem. U.S., Cal. (dir.), Los Angeles (dir.) C.'s of C.; So. Cal. Industry-Edn. Council chmn. bd.), Electronic Industries Assn. (dir., past pres.), Aeronautics Assn., Armed Forces Communications and Electronics Assn. (dir.), Assn. U.S. Army, Nat. Security Indsl. Assn., Am. Ordnance Assn., Am. Radio Relay League, Am. Rocket Soc., Aircraft Owners and Pilots Assn., Nat. Mgmt. Assn. (gold Knight award), Western Electronic Mfrs. Assn., Navy League, Naval Order U.S., U.S. Naval Acad. Alumni Assn. Club: Aero of Southern California. Home: 844 Hillcrest Dr Pomona CA 91766 Office: PO Box 2507 Pomona CA 91766

HORNE, DAVID HAMILTON, publisher; b. Worcester, Mass., Oct 26, 1912; s. Ralph Hamilton and Harriet (Scott) H.; A.B. magna cum laude with honors in English, Clark U., 1942; M.A., U. Mo., 1947; Ph.D., Yale, 1950; m. Elinor Clark, Nov. 6, 1948; children—Susan Hamilton, Beverly Palmer, Shirley Scott. Instr. English, U. Mo., 1942-43, 46-47; instr. English, Yale, 1950-52, univ. series editor, 1958-65, fellow Timothy Dwight Coll., 1962-65; with Yale U. Press, 1954-65, exec. editor, 1961-65; asst. dir. Harvard U. Press, 1966-67, asso. dir., 1967—; pres., treas. Horne Assos., Inc., New Haven, 1960—. Mem. Bibliog. Soc., Conn. Acad. Arts and Scis., Am. Polit. Sci. Assn., Am. Assn. U. Presses, Phi Beta Kappa, Author: The Life and Minor Works of George Peele, 1952. Editor: (Shakespeare) The Tempest, 1955. Home: 65 Deacon Haynes Rd Concord MA 01742 Office: 79 Garden St Cambridge MA 02138

HORNE, JAMES GRADY, educator; b. Ft. Worth, Tex., Apr. 6, 1926; s. James Grady and Mary Louise (Parker) H.; B.Chem. Engring., Tulane U., 1946, M.A., 1952, Ph.D., 1956; m. Margaret Elizabeth Martin, July 16, 1949; children—Karen, Charles, Alan. Asst. prof. U. Ky., 1956-59; asst. prof. U. Ga., 1959-61, asso. prof., 1961-66, prof., 1966—, head, dept. math., 1969—. Served with USNR, 1944-46, 53-55. Mem. Am. Math. Soc., Math. Assn. Am. Home: Route 1 Cleveland Rd Bogart GA 30622

HORNE, JOHN E., ins. co. exec., former govt. ofcl.; b. Clayton, Ala., Mar. 4, 1908; s. John Eli and Cornelia (Thomas) H.; Normal certificate Troy State U., 1928; A.B. with honors, U.Ala. 1933, M.A. (fellow in history 1933-35), 1941, LL.D., 1970; m. Ruth F. Kleinman, July 27, 1938; children—Linda (Mrs. Richard Clark), Susan (Mrs. James K. Ewart). Tchr., Pike County, Ala., 1925-26, Columbiana, Ala., 1928-31; rep. Macmillan Pub. Co., 1935-39, Row, Peterson Pub. Co., 1939-42, 46; adminstrv. asst. to Senator John J. Sparkman of Ala., 1947-51, 54-61; adminstr. Small Def. Plants Administrn., 1951- 53; staff dir. Democratic Senatorial Campaign Com., 1954; asst. campaign mgr. to Adlai E. Stevenson, 1956; exec. dir. Nat. Citizens Com. Kennedy- Johnson, 1960; adminstr. Small Bus. Administrn., 1961-63; mem. Fed. Home Loan Bank Bd., 1963-68 chmn., 1965-68; pres. Investors Mortage Ins. Co., 1969-70, chmn., 1970—; dir. Continental Investment Corp., Boston. Pres. Pi Kappa Alpha Meml. Found., 1967-69. Served from lt. (j.g.) to lt. (s.g.) USNR, 1943-45, capt. Res. Recipient Letter of Commendation for meritorious Navy service, Outstanding D.C. Alumnus award U. Ala., 1965. Mem. Fla. Jr. C. of C., Am. Legion, Sons Confederate Vets., V.F.W., Newcomen Soc., Ala. Hist. Soc., Phi Beta Kappa, Omicron Delta Kappa, Phi Delta Kappa, Kappa Delta Pi, Pi Kappa Alpha (chmn. nat. conv. 1958; chmn. distinguished achievement award com. 1961-62; distinguished achievement award 1966; nat. treas. 1966-68). Elk. Clubs: Nat. Press, Nat. Capital Democratic (dir.), Post Mortem, Burro, Internat., Metropolitan (Washington); University Ala. Alumni (v.p. 1961-62); Algonquin (Boston). Home: 415 Crown View Dr Alexandria VA 22314

HORNE, JOSH L., editor and publisher; b. nr. Whitakers, Nash County, N.C., Dec. 21, 1887; s. Joshua Lawrence and Lula C. (Parker) H.; student Trinity Park Sch., Durham, N.C., 1903-05, Trinity Coll. (now Duke U.), 1905-09; m. Mary A. Thorp, July 17, 1912 (div. 1945); 1 dau., Mary Louise (Mrs. Melvin Jobe Warner): m. 2d, Mildred A. Nicholson, May 3, 1958. Newspaper carrier, corr. and reporter, 1898-1910; city editor Daily Record, Rocky Mount, 1910-11; founder Morning Telegram, 1911, became Evening Telegram, Jan. 1, 1912; former pub. Evening Telegram, from 1911, Sunday Telegram, from 1950; former pres. Rocky Mount Pub. Co., from 1911, radio stas. WCEC and WFMA; dir. Planters Nat. Bank & Trust Com., Carolina Motor Club; pres. Rocky Mount Sanitarium. Mem. Bd. of Aldermen, 1919-20; mem. Airport Commn., 1934—; v.p., dir. Y.M.C.A., 1921—; pres. C. of C., 1924-25 (all of Rocky Mount). Dir. Asso. Press, 1937-50. Mem. State Rural Electrification Authority, 1933-37; chmn. State Bd. Conservation and Devel.; mem. State Advt. Campaign, 1937-50; dir. State N.C. Dept. Archives and History. Pres. N.C. Press Assn., 1930-31; trustee Duke U., High Point Coll. Mem. Am. Soc. Newspaper Editors, Inter Am. Press Assn. Methodist. Clubs: Kiwanis (pres. 1922-23); Nat. Press (Washington); University (Orlando, Fla.). Home: R 2 Whitakers NC 27891 also 1018 E Livingston Orlando FL 32803

HORNE, LENA, singer; b. Bklyn., June 30, 1917; m. Lennie Hayton, Dec. 1947. Dancer, Cotton Club, 1934; toured, recorded with Noble Sissle Orch., 1935- 36; with Ch. Barnet's Band, 1940-41; became cafe society singer; starred in motion pictures Panama Hattie, Cabin in the Sky, Stormy Weather, others; singer popular music; TV appearances include spl. Harry and Lena, 1970. Author: (with Richard Schickel) Lena, 1965.*

HORNE, LOUIS DONALD, business exec.; b. N.Y.C., Feb. 20, 1933; s. Louis G. and Monica (McMorris) H.; B.B.A., Pace Coll., 1955; m. Cathleen M. Hackett, June 5, 1955; children—Patricia Anne, William Donald, Kimberly Susan, Bradley Louis. Sr. accountant Ernst & Ernst, N.Y.C., 1955-58; auditor, plant controller, budget mgr. Hudson Pulp & Paper Corp., N.Y.C., 1958-64; audit mgr., controller, treas., v.p. finance P. Ballantine & Sons, Newark, 1964-69; controller bus. systems and equipment group Litton Industries, Inc., Beverly Hills, Cal., 1970; v.p. finance, treas., dir. Mennen Co., Morristown, N.J., 1971—. Trustee Boston Celtics Basketball Club, 1968-69; treas. Football Coaches Found. N.Y.C. C.P.A., N.Y. Mem. Nat. Assn. Accountants, N.Y. State Soc. C.P.A.'s, Financial Execs. Inst. Home: 176 Briarwood Dr Berkeley Heights NJ 07922 Office: Mennen Co Morristown NJ 07960

HORNE, MARILYN, mezzo-soprano; ed. U. So. Cal.; Mus.D., Rutgers U., 1970; m. Henry Lewis. Operatic debut as Hata in The Bartered Bride, Lo Angeles Guild Opera, La Scala debut in Oepidus Rex, 1969, Met. Opera debut as Adalgisa in Norma, 1970; other roles include Rosina in Barber of Seville, Cleonte in The Siege of Corinth, Isabella in L'Italiana in Algieri; other appearances include Venice Festival (invitation Igor Stravinsky), San Francisco Opera (Marie in Wozzeck), Am. Opera Soc., N.Y.C., for several seasons (including roles in Iphigenie en Tauride, Semiramide), Vancouver Opera (Adalgisa in Norma), Philharmonic Hall, N.Y.C., Covent Garden, London (in Wozzeck); has annual recital at Carnegie Hall; European tour with husband for State Dept., 1963; rec. artist for London, Columbia records; leading exponent florid vocal style. Address: care Met Opera Assn Lincoln Center New York City NY 10018

HORNE, MARK DANIEL, educator; b. Montreal, Can., Sept. 27, 1910 (parents U.S. citizens); s. John Rodbard and May (Hynes) H.; Ph.B., Loyola U., New Orleans, 1934; A.M., La. State U., 1935, Ph.D., 1939; m. Isabel Bouny, Dec. 20, 1937; children—May Alicia (Mrs. James R. Fister), John H., Mark Daniel, Joan (Sister Danielle), Margaret (Mrs. Terry Scafidi), Mary Anne, Michael. Instr., Fortier High Sch., New Orleans, 1935-36; teaching fellow La. State U., 1936-38; mem. faculty Loyola U., New Orleans, 1938—, prof. English, 1949—, chmn. dept. journalism, 1964-66; vis. prof. Armstrong State Coll., Savannah. Ga., summer 1966, La. State U., New Orleans, 1968-69. Served to lt. comdr. USNR, 1942-45. Mem. Am. Assn. U. Profs., Modern Lang. Assn. Am., S. Central Modern Lang. Assn., Holy Name Soc. Catholic. Contbr. profl. jours. Home: 123 Sycamore St Bay St Louis MS 39520 Office: Dept English Loyola Univ New Orleans LA 70118

HORNE, MCDONALD KELSO, Jr., economist; b. Winona, Miss., Apr. 24, 1909; s. McDonald Kelso and Charlotte Louise (Smith-Vaniz) H.; A.B., U. Miss., 1930; A.M., U. N.C., 1932, Ph.D., 1940; m. Mary Elizabeth Cobb, Dec. 9, 1942; children—McDonald Kelso, Robert Chapman. Mng. editor Tupelo (Miss.) Jour., 1934-35; instr. econs., dir. news bur. U. Miss., 1935-36, asst. prof., 1936-37, prof. econs. and dir. bur. bus. research, 1941-42, prof. econs., chmn. dept. econs. and bus. adminstrn., 1947-50, dean Sch. Commerce and Bus. Adminstrn., 1949-50; chief economist Nat. Cotton Council Am., 1950-69; dir. econ. study of U.S. Farmer's future in cotton, 1970; dir. research and information Miss. Unemployment Compensation Commn., 1937-39; cotton market specialist, staff of com. on agr. U.S. Ho. of Reps., 1945-46; mem. fact-finding commn. on north-south wage differential in aluminum case before Nat. Labor Mediation Bd., 1941-42; cotton specialist, staff Bd. Econ. Warfare, part-time 1942; mem. secretariat, fact-finding program on postwar agr. and econ. problems of Cotton Belt, 1945-47; mem. tech. subcom. of cotton and cottonseed adv. com. Agrl. Research and Marketing Act, 1947-56; adv. com. Sec. Agr. Econs. Research, 1958-62; mem. Mgmt.-Labor Textile Adv. Com., 1966-69. Trustee Carrier Found., 1969—. Served to lt. USNR, 1942-45. Mem. Am., So. (v.p. 1950) econ. assns., Conf. Bus. Economists, Phi Delta Theta, Sigma Upsilon, Omicron Delta Kappa, Beta Gamma Sigma, Delta Sigma Pi. Rotarian. Author numerous monographs and articles for profl. and trade jours. Home: 372 Grandview St Memphis TN Office: PO Box 9905 Memphis TN

HORNE, RICHARD CARTER, III, army officer; b. Savannah, Ga., July 21, 1920; s. Richard Carter, Jr. and Lily (Gregg) H.; B.S. in Elec. Engring., Va. Mil. Inst., 1942; grad. U.S. Army Command and Gen. Staff Coll., 1957, Naval War Coll., 1961; m. Mary Elizabeth Payne, Jan. 9, 1943; children—Richard Carter IV, James G.S., John T.P. Commd. 2d lt. U.S. Army, 1942, advanced through grades to brig. gen., 1969; comdr. 38th Div. Signal Corps, World War II; with Spl. Weapons Project, 1949-53; served with Hdqrs. 8th Army, Korea, 1953-60, Hdqrs. NORAD, 1960-63, NATO, Izmir, Turkey, 1963-66, I Field Force Signal O, Vietnam, 1966-68; comdt. U.S. Army Signal Center and Sch., Ft. Monmouth, N.J., 1968—. Decorated Legion of Merit with oak leaf cluster, Bronze Star, Army Commendation medal, Air Force Commendation medal, Joint Services Commendation medal. Mem. Assn. U.S. Army, Armed Forces Communications and Electronics Assn. Episcopalian. Mason. Home: 2 Russel Av Fort Monmouth NJ 07703 Office: Hdqrs USASCS Fort Monmouth NJ 07703

HORNE, ROMAN LEMUEL, former internat. orgn. ofcl.; b. Tryon, N.C., Dec. 14, 1901; s. Bernard Rome and Susan (Westbrook) H.; B.A., Ohio State U., 1928, M.A., 1931, Ph.D., 1936; m. Margaret Reichert Perkins, Nov. 11, 1939; children—Emily Perkins (Mrs. David Ray), Martha Westbrook (Mrs. John P. Mahr), Allen Bernard, Amy Louise. Instr. econs. Mich. State U., 1929-30, U. Buffalo, 1935-36; economist Fed. Res. Bd., 1937-39; chief reports editor TVA, 1939-42; asst. to sec. WPB, 1942-44; economist Treasury Dept., 1944-46; organizing sec. IMF, 1946, dep. sec., 1946-56, sec., 1956-67; adv. dir. Washington-Lee Savs. and Loan Assn., Arlington, Va. Mem. Am. Econ. Assn. Democrat. Unitarian. Club: Internat. (Washington). Author: Farm Business, 1936; (with Marc Rose) Money, 1937. Home: 8736 Old Dominion Dr McLean VA 22101

HORNER, ARTHUR STEWART, gen. contractor; b. Topeka, Feb. 23, 1896; s. Horace Cicero and Gertrude Alice (Turney) H.; student Washburn Coll., 1915-16; B.S., U. Colo., 1922; m. Mary Leah Brewer, June 9, 1923; 1 dau., Joan (Mrs. Carl F. Krueger). Engring. and constrn., 1922-27; owner A.S. Horner Constrn. Co., Denver, 1927—, specialist indsl. plants, power plants and dams, 1942—. Vice pres., dir. Rocky Mountain Osteopathic Hosp., Denver, 1950-52. Mem. Asso. Gen. Contractors Am. (dir. 1945-51, v.p. 1951, pres. 1952), Am. Soc. C.E. (asso.), Colo. Soc. Engrs., Colo. Contractors Assn. (pres. 1940, 44). Home: 3131 E Alameda St Denver CO 80209 Office: 2810 S Havana St Denver CO 80232

HORNER, CHARLES THOMPSON, Jr., army officer; b. Doylestown, Pa., May 6, 1916; s. Charles Thompson and Ida (Cloke) H.; student U.S. Mil. Acad., 1935-36; B.S., U. Pa., 1940; postgrad. Command and Gen. Staff Coll., 1946, Armed Forces Staff Coll., 1946, Army War Coll., 1953-54, U. Pitts., 1960; m. Joan Mary Davy, May 14, 1945; children—Charles Thompson III, Richard W., Colin A., Charlotte M., Michael D. Commd. 2d lt. inf., U.S. Army, 1940, advanced through grades to maj. gen., 1968; comdr. inf. bn. invasion of Sicily and Omaha Beach, France, 1943-44; mem. Gen. Staff Dept. of Army, 1949-53; instr. Inf. Sch., 1958-60, Armed Forces Staff Coll., 1954-57; chief of staff Adv. Group, Vietnam, 1957-58; chief of staff I Corps, Korea, 1967-68; chief of staff Army Materiel Command, Washington, 1970—; comdr. 1st Inf. Brigade, Ft. Benning, 1960-61; comdr. 2d Logistical Command, Okinawa, 1968-70. Decorated D.S.C., D.S.M., Silver Star medal with oak leaf cluster, Bronze Star medal with three oak leaf clusters, Commendation medal with oak leaf cluster; Distinguished Service Order (Brit.). Mem. Assn. U.S. Army, Def. Supply Assn., V.F.W. Club: Army Navy Country (Washington). Home: 1600 S Joyce St Arlington VA 22202 Office: US Army Materiel Command Washington DC 20315

HORNER, DANIEL MEADE, ret. mfg. exec.; b. Oberlin, Pa., May 12, 1906; s. Gordon Leroy and Carrie (Hege) H.; student Gettysburg Coll., 1922-23; M.E., Lehigh U., 1928; m. Wilma Irene Thomas, Aug. 2, 1935; children—Susan Laurie, Edith Bryant. With Gen. Electric Co., 1928-29, Bethlehem Steel Co., 1929-30; with Harsco Corp., and predecessors, Harrisburg, Pa., 1930-68, v.p., 1948-68, now dir.; pres. divisions Harrisburg Steel Co., 1959-68, Taylor-Wharton Co., 1959-68. Bd. mgrs. Harrisburg Hosp.; bd. dirs. Harrisburg area YMCA, Capital Blue Cross. Registered profl. engr., Pa. Mem. Compressed Gas Assn. (pres. 1961), Am. Soc. Metals (pres. York chpt. 1942), Pa. Soc. Profl. Engrs., Engrs. Soc. Pa., Theta Xi. Episcopalian (past vestry, sr. warden). Mason. Clubs: West Shore Country (bd. govs. 1959-62) (Camp Hill); Lauderdale Yacht (Ft. Lauderdale, Fla.). Home: 918 River House Harrisburg PA 17110 Office: Harsco Corp Harrisburg PA 17110

HORNER, GARNETT DENTON, newspaperman; b. Chattanooga, Mar. 22, 1909; s. Charles A. and Elizabeth (Denton) H.; student U. Chattanooga, 1927-30; m. Leota Still Stivers, Sept. 4, 1948. Reporter, Chattanooga News, 1927-31; successively asst. bur. mgr., night mgr. U.P., Atlanta, bur. mgr., Birmingham, Ala., night mgr., N.Y.C., Washington, 1931-37; reporter Washington Star, 1937—, White House corr., 1954—; press attache to Robert D. Murphy, polit. adviser Allied Force Hdqrs. Mediterranean, 1943-44. Mem. White House Corrs. Assn. (pres. 1959-61, sec. 1961—). Club: Nat. Press (Washington). Home: 4811 Albemarle St NW Washington DC 20016 Office: 225 Virginia Av SE Washington DC 20003

HORNER, GEORGE NORMAN, real estate developer exec.; b. N.Y.C., July 19, 1918; s. J. Milton and Edna (Townsend) H.; B.S., N.Y.U., 1961; m. Betty Huston, Nov. 6, 1946; children—John Huston, Peter Townsend. Pub. accountant Hurdman & Cranstoun, N.Y.C., 1941-48; with Handy & Harman, N.Y.C., 1948-71, controller, 1966-71; sec., treas. Electric Thermometers, Inc., Norwalk, Conn., 1965-71; Controller Thermo-Kinetic Corp., Tucson, 1971—. Treas. Edgemont Recreation Com., 1962-63. Treas., v.p., pres. Greenville Republican Club, 1960-63. Served with AUS, 1942-46; ETO. Mem. Financial Execs. Inst. Clubs: Knollwood Country (past sec., bd. govs., chmn. youth activities) (White Plains, N.Y.); Tucson Country. Home: 2710 Kiva Pl Tucson AZ 85715 Office: 6550 E Tanque Verde Tucson AZ 85715

HORNER, H. MANSFIELD, ret. aircraft exec.; b. New Haven, Sept. 12, 1903; s. Leonard S. and Julia Stuyvesant (Barry) H.; B.S., Yale, 1926; D.Eng. (hon.), Rensselaer Poly., (1948; D.Sc., Hillyer Coll., 1956, Trinity Coll., 1959; LL.D., U. Hartford, 1967; m. Lela Thomas Shumate, June 25, 1926; children—Leonard M., Lela Burwell. Pres., dir. United Aircraft Corp., East Hartford, Conn., 1943-56, chmn., chief exec. officer, 1956-68, now chmn. emeritus. Trustee Hartford YMCA, Rensselaer Poly. Inst. Recipient Pres.'s Certificate of Merit, 1948; decorated chevalier French Legion Honor. Home: 105 Bloomfield Av Hartford CT 06105

HORNER, HARRY, dir., designer performing arts; b. Vienna, Austria, July 24, 1910; s. Felix and Gisela (Kohn) H.; archtl. engring. degree, U. Vienna, 1932; grad. Max Reinhardt Sem., State Acad. Theater, 1932; m. Betty Arnold Pfaelzer, Sept. 22, 1938 (dec.); m. 2d, Joan Frankel, 1952; children—James, Christopher, Tony. Came to U.S., 1935, naturalized, 1940. Designer numerous Broadway plays and musicals; designer pageants for N.Y.C. R.R., Cleve., 1937, N.Y. World's Fair, 1939-40; prodns. designed for Broadway include: Eternal Road, 1936, World We Make, Lady in the Dark (mus.), The World of Christopher Blake, 1947, Joy to the World, Me and Molly, 1948, Herod, Family Portrait, Star and Garter; prodns. designed for motion pictures include: Our Town, 1940, A Double Life, The Heiress (Acad. award), 1948, Separate Tables, Born Yesterday, Wonderful Country, The Hustler (Acad. award), They Shoot Horses, Don't They? (Acad. award nominee), 1969, Who is Harry Kellerman, 1970; motion picture dir. 20th Century Fox Films, 1951—; pictures directed include: New Faces, Vicky, A Matter of Life and Death, Man from Del Rio, Wild Party; operas designed and directed include: Dialogues of the Carmelites, 1957, David, 1956, Magic Flute for Met. Opera, 1956; also operas for Vancouver (B.C., Can.) Festivals, San Francisco Opera, others; producer, dir. TV series Royal Canadian Mounted Police, also dir. Readers Digest, Schlitz Playhouse, Shirley Temple Presents, Gunsmoke; pres. Enterprises Films Can., 1964—; mng. dir. Anglo Enterprise Films, London, 1966. Served with USAAF, 1943-45. Recipient award for best moving picture script on a peace theme League of Nations, 1932. Mem. Screen Dirs. Guild, United Scenic Artist Union, Soc. Motion Picture Art Dirs., Acad. Motion Picture Arts and Scis., Canadian Directors Guild. Jewish Religion. Home: 272 Brooktree Rd Pacific Palisades CA 90272 ☆

HORNER, JOHN EDWARD, coll. pres.; b. Passaic, N.J., Dec. 12, 1921; s. William Joseph and Cardera Estelle (Bissell) H.; A.B. cum laude, Drew U. 1943; M.A., Columbia, 1947; PH.D., Ohio State U., 1955; m. Anne Catherine Evans, Aug. 16, 1952; children—Joanne, Jeffrey, Heather, Scott. Tchr. Latin, English, coach Morristown (N.J.) High Sch., 1945-49; Fulbright exchange tchr. and scholar, Latin, English, coach Morristown (N.J.) High Sch., London, Eng., 1949-50; instr. Latin, English, Drew U., 1950-52; asst. prof., dir. athletics and coach Kansas Wesleyan U., 1952-53, asst. to pres., 1953-54; instr., adminstrv. asst. Ohio State U., 1954-56; asst. to pres. U. Omaha, 1956-58, asst. to pres., dean Grad. Div., 1957-58; pres. Hanover Coll., 1958—. Dir. First Nat. Bank, Madison, Ind. Mem. survey com. higher edn. in Neb., 1957; mem. commn. on research and service, cons., examiner N. Central Assn. Colls. and Secondary Schs.; participant leadership tng. project North Central Assn., 1957-58, exec. bd. of commn. colls. and univs.; mem. commn. on students and faculty Assn. Am. Colls.; mem. Ind. Library and Historical Bd.; mem. Nat. Presbyn. Scholarship Com. v.p. Historic Madison, Inc. Named Sagamore of Wabash by Gov. Ind.; Ky. Col. Mem. Ind. State Scholarship Commn., Ind. Conf. Higher Edn. (pres. 1965-66), Ind. Assn. Ch.-Related and Independent Colls. (pres. 1962-63), Classical Assn. Middle West and South, Assn. Higher Edn., Commn. Acad. Freedom and Tenure, A.I.M. (fellow pres.'s council), Presbyn. Coll. Union (pres.), Asso. Colls. Ind. (pres. 1968), Newcomen Soc., Phi Delta Kappa. Presbyn. (ruling elder). Rotarian. Contbr. articles profl. jours. Address: Hanover Coll Hanover IN 47243

HORNER, JOHN EVARTS, internat. orgn. exec.; b. Detroit, July 19, 1916; s. Ralph Burroughs and Helen (Evarts) H.; B.S., Georgetown U., 1937; Diplome, Sorbonne, 1938; Russian lang. and tng. course Cornell U., 1948-49; m. Catherine Daniels, Mar. 5, 1946; children—Jacqueline, Jonathan, Christopher, Willem, Stefanie. Fgn. service officer, 1938-67, vice consul, Dublin, Ireland, 1938-39, 3d sec., vice consul, Wellington, New Zealand, 1939-42, 3d sec., Ottawa, Can., 1943, 2d sec., Ankara, Turkey, 1944-45, 1st sec., Sofia, Bulgaria, attached to Allied Control Commn., 1946-47, 1st sec., Moscow, USSR, 1949-50, 1st sec., Kabul, Afghanistan, 1951-52; assigned to Nat. War Coll., Washington, 1953-54; 1st sec., Paris, 1954-56; with Dept. of State, 1956-58; counselor Am. embassy, Athens, Greece, 1958; Arabic lang. area trainee, 1960-61; consul gen. Am. consulate gen., Dhahran, Saudi Arabia, 1961-64; dir. Office Pub. Services Dept. State, Washington, 1964-66; sr. fellow Tulane U., 1966-67; sec. gen. Internat. Fedn. Multiple Sclerosis Socs., 1967—. Office: 257 Park Av S New York City NY 10010

HORNER, LAWRENCE E., advt. agy. exec. Sr. v.p. Compton Advt., Inc., N.Y.C. Office: 625 Madison Av New York City NY 10022*

HORNER, LORENZO DAVID, III, banker; b. Lynchburg, Va., Dec. 13, 1934; s. Lorenzo David, Jr. and Katherine (Byers) H.; B.A., U. Va., 1956; Grad. degree, Stonier Grad. Sch. Banking, Rutgers U., 1967; m. Jayne Bond, Sept. 10, 1955; children—Valerie Jayne, Victoria Lynn, Julie Bond. With Bank of Va., Richmond, 1959—, exec. v.p., 1969—; pres. Bank of Central Va., Lynchburg, 1966-68; dir. Runnstrom Industries, Miami, Fla., Datatype Corp., Miami. Mem. Va. adv. council Small Bus. Adminstrn., 1967-70. Bd. dirs. Met. Bd. YMCA, Richmond; trustee Found. Ind. Jr. Colls. Va., Va.-Md. Bankers Sch. Served with USNR, 1956-58. Mem. Am. Banking Assn. (state v.p.), Va. Bankers Assn. (pres. young bankers sect.), Va. Skin Divers Assn. (past pres.). Author: Shipwrecks, Skin Divers and Sunken Gold, 1965; Better Scuba Diving for Boys, 1966; The Blockade Runners, 1968; The Treasure Galleons, 1971. Home: Westham Sta Rd Richmond VA 23229 Office: 800 E Main St Richmond VA 23214

HORNER, RICHARD ELMER, corp. exec.; b. Wrenshall, Minn., Oct. 24, 1917; s. Marion Chester and Maude Nancy (Eckert) H.; B.S. in Aero. Engring., U. Minn., 1940; M.S., Princeton, 1947; postgrad. Ohio State U., 1948; m. Jean Margaret Hodgson, June 21, 1941; children—Richard James, Judith Rae. Commd. 2d lt. USAAF, 1940, advanced through grades to col., 1948; comdr. 86th Bomb Squadron, MTO, 1942-43, dir. flight test engring. Wright Field, 1944-45, 47-49, tech. dir. Air Force Flight Test Center, 1950-55; dep. asst. sec. air force, 1955-57, asst. sec. air force for research and devel., 1957-59; asso. adminstr. NASA, 1959-60; sr. v.p. tech. Northrop Corp., Beverly Hills, Cal., 1960-70; pres. E.F. Johnson Co., Waseca, Minn., 1970—. Decorated Silver Star, Air medal with clusters. Fellow Am. Inst. Aeros. and Astronautics (past pres.), Am. Astronautical Soc. Conglist. Home: 905 11th St NE Waseca MN 56093 Office: E F Johnson Co Waseca MN 56093

HORNER, WILLIAM LUDWIG, cons. engr.; b. Stroudsburg, Pa., May 29, 1908; s. Ludwig and Irene (Lander) H.; B.S., U. Pitts., 1928, Petroleum Engr., 1934, Geol. Engr., 1951; m. Elizabeth Berghane, June 24, 1929; childrenWilliam B., David L., Richard A. Student engr. Standard Oil Co. of N.J., 1928-29; petroleum prodn., reservoir and water flood research Humble Oil Co., Forest Oil Corp., 1929-36; developed core analysis, co-founder Core Labs., Inc., 1936-42; with Sunray Oil Corp. (now Sun Oil Co.), 1943- 54, chief engr., 1948, v.p., 1952-54; with Core Labs. Inc., 1954-60, v.p. engring. and cons. dept.; coordinator Citronelle, Ala. Oil Field Unit, 1960-61, unit mgr., 1961-64; oil producer, partner Horner & Smith, Inc., 1964—. Past chmn. of numerous oil operators and engring. coms., 1943-54; mem. Secondary Recovery Adv. and Engring. Commn., Interstate Oil Compact Commn. Registered profl. engr., Tex., Ala. Mem. Ind. Petroleum Assn. Am. (dir. 1961-64), Soc. Petroleum Engrs., Am. Assn. Petroleum Geologists, Sigma Tau, Sigma Gamma Epsilon, Sigma Chi. Presbyn. Clubs: Petroleum (Dallas); Mobile Country, Pine Forest Country (Houston). Contbr. articles in field. Patentee in field. Office: 3210 One Shell Plaza Houston TX 77002

HORNIG, DONALD FREDERICK, univ. pres. b. Milw., Mar. 17, 1920; s. Chester Arthur and Emna (Knuth) H.; B.S., Harvard, 1940, Ph.D., 1943; LL.D., Temple U., 1964, Boston Coll., 1966; D.H.L., Yeshiva U., 1965; D.Sc., Notre Dame, 1965, U. Md., 1965, Rensselaer Poly. Inst., 1965, Ripon Coll., 1966, PMC Colls., 1967, U. Wis., 1967, U. Puget Sound, 1968, Syracuse U., 1968; D.Eng., Worcester Poly. Inst., 1967; m. Lilli Schwenk, July 17, 1943; children—Joanna, Ellen, Christopher, Leslie. Research asso. Woods Hole (Mass.) Oceanographic Instn., 1943-44; scientist, group leader Los Alamos Lab., N.M., 1944-46; asst. prof. chemistry Brown U., 1946-49, asso. prof., 1949-51; prof., 1951-57, dir. Metcalf Research Lab., 1949- 57, asso. dean grad. sch., 1952-53, acting dean, 1953-54; vis. prof. Princeton, 1957, prof. chemistry, 1957-64, chmn. dept., 1958-64, Donner prof. sci., 1959-66; spl. asst. sci. and tech. to Pres., 1964-69; dir. Office Sci. and Tech., 1964-69; chmn. Fed. Council Sci. and Tech., 1964- 69; v.p., dir. Eastman Kodak Co., 1969-70; prof. chemistry U. Rochester, 1969-70; pres. Brown U., Providence, 1970—. Mem. Pres.' Sci. Adv. Com., 1960-69; chmn. 1964-69; chmn. Project Metcalf Office Naval Research, 1951-52. Bd. overseers Harvard Coll., 1964-70; bd. dirs. Overseas Devel. Council; trustee George Eastman House, Manpower Inst. Decorated Order Civil Meric, Distinguished Civilian Service medal (Korea); Guggenheim fellow, 1954-55; Fulbright fellow, 1954-55; recipient Charles Lathrop Parsons award Am. Chem. Soc., 1967, Mellon Inst. award, 1968. Fellow Am. Phys. Soc., Am. Acad. Arts and Scis.; mem. Nat. Acad. Scis., Am. Chem. Soc., A.A.A.S., Am. Philos. Soc., Romanian Acad. (fgn.), Sigma Xi. Author articles sci. jours. Home: 55 Power St Providence RI 02906

HORNIG, JAMES FREDERICK, coll. dean; b. Milw., Feb. 22, 1929; s. Herbert E. and Edna (Hennig) H.; B.A., Harvard, 1950; Ph.D., U. Wis., 1954; m. Evalyn Ortelt, Nov. 1, 1952; children—David, Douglas, Linda. Chemist, E.I. duPont de Nemours & Co., 1956-58; asst. prof. U. Cal. at Riverside, 1958-62; prof. chemistry Dartmouth, 1962—; asso. dean faculty, dean grad. studies, 1964—. Mem. Am. Chem. Soc., Am. Phys. Soc. Home: 10 Occom Ridge St Hanover NH 03755

HORNING, EVAN CHARLES, educator, chemist; b. Phila., June 6, 1916; s. Samuel and Mary (Schnader) H.; B.S., U. Pa., 1937; Ph.D., U. Ill., 1940; m. Marjorie Groothuis, Sept. 25, 1941. Instr., Bryn Mawr Coll., 1940-41; instr. U. Mich., 1941-43, research asso., 1943-45; asst. prof. U. Pa., 1945-47, asso. prof., 1947-50; chief Lab. of Chem. of Natural Products, NIH, Bethesda, Md., 1950-61; prof. chemistry Baylor U. Coll. Medicine, 1961—, chmn. dept. biochemistry, 1962-66, dir. Inst. for Lipid Research, 1966—. DuPont fellow, 1939-40, Rohm & Haas fellow, 1940, Guggenheim fellow, 1958. Fellow N.Y. Acad. Sci.; mem. Am., Swiss chem. socs., Biochem. Soc. (London), Am. Soc. Biol. Chemists, Am. Geriatrics Soc., A.A.A.S., Tex. Acad. Sci. Author: Organic Syntheses, vol. III, 1955; Effects of Drugs on Synthesis and Mobilization of Lipids, 1963; also numerous articles. Devel. gas phase analytical biochem. methods for study of steroids, lipids, urinary acids, glucuronides and other compounds of biol. significance; studies in gas chromatography and gas chromatography-mass spectrometry, and applications in studies of atherosclerosis and related metabolic problems; drug metabolism; isolation and structural studies of naturally occurring compounds. Home: 11610 Starwood Dr Houston TX 77024

HORNOR, FRANK BERKSHIRE, banker; b. Clarksburg, W.Va., July 13, 1923; s. James Lee and Grace (Haymaker) H.; B.A., Duke, 1947; M.B.A., U. Pa., 1948; m. Betty Ball, Sept. 4, 1948; children—Virginia Patton, James Berkshire. Mgmt. trainee Chase Nat. Bank, N.Y.C., 1948-50; asst. v.p. comml. lending Peoples First Nat. Bank of Pitts., 1950-59; v.p., trust officer Union Nat. Bank, Clarksburg, 1959-64; v.p. nat. div. Western Pa. Nat. Bank, Pitts., 1964-70; sr. v.p. comml. lending First Va. Bank, Arlington, 1970—. Bd. dirs. Assn. Indsl. Devel. Harrison County, W.Va., 1962-64, United Cerebral Palsy Pitts., 1968-70; trustee Salem Coll. (W.Va.) Found., 1963-64. Served to lt. (j.g.) USNR, 1943-46; PTO. Mem. W.Va. Bankers Assn. (pres. trust div. 1963-64), Robert Morris Assos., Sigma Alpha Epsilon. Democrat. Methodist. Home: 6736 Melrose Dr McLean VA 22101 Office: 2926 Columbia Pike Arlington VA 22204

HORNSBY, ERNEST C., lawyer; b. Montgomery, Ala., Oct. 8, 1936; s. Ernest Arnold and Kate (Clayton) H.; A.B., Auburn U., 1958; LL.B., U. Ala., 1960; m. Judith Ellen O'Daniel, May 27, 1961; children—Ernest Clayton, Emily Elon. Admitted to Ala. bar, 1960; practice in Tallassee, 1963—; legal counsel Ala. Jaycees, 1969-70; asst. supt. ins. Ala., 1960-63; lectr. annual seminar Ala. Trial Lawyers Assn. Mem. Ala. Senate, 1962-66. mem. Ala., Elmore County (pres. 1968-69) bar assns., Phi Alpha Delta. Democrat. Mem. Christian Ch. (past chmn. bd. sec., tchr. adult Sunday class). Mason (Shriner); mem. Order Eastern Star. Author articles. Home: 609 Camellia Dr Tallassee AL 36078 Office: Old Bank Bldg Tallassee AL 36078

HORNSLETH, POUL, publisher; b. Kingston, Jamaica, Sept. 6, 1918; s. Christian Rasmus and Johanna (Poulsen) H.; A.B., U. Pa., 1940; m. Helen Bennett, Apr. 14, 1941 (div.); children—JoAnn (Mrs. Finn Kai Neilsen), Poul, Helen Faith, Christian Rasmus II. With IBM Corp., Newark, 1940-44; with Forge Mills, Inc., 1945-55; v.p. sales and mgmt. Conde Nast Publs., Inc., N.Y.C., 1955—. Mem. Friar Honor Soc., Delta Kappa Epsilon. Episcopalian. Clubs: Deke (N.Y.C.); Brooklawn Country (Bridgeport, Conn.). Home: Fanton Hill Rd Weston CT 06880 Office: 420 Lexington Av New York City NY 10017

HORNUNG, PAUL ANDREW, sports editor; b. New Bavaria, O., July 18, 1917; s. Andrew Jacob and Gertrude (Wolfe) H.; student Ohio State U., 1935-39; m. Cornelia I. Marshall, Sept. 21, 1940. Sports editor Ohio State U. Student Lantern, Lantern, 1938-39; asso. editor Sundial, 1938-39; sports editor Columbus (O.) Dispatch, 1956—; asso. editor Street and Smith Ann. Yearbook of Coll. Football, New York, 1960—. Ohio rep. Heisman Trophy Com., 1956—. Mem. Football Writers Am. (dir.), Sigma Delta Chi. Club: Agonis. Home: 3995 Mountview Rd., Columbus, OH 43221 Office: 34 S 3d St Columbus OH 43216

HORNYAK, EUGENE AUGUSTINE, bishop; b. Kucura, Backa, Yugoslavia, Oct. 7, 1919; s. Peter and Juliana (Findrik) H.; Ph.B., Pontifical U., Rome, Italy, 1941, S.T.D., 1947; J.C.B., Gregorian U., Rome, 1947. Came to U.S., 1948, naturalized, 1955; came to Eng., 1961. Ordained priest Roman Catholic Ch., Byzantine-Ukranian rite, 1945; asst. priest, Struthers and Warren, O., 1948-49; adminstr. St. Michael's Ch., Newton Falls, O., 1949-50; prof. moral theology, canon law, liturgy, also spiritual dir. Sts. Cyril and Methodius Byzantine Seminary, Pitts., 1950-55; spiritual dir. St. Basil's Ukralnian Minor Seminary, Stamford, Conn., 1958-61; entered Order St. Basil the Great, Can., 1956-57; master novices, also superior St. Josaphat's Monastery, Glen Cove, L.I., 1961; apptd. titular bishop Hermonthis, also aux. to Cardinal Godfrey for Ukrainian Catholics in Eng. and Wales, London, 1961-63, bishop-apostolic exarch for Ukrainian Catholics in Eng. and Wales, 1963—, for Ukrainians in Scotland, 1968—. Mem. Cath. hierarchy Eng., Wales, Scotland; mem. Ukrainian Cath. hierarchy in free world; suffragan bishop to Met. See Westminster, London. Home: 22 Binney St London W1 England Office: 14 Newburgh Rd Acton London W3 England

HOROVITZ, ISRAEL ARTHUR, playwright; b. Wakefield, Mass., Mar. 31, 1939; s. Julius Charles and Hazel (Solberg) H.; fellow Royal Acad. Dramatic Art, London, Eng., 1961- 63; m. Doris Keefe, Dec. 25, 1959; children—Rachael Keefe, Matthew Keefe, Adam Keefe. Am. playwright-in-resident Royal Shakespeare Co., London, 1965; lectr., 1961—. Recipient Vernon Rice award, 1967-68, Drama Desk award, 1967-68, Jersey Jour. best play award, 1968, OBIE award, 1967-68; Rockefeller fellow, 1968. Mem. Actors Studio, New Dramatists Com., Eugene O'Neill Found. Club: Players (N.Y.C.). Author: The Comeback, 1958; The Death of Bernard the Believer, 1960; This Play is About Me, 1961; The Handing of Emanuel, 1962; Jump, 1962; The Killer Dove, 1963; The Indian Wants the Bronx, 1964; It's Called the Sugar Plum, 1965; Line, 1967; Rats, 1967; Schnozzolla, 1968; Chiaroscuro (or Morning), 1968; The World's Greatest Play, 1968; First Season, 1968; Leader, 1969; Morning, Noon and Night, 1969; also film and TV. Contbr. nat. mags.

HOROVITZ, SAMUEL BERTRAM, lawyer, author; b. Chelsea, Mass., Nov. 23, 1897; s. Israel and Bessie (Binksy) H.; A.B. magna cum laude, Harvard, 1919, J.D., 1922; m. Sara Levy, Aug. 7, 1922; 1 son, Seba (both killed in airplane crash, Jan. 1936); m. 2d, Evelyn McCarthy, Nov. 1, 1942; children—Paul Seba, David Carroll. Admitted to Mass. bar, 1922, U.S. Supreme Ct. bar, 1928; chief workmen's compensation dept. Boston Legal Aid Soc., 1922- 32; in pvt. practice specializing in workmen's compensation cases, Boston, 1932—; sr. mem. firm Horovitz, Petkun, Rothschild & Locke, 1942—; workmen's compensation atty. Mass. Fedn. Labor, 1932—; worldwide lectr. on workmen's compensation; asst. prof. law Suffolk U. Law Sch., Boston. Mem. Republican Town Com., Wakefield, 1925-35; mem. Rep. program com., representing labor, 1940. Recipient John Harvard scholarship, 1919. Mem. Am. Trial Lawyers Assn. (co-founder, 1946; editor-in-chief, exec. editor NACCA Law Jour., 1948—), Am. Bar Assn., Internat. Assn. Indsl. Accident Bds. and Commns. (asso. mem.). Republican. Clubs: New Century, Charles River Yacht. Author several books on workmen's compensation. Home: 16 Shuman Circle Newton Center MA 02159 Office: 6 Beacon St Boston MA 02108

HOROWITZ, CHARLES, judge; b. Bklyn., Jan. 5, 1905; s. Harry and Fanny (Mirkin) H.; A.B. magna cum laude, U. Wash., 1925, LL.B. summa cum laude, 1927; B.A. (Rhodes scholar) with 1st class honors, Oxford (Eng.) U., 1929, M.A., 1952; m. Diana Glickman, Mar. 23, 1930; children—Caroline Ann, Elinor Louise. Admitted to Wash. bar, 1927; asso. Preston, Thorgrimson & Turner, now Preston, Thorgrimson & Horowitz, Seattle, 1929-33, mem. firm, 1933-69; acting chief judge div. 1, Wash. Ct. Appeals, 1969-70, chief judge, 1971—; lectr. law U. Wash., 1932-33, 39, 45. Pres. Travelers Aid Soc. Seattle, 1940- 42, Caroline Kline Galland Home for Aged, 1945-46, Friends of Seattle Pub. Library, 1946-47; pres. N.W. br. Am. Assn. UN, 1952-55; mem. Wash. Uniform Law Commn., 1960—, chmn., 1966—; chmn. bd. N.W. Meml. Hosp. Assn., 1957-59, pres., 1959-61. Served with USCGR, World War II. Mem. Am. Law Inst., Am., Wash. State, Seattle (pres. 1957-58) bar assns., Phi Beta Kappa, Order of Coif. Jewish religion (past pres. temple). Home: 3923 E 38th St Seattle WA 98105 Office: IBM Bldg Seattle WA 98101

HOROWITZ, DAVID, banker; b. Drohobicz, Poland, Feb. 15, 1899; s. Sigmund and Fanny (Lichtenstein) H.; student Lwow Coll.; doctor honoris causa Hebrew U., 1967, Tel-Aviv U., 1970; m. Rivka Bobkoff, Aug. 1922; 1 son, Dan. Econ. adviser, sec. Am. Econ. Com. for Palestine, 1932-35; dir. econ. dept. Jewish Agy., Jerusalem, 1935-48; dir. gen Ministry Finance Israel, Jerusalem, 1948-52; gov. Bank Israel, Jerusalem, 1954—; gov. for Israel, Internat. Bank Reconstrn. and Devel., Internat. Finance Corp., Internat. lectr. Tel-Aviv U., 1946-50. Mem. State Council Higher Edn.; mem. exec. council Weizmann Inst. Sci. Bd. govs. Hebrew U., Jerusalem, Tel-Aviv U.; trustee Truman Research Center, Jerusalem. Recipient Israel prize social scis., 1967, Bareli prize, 1958. Mem. Israel Assn. Friendship with Sweden. Devel. Assn. Author: State in the Making, 1953; Hemispheres North and South, 1966; The Economics of Israel, 1967; The Abolition of Poverty, 1969; others. Home: 4 Halamed He Jerusalem Israel Office: 29 Jaffa Rd Jerusalem Israel

HOROWITZ, DAVID CHARLES, correspondent; b. N.Y.C., June 30, 1937; s. Max Leo and Dorothy (Lippman) H.; B.A., Bradley U., 1959; M.S.J., Northwestern U., 1960; CBS fellow, Columbia, 1962-63; m. Judith Ann Rosenthal, July 13, 1964; 1 dau., Victoria Ann. Editor-in-chief Tazewell County (Ill.) Newpaper, 1956; reporter Peoria (Ill.) Jour. Star, 1957-60, Lerner Newspapers and Chgo. City News Bur., 1959-60; newscaster KRNT Radio-TV, Des Moines, 1960-62; newswriter-producer ABC Radio Network, N.Y.C., 1963; far east corr. NBC News, 1963-64; pub. affairs dir. WMCA, N.Y.C., 1964-66; corr., edn. editor NBC News, Los Angeles, 1966—. Dir. Nat. Broadcast Editorial Conf. Patron, Los Angeles County Art Museum; mem. adv. council on pub. information Am. Cancer Soc. Served with USNR, 1954-62. Mem. Acad. Television Arts and Scis., Internat. Radio-Television Soc., Radio-Television News Dirs. Assn., The Guardians, Nat. Edn. Writers Assn., Sigma Delta Chi. Clubs: Friars, Overseas Press America (N.Y.C.). Home: 455 Bonhill Rd Los Angeles CA 90049

HOROWITZ, DAVID H., motion picture co. exec., lawyer; b. N.Y.C., Sept. 11, 1928; s. Abraham and Florence (Bob) H.; A.B., Columbia, 1948, LL.B., 1950; m. Louise Schwartz June 20, 1951; children—Marilyn, Roger, Diana. Admitted to N.Y. bar, 1950; asso.-in-law Columbia Law Sch., 1950-53; law clk. Judge Stanley H. Fuld, N.Y. Ct. Appeals, 1951-52; partner firm Schwartz & Frohlich, N.Y.C., 1952-63; with Screen Gems, Inc., N.Y.C., 1963-68, v.p., gen. counsel, 1966-68; v.p., sec., gen. counsel Columbia Pictures Industries, Inc., N.Y.C., 1968—; mem. faculty N.Y. Law Sch., 1961-62. Mem. Am., N.Y. State bar assns., Assn. Bar City N.Y., N.Y. County Lawyers Assn., Nat. Lawyers Club Washington. Home: 25 Central Park West New York City NY 10023 Office: 711 Fifth Av New York City NY 10022

HOROWITZ, DON ROY, instrument co. exec.; b. Pitts., Mar. 12, 1930; s. Samuel and Clara (Aberman) H.; B.S., U. Pitts., 1952; m. Carole Spiegel, Jan. 29, 1960; children—Cindy, Thomas. Editor, Pitts. Spectator mag., 1951-52; writer Fairchild Publs., 1952-53; pub. relations dir. Dubin. Feldman & Kahn. Inc., 1955-58; pres. Carlton Advt., Pitts., 1959—, Corp. Communications Counselors, Pitts., 1962—, Defensive Instruments, Inc., Pitts., 1968—, Mut. Advt. Agy. Network, Mpls., 1969-70, Homehelp Unlimited, Inc., Pitts., 1969—; v.p. Normda Industries, Inc., San Diego, Cal., 1968—. Served with AUS, 1953-55. Mem. Pitts. Advt. Club, Sales-Marketing Execs., Pi Lambda Phi. Clubs: Press, Westmoreland (Pitts.). Home: 5464 Darlington Rd Pittsburgh PA 15217 Office: 925 Penn Av Pittsburgh PA 15222

HOROWITZ, HAROLD, architect; b. Chgo., Sept. 6, 1927; s. Samuel and Anna (Miller) H.; B.A. in Architecture, Ill. Inst. Tech., 1950; M. Arch., Mass. Inst. Tech., 1951; m. Clara Marie Stastny, Sept. 1, 1950. Research architect Bldg. Research Labs., S.W. Research Inst., Princeton, N.J., 1953-55; tech. dir. Bldg. Research Inst., Nat. Acad. Scis.-NRC, Washington, 1955-63; supervisory architect NSF, Washington, 1963—; lectr., cons. in field. Served with AUS, 1946-48. Mem. A.I.A. (mem. research com. 1965-70; recipient nat. and state awards). Registered architect, N.J., Md. Home: 4 Barkwood Ct Rockville MD 20853 Office: NSF Washington DC 20550

HOROWITZ, HAROLD WILLIAM, educator; b. Los Angeles, June 28, 1923; s. Louis and Clara (Zimring) H.; A.B., U. Cal. at Los Angeles, 1943; LL.B., Harvard, 1949, S.J.D., 1967; LL.M., U. So. Cal., 1954; m. Elizabeth Marmorston, Dec. 28, 1952; children—Lisa Aron, Adam Jonas. Admitted to Cal. bar, 1950; prof. law U. So. Cal., 1950-60; asso. gen. counsel Dept. Health, Edn. and Welfare, 1961-64; mem. President's Task Force on War Against Poverty, 1964; prof. law U. Cal. at Los Angeles, 1964—; dep. gen. counsel Gov. Cal. Commn. on Los Angeles Riots, 1965. Mem. Gov. Cal. Commn. Law of Pre-emption, 1966; nat. adv. com. to legal services program Office Econ. Opportunity, 1965—. Served with USAAF, 1943-46. Mem. Cal. State Bar, Phi Beta Kappa, Phi Eta Sigma, Pi Gamma Mu, Pi Sigma Alpha. Home: 2821 Forrester Dr Los Angeles CA 90064

HOROWITZ, IRVING LOUIS, educator, sociologist; b. N.Y.C., Sept. 25, 1929; s. Louis and Esther (Tepper) H.; B.S.S., City Coll. N.Y., 1951; M.A., Columbia, 1952; Ph.D., Buenos Aires (Argentina) U., 1957; postgrad. fellow Brandeis U., 1958- 59; m. Ruth Lenore Horowitz, 1950 (div. 1964); children—Carl Frederick, David Dennis. Asst. prof. sociology Bard Coll., 1960; asso. prof. social theory Buenos Aires U., 1955-58; chmn. dept. sociology Hobart and William Smith Colls., 1960-63; asso. prof., then prof. sociology Washington U., St. Louis. 1963-69; chmn. dept. sociology Livingston Coll., Rutgers U., 1969—, prof. sociology grad. faculty Rutgers U., 1969—; vis. prof. sociology U. Caracas (Venezuela), 1957, Buenos Aires U., 1959, 61, 63, State U. N.Y., at Buffalo, 1960, Syracuse U., 1961, Rochester U., fall 1962. U. Cal. at Davis, 1966, U. Wis. at Madison, 1967, Stanford, 1968-69; vis. lectr. London Sch. Econs. and Polit. Sci., 1962. Prin. investigator for numerous sci. and research projects. Mem. A.A.A.S., Am. Assn. U. Profs., Am. Philos. Assn., Am. Sociol. Assn., Authors Guild, Centre Internat. pour le Devel. (a founder), Internat. Assn. Philosophy Law and Social Thought, Internat. Studies Assn., Latin Am. Studies Assn., Midwest (chmn. com. professions 1968-69), N.Y. State sociol. socs., Soc. Internat. Devel., Soc. Study Social Problems (chmn. awards com. 1964-66). Author: Idea of War and Peace in Contemporary Philosophy, 1957; Philosophy, Science and the Sociology of Knowledge, 1960; Radicalism and the Revolt Against Reason: The Social Theories of Georges Sorel, 2d edit. 1968; The War Game; Studies of the New Civilian Militarists, 1963; Historia y Elementos de la Sociologia del Connocimento, 1963; The New Sociology; Essays in Social Science and Social Values in Honor of C. Wright Mills, 1964; Revolution in Brazil; Politics and Society in a Developing Nation, 1964; The Rise and Fall of Project Camelot, 1967; Three Worlds of Development; The Theory and Practice of International Stratification, 1966; Professing Sociology; The Life Cycle of a Social Science, 1963; Latin American Radicalism; A Documentary Report on Nationalist and Left Movements, 1969; Sociological Self-Images, 1969; The Knowledge Factory; Student Activism and American Crisis, 1970; Masses in Latin America, 1970; Cuban Communism, 1970. Home: 10 Landing Lane New Brunswick NJ 08903

HOROWITZ, MORRIS A., economist; b. Newark, Nov. 19, 1919; s. Samuel and Anna (Litwin) H.; B.A. in Econs., N.Y. U., 1940; Ph.D. in Econs., Harvard, 1954; m. Jean Ginsburg, July 12, 1941; children—Ruth, Joel. Mem. faculty Northeastern U., 1956—, prof. econs., chmn. dept., 1959—. Home: 5 Riedesel Av Cambridge MA 02138 Office: Northeastern U Boston MA 02115

HOROWITZ, MURRAY M., educator; b. N.Y.C., Aug. 29, 1918; s. Robert and Gusta (Haas) H.; B.A., Bklyn. Coll., 1938, M.A., 1941; Ph.D., Columbia, 1955; m. Adele Miriam Miller, Aug. 20, 1948. Mem. faculty Bklyn. Coll., 1938—, prof. history, 1960—, asso. dean, 1960-69. Served to capt. USAAF, 1943- 46. Mem. Am. Hist. Assn. Author articles, chpts. in books. Home: 463 Beach 142d St Neponsit NY 11694 Office: Brooklyn Coll Brooklyn NY 11210

HOROWITZ, NORMAN HAROLD, educator, biologist; b. Pitts., Mar. 19, 1915; s. Joseph L. and Jeanette (Miller) H.; B.S., U. Pitts., 1936; Ph.D., Cal. Inst. Tech., 1939, research fellow biochemistry, 1940-42, sr. research fellow, 1946; NRC fellow Stanford, 1939-40, research asso., 1942-46; m. Pearl Shykin, June 16, 1939; children—Joel Lawrence, Elizabeth Anne. Teaching fellow biology Cal. Inst. Tech., Pasadena, 1936-39, asso. prof. biology, 1947-53, prof. biology, 1953—; chief bio sci. sect. Jet Propulsion Lab., Pasadena, 1965-70; cons. NASA Fulbright and Guggenheim fellow U. Paris, 1954-55. Mem. Am. Soc. Biol. Chemists, Genetics Soc. Am., A.A.A.S., Nat. Acad. Scis., Am. Acad. Arts and Scis., Phi Beta Kappa, Sigma Xi. Editorial bd. Jour. Biol. Chemistry, 1959-64. Contbr. articles tech. jours. Home: 2495 Brigden Rd Pasadena CA 91104

HOROWITZ, RAYMOND JACK, lawyer; b. N.Y.C., May 7 1916; s. Israel S. and Sadye (Freiman) H.; A.B., Columbia, 1936, LL.B. 1939; m. Margaret Goldenberg, Sept. 22, 1940; 1 dau., Judith. Admitted to N.Y. bar, 1939; practiced in N.Y.C., 1939-41; asst. corp. counsel City of N.Y., 1941-43; asso. Meyer, Wallach & Silverson, N.Y.C., 1943-46; partner McGoldrick, Dannett, Horowitz & Golub and predecessors, N.Y.C., 1946-69; mem. firm Graubard, Moskowitz, McGoldrick, Dannett & Horowitz, 1969—. Vice pres., dir., gen. counsel Allied Maintenance Corp.; dir. Seagrave Corp.; cons. Nat. Housing Agy., 1946-47. Office Housing Expediter, 1947, Temporary State Housing Rent Commn., 1950-51. Mem. Assn. Bar City N.Y., N.Y. County Lawyers Assn., Phi Beta Kappa. Clubs: Lotos, Wings (N.Y.C.). Author: (with others) Building Regulation in New York City, 1944. Home: 930 Fifth Av New York NY 10028 Office: 345 Park Av New York NY 10022

HOROWITZ, SAUL, constrn. co. exec.; b. N.Y.C., May 27, 1897; s. Meyer and Minnie (Simon) H.; A.B., Coll. City N.Y., 1917; postgrad. N.Y. U., 1918; m. Miriam R. Ravitch, Dec. 12, 1922; children—Saul, Alan Paul. Engaged in steel and constrn. bus., 1918-25; pres. HRH Constrn. Corp., N.Y.C., 1925-65, chmn. bd., 1965—. Trustee-at-large Fedn. Jewish Philanthropies, 1951- 58, trustee, 1958—, campaign chmn., 1952-53, chmn. constrn. co., 1954, chmn. bd. com., 1960-; bd. dirs. United Jewish Appeal, 1953—, div. chmn., 1943; div. chmn. Israel Bonds, 1955; founder Albert Einstein Coll. Medicine, 1958, chmn. bldg. com., 1954-58; chmn. builders div. United Hosp. Fund, 1952; chmn. gen. contractors div. Greater N.Y. Fund, 1956; chmn. bldg. and constrn. industry Nat. Found. Infantile Paralysis, 1955—, mem. campaign com., 1958-60; chmn. bldg. industry com. N.Y. Cancer Com., 1953-64; mem. nat. council Joint Distbn. Com., 1954—; chmn. constrn. industry com. Girl Scout Council Greater N.Y., 1956, 59, 60; trustee Asso. YM-YWHA's Greater N.Y., 1958—, chmn. bldg. com., 1958- -, v.p., 1959-61, chmn. trustees, 1961-68, spl. cons. bldg. com. Hadassah-Hebrew U., 1961; mem. nat. adv. council Am. Jewish Com., 1958- -; chmn. bldg. com. Jerusalem YM-YWHA bldg. World Fedn. YM-YWHA's and Jewish Community Centers, 1963—; mem. neighborhood and regional planning bd. Community Council Greater N.Y., 1958-59; asso, campaign chmn. City Coll. Fund., 1959—. Chmn. N.Y. County com. housing N.Y. County Democrat Com., 1960-61. Bd. Am. Friends Wetzman Inst., Rehovath, Israel. Served with USNRF, 1918. Recipient citation Albert Einstein Coll. Medicine, 1955; Alumni Service award Coll. City N.Y., 1957; named Jewish Community Center Man of Year, Nat. Jewish Welfare Bd., 1959; fellow Brandeis U., 1961. Mem. Sigma Alpha Mu (Merit award 1960). Jewish religion (trustee synagogue 1940-60). Club: Harmonie (N.Y.C.). Home: 35 E 76th St New York City NY 10021 Office: 515 Madison Av New York City NY 10022

HOROWITZ, SAUL, Jr., constrn. co. exec.; b. N.Y.C., May 5, 1925; s. Saul and Miriam (Ravitch) H.; grad. Phillips Andover Acad., 1942; student Yale, 1942-43; B.S., U.S. Mil. Acad., 1946; postgrad. Mass. Inst. Tech., 1950; m. Mary Elizabeth Blakeney, Mar. 11, 1950; children—Mary Elizabeth, Saul Mark, Charles James, Sarah Louise. Commd. 2d lt., C.E., U.S. Army, 1946, advanced through grades to capt., 1954; assigned 11th Airborne Div., Japan, 1947-49, 76th Engr. Constrn. Brigade, Korea, 1953-54; resigned, 1954; with HRH Constrn. Corp., N.Y.C., 1954—, exec. v.p., 1958-65, pres., 1965—; chmn. bd. Universal Constrn. Corp., P.R., dir. Consolidated Cigar Corp., 1959-68, Scarsdale Nat. Bank (N.Y.), 1971—; trustee Am. Savs. Bank, N.Y.C. Chmn. campaign Fedn. Jewish Philanthropies, N.Y. State, 1963. Mem. Bd. Edn., Scarsdale, 1964-65; trustee, Scarsdale, 1965-69, mayor, 1969—; mem. Republican Nat. Finance Com., 1969—. Trustee Mt. Sinai Hosp., N.Y.C., 1957—. Decorated Bronze Star, 1954. Mem. Mason Builders and Bldg. Contractors Assn. N.Y. (pres. 1960), Met. Builders Assn. N.Y. (pres. 1963-64), Asso. Gen. Contractors Am. (nat. bd. dirs., chmn. bldg. div.). Clubs: Yale, Harmonie (N.Y.C.); Army and Navy (Washington); Beach Point (Mamaroneck, N.Y.). Home: 7 Old Lyme Rd Scarsdale NY 10583 Office: 515 Madison Av New York City NY 10022

HOROWITZ, SIDNEY, corp. exec.; b. Loch Sheldrake, N.Y., Nov. 21, 1920; s. Abraham and Jennie (Jennig) H.; B.B.A., St. Johns U., 1942; m. Grace Fern Nelson, June 27, 1948; children—Richard Andrew, Joanne Patricia. With Horowitz Bros., Inc., L.I., N.Y., 1945-61, pres., 1954-61; pres., chmn. bd. P & F Industries, Inc., Great Neck, N.Y., 1961—; chmn. bd. Ranchers Packing Corp.; partner Crossways Indsl. Park. Pres. Grace and Sidney Horowitz Found. Served to 1st lt. USAAF, 1943-45. Decorated Air medal with 7 oak leaf clusters, D.F.C. Mem. Nat. Assn. Home Builders (pres.), Nat. Assn. Plumbers (pres.). Club: Glen Head (N.Y.) Country. Home: 111 Wood Hollow Rd East Hills NY 11577 Office: 45 N Station Plaza Great Neck NY 11021

HOROWITZ, STANLEY, business exec.; b. 1928; married. Pres., sec., dir. Horowitz Bros., Inc.; with P & F Industries, Inc., 1962—, sec., exec. v.p., 1970—, also dir. Office: 45 North Station Plaza Great Neck NY 11021•

HOROWITZ, VLADIMIR, pianist; b. Kiev, Russia, Oct. 1, 1904; s. Samuel and Sophia (Bodik) H.; ed. Kiev Conservatory; study under Felix Blumenfeld; m. Wanda Toscanini, Dec. 21, 1933. Made first appearance at age 17; made debut in Europe, 1925; debut in U.S. with N.Y. Philharmonic, Jan. 1928; concert tours of U.S., 1928—. Recipient Grammy award for best classical performance, instrumental soloist or soloists Nat. Acad. Rec. Arts and Scis., 1967; named number 7 in classical field Top Artists on Campus Poll (album sales), 1968. Address: care Columbia Records 51 W 52d St New York City NY 10019

HOROWITZ, WILLIAM, banker, corp. exec.; b. Kansas City, Mo., May 6, 1907; s. Louis and Esther (Peabody) H.; A.B., Yale, 1929, M.A. (hon.), 1965; m. Miriam Botwinik, June 25, 1933; children—Judith, Daniel. Purchasing agt. Botwinik Bros., Inc., New Haven, 1931-40, v.p., 1940—, also dir.; pres., dir. Gen. Bank & Trust Co., New Haven, 1950-70; v.p., dir. radio sta. WELI, New Haven, 1953—, Pyrene Mfg. Co., Newark, 1954-56, Baker Industries, Newark, 1956-66; pres. Gen. Venture Capital Corp., New Haven, 1961—; chmn. bd. Winthrop Bank & Trust Co., New London, Conn., 1964-70; New Haven area adv. bd. chmn. Hartford Nat. Bank & Trust Co., 1970—; pres. Eastern Machine Screw Corp., New Haven, 1967—; dir. Conn. E.T.V. Corp., Hartford Nat. Bank & Trust Co. Pres. Nat. Friends Yale Hillel Found., 1950-56, Jr. Achievement New Haven, 1955-56; mem. Conn. Bd. Edn., 1955—, chmn., 1959—; vice chmn. B'nai B'rith Youth Commn.; mem. New Haven Found. Distbn. Com., 1952-59, chmn., 1958; vice chmn., Conn. del. White House Conf. Children and Youth, 1960; mem. Conn. Study Commn. Higher Edn., 1963-65, Conn. Commn. Higher Edn., 1965-67. Treas. Town Democratic Com., 1949-66. Mem. Yale Corp., 1965-71; trustee Peabody Mus., New Haven. Fellow Branford Coll., Yale (acting master 1971-72); recipient award outstanding community service New Haven B'nai B'rith, 1953; Nat. Youth Commn. award, 1962; Jr. Distinguished Alumnus award; citation for service So. Conn. State Coll.; citation Kappa Delta Pi of Central Conn. State Coll., 1965; Americanism award B'nai B'rith, 1967. Hon. life mem. Conn. P.T.A.; mem. Purchasing Agts. Assn. Conn. (pres. 1945). Jewish religion (pres. synagogue 1946-47). Home: 100 York St New Haven CT 06511 Office: 155 Church St New Haven CT 06510

HORR, WILLIAM HENRY, lawyer; b. Portsmouth, O., Sept. 23, 1914; s. Charles Chick and Effie (Amberg) H.; A.B., Ohio Wesleyan U., 1936; J.D., U. Cin., 1939; m. Marjorie Bell Marshall, Aug. 31, 1940; children—Robert W., Thomas M., Catherine, James C., Elizabeth. Admitted to Ohio bar, 1939; practice in Portsmouth 1939-42, 45—; atty. Skelton, Kahl, Horr, Marhsall & Burton, 1939-42, 45—; spl. agt. FBI, Louisville, Indpls., Newark, 1942-45; substitute judge Municipal Ct., Portsmouth, 1955—; gen. counsel Ohio Wesleyan U., 1966-70. Mem. Portsmouth Bd. Edn., 1947- 60; pres. Portsmouth YMCA. Trustee Ohio U. Portsmouth Br. Recipient Distinguished Service award Portsmouth Jr. C. of C., 1947. Mem. Ohio (past mem. exec. com.), Portsmouth (past pres.) bar assns., Phi Delta Phi, Phi Kappa Psi, Omicron Delta Kappa. Republican. Methodist. Rotarian, Elk. Home: 1106 29th St Portsmouth OH 45662 Office: 428 Masonic Bldg Portsmouth OH 45662

HORRIGAN, ALFRED FREDERIC, coll. pres.; b. Wilmington, Del., Dec. 9, 1914; s. William James and Anna (Kienle) H.; student St. Joseph Coll., Collegeville, Ind., 1928-34; B.A., St. Meinrad (Ind.) Sem., 1940; M.A., Cath. U. Am., 1942, Ph.D., 1944; LL.D., Belmont Abbey Coll., 1961, St. Joseph's Coll., 1966. Ordained priest Roman Catholic Ch., 1940; asst. pastor, Louisville, 1940-41, 44-49; head dept. philosophy Nazareth Coll., Louisville, also part-time prof. philosophy Ursuline Coll., U. Louisville, 1944-49; editor The Record newspaper, 1946-49; first pres. Bellarmine Coll., Louisville, 1949—. Chmn. Louisville-Jefferson County Commn. on Human Relations, 1965-68. Bd. dirs. Brescia Coll., Owensboro, Ky., Louisville Fund, Louisville Community Concerts Assn.; Mem. Nat. Cath. Ednl. Assn. (exec. com. 1956-58, pres. coll. and univ. dept. 1962-64, exec. bd. 1962-68, problems and plans commn. 1962-65), Assn. Am. Colls. and Univs., Am. Cath. Philos. Assn., English Speaking Union. Club: Filson. Author: Metaphysics as a Principle of Order in the University Curriculum, 1944. Editor: Roots of a Catholic College, 1955. Home: 2000 Norris Pl Louisville KY 40205

HORSCH, VADA, retired assn. exec.; b. Woodbine, Ill., Aug. 21, 1906; d. Frederick and Marie Ann (Uhlrich) Horsch; A.B., U. Wis., 1928; m. Bennett H. Horchler, Nov. 3, 1932 (div. 1948). Dir. exec. placement Med. Bur., Chgo., 1928-32; adminstrv. asst. N.A.M., 1932-39, asst. to sec., 1939-47, asst. sec., 1947-66, asst. sec. indsl. relations com., 1935-40, sec. Indsl. Relations Inst., 1940-43, asst. sec. internat. relations com., 1941-48, dir. internat. econ. affairs dept., 1959-66; sec. Internat. Bus. Conf., 1944; treas., asst. sec. Conf. Nat. Orgns., 1947-50, sec.-treas., 1950-64; asst. sec. U.S. Inter-Am. Council, 1950- 54, sec., 1954-66. Mem. bd. Lafayette fellowship program Eisenhower Exchange Fellowships, 1953-67; mem. U.S. delegations to plenary meetings Inter-Am. Council of Commerce and Prodn., Lima, Peru, 1952, Mexico City, 1954, Buenos Aires, Argentina, 1957, Montevideo, Uruguay, 1961, Santiago, Chile, 1964; mem. U.S. delegation Internat. Conf. Mfrs., London, 1960. Decorated Order of Crown (Belgium); chevalier Ordre du Merite Comml., chevalier Legion D'Honneur (France); officer Order of Merit (Italy); National Order Al Merito (Ecuador); Order of Merit (Fed. Republic of Germany). Mem. French C. of C. of U.S. (hon.), Assn. Internat. des Etudiants en Scis. Economiques et Commls. (bd. advisers), Conf. Nat. Orgns. (hon.), Phi Beta Kappa. Home: 949 Palmer Rd Bronxville NY 10708

HORSEY, GRANT, investment and finance co. exec.; b. Buffalo, Oct. 17, 1915; s. J. William and Clara (Banford) H.; B.Comm., McGill U., 1938; m. Eleanor Mae Child, Feb. 17, 1940; 1 dau., Susan (Mrs. Dees). Route salesman Standard Brands, Ltd., Toronto, Can., 1938; jr. audit clk. McDonald, Currie & Co., Montreal, Can., 1938, sr. audit clk., 1941; asst. dist. mgr. Dominion Stores, Ltd., Halifax, N.S., 1939; treas. Apte Canning Sales Corp., Tampa, Fla., 1946; v.p. J. William Horsey Corp., Plant City, Fla., 1946-50, pres., 1950-55; pres. Shirriff-Horsey Corp., Ltd., Toronto, 1955-57; pres. Salada Foods Ltd., Don Mills, Ont., 1957- 64, chmn. bd., chief exec. officer, 1964-67; pres. Wilgran Corp. Ltd., Toronto, 1962—; chmn. bd. DRG Ltd., Toronto, Cantrend Industries, Ltd.; chmn. exec. com. Barker Indsl. Equipment Ltd.; dir. Gen. Bakeries, Ltd., Pilot Ins. Co., Nat. Trust Co. (all Toronto). Trustee-Toronto Western Hosp. Served as lt. Royal Canadian Army., 1943-46. Mem. Theta Delta Chi. Presbyn. Clubs: Toronto, Granite, Donalda, Ontario (Toronto); Tampa Yacht and Country, University (Tampa, Fla.); Canadian (N.Y.C.) Home: 330 Spadina Rd Toronto 4 Ontario Canada Office: 199 Bay St Toronto 1 Ontario Canada

HORSEY, OUTERBRIDGE, former fgn. service officer; b. N.Y.C., Oct. 1, 1910; s. Outerbridge and Mary Digges (Lee) H.; student Downside Sch., Eng., 1921-28; B.A., Trinity Coll., Cambridge (Eng.) U., 1931; S.B., Mass. Inst. Tech., 1933; m. Mary Hamilton Lee, Jan. 2, 1946; children—Mary Lee, Sarah R., Anita C., Outerbridge. Spl. asst. Nat. Emergency Council, 1934-36; sales engr. Autocar Co., Ardmore, Pa., 1936-37; fgn. service officer, 1938-70; vice consul, Naples, Italy, 1938, Budapest, Hungary, 1940-41; 3d sec. Am. embassy, Madrid, Spain, 1942-44; asst. chief div. Western European affairs Dept. State, 1944-48; assigned Am. embassy, Rome, Italy, 1948-52; staff European affairs Dept. State, 1953-56; minister Am. embassy, Tokyo, Japan, 1956-59, Am. embassy, Rome, 1959-62; ambassador to Czechoslovakia, 1963-66; consul gen., Palermo, Italy, 1968-70. Clubs: Metropolitan (Washington); Chevy Chase (Md.). Home: 3305 Dent Pl Washington DC 20007

HORSFALL, JAMES GORDON, plant pathologist; b. Mt. Grove, Mo., Jan. 9, 1905; s. Frank and Margaret Atwood (Vaulx) H.; B.S., U. Ark., 1925, LL.D., 1969; Ph.D., Cornell, 1929; D.Sc., U. Vermont, 1958; D.Agr. honoris causa, Turin Univ. Italy, 1964; m. Sue Belle Overton, June 30, 1927; children—Margaret Eleanor, Anne Vaulx. Asst. plant pathology Cornell, 1925-28, instr., 1928-29; research asso., asst. prof. plant pathology N.Y. State Agr. Exptl. Sta., Geneva, 1929-36, research chief, prof., 1936-39; chief dept. plant pathology and botany Conn. Agr. Exptl. Sta., 1939-50, dir., 1948—; lectr. Yale, 1950-64. Chmn. executive com. Chem.-Biol. Coordination Center, Nat. Research Council, 1952-57; U.S. del. Atoms for Peace Conf., Geneva, 1958; v.p. 2d Internat. Congress Crop Protection, London, Eng., 1949; trustee Biological Abstracts, 1952-58; mem. Nat. Adv. Commn. Food and Fiber, 1965-67; cons. Pres.'s Sci. Adv. Com., 1960-69; chmn. Gov. Conn. Com. on Environmental Policy, 1970; adv. com. 1st Internat. Congress Plant Pathology. Life mem. India Internat. Centre, New Delhi. Decorated Order of Merit of Agr. (France); named Distinguished Alumnus, U. Ark., 1951. Fellow Am. Phytopathology Soc. (pres. 1950), Indian Phytopathol. Soc. (hon.), A.A.A.S. (council 1947-48); mem. Bot. Soc. Am., Am. Acad. of Arts and Scis., Indian Phytopathological Soc., Assn. Applied Biologists of England, Nat. Acad. Scis., Soc. Indsl. Microbiologists (pres. 1954), Accademia Nazionale di Agricoltura (Italy) (corr. asso.), Societa Phytoatria Italy (hon. mem.), also mem. Sigma Xi, Phi Kappa Phi, Alpha Zeta. Clubs: Graduates (pres. 1959-61), Rotary (New Haven, Conn.); Cosmos (Washington, D.C.). Author: Fungicides and their action, 1945; Principles of Fungicidal Action, 1956; also articles sci. jours. Contbr. Ency. of Chem. Technology, Am. Peoples Ency. Co-editor: Plant Pathology, An Advanced Treatise, 3 vols., 1960. Edit. com. Ann. Rev. Plant Physiology, 1957-61; editor Ann. Rev. Phytopathology, 1962-. Home: 49 Woodstock Rd Hamden CT 06517 Office: Conn Agrl Expt Sta 123 Huntington St New Haven CT 06504

HORSKY, CHARLES ANTONE, lawyer; b. Helena, Mont., Mar. 22, 1910; s. Antone J. and Marguerite (Bowden) H.; A.B., U. Wash., 1931; LL.B., Harvard, 1934; m. Barbara Egleston, Oct. 2, 1936; children—Margaret Ellen, Antone (dec.). Clk. to Judge A.N. Hand, N.Y.C., 1934-35; admitted N.Y. bar, 1935; D.C. bar, 1938; atty. Solicitor Gen. Office, 1935-37, 38-39; mem. Covington & Burling, Washington, 1937-38, 39-62, 67—; adv. to President for Nat. Capital Affairs, 1962-67; lectr. U. Va. Law Sch., 1956-62, 68—. Chmn. D.C. Bd. Higher Edn., 1967-70, vice chmn., 1970—. Dir. Atty. Gen.' s Com. Bankruptcy Adminstrn., 1934-40 mem. Nat. Bankruptcy Conf., 1945-62, 67—, chmn., 1954-62; asso. in charge Wash. office. Office Chief of Counsil for War Crimes, 1945-47, asst. prosecutor, Nurnberg, Germany, 1948. Pres. Washington Housing Assn., 1955-62; mem. Commrs. Planning Adv. Council, chmn., 1960-62. Trustee Woodrow Wilson Internat. Center for Scholars, Found for Coop Housing, E. and A. Meyer Found. (pres. 1970—). Fellow Am. Acad. Arts and Scis., Am. Coll. Trial Lawyers; mem. Am. Bar Assn. (chmn. com. legal services and procedures, 1957-59), Fed. Bar Assn., Am. Judicature Soc., Am. Law Inst., Assn. Bar City N.Y., Selden Society, Order of Grizzly, Phi Beta Kappa, Pi Sigma Alpha. Clubs: Cosmos, Harvard, Nat. Lawyers, Metropolitan (Washington). Author: The Washington Lawyer, 1952. Home: 1227 Pinecrest Circle Silver Spring MD 20910 Office: 888 16th St NW Washington DC 20006

HORSLEY, ANDREW BURT, educator; b. Brigham City, Utah, Nov. 23, 1918; s. William Clements and Adella (Burt) H.; A.B., Brigham Young U., 1945, M.A., 1954; Ph.D., U. Muenster (Germany), 1956; m. Faye McBride, Sept. 18, 1940; children—Dee, Raymon, Christine, Linda, John. Prin. piute Latter-day Saints Sem., 1945-46; prin. Cedar City Sem., 1946-53; supr. sem. tchr. tng. Brigham Young U., Provo, Utah, 1953-54, asst. prof., asso. prof., prof. philosophy and religion, 1956—. Mem. Mountain Plains Philos. Conf. Republican. Mem. Ch. of Jesus Christ of Latter-day Saints (past mem. high council, bishop). Kiwanian. Home: 260 East 400 North Provo UT 84601

HORSMAN, REGINALD, educator, historian; b. Leeds, Eng., Oct. 24, 1931; s. Alfred William and Elizabeth (Thompson) H.; came to U.S., 1954, naturalized, 1965; B.A., U. Birmingham (Eng.), 1952, M.A., 1955; Ph.D., Ind. U., 1958; m. Lenore Eileen McNabb, Sept. 3, 1955; children—John, Janine, Mara. Mem. faculty U. Wis.-Milw., 1958—, prof. history, 1964—, chmn. dept., 1970—. Recipient Kiekhofer teaching award U. Wis., 1961; Guggenheim fellow, 1965-66. Mem. Am. Hist. Assn., Orgn. Am. Historians, Am. Assn. U. Profs. Author: The Causes of the War of 1812, 1962; Matthew Elliott: British Indian Agent, 1964; Expansion and American Indian Policy, 1967; The War of 1812, 1969; The Frontier in the Formative Years, 1970. Home: 3548 N Hackett Av Milwaukee WI 53211

HORST, BRUCE EVERETT, mfg. co. exec.; b. Three Rivers, Mich., Feb. 17, 1921; s. Walter and Genevieve (Turner) H.; B.S. in Bus. and Engring. Adminstrn., Mass. Inst. Tech., 1943; m. Patricia Kranish, Oct. 4, 1969; children—Michael, Diane, Mark. With Barber-Colman Co., Rockford, Ill., 1946—, pres., 1965—. Bd. dirs. Rockford YMCA, 1964—, pres., 1965-67. Served to 1st lt. USAAF, 1943-45. Decorated Air medal. Clubs: Ledges Country (Roscoe); Rotary; Forest Hills Country (past sec.) (Rockford). Home: 2903 Spring Creek Rd Rockford IL 61107 Office: 1300 Rock St Rockford IL 61101

HORST, PETER, advt. agy. exec.; b. Benton Harbor, Mich., June 21, 1933; s. George Carl and Dorothy (Scott) H.; student U. Mich., 1951-53, 56-58; m. Patricia Ann Gordon, July 27, 1968; 1 son, Ian Scott. Creative dir. N.W. Ayer & Son, Phila. and Chgo., 1959-65; asso. creative dir. Leo Burnett Co., Inc., Chgo., 1965-68; v.p., creative dir. Henderson Advt. Agy., Inc., Greenville, S.C., 1968-71; pres. Horst, Hughes, McCarthy & Boesch, Inc., San Francisco, 1971—. Home: 301 Panoramic Hwy Mill Valley CA 94941 Office: 153 Maiden Lane San Francisco CA 94108

HORSTICK, WILLIAM WALLACE, bishop; b. Harrisburg, Pa., Jan. 31, 1902; s. John Franklin and Emma (Machen) H.; B.D., Nashotah Theol. Sem., 1929, D.D., 1944, D.C.L., 1969; m. Joan E. Piesen, July 28, 1937; children—Ruth Ariel, Emma May, David Piersen, Mary Alice. Curate, Ch. of the Redeemer (Episcopal), Chgo., 1929-31; rector Trinity Episcopal Ch., Aurora, Ill., 1931-44; bishop Diocese of Eau Claire, Wis., 1944-69, now coadjutor bishop. Trustee Nashotah Theol. Sem.; pres. trustees Roanridge Found. Mem. Newcomen Soc. Republican. Home: 938 N Griffith Rd Oconomowoc WI 53066

HORSTMAN, WILLIAM BERNARD, hotel exec.; b. Parkersburg, W. Va., Jan. 8, 1909; s. Joseph Prosper and Laura Clarke (Gurley) H.; student U. Cin., 1928-34; m. Frances Josephine Russell, Apr. 17, 1949; children—Caroline Frances, Laura Anne. Athletic publicity dir. U. Cin., 1935-36; nat. conv. mgr. Nat. Hotel Mgmt. Co., N.Y.C., 1937; sales and advt. mgr. Congress Hotel, Chgo., 1938, Netherland Plaza Hotel, Cin., 1939-40; promotion mgr. Hollywood Ice Revue, 1948-53; asst. producer, gen. mgr. Olsen & Johnston's Funzapoppin, 1949; v.p., gen. mgr. Cole Bros. Circus, 1950-53; mgr. Chgo. Stadium, now asst. to pres.; v.p., gen. mgr. Bismarck Hotel, Chgo.; pres. Lincoln-Robey Corp. Vice chmn. Midwest Hotel Show, Chgo., 1957, chmn., 1958. Served to lt. comdr. USNR, World War II. Mem. Assn. Theatrical Press Agts. and Mgrs., Lambda Chi Alpha, Omicron Delta Kappa. Mason (K.T., Shriner, Jester). Clubs: Executive (Chgo.); Variety. Home: 401 Hawthorn St Winnetka IL 60093 Office: 171 W Randolph St Chicago IL 60601

HORSTMANN, DOROTHY MILLICENT, physician; b. Spokane, Wash., July 2, 1911; d. Henry J. and Anna (Hunold) H.; A.B., U. Cal., 1936, M.D., 1940; D.Sc. (hon.), Smith Coll., 1961; Dr. Med. Scis. (hon.), Women's Med. Coll. of Pa., 1963. Intern San Francisco City and County Hosp., 1939-40, asst. resident medicine, 1940-41; asst. resident medicine Vanderbilt U. Hosp., 1941-42; Commonwealth Fund fellow, sect. preventive medicine, sch. medicine Yale, New Haven, Conn., 1942-43, instr. preventive medicine, 1943-44, 45-47, asst. prof., 1948- 52, asso. prof., 1952-56, asso. prof. preventive medicine and pediatrics, 1956-61, prof. epidemiology and pediatrics, 1961—; instr. medicine U. Cal., 1944-45; NIH fellow Nat. Inst. Med. Research, London, Eng., 1947-48. Fellow A.C.P.; hon. asso. fellow Am. Acad. Pediatrics; mem. Am. Soc. Clin. Investigation, Am. Assn.

Immunologists, Am. Epidemiological Soc., Am. Pediatric Soc., Assn. Tchrs. Preventive Medicine, Infectious Diseases Soc. Am., Soc. Epidemiologic Research. Home: 11 Autumn St New Haven CT 06511

HORSWILL, ERLE WASSON, lawyer; b. Orofino, Ida., Aug. 11, 1917; s. Erle W. and Gertrude (Earlywine) H.; LL.B., U. Wash., 1940; m. Jeanne C. McCrea, Sept. 18, 1943; children—Ann, Michael, Stephen. Admitted to Wash. bar, 1940, since practiced in Seattle; partner firm Horswill, Keller, Rohrback, Waldo & Moren, 1950—. Mem. for Wash. to bd. advisers on criminal justice act 9th Circuit Ct. Appeals, 1965-68. Bd. regents St. Martin's Coll. Fellow Am. Coll. Trial Lawyers; mem. Am., Wash. (bd. govs. 1964-67), Seattle bar assns. Home: 1244 20th St E Seattle WA 98102 Office: IBM Bldg Seattle WA 98101

HORSZOWSKI, MIECZYSLAW, pianist; b. Lwow, Poland, June 23, 1892; s. Stanislaw and Rose Jeanne (Wagner) H.; pupil of Theodore Leschetizky, Vienna, Austria; Mus.D., Curtis Inst. Music, 1969. Came to U.S. 1941, naturalized, 1948. Concert pianist, 1904—; first recital, N.Y.C., 1906; frequent appearances with major orchs. throughout world; soloist with Toscanini and NBC Orch., 1942, 53; participated annually Casals Festivals, Prades, France and P.R.; faculty Curtis Inst. Music, Phila., 1942—. Office: Care Curtis Inst of Music Philadelphia PA 19103

HORTE, VERNON LYLE, pipeline co. exec.; b. Kingman, Alta., Can., July 12, 1925; s. Thor and Marit (Haugen) H.; B. Sc. in Chem., Engring., U. Alta., 1949; m. Thelma Margaret Boness, Feb. 18, 1950; children—Joan Thelma, Robert Vernon, Douglas Boness. Gas engr. Oil and Gas Conservation Bd., Alta., 1949-52; petroleum engring. cons. De Goyler and MacNaughton, Dallas, 1952-57; with TransCan. Pipelines Ltd., 1957—, pres., dir., 1968—; pres. dir. Western Pipe Lines; dir. Gt. Lakes Gas Transmission Co., Banner Petroleums Ltd., TransCan. Gas Products Served with RCAF, 1943-45. Registered profl. engr., Alta., Tex. Mem. Canadian (bd. dirs.), Am. gas assns., Am. Inst. Mining, Metall. and Petoleum Engrs., Canadian Inst. Mining and Metallurgy, Alta. Soc. Petroleum Geologists. Home: 30 Banstock Dr Willowdale Ontario Canada Office: 150 Eglinton Av E Toronto Ontario Canada

HORTEN, CARL FRANK, textile mfg. co. exec.; b. Fort Lauderdale, Fla., Aug. 19, 1914; s. Joseph Frederick and Phyllis (Gregory) H.; B.S., Geneva Coll., 1936; M.B.A., Harvard, 1938; grad. exec. program, U. N.C., 1959; m. Alice Jeannette Yereance, June 8, 1940; children—Bruce Carl, Lynn Alice, Heather Belle. Sales corr. L. Sonneborn Sons, 1938-40; asst. controller Nashua Mfg. Co., 1940-47; controller Textron So., Inc., 1947-49; with Springs Mills, Inc., Ft. Mill, S.C., 1949—, v.p., 1964-66, treas., 1967—, exec. v. p., 1966—, sec., 1969, also dir.; dir. Carolina Carpet Co. Served to lt. (j.g.) USNR, 1943-46. Home: PO Box 396 Fort Mill SC 29715 Office: Springs Mills Inc Fort Mill SC 29715

HORTON, ALAN WILLIAMS, assn. exec., anthropologist; b. Middletown, Conn., July 31, 1921; s. Douglas and Carol (Williams) H.; B.A., Princeton, 1947; M.A., Harvard, 1953, Ph.D., 1962; postgrad. Am. U., Cairo, 1947-48; m. Dorothy Joan Ryder, Jan. 17, 1951; children—Carol Ryder, James McAfee, Edward Alan Douglas. Instr. Am. U., Cairo, 1948-49, dean Sch. Oriental Studies, 1955-56, dean grad. faculty, 1956-62; mem. Gaza unit Am. Friends Service Com., 1949-50; sr. area officer Gaza dist. UN Relief and Works Agy., 1950, dep. chief dist. officer, Lebanon, 1950-51; asst. dir. N. Syria field session U. Mich., 1953-54; Middle East asso. Am. Univs. Field Staff, Cairo, 1962-68, exec. dir., Hanover, N.H., 1968—; adj. prof. Dartmouth, 1969—. Served with USNR, 1942-46. Decorated Silver Star. Fellow Am. Anthrop. Assn., Middle East Studies Assn., Middle East Inst., African Studies Assn. Home: Lyme Rd Hanover NH 03755 Office: 535 Fifth Av New York City NY 10017 also 3 Lebanon St Hanover NH 03755

HORTON, ALLEN W., chem. co. exec.; b. Chgo., 1912; ed. Mass. Inst. Tech., 1936. Sec., treas. Chevron Chem. Co.; mgr. Chevron Chem. G.m.b.H.; dir. Aditivos Mexicanos, S.A., BP-Cal. Ltd., BP-Cal (Grangemouth) Ltd., Karonite Chem. Co., Ltd., Nippon Petroleum Detergent Co. Ltd., Petrosynthese S.A. Home: 175 29th Av San Francisco CA 94131 Office: 200 Bush St San Francisco CA 94120

HORTON, BAYARD TAYLOR physician; b. Gate City, Va., Dec. 6, 1895; s. Thomas Flurnoy and Ellen Ann (Watkins) H.; B.S., U. Va., 1921, M.D., 1922; M.S., U. Minn. (Mayo Found.), 1928; m. Jane Heyl, June 14, 1922; children—Bayard Taylor, Nancy Ellen, Thomas Nelson. In practice at Emory, Va., 1923-25; prof. biology Emory and Henry Coll., Emory, Va., 1923-25; entered Mayo Found., Rochester, Minn., as fellow in medicine, 1925, instr. in medicine, 1929-34, asst. prof., 1934-37, asso. prof., 1937—, cons. in medicine Mayo Clinic, 1930—, head of sect. clin. investigation, 1940. Served as seaman USN, World War I. Recipient John Horsley prize 000 for research work on "Pyloric Block," U. Va., 1929. Diplomate Am. Bd. Internal Medicine. Fellow A.C.P., Am. Geriatrics Soc., Am. Coll. Allergists; mem. A.M.A., Minn. Soc. Internal Medicine (pres. 1943-44), Am. Soc. for Clin. Investigation, Central Soc. for Clin. Research, N.Y. Acad. Scis., Am. Assn. Study Headache (pres. 1961-63), Phi Beta Kappa, Sigma Xi, Phi Chi, Alpha Omega Alpha. Democrat. Baptist. Author of numerous med. articles, including description of two new disease entities, namely, temporal arteritis (with G.E. Brown and T.B. Magath) and histaminic cephalgia (with A.R. Maclean and W. McK. Craig) (Horton's syndrome). Home: 830 4th St SW Rochester MN 55901 Address:

HORTON, BENJAMIN STEVENS, trucking co. exec.; b. Charlotte, N.C., Jan. 5, 1917; s. Herman Dewitt and Daisy (Eidson) H.; student N.C. State Coll., 1937, Curtis Wright Tech. Inst., 1938; m. Hazel Dees Barefoot, Jan. 4, 1941; children—Hazel Elaine (Mrs. Harry D. Snook), Eloise Gail (Mrs. Thomas M. Hunter, Jr.). With Brown Equipment & Mfg. Co., 1939-62, pres., 1957-62; adminstrv. v.p. Asso. Transp., Inc., 1962-68, vice chmn. bd., 1968—, also dir. Mem. Soc. Automotive Engrs. Mason (Shriner). Home: 5806 Old Providence Rd Charlotte NC 28221 Office: 380 Madison Av New York NY 10017

HORTON, BERNARD FRANCIS, newspaper editor; b. Peabody, Kan., May 26, 1916; s. Frank H. and Lula Elizabeth (Stovall) H.; B.A., U. Wyo., 1938; m. Betty Mildred Wessels, Dec. 20, 1938; 1 son, Gary Francis. Owner, editor, pub. Chugwater News, handset weekly, Wyo., 1938-42; editor No. Wyo. Daily News, Worland, 1942-43, Rawlins (Wyo.) Daily Times, 1946-49; asst. news editor Wyo. Eagle, Cheyenne, 1949-52, news editor, 1952-54, mng. editor, 1955-62, editor, 1962—; columnist Political and Otherwise. Served with AUS, 1943-46; chief pub. relations sect. 97th Inf. Div. ETO; mng. editor Pacific Stars and Stripes, 1946. Mem. Wyo. Press Assn. (pres. 1971—). Home: 3618 Dover Rd Cheyenne WY 82001 Office: 110 E 17th St Cheyenne WY 82001

HORTON, BRIAN ROBERT, journalist; b. Bournemouth, Eng., Apr. 23, 1933; s. Edwin and Celeste (Bouillon) H.; M.A. with honours, Auckland (New Zealand) Univ. Coll., 1954; M.A., Univ. Coll., Oxford (Eng.) U., 1957; m. Sally Georgina Eaton, Feb. 6, 1960; children—Matthew Edwin, Charlotte Mary. With Reuters Ltd., 1957—, chief diplomatic corr., 1962-63, European editor, 1964-65, chief news editor, 1965-67, dep. mng. editor, 1967, editor-in-chief, 1968—. Club: The Reform (London). Home: 12 Rawlings St London SW3 England Office: 85 Fleet St London EC4 England

HORTON, BRUCE WILLIAM, newspaperman; b. Zanesville, O., Oct. 18, 1906; s. Willard and Bessie (Bruce) H.; A.B. cum laude, Salem Coll., 1930; m. Alice Mary Kleinhans, Sept. 28, 1935 (dec. June 1951); children—Robert Bruce, Harry Richard; m. 2d, Hallie Hutten, May 3, 1952. Promotion editor Pitts. Press, 1933- 40; asst. mgr. aviation dept. Gulf Oil Corp., 1940-45; Eastern mgr. Register and Tribune Syndicate, N.Y.C., 1945-59, v.p., gen. mgr., Des Moines, 1960-70. Mem. Laudi Soc. Republican. Presbyn. Club: Nat. Press (Washington). Home: 9449 110th Av Sun City AZ 85351

HORTON, CLAUDE WENDELL, educator; b. Cherryvale, Kan., Sept. 23, 1915; s. Roy Wesley and Marie (Terwilleger) H.; B.A. with honors in Physics, Rice Inst., 1935, M.A. in Physics, 1936; postgrad. Princeton, 1937-38; Ph.D. in Physics, U. Tex., 1948; m. Louise Walthall, Nov. 23, 1938; children—Claude Wendell, Margaret Elaine. Asst. seismologist Shell Oil Co., 1936-37, party chief field crew, 1938-43; research asso. underwater sound lab. Harvard, 1943- 45; research physicist def. research lab. U. Tex., Austin, 1945—, prof. physics, 1953—, acting chmn. dept., 1956-57, chmn. dept., 1957-62, prof. geology, 1965—. Mem. corp. Woods Hole (Mass.) Oceanographic Instn., 1966—. Fellow Acoustical Soc. Am., Am. Phys. Soc., mem. A.A.A.S., Am. Geophys. Union, Soc. Exploration Geophysicists. Home: 3213 Cherry Lane Austin TX 78703

HORTON, MRS. DOUGLAS, see Horton, Mildred McAfee.

HORTON, FRANK, U.S. congressman; b. Cuero, Tex., Dec. 12, 1919; s. Frank J. and Mary (Hathcox) H.; B.A., La. State U., 1941; LL.B., Cornell U., 1947; m. Marjorie Mae Wilcox, Jan. 1, 1945; children—Frank Jefferson III, Steven William. Admitted to N.Y. bar, 1947; asso. firm Johnson, Reif & Mullan and predecessor firm, Rochester, N.Y., 1947-52, partner, 1952-69; mem. 88th-92d U.S. Congresses, 36th Dist. N.Y., mem. house govt. operations com., house select com. on small bus.; mem. congl. task force on earth resources and population. Commr., Commn. on Govt. Procurement, 1969—. Exec. com. Seneca dist. Otetiana council Boy Scouts Am., 1955—; pres. Rochester Community Baseball, Inc., 1957-62. Councilman-at-large Rochester City Council, 1955-61; v.p. 18th Ward Men's Republican Club, 1957. Served from 2d lt. to maj., AUS, 1941-46. Mem. Am., N.Y. (exec. com. young lawyers sect. 1952), Monroe County (sec. 1953-57) bar assns., Fedn. Bar Assns. Western N.Y. (pres. 1956-57), Res. Officers Assn. (past pres.), V.F.W., Am. Legion, Order Coif. Presbyn. (elder, trustee). Mason (33,Shriner). Co-author: How to End the Draft, 1967; A Study of Urban Education in America, 1968. Home: 2123 East Av Rochester NY 14610 Office: Ho of Reps Washington DC 20515

HORTON, FRANK C., lawyer; b. Grenada County, Miss., July 13, 1917; A.B., U. Miss., 1941, J.D., 1941. Admitted to Miss. bar, 1941; now partner firm Daniel, Coker, Horton & Bell, Jackson, Miss. Atty. referee Miss. Workmen's Compensation Commn., 1955-58. Mem. Am., Hinds County bar assns., Miss. State Bar, Miss. Def. Lawyers Assn., Phi Delta Phi. Office: 405 Tombigbee St at S Congress St Jackson MS 39205*

HORTON, GILBERT ROBINSON, architect; b. St. Paul, Nov. 10, 1888; s. Gilbert Lafayette and Annie (Napier) H.; student U. Minn., 1908-09, U. Wash., 1909-10; m. Evangelyn Mae Roberts, Nov. 10, 1913; children—Gilbert Everett, Kent Howard. Practice architecture, Jamestown, N.D., 1913—; prin. works include Jamestown Hosp., 1930-70, Jamestown High Sch., 1963-66, First Fed. Savs. & Loan Assn., Jamestown, 1966, First James River Nat. Bank, Jamestown, 1966. Mem. N.D. Bd. Architecture, 1941-55, pres., 1953-55. Troop cmdr. local Boy Scouts Am., 1927-32; mem. Jamestown City Council, 1925-27; city engr., Jamestown, 1932-37. Fellow A.I.A. (awards N.D. chpt.); mem. Jamestown C. of C. Republican. Episcopalian (sr. warden). Rotarian. Home: Sunny Hills Jamestown ND 58401 Office: Box 1351 Jamestown ND 58401

HORTON, JACK KING, utilities exec.; b. Stanton, Neb., June 27, 1916; s. Virgil L. and Edna L. (King) H.; A.B., Stanford, 1936; LL.B., Oakland Coll. Law, 1941; m. Betty Lou Magee, July 15, 1937; children—Judy, Sally, Harold. Admitted to Cal. bar, 1941; treasury dept. Shell Oil Co., 1937-42; pvt. law practice, San Francisco, 1942-43; atty. Standard Oil Co., 1943-44; sec., legal counsel Coast Counties Gas & Electric Co., 1944-51, pres., 1951- 54; v.p. Pacific Gas & Electric Co., San Francisco, 1954-59; pres. So. Cal. Edison Co., 1959—, chief exec. officer, 1965—, chmn. bd., 1968—; dir. United Cal. Bank, Pacific Mut. Life Ins., Lockheed Aircraft Corp. Trustee U. So. Cal. Mem. State Bar Cal., Tax Found. (trustee), Bus. Council. Clubs: Pacific Union, Bohemian, California, Los Angeles Country. Home: 315 S Windsor Blvd Los Angeles CA 90020 Office: PO Box 351 Los Angeles CA 90053

HORTON, JAMES WRIGHT, lawyer; b. Belton, S.C., Dec. 24, 1919; s. John Aiken and Emmae (Tate) H.; B.A., Furman U., 1942; J.D., Harvard, 1948; m. Eunice Rice, Nov. 20, 1948; children—James Wright, Max Rice, Rex Rice. Admitted to S.C. bar, 1948; partner Nettles & Horton, 1948-52, Rainey, Fant & Horton, 1952-70, Horton, Drawdy, Dillard, Marchbanks, Chapman & Brown, 1970— (all Greenville, S.C.). Pres. United Fund Greenville County, 1959; vice chmn. Greenville County Sch. Trustees, 1968—; pres. Greenville Family and Childrens Service, 1954-55; treas. Salvation Army, 1970-71. Bd. dirs. Family and Childrens Service. Served with USMCR, 1942-46. Decorated Silver Star. Baptist (deacon 1964-69, 71—). Home: 2 Osceola Dr Greenville SC 29605 Office: 307 Pettigru St Greenville SC 29602

HORTON, JARED CHURCHILL, investment co. exec.; b. Greenwich, Conn., Oct. 8, 1924; s. Frederic Jared and Marcelene (Churchill) H.; student Yale, 1942; grad. Packard Jr. Coll., 1948; m. Pauline Elizabeth Finn, June 14, 1947; children—Janette Elizabeth, Cynthia Joan, Allison Jane, Juliana Ruth. With PM Industries, Stamford, Conn., 1948-54; with Alleghany Corp., N.Y.C., 1954—, treas., 1956—, sec., 1959-61, 63—, v.p., 1967—. Served to 1st lt. AUS, 1942-46. Mem. Am. Soc. Corporate Secs. Episcopalian. Home: Coachlamp Lane Greenwich CT 06830 Office: 350 Park Av New York City NY 10022

HORTON, JOHN THEODORE, educator; b. Bolivar, N.Y., Sept. 29, 1902; s. Milton V. and Jeannette (Hatch) H.; B.A. cum laude, U. Buffalo, 1926; A.M., Harvard, 1929, Ph.D., 1935; m. Evelyn B. Williams, June 18, 1935; 1 dau., Anne K. (Mrs. Anne H. Kendzior). Mem. faculty U. Buffalo, 1926- 62, inst., asst. prof., asso. prof., 1926-44, prof., 1944-62, chmn. dept. history and govt., 1948-62; chmn. dept. history State U. N.Y. at Buffalo, 1962-67, now prof. history; vis. lectr. State U. Ia., summers 1946, 47. Chmn. U. Buffalo Nat. Municipal League Com. on Constn. State N.Y., 1937-38; mem. com. Buffalo Town Meeting of Air, 1937-38; organizer, chmn. U. Buffalo Com. Coop. with Brit.-Am. Ambulance Corps, 1940; sec. Niagara Frontier Def. Com., 1940-41; mem. regents' adv. com. historians on History in Curriculum Secondary Schs. N.Y. State, 1949-50; mem. organizing com. Congress Local Hist. Socs., 1955-62. Mem. Am. Hist. Assn., Buffalo, L.I. hist. socs., Am. Assn. U. Profs., S.R. (sometime pres. Buffalo chpt.), Phi Beta Kappa (past chapt. pres.). Episcopalian. Author: James Kent: A Study in Conservatism, 1939 (recipient Albert J. Beveridge prize Am. Hist. Assn. 1939); Old Erie: The Growth of an American Community, 1947; Edward Grotrian Schauroth: A Memoir, 1955. Home: 85 Woodward Av Buffalo NY 14214

HORTON, JOHN TOD, engring. co. exec.; b. Chgo., May 2, 1928; s. Horace Babcock and Phyllis (Fay) H.; Ph.B., U. Chgo., 1946; B.Civil Engring., Rensselaer Poly. Inst., 1952, M.S., 1953; m. Helene Arvanitidi, Jan. 8, 1959; children— Horace H., John M. Instr. Rensselaer Poly. Inst., 1952-53; with Chgo. Bridge & Iron Co., 1955—, mgr. spl. designs and estimates, 1959- 60, v.p. research, 1961-66, exec. v. p., 1966-68, pres., 1968-69, now dir.; dir. Star Shipyards Ltd., Aerovac Corp., Troy, N.Y. Trustee Rensselaer Poly. Inst. Mem. Am. Phys. Soc., Am. Soc. C.E., Sigma Xi, Chi Epsilon, Tau Beta Pi. Home: 348 E 3d St Hinsdale IL 60521 Office: 901 W 22d St Oak Brook IL 60523

HORTON, KENNETH DOUGLAS, railroad ofcl.; b. Purvis, Miss., Oct. 25, 1903; s. John William and Laura E. (Sims) H.; B.S., Miss. State Tchrs. Coll., Hattiesburg, 1925; LL.B., U. Miss., 1929; m. Lois Melba Hales, Dec. 10, 1949; 1 son, Kenneth Douglas. Tchr. high sch., Kinder, La. and Belzoni, Miss., 1925- 26; admitted to Miss. bar. 1929; with G.,M. & O. R.R., 1929—, sec., atty., 1938—; sec., dir. New Orleans Gt. No. Ry. Co., Gulf Transp. Co., GM & O Land Co. Mem. Alpha Tau Omega, Phi Alpha Delta. Home: 34 McPhillips Av Mobile AL 36604 Office: 104 St Francis St Mobile AL 36602

HORTON, LEONARD MEAD, banker; b. Glen Ridge, N.J., Nov. 30, 1906; s. John Marcus and Florence (Crane) H.: B.S., Lehigh U., 1928, LL.D., 1965; m. Gladys M. Wester, May 20, 1932; children—Nancy, William. With Nat. City Co., 1928-30; with Chem. Bank & Trust Co., 1930-49, asst. sec., 1941, asst. v.p., 1943, v.p., 1947-49; v.p., treas., dir. Aubrey G. Langston & Co., Inc., 1949-50, pres., 1959-63, chmn. bd., 1963-70, now dir. Trustee Lehigh U. (chmn. finance com. 1946). Mem. Beta Gamma Sigma, Alpha Chi Rho, Alpha Kappa Psi. Republican. Methodist. Clubs: University, Bond (N.Y.C.); Baltusrol Golf; Ocean (Ocean Ridge, Fla.); Gulf Stream Golf (Delray Beach, Fla.); Short Hills. Home: 40 Montview Av Short Hills NJ 07078 Office: 20 Broad St New York City NY 10005

HORTON, MILDRED MCAFEE, (Mrs. Douglas Horton), educator; b. Parkville, Mo., May 12, 1900; d. Cleland Boyd and Harriet (Brown) McAfee; B.A., Vassar Coll., 1920; M.A., U. Chgo., 1928; student U. Chgo., 1929, 31, 33, Columbia, summers 1924, 32; LL.D., Oberlin Coll., 1936, Williams Coll., 1936, Mt. Holyoke Coll., 1937, Bates Coll., 1937, Boston U., 1940, Wesleyan U., 1940, Women's Coll. N.C., 1942, U. Pa., 1943, N.J. Coll. Women, 1943, Rockford Coll., 1943, Occidental Coll., 1944, Smith Coll., 1944, Tulane U., 1944, U. Buffalo, 1946, Park Coll., 1948, Wellesley Coll., 1950, Middlebury Coll., 1950; L.H.D., Goucher Coll., 1938, Wilson Coll., 1941, Princeton, 1947, Beaver Coll., 1950, U. State N.Y., 1951, Centre Coll., 1954, Colby Coll., 1956; m. Rev. Douglas Horton, Aug. 1945. Tchr. French and English, Monticello Sem., Godfrey, Ill., 1920-21; asst. 8th grade Francis Parker Sch., Chgo., 1921-22; dir. girls' work 4th Presbyn. Ch., Chgo., 1922- 23; acting prof. econs. and sociology Tusculum Coll., Greenville, Tenn., 1923-25, 1 semester, 1926; tutor in econs. Bryn Mawr Summer Sch. for Women in Industry, summer 1927; dean of women, prof. sociology woman's dept. Centre Coll., Danville, Ky., 1927-32; tchr. social scis. Asheville (N.C.) Normal Sch., summer 1930; exec. sec. Asso. Alumnae of Vassar Coll., 1932-34; dean of coll. women Oberlin Coll., 1934-36; pres. Wellesley Coll., 1936-49; dir. NBC, 1950-61, RCA, 1951-61. Pres. Am. Bd. Commrs. for Fgn. Missions, 1959-61; past pres. United Bd. Christian Higher Edn. in Asia; past mem. United Ch. Bd. for World Ministries; past pres. Nat. Social Welfare Assembly, 1950-53; mem. Com. on White House Conf. on Edn., 1955; mem. U.S. Ednl. Mission to Japan, 1946; U.S. del. 12th Gen. Conf. UNESCO, 1962. Co-chmn. Nat. Women's Com. on Civil Rights, 1963-64. Trustee emeritus Northfield Mt. Hermon Sch.; trustee U. N.H. Served from lt. comdr. to capt., dir. Women's Res., USNR, 1942- 46. Address: Randolph NH 03593

HORTON, RALPH, Jr., personnel exec.; b. N.Y.C., Oct. 2, 1916; s. Ralph and Rita (Thompson) H.; grad. Choate Sch., 1935; A.B., Princeton, 1939; m. Rosina Middleton, Apr. 17, 1962; children—Daniel, Ralph, Mark, John. Vice pres. Pride Transp. Co., N.Y.C., 1946-51; spl. promotions exec. Liggett & Myers Tobacco Co., N.Y.C., 1951-60; with Dept. Def., 1961-69, dir. equal employment program Office Sec. Def., 1962-69; pres. Automated Personnel Internat., Norfolk, 1969—; spl. cons. to sec. housing and urban devel., 1967-69. Coordinator John F. Kennedy campaign, 1961, Senator Robert F. Kennedy campaign, 1964. Bd. dirs. Operation Mainstream Concentrated Employment Program. Served to maj. AUS, 1942-46. Recipient Outstanding Service award Dept. Army, 1962. Democrat. Roman Cath. Club: Princeton (Washington). Home: 4552 Bob Jones Dr Virginia Beach VA 23462 Office: Atlantic Nat Bank Bldg Norfolk VA 23510

HORTON, ROBERT EUGENE, coll. pres.; b. Los Angeles, Apr. 8, 1914; s. Henry Hollis and Grace (Wood) H.; B.A. in Math., U. Cal. at Los Angeles, 1936, M.A. in Math., 1947; Ed.D., U. So. Cal., 1959; m. Flora Mae Carlsen, June 14, 1952; 1 dau., Diane (Mrs. Jay R. Weed). Engr., Douglas Aircraft Co., 1937-38; tchr. math. Los Angeles City Schs., 1939-41; asso. math. U. Cal. at Los Angeles, 1946-47; prof. math. Los Angeles City Coll., 1947-60, dean edn. services, 1960-67; pres. Los Angeles Valley Coll., Van Nuys, Cal., 1968—. Bd. dirs. San Fernando Valley Symphony Assn., Com. on the Arts, Los Angeles chpt. A.R.C. Served to 2d lt., U.S. Army, 1936-37, to lt. col., USAAF, 1941-46, 51-53. Mem. Math. Assn. Am., Am. Math. Soc., Van Nuys C. of C. (bd. dirs. 1970—), Phi Delta Kappa, Alpha Sigma Lambda. Rotarian. Asso. editor Math. Mag., 1953-59, 64—, editor, 1959-64. Home: 3418 Vista Haven Rd Sherman Oaks CA 91403

HORTON, WADE HENRY, clergyman; b. Lancaster County, S.C., Sept. 13, 1908; s. Lonnie John and Flonnie Sophronia (Carnes) H.; m. Ruby Gaines, Dec. 24, 1931; children—Wade Henry, Betty Jo, John Clifton, Johnathan David. Ordained to ministry Ch. of God; pastor in McCall, S.C., 1933-34, Union, S.C., 1935-37, Columbia, S.C., 1938-40, Washington, 1941-43, Charlotte, N.C., 1944-45, 48-52, Kannapolis, N.C., 1946-47, Anderson, S.C., 1952; mem. bd. missions Ch. of God, 1948-52, rep fgn. missions field, 1953-58, oversseer of Miss., 1958-60, mem. exec. council, 1953-56, 58-, 1st asst. gen. overseer, 1960-62, gen. overseer, 1962-66, overseer, 1966-68, asst. gen. overseer, 1968—. Bd. dirs. Pentecostal Fellowship N.Am.; adv. council Presidium World Pentecostal Conf. Author: Pentecost Yesterday and Today; The Trinitarian Concept of God. Home: 450 25th St NW Cleveland TN 37311 Office: Keith at 25th St Cleveland TN 37311

HORVAT, HENRY RUDOLPH, educator; b. Duryea, Pa., July 14, 1907; s. Rudolph Joseph and Ida Elizabeth (Bosker) H.; A.B., Mt. St. Mary's Coll., 1927; student Bucknell U., 1929, N.Y.U., 1940; A.M.,

Columbia Tchrs. Coll., 1933, Ed.D., 1946; m. Ida Elinor Wilcom, Aug. 12, 1937. Tchr., Pringle (Pa.) High Sch., 1928-30, Duryea Sr. High Sch., 1930-34; supervising prin. Jenkins Twp. Sch. Dist., Pittston, Pa., 1934-37, Swoyerville (Pa.) Borough Sch. Dist., 1937-42; asst. county supt. Luzerne County schs., Wilkes Barre, Pa., 1942-46; dean students Asso. Colls. Upper N.Y., Mohawk Coll., Utica, 1946-48, Sampson Coll., Geneva, N.Y., 1948-49; adminstrv. asst. to dean acad. adminstrn. Asso. Colls. Upper N.Y., 1949- 50; dean students Champlain Coll., Plattsburg, N.Y., 1950-53; asst. prof. Marquette U., 1953-58; prof. edn., chmn. dept. adminstrn. and supervision St. John's U., 1958-62, dean faculty, 1962-67, dean summer sessions, 1967-68, acting dean Sch. Edn., 1968- 69, prof., 1969—. Del. to UNESCO, Boston, 1962; chmn. Coop. Assn. Colls. and Univs. L.I., 1962-65; mem. planning com. Coll. Assn. Devel. Ednl. Adminstrn. N.Y. 1960-63; v.p. Rockville Diocesan Bd. Cath. Edn. Trustee King's Coll., Wilkes-Barre. Recipient Distinguished Service certificate Pa. dept. Am. Legion, 1945. Mem. Am. Assn. Sch. Adminstrs., Phi Delta Kappa. Co-author: Definition of Professional Terms in Educational Psychology, 1958. Home: 290 Concord Av West Hempstead NY 11552 Office: St John's Univ Grand Central and Utopia Pkwys Jamaica NY 11432

HORVATH, ERNEST VINCENT, textile mfg. co. exec.; b. Budapest, Hungary, Aug. 14, 1902; s. Anton A. and Irene (Nadas) H.; student schs., Budapest; grad. Fiume Export Acad., 1918; divorced; m. 2d, Maria J. Gonzalez, Mar. 1964. Came to U.S., 1919, naturalized, 1926. Chmn., Mt. Clemens Corp.; pres. Neisco, Inc.; pres., dir. Masmo, Inc. Dir. George Junior Republic. Home: 630 Park Av New York City NY 10022 Office: 545 Madison Av New York City NY 10016

HORVATH, GEORGE A., corp. exec.; b. Hungary, 1909; ed. St. Stephen's Coll., 1931. Pres. Mt. Clemens Industries, Inc., Mt. Clemens Corp.; exec. v.p., dir. Nederland Mines, Inc. Home: 1 Beekman Pl New York City NY 10022 Office: 545 Madison Av New York City NY 10022

HORVAY, FRANK DOMINIC, educator; b. Budapest, Hungary, July 2, 1916; s. Gyula and Rose (Pollak) H.; came to U.S., 1936, naturalized, 1942; B.A., U. Ala., 1939, M.A., 1940; Ph.D., Washington U., St. Louis, 1949; m. Vlasta Vesely, July 31, 1944; children—Linda R., Vicki L. Asso. prof. German Wabash Coll., 1947-52; with U.S. govt., 1952-60; prof. German, head dept. fgn. langs. Ill. State U., Normal, 1960-64; prof. German, head dept. Heidelberg (O.) Coll., 1964—. Served with AUS, 1943-46; lt. col. Res. Mem. Modern Lang. Assn. Am., Am. Assn. Tchrs. German, Central States, Midwest modern lang. assns., Am. Assn. U. Profs. (pres. Ill. State U. chpt. 1962-63, pres. Heidelberg Coll. chpt. 1965-66). Rotarian. Contbr. profl. jours. Home: 154 Main St Tiffin OH 44883

HORVITZ, HAROLD, lawyer; b. Chelsea, Mass., June 19, 1902; s. Charles and Annie (Margolis) H.; B.S. in Chem. Engring., Tufts Coll., 1922; LL.B., Harvard, 1925; m. Beatrice Ruth Gerstein, Jan. 12, 1933; children—John Charles, David (dec.), Richard. Admitted to Mass. bar, 1926; spl. asst. to U.S. atty. gen., 1925-26; pvt. practice, Boston, 1926—; partner firm Guterman, Rubin & Rudman, 1934—; lectr. bankruptcy Northeastern U. Law Sch., 1947-52. Dir. Kiddie Products, Inc., Barkley & Barkley & Dexter, Inc., Barkley & Dexter Labs., Inc., Raymond's, Inc. Honorary sec., also mem. Mass. Council on Crime and Correction; vice chmn. Mass. Council Crime and Corrections; past mem. Mass. Jud. Survey Commn. Trustee Nat. Council on Crime and Delinquency; past mem. bd. Health and Hosps., Cambridge, Mass.; mem. bd. Jewish Family and Children's Service, Boston. Fellow Am. Law Inst., Am. Bar Found.; mem. Am., Mass. (pres. 1960-62), Boston bar assns., New Eng. Law Inst. (exec. com.). Home: 152 Brattle St Cambridge MA 02138 Office: 3 Center Plaza Boston MA 02108

HORVITZ, WAYNE LOUIS, cons.; b. Chgo., Oct. 8, 1920; s. Aaron and Gertrude Jeannette (Wayne) H.; A.B., Columbia, 1942; M.S. (Sloan fellow 1952-53), Mass. Inst. Tech., 1953; m. Ann Battie, Aug. 16, 1945; children—William Wayne, Lee Marc, Wayne Bartow, Philip Robert. With Gen. Cable Corp., 1947-57, asso. dir. personnel, 1953-57; with Western Mgmt. Cons., Inc., Phoenix, 1957-60; asst. prof. mgmt. Ariz. State U., 1957-60; v.p. indsl. relations Matson Nav. Co., San Francisco, 1960-67, v.p., Washington, 1967-69; cons. on labor, legislation and pub. affairs, 1969—. Served with AUS, 1942-46. Mem. Indsl. Relations Research Assn., Am. Mgmt. Assn. Clubs: Press, Union League, Commonwealth (San Francisco); Internat. (Washington). Home: 4821 Linnean Av NW Washington DC 20008 Office: 1816 Jefferson Pl NW Washington DC 20036

HORWICH, FRANCES RAPPAPORT, educator; b. Ottawa, O., July 16, 1908; d. Samuel and Rosa (Gratz) Rappaport; Ph.B., U. Chgo., 1929; A.M., Columbia, 1933; Ph.D., Northwestern U., 1942; Pd.D. (hon.), Bowling Green State U., 1954; m. Harvey L. Horwich, June 11, 1931. Tchr. Evanston, Ill., 1929-32; supr. WPA Nursery Schs., Chgo., 1932-35; dir. jr. kindergarten, Winnetka, Ill., 1935-38; dean of edn. Pestalozzi Froebel Tchrs. Coll., 1938-40; counsellor of student tchrs. Chgo. Tchrs. Coll., 1940-43; dir. Hessian Hills Sch., Croton-on-Hudson, N.Y., 1943-45; vis. prof. edn. U. N.C., 1945-46; prof. edn., chmn. dept. Roosevelt U., Chgo., 1946-52; appearing as Miss Frances on Ding Dong Sch., NBC-TV Nursery Sch. Air, 1952-56, WGN-TV, 1957-59, Ind. Television Corp., 1959-65, also writer-producer program; supr. children's programs NBC-TV, 1955-56; lectr., ednl. cons.; ednl. dir. Curtis Pub. Co., 1962-64, cons., 1965; ednl. cons. Field Enterprises Ednl. Corp., 1965-66; dir. children's programming, also 2 daily programs WFLD-TV, Chgo., 1966-68. Bd. dirs. Chgo. Unlimited, 1965-67, Girl Scouts Chgo., 1965-70. Recipient numerous awards and citations for achievement in field. Mem. Nat. Soc. Study Edn., U. S. Nat. Com. Childhood Edn., Nat. Assn. Edn. Young Children (pres. 1948-51), Broadcast Pioneers, A.F.T.R.A., Am. Women in Radio and Television, Internat. Assn. Childhood Edn., N.E.A., Nat. Assn. Mental Health, Am. Assn. Gifted Children, Acad. TV Arts and Scis., Screen Actors Guild, Nat. Assn. of Ednl. Broadcasters, Authors League Am., Internat. Platform Assn., Internat. Reading Assn. Club: Women's Advertising (dir. 1966-67). Author: (series) Ding Dong School Books, 1954—; Miss Frances' All-Day-Long Book, 1954; Have Fun With Your Children, 1954; Miss Frances' Story Book of Manners for the Very Young, 1955; Miss Frances' Storybook of Pets for the Very Young, 1956; The Magic of Bringing Up Your Child, 1959; Safety on Wheels, 1960; Stories and Poems to Enjoy, 1962; From Miss Frances' Desk, 1964; The White House, 1964; also articles. Address: 400 E Randolph St Chicago IL 60601

HORWILL, WILLIAM EDGAR, former corp. exec.; b. Bklyn., July 6, 1904; s. Edward T. and Emilie M. (Wurster) H.; grad. St. Paul's Sch., Concord, N.H., 1921; B.A., Williams Coll., 1925; m. Sylvia E. Turner, Apr. 11, 1942; 1 dau., Sally Evadne. With Stone & Webster, Inc., N.Y.C., 1925-68, asst. sec., 1929-38 sec., 1938-54, v.p., 1954-68; sec. Stone & Webster Engring. Corp., 1938- 54, Stone & Webster Securities Corp., 1938-54; trustee Williamsburgh Savs. Bank. Mayor, Village of Huntington Bay, N.Y., 1946-52. Club: Huntington (N.Y.) Country. Home: Woodside Dr Box 51 Halesite NY 11743

HORWIN, LEONARD, lawyer; b. Chgo., Jan. 2, 1913; s. Joseph and Jeannette (Furhman) H.; B.A., U. Cal. at Los Angeles, 1933; LL.B. cum laude, Yale, 1936; m. Ursula Helene Donig, Oct. 15, 1939; children—Noel S., Leonora M. Admitted to Cal. bar, 1936; practice in Los Angeles, 1936-42; consel Bd. Econ. Warfare, 1942-43; mem. requirements com. WPB, 1942-43; attache embassy, Madrid, Spain, 1943-47; rep. Allied Control Council Germany, 1945-47; pvt. practice, Beverly Hills, Cal., 1947—; counsel Jewish War Vets. U.S. Chmn. com. ct. reorgn. League Cal. Cities, 1963-66; pres. Friends Santa Monica Mountain Parks, 1964-66; dir. communition relations com. Jewish Community-Fedn. Council Los Angeles; chmn. transp. Los Angeles Goals Council, 1966-69; 1st v.p. Beverly Hills Sister City Assn.; mem. challenges com. Claremont Colls.; mem. capital fund com. Yale Law Sch. Councilman, mayor, Beverly Hills, 1962-66. Recipient Beverly Hills Man of Year award, 1964; citation for outstanding achievement So. Cal. Rapid Transit Dist. Bd., 1966. Jewish religion. Home: 434 El Camino Dr Beverly Hills CA 90212 Office: 121 S Beverly Dr Beverly Hills CA 90212

HORWITZ, IRWIN D., educator, physician, surgeon; b. Chgo., Mar. 31, 1920; s. Sol and Belle (Stern) H.; B.S., U. Ill., 1941, M.D., 1943; m. Isabel Morwitz, July 23, 1944; children—Steven, Judd, Clare. Intern Cook County Hosp., Chgo., 1944; resident Ill. Eye and Ear Infirmary, Chgo., 1946-48; practice otolaryngology, Chgo., 1948—; clin. prof. Chgo. Med. Sch., 1969—, head div. otolaryngology, 1969—; chief div. otolaryngology Mt. Sinai Hosp., 1969—, pres. med. staff, 1969—. Served to capt., M.C., AUS, 1944-46. Fellow A.C.S.; mem. A.M.A., Chgo. Otol. and Laryngol. Assn., Am. Acad. Ophthalmology and Otolaryngology, Ill., Chgo. med. socs. Contbr. articles profl. jours. Home: 6628 N Trumbull St Lincolnwood IL 60645 Office: 55 E Washington St Chicago IL 60602

HORWITZ, MARTIN, mining co. exec., lawyer; b. Bklyn., Nov. 3, 1920; s. Ernest and Betty (Weinstein) H.; student Bklyn. Coll., 1942; LL.B., Harvard, 1948; m. Caryl Krieger, June 13, 1945; children—William Eric, Lauren. Admitted to Mass. bar, 1948, N.Y. bar, 1950; gen. counsel U.S. Smelting Refining and Mining Co., 1963-70, chmn. bd., 1965-70, pres., chief exec. officer, 1970—; v.p., gen. counsel Mueller Brass Co., 1965—; dir. Richmond Eureka Mining Co., Ruby Hill Mining Co., U.S. Fuel Co., U.S.S. Ram Exploration Co., U.S.S. Lead Refining Co., Wash. Mining Co. Served to 1st lt., inf., AUS, World War II. Mem. Am. Mining Congress, County Lawyers Assn. N.Y. Clubs: City, Copper (N.Y.C.). Home: 150 E 69th St New York City NY 10021 Office: 235 E 42d St New York City NY 10017

HORWITZ, SOLIS, educator; b. Pitts., Nov. 2, 1910; s. Samuel Abe and Lillian Yetta (Goldman) H.; A.B., U. Pitts., 1930, M.A., 1932; J.D., Harvard, 1936. Admitted to Pa. bar, 1937, D.C. bar, 1953; practice in Pitts., 1937-42; counsel internat. prosecution major criminals, Tokyo, Japan, 1945-48, acting chief counsel, 1948; spl. counsel armed services com. U.S. Ho. Reps., 1949; spl. counsel chmn. NSRB, 1950-51; gen. counsel RFC, 1951-53; counsel com. govt. operations for Army- McCarthy hearings U.S. Senate, 1954; pvt. practice, Pitts. and Washington, 1954-57; counsel majority policy com., also preparedness investigating subcom., armed services com. U.S. Senate, 1957-60; pvt. practice, Washington, 1961; dir. office orgnl. and mgmt. planning studies Office Sec. Def. 1961-64, asst. sec. of def. (adminstrn.), 1964-69; prof. pub. policy U. Pitts., 1968—. Served with AUS, 1942-45. Mem. Am., Fed., Allegheny County bar assns., Harvard Law Sch. Assn., Phi Beta Kappa. Author: Tokyo War Crimes Trial, 1950. Home: 5 Bayard Rd Pittsburgh PA 15213

HORWITZ-BARAK, ABRAHAM, physician; b. Santiago, Chile, Dec. 25, 1910; s. Isidoro Rosemblat Horwitz and Catalina Tolmach Barak; M.D., U. Chile, 1936; M.P.H. (Rockefeller Found. fellow), Johns Hopkins, 1944. Prof. infectious disease U. Chile, 1942, dir. Sch. Pub. Health, 1953-54, part-time prof. preventive medicine, 1957—; epidemiologist Bacteriol. Inst. of Chile, med. officer Enteric Infections Control Program, Santiago; resident physician Herman Kiefer Hosp., Detroit, 1943; prof. epidemiology and infectious diseases Sch. Nursing, Chilean Ministry Welfare and Social Assistance, 1945-50; asst. dir. Nat. Health Service, Santiago, 1954-59; prof. infectious diseases Sch. Medicine, Cath. U. of Chile, 1945-50; lectr. infectious diseases; mem. expert com. rheumatic fever WHO, dir. Pan Am. San. Bur., regional office WHO, Washington, 1959- -. Tech. bd. Milbank Meml. Fund; bd. dirs. Am. Nat. Council for Health Edn. of Public; related dir. Gorgas Meml. Inst. Recipient Lutz Prize Govt. of Sao Paulo; Order Med. Merit (Brazil); Liciaga medal Govt. of Mexico. Mem. Chilean Med. Soc., Chilean Soc. Pub. Health (pres. 1958), Am. Pub. Health Assn. (v.p. 1958-59, Bronfman award 1966), Peruvian (hon.), Bolibian (hon.) socs. pub. health, Mexico-U.S. Border Health Assn., Internat. Union for Health Edn., Delta Omega. Home: 4501 Connecticut Av NW Washington DC 20008 Office: 525 23d St NW Washington DC 20037

HOSACK, ROBERT EWING, educator; b. Smith's Ferry, Pa., May 15, 1911; s. Hermann M. and Helen (Ewing) H.; A.B., Coll. Wooster, 1932; A.M., U. Chgo., 1934; Ph.D., Duke, 1951; m. Nancy McLane Weeks, Aug. 21, 1937; children—Elizabeth, Harriet, Charles. Chmn. dept. social studies Weir High Sch., Weirton, W.Va., 1934-39; instr. polit. sci. Duke, 1941-43; mem. faculty U. Ida., Moscow, 1943—, prof. polit. sci., 1953—, chmn. dept., 1947-59, 69—, head dept. social scis., 1955-69. Mem. W. Va. Edn. Assn. (dir. 1937-39), N.W. Sci. Assn. (trustee 1961-62), Inst. Pacific Relations (pres. Inland Empire br. 1948-49), Am. Polit. Sci. Assn., Pacific N.W. Polit. Sci. Assn. (pres. 1966-67), Am. Assn. U. Profs., Assn. Asian Studies, Phi Beta Kappa, Pi Gamma Mu, Kappa Delta Pi. Presbyn. Co-author: China, 1946; Introduction to Political Science, 1960. Contbr. articles profl. jours. Home: 820 W C St Moscow ID 83843

HOSE, ROBERT HAVEN, indsl. design cons.; b. Sleepy Eye, Minn., Jan. 12, 1915; s. Robert and Grace (Irish) H.; B.Arch., U. Minn., 1937; M.Arch., Mass. Inst. Tech., 1940; m. Anne Runkle, Aug. 26, 1939; children—John Robert, Judith, Barbara Clair. Mem. tech. staff Bell Telephone Labs., N.Y.C., 1939-46; asso., partner Henry Dreyfuss, N.Y.C., 1946-61; owner Robert Hose Assos., Summit, N.J., 1961—; dir. Hampden Mfg. Co., Plainfield, N.J. Registered architect, N.J. Fellow Indsl. Designers Soc. Am. (past pres.); mem. Am. Soc. M.E., Acacia. Republican. Home: 4 Park Slope Mountainside NJ 07092 Office: 382 Springfield Av Summit NJ 07901

HOSELITZ, BERT FRANK, educator, editor; b. Vienna, Austria, May 27, 1913; s. Bela and Anna (Gross) H.; Dr.Juris, U. Vienna, 1936; M.A., U. Chgo., 1946; m. Gunhild Gustafson, May 5, 1945; children—David Carl, Ann Gunhild. Came to U.S., 1939, naturalized, 1945. Instr. econs. Manchester Coll., 1940-41; research asso. Yale, 1943; research asso. U. Chgo., 1944-45, asst. prof. social sci., 1945-47, asso. prof., 1948-53, prof., 1953—; also. prof. econs. Carnegie Inst. Tech., 1947-48. Mem. UN Tech. Assistance Mission to El Salvador, 1952; expert cons. UN and UNESCO, 1953-54; adviser Govt. India on Delhi Master Plan, 1957-58. Mem. Am. Econ. Assn., Royal Econ. Soc., Econ. History Assn., Institut International des Civilizations Differents, Royal Econ. History Soc. Author: Sociological Aspects of Economic Growth, 1960; Sociological Aspect of Economic Development, 1961. Editor: The Progress of Underdeveloped Areas, 1952. Editor, Econ. Devel. and Cultural Change Jour., 1954-61, 65—, Ency. of Social Scis., 1961-62. Contbr. profl. jours. Home: 5318 Hyde Park Blvd Chicago IL 60615

HOSFIELD, GEORGE WILLIAM, food co. exec.; b. Medford, Minn., Nov. 13, 1914; s. Ralph Garfield and E. Emma (Buboltz) H.; B. Chem. Engring., U. Minn., 1939; m. Ruth Margaret Baillie, July 20, 1940; children—William B., Susan J., Margaret J., James R. With Pillsbury Co., 1939—, v.p., 1964-68, group v.p., 1968- -, also dir. Office; Pillsbury Co Minneapolis MN 55402

HOSFORD, WILLARD DEERE, Jr., farm equipment mfr.; b. Omaha, July 21, 1912, s. Willard Deere and Mary Lee (McShane) H.; grad. Phillips Exeter Acad., 1931; B.A., Yale, 1935; m. Mary A. Harding, Feb. 12, 1938; children—Damaris Ann Robertson, Mary Lee Swanson, Willard Deere III. With John Deere Co., Omaha, 1935—, v.p., gen. mgr., 1950—; dir. Deere & Co., Northwestern Bell Telephone Co.; vice chmn. Fed. Res. Bd. Kansas Kansas City. With farm equipment sect. NPA, 1952. Trustee Creighton Hall, Children's Meml. Hosp., Joslyn Art Mus. Clubs: Omaha, Omaha Country; Yale (N.Y.C.); Army and Navy, Chevy Chase (Washington); Jupiter Island, Seminole Golf (Fla.). Home: 8405 Indian Hills Dr Omaha NB 68114 Office: 912 Howard St Omaha NB 68102

HOSHALL, CLIFFORD EARLE, fgn. service officer; b. Md., May 22, 1905; s. Charles E. and Florence May (Turnbaugh) H.; B.A., U. Richmond, 1926; M.A., U. Colo., 1938, Ed. D., 1947; grad. student Johns Hopkins., Columbia, N.Y. U., N.J. State Tchrs. Coll.; m. Edna Mae Hunt, Nov. 28, 1928; children—Edna Erle (Mrs. John Daniher), Mary Anne (Mrs. Eldon Prock), Viola Mae (Mrs. Hans Schoch), Paul C. Tchr., athletic coach, supr. pub. schs., Md. and N.J., 1926-46; instr. edn. U. Colo., 1946-47; prof. edn., head edn. and psychology div. Western State Coll., Gunnison, Colo., 1947-52; prof. edn., chmn. dept. Ohio Wesleyan U., 1952-56; vis. lectr. U. Ind., 1954, Washington Coll., Machias, Me., 1953, Drury Coll., 1955, 56; joined U.S. Fgn. Service, 1956; chief edn. adviser Philippine Govt. for ICA and AID, 1956-63; chief Far East edn. br. AID, Washington 1963- 65, spl. cons. S.E. Asian Ministers Edn. Secretariat, 1966, chief East Asian edn. div., 1967, dep. asst. dir. higher edn., Vietnam, 1967—. Mem. Ohio Tchr. Edn. and Profl. Standards Commn., 1952-56; pres. Ohio Tchr. Edn. Coll. Assn., 1955-56; mem. Colo. Gov's Safety Edn. Com., 1949-52. Dir. religious edn., Ridgewood, N.J., 1931-45. Mem. N.E.A., Assn. Supervision and Curriculum Devel., Assn. Student Teaching, Sigma Phi Epsilon, Phi Delta Kappa, Tau Kappa Alpha, Kappa Delta Pi. Contbr. articles profl. jours. Home: Route 1 Box 62B Hillsboro OR 97123 Office: Saigon USAID Edn APO San Francisco CA 96243

HOSIASSON, PHILIPPE, painter; b. Odessa, Russia, Feb. 15, 1898; s. Hermann and Augusta (Jacobson) H.; ed. law and art history New Russia U., Odessa, 1917-19; m. Olga Bilinkaia, July 25, 1918. One-man shows in Rome, 1921, Berlin, 1922-24, Paris, 1931-55, 61-63, Bergamo, 1968, also at Kootz Gallery, N.Y.C., 1957-59, Martha Jackson Gallery, N.Y.C., 1962, also several salons and internat. shows; rep. permanent collections U.S. and Europe. Served with French Army, 1939-40. Decorated Legion of Honor; recipient Artistic Merit medal, France, 1966. Address: 26 rue Lacretelle Paris 15e France

HOSIER, HAROLD ANCIAL, union ofcl.; b. Holton, Kan., Oct. 30, 1901; s. Franklin Pierce and Rose (Bissell) H.; student pub. schs., Topeka; m. Frieda Stroscher, Feb. 16, 1922; children—Robert, Delbert, Janice (Mrs. Robert Whitcomb), Jewell, Merrillee (Mrs. Victor Soderstrom). Vice pres. Internat. Mailers Union, Denver, 1946-51, pres., 1951—. Mem. Nat. Assn. Unions (pres.). Mason. Address: 2240 Bell Ct Denver CO 80215

HOSKEN, WILLIAM EDWARD, mining co. exec.; b. Oakland, Cal., June 8, 1921; s. William M. and Vera (Medau) H.; student Stanford, 1939-41, U. Cal. at Davis, 1941-42, Harvard Grad. Sch. Bus. Adminstrn., 1942-43, 46; m. Ruth Anne Kirby, Dec. 26, 1942; children—Katherine, Nancy, Edward, Joan, Sarah, Kimberly. With Shell Chem. Corp., 1946-48, Stanford Research Inst., 1948-62; with Cyprus Mines Corp., Los Angeles, 1962—, v.p., 1965—; dir. Image, Inc., Los Angeles; tchr. credit and financial mgmt. Stanford Grad. Sch., 1957-61. Chmn. pub. relations com. Honolulu United Fund, 1955-56. Served to 1st lt. USAAF, 1943-46. Clubs: University, Yacht (Los Angeles); Palos Verdes Tennis. Home: 553 Via Media Palos Verdes Estates CA 90274 Office: 523 W 6th St Los Angeles CA 90014

HOSKINS, D.A., savs. and loan assn. exec. Pres., Atlantic Savs. and Loan Assn., Los Angeles. Office: 5301 Whittier Blvd Los Angeles CA 90022*

HOSKINS, JOSEPH ALOYSIUS, lawyer; b. Kansas City, Mo., Nov. 19, 1912; s. Austin A. and Louise (McCormack) H.; A.B., Rockhurst Coll., Kansas City, Mo., 1933; LL.B., Georgetown U., 1937, LL.M., 1939; m. Mary Elizabeth Nash, June 6, 1940; children—Carroll Louise, Susan Marie. Admitted to D.C. bar, 1936, Mo. bar, 1942; appellate and regional atty. NLRB, 1937-41; chmn. Regional War Labor Bd., 1941-42; practice in Kansas City, Mo., 1942—; sr. partner firm Hoskins, King, McGannon and Hurwitz, 1953. Dir. Mercantile Bank and Trust Co., Kansas City, Mo. Past chmn. bd. regents Rockhurst Coll. Served to lt. USNR, 1943-46. Mem. Am., Mo., Kansas City bar assns., Lawyers Assn. Kansas City, Am. Judicature Soc. Home: 121 W 48th St Kansas City MO 64112 Office: Commerce Bank Bldg Kansas City MO 64106

HOSKINS, LEWIS MALONEY, educator; b. McMinnville, Ore., Feb. 23, 1916; s. Hervey M. and Louise (Maloney) H.; A.B., Pacific Coll., Newberg, Ore., 1938; A.M., Haverford (Pa.) Coll., 1939; Ph.D., U. Mich., 1946; m. Lois Roberts, Sept. 2, 1941; children—Theresa Ann, Laurel Page, Adrienne Ruth, Scott Ellis. Instr. Friends U., Wichita, Kan., 1939-40; teaching fellow U. Mich., 1941-43; dean, prof. history Pacific Coll., 1943-45; served with Friends Ambulance unit and Friends Service unit in China as bus. mgr. of The Changte Hosp., Honan, 1945-46; tchr. St. Johns and Fuh Tan Univ., 1946-48; exec. sec. China unit, Shanghai, 1946- 47, chmn. unit, 1947-48; acting exec. sec. Am. Friends Service Com., Portland, Ore., 1949, personnel sec., Phila., 1949-50, exec. sec., 1950-59; prof. history Earlham Coll., Richmond, Ind., 1959—, chmn. dept., 1963-68; tchr. U. Coll., Nairobi, Kenya, E. Africa, 1966-67. Home: 842 National Rd W Richmond IN 47374

HOSKINS, ROBERT ALAN, investment co. exec.; b. Orange, Cal., July 27, 1934; s. Cortez R. and Leonora (MacAllister) h.; A.B., Occidental Coll., 1955; M.B.A., Stanford, 1957; m. Martha L. Walters, Mar. 29, 1964; 1 dau., Robin L. Account adviser Dean Witter & Co., Santa Ana, Cal., 1957-61; self employed securities tng. cons., 1961-66; v.p., dir. Western Programming Corp., 1966-68; v.p. Penn Securities Co., Santa Monica, Cal., 1968-70; v.p., dir. Pacific Programming Corp., Santa Monica, 1966—; v.p. P-L Co. of Cal. Mem. Nat. Rifle Assn., Kappa Sigma. Club: South Coast Gun (Santa Ana). Author: Securities Training Guide, 1964; Securities License Course, 1966. Contbr. articles profl. jours. Home: 109 W Stevens St Santa Ana CA 92707 Office: 3130 Wilshire Blvd Santa Monica CA 90406

HOSLER, CHARLES LUTHER, Jr., meteorologist, educator; b. Honey Brook, Pa., June 3, 1924; s. Charles Luther and Miriam Deichley (Stauffer) H.; student Bucknell U., 1943-44, Mass. Inst. Tech., 1944-45; B.S., Pa. State U., 1947, M.S., 1948, Ph.D., 1951; m. Gladys Cheesbrough, June 23, 1947 (div.); children—Sharon Elizabeth, David Charles, Lynn Rebecca, Peter William; m. 2d, Anna R. Stahel, July 1, 1971. Faculty, Pa. State U., University Park, 1948—, prof. meteorology, 1960—, head dept., 1961-65, dean Coll. Earth and Mineral Scis., 1965—. Hydrographer, Pa. Dept. Forests and Waters, 1949-59; meteorol. cons., 1950—; vis. prof. colls., lectr. civic and profl. groups; condr. daily TV weather program, 1957—; spl. research microphysics of clouds; cons. Pres. Adv. Com. Weather Control, 1955; adv. com. on meteorology Environmental Protection Agy.; storm fury adv. com. USN. Served to lt. (j.g.) USNR, 1943-46; lt. comdr. Res. Fellow Am. Meteorol. Soc. (councilor); mem. Am. Geophys. Union (award outstanding paper hydrology 1955), Am. Soc. C.E. (weather modification com.), Am. Chem. Soc. (regional lectr. 1971-72), Am. Assn. U. Profs. (v.p. Pa. State U. 1961), A.A.A.S., Sigma Xi (pres. Pa. State U. 1958), Tau Beta Pi, Sigma Gamma Epsilon. Contbr. articles to profl. jours. Home: 1000 Plaza Dr State College PA 16801 Office: Earth and Mineral Scis Pa State U University Park PA 16802

HOSLER, RUSSELL JOHN, educator; b. DuPont, O., Apr. 2, 1906; s. John Henry and Etta (Spitznaugle) H.; A.B., Defiance Coll., 1932; M.A., Toledo U., 1941; Ed.D., Ind. U., 1946; m. Hilda Elizabeth Weible, Dec. 25, 1927 (div. Oct. 1966); children—Philip Eugene, Helen (Mrs. James Ackerman), Russell John; m. 2d, Mary Margaret O'Connell, Aug. 23, 1968. High sch. tchr., Montpelier, O., 1927-34, Fostoria, O., 1934-38, Libbey High Sch., Toledo, 1938-42; asst. prof. commerce Ind. U., 1942-46; faculty U. Wis., Madison 1946—, prof., 1953—, chmn. dept. edn., 1955-59. Recipient John Robert Gregg award, 1966. Mem. Nat. Bus. Edn. Assn. (pres. 1968-69), Nat. Bus. Tchrs. Assn. (pres. 1955), Nat. Assn. Bus. Tchr. Edn. (pres. 1959-61). Co-author: Gregg Shorthand for Colleges, rev. edit., 1958, 65; Gregg Transcription for Colleges, 1959, rev. edit., 1966; Programmed Gregg Shorthand, 1969; Personal Typing, 1969. Contbr. articles to profl. mags. Home: Overlook Dr McFarland WI 53558

HOSLETT, SCHUYLER DEAN, former coll. pres.; b. Sturgeon Bay, Wis., June 3, 1918; s. George and Grace (Schuyler) H.; A.B., Park Coll., 1940; M.A., Ohio State U., 1942, Ph.D., 1949; M. Pub. Adminstrn., Harvard, 1946. Adminstrv. analyst War Dept., 1942-46; asst., then asso. prof. bus. and pub. adminstrn. Cornell U., 1948-51; asso. prof. Columbia, 1951-55; asst. to pres. Reuben H. Donnelley Corp., Chgo., 1955-57, v.p., 1957-61; v.p. Dun & Bradstreet, Inc., 1961-63; cons. Ford Found., 1961—; dean Coll. Bus. Adminstrn., U. Hawaii, 1963-68, former pres. Bryant Coll., Providence, from 1968; lectr. univ., exec. devel. programs, bus. groups on mgmt., 1950—. Dir. Am. Factors, Ltd., Hawaiian Life Ins. Co. Trustee Park Coll.; bd. dirs. Hawaii Council Econ. Edn. Recipient Distinguished Alumnus award Park Coll., 1959. Mem. Am. Mgmt. Assn., Acad. Mgmt., Honolulu C. of C. (bd. dirs.), Hawaii Mfrs. Assn. (bd. dirs.), Hawaii Econ. Assn., Hawaii Soc. Littauer Fellows (chancellor). Clubs: 15, Harvard (Honolulu); Yacht, University (Chgo.); Columbia University (N.Y.C.). Author: Lucretius, 1938; Army Depot Administration, 1945; Human Factors in Management, 2d edit., 1951.

HOSMER, CRAIG, congressman; b. Brea, Cal., May 6, 1915; s. Chester Cleveland and Mary Jane (Craig) H.; A.B., U. Cal., 1937; postgrad. U. Mich., 1938, U.S. Naval Acad., 1941; J.D., U. So. Cal., 1940; m. Marian Caroline Swanson, Feb. 12, 1946; children—Susan Jane, Craig Larkin. Admitted to Cal. bar, 1940, Supreme Ct. bar, 1953; practiced in Long Beach, 1946-47, 49—; spl. asst. U.S. dist. atty. for AEC, Los Alamos, 1948. Mem. 83d-92d Congresses, 32d Dist. Cal., interior and insular affairs and joint com. on atomic energy, ranking minority mem.; adviser U.S. Atoms-for-Peace Delegation, Geneva, 1958, 63, 71; Congl. adviser 18 Nation Disarmament Conf., UN Conf. of Com. on Disarmament. Served to rear adm. USNR, 1941-46. Mem. Am. Nuclear Soc. Editor: U. So. Cal. Law Rev., 1939-40. Home: 1635 E Ocean Blvd Long Beach CA 90802 Office: House Office Bldg Washington DC 20515 also Security Bldg Long Beach CA 90802

HOSNER, JOHN FRANK, educator; b. Gillespie, Ill., Feb. 25, 1925; s. Joseph and Mary (Schust) H.; student So. Ill. U., 1942-43; B.S., Mich. State U., 1948; M.F., Duke, 1950; Ph.D., State U. N.Y., 1957; m. Lola Irene Neal, Aug. 11, 1951; children—Angela Lynn, David Allen. Dist. forester Ill. Div. Forestry, Sparta and Murphysboro, 1948-50; from instr. to asso. prof. forestry So. Ill. U., 1950-57, 59-61; vis. prof. State U. N.Y. at Syracuse, 1958-59; prof., head dept. forestry and wildlife Va. Poly. Inst., Blacksburg, 1961-69, dir. div. forestry and wildlife scis., 1969—. Pres. Ill. Tech. Forestry Assn., 1952-53. Served as officer USAAF, 1943-44. Decorated Air medal. Fellow A.A.A.S.; mem. Soc. Am. Foresters (pres. Blue Ridge chpt. 1963-64), Ecol. Soc. Am., Am. Assn. U. Profs., Am. Forests, Am. Inst. Biol. Scis., Internat. Union Forest Research Orgns., Sigma Xi, Xi Sigma Pi, Phi Sigma. Author: (with others) Regional Silviculture of the United States, 1962; also numerous articles. Home: Lincoln Lane Blacksburg VA 24060

HOSPERS, JOHN, educator; b. Pella, Ia., June 9, 1918; s. John G. and Dena (Verhey) H.; B.A., Central Coll., 1939, D.Litt., 1962; M.A., State U. Ia., 1941; Ph.D., Columbia, 1944. Instr., Columbia, 1946-48; asst. prof., asso. prof. U. Minn., 1948-56; prof. Bklyn. Coll., 1956-66, Cal. State Coll., Los Angeles, 1966-68; dir., prof. philosophy U. So. Cal. Sch. Philosophy, Los Angeles, 1968—; Fulbright research scholar U. London (Eng.), 1954-55; vis. prof. U. Cal. at Los Angeles, 1960-61, 64. Mem. Am. Philos. Assn., Am. Soc. Aesthetics, Mind Assn., Aristotelian Soc., Royal Inst. Philosophy. Author: Meaning and Truth in the Arts, 1946; (with W. Sellars) Readings in Ethical Theory, 1970; Introduction to Philosophical Analysis, 1967; Human Conduct, 1961; Readings in Introductory Philosophical Analysis, 1968; Introductory Readings in Aesthetics, 1969; Artistic Expression, 1970; Libertarianism, a Political Philosophy for Tomorrow, 1971. Home: 8229 Lookout Mountain Av Los Angeles CA 90046

HOSSENLOPP, GEORGE JOSEPH, banker; b. N.Y.C., Mar. 17, 1908; s. John D.A. and Edna (Mcyer) H.; Litt. B., Rutgers, U., 1928; m. Georgia Straub, Oct. 8, 1938; children—John J.A., George Joseph. With credit dept. Guaranty Trust Co., N.Y.C., 1929-33; with N.J. Bank & Trust Co., Passaic, N.J., 1933-70, v.p., 1948-62, sr. v.p., 1962-70; v.p., dir. Hedix Corp.; v.p. dir. Concord Trading Corp. Mem. Aheka council Boy Scouts Am.; chmn. finance com. Salvation Army, Passaic. Mem. Passaic County Bankers Assn. (past pres.), Delta Kappa Epsilon. Club: Pennington (pres. 1962) (Passaic). Home: 29 Lake St Nutley NJ 07110 Office: 657 Main Av Passaic NJ 07110

HOSTERMAN, FRED O., mfg. co. exec.; b. Millheim, Pa., Mar. 16, 1916; s. Fred O. and Barbara (Winegardner) H.; student aero. engring. Bellefonte (Pa.) Sch. Aero., 1934; B.S. in Aero. Engring., Parks Air Coll., East St. Louis, Ill., 1936; m. Carol Henry, Nov. 7, 1958; 1 daughter, Lynn Ann Hosterman; children (by previous marriage)—Barbara, Jane, Fred O. III. From design engr. to design specialist Lockheed Aircraft Corp., 1936-51; with Weston Hydraulics div. Borg-Warner Corp., Van Nuys, Cal., 1951-70, pres., gen. mgr., 1959-61, pres., chief exec. officer, 1961-70; pres., dir. Walfred Co., Inc., Beverly Hills, Cal., 1971—. Mem. aircraft adv. com. to asst. sec. def. for research and devel., 1954-57. Recipient Alumni Merit award St. Louis U., 1959. Mem. Soc. Automotive Engrs. (chmn. So. Cal. sect. 1950-51, v.p. aircraft sect. 1956, chmn. tech. com. A-6A, 1948-57), Am. Ordnance Assn., Van Nuys C. of C. Adv. editor Applied Hydraulics mag., 1949-51. Author papers in field. Home: 22571 Paul Revere Dr Woodland Hills CA 91364 Office: 630 N Foothill Rd Beverly Hills CA 90210

HOSTETLER, PAUL S., educator; b. Butte, Mont., July 9, 1921; s. Ivan Paul and Genevieve (Smith) H.; B.A., Stanford, 1943, M.A., 1949; postgrad. Ind. U., 1957; Ph.D., La. State U., 1964; m. Virginia Sherwood, July 28, 1950 (div.); children—Paul Sherwood, Karen Melissa, David Huntington; m. 2d, Diane Schuldenfrei, Oct. 9, 1971. Mem. faculty Tulane U., 1949-67, prof. theatre and speech, 1965-67, dir. Univ. Theatre, 1960-67, head dept., 1964-67; prof., chmn. dept. theatre Temple U., 1967—. Bd. dirs. La. Civil Liberties Union; trustee Greater New Orleans TV Found. Served with USNR, 1943-46. Mem. Am. Assn. U. Profs., Am. Ednl. Theatre Assn., Speech Communication Assn., Southwest Theatre Conf. (sec. 1957), Nat. Theatre Conf., Screen Actors Guild, Am. Fedn. TV and Radio Artists, Am. Soc. Theatre Research. Asso. editor Quart. Jour. Speech, 1965-68; coll. and univ. editor Players mag., 1959. Contbr. profl. jours. Dir. Am. premier prodn. Friedrich Durrenmatt's The Meteor, 1969. Home: 315 Jefferson Av Haddonfield NJ 08033 Office: Dept Theatre Temple U Philadelphia PA 19122

HOSTETTLER, GORDON FLOYD, educator; b. Kent, O., Mar. 17, 1918; s. Clyde O. and Ocala (Feigert) H.; A.B., Kent State U., 1940, B.S., 1940; M.A., State U. Ia., 1942, Ph.D., 1947; m. R. Joyce Kirsch, Sept. 24, 1943; children—Margaret Gail, Barbara Joyce (twins). Instr. speech State U. Ia., 1942-44, Coe Coll., 1944-45; instr. speech, dir. forensics Temple U., 1945-47, asst. prof., 1947-52, asso prof., 1952-58, prof. speech, 1958-64, chmn. dept. speech and dramatic arts, 1952-64; prof. speech Ohio State U., 1964-66; prof. and chmn. dept. speech Colo. State U., 1966—. Mem. Pa. Speech Assn. (exec. sec. 1949-52, pres. 1963-64), Speech Assn. Eastern States (exec. sec. 1952-54). Author articles in field. Home: 1510 Hillside Dr Fort Collins CO 80521

HOTCHKIS, PRESTON, bus. exec.; b. Los Angeles, June 19, 1893; s. Finlay Montgomery and Flora Cornelia (Preston) H.; A.B., U. Cal. at Berkeley, 1916; postgrad. U. So. Cal. Law Sch., 1916- 17; LL.D., Pepperdine Coll., 1955, Whittier Coll., 1957; m. Katharine Bixby, Dec. 11, 1923; children—Katharine (Mrs. M.F. Allende), Joan (Mrs. Foster), Preston Bixby, John Finlay. Asst. sec., later sec. Cal. Delta Farms, Inc., Los Angeles, 1919-25; admitted to Cal. bar, 1920; asso. in founding Pacific Finance Corp., 1920, Pacific Indemnity Co., 1926; organizer Founders' Ins. Co., 1946; dir., chmn. bd. Fred H. Bixby Ranch Co.; adv. dir. Yosemite Park & Curry Co. Councilman, City San Marino, 1940-55. U.S. rep. Econ. and Social Council UN, 1954-55; grad. mem. Bus. Council; mem. Hoover Commn. Task Force on Fed. Lending Agys., 1954-55, State Cal. Reconstrn. and Reemployment Commn. 1942-47, Gov.'s Tax Com., 1942; chmn. Southland Water Com.; chmn. Local Agy. Formation Commn. Los Angeles County; pres. Colorado River Assn., 1947-52; dir. Cal. Inst. Tech. Assos. Chmn., Navy Relief Soc. campaign So. Cal. (citation Sec. Navy), 1942; mem. tng. within industry com. War Manpower Bd. for So. Cal., 1942-45 (citation War Manpower bd.); mem. War Finance Com. U.S. Treas. Dept. for Cal., 1942-45 (citation Treas. Dept.); chmn. War Chest campaign Greater Los Angeles Area (citation War Chest) 1945; mem. nat. adv. council Girl Scouts U.S.A.; fellow U. Cal., Berkeley; mem. pres.'s council Cal. Inst. Tech.; mem. pres.'s bd. Pepperdine Coll.; chmn. So. Cal. Com. for Radio Free Europe, 1968-70; pres. Goodwill Industries So. Cal., 1967. Del., Republican Nat. Cov. (Cal. rep. resolutions com.) Phila., 1940, Chgo., 1944, San Francisco, 1964, alternate del., 1948-52. Trustee Mills Coll., Good Hope Med. Found., S.W. Mus., Harvey Mudd Coll.; regent U. Cal., 1935-36. Served to ensign USN, 1917-18. Mem. Cal., Los Angeles bar assns., Cal. Alumni Assn. (pres. 1935-36), Cal. State C. of C. (pres. 1942-43), Sigma Nu, Phi Delta Phi. Presbyn. Clubs: California, University (Los Angeles); Valley Hunt (Pasadena); Bohemian, Pacific Union (San Francisco). Home: 1415 Circle Dr San Marino CA 90014

HOTCHKISS, EUGENE III, coll. pres.; b. Berwyn, Ill., Apr. 1, 1928; s. Eugene and Jeanette (Kennan) H.; A.B., Dartmouth 1950; Ph.D., Cornell U., Ithacca, N.Y., 1960, m. Suzanne Ellen Troxell, Nov. 17, 1962; 1 dau., Ellen Sinclair. Asst. to dean Dartmouth, 1953-54, asst. dean, 1954-55, asso. dean, 1958-60; asst. dean Cornell U., Ithacca, N.Y., 1955-58; dean students, lectr. history Harvey Mudd Coll., Claremont, Cal., 1960-63, dean coll., 1962-68; exec. dean Chatham Coll., Pitts., 1968-70; pres. Lake Forest (Ill.) Coll., 1970—. Mem. vis. com. Case Western Res. U., 1968-70. Bd. dirs. Regional Council Internat. Edn., Pitts. Served to lt. (j.g.) USNR, 1950-53 Mem. Phi Beta Kappa, Phi Kappa Phi, Chi Phi. Home: 738 E Rosemary Rd Lake Forest IL 60045

HOTCHKISS, ROBERT SHERMAN, urologist; b. Jamestown, N.Y., 1903; M.D., U. Mich., 1928; m. Olivia Nally, 1937; children—Roberta, Fredrica, Sherman. Intern, Royal Victoria Hosp., Montreal, Que., Can., 1928-29; intern Bellevue Hosp., N.Y.C., 1929-31, resident in urology, 1930-31, now dir. urology Bellevue Hosp., U. Hosp.; asst. attending surgeon in urology N.Y. Hosp.; prof., chmn. dept. urology N.Y. U. Sch. Medicine. Served with USNR, 1942-46. Recipient Lasker award Planned Parenthood Fedn. Am., 1945; 10th Ferdinand C. Valentine Lecture and award N.Y. Acad. Medicine, 1971. Diplomate Am. Bd. Urology. Mem. Assn. Genito-Urinary Surgeons, A.M.A., Am. Urol. Assn., Am. Fertility Soc. (pres. 1965), Bellevue Alumni Assn. (pres.), Phi Rho Sigma. Home: 246 Corlies Av Pelham NY 10803 Office: 566 1st Av New York City NY 10016

HOTCHKISS, ROLLIN DOUGLAS, biochemist, educator; b. South Britain, Conn., Sept. 8, 1911; s. Charles Leverett and Eva (Platt) H.; B.S., Yale, 1932, Ph.D. (Loomis fellow), 1935, Sc.D., 1962; m. Shirley Dawson, June 24, 1933 (div. 1967); children—Paul, Cynthia; m. 2d, Magda Gabor, May 19, 1967. Mem. staff Rockefeller U., N.Y.C., 1935—, prof., 1955- -. Rockefeller Found. fellow Carlsberg Lab., Copenhagen, 1937-38; vis. prof. Mass. Inst. Tech., 1957-58; Dyer lectr. NIH, 1962; vis. prof. dept. genetics U. Cal., Berkeley, 1968; fellow-commoner Corpus Christi Coll., Cambridge (Eng.) U., 1970. Recipient Comml. Solvents award in antibiotics, 1954. Mem. Am. Soc. Cell Biology (councilor 1962-64), Harvey Soc. (pres. 1958-59), L.I. Biol. Assn. (dir.), Am. Soc. Biol. Chemists, Am. Acad. Arts and Scis., Nat. Acad. Sci., Genetics Soc. Am. (pres. 1972), Am. Chem. Soc., A.A.A.S., Am. Soc. Naturalists (v.p. 1965), N.Y. Acad. Scis., Sigma Xi. Contbr. articles to profl. publs. Research immunochemistry bacterial polysaccharides, 1935-37, protein chemistry, 1937-39, (with R.J. Dubos) devel. and purification, chem. study, antibiotics gramicidin and tyrocidine, 1939-43, bacterial metabolism and physiology, peptide synthesis, 1944-47, genetic biochemistry deoxyribonucleic acids, 1947—, developed genetic transformation bacteria to drug resistance and sensitivity, 1951, polarity and heterozygosity in nucleic acid, 1962—. Home: 342 E 67th St New York City NY 10021 Office: Rockefeller U 66th St and York Av New York City NY 10021

HOTCHKISS, SANFORD NORMAN, educator, psychologist; b. Johnstown, Pa., Sept. 26, 1923; s. Raymond Charles and Catherine (Burkhart) H.; B.A., U. Minn., 1949, M.A., 1950, Ph.D., 1959; m. Sally Lou McMurdo, Feb. 13, 1954; children—Charles Montagu, Douglas Logan. Asst. prof. psychology Ia. State U., 1953-54, Kan. State U., 1954-55; project supr. Perceptual Devel. Labs., St. Louis, 1955-57; mgmt. cons. Psychol. Services Pitts., 1957-61, Ernst & Ernst, C.P.A.'s, Cleve., 1961-67; prof. psychology, chmn. dept. Youngstown (O.) State U., 1968—; cons. in field, Vice pres. Regional Council Episcopal Chs. Bd. dirs. Mahoning Country Mental Health Assn.; adv. bd. Youngstown Area Assn. Children with Learning Disabilities. Served with AUS, 1944-46. Mem. Am., Midwestern, Ohio, Pa. psychol. assns., Am. Assn. U. Profs., A.A.A.S. Episcopalian (vestryman, clk.). Home: 213 Mayflower Dr Boardman OH 44512 Office: Dept Psychology Youngstown State U Youngstown OH 44503

HOTCHKISS, WESLEY AKIN, clergyman, educator; b. Spooner, Wis., Jan. 26, 1919; s. Fay W. and Codie L. (Akin) H.; B.A., Northland Coll., Wis., 1944, Th.D., 1958; M.S., U. Chgo., 1948, Ph.D., 1950; D.D., Yankton Coll., 1956; LL.D., Pacific U., 1965; m. Mary Ellen Fink, Sept. 16, 1941; 1 dau., Tannia F. Ordained to ministry Congl. Ch., 1944; research asso. Chgo. Theol. Sem., 1947-49; research dir. Greater Cin. Council Chs., 1949-50; research dir. United Ch. Bd., 1950-55, sec., 1955-58, gen. sec. for higher edn., 1958—. Lectr. geography Coll. City N.Y., 1960—; mem. spl. seminar higher edn. Columbia, 1962—. Trustee Ripon Coll., Dillard U., Fisk U., Northland Coll., Talladega Coll. Served as chaplain AUS, 1945-47. Fellow Assn. Am. Geographers; mem. A.A.A.S., Am. Sociol. Assn., Religious Research Assn. Home: 420 McKinley Terrace Centerport NY 11721 Office: 287 Park Av New York City NY 10010

HOTCHNER, AARON EDWARD, author; b. St. Louis, June 28, 1920; s. Samuel and Sally (Rossman) H.; A.B., LL.B., Washington U., St. Louis, 1941. Admitted to Mo. bar, 1941; practiced law in St. Louis, 1941-42; articles editor Cosmopolitan mag., 1948-50; free lance writer short stories and articles in various mags. including Sat. Eve. Post, Esquire, Readers Digest, 1950—; TV playwright Playhouse 90, 1958-60; adapted major Hemingway works for TV including For Whom The Bell Tolls, 1958, The Killers, 1959; writer screenplay Adventures of a Young Man, 1961. Served to maj. USAAF, 1942-46; NATOUSA. Mem. Mo. Bar Assn., Writers Guild Am., Dramatists Guild, Overseas Press Club. Author: The Dangerous American, 1958; Papa Hemingway: A Personal Memoir, 1966; Treasure, 1970; (plays) The White House, 1964; The Hemingway Hero, 1967; Do You Take This Man?, 1970. Address: 14 Hillandale Rd Westport CT 06880

HOTELLING, HAROLD, mathematician, educator; b. Fulda, Minn., Sept. 29, 1895; s. Clair Alberta and Lucy Amelia (Rawson) H.; A.B., U. Wash., 1919, M.S., 1921; student U. chgo., summer 1920, LL.D., Princeton, 1924; Sc. D. (hon.), U. Rochester, 1963; m. Floy Tracy, Dec. 27, 1920 (dec. Oct. 1932); children—Eric Bell, Muriel (Mrs. Glenn L. Burrows); m. 2d, Susanna Porter Edmondson, June 14, 1934; children—George Alfred, William Edmondson, Edward Rawson, Harold, James Maynard. Employed with weekly newspapers, State of Wash., 1915- 16, 1919; teaching asst. math. U. Wash., 1920-21; fellow in math. Princeton, 1921-22, instr., 1922-24; research asso. Food Research Inst., Stanford, 1924-27, asso. prof. mathematics, 1927-31; research Rothamsted Exptl. Sta., Eng., 1929; prof. econs. Columbia, 1931-46; prof. math. statistics U. N. C., 1946-61, Kenan prof. statistics, 1961-66 Kenan prof. emeritus, 1966—; vis. prof. Indian Statis. Inst., 1939-40, U. Buenos Aires, 1964; vis. lectr. in many Am. and European univs. Organizer, head statis research group Colubmia, 1942-45; cons. NRA, 1933. U.S. Treasury Dept., 1943, U.S. Bur. Budget, 1944-49, N.Y. State Pub. Service Commn., 1949-50, NSF, 1952-54, other. Recipient medal free U. Brussels, 1951. Fellow Econometric Soc. (pres. 1936-37, mem. council 1955-58), Royal Statis. Soc. (hon.), Inst. math. Statis. (pres. 1941, mem. council 1957-60), Royal Econ. Soc., Am. Statis. Assn. (v.p. 1941), Am. Econ. Assn. (distinguished fellow), A.A.A.S. (chmn. sect. K 1942, sect. U 1963, mem. council 1950-61; mem. Social Sci. Research Council (bd. 1945-48), Am. Math. Soc. (mem. council several terms) Am. Assn. U. Profs., Internat. Statis. Inst., Nat. Acad. Sci., Phi Beta Kappa, Sigma Xi (pres. Chapel Hill Chpt. 1957-58), Indian Statis. Congress (pres.), Elisha Mitchell Sci. Soc., (pres. 1954-55). Club: Faculty (pres. Chapel Hill 1963-64). Former asso. editor Annals of Math. Statistics, Econometrica; asso. editor Am. Jour. Econs. and Sociology. Contbr. to sci. publs. Address: Box 2167 Chapel Hill NC 27514

HOTSKO, WILLIAM, banker; b. Nesquehoning, Pa., June 10, 1921; s. Michael and Mary (Goyda) H.; B.S. in Bus. Adminstrn., Bowling Green State U., 1944; m. Altha C. Mallory, Mar. 18, 1950; 1 dau., Mary Beth. Cost accountant Goodyear Tire & Rubber Co., 1947-54; sr. accountant L.R. Sarver, C.P.A., Akron, O., 1954-56; accountant, asst. controller Valley Nat. Bank, Phoenix, 1957- 62, auditor, 1963—; lectr. in field, 1968—. Served with USCGR, 1942. C.P.A., Ariz. Mem. Am. Inst. C.P.A.s, Inst. Internal Auditors, Bank Adminstrn. Inst. (pres. Ariz. 1967-68, bd. dirs. Ariz. 1968-69), Sigma Alpha Epsilon. Home: 4045 E Coolidge St Phoenix AZ 85018

HOTTEL, ALTHEA K., former dean women; b. Lansdale, Pa., Oct. 16, 1907; d. Clarence M. and Antoinette S. (Hallowell) Kratz; B.S., U. Pa., 1929, M.A., 1934, Ph.D., 1940, Litt. D., 1947, 54, 58, 59, 60, LL.D., 1947, 48, 52, 56, 59, L.H.D., 1953, 57; m. Abram Stauffer Hottel, Apr. 5, 1941. Social sci. tchr., Wilmington, Del. 1929-30; staff mem. Social Service Dept., Grad. Hosp., 1930-33; dean instrn., prof. edn. Queens Coll., 1935-36; dean women, lectr. sociology U. Pa., 1936-59, ret., 1959; Dir. commn. on edn. women Am. Council on Edn., 1953-55; chmn. Phila. Commn. Higher Edn., 1963-65; mem. Pa. Bd. Edn., 1968—. Chmn. operating com. War Job Information Center for Women, Phila., 1942-46; mem. nat. com. for Marshall Plan; mem. exec. bd. Citizens Com. for Displaced Persons; chmn. Womens Indsl. Div. Bd. Trade and Phila. C. of C., 1945-46, Bennett fellow, 1934-35; rep. conf. Fedn, U. Women, Europe, Mexico, India, Australia, New Zealand; U.S. rep. social commn. ECOSOC, 1955-61; pres. Virginia Gildersleeve Internat. Fund for U. Women, 1969—. Bd. dirs., v.p. Baldwin Sch., Bryn Mawr, 1947-62. Recipient Phila. Gimbel award, 1947, U. Pa. Alumni award merit, Distinguished Dau. Pa., 1950; Golden Slipper Sq. Club award Phila., 1956. Mem. Am. Assn. U. Women (nat. pres.), Pa. Assn. Women Deans and Counselors, Internat. Fedn. U. Women (pres. 1965-68), Am. Sociol. Soc., World Affairs Council Phila. (v.p.), Phila. Art Alliance, Phi Beta Kappa, Pi Gamma Mu, Pi Lambda Theta, Delta Delta Delta (award 1950), Delta Kappa Gamma. Clubs: Womens University, Faculty. Author: Prosecutions and Treatment of Women Offenders and the Economic Crisis, 1934; How Fare American Women?, 1955; also articles. Participant Round The World Town Meetings of the Air, 1949. Home: 824 Gatemore Rd Bryn Mawr PA 19010

HOTTEL, HOYT CLARKE, educator; b. Salem, Ind., Jan. 15, 1903; s. Louis Weaver and Myrtle (Clarke) H.; A.B., Ind. U., 1922; M.S., Mass. Inst. Tech., 1924; m. Nellie L. Rich, June 11, 1929; children—Louis, Hoyt C., Barbara E., Elizabeth L. Mem. faculty Mass. Inst. Tech., 1927—, prof. fuel engring., 1941-66, Carbon P. Dubbs prof. chem. engring., 1966-68, prof. chem. engring. emeritus, 1968—, dir. of fuels research lab., 1934-68; cons. fuels and combustion; sect. chief on fire warfare Nat. Def. Research Com., 1942-45; chmn. U.S. Com. on Flame Radiation, Nat. Acad. Scis.-NRC Com. Fire Research, 1956-67, Armed Forces Spl. Weapons Project Thermal Panel, 1946-58; v.p. Combustion Inst., 1952-64; mem. adv. panel bldg. research div. U.S. Bur. Standards, 1965-69. Decorated Medal for Merit; King's Medal (Brit.); recipient Wm. H. Walker award Am. Inst. Chem. Engrs., 1945; Egerton Gold medal. Combustion Inst., 1960; Melchett medal Inst. of Fuel (Britain), 1960; Max Jakob award Am. Soc. M.E.-Am. Inst. Chem. Engrs., 1966; Founder's award Am. Inst. Chem. Engrs., 1967. Mem. Am. Chem. Soc., Am. Inst. Chem. Engrs., Am. Soc. M.E., Am. Acad. Arts and Scis., Nat. Acad. Scis., Sigma Xi, Phi Beta Kappa, Phi Gamma Delta. Author: (with G. W. Williams and C. N. Satterfield) Thermodynamic Charts of Combustion Process, 1949, Radiative Transfer, 1949; (with A.F. Sarofin), Radiative Transfer, 1967; also sects. in handbooks and tech. articles on combustion, radiant heat transmission, pyrometry, furnaces, thermodynamics, solar energy utilization. Home: 27 Cambridge St Winchester MA 01890 Office: Mass Inst Tech Cambridge MA 02139

HOTTELET, RICHARD CURT, fgn. corr.; b. N.Y.C., Sept. 22, 1917; s. Richard and Antonie (Heck) H.; B.A., Bklyn. Coll., 1937; student Friedrich-Wilhelm U., Berlin, Germany, 1937-38; m. Ann Delafield, Jan. 21, 1942; children—Antonia Jane, Richard Peter. Fgn. corr. United Press, 1938-42, OWI, London, 1942-44; war and fgn. corr. CBS, London, Moscow, Berlin and Bonn, 1944-56, CBS News, N.Y.C., 1956-60, UN corr. CBS News, 1960—. Recipient Bklyn. Coll. award, 1957. Mem. Assn. Radio News Analysts. Home: Wilton CT 06897 Office: 530 W 57th St New York City NY 10019

HOTTER, HANS, opera singer; b. Offenbach, Germany, Jan. 19, 1909; s. Karl and Crescentia Hotter; ed. Hochschule fuer Musick; m. Helfa Fischer, July 7, 1936; children—Peter, Gabriele. Singer in opera and concerts, 1930—; appearances with opera companies in Germany, Austria, Italy, France, Eng.; mem. Met. Opera Co., 1950-54, San Francisco Opera Co., 1954, 56, Chgo. Lyric Opera, 1960, 61; concert appearances in Europe, U.S., S.Am., Australia, Japan. Address: 41 Osterwaldstrasse 8 Munich 23 West Germany

HOTTUN, C. HENRY, hosp. adminstr. Adminstr. Meth. Hosp., Memphis. Office: 1265 Union Av Memphis TN 38104*

HOTZ, ALFRED JULIUS, educator; b. Quincy, Ill., Nov. 11, 1909; s. Albert James and Emma (Haas) H.; A.B., Heidelberg Coll., 1932; M.A., Ohio State U., 1935; Ph.D., U. Chgo., 1948; m. Margaret Adele, Dec. 24, 1936; chidren—Elizabeth Ann, Kenneth Alan. High sch. tchr., coach, 1935-43; dir. recreation, Lakewood, O., 1943-44; instr. U. Chgo., 1947-48; asst. prof. Triple Cities Coll., 1948-49; became prof. polit. sci., chmn. dept. Western Res. U., 1949, lectr. Salzburg Seminar in Am. Studies, 1953, chmn. citizenship, world affairs grad. program; now prof. polit. sci., chmn. dept. polit. sci. Augustana Coll., Sioux Falls, S.D. Cons. U.S. Dept. State; adviser dept. internat. justice and goodwill Nat. Council Chs. Christ in Am. Mem. Am. Polit. Sci. Assn., Am. Soc. Internat. Law, Am. Assn. U. Profs., Am. Acad. Polit. and Social Sci., Omicron Delta Kappa, Phi Theta Alpha, Pi Sigma Alpha, Theta Alpha Phi. Club: City (dir. 1956-58, treas. 1958) (Cleve.). Author: United Nations: New Perspectives; MIlitary Force; Investment of National Policy; United Nations Peacekeeping Financing. Contbr. to profl. jours. Home: 1909 W 22d St Sioux Falls SD 57105

HOTZ, ROBERT BERGMANN, editor; b. Milw., May 23, 1914; s. Harry Phillip and Emma (Bergmann) H.; B.S., Northwestern U., 1936; m. Joan Willison, Nov. 18, 1944; children—George, Michael, Robert Lee, Harry II. Reporter, Paris edit. N.Y. Herald Tribune, 1936-37; reporter, editor Milw. Jour., 1938-41; news editor McGraw-Hill Pub. Co., Washington, 1946-49; dir. pub. relations Pratt & Whitney Aircraft, Hartford, Conn., 1950-52; editor Aviation Week and Space Tech. mag., N.Y.C., 1953—, Space Tech. Internat., 1958—. Served from 2d lt. to maj. USAAF, 1942-46. Decorated Air medal with oak leaf cluster. Mem. 14th Air Force Assn., White House Corr. Assn., Royal Aero. Soc. (companion), Am. Inst. Aeros. and Astronautics. Clubs: National Press, Caterpillar, Aero. (Washington); Royal Aero. (London); National Space (bd. govs.) (Washington). Author: With General Chennault, the Story of the Flying Tigers, 1943; Pratt and Whitney Aircraft Story, 1950. Editor: Way of a Fighter, Memoirs of Claire Lee Chennault, 1949. Home: Rams Horn Farm Mt Tabor Rd Middletown MD 21769 Office: Nat Press Bldg Washington DC 20004

HOTZE, CHARLES WAYNE, publisher, printer; b. Moline, Ill., Feb. 19, 1919; s. Charles Edmund and Nellie (Gibbs) H.; B.A., U. Ill., 1941; m. Hazel Ann Tebbens, Dec. 20, 1956; children—Karen Ann, Carla Ann. Pres., chmn. bd. Fowle Printing Co., Milw., 1953-55; pres., pub. Clin. Medicine Publs., Inc., Northfield, Ill., 1954—, Med. Digest, Inc., 1955—. C. W. Hotze, Inc., 1957—, Progressive Pharmacist, 1958—, E.E.N.T. Digest, Inc., 1959—, Pediatrics Digest, Inc., 1962—, Psychiatry Digest, Inc., 1962—, Dermatology Digest, Inc. 1963—, Obstetrics-Gynecology Digest, Inc., 1964—, Urology Digest, Inc., 1964- -, Internal Medicine Digest, Inc., 1966—, Surgery Digest, Inc., 1966—, Cardiology Digest, Inc., 1966—, Geriatrics Digest, Inc., 1968—(all Northfield); pres. Modern Sci. Publs., Inc., 1968—. Served to 1st lt. AUS, 1942-45. Mem. Soc. Acad. Achievement, Am. Med. Writers Assn., Pharm. Advt. Club, Midwest Pharm. Advt. Club, S.A.R., Psi Upsilon. Club: Sunset Ridge (Winnetka, Ill.). Home: 1950 Sunset Ridge Rd Northbrook IL 60062 also 305 E 40th St New York City NY 10016 Office: 445 Central Av Northfield IL 60063 also 41 E 42 St New York City NY 20027

HOU, CHI MING, educator; b. Hopei, China, Dec. 3, 1924; s. H.T. and S.C. (Tien) H.; LL.B., Fu Jen U., 1945; M.A., U. Ore., 1949; Ph.D., Columbia, 1954; m. Irene Liu, June 20, 1953; children-Donald, William, Victor. Faculty, Colgate U., Hamilton, N.Y., 1956—, Charles A. Dana prof. econs., 1968- -; research prof. Brookings Instn., 1965-66; research fellow Chinese econ. studies Harvard, 1959-62; Fulbright lectr. econs., Taiwan, 1970- 71. Mem. Am. Econ. Assn., Assn. Asian Studies. Author: Foreign Investment and Economic Development in China 1840-1937, 1965. Contbr. articles profl. jours. Address: 39 Maple Av Hamilton NY 13346

HOUBOLT, JOHN CORNELIUS, physicist; b. Altoona, Ia., Apr. 10, 1919; s. John H. and Hendreika (Van Ingen) H.; B.S., U. Ill., 1940, M.S., 1942; Ph.D., Swiss Fed. Inst. Tech., Zurich, 1958; m. Mary Mooris, June 14, 1949; children—Mary Cornelia, Joanna, Julie. Bridge engr. I.C. R.R., 1940; city engr., Waukegan, Ill., 1941; aero. research scientist NASA, Hampton, Va., 1942- 49; asso. chief dynamic loads div. NACA-NASA, 1949-62, chief theoretical mechanics div. NASA, 1962-63; sr. v.p., dir. Aero Research Assos. Princeton Inc., (N.J.), 1963—; instr. grad. extension div. U. Va., 1944- -, Va. Poly. Inst., 1958—; exchange scientist Royal Aircraft Establishment, Eng., 1949. Dir. Doweave, Inc., 1969—. Mem. Air Force Scientific Adv. Bd. Recipient Rockefeller Pub. Service award, 1956; NASA Exceptional Sci. Achievement award, 1963; AIAA Structures, Structural Dynamics and Materials award, 1967; U. Ill. Distinguished Civil Engring. Alumni award, 1969; U. Ill. Illini Achievement award, 1970. Fellow Am. Inst. Aeros. and Astronautics (v.p. tech.). Asso. editor Jour. Spacecraft and Rockets. Research, numerous reports in aeros., aeroelasticity, structures, atmosphere turbulence, space flight and landing. Home: 105 Elm Rd Princeton NJ 08540 Office: 50 Washington Rd Princeton NJ 08540

HOUBREGS, ROBERT JOHN, basketball team exec.; b. Vancouver, B.C., Can., Mar. 12, 1932; s. John Louis and Mary Strathearn (Gray) H.; came to U.S., 1938; B.A., U. Wash., 1953; m. Ardis Hloha Olson, Apr. 15, 1954; children—Robert John, Todd, Jol, Guy. Profl. basketball player Ft. Wayne Pistons, 1953-58; asst. coach U. Wash., 1958-59; salesman Converse Rubber Co., 1959-69; gen. mgr. Seattle Supersonics Basketball Team, 1969—. Pres. Bob Houbregs Basketball Sch. Named Helms Player of Year, 1953, to Wash. State Hall of Fame Sports, 1969. Mem. Nat. Basketball Assn. Gen. Mgrs. Coach Assn. (treas.), Alpha Sigma Phi. Rotarian. Clubs: Variety, Oval, Big W, Wing Point Golf. Home: Route 5 Box 5474 Bainbridge Island WA 98110 Office: 221 W Harrison St Seattle WA 98118

HOUCHIN, JOHN MARVIN, oil co. exec.; b. Jackson, Miss., Jan. 11, 1909; s. John Chambers and Ada Loraine (Chamblin) H.; B.S., U. Okla., 1934; m. Louise Dodson, Apr. 26, 1930; children—Jane (Mrs. Lee M. Gammill, Jr.), John M., Larry. With Phillips Petroleum Co., 1933 field engr., asst. div. supt., asst. chief engr., dist. supt., asst. gen. supt., gen. supt. prodn. dept., chmn. operating com. exec. dept., 1933-57, v.p., dir., 1957-62, exec. com., 1958, exec. v.p., 1962-67, chmn. exec. com., 1967-68, pres., 1968—; pres., dir. Phillips Marketing Properties, Inc., Phillips Petroleum Internat. Corp., Phillips Petroleum Co. Saudi Arabia; dir. Pacific Petroleums, Ltd., Calgary, Can., Phillips Petroleum Can. Ltd., Calgary, Westcoast Transmission Co., Ltd., Vancouver, Can., Phillips-Imperial Petroleum Ltd., London, Eng., First Nat. Bank, Bartlesville, Okla., First Nat. Bank & Trust Co. Tulsa. Trustee Bartlesville Boys Club, U. Okla. Found. Named to Hall of Fame, Sch. Engring. U. Okla., 1969. Mem. Am. Petroleum Inst. (dir.), Mid Continent Oil and Gas Assn. (dir., exec. com.), Okla. Soc. Profl. Engrs., 25 Year Club Petroleum Industry. Presbyn. Mason. Club: Hillcrest Country. Home: 1529 Hillcrest Dr Bartlesville OK 74003 Office: Phillips Bldg Bartlesville OK 74003

HOUCK, CALVIN BRYAN, advt. exec.; b. Todd, N.C., Apr. 13, 1896; s. Sylvester Lee and Roxie Ann (Walker) H.; A.B., Duke, 1922; m. Margaret Moore McGuire, Aug. 22, 1922; children—William Bryan, Margaret Ann (Mrs. Tenney Saunders Griffin). Prof. grad. study Columbia, 1924-25; tchr. English, High Point (N.C.) Coll., 1925-26; newspaper feature writer, trade paper editor, 1927-28; established Houck and Co., Inc., advt. agy., Roanoke, Va., 1928, now chmn., treas., dir. Trustee Duke U. Served from pvt. to sgt. World War I. Recipient Ann. Silver Medal award Roanoke Valley Advt. Club and Am. Advt. Fedn., 1970. Mem. Duke Alumni Assn. (pres. 1950-51). Presbyn. (deacon). Clubs: Shenandoah Valley, Inc. (Staunton, Va.); Commonwealth (Richmond, Va.); Rotary, Advertising, Country, Shenandoah (Roanoke). Home: 2607 Rosalind Av Roanoke VA 24014 Office: 2013 Jefferson St SW Roanoke VA 24014

HOUCK, GEORGE CLARENCE, mfg. exec.; b. Buffalo, Feb. 17, 1913; s. Christopher George and Emma Louise (Seitz) H.; B.A., Ohio Wesleyan U., 1935; m. June Waldorf, Dec. 25, 1935; children—John Christopher, Ann Louise. Factory auditor Perfection Stove Co., 1936-39; with Harris-Seybold Co. (now Harris- Seybold Co. div. Harris-Intertype Corp.), Cleve., 1939—, beginning as div. controller, successively asst. treas., dir. planning, asst. to pres., v.p. operations, v.p., gen. mgr., dir., 1939-57, pres., 1957—; v.p., dir. Harris-Intertype Corp. Mem. finance com. Graphic Arts Tech. Found. Mem. Nat. Printing Equipment Assn. (dir., v.p.). Club: Union (Cleve.). Home: 12700 Lake Av Lakewood OH 44107 Office: 55 Public Sq Cleveland OH 44113

HOUGAS, ROBERT WAYNE, univ. dean; b. Blythedale, Mo., June 17, 1918; s. Harley Jay and Maude Rebecca (Richardson) H.; B.S., U. Wis., 1941, Ph.D., 1949; m. Janet Margaret Anthony, Aug. 1, 1943. Prof., plant research genetics Dept. Agr., U. Wis.-Madison, 1949-61, asst. dean, dir. Coll. Agr., 1961-66, asso. dean, dir. Coll. Agr., 1966—. Served with USNR, 1942-45. Mem. Potato Assn. Am. (hon. life, sec., dir., v.p., pres.). Home: Cross Plains WI 53528 Office: Agr Hall Coll Agr and Life Scis U Wis Madison WI 53706

HOUGEN, JOEL OLIVER, educator; b. Tacoma, Feb. 26, 1914; s. Johan Olai and Anna (Stockstad) H.; B.S. in Chem. Engring., U. Wis., 1936; M.S., U. Minn., 1946, Ph.D., 1948; m. Alma M. Thorsheim, May 25, 1938; children—Kathryn Elene (Mrs. Richard P. Knutsen), Thomas Joel, Martha Clare (Mrs. David W. Summers), Stephen Thorsheim. Engr., Pan Am. Refining Corp., 1937-41; process engr. Union Oil Co. Cal., 1944-46; systems engr., technologist Monsanto Co., 1956-66; prin., chem. engring. cons. J.O. Hougen & Assos., St. Louis, 1966-67; instr. chem. engring. U. Minn., 1941-44, U. Ill. at Urbana, 1944-48; prof. chem. engring. Rensselaer Poly. Inst., 1948-56; Alcoa prof. U. Tex., Austin, 1967—; cons. in field. Mem. Am. Soc. Engring. Edn., Am. Inst. Chem. Engrs. (Inst. lectr. 1960), Am. Chem. Soc., Instrument Soc. Am. (Instrumentation Tech. award 1970). Lutheran (council). Rotarian. Author: Process Measurements and Control. Contbr. prof. jours. Home: 4210 Cat Hollow Dr Austin TX 78712

HOUGH, CASS SHEFFIELD, mfg. co. exec.; b. Plymouth, Mich., Oct. 4, 1904; s. Edward C. and Louise (Sheffield) H.; A.B., U. Mich., 1925, M.A., 1926; M.B.A., Cleary Coll., 1952; LL.D., John Brown U., 1966; m. Margaret Reid, Oct. 4, 1926 (div. 1952); children—Emily (Mrs. Robert Egan), Cass Sheffield; m. 2d, Rosemary Lappin, July 2, 1952 (div. 1958); 1 son, Christopher; m. 3d, Grethe Bult, 1958 (dec. 1960); m. 4th, Beth Brogdon, June 6, 1960. With Daisy Mfg. Co., Rogers, Ark., 1926-67, exec. v.p., dir., 1945-59, pres., treas., 1959-67, also dir.; pres. James Heddon's Sons, Dowagiac, Mich., 1962- 67; pres. Daisy Heddon div. Victor Comptometer Corp., Rogers, 1967—, dir. parent co.; dir. Town and Country Motor Lodge, Inc., Hoyt Corp., Rogers, Sav-A-Stop Midwest, Inc., Union Nat. Bank Little Rock. Mem. spl. adv. com. on pub. affairs Dept. State, 1970—. Chmn., Ark. Council Econ. Edn., 1967, N.W. Ark. Regional Airport Authority, 1967; mem. Ark. Indsl. Devel. Commn.; chmn. Mich. Aero. Commn., 1947-51. Mayor, Plymouth, Mich., 1951. Trustee John Brown U.; bd. dirs. Culver Ednl. Found., Rogers Meml. Hosp. Assn. Served to col. USAAF, 1940-45; ETO. Decorated Legion of Merit, D.F.C. with cluster, Air medal with 3 clusters; Croix de Guerre (Belgium). Mem. Toy Mfrs. Am. (dir., past pres.), Rogers C. of C., Sportsman Pilots Assn. (past pres.), Quiet Birdmen, Vet. Air Pilots, Alpha Kappa Psi, Pi Delta Epsilon, Sigma Alpha Epsilon. Republican. Episcopalian. Rotarian, Elk. Home: Box 220 Rogers AR 72756 Office: Daisy/Heddon Rogers AR 72756

HOUGH, DONALD, author; b. St. Paul, June 29, 1895; s. Sherwood and Edith Evelyn (Moses) H.; student pub. schs.; m. Harriet Berry, 1922; 1 son, Sherwood. Newspaper reporter, 1920-25; patrolman U.S. Forest Service, 1925; dir. publicity Izaak Walton League Am., also asso. editor Outdoor America mag., 1926-29; vis. asso. prof. mag. journalism sequence State U. Ia. Sch. Journalism, 1956-57; contbr. popular mags.; author books including: Snow Above Town, 1942; Captain Retread, 1944; The Camelephamoose, 1946; Darling, I Am Home, 1946; The Cocktail Hour in Jackson Hole, 1956; The Streetcar House, 1960; The Poet, 1963. Served from pvt. to lt., Signal Corps, U.S. Army, World War I; capt. AC, World War II, overseas; now maj. Res. ret. Democrat.

HOUGH, ELDRED WILSON, coll. dean; b. Carrollton, Ill., Jan. 26, 1916; s. Thomas Crispen and Jennie (Eldred) H.; B.S., U. Ill., 1939; M.S., Cal. Inst. Tech., 1941, Ph.D., 1943; m. Jane Ruth Elder, Dec. 28, 1948; children—Christine Elizabeth, Phyllis Jane, Roger Eldred, Carl Emerson. Research asst. Cal. Inst. Tech., 1941-46, sr. research fellow, 1946-49; sr. research engr. Stanolind Oil & Gas Co., Tulsa, 1949-52; prof. petroleum engring., mem. Grad. Mem. faculty U. Tex., Austin, 1952-61; head dept., prof. petroleum engring., dir. grad. studies Coll. Engring., Miss. State U., 1961-65; asst. dean. Sch. Tech., prof. engring. So. Ill. U., 1965-69; dean Coll. Tech., prof. chem. engring. U. Me., Orono, 1969—; lectr. chem. and petroleum engring. U. Tulsa, 1950-52; petroleum engr.. cons. Gulf Oil Corp., 1953-54; cons. Humble Oil & Refining Co., 1954-61, Jersey Prodn. Research Co., 1961. Registered profl. engr., Cal., Tex. Mem. Am. Chem. Soc., Am. Phys. Soc., Am. Inst. Mining Engrs., Am. Inst. Chem. Engrs., Nat. Soc. Profl. Engrs., Tau Beta Pi. Lion. Contbr. articles profl. jours. Office: Barrows Hall U Me Orono ME 04473

HOUGH, HENRY BEETLE, editor, author; b. New Bedford, Mass., Nov. 8, 1896; s. George A. and Abby Louise (Beetle) H.; B.Litt., Columbia Sch. Journalism, 1918; M.A. (hon.), Yale, 1958; m. Elizabeth Wilson Bowie, June 10, 1920. Mem. pub. relations staff Inst. Am. Meat Packers. Chgo., 1919-20, Western Electric Co., N.Y.C., 1923-26; editor, pub. with wife Vineyard Gazette, Edgartown, Martha's Vineyard, 1920-68, editor, 1968—. Bergen lectr. Yale, 1952-53; dir. Edgartown Nat. Bank. Vice pres. Martha's Vineyard Hosp.; pres. Duke's County Hist. Soc., 1941-49. Served as yeoman 1st class, Naval Intelligence, Washington, 1918-19. Recipient Columbia U. medal for Excellence, 1942. Mem. Thoreau Soc. (pres. 1968- 69), Am. Rose Soc. Co-author Pulitzer prizewinning History of Services Rendered by the American Press, 1917. Author: Martha's Vineyard, Summer Resort, 1936; Country Editor, 1940; (novels) That Lofty Sky, 1941; All Things Are Yours, 1942; Roosters Crow in Town, 1945; Long Anchorage, 1947; Lament for a City, 1960; The Road, 1970; (nonfiction): Once More the Thunderer, 1950; Singing in the Morning, 1951; (with Emma Whiting), Whaling Wives, 1953; An Alcoholic to His Sons, 1954; Thoreau of Walden (biography), 1956; The New England Story, 1957; Great Days of Whaling, 1958; Melville in the South Pacific (juvenile), 1960; The Port, 1963; Vineyard Gazette Reader, 1967; Martha's Vineyard, 1970; (with Alfred Eisenstadt) Tuesday Will Be Different (essays), 1971. Contbr. to leading mags. Home: Edgartown MA 02539

HOUGH, JACK LUIN, educator, geologist; b. Chgo., Mar. 30, 1909; s. Luin Wesley and Margaret (Jones) H.; B.S., U. Chgo., 1932, M.S., 1934, Ph.D., 1940; Sc.D., Western Mich. U., 1969; m. Alice Esther Carlson, May 4, 1934; children—Richard Anton, Barbara Alice. From jr. to asso. geologist Soil Conservation Service, Dept. Agr., 1935-41; research geologist Humble Oil & Refining Co., 1941-42; civilian scientist Bur. Ordnance USN, 1942-43, research asso., 1946-47; supr. oceanographic research Woods Hole (Mass.) Oceanographic Inst., 1943-45; research geologist Standard Oil Devel. Co., 1945-46; oceanographer USN Antarctic Expdn., Antarctica, 1946-47; prof. geology U. Ill., Urbana, 1947-63; prof. oceanography dept. meteorology and oceanography, prof. geology U. Mich., Ann Arbor, 1964—. Head dept. geology and geophysics Indian Inst. Tech., Kharagpur, 1944-45; cons. to govt. and industry, 1950—. Fellow A.A.A.S., Geol. Soc. Am. (Kirk Bryan award 1959, chmn. pub. com. 1964), Sigma Xi (nat. lectr. 1963-64); mem. Am. Assn. Petroleum Geologists, Am. Geol. Inst. (vis. scientist 1966, del. house soc. reps. 1969-71), Am. Geophys. Union (chmn. com. lakes 1947- 53), Am. Soc. Limnology and Oceanography, Soc. Econ. Paleontologists and Mineralogists (editor 1949-61, councillor 1960-61, chmn. pub. com. 1961-63, 71—, pres. 1966- 67). Author: Geology of the Great Lakes, 1958. Contbr. articles to profl. jours. Home: 2104 Pauline Blvd Ann Arbor MI 48103

HOUGH, JOHN E., chmn. Wis. Republican Party; mem. rules com. Rep. Nat. Com. Address: PO Box 591 Janesville WI 53545

HOUGH, JOHN NEWBOLD, educator; b. N.Y.C., Nov. 17, 1906; s. Charles Merrill and Ethel (Powers) H.; A.B., Dartmouth, 1927; M.A., Princeton, 1928, Ph.D., 1931; m. Eleanor Fulton Sloan, Aug. 26, 1930; children—Charles Merrill, Jonathan Sloan. Instr. Greek and Latin, Dartmouth, 1928-29; from instr. to prof. classics Ohio State U., 1931-46; prof., chmn. dept classics U. Colo., 1946—; Fulbright prof. U. Sydney (Australia), 1952. Mem. Am. Philol. Assn., Classical Assn. Middle West and South (sec. 1951-59, pres. 1960- 61), Royal Zool. Soc. New South Wales, Phi Beta Kappa. Author: Scientific Terminology, 1953. Home: 1515 Mariposa Av Boulder CO 80302

HOUGH, MEREDITH CARTER, cosmetic co. exec.; b. Canastota, N.Y. Nov. 26, 1915; s. Ivan Northrup and Ruth (Carter) H.; student St. Lawrence U., 1932-33; B.A., Syracuse U., 1936; m. Mary Daley, June 3, 1935; children—Nancy (Mrs. A. Clifton Rucker), Judith Ann, David Bruce, William Daley, Michael Carter. Dir. personnel Walsh Constrn. Co., 1927-44; gen. mgr. Winthrop div. operation in Brazil, Sterling Drug Co., 1944-54; with Chas. Pfizer & Co., Inc., 1954—, pres. Pfizer de Mexico, 1955-60, pres. div. Coty, Inc., 1964—; v.p. Chas. Pfizer & Co. Internat., also pres. Latin. Am. Mgmt. Center of co., 1967—. Chmn. pharm. industry div. N.Y.C. United Fund drive, 1963. Bd. dirs. Escola Americana, Rio de Janeiro, Escuela Americana, Mexico City, Am. Soc. Mexico City. Clubs: N.Y. Athletic; Rio de Janeiro Country, Itahanga Country (Rio de Janeiro); Chapultapec Country, Bankers (Mexico City). Home: 116 Central Park S New York City NY 10019 Office: 423 W 55th St New York City NY 10019

HOUGH, RICHARD RALSTON, communications co. exec.; b. Trenton, Dec. 13, 1917; s. Douglas R. and Leola A. (Moore) H.; B.S. in Engring., Princeton, 1939, E.E., 1940; m. Jane L. Jackson, Mar. 22, 1941; children—Suzanne L., Richard Ralston, Edith R., William F., Jane L., Robert M. With Bell Telephone Labs., Inc., 1940-57, dir. mil. electronics devel., 1955-57, v.p., 1957, now dir.; asst. chief engr. Am. Tel.&Tel. Co., 1957-59, v.p., 1961-66, pres. long lines dept., 1966—; v.p. operations Ohio Bell Telephone Co., 1959-61, mem. exec. com., dir., 1959-61; chmn. bd. Bellcomm, Inc.; dir. Bell Telephone Can., Ltd., Mountain States Tel.&Tel. Co., Am. Can. Co., Communications Satellite Corp., Allegheny Corp. Chmn., Project Beacon, presdl. task force to study safe and efficient use of airspace. Trustee Turell Fund, Morristown Meml. Hosp., Wilson Coll., Kent Place Sch., Princeton. Recipient Eta Kappa Nu award as Outstanding Young Elec. Engr., 1947. Fellow I.E.E.E.; mem. Princeton Engring. Assn. (exec. bd.), Phi Beta Kappa, Sigma Xi. Home: Van Beuren Rd Morristown NJ 07960 Office: 32 Av of Americas New York City NY 10013

HOUGH, ROBERT LEE, Jr., educator; b. Los Angeles, May 19, 1924; s. Robert Lee and Kathryn (Hindinger) H.; B.A., Pomona Coll., 1949; M.S., Columbia, 1950; Ph.D., Stanford, 1957; m. June Florence Rowley, June 29, 1952; children—Alison, Carol, Timothy, John. Inst. journalism News Bur., Whittier Coll., 1950-51; instr. to prof. English, U. Neb., Lincoln, 1956—, asst., asso. and full dean Coll. Arts and Scis., 1965-70. Served with AUS, 1942-44. Mem. Am. Ass. U. Profs., Modern Lang. Assn., Nat. Council Tchrs. English, Phi Beta Kappa.

Author: The Quiet Rebel, William Dean Howells as Social Commentator, 1959. Editor: James Fenimore Cooper's Satanstoe, 1962; Literary Criticism of Edgar Allan Poe, 1965. Home: 3000 Stratford St Lincoln NB 68502

HOUGH, WILLIAM ROCKWELL, elec. mfg. co. exec.; b. Kalamazoo, July 9, 1907; s. Frank W. and May (Marvin) H.; B.S. in Elec. Engring., U. Mich, 1929; m. Virginia Olds, Apr. 20, 1935; children—Steven, Nancy, Patricia. With Reliance Electric & Engring. Co. (now Reliance Electric Co.), Cleve., 1929- -, v.p. engring., control div., 1953-60, v.p. research, devel. and engring., 1960-69, v.p. tech. bd., 1969—, also dir. Pres. bd. trustees Euclid-Glenville Hosp., 1959-61; trustee Engrs. Found. Ohio. Registered profl. engr., Ohio. Fellow I.E.E.E.; mem. A.A.A.S., Assn. Iron and Steel Engrs., Cleve. Engring. Soc., Ohio Soc. Profl. Engrs., Cleve. Tech. Socs. Council (pres. 1948-49), Tau Beta Pi, Eta Kappa Nu, Tau Kappa Epsilon. Club: Chagrin Valley Country (Cleve.). Contbr. aricles to profl. jours. Home: 14789 Hillbrook Lane Novelty OH 44072 Office: 24701 Euclid Av Cleveland OH 44117

HOUGHTON, AMORY, former ambassador, glass exec.; b. Corning, N.Y., July 27, 1899; s. Alanson Bigelow and Adelaide Louise (Wellington) H.; ed. St. Paul's Sch., Concord, N.H., 1913-17; A.B. Harvard, 1921; LL.D., Hobart and William Smith Colls., Geneva, N.Y., 1947, Alfred (N.Y.) U., 1948, N.Y. U., 1961, Colgate U., 1961, Ohio State U., 1969; D. Eng. (hon.), Rensselaer Poly. Inst., 1949; m. Laura DeKay Richardson, Oct. 19, 1921; children—Elizabeth, Amory, Alanson Bigelow II, James Richardson, Laura DeKay. With Corning Glass Works, 1921—, asst. to pres., 1926-28, exec. v.p., 1928-30, pres., 1930-41, chmn. bd., 1941-61, chmn. exec. com., 1961-64, hon. chmn. bd., 1964—; trust adv. bd. First Nat. Bank, N.Y.C.; dir. Met. Life Ins. Co., Dow Corning Corp., Pitts.-Corning Corp.; ambassador to France, 1957-61. Councillor Nat. Indsl. Conf. Bd.; mem. adv. council State U. N.Y., Bd. dirs. Atlantic Council U.S., Inc.; trustee, mem. Corning Glass Works Found.; trustee Eisenhower Coll., Eisenhower Exchange Fellowships. Inst. Advanced Study, Corning Mus. Glass, Houghton Found., Inc., French Inst.; hon. v.p., mem. nat. exec. bd. Boy Scouts Am. Asst. dep. dir. materials div. OPM, 1941-42; dep. chief, bur. industry brs. WPB, 1942, dir. gen. operations, 1942; dep. chief Mission for Econ. Affairs, 1943- 44. Decorated Order Merit Bernardo O'Higgins (Chile); grand croix Legion de Honneur (France). Mem. Internat. Co. of Co. (exec. com., trustee, mem. U.S. council; v.p. internat. council), France Am. Soc. (chmn. bd.). Republican. Episcopalian. Clubs: Union, University, Harvard, Links, Fifth Avenue (N.Y.C.); Elmira Country, Corning Country, Kittansett (Marion, Mass.); Chevy Chase (Md.); Augusta (Ga.) Nat. Golf; Rolling Rock (Ligonier, Pa.); Metropolitan (Washington); Cotton Bay (Nassau); Eldorado Country (Cal.); La Quinta Country, Seven Lakes Country. Home: The Knoll Corning NY 14830

HOUGHTON, AMORY, Jr., glass works exec.; b. Corning, N.Y., Aug. 7, 1926; s. Amory and Laura DeKay (Richardson) H.; student St. Paul's Sch., Concord, N.H., 1941-45; A.B., Harvard, 1950, M.B.A., 1952; m. Ruth Frances West, June 27, 1950; children—Amory Amory III, Robert West, Sarah, Katherine. With Corning Glass Works, 1951—, v.p., 1957-61, pres., 1961-64, chmn., chief exec. officer, 1964—, also dir.; dir. Corning Glass Works of Can. Ltd., Pitts. Corning Corp., IBM Corp., Dow Corning Corp., Corhart Refractories Co., N.Y. Telephone Co., First Nat. City Bank. Mem. bd. Nat. Indsl. Conf. Bd., Bus. Council; trustee Corning Glass Works Found., Corning Mus. Glass, Episcopal Theol. Sch., Cambridge, Mass., St. Paul's Sch., Concord, N.H. Served with USMCR, 1945-46. Republican. Episcopalian. Clubs: University, Links, Fifth Avenue, Harvard (N.Y.C.); Corning Country; Elmira (N.Y.) Country; Kittansett (Marion, Mass.); Augusta (Ga.) National Golf; Rolling Rock (Ligonier, Pa.); Lyford Cay (Nassau, Bahamas). Home: 33 E 3d St Corning NY 14830 Office: Corning Glass Works Corning NY 14830

HOUGHTON, ARTHUR AMORY, Jr., corp. ofcl.; b. Corning, N.Y., Dec. 12, 1906; s. Arthur Amory and Mabel (Hollister) H.; student St. Paul's Sch., Concord, N.H., 1920-25, Harvard, 1925-29; L.H.D., Lehigh U., 1950, U. Md., 1963; LL.D., U. Rochester, 1952, Alfred U., 1954, Wesleyan U., 1963; Litt.D., Wash. Coll., 1953, Hofstra Coll., 1956, Trinity Coll., 1955, St. John's U., 1966; D.Lit., Beaver Coll., 1957; D.Sc., Hobart and William Smith Colls., 1958, Bucknell U., 1968; D.F.A., Washington and Jefferson Coll., 1971; m. Elizabeth Douglas McCall; children—Jane Olmsted (Mrs. George R. Kneeland), Sylvia Bigelow (Mrs. Richard G. Garrett), Arthur Amory III, Hollister Douglas (Mrs. William D. Haggard III). With mfg. dept. Corning Glass Works, 1929, treas. dept., 1929-30, asst. to pres., 1930-32, v.p., 1935-42, now dir.; curator rare books Library of Congress, 1940-42, mem. trust fund bd., hon. cons. English bibliography; pres. Steuben Glass, N.Y.C., 1933—; dir. N.Y. Life Ins. Co., U.S. Steel Corp.; trustee U.S. Trust Co. of N.Y. Vice pres. Corning Mus. of Glass, Pierpont Morgan Library; past chmn. Philharmonic-Symphony Soc. N.Y.; past vice chmn. Lincoln Center Performing Arts; chmn., pres. Wye Inst.; past chmn. Inst. Internat. Edn.; chmn. Met. Mus. Art. Trustee N.Y. Pub. Library, Rockefeller Found.; hon. trustee, past chmn. Parsons Sch. Design; trustee, past chmn. Cooper Union; hon. curator Keats Collection, Harvard; hon. trustee Inst. Contemporary Art (Boston). Served from capt. to lt. col. USAAF, 1942-45. Decorated officer Legion Honor (France); asso. comdr. Order St. John of Jeruselem; comdr. l'Ordre des Arts et des Lettres; recipient Michael Friedsam medal in indsl. art; Gertrude Vanderbilt Whitney award Skowhegan Sch. Fellow Royal Coll. Art (sr.), Royal Soc. Arts; mem. English-Speaking Union U.S. (dir.-at- large nat. bd.). Episcopalian. Clubs: Century, Union, Harvard, Knickerbocker, Grolier, Fifth Avenue (N.Y.C.). Home: 3 Sutton Pl New York City NY 10022 also Wye Plantation Queenstown MD 21658 Office: 715 Fifth Av New York City NY 10022

HOUGHTON, CHARLES NORRIS, stage dir., author, educator; b. Indpls., Dec. 26, 1909; s. Charles D. Mansfield and Grace (Norris) H.; A.B., Princeton, 1931; D.F.A. (hon.), Denison U., 1959. Stage mgr. on Broadway, 1933-37; stage designer Broadway prodns.: In Clover, Stop-Over, How To Get Tough About It, Whiteoaks, 1937-38, Dame Nature, Waltz in Goosestep, Good Hunting, 1939-40, The Sleeping Prince, 1956; art dir. St. Louis Municipal Opera, 1939-40; dir. Elitch's Gardens Theatre, Denver, 1948-49; dir. Broadway prodns.: Macbeth, 1947; Clutterbuck, 1949; Billy Budd, 1951; bd. dirs. Theatre, Inc., N.Y. C.; lectr. drama, dir. dramatics Princeton, 1941-42; guest prof. drama Smith Coll., 1947; lectr. comparative lit. Columbia, 1948-54; producer, dir. television CBS, 1951-52; adj. prof. drama Barnard Coll., 1954-58; co-mng. dir. Phoenix Theatre, N.Y.C., 1953-63; adj. prof. drama, guest dir. Exptl. Theatre, Vassar Coll., 1959-60, prof. drama, dir. Exptl. Theatre, 1962-67; dean div. theatre arts, prof. State U. N.Y. Coll., Purchase, 1967—. Guggenheim fellow, 1934, 35, 60-61. Trustee Nat. Repertory Theatre. Fellow Am. Acad. Arts and Scis.; mem. Nat. Council Chs. Christ (chmn. adv. com. on drama 1954-57), Nat. Theatre Conf. (pres. 1968-69), Am. Ednl. Theatre Assn., Inst. Advanced Studies in Theatre Arts (mem. adv. council), Phi Beta Kappa. Clubs: Century, Coffee House (N.Y.C.); Bucks (London). Author: Moscow Rehearsals, 1936; Advance from Broadway, 1941; But Not Forgotten, 1951; Return Engagement, 1962. Editor: Masterpieces of Continental Drama, 3 vols, 1963; Great Russian Short Stories, 1958; Great Russian Drama, 1960. Asso. editor Theatre Arts Mag., 1945-48. Contbr. to nat. theatrical mags. Home: 202 Millwood Rd Chappaqua NY 10514 Office: State U Coll Purchase NY 10577

HOUGHTON, DOROTHY DEEMER (Mrs. Hiram Cole Houghton) former govt. ofcl.; b. Red Oak,0Ia., Mar. 11, 1890; d. Horace Emerson and Jeannette (Gibson) Deemer; A.B., Wellesley Coll., 1912; LL.D., Coe Coll., 1942; L.H.D., Tarkio Coll., 1949; Litt.D., Am. U., 1952 D.Sc. in Govt. (hon.), U. Tampa, 1954; m. Hiram Cole Houghton, Dec. 18, 1912 (dec. 1957); children—Horace Deemer, Cole Hayward, Joan (Mrs. John J. Williams), Hiram Clark. Pres., Ia. Fedn. Women's Clubs, 1935-37, Gen. Fedn. Women's Clubs, 1950-52; dep. dir. refugee program and migration ICA, 1953-56; mem. adv. council OCDM, 1957-60. Adviser, alternate del. 5 internat. sessions Intergovtl. Com. European Migration; v.p. Electoral Coll., 1953-57, hon. life chmn.; mem.-at-large nat. commn. UNESCO: mem. bd. UN Internat. Children's Fund; mem. State Bd. Regents Ia., 1939-51. Nat. bd. mem. Women's Med. Coll. Pa.; trustee-at-large Nat. Soc. Crippled Children and Adults; chmn. 1963 project for Internat. Christian U., Tokyo, Japan; mem. adv. com. N.Y. World's Fair, 1964; trustee Washington Pilgrimage; bd. dirs. Library of Red Oak (Ia.), Seminars of Internat. Understanding. Co-chmn. Nat. Citizens for Eisenhower, 1956. Decorated officer Order Orange Nassau (Netherlands); Insignia and Diploma of Gold Cross of Royal Order Beneficence (Greece). Recipient Am. Heritage award Nat. Assn. Home Builders, 1952; Internat. Cup of Goodwill, All Nations Club, 1954; Nansen award for most distinguished service to refugees, Geneva, Switzerland, 1956. Mem. Nat. Assn. Parliamentarians (Ia. dir.), Ia. Safety Council (exec. com.), Congl-Christian Conf. Ia. (asst. moderator), Ia. Hist. Soc. (curator), Nat. Planning Assn. (nat. council), Assn. Bus. and Profl. Women, Am. Assn. U. Women, Pen Women Am., Ia. Library Assn. (pres. 1941-42), D.A.R., P.E.O., Delta Kappa Gamma, Zeta Phi Eta., Pi Beta Phi. Republican. Conglist. Home: Red Oak IA 51566

HOUGHTON, ELIZABETH D. MCCALL, (Mrs. Arthur A. Houghton, Jr.), civic worker; b. Florence, S.C., Feb. 25, 1919; d. Arthur M. and Julia H. (Lachicotte) McCall; B.S., Converse Coll., 1940; m. Arthur A. Houghton, Jr., Jan. 15, 1944; 1 dau., Hollister Douglas (Mrs. William D. Haggard III). Mem. women's council N.Y. Pub. Library, 1950, chmn. women's council, 1964-70, exec. com. of com. for dance, 1957; trustee Poetry Soc. Am., 1960-65; sec.-treas., dir. Keats-Shelley Assn. Am., Inc., 1961—; trustee Converse Coll., Spartanburg, S.C., 1958—, exec. com., 1965—; v.p., trustee Wye Inst., Inc., Centreville, Md., 1964—; trustee Inst. Internat. Edn. N.Y., exec. com., 1968—; bd. mgrs. Hosp. for Spl. Surgery, 1968—; mem. altar guild St. James Ch., N.Y.C., and Old Wye Ch., Wye Mills, Md.; mem. bd. Hammond-Harwood House, Annapolis, Md., 1962-69; mem. Friends Whitney Mus.; bd. dirs. Am.-Italian Soc., 1969—. Republican. Episcopalian. Clubs: Colony, Cosmopolitan (N.Y.C.); Queen Anne's County Garden of Maryland (Centreville). Home: 3 Sutton Pl New York City NY 10022 also Wye Plantation Queenstown MD 21658

HOUGHTON, FRANCIS, advt. exec.; b. Hartford, Conn., June 24, 1927; s. Henry Ernest and Frances Mary (Plaunt) H.; grad. Phillips Exeter Acad., 1945; B.A., Princeton, 1949; m. Averell Turner, June 23, 1961; children—Alan Maclean, Francis David, Nicholas Turner. Account supr. Benton & Bowles, N.Y.C., 1951-58; with Ogilvy & Mather, Inc., N.Y.C., 1959—, copywriter, 1959-61, copy supr., 1961-64, creative mgr., 1964—, mgr. account services, 1969—, sr. v.p., 1966—, also dir.; dir. Inverness Fund. Served with AUS, 1945-47. Club: Racquet & Tennis (N.Y.C.). Home: 315 E 70th St New York City NY 10021 Office: 2 E 48th St New York City NY 10017

HOUGHTON, HARRY ERNEST, business exec.; b. Kitchner, Ont., Can., May 25, 1900; s. William H.E. and Alma Ethel (Leatch) H.; m. 2d, Ethel Maclean, June 10, 1950; children by previous marriage—William Henry, Francis Xavier. Gen. sales mgr. Sesamee Lock Co., 1925-31; v.p., dir. Geyer, Cornell, advt. agy., 1931-37; v.p., dir. sales Brown Co., 1937-45; pres., dir. Muzak Corp.; chmn. bd. Subscription Radio, Inc., Air Music, Inc., Bertgil Music, Inc., 1945-58; dir., pres., chmn. exec. com. Ency. Brit., Inc.; chmn. Ency. Brit. Can., Ltd., EB Canadian Sales Co., EB Latin Am. Sales Co.; dir. Ency. Brit., Ltd. (Eng.), Ency. Brit. Films, Inc., 1958-62, ret.; dir. Internat. Equity Corp., Comcast Corp. Chmn., Historpedia House. Clubs: Tavern (Chgo.); Metropolitan (N.Y.C.); Everglades, Sailfish, Beach (Palm Beach). Home: 141 Barton Av Palm Beach FL 33480 also Houghton Bay Portland Ontario Canada

HOUGHTON, HENRIETTA FLECK, see Fleck, Henrietta.

HOUGHTON, HENRY GARRETT, educator, scientist; b. N.Y.C., Feb. 2, 1905; s. Henry Garrett and Ivy Estelle (Smith) H.; B.S., Drexel Inst. Tech., 1926, D.Sc. (hon.), 1947; S.M., Mass. Inst. Tech., 1927; m. Dorothy Jenness, July 10, 1933. Engring. asst. Bell Telephone Co. of Pa., Phila., 1927-28; research asst. Mass. Inst. Tech., 1928-32, research asso., 1938-39, asst. prof. meteorology, 1939-42, asso. prof., 1942-45, prof. meteorology, head dept., 1945-70, prof. emeritus, sr. lectr. 1970—. Recipient Robert M. Losey award Inst. Aeron. Scis., 1940. Fellow Am. Acad. Arts and Scis., A.A.A.S., Am. Meterol. Soc. (Brooks award 1958, pres. 1946-47, sec. 1954-57), Am. Geophys. Union (pres. meteorology sect. 1964-68); mem. Royal Meteorol. Soc. (hon.), Sigma Xi, Tau Beta Pi. Contbr. sci. papers to profl. lit. Patentee in field. Home: 29 Edmunds Rd Wellesley Hills MA 02181 Office: Mass Inst Tech Cambridge MA 02139

HOUGHTON, LEROY BRYAN, oil co. exec.; b. Whittier, Cal., 1907; s. Roy James and Elizabeth (Hunt) H.; student Whittier Coll., 1925-27, Stanford, 1928-29; B.A., Woodbury Coll., 1930; m. Jane Layton, 1931; 1 dau., Janalee (Mrs. Robert E. Ashford). With Union Oil Co. of Cal., Los Angeles, 1931—, asst. treas., asst. sec., 1946-59, treas. 1959—. Home: 600 Pasqual Av San Gabriel CA 91775 Office: 461 Boylston Av Los Angeles CA 90017

HOUGHTON, WALTER EDWARDS, educator; b. Stamford, Conn., Sept. 21, 1904; s. Walter Edwards and Nancy (Acheson) H.; Ph.B., Yale, 1924, M.A., 1927, Ph.D., 1931; m. Esther Lowrey Rhoads, June 22, 1929; children—Nancy Acheson, Esther Edwards. Instr., Hill Sch., Pottstown, Pa., 1924-25, Phillips Andover Acad., 1927-29; instr., tutor in history and lit. Harvard, Radcliffe Coll., 1931-38, asst. prof., tutor history and lit., 1938-41; asso. prof. English lit. Wellesley Coll., 1942-48, prof. English lit., 1948-69, Sophie C. Hart prof. English, 1957-69. Active in Civil Def., Cambridge and Wellesley, Mass., World War II. Fellow Am. Acad. Arts and Scis.; mem. Conf. Brit. Studies, Am. Assn. U. Profs., Modern Lang. Assn. Author: The Formation of Thomas Fuller's Holy and Profane States, 1938; The Art of Newman's Apologia, 1945; The Victorian Frame of Mind, 1830-70, 1957; The Poetry of Clough, 1963. Editor: (with Hazelton Spencer, Herbert Barrows) British Literature from Blake to the Present Day, 1952; (with G. Robert Stange) Victorian Poetry and Poetics, 1959; The Wellesley Index to Victorian Periodicals, 1824-1900, vol. 1, 1966. Adv. editor Victorian Studies, 1960-69, Victorian Poetry, 1963—. Home: 19 Summit Rd Wellesley MA 02181

HOUGHTON, WOODSON PLYER, lawyer; b. Washington, Apr. 19, 1893; s. Harry Sherman and Alice Virginia (Ballentine) H.; B.A., Washington and Lee U., 1915; LL.B., Georgetown U., 1918; m. Geta Triester, July 21, 1933. Asst. sec. 2d Pan Am. Sci. Congress, 1916-17; admitted to D.C. bar, 1918, since practiced in Wasington; mem. firm Ellis, Houghton and Ellis, 1919- 68, sr. partner, 1948-68; prof. law Nat. U. Law Sch., 1923-26; formerly mem. bd. Mut. Protection Fire Ins. Co., Norfolk, Washington Steamboat Co. Pres. Family Service Assn. (Asso. Charities); mem. bd. Family Welfare Assn. Am., Council Social Agys., Community Chest, D.C. Served as 1st lt. judge adv. gen. corps. U.S. Army. 1918-19, asst. port judge adv., Port Embarkation, Newport News. Va. Mem. Am., D.C. bar assns., DuPont Circle Citizens Assn., S.A.R., Barristers, Sigma Chi, Phi Delta Phi Omicron Delta Kappa. Clubs: Nantucket Yacht; Sankaty Head Golf; Metropolitan; Chevy Chase; 1925 F Street (gov.), Pacific; Wharf Rat. Home: 2337 California St NW Washington DC 20008 Office: 815 Connecticut Av NW Washington DC 20006

HOUK, RALPH GEORGE, profl. baseball co. exec.; b. Lawrence, Kan., Aug. 9, 1919; s. George and Emma (Walters) H.; grad. Lawrence High Sch.; m. Bette Porter, June 3, 1948; children—Donna, Richard, Robert. With N.Y. Yankees orgn., 1939- -, field mgr., 1961-63, gen. mgr., 1963—, v.p., 1965—. Served to capt. AUS, World War II, Elk. Office: Yankee Stadium Bronx NY 10451

HOULAHAN, JAMES JOSEPH, advt. exec.; b. Milton, Mass., Sept. 7, 1907; s. John and Johanna (Curran) H.; A.B. in Bus. Adminstrn., Northeastern U., 1929; m. Marion L. Lyons, June 29, 1935; children—Andrew Paul, Kathleen Johanna. With Paine Webber Co., stock brokers, Boston, 1929-30, Price Waterhouse, Boston, 1930, Lever Bros. Co., Cambridge, Mass., 1930-42; exec. v.p. William Esty & Co., advt. agy., 1942-47, pres. 1947-59, chmn. bd., 1960-67, hon. chmn., 1967—; dir. Coca-Cola Bottling Co. of N.Y. Republican. Roman Catholic. Clubs: Indian Harbor Yacht, Greenwich (Conn.) Country; Edgartown Yacht; Thoroughbred Club Am.; Country of Fla. Home: Round Hill Rd Greenwich CT 06830 Office: 100 E 42d St New York City NY 10017

HOULE, CYRIL ORVIN, educator; b. Sarasota, Fla., Mar. 26, 1913; s. John Louis and Annie Mae (Hescock) H.; A.B., U. Fla., 1934, M.A., 1934; Ph.D., U. Chgo., 1940; Fulbright fellow, U.K., 1950-51; D.H.L., Rutgers U.; LL.D., Fla. State U., Syracuse U.; m. Bettie Eckhardt Totten, May 15, 1947; 1 son, David. Instr. U.Chgo., 1939-42, asst. prof., 1942-45, asso. prof., dean U. Coll., 1945-52, prof., 1952—; vis. instr. U. Cal., 1940; Knapp vis. prof. U. Wis., Milw., 1960; vis. sr. research specialist Oxford U., 1968; dir. UNESCO seminar Sweden, 1950; mem. Nat. Adv. Council on Extension and Continuing Edn. Recipient Tolley medal Syracuse U., 1966; Outstanding Achievement award Assn. Evening Colls., 1967, Nat. Assn. of Public Sch. Adult Educators, 1968. Mem. Phi Beta Kappa, Delta Tau Delta. Clubs: Tavern, University, Quadrangle (Chgo.). Author or co-author: Adult Education, 1937; Armed Services and Adult Education, 1947; Libraries in Adult and Fundamental Education, 1951; The University, the Citizen, and World Affairs, 1956; The Effective Board, 1960: The Inquiring Mind, 1961; Continuing Your Education, 1964; also articles profl. jours. Home: 5510 Woodlawn Av Chicago IL 60637

HOULE, JOSEPH E., educator; b. Hartford, Conn., Oct. 11, 1930; s. Joseph E. and Rena (Cyr) H.; A.B., Cath. U. Am., 1952, M.A., 1954, Ph.D., 1959; m. Constance Deschamps, June 19, 1954; children—Marie, Joseph, Celia, Elizabeth, Amy, Bernice. From instr. to asso. prof. math. Georgetown U., 1953-62; asso. prof. Seton Hall U., 1962-63; prof. math. Pace Coll., N.Y.C., 1963—, chmn. dept., 1963-70, dean Sch. Arts and Scis., 1971—. Danforth asso., 1968—. Fellow N.Y. Acad. Scis. (chmn. div. math. 1968-69); mem. Am. Assn. U. Profs., Math. Assn. Am., Phi Beta Kappa, Sigma Xi. Roman Catholic. Home: 227 Garfield Pl South Orange NJ 07079 Office: Pace Coll Plaza New York City NY 10038

HOUNSHELL, CHARLES DAVID, coll. pres.; b. Rural Retreat, Va., Dec. 19, 1920; s. David Washington and Florence Earhart (Brown) H.; A.B., Emory and Henry Coll., 1942, LL.D., 1968; Ph.D., U. Va., 1950; Ford Faculty fellow, Princeton, 1953-54; m. Elizabeth Jane Yoak, Oct. 9, 1944; children—Jeffrey David (dec.), William Douglas, Elizabeth Anne. Instr. polit. sci. U. Va., 1948-50; mem. faculty Emory U., 1950-66, asso. prof. polit. sci., 1955-66, asso. dean Coll. Arts and Scis., 1960-66; dean Newcomb Coll., prof. polit. sci. Tulane U., New Orleans, 1966- 69; pres. Birmingham-So. Coll., Birmingham, Ala., 1969—. Chmn. region VI, Woodrow Wilson Nat. Fellowship Found., 1957-66, nat. rep., 1962-63, mem. nat. com., 1966-67, chmn. region XII, 1967-69. Served to lt. with USNR, 1942-46; capt. Res. Philip Francis du Pont sr. fellow, 1947-48, research fellow, 1948; summer research scholar Duke Commonwealth Studies Center, 1957; research grantee Emory U. Research Com., 1952, 55, 60, U. Center in Ga., 1955. Mem. Am., So. (exec. council 1954-57, v.p. 1957) polit. sci. assns., Phi Beta Kappa, Omicron Delta Kappa, Democrat. Methodist. Author: The Legislative Process in Virginia, 1951. Book rev. editor Jour. Politics, 1960-62. Home: 816 8th Av W Birmingham AL 35204

HOUNTRAS, PETER TIMOTHY, educator; b. Memphis, Dec. 7, 1927; s. Timothy John and Ethel (Trakas) H.; B.S. cum laude, U. Toledo, 1946; M.A., U. Mich., 1951, Ph.D., 1955; m. Helen Madias, Nov. 21, 1954; children—John, Dean. Instr., U. Mich., 1954-57; asst. prof. psychology and edn. U. Pitts., 1957-59, asso. prof., 1959-61; asso. prof. ednl. psychology, guidance and counseling Northwestern U., Evanston, Ill., 1961-66; prof. counseling and guidance, chmn. dept. U. N.D., Grand Forks, 1966-70; dean of counseling services Eastern Mich. U., Ypsilanti, 1970—; cons. psychologist, 1957—. Regional counseling and testing cons. Bur. Employment Security, U.S. Dept. Labor, 1966—; cons. to U.S. Office of Edn., 1967—. Recipient Distinguished Service Citation, Gov. N.D., 1969. Fellow Am. Psychol. Assn.; mem. Am. Personnel and Guidance Assn., Ill., Midwestern psychol. assns., Assn. Counselor Educators and Suprs., N.D. Guidance and Personnel Assn., Nat. Soc. Study Edn., Psychologists Interested in Advancement Psychotherapy, Am. Ednl. Research Assn., Am. Assn. U. Profs., N.D. Psychol. Assn., Sigma Xi, Psi Chi, Phi Kappa Phi, Phi Delta Kappa, Kappa Delta Pi. Presbyn. (elder). Rotarian. Author: Mental Hygiene, 1961; Manifest Anxiety and Achievement, 1970. Contbr. articles profl. jours. Home: 2970 Aurora St Ann Arbor MI 48105

HOUPHOUET-BOIGNY, FELIX. pres. Republic of Ivory Coast; b. Yamoussoukvo, Ivory Coast, Oct. 18, 1905; ed. Sch. Medicine, Dakar; m. 2d, Marie-Thérèse Brou, 1 dau.; 3 sons, 1 dau., by previous marriage. Doctor for Asst Médicale, 1925-40; pres. Syndicat Agricole Africain, 1944; mem. Constiuent Assembly, 1945- 46, mem. Nat. Assembly, 1946, 51, 56; minister, councilor French Govt., 1959-60; pres. Council 1959-60, pres. Republic of Ivory Coast, 1960—, minister fgn. affairs, 1961, minister interior, def. edn. and agr., 1963; pres. Reassemblement Democratique Africain. Decorated grand cross French Legion of Honor; grand master Nat. Order of Ivory Coast; others. Address: Abidjan Ivory Coast *

HOURANI, GEORGE FADLO, educator; b. Manchester, Eng., June 3, 1913; s. Fadlo and Sumaya (Racy) H.; B.A., Oxford (Eng.) U., 1936; Ph.D., Princeton, 1939; m. Celeste Habib, June 15, 1940. Came to

U.S., 1950, naturalized, 1956. Lectr. classics and philosophy Govt. Arab Coll., Jerusalem, Palestine, 1939-48; prof. Islamic history and philosophy U. Mich., 1950-67; prof. philosophy State U. N.Y., Buffalo, 1967—. Ford Found. area research fellow, 1956- 57; Guggenheim fellow, 1963-64. Mem. Am. Oriental Soc. (asso. editor jour. 1964-70), Am. Philos. Assn., Middle East Inst., Royal Inst. Philosophy (London), Middle East Studies Assn. (pres. 1968). Author: Arab Seafaring in the Indian Ocean in Ancient and Early Medieval Times, 1951; Ethical Value, 1956; Ibn Rushd: (Averroes): Kitab fasl al-maqal, 1959; Averroes on the Harmony of Religion and Philosophy, 1961; Islamic Rationalism-The Ethics of 'Abd al-Jabbar, 1971. Home: 105 Troy Del Way Williamsville NY 14221 Office: Dept Philosophy State U NY at Buffalo Amherst NY 14226

HOURIGAN, ANDREW, Jr., lawyer; b. Wilkes-Barre, Pa., July 14, 1915; s. Andrew and Marie (Quinn) H.; B.A., Princeton, 1937; LL.B., U. Pa., 1940; m. Annette Beasley, Apr. 11, 1945; children—Kathleen, Andrew III, Annette. Admitted to Pa. bar, 1940; partner White, Rowlands & Hourigan, 1948-59, Hourigan, Kluger & Spohrer, 1959—; dir. United Penn Bank Wilkes-Barre, Bertels Metal Ware, Inc., Motor Twins, Inc. Chmn., Nat. Conf. Lawyers and Life Ins. Cos., 1968-69. Campaign chmn. Wyo. Valley Community Chest, 1954; pres. Wyo. Valley United Fund, 1958-60; vice chmn. Mideast adv. council United Community Funds and Councils Am., 1961-64; v.p. Community Services Pa., 1968—; campaign chmn. Wyo. Valley Indsl. Devel. Fund, 1960, v.p. Blue Cross of N.E. Pa., 1963—. Trustee Wilkes Coll., Luzerne County Community Coll.; bd. govs. U. Pa. Law Alumni Soc., 1959-64; Fellow Am. Bar Found., Am. Coll. Probate Counsel; mem. Am. (past chmn. unauthorized practice law com., chmn. com. on confs., Pa. State del.), Pa. (pres.), Luzerne County bar assns., Nat. Legal Aids and Defender Assn. (nat. membership chmn. 1971), Greater Wilkes-Barre C. of C. (past pres.). Republican. Roman Catholic. Club: Westmoreland (Wilkes-Barre); Princeton (N.Y.C.). Home: 1720 Wyoming Av Forty Fort Pa 18704 Office: United Penn Bank Bldg Wilkes-Barre PA 18701

HOURS-MIEDAN, MAGDELEINE, author, art historian; b Paris, France; d. Luciena and Suzanne (Ricard) Miedan; grad. l'Ecole des Louvre, Paris, 1936; grad. student history and philology, Sorbonne, Paris; m. Jacques H Hours, Jan. 10, 1935; children—Antoine, Emmanuel, Laurent. Attachee archeology Louvre Mus., Paris, 1937-47, dept. Oriental archaeology, 1940-44, chief labs., 1947—, curator Nat. Mus. France, 1945—; field trip to Africa to study monuments of cult of Tophet of Salamba, Carthage, 1945- 47; TV prod. Secrets of Masterpieces, 1959—; lectr. Europe, U.S. Decorated chevalier Legion of Honor; officiere Arts and Letters, Chevalier du Mérite pour la Recherche. Fellow Internat. Inst. Conservators (London); mem. Soc. Gens de Lettres, Rocolta Vincianna (Milan), Central Nat. de la Recherche Scientifique (maitre recherche). Catholic. Author: Carthage, 1949; A la Decouverte de la Peinture, 1958; Les secrets des chefs d'oeuvre, 1964. Home: 98 rue de Longchamp Paris 16 France Office: Musee de Louvre Paris France

HOURTOULE, GILBERT OTTO, educator, polit. scientist; b. Newark, June 25, 1924; s. Gilbert and Georgiana (Schumm) H.; A.B., Montclair State Coll., 1947; M.A., Stanford, 1948; Ph.D., Pa. State U., 1953. Instr. Montclair State Coll., 1949-51; asst. prof. Lafayette Coll., Easton, Pa., 1953-61, asst. dean coll., 1958-61; asso. prof., asst. to pres. Montclair State Coll., 1961-63, prof., 1963—, chmn. dept. polit. sci., 1968—; cons. U.S. Commn. Govt. Security, 1956. Served with USAAF, 1943-46. Mem. Am. Polit. Sci. Assn., Am. Acad. Polit. and Social Sci., N.J. Edn. Assn., Pi Sigma Alpha, Pi Gamma Mu, Kappa Delta Pi. Republican. Episcopalian. Mason. Contbr. profl. jours. Office: Montclair State Coll Upper Montclair NJ 07043

HOUSE, ARTHUR STEPHEN, educator; b. N.Y.C., May 1, 1921; B.S., Coll. City N.U., 1942; M.A., U. Denver, 1948; Ph.D. in Speech, U. Ill., 1951; married; 2 children. Instr. speech sci. U. Ill., Champaign-Urbana, 1951-52, research asso. Control Systems Lab., 1952-53; mem. staff speech communication, Acoustics Lab., Mass. Inst. Tech., 1953-57, research lab. electronics, 1959-64; asso. prof. audiology and speech pathology Syracuse U., 1957-59; prof. audiology and speech sci. Purdue U., Lafayette, Ind., 1964—. Mem. com. on hearing, bioacoustics and biomechanics Nat. Acad. Sci.-NRC, 1965-66. Served to sgt. AUS, 1942-46. Fellow Am. Speech and Hearing Assn., Am. Acoustical Soc.; mem. Am. Speech Assn. Office: Sch Elec Engring Purdue U Lafayette IN 47907*

HOUSE, CHARLES STAVER, judge; b. Manchester, Conn., Apr. 24, 1908; s. Herbert Bissell and Sophia (Staver) H.; grad. Williston Acad., 1926; A.B., Harvard, 1930, LL.B., 1933; m. Virginia Mabel Brown, Aug. 5, 1938; children— Carolyn, Arthur, Elizabeth. Admitted to Conn. bar, 1933; partner Day, Berry & Howard, Hartford, Conn., 1936-53; judge Conn. Superior Ct., 1953-65; asso. justice Conn. Supreme Ct., 1965-71, chief justice, 1971—. Dir. Manchester Savs. & Loan Assn. Chmn., Manchester Bd. Edn., 1943-53; vice chmn. Conn. Jud. Council, 1964-65, chmn., 1965—; chmn. Jud. Rev. Council, 1970—. Rep., Conn. Gen. Assembly, 1939, state senator, 1947, 49, Republican leader Senate, chmn. legislative council, 1949; asst. state's atty., 1942-46; legal adviser Gov. Lodge, 1951-53. Hon. trustee Manchester Meml. Hosp. Fellow Am. Bar Found.; mem. Am., Conn. bar assns. Conglist. Mason. Home: Westland St RFD 3 Manchester CT 06040 Office: Supreme Ct Bldg Capitol Av Hartford CT 06101

HOUSE, HERBERT OTIS, educator, chemist; b. Willoughby, O., Dec. 5, 1929; s. Otis W. and Lorraine (Watkins) H.; B.S., Miami U., 1950; Ph.D., U. Ill., 1953; m. Jean Borsick, June 18, 1951; children—Margaret Ann, Mary Ann. Instr. chemistry Mass. Inst. Tech., Cambridge, 1953-55, asst. prof., 1955-59, asso. prof., 1959-64, prof. chemistry, 1964—; cons. McNeil Labs., Union Carbide Chems. Corp. Alfred P. Sloan fellow, 1955- 59. Mem. Am. Chem. Soc. (sec. organic div. 1959—), Chem. Soc. (London, Eng.), Swiss Chem. Soc. Author numerous research publs. Home: 34 Spring Valley Rd Belmont MA 02178 Office: Chemistry Dept Mass Inst Tech Cambridge MA 02139

HOUSE, LOU, host TV program Black Jour., also dir. Council Bio-Med. Careers Tng. Program. Address: care Nat Ednl TV Network 10 Columbus Circle New York City NY 10019*

HOUSE, ROBERT WILLIAM, educator; b. Bristow, Okla., Nov. 28, 1920; s. Richard Morton and Elizabeth (Swartz) H.; B.F.A., Okla. State U., 1941; Mus.M., Eastman Sch. Music, 1942; Ed.D., U. Ill., 1954; m. Esther Jean Hawkins, June 5, 1943; children—R. Edmund, Richard M., Russell L., Kathryn M. Asst. prof. band, cello, wind instruments Neb. State Coll., Kearney, 1946-55; prof. orch., cello and music edn., chmn. music dept. U. Minn., Duluth, 1955-67; dir. Sch. Music, So. Ill. U., Carbondale, 1967—; prin. cellist Duluth Symphony, 1955-67; cons. Ednl. Testing Service, 1962-66. Served with AUS, 1942-46; ETO. Mem. Nat. Assn. Schs. of Music (panel evaluators 1960—, chmn. com. on tchr. edn. in music 1962-66, chmn. com. on ethics, 1970—), Music Educators Research Council (nat. chmn. 1958-60). Author: (with Charles Leonhard) Foundations and Principles of Music Education, 1959, rev. 1972; Instrumental Music for Today's Schools, 1965. Mem. editorial com. Jour. of Research in Music Edn., 1958-70. Home: RR 8 Box 143 Carbondale IL 62901

HOUSE, ROY C., hosp. ofcl.; b. West Liberty, O., July 11, 1917; s. Thomas C. and Myrtle (McLeland) H.; A.B., Evansville (Ind.) Coll., 1939; M.S. in Hosp. Adminstrn., Northwestern U., 1949; m. Elizabeth M. Fritschle, Sept. 11, 1942; children—David R., Janet Sue. Asst. mgr. comml. foods div. Igleheart div. Gen. Foods Corp., Evansville, Ind., 1939-47; resident in adminstrn. Meth. Hosp., Indpls., 1948-69; asst. adminstrn. Samuel Merrett Hosp., Oakland Cal., 1949-50; adminstr. Warm Springs Found. Hosp. Crippled Children, Gonzales, Tex., 1950-54, Marion (Ind.) Gen. Hosp., 1954-57; exec. v.p., chief exec. officer Wesley Med. Center, Wichita, Kan., 1957—. Preceptor, lectr. Northwestern U., 1958-62, Washington U., St. Louis, 1962—. Pres., Austin (Tex.) Hosp. Council, 1953, E. Ind. Hosp. Council, 1956, Hosp. Council Met. Wichita, 1960; pres. Kan. Blue Cross Plan, 1965-66, mem. exec. bd., 1959-66, mem. exec. com., 1963-66, treas., 1964, v.p., 1965; mem. Gov. Kan. Adv. Council Regional Med. Programs, 1965—; treas. Wesley Research Found., 1960—. Recipient Laura Jacken award outstanding grad. hosp. adminstrn. Northwestern U., 1970. Fellow Am. Coll. Hosp. Adminstrs. (regent for Kan. 1966-69, dist. gov. 1971—); mem. Am., Kan. (pres. 1968-69) hosp. assns., Tau Kappa Alpha, Pi Gamma Mu, Alpha Delta Mu. Rotarian, Mason (Shriner). Home: 7002 E 10th St Wichita KS 67206 Office: 550 N Hillside St Wichita KS 67214

HOUSE, SON, (Eddie James Son House) musician; b. Clarksdale, Miss., Mar. 21, 1902; s. James and Maggie (Burns) H.; ed. pub. schs.; m. Evie McGown, Nov. 14, 1934; 1 son by previous marriage, James. Pastor in various churches: started playing, 1927; recording artist for Paramount Records. Address: 61 Greig St Rochester NY 14608

HOUSE, WILSON M., business exec. Chmn., Eastern Express, Inc. Office: 1450 Wabash Av Terre Haute IN 47808*

HOUSEHOLD, GEOFFREY EDWARD WEST, author; b. Bristol, Eng., Nov. 30, 1900; s. Horace W. and Beatrice (Noton) J.; student Clifton Coll., Oxford U.; m. Ilona Zsoldos-Gutmán; children—Geoffrey Andrew, Nicolette Ilona, Anna Celia. Author: (novels) The Third Hour, 1937; Rogue Male, 1939, Arabesque, 1948; The High Place, 1950; A Rough Shoot, 1951; A Time to Kill, 1951; Fellow Passenger, 1955; Watcher in the Shadows, 1960; Thing To Love, 1963; Olura, 1965; The Courtesy of Death, 1967; Dance of the Dwarfs, 1968; (short stories) The Salvation of Pisco Gabar, 1938, Tales of Adventures, 1952, The Brides of Solomon, 1958, Sabres on the Sand, 1967; (autobiography) Against the Wind, 1958. Home: Church Headland Whitchurch Aylesbury England

HOUSEHOLDER, ALSTON SCOTT, educator, mathematician; b. Rockford, Ill., May 5, 1904; s. Earl and Mary (Scott) H.; B.S., Northwestern U., 1925; M.A., Cornell U., 1927; Ph.D., U. Chgo., 1937; D. Natural Sci., Munich Tech. Inst., 1965; m. Eleanor Belle Noonan, Mar. 3, 1926; children—Jaclin (Mrs. Charles E. Christian), John A. Faculty, Washburn Coll., 1930-37, asst. prof., 1931-37; Rockefeller Found. fellow U. Chgo., 1937-39, faculty, 1939-44, asst. prof., 1941-44; sr. research psychophysiologist applied psychology panel NDRC Brown U., 1944-45; math. cons. Naval Research Lab., Washington, 1945-46; sr. mathematician Oak Ridge Nat. Lab., 1946-69; prof. N. Ill. Coll. Optometry, 1940; prof. math. U. Tenn., Knoxville, 1964—. Fellow A.A.A.S., Am. Acad. Arts and Scis.; mem. Am. Math. Soc., Soc. Indsl. and Applied Math. (past pres.), Assn. Computing Machinery (past pres.), Math. Assn. Am. (past v.p.). Author: (with H.D. Landahl) Mathematical Biophysics of the Central Nervous System, 1945; Principles of Numerical Analysis, 1953; The Theory of Matrices in Numerical Analysis, 1964; The Numerical Treatment of a Single Nonlinear Equation, 1970; also numerous articles. Research in math. biology and psychology, numerical analysis. Home: 116 Cahill Lane Oak Ridge TN 37830 Office: U Tenn Dept Math Knoxville TN 37916

HOUSEL, JERRY WINTERS, lawyer; b. Cripple Creek, Colo., Aug. 9, 1912; s. James Robert and Emma (Winters) H.; B.A., U. Wyo., 1935, J.D., 1936; Ph.D., Am. U., 1941; m. Mary Elaine Bever, July 8, 1941; children—James Robert, Jerry Laine, John Ora, Peter Elliott. Amitted to Wyo. bar, 1936; practice in Laramie, Wyo., 1936; teaching fellow Am. U. Grad. Sch., 1937; asst. to U.S. Senator Schwartz, 1937-40; atty. FTC, 1941, War Relocation Authority, 1942; practiced in Cody, Wyo., 1946—. Pres., mem. Wyo. Bd. Law Examiners, 1956-70. Pres., The Bar T L, 1957—; chmn. bd. First State Bank, Cody; dir. First Nat. Bank, Meeteetse, Wyo. mem. Cody City Council, 1950. Served with USNR, 1943-46. Mem. Wyo. State Bar (pres. 1964), Cody C. of C. (pres. 1952), Am. Legion (comdr. Cody post 1951), Am. (ho. of dels. 1965-67), Park County (pres. 1950) bar assns., Am. Judicature Soc. (dir. 1967). Home: 1500 11th St Cody WY 82414 Office: Box 69 Cody WY 82414

HOUSEMAN, JOHN, producer, dir.; b. Bucarest, Rumania, Sept. 22, 1902;; s. Georges and May (Davies) H.; student Clifton Coll., Eng.; m. Joan Courtney, Dec. 1950; children—John Michael, Charles Sebastian. Theatre dir. plays Four Saints in Three Acts, 1934, Valley Forge, 1935, Hamlet, 1936, The Devil and Daniel Webster, 1938, Liberty Jones, 1939, Lutesong, 1947, King Lear, 1951, Corioianus, 1955; producer Macbeth, 1935, Dr. Faustus, 1937, Julius Caesar, 1937, Shoemaker's Holiday, 1938, Native Son, 1940, King Lear, 1964, operas Othello, 1963, Tosca, 1965, The Mines of Sulphur, 1968, Antigone, 1970, The Losers, 1971; artistic dir. Am. Shakespeare Festival, 1956-59, Profl. Theatre Group of U. Cal. at Los Angeles Extension, 1959-63; producing dir. A.P.A. Repertory Co., 1967-69, Phoenix Theatre, 1969—; dir. drama div. Juilliard Sch., N.Y.C., 1967—; producer motion pictures The Unseen, Miss Suzie Slagle's, 1944, The Blue Dahlia, 1945, They Live by Night, 1946, Letter from an Unknown Woman, 1947, The Bad and the Beautiful, 1952, Julius Caesar, 1953, Executive Suite, 1954, The Cobweb, 1955, Lust for Life, 1956, All Fall Down, 1961, Two Weeks in Another Town, 1962, The Dancer's World, 3 by Martha Graham, also (for U.S. Govt.) Tuesday in November, 1944, Voyage to America, 1964. Asso. prof. English drama Vassar Coll., 1937-38; lectr. New Sch. for Social Research, Barnard Coll., others; Regents lectr. U. Cal. at Los Angeles, 1960; Cockefair chair U. Mo., Kansas City, 1971-72. Co-founder, pres. Mercury Theatre, 1937-39; v.p. David O. Selznick Prodns., 1941; chief overseas radio program bur. OWI, 1942-43; producer Paramount Pictures, 1943-46, RKO, 1947-49, Metro-Goldwyn-Mayer, 1950-56; producer CBS-TV, 1956-59, exec. producer TV, Seven Lively Arts, 1957, Playhouse 90, 1958-59, The Great Adventure, 1963; radio editor Mercury Theatre of the Air; writer Helen Hayes Theatre. Mem. Author's League, Writers Guild, Screen Producers Guild, Actor's Equity, Nat. Theatre Conf. (pres. 1970-71), Internat. Theatre Inst. U.S. (v.p. 1968-70). Club: Century Assn. (N.Y.C.). Address: 565 S Mountain Rd New York City NY 10001

HOUSER, DONALD LEE, clergyman; b. Ruffsdale, Pa., Nov. 14, 1909; s. William P. and Mary E. (Bryan) H.; A.B., Gettysburg Coll., 1931; B.D., Mt. Airy Theol. Sem., 1935; D.D., Thiel Coll., 1949; student U. Pitts., 1934; m. Johanna K. Erickson, Aug. 30, 1939; children—William J., Joan L. Ordained to ministry Lutheran Ch., 1935; pastor Messiah Luth. Ch., Wesleyville, Pa, 1935-45; missionary supt. Pitts. Synod Luth. Ch., 1945-54; asst. sec. English mission Bd. Am. Missions, United Luth. Ch., 1954-55, sec. English missions, 1955-57, exec. sec. Bd. Am. Missions, 1958-62; exec. sec. Bd. Am. Missions, Luth. Ch. Am., 1963—. Pres. Erie Conf., Pitts. Synod Luth. Ch., 1938-41, mem. synodical bd. Am. missions, 1942-45; del. United Luth Ch. Conv., 1940, 44, 46, 48, 50, 52 56; mem. commn. 16 orgnl. structure United Luth. Ch., 1954-56. Trustee Thiel Coll., 1942- 45. Mem. Sigma Alpha Epsilon. Home: 6100 S Madison St Hinsdale IL 60521 Office: 327 S LaSalle St Chicago IL 60604

HOUSER, DOUGLAS GUY, lawyer; b. Oregon City, Ore., July 11, 1935; s. Roy B. and Shirley (Knight) H.; B.A., Willamette U., 1957; J.D., Stanford, 1960; m. Lucy Anne Latham, Sept. 1, 1961; children—Brooks Bonham, Bradley Knight, Anne Elizabeth. Admitted to Ore. bar, 1960; practice in Portland, 1961—; partner Bullivant, Wright, Johnson, Pendergrass & Hoffman, 1965—. Prosecutor, Ore. State Bar in disciplinary proceeding, 1965, chmn. com. on continuing legal edn., 1969—; asst. sec., dir. BRS, Inc., Sports- Tek, Inc. Legal adviser Portland Sch. Dist. 1 Race and Edn. Com., 1963-64; mem. Eagle bd. Columbia-Pacific council Boy Scouts Am., 1963—; chmn. lawyers sect. Multnomah County United Good Neighbors, 1970—. Vice pres., bd. dirs. Waverley Childrens Home: Recipient certificate of appreciation Sch. Dist. 1 for work on race and edn. legal subcom., 1964. Mem. Am., Ore. (plaque of appreciation 1969, bd. bar examiners 1971—), Multonomah County bar assns., Nat. Assn. R.R. Trial Counsel, Ore. Assn. Def. Counsel, Def. Research Inst., Am. Judicature Soc., Portland C. of C., Willamette U. Alumni Assn. (pres. elect, mem. exec. bd.), Beta Theta Pi, Phi Delta Phi, Omicron Delta Kappa, Pi Gamma Mu. Republican. Episcopalian. Panelist television series Legally Speaking, 1969—. Home: 2939 SE Tolman St Portland OR 97202 Office: Pacific Bldg Portland OR 97204

HOUSER, F. DOUGLASS, business exec.; b. 1905; B.S. in Mech. Engring., Princeton, 1928. With Hobart Mfg. Co., 1928—, sec., 1956-68, chief engr., 1945—, v.p., 1959—, sec. bd., 1968—, dir., 1953—. Address: Hobart Mfg Co World Headquarters Av Troy OH 45373

HOUSER, JOHN W., lawyer, former hotel exec.; b. Ames, Ia., Dec. 7, 1909; s. John Twin and Grace (Harper) H.; A.B., U. So. Cal., 1931, LL.B., 1934; m. Polly White, Mar. 27, 1937; children—Julie Margaret, John Comet. Admitted to Cal. bar, 1934; practiced with Houser, Houser and Houser, Long Beach, Cal., 1934-37; with SEC. Washington, 1937-43, becoming asst. dir., 1941, dir. utilities div., 1942; with Bd. Econ. Warfare, 1943- 44; agt. for Bell Telephone System in patent licensing matters, 1946-48; exec. v.p., dir. Hilton Hotels Internat., 1948-57; v.p. Hilton Hotels Corp., 1952-57; v.p. charge domestic and fgn. travel Am. Express Co.; cons. internat. trade and travel, 1962—; cons. Canadian Pacific Hotels, 1966—; builder, owner Young Island off St. Vicent, W.I. Spl. rep. West Africa; lt., 4th Marine Aircraft Wing, serving in Pacific as intelligence officer, 1944-45. Mem. Am. Bar Assn., Beta Theta Pi, Phi Alpha Delta. Home: PO Box 343 Sterling Forest Tuxedo NY 10987 Office: 77 Park Av New York City NY 10016

HOUSER, ROBERT NORMAN, ins. co. exec.; b. Bloomfield, Ia., Sept. 21, 1919; s. Charles B. and Venna C. (Bartholomew) H.; B.A. summa cum laude, U. Ia., 1947; m. Doris V. Miller, Dec. 18, 1943; children—Theodore Alan, Judith Eileen, James Robert. With Bankers Life Co., 1936-38, 40-43, 47—, asst. actuary, 1953- 60, asso. actuary, 1960-63, 2d v.p., actuary, 1963-68, v.p., actuary, 1968-71, v.p., chief actuary, 1971—. Served to 1st lt. USAAF, 1943-45, USAF, 1951-52. Decorated D.F.C., Air medals. Fellow Soc. Actuaries; mem. Pub. Health Nursing Assn. (bd. dirs. Des Moines), Phi Beta Kappa. Baptist (gen. conf. home mission bd.). Home: 2412 48th St Des Moines IA 50310 Office: 711 High St Des Moines IA 50307

HOUSER, THOMAS JAMES, govt. ofcl.; b. Chgo., June 28, 1929; s. Thomas and Mayme (Mikulecky) H.; student Mich. State Coll., 1947-48; A.B., Hanover Coll., 1951; postgrad. Advanced Sch. Internat. Studies, Washington, 1951-52; J.D., Northwestern U., 1959; m. JoAnn Ochsenhirt, Nov. 20, 1954; children— Deborah, Deneen, David. Admitted to Ill. bar, 1959—; practice in Chgo., 1959-69; atty. Assn. Western Rys., 1959-61; commerce counsel C.B.& Q. R.R., 1961-66; spl. counsel Sen. Charles H. Percy, 1966-67; counsel Leibman, Williams, Bennett, Baird & Minow, 1967-69; dep. dir. Peace Corps, Washington, 1969-71; commr. FCC, Washington, 1971—. Wheeling Twp. Republican committeeman, 1962- 66; chmn. Cook County Rep. Exec. Com., 1964-66; campaign mgr. for senatorial candidate Charles H. Percy, Ill., 1966. Served with U.S. Army, 1954-56. Recipient Alumni Achievement award Hanover Coll., 1970. Mem. Nat. R.R. Transp. Inst. (sec., mem. exec. com.), Am., Chgo. bar assns. Clubs: Economic, Union League (Chgo.); Federal City (Washington). Author: To Be Or Not To Be a Candidate. Home: 2231 Laurel Ridge Rd Vienna VA 22180 Office: FCC Bldg 1919 M St NW Washington DC 20554

HOUSER, WILLIAM DOUGLAS, naval officer; b. Atlanta, Nov. 11, 1921, s. Harry M. and Berenice (Horton) H.; B.S., U.S. Naval Acad., 1941; postgrad. U. Md., 1949-50, U.S. Naval War Coll., 1958-59, Harvard Bus. Sch., 1963; M.S., George Washington U., 1968; m. Betty Lou Worrall, Mar 11, 1946; children—Cynthia L., Gayle L., Francie L. Commd. ensign USN., 1941, advanced through grades to rear adm., 1966; comdr. fighter squadron Korean War and aircraft carrier U.S.S. Constellation in Viet Nam, 1966; mil. asst. to sec. def., 1962-63; mem. joint staff Joint Chiefs of Staff, 1960-62, 67-68; dir. aviation plans and requirements USN, Washington, 1968-70; comdr. Carrier Div. Two, U.S. Atlantic Fleet, 1970—. Decorated Legion of Merit with three gold stars, Bronze Star, Air Medal with gold star. Methodist. Home: 796 Woodcrest Rd Key Biscayne Miami FL 33149 Office: Carrier Div Two FPO New York City NY 09501

HOUSEWORTH, RICHARD COURT, banker; b. Harveyville, Kan., Jan. 18, 1928; s. Court Henry and Mabel (Lynch) H.; B.S., U. Kan., 1950; m. Laura Louise Jennings, Nov. 1, 1952; children-Louise, Lucile, Court. Mgmt. trainee Lawrence (Kan.) Nat. Bank, 1951-52; pres. 1st Nat. Bank, Harveyville, 1952-55; sr. v.p. Ariz. Bank, Tucson, 1955—. Vice pres. Better Bus. Bur.; bd. dirs. Pacific Coast Banking Sch. U. Wash., Barrow Neurol. Found., Phoenix. Served with U.S. Army, 1946-48. Recipient 1st Distinguished Service award Scottsdale Jr. C. of C., 1962. Mem. Robert Morris Assos. (dir. Ariz. chpt.), Tucson C. of C. (pres.), Am. Inst. Banking (past pres. Maricopa chpt.), Phi Delta Theta. Republican. Episcopalian. Rotarian. Clubs: Old Pueblo, Tucson Country (Tucson). Home: 5901 E Miramar St Tucson AZ 85715 Office: 160 N Stone Av Tucson AZ 85703

HOUSEWRIGHT, RILEY DEE, microbiologist; b. Wylie, Tex., Oct. 17, 1913; s. Jick and Lillie (Townsend) H.; B.S., N. Tex. State Coll., 1934; M.A., U. Tex., 1938; Ph.D., U. Chgo., 1944; postgrad. Cambridge (Eng.) U., 1950; m. Marjory Bryant, June 10, 1939 (dec. July 1962); 1 son, Kim Bryant; m. 2d, Artemis Skevakis Jegart, Aug. 1969. Pub. sch. tchr., Tex., 1934-36; instr. S.W. Tex. State Coll., also in San Marcos, Tex., 1937-41; chief microbial physiology and chemotherapy br., Ft. Detrick, Md., 1946-50, dep. chief, chief med. bacteriology div., 1950-56, sci. dir. U.S. Army Biol. Labs., 1956-70; v.p., sci. dir. Microbiol. Assos. Inc., Bethesda, Md., 1970—. Mem. adv. com. to sci. dir. Inst. Microbiology, Rutgers U., 1959-67; mem. panel on regulatory biology NSF, 1967-70. Bd. assos. Hood Coll., Frederick, Md. Served to lt. (j.g.) USNR, 1944-46; capt. Res. ret. U.

Chgo. fellow, 1941-42; John and Mary E. Markle fellow, 1942-43; scholarship Am. Mgmt. Assn., 1957; recipient U.S. Patent awards, 1959; Meritorious Civilian Service award Dept. Army, 1962, 64; Distinguished Alumni citation N. Tex. State U., 1965; Exceptional Civilian Service award Dept. of Army, 1968. Diplomate Am. Bd. Microbiology. Fellow Am. Acad. Microbiology, A.A.A.S., N.Y. Acad. Scis.; mem. Am. Soc. Microbiology (pres. 1965-66, Barnett E. Cohen award Md. br. 1967), Soc. Gen. Microbiology (Eng.), Soc. Exptl. Biology and Medicine, Research Soc. Am. Club: Cosmos (Washington). Author chpts. in book, articles. Editor Bacteriol. Proc., 1957-59. Home: 147 Fairview Av Frederick MD 21701 Office: 4733 Bethesda Av Bethesda MD 20014

HOUSEWRIGHT, WILEY LEE, educator; b. Wylie, Tex., Oct. 17, 1913; s. Jick and Lillie (Townsend) H.; B.S., N. Tex. State U., 1934; M.A., Columbia, 1938; Ed.D., N. Y. U., 1943; m. Lucilla Elizabeth Gumm, Dec. 27, 1939. Dir. music pub. schs., Tex., N.Y., 1934-41; lectr. music N.Y. U., 1942-43; asst. prof. U. Tex., 1946-47; faculty Fla. State U., Tallahassee, 1947—, prof. music, 1948—, Distinguished prof., 1961-62, dean Sch. Music, 1966—. Vis. summer prof. U. Mich., 1960, U. Ind., 1955; Fulbright scholar, Japan, 1956-57. Mem. U.S. nat. com. for UNESCO, 1958; music adv. panel internat. cultural presentations program State Dept., 1958—; adv. bd. humanities and arts Ford Found., 1958—. Served to 1st lt. AUS, 1943-46. Decorated Distinguished Service citation. Ford Found. grantee, 1966-68. Recipient Distinguished Alumni citation No. Tex. State U., 1967. Mem. Music Educators Nat. Conf. (pres. 1968-70), Am. Musicological Soc., Music Tchrs. Nat. Assn., Internat. Soc. Music Edn., Music Library Assn., Pi Kappa Lambda, Phi Delta Kappa, Phi Mu Alpha. Editor: Birchard Music Series, vols. I-VI, 1962; chmn. editorial bd. Music Educators Jour., 1957-66; editorial asso. Jour. Research Music Edn., 1953-62, choral music rev. editor, 1955-57. Home: 515 South Ride Tallahassee FL 32303

HOUSH, CHARLES LEIGHTON, newspaper editor; b. Des Moines, Oct. 19, 1911; s. Charles A. and Madeleine (Ghormley) H.; B.A., Drake U., 1932; m. Alice Elizabeth Harter, Sept. 5, 1933; children—David Leighton, Cynthia Helen. Mem. staff Des Moines Register & Tribune, 1932—, exec. sports editor, 1947-65, sports editor, 1965—. Mem. Drake Relays Com., 1953—. Served to lt. USNR, World War II. Mem. Sigma Delta Chi, Alpha Tau Omega. Conglist. (bd. deacons 1966-68). Club: Embassy. Home: 5828 Pleasant Dr Des Moines IA 50212 Office: Register & Tribune Des Moines IA 50309

HOUSKA, CHARLES ROBERT, educator; b. Cleve., May 16, 1927; s. Charles and Anna (Gehrke) H.; S.B. in Physics, Mass. Inst. Tech., 1951, S.M. in Metallurgy, 1954, Sc.D. in Metallurgy, 1957; m. Mary Frances Dittmer, Aug. 20, 1953; children—Catherine Mary, Robert Bradford, Susan Sanford. Mem. research staff dept. physics Mass. Inst. Tech., 1951-52, dept. metallurgy, 1957-59; mem. research staff Union Carbide Research Inst., Tarrytown, N.Y., 1959-63; asso. prof. Va. Poly. Inst. and State U. at Blacksburg, 1963-65, prof., 1965-69, prof., head metals and ceramic engring., 1969—. Served with USNR, 1945-46. Mem. Am. Inst. Mining, Metall. and Petroleum Engrs., Am. Crystallographic Assn., Sigma Xi, Alpha Sigma Mu. Contbr. articles profl. jours. Home: Route 3 Box 64 Blacksburg VA 24060

HOUSMAN, KENNETH ALFRED, r.r. exec.; b. N.Y.C., Nov. 16, 1925; s. A.J. and Ruth (Sorely) H.; diploma Mt. Hermon (Mass.) Sch., 1943; B.A. cum laude, Harvard, 1947; m. Patricia Eagan, July 31, 1949; children—Jeffrey, Pamela Ann. Engaged in efficiency study for Govt. Cal., 1965-67; mgr. pub. affairs Union Carbide Corp., 1967-69; asst. postmaster gen. for personnel Post Office Dept., 1969-71; v.p. Amtrak-Nat. R.R. Passenger Corp., Washington, 1971—. Mem. Am. Philatelic Soc., Soc. Bur. Issues Assn. Mason. Home: 7104 Arrowood Rd Bethesda MD 20034 Office: 955 L'Enfant Plaza Washington DC 20024

HOUSSAY, BERNARDO ALBERTO, sci. investigator; b. Buenos Aires, Argentina, Apr. 10, 1887; s. Alberto and Clara (Lafont) H.; Pharmacist, 1904; M.D., Buenos Aires, 1911; Dr. Honoris causa in medicine, univs. of Paris, 1935, Montreal, 1946, Lyon, 1946, Geneva, 1946, Asución, 1943, Catholic of Chile, 1942, Montevideo, 1948, Brussels, Catholic of Louvain, 1949, Strasbourg, 1949, also Düsseldorf, Montpellier, Alger, Brazil, Venezuela, Salamonco; hon. degrees in scis., Harvard, 1936, Saõ Paulo, 1936, Oxford, 1947, Mexico, Toronto, Columbia, N.Y., Cambridge, 1961; L.H.D., Georgetown U.; LL.D., U. Glasgow; Dr. honoris causa med. scis., U. Orienta; Dr. honoris causa chemistry, U. Nacional del Sud; m. Maria Angelica Catán, Dec. 22, 1920; children—Alberto Bernardo, Héctor Emilio José, Rául Horacio. Prof. physiology Vet. Faulty, Buenos Aires, 1910-19, Faculty Medical Scis., 1919-43, 45-46, 55-57; hon. prof. faculties of med. univs. of Montevideo, Santiago, Bogota, Lima, Brazil, Bahia, Porto Alegre, Recife, La Habana, Concepcion (Chile), Venezuela, Minas Gerais, San Carlos, de Guatemala, Vet. Sch., Buenos Aires and Lima; faculty sci., Lima; Hitchcock prof. U. Cal., 1948; formerly research prof. physiology Faculty Med. Scis., Buenos Aires, now dir. Inst. Biology and Exptl. Medicine. Decorated Order Merit of Chile, grand officer Order Merit (Italy), Order Belgian Crown, grand cross Order Merit of Germany, Isabel la Catolica, comdr. Legion of Honor, officer Order of Leopold, Order de San Gregorio Magno (Vatican), Gran Cruz al merito con placa de la Orden Militar Soberanade Malta, gran oficial Order Holandesa de Orange y Nassua, segunda clase Orden Sol Naciente del Japan; also numerous other decorations and awards; recipient Nat. Award Scis., Buenos Aires, 1923; Banting medal Am. Diabetes Association, 1946; research award Am. Pharm. Mfrs. Assn., 1947; Baly medal Royal Coll. Physicians London, 1947; Nobel prize for physiology and medicine, 1947; James Cook medal, Sidney, 1948; Dale medal Soc. for Endocrinology, London; Weizmann prize in scis. and humanities. Charles Mickle fellow, Toronto, 1945. Fgn. asso. mem. Nat. Acad. Scis. (U.S.), Royal Soc. London, Am. Philos. Soc., Swedish Acad. Scis., Acad. Medicine Paris, Acad. Sci. Paris, Deutsche Akademie für Naturforschung, Royal Acad. Medicine Belgium, Academia Nazionale dei Lincei (Italy), Academia Inst. Egypt, Ciencias Exactas, Fisicas y Naturales Lima; hon. mem. acads. medicine of Rio de Janeiro, Madrid, Mexico, N.Y., Lombardia, Bogota, Washington, Am. Physiol. Soc. (Gt. Britain), Italian Soc. Physiology, Royal Soc. Edinburgh, Harvey Soc. N.Y., Mus de la Plata Argentina, Acad. Scis. Cordoba, numerous sci. socs.; pres. Argentine Soc. Biology; past pres. Argentine Assn. Advancement Sci., Nat. Acad. Medicine Buenos Aires, Internat. Union Philosophy of Scis. Physiology and Pharmacology Soc. Israel, Weizmann Inst. Scis., Assn. Am. Physicians. Author numerous sci. papers. Home: Viamonte 2790 Buenos Aires Argentina Office: Obligado 2490 Buenos Aires Argentina

HOUSTON, BENJAMIN FRANKLIN, investment banker; b. McKinney, Tex., Jan. 14, 1905; s. Dick Frank and Maggie (Furr) H.; student Okla. State U., 1924-26, U. Tex., 1927; m. Mary McClevey, June 10, 1930; 1 dau., Nancy (Mrs. Fortson). Vice pres. Dallas Union Trust Co., 1936-58; pres. Dallas Union Securities Co., Inc., 1958-66; vice chmn. bd. Rotan Mosle-Dallas Union, Inc., 1966—. Mem. N.Y., Am., Midwest stock exchanges. Served to lt. USNR, 1942-44. Mem. Investment Bankers Assn. (vice chmn. Tex. 1958-59, chmn. 1959-60, gov. Tex. group 1963-66) Kappa Alpha, Alpha Kappa Psi. Clubs: Country, Petroleum, City. Office: 1st Nat Bank Bldg Dallas TX 75202

HOUSTON, BRYAN, ret. business exec.; b. San Antonio, Tex., Aug. 26, 1899; s. Reagan and Martha (Green) H.; student U. Tex., 1920-21; m. Ruth Hamilton, 1926; children—Ruth, Betty; m. 2d, Shirley Deal, 1936; m. 3d, Barbara Mack, 1954. Service sta. operator Magnolia Petroleum Co., San Antonio, Tex., 1916-17, Stillman, Pa., 1921-22; cost accountant Tidewater Oil Co.; asst. sales mgr., Standard Oil Co. (Ohio), Cleve., 1930-35; pres. Houston and Wishar, cons., Cleve. 1935-36; v.p. Young and Rubicam, Inc., New York City, 1936-46; exec. v.p., gen. sales mgr. Pepsi-Cola Co., Long Island City, N.Y., 1946-48, dir. information Econ. Adminstrn., Washington, 1948; became exec. v.p. Sherman and Marquette, Inc., 1950; former chmn. bd. Bryan Houston, Inc., N.Y.C.; chmn. bd. Fletcher Richards Co., Inc. until 1971. Served in USN, 1917-19; served as asst. dir. purchases div. Army Service Forces, Washington, 1942-43; asst. dir. for contract terminations, 1943; asst. dir. for property disposal, readjustment div., 1944; dep. dir. for rationing OPA, Washington, 1943-44; asst. dir. Bur. Pub. Relations, War Dept., 1944-45. Republican. Episcopalian. Clubs: Sleepy Hollow Country; Army-Navy (Washington). Home: 734 Sleepy Hollow Rd Briarcliff Manor NY 10510

HOUSTON, CHARLES SNEAD, physician, educator; b. N.Y.C., Aug. 24, 1913; s. Oscar Remple and Nellie Snead (Macdonald) H.; A.B., Harvard, 1935; M.D., Columbia, 1939; m. Dorcas Tiemeyer, July 2, 1941; children—Dorcas Scott, Robin Macdonald, David Lewis Ruffner. Intern medicine Presbyn. Hosp., N.Y.C. 1939-41; practiced, Exeter, N.H., 1947-56, Aspen, Colo., 1957-62; mem. staff Exeter Hosp., Manchester VA Hosp., 1947-56, Valley View Hosp., Pitkin County Hosp., 1956-62; dir. for India, Peace Corps, 1962-64, spl. asst. to dir. charge med. program devel., Washington, 1965-66; prof., chmn. dept. community medicine Coll. Medicine, U. Vt., Burlington, 1966—. Mem. Gov's Commn. Environmental Quality, 1969, Vt. Perticide Adv. Council, 1970. Spl. research high altitude tng., acclimatization to heights; co-leader Brit.-Am. Himalayan Expdn., 1936; leader 1st and 3d Am. expdns. to K-2, 1938, 53; first Am. reconnaissance Mt. Everest, 1950; dir. Mt. Logan High Altitude Physiology Project, 1968—. Served to comdr. USNR, 1941-46; flight surgeon. Diplomate Am. Bd. Internal Medicine. Fellow A.C.P. Author: (with Robert H. Bates, others) Five Miles High, 1939; (with Robert H. Bates) K- 2 The Savage Mountain, 1954. Home: 77 Ledge Rd Burlington VT 05401

HOUSTON, CLIFFORD GRANVILLE, ednl. psychologist; b. Sugar City, Colo., Mar. 5, 1903; s. Elmer Grey and Bertha Maude (Ellis) H.; A.B., A.M., Ph.D., U. Colo.; student Columbia, 1930, 1936; m. Shirley Laura Sickenberger, June 14, 1931; children—Jerry Lee, Barrie Kent. Pub. sch. tchr., 1921-23; instr. psychology and edn., jr. coll., 1929-31; pres. jr. coll., prof. psychology and edn., 1931-37; dir. div. of extension and adult edn. U. Colo., Boulder, 1937-47, dean of summer quarter and prof. of edn., 1939-47, dean of students and dir. student personnel, 1947-57, prof. edn., 1957—, dir. summer sessions, 1950-55. Served as comdr. USNR; officer in charge selection requirements, Bur. Naval Personnel. Mem. Am. Coll. Personnel Assn., Am. Psychol. Assn., Kappa Delta Pi, Phi Delta Kappa, Kappa Sigma. Home: 3840 Armer Dr Boulder CO 80303

HOUSTON, EDWARD J., lawyer; b. 1918; B.A., U. Toronto, 1947; degree in law, Osgoode Hall, 1950. Admitted to Ont. bar, 1950; partner firm Soloway, Wright, Houston, McKimm, Killern, Greenberg & Citron, Ottawa, Ont., Can. Apptd. Queen's Counsel, 1961. Mem. Canadian Bar Assn., County Carleton Law Assn., Advocates Soc. Ont. (v.p. 1968-70). Office: 170 Metcalfe St Ottawa 4 Ontario Canada*

HOUSTON, HOWARD EDWIN, govt. ofcl.; b. Ia., Nov. 2, 1910; s. Frederick L. and Ida C. (Woodard) H.; A.B., Columbia, 1932; m. Frances G. Crawford, Sept. 9, 1939; children—Frederick W., Molly C. Dir. Bradley Home, Meriden, Conn., 1935-54; dep. dir. U.S. Tech. Coop. Mission to India, 1955-56, minister- dir., 1957-59; dir. econ. affairs, dir. AID, Am. embassy, Seoul, Korea, 1970—. Dir. Meriden Trust and Safe Deposit Co., Meriden Savs. Bank; mem. asso. bd. Conn. Bank and Trust Co. Chmn. Gov. Conn. Commn. Med. Edn., 1952; commr. welfare, Conn., 1953-54. Mayor, Meriden, 1948-51, 62-63. Bd. dirs. Meriden Hosp. Chmn. India com. Asia Soc., 1961; v.p. World Edn., Inc., 1964. Mem. Republican State Central Com., 1960-66; del. Conn. Constl. Conv., 1965. Trustee Colby Jr. Coll.; corporator Marine Biol. Lab., Woods Hole, Mass. Served from pvt. to 1st lt., AUS, 1943-46; PTO; capt. Res. Mem. Meriden Music Assn. (past pres.), Psi Upsilon (past pres. Lambda chpt.). Republican. Episcopalian. Clubs: University (N.Y.C.); Hartford (Conn.); Home, Rotary (past pres.) (Meriden); Woods Hole (Mass.) Golf; Quissett (Mass.) Yacht; Shuttle Meadow (Conn.) Country. Home: Preston Notch Farm Meriden CT 06450 also Quissett Harbor Woods Hole MA 02543 also 16 Sutton Pl New York City NY 10022 Office: Am Embassy Seoul Korea

HOUSTON, HOWARD EDWIN, govt. ofcl.; b. Ryan, Ia., Nov. 2, 1910; s. Frederick L. and Ida (Woodard) H.; A.B., Columbia, 1932; m. Frances Gregory Crawford, Sept. 9, 1939; children—Frederick Woodard, Molly Crawford. Dir. Bradley Home, Meriden, Conn., 1935-54; commr. pub. welfare State Conn., 1953-54; dep. dir. U.S. tech. cooperation mission to India, 1955-56, minister dir., 1957-59; dir. AID/Korea, econ. counselor Am. embassy, Seoul, Korea, 1970-71; minister, dir. AID mission to India, 1971—. Dir. Meriden Trust & Safe Deposit Co., Central Bank for Savs., Meriden; mem. asso. bd. Conn. Bank & Trust Co., Meriden. Chmn. Gov.'s Com. on Med. Edn., 1952; v.p. World Edn., 1964. Mayor, Meriden, 1948-51, 62-63; mem. Conn. Republican Central Com., 1960-66; del. Conn. Constl. Conv., 1965. Bd. dirs. Meriden Hosp.; mem. corp. Marine Biol. Lab., Woods Hole, Mass.; trustee Colby Jr. Coll., New London, N.H. Served to 1st lt. AUS, 1943-46; PTO. Mem. Asia Soc. (chmn. India com. 1961), Inst. Social Scis., Fgn. Policy Assn., Psi Upsilon. Republican. Episcopalian. Rotarian. Clubs: Woods Hole (Mass.) Golf; Quissett Mass. Yacht (Woods Hole); Shuttle Meadow Golf (Ct.); Home (New Britain, Conn.); Hartford; University (N.Y.C.). Home: Preston Notch Farm Meriden CT 06450

HOUSTON, JAMES GARFIELD, lawyer; b. Pitts., Sept. 22, 1881; s. James Wilson and Sarah (McCutcheon) H.; A.B., U. Pitts., 1903, LL.B., 1906, M.A., 1918, L.L.D., 1956; m. Grace Preston, June 30, 1926. Admitted to Pa. bar, 1906; pvt. practice law, Pitts., 1906—; partner Blaxter, O'Neill & Houston, 1937—. Asso. prof. law U. Pitts., 1912-38. Served as maj., asst. adj. 18th Inf. Div., U.S. Army, 1917-18. Mem. Allegheny County (pres. 1950- 51), Am., Pa. bar assns., Phi Delta Theta, Phi Delta Phi. Presbyn. (trustee). Club: Duquesne. Home: 116 Bayard Pl Pittsburgh PA 15213 Office: 1 Oliver Plaza Pittsburgh PA 15222

HOUSTON, JOE BENNETT, lawyer; b. Clarksville, Ark., Sept. 14, 1901; s. Arthur P. and Selma Houston; m. Aug. 12, 1923; children—Patricia J. (Mrs. Charles H. Ostrander), Robert A. Admitted to Okla. bar, 1928, since practiced in Tulsa; mem. firm Houston, Klein and Davidson, 1945—; judge pro tem Probate Ct., summer term; spl. justice Okla. Supreme Ct., 1948. Sec.-treas., gen. counsel, dir. Gt. Yellowstone Corp. Mem. Am., Okla, Tulsa County bar assns., Tulsa C. of C. (pres. govtl. affairs com. 1952, 53, chmn. com. to study new form of city govt. 1954), Am. Coll. Probate Counsel (mem. bd. 1948—, pres. 1952- 55). Clubs; Tulsa, Tulsa Country. Home: 4221 E 40th Pl Tulsa OK 74135 Office Drew Bldg Tulsa OK 74103

HOUSTON, JOHN ALBERT, educator; b. Spokane, Dec. 24, 1914; s. John Alexander and Ethel (Robinson) H.; A.B. in Econs., Stanford, 1936, M.A. in Internat. Relations, 1947; Ph.D. in polit. sci., U. Mich., 1951; m. Marjorie Anne Robinson, Aug. 14, 1939 (dec. Sept. 1968); children—Alexandra Louise (Mrs. Lee Benham), John Alexander II, Ann Celeste; m. 2d, Pollyanna Turner, Nov. 1, 1969. Ins. broker Johnson & Higgins, San Francisco, 1936-37; case aide Cal. Relief Adminstrn., 1938-40; asst., then asso. prof. polit. sci. U. Miss., 1949-54, faculty Knox Coll., Galesburg, Ill., 1954—, prof. polit. sci., 1957—, Philip Sydney Post distinguished prof., 1961—. Sec.-treas. Midwest Collegiate Athletic Conf., 1961—. Mem. Galesburg Planning Commn., 1956-57. Served to lt. comdr. USNR, 1941- 45. Social Sci. Research Council fellow, 1956. Mem. Am. Polit. Sci. Assn., Midwest Conf. Polit. Scientists, Omicron Delta Kappa, Pi Sigma Alpha, Scabbard and Blade, Sigma Alpha Epsilon. Author: Latin America in the United Nations, 1956. Book rev. editor Midwest Jour. Polit. Sci., 1962-65. Home: 191 Fair Acres Dr Galesburg IL 61401

HOUSTON, JOHN COATES, Jr., bus. exec.; b. Paterson, N.J., Jan. 17, 1909; s. John Coates and Elizabeth (Sullivan) H.; student Phillips Andover Acad., 1923-27; student Yale, 1927-29; m. Elizabeth Ellis, Feb. 25, 1929. Asso. with Fed. Water Service Corp. subsidiary cos.: asst. mgr. Rochester (N.Y.) & Lake Ontario Water Co., 1929-30; asst. mgr. Chester (Pa.) Water Co., 1930-31; asst. v.p. Western N.Y. Water Co., Buffalo, 1931-37; treas. R.P. Adams Co., Inc., Buffalo, 1937-42; held various positions then dir. Program Controls Bur., WPB, Washington, 1942-45, Civilian Prodn. Adminstrn., Washington, 1945-47; chmn. nat. prodn. urgency com., World War II, mem. com. appointed to advise on plans and policies of reconversion period; v.p. Stacom Industries, Inc., L.I., N.Y., 1948-50; asst. to asst. to pres., The White House, Washington, 1950-51; exec. vice chmn. Munitions Bd., 1952, acting chmn., 1953; adviser on mil. procurement Hoover Commn. on Fed. Govt. Orgn., 1954-55; indsl. cons., 1955; pres. Frederick Electronics Corp. (Md.). Home: Spring Rise Farm Lewistown MD 21701 Office: Frederick MD 21701

HOUSTON, MAX DALE, hotel chain exec.; b. Ottumwa, Ia., Nov. 21, 1921; s. Claud Francis and Stella (Bodkins) H.; student Northwestern U., 1939-40; m. Betty Marie Spang, Sept. 7, 1946; children—Daniel, Michael, David, Mary, Timothy, Teresa. With Pick Hotels Corp., 1951—, v.p., 1969—, v.p., gen. mgr. Pick-Fort Shelby Hotel Co., Detroit, 1966—. Trustee Chgo. Hotel Employees Pension Trust, Chgo. Employees Health and Welfare Plan. Served with USAAF, 1942-45; ETO. Decorated D.F.C., Air Medal with 6 oak leaf clusters; Mem. Detroit Hotel Assn. (pres. 1969), Mich. Hotel Assn. (1st dist. v.p. 1967-69), Detroit C. of C., Am. Hotel and Motel Assn., Detroit Conv. Bur., Am. Legion, Econ. Club Detroit. K.C. Address: Pick-Fort Shelby Hotel 525 W Lafayette St Detroit MI 48226

HOUSTON, NORMAN OLIVER, ins. co. exec.; b. San Jose, Cal., Oct. 16, 1893; s. Oliver James and Lilian L. Houston; ed. U. Cal. At Berkeley, U. So. Cal.; LL.D., Bethune- Cookman Coll., 1951, Wilberforce U., 1951; m. Edythe A. Pryce; children—Norman B., Ivan J., Elizabeth Jean. Co-founder, dir. Golden State Mut. Life Ins. Co., Los Angeles, 1925—, controller, 1945-49, pres., 1945-66, chmn. bd., bd., 1967—; Mem. Town Hall, Los Angeles; mem. Joint Com. on Urban Problems. Bd. dirs. World Affairs Council, S.W. Community Hosp., Crippled Children Soc., Children's Home Soc., Internat. Student Center, Los Angeles, Internat. Exec. Service Corps, Nat. Recreation and Park Assn.; v.p., bd. dirs. Nat. Conf. Christians and Jews; bd. mgrs. Los Angeles YMCA. Served to lt. 92d Div., U.S. Army, 1917-19; AEF in France. Mem. Am. Mgmt. Assn., Life Office Mgmt. Assn. Inst. (asso.), Ins. Accounting and Statis. Assn., Nat. Ins. Assn. (pres. 1950-52), Los Angeles Urban League, Cal. State C. of C. (dir.), Am. Legion (past comdr.), V.F.W., Kappa Alpha Psi, Sigma Pi Phi. Mem. A.M.E. Ch. (trustee). Home: 4230 Parva Av Los Angeles CA 90027 Office: 1999 W Adams Blvd Los Angeles CA 90018

HOUSTON, RALPH HUBERT, educator; b. Lewisville, Tex., June 17, 1910; s. Moses Walter and Pearl (Stover) H.; B.A., North Tex. State U., 1930; M.A., U. Tex., 1934, Ph.D., 1946; m. Francys McNew, Dec. 25, 1933; 1 dau., Susan (Mrs. William G. Reid). Tchr., Big Spring (Tex.) pub. schs., 1930-36; asst. prof. English Southwest Tex. State U., 1937-41, asso. prof., 1941-46, prof., 1946—, chmn. dept. English, 1958-65, dean Sch. Liberal and Fine Arts, 1965-70. Served to maj. USAAF, 1942-46, USAF, 1950-52. Mem. Modern Language Assn., Am. Assn. U. Profs. Tex. Conf. Coll. Teachers of English (pres. 1967), Tex. Folklore Soc. (pres. 1971). Episcopalian. Home: 217 W Wood St San Marcos TX 78666

HOUSTON, ROBERT STROUD, educator; b. Monroe, N.C., May 11, 1923; s. Robert Stroud and Mary (Rawlins) H.; B.Engring., N.C. State U., 1948; M.S., 1950; Columbia, Ph.D., 1954; m. Maxine Mary Brand, June 19, 1952; 1 dau., Kelly Ann. Geol. engr. Atlantic Refining Co., 1948-49; geologist TVA-N.C. Dept. Constrn. Devel., 1949-50; mem. faculty U. Wyo., 1953—, prof. econ. geology, head dept., 1967—; geologist U.S. Geol. Survey, 1953-57, 67—, Geol. Survey Wyo., 1957-64. Served with USAAF, 1942-45. Fellow Geol. Soc. Am.; mem. Am. Assn. Petroleum Geology, Soc. Econ. Geologist, Am. Geophys. Union, Soc. Econ. Paleontologists and Mineralogists, Wyo. Geol. Assn., Sigma Xi, Tau Beta Phi. Author papers in field. Home: 1410 Sublette St Laramie WY 72070

HOUSTON, VICTOR MONTGOMERY, educator; b. Marionville, Mo., Apr. 11, 1903; s. Alfred Traugett and Louise (Wissman) H.; B.S., U. Mo., 1926, M.A., 1930; Ed.D., Columbia, 1936; m. Jo Rickman, June 5, 1927. Pub. sch. tchr., adminstr., 1922-35; asso. prof. edn. Ill. State Normal U., 1936-43, prof., head dept. edn., 1943-45, prin. U. High Sch., 1945-50, head dept. edn. and psychology, dir. div. secondary edn., 1950-52; chmn. div. edn. and psychology, coordinator summer session and extension Chico (Cal.) State Coll., 1952-55, dean ednl. services and summer sessions, 1955-68, prof. edn., 1968—. Cons. ednl. groups on curriculum problems and community devel., Ill., Mo., Cal.; asso. dir. Ill. Secondary Curriculum Program, 1947-50. Mem. Cal. Secondary Sch. Adminstrs., Nat. Assn. Secondary Sch. Prins., Phi Delta Kappa, Kappa Delta Pi. Methodist. Rotarian. Contbr. articles profl. periodicals. Home: 844 Arbutus Av Chico CA 95926

HOUSTON, WILLIAM VERMILLION, former univ. ofcl.; b. Mt. Gilead, O., Jan. 19, 1900; s. William and Lena May (Vermillion) H.; B.A., Ohio State U., 1920, B.S. in Edn., 1920, Ph.D., 1925, D.Sc., 1950; S.M., U. Chgo., 1922; LL.D., U. Cal., 1956; m. Mildred Harriet White, June 6, 1924; 1 dau., Harriet Anne (Mrs. Harold Coley). Nat. research fellow Cal. Inst. Tech., 1925-27, asst. prof. physics, 1927-31, prof., 1931-46; dir. spl. studies div. war research Columbia, 1942-46; pres. Rice Inst., 1946-61; chancellor Rice U., Houston, 1961, hon. chancellor, 1961—. Vis. prof. Rockefeller Inst., 1963—. Mem. bd. NSF. Guggenheim fellow, 1927-28 Mem. Am. Acad. Arts and Scis., Nat. Acad. Scis., Am., Tex. philos. socs., Am. Phys. Soc., Phi Beta

Kappa, Sigma Xi, Tau Beta Pi. Republican. Presbyn. Clubs: Cosmos; Bayou (Houston). Author: Principles of Mathematical Physics, 1934; Principles of Quantum Mechanics, 1951. Contbr. articles to Phys. Rev.

HOUSTON, WINFREY DAVID, lawyer; b. Stillwater, Okla., June 1, 1926; s. Oscar D. and Lillian (Holbrook) H.; B.A., Okla. State U., 1948; J.D., Okla. U., 1950; m. Barbara Ann Lowrey, Nov. 26, 1950; children—Ann Carol, David L., Nancy C., Mary L. Admitted to Okla. bar, 1950, since practiced Stillwater; partner Fitzgerald, Houston & Worthington, 1967—. Served with USAAF, 1944-46; ETO. Named Outstanding Young Man of Year, Jr. C. of C., 1962. Mem. Am. (com. law office mgmt. gen. practice sect. 1969—, ho. dels., 1968-70, conferee 1st conf. problems effecting practice of law, gen. practice sect. 1969), Okla. (pres. 1969), Payne County (pres. 1956) bar assns., Okla. Bar Found. (patron). Presbyn. (elder 1964-67). Club: Lion. Home: 2205 W 4th Av Stillwater OK 74074 Office: 111 W 8th Av Stillwater OK 74074

HOUTCHENS, BARNARD, lawyer; b. Johnstown, Colo., Aug. 5, 1911; s. Everet Harrison and Evelyn Mary (Barnard) H.; B.A., U. Neb., 1933, LL.B., 1935; LL.D., U. No. Colo. at Greeley, 1963; m. Margaret Belle Colvin, Dec. 27, 194O; children—John Barnard, Marilyn (dec.). Admitted to Colo. bar, 1935, since practiced in Greeley; city atty. Greeley, 1941-47, 49-50. Pres. bd. dirs. United Bank, Greeley; dir. Meroco Broadcasting Co., Noffsinger Mfg. Co., Wilshire Land Co., Miner & Miner Cons. Engrs., Inc. (all Greeley). Mem. bar com. Colo. Bd. Law Examiners, 1948—. Trustee State Colls. Colo., 1948-65, pres. bd., 1964-65; nat. sec.-treas. Assn. Gov. Bds. State Univs. and Allied Instns., 1960-62. Fellow Am. Coll. Trial Lawyers; mem. Am., Colo., Weld County (pres. 1946-47) bar assns., Greeley Jr. (life), Greeley (pres. 1951-52) chambers commerce, Blue Key, Sigma Chi. Rotarian, Elk (past exalted ruler Greeley), Mason. Home: 814 19th St Greeley CO 80631 Office: 1007 9th Av Greeley CO 80631

HOUTHAKKER, HENDRIK SAMUEL, educator; b. Amsterdam, Netherlands, Dec. 31, 1924; s. Bernard and Marion (Lichtenstein) H.; D.Econs., U. Amsterdam, 1949; m. Anna-Teresa Tymieniecka, Sept. 8, 1955; children—Louis, Isabella, Jan Nicolas. Came to U.S., 1951, naturalized, 1966. Mem. research staff dept. applied econs. U. Cambridge (Eng.), 1949-51; research staff Cowles Commn. Research Econs., U. Chgo., 1952-53; from acting asso. prof. to prof. econs. Stanford, 1954-60; prof. econs. Harvard, 1960—. Sr. staff economist Council Econ. Advisers, 1967-68, now mem. council, 1969—; vis. prof. U. Tokyo, 1955, Mass. Inst. Tech., 1957-58; cons. U.S. Treasury Dept., 1961-67. Bd. dirs. Netherlands-Am. Found. Fellow Econometric Soc. (pres. 1967), Am. Statis. Assn.; mem. Am. Econ. Assn. (John Bates Clark medal 1963), Internat. Statis. Inst., Am. Acad. Arts and Scis., Royal Netherlands Acad. Scis. Author: (with S.J. Prais) The Analysis of Family Budgets, 1955; (with Lester D. Taylor) Consumer Demand in the United States, 1966, 70; Economic Policy for the Farm Sector, 1967. Contbr. articles to profl. jours. Editor: Rev. of Econs. and Statistics, 1971—. Home: 348 Payson Rd Belmont MA 02178 Office: Littauer Center Harvard U Cambridge MA 02138*

HOUZE, ROBERT ALVIN, librarian; b. Buffalo, Apr. 10, 1918; s. Herbert Alvin and Ruth (Best) H.; A.B., U. Denver, 1940, B.S. in Library Sci., 1941; M.S., Tex. A. and M. U., 1969; m. Mary Myrtle Payne, Oct. 14, 1944; children—Robert A., Martha Jane. Order librarian U. Denver, 1941-42; librarian vet. Colo. A. and M. Coll., 1942; librarian Longmont (Colo.) Pub. Library, 1945-46; acquisitions librarian U. Tex., 1946-49; acting librarian Tex. A. and M. U., 1949-51, librarian, 1951-58, library dir., 1958-65; dir. libraries Trinity U., San Antonio, 1965—. Vis. lectr. library sci. Tex. Woman's U., summers 1966, 70, 71; library cons. Served with F.A., U.S. Army, 1942-45. Mem. Am., Tex., Southwestern, Bexar County (pres. 1967-68) library assns., Tex. Consortium for Microfilming, Mexican Archival Resources (pres. 1969-71), Council Research and Acad. Libraries San Antonio (pres. 1968- 69). Presbyn. Rotarian (past pres.). Contbr. to Tex. Library Jour. Address: Library Trinity U 715 Stadium Dr San Antonio TX 78212

HOVDE, CARL FREDERICK, coll. dean; b. Meadville, Pa., Oct. 11, 1926; s. Bryn J. and Theresse (Arneson) H.; B.A., Columbia, 1950; M.A., Princeton, 1954; Ph.D., 1956; m. Jane Hale Norris, Aug. 29, 1960; children—Katherine Hale, Sarah Theresse, Peter Bryn. Instr. English, Ohio State U., 1955-58; vis. lectr. U. Muenster (W. Germany), 1958-60; mem. faculty Columbia, N.Y.C., 1960- -, asso. prof. English, 1964-69, prof. English, 1969—, dean coll., 1968—; vis. prof. U. Guanabara (Brazil). 1964. Served with AUS, 1944-46. Home: 460 Riverside Dr New York City NY 10027

HOVDE, FREDERICK LAWSON, univ. pres.; b. Erie, Pa., Feb. 7, 1908; s. Martin Rudolph and Julia Essidora (Lawson) H.; B.Chem. Engring., U. Minn., 1929, LL.D., 1956; Rhodes Scholar from N.D., Oxford U., 1929-32, B.A., B.Sc., 1932, M.A., 1942, D.C.L., 1957; D.Sc., Hanover Coll., 1946, Case Inst. Tech., 1948, Tri-State Coll., 1967; LL.D., Wabash College, 1946, N.D. Agrl. Coll., 1949, N.Y. U., 1951, Mich. State U., 1955, Northwestern U., 196O, U. Notre Dame, 1964, Ball State U., 1965, Ind. State U., 1966; D.Ed., Valparaiso U., 1967; D.Eng., Rose Poly. Inst., 1948; L.H.D., U. Cin., 1956; Pd.D., Findlay Coll., 1961; Dr. Honoris Causa, U. Rural do Estado de Minas Gerais (Brazil), 1965; m. Priscilla Boyd, Aug. 23, 1933; children—F. Boyd, Jane (Mrs. D. R. Price), Linda (Mrs. Louis Buehler II). Asst. to dir. Gen. Coll., U. Minn., 1932- 36; asst. to pres. U. Rochester (N.Y.), also exec. sec. Rochester prize scholarships, 1936-41; head London mission OSRD, 1941- 42; exec. asst. to chmn. Nat. Def. Research Com., 1942-43, chief div. 3, 1943-45; pres. Purdue U., 1946—. Chmn. guided missiles com. Research and Devel. Bd., 1947-49; chmn. bldg. research adv. bd. NRC, 1950- 52; mem. bd. fgn. scholarships Dept. State, 1951-55, chmn., 1953-55; cons. Nat. War Coll., 1953-55. Dir. Gen. Electric Co., Investors Mut., Inc., Investors Stock Fund, Inc., Investors Selective Fund, Inc., Investors Variable Payment Fund, Inc., Ednl. Facilities Labs., Inc., Inland Steel Co. Bd. dirs. Culver Ednl. Found.; trustee Carnegie Fund for Advancement of Teaching; mem. President's Com. on Edn. Beyond High School; chmn. Pres.'s Task Force Com. on Educations, 1961; mem. sci. advisory panel Dept. of Army, 1952-6O, chmn., 1956-58; mem. study com. on fed. aid to agr. Commn. Intergovtl. Relations, 1954; mem. bd. visitors Air Force Acad., 1961-63, U.S. Mil. Acad., 1965-67. Decorated comdr. Order So. Cross (Brazil); recipient President's Medal for Merit, King's Medal for Service in Cause of Freedom; Washington award Western Soc. Engrs., 1968. Mem. Assn. Land-Grant Colls. and Univs. (pres. 1953-54), A.A.A.S., Phi Delta Theta, Phi Lambda Upsilon, Tau Beta Pi, Sigma Xi. Home: 515 S 7th St Lafayette IN 47901

HOVDE, HOWARD T., educator, cons.; b. Des Moines, Nov. 24, 1899; s. Charles M. and Emelie Louise (Thrune) H.; B.S. in Econs., Wharton Sch. Finance and Commerce, U. Pa., 1922, Ph.D., Grad. Sch., 1930; m. Katheryn Desire Newbury, Feb. 28, 1925 (div. Mar. 1958); 1 son, Nelson Newbury. Mem. faculty Wharton Sch. Finance and Commerce, U. Pa., 1922-44; cons. Bur. Fgn. and Domestic Commerce, Dept. of Commerce, Washington, 1942-44; lectr. Am. U., Washington, 1944; research prof. Grad. Sch. Bus. Adminstrn., Harvard, 1944-45; head marketing and sales adminstrn. dept. Biarritz Am. U., U.S. War Dept., France, 1945- 46; negotiator on Belgium war debts Office Fgn. Liquidation Commn., U.S. State Dept., Paris, France, 1946; exec. dir. Nat. Wall Paper Wholesalers Assn. 1947-52; v.p. Econometric Inst. Inc., 1952-58: v.p., treas. Coordinated Marketing Mgmt. Corp., 1958-60, Market Penetration Corp., 1958-6O; prof. marketing Drexel Inst. Tech., Phila., 196O-66; Distinguished vis. prof. marketing Coll. Bus. Adminstrn., Kent (O.) State U., 1966-68; vis. prof. marketing Coll. Bus., No. Ill. U., 1968-69; prof. marketing U. Fla., 1969- 70; prof. marketing Coll. Bus., No. Ill. U., 1970—; cons., research work, 1931—. Sec., Econometric Specialists, Inc., 1953-58; trustee Nat. Wholesalers' Assn. Pres. Am. Marketing Assn., 1941. Ednl. dir. Seagram Distillers Corp., New York; staff mem. Phila. Evening Bull. Mem. Wholesale Trade Adv. Com., U.S. Dept. Commerce. Formerly research asso. The Psychol. Corp. and mem. adv. staff Inst. Pub. Relations, Inc. Fellow Am. Psychol. Assn.; mem. Am. Econ. Assn., Nat. Assn. Bus. Economists, Sales Exec. Club. Club: Poor Richard. Author or editor of publs. Marketing in Our American Economy; National Advertising in Newspapers; Payroll Policies in Philadelphia; Wholesaling in Our American Economy; and other monographs. Contbr. to trade jours, including Bus. Week, Printer's Ink, Sales Mgmt., Jour. Marketing, Jour. Applied psychology. Home: 145 Barnegat Blvd Beachwood NJ 08722 Office: No Ill U DeKalb IL 60115

HOVE, ADOLPH MAGNUS, utility exec.; b. Stoughton, Wis., Aug. 11, 1909; s. John Edwin and Marie (Skough) H.; B.A., U. Wis., 1930; m. Helen D. Moller, June 5, 1937; children—Randall A., Craig M. Chief engr. Dominion Natural Gas Co. Ltd., Brantford, Ont., Can., 1953-58; now exec. v.p. No. & Central Gas Corp., Ltd., Toronto, Ont. Served to lt. (s.g.) USNR, 1943-46. Mem. Natural Gas and Petroleum Assn. Ont. (dir.), Assn. Profl. Engrs. Ont. Lutheran. Office: Toronto-Dominion Centre Toronto 1 Ontario Canada*

HOVEL, CLEO, exec. v.p. Campbell-Mithun, Inc. Address: 1 E Wacker Dr Chicago IL 60601

HOVERMAN, RUSSEL MAAS, banker; b. Bklyn., Jan. 15, 1918; s. John Henry and Caroline (Koster) H.; B.S. in Econs., U. Pa., 1938; grad. Am. Inst. Banking, 1940; M.B.A., N.Y.U., 1950; m. Mary Jean Mahan, Nov. 6, 1943; children-John R., James M., Stephen K. With Williamsburgh Savs. Bank, Bklyn., 1938—, exec. v.p., 1968—, trustee, 1969—. Past pres. Savs. Banks Auitors and Comptroller Forum N.Y. State. Past pres. Sch. Bd., Seaford, N.Y. Served to lt. comdr. USNR, 1941-47. Mem. Alpha Sigma Phi (Delta Xi award 1968). Lutheran. Club: Southward Ho Country (Brightwaters, N.Y.). Home: 1820 Jackson Av Seaford NY 11783 Office: 1 Hanson Pl Brooklyn NY 11217

HOVET, THOMAS, Jr., educator polit. scientist; b. Helena, Mont., Feb. 4, 1923; s. Thomas and Elizabeth (Strauss) H.; B.A., U. Wash., 1948; M.A., N.Y. U., 1949; Ph.D., Victoria Univ. Coll., U. New Zealand, 1954; m. Erica Steinleitner, Sept. 6, 1957; children—Lisa, Heather. Employment interviewer Wash. Dept. Employment Security, 1949; dist. crew leader Census Bur., 1950; research asso. Internat. Studies Group, Brookings Instn., 1951-53; instr. govt. N.Y. U., 1953-54; asst. prof. govt. Miami U., Oxford, O., 1954-56; mem. faculty N.Y. U., 1956-66, prof., 1962-66; prof. polit. sci. U. Ore., Eugene, 1966—, head dept., 1968-7O; cons. State Dept., 1966. Vice pres. UN Assn. Ore., 1968—, Taraknath Das Found., 1957—; rep. Am. Civil Liberties Union to UN, 1962-66. Chmn. Lane County (Ore.) Democratic Party, 1968-69; chmn. 4th Congl. Dist. Dem. Party Ore., 1968. Bd. dirs. Internat. League Rights of Man. 1964-66. Served with AUS, 1942-46. Fulbright scholar, 1950-51; recipient Ersted award distinguished teaching U. Ore., 1968; Danforth Asso., 1964-66. Mem. Western Am., Internat. polit. sci. assns., Am., Indian socs. internat. law, Internat. Studies Assn., African Studies assn. Author: Legislative History and Subject Analysis-Documents of the United Nations Conference on International Organization, Vol. VXI, in English, 1956, Vol. XXII, in French, 1956; (with Waldo Chamberlin and Richard H. Swift) Chronology of the United Nations, 1959; Bloc Politics in the United Nations, 1960; (with Waldo Chamberlin) A Chronology and Fact Book of the United Nations, 1941-1961, 1961; (with others) A Guide to the Use of United Nations Documents, 1962; Africa in the United Nations, 1963; (with Waldo Chamberlin and Erica Hovet) Chronology and Fact Book of the United Nations, 1941-64, 1964; (with others) Primacy of Politics in Africa, 1966; (with Waldo Chamberlin and Erica Hovet) Chronology and Fact Book of the United Nations, 1941-70, 1970. Editor: with Waldo Chamberlin and Richard N. Swift) Annual Review of the United Nations, 1959, Annual Review of the United Nations, 1960. Home: 3204 Fillmore St Eugene OR 97405

HOVEY, PHILIP LEONARD, paper co. exec.; b. Sherbrooke, Que., Can., June 23, 1917; s. Rex William and Lesley Marion (Duncalfe) H.; B.S., Sheffield Sci. Sch., Yale, 1939; m. Femke Vanderzee, Feb. 19, 1944; children—Diana Lesley, Karen Beatrice, Philip Rex, Richard Vanderzee. With Oxford Paper Co., 1939—, mill mgr., Miami, 1948-51, asst. v.p. mfg., 1954-57, v.p. mfg., 1957-61, v.p. operations, 1961-62, dir., 1960-62; pres. Fraser Cos. Ltd., Edmundston, N.B., Can., 1962-68, Fraser Paper Ltd., Madawaska, Me., 1962-68, also dir.; prin. James G. Bronson Assos., N.Y.C., 1968—. Mem. Delta Psi. Home: 1007 SE 11th St New York City NY 10016 Office: 437 Fifth Av New York City NY 10016

HOVEY, RICHARD BENNETT, author, educator; b. Cin., July 28, 1917; s. George B. and Kathryn (Bennett) H.; student Columbia, 1935-36; A.B., U. Cin., 1942; M.A., Harvard, 1943, Ph.D., 1950; m. Marcia L. Johnson, Aug. 20, 1955; 1 son, Daniel R. Instr. U. Cin., 1943-46, U. Pa., 1949-55; asst. prof. Western Md. Coll., Westminsster, 1955-57, asso. prof., 1957-60; asso. prof. U. Md., 1960-68, prof., 1968—. Ford Found. fellow, 1951-52. Mem. Nat. Council Tchrs. of English, Coll. English Assn., Phi Beta Kappa. Unitarian. Author: John Jay Chapman; an American Mind, 1959; Hemingway; the Inward Terrain, 1968. Contbr. to books, also articles in field to popular and tech. mags. Adv. editor Hartford Studies in Literature. Home: 4320 Van Buren St Hyattsville MD 20782

HOVEY, WALTER READ, educator, art critic; b. Springfield, Mass., July 21, 1895; s. Albert Henry and Sarah Elizabeth (Heywood) H.; A.B., Yale, 1918; M.A., Harvard, 1926; Carnegie Found. fellow, 1926; A.F.D. (hon.), Coll. Wooster (O.), 1966. Asst. prof. fine arts U. Pitts., 1927-39, prof., head dept. fine arts, 1939-67, developed fine arts library and art gallery, Henry Clay Frick prof., dir. Henry Clay Frick Fine Arts Bldg., 1965-67; distinguished prof. fine arts Point Park Coll., Pitts., 1967—; vis. lectr. Reading (Pa.) Mus. and Art Gallery, 1970-71. Specialist U.S. Dept. State to Near East, Pakistan and Ceylon, 1954-55. Bd. dirs. Pitts. Playhouse, Westmoreland County Mus. Art, Greensburg, Pa., Hammond Mus., North Salem, N.Y. Served with mobile hosp. unit, AEF, 1916-18. Named Man of Year in Art, Pitts. Jr. C. of C., 1964. Mem. Coll. Art Assn., Asso. Artists Pitts., Pitts. Bicentennial Assn. Republican. Clubs: University, Faculty, Pittsburgh Golf (Pitts.). Author: Potteries and Porcelains in the Frick Collection, 1955. Contbr. profl. jours. and art publs. Home: 5732 Kentucky Av Pittsburgh PA 15232

HOVEYDA, AMIR ABBAS, premier of Iran; b. Tehran, Iran, Feb. 1919; s. Habiballah and Fatemeh (Afsar-ol-Molouk) H.; degrees in econs., polit. science and history, univs. of Paris and Brussels; m. Leyla Emami-Khoi, 1966. With Iranian Diplomatic Service, 1943-48; attache Iranian embassy, Paris, France, 1945-47; 2d sec. Iranian Mission to Germany, 1947-51; pvt. sec. to minister fgn. affairs, 1951; cousellor Iranian embassy, Ankara, Turkey, 1957, head various depts. Office UN High Commr. for Refugees, 1951-57; asst. to bd. chmn., gen. mng. dir. Nat. Iranian Oil Co., 1958, mem. bd., head adminstrn. orgn., 1961-64; minister finance of Iran, 1964-65, prime minister, 1965—. Home: 5 Cyrus St Darrous Tehran Iran Office: Office of Prime Minister Tehran Iran

HOVGARD, CARL, former publisher; b. Parsons, Kan., Oct. 1O, 1905; s. Christopher and Gyda (Holm) H.; A.B., Coll. Emporia, 1928; LL.D., Parsons U., 1940. Founder, Research Inst. Am., N.Y.C., 1935, pres., 1935-67: engaged in oil exploration and prodn., hdqrs. Abilene, Tex.; partner Nat. Law Press, N.Y.C., 1940-67, Hovgard- Johnson Oil Co., Abilene, Tex., 1953—; owner Worthree Mines (tungsten), Kingman, Ariz., 1953-60, Nevins Yacht Yard, City Island, N.Y., 1954-59; dir. Flight Safety, Inc., Am. Avitron, Inc. Trustee Parsons Coll., 1948- 64. Republican. Methodist. Clubs: Union League (pres.), N.Y. Yacht, Wings (N.Y.C.); American Yacht (commodore 1957-58) (Rye, N.Y.); Desert Forest Golf (Carefree, Ariz.); Cruising of Am.; Royal Swedish Yacht (Stockholm); Royal Ocean Racing (London, Eng.); Royal Norwegian Yacht (Oslo); Royal Danish Yacht. Comml. pilot with instrument rating; Class B. winner Bermuda Yacht Race, 1954; skipper Yacht Circe 1955 Trans-Atlantic race King of Sweden Cup, 1966 Trans- Atlantic race to Denmark. Home: Carefree AZ 85331 Office: 589 Fifth Av New York City NY 10017

HOVHANESS, ALAN, composer; b. Somerville, Mass., Mar. 8, 1911; s. Haroutioun and Madeleine (Scott) Hovhaness Chakmakjian; student New Eng. Conservatory Music, 1932-34; Mus.D. (hon.), U. Rochester, 1958, Bates Coll. Condr. concerts of original orchestral music Symphony Hall, Boston, 1946, Carnegie Hall, N.Y.C., 1947. Composer: (concertos) Lousadzak, 1944, Elibris, 1944, Tzaikerk, 1945, no. 1, Arevakal, 1951, Khaldis, 1952, no. 6, 1953, Talin, 1953, no. 7, 1953, Hanna (ballet), 1953; (cantatas) Avak the Healer, 1946, 30th Ode of Solomon, 1947, Vartan Symphony, 1950, Easter Cantata, 1953, Shepherd of Israel, 1953, Glory to God, 1954; (ballet) Ardent Song, 1954; (symphony) Vision from High Rock, 1954, Symphony no. 15, Silver Pilgrimage, Symphony no. 16 for strings and Korean harp, Symphony no. 19 Vishnu (commd. N.Y. Philharmonic), 1967; Symphony no. 22 City of Light, 1971; incidental music for play The Flowering Peach, 1955; Magnificat, 1958; (opera) Burning House; (dance-opera) Lady of Light, 1969, And God Created Great Whales, 1970; music for NBC-TV films: Assignment India, Southeast Asia. Guggenheim fellow (2); Fulbright research scholar to India; Rockefeller grantee for mus. research in Japan, 1962-63. Recipient awards Nat. Arts and Letters, Fromm Music Found. Address: care C F Peters Corp 373 Park Av S New York City NY 10016

HOVING, THOMAS PEARSALL FIELD, museum dir.; b. N.Y.C., Jan. 15, 1931; s. Walter and Mary (Osgood) H.; grad. Hotchkiss Sch., Lakeville, Conn., 1949; B.A., Princeton, 1953, M.A., 1958, Ph.D., 1959; L.H.D., Hofstra U.; LL.D., Pratt Inst.; m. Nancy Melissa Bell, Oct. 3, 1953; 1 dau., Petrea Bell. Mem. staff Medieval Met. Mus. Art and The Cloisters, 1959-65, curator, 1965-66; commr. parks, N.Y.C., 1966-67, adminstr. recreation and cultural affairs, 1967; dir. Met. Mus. Art. Dir., IBM Internat. Mem. N.Y. State Council Arts; chmn. Nat. Citizens Com. for Broadcasting; mem. editorial bd. Pub. Broadcast Lab. Recipient Bronze medal Citizens Budget Comm., 1967; Cue mag. award, 1966; Distinguished Achievement award Advt. Club N.Y. Mem. A.I.A. Home: 150 E 73d St New York City NY 10021 Office: Metropolitan Museum Art Fifth Av and 82d St New York City NY 10028

HOVING, WALTER, corp. exec.; b. Stockholm, Sweden, Dec. 2, 1897; s. Johannes and Helga (Adamsen) H.; Ph.B., Brown U., 1920; L.H.D., L.I. U., 1966; LL.D., Pratt Inst., 1966; m. Mary Osgood Field, Nov. 4, 1924; children—Petrea Field, Thomas Pearsall; m. 2d, Pauline V. Rogers, Apr. 30, 1937. With R.H. Macy & Co., N.Y. C., 1924-32, v.p., 1928-32; v.p. Montgomery Ward & Co., 1932-36, dir., 1934-36; pres. Lord & Taylor, N.Y.C., 1936-45; pres. Hoving Corp., 1946-60; pres. Bonwit Teller, Inc., 1950-60; chmn. bd. Tiffany & Co., N.Y.C., 1955—. Chmn. organizing com. U.S.O., pres., 1940, chmn. bd., 1941-48; chmn. bd. U.S.O. Camp Shows, 1941-48; pres. Salvation Army Assn. N.Y., 1939-60; chmn. drive Salvation Army Citizens Appeal, 1939; nat. chmn. United Negro Coll. Fund, 1944; chmn. N.Y.C. Anti-Sales Tax Com., 1943, 63. Asst. campaign mgr. nat. Republican presdl. campaign, 1944. Served with USNR, 1918-19. Recipient Distinguished Service Cross, Salvation Army, 1942; decorated chevalier Legion of Honor (France); Order of Merit of the Italian Republic; M. Freedman gold medal N.Y. Archtl. League, 1967. Mem. Commerce and Industry Assn. N.Y. (pres. 1948-50), Nat. Retail Mchts. Assn., Fifth Av. Assn. (pres. 1939-45, chmn. bd. 1946-52), Nat. Inst. Social Scis. (pres. 1953-56), Asso. Alumni Brown U. (pres. 1939- 40), Delta Kappa Epsilon. Episcopalian (sr. warden). Mason (32). Clubs: Deepdale Golf; Cammarian (Brown U.); Racquet and Tennis, River (N.Y.C.); Brook; Southampton. Author: Your Career in Business, 1940; The Distribution Revolution, 1960. Home: 435 E 52d St New York City NY 10022 Office: 2 E 57th St New York City NY 10022

HOVLAND, CLARENCE WARREN, educator; b. Chgo., Aug. 17, 1918; s. Ole C. and Augusta (Anderson) H.; B.A., Lawrence Coll., 1940; B.D., Yale, 1943, Ph.D., 1950; m. Suzanne Tillson, Aug. 19, 1950; children—Jeremy Hunt, Anne Marit. Ordained to ministry Congl.-Christian Ch., 1943; faculty Ore. State U., Corvallis, 1949—, prof. philosophy and religion, chmn. dept. religious studies, 1957—. Dir. Am. Friends Service Com. projects, 1954, 56; chmn. N.W. Conf. Religion and Higher Edn., 1955. Mem. exec. com. N.W. YMCA regional council. Danforth Asso., 1952-56; Danforth grantee Harvard, 1957. Recipient Danforth Asso. award Harvard, 1963-64, Outstanding Tchr. award Ore. State U., 1963; Asian Study and Travel grantee, 1967-68. Served as chaplain USNR, 1946-49. Mem. Phi Beta Kappa, Phi Theta Kappa, Sigma Phi Epsilon. Democrat. Co-author: Studies in the Reformation, 1962. Contbr. profl. jours. Home: 4830 SW West Hills Rd Corvallis OR 97330

HOVNANIAN, H. PHILIP, med. sci. research co. exec.; b. Aleppo, Syria, Dec. 17, 1920; s. Philip and Rosa (Jebejian) H.; B.S., Am. U., Beirut, 1942, postgrad. 1945-47; postgrad. Brown U., 1947-49; M.S., State Coll., Boston, 1951; m. Siran Norian, June 10, 1948; children—Rosemary Janice, Joan Anita, John Philip. Prin. investigator, research grant Nat. Heart Inst., NIH; faculty dept. physics Am. U., Beirut, 1942-47, Brown U., 1947-49; sr. engr. Western Electric Co., Haverhill, Mass., 1951-52; asst. chief engr. Calidyne Co., Winchester, Mass., 1952-53; sr. physicist, project head, asst. research dir. Boston Electronics div. Norden-Ketay Corp., 1953-56; partner, research and devel. dir. physics Neutronics Research Co., Waltham, Mass., 1956-58; sr. staff scientist Avco Corp., 1958, mgr. med. sci. dept., 1959-66; mgr. lunar biosci. NASA, Washington, 1966-67; mgr. biomed. engring. and biophysics Kollsman Instrument Corp., Syosset, N.Y., 1967-68; v.p., dir. biomed. products Cavitron Corp., 1969—; dir. Ponti Instruments Inc., Milab, Inc. Guest lectr. biomed. engring. Northeastern U., Mass. Inst. Tech., Harvard Study Group on Biomed. Engring.; research asso. in surgoresearch Lahey Clin. Found. Registered profl. engr., N.Y., Mass. Fellow Inst. Physics (Brit.), Phys. Soc. (Brit.); mem. Optical Soc. Am., Am. Inst. Physics, I.E.E.E. (profl. group biomed. electronics), Internat. Fedn. Med. Electronics, Biomed. Engring. Soc., Research Soc. Am., Internat. Microscopy Assn., Am. Inst. for Ultrasound in Medicine, Am. Soc. Microbiology N.Y. Acad. Scis., A.A.A.S., Assn. for Advancement Med. Instrumentation, Am. Dental Trade Assn. (com. on dental materials and devices), Am. Inst. Biol. Scis. Conglist. (chmn. bd. trustees). Mason. Club: Centerport Yacht. Contbr. tech. papers to profl. jours. Patentee in field. Home: 105 Old Field Rd Huntington NY 11743 Office: 11-40 Borden Av Long Island City NY 11101

HOVORKA, FRANK, educator; b. Cernikovice, Czechoslovakia, Aug. 5, 1897; s. Frank and Anna (Pavlova) H.; A.B., Ia. State Tchrs. Coll., 1922; M.S., U. Ill., 1923, Ph.D., 1925; m. Sophie Paul Nickel, June 12, 1926. Came to U.S., 1913, naturalized, 1923. Prof. chemistry Western Res. U., 1942-54, dir. chem. labs., 1942-58, chmn. dept. chemistry, 1950-58, 62-64, Hurlbut prof. chemistry, 1954-68, prof. emeritus, cons. dept., 1968—; research research asso. Argonne Nat. Lab., 1954-62. Western Res. U. rep. council sponsoring instns. Asso. Midwest Univs., 1947-58, dir., 1958-62. Recipient Distinguished Tchrs. award Mfg. Chemists Assn., 1963; Alumni Achievement award State Coll. Ia., 1964; Distinguished Service award Cleve. Tech. Socs. Council, 1969. Fellow A.A.A.S., Electrochem. Soc., Soc. Chem. Industry (Gt. Britain), Chem. Soc. London; mem. Am. Chem. Soc., Faraday Soc. (Eng.), Am. Assn. U. Profs., N.E.A., Sigma Xi, Phi Lambda Upsilon, Pi Mu Epsilon, Epsilon Chi, Alpha Chi Sigma. Republican. Contbr. articles phys. chemistry, electrochemistry, ultrasonics. to profl. jours. Home: 2593 Exeter Rd Cleveland Heights OH 44118 Office: Dept Chemistry Case Western Res U Cleveland OH 44106 OH 44106

HOWARD, ARNE TORKEL, educator, economist; b. Oslo, Norway, Nov. 5, 1915; s. Conrad N. and Borghild (Olsen) H.; came to U.S., 1922, naturalized, 1941; B.B.A., Baylor U., 1947; M.B.A., Denver U., 1948; grad. student Northwestern U., DePaul U.; m. Marion Margaret Herr, Aug. 21, 1948; children—Timothy W., Bruce D., Craig S., Sharon Joy. Accountant Berwind Co., Chicago, 1938- 41; mem. faculty Wheaton (Ill.) Coll., 1948—, prof. econs., 1948—, chmn. dept. econs. and bus. adminstrn., 1954—. Served to maj. USAAF, 1941-46. Mem. Am. Accounting Assn., Am. Econ. Assn., Am. Assn. U. Profs. Republican. Baptist (moderator). Author articles. Home: 408 E Evergreen St Wheaton IL 60187

HOWARD, ARTHUR DAVID, educator; b. N.Y.C., Aug. 9, 1906; A.B., N.Y. U., 1929, M.S., 1931; Ph.D., Columbia, 1937; m. Julia Salter, Nov. 29, 1947. Instr., Washington Sq. Coll., N.Y. U., 1932-41; instr. univ. extension Columbia, 1932-41; cartographic engr. U.S. Coast and Geodetic Survey, Washington, 1942-44, OSS, 1944-46, U.S. Geol. Survey, 1946-48; prof. geology Stanford, 1948—, now emeritus, chmn. dept. geology, 1959-60, 63-65, on leave of absence to teach in Brazil, 1960-62. ICA cons. Chinese Petroleum Corp., summer 1960; vis. prof. Fed. U. Rio de Janeiro, Brazil, 1970; geologist Navy Antarctic Expdn., 1946-47. N.Y. U. del. Internat. Geol. Congress, Moscow, 1937; Stanford del. 19th Geol. Congress, Algiers, 1952. Recipient emblem for meritorious civilian service OSS, 1945; A. Cressey Morrison prize N.Y. Acad. Sci., 1935; Congl. Antarctic medal, 1970; antarctic glacier named in his honor, 1961. Mem. Geol. Soc. Am. (chmn. geomorphology div. 1968-69) Am. Soc. Photogrammetry, Internat. Geog. Union (com. for study erosion surfaces), Am. Polar Soc., Am. Assn. Petroleum Geologists (distinguished lectr. 1950), Arctic Inst. N.Am., Sigma Xi. Author: History of the Grand Canyon of the Yellowstone, 1937; Cenozoic History of Northeastern Montana and Northwestern North Dakota, 1960; Evolution of the Landscape of the San Francisco Bay Region, 1962. Contbr. articles to profl. jours. Home: 934 Creek Dr Menlo Park Stanford CA 94305 Office: Stanford U Stanford CA 94305

HOWARD, ARTHUR ETHELBERT, Jr., lawyer; b. Hartford, Conn., Dec. 28, 1891; s. Arthur Ethelbert and Mary (Bagley) H.; B.A., Yale, 1914, LL.B., 1917; m. Winifred S. Merrill, Sept. 6, 1920. Admitted to Conn. bar, 1917; practice of law, Hartford, 1919—; with firm Howard, Kohn, Sprague and Fitzgerald; asst. clk. bills Conn. Legislature, 1923; asso. judge Ct. of Common Pleas, 1925-31; asst. corp. counsel City of West Hartford, Conn., 1931-39. Served with USN, 1917-18. Mem. Am., Conn., Hartford bar assns., Phi Beta Kappa, Phi Delta Phi, Zeta Psi. Clubs: University (past pres.), Choral (past pres.) (Hartford). Home: 52 Robin Rd West Hartford CT 06007 Office: 229 Buckingham St Hartford CT 06106

HOWARD, AUGUST, editor, polar historian; b. N.Y.C., Jan. 2, 1910; s. Solomon and Rose (Belinky) Horowitz; student Townsend Harris Hall Coll. City N.Y., 1927; postgrad. N.Y. U., 1931; m. Rose Miller, Feb. 15, 1941; children—Alan, Doris. Pub. relations officer nat. council Boy Scouts Am., 1928-70. Editor, pub. Little Am. Times, pub. privately for friends and relatives of 2d Byrd expdn. and Lincoln Ellsworth Trans- Antarctic Flight expdn., 1933-35; editor Polar Times, 1935—. Founder Am. Polar Soc., 1934, sec., 1934—. Cape Howard in Antarctic named in his honor. Expert on polar history and activities. Home: 98-20 62d Dr Rego Park NY 11374

HOWARD, BAILEY KNEIRIEM, publisher; b. Jamestown, Mo., Oct. 25, 1914; s. Moran Elmo and Anna Oliva (Kneiriem) H.; student U. Mo., 1934-35, USAF Sch. Applied Tactics, Combat Intelligence Sch., Orlando, Fla., 1943; m. Virginia Louise Enochs (div. 1946); m. 2d, Frankie Louise Canaday, Nov. 5, 1949; 1 dau., Stacey Ann. Reporter, Kansas City (Mo.) Jour. Post, 1935- 37; sales mgr. Marshall Hughes Co., Kansas City, 1937-38, T.G. Nichols Co., 1938-40; Ia. div. mgr. Roach Fowler Co., 1940-42; asst. gen. sales mgr. Quarrie Corp., Chgo., 1946-50; gen. sales mgr. ednl. div. Field Enterprises, Inc., Chgo., 1950-53, v.p., gen. sales mgr., 1953-57, sr. v.p. Ednl. Corp., 1957, exec. v.p., 1957, pres., 1957-64, pres., chief exec. officer, 1964-66, pres. parent corp., 1966-68, pres., chief exec. officer, 1968-70, chmn. bd., chief exec. officer, 1970—, also dir., chmn. exec. com.; pres., chief exec. officer newspaper div. (Chgo. Sun-Times, Chgo. Daily News); pres., dir. Field Enterprises Realty Corp., World Book Ednl. Ins. Co.; chmn. exec. com. Field Creations, Chgo., Atlanta; dir. Field Ednl. Enterprises of Australasia, Pty., Ltd., Il Libro del Mondo, S.p.A., Rome, Field Ednl. Italia, Aprilia, World Book Ency. Sci. Service, Inc., Houston; dir., mem. exec. com. GAF Corp.; dir. Field Communications Corp., Met. Printing Co., Elk Grove Village, Ill., Mainstique Paper & Pulp Co. (Mich.), Pubs.-Hall Syndicate N.Y.C., World Book Ency., Inc., FSC Paper Co., Alsip, Ill. Pres., bd. dirs. Field Enterprises Charitable Corp., Racing for Charities, Trotting for Charities, Inc. (both Chgo.); trustee, regent Lincoln Acad. Ill.; bd. dirs. exec. com. Chgo. Lyric Opera Co.; trustee Field Estate; founder numerous scholarship, cultural, fellowship funds; mem. Chgo. Natural History Mus. Mem. Bus. and Industry Execs. for Johnson, 1964; chmn. Kerner Com. 1000, Chgo., 1965- 66. Served as capt. Combat Intelligence Corps, USAAF, 1942-45. Mem. Am. End. Pubs. Inst., English-Speaking Union, Chgo. Art Inst. (life), Chgo. Hist. Soc. (life), Newcomen Soc. N.Am., Hon. Order Ky. Cols. Clubs: Private Turf (Santa Anita, Arcadia, Cal.); Marco Polo (N.Y.C.); Turf (Hollywood, Cal.); Kona Kai (San Diego); Tavern, Racquet, Saddle and Cycle, Chicago, Chicago Press (Chgo.); Federal City (Washington); Lakeside Golf (North Hollywood, Cal.); Post and Paddock (pres., dir. Arlington Heights, Ill.); Beverly Hills (Cal.).; many others. Home: 1550 Lake Shore Dr Chicago IL 60610 also: 13741 Mulholland Dr Beverly Hills CA 90210 Office: 401 N Wabash Av Chicago IL 60611 also 14545 Victory Blvd Van Nuys CA 91401

HOWARD, BERNARD EDSON, advt. exec.; b. Kalamazoo, Oct. 15, 1905; s. Norman E. and Laura Jane (Weed) H.; extension student U. Minn., 1926-28; m. Alice Agnes Houska, Nov. 24, 1927; 1 son, Gerald Stevens. Reporter, East Side Jour., St. Paul, 1925-26; advt. mgr. Merrill Greer Chapman Co., St. Paul, 1926-27, Montgomery Ward, St. Paul, 1928-30; sales promotion mgr. MW Savage Co., Mpls., 1930-32; advt. mgr. Adlerika Co., St. Paul, 1932-38; copywriter Campbell Mithun Inc., Mpls., 1938-43; creative chief Batten Barton Durstine and Osborn, Los Angeles, 1943-45, Elwood Robinson Advt., Los Angeles, 1945-48; creative chief Campbell Mithun Inc., Chgo., 1949-51, then sr. v.p. Served to capt. AUS, World War II. Conglist. Club: Edina (Minn.) Country. Home: 4510 Lakeview Dr Minneapolis MN 55424

HOWARD, BION BRADBURY, educator; b. Paris, France, Oct. 28, 1912 (parents Am. citizens); s. Bion B. and Lucile (Jones) H.; came to U.S., 1914; Ph.B., U. Chgo., 1933; M.B.A., Northwestern U., 1940, Ph.D., 1950; m. Lita Dickerson, Dec. 24, 1940; children-Bion Dickerson, Julia. Asst. buyer Montgomery Ward & Co., 1933-36; lectr. Northwestern U. Sch. Bus., Evanston, Ill., 1947- 50, asst. prof., 1950-51, asso. prof., 1951-56, prof., 1956—, Nathan and Mary Sharp prof. finance, 1962—; vis. prof. Stanford Grad. Sch. Bus. Adminstrn., 1954-55, U. Va., 1971-72. Dir. Cardiff Industries, United Wirecraft Co., Chgo., Densitronics, Columbus, O., Consumer Display Corp., Chgo. Economist, price exec. consumer durable goods br. OPA, Washington, 1942-46; div. economist, asso. div. dir. consumer durable goods div. OPS, Washington, 1951. Mem. Am. Finance Assn. (dir. 1959-60, pres. 1962), Am. Econ. Assn., Am. Risk and Ins. Assn., Investment Analysts Soc. Chgo., Phi Beta Kappa, Beta Gamma Sigma, Delta Kappa Epsilon. Club: University (Chgo.), Author: (with Miller Upton) Introduction to Business Finance, 1953. Co-author: Managerial Problems in Finance, 1964; The Individual Marriage and the Family, 1967. Contbr. articles profl. publs. Home: 2745 Lawndale Av Evanston IL 60201

HOWARD, BUSHROD BRUSH, former oil co. exec.; b. Annapolis, Md., Nov. 18, 1889; s. Thomas Benton and Anne Jacob (Claude) H.; student St. John's Coll., 1905-06; B.S., U.S. Naval Acad., 1911; m. Esther Margaret Green, Apr. 23, 1913 (dec.); children—Thomas Benton, Margaret (Mrs. David L. Roscoe, Jr.), Bushrod Brush, Peter; m. 2d, Mrs. Margaret Cobb Perkins, July 28, 1939. Joined marine dept. Standard Oil of N.J., 1920, apptd. fgn. rep., Paris, France, 1922, mng. operator Sociĕtĕ Auxiliare de Transports, 1925, dir. L'Economique and Bedford Petroleum Co., Paris, 1926, London rep. Standard Shipping Co., 1929, asst. to gen. mgr. marine dept., N.Y.C., 1934, asst. gen. mgr., 1938, gen. mgr., 1939, dir. co., 1945-54. Served to lt. comdr. U.S. Navy, 1907-19. Episcopalian. Club: University (N.Y.C.). Address: 14 Legare St Charleston SC 29401

HOWARD, CY, TV writer, producer. Writer radio sta. WBBM; exec. prod., writer situation comedy Fair Exchange, CBS-TV; other shows include My Friend Irma, Life with Luigi, Harrigan and Son, Guestward Ho; assisted writing for motion picture Around the World in 80 Days; author, screen-writer, asst. prod., dir. That's My Boy; also wrote comedy for Jack Benny, Milton Berle, Danny Thomas, Eddie Cantor. Address: care CBS-TV 485 Madison Av New York City NY 10022*

HOWARD, DAGGETT HORTON, lawyer; b. N.Y.C., Mar. 20, 1917; s. Chester Augustus and Olive Ree (Daggett) H.; B.A. magna cum laude, Yale, 1938, J.D., 1941; m. Patricia McClellan Exton, Sept. 1950; children—Daggett Horton, Jeffrey, David, Patricia. Admitted to N.Y. bar, 1942, D.C. bar, 1961; legal staff Root, Clark, Buckner & Ballantine, N.Y.C., 1941-43; legal staff Lend Lease Adminstrn., Fgn. Econ. Adminstrn., 1943-44; exec. asst. to spl. counsel to Pres., White House, 1945; legal adviser Fgn. Econ. Adminstrn., also Dept. State, 1945-47; internat. atty., asst. chief internat. and rules div. CAB, 1947-52; asso. gen. counsel Dept. Air Force, 1952-56, dep. gen. counsel, 1956-58; gen. counsel FAA, 1958-62; partner Cox, Langford & Brown, Washington, 1962-66, Howard, Poe & Bastian (formerly Howard & Poe), Washington, 1966—. Past mem. policy com. Daniel and Florence Guggenheim Aviation Safety Center; corporate mem. Children's Hosp. of D.C. Bd. dirs. Audubon Naturalist Soc. Recipient Exceptional Civilian Service award Dept. Air Force, 1958; Distinguished Service award FAA, 1962. Mem. Yale Law Sch. Assn. Washington, Corbey Ct., Fed., Am. bar assns., Nat. Lawyers Club, Phi Beta Kappa, Alpha Sigma Phi. Clubs: Yale, Federal City, National Capital Democratic (Washington); Chevy Chase (Md.) Bd. editors Yale Law Jour. Home: 4554 Klingle St NW Washington DC 20016 Office: 1701 Pennsylvania Av NW Washington DC 20006

HOWARD, DONALD F., univ. dean; B.A., U. No. Ia.; M.A., Ph.D., U. Ia. Prof. history, dean Coll. Bus. and Behavioral Scis., U. No. Ia., Cedar Falls. Office: Coll Bus and Behavioral Scis U No Ia Cedar Falls IA 50613*

HOWARD, DONALD ROY, educator, author; b. St. Louis, Sept. 18, 1927; s. Albert and Emily (Johnson) H.; A.B. summa cum laude, Tufts U., 1950; M.A., Rutgers U., 1951; Ph.D., U. Fla., 1954. Mem. faculty Ohio State U., 1955-63, U. Cal. at Riverside, 1963-66, at Los Angeles, 1966-67; prof. English, Johns Hopkins, Balt., 1967—. Served with USNR, 1945-46, Fulbright research fellow, Italy, 1960; Am. Council Learned Socs. fellow, 1964; Guggenheim fellow, 1969-70. Mem. Modern Lang. Assn., Medieval Acad. (councillor 1969), Am. Assn. U. Profs., Phi Beta Kappa. Author: The Three Temptations: Medieval Man in Search of the World, 1966; Critical Studies of Sir Gawain and the Green Knight, 1968; Chaucer, Canterbury tales, A Selection, 1969; also articles. Mem. editorial bd. Speculum, ELH (English Literary History). Address: English Dept Johns Hopkins Baltimore MD 21218

HOWARD, DONALD STEVENSON, educator; b. Tokyo, Japan, Sept. 22, 1902 (parents U.S. citizens); s. Alfred Taylor and May Day (Stevenson) H.; A.B., Otterbein Coll., 1925, L.H.D., 1947; A.M., U. Denver, 1931; Ph.D., U. Chgo., 1941; m. Bernice Norris, June 12, 1929; children-John Alfred, Margery Gertrude, Robert Hamilton. Community orgn. work, Pueblo, Colo., 1927-31; dir. adult activities U. Chgo. Settlement, 1931-34; dir. social welfare survey, Colo., 1934; dir. research, statistics Colo. Emergency Relief Adminstrn., 1934; regional statician WPA, part-time faculty U. Denver, 1935-36; research asso., later dir. dept. social work adminstrn. Russell Sage Found., 1936-48; intermittently faculty dept. pub. welfare adminstrn., internat. relief adminstrn. Hunter Coll., Bklyn. Coll., 1936-40, N.Y. Sch. Social Work, Columbia, 1940-48; staff UNRRA Council, later dir. welfare, research and planning, Washington, devel. welfare program various European countries, chief welfare officer charge health, welfare, displaced persons services, China, 1943-46; prof. U. Cal. Sch. Social Welfare, Los Angeles, 1948—, dean, 1948-60. Chmn., Cal. Gov.'s Adv. Com. on Children and Youth; counsel on social security Senate Finance Com., 1947-48; chmn. Nat. Council State Coms. for Children and Youth, 1958-60; vice chmn. White House Conf. on Children and Youth, 1960; mem. Los Angeles County Mental Health Adv. Bd. Mem. Am. (pres. 1948- 50), Nat. assns. social workers, Nat. (1st v.p. 1949-50), Cal. (pres. 1950-52), Internat. (exec. com. 1948-57, ednl. dir. social welfare study tours), confs. social work, Nat. Council Chs. Christ Am., Am. Pub. Welfare Assn., Nat. Rehab. Assn., Council Social Work Edn., Internat. Assn. Schs. Social Work (mem. bd.), Cal. (v.p.), Los Angeles County (bd.) assns. for mental health, Pi Gamma Mu, Phi Delta Kappa. Methodist. Author: WPA and Federal Relief Policy, 1943; Social Welfare-Values, Means and Ends, 1969. Contbr. to books, articles to profl. jours. Adv. editor social welfare Ency. Americana. Home: 10801 Wellworth Av Los Angeles CA 90024

HOWARD, EDGAR, Jr., educator; b. Westerly, R.I., Aug. 14, 1922; Sc.B., Brown U., 1943; Ph.D., U. Ill., 1946; married, 1953; 3 children. Pitts. Plate Glass Co. fellow Harvard, 1946-47; instr. chemistry Temple U., Phila., 1947-49, asst. prof., 1949-55, asso. prof., 1955-63, prof., 1963—, chmn. dept., 1963-68. Office: Dept Chemistry Temple U Philadelphia PA 19122

HOWARD, EDGAR N., pipeline co. exec.; b. 1926; B.B.A., U. Tex., 1948; married. With Price Waterhouse & Co., C.P.A.'s, 1948-50; sr. accountant W.M. Briscoe, 1950-52, Peat, Marwick, Mitchell & Co., C.P.A.'s, Houston, 1952-60; asst. controller Transwestern Pipeline Co., Houston, 1960-64, controller, asst. treas., 1964—. Served with AUS, 1950-52. C.P.A., Tex. Office: PO Box 2521 Houston TX 77001*

HOWARD, EDWARD ALLEN, librarian; b. Erlanger, Ky., May 10, 1931; s. William Edward and Betty (Smiley) H.; B.A., U. Louisville, 1953; M.S., U. Ill., 1956; m. Phyllis Vincent Forster, May 16, 1959; children—Randall, Kim. Film librarian Louisville Free Pub. Library, 1953-54; research asst. U. Ill. Grad. Library Sch. U. Ill., 1954-56; head fine arts div. Topeka Pub. Library, 1956-58; city librarian Lawrence (Kan.) Pub. Library, 1958-62; dir. Evansville (Ind.) Pub. Library and Vanderburgh County Pub. Library, 1962—. Cons. Kan. State Library, 1957-59. Chmn. Nat. Library Week in Kan., 1960; mem. adv. council Sr. Citizens, 1962—; mem. Mayor's Human Relations Commn., Evansville, 1964-69. Bd. dirs. Heart Assn. Mem. Am., Ind. (pres. elect), library assns., Pi Kappa Phi, Pi Delta Epsilon. Republican. Unitarian. Kiwanian. Home: 5917 Oak Hill Rd Evansville IN 47711 Office: 22 SE 5th St Evansville IN 47708

HOWARD, EDWARD DOUGLAS, II, investment co. exec.; b. Chgo., July 9, 1907; s. Lewis Edward and May Agnes (Countiss) H.; A.B., Williams Coll., 1928; m. Barbara Requa Lewis, Feb. 11, 1932; children—Edward Douglas III, Barbara Anne, James Lewis. Engaged in banking and investment bus., Buffalo, 1928-41; v.p. Schoellkopf, Hutton & Pomeroy, Inc., Buffalo, 1945-47; with Niagara Share Corp., Buffalo, 1948—, pres., 1961—, also dir. Chmn. bd. dirs., chmn. finance com. Med. Found. Buffalo. Served to lt. comdr. USCGR, 1941- 45. Mem. N.Y. Soc. Security Analysts, Nat. Assn. Closed-End Investment Cos. (dir.), Buffalo C. of C., Am. Arbitration Assn. (nat. panel arbitrators), Delta Phi. Clubs: Williams (N.Y.C.); Saturn, Mid-Day (Buffalo); Clarksburg (Eden). Home: 9500 E Eden Rd Eden NY 14057 Office: 70 Niagara St Buffalo NY 14202

HOWARD, ERNEST B., med. adminstr., physician; b. Boston, Feb. 5, 1910; A.B., Harvard, 1931, M.P.H., 1941; M.D., Boston U., 1936. Intern medicine Boston City Hosp., 1936-37; mem. staff A.M.A., 1948—, asst. exec. v.p., 1957-69, exec. v.p., 1969—. Home: 1980 Pheasant Trail Palatine IL 62451 Office: 535 N Dearborn St Chicago IL 60610

HOWARD, EUGENE MERRILL, banker, assn. ofcl.; b. Danville, Ill., Sept. 21, 1908; s. William Tecumsch and Alice (Smith) H.; student Ind. U., 1941-45; grad. Rutgers U. Grad. Sch. Banking, 1948, Am. Inst. Banking, 1946; m. Marjorie Wildason, Nov. 17, 1928; 1 son, Thomas Eugene; m. 2d, Loretta Mea Herndon, Nov. 28, 1945; 1 dau., Laura Jean. With Am. Fletcher Nat. Bank & Trust Co., and predecessor, Indpls., 1926—, sr. loan officer, 1950- 54, v.p., 1954-67, sr. v.p., 1967—. Mem. Robert Morris Assos. (pres. Ohio Valley chpt., 1954-55, nat. dir., 1956-60 nat. pres. 1962-63), Am. Inst. Banking (pres. Indpls. 1947-48). Clubs: Indpls. Athletic, Columbia (Indpls.). Home: 6225 N Sherman Dr Indianapolis IN 46220 Office: Fidelity Bldg Indianapolis IN 46209

HOWARD, FONTAINE MAURY, lawyer; b. Autagaville, Ala., Sept. 18, 1908; s. Fontaine Maury and Mary (O'Brien) H.; A.B., Birmingham So. Coll., 1929; LL.B., Jones Law Sch., 1935; postgrad. Harvard Law Sch., 1946; m. Janet Evelyn Poole, Nov. 20, 1946; children—Richard F., Jennifer M. Pub. sch. tchr., 1929-38; admitted to Ala. bar, 1939, since practiced in Montgomery; partner firm Capell, Howard, Knabe & Cobbs, 1946—. Pres., Montgomery Estate Planning Council, 1960; chmn. Fed. Tax Clinic Com., 1958. Vice pres. Montgomery United Appeal, 1965-69. Trustee Birmingham So. Coll. Mem. Am., Montgomery (pres. 1959) bar assns., Newcomen Soc. Methodist (chmn. ofcl. bd. 1966, chmn. trustees 1968-69). Kiwanian. Chief editorial adv. bd. Ala. Lawyer, 1969—. Home: 3338 Allendale Pl Montgomery AL 36111 Office: Box 2069 Montgomery AL 36104

HOWARD, FRANCES ELLIOT lawyer, corp. exec.; b. Kent, O., 1922. Admitted to Massachusetts bar, 1944; practiced in Boston, 1947--. Home: 23 Beacon St Boston MA 02107

HOWARD, FRANK JAMES, ret. athletic dir.; b. Barlow Bend, Ala., Mar. 25, 1909; s. Augustus Taylor and Leota (McConnell) H.; B.A. in Bus. Adminstrn., U. Ala., 1931; m. Anna Eliza Tribble, Aug. 23, 1933; children—Alice (Mrs. Bobby McClure), Frank James. Line coach Clemson U., 1931-40, head football coach, athletic dir., 1940-69; univ. team has played in Gator Bowl, 1949, 52, Orange Bowl, 1951, 57, Sugar Bowl, 1959, Bluebonnet Bowl, 1959; mem. coaching staff Blue-Gray Game, 1941, 52, 59, 69, East-West Shrine Game, 1960, 62; coach So. squad North-South Game, 1961, 68. Mem. rules com. Nat. Collegiate Athletic Assn., 1960-65. Named to Jason (S.C.) Hall of Fame, Hula Bowl, 1970. Mem. Omega Delta Kappa. Home: 102 Bradley St Clemson SC 29631

HOWARD, GLENN WILLARD, educator; b. Grants Pass, Ore., Apr. 5, 1906; s. George E. and Estelle E. (Anderson) H.; A.B., U. Ore., 1928; M.A., Columbia, 1929, Ph.D., 1937; m. Thelma E. Akey, Sept. 8, 1931; children—Glenn W., Gordon E., Katherine E. Instr. hygiene Townsend Harris Hall, Coll. City N.Y., 1929; chmn. dept. health and phys. edn. Seth Low, Jr. Coll., Columbia, 1929- 36, instr. hygiene, 1929-36; vis. prof. phys. edn. Purdue U., summer 1936; asst. prof., then asso. prof. phys. edn. Ohio State U., 1936-45, survey staff bur. ednl. research; vis. prof. phys. edn. U. Tex., summer 1940, U. Cal., 1946; asso. prof. Queens Coll., 1945-52, prof. health and phys. edn., 1953—, chmn. dept. health and phys. edn., 1945-56, dir. Sch. Gen. Studies, 1956-62, adminstrv. head, 1964-65, dean adminstrn., 1962—. Chmn. com. coll. phys. edn. and health instrn. of wartime commn. U.S. Office Edn., 1942; spl. cons. bd. examiners Bd. of Edn., N.Y.C., 1947, spl. examiner, 1955-58; v.p. Met. Inter-Collegiate Soccer Conf., 1950-51, pres., 1951-52; del. Internat. Congress on Essentials of Phys. Edn. for Youth, 1954. Bd. dirs. Greater N.Y. Council Fgn. Students, 1961- -. Mem. Nat. Coll. Phys. Edn. Assn. for Men (chmn. hist. records com. 1963), Am. Mgmt. Assn., Coll. Phys. Edn. Assn. (pres. 1950), Am., N.Y. (chmn. com. on profl. preparation

1946) assns. health, phys. edn. and recreation, Assn. for Higher Edn., Greater N.Y. Council for Fgn. Students (treas. 1968—), Nat. Soc. for study of Edn., N.E.A., Child Service League (pres. 1962), Assn. U. Evening Colls., Bldg. Research Inst., Phi Beta Kappa, Phi Delta Kappa. Methodist (trustee; chmn. commn. on edn. 1964-65, mem. adminstrv. bd. 1969—). Author: (with Edward Masonbrink) The Administration of Physical Education, 1963. Contbr. profl. publs. Home: 11 Eastland Dr Glen Cove NY 11542 Office: Queens Coll Flushing NY 11367

HOWARD, HAROLD HILL, chem. co. exec.; b. Holden, Mo., Dec. 21, 1916; s. Albert Earl and Gail Grace (Hill) H.; B.S. in Edn., Central Mo. State Coll., 1938; m. Anne E. Wagoner, June 1, 1941; 1 son, David Douglas. Purchasing agt. Zellerbach Paper Co., Kansas City, Mo., 1938-42; v.p. purchasing Wagoner Electric, Nashville, 1947-49; with Thompson-Hayward Chem. Co., Kansas City, Mo., 1949—. sr. v.p. sales and operations, 1969—. Served with USCGR, 1942-45. Mem. Nat. Agrl. Chem. Assn. (mem. bd. 1969—), Sales and Marketing Execs. Methodist. Club: Kansas City. Home: 8950 E 61st Raytown MO 64133 Office: 5200 Speaker Rd Kansas City KS 66106

HOWARD, HARRY NICHOLAS, educator; b. Excelsior Springs, Mo., Feb. 19, 1902; s. Alpheus M. and Lois A. (Foster) H.; A.B., William Jewell Coll., 1924; A.M. (Gregory fellow), U. Mo., 1927; Ph.D., U. Cal. at Berkeley, 1930; m. Virginia Faye Brubaker, Aug. 13, 1932; children—Robert Wendell, Norman Foster. Research asst. Eastern European history U. Cal., 1928- 29; asst. prof. history U. Okla., 1929-30; asst. prof. history Miami U., 1930-37, asso. prof., 1937-40, prof., 1940-42; vis. prof. several univs., summers 1930-41; with Dept. of State, 1942-62, head East European unit Div. Territorial Studies, 1942-45, expert on internat. orgn., 1945-46, chief Near East Research br. Office Near Eastern and African Affairs, 1946-47, adviser div. Greek, Turkish and Iranian Affairs, 1947-49, adviser U.S. dels., cons. investigation concerning Greek frontier incidents, 1947-50, spl. UN com. on Balkans; UN adviser Bur. Nr. East, S. Asian, African Affairs, 1949-56; acting U.S. rep. adv. commn. for Palestine refugees UN Relief and Works Agy., 1956-62, spl. asst. to commr. gen., 1962-63; prof. Middle East studies Am. U. Sch. Internat. Service, Washington, 1963-68, adj. prof. Middle East studies, 1968—. Vis. prof. internat. relations Columbia, 1955; program chmn. Nr. East and N. Africa area studies Fgn. Service Inst., Dept. State, summer 1966, 71-72, faculty adviser, 1967-68; lectr. Middle East, U.S. Army War Coll., Carlisle, Pa., 1971-72. Gov., Middle East Inst., 1963- -; bd. dirs. Am. Nr. East Refugee Aid, 1968—. Recipient Citation of Achievement, William Jewell Coll., 1947; Distinguished Alumni award Pi Kappa Delta; decorated comdr. Royal Order Phoenix (Greece). Member nat., state, local profl. assns. Author numerous books in field internat. politics, dealing primarily with Balkan area including The King-Crane Commission An American Inquiry in the Middle East, 1963. Contbr. to Ency. Brit., Ency. Americana. Asso. editor Middle East Jour., 1963—. Contbr. numerous articles to profl. jours. Home: 6508 Greentree Rd Bradley Hills Grove Bethesda MD 20034 Office: Am U Massachusetts and Nebraska Avs Washington DC 20016

HOWARD, HILDEGARDE (Mrs. Henry Anson Wylde), paleontologist; b. Washington, Apr. 3, 1901; d. Clifford and Hattie Sterling (Case) Howard; A.B., U. Cal. 1924, A.M., 1926, Ph.D., 1928; m. Henry Anson Wylde, Feb. 6, 1930. Asst. in zoology U. Cal., Los Angeles, 1924-25; teaching fellow paleontology U. Cal., 1925-26, research fellow zoology, 1927-28; research asst. Los Angeles County Mus. Natural History, 1924-25, 28, avian paleontologist, 1929-38, curator avian paleontology, 1939-51, chief curator sci. div., 1951-61, research asso., 1961—; research asso. avian paleontology Santa Barbara Mus. Natural History, 1956—, Western Speleological Inst., 1958—. John Simon Guggenheim Found. fellow, 1962-63. Fellow Geol. Soc. Am., Am. Ornithol. Union (Brewster Meml. award in ornithology 1953), A.A.A.S., So. Cal. (pres. 1957-59), Cal. acads. sci.; mem. Cooper Ornithol. Soc. (life), Soc. Vertebrate Paleontology, Phi Beta Kappa, Sigma Xi, Phi Sigma. Author several monographs, including Fossil Evidence of Avian Evolution, 1950; A New Wading Bird from the Eocene of Patagonia, 1955; Handbook on Fossil Birds, 1955, 2d edit., 1962; A Gigantic Toothed Marine Bird from the Miocene of California, 1957; A New Species of Passerine Bird from the Miocene of California, 1957; Miocene Sulids from Southern California, 1958; Avian Census of Individual Pits at Rancho La Brea, 1962; Fossil Birds from the Anza-Borrego Desert, 1963; Fossil Anseriformes, 1964; Pliocene Birds from Chihuahua, Mexico, 1966; Tertiary Birds from Laguna Hills, Orange County, California, 1968; Avian Fossils from three Pleistocene Sites in Central Mexico, 1969; A Review of the Extinct genus, Mancalla, 1970; Pliocene Avian Remains from Baja California, 1971. Editor: Los Angeles County Mus. Contbns. in Sci., 1957-61. Contbr. articles to sci. jours. Address: Los Angeles County Mus Natural History 900 Exposition Blvd Los Angeles CA 90007

HOWARD, HOWELL HOFFMAN, lumber co. exec.; b. Evanston, Ill., Sept. 27, 1927; s. Howell Hoffman and Loretta (Hines) H.; B.S., Yale, 1950; m. Mimi Foss, Oct. 29, 1951; children—Howell Hoffman, Mark Maxwell, Lynn Foss, Paul Wilson, Douglas. With Edward Mines Lumber Co., 1950—, treas., 1957—, exec. v.p., 1960-63, pres., 1963—; dir. 1st. Nat. Bank, Winnetka, Ill. Bd. dirs. Ill. State C. of C. Home: 39 Indian Hill Rd Winnetka IL 60093 Office: 200 S Michigan Av Chicago IL 60604

HOWARD, HUMBERT LINCOLN, artist; b. Phila., July 12, 1915; s. David and Ethel (Morgan) H.; student Howard U., 1932-34, U. Pa., 1934-35, Barnes Found., 1959-61; m. Beatrice Wood, June 10, 1938; children—David D., Humbert J. Instr., Cheltenham Art Center, 1962-66, Allens Lane Art Center, 1967-71; exhibited in one man shows at Pyramid Club, 1958, Phila. Art Alliance, 1956, 58, Howard U., 1959, Newman Gallery, 1962, Grabar Gallery, 1968; exhibited in group shows at Pa. Acad. Fine Arts, 1951-54, 61, 69, Pa. Acad. Living Phila. Artists Show, 1956, Phila. Art Alliance, 1958, Afro-Am. Exhbn. N.Y.C. Coll., 1967, Pa. Acad. Fine Arts, Phila. Mus. Art Arts Festivals, Green Hill, 1969, McCleaf Gallery, Phila., 1970; represented in permanent collections at Pa. Acad. Fine Arts, Phila. Civic Mus., Howard U., Sterne Sch. Recipient Purchase prize Pa. Acad. Fine Arts, 1951, Outstanding Achievement in Art award Am. Exhibiting Artists, 1965, Woodmere, Van Sciver Meml. prize, 1968; Reproduced in American Negro Art by Cedric Dover, 1960; The Barnes Foundation-Reality vs. Myth by Gilbert M. Cantor, 1963; Ebony Mag., 1963; 100 Years After the Emancipation by Jack Saunders, 1965. Mem. Artists Equity, Phila. Art Alliance, Pa. Acad. Fine Arts, Phila. Mus. Art, Omega Psi Phi. Club: Peale (Phila.). Writer feature articles in Sunday Bull., 1969-70. Home: 3411 Hamilton St Philadelphia PA 19104 Studio: 1601 Walnut St Philadelphia PA 19102

HOWARD, JACK, business exec.; b. Santa Ana, Cal., Aug. 26, 1924; s. Floyd Willie and Inez (Cooley) H.; A.B., U. Cal. at Berkeley, 1948, M.A., U. Cal. at Los Angeles, 1952; m. Margaret Anne McKinnon, Aug. 25, 1950; children—Marc, Anne. Reporter, Springfield (O.) Daily News, 1949-51; labor editor San Francisco Chronicle, 1952-60; chief investigator govt. information subcom. U.S. Ho. of Reps., 1960-63; spl. asst. to undersec. of Labor, 1963-64, adminstr. Neighborhood Youth Corps, 1964-66, adminstr. Bur. of Work Programs, 1966-67, spl. asst. to sec. Labor, 1968; with Ednl. Scis. Programs, Inc., N.Y.C., 1969-71; asst. to pub. Ency. Brit., N.Y.C., 1971—. Internat. v.p. Am. Newspaper Guild-AFL-CIO, 1957-60. Served with AUS, 1943-46. Congl. fellow Am. Polit. Sci. Assn., 1957-58. Recipient Distinguished Service award Dept. Labor, 1965. Mem. Am. Civil Liberties Union, Sigma Delta Chi, Pi Sigma Alpha. Home: 520 La Guardia Pl New York City NY 10012 Office: 342 Madison Av New York City NY 10017

HOWARD, JACK ROHE, newspaperman; b. N.Y.C., Aug. 31, 1910; s. Roy Wilson and Margaret (Rohe) H.; grad. Phillips Exeter Acad., 1928; A.B., Yale, 1932; m. Barbara Belfe, Apr. 5, 1934 (dec. 1962); children—Pamela, Michael; m. 2d, Eleanor Sallee Harris, 1964. Reporter, Japan Advertiser, Tokyo, Shanghai (China) Evening Post and Mercury, 1932-33; reporter Indpls. Times, 1933-34; asst. telegraph editor, telegraph editor and news editor Washington Daily News, 1935; with program dept. radio sta. WNOX, Knoxville, Tenn., and Washington and N.Y.C. offices Continental Radio Co. (now Scripps- Howard Broadcasting Co.), 1936-39; asst. exec. editor Scripps-Howard Newspapers, 1939-42, 1945-48, gen. editorial mgr., 1948—; pres., dir., exec. com. mem. Scripps-Howard Newspapers (E. W. Scripps Co.), 1953-; pres., dir. chmn. exec. com. Scripps-Howard Broadcasting Co., 1937-42, 45—; dir. Trans World Air-lines, Inc.; mem. Midtown adv. bd. Chem. Bank N.Y. Dir. Boys' Clubs Am. Commd. lt. (j.g.), USNR, 1942; active duty Washington, 1943, sea duty, PTO, 1944-45; now lt. comdr. USNR ret. Mem. Am. Soc. Newspaper Editors, Am. Newspaper Pubs. Assn. (dirs), Inter Am. Press Assn. (pres. 1965-66, mem. adv. Council), Phillips Exeter Alumni Assn. (pres. 1958-60), Beta Theta Pi, Sigma Delta Chi. Clubs: Dutch Treat Yale River, Pilgrams (N.Y.C.); Overseas Writers, Nat. Press (Washington); Bohemian (San Francisco); Seawanhaka Corinthian Yacht, (Oyster Bay, N.Y.). Address: 200 Park Av New York City NY 10017

HOWARD, JAMES J., congressman; b. Irvington, N.J., July 24, 1927; s. George P. and Bernice M. Howard; B.A., St. Bonaventure U., 1952; M.Ed., Rutgers U., 1958; m. Marlene Vetrano; children—Kathleen (Mrs. Raymond Lowther), Lenore, Marie. Tchr., acting prin. Wall Twp. (N.J.) Sch. System, 1954-64; mem. 89th to 92d congresses 3d Dist. N.J. Served with USNR. World War II: UTO. Mem. Nat., N.J. (del. assembly), Monmouth County (past pres.) edn. assns. Democrat. Address: House Office Bldg Washington DC 20515

HOWARD, JAMES MERRIAM, Jr., educator; b. Morristown, N.J., Feb. 9, 1922; s. James Merriam and Gertrude Laura (Hunter) H.; grad. Morristown Sch., 1938; student All Saints Sch., Bloxham, Eng., 1938-39; A.B., Yale, 1943; A.M., Harvard, 1952; Litt.D., Lafayette Coll., 1965; m. Sarah Saymour, Sept. 25, 1942 (dec. 1945); 1 son, James Merriam III; m. 2d. Selena Tatlock, Nov. 19, 1949; children—Alida Babcock, Mary Carrington, Eleanor Tatlock. Faculty Lawrenceville (N.J.) Sch., 1945-64, master Cleve. House, 1952-64; headmaster Blair Acad., Blairstown, N.J., 1954—. Trustee Trenton State Coll., Council Religion Ind. Schs., Warren County Childrens Com. Served to 1st lt. USMCR, 1942-45. Mem. Headmasters Assn., Phi Beta Kappa. Author articles. Home: Sharpe House Blairstown NJ 07825

HOWARD, JAMES STEPHEN, III, steel co. exec.; b. Schenectady, July 7, 1921; s. James Stephen, Jr. and Marjorie (Tillema) H.; grad. Bentley Coll. Accounting and Finance, Boston, 1942; postgrad. Boston Tchrs. Coll., 1946, Northwestern U., 1947; grad. Dartmouth Grad. Sch. Credit and Financial Mgmt., 1957; m. Ruth Gillis, 1944; children—James S., Roger A., Judy H., Holly R. Accountant, Price Waterhouse & Co., Boston, 1942-50; with Johnson Steel & Wire Co., Worcester, Mass., 1950-58, asst. treas., 1952-58; with Pitts. Steel Co., 1958-69, comptroller, asst. treas., 1964-68, v.p., comptroller, 1968-69; v.p., comptroller Wheeling Pitts. Steel Corp., Pitts., 1969—; v.p., dir. Pitts. Canfield Corp.; dir. Glaros Products, Inc. Bd. dirs. Pa. Economy League, 1959-69. Pres., Harmony (Pa.) Merged Sch. Dist., 1962-65; mem. S.W. Butler County Sch. Authority, 1964—; chmn. bd. auditors Cranberry Twp., Butler County, 1965-69. Bd. dirs. Jr. Achievement S.W. Pa.; bd. dirs., sec. Blue Cross Western Pa., 1969—. Served to 1st lt. AUS, World War II; ETO. Decorated D.S.C., Silver Star, Bronze Star, Purple Heart. C.P.A., Mass., Pa. Mem. Financial Execs. Inst. (bd. dirs., pres. 1971-72), Am. Iron and Steel Inst., Nat. Assn. Accountants, Mass. Soc. C.P.A.'s, Am. Inst. C.P.A.'s, Pa. Soc., Newcomen Soc. Clubs: Pittsburgh, Duquesne (Pitts.). Home: RD 1 Evans City PA 16033 Office: PO Box 118 Pittsburgh PA 15230

HOWARD, JAMES WEBB, investment banker; b. Evansville, Ind., Sept. 17, 1925; s. Joseph R. and Velma (Cobb) H.; B.S. in Mech. Engring., Purdue U., 1940; postgrad. Akron (O.) Law Sch., 1950-51, Cleve. Marshall Law Sch., 1951-52; M.B.A., Western Res. U., 1962; m. Phyllis Jean Brandt, Dec. 27, 1948; children—Sheila Rae, Sharon Kae. Jr. project engr. Firestone Tire & Rubber Co., Akron, 1949-50; gen. foreman Cadillac Motor Car div. Gen. Motors Corp., 1950-53; mgmt. cons. M.K. Sheppard & Co., Cleve., 1953- 56; plant mgr. Lewis Welding & Engring. Corp., Bedford, O., 1956-58; underwriter The Ohio Co., Columbus, 1959; chmn. Growth Capital, Inc., Chgo., 1960—, Meister Brau, Inc., Chgo., 1966—; dir. North Bank. Co-chmn. Chgo. com. Ill. Sesquicentennial Com. Bd. dirs. Rehab. Inst., Chgo., Boy Scouts, Chgo., Boys' Clubs, Chgo. Mercy Hosp. Served with AUS, 1943-47. Decorated Parachutist badge, Combat Inf. badge. Registered profl. engr., Ind., Ohio. Mem. Am. Soc. M.E., Nat. Assn. Small Bus. Investment Companies (past pres.), Cleve. Soc. Security Analysts, Grad. Bus. Alumni Assn. Western Res. U. (past gov.), Tau Kappa Epsilon, Pi Tau Sigma, Beta Gamma Sigma. Republican. Presbyn. Mason. Clubs: Lake Shore, Chicago Athletic, Racquet, 100. Home: 505 Lake Shore Dr Chicago IL 60611 Office: 1000 W North Av Chicago IL 60622

HOWARD, JOHN ADDISON, coll. pres.; b. Evanston, Ill., Aug. 10, 1921; s. Hubert Elmer and Edith (Sackett) H.; student Princeton, 1939-42; B.S., Northwestern U., 1947, M.A., 1949, Ph.D., 1962; m. Janette Marie Nobis, Aug. 11, 1951; children—Marie Starr, Steven Lamson, Martha Nobis, Katherine Louise. Instr. French, Palos Verdas Coll., Rolling Hills, Cal., 1947-49, dean students, 1949-51, v.p., 1950-51, pres., 1951-55; exec. vice chmn. Pres.'s Com. on Govt. Contracts, 1956-57; pres. Rockford (Ill.) Coll., 1960—. Mem. U.S. Commnn. on Marijuana and Dangerous Drugs, 1971—, Pres.'s Task Force on Priorities in Higher Edn., 1969-70. Bd. dirs. Lincoln Acad. Served to 1st lt. AUS, 1942-45. Decorated Silver Star with oak leaf cluster, Purple Heart with oak leaf cluster. Recipient Horatio Alger award, 1967. Mem. Am. Assn. Presidents Ind. Colls. and Univs. (pres. 1969—), Phila. Soc. (dir.), Phi Beta Kappa (hon.). Rotarian. Clubs: Rockford Country; Princeton (N.Y.C.); University (Chgo.); Bohemian (San Francisco). Home: 2120 Harlem Blvd Rockford IL 61103

HOWARD, JOHN BRIGHAM, lawyer; b. Edgewood, Pa., June 9, 1912; s. Lemuel Frederic and Anna (Kimm) H.; B.S. summa cum laude, Harvard, 1933, Ph.D., 1936; postgrad. Cal. Inst. Tech., 1933-34; J.D. cum laude, U. Chgo., 1942; m. Dorothy Koch, June 5, 1937 (dec. Oct. 1966); children—Elizabeth K., Frederic K., Theodore B., Catherine M.; m. 2d, Margaret Betz, Sept. 12, 1970. Jr., Harvard Soc. Fellows, 1936-39; admitted to Ill., D.C., Supreme Ct. bars; asst. legal adviser Dept. State, 1946-47, adviser U.S. delegation to U.N. Atomic Energy Commn., 1946; counselor Am. Mission Aid to Greece, 1947, dep. chief, 1948; cons. Congl. relations ECA, 1948-49; special asst. to sec. of state, 1949-50; regional planning adviser Nr. East, S. Asia, Africa affairs, Dept. State, 1950-51; dep. dir., dir. div. overseas activities Ford Found., 1952-54, dir. internat. tng. and research, 1955-67; pres., trustee Internat. Legal Center, 1967—. Mem. Council on Fgn. Relations, Am. Soc. Internat. Law, Assn. Bar N.Y.C., Am. Bar Assn., Phi Beta Kappa, Phi Delta Phi. Club: University. Contbr. articles to profl. jours. Home: 86 Edgemont Rd Scarsdale NY 10583 Office: 866 UN Plaza New York City NY 10017

HOWARD, JOHN CONLAN, steel co. exec.; b. Dover, N.J., Oct. 14, 1910; s. John James and Mary (Conlan) H.; B.S. in Econs., Wharton Sch. U. Pa., 1934; m. Mary Elizabeth Loughery, Oct. 10, 1939; children—John L., Thomas H., Neal J. and William J. (twins). With E.J. Lavino Co., 1934-36, U.S. Rubber Co., 1936-44, Office Def. Transp., 1942-44; with Bethlehem Steel Corp., 1944- -, asst. v.p., 1963-65, v.p. transp., 1965—. Mem. Pa. Soc., Am. Iron and Steel Inst. (chmn. traffic com.), Nat. Freight Traffic Assn., Nat. Indsl. Traffic League, N.Y.C., Phila. traffic clubs, Transp. Assn. Am. (dir.), Transp. Data Coordinating Com. (dir.), Phi Kappa Psi, Pi Gamma Mu. Clubs: Racquet (Phila.); University, Sky (N.Y.C.); Bethlehem, Saucon Valley Country (Bethlehem). Home: Saucon Valley Rd Bethlehem PA 18015 Office: 701 E 3d St Bethlehem PA 18016

HOWARD, JOHN DON, cons.; b. Estherville, Ia., June 3, 1903; s. Willis Vernon and Amelia Elizabeth (Nancolas) H.; B.S. in Elec. Engring., Ia. State U., 1925; m. Nita Knowles, Dec. 28, 1926; 1 son, Richard K. Engr., Westinghouse Electric Corp., 1925-34; with Wis. Power & Light Co., Madison, 1934-41, 43-68, exec. v.p., 1962-65, pres., 1965-68, also dir.; past pres., dir. S. Beloit Water, Gas & Electric Co., Wis. Valley Improvement Co.; v.p., dir. Wis. River Power Co., 1955-68; past dir. Atomic Power Devel. Assos. Dist. mgr. WPB, 1941-43; chmn. sponsored student com. Am. Power Conf., 1962-68; mem. Assn. Edison Illuminating Cos. Mem. Mayor's Govtl. Services Com. Registered profl. engr., Wis. Mem. I.E.E.E., Edison Electric Inst., Nat. Soc. Profl. Engrs., Wis. Utilities Assn. (pres., dir. 1963), Am. Gas Assn., Kappa Sigma, Eta Kappa Nu. Conglist. (trustee). Mason (Shriner), Kiwanian; mem. Order Eastern Star (past patron). Clubs: Madison, Nakoma Golf, Four Lakes Yacht, Forest Lakes Country. Home: 3622 Collins St Sarasota FL 33580 also 10 Heritage Circle Madison WI 53711

HOWARD, JOHN EAGER, physician, educator; b. Baltimore County, Md., Aug. 27, 1902; s. John Duvall and Mary Greenwood (Smith) H.; grad. Hill Sch., 1920; A.B., Princeton, 1924; M.D., Johns Hopkins, 1928; m. Lucy James Iglehart, June 30, 1928; children—John Eager (dec. 1971), William James, Lucy Anne Calhoun. Intern, Mass. Gen. Hosp., Boston, 1928-30; asst. resident Johns Hopkins Hosp., 1930-32, now mem. staff; practice medicine, Balt., 1934—; chief medicine Union Meml. Hosp., 1957—; prof. medicine Johns Hopkins, 1960-68, prof. emeritus, 1968—. Recipient Distinguished Achievement award Modern Medicine 1964; Passano award, 1968. Mem. Assn. Am. Physicians, Endocrine Soc. (pres. 1960-61), Am., Md. (pres. 1961-62) socs. internal medicine, Am. Clin. and Climatol. Assn., Balt. City Med. Soc., Interurban Clin. Club. Home: Waverly RFD 1 Lutherville MD 21093 Office: Johns Hopkins Hosp Baltimore MD 21205

HOWARD, JOHN GORDON, clergyman; b. Tokyo, Japan, Dec. 3, 1899 (parents U.S. citizens); s. Alfred Taylor and May Day (Stevenson) H.; A.B., Otterbein Coll., Westerville, O., 1922; B.D., United Theol. Sem., Dayton, O., 1925; A.M., N.Y.U., 1927; student Ohio State U., 1927-28; D.D., Otterbein Coll., 1936; LL.D., Albright Coll., 1952; Litt.D., Lebanon Valley Coll., 1969; L.H.D., Ind. Central Coll., 1970; m. Rhea McConaughy, July 22, 1924; children—Gloria Mae, Sarah Ellen; m. 2d, Katharine H. Shannon, Feb. 9, 1967. Nat. dir. young people's work United Brethren Ch., 1927-40; editor ch. sch. publs., 1940-45; pres. Otterbein Coll., 1945-57; bishop East Central area Evang. United Brethren Ch., Pitts., 1957-68; bishop Phila. area United Methodist Ch., 1968—. Bd. dirs. Pa., Phila. councils of chs. Past chmn. Ohio-W.Va. bd. YMCA, interracial commn. nat. council YMCA; pres. Ohio Council Chs., 1952-55; sec. Church Union Commn., United Brethren Ch. Mason. Clubs: Union League (Phila.); University (Pitts.); Civitan (Dayton, O.); Rotary (Wilkinsburg, Pa.). Author: When Youth Worship, 1940; The Successful Sunday Sch., 1940; A Catechism for Youth, 1942; Christian Belief for Christian Youth, 1950; Small Windows in a Big World, 1969. Home: 1801 Kennedy Blvd Philadelphia PA 19103 Office: 1701 Arch St Philadelphia PA 19103

HOWARD, JOHN RAYMOND, coll. pres.; b. McGuffey, O., Nov. 6, 1922; s. Jack Rebel and Pauline (Wies) H.; A.B., U. Pa., 1947, M.A., 1948; LL.D., Parsons Coll., 1960; L.H.D., Pacific U., 1970; Ruth Marie Hanners, Dec. 23, 1945; children—John Randolph, Linda Seely, Rebecca Lynn. Research asst. Pa. Hist. Soc., 1946; instr. polit. sci. U. Pa., 1948-57, coach debate team, 1949-52, asst. to exec. v.p., 1951-54, bus. mgr., 1955-57; bus. mgr. Lake Forest Coll., 1957-58, v.p. bus. and finance, 1958-59, acting pres., 1959-60; pres. Lewis and Clark Coll., Portland, Ore., 1960—. Dir. Portland br. Fed. Res. Bank San Francisco. Mem. Pres's Comm. Observance 25th Anniversary UN, 1970; mem. Mayor's Citizen's Exec. Com.; regional health adv. bd. Health, Edn. and Welfare. Trustee Physicians and Surgeons Hosp. Pres. Chester County (Pa.) Fedn. Young Republican Clubs, 1950-55. Mem. Nat. Commn. on Accrediting, bd. Christian edn. United Presbyn. Ch. U.S.A., Nat. Presbyn. Coll. Scholarship Com. Past vice chmn. Ore. Ednl. Coordinating Council ; mem. higher commn. N.W. Assn. Secondary and Higher Schs. Served to lt. (j.g.) USNR, 1942-46. Mem. Am. Polit. Sci. Assn., C. of C. (past dir.), Phi Delta Theta, Delta Sigma Rho, Pi Gamma Mu, Pi Sigma Alpha. Clubs: Rotary (pres. 1968-69), City (Portland); Waverley Country (past gov.), University. Home: 12746 SW Iron Mountain Blvd Portland OR 97219

HOWARD, JOHN TASKER, educator; b. Paris, France, June 7, 1911 (parents U.S. citizens); s. Rossiter and Alice (Woodbury) H.; student Antioch Coll., 1928-31; B.F.A., Yale 1934; B.Arch., Mass. Inst. Tech., 1935, M.C.P., 1936; traveling fellow in regional planning, 1936-37; m. Eleanor M. Robb, Dec. 26, 1940; children—John T., Jr., Margaret Alice. Research asst. N.E. Regional Planning Commn., Boston, 1935-36; city planner Regional Assn. of Cleve., 1937-42; lectr. in city planning Western Res. U., 1939-49; planning dir. Cleve. City Planning Commn., 1942-49; partner Adams, Howard & Greeley, city planning cons., Boston, Cleve., Hartford, Los Angeles, San Francisco Bay Area, Washington and other U.S. cities and towns, 1949-63, Adams, Howard & Oppermann, city planning cons., 1964-69; asso. prof. city planning Mass. Inst. Tech., 1949-57, prof., 1957—, head dept. city and regional planning, 1957-70. Mem. exec. com. Hwy. Research Bd., 1962-68; bd. consultants Eno Found. for Transp. Research, 1962—. Hon. asso. Cleve. chpt. A.I.A.; recipient Yale medal distinction in Arts, 1959. Mem. Assn. Collegiate Schs. of Planning (pres. 1960), Am. Soc. Planning Ofcls. (dir. 1947-50), Am. Inst. Planners (pres. 1954-56, distinguished service award 1963), Ohio Planning Conf. (pres. 1948). Home: 741 Washington St Annisquam MA 01930 Office: Mass Inst Tech Cambridge MA 02139 ☆

HOWARD, JOHN ZOLLIE, editor; b. Gainesboro, Tenn., Dec. 20, 1897; s. John W. and Lizzie (Van Hooser) H.; B.A., U. Tenn., 1924; m. Jessie Magill, Oct. 28, 1920; children—Joseph E., William Edwin. Instr., U. Tenn., 1924-25; reporter, Sunday editor, city editor Knoxville News-Sentinel, 1925-40; mng. editor Memphis Pres-Scimitar, 1940-64, asso. editor and editor editorial page, 1964—. Treas., The Goodfellows of Memphis, Inc. Presbyn. Home: 896 Robin Hood Lane Memphis TN 38111 Office: 495 Union Av Memphis TN 38101

HOWARD, JOSEPH LEON, naval officer; b. New Haven, Dec. 21, 1917; s. Benjamin Ely and Eva (Burban) H.; student San Diego State Coll., 1935-38; A.B. in Econs., U. Cal. at Berkeley, 1940; grad. Naval War Coll., 1948-49, Harvard Advanced Mgmt. Program, 1963; m. Irene Elizabeth Silver, Oct. 17, 1942; children—Michael Edward, Kenneth Lee, John Wayne. Commd. ensign USN, 1940, advanced through grades to rear adm., 1967; asst. dir. purchase div. Bur. Supplies and Accounts, Dept. Navy, 1949-52; spl. asst. to chief naval operations, 1957-59; various planning and operational positions inventory mgmt., depot operations Navy Dept.; dep. chief naval materiel, 1966-68; dir. procurement Office Asst. Sec. Navy, 1965-67; dep. dir. def. supply agy. Def. Contract Adminstrn. Services, 1968-70; comdg. officer NSC, Charleston, S.C., 1970—. Decorated Legion of Merit with gold star, Bronze Star with Combat V. Mem. Am. Profl. Writers Assn., Armed Forces Writers League, Nat. Contract Mgmt. Assn. (bd. advisers 1966—), Cal. State Soc., Mil. Order Carabao, Nat. Def. Transp. Assn., Naval Hist. Found., Naval Inst., Soc. Logistics Engrs. (charter, exec. bd., v.p. tech.). Mason (32). Clubs: Harvard Business School (dir. Washington); Army-Navy Country (bd. govs., exec. com., finance com. 1964-68 Arlington, Va.). Author: Our Modern Navy, 1961. Contbr. articles to profl., trade jours. Home: Qtrs F Naval Base Charleston SC 29408 Office: Comdg Officer NSC Charleston SC 29408

HOWARD, KENNETH JOSEPH, Jr., actor; b. El Centro, Cal., Mar. 28, 1944; s. Kenneth Joseph and Martha Carey (McDonald) H.; A.B., Amherst Coll., 1966; postgrad. Yale Sch. Drama, 1966-68. Appeared Broadway debut as Karl Kubelik in Promises, Promises, 1968-69; appeared as Thomas Jefferson in 1776 (Theatre World award), 1969; co-starred with Liza Minnelli in Otto Preminger film Tell Me That You Love Me, Junie Moon, Paramount Pictures, 1970; appeared as Paul Reese in Child's Play (Tony award), 1970—. Home: 333 E 75th St New York City NY 10021

HOWARD, LAWRENCE CABOT, univ. dean; b. Des Moines, Apr. 26, 1925; s. Charles P. and L. Maude (Lewis) H.; B.A., Drake U., 1949; M.A., Wayne U., 1950; Ph.D., Harvard, 1956; m. Elizabeth Fitzgerald, Feb. 14, 1953; children—Jane, Susan, Laura. Instr., then asst. prof. Hofstra U., 1956-58; asst. prof. Brandeis U., Waltham, Mass., 1958-63; asso. dir. Peace Corps, Philippines, 1961-63; asso. dir. Center on Innovation, N.Y. State Dept. Edn., 1964; dir. Inst. Human Relations, U. Wis., Milw., 1964-67; v.p. Danforth Found., 1967-69; prof. pub. and internat. affairs, dean Grad. Sch. Pub. and Internat. Affairs, U. Pitts., 1969—. Cons., U.S. Office Edn., State Dept. Bur. External Research; mem. research and adv. bd. Com. Econ. Devel., 1970—; mem. nat. adv. commn. Tchrs. Corps., 1967-69; mem. Pitts. World Affairs Council, 1969—, Pitts. History and Landmarks Found. Trustee Church Soc. for Coll. Work, Drake U., St. Augustine Coll., Harvard Grad. Soc. for Advancement of Study and Research. Served with AUS, 1943-45. Named Man of Year, Alpha Phi Alpha, 1949. Mem. Phi Beta Kappa. Contbr. articles to profl. jours. Home: 4200 Centre Av Pittsburgh PA 15213

HOWARD, LAWRENCE VAUGHAN, educator; b. Gastonburg, Ala., July 28, 1900; s. Albert H. and Annie P. (Vaughan) H.; A.B., Birmingham-So. Coll., 1920; M.A., U. Chgo., 1926, Ph.D., 1931; m. Purcell C. Corley, Sept. 4, 1929; children—Keren, Lawrence. High sch. tchr., 1920-24; asso. prof., then prof. polit. sci. Coll. William and Mary, 1928-37, asst. to pres., acting dean of men, 1932-34; prof. U. Md., 1937-43; historian USAAF, 1943-44; prof., dir. bur. pub. adminstrn. U. Ga., 1944-47, also exec. dir. Agrl. and Indsl. Devel. Bd. Ga.; prof. polit. sci. Tulane U., New Orleans, 1947-66, prof. emeritus, 1966—, chmn. dept. polit. sci., 1947-64; cons. La. Div. Employment Security, 1949-52; dir. So. Assembly, 1957-66. Mem. charter adv. com. City New Orleans, 1961; Ga. com. Nat. Council Crime and Delinquency, 1968—. Bd. mgrs. Delgado Trades and Tech. Inst. Served with U.S. Army, 1918. Mem. Am., So. polit. sci. assns., Am. Soc. Pub. Adminstrn., Phi Beta Kappa, Omicron Delta Kappa, Pi Sigma Alpha, Alpha Tau Omega. Co-author: Current American Government, 1943; Presidential Politics in Louisiana, 1952; Civil Service Development in Louisiana, 1956; Government in Metropolitan New Orleans, 1960. Contbr. articles profl. jours. Home: 3916 E Brookhaven Dr NE Atlanta GA 30319

HOWARD, LEE MILTON, physician; b. India, Nov. 9, 1922 (parents Am. citizens); s. John A. and Grace Mary (Lemen) H.; B.Sc., Baylor U., 1945; M.D., Johns Hopkins, 1947, M.P.H., 1958, D.P.H., 1959; m. Maxwell C. Croft, June 22, 1946; children—Regan Ellis, Christine Baker, Kirk Anderson, Gene Reid. Med. and surg. resident Church Home Hosp., Balt., 1947-50; mem. med. staff Clough Meml. Hosp., Ongole, Andhra, India, 1950-53; dir. Victoria Meml. Hosp., Warangal, Andhra, India, 1953-56; physician Med. Care Clinic, Johns Hopkins Hosp., 1957; U.S. adviser on malaria, Philippines, 1960- 62; U.S. regional malaria adviser Far East AID, 1962-64; chief malaria br. health div. AID, Washington, 1964-66; dep. dir. health service Office Tech. Coop. and Research, 1966-67, dir., 1967, dir. Office Health, Tech. Assistance Bur., 1969; mem. expert co. on malaria WHO, 1966-67, chmn. com., 1970, adviser parasitic diseases, 1970, mem. U.S. delegation, 1969, 70; vis. asso. prof. parasitology Inst. Hygiene U. Philippines, 1960—. Vis. lectr. Johns Hopkins U. Sch. Pub. Health. Mem. U.S. delegation, directing counsel Pan Am. Health Orgn., 1969, 70. Research fellow U.S. Armed Forces Epidemiological Bd., 1958-59. Diplomate Am. Bd. Preventive Medicine. Fellow Am. Pub. Health Assn., Royal Soc. Tropical Medicine and Hygiene; mem. Am. Soc. Tropical Medicine and Hygiene, Philippine Pub. Health Assn. Home: 621 Goldsborough Dr Rockville MD 20850 Office: Office Health Tech Assistance Bur AID Dept State Washington DC 20203

HOWARD, LEON, educator; b. Talladega, Ala., Nov. 8, 1903; s. Percy L. and Georgia (Heacock) H.; A.B., Birmingham-So. Coll., 1923; A.M., U. Chgo., 1926, L.H.D., 1961; Ph.D., Johns Hopkins, 1929; Ph.D. (hon.), Abo Akademi, Finland, 1968; m. Henrietta Starr, Mar. 6, 1931; children—Mary Morris, Charles Malone, Kathleen. Newspaper work, tchr. prep. schs., Ala., Ga., 1923-26; instr. English, Johns Hopkins, 1927-30; instr. English, Pomona Coll., 1930-32, asst. prof., 1932-37; Internat. Research fellow Henry E. Huntington Library, 1937-38; asso. prof. English, Northwestern U., 1938-43, prof., 1943-50, Morrison prof. English, 1945-50; prof. English, U. Cal. at Los Angeles, 1950- 71. Vis. prof. Tokyo U., summers 1951, 54, Centre Universitaire Mediterranean, summer 1957, U. N.M., Albuquerque, 1972—. Fulbright lectr. U. London, 1956-57, U. Copenhagen, 1960, Australia, 1963, Germany and Switzerland, 1964; Guggenheim fellow, 1944-45; sr. research fellow Newberry Library, 1966. Mem. Am. Acad. Arts and Scis., Modern Lang. Assn. Am., Am. Studies Assn., Phi Beta Kappa. Democrat. Episcopalian. Author: The Connecticut Wits, 1943; Herman Melville: a Biography, 1951; Victorian Knight-Errant: A Study of the Early Literary Career of James Russell Lowell, 1952; Literature and the American Tradition, 1960; The Mind of Jonathan Edwards, 1963. Contbr. articles to profl. publs. Home: 1200 Calle del Sol Albuquerque NM 87106

HOWARD, MILO BARRETT, Jr., state archivist; b. Montgomery, Ala., Oct. 21, 1933; s. Milo Barrett and Josepha (Key) H.; B.A., Ala. Poly. Inst., 1955; M.A., Auburn U., 1960. With Ala. Dept. Archives and History, 1958—, dir., 1967—; instr. U. Ala., 1964-68, Auburn U., 1968—. Chmn., Ala. Hist. Commn.; mem. Ala. Sesquicentennial Commn.; historiographer Episcopal Diocese Ala.; mem. Montgomery Hist. Devel. Commn., Ala. Am. Revolution Bicentennial Commn.; chmn. State Capital Preservation Commn. Served to 1st lt. AUS, 1955-57. Recipient Distinguished Service award Montgomery Jr. C. of C., 1967. Mem. Ala. Hist. Assn. (treas. 1956-64, 66—, pres. 1965-66), Soc. Am. Archivists, Newcomen Soc., Theta Chi. Episcopalian (vestryman 1963-66, 67-70, jr. warden 1968-69, sr. warden 1969-70, treas. 1971-72). Rotarian. Author: (with R.R. Rea) Memoire Justificatif of the Chevalier Montant de Monberaut, 1965. Contbr. articles to profl. jours. Home: 802 Felder Av Montgomery AL 36106 Office: Ala Archives and History Dept Montgomery AL 36104

HOWARD, NATHANIEL RICHARDSON, former newspaper editor; b. Arlington, Columbus, O., Apr. 23, 1898; s. Carlos Newton and Anne McKennan (Richardson) H.; student Oberlin Coll., 1915-18; m. Marjorie Norton, Sept. 13, 1918 (dec. Dec. 1928); children—Mary Anne, Marjorie Norton; m. 2d, Edith E. Moriarty, July 17, 1930. Reporter, Cleve. News, 1917, editor, 1937-60; with Cleve. Plain Dealer, 1918-37, mng. editor, 1930-37, contbg. editor, 1960-63; dir. A.P., 1952-60. Asst. dir. press U.S. Office Censorship, Washington, 1942-43. Trustee St. Luke's Hosp., Cleve. Mem. Am. Soc. Newspaper Editors (pres. 1947-48). Republican. Conglist. Clubs: Advertising, Union (Cleve.); Cosmos (Washington). Author: Trust for All Time, 1963; The George M. Humphrey Basic Papers, 1965. Home: 2227 S Overlook Rd Cleveland Heights OH 44106

HOWARD, PENDLETON, law educator; b. Ottawa, Kan., Sept. 2, 1894; s. Byron Gilbert and Gertrude (Pendleton) H.; LL.B., U. Tex., 1917; A.B., Columbia, 1921, A.M., 1924, Ph.D., 1931; m. Sarah Bridgers, July 26, 1926. Admitted to Tex. bar, 1917, N.Y. bar, 1921, Ida. bar, 1936; Practiced law, Dallas, 1917, N.Y. 1921-29; asst. dist. atty. N.Y. County, 1922-27; lectr. polit. sci. Columbia, 1924-27, Curtis fellow in pub. law, 1926-27, lectr. law, 1928-29; prof. law U. Ida., 1929- 45, dean Coll. Law, 1934-45; prof. law U. So. Cal., 1945-66, prof. emeritus, 1966—. Vis. prof. law Northwestern U., 1933-34, summers 1930, 34, U. So. Cal., summers 1931, 41, U. Ore., summer 1939, U. Mo., summer 1945, U. N.C., summer 1951, made survey of adminstrn. criminal justice in Eng. under auspices Council for Research in Social Scis., Columbia, U 1927-28. Mem. for Ida., Nat. Conf. Commrs. on Uniform State Laws, 1936-45; arbitrator Nat. War Labor Bd. in various wage disputes in lumber and mining industries Pacific N.W., 1942-43; research asso., adv. com. on rules fed. criminal procedure Supreme Ct. U.S., 1942. Served as 2d. lt. AS, U.S. Army, World War I. Mem. Order of Coif, Delta Chi, Phi Alpha Delta, Delta Sigma Rho, Sigma Delta Chi. Democrat. Presbyn. Author: Criminal Justice in England—A Study in Law Administration, 1931; (with D.O. McGovney) Cases on Constitutional Law, 1954. Contbr. to Ency. Social Sci., also articles to legal jours. Home: 400 S Burnside Av Los Angeles CA 90036

HOWARD, RHEA, newspaper pub.; b. Wichita Falls, Tex., July 25, 1892; s. Ed and Jettie Lee (Maloney) H.; student Trinity U., Waxahachie, Tex., 1910-11, Eastman Coll., Poughkeepsie, N.Y., 1912; m. Kathleen Benson, Oct. 22, 1913; 1 dau., Anna Katherine (Mrs. James B. Barnett). With Times Pub. Co. (Wichita Daily Times, Wichita Falls Record News), 1913—, pres., 1948—; v.p., dir. Wichita Water Irrigation Dist.; dir. Burlington No. Ry. Bd. dirs. Wichita Falls United Fund, Tex. Law Enforcement Found., River Valley Assn., Midwestern U. Found., Wichita Falls Bd. Commerce and Industry, YMCA, Wichita Falls Art Mus., N. Tex. Rehab. Center, A.R.C., Wichita County Child Welfare and Devel. Found., Wichita Falls Symphony, Tex. Council for Higher Edn., Woman's Forum. Mem. Tex. State Democratic Exec. Com.; del. nat. conv., 1952, 56, 60, 64. Named Pub. of Year, Headliners Club, 1960. Mem. National Press Club, Am. Soc. Newspaper Editors, Tex. Daily Newspaper Assn., N. Tex. Oil and Gas Assn. (dir.), Am., So. newspaper pubs. assns., C. of C. (dir.), Asso. Press, Sigma Delta Chi. Democrat. Presbyn. Mason (K.T., Shriner, 32). Clubs: President's, Wichita Falls Country. Home: 2105 Berkley Dr Wichita Falls TX 76307 Office: 1301 Lamar St Wichita Falls TX 76301

HOWARD, RICHARD ALDEN, botanist; b. Stamford, Conn., July 1, 1917; s. Charles Frederick and Augusta Grace (Barker) H.; A.B., Miami U., Oxford, O., 1938; M.A., Harvard, 1940, Ph.D., 1942; m. Elizabeth Solie, Feb. 14, 1944; children—Jean Elizabeth, Barbara Jo, Bruce Richard, Philip George. Jr. fellow Soc. of Fellows, Harvard, 1942, 46-47, asst. prof. biology, 1948-53, Arnold prof. botany, prof. dendrology, dir. Arnold Arboretum, 1954—; curator N.Y. Bot. Garden, 1947-48; asst. prof. botany; head dept. U. Conn., 1953-54. Cons. Arctic Dessert, Tropic Information Center, USAF, 1946-. Served from pvt. to capt. USAF, 1942- 46; organized and directed Jungle Survival Program, Sch. Applied Tactics, Orlando, Fla. Decorated Legion of Merit. Mem. Internat. Assn. Botanic Gardens (pres. 1950-64), Bot. Soc. Am., Am. Soc. Plant Taxonomists (treas. 1949-53), Am. Acad. Arts and Scis.; Am. Inst. Biol. Scis., N.E. Bot Club (pres. 1952-53), Sigma Xi. Author: 999 Survived, Analysis of survival experiences in S.W. Pacific, 1949; Sun, Sand and Surviaval, 1953; Down in the North, 1953; sci. papers in field. Research in systematic botany and plant morphology and studies of vegetation and distbn. plants in Caribbean area, West Indian Islands, numerous field expdns. to Caribbean Islands, Mexico, C.A.M. Home: 137 Wellesley St Weston MA 02193 Office: Arnold Arboretum Jamaica Plain MA 02130

HOWARD, RICHARD FOSTER, museum ofcl.; b. Plainfield, N.J., July 26, 1902; s. Lawrence Riggs and Nina Margaret (Kellogg) H.; B.S., Harvard, 1924, postgrad. 1929-31; postgrad. Cornell U., summer 1930, Inst. Human Relations, Yale, 1931; m. Anne Okeson, Sept. 3, 1925; 1 dau., Margaret Anne; m. 2d, Frances Flanders, Dec. 17, 1932; m. 3d, Helen Boswell, Oct. 14, 1943 (dec. 1969); 1 son, James Boswell; m. 4th, Ethel Dunnan Booker, Feb. 28, 1970. Tchr., The Hill Sch.; Pottstown, Pa., 1924-26, Arnold Sch., Pitts., 1926-27, Chestnut Hill Acad., Phila., 1927-29; staff psychologist Pa. Mus. Art, 1932-35; dir. Dallas Mus. Fine Arts, 1935-42; lectr. art So. Meth. U., 1936-42; instr. art Hockaday Jr. Coll., Dallas, 1937-39; dir. Des Moines Art Center, 1948-49, Birmingham (Ala.) Mus. Art, 1950- -. Served from capt. to lt. col. F.A., AUS 1942-44, chief monuments, fine arts and archives sect. Office Mil. Govt. U.S., 1946-48. Mem. Am. Fedn. Art, Washington, Am. assns. museums, Western Assn. Art Mus. Dirs., Mil. Order Loyal Legion U.S., Sigma Alpha Epsilon. Conglist. Contbr. articles to profl. jours. Home: 3920 9th Ct S Birmingham AL 35222 Office: Birmingham Mus Art Oscar Wells Meml Bldg Birmingham AL 35203

HOWARD, ROBERT ADRIAN, physicist, educator; b. Los Angeles, Feb. 23, 1913; s. Robert and Mary (Taylor) H.; B.S., Cal. Inst. Tech., 1934, M.S., 1935; Ph.D., Washington U., St. Louis, 1938; m. Jane Elizabeth Morgens, June 2, 1939 (dec. 1966); children—Eileen (Mrs. Ernest Manes), Brian, Donald, Kathleen; m. 2d, Phyllis I. Mummery, 1971. Research physicist Carter Oil Co., Tulsa, 1939-41; staff mem. Radiation Lab., Mass. Inst. Tech., 1942-45; staff mem. Hydrodynamics Lab., Cal. Inst. Tech., 1946-47; prof. physics U. Okla., Norman, 1947—. Cons. Ramo-Wooldridge Corp., 1955-57; dir. Instituto Central de Fisica, Universidad de Concepcion, Chile, 1962-64; guest scientist Institut für Hochenergiephysik, U. Heidelberg, 1969-70. Fellow Okla. Acad. Sci.; mem. Am. Phys. Soc., Am. Assn. Physics Tchrs., Am. Assn. U. Profs. (past chpt. pres.), Sigma Xi, Sigma Pi Sigma, Tau Beta Pi. Author: (with others) Radiation Laboratory Technical Series, 1948; Nuclear Physics 1963. Patentee microwave field. Home: 711 W Timberdell Rd Norman OK 73069 Office 440 W Brooks St Norman OK 73069

HOWARD, ROBERT BOARDMAN, sculptor, painter; b. N.Y.C., Sept. 20, 1896; s. John Galen and Mary Robertson (Bradbury) H.; student Art Students League N.Y.C., 1916-17; study, travel in Europe, 1919-22; m. Adaline Kent, 1930; children—Ellen Kent, Galen H. Designer, executor murals, sculpture, 1922—; sculpture in wood and iron, murals Yosemite Nat. Park, 1929-36; murals, sculpture, San Francisco Stock Exchange, 1938-39; ann. shows San Francisco Mus. Art, Whitney Mus. Am. Art; one-man shows Mills Coll., 1945, Legion of Honor, San Francisco, 1946, U. Cal. at Berkeley, 1947, Cal. Sch. Fine Arts Gallery, 1956, Salon de Mai, Paris, France, 1962, 63, Seattle Expn., 1962, San Francisco Mus. Art, 1963, U. Cal. at Santa Cruz, 1968, San Francisco Art Commn. (award), 1971; sculpture Acad. Scis., San Francisco, IBM, San Jose. Mem. San Francisco Art Commn., 1950-54. Served with U.S. Army in France, 1918-19. Recipient awards, painting or sculpture, San Francisco Art Inst., 1923, 24, 37, 41, 43, 44, 46, 51, San Francisco Art Festival, 1952, Chgo., 1947-48, Crocker prize, 1955. Mem. San Francisco Art Inst. Studio: 521 Francisco St San Francisco CA 94133

HOWARD, ROBERT BRUCE, educator; b. St. Paul, Dec. 25, 1920; s. Willard Samuel and Edna (Bole) H.; B.A., U. Minn., 1942, M.B., 1944, M.D., 1945, Ph.D. in Medicine, 1952; m. Lorraine Leavitt, Mar. 21, 1942; children—Gregory, David, Carol, Irene, Bradley. Faculty, U. Minn., Mpls., 1948—, instr. medicine, asst. prof., asso. prof., dir. continuation med. edn., asso. dean med. scis., 1948-58, dean med. scis., prof. medicine, 1958-70, prof. medicine, dir. med. edn. U. Teaching and Research Unit, Northwestern Hosp., 1971—. Trustee, past sec.-treas. Minn. Med. Found. Fellow A.C.P.; mem. Assn. Am. Med. Colls. (chmn. 1970), Am., Minn. med. assns., Minn. Acad. Medicine, Minn., Mpls. socs. internal medicine, Phi Beta Kappa, Alpha Omega Alpha. Home: 2243 W Hoyt St St Paul MN 55108 Office: Northwestern Hosp Minneapolis MN 55407

HOWARD, ROBERT LEE, conveyor co. exec.; b. Louisville, Aug. 28, 1911; s. John Thomas and Ernestine Amelia (Fehler) H.; student U. Louisville, 1929, evenings 1934- 37; m. Marie Jarboe, Oct. 30, 1931; children—Robert Lee, Patricia Sheeran. With Logan Co., Louisville, 1938-67, v.p., controller, 1956-63, v.p., sec., 1963-67, also dir.; v.p., treas. Seamco Conveyor Co., 1967- -; pres., treas. Service Erection & Machine Co. Treas., Jr. Achievement Louisville, 1959, pres., 1960-62, nat. bd. dirs., 1961- -; active fund raising drives Community Chest, Ky. Crippled Children's Assn., local A.R.C., Heart Assn. Mem. Nat. Assn. Credit Mgmt. (pres. Louisville 1958, dir., v.p. central div. 1961, nat. pres. 1964-65), Adminstrv. Mgmt. Soc. (pres. Louisville 1957, Merit award 1961), Financial Execs. Inst. Am. Mem. Christian Ch. (deacon). Rotarian. Club: Wildwood Country (past pres. Louisville). Home: 3421 Mt Rainier Dr Louisville KY 40222 Office: 3918 Bardstown Rd Louisville KY 40218

HOWARD, ROBERT PIKE, investment banker; b. Phila., Oct. 12, 1922; s. Edgar Billings and Elizabeth (Newhall) H.; grad. St. Paul's Sch., Concord, N.H., 1941; B.A., Yale, 1945; m. Carolyn Beth Schwing, Nov. 27, 1946; children—Scott Pike, Carolyn Newhall, Peter Schwing. With traffic dept. Miss. Shipping Co., 1946-50; with ocean rate dept. Ins. Co. N.Am., 1950-53; with Howard, Weil, Labouisse, Fredericks & Co., New Orleans, 1954—, sr. v.p., mgr. trading dept., 1956—. Bd. dirs. Howard Meml. Library. Served to capt. USMCR, 1941-46, 53-54. Mem. Nat. Assn. Securities Dealers (chmn. bus. conduct com. dist. 5). Home: 1435 2d St New Orleans LA 70130 Office: 211 Carondelet St New Orleans LA 70130

HOWARD, ROBERT STAPLES, newspaper pub.; b. Wheaton, Minn., Oct. 23, 1924; s. Earl Eaton and Helen Elizabeth (Staples) H.; student U. Minn., 1942, 45; m. Lillian Irene Crabtree, Sept. 2, 1945; children—Thomas, Andrea, William, David. Pres., Howard Publs. (8 daily newspapers). Served as pvt. AUS, 1942-43, 2d lt. USAAF, 1944-45. Home: PO Box 1337 Rancho Santa Fe CA 90670 Office: PO Box 570 Oceanside CA 92054

HOWARD, ROBERT WEST, author; b. Addison, N.Y., Apr. 7, 1908; s. Charles James and Clare Jane (West) H.; ed. pub. high schs., N.Y.; m. Alice Harriet Barrett, 1938 (div. Oct. 1947); children—Elizabeth Barrett, David James; m. 2d, Anna Margaret Taylor, Nov. 8, 1947 (div. Mar. 1958); 1 dau., Margaret; m. 3d, Elizabeth Zimmermann, May 24, 1958. Newspaper reporter various N.Y. dailies, 1927-36; asst. state editor Fed. Writers Project, N.Y. State, 1936, asst. state dir., 1937; free-lance writer, N.Y., 1937-38; asso. editor Farm Jour., Phila., 1938-43; editor in chief Pathfinder mag., Washington, 1943-45; v.p. Lyme Found., Hartford, Conn., 1945; v.p. Antioch Coll., 1949; roving editor Am. Meat Inst., 1954-59; editor N.Y. Brand Book, 1970—. Recipient Distinguished Service award Am. Inst. Cooperation, 1948. Club: Nat. Press. Author: Two Billion Acre Farm, 1945; The Real Book About Farms, 1952; (with Paul L. Essert) Educational Planning By Communities, 1952; Toward Mental Democracy, 1954. Editor and contbr. This is The West, 1956-57 (Spur and Maggie awards, 1958); This is the South, 1959; (With Oren Arnold) Rodeo-Last Frontier of Old West, 1959; The Bench Mark, 1960; Hoofbeats of Destiny, 1960; The Great Iron Trail, 1962; The Race West, 1962; The Wagonmen, 1964; The Flag of the Dreadful Bear, 1965; The Horse in America 1965; Eli Whitney, 1966; The Boatmen, 1967; First Book of Farms, 1968; Thundergate: The Forts of Niagara, 1968; The South Pass Story, 1968; The First Book of Niagara Falls, 1969. Contbr. The Wonderful World of Books, 1953, Ency. Brit., 1964, World Book, 1965, Childcraft, 1965, also nat. mags. Home: 30 Doncaster Rd Rochester NY 14623

HOWARD, RONALD ARTHUR, educator; b. N.Y.C., Aug. 27, 1934; s. William McG. and Susan (Gault) H.; S.B. in Elec. Engring. and Econs., Mass. Inst. Tech., 1955, S.M. in Elec. Engring., 1956, E.E., 1957, Sc.D. in Elec. Engring., 1958; m. Polly Avery Hatheway, Sept. 17, 1955; children—Kim Elizabeth, David Randall, John Avery, Robert Andrew. Asst., then asso. prof. elec. engring. and indsl. mgmt. Mass. Inst. Tech., 1958-65; prof. engring. econ. systems Stanford, 1965—; cons. Arthur D. Little, Inc., 1956-64, Gen. Electric Co., 1964—, Stanford Research Inst., 1965—, Xerox Corp., 1971—. Sr. mem. I.E.E.E.; mem. Inst. Mgmt. Scis. (pres. 1967, editor jour. 1964—), Operations Research Soc. Am. (asso. editor jour. 1964-70, dept. editor 1970—). Author: Dynamic Programming and Markov Processes, 1960; Dynamic Probability Systems, 2 vols., 1971. Home: 646 Tennyson Av Palo Alto CA 94301 Office: Engring-Economic Systems Stanford Univ Stanford CA 94305

HOWARD, ROY JOSEPH, educator; b. Shreveport, Mar. 19, 1925; s. Lewis Benton and Felicie (Dauterive) H.; B.A., Woodstock Coll., 1948, licentiate philosophy, 1949, M. Teaching, 1950; licentiate theology, Facultes St. Albert, Louvain, Belgium, 1956; Ph.D., U. Louvain, 1960; m. Sonja Sylvia Valderhaug, Sept. 13, 1962; children—Stacy Lynn, Karin Michelle, Stephen Roy. Tchr., Jesuit High Sch., New Orleans, 1949-52; asso. prof. philosophy Spring Hill Coll., Mobile, 1957-58, 60-62; mem. faculty San Diego (Cal.) State Coll., 1963—, prof. philosophy, 1969—. Author: Liturgical Retreat, 1959. Home: 1406 Monument Hill Rd El Cajon CA 92020 Office: Dept Philosophy San Diego State Coll San Diego CA 92115

HOWARD, TRAVIS GLENN, banker; b. Bairdstown, Tex., Mar. 4, 1920; s. Gaither Artis and Nita (Kennemer) H.; B.B.A., U. Tex., 1947; m. Alice Marie Kost, June 17, 1949; children—Travis Glenn, Gary Neal. Agt., Internal Revenue Service, 1947-60; with Tex. Nat. Bank Commerce, and predecessor, Houston, 1960—, auditor, 1962-65, comptroller, 1965-70, v.p., 1970—. Served with USNR, 1942-45; PTO. C.P.A., Tex. Baptist. Home: 13319 Indian Creek Houston TX 77024 Office: 712 Main St Houston TX 77001

HOWARD, TREVOR, actor; b. Kent, Eng., Sept. 29, 1916; student Clifton Coll., (Bristol, Eng.), also Royal Acad. Dramatic Art. Stage debut in Revolt in a Reformatory, 1933; appeared in Old Vic prodns. Taming of the Shrew, The Anatomist; screen debut in The Way Ahead, 1943; motion pictures include Brief Encounter, Way to the Stars, So Well Remembered, Passionate Friends, Golden Salamander, Odette, Outcast of the Islands, The Gift Horse, Run for the Sun, Around the World in 80 Days, Roots of Heaven, Sons and Lovers, Charge of the Light Brigade, Interpol, Manuel, The Key, Mutiny on the Bounty, 1962, Operation Crossbow, Von Ryan's Express, Morituri, Eagle in a Cage, The Liquidator, The Poppy is also a Flower, The Lion, Man in the Middle, Pretty Polly. Served with British Army, World War II. Recipient TV Emmy award for best actor in The Invincible Mr. Disraeli, 1963. Address: Rowley Green Arkley Hertsfordshire England

HOWARD, WILLIAM ALLEN, physician; b. New Orleans, July 12, 1912; s. A. Allen and Ellie Kate (Elgin) H.; M.D., Tulane U., 1934; m. Marion McAlpine Rowcliffe, Sept. 5, 1947; children—Marion McNeill, Alison Rowcliffe, William Rowcliffe. Intern, asst. resident U. Ia. Hosp., 1934-36; asst. resident pediatrics Strong Meml. Hosp., chief resident pediatrics Childrens Hosp. of D.C., 1937-38; teaching fellow Georgetown U. Med. Sch., 1938-39; practice medicine, specializing in pediatrics and allergy, Washington, 1939—; instr., asst. prof., prof. pediatrics George Washington U. Med. Sch., 1946-67, chmn. dept., 1959-67, clin. prof. pediatrics, 1967—; sr. attending pediatrics, chief of allergy Childrens Hosp. D.C., also bd. dirs., trustee. Chmn. sub bd. Pediatric Allergy, 1967-71. Served to lt. col. AUS, 1942-46. Decorated Legion of Merit. Fellow Am. Acad. Pediatrics (chmn. dist. III, mem. exec. bd.), Am. Acad. Allergy, So. Soc. for Pediatric Research; mem. A.M.A., D.C. Med. Soc., Soc. Med. Cons. to Armed Forces (past pres.), Phi Chi, Alpha Omega Alpha, Pi Kappa Phi. Clubs: Metropolitan (Washington); Chevy Chase. Contbr. articles profl. jours. Home: 3714 Cardiff Ct Chevy Chase MD 20015 Office: 4100 Cathedral Av NW Washington DC 20016

HOWARD, WILLIAM EDWARDS, former banker; b. Salisbury, Md., June 27, 1904; s. William Edwards and Eunice (Morgan) H.; A.B., U. Del., 1924; m. Evelyn Sale, Mar. 17, 1934; children—Macon Lee, Julia Morgan, Evelyn Sale. Asst. cashier Mchts. Nat. Bank, Hampton, Va., 1924-28; nat. bank examiner, 1928-30; asst. cashier McDowell County Nat. Bank, Welch, W.Va., 1930-32; pres., dir. Braddock Nat. Bank (Pa.), 1932-47; v.p., dir. Wilkinsburg Bank (Pa.), 1938-47; v.p. Mellon Nat. Bank & Trust Co., Pitts., 1947-63, sr. v.p., 1963-69; now ret.; pres. Columbia Corp., Pitts.; trustee Dollar Savs. Bank of Pitts.; dir. Kennametal, Inc., Latrobe, Pa., White Cross Stores, Inc., Pitts., O. Hommel Co., Union Title Guaranty Co., H.H. Robertson Co., Pitts., Latrobe Steel Co. (Pa.), Mchts. Despatch Transp. Corp., N.Y.C., Despatch Shops, Inc., N.Y.C., Fisher Sci. Co., Pitts., Lake Erie & Eastern R.R. Co., Pitts., Ry. Maintenance Corp., Pitts. Bd. dirs., exec. v.p. Braddock Gen. Hosp.; bd. dirs., treas. Western Pa. Conservancy; trustee, treas. Valley Sch. Ligonier (Pa.), Community Coll. Allegheny County. Vice chmn., mem. finance com., treas. United Fund Allegheny County; treas., mem. exec. com. Pitts. Urban Transit Council, Nat. Transp. Center, Pitts.; vice chmn. bd. Nature Conservancy. Episcopalian. Mason (Shriner). Home: 3955 Bigelow Blvd Pittsburgh PA 15213 Office: Mellon Bank Bldg Mellon Sq Pittsburgh PA 15230

HOWARD, WILLIAM JACK, corp. exec.; b. Kimball, Neb., Aug. 25, 1922; s. Carl G. and Agnes (Forsling) H.; B.S. in Mech. Engring., N.M. State U., 1946; postgrad. U. N.M., 1947-50; m. Georgia S. Holt, June 26, 1946; children—Melissa, Andrew Jay. With engring. div. Sandia base Los Alamos Sci. Lab., 1946-56, dept. mgr., 1949-56; with Sandia Livermore (Cal.) Lab., 1956-63, dir. systems devel., 1957-63; chmn. mil. liaison com. AEC, also asst. to sec. def. for atomic energy, 1963-66; v.p. Sandia Corp. Albuquerque, 1966—. Vice pres. Livermore C. of C., 1958. Served to capt., inf., AUS, 1943-46; ETO, P. I. Decorated Bronze Star with combat V, Purple Heart, Combat Inf. Badge; recipient Distinguished Pub. Service medal Dept. Def., 1966. Mem. Am. Soc. M.E., Am. Inst. Aeros. and Astronautics, Am. Ordnance Assn. Home: 920 McDuffie Circle Albuquerque NM 87110 Office: Sandia Corp PO Box 5800 Albuquerque NM 87115

HOWARD, WINIFRED TOYA, oil and chem. co. exec.; b. Tallahassee, Apr. 3, 1925; s. Winifred Toya and Evelyn (Russ) H.; B.A., Western Res. U., 1949; student U. Fla.; m. Ruth Bandy, July 18, 1953; children—Samuel Bryan, Timothy Russ, Paul Lee. Asso. prof. bus. adminstrn. Fla. So. Coll., Lakeland, 1955-56; gen. credit mgr. White Industries, 1956-58; area credit mgr. J.C. Penney Co., 1958-59; mem. treasury and sales finance staff Chrysler Corp., 1960-61; mgmt. cons., 1965-67; div. treas. Amerada-Hess Corp., Hudson Petroleum Corp., 1961-69; asst. treas. Hess Oil and Chem. Corp., 1969—. Vice pres., dir. United Fund Central Jersey, 1969. Served with USNR, World War II, Korea. Mem. Am. Mgmt. Assn., Nat. Research Credit Found., Am. Petroleum Credit Assn., Internat. Consumers Credit Assn., Pi Kappa Phi, Pi Gamma Mu. Baptist. Home: 58 Wellington Rd East Brunswick NJ 08816 Office: 1 Hess Plaza Woodbridge NJ 07095

HOWARD, WINSTON STANLEY, lawyer; b. Des Moines, Oct. 15, 1907; s. William Shadrick and Amanda (Sandstrom) H.; student U. Neb., 1925-26; J.D. cum laude, U. Wyo., 1930; m. Marguerite Blair, June 7, 1933; children—Alan Blair, Joan. Admitted to Wyo. bar, 1930, Colo. bar, 1935; practice in Big Horn County, Wyo., 1931-35, Denver, 1935—; partner firm Dawson, Nagel, Sherman & Howard, 1939—. Chmn. bd. dirs. Continental Nat. Bank; dir. MSI Industries, Inc., Blvd. Nat. Bank, Tri State Finance Co. Pres. bd. trustees Temple Buell Coll., Swedish Med. Center; bd. dirs. Denver Technol. Center, Inc.; dir. Nat. Western Stock Show Assn.; Denver adv. bd. Salvation Army. Served from lt. to lt. comdr., USNR, 1944-46. Recipient Others award Salvation Army, 1962, Distinguished Alumni award U. Wyo., 1967. Mem. Am., Colo. (past gov.), Denver bar assns., Denver, Englewood chambers commerce, Sigma Nu, Delta Sigma Rho. Republican. Episcopalian (former vestryman, warden). Clubs: Denver, Kiwanis (past pres.), Mile High (Denver); Garden of the Gods (Colorado Springs, Colo.). Home: 4860 S Dahlia St Littleton CO 80120 Office: First Nat Bank Bldg Denver CO 80202

HOWARD-FLANDERS, PAUL, educator; b. Bristol, Eng., June 30, 1919; s. Leonard Richard and Millicent (Franks) H-F.; B.S., London U., Eng., 1940, Ph.D., 1956; M.A., Yale, 1964; m. June Daphne Cain, Sept. 23, 1950; children—Rob Stewart, Mark Richard. With Med. Research Council exptl. radio-pathology unit Hammersmith Hosp., London, 1953-59; asso. prof. radiobiology Yale, New Haven, 1959-63, prof. radiobiology and molecular biophysics, 1963—. Mem. research adv. council Am. Cancer Soc., 1963—. Mem. editorial bd. Jour. Bacteriology, 1966-70. Contbr. articles profl. jours. Office: 333 Cedar St New Haven CT 06510

HOWARTH, ANTHONY JONATHAN, educator; b. Colchester, Eng., Sept. 10, 1933; s. Frank and Kathleen Mary (Ball) H.; came to U.S., 1947, naturalized, 1956; B.A., Yale 1955; M.A., Columbia, 1967, Fordham U., 1970; m. Marna Dundes, Dec. 24, 1956; children—Andrew, Dianne, Roger. Mem. staff Cleve. Press, 1951-55, Lancaster (Pa.) Intelligencer-Jour., 1959-60; wire editor Indpls. Times, 1960-62; editorial writer N.Y. World-Telegram & Sun, 1962-66, features editor, 1966; tchr. Woodlands High Sch., Hartsdale, N.Y., 1966—. Home: 161 Mendham Av Hastings-on-Hudson NY 10706 Office: Woodlands High Sch Hartsdale NY 10530

HOWARTH, THOMAS, telephone co. exec.; b. Eng., June 2, 1921; s. Frank and Mary Elizabeth (Conner) H.; B.C.S., Benjamin Franklin U., 1946, M.C.S., 1947; m. Eleanor Louise King, Feb. 4, 1942; 1 son, Thomas King. Came to U.S., 1926, naturalized, 1936. With Springfield Nat. Bank (Mass.), 1939-42; C.P.A., Washington, 1946-57; sec., treas. Nat. Coal Assn., Washington; treas. Fuels Research Council, Inc., Washington, 1957-70, Coal Exporters Assn. U.S., Inc., 1959-70; asst. treas. Bituminous Coal Research, Inc., 1960-70; asst. to exec. v.p. U.S. Ind. Telephone Assn., Washington, 1970—; instr. accounting Am. Inst. Banking, Washington, 1948-57. Served with USNR, 1942-45. Mem. Inst. Orgn. Mgmt. (chmn. bd. regents 1969-70), Am., D.C. insts. C.P.A.'s. Episcopalian (chmn. dept. finance Diocese Washington 1964-67, treas. 1969—, parish treas., vestryman, sr. warden). Mason (Shriner). Clubs: Burning Tree (Bethesda, Md.); Argyle Country (Silver Spring, Md.). Home: 1505 Live Oak Dr Silver Spring MD 20910 Office: 438 Pennsylvania Bldg 425 13th St NW Washington DC 20004

HOWE, ALBERT SPAULDING, Jr., corp. exec.; b. Brookline, Mass., Apr. 24, 1906; s. Albert Spaulding and Belle (Forbes) H.; A.B., Harvard, 1927, M.B.A., 1929; m. Isabel Sproul, May 3, 1924 (div. 1934); m. 2d, Dorothy Hutchinson, July 19, 1935; children—Albert Spaulding III, Julia Forbes (Mrs. Rodman Rhodes), Thomas Hutchinson, Doria Waller. Instr., Harvard Bus. Sch., 1929-30; asst. to Jean Monnet, N.Y.C., 1930-35, to A. F. Adams, N.Y.C., 1935-43; chmn. Autoflight Corp., N.Y.C., 1943-45; pres. Howe & Fant, Inc., Norwalk, Conn., 1945-59; pres. Cellular Concrete Co., Darien, Conn., 1962—; Chmn. bd. Roxbury Carpet Co., Saxonville, Mass., 1963-65. Trustee New Eng. Inst., Ridgefield, Conn., Thomas Sch., Rowayton, Conn., Stamford (Conn.), Darien, New Canaan Community Mental Health Center, Inc., Franklin S. DuBois Day Treatment Center, Stamford, Rockledge Inst., Darien. Republican. Conglist. Club: Wee Burn Country (Darien). Address: 180 Long Neck Point Darien CT 06820

HOWE, DAVID LEONARD, machinery mfg. co. exec.; b. Grand Rapids, Mich., Oct. 17, 1926; s. Leonard F. and Beulah (Joyce) H.; A.B., U. Mich., 1949, J.D., 1952; m. Helene Aldrich VanDyke, Aug. 5, 1948; children—Eric VanDyke, Kristen Aldrich, Steven Edward. Admitted to Mich. bar, 1952; research asso. law sch. U. Mich., Ann Arbor, 1952-56, lectr. bus. law Sch. Bus. Administrn., 1953-56; corp. and financial counsel Clark Equipment Co., Buchanan, Mich., 1956-60, asst. sec., 1960-62, asst. treas., 1962-69, v.p., treas., 1969—; dir. First Nat. Bank Southwestern Mich., Niles, Garden City Fan & Blower, Niles, CTS Corp., Elkhart, Ind. Served with USNR, 1944-46. Mem. Am. Bar Assn., Financial Execs. Inst., Comml. Law League Am., Nat. Found. Consumer Credit, Am. Mgmt. Assn. Home: 1455 Ottawa Trail Niles MI 49120 Office: 324 E Dewey Av Buchanan MI 49107

HOWE, EUNICE SIMM, (Mrs. Henry Dunster Howe), lawyer, mem. Republican Nat. Com.; b. Belmont, Mass., Apr. 24, 1918; d. A. Glenn and Mary Eliza Simm; student Geneva Coll. (Switzerland), 1936- 37; A.B., Mt. Holyoke Coll., 1938; J.D., Boston U., 1941; postgrad. George Washington U.; m. Henry Dunster Howe, Feb. 9, 1946; children—Eunice Dunster, Maryalice Boardman. Admitted to Mass. bar, 1941; practiced in Boston, 1941—; asst. atty. gen. Mass., 1941-44; counsel Mass. Div. Employment Security, 1946-47; mem., chmn. com. consumer edn. Mass. Consumers Council, 1965—; chmn. Consumer Adv. Council, 1970—; mem. Mass. Council Crime and Correction; mem. Legislative Commn. Revision Mass. Criminal Law. Chmn. bequest, annuities com. Mt. Holyoke Coll., 1960—, chmn. alumni fund com., 1961-63, trustee, 1970—. Mem. Rep. Nat. Com. of Mass., 1968—; hon. pres. Mass. Fedn. Rep. Women. Served to lt. (j.g.) USNR, World War II. Recipient Alumnae medal of honor Mt. Holyoke Coll., 1968; Woman of Yr., Greater Boston Bus. and Profl. Womens Club, 1970. Episcopalian (mem. corp.). Home: 6 Woodbine Rd Belmont MA 02178

HOWE, FREDERIC WILLIAM, Jr., ret. business exec.; b. Providence, July 8, 1905; s. Frederic William and Ruth Woodcock (Stone) H.; A.B., Williams Coll., 1926; student Lowell Textile Inst., 1927; m. Mary F. Washburn, June 7, 1927; children—Frederic William, Barbara Rhodes; m. 2d, Winifred E. Bowler, Jan. 2, 1934; 1 dau., Elisabeth S.; m. 3d, Muriel E. Johnstone, Feb. 23, 1950. Sales trainee Crompton & Knowles, Corp., Worcester, 1927-34, office staff. Phila., 1934-35, So. mgr., Charlotte, N.C., 1935-43, v.p., Worcester, 1943-53, dir., 1941—, gen. sales mgr., 1948-53, pres., gen. mgr., 1953-69, bd. chmn., 1969-70; dir. Compo Industries, Ware Knitters, Worcester County Nat. Bank, Societa Nebiolo, Italy; trustee Peoples Mechanics Savs. Bank, Worcester. Bd. dirs. Mass. Taxpayers Found.; trustee Meml. Hosp., Clark U., Worcester. Mem. S.A.R., Alpha Delta Phi. Clubs: Worcester, Tatnuck Country (Worcester); Williams, Union League (N.Y.C.). Home: Thompson Rd New Braintree MA 01531 also 5 Beekman Pl New York City NY 10022

HOWE, GORDON, profl. hockey club exec.; b. Saskatoon, Sask., Can., Mar. 31, 1928; s. Albert Clarence and Katherine (Schultz) H.; student pub. schs. Can.; m. Colleen Janet Joffa, Apr. 15, 1953; children—Marty Gordon, Mark Steven, Cathleen Jill, Murray Albert. Came to U.S., 1944. Profl. hockey player with Detroit Red Wings Hockey Club, Nat. Hockey League, 1944—, now v.p. Vice pres., dir. Nat. Investors Life Ins. Co.; asst. to pres. Norin Corp.; sports adviser T. Eaton Co.; dir. Calderone-Curran Ranches, Jr. Wings Hockey Club. Chmn. March of Dimes Found., Mich. Arthritis Found. Recipient Order of Can. medal, 1971; named Canada's Athlete of Year, 1963; holder Hart Meml. Trophy, Art Ross Trophy, Lester Patrick Trophy; 12 times 1st All Star Team, 9 times 2d All Star Team. Conglist. Author: Hockey, Here's Howe; Gordie Howe, No. 9. Office: Olympia Stadium 5920 Grand River Detroit MI 48208

HOWE, HAROLD, banker; b. Chapman, Kan., Feb. 24, 1901; s. Michael Maurice and Margaret Ann (Kiley) H.; B.S. in Agr., Kan. State Coll., 1922; M.S., U. Md., 1923; Ph.D., U. Wis., 1937; LL.D., St. Benedicts Coll., 1950; m. Ruth Riordan, June 23, 1930; children—Philip, Barbara. Asst. in soils Md. Agrl. Exptl. Sta., 1922-23; asst. in agrl. econs. Wis. Agrl. Exptl. Sta., 1924-25; instr. agrl. econs. Kan. State Coll., Manhattan, 1925-27, asst. prof., 1927-30, asso. prof., 1930-34, prof., 1934-64; dean Grad. Sch., St. Louis U., 1964-67; project mgr. UN Devel. Program 80, Turrialba, Costa Rica, 1968-70; sr. v.p., dir. Kan. State Bank, Manhattan, 1970—. Cons. Nat. Resources Planning Bd., 1938-43. City commr. Manhattan, 1951-55, mayor, 1953-54. Mem. exec. com., council on grad. work Assn. Land Grant Colls. and Univs., 1948-52, chmn. council on grad. work, 1950-51. Bd. dirs. Kan. Soc. for Crippled Children, 1945-64; trustee Nat. Soc. Crippled Children and Adults, 1957-60. Mem. Phi Kappa Phi, Alpha Zeta, Gamma Sigma Delta, Pi Kappa Delta, Phi Kappa Theta. Democrat. Roman Catholic. Author numerous bulls and papers on pub. finance, land econs. Home: 2437 Anderson Av Manhattan KS 66502

HOWE, HELEN, author, monologuist; b. Boston, Mass., Jan. 11, 1905; d. Mark Antony De Wolfe and Fanny Huntington (Quincy) Howe; grad. Milton Acad., 1922; student Radcliffe Coll., 1923-24; m. Alfred Reginald Allen, May 31, 1946. Appeared in recitals of character sketches of own authorship in 45 states, since 1936; solo appearances, New York and London theatres, and supper clubs. Episcopalian. Clubs: P.E.N., Cosmopolitan (New York). Author: (novels): The Whole Heart, 1943; We Happy Few, 1946; The Circle of the Day, 1950; The Success, 1956; The Fires of Autumn, 1959; (biography) The Gentle Americans, 1965. Address: 1158 Fifth Av New York City NY 10029

HOWE, HERBERT MARSHALL, educator; b. Bristol, R.I., Mar. 21, 1912; s. Wallis Eastburn and Mary Emily (Locke) H.; grad. St. George's Sch., 1930; A.B., Harvard, 1934; M.A., U. Wis., 1941, Ph.D., 1948; m. Evelyn Grace Mitchell, Sept. 6, 1941; children—Evelyn Mitchell, Herbert Marshall, Emily Judson. Tchr., Latin, biology Brooks Sch., North Andover, Mass., 1934-40, Latin, history Pomfret (Conn.) Sch., 1942-48; faculty U. Wis., Madison, 1948—, prof. classics, 1956—, chmn. dept., 1954-68. Mem. Am. Philol. Assn., Am. Inst. Archaeology, Logos. Episcopalian. Author: (with P.L. MacKendrick) Classics in Translation, 1952; (with W.R. Agard) Medical Greek and Latin, 1955; Ancient Religion and the Early Church, 1968. Home: 2011 Chadbourne Av Madison WI 53705

HOWE, IRVING, author, historian, critic; b. N.Y.C., June 11, 1920; s. David and Nettie (Goldman) H.; grad. Coll. City N.Y.; m. Arien Hausknecht; 1 son, Oned. Tchr. English, Brandeis U., 1953-61, Stanford; 1961-63; prof. English, City U. N.Y. at Hunter Coll., 1963—, Distinguished prof., 1970—. Christian Gauss seminar chair prof. Princeton, 1954. Recipient Longview Found. prize for lit. criticism; Nat. Inst. Arts and Letters award. Kenyon Rev. fellow for lit. criticism, 1953; Bollingen Found. fellow; Guggenheim fellow, 1971. Served with AUS, World War II. Author: Sherwood Anderson: A Critical Biography; William Faulkner: A Critical Study; Politics and the Novel: A World More Attractive, 1963; Steady Work., 1966; The Decline of the New, 1969. Co-author: The UAW and Walter Reuther; The American Communist Party: A Critical History; The Radical Papers, 1966. Editor: (periodical) Dissent; Essential Works of Socialism, 1971; co-editor A Treasury of Yiddish Poetry, 1971. Contbr. to Harper's, N.Y. Times Book Rev. Address: Dept of English Hunter Coll New York City NY 10021

HOWE, JAMES WONG, cinematographer; b. Kwangtung, China, Aug. 28, 1899; s. Wong How and Dang Shee; brought to U.S., 1904; ed. high sch., Pasco, Wash.; m. Sanora Babb, Sept. 16, 1949. Asst. camerman Lasky Studios, Hollywood, Cal., 1917-22, dir. photography, 1922—; first film, Drums of Fate, others include Body and Soul (Look award 1947), Rose Tatoo (Acad. award 1955, Look award 1955), Picnic (Look award 1955), Song Without End, Hud (Academy award 1963), The Outrage, Hombre, Seconds, 1967, The Heart is a Lonely Hunter, 1968, The Molly, Maquires, 1969. Recipient Medal of Honor, George Eastman Festival Film Artists, 1957; 16 Oscar nominations. Mem. Acad. Motion Picture Arts and Scis., Internat. Photographers Am., Am. Soc. Cinematographers, Dirs. Guild Am., Chinese Hist. Soc., Delta Kappa Alpha. Home: 1562 Queens Rd Hollywood CA 90069 Office: care Internat Photographers 7715 Sunset Blvd Hollywood CA 90069

HOWE, JOHN EDGAR, educator, lawyer; b. Newport, Ky., Jan. 22, 1919; s. Allie Everett and Martha Elizabeth (Herget) H.; A.B., Western Ky. State Coll., 1940; LL.B., U. Ky., 1943; LL.M., U. Mich., 1943; m. Margaret N. Osborne, May 31, 1940; children—Jeanne, Jay, Martha. Admitted to Ky. bar, 1943, Kan. bar, 1960; mem. firm Howe & Clay, Mt. Sterling Ky., 1943-46; asst. prof. law Creighton U., 1946-52; asso. prof. law St. Louis U., 1952-55, prof., asst. dean, 1955-59; prof. law Washburn U., Topeka, 1959—, former dean Law Sch. Kan. commr. on uniform state laws, 1961—. Mem. Am., Kan., Ky. bar assns. Home: 1346 Wayne St Topeka KS 66604

HOWE, JOHN PERRY, educator, research dir.; b. Groton, N.Y., June 24, 1910; s. Mather Crain and Belle Gertrude (Smith) H.; B.S., Hobart Coll., 1933; Ph.D. (Jesse Metcalf fellow 1935-36), Brown U., 1936; m. Marilyn Leilani Evans, Dec. 27, 1941; children—Roger Evans, Susan Lee, Nancy Kathleen, John Alton. Instr. chemistry Ohio State U., 1936-38; asst. prof. phys. chemistry Brown U., 1938-42; research asso. metall. lab. Manhattan Dist., U. Chgo., 1942-44, asso. dir., gen. research and devel. nuclear reactors, 1945; mgr. metallurgy sect. Knolls Atomic Power Lab., Gen. Electric Co., 1945- 52; research energy conversion and storage Gen. Electric Research Lab., 1952-53; sect. chief reactor materials Atomics Internat., 1953-57, dir. research dept., 1957-61; Ford prof. engring., dir. dept. engring. physics and materials sci. Coll. Engring., Cornell U., 1962-64, dir. dept. engring. physics, 1965-67; staff mem. Inst. for Def. Analyses, Arlington, Va., 1967-68; asst. lab. dir., chmn. metallurgy Gulf Gen. Atomic, Inc., 1968-69, asso. dir. research and devel., 1970-71, tech. dir. advanced reactors div., 1971—. Com. sr. reviewers div. classification AEC, 1952-67, editorial adv. bd. reactor handbook, 1953-63, mem. bd. atomic safety and licensing, 1965-69; adviser AEC delegation, also vice chmn. session radiation effects Geneva (Switzerland) Conf. Peaceful Uses of Atomic Energy, 1955, del., 1958; mem. chemistry adv. com. Air Force Office Sci. Research, 1957-64; cons. spl. com. fundamental research in connection study made for Air Force, Nat. Acad. Scis., 1957- 58; cons. materials adv. group Inst. Def. Analyses, 1960; mem. sci. adv. group Air Force Office Aerospace Research, 1963-71; vis. com. nuclear engring. div. Brookhaven Nat. Lab.; vis. com. solid state div. Oak Ridge Nat. Lab. Fellow Am. Phys. Soc., A.A.A.S., Am. Nuclear Soc., Am. Inst. Chemists, Am. Soc. Metallurgy; mem. Am. Chem. Soc., Am. Inst. Mining and Metall. Engrs., Inst. Metals, Am. Ceramic Soc., Phi Beta Kappa, Sigma Xi. Editor: (with R. Smith) Beryllium Oxide: Proc. First Internat. Beryllium Oxide Conf., Australian Atomic Energy Establishment, Sydney, 1963; (with Dr. M. Finniston) Progress in Nuclear Energy, series V. vols. 1-4, 1955-62; (with R.W. Cahn, P. Lacombe) Jour. Nuclear Materials, 1958-66; editorial adv. bd. Program Solid State Chemistry, 1970—. Home: 6627 Avenida de las Pescas La Jolla CA 92037 Office: Gulf Gen Atomic Inc PO Box 608 San Diego CA 92112

HOWE, JOHN STROTHER, banker; b. Milton, Mass., Feb. 9, 1914; s. James C. and Letitia (Lemon) H.; A.B., Harvard, 1936; m. Frances Fairfax Hovey, Nov. 18, 1939; children—Peter Fairfax, Emily Dexter. With E.B. Smith & Co., Smith, Barney & Co., 1936-42, Webster & Atlas Nat. Bank, Rockland-Atlas Nat. Bank, Boston, 1947-56; treas. Provident Instn. for Savs., Boston, 1956-58, pres., trustee, 1958—; dir. State St. Bank & Trust Co., Boston, Savs. Bank Investment Fund, Bankers Data Processing, Inc. Trustee Browne and Nichols Sch., Mass. Eye and Ear Infirmary; bd. dirs. Better Bus. Bur. Eastern Mass., Travelers Aid Soc. Boston, Mass. Taxpayers Found., Mass. Bay United Fund. Served from pvt. to capt., AUS, 1942-46. Mem. Greater Boston C. of C. (dir.). Home: 92 Mt Vernon St Boston MA 02108 Office: 36 Temple Pl Boston MA 02111

HOWE, JOSEPH WARNER, educator; b. Omaha, Jan. 19, 1902; s. Homer and May Miller (Lewis) H.; B.E., State U. Ia., 1924, M.S., 1925; m. Luceille Muriel Denis, Sept. 4, 1929; children—Joseph Dennis, Judith Annetta. Asst. to san. engr., Chgo., 1925; asst. engr. Miss. River Power Co., Keokuk, Ia., 1925-27; instr. dept. theoretical and applied mechanics U. Ill., 1927-29; asst. prof. dept. mechanics and hydraulics State U. Ia., 1929-38, asso. prof., 1938-42, prof., head dept., 1942-71. Chief of party flood control studies U.S. Engr. Corps, summers 1928, 29, 30; cons. engr. Ia. Inst. Hydraulic Research. Mem. Ia. Natural Resources Council. Mem. Am. Soc. C.E., Ia. Engring. Soc., Am. Soc. Engring. Edn., Am. Water Resources Assn., Am. Assn. U. Profs., Am. Geophys. Union, Tau Beta Pi, Sigma Xi, Chi Epsilon, Theta Tau. Rotarian. Club: Triangle (Iowa City). Co-author: Basic Mechanics of Fluids, 1953. Editor: Ia. Studies in Engring. Bulls. Home: 1635 Ridge Rd Iowa City IA 52240

HOWE, LAURENCE LUVERNE J., ret. investment banker; b. Ogden, Ia., Jan. 30, 1898; s. Harrison Dyer and Della (Vernon) H.; student Coe Coll., Cedar Rapids, Ia., 1916-18, LL.D., 1963; m. Claribel Dawson, Sept. 4, 1924; children—Susanne (Mrs. Val Nolan), Nancy (Mrs. Walter Houston). Engaged in investment bus., 1920—; with John Nuveen & Co., Inc., Chgo., 1936—, partner, 1945—, chmn. bd., 1953-69; dir. Thomas Industries, Louisville, Barnett Bank of Winter Haven, N.A. (Fla.). Trustee Shimer Coll., Mt. Carroll, Ill., Coe Coll., Cedar Rapids, Ia. Served to 1t., pilot, USSC, 1918-19. Clubs: Municipal Bond, Bond, Attic, Chicago, Mid-America, Racquet (Chgo.); Bankers (N.Y.C.); Barrington Hills (Ill.) Country; Lake Region Yacht and Country (Winter Haven). Home: Mountain Lake Lake Wales FL 33853 Office: Barnett Bank Winter Haven FL 33880

HOWE, LAWRENCE, mfg. co. exec.; b. Evanston, Ill., Nov. 16, 1921; s. Lawrence and Hester (Davis) H.; A.B., Harvard, 1942; J.D., U. Chgo., 1948; m. Ellen G. Vaughan, Feb. 22, 1943; children—James, Ellen, Eliza, Samuel. Admitted to Ill. bar, 1948; asso. firm Pope & Ballard, Chgo., 1948-52; asso., then partner firm Vedder, Price, Kaufman & Kammholz, Chgo., 1952-66; v.p., sec. Bell & Howell Co., Chgo., 1966-71, sr. v.p., dir., 1971—. Pres., Village of Winnetka, Illa., 1964-68. Served to lt. USNR, 1942-45. Home: 175 Chestnut St Winnetka IL 60093 Office: 7100 McCormick Rd Chicago IL 60645

HOWE, QUINCY, journalist; b. Boston, Aug. 17, 1900; s. Mark Antony DeWolfe and Fanny Huntington (Quincy) H.; A.B., Harvard, 1921; postgrad. Christ's Coll., Cambridge, Eng., 1921-22; m. Mary L. Post, May 14, 1932; children—Quincy, Mabel Davis. With Atlantic Monthly Co., 1922-28; editor of Living Age, 1929-35; with Simon & Schuster, Inc., pubs., 1935-42; news analyst CBS, 1942-49, in TV, 1949-50; asso. prof. U. Ill., Sch. Journalism, news analyst Sta. WILL, 1950- 54; news analyst ABC, 1954-63, Radio N.Y. World Wide, 1966-70; editor Atlas, mag. of World Press, 1961-65. Pres., Nat. Bd. Rev. Motion Pictures Recipient George Foster Peabody award for radio-TV news analysis, 1955; Overseas Press Club award for radio-TV news analysis, 1959; Columbia-Catherwood award for responsible internat. journalism, 1962. Mem. Assn. Radio-TV News analysts, Sigma Delta Chi. Club: Century. Author: World Diary (1929-34), 1934; England Expects Every American to Do His Duty, 1937; Blood Is Cheaper Than Water, 1939; The News and How to Understand It, 1940; A World History of Our Own Times, vol. I The World We Lost: From the Turn of the Century to 1918, Armistice, 1949; vol. II The World Between the Wars, From the 1918 Armistice to the Munich Agreement, 1953. Home: 108 E 82d St New York City NY 10028

HOWE, RICHARD ESMOND, Jr., educator, musician; b. Murray, Utah, Apr. 30, 1927; s. Richard Esmond and Louise (Hill) H.; student U. Utah, 1946; B.S. in Music, Juilliard Sch. Music, 1951, M.S. in Music, 1952; student U. Florence (Italy), 1952-53; D.Mus. Arts, Eastman Sch. Music, 1956; m. Agnes Jensen, May 31, 1949; 1 dau., Mary Katherine. Mem. faculty Grinnell (Ia.) Coll., 1956—, prof. music, 1963—, chmn. dept., 1959-62, 65-67, 70—, chmn. div. humanities, 1971—. Served with USNR, 1945-46. Fulbright grantee, Italy, 1952-53, 53-54. Mem. Am. Musicol. Soc., Coll. Music Soc. Spl. research keyboard music of Baldassare Gallupi. Contbr. articles to mus. jours. Home: 1414 Broad St Grinnell IA 50112

HOWE, ROBERT MILTON, educator; b. Oberlin, O., Aug. 28, 1925; s. Carl E. and Nettie (Gregory) H.; A.B. in Physics, Oberlin Coll., 1947; B.S. in Elec. Engring., Cal. Inst. Tech., 1945; M.S. in Physics, U. Mich., 1948; Ph.D., Mass. Inst. Tech., 1950; m. Joan F. Craig, Sept. 7, 1947; children—Jacqueline, Julie, Randall, Rawleigh. Faculty dept. aerospace engring. U. Mich., Ann Arbor, 1950—, asso. prof., 1954-57, prof., 1957—, chmn. dept., 1968—. Cons. Gen. Motors Corp., Singer Co., Reliance Electric Co., others. Dir. Reliance Electric Co., Cleve. Served with USNR, 1943-46. Mem. I.E.E.E., Am. Inst. Physics, Am. Inst. Aeros. and Astronautics, Simulation Councils (1st nat. chmn.), Phi Beta Kappa, Sigma Xi, Tau Beta Pi. Research and publs. in analog and hybrid computation, flight simulation and automatic control. Home: 485 Rock Creek Dr Ann Arbor MI 48104

HOWE, STEWART SAMUEL, publicist, ednl. adminstr.; b. Streator, Ill., Oct. 25, 1905; s. Orion Harrison and Ethel Irene (Elder) H.; A.B., U. Ill., 1928, M.Journalism (hon.), 1937. Reporter, Times-Press, Streator, 1923-27, city editor, 1927-28; advt., promotion L.W. Ramsey Co., 1928-30; established Stewart Howe Alumni Service, Inc., 1930, pres., 1930—, also pres., treas. affiliated firms; pub. relations officer 9th Naval Dist., Navy Dept., 1942-43; recruiting publicity WAC, Young & Rubicam, Inc., N.Y.C., 1944; account exec. John Price Jones Corp., 1944- 49; regional dir. U. Mich. Meml.-Phoenix Project, 1949-52; v.p. Ill. Inst. Tech., Armour Research Found., Chgo., 1952-58; asst. to pres. for devel. Fordham U., N.Y.C., 1958-59; pres. Recorder Pub. Co., Columbus, O., 1951; pres., dir. Frat. Service, Inc., Evanston, Frat. Mags. Assn.; Inc., Stewart Howe Services, Inc., Evanston, 1963—, Howe Service, Inc., N.Y.C. and Champaign, Ill., 1945—; pres., dir. Columbia Bus. Service, Inc. (Mo.), 1960—; pres. Copy & Mailing Services, Inc., O., 1961—, Ind., 1965—. Regional rep. Ill. U.S.O. Mem. Nixon-Agnew nat. campaign pub. relations adv. com., 1968. Trustee, chmn. Stewart Howe Found.; governing mem. U. Ill. Found. Life mem. Nat., Ill., Chgo. Evanston hist. socs.; mem. Pub. Relations Soc. Am. (nat. bd. 1957-58), Am. Coll. Pub. Relations Assn. (nat. bd. 1956-58), Chgo. Soc. Fund Raising Execs. (dir.), Nat. Ednl. Devel. Officers Assn. (pres. 1956), Pub. Relations Clinic, Alpha Gamma (trustee), Skull and Crescent, Kappa Sigma, Sigma Delta Chi, Phi Eta Sigma (nat. pres. 1927), Kappa Tau Alpha. Clubs: Press, Executive, Headline, Tavern, University (Chgo.); N.Y. Athletic, University (N.Y.C.). Contbr. articles to ednl. publs. Office: 1462 Chicago Av Evanston IL 60201

HOWE, THOMAS CARR, museum dir.; b. Kokomo, Ind., Aug. 12, 1904; s. Thomas Carr and Jennie (Armstrong) H.; A.B. magna cum laude, Harvard, 1926, postgrad. Sch. Architecture, 1927-28, M.F.A., 1929, postgrad., 1929-31; D.F.A. (hon.), Cal. Coll. Arts and Crafts, Oakland, 1969; m. Francesca Craft Deering, Apr. 9, 1932; 1 dau., Francesca Deering. Tutor, instr. dept. fine arts Harvard, 1927-28; asst. dir. Cal. Palace Legion of Honor (Mus. Fine Arts), San Francisco, 1931-39, dir., 1939-68, dir. emeritus, 1968—. Vice chmn. com. pub. works of art project, San Francisco, 1934; spl. art commr. Golden Gate Internat. Expn., San Francisco, 1940; cultural affairs officer High Commr. Germany, 1950-51; mem. U.S. fine arts com. Brussels Internat. Expn., 1958; mem. Fine Arts Com. for White House; mem. Smithsonian Art Commn.; art adviser Hearst Castle, San Simon, Cal.; adv. council Art Mus. Princeton, 1969; chmn. Nat. Collection Fine Arts. Smithsonian Instn., 1970. Served as lt. comdr. USNR, 1945-46; dep. chief monuments, fine arts, archives sect. U.S. Forces, Germany and Austria. Decorated chevalier Legion of Honor (France); officer Order Orange-Nassau (Holland). Carnegie fellow, 1928. Mem. Assn. Am. Art Mus. Dirs. (pres. 1960-61), Am. Fedn. Arts (trustee), Western Assn. Art Mus. Dirs. (pres. 1941-42), Phi Beta Kappa. Republican. Mem. Disciples Christ Ch. Clubs: Century, Harvard (N.Y.C.); Bohemian (San Francisco). Author: Salt Mines and Castles, 1946. Contbr. articles to profl. publs. Home: 2709 Larkin St San Francisco CA 94109 Office: 1485 Pacific Av San Francisco CA 94109

HOWE, WARREN ASQULTH, educator; b. Custar, O., June 16, 1910; s. David Newton and Clara Susan (Werking) H.; B.S. in Bus. Adminstrn., Bowling Green State U., 1943; M.B.A., U. Toledo, 1946; Ph.D. in Accounting. Ohio State U., 1954; m. Edith Lucille Miller, Feb. 2, 1936. Asst. prof. accounting U. Toledo, 1946-54, Bowling Green State U., 1954-55; prof. accounting Temple U., 1955—. Vice pres. Howe-Williamson, Inc.; exec. v.p., vice chmn. bd. Exec. Sales Service Corp. Mem. Financial Execs. Inst., Internat. Platform Assn., Am. Assn. U. Profs., Am. Accounting Assn., Inst. Internal Auditors, Beta Gamma Sigma. Beta Alpha Psi (faculty v.p. Alpha Phi chpt. 1956-68). Author: Cost Accounting; (with Carlson) Workbook of Study Guides for Use with Accounting Principles, rev. edit., 1961; also articles. Home: 7812 Haines Rd Cheltenham PA 19012 also 538 W Shore Dr Brigantine NJ 08203 Office: Dept Accounting Temple U Philadelphia PA 19122

HOWELL, A. CLEWIS, banker; b. Ithaca, N.Y., 1924; grad. U. Fla., 1949. Pres., Marine Bank & Trust Co., Tampa, Fla.; chmn., pres. Midway Bank at Tampa; chmn. 1st Fla. Bancorp.; dir. Founders Life Assurance Co., Reeves Fences, Inc., Commerce Bank of Tampa, Founders Financial Corp. Sec. Myrtle Hill Meml. Park, Inc. Trustee U. Tampa. Home: 924 Golf View St Tampa FL 33609 Office: Madison and Franklin Sts Tampa FL 33602*

HOWELL, ALVIN HAROLD, engr.; b. Sedgwick, Kan., Feb. 5, 1908; s. George Alfred and Gertrude (Johnson) H.; B.S., U. Kan., 1929: student Union Coll., Schenectady, 1929-30; M.S., Mich. Coll. Mining and Tech., 1934; Sc.D., Mass. Inst. Tech., 1938; m. Helen Whitney, Sept. 7, 1934; children—Elizabeth, Alvin Harold, John Arthur, Gordon Howard. Test engr. Gen. Electric Co., Schenectady, 1929-30; instr. Mich. Coll. Mining and Tech., 1931-34, research geophys. prospecting methods, summers 1931-34; research asso. Mass. Inst. Tech., 1939-40, vis. prof., adminstrv. officer Radar Sch., 1942-43; asst. prof. elec. engring. Tufts U., 1940-41, asso. prof., head dept., 1941-43, prof., head dept., dir. research dept. elec. engring., 1943-70, dir. Balloon Astronomy Lab., 1970—; devel. rocket and balloon type instrumentation; dir. Doble Engring. Co., 1960—, v.p., 1961-63. Mem. NRC. Recipient Exceptional Service award USAF, 1955. Registered profl. engr., Mass. Mem. I.E.E.E., Am. Phys. Soc., A.A.A.S., Am. Assn. U. Profs., Am. Soc. Engring. Edn., Sigma Xi, Eta Kappa Nu, Tau Beta Pi. Baptist. Author: (with others) Principles of Radar, 1944. Contbr. articles to profl. publs. Developer balloon-borne telescope for tracking planets and stars. Home: 12 Lincoln St Arlington MA 02174 Office Tufts U Medford MA 02155

HOWELL, ARTHUR, lawyer; b. Atlanta, Aug. 24, 1918; s. Arthur and Katharine (Mitchell) H.; A.B., Princeton, 1939; LL.B., Harvard, 1942; m. Caroline Sherman, June 14, 1941; children—Arthur, Caroline, Eleanor, Richard, Peter, James. Admitted to Ga. bar, 1942; with F.M. Bird (name changed to Bird & Howell, 1945, then to Jones, Bird & Howell, 1959), asso., 1942- 45, partner, 1945—. Dir., gen. counsel Atlantic Steel Co.; v.p., dir. Creomulsion Co.; dir. Alpha Fund, Inc., Computer Mgmt., Inc., Southwest Investors, Inc. Pres. Met. Atlanta Community Services, 1956, dir., 1953—; pres. Community Planning Council, 1961-63; gen. chmn. United Appeal, 1955; spl. atty. gen. State Ga., 1948-55; spl. counsel Univ. System Ga., State Sch. Bldg. Authorities, 1951-70; adv. com. Ga. Corporate Code, 1967—; chmn. Atlanta Adv. Com. Parks. Trustee Princeton, 1964-68, Atlanta Speech Sch., Oglethorpe (past chmn.), Morehouse colls., Westminister Schs., Atlanta, Episcopal High Sch., Alexandria, Va. Mem. Inst. Internat. Edn. (exec. com.), Am. Law Inst., Am., Ga., Atlanta bar assns., Lawyers Club of Atlanta (past pres.), Am. Judicature Soc., Soc. Colonial Wars, Phi Beta Kappa. Presbyn. (deacon, trustee). Clubs: Capital City, Piedmont Driving, Commerce; Homosassa Fishing; Nassau (Princeton, N.J.); Princeton (N.Y.C.). Home: 3727 Tuxedo Rd NW Atlanta GA 30305 Office: Haas-Howell Bldg Atlanta GA 30303

HOWELL, BENJAMIN FRANKLIN, Jr., geophysicist, educator; b. Princeton, N.J., June 12, 1917; s. Benjamin Franklin and Claire M. (Mead) H.; A.B., Princeton, 1939; M.S., Cal. Inst. Tech., 1942, Ph. D., 1949; m. Constance M. Benson, June 30, 1943; children—Barbara Carolyn, Catherine Ann (dec.), Bonnie Andrea, James Benjamin. Research engr. div. war research U. Cal. at San Diego, 1942-45; geophysicist United Geophys. Co., 1946-49; faculty Pa. State U., 1949—, prof. geophysics, 1953—, head dept. geophysics and geochemistry, 1949-63, asst. dean Grad. Sch., 1968-70, asso. dean, 1970—. Chief cons. seismologist Vibratech Engring. Co., Hazleton, Pa., 1955-69. Fellow Am. Geophys. Union (sec. sect. tectonophysics 1956-59, sect. seismology 1959-63), Geol. Soc. Am.; mem. soc. Exploration Geophysics, European Soc. Exploration Geophysicists, Seismol. Soc. Am. (pres. 1963-64), Assn. Geol. Tchrs., Pa. Acad. Scis., Phi Beta Kappa, Sigma Xi. Baptist. Author: Introduction to Geophysics, 1959. Editor: Contributions in Geophysics in Honor of Beno Gutenberg, 1958. Home: 308 W Prospect Av State College PA 16801 Office: Grad Bldg University Park PA 16802

HOWELL, BENJAMIN RANDOLPH, ret. lawyer; b. Roswell, N.M., Sept. 20, 1900; s. Mark and Leona (Randolph) H.; LL.B., U. Tex., 1925; m. Romaine Safford, Apr. 30, 1931; children—Margaret Safford (Mrs. James M. Langford), Mark Franklin. Admitted to Tex. bar, 1925, since practiced in El Paso; former mem. Jones, Hardie, Grambling and Howell. Former v.p., dir. El Paso Natural Gas Company. Mem. Tex. Bd. Edn., 1957—, chmn., 1969—. Served as col. AUS, 1940-45. Decorated Legion of Merit. Mem. Am., Tex. (dir. 1946-48), El Paso (pres. 1952) bar assns., Nat. Assn. State Bds. Edn. (area v.p. 1970-71), Tex. Research League (dir.), Pi Kappa Alpha, Phi Delta Phi. Episcopalian. Club: El Paso. Home: 1225 Cincinnati St El Paso TX 79902

HOWELL, CHARLES ROBERT, former congressman, former state ofcl.; b. Trenton Apr. 23, 1904; s. Robert Wilson and Harriet Newton (Bumsted) H.; grad. Hoosac Sch., Hoosick, N.Y., 1923; student Princeton, 1923-24, U. Pa., 1936-37; m. Inez Wood Howe, Oct. 3, 1928. Ins. broker, Trenton, 1928-54; elected to N.J. Ho. Assembly, 1944, 45; mem. 81st to 83d Congresses, 4th N.J. Dist.; former N.J. commr. banking and ins. Democratic state chmn. 1953; Dem. candidate U.S. Senate, 1954; pres. Bank of Manalapan, N.J.; bd. mgrs. U.S. Savs. Bank, Newark. C.L.U., N.J. Mem. Trenton (past pres.), N.J. (past v.p.) assns. life underwriters, Nat. Assn. Suprs. State Banks (past pres.), Nat. Assn. Ins. Commrs. (past pres.). Episcopalian. Introduced original fair employment practices bill in N.J. legislature, 1945. Home: East Curlis Av Pennington NJ 08534

HOWELL, DARIEL ELZA, educator; b. Montebello, Cal., Dec. 27, 1910; s. Elza Thomas and Elizabeth (Lambert) H.; B.S., U. Cal. at Berkeley, 1933, M.S., 1934, Ph.D., 1939; m. Mary Carleen Williamson, Aug. 10, 1940; children—Thomas William, Kathleen Elizabeth, Susan Mary. Asst. med. entomologist U. Cal. at Berkeley, 1933-39; field aid Cal. Dept. Agr., 1939; asst. prof. entomology Okla. State U., 1939-42, asso. prof., 1943-46, prof., 1946—, head dept. entomology, 1952-70, also acting dean Grad. Sch. Collaborator, Bur. Animal Industry, U.S. Dept. Agr., 1939-46. Served from lt. (j.g.) to lt. comdr. Med. Service Corps, USNR, 1943-46; capt. Res. Decorated Bronze Star. Mem. Entomol. Soc. Am. (v.p. 1950-51, pres. 1953-54, governing bd. 1964-67), Nat. Acad. Study Group on Animal Diseases in Africa, Assn. Research Workers, Animal Diseases So. States (sec.-treas. 1947-48, v.p., 1948-49, pres. 1949-50), Am. Soc. Tropical Medicine, Central States Entomol. Soc. (pres. 1965-66), Southwestern Assn. Naturalists, Am. Soc. Parasitologists, Okla. Acad. Sci. (sec.-treas. 1953-55, v.p. 1955-56, pres. 1956-57), A.A.A.S., Phi Kappa Phi (chpt. pres. 1965-66). Methodist. Lion. Mem. editorial bd. Jour. Econ. Entomology. Home: 147 S Redwood Dr Stillwater OK 74074

HOWELL, DAVID J., lawyer; b. Maryville, Mo., May 26, 1887; s. David J. and Elizabeth Elvira (Stewart) H.; student U. Kan., 1905-06; LL.B., U. Mo., 1908; m. 2d, Catharine Campbell, Oct. 21, 1933. Admitted to Wyo. bar, 1908, began practice at Cheyenne; asst. pros. atty. Laramie County, 1911-12; asst. U.S. atty., 1914-21; atty. gen. of Wyo., 1923-26; counsel Reconstrn. Finance Corp., 1933-35. Mem. Wyo. Soc. S.A.R. (pres. 1925). Democrat. Mason (32, Shriner). Home: 2453 Riverside Dr Santa Ana CA 92706

HOWELL, EDGAR MCPHERSON, museum curator; b. Richmond, Va., July 16, 1915; s. George Cook and Anne (McPherson) H.; B.A., Princeton, 1938; m. Winfred Harriet Harward, July 17, 1942; children—Harriet Vandegrift, Edgar McPherson, Charles Jarrett McPherson. Historian, Office Chief Mil. History, Dept. Army, 1949-56; curator div. mil. history, chmn. dept. nat. and mil. history U.S. Nat. Museum, Smithsonian Instn., 1956—. Served to maj., F.A., U.S. Army, 1940-49. Author: The Soviet Partisan Movement, 1941-44, 1956; (with J. D. Campbell) American Military Insignia, 1800-1851, 1963; (with D. E. Kloster) United States Army Headgear to 1854, 1968. Editor: Uniform Regulations for the Army of the United States, 1961, 1961. Episcopalian. Home: 307 Poplar Dr Falls Church VA 20046 Office: Smithsonian Instn Washington DC 20025

HOWELL, ELSWORTH SEAMAN, publisher; b. N.Y.C., Dec. 4, 1915; s. Clarence Seaman and Josephine Polhemus (Weller) H.; student N.Y. U., 1935-36; m. Elizabeth Roper, July 27, 1940; children—Jean Elizabeth (Mrs. Bernard J. Salembier, Jr.), Maureen Anne (Mrs. Norman Nicoll Snow). Asst. editor Book of Knowledge, 1934-36; editor L'Encyclopedie de la Jeunesse, 1936- 37; mgr. mail order sales Grolier Soc., Inc., N.Y.C., 1939-46, v.p., 1947-59; pres., dir. Grolier Enterprises, Inc., N.Y.C., 1960-66, chmn. bd., 1967-68; chmn. bd. House of Grolier Ltd. (London), 1966—; v.p. Grolier Internat., 1966-69, exec. v.p., 1969—; pres., dir. Howell Book House, Inc.; dir. Grolier Ednl. Corp., Grolier Soc. Ltd. (London), 1966—; v.p., dir. Franklin Watts, Inc.; sec., dir. Americana Interstate Corp.; v.p., dir. Grolier, Inc., 1960—, mem. exec. com., 1966—; columnist Popular Dogs mag., 1955-66; pub. New Knowledge of Dog Behavior, 1963. Pres., Allwood Homeowners Assn., Darien, Conn., 1963-65. Recipient award Direct Mail Advt. Assn., 1954; Gaines' Dogdom's Man of Year award, 1970. Mem. English Setter Assn. Am. (past pres.). Clubs: Wee Burn Country (Darien); Dutch Treat, Am. Kennel (del., judge N.Y.C.). Author: (with D.H. Tuck) The New Complete English Setter, 1964. Home: 6 Tinywood Rd Darien CT 06820 also 111 E 56th St New York City NY 10022 Office: 575 Lexington Av New York City NY 10022

HOWELL, EVERETTE IRL, educator; b. Shelby, Miss., Jan. 4, 1914; s. Thomas Daniel and Helen Lundy (Eason) H.; B.A., Miss. Coll., 1936; M.S., Vanderbilt U., 1937; Ph.D., U. N.C., 1940; m. Beverly Ione McLaurin, June 12, 1943; children—Everette Irl, Marcia Marie, Beverly Jeannine. Prof. phys. sci. Belhaven Coll., 1940-48; prof., head dept. physics Miss. State U., 1948- -; summer teaching physics dept. Vanderbilt U., 1946, U. Fla., 1947; summer research participant Oak Ridge Nat. Lab., 1950, 51. Mem. Am. Inst. Physics, Am. Phys. Soc., Am. Assn. Physics Tchrs., Miss. Acad. Scis., Sigma Xi, Phi Kappa Phi. Presbyn. (elder). Contbr. articles sci. publs. Home: Blackjack Rd State College MS 39762

HOWELL, FRANCIS CLARK, educator; b. Kansas City, Mo., Nov. 27, 1925; s. E. Ray and Myrtle (Clark) H.; M.A., U. Chgo., 1951, Ph.D., 1953; m. Betty Ann Tomsen, June 17, 1955; children—Brian David, Jennifer Clare. Mem. faculty Washington U. Sch. Medicine, St. Louis, 1953-55; prof. anthropology U. Chgo., 1955-70, U. Cal. at Berkeley, 1970—. Served with USNR, 1944-46. Contbr. articles to profl. jours. Home: 1994 San Antonio Rd Berkeley CA 94707

HOWELL, FRANKLIN E., business exec.; b. Centerville, Ind., June 10, 1913; s. Frank W. and Bertha (Lewis) H.; student Purdue U., 1929, Miami Jacobs Bus. Coll., 1934; m. Betty Jane Wiley, Mar. 5, 1936; 1 dau., Joan (Mrs. Samuel E. Long). Asst. to pres. Eureka Vacuum Cleaner Co., 1936-42; div. sales mgr. AMP, Inc., Harrisburg, Pa., 1942-46, v.p. indsl. sales div., 1957- -; sales mgr. Leonard div. Am. Motors Co., Detroit, 1946-54; v.p. sales Crosley Bendix div. Avco Corp., Cin., 1954-57. Home: 244 N 36th St Camp Hill PA 17011 Office: Eisenhower Blvd Harrisburg PA 17111

HOWELL, GEORGE BEDELL, diversified co. exec.; b. Schenectady, Sept. 19, 1919; s. Jess M. and Grace (Gerhaeusser) H.; B.S. in Adminstrv. Engring. (N.Y. State and Univ. scholar), Cornell U., 1942; m. Mary Barbara Crohurst, July 10, 1944; children—Raymond Gary, Terry Barbara, Janice Patricia, Nancy Jo, George Bedell. With Gen. Electric Co., 1946-59; v.p. mfg. Leece Neville Co., Cleve., 1959-61, Royal Electric Co., Pawtucket, R.I., 1961-62; dir. operations packaging equipment and product devel. Acme Steel Co., 1962-64; v.p. adminstrv. service Interlake Steel Corp., Chgo., 1964-66, v.p. internat. div., also v.p. Acme Products div., 1966-70; chief exec. officer dir. Golconda Corp., Chgo., 1970—; pres. Bastian Blessing Inc.; dir. Nat. Bank of Oakbrook. Trustee

Village of Oak Brook, Ill., 1965—. Served to maj. AUS, 1942-46; ETO. Mem. Am. Mgmt. Assn., Ill. C. of C. Clubs: Chicago Athletic; Oak Brook Polo. Home: 5 Brighton Lane Oak Brook IL 60521 Office: 8550 W Bryn Mawr Av Chicago IL 60631

HOWELL, HANNAH JOHNSON, librarian; b. Oskaloosa, Ia., June 22, 1905; d. Irving Culver and Mary Hortense (Burnside) Johnson; student Penn Coll., Oskaloosa, 1924-25; Ph.B., U. Chgo.; 1927; B.L.S., Columbia, 1928; student N.Y.U. Inst. Fine Arts, also lectures N.Y. Hist. Soc., 1940-41; m. Henry Wilson Howell, Jr., June 5, 1947. Reviser summer library sch. U. Ia., 1928; research asst. Frick Art Reference Library, N.Y.C., 1928-34, head reference dept., 1935-47, asst. librarian, 1942-47, chief librarian, 1947-70, cons. librarian, 1970—. Mem. hon. com. nat. capital sesquicentennial commn. exhbn., Am. Processional, Corcoran Gallery Art, 1950; patroness benefit exhbn. paintings for Smith Coll. Collection, Knoedler Galleries, N.Y.C., 1953. Mem. A.L.A., U. Chgo. Alumnae Assn. (pres. N.Y. chpt. 1932-37). Presbyn. Clubs: Columbia U. (chmn. ladies com. 1942-44), Cosmopolitan (mem. library com. 1946-49) (N.Y.C.). Home: 151 E 83d St New York City NY 10028 Office: 10 E 71st St New York City NY 10021

HOWELL, HENRY WARDWELL, mgmt. cons.; b. Sewickley, Pa., Jan. 27, 1910; s. Alleyne C. and Rosalie (Wardwell) H.; grad. St. Paul's Sch., 1928; A.B., Yale, 1932; m. Margaret Grant Noyes, Sept. 13, 1936; children—Janet (Mrs. Reddock), Henry Wardwell, David, Clinton. Syndicate mgr. Bonbright & Co., N.Y.C., 1932-42; renegotiator USAAF, 1942- 44; fgn. trade cons. Fgn. Econ. Adminstrn., 1944-45; v.p. Middle East Co., Cairo, Egypt, 1945-47; cons., mgr. exec. recruiting dept. McKinsey & Co., N.Y.C., 1948-51; pres. Ward Howell Assos., Inc., N.Y.C., 1951—, Howell-Am. Corp., 1952—. Bd. dirs. Deafness Research Found.; trustee Hobart and William Smith Colls. Mem. Assn. Exec. Recruiters (dir.). Republican. Episcopalian. Clubs: Yale, Sky (N.Y.C.); Woodway Country; St. Croix (V.I.) Country. Home: 68 Gerrish Lane New Canaan CT 06840 Office: 122 E 42d St New York City NY 10017

HOWELL, HILTON HATCHETT, lawyer; b. Waco, Tex., Jan. 10, 1928; s. Hilton Emory and Louise (Hatchett) H.; B.A., Baylor U., 1948, LL.B., J.D.; m. Donna Massengill, Apr. 8, 1961; children—Hilton Hatchett, Brian Emory. Admitted to Tex. bar, 1951, since practiced in Waco; partner firm Naman, Howell, Smith & Chase, 1955—. Dir. First Nat. Bank Waco, KWTX Broadcasting Co., Texoma Broadcasters, Inc., Word, Inc. Bd. dirs. Tex. Baptist Found., trustee Cooper Found., Waco YMCA. Served with USAF, 1953-55. Fellow Tex. Bar Found.; mem. Am. Bar Assn., State Bar Tex. (chmn. Pub. information com. 1959-60, pub. relations com. 1970, adv. com. pub. relations 1970), Internat. Assn. Ins. Counsel, Am. Counsel Assn., Tex. Assn. Def. Counsel, Baylor Ex-Student Assn. (bd. dirs.), Phi Alpha Delta. Baptist (deacon). Home: 2508 Lake Air Dr Waco TX 76710 Office: First Nat Bldg Waco TX 76701

HOWELL, JAMES THEODORE, med. cons., internist; b. Ironton, O., Dec. 15, 1919; s. Leonard G. and Fay (Henry) H.; A.B., Miami U., 1941; M.D., U. Cin., 1944; m. Sarah Lee Dunn, May 26, 1951; 1 dau., Mary Lee. Intern, resident Henry Ford Hosp., Detroit, 1944; practice of medicine, 1944-65, specializing internal medicine, 1945-65; chief 7th Med. Service Henry Ford Hosp., Detroit, 1950-65, exec. dir., 1965-69; prin., nat. dir. health and med. affairs Peat Manwick Mitchell & Co., Washington, 1970—. Trustee Mich. Hosp. Service, Nat. Health Council; mem. Nat. Adv. Council on Regional Med. Programs. Diplomate Am. Bd. Internal Medicine. Fellow A.C.P., Am. Coll. Hosp. Adminstrs.; mem. Council Med. Adminstrn. (pres. 1958), Assn. Hosp. Dirs. Med. Edn., Assn. Am. Med. Colls., A.M.A., Am. (trustee), Mich. (trustee) hosp. assns., Internat. Hosp. Fedn., Soc. Med. Adminstrs, Am. Pub. Health Assn., Omicron Delta Kappa, Beta Theta Pi, Nu Sigma Nu. Presby. (trustee). Contbr. articles profl. jours. Home: 7401 Masters Dr Potomac MD 20854 Office: 1025 Connecticut Av NW Washington DC 20036

HOWELL, JANET K. GREGG, (Mrs. Alfred Corey Howell), former publisher; b. Urbana, Ill., Aug. 28, 1903; d. David and Kate Ruth (Neal) Kinley; A.B., U. Ill., 1924; grad. study U. Cal., 1925; m. John Robert Gregg, Oct. 23, 1930 (dec. Feb. 1948); children—Kate Kinley (Mrs. Duncan Ward Smith), John Robert; m. 2d, Alfred Corey Howell, Jan. 7, 1950. Vice pres. Gregg Pub. Co., 1938-48, pres., 1948, mem. bd. dirs., 1949; editor The Gregg Writer, Bus. Edn. World; v.p. Gregg Coll. Chgo., 1941-48, pres., 1948; chmn. bd. The Gregg Schs., Ltd., 1948, retired. Mem. U. Ill. Found. 1959—. Episcopalian. Democrat. Clubs: Nat. Arts (gov. 1950—); Cosmopolitan. Mem. Kappa Alpha Theta, Alpha Iota (hon.), Mortar Bd. Home: 18 Graenest Ridge Rd Wilton CT 06897

HOWELL, JOHN I., banker; b. Pitts., 1917; ed. Yale, 1939. Chmn. bd. J. Henry Schroder Banking Corp., N.Y.C., Schroder Trust Co., N.Y.C.; dir. Ward Howell Assos., Internat. Holding Corp., Dominick Fund, Inc., Schroders, Ltd., London, Schroders, Inc., N.Y.C., United Cal. Bank Internat., N.Y., Schroder Capital Corp., N.Y.C., Am. Internat. Group, Inc., N.Y.C. Trustee Internat. House, N.Y. Home: Mayfair Lane Greenwich CT 06830 Office: 57 Broadway New York City NY 10006

HOWELL, JOHN MCDADE, educator; b. Five Points, Ala., Jan. 28, 1922; s. John William and Bettie Mae (Lee) H.; A.B., U. Ala., 1948, M.A., 1949; Ph.D., Duke, 1954; m. Gladys Evelyn David, Aug. 9, 1952; children-David Noble, Joseph Lee. Instr., U. Ida., 1950; instr. Randolph-Macon Woman's Coll., Lynchburg, Va., 1951-52; instr. Duke, 1952-53; asst. prof. Sweet Briar Coll., Lynchburg, 1953-54; asst. prof. Memphis State U., 1954-57; asso. prof. E.Carolina U., Greenville, N.C., 1957-61, prof., 1961—, chmn. polit. sci. dept., 1963-66, dean Coll. Arts and Scis., 1966-69, dean Grad. Sch., 1969—. Served with USAAF, 1942-45. Decorated Bronze Star medal. Mem. Am. Soc. Internat. Law, Am., So. polit. sci. assns., Phi Beta Kappa, Phi Kappa Phi, Pi Sigma Alpha. Contbr. chpts. to The International Law Standard and Commonwealth Developments, 1966; De Lege Pactorum, 1970. Contbr. articles profl. jours. Home: 132 E Longmeadow Rd Greenville NC 27834

HOWELL, JOHN OWEN, Jr., retail mcht.; b. Nashville, Feb. 7, 1925; s. John Owen and Margaret Lee (Bowden) H.; student Middle Tenn. State Coll., 1946-47; m. Margaret Sue Stephens, Apr. 4, 1946; children—Frances Lee, Stephen Owen, Susan Lynn. With Genesco, Inc., Nashville, 1947—, successively purchasing agt. mfg. plants, style and cost engr. retail div., style dir., mdse. mgr., 1947- 58, pres. Flagg Bros. div., 1958—, pres. Holiday-Wise div., 1961—, also dir., mem. exec. com., bd. govs. Genesco, Inc., exec. v.p., 1968-69, pres., chmn. finance com., 1969—; dir. 3d Nat. Bank of Nashville, Am. Security Real Estate Investment Trust. Pres., Youth, Inc. Bd. dirs., v.p. United Givers Fund of Nashville; pres. bd. trustees Bethel Coll. Served with USNR, 1943-46. Mem. Volume Footwear Retailers Assn. (pres., dir.), Nashville Area C. of C. (gov.). Presbyn. (elder). Clubs: Bluegrass Yacht and Country (Hendersonville, Tenn.); Belle Meade Country (Nashville). Home: 4006 Brush Hill Rd Nashville TN 37216 Office: 111 7th Av N Nashville TN 37206

HOWELL, ROBERT JAMES, educator; b. Salt Lake City, Sept. 13, 1925; s. Elmer Virgil and Stella Myrtle (Knight) H.; student Wash. State U., 1944; B.A., U. Utah, 1948, M.A., 1949, Ph.D., 1951; m. Mary Winnie Raiford, Aug. 16, 1946; children—Carol Ann, Peggy Lynne, Robert Bruce. Instr. psychology Fresno State Coll., 1951-52; faculty Brigham Young U., Provo, Utah, 1952—, prof. psychology 1960—, chmn. dept., 1961-68, dir. clin. tng., 1968—. Sr. psychologist Utah State Hosp., 1958-60, cons., dir. psychol. tng., 1960-61; cons. Utah State Prison, 1961—; staff psychologist Patton State Hosp., 1965-66; research specialist Center for Tng. in Community Psychiatry, Los Angeles, 1968-69. Served with USAAF, 1943-46. Fellow Am., Utah (pres. 1963-64) psychol. assns.; mem. Rocky Mountain Psychol. Assn., Sigma Xi, Phi Kappa Phi, Psi Chi. Home: 2761 North 1200 East Provo UT 84601

HOWELL, ROGER, Jr., coll. pres.; b. Balt., July 3, 1936; s. Roger and Katherine (Clifford) H.; A.B. summa cum laude, Bowdoin Coll., 1958; B.A. (Rhodes scholar), St. Johns Coll., Oxford (Eng.) U., 1960, M.A., D.Phil., 1964; LL.D., Nasson Coll., Colby Coll., 1970; L.H.D., U. Me., 1971; m. Marcla Lunt, June 11, 1966; children—Tracy Walker, Ian Christopher. Jr. instr. history Johns Hopkins, 1960-61; research fellow, tutor final honour sch. modern history St. John's Coll., Oxford U., 1961-64, jr. dean arts of coll., 1962-64; tutor history and polit. theory Oxford U. Internat. Grad. Summer Sch., 1962-63, W.E.A. lectr. delegacy extramural studies, 1963-64; faculty Bowdoin Coll., 1964—, prof. history, 1968—, chmn. dept., 1967-68, acting dean coll., 1968-69, pres., 1969- -. Vis. prof. U. Me., 1968-69, mem. higher edn. planning commn., 1969—; pres. WCBB (Colby-Bates-Bowdoin Ednl. Telecasting Corp.), 1969-71. Bd. dirs. Allagash Group, Coast Heritage Trust; trustee Waynflete Sch., Portland, Me., Regional Meml. Hosp., Brunswick. Recipient Outstanding Young Man of Year award Me. Jr. C. of C., 1970, New Eng. Jr. C. of C., 1970. Fellow Royal Anthrop. Inst. Gt. Britain and Ireland, Royal Hist. Soc.; mem. Hist. Assn. Gt. Britain, Am. Hist. Assn., Past and Present Soc., Econ. History Soc., Soc. Antiquaries Newcastle, Stubbs Soc. (Oxford U.), Scottish History Soc., Soc. d'Etude du XVIIe siecle, Conf. Brit. Studies (exec. com. 1967-69), New Eng. Conf. Brit. Studies (exec. sec. 1967-69, hon. pres. 1969-70), Renaissance Soc. Am., Am. Assn. Advt. Agys. Ednl. Found. (chmn. acad. adv. com. 1970—), Phi Beta Kappa. Rotarian. Clubs: St. Botolph (Boston); Hamilton Street (Balt.); United University (London), London Scottish Rugby; Oxford Union; University (N.Y.). Author: Newcastle upon Tyne and the Puritan Revolution, 1967; Sir Philip Sidney: The Shepherd Knight, 1968; also articles. Editor: Prescott: The Conquest of Mexico, Etc., 1966; British Studies Monitor, 1969—. Home: 85 Federal St Brunswick ME 04011

HOWELL, THOMAS WILLIAM, musician; b. Cin., Nov. 29, 1948; s. Richard Hirst and Mary Phyllis (Shofner) H.; B.Mus., Juilliard Sch. Music, 1961 1971. 2d French horn Am. Symphony Orch. conducted by Leopold Stokowski, 1970-71; asso. 1st horn Chgo. Symphony Orch., 1971—; mem. Chgo. Symphony Woodwind Quintet. Home: 1 E Scott St Chicago IL 60610 Office: 220 S Michigan Av Chicago IL 60604

HOWELL, WILBUR SAMUEL, educator; b. Wayne, N.Y., Apr. 22, 1904; s. Wood Augustus and Edna (Hanmer) H.; A.B., Cornell U., 1924, M.A., 1928, Ph.D., 1931; grad. study U. of Paris, 1928-29; m. Charlotte Coombe, June 26, 1928 (dec. April 5, 1956); 1 son, Samuel Coombe; m. 2d, Cecilia Jonkman van Eerden, June 27, 1962; Instr. pub. speaking Ia. State Coll., 1924-25, Washington U., 1925-27, Cornell U., 1929-30, Harvard, 1930-33; asst. prof. Dartmouth, 1933-34; asst. prof. Princeton, 1934-40, asso. prof., 1940-55, prof. rhetoric and oratory, 1955—, acting chmn. department of English Summer Sch., 1947, clerk university faculty, 1958- 68, sr. fellow Council Humanities, 1966; visiting professor Stanford U., summer 1958. Foreman Mercer County (N.J.) Grand Jury, 1944. Guggenheim fellow. 1948-49, 57-58; Huntington Library fellow, 1951-52, 62-63. Mem. Princeton Police Res., 1941-45; instr. A.S.T.P., 1943-45. Mem. Modern Lang. Assn., Speech Communication Assn., Renaissance Soc. Am., Am. Assn. U. Profs., N.J. Edn. Assn. (parliamentarian 1938, 41), Phi Beta Kappa, Delta Sigma Rho, Pi Kappa Phi. Democrat. Episcopalian. Club: Nassau. Author: The Rhetoric of Alcuin and Charlemagne, 1941; Problems and Styles of Communication, 1945; Fenelon's Diaglogues on Eloquence, 1951; Logic and Rhetoric in England: 1500-1700, 1956; Eighteenth-Century British Logic and Rhetoric, 1971; also articles and reviews profl. jours., publs. Editor-in-chief quar. jour. Speech, 1954-56. Contbr. Ency. Brit. Home: 20 Armour Rd Princeton NJ 08540

HOWELL, WILLIAM KENNETH, lawyer, ins. co. exec.; b. Columbus, O., Apr. 7, 1906; s. William and Gerda (Powell) H.; A.B., Ohio State U., 1927, LL.B., 1929, J.D., 1967; m. Virginia Mae LeConey, May 2, 1927; children—Larry, Brian, Jeffrey. Admitted to Ohio bar, 1929; practice in Columbus, 1929-37; with Nationwide Ins. Cos., Columbus, 1937—, now sr. v.p., gen. counsel Nationwide Mut. Ins. Co., Nationwide Mut. Fire Ins. Co., Nationwide Life Ins. Co., Nationwide Gen. Ins. Co.; v.p., gen. counsel Nationwide Devel. Co., Nationwide Premium Accounts, Inc., Nationwide Consumer Services, Inc., Approved Consumer Discount Co., Nationwide Consumer Credit Corp., Heritage Securities, Inc., Nat. Services, Inc., Nationwide Research Center, Inc., Nationwide Transport, Inc., Nationwide Communications, Inc., gen. counsel United Redevel. Corp. Mem. Ohio Traffic Safety Council, 1941-46, Pres.'s Hwy. Safety Conf., 1946. Vice pres., gen. counsel Nationwide Found. Mem. Am., Ohio, Columbus (sec. 1935-37) bar assns., Am. Land Title Assn., Ohio Title Assn., Assn. Life Ins. Counsel, Am. Life Conv., Am. Judicature Soc., U.S. Power Squadrons, U.S. Coast Guard Aux., Delta Theta Phi. Clubs: Lawyers (pres. 1932), University (Columbus); Catawba Island (Port Clinton, O.). Home: 1649 Sundridge Dr Columbus OH 43221 Office: 246 N High St Columbus OH 43216

HOWELL, WILLIAM M., lawyer; b. Jacksonville, Fla., Dec. 4, 1921; s. Charles Cook and Clara (Moffitt) H.; student Davidson Coll., 1939-41; B.A., U. Fla., 1943, LL.B., J.D., 1947; m. Margaret Ann Fisher, Feb. 20, 1950; children—William Robert, Margaret M., Chanley Taylor. Admitted to Fla. bar, since practiced in Jacksonville; men. firm Howell, Kirby, Montgomery & Diainto. Served with USAAF, 1943-45. Mem. Nat. Assn. Ins. Counsel, Fla. Def. Lawyers Assn. Republican. Presbyn. (elder, deacon). Author articles. Home: 4942 Ortega Forest Dr Jacksonville FL 32210 Office: Gulf Life Tower Jacksonville FL 32207

HOWELL, WILLIAM SMILEY, educator; b. Center Twp., Rock Co., Wis., Apr. 13, 1914; s. William Owen and Cora Del Myra (Smiley) H.; student Beloit Coll., 1931-32; B.S., U. Wis., 1935, M.A., 1938, Ph.D., 1942; m. Jessie Irene Walker, Apr. 23, 1935; children—Mark William, Craig Walker. Instr. Lake Geneva (Wis.) High Sch., 1935-37; instr. speech, dir. debate U. S.D., 1938-40; civilian ednl. cons. Tech. Tng. Command, USAAF, Truax Field Madison, Wis., 1942-45; asst. prof., dir. forensics U. Minn., 1945-49, asso. prof., dir. forensics, 1949-54, prof., chmn. dept. speech and theater arts, 1954-59, prof., asso. chmn. dept. speech, theater arts, 1959- 64, prof. speech communication, 1964—; vis. prof. U. of Hawaii, 1967. Mem. Am. Assn. U. Profs., Speech Communication Assn. (pres. 1971), Central States Speech Assn., Delta Sigma Rho, Phi Kappa Phi, Gown-in-Town. Club: Campus (Mpls.). Author: (with Winston Brembeck) Persuasion, A Means of Social Control, 1952; (with Donald K. Smith) Discussion, 1956; (with David W. Thompson and Donald K. Smith) Speech-Debate-Drama, 1968; (with others) Interpersonal Communication in the Modern Organization, 1969; (with Ernest G. Bormann) Presentational Speaking for Business and the Professions, 1971. Home: 2546 39th Av S Minneapolis MN 55406

HOWELL, WILLIAM TALBOT, govt. ofcl.; b. Carlisle, Ky., Feb. 28, 1913; s. John Hadden and Mary Stuart (Congleton) H.; student Southeastern U., 1936-39; m. Edith Louise Harden, Feb. 22, 1939; children—Jean (Mrs. Larry Row), Martha (Mrs. Richard Stover), Kathyn (Mrs. Richard Hathaway). Admitted to D.C. bar, 1941; with office of Treas. U.S., 1936—, dep. treas., 1957—. Served to lt. USNR, 1942-45. Home: 2305 N Sibley St Alexandria VA 22311 Office: Treasury Dept Washington DC 20225

HOWELLS, JOHN ANDREW, machine tool co. exec.; b. Christopher, Ill., Mar. 22, 1918; s. George and Nellie (Humble) H.; B.S., Ohio State U., 1940; m. Lucille E. Rigel, Oct. 1, 1949; children—John Andrew, Raye Rigel. Accountant, Youngstown Sheet & Tube Co. (O.), 1940-41; auditor RFC, Cleve., 1941-53; with corp. loans dept. Central Nat. Bank, Cleve., 1953-56; auditor Warner & Swasey Co., Cleve., 1956-62 controller, 1962—. Bd. dirs. Brentwood Hosp., Cleve., 1967—; bd. dirs. Friendly Inn Settlement House, Cleve., 1962-68, chmn., 1966-68. Served to maj., arty., AUS, 1942-46; ETO. C.P.A., Ohio. Mem. Financial Execs. Inst., Financial Council Machinery and Allied Products Inst. Baptist. Mason (Shriner). Home: 2066 Newcome St Cleveland OH 44143 Office: 11000 Cedar Av Cleveland OH 44106

HOWELLS, WILLIAM WHITE, anthropologist, educator; b. N.Y.C., Nov. 27, 1908; s. John Mead and Abby Macdougall (White) H.; grad. St. Paul's Sch., 1926; S.B., Harvard, 1930, Ph.D., 1934; m. Muriel Gurdon Seabury, June 15, 1929; children—Muriel Gurdon (Mrs. Richard E. Metz), William Dean II. Asst. prof. anthropology U. Wis., 1939-46, asso. prof., 1946-48, prof., 1948- 54, prof. integrated liberal studies, 1948—54; prof. anthropology Harvard, 1954—, also curator somatology, faculty Peabody Mus., 1955—, faculty Mus. Comparative Zoology, 1966—. Served as lt. USNR, 1943-46. Recipient Viking Fund medal in phys. anthropology, 1954. Fellow Am. Acad. Arts and Scis., Am. Anthrop. Assn. (pres. 1951), A.A.A.S.; mem. Am. Assn. Phys. Anthropologists, Nat. Acad. Sci., Austrian Acad. Scis.; corr. mem. Geog. Soc. Lisbon, Antrhop. Soc. Paris, Anthrop. Soc. Vienna (hon.). Clubs: Somerset, Tavern (Boston); Century (N.Y.C.); Harvard Faculty. Author: Mankind So Far, 1944; The Heathens, 1948; Back of History, 1954; Mankind in the Making, 1959, rev. edit., 1967. Editor: Early Man in the Far East, 1949; Ideas on Human Evolution, 1962; Am. Jour. Phys. Anthropology, 1949-54; asso. editor Human Biology, 1955—, Am. Naturalist, 1967-70. Contbr. articles to sci., gen. publs. Home: Kittery Point ME 03905 Office: Peabody Mus Cambridge MA 02138

HOWER, FELIX, advt. exec.; b. N.Y.C., Sept. 6, 1911; s. Louis and Bertha (Mittledorf) H.; B.S., U. Detroit, 1932; m. Roslyn Greenberg, Aug. 24, 1941; children—Barbara, Dale. With Bass-Luckoff, Detroit, 1936-40; with W.B. Doner & Co., Detroit, 1945—, exec. v.p. 1963—. Served with AUS, 1942-45. Mem. Detroit Conv. Bur. (dir.), Adcraft Club Detroit, Am. Assn. Advt. Agys. (gov. Mich.). Clubs: Tam O'Shanter Country, Standard (Detroit). Home: 29660 Middlebelt Farmington MI 48024 Office: 26711 Northwestern Hwy Southfield MI 48075

HOWER, FRANK BEARD, Jr., banker; b. Louisville, Nov. 26, 1928; s. Frank Beard and Katharine (Coffman) H.; A.B., Centre Co., Danville, Ky., 1950; m. Virginia W. Barker, Dec. 30, 1954; children—Frank Beard III, William. With Liberty Nat. Bank, Louisville, 1950—, exec. v.p., 1967-71, pres., 1971—, also dir. Commonwealth Life Ins. Co., Falls City Brewing Co., Louisville, Louisville Title Ins. Co. Mem. Ky. Registry of Election Finance, 1966-70, Ky. Econ. Progress Commn., 1964-70; mem. Dept. Commerce Regional Export Expansion Council; gen. chmn. United Appeal, 1969. Bd. dirs. Bellarmine Coll., Louisville Childrens Hosp.; bd. overseers U. Louisville; trustee Ky. Ind. Coll. Found. Served as 2d lt. USMCR, 1951-52; Korea. Mem. Am., Ky. bankers assns., Robert Morris Assos. Republican. Presbyn. Clubs: Louisville Country, Pendennis, Wynn- Stay, River Valley (Louisville). Home: 613 Maryhill Lane Louisville KY 40207 Office: 416 W Jefferson St Louisville KY 40202

HOWER, RALPH M., educator, business cons.; b. Salina, Kan., Aug. 25, 1903; s. Edward Charles and Etta (Kistler) H.; A.B., U. Kan., 1925; B.A., Oxford U., 1928, M.A., 1953; D.C.S., Harvard, 1935; Dr. Philosophy and Letters, U. Navarra (Spain), 1967; m. Elizabeth Niven, June 27, 1928; children—Alison Mary Steuart, Robert Kistler. Instr. econs. U. Kan., 1928-30; research asst. business history Harvard, 1930-34, instr. bus. history, 1934-35, asst. prof., 1935-46, asso. prof., 1946-49, prof. bus. adminstrn., 1949-70, prof. emeritus, 1970—; prof. Mgmt. Devel. Inst., Lausanne, Switzerland, 1960-61. Cons. adminstrn., exec. devel. several orgns. and corps.; mem. adv. com. Instituto de Estudios Superiores de la Empressa, Barcelona, Spain. Pres. Community Council of Weston, Mass., 1947-49. Bd. Assesors, Weston, Mass., 1955-60. Trustee Bus. History Found. Served to col. Q.M.C., AUS, 1942-46; ETO. Decorated Bronze Star (U.S.); Legion of Honor, Cross of War with gold star (France). Mem. Am. Assn. Rhodes Scholars, Phi Beta Kappa, Beta Theta Pi. Episcopalian. Club: Harvard (N.Y.C.). Author: The Preservation of Business Records, 1937; The History of an Advertising Agency, 1939, rev. edit., 1949; The History of Macy's of New York, 1943; The Administrator (with John Desmond Glover), 1949, rev. edit., 1963; (with Charles D. Orth 3d) Managers and Scientists, 1963. Home: 467 Concord Rd Weston MA 02193 Office: Baker Library Soldiers Field Boston MA 02163 ☆

HOWERTON, GEORGE, educator; b. Milton, Ky., Oct. 28, 1905; s. David Ham and Sara (Sutton) H.; A.B., William Jewell Coll., 1926; A.M., Columbia, 1940; Ph.D., Northwestern U., 1950; Dupre (Paris); m. A'Louise Trester, Sept. 4, 1940. Faculty, Northwestern U., Evanston, Ill., 1939-71, dir. choral activities, 1939-54, prof. hist. music, 1950-71, dean Sch. Music, 1951-71. Governing mem. Chgo. Symphony Orch. Assn.; nat. co-chmn. Central Opera Service; nat. co-chmn., exec. com. Met. Opera Nat. Council, N.Y.C. Life trustee Ravinia Festival Assn. Chgo. Recipient Steinway award, 1967. Mem. Pi Kappa Lambda (nat. pres. 1960-66), Kappa Alpha, Phi Mu Alpha. Clubs: University, Cliff Dwellers, Arts (Chgo.); University (Evanston). Author: The Use of Victor Records in the High School Choral Training Program (pamphlet), 1944; (with Traugott Rohner) Fundamentals of Music Theory, 1943; Technique and Style in Choral Singing, 1957; (with Donald J. McGinn) Literature as a Fine Art, 1958. Home: Longview Farm Wadsworth IL 60083

HOWERY, BILL NELSON, r.r. exec.; b. Cherokee, Ia., May 6, 1915; s. Robert Richard and Ossie Margaret (Nelson) H.; grad. Advanced Mgmt. Program, Harvard, 1956; m. Geraldine Louise Francisco, June 6, 1937; children—Judith, William, Sandra, Nancy, Robert. With C.G.W.R.R., 1936-60, beginning as brakeman, successively condr., asst. trainmaster, trainmaster, asst. supt., asst.

gen. mgr., 1936-57, gen. mgr., 1957-60; v.p., gen. mgr. St. Paul Union Depot & Minn. Transfer Ry. Co., 1960-64, Mpls., Northfield & So. Ry., 1964—. Mason. Club: Minneapolis Athletic. Home: 5210 Villa Way Edina MN 55436 Office: 911 Hennepin Av Minneapolis MN 55403

HOWERY, VICTOR IRVING, educator; b. South Wayne, Wis., Apr. 13, 1916; s. Clinton Victor and Helen Islonia (LaDue) H.; B.S., Wis. State Coll., 1941; Ph.M., U. Wis., 1946, M.S. in Social Work, 1948, PhD., 1949; m. Garnett Eleanor Schroeder, Feb. 26, 1949; children—Carla Beth, Marcia Islonia. Social worker, LaFayette County, Wis., 1934-36; tchr. Blanchardville (Wis.) Elementary and Jr. High Sch., 1936-40; cons. edn. Wis. Dept. Pub. Welfare, Madison, 1948-49; cons., counselor pub. sch. system Cedar Rapids, Ia., 1949-50; asst., asso. prof. U. Wis. Sch. Social Work, Madison, 1950-52; prof. social work, 1962-68; dir., dean Sch. Social Work U. Wash., Seattle, 1952-62; prof. Wis. State U., Eau Claire, 1968—. Mem. profl. adv. coms. Rehab. Edn. Project, Wash. Bd. Health, research sect. Wash. Dept. Pub. Assistance, alcoholism div. Wash. Dept. Health, Gov. Wash. Panel Mental Retardation, Gov. Wash. Council Aging, Seattle Speech and Hearing Center, Office Vocational Rehab., Dept. Health, Edn. and Welfare, Tb Assn.; mem. adv. panel social work edn. Nat. Inst. Mental Health. Bd. dirs. Council Social Work Edn., Nat. Conf. Social Welfare. Chmn. study com. chmn. Council Planning Affiliates Seattle United Good Neighbors, 1961-62. Served with AUS, 1941-45. Mem. Nat. Assn. Social Workers (dir., com. chmn.), Am. Assn. U. Profs., Am. Civil Liberties Union. Home: 4945 Black Oak Dr Madison WI 53711

HOWES, BENJAMIN DURWARD, jeweler; b. Clinton, Ia., June 19, 1899; s. Benjamin Durward and Helen (Sanborn) H.; student Stanford, 1916-18; m. Maxine Eccleston, Nov. 16, 1921; children—Benjamin Durward III, Doreen Eccleston (Mrs. R.S. Hambleton), Maxine Sanborn (Mrs. Brice Toole, Jr.). Partner, B.D. Howes & Son, retail jewelers, 1919-39, pres., 1939-58, chmn. bd., 1958—. Chmn., Orthopedic Council, 1970—, Met. Traffic and Transit Com., 1950. Mem. Los Angeles (pres. 1934-35), Cal. (pres. 1936-37), retail jewelers assns. Los Angeles Retail Code Authority (vice chmn. 1934-35), Am. Nat. Retail Jewelers Assn. (v.p. 1944-46, pres. 1946, chmn. nat. adv. council 1948-49), Los Angeles (mem. bd. 1936-39, 48-49), U.S. Jr. (pres. 1930-31), Internat. Jr. (chmn. 1931-32), Wilshire (pres. 1945) chambers commerce, Wilshire Blvd. Assn. (pres. 1948-49), Econ. Round Table (founder, pres. 1932), Los Angeles Better Bus. Bur., Alpha Tau Omega. Republican. Conglist. Author: Birthdays in the News, over NBC radio stas., also column Today's Famous Birthdays, Los Angeles Times, 1939-41; founder, editor Am. Women (biog. dict. notable women), America's Young Men (biog. dict. outstanding young men). Rotarian (pres. 1951-52). Home: 1120 S El Molino Av Pasadena CA 91106 Office: 3100 Wilshire Blvd Los Angeles CA 90010

HOWES, BENJAMIN DURWARD, III, jewelry co. exec.; b. Los Angeles, Oct. 31, 1922; s. Durward and Maxine (Eccleston) H.; student Stanford, 1941-42; B.S. in Bus. Adminstrn., U. So. Cal., 1943; m. Cynthia Marble, May 25, 1951; children—Cynthia Marble, Dana Belinda, Mellisa Sanborn (dec.), Durward IV, Mary Devin, Daryl Brett. With B.D. Howes & Son, retail jewelers, Pasadena, Los Angeles, Santa Barbara, Newport Beach, Cal. and Phoenix, 1946—, pres., 1957—. Chmn. bd. jewelery Industry Council, 1970-71. pres. Pasadena-Altadena Community Chest, 1960, 61. Trustee, exec. com. Republican Assos. Served to lt. (j.g.) USNR World War II. Recipient Distinguished Service award as Outstanding Young Man in Pasadena, U.S. Jr. C. of C., 1957. Mem. Young Presidents Orgn. (chmn. San Gabriel 1964-65), Retail Jewelers Am. (pres. 1963-65), Cal. Retail Jewelers Assn. (pres. 1950), Cal. Jr. (v.p. 1949), Pasadena Jr. (pres. 1951-52) Pasadena (v.p.), Los Angeles Area (dir., v.p. 1971) chambers commerce, Los Angeles Breakfast Panel (founder, past pres.), Psadena Tournament Roses Assn., U. So. Cal. Alumni Assn. (bd. govs.), Alpha Delta Sigma, Kappa Alpha. Republican. Episcopalian. Rotarian (pres. 1967-68, dir. Pasadena). Home: 1145 Oak Grove Av San Marino CA 91108 Office: 336 Lake Av Pasadena CA 91101

HOWES, OLIVER P., lawyer; b. New Rochelle, N.Y., 1927; B.A., N.Y. U., 1950; LL.B., Columbia, 1953. Admitted to N.Y. State bar, 1953; partner Nims, Halliday, Whitman, Howes, Collison and Isner, N.Y.C. Mem. Am. Bar Assn. Office: 60 E 42d St New York City NY 10017•

HOWES, RAYMOND FLOYD, educator; b. Ithaca, N.Y., Apr. 28, 1903; s Charles Henry and Eleanor (Titchener) H.; A.B., Cornell U., 1924; M.A., U. Pitts., 1926; L.H.D., Northeastern U., 1960; m. Louise Atilla Riley, June 18, 1927; children—Raymond Tichener, Bradford Riley. Instr. English, U. Pitts., 1924-26; instr. English, Washington U., St. Louis, 1926-29, asst. prof., 1929-36, dir. news bur., 1931-36, dir. forensics, 1927-36; asst. to exec. sec. Cornellian Council, Cornell U., 1936-38, asst. to dean Coll. Engring., 1937-41, asst. to provost, 1941-42, acting dir. pub. information, 1942-43, instr. engring. journalism, 1940-42, adminstrv. asst. to v.p., 1946-48, sec. univ., 1948-51; staff asso. Am. Council on Edn., Washington, 1951-62; asst. to chancellor U. Cal., Riverside, 1962-66; dir. publicity and pubis. Claremont (Cal.) Grad. Sch. and U. Center, 1966-68. Served from lt. to comdr. USNR, 1943-46. Mem. Delta Sigma Rho, Sigma Delta Chi, Omicron Delta Kappa, Alpha Phi Omega. Club: Savage (Ithaca). Author: (with Richard W. Armour) Coleridge the Talker, 1940; Sikes the Good Teacher, 1941; A Cornell Notebook, 1971. Editor: Women in the Defense Decade, 1952; Causes of Public Unrest Pertaining to Education, 1953; Toward Unity in Educational Policy, 1953; Higher Education and the Society It Serves, 1957; Vision and Purpose in Higher Education, 1963; The Educational Record, 1951-62; Toward Better Preparation of College and University Administrators, 1964; editor, co-author Debating, 1931; Our Cornell, 1939; Historical Studies of Rhetoric and Rhetoricians, 1962; asso. editor Quar. Jour. Speech, 1933-36. Contbr. articles to periodicals. Home: 149 Nisbet Way Riverside CA 92507

HOWIE, GEORGE WILLIAMSON, traffic and transp. engr.; b. Portland, Ore., Aug. 19, 1908; s. George Williamson and Christina (Steele) H.; B.S., Ore. State U., 1932; certificate in hwy. traffic Yale, 1946; m. Alberta Steele, Mar. 27, 1931; children—Gordon G., Kathelyn Ann (Mrs. Michael Carroll Doyle), Douglas A., Susan C. (Mrs. Alan Hirsch). Editor publs., transp., pub. utility work, 1932-38; jr. engr., statistician Bur. Traffic Engring., Portland, 1939-43; asst. city traffic engr., Portland, 1943-48; city traffic engr., Cin., 1949- 64; dir. dept. pub. utilities, 1954-64; transp. engr. Eastern region DeLeuw, Cather & Assos., N.Y.C., 1964-68, partner- in-charge N.Y. office, 1967-68; v.p. Winko-Matic Signal Co., Inc., Avon Lake, Ohio, 1968-69; engr.-planner Washington Suburban Transit Commn., Silver Spring, Md., 1969—; chmn. interim coordinating com. Ohio-Ky. Ind. Regional Transp. and Devel. Study, 1962-64; guest lectr. Yale, Northwestern U., Ohio State U., Purdue U., U. Tenn., U. Cin., U. Ill., U. Wis., Ore. State U.; cons. Nat. Com. Urban Transp.; mem. com. sch. crossing protection, Am. Assn. State Hwy. Ofcls. Pres. Yale Traffic Bur. Alumni, 1960; chmn. com. urban volume characteristics Hwy. Research Bd., 1950-59; vice chmn. engring. sect. Pres.'s Hwy. Safety Conf., 1958; chmn. traffic signal tech. com. Nat. Joint Com. Uniform Traffic Control Devices, 1959-61, vice chmn. research, 1962-63. Registered profl. engr., Ohio, Conn., Va., N.Y., D.C. Mem. Inst. Traffic Engrs. (pres. 1965, chmn. roadway sign lighting com., past dist. dir.), Illuminating Engring. Soc. (chmn. roadway sign lighting com.), Internat. Commn. Illumination, Am. Soc. C.E. (past program chmn. Nat. Transp. Conf.), Nat. Acad. Sci. (hwy. research bd.), Lambda Chi Alpha. Methodist. Mason (Shriner); mem. Order Eastern Star. Mem. editorial bd. Traffic Engring. Handbook, 1959-62. Home: 9613 Lorain Av Silver Spring MD 20901 Office: 8720 Georgia Av Silver Spring MD 20910

HOWISON, JEAN PIERRE, steel co. exec.; b. Montreal, Que., Can., Jan. 25, 1933; s. Alfred and Cecile (Racette) H.; B.Commerce, Loyola Coll., Montreal, 1948-56; chartered accountant, McGill U., 1959; m. Dorothy Harris, Nov. 14, 1960; 1 son, Robert. Asst. treas. Davie Shipbldg. Ltd., Lauzon, Que., 1959-65; treas. Sidbeec, Montreal, 1966—; treas., controller Dominion Steel & Coal Corp., Montreal, 1968—. Mem. Canadian Inst. Chartered Accountants. Home: 4 Hazel Dollar Des Dr Ormeaux Quebec Canada Office: 507 Pl D'Armes Montreal Quebec Canada

HOWISON, JOHN MCCOUL, fgn. service officer; b. Bogata, Tex., Jan. 11, 1925; s. William Clatterbuck and Raviah (Sullivan) H.; student Kilgore (Tex.) Coll., 1941- 45; A.B., Harvard, 1947; student Princeton, 1951-52; m. Joan Carney, June 16, 1954; children—Martha Lynne, John Neil, Stephen Carney. Joined U.S. Fgn. Service, 1947; 3d sec., Kabul, 1947-49; vice consul, Istanbul, 1950; 2d sec., Ankara, 1950-51, Tehran, 1952-54; desk officer Afghanistan and Pakistan, State Dept., 1954-58; 1st sec. mut. def. affairs officer, Rome, 1958-61; prin. officer, Tabrix, Iran, 1961-63; assigned Naval War Coll., 1963-64; dep. dir. Office Greek, Turkish and Iranian affairs State Dept., 1964-66, country dir. for Turkish affairs, 1966-68; dep. chief mission Am. embassy, Monrovia, Liberia, 1968—. Served with USAAF, 1943-45. Address: Am Embassy Monrovia Liberia

HOWLAND, ARTHUR LLOYD, educator; b. Phila., Pa., Jan. 13, 1908; s. Arthur Charles and 1931; Ph.D., Princeton U., 1933; m. Jean Smith, Dec. 15, 1938; children- -Sarah, Emily, Nicholas K. Instr. geology Northwestern U., 1933-39, asst. and asso. 1939-50, prof., 1950—, chmn. dept. geology 1945-69; asst. geologist, U.S. Geol. Survey, 1940-43, asso. geologist, 1943- 44, geologist, 1944-54; geologist Newfoundland Geol. Survey, 1938. Fellow Am. A.A.A.S., Geol. Soc. Am., Mineral Soc. Am.; mem. Soc. Econ. Geologists, Chgo. Acad. Scis. (sci. gov.), Delta Phi, Sigma Xi. Contbr. articles sci. jours. Address: Dept Geology Northwestern U Evanston Il. 60201

HOWLAND, HAROLD EDWARD, govt. ofcl.; b. Pitts., Aug. 18, 1913; s. Charles and Sara (Girson) H.; B.S. with high honor, U. Pitts., 1936, Litt.M., 1937, LL.D., 1965; m. Elizabeth Jetson Spell, Oct. 4, 1942; children—Carol, Harold Edward, Charles. Instr. biology U. Pitts., 1936-37; high sch. tchr. scis. and history, Pa., 1937-41; asst. prin., then prin. Landon Jr.-Sr. High Schs., Jacksonville, Fla. and Monongahela, Pa., 1946-48; ednl. adviser high commr. U.S. Allied Commn. for Austria, 1948-50; chief branches depts. cultural and ednl. exchange service State Dept., 1951- 59; cultural attache Am. embassy, Tel Aviv, Israel, 1959-61; dir. fgn. student affairs staff Dept. State 1961-64, dir. Office Far Eastern Programs, 1964-65; dep. asst. sec. of state Bur. Ednl. and Cultural Affairs, Dept. State, Washington, 1965-67; Am. consul gen., Amsterdam, Netherlands, 1967—. Bd. dirs. Boys Club Underprivileged Boys, Pitts., 1935-40. Served to maj. AUS, 1941-46; lt. col. Res. Recipient citation for outstanding services U.S. Allied Commn. Austria, 1950, State Dept., 1953, 57, 64. Mem. N.E.A., Nat. Assn. Secondary Sch. Prins., Kappa Phi Kappa, Phi Sigma. Editor: American Life and Literature. Author articles in field. Home: 406 Dove Circle SW Vienna VA 22180 Office: Museumplein 19 Amsterdam Netherlands APO New York City NY 09159

HOWLAND, JOHN PARTRIDGE, textile co. exec.; b. Boston, July 29, 1910; s. Joseph Briggs and May (Partridge) H.; grad. Newton Country Day Sch.; B.A., Conn. Wesleyan U., 1933; student Harvard Bus. Sch., 1935; m. Virginia Wynans Myer, Apr. 26, 1941; children—John Partridge II, Judith B. (Mrs. Peter N. Pund), Randolph M. With Pepperell Mfg. Co., N.Y.C., 1935-48, asst. treas., 1946-48, v.p., 1948; with Woodward, Baldwin & Co. Inc., N.Y.C., 1948-64, v.p., 1948-55, exec. v.p., 1955-57, pres., 1957-58, pres., chmn. bd., 1958-64; pres. Erwin Mills div. Burlington Industries, N.Y.C., 1964-67; dir. Burlington Industries, 1966, exec. v.p., 1967-68; pres., dir. West Point Pepperell, N.Y.C., 1968—. Served to lt. comdr. USNR, 1942-46. Home: 40 Old Farm Rd Darien CT 06820 Office: 111 W 40th St New York City NY 10018

HOWLAND, RICHARD HENRY, educator; b. Grand Rapids, Mich., Mar. 27, 1925: s. Henry James and Wilma (Rauser) H.; A.B., U. Mich., 1949, Ph.D., 1964; M.S., Simmons Coll., 1950; m. Marilyn Ruth Michaels, June 14, 1957; children—Carol Dawn, Michael Richard, Richard James, Mark Richard, Douglas Richard, John Richard. Distributive edn. tchr. and coordinator, Grand Rapids, 1950-55; asso. prof., head marketing dept. Ferris State Coll., Big Rapids, Mich., 1955-64; prof., head marketing dept. No. Ill. U., DeKalb, 1964—. Founder, 1965, since pres. Four-Way Seiling, DeKalb; pres. R.H. Howland & Assos., 1965—, Howland Enterprises, 1963—. Served with USAAF, World War II. Decorated Air medal with 6 oak leaf clusters. Mem. Am. Marketing Assn., Sales- Marketing Execs. Chgo., Midwest Bus. Adminstrn. Assn., Mich. Pine Growers Assn., Delta Sigma Pi (Delta Sig of Year 1970), Beta Gamma Sigma. Republican. Conglist. Elk. Co-author: Principles of Marketing, 1961, author Salesmanship, 1971. Home: 364 Rolfe Rd DeKalb IL 60115

HOWLAND, RICHARD HUBBARD, archtl. historian; b. Providence, Aug. 23, 1910; S. Carl Badger and Cora Augusta (Hubbard) H.; A.B., Brown U., 1931, also hon. doctor's degree; A.M., Harvard, 1933; Ph.D., Johns Hopkins, 1946. Fellow Agora excavations, Athens, Greece, 1936-38; instr. Wellesley Coll., 1939-42; chief pictorial records sect. OSS, 1943-44; organizer dept. history art Johns Hopkins, 1947, chmn. dept., 1947- 56; pres. Nat. Trust for Historic Preservation, 1956-60; chmn. dept. civil history Smithsonian Instn., Washington, 1960-67, spl. asst. to sec. instn., 1968—. Mem. bldg. com. Nat. Cathedral, Washington; chmn. mng. com. Am. Sch. Classical Studies, Athens, founding mem. Am. Com. Internat. Commn. Historic Sites and Monuments. Trustee L.A.W. Found., Sotterley Found., Evergreen Found. Mem. Fellows in Am. Studies, Soc. Archtl. Historians (dir.), Irish Georgian Soc. (trustee), Archaeol. Inst. Am., Soc. Cincinnati (hon.), Phi Gamma Delta. Clubs: Century Assn. (N.Y.C.); 14 West Hamilton Street (Balt.); Arts, Metropolitan, 1925 F Street, Cosmos (Washington). Author: (with Elanor Spencer) Architecture of Baltimore, 1954; Greek Lamps and Their Survivals, 1958. Home: 1516 33d St Washington DC 20007 Office: Smithsonian Instn Washington DC 20560

HOWLAND, RICHARD LEVAN, architect; b. Kingston, N.Y., Dec. 16, 1912; s. Van L. and Ruth (Quick) H.; student Cazenovia Sem., 1923-29; B.Arch., Syracuse U., 1937; m. Gertrude Anna Glass, Sept. 5, 1938; children—William C., Catherine C. (Mrs. Robert A. Bonner), Teresa A. (Mrs. Steven S. Levine), Laura M. Architect asso. firm W. P. Beardsley, Auburn, N.Y., 1945-49; edn. cons. Conn. Dept. Edn., Hartford, Conn., 1949-55; pvt. practice architecture, West Hartford, Conn., 1955-60; architect sch. bldgs. Conn. State Dept. Edn., Hartford, Conn., 1960-66, chief Bur. Sch. Bldgs., 1966—. Mem. Mt. St. Joseph Acad. Bldg. Com., 1965; mem. bldg. com. Children's Museum of Hartford, 1966. Fellow A.I.A., Northeast Council Schoolhouse Constrn. Republican. Roman Cath. Club: Internat. Torch Home: 25 Foxcroft Rd West Hartford CT 06119 Office: State Office Bldg Hartford CT 06115

HOWLAND, WILFRED GLENROY, ins. co. exec.; b. Concord, N.H., Mar. 21, 1919; s. Wilfred B. and Gladys (Southard) H.; A.B., Bates Coll., 1940; J.D. cum laude, Harvard 1943; m. Elizabeth Burnes Joubert, Mar. 17, 1942; children—Wendy, Pamela. Admitted to Mass. bar, 1947; asso. Nutter, McClennen & Fish, Boston, 1947-50; gen. counsel Springfield Ins. Co., 1950-52, sec., 1952- 55; v.p., dir. Springfield-Monarch Ins. Cos., 1955-62; v.p., dir. marketing Providence Wash. Ins. Group, 1962-67; 2d v.p. State Mut. Life Assurance Co. Am., 1968—; v.p., corporate sec. Hanover Ins. Co., Mass. Bay Ins. Co., Cal-Comp Ins. Co.; pres. AMGRO, Inc.; dir. Conval, Inc. Served from pt. to lt. AUS, 1941-46. Mem. Fed., Am., Mass. bar assns., Harvard Law Sch. Assn., Newcomen Soc., Royal Philatelic Soc. Clubs: R.I. Country, Worcester Country, Collectors', New York Downtown Athletic; Southboro Tennis. Home: 17 Red Gate Lane Southboro MA 01772 Office: 440 Lincoln St Worcester MA 01605

HOWLAND, WILLIAM FRANKLIN, Jr., lawyer, govt. ofcl.; b. Townsville, N.C., Nov. 21, 1909; s. William Franklin and Mary (McIntosh) H.; A.B., Duke, 1930, LL.B., 1933; m. Verdye Catherine Jackson, Sept. 19, 1937; children—Billie Catherine, William Franklin, David Jackson. Admitted to N.C. bar, 1933, Va. bar, 1947; pvt. practice, Henderson, N.C., 1933-36; U.S. probation officer, Raleigh, N.C., 1936-43; chief U.S. probation officer U.S. Dist. Ct., Roanoke, Va., 1943-55; mem. U.S. Bd. of Parole, Washington, 1955—. Served from lt. (j.g.) to lt., USNR, 1944-46; lt. comdr. Res. Mem. Fed. Probation Officers Assn., N.C., Va., U.S. Dist. Ct. bar assns., Duke U. Alumni Assn. (1st alumni pres. class 1930), U.S. Supreme Ct., Am. Bar Alpha. Baptist. Clubs: Rotary (Raleigh and Roanoke, Va.); Civitan (Roanoke, Va.). Home: 1301 Dogwood Dr Alexandria VA 22302 Office: HOLC Bldg Washington DC 20001

HOWLAND, WILLIAM GOLDWIN CARRINGTON, lawyer; b. Toronto, Ont., Can., Mar. 7, 1915; s. Goldwin William and Margaret (Carrington) H.; B.A., U. Toronto, 1936; LL.B., Osgoode Hall Law Sch., 1939; m. Margaret Patricia Greene, Aug. 20, 1966. Read law with Rowell, Reid, Wright & McMillan, 1936-39; called to bar, Ont., 1939; practice in Toronto, 1939—; asso. McMillan & & Binch, 1936—, partner, 1948—; bencher Law Soc. Upper Can., 1960, 65, life bencher, 1969—, treas. (head), 1968-70. Chmn. bd. Gruen Watch Co. of Can., Ltd.; pres. Eve, Ltd.; dir. Gruen Industries, Inc., Monarch Investments, Ltd., Monarch Constrn., Ltd., Taylor Woodrow of Can., Ltd., Radley Investments, Ltd., Kent Cambridge, Ltd., Zenith Radio Corp. of Can., Ltd., A.I. and P. Can. Properties, Ltd., Kerr Bros., Ltd., Bourns (Can.), Ltd., Franklin Electric of Can., Ltd., St. Hilda's Investments, Ltd., Pyrotenax of Can., Ltd., P.A. Monaghan Holdings, Ltd., B.D. Wait Co., Ltd., Credit Heights, Ltd. Nat. pres. UN Assn. in Can., 1959-60. Bd. govs. Upper Can. Coll. 1968-70; mem. senate York U., 1968. Served to capt. Canadian Army, 1942-45. Mem. Canadian Bar Assn., Canadian Inst. Internat. Affairs, Univ. Coll. Alumni Assn. (past pres.), Delta Upsilon, Phi Delta Phi. Anglican. Author: Special Lectures, Law Society of Upper Canada, 1951; (with Marriott) Practice in Mortgage Actions in Ontario, 1960; Engaged on Falconbridge & Howland, Law of Mortgages, 4th edit. Home: 2 Bayview Wood Toronto 12 Ont Can Office: 20 King St W Toronto 105 Ont Can

HOWLAND, WILLIAM STAPLETON, educator, anesthesiologist; b. Savannah, Ga., July 21, 1919; s. William and May (Stapleton) H.; B.S. Notre Dame U., 1941; M.D., Columbia, 1944; m. Gail Margaret Ryan, Nov. 15, 1965; children—Karen, William Stapleton. Surg. intern Grady Hosp., Atlanta, 1944-45, asst. resident urology, 1945-46; asst. resident anesthesiology Presbyn. Hosp., N.Y.C., 1948-50, asst. anesthesiologist, 1950-52, asso. staff anesthesiologist, 1952-53; staff anesthesiologist, chmn. dept. anesthesiology Meml. Hosp., N.Y.C., 1953—, dep. chief med. officer, 1967—; asst. prof. anesthesiology Columbia, 1953; asso. prof. surgery Sloan Kettering div. Cornell U. Med. Coll., N.Y.C., 1954-55, head exptl. surgery, 1967—, asso. prof. surgery, 1955-68, prof. anesthesiology, 1968—, chmn. dept. anesthesiology, 1953—. Served to capt., M.C., AUS, 1946-48; chief urology sect. 121st Gen. Hosp., Bremerhaven, Germany, 1946-48. Mem. Nat. Bd. Med. Examiners, Meml. Hosp. Med. Bd. (pres. 1966, 67, 68-69), Am., N.Y. State (v.p. 1958, pres. 1966) socs. anesthesiologists, N.Y. Acad. Medicine, N.Y. Acad. Sci. Contbr. articles profl. jours. Home: 430 E 67th St New York City NY 10021

HOWLETT, CAROLYN SVRLUGA, art educator; b. Berwyn, Ill., Jan. 1914; d. John and Josephine (Blazina) Syriuga; student U. Chgo., 1933-36; B.Art Edn., Art Inst. Chgo., 1937, M.Art Edn., 1952; M.A., Northwestern U., 1953; m. James Howlett, July 15, 1939. Art instr. Oak Park (Ill.) pub. schs., 1934-37; art dir. Libertyville High Sch., 1937-43; instr. design, crafts, weaving, edn. Sch. of Art Inst., Chgo., 1935-43, head jr. sch., 1943-53, head art edn. dept., 1943-63, prof. art edn., 1955-70, prof. emeritus, 1970—, asso. dean, 1963-65; ednl. cons. fine arts design, art edn., also artist free lance designer and lecturer, 1934—; exhibited paintings and photographs Pan Am. and Internat. exhibits at Chgo. Hist. Soc., Art Inst. Chgo., Findlay Galleries, Chgo., Riverside Mus., N.Y.C., Mus. Sci. and Industry, Chgo., Press Club, others Tech. cons. arts and skills war program A.R.C., 1943-45 Mem. Nat., Ill. (pres. 1962) art edn. assns., Am. Fedn. Arts, Western Arts Assn., Chgo. Soc. Artists, Nat. Com. Art Edn. Club: The Arts (profl. mem. Chgo.). Author: Art Education Bibliography, 1959; author tchrs. guide Orientation to the Visual Arts, 1966. Contbr. articles on handicraft and basketry World Book Ency., 1945, 59, chpt. in Childcraft Ency., 1949; also articles art publs. Home: 336 Coonley Rd Riverside IL 60546 Office: Chicago Art Inst Chicago IL 60603

HOWLETT, DUNCAN, clergyman; b. Newton, Mass., May 15, 1906; s. Albert D. and Ella (Murdoch) H.; S.B., Harvard Coll., 1928, LL.B., 1931; S.T.B. cum laude, Harvard Div. Sch., 1936; LL.D., Emerson Coll., Boston, 1957, Meadville Theol. Sch., 1958; D.D., U. Chgo., 1958; spl. studies U. Me. Sch. Forest Resources, 1970-71; m. Margaret L. Merritt, June 30, 1931 (dec. Sept. 2, 1933); 1 dau., Margaret Lawrence (Mrs. Richard Hasty); m. 2d, Carolyn Abbott Chance, Apr. 26, 1943; children—Albert, Richard, Carolyn. Admitted to Mass. bar, 1931; gen. practice of law, Holyoke, Mass., 1931-33; student asst. 2d Unitarian Ch., Salem, Mass., 1933-34, asst. minister, 1934-35, minister, 1935-38; minister 1st Cong. Soc. (Unitarian), New Bedford, Mass., 1938- 46; minister 1st Ch. Boston, 1946-58, All Souls Unitarian Ch., Washington, 1958-68. Mem. Harvard U. Bd. Overseas' Com. To Visit Divinity Sch., 1940-62; chmn. D.C. adv. com. U.S. Commn. on Civil Rights, 1962-65; chmn. Ch. and its Leadership Commn., Unitarian Universalist Ch.; chmn. Washington adv. com. dept. social responsibility Unitarian Universalist Assn.; mem. D.C. Commrs. Youth Council, 1959-64, D.C. Crime Commn., 1962-63. Mem. Hubert Humphrey campaign staff, 1968. Mem. Soc. Am. Foresters. Clubs: Nat. Press, Cosmos (Washington); Harvard (New Bedford) (past pres.). Author: Man Against the Church, 1954; The Essenes and Christianity, 1957; The

Fourth American Faith, 1964; No Greater Love, 1966. Contbr. to Voices of Liberalism, Vol. 1, 1947; Contemporary Accents in Liberal Religion, 1960. Home: Center Lovell ME 04016

HOWLETT, HAROLD HENRY, communications co. exec.; b. Merrill, Wis., Dec. 3, 1914; s. James and Louise (Buelow) H.; student Northwestern U., 1938-40, U. Del., 1940-42; m. Helen Hope, Sept. 17, 1938; 1 dau., Hope Adams. Sec., Theodore Gary & Co., also sec. and/or asst. sec. subsidiary cos., 1935-56; asst. sec. Gen. Telephone Corp., 1956-60; sec. Gen. Telephone & Electronics Corp., 1960—, also sec. and/or asst. sec. numerous subsidiary and affiliated cos. Served with USMCR, 1943- 46. Mem. Am. Soc. Corp. Secs., Ind. Telephone Pioneers Assn. Home: 314 Haviland Rd Stamford CT 06903 Office: 730 3d Av New York City NY 10017

HOWLETT, RICHARD JAMES educator, biologist; b. Ames, Ia.; B.A., Ia. State U., 1936, M.A., 1937, Ph.D. with honors, 1940. Instr., Ia. State U., 1946-47; asst. prof. biology Johns Hopkins, 1947-50, asso. prof., 1950-62, prof., 1962--, chmn. dept., 1963-69; vis. lectr. Stanford, 1970-71. Active Boy Scouts Am., 4-H Club. Served with AUS, 1940-46. Mem. Am. Soc. Biologists, Md. Biologists, A.A.A.S., Am. Acad. Arts and Scis., Phi Beta Kappa. Home: 48936 W Hancock Blvd Baltimore MD 20206

HOWLETT, WILLIAM PORTER, industrialist; b. Warren, Pa., May 1, 1916; s. Grayle W. and Ruth (Temmel) H.; student Drake U., Phoenix Jr. Coll., Northwestern U., 1934- 46; m. Ruth Brennan, Jan. 3, 1940; children—Timothy Reed, Merrily Jo, Ruth Landry. Newspaper and pub. relations positions, Chgo., 1937-40; pub. relations work Carl Byoir & Assos., N..Y.C., 1940-45, v.p., account exec., 1946-50; asst. to chmn. bd. Willys-Overland, Toledo, 1945; exec. v.p., pres. Nesco, Inc., Chgo., 1950-52; gen. mgr. O-Cel-O div. Gen. Mills, Inc., Buffalo, 1954-57; v.p. operations Consol. Foods Corp., Chgo., 1957, pres., 1962-68, chmn. bd., chief exec. officer, 1968-69; pres., owner William Howlett, Inc., Winnetka, Ill., 1969—. Home: 302 White Oak Lane Winnetka IL 60093 Office: 833 Elm St Winnetka IL 60093

HOWLEY, FRANK LEO, writer; b. Hampton, N.J., Feb. 4, 1903; s. Dennis Walter and Mary (Sheehan) H.; B.S. in Commerce, N.Y. U. 1925, LL.D., 1950; postgrad. Sorbonne, Paris, France, 1929-31, Parsons Sch. Design, Paris, 1930; LL.D., St. Joseph's Coll., 1949; M.D. (honoris causa), Free U. Berlin, 1954; m. Edith Jenkins Cadwallader, Sept. 26, 1934; children—Dennis, Peter, William, Frances. Asst. supt. Hudson River Dayline, 1925; advt., sales exec. Strathmore Paper Co., 1926-29; adv. exec. Gray & Rogers Co., 1931-37; pres. Frank Howley Advt. Co., 1937- 40; founder Free U. Berlin, 1948; lectr., writer, cons. internat. affairs, 1949-53; v.p. N.Y. U., 1952-67; v.p. Bache & Co., N.Y.C., 1967-68; permanent panel mem. Answers for Ams., WABC-TV. Mem. Citizens Com. for a Free Cuba, Am. Com. to Preserve Abu Simbel. Served as brig. gen. U.S. Army, 1940-49; assigned cav., 1940; comdg. officer Rising Sun Sch. Aero., 1940; staff, faculty cav. sch. 1941-43; exec. officer 3rd cav. mechanized, 1943; dir. civil affairs, Cherbourg, France, also Paris, 1944; with U.S. Mil. Govt., Berlin, Germany, 1945-49; U.S. comdt. Berlin Allied Kommandatura, 1945- 49. Decorated D.S.M., Legion of Merit; Legion of Honor, Croix de Guerre with 3 palms (France); Mil. Cross (Belgium); knight comdr. cross (Fed. Republic Germany). Mem. Am. Riding Assn. Berlin (pres., founder 1947), Newcomen Soc. N.Am., Perstare et Praestare, Phi Beta Kappa, Psi Upsilon, Alpha Kappa Psi, Alpha Delta Sigma. Clubs: Die Steuben-Schurz-Gesellschaft E.V. Berlin, Spring Valley Hounds, University, Racquet, Cricket (Phila.); West Chester, Golf and Country, West Chester Hunt, Midday. Author: My Four Years' War with the Reds, 1950; Berlin Command, 1950; How Big is Russia's Bluff?, 1951; Characteristics of Russian Leaders, 1952; Your War for Peace, 1953; Revolt in North Africa, 1956; Formosa-War of Peace, 1956; Peoples and Policies, 1959; Behind the Terror in African Angola, 1961; An African Alamo, 1962; Berlin and the Western Cause, 1963; The African State That Tried To Help Itself, 1964; Eisenhower's Tragic Mistake, 1970; Turmoil in American Education, 1970. Competitor in international horse jumping events, Lucerne, Switzerland, 1946, Aachen, Germany, 1947; winner Coupe de Berlin, 1946-48. Columnist, Shooting Straight. Home: PO Box 147 Madison NJ 07940 Office: care University Club New York City NY 10019

HOWLEY, LEE CHRISTOPHER, illuminating co. exec., lawyer; b. Cleve., June 16, 1910; s. Christopher J. and Emily A. (Smith) H.; B.A., Wittenberg Coll., 1932; LL.B., Western Res. U., 1935; m. Jean H. Hauserman, June 5, 1937; children—Tim (dec.), Dan, Kate, Lee, Tom. Admitted to Ohio bar, 1935, pvt. practice, Cleve., 1935-39; asst. U.S. dist. atty., 1939-45; law dir. City of Cleve., 1945-51; v.p., gen. counsel Cleve. Electric Illuminating Co., 1951—; chmn. bd. Elyria Spring & Splty. Co.; nat. pres. Ducks Unlimited, Inc.; dir. E.F. Hauserman Co., Continental Bank; West Side Fed. Savs. & Loan, Wenham Trucking Co.; chmn. bd. Revco, D.S., Inc., 1969—; trustee U.S. Realty Investments. Vice pres. Cleve. Zoo; past pres., dir. Cath. Charities Corp.; v.p., dir. Cleve. Conv. and Visitors Bur.; chmn. bd. dirs. Kaiser Community Health Found. Recipient certificate of recognition for achievements in field of good govt. Cleve., U.S. Jr. chambers commerce, 1954; named hon. commr. Cleve. Mounted Police; hon. bn. chief City of Cleve. Fire Dept. Mem. Am., Ohio, Cuyahoga County, Cleve. bar assns., Edison Electric Inst., Am. Mgmt. Assn., Nat. Assn. Elec. Contractors, N.A.M., Ohio C. of C., Newcomen Soc., Phi Gamma Delta, Delta Theta Phi. Clubs: Cleveland Athletic, City, Union, Vermilion Yacht. Home: 5430 Portage Dr Vermilion OH 44089 Office: PO Box 5000 55 Pub Sq Cleveland OH 44101

HOWLEY, ROGER, book publisher; b. Ithaca, N.Y., Nov. 28, 1925; s. Patrick and Alice (Hester) H.; A.B., Cornell U., 1949; m. Leona Punch, Oct. 7, 1961. Univ. rep., sr. editor, London (Eng.) editorial rep. Macmillan Co., 1950-62; editor-in-chief Johns Hopkins Press, 1962-63; dir. Cornell U. Press, Ithaca, also Comstock Pub. Assos., 1963—; chmn. Cornell U. Press, Ltd., London, Eng., 1969—, Internat. Book Export Group, London, 1971—. Cons. pub. in Indonesia, Ford Found., 1968. Served with USNR, 1943-46. Mem. Assn. Am. U. Presses, Assn. Am. Pubs. (council gen. pub. div. 1970—). Home: 303 Valley Rd Ithaca NY 14850 Office: Cornell U Press Cornell U Ithaca NY 14850

HOWORTH, LUCY SOMERVILLE, lawyer; b. Greenville, Miss., July 1, 1895; d. Robert and Nellie (Nugent) Somerville; A.B., Randolph-Macon Womans Coll., 1916; grad. student, Columbia, 1918; J.D. summa cum laude, U. Miss., 1922; m. Joseph Marion Howorth, Feb. 16, 1928. Asst. in psychology Randolph-Macon Womans Coll., 1916-17; gauge insp. Allied Bur. Air Prodn., N.Y. City, 1918; indsl. research nat. bd. YMCA, 1919-20; admitted to Miss. bar, 1922, U.S. Supreme Ct. bar, 1934; gen. practice firm Howorth & Howorth, Cleveland, Greenville, and Jackson, Miss., 1922-34; U.S. commr. So. Jud. Dist. Miss., 1927-31; asso. mem. Bd. Vet. Appeals, Washington, 1934-43; legislative atty. VA, 1943-49, v.p., dir. VA Employees Credit Union, 1937-49; asso. gen. counsel War Claims Commn. 1949-52, dep. gen. counsel, 1952-53, gen. counsel, 1953-54; partner James Somerville & Assos., overseas trade and devel., 1954—; atty. Commn. on Govt. Security, 1956-57; pvt. law practice, Cleveland, Miss., 1958—. Mem. nat. bd. cons. Women's Archives, Radcliffe Coll.; mem. lay adv. com. study profl. nursing Carnegie Corp. N.Y., 1947-48. Chmn., Miss. State Bd. Law Examiners, 1924-28; rep. Hinds County, Miss. State Legislature, 1932-36, chmn. Ho. Reps. com. pub. lands, 1932-36. Treas. com. for econ. survey Miss., 1928-30; mem. Research Commn. Miss., 1930-34. Keynote speaker White House Conf. on Women in Postwar Policy Making, 1944, at conf. on opening 81st Congress. Mem. Am. Assn. U. Women (nat. dir., 2d v.p. 1951-55, mem. found. 1960-63), Nat. Fedn. Bus. and Profl. Women's Clubs (nat. dir.; rep. to internat. 1939, chmn. internat. conf. 1946), Nat. Assn. Women Lawyers, D.A.R., Daus. Am. Colonists, Am. Legion Aux. (past sec. Miss. dept.), Assembly Women's Orgns. for Nat. Security (chmn. 1951-52), Phi Beta Kappa, Pi Gamma Mu, Phi Delta Delta, Alpha Omicron Pi, Delta Kappa Gamma. Democrat (del. nat. conv., 1932). Methodist. Club: Soroptimist (Washington). Editor: Fed. Bar Assn. News, 1944; asso. editor Fed. Bar Assn. Jour., 1943-44. Contbr. articles profl. jours. Address: 515 S Victoria Av Cleveland MS 38732

HOWORTH, M. BECKETT, orthopedic surgeon; b. West Point, Miss.; s. Benjamin M. and Wllie Capel (Beckett) H.; B.S., U. Miss., 1921; M.D., Washington U., 1925; Med. Sci. D., Columbia, 1933; m. Marjorie Maye Meehan. Intern, Presbyn. Hosp., N.Y.C., 1925-27, attending surgeon fracture service, 1933; intern N.Y. Orthopedic Hosp., 1927-29, asst. attending surgeon, 1934-51; asso. vis. orthopedic surgeon Bellevue, 1951—; vis. orthopedic surgeon Welfare Hosp. Chronic Dis., 1939, 40; cons. orthopedist Vanderbilt Clinic, N.Y.C., 1931-49, Roosevelt Hosp., 1935—; asso. clin. prof. orthopedic surgery Columbia Coll. Phys. and Surg., 1936-51, lectr. orthopedic phys. and occupational therapy, 1944-50, lectr. nursing edn. Tchrs. Coll., 1938-50; clin. prof. orthopedics N.Y. U. Postgrad. Med. Sch., 1951—; lectr. orthopedic surgery Yale, 1959—; cons. orthopedic surgeon Greenwich (Conn.) Hosp., 1949-52, chief orthopedic dept., 1952—; cons. orthopedic surgeon No. Westchester Hosp., Mt. Kisco, N.Y., 1949-63, Stamford (Conn.) Hosp., 1959—, Newington (Conn.) Children's Hosp. Mem. adv. bd. Assn. Aid Crippled Children, 1946-53, Rehab. Center, 1950-70. Fellow A.C.S.; mem. Assn. Bone and Joint Surgeons, Pan Pacific Surg. Assn. (v.p. orthopedics 1963-66), Internat., Am. (v.p. 1962, pres. 1963), Can., New Zealand (corr.), Japanese orthopedic assns., Internat. Soc. Orthopedics and Traumatology, Orthopedic Corr. Club, A.A.A.S., Am. Assn. Phys. Anthropology, A.M.A., Orthopedic Research Soc., Am. Acad. Orthopedic Surgeons, Interurban Orthopedic Club, N.Y. Acad. Medicine; hon. mem. Turkish, Western Pacific, La., New Eng. orthopedic assns., Latin-Am., Chilean, Guatemalan socs. orthopedics and traumatology, Alpha Omega Alpha. Methodist. Rotarian. Clubs: Am. Alpine (N.Y.C.); Appalachian Mountain (Boston); Alpine of Canada; Sierra (San Francisco); Rhino; Spectators. Author: Textbook of Orthopedics, 1952; Examination and Diagnosis of the Spine and Extremities, 1962; Injuries of the Spine, 1964. Contbr. numerous articles to med., nursing jours.; also articles on mountaineering. Home: New Canaan CT Office: 49 Lake Av Greenwich CT 06830

HOWREY, EDWARD F., lawyer; b. Waterloo, Ia., Sept. 6, 1903; s. Benjamin J. and Ada C. (McStay) H.; A.B., U. Ia., 1925; J.D. with honors, George Washington U., 1927; m. Jane Pickett Gould, Nov. 10, 1933. Admitted to D.C., Ia. bars, 1927, Va., 1938; with U.S. Dept. Justice, 1927-29; asso. Sanders, Childs, Bob & Wescott, Washington, 1929-37, partner successor firm Sanders, Gravelle, Whitlock & Howrey, 1937-53; chmn. FTC, 1953-55; practice law, Washington, 1955—; partner Howrey, Simon, Baker & Murchison. Fellow Am. Coll. Trial Lawyers, Am. Bar Found.; mem. Am. Soc. Internat. Law, Internat. Bar Assn., Am. Judicature Soc., Acad. of Polit. Sci., English Speaking Union, Am. Bar Assn., Phi Kappa Psi, Phi Delta Phi, Order of Coif. Republican. Episcopalian. Clubs: City Tavern, Metropolitan, Chevy Chase (Washington); Fairfax Hunt. Home: St Brides Upperville VA 22176 Office: 1707 H St NW Washington DC 20006

HOWSAM, ROBERT BASIL, coll. dean; b. Tessier, Sask., Can., Aug. 28, 1916; s. Luther Frank and Elva Myrtle (Sutton) H.; B.Ed. magna cum laude, U. Sask., 1948, M.Ed., 1950; Ed.D., U. Cal. at Berkeley, 1956; m. Muriel May Ford, June 22, 1945; children—Patricia Ellen, Marilyn Rose, Robert Gary, William Alan. Came to U.S., 1956. Elementary sch. tchr., 1936-47; vice prin. Saskatoon pub. schs., 1940-47; lectr. U. Sask., 1949-50, part-time, 1948-49, 51- 56, prin. univ. demonstration sch., 1951-56; asst., then asso. prof. ednl. adminstrn. U. Cal. at Berkeley, 1956-60; prof. ednl. adminstrn., asso. dean grad. studies Coll. Edn., U. Rochester, 1960-66; dean Coll. Edn., U. Houston (Tex.), 1966—. Cons. to sch. systems, N.Y., Cal., Alaska. Served with RCAF, 1941-45. Mem. Am. Assn. Sch. Adminstrs., N.E.A., Nat. Soc. Study Edn., Am. Assn. U. Profs., Phi Delta Kappa, Phi Kappa Phi, Kappa Delta Pi. Author monographs, articles. Home: 5215 Loch Lomond Dr Houston TX 77035

HOWSAM, ROBERT LEE, profl. baseball exec.; b. Denver, Feb. 28, 1918; s. Lee W. and Mary (Creley) H.; student U. Colo., 1936-38; m. Janet Johnson, Sept. 15, 1939; children—Edwin, Robert Lee. Gen. mgr., pres. Denver Bears Baseball Club, 1947-60; pres. Denver Broncos Football Club, 1960-61, Howsam- Brown, Inc., Denver, 1961-63; asst. v.p. Westamerica Securities Co., Denver, 1963-64; became gen. mgr., dir. St. Louis Nat. League Baseball Club, 1964; now gen. mgr. exec. v.p. Cin. Reds, Inc. Mem. Mayor Denver Exec. Sports Com.; past bd. dirs., v.p. Am. Assn., Denver, Old Timers Baseball Assn., Denver. Chmn., Gov. Colo. Conf. on Met. and Urban Problems; past chmn. Colo. Planning Commn.; chmn. Denver and Colo. Crusade for Freedom Planning Commn.; chmn. Denver and Colo. Crusade for Freedom, 1952-53; past asso. U. Denver; past dir., v.p. Denver area council Boy Scouts Am.; past mem. bd. mgmt. Denver YMCA. Served with USNR, 1941-46. Recipient Minor Leaguer Exec. of Year award Sporting News, 1951, 56; named one of Colo.'s five Outstanding Young Men, Colo. Jr. C. of C., 1951; Denver's Young Man of Year, Jr. C. of C., 1952; Gold Nugget award Nugget Boosters Club, 1954; Legion of Merit, Order DeMolay, 1955. Mem. Am. Legion (past post comdr.). Rotarian, Elk; hon. Shriner. Clubs: Press (life), Denver Country, Executive (past pres.), Pinehurst Country, Rolling Hills Country (first ann. Personality and Sports award 1956 Denver); Hyde Park Country, Queen City, Cincinnati. Office: 100 Riverfront Stadium Cincinnati OH 45202*

HOWSE, ERNEST MARSHALL, clergyman, author; b. Twillingate Nfld., Can., Sept. 29, 1902; s. Charles and Elfreda (Palmer) H.; student Meth. Coll., St. John's, Nfld., 1919-20, Albert Coll., Belleville, Ont., Can., 1924-25; student Dalhousie U., Halifax, N.S., 1929; B.A., Pine Hill Div. Hall, Halifax, 1931; S.T.M., Union Sem., N.Y., 1932; Ph.D. in History, U. Edinburgh (Scotland), 1932; D.D, United Coll., (Man.), 1948, Laurentian U., 1964, Victoria U., Toronto, Ont., 1967; D. Litt., Nfld. Meml. U., 1965; D.D., Pine Hill Div. Hall, 1966; m. Esther Lilian Black, Sept. 17, 1932; children—Margery (Mrs. Raymond Dyer), David C. Napier, George Arthur. Ordained to ministry United Ch. Can., 1931; pastor Beverly Hills (Cal.) Presbyn. Ch. 1934-35, Westminister United Ch., Winnipeg, Man., 1935-48, Bloor Street United Ch., Toronto, 1948—. Participant, newspaper corr. 1st Assembly World council Chs., Amsterdam, Holland, 1948, 2d Assembly, Evanston, Ill., 1954, 3d Assembly, New Delhi, India, 1961, press rep. 4th Assembly, Uppala, Sweden, 1968; del. 1st Muslim-Christian convocation, Bhamdoun, Lebanon, 1954, Christian co-pres. Continuing Com. on Muslim-Christian Cooperation, 1955-64; pres. Toronto conf. United Ch. Can., 1961-62; moderator 21st Gen. Council, United Ch. Can., 1964- 66; mem. Exec. World Meth. Council; Canadian del. 1st World Conf. Religion and Peace, Japan, 1970. Named hon. citizen, Seoul, Korea. Mem. Internat. Meth. Hist. Soc. (v.p. 1966). Club: Empire (dir.). Author: Our Prophetic Heritage, 1945; The Law and the Prophets, 1947; Saints in Politics, 1952, 2d edit., 1960; Story of the English Bible, 1952; Spiritual Values in Shakespeare, 1955, paperback edit., 1964; The Lively Oracles, 1956; People and Provocations, 1965; also weekly feature articles syndicated in Canadian newspapers, articles in mags. and other periodicals. Home: 29 Eastbourne Av Toronto 7 Ontario Canada also Lake of Bays Baysville Ontario Canada

HOWSE, ROBERT DAVIS, business exec.; b. Chgo., Apr. 15, 1908; s. Richard George and Editha (Davis) H.; A.B., Yale, 1930; m. Eliose Smith, 1931; 1 dau., Judith Ann (Mrs. Onthank). With Agfa Ansco Corp., Binghamton, N.Y., 1930-33, Literary Digest, Detroit office, 1933-37, Melvyn J. Evans Co., Chgo., 1937-40; pres. Argus, Inc., Ann Arbor, 1940-49; pres. Electro-Phys. Labs., Inc., Stamford, Conn., 1950-52; exec. v.p. Waterman Pen Co., Inc., Seymour, Conn., 1952-54, pres., dir., 1954-59; v.p. Sterling Precision Corp., N.Y.C., 1959-62; exec. v.p. Edward Weck & Co., Inc., Long Island City, 1963-66, pres., 1966—, also dir.; Arnold Bakers, Inc., Greenwich, Conn. Republican. Clubs: Yale (N.Y.C.); Greenwich Country. Home: 20 Church St Greenwich CT 06830 Office: 49-33 31st Pl Long Island City NY 11101

HOWSE, W.L., Jr., religions educator; b. Fayetteville, Tenn., Feb. 26, 1905; s. William Lewis and Emma (Paulk) H.; A.B., Union U., 1926, M.A. magna cum laude, Baylor U., 1932, M.R.E., Southwestern Bapt. Theol. Sem., 1934, D.R.E. cum laude, 1937; L.H.D., Hardin-Simmons U., 1948; LL.D., Union U., Jackson, Tenn., 1958: m. Genevieve Morgan, Oct. 28, 1930; 1 son, William Lewis III. Ednl. dir. Broadway Bapt. Ch., Ft. Worth, 1927-30; minister religious edn. Broadway Bapt. Ch., 1935-45; from instr. to prof. Southwestern Bapt. Theol. Sem., Ft. Worth, 1932-54; dir. edn. div. Sunday Sch. Bd. So. Bapt. Conv., Nashville, 1954-71, programming cons. East Asia area Fgn. Mission Bd., 1971—. Mem. Childrens Hosp. Bd., Ft. Worth, 1948-51; pres. Tex. Bapt. Sunday Sch. Conv., 1947-51; pres. Tex. Bapt. Tng. Union, 1929-30, pres. exec. bd., 1937-38; pres. Southwestern Bapt. Religious Edn. Assn., 1941, Inter-Agy. Council So. Bapt. Conv., 1957-58. Bd. dirs. Ft. Worth Community Chest. Mem. Nashville C. of C., Sigma Alpha Epsilon, Kappa Delta Pi. Author several books, pamphlets. Home: 3000 Hillsboro Rd Nashville TN 37215

HOWSON, JAMES DAY, lawyer; b. Wayne, Pa., Dec. 7, 1910; s. Charles Henry and May Day (Yeatts) H.; B.A., Williams Coll., 1932; LL.B., U. Pa., 1935; m. Elizabeth Janquett, Feb. 14, 1942; children—James Day, Jane Jaquette. Admitted to Pa. bar, 1936; mem. firm Howson & Howson, Phila., 1936-65. Bd. dirs. YMCA, Phila. Served with USNR, 1942-44. Mem. Am., Pa., Phila. bar assns., Phila. Patent Law Assn., Mil. Order Fgn. Wars, Theta Delta Chi. Presbyn. (elder). Home: 311 Windsor Av Wayne PA 19087 Retired.

HOWZE, HAMILTON HAWKINS, former army officer; b. West Point, N.Y., Dec. 21, 1908; s. Robert Lee and Anne Chifelle (Hawkins) H.; B.S., U.S. Mil. Acad., 1930; postgrad. Command and Gen. Staff Coll., 1945; grad. Nat. War Coll., 1949; m. Mary Ingraham Henry, Mar. 28, 1936; children—William Gray, Guy Rodgers. Commd. 2d lt. Cav., U.S. Army, 1930, advanced through grades to gen.; jr. officer 3d, 6th, 7th, 26th Cav. Regts., 1930-41; assigned 91st Cav. Reconnaissance Squadron, 1st Cav. Div., Ft. Bliss, Tex., 1941-42; asst. chief staff for operations 1st Armored Div., Eng., North Africa, 1942- 43; exec. 13th Armored Regt., then comdr. bn. and comdr. regt., 1943-44; comdr. Combat Command A, 1st Armored Div., Italy, 1944-45; chief dept. tactics Cav. Sch., Ft. Filey, Kan., 1945, dir. instrn., 1946-48; mem. intelligence div. Army Gen. Staff, 1949-51 chief prodn. div., 1951-52; asst. div. comdr. 2d Armored Div., Germany, 1952-54; dep. chief staff for operations 7th Army, Europe, 1954-55; chief Army Aviation Div. G-3, Dept. Army, 1955; dir. army aviation Office Dep. Chief Staff Mil. Operations, 1956-58; comdg. gen. 82d Airborne Div., Fort Bragg, N.C., 1958-59; chief mil. adv. group, Korea, 1959-61; comdg. gen. XVIII Airborne Corp., Ft. Bragg, N.C., 1961-63; comdr.-in-chief UN Command, comdr. U.S. Forces, Korea, comdg. gen. 8th U.S. Army, Korea, 1963-65; v.p. Bell Helicopter Co., Ft. Worth, 1965-70, cons., 1971—; cons. Gen. Electric Co., 1971—. Decorated D.S.M., Silver Star, Legion of Merit with cluster, Bronze Star with V; Mil. Cross (Italy); Korean Order of Merit 1st class. Mem. Assn. Grads. U.S. Mil. Acad. Club: Nat. Aviation (Washington). Home: 2209 Canterbury Dr Fort Worth TX 76107 Office: Bell Helicopter Co Fort Worth TX 76107

HOXENG, RAYMOND BENNETT, business exec.; b. Volin, S.D., Aug. 13, 1919; s. Alfred J. and Huldah (Peterson) H.; B.A. magna cum laude, Yankton Coll., 1940; student Ia. State U., 1940-42, U. Pitts., 1945-47; Ph.D., Case Inst. Tech., 1949; m. Helen Louise Paul, Aug. 9, 1943; children—David Earl, Holly Sue. Research asso. Manhattan Project, Ia. State U. and U. Chgo., 1942-45, Alcoa Aluminum Research Lab., 1945-47; Research fellow Case Inst. Tech., 1947-51; asst. to dir. research U.S. Steel Corp., 1951-61, dir. research Am. Steel and Wire div., 1961-63; v.p. planning and devel. Clarkson Coll., Potsdam, N.Y., 1963-65; became pres. Inter Am. U. P.R., San German, 1965; now v.p. Wood & Tower, Inc., Princeton, N.J. Mem. adv. com. St. Lawrence County Nat. Bank, Potsdam, 1964-65. Township commnr., Mt. Lebanon, Pa., 1959-61. Mem. Am. Soc. Metals, Nat. Assn. Corrosion Engrs. (past chmn. publs. com., past pres. Cleve. sect.), Sigma Xi, Phi Lambda Upsilon. Presbyn. Office: 90 Nassau St Princeton NJ 08540

HOXIE, RALPH GORDON, educator, author; b. Waterloo, Ia., Mar. 18, 1919; s. Charles Ray and Ada May (Little) H.; B.A., Ia. State Tchrs. Coll., 1940; M.A., U. Wis., 1941; Ph.D., Columbia, 1950; LL.D., Chung-ang Univ., 1965; Litt.D., D'Youville Coll., 1966; m. Louise Lobitz, Dec. 23, 1953. Roberts fellow Columbia, 1946-47, Roberts travelling fellow, 1947-48, asst. to provost, 1948-49; asst. prof. history, gen. editor Social Sci. Found., asst. to chancellor U. Denver, 1950-53; project asso. Columbia Bicentennial History, 1953-54; dean Coll. Liberal Arts and Scis., L.I.U., 1954-55, acting dean C. W. Post Coll., L.I.U., 1954-55, dean, 1955-60, provost, 1960-62, pres., 1962-68, chancellor L.I. U., 1964-68, cons., 1968-69; chmn. edn. council, provost, acting headmaster Sands Point Country Day Sch.-Fetsch Acad.; cons. Franklin Nat. Bank, 1968-69; pres. Center for Study of Presidency, 1969—. Pub. mem. Fgn. Service Officer Selection Bd., U.S. Dept. State; vis. lect. Columbia, U. Colo., Colo. A. and M. Coll., U. Wyo., Colo. Coll. Edn., Naval War Coll., Northwestern U. Bd. govs. La Banque Continentale br. Franklin Nat. Bank. Bd. dirs. United Fund L.I., Bklyn. Inst. Arts and Scis., Tibetan Found., Am. Friends Chung-ang U. (pres.), L.I. Council Alcoholism, Bklyn. chpt. A.R.C. Greater N.Y.; trustee Kosciuszko Found. N.Y., Mackinac Coll., N. Shore chpt. Am. Assn. UN, Downtown Bklyn. Assn., Council Higher Ednl. Instns. N.Y.C.; mem. adv. bd. L. I. Air Res. Center; mem. adv. council Robert A. Taft Inst. Govt.; sec. Nassau County Commn. on Govt. Revision; co-chmn. Nassau-Suffolk Conf. Christians and Jews; dir., pres., Great-N.Y. Council Fgn. Students; bd. govs. Human Resources Center. Served from pvt. to capt. USAAF, 1942- 46; North Pacific 11th Air Force; brig. gen. Res.

Decorated Meritorious Service medal, numerous other medals; recipient Distinguished Service medal City N.Y., 1966: Paderewski Found. Man of Yr. award, 1966; Eloy Alfaro Internat. Found. Republic Panama Man of Year award, 1966; Alumni Achievement award U. No. Ia.; decorated Korean Cultural medal. Fellow Am. Studies Assn. Met. N.Y.; mem. Am. Hist. Assn., Am. Polit. Sci. Assn., Acad. of Polit. Sci., Navy League, Air Force Assn., Res. Officers Assn. (pres. Mitchel chpt.), V.F.W., L. I. Assn. (mem. bd. dirs.), Kappa Delta Pi, Pi Gamma Mu, Alpha Sigma Lambda, Delta Sigma Pi, Gamma Theta Upsilon. Republican. Episcopalian. Clubs: Century Assn., Metropolitan, Columbia Univ. Men's Faculty (N.Y.C.), Metropolitan (Washington), Brooklyn, Montauk (Bklyn.); Old Westbury Golf and Country and Mill River (hon.). Author: John W. Burgess, American Scholar, 1950; (with others) A History of The Faculty of Political Science, Columbia University, 1955. Editor: Frontiers for Freedom, 1952; The White House: Organization and Operations, 1971. Contbr. Freedom and Authority in Our Time (with others), 1953; also profl. jours. Home: 2 Red Ground Rd Old Westbury NY 11568 Office: 17 E 80th New York City NY 10021

HOY, HARRY EUGENE, educator, geographer; b. Lincoln, Neb., June 10, 1908; s. Ernest W. and Melissa Ann (Wells) H.; B.S., U. Neb., 1929, A.M., 1933, Ph.D., 1940; m. Eldora C. Larsen, Aug. 14, 1930; children—Don Roger, Douglas Stuart. Instr., U. Ill., 1937-40, asso. prof. Mich. State Normal Coll., Ypsilanti, 1940-42, 43-45; cartographer OSS, Washington, 1942-43; field technician, explorer Amazon Basin, Peru and Brazil, 1943; asst. prof. Western Res. U., Cleve., 1945-46; asso. prof. U. Okla., Norman, 1946-48, prof. geography, 1948—, chmn. dept., 1948-56, cons. prof. dept. biostatistics and epidemiology Med. Center, U. Okla., Oklahoma City. Vis. prof. geography U. Leicester, Eng., 1970; Fulbright lectr. U. Cai, Egypt, 1961-62; geog. research, Costa Rica, El Salvador, summer 1965; research contractor Office Q.M. Gen., 1949-52; asso. dir. Office Naval Research Project, Boreal Fringe, Arctic, 1952-54. Fellow Okla. Acad. Sci.; mem. Assn. Am. Geographers, Am. Geog. Soc., S.W. Social Sci. Assn., Sigma Xi. Methodist. Lion. Co-author social studies series. Contbr. articles to profl. jours. Home: 1515 SE 48th Route 2 Norman OK 73069

HOY, JUSTIN EUGENE, telephone co. exec.; b. St. Mary's, Kan., Nov. 19, 1900; s. Andrew E. and Justine (Mueller) H.; A.B., St. Mary's Coll., 1929; student St. Thomas Coll., St. Paul, 1928; m. Margaret Shepard, July 25, 1942; children—Margaret Lannon, Justin Eugene, Katherine, Susan, Michaela, Gregory. With Southwestern Bell Telephone Co., 1929—, comml. operations engr., 1960-61; v.p. pub. relations, 1961—; guest lectr. econ. seminar Drury Coll., Springfield, Mo.; mem. faculty exec. devel. program Tex. A. and M. Coll. Mem. Pub. Relations Soc. Am., Newcomen Soc. N. Am. Clubs: Media (bd. dirs.), Press (St. Louis). Home: 57 Clermont Lane St Louis MO 63124 Office: 1010 Pine St St Louis MO 63101

HOY, PATRICK HENRY, corp. exec.; b. Mpls., Mar. 3, 1914; s. Patrick H. and Mary (Walsh) H.; student U. Minn., 1933-35; m. Betty Bergman, July 1, 1944; children—Patrick Devin, Christopher Peter, Timothy. Sales mgr. Commander Larabee Milling Co., Mpls., 1930-40; v.p., gen. mgr. Amber Mills, 1940-43; exec. asst. to pres. Hotel Sherman, 1946-49, became exec. v.p., gen. mgr., 1949, also dir.; exec. asst. to pres. Hotels Ambassador, Chgo., 1946-49; became v.p. Ambassador East, Inc., 1949; pres. Hotel Sherman, Inc., and Ambassador East, Inc., Chgo., 1955- 60; pres. Material Service div. Gen. Dynamics Corp., 1960-69; vice chmn., exec. v.p. Penn-Dixie Cement Corp., from 1969, now represenative; sr. v.p. Gen. Dynamics Corp., 1960—. Vice pres. Mexico Hotels, Ltd., 1946-52; dir. Union Asbetos & Rubber Co. Served with USN, 1942-46. Home: Arrowhead Home 1335 N Astor St Chicago IL 60610 Office: Penn Dixie Cement Co 875 N Michigan Av Chicago IL

HOY, WILLIAM IVAN, educator; b. Grottoes, Va., Aug. 21, 1915; s. William I. and Ileta (Root) H.; student Lees-McRae Coll., 1933-34; B.A., Hampden-Sydney Coll., 1936; B.D., Union Theol. Sem., 1942; S.T.M., Bibl. Sem. N.Y., 1949; Ph.D., U. Edinburgh, 1952; m. Wilma J. Lambert, Apr. 29, 1945; children—Doris Lambert, Martha Virginia. Tchr. high sch., Va., 1936-39; interim pastor Asheboro (N.C.) Presbyn. Ch., 1948, 52-53; asst. prof. Bible, Guilford Coll., 1947-48; asst. prof. religion U. Miami, 1953-57, asso. prof., 1957-63, prof., 1963—, acting chmn. dept. religion, 1958- 60, chmn., 1960—. Moderator Presbytery of Everglades, 1960-61, stated clk., 1968—; pres. Greater Miami Ministerial Assn., 1964; adv. mem. bd. dirs. Greater Miami Council Chs., 1964; mem. bd. Christian edn. Presbyn. Ch. U.S., 1969—; v.p., bd. dirs. Met. Fellowship Chs., v.p. 1970—. Served from ensign to lt. comdr., USNR, 1942-45; comdr. Res. Decorated Purple Heart. Mem. Soc. Bibl. Lit., Am. Acad. Religion, Am. Soc. Ch. History, Studiorum Novi Testamenti Societas, Scottish Ch . History Soc., Soc. for Sci. Study Religion, Religious Research Assn., Res. Officers Assn. (past nat. chaplain, nat. councilman 1965-66, pres. Fla. dept. 1965-66, v.p. for navy dept. Fla.), Phi Kappa Phi, Omicron Delta Kappa, Lambda Chi Alpha, Alpha Psi Omega. Rotarian. Co-author: History of the Chaplains Corps, USN, Volume 6; also articles and book reviews in various publications. Home: 5881 SW 52d Terrace Miami FL 33155 Office: Box 8264 Coral Gables FL 33124

HOYER, HARVEY CONRAD, clergyman; b. Clay Co., S.D., July 21, 1907; s. Gust and Johannah (Norder) H.; student U. S.D., 1925-28; A.B., Augustana Coll., 1931, D.D., 1950; B.D., Augustana Theol. Sem., 1936; m. E. Margaret Larson, Sept. 3, 1930; children—Gustav Adolph, Helen JoAnn, Ruth, Marcus Conrad, Bernard Eric. Ordained to ministry Luth. Ch., 1936; grad. sch. tchr., S.D., 1926-29; prin. Mission Hill Sch., S.D., 1931-32; pastor Central Luth. Ch., Madison, Wis., 1936-40, Calvary Luth. Ch., Chgo., 1940-42; pres. Ill. Conf. Luther League, 1938-42; v.p. Augustana Synod Luther League, 1947-49; exec. sec. Div. Am. Missions, Nat. Luth. Council 1942-60; asso. exec. sec. div. home missions Nat. Council Chs. of Christ in U.S.A., 1960-64, asso. exec. sec. dept. for councils of chs., 1965-70; asso. exec. dir. Commn. Regional and Local Ecumenicism, 1970—. Organizer Luth. Ch.'s ministry to temp. def. communities, 1942, Nat. Luth. Council's dept. chmn. for Christian approach to Jewish people, 1946, Christian Ministry to Nat. Parks, Nat. Council of Chs. 1957-60. Mem. Assn. Council Secs. (v.p. 1964-65, editor Jour.). Author, co-author books, pamphlets, latest: Go Into all the World, 1951; Ministering to People-on- the-move, 1952; Mission Fields U.S.A., 1956; Heritage and Horizons in Home Missions, 1960; Ecumenopolis-USA, 1971; also articles. Editor: Am. Missions Together, 1946-60; Redeeming the Time, 1949; Christ for the Moving Millions, 1955; Adventuring in American Missions, 1955; Church Planning for Mission in Today's World, 1967. Home: 50 Harrington St Bergenfield NJ 07621 Office: 475 Riverside Dr New York City NY 10027 ☆

HOYER, VINCENT EDGAR, ins. co. exec.; b. Metuchen, N.J., Dec. 13, 1924; s. Waldemar R. and Nellie (Miller) H.; B.S. magna cum laude, Rider Coll., 1948; m. Doris E. Sprague, Aug. 21, 1948; children—Gary Vincent, Dwight Waldemar, Gregg Wilbur, Mark David, Kevin Sprague, Elizabeth Ann. With N.J. Mfrs. Ins. Co., Trenton, 1948—, asst. treas., 1956-62, v.p., 1963-66, pres., dir., 1966—. Served to 1st lt. USAAF, World War II. Presbyn. (deacon, elder). Home: Harbourton NJ 08534 Office: PO Box 2708 Sullivan Way Trenton NJ 08607

HOYLE, FRED, educator; b. Yorkshire, Eng., June 24, 1915; s. Benjamin and Mabel (Pickard) H.; M.A., Emmanuel Coll., Cambridge U., 1939; m. Barbara Clark, Dec. 28, 1939; children—Geoffrey, Elizabeth Jeanne (Mrs. Richard A. Lowndes). Fellow St. John's Coll., Cambridge U., 1939—, univ. lectr. math., 1945-58, Plumian prof. astronomy and exptl. philosophy, 1958—, Palomar observatories, 1956—. Mayhew prizeman in math. tripos, 1936, Smith's prizeman, 1938; recipient Kalinga prize UNESCO, 1967. Fellow Royal Soc., Royal Astron. Soc.; mem. Am. Acad. Arts and Scis.; fgn. asso. Nat. Acad. Scis. Author: Some Recent Researches in Solar Physics, 1949; The Nature of the Universe, 1950; A Decade of Decision, 1953; Frontiers of Astronomy, 1955; (novel) The Black Cloud, 1957; (novel) Ossian's Ride, 1959; Astronomy, 1962; (play) Rockets in Ursa Major, 1962; (TV play) A for Andromeda, 1962; (novel) Fifth Planet, 1963; Of Men and Galaxies, 1964; (with J. Elliot) (novel) Andromeda Breakthrough, 1964; Galaxies, Nuclei and Quasars, 1965; Man in the Universe, 1966; (novel) October First Is Too Late, 1966; (with G. Hoyle) Rockets in Ursa Major, 1969, Seven Steps to the Sun, 1970, The Molecule Men, 1971; also papers. Address: Inst Theoretical Astronomy Madingley Rd Cambridge England

HOYMAN, HOWARD STANLEY, health educator; b. Lancaster, O., Jan. 21, 1902; s. Oscar and Kathryn (Vollmer) H.; B.S., Ohio State U., 1931, grad. student. 1937-38; M.S., Columbia, 1932, Ed.D., 1947; grad. student Stanford, 1937-38, Sch. Pub. Health, U. Mich., 1938-39; m. Helen Elizabeth Huffman, Aug. 11, 1937 (div.); children—Robert James, William George, Ellen Kate; m. 2d, Annelis Strange Jensen, June 9, 1962. X-ray technician USN Hosp., Pensacola, Fla., 1925-28; mem. Miller Municipal Recreation Park, Lancaster, O., summers 1929-31; instr. U. Ore., 1932-36, coach varsity, freshman swimming teams, 1933-39, 1941-43, asst. prof., 1936-40, asso. prof., 1940-45, prof. health edn., head div. health edn., 1946-49; prof. health edn., head div. health edn. U. Ill., 1949-70, co-sponsor, sr. mem., exec. com. Center Human Ecology. Mem. exec. com. Ill. Joint Com. Sch. Health; chmn. Ill. Sex Edn. Adv. Bd.: mem. conf. on profl. preparation health edn. students Fed. Security Agy., Office Edn., Washington, 1949, nat. conf. on grad. study health edn., phys. edn., recreation Pierre Marquette State Park, Ill., 1950 mem. 2d, 7th to 10th nat. confs. physicians, schs. A.M.A., Bur. Health Edn. of Ill.; mem. Ore. Joint Com. Health, Phys. Fitness, Ill. Joint Com. Sch. Health, Phys. Fitness, Ill. Com. Med. Residencies in Pub. Health; del. Internat. Health Conf., Rome, Italy, 1955. Fellow Am. Pub. Health Assn. (governing council 1961-62, chmn. sch. health sect.), Am. Sch. Health Assn. (governing council, chmn. new film com., mem. nat. research council, distinguished service award); mem. Lane County Pub. Health Assn. (trustee), Am. Social Hygiene Assn., A.A.H.P.E.R., Am. Assn. U. Profs., Ill. Pub. Health assn., Ill. Health and Phys. Edn. Assn., Nat. Phys. Edn. Com., Royal Soc. Promotion Health Eng., Am. Acad. Phys. Edn., New Assn., Am. Nat. Council for Health Edn. of Pub., Internat. Union for Health Edn. of Pub., Phi Beta Kappa, Phi Kappa Phi. Republican. Methodist. Author: Developing Health Instruction in Oregon High Schools, 1940; Health Guide Units for Oregon Teachers, 1945; Your Health and Personality, 1948; Functional Health Teaching, 1949, rev. 1962; (with others). Your Health and Safety. 1956; others. Collaborator: (film) Human Growth; Graphic Health Charts, 1949, rev. 1963. Asso. editor Jour. A.A.H.P.E.R., Jour. Sch. Health. Contbr. articles profl. jours. Home: 805 Haines Blvd Champaign IL 61820

HOYME, CHAD EARL, forest products co. exec.; b. Sioux Falls, S.D., Nov. 6, 1933; s. Knute Odell and Martha (Johnson) H.; B.S. in Bus. Adminstrn., U. S.D., 1956; m. Carolyn Ella Robson, June 21, 1958; children—Christopher, Beth, Amy, Tod. Accounting mgr. Cargill Inc., Mpls., 1956-63; chief accountant Northwest Paper Co., Cloquet, Minn., 1963-65; budget dir. Potlatch Forests, Inc., Lewiston, Ida., 1965-67, corp. controller, 1968—. Mem. exec. com. Twin County United Fund, Lewiston, 1967-70. Mem. Bd. Edn. Lewiston. Mem. Republican State Central Com. Ida., 1968—. Served to 2d lt. AUS, 1956. Lutheran. Elk. Home: 2624 Sunset Dr Lewiston ID 83501 Office: PO Box 1016 Lewiston ID 83501

HOYT, AUSTIN, U.S. judge; b. Beacon, N.Y., Apr. 26, 1915; s. Ferdinand Augustus and Beatrice (Watson) H.; student U. Ala., 1933-34, St. John's U., 1934-35; LL.B., U. Va., 1938; m. Margaret Llewellyn Carter, Nov. 11, 1939; children—John Carter, Julia Vail, Dale Llewellyn. Admitted to D.C. bar, 1939, N.Y. bar, 1940, Colo. bar, 1949; atty. REA, 1938-40; pvt. practice, Beacon, 1940-42; spl. asst. U.S. atty. gen., 1942-49; asst. chief compromise sect., tax div. Dept. Justice, 1946-49; mem. firm Ziegler & Hoyt, Colorado Springs, Colo., 1949-54, Hoyt & Gallagher, 1954- 59; judge dist. ct. 4th Jud. Dist. Colo., 1959-61; judge U.S. Tax Ct., 1962—. Pres., Colorado Springs Symphony Assn., 1958-60, Colorado Springs Sch. for Girls, 1961-62. Served to lt. USNR, 1943-46. Mem. U. Va. Law Sch. Alumni Assn. (council 1965-68, pres. Washington area chpt. 1966-67), Am., Colo. bar assns., Am. Judicature Soc., Soc. Mayflower Descs., Order of Coif, Phi Delta Theta, Phi Alpha Delta. Editorial bd. Va. Law Rev., 1937-38. Home: Prospect Hill Tidewater Trail Fredericksburg VA 22401 Office : US Tax Court Washington DC 20044

HOYT, CLAIRE CLINTON PATTERSON, clergyman; b. Storm Lake, Ia., Feb. 2, 1906; s. Fred and Eva (Patterson) H.; B.A., Upper Ia. U., 1928; B.D., Garrett Bibl. Inst., 1930; M.A., Northwestern U., 1931; LL.D., Ia. Wesleyan Coll., 1966; m. Velna Oliver Garner, Nov. 25, 1961; children—Betty Fern (Mrs. Joseph W. Lathrop), Marilyn Rae (Mrs. William O. Schroeder). Ordained to ministry Meth. Ch.; pastor in Ia., 1923-26, Wyo., 1931-42, 45-54, Neb., 1942-45; treas. Rocky Mountain Conf., 1959-63; asso. gen. sec. Gen. Bd. Pensions, Meth. Ch., 1963-64, gen. sec. bd., 1964—, mem. exec. com., 1954-63; founder, instr. Wyo. Sch. Religion, 1936-42; spl. instr. Iliff Sch. Theology, 1960-61. Chaplain, Wyo. Senate, 1951; mem. joint commn. on Evang. U.B.- Meth. Ch. Union; mem. World Meth. Council; cons. Nat. Council Chs.; pres. Council Secs., 1970-71, Ch. Pensions Conf., 1969-70, Continuing Coordinating Com., 1970-71. Chmn., Albany County (Wyo.) chpt. A.R.C., 1940; vice chmn. Cornhusker council Boy Scouts Am., 1944; mem. Pueblo (Colo.) Welfare Council, 1955-59. Rotarian. Contbr. articles to religious publs. Home: 648 Sheridan Rd Evanston IL 60202 Office 1200 Davis St Evanston IL 60202

HOYT, EDWIN CHASE, educator; b. Commack, N.Y., Aug. 3, 1916; s. Edwin C. and Maria Louisa (Moran) H.; grad. Middlesex Sch., 1934; A.B., Harvard, 1938, LL.B., 1942; Ph.D., Columbia, 1958; m. Mary P. Hazard, Aug. 1, 1953 (div. 1968); children—William B., Maria Louisa, Emily Elizabeth. Admitted to N.Y. bar, 1942; asst. dist. atty. N.Y. County, 1947-48, 48-51; research analyst State Dept., 1948; practice law, N.Y.C., 1951-54; lectr. internat. law Columbia, 1956-57; vis. asst. prof. Hamilton Coll., Clinton, N.Y., 1957-58, vis. asso. prof., 1958-59; research fellow U. Mich. Law Sch., 1959-60; asso. prof. polit. sci. U. N.M., 1959-66, chmn. dept., 1960-69, prof., 1966—. Served to capt., inf., AUS. 1942-46. Author: The Unanimity Rule in the Revision of Treaties, 1959; National Policy and International Law, 1966; also articles. Home: 808 Lafayette Dr NE Albuquerque NM 87106

HOYT, EVERETT W., ret. advt. exec.; b. New Haven, Apr. 28, 1905; s Charles W. and Effie (Smith) H.; grad. Phillips Exeter Acad., 1923; B.A., Yale, 1927; m. Elizabeth Sayer, Feb. 22, 1935; children—Charles E., Anthony S., William W. With Charles W. Hoyt Co., 1927-66, pres., 1942-66; chmn. bd. Rumrill- Hoyt, Inc., 1966-67, chmn. exec. com., 1967-70, dir., now ret. Mem. Squadron A Assn. Clubs: Huntington (L.I.) Country; Ekwanok Country (Manchester, Vt.); Yale (N.Y.C.). Home: 71 Cove Rd Oyster Bay NY 11771 Office: 380 Madison Av New York City NY 10017

HOYT, FRANKLIN KNIBLOE, book publisher; b. Indpls., Sept. 11, 1907; s. Franklin Sherman and Mabel (Knibloe) H.; grad. Phillips Andover Acad., 1926; A.B., Williams Coll., 1930; LL.B., Northeastern U., 1937; m. Alice Laura Potter, May 23, 1931; children—Franklin Sherman II, Alice Taylor (Mrs. Daniel M. Hall), Marian Knibloe. Admitted to Mass. bar, 1937; with Houghton Mifflin Co., Boston, 1930—, now v.p. finance and adminstrn., dir.; chmn. bd. Newton Co-op. Bank; corporator Boston 5 ☆ Savs. Bank; dir. Am. Mut. Liability Ins. Co., Am. Mut. Ins. Co. of Boston, AM Life Ins. Co., Arkwright-Boston Mfrs. Mut. Ins. Co., Mut. Boiler & Machinery Ins. Co., Keystone Apollo Fund, Inc. Alderman, City of Newton, 1947-50. Bd. dirs. Stone Inst. and Newton Home for Aged People, 1951—, pres., 1951-57, v.p., 1958—; chmn. corp. Simmons Coll.; trustee Pierce Coll., Greece. Mem. Boston Bar Assn., Sigma Phi. Republican. Conglist. Clubs: Brae Burn Country (past v.p., dir. West Newton, Mass.); Duxbury (Mass.) Yacht (past commodore, dir.); Williams (N.Y.C.). Home: 279 Fuller St West Newton MA 02165 Office: 2 Park St Boston MA 02107

HOYT, GERALD A., telegraph corp. exec.; b. Thayer, Kan., Oct. 29, 1914; s. Calvin Rae and Marie (Rich) H.; B.S. in Elec. Engring., Kan. State Coll., 1941; m. Doreen Bowers, Sept. 18, 1937; 1 dau., Mary Elaine (Mrs. Jack Delay). With Gen. Electric Co., 1941-67, v.p., gen. mgr. def. electronics div., 1962-67; exec. v.p. Western Union Telegraph Co., N.Y.C., 1967-70, now exec. v.p. Western Union Corp., 1970—, also dir. Office: 60 Hudson St New York City NY 10013

HOYT, HENRY HAMILTON, pharm. co. exec.; b. N.Y.C., June 28, 1895; s. Frank A. and Susan (Gardiner) H.; Litt. B., Princeton, 1917; m. Anna Orcutt, June 1925; children—Henry Hamilton, Charles O., Suzanne K. Partner, A.D. Strauss & Co., 1925-30; with Carter-Wallace, Inc. (formerly Carter Products, Inc.), N.Y.C., 1930—, dir., 1930—, pres., now chmn.; dir. Canalco, Inc., Rockville, Md.; hon. dir. Bank of N.Y. Hon. trustee Hosp. Center at Orange (N.J.). Served as capt. with 2d Div. U.S. Army, 1917-19; AEF. Clubs: University, Union League (N.Y.C.); Baltusrol Golf (Springfield, N.J.); Oyster Harbors (Osterville, Mass.); Lyford Cay (Nassau, Bahamas). Home: 41 Lake Rd Short Hills NJ 07078 Office: 767 Fifth Av New York City NY 10022

HOYT, HERMAN ARTHUR, pres. theol. sem.; b. Greenfield, Ia., Mar. 12, 1909; s. Clarence Lyman and Anna Leola (Dorsey) H.; A.B., Ashland Coll., 1932; B.Th. summa cum laude, Ashland Theol. Sem., 1935; postgrad. U. Mich. Grad. Sch., summer 1935; B.D., Grace Theol. Sem., 1937, M.Th., 1939, D.Th., 1946; LL.D., Bryan Coll., Tenn., 1963; m. Harriet Lucile Fitz, Aug. 30, 1930; children—Joseph Paul, Edwin Max. Prof., N.T. and Greek, sec. faculty Ashland Theol. Sem., 1935-37; faculty Grace Theol. Sem., 1937—, prof. N.T., Greek, 1937-62, dean, 1948-62, pres., prof. Christian theology, 1962—. Moderator, Brethren Ch., 1940-41, 43-44. Pres. trustees Brethren Missionary Herald Co., 1940-51, trustee, 1951- 66; trustee Bryan Coll.; trustee Christian League Handicapped, 1956—, pres., 1959—; bd. dirs. Winona Lake Christian Assembly, 1962—, pres. corp., chmn. bd. 1968; bd. dirs. Am. Assn. Jewish Evangelism. Mem. Town Bd. Winona Lake, 1942-48. Mem. N.E.A., Evang. Theol. Soc. Kiwanian. Author: This Do in Remembrance of Me, 1947; All Things Whatsoever I Have Commanded, 1948; Exposition of Romans, 1950; Exposition of Hebrews, 1951; Exposition of Revelation, 1953; Then Would My Servants Fight, 1956; The New Birth, 1961; Trip to Europe and Near East, 1967; The End Times, 1969. Contbr. articles to Wycliffe Bible Ency. Home: Box 785 Winona Lake IN 46590

HOYT, HOMER, cons., real estate economist; A.B., U. Kan., 1913, A.M., 1913; J.D., U. Chgo., 1918, Ph.D. in Econs., 1933; m. Gertrude O'Neill, Aug. 13, 1941; 1 son, Michael. Admitted to Ill., D.C., U.S. Supreme Ct. bars; instr. econs. Beloit Coll., 1917-18; economist War Trade Bd., Washington, 1918-19; prof. econs. U. Del., 1919-20; statistician Am. Tel.&Tel. Co., N.Y.C., 1920-21; asso. prof. econs. U. N.C., 1921-23, U. Mo., 1924-25; real estate broker, economist, Chgo., 1925-34; prin. housing economist FHA, 1934-40; dir. research Chgo. Plan Commn., 1941- 43; dir. econ. studies Regional Plan Assn., N.Y.C., 1943-46; pres. Homer Hoyt Assos., Washington, 1946—. Vis. prof. land econs. Mass. Inst. Tech., Columbia, 1944-46. Mem. Am. Inst. Real Estate Appraisers (George L. Schmutz award 1964), Am. Econ. Assn., Am. Statis. Assn., Am. Hist. Assn., Washington Real Estate Bd., Fairfax C. of C., Phi Beta Kappa, Lambda Alpha, Delta Sigma Rho. Author: One Hundred Years of Land Values in Chicago, 1933; Structure and Growth of Residential Neighborhoods in American Cities, 1939; World Urbanization, 1962; According to Hoyt, 1966, rev., 1970; (with Arthur M. Weimer) Real Estate, 1939, rev., 1966, Urban Land Use Requirements 1968-2000, 1968, People, Profits, Places, 1969. Cons. editor Land Econs., Traffic Quar. Contbr. numerous articles to profl. jours. Address: 2939 Van Ness St NW Washington DC 20008

HOYT, KENNETH BOYD, educator; b. Cherokee, Ia., July 13, 1924; s. Paul Fuller and Mary Helen (Tinker) H.; B.S., U. Md., 1948; M.A., George Washington U., 1950; Ph.D., U. Minn., 1954; m. Phyllis June Howland, May 25, 1946; children—Andrew Paul, Roger Alan, Elinore Jane. Tchr., counselor Northeast (Md.) High Sch., 1948-49; dir. guidance Westminster (Md.) High Sch., 1949-50; teaching asst. U. Minn., 1950-51, instr. ednl. psychology, 1951-54; asst. prof. U. Ia., Iowa City, 1954-57, asso. prof., 1957-60, prof. edn., 1961-69; dir. Splty. Oriented Student Research Program, prof. edn. U. Md., Silver Spring, 1969—. Cons. Ordnance Civilian Personnel Agy., 1954-60, Ia. Dept. Pub. Instrn., 1954-69, U.S. Dept. Labor, 1956-68, 65—, U.S. Office Edn., 1958—. Served with AUS, 1943-46. Mem. Am. Personnel and Guidance Assn. (pres. 1966-67), Am. Psychol. Assn., Am. Vocational Assn., Assn. for Counselor Edn. and Supervision (Distinguished Service award 1965), Nat. Vocational Guidance Assn., Am. Sch. Counselors Assn., Am. Coll. Personnel Assn., Phi Delta Kappa. Author: (with L.A. Van Dyke) The Drop-Out Problem in Iowa High Schools, 1958; (with C.P. Forehlich) Guidance Testing, 1960; Selecting Employees For Developmental Opportunites and Guidance Services; Suggested Policies For Iowa Schools, 1963. Editor: Counselor Education and Supervision, 1961-65. Mem. editorial bd. Personnel and Guidance Jour., 1960-63. Contbr. articles to profl. jours. Home: 311 Colesville Manor Dr Silver Spring MD 20904

HOYT, LESTER HAROLD, pathologist; b. Scranton, Ia., Sept. 28, 1911; s. Delmer L. and Clara J. (Allen) H.; A.B., Simpson Coll., 1933; M.D., State U. Ia., 1937; postgrad. Wayne State U., 1940-41, Ind. U., 1965, U. S.C., 1956-57, Purdue U., 1966; m. Esther L. Harding, Oct. 9, 1938; children—Judy Anne (Mrs. Ronald Taylor), Mary Jane (Mrs. Steven May), Joseph Delmer, Lois Jean (Mrs. Richard Lewis). Intern, Meth. Hosp., Madison, Wis., 1937- 38, resident in pathology, 1938-40; resident in pathology Ford Hosp., Detroit, 1940-41;

patholgist Oakdale (Ia.) Sanitorium, 1942-43; practice medicine specializing in pathology, Indpls., 1943—; asst. clin. prof. clin. pathology Ind. U. Sch. Medicine, 1952—. Bd. dirs. Blue Cross Ind. Diplomate Am. Bd. Pathology. Fellow Am. Soc. Clin. Pathologists (sec.- treas. 1960-66), Coll. Am. Pathologists (a founder); mem. A.M.A., Pan Am., Ind. (del. 1952—, treas. 1967—) med. assns., Marion County Med. Soc., Ind. Assn. Pathologists (past pres.), Internat. Acad. Pathology, Am., Ind. assns. blood banks, Am. Acad. Forensic Scis., Community Blood Bank Marion County (dir., past pres.), Am. Cancer Soc. (past com. chmn. Ind. div.), Am. Soc. Human Genetics, Soc. Nuclear Medicine, Acad. Internat. Medicine, Sigma Xi, Phi Chi, Epsilon Sigma, Beta Beta Beta. Mem. Christian Ch. (elder). Mason, Rotarian. Clubs: Columbia; Indiana Gun; Conservation; Riviera; Flying Physicians. Contbr. articles to profl. jours. Home: 6502 Landborough Dr S Indianapolis IN 46220 Office: 1604 N Capitol Av Indianapolis IN 46202

HOYT, NELLY SCHARGO, (Mrs. N. Deming Hoyt), educator; b. Nicolaev, Russia, Jan. 15, 1920; d. Simon S. and Vera (Rivkind) Schargo; Bacc. es Lettres, Musee de l'Homme, 1939, certificate Anthropologie, 1940; B.A., Smith Coll., 1943; M.A., Columbia, 1944, Ph.D., 1946; m. N. Deming Hoyt, Sept. 7, 1946; children—Susan, Victor. Came to U.S., 1941, naturalized, 1946. Research analyst U.S. Mission to UN, 1946-48; cons. research in comtemporary cultures Columbia U. Mus. Natural History, 1949-53; prof. dept. history Smith Coll., 1949—; editor Smith Coll. Studies in History, 1961—. Mem. Societe du Dixhuitième Siècle. Author: (with T. Cassirer) Selections From Diderot's Encyclopedia, 1965; History in the Encyclopédie, 2d edit., 1970; Study of Culture at a Distance, 1950. Contbr. articles profl. jours. Home: 89 Maynard Rd Northampton MA 01060

HOYT, PALMER, newspaper cons.; b. Roseville, Ill., Mar. 10, 1897; s. Edwin Palmer and Annie (Tendler) H.; A.B., U. Ore. 1923; LL.D., Linfield Coll., 1940, Whitman Coll., 1942, William Jewell Coll., 1955, U. N.M., 1965; m. Cecile De Vore, May 18, 1921 (div. 1949); children—Edwin Palmer II, Charles Richard; m. 2d, Helen May Taber, Nov. 7, 1950; 1 son, Lincoln; foster sons, Monty, Gregory Byrd, Wesley Winfield. Telegraph and sports editor East Oregonian, Pendelton, 1923-26; copy reader Oregonian, Portland, 1926-28, reporter, 1928- 29, drama editor, 1929-31, night editor, 1931-32, exec. news editor, 1932-33, mng. editor, 1933-38, editor, pub., 1939-46; pub., editor Denver Post, 1946-70; ret., 1970. Dir. Guaranty Bank & Trust Co. Domestic dir. OWI, 1943; mem. Pres.'s Air Policy Commn., 1947, Nat. Citizen's Commn. for Pub. Schs.; mem. U.S. Adv. Commn. Information, 1965—. Campaign chmn. Denver Community Chest, 1948, pres., 1949; chmn. Red Cross War Fund 1945; regional chmn. War Bond Com., 1941-43. Bd. dirs. Nat. Cowboy Hall Fame, Bur. Advt. Served with U.S. Army, A.E.F. in France, World War I. Mem. Ore. Press Conf. (pres. 1942), Ore. Newspaper Pubs. Assn. (pres. 1943-45), mem. Advt. Fedn. Am. (dir.), Chi Psi, Sigma Delta Chi (nat. pres. 1941-42), Sigma Upsilon, Hammer and Coffin. Republican. Rotarian. Baptist. Clubs: Cherry Hills, Denver, Denver Athletic, Denver Country. Office: Denver Club Bldg 518 17th St Denver CO 80202

HOYT, RALPH MELVIN, lawyer; b. Columbus, Wis., Jan. 14, 1890; s. Judson E. and Edith (Evans) H.; A.B., U. Wis., 1910, LL.B., 1912; m. Dorothy Louise Taylor, Apr. 14, 1917 (dec. 1960); children—Hamilton Taylor, Stuart Evans. Admitted Wis. bar, 1912; asst. sec. R.R. Commn. Wis., 1912-14; pvt. practice law, Milw., 1914-20, 23-30, 34—, now mem. law firm Shea, Hoyt, Greene, Randall & Meissner; dep. atty. gen. State Wis., 1921-22; pres. Title Guaranty Co., Wis., 1930-34. Bd. dirs. Asso. Hosp. Service (Wis. Blue Cross); chmn. bd. trustees Milw.-Downer Coll., 1949-62. Mem. Am. (com. on adminstrv. law 1936-37, 41-46, chmn. com. on adminstrv. agys. and tribunals in sect. jud. adminstrn. 1937-41, mem. council sect. adminstrv. law 1948-52), Wis., Milw. (pres. 1939-40) bar assns., Order of Coif, Phi Beta Kappa, Sigma Nu, Phi Alpha Delta. Republican. Episcopalian. Mason. Clubs: Milwaukee, Milwaukee Country, City. Contbr. articles to law reviews. Home: 2428 E Linnwood Av Milwaukee, WI 53211. Office: 735 N Water St Milwaukee WI 53202

HOYT, ROBERT LEON, business exec.; b. Batavia, N.Y., Jan. 18, 1927; s. Leon E. and Edna (Gilliatt) H.; B.S. in Accounting, U. Buffalo, 1949; m. Beverly Calmes, Oct. 11, 1947; children—Margaret, Joanne, William, Robert. Agt., Internal Revenue Service, Rochester, N.Y., 1949-57; with Pfaudler Permutit, Inc., 1957-65, controller, 1965; treas. Ritter Pfaudler Corp., Rochester, 1965-69; sr. v.p., sec., treas., dir. United Bancshares of Fla., Inc., Miami Beach, Fla., 1969—. Served with USNR, 1944-46. Mem. Tax Execs. Inst., Financial Analysts Soc., Financial Execs. Inst., Greater Miami C. of C., Econ. Soc. S. Fla. Home: 5900 Killian Dr Miami FL 33156 Office: 1111 Lincoln Rd Mall Miami Beach FL 33139

HOYT, ROSALIE CHASE, physicist, educator; b. N.Y.C., May 20, 1914; B.A., Columbia, 1940; M.A., Bryn Mawr Coll., 1941, Ph.D. in Physics, 1945. Instr. physics U. Rochester, 1945-48; instr. physics Bryn Mawr (Pa.) Coll., 1941-45. asst. prof. 1948-52, asso. prof., 1952, now prof. Mem. Am. Phys. Soc. Research on bioelectric instrumentation, nerve models, counters and detectors for nuclear research. Address: Dept. of Physics Bryn Mawr College Bryn Mawr, PA.*

HOYT, SAMUEL LESLIE, metall. cons.; b. Mpls. May 29, 1888; s. Alphonso Orlando and Hulda Lucretia (Hunt) H.; E.M., U. Minn., 1909; postgrad. Columbia, 1909-11, Royal Inst. Tech., Charlottenburg, Germany, 1911-13; Ph.D., Columbia, 1914; Sc.D., S.D. Sch. Mines and Tech., 1955; m. Jane Woodruff, Jan. 1, 1913; 4 sons; m. 2d, Edyth S. Armstrong, Nov. 1946; m. 3d, Kay W. Dowd, Nov., 1966. Asso. prof., founder dept. metallography U. Minn., 1913-19; metall. engr. Gen. Elec. Co., 1919-30; metallurgist A.O. Smith Corp., 1931-34, dir. metall. research, 1934-39, cons., 1939-41; tech. adviser Battelle Meml. Inst., Columbus, O., 1939-53; metall. cons. indsl. research to producing and fabricating cos., govt. agys., 1953-59; staff rep. research and engring. div. Dept. Def., Frankfurt, Germany, 1959-60, metall. cons., 1960—; staff cons. Anamet Labs., Berkeley, Cal., 1968—. Priestley lectr. Pa. State U., also ann. and meml. lectures; developer carboloy; inventor, developer Smith Alloy 10, heat resistant alloy, developer low alloy steel otiscoloy, welding, metallurgy, steel procurement, failure analysis, gen. metall. research; sci. cons. ALSOS Mission, 1945. Mem. sci. adv. council Picatinny Arsenal; mem. NRC Commn. on Ship Steel. Recipient Outstanding Achievement award, medal U. Minn. Fellow Am. Soc. Metals (metall. Milestone for 1928 for work on carboloy 1963, trustee); mem. Am. Inst. Metall. Engrs. (Legion of Honor, com. phys. chemistry steel making), Am. Welding Soc., Inst. Metals, Welding Research Council, Am. Ordnance Assn., A.A.A.S., Iron and Steel Inst. Eng., Sigma Xi, Delta Tau Delta. Author tech. books, latest; Metal Data, 1952. Office: 88 Purdue Av Berkeley CA 94708 ☆

HROMADKO, GEORGE, chem. co. exec.; b. Pole, Czechoslovakia, Sept 4, 1920; s. Francis and Albina (Nietsche) H.; student Univ. Aix-Marseille (France), 1936; Dr. Law, Masaryk U., 1946; M.S., Columbia, 1959; m. Vera Tichopad, Aug. 17, 1946; children—Hanna, Vera. Came to U.S., 1957, naturalized, 1962. With Babcock-Wilcox, 1958-59; successively internat. controller, dir. finance internat., v.p. finance internat., v.p., treas. Warner-Lambert Co., Morris Plains, N.J., 1959—; lectr. Rutgers U., Pace Coll., Am. Mgmt. Assn. Mem. Pharm. Mfrs. Assn., N.A.M. Office: 201 Tabor Rd Morris Plains NJ 07950

HRONES, JOHN ANTHONY, educator; b. Boston, Sept 28, 1912; s. Emil and Olga Victoria (Cech) H.; S.B., Mass. Inst. Tech., 1934, S.M., 1936, Sc.D., 1942; m. Margaret Baylis, June 17, 1938; children—Janet H. Roach, Stephen Baylis, Mary H. Parsons, John Anthony. Asst. factory mgr. Coldwell Lawnmower Co., Newburgh, N.Y., 1937-39; asst. mech. engring. dept. Mass. Inst. Tech., 1934-36, instr., 1936-37, 39-41, asst. prof., 1941-45, asso. prof., 1945-48, prof. mech. engring., 1948, head machine design div., 1946, dir. Dynamic Analysis and Control Lab., 1950; v.p. for acad. affairs Case Inst. Tech., Cleve., 1957-67, acting pres., 1963, provost, 1964-67, provost sci. and tech. Case Western Res. U., 1967—. Cons. automatic control and machine design, 1939—; pres. ChiCorp., 1967-68, chmn., 1967—. Bd. dirs. Cleve. Mus. Nat. History; trustee Asian Inst. Tech. Chmn., Univ. Circle Research Center Corp.; pres. A.I.T. Found. Mem. Newcomen Soc., Am. Soc. M.E., Am. Soc. Engring. Edn., Am. Acad. Arts and Scis., Inst. for Def. Analyses (trustee), Sigma Xi, Tau Beta Pi, Pi Tau Sigma. Club: Cleveland Skating (trustee). Author: (with Nelson) Analysis of the Four Bar Linkage, 1951. Contbr. articles to engring. publs. Home: 2957 Sedgewick Rd Shaker Heights OH 44120 Office: Case Western Res U Cleveland OH 44106

HRUBY, FRANK M., musican, critic, educator; b. Emporia, Kan., June 29, 1918; s. Frank and Eva (Ptacek) H.; B.Mus., U. Rochester, 1940, M.Mus., 1941; m. Pollee Menoher Phipps, May 10, 1945; children—F. Michael, George P., David A., Faith A., Mark S. Head composition and theory dept. Miss. So. Coll., 1946-48; mus. dir. Cain Park Summer mus. comedy prodns., Cleveland Heights, O., 1946-56; condn. Singer's Club Cleve., 1956-65; chmn. music and humanities dept. Univ. Sch., Shaker Heights, O., 1948-70, humanities faculty, 1970—; music critic, columnist Cleve. Press, 1956—. Music cons. Ednl. Research Council, Cleve., 1965-66. Served to lt. USNR, 1942-45. Mem. Music Educators Nat. Conf., Music Critics Assn. Contbr. to Musical Am., 1956-60. Composer: String Quartet, 1953; (plays-with music for children) Freddie and His Fiddle, 1952, Hiccupping Princess, 1953, Emperor's New Clothes, 1954; Clarinet Quartet, For the Birds, 1956. Home: 2350 Beachwood Blvd Cleveland OH 44122

HRUBY, NORBERT JOSEPH, educator, coll. adminstr.; b. Cicero, Ill., Feb. 4, 1918; s. Thomas John and Marie Frances (Rychtik) H.; P.B., Loyola U., Chgo., 1939, M.A., 1941, Ph.D., 1951; postgrad. drama Yale, 1946-47; m. Dolores Marie Smith, June 19, 1943; children—Michael G., Monica M., Patricia A. Instr. English, Loyola U., Chgo., 1947-48, asst. dean Coll. Commerce, 1948-51, dir. pub. information, 1951-55; dir. radio and TV, U. Chgo., 1955-58, asso. dean Univ. Coll., 1958-62; v.p. Mundelein Coll., Chgo., 1962-69; pres. Aquinas Coll., Grand Rapids, Mich., 1969—. Ednl. cons., dir. coll. self-studies, 1966—; cons. communications Am. Mut. Ins. Alliance, 1960-70; co-planner in founding Chgo. Ednl. TV Assn. channel WTTW, 1951-54; asso. dir. Court Theatre, Chgo., 1957-62; dir. Faustus, 1957, The Cenci, 1958, Francesca da Rimini, 1959, Six Characters in Search of an Author, 1961; producer, dir., author radio and TV series Loyola U., U. Chgo., 1951-58; pub. relations cons. Forest Preserve Dist., Cook County, Ill., 1958-62; founder Assn. Community Theatres of Chgo., 1961, exec. sec., 1961-62. Officer, Grand Rapids Area Council Chs. Bd. dirs. Grand Rapids Symphony. Served to capt. AUS, 1942-46. Recipient 5 nat. awards for network and syndicated radio series prodns. U. Chgo., 1956-58. Mem. Nat. Cath. Ednl. Assn. (exec. com.), Blue Key, Alpha Sigma Nu, Pi Gamma Mu. Roman Catholic. Home: 245 Briarwood Av SE Grand Rapids MI 49506

HRUSKA, ROMAN LEE, U.S. senator; b. David City, Neb., Aug. 16, 1904; s. Joseph C. and Caroline (Dvorak) H.; student U. Omaha, 1923-25; LL.B., Creighton U., 1929, LL.D., 1958; LL.D., Doane Coll. (Neb.), 1963; H.H.D., Coe Coll. (Ia.), 1964; m. Victoria Kuncl, Sept. 24, 1930; children— Roman Lee, Quentin, Jana. Admitted to Neb. bar, 1929, since practiced in Omaha; county commr. Douglas County, Neb., 1944-52; mem. 83d Congress, 2d Neb. Dist.; U.S. senator from Neb., 1954—. Mem. adv. com. Neb. Bd. Control, 1947-52. Regent, U. Omaha, 1950-57. Mem. Nat. (v.p.), Neb. (pres.) assns. county ofcls., Am., Neb., Omaha bar assns. Mason (Shriner), Kiwanian. Home: 2139 S 38th St Omaha NB 48105 also 2429 N Lincoln St Arlington VA 22207 Office: Senate Office Bldg Washington DC 20510

HRYCAK, PETER, educator; b. Przemysl, Poland, July 8, 1923; s. Eugene and Ludmyla (Dobrzanska) H.; came to U.S., 1949, naturalized, 1956; student U. Tubingen (Germany), 1946-48; B.S. with high distinction, U. Minn., 1954, M.S., 1955, Ph.D., 1960; m. Rea Meta Limberg, June 13, 1949; children—Maria, Michael Paul, Orest W.T., Alexandra Martha. Instr., U. Minn., Mpls., 1955-60; mem. tech. staff Bell Telephone Labs., Murray Hill, N.J., 1960-65; sr. project engr. Curtiss-Wright Corp., Woodridge, N.J., 1965; asso. prof. mech. engring. Newark Coll. Engring., 1965-68, prof., 1968—. Recipient NASA grant, 1967-68. Mem. Am. Soc. M.E., Am. Inst. Aeros. and Astronautics, Am. Soc. Engring. Edn., Ukrainian Engrs. Soc. Am. (pres. 1966-67), N.Y. Acad. Scis., Pi Tau Sigma, Tau Beta Pi, Sigma Xi. Contbr. articles profl. jours. Home: 19 Roselle Av Cranford NJ 07016 Office: 323 High St Newark NJ 07102

HSIA, DAVID YI-YUNG, physician, educator; b. Shanghai, China, Aug. 22, 1925; s. Ching-Lin and Wai-Tsung (New) H.; came to U.S., 1940, naturalized, 1960; A.B., Haverford Coll., 1944; M.D., Harvard, 1948; m. Hsio-Hsuan Shih, July 23, 1949; children—David, Judith Ann, Lisa, Peter. Intern, Charity Hosp., New Orleans, 1948-49; asst. resident pediatrics Childrens Hosp., Phila., 1949-50, N.Y. Hosp., 1950-51; research fellow pediatrics Harvard Med. Sch., 1951-53, instr. pediatrics, 1953-56; research asst. Galton Lab., Univ. Coll., London, 1956-57; faculty Northwestern U., 1957-69, prof. pediatrics, 1960-69, now lectr.; prof., chmn. dept. pediatrics Loyola U.-Stritch Sch. Medicine, Chgo., 1969—; chief pediatrics Loyola U. Hosp., 1969—; cons. pediatrics at Children's Meml., St. Joseph's Evanston, Cook County hosps. Bd. dirs. Am. Bur. Med. Aid to China; bd. dirs. Cook County chpt. Nat. Found., 1959—, mem. sci. adv. com., 1967—. Recipient Mead Johnson award pediatric research, 1965; City of Hope award, 1970. Mem. Soc. Pediatric Research, Central Soc. Clin. Research, Soc. Exptl. Biology and Medicine, Am. Pediatric Soc., Sigma Xi, Alpha Omega Alpha, Phi Beta Kappa. Author: Inborn Errors of Metabolism, 2d edit., 1966; Human Developmental Genetics, 1968. Home: 2752 Bennett St Evanston IL 60201 Office: 2160 S 1st Av Maywood IL 60153

HSIANG, WU-CHUNG, educator. Prof. math. Yale. Office: 1 Hillhouse Av New Haven CT 06520

HSIAO, CHIH-CHUN, scientist, educator; b. Peking, China, Oct. 23, 1919, s. P.Y. and P.L. (Tuan) H.; came to U.S., 1943, naturalized, 1954; B.S., Yenching U., Tsinghua U., 1941; S.M., Mass. Inst. Tech., 1944, Ph.D., 1948; postgrad. U. Colo., summer 1945; m. Joyce Chao-Ying Yuan, Aug. 6, 1953; children—Karen K.J., Caroline K.L., Nina K.L., Albert K. C. Asst. prof., asso. prof. Pa. State U., 1946-53; prin. research physicist Jones & Laughlin Research Lab., 1953-55; asso. prof., prof. U. Minn., Mpls., 1955—. Sr. vis. prof. U. Cambridge (Eng.), 1968-69. Mem. Am. Phys. Soc., Soc. Natural Philosophy, Soc. Engring. Sci., Sigma Xi, others. Research on structure and behavior metallic and polymeric solids, mechanics in molecular biology, viscoelasticity, continuum mechanics with microstructure, strength and fracture, physics and mechanics of solids, bio-systems. Home: 3131 Shoreline La St Paul MN 55112 Office: Inst Tech U Minn Minneapolis MN 55455

HSU, FRANCIS LANG KWANG, educator; b. Chuang Ho, China, Oct. 28, 1911; s. Chung-ting and Lee (Shih) H.; B.A., Shanghai U., 1933; Ph.D., U. London, 1940; m. Vera Y.N. Tung, Apr. 26, 1943; children—Eileen Y.N., Penelope S.H. Asst. prof. to prof. anthropology, sociology Nat. Yunnan U., Kumming, China, 1941-44; lectr. Columbia, 1944-45; acting asst. prof. Cornell U., 1945-47; asst. prof., asso. prof. anthropology Northwestern U., Evanston, Ill., 1947-55, prof., 1955—, also chmn. dept. field expdns. to Shansi, North China, 1936, West Yunnan, Southwestern China, 1941-42, 1943, Hawaii, 1949-50, India, 1955-57, Japan, 1964-65. Chinese labor cons. Bur. Labor Statistics, U.S. Dept. Labor, 1945; vis. prof. Kyoto U., 1964-65, U. Hawaii, 1969-70. Viking Fund fellow, 1944-45, Viking Fund grantee, 1949- 50, 55-57; Social Sci. Research Council fellow, 1949-50; Rockefeller Found. fellow, 1955-57; Carnegie Corp. grantee, 1964-65; sr. specialist East-West Center, 1969-70. Fellow Am. Anthrop. Assn. Author: Under the Ancestors Shadow, 1948; Religion, Science and Human Crises, 1952; Americans and Chinese, Two Ways of Life, 1953; The Study of Literate Civilizations 1969; Kinship and Culture, 1971. Editor: Aspects of Culture and Personality, 1954; Psychol. Anthrop.: Approaches to Culture and Personality, 1961; Clan, Caste and Club: A Comparative Study of Chinese, Hindu and Am. Ways of Life. 1963; Americans and Chinese, Purpose and Fulfillment in Great Civilizations, 1970. Asso. editor Internat. Jour. Comparative Sociology; adv. editorial bd. Internat. Jour. Social Psychiatry. Contbr. articles to profl. publs. Home: 310 Wesley Av Evanston IL 60202

HSU, IMMANUEL CHUNG YUEH, educator; b. Shanghai, China, May 6, 1923; s. Thomas K.S. and Mary (Loh) H.; B.A., Yenching U., China, 1946; M.A., U. Minn., 1950; Ph.D. (Harvard-Yenching fellow), Harvard, 1954; m. Dolores Menstell, Apr. 14, 1962; 1 son, Vadim Menstell. Came to U.S., 1949, naturalized, 1962. Postdoctoral research fellow Harvard, 1955-58, vis. asso. prof. history, vis. prof. history Summer Sch., 1961, 64, 68; asst. prof. history U. Cal. at Santa Barbara, 1959-60, asso. prof., 1960-65, prof., 1965—, chmn. history dept., 1970—. Guggenheim fellow, 1962-63. Mem. Am., Pacific hist. assns., Assn. for Asian Studies, Assn. for Ch'ing Studies. Author: Intellectual Trends in the Ch'ing Period, 1959; China's Entrance into the Family of Nations, 1960; The Ili Crisis: A Study of Sino-Russian Diplomacy, 1871-1881, 1965; The Rise of Modern China, 1970. Editor: Readings in Modern Chinese History, 1971. Office: Dept History U Cal Santa Barbara CA 93106

HSU, JOHN TSENG HSIN, educator, cellist; b. Swatow, China, Apr. 21, 1931; s. Benjamin D.H. and Lucy (Ma) Zi; came to U.S., 1949, naturalized, 1961; Mus.B., New Eng. Conservatory Music, Boston, 1953, Mus.M., 1955, Mus.D. (hon.), 1971; m. Martha Russell, July 31, 1968. Music faculty Cornell U., cellist U. Trio, Ithaca, N.Y., 1955—, prof., 1966—, chmn. dept. music, 1966-71; active as viola de gamba recitalist; toured throughout Europe, Am. Fellow Cornell Soc. for Humanities, 1971-72. Mem. viola da gamba socs. Am. and Eng., Pi Kappa Lambda. Recorded by Musical Heritage Soc., N.Y.C., Disques Alpha, Brussels, Da Camera Schallplatten- edition, Mannheim, Germany. Home: 713 Hanshaw Rd Ithaca NY 14850

HU, SZE-TSEN, educator; b. Huchow, China, Oct. 9, 1914; s. Hsiao Tang and Su Mei (Tang) H.; B.Sc., Nat. Central U., China, 1938; Ph.D., U. Manchester (Eng.), 1947, D.Sc., 1959; m. Shia Zong Wang, Mar. 14, 1948 (dec. 1962); children—Herman, Charlotte. Came to U.S., 1949, naturalized, 1955. Mem. Inst. Advanced Study, Princeton, 1950-52; asso. prof. Tulane U., 1952- 55; prof. U. Ga., 1955-56, Wayne State U., 1956-60, U. Cal. at Los Angeles, 1960—; cons. Lockheed Aircraft Corp., 1959-64. Mem. Am. Math. Soc., Math. Assn. Am., London Math. Soc., Soc. Math. de France, Soc. Math. de Belgique, Wiskundig Genootschap re Amsterdam, Sigma Xi. Author: Homotopy Theory, 1959; Elements of General Topology, 1964; Theory of Retracts, 1965; Elements of Modern Algebra, 1965; Threshold Logic, 1965; Introduction to General Topology, 1966; Homology Theory, 1966; Introduction to Contemporary Mathematics, 1966; Elements of Real Analysis, 1967; Introduction to Homological Algebra, 1968; Cohomology Theory, 1968; Mathematical Theory of Switching Circuits and Automata, 1968; Elementary Functions and Coordinate Geometry, 1969; Diffentiable Manifolds, 1969; also numerous articles. Home: 1076 Tellem Dr Pacific Palisades CA 90272 Office: Dept Math U Cal at Los Angeles Los Angeles CA 90024

HUANG, A. BEN, educator; b. Taipei, Taiwan, China, July 1, 1935; s. Yu Shen and Yen (Yen) H.; B.S., Nat. Taiwan U., 1957; M.S., U. Ill., 1961, Ph.D., 1963; m. Mavis Y. Juang, Dec. 19, 1964; 1 dau., Erica Yen-Ling. Came to U.S., 1959, naturalized, 1971. Teaching asst. U. Ill., 1959-60, research asst., 1960-63; asst. prof. U. Ala., 1963-64; asso. prof. Ga. Inst. Tech., Atlanta, 1964-68, prof., 1968—; cons. Coll. Engring. Nat. Taiwan U., 1969—. Served to 2d lt. Chinese Air Force, 1957-59. Recipient Mamie A. Ferst Meml. Sigma Xi Research award, 1967. Mem. Am. Inst. Aeros. and Astronautics, Am. Phys. Soc., Sigma Xi. Contbr. articles profl. jours. Home: 3134 Woodrow Way NE Atlanta GA 30319

HUBACHEK, FRANK BROOKES, lawyer; b. Mpls., Aug. 10, 1894; s. Frank R. and Nellie A. (Brookes) H.; A.B., U. Minn., 1915, LL.B., 1922; postgrad. Harvard Law Sch., 1915-17; L.H.D., Cornell Coll., 1962; LL.D., Beloit Coll., 1970; m. Marjorie Mix, Dec. 25, 1917; children—Marjorie Ann (Mrs. William H. Watkins, Jr.), Frank Brookes. Admitted to Minn. bar, 1922, Ill. bar, 1929; partner Hubachek & Schall, Mpls., 1922-24, pvt. practice, 1924-34; mem. firm Hubachek, Kelly, Rauch & Kirby and predecessor firms 1934-69; dir. Household Finance Corp., 1925-67, chmn. exec. com., 1934-66. Cons. OPA, Washington, alternate price adminstr.; cons. Com. under Presdl. order 8843, 1941-43. Mem. Bd. Edn. Glencoe, Ill., 1932-36. Pres., trustee Wilderness Research Found., Lakeland Found.; v.p., trustee Art Inst. Chgo. until 1970, now life trustee; trustee Gads Hill Center, now hon.; Served with ambulance corps, French Army, 1917; lt. (j.g.), pilot U.S.N.A.S., 1918, U.S.N.R.F., 1919-22. Mem. Am. Forestry Assn. (Nat. award for service in conservation 1957), Am., Ill., Chgo. bar assns., Phi Delta Phi, Phi Kappa Psi. Republican. Baptist. Mason. Clubs: Chicago, University, Mid-America, Skokie Country (Chgo.); Minneapolis, 1938. Author: Annotations on Small Loan Laws, Russell Sage Found., 1938. Contbr. law rev. articles. Home: 635 Washington Av Glencoe IL 60022 Office: Prudential Plaza Chicago IL 60601

HUBATA, JOSEPH ALLEN, physician; b. Chgo., Oct. 18, 1904; s. Joseph and Anna Barbara (Herda) H.; A.B., Oberlin Coll., 1926; M.D., Ill. Coll. Medicine, 1932; hon. degree in med. research U. Terroni, Italy; m. Onelia T. Magnabosco, Dec. 26, 1943; 1 dau., Kerry Celeste. Intern, Englewood Hosp., Chgo., 1932-33; pvt. practice, Chgo., 1933-46; indsl. med. staff Internat. Harvester Co., 1938-46; med. dir., indsl. Armour & Co., 1946-50; med. dir. Armour Pharm.

Co., 1950-70; instr. dept. medicine Rush Med. Sch., 1935-37, med. staff Am., Englewood hosps., Chgo. Maj., M.C., Ill. State Guard, 1941-46. Trustee Valmora Sanitorium. Named chevalier Republic of Haiti, comdr. Order of Merit, Toussaint Louverture (Haiti). Mem. A.M.A., Am. Geriatric Soc., Am. Heart Assn., Am. Med. Writers Assn., Royal Soc. Indsl. Health and Hygiene, Ill. Med. Assn., Chgo. Med. Soc., Central States Soc. Indsl. Medicine and Surgery, Acad. Occupational Medicine, Ill. Med. Soc. Home: 2001 Sherman Av Evanston IL 60201 Office: Am Hosp 850 Irving Park Rd Chicago IL 60613

HUBAY, CHARLES ALFRED, surgeon, educator; b. Chagrin Falls, O., Jan. 23, 1918; s. Stephan and Mary Elizbaeth (Szitar) H.; A.B., Adelbert Coll., 1940; M.D., Western Res. U., 1943; m. Gladyce E. Jones, Sept. 8, 1945; children—Charles Alfred, William C., Thomas A. Intern, Univ. Hosps., Cleve., 1943-44, resident, 1946-50; practice medicine, specializing in surgery, Cleve., 1950—; prof. surgery Western Res. U., 1965—, dir. gen. surgery, 1965- -; asso. surgeon Highland View Hosp. Served with AUS, 1944-46; ETO. Diplomate Am. Bd. Surgery. Mem. A.C.S., Am., Central surg. assns., Soc. U. Surgeons. Contbr. articles to profl. jours. Home: 33325 Woodleigh Dr Cleveland OH 44124 Office: 2065 Adelbert Rd Cleveland OH 44106

HUBBARD, ALLEN SKINNER, lawyer; b. Auburn, N.Y., Jan. 31, 1891; s. Rev. William H. and Elizabeth Allen (Skinner) H.; A.B., Yale, 1911; LL.B., Harvard, 1914; m. Harriet E. Richardson, Dec. 24, 1913; children—Allen Skinner, David Richardson, Elizabeth (Mrs. Gordon D. Scott), Charlotte (Mrs. H. H. Hugo Fries), William Skinner (dec.). Admitted to N.Y. bar, 1915; with Stetson, Jennings & Russell, N.Y.C., 1914-17; asso., later partner Hughes, Rounds, Schurman & Dwight, 1917-37; partner firm Hughes, Hubbard & Reed, and predecessors, 1937—. Mem., treas. Metro. Rapid Transit Commn., 1954-59. Served as pvt., 41st Tng. Battery, U.S. Army, 1918. Mem. Am., N.Y. State bar assns., Assn. Bar City of N.Y. (exec. com. 1951-55), N.Y. County Lawyers Assn., New Eng. Soc. City of N.Y. (pres. 1950), Alpha Delta Phi. Republican. Presbyn. Clubs: University, Dowtown Assn. (N.Y.C.); Blind Brook (Port Chester, N.Y.). Home: 1 E 66th St New York City NY 10021 Office: 1 Wall St New York City NY 10005

HUBBARD, CHARLOTTE MOTON, former govt. ofcl.; b. Hampton, Va., Nov. 27, 1912; d. Robert Russa and Jennue Dee (Booth) Moton; B.S. in Edn., Boston U., 1934, postgrad. Sch. Edn., summer 1939; D.C.L., New Eng. Coll., Henniker, N.H., 1965; m. Maceo Hubbard, Dec. 29, 1945. Instr., asso. prof. health and phys. edn. Hampton Inst., 1934-41, asso. dir. dance group, 1936-41; recreation rep. Office Community War Services, FSA, 1942-45; community relations adviser Girl Scouts U.S.A., N.Y.C., 1945-49; dir. field relations Tuskegee Inst., 1950-52; mat. rep. div. pub. relations, polit. action com. CIO, 1952; pub. relations asst. United Givers Found, Washington, 1958-63; officer-in-charge community meetings Bur. Pub. Affairs, State Dept., 1963, coordinator women's activities Office Community Adv. Services, 1963-64; dep. asst. sec. state for pub. affairs, 1964-70. Mem. community relations com. Girl Scouts U.S.A., 1951-52; cons. Inter-group Relations for Recreation Workers, 1953-54; mem. pub. relations com. Washington Urban League, 1956-58, youth incentives and edn. com., 1958-60; pub. relations com. Washington YWCA, 1960-64, mem. bd., 1961-64; co-chmn. Washington campaign United Negro Coll. Fund, 1965. Adv. bd. Washington chpt. Am. Friends Service Com., 1951-54; mem. bd. Southeastern U., Washington, 1965—, Davis Meml. Goodwill Industries, Arthritis and Rheumatism Assn. Mem. Women's Nat. Democratic Club. Recipient Outstanding Alumni award Tuskegee Inst., 1965; Alumnae award Boston U., 1968—. Mem. Am. Women in Radio and Television (mem. bd. Washington 1965-66), Nat. Conf. Christians and Jews, N.A.A.C.P., League Women Voters, Theta Sigma Phi. Home: 1830 16th St NW Washington DC 20009

HUBBARD, CORTLANDT VAN DYKE, author; b. Newton Centre, Mass., June 4, 1912; s. Robert Arnold and Nancy Morrison (Holland) H.; student Phillips Exeter Acad., 1927-30; A.B., Harvard Coll., 1934, student Law Sch., 1934-35; m. Margaret Douglas Gribbel, June 4, 1938; children—Cortlandt Van Dyke, Margaret Douglas, Louisa Van Dyke. Began writing, 1935. Served as lt. comdr. USNR, World War II. Mem. Pa. Soc. Sons Revolution, Colonial Soc. Pa., Phila. Soc. Preservation Landmarks, Mil. Order Fgn. Wars, St. Andrews Soc., Soc. Colonial Wars. Clubs: Penn, Phila. Cricket, Harvard. Author: (with Harold D. Eberlein) Diary of Independence Hall, 1948; American Georgian Architecture, 1952; Historic Houses of George-Town and Washington City, 1958; Historic Houses and Churches of Delaware, 1961; others 1937-44; also articles; photographic illustrator. Home: 860 E Manatawna St Roxborough Philadelphia PA 19128 Office: 2201 Chestnut St Philadelphia PA 19103 ☆

HUBBARD, DAVID ALLAN, educator, clergyman; b. Stockton, Cal., Apr. 8, 1928; s. John King and Helena (White) H.; B.A., Westmont Coll., Cal., 1949; B.D., Fuller Theol. Sem. Pasadena, 1952, Th.M., 1954; Ph.D., St. Andrews U. (Scotland), 1957; m. Ruth Doyal, Aug. 12, 1949; 1 dau., Mary Ruth. Ordained to ministry Conservative Bapt. Assn., 1952; lectr. O.T., St. Andrews U., 1955-56; asst. prof. Bible and Greek, Westmont Coll., 1957, chmn. dept. Bibl. studies and philosophy, 1958-63; interim pastor Montecito (Cal.) Community Ch., 1960-62; pres., prof. O.T., Fuller Theol. Sem., 1963—; exec. v.p. Gospel Broadcasting Assn., 1969—. Speaker, The Joyful Sound, internat. radio broadcast, 1969—; Tyndale O.T. lectr., Cambridge, Eng., 1965. Chmn., Pasadena Urban Coalition, 1967-71. Mem. Am. Acad. Religion, Soc. Bibl. Lit., Pasadena C. of C. Rotarian. Author: With Bands of Love, 1968; (with others) Is God Dead?, 1966; Is Life Really Worth Living?, 1969; What's God Been Doing All This Time?, 1970; What's New?, 1970; Does the Bible Really Work?, 1971; Psalms for All Seasons, 1971. Contbg. editor Eternity mag. Contbr. articles to dictionaries, mags. Home: 1925 N Grand Oaks Av Altadena CA 91001 Office: 135 N Oakland Av Pasadena CA 91101

HUBBARD, FREDERIC GEORGE, hosp. dir.; b. Cogswell, N.D., Apr. 17, 1921; s. Frederic George and Olga (Johnson) H.; B.A., U. N.D., 1948; M. Hosp. Adminstrn., U. Minn., 1950; m. Phyllis Annette Sanderson, Jan. 19, 1952; children—Hilary Warren, Lisa Louise. Adminstrv. asst. Vancouver Gen. Hosp., 1951-52, asst. dir., 1952-55; instr. U. B.C., 1952-55; dir. adminstrn., dept. health and hosps., Denver, 1955-59; dir. Balt. City Hosps., 1959—; clin. preceptor grad. course hosp. adminstrn. U. Minn., Mpls.; preceptor grad. course hosp. adminstrn. George Washington U.; asso. Johns Hopkins U. Chmn. Combined Health Appeal, 1966; bd. Md. Comprehensive Health Planning; mem. Balt. Areawide Health Planning Com., Md. Regional Med. Program. Pres. Md. Hosp. Edn. and Research Found. Served from pvt. to capt., Med. Adminstrv. Corps, 1942- 45. Mem. Hosp. Council Md., Md., Del., D.C. (dir.), Am. hosp. assns., Am. Coll. Hosp. Adminstrs. Episcopalian. Mason. Contbr. profl. articles hosp. jours. Home: Box 323 Manor Rd Glenarm MD 21057 Office: 4940 Eastern Av Baltimore MD 21224

HUBBARD, FREDERICK DEWAYNE, musician; b. Indpls., Apr. 7, 1938; student mellophone in high sch. Player trumpet, fluegelhorn, piano; with Montgomery Bros., Indpls., then with Sonny Rollins, Slide Hampton. J.J. Johnson, Quincy Jones; mem. Art Blakey's Jazz Messengers. 1961; tours of Europe, Japan, Austria; appeared Berlin Jazz Festival, 1965; played with Quincy Jones in soundtrack for film The Pawnbroker; recording artist for Blue Note, Impulse records. Recipient Down Beat New Star award for trumpet, 1961. Address: 919 Park Pl Brooklyn NY*

HUBBARD, HONORE C., lawyer; b. Brooklyn, Wis., Jan. 19, 1901; B.S., U. Wis., 1922, M.S., 1934; J.D., De Paul U., 1928. Admitted to Ill. bar, 1928; mem. firm Wolfe, Hubbard, Leydig, Voit and Osann, Chgo. Office: 1 N La Salle St Chicago IL 60602*

HUBBARD, JAY WARREN, marine corps officer; b. San Francisco, June 16, 1922; s. Benjamin Franklin and Molly Adeline (Wilkins) H.; B.S., U. Omaha, 1960; M.S. in Internat. Affairs, George Washington U., 1966; student Air Command Staff Coll., 1952, Command Staff Coll., 1962, Nat. War Coll., 1966; m. Dorla Dean Kerr, Jan. 10, 1943; children—Clinton L., Diana D., Glenn W., Brad A. Joined USMC, 1940, commd. 2d lt., 1942, advanced through grades to brig. gen., 1968; inf. officer, World War II; fighter pilot, Korean Conflict; attack group comdr., Vietnam, 1966-67; dir. information, 1968-71; comdg. gen. Marine Air Res. Tng., Glenview, Ill., 1971—. Active youth activities. Decorated Silver Star, Legion of Merit, (3), D.F.C., Air medal (10) Navy Commendation medal, Purple Heart. Home: Quarters G NAS Glenview IL 60026 Office: HQ 4th MAW/MARTC NAS Glenview IL 60026

HUBBARD, JESSE DONALD, educator; b. nr. Sardinia, Ind., May 2, 1920; s. Jesse Wilmar and Emma Susan (Dieringer) H.; A.B., DePauw U., 1943; M.D., Johns Hopkins, 1951; m. Dorothy Emma Drake, June 6, 1948; children—Richard, Joseph, Debra, Jean. Intern, resident Union Meml Hosp., Balt., 1951-54; resident Ind. U. Med. Center, Indpls., 1954-56, mem. faculty, 1956—, prof. pathology, 1968—, also pathologist. Served with USAAF, 1943-46. Mem. A.M.A., Am. Soc. Clin. Pathologists. Home: 4330 Black Oak Dr Indianapolis IN 46208

HUBBARD, JOHN BARRY, banker; b. Sweetwater, Tex., Mar. 16, 1917; s. John Howard and Shirley (McCarty) H.; B.B.A., U. Tex., 1939, LL.B., 1940; m. Virginia Marie Olsen, Dec. 10, 1943; children—Carol Ann (Mrs. Sam Houston Lane III), Virginia Sue (Mrs. Kenneth Nolan Tarlton), Jean Ellen, John Barry. With FBI, U.S. Dept. Justice, 1940- 53; sr. v.p., trust officer Ft. Worth Nat. Bank, 1953—; sr. v.p. Fort Worth Nat. Corp. Faculty, Southwestern Grad. Sch. Banking So. Meth. U. Treas., bd. dirs. Longhorn council Boy Scouts Am., Girls Service League. Mem. Tex., Tarrant County bar assns., Tex. Bankers Assn. (past pres. trust sect.). Mem. Christian Ch. Home: 6491 Woodstock Rd Fort Worth TX 76116 Office: 800 Main St Fort Worth TX 76102

HUBBARD, JOHN INGRAM, educator; b. Wellington, New Zealand, Dec. 1, 1930; s. John and Anne (Ingram) H.; B.Med. Sci., U. New Zealand, 1952; B.A. with 1st class honours in Physiology, Oxford (Eng.) U., 1954, M.A., B. Medicine and Surgery, 1957, M.D., 1968; Ph.D., Australian Nat. U., 1961; m. Patricia Margaret Sargent, July 17, 1954; children—Jennifer, Caroline, Andrew, Linda, Alastair. Came to U.S., 1967. Demonstrator physiology U. Otago, Dunedin, New Zealand, 1951-52; house physician and surgeon Radcliffe Infirmary, Oxford, U., 1957-58; mem. faculty John Curtin Med. Sch., Australian Nat. U., 1961-67; prof. biol. engring. Northwestern U., 1967—. Mem. expdn. Billabong to Great Barrier Reef, 1966. Mem. Physiol. Soc., Am., Australian (past mem. council. archivist) physiol. socs., A.A.A.S., N.Y. Acad. Scis., Soc. Bibliography Natural History, Soc. Neurosci. (orgn. sec. Chgo. chpt.), Internat. Union Physiol. Scis. (archivist). Author papers, revs., monographs. Home: 1564 Asbury St Evanston IL 60201

HUBBARD, JOHN PERRY, physician; b. Phila., Oct. 26, 1903; s. Russell Sturgis and Elizabeth Russell (Perry) H.: grad. Milton Acad., 1921; A.B., Harvard, 1925, M.D., 1931; m. Dorothy Allen, June 30, 1933; children—Elizabeth (Mrs. Phillip Edgerton), Florence Allen (Mrs. John S. Lloyd III). Intern Children's Hosp., Boston, 1931-34; Rockefeller travelling fellow, 1934-35; staff physician medicine and pediatrics St. Luke's Hosp., Tokyo, Japan, 1935; Commonwealth research fellow, 1936-37; instr. med. sch. Harvard, also asso. physician Children's Hosp. of Boston, and pvt. practice of medicine, 1937-42; dir. study of child health services for Am. Acad. Pediatrics in cooperation with USPHS and U.S. Children's Bur., 1945-49; George S. Peper prof. pub. health and preventive medicine U. Pa. Sch. Medicine, 1950-66, emeritus prof., 1966—. Nat. cons. med. edn. USAF, 1963—. Exec. dir. Nat. Bd. Med. Examiners, 1950-67, pres., dir., 1967—; dir. Media Medica, Inc., 1968—. Vice pres. Harvard Med. Alumni Council, 1962-65; pres. Am. Bd. of Med. Specialties, 1970—. Served from maj. to col. M.C. AUS, 1942- 45, chief med. service, Mitchell Field, N.Y., 1942-43, attached to SHAEF, mil. govt., pub. health, 1943-45, chief pub. health sect. Mil. Mission to France and Denmark. Decorated Order of Danneborg (Denmark); recipient award merit Am. Heart Assn., 1966. Fellow A.C.P., Am. Pub. Health Assn.; mem. A.M.A., Am. Heart Assn. bd. dirs., 1960-63), Heart Assn. Southeastern Pa. (pres. 1959- 60), Am. Acad. Pediatrics, Soc. Pediatrics. Soc, Pediatric Research, Am. Pediatric Soc., Soc. Med. Cons. World War II. Club: Harvard (Boston and Phila.). Author: Early Detection and Prevention of Disease; Multiple Choice. Home: Gladwyne PA Office: 3930 Chestnut St Philadelphia PA 19104

HUBBARD, JOHN RANDOLPH, univ. pres.; b. Belton, Tex., Dec. 1, 1918; s. Louis Herman and Bertha (Altizer) H.; A.B., U. Tex., 1938, A.M., 1939, Ph.D., 1950; m. Lucille Luckett, Jan. 29, 1947; children—Elisa, Melisse, Kristin. Pvt. sec. to ICC commr., 1938-41; teaching fellow U. Tex., 1946-48; vis. asst. prof. Brit. history La. State U., 1948; asst. prof. European history Tulane U., 1949-52; vis. asst. prof. European history Yale, 1952-53; asso. prof. European history Tulane U., 1953-58, prof. 1958-65, dean Newcomb Coll., 1953-65; chief edn. adviser AID, India, 1966-69; v.p. for acad. affairs, provost U. So. Cal., 1969-70, pres., 1970—. Mem. bd. Tulane-Lyceum Assn., 1953-65, Isidora Newman Sch., 1953-65; mem. Region 12 selection com. Woodrow Wilson Fellowship Program, also chmn., 1955-65; mem. bd. U.S. Edn. Found., India; mem. Indian adv. bd. Women's Coll. Faculty Exchange program; pres. bd. Am. Internat. Sch., New Delhi. Served as an aviator in USN, 1941-46; flight instr. and patrol plane comdr. Atlantic and Pacific fleets; lt. comdr. Res. Decorated Distinguished Flying Cross, 4 Air Medals; Chevalier des Palmes Academiques; Stella della Solidarietá Italiana (Italy). Mem. Am., Miss. Valley, So. (exec. council 1953-56) hist. assns., Anglo-Am. Hist. Soc., Phi Delta Kappa, Delta Kappa Epsilon, Omicron Delta Kappa. Clubs: Royal Aero (London, Eng.); Boston (New Orleans). Contbr. articles and revs. to Jour. Modern History, other ednl. jours. Home: 1500 Chelsea Rd San Marino CA 91108 Office: U So Cal Los Angeles CA 90007

HUBBARD, LESLIE STODDARD, poultry industry exec.; b. Walpole, N.H., Apr. 25, 1904; s. Ira Stoddard and Gertrude (Lamb) H.; B.S. in Mech. Engring., U. N.J., 1927; m. Iola Muriel McCracken, Sept. 23, 1932; children—Marcia Leslie, John Cooper. Engr., N.Y. Telephone Co., Syracuse, N.Y., 1927-28; mgr. Niagara Poultry Farm, Ransomville, N.Y., 1928-32; mgr. Hubbard Farms Inc., Lancaster, Pa., 1932-56, v.p., 1955-69, chmn. bd., 1969—, also dir.; chmn. bd. Hubbard Europoultry S.A., 1962-64; dir. Hubbard Europoultry S.A., Oudenaarde, Belgium. Pres., Poultry and Egg Nat. Bd., 1955-56; mem. U.S. delegation Worlds' Poultry Congress, 1951, 66. Bd. dirs. Citizen Scholarship Found. Am.; bd. dirs. Lancaster Gen. Hosp., 1938-62, pres., 1952-54. Named Poultryman of Year in Pa., 1957; named Hon. Keystone Farmer, Future Farmers Am., 1950. Mem. N. Eastern Poultry Producers Council (pres. 1946-47), Pa. (pres. 1949-51), Nat. (pres. 1948-52) poultry producers fedns., Am. Poultry and Hatchery Fedn. (pres. 1965-68, treas. 1968-69). Presbyn. Mason. Club: Beverly Yacht (Marion, Mass.). Home: Sparhawk Hill Walpole NH 03608 Office: Hubbard Farms Inc Walpole NH 03608

HUBBARD, LLOYD CLAYTON, computer products co. exec.; b. Huntington Park, Cal., Sept. 26, 1923; s. Herbert L. and Margaret (Grier) H.; B.S., U. Cal. at Los Angeles, 1949; m. Bette A. Hunter, June 12, 1943; children—Gregory, Laurie, Kristen. With IBM Corp., 1949-70, br. mgr., Houston, 1962-63, distbr. mgr., Dallas, 1963-66, dir. marketing research and forcasting White Plains, N.Y., 1966-68, systems mgr., Boca Raton, Fla., 1968-70; pres. Tracor Data Systems Co., Austin, Tex., 1970—; dir. Berkeley Sci. Labs., Peripherials Gen. Corp., Remcom Systems, Inc. Served with USNR, 1942-46. Mem. Tau Beta Pi. Home: 7209 Mesa Dr Austin TX 78731 Office: 4201 Ed Bluestien Blvd Austin TX 78721

HUBBARD, ORVILLE LISCUM, city ofcl.; b. Union City, Mich., Apr. 2, 1903; s. Ralph Star and Sylvia Elizabeth (Hart) H.; student Ferris State Coll., 1925-26; LL.B., Detroit Coll. Law, 1932; extension courses Henry Ford Community Coll., U. Mich.; m. Fay Velma Cameron, July 20, 1927; children—James, Frank, Nancy Anne, John Jay, Henry Ford. Admitted to Mich. bar, 1932; stenographer Ford Motor Co., 1925; reporter Wall Street Jour., 1929-34; U.S. Army reserve officer, 1930-37; Mich. state trooper, 1942-45; asst. Atty. Gen. Mich., 1939-40; mayor of Dearborn, Mich., 1941—. Republican precinct del., 1932—; mem. Wayne County Bd. Suprs., 1942-68; del. Rep. Nat. Conv., 1952, alternate del., 1940. Served as sgt. USMCR, 1922-25. Recipient Distinguished Citizen award Dearborn C. of C., 1962. Mem. Dearborn Bar Assn. (pres.). Republican. Club: Dearborn Exchange. Holder nat. record longest full-time mayor. Founder first out-of-state apt. bldg. for retirees, Dearborn Towers, Clearwater, Fla., also Camp Dearborn. Home: 7055 Mead Dearborn MI 48126 Office: 13615 Michigan Av Dearborn MI 48126

HUBBARD, PAUL GAYLORD, educator; b. Virginia, Minn., Aug. 6, 1921; s. Paul G. and Mary Jane (Freebury) H.; A.B., Wabash Coll., 1943; M.A., U. Ill., 1945, Ph.D., 1949; m. Henrietta Kamarit, Sept. 7, 1947. Instr., Galesburg br. U. Ill., 1947-49; research asst. to U.S. Congressman Judd, 1949-50; mem. faculty Ariz. State Coll., Tempe, 1950-59, asso. prof. history, 1956-59; prof. history, chmn. dept. Ariz. State U., 1959—. Ariz. adviser for Ariz. and The West Jour., 1959—. Mem. Am. Hist. Assn., Orgn. Am. Historians, Phi Beta Kappa, Phi Kappa Phi, Lambda Chi Alpha. Home: 137 W Palmcroft Dr Tempe AZ 85281

HUBBARD, PAUL STANCYL, Jr., educator; b. St. Petersburg, Fla., July 15, 1931; s. Paul Stancyl and Lee (Wilkerson) H.; B.S., in Physics, U. Fla., 1953; A.M., Harvard, 1954, Ph.D., 1958; m. Carol Sylvia Martyn, June 8, 1957; children—Carol Lee, Philip Martyn. Asst. prof. physics U. N.C. at Chapel Hill, 1958-63, asso. prof., 1963-68, prof., 1968—, asso. dean Grad. Sch., 1969—. Sloan research fellow, 1962-66; NSF sr. postdoctoral fellow Clarendon Lab., Oxford, Eng., 1964-65. Mem. Am. Phys. Soc., Am. Assn. Physics Tchrs., A.A.A.S., Am. Assn. U. Profs., Phi Beta Kappa, Sigma Xi. Contbr. articles on nuclear magnetic resonance and relaxation profl. jours. Home: 1710 Audubon Rd Chapel Hill NC 27514

HUBBARD, PERRY, lawyer; b. Tarrant, Ala., Mar. 17, 1921; s. Lex Walter and Elrine (Perry) H.; B.S. in Commerce and Bus. Adminstrn., U. Ala., 1943, LL.B., 1945; m. Carolyn Louise Gates, Nov. 26, 1942; children—Perry, Carolyn Lex, Kathryn Rush, Edward Haigler. Admitted to Ala. bar, 1945; practice in Birmingham, 1945-48; asst. prof. law U. Ala. Law Sch., 1948-49; practice in Tuscaloosa, 1949—; partner firm Hubbard & Waldrop, 1967—; adj. prof. law U. Ala. Law Sch., 1949—; gen. counsel, dir. Cotton States Life Ins. Co. Mem. local SSS, 1951—. Bd. dirs., v.p. Met. YMCA. Mem. Am., Ala. (chmn. practice and procedure sect. 1967-68) bar assns., Ala. Law Inst. (council 1968—). Home: 15 Parkwood St Tuscaloosa AL 35401 Office: 2319 8th St Tuscaloosa AL 35401

HUBBARD, PHILIP GAMALIEL, engr., educator; b. Macon, Mo., Mar. 4, 1921; s. Philip Alexander and Rosa Belle (Wallace) H.; B.S. in Elec. Engring., U. Ia., 1946, M.S., 1949, Ph.D., 1954; D. Humanities (hon.), St. Ambrose Coll., 1969; m. Synnonna Marie Griffin, May 3, 1943; children—Philip Gamaliel, Christine, Michael Laurence, Richard Charles, Peter David. Research engr. Ia. Inst. Hydraulic Research, 1946-65; pres. Hubbard Instrument Co., Iowa City; from asst. to full prof. Mechanics and Hydraulics engring. U. Ia., 1946—, vice provost, dean acad. affairs, 1966—. Cons. research instrumentation; cons. OAS, Argentina, 1962. Mem. adv. bd. Danforth Found.; bd. dirs. S.E. Ia. Goodwill Industries. Served with AUS, 1943-45. Fulbright scholar, Uruguay, 1962-68. Registered profl. engr., Ia. Mem. Am. Soc. Engring. Edn. (mem. projects bd.; vis. engr. to NSF, 1956-66), Sigma Xi, Tau Beta Pi, Eta Kappa Nu, Phi Lambda Upsilon, Omicron Delta Kappa. Methodist (past supt.). Kiwanian (past chpt. pres.). Home: 4 W Park Rd Iowa City IA 52240

HUBBARD, ROBERT MERRILL, chem. engr., educator; b. Indpls., Nov. 3, 1909; s. Harry Niles and Flora (Merrill) H.; B.S.E., U. Mich., 1931, M.S.E., 1932, Ph.D., 1940; m. Frances Edmonds Johnson, June 18, 1952. Chem. engr. in process devel. work Solvay Process Co., Hopewell, Va., 1936-41, Koppers Co., Pitts., 1941-46; faculty U. Va., Charlottesville, 1946—, prof., 1947—, chmn. dept. chem. engring., 1946-63, also dir. engring. expt. sta., 1951-56, cons. engr. Mem. Am. Inst. Chem. Engrs., Am. Chem. Soc., Am. Soc. Engring. Edn., Va. Acad. Sci., Instrument Soc. Am. Home: 311 Montebello Circle Charlottesville VA 22903

HUBBARD, RUDOLPH TREZVANT, orgn. exec.; b. Plant City, Fla., Dec. 29, 1902; s. George Franklin and Catherine Amelia (Draughon) H.; A.B., Duke, 1926; m. Janice Little Montgomery, Mar. 4, 1927; children—Rudolph Franklin, Marilyn Kay. Tchr. history and journalism, athletic coach Berryhill High Sch., Charlotte, N.C., 1926-28; in various depts. Walker & Co., outdoor advt. firm, Flint, Mich., 1928-43, mgr. br. office, Saginaw, Mich., 1943-45; exec. sec. Civitan Internat., editor Civitan mag., Birmingham, Ala., 1945-71, controller, 1971—. Mem. bd. Crippled Children's Soc. Jefferson County; mem. nat. adv. council Boy Scouts Am.; mem. Gov.'s Safety Com. Ala. Recipient Distinguished Civic Service award Flint C. of C., 1942; Get Out the Vote award Am. Heritage Found., 1952; Crusade for Freedom award, 1954; George Washington Honor award Freedoms Found., 1968; Honor Key Civitan Internat., 1971. Mem. Flint, Saginaw, Bay City, Mich. chambers of commerce. Methodist. Clubs: Saginaw Golf and Country, Saginaw Civitan (sec.- treas. 1939-40, lt. gov. 1943-44, gov. north central dist. Civitan Internat. 1944-45), Flint Advertising and Sales (dir.), So. Indsl. Editors Assn., Birmingham (Ala.) Civitan. Methodist (chmn. bd. stewards 1954-56, pres. Meth. men 1966-67, ch. sch. supt. 1967-69). Clubs: Relay House, The (Birmingham). Home: 1317 44th St W Birmingham AL 35208 Office: Civitan Bldg 115 N 21st St Birmingham AL 35203

HUBBARD, RUSSELL STURGIS, bishop; b. Germantown, Pa., Sept. 8, 1902; s. Russell Sturgis and Elizabeth Russell (Perry) H.; student St. George's Sch., R.I., 1915-20; A.B., Harvard, 1924; B.D., Va. Theol. Sem., 1927, D.D., 1949; student Trinity Coll., Cambridge, Eng., 1924-25; LL.D., (hon.), Gonzaga Univ., Spokane; m. Anna Catherine Pratt, Nov. 3, 1928; children—Ann Perry (Mrs. P.T. Austin), Jane Parkinson (Mrs. John Keydel), Judith Bradbury (Mrs. Thomas Osgood), Russell, Catherine Carroll (Mrs. Richard A. Burke). Ordained deacon, Episcopal Ch., 1927, priest 1928; consecrated bishop, 1948; asst. St. John's Ch., Waterbury, Conn., 1927-29; priest in charge St. Paul's Ch., Vermillion, S.D., 1929-32; rector St. Martin's Ch., Providence, 1932-41, St. Saviour's Ch., Bar Harbor, Me., 1942-48; canon missioner Diocese of Me., 1943-48; suffragan bishop Diocese of Mich., 1948-54; bishop of Spokane, 1954-67. Rotarian. Address: Sunland Route 2 Box 88 Sequim WA 98382

HUBBARD, W.C., radio co. exec.; b. 1923; B.S., U. Ky., 1947; married. With Collins Radio Co., Dallas, 1953—, mgr. accounting dept., 1955-61, controller Cedar Rapids office, 1961-68, corporate controller, 1968—, v.p., 1971—, also dir. Served to 1st lt. AUS, 1950-53. Office: 1200 N Alma Rd Dallas TX 75215*

HUBBARD, WILLIAM NEILL, Jr., pharm. co. exec.; b. Fairmont, N.C., Oct. 15, 1919; s. William Neill and Mary Emma (Fenegan) H.; A.B., Columbia, 1942; postgrad. U. N.C. Sch. Medicine; M.D., N.Y. U., 1944; m. Elizabeth Terleski, Dec. 28, 1945; children— William Neill III, Michael J., Mary E., Elizabeth A., Susan E. Mem. house staff 3d med. div. Bellevue Hosp., N.Y.C., 1944-50; instr. medicine N.Y. U., 1950-53, asst. prof., 1953-59, asst. dean, then asso. dean N.Y. U. Coll. Medicine, 1951-59; dean U. Mich. Med. Sch., 1959-70, asso. prof. internal medicine, 1959-64, prof., 1964-70, dir. U. Mich. Med. Center, 1969-70; gen. mgr. pharm. div., v.p. Upjohn Co., 1970—. Cons. USPHS; mem. Nat. Adv. Commn. on Libraries, 1966-68; med. adv. com. W.K. Kellogg Found., 1959-67; mem. Gov.'s Adv. Com. on Edn. Health Care, 1965-69. Chmn. bd. regents Nat. Library of Medicine, 1965-67. Fellow A.C.P.; mem. Harvey Soc., N.Y. Acad. Medicine, Soc. Alumni Bellevue Hosp., Mich. Med. Soc. (mem. council 1960-62), A.M.A., Kalamazoo Acad. Medicine, Am. Soc. Clin. Pharmacology and Therapeutics, Assn. Am. Med. Colls. (pres. 1966-67) Nat. Fund Med. Edn. (dir.), Sigma Xi, Alpha Omega Alpha. Home: 1401 Lama Rd Kalamazoo MI 49001

HUBBEL, STANLEY W., banker; b. Ridgefield Park, N.J., Oct. 3, 1910; s. Walter L. and Julia Wells (Preston) H.; B.A., Cornell U., 1932; m. 2d, Charlotte Knott, Jan. 22, 1949; children by previous marriage—Judith Ann Wells (Mrs. William Secor), Shelley Lynn (Mrs. Daniel Rubin). With Chase Manhattan Bank, N.Y.C., 1932-41; with Marine Midland Bank-N.Y., N.Y.C., 1945—, adminstrv. v.p., 1964, sr. v.p., 1964-70, exec. v.p. adminstrn., 1970—. Active Ho-Ho-Kus (N.J.) Community Chest. Served to lt. comdr. USNR, 1941-46. Clubs: Cornell, City Midday (N.Y.C.). Home: 418 Braeburn Rd Ho-Ho-Kus NJ 07423 Office: 200 E 64th St New York City NY 10021

HUBBELL, DELMER FULLERTON, Jr., banker; b. Syracuse, N.Y., Mar. 23, 1913; s. Delmer Fullerton and Agnes Lawrence (Hanchett) H.; student Northwestern U., 1931-34; m. Adelaide Amelia Sullivan, Sept. 28, 1946. Counter man to dept. head F.G. Shattuck Co., 1935-42; commodity loan clk. Chase Nat. Bank, N.Y.C., 1945-53; with M.&T. Discount Corp., N.Y.C., 1953—, pres., 1961—, also dir.; v.p. Mfrs. & Traders Trust Co., Buffalo, 1960—. Served with USAAF, 1942-45. Mem. Bankers Assn. for Fgn. Trade, Beta Theta Pi, Sigma Delta Chi. Republican. Club: Wall Street (N.Y.C.). Home: 300 E 74th St New York City NY 10021 Office: M & T Discount Corp 1 Chase Manhattan Plaza New York City NY 10005

HUBBELL, ERNEST, lawyer; b. Trenton, Mo., Aug. 28, 1914; s. Platt and Maud Irene (Ray) H.; student Trenton Jr. Coll., 1932-34; LL.B., Georgetown U., 1938; m. Nevah Smith, Apr. 25, 1943; 1 son, Platt Thorpe. Admitted to Mo. bar, 1938: practiced in Trenton, 1938-39, Jefferson City, 1939-42, Kansas City, 1947—; asst. atty. gen. Mo., 1939-42; pvt. practice, 1947—; lectr. U. Mo. at Kansas City, 1952-54. First chmn. bench, bar com. 16th Jud. Circuit Ct., Kansas City, 1964—. Trustee Kansas City Art Inst. Legal Aid and Defender Soc. Greater Kansas City. Served with USAAF, 1942-44; to capt. AUS, 1944-46. Mem. Am., Mo. (past pres.) trial lawyers assns., Am., Mo., Kansas City (past pres.) bar assns., Lawyers Assn. Kansas City, Lawyers Assn. St. Louis, Nat. Council on Crime and Delinquency (chmn. Kansas City com.), Archaeol. Inst. Am., S.A.R. Democrat. Episcopalian. Clubs: Kansas City, Carriage, Editor: Missouri Trial Lawyers Assn. Bull., 1955; asso. editor Am. Trial Lawyers Assn. Law Jour., R.R. Law, 1951—. Home: 1210 W 63d St Kansas City MO 64113 Office: Power and Light Bldg Kansas City MO 64105

HUBBELL, GEORGE WESLEY, banker; b. Bridgeport, Conn., Aug. 1, 1906; s. Walter A. and Maud (Mosher) H.; student Milford Sch., 1925-26, U. of South, 1926-27, Stonier Grad. Sch. Banking, 1946-48; m. Alma Hand, Oct. 11, 1928; 1 dau., Suzanne (Mrs. Richard L. Chantland). With City Savs. Bank, Bridgeport, 1927—, dir. (trustee), 1959. dir. corporator, 1960, pres., treas., 1963—; dir. Conn. Nat. Bank. Mem. Planning and Zoning Commn., Easton, 1949-67; mem. Sch. Bldg. Com., Easton, 1962-67. Bd. assos. U. Bridgeport; bd. dirs. Easton Pub. Health Nurses Assn. Mem. Bridgeport C. of C., Newcomen Soc. N.Am. Clubs: Algonquin, Exchange (Bridgeport). Home: 134 Sunny Ridge Rd Easton CT 06612 Office: 948 Main St Bridgeport CT 06603

HUBBELL, JOHN WILLIAM, business exec.; b. Washington, Dec. 2, 1899; s. John Edmund and Mae (Main) H.; A.B., Dartmouth Coll., 1921; m. Ruth Seanor, Sept. 20, 1934; children—John W., Jean Susan, Patricia. Salesman, Colgate & Co., N.Y.C., 1921-25; Butterick Pub. Co., 1925-27; sales Curtis Pub. Co., N.Y.C., 1927-29; with Simmons Co., N.Y.C., since 1929, promotional mgr., 1929-32, advt. dir. and promotional mgr., 1932-48, v.p. since 1948, dir.; v.p., dir. Movies Enroute, Inc. Served as pvt., inf., U.S. Army 1918; lt. col., in charge Army's Overseas Motion Picture Service, Signal Corps, AUS, 1943-45; overseas part of 1944 and 1945. Hon. life dir., past chmn. bd. Brand Names Found. Trustee United Hosp. Westchester County, N.Y., Nat. Coordinator Polio (advt. council). Recipient Wentworth bowl for distinguished Dartmouth service. Mem. Home Furnishing Council (pres.), Nat. Assn. Bedding Mfrs. (trustee, pres.). Mem. Presbyn. Ch. Clubs: Union League (v.p.), Circus Saints and Sinners, Banshees, Sales Executives (past pres., dir.) (N.Y.C.); Ekwanok Country; Manursing Island, Apawamis Country (Rye, N.Y.); Pilgrims of U.S. Gov. U.S. Seniors Golf Assn. Home: Windcrest Rd Rye NY 10580 Office: U S Geol Survey Washington DC 20242

HUBBELL, LESTER EARLE, former naval officer; b. Hackensack, N.J., Sept. 24, 1916; s. Lester Sprague and Margaret (Malure) H.; B.S., Ga. Sch. Tech., 1938; m. Katharine Jean Bush, May 11, 1946; children—Lester Woodrow, Katherine Jean, Michael Lee. Commd. ensign USN, 1938, advanced through grades to rear adm., 1966; comdr. Destroyer Div. 262, 1956, Destroyer Squadron 15, 1962, Fleet Air Def. Tng. Center, Dam Neck, Va., 1958; chief staff Pacific Fleet Cruiser-Destroyer Force, 1963; chief staff sec. navy retention task force Office Sec. Navy, 1965; dir. uniformed services compensation and career devel. Office Sec. Def., 1966-69; comdr. Cruiser-Destroyer Flotilla 6, 1969-71; ret., 1971. Address: 5306 Camberley Av Bethesda MD 20014

HUBBERT, MARION KING, geologist, geophysicist b. San Saba, Tex., Oct. 5, 1903; s. William Bee and Cora Virginia (Lee) H.; student Weatherford Coll., 1921-23; B.S., U. Chgo., 1926, M.S., 1928, Ph.D., 1937; m. Miriam Graddy Berry, Nov. 11, 1938. Asst. geologist Amerada Petroleum Corp., Tulsa, summer 1926, 1927-28; teaching asst. geology U. Chgo., 1928-30; instr. geophysics Columbia, 1930-40; geophysicist Ill. Geol. Survey, summers 1931-32, 35-37; asso. geologist U.S. Geol. Survey, summer 1934; pvt. research, writing, 1940- 41; sr. analyst Bd. Econ. Warfare, Washington, 1942-43; research geophysicist Shell Oil Co., Houston, 1943-45, asso. dir. research, 1945-51, chief cons. gen. geology, 1951-55; cons. gen. geology Shell Devel. Co., 1956-64; vis. prof. geology and geophysics Stanford, 1962-64, prof., 1964-68; vis. prof. geography Johns Hopkins, spring 1968; research geophysicist U.S. Geol. Survey, 1964—. Mem. U.S. delegation UN Sci. Conf. Conservation and Utilization Resources, Lake Success, N.Y., 1949; mem. com. geophysics Nat. Council, adviser Office Naval Research, 1949-51, mem. com. Disposal Radioactive Waste Products, 1955-63; mem. Adv. Selection Com. for Allowing Grants under Fulbright Act, 1950-51; mem. vis. com. earth scis. Mass. Inst. Tech., 1958-60; mem. earth scis. adv. panel NFS, 1953-57, chmn., 1954- 57; vis. lectr. Mass. Inst. Tech., 1959; regents lectr. U. Cal., Los Angeles, 1960; chmn. div. earth scis. Nat. Acad. Scis.-NRC, 1963-65; nat. adv. bd. U. Nev. Desert Research Inst., 1967—; mem. com. resources and man NRC, 1966-70. Trustee, sec. Population Reference Bur. Recipient Lucas medal Am. Inst. Mining, Metall. and Petroleum Engrs., 1971. Fellow Am. Acad. Arts and Scis., A.A.A.S., Geol. Soc. Am. (Day medal 1954, council 1947-49, pres. 1962), Internat. Union Geol. Scis. (U.S. nat. com. 1961-64); mem. Am. Assn. Petroleum Geologists (Distinguished lectr. U.S. and Can. 1945, 52), Am. Geophys. Union, Soc. Petroleum Engrs. (Distinguished lectr. 1963-64), Soc. Expln. Geophysicists (hon. life), NAS, Sigma Xi, Gamma Alpha. Club: Cosmos (Washington). Author: Theory of Ground-Water Motion, Energy Resources; co-author: Resources and Man. Editor: Geophysics, 1947-49; asso. editor Jour. Geology, 1958—, Bull. Am. Assn. Petroleum Geologists, 1955—. Contbr. articles to profl. jours. Home: 5208 Westwood Dr Washington DC 20016 Office: US Geol Survey Washington DC 20242

HUBBS, CHARLES TAYLOR, newspaper editor; b. Amsterdam, N.Y., Oct. 15, 1926; s. Hazlett D. and Carolyn (Taylor) H.; student Severn Sch., 1943-44, Cornell U., 1947-49, Carnegie Inst. Tech., 1949-51; m. Vi Shamblin, Nov. 21, 1953; children—Elizabeth R. (dec. Feb. 1958), Holly K., Heather. City editor Daily Blade-Tribune, Oceanside, Cal., 1956-58; mng. editor Daily News, Lewistown, Mont., 1958-59; mem. staff Cin. Enquirer, 1959—, asst. to editor, 1964, mng. editor, 1964—. Pres. lay adv. bd. Mt. Alverno Sch. Boys. Served with AUS, 1944-46; ETO; with USMC, 1951-55. Mem. A.P. Mng. Editors (dir. 1970—), A.P. Soc. Ohio (trustee 1970-71), Theta Delta Chi. Home: 986 Hickok Lane Cincinnati, OH 45238 Office: 617 Vine St Cincinnati OH 45202

HUBBS, RONALD M., ins. co. exec.; b. Silverton, Ore., Apr. 27, 1908; s. George W. and Ethel (Burch) H.: B.A., U. Ore.; m. Margaret S. Jamie, Sept. 9, 1935; 1 son, George J. With St. Paul Fire & Marine Ins. Co., 1936—, beginning as spl. agt. Pacific Northwest, successively agy. supt. Pacific dept., gen. mgr. So. Cal. br., asst. to pres., 1948-52, v.p., 1952-59, exec. v.p., 1959-63, pres., 1963-69, chmn., 1969—; chmn., dir. St. Paul Mercury Ins. Co., 1969—; pres., dir. The St. Paul Cos., Inc.; dir. Western Life Ins. Co., 1st Trust Co. of St. Paul, St. Paul Fire & Marine Ins. Co., Econs. Lab., Burlington No. Ry., Toro Mfg. Co., Northwestern Bell Telephone Co. Dir. Twin City Area Ednl. TV Corp., Miller Hosp., St. Paul; trustee Carleton Coll., William Mitchell Coll. Law, James J. Hill Library, Haynes Found; consultative council U. Minn. Sch. Bus. Adminstrn. Served 1st lt. to col. AUS, World War II. Decorated Legion of Merit. Mem. Ins. Inst. Am. (vice chmn.), AFIA World Wide Ins. (chmn.), Am. Inst. Property and Liability Underwriters (vice chmn.), Minn. Hist. Soc. (1st v.p.), Alpha Tau Omega, Phi Delta Phi, Scabbard and Blade, Friars. Episcopalian (trustee diocese Minn.). Clubs: Somerset Country; Minnesota. Home: 1410 Edgcumbe Rd St Paul MN 55116 Office: 385 Washington St St Paul MN 55102

HUBEL, DAVID HUNTER, educator, physiologist; b. Windsor, Ont., Can., Feb. 27, 1926 (parents Am. citizens); s. Jesse Harvey and Elsie (Hunter) H.; B.Sc., McGill U., 1947, M.D., 1951; A.M. (hon.), Harvard, 1962; m. Shirley Ruth Izzard, June 20, 1953; children—Carl Andrew, Eric David, Paul Matthew. Intern, Montreal Gen. Hosp., 1951-52; asst. resident neurology Montreal Neurol. Inst., 1952-53, fellow clin. neurophysiology, 1953-54; asst. resident neurology Johns Hopkins Hosp., 1954-55; sr. fellow Johns Hopkins, 1958- 59; faculty Harvard Med. Sch., 1959—, George Berry prof. physiology, chmn. dept., 1967-68, George Berry prof. neurobiology, 1968- -. George M. Bishop lectr. exptl. neurology Washington U., St. Louis, 1964; Jessup lectr. biol. scis. Columbia, 1970. Sr. fellow Harvard Soc. Fellows. Served with AUS, 1955-58. Recipient Research to Prevent Blindness Trustees award, 1971. Fellow Am. Acad. Arts and Scis.; mem. Nat. Acad. Sci., Am. Physiol. Soc. (Bowditch lectr. 1966). Research brain mechanisms in vision. Home: 98 Collins Rd Waban MA 02168 Office: 25 Shattuck St Boston MA 02115

HUBENKA, LLOYD JOHN, educator; b. Omaha, Jan. 1, 1931; s. Lloyd John and Emma (Dobrovolny) H.; B.A., Creighton U., 1952, M.A., 1959; Ph.D., U. Neb., 1966; m. Beverly Ann Conkling, Feb. 14, 1953; children—Jayne, Evan, Naomi, Sara. Faculty, Creighton U., Omaha, 1958—, asso. prof., 1966-68, prof., 1968—, chmn. English dept., 1966—. Served to maj. AUS, 1952-56; Korea. Decorated Commendation medal. Fellow Nat. Endowment for Humanities, 1968. Mem. Modern Lang. Assn., Nat. Council Tchrs. English, Assn. Depts. English, Am. Assn. U. Profs. Editor: Unto This Last (John Ruskin), 1968. Home: 4115 N Post Rd Omaha NB 68112

HUBENTHAL, KARL SAMUEL, editorial cartoonist; b. Beemer, Neb., May 1, 1917; s. George W. and Perna (Jackson) H.; student Chouinard Art Sch., 1935; m. Elsie Helene Litschke, Sept. 10, 1940; children—Karen Elaine Hubenthal (Mrs. Wallace Chappell), Kathleen Eve. Mem. staff art dept. Los Angeles Evening Herald-Express, 1935, artist sports cartoons, 1939-44; free lance comml. art, mag. illustration, N.Y.C., Los Angeles, 1946-49; sports cartoonist Los Angeles Examiner, 1949-56, editorial cartoonist, 1952—; editorial cartoonist syndicated Hearst Newspapers, 1952—; story illustration, cover art. advt. Drawings West Coast publs. Served with USMCR, 1944-46. Named Best Sports cartoonist, World's Fair, N.Y.C., 1940; recipient Freedom Found. award, 1951-53, 55-61, 63-70, Grand award, 1962; Nat. Headlinerss award for outstanding achievement in journalism, 1959; Helms Athletic Found. medal, 1964. Mem. Marine Corps Newsmen's Assn., Nat. Cartoonists Soc. (Nation's Best Editorial Cartoonist 1962, 68, 70), Soc. Illustrators (pres. 1958-59), Assn. Am. Editorial Cartoonists (pres. 1963-64), Sigma Delta Chi, Kappa Tau Alpha. Clubs: Art Directors, Press (Los Angeles); San Moritz (Lake Gregory, Cal.). Home: 16863 Marmaduke Pl Encino CA 91316 Office: 1111 S Broadway Los Angeles CA 90015

HUBER, SISTER ALBERTA, coll. pres.; b. Rock Island, Ill., Feb. 12, 1917; d. Albert and Lydia (Hofer) Huber; B.A., Coll. St. Catherine, St. Paul, 1939; M.A., U. Minn., 1945; Ph.D., U. Notre Dame, 1954. Faculty, Coll. St. Catherine, 1940- -, prof. English, 1953—, chmn. dept., 1960-63, acad. dean, 1962-64, pres., 1964—. Exec. com. Minn. Citizens Com. on Ct. Reform. Bd. dirs. Minn. Internat. Center; trustee Fontbonne Coll., St. Louis; St. Paul Opera Assn., St. Joseph's Hosp., St. Paul; hon. bd. dirs. Minn. Orch. Assn. Home: 2004 Randolph Av St Paul MN 55116

HUBER, AUGUST, investment co. exec.; b. N.Y.C., Nov. 19, 1911; s. August G. and Lillie (Schneider) H.; student Am. Inst. Banking, N.Y. Inst. Finance; m. Alice E. Mallinson, Apr. 24, 1941; children—William A., Robert H. Partner Spencer Trask & Co., Inc., N.Y.C., 1958-68, sr. v.p., 1968-69, pres., 1969—, chief exec. officer, 1971—; trustee Peoples Savs. Bank of Yonkers; dir. Midwest Stock Exchange Service Corp., 1966-68, Tex. Oil & Gas Corp. Bd. govs. Am. Stock Exchange, 1960-66, vice chmn. bd. govs., 1964-66. Mem. N.Y. Soc. Security Analysts. Clubs: Economic, Downtown Athletic, Bond of N.Y., Recess (N.Y.C.); Sleepy Hollow Country (Westchester, N.Y.). Home: River Rd Scarborough NY 10510 Office: 60 Broad St New York City NY 10004

HUBER, CARL PARKER, physician, educator; b. Ann Arbor, Apr. 8, 1903; s. Carl and Luch Ann (Parker) H.; A.B., U. Mich., 1924, M.A., 1925, M.D., 1928, Peterson fellow, 1933-35; m. Marion Elizabeth Kubik, June 20, 1929; children G. Carl. Mariel Stow, David Garrett. Instr. obstetrics and gynecology U. Mich., 1930-36, U. Chgo., 1936-38; attending obstetrician, gynecologist Chgo. Lying-In Hosp., 1936-38; asst. prof. obstetrics and gynecology Ind. U. Sch. Medicine, 1938-44, asso. prof., 1944-48, prof. since 1948, also chmn. dept.; cons. obstetrician Ind. State Bd. Health, 1938—. Diplomate Am. Bd. Obstetrics and Gynecology (bd. dirs. 1956—, pres., 1964-66, chmn. 1968-70). Mem. N.D. (hon.), Indpls. Obstet. and gynecol. socs., Am. , Chgo. gynecol. socs., Central Assn. Obstetricians and Gynecologists, Am. Assn. Obstetricians and Gynecologists, Am. Coll. Obstetrics and Gynecology (pres. 1952), Am. Com. Maternal Welfare (nd. dirs. 1946—), Sigma Xi, Alpha Sigma Phi, Phi Rho Sigma, Phi Sigma, Alpha Omega Alpha. Author med. articles. Home: 490 Westwood Rd Indianapolis, IN 46240. Office: 1100 W Michigan St Indianapolis IN 46202

HUBER, EDWARD FREDERICK, lawyer; b. Paterson, N.J., Apr. 1, 1906; s. William and Barbara (Zucker) H.; A.B., Fordham U., 1926, LL.B., 1929; m. Mary Elizabeth Fallon, July 26, 1951; children—Barbara, Anne Marie, Catherine, Edward, Mary Liz, William, George, John, Mary Louise, Mary Theresa. Admitted to N.Y. bar, 1929; asso. Travis, Brownback & Paxson, N.Y.C., 1929-37, partner, 1937-43; partner Dean, Magill & Huber, N.Y.C., 1946-54, Holland, Huber & Banigan, Chgo., 1949-54, Naylon, Aronson, Huber & Magill, N.Y.C., 1954- 67, Naylon, Huber, Magill, Lawrence & Farrell, N.Y.C., 1967—. Served to capt. AUS, 1944-47. Mem. Am., N.Y. bar assns., Judge Advs. Assn., Cath. Lawyer's Guild. Home: 11 Iden Av Larchmont NY 10538 Office: 61 Broadway New York City NY 10006

HUBER, EDWARD WILLIAM, former brewer; b. Chgo., May 1, 1905; s. Frederick and Mina (Schmidt) H.; Master Brewer, Wahl Inst. Brewing Tech., Chgo., 1936; m. Dorothea Wollenberg, May 29, 1926; 1 son, Curtis E. Asst. master brewer Roosevelt Brewing Co., Chgo., 1933-37; master brewer Prima-Bismarck Brewing Co., 1937-44; v.p., master brewer Miller Brewing Co., Milw., 1944-54, sec., dir., 1954, master brewer, exec. v.p., 1956-71. Mem. tech. adv. com. U.S. Brewers Assn. Mem. Master Brewers Assn. Am. (nat. tech. chmn., past nat. pres.), Malting Barley Improvement Assn. (dir., Cin. Achievement award 1961), Am. Soc. Brewing Chemists, Malt Research Inst., Brewing Industries Research Inst. (pres.), Inst. Brewing London, Milw. Master Brewers Assn. (past pres.), Milw. Assn. Commerce. Lutheran. Clubs: Blue Mound Golf and Country, Wisconsin (Milw.). Contbr. articles to research publs. Home: PO Box 27 Oconomowoc WI 53066

HUBER, FREDERICK ROLAND, coll. pres.; b. Los Angeles, Nov. 26, 1914; s. Roland A. and Irene M. (Lynch) H.; A.B., U. Cal. at Los Angeles, 1937; M.A., U. So. Cal., 1940, Ed.D., 1955; 1 dau., Clare Ann; m. 2d, Helen E Phelps, Aug. 1, 1970. Instr., adminstr. Cal. pub. schs., 1940—; dean men Orange Coast Coll., Costa Mesa, Cal., 1948-56; dir. Palo Verde Coll., Blythe, Cal., 1956-58; pres. Monterey Peninsula Coll., 1958-64; pres. Palomar Coll. San Marcos, Cal., 1964—. Lectr. summers U. Conn., 1964, U. Ariz., 1971. Sec., Palomar Coll. Devel. Found.; co-chmn. City Escondido Gen. Plan; with Greater San Luis Rey Planning and Devel. Council. Adv. bd. U. Cal. Extension, San Diego. Served to maj., inf. AUS, World War II; col. Res. Mem. N.E.A., Cal. Tchrs. Assn., Am. Council Edn., Nat. Soc. Study Edn., Nat., Cal. assn. secondary sch. prins., Res. Officers Assn., Am. Assn. Jr. Colls., Cal. Jr. Coll. Assn., Phi Delta Kappa, Delta Epsilon. Rotarian. Home: 1120 E Washington Escondido CA 92025

HUBER, HOWARD R., corp. exec.; b. 1924; married. Asst. transfer agt. S.P. Co., 1945—; v.p., treas. Pacific Fruit Co., 1945—, also dir.; pres., treas. H.F. Floyd Co. Address: 116 New Montgomery St San Francisco CA 94105

HUBER, JOHN FRANKLIN, educator; b. Ann Arbor, Mich., Nov. 8, 1904; s. Gothelf and Lucy (Parker) H.; A.B., U. Mich., 1925, M.A., 1928, M.D., 1929; Ph.D., 1933; m. Gladys Boutillier, Apr. 10, 1933; children—Candace, John Parker. From asst. to instr. anatomy U. Mich., 1926-36; faculty Temple U. Sch. Medicine, Phila., 1936—, prof. anatomy, 1944—, chmn. dept., 1944-70; spl. asst. to dean, 1971—. Mem. Am. Assn. Anatomists (2d v.p. 1964-66), Council Med. TV (chmn. 1962), Audio-Visual Conf. Med. and Allied Scis. (pres. 1963-67), A.M.A., Phila. Coll. Physicians, Nat. Audio-visual Assn., Biol. Photog. Assn., Mexican Soc. Anatomy, Phi Beta Kappa, Sigma Xi, Alpha Omega Alpha, Pi Delta Epsilon, Phi Kappa Phi, Phi Sigma, Phi Rho Sigma (pres. 1960-64), Alpha Sigma Phi. Rotarian. Co-author motion picture on bronchopulmonary segments. Home: 454 Moreno Rd Wynnewood PA 19096 Office: 3400 N Broad St Philadelphia PA 19140

HUBER, JOHN RICHARD, economist, educator; b. Dayton, O., Feb. 8, 1909; s. John G. and Mattie (Hott) H.; A.B., Coll. of Wooster, 1931; M.A., Princeton, 1933, Ph.D., 1937; m. Katherine Haas, June 30, 1934; children—Thomas Thomas Edward, John G., William Richard, Michael Ramey. Asst. prof. econs. Emory U., 1934- 39; mem. faculty U. Wash., 1939—, prof. econs., exec. officer dept. econs., 1948—; Fulbright prof. Nagoya (Japan) U., 1955-56. Served with OSS, 1941-45, economist, intelligence officer, spl. asst. to Am. minister, Stockholm, Sweden, 1944-45; vis. econ. cons. SCAP, Tokyo, Japan, summers 1949, 50, 51; chief R.R. Nathan Assos. Econ. Adv. Team, Govt. Afghanistan, 1961-63. Fellow Belgian- Am. Ednl. Found., 1938; Fulbright Scholar Japan, 1955- 56. Recipient Medal of Freedom award, War Dept., 1945. Mem. Am. Assn. U. Profs., Am. Econ. Assn., Western Econ. Assn., Phi Beta Kappa. Author articles econ. jours. Home: 11509 12th St N W Seattle WA 98177

HUBER, PAUL SPEER, Jr., newspaper pub.; b. Norfolk, Va., Mar. 14, 1921; s. Paul Speer and Elizabeth (Lingamfelter) H.; student Norfolk (Va.) Acad.; grad. Woodberry Forest Sch.; student U. N.C.; m. Sarah Jane Booth, Sept. 17, 1948; children—Paul Speer III, Peter McPherson. With Landmark Communications, Inc., 1947—, now pres. and dir.; dir. WTAR Radio Corp., Norfolk Savs. & Loan, United Va.Bank-Seaboard Nat. Vice pres. Area United Communities Fund. Dir. Leigh Meml. Hosp. Home: 1415 Daniel Av Norfolk VA 23505 Office: 150 W Brambleton Av Norfolk VA 23510

HUBER, ROBERT BRUCE, educator; b. Huntington, Ind., June 12, 1909; s. Henry Casper and Olive Maude (Harris) H.; A.B., Manchester Coll., 1930; M.A., U. Mich., 1934; Ph.D., U. Wis., 1942; m. Isabel Nickey, Oct. 27, 1933; 1 dau., Mary Susan. Tchr., Churubusco (Ind.) High Sch., 1930-32, Mishawaka (Ind.) High Sch., 1932-34; asst. prof. speech Manchester Coll., 1934-35; instr. speech Ind. U., 1934-41; asst. U. Wis., 1941-42; asst. prof. speech U. Ore., 1942-43; chmn. dept. U. Vt., Burlington, 1946-66, prof., 1950-66, Lawrence prof. forensics, 1966—; summer lectr. U. Wis., 1946, U. So. Cal., 1952, U. Del., 1970. Town moderator, Shelburne, Vt., 1955—. Served as navigator USNR, 1943-46. Mem. speech assns. Am. (nat. council 1951, legis. assembly 1959-62), Eastern States (pres. 1951), New Eng. Speech Assn. (pres. 1950), Am. Forsenic Assn. (pres. 1963-65), Vt. Speech and Hearing Assn. (pres. 1957-59), Tau Kappa Alpha (1st v.p. 1960-63). Author: Influencing Through Argument, 1963. Home: RFD 2 Shelburne VT 05482

HUBER, ROBERT W., corp. exec.; b. 1914; B.S. in Bus. Adminstrn. Ohio State U. 1939; married. Accountant, Buckeye Union Casualty Co., 1940-42; with Konopak & Dalton, 1946-50; with Libbey Owenss Ford Co., 1951—, treas., 1960—. Served to capt. AUS, 1942-46. Address: 811 Madison Av Toledo OH 42624.*

HUBER, WILLIAM H., ednl. adminstr.; b. Harrisburg, Pa., Apr. 18, 1922; s. William H. and Sarah Catherine (Peace) H.; A.B., Ohio State U., J.D., 1947; m. Sarah Hughes Douglass, Oct. 5, 1942; 1 dau., Sarah Kathryn. Admitted to Ohio, N.M. bars; former instr. U. N.M., Albuquerque, prof. bus. adminstrn., 1960—, dir. U. Coll., 1957-65, dir. U. Coll. and Counseling Center, 1965-71, acting dean Coll. Bus. Adminstrn., 1968-69, dean U. Coll., 1971—. Mem. Am., N.M. bar assns., Phi Kappa Phi, Alpha Kappa Psi, Blue Key. Author: (with R.K. Evans) The Business Venture in New Mexico, 1952. Home: 2811 Campus Blvd NE Albuquerque NM 87106

HUBERT, FRANK WILLIAM RENE, coll. dean; b. Milam County, Tex., June 2, 1915; s. Jonce Sherod and Lura Gertrude (White) H.; B.A., U. Tex., 1938, M.A., 1946, Ph.D., 1950; m. Mary Julia Glidden, June 15, 1940; children—Frank William Rene, Mary Katherine. Dir., Lutcher Stark Boys, Inc., Orange, Tex., 1938-44; prin., dir. secondary edn. Stark Sr. High Sch., Orange, Tex., 1946-48; research fellow, curriculum and instrn. U. Tex., 1948-49; adminstv. asst. Found. Sch. Program Act div. Tex. Auditor's Office, Austin, 1949-50, dir. div., 1949-50; dir. div. profl. standards, also div. tchr. edn. Tex. Edn. Agy., Austin, 1950-55; supt. schs. Orange Ind. Sch. Dist., 1955-59; dean Tex. A. and M. U. Sch. Arts and Scis., College Station, 1959-65, dean Coll. Liberal Arts, 1965-69, Coll. Edn., 1969—, dir. basic div., 1959-60. Exec. sec. Tex. Bd. Exam. Tchr. Edn., 1952-55; mem. com. 75, U. Tex.; pres. Tex. Conf. Tchr. Edn., 1959; mem. Nat. Council Accreditation Tchr. Edn., 1953-55; v.p. S.W. Ednl. Devel Corp., 1966-67, pres., 1967-68; dir. Bank of A & M. Mem. Nat. Adv. Commn. on Mexican-Am. Edn., 1967-69, U.S. Office Edn.; adv. council U.S. Command and Gen. Staff Coll., 1970—; pres. Corp. Research and Engring. in Edn., 1969—; mem. Gov.'s Com. Pub. Edn., 1966-69; mem. charter change commn. Orange, 1958. Served with AUS, 1944-46. Mem. Nat., Orange (pres. 1943-44) edn. assns., Assn. Tex. Colls. and Univs. (pres. 1965-66), Am., Tex. assns. sch. adminstrs., Am. Acad. Polit. and Social Sci., Nat. Assn. State Dirs. Tchrs. Edn. and Certification, Tex. Tchrs. Assn. (chmn. com. tchr. edn. and profl. standards 1955-60), Phi Kappa Phi, Phi Delta Kappa. Rotarian. Club: Briarcrest Country. Home: 2404 Morris Lane Bryan TX 77801 Office: Tex A and M U College Station TX 77840

HUBIN, VINCENT JOSEPH, educator; b. N.Y.C., July 26, 1918; s. Patrick and Mary (Quinn) H.; B.S., N.Y.U., 1947, M.B.A., 1948, Ph.D., 1959; m. Irene Schuster, July 21, 1953. Instr. N.Y.U., 1949-59; prof. real estate econs. Fairleigh Dickinson U., 1959—; Pres. Hubin Assos., real estate cons. and brokers, 1950—; assessor Borough Saddle River, N.J., 1960-71. Served with AUS, 1942-45. Home: 211 W Saddle River Rd Saddle River NJ 07458 Office: Farleigh Dickinson U Rutherford NJ 07070

HUBLEY, GEORGE WILBUR, Jr., govt. ofcl.; b. Louisville, Aug. 19, 1910; s. George Wilbur and Sara Shelby (Wolfe) H.; A.B., U. Louisville, 1933; postgrad. U. Chgo., 1933- 35; m. Alice Gordon Barrickman, Jan. 1, 1938; children—George Wilbur III, Gordon Grant, Todd McAlister. State coordinator research projects WPA, Louisville, 1937-38; regional coordinator research projects Fed. Works Agys., Chgo., 1939-41; fed. coordinator research projects, nat. dir. pub. health research assistance, liaison officer USPHS, Washington, 1941-42; dir. research Ky. C. of C., Louisville, 1946-47; pres. Mgmt. Cons., Inc. Ky., Louisville, 1947; exec. dir. Ky. Agrl. and Indsl. Devel. Bd., 1948-53; exec. v.p. Ohio Valley Improvement Assn., 1953-55; econ. devel. planners states Ky., N.M. also city Atlanta; commr. econ. devel. Commonwealth Ky., 1956- 60; dir. Md. Dept. Econ. Devel. Md., 1960-67, mem. Md. Commn. on N.Y. World's Fair, 1964-65, Md. Regional Export Council, 1963-67; asst. commr. for econ. devel. Bur. Indian Affairs, Dept. Interior, Washington, 1967-70, chief indsl. and tourism devel., 1970—. Chmn., Ky. Small Bus. Commn., 1952-53; past mem. Md. Regional Export Expansion Council. Served from capt. to lt. col. AUS, 1942-46. Mem. Nat. Planning Assn. (dir.), Ky. Hist. Soc., Assn. State Econ. Devel. Agys. (nat. pres. 1959-60), So. Assn. state Planning and Devel. Agys. (pres. 1952), Am. Indsl. Devel. Council, Am. Acad. Polit. and Social Scis., S.A.R. Clubs: Filson (Louisville); National Aviation (Washington). Contbr. articles to profl. jours. Home: 189 Defense Hwy Annapolis MD 21401 Office: US Dept Interior Bur Indian Affairs Washington DC 20242

HUBNER, ROBERT WILMORE, business machines co. exec.; b. Seattle, Mar. 21, 1918; s. Robert G. and Thurza (Wilmore) H.; student U. Wash., 1937-41; m. Katherine L. Huick, Apr. 4, 1942; children—Melissa, Robert Wilmore. With IBM, 1941-43, 43—, dir. recruitment, 1956, exec. asst. to exec. v.p., 1957, sales mgr. data processing div., 1957-59, exec. asst. to chmn. bd., 1959-61, dir. marketing, 1961-65, v.p. marketing, 1965-68, v.p., group exec., 1968—; dir. Marine Midlands Bank of Southeastern N.Y. Trustee Marketing Sci. Inst. Served with AUS, 1943. Mem. Am. Marketing Assn. Clubs: N.Y. Yacht (N.Y.C.); Tokeneke (Darien, Conn). Home: Burler's Island Darien, CT 06820. Office: IBM Armonk NY 10504

HUBNER, ROLAND FORREST, physician; b. Avon, S.D., Apr. 10, 1910; s. William A. and Emma (Mattis) H.; B.S. in Medicine, U. S.D., 1931; M.D., U. Neb., 1933; m. Laverne Hendrickson, May 12, 1935; children-Sandra K. (Mrs. Victor Johnson), Jay William. Intern Ancker Hosp., St. Paul; resident Swedish Hosp., Mpls.; practice in Scotland and Tripp, S.D., 1933-40, Yankton, S. D., 1940-42, 45—; mem. staff Med. Clinic, Yankton, 1946—. Dir. First Dakota Nat. Bank, Yankton. Mem. Yankton City Sch. Bd., 1953-56, Yankton County Sch. Bd., 1955-63; mem. S.D. Regents of Edn., 1961—, chmn., 1962-65; chmn. S.D. Higher Edn. Facilities Commn., 1964—; mem. bd. trustees of Yankton Coll., 1962—; mem. S.D. Bldg. Authority, 1967—. Served with USAAF, 1942-45. Mem. Am., S.D. med. assns., Internat. Coll. Surgeons, Yankton C. of C. (past bd. dirs.). Lutheran. Mason, Elk. Home: 703 W Riverside St Yankton SD 57078 Office: 1104 W 8th St Yankton SD 57078

HUBSHMAN, HENRY M., Jr., banking exec.; b. N.Y.C., Nov. 21, 1925; s. Henry M. and Sylvia (Cohen) H.; grad. Phillips Acad., Andover, Mass, 1942; B.A., Yale, 1945; m. Barbara Chalk, June 12, 1953; children—Kathryn, Peter, James. Sr. v.p. 1st Nat. City Bank, N.Y.C., 1965—; chmn. FNCB Capital; dir. D.C. Transit System (Washington). Bd. dirs. H. and S. Hubshman Found., Phillips Acad. Andover Alumni Assn. N.Y.C., Nightingale-Bamford Sch. Served with USNR, 1943-46; PTO. Home: 1010 Fifth Av New York City NY 10028 also 1037 Constable Lane Mamaroneck NY Office: 399 Park Av New York City NY 10022

HUCK, F. G., pulp and paper com. exec.; b. Sask., Can., 1913. Vice pres., controller Bowaters Newfoundland Pulp & Paper Mills, Ltd.; pres. Newfoundland Export & Shipping Co., Ltd.; controller Bowater Power Co., Ltd., Bowaters Mersey Paper Co., Ltd.; treas. Bowaters Canadian Corp. Ltd.; dir. Bay of Islands Hotel Co., Ltd., Corner Brook Sales Co. Ltd., Indsl. Equipment & Supplies, Ltd. Home: 11 Cobb Lane Corner Brook Newfoundland Canada *

HUCK, JOHN WENZEL, assn. exec.; b. Chgo., Nov. 1, 1916; s. Claude Alexander and Margaret Columbia (John) H.; grad. Phillips Exeter Acad., 1934; A.B., Dartmouth, 1938; M.A., Columbia, 1940; postgrad. U. Chgo., 1940-41; L.H.D., Lincoln U., 1966; m. Dorothy Elizabeth Montgomery, Oct. 10, 1942; children-Geoffrey James, Christopher Claude, Stuart Montgomery. Dir. med. devel. U. Chgo., 1946-55; founder John W. Huck & Assos., Chgo., 1955-60; exec. dir. Asso. Colls. Ill., 1961—. Dir. Chgo. Extruded Metals Co. Sec. U. Chgo. Cancer Research Found., 1948-56; sec.-treas. Cancer Research Found., Inc., 1954-56; mem. citizens bd. Loyola U.; bd dirs. Oscar Mayer Found., 1969—; dir. St. Paul's House, 1949—; dir. Better Govt. Assn. Served as capt. Ordnance AUS, 1941-46. Mem. Phi Sigma Kappa. Republican. Club: Union League (Chgo.). Home: 10856 Longwood Dr Chicago IL 60643 Office: 343 S Dearborn St Chicago IL 60604

HUCK, RALPH FRANCIS, lawyer; b. Quincy, Ill., Mar. 8, 1903; s. Oscar P. and Eda (Burge) H.; student U. Ill., 1921-23; LL.B., U. Mich., 1926; m. Catherine Hunter, July 28, 1928. Admitted to Ill. bar, 1926; with firm Chapman & Cutler, Chgo., 1926—, partner 1943—. Dir. Harris Trust & Savs. Bank Chgo. Mem. Order of Coif. Home: 520 Oak St Winnetka IL 60093 Office: 111 W Monroe St Chicago IL 60603

HUCKABA, CHARLES EDWIN, educator; b. Huntingdon, Tenn., Oct. 20, 1922; s. Oscar Franklin and Fannie (Austin) H.; B.S., Vanderbilt U., 1944; M.S., Mass. Inst. Tech., 1947; Ph.D., U. Cin., 1953; m. Ann Coleman Dickerson, June 12, 1946; children—Charles David, Carol Ann. Asso. prof. chem. engring. Lamar State Coll. Tech., 1952-55; asso. prof. chem. engring. U. Fla., 1955-63; prof., chmn. chem. engring. dept. Drexel Inst. Tech., 1963-67; vis. prof. chem. engring. Columbia, 1967-68, sr. research asso. 1968-69, prof. rehab. medicine, 1969—. Cons. shipbuilding div. Bethlehem Steel Co., 1952-56, Thermal Research & Engring. Corp., 1965-67, Foxboro Co., 1970—; Year-In-Industry educator E.I. duPont de Nemours & Co., Inc., 1961-62. Registered profl. engr., Pa. Recipient Distinguished Engring. Alumnus award U. Cin., 1971. Fellow Am. Inst. Chemists; mem. N.Y. Acad. Scis., Am. Inst. Chem. Engrs., Am. Soc. Engring. Edn., Instrument Soc. Am., Sigma Xi, Tau Beta Pi, Phi Lambda Upsilon. Home: 309 W 57th St New York City NY 10019 Office: Box 114 P H Columbia-Presbyn Med Center New York City NY 10032

HUCKABY, GARY CARLTON, lawyer; b. Lanett, Ala., July 12, 1938; s. Carl W. and Mary E. (Meriwether) H.; B.A., U. Ala., 1960, J.D., 1962; m. Jeanne Davey, Feb. 23, 1963; children—Gary Carlton, John Stephen, Michael Stewart. Admitted to Ala. bar, 1962; law clk. to justice Ala. Supreme Ct., 1962; asst. to U.S. Senator Lister Hill, 1963; practice in Huntsville, 1966—; mem. firm Smith & Huckaby, 1967—; part-time instr. U. Ala. in Huntsville, 1969. Mem. Huntsville Indsl. Expansion Com., Huntsville-Madison County Mental Health Assn.; pres. Madison County Heart Div., 1970-71. Vice pres. Madison County Young Democrats, 1969-70; mem. Madison County Democratic Exec. Com., 1970—. Bd. dirs. United Cerebral Palsy Assn. Huntsville, 1970-71. Served to capt. USAF, 1963-66. Mem. Am., Ala. bar assns., Am., Ala. trial lawyers assns., Farrah Law Soc., Pi Kappa Phi (pres. 1962- 63), Omicron Delta Kappa, Phi Alpha Delta. Episcopalian. Home: 1200 Kennamer Dr Huntsville AL 35801 Office: State Nat Bank Bldg Huntsville AL 35801

HUCKER, CHARLES OSCAR, educator, author; b. St. Louis, June 21, 1919; s. Edward Christian and Kate (Bond) H.; B.A. with high honors, U. Tex., 1941; Ph.D. with honors, U. Chgo., 1950; m. Myrl C. Henderson, Feb. 12, 1943; Instr., U. Chgo., 1950-54, asst. prof., 1954-56; asso. prof. U. Ariz., 1956-58, prof., 1958-61; prof. Oakland U., Rochester, Mich., 1961-65; prof. Chinese and history, chmn. dept. Far Eastern langs. and lits. U. Mich., Ann Arbor, 1965—. Cons., U.S. Office Edn., 1960, 65, 66, Ford Found., 1962-63; cons. or vis. lectr. various colls. and univs. Served to maj. USAAC, 1942-46; PTO. Decorated Bronze Star; postdoctoral fellow Rockefeller Found., 1952-54; sr. fellow Nat. Endowment for Humanities, 1968-69. Mem. Assn. for Asian Studies (sec. 1966-68, dir. 1960-63), Am. Oriental Soc., Am. Hist. Assn., Phi Beta Kappa, Phi Alpha Theta. Author: Chinese History: A Bibligraphic Review, 1958; The Traditional Chinese State In Ming Times, 1961; China: A Critical Bibliography, 1962; The Censorial System of Ming China, 1966; (with others) Chinese Thought and Institutions, 1957; (with others) Confucianism in Action, 1959. Editor: Chinese Government in Ming Times: Seven Studies, 1969. Home: 1918 Day St Ann Arbor MI 48104

HUCKER, GEORGE JAMES, bacteriologist, educator; b. Cascade, Ia., Aug. 19, 1893; s. James Burleigh and Esther (Pangburn) H.; student Upper Ia. U., 1912-13; B.S., Lenox Coll., 1915; postgrad. Cornell U., 1920-21; A.M., Columbia, 1916; Ph.D. (Cutler fellow), Yale, 1924; D.H.L. (hon.), Hobart and William Smith Colls.; m. Alice Mackenzie, Sept. 4, 1917 (dec. May 1965); m. Marjorie Cook, Apr. 9, 1966. Instr. biology, Allegheny Coll., 1916-17, asst. prof., 1917-38; spl. agt. U.S. Dept. Agr., 1918; asst. bacteriologist N.Y. State Agrl. Expt. Sta., Geneva, 1919-22, asso. research bacteriologist, 1922-29, chief in research, 1929—; asst. prof. Cornell U., 1922-29, prof. bacteriology, 1929—. Mem. Internat. Edn. Bd., Copenhagen, London, Paris, 1926-27; editor Food Research, 1936-49; mng. editor Food Tech.; cons. New Zealand Govt., 1938; mem. Nat. Nutrition Adv. Com., 1940-50. Past chmn. Rochester (N.Y.) State Hosp. Regional Planning Council. Past pres. bd. dirs. Rochester Regional Council Hosps.; trustee Coll. Center Finger Lakes. Served as lt. San. Corps, AEF, 1918-19. Fellow Am. Pub. Health Assn.; mem. Inst. Food Technologists (ex-pres.), Newcomen Soc., Soc. Am. Bacteriologists, Internat. Milk Sanitarians. Republican. Presbyn. Rotarian. Clubs: University (dir., past pres.), Torch (past pres., dir.). Contbr. numerous articles to sci. jours. Home: 6 Sunset Dr Geneva NY 14456 Office: NY State Agrl Expt Sta Geneva NY 14456

HUDDLESON, EDWIN EMMET, Jr., lawyer; b. Oakland, Cal., Jan. 28, 1914; s. Edwin Emmet and Gertrude (Conahan) H.; A.B. Stanford, 1935; LL.B., Harvard, 1938; m. Mary Taeusch, July 21, 1941; children—Michael Stephen (dec.), Edwin Emmet III, Mary Catherine. Admitted to Cal. bar. 1939; law clk. to Judge A.N. Hand, 1938-39; atty. Office Solicitor Gen., 1939-40; law clk. Mr. Justice Frank Murphy, 1940; dir. spl. projects staff Office Asst. Sec. Intelligence, State Dept., 1946; dep. gen. counsel AEC, 1947-48; mem. firm Cooley, Crowley, Gaither, Godward, Castro & Huddleson, San Francisco, 1949—. Dir. Raychem Corp., Varian Assos., U.S. Leasing Internat., Inc.; trustee Aerospace Corp., Mitre Corp., RAND Corp. Trustee Center for Advanced Study Behavioral Scis., Riverside Research Inst., System Devel. Found. Served to lt. col. AUS, 1941-46; PTO. Decorated Legion of Merit. Mem. Phi Beta Kappa. Pres., Harvard Law Rev., 1937-38. Home: 2201 Bywood Dr Oakland CA 94602 Office: Alcoa Bldg 1 Maritime Plaza San Francisco CA 94111

HUDDLESTON, GEORGE, Jr., former congressman, aircraft co. exec.; b. Birmingham, Ala., Mar. 19, 1920; s. George and Bertha (Baxley) H.; A.B. magna cum laude, Birmingham-So. Coll., 1941; LL.B., U. Ala., 1948; m. Alice Jeanne Haworth; children—George III, Margaret, Nancy. Admitted to Ala. bar, 1948, D.C. bar, 1965; dep. circuit solicitor 10th Jud. Circuit, 1948-49; asst. U.S. atty. No. Dist. Ala., 1949-52; practice law, Birmingham, 1952-54; mem. 84th-87th Congresses, 9th Dist. Ala., mem. 88th Congress at large, Ala.; Washington counsel N.Am. Rockwell Corp., 1965—. Served to capt. USNR, World War II. Mem. Am. Legion (dep. comdr. Ala. 1950-51), Phi Beta Kappa, Phi Delta Phi. Editor: Index to Ofcl. Procs. Ala. Constl. Conv. of 1901, 1948. Home: Kinross Middleburg VA 22117 Office: 1629 K St NW Washington DC 20006

HUDDLESTON, JACKSON NOYES, lawyer; b. Creston, Wash., Nov. 18, 1908; s. Samuel L. and Agnes (Noyes) H.; A.B., U. Ill., 1930; LL.B., Harvard, 1933; m. Rita E. Bussell, Nov. 3, 1934; children—Jackson Noyes, Rita Ellen. Admitted to W.Va. bar, 1933, since practiced Huntington; asso. partner Huddleston, Bolen, Beatty, Porter & Copen and predecessor firms, 1933—; past pres., dir. Huntington Indsl. Corp.; dir. First Huntington Nat. Bank, Multi-State Build-Lease Co., Guyan Eagle Investment Co., Huntington Pub. Co., Kelly-Hatfield Land Co., First Huntington Co.; sec., dir. Modern Health Care, Inc.; Dist. chmn. Am. Bar Found., 1953. Charter mem. Huntington Galleries. Fellow Am. Bar Found., Am. Coll. Probate Counsel; mem. Am. Law Inst., Am. Judicature Soc., Am. (chmn. W.Va. membership com. jr. bar conf.), W.Va., Inter-Am., Cabell County bar assns., W.Va. State Bar (pres. 1957-58), Nat. Probation and Parole Assn. (local chmn. 1952-53), Newcomen Soc., C. of C., S.A.R. Methodist. Club: Guyan Golf and Country. Home: 225 High Dr Huntington WV 25705 Office: 1st Huntington Nat Bank Bldg Huntington WV 25722

HUDDLESTON, KENNETH EARL, assn. exec.; b. Covington, Ky., Sept. 3, 1915; s. Edward Charles and Agnes (Howard) H.; student Transylvania Coll., 1935-36, U. Cin., 1937; student orgn. mgmt., Northwestern U., 1955; certificate orgn. mgmt., Mich State U., 1957; m. Stella Rosa Dell Hiller, May 13, 1945; children—Rebecca Howard, Kim Ardene, Jan Aline. Freelance radio writer, Cin., 1936-37; pub. Bellevue-Dayton Pub. Co. (Ky.), 1938; ednl. radio program supr. U. Ky., 1939; dir. pub. service, ednl. dir. radio sta. WNOX, Knoxville, Tenn., 1940-42; with Dept. Agr., 1943-44, 44-49, 50-53, information specialist Soil Conservation Service, Washington, 1949-53; editor Nat. County Agent, also Vo-Ag Tchr., Phila., 1948; cons. Ware Bros. Pub. Co., 1949-51; asst. exec. sec., dir. pub. relations Farm Equipment Inst., Chgo., 1953-60; exec. sec., treas., Forest Products Research Soc., also bus. mgr. Forest Products Jour., Madison, Wis., 1960- -; trustee Forest Products Research Soc. Group Life Ins. Program, 1963- -. Mem. Am. Soc. Assn. Execs., Chgo. Forum Trade Assn. Execs. (past dir.), Chgo. Agrl. Club (past pres.), Nat. Wood Council. Presbyn. Mason, Rotarian. Contbr. articles profl. jours. Home: 4702 Odana Rd Madison WI 53711 Office: 417 N Walnut St Madison WI 53705

HUDDLESTON, TREVOR, clergyman; b. June 15, 1913; s. Capt. Sir Ernest Huddleston; student Christ Church Oxford, Wells Theol. Coll.; B.A., Oxford, 1934, M.A., 1937; D.D., Aberdeen U., 1956. Ordained to ministry P.E. Ch., deacon, 1936, priest, 1937; joined Community of Resurrection; apptd. priest in charge Sophiatown, Orlando Anglican missions, diocese of Johannesburg, 1943; provincial C.R., 1949-55, guardian of novices Community of Resurrection, Mirfield, Yorkshire, 1956-58; prior London House, 1958-60; bishop, Masasi, East Africa, 1960-69; suffragen bishop of Stepney, 1969- -. Recipient Anisfield-Wolf award. Club: Nab Working Men's (Mirfield) Author: Naught for your Comfort, 1956; The True and Living God; God's World. Address: care 400 Commercial Rd London E1 England

HUDDY, JOHN DENNIS, film critic; b. Pitts., Sept. 10, 1943; s. Norman Walter and Anna (Mergen) H.; student Ohio State U., 1960-66; m. Erica Trevor-Michaels, Apr. 12, 1969; 1 dau., Juliet Ann-Marie. Movie critic, columnist The Columbus (O.) Dispatch, 1965-69; corr. Variety, Columbus, 1968-69; critic-columnist Entertainment World mag., Los Angeles, 1969-70; pres., exec. producer Juliet TV Prodns., Miami and Columbus, 1969—; film and popular music critic Miami Herald, also entertainment editor, 1969-70; cons. pub. relations Performing Arts Mgmt., Columbus, 1968-70; host The Miami Scene TV program. Served with USMC, 1964-65. Recipient William Randolph Hearst prize for investigative reporting, 1964. Mem. Sigma Delta Ch. Club: Press (Ohio). Author: (screenplay) Commune. Home: 700 N E 23d St Miami FL 33137 Office: 1 Herald Plaza Miami FL 33101

HUDGINS, DANIEL EDWARD, lawyer; b. Marion, N.C., May 27, 1907; s. Daniel Edward and Josephine (Carter) H.; student Woodberry Forest Sch., Orange, Va., 1923-24; A.B., U. of N.C., 1928, student Law Sch., 1929; Jurisprudence degree, Oxford (Rhodes Scholar), 1931; m. Polly Fulford, Dec. 26, 1931 (dec. Apr. 1939); children—Margaret Anne, Edward; m. 2d, Elizabeth Banner, June 21, 1941; 1 dau., Elizabeth Banner. Admitted to N.C. bar, 1929; asso. law firm Brooks, Parker, Smith & Wharton, Greensboro, N.C., 1931-32; mem. firm Smith, Wharton & Hudgins, 1933-41; practiced individually, 1941-45; sr. mem. Hudgins & Adams, 1945-55, ret. 1955; sr. v.p., gen. counsel and dir. Jefferson Standard Life Ins. Co.; gen. counsel, dir. Jefferson-Pilot Corp.; dir. Burlington Industries, Inc. Mem. N.C. State Senate, 1943-45; chmn. Guilford County Bd. of Elections, 1939-43; chmn. bd. edn., Greensboro, 1947-55. Pres. Children's Home Soc. of N.C., 1956-58; pres. Greenboro United Fund, 1958- 59. Mem. Am., N.C., Greensboro bar assns., Assn. Life Ins. Counsel (pres. 1963-64), S.A.R. (pres. Gen. Greene chpt. 1948), Phi Beta Kappa, Kappa Sigma, Phi Delta Phi. Democrat. Episcopalian. Clubs: Rotary, Greensboro Country. Home: 1606 Nottingham Rd Greensboro NC 27408 Office: Jefferson Standard Bldg Greensboro NC 27408

HUDGINS, SAMUEL EDWARDS, accountant; b. New Brockton, Ala., Mar. 4, 1929; s. John Edward and Mary (Fowler) H.; B.S., U. Ala., 1951; m. Janet Epting, Nov. 22, 1951; children—Jan, Julie, John.

Staff accountant Arthur Andersen & Co., Atlanta, 1951-57, mgr., 1957-60, mgr., Chattanooga office, 1960-62, partner charge Chattanooga office, 1962—. Treas. Jr. Achievement of Chattanooga, 1966; pres. Hamilton County unit Am. Cancer Soc., 1966. Served with USNR, 1946-48. C.P.A., Ga., Tenn. Mem. Am. Inst. C.P.A.'s, Tenn. Soc. C.P.A.'s, Nat. Assn. Accountants (pres. Chattanooga chpt. 1966), Chattanooga C. of C. (dir.). Presbyn. Clubs: Chattanooga Golf and Country, Mountain City (Chattanooga). Office: Maclellan Bldg Chattanooga TN 37402

HUDGINS, WILLIAM COLES, telephone co. exec.; b. Norfolk, Va., Dec. 26, 1906; s. William R. and Addie (Lee) H.; B.S. in Mining Engring., Va. Polytech. Inst., 1928; m. Reba T. Clarkson, June 22, 1934; children—Ann Sayre (Mrs. Edward S. Newton), William Coles. Gen. plant mgr. Chesapeake & Potomac Telephone Co., Balt., 1949-51; asst. v.p. labor relations for Bell System, Am. Tel. & Tel. Co., 1951-53; v.p. personnel Mountain States Tel. & Tel. Co., Denver, 1953-58, v.p. operations, now exec. v.p., dir.; dir., mem. exec. com. 1st Nat. Bank Denver. Dir., v.p. Boys Clubs Denver; trustee Denver United Way (chmn. 1967), Denver Art Mus. Mem. C. of C. (former group v.p., dir., chmn. steering com.). Clubs: Denver Athletic, Lions (past pres.), University, Denver, Denver Country (Denver); Annapolis (Md.) Yacht, Gyro. Home: 4949 E 6th Av Pkwy Denver, CO 80220. Office: 931 14th St Denver CO 80202

HUDNALL, JARRETT, Jr., educator; b. Rhome, Tex., Oct. 6, 1931; s. Jarrett and Katherine (Wilson) H.; student Arlington State Coll., 1948-50; B.B.A., U. Tex., Austin, 1953, M.B.A., 1956; Ph.D., U. Ala., 1966; m. Sarah Ruth Warren, Nov. 24, 1955; children—Jarrett Joseph, William Warren, Katherine Lee, Thomas Wilson. Lectr., U. Tex., 1955-56; asst. prof. Arlington State Coll., 1956-58; instr. U. Ala., 1958-61; asst. prof. La Tech. U., 1961-62, asso. prof. marketing, 1962-67, prof., head dept. bus. 1967—; cons. firms in chem. fertilizer, petroleum, farm equipment mfg., distbg. bus. Served to lt. AUS, 1953-55. Gulf Oil Corp. fellow, 1963. Mem. Am., So. marketing assns., S.W. Social Sci. Assn., Beta Gamma Sigma, Alpha Kappa Psi. Democrat. Baptist. Author: (with A.L. Seeyle) Compensation of Retail Department Store and Specialty Store Salesman in Major Texas Cities, 1957; Attitudes of Gulf Service Station Dealers Toward Minor Tuneup and Repair Work, 1963; An Economic Analysis of Income and Employment in a Four-State Deep South Region, 1950-1960, 1966. Home: 1003 Lakeview Av Ruston LA 71270

HUDNUT, WILLIAM HERBERT, Jr., clergyman; b. Youngstown, O., May 29, 1905; s. William Herbert and Harriet (Beecher) H.; A.B., Princeton, 1927, D.D., 1967; B.D., Union Theol. Sem., 1930; D.D., Blackburn Coll., 1940; LL.D., Huron Coll., 1960; L.H.D., Pikeville Coll., 1964; m. Elizabeth Kilborne, Nov. 21, 1931; children—William Herbert III, Robert Kilborne, David Beecher, Stewart Skinner, Harriet Katharine, Thomas Cushman. Ordained to ministry Presbyn. Ch., 1930; dir. religion The Hill Sch., Pottstown, Pa., 1930-32; pastor Glendale Presbyn. Ch., Cin., 1932-40; First Presbyn. Ch., Springfield, Ill., 1940-46; Third Presbyn. Ch., Rochester, N.Y. 1946-64; nat. chmn. Presbyn. 50 Million Fund, 1964-67; interim pastor Chevy Chase (Md.) Presbyn. Ch., 1967-69, 1st Ch., Evanston, Ill., 1970, Brick Ch., N.Y.C., 1970-71. Dir. McCormick Theol. Sem., Chgo., 1942-49; pres. Westminister Found. N.Y. 1947-53; mem. nat. student commn. YMCA, 1946-57; mem. Presbyn. U.S.A. Gen. Council, 1950-58, 64-67. Bd. dirs. Union Sem., N.Y.; mem. bd. Nat. Missions Presbyn. Ch. U.S.A., 1962- 64. Clubs: Princeton (N.Y.C.); Rochester City (pres. 1952-53), Rochester Country, University. Home: Windover North Creek NY 12853 Office: 62 E 92d St New York City NY 10028

HUDON, CHARLES WILLIAM, wire and cable co. exec.; b. Richmond, Ind., Feb. 19, 1909; s. Charles W. and Ella (Warren) H.; grad. Northwestern U., 1935; m. Sylvia C. Clawson, Feb. 26, 1938 (dec. May 1966); children—Karen, Gail (Mrs. John Murray); m. 2d, Leone Modine Clark. With Belden Mfg. Co. (co. name changed to Belden Corp.) 1928—, now sr. v.p., treas., sec., dir.; chmn. bd. Complete Reading Elec., Mid-States Indsl. Corp. Mem. Newcomen Soc. N.Am., Ill. Mfrs. Assn., Nat. Elec. Mfrs. Assn., Ill. Mfrs. Costs Assn. (pres. 1963-64, chmn. adv. bd. 1964—). Clubs: Economic (Chgo.); Glen Oak. Home: 281 Merton Av Glen Ellyn, IL 60137. Office: 415 S Kilpatrick Av Chicago IL 60624

HUDSON, ANDREW, art critic, painter; b. Birmingham, Eng., July 9, 1935; s. John Christipher and Audrey (Turner) H.; student Malvern Coll., Eng., 1948- 53; B.A., Oxford (Eng.) U., 1957; postgrad. Slade Sch. Fine Art, London, Eng., 1957-59, U. Sask. (Can.), 1961-62. Came to U.S., 1965. Tchr. art extension div. U. Sask., 1962-65; exhibited one man shows James Art Studio, Sask., 1962, Galerie du Siecle, Montreal, Que., 1965; rep. permanent collection Nat. Gallery Can. Ottawa; art critic Washington Post, 1965, now art editor. Contbr. articles, revs. to art jours. Office: 1515 L St N W Washington DC 20005

HUDSON, ANTHONY WEBSTER, govt. ofcl.; b. Durham, N.C., Mar. 23, 1937; s. Emanuel and Adele (Nixon) H.; student Rutgers U., 1954-59, Columbia, 1960-62, George Washington U., 1967—; m. Glenda Buchanan, Jan. 18, 1964; children—April Lynn, Verna Lea. Personnel mgmt. specialist U.S. Civil Service Commn., N.Y.C., 1962-65, tng. officer personnel div., Washington, 1966, tng. officer Bur. Tng., 1967, coordinator Project 250 Bur. Tng., 1968-70, dir. personnel, 1970—; asso. mem. Govt. Services, Inc., Washington; instr. U.S. Dept. Agr. Grad. Sch. Served from 2d lt. to 1st lt., arty., U.S. Army, 1959-60. Recipient Spl. citation U.S. Civil Service Commn., 1969, William A. Jump Meml. award, 1970. Mem. Am. Soc. Tng. and Devel. (exec. bd., chmn. community services 1966-68), D.C. Sociol. Soc., Am. Personnel and Guidance Assn., Soc. Personnel Adminstrn. (exec. com. 1971—), Phi Sigma Delta. Conglist. Club: Rutgers (Washington). Contbr. to Ency. of Edn., 1971. Home: 7309 Pinehurst Pkwy Chevy Chase MD 20015 Office: 1900 E St NW Washington DC 20415

HUDSON, ARTHUR PALMER, educator; b. Palmer's Hall, Miss., May 14, 1892; s. William Arthur and Lou Garnett (Palmer) H.; B.S., U. Miss., 1913, A.M., 1920; A.M., U. Chgo., 1925; Ph.D., U. N.C., 1930; m. Grace McNulty Noah, Sept. 12, 1916; children—William (dec.), Margaret Louise (Mrs. Almand R. Coleman), Ellen Noah (Mrs. Richard B. Vowles). Prin., Gulfport (Miss.) High Sch., 1913-18; supt. schs., Oxford, Miss., 1919-20; asst. prof. English, U. Miss., 1920-24, asso. prof., 1924-27, prof., 1927-30; asso. prof. English, U. N.C., Chapel Hill, 1930- 35, prof., 1935-51, Kenan prof., 1951-63, Kenan prof. emeritus, 1963—. Prof. English, U. Fla., summers 1938-39. Recipient Smith research prize U. N.C., 1930; fellow in humanities Gen. Edn. Bd., Rockefeller Found., 1934-35. Fellow Am. Folklore Soc., Soc. Am. Historians; mem. Vanderbilt Conf. Humanities (exec. com.), N.C. Folklore Council (chmn.), N.C. (Brown-Hudson award 1970, v.p., sec.-treas.), Miss. (hon. life), Southeastern (exec. com.) folklore socs., South Atlantic Modern Lang. Assn. Am., Modern Lang. Assn., Am. Coll. English Assn., Nat. Folk Festival Assn., Phi Beta Kappa. Democrat. Episcopalian. Author, editor, 1937—; publs. include: Folklore and Folksongs in Dictionary of Am. History, 1940; Folklore, in a Literary History of the U.S. (editors: Robert Spiller, Willard Thorp, others), 1948; Am. Popular Literature in Chambers Ency.; vols. II, III of Frank C. Brown Collection of North Carolina Folklore (with H.M. Belden), 1952; Folklore in American Literature (with John T. Flanagan), 1958; Folklore Keeps the Past Alive, 1962; Songs of the Carolina Charter Colonists (1663-1763), 1962. Editor: N.C. Folklore, 1954-64. Contbr. folklore, articles to profl. jours. Home: 710 Greenwood Rd Chapel Hill NC 27514 ☆

HUDSON, BENJAMIN FRANKLIN, Jr., educator; b. Selma, Ala., Aug. 30, 1917; s. Benjamin Franklin and Geneva (Jackson) H.; A.B., Fisk U., 1946; M.A., U. Mich., 1947, Ph.D., 1958; diplome, U. Paris (France), 1952; m. Ellen Webb, Apr. 15, 1943; 1 son, Richard Byron. Mem. faculty N.C. Coll., 1948-59, asso. prof. French, 1958-59; prof. French, chmn. dept. modern fgn. langs. Southern U., 1959-61; prof. French, chmn. dept. Atlanta U. 1961—; dir. Nat. Def. Edn. Act Summer Lang. Inst., 1961, 63, 64. Chpt. pres. Nat. Assn. Retarded Children. Served with AUS, 1942-46; ETO. Carnegie grantee, 1949; Fulbright fellow, 1951; Danforth teaching fellow, 1956. Mem. Am. Assn. U. Profs., Modern Lang. Assn., Am. Assn. Tchrs. French, Nat., Ga. edn. assns., Alpha Phi Alpha. Home: 502 Harlan Rd S W Atlanta GA 30311

HUDSON, BRADFORD BENEDICT, educator; b. San Jose, Cal., Dec. 8, 1906; s. Charles Bradford and Grace (Barnhisel) H.; B.A., Stanford, 1930; Ph.D. In Psychology, U. Cal. at Berkeley, 1947; m. Mary Elizabeth MacLaughlin, May 20, 1937; 1 dau., Annis Bradford. Research asst. NRC contract Princeton, 1941-43; mem. assessment bd. OSS, 1943-45; chief personnel and survey sect. CIA, 1946- 47; mem. faculty Rice U., 1948—, prof. psychology, 1955—. Dir. Middle East Cross-Cultural Research Program, 1952-58; asst. program dir. NSF, 1961-62. Bd. dirs. Settlement House Program, Houston, 1949-54. Fellow Am. Psychol. Assn.; mem. Southwest, Tex. psychol. assns., Middle East Inst., Am. Assn. U. Profs. Author monographs. Home: 19827 White Dove Trail Crosby TX 77532 Office: Rice U Houston TX 77001

HUDSON, CHARLES LOWELL, physician; b. Merill, Mich., Aug. 5, 1904; s. James Harvey and Sophia (Dunn) H.; A.B., magna cum laude, Alma (Mich.) Coll., 1924, LL.D., 1967; M.D. cum laude, U. Mich., 1930; m. Ruth Strong, Sept. 29, 1937; children—Judith Harvey (Mrs. Colby), Charles Lowell, Mary. Intern, U. Hosps., Cleve., 1930-31, asst. resident, 1931-32, chief resident medicine, 1934-35, asst. physician, 1935-56, asso. physician, physician charge out-patient dept., 1956-62; research fellow pharmacology and kidney physiology U. Pa., 1932-34; faculty Case Western Res. U., 1935-63, asso. clin. prof. medicine, 1956-68, asso. clin. prof. preventive medicine, 1958-63, prof. health and dir. univ. health service, 1958-61; asso. prof. medicine Cleve. Clin. Ednl. Found., 1962- 69; pvt. practice Cleve., 1937-69; sr. cons. Cleve. Clinic, 1968-69, sr. cons. emeritus, 1969—, coordinator health care programs, 1970—; sr. attending physician Cleve. VA Hosp., 1946-62. Mem. adv. com. medicine Blue Cross Northeast Ohio, 1955-67, citizens hosp. study com., 1955-61; active Cleve. Welfare Fedn., 1953—, mem. chronically ill com., 1955-67, chmn. com. home care plans, 1955-56, trustee, 1962-67, com. health plan and devel., 1969—; mem. com. profl. problems Cleve. Hosp. Council, 1955, mem. com. community resources nursing edn., 1961; mem. com. careers Nat. League Nursing, 1958-61, program rev. com., trustee, 1969—. Served to lt. col. M.C., AUS, World War II. Recipient award Cuyahoga County Med. Soc., 1958. Diplomate Am. Bd. Internal Medicine. Mem. A.C.P., A.M.A. (pres. 1966-67, numerous coms. and councils), Cleve. Acad. Medicine (pres. 1952-53), Ohio Med. Assn. (pres., chmn. council, speaker ho. of dels. 1955-56, chmn. com. govt. relations 1956-62), Cleve. Med. Library Assn. (pres. 1962-63), Pasteur Club, Nat. Acad. Scis. (panel on health services 1968—), Galens Soc., Alpha Omega Alpha, Phi Kappa Phi. Presbyn. Home: 13605 Shaker Blvd Cleveland OH 44120 Office: Cleveland Clinic 2020 E 93d St Cleveland OH 44106

HUDSON, CHARLES MELL, educator; b. Nashville, Mar. 8, 1912; s. Charles M. and Nell (Dortch) H.; B.A., Vanderbilt U., 1933, M.A., 1934; Ph.D. in English, Yale, 1943; m. Clara Marksbury, June 12, 1954. Instr. English, Lafayette Coll., 1938- 39; faculty U. Mo., Columbia, 1939—, prof. English, 1954—, chmn. dept., 1956- 60, 65-67. Mem. Modern Lang. Assn., Phi Beta Kappa. Democrat. Baptist. Editor: (with Clark, Pace, Dickinson) English Literature: A College Anthology, 1960. Home: 12 E Stewart Rd Columbia MO 65201

HUDSON, DONALD ELLIS, educator; b. Alma, Mich., Feb. 25, 1916; s. Albert W. and Ruth (Ellis) H.; B.S., Cal. Inst. Tech., 1938, M.S., 1939, Ph.D., 1942. Prof. mech. engring. and applied mechanics Cal. Inst. Tech., Pasadena, 1941—. Mem. Am. Soc. M.E., Am. Soc. for Engring. Edn., Soc. Exptl. Stress Analysis, Am. Geophys. Union, Seismol. Soc. Am. (pres., dir., editorial com.). Author: (with G.W. Housner) Applied Mechanics, Statics and Dynamics, 1949-50. Office: 1201 E California St Pasadena CA 91109

HUDSON, EARL ROSS, advt. exec., b. Boston, Jan. 10, 1909; s. Rollo and Laura (Austrup) H.; B.S. in Bus. Adminstrn., Boston U., 1931; postgrad. banking and finance N.Y. U., 1939; m. Gladys Macafee, Apr. 16, 1932; children—Ross D., Peter M. With trust dept. N.Y. Trust Co., 1935-41; with Kennedy Sinclaire, Inc., financial advt. agy., Wayne, N.J., 1941—, pres., 1954—, chmn. bd., 1971—, also dir. Faculty trust schs. various state bank assns.; adv. bd. Bank N.J. Bd. visitors Boston U. Coll. Bus. Adminstrn. Served as air combat intelligence officer USNR, 1943-46. Mem. Bank Marketing Assn. Clubs: Upper Ridgewood (N.J.) Tennis; East Chop (Mass.) Assn. (dir.). Contbr. articles to trade jours. Home: 355 Godwin Av Ridgewood NJ 07470 Office: 524 Hamburg Turnpike Wayne NJ 07470

HUDSON, EDWARD JOSEPH, constrn. co. exec.; b. Newark, Mar. 13, 1904; s. Wilbur E. and Marion (Dooley) H.; M.E., Stevens Inst. Tech., N.J., 1926, D.Eng., 1953; m. Cecil Amelia Blaffer, Aug. 7, 1945; children—Edward Joseph, Robert Lee. Pres., chmn. bd. Hudson Engring. Corp., Houston, 1934—; chmn. bd. J. Ray McDermott & Co., Inc., New Orleans, 1969—; dir. Gulf Resources & Chem. Corp., Houston. Pres., Hudson Found. Del., Republican Nat. Conv., 1968. Bd. dirs. St. Joseph Hosp. Found., Houston; trustee Houston Mus. Fine Arts, Stevens Inst. Tech. Registered profl. engr., Tex. Mem. Am. Petroleum Inst., Beta Theta Pi. Clubs: River Oaks Country, Petroleum, Ramada (Houston); Sleepy Hollow Country (N.Y.C.); Boston (New Orleans). Home: 5449 Tupper Lake Houston TX 77027 Office: 5900 Hillcroft St P O Box 36100 Houston TX 77036

HUDSON, ELLWOOD FRANKLIN, banker; b. Camden, N.J., Feb. 27, 1931; s. Leonard and Esther (Ross) H.; B.A., U. Pa., 1962; student U. Wis., 1968; m. Emily Harvey Huber, Nov. 14, 1965; 1 son, John Steven. Examiner, Fidelity Bank, Phila., 1957-63; sr. examiner First Nat. Bank S. Jersey, Pleasantville, N.J., 1963, asst. auditor, 1964, auditor, 1964-66; asst. auditor United Va. Bank State Planters, Richmond, Va., 1967-69, auditor, 1969-70; gen. auditor United Va. Bankshares, Inc., Richmond, 1970—. Named One of Outstanding Young Men of Am., U.S. Jaycees, 1967. Mem. Inst. Internal Auditors (v.p. Richmond chpt.), Fidelity Bank Employees Assn. (pres. 1963), N.J. Jaycees (treas. 1966). Home: 9311 Brundidge Rd Richmond VA 23235 Office: 900 E Main St Richmond VA 23219

HUDSON, GEORGE ELBERT, research physicist; b. Pitts., Apr. 25, 1916; s. George Elbert, Jr., and Mary Jane (Wilson) H.; B.S., George Washington U., 1938; Sc.M., Brown U., 1940, Ph.D., 1942; m. Olive Gallant, June 24, 1939; children—George, Brian, Nancy. Vis. prof. physics Georgetown U., 1943-44; asso. prof. physics N.Y. U., 1946-49, prof. physics, 1949-63; physicist Taylor Model Basin, U.S. Navy, 1942-46; dir. research Smyth Research Assos., 1956-57; cons. Naval Ordnance Lab., 1957- 59, Brookhaven Nat. Lab., 1958-61, Woods Hole Oceanographic Instn., 1959- 61, Avco Corp., 1961-62; cons. Nat. Bur. Standards, 1962-63, asst. chief radio physics div., Boulder, Colo., 1963-67, cons. time and frequency div., Inst. Basic Standards, Nat. Bur. Standards, 1967-71; sr. research cons. Naval Ordnance Lab., 1971—. Adj. prof. physics Denver U., 1965-69. Fellow Am. Phys. Soc., A.A.A.S.; mem. Washington Philos. Soc., Sigma Xi, Sigma Pi Sigma, Delta Tau Delta. Club: Cosmos (Washington). Contbr. articles physics and math. profl. publs. Home: 750 Cascade Av Boulder CO 80302 Office: Naval Ordnance Laboratory White Oak-Silver Spring MD 20910

HUDSON, HAROLD JORDON, Jr., ins. co. exec.; b. Kansas City, Mo., Mar. 10, 1924; s. Harold Jordan and Fannie (Jenkins) H.; B.S., U. Mo., 1945, LL.B., 1948; grad. Advanced Mgmt. Program Harvard, 1968 m. Patricia Louise Orr, Oct. 1, 1949. Admitted to Mo. bar, 1948; practice in Kansas City until 1952; atty. Comml. Union Co., Kansas City, 1952-53, Cleve., 1953-56; atty. Gen. Reins. Corp., N.Y.C., 1956-58, asst. sec., 1958-61, sec., 1961-62, v.p., 1963-68, sr. v.p., 1968-70, pres., 1970—, also dir.; dir. Herbert Clough, Inc., North Star Reins. Corp., Gen. Reassurance Co. Mem. Mo. Bar, Phi Delta Phi, Kappa Alpha. Clubs: Union League (Chgo.); Metropolitan (N.Y.C.). Home: 420 E 51st St New York City NY 10022 Office: 400 Park Av New York City NY 10022

HUDSON, HARRIET DUFRESNE, coll. dean; b. Kirby, Pa., July 14, 1912; d. William Mestrezat and Florence Ronald (Barclay) Hudson; student Blackburn Coll., 1929-30, LL.D., 1957; A.B., Wellesley Coll., 1933; M.A., U. Chgo., 1936, Ph.D., 1950. Grader Harvard Grad. Sch. Bus. Adminstrn., 1937-39; instr. econs. and sociology Pine Manor Jr. Coll., 1939-42, Mt. Holyoke Coll., 1942-47; asst. prof. econs. U. Ill., Urbana, 1948-53; prof. econs., dean coll. Randolph-Macon Woman's Coll., Lynchburg, Va., 1953—. Bd. dirs. Tuition Exchange, 1957-68; trustee Coll. Entrance Examination Bd., 1963-66. Mem. Am. Econ. Assn., Indsl. Relations Research Assn., Am. Assn. U. Women, So. Econ. Assn., Am. Council on Edn. (com. on coll. teaching 1959-61), Assn. for Higher Edn. (exec. com. 1959-61), So. Assn. Colls. and Schs. (com. on standards and reports 1960-70, exec. council commn. on colls. 1971—), Alliance Francaise, P.E.O. Presbyn. Home: 232 Norfolk Av Lynchburg VA 24503

HUDSON, HARRY TATE, oil co. exec.; b. Toronto, Ont., Can. Dec. 26, 1914; s. George William and Alice (White) H.; grad. high sch.; m. Merle Lois Rands, Sept. 16, 1939; children—Gerald, Robert, Paul. Profl. musician, 1934-40; office mgr. Texaco, Montreal, Que., Can., 1941-47 statistician, 1948- 57, mgr. econs., 1958-67, treas., 1968—. Active Boy Scouts Can. Mem. United Ch. Can. (chmn. music com., carilloneur). Home: 245 Sanford Av St Lambert Quebec Canada Office: 1425 Mountain St Montreal Quebec Canada

HUDSON, HINTON GARDNER, lawyer; b. Smithfield, N.C., Nov. 1, 1896; s. James Buchanan and Sarah Agnes (Woodall) H.; A.B., U. N.C., 1916; LL.B., Harvard, 1919; m. Margaret Baggs, Aug. 6, 1927; children—Margaret (Mrs. John M. Blades), Hinton Gardner, Gordon L. Admitted to N.C. bar, 1919, since practiced in Winston-Salem; sr. partner of firm Hudson, Petree, Stockton, Stockton & Robinson; lectr. law Wake Forest Coll., 1963. Mem. N.C. Gen. Statutes Commn., 1960-70, chmn., 1967-70. Rep. Gen. Assembly N.C., 1943-45. Served with USN, 1918. Recipient spl. resolutions of Commendation for 10 Years Service on N.C. Gen. Statutes Commn. (including 1st rewriting of Rules Civil Procedure since 1868), from N. C. Gen. Assembly, N.C. State Bar and N.C. Bar Assn., 1970. Mem. Am., N.C., Forsyth County (past pres.), Forsyth County Jr. (founder, past pres.) bar assn., N.C. State Bar (councillor 1959- 68), Phi Beta Kappa. Democrat. Methodist. Clubs: Forsyth Country (pres. 1957), Winston-Salem Torch. Home: 303 Arbor Rd Winston-Salem NC 27104 Office: Reynolds Bldg Winston-Salem NC 27101

HUDSON, JESSE TUCKER, Jr., banker; b. Roanoke, Va., Sept. 25, 1920; s. Jesse Tucker and Bernice (Ragland) H.; B.A. in Econs., U. Va., 1945, postgrad. in econs., 1946; m. Bert Browning Wood, June 9, 1944; children—A. Gregory, David Wood, Amy Jean. Staff asso. T. Coleman Andrews & Co., Richmond, Va., 1946-49; sr. accountant A.M. Pullen & Co., Richmond, 1949-54; asst. controller Millers Rhoads, Inc., Richmond, 1954-59; comptroller, asst. treas. U. Pitts., 1959-64, vice chancellor finance, 1964; v.p. finance, treas. Colonial Stores, Inc., Atlanta, 1964-69; v.p. finance, adminstrn., dir. Davis Food Service, Inc., Atlanta, 1970-71; v.p.-finance S.E. Banking Corp., Miami, Fla., 1971—. Pres., Richmond Young Republican Club, 1947-48, Young Rep. Club Va., 1948-49; alternate del. Rep. Nat. Conv., 1948. Served to maj. AUS, 1941-45. Mem. Am. Econ. Assn., Financial Execs. Inst., Am. Mgmt. Assn., Nat. Assn. Accountants. Home: 735 Coronado Av Coral Gables FL 33143 Office: 100 S Biscayne Blvd Miami FL 33131

HUDSON, JOHN ALLEN, librarian; b. Beaumont, Tex., May 14, 1927; s. Walter Byron and Bessie (Aman) H.; B.A., U. Tex. at Austin, 1951, M.A., 1954; M.L.S., Case Western Res. U., 1957; m. Genevieve Lynch, Jan. 3, 1948. Librarian journalism and newspaper collection U. Tex. at Austin, 1951-54; state dir. library extension Tex. State Library, Austin, 1954-56; univ. librarian U. Tex. at Arlington, 1957—. Pres. Texas Council. State Coll. Librarians, 1968—. Trustee Arlington (Tex.) Pub. Library. Served with USNR, 1944-45. Mem. Am., Southwestern, Tex. library assns., Am. Hist. Assn., Southwestern Social Sci. Assn. Author: (with George Wolfskill) All but the People: Franklin D. Roosevelt and His Critics, 1933-39, 1969. Home: 1409 Juanita Dr Arlington TX 76013

HUDSON, JOHN IMBODEN, Jr., former editorial cartoonist; b. Portsmouth, O., Mar. 8, 1899; s. John Imboden and Lizzie (Doty) H.; student Chgo. Acad. Fine Arts, Columbus (O.) Art Sch., Western Res. U.; m. Florence Maria Spencer, Sept. 20, 1929; 1 dau., Mrs. Martha Casey. Editorial cartoonist Columbus Citizen, 1924-42; editorial artist and cartoonist Toledo Blade, 1942-45; cartoonist Erie (Pa.) Dispatch Herlad, 1945-47; editorial cartoonist Cleve. News, 1947- 6O, Phoenix Gazette, 1960-69, ret., 1969. Served with F.A., U.S. Army, 1918. Rep. permanent collections Mo. Hist. Soc., Huntington Park Library, U. Cal at Los Angeles, Syracuse U., Archives Am. Art. Detroit, Albert T. Reid Cartoon Collection U. Kan., U. Mo. Sch. Journalism. Recipient Freedoms Found. award 1964-66, Best Editorial Cartoon Cleve. Newspaper Guild, 1949, 52, 53, 55-57, Best Cartoon award Ariz. Press Club, 1960. Mem. Nat. Cartoonist Soc., Assn. Am. Editorial Cartoonists. Home: 6333 Mt Ada Rd San Diego CA 92111

HUDSON, JOSEPH A., banker; b. 1911; student Syracuse U., mgmt. clinic U. Rochester, Rutgers U. Grad. Sch. Banking; married. With Universal Credit Corp., Watertown, N.Y., 1936-41, Cornell Theatres, Inc., 1946; br. mgr. Installment Credit Corp., N.Y.C.,

1946-48; with Lincoln-Rochester Trust Co., 1948-70, sr. v.p., 1965-70; adminstrv. v.p. Lincoln First Banks Inc. Served with AUS, 1941-46. Address: 183 E Main St Rochester NY 14603

HUDSON, JOSEPH LOWTHIAN, Jr., merc. co. exec.; b. Buffalo, July 4, 1931; s. Joseph L. and Elizabeth (Gilbert) H.; B.A., Yale, 1953; m. Jean Bent Wright, Aug. 9, 1952; children—Joseph L. IV, Jean Croy, Richard Webber, Louise Wright. Exec. trainee J.L. Hudson Co., Detroit, 1953-54, asst. to gen. mgr., 1956, v.p., asst. gen. mgr., 1957, v.p., gen. mgr., 1957-61, pres., 1961—, also dir.; vice chmn., dir. Dayton Hudson Corp.; dir. Nat. Bank of Detroit, Mich. Bell Telephone Co., Detroit Edison Co.; dir., mem. exec. com. Asso. Merchandising Corp. Past chmn., dir. Met. Fund; past chmn. New Detroit Com. Pres., Eloise and Richard Webber Found.; v.p., dir. United Found.; trustee Hudson-Webber Found., Univ.-Liggett Sch. and Founders Soc., Detroit Inst. Arts; trustee, vice chmn. Harper Hosp. Served to 1st lt. AUS, 1954-56. Recipient Distinguished Service award Detroit Jr. C. of C. 1960; Layman's Spl. Civic Leadership award Met. Detroit Council Chs., 1968; B'nai B'rith Humanitarian award, 1970. Clubs: Country Club of Detroit, Detroit Athletic, Detroit; Grosse Pointe Club; Minneapolis. Office: 1206 Woodward Av Detroit MI 48226

HUDSON, KEITH PANTING, corp. exec. b. Robin, Ida., Feb. 7, 1914; s. Parley Robins and Frances (Panting) H.; B.S., U. Utah, 1935; student George Washington U., 1938-40; m. Arlene Good, Sept. 3, 1944; children—Kay, Lynne, Joan, Anne, Gail. With S & W Fine Foods, Inc., San Francisco, 1958-63, exec. v.p., 1962-63, also dir.; v.p., dir. DiGiorgio Fruit Corp., 1958-63, R.S.P. Car Co., 1959-63; pres., dir. Klamath Lumber & Box Co., Inc., 1958-63; v.p. finance Weber Showcase & Fixture Co., Inc., Los Angeles, 1963-65; v.p. Dillingham Corp., Honolulu, 1965-69, sr. v.p. adminstrn. and corporate devel., 1969—, also dir.; dir. Cal. Liquid Gas Corp., Dillingham Petroleum Corp., Maui Divers Hawaii Ltd. Mem. Financial Execs. Inst. (pres. San Francisco 1963-64, dir. Hawaii 1965-66), Am. Mgmt. Assn., Honolulu C. of C., Hawaii Mfrs. Assn. (pres., dir.). Clubs: Commonwealth, Mzuri Safari (San Francisco); Toastmasters (pres. Walnut Creek 1961); Oahu Country, Waialae Country (Honolulu). Home: 161 Wailupe Circle Honolulu HI 96821 Office: P O Box 3468 Honolulu HI 96801

HUDSON, KENNETH EUGENE, artist; b. Xenia, O., Dec. 28, 1903; s. George Ernest and Anna (Scott) H.; student Ohio Wesleyan U., 1921-23; B.F.A., Yale, 1927; m. Gwendolyn Belle Mills, June 28, 1925; 1 dau., Ann Lee. Studio asst. to Eugene F. Savage, mural painter, 1925-26; asst. prof. U. Ore. Sch. Fine Arts, 1927-29; prof., chmn. fine arts dept. U. Mo. Sch. Fine Arts, 1927-38, residence in Europe, chiefly Brussels, Belgium, 1935-36; dean St. Louis Sch. Fine Arts, Washington U., 1938-69, dean emeritus, 1969—, dean schs. architecture and fine arts, 1952-53. Mural paintings: 6 panels in dormitory U. Ore.; Hendrix Hall, U. Mo.; 12 panels council chamber Municipal Bldg., Columbia, Mo.; triptychs, Citizens Com. for Army and Navy. Pres., Nat. Assn. Schs. Design, 1953-55. Fellow Belgian-Am. Ednl. Found. Fellow Nat. Assn. Schs. Art; mem. Phi Delta Theta. Home: 7900 Stanford Av St Louis MO 63130

HUDSON, L. DENIS, Canadian financial exec.; b. Dec. 21, 1924; ed. Laval U., also U. Toronto. With econ. policy div. Dept. Finance, Ottawa, 1948-51; financial sec. Permanent Canadian Mission to NATO, 1952-54; with internat. and econ. div. Dept. Finance, Ottawa, 1954-60; dir. policy and planning coordination External Aid Office, 1960-61; alt. dir. Internat. Monetary Fund, Internat. Bank Reconstrn. and Devel., Internat. Devel. Assn., 1961-64, exec. sec. for Can., Ireland and Jamaica, 1965—. also asst. dir. gen. external aid office, Ottawa; financial counsellor Canadian embassy, Washington, 1961-64; dir. internat. programs div. Dept. Finance, Ottawa, 1964—. Address: care Dept Finance Ottawa Ontario Canada

HUDSON, NOEL PAUL, educator; b. Lincoln, Ill., Jan. 9, 1895; s. George Gary and Delia Ann (Herndon) H.; A.B., James Millikin U., 1917, Sc.D. (hon.), 1951; Ph.D., U. Chgo., 1923; postgrad. Rush Med. Coll., 1920-24; M.D., Harvard, 1925; Sc.D., Ohio State U., 1965; m. Emily Madlin, June 11, 1925; children—Robert Paul, Stephen Perry. Asst. pathologist Boston City Hosp., 1925-27; yellow fever research Rockefeller Found., 1927-30; prof. dept. bacteriology U. Chgo., 1930-35; prof., chmn. dept. bacteriology Ohio State U., 1935-46, dean Grad. Sch., 1946-56, asst. dean Coll. Medicine, 1956-61, research prof. dept. bacteriology, 1946-61, prof. emeritus microbiology, 1961—. Rep. Rockefeller Found., London, Eng., 1940-41 in war health program-on leave from Ohio State Univ. Served from pvt. to 2d lt. San. Corps, U.S. Army, AEF, 1918-19; on leave from Ohio State U. to serve with War Dept. as civilian cons., 1943-45. Fellow Am. Pub. Health Assn., A.A.A.S., Ohio Acad. Scis., Am. Acad. Microbiology, Am. Soc. Tropical Medicine and Hygiene (pres. 1942-43); mem. Soc. Am. Bacteriologists, Assn. Grad. Schs. (sec.-treas. 1948-51, pres. 1953-54), Am. Assn. U. Profs., Ohio Acad. Med. History (pres. 1963-64), Phi Beta Kappa, Sigma Xi, Gamma Alpha, Alpha Omega Alpha, Alpha Kappa Kappa, Tau Kappa Epsilon. Conglist. Contbr. numerous articles to sci., ednl. jours. Home: Wesley Manor Jacksonville FL 32223 ☆

HUDSON, PHILIP GRAYDON, educator; b. Phoenix, Aug. 27, 1909; s. James Elisha and Eunice (Johnson) H.; B.S., U. Ariz., 1930, M.S., 1933; Ph.D., U. Ill., 1938; m. Irene Tatum, Sept. 1, 1934 (dec. 1942); children—Phyllis Rose (Mrs. Paul A. Bering), Philip Graydon, Kathryn Jeanne; m. 2d, Edna Earle Moore, Aug. 11, 1943. Instr. econs. U. Ariz., Tucson, 1938-42, asst. prof., 1942-48, asso. prof., 1948-53, prof., 1953—, dept. head, 1958-65, dir. grad. studies, 1965—; price analyst OPA, Washington, 1942-43; cons. Employment Security Commn. Ariz., Ariz. Dept. Property Evaluation. Incorporator, Saguaro Credit Union. Served to lt. comdr. USNR, 1943-46. Recipient Faculty Recognition award Tucson Retail Trade Bur., 1966, Creativity in Teaching award U. Ariz. Found., 1970. Mem. Am., Western econ. assns. Nat. Tax Assn., Ariz. Acad., Phi Beta Kappa. Kiwanian. Club: Conquistador (past pres.) (Tucson). Author: (with others) The Economy of Arizona, 3d edit., 1970. Contbr. articles profl. jours. Home: 2141 E Edison St Tucson AZ 85719

HUDSON, RALPH PERCY, physicist; b. Wellingborough, Eng., Oct. 14, 1924; s. Harold and Ada (Jenkinson) H.; B.A., Merton Coll., Oxford U., 1944, M.A., 1949, Ph.D., 1949; m. Nancy Brisby, July 9, 1947; children—Geoffrey R., Wendy E. Came to U.S. 1949, naturalized, 1960. Sci. officer U.K. Ministry Supply, Birmingham, Eng., Montreal, Que. and Chalk River, Can., 1944-46; vis. lectr. Purdue U., 1949-50, asst. prof., 1950-51; with Nat. Bur. Standards, Washington, 1951—, chief cryogenic physics sect., 1954-61, chief heat div., 1961—. Mem. U.K. Home Guard, 1941-43, U.K. Atomic Energy Program, 1944-46. Recipient Silver, Gold medals Dept. Commerce, 1957; Samuel Wesley Stratton award Nat. Bur. Standards, 1964. Guggenheim fellow, 1960-61. Fellow Am. Phys. Soc., Franklin Inst. (John Price Wetherill medal 1962); mem. Philos. Soc. Washington, Sigma Xi. Spl. research behavior matter near absolute zero temperature. Home: 3101 Aberfoyle Pl NW Washington DC 20015 Office: Nat Bur Standards Washington DC 20234

HUDSON, ROBERT, sculptor; b. Salt Lake City, Sept. 8, 1938; student San Francisco Art Inst., 1962-63; M.F.A.; m.; 2 children. Exhibited one-man shows including Batman Gallery, San Francisco, 1961, Allan Frumkin Gallery, N.Y.C., 1965, Nicholas Wilder Gallery, Los Angeles, 1967; group shows Oakland Art Mus., 1961, 63, La Lolla, 1961, Whitney Mus., 1964, 65, 67, 68, Los Angeles County Mus., 1967, San Francisco Mus. Art; instr. San Francisco Art Inst., 1964-65, chmn. sculpture and ceramic dept., 1965-66; asst. prof. U. Cal. at Berkeley, 1966—. Recipient purchase prize San Francisco Art Festival, 1961, San Jose State Coll., 1964, prize San Francisco Mus. Art, 1963. Home: Stinson Beach CA 94970 Office: care Allan Frumkin Gallery 41 E 57th St New York City NY 10022 also Nicholas Wilder Gallery Los Angeles CA 90028

HUDSON, ROBERT CLIVE, mfr.; b. Ganges, Mich., Jan. 19, 1900; s. Herbert D. and Delia (Kenter) H.; student U. Minn., 1917-20; m. Margaret Simons, Nov. 17, 1926; children—Robert C., Margaret Carolyn (Mrs. Dean R. Doll). Vice pres. H.D. Hudson Mfg. Co., Chgo., 1933-43, now chmn., treas.; pres., treas. Lowell Mfg. Co., 1943-53; dir. Lake Shore Nat. Bank. Clubs: Chicago Athletic, Lake Shore (Chgo.); Knollwood (Lake Forest, Ill.). Home: 396 Kelling Lane Glencoe IL 60022 Office: 589 E Illinois St Chicago IL 60611

HUDSON, ROBERT DADE, lawyer; b. Nashville, Mar. 24, 1900; s. Washington E. and Annie (Dade) H.; student Henry Kendale Coll., Tulsa; LL.B., Vanderbilt U., 1922; m. Dorothy Vensel, Oct. 16, 1926; 1 dau., Shirley A. (Mrs. Brown). Admitted to Okla. bar, 1922, since practiced in Tulsa: mem. firm Hudson, Wheaton & Brett, and predecessors; judge Ct. Commons Pleas, Tulsa County, 1923-26, Dist. Ct. 21st Jud. Dist. of Okla., 1926-29. Mem. Am., Okla., Tulsa County (pres. 1943) bar assns., Phi Alpha Delta. Home: Tulsa OK Office: Hudson Wheaton & Brett Ritz Bldg Tulsa OK 74101

HUDSON, ROBERT LITTLETON, newspaper exec.; b. St. Petersburg, Fla., Oct. 4, 1925; s. Grover Cleveland and Winifred (Root) H.; student U. Ga.; m. Martha Russ, Jan. 10, 1949; 1 son, Robert Cleveland. Sports writer St. Petersburg Times, 1948-52; sports writer Tampa Tribune (Fla.), 1953-54, sports editor, 1954-59, state editor, 1960-65, asst. mng. editor, 1965-66, mng. editor, 1966—; chmn. U.P.I. Conf., 1968, v.p. AP, Fla., 1970. Mem. U.S.O. Council, Fla. Bd. dirs. U.S. Fla. Found. Named Fla.;s Sports Writer of Year, Fla. Sports Writers Assn. 1958; recipient Tampa C. of C. Sports ward, 1958. Mem. Fla. Sports Writers Assn. (pres. 1957), Sigma Delta Chi (pres. 1968). Democrat. Episcopalian. Club: Downtown Sertoma (Tampa). Home: 3003 Emerson St Tampa FL 33609 Office: PO Box 191 Tampa FL 33601

HUDSON, ROCK, (Roy Fitzgerald) motion picture actor-producer; b. 1925; hon. Doctor Arts, Marietta (O.) Coll., 1957; ed. high sch., Winnetka; m. Phyllis Gates (div. 1958). Motion picture debut in Fighter Squadron; others include Winchester 73, Iron Man, Bright Victory, Bend in the River, Magnificent Obsession, All That Heaven Allows, Giant (Acad. award nomination), Something of Value, A Farewell to Arms, This Earth is Mine, Pillow Talk, Come September, Lover Come Back, The Spiral Road, A Gathering of Eagles, Send Me No Flowers, Strange Bedfellows, Blindfold, Seconds, Tobruk, Ice Station Zebra, A Fine Pair, Darling Lill, The Hornet's Nest, Pretty Maids All in a Row, McMillan and Wife. Christmas Seal chmn., 1970. Served with USNR, 1941-46. Recipient Look mag. award, 1956; Exhibitor Laurel awards, 1958- 66; Bambi awards, Germany, 1958-65; Golden Globe award as world favorite film actor Hollywood Fgn. Corrs. Assn., 1958, 60-62; King David award, 1970. Address: care Allan Ingersoll & Webber 1901 Av of Stars Los Angeles CA 90067

HUDSON, ROY DAVAGE, educator; b. Chattanooga, June 30, 1930; s. Roy and Everence (Wilkerson) H.; B.S., Livingstone Coll., 1955; M.S., U. Mich., 1957, Ph.D., 1962; M.A., Brown U., 1968; m. Constance Joan Taylor, Aug. 31, 1956; children—Hollye Lynne, David Kendall. Prof. pharmacology U. Mich. Sch. Medicine, 1961-66; prof. med. sci. Brown U. Sch. Medicine, 1966-70, asso. dean grad. sch., 1966-69; pres. Hampton Inst., 1970—; mem. screening com. Danforth Grad. Fellowship, 1962—. Mem. R.I. Commn. Econ. Devel., 1967-69, R.I. Urban League scholarship com., 1966-70. Bd. dirs. Afro-Am. Soc. Conn. Coll. Served to staff sgt. USAF, 1948-52. Recipient Livingstone Coll. distinguished alumni award; Danforth Grad. fellow, 1955-61. Mem. Am. Soc. Pharmacology and Exptl. Therapeutics, N.A.A.C.P., A.A.A.S., Sigma Xi, Phi Kappa Phi, Phi Sigma, Beta Kappa Chi. Contbr. articles profl. jours. Home: 612 Shore Rd Hampton VA 23368

HUDSON, THOMAS P., banker. Pres., chmn. bd. First Am. Nat. Bank Wausau (Wis.). Office: 500 3d St Wausau WI 54401*

HUDSON, WAYNE D., lawyer; b. Bellevue, Ida., Oct. 2, 1919; s. Arthur Logan and Fern (Hartfield) H.; B.S., U. Ida., 1942; LL.B., Stanford, 1950; LL.M., N.Y. U., 1951; m. Patricia Ann Dunn, Dec. 25, 1950; children- Kathleen, Susan, Curtis. Research entomologist Standard Oil Co., 1947; asso. prof. law Stanford, 1951-60; dep. atty. gen. Cal., 1952-56; mem. Hancock, Elkington & Rothert, 1956-59; gen. counsel Foremost Daires, Inc., San Francisco, 1959-61, sec., gen. counsel, 1961-69, v.p., 1966-69; gen. counsel, v.p., sec. Foremost-McKesson, Inc., 1969—. Served as capt. USMCR, 1942-47. Unitarian. Club: Commonwealth of California. Home: 320 42d Av San Mateo CA 94403 Office: 111 Pine St San Francisco CA 94111

HUDSON, WILLIAM BURCHELL, Jr., constrn. co. exec.; b. Phila., Apr. 3, 1919; s. William Burchell and Ida E. (Rothenberger) H.; B.S. in Chem. Engring., Drexel Inst. Tech., 1941; postgrad. N.Y. U., Poly. Inst. Bklyn.; m. Maybelle M. Schleicher, June 25, 1944; children—Paul S., Diana E. With Foster-Wheeler Corp., 1941-60, mgr. petroleum refinery dept., 1953-59, mgr. fgn. operations, 1959-60; v.p. Arthur G. McKee & Co., Cleve., 1960-61, exec. v.p., dir., 1961-63, sr. v.p., dir., mem. exec. com., 1963-67, exec. v.p., dir., mem. exec. com., 1967-70, group v.p., dir., 1970—; dir., mem. exec. com. Compagnia Technica Industrie Petroli, Rome, Italy, 1966—. Mem. Am. Inst. Chem. Engrs., Cleve. Engring. Soc. Presbyn. Clubs: Economic (N.Y.C.); University, Shaker Heights Country (Cleve.). Home: 16714 Fernway Rd Shaker Heights OH 44120 Office: 2300 Chester Av Cleveland OH 44114

HUDSON, WILLIAM HARRY, railroad cons.; b. Pine Bluff, Ark., Dec. 31, 1903; s. William Hamilton and Tennessee Gossit (Byrd) H.; B.S. in Civil Engring., Washington U., St. Louis, 1926; grad. Harvard Advanced Mgmt. Program, 1954; m. Sadie Moon, 1933; 1 dau., Gail (Mrs. John B. White III). With St. Louis S.W. Ry. Co., 1926-69, v.p., gen. mgr., 1957-65, v.p., 1965-69; r.r. cons., Tyler, Tex., 1969—; dir. Southside State Bank, Tyler. Mem. Am. Ry. Engring. Assn., Am. Soc. C.E., Sigma Nu. Presbyn. (deacon). Mason (32, K.T., Shriner). Clubs: Willowbrook Country (Tyler). Home: 207 Mockingbird Lane Tyler TX 75701 Office: PO Box 3485 Tyler TX 75701

HUDSON, WILLIAM NOEL, ednl. adminstr.; b. Taylorville, Ill., Oct. 7, 1912; s. William and Lillie (Freeman) H.; B.A., James Millikin U., 1938; postgrad. George Williams Coll., 1939, Columbia, 1944; m. Margaret Ann Waldron, July 24, 1939; children-Judith Ann (Mrs. Glenn T. Dallas), Joda Sue (Mrs. David F. Marano). Sec., Decatur (Ill.) YMCA, 1933-38; gen. supt. Chgo. Boys Clubs, 1938-42; dir. operations U.S.O., N.Y.C., 1942-45; exec. v.p., asst. treas. Fedn. Protestant Welfare Agys., N.Y.C., 1945-54; exec. v.p. Protestant Childrens Service, N.Y.C., 1946-48; exec. dir. Protestant Fund Greater N.Y., 1947-48; acting exec. dir. Welfare Council N.Y.C., 1950-51; adminstrv. v.p. Tamblyn & Brown, Inc., pub. relations, N.Y.C., 1954-60, v.p. for devel. Rensaelaer Poly. Inst., 1960-64; dir. devel. Colgate U., 1964-68; v.p. devel. and relations Niagara (N.Y.) U., 1968—. Pres., N.Y. State Welfare Conf., 1952-54; mem. N.Y.C. Commn. Foster Care Children, 1947-54, Greater N.Y. Fund Distbn. Com., 1947-54, Mayor N.Y.C. Com. Pub. Assistance, 1948-49; reconstrn. com. Welfare Council N.Y.C., 1949-50; dir. federated hosp. campaign, Camden, N.J., 1956-57, program for united engring. center at UN Plaza, 1957-58, Mem. Pub. Relations Soc. Am., Nat. Assn. Social Workers, Sigma Alpha Epsilon, Alpha Omega. Clubs: Engineers' Bankers, N.Y., Athletic (N.Y.C.); Niagara Falls Country, Niagara. Home: 738 The Circle Lewiston NY 14092

HUDSON, WILLIAM THOMAS, govt. ofcl.; b. Chgo., Dec. 14, 1929; s. Cornelius and Mary (Palmer) H.; B.S., Northwestern U., 1953; M.A. in Polit. Sci., U. Chgo., 1954. Claims authorizer Bur. Retirement and Survivors Ins., Social Security Adminstrn., Dept. Health, Edn. and Welfare, Chgo., 1956-63, employee devel. officer Hdqrs. Retirement and Survivors Ins., Balt., 1963-64, spl. asst. for EEO to dir. bur., 1964-65, contract operations specialist Bur. Health Ins., 1965-66, dep. EEO officer Office Sec. Dept. Health, Edn. and Welfare, Washington, 1966-67; program mgr. Internal EEO Program, Office Sec., Dept. Transp., Washington, 1967-70; chief Office Civil Rights, USCG, Washington, 1970—; detailed to Pres.'s Com. on Equal Employment Opportunity, Washington, 1964-65; resource cons. Nat. Urban League Conv., 1970. Served with U.S. Army, 1954-56. Mem. Nat. Assn. Human Rights Workers, Phi Delta Kappa. Home: 700 7th St SW Washington DC 20024 Office: 400 7th St SW Washington DC 20591

HUDSON, WINTHROP STILL, clergyman, educator; b. 1911; s. Grant Martin and Mildred (Gilchrist) H.; B.A., Kalamazoo Coll., 1933, D.D., 1958; B.D., Colgate Rochester Div. Sch., 1937; Ph.D., U. Chgo., 1940; m. Mildred Lois Austin, June 23, 1934; children—Judith Ann, Susan Camille. Ordained to ministry Bapt. Ch., 1937, minister York (N.Y.) Ch., 1935-37, Normal Park Ch., Chgo., 1937-42; instr. Colgate Rochester Div. Sch., 1942-44, adminstrv. asso., 1947-48, James B. Colgate prof. history of Christianity, 1948—; prof. history U. Rochester, 1970—; asso. prof. U. Chgo., 1944-47. Recipient Susan Colver Rosenberg award for meritorious research, 1940. Mem. Am. Soc. Ch. Hist. (pres. 1948, sec. 1955-60), Am. Bapt. Hist. Soc. (pres. 1955-66), Am. Hist. Assn. Author: John Ponet-Advocate of Limited Monarchy, 1942; The Great Tradition of the American Churches, 1953; The Story of the Christian Church, 1958; Understanding of Roman Catholicism, 1959; American Protestantism, 1961; Religion in America, 1965; Nationalism and Religion in America, 1970. Editor: Christian Leadership in a World Society, 1946; Henry Scougal's Life of God in the Soul of Man, 1948; Roger Williams Experiments of Spiritual Life and Health, 1951; Baptist Concepts of the Church, 1959; Nationalism and Religion in America, 1971. Home: 159 Rockingham St Rochester NY 14620

HUDSPETH, EMMETT LEROY, educator, physicist; b. Denton, Tex., Dec. 3, 1916; s. Junia Evans and Ethel Leonis (Burns) H.; A.B., Rice Inst., 1937, M.A., 1938, Ph.D., 1940; m. Mary Alice Barnes, Dec. 2, 1944; children—John, Philip, Anne, Paul. Fellow physics Rice Inst., 1937-40; fellow Bartol Research Found., 1940- 41, asst. dir., 1946-50; staff mem. radiation lab. Mass. Inst. Tech., 1941-45; prof. physics U. Tex., Austin, 1950—; dir. Nuclear Physics Lab., 1950—. Research nuclear physics, disintegration of light elements, energy levels of nuclei and others; cons. USN, 1943-45; adviser Sec. War, 1942; com. on Undersea Warfare, 1947-49; sci. adv. com. Radiobiol. Lab., U. Tex. and USAF, 1954-58. Fellow Am. Phys. Soc., A.A.A.S.; mem. Phi Beta Kappa, Sigma Xi. Contbr. articles to profl. jours. Home: 6104 Janey Dr Austin TX 78731

HUEBER, FRANCIS MAURICE, paleobotanist; b. Sand Springs, Okla., Feb. 27, 1929; s. Maurice Miron Reed and Ema Lina (Schneider) H.; B.S magna cum laude, Butler U., 1956; M.S., Cornell U., 1959, Ph.D. (NSF fellow), 1960. Instr. dept. botany Cornell U., 1960-61; geologist-paleobotanist Geol. Survey Can., Ottawa, Ont., 1961-62; geologist-paleobotanist div. paleobotany Smithsonian Instn., Wash., 1962—. Served with inf. AUS, 1951-52. John E. Potzger Meml. scholar, 1956. Mem. Bot. Soc. Am., geol. socs. Am., Washington, Internat. Assn. Plant Taxonomy, Paleontol. Assn. London, Phi Kappa Phi. Home: 4806 Morgan Dr Chevy Chase MD 20015 Office: Div Paleobotany Smithsonian Instn Washington DC 20560

HUEBNER, CARL H., ins. co. exec.; b. 1912; B.S. in Civil Engring., Newark Coll., Engring., 1932; married. With real estate mgmt. firm, Newark, 1932-35; with Met. Life Ins. Co., N.Y.C., 1935—, asst. v.p., 1958-61, 3d v.p., 1961-63, 2d v.p., 1963-66, v.p., 1966-69, sr. v.p. real estate finance, 1969—; trustee Empire Savs. Bank N.Y. Office: 1 Madison Av New York City NY 10010*

HUEBNER, HERBERT ALLOWAY, lawyer; b. Washington, Mar. 21, 1902; s. Francis C. and Anna (Alloway) H.; A.B., U. So. Cal., 1923, postgrad. law sch., 1923-25; m. Lorna C. Pierce, June 18, 1925; 1 son, Harlan Pierce. Admitted to Cal. bar, 1926, U.S. Supreme Ct. bar, 1934, N.Y. bar, 1936; patent counsel and pub. relations rep. Consol. Film Industries and affiliated cos., N.Y., 1930-37; gen. counsel Republic Pictures, Los Angeles, 1937; pvt. practice patent law, Los Angeles, 1938—. Mem. Regional Export Expansion Council, 1963-64. Mem. Am., Cal. (chmn. patent conf. 1951-52), Los Angeles bar assns., Am. Patent Law Assn. Republican. Presbyn. Mason (32 K.T., Shriner, grand orator Cal. 1954, grand master 1970-71), Rotarian. Clubs: Jonathan, Lakeside, Eldorado Country (Palm Desert, Cal.). Contbr. articles on masonry, patents to various publs. Home: 1850 N Whitley Av Hollywood CA 90028 Office: 610 S Broadway Los Angeles CA 90014

HUEBNER, JOHN MUDIE, lawyer, ins. exec.; b. Kingston, Ont., July 25, 1911 (parents U.S. citizens); s. Solomon Stephen and Ethel Elizabeth (Mudie) H.; B.S., U. Pa., 1931, J.D., 1934; m. Elizabeth Converse, Sept. 23, 1935; children—John Stephen, Bernard Converse. Admitted to Pa. bar, 1934; various positions in law underwriting and ins. operations Penn Mut. Life Ins. Co., Phila., 1934-49, v.p., 1950-56, sr. v.p., 1957—, in charge agy. operations, 1958-68, sr. v.p., chmn. operations com., 1968- -. Bd. mgrs. Hosp. U. Pa. Bd. dirs. Pa. Plan Devel. of Scientists in Med. Research. Served as lt. USNR, 1943-46. Mem. Juristic Soc., Home Office Life Underwriters Assn. (pres. 1957-58), Zeta Psi. Clubs: Union League (Phila.); Merion Cricket. Contbr., cons. editor ins. publs., textbooks. Home: 150 Anton Rd Wynnewood PA 19096 Office: 530 Walnut St Philadelphia PA 19105

HUEBNER, ROBERT JOSEPH, med. research scientist; b. Cin., Feb. 23, 1914; s. Joseph Frederick and Philomena (Brickner) H.; student Xavier U., 1932-35, U. Cin., 1937-38; M.D., St. Louis U., 1942; LL.D., U. Cin., 1965; D.Sc. (hon.), Edgecliff Coll., 1970, U. Parma, Italy, 1970; m. Grace Berdine Sept. 29, 1939; children—Elizabeth, Frances, Geraldine, James, Virginia, Roberta, Edward, Louise, Daniel. Commd. jr. asst. surgeon USPHS, 1942, advanced through grades to med. dir., 1953; mil. duty Alaskan area USCG, 1943- 44; virus and rickettsial disease research NIH, 1944—, chief virus sect., 1949-56, chief lab. infectious disease Nat. Inst. Allergy and Infectious Diseases, 1956-68, chief viral carcinogenesis br. Nat. Cancer Inst., Bethesda, Md., 1968—. Gehrman lectr. U. Ill., 1955, Eli Lilly lectr., 1957; Gudakunst lectr. U. Mich., 1958, Harvey lectr., 1960, Puckett lectr., 1960. Recipient Bailey K. Ashford award, 1949; certificate merit St. Louis U., 1949; James D. Bruce Meml. award, 1964; Pasteur medal, 1965; Distinguished Service medal USPHS, 1966; Howard Taylor Ricketts award, 1968; Nat. medal Sci., 1969; Kimble award, 1970; Rockefeller award, 1970; Guido Lenghi award 1971. Fellow Am. Pub. Health Assn., N.Y. Acad. Scis.; mem. Nat. Acad. Scis., A.A.A.S., Am. Assn. Immunologists, Am. Epidemiol. Soc., Fedn. Am. Socs. Exptl. Biology and Medicine, Wash. Acad. Sci. (award biol. scis. 1949), Internat. Union Against Cancer Infectious Diseases Soc. Am., Am. Acad. Microbiology, Am. Assn. Cancer Research, A.M.A., Md. Angus Assn. (pres. 1959-60), Sigma Xi, Alpha Omega Alpha. Contbr. numerous articles to profl. jours. Home: Hidden Hills Farm Ijamsville MD 21754 Office: Viral Carcinogenesis Br Nat Cancer Inst Bethesda MD 20014

HUEGEL, L. JAMES, coal co. exec.; b. Lancaster, Pa., May 29, 1916; s. Leo Joseph and Mary (Gallagher) H.; A.B., Franklin and Marshall Coll., 1938; LL.B., U. Pa., 1943; m. Helen L. Derr, Oct. 4, 1947; children—Stephen Geary, Frances Perrin, Daniel James Admitted to Pa. bar, 1944, Md. bar, 1948; asst. solicitor Pa. R.R., 1944-47; asst. gen. counsel B. & O. R.R., 1947- 55; with Consol. Coal Co., Pitts., 1955—, exec. v.p. marketing and transp., 1966—, also dir. Bd. dirs. Carlow Coll., Pitts.; trustee, overseer Franklin and Marshall Coll., 1966—. Mem. Am., Pa. bar assns., ICC Practitioners Assn. Clubs: Duquesne, Field (pres. 1966-68, dir.), Laurel Valley Golf (Pitts.); Pinnacle (N.Y.C.). Home: 208 Foxhurst Dr Pittsburgh PA 15238 Office: 1 Oliver Plaza Pittsburgh PA 15222

HUEGLI, ALBERT GEORGE, univ. pres.; b. Detroit, June 7, 1913; s. Albert George and Lydia (Reif) H.; B.D., Concordia Sem., St. Louis, 1936, D.D., 1968; M.A., U. Mich., 1937; B.Ed., Wayne U., 1938; Ph.D., Northwestern U., 1944; LL.D., Concordia Tchrs. Coll. 1964; m. Rae Merritt, Jan. 2, 1941; children—Karen Michele (Mrs. Robert A. Buethe), Jon Merritt. Ordained to ministry Luth. Ch., 1936; asst. prof. history and polit. sci. St. John's Coll., 1938-40; faculty Concordia Tchrs. Coll., River Forest, Ill., 1940-44, prof. history and polit. sci., 1944, dean students, 1944-55, acad. dean, 1955-61, dir. grad. div., 1957-61; v.p. acad. affairs Valparaiso (Ind.) U., 1961-68, acting pres., 1968, pres., 1968—. Vis. asso. prof. polit. sci. Northwestern U., summers 1947, 1948; examiner, cons. N. Central Assn., 1961—. Mem. bd. higher edn. Luth. Ch. Mo. Synod, 1964-69, chmn., 1967-69; pres. Luth. Ednl. Conf. N.Am., 1970-72. Mem. N.E.A., Am. Acad. Polit. and Social Sci., Am. Polit. Sci. Assn., Luth. Edn. Assn. Author: (with R.B. Posey) Government for Americans, 2d edit., 1965. Editor: Church and State Under God, 1964. Home: 1401 Linwood Valparaiso IN 46383

HUEGLI, RICHARD FREDERICK, social planner; b. Detroit, June 26, 1915; s. Albert George and Lydia (Reif) H.; B.D., Concordia Sem., St. Louis, 1938; M.S.W., Wayne State U., 1945, M.P.A. (Voekler scholar), 1947; m. Marion L. Baetz, Sept. 20, 1941; children—Richard Frederick, Bruce Albert, Joyce Ann. Met. dir. Detroit War Chest and Community Chest, 1940-50; asst. dir. United Community Service Met. Detroit, 1951-57, mng. dir., 1958-68, exec. v.p., 1968—. Commr., Met. Detroit Plan Commn., 1961- 67, bd. mem. Mayor's Com. for Human Resources Devel., 1965—. Mem. Detroit-Wayne County Mental Helath Bd., 1964—. Trustee, mem. exec. com. Nat. Health and Welfare Retirement Assn., 1960—; trustee Oakland Housing; bd. regents Mich. Luth. Coll., 1962-70; trustee Student Aid Found., 1951- 63, chmn. 1963—; trustee New Detroit, Luth Ch.-Mo. Synod Found. Wheat Ridge Found. Recipient Wayne Distinguished Alumni award, 1966; award of merit Nat. Assn. Social Workers, 1959. Mem. Wayne State U. Alumni Assn. (pres. 1968). Clubs: Detroit, Torch, Prismatic (Detroit). Home: 10 Radnor Circle Grosse Pointe MI 48236 Office: 51 W Warren St Detroit MI 48201

HUEHL, WALTER HAROLD, life ins. co. exec.; b. Chelsea, Mich., Oct. 22, 1902; s. Benjamin and Bertha (Finkbeiner) H.; A.B. in Actuarial Sci. and Bus. Adminstrn., U. Mich., 1923; m. N. Kathryn Kirkpatrick, Nov. 30, 1946; children— Judith Anne, Janet Kathryn. Asst. actuary Security Life Ins. Co., Chgo., 1923- 24; actuary Ind. Ins. Dept., 1924-27; with Indpls. Life Ins. Co., 1927—, exec. v.p., 1949, pres., 1949—. Dir. Inst. Life Ins., 1962-66; v.p. Assn. Ind. Legal Res. Life Ins. Cos., 1957-59, pres., 1959-61. Mem. Mayor Indpls. Citizens Adv. Com. Civil City Budget, 1957—; pres. Indpls. YMCA, 1955-57; pres. bd. Franklin United Meth. Home, 1969—. Bd. dirs. United Fund Greater Indpls., Jr. Achievement Indpls., Indpls. C. of C., Indpls. Hosp. Devel. Assn. Served as maj. USAAF, 1942-45. Asso. mem. Soc. Actuaries. Mason (Shriner), Kiwanian. Clubs: Indianapolis Athletic, Meridian Hills Country, U. Mich. (Indpls.). Home: 5260 N Pennyslvania St Indianapolis IN 46220 Office: 2960 N Meridian St Indianapolis IN 46208

HUENEMANN, RUBEN HENRY, clergyman; b. Waukon, Ia., Jan. 15, 1909; s. William and Mary (Hansmeier) H.; A.B., Luther Coll., Decorah, Ia., 1933; B.D., Mission House Sem., Plymouth, Wis., 1936; postgrad. Washington U., also Pacific Sch. Religion, Berkeley, Cal.; D.D., Franklin and Marshall Coll., 1954; m. Clara James, Aug. 19, 1936; children—Robert Gilchrist, Ralph William, Carol Ruth, Grace Noel. Tchr. rural schs., S.D., 1927-29; ordained to ministry Evang. and Ref. Ch., 1936; pastor St. Stephen's Ch., Juneau, Wis., 1936-38, Salem Ch., St. Louis, 1938-44, Zion Ch., Lodi, Cal., 1944-54, Grace Ch., Milw., 1954-58, Faith Ch., Milw., 1958-60; pres. United Theol. Sem. of Twin Cities, Mpls., 1960-70; conf. exec. Ore. Conf. United Ch. Christ, Portland, 1970—. Pres. Cal. Synod Evang. and Ref. Ch., 1950-54; moderator Gen. Synod Tiffin, O., 1953; mem. theol. com. United Ch. Christ. Mem. Nat. Council Chs. (gen. bd. 1966-69). Contbr. denominational periodicals. Address: 7111 S E Harrison Ct Portland OR 97215

HUESTIS, CHARLES BENJAMIN, ednl. adminstr.; b. Seattle, Jan. 27, 1920; s. Claude Erwin and Eloise Marie (Petitt) H.; student Griffin Murphy Coll., Seattle, 1938-39, U. Cal. at Berkeley, 1946; m. Kathryn Alice Porter, Mar. 1, 1942; children—Stephen Porter, Jeffrey Charles, Robin Rebecca. With Seattle First Nat. Bank, 1941; accountant Rheem Mfg. Co., Richmond, Cal., 1946- 51, chief accountant aircraft div., Downey, Cal., 1951-54, comptroller company, 1954-56; v.p. treas. Hall-Scott Inc., Berkeley, Cal., 1956 exec. v.p., dir., treas., 1956-57; adminstrv. cons. Overseas Nat. Airways, Oakland, Cal., 1957-58; controller Hughes Aircraft Co., El Segundo div., 1958-59, Tucson div., 1959, treas., dir. finance co. 1959-66, chmn. finance com., 1959-66, v.p., 1962-66; v.p., treas., dir. Am. Mt. Everest Expdn., 1963, Inc., Santa Monica, Cal., 1962-67; v.p. bus. and finance Duke U., Durham, N.C., 1966—. Dir. Technomics, Inc., Falls Church, Va., Durham Investment Corp. Dir. Santa Barbara (Cal.) Research Center, 1959-66; dir., mem. exec. com. Research Triangle Found., Research Triangle Park, N.C.; trustee Research Triangle Inst., Research Triangle Park. Mem. Archaeol. Inst. Am. Clubs: Sierra (treas. and dir.); Explorers. Home: 1803 Woodburn Rd Durham NC 28301 Office: Duke U Durham NC 27706

HUESTON, MICHAEL JOSEPH, publishing co. exec.; b. Phila., May 12, 1907; s. Michael A. and Leonore (Ferry) H.; grad. high sch.; m. Blanche K. Kimenhour, Oct. 26, 1940; children—Robert Francis, Michael Joseph. With Curtis Pub. Co., Phila., 1923—, adminstrv. asst. N.Y. operations, 1964, v.p. editorial and adminstrn., 1964-66, v.p. editorial and advt. adminstrn., div. mgr. corp. prodn. control, 1966—. Bd. dirs. Dorchester House, Boston, 1962- -. Served with USMCR, 1944-45. Mem. Periodical Pub. Assn. (bd. dirs. 1966), Roman Cath. Club: Lantern (sec.-treas. 1961, pres. 1962) (Boston). Home: 1958 Beacon St Waban MA 02168 Office: Curtis Publishing Co Independence Sq Philadelphia PA 19105

HUETER, ERNEST BOYD, bakery exec.; b. San Francisco, June 15, 1920; s. Ernest Claus and Lauretta (Boyd) H.; B.J., U. Mo., 1942; grad. student U. Cal. at Los Angeles, 1948; m. John Adele LeBrun, Aug. 3, 1947; children— Ernest Ross, Kristin Joan. Free lance comedy writer, 1946; pres., chief exec. officer Interstate Bakeries Corp. (co. name changed to Interstate Brands Corp.), Kansas City, Mo., 1947—. Dir. Starlight Theater. Served with AUS, 1942-45; PTO. Mem. Am. Bakers Assn. (bd. govs.), Am. Mgmt. Assn. (bd. dirs.), Kansas City C. of C., Sigma Delta Chi, Beta Theta Pi. Mason (K.T., Jester, Shriner). Clubs: Saddle and Sirloin (Leawood, Kan.); Mission Hills Country; Kansas City.‡

HUFF, CLAY G., scientist; b. Cory, Ind., Sept. 10, 1900; s. Howard and Estella May (Coble) H.; student Ind. State Tchrs. Coll., 1918-21; A.B., Southwestern (Kan.) Coll., 1924; Sc.D., Johns Hopkins, 1927; m. Florence May Clark, Sept. 1, 1927; children—Eskin, Elaine. NRC fellow Harvard Med. Sch., 1928-30; asso. prof. zoology, U. Ga., 1927-28; asst. prof. parasitology U. Chgo., 1930-36, asso. prof., 1936- 41, prof., 1941-47; dir. dept. parasitology Naval Med. Research Inst., Bethesda, 1947-69, ret., 1969. Recipient Distinguished Civilian service awards Navy, Dept. Def., 1958. Mem. Nat. Malaria Soc. (v.p. 1945-46), Am. Soc. Parasitologists, (v.p. 1946-47, pres. 1955), Am. Acad. Tropical Medicine (Theobald Smith award 1947, sec. 1949-52), Am. Soc. Tropical Medicine and Hygiene (pres. 1962-63), A.A.A.S., Sociedad Mexicana de Historia Natural, Sigma Xi. Author: Parasitology (with Hegner, Root, Augustine), 1938; A Manual of Medical Parasitology, 1943. Home: 411 Key West Dr Charlottesville VA 22901

HUFF, CLAYTON, advt. exec.; b. Martinsville, Ind., June 18, 1914; s. Bryon and Martha (Clayton) H.; A.B., DePauw U., 1935; M.B.A., Harvard, 1937; m. Margaret Warner, Aug. 12, 1939, children—Joseph, Patricia, William, Robert. With Chrysler Corp., 1937-40, J. Stirling Getchell, Inc., 1940-42, J. Walter Thompson Co., 1942-44, 46-47; asst. treas. Compton Advt., Inc., 1947-52; treas. Batten, Barton, Durstine & Osborn, Inc., N.Y.C., 1962—, v.p., 1956—, dir., mem. exec. com., 1970—. Served to lt. (j.g.) USNR, 1944-46. Mem. Sons of Ind. (bd. govs. N.Y.), Beta Theta Pi, Phi Eta Sigma. Clubs: Harvard, Harvard Business School (N.Y.C.); Pelham Country (past treas., bd. govs.). Home: 925 Edgewood Av Pelham Manor NY 10803 Office: 383 Madison Av New York City NY 10017

HUFF, GEORGE CHARLES, ednl. adminstr.; b. Des Moines, Ia., Feb. 15, 1906; s. Charles Porter and Bertha Grace (Allen) H.; B.S. in Commerce, Drake U., 1928; M.S., State U. Ia., 1929, Ph.D., 1935; student Marine Biol. Lab., 1932, U. Chgo., 1935; m. Ella Cecelia Sipple, Sept. 6, 1933 (dec. 1964); children—Marian Elaine, Dennis Karl; m. 2d, Ivadel T. Picht, Sept. 2, 1967. Asst. dir. Mus., State U. Ia., 1929-32; asst. prof. biology, Drake U., Des Moines, Ia., 1933-34, prof. and acting chmn. biology dept., 1934-35, prof. and chmn. dept., 1935-55, acting dean Coll. Liberal Arts, 1949-51, 54-55, v.p. academic adminstrn., 1955-67, v.p. spl. programs, 1967—. Mem. A.A.A.S., Am. Soc. Parasitology, Am. Micros. Soc., Ia. Acad. Sci., Sigma Xi, Gamma Alpha, Delta Sigma Pi, Phi Beta Kappa. Republican. Methodist. Mason (32). Clubs: University, Prairie (Des Moines). Contbr. to scientific jours. Home: 6114 Windsor Dr Des Moines, IA 50312.

HUFF, GERALD BOONE, mathematician; b. Ft. Worth, Tex., May 23, 1909; s. Stephen Barr and Ella Sandidge (Furman) H.; A.B., So. Meth. U., 1929, A.M., 1930, D.Sc., 1966; Ph.D., U. Ill., 1935; m. Helen May Comstock, Jan. 1, 1933; children—Daniel Alan, Mary Helen. Instr., Southwestern U., Georgetown, Tex., 1930-31; asst. in mathematics U. Ill., 1931-35; asst. prof., asso. prof. So. Meth. U., 1935- 44; vis. lectr. U. Tex., 1944-45; asso. prof., prof. U. Ga., 1946—, head dept. math., 1952- 59, grad. dean, 1959-68. Research fellow Harvard, 1948-49. Mem. Am. Math. Soc., Math. Assn. Am., Ga. Acad. Sci., Am. Assn. Univ. Profs., Phi Beta Kappa, Sigma Xi. Democrat. Methodist. Home: 340 Milledge Circle Athens GA 30601

HUFF, ISAAC CLEVELAND, Jr., trade assns. exec.; b. Bertram, Tex., Sept. 30, 1908; s. Isaac Cleveland and Kathryn (Alter) H.; student N.M. A. and M. Coll., 1926-27, Tyler (Tex.) Comml. Coll., 1928; m. Mildred Morton, Aug. 24, 1930; 1 dau., Jo Ann (Mrs. T. A. Green). Asst. sec., office mgr. Pawnee Oil Prodn. Co., Tulsa, 1928-32; self employed, 1932-34; office mgr. Cree & Hoover Drilling Co., Pampa, Tex., 1934-41; with Ind. Petroleum Assn. Am., Tulsa, 1941—, exec. mgr., sec., 1954—, also dir., mem. exec. com. Mem. Tulsa C. of C. (petroleum exec. com., nat. affairs com.), Am. Soc. Assn. Execs., Am. Petroleum Inst. Clubs: Rolling Hills Country, University (Tulsa). Home: 3804 E 58th St Tulsa OK 74135 Office: Box 1019 Tulsa OK 74101

HUFF, STANLEY EUGENE, dermatologist; b. Bremen, Ind., June 5, 1918; s. Otho H. and Gertrude M. (Nufer) H.; B.S., U. Notre Dame, 1940; M.D., Northwestern U., 1944; M.S. in Dermatology, U. Minn., 1949; m. Helen Leonard, Oct. 30, 1946; childrenJohn, Margaret, Thomas, Stephen, Katherine, Mary. Intern Wesley Meml. Hosp., Chgo., 1944; pvt. practice, Evanston, Ill., 1950—; mem. staff Evanston Hosp.; asso. prof. dermatology Northwestern U. Med. Sch. Vice pres. Evanston United Fund, 1960-62. Served with M.C., AUS, 1944-46. Mem. Am. Acad. Dermatology (pres. 1968), Am. Dermatol. Assn., Soc. Investigative Dermatology, A.M.A., Evanston C. of C. Kiwanian. Home: 454 Sheridan Rd Winnetka IL 60093 Office: 636 Church St Evanston IL 60201

HUFF, WILLIAM NATHAN, educator; b. Bryn Mawr, Pa., Dec. 20, 1912; s. William Bashford and Helen Elizabeth (Schaeffer) H.; A.B., Haverford Coll., 1935; M.A., U. Pa., 1937, Ph.D., 1947; m. Mary Cathern Albin, June 12, 1938; children—Marian (Mrs. W. Max Reno), William Gregg, Cynthia Anne. Instr., Northwestern U., 1940-41, U. Neb., 1943-44, Rochester U., 1944-46; faculty math. U. Okla., Norman, 1946—, chmn. dept., 1955-61, prof., 1961—. Recipient U. Okla. Found. teaching award, 1954, Regents award superior teaching, 1970. Mem. Math. Assn. Am., Am. Math. Soc., Phi Beta Kappa (chmn. S. Central dist. 1970-73), Sigma Xi. Republican. Presbyn. Contbr. articles to profl. jours. Home: 1600 Normandie St Norman OK 73069

HUFF, ZACHARY TAYLOR, former coll. adminstr.; b. Ellis County Tex., Nov. 18, 1895; s. Z.T. and Lula Addie (Smyth) H.; A.B., Baylor U., 1925; A.M., Columbia, 1929; Ph.D., U. Tex., 1936; m. Laura Jane Stinson, June 28, 1927; 1 dau., Leta Lu. Various positions stock farming, wholesale produce, ins. and banking; dean Wayland Coll., 1925-38; dean Howard Payne Coll., 1938-60, academic v.p., 1955-60. Mem. N.E.A., Am. Assn. Sch. Adminstrs., Tex. Acad. Sci., Nat. Soc. Study Edn., Nat. Assn. Secondary Sch. Prins., Phi Delta Kappa. Baptist (deacon; tchr. men's Sunday sch. class, Sunday sch. lesson weekly over radio; writer weekly Sunday sch. lesson for newspaper). Rotarian (past pres.). Address: 1903 7th St Bronwood TX 76801

HUFFAKER, CLAIR, author Nobody Loves a Drunken Indian; War Wagon. Address: care David McKay Co Inc 750 3d Av New York City NY 10017

HUFFINE, SHERMAN ROBISON, brewing co. exec.; b. Seattle, Wash., Mar. 26, 1908; s. Charles W. and Maude I. (Robison) H.; LL.B., U. Wash., 1930, J.D., 1968; LL.M., N.Y. U., 1935; m. Clara Louise Schmidt, Oct. 16, 1937; children—Louise, Richard S., Robert R. Admitted to Wash. bar, 1930, N.Y. bar, 1936; with legal dept. Stone & Webster, Inc., N.Y.C., 1930-42; asst. sec. Stone & Webster and Blodget, Inc., N.Y.C. 1938-42; sec. Olympia Brewing Co. (Wash.), 1942—, v.p. legal, 1964—, also dir.; dir. Gen. Metalcraft, Inc., Portland, Ore. Trustee Automobile Club Wash., 1957—; mem. Wash. Arts Commn., 1965—; mem. tourist adv. com. Wash. Dept. Commerce and Econ. Devel., 1965—. Trustee Olympia Fine Arts Build; sec., trustee Olympia-Tumwater Found., 1957—, Design for Wash., 1964—, Wash. Research Council, 1954- -. trustee W. Coast Stationary Engrs. Health and Welfare Trust, Seattle Symphony Orch., Seattle Opera Assn. (v.p. 1968—). Mem. Order of Coif, Delta Upsilon, Phi Alpha Delta. Elk, Kiwanian. Home: PO Box 304 Olympia WA 98501 Office: PO Box 947 Olympia WA 98501

HUFFINES, ROBERT LUTHER, Jr., business exec.; b. Rocky Mountain, N.C., Apr. 19, 1905; s. Robert Luther and Carrie Elizabeth (Whitehead) H.; student U. N.C., 1923-24, Phila. Textile Inst., 1925-26; m. Eleanor M. Lilly, Oct. 25, 1933 (died May 22, 1959); children—Robert L., Hannah Pickett, Calvert Whitehead; m. Jane Hoyt Welles, Apr. 16, 1961. Joined Burlington Mills, 1941; pres. Burlington Mills Corp. of N.Y., 1947-53; pres. Textron, Inc., 1953-54; chmn. bd., pres. Robbins Mills, Inc., 1954; and following merger; pres. Textron-Am. Co., 1955; chmn. exec. com., dir. Am. Steel & Pump, until 1966; chmn. Cherokee Securities Corp.; pres. B.S.F. Co., until 1966, Fairways Devel. Corp.; chmn. Serrick Corp., 1960-66; dir. Textron, Inc., Am. Broadcasting-Paramount Theatres, Inc.; chmn. Columbia Yacht Corp., 1966-67; pres. Millcraft Corp., until 1966, Clankton Mills, Inc., 1964-66. Chmn. Robert L. Huffness Jr. Found. Inc. Mem. Delta Kappa Epsilon. Methodist. Clubs: Union League (N.Y.C.); Blind Brook (Port Chester, N.Y.); Edgartown Yacht; Charlotte City, Country of N.C. (Pinehurst). Home and office: Box 979 Southern Pines NC 28387

HUFFMAN, ARTHUR VINCENT, criminologist; b. New Holland, Ill., Feb. 7, 1912; s. Oliver Edum and Ella (Stonecipher) H.; A.B., McKendree Coll., 1935; M.A., U. Ill., 1940; m. Mary Phyllis Wittman. Asst. sociology U. Ill., 1938-40; adviser Royal Afghan Govt., Kabul, Afghanistan, 1942-49; supervising sociologist, div. state criminologists Dept. Pub. Safety, Joliet, Ill., 1949-61, state criminologist, 1961-70; chief profl. services Ill. Dept. Corrections, Springfield, 1970—. Asso. exec. dir. Ill. Sex Offenders Commn., 1952-56; lectr. Moran Meml. Inst. Crime and Delinquency, St. Lawrence U., summer 1961-66; exec. dir. Gov.'s Com. Criminal Justice, spl. asst. to dir. Ill. Dept. Pub. Safety, 1967-69; mem. Ill. Law Enforcement Commn., 1969—. Mem. profl. adv. com. John Howard Assn. (award 1964). Bd. dirs. Goodwill Industries, YMCA. Recipient Merit award for distinguished achievement in pub. service Am. Assn. Criminology, 1963. Fellow Am. Sociol. Assn., Royal Central Asian Soc. (London), Am. Soc. Criminology; mem. Ill. Acad. Criminology (exec. bd., v.p.), Am. Correctional Assn. (dir.), Med. Correctional Assn. (v.p.), Nat. Council Crime and Delinquency, Pi Kappa Delta, Alpha Kappa Delta, Alpha Psi Omega. Mason (K.T.). Editorial bd. Jour. Social Therapy and Corrective Psychiatry; criminology editorial cons. Jour. Criminal Law, Criminology and Police Sci. Contbr. articles to profl. jours. Home: 1309 S Douglas Av Springfield IL 62704 Office: State Armory Bldg Springfield IL 62706

HUFFMAN, BURNSIDE ELIJAH, Jr., army officer; b. Columbus, Ga., Jan. 12, 1920; s. Elijah B. and Lucy (Watson) H.; B.S., U.S. Mil. Acad., 1941; M.A., George Washington U., 1965; m. Margaret Katherine Uncles, July 22, 1950; children—Lucy Elaine, Elizabeth Banks, Rebecca Ann, John Uncles. Commd. 2d lt. U.S. Army, 1941, advanced through grades to maj. gen., 1969; instr. math., asst. prof. U.S. Mil. Acad., 1952-55; student Command and Gen. Staff Coll., Ft. Leavenworth, Kan., 1955-56, U.S. Army War Coll., Carlisle Barracks, Pa., 1959-60; comdg. officer 2d Div. Arty., chief of staff 2d Inf. Div., Ft. Benning, Ga., 1963-65; dir. gunnery dept. Arty. Sch., Ft. Sill, Okla., 1965-66; G-3 8th U.S. Army, Korea, 1966-68; arty. comdr., chief of staff II Field Force, Vietnam, 1969; sr. army mem. Weapon Systems Evaluation Group, OSD, Washington, 1969—. Decorated Legion of Merit with oak leaf cluster, Bronze Star medal with oak leaf cluster, Air medal, Army Commendation medal with two oak leaf clusters. Home: 6018 Balsam Dr McLean VA 22101 Office: Weapon Systems Evaluation Group OSD 400 Army Navy Dr Arlington VA 20301

HUFFMAN, GEORGE LANGFORD, packaging co. exec.; b. Ontario, Can., Sept. 8, 1910; s. Clarence W. and Jane E. (Cundle) H.; came to U.S., 1928, naturalized, 1936; B.Mech. Engring., U. Detroit, 1933; m. Erline L. Crawford, Aug. 21, 1937; children—George Langford, Ruthann (Mrs. David M. Phillips), Pamela (Mrs. Paul S. Gerber), Larry. With Ex-Cello-O Corp., 1934—, v.p. packaging equipment group, 1964—; dir. Conveyor Specialities Co., Elopak Ltd., Norway. Dir. Nat. Assn. Diary Equipment Mfrs., 1957-59, Nat. Diary Council, 1965—; bd. dirs. Diary and Food Industry Supply Assn., 1956—, v.p., 1964-65, pres., 1966-68. Bd. dirs. Protect Hope in Mich., 1964—, vice chmn., 1967-68, pres., 1968—. Club: Detroit Golf. Home: 7305 Deep Run Birmingham MI 48010 Office: 1200 Oakman Blvd Detroit MI 48232

HUFFMAN, GERALD HARLEY, govt. ofcl.; b. Union County, O., Apr. 3, 1913; s. Harley Thurman and Margery (Fry) H.; B.S. in Agr., Ohio State U., 1936; M.P.A., Harvard, 1949; m. Veva Iris Graig, Sept. 3, 1941; 1 dau., Nancy Mae. Instr. vocational agr., Williamsburg, O., 1937; agrl. agt. Ohio Agrl. Extension Service, 1938-49; extension service specialist, agrl. div. ECA mission to Rome, Italy, 1949-54; U.S. Regional Office, Paris, France, 1954-62; adminstrn., field rep., asst. adminstr. programs, also dep. adminstr. Fed. Extension Service, Dept. Agr., Washington, 1954-62; cons. Ford Found., 1959; U.S. commr. Joint Commn. Rural Reconstrn., Taipei, Taiwan, 1962-69; asso. dir. AID, Saigon, Vietnam, 1969—. Served to lt. (j.g.) USNR, 1944-46; MTO. Decorated Aus. Ordres de Chavalierie (France), 1954. Home: 1771 Cambridge Blvd Columbus OH 43212

HUFFMAN, HORACE MCKEE, Jr., mfg. co. exec.; b. Dayton, O., Aug. 8, 1914; s. Horace McKee and Mary (Reynolds) H.; B.A., Dartmouth, 1936; m. Jane Elizabeth Boggs, Oct. 2, 1937; children—Stephen R., William Anthony, Micheal G., Elizabeth Lee. Sales mgr. Huffman Mfg. Co., Dayton, 1937-39, v.p., works mgr., 1939-42, pres., gen. mgr., 1942-61, chmn. 1961—; partner HKL, Inc., Hukela, Inc.; dir. Winters Nat. Bank & Trust Co. Pres. Cox Arboretum; bd. dirs. Dayton Art Inst. Republican. Episcopalian. Club: Moraine Country (bd. govs.) (Dayton). Home: 4418 Moraine Ridge Lane Dayton OH 45429 Office: PO Box 1204 Dayton OH 45401

HUFFMAN, JASPER ABRAHAM, clergyman, educator, author; b. Elkhart County, Ind., Feb. 28, 1880; s. John W. and Martha (Howenstine) H.; grad. Bonebrake Theol. Sem., 1909; A.B., Bluffton (O.) Coll., 1915; B.D., McCormick Theol. Sem., 1919;D.D., Taylor U., 1920; m. Elizabeth D. Lambert, May 5, 1901 (dec. 1949); children—David Paul, Martha Emma (dec.), S. Lambert, John Abram; m. Olive May Sando, Jan. 1, 1951 (dec.1969). Ordained to ministry, United Missionary Ch., 1904; dean Taylor U. Sch. Religion, 1936-45. Mem. extension faculty Ind. State Normal Sch., 1925; dean Winona Lake Sch. Theology (summer sch.), 1926-39, pres., 1939-54, emeritus, 1954; dean dept. Bible, Bethel Coll., 1954—; ednl. cons. May K. Houck Found., Sarasota, Fla., 1960—. Mem. staff of joint expn. for Palestinian excavation of Xenia Theol. Sem. and Am. Sch. for Oriental Research, 1930. First pres. World-Wide Bible Readers' Fellowship, 1946. Editor: Gospel Banner, 1913-25, Bethel series of Sunday Sch. lit. 1911-51; critical editor of Higley Sunday Sch. Lesson Commentary, 1937—, editor- in-chief, 1960—; editor-in-chief Living Bible Series and Study, Six Year Cycle, Covering Entire Bible, 1963—. Author numerous books, 1904- 45; later publs. include: The Stone Cry Out, 1946; Golden Treasures from the Greek New Testament for English Readers, 1951; The Meanings of Things Believed by Christians, 1953; The Revised Standard Version; An Appraisal, 1953; Our Lord's Unique Person, 1955; An Untold Miracle Story Concerning The Revised Standard Version; The Biography of A Soul-Judas, 1957; A Comprehensive System of Christian Doctrine, 1959; Straight Through the Bible in Two Years, 8 vols., 1963; Seventy Years with Pen, Pointer and Pulpit, 1968; Profile of a Modern Penticostal Movement, 1968. Kiwanian. Home: Swiss Village Berne IN 46711

HUFFMAN, JOHN WILLIAM, gynecologist; b. Gowrie, Ia., June 8, 1903; s. George Foreman and Ora (Dicus) H.; A.B., U. Ariz., 1924; M.S., Northwestern U., 1929, M.D., 1930; m. Florence Kearns, 1930 (div. 1958); children—John, Joan (Mrs. George Ellis), Mary (Mrs. Igor Drobocky); m.2d, Marilyn Moehling, Aug. 4, 1960. Intern Cal. Hosp., Los Angeles, 1929-30; gen. practice medicine, Tucson, 1930-35; resident in gynecology Passavant Meml. Hosp., Chgo., 1935-37; house officer Boston Lying-In Hosp., 1937; clin. asst. to prof. obstetrics and gynecology Northwestern U. Med. Sch., Chgo., 1938—; attending obstetrician, gynecologist Passavant Meml. Hosp., 1938—; attending gynecologist, head dept. gynecology emeritus Children's Meml. Hosp., Chgo. Served from Lt. comdr. to comdr., USNR, 1943-45. Fellow A.C.S., Am. Coll. Obstetricians and Gynecologists, Am. Acad. Pediatrics; mem. Soc. Exptl. Biology and Medicine, Central Assn. Obstetricians and Gynecologists, Pan Pacific Surg. Assn., Chgo. Gynecology Soc., A.M.A., Ill. Obstet. and Gynec. Soc. (hono), Sigma Xi, Pi Kappa Epsilon, Phi Delta Theta, Phi Chi, Pi Delta Epsilon. Episcopalian. Club: Chicago Literary. Author: Gynecology and Obstetrics, 1962; The Gynecology of Childhood and Adolescence, 1968. Home: 202 E Walton St Chicago IL 60611 Office: 720 N Michigan Av Chicago IL 60611

HUFFMAN, NORMAN ARA, educator; b. Hickory, N.C., Jan. 15, 1909; s. Ara Eliab and Bessie (Payne) H.; A.B., Duke, 1930, A.M., 1932, B.D., 1933; S.T.M., Harvard, 1934, post-doctoral scholar Div. Sch., 1969-70; Ph.D., Brown U., 1936; m. Esther S. Wright, June 8, 1932. Ordained to ministry Meth. Ch.; pastor, Huntersville, N.C., 1936, Lilesville, N.C., 1937, Waxhaw, N.C., 1938-40; asso. prof., head dept. religion Wesleyan Coll., Macon, Ga., 1941-46; prof., head dept. religion Willamette U., 1946—. Mem. archeol. expdn. of Harvard and Brown univs. to Van, Turkey, 1939. Fulbright research fellow, Italy, 1950-51. Mem. Soc. Bibl. Lit., Am. Acad. Religion, Am. Schs. Oriental Research, Phi Beta Kappa. Contbr. to Quantalacumque (R.P. Casey and others, editors), 1937, also articles to journ. Mem. Internat. New Testament Manuscript Project; cons. The Greek New Testament (United Bible Socs.), 1966. Office: Williamette U Salem OR 97301

HUFFMAN, ROBERT ALLEN, lawyer; b. Havelock, Neb., May 1, 1921; s. Orville Frank and Stella (Winkler) H.; J.D., U. Ariz., 1952; m. Ruth Jane Hicks, Dec. 30, 1946; children—Robert Allen, Margaret Jane, William Hicks, Elizabeth Kay. Admitted to Okla. bar, 1952, Ariz. bar, 1952; asso. atty. Huffman, Arrington, Scheurich & Kincaid and predecessors, Tulsa, 1952-54, partner, 1954-61, sr. partner, 1961—; gen. counsel Okla. Natural Gas Co. Chmn. bd. Republic Nat. Bank of Tulsa. Bd. dirs., exec. v.p. Tulsa Charity Horse Show. Served to capt. AUS, 1940-47. Decorated Combat Inf. badge, Bronze Star medal, Purple Heart. Mem. Am., Ariz., Okla., Tulsa County bar assns., Met. Tulsa C. of C., Phi Delta Phi. Republican. Presbyn. Clubs: Southern Hills Country, Summit, Tulsa (Tulsa); Tower (Oklahoma City). Home: 3139 S Atlanta St Tulsa OK 74105 Office: Okla Natural Bldg Tulsa OK 74119

HUFFMAN, ROY ELWOOD, univ. ofcl.; b. Highwood, Mont., Apr. 12, 1916; s. James L. and Gladys (Fuller) H.; B.S., Mont. State Coll., 1938; M.S., U. Md., 1939; Ph.D., U. Wis., 1952; m. Menga Herzog, July 2, 1939; children—Marjorie Ellen, Menga Elizabeth, James Lloyd. Agrl. economist FSA, Dept. Agr., 1939-42; instr. agrl. econs., asst. prof., asso. prof. Mont. State U., 1942-53, prof., head agrl. econs. and rural sociology, 1953-58, dean agr., 1958-65, v.p. for research, 1965—. Cons. Pres.'s Mo. Basin Survey Commn., 1952, Task Force on Water Resources and Power, Hoover Commn., 1954, Mo. River Basin Planning, Dept. Interior, 1964-65; sci. adviser Gov. Mont., 1969—; bd. cons. Columbia Basin, 1961; Mont. commr. on higher schs. N.W. Assn. Secondary and Higher Schs., 1969—. Served to lt. USNR, 1943-46. Mem. Am., Western farm econ. assns., Mont. Acad. Sci., Phi Kappa Phi, Alpha Zeta, Pi Kappa Delta. Methodist. Kiwanian. Home: 2609 Highland Blvd Bozeman MT 59715

HUFFMAN, SAM HOUSTON, retired actuary; b. Eliasville, Tex., Apr. 14, 1906; A.B., U. Fla., 1927; M.S., U. Ia., 1929; m. Florence Margaret Holsteen, Sept. 4, 1929; children—Sam Houston, Margaret Rose Joiner, Joseph Holsteen. Instr., U. Fla., 1930-31; actuarial supr. Met. Life Ins. Co., 1931-43; asst. group sec. State Mut. Life Assurance Co., 1946-47; group sec. Northwestern Nat. Life Ins. Co., 1948-52; actuary, mgr. The Wyatt Co., Dallas, 1952-55, v.p., 1955-70, dir., 1958-71, chmn. bd., 1970-71; retired, 1971. Served as maj. AUS, World War II. Fellow Conf. of Actuaries in Pub. Practice; mem. Soc. Actuaries (asso.), Am. Acad. Actuaries, Sigma Xi, Phi Kappa Tau, Phi Kappa Phi, Kappa Delta Pi. Home: Route 1 Box 751 Punta Gorda FL 33950 Office: Republic Nat Bank Tower Dallas TX 75201

HUFFMAN, WILLIAM CHARLES, univ. dean; b. Columbus, O., June 2, 1910; s. Charles Houston and Laura Elizabeth (Craig) H.; B.S., Ohio State U., 1931, M.A., 1941; postgrad. Miami U., 1938, U. Cin., 1948, Harvard Bus. Sch., 1944; Ph.D., Northwestern U., 1949; m. Virginia Lee Ryle, Aug. 9, 1941; children—Deborah Elizabeth, Cynthia Ann, Diana Lee. Tchr., coach high sch., Waynesville, O., 1932-33, Danville, Ky., 1933-36, Holmes High Sch., Covington, Ky., 1936-42; faculty econs., mgmt. U. Louisville, 1947—, prof., 1965—, acting head econs. dept., summers 1950-51, dir. div. adult edn., 1952-57, dean summer session, 1955—, acting dean Coll. Arts and Scis., 1955, dean Univ. Coll., 1957—. Mem. adv. com. Ky. Authority Ednl. TV. Mem. Louisville-Jefferson County Planning Commn. Served from pvt. to 1st lt. USAAF, 1942-46. Mem. Assn. U. Evening Colls. (pres. 1967-68), Nat. Assn. Colls. and U. Summer Sessions, Purchasing Mgmt. Assn. (econ. adviser 1951), Adult Edn. Assn. U.S. (state dir. membership, state coordinator pub. relations 1954-57), Sales Exec. Council Louisville, Louisville C. of C., Phi Kappa Tau. Episcopalian (vestryman). Rotarian. Club: Advertising (dir.). 5314 Hempstead Rd Louisville KY 40207

HUFFMAN, WILLIAM PHILLIPS, business exec.; b. Dayton, O., June 26, 1890; s. Torrence and Annie Eliza (Beckel) H.; B.S., Denison U., 1911; m. Elizabeth M. Kier, July 1, 1969. Accountant, Dayton Engring. Labs. Co., 1912-15; head order dept. Domestic Engring. Co., Dayton, 1916; sec.-treas. Buckeye Iron & Brass Works, Dayton, 1917-36, pres., 1936-65; pres. State Fidelity Fed. Savs. & Loan Assn., 1949-64, vice chmn., 1964-71; dir. City Transit Co., Midwest Securities Investment, Inc., Home Av. R.R. Co. Trustee Dayton Art Inst., Denison U., Woodland Cemetery Assn. Mem. C. of C., Sigma Chi. Clubs: Dayton City, Dayton Country, Moraine Country. Home: 2622 Ridgeway Rd Dayton OH 45419 Office: Gas & Electric Bldg Dayton OH 45402

HUFFSTETLER, PALMER EUGENE, transp. co. exec., lawyer; b. Shelby, N.C., Dec. 21, 1937; s. Daniel S. and Ethel (Turner) H.; B.A., Wake Forest U., 1959, LL.B., 1961; m. Mary Ann Beam, Aug. 9, 1958; children—Palmer Eugene, Ben Beam. Admitted to N.C. bar, 1961; practice law, Kings Mountain, N.C., 1961-62, Raleigh, N.C., 1962-64; with State Farm Ins. Co., Orlando, Fla., 1962; legal counsel Carolina Freight Carriers Corp., Cherryville, N.C., 1964—, sec., 1969—, also dir. Chmn., Cherryville Zoning Bd. Adjustment, 1967-70. Mem. N.C. State Bar, Am., N.C. bar assns. Methodist (mem. adminstrv. bd. 1965-69, chmn. adminstrv. bd. 1969-70, trustee 1970—). Rotarian (past pres.). Home: Roy Eaker Rd Cherryville NC 28021 Office: Carolina Freight Carriers Corp Cherryville NC 28021

HUFNAGEL, CHARLES ANTHONY, surgeon; b. Louisville, Aug. 15, 1916; s. Charles John and Lucine (Kirst) H.; B.S., U. Notre Dame, 1937; M.D., Harvard U., 1941; D.Sc. (hon.), Georgetown U., 1966; m. Katherine Moulton, 1944; children—Katherine Lucina, Judith Ann. Dir. lab. for surg. research Harvard Med. Sch., 1949-50; prof. surg. research, asso. prof. surgery Georgetown U. Med Sch., Washington, 1950-59, prof. surgery, 1959—, chmn. dept. surgery, 1969—, dir. surg. research lab.; chmn., prof. surgery Georgetown U. Med. Center. Recipient distinguished service award to 10 outstanding young men Nat. Jr. C. of C., 1949; named Notre Dame Man of Year, Boston, 1949; distinguished service award Ind. Jr. C. of C., 1949; named Notre Dame Man of the Year, 1953; distinguished service medal Washington Cosmopolitan Club, 1954; Modern Medicine award, 1961; T. and S. Cummings Humanitarian award, 1965; Mendel medal Villanova U., 1965; distinguished service award Am. Heart Assn., 1969; Wisdom award Honor, mem. Wisdom Hall Fame, 1970; James F. Mitchell Internat. award for heart and vascular research, 1970. Diplomate Am. Bd. Surgery, Am. Bd. Thoracic Surgery, Pan Am. Med. Assn. Fellow A.C.S.; mem. Am. Assn. Thoracic Surgery, Am. Heart Assn. (exec. com. cardiovascular surgery sect.). Soc. Univ. Surgeons, Am. Surg. Assn., Am. Assn. U. Profs., A.M.A., So. Surg. Assn., Internat. Soc. Cardiovascular Surgery, Am. Soc. Nephrology, Soc. Thoracic Surg., Soc. Vascular Surgery, A.A.A.S., Am. Fedn. Clin. Research, Am. Coll. Chest Physicians (gov.), So. Med. Assn., N.Y. Acad. Scis., Soc. Artifical Organs, Am. Thoracic Assn., Eastern Surg. Assn., Am. Coll. Cardiology (gov. 1966), Internat. Soc. Surgery, Allen O. Whipple Surg. Soc., So., Pan Pacific med. assns., Assn. Med. Writers, Royal Acad. Medicine (Spain), Coll. Surgeons (Ecuador, Colombia, Cuba), S.E. Surg. Assn., Soc. for Cryobiology, Phi Beta Kappa, Alpha Omega Alpha. Asso. editor Am. Jour. Surgery; editorial bd. Am. Family Physician. Home 4240 Nebraska Av NW Washington DC 20007 Office: 3800 Reservoir Rd Washington DC 20007

HUFSTEDLER, SHIRLEY MOUNT, (Mrs. Seth M. Hufstedler), U.S. judge; b. Denver, Aug. 24, 1925; d. Earl Stanley and Eva (Von Behren) Mount; B.B.A., U. N.M., 1945; LL.B., Stanford, 1949; LL.D., U. Wyo., 1970, Gonzaga U., 1970, Occidental Coll., 1971; m. Seth Martin Hufstedler, Aug. 16, 1949; 1 son, Steven Mark. Admitted to Cal. bar, 1950; mem. firm Beardsley, Hufstedler & Kemble, Los Angeles, 1951-61; pvt. practice, Lo Angeles, 1961; judge Superior Ct., County Los Angeles, 1961-66; justice Ct. Appeal 2d Dist., 1966-68; circuit judge U.S. Ct. Appeals 9th Circuit, 1969—. Trustee Inst. Ct. Mgmt.; bd. councilors U. So. Cal. Law Center. Mem. Am., Los Angeles bar assns., Women Lawyers Assn. (pres. 1957-58), Am. Judicature Soc., Am. Law Inst., Order of Coif. Mem. staff Stanford Law Rev., 1947-49, articles and book rev. editor, 1948-49. Home: 720 W Inverness Dr Pasadena CA 91103 Office: US Courthouse Los Angeles CA 90012

HUFTY, PAGE, financier; b. Washington, July 6, 1907; s. Malcolm and Mary (Page) H.; grad. Devitt Prep. Sch., Washington, 1925; m. Frances Archbold, Apr. 25, 1932; children—John Archbold, Mrs. Alexandra Page De Atucha Reynal, Frances Archbold (Mrs. Carter R. Leidy, Jr.), Page Lee, Mary Page. Pres., Virginia-Fla. Holding Corp., Palm Beach, Fla., 1958, Delaware Manitoba Corp., Palm Beach, 1958—, Vancouver-Del. Corp., Palm Beach, 1958—; pres., dir. Nat. Capital Warehouse Corp., Washington, 1942—; dir. First Nat. Bank, Palm Beach, Baldwin Securities Corp., N.Y.C. Trustee Blood Research Found.; hon. trustee Columbia Hosp. for Women, Washington; trustee Columbia Lighthouse for Blind, Palm Beach County Crippled Childrens Soc., Columbia Polytech. Inst. for Blind, Washington, Hufty Found. bd. dirs. Everglades Protective Syndicate, Inc. Clubs: Everglades (bd. govs.), Bath and Tennis (gov.), Seminole Golf (Palm Beach); Brook, River, West Side Tennis (N.Y.C.); Burning Tree, Chevy Chase, Metropolitan, University (Washington). Address: 7600 River Rd Washington DC 20034 also 330 Island Rd Palm Beach FL 33480

HUG, ARTHUR J., Jr., banker; b. N.Y.C., 1922; ed. Hofstra U., 1953. Pres. L.I. Trust Co., Garden City, N.Y. Bd. dirs. L.I. Assn. Mem. L.I. Bankers Assn. (past pres., dir.). Home: 121 Whitehall Blvd Garden City NY 11530 Office: 1401 Franklin Av Garden City NY 11530

HUG, PROCTER RALPH, Jr., lawyer; b. Reno, Mar. 11, 1931; s. Procter Ralph and Margaret (Beverly) H.; B.S., U. Nev., 1953; LL.B., J.D., Stanford, 1958; m. Barbara Va Meter, Apr. 4, 1954; children—Cheryl Ann, Protecter James, Elyse Marie. Admitted to Nev. bar, 1958, since practiced in Reno; mem. firm Woodburn, Forman, Wedge, Blakey, Folsom & Hug, 1963—; chmn. Nav. State Bar Com. on Jury Inst. Vice pres., dir. Nev. Tel. & Tel. Co. Vice pres. Young Democrats Nev., 1960-61. Chmn. bd. regents U. Nev.; bd. visitors Stanford Law Sch. Served to lt. USNR, 1953-55. Recipient Outstanding Alumnus award U. Nev., 1967. Mem. Am. Bar Assn. (state del.), Nat. Assn. Coll. and Univ. Attys. (past mem. exec. bd.), U. Nev. Alumni Assn. (past pres.), Stanford Law Soc. Nev. (pres.). Home: 2095 Regent St Reno NV 89502 Office: 1 E First St Reno NV 89501

HUG, RUSSELL JOHN, food co. exec.; b. Canton, O., Apr. 21, 1904; s. John Leo and Mary (Seikel) H.; student Ohio State U.; m. Bernadette Fox, 1934. With Gen. Baking Co., Canton, O., 1932-64, pres., 1956-64; exec. v.p. Ward Foods, Inc., 1964-71. Mem. Am. Inst. Baking (cons., dir. 1971—, past chmn.). Club: Union League (N.Y.C.). Home: 13 Linda Rd Port Washington Nassau Co NY 12123

HUGANIR, GEORGE HENRY, Jr., univ. dean; b. Phila., July 30, 1912; s. George Henry and Edna (Lewis) H.; A.B., Temple U., 1938; M.A., U. Pa., 1942, Ph.D., 1958; m. Helen N. Rambo, June 19, 1943; children—Jeffrey, Holly, Richard, Bruce. Tchr. secondary schs., Norristown, Pa., 1938-42; faculty Moses Brown Sch., Providence, 1942-43; employment mgr. Bendix Aviation Corp., N.Y.C., 1943-46; asst. registrar, instr., asst. prof., asso. prof., prof., chmn. dept. sociology and anthropology Temple U., Phila., 1946-58, vice provost, 1958-60, dean Grad. Sch., 1960-71, spl. asst. to pres., 1971—. Ednl. cons. State Farm Ins. Co., Citizen's Council of Montgomery County. Bd. dirs. Montgomery County Citizens Council; v.p. bd. Montgomery County Library. Fellow Am. Sociol. Assn.; mem. Am. Assn. U. Profs., Am. Acad. Polit. and Social Scis. Home: Locust Lane Norristown PA 19401 Office: Temple U Philadelphia PA 19122

HUGGARD, VINCENT P., govt. ofcl.; b. N.Y.C., Aug. 10, 1917; s. Joseph Michael and Kathryn (Kane) H.; ed. Am. U.; m. Dorothy Frances Travers, Sept. 3, 1938; children—Thomas, Jacqueline (Mrs. David Wyatt), Sister Mary Dorothy, Michael, Karen Ann (Mrs. Ernest Mata), Paul. Mgr. army affairs RCA, 1961-62; with Dept. Army, 1940-60, 62—, prin. dep. asst. sec. army for installations and logistics, 1967—. Chmn. bd. advisers devel. fund Patton Mus. Served with AUS, 1944-45. Recipient Exceptional Service medal Dept. Army (2). Home: 9100 Friars Rd Bethesda MD 20034 Office: Pentagon Washington DC 20310

HUGGINS, CHARLES, educator; b. Halifax, N.S., Can., Sept. 22, 1901; s. Charles Edward and Bessie (Spencer) H.; B.A., Acadia U., 1920, D.Sc., 1946; M.D., Harvard, 1924; M.Sc., Yale, 1947; D.Sc., Washington U., St. Louis, 1950, Leeds U., 1953, Turin U., 1957, Trinity Coll., 1965, Wales, 1967; LL.D., U. Aberdeen, 1966, York U., Toronto, U. Cal. at Berkeley, 1968; D.P.S., George Washington U., 1967; Sigillium Magnum, Bologna U., 1964; m. Margaret Wellman, July 29, 1927; children—Charles Edward, Emily Wellman. Intern in surgery U. Mich., 1924-26, instr. surgery, 1926-27; with U. Chgo., 1927—, instr. surgery, 1927-29, asst. prof., 1929-33, asso. prof., 1933-36, prof. surgery, 1936—, dir. Ben May Lab. for Cancer Research, 1951-69, William B. Ogden Distinguished Service prof., 1962—, chancellor Acadia U., Wolfville, N.S., 1971—; Macewen lectr. U. Glasgow, 1958. Trustee Worcester Found. Exptl. Biology. Decorated Order Pour le Mérite (Germany); Order of The Sun (Peru). Recipient Am. Urol. Assn. award for research on male genital tract, 1948; Francis Amory award for cancer research, 1948; A.M.A. gold medals for research, 1936, 40, Société Internationale d'Urologie, 1948; Am. Cancer Soc. award, 1953; Bertner award M.D. Anderson Hosp., 1953; award Am. Pharm. Mfrs. Assn., 1953, gold medal Am. Assn. Genito Urinary Surgeons, 1955, Borden award Assn. Am. Med. Colls., 1955, FRCS (hon.), Edinburg, 1958, London, 1959; Confort Crookshank award Middlesex Hosp., London, 1957; Charles Mickel fellow Toronto U., 1958; Cameron prize Edinburg U., 1958; Valentine prize N.Y. Acad. Medicine, 1962; Hunter award Am. Therapeutic Soc., 1962, Lasker award for med. research, 1963, gold medal for research Rudolf Virchow Soc., 1964, Laurea and award Am. Urol. Assn., 1966; gold medal in therapeutics Worshipful Soc. Apothecaries of London, 1966; Gairdner award, Toronto, 1966; Nobel prize for medicine, 1966; Chgo. Med. Soc. award, 1967; Centennial medal Acadia U., 1967; Hamilton award Ill. Med. Soc., 1967. Fellow A.C.S. (hon.); mem. Am. Philos. Soc., Nat. Acad. Scis. (Charles L. Meyer award for cancer research 1943), Am. Assn. Cancer Research, Canadian Med. Assn. (hon.), Alpha Omega Alpha. Home: 5759 S Kenwood Av Chicago IL 60637 Office: 950 E 59th St Chicago IL 60637

HUGGINS, CHARLES EDWARD, surgeon, cryobiologist, b. Chgo., May 7, 1929; s. Charles Brenton and Margaret (Wellman) H.; Ph.B., U. Chgo., 1947; M.D. cum laude, Harvard, 1952; m. Nancy Tienhaara, June 1, 1952; children—Elizabeth Ann, Margaret Ruth, Nancy Wellman, Charles Edward, Gordon Spencer. Surg. intern Mass. Gen. Hosp., 1952-53, surg. resident, 1953-60, asst. surgery, 1960-64, asst. surgeon, also asst. dir. blood bank and transfusion service, 1964- 67, asso. dir. blood bank and transfusion service, 1969—, chief surg. low temperture unit, 1969—, asso. vis. surgeon, 1968—; instr., then clin. asso. surgery Harvard Med. Sch., 1960-63, 64-68, asst. prof. surgery, 1968-69, asso. prof. surgery, 1969—. Served as lt. M.C., USNR, 1954-56. Moseley Traveling fellow, 1958-59; clin. fellow Am. Cancer Soc., 1959-60. Diplomate Am. Bd. Surgery. Fellow A.C.S.; mem. Soc. Cryobiology (gov. 1965-66, pres. 1968), Internat. Soc. Blood Transfusion, Soc. Univ. Surgeons, A.M.A., Soc. Internat. de Chirurgie, Mass. Med. Soc., Am. Assn. Blood Banks, Alpha Omega Alpha. Home: Monument St Concord MA 01742 Office: Mass Gen Hosp Boston MA 02114

HUGGINS, EDDIE LOU THOMPSON, TV newswoman; b. St. Joseph, Mo., Aug. 14, 1935; d. Edward William and Blanch (Payne) Thompson; student U. Neb., 1955-57; B.S., State U. N.Y. at Plattsburgh, 1963; postgrad. Temple U., 1969—; divorced; children—H. Edward, Laurie Linn. Nurse Flower-Fifth Av. Hosp., Bellevue Hosp., actress The Doctors, NBC-TV, model, N.Y.C., 1964-65; TV spl. feature reporter Evening News, Anchor Morning News, consumer reporter Right On, on-air TV comml. performer WCAU-TV, Phila., 1965—; spl. cons. Phila. Army Nurse Corps, 1969-71. Chmn. mother's march Phila. Assn. Retarded Children, 1970-71; asst. dir. Restitution Fund Commn., Episcopal Diocese of Pa., 1970—. Mem. Am. Nursing Assn., Black Communicators Phila., Kappa Delta Pi, Sigma Delta Chi. Contbr. editor Today's Girl mag., 1971—. Home: 2200 Benjamin Franklin Pkwy Philadelphia PA 19130 Office: WCAU-TV City Line Av Philadelphia PA 19131

HUGGINS, EDWIN VIRGIL corp. exec.; b. Madison, Wis., Sept. 28, 1907; s. Owen R. and Clementina (Michel) H.; Ph.B., Yale, 1929, LL.B., 1932, m. Leonora Ornston, Sept. 2, 1933; children—Robert Michel, Judith Lee (Mrs. Harry Balfe II), Kenneth, Janet (Mrs. Daniel Taylor). Admitted to N.Y. bar, 1934; asso. atty. Cravath, de Gersdorff, Swaine & Wood, 1932-40; atty. Rohm & Haas Co., Phila., 1940-43; atty. Westinghouse Electric Corp., 1943—, in charge N.Y. office law dept., 1945-51, corp. sec., 1948- 51, 54-57, v.p. corporate affairs, 1953-63, chmn. exec. com., 1958-61, exec. v.p., 1961-63, dir., 1951, 55, 57- 63, now sr. cons.; chmn., dir. Westinghouse Broadcasting Co., 1954-63, Westinghouse Electric Internat. Co., 1957-63; dir., vice chmn. Industria Electrica de Mexico; dir. Canadian Westinghouse Co., Ltd., Jaspar- Westinghouse Ateliers, S.A. (Liege, Belgium); vice chmn., dir. TV Advt. Reps., Inc., 1959-63; pres. Automated Spltys., Inc., Charlottesville, Va., 1964-65; chmn. dir. Renwell Industries, Inc., 1965-66; chmn., pres., dir. Gulf States Land & Industries, Inc., 1968-70. Asst. sec. USAF, 1952-53; exec. dir. Met. Airlines Com., 1966-67; mem. Def. Industry Adv. Com., 1962-67, vice chmn., 1962-64. Pres., Pocomo Area Assn., Nantucket, Mass., 1968-71. Trustee Nantucket Conservation Found., Mem. Nat. Secutiry Indsl. Assn. Home: 22 Canterbury Lane Summit NJ 07901 Office: 120 Broadway New York City NY 10005

HUGGINS, NATHAN IRVIN, educator; b. Chgo., Jan. 14, 1927; s. Winston J. and Marie (Warsaw) H.; A.B., U. Cal. at Berkeley, 1954, M.A., 1955; A.M., Harvard, 1959, Ph.D., 1962; m. Brenda Smith Spigner, July 18, 1971. Asst. prof. Cal. State Coll. at Long Beach, 1962-64, Lake Forest (Ill.) Coll., 1964-66; asst. prof., then asso. prof. U. Mass.-Boston, 1966-70; prof. history Columbia, 1970—. Commnr.

Mass. Tchr. Corps Com., 1968-69. Pres. Museum Afro-Am. History, Boston, 1967-69. Bd. dirs. Children's TV Workshop, 1970—; trustee Howard Thurman Ednl. Trust, 1968—. Served with AUS, 1945-46. Mem. Am. Hist. Assn., Orgn. Am. History, Assn. Study Negro Life. Author: Protestants Against Poverty, 1971; Harlem Renaissance, 1971. Co-editor: Key Issues of the Afro-American Experience, 1971. Home: 410 Riverside Dr New York City NY 10025

HUGGINS, RICHARD EMMETT, interstate moving co. exec.; b. Indpls., July 25, 1910; s. Emmett S. and Florence (Moore) H.; M.S., Butler U., 1931; LL.B., Ind. U., 1935; m. Louise Eickhoff, June 8, 1935; children—Linda Jane, Andrea Louise. Admitted to Ind. bar, 1934; adjuster Ind. Ins. Co., 1932-35; with Aero Mayflower Transit Co., Inc., Indpls., 1935—, sec., 1962—, also dir.; dir. Ind. Ins. Co., Hogan Transfer and Storage Corp. Republican. Presbyn. (trustee, deacon, elder). Mason (Shriner), Kiwanian (bd. dirs. Indpls.). Club: Indpls. Athletic. Home: 6347 Macatuck Dr Indianapolis IN 46220 Office: 863 Massachusetts Av Indianapolis IN 46204

HUGGINS, ROLLIN CHARLES, Jr., lawyer; b. Berwyn, Ill., Oct. 11, 1931; s. Rollin Charles and Helen (Smith) H.; A.B., Knox Coll., 1953; LL.B., Harvard, 1958; m. Charlotte Harrison, Apr. 26, 1952; children—Cynthia C., Shirley A., John C. Admitted to Ill. bar, 1958, since practiced in Chgo.; partner Bell, Boyd, Lloyd, Haddad & Burns, 1958—. Served to 1st lt. AUS, 1954-56. Mem. Am., Ill., Chgo. bar assns., Phi Beta Kappa, Beta Theta Pi. Home: 700 Greenwood Av Wilmette IL 60091 Office: 135 S LaSalle St Chicago IL 60603

HUGGINS, SARA ESPE, educator; b. Denver, June 29, 1913; d. Paul Albert and Ethel (Benton) Espe; A.B., Aurora Coll., 1934; M.S., U. Ill., 1936; Ph.D., Western Res. U., 1939; m. Russell Arno Huggins; children—James, George. Instr. biology Paine Coll., 1946-47; faculty U. Houston, 1947—, prof. biology, 1953—, chmn. dept., 1952-64. Mem. Am. Assn. U. Profs., Sigma Xi, Phi Kappa Phi. Home: 4811 Palmetto St Bellaire TX 77401 Office: U Houston Houston TX 77004

HUGGINS, WILLIAM HERBERT, educator; b. Rupert, Ida., Jan. 11, 1919; s. William John and Alafretta Evelyn (Roraback) H.; B.S., Ore. State Coll., 1941, M.S., 1942; Sc.D., Mass. Inst. Tech., 1953. Instr. elec. engring. Ore. State Coll., 1942- 44; spl. research asso. radio research lab. Harvard, 1944-46; supervising scientist Air Force Research Center, Cambridge, Mass., 1946- 54; research asso. Mass. Inst. Tech., 1949-54; Westinghouse prof. elec. engring. Johns Hopkins, 1954—, chmn. dept., 1970—. Cons. editor Addison-Wesley Pub. Co., 1957-60, Blaisdell Pub. Co. 1961-65; cons. Rand Corp., 1955—. Recipient decoration for exceptional civilian service USAF, 1954; Browder J. Thomson Meml. prize Am. I.R.E., 1948; Lindback Found. award for distinguished teaching, 1961; Western Electric Fund award Am. Soc. Engring. Edn., 1965. Fellow I.E.E.E. (Edn. medal 1966), Acoustical Soc. Am.; mem. A.A.A.S., Operations Research Soc. Am., Nat. Acad. Engring., Soc. Indsl. and Applied Math., Sigma Xi, Phi Beta Kappa. Home: 2813 St Paul St Baltimore MD 21218

HUGHART, STANLEY PARLETT, educator, mathematician; b. Spokane, Mar. 17, 1918; s. Robert Samuel and Ruth (Myrell) P.; B.S. magna cum laude, Whitworth Coll., Spokane, 1940; Ph.D., Cal. Inst. Tech., 1954; m. Dorothy Martin, Aug. 3, 1941. Instr. math. Princeton, 1943-44; instr., then asst. prof. math. U. Chgo., 1944- 54; mem. faculty Sacramento State Coll., 1954—, prof. math., 1962—, chmn. dept. math., 1958-63, 66-68. Mem. Math. Assn. Am., Am. Math. Soc. Home: 5814 River Oak Way Carmichael CA 95608

HUGHES, ANDREW WESLEY, mfg. exec.; b. Cloquet, Minn., May, 10, 1912; s. William Edward and Helga (Swendby) H.; student U. Minn., 1931-32; m. Gladys Ethel Fredrickson, Oct. 7, 1933; 1 son, Richard. Constrn. worker P.J. Walker Co., Los Angeles, 1933; mechanic Kittoe & Hardiman Co., 1934; constrn. foreman Westco Constrn. Co., 1935; paymaster Republic Steel Corp., Stevenson, Minn., 1936; asst. chief ore grader Oliver Iron Mining Co., Hibbing, Minn., 1938-43; with Rheem Mfg. Co., 1944—, gen. mgr. jet. engine container dept., Sparrows Point, Md., 1949-52, asst. to comptroller, Linden, N.J., 1952-53, gen. mgr. Eastern div., 1953-56, comptroller, N.Y.C., 1956-62, treas., 1963-64, v.p., treas., 1964—, also dir.; dir. Saiar-Argentina, Rheem Peruana, Lima, Peru. Chmn., Christian Bus. Men's Com. Internat. Bd. dirs. Christian Nats. Evangelism Commn. Mem. Am. Mgmt. Assn., Financial Execs. Inst., Nat. Assn. Accountants, N.Y. Bible Soc. (bd. mgrs.). Presbyn. (elder). Contbr. articles to profl. jours. Home: 35 Sutton Pl New York City NY 10022 Office: 400 Park Av New York City NY 10022

HUGHES, ARTHUR HOWARD, coll. adminstr.; b. Dayton, O., May 23, 1906; s. Arthur Lewis and Stella Jeanette (Peters) H.; A.B., Johns Hopkins, 1927, A.M., 1929, Ph.D., 1931; L.H.D., Trinity Coll., 1946; student in Vienna, 1928, 30; m. Laura Ellen Kenealy, July 30, 1940; children—Kathleen, David. Instr. in German, Johns Hopkins U., 1928-30; instr. George Washington U., 1930- 31, asst. prof., 1931-34; instr. in German, Trinity Coll., Hartford, Conn., 1935-38, asst. prof., 1938-43, asso. prof., 1943-45, prof. Modern langs., 1945—, dean coll., 1941-64, acting pres., 1943-45, 51-53, v.p., 1954-70, spl. asst. to pres., 1970—. Nat. scholarship dir. UNICO, 1968—. Corporator Hartford Hosp., Hartford Pub. Library; bd. dirs. Hartford (Conn.) Hosp. Assn. Chmn. Commn. on City Plan, Hartford, 1959-61, commr., 1957—. Mem. Am. Name Soc., Am. Geog. Soc., Eastern Assn. Coll. Deans, Nat. Assn. Fgn. Student Advisers, Conn. Audio-Visual Edn. Assn., Mod. Lang. Assn. Am., Soc. Colonial Wars, New Eng. Modern Lang. Assn., Am. Assn. U. Profs., Phi Beta Kappa, Phi Gamma Mu, Delta Phi Alpha. Episcopalian. Club: Hartford. Contbr. to lit. and philol. jours. Home: 73 Vernon St Hartford CT 06106 Office: Trinity Coll Hartford CT 06106

HUGHES, AUTHOR ERNEST, Jr., educator; b. Hoopeston, Ill., Nov. 4, 1929; s. Arthur Ernest and Nora (Cleveland) H.; B.S., Eastern Ill. U., 1951; M.A., Colo. State Coll., 1954; Ph.D., U. Ia., 1960; m. Marjorie Ann Herman, Aug. 21, 1956; children—James Gregory, Timothy Charles, John Andrew, Susan Marie. High sch. bus. tchr., 1951-54; coll. bus. tchr. 1954-66; dean No. Ariz. U. Coll. Bus., Flagstaff, 1966-69, v.p., provost, 1969—. Cons. in systems field. Bd. dirs. Flagstaff Salvation Army. Mem. Ariz. Acad., Am. Assn. Jr. Colls. (adv. bd.), Beta Gamma Sigma, Phi Kappa Phi, Delta Pi Epsilon, Delta Sigma Pi. Kiwanian. Co-author: Automated Data Processing, 1969. Home: 1415 N Aztec St Flagstaff AZ 86001

HUGHES, BLAKE, publishing co. exec.; b. N.Y.C., June 24, 1914; s. Ferdinand Holme and Ines (De Cordova) H.; A.B. summa cum laude, Dartmouth Coll., 1936; degre de civlisation Sorbonne U., Paris, France, 1935; postgrad. Columbia, 1936-37; m. Betty Jean Wolf, Aug. 26, 1951; children—Diane Elizabeth, Brian Blake. Salesman Edward B. Smith & Co., Smith, Barney & Co., investment bankers, N.Y.C., 1936-38; salesman N.Y. Life Ins. Co., N.Y.C., 1939-40; promotion mgr. Engring. News Record, Constrn. Methods McGraw-Hill Inc., N.Y.C., 1947-50; promotion mgr., dir. marketing Archtl. Record, F.W. Dodge Corp., N.Y.C., 1951-61, asso. pub. Archtl. Record, Mc Graw Hill Inc., 1961-68, pub., 1968—; pub. Archtl. Record Books, 1970—, Archtl. Record News Letter, 1970—. Trustee Unity (Me.) Coll., 1970—. Served to lt. USNR, 1940-45. Decorated Order Fatherland War (Russia). Mem. Phi Beta Kappa, Delta Sigma Rho. Episcopalian (vestryman). Club: Architectural League N.Y., Sales Execs Club (N.Y.C.). Home: 25 Chestnut Dr Hastings-on-Hudson NY 10706 Office: 330 W 42d St New York City NY 10036

HUGHES, CARL WILSON, army med. officer; b. Eminence, Mo., June 29, 1914; s. Stephen Mitchel and Sarah (Ward) H.; A.B., U. Mo., 1939; M.D., U. Tenn., 1944; m. Eleanor Naomi Hulseweh, June 13, 1943; children—Elaine Leslie, Debra Lenor. Intern, Bapt. Meml. Hosp., Memphis, 1944; resident John Gaston Hosp., Memphis, 1945-46; commd. 1st lt. M.C., U.S. Army, 1946, advanced through grades to maj. gen., 1970; asst. chief, later chief surg. service 57th Field Hosp., Wurzburg, Germany, 1946-47; chief surg. service 385th Sta. Hosp., Nurnberg, Germany, 1948-49; surg. resident Walter Reed Army Hosp., 1949-52; vascular surg. cons. 8th Army, mem. surg. research team U.S. Army, Korea, 1953; dir. div. surgery Walter Reed Army Inst. Research, chief peripheral vascular surgery Walter Reed Hosp., 1954-57; chief gen. surgery staff, later chief dept. surgery Tripler Gen. Hosp., Honolulu, 1957-61; chief dept. surgery Madigan Gen. Hosp., Tacoma, 1961-64, Letterman Gen. Hosp., San Francisco, 1964-65; chief dept. surgery Walter Reed Gen. Hosp., 1965-69, comdg. gen., 1969-71; comdg. gen. Tripler Gen. Hosp., chief surgeon U.S. Army, Pacific, 1971—; cons. vascular surgery surgeon gen., 1965-71. Clin. asso. prof. surgery U. Wash. Sch. Medicine, Seattle, 1962-64; asso. clin. prof. surgery George Washington U. Sch. Medicine, 1966-71. Decorated Bronze Star; Legion of Merit with oak leaf cluster. Named comdr. Most Noble Order Crown Thailand; recipient Sir Henry Wellcome award, 1958; Arthur M. Shipley award, 1968; citation of merit U. Mo. Alumni Assn. and Sch. Medicine, 1970. Diplomate Am. Bd. Surgery. Mem. A.C.S., Soc. Vascular Surgery, Am. Assn. Surgery Trauma, So., Am. surg. assns., A.M.A., Assn. Mil. Surgeons U.S. Author, co-author 2 books, numerous articles. Home: Tripler Gen Hosp Honolulu HI 96438

HUGHES, CHARLES CAMPBELL, educator; b. Salmon, Ida., Jan. 26, 1929; s. Charles Frederick and Grace (Campbell) H.; A.B. magna cum laude, Harvard Coll., 1951; M.A., Cornell U., 1953, Ph.D., 1957; m. Jane Ellen Murphy, Feb. 6, 1951 (div. July 1962); m. 2d, Patricia Diane Devereux, Aug. 8, 1964 (div. May 1969); m. 3d, Leslie Ann Medert, Mar. 7, 1970. Asso. dir., sr. research asso. Cornell Program in Social Psychiatry Cornell U., 1957-61, asst. prof. anthropology Dept. Psychiatry Cornell U. Med. Coll., 1959-61; fellow Center for Advanced Study in Behavioral Scis., Stanford, Cal., 1961-62; dir. African Studies Center, Mich. State U., 1962-70, asso. prof., 1962-64, prof., 1964—, prof. anthropology and psychiatry, 1970—. Fellow Am. Anthropol. Assn., Soc. Applied Anthropology (pres. 1969-70), Am. Sociol. Assn., African Studies Assn., Arctic Inst. North Am., A.A.A.S.; mem. Am. Ethnol. Soc., Phi Beta Kappa, Sigma Xi, Phi Kappa Phi. Co-author: An Eskimo Village in the Modern World, 1960; People of Cove and Woodlot, 1960; Psychiatric Disorder Among the Yoruba, 1963. Home: 2900 Northwind Dr East Lansing MI 48823

HUGHES, CLIFFORD EVANS, lawyer; b. Dawn, Mo., Nov. 18, 1894; s. Joseph and Sarah (Evans) H.; A.B., U. So. Cal., 1919, J.D., 1921; m. Sarah Burton, Oct. 29, 1923; children—Clifford Burton, Warren Burton. Admitted to Cal. bar, 1921, U.S. Supreme Ct. bar, 1941; since practiced in Los Angeles; formerly sr. partner, now of counsel Meserve, Mumper & Hughes; chmn. Chrysons, Ltd., Burbank, Cal., 1944-68; sec.-treas. firm Royalties, Inc., 1936—. Former trustee, past pres. Beverly Hills Sch. Bd.; fellow U. So. Cal., bd. counsellors. Civic center com., Beverly Hills, 1954, oil and gas com., 1955, freeway com., 1953, citizens adv. com. on master planning, 1959—; sec. Home Owners Assn., 1925-40, Taxpayers Assn., 1931-35; life mem. adv. bd. Salvation Army, Los Angeles. Bd. dirs. (life) Better Bus. Bur. Served with inf. AEF, 1917-18. Recipient award of merit U. So. Cal., 1964. Mem. Am., Los Angeles County bar assns., State Bar Cal., Gen. Alumni Assn. U. So. Cal. (pres. 1934), 91st Div. Assn. (past sec.), Am. Legion (past sec.), V.F.W., C. of C., (past sec.), Legion Lex, Skull and Dagger, Phi Delta Phi, Chi Phi. Republican Episcopalian. (sr. warden). Clubs: Bel Air Bay (past pres. Santa Monica); University (past pres. Los Angeles); Trojan (past pres.); Irvine Coast Country. Home: 2525 Ocean Blvd Corona del Mar CA 92625 Office: 612 S Flower St Los Angeles CA 90017

HUGHES, DANA THOMAS, pub. relations exec.; b. Glen Ridge, N.J., July 8, 1922; s. Ellsworth Guy and Marjorie (Meihr) H.; B.A., Lafayette Coll., 1949; postgrad. Lehigh U., 1950-51, Cornell U., 1953-54; m. Barbara Harrison, Sept. 6, 1947; children—Richard Douglas, Susan Barbara. Adminstrv. asst. Dixie Cup Co., Easton, Pa., 1949-52; writer Am. Locomotive Co., 1952-54, dir. information, 1954-56, dir. pub. relations, 1956-59; partner Dana Hughes Associates, Phila., 1959-62; mgr., Rumrill Co., Inc., pub. Relations, Rochester, N.Y. office, 1962-64; v.p., gen. mgr. Burson-Marsteller Internat. Pub. Relations Cons., Pitts. br., 1964—. Bd. dirs. Opportunities Industrialization Center, Inc., Pitts., Pitts. Coordinating Council. Served with USMCR, 1942-45. Mem. Pub. Relations Soc. Am. (pres. Pitts. 1971). Press Club. Presbyn. Clubs: Allegheny, Duquesne, University (Pitts.). Contbr. profl. jours. Home: 15 Thornwood Dr Pittsburgh PA 15228 Office: 1 Oliver Plaza Pittsburgh PA 15222

HUGHES, DAVID GRATTAN, educator, musicologist; b. Norwalk, Conn., June 14, 1926; s. George P. and Elizabeth (Lennox) H.; A.B., Harvard, 1949, A.M., 1954, Ph.D., 1956; m. Janet Brandon, Apr. 29, 1953; children—Catherine E.C., Anne A.M. Faculty, Harvard, 1956—, prof. music, 1964—, chmn. dept., 1961-65. Vis. asst. prof. history music Yale, 1957-58. Mem. adv. com. Berkshire Music Center, 1962-67. Served with AUS, 1944-46. Mem. Am. (council 1962-64, 66-68, editor jour. 1960-63, editorial bd. 1963- 69), Internat. musicological socs., Mediaeval Acad. Contbr. articles, revs. mediaeval music to profl. jours. Editor: Instrumental Music, a Conference at Isham Memorial Library, 1959. Compiler: (with John R. Bryden) An Index of Gregorian Chant, 2 vols., 1970. Home: 25 Day School Lane Belmont MA 02178 Office: Music Bldg Harvard U Cambridge MA 02138

HUGHES, DAVID H., architect; b. Phila., Nov. 8, 1918, s. David A. and Anne (Wright) H.; B.A., Yale, 1941, B.F.A., 1948; m. Ruth Noel Hurley, Dec. 24, 1942; children—David, Wilson, Anne, Cecily, Ruth, Ian, Peter, Graeme. With Skidmore, Owings & Merrill, N.Y.C., 1948—, gen. partner, 1958—. Treas. internat. council Mus. Modern Art. Served with AUS, 1941-42; from 2d lt. to capt. USAAF, 1942-46; ETO. Decorated Air medal (8). Mem. A.I.A., Yale Arts Assn. (pres. 1966-70), Am. Soc. Planning Ofcls., Soc. Archtl. Historians, Archtl. League. Clubs: Yale (N.Y.C); Belle Haven, Stanwich (dir. Greenwich). Home: Crown Lane Greenwich CT 06830 Office: 400 Park Av New York City NY 10022

HUGHES, EARL MULFORD, agrl. co. exec.; b. Woodstock, Ill., Sept. 6, 1907; s. Earl Christopher and Mary Magdalene (Wiedrick) H.; B.S. in Agr., U. Ill., 1929; Ph.D., N.Y. State Coll. Agr. at Cornell U., 1938; m. Mildred Margaret Shuman, Feb. 20, 1932; children—Helen Shuman, Robert Christopher, Earl Mulford. Farm laborer, 1924-25; with father, Woodstock, 1929-34; asst. in marketing Cornell U., 1934-38; asst. prof. agrl. econs. U. Ill. Extension Coll. Agr., 1938-42; partner Hughes Seed Farms, 1942—; farmer, also fieldman Farm Mgmt. Service, 1942-43; farmer, Woodstock, 1944-55; cons. to sec. agr., 1954; adminstr. Commodity Stblzn. Service, exec. v.p. CCC, Washington, 1955-56, mem. adv. bd., 1957-61, chmn., 1957-61; chmn. bd. Hughes Hybrids Inc., 1967—; dir. 1st Nat. Bank of Woodstock (Ill.), Country Mut. Casualty Co., Country Life Ins. Co., Ill. Bell Telephone Co. Mem. sch. bd. Rural Community Consol. Sch. Dist. 10, Woodstock, 1946-55; mem. Woodstock Community High Sch. Bd., 1952-55; mem. U. Ill. Found.; mem. Univ. Civil Service Merit Bd. Ill., 1963-69. Trustee Farm Found., Found. Am. Agr., Univs. Retirement System Ill.; trustee U. Ill., 1956—, pres., 1969—. Recipient Distinguished Service award Ill. Soc. Farm Mgrs., Rural Appraisers, 1968; award of merit U. Ill. Coll. Agr., 1968; award for service to agr. and people State Ill., Ill. Extension Advisers Assn., U. Ill. Coll. Agr., 1970. Mem. Am. Farm Bur. Fedn., Ill. Agrl. Assn. (chmn. pub. relations com. and legislative com. 1953-54), McHenry County Farm Bur., Ill. Found. Seeds Inc., Ill. Crop Improvement Assn., Am. Seed Trade Assn., Alpha Zeta, Gamma Sigma Delta, Farmhouse. Methodist. Address: 206 N Hughes Rd Woodstock IL 60098

HUGHES, EDWARD HUNTER, editor, writer; b. Ashland, Ky., Aug. 20, 1921; s. Paul Jones and Jessie Lee (Owens) H.; A.B., Centre Coll. Ky., 1943; M.A., Harvard, 1947; m. Mary J. Stanford, Jan. 15, 1955 (dec.). Reporter, Washington bur. Wall Street Jour., 1947-50, reporter, Europe, Middle East and Africa, 1950-53, fgn. editor, 1953-54; Africa bur. chief Time Inc., 1954-56, Germany and Eastern Europe bur. chief, 1956-59, writer, 1959-62, sr. editor, 1962-68, Middle East bur. chief, 1968-70. Served with AUS. 1944-45; ETO. Address: care Hotel St Georges Beirut Lebanon

HUGHES, EDWARD THOMAS, clergyman; b. Lansdowne, Pa., Nov., 13, 1920; s. Charles Valentine and Kathryn Mary (Mingey) H.; B.A., St. Charles Sem., Overbrook, Phila., 1944; M.A., U. Pa., 1953. Ordained priest Roman Cath. Ch., 1947; tchr. St. James High Sch., Chester, Pa., 1947-54; asst. rector Immaculate Conception Ch., Jenkintown, Pa., 1954-56; vice rector St. Charles Sem., 1956-60; asst. supt. schs. Archdiocese Phila., 1960-61, became supt. schs., 1961; mem. faculty U. Villanova, 1958-59. Mem. Commn. Higher Edn. Phila.; dir. exec. com. sta. WHYY. Recipient LaSalle Coll. Centennial medal in edn., 1962; named domestic prelate, 1962. Mem. Nat. Cath. Ednl. Assn., Cath. Ednl. Assn. Pa. Home: 1 Fatima Dr Secane PA 15953

HUGHES, ELINOR LAMBERT, drama editor, critic; b. Cambridge, Mass., Mar. 3, 1906; d. Hector James and Elinor (Lambert) H.; ed. Buckingham Sch., Cambridge, 1915-20, May Sch., Boston, 1920-23; A.B., Radcliffe Coll., 1927; m. David D. Jacobus, July 14, 1957; stepchildren—David P. Jacobus, John H. Jacobus. Asst. in drama dept. Boston Herald-Traveler, 1929- 34, drama and film editor and critic, 1934-66; lectr. on drama and film criticism. Mem. Soc. Preservation of N.E. Antiquities, Inst. Contemporary Art. Republican. Unitarian. Clubs: Women's City (Boston). Author: Famous Stars of Filmdom (Men) and Famous Stars of Filmdom (Women), 1932; Passing Through to Broadway, 1948. Blank verse rev. of Shakespearean prodns. included in Best News Stories of 1937-38. Home: 24 Academy Lane Bellport NY 11713

HUGHES, EMMET JOHN, author, journalist; b. Newark, Dec. 26, 1920; s. John L. and Grace (Freeman) H.; A.B. summa cum laude, Princeton, 1941; m. Katherine Nouri; children—Caitlin, (by previous marriage) John, Mary L., Kathleen F. Press attache Am. embassy, Madrid, 1942-46; fgn. corr., chief Rome bur. Time-Life, 1946-48, chief Berlin bur., 1948-49; articles editor Life mag., 1949-52; speech writer nat. campaign Dwight D. Eisenhower, 1952; adminstrv. asst. to Pres. Eisenhower, 1953; spl. European corr. Life mag., 1954-56; speech writer Eisenhower campaign, 1956; mem. bd. editors Fortune mag., 1956-57; chief fgn. corr. Time-Life, 1957-60; sr. adviser pub. policy to Rockefeller Family, 1960-63; columnist, editorial cons. Newsweek and Washington Post, 1963-68; spl. asst. to Gov. Nelson Rockefeller, N.Y.C., 1968-70; prof. politics Eagleton Inst., Rutgers U., 1970—. Roman Catholic. Author: The Church and The Liberal Society, 1943; Report From Spain, 1947; America the Vincible, 1959; The Ordeal of Power, 1963. Home: 9 Olden Lane Princeton NJ 08540 Office: care Gov Nelson Rockefeller 22 W 55th St New York City NY 10019

HUGHES, ERIC MILTON, fgn. service officer; b. New Albany, Miss., Jan. 19, 1914; s. Clyde and Erena (Strum) H.; m. Mary Fay Oliver, Apr. 25, 1947; children— Marilyn, Patricia. Salesman, 1932-41; civilian employee U.S. Govt. in Europe, 1946-52; joined U.S. fgn. service, 1950; dep. dir. U.S. Escapee Program for Europe, Middle East, Germany, 1952-57; specialist refugee affairs State Dept., Washington, 1957-60; asst. adviser refugee affairs, 1960-62; consul gen. Belfast, No. Ireland, 1962-65; dep. refugee coordinator AID, Saigon, Vietnam, 1965-66, refugee coordinator, 1966; asst. dir. for refugees Office Civil Operations, Am. embassy, Saigon, Vietnam, 1966-67; dep. dir. Visa Office, Dept. State, Washington, 1967-69, dir. Office Spl. Consular Services, 1970—. Adviser U.S. del. 6th session exec. com., 4th session gen. council Internat. Refugee Orgn., Geneva, 1949, 7th session exec. com., 5th session gen. council, Geneva, 1950, 10th session exec. com., 8th session gen. council, Geneva, 1951; adviser U.S. delegation provisional intergovtl. com. Movement of Migrants from Europe, Geneva, 1952; adviser U.S. delegation 13th session exec. com., 11th session council Intergovtl. Com. European Migration, Geneva, 1959, 15th session exec. com., 12th session council, Naples, 1960, 16th session exec. com., 13th session council, Geneva, 1960, 14th to 15th session councils, Geneva, 1961. Served to maj. with AUS, 1941-46; lt. col. Res. Decorated Bronze Star (U.S.); medal of Merit 1st class (Czechoslovakia); Croix de Guerre (Belgium). Mem. Am. Fgn. Service Assn. Home: 2601 Woodley Pl Washington DC 20008 Office: Dept State Washington DC 20520

HUGHES, EVERETT CHERRINGTON, sociologist, educator; b. Beaver, O., Nov. 30, 1897; s. Charles Anderson and Jessamine Blanche (Roberts) H.; A.B., Ohio Wesleyan U., 1918; Ph.D., U. Chgo., 1928; LL.D., Sir George Williams U., Boston Coll., Queen's U., McGill U.; L.H.D., Mich. State U., Ohio Wesleyan U.; m. Helen Gregory MacGill, Aug. 18, 1927; children—Helen MacGill Cherrington, Elizabeth Gregory Roberts. Asst. prof. sociology McGill U., Montreal, Que., Can., 1927-38; Social Sci. Research Council fellow, research in Germany, 1931-32; asst. prof. U. Chgo., 1938-43, asso. prof., 1943-49, prof., 1949-61, chmn. dept. sociology, 1952-56; prof. sociology Brandeis U., Waltham, Mass., 1961-68, prof. emeritus, 1968—; prof. sociology Boston Coll., Chestnut Hill, Mass., 1968—; vis. prof. McGill U., Université de Montréal, 1965. Fellow A.A.A.S., Am. Sociol. Assn. (pres. 1962-63), Am. Anthrop. Assn., Am. Acad. Arts and Scis.; mem. Soc. Applied Anthropology (pres. 1950-51), Canadian Sociology and Anthropology Assn. (hon. pres.), Eastern Sociol. Soc. (pres. 1968-69), Alpha Sigma Phi. Democrat. Episcopalian. Author: (with R. E. Park, A. B. Hollingshead, H. Blumer, E. B. Reuter and R. Fuller) Outlines of Sociology, 1940; French Canada in Transition, 1943; Reccontre de deux mondes, 1945; Where Peoples Meet: Racial and Ethnic Frontiers (with Helen Hughes), 1952; Men and Their Work, 1958; (with Helen MacGill Hughes and Irwin Deutscher) Twenty Thousand Nurses Tell their Story, 1958; (with Howard S. Becker and Blanche Geer) Boys in White: Student Culture in Medical School, 1961; Making the Grade, The Academic Side of College Life, 1968; The Sociological Eye,

Collected Papers on Social Institutions, Race Relations, Work, and Sociological Method, 1971. Editor: Race: Individual and Collective Behavior (with E. T. Thompson), 1958; the Sociological Eye, 1971. Editor Am. Jour. Sociology, 1952-60; also contbr. Home: 27 Shepard St Cambridge MA 02138 Office: Dept Sociology Boston Coll Chestnut Hill MA 02167

HUGHES, EVERETT CLARK, educator; b. Wadena, Minn., Nov. 22, 1904; s. Albert B. and Pearl Sylpha (Moses) H.; B.A. in Chemistry, Carleton Coll., Northfield, Minn., 1927; Ph.D., Cornell U., 1930; m. Ruth Scherer, Aug. 3, 1907; children—Mary Alice (Mrs. Donald P. Allen), Kathleen (Mrs. Frederick D. Barker III), Robert, Bruce, Randolph. Research chemist Standard Oil Co. (O.), Cleve., 1930-44, chief chem. and phys. research div., 1944-54, mgr. research div., 1954-60, v.p., 1960-69; research dir., research asso. dept. surgery (otolaryngology) Sch. Medicine U. So. Cal., Los Angeles, 1970—. Fellow A.A.A.S., Am. Inst. Chemists (chem. Pioneer of 1971 award); mem. Am. Chem. Soc., Am. Petroleum Inst., Clve. Assn. Research Dirs., Soc. Chem. Industry, Phi Beta Kappa, Sigma Xi, Alpha Chi Sigma. Contbr. articles profl. jours. Patentee in field. Home: 1225 Charles St Pasadena CA 91103 Office: Sch Medicine U So Cal Hoffman Research Bldg 2025 Zonal Av Los Angeles CA 90033

HUGHES, FELIX TURNER, mfg. exec.; b. Chgo., Mar. 3, 1912; s. Felix Turner and Elizabeth Wheeler (Curtis) H.; grad. Pomfret Sch., 1930; B.A., Yale, 1934; m. Esther Kneeland, Sept. 4, 1935; children—David K., Elizabeth C. (Mrs. Richard R. Standel, Jr.), Lisa B. (Mrs. Eugene A. Peyroux, Jr.). With Pitts. Plate Glass Co. (co. name changed to PPG Industries, Inc. 1968), 1934—, trainee, mgr., Mobile, Columbus, O., Atlanta, asst. mgr. plate glass sales Gen. Office, mgr., Nashville, Memphis, asst. to v.p., 1934-57, v.p. merchandising div., 1957-64, gen. mgr. of merchandising div., 1961-64, v.p. gen. sales, glass div., 1964—; dir. Pitts. Corning Corp., 1958—. Trustee Mercy Hosp., Pitts. Mem. Delta Kappa Epsilon, Wolf's Head Sr. Soc. Clubs: Fox Chapel Golf, Duquesne (Pitts.); Laurel Valley Golf (Ligonier, Pa.). Home: 150 Forest Dr Pittsburgh PA 15238 Office: 1 Gateway Center Pittsburgh PA 15222

HUGHES, FRANK CLAYTON, univ. dean; b. Ada, Okla., Nov. 28, 1915; s. Walter Nathaniel and Winnie Irene (Cales) H.; B.F.A., U. Okla., 1937, M.M.E., 1939; Mus.M., U. Rochester, 1949, Ph.D., 1955; m. Barbara Belle Germany, June 4, 1942; children—Clayton Frank, Marjorie Lee. Faculty mem. U. Okla., 1938-56, then Eastman Sch. Music of U. Rochester, Nazareth Coll., Trinity U., San Antonio; dean Sch. Fine Arts, Tex. Christian U., 1960—. Served to 1st lt. AUS, W.W. II; lt. col. Res. Mem. Internat. Council Fine Arts Deans, Tex., Ft. Worth music tchrs. assns., Tex. Music Educators Assn., Music Educators Nat. Conf., Music Tchrs. Nat. Assn., Alpha Psi Omega, Pi Kappa Lambda, Kappa Kappa Psi (hon.), Sigma Alpha Eta, Phi Mu Alpha Sinfonia. Rotarian. Home: 3905 Lynncrest Dr Fort Worth TX 76109

HUGHES, FRED, newspaper publisher; b. Grand Rapids, Mich., Aug. 16, 1915; s. Fred G. and Mary Jane (McKay) H.; A.B., U. Mo., 1937, LL.B., 1939; postgrad. U. Wis., 1938-39; m. Rebekah Blair, Jan. 2, 1942; children—Sallie E., Mary Jane. Admitted to Mo. bar, 1939; practice of law, Joplin, 1939-41; spl. agt. FBI, 1941-46; asst. gen. mgr. Joplin Globe Pub. Co., 1946-59, gen. mgr., dir., 1959—; pres., 1964—; dir. Mid-Continent Telecasting, Inc. (KOAM-TV), First Nat. Bank, Joplin. Pres. Joplin YMCA, 1959-61, Jasper County Jr. Coll., 1964—, Mo. Good Rds. Assn., 1964-66. Pres. bd. regents Mo. So. Coll., 1964—. Mem. Am. Newspaper Pubs. Assn., Inland Daily Press Assn. (pres. 1965). Presbyn. Rotarian (past pres.). Home: 601 N Wall St Joplin MO 64801 Office: 117 E 4th St Joplin MO 64801

HUGHES, FREDERIC JOHN, army med. officer; b. Plainfield, N.J., Mar. 21, 1914; s. Frederic John and Loretta (Flanagan) H.; grad. Loomis Sch., Windsor, Conn., 1932; A.B., Cornell U., 1935, M.D., 1938; postgrad. U. Minn. Med. Sch., 1948- 49; m. Martha Hedman, Oct. 5, 1940; children—Gretchen, Dorothy. Intern, then resident Cornell-N.Y. Hosp., 1938-41; commd. 1st lt. M.C., U.S. Army, 1941, advanced through grades to maj. gen., 1969; assigned Stark Gen. Hosp., Charleston, S.C., 1941-44, Med. Field Service Sch., 1944, 31st Med. Tng. Bn., Camp Grant, Ill., 1944; comdg. officer 15th Med. Tng. Bn., Ft. Lewis, Wash., 1944; exec. officer 304th Gen. Hosp., Ft. Knox, Ky., 1944-45; dep. surgeon, then surgeon Hdqrs. MARBO, Western Pacific Base Command, Saipan, 1945-47; comdg. officer 22d Sta. Hosp., Guam, 1947-48; assigned Walter Reed Army Med. Center, 1948-49; asst. chief Tb service Fitzsimmons Gen. Hosp., Denver, 1949-52, resident cardiovascular disease, 1953-54; chief cardiovascular disease service, asst. chief dept. medicine Tripler Army Hosp., Honolulu, 1954-57; chief gen. med. service, chief dept. medicine, chief profl. service Letterman Gen. Hosp., San Francisco, 1957-61; chief med. cons., directorate profl. service Office Surgeon Gen., 1961-62, dir. profl. service, 1962-66; comdg. gen. William Beaumont Gen. Hosp., El Paso, Tex., 1966-67, Walter Reed Gen. Hosp., 1967-69, Letterman Gen. Hosp., San Francisco, 1969-70; chief surgeon, comdg. gen. U.S. Army Med. Command, 7th Army Hdqrs., Europe, 1970—. Decorated Legion of Merit with 2 oak leaf clusters; D.S.M. Diplomate Am. Bd. Internal Medicine. Mem. A.M.A., A.C.P., Am. Fedn. Clin. Research, Assn. Mil. Surgeons, Am. Clin. and Climatol. Assn., Theta Xi, Nu Sigma Nu, Phi Kappa Phi, Alpha Omega Alpha. Republican. Home: 1000 O'Reilly Av San Francisco CA Office: APO New York City NY 09403

HUGHES, GEORGE JAMES, banker; b. Long Branch, N.J., Sept. 22, 1914; s. Ernest and Elizabeth (Forde) H.; student N.Y. U. Sch.-Commerce, 1935-46; grad.. Stonier Sch. Banking, 1951-53; m. Laura G. Peters, Mar. 28, 1942; children—Patricia Jane (Mrs. Michael J. Brennan), James Michael. With Chase Nat. Bank, 1931-55, 2d v.p., 1952-55; asst. v.p. Chase Manhattan Bank, 1955-56; pres., dir. Met. Bank Miami (Fla.), 1956-61; pres., dir. Pan Am. Bank Miami, 1961-62; exec. v.p., dir. Citizens Nat. Bank, Englewood, N.J., 1962-68; chmn., pres., dir. Atlantic Bank N.Y., N.Y.C., 1968—; pres., dir. Atlantic Enterprises, Inc.; 2d v.p., dir. N.B.G. Enterprises, Ltd., Montreal, Que., Can. Trustee John Marshall Inst. Taxation. Served with AUS, 1943-45. Mem. C. of C. of Ams. (pres. 1960-61, hon. life pres.). Kiwanian. Home: 66 S Terrace St Short Hills NJ 07078 Office: Atlantic Bank of NY 960 Av of Americas New York City NY 10001

HUGHES, GEORGE ROBERT, educator; b. Wymore, Neb, Jan. 12, 1907; s. Evan and Pyne (Jones) H.; A.B., U. Neb., 1929; B.D. (Nettie F. McCormick fellow 1932-34), McCormick Theol. Sem., 1932; Ph.D., U. Chgo., 1939; m. Maurine Gwendolyn Hall, May 10, 1932. Research asst. Oriental Inst., U. Chgo., 1934-42, research asso., epigrapher Inst. Epigraphy Survey, Luxor, Egypt, 1946- 48, field dir., 1949-64; asst. prof. Egyptology U. Chgo., 1948-55, asso. prof., 1955-61, prof., 1961—, dir. Oriental Inst., 1968- -; ordained to ministry Presbyn. Ch., 1932. Signal Intelligence service, Washington, 1942-46. Wilbour fellow Bklyn. Museum, 1966. Fellow Deutsches Archaeologisches Inst.; mem. Am. Oriental Soc., Egypt Exploration Soc., Am. Research Center Egypt, Phi Beta Kappa. Club: Quadrangle (U. Chgo.). Author: Saite Demotic Land Leases, 1952. Co-author: Reliefs and Inscriptions at Karnak I, 1954; Medinet Habu V, 1957; Medinet Habu VI, 1962; Medinet Habu VII, 1964; The Beit el-Wali Temple of Ramesses II, 1967. Home: 5613 Woodlawn Av Chicago IL 60637

HUGHES, GORDON A., market analyst; b. Mpls., Oct. 3, 1905; s. Ainslie Henry and Bernice C. (Brown) H.; grad. Macalaster Coll., 1926; B.S. in Bus. Adminstrn., U. Minn., 1928; M.B.A. in Marketing, Temple U., 1959; m. Elizabeth S. Nease, June 15, 1931; children—Patricia Ann, Richard Gordon. With Nat. Lead Battery Co., St. Paul, 1928-29, Mpls. Tribune Co., 1929-36, Lord & Thomas, Chgo., 1936-40; dir. market analysis dept. Gen. Mills, Inc., Mpls., 1940-55; dir. marketing research, sr. merchandising research adviser Scott Paper Co., 1954-68, ret., 1968; vis. lectr. Temple U., Sch. Bus. Adminstrn., 1968—. Dir. Advt. Research Found., N.Y.C. Research adv. com. Council Social Agys., Mpls.; bus. statistics com. U.S. C. of C., Washington; chmn. census adv. com. Bur. Census. Chmn. bd. Charles Coolidge Parlin award, 1963, 65. Mem. Am. Marketing Assn. (pres. 1951-53), Research Dirs. Adv. Com., Nat. Indsl. Conf. Bd., Alathean Soc., Market Research Council. Presbyn. Mason. Author articles advt. and research subjects trade jours.; contbg. author Handbook of Modern Marketing. Home: 101 W Possum Hollow Rd Wallingford PA 19086 Office: Temple U Speakman Hall Philadelphia PA 19122

HUGHES, HAROLD EVERETT, U.S. senator; b. Ida Grove, Ia., Feb. 10, 1922; s. Lewis C. and Etta E. (Kelly) H.; student State U. Ia., 1940-41; m. Eva Mae Mercer, Aug. 23, 1941; children—Connie (Mrs. Dennis Otto), Carol (Mrs. Gerald Medlin), Phyllis. Engaged in transp. and ins., 1946- 58; commnr. commerce Ia., 1958-63; gov. of Ia., 1963-69; U.S. senator from Ia., 1969—. Democratic candidate for gov. Ia., 1960. Served with AUS, 1942-45. Mem. Am. Legion. Methodist. Mason (Shriner). Home: 813 Carrie Ct McLean VA 22101 also Ida Grove IA Office: New Senate Office Bldg Washington DC 20510

HUGHES, HAROLD KENNETH, educator, physicist; b. N.Y.C., Dec. 31, 1911; s. John Watt and Rachel E. (Mulgrew) H.; A.B. (scholarship 1930-33), Columbia, 1934, M.A., 1943, Ph.D., 1948; m. Mildred M. Wells, July 22, 1936; children—Phyllis L. (Mrs. Arnold S. Rojakovick), Marilyn P. (Mrs. Gary S. Patrik). Asst., then instr. physics Columbia, 1935-40; asst. prof. physics, head dept. U. Newark, 1940-45; with radiation lab. Columbia, 1944-45; with tech. service dept. Socony Mobil Oil Co., 1945-52; group leader research labs. Celanese Corp. Am., 1952-53, head dry spinning research sect., 1953-55, supt. tech. extrusion dept., 1955-57; dir., mfg. devel. extrusion, 1957-58; asst. tech. dir. Markite Corp., 1958-59; dir. physics research, central research and engring. div. Continental Can Co., 1959- 62; mem. faculty Ind. State U., Terre Haute, 1962-69, prof. physics, 1962-69, chmn. dept., 1962-69; dir. research Midwest Devel. Found., 1966-69; v.p. acad. affairs State U. N.Y., Potsdam, 1969—; co- chmn. creative sci. program, seminar on cybernetics N.Y.U., 1958—; cons. in field, 1940—. Fellow Am. Phys. Soc.; mem. Soc. Applied Spectroscopy (pres. 1950-51), Am. Chem. Soc., Am. Assn. Physics Tchrs. (chmn. Ind. sect. 1964-65), A.A.A.S., Indpls. Sci. and Engring. Found., Phi Beta Kappa, Sigma Xi. Author numerous articles in field. Home: 12236 Hannawa Rd Potsdam NY 13676

HUGHES, HARRY CLARENCE, supply co. exec.; b. Crawfordsville, Ind., May 21, 1909; s. Clarence L. and Romania (Smith) H.; student Rollins Coll., 1925-27; m. Pauline Beecher, Nov. 30, 1935; children—Vincent Smith, David Henry. With Hughes Supply Inc., Orlando, Fla., 1928—, pres., 1970—; dir. First Nat. Bank Orlando, First at Orlando Corp. (also v.p.), Am. Fed. Savs. & Loan Assn., all Orlando. Pres. Boys' Clubs Orange County, 1958; mem. Judicial Council Fla., 1959-60, Fla. Council of 100, 1966—. Bd. dirs. Fla. Tech. U. Found., Orlando; gov. Orange Meml. Hosp., Orlando. Mem. Purchasing Agts. Assn. Fla., C. of C. Greater Orlando (past pres.). Clubs: University, Orlando Country, Bay Hill (Orlando). Home: 705 Valencia Av Orlando FL 32804 Office: 521 W Central Blvd Orlando FL 32802

HUGHES, HARRY HERBERT, mgmt. cons.; b. Linden, Pa., Dec. 1, 1905; s. Harry H. and Laura (Kulp) H.; B.S., Pa. State Coll., 1926; m. Mary Brestel, Oct. 2, 1932. Editor, Minerals Yearbook, U.S. Bur. Mines, 1930-41; Washington rep. Studebaker Corp., 1944-54; established European offices Porter Internat. Co., Brussels, Belgium, 1954-57, v.p. for Europe, 1954-57; dep. adminstr. Bus. and Def. Service Adminstrn., Dept. Commerce, Washington, 1958-61; with Hughes, Sears & Shiver, Inc., govt. relations cons., Washington, 1961—. Charge strategic materials in Europe for Marshall Plan, ECA, 1948-51. Mem. Beta Theta Pi. Club: Cosmos (Washington). Home: 14506 Fiske Dr Silver Spring MD 20906

HUGHES, HENRY STUART, educator; b. N.Y.C., May 7, 1916; s. Charles Evans and Marjory (Stuart) H.; A.B. summa cum laude, Amherst Coll., 1937; M.A., Harvard, 1938, Ph.D., 1940; L.H.D., Amherst Coll., 1967; m. Suzanne Rufenacht, Dec. 28, 1949 (div. 1963); children—Sandara Latham, Kenneth Stuart; m. 2d, Judith B. Markham, Mar. 26, 1964; 1 son, David Markham. Instr. Brown U., 1940-41; chief div. research for Europe, Dept. State, 1946-48; asst. prof. Harvard, 1948-52, prof., 1957-69, Gurney prof. history polit. sci., 1969—; asso. prof. Stanford, 1952-55, prof., head dept. history, 1955-56; vis. mem. Inst. Advanced Study, Princeton, N.J., 1950; Bacon exchange prof. U. Paris, 1967. Independent candidate for U.S. Senate, 1962. Co-chmn. Nat. Com. for a Sane Nuclear Policy, 1963-67, chmn., 1967-70. Fellow Center Advanced Study Behavioral Scis., Stanford, 1957. Served from pvt., F.A., to lt. col., OSS, AUS, 1941-46. Decorated Commendatore dell'Ordine della Corona D'Italia; Cavaliere ufficiale al merito della Repubblica Italiana. Guggenheim fellow, 1955, 58. Mem. Am. Hist. Assn., Am. Acad. Arts and Scis., Phi Beta Kappa. Author: An Essay for Our Times, 1950; Oswald Spengler: A Critical Estimate, 1952; The United States and Italy, 1953; Consciousness and Society, 1958; Contemporary Europe: A History, 1961; An Approach to Peace, 1962; History as Art and as Science, 1964; The Obstructed Path, 1968. Address: Harvard U Cambridge MA 02138

HUGHES, HOWARD ROBARD, manufacturer, aviator, motion picture producer; b. Houston, Dec. 24, 1905; s. Howard Robard and Alene (Gano) H.; ed. Thacher Sch., Ojai, Cal., Fessenden Sch., West Newton, Mass., Rice Inst., Houston, Cal. Inst. Tech.; m. Jean Peters, 1957 (div. 1971). Owner Hughes Tool Co., Houston; pres. Hughes Aircraft Co., Culver City, Cal. Trustee Howard Hughes Med. Inst. Pictures produced include Hell's Angels, Scarface, Front Page, The Outlaw. Clubs: Los Angeles Country, Wilshire Country, Lakeside Golf, Westchester Country, Aviation Country. In plane of own design established world's land plane speed record, 352 miles per hour, Sept. 13, 1935; transcontinental record, 7 hrs. 28 min., Jan. 19, 1937; world flight record, 91 hrs. 14 min. 28 sec., July 10-14, 1938; designed, built and flew world's largest plane, Nov. 2, 1947. Awarded Harmon Trophy, 1938; Collier trophy, 1939, Octave Chanute Award, 1940, Congressional Medal, 1941. Office: Humble Bldg Houston TX 77002

HUGHES, JAMES A., business exec., b. N.Y.C., Dec. 19, 1912; s. James A. and Dawn (Eggleston) H.; A.B., Dartmouth, 1935; LL.B., Yale, 1938; m. Elizabeth Sherman, Feb. 2, 1940; children—Anne Sharon, James S., Harriette, Timothy. With Am. Ship Bldg. Co., 1940-44, Dresser Industries, 1944-48; v.p. Affiliated Gas Equipment, Inc., 1948-55; v.p. Diamond Alkali Co., 1955-60, exec. v.p., dir., 1960-63, vice chmn., 1963—; pres. Diamond Shamrock Corp., 1967-71, chmn. bd., 1971—; dir. White Motor Corp., 1st Realty Corp., Terra Internat., Inc. Trustee Univ. Sch.; chmn. bd. trustees Cleve. Clinic Found. Mem. Delta Kappa Epsilon. Clubs: Union, Kirtland, Pepper Pike (Cleve.); Yale (N.Y.C.). Home: 2762 Center Rd Cleveland OH 44124 Office: Union Commerce Bldg Cleveland OH 44114

HUGHES, JAMES DONALD, air force officer; b. Balmville, N.Y., July 7, 1922; s. Edward A. and Alice Frances (Cooney) H.; B.S., U.S. Mil. Acad., 1946; grad. Flying Sch., Stewart Field, N.Y., 1946; M.S. in Internat. Affairs, George Washington U., 1966; grad. Nat. War Coll., 1966; m. Mary Elizabeth Masterson, June 4, 1946; children—Donna, Michael, Karen, Robert. Various assignments, U.S, 1946-55; assignment officer, assignment div. dir. mil. personnel Hdqrs. USAF, 1957-61; aide to v.p. of U.S., 1961-62; evaluation officer Hdqrs. 31st Tactical Fighter Wing, George AFB, Cal., 1961, squadron operations officer 306th TACFRON, 1961, wing plans officer Hdqrs. comdr. 31st CAMRON, 1962; air liaison officer Hdqrs. 2d ADVON, Tan Son Nhut, Vietnam, 1962, asst. operations officer, Hdqrs. 2d Air Div., 1962-63, chief spl. operations br. Hdqrs. 2d Air Div., 1963; personnel staff officer dept. personnel planning Hdqrs. USAF, 1963, asst. exec., 1963-65; dep. for test and evaluation 4525th Fighter Weapons Wing, Bellis AFB, Nev., 1966, vice comdr., 1966-68; dir. safety Hdqrs. USAFE, Lindsey AS, Germany, 1968; mil. asst. to President Nixon, 1969—. Decorated Air Medal with 9 oak leaf clusters, D.F.C. with oak leaf cluster, Bronze Star, Purple Heart. Home: Quarters 4776 Command Lane Andrews AFB Washington DC 20331 Office: The White House Washington DC 20500

HUGHES, JAMES GILLIAM, physician; b. Memphis, 1910; M.D., U. Tenn., 1935; m. Jane Barker, Mar. 1, 1935; children—Allen Holt, Jane Caroline, Sarah Elizabeth, Anne Louise. Intern John Gaston Hosp., Memphis, 1935-37, pediatric resident, 1938-39; pediatric resident Children's Meml. Hosp., Chgo., 1937-38; postgrad. lectr. pediatrics Okla. State Med. Assn., sponsored by Commonwealth Fund, 1940-42; pvt. practice pediatrics, Memphis, 1939, 46- 52; prof. pediatrics U. Tenn., 1952-, chmn. dept., 1960-; chief staff Le Bonheur Children's Hosp., Memphis, 1959-60; pediatrician-in-chief City of Memphis Hosps., 1960—. Cons. Surgeon Gen., U.S. Army, 1954, 69, 70, WHO, 1955, 56, 58, Rockefeller Found., 1956, AID, 1963; hon. prof. U. San Carlos, Guatemala, U. Guadalajara, Mexico; mem. Com. on Certification in Child Psychiatry, 1960-66. Served from capt. to col., M.C., AUS, 1942-46; comdg. officer 330th Gen. Hosp., U.S. Army Res., 1947-66; promoted to brig. gen. M.C., U.S. Army Res., 1966; spl. asst. to surgeon gen. U.S. Army Res. Affairs, 1966-70. Decorated Legion of Merit with oak leaf cluster. Diplomate Am. Bd. Pediatrics (dir. 1953-59, ofcl. examiner 1959—). Mem. Am. Pediatric Soc., Soc. Pediatric Research, So. Soc. Pediatric Research, Am. Acad. Pediatrics (dir. 1959-64, pres.-elect 1964, pres. 1965), Soc. Med. Cons. Armed Forces, Alpha Omega Alpha, Kappa Sigma, Omicron Delta Kappa, Phi Chi; hon. mem. pediatric socs. Argentina, Uruguay, Colombia, Venezuela, Cuba, Guatemala, Mexico. Episcopalian. Clubs: Memphis Country, University. Author: Pediatrics in General Practice, 1952; Synopsis of Pediatrics, 1963, 3d edit., 1971. Contbr. tech. papers med. lit. Home: 175 W Chickasaw Pkwy Memphis TN 38111 Office: 848 Adams Av Memphis TN 38105

HUGHES, JAMES JOHN, mfr. coin machines, b. Boston, Sept. 19, 1933; s. Cyril Anthony and Anna (Boles) H.; B.S., Suffolk U., 1959; student Bentley Coll. Acctg., 1950-52; m. Sheila Smith, Aug. 11, 1962; children—Elizabeth M., Terrence L., Sara A. Budget mgr. The Seeburg Corp., Chgo., 1965-67, asst. controller, 1967-69, v.p.-controller, 1969-71, v.p. adminstr., 1971—, dir., 1970—. Served with USMC, 1953-56. Home: 18100 San Diego St Homewood IL 60430 Office: 1500 N Dayton St Chicago IL 60622

HUGHES, JAMES ROBB, banker; b. Utica, N.Y., May 10, 1909; s. James Robb and Mary Elizabeth (Gerorge) H.; A.B., Hamilton Coll., 1931; M.B.A., Harvard, 1933; m. Sarah Collins, Oct. 5, 1935; 1 dau., Sarah P. (Mrs. David A. Brown). With Savs. Bank of Utica, 1935—, trustee, 1948—, pres., 1957-70, chmn. bd., chief exec. officer, 1970—; dir. Comml. Travelers Mut. Ins. Co., Instl. Investors Mut. Fund. Trustee Munson-Williams-Proctor Inst., Utica Pub. Library; bd. dirs. Utica YMCA, Hosp. Plan, Utica Coll. Found., Frederick B. Rutter Meml. Served as lt. USNR, 1943-46. Mem. Utica C. of C., Empire State C. of C., Mil. Order World Wars, Alpha Delta Phi. Rotarian. Clubs: Ft. Schuyler, Yahnundasis Golf, Sadaquada Golf (Utica). Home: 42 Woodberry Rd New Hartford NY 13413 Office: 233 Genesee St Utica NY 13501

HUGHES, JOHN CHAMBERLAIN, lawyer; b. Ft. Pierre, S.D., May 22, 1915; s. Felan T. and Florence (Chamberlain) H.; teaching certificate Eastern State Tchrs. Coll., Madison, S.D., 1935; LL.B., U. S.D., 1940; m. Marjorie Anstey, Jan. 31, 1948; children—Mary Kay, Patricia Ann, Bridget. Admitted to Alaska bar, 1947; practice in Kodiak, 1947-51, Anchorage, 1951—; mem. law firm Hughes, Thorsness, Lowe, Gantz & Clark, and predecessor firms, 1951—. Pres. Tri-Lex, Inc., Anchorage, 1960—; sec., dir. Pago Investment Co., Anchorage, 1958—; dir. People's Bank & Trust Co. Pres. Kodiak Ind. Sch. Dist., 1948-51; mem. Alaska Territorial Banking Bd., 1951-52; mem. Anchorage Borough Sch. Dist., 1960-69, pres., 1964-65; mem. Alaska Draft Bd., 1959—. Bd. dirs. Alaska Sch. Bds. Assn., 1964-69, pres., 1967-69; mem. Anchorage Estate Planning Council, 1962—, past pres.; mem. Alaska Ednl. Broadcasting Commn. Served with U.S. Merchant Marine, 1943-45. Mem. Pioneer of Alaska. Republican. Roman Catholic. Elk, Lion (pres. Anchorage 1961-62). Home: 511 9th Av Anchorage AK 99501 Office: 807 G St Anchorage AK 99501

HUGHES, JOHN FRANCIS, financial exec.; b. N.Y.C., Sept. 18, 1915; s. Charles E. and Kathryn (Foley) H.; A.B., Fordham U., 1937; M.B.A., Harvard, 1940; m. Rita A. Jackson, June 15, 1942; children—John Francis, William C., Kenneth M., Brian E., Marie Ann. Accounting clk. Gen. Foods, N.Y.C., 1940-41; mill cost accountant Deering Milliken, Union, S.C., 1941-42; comptroller staff Standard Brands, Inc., N.Y.C., 1946-53; comptroller, treas., v.p. Perkin-Elmer Corp., Norwalk, Conn. 1953-. Rep., Town Meeting Westport (Conn.), 1957-58, 59-61. Trustee, mem. exec. bd. New Eng. Pub. Expenditure Council. Served to capt. AUS, 1942-45. Mem. Financial Execs. Inst. (dir.; pres. So. New Eng. chpt. 1965-66), Nat. Assn. Accountants. Home: 4 Little Lane Westport CT 06880 Office: Main Av Norwald CT 06651

HUGHES, JOHN GILLIAM, Jr., educator; b. Clinton, Ky., July 7, 1921; s.. John Gilliam and Beulah Etta (Brown) H.; student Carson-Newman Coll., 1939-41, Conservatoire Nationale de Paris, 1945; B.A., Southwestern at Memphis, 1947; M.S., Juilliard Sch. Music, 1949; postgrad. N.Y.U., 1952; Ph.D. (So. Fellowships Fund fellow), Fla. State U., 1961; postgrad. Academia Musicale Chigiana, 1961. Chmn. div. fine arts Union U., Jackson, Tenn., 1952-68; chmn. div. fine arts U. Ark., Little Rock, 1968—; pvt. music tchr., Great Neck, N.Y., Memphis. Served with AUS, 1943-46. Mem. Am. Musicol. Soc., Soc. for Ethnomusicology, Am. Guild Organists, Am. Choral Dirs. Assn. Composer: (anthem) Isaiah's Vision, 1967—. Home: 5 Malcolm Cove Little Rock AR 72209

HUGHES, JOHN HENRY, lawyer, state senator; b. Syracuse, N.Y., Apr. 1, 1904; s. Thomas P. and Susan (Eagan) H.; LL.B., Syracuse U., 1928; m. Mary Loraine Porter, Feb. 26, 1938; children—Mary H. (Mrs. Thomas Francis Dolan III), Suzanne (Mrs. Thomas Francis

Quinlan), Thomas Porter. Admitted to N.Y. State bar, 1929, Fed. Ct. bar, 1929, U.S. Supreme Ct. bar, 1942; mem. firm Mackenzie, Smith Lewis, Michell & Hughes, and predecessor, Syracuse, 1928—; mem. N.Y. State Senate, 1947—, chmn. jud. com.; chmn. N.Y. Legislative Com. Crime. Bd. dirs. Syracuse Transit Corp.; trustee Onondaga County Savs. Bank, Syracuse; dir. P. & F. Industries. Chmn. Onondaga County Republican. Com., 1960-63. Bd. dirs. United Cerebral Palsy Assn. of Syracuse, Inc., Community-Gen. Hosp., Onondaga County chpt. Assn. for Help Retarded Children, Youth Devel. Center, Syracuse U. Fellow Coll. Trial Lawyers; mem. Am., N.Y. State, Onondaga County (past pres.) bar assns., Fedn. Bar Assns. 5th Jud. Dist. (past pres.), Am. Judicature Soc., Am. Bar Found., Internat. Assn. Ins. Counsel, Phi Delta Phi, Sigma Nu. Republican. Clubs: University, Century, Onondaga Golf and Country (Syracuse). Home: 311 Brookford Rd Syracuse NY 13224 Office: Onondaga County Savings Bank Bldg Syracuse NY 13202

HUGHES, JOHN LAWRENCE, publisher; b. N.Y.C., Mar. 13, 1925; s. John Chambers and Margaret (Kelly) H.; grad. St. Paul's Sch., Concord, N.H., 1943; B.A., Yale, 1949; m. Rose Marie Pitman, Nov. 27, 1947; children—Alexandra, Timothy, Christopher, Ian. Reporter, Nassau Review Star, Rockville Centre, L.I., N.Y., 1949; asst. sr. editor Pocket Books, Inc., N.Y.C., 1949-59; v.p. Washington Sq. Press, 1958; v.p. William Morrow & Co., Inc., N.Y.C., 1960-65, pres.,1965—, also dir.; exec. v.p., dir. Fielding Publs., Inc., N.Y.C., 1968—; dir. Scott-Foresman and Co., Chgo., Avery- Hand, Inc., Westport Conn., Apollo Editions, Inc., N.Y.C. Trustee Unquowa Sch., Fairfield, Conn., Pequot Library, Southport, Conn., N. Country Sch., Lake Placid, N.Y. Served to 1st lt. USMCR, 1943-46, 51. Home: 750 Harbor Rd Southport CT 06490 Office: 105 Madison Av New York City NY 10016

HUGHES, JOHN MCCALL, insurance exec.; b. West Long Branch, N.J., Sept. 8, 1907; s. Richard Robert and Annie (Van Note) H.; Ph.B., Brown U., 1933; m. Dorothy Hanson, Jan. 13, 1934; children—Richard R., Gail M. With Bankers Trust Co., N.Y.C., 1933-39; auditor Merc.-Commerce Bank & Trust Co., St. Louis, 1939-43; asst. to exec. v.p. Mut. Life Ins. of N.Y., N.Y.C., 1943- 45, controller, 1945-52, v.p., controller, 1952-59, exec. v.p., 1959-67, pres., 1967—; trustee Mut. of N.Y., 1961—. Mem. Financial Execs. Inst. (pres. 1958-59, chmn. bd. 1959-60), Phi Delta Theta. Clubs: University, Brown, The Board Room (N.Y.C.); Mount Kisco (N.Y.) Country. Home: Old Wagon Rd Mount Kisco NY 10549 Office: 1740 Broadway New York City NY 10019

HUGHES, JOSEPH D., lawyer, found. exec.; b. Dothan, Ala., June 20, 1910; s. Robert T. and Ora (Domingus) H.; B.S., Auburn U., 1931; J.D. with highest honors, George Washington U., 1934; LL.M., Georgetown U., 1936; grad. Sch. Public Affairs, Am. U. 1937; LL.D., Waynesburg Coll., 1956, Auburn U. 1962; m. Jane Blackistone, Nov. 29, 1934; children—Thomas Mifflin, Gordon, Gerard. Admitted to D.C. bar 1934, Pa. bar. 1950; with U.S. Dept. State, 1934-35, Treasury Dept., 1936-37, Bur. Internal Revenue, 1937-40, Pitts. Plate Glass Co., 1940-46; gov., v.p. T. Mellon & Sons, Pitts., 1946—. Adminstrv. trustee Richard King Mellon Found.; trustee Auburn U. Found., George Washington U., P.E. Theol. Sem. in Va., Western Pa. Hosp., Pitts. Zool. Soc.; bd. dirs. Nat. Wildlife Fedn., Max McGraw Wildlife Found.; mem. Councils on Founds., Inc.; dir. Corp. for Pub. Broadcasting. Served with AUS, 1942-46; chmn. Japanese- Am. Joint Bd., 1943-44. Civilian aide to sec. of army, 1955-63; Sigma Phi asst. adj. gen. Commonwealth Pa., 1963-; brig. gen. Pa. N.G. Decorated Legion of Merit. Mem. Am., Pa., Allegheny County bar assns., Bar Assn. City N.Y., Am. Law Inst., Conf. Bd. (mem. sr. execs. adv. council), Sigma Phi Epsilon, Phi Delta Phi, Order of Coif. Republican. Episcopalian. Clubs: Duquesne (Pitts.); Metropolitan (Washington); Links (N.Y.C.); Chevy Chase (Md.); Laurel Valley Golf (Ligonier, Pa.). Home: 1331 Bennington Av Pittsburgh PA 15217 Office: 525 William Penn Pl Pittsburgh PA 15219

HUGHES, JOSEPH KENNETH, bus. exec.; b. Leonard, Tex., 1927; s. Medford F. and Ina M. (Akins) H.; student N. Tex. State Coll.; B.A., So. Meth. U., 1948; m. Betty Penry, Feb. 26, 1949; childrenTimothy J., Mark D. Writer, then asst. city editor Dallas Times Herald, 1948-53; mgr. Dallas office Harshe-Rotman, Inc., pub. relations, 1953-55; account exec., v.p., mgr. Dallas office Grant Advt., Inc., 1956-64, exec. v.p., 1964-68; v.p. franchise Dr. Pepper Co., 1968-69, v.p. marketing services, 1969-70, v.p. marketing, 1970—. Mem. Assn. Broadcast Execs. Tex., Dallas Advt. League, Sigma Delta Chi. Club: Dallas Press (charter, dir. 1952-53). Home: 3420 Wentwood Dr Dallas TX 75225 Office: Dr Pepper Co PO Box 5086 Dallas TX 75222

HUGHES, JOSEPH P., grocery co. exec.; b. Atlantic City, N.J., 1906; Chmn. Certified Grocers of Cal. Ltd., Los Angeles; pres. Hughes Markets Inc., Hughes Market No. 2, Inc.; Hughes Coldwater, Sherman Oaks, Cal.; dir. Spartan Grocers Inc., Hughes Realty, Inc. Bd. dirs. Los Angeles Beautiful. Mem. Food Employers Council (dir.), Nat. Assn. Retail Grocers (dir.). Office: 2716 San Fernando Rd Los Angeles CA 90065

HUGHES, LEO, educator; b. Carlyle, Ill., Nov. 20, 1908; s. Peter William and Florence (Ogle) H.; B.A., U. Ill., 1933, M.A., 1934, Ph.D. (fellow 1934-35), 1938; m. Mildred Robert, Aug. 25, 1936; childrenBarbara Jane (Mrs. Jerrold S. Buttrey), Robert Lee. Teaching asst. U. Ill., 1935-38; mem. faculty U. Tex., 1938-, prof. English, 1956-, asso. dean Grad. Sch., 1959-65; vis. prof. N.Y.U., summers 1949, 58, Rice U., 1961-62. Fellow Folger Library, 1953, 66; Guggenheim fellow, 1956-57. Decorated knight Comdr. St. Gregory, 1965. Mem. Modern Lang. Assn., Phi Beta Kappa. Democrat. Catholic. Author: A Century of English Farce, 1956; The Drama's Patrons, 1971. Editor: (with A.H. Scouten) Ten English Farces, 1948. Home: 902 W 31st St Austin TX 78705

HUGHES, LLOYD LYNNELL, hosp. adminstr.; b. Independence, Kan., Sept. 6, 1920; s. Lloyd Lowrey and Jess (O'Connell) H.; A.B., Washburn U., 1942, LL.B., 1947; M.H.A., U. Minn., 1951; m. Isabel Neiswanger, June 28, 1947; children—Lucinda, Nancy, Melissa, David Lloyd. Admitted to Kan. bar, 1947; asst. gen. counsel Kan. Corp. Commn., 1947-49; asst. dir. R.I. Hosp., 1951-56; supt. U. Wis. Hosp., 1957-60; dep. dir. R.I. Hosp., 1960-62, exec. dir., 1962-70, exec. v.p., 1970—; asso. prof. hosp. adminstrn. U. Wis., 1958-60; clin. preceptor U. Minn. program hosp. adminstrn., 1958-60, 62. Mem. Gov.'s Commn. on Heart Disease, Cancer and Stroke; rep. Council of Teaching Hosps. to Am. Assn. Med. Coll., 1969-72. Served with AUS, 1943-46. Mem. Hosp. Assn. R.I. (pres. 1967-69), New Eng. Hosp. Assembly (trustee 1969-73), Am. Coll. Hosp. Adminstrs., Am. Hosp. Assn. (del. 1971-73). Episcopalian. Home: 26 Melrose Av Barrington RI 02806 Office: 593 Eddy St Providence RI 02903

HUGHES, LOWELL R., physician; b. Dingle, Ida. Feb. 11, 1920; s. Robert Richard and Margaret (Dayton) H.; B.S., U. Utah, 1941; M.D., U. Pa., 1943, certificate neurology and psychiatry, 1950; m. Henrietta Zebreski, Apr. 6, 1946; children-Brownyn, Richard, Kathryn, Beverly, Lowell. Intern Latter-day Saints Hosp., Salt Lake City, 1944-45; resident psychiatry Western State Hosp., Ft. Steilacoom, Wash., 1945-46; resident psychiatry No. State Hosp., Sedro Wooley Wash., 1948-4Q, asst. supt., 1950-51, 54- 61; pvt. practice, Tacoma, 1951-54, Mt. Vernon, Wash., 1961-62; supt. Nev. State Hosp., Reno, 1962-66; clin. instr. psychiatry U. Wash., 1950-51; now gen. med. practice, Porterville, Cal. Mem. Nev. Health Facilities Adv. Council, 1965-. Served to capt., M.C., AUS, 1946- 48. Mem. Am., Nev. med. assns., Washoe County Med. Soc., Am. Psychiat. Assn. Home: 32300 River Island Dr Porterville CA 93257 Office: 164 W Putnam Av Porterville CA 93257

HUGHES, MILDRED B., city ofcl.; b. Shelby County, Ill.; dJohn Adams and Martha (Lockwood) Barding; ed. Sacred Heart Acad., Springfield, Ill., and Northwestern U.; Masters degree, Ariz. State U.; m. James E. Hughes, July 5, 1923 (dec. Jan. 1964); 1 dau., Mary Beth (Mrs. Taber Loree Collins). Asst. sales dir. Hughes & Co., 1921, mng. dir. Richmond (Va.) office, 1922; dir. sales, James H. O'Hara Co., 1926-27; in govtl. relations, Washington, 1929-34; exec. in internat. relations fields, N.Y.C., 1934- 62; exec. v.p. Far East Am. Council of Commerce and Industry, Inc., 1943- 62, bd. dirs., 1948-63; dir. alcohol and drug abuse sect. Ariz. Dept. Health, until 1970; coordinator Phoenix City Drug Abuse Services, 1970—; economist-adviser, specializing Asia-U.S. econ. affairs. Nat. vice chmn. China Emergency Relief Com., 1940, Nat. Com. United China Relief, 1941. Mem. adv. com. U.S. World Trade Fair, 1957- 62. Decorated Most Exalted Order White Elephant (Thailand), 1956. Mem. Asia Soc., Japan Soc., Pan Pacific S.E. Asia Women's Assn. Contbr. surveys and articles to Fortune mag., Jour. Commerce, profl. publs. Address: 5648 W. Meadowbrook Av Phoenix AZ 85031

HUGHES, PARKER KELLUM, obstetrician and gynecologist; b. Meridian, Tex., Feb. 9, 1914; s. Julian and Mary (Kellum) H.; student Drake U., 1932-34; M.D., State U. Ia., 1938; m. Martha Housh, July 31, 1937; children—Judith (Mrs. Richard A. Miller), Mary (Mrs. W. Michael Williams). Intern U. Kan. Hosp., 1938- 39; intern, then resident N.Y. Lying-In Hosp., 1939-41, Charity Hosp., New Orleans, 1941-42, 46; chief obstetrics and gynecology Ia. Methodist Hosp., Des Moines, 1948-54, 65-70, chief staff, 1963-64. Bd. dirs. Des Moines YMCA, 1962—, Med. Facilities Planning Council, Des Moines, 1966-69. Served to capt. AUS, 1942-46. Diplomate Am. Bd. Obstetricians and Gynecologists. Founding fellow Am. Coll. Obstetricians and Gynecologists (chmn. com. gynecol. practice 1971—); mem. Central Assn. Obstetricians and Gynecologists (v.p. 1966-67), A.M.A., Ia., Polk County (pres. 1965) med. socs. Home: 5226 Woodland St Des Moines IA 50312 Office: 3200 University Av Des Moines IA 50311

HUGHES, PAUL LESTER, educator, author; b. Cedar Rapids, Ia., Nov. 25, 1915; s. Harry and Theresa (Reilly) H.; B.A., Coe Coll., 1941; M.A. in History, State U. Ia., 1947, Ph.D., 1951; m. Virginia A. Schnare, Oct. 6, 1942. Instr., State U. Ia., 1947-51; mem. faculty DePaul U., 1952-67, prof. history, 1961-67; chmn. dept. history and polit. sci., 1965-67; prof. history Wis. State U., Whitewater, 1967-. Served with USAAF, 1941-45. Mem. Am., Hist. assn. Author: Tudor Royal Proclamations, The Early Tudors 1485-1533, vol. I, 1964; The Later Tudors 1553- 1587, vol. II, 1966; The Later Tudors 1588-1603, vol. III, 1967; Crown and Parliament in Tudor-Stuart England, 1959; Readings in Western Civilization, 1956; European Civilization: Basic Historical Documents, 1965. Home: 240 Woodland Dr Whitewater, WI 53190.

HUGHES, PHILLIP SAMUEL, social scientist; b. Chgo., Feb. 26, 1917; s. Arthur Samuel and Beulah (Blish) H.; B.A., U. Wash., 1938, grad. student sociology, 1940; m. Jean Evans, July 9, 1938; children—Suzanne, Patricia, Michael, Shirley. Various positions State of Wash., 1938-43, chief research and statistics, dept. social security, 1942-43; sr. labor market analyst War Manpower Commn., Seattle, 1943-44; with VA, Seattle, 1946-49, chief research and statistics, 1946-49; with U.S. Bur. Budget, 1949-69, dep. chief Office Legistative Reference, 1956-59, asst. dir. legislative reference, 1959-66, dep. dir. of bureau, 1966-69; acting pres. Nat. Inst. Pub. Affairs, 1970-71; sr. fellow Brookings Instn., 1971—; cons. U.S. Office Mgmt. and Budget, Ford Found., conservation orgns. Bd. dirs. YMCA Met. Washington, 1961—, asst. treas., 1965—. Served with USNR, 1944-45. Recipient Career Service award Nat. Civil Service League, 1962; Distinguished Service award Bur. of Budget, 1965. Mem. Am. Soc. Pub. Adminstrn. (nat. council), Nat. Acad. Pub. Adminstrn., Wilderness Soc., Potomac Appalachian Trail Club, Delta Upsilon. Unitarian (bd. trustees Unitarian-Universalist Assn. Am. 1970—). Home: 3710 Taylor St Chevy Chase MD 20015 Office: 1225 Connecticut Av Washington DC 20025

HUGHES, RAYMOND HARGETT, educator, physicist; b. Walla Walla, Wash., June 1, 1927; s. Clifford R. and Frances (Hargett) H.; A.B., Whitman Coll., 1949; M.S., U. Wis., 1951, Ph.D., 1954; m. Olive Jane Wipson, Feb. 8, 1952; children—Diane Frances, Marshall Raymond, Clayton Wipson, Randall Clifford. Mem. faculty dept. physics U. Ark., Fayetteville, 1954—, prof., 1965—. Fellow Am. Phys. Soc.; mem. Phi Beta Kappa, Sigma Xi. Research, publs. in atomic structure and spectra, atomic collisions, atomic radiative processes. Home: 2510 Wedington Dr Fayetteville AR 72701

HUGHES, RICHARD ARTHUR WARREN, author: b. Weybridge, Eng., Apr. 19, 1900; s. Arthur and Louisa Grace (Warren) H.; student Charterhouse Sch., 1913-18; B.A., Oriel Coll., Oxford (Eng.) U., 1922; D.Litt. (hon.), U. Wales; m. Frances Catharine Ruth Bazley, Jan. 8, 1932; children—Robert Elistan-Glodryd, Penelope, Lleky Susannah, Catharine Phyllida, Owain Gardner Collingwood. Author: (plays) The Sisters' Tragedy, produced London, 1922, A Comedy of Good and Evil, produced London, 1924 (revived and produced in N.Y.C. as Minnie and Mr. Williams, 1948); co-founder Portmadoc Players, Welsh theatrical co., 1923; 1st vice chmn. Welsh Nat. Theatre Co.: for 3 years Gresham prof. of rhetoric, London; author of radio plays, 1924—, including Danger, 1st radio play in world, 1924, also sundry film scripts. Served in Brit. Admiralty, 1940-45. Decorated Order Brit. Empire. Author: Gipsy Night and Other Poems, 1922; The Sisters' Tragedy and Other Plays, 1922; A Moment of Time (collected stories), 1926; Confessio Juvenis (poems), 1926; Plays, 1928; A High Wind in Jamaica (The Innocent Voyage), 1929; The Spider's Palace (children's stories), 1931; In Hazard, 1938; Don't Blame Me (children's stories), 1940; vol. in ofcl. history of the war (civil series) The Administration of War Production (with J.D. Scott), 1956; The Fox in the Attic, Vol. 1 of The Human Predicament, 1961; Gertrude's Child (children's story), 1966; Plays, 1966. Home: Mor Edrin Talsarnau Merioneth Wales Office: care Harper & Row Publishers 49 E 33d St New York City NY 10016

HUGHES, RICHARD JOSEPH, past gov. of N.J., lawyer; b. Florence, N.J., Aug. 10, 1909; s. Richard Paul and Veronica (Gallagher) H.; student St. Charles Coll., 1926-28, St. Joseph's Coll., 1928; LL.B., N.J. Law Sch., 1931; m. Miriam McGrory (dec.); children—Richard P., Robert F., John, Mary; m. 2d, Elizabeth Sullivan Murphy, May 7, 1954; stepchildren—Michael Murphy, Patrick Murphy, Timothy Murphy; children—Brian, Helen, Thomas M. Admitted to N.J. bar, 1932; asst. U.S. atty. Dist. N.J., 1939-45; partner firm Lord & Hughes, Trenton, 1945-48; judge Mercer County (N.J.) Ct., 1948-52; judge Superior Ct. N.J., 1952-59, also assignment judge Union County; gov. N.J., 1961-70; partner firm Hughes, McElroy, Connell, Foley & Geiser, Newark, 1970—. Mem. Am. (chmn. commn. on correctional facilities and services), N.J., Mercer County (pres. 1953-54), Essex County bar assns. Democrat. Roman Cath. Home: 90 Westcott Rd Princeton NJ 08540 Office: 24 Commerce St Newark NJ

HUGHES, ROBERT HARRISON, univ. regent, sugar co. exec.; b. Puunene, Hawaii, Mar. 23, 1917; s. Robert Edwin and Alice Thayer (Walker) H.; B.Sc. in Sugar Tech., U. Hawaii, 1938; student La. State U., 1939; grad. Advanced Mgmt. Program, Harvard, 1955; m. Nadine Jeannette Hegler, Aug. 24, 1940; children—Robert Lawrence, Linton Alice, Carole Nadine. With Hawaiian Comml. & Sugar Co., 1939-65, sugar mill supt., 1951-63, prodn. mgr., 1963-65; v.p. tech. services C. Brewer & Co., Ltd., Honolulu, 1965-69, sr. v.p. Hawaiian operations, 1969—, dir. subsidiaries, 1966—; dir. Cal. & Hawaiian Sugar Co. 1971—. Bd. regents U. Hawaii, 1961-66; trustee Hawaii Conf. Found., 1969—, pres., 1966, U. Hawaii Found., 1963-65, pres., 1967-69. Pres. Hawaii conf. United Ch. of Christ, 1962-63, trustee, 1966—. Rotarian (pres. Maui 1953-54). Home: 618 Kuana St Honolulu HI 96816 Office: PO Box 3470 Honolulu HI 96801

HUGHES, ROBERT JOHN, journalist; b. Neath, Wales, Apr. 28, 1930; s. Evan John and Dellis (Williams) H.; ed. Stationers Company Sch., London, Eng.; Nieman fellow Harvard, 1961-62; m. Vera Elizabeth Pockman, Aug. 20, 1955; children—Wendy Elizabeth, Mark Evan. Came to U.S., 1954, naturalized, 1965. Reporter, editor English and S. African newspapers and news agys., 1946-54; with Christian Sci. Monitor, 1954—, Far Eastern corr., 1964—; TV and radio corr. Westinghouse Broadcasting Co., 1963—. Recipient Pulitzer prize for internat. reporting, 1967. Author: The New Face of Africa, 1961; Indonesian Upheaval, 1967; also articles. Home: 4 S Bay Rd Repulse Bay Hong Kong Office: Central Bldg Pedder St Hong Kong

HUGHES, ROBERT NATHANIEL, ins. co. exec.; b. Atlanta, Oct. 10, 1917; s. William Denson and Susan (Flynn) H.; student Emory U., 1935-36; m. Maria Dendy Maret, Sept. 13, 1947; children—Mariah Dency, Sara Susan, Robert III. Mgr., S.E. dept. Asso. Aviation Underwriters, Atlanta, 1946-49; sr. v.p., dir. No. Ins. Co., N.Y.C., 1949-66; v.p. Am. Home Assurance Co., N.Y.C., 1969—; pres., dir. Nat. Union Fire Ins. Co., Pitts., 1969—; dir. Lexington Ins. Co., Boston, Nat. Union Life Ins. Co., Birmingham, Fire Ins. Co. of Pa., N.Y.C. Served to capt. USAAF, 1941-46. Home: 41 Knob Hill Dr Summit NJ 07901 Office: 102 Maiden Lane New York City NY 10005

HUGHES, ROY E., materials co. exec.; b. Zwingle, Ia.; s. Elmer C. and Lottie (Datisman) H.; m. Marion Gilbert, Nov. 27, 1959; childrenGayle E. (Mrs. Gary McCue), Steven Hughes. With Consol. Vultee Aircraft Co., 1941-49; self- employed, 1941-51; now sr. v.p. Whittaker Corp., Los Angeles, also dir. Home: 16381 Ardsley Circle Huntington Beach CA 92647 Office: 9229 Sunset St Los Angeles CA 90069

HUGHES, ROY ELWARD, mfg. co. exec., b. Hoisington, Kan., Dec. 31, 1924; s. Delbert Littrell and Louella (Woodward) H.; B.S., Phillips U., Enid, Okla., 1949; M.B.A., Stanford, 1955; m. Dorothy Janet Sites, Jan. 6, 1946; children—Carol Jeanne (Mrs. Carleton James Howard), and Janet Lynn. With Kaiser Industries Corp., Oakland, Cal. 1957—, controller, 1961- 67, v.p., controller, 1967-68, v.p. corporate planning, 1968-69, exec. v.p., 1969—; dir. Am. Motors Corp. Bd. dirs. Kaiser Found. Hosps., Kaiser Found. Health Plan. Served to 1st lt., pilot, USAAF, 1943-45, USAF, 1951- 53. C.P.A., Cal. Home: 974 Arbor Dr San Leandro CA 94577 Office: 300 Lakeside Dr Oakland CA 94612

HUGHES, SARAH TILGHMAN, judge, orgn. exec.; b. Balt. Aug. 2, 1896; d. James Cooke and Elizabeth (Haughton) Tilghman; A.B., Goucher Coll., 1917, LL.D., 1950; LL.B., George Washington U., 1922; LL.D., So. Meth. U., Ind. State U., 1967; m. George E. Hughes, Mar. 13, 1922. Tchr., Salem Acad. and Coll., Winston-Salem, N.C., 1917-19; police woman Met. Police Dept. Washington, 1919-22; admitted to Tex. bar, 1922, practiced in Dallas, 1922-35; mem. Tex. Legislature, 1931-35; judge 14th Dist. Ct. of Tex., 1935-61, U.S. Dist. Ct., No. Dist. Tex., 1961—; Active Nat. Fedn. Bus. and Profl. Women's Clubs, 1931—, lst. v.p., 1948-50, pres., 1950-52; v.p. Internat. Fedn. Bus. and Profl. Women, 1953-59. Mem. nat. commn. UNESCO. Past trustee Goucher Coll.; trustee Bishop Coll. Mem. State Bar of Tex., Am., Dallas bar assns., Am. Judicature Soc., Nat. Assn. Women Lawyers, Am. Assn. U. Women, Phi Beta Kappa, Delta Sigma Rho, Kappa Beta Pi, Delta Gamma, Delta Kappa Gamma (hon.). Democrat. Episcopalian. Home: 3816 Normandy St Dallas TX 75205 Office: US Court Dallas TX 75202

HUGHES, THOMAS GERALD, chem. co. exec.; b. Oakland, Cal., Aug. 18, 1908; s. Thomas Robert and Jessie (Darneal) H.; student San Francisco Inst. Accountancy, 1926-30; m. Marie Frances Linder, Aug. 18, 1945. With Standard Oil Co. of Cal., 1930—, chmn., dir. Chevron Chem Co., San Francisco, 1966—; dir. BP-Cal., Ltd., BP-Cal. (Grangemouth), Ltd., Societe Calgil, Societe Californie-Atlantique, Karonite Chem. Co., Ltd., Nippon Petroleum Detergent Co., Ltd., Orobis, Ltd., Orogil S.A., Coromandel Fertilisers, Ltd., Aditivos Mexicanos. Mem. A.A.A.S., Mfg. Chemists Assn. (dir.), San Francisco Stock Exchange Club, Cercle de l'Union. Home: 361 La Salle Av Piedmont CA 94610 Office: 225 Bush St San Francisco CA 94120

HUGHES, THOMAS LOWE, found. exec.; b. Mankato, Minn., Dec. 11, 1925; s. Evan Raymond and Alice (Lowe) H.; B.A. summa cum laude, Carleton Coll., 1947; B.Phil. in Politics (Rhodes scholar), Balliol Coll., Oxford (Eng.) U., 1949; J.D., Yale, 1952; student U. Minn. Law Sch.; m. Jean Reiman, May 7, 1955; children—Thomas Evan, Allan Cameron. Admitted to Minn. bar, 1952; U.S. Supreme Ct., 1960; U.S. Dist. Ct. D.C., 1968; profl. staff mem. U.S. Senate Subcom. on Labor and Labor-Mgmt. Relations, Com. on Labor and Pub. Welfare, 1951-52; asso. prof. polit. sci. and internat. relations U. So. Cal., 1953, Trinity Coll., Tex., 1954, George Washington U., 1957-58; exec. sec. to gov. of Conn., 1954-55; legislative counsel Sen. Hubert Humphrey, 1955-58; adminstrv. asst. U.S. Rep. Chester Bowles, 1959-60; spl. asst. to under sec. state Dept. State, 1961, dep. dir. intelligence and research, 1961- 63, dir. intelligence and research with rank of asst. sec. state, 1963-69; minister, dep. chief mission Am. embassy, London, 1969-70; planning and coordination staff Dept. State, 1970-71; pres., trustee Carnegie Endowment for Internat. Peace, 1971—. Visitor, Middle East Inst., U. Chgo.; mem. adv. council Woodrow Wilson Sch., Princeton. Staff asst. Democratic Nat. Conv., 1944, 52, 56, staff dir. platform com., 1960. Served to maj. Judge Adv. Gen.'s Dept., USAF, 1952-54. Mem. N.Y. Council Fgn. Relations, Inst. Strategic Studies London, Am. Assn. Rhodes Scholars, Am. Polit. Sci. Assn., Am. Soc. Internat. Law, Am. Fgn. Service Assn., Am. Bar Assn., Fgn. Policy Assn., UN Assn., Phi Beta Kappa, Phi Delta Phi. Episcopalian. Clubs: Yale (N.Y.C.); Oxford (Eng.) Union. Contbr. articles nat. periodicals. Home: 5636 Western Av Chevy Chase MD 20015 Office: UN Plaza at 46th St New York City NY 10017

HUGHES, VERNON WILLARD, physicist, educator; b. Kankakee, Ill., May 28, 1921; s. Willard Vernon and Jean (Parr) H.; A.B., Columbia, 1941, Ph.D. (NRC fellow), 1950; M.S., Cal. Inst. Tech.,

1942; M.A., Yale, 1960; m. Inge Michelson, Sept. 22, 1950; childrenGareth Albert, Emlyn Willard. Research asso. Radiation Lab., Mass Inst. Tech., 1942-46; instr., lectr. physics Columbia, 1949-52, vis. asso. prof., 1958-59; asst. prof. physics U. Pa., 1952-54 asst. prof. Yale, 1954-57, asso. prof., 1957-60, prof., 1960-69, Donner prof. physics, 1969-, asso. chmn. physics dept., 1960- 61, chmn., 1961-69; cons. Inst. Space Studies, NASA, Oak Ridge Nat. Lab. Trustee Asso. Univs., Inc. Fellow Am. Acad. Arts and Scis., Am. Phys. Soc.; mem. Nat. Acad. Sci. Home: 37 Loomis Pl New Haven CT 06511

HUGHES, WALTER LEE, Jr., educator; b. Trenton, Nov. 19, 1915; s. Walter Lee and Jewell (Dawes) H.; B.S., Mass. Inst. Tech., 1937, Ph.D., 1941; m. Eleanor M. Ryan, June 1, 1945; childrenMary Lee, Judith E. Fellow protein chemistry Harvard, 1940-42, research asso. phys. chemistry, 1942-46, asso., then asst. prof., 1946-53; asso. prof. Johns Hopkins, 1953-55; head div. microbiology, med. research center Brookhaven Nat. Lab., 1955- 58, head div. biochemistry, 1958-63; prof. physiology, chmn. dept. Tufts U. Sch. Medicine, 1963-. Dir. Harvard Apparatus Co. Mem. exec. com. Blood Research Found. Moore Travelling fellow, 1937-38; Guggenheim fellow, 1951-52. Mem. Am. Acad. Arts and Scis., Am. Physiol. Soc., Am. Soc. Biol. Chemists, Soc. Gen. Physiology, Sigma Xi. Home: 90A Chestnut St Boston MA 02108 Office: 136 Harrison Av Boston MA 02111

HUGHES, WILLIAM FRANK, educator, mech. engr.; b. Ash, N.C., Oct. 20, 1930; s. Olan T. and Elma (Frink) H.; B.S., Carnegie Inst. Tech., 1952. M.S. 1953, Ph.D., 1955; m. Jane Thomas, June 27, 1959; children—Christopher T., Eric Olan. NSF postdoctoral fellow Cambridge (Eng.) U., 1957-58; mem. faculty Carnegie-Mellon U., Pitts., 1955—, prof. mech. and elec. engring., 1966—, co- ordinator space scis. program, 1963—. Fulbright lectr. U. Sydney (Australia), 1963. Mem. Am. Soc. M.E., Am. Phys. Soc., Am. Geophys. Union, Soc. Automotive Engrs., Sigma Xi, Tau Beta Pi, Pi Tau Sigma, Phi Kappa Phi. Author: (with F.J. Young) Electromagnetodynamics of Fluids, 1966; also articles. Research in magneto-fluid mechanics, lubrication and friction, space scis., fluid mechanics. Home: RD 3 Cambridge Springs PA 16403

HUGHES, WILLIAM FRANKLIN, Jr., ophthalmologist; b. Indpls., Apr. 18, 1913; s. William F. and Alta (Rentschler) H.; A.B., Amherst Coll., 1934; M.D., Johns Hopkins, 1938; m. Wanema Dickey, June 28, 1941 (dec. 1969); children-William Franklin III, Jacqueline Alter, Sarah Lee; m. 2d, Jane M. Stockdale, 1970. Intern, asst. resident and resident in ophthalmology Johns Hopkins, 1938-44, asst. prof. ophthalmology, 1944-46, research work, 1941-46; pvt. practice in ophthalmology, Ind. U. Sch. of Medicine, 1946-47; prof. ophthalmology, U. Ill., 1947—, head dept., 1947-58; ophthalmologist-in-chief Research and Ednl. Hosps. and Ill. Eye and Ear Infirmary, 1947-58; chmn. dept. ophthalmology Presbyn.-St. Luke's Hosp., Chgo., 1956—; prof. ophthalmology Rush Med. Coll., 1971—. Past mem. ophthalmology com. NRC. Mem. A.M.A., Am. Bd. Ophthalmology, Assn. for Research in Ophthalmology (trustee, 1949-55), Am., Chgo. (past pres.) ophthal. socs., Inst. of Med. Chgo., Billings Med. Club of Chgo. (pres. 1965), Sigma Xi, Alpha Kappa Kappa, Phi Kappa Psi. Club: University (Chgo.). Author: Office Management of Ocular Diseases, 1953. Mem. editorial bds. Archives of Ophthalmology, 1951-62, Jour. Am. Geriatrics Soc. Editor: Yearbook Ophthalmology, 1959—. Author articles on chem. burns of the eyes, cataract extraction, beta irradiation, retinal detachment, corneal diseases and corneal transplantation. Home: 4073 Bunker Lane Wilmette IL 60091 Office: 1753 W Congress Pkwy Chicago IL 60612

HUGHES, WILLIAM LEWIS, elec. engr., educator; b. Rapid City, S.D., Dec. 2, 1926; s. Clarence William and Newell (Chase) H.; B.S. in Elec. Engring., S.D. Sch. Mines and Tech., 1949; M.S., Ia. State U., 1950, Ph.D., 1952; m. Stella Marie Platt, June 9, 1950; childrenElizabeth Helen, James Edward, Judith Lee, Michael George. Broadcast and TV engr., 1946-49; mem. faculty Ia. State U., 1949-60; prof. elec. engring., 1959-60; prof. elec. engring., head Sch. Elec. Engring., Okla. State U., 1960—. Mem. indsl. com. TV frequency allocation studies FCC, 1957-59. Served with USNR, World War II. Fellow I.E.E.E.; mem. Am. Soc. Engring. Edn., Sigma Xi, Sigma Tau, Tau Beta Pi, Eta Kappa Nu, Pi Mu Epsilon. Author: Nonlinear electrical Networks, 1960; also articles; co-author Lines, Waves and Antennas, 1961. Patentee nonlinear systems, color TV systems, direct energy conversions systems. Home: 712 Lakeshore Dr Stillwater OK 74074

HUGHES, WILLIAM NOLIN, educator; b. Raymond, Wash., May 21, 1918; s. William Garfield and Rhea (Cheshire) H.; B.A., U. Wash., 1941; M.A., Northwestern U., 1952, Ph.D., 1955; m. Diane Krueger, Aug. 23, 1953; children-Megan Rhea, Michael William, William Richard. Staff writer, pub. relations Boeing Aircraft Co., Seattle, 1941-46; asst. to labor adviser U.S. Element, Allied Commn. for Austria and ECA, Vienna, 1946-50; instr. German, U. Mich., 1955-60; asst. prof. German, Columbia, 1960-63; asso. prof. German, Mich. State U., East Lansing 1963-65, prof. German, chmn. dept. German and Russian, 1965—. Mem. Modern Lang. Assn. (asso. bibliographer), Mich. Fgn. Lang. Assn. (past pres.), Internat. Arthur Schnitzler Gesellschaft, Thomas Mann Gesellschaft, Delta Phi Alpha. Contbr. articles profl. jours. Home: 513 Ardson Rd East Lansing MI 48823

HUGHES, WILLIAM PULASKI, fgn. service officer; b. Lytle, Tex., Sept. 16, 1911; s. Harry Davis and Clarkie Lee (Riley) H.; B.B.A., Baylor U., 1934; M.B.A., Harvard, 1938, grad. Advanced Mgmt. Program, 1950; m. Elizabeth Oswald, June 18, 1937; children—Clark, Joe Kelly, Craig. Comptroller, Gallaudet Coll., 1938-41; underwriting supr. FHA, 1941-42; staff Office of Coordinator Inter-Am. Affairs, Honduras and Brazil, Dept. of State, 1942-44, analyst Dept. of State, 1945-47, attache, Mexico City, 1947-49, exec. dir. Bur. Inter- Am. Affairs, 1949-51; mem. Mexico-U.S. Internat. Boundary and Water Commn., 1951-54, dir. Office Fgn. Bldgs., directed design and constrn. 42 embassies and consulates, including London, New Delhi, Oslo, Lima, The Hague, Athens, Accra, Leopoldville, Lagos, 1954-61, dir. U.S. operations mission to Bolivia, 1961-63; consul gen. Ciudad Juarez, Mexico, 1963—. Home 5525 Westside Rd El Paso TX 79932 Office: Am Consulate General Ciudad Juarez Mexico

HUGHES, WILLIAM S., investment banker; b. St. Louis, 1904; ed. U. Cal. at Los Angeles, 1929. Pres., dir. Wagenseller & Durst, Inc.; dir. Pacific Outdoor Advt. Co. Home: 1165 Rosalind Rd San Marino CA 91108 Office: 626 S Spring St Los Angeles CA 90014*

HUGHEY, M. STANLEY, ins. co. exec.; b. Greenville, Ill., Aug. 11, 1917; s. Elmer and Nelle (Thacker) H.; student Greenville Coll., 1934-37; B.A., U. Ill., 1938; M.B.A., Northwestern U., 1947; m. M. Elaine Cartmell, July 7, 1939; children—Karen (Mrs. Kenneth A. Childs), Thomas, Michael, Linda. With Kemper Ins. Group, Chgo., 1938—, v.p. Kemperco, 1968—; v.p. Lumbermens Mut. Casualty Co., Chgo., 1959-63, exec. v.p., 1963—; v.p. Am. Motorists Ins. Co., Chgo., 1959-63, exec. v.p., 1963—; v.p. Am. Mfrs. Mut. Ins. Co., Chgo., 1959—, Fed. Mut. Ins. Co., Decatur, Ill., 1959—, Fidelity Life Ins. Co., 1969—, Fed. Kemper Life Ins. Co., 1969—; dir. Tower Finance Co., DeMoulin Bros. & Co., Greenville, Kemperco Re. Mem. New Trier Sch. Bd. No. 203, Winnetka, Ill.; dir. Ins. Sch. Chgo. Served with Supply Corps, USNR, 1945-46. Fellow Casualty Actuarial Soc.; mem. Newcomen Soc. N.Am. Presbyn. Clubs: Economic, Executive, Wilson Avenue Toastmasters (Chgo.); Michigan Shores (Wilmetté). Home: 711 Laurel Av Wilmette IL 60091 Office: 4750 N Sheridan Rd Chicago IL 60640

HUGHLETT, ROBERT BROOKS, dentist; b. Grand Junction, Colo., Apr. 16, 1918; s. Hugh Brooks and Fern (Fancher) H.; student U. Tampa, 1936-38; D.D.S., U. Tenn., 1942; m. Doris Nelms, Sept. 10, 1939; children—Marjorie, James, Carolyn, Patricia, Pamela. Dental cons. Ala. Health Dept., 1942-43; gen. practice dentistry, Tampa, Fla., 1946—; pres. Hillsborough County Dental Research Clinic, 1954; mem. Fla. Bd. Dental Examiners, 1952-56; pres. Hughlett & Garrett, Inc., Tampa, 1959—. Served to lt. USNR, 1943-46. Recipient Faculty medal U. Tenn., 1942. Fellow Am. Coll. Dentists; mem. Am., Fla. (pres. 1971-72, chmn. council legislation 1956-69; Dentist of Year award 1965), West Coast, Hillsborough County dental socs., Am. Prosthodontic Soc., Omicron Kappa Upsilon. Home: 1701 Park Circle Tampa FL 33610 Office: 5420 Florida Av Tampa FL 33604

HUGHSTON, HAROLD VAUGHAN, lawyer; b. Tuscumbia, Ala., Aug. 15, 1915; s. Hubert H. and Lutie (Vaughan) H.; LL.B., U. Ala., 1940; m. Lucy Caroline Allison, Sept. 18, 1948; children-Lutie Caroline, Lucy Ann, Harold Vaughan, James Dowlen. Admitted to Ala. bar, 1940; practice in Tuscumbia, 1940-42, 46—; mem. firm Smith, Hughston & Tompkins, 1946-47; judge Colbert Law and Equity Ct., 1947; circuit judge 11th Judicaial Circuit and 31st Judicial Circuit, 1948-55; mem. firm Kirk, Rather & Hughston, 1955—. Dir. First Nat. Bank in Tuscumbia, Sheffield Fed. Savs. & Loan Assn., New Southland Nat. Life Ins. Co., Nat. Telephone of Ala., Inc. Solicitor, Colbert County, 1942; city atty., Tuscumbia, 1965—; atty. Colbert County Sch. Bd., 1965—; chmn. Tuscumbia Bd. Edn., 1967—. Served to capt., Judge Adv. Gen. Corps, AUS, 1942-46; ETO, MTO. Mem. Ala., Colbert County, 31st Judicial Circuit (pres.) bar assns., Farrah Law Soc., Nat. Alumni Assn. U. Ala. (pres.), Kappa Alpha, Phi Delta Phi. Presbyn. (elder). Kiwanian, (dist. gov. 1955). Home: 805 E 4th St Tuscumbia AL 35674 Office: Old State Nat Bldg W 6th St Tuscumbia AL 35674

HUGIE, ELDON RIGGS, lawyer, business exec.; b. Logan, Utah, July 17, 1932; s. Albert, Jr. and Edna (Riggs) H.; B.S. cum laude, Utah State U., 1954; LL.D., U. Cal., Berkeley, 1960; m. Cleo Tibbitts, June 29, 1951; children-Michael Eldon, Susan Kaye, Robert Eldon and David Eldon (twins), Patti Jean. Admitted to Cal. bar, 1960, since practiced in Bakersfield and Monterey; partner Darling & Hugie, 1964-68; v.p., gen. counsel, dir. Fat City Corp., Monterey, 1968—; tchr. taxation Bakersfield Coll., 1967-68. Served to capt. USAF, 1954-57. Distinguished Mil. Grad. Air Force ROTC, Utah State U., 1954. C.P.A., Cal. Mem. Am., Kern County (past v.p.), Monterey County bar assns., State Bar Cal., State Bar Utah, Cal. Soc. C.P.A.'s, U. Cal. Law Sch. Alumni Assn.. (past dir.), Phi Kappa Phi. Mem. Ch. of Jesus Christ of Latter-day Saints. Home: 22651 Equipoise Rd Monterey CA 93940 Office: 2460 Garden Rd Monterey CA 93940

HUGILL, ELBERT ABRAM, Jr., lawyer; b. Berkeley, Cal., June 7, 1908; s. Elbert A. and Grace (Creider) H.; A.B., U. Cal., Berkeley, 1930, LL.B., 1933; m. Barbara-Lu White, Dec. 16, 1933; childrenPerry Ann (Mrs. Richard Compton Kurtz), Steven Elbert. Admitted to Cal. bar, 1933, N.Y. bar, 1951; ret. as v.p. and sec. Shell Oil Co., 1968; spl. asst. to pres. Kennecott Copper Co., N.Y.C., 1968-71; partner firm Brown, Wood, Fuller, Caldwell & Ivey. Trustee, Bronxville, N.Y., 1955- 59, mayor, 1959-65. Mem. Am., Cal., N.Y. State bar assns., Order of Coif, Delta Theta Phi, Alpha Kappa Lambda. Republican. Address: 89 Seaview Av Piedmont CA 94611

HUGUS, Z. ZIMMERMAN, Jr., educator; b. Washington, Aug. 14, 1923; s. Z. Zimmerman and Marguerite (Weaver) H.; B.A., Williams Coll., 1943; Ph.D., U. Cal. at Berkeley, 1949; m. Nancy Anne Regin, June 25, 1947; children—Carily, Z. Zimmerman III, Richard Regin, Patricia Helen. Research fellow, instr. U. Cal. at Berkeley, 1949-52; mem. faculty U. Minn., 1952-67. prof., chief inorganic chemistry, 1963-67; prof., head chemistry N.C. State U., Raleigh, 1967—. Served with USNR, 1944-46. Fellow A.A.A.S.; mem. Am. Chem. Soc., Am. Assn. U. Profs., Sigma Xi, Phi Beta Kappa, Phi Lambda Upsilon, Alpha Chi Sigma, Phi Delta Theta. Home: 1201 Glen Eden Dr Raleigh NC 27609

HUIE, WILLIAM BRADFORD, author; b. Hartselle, Ala., Nov. 13, 1910; s. John Bradford and Margaret Lois (Brindley) H.; A.B., U. of Alabama, 1930; m. Ruth Puckett, Oct. 27, 1934. Author: Mud on the Stars, 1942; The Fight for Air Power, 1942; Can Do; The Story of the Seabees, 1944; From Omaha to Okinawa, 1945; The Case Against the Admirals, 1946; The Revolt of Mamie Stover, 1951; The Execution of Private Slovik, 1954; The Crime of Ruby McCollum, 1956; Wolf Whistle, 1959; The Americanization of Emily, 1959; The Hero of Iwo Jima, 1960; Hotel Mamie Stover, 1963; The Hiroshima Pilot, 1964; Three Lives for Mississippi, 1965; The Klansman, 1967; He Slew the Dreamer, 1969; In the Hours of Night, 1972; also numerous mag. articles and stories. Mem. Phi Beta Kappa. Home: Hartselle AL 35640

HUIE, WILLIAM ORR, educator; b. Arkadelphia, Ark., Sept. 15, 1911; s. Robert W., Jr. and Minnie Belle (Smith) H.; B.A., Henderson (Ark) State Tchrs. Coll., 1932; LL.B., U. Tex., 1935; S.J.D., Harvard, 1953; m. Hugh Mae Wolff, Aug. 27, 1935 (dec. Jan. 1970); children-William Orr, Robert Wolff. Admitted to Tex. bar, 1935; mem. faculty U. Tex. Law Sch., 1936-, prof. law, 1946, Sylvan Lang prof., 1965-; vis. prof. U. Cal. at Berkeley, summer 1956, U. Cal. at Los Angeles, summer 1961, Harvard, 1961-62; with firm Greenwood, Moody & Robertson, Austin, 1935-36; sr. atty. OPA, 1942-43. Served with USNR, 1943-46. Research fellow Harvard Law Sch., 1939-40. Mem. Chancellors, Order of Coif, Phi Delta Phi. Democrat. Methodist. Contbr. legal jours., also author casebooks. Home: 3401 Barranca Circle Austin TX 78731.

HUIE, WILLIAM STELL, lawyer; b. College Park, Ga., Dec. 23, 1930; s. Wm. M. and Nannie Lou (Stell) H.; LL.B., Emory U., 1953; m. Madaline Johnson, June 26, 1953; children—Helen Claire, Sarah Fort. Admitted to Ga. bar, 1952, since practiced in Atlanta; mem. firm White, Schwall & Heuett, 1955-57; pvt. practice, 1957-59; partner Huie & Etheridge, 1959-60, Huie, Etheridge & Harland, 1960-67, Huie & Harland, 1967—; lectr. Emory U. Law Sch., 1957- 60, Dental Sch., 1959-68. Dir. Am. Bus. Products, Inc., Johnson Mfg. Co. Pres., bd. dirs. Ga. YMCA, Atlanta Phi Delta Theta Alumni Club; bd. dirs. Presbyn. Found., Westminster Schs. Served as 1st lt., Judge Adv. Gen. Corps, AUS, Korea. Mem. Am., Ga. (bd. govs.), Atlanta (pres.) bar assns., Lawyers Club Atlanta, Am. Judicature Soc., Atlanta Lawyers Found., Bryan Soc., Atlanta Emory U. Alumni Club (pres.), Phi Delta Theta, Phi Delta Phi, Omicron Delta Kappa. Presbyn. (elder, deacon). Home: 363 Manor Ridge Dr NW Atlanta GA 30305 Office: Fulton Fed Bldg Atlanta GA 30303

HUITT, RALPH KINSLOE, assn. exec.; b. Corsicana, Tex., Jan. 8, 1913; s. John Delloyd and Birdie (Wright) H.; A.B., Southwestern U., 1934; Ph.D., U. Tex., 1950; m. Winnie Mavis Smith, Jan. 8, 1938; children—Frank Smith, Cynthia Beth. Boys work sec. Beaumont (Tex.) YMCA, 1934-42; asst. prof. Lamar Coll., Beaumont, 1942-46; asst. prof. polit. sci. U. Wis., 1949-54, asso. prof., 1954-59, prof., 1959-65; legislative asst. to Sen. William Proxmire, 1958; asst. sec. for legislation U.S. Dept. HEW, Washington, 1965-69; guest scholar Brookings Instn., 1969; exec. dir. Nat. Assn. State Univs. and Land Grant Colls., Washington, 1970—; vis. prof. U. Okla. Served with USNR, 1943-46. Named distinguished alumnus, Southwestern U., 1970. Mem. Am. Polit. Sci. Assn. (exec. com. 1958-59), Phi Delta Theta. Democrat. Methodist. Author: (with Robert L. Peabody) Congress: Two Decades of Analysis, 1969. Contbr. articles profl. jours. Home: 5223 Reno Rd Washington DC 20015 Office: 1 Dupont Circle Washington DC 20036

HUIZENGA, CHARLES B., mfg. exec.; b. Kalamazoo, June 26, 1917; s. Fred and Wilhelmina (Klimp) H.; B.S. in Mech. Engring., U. Mich., 1939; m. Muriel E. Whiteman, Oct. 11, 1941; children—Duane C., Douglas L. Asst. mgr. prodn. control King Seely Corp., Ann Arbor, Mich., 1939-41; asst. chief engr. Consol. Steel Corp., 1941-47; dir. Kawneer Co., Niles, Mich., Kawneer de Mexico, South Bend Screw; v.p. Amax; pres. Amax Aluminum Co.; dir. Garden City Fan, Inc., 1st Nat. Bank Southwestern Mich. Mem. Nat. Indsl. Conf., Nat. Mgmt. Assos., U. Mich. Alumni. Presbyn (pres.). Lion. Address: 1440 Cedar Niles MI 49120

HUJER, KAREL, astronomer, educator; b. Zelezny Brod, Czechoslovakia, Sept. 18, 1902; s. Filip and Frantiska (Palounkova) H.; student U. London, 1924-25, Yerkes Obs., U. Chgo., 1926-30; D.Sc., U. Prague, 1932; m. Harriet Hunt, Oct. 4, 1939. Came to U.S., 1938, naturalized, 1949; Prof. physics and astronomy Ia. Wesleyan Coll., 1942-43; asst. prof. physics and astronomy Mich. State U., 1943-46; prof. astronomy and physics U. Tenn., Chattanooga, 1946-69, Guerry prof. astronomy and physics, 1969-, also head Jones Obs.; lectr. Indian univs. and colls., 1934-35. Fellow Royal Astron. Soc. London, A.A.A.S.; mem. Internat. Union History and Philosophy of Sci., Czech Astron. Soc., Soc. Astronomique de France, Astron. Soc. of Pacific, History of Sci. Soc., Royal Astron. Soc. Can., Am. Assn. Physics Tchrs., Am. Phys. Soc., Barnard Astron. Soc., Sigma Xi, Sigma Pi Sigma. Club: Torch (Chattanooga). Contbr. articles sci. jours., chpts. to books. Research history of astronomy and physics. Home: 216 Hillcrest Av Chattanooga TN 37411

HUKE, ROBERT EDWARD, educator, geographer; b. Newton, Mass., Mar. 3, 1925; s. Benjamin F. and Sarah (Alexander) H.; B.A., Dartmouth, 1948; Ph.D., Syracuse U., 1953; m. Eleanor Havko, July 4, 1950; childrenBeverly Hlakyi, Deborah Ann, Patricia Ann. Mem. faculty Dartmouth, 1953-, prof. geography, 1962-, chmn. dept., 1967-; Fulbright prof. U. Philippines, 1955-56, 62-63. Mem. Commn. Coll. Geography; chmn. Com. Computer Assisted Instrn. Pres. Upper Valley Devel. Council. Chmn. Norwich (Vt.) Republican Town Com. Served with USMCR, 1942-46. Lion (past pres. Norwich). Author: Shadows on the Land, and Economic Geography of the Philippines, 1963, also monographs. Editor; Dartmouth Publs. in Geography. Home: Partridge Hill Norwich VT 05055 Office: McNutt Hall Dartmouth Coll Hanover NH 03755

HULBARY, ROBERT LOUIS, educator, botanist; b. Madelia, Minn., July 24, 1916; s. William Harold and Olive Myrtle (Cox) H.; B.A., U. Ill., 1939; Ph.D., Columbia, 1943; m. Mary Brierly Nelson, June 15, 1940; 1 son, William Edward. Teaching fellow, then lectr. botany Columbia, 1939-44; mem. faculty U. Ia., 1946- -, prof. botany, 1961—, chmn. dept., 1962—. Chmn. U. Ia. chpt. A.R.C., 1954. Served to lt. (j.g.) USNR, 1944-46; PTO. Fellow A.A.A.S.; mem. Bot Soc. Am. (sec. central states sect. 1952-54, sec. teaching sect. 1953- 56), Phycol. Soc. Am., Am. Microscopic Soc., Internat. Soc. Plant Morphology, Ia. Acad. Sci. (pres. 1961), Sigma Xi. Home: 406 Whiting Av Iowa City IA 52240

HULBERT, MARSHALL BRANDT, coll. ofcl.; b. Oshkosh, Wis., May 23, 1905; s. Chester Cephas and Anna (Brandt) H.; A.B., Lawrence Coll., 1926, Mus.B., 1932; M.A., Columbia, 1939; Ph.D., Northwestern U., 1948; student voice Frank La Forge, N.Y.C.; m. Ruth Logan, July 12, 1944; 1 dau., Ann Logan. Tchr. social sci., Wausau, Wis., 1926-30; sec. Lawrence Conservatory Music, 1932-43; asso. prof. music Lawrence U., Appleton, 1939, asst. dean, 1943- 45, dir. admissions, 1945-58, dean administrn., 1948-54, dean coll., 1954-61, v.p., 1961-70, dir. fgn. studies, 1966-70, Mary Mortimer prof. liberal arts, 1970—. Cons. Asso. Colls. Midwest, 1970—; bus. mgr. Lawrence European Tour, 1936. Choral dir. First Presbyn. Ch., Neenah, Wis., 1938-60. Mem. Am. Assn. U. Profs., Assn. Coll. Admissions Counselors, Phi Beta Kappa, Phi Mu Alpha-Sinfonia. Methodist. Home: 70 S Meadows Dr Appleton WI 54911

HULBURT, HUGH MCKINNEY, chem. engr.; b. Nashua, N.H., Oct. 27, 1917; s. Clarence Hellings and Alice (McKinney) H.; B.A., Carroll Coll., Waukesha, Wis., 1938; M.S., U. Wis., 1940, Ph.D., 1942; NRC fellow chemistry, Princeton, 1942-43; m. Ann Podlucky, June 30, 1940; children—Susan (Mrs.Stephen A. Wadelton), Margery Ann; m. 2d, Pauline Podlucky, Dec. 1, 1956; 1 son, William Hugh. Sr. research chemist Shell Oil Co., 1943-44; instr. Hunter Coll., 1944-46; asst. prof., then asso. prof. chemistry and chem. engring. Cath. U. Am., 1946-51; supr. engr., then dir. research and devel. Chem. Constrn. Co., N.Y.C., 1951-56; with Am. Cyanamid Co., 1956-63, dir. phys. research, central research div., 1959-63; prof. chem. engring. Northwestern U., 1963—, chmn. dept., 1964-70; Reilley lectr. U. Notre Dame, 1967; vis. prof. Swiss Fed. Tech. Inst., 1971; cons. in field. Mem. Am. Inst. Chem. Engrs. (inst. lectr. 1962), Am. Chem. Soc., Am. Phys. Soc., Faraday Soc., Electrochem. Soc., Catalysis Club N.Y. (pres. 1962), Sigma Xi. Author papers in field. Editor: IEC Process Design and Development, 1962—. Home: 2040 Thornwood Av Wilmette IL 60091 Office: Dept Chem Engring Northwestern Univ Evanston IL 60201

HULEN, ELMER CULBERTSON, fgn. service officer; b. Horse Cave, Ky., Feb. 15, 1919; s. Elmer Culbertson and Natalie (Edwards) H.; B.S., Davidson Coll., 1940; M.B.A., Harvard, 1947; postgrad. Yale, 1958, U. Wash., 1958-59; m. Mary Frances Fulcher, Dec. 27, 1958; children-Natalie, Sarah, Anne Macklin. Joined U.S. Fgn. Service 1947; assigned in Saudi Arabia, 1947-49, Greece, 1950-52, Korea, 1952-54, 59-61, Can., 1955-57, State Dept., 1958-59; chief N.E. Asia div. Bur. Intelligence, State Dept., 1961-65; 1st sec. Am. embassy, Rawalpindi, Pakistan, 1965-69, Manila, Philippines, 1969—. Served with AUS, 1941-46. Mem. Phi Beta Kappa. Club: University (Washington). Address: Am. Embassy Manila Philippines.

HULET, ERVIN KENNETH, nuclear chemist; b. Baker, Ore., May 7, 1926, s. Frank E. and Marjorie (Suiter) H.; B.S., Stanford, 1949; Ph.D., U. Cal. at Berkeley, 1953; m. Betty Jo Gardner, Sept. 10, 1949; childrenCarri, Randall Gardner. AEC grad. student Lawrence Radiation Lab., Berkeley, Cal., 1949-53, research chemist radiochemistry div., Livermore, 1953-66, group leader, 1966-. Served with USNR, 1944-46. Fulbright scholar, Norway. Home: Calle los Collados Diablo CA 94528. Office: Lawrence Radiation Lab U Cal Livermore CA 94550

HULETT, CHARLES WILBUR, transfer and storage co. exec.; b. Indpls., July 27, 1917; s. Charles and Bertha Louise (Wilson) H.; ed. Butler U., 1939; LL.B., Ind. U., 1947; m. Dorothy Mae Srader, Mar.

30, 1941; 1 son, Robert Srader. Admitted to Ind. bar, 1947, Interstate Commerce Commn., 1960; with Aero Mayflower Transit Co., Inc., Indpls., 1946—, claim adjuster, 1946, asst. to v.p., 1947-54, asst. sec., also operations mgr., 1954-57, v.p. operations, 1957-69, pres. Hogan Transfer & Storage (prin. subsidiary), 1969, exec. v.p., 1970—, also dir., mem. exec. com. Served to 1st lt. inf. AUS, 1942-46. Mem. Am. Movers Conf. (dir.), Indpls., Ind. bar assns., Tau Kappa Alpha, Delta Tau Delta. Republican. Presbyn. Rotarian. Clubs: Indpls. Athletic, Columbia, Athenaeum. Home: 7950 Meridian Hills Lane Indianapolis IN 46240 Office: 863 Massachusetts Av Indianapolis IN 46204

HULETT, JAMES EDWARD, Jr., sociologist; b. Hattiesburg, Miss., June 30, 1909; s. James Edward and Anna Pauline (Schneider) H.; A.B., Miss. Coll., 1929; M.A., U. Wis., 1935, Ph.D., 1939; m. Jo Day, Sept. 3, 1937; 1 son, David Todd. Asso. social psychologist Dept. Agr., 1939-40; asst. prof. sociology U. Ill., Urbana, 1940-50, asso. prof., 1950-57, prof., 1957—, chmn. dept. sociology and anthropology, 1953-59, mem. grad. faculty in communications, 1963-71, acting head dept. sociology, 1968-69. Visiting prof. sociology U. Ala., summer 1939. Sr. research asst. WPA, 1934-35; clin. psychologist OSS, 1944-45. Fellow Am. Psychol. Assn., A.A.A.S., Am. Sociol. Assn.; mem. Am., Midwest sociol. socs. Unitarian. Editor: (with Ross Stagner) Problems in Social Psychology, 1951; A Symbolic Interactionist Model of Human Communication, 1966. Contbr. articles to profl. jours. Home: 105 W Pennsylvania Av Urbana IL 61801

HULFORD, CLARENCE LESTER, banker; b. Seattle; s. Morton A. and Margaret Ann (McKinnon) H.; B.A., U. Wash., 1935. With Hughbanks, Inc., Seattle, 1934-41, with Northwest Airlines Inc., Seattle, 1941-45; Nat. Bank Commerce, Seattle, 1947—, sr. v.p., 1965—; pres., dir. Internat. Bank Commerce, Seattle, 1969—, exec. v.p., dir. Nat. Bank Commerce Seattle (Internat.), N.Y.C., 1969—. Mem. Banker's Assn. Fgn. Trade, Nat. Export Expansion Council, Western Internat. Trade Group, Japan-Am. Soc. Episcopalian. Rotarian. Home: 1935 10th Av Seattle WA 98102 Office: 1100 2d Av Seattle WA 98124

HULINGS, ALBERT DEWAYNE, window mfg. co. exec.; b. Elmdale, Mont., June 9, 1913; s. Russell M. and Pearl (Ross) H.; B.A., Carleton Coll., Northfield, Minn., 1936; m. Mary Elizabeth Andersen, May 20, 1938; children—Mary (Mrs. John D. Rice), Martha (Mrs. Arthur Kaemmer). With Andersen Corp., Bayport, Minn., 1937—, dir., 1943—, exec. v.p., 1967-68, pres., 1968—; dir. Ponderosa Pine Woodwork Assn.; mem. investment com. trust dept. First Nat. Bank of Mpls. Vice pres., bd. dirs. Indianhead council Boy Scouts Am.; past bd. dirs. Sci. Mus. St. Paul, St. Paul Council Arts and Sci.; v.p., trustee Bayport Found.; pres. bd. mgrs. Lakeview Meml. Hosp.; trustee Carleton Coll., Andersen Pension Fund, Andersen Deferred Profit Sharing Fund. Recipient Carleton Alumni Achievement award, 1956, Silver Beaver award Boy Scouts Am., 1965, Jaycee Boss of Year award Stillwater chpt., 1970. Republican. Conglist. Lion. Clubs: Stillwater Golf; St. Paul Athletic, Minnesota (St. Paul); Apostle Island Yacht (Bayfield, Wis.); Minneapolis. Home: The Point Bayport MN 55003 Office: Bayport MN 55003

HULL, ANSON ELDER, lawyer; b. Springfield, O., Aug. 22, 1915; s. George A. and Ethel (Cultice) H.; A.B., Ohio State U., 1938, LL.B., J.D., 1940; m. Dorothy M. Mitchell, Dec. 7, 1940; children—William A., Joseph W. Admitted to Ohio bar, 1940, since practiced in Springfield; pvt. practice, 1940-42; exec. dir. OPA, 1942-44; asso., sr. partner Martin, Browne, Hull & Harper, 1944—. Dir. Springprint Paper Products Co. 1st pres. Clark County Regional Planning Bd., 1955-57; chmn. Clark County Regional Mental Health and Retardation Bd., 1968—. Mem. Am., Ohio, Clark County bar assns., Clark County Law Library Assn. (treas.). Republican. Methodist. Kiwanian. Club: Sertoma (pres.) (New Carlisle, O.). Home: 95 S Tecumseh St Springfield OH 45506 Office: 1st Nat Bank Bldg Springfield OH 45502

HULL, DAVID CARLOCK, petro chem. co. exec.; b. Marion, Va., Dec. 15, 1908; s. Wythe M. and Clyde (Carlock) H.; B.S., Emory and Henry Coll., Emory, Va., 1930, D.Sc., 1969; M.S., U. Tenn., 1931; m. Nola C. Murray, Sept. 17, 1933; children-Betty Jane (Mrs. Earl Roberts, Jr.), David Carlock. Chemist, supt. acetic anhydride dept., supt. acid div., prodn. mgr. Clinton Engring. Works, Tenn. Eastman Co., Kingsport, 1931-50; mgr., v.p. Tex. Eastman Co. div. Eastman Kodak Co., Longview, 1950-63, pres., 1963—; pres., dir. First Fed. Savs. & Loan Assn., dir. First Nat. Bank, Longview. Bd. dirs. Longview YMCA; bd. mgrs. Good Shepherd Hosp.; mem. Engring. Found., U. Tex., Austin. Mem. Tex. Mfrs. Assn. (dir.), Am. Chem. Soc., Am. Inst. Chem. Engrs. Methodist. Patentee in field. Home: 1104 Yates Dr Longview TX 75601 Office: P O Box 7444 Longview TX 75601

HULL, DAVID RYERSON, electronics mgmt. cons.; b. Newton, N.J., Oct. 29, 1903; s. David R. and Carrie F. (Ayers) H.; B.S., U.S. Naval Acad., 1925; M.S., Harvard, 1933; m. Flora E. Keeher, May 9, 1927; children-David R., Kathryn A. Commd. midshipman USN, 1925, advanced through grades to capt., 1948; asst. tech. dir. Internat. Tel. & Tel. Corp., 1948-50; v.p. Fed. Tele-communication Labs., Inc., Nutley, N.J., 1948-50; exec. v.p. Capehart-Farnsworth Corp., 1949-50; v.p., dir. Radio Electronic TV. Mfg. Assn., 1956-58; dir. Armed Forces Communications and Electronics Assn., 1956-64; dir. Tech. Operations, Inc., 1956-60; dir. Raytheon- Can., Ltd., 1956-60, gen. mfg. equipment operations Raytheon Co., 1950-58, v.p. corporate relations, 1958-60; exec. v.p. Hoffman Electronics Corp., 1960-62; asso. Boyden Assos., Inc., mgmt. cons., 1962-63; cons., 1963-; pres. Delray Properties, Inc., Delray Beach, Fla., 1963-69; dir. engring. Electronic Industries Assn., 1965-70, cons. to pres., 1970—; dir. Globe-Union, Inc., Astronautics Corp. Am., Mycalex Corp. Am., Yardney Electric Corp., Epsco, Inc. Decorated Legion of Merit. Fellow I.E.E.E., Acoustical Soc. Am.; mem. Am. Inst. Physics, Soc. Naval Engrs., U.S. Naval Inst., Electronic Industries Assn. (pres., dir. 1958-60, hon. mem.; medal of honor 1960). Mason. Clubs: Army-Navy (Washington); Coral Ridge Yacht (Ft. Lauderdale, Fla.). Address: 1900 S Ocean Blvd Pompano Beach FL 33062

HULL, DENISON BINGHAM, architect; b. Chgo., Mar. 25, 1897; s. Morton Denison and Katharine Louise (Bingham) H.; A.B., Harvard, 1919, M.Arch., 1923; L.H.D., Meadville, 1965; m. Marion Emily Walker, May 29, 1926; children—Morton Denison, Lyman Walker, Katherine Bingham, Eunice Larned. Practicing architect independently since 1927; prin. bldgs. include First Unitarian Ch., Meadville Theol. Sch., Chgo., Ill. Coll. Library, Jacksonville, Restoration Old First Ch., Bennington, Vt.; installed, designed 1st radiant heating system in Middle West, 1937; treas., dir. 208 S. LaSalle St. Corp., Chgo., 1945-67, pres., 1967-. Chmn. Chgo. com. Fight for Freedom, Inc., 1941-42; commr. Winnetka Park Bd., 1939-45, pres., 1940, v.p., 1941-45; candidate for Republican nomination for Congressman-at-large, 1942. Dir., treas. Legislative Voters League of Ill., 1938-39, sec., 1939-42; bd. mem. Library Internat. Relations, 1937-38, governing mem., 1946-49; trustee Provident Hosp., Chgo., 1930; dir. Evanston (Ill.) Hosp., 1949-54; dir. Harvard Alumni Assn., 1954-58; pres. trustees Music Center N. Shore, 1953-61; dir. North Shore Country Day Sch., Winnetka, 1938-52, pres., 1945-46; trustee First Unitarian Soc., Chgo., 1936-44, Hunt Servants Benefit Found., 1853-63; past mem. vis. com. Sch. Design and Visual Arts, Harvard; vis. com. div. humanities U. Chgo.; trustee, vice chmn., chmn., treas. Meadville Theol. Sch. Lombard Coll., 1938-67; trustee Am. Farm Sch., Thessaloniki, Greece, 1969—. Mem. adv. com. on manufacture of hearing aids WPB, 1942. Served to 2d lt. 70th Inf., U.S. Army, 1918-19. Decorated Gold Cross Order Phoenix, Greece. Mem. A.I.A. (treas. Chgo. chpt. 1934-36, 1st v.p., dir. 1936-38), Harvard Found. for Advanced Study and Research (mem. council 1952-63), Harvard Alumni Assn. (dir. 1954-55), Art Inst. Chgo. (governing life mem.); mem. Archaeol. Inst. Am. (exec. com. Chgo. soc. 1968), Masters of Foxhounds Assn. Am. Clubs: Indian Hill (Winnetka, Ill.); Harvard (pres. 1963), University, Cliff Dwellers (Chgo.); Fox River Valley Hunt (Barrington, Ill.). Author: Thoughts on American Fox-Hunting, 1958; Aesop's Fables Told by Valerius Babrius, 1960; Hounds and Hunting in Ancient Greece, 1964; articles and verse in Greek Heritage; also articles archtl. jour. Office: 77 W Washington St Chicago IL 60602

HULL, DONALD FRANKLIN, ret. army officer; b. Greenville, Ill., Sept. 22, 1913; s. Thomas Burton and Lillian (Turley) H.; B.S., U.S. Mil Acad., 1939; student Columbia Sch. Edn., 1945-46; m. Dorothy Cavanagh, June 13, 1939; children—Dorothy Ann (Mrs. John M. Carrick), Dona Maria, Donald Franklyn, Deborah Jean. Commd. 2d lt. U.S. Army, 1939, advanced through grades to col., 1961; with Airborne Inf., World War II; gen. staff officer, 1943-45; dir. phys. edn. U.S. Mil. Acad., 1945-47; sports and recreation officer European Command, 1947-50; Army sports and Olympic rep., 1950-57, 58-60; UN sports officer, Korea, Japan, Okinawa, 1957-58; Adj. Gen. Corps officer U.S. Modern Pentathlon, 1960-61, ret., 1962; nat. exec. dir. Amateur Athletic Union U.S., 1962-71. Home: 135 Westervelt Pl Cresskill NJ 07626

HULL, EUGENE DELOSS, elevator co. exec.; b. Wolf Lake, Ind., Sept. 27, 1920; s. Henry E. and Merle M. (Zentz) H.; B.S. in Bus. Adminstrn., U. Notre Dame, 1947; M.B.A., Harvard, 1948; div. With Otis Elevator Co., N.Y.C., 1948. sr. v.p., 1968—, dir., 1968—. Served to 1st lt AUS, 1943-46. Clubs: The Chicago; University, Harvard New York Yacht (N.Y.C.); Essex Country (Manchester, Mass.). Home: 200 E 66th St New York City NY 10021 Office: 260 11th Av New York City NY 10001

HULL, GORDON, advt. agy. exec.; b. N.Y.C., Jan. 3, 1916; s. Edward G. and Ethel (Keen) H.; m. Elizabeth Libertucci, Nov. 11, 1950; children-Libbie, Jeffrey and Douglas (twins). Freelance newspaper reporter, N.Y.C., 1934-43; life ins. editor Ins. Adv., N.Y.C., 1946-47; editor The Pelican, 1947-51; sales service mgr. Mut. Benefit Life Ins. Co., Newark, 1950-51, dir. sales services, 1951-59, dir. advt., sales devel., 1959-61; account exec. Compton Advt., Inc., N.Y.C., 1961-62, v.p., 1962-65, v.p., account supr., 1965, sr. v.p., mgmt. supr., 1966—. Vice chmn. nominating com. Bd. Edn., Mountain Lakes, N.J., 1956. Served with Signal Corps, AUS, 1942-46; ETO, PTO. Mem. October Tennis League N.J. (founder, pres. 1963- 66). Clubs: Orange Lawn Tennis (South Orange), Park Lakes Tennis (past pres.) (Mountain Lakes). Home: 33 Crystal Rd Mountain Lakes NJ 07046 Office: 625 Madison Av New York NY 10022

HULL, HADLAL AUSTIN, govt. ofcl.; b. New London, Conn., May 30, 1914; s. Charles and Grace (Stoddard) H.; A.B., Yale, 1936, LL.B., 1939; m. Anne Dalrymple, July 14, 1939; children—Charles Hadlai, John Dalrymple, Thomas Stoddard. Admitted to N.Y. bar, 1940; asso. Sullivan & Cromwell, 1939- 41; asst. sec. Minn. & Ont. Paper Co., Mpls., 1946-49, sec., 1949-51, sec.-treas. 1951-55; dir., treas. Dayton Co., 1955-60, v.p., treas., 1960-69, sr. v.p., dir., Dayton Hudson Corp., 1969-71; asst. sec. for manpower and res. affairs Dept. Army, Washington, 1971—; past mem. trust com. 1st Nat. Bank Mpls.; past dir. Northwestern Nat. Life Ins. Co. Trustee Mpls. Soc. Fine Arts. Served to comdr. USNR, 1941-45. Clubs: Minneapolis; Woodhill Country (trustee); Kitchi Gammi (Duluth, Minn.). Home: 2700 Virginia Av NW Washington DC 20037 Office: Pentagon Washington DC

HULL, HAROLD COTTERMAN, banker; b. Dayton, O., Mar. 21, 1908; s. Ora L. and Lulu (Kirkpatrick) H.; B.S. in Commerce, U. Cin., 1931; m. Dorothy Logan Hammitt, Aug. 22, 1931; children—Carolyn (Mrs. Myron D. Peterson), Harold Cotterman. Dist. mgr. Remington-Rand, Inc., Birmingham, Ala., 1931-39; bus. rep. C.I.T. Corp., Nashville, 1940- 43, 46-47; sr. v.p. Commerce Union Bank, Nashville, 1947—. Served as lt. comdr. USNR, 1943-45. Mem. Alpha Tau Omega. Episcopalian. Mason (Shriner.) Clubs: Richland Country; Nashville City. Home: 201 Olive Branch Rd Nashville TN 37205 Office: 400 Union St Nashville TN 37219

HULL, HARRY, orgn. exec.; b. Athens, Ga., Jan. 18, 1912; s. Harry and Anne Spann (Burnett) H.; B.S., U.S. Naval Acad., 1932; student Naval Postgrad. Sch., 1939-41; grad. Advanced Mgmt. Program. Harvard, 1954; m. Louisa Catherine Adams Clement, Aug. 19, 1943; children—Harry III, Kimball Erskine Clement, Louisa Catherine Adams. Commd. ensign U.S. Navy, 1932, advanced through grades to rear adm., 1961; comdr. submarine U.S.S. Thresher, World War II, destroyer U.S.S. Orleck, 1948-50, ammunition ship U.S.S. Firedrake, 1952-53, amphibious cargo ship U.S.S. Merrick, 1953-54, cruiser U.S.S. Macon, 1957-58; comdr. Mil. Sea Transp. Service, Atlantic area, 1961-63; comdr. cruiser destroyer flotilla 10, 1963-64; dir. shore activities, devel. and control div. Office Chief Naval Operations, 1964-67, ret., 1967; exec. dir. Internat. Center New Eng., Inc., Boston, 1967—. Mem. adv. council North Bay council Boy Scouts Am. Decorated Navy Cross. Episcopalian. Home: Uplands Highland Av Manchester MA 01944 Office: 470 Atlantic Av Boston MA 02210

HULL, HARVARD LESLIE, corp. ofcl.; b. Holstein, Neb., Oct. 23, 1906; s. Joel Leslie and Caroline Evangeline (Larsen) H.; A.B. with distinction, Neb. Wesleyan U., 1927; Ph.D. in Physics, Columbia, 1933; m. Alta Zera Jones, June 9, 1928; childrenGwen Alta (Mrs. Stanley A. Framburg, Jr.), Janet Barbara (Mrs. Edward J. Clark). Project engr. Sperry Gyroscope Co., Bklyn, 1933-35, research engr., 1935-40, dir. remote control devel., 1940-43; introduced new equipment Sperry Gyroscope Co., Ltd., Eng., 1934, 35-36; dir. process improvement electromagnetic process of separation Uranium 235, Tenn. Eastman Corp., Oak Ridge, 1943- 46; asso. dir. Argonne Nat. Lab., Chgo., 1946-49, dir. remote control engring. dev., 1949-53; v.p. research and devel. div. Capehart- Farnsworth Co., Ft. Wayne, 1953-54; pres. Farnsworth Electronics Co., Co. div. Internat. Tel.&Tel. Corp., Ft. Wayne, 1954-56; v.p. Litton Industries, Beverly Hills, Cal., 1956-57; pres. Hull Assos., Chgo., 1957-; dir., pres. Chgo. Aerial Industries, Inc., Barrington, Ill., 1962-64, Internat. Tech. Corp., Western Springs, Ill.; dir. Central Research Labs., Inc. Dir. research Aero-Space Inst., Chgo. Fellow Am. Inst. Aeros. and Astronautice (asso.); mem. I.E.E.E. (sr.); Am. Nuclear Soc., A.A.A.S., Am. Phys. Soc., Nat. Telemetering Conf. (chmn., 1956), Sigma Xi, Phi Kappa Phi, Theta Chi. Conglist. Club: Executives. Address: 5223 Caroline Av Western Springs IL 60558

HULL, JAMES MERIWETHER, lawyer; b. Augusta, Ga., Oct. 6, 1885; s. James Meriwether and Mary Baldwin (Lyon) H.; student U. Ga., U. Va.; m. Marion Stewart Phinizy, Nov. 10, 1909; childrenStewart Phinizy, Mary (Mrs. Darwin H. Boyd), James Meriwether. Admitted to Ga. bar, 1907, since practiced in Augusta; sr. mem. firm Hull, Towill, Norman, Barrett & Johnson, 1922—. Dir. First Nat. Bank & Trust Co. Augusta, Augusta Rialto Co., Fine Products Co., Inc., Ga. & Fla. Ry. Co. Pres., Met. Augusta Found., Ga.-Carolina council Boy Scouts Am.; hon. pres. Jr. Achievement Augusta. Served as 1st lt. U.S. Army, World War I. Fellow Am. Bar Found., Am. Coll. Trial Lawyers; mem. Phi Delta Phi, Delta Tau Delta. Episcopalian (sr. warden). Rotarian (charter pres. Augusta). Clubs: Augusta National Golf, Augusta Country, Pinnacle. Home: 1965. Address: 1107 Peachtree Rd Augusta GA 30904 Office: First Nat Bank Bldg Augusta GA 30903

HULL, JAMES RICHARD, hosp. supply co. exec.; b. Keokuk, Ia., Dec. 5, 1933; s. James Robert and Alberta Margaret (Bouseman) H.; B.A., Ill. Wesleyan U., 1955; J.D., Northwestern U., 1958; m. Patricia M. Kiesner, June 14, 1958; children—Elizabeth, James, David. Corporate sec., v.p. Honeggers & Co., Inc., Fairbury, Ill., 1959-65, also dir.; with Am. Hosp. Supply Corp., Evanston, Ill., 1965—, now corporate sec., sr. atty. Mem. alumni council fund raising Ill. Wesleyan U. Mem. Am., Ill., Chgo. bar assns., Am. Soc. Corporate Secs., Sigma Chi. Club: Legal (Chgo.). Home: 2603 Oak St Northbrook IL 60062 Office: 1740 Rdge Av Evanston IL 60204

HULL, JEROME WEBSTER, telephone co. exec.; b. Aberdeen, Wash., May 7, 1912; s. Jerome Webster and Caroline Nancy (Berry) H.; student Stanford, 1934; A.B., Occidental Coll., 1935; m. Lucille Mae Spelts, Jan. 31, 1942; childrenParticia Ann (Mrs. George Cavender), Victoria Jean (Mrs. Paul Edward Hazelrig), Carolyn Marie. Asst. v.p. Am. Tel. & Tel. Co., 1959-60; v.p., gen. mgr. Pacific Tel. & Tel. Co., 1960-61, v.p. operations, 1962-66, exec. v.p., 1966-68, pres., 1968-70, also dir. Trustee Occidental Coll.; bd. dirs. Golden Gate chpt. A.R.C. Mem. San Francisco C. of C. (dir.). Presbyn. Clubs: Stock Exchange, World Trade (dir.) (San Francisco); California (Los Angeles); Stanford (Cal.) Golf; Olympic; Burlingame (Cal.) Country. Home: 5 Lupine Way Hillsborough CA 94010

HULL, JOHN DANIEL, Jr., educator; b. Mountain Grove, Mo., Mar. 11, 1900; s. John Daniel and Nancy Susan (McQuitty) H.; B.S., U. Mo., 1920; A.M., U. of Chgo., 1923; Ph.D., Yale U., 1933; LL.D., Drury Coll., 1964; m. Alene Oliver, Dec. 21, 1924; childrenNancy Susan (Mrs. Willis A. McCracken), John Daniel III. Prin. high sch., Mountain Grove. Mo., 1918-19. Sullivan, Ind., 1920-24. Springfield, Mo., 1924-41, Shortridge High Sch., Indpls., 1941-47; with U.S. Office of Edn., 1947-64, chief secondary schs., 1952-55, dir. instrn. services, 1955-64; instr. Grad. Sch. Drury Coll., 1965-68; prof. edn. adminstrn., summers, S.W. Mo. State, Drury, La. State U., U. Buffalo, Yale, U. Mo., N.Y. U., George Washington U., U. Wyo., Syracuse U. Mem. high sch. curriculum com. Mo. State Dept. Edn., 1937-41, curriculum com. Ind. State Dept., 1943-47; exec. sec. Nat. Commn. on Life Adjustment Edn. for Youth, 1947-53; cons. to Dependent Schs., U.S. Army in Europe, 1952-53. Trustee Long Coll. for Women, Hanover Coll., 1944-47. Chmn. U.S. Delegation to Internat. Conf. on Secondary Edn., Chile, 1955. Chmn. Springfield chpt. A.R.C., 1968, 69; treas. Greene County Humane Soc., 1968—. Recipient Shattuck Sch. Centennial Citation, 1958, for service to secondary edn. Mem. Nat. Assn. Secondary Sch. Prins. (curriculum com. 1946-51, nat. com. for nat. council social studies 1941-45), Ind. State Mental Hygiene Soc. (exec. com. 1944-47), N.E.A., Headmasters Assn. (hon.), Phi Delta Kappa, Kappa Alpha. Presbyn. Clubs: Rotary, Univ., Hickory Hills Country. Author: A Primer of Life Adjustment Education, 1949; Offerings and Enrollments in High School Subjects (with Grace Wright), 1948-49; American High School Administrations (with French and Dodds), 1951, rev., 1957, (with Austin and French), 1962. Editor: Why Do Boys and Girls Drop Out of School and What Can We Do About It, 1950; Vitalizing Secondary Education, 1951; Improving School Holding Power, 1951; A Look Ahead in Secondary Education, 1954; Teaching Fast and Slow Learners in High School (with Arno Jewett), 1954. Contbr. to ednl. jours. Address: 2222 Englewood Rd Springfield MO 65804

HULL, JOHN KENNETH, airplane co. exec.; b. Pocatello, Ida., Feb. 20, 1901; s. John J. and Anne (Carroll) H.; student U. Ida., 1918, U. Cal. at Los Angeles, 1921, U. So. Cal., 1924; m. Helen Virginia Kirk, Aug. 18, 1925; children—John Kenneth, Caroline (Mrs. William B. Chase). Jr. v.p. Cal. Bank, 1924-41; supr. statistics Lockheed Aircraft Corp., 1941, asst. dir. contract mgrs., 1945-55, asst. gen. parts and service mgr., 1945-46, pres. Lockheed Aircraft Service Corp., 1949- 59; asst. gen. fgn. mgr. base operations Lockheed Overseas Corp., 1941- 45, pres., 1950-59; v.p. gen. mgr. Lockheed Service Corp., 1947-49, pres., 1949-58; pres., mng. dir. Lockhead Internat., 1959-62, cons., 1962-66; self employed, 1966; pres. Air Cal., 1966-68, now dir.; pres. Mohr Labs., Inc., Orange, Cal., 1968—, also dir. chmn. bd. Air Colo.; pres., chmn. bd. Lite-Ron Industries, Irvine, Cal.; dir. Radiant Industries, Copaltronics Corp., Los Angeles. Asso. mem. Cal. Republican Central Com. 1967-68. Bd. dirs. Care, Los Angeles County Mus. Alliance; mem. Friends of Harvey Mudd Coll., Friends Claremont Colls., Friends Huntington Library, Los Angeles County Art Museum, San Antonio Community Hosp. Assn. Mem. Los Angeles World Affairs Council, Econ. Roundtable. Clubs: Balboa Bay (Newport Beach, Cal.); California (Los Angeles); Trojan. Home: 133 Venezia Lido Isle Newport Beach CA 92660 Office: Mohr Labs Inc 210 Emerson Orange CA 92667

HULL, MCALLISTER HOBART, Jr., educator, physicist; b. Birmingham, Ala., Sept. 1, 1923; s. McAllister Hobart and Grace (Johnson) H.; B.S. with highest honors, Yale, 1948, Ph.D. in Physics, 1951; m. Mary Muska, Mar. 23, 1946; children—John McAllister, Wendy Ann. From instr. to asso. prof. physics Yale, 1951-66; prof. physics, chmn. dept. Ore. State U., 1966-69, State U. N.Y. at Buffalo, 1969—; adviser to supt. schs., Hamden, Conn., 1958-65. Bd. dirs. Western N.Y. Reactor Facility. Served with AUS, 1943-46. Faculty fellow Yale, 1964-65. Fellow Am. Phys. Soc.; mem. Am. Assn. Physics Tchrs. (chmn. Ore. sect. 1967-68). Author papers, books, chpts. in books, articles in encys. Home: 63 Columbia Dr Williamsville NY 14221 Office: Hochstetter Hall State Univ New York Buffalo NY 14214

HULL, RAYMOND HORACE, writer, lectr.; b. Shaftesbury, Eng., Feb. 27, 1919; s. Edgar John and May (Coates) H.; ed. pub. schs. Laborer, folk-singer, saw operator, puppeteer and other miscellaneous jobs, 1937-65; pres. Raymond Hull Enterprises, Ltd., 1970—; writer of articles, books, plays, poetry, song lyrics, radio and television scripts; lectr. on non-fiction books, articles and playwriting. Pres. Gower Point Property Owners' Assn., 1969—; v.p. Vancouver Center Progressive Conservative Assn., 1965-66. Mem. Canadian Authors Assn., Vancouver Arts Club, Canadian Anti-Dog Soc. (pres.). Club: Men's Canadian. Author: Profitable Playwriting, 1968; Writing for Money in Canada, 1969; Tales of a Pioneer Surveyor, 1970; Successful Public Speaking, 1971; (with Jack Sleight) Home Book of Smoke Cookery and Smoke Curing, 1971; How to Get What You Want, 1969; (with Laurence J. Peter) The Peter Principle, 1969; (with Stanley F. Anderson) The Art of Making Wine, 1968, The Art of Making Beer, 1971; (with Olga Ruskin) Gastown's Gassy Jack, 1971. Address: 1703-1200 Alberni St Vancouver 5 British Columbia Canada

HULL, ROBERT LESLIE, musician; b. N.Y.C., Feb 11, 1916; s. O. Leslie and Myrtle (Patterson) H.: student Ashland (O.) Coll., 1933-37; Mus.B., U. Rochester, 1939, Mus.M., 1941; Ph.D., Cornell U., 1945; m. Jeanne Bredbenner, July 17, 1942. Asst. prof. music Duke, 1943-47; asso. prof., dir. univ. music Cornell U., 1947-56; dir. Elmira (N.Y.) Civic Chorus; dean Sch. Fine Arts. Tex. Christian U., 1956-59; mus. dir., conductor Fort Worth Symphony and Ballet Socs., 1959-63; vis. prof. U. Kan., 1964; dean Coll. Fine Arts, U. Ariz., 1964—; condr. Ariz. Chamber Orch., 1967—; condr. profl. recs. Concert Hall Soc., Handel Soc. Records, Inc. N.Y.C.; guest condr. Pitts., Buffalo, Rochester, Phoenix, Tucson symphonies. Mem. Ariz. Commn. Arts and Humanities. Mem. bd. Tucson Symphony Soc. Winner profl. div. N.C. Composers Contest, 1947. Mem. Am. Symphony Orch. League (exec. bd. 1955-57), Music Tchrs. Nat. Assn., Am. Musicol. Soc., Tucson Arts Council, Nat. Council Fine Arts Deans, Am. Assn. U. Profs., Simfonia, Phi Mu Alpha. Mem. Christian. Ch. Home: 5403 Via Alcalde Tucson AZ 85718

HULL, ROGER, James, life ins. exec.; b. State College, Miss., Nov. 17, 1907; s. David Carlisle and Madge Cook (Wilson) H.; student Miss. State Coll., 1924-25; A.B., Ky. Wesleyan Coll., 1928, L.H.D., 1957; LL.D., Wheaton Coll., 1963, Houghton Coll., 1963; m. Rosalie Paschal, Dec. 31, 1932; childrenJames Roger, Rosemary (Mrs. David Mace), Elizabeth (Mrs. David E. Hall). With Mut. Life Ins. Co. N.Y., 1928—, dist. mgr., Nashville, asst. Supt agys. home office, v.p., mgr. agys., 1941-50, exec. v.p., 1950- 59, trustee 1950—, pres., 1959-67, chmn. 1967—; dir. Dun & Bradstreet, Inc., Hart Schaffner & Marx, Centennial Ins. Co.; trustee Atlantic Mutl Ins. Co. Chmn. life trustee Am. Coll. Life Underwriters. Mem. Nat. Indsl. Conf.; bd. mem. adv. bd. Salvation Army. C.L.U., 1934. Presbyn. (trustee U.P. Found.). Clubs: Links, River (N.Y.C.); Wee Burn Country (Darien). Home: 317 Hollow Tree Ridge Rd Darien CT 06820 Office: 1740 Broadway New York City NY 10019

HULL, WILLIAM HENRY, publishing co. exec., orgn. ofcl.; b. Boonville, Mo., Oct. 29, 1918; s. Aubrey Grant and Mary Ann (Moore) H.; A.B. in English and Art, Central Coll., Fayette, Mo., 1940; M.A. in English, So. Meth. U., 1941; m. Carol Louise Hanson, Aug. 16, 1943; children—Judith Lynn (Mrs. E.T. Lindberg), Pauline Ann (Mrs. Patrick Conn). Chmn. English dept., humanities div. Kemper Mil. Sch., Boonville, 1941-46; prof. English, Mankato (Minn.) State Coll., 1946-47; bus. mgr., pub. relations mgr. Postgrad. Medicine jour., McGraw-Hill, Inc., Mpls., 1948-68, marketing services mgr., 1968-71, circulation mgr., 1971—. Free lance garden writer. Mem. Men's Garden Clubs Am., 1952—, pres. Mpls., 1958, nat. bd. dirs., 1956- -, nat. v.p., 1961-63, nat. pres., 1964, chmn. adv. bd., 1965. Recipient bronze medal Men's Garden Club of Mpls., 1966; silver medal Men's Garden Clubs Am., 1966. Mem. Minn. Press Club (charter), Garden Writers Assn. Am., Alpha Phi Omega, Pi Delta Epsilon. Mason. Author: Public Relations for the Pharmacist, 1955; Buying Fruits and Vegetables, 1957. Editor: The Garden Spray, 1966-70. Contbr. articles to profl. jours. Home: 6833 Creston Rd Edina MN 55435 Office: 4015 W 65th St Minneapolis MN 55424

HULL, W. R., Jr., congressman; b. Weston, Mo., Apr. 17, 1906; student pub. schs.; children-Susan (Mrs. Floyd Hudson), W.R., III. Co-owner Hulls' Tobacco Warehouse, Weston, Mo.; dir. First Nat. Bank, Leavenworth, Kan.; mem. 84th-92d Congresses, 6th Mo. Dist. Past v.p., dir. Kansas City Area council Boy Scouts Am. Former mayor, Weston, Mo. Mem. C. of C. (past Pres.). Democrat. Mem. Christian Ch. (deacon). Home: Weston MO 64098 Office: House Office Bldg Washington DC 20515

HULM, JOHN KENNETH, physicist; b. Southport, Eng., July 4, 1923; s. James and Frances Elizabeth (Goodall) H.; B.A. in Natural Scis., Gonville and Caius Coll., Cambridge (Eng.) U., 1943, M.S. in Physics, 1948, Dept. Sci. and Indsl. Research (research fellow), Ph.D., 1949; m. Joan Audrey Beatrice Askham, Sept. 25, 1948; children—Clair Frances, Carol Anne, Cherie, Megan, John Allen. Came to U.S., 1949, naturalized, 1957. Union Carbide research fellow U. Chgo., 1949-51, asst. prof. physics, 1951-54; mem. staff Westinghouse Research Labs., 1954—, dir. solid state research, 1967—. Mem. sci. edn. adv. com. NSF. Sci. officer RAF, 1943-46. Recipient John Price Wetherill medal Franklin Inst. Fellow Am. Phys. Soc.; mem. Pitts. Phys. Soc. (pres. 1962-63). Home: 5636 Woodmont St Pittsburgh PA 15217 Office: Westinghouse Research Labs Pittsburgh PA 15235

HULME, KATHRYN CAVARLY, author; b. San Francisco, Jan. 6, 1900; d. Edwin Page and Julia Frances (Cavarly) Hulme; student U. Cal., 1918-21; spl. courses Columbia Sch. Journalism, 1922, Hunter Coll., 1923. Publicity dir. Ask Mr. Foster, travel service, 1935-43; dep. dir. UNRRA, U.S. Zone Germany, 1945-47; U.S. zone chief emigration displaced persons Internat. Relief Orgn., 1947-51. Roman Catholic. Author: Arab Interlude, 1931; Desert Night, 1933; We Lived as Children, 1939; The Wild Place (Atlantic nonfiction award 1953), 1953; The Nun's Story (Nat. Council Women of U.S. award 1957), 1956; Annie's Captain (biography), 1961; Undiscovered Country, 1966. Home: Waialua Homesteads Kauai HI 96791

HULME, MILTON G., investment co. exec.; b. New Brighton, Pa., July 20, 1899; s. George Milton and Caroline (Schumacher) H.; ed. U. Pitts., m. Helen B. Cloherty, Aug. 27, 1924. Personnel dept. Goodyear Tire & Rubber Co., Akron, O., 1918-19; with Glover & MacGregor, investment banker 1920, v.p., 1931, pres., 1936—, also dir., dir. Drake Realty Co.; chmn. bd. Hulme, Applegate & Humphery, Inc., Thorofare Markets, Inc., Pitts. Brewing Co.; dir. Heppenstall Co., Mellon Stuart Co., Reading & Bates Offshore Drilling Co., Fuqua Industries. Mem. exec. council Boy Scouts Am., Western Pa. Bd. dirs. Boys Clubs Am., Civic Light Opera. Recipient Horatio Alger Award, 1958. Mem. Investment Bankers Assn. Am. Clubs: Duquesne; Fox Chapel Golf, University; Lauderdale Yacht, Pike Run Country; Rolling Rock; Inverarry Lago Mar Golf. Home: 154 N Bellefield Av Pittsburgh PA 15213 also RR3 Ligonier PA 15658 Office: Union Trust Bldg Pittsburgh PA 15219

HULSBOS, CORNIE LEONARD, educator; b. Given, Ia., Aug. 23, 1920; s. Neal and Elizabeth (Van Klaveran) H.; B.S., Ia. State U., 1941, M.S., 1949, Ph.D., 1953; m. Elsie Marthe Hallas, June 21, 1945; children—Susan, Betty, David. With Am. Bridge Co., 1941-46; faculty Ia. State U., 1946-60, prof. civil engring., 1957-60; research prof. civil engring., chmn. structural concrete div. Fritz Engring. Lab., Lehigh U., 1960-65; prof. civil engring., chmn. dept. U. N.M., Albuquerque, 1965—. Mem. com. concrete superstructures Hwy. Research Bd., 1962—, chmn., 1971—, mem. com. field testing bridges, 1965- -; mem. adv. panel C-12, Nat. Coop. Hwy. Research Program, 1964—. Registered profl. engr., Ia. Fellow Am. Soc. C.E. (sec. treas. Ia. sect. 1957-60, 1st v.p. Lehigh Valley sect. 1964-65, chmn. Albuquerque br. 1968-69); mem. Am. Concrete Inst., Am. Soc. Engring. Edn., Sigma Xi, Tau Beta Pi, Phi Kappa Phi, Chi Epsilon, Pi Mu Epsilon. Home: 7608 Palo Duro Av NE Albuquerque NM 87110

HULSE, FRANK WILSON, airline exec.; b. North Augusta, S.C., Sept. 12, 1912; s. Frank Wilson and Vivian (Chastaine) H.; B.S., Ga. Inst. Tech., 1934; m. Mary Jemison Cobb, Apr. 11, 1940; children-Mary Cobb (Mrs. Frank M. Young), Frank Wilson IV. Comml. pilot. Augusta, Ga., 1927-34; asst. airport mgr., Augusta, 1934-35; sta. mgr. Delta Airlines, 1935-36; pres. So. Airways of Ga., 1936-43; founder, pres. So. Airways, Inc., Birmingham, Ala., 1943-, providing local airline service in Eastern U.S., 1949—; chmn. bd. So. Airways Co., Atlanta and Orlando, Fla., 1950—, chmn. asso., local transport airlines, 1964—; dir. Fuqua Industries, Am. Fidelity Life Ins. Co. Mem. Ala. Aviation Commn., 1939-40; mem. Chief Execs. Forum; mem. com. def. transp. Nat. Rivers and Harbors Congress; mem. bd. nominations Aviation Hall Fame. Decorated by Brit. Govt. for tng. RAF pilots, World War II. Mem. Nat. Aerospace Services Assn. (mem. bd., past chmn.), U.S. (mem. transp. com.), Birmingham (mem. aviation com.) chambers commerce, Am. Helicopter Soc., Ga. Tech. Nat. Alumni Assn. (trustee). Episcopalian. Clubs: Wings (N.Y.C.); Aviation (Washington). Home: 3624 Ridgeview Dr Birmingham AL 35213 Office: So Airways Inc Atlanta Airport Atlanta GA 30320

HULSEBOSCH, CHARLES JOSEPH, food co. exec.; b. N.Y.C., Dec. 14, 1933; s. Albert J. and Marie (Gough) H.; A.B., Dartmouth, 1955, M.B.A., Amos Tuck Sch., 1956; m. Elizabeth Ferguson, July 6, 1957; childrenAlbert, Daniel, Joseph, Kristine, Thomas, Howard, John. Financial analyst Ford Motor Co., 1956-60; from budget mgr. to controller Renault, Inc., N.Y.C., 1960-63; with United Fruit Co., 1963-69, treas., 1967-69, v.p. treas. Libby, McNeill & Libby, 1969—. Mem. membership com. Boston Mus. Sci., 1966. Mem. Financial Execs. Inst., Newcomen Soc., Zeta Psi. Republican. Roman Catholic. Clubs: Executives, Dartmouth (dir.) (Chgo.). Home: 401 52d Pl Western Springs IL 60558 Office: 200 S Michigan Av Chicago IL 60604

HULSEN, ROBERT BENNARD, animal feed co. exec.; b. East Moline, Ill., Aug. 3, 1913; s. Bennard and Maggie (Sullivan) H.; student Augustana Coll., 1932-33; A.B., Culver-Stockton Coll., 1937, LL.D., 1970; m. Virginia Rosetta Stoermer, June 4, 1938; children—Linda (Mrs. Stephen R. Daniel), Sue Mary, Michael Robert, Mark Stephen. With Moorman Mfg. Co., Quincy, Ill., 1937—, pres., chmn. bd., 1964—, also dir.; dir. Quincy Soybean Co., Merc. Trust & Savs. Bank, Quincy. Vice pres., trustee Blessing Hosp.; v.p. John Howard Assn.; bd. dirs. Moorman Found., Moorman Co. Fund, Nat. 4-H Service Com., Villages, Topeka, Erroke Indian Mus.; trustee Menninger Found., Topeka. Recipient Hon. State Farmer degree Ill. Future Farmers Assn. Mem. Nat., Ill. Audubon socs., Am. Mus. Natural History, Southwestern Assn. Indian Affairs, Nat. Wildlife Fedn., Ill. C. of C. (v.p., dir.), Am. Feed Mfrs. Assn. (dir.). Home: 7 Kentucky Rd Quincy IL 62301 Office: 1000 N 30th St Quincy IL 62301

HULSEY, BURL B., Jr., corp exec.; b. Forney, Tex., 1917; ed. Tex. A. and M. U., 1939. Pres., chief exec. officer Tex. Electric Service Co. Home: 3645 Bellaire Dr S Fort Worth TX 76109 Office: PO Box 970 Fort Worth TX 76101*

HULSEY, WILLIAM HANSELL, mortgage banker, art collector; b. Carbon Hill, Ala., May 2, 1901; s. John Balus and Gabriella (Hansell) H.; student pub. schs., m. Susan Mabry, July 21, 1934. Pres., Garber, Cook & Hulsey, Inc., Birmingham, Ala., 1937—; chmn. bd. Realty Mortgage Co., Birmingham, 1952-68, Ingalls Iron Works Co., Birmingham, 1961, Ingalls Shipbuilding Corp., Birmingham, 1961; dir. Birmingham Trust Nat. Bank. Co- founder Hulsey Art Collection, Birmingham. Gen. chmn. Community Chest Campaign, 1955-56; chmn. Capital Funds drive YWCA, 1948, later chmn. exec. com. Bd. dirs. Community Chest, Indsl. Water Bd. Birmingham, Birmingham Mus. Art, Eye Found. Hosp., Birmingham Symphony; trustee, exec., finance coms. Birmingham So. Coll. Served to maj. USAAF, 1942-45. Episcopalian. Rotarian. Clubs: Birmingham Country (past pres.), Mountain Brook, Club (Birmingham); Relay House, Downtown. Home: 2980 Cherokee Rd Birmingham Al 35213 Office: Bank for Savs Bldg Birmingham AL 35203

HULSIZER, ROBERT INSLEE, Jr., educator, physicist; b. East Orange, N.J., Nov. 25, 1919; s. Robert Inslee and Dorothy Joy (Price) H.; B.S., Bates Coll., 1940; M.A., Wesleyan U., Middletown, Conn., 1942; Ph.D., Mass. Inst. Tech., 1948; m. Bernice Lord, June 21, 1941 (div. July 1965); childrenStephen, Ann, Deborah, Cynthia: m. 2d, Carol K. Ascher, May 27, 1967. Staff mem. Radiation Lab., Mass. Inst. Tech., 1942-46, grad. research nature cosmic rays, 1946-49; research cosmic rays U. Ill., 1949-51, devel. computer control naval air def. situation Control Systems Lab., 1951-57, research low temperature physics, 1957-60; research elementary particle physics and computer aids to data analysis, 1960—; prof. physics Mass. Inst. Tech., 1964—, dir. Edn. Research Center, 1964-68. Cons. Office Naval Research Center, 1957-59; mem. steering com. Phys. Sci. Study Com., 1959-64; mem. Commn. Coll. Physics, 1960-66, chmn. panel selection fellowships in physics NSF, 1962- 65. Fellow Am. Phys. Soc.; mem. Am. Assn. Physics Tchrs., Am. Assn. U. Profs. Editor vol. 22, Electronic Time Measurements of Radiation Laboratory Technical Series, 1946. Home: 31 Maple St Lexington MA 02173

HULSMAN, CARL HENRY, mfg. co. exec.; b. Medina, O., Feb. 21, 1929; s. John Ernest and Louise (Kirstein) H.; B.S. magna cum laude, Kent State U., 1955; m. Jane Gay Tripp, Sept. 4, 1954; children—John Charles, Ann Elizabeth, Jean Ellen. Pub. accountant Walthall & Drake, Cleve., 1955-62; controller Work Wear Corp., Cleve., 1962—. Served with inf., U.S. Army, 1946-52. Mem. Ohio Soc. C.P.A.'s, Beta Gamma Sigma. Home: 618 Humiston Dr Bay Village OH 44140 Office: 1768 E 25th St Cleveland OH 44114

HULT, MILTON, former dairy orgn. exec.; b. Rockford, Ill.; s. Carl Albert and Mary Louise (Danielson) H.; B.S. Knox Coll., 1919; M.B.A., Harvard Sch. Bus. Adminstrn., 1921; m. Ruth Hitzhusen Buckner, Feb. 16, 1948 (dec. Aug. 1963); m. 2d, Alice Marian Cooley, Oct. 5, 1968. Pres., Superior Dairy Co., Davenport, Ia., 1921-36, Internat. Assn. Milk Dirs., Chgo., 1934-36; pres. Nat. Dairy Council, Chgo., 1936-68, pres. emeritus, 1968-. Cons. U.S. Govt., Internat. Exec. Service Corps; chmn., pres., dir. Dairy Soc. Internat., 1950-68. Del. USA to Internat. Dairy Congresses, The Hague, 1953, Rome, 1956, London, Eng., 1959; mem. food industry adv. com. Nutrition Found. Recipient Goodrich award for contbn. to Am. agr. N.Y. World's Fair, 1940, Knox Achievement award, 1956; Distinguished Service award Am. Dairy Sci. Assn., 1968. Mem. Phi Gamma Delta, Delta Sigma Rho, Sigma Delta Chi. Mason (32, Shriner). Club: Lake Shore (Chgo.). Contbr. articles, bulls. on dairy industry and govt.-industry relations. Home: 1360 Lake Shore Dr Chicago, IL 60610. Office: 111 N Canal St Chicago IL 60606

HULTBERG, JOHN, artist; b. Berkeley, Cal., Feb. 8, 1922; s. John Waldemar and Mabel Olive (Hammer) H.; A.B., Fresno State Coll., 1943; student Cal. Sch. Fine Arts, 1947-49, Art Students League, N.Y.C., 1949-51; m. Hilary Editha Blesh, June 9, 1948 (div. 1956); children—Carl Rudolph, Stephanie Maria; m. 2d, Joyce Elbert, 1959 (div. 1960); m. 3d, Lynne Drexler, 1961. Exhibited San Francisco Mus. Art. 1947-49, Los Angeles Mus., 1949, New Talent show Mus. Modern Art, 1952; one man shows Korman Gallery, N.Y.C., 1953, Martha Jackson Gallery, N.Y.C., 1955, Corcoran Gallery, Washington, 1955, Butler Art Inst., Ohio, 1955, UN Exhibit, San Francisco, 1955, Galerie Rive Droit, Paris, 1954-55, Galerie Nina Dausset, Paris, 1954, Galeria Spazio, Rome, 1955, Mus. Modern Art, Rome, 1955, Guild Hall, East Hampton, N.Y., 1955, I.C.A., London, 1956, others; rep. in collections Met. Mus. Art, Whitney Mus., Roy R. Neuburger, Edward Root, Michel Tapie. Served as lt. (j.g.) USNR, 1943-46. Recipient prize San Francisco Mus. watercolor ann., 1948; prize San Francisco oil ann., 1941; hon. mention Los Angeles Centennial painting exhibit, 1949; 1st prize Corcoran Biennial Exhibit, Washington, 1955; prize Congress for Cultural Freedom Exhbn. for painters under 35, Europe, 1955; hon. mention Carnegie Internat. Ex-hon., 1955; Norman Harris medal at 65th ann. exhbn. Art Inst. Chgo. Albert Bender fellow, San Francisco, 1949; Guggenheim Fellow, 1956. Office: Martha Jackson Gallery 32 E 69th New York City NY 10021

HULTEN, C. PAUL, banker; b. San Francisco, 1918; grad. Golden Gate Coll., 1952. Exec. v.p. Western Bancorp., Los Angeles. Home: 6515 Nancy Rd Miraleste CA 90732 Office: 600 S Spring St Los Angeles CA 90014*

HULTENG, JOHN LINNE, educator; b. Grand Forks, N.D., Apr. 1, 1921; s. John Linne and Ragnhild (Anderson) H.; Ph.B., U. N.D., 1943; M.S., Columbia, 1947; postgrad. (Nieman fellow). Harvard, 1949-50; m. Elizabeth Jean Rucker, June 18, 1947; children-Robert Gordon, Karen Elizabeth, Richard John. Reporter, sports editor Grand Forks Herald, 1942-43; editorial writer, fgn. corr., chief editorial writer, columnist Providence Jour. and Evening Bull., 1947-55; faculty U. Ore., Eugene, 1955—, prof. journalism, 1961—, dean Sch. Journalism, 1962-68. Vis. prof. Stanford, 1970-71. Served to 1st lt. USAAF, 1943-46. Pulitzer traveling scholar Columbia, 1947-48. Recipient Ersted award for distinguished teaching U. Ore., 1961; Nat. Sigma Delta Chi award for distinguished teaching, 1970. Mem. Am. Assn. Schs. and Depts. Journalism (pres. 1966-67), Am. Assn. U. Profs., Assn. Edn. Journalism, Phi Beta Kappa, Alpha Delta Sigma, Kappa Tau Alpha, Sigma Delta Chi. Author: (with R. Paul Nelson) The Fourth Estate, 1971. Contbr. articles to mags., profl. jours., anthologies. Home: 1665 Fairmount Blvd Eugene OR 97403

HULTGREN, HERBERT NILS, educator, physician; b. Santa Rosa, Cal., Aug. 29, 1917; s. Adolf W. and Hilda (Hakanson) H.; Jr. certificate, Santa Rosa Jr. Coll., 1937; A.B., Stanford, 1939, M.D., 1942; m. Barbara Brooke, Aug. 7, 1948; children—Peter B., Bruce H., John B. Intern, San Francisco Gen. Hosp., 1942-43; resident medicine Stanford Hosp., 1943-44, resident pathology, 1946-47; fellow cardiology Thorndike Meml. Lab., Boston, 1947-48; instr. medicine Stanford, 1948-51, asst. prof., 1951-55, asso. prof., 1955-67, prof., 1967—. Chmn. written exam. com. Bd. Cardiovascular Disease, 1969—. Served from 1st lt. to capt., M.C., AUS, 1944-46; ETO. Markle scholar in med. sci., 1951-56. Mem. Western Soc. Clin. Research (pres.), Western Assn. Physicians (pres.), Assn. U. Cardiologists (pres.), Phi Beta Kappa. Contbr. articles profl. jours. Home: 827 San Francisco Ct Stanford CA 94305 Office: Palo Alto VA Hosp Palo Alto CA 94305

HULTGREN, KENNETH WESLEY, lumber co. exec.; b. Mpls., Dec. 12, 1913; s. Einer E. and Minerva (Lindquist) H.; student MacPhail Sch. Music, Mpls., 1935-38, U. Minn., 1935-42; grad. Advanced Mgmt. Program Harvard, 1968; m. Marcy Lucille Wilson, Sept. 28, 1940; children-Kenneth Wesley, Alan McNair. Accountant, Gen. Mills, Inc., 1932-42; asst. credit mgr., gen. credit mgr. Dayton Co., Mpls., 1942-55; from gen. credit mgr. to treas. Roddis Plywood Co., Marshfield, Wis., 1955-60; with Weyerhaeuser Co., Tacoma, 1960, treas., 1967—. Conf. lay leader Minn. Meth. Ch.; div. chmn. United Good Neighbors, Tacoma. Bd. dirs. Tacoma Symphony. Served with AUS, 1943-46. Mem. Nat. Office Mgrs. Assn., Nat. Assn. Credit Mgmt. (chmn. bldg. materials group 1966). Home: 1714 Karl Johan Rd Tacoma WA 98465 Office: Tacoma Bldg Tacoma WA 98401

HULTGREN, RALPH RAYMOND, educator; b. Spokane, Wash., Sept. 7, 1905; s. Charles August and Augusta (Benson) H.; B.S., U. Cal., 1928; M.S., U. Utah, 1929; Ph.D., Cal. Inst. Tech., 1933; m. Lesta Teresa Wood, June 11, 1933; children—Neilen Wood, Glen Owen, Eric Carl. Research fellow NRC, Mass. Inst. Tech., 1933-35; advanced from instr. to asst. prof. metallurgy Harvard, 1935-41; with U. Cal., Berkeley, 1941—, asst. prof., asso. prof., 1941-48, prof. metallurgy, 1948—, asst. dean Coll. Engring., 1958-61, chmn. dept. mineral technology, 1961-65. Past chmn. U.S. Calorimetry Conf. Mem. Mechanics Inst. San Francisco (trustee), Am. Inst. Mining and Metall. Engrs., Phi Beta Kappa, Sigma Xi. Author: Fundamentals of Physical Metallurgy; Selected Values of Thermodynamic Properties of Metals and Alloys, 1963; Selected Values of Thermodyamic Properties and Phase Diagrams of Copper and Some Binary Copper Alloys, 1971. Home: 1501 LeRoy Av Berkeley CA 94708

HULTGREN, WARREN CURTIS, clergyman; b. Mpls., Dec. 16, 1920; s. David Clarence and Myrtle Elvina (Hansen) H.; B.A., Hardin-Simmons U., 1947; B.D., Southwestern Baptist Theol. Sem., 1950; D.D. (hon.), U. Corpus Christi, 1954; m. Wanda Lee Wadsworth, Sept. 3, 1946; childrenLanda Lee, Warren Curtis, Howard Madison. Ordained to ministry Bapt. Ch., 1944; pastor in Corpus Christi, 1950-55, Lake Charles, La., 1955-57, First Bapt. Ch., Tulsa, 1957-. Mem. Downtown Tulsa Unlimited; chmn. Okla. com. Nat. Library Week, 1964. Trustee Okla. Bapt. U., Hillcrest Med. Center, Tulsa. Fellow Royal Geog. Soc. Gt. Britain; mem. Am. Schs. Oriental Research. Rotarian. Home: 3127 S Lewis St Tulsa OK 74105 Office: First Baptist Ch 4th at Cincinnati St Tulsa OK 74103

HUMANN, WALTER JOHANN, corp. exec.; b. Dallas, May 30, 1937; s. Walter Christoph and Lois (Smith) H.; B.S. in Physics, Mass. Inst. Tech., 1959; M.B.A., Harvard, 1961: J.D., So. Meth. U., 1967; m. Beatrice Josephine Read, July 31, 1959; children—Walter John, David Andrew, Lisa Kathleen. Gen. mgr., asst. to pres. Dorsett Electronics Co., Oklahoma City, 1962-63; with project mgmt. office Ling-Temco-Vought, Inc., Dallas, 1963-66; partner GOF & Co., Dallas, 1964-66; admitted to Tex. bar, 1966; asst. to postmaster gen., 1966-67; corp. sec., asst. treas. LTV Aerospace Corp., 1968-69, v.p., sec., gen. counsel, 1970—; dir. LTV Edn. Systems, Inc., 1969—; sec. Computer Tech. Inc., 1966-70. Mem. Task Force on Govt. Goals for Dallas Program, 1960- 69, Task Force on Dallas Edn.; commr. Pres.'s Commn. White House Fellows, 1968-69; mem. Sec. Labor Adv. Bd. Employment Security, 1968-70; chmn. Dallas. C. of C. task force on Dallas Sch. System, 1971—; pres. White House Fellows Assn., 1968-69; founder, 1968, nat. chmn. Citizens for a Postal Corp. White House fellow, 1966-67. Named Outstanding Young Man of Dallas, Dallas Jr. C. of C., 1969, named 1 of 5 outstanding Young Texans, 1970; 1 of Am.'s Ten Outstanding Young Men, U.S. Jr. C. of C., 1970. Mem. Am., Tex., Dallas bar assns., Am. Soc. Corp. Secs., Sigma Xi, Sigma Alpha Epsilon. Episcopalian. Clubs: Dervish, Dallas 40, Dallas Forum (Dallas). Home: 3533 Stanford St Dallas TX 75225 Office: PO Box 5003 LTV Tower Dallas TX 75222

HUMBER, JOHN DAVIS, physician; b. Greenville, N.C., Dec. 5, 1895; s. Robert Lee and Lena Clyde (Davis) H.; B.S., Wake Forest (N.C.) Coll., 1917; M.D., Tulane, 1920; spl. studies U. Wis., 1915, Harvard, 1916, Yale, 1917-18; m. Agnes Frolli, June 4, 1928 (dec.); m. 2d, Roberta Marr. Asst. in anatomy Wake Forest Coll, 1916-17; supt. So. Pacific Gen. Hosp., San Francisco, 1927-38; specialist in cancer research; co-discoverer of Coffey-Humber treatment for cancer. Served in U.S. Navy, World War I. Vice chmn. charge Red

Cross Disaster Relief of West Portal Dist. San Francisco; gen. chmn. Amaranth War Effort Program for State of Cal. Supreme royal patron, Order of Amaranth, Inc., 1945-46; pres. bd. dirs., Amaranth Found., Cal. Bd. dirs. Bett-Health Found. of Cal. Mem. A.M.A., Cal. Med. Assn., San Francisco County Med. Soc., Am. (founder; past chpt. pres.), Cal. (chpt. pres.) acads. gen. practice, Assn. Am. Physicians and Surgeons, World Med. Asso. (founder), S.A.R., Alpha Kappa Kappa. Democrat. Baptist. Mason (Shriner); member Order Eastern Star, Royal Order Caritas (pres. supreme council). Clubs: West O'Twins Peaks Lions (pres., 1946-47) (San Francisco). Co-author: (with W.B. Coffey), Angina Pectoris, 1927. Contbr. papers on malignancy. Home: 310 Arballo Dr San Francisco CA 94132 Office: 909 Hyde St San Francisco CA 94109 ☆

HUMBERSTONE, JOSEPH HOWARD, engr., business exec.; b. Toledo, Oct. 25, 1909; s. Ernest Howard and Pauline (Gildemeister) H.; B.Met.E., Ohio State U., 1931, D.Sc. (hon.), 1962; m. Mary Ida Thomas, Oct. 23, 1933; 1 dau., Susan. Devel. engr. Gen. Electric Co., 1932-38; with Arcrods Co., N.Y.C., 1939-61; with Air Reduction Co. Inc., 1948—, v.p., 1951—, group v.p., dir., 1963—; dir. Nat. State Bank, Elizabeth, N.J. Mem. war metallurgy com. NRC, 1942-44. Mem. Am. Welding Soc. (pres. 1954-56), Am. Ordnance Assn., Nat. Security Indsl. Assn., Nat. C. of C., Compressed Gas Assn., Soc. Naval Architects and Marine Engrs., Am. Iron and Steel Inst., Internat. Inst. Welding, Kappa Sigma. Clubs: Greenwich (Conn.) Country; Engineers (N.Y.C.); Blind Brook (Port Chester, N.Y.); Duquesne (Pitts.). Office: 150 E 42d St New York City NY 10017

HUMBERT, REUBEN LEE, educator; b. Harrisonburg, Va., Aug. 22, 1900; s. Joseph Lee and Fannie May (Armentrout) H.; student Washington and Lee U., 1918; B.A., Bridgewater (Va.) Coll., 1922; postgrad. Columbia, summer 1923; M.A., U. Mich., 1926; LL.B., Blackstone Coll. Law, 1931, J.D., 1933; m. Louise White Swope, Aug. 24, 1929; 1 son, Wilson Lee. Prin., Timberville (Va.) High Sch., 1922-24; asst. Detroit Bur. Govt. Research, 1925; sec. Harrisonburg C. of C., 1926-28; exec. sec. Va. Poly. Inst., 1928-44, prof. econs., pub. adminstrn., 1942-61, prof. bus. adminstrn., 1961- 70, prof. emeritus, 1970—, head dept. bus. adminstrn., 1961-68; admitted to Va. bar, 1932. Sec.-treas. Blacksburg Community Concert Assn., 1936-69; exec. officer Radford Regional Def. Council, 1941; mem. Blacksburg Bd. Zoning Appeals, 1954—, chmn., 1965—; mem. Blacksburg Town Council, 1936-42, 50-54. Bd. dirs. Roanoke Symphony Soc. Served to maj. AUS, 1942-46; lt. col. Res. Mem. Va. Bar, So. Econ. Assn., Alpha Kappa Psi (regional dir. 1956-64, Distinguished Service award 1952), Omicron Delta Kappa, Delta Sigma Rho, Tau Kappa Alpha. Democrat. Episcopalian (vestryman, treas.). Mason, Rotarian. Club: University (pres., treas. 1933-38 Blacksburg). Editor, co- author: Virginia: Economic and Civic, 1933. Home: 704 Draper Rd Blacksburg VA 24060

HUMBERT, RICHARD BERNARD, engring. and constrn. co. exec.; b. St. Cloud, Minn., Feb. 5, 1924; s. Joseph and Mary (Roering) H.; student St. John's U., Collegeville, Minn., 1942-43; B.S., U.S. Coast Guard Acad., 1946; LL.B., Harvard, 1952; m. Constance Cruger, June 7, 1952; children—Richard Bernard, Jennifer Elizabeth, Gretchen Mary. Commd. ensign USCG, 1946, advanced through grades to lt., 1949; resigned, 1949; admitted to Cal. bar, 1952; with firm Schulthesus & Laybourne, Los Angeles, 1952-55; asso. counsel Fluor Corp., Ltd., Los Angeles, 1955-58; partner firm Voegelin, Barton, Harris & Callister, Los Angeles, 1958-67; v.p., sec., gen. counsel Fluor Corp., Ltd., 1967—. Campaign chmn. Los Angeles Heart Assn., 1968-69. Trustee Fluor Found. Mem. N.A.M., Am. Soc. Corporate Secs., Am., Fed., Cal., Los Angeles County bar assns. Home: 825 San Marino Av San Marino CA 91108 Office: 2500 S Atlantic Blvd Los Angeles CA 90022

HUME, DAVID, lawyer; b. Eagle Pass, Tex., Oct. 2, 1915; s. David E. and Lupita (James) H.; B.A., U. Tex., 1937; student Temple U. Sch. Law, 1939-41; LL.B. with honors, So. Meth. U. Sch. Law, 1939-41; LL.B. with honors, So. Meth. U., 1946; m. F. Arlee Eaton, Aug. 28, 1943 (div.); children-David III, Stephen; m. 2d, Margaret Williams, June 19, 1966; 1 dau., Marge Ann. Admitted to Tex. bar, 1946, D.C., Md. bars, 1954, U.S. Supreme Ct., 1948, also Ct. Mil. Justice, FCC, ICC; trial atty. U.S. Dept. Justice, 1947, spl. asst. to atty. gen. U.S., 1948; with firm Steptoe & Johnson, Washington, 1954-58; mem. firm Hume & Stewart, Washington, 1958-65, Hume & Hume, Eagle Pass, Tex., 1965—. Hon. cons. to Consulate of Republic of Mex., 1970. Rep. Am. Bar Assn., 12th Inter-Am. Bar Assn. conv. Bogota, Colombia, 1961. Mem. Md. Bd. Natural Resources. Chmn. Democratic Party So. Md., 1958, treas., 1958- 60; mem. Dem. Nat. Adv. Council, 1958-60; candidate for Gov. Md., 1962. Bd. dirs. Balt. Civic Opera. Served with Submarine Service, USNR, World War II, Korean War; capt. Res. Decorated Bronze Star. Mem. Am., Inter- Am., Md. bar assns., Tex. Trial Lawyers Assn., State Bar Texas, Border Bar Assn. (dir.), Judge Adv. Assn. Am. Vets. Com., Am. Legion, Navy League, S.A.R., Md. Hist. Soc., Izaak Walton League. Clubs: Terrapin (U. Md.); Jefferson Island (St. Mary's County, Md.); Marlboro Hunt (Prince George's County, Md.); Taylor's Landing Rod and Gun (Washington County, Md.); Hawthorne Country (Charles County, Md.). Author numerous articles on conservation, govt. and agrarian reform, Latin Am. Home: Eagle Pass TX 78852 Office: Hume & Hume Eagle Pass TX 78852

HUME, DAVID MILFORD, surgeon, educator; b. Muskegon, Mich., 1917; B.S., Harvard, 1940; M.D., U. Chgo., 1943. Surg. intern Peter Bent Brigham Hosp., Boston, 1943-44, surg. asst. reisdent, 1944-45, 48-49, Harvey Cushing fellow, 1948-50, chief resident surgery, 1950-51, jr. asso. surgeon, 1951-54, asso. surgeon, 1954-56; from instr. surgey to asst. prof. Harvard, 1950-56; mem. faculty Med. Coll. Va., 1956-, now Stuart McGuire prof. surgery, chmn. dept. Served to lt. comdr., M.C., USNR, 1945-46, 53-54. Diplomate Am. Bd. Surgery. Fellow A.C.S.; mem. A.M.A., Halsted Surg. Soc., A.A.A.S., Soc. Univ. Surgeons, Am. Soc. Clin. Investigation, Am., So. surg. assns., Soc. Vascular Surgeons, Am. Soc. Exptl. Pathology, Endocrine Soc. Address: 1200 Broad St Richmond VA 23219

HUME, DAVID NEWTON, chemist, educator; b. Vancouver, B.C., Can., Dec. 22, 1917; s. John Noble and Elizabeth (Newton) H.; student Los Angeles City Coll., 1935- 37; B.A., U. Cal. at Los Angeles, 1939, M.A., 1940; Ph.D. (Du Pont fellow), U. Minn., 1943; postgrad. (NSF fellow) Swiss Fed. Inst. Tech., 1964-65; m. Aloyse Bottenwiser, July 20, 1941; children-Robert, Rebecca. Research asso. U. Chgo. Metall. Lab., 1943; group leader, sect. chief Clinton Labs., AEC, 1943-46; asst. prof. chemistry U. Kan., 1946-47, asst. prof. Mass. Inst. Tech., 1947-50, asso. prof., 1950-59, prof., 1959—. Indsl. cons., adv. com. analytical chemistry Oak Ridge Nat. Lab.; adv. panel for chemistry NSF; mem. com. for analytical chemistry NRC; com. on equilibrium data Internat. Union Pure and Applied Chemistry; adv. editor McGraw-Hill Advanced Chemistry Series; mem. adv. council Coll. Chemistry, 1961-69. Guggenheim fellow Tech. U. Denmark, Copehegen, 1954-55. Mem. Am. Chem. Soc. (Fisher award in analytical chemistry 1963), Am. Acad. Arts and Scis., Sigma Xi, Phi Lambda Upsilon. Home: 1 Sylvan Rd Wellesley Hills MA 02181. Office: 77 Massachusetts Av Cambridge MA 02139

HUME, JAMES PICKRELL, lawyer; b. Washington, June 4, 1901; s. Thomas L. and Laura Gertrude (Cox) H.; student chem. engring. George Washington U., 1921-22, LL.B., 1926; m. Marion McFadden, Mar. 17, 1933; children—Andrew, Anthony, Alexander. Asst. examiner U.S. Patent Office, 1922-26; admitted to D.C. bar, 1926, Ill. bar, 1927; asso. Wilkinson, Huxley, Byron & Knight, 1926- 30, partner, 1930-47; partner Wilkinson, Huxley, Byron & Hume, Chgo., 1947-56; partner Hume, Groen, Clement & Hume, now chmn. bd. Hume, Clement, Hume & Lee Ltd.; past mem. faculty Lawyers Inst., John Marshall Law Sch. Mem. citizens bd. U. Chgo.; mem. Chgo. Crime Commn., chmn. bd. dirs. Aspen Valley Improvement Assn.; past. pres. bd. Latin Sch. Chgo.; past mem. bd. Chgo. Council on Fgn. Relations; bd. dirs. Music Assos. of Aspen, Aspen Hist. Soc., Chgo. Hearing Soc. (past pres.). Fellow Am. Bar Found., Am. Coll. Trial Lawyers; mem. Chgo. Bar Found. (mem. bd.), Chgo. Orchestral Assn., Am. Bar Assn. (del., past chmn. sect. on patent, trademark and copyright law), Chgo. Bar Assn. (past mem. bd. mgrs. and chmn. patents and trademarks), Am. (past chmn. nat. council patent law assns. and past pres.), Chgo. (pres.) patent law assns., Bar Assn. 7th Fed. Circuit (mem. Library com., bd. dirs.), Internat. Patent and Trademark Assn. (exec. com.), U.S. Trademark Assn., Delta Tau Delta, Phi Delta Phi. Episcopalian (vestryman). Clubs: Law, Wayfarers, Tavern, Cliff Dwellers, University (Chgo.); Metropolitan (Washington). Home: 1350 N State St Chicago IL 60610 Office: One First Nat Plaza Chicago IL 60603

HUME, JAQUELIN HOLLIDAY, food preserving exec., art mus. ofcl.; b. Harbor Point, Mich., July 17, 1905; s. George Edgar and Lucy (Holliday) H.; grad. Phillips Exeter Acad., 1924; A.B., Princeton, 1928; M.B.A., Harvard, 1930; m. Caroline Elizabeth Howard, Feb. 20, 1935; childrenPatricia Howard, William Jaquelin, Carol Elizabeth, George Holliday. Exec. v.p. Basic Vegetable Products, Inc., San Francisco, 1933-60, pres., 1960—, also dir.; chmn., dir., former pres. Am. Potato Co., San Francisco; dir. Leslie Salt Co. Chief of protocol No. Cal. Chmn.; No. Cal. Reagan for Gov. Finance Com.; chmn. No. Cal. Nixon-Agnew Finance Com.; mem. Republican Nat. Finance Com. Bd. dirs. Found. for Asian Art, San Francisco Opera Assn.; trustee, former pres. San Francisco Mus. Art; v.p., trustee Pacific Med. Center. Mem. San Francisco C. of C. Home: 3355 Pacific Av San Francisco CA 94118 Office: 120 Montgomery St San Francisco CA 94104

HUME, JOHN CHANDLER, educator, physician; b. Bklyn., May 16, 1911; s. John C. and Elizabeth K. (Lynch) H.; B.A., Princeton, 1932; M.D., Vanderbilt U., 1936; M.P.H. (Rockefeller Found. fellow), Johns Hopkins, 1947, Dr.P.H., 1951; m. Amelia E. Brown, Sept. 9, 1933: children—John Chandler, William P., Susan F. (Mrs. Thomas C. Wimsatt). Med. intern Vanderbilt U. Hosp., 1936-37; acting dir. Hardin County Health Dept., 1937-38; clinician, acting dir. Tri-County Venereal Disease Control Demonstration, Brunswick, Ga., 1938-39; pvt. practice medicine, 1939-42; commd. asst. surgeon USPHS, 1942, advanced through grades to med. dir., 1955, resigned, 1961; dir. venereal disease div. Wilmington City and New Hanover County Health Dept., N.C., 1942- 44; chief bur. venereal disease control W.Va. Dept. Health, Charleston, 1944-46; research asso. Johns Hopkins Sch. Hygiene and Pub. Health, 1947- 51, asso. prof., 1951-55, asst. dir., 1948-55, prof., pub. health adminstrn., 1961—, chmn. dept. pub. health adminstrn., 1961-69, asso. dean, 1961-67, dean 1967—; lectr. medicine Johns Hopkins Sch. Medicine, 1947-55, chief venereal disease div. (p.m.) med. clinic Johns Hopkins Hosp., 1947-55; chief venereal disease control div. Md. Dept. Health, Balt., 1952-55. Chief health div. U.S. Tech. Coop. Mission to India, ICA 1955-61; cons. WHO, 1950-55, USPHS, 1950- 55; chmn. Am. Bd. Preventive Medicine, 1967—; mem. Residency Rev. Com. for Preventive Medicine, 1963—, Adv. Bd. Med. Spltys., 1964- 69, Pub. Health Service Nat. Adv. Council Pub. Health Tng., 1966-70; mem. Nat. Commn. on Venereal Disease, Dept. Health, Edn. and Welfare, 1971—; trustee, 1st v.p. Pan-Am. Health and Edn. Found., 1970—. Served to col. M.C., USAF Res., 1962—. Fellow Am. Coll. Preventive Medicine, Am. Pub. Health Assn. (governing council 1962-70); mem. Am. Venereal Disease Assn. (pres. 1969-70), Assn. Schs. Pub. Health (pres. 1970-71), Md. Pub. Health Assn. Am. Social Health Assn. (dir. 1969—), Am. Soc. Tropical Medicine and Hygiene, Assn. Tchrs. Preventive Medicine, Am. Assn. World Health (dir. 1970—); hon. mem. Indian Pub. Health Assn., Venezuelan Soc. Dermatology and Syphilology. Clubs: Cosmos (Washington); Johns Hopkins, 14 West Hamilton Street (Balt.); Princeton (N.Y.C.) Home: 317 Tuscany Rd Baltimore MD 21210 Office: 615 N Wolfe St Baltimore MD 21205

HUME, JOHN E. N., Jr., newspaper editor; b. Schenectady, Sept. 10, 1915: s. John E. N. and Anna Cady (Smith) H.; grad. Albany (N.Y.) Acad., 1933; B.S., U. Va., 1937; m. Marion Stewart Hume, Apr. 15, 1939; children- John E.N. III, Bryce Stewart II. With Schenectady Gazette, corr., 1930-37, reporter and photographer, 1937-40, city editor, 1940- 46, editor, 1946—, also sec. Mem. Am. N.Y. State socs. newspaper editors, N.Y. State Pubs. Assn., Am. Ordnance Assn., Schenectady C. of C. (dir. 1945), Beta Theta Pi. Republican. Episcopalian. Mason. Clubs: Mohawk, Mohawk Golf, Saratoga Reading Rooms. Home: 2029 Lexington Pkwy Schenectady, NY 12309 Office: 332 State St Schenectady NY 12301

HUME, PATRICK HENRY, lawyer; b. Washingtonn, Mar. 17, 1911; s. Thomas L. and Laura G. (Cox) H.; LL.B., George Washington U., 1933, M.P.L., 1934; m. Helen Galt Minnigerode, Dec. 22, 1956; 1 dau., Patricia (Mrs. Sham Lal Shridhar- Gautam). Admitted to D.C. bar, 1935, also U.S. Supreme Ct.; patent atty. Am. Steel & Wire Co., Cleve., 1935-39; chmn. com. on patentable devels. U.S. Steel Corp. subsidiaries, 1938-41; counsel Fay, Golrick & Chilton, Cleve., 1941-46; partner firm Nielsen & Hume, Washington, 1947-51; partner Hume, Clement, Hume & Lee, Chgo., 1952—. Dir. Preformed Line Products Co., Cleve., 1954-57; patent counsel U.S. Gypsum Co., Maytag Co., Stanray Corp. Trustee Adler Planetarium and Astro-Sci. Center; charter mem. Great Lakes Found. Served to lt. USNR, 1943-46; PTO. Decorated Purple Heart, Mem. Am., Ill. State, Chgo. bar assns., Am., Chgo. (bd. mgrs.) patent law assns., Am. Judicature Soc., Soc. History Tech., Field Mus. Natural History, Art Inst. Chgo., Mus. Contemporary Art. Home: 210 E Pearson St Chicago IL 60611 also 3830 Macomb St Washington DC 20016 Office: One First Nat Plaza Chicago IL 60670

HUME, PAUL CHANDLER, music editor; b. Chgo., Dec. 13, 1915; s. Robert Woolsey and Katherine English (Rockwell) H.; ed. U. Chgo., 1937; D. Mus. (hon.), Thiel Coll., 1968; m. Ruth Fox, Dec. 29, 1949; children—Paul, Michael, Ann, Peter. Music editor Washington Post, 1947—; prof. music, dir. glee club Georgetown U., 1950—; organist and baritone, 1936—; solo, oratoric and opera appearances in Chgo. and Washington, 1936—. Mem. Am. Assn. U. Profs., Music Critics Assn. (exec. com. 1962-63), Lit. Soc. Author: Catholic Church Music, 1956; (with Mrs. Hume) The Lion of Poland, 1962, King of Song, 1964. Co-editor: Hymnal of Christian Unity, 1964. Home: 3625 Tilden St N W Washington DC 20008 Office: 1515 L St N Washington DC 20005

HUME, ROBERT IBELLE, former publishing co. exec.; b. New Britain, Conn., Apr. 5, 1912; s. George Arthur and Bethel (Ibelle) H.; grad. Morse Coll., Hartford, Conn., 1932; m. Blanche Feder, June 24, 1939; children-Beverly Jean (Mrs. Beverly Hume James), and Barbara Jane (dec.). Accountant, A. K. Hall Co., C.P.A.'s, Hartford, 1932-33, Aetna Brewing Co., Hartford, 1933-36; div. office and credit mgr., Firestone Tire & Rubber Co., 1936- 37; with Bond Electric div. Winchester Repeating Arms, Co., 1937-39; partner Baker Goodyear & Co., C.P.A.'s, New Haven, 1939-43; with Cowles Communications, Inc., N.Y.C., 1943-71, treas., 1966-71; ind. cons. in labor relations and finance, 1971—. Bd. dirs. Westchester County YMCA, Camp Sloane. C.P.A., Conn. Mem. Am. Inst. C.P.A.'s Conn. Soc. A.P.A.'s Conglist. (past treas.). Club: Scarsdale Golf. Home: 40 Downer Av Scarsdale NY 10583 Office: 488 Madison Av New York City NY 10022

HUME, ROBERT REES, lawyer; . Bklyn., Mar. 4, 1915; s. Charles B. and Elizabeth (Rees) H.; B.B.A., St. Johns U., 1937; LL.B., St. Lawrence U., 1942; m. Margaret Blue, June 12, 1937; children—Duncan B., Cameron R. Admitted to N.Y. bar, 1942; practice in N.Y.C., 1962—; with law dept. Am. Surety Co. of N.Y., 1933-52; sec., gen. counsel Seaboard Surety Co., 1952-62; partner Hart, Hume & Engleman, 1962-66, Hart & Hume, 1966—; lectr. Am. Mgmt. Assn., N.Y. State Bar Assn., Practicing Law Inst. Dir. Unity Fire Ins. Co., Gen. Security Assurance Corp. of N.Y., 72d St. East Corp., Shell Equipment Corp., Telemar Homes, Inc., Crestview on Hudson, Inc. Mem. Charter Revision Commn., Stamford, Conn., 1963. Served with AUS, 1944. Mem. Am. Arbitration Assn., Am. (com. chmn.), N.Y. State bar assns., Internat. Assn. Ins. Counsel (mem. exec. com., chmn. fidelity and surety com.), Phi Delta Phi. Contbr. articles profl. jours. Home: 320 E 72d St New York City NY 10021 Office: 10 E 40th St New York City NY 10016

HUME, WARREN CHARLES, mfg. co. exec.; b. Chgo., June 14, 1916; s. Charles and Genevieve (Keller) H.; A.B. Rollins Coll., 1939, LL.D., 1970; student Grad. Sch. Bus. Mich. State U., 1948-50, M.B.A.; grad. Advanced Mgmt. Program Harvard, 1956; m. Augusta Yust, June 5, 1939; children—David, Nicholas, Christina. With IBM Corp., 1939—, div. v.p., regional mgr., Chgo., 1960-61, div. v.p., gen. mgr., White Plains, N.Y., 1961, pres. data processing div., White Plains, 1961-65, corp. v.p., group exec. 1965-67, sr. v.p., 1967—; dir. IBM World Trade Corp., Indian Head Corp. Bd. dirs. United Fund, Westchester Heart Fund. Served with USNR, 1942-46; PTO. Contbr. articles to profl. jours. Home: 75 Cowdin Rd Chappaqua NY 10514 Office Old Orchard Rd Armonk NY 10504

HUMELSINE, CARLISLE HUBBARD, found. exec.; b. Hagerstown, Md., Mar. 12, 1915; s. Charles Ellsworth and Anna Barbara (McNamee) H.; A.B., U. Md., 1937; LL.D. (hon.) Coll. of William and Mary, 1963, Hampden-Sydney Coll., 1970; m. Mary Miller Speake, Aug. 16, 1941; children—Mary Carlisle, Barbara Anne. Editor publs., spl. asst. to pres. U. Md., 1937- 41; dir. personnel Colonial Williamsburg, 1945-46, now pres. Colonial Williamsburg Found.; dir. Office Departmental Adminstrn., U.S. Dept. State, 1946-47, exec. sec., 1947-50, dep. under-sec. state, 1950; spl. asst. to sec. state at meeting Council Fgn. Ministers, London, 1947. Dir. N.Y. Life Ins. Co., Grand Teton Lodge Co., Caneel Bay Plantation, Chesapeake & Potomac Telephone Co., United Bankshares, Inc., Sleepy Hollow Restoration, Inc., Garfinckel, Brooks Bros., Miller & Rhoads. Bd. dirs. Mariner's Mus.; mem. bd., exec. com. Nat. Trust for Historic Preservation; pres. Va. Mus. Fine Arts; past chmn. Va. State Conservation and Econ. Devel. Commn., 1965-67; hon. cons. Robert E. Lee Meml. Found.; former chmn. Am. Revolution Bicentennial Commn.; v.p., mem. exec. com. Jamestown Corp. Bd. dirs. Jamestown Found. Served from lt. to col. AUS, 1941-45. Decorated D.S.M., Bronze Star medal. Mem. Alpha Tau Omega, Omicron Delta Kappa, Pi Delta Epsilon. Democrat. Episcopalian. Clubs: F Street (Washington); Commonwealth, Forum (Richmond). Home: Coke-Garrett House Williamsburg VA 23185 Office: Colonial Williamsburg Found Williamsburg VA 23185

HUMENSKY, JOHN JOSEPH, clergyman, assn. exec.; b. Youngstown, O., Apr. 13, 1907; s. Michael and Mary (Javorsky) H.; student St. Procopius Coll., 1925-27, St. Mary Sem., Gregorian U., 1932-34; S.T.D., Propaganda de Fide U.; 1932; Ph.D., Cath. U. Am., 1937. Ordained priest Roman Cath. Ch., 1932; pastor Sts. Anthony and Bridget Ch., Cleve., 1937-56, Nativity B.V.M. Ch., Cleve., 1956-68; Sts. Cryril and Methodius Ch., 1968—; diocesan dir. hosp. Cleve., 1949-68, cons., 1968- -. Mem. Fed. Hosp. Council, 1964-69, Joint Commn. Accreditation Hosps. 1964- 69. Mem. Am. Hosp. Assn., Cath. Hosp. Assn. U.S. and Can. (pres. 1959- 60). K.C. (4). Address: 12608 Madison Av Lakewood OH 44107

HUMES, BERNARD JAMES, communications cons.; b. Troy, N.Y., July 27, 1907; s. Joseph and Anne (Igoe) H.; student pub. schs., Troy; m. Elfriede Mainka, Sept. 26, 1950. With Am. Ry. Express Co., 1926-28; post office insp. Ry. Mail Service, 1928-42; postal adviser Office Mil. Govt. for Germany, also U.S. rep. Quadripartite Postal Com., Allied Control Authority, Berlin, 1946-47; U.S. rep. Bizonal and Trizonal posts coms., Berlin and Frankfurt, Germany, 1948-50; dep. chief communications div., postal adviser Office U.S. High Commr. for Germany, 1948-50; communications cons. Dept. State, 1951, diplomatic mail and courier officer, 1952-54, officer charge diplomatic mail, chief Diplomatic Courier Service, 1955- 58, also consul, sec. Diplomatic Service; 1st sec. Am. embassy, Belgrade, 1959-61; chief regional diplomatic courier officer for Europe Middle East and Africa, 1961-67; ofcl. Couriers Worldwide, Inc.; 1967—; sr. partner Communications Systems Analysts, Washington, 1967—. Served from capt. to col. AUS, 1942-46; chief postal operations ETO. Mem. Fgn. Service Assn., Diplomatic Courier Assn. Clubs: Foreign Service, Dacor (Washington). Home: 3529 Slade Run Dr Falls Church VA 22042 Office: 1028 Connecticut Av Washington DC 20036

HUMES, JOHN P., U.S. ambassador; b. N.Y.C., July 21, 1921; grad. St. Paul's Sch.; A.B., Princeton, 1943; LL.B., Fordham U., 1948. Admitted to N.Y. bar, 1948, and practiced in N.Y.C.; ambassador to Austria, 1969—. Mem. Assn. Bar City N.Y., Am., Internat., N.Y. State bar assns., Delta Theta Phi. Address: care American Embassy Vienna Austria.*

HUMES, WILLIAM BROWN, business exec.; b. Altoona, Pa., Mar 15, 1918; s. Frank W.B. and Anna M. (Burley) H.; S.B. in Chemistry, Harvard, 1949; m. Geraldine L. Hart, Aug. 31, 1946 (dec. Oct. 1966); childrenKathryn Hart, Steven William; m. 2d, Alda M. Brown, June 9, 1968. Dir. research Nat. Research Corp., Boston, 1940-44; engr. Ford, Bacon & Davis Co., Oak Ridge, 1944- 45; exec. Union Carbide Corp., 1945-66; v.p. Bell & Howell Co., Chgo., 1966-67; pres. 2000, Inc., Los Angeles, 1968—. Club: Larchmont Yacht. Home: 9340 Readcrest Dr Beverly Hills, CA 90210. Office 1720 Pontius Av Los Angeles CA 90025

HUMESTON, EDWARD JUDSON, Jr., educator; b. Phila., Dec. 12, 1910; s. Edward Judson and Pauline (Benedict) H.; A.B., Hamilton Coll., 1932; M.A., Princeton, 1934, Ph.D., 1942; B.S., L.S., Peabody Coll., 1946; m. Mary Campbell Leiphart, Dec. 19, 1942; children-Mary Rand, Edward Judson III, Everitt Wade. Master, Taft Sch., 1934-36; tchr. French, Spanish, Princeton Tutoring Sch., 1936-37, Hollins Coll., 1937-42; librarian Kan. State Tchrs. Coll., Pittsburg, 1946-48; asso. prof. library sci. U. Tex., 1948-53; head dept. library sci. U. Ky., 1953-59; dir. students Grad. Sch. Library Sci.,Drexel Inst. Tech., Phila., 1959-62, dir. curriculum, 1962-64; dean grad. library sch. U. R.I., Kingston, 1964—. Served with USAAF, 1942-45. Mem. Am., R.I. library assns., Assn. Coll. and Reference Libraries, Phi Kappa Phi, Alpha Delta Phi. Presbyn. Editor: Tex. Library Jour.,

1951-53; Assn. Am. Library Schs. Newsletter, 1953-58. Home: 5 Hazelton Rd Barrington RI 02806 Office: 74 Lower College Rd Kingston RI 02881

HUMKEY, WALTER, lawyer; b. Lebanon, Ky., June 26, 1912; s. Walter Bernard and Hayes (Osborne) H.; B.B.S., U. Fla., 1936, LL.B., 1938; m. Rosemary Voulair Erskine, Nov. 22, 1939; children—Barbara Ann, Joseph Erskine. Admitted to Fla. bar, 1939; exec. sec. Fla. Lumber and Mill Work Assn., 1938; asso. atty. with Fred Noble, Jacksonville, 1939-40, with Herbert Fribelman, Miami, 1941-42, with Cody, Fowler, Miami, 1941-42; sr. mng. partner Fowler, White, Humkey, Burnett, Hurley & Banick, Miami, 1946—. Dir. City Nat. Bank Miami. Active Miami United Fund. Bd. dirs., v.p. Dade County Citizens Safety Council; bd. dirs., chmn. Dade County chpt. Am. Red Cross, 1968; trustee U. Fla. Law Center. Served with USNR, 1942-45. Mem. Fla. Bar (gov. 1953-57), Am., Dade County (pres. 1952-53) bar assns., Am. Coll. Trial Lawyers, Internat. Assn. Fedn. Ins. Counsel, Sigma Alpha Epsilon, Phi Delta Phi. Democrat. Club: Riveria Country, Surf, Committee of 100 (Miami Beach); Miami (Miami). Home: 6160 Chapman Field Dr Miami FL 33156 Office: City Nat Bank Bldg Miami FL 33130

HUMLHANZ, ALBERT FRANK, mfg. co. exec.; b. Chalfont, Pa., May 21, 1924; s. William and Mary (Neubert) H.; grad. Pierce Sch. Bus. Adminstrn., Phila., 1947; m. Kathryn Crouthamel, Nov. 23, 1946; children—Kathleen (Mrs. Samuel B. Cupp, Jr.), Donna (Mrs. Richard C. Brown). Treas., controller Keasbey & Mattison Co., Ambler, Pa., 1948-62; controller Norwalk Truck Lines (O.), 1962-64; v.p. finance Jones Motor Co. Inc., Spring City, Pa., 1964—. Served with AUS, 1943-44. Mem. Nat. Assn. Accountants, Nat. Adminstrv. Soc. Home: Coventry East Apts Vaughan Rd Pottstown PA 19464 Office: Jones Motor Co Inc Bridge St and Schuylkill Rd Spring City PA 19475

HUMMEL, ARTHUR WILLIAM, Jr., fgn. service officer; b. Fenchow, China, June 1, 1920; s. Arthur William and Ruth Emily (Bookwalter) H.; student Antioch Coll., 1937-39, Coll. of Chinese Studies, Peking, 1940-41; M.A., U. Chgo., 1949; m. Betty L. Fristenberger, May 31, 1951; children—Timothy A., William A. English tchr. Fu Jen Middle Sch., Peking, 1941; interned by Japanese, 1941-44; escaped, 1944, mem. Chinese guerrilla unit, 1944-45; liaison officer UNNRA, Tientsin, China, 1945-46; staff lectr. United Service to China, N.Y.C., 1946-47; intelligence analyst officer naval Intelligence, 1950; fgn. affairs officer Dept. of State, 1950-52; consul, dep. pub. affairs officer, Hong Kong, 1952, pub. affairs officer, 1953-55; attache, dep. pub. affairs officer Am. embassy, Tokyo, Japan, 1955-57; attache, pub. affairs officer Am. embassay, Rangoon, Burma, 1957-60; Nat. War Coll., 1960-61; dep. dir. Voice of Am., 1961-63; dep. asst. U.S. sec. of state for cultural and ednl. affairs, 1963-65; dep. chief of mission Am. embassy, Taipei, Taiwan, 1965-68; Am. ambassador, Rangoon, Burma, 1968—. Recipient Arthur S. Fleming award, 1959. Mem. Far Eastern Assn., Phi Beta Kappa. Home; 4923 Essex Av Chevy Chase MD 20015 Office: Dept State Washington DC 20521

HUMMEL, CHARLES FREDERICK, architect; b. Boise, Ida., June 21, 1925; B. Arch., Cath. U. Am.; 1950; M.S., Columbia, 1953; m. Calista F. Ward, June 8, 1951; children—Michael, Mary Catherine, John, Joan. Mem. firm Hummel, Hummel, Jones & Shawver, and predecessor, Boise; prin. works include C.F. Hummel residence, Boise, 1956, St. John's Cath. Chapel, 1958, St. Peter and Paul Rectory, Greangeville, 1959, Mountain States Wholesale Warehouse, 1960, Coll. Courts Dorm. and North End Shopping Center, Boise, 1961, Boise Jr. Coll. Library, Bishop Kelly High Sch. Boise, 1964. Mem. Ida. Bd. Archtl. Examiners. Mem. Boise City Plan Commn., Ada County Zoning Commn., Boise. Served to 2d lt. AUS, 1943-45, 51-52. Mem. A.I.A. (dir. Ida. chpt. 1960-61), Boise Art Assn. (pres. 1962-64). K.C., Elk. Club: Arid. Home: 305 Mobley Dr Boise ID 83706 Office: 1324 Idaho St Boise ID 83702

HUMMEL, CHARLES RONALD, restaurant chain exec.; b. Detroit, Apr. 22, 1938; s. Charles R. and Anne Veronica (Norton) H.; B.A. cum laude, Princeton, 1960; M.B.A., Harvard, 1960-62; m. Anne Steele Hummel, July 6, 1963; children—Cynthia B., Krista A., Hans Charles. Research asst. Harvard Bus. Sch., 1962-63; with Gen. Foods Corp., 1963—, dir. corporate financial planning and analysis, 1970-71, v.p. finance subsidiary Burger Chef Systems, 1971—, also dir. Vice pres., mem. bd. United Fund No. Westchester, N.Y., 1970; chmn. schs. and scholarship com. No. Westchester, Princeton, 1970. Club: Cap and Gown. Contbg. author: Financial Executive's Handbook, 1970. Home: 8148 N Oakland St Indianapolis IN 46202 Office: 1348 W 16th St Indianapolis IN 46202

HUMMEL, DON, lawyer, govt. ofcl.; b. Cin., Sept. 9, 1907; s. Louis Gotlob and Enma (Yockey) H.; A.B. in Polit. Sci. and History, U. Ariz., 1930; J.D., U. Mich., 1933; m. Eugenia Mitchell, Dec. 27, 1947; children—Donna, Diane, Clifford, Charlene. Admitted to Cal. bar, 1933, Ariz. bar, 1934; with firm Hummel, Hummel & Wyatt, Tucson, 1933-56; investigator, field agt. WPA, 1936-40; field agt. charge investigation div. Rocky Mountain and Southeastern regions OPA, 1940-42; asst. U.S. atty. Dist. Ariz., 1947- 51; pres. Lassen Nat. Park Co., 1933-42, 46-61, Mt. McKinley Nat. Park Co., 1958-66, Glacier Park, Inc., 1961—. Vice chmn. Adv. Commn. on Inter- Govtl. Relations, 1962—; chmn. U.S. delegation Inter-Am. Municipal Congress, 1960, Internat. Congress Local Authorities, 1960; pres. League Ariz. Cities and Towns, 1956, Am. Municipal Assn., 1960-61; chmn. Western Conf. Nat. Park Concessioners, 1960-66; chmn. exec. com. bd. dirs. Yosemite Park and Curry Co., 1970—; v.p. operations U.S. Natural Resources, 1970—. Mayor, Tucson, 1955-62; commr. Ariz. Power Authority, 1965-66, U.S.-Mexico Border Devel. Commn., 1966-69; asst. sec. renewal and housing Dept. Housing and Urban Devel., Washington, 1966-69. Del. Democratic Nat. Conv. 1956, 60. Served to lt. col. USAAF, World War II. Decorated Bronze Star, Legion of Merit; 2 chinese Govt. awards. Named Man of Year in Ariz., Nat. Conf. Christians and Jews, 1960; recipient commendation Adv. Commn. Inter- Govtl. Relations, 1961. Mem. Am. Arbitration Assn. (panelist), Am., Cal., Ariz. bar assns,, Am. Legion, V.F.W. Presbyn. (trustee). Elk, Kiwanian. Home: 40 Calle Encanto Tucson AZ 85716

HUMMEL, EDWARD AARON, govt. ofcl.; b. Gackle, N.D., Mar. 26, 1909; s. John and Emma (Odenbach) H.; B.A., N.D. State Tchrs. Coll., Valley City, 1930; M.A., U. Colo., 1931; postgrad. U. Minn., 1932-35; m. Vibekke Kjelland, Aug. 30, 1932; children-John Olaf, Kathrine Marie (Mrs. Felix Fegette). Tchr. pub. schs., N.D., 1928-30; historian, regional office Nat. Park Service, Omaha, 1935-42, regional dir., San Francisco, 1963-66, asst. dir. Nat. Park Service, 1966-68, asso. dir., 1968—; supt. Fredericksburg and Spotsylvania Nat. Mil. Park, 1942- 43, 46, Colonial Nat. Hist. Park, Yorktown, Va., 1946-52, Great Smoky Mountain Nat. Park, 1952-58, Glacier Nat. Park, 1958-62. Served from lt. (j.g.) to lt. USNR, 1943-46. Home: 6605 Spring Rd Springfield VA 22150 Office: Dept Interior Nat Park Service Washington DC 20240

HUMMEL, LAWRENCE EDGAR, physician; b. Darien Center, N.Y., Apr. 22, 1903; s. Edward Eugene and Ida M. (Meyer) H.; B.S., U. Buffalo, 1926; M.D., Harvard, 1931; postgrad. Schwabing-Krankenhaus, Munich, Germany, 1932; m. Dorothy Hayes, Oct. 14, 1939; children—Margaret Ellen, Dorothy May. Intern, Mass. Gen. Hosp., Boston, 1931-32, St. Luke's Hosp., N.Y.C., 1933-35; resident Lenox Hill Hosp., N.Y.C., 1935; research Hosp. Rockefeller Inst. Med. Research, N.Y.C., 1935-36, resident, 1936-37; practice medicine specializing in internal medicine, hematology, Buffalo, 1937-57, part time 1957-70; supt. Edward J. Meyer Meml. Hosp., 1957-70, also attending physician; asst. dean U. Buffalo Sch. Medicine, 1939-44, asst. prof. medicine, 1939-63, asst. clin. prof. medicine, 1963—, chmn. com. dept. medicine, 1939-46, ex-officio mem. exec. com., 1961-63; med. dir. Buffalo Regional Red Cross Blood Bank, 1950-57; cons. physician Millard Fillmore Hosp., asso. physician Buffalo Gen. Hosp. Mem. exec. bd. Community Welfare Council, 1960-69; bd. mem. Blue Cross Western N.Y., 1970. Diplomate Am. Bd. Internal Medicine, Nat. Bd. Med. Examiners. Fellow A.C.P., Internat. Soc. Hematology; mem. Am., Western N.Y. (past dir., chmn. com. profl. services) hosp. assns., Hosp. Assns. N.Y. State, A.M.A., Harvey Soc., Pan Am. Med. Assn., N.Y. State, Erie County med. socs., Buffalo Acad. Medicine, Med. Union Buffalo, Sigma Xi. Contbr. articles to profl. jours. Home: 9691 Knoll Rd Eden NY 14057

HUMMEL, MARTIN HENRY, Jr., advt. exec.; b. Glen Ridge, N.J., May 7, 1927; s. Martin Henry and Florence (Lanken) H.; A.B., Cornell U., 1949; m. Evelyn Mayer, Sept. 19, 1953; childrenMartin Henry III, Patricia Katherine. With Vick Chem. Co., 1949-50, J. Walter Thompson, 1950-51, Crowell-Collier Pub. Co., 1952-57; with Sullivan, Stauffer, Colwell and Bayles, Inc., N.Y.C., 1957- -, exec. v.p., 1968—, also dir.; vice chmn., mng. dir. SSC & B- Lintas Internat., Ltd.; mem. faculty Am. Mgmt. Assn., 1968. Dir. various N.J. Republican state and county polit. campaigns, 1953-57, 60; mem. Bloomfield (N.J.) Zoning Bd., 1953-55. Served with AUS, World War II. Mem. Am. Assn. Advt. Agys., Cornell U. Council. Clubs: Cornell (chmn. membership com. 1969, admissions com. 1965-69), Cloud, Overseas Press (N.Y.C.). Home: 50 Holland St London W8 England Office: 575 Lexington Av New York City NY 10022

HUMMER, DONAL, lawyer; b. Defiance, O., Feb. 19, 1924; s. Ecdward M. and Clara (Krotz) H.; J.D., U. Notre Dame, 1948; m. Nancy Marie Garner, July 26, 1947; children-Mary Cliare, William Garner, Suzanne, Donald, Edward Mark II. Admitted to Ohio bar, 1948, since practiced in Toledo; partner firm Marshall, Melhorn, Bloch & Belt., 1955—. Dir, Lathrop Co. Sec. Maumee Valley Country Day Sch., 1964—; asst. sec. Boys Club Toledo, 1958—. Trustee Luella Cummings Sch., 1960—. Served to lt. (j.g.) USNR, 1944- 46. Recipient award of merit Ohio Legal Center Inst., 1967, Fed. Bar Columbus, 1970. Mem. Am., Ohio, Toledo (exec. com. 1966—) bar assns. Clubs: Toledo (bd. dirs. 1966—, pres. 1968—), Toledo Country; Belmont Country, Belmont Gun (pres. 1970—) (Perrysburg, O.). Home: Eagle Point Rossford OH 43460 Office: Nat Bank Bldg Toledo OH 43604

HUMPERDINCK, ENGELBERT, see Dorsey, Arnold George,

HUMPHREY, ARTHUR EARL, educator; b. Moscow, Ida., Nov. 9, 1927; s. Samuel Earl and Iris May (Rowe) H.; B.S. in Chem. Engring., U. Ida., 1948, M.S., 1950; Ph.D., Columbia, 1953; M.S. in Food Tech., Mass. Inst. Tech., 1959; m. Sheila Claire Darwin, June 13, 1951; children—Andrea Lynn, Allyson Dawn. Faculty, U. Pa., Phila., 1953—, prof. chem. engring., dir. Sch. Chem. Engring., 1961—. NSF sci. tchr. fellow Mass. Inst. Tech., 1957-58; Fulbright lectr. U. Tokyo (Japan), 1963, U. New South Wales (Australia), 1970; guest lectr. Inst. Biology, Czechoslovakian Acad. Sci., 1964, Tech. Inst., Budapest, 1966; cons. Merck Sharp & Dohme, 1957-63, Merck Chem. Co., 1963-64, Sun Oil Co., 1961-68, Bioferm, 1964-67, Cryotherm, 1966-67, Fermentation Design, 1967—, E.R. Squibb, 1967—, Air Products, 1971—. Vice pres. Keystone Trails Assn., 1962-67; councilor Appalachian Trail Conf., 1961-67; chmn. space sci. panel Nat. Acad. Sci.; co-chmn. 3d Internat. Fermentation Symposium; mem. engring. adv. bd. NSF; mem. single cell protein working group Pan Am. Union-WHO-FAO-UN. Recipient Outstanding Tchr. award U. Pa., 1959. Mem. Internat. Assn. Microbiol. Socs. (sec.-gen. econ. and applied microbiology), Am. Chem. Soc. (chmn. div. microbial. chem. and tech. 1967), Am. Inst. Chem. Engrs. (v.p. food and bioengrig. div. 1971), Franklin Inst., Japanese Soc. Fermentation Tech., Soc. Am. Microbiologists, Sigma Xi, Sigma Tau. Clubs: Philadelphia Trail, Horse-Shoe Trail (Phila.); Appalachian Mountain (Boston). Author: Biochemical Engineering; also ann. Fermentation Rev., 1960-64. Contbr. articles to profl. jours. Home: 441 S Feathering Rd Media PA 19036 Office: Towne Bldg U Pa Philadelphia PA 19104

HUMPHREY, CHAMP, former advt. exec.; b. Herrin, Ill., Mar. 14, 1911; s. Christopher C. and Julia Ann (Worsham) H.; student LaSalle Extension div. U. Chgo.; m. Louise Fallon, Aug. 12, 1939; children—Stephen, James, Richard. With Brown & Colombo, wholesale and retail grocery, Herrin, 1928-38; with Garner Advt. Co., St. Louis and N.Y.C., 1938-70, v.p. charge account service, 1959-60, exec. v.p. account service, 1960-64, pres., 1964-67, chmn. bd., 1967-70. Home: 16 Shagbark Rd Darien CT 06820 Office: 90 Park Av New York City NY 10016

HUMPHREY, EDWARD, editor; b. South Norwalk, Conn.; s. Fred Robert and Natalie Charles (Gates) H.; student U. Buffalo; B.A., Columbia, M.A., Ph.D. Instr. English, L.I. U.; mng. editor Richards Topical Ency., 1950-55; editor Grolier Classics, 1955; exec. editor Book of Knowledge, 1955-61; editor in chief Am. Peoples Ency., N.Y.C., 1961-; dir. Grolier Publs. in French. Served to capt. USAAF, 1941-46. Home: 205 E 69th St New York City NY 10021 Office: 575 Lexington Av New York City NY 10022

HUMPHREY, EDWARD WILLIAM, surgeon, educator; b. Fargo, N.D., Dec. 6, 1926; s. Edward W. and Minnie (Ramstad) H.; B.A., U. Minn., 1948, M.D., 1951, Ph.D. in Physiology, 1959; m. Noreen Sander, Sept. 23, 1950; children—Katherine Lisa, Joan Karen. Faculty, U. Minn., Mpls., 1958—, prof. dept. surgery, 1965—; mem. staff VA Hosp., Mpls., 1958—, chief surg. service, 1962—. Mem. A.C.S., Minn. Surg. Soc., Central Surg. Assn., Soc. Univ. Surgeons, Am. Physiol. Soc., Am. Soc. Cell Biology, Am. Assn. Thoracic Surgery, Soc. Exptl. Biology and Medicine, Sigma Xi, Alpha Omega Alpha. Research, publs. in field cancer; chemotherapy of cancer; electrolyte flux in various tissues; thoracic surgery. Home: 9734 Russell Circle Minneapolis MN 55431 Office: VA Hosp 48th Av and 54th St Minneapolis MN 55417

HUMPHREY, FRED A., physician; b. Broken Bow, Neb., Mar. 16, 1896; s. A.R. and Nellie (Nightengale) H.; B.Sc., U. Neb., 1919, M.D., 1921; m. Violet Osborne, June 19, 1921; children-Betty Clee (Mrs. T.M. Snow), Robert N. Practice medicine, Ft. Collins, Colo., 1922—; mem. staff Poudre Valley Meml. Hosp., Ft. Collins. Dir. Woodward Governor Co., United Bank Ft. Collins. Trustee Colo. Blue Shield, 1952-67. Mem. Am. Acad. Gen. Practice (v.p., exec. com. 1951), A.M.A. (chmn. council on rural health 1959-63), Colo, (pres. 1949-50), Larimer County (pres. 1935) med. socs., Am. Legion (past post comdr.). Mason (32 Shriner), Elk (past exalted ruler). Home: 837 Juniper Lane Ft Collins CO 80521 Office: 1224 Doctors Lane Fort Collins CO 80521

HUMPHREY, GEORGE DUKE, educator; b. Tippah County, Miss., Aug. 30, 1897; s. John Washington and Louis Isoble (Cheeves) H.; grad. State Tchrs. Coll., Hattiesburg, Miss., 1922; B.A., Blue Mountain (Miss.) Coll., 1929; M.A., U. Chgo., 1931; Ph.D., Ohio State U, 1939; LL.D., Ohio Wesleyan U., 1959, U. Wyo., 1964; Litt.D., U. Ariz., 1962; m. Josephine Robertson, Apr. 15, 1925 (dec. Sept. 1971); 1 son, John Julius. Began as pub. sch. tchr. in Miss.; later prin. consol. sch., 3 sessions; supt. Ripley (Miss.) Sch. Dist., 4 sessions; prin. Agrl. High Sch., Tippah County, 1923; county supt. edn., Tippah County, 1924-30; supt. city schs., Kosciuko, Miss., 1931-32; high sch. supr. State of Miss., 1932-33; pres. Miss. State Coll., 1934-45; pres. U. Wyo., 1945-64, pres. emeritus, 1964-, adminstr. Sch. Am. Studies, 1964- 68; instr. in edn. Furman U., Greenville, S.C., summer 1932; local dir. 4 state summer normals Blue Mountain Coll.; instr. history Miss. summer normals, 3 years. Mem. State Vocational Bd.; pres. Southeastern Athletic Conf., 1938-40, mem. exec. com., 1937- 40, 43-45; cons. to adv. panel on regional materials of instrn. TVA, 1941-44; mem. Nat. Commn. on Accrediting, 1961-64, pub. mem. Regional War Labor Bd., 1943- 45; pres. So. Assn. Colls. and Secondary Schools, 1942-45, chmn. postwar ednl. com., 1944-45; cons. edn. policies commn. N.E.A., 1936-48; mem. exec. com. Assn. Land Grant Colls., 1944-46, mem. com. on irrigated agr. and water resources, 1948-56, chmn., 1948-55; mem. bd. NSF, 1950-62; spl. cons. on reorgn. Bur. Entomology and Plant Quarantine, U.S. Dept. of Agr., 1951; adviser U.S. Dept. Interior on saline water program, 1952-62; cons. reorgn. saline water div., 1958; chmn. Western Interstate Commn. for Higher Edn., 1954-55; chmn. Freedom Found. Award Jury, 1954. Mem. N.E.A., Am. Assn. Sch. Adminstrs., Assn. Adult Edn., Miss. Edn. Assn. (mem. legislative com. 1928-45, dir. 1929-32, pub. relations com., 1935-40, vocations commn. 1943-45), Miss Forestry and Chemurgic Assn. (dir. 1944-45), Miss. County Supts. Assn. (past chmn.), Miss. City Sch. Supts. Assn. (dir. 1931-32), Miss. Assn. Colls., (pres. 1940-41), Am. Council on Edn. (com. on So. regional studies and edn. 1944-45), Am. Assn. for Adult Edn. (mem. exec. council 1946), Wyo. Edn. Assn. (mem. exec. com. 1945—), Nat. Assn. State Univs. (chmn. mil. affairs com. 1947-48, v.p. 1959-60, pres. 1960-61), Assn. Land Grant Colls. and Univs. (chmn. council, pres. 1956-57), Assn. Am. Colls. (dir. 1954-61, v.p. 1958, pres. 1959), Scabbard and Blade, Iota Lambda Sigma Kappa Sigma, Blue Key, Omicron Delta Kappa, Phi Delta Kappa. Methodist. Mason (K.T., Shriner). Clubs: Cosmos, Laramie Country, Denver. Address: 1502 Shields Laramie WY 82001

HUMPHREY, GEORGE NORWOOD, musician; b. Bellaire, O., Aug. 25, 1940; s. George Latham and Mabel May (Long) H.; grad. N.E.C. of Music, 1929; student Curtis Inst. Music, 1930-31; m. Mildred Martha Weber, Oct. 2, 1929; children—George Lee, John Robert, Eric Richard. With Mpls. Symphony Orch., 1929-30; with Boston Symphony Orch., 1934—; mem. research group Mass. Inst. Tech., 1961-64; mem. missions State Dept., Iceland, 1955, 56, 57, 58, 59; Am. rep. Japan Philharmonic Orch., 1968. One man photog. shows, Boston, N.Y., Phila., Washington, also libraries in New Eng. Patentee musical accessory. Home: 82 Wollaston Av Arlington MA 02174 Office: Symphony Hall Boston MA 02115

HUMPHREY, GEORGE THOMAS, mfg. co. exec.; b. Dallas, Dec. 23, 1917; s. George T. and Pearl (Hamilton) H.; student U. Tex., 1936-39, U. Pitts., 1955; m. Jane Wolverton, Apr. 27, 1940; children—Judith (Mrs. Richard Conley), George Thomas III, Carolyn (Mrs. William H. Avery), Gretchen, Nancy, Jill. Sales trainee Timken Roller Bearing Co., Dallas, 1939- 40, asst. to br. mgr., asst. gen. mgr., Canton, O., 1951-57, gen. mgr., 1957-64; exec. asst. to pres. automotive divs. Rockwell-Standard Corp., 1964-65, v.p. marketing, 1965-66, v.p., gen. mgr. automotive products divs., 1966-67, pres. aircraft divisions, Pitts., 1967-69; sr. v.p. Beech Aircraft Corp., Wichita, Kan., 1969—, also dir.; dir. B.C. Bearing Engring. Ltd., Beechcraft Hawker Corp. Mem. Automotive Service Industry Assn. Bearing Distbrs. Assn. (vice chmn. 1963-64), Am. Mining Congress (bd. govs. 1963-64), Soc. Automotive Engrs. Clubs: Detroit Athletic; Orchard Lake (Mich.) Country; Economic (Detroit); Duquesne (Pitts.); Wichita Country. Home: 202 N Rock Rd Wichita KS 67206 Office: 9709 E Central Wichita KS 67207

HUMPHREY, GILBERT WATTS, business exec.; b. Saginaw, Mich., July 4, 1916; s. George Magoffin and Pamela (Stark) H.; A.B., Yale, 1939, LL.B., 1942; m. Louise Ireland, Dec. 27, 1939; children—George Magoffin II, Margaret, Gilbert Watts. Admitted to Ohio bar, 1946; practiced law with Jones, Day, Cockley & Reavis, 1946-47; joined M.A. Hanna Co., 1948, pres., 1960-61, chmn. bd., 1961-65, dir., chmn. bd., mem. exec. com. Hanna Mining Co., dir. affiliated cos.; dir., chmn. exec. com. Nat. Steel Corp.; dir. Southwire Co., Sun Life Assurance Co. Can., Gen. Electric Co., Nat. City Bank Cleve., Texaco, Inc., Massey-Ferguson, Ltd., Gen. Reins. Corp. Mem. bd. overseers Case Western Res. U.; trustee, v.p., exec., com. U. Hosps. Cleve. Clubs; Union, Tavern, Chagrin Valley Hunt, Pepper Pike Country, Kirtland Country, Clevelander (Cleve.); Pacific Union (San Francisco); Links (N.Y.C.); Augusta National (Ga.); Cypress Point (Pebble Beach, Cal.). Home: Hunting Hill River Rd Chagrin Falls OH 44022 Office: 100 Erieview Plaza Cleveland OH 44114

HUMPHREY, HARRY JAMES, govt. ofcl.; b. Washington, Mar. 18, 1910; s. Ernest Randolph and Mary Agnes (Hutchison) H.; B.C.S., Ben Franklin U., 1933; m. Lillian Frances Harbaugh, Apr. 4, 1931 (dec. Nov. 1970); children—Lou Ann (Mrs. John Aubrey Parrott), Harriett (Mrs. Joseph Barish). With Govt. Printing Office, Washington, 1928—, dep. controller, 1961-66, adminstrv. asst., 1966-70, dep. pub. printer, 1970—. Recipient Distinguished Service award Govt. Printing Office, 1970. Mem. Columbia Typographical Union. Methodist. Club: Chesapeake Country (Lusby, Md.). Home: 2816 S Joyce St Arlington VA 22202 Office: Govt Printing Office N Capital & H Sts Washington DC 20401

HUMPHREY, HUBERT HORATIO, Jr., U.S. senator, former vice pres. U.S.; b. Wallace, S.D., May 27, 1911; s. Hubert Horatio and Christine (Sannes) H.; student Denver Coll. Pharmacy, 1932-33; A.B., U. Minn., 1939; A.M., La. State U., 1940; postgrad. U. Minn., 1940-41; recipient numerous hon. degrees; m. Muriel Fay Buck, Sept. 3, 1936; children—Nancy Faye (Mrs. C. Bruce Solomonson), Hubert Horatio III, Robert Andrew, Douglas Sannes. Pharmacist with Humphrey Drug Co., Huron, S.D., 1933-37; asst. instr. polit. sci. La. State U., 1939-40, U. Minn., 1940-41; mem. adminstrv. staff WPA, later head state div.; asst. state supr. adult edn., chief war services sect., dir. tng. re-employment div., 1941-43; asst. regional dir. War Manpower Commn., 1943; vis. prof. polit. sci. Macalester Coll., St. Paul, 1943-44; state campaign mgr. Roosevelt-Truman Com., 1944; mayor City of Mpls., 1945-48; U.S. senator from Minn., 1948-64, 70—, elected senate majority whip, 1961; vice pres. U.S., 1965-69. U.S. del. UN, 1956-58; del. UNESCO Conf., Paris, 1958. Hon. chmn. Pres.'s Council on Equal Opportunity, Pres.' Com. on Equal Employment Opportunity, Nat. Aeros. and Space Council, Peace Corps Adv. Council; mem. Nat. Security Council. Bd. regents Smithsonian Instn. Recipient Jr. Assn. of Commerce award for Outstanding Minneapolitan, 1945; named Outstanding Young Man in State, Minn. Jr. Assn. of Commerce, 1945. Mem. Am. Polit. Sci. Assn., Pub. Adminstrn. Soc., Am. Acad. Arts and Scis., Phi Beta Kappa, Delta Sigma Rho. Democrat. Active in fusing Democratic and Farm Labor parties. Home: 550 N St SW Washington DC 20024

HUMPHREY, JOHN, curator San Francisco Museum Art. Address: San Francisco Museum Art McAllister St at Van Ness Av Francisco CA San Francisco CA 94102*

HUMPHREY, JOHN PETERS, internat. ofcl., educator; b. Hampton, N.B., Can., Apr. 30, 1905; s. Frank M. and Elizabeth (Peters) H.; student Mount Allison U., Sackville, N.B., 1921-23; B.Com., McGill U., 1925, B.A., 1927, B.C.L., 1929, Ph.D., 1942; postgrad. U. Paris, 1929-30; Dr. honoris causa U. Algiers, 1945; Dr. Social Scis. honoris causa, U. Ottawa (Can.); LL.D., Carleton U., 1968, St. Thomas U., 1971; m. Jeanne Godreau, Sept. 3, 1929. Admitted to Can. bar, 1930, practiced in Montreal with firm Wainwright, Elder & McDougall, 1930-36; faculty McGill U., 1936-46, 66-71 Gale prof. Roman law, 1946; now vis. prof. law U. Toronto; became dir. div. human rights UN Secretariat, N.Y.C., 1946; exec. sec. UN Conf. on Freedom of Information, 1948, on Protection of Refugees, 1951, on Protection of Stateless Persons, 1954, on UN Slavery Conf., 1956; chmn. N.Y. br. Canadian Inst. Internat. Affairs; prin. sec. UN Commn. to Vietnam, 1963; nat. pres. UN Assn. in Can., 1968-70; mem. UN Sub- Commn. on Preventions Discrimination and Protection Minorities, chmn., 1970-71; mem. Royal Commn. on Status Women in Can., 1968-70. Carnegie fellow internat. law U. Paris, 1936-37. Author: The Inter-American System: a Canadian View, 1942. Contbr. articles to Am., Brit., Canadian publs. Home: 1455 Sherbrooke St W Montreal Quebec Canada

HUMPHREY, JOHN W., mfg. exec.; b. Brighton, Mich., Sept. 28, 1902; s. John B. and Mabel (Tunis) H.; grad. indsl. engring. U. Mich., 1924; m. Virginia Schachne, Nov. 15, 1928; children—John W., Holly B., Heather C. Sales, indsl. engr. Athol Mfg. Co. (Mass.), 1924-27; indsl. engr. Gen. Motors Corp., 1927-33, factory mgr. Sunlite Electric div., Warren, O., Delco Products div., Dayton, O., 1933-40; factory mgr. Nat. Cash Register, Dayton, 1940-45; v.p. in charge mfg. Internat. Tel.&Tel., N.Y.C., 1946- 47; cons. engr., propr., pres. Philip Carey Mfg. Co., 1948-67; past chmn. bd. Philip Carey Corp., 1967-68. Pres., Action Housing Greater Cin. Bd. dirs. Central Clinic of U. Cin., Cin. br. Fed. Res. Bd., Ohio Capital Fund, Inc., Ohio Presbyn. Homes. Mem. C. of C. Clubs: Queen City, Commercial. Home: 835 Ivy Av Glendale OH 45246 Office: Fed Res Bank Bldg Cincinnati OH 45202

HUMPHREY, JOSEPH HARRISON, securities co. exec.; b. St. Louis, Aug. 30, 1908; s. Joseph Harrison and Contessa Maria (Clerico) H.; B.A., Washington U., St. Louis, 1929; M.B.A., Harvard, 1934; m. Nancy Patricia Powell, June 26, 1936; children—Joseph Harrison III, Nancy Patricia. With Calvin Bullock Ltd., N.Y.C., 1936—, pres., 1955—; v.p., dir. Dividend Shares Co., 1955—, Bullock Fund, 1965—; pres., dir. Nation-Wide Securities Co., 1955—, Carriers & Gen. Corp., 1955—. Trustee Queens County Savs. Bank. Mem. Pilgrims U.S. Club: Recess (N.Y.C.). Author: (with Lester Plum) Investment Analysis and Management, 1950. Home: 35-21 159th St Flushing NY 11358 Office: 1 Wall St New York City NY 10005

HUMPHREY, LOUISE BEUTNER, mem. Republican Nat. Com.; b. White Lake, S.D., June 11, 1905; d. August and Louise (Nihart) Beutner; B.A., Yankton (S.D.) Coll., 1927; m. Bert Humphrey, Dec. 24, 1927; 1 dau., Mary Louise (Mrs. Richard K. Stanley). Instr. high sch., White River, S.D., 1927-28, 33-34; assessor Mellette County, 1929-30; supr. West River agrl. census White River, 1954. Vice chmn. Mellette County Republican Com., 1935-45; mem. bd. S.D. Fed. Rep. Women's Club, 1954; del. Rep. Nat. Conv., 1948, mem. rules com., 1968; mem. S.D. Legislature, 1958-62; mem. Rep. Nat. Com. for S.D., 1964—. Mem. S.D. Centennial Commn., 1961, Joseph Ward Commn., 1961, S.D. Ct. Study Commn., 1962, Gov's. Adv. Com. Govt. Status of Women. Trustee, mem. corporate bd. Yankton Coll. Active local drives Am. Cancer Soc., A.R.C., Girl Scouts U.S.A. Mem. Rosebud Geol. Soc., Cowbelles, Stockgrowers, White River Devel. Assn., Am. Legion Aux., Bus. and Profl. Women's Club, Am. Assn. U. Women. Club: Women's (2d dist. S.D. pres.). Address: White River SD 95757

HUMPHREY, LUCIE KING, mem. Republican Nat. Com.; b. Mokelumne Hill, Cal., Feb. 23, 1911; d. Ralph Mower and Mabel (Plumb) King; A.B., U. Nev., 1931; m. Marvin Bender Humphrey, Sept. 14, 1932; children—Joseph, Barbara (Mrs. F.E. Redman), Sarah (Mrs. Robert H. White), Ellen. Sch. tchr., 1931-32; mem. Nev. Fedn. Rep. Women 1950—, pres., 1950-53; pres. Reno Rep. Women's Club, 1963-67; mem. Rep. Nat. Com. for Nev., 1968—. Bd. dirs. Sierra Nev. Reno Girl Scouts, 1944-66, pres., 1946-48; pres. Nev. Campus YWCA, bd., 1950-51. Mem. Nev. Hist. Soc., Nev. Hort. Soc., Gamma Phi Beta (local alumnae pres. 1933, house corp. pres. 1958-60). Episcopalian. Club: Monday (pres. 1946—) (Reno). Home: 30 Suda Way Reno NV 89502

HUMPHREY, MURIEL FAY BUCK, (MRS. HUBERT HORATIO HUMPHREY); b. Huron, S.D., Feb. 20, 1912; d. Andrew E. and Jessie May (Pierce) Buck; student Huron Coll., 1931-32; m. Hubert Horatio Humphrey, Sept. 3, 1936; children-Nancy (Mrs. C. Bruce Solomonson), Hubert Horatio III, Robert, Douglas. Home: 550 N St SW Washington DC 20024

HUMPHREY, NEIL DARWIN, univ. chancellor; b. Idaho Falls, Ida., May 20, 1928; s. Clair Pierce and Freda (Hatfield) H.; B.A. in Polit. Sci., Ida. State U., 1950; M.S. in Govt. Mgmt., U. Denver, 1951; m. Mary Pat Smith, Aug. 21, 1950; children—Ann Marie, Therese Claire. Research asst. Colo. Pub. Expenditure Council, 1951-52, research assistant, acting director Colo. Municipal League, 1952-53; mgr. Golden (Colo.) C. of C., 1953; dir. legislation and research, asst. treas. Denver C. of C., 1954-55; ex. sec. Nev. Taxpayers Assn., 1955-59; budget dir. Nev., 1959-61; bus. mgr. U. Nev., 1961-64, v.p. finance, 1964-67, acting pres., 1967-68; chancellor U. Nev. System, 1968—. Mem. Delta Sigma Pi, Pi Sigma Alpha, Phi Kappa Phi. Home: 1395 Webster Way Reno NV 89509

HUMPHREY, PATRICK L., ins. co. exec.; b. Shelbina, Mo., May 19, 1908 s. George W. and Gertrude (List) H.; B.S., U.S. Naval Acad., 1929; postgrad. State U. Ia., 1933-34; m. Peggy Jane Doyle, Apr. 20, 1935; children—Marliyn (Mrs. Leon Lants, Jr.,) Jan. With Kansas City Life Ins. Co. (Mo.), 1930—, now v.p., actuary. Served to lt. USNR, 1942-45. Fellow Soc. Actuaries. Home: 3616 W 63d St Prairie Village KS 66208 Office: 3520 Broadway Kansas City MO 64141

HUMPHREY, PERCY, jazz trumpeter; b. New Orleans, Jan. 13, 1905. Played with Eureka Brass Band, then with Kid Howard in Chgo., 1929; engaged in odd jobs during 1930s; retired 1939, returned to music 1946; worked with George Lewis, 1953; leader Eureka Brass Band; recordings with Eureka Band, also George Lewis and Paul Barharin. Address: 235 W 46th St New York City NY 10036*

HUMPHREY, RICHARD SEARS, Jr., advt. exec.; b. Boston, Dec. 22, 1925; s. Richard Sears and Maion VanBuren (Emmons) H.; A.B., Harvard, 1947; m. Linda Dwyer Stroh, June 11, 1966; children—Joan F., Katherine V.I., Brooks S., Diane E., Wendy S., Richard Sears III. With Reach McClinton & Co., 1958—, pres. Boston co. Humphrey Browning MacDougal Inc., 1970—. Served with USNR, 1944-47, 51-53. Home: 450 Essex St Beverly MA 01915 Office: 3 Center Plaza Boston MA 02108

HUMPHREY, ROBERT CLAYTON, banker; b. Moweaqua, Ill., July 12, 1918; s. Clayton E. and Zoe (Hudson); H. B.S. in Finance, U. Ill., 1940; postgrad. Northwestern U., 1940-42; grad. Rutgers U. Grad. Sch. Banking, 1954; m. Vivian Anderson, Mar. 15, 1941; children—Susan, Michael, Matthew. Vice pres. Comml. Nat. Bank, Peoria, Ill., 1946-62; pres., dir. State Nat. Bank, Evanston,. Ill., 1962—; dir., mem. finance com. Washington Nat. Ins. Co.; dir. Washington Nat. Corp. Bd. assos. Northwestern U., 1963—. Served to lt. USNR, 1943-46. Rotarian. Clubs: University (Evanston); Bankers, Economic (Chgo.); Westmoreland Country (Wilmette, Ill.). Home: 9401 Hamlin Av Evanston IL 60203 Office: 1603 Orrington Av Evanston IL 60204

HUMPHREY, ROBERT LEE, business cons.; b. Muskogee, Okla., Mar. 9, 1907; s. Walter Glenn and Pearl Rosamond (Hedges) H.; student U. Colo., 1925-26, U. Okla., 1927- 28; m. Irene Elizabeth Utley, Jan. 25, 1930; children—Robert Lee, Gary Knight. Sales promotion dir. Dallas News, 1930-35; nat. advt. mgr. Ft. Worth Press, 1935-37; dir. sports and entertainment Pan Am. Expo, Dallas, 1937; sales promotion dir. Houston Chronicle, 1937-39; v.p., gen. mgr. Assoc. Pubs., Inc., Dallas, 1939-45; mgr. sales personnel oilwell supply div. U.S. Steel, New Orleans, Houston, Dallas, 1946-51; nat. dir. pub. affairs N.A.M., Washington, N.Y.C., 1951-63; pres. Bus.-Industry Polit. Action Com., N.Y.C., 1963—; legislative, govt. relations cons. Mem. Am. Olympic Com., 1935-37; organizer, dir. first Pan Am. Games, 1937; pres. S.W. Amateur Athletic Union; dir., mem. exec. com. Nat. Amateur Athletic Union. Served from lt. to lt. col., USAAF, 1942-46. Episcopalian. Clubs: Dallas Athletic; New Orleans Country, Petroleum (New Orleans); Cornell, Knollwood Country, Rockefeller Center (N.Y.C.); Washington Golf and Country (Va.); International (Washington); Milbrook Country (Greenwich, Conn.). Home: 203 James Thurber Ct Falls Church VA 22046 Office: 1747 Pennsylvania Av NW Washington DC 20006

HUMPHREY, STANLEY MAGOUN, mgmt. cons.; b. Swampscott, Mass., May 30, 1906; s. Clarence B. and Bessie (Stanley) H.; B.S., Mass. Inst. Tech., 1928; m. Anne C. Bauer, Sept. 30, 1934; children—Stanley C., Lynne B. Engr., Sylvania Electric Products, Salem, Mass., Emporium, Pa., 1928-34; v.p. engring. Taylor Winfield Corp., Warren, O., 1934-44; partner Booz, Allen & Hamilton, 1944—, now corporate staff. Mem. I.E.E.E., Am. Soc. M.E. Address: Booz Allen & Hamilton 135 S LaSalle St Chicago IL 60603

HUMPHREY, WAYMAN EARL, gas co. exec.; b. Dixon, Mo., Nov. 1, 1911; s. Eather Arwine and Ollie (Elkins) H.; grad. Okla. Sch. Accountancy, Law and Finance, 1939; m. Hallie Elizabeth Miller, Aug. 26, 1934; children—Sandra (Mrs. Ray Garnett Collins III), Linda (Mrs. Robert Luther Martin). With Okla. Natural Gas. Co., Tulsa, 1941—, dist. v.p., Shawnee, 1959-64, financial v.p., 1964- 67, exec. v.p., 1967—, also dir.; dir. Republic Nat. Bank. Mem. Tulsa Area Health and Hosp. Planning Council, 1967—. Bd. dirs. Tulsa Council Camp Fire Girls; trustee, mem. exec. com. Okla. Pub. Expenditures Council. Mem. Ind. Petroleum Assn. Am., Ind. Natural Gas Assn. Am., Am., So. gas assns., Okla. (v.p., dir., mem. exec. com.), Tulsa, Oklahoma City chambers commerce. Democrat. Episcopalian. Clubs: Tulsa, Plaza, Summit, Southern Hills Country (Tulsa); Tower (Oklahoma City). Home: 2630 E 65th Pl Tulsa OK 74105 Office: 624 S Boston Av Tulsa OK 74119

HUMPHREY, WILLIAM, novelist. Author: Home from the Hill, 1958; the Ordways, 1965; Time and Place, 1968; Spawning Run, 1970. Address: care Alfred A Knopf Inc 201 E 50th New York City NY 10022*

HUMPHREY, WILLIAM GREY, textile co. exec.; b. Clark, N.C., July 1, 1922; s. Jay Lee and Rose (Pittman) H.; B.S. in Textiles, N.C. State Coll., 1952; m. Maclyn Mackie, Aug. 30, 1950; children—MacLyn, Monta, William Grey. With Deering Milliken, Inc., 1951—, pres. fine goods mfg. div., 1962—; v.p. Pacolet Industries, Inc., Pacolet Mills, S.C., 1962-63, exec. v.p., 1963- 64, pres., 1964—, also dir.; pres., dir. Cotton Blossom Corp., Spartanburg, S.C.; pres. Gayley Rico Co., P.R.; v.p. Gayley Wycombe Corp. (Pai); v.p., treas. Clemson Industries, Marietta, S.C.; v.p., treas., dir. Lockhart Power Co.; dir. Magnolia Industries, Inc., Piedmont Motor Lines, Inc., Deering Milliken Research Corp., Deering Milliken Service Corp., Peoples Nat. Bank (Greenville, S.C.). Co- chmn. textile div. Greenville County United Fund Campaign, 1963. Mem. Am. Textile Mfrs. Inst., S.C. Textile Mfrs. Inst. (dir.). Baptist. Clubs: Poinsett, Green Valley Country (Greenville); Piedmont, Spartanburg Country (Spartanburg); Union League (N.Y.C.). Home: 1305 Pinecrest Rd Spartanburg SC 29302 Office: PO Box 1926 Spartanburg SC 29301

HUMPHREY, WILLIAM RIVERIUS, Jr., food co. exec.; b. Greenwood, Miss., July 18, 1915; s. William Riverius and Susan (Baird) H.; B.A., Yale 1936; postgrad. Advanced Mgmt. Program, Harvard, 1957; m. Marjorie Ann Goodwin, Nov. 5, 1955; childrenAnn, William Riverius III, Andrew, Kathryn. With Gen. Mills, Inc., Mpls., 1936-, asst. mgr. flour div., 1961-62, gen. mgr. flour div., 1962-, v.p., 1962-. Mem. exec. com. for Minn., Upper Midwest Research and Devel. Council. Bd. dirs. United Fund Hennepin County, Highcroft Sch. Served to capt. AUS, 1941-45. Mem. Millers Nat. Fedn. (dir., exec. com.), Delta Kappa Epsilon. Republican. Episcopalian. Clubs: Minneapolis; Woodhill (Wayzata). Home: 425 Highcroft Rd Wayzata MN 55391 Office: 9200 Wayzata Blvd Minneapolis MN 55440

HUMPHREYS, CECIL CLARENCE, univ. pres.; b. Paris, Tenn., May 17, 1914; s. Robert Lee and Cecil Clara (Huggins) H.; B.S., M.A., U. Tenn.; Ph.D., N.Y.U., 1957; LL.D., Southwestern at Memphis, 1966; m. Florence Van Natta, Jan. 22, 1949; children—Robert Hunter, Cecil Clarence. Mem. faculty Memphis State U., 1937-41, 47—, dir. Grad. Sch., 1959-60, pres., 1960—; dir. Union Planters Nat. Bank; spl. agt. FBI, 1942-44, 46-47. Mem. bd. Memphis and Mid-South Med. Center; commr. Goodwyn Inst.; Tenn. chmn. Nat. Found., 1966-68. Served to lt. (j.g.) USNR, 1944-46. Recipient Americanism award Nat. Football Hall of Fame, 1966. Mem. Internat. Assn. U. Presidents, Am. Legion, Mil. Order World Wars, Memphis Area C. of C. (dir.), Sigma Chi. Presbyn. (deacon). Clubs: University (Memphis), Rotary. Home: 4035 Grandview Av Memphis TN 38111

HUMPHREYS, EDWIN WARD, tobacco co. exec.; b. Henderson, Ky., July 17, 1910; s. Llewelyn and Vashti (Ward) H.; B.S. in Metall. Engring., U. Ky., 1932; m. Susan Gaines Grover, Sept. 22, 1934; childrenEleanor (Mrs. Robert E. Milward), Edwina (Mrs. Audry W. Simmons, Jr.). Foreman in tobacco processing and maintenance, Lexington, Ky., Wilson, N.C., 1934-37; tobacco buyer, 1938-45; with Universal Leaf Tobacco Co. and subsidiaries, 1956-, v.p. charge operations, 1955-65, sr. v.p., 1966-, also dir.; v.p. subsidiary Southwestern Tobacco Co.; dir. Greeneville Redrying Co., Southwestern Tobacco Co., Rudolph Hach Co. Recipient Centennial Alumni award U. Ky., 1965. Mem. Tobacco Assn. U.S. (pres. 1951-53, dir.), Phi Delta Theta. Presbyn. (elder). Clubs: Jiggers; Idle Hour Country (Lexington); Country of Va., Commonwealth, Rotunda (Richmond). Home: RFD 3 Georgetown KY 40324 Office: 201 S 3d St Richmond VA 23219

HUMPHREYS, GEORGE HOPPIN, II, surgeon; b. N.Y.C., Nov. 22, 1903; s. John S. and Marie Mitchell (Champney) H.; B.A., Harvard, 1925, M. D., 1929; D.M.S., Columbia, 1935; m. Edith Sturgis, 1930; children—John Sanford, Cornelia, Edith Barnes. Intern, Presbyn. Hosp., N.Y.C., 1930-32; fellow, 1932-35; asst. surgery, Coll. Phys. and Surg., Columbia, 1932-34, instr. surgery, 1934- 40, asst. prof. clin. surgery, 1940-46, asst. dean, 1944-46, Valentine Mott prof. surgery, 1946-69, emeritus, 1969—; attending surgeon Presbyn. Hosp., 1946-69, dir. surg. service, 1946-69, cons., 1969—; côns. surgeon Vassar Bros. Hosp., Poughkeepsie, N.Y., 1948, Harlem, St. Luke's hosps. N.Y.C. Trustee Mary Imogene Bassett Hosp., Cooperstown, N.Y. Diplomate Am. Bd. Surgery; founder mem. Am. Bd. Thoracic Surgery. Fellow A.C.S.; mem. N.Y. Soc. Thoracic Surgery, Inter-Soc. Surgery, Am., Internat. cardio-vascular socs., A.O. Whipple Soc., Am. Coll. Chest Physicians, Soc. U. Surgeons, Am. Assn. Thoracic Surgery, Harvey Soc., N.Y. Acad. Medicine, A.M.A., N.Y., Pan Pacific, Am. surg. socs., Soc. Clin. Surgery, Practitioners Soc., Am. Heart Assn., Halsted Soc., Am. Acad. Pediatrics. Contbr. articles to med. jours. Home: 1211 Park Av New York City NY 10028 Office: 161 Ft Washington Av New York City NY 10032

HUMPHREYS, HENRY SIGURD, organist, composer, music critic; b. Vienna, Austria, Nov. 27, 1909; (father U.S. citizen); s. J. Mitchell and Johanna (Rauscher) H.; Mus.B., Coll. Music, Cin., 1941, Mus.M., 1945; A.M. in German Lit., U. Cin., 1948; m. Mary Sue Johston, June 33, 1933; children—Karen Patricia (Mrs. Donald Sprague). Prof. music theory Coll. Music, Cin., 1946-51; music and drama critic Cin. Times-Star, 1951-58, Cath. Telegraph, Cin., 1958-61; music editor Cin. Enquirer, 1962-70; asso. prof. composition, organ and theory, composer-in-residence Coll. Mt. St. Joseph, Cin., 1964—; founder, dir. Don Bosco Collegiate Inst., Cin., 1961-62. Mem. A.S.C.A.P., Musicians Union, Music Critics Assn. Am. (charter), Am. Guild Organists, Cordelian Soc., Jongleurs de Dieu (founder). Composer: (opera) Mayerling, 1957; (tone poem) Waste Land, 1958. Editor: Civil War Song Anthology, 1961; (cantata) Miracle at Grodno, 1965; (with Cecil Hale (musical) Audubon, or Wings Over the Wilderness, 1966; (opera) Joan of Arc at Reims, 1967; Prometheus of the Andes, 1970. Home: 5661 Delhi Rd Cincinnati OH 45238 Office: Coll Mt St Joseph Cincinnati OH 45051

HUMPHREYS, HERBERT, mfr. edible oil products; b. Memphis, Dec. 29, 1907; s. Hugh and Elise Flournoy (Selden) H.; student Ga. Inst. Tech., 1926-27, Southwestern U., 1927-28; children by previous marriageHugh, Lyn S., Gelles, Lele H. Weaver; m. 2d, Wilda M. Mathis, Jan. 10, 1946; 1 son, Herbert. Co- founder Hum Ko Co., Memphis, 1930, pres., 1930-53; company merged with Nat. Dairy Products Corp., 1953, now chmn. div.. dir. corp.; dir. First Nat. Bank, Memphis, Ill. Central Railroad, Chgo., Ellis-Bagwell Drug Co., Memphis, Downtowner Corp., Memphis. Trustee Crippled Childrens Hosp., Memphis; vice chmn. trustees Memphis U. Sch. Served to lt. comdr. USNR, 1942-45. Episcopalian (vestry). Clubs: Hunt and Polo, Memphis Country, University, Tennessee, Summit (Memphis); University (Washington); Gulf Stream (Fla.) Bath and Tennis; Key Largo (Fla.) Anglers; Delray Beach (Fla.) Yacht. Home: 6058 Shady Grove Rd Memphis TN 38117 Office: Sterick Bldg Memphis TN 38103

HUMPHREYS, JAMES W., former air force officer, surgeon, assn. exec.; b. Fredericksburg, Va., May 28, 1915; s. James William and Josephine (Rooks) H.; B.S. in Chem. Engring., Va. Mil. Inst., 1935; M.D., Med. Coll. Va., 1939; M.S., U. Colo., 1951; m. Josephine Bailey, Aug. 18, 1943; children—Jean Elizabeth, Josephine III. Intern, surg. resident Cin. Gen. Hosp.; commd. 1st lt. M.C., U.S. Army, 1940, advanced through grades to maj. gen. USAF, 1965; comdr. USAF Hosp., Wright-Patterson AFB, O., 1957-60, Wilford Hall USAF Hosp., San Antonio, 1960-65, surgeon, chief med. spltys., dir. land-based med. recovery facilities Project Mercury, 1960-63; cons. bioastronautics Project Gemini, 1964-65; asst. dir. for pub. health U.S. AID, Vietnam, 1965-67; dir. space medicine Manned Space Flight, Hdqrs. NASA, 1967-70, dir. life scis., 1970-71; sec.-treas. Am. Bd. Surgery, Phila., 1971—. Decorated D.S.M. with oak leaf cluster, Legion of Merit with oak leaf cluster, Air medal with oak leaf cluster (U.S.); Order of Merit (Iran); Nat. Order, Cross of Valor with palm, Medal of Honor, Mil. Civil Action medal (Vietnam); Order Sikathuna (Philippines); Missione Medico Gold medal (Milan, Italy); recipient NASA medal for exceptional sci. achievement. Boynton award Am. Astronautical Soc. Diplomate Am. Bd. Surgery. Fellow A.C.S., Aerospace Med. Assn. (Bauer award), Am. Coll. Chest Physicians; mem. Assn. Mil. Surgeons U.S., A.M.A., Soc. Air Force Clin. Surgeons, Soc. Air Force Flight Surgeons, Pan Am. Med. Assn., Southwestern Surg. Congress, Alpha Omega Alpha. Home: 680 Harwick Rd Strafford PA 19087 Office: Am Bd Surgery 1617 John F Kennedy Blvd Philadelphia PA 19102

HUMPHREYS, JOHN ROSS, banker; b. Jefferson, Tex., July 30, 1901; s. Charles and Leona (Smith) H.; student pub. schs., corr. univ. courses; m. Rose Syble Rogers, Apr. 25, 1921; 1 son, John Ross. From clk. to bank officer, various banks in Okla., 1919-30; automobile sales bus. and hotel operator, Okla., 1930- 35; auditor Halsted Exchange Nat. Bank, Chgo., 1935-39; asst. cashier Central Nat. Bank, Chgo., 1939-47, pres., 1967, now hon. chmn., dir. Mem. Chgo. Land Clearance Commn., 1953—, chmn., 1954—. Mem. Ill. Bankers Assn. (pres. Chgo. 1962-63). Clubs: Medinah Country; Union League (Chgo.). Home: 5510 Sheridan Rd Chicago IL 60640 Office: 728 Roosevelt Rd Chicago IL 60607

HUMPHREYS, LLOYD GIRTON, research psychologist; b. Lorane, Ore., Dec. 12, 1913; s. John Pryor and Gertrude (Stephenson) H.; B.S., U. Ore., 1935; M.A., Ind. U., 1936; Ph.D., Stanford, 1938; m. Dorothy Jane Windes, Dec. 27, 1937; children—John Daniel, Michael Stephenson, Margaret Anne, Susan Jeanne. Instr., Northwestern U., 1939-42, asst. prof., 1945-46; asso. prof. U. Wash., 1946-48; asso. prof. Stanford, 1948-51; research psychologist USAF, San Antonio, 1951-57; prof. U. Ill., Urbana, 1957-70, chmn. dept. psychology, 1959-69; asst. dir. for edn. NSF, Washington, 1970—. Served to capt. USAAF, 1942-45. Mem. A.A.A.S. (chmn. sect. I, v.p. 1963), Am. Psychol. Assn. (pres. div. mil. psychology 1957-58, div. evaluation and measurement, 1960-61), Psychometric Soc. (pres. 1959-60), Soc. Exptl. Psychologists, Psychonomic Soc. (a founder, chmn. governing bd. 1962-63), Phi Beta Kappa, Sigma Xi, Beta Gamma Sigma, Phi Delta Kappa, Delta Upsilon. Initiated profl. curriculum and degree in clin. psychology, 1967. Editor Psychol. Bull., 1964-68, Am. Jour. Psychology, 1968—. Home: 12101 Glen Mill Rd Potomac MD 20640 Office: Nat Sci Found Washington DC 20550

HUMPHREYS, MABEL GWENETH, educator; b. Vancouver, B.C., Can., Oct. 22, 1911; d. Richard and Mabel Jane (Thomas) H.; B.A., U. B.C., 1932; A.M., Smith Coll., 1933; Ph.D., U. Chgo., 1935. Came to U.S., 1932, naturalized, 1941. Instr. math., physics Mt. St. Scholastica Coll., Atchison, Kan., 1935-36; instr. math. Newcomb Coll., Tulane U., New Orleans, 1936-41, asst. prof., 1941-49; asso. prof. math. Randolph-Macon Woman's Coll., 1949-50, became prof., chmn. dept., 1950, later Larew prof. math. Mem. Am. Math. Soc., Math. Assn. Am., Can. Math. Congress, Am. Assn. U. Profs., Am. Assn. U. Women, Sigma Xi. ‡

HUMPHREYS, PRISCILLA COBB (Mrs. Irvin Wendell Humphreys), Republican nat. committeewoman; b. Huntington, W.Va., Apr. 28, 1912; d. James Edward and Bertie Mae (Esque) Cobb; student Marshall U., 1930-33; m. Irvin Wendell Humphreys, Feb. 9, 1936; childrenDavid Wendell, Bertie Anne, John Edward. Troop leader Girl Scouts Am., 1952-56; pres. Alpha Xi Delta Mother's Club, 1962; vice chmn., bd. dirs. art dept. Huntington Woman's Club. Second v.p. Cabell Country Republican Woman's Club, 1958-60, pres., 1960-62; vice chmn., committeewoman at large Cabell County Rep. Exec. Com., 1963-, mem. finance com., 1965; Rep. nat. committeewoman for W.Va., 1964-; bd. dirs. Rep. Youth Tng. Camp, 1965. Bd. dirs. local YWCA. Mem. W.Va. Wholesalers Aux. (pres.). Baptist. Address: 1546 16th St Huntington WV 25701

HUMPHREYS, ROBERT LEE, advt. agy. exec.; b. Burbank, Cal., Dec. 30, 1924; s. Robert Elmer and Nancy Lucille (Gum) H.; B.S., U. Cal., Los Angeles, 1947; m. Marie Dorthea Wilkinson; children-Dina Lizette, Gia Monique. Formerly merchandising rep. for Life mag., Los Angeles: promotion mgr. Fortune mag., N.Y.C., Time, Inc.. 1947-50; copywriter Batten, Barton, Durstine & Osborne, Los Angeles, 1950-51; account exec., account supr. Foote, Cone & Belding, Los Angeles, 1951-56, v.p., account group mgr., 1956-61; exec. v.p. charge Western operations, dir. Grey Advt., Inc., Los Angeles, 1962—. Chmn. fund raising com. YMCA, 1958-63; mem. Los Angeles County Sheriffs Pub. Relations Adv. Group, 1959-; mem. World Affairs Council, 1962—. Vice chmn. bd. trustees U. Cal. Los Angeles Found. Served to lt. (j.g.) USNR, 1943-46. Mem. Am. Assn. Advt. Agys. (gov.), Bel Air Assn., Inst. Fine Arts, Los Angeles Copy Club (past pres.), Phi Gamma Delta (v.p.). Clubs: Bel Air Country, California, Sierra. Home: 10606 Chalon Rd Los Angeles CA 90024. Office: 3435 Wilshire Blvd Los Angeles CA 90005

HUMPHREYS, WARD COOK, mfg. co. exec.; b. Stockton, Cal., Mar. 31, 1909; s. Charles Ward and Mary Adelaide (Woodbridge) H.; grad. Western Sch. Bus., 1924; m. June Elizabeth Coles, July 3, 1939. With Kaiser Corp., and affiliates, 1942- , v.p. Kaiser Bauxite Co., 1961-, v.p. charge govt. relations Kaiser Industries Corp., 1962-, v.p. Kaiser Services, Inc., 1962-; v.p., dir. Queensland Alumina Security Corp., 1965-, Kaiser Aluminum & Chem. Internat. Co., 1965-. Home: 7304 Marbury Rd Bethesda MD 20014 Office: 900 17th St NW Washington DC 20004

HUMPHRIES, JACK WOOD, univ. adminstr.; b. Mabank, Tex., Sept. 9, 1936; s. Ode Robert and Lila (Wood) H.; A.A., Henderson County Jr. Coll., 1956; B.A., Baylor U., 1958, M.A., 1962; Ph.D., Tex. A. and M. U., 1969; m. Sharon Ann Ridenhour, Jan. 31, 1959; children—Jeffery Marshall, Joel Mark, Jonathan Maury. Tchr., LaVega High Sch., Waco, Tex., 1958-60; instr. history, chmn. dept. Alvin (Tex.) Jr. Coll., 1960-65; asst. dir. admissions, instr. history Sam Houston State U., Huntsville, Tex., 1965-66, dean Sch. Humanities, 1969-71, v.p. univ. affairs, 1971—; adminstrv. asst. to dean Coll. Liberal Arts, Tex. A. and M. U., 1966-69; asso. dir., mem. state adv. com. Summer Seminar on Acad. Adminstrn., Assn. Tex. Colls. and Univs., Austin, 1967—. Mem. Am. Assn. Higher Edn., Nat. Soc. Study Edn., Am. Studies Assn., Phi Delta Kappa, Phi Theta Kappa. Mem. Christian Ch. Rotarian. Club: Forest Hills (Huntsville). Editor: The Academic Administrator, 1967; The Academic Administrator, 1968; Powers and Responsibilities in Academic Governance, 1969. Home: 204 Pine Valley Huntsville TX 77340

HUMPHRY, JAMES, III, librarian, bus. exec.; b. Springfield, Mass., July 21, 1916; s. James and Elizabeth Lucy (Ames) H.; A.B., Harvard, 1939; M.S., Columbia, 1941; m. Priscilla Eaton, Dec. 26, 1942; children—Susan (Mrs. Michael C. Fitch), Elizabeth Ames. Reference asst. N.Y. Pub. Library, 1939-41, 46, chief map div., 1946; librarian, prof. bibliography Colby Coll., bus. mgr. Coll. Press, 1947-57; chief librarian Met. Mus. Art, 1957-68; v.p. H.W. Wilson Co., Bronx, 1968—, also dir., 1965—. Cons. Am. Heritage, 1965-68, John Wiley & Sons, 1966—; lectr. Columbia Sch. Library Service, 1967-68; library cons. Council Advancement Small Colls., 1956; coordinator Me. Library Assn. for A.L.A. sponsored Library Services bill, 1948-49, 55-57; nat. bd. Library Presdl. Papers, 1967-69; adminstr. grants-in-aid program N.Y. State Council Arts, 1967-68; trustee, chmn. adv. com. Archives Am. Art, 1967—; mem. fine arts vis. com. Harvard, 1967—; mem. adv. council St. John's U. Congress for Librarians, 1963-67. Bd. dirs. Huguenot YMCA; trustee N.Y. Met. Reference and Research Library Agy., 1967—. Served with AUS, 1942-46, as maj., 1951-54; lt. col. Res. Mem. A.L.A. (councilor 1959-63, 67-69, chmn. com. on Wilson index reference services div. 1959-65, mem. subscription books com. 1963-66), Met. Mus. Art Employees Assn. (pres. 1961-63, gov. 1958-66), Res. Officers Assn. U.S., Me. Library Assn. (pres. 1955-56), Am. Assn. Museums (chmn. library group), Archons of Colophon (convener 1963-65), N.Y. Library Assn. (cons.), Spl. Libraries Assn. (chpt. vice chmn., chmn. mus. group 1962-64, N.Y. conf. chmn. 1967), Assn. Coll. and Research Libraries (pres., dir. 1966-69), Internat. Council Museums (corr.). Clubs: Grolier; N.Y. Library (council 1959-67, pres. 1965-66). Compiler: Library of Edwin Arlington Robinson, 1950. Editor: (with Carl J. Weber) Fitzgerald's Rubaiyat, 1959. Contbr. articles to mags., jours. Home: 10 Ridge Rd New Rochelle NY 10804 Office: 950 University Av Bronx NY 10452

HUMPHRY, JOHN AMES, librarian; b. Springfield, Mass., July 21 1916 s. James and Elizabeth (Ames) H.; A.B. in Econs., Harvard, 1939, postgrad. Grad. Sch. Arts and Scis., 1942-43; B.S. in L.S., Columbia, 1941; m. Elizabeth Daniell, Sept. 13, 1941; childrenJonathan Ames, Keith Daniell. Gen. asst. Harvard Coll. Library, 1939-40, 41-44; part-time gen. asst. N.Y. Pub. Library, 1940-41; field service cons. OSRD, Office Chief Naval Operations, 1944-46; dir. book processing Enoch Pratt Free Library, Balt., 1946-48; dir. City Library, Springfield, Mass., 1948-64; exec. dir. Springfield Library and Museums Assn., 1960-64; dir. Bklyn. Pub. Library, 1964-67; state librarian, asst. commr. libraries N.Y. State Dept. Edn., 1967—. Dir. Forest Press, Inc. Spl. cons. operations evaluation group Office Chief Naval Operations, Dept. Def., 1951-53; asso. pub. library adminstrn. Simmons Coll. Sch. Library Sci., 1952-54; mem. Mass. Library Devel. Com., 1957-59, chmn., 1959; mem. Mass. Bd. Library Commrs., 1957-64; mem. edn. com. Citizens Action Commn. of Springfield, 1958-62; vis. lectr. Am. Internat. Coll., 1959-61; dir. Brown U. study to coordinate library service in R.I. Incorporator, United Fund Greater Springfield Inc.; adv. bd. Springfield Goodwill Industries; adv. bd. Springfield Motion Picture Council, 1950-64; mem. adv. council Springfield Coll. Community Tensions Center, 1958-63; sec.-treas. Phillips Lecture Fund Com., 1956-64; mem. adv. com. on sch. library standards N.Y. State Edn. Dept., 1966—; adv. council Office Urban Library Research, Wayne State U. Trustee N.Y. Met. Reference and Research Library Agy. Mem. A.L.A. (chmn. membership com. 1958-64, councilor 1960-64), New Eng. (bd. 1953-54), Mass. (exec. bd. 1949-63, pres. 1957- 58), N.Y (mem. legislative com. 1964) library assns., Am. Assn. State Libraries (pres. 1968-69), Council Library Resources (dir.), UN Assn., (librarian's adv. council 1948-50), Am. Econ. Assn., New Eng. Hist. and Geneal. Soc., World Affairs Council Conn. Valley (past treas.). Clubs: Automobile, Western Mass. Library, Melvil Dui Chowder and Marching Assn., N.Y. Library, Archons of Colophon (N.Y.C.); Harvard (Springfield). Home: 2316 Rosendale Rd Schenectady NY 12309 Office: State Edn Dept Albany NY 12224

HUMPHRYS, CHARLES MEREVALE, financial exec.; b. Baxterly, Eng., Jan. 21, 1921; s. Percy and Helen (Minchiner) H.; student Lancing Coll., 1934-38. Sec., treas., dir. Kelly Douglas & Co., Ltd., Vancouver, B.C., Can., 1966-. Served with RCAF, 1939-45. Mem. Financial Execs. Inst., Canadian Chartered Accountants Inst. Home: 6187 McCleery St Vancouver 13 British Columbia Canada Office: Box 3051 Vancouver British Columbia Canada

HUND, JAMES MADDEN, educator; b. Detroit, Apr. 27 1922 s. Henry E. and Emma L. (Madden) H.; student Stanford, 1940-41; A.B., Amherst Coll., 1943; M.A. in Econs., Princeton, 1952, Ph.D., 1954; m. Nancy Ione Black, June 10, 1950 (dec. Apr. 1967); children—Marcia Ione, Gretchen Elizabeth; m. 2d, Barbara M. Roberts, June 6, 1969. Asso. with Reo Motors, Inc., 1946-50; mem. faculty Clark U., 1954-57; mem. faculty Emory U., 1957—, prof. bus. adminstrn., 1961—, dean Grad. Sch. Bus., 1965-68. Mem. N.Y. Met. Regional Study, 1957-58. Served as officer USNR, 1944-46. Mem. Am., So. econ. assns., Acad. Mgmt., Chi Psi. Methodist. Author articles, contbr. books. Home: 1535 Victoria Falls Dr NE Atlanta GA 30329

HUNDLEY, JAMES MANSON, assn. exec.; b. Summitville, Ind., Apr. 17, 1915; s. Frank Martin and Mabelle Moselene (Johnson) H.; B.S., Ind. U., 1937, M.D. (McLanden research fellow), 1940; m. Grethel Ann Hendricks, Apr. 19, 1940; children—Phyllis, Marjorie, June, Joyce, Frank. Intern, Marine Hosp., N.Y.C., 1940-41; officer USPHS, 1941-66, dist. health officer Ind. Bd. Health, 1941-42, bubonic plague control, San Francisco, Tacoma, Western states, 1942-43, nutrition research NIH, 1944, med. officer USCG and PTO, 1944-45; with NIH, 1945-56, chief nutrition sect., 1948-50, chief lab. biochemistry and nutrition, 1950-53, chief lab. research Nat. Inst. Arthritis and Metabolic Diseases, Bethesda, Md., 1953-56; cons. nutrition NSRB, 1950-51, FCDA, 1951-56; FAO nutrition adviser to UNICEF, 1956-58; spl. asst. internat. affairs NIH, 1958-59; asst. Surgeon Gen. USPHS, 1960-66; exec. dir. Inst. Med. Scis., Presbyn. Med. Center, San Francisco, 1966-68; exec. dir. Am. Heart Assn., N.Y.C., 1968—. Recipient Fleming award Washington C. of C., 1954. Fellow Am. Pub. Health Assn.; mem. Am. Dietetic Assn., Am. Inst. Nutrition, A.A.A.S., N.Y., Wash. acads. scis., Sigma Xi, Alpha Omega Alpha. Asso. editor Nutrition Rev., 1948-50. Contbr. articles to profl. jours. Home: 91 Akbar Rd Stamford CT 06902 Office: 44 E 23d St New York City NY 10010

HUNDLEY, JOHN ROBINSON, Jr., steel co. exec.; b. St. Louis, Jan. 29, 1917; s. John Robinson and Emily (Shewell) H.; B.Sc. in Bus. Adminstrn., Washington U., St. Louis, 1939; m. Shirley Conrad, May 2, 1941; children—John Robinson III, Nancy Conrad (now Mrs. William F. Hecker), Stephen Thomas. Asst. v.p. Stouffer Corp., 1945-47; personnel dir. Owens-Ill. Glass Co., 1939-42; dir. indsl. relations Granite City Steel Co. (Ill.), 1947-63, v.p., 1963- -; dir. Cemrel, Inc. Mem. Ill. Gov.'s Com. on Unemployment, 1961; pub. mem. Ill. Commn. Aged and Aging, 1958-62; adv. com. Mo. Manpower Tng. and Devel. Act, 1962—; chmn. Civil Service Commn. Met. Sewer Dist. St. Louis and St. Louis County; mem. citizens adv. com. Ill. State Bd. Higher Edn. chmn. Tri Cities United Fund., 1964-65. Bd. dirs. Washington U., 1958-61, Works Opportunities Unltd.; adv. bd. So. Ill. U. Served to col. USAAF, World War II. Decorated Air medal; recipient spl. merit award for outstanding community service St. Louis Indsl. Relations Club, 1959. Mem. Am. Iron and Steel Inst., Indsl. Relations Club St. Louis (past pres.), Ill. C. of C., Newcomen Soc. Presbyn. (elder). Clubs: Mo. Athletic, Old Warson Country. Home: 10 Roan Lane St Louis MO 63124 Office: Granite City Steel Co Granite City IL 62040

HUNDLEY, JOHN WALKER, found. exec.; b. Highstown, N.J., July 4, 1899; s. H. Rhodes and Mabel Parker (Lewis) H.; student Cornell U., 1917-18; Ph.B., Denison U., 1919; m. Eleanor Rothschild, Mar. 24, 1932; 1 dau., Sally Lewis (Mrs. Robert Alan Bear). Asst. service dir. Oneida Truck Co., Green Bay, Wis., 1919- 21; salesman No. Bond & Mortgage Co., Green Bay, 1921-22; baritone with Am. Opera Co., 1922-23; appeared in Broadway mus. prodns. Little Jesse James, Merry, Merry, Just Fancy, Just a Minute, Polly, Spring Is Here, Heads Up, Walk a Little Faster, 1924-34; gen. mgr., advt. mgr. Secrets of Smartness-Corr. Sch. Course for Women, 1935-38; network announcer, producer-writer, asst. dir. broadcasts-short wave dept. CBS Radio, 1938-48; charge day-time programming, mgr. network program services, mgr. client relations-network operations, mgr. sales devel. prodn. sales, editor program practices CBS-TV, 1948-65; pres. John Walker Hundley Enterprises, cons., adv., services, N.Y.C., 1965-66; exec. dir. Belle W. Baruch Found., N.Y.C., 1966-69; dir. Found. Adv. Services, Inc., 1970—; cons. Catalyst for Environmental Quality mag.; mem. environmental edn. adv. bd. Doubleday & Co., Inc. Mem. nat. exec. bd. Muscular Dystrophy Assn. Am. Bd. dirs., v.p. Percy Williams Home. Recipient citations Nat. Assn. Mental Health, 1952, Nat. Conf. Christians and Jews, 1951, Crusade for Freedom, 1950, Community Chest Am., 1950, Muscular Dystrophy Assn. Am., 1959-61, Denison U. Alumni citation, 1955. Mem. N.Y. County Grand Jury Assn., Beta Theta Pi, Phi Mu Alpha, Sinfonia. Clubs: Lambs (bd. dirs.), Players (N.Y.C.). Home: 168 E 74th St New York City NY 10021 Office: 274 Madison Av New York City NY 10016

HUNDLEY, KERMIT EDWIN, banker; b. Charleston, W.Va., June 20, 1925; s. Roy and Gladys (Jeffrey) H.; B.S. cum laude, Morris Harvey Coll., 1949; LL.B. magna cum laude, Washington and Lee U., 1953; m. Rosa Lee Nicely, Nov. 27, 1947; children-Patrick Lee, Carol Beth. Asst. trust officer Charleston Nat. Bank (W.Va.), 1950-56; sr. v.p., exec. trust officer Houston Bank & Trust Co., 1956-68; vice chmn. bd., chief exec. officer Citizens Bank & Trust Co., Park Ridge, Ill., 1968—; dir. Royal Nat. Bank, N.Y.C.; instr. S.W. Grad. Sch. Banking. Served with USAAF, 1948-49. Mem. Am. Bar Assn., State Bar W.Va., Houston Financial Analysts Soc., Houston Bus. and Estate Planning Council (pres.), Corp. Fiduciary Assn., Kanawha Valley Accountants Assn., Phi Beta Kappa, Order of Coif. . Author articles.

HUNEYCUTT, MAEBURN BRUCE, univ. dean; B.A., U. N.C., 1946, M.A., 1949, Ph.D., 1956. Dean Coll. Liberal Arts, U. Miss. Office: Coll Liberal Arts U Miss University MS 38677*

HUNGATE, ROBERT EDWARD, bacteriologist, educator; b. Cheney, Wash., Mar. 2, 1906; s. Joseph W. and Winona (Terpening) H.; A.B., Stanford, 1929, Ph.D., 1935; m. Alice Wolcott, Feb. 3, 1933; children—Robert, Dan, Harriet. Instr. biology Stanford, 1930-35; instr. zoology U. Tex., 1935-38, asst. prof. 1938-43, asso. prof., 1943-45; asso. prof. bacteriology Wash. State Coll., 1945- 49, prof. 1949-56; prof. bacteriology U. Cal. at Davis, 1956—, chmn., 1956-62, faculty research lectr., 1966. Vis. scientist Sheffield U., 1962-63; vis. investigator East Africa Vet. Research Orgn., Muguga, Kenya, summer 1957. Guggenheim fellow Cornell U., 1950; Fulbright fellow, New Zealand, 1969. Mem. Am. Soc. Microbiology (pres. 1970-71), Am. Soc. Protozoologists, Am. Soc. Naturalists, A.A.A.S., Am. Acad. Microbiology, Am. Inst. Biol. Scis., Sigma Xi, Phi Beta Kappa, Phi Kappa Phi, Phi Zeta. Author: The Rumen and Its Microbes, 1966. Contbr. numerous articles to profl. jours. Home: 801 Anderson Rd Davis CA 95616

HUNGATE, ROBERT PAUL, educator; b. Omaha, Oct. 8, 1925; s. Paul A. and Eva (Van Doren) H.; B.A., U. Wash., 1951; Ph.D., U. Cal. at Los Angeles, 1961; m. Marguerite L. Rouse, June 10, 1948; children—Deborah Ruth, Robert Paul, Philip Charles. Spl. agt. FBI, 1952-53; pvt. industry, 1953-55; asst. head exec. program U. Cal., Los Angeles, 1955-61; asso. prof. finance, dir. Bur. Bus. Research, San Diego State Coll., 1961-65; prof. finance, dean Sch. Bus. Adminstrn., Wis. State U., Oshkosh, 1965-69; prof. finance, dean Sch. Bus. Adminstrn., San Diego State Coll., 1969—. Cons. in field, 1961—. Served with Aus, 1943-46. Mem. Am. Finance Assn., Am. Econs. Assn., Phi Beta Kappa, Beta Gamma Sigma. Author: Interbusiness Financing, 1962; (with D.C. Bridenstine) Money and Finance, 1964. Home: 11401 Meadow Creek Rd El Cajon. CA 92020 Office: San Diego State Coll San Diego CA 92115

HUNGATE, WILLIAM LEONARD, congressman; b. Benton, Ill., Dec. 14, 1922; s. Leonard Wathen and Maude Irene (Williams) H.; A.B., U. Mo., 1943; LL.B., Harvard, 1948; LL.D., Culver-Stockton Coll., Canton, Mo., 1968; m. Dorothy N. Wilson, Apr. 13, 1944; chilren—William David, Margie Kay (Mrs. Branson L. Wood III). Admitted to Mo. bar, 1948, Ill. bar, 1949, U.S. Supreme Ct., 1960; gen. practice, Troy, Mo., 1948—; sr. partner firm Hungate and Grewach, 1956—; pros. atty. Lincoln County, Mo., 1951-55; spl. asst. Atty. Gen. of Mo., 1958-64; research adminstrn. criminal justice in U.S., Am. Bar Found., 1956; mem. 88th- 92d congresses, 9th Dist. Mo., mem. judiciary com., select com. on small bus., D.C. com. Mem. Ill., Fed., Mo., D.C. bar assns., Harvard Law Sch. Assn. Mo. (pres. 1962-64). Kiwanian (pres. Troy 1951, lt. gov. 1959). Home: 755 Cap-au-Gris Troy MO 63379 Office: House Office Bldg Washington DC 20515

HUNGERFORD, CYRUS COTTON, cartoonist; b. Manilla, Ind.; s. Addison J. and Florence (Cotton) H.; Dr. Arts, Washington and Jefferson Coll., 1945; m. Dorothy Evans, Nov. 29, 1966. Newspaper cartoonist Pitts. Sun, 1912-27, Pitts. Post-Gazette, 1927—; European cartoon news assignments, 1923, 37, 47, 53. Recipient Nat. Headliners award, 1947; Freedoms Found award, 1953; Lincoln Nat. Life Found. award, 1957; Pitts. Jr. C. of C. award, 1957; award for excellence in journalism Gov.'s Com. 100,000 Pennsylvanians, 1970. Hon. mem. Omicron Delta Kappa, Sigma Delta Chi. Club: University. Home: Bigelow Apts Bigelow Sq Pittsburgh PA 15219 Office: 50 Blvd of Allies Pittsburgh PA 15222

HUNGERFORD, HERBERT EUGENE, educator; b. Hartford, Conn., Oct. 3, 1918; s. Herbert Eugene and Doris (Emmons) H.; B.S. in Physics, Trinity Coll., Hartford, 1941; M.S. in Physics, U. Ala., 1949; Ph.D. in Nuclear Engring., Purdue U., 1964; part-time grad. student, U. Tenn., 1951-55, Wayne State U., 1956-61; m. Edythe Lugene Green, Nov. 4, 1949. Tchr. sci. Brent Sch., Baguio, P.I., 1941; prisoner of war, 1941-45; tchr. math. Choate Sch., 1945-46; head physics dept. Marion Mil. Inst., 1946-48; grad. instr. U. Ala., 1948-49; physicist Oak Ridge Nat. Lab., 1950-55; shielding specialist, head shielding and health physics sect. Atomic Power Devel. Assos., 1955-62; research asso. Purdue U., 1963-64, asso. prof., 1964—, prof. nuclear engring., 1968—; cons. in field. Recipient Presdl. citation Kiwanis Internat., 1970. Mem. Am. Nuclear Soc. (sec. shielding and dosimetry div. 1960-62, div. vice chmn. 1969-70, div. chmn. 1970-71), Am. Phys. Soc., Helath Physics Soc., Am. Assn. Physics Tchrs., Am. Soc. Engring. Edn., Sigma Xi, Sigma Pi Sigma. Author chpts. in books, articles. Inventor lattice model stochastic radiation transp.; pioneer use of serpentine and calcium borate as high temperature shield materials. Home: 7 Knoll Crest Ct Route 9 West Lafayette IN 47906 Office: Dept Nuclear Engring Purdue Univ Lafayette IN 47907

HUNGERFORD, RICHARD H., educator; b. Concord, Mich., Sept. 3, 1903; s. Harold H. and Eva (Tewksbury) H.; A.B., Albion (Mich.) Coll., 1927; A.M., U. Mich., 1931. With Detroit pub. schs. system, 1922-42, supr. spl. edn., 1939-42; dir. Bur. for Children with Retarded Mental Devel., N.Y.C., 1942-53; supt. Laconia (N.H.) State Sch., 1953- 60; exec. dir. Gulf Bend Center for Children and Youth, 1963-66; exec. dir. mental health-mental retardation services Diocese Galveston- Houston, 1966-68; vis. prof. spl. edn. Boston U., 1968-71; project dir. Work Opportunity Center, West Springfield, Mass., 1971—; originator program occupational edn. for mentally retarded. Mem. Am. Assn. on Mental Deficiency (former pres.). Co-founder (with Chris J. DeProspo) Occupational Education, 1943-50. Editor: Am. Jour. Mental Deficiency, 1948-59. Home: 32 Park Av West Springfield MA 01089 Office: 166 South Blvd West Springfield MA 01089

HUNKELE, JOHN J., motel exec.; b. Napoleon, N.D., Apr. 4, 1929; s. Leo and Stefina (Walter) H.; A.A., Bismarck Jr. Coll., 1954; B.A., Mich. State U., 1956; m. Phyllis R. Krzmarzick, June 18, 1954; children—Benita M., Barbara A., Lynn M., Patricia J., Lisa M., Jeanine S., John J., Jennifer S. Front office clk. Grand Pacific Hotel, Bismarck, N.D., 1947-48, front office clk., supr., 1952-54; resident mgr. Medea Hotel-Mineral Baths, Mt. Clemens, Mich., 1956; mgr. food dept. Sherman Hotel, Aberdeen, S.D., 1956-60; div. mgr. Prudential Ins. Co., 1960-62; innkeeper, gen. mgr. Holiday Inn, Bismarck, 1962—. Chmn. Tourist and Conv. Com. Bd.dirs. Old West Trail Found.; mem. lay adv. bd. St. Alexius Hosp., Bismarck. Served with USAF, 1948-52. Recipient Key Man award Aberdeen Jr. C. of C.; named Innkeeper of Year, Holiday Inn, Inc., 1969, Hall of Fame, Hospitality Mags., 1970. Mem. N.D. Food and Lodging Assn. (dir.), Bismarck Jr. Coll. Alumni Assn. (past pres.), Bismarck C. of C. (dir., exec. com.), N.D. Hotel and Motel Assn. (past pres.), D.A.V., Am. Legion, Sigma Pi Eta. Roman Catholic (pres. bd.). Elk, K.C. Home: 1006 N 5th St Bismarck ND 58501 Office: Holiday Inn East of Memorial Bridge Bismarck ND 58501

HUNKIN, WILLIAM JAMES II, constrn. co. exec.; b. Montgomery, Ala., Jan. 5 1920 s. Samuel Everett and Margaret (Perry) H.; grad. Manlius (N.Y.) Sch., 1939; C.E., Cornell U., 1943; m. Barbara Horner, Oct. 8, 1942; children—Margaret Ann (Mrs. J.D. Crow), Samuel Everett II, Elizabeth. With Hunkin-Conkey Conkey Constrn. Co., Cleve., 1945—, pres., 1958—; dir. Society Nat. Bank Cleve., Society Corp., Medusa Portland Cement Co.; adv. bd. Liberty Mut. Ins. Co. Mem. Ohio Republican Finance Com. Bd. dirs. Greater Cleve. Growth Bd., Fenn Found., Fenn Ednl. Found. Served to capt. USAAF, World War II. Decorated D.F.C., Air Medal with 8 clusters. Mem. The Beavers, The Moles, Soc. Am. Mil. Engrs. Clubs: Union, Tavern, Pepper Pike, Kirtland Country (Cleve.); Kitchi Gammi (Duluth); Cornell (N.Y.C.).‡

HUNLEY, H. MARTIN, Jr., lawyer; b. Gretna, La., June 22, 1918; B.A., La. State U., 1938; LL.B., Tulane U., 1947. Admitted to La. bar, 1947; mem. firm Lemle, Kelleher, Kohlmeyer, Matthews & Schumacher, New Orleans. Mem. Am., La., New Orleans bar assns., Internat. Assn. Ins. Counsel, Nat. Assn. Railroad Trial Counsel, Order of Coif, Phi Delta Phi. Editor-in-chief Tulane Law Rev., 1947. Office: 1800 Nat Bank Commerce Bldg New Orleans LA 70112*

HUNNEMAN, ROBERT INGLE, lawyer; b. Brookline, Mass., Nov. 21, 1905; s. Carleton and Annie Wilson (Ingle) H.; A.B., Harvard, 1928, LL.B., 1931. Admitted to Mass. bar, 1931, since practiced in Boston; asso. Palmer & Dodge, 1931—, mem. firm, 1941—; trustee

Brookline Savs. Bank. Served with AUS, 1941, to comdr. USNR, 1942-45. Trustee Radcliffe Coll., Noble and Greenough Sch. (treas. 1947- 71); trustee, treas. Ella Lyman Cabot Trust; trustee, clk. Joslin Diabetes Found. Clubs: Country (Brookline); Union, Harvard, Harvard Travelers (Boston). Home: 191 Clyde St Brookline MA 02147 Office: 28 State St Boston MA 02109

HUNNICUTT, CLARENCE WILLIAM, educator; b. Whittier, Cal., Aug. 19, 1907; s. Jesse Faulkner and May (Williams) H.; B.S., U. Ariz., 1930, M.A., 1931; Ed. D., Stanford, 1942; m. Lillie McAlister, June 1, 1932 (dec. Sept. 1954); childrenAlice Lucile (Mrs. Richard L. Entin), William McAlister, Charles Gilbert, Karl Sands; m. 2d, Ardelle Whitman, Oct. 25, 1958. Sch. prin., Scottsdale, Ariz., 1930-38; curriculum coordinator, Santa Barbara County, Cal., 1939-40; head elementary edn. Syracuse U., 1940-67, asst. prof., 1940-44, asso. prof., 1944-47, prof., 1947-67; mem. faculty U. S. Fla., Tampa, 1967-; mem. summer staff U. N.C., 1939, Drake U., 1940, U. Ill., 1950, U. So. Cal., 1960; vis. prof. Stanford, 1952-53, U. Philippines, 1953-54; pub. sch. ednl cons., N.Y.C., 1940-41, Caddo Parish, La., 1948, Dade County, Fla., 1951, Corpus Christi, Tex., 1951, Manteca, Cal., 1953, Tulsa, 1956, Oklahoma City, 1957-58, 60, Los Angeles County, Cal., 1961, 63; cons. Coronet Films, Handwriting Found; cons. AID-ROCAP textbook project Central Am., 1965-70. Mem. N.E.A., Nat. (dir.), N.Y. State (past pres.) assns. supervision and curriculum devel., Nat. Council Social Studies, Assn. Higher Edn., Am. Edn. Research Assn. Kiwanian. Author: Answering Children's Questions, 2d edit., 1954. Sr. author: Singer Social Studies Series, 30 titles, 1957—. Co-author: What Does Research Say About Arithmetic, 2d edit., 1958; Research in the Three R's, 1958. Also editor 6 books. Home: 11507 Carrollwood Dr Tampa FL 33618

HUNNICUTT, GAYLE, actress; b. Tex.; grad. U. Cal. Former model; appeared in movies P.J., Eye of the Cat, Marlowe, Fragment of Fear, The Freelance. Address: Universal City Studios Inc 100 Universal City Plaza Universal City CA 91608*

HUNNINGHER, BENJAMIN, educator; b. Vlissingen, The Netherlands, Apr. 15, 1903; s. Christiaan and Aleida G. J. (ten Cate) H.; Ph.D., Utrecht U., 1931; m. Anna M.L. Korthals van Schooten, Dec. 30, 1932; children—Louise Victoire, Joannes George Christiaan, Reinout Eduard. Tchr., Dutch lit. and history City Coll., Amsterdam, The Hague, 1932; critic, theater and fine arts, Amsterdam, 1935; govt. adviser head theater dept. Ministry Edn. and Arts, The Hague, Holland, 1945-48; Queen Wilhelmina prof. Columbia, 1948-64; prof. history theatre arts U. Amsterdam, 1964—. Decorated comdr. Order of Crown (Belgium). Rockefeller Found. fellow, 1946; J.S. Guggenheim Found. fellow, 1961. Author: Life and Work of Dutch Dramatist, H. J. Schimmel, 1931; Theater and Education, 1946; Theater and Realisme, 1947; Dutch Theater, 1940, 1949; Medieval Liturgy and the Theater, 1954; The Origin of the Theater, 1955; The Theater of Dionysus Eleuthereus, 1956; The Amsterdam Theatre of 1637, 1959; The Idea in American Drama, 1963; The Mirror of Baroque Theatre, 1964. Contbr. to theatrical and art jours. Home: 21 Roemer Visscherstr Amsterdam The Netherlands Office: U Amsterdam Inst for Dramatic Art N Doelenstr 16 Amsterdam The Netherlands

HUNSAKER, JEROME CLARKEL aero. engr.; b. Creston Ia., Aug. 26, 1886; s. Walter J. and Alma (Clarke) H.; grad. U.S. Naval Acad., 1908; M.S., Mass. Inst. Tech., 1912, D.Sc., 1916; D.Sc., Williams Coll., 1943, Adelphi Coll., 1955; D. Eng., Northeastern U., 1945; m. Alice Porter Avery, June 26, 1911 (dec. 1966); children-Mrs. Sarah P. Swope, Jerome Clarke, James (dec.), Mrs. T.A. Bird. Officer, later advancing to comdr. Constrn. Corps, USN, 19O9-26; instr. aero. engring. Mass. Inst. Tech., 1912-16; in charge aircraft design Navy Dept., Washington, designed airship Shenandoah, and flying boat NC4, (1st to fly Atlantic), 1916-23; asst. naval attaché, London, Paris, Berlin, Rome, 1923-26; asst v.p. Bell Telephone Labs. (wire and radio services for airways), 1926-28; v.p. Goodyear Zeppelin Corp., 1928-33; head depts. aero. engring. and mech. engring. Mass. Inst. Technol., 1933- 51, now prof. emeritus. Mem. Guggenheim Medal Bd., Sperry Medal Bd. Served to capt. USNR ret. Chmn. Nat. Adv. Com. Aeros., 1941-56. Awarded Navy Cross, Medal for Merit (U.S.); Legion of Honor (France); Daniel Guggenheim medal, Franklin medal; Wright Brothers medal; Godfrey L. Cabot Trophy, 1950; Langley Medal, 1955; Gold Medal of Royal Aero. Soc. (Gt. Britain), 1957; Navy award for distinguished public service, 1958; Stratton award Swiss Soc., 1969. Fellow Am. Phys Soc., Am. Acad. Arts and Scis.; hon. fellow Inst. Aero. Scis., Royal Aero. Soc. Britain, Imperial Coll. Sci. (London); hon. mem. Am. Soc. M.E., Instn. Mech. Engrs. (London); mem. Am. Soc. Naval Architects and Marine Engrs., Am. Soc. Automotive Engrs., Nat. Acad. Scis., Am. Philos. Soc., Delta Kappa Epsilon, Sigma Xi. Clubs: Century (N.Y.C.); Army and Navy (Washington); St. Botolph (Boston). Contbr. to profl. jours. Home: 10 Louisburg Square Boston MA 02108 Office: Mass Inst Tech Cambridge MA 02139

HUNSAKER, NEVILLE CARTER, educator; b. Honeyville, Utah, Dec. 11, 1907; s. Israel and Rosa (Carter) H.; B.A., U. Utah, 1930; M.A. (Willard D. Thompson scholar), U. Cal. at Berkeley, 1932; Ph.D., Rice U., 1948; postgrad. U., Ill., 1959-60; m. Annie Peterson, Sept. 19, 1935; childrenWorthen, Calvin, Gloria, Hedy, Jesse. Computor, Rieber Labs., Los Angeles, Houston, 1934-38; instr. math. U. Houston, 1938-41; faculty Utah State U., Logan, 1941—, prof. math., 1953—, head dept., 1956—. Vis. prof. U. Hawaii, summer 1962. Mem. Am. Math Soc., Math. Assn. Am., Nat. Council Tchrs. Math. Home: 1063 N 2d East Logan UT 84321

HUNSAKER, RALPH EARL, lawyer; b. Mesa, Ariz., Dec. 26, 1936; s. Homer D. and Lora (Ellsworth) H.; B.S., U. Ariz., 1959, J.D., 1962; m. Martha Jo Anderson, Aug. 16, 1958; children—Gary Marlon, Craig Earl, Mark Allen. Admitted to Ariz. bar, 1962, since practiced in Phoenix; atty. O'Connor, Cavanagh, Anderson, Westover, Killingsworth & Beshears, 1962—; atty. Ariz. Insterstate Stream Commn. Mem. Am., Ariz., Maricopa County bar assns., Phoenix C. of C., Am. Arbitration Assn., Sigma Alpha Epsilon, Phi Delta Phi. Democrat. Mem. Ch. of Jesus Christ of Latter-day Saints. Clubs: Arizona, Lawyers (Phoenix). Home: 4624 E Exeter St Phoenix AZ 85018 Office: 3003 N Central St Phoenix AZ 85012

HUNSBERGER, ISAAC MOYER, univ. dean, chemist; b. Quakertown, Pa., Aug. 3, 1921; s. A.F. and Eliza (Moyer) H.; B.S., Lehigh U., 1943, M.S., 1946, Ph.D., 1948; AEC postdoctoral fellow organic chemistry U. Ill., 1948-49; m. Elizabeth Rita Ochnich, Mar. 19, 1944; children—Donald Moyer, Elizabeth Anne, Gretchen, Mark, Carol, Luke, Heidi. Asst., then asso. prof. chemistry Antioch Coll., 1949-55; asso. prof. Fordham U., 1955-60; head dept. chemistry U. Mass., 1960-61, dean Coll. Arts and Scis., research prof. chemistry, 1961-69; program adviser edn. Ford Found., Pakistan, 1969-71; dean Coll. Arts and Scis., State U. N.Y. at Albany, 1971—; spl. research chemistry sydnones, reactions sulfoxides and N-oxides. Mem. com. modern methods handling chem. information NRC, 1959-65. Served with USAAF, 1943-45. Decorated D.F.C., Air medal with 5 oak leaf clusters. Fellow A.A.A.S., Am. Inst. Chemists; mem. Am. Chem. Soc., Am. Assn. U. Profs., Phi Beta Kappa, Pi Mu Epsilon, Phi Eta Sigma, Phi Lambda Upsilon. Author: (with others) Survey of Chemical Notation Systems, 1964. Contbr. articles to profl. jours. Editor sect. 36, Chem. Abstracts, 1960-64. Home: 38 Hiawatha Dr Guilderland NY 12084

HUNSCHER, HELEN ALVINA (Mrs. H.P. Wilkinson), educator, nutritionist; b. Gates Mills, O., Aug. 5, 1904; d. Ernest Henry and Cora Annis (Knapp) Hunscher; A.B., Ohio State U., 1925; postgrad. (fellow in nutrition research), Merrill-Palmer Sch., Detroit, 1926- 27, Laura Spelman Rockefeller fellow, 1927-28; Ph.D.(NRC fellow), U. Chgo., 1932; m. Howard Paul Wilkinson, Dec. 23, 1939; childrenJeanne (Mrs. Mark E. Goeble), James H. Asst. in nutrition research Merrill-Palmer Sch. and Children's Hosp. Mich., 1928-29; instr. home econs. U. Chgo., 1930-31; asso. in research Children's Fund Mich., Detroit, 1931-37; profl. lectr. in nutrition Wayne U., Detroit, 1931-37; prof., chmn. home econs. Case Western Res. U., Cleve., 1937-63, chmn. nutrition, 1963- Mem. spl. med. adv. group VA, 1948-54. Mem. Am. Bd. Nutrition, Am. Dietetic Assn. (Copher award 1958, pres. 1947-48), Am. Home Econs. Assn. (chmn. food and nutrition div. 1945-46), Am. Inst. Nutrition, Am. Chem. Soc., Pub. Health Assn., Soc. for Exptl. Biology and Medicine, Soc. for Research in Child Devel., A.A.A.S., Sigma Xi, Phi Beta Kappa, Sigma Kappa, Phi Upsilon Omicron, Omicron Nu, Iota Sigma Pi. Episcopalian. Contbr. articles to profl. jours. Author: Gates Mills and a History of Its Village Church. Home: Gates Mills OH 44040 Office:: Case Western Res U Cleveland OH 44106

HUNSUCKER, ROBERT D., gas co. exec.; b. 1925; ed. Washburn U., 1952; married. Asst. treas. Panhandle Eastern Pipeline Co., 1952-66; v.p., treas. Trunkline Gas Co., 1966-. Address: 3000 Bissonet Av. Houston TX 77005.*

HUNT, ALBERT A., utility exec.; b. 1923; B.A., Stanford, 1947; married. With So. Cal. Gas Co., 1947-68; controller, treas., ir. So. Counties Co. Cal., 1968-70; controller, treas. Pacific Lighting Service Co. Cal., 1970—. Served with USMCR and USNR, 1943-46. Address: PO Box 54790 Terminal Annex Los Angeles CA 90054

HUNT, ALFRED MORTIMER, aluminum exec.; b. Pitts., Apr. 2, 1919; s. Roy Arthur and Rachel McMasters (Miller) H.; grad. St. Paul's Sch., 1938; A.B., Yale, 1942. With Massena (N.Y.) works Aluminum Co. Am., 1942-45, New Kensington (Pa.) works, 1945-47, Alcoa (Tenn.) works, 1948, Cleve. works, 1948-50, dir., 1949—, asst. sec., 1950-52, sec. 1952—, v.p., 1963—; pres., dir. Delcalo, Inc.; dir. Alcoa Properties, Inc., Alcoa Service Corp., Allendale Mut. Ins. Co., Alcoa Castings Co., Columbia River Orchards Co. Mem., sec. Republican Finance Com. Allegheny County. Trustee P.E. Diocese Pitts., Carnegie Inst., Duke, Hunt Found., Helen Clay Frick Found.; bd. dirs., sec. Pitts. Regional Planning Assn.; bd. dirs. Alcoa Found., ACTION-Housing, Inc., Pitts. History and Landmarks Found., Bishop's Fund. Mem. Carnegie Hero Fund Commn.; mem. sponsoring com. Allegheny Conf. on Community Devel. Mem. Masters of Foxhounds Assn. Am., Nat. Steeplechase and Hunt Assn., Am. Inst. Mining and Metall. Engrs. (jr.), Newcomen Soc. Eng., Engrs. Soc. Western Pa., Pa. Soc., Am. Soc. Metals, Am. Soc. Corporate Secs., Pitts. Bibliophiles, Berzelius, Chi Psi. Episcopalian. Clubs: Pittsburgh Golf, Fox Chapel Golf, Rolling Rock, Duquesne, University, Allegheny Country, Harvard-Yale- Princeton (P.Hs.); Yale (N.Y.C.); Chagrin Valley Hunt (Cleve.); Rolling Rock Hunt. Home: 4875 Ellsworth Av Pittsburgh PA 15213 Office: Alcoa Bldg Pittsburgh PA 15219

HUNT, ALMA FAY, missions exec.; b. Roanoke, Va., Oct. 5, 1909; d. William Otis and Mary Myrtle (Wertz) Hunt; B.S., Farmville (Va.) State Tchrs. Coll., 1941; A.M., Columbia, 1947; D.H.L., William Jewell Coll., 1958. Tchr., Roanoke (Va.) County Schs., 1929-31, prin., 1931-32, Roanoke City Sch., 1932-44; dean women William Jewell Coll., Liberty, Mo., 1944- 48; exec. sec. Woman's Missionary Union, Aux. So. Bapt. Conv., Birmingham, Ala., 1948—, trustee, 1953- 56; sec. bd. trustees Carver Sch. Missions and Social Work, 1948- 57; mem. women's dept. Bapt. World Alliance, 1950-60, 65—, relief com., 1950-60; mem. exec. com. N. Am. Bapt. Women's Union, 1950—, pres., 1965-67; mem. commn. religious liberty Bapt. World Alliance, 1961-65, commn. on evangelism and missions, 1966—, co-chmn., 1970—; v.p. Bapt. World Alliance, 1970—; mem. Bapt. Joint Com. on Pub. Affairs, 1958—; mem. N. Am. Bapt. Fellowship, 1971—; bd. dirs. So. Bapt. Found., 1970—. Mem. Nat. Multiple Sclerosis Soc. (exec. bd. Ala. chpt. 1953-58), Nat. Assn. of Deans Women, Kappa Delta Pi. Clubs: Kenilworth, Bibs Book Review. Author: Woman's Missionary Union; History of Woman's Missionary Union. Home: 745 Canyon Creek Lane Birmingham AL 35216 Office: 600 N 20th St Birmingham AL 35203

HUNT, ANDREW DICKSON, Jr., coll. dean, physician; b. N.Y.C., Oct. 1, 1915; s. Andrew D. and Elizabeth (Pinney) H.; B.S., Haverford Coll., 1937; M.D., Cornell U., 1941; m. Lotta H. Mayberry, Dec. 20, 1940; children—George M., Elisabeth H., Judith P., Lotta R. Rotating intern, then resident pediatrics U. Pa. Hosp., 1941- 43; chief resident, then asst. dir. clinics Children's Hosp. Phila., 1946-50, dir. clinics, 1950-52; mem. U. Pa. Sch. Medicine, 1948-52, asst. prof. pediatrics, 1952; dir. pediatric services Hunterdon Med. Center, Flemington, N.J., 1952-59; asst. vis. physician Bellevue Hosp., N.Y.C., 1952-59; asst. prof. clin. pediatrics, then asst. prof. pediatrics N.Y.U. Coll. Medicine, 1952-59; asst. prof. pediatrics Stanford Sch. Medicine, 1959-64; dir. ambulatory services Stanford Med. Center, 1959-64; prof. pediatrics, dean Coll. Human Medicine, Mich. State U., 1964-. Vice pres. Pa. Assn. Retarded Children, 1949-52; mem. med. adv. com. W.K. Kellogg Found., Battle Creek, Mich., 1966-68; chmn. adv. council Mich. State Comprehensive Health Planning, 1968—; vice pres. Mich. League for Human Services, 1970—. Vice pres. Community Council No. Santa Clara County, Cal., 1960-62, pres., 1962-64; mem. Human Rights Commn., Palo Alto, Cal., 1962-64. Served to capt. M. C., AUS, 1943-46. Diplomate Am. Bd. Pediatrics. Mem. Soc. for Pediatric Research (emeritus), Am. Pediatric Soc., A.A.A.S., Am. Acad. Pediatrics, Am. Pub. Health Assn., A.M.A. Contbr. med. jours. Home: 510 Northlawn East Lansing MI 48823

HUNT, CARLTON CUYLER, Jr., physiologist, educator; b. Waterbury, Conn., Aug. 11, 1918; s. Carlton Cuyler and Adele F. (Weidemann) H.; B.A., Columbia U., 1939; M.D., Cornell U., 1942; m. 2d, Marion Hall, July 3, 1965. Intern, N.Y. Hosp., 1942-43, asst. resident, 1946; research fellow Cornell U., 1946-48, instr. physiology, 1948; sr. fellow NRC, 1948-52; asst. prof. Johns Hopkins, 1951-52; asso. Rockefeller Inst., 1952-55; prof. physiology Albert Einstein Coll. Medicine, 1955-57; prof. physiology, chmn. dept. U. Utah, 1957-64, Yale Sch. Medicine, 1964, 68; prof., head dept. physiology and biophysics Washington U. Sch. Medicine, St. Louis, 1967- -. Hon. research asso. U. Coll., London, Eng., 1962-63; spl. research sensory receptors. Mem. adv. panel NSF, 1958-59, NIH, 1959-62. Served as med. officer AUS, 1943-46. Mem. Harvey Soc., Am. Physiol. Soc. Home: 42 Westmoreland Pl St Louis MO 63108

HUNT, CHARLES BROWNLOW, Jr., coll. dean, musician; b. Nashville, July 20, 1916; s. Charles Brownlow and Mary Agnes (Buquo) H.; student Northwestern U., 1936; B.S., M.A., Peabody Coll., 1938; postgrad. Eastman Sch. Music, 1941; Ph.D., U. Cal. at Los Angeles, 1949; m. Anna Lillian Vann, Aug. 20, 1938; children—Charles Hunt III, Carol Vann. Faculty, Peabody Coll., 1940—, prof. music, head div. music, 1955—, dir. Sch. Music, 1963-65, dean Grad. Sch., 1965—. Band dir. U. Cal. at Los Angeles, 1947-49; prin. clarinetist Nashville Symphony Orch., 1946-61. Mem. Council Grad. Schs. U.S., chmn. com. on membership, 1969—. Pres. Nashville Symphony Assn., 1971—. Served with USNR, 1945-46. Mem. Music Educators Nat. Conf., Nat. Assn. Schs. Music (commn. curricula 1958-60, pres. 1962-65, exec. com., hon. life). Home: 1500 Clairmont Pl Nashville TN 37215

HUNT, CHARLES BUTLER, geologist; b. West Point, N.Y., Aug. 9, 1906; s. Irvin Leland and Annie (Butler) H.; A.B., Colgate U., 1928; postgrad. Yale, 1928-30; m. Alice Parker, Oct. 20, 1930; children—Eugene Parker, Anne Butler (Mrs. John MacDonald). With U.S. Geol. Survey, 1930-53, 55-61; prof. geography Johns Hopkins, 1961—; exec. dir. Am. Geol. Inst., 1953-55; adv. panel Earth Sci. Div. NSF, 1960-63, chmn., 1962-63, divisional com. math. and phys. sci., 1964-65. Recipient Dept. Interior Distinguished Service award. Mem. Phi Beta Kappa. Author: Physiography of United States. Address: Geog Dept Johns Hopkins U Baltimore MD 21218

HUNT, CLARENCE STUART, lawyer; b. San Jose, Cal., July 24, 1904; s. Rockwell Dennis and Nancy Seavey (Stuart) H.; A.B., U. So. Cal., 1925, J.D., 1927; m. Leota Clair Jardon, June 30, 1932; children-Dennis Martin, Sandra Clair. Admitted to Cal. bar, 1927; dep. dist. atty. Los Angeles County, 1928- 43; practice in Long Beach, 1945—; sr. partner firm Ball, Hunt, Hart, Brown & Baerwitz, 1946—. Mem. Cal. Jud. Council, 1968-71. Bd. dirs. Western Center Law and Poverty, 1968-70. Bd. dirs. Santa Catalina Island Tuna Club Found. Served to lt. comdr. USNR, 1943-45. Mem. State Bar Cal. (bd. govs. 1963-66), Am. Coll. Trial Lawyers, Am., Long Beach (past pres.), Los Angeles County (past dir. profl. field-united crusade) bar assns., Soc. Cal. Def. Counsel, Native Sons Golden West (past pres.). Mem. Community Ch. Clubs: Pacific Coast, Long Beach Yacht (Long Beach); Tuna (Avalon, Caltalina Island); Southern Cal. Tuna; Light Tackle Marlin. Home: 232 Claremont Av Long Beach CA 90803 Office: 120 Linden Av Long Beach CA 90802

HUNT, DOUGLASS, univ. ofcl.; b. Winston-Salem, N.C., 1924; s. John Douglas and Kate Thelma (Harrell) H.; A.B., U. N.C., 1946; LL.B., Yale, 1951; m. Mary Jane Abdill, 1952; children—Lloyd Abdill, John Douglass III, Amanda Caroline, Arthur Laurence. Admitted to D.C. bar, 1952, also U.S. Supreme Ct.; asso. firm Gardner, Morrison and Rogers, Washington, 1951-61; spl. asst. to undersec. treasury, 1961-65, to sec. treasury, 1965-69; v.p. for finance Columbia, 1969—. Mem. council on fed. relations Assn. Am. Universities, 1970—; mem. tax com. Am. Council on Edn., 1971—. Chmn. Alexandria City Democratic Com., 1959-61. Served with AUS, 1946-48. Mem. Phi Beta Kappa. Home: 108 Bellair Dr Dobbs Ferry NY 10522 Office: Columbia U New York City NY 10027

HUNT, E. GEORGE, business exec.; b. 1920; married. With Diversey Corp., 1949—, v.p. U.S. chem. operations, 1966-69, exec. v.p., 1969, pres., dir., 1969—. Office: 212 W Monroe St Chicago IL 60606*

HUNT, E. JANSEN, investment banker; b. Yonkers, N.Y., May 28, 1901; student Columbia, Brown U. Successively with W.A. Harriman and Co., John Nickerson and Co., G.E. Garrett and Co.; now partner White Weld and Co., N.Y.C. Bd. dirs. Better Bus. Bur., N.Y.C., Madison Square Boys Club, N.Y.C.; trustee Brown U., Yankton Coll. Clubs: Sky, Bond, Knickerbocker, DKE, Stock Exchange Lunch, Pilgrims (N.Y.C.); Manhasset Bay Yacht Club (Port Washington, N.Y.); Pacific Union (San Francisco); Hope (Providence); Montego Bay (Jamaica, W.I.) Yacht. Address: 20 Broad St New York City NY 10005

HUNT, EARL GLADSTONE, Jr., bishop, coll. pres.; b. Johnson City, Tenn., Sept. 14, 1918; s. Earl Gladstone and Tommie Mae (DeVault) H.; B.S., East Tenn. State Univ., 1941; B.D., Emory U., 1946; D.D., Tusculum Coll., 1956; LL.D., U. Chattanooga, 1957; D.C.L., Emory and Henry Coll., 1965; D.D., Duke, 1969; m. Mary Ann Kyker, June 15, 1943; 1 son, Earl Stephen. Ordained to ministry Meth. Ch., 1944; pastor Sardis Meth. Ch., Atlanta, 1942-44; asso. pastor Broad Street Meth. Ch., Kingsport, Tenn., 1944-45, Wesley Meml. Meth. Ch., Chattanooga, 1945-50, First Meth. Ch., Morristown, Tenn., 1950- 56; pres. Emory and Henry Coll., 1956-64; resident bishop Charlotte Area, United Meth. Ch., 1964—. Participant Meth. series Protestant Hour, nationwide broadcast, 1956; mem. Meth. Gen. Bd. Edn., 1956-68; bd. fellows Interpreters' House, Inc., 1967—; del. Meth. Gen. Conf., 1956, 60, 64, S.E. Jurisdictional Conf., 1952, 56, 60, 64. Bd. dirs. Holston Meth. Home, 1952-56; trustee Brevard Coll., Emory U., Greensboro Coll., High Point Coll., Pfeiffer Coll., Lake Junaluska Meth. Assembly; mem. bd. mgrs. Charlotte Meth. Home; chmn. gen. com. on family life United Meth. Ch., also mem. gen. bd. laity and gen. com. ecumenical affairs; pres. Inst. Homiletical Studies, Inc.; trustee Bennett Coll.; mem. Com. One Hundred, Emory U. Named young man of year, Morristown Jr. C. of C., 1952. Mem. Pi Kappa Delta. Home: 3912 Beresford Rd Charlotte NC 28211 Office: Cole Bldg 207 Hawthorne Lane Charlotte NC 28204

HUNT, EVERETTE HOWARD, Jr., pub. relations exec., author, govt. ofcl.; b. Hamburg, N.Y., Oct. 9, 1918; s. Everette Howard and Ethel Jean (Totterdale) H.; A.B., Brown U., 1940; m. Dorothy L. Wetzel, Sept. 7, 1949; children—Lisa Tiffany, Kevan Totterdale, Howard, David. Movie script writer, editor March of Time, 1942-43; war corr. Life mag., 1943; screen writer, 1947-48; attache Am. embassy, Paris, France, 1948-49, Vienna, Austria, 1949-50, Mexico City, 1950-53; polit. officer Far East Command, Tokyo, Japan, 1954-56; 1st sec., consul Montevideo, Uruguay, 1957-60; cons. Dept. Def., 1960-65; with Dept. State, Washington, 1968-70; v.p., dir. Robert R. Mullen & Co., Washington, 1970-71; cons. to the Pres., 1971—. Served with USNR, 1940-42; to 1st lt. USAAF, 1943-46. Guggenheim fellow, 1946. Clubs: Brown University (N.Y.C.); Army and Navy, Lakewood Country (Washington). Author 44 novels, 1942—, pseudonyms Robert Dietrich, John Baxter, Gordon Davis. Contbr. fgn. affairs and polit. jours. Home: Witches Island 11120 River Rd Potomac MD 20854 Office: The White House Washington DC

HUNT, FLOYD PHILIP, glass co. exec.; b. Branchport, N.Y., Jan. 20, 1920; s. Floyd Prentiss and Edna Louise (Smith) H.; B.S., Cornell U., 1943; m. Doris H. Herter, June 31, 1947; children—Janet Evelyn, Arthur Clarendon, Eugene Herter, Claire Elise, David Prentiss. With E.C. Brown Co., Rochester, N.Y., 1945-49; with Corning Glass Works, 1949—, plant mgr., Albion, Mich., 1962-63, v.p., dir. lighting div., Corning, N.Y., 1963—. Served with USAAF, 1943-45. Mem. Empire State C. of C. (dir.), Alpha Sigma Phi. Home: 126 Grace Blvd Painted Post NY 14870 Office: Corning Glass Works Corning NY 14830

HUNT, FREDERICK VINTON, educator, physicist; Barnesville, O., Feb. 15, 1905; s. Fred and Ella (Shipley) H.; A.B., Ohio State U., 1924, B.E.E., 1925, D.Sc. (hon.), 1970; M.A., Harvard, 1928, Ph.D., 1934, S.D. (hon.), 1945; m. Katharine Buckingham, Nov. 25, 1932; 1 son, Thomas Kintzing. Grad. asst. physics Ohio State U., 1924-25; asst. in physics Harvard, 1927, 28-29, instr., 1929-34, instr. physics and communication engring., 1934-37; tutor in div. phys. scis.,

1931-38, asst. prof. physics and communication engring., 1937- 40, asso. prof., 1940-46, Gordon McKay prof. applied physics, 1946-71, prof. emeritus, 1971—, Rumford prof. physics, 1953-71, emeritus, 1971—; dir. Underwater Sound Lab., 1942- 46, chmn. dept. engring. sci. and applied physics, 1946-49; now with marine phys. lab. Scripps Inst. Oceanography, U. Cal. at San Diego. Recipient Presdl. medal merit, 1947; Emile Berliner award, 1954, Publs. award, 1956, John H. Potts medal, 1965 (all Audio Engring. Soc.); Pioneers Underwater Acoustics medal, 1965, Gold medal, 1969 (all Acoustical Soc. Am.; Distinguished Pub. Service award USN, 1970. Fellow Am. Acad. Arts and Scis., Acoustical Soc. Am. (exec. council 1938-41, editorial bd. 1940-45, pres. 1951-52), Am. Phys. Soc., I.R.E., Audio Engring. Soc. (hon., bd. govs. 1963-65, pres. 1969-70), Phi Beta Kappa, Tau Beta Pi, Sigma Xi, Eta Kappa Nu, Sigma Nu. Club: Cosmos (Washington). Author: Electroacoustics. Contbr. papers to profl. lit. Home: 2621 Calle del Oro LaJolla CA 92037 Office: Marine Phys Lab Scripps Inst Oceanography U Cal at San Diego San Diego CA 92152

HUNT, G. CARLETON, film lab. exec.; b. Bridgeport, Conn., Jan. 5, 1908; s. Henry Bishop and Estelle (Lynch) H.; ed. Miami (Fla.) pub. schs.; m. Una Young, May 25, 1929; children—Guy C., Roger H. With Warner Bros. Theatres, 1929-35, New Eng. Theatres, 1935-38; with stage groups, 1938-41; with RKO Studios, Hollywood, Cal., 1941-51; sec., gen. mgr. Unicorn Theatres, San Francisco, 1952-53; pres. Gen. Film Labs., Hollywood, Cal., 1953-62; chmn. bd. dirs. Pacific Industries Inc., San Francisco, 1956-62; pres. Glen Glenn Sound Co., Hollywood, 1962-64, chmn. bd. dirs., 1964—; pres. DeLuxe Gen. Inc., Hollywood and N.Y.C. Fellow Soc. Motion Picture and TV Engrs. (pres. 1967-68); mem. Acad. Motion Picture Arts and Scis., Am. Soc. Cinematographers, TV Acad. Arts and Scis., Navy League, Motion Picture Pioneers, Variety N.Y. Mason (Shriner). Clubs: Jonathan; Catalina Island Yacht; Cal. Yacht; N.Y. Athletic; Bel Air Country; Balboa Bay. Home: 21536 Pacific Coast Hwy Malibu CA 90265 Office: 1546 N Argyle Av Hollywood CA 90028

HUNT, GEORGE HALSEY, physician; b. Newton, Mass., May 31, 1903; s. Rolla Elijah and Nellie (Tillinghast) H.; A.B., Brown U., 1924; M.D., Columbia, 1928; m. Mildred L. Gertzen, Jan. 22, 1932; 1 dau., Barbara T. (Mrs. Herbert S. Ketay). Intern, jr. fellow in surgery Presbyn. Hosp., N.Y. C., 1928- 32; pvt. practice medicine, Red Bank, N.J., 1932-36; entered regular corps, USPHS, 1936; commd. p.a. surgeon (capt.), 1936, advanced through grades to med. dir. (col.), 1949; asst. chief, chief surg. services, marine hosps, USPHA, 1936-45, asst. chief, div. hosps., 1947-49, chief div. hosps., 1949-52, asst. surgeon gen., asso. chief, Bur. Med. Services, 1952-56; dir. Center for Aging Research, 1956-58; chief div. Gen. Med. Scis., 1958-62; asso. dir. Ednl. Council for Fgn. Med. Graduates, Phila., 1962, exec. dir., 1963—. Bd. trustees Med. Service of D.C., Inc., 1948-57, 59-62. Diplomate Am. Bd. Surgery. Fellow A.C.S. (gov. 1948-57), Am. Pub. Health Assn.; mem. A.A.A.S., Am. Hosp. Assn. Home: 623 Spruce St Philadelphia PA 19106 Office: 3930 Chestnut St Philadelphia PA 19104

HUNT, GEORGE PINNEY, mag. editor; b. Phila., July 17, 1918; s. Andrew Dickson and Elizabeth (Pinney) H.; B.A., Amherst Coll., 1939; m. Anita Eller, Apr. 2, 1942; children—Donna Elizabeth, George Pinney, Margaret de la Barre. With Time Inc., 1941—, mem. staff Life mag., 1948-69, asst. mng. editor, 1955-61, mng. editor, 1961-69. Chmn. Amherst Alumni News, 1959—. Chmn. Fusion-Economy Party, Huntington, N.Y., 1959-61, dir., 1957-68. Served to maj. USMCR, 1941-45; PTO. Decorated Navy Cross, Silver Star. Mem. Psi Upsilon. Episcopalian. Clubs: Century, River, N.Y. Yacht (N.Y.C.); Deep Sea (Montauk); Army-Navy (Washington). Author: Coral Comes High, 1946; Story of the U.S. Marines, 1950. Home: 266 Southdown Rd Huntington NY 11743 Office: Time Inc Rockefeller Center New York City NY 10020

HUNT, HAROLDSON LAFAYETTE, oil producer; b. Vandalia, Ill.; ed. pub. schs; m. Lyda Bunker (dec. May 1955); m. 2d Ruth Ray Wright, Nov. 1957. Oil producer Hunt Oil Co. Established Facts Forum and Life Line, founds. Producing radio and TV programs on nat. issues. Democrat. Baptist. Author 8 books. Address: 4009 W Lawther Dr Dallas TX 75218

HUNT, HEROLD CHRISTIAN, educator; b. Northville, Mich., Feb. 9, 1902; s. George E. and Katherine E. (Herold) H.; A.B., U. Mich., 1923, M.A., 1927; Ed.D., Tchrs. Coll., Columbia, 1940; LL.D., Park Coll., Parkville, Mo., 1947, Western Mich. Coll. Edn., Kalamazoo, 1947, Wis. U., 1951, St. Louis U., 1955; L.H.D., Mo. Valley Coll., 1966; m. Isabel Lucile Wright, Aug. 24, 1927; 1 son, Douglas Wright. Tchr. social studies Hastings (Mich.) Pub. Sch., 1923-27; prin. St. Johns (Mich.) High Sch., 1927-28, 1929-31; asst. cashier and trust officer St. Johns Nat. Bank, 1928-29; supt. schs., St. Johns, 1931-34, Kalamazoo, 1934-37, New Rochelle, N.Y., 1937-40, Kansas City, Mo., 1940-47; gen. supt. city schs., Chgo., 1947-53; prof. edn. Grad. Sch. Edn. Harvard, 1953-70, Charles William Eliot prof. of edn. emeritus, 1970—; under sec. of health, edn. and welfare, 1955-57; instr. summer session Columbia, 1938, U. Chgo., 1944; lectr. summer session U. Colo., 1942, 45, U. Kansas City, 1943-44, 46, 47, Northwestern U., 1944, U. Denver, 1945, U. Wis., 1946, 48, Okla. A. and M. Coll., 1946. Pres. Am. Assn. Sch. Adminstrs., 1947-48, 1st v.p., 1948-49; 2d v.p., Nat. Congress Parents and Tchrs., 1948-51; chmn. Am. Council on Edn., 1948-49, chmn. bd. trustees Ednl. Testing Service, 1949- 50; chmn. accrediting comm. Nat. Home Study Council: mem. 1943 yearbook commn., chmn. 1948 yearbook commn. Am. Assn. Sch. Adminstrs.; mem. 1943 yearbook commn. Sch. Pub. Relations Assn., 1946 yearbook commn. Nat. Soc. for Study Edn.; mem. Am. Council on Edn.'s commn. to Study implications of Armed Services Ednl. Program, Commn. on internat. edn. and cultural relations; commn. on edn. orgns. Nat. Conf. Christians and Jews. Bd. dirs. Nat. Safety Council; v.p., mem. exec. bd. nat. council Boy Scouts Am. Recipient Am. Edn. award, 1958; Silver Beaver, Antelope, Buffalo awards Boy Scouts Am. Mem. Soc. Mayflower Descs., Soc. Colonial Wars, N.E.A. (life), Horace Mann League Am., S.R., Phi Delta Kappa, Pi Delta Epsilon. Mason. Dist. gov. 35th Dist. Clubs: Rotary (pres. Kansas 1946-47); University, Rotary (Chicago); Faculty (Harvard U.); Harvard (Boston); Cosmos (Washington). Episcopalian. Rep. Author: (with Paul R. Pierce) The Practice of School Administration, 1958; (with R. Oliver Gibson) The School Personnel Administrator, 1965. Cons. to World Book Ency.; editorial adviser Houghton Mifflin Co.; ednl. articles. Home: 5 Lantern Lane Lexington MA 02173 Office: Larsen Hall Grad Sch Edn Harvard U Cambridge MA 02138

HUNT, HOWARD BEEMAN, physician; b. Winthrop, N.Y., Sept. 23, 1902; s. Levi Luther and Chloe (Beeman) H.; A.B., U. Cal., 1922, A.M., 1926; M.D., Harvard, 1927 m. Harriet Newton, Mar 29, 1930; children-Chloe Mae (Mrs. Robert Bratton), R. Thomas Newton. Intern surgery, radiology U. Mich., 1927- 29; teaching fellow physiology Harvard, 1926-27; instr. roentgenology U. Mich., 1929-30; chmn. dept. radiology U. Neb. Coll. Medicine, 1930—; radiologist U. Neb. Hosp. Cons. Neb. Meth. Hosp., Omaha VA Hosp., Children's Meml. Hosp., Blair Community Hosp. Bd. dirs. Neb. Med. Service Plan, Am. Cancer Soc. Fellow Am. Coll. Radiology (past bd. chancellors); mem. A.M.A., Am. Radium Soc. (past pres.), Soc. Nuclear Medicine, Rocky Mountain Radiol. Soc. (past pres.), Assn. Univ. Radiologists, Radiol. Soc. N. Am. (1st v.p. 1955), Faculty Radiologists, Am. Soc. Therapeutic Radiologists, Am. Roentgen Ray Soc., Sigma Xi, Alpha Omega Alpha, Phi Chi, Phi Beta Kappa. Home: 7541 Shirley St. Omaha NB 68105 Office: U Neb Coll Medicine Omaha NB 68105

HUNT, HOWARD FRANCIS, psychologist; b. Morgantown, W.Va., May 29, 1918; s. Harrison R. and Jane (Fisher) H.; A.B., Mich. State Coll., 1940; Ph.D., U. Minn., 1943; m. Ida Altman, Aug. 16, 1941; children—Carol Ann, William H., Steven C., John H. Instr. psychology U. Minn., 1943-44; asst. prof. psychology Stanford, 1946-48; asso. prof. U. Chgo., 1948-54, prof., 1954, chmn. dept. psychology, 1955-62; chief psychiat. research N.Y. State Psychiat. Inst., N.Y.C., 1962—; prof. med. psychology Coll. Phys. and Surg., 1962—; prof. psychology Columbia, 1962—; fellow Center for Advanced Study in Behavioral Sci., 1959-60. Chmn. psychopharmacology rev. com. Nat. Inst. Mental Health, 1958-61, mem., 1971—, mem. bd. sci. counselors, 1961-65. Bd. dirs. Children's Village, Dobbs Ferry, N.Y. Served from ensign to lt. (j.g.) USNR, 1944-46. Diplomate clin. psychology Am. Bd. Examiners Profl. Psychology. Fellow Am. Psychol. Assn., A.A.A.S., N.Y. Acad. Scis.; mem. Am. Psychopath. Assn. (treas. 1964-65), Eastern Psychol. Assn., Sigma Xi, Phi Kappa Phi, Kappa Sigma. Mem. editorial bd. Jour. Abnormal Psychology, Jour. Psychiat. Research, Internat. Jour. Neuropharmacology. Editorial adviser psychology Ency. Brit., 1957—. Editor: Dorsey Press Psychology Series; Jour. Abnormal Psychology, 1964-70. Home: Ardsley Park Irvington-on-Hudson NY 10503 Office: 722 W 168th St New York City NY 10032

HUNT, IRENE, author; b. Newton, Ill.; d. Franklin Pierce and Sarah (Land) Hunt; A.B., U. Ill., 1939; M.A., U. Minn., 1945. Elementary sch. tchr., Oak Park, Ill., 1934-45; instr. psychology U. S.D., 1947-52; now dir. lang. arts Cicero (Ill.) Pub. Schs. Recipient Newberry award, 1966. Author: Across Five Aprils, 1964; Up A Road Slowly, 1966; Trail of Apple Blossoms, 1968. Home: 2800 Lincoln St North Riverside IL 60546 Office: 5110 W 24th St Cicero IL 60650

HUNT, JAMES CLAY, Jr., educator; b. Lexington, Ky., Jan. 28, 1915; s. James Clay and Margaret (Scott) H.; A.B., U. Ky., 1934, M.A., 1935; Ph.D., Johns Hopkins U., 1941. Instr. English, Wayne State U., 1939-41; instr. English, Williams Coll., 1941-42, 1946-48, asst. prof., 1948-54, asso. prof., 1954-58, prof., 1958-71, John Hawley Roberts prof. English, 1971—. Served with USNR, 1942-46. Mem. Modern Language Assn., Renaissance Soc. Am., Phi Beta Kappa. Democrat. Author: Donne's Poetry, 1954. Home: Box 621 Williamstown MA 01267

HUNT, JAMES ROBERT, librarian; b. West Brownsville, Pa., May 5, 1925; s. James Clarence and Jesse (Sharp) H.; Ph.B., U. Detroit, 1951, M.A. in Polit. Sci., 1955; M.A. in L.S., U. Mich., 1959; m. Gloria Solli, June 26, 1954; children—Christopher James, Màrya Madeline, Megan Maura, Shelagh Maureen, Matthew Becket, Deirdre Mór. Co-mgr. Madonna Book Shop, Detroit, 1951-56; bookmobile librarian Wayne County (Mich.) Library, 1956-57, adminstrv. asst. to librarian, 1958-60, head central services, 1960-62; asst. state librarian Mich. State Library, Lansing, 1962-64; state librarian, asst. supt. library services Hawaii Dept. Edn., Honolulu, 1964-70, acting dep. supt. edn., 1970-71, state librarian, 1971—. Mem. library tech. com. Lansing Community Coll.; chmn. Hawaii Gov's. Com. State Library Resources, 1964; adv. com. U. Hawaii Grad. Library Sch., 1962—; mem. Gov.'s Com. on Hawaiian Textbook Materials, 1971—. Mem. A.L.A. (life), Mich. (chmn. library adminstrn. sect. 1961-62), Hawaii (A.L.A. rep. 1964- 68) library assns., Hawaiian Hist. Soc., Friends of Library, Am. Soc. Pub. Adminstrn. (sec. Honolulu chpt. 1966—). Contbr. articles to profl. publs. Office: PO Box 2360 Honolulu HI 96804

HUNT, JAMES WESLEY, assn. exec.; b. Wellborn, Fla., Aug. 11, 1927; s. Richard W. and Carrie (Jernigan) H.; A.B., U. Chattanooga, 1950; grad. inst. for Orgn. Mgmt., U. N.C., Chapel Hill, 1957; postgrad. Ga. Inst., Athens, 1964-65; m. Jacqueline Williams, Oct. 31, 1959; children—Leslie Ruth, Richard Stevenson, Kimberly Anne, James Patrick, Susan Paige. Indsl. devel. agt. Carolina Power & Light Co., Florence, S.C., 1957-59; mgr. Union County (S.C.) C. of C., 1959; mgr. indsl. com. of 100 Greater Chattanooga C. of C., 1959-63, exec. v.p., 1963—. Instr. insts. U. Ga., U. Colo., Mich. State U., 1969-70. Cons., Ch. and Urban Life Steering Com., 1967-70; mem. adv. com. Chattanooga State Tech. Inst., 1968-70; mem. adv. com. U. Tenn. at Chattanooga Mgmt. Devel. Seminar, 1965-70; mem. Mayor's Manpower Adv. Com., 1969-70; mem. allocations com. United Fund, 1969-70; mem. Met. Council for Community Services, 1967-70. Bd. dirs. YMCA. Served with USNR, 1945-46. Mem. Chattanooga Chamber Found. (exec. v.p., sec.), Tenn. Assn. C. of C. Execs. (past pres.), Insts. for Orgn. Mgmt. (bd. regents), Am. C. of C. Execs., So. Assn. C. of C. Execs. (dir.), Sales and Marketing Execs. Assn. Methodist (steward 1956-59, 67-70, Sunday Sch. tchr. 1966-69, chmn. ecumenical affairs 1968-70). Rotarian. Home: 818 Brynwood Dr Chattanooga TN 37415 Office: 819 Broad St Chattanooga TN 37402

HUNT, JOHN DAVID, banker; b. Worcester, Mass., May 2, 1925; s. John J. and Honorea B. (Tully) H.; A.B., Brown U., 1949; postgrad. Williams Coll. Sch. Banking, 1960; m. Claire A. Sullivan, June 25, 1949; children—Barbara A., Kathryn R. Accountant, Harry W. Wallis & Co., Worcester, 1949-50; with Worcester County Nat. Bank, 1952—, asst. v.p., 1959-61, v.p., 1961-69, sr. v.p., 1969—, loan officer, 1961-65, chmn. loan review com., 1961—, sr. loan officer, 1965—; dir. RSC Industries, Wornat Devel. Corp., Worcester Bus. Devel. Corp., Worcester Capital Corp. Instr. Am. Inst. Banking, 1957-60. Mem. adv. bd. Notre Dame Acad.; bd. dirs. United Cerebral Palsy Assn. Worcester County, 1957-67, Worcester Better Bus. Bur., 1964-69, Cath. Charities Worcester; trustee, corporator Hahnemann Hosp.; corporator St. Vincent Hosp. Served to lt. USNR, 1943-47, 50-52. Recipient Outstanding Young Man award Worcester County, 1961. Mem. Am. Inst. Banking, Robert Morris Assos. (bd. govs. 1966-71, pres. New Eng. chpt. 1969-70), Alpha Delta Phi. Republican. Roman Catholic. Clubs: Economic of Worcester, Worcester County Brown, First Friday, Worcester, Worcester Country. Home: 14 Spring Valley Rd Worcester MA 01609 Office: 446 Main St PO Box 529 Worcester MA 01608

HUNT, JONATHAN KEVIN, Jr. chemist, educator; b. Chicago, 1928; B.S. in Physics, Yale, 1950; Ph.D. in Chemistry, Harvard, 1956; m. Sally Ann Jones, July 5, 1957; children--Kenneth J., Nancy A. Chemist, Acme Chem. Co., Blue Island, Ill., 1950-51; director of Research Lab., Indsl. Chemicals Corp., Cambridge, Mass., 1956-60; project coordinator environmental sect. Steinmetz Assos., Chgo., 1960-61; v.p. for research Bauer Bros. Chem. Co., Inc., Memphis, 1961-64; asst. prof. chemistry Washington U., St. Louis, 1964-66, asso. prof., 1966-70, prof., 1970--, head of chemistry dept., 1970-71. Vis. prof. So. Ill. U., summer 1967, U. of Ore., 1969. Scoutmaster, Boy Scouts America, University City, Mo., 1968-70. Bd. dirs. Rest Haven Home for Elderly, 1960-61; trustee of the Lutheran Hosp., 1965-71. Served from lt. to capt., AUS, 1951-53. Mem. Am. Chem. Soc., Sci. Research Soc. Am. (chpt. treas. 1967), American Instititute Chemists, Ecological Soc. Am. (chpt. sec.), Sigma Xi. Author: (with others) Basic Inorganic Chemistry, 1971. Contbr. articles to profl. jours., encys., also chpts. to books. Home: Fairfax Apts 7291 Windermere Dr University City MO 63105 Office: Dept Chemistry Washington University St Louis MO 63130

HUNT, JOSEPH MCVICKER, psychologist; b. Scottsbluff, Neb., Mar. 19, 1906; s. Robert Sanford and Carrie Pearl (McVicker, nee Loughborough) H.; A.B., U. Neb., 1929, A.M., 1930, D.Sc., 1967; Ph.D., Cornell U., 1933; Sc.D., Brown U., 1958; m. Esther Dahms, Dec. 25, 1929; children—Judith Ann, Carol Jean. Tng. and research, 1929-36; instr. to asso. prof. Brown U., 1936-46; research cons. Inst. Welfare Research, Community Service Soc. N.Y., 1944-46, dir., 1946-51; lectr. Columbia Tchrs. Coll., 1948-50; adj. prof. Grad. Sch. N.Y. U., 1950-51; prof. psychology U. Ill., 1951-67, prof. psychology and edn., 1967—. Cons. VA Hosp., Danville, Ill.; dir. Coordination Center, Nat. Lab. Early Childhood Edn., 1967-68, mem. adv. bd., 1968-70. Chmn., White House Task Force Child Devel., 1966-67. Trustee Am. Psychol. Found., 1952-59, pres. 1953-54, 58-59; trustee Rocky Ridge Music Center Found., 1963—. Recipient awards for excellence in research Am. Personnel and Guidance Assn., 1950, 60, Research Career award Nat. Inst. Mental Health, 1962—. Certified Am. Bd. Profl. Psychology. Fellow Am. Psychol. Assn. (pres. 1951-52, pres. div. clin. psychology 1968- 1969), A.A.A.S.; mem. Am. Statis. Assn., Am. Acad. Psychotherapists, Eastern Psychol. Assn. (pres. 1947-48), Am. Sociol. Assn., Sigma Xi, Psi Chi, Phi Kappa Psi. Unitarian. Editor: Personality and the Behavior Disorders (2 vols.), 1944; Jour. Abnormal and Social Psychology, 1950-55. Author: (with L.S. Kogan) Measuring Results in Social Casework: A Manual on Judging Movement, 1950; (with Blenkner, Kogan) Testing Results in Social Casework: A Field Test of the Movement Scale, 1950; (with Kogan, Bartelme) A Follow-Up Study of the Results of Social Casework, 1953; Intelligence and Experience, 1961; The Challenge of Incompetence and Poverty, 1969. Contbr. articles, papers to profl. lit. Home: 1807 Pleasant Circle Urbana IL 61801

HUNT, LAMAR, pres. Kansas City Chiefs of Am. Football League. Address: 4231 Armstrong Parkway Dallas TX 75205*

HUNT, LESTER WILLIAM, ednl. cons.; b. Rosalie, Neb., June 19, 1925; s. Lester Wesley and Blance Hazel (Johnson) H.; B.Sc., U. Neb., 1949, M.A., 1950, Ed.D., 1959; m. Shirley Ann Crouse, July 7, 1946; children—Cheryl Dec, Janice Kay, Nancy Ann; m. 2d, Nancy Winston Hailey Elson, July 2, 1970. Supt. schs., Maywood, Neb., 1950-51, Axtell, Neb., 1951- 55; dir. sch. dist. reorgn. and cons. sch. facilities planning Neb. Dept. Edn., 1955-58, dir. research, 1959; dean adminstrn., prof. edn. Neb. State Tchrs. Coll., 1959-63: exec. v.p. Wis. State U., Eau Claire, 1963-70; ednl. facility specialist San Diego State Coll. Found., 1970—; cons. to Ministry Edn. and Culture, Govt. of Brazil, 1970—; vis. prof. ednl. adminstrn. U. Wis., Madison, 1968- 69. Exec. Overland Trails council Boy Scouts Am.; mem. Gov. Neb. Conf. on Youth, 1962; mem. mayors' adv. council, Kearney; community adv. com. on TV. Served to 1st lt. AUS, 1943-46; mem. Neb. N.G., 1955-59. Mem. Am., Neb. assns. sch. adminstrs., Council of Ednl. Facility Planners, Neb. Schoolmasters Club, Assn. Higher Edn., N.E.A., Midwest Workshop on Rural Edn., Midwest Adminstrv. Coop. Study Council (exec. com.), Phi Delta Kappa. Home: Praia Flamengo 194/603 Rio de Janeiro Brazil Office: USAID/Rio de Janeiro/SDS APO New York City NY 09676

HUNT, LORD OF LLANVAIR WATERDINE; b. Simla, India, June 22, 1910; s. Cecil Edwin and Ethel (Crookshank); student Marlborough Coll., 1924-28, Royal Mil. Acad., Sandhurst, 1928- 29; D.C.L., univs. of Durham and Aberdeen; LL.D., U. London, 1954; m. Joy Mowbray-Green, Sept. 3, 1936; children—Sally, Susan, Prudence, Jennifer. Commd. 2d lt. Brit. Army, 1930; T/Brigadier, 1953; served in India and Burma, 1930-37, Indian police secondment, 1934-35, 38-40; bn., brigade comdr., W. Desert, Italy, Greece, 1943-45; staff appointments Middle East, Central Europe, Germany, 1946-52; asst. comdt. Army Staff Coll., 1953-55; rector Aberdeen U., 1963-66; chmn. Parole Bd., 1968—; pres. Council for Vols. Overseas, 1969—. Past pres. Brit. Mountaineering Council; pres. Nat. Ski Found. Gt. Britain, 1968—. First dir. The Duke of Edinburgh's Award Scheme, 1956-66. Decorated Indian Police Medal, Distinguished Service Order, comdr. Order Brit. Empire, knighted, 1953; Order Gurkha Right Hand 1st class (Nepal); recipient Indian Everest Medal, 1953, Hubbard medal Nat. Geog. Soc., Lawrence medal, Livingstone medal, Founders medal Royal Geog. Soc., Cullum medal Am. Geog. Soc., Gold medal French Geog. Soc., Gold medal Royal Geog. Soc. of Antwerp. Clubs: Alpine (past pres.), Climbers (past pres.). Author: The Conquest of Everest, 1953; The Red Snows, 1959. Home: Highway Cottage Aston Henley-on-Thames England

HUNT, LOIS soprano; b. York, Pa., Nov. 26, 1925; d. Matthew and Bertie (Jacobson) Marcus; Registered Dental Hygienist, U. Pa., 1943; m. Morton M. Hunt, Aug. 10, 1946 (div. 1965); 1 son, Jeffrey M. Concert debut, Phila., 1946; operatic debut, Central City, Colo., 1947; Broadway mus. debut in Buttrio Square, 1953; maj tv and radio appearances, 1950-, including Voice of Firestone, Bell Telephone Hour, Tonight Show; leading soprano Met. Opera Co., 1949-53; Broadway appearance in Sound of Music, 1961-62; active concerts, summer theatre, 1950—; rec. artist Columbia Records. Winner, Met. Opera Auditions of Air, 1949. Mem. Am. Guild Mus. Artists, A.F.T.R.A., Actors Equity Assn., Am. Guild Variety Artists. Home: 75 Central Park W New York City NY 10023 Office: care Kolmar-Luth 1776 Broadway New York City NY 10023

HUNT, PEARSON, educator; b. S.I., N.Y., Dec. 10, 1908; s. William Floyd and Julia (Pearson) H.; Ph.B., Yale, 1930; M.B.A., Harvard, 1933, D.C.S., 1939; m. Mary Merrill Towne, May 25, 1935 (div. 1962); childrenMerrill, Lucy; m. 2d, Edna B. Homa, Aug. 14, 1962; 1 son, David. Research asst. Harvard Bus. Sch., 1934-35, asst. prof. finance, 1940-46, asso. prof., 1946-50, prof. bus. adminstrn. 1950-68, Edmund Cogswell Converse prof. finance and banking, 1968—; on leave as dean and prof. Istatuto Post-Universatario per lo Studio dell Organizzazione Aziendale, Torino, Italy, 1953-55; instr. econs. Yale, 1935-40; prof. econs. Albertus Magnus Coll., New Haven, 1936-40; staff mem. radiation lab. Mass. Inst. Tech., 1944-45; vis. lectr. U. Toronto, 1949, U. Minn., 1949; vis. prof. indsl. adminstrn. Carnegia Inst. Tech., 1950; dir., treas. de Cordova and Dana Mus. and Park, Lincoln, Mass., 1949-53; vis. prof. adminstrn. Internat. Center for Advancement Mgmt. Edn., Stanford, 1962-63; vis. lectr. U. So. Cal., 1963; vis. prof. U. Cal. Los Angeles, 1963; Leatherbee lectr. Harvard, 1964—. Eisenhower Exchange fellow to Europe, 1957-58. Mem. Am. Finance Assn. (v.p. 1952), Am. Econ. Assn., Phi Beta Kappa, Delta Sigma Rho. Author: (latest) (with C.M. Williams, G. Donaldson) Basic Business Finance, 1961; Cases in Financial Management, 1960; Financial Analysis in Capital Budgeting, 1964; (with Victor L. Andrews) Financial Management: Cases and Readings, 1968. Contbr. articles to profl. jours. Home: 3 Bowdoin Street Cambridge MA 02138 Office: Harvard Bus Sch Soldiers Field Boston MA 02163

HUNT, PETER HULS, theatrical dir.; b. Pasadena, Cal., Dec. 16, 1938; s. George Smith and Gertrude (Ophuls) H.; grad. Hotchkiss Sch., 1957; B.A., Yale, 1961, M.F.A., 1963; m. Virginia Osborn, Jan. 19, 1965. Lightning designer, dir. Williamstown Theatre, 1957-68; designer lighting many Broadway and Off-Broadways prodns.; dir. Booth, 1969, 1776, 1969. Recipient Tony award, 1969. Address: 433 W 21st St New York City NY 10011

HUNT, REED OLIVER, former mfg. exec.; b. Wollochet Bay, Wash., Oct. 12, 1904; s. Arda Roy and Edna Elisabeth (Oliver) H.; student Smith Sch. Nav., Seattle, 1923-24, Harvard Advanced Mgmt. Program, 1951; m. Sarah Elizabeth Trombley, Mar. 23, 1926; children—Reed Oliver, Patricia (Mrs. Jack Gordon Nevin). Deck hand, purser, mate, master Puget Sound and deep sea vessels, various cos., 1916-27; clk., accountant, asst. office mgr. Crown Zellerbach Corp., Pulp & Paper Mills, 1927-35, office mgr., 1935-43, asst. to v.p. in charge mfg. hdqrs. parent co., San Francisco, 1943-46, asst. gen. mgr. mfg., 1946-51, v.p. mfg., 1952-54, v.p. operations, 1954-56, dir., exec. v.p., 1956-70, pres., chief exec. officer, 1959-63, chmn. bd., chief exec. officer, 1963-69, chmn. exec. com., 1969, now dir.; dir. Canadian Imperial Bank of Commerce, Toronto, Union Oil Co., Singer Co., N.Y. Chmn., President's Commn. Financial Structure and Regulation. Vice pres., dir. Crown Zellerbach Found. Republican. Episcopalian. Clubs: Commonwealth, Pacific Union (San Francisco); Ranier (Seattle). Home: Box 366 Gig Harbor WA 98335

HUNT, RICHARD HOWARD, sculptor; b. Chgo., Sept. 12, 1935; s. Cleophus Howard and Etoria Inez (Henderson) H.; studied sculpture with Nelli Bar, 1950-53; student U. Chgo., 1953-55; B.A.E., Art Inst. of Chgo.; m. Betty Marjorie; 1 dau. Cecilia Elizabeth. Exhibited Artists of Chgo. and Vicinity exhbn., 1955-56, 62nd, 63d, 64th Am. exhbns. Art Inst. Chgo., Carnegie Internat. Pitts., 1958, Mus. Modern Art, N.Y.C., 1959; one man exhibits Alan Gallery, N.Y.C., 1960, B.C. Holland Gallery, Chgo., 1963; works in permanent collections Mus. Modern Art, N.Y.C., Whitney Mus., N.Y.C., Albright Gallery, Buffalo, Art Inst. Chgo., Nat. Mus. Israel, Alan Gallery, N.Y.C., 1956, 58, Houston Mus., 1957, Whitney Mus., 1958, Mus. Modern Art, N.Y.C., 1957; vis. artist Yale, 1964, Chovinard Art Sch., 1964-65. Served with U.S. Army. Recipient Frank G. Logan medal and prize, 1956, Pauline Palmer prize, 1957, James Nelson Raymond traveling fellowship, 1957, Logan medal and prize Artists of Chgo. and Vicinity show, 1961. John Simon Guggenheim fellow, 1962-63. Address: 1503 N Cleveland Av Chicago IL 60610

HUNT, RICHARD NASH, geologist; b. Chgo., Apr. 16, 1893; s. George Edwin and Lulu Mary (Taylor) H.; A.B., U. Wis., 1915, grad. student, 1915-17; m. Grace Lee Prior, July 6, 1929; children—John Prior, Jeremy Stone. Geologist E.J. Longyear and Co., also Longco Oil Co., 1917, Utah Consol. Mining Co., Bingham, 1917-20; cons. geologist, Los Angeles, 1920-29, Palo Alto, Cal., 1930-38; geologist U.S. Smelting, Refining and Mining Co., Los Angeles and Salt Lake City, 1925-29, chief geologist, Salt Lake City, 1938—, v.p., dir., 1952—; v.p., dir. Hecla Mining Co., 1954—. Mem. Am. Inst. Mining, Metall. and Petroleum Engrs. (hon.), Soc. Econ. Geologists, Geol. Soc. Am., Am. Assn. Petroleum Geologists, Ind. Petroleum Assn. Am., Phi Beta Kappa, Sigma Xi. Presbyn. Club: Alta (Salt Lake City). Home: 2684 E Hillsden Dr Salt Lake City UT 84117

HUNT, ROBERT E., banker; b. Waterloo, Ia., Dec. 28, 1910; s. Ernest A. and Addie (Kimball) H.; A.B., Lawrence Coll., 1932; M.B.A., Harvard, 1934; LL.B., Kent Coll. Law, Chgo., 1938; m. Florence I. Walsh, Nov. 30, 1940; children—Charles A., Sarah. With No. Trust Co., 1934—, sr. v.p. charge banking dept., 1963-66, exec. v.p., 1966—. Mem. Ill. Bd. of Banks and Trust Cos., 1966—. Chmn., Chgo. Heart Fund drive, 1956; mem. vis. com. div. social scis. U. Chgo. Bd. dirs. Chgo. Heart Assn.; bd. dirs., chmn. finance com. N. Shore Country Day Sch.; bd. dirs. Mid-Am. chpt. A.R.C. Served to maj. USAAF, World War II. Mem. Res. City, Ill. (bd. govs., chmn. bank mgmt. com. Chgo. dist.) bankers assns., Nat. Recreation Assn. Clubs: Commonwealth (bd. dirs.), Chicago, Economic, University (Chgo.); Indian Hill (Winnetka); Detroit. Home: 333 Willow Rd Winnetka IL 60093 Office: 50 S LaSalle St Chicago IL 60690

HUNT, ROBERT FREDERICK, aircraft co. exec.; b. Cheltenham, Eng., May 11, 1918; s. Arthur and Kathleen Alice (Cotton) H.; student Cheltenham and North Gloucestershire Tech. Coll., 1935-40; m. Joy Patricia Molly Harding, June 28, 1947; children—Jacqueline Anne (Mrs. Peter Heywood), Pamela Kathleen, Margaret Joy, Alexandra Carol. Apprentice, Dowty Equipment, Ltd., 1935-40, chief instr. Co.'s Sch. Hydraulics, 1940-46, export mgr., 1946-49, v.p., gen. mgr. Dowty Con. Ltd., 1949-54, pres., 1954-56; dep. chmn. Dowty Group, Ltd., Cheltenham, 1956—. Chmn., Cheltenham Hosp. Group Mgmt. Com. Fellow Royal Aero. Sci.; mem. Soc. Brit. Aerospace Cos. (pres. 1967-68), AFCAI. Club: New (Cheltenham). Home: 5 Charlton Park Gate Cheltenham GL53 7DJ England Office: Arle Ct Cheltenham GL51-OTP England

HUNT, ROBERT LEWIS, banker; Newark, Jan 10, 1921; s. Lewis W. and Evelyn (Widman) H.; student U. Cal. at Los Angeles, 1939-42; LL.B., U So. Cal., 1948; m. June Tornay, Dec. 21, 1946; children—Robert Lewis II, Randall Douglas, Stephanie Tornay. Admitted to Cal. bar, 1948; partner firm Hunt and McCann, Beverly Hills, Cal. and Los Angeles, 1948-57; with Security Pacific Nat. Bank, Los Angeles, 1957—, gen. counsel, 1964-69, sr. v.p., 1967-69, exec. v.p., 1969—. Trustee, treas. Los Angeles Orthopaedic Found. and Orthopaedic Hosp., 1965—. Served with inf. AUS, World War II. Mem. Am., Cal., Los Angeles County bar assns., State Bar Cal. (conf. dels. 1957—, mem. exec. com. 1968—), Order of Coif, Sigma Chi, Phi Delta Phi, Phi Kappa Phi. Clubs: Republican Assos., Chancery, California (Los Angeles). Office: 215 W 6th St Los Angeles CA 90014 Mailing Address:

HUNT, RUSSELL FRANK, lawyer, banker; b. Wagoner, Okla., Apr. 27, 1909; s. W.T. and Martha (Rose) H.; student U. Okla., 1928-29; LL.B., Cumberland U., 1931; m. Margaret Kerr, Mar. 30, 1932; 1 son, Russell Kerr. Admitted to Okla. bar, 1931, since practiced in Tulsa; v.p. First Nat. Bank & Trust Co. of Tulsa, 1950-55, exec. v.p. 1955-66, vice chmn., 1966—; dir. Am. Gen. Life Ins. Co. Okla. Chmn., Okla. Ordnance Works Authority; mem. Tulsa Urban Renewal Authority, Tulsa Community Chest. Mem. Tulsa C. of C. (past pres., dir.), Res. City Bankers Assn. Clubs: Southern Hills (past pres., dir.), Tulsa (past dir.) (Tulsa). Home: 2916 S Yorktown Tulsa OK 74114 Office: Box 1 Tulsa OK 74101

HUNT, SAMUEL E., Jr., grain co. exec.; b. Red Lake Falls, Minn., Feb. 1, 1916; s. Sam E. and Maude (Findeisen) H.; B.B.A. with distinction, U. Minn., 1937; m. Marcia Kundert, Aug. 5, 1937; children—Thomas and Donald (twins), Penelope, Patricia. With Cargill, Inc., Mpls., 1943-57; with Central Soya Co., Inc., Ft. Wayne, Ind., 1957—, v.p. grain div., 1963—. Bd. dirs. Family and Childrens Service Ft. Wayne. Mem. Chgo. Bd. Trade, Phi Beta Kappa, Beta Gamma Sigma. Conglist. Home: 4311 Old Mill Rd Fort Wayne IN 46807 Office: Fort Wayne Bank Bldg Fort Wayne IN 46802

HUNT, THELMA, educator; b. Aurora, Ark., Nov. 30, 1903; d. Jay Guy and Ollie Allan (Spurlock) Hunt; A.B., George Washington U., 1924, M.A., 1925, Ph.D., 1927, M.D., 1935; m. Ernest Alfred Healy, Jr., Mar. 15, 1942. Research asst. psychol. tests Civil Service Commn., 1923-27; instr. psychology Middle Tenn. State Coll., 1927-28; faculty psychology George Washington U., 1928—, prof., 1939—, chmn. dept., 1940-64; dir. Center for Psychol. Service, Washington 1937—; cons. personnel research br. War Dept., 1942-44, D.C. Nursing Sch., 1941—. Diplomate Am. Bd. Examiners in Profl. Psychology. Fellow Am. Psychol. Assn., A.A.A.S. Author: Measurement in Psychology, 1936; Nursing Aptitude Tests, 1944; Social Intelligence Test, 1949. Home: 3517 Macomb St NW Washington DC 20016

HUNT, VERE LOUIS, mfg. co. exec.; b. Syracuse, N.Y., Sept. 10, 1908; s. John E. and Mildred F. (Haar) H.; grad. Phillips Exeter Acad., 1927; A.B., Williams Coll., 1931; m. Elizabeth Ann Sulivan, Apr. 25, 1943; children—Richard V., Mary Barbara. With Bankers Trust Co., N.Y.C., 1931-40, Gen. Motors Acceptance Corp., Syracuse, N.Y., 1940; asst. to pres. Prosperity Co., Inc., Syracuse, 1940-56; with Carrier Corp., Syracuse, 1956—, treas., 1960—; chmn. v.p. Carrier Distbn. Credit Corp., Syracuse, 1962—. Vice pres., treas., dir. Onondaga Indsl. Devel. Corp. Past treas., bd. dir. Syracuse chpt. A.R.C.; bd. dirs. Syracuse Community Housing Devel. Corp. Served with USAAF, 1942-45. Mem. Syracuse Assn. Credit Mgmt. (past v.p., dir.), Air and Refrigeration Inst. (past v.p.), Greater Syracuse C. of C. (past v.p., dir.), Chi Psi. Roman Catholic. Club: Cavalry (Manlius, N.Y.). Home: 507 N Manlius St Fayetteville NY 13066 Office: Carrier Corp Carrier Pkwy Syracuse NY 13201

HUNT, WALTER SKELLIE, Jr., orthopedic surgeon; b. Troy, N.Y., Jan.1, 1917; s. Walter Skellie and Ruth Margaret (White) H.; B.S., U. N.C., 1937; M.B., Northwestern U., 1939, M.D., 1940; m. Miriam Pepper Hall, Oct. 28, 1938; children—Walter Skellie, Kemp Neal, William Hall. Intern Rex Hosp., Raleigh, N.C., 1939- 40; resident orthopedic surgery Passavant Wesley, Children's Meml. hosps., Chgo., 1946-48; attending orthopedic surgeon Rex and Wake Meml. hosps.; dir. crippled children's clinics, New Bern and Raleigh, N.C., 1950—, Smithfield, N.C., 1955—; asst. clin. prof. orthopedic surg. Med. Sch., U. N.C. Served from 1st lt. to maj., M.C., U.S. Army, 1940-45; PTO. Recipient gov.'s award as N.C.'s Outstanding Physician of Yr. in treatment of the handicapped, 1965. Diplomate Am. Bd. Orthopedic Surgery. Fellow A.C.S., Am. Acad. Orthopedic Surgeons, So. Med. Assn.; mem. A.M.A., N.C. Orthopedic Assn. (sec. 1955, pres. 1957). Author articles, treatises profl. jours. Home: Route 1 Box 335 Raleigh NC 27609 Office: 600 Wade Av Raleigh NC 27605

HUNT, WILLIAM ALVIN, psychologist; b. Hartford, Conn., Nov. 10, 1903; s. Alvin Ashbell and Mabel Stetson (Hodges) H.; A.B., Dartmouth, 1928; A.M., Harvard, 1929, Ph. D., 1931; m. Edna Reeve Bossen, June 15, 1929 (dec. Apr. 1959); m. 2d, Diana Bengston Theobald, Dec. 19, 1960; 1 dau., Margit. Instr., Dartmouth, 1931-33; asst. prof. Conn. Coll. for Women, 1933-37; prof. Wheaton (Mass.) Coll., 1938-45; prof. psychology Northwestern U., 1945-67, chmn. dept. psychology, 1951-67; prof. psychology Loyola U., Chgo., 1967—. Cons. clin. psychol. Surgeon Gen. Army, VA, 1946—; cons. Asst. Sec. Def., 1954—, Army Sci. Adv. Panel, 1956—; cons. clin. psychol. Surgeon Gen. Navy, 1958-; cons. Nat. Security Agy., 1962—. Served as comdr. USNR, World War II. Fellow Am. Psychol. Assn. (Outstanding Clin. award 1967, pres. div. clin. psychology 1954); mem. Soc. Exptl. Psychology, Phi Beta Kappa, Sigma Xi, Alpha Delta Phi. Asso. editor Jour. Clin. Psychology, 1945—. Contbr. articles to jours. Home: 2815 Sheridan Rd Evanston IL 60201

HUNT, WILLIAM DUDLEY, Jr., architect, editor, pub.; b. New Orleans, Mar. 23, 1922; s. William Dudley and Ruth (Lee) H.; B.S., Jacksonville State U., 1949; B.Arch., Tulane U., 1957; m. Gwendolyn Pratt Munson, June 19, 1954; children—William Dudley III, Walter W., Ruth Lee, Stephen Clarendon Munson, Gwendolyn Munson, John Morgan. Practice architecture William Dudley Hunt, Jr., New Orleans, Pensacola, Fla., N.Y.C., 1954-64; sr. editor Archtl. Record mag., N.Y.C., 1958-63; pub. A.I.A. Jour. mag., Washington, 1963—; cons. editor archtl., related books McGraw-Hill, 1965—; pub. dir. A.I.A., 1970—, acting dep. exec. v.p., 1970—; archtl. cons. to bldg. industry firms and assns.; asst. prof. Jacksonville State U., 1948-53; instr. Tulane U., 1953-58. Dir. Prod. Systems for Architects and Engrs., Inc., 1970—. Mem. Archtl. Rev. Bd., Rye, N.Y., 1963. Served with USAAF, 1942-45. Recipient Dallas Mus. Fine Arts Furniture Design award, 1958. Fellow A.I.A.; mem. N.Y. State Assn. Architects, Archtl. League N.Y., Engrs. Club N.Y., Authors Guild, Authors League Am., Assn. Collegiate Schs. of Architecture, Chi Phi, Tau Sigma Delta. Republican. Episcopalian. Author: Contemporary Curtain Wall, 1958; Total Design in Architecture, 1971. Author, editor: Hotels, Motels, Restaurants and Bars, 1960; Hospitals, Health Centers and Clinics, 1961; Office Buildings, 1961; Comprehensive Architectural Services, 1965; Creative Control of Building Costs, 1967. Contbr. articles profl. jours. Home: 7404 MacKenzie Ct Bethesda MD 20034 also River's Edge Route 3 Box 229 Gloucester VA 23061 Office: 1785 Massachusetts Av NW Washington DC 20036 also 32 W 40th St New York City NY 10018

HUNT, WILLIAM H., mfg. co. exec.; b. Madison, Wis., July 23, 1909; s. Walter H. and Henrietta (Milhaupt) H.; grad. Wis. State U., 1929; m. Mago Ann Dolan, July 27, 1932; 1 son, William Boynton. Tchr. gen. sci. and physics, coach, athletic dir. Algoma (Wis.) High Sch., 1929-35; sales trainee Algoma Plywood & Veneer Co., 1935-38; with U.S. Plywood Corp., 1938-57, v.p. charge sales, also dir., mem. exec. com., 1953-57; v.p. charge plywood, splty. sales Ga. Pacific Corp., 1957-64, exec. v.p., 1964-70, mem. exec. com., 1969—, pres., 1970—, also dir. Mem. Nat. Forest Products Assn. (dir.). Home: 2323 SW Park Pl Portland OR 97205 Office: 900 SW 5th Portland OR 97204

HUNTER, ALLAN OAKLEY, govt. ofcl.; b. Los Angeles, June 15, 1916; s. Henry Allan and Janet (Oakley) H.; A.B., Fresno State Coll., 1937; J.D., U. Cal. at Berkeley, 1940; m. Loberta Geene Taylor, Jan. 15, 1949; children—Genella (Mrs. Harold Williamson), Janet Oakley, John Henry, Allan Oakley. Spl. agt. FBI, 1940-44; admitted to Cal. bar, 1940; pvt. practice in Cal., 1946-50, 58-69; gen. counsel HHFA, 1955-57; pres., dir. Fed. Nat. Mortgage Assn., 1970—. Chmn. Cal. Com. Housing and Community Devel., 1967-69. Mem. U.S. Ho. of Reps., 12th Dist. Cal., 1951-54. Bd. councillors U. So. Cal. Center Urban Affairs, 1969—. Served with USNR, 1944-46. Mem. Am., Fed. bar assns., State Bar Cal., Phi Delta Phi, Sigma Chi. Clubs: Congressional Country, Metropolitan (Washington). Home: 4937 Crescent St Chevy Chase MD 20016 Office: 1133 15th St NW Washington DC 20005

HUNTER, BARBARA WAY, pub. relations exec.; b. Westport, N.Y., July 14, 1927; d. Dr. Walter Denslow and Hilda (Greenawalt) Way; B.A., Cornell U., 1949; m. Austin F. Hunter, Jan. 24, 1952; children—Kimberley Way, Victoria Meigs. Asso. editor Food Field Reporter of Topics Pub. Co., N.Y.C., 1949-51; publicist Nat. Dairy Products Corp., N.Y.C., 1951-53; account exec. Sally Dickson Assos., N.Y.C., 1953-56; with Dudley-Anderson-Yutzy Pub. Relations, Inc., N.Y.C., 1956—, asso., 1964-68, partner, 1968-70, exec. v.p., 1970—. Recipient Sparkplug award Internat. Food Service Mfrs. Assn., 1970, silver anvil Pub. Relations Soc. Am., 1966. Mem. Pub. Relations Soc. Am., Internat. Food Service Mfrs. Assn., Mortar Bd., Kappa Kappa Gamma. Mem. Community Ch. of N.Y. Home: 137 E 38th St New York City NY 10016 Office: 551 Fifth Av New York City NY 10017

HUNTER, BYNUM MERRITT, lawyer; b. Greensboro, N.C., June 13, 1925; s. Hill McIver and Annie (Merritt) H.; A.B., U. N.C., 1945, J.D., 1949; m. Ann Fulenwider, June 22, 1957 (div. 1968); children—Ann Shirley, Mary Parker; m. 2d, Mary Lane Yancey, Aug. 7, 1969. Admitted to N.C. bar, 1949, since practiced in Greensboro; partner Smith, Moore, Smith, Schell & Hunter. Served with USNR, 1943-46, 51-53. Fellow Am. Coll. Trial Lawyers; mem. Internat. Assn. Ins. Counsel, Am. Judicature Soc., Am., Greensboro (pres. 1965-66) bar assns., Zeta Psi, Phi Delta Phi. Rotarian. Home: 2210 Carlisle Rd Greensboro NC 27408 Office: Jefferson Bldg Greensboro NC 27402

HUNTER, CHARLES AXTELL, Jr., physician; b. State Coll., Pa., May 26, 1922; s. Charles Axtell and Bessie (Hildreth) H.; A.B., U. Kan., 1944, M.D., 1946; m. Lila Jean Doughman, July 28, 1945; children—Patricia Ann. Joan Leslie. Intern, U. Kan. Med. Center, 1946-47, resident pathology, 1947-48, resident obstetrics, gynecology, 1950-53; practice medicine, specializing in obstetrics and gynecology; instr. obstetrics and gynecology U. Kan., 1952-53, asst. prof., 1953-57, asso. prof., 1957-58; asso. prof. obstetrics and gynecology Ind. U. 1958-61; prof., chmn. dept. obstetrics and gynecology Sch. Medicine, U. Wash., Seattle, 1961-69; prof., chmn. dept. obstetrics and gynecology Ind. U. Med. Center, Indpls., 1969—. Served to capt., M.C., U.S. Army, 1948-50. Recipient Ann. prize Central Assn. Obstetricians and Gynecologists, 1959, Found. prize Am. Assn. Obstetricians and Gynecologists, 1960. Diplomate Am. Bd. Obstetricians and Gynecology. Mem. A.C.S., Am. Coll. Obstetrics and Gynecology (sec.), Am. Assn. Obstetricians and Gynecologists (mem. exec. council, sec., com. chmn.), Soc. Gynecologic Investigation, Assn. Profs. Gynecology and Obstetrics (v.p.), A.M.A., Ind., Marion County med. socs., N.Y. Acad. Scis., Sigma Xi. Home: 5218 Nob Lane Indianapolis IN 46226 Office: 1100 W Michigan Indianapolis IN 46202

HUNTER, CHARLES FRANCIS, educator; b. Morely, Mo., Oct. 24, 1913; s. John Jackson and Nancy (McMullin) H.; B.S., in Edn., A.B., S.E. Mo. State Coll., Cape Girardeau, 1935; Ph.M., U. Wis., 1937; Ph.D., Cornell U., 1942; m. Virginia Ann Ricker, June 18, 1944; childrenStephen, Andrew, Timothy, Julie. Asst. prof. speech U. Mo., 1942-44; dir. radio U. Mo. at Kansas City, 1945-47; asst. prof. radio Northwestern U., 1947, prof., chmn. dept. radio-TV-film, 1958—; edn. producer NBC, Chgo., 1952-64; area coordinator Midwest program airborne TV, Lafayette, Ind., 1961-64; joint prof. edn. Sch. Edn., Northwestern U. 1964—; cons. in field, 1960—. Recipient 1st award (for Live and Learn) Inst. Edn. by Radio-TV, Ohio State U., 1954. Mem. Speech Assn. Am., Central States Speech Assn., Assn. Profl. Broadcast Edn., Internat. Broadcasters Soc. (adv. bd. editors). Author articles in field. Home: 2031 Old Willow Rd Northfield IL 60093 Office: Dept Radio-TV-Film Sch of Speech Northwestern U Evanston IL 60201

HUNTER, CLARENCE E., govt. ofcl., ret.; b. Wellsburg, N.Y., Sept. 2, 1884; s. Wilmot and Clara (Emerick) H.; grad. Schissler Coll. Bus., Norristown, Pa., 1901; night courses in engring. Drexel Inst., Phila.; m. Sara Jane Landis, Jan. 10, 1905. Stenographer, Hale and Kilburn Mfg. Co., Phila., 1901; credit mgr. N.Y. Trust Co., 1921, asst. treas., 1922, asst. v.p., 1926, v.p. charge fgn. bus., 28-49; ret., 1949; dir. Walter Kidde and Co., Inc., Belleville, N.J., 1943-53; chief ECA spl. mission to Netherlands, 1949-51, Mut. Security Adminstrn. spl. mission for econ. coop., Netherlands, 1952-53; U.S. Treasury rep. U.S. mission to NATO, OECD, 1953-61. Dir. Council on Fgn. Relations, N.Y.C., 1942-53; councillor Nat. Indsl. Conf. Bd. Decorated comdr. Order of Lion (Finland), grand cross Order of Orange Nassau (Netherlands). Republican. Episcopalian. Mason (32). Clubs: Metropolitan (N.Y.C.); Metropolitan (Washington); St. Cloud Golf (Garches, France); Union Interalliee (Paris). Address: Hotel Meurice Paris 1 France also The Barclay Philadelphia PA 19103

HUNTER, DAVID ROBERT, clergyman, educator; b. Pitts., Sept. 25, 1910; s. John and Mabelle May (Fife) H.; A.B., Westminster Coll., 1932; B.D., Union Theol. Sem., N.Y.C., 1935; Ed.D., Harvard, 1952; D.D., Rikkyo (St. Paul's) U., Tokyo, Japan, 1958; m. Jewell Peterson, Mar. 21, 1935 (div. 1962); children—Joan Peterson (Mrs. Richard L. Manzelmann), David Peterson, Sara Lowell (Mrs. Charles Kellogg Hudson, Jr.), Stephen Jonathan; m. 2d, Carman St. John Wolff, Apr. 24, 1965. Ordained to ministry Congl. Ch., 1935, as deacon P.E. Ch., 1940, priest, 1940; chaplain State Infirmary, Tewksbury, Mass., 1935-38, Mass. Gen. Hosp., Boston, 1938-42; lectr. Episcopal Theol. Sch., Cambridge, Mass., 1936-42, 48-52; rector Trinity Episcopal Ch., Bridgewater, Mass., 1939- 41, Ch. of Holy Spirit, Boston, 1941-45; exec. sec. dept. Christian edn. Diocese of Mass., 1945-52, dir. dept. Christian edn. P.E. Ch., 1952- 63; dep. gen. sec. Nat. Council of Chs., N.Y.C., 1963—; lectr. Union Theol. Sem., N.Y.C., 1965. Pres., Seabury Press, 1952-57, vice chmn. bd., 1957-63; mem. joint commn. on edn. World Council Chs. and World Council Christian Edn., 1964-68; mem. bd. Nat. Tng. Labs., 1955-61; mem. program unit edn. and communication World Council of Chs., 1971—, cons. com. on The Church and Jewish people, 1971—. Mem. Mass. Gov.'s Commn. on Racial Discrimination, 1948-52. Mem. Religious Edn. Assn. (chmn. 1953-57, pres. 1966-69), World Council Christian Edn. (program chmn. 1958-67, bd. mgrs. 1967-71), Nat. Council Chs. (chmn. commn. gen. Christian edn., mem. gen. bd. 1960-63), Alpha Sigma Phi, Tau Kappa Alpha. Author: Christian Education as Engagement, 1963. Editorial bd. Religion in Life, 1966—. Home: 196 Carroll St Brooklyn NY 11231 Office: 475 Riverside Dr New York City NY 10027

HUNTER, DONALD FLEMING publisher; b. Toronto, Ont., Can., Jan. 22, 1911; s. Horace T. and Christine (Fleming) H.; student U. Toronto, 1930; m. Mary Holton, May 29, 1937; children—Donald Holton, Mary Margaret. Chmn. Maclean-Hunter, Ltd., Toronto, 1970—; chmn. Maclean-Hunter Pub. Corp., Chgo., Greatlakes Broadcasting System Ltd., Nat. Automotive Pubs. Ltd., Design Craft Ltd.; dir. Shoreacres Broadcasting Co. Ltd., CFCN Television, Ltd., Voice of the Prairies, Ltd., Maclean-Hunter Cable TV Ltd., Huron Cable TV Ltd., Orillia Broadcasting Ltd., Toronto Dominion Bank. Served to maj. Canadian Army, 1940-45. Home: 237 Warren Rd Toronto 195 Ontario Canada Office: 481 University Av Toronto 101 Ontario Canada

HUNTER, E. ALLAN, electric co. exec. ; b. Grantsville, Utah, May 27, 1914; s. James Austin and Francis (Fraser) H.; B.S. in Elec. Engring., U. Utah, 1937; postgrad. U. Mich., 1955; m. Helen Spindler, July 12, 1941; children—Edward Allan, James Scott. With Utah Power and Light Co., Salt Lake City, 1937—, various positions including asst. to pres., comml. mgr., 1937-62, v.p., 1963-68, asst. gen. mgr., dir., 1966-68, pres., chief exec. officer, 1969—; pres., dir. Western Colo. Power Co., 1969—. Mem. adv. council Weber State U. Sch. Bus. and Econs., Brigham Young U.; campaign chmn. Utah United Funds, 1968-69. Trustee Utah Blue Cross; bd. dirs. Ballet West. Served from 1st lt to maj., AUS, 1942-46; ETO. Decorated Bronze Star, Purple Heart; recipient Utah Engr. in Industry, 1968. Registered profl. engr., Utah. Mem. Salt Lake Area C. of C. (1st v.p. 1970, bd. govs.), Electric Heating Assn. (dir.), Nat. Soc. Profl. Engrs. (past pres. local chpt.), Utah Mfrs. Assn. (dir.), N.W. Electric Light and Power Assn. (past dir.). Mem. Ch. of Jesus Christ of Latter-day Saints. Clubs: Alta, Weber, Rotary (Salt Lake City). Home: 4234 Neptune Dr Salt Lake City UT 84117 Office: 1407 W North Temple St PO Box 899 Salt Lake City UT 84110

HUNTER, EDGAR HAYES, architect; b. Hanover, N.H., Aug. 1, 1914; s. Edgar Hayes and Edna H. (Hill) H.; grad. Deerfield Acad., 1933; B.A., Dartmouth, 1938, M.A., 1954; M.Arch., Harvard, 1941;

m. Margaret Greenough King, May 8, 1943; children—Christopher King, Margaret Greenough. Instr. naval architecture Mass. Inst. Tech., 1941-42; underwater gear design Boston, N.Y. navy yards, 1942-45; partner E.H. & M.K. Hunter, Hanover, N.H., 1945-66; v.p., dir. Raleigh (N.C.) office Lyles, Bissett, Carlisle & Wolff, Columbia, S.C., 1966-69; partner E.H. & M.K. Hunter, Raleigh, 1969—; v.p. Cricket Corp., Winston-Salem, N.C., 1970—; exhibited in Munich, Germany, 1958; traveling exhibit U.S. colls. and museums, 1963-66. Prof. architecture Dartmouth, 1946-66; lectr. N.C. State U., 1968-69; archtl. cons. N.C. Higher Edn. Facilities Commn., 1969-70; chmn. publ. com. N.C. Architect, 1969—. Mem. Hanover Town Planning Commn., 1964-66; mem. adv. council N.C. Higher Edn. Facilities Commn., 1968—. Bd. dirs. Raleigh Chamber Music Guild, Raleigh Children's Theatre, Recipient Progressive Architecture award, 1946, 47; award N.H. State Office Bldg. Competition, 1950. Mem. A.I.A., Newcomen Soc., N.C. Land Use Congress. Mem. Ch. of Christ. Club: North Hills (Raleigh). Important works include Out Patient Clinic, N.H. State Hosp., 1954, Toll Collectors Sta. and Canopies, Everett and Spaulding turnpikes, N.H., 1955, Lutheran Ch., 1962, Arts Center and Sci. Bldg., Colby Jr. Coll., New London, N.H., 1962, Stratton Mountain Site Planning, Vt., 1961, Loon Mountain Ski Area, Lincoln, N.H., 1966, dormitory Conn. Coll. for Women, New London, 1964, classroom bldg. and dormitories Bridgton Acad., Me., 1965, apts. and classroom bldg. Dartmouth, 1958, N.C. State Fair planning, 1970, Sugar Mountain land planning, 1969, Campus Plan for N.C. Central U., 1971, relocatables Cricket Corp., 1970. Home: 1108 Manchester Dr Raleigh NC 27609 Office: 4224 Six Forks Rd Raleigh NC 27609

HUNTER, EDWARD, editor, author; b. N.Y.C., July 2, 1902; s. Edward and Rose (Weiss) H.; self educated; m. Tatiana Pestrikoff, June 30, 1932 (div. May 1961); children—Robert, Tate Ann. Reporter and news editor of various newspapers, including Newark Ledger, New Orleans Item, N.Y. Post, N.Y. American; reporter Paris edit. Chgo. Tribune, 1924-25; news editor Japan Advertiser, Tokyo, 1927; editor Hankow (China) Herald, 1928- 29, Peking Leader, 1929-30; covered Japanese conquest of Manchuria, Spanish Civil War, Italian conquest of Ethiopia, Internat. News Service, 1931-36; Chmn. Anti-Communist Liaison, Inc., 1962—; also publisher- editor of monthly TACTICS. Cons. psychol. warfare USAF, 1953-54. Served as propaganda warfare specialist AUS, with morale operations sect. OSS, Asia, World War II. Author: Brain-Washing in Red China, 1951, rev. edit., 1971; Brainwashing; The Story of Men who Defied It, 1956, reprinted, 1971; The Story of Mary Liu, 1957; The Black Book on Red China, 1958; The Past Present: A Year in Afghanistan, 1959; In Many Voices: Our Fabulous Foreign-Language Press, 1960; Attack by Mail, 1963. Contbr. articles on psychol. warfare, polit. extremism numerous periodicals. Clubs: Overseas Press, Silurians. Address: 320 N George Mason Dr Arlington VA 22203

HUNTER, EDWIN D., mng. editor Houston Post. Address: 2410 Polk Av Houston TX 77001*

HUNTER, EDWIN FORD, Jr., U.S. judge; b. Alexandria, La., Feb. 18, 1911; s. Edwin Ford and Amelia (French) H.; student La. State U., 1930-33; LL.B., George Washington U., 1938; m. Shirley Kidd, Nov. 9, 1941; children—Edwin Kidd, Janin, Kelley. Admitted to La. bar, 1938. mem. Smith, Hunter, Risinger & Shuey, Shreveport, 1940-53. Mem. La. Legislature, 1948-52; exec. counsel Gov. La., 1952; mem. La. State Mineral Bd., 1952; now judge U.S. Dist. Ct., Western Dist. La. Served as lt. USNR 1942-45. Mem. Am. Bar Assn. (La. state chmn. jr. bar sect. 1945), Am. Legion (post comdr. 1945, judge adv. Dept. La. 1948), Sigma Chi. Roman Catholic. Home: 1000 Bayou Oaks Lane Lake Charles LA 70601 Office: PO Box 1337 Lake Charles LA 70601

HUNTER, ELMO BOLTON, U.S. judge; b. St. Louis, Oct. 23, 1915; s. David Riley and Della (Bolton) H.; A.B., U. Mo., 1936, LL.B., 1938; Cook Grad. fellow, U. Mich., 1941; m. Shirley Arnold, Apr. 5, 1952; 1 dau., Nancy Ann (Mrs. Ray Lee Hunt). Admitted to Mo. bar, 1938; practiced in Kansas City, 1938- 51; sr. asst. city counselor, 1939-40; partner Sebree, Shook, Hardy and Hunter, 1945-51; state circuit judge Mo., 1952-56; Mo. appellate judge, 1956-65; fed. dist. judge, 1965—; instr. law U. Mo., 1952-62. Mem. Bd. Police Commrs., 1949-51. Trustee Kansas City U., Sch. of Ozarks. Served to 1st lt. M.I., AUS, 1943-46. Recipient First Annual Law Day award U. Mo., 1964. Mem. Am., Fed., Mo. bar assns., Am. Judicature Soc. (bd. govs., mem. exec. com., pres.), Order of Coif, Phi Beta Kappa, Phi Delta Phi. Presbyn. (elder). Contbr. articles profl. jours. Home: 1234 W 68th Terrace Kansas City MO 64113 Office: 811 Grand Av Kansas City MO 64106

HUNTER, EVAN (pseudonym Ed McBain), author; b. N.Y.C., Oct. 15, 1926; s. Charles F. and Marie (Coppola) Lombino; student Cooper Union, 1943-44; B.A., Hunter Coll., 1950; m. Anita Melnick, Oct. 17, 1949; children—Ted, Mark, Richard. Author: The Blackboard Jungle, 1954; Second Ending, 1956; Strangers When We Meet, 1958; A Matter of Conviction, 1959; The Remarkable Harry, 1960; The Wonderful Button, 1961; Mothers and Daughters, 1961; Happy New Year, Herbie, 1963; Buddwing, 1964; The Paper Dragon, 1966; A Horse's Head, 1967, Last Summer, 1968; Sons, 1969; Nobody Knew They Were There, 1971; also mystery novels under pseudonym Ed McBain which became basis for weekly TV series: 87th Precinct: Cop Hater, The Mugger, The Pusher, 1956; The Con Man, 1957; Killer's Choice, Killer's Payoff, Lady Killer, 1958; Killer's Wedge, 'Til Death, King's Ransom, 1959; Give the Boys a Great Big Hand, The Heckler, See Them Die, 1960; Lady, Lady, I Did It!, 1961; The Empty Hours, Like Love, 1962; Ten Plus One, 1963; Ax, 1964; The Sentries, 1965; He Who Hesitates, 1965; Doll, 1965; Eighty Million Eyes, 1966; Fuzz, 1968; Shotgun, 1969; Jigsaw, 1970; Hail, Hail, the Gang's All Here , 1971; writer screenplays: Strangers When We Meet, 1960; The Birds, 1962. Served with USNR, 1944-46. Named Lit. Father of Year, 1961. Mem. Phi Beta Kappa. Address: care Scott Meredith Literary Agency Inc 580 Fifth Av New York City NY 10036

HUNTER, FRANK ADDISON III, film and drama critic; b. St. Louis, Dec. 5, 1931; s. Frank Addison, Jr. and Olive (Robinson) H.; student Washington U., St. Louis, 1954; m. Teresa McCarthy, Aug. 30, 1952; children—Angela, Mark. With Hunter Packing Co., E. St. Louis, Ill., 1952-60, asst. to mgr. carload sales and pork procurement dept., 1956-60; film and drama critic St. Louis Globe-Democrat, 1960—. Mem. Sigma Alpha Epsilon. Club: Metropolitan Press (St. Louis). Home: 140 Linden Av Clayton MO 63105 Office: St Louis Globe-Democrat 12th at Delmar Blvd St Louis MO 63102

HUNTER, FRANK HERBERT, broker; b. Pitts., Oct. 22, 1901; s. David Jr. and Elizabeth (Crow) H.; A.B., Amherst Coll., 1924, J.D., U. Pitts., 1927; m. Josephine Wittmer, June 15, 1926; children—Barbara Josephine (Mrs. A. W. Moore), David Wittmer, Peter Crow. Admitted to Pa. bar, 1927; practicing atty., 1927- 28; securities investment bus., 1929—; with McKelvy and Co., Pitts., 1932-69, partner, 1941-69; pres. Parker/Hunter, Inc., 1969—. Bd. govs. N.Y. Stock Exchange, 1962-65. Mem. Investment Bankers Assn. Am. (chmn. W. Pa. group), Allegheny County Bar Assn., Nat. Assn. Securities Dealers (chmn. bd. govs. 1956), Pa. Soc. Republican. Presbyn. Clubs: N.Y. Stock Exchange Luncheon; Bond, University, Duquesne (Pitts.); Fox Chapel Golf. Home: 2690 Oak Hill Dr Allison Park PA 15101 Office: Union Trust Bldg Pittsburgh PA 15219

HUNTER, FRANK RHODES, Jr., lawyer, educator; b. Norfolk, Va., Nov. 21, 1913; s. Frank Rhodes and Ethel Melvina (Heltman) H.; student U. Md.; B.S. in Engring., George Washington U., 1939, J.D. with honors, 1945; m. Barbara Pace, Mar. 31, 1939; 1 son, William Pace. Pvt. engring. work, engring. positions U.S. Govt., 1938- 46; admitted to D.C. bar, 1946, U.S. Supreme Ct. bar, 1960, U.S. Ct. of Appeals bar, 1946; legal adviser U.S. Maritime Commn., 1946-50; asst. gen. counsel Subversive Activities Control Bd., 1950-59, gen. counsel, 1959-69; asso. prof. law U. Fla. Coll. Law, 1969—. Mem. Fed. Bar. Assn., Phi Alpha Delta. Methodist (ofcl. bd.). Home: 5232 Shadow Lane Dr Sarasota FL 33581

HUNTER, GEORGE CAMERON, architect; b. Berkeley Springs, W.Va., Dec. 29, 1912; s. George Cameron and Bessie (Harmison) H.; B.S. in Architecture, U. Va., 1935; m. Lillian Janet Miller, June 18, 1938; children—Martha Sue, Mary Ann (Mrs. James Robert Eccles). Asst. architect Nat. Park Service, 1935-41; designer, architect W. Va. Conservation Commn., 1941-42; asso. architect Def. Plant Corp., Charleston, W. Va., 1942-45; draftsman Glen C. Hancock, 1945-49, Tucker & Silling, 1949-51, Asso. Housing Architects, 1951-52; chief draftsman, Grerfe & Daley, 1952-55; partner firm Hunter & Spurling, 1955-57; owner firm G. Cameron Hunter, Architect, 1957-66; partner firm G. Cameron Hunter and Zando, Martin & Milstead, Architects and Engrs., Princeton, W. Va., 1966—. Mem. Princeton Planning and Zoning Commn. Mem. A.I.A. (pres. W. Va. 1962-63), Princeton C. of C. (bd. dirs.), W. Va. Bd. Architects (sec.), Scarab, Theta Chi. Methodist (v.p. adminstrv. bd. trustee). Rotarian (pres. Princeton), Elk. Clubs: Toastmaster (Princeton); University (Bluefield, W.Va.). Home: 11 Grandview Pl Princeton WV 24740 Office: 1422 Main St Princeton WV 24740

HUNTER, GEORGE WILLIAM, educator; b. Jenkintown, Pa., Sept. 29, 1911; s. Joseph Walker and Esther (Thomas) H.; A.B., Lincoln U., 1931; A.M., Columbia, 1933; Ph.D., Pa. State U., 1946; m. Anna Elizabeth DeCosta, July 12, 1932; children—Georgianna (Mrs. George B. Price), George William. Instr. chemistry Lincoln U., 1931; asst. prof. sci. and math. Tex. Coll., 1933; asst. prof. chemistry Prairie View Coll., 1934; prof. sci. St. Phillip Jr. Coll., San Antonio, 1935; med. social worker N.Y. Dept. Welfare, 1937-40; lab. technician Coll. City N.Y., 1940-42; prof. chemistry, head dept. Hampton Inst., 1942-48, Md. State U., 1948-51; prof. chemistry S.C. State Coll., 1951-56, prof. natural sci., head dept., 1959-63, dean, 1963-71; prof. chemistry Agr. and Tech. Coll., 1956-59; dir. NSF In-Service and Summer Inst., 1959-65; sci. cons. Claflin Coll., 1958-63. Dir. Am. Fed. Savs. & Loan Corp. Dist. chmn. S.C. Boy Scouts, 1951-54, N.C. Boy Scouts, 1956-59. GEB Fellow, 1945-46. Fellow Am. Inst. Chemistry, A.A.A.S.; mem. Nat. Tech. Assn., Nat. Inst. Sci., Am. Oil Chemists Soc., Sigma Xi, Phi Kappa Phi, Phi Lambda Upsilon, Gamma Sigma Delta, Beta Kappa Chi, Delta Mu Delta, Alpha Mu Gamma. Home: Rte 1 Box 782 Orangeburg SC 29115 Office: S C State Coll Orangeburg SC 29115

HUNTER, GROVER CLEVELAND, Jr., educator, dentist; b. La Grange, Ga., July 26, 1915; s. Grover Cleveland and Mary (Hines) H.; A.B., Emory U., 1936, D.D.S., 1940; M.S., U. Ill., 1941; m. Betty Jean Silver, Oct. 16, 1942; children—James Milton, Jean Ann, Carolyn Jane. Successively asso., asso. prof., prof. oral pathology Emory U., 1941-52; prof., head dept. peridontology and oral pathology U. N.C., 1952-69, prof., chmn. dept. periodontics, 1969—. Diplomate, Am. Bd. Oral Pathology. Fellow Am. Acad. Oral Pathology; mem. Am. Dental Assn., Internat. Platform Assn., So. Acad. Periodontology (past pres.), N.C. Dental Soc., Am. Coll. Dentists, Am. Acad. Periodontology, A.A.A.S., Phi Beta Kappa, Omicron Kappa Upsilon. Co-author: Periodontics for the Dental Hygienist, 1968. Contbr. articles profl. jours., chpts. to several textbooks in field, poems to N.Y. Times and Emory U. Quar. Home: 3607 Hope Valley Rd Durham NC 27707 Office: Dental Bldg Chapel Hill NC 27514

HUNTER, HENRY HAMILTON, chem. co. exec.; b. Pitts., Apr. 17, 1922; s. Henry Phipps and Marjorie (Hamilton) H.; student Williams Coll., 1940-41; B.J., U. Mo., 1948; m. Diane Webb, Feb. 7, 1959; children—Hyatt Hamilton, Alison Webb, Henry Hamilton. Asst. city editor (Champaign (Ill.) News Gazette, 1949; editor Irving-Cloud Pub. Co., Cleve, 1950; asst. pub. relations dir. Ross Roy Inc., Detroit, 1950-51; asst. pub. relations dir. Grant Advt., N.Y.C., 1951-54; with Olin Mathieson Chem. Corp., 1954—, dir. marketing services, 1963-64, v.p. marketing services, 1964-67, v.p. pub. relations and communications, 1967—. Pub. relations com. U.S. Com. for UN. Bd. dirs., v.p. Stamford United Fund. Served with USMCR, 1941-45. Mem. Pub. Relations Soc. Am., Airplane Owners and Pilots Assn., Soaring Soc. Am., Assn. Nat. Advertisers (dir.). Clubs: New Canaan Field; N.Y. Yacht; Madison (Conn.) Country; Sachems Head Yacht. Home: 125 Greenley Rd New Canaan CT 06840 Office: 460 Park Av New York City NY 10022

HUNTER, HOLLAND, educator, economist; b. Evanston, Ill., July 6, 1921; s. Harry Holland and Hester (Walrath) H.; B.S., Haverford Coll., 1943; M.A., Harvard, 1947, Ph.D., 1949; m. Helen Taft Manning, Jan. 31, 1946; children—Ann Herron, Barbara Walrath, Christine Manning, Timothy White. Price analyst OPA, 1943-44; requirements analyst FEA, New Delhi, India, 1944-45; teaching fellow Harvard, 1946-48; faculty Haverford (Pa.) Coll., 1948—, prof. econs., chmn. dept., 1963—. Cons. in field, 1950—: Brookings Instn. research prof., 1962-63, mem. sr. staff, 1965-66. Committeeman, Haverford Twp. Democratic Com., 1953-63. Trustee Baldwin Sch., Haverford Friends Sch., Fountain Valley Sch. Guggenheim fellow, 1959-60. Mem. Am. Assn. Advancement Slavic Studies (pres., v.p., dir.), Am. Econ. Assn., Assn. Asian Studies. Mem. Soc. Friends (chmn. nominating com. Haverford monthly meeting 1969—). Author: Soviet Transportation Policy, 1957; Soviet Transport Experience, 1968. Home: Featherbed Lane Haverford PA 19041

HUNTER, HOWARD LOUIS, ret. coll. dean; b. Fulton, N.Y., June 17, 1904; s. Robert Bates and Belle Madeleine (Mosher) H.; Chem.B., Cornell U., 1925; Ph.D., (Heckscher research fellow 1927-28), 1928; student Mass. Inst. Tech., 1939; m. Roxana Wulliams Eaton, Oct. 19, 1932; children—Nancy Roxanna (Mrs. James E. Padgett), Robert Eaton. Asst. prof. chemistry Clemson Coll., 1928-31, acting prof. textile chemistry, 1931- 32, asso. prof., head inorganic chemistry div., 1932-41, prof. chemistry, 1945-46, prof. chemistry, dean Sch. Chemistry and Geology, 1946-55; dean Coll. Arts and Scis., Clemson U., 1955-69; councilor Oak Ridge Inst. Nuclear Studies, 1952-69. Served with C.W.S. in Devel. lab. Mass. Inst. Tech., 1941-45; lt. col. Chem. Corps Res. Fellow A.A.A.S., Am. Inst. Chemists; mem. S. C. Acad. Sci., Am. Chem. Soc. (councilor Western Caronnas sect.), Phi Kappa Phi, Sigma Xi, Phi Kappa Psi, Alpha Chi Sigma. Presbyn. Club: Fellowship, S.C. Forum. Author: Laboratory Manual in General Chemistry, 1947. Contbr. articles in tech. mags. Researcher on rare element chemistry. Home: Box 952 Clemson SC 29631

HUNTER, HOWARD WILLIAM, ch. ofcl.; lawyer; b. Boise, Ida., Nov. 14, 1907; s. John William and Nellie Marie (Rasmussen) H.; J.D., cum laude, Southwestern U., 1939; m. Clara May Jeffs, June 10, 1931; children—Howard William, John Jacob, Richard Allen. Engaged in banking in Cal., 1928-34; admitted to Cal. bar, 1939, practiced in Los Angeles until 1959; mem. council of 12, Ch. of Jesus Christ of Latter-day Saints, 1959—, also mem. ch. bd. edn. Dir. Beneficial Life Ins. Co., Salt Lake City, Watson Land Co., Los Angeles, Utah Home Fire Ins. Co., Heber J. Grant & Co., Continental Bank & Trust Co. Pres., Polynesian Cultural Center, Hawaii. Trustee Brigham Young U. Mem. Cal., Utah bar assns., Geneal. Soc. Utah (pres.). Home: 2833 Sherwood Dr Salt Lake City UT 84108 Office: 47 E South Temple Salt Lake City UT 84111

HUNTER, JACK CORBETT, city ofcl.; b. Youngstown, O., Mar. 13, 1930; s. Charles E. and Margaret C. (Higgins) H.; degree U. Denver; postgrad. Youngstown State U.; grad. degree Kent State U.; Instr. Youngstown State U.; asst. trust officer Mahoning Nat. Bank; ward councilman, 2 terms; mayor City of Youngstown, 1970—. Mem. Republican State Central Com. of Ohio; alternate del. Rep. Nat. Conv., 1968. Trustee Youngstown U. Served with USMCR. Mem. Navy League, Phi Sigma Alpha. Home: 467 W Boston Av Youngstown OH 44511 Office: City Hall Bldg Boardman and Phelps St Youngstown OH 44503

HUNTER, JAMES, educator: b. Glasgow, Scotland, Dec. 20, 1921; s. David Constable and Margaret (Wink) H.; came to U.S., 1930, naturalized, 1938; B.A., Carnegie Inst. Tech., 1943; M.A., Duquesne U., 1946; Ph.D., Eastman Sch. Music, 1958; pupil Jean Langlais, Paris, 1967; m. Lois J. Stuckey, June 11, 1951; children—Craig Edward, Bradley Frederick. Faculty, Duquesne U. Sch. Music, 1946-, prof. music, 1958-; organist, dir. music Westminster Presbyn. Ch., 1960—; recitalist throughout U.S., 1943- -. Vice pres. Musicians Club Pitts., 1964-65; chmn. music com. Mendelssohn Choir Pitts., 1963-64. Mem. Phi Kappa Phi, Phi Mu Alpha. Author: A Dorian Trypych (Symphony for Orch.), 1958; others. Home: 525 Roslyn Pl Pittsburgh PA 15232

HUNTER, JAMES M., architect; b. Omaha, Neb., Apr. 19, 1908; s. Edgar William and Ida L. (Bogue) H.; student Ia. State Coll., 1927-30; B. Arch., U. Ill., 1936; m. Madelyn J. Engleman, Feb. 5, 1937; children—John David, and Janet Diane (Mrs. Ward Powers). Engaged in practice of architecture, 1940- -; firm James M. Hunter and Assos., Boulder, Colo., 1945—; planner, architecture Colo. State U., Ft. Lewis Coll., Tarkio (Mo.) Coll., Regis Coll., Denver; architect in residence Am. Acad., Rome, 1963; vis. prof. architecture U. Colo. Mem. adv. bd. Assn. Applied Solar Energy, U. Colo. Sch. Architecture; mem. pub. adv. panel on archtl. services Gen. Services. Adminstrn., 1965; chmn. archtl. jury Dept. Health, Edn. and Welfare, 1966. Served as lt. (j.g.) USNR, World War II, Recipient award of merit A.I.A., 1955, regional awards, 1954, 55, 56, 57, 58, 60, 62, 65, 67; award N.Y. Archtl. League, 1954, 55; Church Archtl. Guild Am., 1956, 58. Registered architect Colo., Wyo., Neb. Fellow A.I.A. 2d v.p. 1960-61, past nat. chmn. com. on edn., nat. chmn. com. on profession, regional dir. Rocky Mountain region 1964-67; past pres. Colo. chpt.); mem. Colo. Bd. Examiners of Architects (past pres.), Colo. Soc. Architects (past pres.). Mason. Rotarian. Home: 1505 Mariposa Av Boulder CO 80302 Office: 1110 Pearl St Boulder CO 80302

HUNTER, JAMES WILSON, clergyman; b. Balt., Apr. 4, 1904; s. William Curtis and Beryl Gertrude (Wilson) H.; A.B., John Hopkins, 1925; B.D., Va. Theol. Sem., Alexandria, 1928, D.D., 1948; m. Nancy McCormick Wattles, Oct. 18, 1928; children—Nancy Wattles, Sally Wilson, James Wilson. Student in charge St. Barnabas Episcopal Ch., Sykesville, Md., 1926-27, deacon in charge, 1927-28, priest in charge 1928-30; rector St. Andrew's, Ft. Thomas, Ky., 1932-38; minister in charge St. Stephen's, Latonia, Ky., 1932-38; rector St. Andrew's, Louisville, 1938-46; rector St. Mark's, San Antonio, Tex., 1946-48; elected bishop coadjutor Episcopal Missionary Dist. of Wyo., 1947, consecrated, Laramie, Wyo., 1948; bishop Missionary Dist. of Wyo., 1949-69. Mem. standing com. Diocese of Lexington and Ky. (pres.), standing com., Diocese of W. Tex., Council of Social Agys. of Louisville (pres. 1944-45), Council of Chs., San Antonio; chmn. program and budget com. Protestant Episcopal Church, 1961, mem. nat. council, 1961—; del. Gen. Conv. of Episcopal Ch., 1934, 37, 40, 43, 46. Clubs: Rotary (San Antonio); Optomist (Newport, Ky.). Home: 1902 Thornburgh Dr Laramie WY 82070

HUNTER, JOHN, appliance mfg. co. exec.; b. Fitchburg, Mass., Sept. 22, 1914; s. Robert and Helen (Ramage) H.; student Bentley Coll., 1946-48; m. Ruth E. Ballard, Sept. 16, 1950. Accountant Whirlpool Corp., Benton Harbor, Mich., 1948-51, chief accountant aircraft div., La Porte, Ind., 1951-53, div. controller service div., 1953-68, corp. controller adminstrv. center, Benton Harbor, Mich., 1968—. Treas. St. Joseph (Mich). Meml. Hosp. Served with USAAF, 1942-45. Mem. Financial Execs. Inst. (nat. dir. 1970—). Home: 1360 Point O'Woods Dr Benton Harbor MI 49022 Office: Whirlpool Corp Adminstrv Center Benton Harbor MI 49022

HUNTER, JOHN, Jr., banker; b. Kelty, Fifeshire, Scotland, Feb. 11, 1925; s. John and Mary (Wallace) H.; came to U.S., 1931, naturalized, 1939; B.A. cum laude, Ithaca Coll., 1949; student Alfred U., summer 1951; M.S. in Edn., St. Bonaventure U., Olean, N.Y., 1954; grad. Mgmt. Inst., N.Y. U., 1955; m. Sylvia J. Wightman, June 30, 1951; children—James D., Nancy J., Judith L., Linda C. With Chase Manhattan Bank, 1954-60; asst. sec., asst. v.p., v.p. Lincoln Rochester Trust Co., (N.Y.), 1960-65; exec. v.p., dir. First Nat. Bank Rochester, 1965-66; pres., chief exec. officer, chmn. bd. Vt. Nat. Bank. 1967- -; v.p. Hunter Broadcasting, Inc., Burlington, Vt., 1964—, Hunter Broadcasting Inc., Kingston, N.Y., 1966—; dir. Durham's, Housing Projects Enterprises, Inc., Montpelier. Mem. Gov. Vt. Council Econ. Advisers, 1968; mem. regional adv. com. First Nat. Bank Region, 1968-70; mem. Brattleboro Sch. Facilities Com., Vt. Econ. Coordinating Com., 1971—. Trustee Village of Webster, N.Y., 1965-66; treas. Monroe County Republican Club, 1964- 66. Bd. corporators Brattleboro Meml. Hosp. Served with USMRC, 1942-45. Decorated Air Medal with 2 gold stars. Rotarian. Home: 71 Western Av Brattleboro VT 05301 Office: 100 Main St Brattleboro VT 05301

HUNTER, JOHN ANDERSON, univ. pres.; b. Donner, La., Apr.23, 1914; s. John Anderson and Minnie Lee (Steinwinder) H.; B.S., Davidson Coll., 1934; M.A., La. State U., 1947, Ph.D., 1949; m. Doris Paine, June 13, 1937; children—David M., John Anderson. Tchr.-coach Gulf Coast Mil. Acad., 1934-37; geophysicist Stanolind Oil & Gas Co., 1937-39; ednl. adviser Civilian Conservation Corps., 1939-41; comdt. cadets Gulf Coast Mil. Acad., 1941-43; dir. classified personnel La. State U., 1947-49; supr. La. Dept. Edn., 1949- 51; registrar La. State U., 1951-56, dean jr. div., 1956-59, dean student services, 1959-62, pres., 1962—, prof. adn., 1959. Dir. Atlanta bd. Fed. Reserve Bank, 1964-69. La. coordinator So. Regional Edn. Bd., exec. com., 1962-66, commn. on higher ednl. opportunity in South, 1966—; mem. Nat. Citizens Com. for Community Relations, 1964—; adv. bd. Our Lady of the Lake Hosp., Baton Rouge. Served with USNR, 1943-46. Mem. Council So. Univs., So. Assn. Colls. and Schs. (pres. 1963- 64), Am. Assn. Collegiate Registrars and Admissions Officers, So. Assn. Land-Grant Colls. and State Univs. (pres. 1964-65), La. Hist. Assn., La. Registrars Assn. (past pres.), S.A.R., Am. Council on Edn., Cabot Corp. Scholarship Com., Nat. Assn. State Univs. and Land Grant Colls., Southeastern Conf. (pres. 1968), La. Beta Club Council, La. Sch. Bds. Assn. (hon.), N.E.A., La. Tchrs. Assn., La. Fulbright Scholarship Com., So. Assn. Coll. and Univ. Registrars (past pres.), Am. Radio Relay League, Am. Legion, Omicron Delta Kappa, Phi Kappa Phi, Phi Delta Kappa, Kappa Phi Kappa, Kappa Delta Pi, Phi Eta Sigma, Sigma Phi Epsilon, Gamma

Beta Phi, Alpha Sigma Lambda, Phi Mu Alpha. Democrat. Episcopalian. Mason (33, Shriner). Clubs: Camelot (gov. 1967—), Pickwick; International House (New Orleans). Author: A Handbook for Louisiana School Board Members, 1949; Teacher Welfare Laws of Louisiana, 1956; School Board Service, 1961; Progress and Promise, 1967. Contbr. articles to prof. jours. Home: 2959 E Lakeshore Dr Baton Rouge LA 70808

HUNTER, JOHN B., aircraft co. exec. Vice pres., controller Canadair Ltd. Office: PO Box 6087 Montreal 101 Quebec Canada*

HUNTER, JOHN B., Jr., mfg. co. exec.; b. Evanston, Ill., Oct. 1, 1916; s. John B. and Gladys (Burns) H.; B.A., Yale, 1938; grad. Advanced Mgmt. Program, Harvard, 1968; m. Anne Miller Murdoch, Sept. 19, 1947; children—Francis G., Amy B. With Nat. Biscuit Co., 1938-40, Procter and Gamble Co., 1940-60; with B.F. Goodrich Indsl. Products Co. div. B.F. Goodrich Co., 1960—, v.p. marketing, 1965—. Bd. dirs. Assn. Nat. Advertisers, 1963—, chmn. bd., 1966; bd. dirs. Bur. Publs. Audit, 1965—, sec. bd., 1967; bd. dirs. Advt. Council; mem. Nat. Marketing Adv. Council. Exec. com. Akron area Boy Scouts Am., 1961—. Trustee Childrens Hosp., Akron, 1965—. Served to maj. USAAF, 1941-46. Mem. Am. Mgmt. Assn., Detroit Advt. Assn. Episcopalian. Clubs: Country of N.C.; Portage Country (Akron); Cincinnati Country; Chicago; Yale (N.Y.C.). Home: 384 S Rose Blvd Akron OH 44313 Office: 500 S Main St Akron OH 44318

HUNTER, JOHN MCNEILE, educator; b. Woodville, Tex., Jan. 23, 1901; s. John Alexander and Mary Evelyn Victoria (Edwards) H.; S.B., Mass. Inst. Tech., 1924; M.S., Cornell, 1927, Ph.D., 1937; m. Ella Louise Stokes, Sept. 10, 1929; 1 dau., Jean Evelyn. Instr. physics Prairie View Coll., 1924-45; instr. elec. engring. Va. State Coll., 1925-26, asst. prof., 1926, prof., head dept. physics, 1927—, chmn. sci. math. unit, 1930-40, acting dean, 1931- 32, 34-35, dir. Div. Grad. Studies, 1939—, dean Coll., 1957- -; civilian supr. instrn. Engrs. Specialist Sch., 1942-43, instnl. rep. Engring., Sci. Mgmt. War Tng., 1942-45; pres. Nat. Inst. Sci., 1944-45. Trustee St. Paul's College. Fellow A.A.A.S.; mem. Am. Phys. Soc., Am. Assn. U. Profs., Am. Assn. Physics Tchrs., Am. Tchrs. Assn., Sigma Xi, Sigma Pi Sigma, Kappa Alpha Psi, Sigma Pi Phi, Kappa Mu Epsilon. Episcopalian. Author articles ednl. jours. Home: Va State Coll Petersburg VA 23803

HUNTER, JOHN PITMAN, Jr., apparel mfr.; b. Tupelo, Miss., Nov. 4, 1923; s. John Pitman and Alice (Adams) H.; B.S., Mass. Inst. Tech., 1947; m. Ann Egelston, Dec. 17, 1944; children—Alice Ann, Bonnie, John Pitman III, Dean, Rebecca. Partner, Hunter-Sadler Co., Tupelo, 1948-60; with Oxford Mfg. Co., Inc., Atlanta, 1950—, exec. v.p., 1955-62, became pres., 1962, now v.p., dir. Served with C.E., AUS, 1942-45. Home: 758 W Paces Ferry Rd NW Atlanta GA 30305 Office: 15 Spring St NW Atlanta GA 30303

HUNTER, JOHN ROBERT, Jr., architect; b. Hollidaysburg, Pa., July 11, 1898; s. John Barr and Nancy Catharine Law (Gardner) H.; student Pa. State U., 1918-22; m. Thelma Vera Davis, Dec. 16, 1922; children—John Davis (dec.), Joan Davis (Mrs. Douglas F. Melville). Pvt. practice architecture, Hollidaysburg, Pa., 1922-27; partner Hunter and Caldwell, Altoona, Pa., 1927-51, Hunter, Campbell and Rea, Altoona and Johnstown, Pa., and predecessor, 1951-63; prin. works include ednl. bldgs. Juniata Coll., St. Francis Coll. of Loretto, Pa. State U., other pub., ednl., indsl. bldgs.; co-ordinator gen. state auth. bldg. program Pa. State U., 1936-39; contract engr. E.I. DuPont de Nemours and Co., 1942-45; mem. adv. bd. Central Pa. Nat. Bank. Mem. indsl. and profl. adv. council Pa. State U., also mem. adv. bd. Altoona campus. Served with S.A.T.C., World War I. Fellow A.I.A.; mem. Pa. Forestry Assn. (dir.), Pa. Soc. Architects, Outdoor Writers Assn. Am., Am. Legion, Pa. Soc. N.Y., Scarab, Alpha Chi Rho (trustee, nat. pres. 1948-50, pres. nat. ednl. found. 1953-57, chmn. bd. 1957-59), Alpha Rho Chi (hon.). Mason (32, Shriner, Jester), Kiwanian. Clubs: Blairmont Country (pres.); Pittsburgh Athletic Assn. Home: Blairmont Terrace Hollidaysburg PA 16648 Office: 3601 Fifth Av Altoona PA 16602

HUNTER, JOHN STUART, educator, statistician; b. Holyoke, Mass., June 3, 1923; s. John and Irene (Robinson) H.; Ph.D. in Exptl. Statistics, N.C. State U., 1954, M.S. in Engring. Math., 1949, B.S. in Elec. Engring., 1947; m. Edna Taylor Martz, Sept. 19, 1952; children—Jean Bartlett, William Mark, Anne Robinson. Staff statistician Am. Cyanamid Co., 1954-59; with Statis. Techniques Research Group, 1957-59, Math. Research Center, U. Wis., 1959- 61; asso. prof. Princeton, 1962-67, prof. statistics, 1968—; statistician in residence U. Wis., 1967-68. Cons., lectr. in field. Served with AUS, 1942-46. Fellow Am. Statis. Assn., Am. Soc. Quality Control (Shewhart medalist 1971); mem. Biometrics Soc., Inst. Math. Statistics, Am. Inst. Chem. Engrs., Am. Soc. Testing Materials, Am. Soc. Ind. Engrs., Am. Assn. U. Profs., Royal Statis. Soc., Internat. Statistics Inst. Episcopalian. Founding editor Technometrics, 1959-63. Home: 100 Bayard Lane Princeton NJ 08540

HUNTER, KENNETH EDWARD, space sci. co. exec.; b., Penetang, Ont., Can., July 29, 1922; s. Herbert N. and Marion (Roberts) H.; B.A.Sc. in Engring. Physics, U. Toronto, 1948, M.A. in Physics, 1949; m. Ruth Steele, Apr. 2, 1949 (dec.); children—Christopher I., Paul K., Stephen T., Laurie Anne; m. 2d, R. Frances Taylor, May 18, 1962 (div. Dec. 1970). Came to U.S., 1949, naturalized, 1958. Project mgr. Newmont Mining Corp., N.Y.C., 1949-52; chief geophysicist Tsumeb Corp., Ltd. (S.W. Africa), 1952-55; mgr. geophysics div. Hycon Mfg. Co., Monrovia, Cal., 1955-58, ngr. spl. equipment div., 1958-60, v.p., 1960-62, v.p., gen. mgr., 1962-63, pres., 1963-71; exec. v.p. Actron Industries, Inc., 1971—; dir. Linkabit Corp. chmn. bd. United Detector Tech. Bd. dirs. City of Hope; trustee Job Resources and Ednl. Center, U.S.-South Africa Leader Exchange Program Found. Served with Signal Corps, Canadian Army, World War II. Mem. Soc. Exploration Geophysicists, Am. Geophys. Union, Am. Rocket Soc., Am. Phys. Soc., Am. Soc. Oceanography. Democrat. Home: 2047 San Pasqual St Pasadena CA 91107 Office: 700 Royal Oaks Dr Monrovia CA 91016

HUNTER, KERMIT HOUSTON, univ. dean, writer; b. Hallsville, W.Va., Oct. 3, 1910; s. Otis John and Lillian Elizabeth Robinson (Farley) H.; B.A., Ohio State U., 1931; M.A. in Theatre, U. N.C., 1949, Ph.D. in English Lit., 1955; D.Litt., Emory and Henry Coll., 1958; L.H.D., Okla. Christian Coll., 1971; m. Josephine Christison, Sept. 6, 1952. Successively newspaper reporter, c. of c. sec., choir dir., organist, and piano study Juilliard Inst., 1931-40; bus. mgr. N.C. Symphony Orch., 1946; prof. drama Hollins Coll., Va., 1956-64; dean Meadows Sch. Arts, So. Meth. U., 1964—; author, prod. more than 30 hist. dramas, especially Unto These Hills, 1950—. Vice pres. Allied Restoration Co., Inc., Dallas. Bd. dirs. Dallas Symphony Soc., Dallas Jr. League, Dallas Met. Opera Assns. Served to lt. col. AUS, 1940-45. Decorated Legion of Merit. Mem. Modern Lang. Assn., Am. Theatre Assn., Assn. Arts Councils Am., Beta Theta Pi. Rotarian. Home: 13322 Peyton Dr Dallas TX 75240 Office: Meadows Sch Arts So Meth U Dallas TX 75222

HUNTER, KIM (Janet Cole), actress; b. Detroit, Nov. 12, 1922; d. Donald and Grace Mabel (Lind) Cole; student pub. schs., acting with Charmine Lantaff Camine, 1938-40, Actors Studio; m. William A. Baldwin, Feb. 11, 1944 (div. 1946); 1 dau., Kathryn Emmett (Mrs. David N. Rosen); m. 2d, Robert Emmett, Dec. 20, 1951; 1 son, Sean Emmett. Made 1st stage appearance, 1939, played in stock, 1940-42; Broadway debut in A Streetcar Named Desire, 1947; appeared in Two Blind Mice (tour), 1950; Darkness at Noon (N.Y.C.), 1951; The Chase, 1952 (N.Y.C.), They Knew What They Wanted (tour), 1952; The Children's Hour (Revival) (N.Y.C.), 1952; The Tender Trap (N.Y.C.), 1954; Write Me a Murder (N.Y.C.), 1961; Weekend, (N.Y.C.), 1968; The Penny Wars (N.Y.C.), 1969; And Miss Reardon Drinks a Little (tour), 1971-72; frequent appearances summer stock and repertory theater, 1940—; appeared Am. Shakespeare Festival, Stratford, Conn., 1961; made film debut in The Seventh Victim, 1943; other motion pictures include: When Strangers Marry (re-released as Betrayed), 1944, You Came Along, 1945, A Canterbury Tale, 1949, Stairway to Heaven, 1946, A Streetcar Named Desire, 1951, Anything Can Happen, 1952, Deadline U.S.A., 1952, Storm Center, 1956, Bermuda Affair, 1957, The Young Stranger, 1957, Money, Women, and Guns, 1958, Lilith, 1964, Planet of the Apes, 1968, The Swimmer, 1968, Beneath the Planet of the Apes, 1970; Escape from the Planet of the Apes, 1971; made TV debut on Actors' Studio program, 1948; numerous TV appearances include: Requeim for a Heavyweight, 1956, The Comedian, 1957 (both on Playhouse 90), Give Us Barabbas on Hallmark Hall of Fame, 1961, 63, 68, 69; recorded From Morning 'Til Night (and a Bag Full of Poems), RCA Victor, 1961, Come, Woo Me:, Unified Audio Classics, 1964. Lectr., High Sch. for Performing Arts, N.Y.C., Friends Sem., N.Y.C., 1961, S.D. U., 1965, Lehigh U., 1965, ANTA In-Tchrs.-Service, N.Y.C., 1965, High Sch. Music and Art, N.Y.C., 1968. Recipient Donaldson award for best supporting actress in A Streetcar Named Desire, 1948, also, on Variety N.Y. Critics Poll, 1948, for film version, 1952; won Acad. awards, LOOK award, Hollywood Fgn. Corrs. Golden Globe award. Mem. Acad. Motion Picture Arts and Scis., ANTA, A.E.A. (council 1953-59), Screen Actors Guild, A.F.T.R.A. Home: 42 Commerce St New York City NY 10014

HUNTER, KRISTIN ELAINE EGGLESTON (Mrs. John I. Lattany), author; b. Phila., Sept. 12, 1931; d. George Lorenzo and Mabel (Manigault) Eggleston; B.Ed., U. Pa., 1951; m. John I. Lattany, June 22, 1968. Advt. copywriter Lavenson Bur. Advt., Phila., 1952-59; information officer City of Phila., 1963-64, 65-66, Minority of One TV documentary, 1955; dir. comprehensive health services Temple U., Phila., 1971—. John Hay Whitney fellow, 1959-60; recipient Phila. Athenaeum award, 1964; recipient Nat. Council on Interracial Books for Children award, 1968; recipient Best Mag. Reporting award Sigma Delta Chi, 1968. Mem. Phila. Art Alliance, Assn. Alumnae U. Pa. (dir. 1970-72). Author: God Bless the Child, 1964; The Landlord, 1966; The Soul Brothers and Sister Lou, 1968; Boss Cat, 1971; contbr. article Pray for Barbara's Baby, Phila. mag., 1968. Office: care Horace Matson Co 22 E 40th St New York City NY 10016

HUNTER, LEE, automotive equipment mfg. co. exec., inventor; b. St. Louis, Apr. 27, 1913; s. Lee and Ollie (Stark) H.; ed. Westminster Coll., Fulton, Mo., Washington U., St. Louis; m. Jane Franklin Brauer, 1959; stepchildren—Arthur J. Brauer, Stephen F. Brauer. Draftsman, designer Herman Body Co., 1935-36; founder Lee Hunter Jr. Mfg. Co., 1936; pres. Hunter-Hartman Corp., 1937-42; pres. Hunter Engring. Co., Bridgeton, Mo., 1947-55, chmn. bd., 1955—; pres. Hunter Aviation Co., 1955-60. Served to 1st lt., C.E., AUS, 1942-46. Mem. Phi Delta Theta. Presbyn. Clubs: St. Louis; Bellerive Country, Strathalbyn (St. Louis County). Inventor 1st rapid battery chargers; lever theory balancing; 1st on car mech. wheel balancer; wheel alignment, automotive equipment. Home: Hunter Farms 13501 Ladue Rd St Louis County MO 63141 Office: Hunter Engring Co 11250 Hunter Dr Bridgeton MO 63042

HUNTER, LEONARD LEGRANDE, architect; b. Charlotte, N.C., Mar. 22, 1905; s. Leonard LeGrande and Bess (Wiley) H.; student U. N.C., 1923-24; B.Arch., U. Pa., 1928, M.Arch., 1929; m. Kate Greene Heard, Sept. 1, 1934; children—Leonard LeGrande III, Laura Wiley. Architect, Oriental Inst., U. Chgo., Luxor, Egypt, 1929-31; asst. prof. design Ga. Sch. Tech., Atlanta, 1931-32; Henry Gillette Woodman scholar architecture U. Pa. in Europe, 1932-33; pvt. practice architecture Atlanta, 1933-34; designer supervising architect's office of Procurement Div., Treasury Dept. (reorganized as supervising architect's office, Fed. Works Agy. 1939), 1934-42, asst. chief design, 1946-49; with pub. bldgs. service Gen. Services Adminstrn., Washington, 1949-63, 66-70, supervising architect, 1956-62, asst. commr. design and constrn., 1966-70; exec. v.p. John Carl Warnecke & Assos., San Francisco, 1962-66, v.p. new bus. and pub. relations, 1970—. Mem. Gov.'s Adv. Com. for Design Hawaiian State Capitol, 1960. Served to comdr., C.E., USNR, 1942-46. Recipient Faculty medal U. Pa., 1928, Meritorious Service award Gen. Services Adminstrn., 1960. Fellow A.I.A.; mem. Sigma Xi, Tau Sigma Delta. Home: 196 Twin Peaks Blvd San Francisco CA 94114 Office: 61 New Montgomery St San Francisco CA 94105

HUNTER, LOUIS JAMES, mgmt. cons.; s. Harry and Elizabeth (Maddocks) H.; student pub. schs.; Boston; m. Marie Helen Atwater, June 19, 1912; children—Elizabeth (Mrs. F.G. Hicks), Robert Louis, Ruth (Mrs. Johnson). Treas., dir. Carter's Ink Co.; v.p., dir. Sagendorph Investment Co., dir. Putnam Equities, Inc., Preston Moss Fund. Inc., Putnam Investors Fund, Putnam Duofund Inc., Putnam Mayflower Fund, Putnam Vista Fund, Inc., Putnam Voyager Fund, Inc.; trustee Putnam Income Fund, George Putnam Fund of Boston, Putnam Growth Fund. Treas., trustee Univ. Hosp., Boston U. Med. Center. Clubs: Union, Down Town, Algonquin (Boston). Home: 172 Beacon St Boston MA 02116 Office: 75 Federal St Boston MA 02110

HUNTER, LOUIS NATHANIEL, assn. exec., b. Brampton, Ont., Can., Aug. 27, 1903; s. John Henry and Elizabeth Jane (Frazer) H.; B.S. in Mech. Eng., U. Toronto, 1925; m. Eileen Mary Magennis, Aug. 24, 1940; 1 dau., Mary Patricia. Registered profl. engr., Pa. Engr., Bryant Heater Co., Cleve., 1926-30; engr. Nat. Radiator Co., Johnstown, Pa., 1930- 60, v.p. charge research, 1941-55, sr. v.p. engring. and research, 1955-60; dir. engring. Plumbing Heating and Air Conditioning Group, Crane Co.; mng. dir. Air-Conditioning and Refrigeration Inst., Arlington, Va., 1964—. Mem. cast iron boiler industry adv. com. WPB, 1942, cons. plumbing and heating div., 1942-43. Fellow Am. Soc. M.E. (low pressure boiler code com. 1940—), Am. Soc. Heating, Refrigerating and Air-conditioning Engrs. (chmn. com. on research 1948-49, mem. council 1951, pres. 1954); mem. Steel Boiler Inst. (chmn. engring. com. 1943-60), Pa. Boiler Adv. Bd., Inst. Boiler and Radiator Mfrs. (chmn. com. research 1940, 47-48, 55-63), Air Pollution Control Assn. (past dir.), Air Conditioning and Refrigeration Inst. (treas. 1958, pres. 1963). Presbyn. Contbr. articles to tech., trade mags. Home: 8930 Colesbury Pl Fairfax VA 22030 Office: 1815 N Fort Myer Dr Arlington VA 22209

HUNTER, MARGARET KING, architect; b. Balt., May 13, 1919; d. Talmage Damron and Margaret Julie (Greenough) King; A.B., Wheaton Coll., 1941; postgrad. Smith Coll. Sch. Architecture, 1941-42; postgrad. Harvard Grad. Sch. Design, 1942-45; m. Edgar Hayes Hunter, May 8, 1943; children—Christopher King, Margaret Greenough. Draftsman, H.V. Lawrence, landscape architect, Mass., 1940; draftsman Antonin Raymond, Architect, N.Y.C., 1942-43; designer Raymond Loewy, N.Y.C., 1943; partner E.H. & M.K. Hunter, Architects-Planners, Hanover, N.H., 1945-66, Raleigh, N.C., 1969—; owner Heritage Antiques, Raleigh, 1971—; writer Pencil Points, 1942-45; traveling exhibit, 1963-66; design instr. N.C. State U., 1968; lectr., writer architecture, conservation, 1945—. Chmn. Dance Com., Hanover, 1964-66; v.p. Culture Arts for Students, Raleigh, 1970; N.H. del. 1st Internat. Conf. Women Engrs. and Scientists, 1964; mem. edn. com. N.C. Land Use Congress, 1971. Recipient Progressive Architecture Mag. award, 1946, 47; award N.H. State Office Bldg. Competition, 1950. Mem. A.I.A. (chmn. pub. relations N.H. chpt. 1953-54), Soc. Women Engrs., Soil Conservation Soc., Constrn. Specifications Inst. Baptist. Club: North Hills (Raleigh). Important works include Laconia (N.H.) State Sch. Dormitories, 1955, N.H. Toll Rd. Structures, 1955, Children's Study Home, N.H. State Hosp., 1954, apts. and classroom bldg. Dartmouth, 1960, House for Life mag., 1956, Colby Jr. Coll. Art Center and Sci. Bldg., New London, N.H., 1962, classroom bldg. Dormitories Bridgton Acad., Me., 1964, Loon Mountain Ski Area, Lincoln, N.H., 1966, dormitory Conn. Coll., New London, 1965, twenty year campus plan N.C. Central U., Durham, 1971, Student Internat. Meditation Soc., Acad., Santa Barbara, Cal. Home: 1108 Manchester Dr Raleigh NC 27609 Office: 4224 Six Forks Rd Raleigh NC 27609

HUNTER, MARSHALL KEITH, banker; b. Elberton, Ga., Oct. 26, 1901; s. Herman Park and Emma (Stillwell) H.; student Ga. Inst. Tech., 1919-20; m. Carter Jaudon, Apr. 26, 1927; 1 dau., Carter Jaudon (Mrs. Fred Williams). Clk., Fed. Res. Bank, Atlanta, 1920; mgr. Miami Credit Agy. (Fla.), 1923; mgr. credit dept. Bank Biscayne Bay (Fla.), 1923-25, First Nat. Bank, Atlanta, 1926- 31; pres. First Nat. Bank and Trust Co., Macon, Ga., 1931-33, Liberty Nat. Bank and Trust Co., Savannah, Ga., 1934-45; v.p. Trust Co. Ga., Atlanta, 1935-41; pres. First Nat. Bank Anniston (Ala.), 1946-66, chmn. bd., 1966—; dir. Ala. Power Co., Tape-Craft, Inc. Mem. Anniston Bd. Edn., 1962; chmn. Anniston United Fund Co., 1956; vice chmn. nat. fund A.R.C., 1962; chmn. 3d Army Adv. Com. Anniston Area, 1954—. Served to lt. col. AUS, 1941-45; ETO. Named Man of Year, Anniston C. of C., 1956; recipient Outstanding Civilian Service medal Dept. Army, 1966. Mem. Am. Ordnance Assn., Ala., (dir.), Anniston (pres. 1952-53) chambers commerce. Presbyn. (trustee). Rotarian (pres. Anniston 1951-52). Home: Berry Manor Apts Anniston AL 36201 Office: First Nat Bank Anniston AL 36201

HUNTER MELVIN JASPER, organic chemist; b. Hamilton County, O., Aug. 11, 1909; s. C. Sargent and Margaret C. (Hoock) H.; B.S., Antioch Coll., 1933; Ph.D., McGill U., 1939; m. Naomi Mary Bowen, Nov. 11, 1939; children—Willard Bowen, Ruth Ann. Research chemist Dow Chem. Co., 1933-36, group leader, 1939-45; basic research on structure of lignin McGill U., 1936-39; asst. dir. research Dow Corning Corp., Midland, Mich., 1945-47; dir. research, 1947- 63; v.p., dir. research Dow Corning Corp., Midland, Mich., 1945-47, dir. research, 1947-63, v.p., dir. research, 1963-65, v.p. for research and devel., 1965—. Mem. Am. Chem. Soc. (chpt. pres. 1952), Am. Inst. Chem. Engrs., Indsl. Research Inst., Research Soc. Am. Methodist (trustee). Developed process for use of silicone fluids to produce a high vacuum, influenced devel. numerous silicone products, glass fiber silicone compositions for indsl. products. Clubs: Saginaw Valley Torch; Midland Kiwanis. Home: 4440 Gladding Ct Midland MI 48640

HUNTER, OSBORNE F mfg. exec.; b. Lima, O., Apr. 1, 1932; B.S., U. San Francisco, 1954; M.S., Stanford University, 1956; m. Rosemarie Lois Brown, May 15, 1955; 1 son, Anthony Robinson. Sales rep. Ames-Brockton Fabricated Products, Akron, O., 1956-58, sales mgr. Coshocton, Ohio, 1959-61, gen. manager plant, 1961-68, v.p. sales, 1968--. Instr. bus. Coshocton Jr. College, 1968-69. Secretary Coshocton YMCA, 1960-61; active Boy Scouts of America. Named Man of Year, Coshocton Junior Chamber of Commerce, 1968. Mem. Coshocton C. of C. (vice president 1967-68, pres. 1969-70), English Speaking Union, Coshocton Sertoma Club, Nat. Assn. Mfrs., Sales Executives Institute, Phi Beta Kappa, Sigma Chi, Phi Mu. Democrat. Mem. Christian Ch. (lay leader). Mason (32, Shriner). Clubs: Coshocton Country, Coshocton City, Running Deer Country. Home: 2d Av Coshocton OH Office: 3d Av Coshocton OH

HUNTER, PAUL ROBINSON, architect; b. Buffalo, Ill., June 29, 1906; s. Guy Lester and Clara Charlotte (Robinson) H.; student U. Cal. at Los Angeles, 1924-26; B.Arch., U. Pa., 1931; m. Helen Sabin Houston, Feb. 12, 1932; children—Paul Robinson, Frederic Houston, Helen Sabin (Mrs. F.S. Dutton, Jr.). With archtl. offices Hunt & Chambers, Los Angeles, 1931-36, Roland E. Coate, Los Angeles, 1936-39; partner Hunter and Reichardt, Los Angeles, 1939-42, Hunter and Benedict, Los Angeles, 1957-66; pvt. practice, Los Angeles, 1942-56, 66—; ext. lectr. U. Cal., 1945, Coll. Arch., U. So. Cal., 1947; prin. works include Dickson Art Center at U. Cal. at Los Angeles, 1952, Aquatorium, City of Commerce, 1961, Monterey Park Hdqrs. Facilities, So. Counties Gas Co., 1963. Mem. Los Angeles Citizens Urban Renewal Adv. Com., 1957—. Recipient awards for design So. Cal. chpt. A.I.A. for horticulture bldgs. U. Cal. at Los Angeles, 1946, nursery Childrens Home Soc., 1946, pre-sch. bldg. Berkeley Hall Sch., 1954, Christian Sci. Ch., Anaheim, Cal., 1957. Fellow A.I.A. (pres. So. Cal. chpt. 1956); mem. Los Angeles C. of C., Town Hall Los Angeles, Delta Upsilon, Tau Sigma Delta. Author: (with Walter Reichardt) Residential Architecture in Southern California, 1939; Plastics in Building, 1946; also articles. Home: 5669 6th St Los Angeles CA 90036 Office: 3670 Wilshire Blvd Los Angeles CA 90005

HUNTER, PHELAN HENDRICK, former oil exec.; b. Macon, Miss., Jan. 28, 1905; s. Phelan H. and Josephine Hunter; student Castle Heights Mil. Acad., Lebanon, Tenn.; B.A., U. Miss.; student Tulane U.; LL.B., Loyola U.; m. Theresa Irvine, July 3, 1937; children—Frances (Herron), Harriet Hendrick, David Phelan. Pres. Interstate Oil Pipe Line Co., Shreveport, 1955-62; pres., dir. Humble Pipe Line Co., Houston, 1962-70. Home: 2701 Westheimer Houston TX 77005

HUNTER, RALPH WILLIAM, physician; b. Hanover, N.H., Dec. 3, 1908; s. Edgar Hayes and Edna Elisabeth (Hill) H.; grad. Phillips Exeter Acad., 1927; A.B., Dartmouth, 1931, student Med. Sch., 1930-32; M.D., Johns Hopkins, 1934; m. Ann Harlow Wilkinson, June 23, 1945; children—Sally Wilkinson, Jane Harlow, Ralph William, John Greenleaf, Martha Stark; m. 2d, Elizabeth Gibson Morrison, July 27, 1960; stepchildren—Donald M. Morrison, Elizabeth M. Morrison, William L. Morrison. Grad. tng. in medicine and neurology Johns Hopkins Hosp., Balt., 1934-36, Royal Victoria Hosp., Montreal, Can., 1936-37, Dartmouth Med. Sch., 1938-39, Mass. Gen. Hosp., Boston, 1938-39; neurologist Hitchcock Clinic, Hanover, N.H., 1939—; asst. prof. neuroanatomy and neurology Dartmouth Med. Sch., 1946- 61, asso. clin. prof. neurology, 1961-70, clin. prof. neurology, 1970—. Charter trustee Dartmouth. Served from lt. (j.g.) to comdr. M.C., USNR, 1941-46. Mem. Am. Acad. Neurology, Assn. Research Nervous and Mental Diseases, Phi Beta Kappa, Phi Delta Theta, Alpha Kappa Kappa. Home: Hemlock Rd Hanover NH 03755 Office: 2 Maynard St Hanover NH 03755

HUNTER, ROBERT E., mfg. co. exec.; b. Nunda, N.Y., June 12, 1911; s. Ernest Floyd and Looloo Belle (Moore) H.; A.B., U. Mich., 1934; m. Mary Catherine Houk, Aug. 29, 1936; children—David,

Harley, R. Scot, Bruce. Engaged in bus. mgmt. Graham-Paige Motors Corp., 1934-37, Pontiac Motors div. Gen. Motors Corp., 1937-41; engaged in indsl. relations Nat. Tube Co., 1941-43; with Gen. Motors Corp., 1943-68, indls. relations and sales Electro-Motive div., 1943-49, dir. sales Gen. Motors Diesel Ltd., 1949-55, gen. sales mgr. diesel engine div., 1955-63, gen. mgr. Euclid div., 1963-68; chmn. bd., pres. Philco-Ford Corp., Phila., 1968-70; v.p. Ford Motor Co., 1968-70; dir., chmn. exec. com. chief exec. officer The Weatherhead Co., 1970—; dir. White Motor Co., 1971—, Ann Arbor Hockey League (Mich.), 1960-63. Mem. indsl. adv. bd. Opportunities Industrialization Center, Phila. Pres. La. Grange Park (Ill.) Community Chest, 1947-48; mem. Businessmen's Interracial Com., Cleve., 1966-68, 71—. Bd. dirs. Victorian Order Nurses, Hudson, Que., 1953. Mem. Am. Road Builders Assn. (dir. 1965-68). Club: Union (Cleve.). Home: Bratenahl Pl Bratenahl OH 44108 Office: Weatherhead Co 300 E 131st St Cleveland OH 44108

HUNTER, ROBERT GRAMS, educator; b. Milbank, S.D., Nov. 12, 1927; s. Donald Raymond and Esther (Grams) H.; B.A., Harvard, 1949; M.A., Columbia, 1957, Ph.D., 1962; m. Anne Ziesmer, Aug. 25, 1956; children—Timothy, Catherine. Instr., Robert Coll., Istanbul, Turkey, 1949-52; instr., asst. prof., asso. prof. Dartmouth, 1959-70; Kenan prof. English, Vanderbilt U., Nashville, 1970—. Served with AUS, 1952-54. Author: Shakespeare and the Comedy of Forgiveness, 1965. Home: 3612 Hampton Av Nashville TN 37215

HUNTER, ROBERT THOMAS, state justice; b. Lawton, Okla., Sept. 29, 1907; s. Alfred Lewis and Nancy Jane (Fisher) H.; LL.B., U. Wash., 1934; m. Helen Maureen Neary, Dec. 25, 1938; children—Janice Kathleen, Marilyn, Patricia, Robert T. Admitted to Wash. bar, 1935; practiced law, 1935-46; formerly judge Superior Ct., Grant and Douglas counties, Wash., now justice Supreme Ct. of Wash. Odd Fellow (past grand master). Home: 1402 Rolling Hills Terrace Olympia WA 98501 Office: Temple of Justice Olympia WA 98501

HUNTER, RODERICK OLIVER ALEXANDER, ins. co. exec.; b. Mather, Man., Can., Dec. 12, 1915; s. John Oliver and Ida (McLean) H.; B.A., U. Man., 1937; LL.B., U. Man. Law Sch., 1941; m. Doris Audrey Moffat, Dec. 26, 1942; children—Roderick George, John David, Richard Craig. Called to Man. bar, 1942; mem. firm Parker, Parker, Hunter & Hamlin, Winnipeg, Man., 1945-46; with Great-West Life Assurance Co., Winnipeg, 1947-71, sec., 1953-62, v.p., sec., 1962-71, also dir.; v.p. James Richardson & Sons, Ltd., Winnipeg, 1971—. Campaign chmn. United Way Greater Winnipeg, 1966; mem. univ. grants commn. Province Man., 1967. Served to lt. comdr. Royal Canadian Navy, 1941-45. Mem. U. Man. Alumni Soc. (past pres.), Assn. Life Ins. Counsel (past pres.), Canadian, Man. bar assns., Man. Law Soc., Mem. United Ch. Clubs: Manitoba; St. Charles Golf and Country; Winnipeg Winter. Home: 346 Oxford St Winnipeg Manitoba R 3M 3J7 Canada Office: Richardson Bldg 1 Lombard Pl Winnipeg 1 Manitoba Canada

HUNTER, ROSS, motion picture producer; b. Cleve., May 6, 1924; s. Isadore and Anna (Rosen) Fuss; M.A., Western Res. U. Sch. tchr., Cleve., 1942-43; actor for Columbia Pictures, 1944-47; producer plays, 1947-50; asst. producer Universal Pictures, 1951-52, producer, 1953—; movies include The Art of Love, Madame X, Thoroughly Modern Millie, 1967, Midnight Lace, Flower Drum Song, The Chalk Garden, Rosie, Airport.

HUNTER, SAM, art critic, educator; b. Springfield, Mass., Jan. 5, 1923; s. Morris and Lottie (Sherman) H.; A.B., Williams U., 1943; student U. Florence (Italy), 1949-51; m. Edys Merrill, July 22, 1954; children—Emily C., Alexa J. Art critic N.Y. Times, 1947-49; editor Harry N. Abrams, Inc., art books publisher, N.Y.C., 1952-53; lectr. Barnard Coll., also asst. prof. U. Cal. at Los Angeles, 1955-57; curator Mus. Modern Art, 1956-58; chief curator, acting dir. Mpls. Inst. Arts, 1958-60; dir. Rose Art Mus., Poses Inst. Art, Brandeis U., Waltham, Mass., 1960-65, asso. prof. art history dept., 1963-65; dir. Jewish Museum, N.Y.C., 1965-58; vis. prof. Cornell U., 1967-69; lectr. New Sch. Social Research, N.Y.C., 1967-68; Regent's prof., vis. critic U. Cal. at Riverside, 1968; vis. critic State U. N.Y., 1968-69; prof. art and archeology Princeton, 1969—. Dir. Am. Art since 1950 exhbn., Seattle World's Fair, 1962; juror Internat. Art Jury 32d Venice Biennale, Italy, 1964; exec. dir. study visual arts in pub. higher edn. Bd. Higher Edn., Mass., 1968-69; dir. critic's choice program N.Y. State Council on Arts, 1968-69. Served as lt. (j.g.) USNR, 1944-46. J.S. Guggenheim Meml. fellow, 1971-72. Mem. Coll. Art. Assn., Phi Beta Kappa. Author: Jackson Pollock, 1956; Modern French Painting, 1956; Picasso: Cubism to the Present, 1957; David Smith, 1957; Piet Mondrian, 1958; Joan Miro: His Graphic Work, 1958; Modern American Painting and Sculpture, 1959; Hans Hofmann, 1963; Larry Rivers, 1969; New Art Around the World, 1966; Avant- Garde Painting in America, 1970; Josef Albers, 1971. Contbr. sect. on Am. painting to Art Since 1945, 1958; James Brooks, 1963; New Directions in American Painting, 1964. Home: 451 West End Av New York City NY 10024 Office: McCormick Hall Princeton Univ Princeton NJ 08540

HUNTER, THOM HUGH, sem. ofcl.; b. Johnstown, Pa. Aug. 28, 1918; s. Thomas and Jeannie (McBlain) H.; B.A., Park Coll., 1942, LL.D., 1966; diploma McCormick Theol. Sem., 1944; D.D. (hon.), Monmouth Coll., 1962; m. Ruth Rinehart, Aug. 26, 1944; children—Jennifer Ruth, Hilary Anne, Hugh McBlain. Ordained to ministry Presbyn. Ch., 1944; chaplain Cornell U., Ithaca, N.Y., 1946-49, U. Ore. at Eugene, 1949-54, U. Tex. at Austin, 1954-57; dir. ch. relations McCormick Theol. Sem., Chgo., 1957-59, v.p., lectr. ch. and higher edn., 1959—. Theol. edn. cons., dept. ministerial relations U.P. Ch. U.S.A.; pres. Chgo. Faculties Union. Mem. exec. bd. Assn. Chgo. Theol. Schs.; sec. Chgo. Theol. Inst. Served with USNR, 1944-46. Mem. Assn. Presbyn. U. Pastors (past pres.), Am. Soc. Ch. History (past pres.), N.W. Conf. Religion in Higher Edn. (past pres.), Council Theol. Edn., Park Coll. Alumni Assn. (past nat. pres.). Home: 3412 63d St Woodridge IL 60515

HUNTER, THOMAS HARRISON, physician, educator; b. Chgo., Oct. 12, 1913; s. Edwin Llewellyn and Argyra (Harrison) H.; A.B. cum laude, Harvard, 1935, M.D. cum laude, 1940; Henry fellow Cambridge (Eng.) U., 1935-38; m. Anne E. Fulcher, Mar. 6, 1943; children—Charles, Elizabeth, William, Thomas, Peter. Intern, resident Presbyn. Hosp., N.Y.C., 1942-45, asst. physician, 1945-47; instr. medicine Columbia, 1945-47; asst. and asso. prof. medicine Washington U. Sch. Medicine, 1947-53, asst. dean, 1947-52, asso. dean, 1952-53; dean Sch. Medicine, U. Va., 1953-64, prof., 1953—, chancellor for med. affairs, 1964—; cons. USPHS; temporary staff mem. Rockefeller Found., 1962-63. Mem. Nat. Arthritis and Metabolic Disease Council NIH. Mem. vis. com. Western Res. U. Med. Sch.; bd. overseers Harvard, 1956-62. Mem. Assn. Am. Physicians, Am. Clin. and Climatol. Soc., Am. Soc. Clin. Investigation, A.A.A.S., A.M.A., Am. Acad. Arts and Scis., Assn. Am. Med. Colls. (pres. 1960, chmn. com. on internat. relations in med. adn., Raven Soc., Phi Beta Kappa, Sigma Xi, Alpha Omega Alpha. Contbr. to Cecil's The Textbook of Medicine, 1951. Home: Big Oaks Cismont VA 22928 Office: School of Medicine U Va Charlottesville VA 22904

HUNTER, WILLIAM ANDREW, educator; b. North Little Rock, Ark., Sept. 6, 1913; s. W.J.C. and Jessie Dorothy (Berry) H.; B.S., Wilberforce U., 1936; M.S., Ia. State U., 1948, Ph.D., 1952; m. Alma Rose Burgess, June 6, 1938. Substitute tchr. Pulaski County (Ark.) schs., 1933-34; tchr. math. and sci. Dunbar High Sch., Little Rock, 1936-40; instr. Dunbar Jr. Coll., 1940-42; tchr. Dunbar High Sch., 1946; mem. faculty Tuskegee Inst., 1950—, now prof. edn., 1956—, dean Sch. Edn., 1959—. Mem. White House Conf. Higher Edn.; mem. Commn. Tchr. Edn. and Profl. Standards; adv. council early childhood edn. So. Edn. Found; v.p., dir. Southeastern Edn., Lab. Active United Negro Coll. Fund, Tuskegee Civic Assn. Served with AUS, 1942-46. Mem. Am., Ala. tchrs. assns., Am. Assn. Sch. Adminstrs., Am. Assn. U. Profs., Assn. Higher Edn., Assn. Curriculum Devel., N.E.A., So. Council Tchr. Edn., Assn. Sch., Coll. and U. Staffing, Ala, Council Tchr. Edn. (commn. on tchr. edn. and profl. standards), Am. Assn. Colls. Tchr. Edn. (exec. com.), Beta Kappa Chi, Phi Delta Kappa, Kappa Alpha Psi, Sword and Shield. Contbr. books. Home: 140 Colvert St Tuskegee Institute AL 36088

HUNTER, WILLIAM CARROLL, ret. govt. ofcl., lawyer; b. White Hall, Md., Aug. 12, 1886; s. Charles C and Mary R. (Slade) H.; LL.B., U. Md., 1910. Sec. to dean Md. U. Law Sch., 1910-13; admitted to Md. bar, Jan. 10, 1911; asso. law firm Haman, Cook, Chestnut and Markell, Balt., 1913-15; pvt. practice, Balt., 1916-33; atty. U.S. Dept. Agr., Washington, 1933- 53, solicitor, (gen. counsel), 1946-53; now ret. Served as 2d lt. F.A., U.S. Army, World War I. Democrat. Presbyn. Clubs: Loudoun (Va.) Hunt; Fairfax (Va.) Hunt. Home: Purcellville VA 22132

HUNTER, R. B., meat packing co. exec.; b. Syracuse, N.Y., Jan. 31, 1911; s. Bruce E. and Jessie (Lockwood) H.; student Syracuse U., Powelson Inst. Accountancy; m. Gladys Cooper, May 1, 1937; children—Jill (Mrs. Robert Essig), Robert B. With Tobin Packing Co., Inc., Rochester, N.Y., 1943—, now treas., v.p., dir. C.P.A., N.Y. Mem. Am. Inst. C.P.A.'s, N.Y. State Soc. C.P.A.'s, Tax Execs. Inst. Home: 81 Daytona Av Webster NY 14580 Office: 900 Maple St Rochester NY 14611

HUNTHAUSEN, RAYMOND GERHARDT, bishop; b. Anaconda, Mont., Aug. 21, 1921; s. Anthony Gerhardt and Edna (Tuchscherer) H.; A.B., Carroll Coll., 1943; A.B., St. Edward's Sem., 1946; M.S., Notre Dame U., 1953; LL.D., De Paul U., 1960; student summers St. Louis U., Cath. U., Fordham U. Ordained priest Roman Cath. Ch., 1946; instr. chemistry Carroll Coll., 1946-57, football and basketball coach, 1953-57, pres., 1957-62; bishop of Helena (Mont.) Diocese, 1962—. Mem. Am. Chem. Soc. Home: 612 Harrison St Helena MT 59601

HUNTING, CONSTANCE COULTER, pub. co. exec., author; b. Providence, Oct. 15, 1925; d. Walter D. and Mildred A. (Farrill) Coulter; B.A., Brown U., 1947; spl. student piano New Eng. Conservatory, Boston, 1950; m. Robert Stilwell Hunting, Aug. 28, 1948; children—Robert Samuel Coulter, Miranda Willson. Tchr. various univs.; propr. Puckerbrush Press, Orono, Me., 1970—. Bd. dirs. Bangor (Me.) Symphony. Recipient Sesquicentennial Poetry prize Ind., 1968; Ind. U. Writers prize poetry, 1970. Author: (poetry collection) After the Stravinsky Concert, 1969; also poems, stories, criticisms, revs. Address: 76 Main St Orono ME 04473

HUNTINGTON, ANNA HYATT, (Mrs. Archer M. Huntington), sculptor; b. Cambridge, Mass., Mar. 10, 1876; d. Alpheus and Audella (Beebe) Hyatt; ed. pvt. sch. the Misses Smith, Cambridge, Art Students' League, N.Y.C.; pupil of H.A. McNiel and Gutzon Borglum; D.F.A., Syracuse U., 1932; m. Archer M. Huntington, 1923. Works include small bronzes, in over 200 museums and art galleries including Don Quixote, N.Y.C.; stag, Oglesby Park, Wheeling, W.Va.; Don Quixote, also Stallions, Brookgreen Gardens, S.C.; Stallions, San Marcos, Tex.; Torchbearers statue, Madrid, Spain, 1955; Torch Bearers statue, Havana, Cuba, 1956; Sybil Ludington statue, Carmel, N.Y., 1961; Lincoln statue, Worlds Fair, N.Y.C., 1964-65. Hon. mention, Paris Salon, 1910; recipient many awards and prizes 1910-40; Nat. Sculpture Soc. spl. medal of honor, 1940; Allied Artists gold medal of honor, 1952; Nat. Academician; Sorolla medal for art Hispanic Soc. Am., 1957; Humanist Rosicrucian Order, Son Jose, 1960; Chevalier Legion of Honor (France), 1922; Officer, 1933; Citizen of Blois, France, 1922. Grand Cross of Alfonso XII (Spain), 1929: Certificate of Honor for El Cid, San Diego, Cal., 1933; Grand Cross of Isabella the Catholic, 1954; Woman of the Americas, 1958; hon. citizen of Cuba, 1958. Fellow Nat. Sculpture Soc. (hon.), Internat, Inst. Arts Letters, 1957; hon. mem. Instituto de Cultura Hispanica, Accademia Culturale Adriatica, Internat. Studia Scientarium Literarumque; mem. Real Academia de Bellas Artes de San Jorge (corr.), Fedn. of Arts, Nat. Inst. Arts and Letters, Hispanic Soc. Am. (v.p., trustee) Am. Acad. Arts and Letters, Spanish Acad. San Fernando (corr.). Home: Bethel CT 06801 ☆

HUNTINGTON, CHARLES ELLSWORTH, educator, biologist; b. Boston, Dec. 8, 1919; s. Ellsworth and Rachel (Brewer) H.; B.A., Yale, 1942, Ph.D., 1952; m. Louise Chapin Slater, Dec. 22, 1956; children—George Slocum, William Ellsworth, Katherine Chapin, Sarah Clarke. Instr. to prof. biology Bowdoin Coll., Brunswick, Me., 1953—; dir. Bowdoin Sci. Sta., Kent Island, Grand Manan, New Brunswick, 1953—. Mem. Harpswell Sch. Com., 1966-69. Bd. dirs. Me. Sch. Adminstrv. Dist. No. 75. Served with USNR, 1942-46. Guggenheim fellow, 1963-64. Mem. A.A.A.S., Am. Inst. Biol. Sci., Soc. Study Evolution, Am., Brit. ornithologists unions, Wilson, Cooper ornithol. socs., Northeastern Bird-Banding Assn. (pres. 1962-67), Sigma Xi. Democrat. Unitarian. Home: RFD 1 South Harpswell ME 04079 Office: Dept Biology Bowdoin Coll Brunswick ME 04011

HUNTINGTON, DAVID HANS, coll. pres.; b. Westford, N.Y., Mar. 19, 1926; s. Lowell S. and Meta C. (Juergensen) H.; B.S., Cornell U., 1946, M.S., 1948, Ph.D., 1953; m. Mary E. Cary, July 17, 1949; children—Scot L., Debra D. Asst. prof. agrl. engrng. U. Me. Coll. Agr., 1953-56, asso. prof., 1957, asso. prof., asst. to dean, 1957-61, asst. dean, 1961-63, asso. dean, 1963-64; pres. Agrl. and Tech. Coll. State U. N.Y., Alfred, 1964—. Mem. council of presidents State U. N.Y., also chancellor's panel on univ. purposes. Exec. bd. Steuben Area council Boy Scouts Am. Served to ensign USNR, 1944-47. Mem. Am., N.Y. State (past pres.) assns. jr. colls. Rotarian. Home: 9 Reynolds St Alfred NY 14802

HUNTINGTON, DAVID MACK GOODE, found. adminstr.; b. Millsboro, Del., Dec. 18, 1926; s. M. Paul St. Agnan and Lona Marie (Goode) H.; A.B., Harvard, 1949, Ed.M., 1954; m. Mary Elizabeth Putman, Dec. 3, 1955; children—James Barrett, Sarah Phelps, Samuel Porter. Adminstrv. asst. customer relations Irving Trust Co., N.Y.C., 1949-52; supr., speech therapist Martin Hall, Bristol, R.I., 1952-55; asst. dir. Office Student Placement, Harvard, 1955-59; dir. placement, asso. dean students Grad. Sch. Bus., U. Chgo., 1959-64, asso. dir. devel. Office Pres., 1965-67, dir. devel., asst. to dean div. biol. scis., exec. dir., sec. Cancer Research Found., 1967-69; dir., sec. Milw. Found., 1970—; sec. Faye McBeath Found., 1970—; adminstr. Walter and Olive Stiemke Found., 1970—. Incorporator, Porter-Phelps-Huntington Found., Hadley, Mass. Served with AUS, 1945-46. Episcopalian. Club: University (Milw.). Home: 4043 N Lake Dr Shorewood WI 53211 Office: 110 E Wisconsin Av Milwaukee WI 53202

HUNTINGTON, FRANCES CARPENTER (Mrs. William Chapin Huntington), author; b. Washington, Apr. 30, 1890; d. Frank G. and Joanna (Condict) Carpenter; A.B., Smith Coll., 1912; m. William Chapin Huntington, 1920 (dec. 1958); children—Joanna Carpenter (Mrs. Huntington Noel), Edith Chapin (Mrs. David Benton Williams). Traveled and collaborated with Frank G. Carpenter on tours of investigation in China, Japan, Korea, Egypt and Near East, Europe and Alaska. Trustee Smith Coll., 1936-1944. Fellow Royal Geog. Soc. London; mem. Internat. Soc. Woman Geographers (pres., 1939-42), Alumnae Assn. Smith Coll. (pres. 1932-35). Club: Cosmopolitan (N.Y.). Author (under name of Frances Carpenter): (with Frank G. Carpenter) The Foods We Eat, 1925, The Clothes We Wear, 1926, The Houses We Live In, 1926; Ourselves and Our City, 1928; The Ways We Travel, 1929; Tales of a Basque Grandmother, 1930; Our Little Friends of Eskimo Land, 1931; Our Neighbors Near and Far, An Elementary Geography, 1932; Tales of a Russian Grandmother, 1933; Our Little Friends of the Arabian Desert; My Geography Work Book, 1934; Our Little Friends of the Netherlands 1935; Our Little Friends of Norway, 1936; Our Little Friends of China, 1937; Tales of a Chinese Grandmother, 1937; Our Little Neighbors at Work and Play, An Introduction to Geography, 1939; Tales of a Swiss Grandmother, 1940; Our Little Friends of Switzerland, 1941; Our South American Neighbors, 1942; The Pacific-Its Lands and Peoples, 1944; Canada and Her Northern Neighbors, 1945; Tales of a Korean Grandmother, 1947; Children of Our World, An Elementary Geography, 1949; Caribbean Lands: Mexico, Central America and the West Indies, 1949; Wonder Tales of Horses and Heroes, 1952; Wonder Tales of Dogs and Cats, 1955; Our Homes and Our Neighbors, A Home Geography, 1956; Pocahontas and Her World, 1957; Holiday in Washington, 1958; Wonder Tales of Seas and Ships, 1959. Editor: Carp's Washington, 1960; The Elephant's Bath TubAsian Folk Tales, 1962; African Wonder Tales, 1963; The Mouse Palace, 1964; The Story of Korea, 1958; South American Wonder Tales, 1969; People from the Sky; Ainu Tales from Northern Japan, 1971. Home: 2101 Connecticut Av NW Washington DC 20008

HUNTINGTON, HILLARD BELL, physicist; b. Wilkes-Barre, Pa., Dec. 21, 1910; s. Frederick L. and Gertrude (Bell) H.; B.A., Princeton, 1932, M.A., 1933, Ph.D., 1941; m. Ruth Smedley Wheeler, June 24, 1939; children—Frederic Wright, Hillard Griswold, David Champion. Teaching asst. U. Pa., 1941; physics instr. Washington U., 1941-42; staff mem. Radiation Lab., Mass. Inst. Tech., 1942-46; asst. prof. Rensselaer Poly. Inst., Troy, N.Y., 1946-48, asso. prof., 1948- 50, prof., 1950—, chmn. dept. physics, 1961-69. Vis. prof. Yale, 1960- 61, Cornell U., 1968-69. Fellow Am. Phys. Soc. (chmn. div. solid state physics 1966-67); mem. Fedn. Am. Scientists, Sigma Xi. Home: 219 Pinewoods Av Troy NY 12180

HUNTINGTON, SAMUEL PHILLIPS, educator; b. N.Y.C., Apr. 18, 1927; s. Richard T. and Dorothy S. (Phillips) H.; B.A., Yale, 1946; M.A., U. Chgo., 1948; Ph.D., Harvard, 1951; m. Nancy Alice Arkelyan, Sept. 8, 1957; children—Timothy Mayo, Nicholas Phillips. Instr. govt. Harvard, 1950-53, asst. prof. govt., 1953-58, prof. govt., 1962—, Thomson prof. govt., 1967—, chmn. dept. govt., 1967-69, 70-71; research asso. def. policy Brookings Instn., Washington, 1952-53; faculty research fellow Social Sci. Research Council, N.Y.C., 1954-57; asst. dir. Inst. War and Peace Studies, Columbia, 1958-59, research asso., 1958-63, asso. dir., 1959-62, asso. prof. govt., 1959-62, Ford research prof., 1960-61; research asso. Center Internat. Affairs, Harvard, 1963-64, faculty mem., 1964—, exec. com., 1966—. Fellow, Center for Advanced Study in Behavioral Scis., Stanford, 1969-70. Cons. numerous govt. agys. Chmn. Council on Vietnamese studies S.E. Asia Devel. Adv. Group, 1966-69; mem. Presidential Task Force on Internat. Devel., 1969-70. Trustee Internat. Devel. Found. Served with AUS, 1946-47. Recipient Silver Pen award Jour. Fund, 1960. Fellow Am. Acad. Arts and Scis.; mem. Am. Soc. Pub. Adminstrn., Internat. Polit. Sci. Assn., Council Fgn. Relations, Inst. Strategic Studies, Am. Polit. Sci. Assn. (mem. council 1969-71). Club: Cosmos (Washington). Author: The Soldier and the State, 1957; The Common Defense, 1961; Political Order in Changing Societies, 1968. Co-author: Political Power: USA-USSR, 1964. Editor: Changing Patterns of Military Politics, 1962. Co-editor: Foreign Policy (quarterly), 1970—; Authoritarian Politics in Modern Society: The Dynamics of Established One-Party Systems, 1970. Contbr. articles to profl. jours. Home: 52 Brimmer St Boston MA 02108 Office: 6 Divinity Av Cambridge MA 02138

HUNTINGTON, THOMAS FOSTER, financial co. exec.; b. Roselle, N.J.. Apr. 14, 1920; s. Henry Strong and Edith Marguerite (Foster) H.; B.S. in Mech. Engring. cum laude, Princeton, 1942; M.B.A. with distinction, Harvard, 1946-47; m. Pauline Herrick, Sept. 28, 1946; children—Ellen Foster, Louisa Boulton, Deborah Lawrence. Engr., Pratt & Whitney Aircraft, 1942-45; plant supt., exec. asst. to pres., asst. div. gen. mgr. Personal Products Corp. div. Johnson & Johnson, Inc., 1947-57; prin. asso. Cresap, McCormick Paget, 1957-59; v.p., exec. asst. to pres. Trans World Airlines, Inc., N.Y.C., 1959-60, v.p. orgn. and procedures, 1961-63, v.p. spl. services div., 1963-68, v.p. sales and services, 1968-70; v.p. mfg. and merchandising CIT Financial Corp., N.Y.C., 1970—. Trustee, mem. exec. com. Robert Coll., Istanbul, Turkey, Near East Coll. Assn. Clubs: Princeton (N.J.) Charter (bd. govs.); Princeton (N.Y.C.). Home: 73 Allison Rd Princeton NJ 08540 Office: 605 3d Av New York City NY 10017

HUNTLEY, CHARLES WILLIAM, educator; b. Schenectady, July 23, 1913; s. Charles Henry and Caroline Alice (Ritter) H.; A.B., Union Coll., 1934; A.M., Ph.D., Harvard, 1938; m. Lee Hoffman, June 15, 1938; children—Deborah Lee, Elizabeth Meriwether. Instr. psychology Flora Stone Mather Coll., Western Res. U., Cleve., 1938-41, asst. prof. psychology Adelbert Coll., 1941-44, prof. psychology, 1944-47, dean coll., 1941- 47; dean coll. Union Coll., Schenectady, 1947-64, prof. psychology, 1947—, chmn. dept., 1962—, sec. coll., 1964—. Armed Services rep. Western Res. U., 1942-44; mem. commn. on higher edn. Middle States Assn. Colls. and Secondary Schs., 1970—. Fellow Am. Psychol. Assn.; mem. Sigma Xi, Phi Beta Kappa, Theta Delta Chi. Contbr. articles to profl. jours. Home: Union Coll Campus Schenectady NY 12308

HUNTLEY, CHESTER ROBERT, (Chet) news commentator; b. Cardwell, Mont., Dec. 10, 1911; s. P.A. and Blanche (Tatham) H.; student Mont. State Coll., 1929-32, Cornish Sch. Arts, Seattle, 1932-33; B.A., U. Wash., 1934; hon. degrees Mont. State Coll., Boston U., Franklin and Marshall Coll.; m. Ingrid Rolin, Feb. 23, 1936; children—Sharon, Leanne; m. 2d, Tipton Stringer, Mar. 7, 1959. With radio sta. KPCB, Seattle, 1934-36; news broadcaster KHQ, Spokane, Wash., 1936, KGW, Portland, Ore., 1937, KFI, 1937-39, CBS, 1939-51, ABC (all Los Angeles), 1951-55, NBC, N.Y.C., 1955-70; commentator syndicated news commentaries Horizon Communications, 1970—. Recipient numerous awards for radio-TV journalism ‡

HUNTLEY, GEORGE HAYDN, educator; b. Endicott, Wash., July 14, 1905; s. George Henry and Martha (Logsdon) H.; S.B., Harvard, 1927, A.M., 1930, Ph.D. (Circolo Italiano fellow, Bacon traveling fellow), 1933; m. Nella Davigo, July 13, 1934; children—John, Mary, Margaret. Instr., Washington U., St. Louis, 1932-36, asst. prof., 1936-38; asst. prof. U. Chgo., 1938-46; vis. prof. U. So. Cal., summer, 1945; asso. prof. art Northwestern U., Evanston, Ill., 1946-48, prof., 1948—. Bd. editors Art Bull., 1940-60; editor Coll. Art Jour., 1942-44, adv. editor, 1944-60, exec. sec. Newberry Library Conf. Renaissance Studies, 1954. Mem. council Chgo. Conf. of UNESCO, 1963. Fulbright Research fellow, Italy, 1950-51. Mem. Midwestern Coll. Art Conf. (pres. 1944-45, sec. 1946-47), Coll. Art Assn. (v.p. 1947-49), Delta Upsilon. Author books on art. Home: 109 4th St Wilmette IL 60091 Office: Northwestern U Evanston IL 60201

HUNTLEY, HARLAN HARRISON, textile co. exec.; b. Madison, Wis., Apr. 8, 1928; s. William E. and Ruth (Grose) H.; B.S. with honors, U. Wis., 1952, J.D. with honors, 1954; m. Marjorie Ann English, June 2, 1954; children—Ruth Ann, Kristen Sue, Scott Harlan. Admitted to Wis. bar, 1954, Va. bar, 1959, Pa. bar, 1963; atty., asst. sec. TVA, 1954-56; atty. Reynolds Metals Co., 1956- 62; asst. gen. counsel Sealtest Foods div. Nat. Dairy Products Corp., 1962-66; sr. atty. Am. Home Products Corp., 1966-67; sec., asso. gen. counsel Dan River Inc., 1967—. Served with USN, 1946-47. Mem. Am., Phila., Danville, Va. bar assns., Wis. State Bar, Am. Soc. Corporate Secs., Order of Coif, Artus. Club: Danville Golf. Author article. Home: 127 Westwood Dr Danville VA 24541 Office: 2291 Memorial Dr Danville VA 24541

HUNTLEY, ROBERT EDWARD ROYALL, univ. pres.; b. Winston-Salem, N.C., June 13, 1929; s. Benjamin F. and Elizabeth (Royall) H.; B.A., Washington and Lee U., 1950, LL.B., 1957; LL.M., Harvard, 1962; m. Evelyn Whitehurst, 1954; children—Martha, Catherine, Jane. Admitted to Va. bar, 1957; asso. firm Boothe, Dudley, Koontz and Boothe, Alexandria, Va., 1957-58; asst. prof. law Washington and Lee U., Lexington, Va., 1958-59, asso. prof. law, 1959-64, prof. law, 1964—, dean Sch. Law, 1967-68, pres., 1968—. Mem. Va. State Bd. Edn., 1969—. Bd. dirs. George C. Marshall Research Found., 1969—. Served with USN, 1950-53. Mem. Am., Va. State bar assns., Phi Beta Kappa, Order of Coif, Omicron Delta Kappa, Phi Delta Phi, Delta Tau Delta. Home: 2 University Pl Lexington VA 24450

HUNTON, BENJAMIN LACY, govt. ofcl.; b. Washington, Nov. 25, 1919; s. Benjamin Holden and Evelyn (Lacy) H.; A.B., Howard U., 1940; M.A., 1942; Ph.D., Am. U., 1954; m. Kelsy Jean Cooper, June 10, 1961; 1 son, Benjamin Lorimer. Tchr., Washington pub. schs., 1942-51, supr., dir., 1951-58, asst. to asst. supt. jr.-sr. high schs., 1958-66; area dir. Equal Ednl. Opportunity Program, Dept. Health, Edn. and Welfare, 1966-69; ofcl. Job Corps Program, Dept. Interior, 1969-70, asst. dir. Bur. Mines, 1970—. Served with AUS, 1942-49. Mem. Assn. U.S. Army, Am. Fedn. Govt. Employees, AMVETS, Res. Officers Assn. Republican. Roman Catholic. Home: 7737 Ardmore-Ardwick Rd Hyattsville MD 20784 Office: 18th and E Sts NW Washington DC 20240

HUNTON, EPPA, IV, lawyer; b. Richmond, Va., July 31, 1904; s. Eppa, Jr., and Virginia Semmes (Payne) H.; B.A., U. Va., 1925, LL.B., 1927; m. Caroline Homassel Marye, Sept. 28, 1936 (dec. July 15, 1962); children—Caroline (Mrs. John H. High), Virginia (Mrs. Randolph F. Totten), Eppa. Admitted to Va. bar, 1926, D.C. bar, 1926; asso. firm Hunton, Williams, Anderson & Gay, 1927-34; partner Hunton, Williams, Gay, Powell & Gibson and predecessors, Richmond, 1934—; pres., dir., counsel Blvd. Bridge Corp., Brown Oil Corp.; dir. First & Mchts. Nat. Bank. Corp. Bd. visitors Med. Coll. Va., 1932-51, 54-58, 59-63, 64-68, chmn. exec. com., 1954-58, 65-68, chmn. bd., 1960-63; bd. visitors Va. Commonwealth Univ., 1968-70, vice rector, 1968-69, rector, 1969-70; trustee Richmond Eye Hosp., 1953—. Served from 1st lt. to maj., AUS, 1942-46. Decorated Bronze Star. Mem. Am., Va., Richmond bar assns., Soc. Cincinnati in Va. (v.p. 1970—), Va. Hist. Soc. (exec. com. 1946—, pres. 1966-69), Delta Kappa Epsilon, Phi Delta Phi. Democrat. Episcopalian. Clubs: Farmington (Charlottesville); Downtown, Commonwealth, Country of Va., German (pres. 1968-70). Home: 6705 River Rd Richmond VA 23229 Office: 700 E Main St Richmond VA 23212

HUNTRESS, KEITH GIBSON, educator; b. South Portland, Me., May 6, 1913; s. Frederick W. and Caroline (Lowell) H.; B.A., Wesleyan U., Middletown, Conn., 1935, M.A., 1936; Ph.D., U. Ill., 1942; m. Ida E. Schaub, June 8, 1940; children—Deborah E. (Mrs. Stephen Adams), Jonathan K., Alison D., Margaret E., Bethany G. Asst. underwriter Travelers Ins. Co., 1936-37; grad. asst. English, U. Ill., 1937-41; instr. English, Ia. State U., 1941-42, asst. prof., 1942- 44, asso. prof., 1944-46, prof., 1946-65, Distinguished prof. sci. and humanities, 1965—. Recipient Alumni award for teaching Wesleyan U., 1965. Mem. Am. Assn. U. Profs., Modern Lang. Assn., Ia. Coll. Conf. English, Phi Beta Kappa, Phi Kappa Phi (hon.), Phi Nu Theta. Author: Of Time and Truth, 1946; Analysis of Propaganda, 1949; Minimum Essentials for Good Writing, 1952; Ideas and Backgrounds, 1957; Murder of an American Prophet, 1960; Design for Reading, 2d edit., 1969. Home: 509 Ash Av Ames IA 50010

HUNTSMAN, JON MEADE, govt. ofcl.; b. Blackfoot, Ida., June 21, 1937; s. Alonzo Blaine and Kathleen (Robison) H.; B.S., U. Pa., 1959; M.B.A., U. So. Cal., 1964; m. Karen Christina Haight, June 20, 1959; children—Jon Meade, Peter Riley, Christena Karen, Kathleen Ann, David Haight, Paul Christian, James Haight. Exec. v.p., dir. Olson Bros., Inc., North Hollywood, Cal., 1961-68; pres., dir. Dolco Packaging Corp., North Hollywood, 1968-70; founder, pres., chmn. bd. Continental Dynamics, Inc., Los Angeles, 1966-71, Huntsman Container Corp., Los Angeles, 1971—; co-founder, dir. Huntsman Container Corp., Huntsman Capital Corp., Continental Dynamics, Inc. Mem. Nat. Task Force on Youth Devel. and Juvenile Delinquency, 1970; asso. adminstr. social and rehab. service Dept. HEW, Washington, 1970; spl. asst. to President Nixon, also staff sec., 1971—. Council rep. Boy Scouts Am. Served as lt., USNR, 1959-61. Recipient Internat. Balfour award Sigma Chi, 1959, Spoon award U. Pa., 1959; Zellerbach Found. fellow, 1958. Mem. Ch. of Jesus Christ of Latter-day Saints (mem. bishopric and high council). Club: Lakeside Golf (Hollywood). Home: 5315 Falmouth Rd Washington DC 20016 Office: The White House Washington DC 20005

HUNTZICKER, HARRY NOBLE, chemist, mfr.; b. Omaha, June 29, 1906; s. Albion Clinton and Annabelle (Noble) H.; B.S., Macalester Coll., 1927; M.S., U. Wis., 1930, Ph.D., 1932; m. Mildred Harriet Carlson, Aug. 14, 1934; children—Jon Noble, James Frederick. Sr. teaching asst. chemistry dept. U. Wis., 1930- 32; high sch. tchr. chemistry, Rockford, Ill., 1932-35; with U.S. Gypsum Co., Chgo., 1935-56, research chemist, research supr. gypsum and lime products, tech. products mgr., prodn. mgr. lime plants, mgr. research and devel. labs., dir. research and devel., v.p. charge research and devel.; exec. v.p. Am.-Marietta Co., 1956-61, dir., 1961; v.p., dir. Martin Marietta Corp., 1961-66, pres. constrn. materials div., 1952-66; pres. Portland Cement Assn., Skokie, Ill., 1966—. Mem. bldg. research adv. bd. NRC, Nat. Acad. Scis., 1953; bd. govs. Bldg. Research Inst., 1954. Trustee Macalester Coll., St. Paul. Mem. Am. Standards Assn., Am. Chem. Soc., Am. Soc. Testing Materials, Am. Soc. Engring. Edn., Am. Concrete Inst., Sigma Xi, Phi Lambda Upsilon, Alpha Chi Sigma. Republican. Presbyn. Clubs: Mid-America (Chgo.); Westmoreland Country (Wilmette, Ill.). Patentee in field. Home: 9424 Monticello Av Evanston IL 60203 Office: Portland Cement Assn Old Orchard Rd Skokie IL 60076

HUNZEKER, HUBERT LA VON, educator; b. Pawnee City, Neb., Nov. 12, 1920; s. Clyde F. and Lily (Branek) H.; A.B., Peru State Coll., 1948; M.S., Ia. State Coll., 1950; Ph.D., U. Mich., 1969; m. Gladys Gloria Deters, Apr. 26, 1943; children—Mary Patrice, Lisa Elizabeth, James Hubert, Peter David. Instr. math. Ohio U., 1950-52; asst. prof. DePauw U., 1953-57; asst. prof. math. U. Neb., 1958-62; prof., head dept. math. U. Omaha, 1962-68; prof., head dept. math. Mich. Technol. U., 1968-71, prof. math., 1971—. Served with USNR, 1941-43. Mem. Am. Math. Soc., Math. Assn. Am., Am. Assn. U. Profs., Sigma Xi, Sigma Tau. Home: Canal Rd Box 244 Houghton MI 49931

HUNZIKER, RICHARD OVERTON, former air force officer; b. Los Angeles, July 6, 1916; s. Eugene P. and Josephine (Crutsinger) H.; B.S., U. Ariz., 1948; grad. Nat. War Coll., 1958; m. Margaret Bailard, Sept., 1945; children—John R., Russell L. Commd. 2d lt. USAAF, 1942, advanced through grades to maj. gen., 1966; fighter pilot in Africa, Italy, France, Sicily, Malta and Corsica, World War II; wing comdr. Europe, U.S., 1942-57; dir. materiel 2d Air Force, SAC, Barksdale AFB, La., 1958-60; comdr. 21st Strategic Aerospace Div., Forbes AFB, Kan., 1960-62; dep. comdr. 1st Strategic Aerospace Div., Vanderberg AFB, Cal., 1962-65; comdr. 821st Strategic Aerospace Div., Ellsworth AFB, S.D., 1965; dep. dir. operations SAC, Offutt AFB, Neb., 1965-66; dir. materiel, 1966-68; dep. insp. gen. for inspection and safety Hdqrs. USAF, Norton AFB, Cal., 1968-69, ret., 1969. Decorated D.S.M. with oak leaf cluster, Silver Star, Legion of Merit, D.F.C. with 2 oak leaf clusters, Air medal with 13 oak leaf clusters; Croix de Guerre with palm and star (France). Author: Crested Ice, The Story of the Recovery of the Atomic Weapons at Thule, Greenland, 1968. Home: PO Box 518 Carpenteria CA 93013

HUPFELDT, WILLIAM GEORGE, meat packing co. exec.; b. Balt., Mar. 20, 1926; s. William C. and Letta (Schluderberg) H.; B.S. in Commerce, U. Va., 1951; m. Nancy M. Kidder, June 12, 1951; children—Susan K. and Christopher (twins), William George, Juliet B. With Schluderberg-Kurdle Co., Inc., Balt., 1951—, pres., 1964—; sec. Frank Research Corp., 1960—. Trustee Boys' Latin Sch., Balt. Mem. Eastern Meat Packers Assn. (pres. bd. dirs.), Boys' Latin Sch. Alumni Assn. (pres.), U. Va. Alumni Assn. (past pres. Md. chpt.). Home: 500 Overhill Rd Baltimore MD 21210 Office: 3800 E Baltimore St Baltimore MD 21224

HUPP, JAMES LLOYD, historian, archivist; b. Hemlock, O., Jan. 5, 1891; s. James Linley and Linnie (Powell) H.; B.S., Ohio U., 1916; A.M., Columbia, 1919; Ph.D., Ohio State U., 1931; m. Luella E. Sherwood, June 8, 1918; children—Virginia (Mrs. Grant W. Speer), James Sherwood, Robert William. Assoc. prof. edn. W.Va. Wesleyan Coll., 1942-43, prof. edn. and psychology, dean students, 1943-55, prof. edn., 1955-61, chmn. div. applied arts and scis., chmn. dept. edn., 1959-61, dir. dept. archives and history 1961—. Historian, archivist W.Va., 1961—; sec.-treas. W.Va. Hist. Commn., 1961-67, W.Va. Antiquities Commn., 1965—; exec. sec. W.Va. Hist. Soc., 1961—, dir. dept. archives and history, 1961—. Dir. adult work Bd. Edn. W.Va. Conf. Meth. Ch., 1943-53, adv. council adult edn., bd. edn. Gen. Conf. Meth. Ch.; editor adult edn. dept. Christian Edn. Bull. Mem. N.E.A., Soc. for Advancement Edn., Nat. Soc. for Study Edn., Am. Assn. State and Local History, A.A.A.S., Soc. Archtl. Historians, Am. Acad. Polit. and Social Sci., Am. Assn. U. Profs., So. Conf. Ednl. Fund (sec. bd. dirs.), Am. Assn. UN, Internat. Council Religious Edn., W.Va. Soc. S.R. (past pres.), W.Va. Philos. Soc. (past pres.), Nat. Trust Historic Preservation, Nat. Geneal. Soc., W.Va. Archeol. Soc., Phi Delta Kappa. Mason (K.T.), Rotarian. Author: (with C.P. Smith) Items Found on Report Forms in Use in Schools in the U.S., 1929; Administrative Problems in the Field of History Teaching, 1932; William Torrey Harris: Teacher, Adminstrator, Philosopher and Writer, 1933; (with C.H. Roberts, R.G. Wood) The Ohio Survey of the Social Sciences, 1934; Eliminating Discrimination, 1950; What Influences Students to Prepare to Teach on the Secondary Level?, 1951; James Rumsey's Memorial in London, 1957; The Movement for West Virginia Statehood, 1962; The West Virginia Flag: It's Development and Meaning, 1962; Storehouse of Treasurers, 1964; The Movement for the Formation of the West Virginia Department of Archives and History, 1966. Contbr. articles for profl. jours., bulls. Home: 57 Meade St Buckhannon WV 26201 Office: Dept Archives and History State Capitol Charleston WV 25305

HURD, CUTHBERT C., mathematician; b. Estherville, Ia., Apr. 5, 1911; s. Harland Corwin and Olive Grace (Long) H.; A.B., Drake U., 1932, LL.D., 1967; M.S., Ia. State Coll., 1934; Ph.D., U. Ill., 1936; m. Bettie Jane Mills, June 20, 1941; children—Steven, Diana, Susan, Elizabeth, Victoria. Asst. prof. math. Mich. State Coll., 1936-42; dean Allegheny Coll., 1945-47; tech. research head Union Carbide & Carbon Corp., Oak Ridge 1947-49, now cons.; dir. applied sci. dept. IBM, 1949-53, dir. applied sci. div., 1953-55, dir. electronic data processing machines, 1955-56, dir. automation research, 1956-60, dir. control systems, 1961-62; chmn. bd. Computer Usage Co., Inc., N.Y.C., 1962—. Mem. adv. com. Center Computer Scis. and Tech., Inst. Applied Tech., Nat. Bur. Standards; mem. computation com. NRC; chmn. computer sci. adv. com. Stanford; mem. adv. council to depts. econs. and sociology Princeton. Trustee Drake U., Johnston Coll.; mem. devel. bd. Mass. Inst. Tech. Served at lt. comdr. USCGR, 1942-45. Fellow A.A.A.S.; mem. Inst. Mgmt. Scis. (past v.p., founder), Am. Math. Soc., Am. Meteorol. Soc., Biometric Soc., Am. Soc. Quality Control, Am. Statis. Assn., Assn. Computing Machinery (council), Econometric Soc., English Speaking Union, Indsl. Math. Soc., Inst. Math. Statistics, Math. Assn. Am. (com. on profl. opportunities), N.Y. Acad. Sci., Operations Research Soc. Am., Soc. Advancement Gen. Systems Theory, Soc. Indsl. and Applied Mathematics, Phi Beta Kappa, Sigma Xi, Phi Kappa Phi. Clubs: University, Metropolitan, University (N.Y.C.). Home: 332 Westridge Dr Portola Valley CA 94025 Office: 851 Welch Rd Palo Alto CA 94304

HURD, EDWIN CECIL, oil co. exec.; b. Marquis, Sask., Can., July 3, 1914; s. Francis Edwin and Hattie D. (Tanner) H.; B.A., U. Sask., 1932, B.Sc. in Chem. Engring., 1934; grad. Advanced Mgmt. Program, Harvard, 1960; m. Helen Z. Edick, May 29, 1937; children—Frances Pat, Penelope Jane, Randall Eugene. Various positions British Am. Oil Co., Ltd., Moose Jaw, Sask., also Montreal, Toronto, 1934-49, asst. to gen. mgr. refineries, 1947-49; indsl. engr. Coop. Refinery Assn., Kansas City, Mo., 1950-51; refinery supt. Mercury Oil Refinery Co., Oklahoma City, 1951-52; mgr. oil movements Trans Mountain Oil Pipe Line Co., Vancouver, B.C., 1953-58, v.p., 1958-60, pres., 1960—; pres., dir. Trans Mountain Oil Pipe Line Corp., Trans Mountain Housing, Ltd., Alpac Constrn. & Surveys, Ltd. Mem. Engring. Inst. Can., Am. Petroleum Inst., Assn. Oil Pipe Lines, Canadian Power Squadron. Mason, Home: 22271 88th Av RR 5 Langley British Columbia Canada Office: 400 E Broadway Vancouver 10 British Columbia Canada

HURD, FREDERICK WILLIAM, traffic engr., assn. ofcl.; b. Troy, Mo., Aug. 24, 1907; s. Fred Arthur and Mary Emelie (Howing) H.; B.S., C.E. in Civil Engring., U. Mo., 1934; certificate traffic engring. Bur. St. Traffic Research, Yale, 1939; m. Ida Mae Richmond, June 23, 1933; children—Marilyn Helen (Mrs. Richard C. Hannah), Frederick William. Engr., traffic engr. safety bur. Mo. Hwy. Dept., 1927-42; asst. safety engr. Wayne County (Mich.) Rd. Commn., 1942; asst. to dir. Mich. Safety Commn., 1942-43; traffic engr. Mich. Hwy. Dept., 1943-35; asst. prof. Bur. Hwy. Traffic, Yale, 1945-55, dir. bur., 1955-68; prof., dir. B.H.T, Pa. State U., 1968—. Pres., Inst. Traffic Engrs., 1964; chmn. dept. traffic and operations Hwy. Research Bd., Nat. Acad. Scis., 1961-63; chmn. Conn. Safety Commn., 1966-67; mem. accident prevention study sect. NIH, 1962-65; adv. com. Pres.'s Com. Traffic Safety, 1964-66. Registered profl. engr., Conn. Recipient T.M. Matson Meml. award for outstanding contbn. to advancement traffic engring., 1969. Mem. Tau Beta Pi, Phi Kappa Phi, Phi Gamma Delta. Co-author: Traffic Engineering, 1955. Contbr. profl. jours. Home: 1650 Glenwood Circle State College PA 16801 Office: Sackett Bldg Pa State U University Park PA 16802

HURD, JAMES BRADDOCK, physician; b. Chgo., Mar. 29, 1921; s. Max Harold and Eunice (Braddock) H.; A.B., Amherst Coll., 1942; M.D., Northwestern U., 1946; M.Sc. in Pathology, 1950; m. Jean Wescott, June 12, 1943; children—Barbara Wescott, Ann Braddock, Janet Darrow. Intern Evanston (Ill.) Hosp., 1945- 46; fellow pathology Cook County Hosp., Chgo., 1948-49, resident medicine, 1950-51; fellow medicine New Eng. Deaconess Hosp., Boston, 1949-50; pvt. practice, Chgo., 1951—; mem. sr. attending staff Chgo. Wesley meml. Hosp., 1957—, chief med. service D, 1961—, sec. staff, 1961-64, vice chief staff, 1964-66, chief staff, 1966—; mem. faculty Northwestern U. Med. Sch., 1951-, asst. prof. internal medicine, 1965- 71, asso. prof., 1971—. Served to capt. M.C., AUS, 1946-48. Mem. Am. Diabetes Assn. (bd. dirs. 1961—, chmn. com. affiliates 1963—, chmn. assembly affiliate dels. and state govs. 1961-63, v.p. 1968, pres. 1970-71), Diabetes Assn. Greater Chgo. (bd. dirs. 1952—, pres. 1959-61, chmn. camp. com. 1952—), A.M.A., Joslin Soc. Republican. Clubs: Economic (Chgo.); Glen View (Golf, Ill.). Home: 362 8th St Des Plaines IL 60016 Office: 222 E Superior St Chicago IL 60611

HURD, JOHN G., U.S. ambassador to Venezuela. Address: American Embassy Caracas, Venezuela.*

HURD, PETER, artist; b. Roswell, N.M., Feb. 22, 1904; s. Harold and Lucy Chew (Knight) H.; student U.S. Mil. Acad., 1921-23, Haverford Coll., 1923-24, Pa. Acad. Fine Arts, and under N.C. Wyeth, 1924-26; D. Fine Arts, Tex. Technol. Coll.; LL.D., N.M. State U., 1968; m. Henriette Wyeth, June 29, 1929; children—Peter Wyeth, Carol (Mrs. Peter W. Rogers), Michael. Represented in collections Met. Mus., N.Y.C., Nat. Gallery (Edinburgh), Rochester, N.Y., Wilmington, Del., Chgo., Andover, Mass., Kansas City, Bklyn., Honolulu, Roswell, N.M., Mpls., Dallas, Neward museums, Ft. Worth Club collection; 16 fresco panels in mus. Tex. Technol. Coll.; fresco murals in U.S. P.O. Big Spring, Tex., Alamogordo, N.M., mural panel Prudential Ins. Co. Bldg., Houston; retrospective show Amon Carter Mus., Ft. Worth, Legion of Honor, San Francisco, 1964-65; portrait Pres. Johnson for White House Hist. Assn. (now in permanent collection Nat. Portrait Gallery Washington). Mem. Nat. Fine Arts Commn., 1959-63. Winner competition for 3 mural panels in U.S. Terminal Annex P.O., Dallas, 1938. Awarded 1st prize 16th Internat. Watercolor Exhbn., Chgo. Art Inst., 1937; elected asso. Nat. Acad., 1941, N.A., 1942—. Mem. Assn. Grads. U.S. Mil. Acad., Wilmington Soc. Fine Arts, Am. Watercolor Soc. Club: Century Assn. Book illustrator. with USAAF in Eng., 1942, U.S. Air Transport Command in S. Am., Africa, India, Arabia and Italy in 1944 as war corr. for Life Mag. Home: Sentinel Ranch San Patricio NM 88348

HURD, ROBERT C., educator; b. Mt. Vernon, Wash., Mar. 7, 1922; s. Edward Lee and Jennie (Deichman) H.; B.S., Pacific U., 1946; M.S., Wash. State U., 1950, Ph.D., 1953; m. Virginia I. Marshall, June 25, 1950; children—Mary Margaret, Elizabeth Anne, Stephen Robert, Roberta Louise. Instr. biology Pacific U., 1946-48; mem. faculty Wash. State U., 1948-53; mem. faculty Gonzaga U., 1953—, chmn. dept. biology, 1957—, prof. biology, 1961—; instr. microbiology Sacred Heart Sch. Nursing, Spokane. Episcopalian. Home: W 3805 Welle St Spokane WA 99208

HURLBERT, LEROY HEQUEMBOURG, toiletries co. exec.; b. Dunkirk, N.Y., Apr. 6, 1913; s. John L. and Helen M. (Hequembourg) H.; B.A. with honors, Yale, 1934, LL.B., 1937; m. Virginia J. Canavan, Oct. 17, 1939 (dec. Oct. 1962); 1 dau., Barbara J. (Mrs. Robert Cantwell); m. 2d, Patricia W. Crowder, June 21, 1963. Admitted to N.Y. bar, 1937; asso. firm Moot, Sprague, Marcy & Gulick, Buffalo, 1937-46; partner firm Moot, Sprague, Macry, Landy, Hurlbert & Fernbach, Buffalo, 1946-62; v.p., gen. counsel, sec. Colgate-Palmolive Co., N.Y.C., 1962—, also dir.; gen. counsel Wildroot Co., 1946-61; counsel Hilton Hotels Corp., 1969-62. Vice pres. Buffalo Philharmonic Orch. Soc., 1959-62, dir., 1956-62; adv. bd. D'Youville Coll., Buffalo, 1962—. Served to lt. USNR, 1943- 46. Mem. Am. Law Inst., Am., N.Y. bar assns., Assn. Bar City N.Y., S.A.R. Mason. Clubs: Canadian, River, Yale (N.Y.C.); Saturn (Buffalo); Lyford Cay (Bahamas). Home: 435 E 52d St New York City NY 10022 Office: 300 Park Av New York City NY 10022

HURLBURT, ALLEN FREEMAN, art dir., designer; b. Bridgeport, Conn., Oct. 24, 1910; s. James Edward and Minnie Viola (Smith) H.; B.S. in Econs., U. Pa., 1932; m. Regina Victoria Rowe, May 29, 1953. Art dir. Bur. Advt., 1937-43, NBC, 1946-51; art dir. Look mag., 1952-67, mem. editorial bd., 1953—; editorial adviser, 1970—; v.p. Cowles Communications, Inc., 1962—, dir. design, 1968—, editorial adviser, 1970—; work exhibited Ann. Exhbn. Advt. Art. 1938-65, Graphic Ann., 1950, 51, 53, Internat. Poster Ann., 1953, exhbn. 43 Am. Typographers, 1957, Mus. Modern Art, 1965. Dir. Internat. Design Conf., 1963-66. Served as 2d lt., inf. AUS, 1943-46. Recipient gold medal awards Ann. Exhbn. Editorial and Advt. Art, Art Dirs. Club, 1948-49, 55, 61-70; named Art Dir. of Year, Nat. Soc. Art Dirs., 1965-66. Fellow Royal Soc. Arts; mem. Am. Inst. Graphic Arts (pres. 1968-69), Art Dirs. Club N.Y.C. (v.p.). Contbr. articles to profl. jours. Author: Publication Design, 1971. Home: 10 W 66th St New York City NY 10023 Office: 488 Madison Av New York City NY 10022

HURLBURT, WILLIAM BLAIR, lawyer; b. Mt. Vernon, Ia., Apr. 19, 1892; s. Rollo Franklin and Mary Halsey (Blair) H.; A.B., U. Ia., 1914, LL.B., 1915; m. Alice Fay Willard, Apr. 6, 1918 (dec.); one son, Willard Blair. Admitted to Ia. bar, 1915 and since practiced des Moines; mem. firm Hurlburt, Blanchard, Cless & Porter and predecessor firm; special asst. U.S. attorney and gen. hearing officer, conscientious objector cases for So. Dist. Ia. 1944-56. Served as 1st lt. Inf., 85th division U.S. Army, World War I. Mem. Am., Ia. State (bd. govs 1950-51) and Polk County (pres. 1949-50) bar assns., Sigma Alpha Epsilon (pres. 1914, province sec. 1916-17), Phi Delta Phi, Sigma Delta Chi. Clubs: Des Moines, Hyperion Field (past pres.). Home: 2606 Forest Dr Des Moines IA 50312 Office: Paramount Bldg Des Moines IA 50309

HURLBUT, CORNELIUS SEARLE, Jr., educator, mineralogist; b. Springfield, Mass., June 30, 1906; s. Cornelius S. and Marion (Adams) H.; A.B., Antioch Coll., 1929; A.M., Harvard, 1932, Ph.D., 1933; m. Anna Dawson, June 18, 1932 (dec. 1954); children—Cornelius Searle IV, Patricia Anne, Marcus Dawson; m. 2d, Margaret Richards Carver, 1956. Instr. petrography Harvard, 1933-34, instr. mineralogy, 1935-40, asso. prof. mineralogy, 1941-53, prof. mineralogy, 1954—. Vice pres. Cambridge Thermionic Corp. Fellow Geol. Soc. Am., Mineral. Soc. Am. (pres. 1963), Am. Acad. Arts and Scis.; mem. Brit. Mineral Soc., Soc. Econ. Geologists, Geochem. Soc., Japanese Mineral Soc. Conglist. Author: Minerals and How to Study Them, 1949; (with Henry E. Wenden) The Changing Science of Mineralogy, 1964; Minerals and Man, 1968; Manual of Mineralogy, 1971. Home: 53 Woodbine Rd Belmont MA 02178 Office: Geol Mus Cambridge MA 02138

HURLBUT, JOHN BINGHAM, educator, lawyer; b. Omro, Wis., Jan. 2, 1906; s. Wilbur Edson and Lulu Marie (Bingham) H.; student U. Wis., 1922-24; A.B., U. Cal. at Los Angeles, 1928; M.A., Stanford, 1929, LL.B., 1934; m. Elizabeth Harriet Harrison, Aug. 27, 1934; children—John Bingham, Mary Elizabeth. Admitted to Cal. bar, 1934, Supreme Ct. bar, 1952; practice O'Melveny, Tuller & Myers, Los Angeles, 1934-37; asso. prof. law Stanford, 1937-42, prof., 1942-71, asst. dean sch. law, 1941-46, Jackson Eli Reynolds prof. law, 1959-71, emeritus, 1971; prof. law Hastings Coll. of Law, U. Cal., 1970—; Fulbright vis. lectr. law U. Tokyo, 1959-60; law lectr. Keio U. Japanese Legal Tng. and Research Inst., 1960. Served as lt. comdr., USNR, 1942-45. Mem. Am. Law Inst., Nat. Coll. Athletic Assn. (past v.p.), Phi Beta Kappa, Phi Alpha Delta, Alpha Tau Omega, Order of Coif. Republican. Club: Bohemian (San Francisco). Home: 430 El Escarpado Stanford CA 94305

HURLBUT, OREN EUGENE, former army officer; b. Brookfield, Mo., Dec. 4, 1911; s. Oren M. and Ida (Frakes) H.; B.S., U.S. Mil. Acad., 1933; postgrad. Indsl. Coll. Armed Forces, 1955; m. Pauline Bartels, Dec. 30, 1936; children—Susan P., Sara J., Sandra L., Stephen B. Commd. 2d lt. U.S. Army, 1933, advanced through grades to lt. gen., 1969; assigned U.S. Mil. Acad., 1947-50; stationed Pentagon, Washington, 1950-54, Europe, 1955-58; comdr. Springfield (Mass.) Armory, 1958-59; comdr. Weapons Command Ill., 1959-61; 8th Army, Korea, 1961-62; dir. logistics Continental Army Command, 1962-66; dir. logistics U.S. Army, Pacific, 1966-68; comdg. gen. U.S. Army Weapons Command, Rock Island, Ill., 1968-69; army mem. joint logistic rev. bd. Office Sec. Def., 1969-70, ret., 1970. Decorated D.S.M., Bronze Star medal, Philippine medal Merit. Home: 4440 Lindell Blvd St Louis MO 63108

HURLEIGH, ROBERT FRANCIS, broadcasting co. exec.; b. Fairmont, Maryland, July 28, 1912; s. Robert Francis and Elizabeth Nancy (Lankford) H.; student McDonogh Mul. Sch.; m. Marjorie Marie Peterson, Oct. 7, 1939; children—Maryland Beth, Robert Blake, Robin Marie, Steven Lankford, Jan Theresa. News Editor radio sta. WOL, Washington, 1934-35, WCAO, Balt., 1935-36, WFBR, 1936-41; central div. mgr. Asso. Press Radio, 1941-43; news analyst C.B.S., Chgo., 1943-45; dir. news radio sta. WGN and midwest bur. chief M.B.S., 1945-53 dir. Washington operations, 1953-57, v.p., 1957-59, pres., 1959-66; exec. v.p. Nat. Forum, N.Y.C., 1966—. Mem. Sigma Delta Chi. Roman Catholic. Clubs: Nat. Press, Kenwood Country. Office: 444 Madison Av New York City NY 10022

HURLEY, DANIEL FRANCIS, fed. labor mediator; b. Hartford, Conn., Nov. 21, 1911; s. Daniel Cornelius and Catherine Mary (Cunningham) H.; student Trinity Coll., Hartford, Conn., 1929-30, Cleve. Coll. Western Res., 1947-48; LL.B., Northeastern U., 1954; m. Mary Lou Crescence De Wan, Feb. 27, 1943; children—Patricia Lee, Daniel Michael, Tarasia. Substitute clk. P.O., Hartford, 1930-32; moulder Colt Patent Firearms Co, Hartford, 1935-36; labor relations adviser Am. Fedn. Actors, N.Y.C., 1936-39; commr. U.S. Conciliation Service, Dept. Labor, Washington, 1939-41, resident commr., Cleve., 1941-44, regional supr. for service, Cleve., 1944-46, asst. regional dir., 1946-47 (entire service transf. to Fed. Mediation and Conciliation Service, 1947), regional dir., Boston, 1948-54, commr., 1954—; admitted to Mass. bar 1954. Instr., Univ. Coll., Northeastern U., Boston. Recipient Cardinal Cushing award for excellence labor mgmt. as rep. of pub., 1967. Mem. Indsl. Relations Research Assn. (sec.-treas. Boston chpt. 1968-71), Boston (pres. 1971—), Fed. bar assns. Roman Catholic. K.C. Clubs: University (Cleve.). Contbr. articles to profl. jours. Home: Yorkshire Rd RFD 1 Dover MA 02030 Office: JFK Fed Bldg Boston MA 02203

HURLEY, DONALD JOSEPH, lawyer; b. Gardner, Mass., May 4, 1907; s. Cornelius Joseph and Rose (O'Loughlin) H.; A.B. magna cum laude, Harvard, 1928, LL.B., 1931; m. Miriam Greene, Aug. 28, 1937; children—Cornelia Greene, Donald, Jr., Stephen Nash, Rosamond Page. Admitted to Mass. bar, 1931; with Goodwin, Proctor & Hoar, Boston, 1931—, partner, 1939—; also counsel Mass. Pardon and Parole Commn., 1938-40; spl. counsel gov. Mass. in preparation of charter Mass. Bus. Devel. Corp., 1953; chmn., dir. Merrimac Paper Co., Inc., Aquamac Corp., Northkraft Industries, Inc.; dir., clk. Stop & Shop, Inc.; pres., dir. Mass. Business Devel. Corp.; trustee, mem. bd. inv. Charlestown Savs. Bank; trustee City Investing Mortgage Group; dir., mem. exec. com. Boston Safe Deposit and Trust Co., Boston Co., Inc.; sec. Fed. Street Capital Corp.; dir. Equitable Fire Ins. Co., Boston Old Colony Ins. Co., Boston Indemnity Ins. Co. J.L. Hammett Co., Lilly Chem. Products, Inc., Putnam Duofund. Inc., Putnam Equities Fund, Inc., Putnam Vista Fund, Inc., Putnam Investors, Inc., Putnam Income Fund, Carling Brewing Co., Inc., Continental Corp., Continental Ins. Co., Fidelity and Casualty Ins. Co. N.Y., Niagara Fire Ins. Co., Putnam Mariner Fund, Putnam Voyager Fund, Seaboard Fire & Marine Ins. Co., Texstar Corp. Trustee Civic Found. Boston, Boston U., Boston Urban Found., George Putnam Fund Boston, Putnam Growth Fund, New Eng. Aquarium; mem. corp. Mass. Gen. Hosp., Mus. Sci.; former dir. Harvard Alumni Assn. Chmn. Boston Mid-Century Jubilee 1960—; gen. chmn. 25th reunion Harvard Class of 1928, 1953; chmn. Mayor's Com. of 100 for Civic Progress in Boston. Pres., dir. Com. of Permanent Charity Fund of Boston, Inc.; dir. Internat. Center of New Eng., Inc., overseer Boy's Clubs Boston, Inc.; trustee Lowell Tech. Inst., 1955-58, Plimoth Plantation. Served from lt. to lt. comdr. USNR, 1943-46. Mem. Greater Boston C. of C. (pres. 1954-56, chmn. exec. com. 1957, dir. 1949-66). Am. Law Inst., Am., Boston bar assns. Clubs: Union (Boston); Harvard (N.Y.C.); Weston (Mass.) Golf; Edgartown Reading Room (Martha's Vineyard, Mass.). Home: 41 Aberdeen Rd Weston MA 02193 Office: 28 State St Boston MA 02109

HURLEY, FRANK HOUSE, univ. dean; b. Houston, Jan. 12, 1912; s. Frank House and Clara Brady (Hauptman) H.; B.A., Rice U., 1933, M.A., 1935, Ph.D. in Chemistry, 1937; m. Frances Kemp, Apr. 26, 1951. Instr. chemistry Rice U., 1937-42; faculty Reed Coll., 1942-51, asso. prof. chemistry, 1946-51, dean men, 1943-51; mgr. coll. relations and personnel devel. Am. Cyanamid Co., N.Y.C., 1951-61; dean faculty arts and scis. Western Res. U., 1961-67, dean grad. studies Case Western Res. U., Cleve., 1967—. Trustee Cleve. Inst. Art, Cleve. Play House, Cleve. Inst. Music, Karamu Ho. Mem. Am. Chem. Soc., Eastern Coll. Personal Officers, Phi Beta Kappa, Sigma Xi. Home: 2472 Overlook Rd Cleveland Heights OH 44106 Office: Case Western Res U Cleveland OH 44106

HURLEY, JOHN FRANCIS, food co. exec.; b. Boston, Aug. 14, 1917; s. Charles and Nora (Burke) H.; m. Mary Louise McEntee, Apr. 7, 1947; children—Lawrence, Gregory, Maureen, Marilynn, Carol, Brian, David, John, Patrick, Michael. With Kellogg Co., Battle Creek, Mich., 1938-42, 46—, v.p., 1960-62, exec. v.p., 1962-68, asst. to pres., 1958-68, also dir.; pres. Kellogg Internat., 1968—. Served with USMCR, 1942-46. Home: 145 Smithfield Rd Battle Creek MI 49015 Office: Kellogg Co Battle Creek MI 49015

HURLEY, KENNETH DUANE, coll. pres.; b. Riverside, Cal., Aug. 19, 1915; s. P.B. and Polly (rice) H.; A.A. Riverside Coll., 1936; A.B., Salem Coll., 1938; A.M., U. So. Cal., 1952; LL.D., Alderson-Broaddus Coll., 1956, Southeastern U., 1959; Pd.D., Milton Coll., 1956; D.Ed., Waynesburg Coll., 1960; postgrad. U. Cal.; m. Shireen Twogood, Aug. 14, 1937; children—Terry Anne, Cathrine Sue, Rebecca, Penelope. Tchr. English, speech, stagecraft, dramatics Marysville (Cal.) High sch., 1939-45; radio announcer KMYC, Marysville, 1943-45; editor Sabbath Recorder, Plainfield, N.J., 1945-47; chmn. speech arts dept. El Monte (Cal.) High Sch., 1947-51; pres. Salem Coll. (W.Va.), 1951—. Radio counselor Cal. Boys State, 1944; pres. Marysville Jr. C. of C., 1944-46; exec. com. Boy Scouts Am.; chmn. W.Va. Broadcasting Authority. Mem. Cal. Scholastic Fedn., Assn. for Edn. by Radio and TV, United Church Men (bd. mgrs.), W.Va. Edn. Assn., W.Va. Found. Ind. Colls., Council for Advancement Small Colls. (founder, past pres.), N.E.A., W.Va. Assn. Coll. and Univ. Presidents (pres. 1966). Kiwanian. Home: 63 Terrace Av Salem WV 26426

HURLEY, LAUREL, singer; b. Allentown, Pa., Feb. 14, 1927; d. Walter James and Viola (Burd) Hurley; student pub. schs., Allentown; m. John Peter Butz, May 6, 1949; children—James Harold, Laurie, Amy, Deborah. Stage debut as dancer, age of 2 1/2 Lyric Theater, Allentown, Pa.; professional debut as Kathie in Student Prince, Broadway, 1943, toured with Student Prince, U.S., Can., 1943-46; operatic debut as Norina in Don Pasquale, Hartford, Conn., 1950; toured as Mimi in La Boheme, 1950; soprano leads, Central City Opera Festival, 1951; Town Hall recital debut, 1951; N.Y. City Opera debut as Zerlina in Don Giovanni, 1952: Met. Opera debut as Oscar in Un Ballo Maschera, 1955. soprano leads in La Perichole, Don Pasquale, and Magic Flute, Der Rosenkavalier, Don Giovanni, Rigoletto, others; appearances NBC-TV in Marriage of Figaro, Hansel and Gretel, La Sonnambula, Magic Flute, I Puritani; soloist with the Tel Aviv Philharmonic; singer light opera roles, summer theater. Recipient Jr. award Nat. Fedn. Music Clubs, 1942-44, Pa. Young Artists award, Nat. Fedn. Music Clubs, 1945-47; Kathryn Turney Long opera scholarship Met. Opera, 1949; Walter W. Naumburg Found. award, 1951. Named Pa. State Ambassador, by Gov., on nomination of Allentown C. of C., 1954. Hon. mem. Sigma Alpha Iota, Sigma Kappa; mem. Actors Equity Assn., Am. Guild Musical Artists, Am. Fedn. TV and Radio Artists. Office: care Metropolitan Opera Assn Lincoln Center New York City NY 10023

HURLEY, LEONARD F., business exec.; b. Michie, Tenn., Feb. 28, 1898; s. William P. and Cora Bell (Donnell) H.; A.B., U. Tenn., 1923; m. Frances Lewis, Oct. 15, 1934; children—Donnell Lewis, Leonard F., Margaret Faye. Salesman, Nat. Cash Register, 1923-24; ins. broker, 1924-29; sec. M.F. Flenniken & Co., 1929-31; v.p., co-owner Morgan & Hurley, Inc., 1931-42; pres. Hurley & Assos., Inc., 1942-66, chmn. bd., 1966—; sec. Stallworth, Inc., 1948—; sec. 7-Up Bottling Co. of Knoxville, Inc., 1935-70; v.p. 7-Up Bottling Co. of Corbin, Ky., 1937—; v.p. Ins. Services of Fla., Inc.; chmn. bd. Mid States Underwriters, Inc., 1965-69, Broome, Stuart & Myers, Inc., 1965—. Treas. sch. religion U. Tenn., mem. Century Club and Pres.'s Club U. Tenn., mem. bd. alumni advisers 1969-70; pres. Knoxville Council Chs., 1953-54; chmn. quota com. United Fund, 1953; pres. So. area council YMCA, 1951-53, v.p. nat. council, 1952-53, mem. internat. com., 1950—, del. world alliance, 1957, bd. dirs., 1957-63. Presbyn. (mem. session bd.). Home: 484 Cherokee Blvd Knoxville TN 37919 Office 1209 Euclid Av Knoxville TN 37921

HURLEY, MARIE V., librarian; b. Elmira, N.Y., Dec. 25, 1910; d. Daniel Joseph and Olga (Hauenstein) Hurley; B.S., Elmira Coll., 1932; B.S. in L.S., Columbia, 1933. Sch. and Reference librarian N.Y.C. Pub. Library, 1933-42; librarian Riverdale (N.Y.) Neighborhood and Library Assn., 1942-46; asst. librarian U.S. Information Library, Sydney, Australia, 1946-47; librarian S. Euclid-Lyndhurst (O.) Pub. Library, 1948-52; br. librarian Cuyahoga County (O.) Pub. Library, 1952-54; asst. dir. Ferguson Library, Stamford, Conn., 1954-65, dir., 1965—. Bd. dirs. Stamford Forum World Affairs, 1960—, Stamford Mental Health Assn., 1959-65, Womens Nat. Book Assn., 1955-60. Mem. Am., New Eng., Conn. (pres. 1967-68) library assns. Home: 140 Sylvan Knoll Rd Stamford CT 06902 Office: 96 Broad St Stamford CT 06901

HURLEY, MARK JOSEPH, bishop; b. San Francisco, Dec. 13, 1919; s. Mark J. and Josephine (Keohane) H.; student St. Joseph's Coll., Mt. View, Cal., 1939, St. Patrick's Sem., Menlo Park, Cal., 1944; postgrad. U. Cal. at Berkeley, 1943-45; Ph.D., Cath. U. Am., 1947; J.C.B., Lateran U., Rome, 1962; LL.D., U. Portland, 1971. Ordained priest Roman Cath. Ch., 1944; asst. supt. schs. Archdiocese San Francisco, 1944-51; tchr. Serra High Sch., San Mateo, Cal., 1944; prin. Bishop O'Dowd High Sch., Oakland, Cal., 1951-58, Marin Cath. High Sch., Marin County, Cal., 1959-61; supt. schs. Diocese Stockton, Cal., 1962-65, chancellor, diocesan counsultor, 1962-65; asst. chancellor Arcdiocese San Francisco, 1965-69, vicar gen., 1957-69; titular bishop Thunusuda, aux. bishop San Francisco, 1967-69; bishop Santa Rosa, Cal., 1969—; pastor St. Francis Assisi Ch., San Francisco, 1967—. Prof. grad. schs. Loyola U., Balt., 1946, U. San Francisco, 1948, San Francisco Coll. Women, 1949, Dominican Coll., Rafael, Cal., 1949, Cath. U. Am., 1954. Del., Conf. Psychiatry and Religion, San Francisco, 1957; mem. bd. Cal. Com. on Study Edn., 1955-60; del.-at-large Cal., White House Conf. on Youth, 1960; Cath. del., observer Nat. Council Chs., Columbus, O., 1964; del. edn. conf. German and Am. educators, Nat. Cath. Edn. Assn., Munich, Germany, 1960; mem. commns. sems., univs. and schs. II Vatican Council, Rome, 1962-65; mem. commn. Christian formation U.S. Cath. Conf. Bishops, 1968; asst. archdiocesan coordinator Campaign on Taxation Schs. Cal., 1958, Rosary Crusade, 1961; adminstr. Cath. Sch. Purchasing Div., 1948-51, St. Eugene's Ch., Santa Rosa, Cal., 1959, St. John's Ch., San Francisco, 1961; syndicated columnist San Francisco Monitor, Sacramento Herald, Oakland Voice, Yakima (Wash.) Our Times, Guam Diocesan Press, 1949-66; TV speaker and panelist, 1956-67; mem. U.S. Bishops' Press Panel, Vatican Council, 1964-65, U.S. Bishops' Com. on Laity, 1964, U.S. Bishops' Com. Cath.-Jewish Relationships, 1965—, U.S. Bishops' Com. on Ecumenical and Interreligious Affairs, 1970; mem. Conf. Maj. Superiors of Men, 1970; chmn. citizens Com. for San Francisco State Coll., 1968—; mem. adminstrn. bd. Nat. Conf. Cath. Bishops, 1970. Trustee N.Am. Coll., Rome, 1970. Author: Church State Relationships in Education in California, 1948; Commentrary on Declaration on Christian Education in Vatican II, 1966; Report on Education in Peru, 1965. Address: PO Box 1499 Santa Rosa CA 95403

HURLEY, MORRIS ELMER, Jr., coll. dean; b. Berkeley, Cal., Mar. 26, 1920; s. Morris Elmer and Alice Grace (Johnson) H.; A.B., Harvard, 1941, M.B.A., 1943; Ph.D., Syracuse U., 1956; m. Jeanne Marie Bassett, Jan. 31, 1943; children—Morris Elmer III, James, Richard, Steven, Robert. Asst. dean Coll. Bus. Adminstrn., Syracuse U., 1946-53, acting dean, 1953-54, dean, 1954-58, instr., 1945- 48, asst. prof., 1948-53, asso. prof., 1953-57, prof., 1957-60; prof. Istituto Direzionale ENI, San Donato Milanese, 1958, IPSOA Istituto Post-Universitaire Torino, Italy, 1959-61; cons. prof. IBM Exec. Sch. Blaricu, Holland, 1960-61; dir. Mgmt. Edn. Programs, Berkeley, Cal., 1961-71; dean Sch. Pub. Affairs, Golden Gate Coll., San Francisco, 1971—; asso. economist with N.Y. dept. Commerce, 1948; research aide Study for the Ford Found., 1949; cons. U.S. Internal Revenue Service, 1957. Dir. Portsmouth (Va.) Community Chest, 1944-46, Frank S. Hiscock Legal Aid Soc., Syracuse, 1951-54; mem. Syracuse city planning commn., 1957-58. Served from ensign to lt., USNR, 1943-46; mem. res. Mem. Am. Econ. Assn., Acad. Mgmt., Acad. Polit. and Social Sci., A.I.M., Financial Execs. Inst., Am. Finance Assn., Am. Statis. Assn., Assn. Higher Edn., Am. Assn. U. Profs., George F. Baker Scholars, Phi Beta Kappa, Beta Gamma Sigma, Pi Eta, Sigma Iota Epsilon, Alpha Kappa Psi. Author: Elements of Business Administration, 1953; Staff Notes, 1953; Economic Development Regionalism, 1956; Business Administration, 2d edit. 1960: Teaching Notes, 1960. Home: 36 Greenbank Av Piedmont CA 94611 Office: 536 Mission St San Francisco CA 94105

HURLEY, PATRICK MASON, educator; b. Hong Kong, China, Jan. 12. 1912; s. F.C. Maso and Anne (Peacock) H.; B.A., U. B.C., 1934, B.A.S., 1934; Ph.D., Mass. Inst. Tech., 1940; m. Margaret Macurda, Aug. 9, 1941; childrenDavid, Peter, Pamela. Came to U.S., 1937, naturalized, 1943. Geologist, mining engr., B.C., 1933-37; research asso. Mass. Inst. Tech., 1940-42, asst. prof. geology, 1946-51, exec. officer geology dept., 1951—, prof., 1953—. Research asso. Nat. Def. Research Com., 1942-45; cons. mineral exploration and evaluation. Research contracts AEC, Office Naval Research. Fellow Geol. Soc. Am., Am. Acad. Sci., Am. Geophys. Union; mem. Am. Inst. Mining Engrs., Sigma Xi. Conglist. Author: How Old is the Earth, 1959. Contbr. articles to sci. jours. Home: 36 Oakmount Circle Lexington MA 02173 Office: Mass Inst Tech Cambridge MA 02139

HURLEY, RUBY, assn. exec.; b. Washington; d. Edward and Alice (Patterson) Ruffin; student Miner Tchrs. Coll., Terrell Law Ch. Nat. youth sec. N.A.A.C.P., 1943-51, regional coordinator, 1951-52, Southeast regional dir., Atlanta, 1952—. Active YWCA. Recipient Citizen of Year award Birmingham chpt. Omega Psi Phi, 1953; award for spl. distinction civil and human rights Friends of Nat. Council Negro Women, 1957; First Medgar Evers award Capital Press Club, Washington; Freedom award West Coast region N.A.A.C.P., Berkeley, Cal.; Distinguished Service award Savannah State Coll. chpt. N.A.A.C.P.; award for Outstanding Contbns. in Fight for Freedom, Region V N.A.A.C.P. and Fla. conf. Quarter of Century Service to N.A.A.C.P. award; named Woman of Year, Utility Club, N.Y.C., 1968; mem. Chgo. Defender Honor Roll of Democracy. Mem. So. Interagy. Conf. Methodist (mem. conf. bd. Christian social concerns). Home: 3775 Gordon Rd SW Atlanta GA 30331 Office: 970 Hunter St SW Atlanta GA 30314

HURLEY, THOMAS EDWIN, ch. ofcl.; b. Des Moines; s. Thomas Edwin and Gertrude (Smith) H.; student Thacher Sch., Ojai, Cal.; A.B. Yale; C.S.B., Mass. Metaphysics Coll., 1931; m. Mrs. Mildred Tritle Smott, Feb. 14, 1945. Bond business Chgo., 1922-25; Christian Science practitioner and teacher; mem. Board of Lectureship of The First Church, of Christ Scientist, Boston, 1938-47. 1950-52; first reader The Mother Ch., 1st Ch. of Christ Scientist, Boston, 1947-50; mgr. com. on publ., 1952-53; dir. Mother Ch., 1953-71. Served 2d lt. field arty. U.S. Army, 1918. Mem. Psi Upsilon. Clubs: Wianno (Osterville); Algonquin (Boston); Elihu (Yale). Home: 274 Beacon St Boston MA 02116

HURLEY, WILLIAM EMMETT, lawyer; b. Pettibone, N.D., Mar. 26, 1931; s. William Emmett and Florence (Daly) H.; B.S., U. Ore., 1952, J.D., 1956; m. Barbara L. Metcalf. June 20, 1953; children-Anne, Mary, Jean, Sarah. Admitted to Ore. bar, 1956, since practiced in Portland; asso. Collier, Bernard, Bernard & Edwards, 1956-59; mem. firm Bernard & Hurley, 1959—; instr. law Northwestern Coll. Law, 1957-61. Served to 2d lt., inf., U.S. Army, Korean War. Mem. Order of Coif, Phi Beta Kappa, Chi Psi, Phi Alpha Delta. Home: 1089 S W Westwood Dr Portland OR 97201 Office: 905 Standard Plaza Portland OR 97204

HURLEY, WILLIAM MARVIN assn. exec.; b. Hector, Ark., Apr. 19, 1906; s. James Henry and Onie (Turnbow) H.; student Ark. Poly. Coll., 1925-28; B.A., U. Ark., 1929, M.A., 1930; m. Marjorie Sue Caldwell, June 17, 1934; children—James Franklin, Gerald Marvin. Instr. journalism, editor Ark. Alumnus, U. Ark., 1929-35; publicity mgr. Tulsa C. of C., 1935-37, indsl. mgr., asst. gen. mgr., 1938-41; exec. v.p. U.S. Jr. C. of C., St Louis, 1937- 38; gen. mgr. Lincoln (Neb.) C. of C., 1941-43; asst. gen. mgr. Houston, C. of C., 1945-50, exec. v.p., 1951—. Bd. dirs. Houston Symphony Soc., Houston Livestock Show, Jr. Achievement Houston, Houston Port Bur. Exec. v.p. Nat. Space Hall of Fame; chmn. Nat. Improved Mail Service; mem. Regional Export Expansion Council. Served as lt. col. C.E., AUS, 1943-45. Decorated Legion of Merit (U.S.); Royal Order of Vasa (Sweden); knight Order Leopold II (Belgium); Distinguished Alumnus citation U. Ark., 1955; Freedoms Found. award, 1953, 55, 56, 62, 65, 66, 68, 69; mem. Hall Distinction, Ark. Poly. Coll. Mem. Am. Soc. Oceanography (dir.), U.S. C. of C. (chmn. regents Insts. Orgn. Mgmt. 1961-62), Am. C. of C. Execs. (pres. 1958), So. Assn. C. of C. Execs. (pres. 1954), Nat. Inst. Comml. and Trade Orgn. Execs. (pres. 1954), Southwestern C. of C. Inst. (pres. 1952), Tex. C. of C. Mgrs. (pres. 1963-64), Lambda Chi Alpha, Kappa Tau Alpha. Democrat. Methodist (past chmn. ofcl. bd.), Kiwanian (past pres.). Clubs: Houston, Lakeside Country. Author: Chamber of Commerce Administration, 1942; Chamber of Commerce Management, 1960; Decisive Years for Houston, 1966. Editor: Am. C. of C. Execs. Jour., 1962. Home: 914 Wild Valley Rd Houston TX 77027 Office: Chamber of Commerce Bldg PO Box 53600 Houston TX 77052

HURLOCK, ELIZABETH BERGNER, author, lectr.; b. Harrisburg, Pa., July 4, 1898; d. William Spry Turner and Catharine Mary (Bergner) Hurlock; A.B., Bryn Mawr (Pa.) Coll., 1919, A.M., 1922; Ph.D., Columbia, 1924; m. Irland McKnight Beckman, Dec. 21, 1931; childrenDaryl (dec.), Gail McKnight. Mem. psychology dept. Columbia, 1924-46, asso. psychology, 1940-46, departmental rep. for univ. undergrads., asst. to adviser women students, 1926-46; asso. psychology U. Pa., 1949, asso. in ednl. psychology Sch. Edn., 1959-67. Fellow Am., Eastern psychol. assns., A.A.A.S.; mem. Am. Assn. U. Profs., Gerontological Soc., Nat. Assn. for Better Radio and Television, Am. Assn. U. Women, Sigma Xi. Episcopalian. Clubs: Bryn Mawr; Philadelphia Cricket. Author: numerous books on children including Child Growth and Development, 4th edit., 1970; Adolescent Development, 3d edit., 1966; Child Development, 5th edit., 1972; Developmental Psychology, 3d edit., 1968; A Guide and Record of Your Baby's Early Years, 1952; Guideposts to Growing Up, 1954; Personality Development, 1971; also series of eleven ednl. sound films and five film strips Child Development, 1950, 55; Adolescent Development, 1953, Adolescent Psychology, 1954. Child tng. editor: Today's Health, A.M.A., 1947- 59; syndicated newspaper column As We Live, in newspapers throughout country, 1947-58. Mem. editorial staff Jour. Adolescence, 1966-68. Address: 1900 Rittenhouse Sq Philadelphia PA 19103

HUROK, SOL, impresario ballets and concerts; b. Pogar, Russia, Apr. 9, 1888; s. Israel and Naomi Hurok; ed. Russian schs.; H.H.D., Boston U. 1958, Wayne U., 1960; m. Emma Runitch, 1933; 1 dau. by former marriage, Ruth. Came to U.S. in 1905, naturalized, 1914. Began as mgr. weekly concerts, Hippodrome, N.Y.C., 1915; has since been impresario for many famous ballets, musicians, dancers, including Anna Pavlova, Feodor Chaliapin, Isadora Duncan, Russian Ballet, Ballet Theatre, Marian Anderson, Artur Rubinstein, Jan Peerce, Mischa Elman, Gregor Piatigorsky, Isaac Stern, Grace Bumbry, Mary Costa, Roberta Peters, Leonard Warren, The Old Vic, Andres Segovia, Victoria de los Angeles, Fritz Reiner, William Steinberg, Jerome Hines, Alexis Weissenberg, Nicolai Gedda, Nathan Milstein, Royal Ballet (Margot Fonteyn and Rudolf Nureyev), Stuttgart Ballet; presented Emlyn Williams on stage as Charles Dickens, 1952-70, Jean-Louis Barrault in French plays, 1952-53, 57; Comedie Francaise, 1956, 61, 70, Moiseyev Folk Ballet, 1958-70, Theatre Nat. Popularie, 1958, Bolshoi Ballet, Maryinsky Ballet, 1961; Ballet Folklorico of Mexico, Royal Danish Ballet, Mazowsze, Romanian Folk Ballet; cons. in field NBC-TV, 1955—. Decorated chevalier and officer French Legion of Honor; comdr. Order Brit. Empire, 1960; recipient other awards. Autobiography: Impresario. Motion Picture titled Tonight We Sing. Address: 1370 Av of Americas New York City NY 10019

HURRELL, PAUL M., educator. Prof. philosophy Mich. State U. Office: Dept Philosophy Mich State U East Lansing MI 48824*

HURSON, DANIEL L., life ins. co. exec.; b. Washington, 1920; ed. Georgetown U., 1942, Harvard Bus. Sch., 1947. Pres., chmn. bd. Acacia Mut. Life Ins. Co. Pres., trustee Cosmopolitan Charities. Home: 312 St Lawrence Dr Silver Spring MD 20901 Office: 51 Louisiana Av NW Washington DC 20001

HURST, DAVID CHARLES, educator; b. Bozeman, Mont., Aug. 25, 1928; s. John Wildeboor and Frances Lucile (Stevens) H.; B.S., Mont. State Coll., 1950; M.S., N.C. State Coll., 1957, Ph.D., 1962; m. Elsbe Hermine van Dam, Mar. 16, 1954; children—Mary Lucile, Sandra Lee. Research asst. phys. sci. U.S. Army, 1951-52; grad. asst. N.C. State Coll., 1953-57; asso. prof. statistics Va. Poly. Inst., 1957-65; asso. prof., chmn. dept. biostatistics U. Ala., 1965-70, prof., chmn. dept., 1970—, cons. Ala. Heart Assn., Ala. Tech. Assistance Corp. NIH. fellow, 1953-57. Mem. Am. Statis. Assn., Biometric Soc., Inst. Math. Statistics, Va. Acad. Sci., A.A.A.S., Sigma Xi, Phi Eta Sigma, Pi Mu Epsilon. Methodist. Home: 2821 Vestavia Forest Pl Vestavia AL 35216 Office: Univ Alabama Birmingham AL 35233

HURST, HAROLD EMERSON, educator; b. Weld County, Colo., June 20, 1912; s. Frank North and Anna Marguerite (Stubbert) H.; A.B., U. Colo., 1936, LL.B., 1938; M.S. in Govt. Mgmt. (Alfred P. Sloan Found fellow), U. Denver, 1940; m. Esther Carolyn Walter, July 26, 1938; childrenHarold Frank, Janet Marie, Pamela Ann. Admitted to Colo. bar, 1938; dir. research Citizens Tax League Ohio, 1940-41; chief staff services Colo. Dept. Revenue, 1941- 42; cons. Ark. Pub. Expenditures Council, 1946-47; asso. prof. law U. Denver, 1947-50, prof., 1950-, dean Coll. Law, 1961-65. Served with USNR, 1942-46. Mem. Am., Colo. (gov.), Denver bar assns., Am. Judicature Soc., Assn. Am. Law Schs. (chmn. round table council on multiple div. schs.),Phi Alpha Delta. Contbr. articles to profl. jours. Home: 3055 Robin Way Denver CO 80222

HURST, JAMES WILLARD, educator; b. Rockford, Ill., Oct. 6, 1910; s. James Dominick and Mabel (Weinert) H.; A.B., Williams Coll., 1932; LL.B., Harvard, 1935, research fellow, 1935-36; m. Frances Wilson, Aug. 20, 1941; childrenThomas Robert, Mary Deborah. Admitted to Ill. bar, 1936; law clk. Justice Brandeis, U.S. Supreme Ct., Oct. term 1936; instr. law U. Wis., 1937-38, asst. prof., 1938-41, asso. prof., 1941-46, prof. law, 1946. Vis. prof summer sessions law schs. Northwestern, 1939, 40, Stanford, 1950, 62, U. Utah, 1952; (leave of absence 1942-46); Pitt prof. Am. history and instns. U. Cambridge (Eng.), 1967-68, fellow Trinity Hall, 1967-68. Staff gen. counsel's office Bd. Econ. Warfare, 1942-43. Served to lt. USNR, 1943-46. Mem. Am. Philos. Soc; Wis. Hist. Soc., Am. Acad. Arts and Scis Phi Beta Kappa, Phi Delta Phi, Order of Coif. Democrat. Conglist. Author books pertaining to law including: The Growth of American Law; The Law Makers, 1950; Law and the Conditions of Freedom, 1956; Law and Social Process in U.S. History, 1960; Law and Economic Growth, 1964; Justice Holmes on Legal History, 1964; The Legitimacy of the Business Corporation, 1970. Contbr.; in the United States, 1971. Contbr.: Supreme Court and Supreme Law (Cahn), 1954, various law revs, Home: 3972 Plymouth Circle Madison WI 53705

HURST, JOHN WILLIS, cardiologist; b. Cooper, Ky., Oct. 21, 1920; s. John M. and Verna (Bell) H.; B.S., U. Ga., 1941; M.D., Med. Coll. Ga., 1944; m. Nelie Wiley, Dec. 20, 1942; children—John, Steve, Phil. Intern, U. Hosp. Med. Coll. Ga., 1944-45, asst. resident, 1945-46; cardiac fellow Mass. Gen. Hosp., 1947- 49; practice medicine, specializing in cardiology, Atlanta, 1949- -; teaching, research fellow cardiology Sch. Medicine Harvard, 1948-49; fellow cardiology Sch. Medicine Emory U., Atlanta, 1950-51, instr., 1951-53, asso. in medicine, 1953-56, asst. prof., 1956-57, prof., chmn. dept. medicine, 1957—, dir. Postgrad. Teaching Program, 1956—; regional cons. cardiology VA Hosp., Atlanta, 1951—; chief of medicine Grady Meml. Hosp., Atlanta, 1957—. Mem. Presidents Com. on Heart Diseases, Cancer and Stroke, 1965—; mem. Nat. Adv. Heart and Lung Council, 1967-71. Served to capt. U.S. Army, 1946-47; to comdr. USNR, 1954-55. Diplomate Am. Bd. Internal Medicine, Am. Bd. Cardiovascular Disease (chmn. subsplty. bd. cardiovascular disease 1967-70). Fellow A.C.P., Am. Coll. Cardiology; mem. A.M.A., Ga., Fulton County med. assns., Am. (pres. 1971-72), Ga. (past pres.) heart assns., Am. Fedn. Clin. Research, Assn. Profs. Medicine, Assn. Am. Physicians, Assn. U. Cardiologists, So. Soc. Clin. Research, Am. Clin. and Climatological Assn., Alpha Omega Alpha. Author: (with G.C. Woodson) Atlas of Spatial Vector Electrocardiography, 1952; Cardiac Resuscitation, 1960; (with R. Bruce Logue) The Heart, 1966. Editor: (with N. K. Wenger) Electrocardiographic Interpretation, 1963. Mem. editorial bd. Am. Heart Jour., 1964—. Contbr. articles to med. jours. Home: 45 Blackland Rd N W Atlanta GA 30305 Office: 69 Butler St S E Atlanta GA 30303

HURST, M.L., ins. co. exec.; b. Fort Scott, Kan., 1892; ed. U. Tenn., 1911. Treas., dir. Western Casualty & Surety Co., Fort Scott; partner West & Co.; treas., dir. Western Fire Ins. Co., Western Indemnity Co. Trustee, Western Casualty and Surety Co. Employees Profit-Sharing Trust. Home: 505 Sunset Dr Fort Scott KS 66701 Office: 14 E 1st St Fort Scott KS 66701

HURST, THOMAS, supermarket exec.; b. 1910; married. Owner grocery store, Montclair, N.J., 1933-42; with Eastern Aircraft Corp., Bloomfield, N.J., 1942-45; partner Tom's Shop-Rite Co., 1946-60; past pres. Broughton Shop-Rite Supermarket Inc., Bloomfield; now sec., dir. Supermarkets Gen. Corp. Address: 1 Commerce Dr Cranford NJ 07016*

HURST, VERNON JAMES, geologist, educator; b. Glenmore, Ga., July 18, 1923; s. Lonnie T. and Essie (Arnold) H.; student U. S.D., 1943, S.D. State Coll., 1944; B.S., U. GA., 1951; M.S., Emory U., 1952; Ph.D., Johns Hopkins, 1954; m. Julia Corneil Wells, Nov. 5, 1950; childrenMarc V., Karen Anne. Geol. cons., bldg. contractor, Alaska, 1946-50; geologist N.J. Zinc Co., 1951; geologist, chief mineralogist Ga. Dept. Mines, Mining and Geology, 1956- 61; prof., head dept. geology U. Ga., Athens, 1961-69, chmn. phys. scis. div., 1966-69, research prof. geology, 1969—. Cons. geologist Alaska, Colombia, Panama, P.R., Honduras; pres Research Analysis, Inc. Past mem. Environmental Scis. Panel, NSF; mem. marine resources adv com. Coastal Plains Regional Commn. Trustee Coastal Plains Center for Marine Devel. Services; past chmn. bd. govs. Center for Research in Coll. Instrn. of Sci. and Math. Served with USAAF, 1943-46; ETO, PTO. Fellow Geol. Soc. Am. (past chmn. S.E. sect.), Mineral. Soc. Am.; mem. Ga. Acad. Sci. (past pres.), Soc. Econ. Geologists, Ga. Geol. Soc. (pres.), Geologesche Vereunigung, Societe Francaise de Mineralogie et Cristallographie, Southeastern Assn. Spectrogrophers, Sigma Xi. Democrat. Presbyn. Kiwanian. Home: 445 Westview Dr Athens GA 30601

HURST, VICTOR, univ. adminstr.; b. Rutherford, N.J., May 6, 1915; s. Albert Edward and Sarah (Schaefer) H.; B.S., Rutgers U., 1938, M.S., 1940; Ph.D., U. Mo., 1948; m. Henrietta A. Goerler, Nov. 28, 1942; children—William T., Ann V., Ruth M., Ellen R. Faculty, Clemson (S.C.) U., 1948—, alumni prof. dairy sci., 1961-65, dean univ., v.p. acad. affairs, 1966—. Active Boy Scouts Am. Served with USCGR, 1942-46. Mem. Sigma Xi, Alpha Zeta, Gamma Sigma Delta, Phi Kappa Phi, Alpha Epsilon Delta, Delta Upsilon. Home: 210 Grove Dr Clemson SC 29631

HURST, WILLIAM DALY, govt. ofcl.; b. Parowan, Utah, Oct. 5, 1915; s. William M. and Katie (Daly) H.; B.S. in Forestry, Utah State U., 1938; m. Emma Johanson, Mar. 19, 1941; children—William J., Kathleen (Mrs. Dean T. Hughes), Linda (Mrs. Bryant D. Nelson), Helen, Carl J. With Forest Service, Dept. Agr., 1938—, regional forester, Albuquerque, 1966—. Served with AUS, 1945-46. Recipient Silver Beaver award Boy Scouts Am., 1962, Bridger award Utah State U., 1962, Superior Service award Dept. Agr., 1968. Mem. Am. Soc. Range Mgmt. (pres. 1970), Soc. Am. Foresters, Soil Conservation Soc. Am. Mem. Ch. of Jesus Christ of Latter Day Saints. Rotarian. Home: 7708 Sierra Av NE Albuquerque NM 87110 Office: 517 Gold Av SW Albuquerque NM 87101

HURST, WILLIAM DONALD, civil engr.; b. Winnipeg, Can., Mar. 15, 1908; s. William and Magdalena (Unger) H.; B.S. in Civil Engring., U. Man., 1930; C.E., Va. Poly. Inst., 1931; m. Gytha Johnson, June 2, 1934; childrenMarilyn Ragna (Mrs. Paul C. White), William Helgi Donald. Teaching fellow civil engring. Va. Poly. Inst., 1930-31; resident engr. Office Engr., Engr. Water Works, City of Winnipeg, 1931-44, asst. city engr., 1944, commr. pub. works & bldgs., 1944—; sec., engr., bd. engrs. Greater Winnipeg San. Dist., 1935-39; chmn. bd. commrs. Greater Winnipeg Water and San. Dists., 1948-60; commr. Winnipeg-St. Boniface Harbor Commn.; chmn. River and Streams Authority, 1952-. Chmn. Winnipeg Parking Authority; mem. Winnipeg Traffic Commn., Man. Floodway Authority. Served as capt. Royal Can. Engrs. Res., 1939-44. Named Top Ten Public Works Man of Year, Kiwanis Internat. and Am. Pub. Works Assn., 1962 Registered engr., Man., Minn.; chartered engr., Gt. Britain. Diplomate Am. Acad. San. Engrs. Fellow Am. Soc. C.E., Instn. Municipal Engrs. (Gt. Britain); mem C. of C., Assn. Profl. Engrs. Province Man. (pres. 1951), Engring. Inst. Can. (chmn. Winnipeg br. 1938, 51, councillor 1958-59), Am. Pub. Works Assn. (Samuel A. Greeley award 1961, pres. 1958-59, vice chmn. research found.), Am. Water Works Assn. (past dir., past pres., George Warren Fuller award), Inst. Municipal Engring. (pres. 1966- 67), Instn. Water Engrs. Gt. Britain (hon.), Winnipeg Symphony Orch. (pres. 1955-56), Phi Delta Theta. Mem. United Church of Can. Clubs: Manitoba, Scientific (Winnipeg); Collectors (N.Y.C.); Canadian. Contbr. tech. articles profl. jours. Home: 67 Kingway Winnipeg 9 Manitoba Canada Office: Civic Centre Winnipeg 2 Manitoba Canada

HURT, JOHN JETER, Jr., editor; b. Conway, Ark., Apr. 19, 1909; s. John Jeter and Ethelyn (Lovell) H.; A.B., Union U., Jackson, Tenn., 1931; LL.D., Mercer U., 1955; m. Doris Oglesby, June 10, 1935; children—John Jeter III, Robert Hamilton. Reporter, Comml. Appeal, Memphis, 1930-31, Jackson Sun, 1931- 36; staff A.P., Nashville, 1936-40, bur. mgr., Chattanooga, 1940-43, Memphis, 1943-46, editor gen. desk, N.Y.C., 1946, Atlanta, 1946-47; editor Christian Index, Atlanta, 1947-66, Bapt. Standard, Dallas, 1967—. Mem. pub. relations adv. com. So. Bapt. Conv., 1960-62, chmn., 1960. Trustee Ams. United. Mem. So. Bapt. Press Assn. (past pres.), Union U. Alumni Assn. (past pres.), Alpha Tau Omega. Baptist. Home: 10019 Bodeker St Dallas TX 75230 Office: 2222 San Jacinto Dallas TX 75221

HURT, ROBERT FRANCIS, aerospace mfg. co. exec.; b. Cicero, Ill., Aug. 23, 1916; s. Rudolph B. and Antoinette (Svoboda) H.; B.S. in Mech. Engring., Purdue U. 1938, Ph.D. in Engring. (hon.), 1964; m. Jean Pope, Aug. 27, 1938; children—Barbara Jean, Nancy Carole. Plant engr. Douglas Aircraft Co., 1939-44; asst. gen. mgr. Pacific Fabricating Co., 1944-45; prodn. supt. Simpson Steel Co., 1945-46; prodn. mgr. Robert H. Clark Co., 1946-51; chief sales engr. Airquipment Co., also Weber Aircraft Co., 1951; with Lockheed Aircraft Corp., 1951-66, v.p., 1963-66, pres. Lockheed Propulsion Co., 1961-66; former pres. Twin Industries Corp. div. Wheelabrator Corp., v.p. parent corp., from 1967. Bd. dirs. La Canada (Cal.) chpt. A.R.C. Mem. Soc. Automotive Engrs., Am. Soc. M.E., Am. Inst. Aero. and Astronautics, Am. Ordnance Assn., Air Force Assn., Sigma Chi. Home: 4909 Winding Lane Clarence NY 14031

HURVICH, LEO MAURICE, exptl. psychologist; b. Malden, Mass., Sept. 11, 1910; s. Julius S. and Celia (Chikinsky) H.; A.B., Harvard, 1932, M.A., 1934, Ph.D., 1936; m. Dorothea Jameson, Oct. 23, 1948. Asst. psychology Harvard, 1936-37, instr., 1937-40, research Bus. Sch., 1940-47; research psychologist Eastman-Kodak Co., 1947-57; prof., chmn. dept. psychology Washington Sq. Coll., N.Y. U., 1957-62; prof psychology, mem. Inst. Neurol. Scis, U. Pa., Phila., 1962—. Vis. prof. psychology Columbia U., 1971-72. Adv. mem. Nat. Acad. Scis.-NRC Vision Com. Co-recipient Howard Crosby Warren award Soc. Exptl. Psychologists, 1971. Guggenheim fellow 1964-65. Fellow A.A.A.S., Optical Soc. Am., N.Y. Acad. Sci., Am. Psychol. Assn.; mem. Psychonomic Soc., Soc. Exptl. Psychologists, Eastern Psychol. Assn., Soc. for Neurosci., Internat. Brain Research Orgn., Assn. for Research in Vision and Ophthalmology, Intersoc. Color Council, Am. Assn. U. Profs., Phi Beta Kappa, Sigma Xi. Author: (with D. Jameson) The Perception of Brightness and Darkness, 1966. Editor: (with D. Jameson) Visual Psychophysics, Handbook of Sensory Physiology, 1972. Contbr. to various research publs., profl. jours. Mem. adv. bd. editors Vision Research. Home: 286 St James Pl Philadelphia PA 19106

HURVIS, JOHN THOMAS, advt. exec.; b. Hagerstown, Md., Aug. 7, 1938; s. Al and Alice (Friend) H.; B.A., Lawrence U., 1960; student U. Madrid (Spain), 1958, U. Barcelona (Spain), 1961; M.B.A., U. Cal. at Berkeley, 1962; m. Julie Ann Esch, June 22, 1963; children—Sara Elizabeth, Christina Marie. Pres., F & H Internat. Market Devel. Corp., N.Y.C., 1965, Hurvis, Binzer & Churchill, Inc., Chgo., 1965—; treas Alameda Broadcasting Inc., Fremont, Cal.; dir. Cosmet, Haven Enterprises, Applied Biochemists. Served with AUS, 1962-63. Home: 343 Country Lane Glenview IL 60025 Office: 520 N Michigan Av Chicago IL 60611

HURWICH, RUDOLPH, corp. exec.; b. Chgo., 1921; ed. Mass. Inst. Tech., 1943. Chmn. bd., chmn. exec. com., exec. officer, dir. Dymo Industries, Inc.; pres., dir. Dymo of Can., Ltd.; dir. Elliott Bus. Machines, Inc. Pres., dir. Pacifica Found. Address: Box 1030 Berkeley CA 94701*

HURWITCH, ROBERT ARNOLD, fgn. service officer; b. Worcester, Mass., Oct. 15, 1920; s. Frank and Sema (Sorin) H.; B.A., U. Chgo.; m. Saralee Pilot, Jan. 10, 1945; childrenJan, Paula, Carol, Sally. Joined U.S. Fgn. Service, 1950; assigned Lima, Peru, 1951-53, Hamburg and Bonn, Germany, 1953-56, Bogota, Colombia, 1956-60, State Dept., 1960-63, Sr. Seminar Fgn. Policy, 1963-64, Santiago, Chile, 1964; dep. chief mission, La Paz, Bolivia, 1964-66; dep. chief mission, Vientiane, Laos, 1967-69, dep. asst. sec. state, Washington, 1969—. Served to capt., inf., AUS, 1943 -47. Recipient Distinguished Service award State Dept., 1963, Commendable Service award, 1962. Decorated Bronze Star with oak leaf cluster. Mem. Fgn. Service Assn. Jewish religion. Address: care Bur Inter-Am Affairs State Dept Washington DC 20525

HURWITZ, DAVID, physician, educator; b. Boston, Aug. 18, 1905; s. Max and Rose (Goldsmith) H.; B.S. cum laude, Harvard, 1925, M.D., 1929; m. Pearl Birnbaum, Sept. 9, 1928; children-R. Michael, Stephen J., Alfred L., Julie B. (Mrs. Michael Seelig). Intern Boston City Hosp., 1929-31; resident U. Chgo. Clinics, 1931; practice medicine, specializing in internal medicine, Cambridge, Mass., 1934—; chief Diabetes Clinic, Boston City Hosp., 1950—; chief div. medicine Mt. Auburn Hosp., Cambridge, 1951—, dir. med. edn., 1963—; vis. physician Harvard Med. Service, Boston City Hosp., 1956—; med. dir. Med. Service, Boston City Hosp., 1956—; med. dir. Polaroid Corp., 1961—; clin. prof. medicine Harvard Med. Sch., 1967—, mem. admissions com., 1966-67; mem. Recess Commn. to Study 1967—, mem. admissions com., 1966-67; mem. Recess Commn. to Study Establishment of Med. and Dental Sch., U. Mass., 1952- 55. Diplomate Am. Bd. Internal Medicine. Mem. A.M.A., Mass., Middlesex South Dist. med. socs., Am., New Eng. (past pres.) diabetes assns., Aesculapian Club. Author papers on diabetes. Home: 38 Cumberland Av Brookline MA 02146 Office: 330 Mt Auburn St Cambridge MA 02138

HURWITZ, HENRY, Jr., physicist; b. N.Y.C., Dec. 25, 1918; s. Henry and Ruth (Sapinsky) H.; A.B., Cornell U., 1938; M.A., Harvard, 1939, Ph.D., 1941; m. Jean Klein, 1944 (div.); 1 son, Barry I.; m. 2d, Alma Rosenbaum, Apr. 15, 1951; children-Robin Elaine, Julia Lea, Wayne Mark. Instr. physics Cornell U. 1941-44; research asso. Los Alamos Sci. Lab. 1944-46; Knolls Atomic Power Lab. Gen. Electric Co., 1946- 56, cons. physicist in charge of ANARPA, 1956, mgr. nucleonics and radiation sect. Research Lab., 1957-68, mgr. theory and systems br. Research and Devel. Center, 1968-. Recipient AEC Ernest Orlando Lawrence award, 1961. Fellow Am. Phys. Soc., Am. Nuclear Soc., A.A.A.S., N.Y. Acad. Scis.; mem. Phi Beta Kappa, Sigma Xi. Editorial bd. Procs. I.E.E.E. Office: Research and Devel Center Gen Electric Co P O Box 8 Schenectady NY 12301

HURWITZ, JERARD, educator, biochemist; b. N.Y.C., Nov. 20, 1928; s. Hyman and Dora (Garbarsky) H.; A.B., Ind. U., 1949; student Coll. City N.Y., 1945-47; Ph.D., Western Res. U., 1953; m. Muriel F. Gould, June 25, 1950; childrenJodie Linda, Deena Ruth. Research, Nat. Inst. Med. Research, Mill Hill, Eng., 1953-54, NIH, 1954-56; instr. microbiology Washington U. Sch. Medicine, St. Louis, 1956-58; asst. prof. microbiology, then asso. prof. N.Y.U. Sch. Medicine, 1958-63; John Reed Kilpatrick prof. molecular biology Albert Einstein Coll. of Medicine, 1963-66, prof. chmn. dept. development biology and cancer, 1966—; postdoctoral fellow Am. Chemical Soc. 1953-56, prof., 1963—. Sr. postdoctoral fellow NIH, 1957-63; recipient Eli Lilly award in biochemistry, 1962; Sigma Xi award N.Y.U., 1962. Mem. Fedn. Am. Biol. Scientists, Biochem. Soc. Eng., Sigma Xi. Home: 18 Darwood Pl Mount Vernon NY 10553 Office: Albert Av Coll Medicine Eastchester Av and Morris Park Ave Bronx NY 10461

HURWITZ, LAWRENCE NEAL, investment co. exec.; b. Austin, Tex., Mar. 21, 1939; s. John and Sarah Ruth (Blumenthal) H.; student U. Tex., 1957-59; M.B.A. with distinction, Harvard, 1961. With research dept. Harvard, 1961-62; asst. to v.p. Atlantic Research Corp., 1962-65; comptroller TelAutograph Corp., 1965; dir. Gen. Artists Corp., 1965-69; pres. Sprayregen & Co., N.Y.C., 1969—; vice chmn., mem. exec. com. Empire Life Ins. Co. Am.; dir., mem. exec. com. Old Town Corp., Stratton Group Ltd., Sayre & Fisher Co., Tech. Tape, Inc., DFI Communications Inc., Columbia Gen. Corp., Cal. Data Systems Corp.; dir. Indsl. Electronic Hardware Corp., Bloomfield Bldg. Industries, Inc., Apollo Industries, Inc., Aberdeen Petroleum Corp., Investors Book Club, Inc., Ling Fund, Am. Land Co., Pacific Nutrient & Chem. Corp., N. Lake Corp., Dataromen, Inc., Merada Industries, Inc. AK Electric Corp., Aerocon, Inc., Hallmark Communications, Inc., Detroit Gray Iron & Steel Foundries, Inc., Financial Tech., Inc., Wid's Films & Film Folks, Investors Preferred Life Ins. Co., Langdon Group, Inc., Essex Systems Corp., Chelsea Nat. Bank, Newport Chem. Industries, Inc. Contbr.: How to Invest in Letter Stock, 1970; Spin-Offs and Shells, 1971. Home: 30 Park Av New York City NY 10016 Office: 200 Park Av New York City NY 10017

HUSA, KAREL, educator, composer, condr.; b. Prague, Czechoslovakia, Aug. 7, 1921; s. Karel and Bozena (Dongresova) H.; diploma summa cum laude, Conservatory and Acad. Music (Prague), 1945, 47; grad. Conservatoire de Paris (France), 1948; license for conducting Ecole Normale de Paris, 1947; m. Simone Perault, Feb. 2, 1952; children—Catherine, Annette, Elizabeth, Caroline. Came to U.S., 1954, naturalized, 1959. Condr., Prague Orch., 1945-46; guest condr. orchs. in Hamburg, Brussels, Paris, Zurich, Suisse Romande, London, Stockholm, Cin., Buffalo N.Y.C., Rochester, N.Y., Balt., Syracuse, N.Y.; faculty Cornell U., Ithaca, N.Y., 1954—, prof. music, 1954—, dir. univ. symphony and chamber orchs., 1956—. Guggenheim fellow, 1964. Life fellow Internat. Inst. Arts and Letters; mem. Am. Music Center (Yaddo fellow), Internat. Soc. Contemporary Music, French Soc. Composers, Am. Fedn. Musicians, Kappa Gamma Psi (hon.), Kappa Kappa Psi (hon.). Composer: Symphony, 1953; Fantasies for Orchestra, 1957; Divertimento for Brass, 1959; Poem for Viola and Orchestra, 1959; Elegy and Rondeau for Saxophone and Orchestra, 1961; Mosaiques for Orchestra, 1961; Fresque for Orchestra, rev., 1964; Sonatina for piano, 1943; Sonatina Violin and Piano, 1945; Sonata for Piano, 1949; Evocations of Slovakia for Clarinet, Viola and Cello, 1951; Eight Duets for Piano, 1955; Twelve Moravian Songs, 1956; Poem for Viola and Piano, 1962;

Serenade for Woodwind Quintet and Orchestra, 1963; Concerto for Brass Quintet and Orch., 1965; Trio (flute, clarinet, bassoon), 1966; Music for percussion, 1966; Concerto (alto saxophone, concert band), 1967; String quartet No. 3, (Pulitzer prize 1969), 1968; Music for Prague, 1968; Apotheosis of this Earth, 1970; others. Recipient prize Prague Acad. Arts, 1948; French Govt. award, 1946, 47; L. Boulanger award, 1952; Guggenheim fellow, 1964-65: recipient Pulitzer prize for music, 1969. Editor French Barok Music: Reconstructions of old French barok works by Lully and Delalande, 1961-68. Home: 333 The Parkway Ithaca NY 14850

HUSAK, GUSTAV, Czechoslovakian politician; b. Jan. 10, 1913; ed. Law Faculty, Comenius U., Bratislava. Jr. lawyer, Bratislava, 1938-42; officer worker, 1943- 44; took part in Slovak Nat. Rising; commnr. interior, 1944-45, transp. and tech., 1945-46; chmn. bd. commnrs., 1946-50; commnr. agr., 1948; dept. head central com. Communist Party Slovakia, 1950-51; polit. prisoner, 1951-60; engaged in bldg. works, Bratislava, 1960-63; sci. worker Inst. Law, Slovak Acad. Scis., 1963-68; dep. premier, 1968—. Mem. 5th illegal central com. Communist Party Slovakia, also mem. central com. and presidium, dep. chmn. Communist Party Slovakia, 1943- 44; mem. central com. and presidium central com. Communist Party Slovakia, 1945-50; mem. central com. Communist Party Czechoslovakia, 1945, 49-51; mem. Slovak Nat. Council, 1945-50, Nat. Assembly, 1945-51; 1st sec. presidium of Central Com. Communist Party Czechoslovakia. Decorated Klement Gottwald Order (Czechoslovakia), others. Author: On the Agricultural Problem in Slovakia, 1949; The Struggle for Tomorrow, 1948; Evidence on Slovak National Rising, 1964. Address: Presidium of the Govt Prague I nabr kpt Jarose 4 Czechoslovakia*

HUSBAND, ALEXANDER CHAPMAN, cons. engr.; b. Troy, N.Y., Mar. 27, 1914; s. James A. and Ann (Anderson) H.; B.N.S., U. S. Naval Acad., 1935; M.C.E., Rensselaer Poly. Inst., 1940; grad. Advanced Mgmt. Program, Harvard Bus. Sch., 1961; D. Engring., Rensselaer Poly. Institute, 1967; m. Mary Hodges Bacon, July 26, 1941. Commd. ensign, U.S. Navy, 1935, advanced through grades to rear adm., 1963-, staff civil engr. Comdr. Amphibious Force, Pacific Fleet, 1946-47, officer charge constrn. Aleutians, 1950, commanding officer constrn. battalion center, Davisville, R.I., 1955, dist. pub. works officer First Naval Dist., 1958; dir. European-Mid East div. Bur. Yards and Docks, 1962-64; dep. chief civil engrs. Navy Dept., 1964-65, comdr. Naval Facilities Engring. Command and chief Civil Engrs., 1965-69; v.p. constrn. Consol. Edison Co., N.Y.C., 1969-71; cons. engr., 1971—. Decorated D.S.M., Legion of Merit, Bronze Star medal with Combat V. Registered profl. engr., R.I., N.Y., Conn. Fellow Am. Soc. C.E.; mem. Soc. Am. Mil. Engrs. (past nat. pres.), Nat. Soc. Profl. Engrs., Sigma Xi, Newcomen Soc. Clubs: Essex, Union League N.Y. Yacht (N.Y.C.); Army-Navy Country (Washington). Home: Ayers Point Rd Box 204 Old Saybrook CT 06475 Office: care BESCO 80 E 42d St New York City NY 10017

HUSBAND, ARTHUR KENNETH, physician; b. Hoboken, N.J., Nov. 27, 1911; s. Arthur Cyril and Ida (Steinel) H.; B.A., U. Pa., 1935; M.D., C.M., McGill U., 1940; m. Eleanor Whiteley, Feb. 11, 1937; childrenEleanor Lynn (Mrs. Richard Singer Latimer), Karen Ann (Mrs. Max David Hedgecoth), Arthur Kenneth. Rotating intern Waterbury (Conn.) Hosp., 1940-41; resident in pediatrics N.C. Baptist Hosp., Bowman Gray Sch. Medicine, 1951-53; practice medicine specializing in pediatrics, Kingsport, Tenn., 1943-63; supt. Greene Valley Hosp. and Sch., Greenville, Tenn., 1963-66; dir. Tampa (Fla.) Diagnostic and Evaluation Clinic, 1966-; lectr. U. South Fla., Univ. of Fla. Mem. Fla. Com. on PKU and other Metabolic Diseases; cons. United Cerebral Palsy, Tampa, 1966—; a founder Palmer Meml. Center for Cerebral Palsy, 1948. Mem. A.M.A., Tenn., So. med. assns., Greene County Med. Soc., Am. Assn. on Mental Deficiency, Am. Acad. Mental Retardation, Assn. Med. Supts. Mental Hosps., Nat. Rehab. Assn. Contbr. articles on mental retardation med. jours. Home: 104 N Jupiter Av Clearwater FL 33515 Office: 4420 Tampa Bay Blvd Tampa FL 33614

HUSBAND, RICHARD WELLINGTON, educator; b. Hanover, N.H., Aug. 8, 1904; s. Richard W. and Helene (Borgman) H.; A.B., Dartmouth, 1926; M.A., Stanford, 1927, Ph.D., 1929; m. Dorothy Anderson, Sept. 15, 1935; 1 son, Richard Wellington. Asst. prof. psychology U. Wis., 1929-41; indsl. relations U.S. Steel Corp., 1942-45; prof. psychology Ia. State Coll., 1946-53, Fla. State U., 1954--. Chmn. Fla. State Bd. Examiners Psychology, 1958-63. Mem. Am. (pres. div. teaching of psychology, 1954-55, mem. counsel 1964-67), Southeast, Fla. (pres. 1957-58) psychol. assns. Author: Applied Psychology, 1948; The Psychology of Successful Selling, 1952. Contbr. articles profl. jours. Address: Psychology Dept Florida State U Tallahassee FL 32303

HUSE, CHARLES WELLS, ret. business exec.; b. Chgo., Aug. 24, 1905; s. Charles Gammon and Juanita (Wells) H.; student Am., Swiss, English schs.; m. Eda Sherman, Sept. 27, 1941. Editorial staff Hutchinson & Co., pubs., London, Eng., 1924-25; staff London office North Am. Newspaper Alliance, 1925-26; editorial staff The Advertiser, Tunbridge Wells, Eng., 1926-27, Boulevardier, Paris, 1928, Chronicle, San Francisco, 1929-30, and Examiner, 1931-37; dir. pub. relations Columbia Steel Co., San Francisco, 1937-50; dir. pub. relations U.S. Steel Corp., Western Dist., San Francisco, 1950-52, adminstrv. asst., office asst. to chmn., N.Y.C., 1953-56, dir. pub. relations adminstrn., 1956-64, v.p. pub. relations, N.Y.C., 1964, v.p. West, San Francisco, 1964-70; ret., 1970. Trustee San Francisco Bay Area Council; dir., mem. exec. com. San Francisco chpt. A.R.C., 1951-52, bd. dirs. Golden Gate chpt.; bd. dirs. Cal. Anti-Litter League; adv. bd. No. Cal. Industry-Edn. Council; pres. bd. dirs. Ind. Colls. of No. Cal. Served as capt. USMC, World War II, Commd. maj. Res., 1951. Mem. Newcomen Soc. N.A., Pub. Relations Soc. Am., Am. Iron and Steel Inst., American Newspaper Guild (v.p. San Francisco-Oakland chpt. 1936-37), Downtown Assn. (dir. 1951-52); Cal., San Francisco chambers of commerce, Cal. Mfrs. Assn. (pres. 1969, mem. exec. com. 1970), Bay Area Urban League (dir.), Federated Employers Bay Area (gov.), Cal., Utah hist. socs., Pub. Relations Roundtable San Francisco, World Affairs Council No. Cal. Mason (Shriner). Clubs: Pacific Union, Press (San Francisco); Burlingame (Cal.) Country; Commonwealth of Cal. Home: 2006 Washington St San Francisco CA 94109

HUSHING, WILLIAM COLLINS, corp. exec.; b. St. Louis, Jan. 22, 1918; s. Sumner Kinney and Anne (Sandner) H.; B.S. in Elec. Engring., U.S. Naval Acad., 1939; M.S. in Naval Constrn. and Engring., Mass. Inst. Tech., 1944; student Harvard Bus. Sch., 1962; D.Sc. (hon.), U. N.H., 1968; m. Mary Hardy, Jan. 10, 1946; children—Druscilla, Rebecca Ann. Commd. ensign U.S. Navy, 1939, advanced through grades to rear adm., 1967; aide, spl. asst. to chief Bur. Ships, 1955-57; indsl. engr., comptroller U.S. Naval Shipyard, Mare Is., Cal., 1957-60; supr. shipbldg. U.S. Navy, Electric Boat div. Gen. Dynamics Corp., Groton, Conn., 1960-64; comdr. Naval Shipyard, Portsmouth, N.H., 1964-69; retired, 1969; exec. v.p. Bath Iron Works, 1969-70; pres. Forster Mfg. Co., Inc., 1970—. Cons. in field. Decorated Navy Commendation medal, Legion of Merit with Star. Mem. Am. Soc. Naval Engrs., Soc. Naval Architects. Lutheran. Home: 1111 Washington St Bath ME 04530 Office: Wilton ME 04107

HUSKEY, HARRY DOUGLAS, educator; b. Whittier, N.C., Jan. 19, 1916; s. Cornelius and Myrtle (Cunningham) H.; B.S., U. Ida., 1937; student Ohio U., 1937-38; M.A., Ohio State U., 1940, Ph.D., 1943; m. Velma Elizabeth Roeth, Jan. 2, 1939; childrenCarolyn, Roxanne, Harry Douglas, Linda. Temp. prin. sci. officer Nat. Phys. Labs., Eng., 1947; head machine devel. lab. Nat. Bur. Standards, 1948, asst. dir. Inst. Numerical Analysis, 1948-54; asso. dir. computation lab. Wayne U., Detroit, 1952-53; asso. prof. U. Cal. at Berkeley, 1954-58, prof., 1958-68, vice chmn. elec. engring., 1965-66; prof. information and computer sci. U. Cal. at Santa Cruz, 1968—; vis. prof. Indian Inst. Tech., Kanpur (Indo-Am. program), 1963-64, 71, Delhi U., 1971; cons. computer div. Bendix, 1954-63; vis. prof. Mass. Inst. Tech., 1966. Mem. computer sic. panel NSF, Naval Research Adv. Com.; cons. on computers for developing countries UN, 1969-71. Fellow A.A.A.S., I.E.E.E. (editorial bd., editor-in-chief computer group 1965-71), Brit. Computer Soc.; mem. Am. Math. Soc., Math. Assn. Am., Assn. Computing Machinery (pres. 1960-62), Am. Fedn. Information Processing Socs. (governing bd. 1961-63), Sigma Xi. Co-editor: Computer Handbook, 1962. Home: 656 High St Santa Cruz CA 95060

HUSKINS, J. FRANK, judge; b. Burnsville, N.C., Feb. 10, 1911; s. Joseph Erwin and Mary Etta (Peterson) H.; student Mars Hill Jr. Coll., 1927-29; A.B., U. N.C., 1930, postgrad. Law, 1930-32; m. Ruth H. McNeill, Oct. 20, 1963; stepchildren—Robert Glenn and Ruth Elizabeth (Mrs. Melvin Webb II) McNeill. Admitted to N.C. bar; mayor, Burnsville, N.C., 1939-42; rep. from Yancey County, N.C. Gen. Assembly, 1947, 49; judge Superior Ct., N.C., 1955-65; dir. Adminstv. Office of Cts. of N.C., 1965-68; asso. justice N.C. Supreme Ct., Raleigh, 1968—. Chmn., N.C. Indsl. Commn., 1949-55. Served to lt. comdr. USNR, 1942-46. Mem. N.C., Wake County bar assns., Am. Judicature Soc., Nat. Conf. Ct. Adminstrv. Officers, Am. Legion, Raleigh Execs. Club. Home: 3204 Beaufort St Raleigh NC 27609 Office: Justice Bldg Raleigh NC 27601

HUSKINS, WILLIAM EVERETT, Jr., airlines exec.; b. Mpls., Feb. 10, 1925; s. William Everett and Bertha (Haukebo) H.; B.Aero, Engring., U. Minn., 1945; m. Shirley Eloise Larson, June 24, 1950; children—Deborah Lavonne, William Charles. With N.W. Airlines, Inc., 1946—, operations mgr. Orient Region, Tokyo, Japan, 1955-59, asst. to pres., 1959-61, v.p. Orient region, 1961-67, v.p. communications and computer services, 1967—. Registered profl. engr., Minn. Beta Theta Pi, Tau Omega. Mason: mem. Order Eastern Star. Home: Route 4 Box 493 Excelsior MN 55331 Office Northwest Airlines Inc Mpls-St Paul Internat Airport Saint Paul MN 55111

HUSMANN, RONALD HUGH, actor; b. Rockford, Ill., June 30, 1937; s. Bernard John and Emma Dorthea (Ohlhues) H.; B.S. in Speech, Northwestern U., 1959; m. Patsy Devine Peterson, Dec. 6, 1959; children—Mark David, Andrew John, Gregory Adam. Broadway appearances include Fiorello, 1959, Tenderloin, 1960, All American, 1962; films include Love Has Many Faces, 1963; TV appearances include Steve Allen Show, 1963, Days of Our Lives, 1966-67, As the World Turns, 1971, Search for Tomorrow, 1971; On the Town, 1971; stage roles Dame at Sea, 1970, Lonely Ladies Kind Gentlemen, 1970. Recipient Blum Theater world award, 1960. Lutheran. Office: care Agy Performing Arts Inc 120 W 57th St New York City NY 10019

HUSS, ALVIN J., corp. exec.; b. 1904; student Washington U., St. Louis; married. Pres. Huss Lumber Co., 1929-65, Huss Ontonogan Pulp & Paper Co., 1955-62; company merged with Hoerner Boxes Inc., 1962; with Hoerner Waldorf Corp., 1962—, chmn. bd., 1967—, also dir.; dir. State Nat. Bank, Evanston, Ill. Address: 2250 Wabash Av St Paul MN 55114

HUSSEIN IBN TALAL, King of Jordan; b. Jordan, 1935; student Harrow Sch., Sandhurst Mil. Acad., Eng., and Victoria Coll., Alexandra, Egypt; m. Queen Sherifa Dina Abdul Hamid el-Aoun (div. 1957); 1 dau., Amman; m. 2d, Princess Muna, 1961; 2 sons, 2 daus. (twins). Succeeded to throne of Jordan, 1952. Address: Royal Palace Amman Jordan

HUSSEY, ALLEN SANBORN, educator; b. Concord, N.H., Jan. 27, 1918; s. Percy Brookes and Helen (Greene) H.; B.S., U. N.H., 1939, M.S., 1941; Ph.D., Ohio State U., 1946; m. Charlotte Louise Bronson, Sept. 2, 1941; children—Frederick Bronson, Eileen Jacklyn, Stephen Robert, Margaret Ellen, Christopher Allen. Research chemist Armstrong Cork Co., Lancaster, Pa., 1941-42; research engr. Battelle Meml. Inst., Columbus, O., 1945; instr., asst. prof., asso. prof. Northwestern U., 1945-62, prof., 1962—, asst. dean Coll. Arts and Scis., 1963-68. Mem. Am. Chem. Soc., A.A.A.S., Catalysis Soc. Am., Sigma Xi, Phi Kappa Phi, Phi Lambda Upsilon. Club: Catalysis (past pres.) (Chgo.). Contbr. articles profl. jours. Home: 2505 Hartzell St Evanston IL 60201

HUSSEY, GEORGE FREDERICK, Jr., naval officer; b. Brookline, Mass., June 15, 1894; s. George Frederick and Kate Willard (Nash) H.; grad. with distinction U.S. Naval Acad., 1916, student, ordnance, Postgrad. Sch., 1921-23; m. Phebe Nell Tidmarsh, Mar. 23, 1929; children—George Frederick III (dec.), William Tidmarsh. Commd. ensign USN, 1916, advancing through grades to vice adm., 1945; served in U.S.S. Penn., 1916-20; several naval assignments including: comdr. Destroyer Div. 24, 1939-41, Mine Squadron 3, 1941-42, Offshore Patrol of Pearl Harbor, 1941-42, dir. prodn. div. Bur. Ordnance, 1942-43, asst. chief (rear adm.), Bur. Ordnance, 1943, chief, 1943-47, ret. for phys. disability. Mng. dir., sec. Am. Standards Assn., Inc., 1948-61, hon. mem., 1961; v.p. Internat. Orgn. for Standardization, 1958-61. Mem. adv. council on devel. Norwalk Hosp.; mem. adv. bd. New Eng. Inst. Med. Research, Community Coll., Norwalk, 1961-67, regional council, 1967—; dir. Sr. Personnel Placement Bur., 1966—. Mem. exec. com. Conn. Red Cross Blood Program, chmn., 1967-69; chpt vice chmn., chmn. blood program com. Norwalk-Wilton chpt. A.R.C. Decorated D.S.M., hon. comdr. mil. div. Order Brit. Empire; recipient Blandy gold medal, 1958, Distinguished Service to Def., 50th Anniversary Gold medal, 1969 (both Am. Ordnance Assn). Fellow Standards Engrs. Soc.; mem. Am. Ordnance Assn. (pres. 1955- 56), Naval Acad. Assn. N.Y. (pres. 1950-51), U.S. Naval Acad. Alumni Assn. (pres. 1953-55), Am. Soc. M.E., Am. Soc. Assn. Execs. Clubs: Army and Navy, Army-Navy Country (Washington); University, N.Y. Yacht (N.Y.C.). Spl. editor naval terms Websters' Internat. Dictionary, 2d edit., 1st printing, 1934. Home: 372 Chestnut Hill Rd Norwalk CT 06851 ☆

HUSSEY, HUGH HUDSON, physician, editor; b. Washington, Nov. 12, 1910; s. Hugh Hudson and Laura (Klinge) H.; B.S., Georgetown U., 1932, M.D. magna cum laude, 1934, L.H.D., 1964; m. Wilhelmina Catherine Gude, July 27, 1935; 1 son, John Christopher. Rotating intern Georgetown U. Hosp., 1934-35, fellow medicine, 1935-36, vis. physician, 1946-62, chmn. dept. medicine, physician-in-chief, 1956-58; instr. clin. medicine Georgetown U. Sch. Medicine, 1936-41, asso. clin. Prof. medicine, 1941-47, asso. prof. med., 1948-56, prof., chmn. dept. preventive medicine and pub. health, 1953-56, prof. medicine, 1956-62, dean, 1958- 62; dir. div. sci. activities A.M.A., 1963-69, dir. div. sci. pubs. and editor jour., 1970—; asso. physician Georgetown div. D.C. Gen. Hosp., 1936-39, vis. physician, chief Georgetown Med. div., 1940-58. Mem. (rep. A.M.A.) in div. med. scis. NRC, 1960—, mem. exec. com., 1963—, drug research bd., 1963—, policy adv. com. of drug efficacy study, 1966-69. Bd. regents Georgetown U., 1967—. Diplomate Am. Bd. Internal Medicine. Fellow A.C.P.; mem. A.M.A. (bd. trustees 1956-62, chmn. bd. trustees 1961-62), Georgetown Clin. Soc., (emeritus), Am. Heart Assn., Nat. Soc. Med. Research (dir.), So. Soc. Clin. Research, Alpha Omega Alpha. Episcopalian. Club: Cosmos (Washington). Med. editor GP, 1951-59; asso. editor Med. Annals D.C., 1940-56. Home: 30 E Division St Chicago IL 60610 Office: 535 N Dearborn St Chicago IL 60610

HUSSEY, KEITH MORGAN, educator; b. Rock Island, Ill., Dec. 2, 1908; s. Ernest Samuel and Diana Hill (Stow) H.; A.B., Augustana Coll., 1936; M.S., La. State U., 1939, Ph.D., 1940; m. Lillian Alberta Pepping, Dec. 26, 1937; children—Michael Keith, Patricia Ann. Instr., U. Houston, 1940-42; asst. prof., asso. prof. Okla. U., 1945-49; faculty Ia. State U., Ames, 1949—. prof. geology, 1954—, head dept., 1961—. Spl. research micropaleontology of Gulf Coast, geomorphology and stratigraphy of Colo., Wyo., Ia, No. Alaska; vis. geoscientist lectr. Am. Geol Inst., 1960-62. Dir. Earth Sci. Tchr. Tng. Program. Served with USAAF, World War II. Fellow Geol. Soc. Am., Ia. Acad. Sci.; mem. Geol. Soc. Ia. (pres. 1967-68), Augustana Coll. Alumni (dir.), Am. Assn. Petroleum Geologists (regional rep. 1967-69), Arctic Inst. N.Am., A.A.A.S., Am. Assn. U. Profs., Wyo. Geol. Assn., Nat. Assn. Geology Tchrs. (pres. central sect. 1958), Sigma Xi, Phi Kappa Phi. Contbr. articles to profl. jours. Co-editor: Dictionary of Geological Terms, 1961. Home: 1910 Meadowlane Av Ames IA 50010

HUSSEY, RUTH, actress; b. Providence, R.I., Oct. 30, d. George and Julia (Corbett) H.; student Pembroke Coll., Doctor of Fine Arts (hon.), 1950; student U. Mich; m. C. Robert Longenecker, 1942; children—George R., John W., Mary Elizabeth. Appeared with Providence Players, 1933-35; summer stock co. in Mich., 1934-35; on Broadway in State of the Union, 1945; motion pictures: Madame X, 1937; The Women, 1939; Susan and God, 1940; The Philadelphia Story, 1940; H. M. Pulham, Esq., 1941; (star) I Jane Doe, 1947; (co-star) The Great Gatsby, 1948; Flight Command, 1940; The Uninvited, 1943; (Broadway play) Goodbye My Fancy, 1949; (motion pictures), Louisa, 1950; Mr. Music, Woman of the North Country, Stars and Stripes Forever, The Lady Wants Mink, 1952; and Joyful Hour (TV films); star TV Shows Ford Theatre, Studio One, Elgin Theatre, Lux Video, Producers Showcase, Shower of Stars, Hitchcock Presents, Playrights; guest star Marcus Welby series, 1971; co-star with Bob Hope-Lucille Ball in Facts of Life (motion picture), 1960. ‡

HUSSEY, WILLIAM BERTRAND, fgn. service officer; b. Bellingham, Wash., Oct. 23, 1915; s. Bertrand Brokaw and Ruth (Axtell) H.; B.S., Boston U., 1938; grad. student, U. Cal. at Los Angeles, 1939-40; m. Fredricka Boone, Dec. 31, 1940 (div. 1957); children—Christina, Pamela, Eva, William Bertrand, Peter; m. 2d, Piyachart Bunnag, May 20, 1959, Instr. journalism, housemaster Berkeley Hall Sch., Beverly Hills, Cal., 1939-40; asst. housing mgmt. supr. U.S. Housing Authority, 1941-42; chmn. London (Eng.) Liaison Group, also State Dept. rep., 1948-52; spl. State Dept. rep., Rome, Italy, 1949, Paris, France, 1950; chmn. regional conf., Dhahran, Saudi Arabia, 1949; chief civil-mil. relations sect., Munich, Germany, 1952-53; adminstrv. officer, Frankfurt, Germany, 1953-55; attache, Rangoon, Burma, 1955-56; consul, Chiengmai, Thailand, 1957-59; acting dep. chief plans and devel. staff, bur. ednl. and cultural affairs State Dept., 1959-60, dep. chief cultural presentations div., 1960-61; mem. delegation regional confs. in Beirut, Lebanon and Kampala, Uganda, 1960; group discussion leader Nat. Strategy Seminar, Asilomar, Cal., 1960; counselor of embassy, Lome, Republic Togo, 1961-65, Blantyre, Malawi, 1965-66; chargé d'affaires Am. embassy Maseru, Lesotho, 1966-67, Port Lours, Mauritius, 1967-68; UN rep. Western Pacific, Apia, Western Samoa, 1969—. Served with U.S. Merchant Marine, 1930-33; served to lt. comdr. USN, 1942-48; ETO, PTO; capt. Res. Recipient Superior Service award Sec. of State, 1968. Mem. S.A.R., Naval Hist. Found., Nantucket Hist. Assn., Alpha Delta Phi. Christian Scientist. 313 Barton Way Menlo Park CA 94025

HUSSON, CHESLEY HAYWARD, Sr., former coll. pres.; b. Lynn, Mass., Mar. 14, 1903; s. George Edwin Parsons and Lillian (Rendell) H.; B.S., Mass. State Tchrs. Coll., Salem, 1926; M.S., U. Me., 1939; fellowship diploma Nat. Coll., Ont., Can.; M.B.A. (hon.), Spencerian Coll., Milw., 1965; D.Sc. in Bus. Adminstrn., Drake Coll., Fla., 1968; m. Dorothy Bell, May 30, 1927; children—Chesley Hayward, Roy George, Paul Edwin. Prin., Me. Sch. Commerce, Bangor, 1926-33, pres., 1933-48; pres. Husson Coll., Bangor, 1948-69. Mem. Nat. Accrediting Commn. for Bus. Schs., 1955-60, chmn., 1957-59; dir. Bus. Edn. Research Assos. Bd. dirs. Bangor YMCA, Bangor Community Chest; treas. Sch. Children's Fund Com., 1950-68; mem. Me. Small Bus. Adv. Council, 1967—. Mem. United Bus. Schools Assn., Nat. Assn. Bus. Schs., N.E. Bus. Coll. Assn. (pres. 1958), Eastern, Nat. bus. tchrs. assns., Me. Tchrs. Assn., Nat. Assn. Secondary Sch. Prins., Bangor C. of C. (dir.), Bangor Execs. Club (pres. 1956-57), Am. Assn. Specialized Colls., Am. Assn. Ind. Coll. and U. Presidents, Kappa Delta Phi, Kappa Phi Kappa, Pi Rho Zeta (nat. gov. 1966-68). Methodist. Lion, Mason (Shriner). Club: Triangle (Bangor). Home: Green Lake ME 04440

HUST, RAYMOND ALFRED, lawyer; b. Salt Lake City, June 3, 1913; s. Alfred F. and Charlotte (Zimmerman) H.; student U. Utah, 1931-33; LL.B., George Washington U., 1938; m. Suzanne Martin, Sept. 2, 1937; childrenEdward Randolph, Stephen Marshall. Admitted to D.C. bar, also N.Y. bar; counsel Fed. Deposit Ins. Corp., 1938-41; practice in Syracuse, N.Y., 1941-; now sr. partner firm Hancock, Ryan, Shove & Hurst; gen. counsel Mfrs. Assn. Syracuse. Dir. Gen. Lab. Assos., Inc., Climax Mfg. Co., First Fed. Savs. & Loan Assn. Syracuse, Will & Baumer Candle Co., Inc., Baldwin-Hall Co., Inc., C.E. Chappell & Sons, Inc. Mem. Mayor Syracuse Commn. for Youth, 1963, Community Found. Syracuse and Onondaga County, 1967, UN Assn. Lawyers Program, 1967; co-chmn. Citizens Com. Mental Health. Bd. dirs. Citizens Found., 1947-; pres., dir. Child and Family Service Syracuse and Onondaga County, 1957-63, Syracuse Dispensary, 1957-64; trustee Syracuse U. Library Assn., 1961-. Mem. Am., N.Y., Onondaga County (pres.1961-62) bar assns., Am. Judicature Soc. Clubs: Onondaga Golf and Country; Century; University. Home: 211 Dewitt Rd Syracuse NY 13214 Office: Hills Bldg Syracuse NY 13202

HUSTED, JAMES WILLIAM, former lawyer; b. Peekskill, N.Y., May 15, 1896; s. James William and Louise W. (Spaulding) H.; B.A., Yale, 1918; post grad. Harvard Law Sch., 1919- 20; LL.B., Columbia, 1924; m. Alice Dodge, Oct. 2, 1926; 1 son, James William. With New Eng. Pin Co., Winsted, Conn., 1920-22; admitted to N.Y. bar, since practiced in N.Y.C.; asso. with firm Winthrop, Stimson, Putnam & Roberts, 1924-30, partner, 1930-69. Hon. trustee Mus. Modern Art, No. Westchester Hosp.; trustee Winifred Masterson Burke Relief Found. Mem. Am., N.Y. State bar assns., Assn. Bar City N.Y. Clubs: Century Assn., Knickerbocker (N.Y.C.). Home: RD 2 Box 499 Bedford NY 10506

HUSTED, RALPH WALDO, utility exec.; b. Martinsville, Ill., Apr. 2, 1911; s. Seth and Mary (Church) H.; LL.B., Benjamin Harrison Law Sch., 1936; m. Margaret Walden, Mar. 18, 1937; children—Catherine

(Mrs. William R. Burleigh), David W. Admitted to Ind. bar, 1935; with Indpls. Power & Light Co., 1929—, sec., counsel, 1957-64, v.p. legal, sec., 1964—, also dir.; dir. Fletcher Av. Savs. & Loan Assn., Indpls. Trustee Liberty Fund, Indpls. Mem. Indpls., Ind., Am. bar assns. Home: 727 N Audubon Rd Indianapolis IN 46219 Office: 25 Monument Circle Indianapolis IN 46206

HUSTED, WALTER, mag editor; b. Bklyn., Feb. 7, 1906; student Columbia, 1922-23, N.Y. U., 1923-25; m. Margaret Denton, July 30, 1927; 1 dau., Myra. Reporter, Bklyn. Eagle, 1925-26, Des Moines Register, 1926-29, A.P., 1929-31; copy reader N.Y. World-Telegram, 1931-34; night editor N.AM. Newspaper Alliance, 1934-40; gen. news editor U.S. News & World Report, 1940-. Mem. Am. Inst. Graphic Arts, Early Am. Industries Assn. Club: National Press (Washington). Home: 6021 Franconia Rd Alexandria VA 22310 Office: 2300 N St NW Washington DC 20037

HUSTON, CHARLES LUKENS, Jr., steel exec.; b. Coatesville, Pa., May 19, 1906; s. Charles Lukens and Annie (Stewart) H.; grad. Hill Sch., Pottstown, Pa., 1924; B.S., Princeton, 1928; postgrad. Mass. Inst. Tech., 1929, U. Cin., evenings 1931-32; m. Nancy E. Gardner, June 14, 1933; children—Charles L. III, Nancy Elizabeth (Mrs. Richard L. Hansen), Elinor (Mrs. Charles B. Chadwick). With Armco Steel Corp., Middletown, O., 1929-39, mem. personnel relations staff, 1934-39; dir. personnel relations Lukens Steel Co., Coatesville, Pa., 1939-42, asst. to pres., 1942-43, exec. asst. to pres., 1946-49, v.p., 1948-49, pres., 1959-69, chmn. bd., chief exec. officer, 1969—, also dir., chmn. exec. com.; pres. Lukenweld, Inc., 1943-46; dir., chmn. bd. Alleghany Ore & Iron Co.; dir. Marine Midland Grace Trust Co. N.Y., Newport News Shipbuilding & Dry Dock Co. Va. industry panel mem. Nat. War Labor Bd., 1942-43. Trustee Drexel Inst. Tech., chmn., 1967-71; mem. bd. mgrs. Coatesville Hosp., 1940-58; dir., past pres. Family Service Chester County. 1947-50; chmn. Pa. Adv. Council on Mental Health Constrn., 1965-68. Mem. Am. Iron and Steel Inst. (dir.), Nat. Planning Assn. (Canadian-Am. com. 1959-65), N.A.M. (faculty Boca Raton Inst. 1947, mem. indsl. relations com. 1946-55, taxation com. 1955-56), Princeton Alumni Council (exec. com. 1954-59, rep. at large 1958-63), Am. Mgmt. Assn. (exec. com. 1946-47, gen. mgmt. council 1950-56), Franklin Inst., Phila. C. of C. (exec. com. 1963-69), Delta Psi. Presbyn. Clubs: Quadrangle (Princeton); Merion Cricket (Haverford, Pa.); Gulph Mills Golf; Midday, Racquet (Phila.); Nantucket Yacht; Princeton (N.Y.C.). Home: Jaffrey Rd R D 2 Malvern PA 19355 also Nantucket MA 02554 Office: Coatesville PA 19320

HUSTON, HARRIS HYDE, legal cons.; b. Pickaway County, O., July 20, 1907; s. Edwin Minor and Lulu Beatrice (Hyde) H.; A.B., Dartmouth, 1929; LL.B., U. Dayton, 1933; m. Hazel Frances Rollins, Dec. 18, 1948; children—Robert Hyde, Linda Rollins. Admitted to Ohio bar, 1933, D.C. bar, 1970, also U.S. Supreme Ct.; asso. Mattern & Sheridan (later Sheridan & Jenkins), later partner Jenkins & Huston, Dayton, O., 1933-40; spl. agt. FBI, 1941-46; asso. dir. surveys and investigations, staff appropriations com. U.S. Ho. of Reps., 1947-48, dir. surveys and investigations, staff appropriations com., 1953-57; dir. tng. Office Spl. Investigations, insp. gen., Dept. Air Force, 1949-52; spl. asst. to under-sec. for adminstrn. Dept. State, 1953. dep. adminstr. bur. security and consular affairs, 1957-60, acting adminstr., 1961; Am. consul gen. Curacao, Netherlands Antilles, 1962-69; legal cons., 1969—. Mem. Harvard Assos. Police Sci., Sociëteit de Gezelligheid, Chi Phi. Clubs: Belle Haven Country, ABC (Alexandria, Va.). Address: 619 29th Rd S Arlington VA 22202

HUSTON, JAMES ALVIN, educator, historian; b. Fairmount, Ind., Mar. 24, 1918; s. Alva Merrill and Nettie (Caskey) H.; A.B. with honors, Ind. U., 1939, A.M., 1940; Ph.D., N.Y. U., 1947; postgrad Oxford (Eng.) U., 1945, U. Fribourg (Switzerland), 1951; m. Florence Ethel Webb, Dec. 29, 1946; children—Nita Diane, James Webb. Faculty, Purdue U., 1946—, prof. history, 1960—; Ernest J. King prof. maritime history Naval War Coll., 1959-60. Vis. prof. fgn. affairs Nat. War Coll., 1966-67, 71-72; cons. Office Chief Mil. History, Dept. Army, 1948, 50. Mem. exec. bd. Harrison Trails council Boy Scouts Am., 1965—; pres. congregation Fed. Ch. W. Lafayette, 1969-70, mem. bd. higher edn. Disciples of Christ, 1970—. Served to capt. Inf., AUS, 1942-46; ETO; 1951-53, col. Res. Decorated Bronze Star with oak leaf cluster. Penfield fellow N.Y. U., 1940-42; NATO fellow, 1964, 66. Mem. Am. Hist. Assn., Orgn. Am. Historians, Ind. Acad. Social Scis. (pres. 1966-67), Inst. Strategic Studies, Inst. World Affairs, Internat. Studies Assn., Am. Assn. U. Profs. (pres. Purdue chpt. 1960-61), Lafayette Geog. Soc. (pres. 1958-59), Phi Beta Kappa (pres. Purdue chpt. 1970-71), Phi Delta Kappa, Omicron Delta Kappa, Alpha Phi Omega, Phi Eta Sigma, Acacia. Rotarian. Club: Parlor of Lafayette (pres. 1970-71). Author: Combat History of the 134th Infantry, 1948; Biography of a Battalion, 1950; Across the Face of France, 1963: The Sinews of War, 1966; NATO Strategy and Logistics; Out of the Blue: U.S. Army Airborne Operations in World War II, 1972. Contbr. articles to profl. jours. Home: 914 Vine St West Lafayette IN 47906 Office: Dept History Purdue U Lafayette IN 47907

HUSTON, JOHN, writer, motion picture dir.; b. Nevada, Mo., Aug. 5, 1906; s. Walter and Rhea (Gore) H.; m. Evelyn Keyes, July 23, 1946; m. 2d, Enrica Soma, 1949 (dec. 1969); children—Walter Anthony, Anjelica. At various times during early career became reporter, editor to picture mag., artist (painter), writer, actor; became writer Warner Brothers Studios, 1938; collaborator: The Amazing Dr. Clitterhouse, 1938, Juarez, 1939, Dr. Ehrlich's Magic Bullet, 1940, High Sierra, also Sergeant York, 1941; dir. The Maltese Falcon, 1941, In This Our Life, 1942, Across the Pacific, 1942; writer and collaborator in prodn. of screen play, Three Strangers, 1945; dir. Key Largo, 1948, The Treasure of Sierra Madre, 1949 (awards for dir., writer Acad. Motion Picture Arts and Sciences, also New York Film Critics award, for best direction of year), Heaven Knows, Mr. Allison, Roots of Heaven, The Unforgiven, The Barbarian and the Geisha, The Misfits, Freud, The List of Adrian Messenger, Night of the Iguana, The Bible, Reflections in a Golden Eye, Casino Royale, Sinful Davey, A Walk with Love and Death, The Kremlin Letter; dir. Broadway play, A Passenger to Bali, 1939; dir. (collaborated in writing) In Time To Come (received N.Y. Drama Critics Circle award); dir. Broadway prodn. of Jean Paul Sarte's play, No Exit, 1945; dir. opera The Mines of Sulphur, La Scala, 1966; producer-dir. We Were Strangers (Horizon Films, which founded with S. P. Eagle); writer and dir. Metro-Goldwyn-Mayer since 1949. Received 1949 One World Award. Served with U.S. Army, 1942-45; disch. with rank of major; assigned filming World War II documentaries: Report from the Aleutians; Let There Be Light; and The Battle of San Pietro. Recipient Screen Dirs. Guild award for the Asphalt Jungle, 1950; named best dir. of the year for Moby Dick, New York Film Critics, 1956; recipient award, Nat. Bd. Review of Motion Pictures, 1956; Silver Laurel award Screen Writers Guild, 1963; Silver Dirs. Guild award for Night of the Iguana, 1964; Martin Bubor award, David di Donatello award for The Bible, 1966; Motion Pictures Exhibitors' Internat. Laurel award for Reflections in a Golden Eye, 1968. Address: St Clerans Craughwell County Galway Ireland

HUSTON, JOHN ALBERT, mfg. co. exec.; b. Birmingham, Mich., May 4, 1920; s. Joseph Clark and Clara Amanda (Maynard) H.; A.B., U. Mich., 1941, J.D., 1947; m. Mary McClellan Barnhardt, Oct. 7, 1950; children—John A., Margaret G., James M. Admitted to N.Y. bar, 1948; with firm Chadbourne, Park, Whiteside & Wolff, and predecessors, N.Y.C., 1947-59; with Sperry Gyroscope Co., div. Sperry Rand Corp., N.Y.C., 1959-68, v.p. legal, 1963-68; asst. gen. counsel Sperry Rand Corp., 1968—. Asso. counsel minority staff com. style and arrangement N.Y. State Constl. Conv., 1967; Democratic dist. leader, Harrison, N.Y., 1954-58; Dem. county committeeman, Manhasset, N.Y., 1969- -. Served with AUS, 1942-45. Mem. Am., Nassau County bar assns., Phi Beta Kappa, Order of Coif, Delta Sigma Rho, Phi Kappa Phi. Episcopalian. Club: Port Washington Yacht. Home: 240 Ryder Rd Manhasset NY 11030 Office: 1290 Av of the Americas New York City NY 10019

HUSTON, LUTHER ALLISON, author, journalist; b. Paulina, Ia., Nov. 18, 1888; s. Luther Allen and Alice (Noble) H.; student U. So. Cal., 1908-11; m. Dora Lee Carey, Feb 15, 1929; 1 dau., Ann Noble. Reporter, Bellingham (Wash.) Herald, 1912-14, Seattle Times, 1914-17; reporter, bur. mgr., fgn. corr., news editor, sales mgr. Internat. News Service, 1917-34; city editor Washington Post, 1934-35; bur. mgr., staff corr. Washington bur. N.Y. Times, 1935-57; dir. pub. information Dept. Justice, Washington 1957-61, asst. to dir. Am. Bar Assn., Washington, 1961-63; with Ernest Wittenberg Assos., pub. relations, 1964-65; Washington corr., editor and pub., 1966—. Recipient George Polk Meml. award, 1954. Fellow Sigma Delta Chi (Wells key 1949, nat. pres. 1947-48). Episcopalian. Club: National Press (gov. 1952-57, chmn. 1957). Author: Pathway to Judgment, A Study of Earl Warren, 1966; The Department of Justice, 1967. Home: 4000 Tunlaw Rd NW Washington DC 20007 Office: Nat Press Bldg Washington DC 20004

HUSTON, PAUL EGER, psychiatrist; b. Delphos, O., Aug. 18, 1903; s. William A. and Anna (Eger) H.; B.S., Purdue U., 1926; M.A., Harvard, 1928, Ph.D. in Abnormal Psychology, 1937; M.D., Yale, 1939; m. Margaret Ann Flinn, Feb. 22, 1932 (dec. June 1965); children—John, David. Exptl. psychologist Worcester Research Found., 1930-35; asst. prof. psychiatry U. Ia., 1943-48, asso. prof., 1949-51, prof., 1952-71, head dept. psychiatry, 1955-56, dir. 1956-71, prof. emeritus, 1971—; asst. dir. Ia. Psychopathic Hosp. Iowa City, 1953-56, dir. 1956-71; spl. cons. to Nat. Inst. Mental Health, 1950-55, dir. Ia. Mental Health Authority, 1956-68. Mem. joint information service exec. com. Am. Psychiat. Assn. and Nat. Assn. Mental Health. Diplomate Am. Bd. Psychiatry and Neurology. Mem. Ia. Neuropsychiat. Assn. (pres. 1948-49), Am. Psychiat. Assn. (chmn. com. on relations with psychology), Group of Advancement Psychiatry (chmn. com. on psychopathology 1950-54, asst. sec. 1956-69), Am. Psychopathologic Assn. Contbr. research papers to profl. lit. Home: 223 Lucon St Iowa City IA 52240 Office: Psychopathic Hosp Iowa City IA 52240

HUSTON, VINCENT GEORGE, ret. air force officer; b. Norristown, Pa., May 23, 1914; s. Edward and Frances (Mills) H.; student Drexel Inst. Tech., 1932-38; grad. Armed Forces Staff Coll., 1948, Advanced Mgmt. Program, Harvard, 1958; m. Mary Livingston, August 29, 1941; one dau., Patricia. Joined Nat. Guard, 1938, grad. Flying Sch., USAAF, 1939, commd. 2d lt. USAAF, 1939, advanced through grades to maj. gen. USAF, 1964; ret., 1971; various assignments, U.S. and PTO, 1939-45; assigned directorate procurement and prodn. Hdqrs. Air Material Command, Wright Field, O., 1945-47; asst. chief insp. sect., Wright Field, 1947-48, chief aero. equipment sect., 1948; chief maintenance Hdqrs. SAC, Offutt AFB, Neb., 1948-52; air force dep. dir., mil. application div. AEC, 1952-55; dep. dir. directorate nuclear systems Hdgrs. Air Research and Devel. Center, Wright-Patterson AFB, 1955-57; comdr. 3079th Aviation Depot Wing. also asst. spl. weapons Hdqrs. Material Command, Wright-Patterson AFB, 1957-60; comdr. Air Material Forces, Pacific, Japan, 1960-62; asst. chief staff material Hdqrs. Pacific Air Forces, 1962-64; comdr. Air Force Eastern Test Range, Patrick AFB, Fla., 1964-67; dep. chief staff operations Hdqrs. Air Force Systems Command, also comdr. nat. range div., mgr. manned space Flight support operations, 1969-71; chief mil. assistance adv. group, Rome, Italy, 1971—. Decorated D.S.M. with oak leaf cluster, Legion of Merit with oak leaf cluster, Air medal, Bronze Star: Order Rising Sun (Japan); Order Cloud and Banner (China). Recipient Outstanding Leadership medal NASA, 1966. Mem. Order Daedalians. Home: care D W Griffith 1435 E 36th St Tulsa OK 74105

HUTAFF, G. HARRY, banker; b. San Francisco, Sept. 24, 1918; s. J. Harry and Mabel (Troppmann) H.; m. Mildred Ada Mowll, Aug. 31, 1940; childrenDouglas Wayne, Mark Charles, Debra Joan. Asst. cashier Bank of Am., 1936-48; operations analyst Bank of Hawaii, 1948-51; v.p., cashier Bank of Cal., N.A., 1951-64; sr. v.p., controller First Hawaiian Bank, Honolulu, 1964—. Mem. Am. Mgmt. Assn., Am. Soc. Personnel Adminstrn., Nat. Assn. Accountants, Financial Execs. Inst. (dir. Hawaii chpt.). Clubs: Oahu Country (Honolulu); Mid. Pacific Country. Home: 1169 Lunahaneli Pl Kailua HI 96734 Office: PO Box 3200 Honolulu HI 96801

HUTCHENS, FRANCIS CASE, ret. lawyer; b. Pender, Neb., Dec. 27, 1903; s. Frank B. and Helen (Case) H.; A.B., Stanford, 1923; LL.B., Harvard, 1926; m. Kathleen Shuman, Dec. 27, 1935; children—Sara C., Susan M. Admitted to Cal. bar, since practiced in San Francisco; mem. Morrison, Foerster, Holloway, Clinton & Clark (formerly Morrison, Foerster, Holloway, Shuman & Clark), 1944-68; admitted to bar U.S. Supreme Ct. 1932. Hon. trustee Starr King Sch. of Ministry, 1957—; trustee Cal. Acad. Scis., 1961—. Mem. Am. Bar Assn., Am. Law Inst., Phi Beta Kappa. Republican. Unitarian. Club: Bohemian (San Francisco). Home: 2240 Hyde St San Francisco CA 94109

HUTCHENS, JOHN KENNEDY, journalist, editor; b. Chgo., Aug. 9, 1905; s. Martin Jay and Leila (Kennedy) H.; A.B., Hamilton Coll., 1926, Litt.D., 1951; m. Katherine Regan Morris (dec); children-Anne, Timothy; m. 2d, Marjorie Kohl Brophy stepchildren—Janice, Peter. Reporter Daily Missoulian and Sentinel, Missoula, Mont. 1926- 27; reporter, film critic, asst. drama editor N. Y. Evening Post, 1927-28; asst. editor Theatre Arts mag., 1928-29, drama critic, 1929-32; drama staff N.Y. Times, 1929-32, 34-38, radio editor, 1941-44; drama critic Boston Eve. Transcript, 1938-41; asst. editor N.Y. Times Book Review, 1944-46, editor, 1946-48; book news columnist, reviewer N.Y. Herald Tribune, 1948-56, daily book reviewer, 1956-63; mem. editorial bd. Book-of-the Month Club, 1963—. Mem. P.E.N., Am. Center, Authors Guild (mem. council). Authors League of Am. (mem. council), Sigma Phi. Democrat. Clubs: Dutch Treat, The Players (N.Y.C.); Shenorock (Rye, N.Y.) Author: One Man's Montana: An Informal Portrait of a State, 1964. Editor: The American Twenties: A Literary Panorama (anthology), 1952. Contbr. Sat. Rev. Home: 306 Milton Rd Rye NY 10580 Office: Book-of-the-Month Club 280 Park Ave New York City NY 10017

HUTCHENS, JOHN OLIVER, physiologist; b. Noblesville, Ind., Nov. 8, 1914; s. Bernayse E. and Della M. (Moore) H.; A.B., Butler U., 1936; Ph.D., Johns Hopkins, 1939; m. Eleanore M. Mothersill, June 3, 1939; children-Margaret A., Judith M., Helen Louise. Nat. research fellow biol. sci. dept. biol. chemistry Harvard Med. Sch., 1939- 40; Johnston scholar dept. biology, Johns Hopkins, 1940-41; instr. physiology U. Chgo., 1941, asst. prof. physiology, 1946, asso. prof. 1946-52, prof., 1952—, chmn. dept., 1946-58, dir. toxicity lab., 1946- 48, prof. pharmacology and physiology, asso. dir. toxicity lab., 1970—.Temporary sci. liaison officer Office Naval Research, London, 1954; cons.-examiner North Central Assn. Colls. and Secondary Schs., 1967—, mem. corp. Marine Biol. Lab. Served to maj. as tech. dir. toxicol. research, med. div. AUS, 1945-46. Fellow A.A.A.S., N.Y. Acad. Sci., mem. Biochem. Soc. (Britain), Soc. Gen. Physiologists, Am. Assn. U. Profs., Chem. Warfare Assn., Am. Physiol. Soc., Soc. for Exptl. Biology and Medicine, Phi Beta Kappa, Phi Kappa Phi, Sigma Xi, Gamma Alpha, Phi Eta Sigma, Blue Key. Methodist. Club: Quadrangle. Contbg. author: Handbook of Biochemistry, 1968. Home: 5633 Drexel Av Chicago IL 60637

HUTCHENS, JOSEPH WARREN, bishop; b. Elnora, Ind., Jan. 20, 1910; s. Ezra Lewis and Hallie (Wyeth) H.; A.B., Evansville (Ind.) Coll., 1933; S.T.B., Gen. Theol. Sem., N.Y.C., 1937; S.T.D., Berkeley Div. Sch., 1962; D.D., Trinity Coll., 1962, Evansville Coll., 1965; m. Carolyn Permelia Hilton, Nov. 19, 1940; children—Margaret Wyeth, Mary Ruth. Ordained to ministry Episcopalian Ch., 1937; asst., also dir. edn. St. Luke's Ch., Evanston, Ill., 1937-39; asst. St. Johns Parish, Bridgeport, Conn., 1939-40, rector, 1940-62; Suffragan bishop Episcopal Diocese Conn., 1962-71, bishop, 1971—. Pres., Donations and Bequests, Inc., Ch. Scholarship Soc., Episcopal Acad., Cheshire, Conn., chpt. pres. Christ Ch. Cathedral; chmn. bd. St. Margaret's Sch., Waterbury, Conn., Episcopal Ch. at Yale, Camp Washington, Inc., Episcopal Social Service, Inc.; trustee Ch. Homes, Inc. Mem. Alpha Tau Omega, Tau Kappa Alpha. Republican. Clubs: Hartford, University (Hartford). Home: 28 Fernwood Rd West Hartford CT 06007 Office: 1335 Asylum Av Hartford CT 06105

HUTCHENS, RAYMOND PAUL, educator, lawyer; b. Ohio, Jan. 29, 1913; s. John Harvey and Nellie (Prine) H.; student Ohio State U., 1931-32; B.S. in Edn., Wilmington Coll., 1936; M.A., Miami U., 1942; J.D., Salmon P. Chase Coll., 1948; Ph.D., U. Ottawa (Can.), 1960; postgrad. Sorbonne, Paris, U. Cin.; m. Rachel Emily Gieringer, 1938; children—Paula Rae, James Ray. Tchr. pub. schs., Warren County, O., 1934-35; tchr., adminstr. pub. schs., Butler County, 1935-39, Hamilton County, O., 1939-42, 46-47; faculty Salmon P. Chase Coll. Sch. Commerce, summer 1947, dir., dean adminstrn., 1947-50, dean coll., 1950-51, pres., 1951, hon. pres., dean, prof. law, 1952-68; vis. prof. Cumberland Sch. Law, Samford U., Birmingham, Ala., 1967- 68, asst. dean, prof. law, 1968-71, asso. dean, prof. law, 1971—. Admitted to Ohio bar, 1948, Ala. bar, 1971. Served with AUS, 1942-45, with USNR, 1948-61. Mem. Am. Bar Assn., Birmingham Bar (asso.), V.F.W., Delta Sigma Phi, Kappa Delta Pi, Phi Alpha Delta, Phi Delta Kappa, Phi Delta Phi (hon.). Mason. Home: 2201 Montreat Circle Birmingham AL 35216

HUTCHENS, TYRA THORNTON, educator, physician; b. Newberg, Ore., Nov. 29, 1921; s. Fred G. and Bess (Adams) H.; B.S., U. Ore., 1943, M.D., 1945; m. Betty Lou Gardner, June 7, 1942; children—Tyra Richard, Robert Jay, Rebecca. Intern., Minn. Gen. Hosp., Mpls., 1945-46; AEC postdocotral research fellow Reed Coll., Med. Sch. U. Ore., 1948-50; NIH postdoctoral research fellow Med. Sch. U. Ore., 1951-53, mem. faculty, 1953—, prof., chmn. dept. clin. pathology, 1962- -, prof. radiotherapy, 1963—, allied health edn. coordinator, 1969—. Cons. radioisotopes St. Vincent Hosp., 1957-67, Providence Hosp., 1952-60; vis. lectr. radiobiology Reed Coll., 1955, 56. Mem. adv. bd. Ore. Regional Med. Program, 1968—; mem. statuatory radiation adv. com. Ore. Bd. Health, 1957-69, chmn., 1967-69; mem. Ore. Health Manpower Council. Served to lt. (j.g.) M.C., USNR, 1946-48. Diplomate Am. Bd. Pathology; charter mem. Acad. Clin. Lab. Physicians and Scientists, Soc. Nuclear Medicine; mem. Ore. Pathologists Assn. (pres. 1968), Pacific N.W. Soc. Nuclear Medicine (pres. 1958), A.M.A., Coll. Am. Pathologists (bd. govs. 1967-71), exec. com., Am. Soc. Clin. Pathologists (bd. registry med. technologists 1967-71), Assn. Am. Med. Colls., A.A.A.S., Phi Beta Kappa, Sigma Xi, Alpha Omega Alpha. Research, publs. radioactive carbon tracer studies of lipid metabolism, clin. radioisotope techniques. Home: 7821 SW 51st St Portland OR 97219

HUTCHERSON, ROBERT, (Bobby) vibraharpist, marimbaist; b. Los Angeles, Jan. 27, 1941; student Terry Trotter and Dave Pike. Worked in San Francisco with Al Grey-Billy Mitchell combo; played Birdland, N.Y.C., 1961; played with combos in N.Y.C., then returned to West Coast, 1965; reocrding artist for Blue Note, BN records. Recipient Down Beat Critics Poll award as new star, 1964, Jazz mag. poll, 1966. Address: 2905 Sterling Pl Altadena Ca 91001*

HUTCHESON, AMY MARGARET, librarian; b. Chiliwack, B.C., Can., Apr. 16, 1913; d. Charles and Annie (Brock) Hutcheson; B.A., U. B.C., 1945; diploma Library Sch. U. Toronto, 1938, Jr. librarian Hamilton (Ont., Can.) Pub. Library, 1938- 40; children's librarian Fraser Valley Regional Library, Abbotsford, B.C., Can., 1940-41; children's librarian New Westminster (B.C., Can.) Pub. Library, 1942-54, chief librarian, 1954—. Mem. B.C. Bd. Certification Profl. Librarians, 1961-69. Named Woman of Year, New Westminster Bus. and Profl. Women's Club, 1965. Mem. Canadian (councilor 1957-60, pres. 1967-68), B.C. (pres. 1949-50), Am. library assns., Canadian Assn. Children's Librarians (pres. 1950-51), Assn. des Bibliothecaires de Langue Francaise, New Westminster C. of C, Office: 716 6th Av New Westminster British Columbia Canada

HUTCHESON, HAROLD LEO univ. adminstr.; b. Castana, Ia., Sept. 26, 1916; s. Leslie G. and Sadie (Moss) H.; B.A., Neb. State Coll., 1948; M.A., U. Neb., 1954, D.Ed., 1957; m. Hazel Z. Moore, Dec. 11, 1943; childrenGayle Jolon, Rex Allison. High sch. sci. tchr., Oakdale, Neb., 1948-49, high prin., 1949- 50; supt. schs., Atkinson, Neb., 1951-55; instr. sch. adminstrn. U. Neb., 1955-57; dir. tchr. edn. Neb. State Coll., Peru, 1957-59; v.p. for devel. and services, dean Coll. Edn., Wis. State U., Platteville, 1959—. Inaugurated project PITCH, program tng. tchrs. for culturally deprived children, 1963; planned coll. campus, Richland Center, Wis., 1965. Exec. sec. S.W. Wis. Sch. Study Council, 1962; mem. Wis. Sch. Health Council, 1965-, Wis. Vocational Edn. Adv. Council, 1963—. pres. city council, Peru, 1958; exec. bd. Wis. P.T.A., 1965—; chmn. Platteville Community Chest drive, 1963. Pres. bd. dirs. Grant County (Wis.) Guidance Center, 1960-62; bd. dirs. U.S. Grant council Boy Scouts Am. Served as officer C.E., AUS, 1941- 46. Mem. Wis. Dirs. Tchr. Edn. (pres. 1966), N.E.A., Assn. Wis. State Univ. Faculties, Alpha Psi Omega, Pi Gamma Mu, Pi Kappa Delta, Lambda Delta Lambda. Home: 455 Madison St Platteville WI 53818

HUTCHESON, JOHN A., former corp. exec.; b. Park River, N.D., Jan. 21, 1905; s. William James and Janet (Avery) H.; B.S., U. N.D., 1926, D.Sc., 1943; m. Grace Nicholson, Dec. 29, 1931; 1 dau., Patricia Joan. With radio engring dept. Westinghouse Electric Corp., 1926-34, designed radio transmitting equipment for naval and mil. purposes, responsible for liaison between radio dept. of Westinghouse and patent and legal depts. Westinghouse and other cos., 1934-37, sect. engr. in charge television for Westinghouse, 1937-40, mgr. radio engring dept., 1940-43, asso. dir. research, 1943-49, dir. research and v.p., 1949-55, v.p. engring., 1955-62, v.p. planning atomic def. and space group, 1962-65; chmn. div. engring. NRC, 1965-70. Mem. I.E.E.E., Sigma Xi (hon.), Sigma Tau. Home: 946 Osage Rd Pittsburgh PA 15243

HUTCHESON JOSEPH C., Jr., judge; b. Houston, Oct. 19, 1879; s. Joseph Chappell and Mildred (Carrington) H.; ed. Bethel (Va.) Mil. Acad., U. Va.; LL.B., U. Tex., 1900; m. Anne Elizabeth Weeden, Dec. 21, 1905; children-Joseph C. III, Mary Pye. Practiced law, Houston, 1900- 18; mem. successively Hutcheson, Campbell & Hutcheson, Hutcheson & Hutcheson , Hutcheson & Bryan; chief legal adviser City of Houston, 1913-17; mayor Houston, 1917-18; U.S. dist. judge, So. Dist. Tex., 1918-30; U.S. circuit judge, Fifth Circuit, Houston, 1931—, chief judge, 1948-59, U.S. sr. circuit judge, 1964—. Mem. council Am. Law Inst.; Am. chmn. Anglo-Am. Com. of Inquiry, 1945-46; mem. adv. com. Nat. Assn. Legal Aid Orgns.; State of Tex. chmn. Am. Bar Assn. Spl. Com. on Restoration of Inns of Ct. Mem. Am., Tex., Harris County bar assns., Houston Philos. Soc., Philos. Soc. Tex., Order of Coif, Kappa Sigma. Presbyn. Club: Country (River Oaks). Author: Law as Liberator; Judgment Intuitive. Address: 500 Lovett Blvd Houston TX 77006

HUTCHESON, JOSEPH CHAPPELL, III, lawyer; b. Houston, Jan. 5, 1907; s. Joseph Chappell and Anne Elizabeth (Weeden) H.; grad. Phillips Acad., 1924; B.A., U. Va., 1928; LL.B., U. Tex., 1931; m. Mary Catherine Jacob, Feb. 18, 1933. Admitted to Tex. bar, 1931; partner firm Baker & Botts, and predecessors, Houston, 1946—. Dir. Schlumberger Ltd. Mem. chancellor's council U. Tex. System. Bd. mgrs. Schlumberger Found. Served to maj. AUS, 1942- 46; ETO. Mem. Am. Law Inst., Am. Bar Assn., Mid-Continent Oil and Gas Assn., Order of Coif, Phi Delta Phi, Kappa Sigma. Home: 3601 Inverness Dr Houston TX 77019 Office: One Shell Plaza Houston TX 77002

HUTCHESON, MAURICE ALBERT, union ofcl.; b. Saginaw County, Mich., May 7, 1897; s. William L. and Bessie Mae (King) H.; student pub. schs.; m. Ethel Hyatt, Oct. 23, 1926. Apprenticeship carpentry, 1914-18; joined United Brotherhood of Carpenters and Joiners of Am., 1914, auditor, 1928-38, 1st gen. v.p., 1938-52, gen. pres., 1952—. Served as carpenters mate USN, World War I. Republican. Mason (32). Home: Milan IN 47031 Office: 101 Constitution Av NW Washington DC 20001

HUTCHESON, ROBERT HENRY, physician; b. Henning, Tenn., Mar. 11, 1900; s. James Albert and Rosa (Barrier) H.; M.D., Univ. of Tenn., 1930; M.P.H., Johns Hopkins Sch. of Hygiene, 1934; m. Elisabeth Ford, Feb. 29, 1924; 1 son, Robert Henry. Interne Marine Hosp., Norfolk, Va., 1930-31; asst. dir. health dept. various countries; dir. local health services Tenn. State Dept. Pub. Health, Nashville, 1935-40, asst. comr., 1940-43, commr. and mem. cabinet, 1943-69, ret., 1969; dir. Williamson County Dept. Pub. Health, 1969—; mem. Tenn. Tb Hosp. Commn., 1943-69; exec. officer Tenn. State Licensing Bd. for the Healing Arts, 1947-69; chmn. Tenn. State Hosp. Licensing Bd., 1947-69. Diplomate Am. Bd. Preventive Medicine and Public Health, Pub. Health Physician. McCormack award by state and territory Health Officers Assn., 1957. Bd. dirs. mem. medical and scientific com. Tenn. div. Am. Cancer Soc. Mem. State and Terr. Health Officers Assn. (past chmn. com. on federal relations, pres. 1949), Am. Pub. Health Assn. (past sec.-treas. and pres. So. br.), Tenn. State Med. Assn., Tenn. Pub. Health Assn., Williamson County Med. Soc., Regional Adv. Council on Nuclear Energy, So. Interstate Nuclear Bd., Kappa Alpha, Alpha Omega Alpha. Democrat. Methodist. Home: 207 Lewisburg Av Franklin TN 37064 Office: Cordell Hull Bldg Nashville TN ☆

HUTCHESON, THOMAS BARKSDALE, Jr., educator; b. Christiansburg, Va., Nov. 4, 1926; s. Thomas Barksdale and Rosilie (Stockard) H.; B.S., Va. Poly. Inst., 1950; M.S., N.C. State U., 1952, Ph.D., 1956; m. Frances Elizabeth McEver, Jan. 16, 1954; children—Elizabeth McEver, Thomas Barksdale III, Joel Collier. Instr. agronomy dept. N.C. State U., Raleigh, 1952-54; asst. prof. agronomy U. Ky., Lexington, 1956-59, asso. prof., 1959-64; prof. agronomy Va. Poly. Inst., Blacksburg, 1964-67, prof., head dept. agronomy, 1967—. Served with AUS, 1945-46. Fellow Am. Soc. Agronomy; mem. Soil Sci. Soc. Am., Sigma Xi, Alpha Zeta, Phi Kappa Phi, Epsilon Sigma Phi, Phi Sigma, Gamma Sigma Delta. Presbyn. (elder). Rotarian. Editorial bd. Tobacco Science, 1969—, Agronomy Jour., 1970—, Soil Sci. Soc. Am. Proceedings, 1970—. Home: 402 E Hemlock Dr Blacksburg VA 24060

HUTCHIN, CLAIRE ELWOOD, Jr., army officer; b. Decatur, Ill., Jan. 9, 1916; s. Claire Elwood and Helen Josephine (Francis) H.; B.S., U.S. Mil. Acad., 1938; grad. Army War Coll., 1953; m. Katharine Porter Steel, June 15, 1938; children—Katharine Keen (Mrs. Ronald J. Menhennet), Claire Elwood III, William Ellis, Marion Belt. Commd. 2d lt. U.S. Army, 1938, advanced through grades to lt. gen., 1967; asst. to Gen. of Army Marshall on Presdl. mission to China, 1946; exec. officer Gen. Wedemeyer on mission to China/Korea, 1947; comdg. officer 1st Bn., 23d Inf., Korea, 1950-51; asst. to Adm. Radford chmn. Joint Chiefs Staff, 1953-57; comdg. officer 12th Inf., 1957-58; chief staff VII Corps, Europe, 1960; dir. plans and policy Dept. Army, 1960-63; comdg. gen. 4th Inf. Div., Ft. Lewis, Wash., 1963-65; dep. chief staff Pacific Command, 1965-67, chief of staff Pacific Command, 1967-69; comdg. gen. V U.S. Corps, Europe, 1969-71, 1st U.S. Army, Fort George Meade, Md., 1971—. Mem. exec. bd. Mt. Rainier council Boy Scouts Am., 1963-65, Aloha council, 1965-69, Balt. council, 1971—, mem. Nat. bd., 1970—, v.p. N. Atlantic council, chmn. Silver Beaver awards com., 1970-71; chmn. Combined Fed. Fund Campaign, 1971—. Decorated D.S.C. with oak leaf cluster, D.S.M., Silver Star, Legion of Merit with 5 oak leaf clusters, Bronze Star, Purple Heart with oak leaf cluster; various fgn., unit and service awards. Mem. Assn. Grad. U.S. Mil. Acad., Assn. U.S. Army, Assn. U.S. Army War Coll. Home: Quarters 1 Fort Meade MD 20755 Office: Hdqrs 1st US Army Fort George Meade MD 20755

HUTCHINGS, FRANCIS STEPHENSON, former coll. pres.; b. Northfield, Mass., Aug. 17, 1902 s. William James and Anna Laura (Murch) H.; student Oberlin Acad., 1915-16; A.B., Oberlin Coll., 1923; LL.D., 1948; A.M., Yale, 1933; LL.D., Lake Forest Coll., 1935, U. Ky., 1944; m. Louise Gilman, Feb. 22, 1934; children—Anne (Mrs. Bruce McManus), Francis, William Maynard, Robert Lawrence. Instr. Oberlin-Shansi Meml., Taikuhsien, China, 1922-24, Yale-in-China Assn., Changsha, China, 1925-27, Shantung Christian U., Tsinan, China, 1927- 28; rep. Am. Trustees of Yale-in-China Assn., 1928-39; pres. Berea Coll. 1939-67, pres. emeritus, 1970—; rep. trustees Yale in China Assn., Hong Kong, 1967-70. Exec. sec. Changsha (China) Internat. Relief Com., 1938-39; trustee (hon.) Yale-in-China Assn. Mem. U.S. Citizens Commn. for NATO, 1961-62, Pres.'s Adv. Commn. on Rural Poverty, 1966-67. Trustee Pine Mountain Settlement Sch., E.O. Robinson Mountain Fund. Conglist. Home: Berea Coll Berea KY 40403

HUTCHINGS GEORGE HENRY food co. exec.; b. Fort Worth, June 23, 1922; s. George H. and Emma (Harder) H.; student Tex. A. and M. Coll., 1940-42; m. Edith Van Gils, Mar. 23, 1946 (dec.); childrenMark Dennis, Lisa Ellen; m. 2d, Elizabeth T. Storey, Apr. 10, 1968. Analyst marketing research Frito Food Mfg., Dallas, 1946-, mgr. marketing research, Los Angeles, 1946-57, div. sales mgr., San Mateo, Cal., 1958-60, div. gen. mgr., 1961, v.p., 1961- 62, v.p. for operations Western zone, 1962—; pres. Nalley's, Inc., Tacoma, 1964, pres. Nalley's div. W.R. Grace & Co., 1966—; dir., mem. exec. com. Puget Sound Nat. Bank, Tacoma. Trustee Charles Wright Acad., Tacoma. Served to capt. USAAF, 1942-46. Decorated D.F.C., Air medal with 7 clusters. Mem. Tacoma C. of C. (dir.). Presbyn. Mason. Home: 12711 Av du Bois Tacoma WA 98498 Office: 3303 S 35th St Tacoma WA 98409

HUTCHINGS, HAROLD EMERSON, newspaper editor; b. Effingham, Ill., Apr. 22, 1907; s. John Charles and Elizabeth Hankins (Francis) H.; B.S. in Journalism, U. Ill., 1929; m. Sue Louise Austin, June 7, 1930; 1 son, John Austin. Reporter, feature writer, then city editor Champaign (Ill.) News-Gazette, 1929-32; mem. staff Chgo. Tribine, 1934—, N.Y. corr. for Chgo. Tribune Press Service, 1946-62, bus. editor, 1962-63, city editor, 1963-67, asst. mng. editor, 1967-68, asst. to editor, 1969-70, exec. editor, 1971—. Served to lt. col. AUS, 1941-45. Mem. Sigma Delta Chi. Republican. Conglist. Clubs: Overseas Press (N.Y.C.); Chicago Press, Tavern (Chgo.). Home: 1215 Croft Lane Evanston IL 60202 Office: Chicago Tribune 435 N Michigan Av Chicago IL 60611

HUTCHINGS, IMRI J., food co. exec.; b. South Jordan, Utah, Apr. 5, 1909; s. Joseph N. and Elizabeth Ann (Bird) H.; B.S., Brigham Young U., 1932, M.S., 1933; Ph.D., Rutgers U., 1936; m. Bernice Page, Aug. 28, 1933 (dec. Aug. 1964); children—Paul Norman, Janet Elizabeth, Alan Page, Mary Elaine; m. 2d, Helen L. Xezones, Sept. 3, 1965. Tech. dir. Grocery Store Products Co., 1936-47; with H.J. Heinz Co., Pitts., 1947—, mgr. food research, 1961-62, mgr. research, 1962-64, gen. mgr. research, 1964-65, gen. mgr. research and devel., 1965—. Fellow A.A.A.S., Am. Inst. Chemists; mem. Inst. Food Technologists (pres. 1960-61), Am. Chem. Soc., Am. Water Works Assn., Am. Soc. Microbiologists, N.Y. Acad. Scis., Am. Assn. Cereal Chemists, Sigma Xi, Phi Tau Sigma. Mem. Ch. of Jesus Christ of Latter-day Saints. Club: Pittsburgh Chemists. Home: 8250 Brittany Pl Briarwood Pittsburgh PA 15237 Office: PO Box 57 Pittsburgh PA 15230

HUTCHINGS, PAUL RAYMOND, trade union exec.; b. Milw., July 4, 1909; s. Raymond Hallock and Clara Marie (Ebert) H.; student U. Wis., 1928-31; B.E., Milw. State Tchrs. Coll., 1933; grad. study George Washington U., 1938-39; m. Lorna Backey, Aug. 27, 1940; children—Lynn, Paul. Code labor adviser, labor adv. bd. N.R.A., 1934-36; organizer Office Workers Union, A.F. of L., Milw., 1936; asst. research dir. Internat. Assn. Machinists, A.F. of L., 1937- 41, research dir., 1941-43; pres. Office Employes Union, A.F. of L., Washington, 1938-42, sec.-treas. Internat Council, 1942-45; pres., chmn. exec. bd. Office Employes Internat. Union, A.F. of L. 1945-53, research dir. metal trades dept., 1954—; cons. labor affairs Fgn. Operations Adminstrn., 1954. Mem. Tau Kappa Epsilon. Author: Handbook on the National Labor Relations Board, 1937; International Association Machinists, The Wagner Act After Ten Years, 1945, Bureau National Affairs (contbr. chpt. Effect on the Trade Union). Editor, Office Worker, 1943-53. Home: 2132 N Troy St Arlington VA 22201 Office: AFL/CIO Bldg Washington DC 20006

HUTCHINGS, WILLIAM LAWRENCE, educator; b. Lehi, Utah, Oct. 2, 1903; s. William Ely and Alice (Naylor) H.; student U. Chgo., 1924-26; A.B., U. Cal. at Ph.D., 1935; m. Phyllis Hayford, May 27, 1934 (dec. 1965); 1 dau., Lucy. Teaching asst. U. Cal. at Berkeley, 1932-34; from instr. to asso. prof. math. Rollins Coll., 1935-43; mem. faculty Whitman Coll., 1943—, Alexander J. Anderson prof. math., 1947—, chmn. dept., 1947-69. Home: 825 Newell St Walla Walla WA 99362

HUTCHINS, CURTIS MARSHALL, business exec.; b. Boston, Apr. 23, 1907; Charles P. and Lena (Curtis) H.; student Country Day Sch., Newton, Mass.; A.B., Williams Coll., 1928; forestry student U. Me., LL.D., 1951; M.S. (hon.), Colby Coll., 1949; m. Ruth Rich, Feb. 28, 1931; children-Hilda, Christopher, Hope. Pres., Dead River Co., Bangor, Me., 1935-57, chmn., 1947—; pres. Bangor and Aroostook R.R. Co., 1948-57, chmn., 1952-58, 65, dir., 1952-58, 64-65; pres. St. Croix Paper Co., 1959-63; dir. Merril Trust Co., Bangor, Scott Paper Co., Phila., State Street Bank & Trust Co., Boston, Northeast Airlines, Inc., Boston, Mass., Guilford Industries, Inc. (Maine), Bangor Punta Corp. Mem. City Council of Bangor, 1941-43, chmn., 1943; mem. Me. State Legislature, 1943; mem. New Eng. Council, pres., 1954; dir. Assn. Am. R.R.'s, 1951-54; mem. Me. Environmental Improvement Commn. Mem. U.S. C. of C. (chmn. natural resources com.), Phi Beta Kappa. Clubs: Penobscot Valley Country, Tarrantine (Bangor); Union (Boston); Pinnacle, Brook (N.Y.C.); The Country (Brookline, Mass.). Home: 300 Kenduskeag Av Bangor ME 04401 Office: 55 Broadway Bangor ME 04401

HUTCHINS, FRANK MCALLISTER, advt. exec.; b. Rochester, N.Y., July 7, 1922; s. Francis Irving and Barbara Woodward (Arnold) H.; diploma Phillips Exeter (N.H.) Acad., 1941; A.B., Dartmouth, 1947, M.C.S., 1948; m. Jeanne Mathilda Bahn, Aug. 24, 1945; children—Katharine Arnold, Virginia Ann, Patricia Arms, Constance Anne. Editor-in-chief Dartmouth Yearbook, 1943; local advt. mgr. Dartmouth Daily Newspaper, 1946-47, bus. mgr., 1947-48; account exec. Hutchins Advt. Co., Inc., Rochester, 1948-50, v.p., gen. mgr., 1950, pres., treas., from 1951, now chmn. bd., chief exec. officer; pres., treas. Hutchins Advt. Co. of Can., Ltd., Toronto; dir. Dollinger Corp., Sykes Datatronics Corp., Quinby & Co., Inc. (all Rochester), Armotek Industries, Inc., Palmyra, N.J. Bd. dirs. Men's Service Center, Highland Hosp. (both Rochester), Monroe County Fair and Recreation Assn.; bd. dirs., v.p. Community Chest Rochester, Monroe County; bd. dirs., pres. YMCA Rochester, Monroe County; trustee Rochester Inst. Tech., George Eastman House; alumni council Dartmouth. Served with OSS, AUS 1943-45, 2d lt. inf., 1945-46. Mem. Rochester C. of C., Rochester Advt. Council (chmn. bd. 1957), Rochester Conv. and Publicity Bur., Rochester Jr. C. of C. (pres. 1952-53), Theta Delta Chi. Episcopalian (vestryman, warden). Clubs: Dartmouth (pres. 1951- 52), University, Rochester Country (pres. 1960-61, bd. stewards) (Rochester); Genesee Valley; Nat. Sales Execs. Home: 75 Indian Spring Lane Rochester NY 14618 Office: Midtown Tower Rochester NY 14604

HUTCHINS, HERIOT CLIFTON, educator; b. Grafton, Mass., Nov. 13, 1909; s. Ernest Leslie and Bertha Miller (Spooner) H.; B.S., Springfield Coll., 1930; M.A., U. Wis., 1932, Ph.D., 1934; m. Alice Chatelain, July 17, 1937; children—David, Alan. Research asst. Com. Youth Problems U.S. Office Edn., Washington, 1934-36; asst. sec. ednl. policies commn. N.E.A., Washington, 1936-40; prof. edn. Willamette U., Salem, Ore., 1940-44; field rep. Nat. Recreation Assn., N.Y.C., 1944-52; prof. edn. U. Wis., 1952—, chmn. dept. curriculum and instrn., 1967-69; Wis. state chmn. North Central Assn., 1959-64. Fellow A.A.A.S.; mem. Am. Assn. Sch. Adminstrs., N.E.A. Author: Social Services and the Schools, 1939. Contbr. articles profl. jours. Home: 4629 Keating Terrace Madison WI 53711

HUTCHINS, LEE MILO, plant pathologist; b. Fennville, Mich., Apr. 21, 1888; s. Henry Hudson and Harriet C. (Robertson) H.; B.S., Mich. State Coll., 1913; student U. Montpelier, 1919; Ph.D., Johns Hopkins, 1924; student Wageningen and Paris, 1930. Asst. pathologist, bur. plant industry, soils and agrl. engring U.S. Dept. Agr., 1914-17, through grades to sr. pathologist, 1919-41, in charge field labs. fruit disease investigation, 1921-41, head pathologist in charge div. forest pathology, 1941-53, chief, div. forest disease research Forest Service, 1945-55, collaborator in U.S. Dept. Agr., pathologist with FAO of UN in Yugoslavia, 1956, with Wis. Alumni Research Found., 1957; investigator diseases of cacao Am. Cocoa Research Inst. and Interam. Inst. of Agrl. Scis., Turrialba, Costa Rica, 1958—. Served as lt. San. Corps, U.S. Army, 1917-19. Received Superior Service award from U.S. Dept. Agr., 1955; Alumni award for Meritorious Service from Mich. State Coll., 1955. Fellow Am. Phytopath. Soc. (pres. 1942); mem. Bot. Soc., Bot. Soc. Wash. (pres. 1952), Soc. Foresters, Plant Physiologists, Soc. Hort. Sci., Soc. of Comp. Patholofy (France), French Botanical Soc., Hort. Soc. France (hon.), Wash. Acad. Sci., Sigma Xi. Club: Cosmos (Washington). Author tech. papers on virus disease of fruit trees, oxygen-supplying power of soil, gall diseases of cacao. Home: 2727 29th St NW Washington DC 20008 Office: Horticultural Corps Research Plant Industry Sta Beltsville MD 20705

HUTCHINS, MAUDE PHELPS MCVEIGH, sculptor, author; b. N.Y.C.; d. Warren Ratcliffe and Maude (Phelps) McVeigh; prep. edn. St. Margaret's Sch., Waterbury, Conn.; B.F.A., Yale, 1926; m. Robert Maynard Hutchins, 1921 (div.); childrenMary Frances Ratcliffe, Joanna Blessing, Clarissa Phelps. One-man shows Cosmopolitan Club. N.Y.C., Grand Central Art Galleries, Renaissance Soc. U. Chgo., St. Louis Mus., Wildenstein Galleries, N.Y.C., San Francisco Mus. Art. Toledo Mus. Art. Quest Art Galleries, Chgo., ann., 1930-39, Roullier Art Galleries, Chgo., 1942-48; works exhibited New Haven Paint and Clay Club. Bklyn. Mus., Nat. Assn. Women Painters and Sculptors, Chgo. World's Fair Show Modern Art, others; sculptor representing Ill., 3d ann. nat. exhbn. Am. art, Am. Fine Arts Soc. Galleries, N.Y.C.; sculptured head of Henry Morgenthau, Sr., now Library of Congress, Profl. life mem. Grand Central Art Galleries. Episcopalian. Author: (with Mortimer Jerome Adler), Diagramatics, 1932; (novels) Georgiana, A Diary of Love (also pub. Eng., Italy, Germany, Japan, Denmark), Love is a Pie. My Hero (also pub. Eng., Germany), Memoirs of Maisie (also published in Germany), Victorine: The Elevator, 1962; Honey on the Moon; Blood on the Doves; The Unbelievers Downstairs. Contbr. to Poetry, New Yorker, New Directions Ann., Accent, Kenyon Rev., Foreground. Mademoiselle, Quar. Rev. Lit., Quest, Harper's Bazaar, Vogue, O. Henry Prize Stories, Ramparts. Home: 1046 Pequot Rd Southport CT 06490

HUTCHINS, ROBERT MAYNARD, fund exec.; b. Bklyn., Jan. 17, 1899; s. William James and Anna Laura (Murch) H.; student Oberlin Coll. 1915-17; A.B., Yale, 1921, hon. A.M., 1922, LL.B., 1925; LL.D., W.Va. U., Lafayette Coll., Oberlin Coll., 1929, Williams Coll., 1930, Berea Coll., 1931, Harvard, 1936, Tulane U., 1938; hon. doctoral degrees, U. Copenhagen, 1946, U. Ill., 1947; LL.D., U. Frankfurt, 1948, U. Stockholm, 1949, Rollins Coll., 1950. U. Chgo., 1951, Colby Coll., 1956, U. Rochester, 1958, Lewis and Clark Coll., 1967; D.Litt., Georgetown U., 1964, Hebrew Union Coll., 1964; m. Maude Phelps McVeigh (div.); children—Frances Ratcliffe, Joanna Blessing, Clarissa Phelps; m. 2d, Mrs. Vesta Sutton Orlick. Master English, history Lake Placid (N.Y.) Sch., 1921-23; sec. Yale, 1923-27; lectr. Yale Law Sch., 1925-27, acting dean, 1927-28, dean, 1928-29, prof. law, 1927-29; pres. U. Chgo., 1929-45, chancellor 1945-51; asso. dir. Ford Found., 1951-54; chief exec. officer Fund for the Republic, 1954—, Center for Study Democratic Instns.; dir. Ency. Brit., Inc., Ency. Brit. Films, Inc. Served in ambulance service U.S. Army, 1917-19; Italian Army, 1918-19. Decorated Croce di Guerra (Italian), 1918; officer Legion 1969. Honor, 1938; receipient Goethe medal, 1948; Aspen Founders award, 1960. Mem. Chgo. Bar Assn., Phi Beta Kappa, Order of Coif. Clubs: University, Tavern (hon.) (Chgo.). Author: No Friendly Voice, 1936; The Higher Learning in America, 1936; Education for Freedom, 1943; St. Thomas and the World State. 1949; Morals, Religion and Higher Education, 1950; The Democratic Dilemma, Some Questions about Education in North America, The Great Conversation, 1951; The Conflict in Education, 1953; The University of Utopia, 1953; Freedom, Education and The Fund, 1956; Some Observations on American Education, 1956; The Learning Society, 1968; Dr. Zuckerkandl, 1968. Bd. editors Ency. Brit., 1946—. Address: P O Box 4068 Santa Barbara CA 93103

HUTCHINS, ROBERT SENGER, architect; b. Oakland, Cal., Dec. 13, 1907; s. Thomas Boyd and Alice Louise (Senger) H.; A.B., U. Cal., 1928; B.Arch., U. Pa., 1929, M.Arch., 1930; m. Evelyn Reed (Brooks), Oct. 12, 1934; children—Robert Ayer, Elizabeth O. (Mrs. Michael H. Bronnert). Apprentice, Delano & Aldrich, N.Y.C., 1930-33; pvt. practice architecture, N.Y.C., 1933-37, Moore & Hutchins Partnership, 1937—, specializing ednl., govtl., instnl., residential architecture; works include: campus plans and numerous bldgs., Goucher Coll., Balt., N.Y. U., Harpur Coll., Binghamton, N.Y., St. Lawrence U., Canton, N.Y., S.I. Community Coll., N.Y., St. Timothy's Sch., Balt., Cazenovia (N.Y.) Coll.; also numerous other schs., colls., univs., chs. Prin. works include: permanent mil. cemetery U.S. Battle Monuments Commn., Carthage, North Africa, U.S. Ambassador's Residence, Dakar, Senegal, IBM Ednl. Bldg., Endicott, N.Y., Village Hall, Garden City, N.Y., Community Ch., Glen Rock, N.J., Grad. Sch. Bus. Columbia; supervising architect Vassar Coll., 1960—. Dir. bldg. services U.S.O., 1942-46; com. bldgs. and furnishings services Nat. Council YMCA; bd. consultants Sch. Architecture Columbia, 1954-55; cooperating com. Sch. Architecture Syracuse U., 1958—, mem. Commn. on Ch. Bldg., Diocese N.Y., 1965—. Trustee St. Tomothy's Sch., 1953-67, pres., 1956- 60; trustee Mary I. Bassett Hosp., Cooperstown, Barnard Coll., 1955—, Cathedral St. John the Divine, N.Y.C., 1964-70; bd. dirs. Farmers Mus., Cooperstown, Morningside Heights, N.Y.C. Licensed architect, N.Y., Conn., N.J., Md., Va. Winner Goucher Coll. competition, 1938, Village Hall Competition, Garden City, N.Y., 1950. Fellow A.I.A. (pres. N.Y. chpt. 1954-56, chmn. edn. com. 1966- 68); mem. N.Y. State Hist. Assn. (trustee), N.A.D., Municipal Art Soc. N.Y., N.Y. State Assn. Architects, Nat. Trust for Historic Preservation, Soc. Archtl. Historians. Episcopalian. Club: Century Assn. Home: 1220 Park Av New York City NY 10028 Office: 800 2d Av New York City NY 10017

HUTCHINS, ROSS ELLIOTT, entomologist; b. Ruby, Mont., Apr. 30, 1906; s. Elliott J. and Helen M. (Pierce) H.; B.S., Mont. State Coll., 1929; M.S., Miss. State Coll., 1931; Ph.D., Ia. State Coll., 1935; m. Annie L. McClanahan, June 5, 1932. Faculty, Miss. State U., 1929-68, prof. entomology emeritus, 1968—; entomologist, exec. officer Miss. Plant Bd., 1951—. Served to lt. comdr. USNR, 1943-45. Mem. Miss. Entomol. Soc., Am. Entomol. Assn., Sigma Xi, Phi Kappa Phi Author: Insects: Hunters and Trappers; Strange Plants and Their Ways; Insect Builders and Craftsman; Wild Ways; This Is a Leaf; This is a Flower; This is a Tree; The Amazing Seeds; Travels of Monarch X; Insects; Plants Without Leaves; Caddice Insects; The Last Trumpeters; The Ant Realm; Island of Adventure: The World of Dragonflies and Damselflies; Adelbert The Penguin, Galls and Gall Insects; Little Chief of the Mountains; The Mayfly; Hop, Skim and Fly; Insetti Cacciatori; Saga of Pelorus Jack, Scaley Wings, The Cicada, Hidden Valley of the Smokies. Home: Starkville MS 39759 Office: Drawer EH State College MS 39762

HUTCHINSON, ALEXANDER, ins. exec.; b. Dover Plains, N.Y., Sept. 10, 1908; s. Harbison and Emily (Smith) H.; C.L.U., 1948; m. Lucille Brusie, June 6, 1931; children—Ann (Mrs. Charles Winterling), Heather (Mrs. Bruce Hemer), Jon H., Holly. Joined Met.

Life Ins. Co., 1933, supt. agencies, 1953-58, 2d v.p., 1958-60, v.p., later exec. v.p. marketing and field mgmt. Trustee Life Underwriter Tng. Council, 1956—, pres., 1960-61; trustee Am. Coll. Life Underwriters. Mem. Nat. Assn. Life Underwriters, Life Ins. Agy. Mgmt. Assn. N.Y.C. Sales Execs. Club. Conglist (deacon). Mason. Home: 300 Martine Av White Plains NY 10601

HUTCHINSON, BRIAN, British diplomat; b. Birmingham, Eng., Aug. 19, 1920; s. Brian and Olga Hutchinson; M.A., Queen's Coll. Oxford U. (Eng.), 1947; m. Jean Fisher, Oct. 10, 1949; children—Martin Oliver, Virginia Mary. Consul from Eng., Washington. Served with Brit. Army, 1940-45. Home: 4901 Dorset Av Chevy Chase MD 20015

HUTCHINSON, DOROTHY HEWITT, former assn. exec.; b. Middletown, Conn., Oct. 16, 1905; d. Joseph William and Evelyn (Clark) Hewitt: B.A., Mt. Holyoke Coll., 1927; Ph.D., Yale, 1932; m. R. Cranford Hutchinson, Sept. 7, 1933; childrenRobert Cranford, Hewitt, Evelyn Clark, Instr. zoology Albertus Magnus Coll., 1932-33; editor Index Advance Abstract Service, Wistar Inst. Pres. publs., 1939- 59; journey of friendship home-to-home around the world, auspices Soc. Friends, 1954; served speakers burs. World Affairs Council Phila., Phila. Peace Center, United World Federalists, 1954-69; pres. U.S. sect. Women's Internat. League for Peace and Freedom, 1960-65, internat. chmn., 1965-68. Contbr. articles on religious subjects, pamphlets on internat. affairs. Address: Jump Off Rd Sewanee TN 37375

HUTCHINSON, EDMOND CARLTON, research co. exec.; b. Rosemark, Tenn., Nov. 23, 1913; s. Lawrence E. and Sue (McFerrin) H.; B.A., Southwestern at Memphis, 1936, D.C.L., 1963; M.A., U. Va., 1937, Ph.D., 1954; postgrad. Va. Poly Inst., 1937-38; m. Minnie Ingram, Dec. 29, 1938; children—Edmond Carlton, David Michael. Economist, analyst R.R. Retirement Bd., 1938-42; chief producers and analysis sect. WPB, 1942-43; provincial dir.-gen. finance Iranian govt., 1944-46; mgmt. analyst Civilian Prodn. Administrn., 1946, Dept. Commerce, 1946-47; financial analyst, chief financial policy unit, dept. chief pub. finance div., chief price and distbn. div. SCAP, Japan, 1947-51; asso. chief monetary affairs staff Dept. State, Washington, 1952-53; area chief, dep. chief internat. div., staff asst. to budget dir., spl. asst. nat. security and fgn. econ. affairs Bur. Budget, Washington, 1953-58; asst. dep. mng. dir. operations Devel. Loan Fund, Washington, 1958-60; mgr. financial projects Internat. div. RCA, N.Y.C., 1960-61; asst. adminstr. charge bur. for Africa and Europe, AID, Dept. State, Washington, 1961-66; mem. research council, chmn. exploratory devel. group, v.p. Research Analysis Corp., McLean, Va., 1967—. Recipient award for exceptional service Devel. Loan Fund, 1960. Mem. Am. Econ. Assn. Democrat. Presbyn. Home: 9619 Hillridge Dr Kensington MD 20795 Office: Research Analysis Corp McLean VA 22101

HUTCHINSON, EDWARD, congressman; b. Fennville, Mich., Oct. 13, 1914; s. Marc C. and Wilna (Leland) H.; A.B., U. Mich., 1936, J.D., 1938; m. Janice Eleanor Caton, Sept. 19, 1959. Admitted to Mich. bar, 1938; mem. Mich. Ho. of Reps. from Allegan County, 1946-50, Senate from 8th Senatorial Dist., 1951-60; del., v.p. Mich. Constl. Conv., 1961-62; mem. 88th-92d Congresses, 4th Dist. Mich. Served with AUS , 1941-46. Republican. Home: 662 W Main St Fenncille MI 49408 Office: House Office Bldg Washington DC 20515

HUTCHINSON, EDWARD PRINCE, educator, demographer, author; b. Auburn, Me., Jan. 3, 1906; s. Frederick William and Agnes (Prince) H.; A.B., Bowdoin Coll., 1927; Ph.D., Mass. Inst. Tech., 1933; postdoctoral student, U. Stockholm, 1933- 35, London Sch. Econs., 1935; m. Louise Forbes, Jan. 6, 1940 (dec. 1962); children—Joan, John. Asst., instr. Harvard Sch. Pub. Health, 1929-32; fellow Social Sci. Research Council, 1933-35; instr. sociology Harvard, 1935-40; sr. research technician Nat. Resources Planning Bd., Exec. Office of Pres., 1942-43; supr. research Immigration and Naturalization Service, 1943-45; asso. prof., prof. sociology U. Pa., 1945—; cons. Dept. of Agriculture, Census Bureau, U.N. , Dept. of State. Fellow library of Congress, 1940; Guggenheim fellow, 1941-42, 56-57; Fulbright fellowship screening com. Com. Internat. Exchange of Persons, 1958-62; Nat. Sci. Found. fellowship panel Nat. Acad. Scis., 1959-65. Mem. Am. Immigration, Citizenship Conf. (dir., chmn. research com.; editor of Immigration Research Digest 1960-68), A.A.A.S., (sec. sect. social and economic scis. 1936-44), Population Assn. Am. (past dir., treas., v.p.), Union Internationale pour l'Etude Scientifique de la Population, Phi Beta Kappa, Delta Upsilon. Author: Studies of Differential Fertility in Sweden (with K. A. Edin), 1935; Guide to the Official Population Data and Vital Statistics of Sweden, 1943; Current Problems of Immigration Policy, 1949; Immigrants and Their Children, 1850-1950, 1956; The Population Debate, 1967. Home: West Beechtree Lane Strafford Wayne PO PA 19087 Office: Dept Sociology U Pa Philadelphia PA 19104

HUTCHINSON, ERIC, educator; b. Morton, Eng., Dec. 25, 1920; s. Fred and Winifred (Parrish) H.; B.A., Cambridge (Eng.) U., 1941, M.A., 1944, Ph.D., 1945; m. Lilian May Tribe, Sept. 19, 1942. Came to U.S., 1946, naturalized, 1959. Lectr. Sheffield (Eng.) U., 1946-48; asst. prof. colloid chemistry Fordham U., 1948-49; postdoctoral fellow Stanford, 1946-48, asst. prof., 1949-54, prof., 1959—. Mem. Am. Phys. Soc., Faraday Soc., Sigma Xi. Rotarian. Author: Chemistry of the Elements, 1959; Physical Chemistry, 1962; Solubilization, 1955. Contbr. profl. jours. Home: 340 Churchill St Palo Alto CA 94301 Office: Chemistry Dept Stanford U Stanford CA 94305

HUTCHINSON, EVERETT, lawyer; b. Hempstead, Tex., Jan. 2, 1915; s. Neely E. and Lida (Hosmer) H.; B.B.A., U. Tex., 1939, LL.B., 1940; m. Elizabeth Stafford, Dec. 16, 1944; children—Stafford, Ann. Admitted to Tex. bar, 1939, D.C. bar, 1963; preacticed in Hempstead, 1940-42; asst. atty. gen. Tex., 1949-51; pvt. practice law, Austin, 1952-55; commr. ICC, Washington, 1955-65, chmn. commn., 1961; pres. Nat. Assn. Motor Bus Owners, 1965-67; under-sec. transp., 1967-68; partner Fulbright, Crooker & Jaworski, Washington, 1968—. Mem. Council Adminstrv. Conf. U.S., 1961-62. Mem. Tex. Ho. of Reps., 1941-45. State orgn. dir. Young Democrat Clubs of Tex., 1939-40. Served from apprentice seaman to lt. USNR, 1942-45; capt. Res. Mem. Bar Assn. D.C., Am., Fed. bar assns., Motor Carrier Lawyers Assn., ICC Practitioners, Nat. Def. Transport Assn., State Bar Tex., Friar Soc., Tex. Soc. Washington, Sigma Phi Epsilon. Episcopalian. Clubs: Metropolitan, Internat., Nat. Lawyers (Washington). Home: 5401 Albemarle St Washington DC 20016 Office: 1140 Connecticut Av NW Washington DC 20036

HUTCHINSON, FRANKLIN, biophysicist, educator; b. Bklyn., Feb. 29, 1920; s. Franklin and Marjorie (Rollhaus) H.; B.S., Mass. Inst. Tech., 1942; Ph.D., Yale, 1948; m. Edith Arnold Pringle, Sept. 16, 1944; childrenBruce, Franklin IV, Alexander, Mary Candace. With radiation lab. Mass. Inst. Tech., 1942- 45; instr. radiology, biophysics Yale, 1948-51, asst. prof. physics, 1951-56, asso. prof. biophysics. 1956-60, prof., 1960—, chmn. dept. molecular biology, biophysics, 1960-63, chmn. dept. molecular biophysics, 1967-69. Cons. radiation physics Grace-New Haven Hosp., Hartford Hosp.; chmn. biophysics tng. study sect. NIH, 1962-64. Guggenheim fellow King's Coll., London 1963-64. Mem. A.A.A.S., Biophysics Soc., Am. Phys. Soc., Radiation Research Soc., Fedn. Am. Scientists. Home: 862 Grassy Hill Rd Orange CT 06477

HUTCHINSON, GEORGE EVELYN, educator, biologist; b. Cambridge, Eng., Jan. 30, 1903; s. Arthur and Evaline D. (Shipley) H.; ed. Greshams Sch., Holt Norfolk, U., Cambridge. Came to U.S., 1928, naturalized, 1941. Sr. lectr. zoology U. Witwatersrand Union, South Africa, 1926-28; instr., advancing to prof., Sterling prof. zoology Yale, 1928-71, prof. emeritus, 1971—. Author: The Clear Mirror, 1936; The Itinerant Ivory Tower, 1953; A Treatise on Limnology, vol. 1, 1957, vol. 2, 1967; A Preliminary List of the Writings of Rebecca West, 1912-51, 1957; The Enchanged Voyage, 1962; The Ecological Theater and the Evolutionary Play, 1965, Contbr. numerous sci. papers on aquatic insects, limnology, biogeochemistry to profl. lit. Home: 269 Canner St New Haven CT 06511

HUTCHINSON, HOWARD, holding co. exec.; b. St. Clairsville, O., May 4, 1913; s. Joseph and Florence (Woodcock) H.; student pub. schs.; m. Selma Grace Henderson, June 14, 1933; children—Shirley Jean (Mrs. Richard C. Laudick), Howard Hayes; m. 2d, Mabel E. Crawford, Dec. 20, 1969. With Nationwide Ins. Cos. (formerly Farm Bur. Ins. Cos.), Columbus, O., 1932-68, dir. agys., 1948-51, v.p. sales, 1951, v.p. operations, 1951-54, v.p. ins. operations, 1954-62, sr. v.p., 1962-68; exec. v.p., dir. Nationwide Corp., Columbus, 1968—; pres., dir. Nat. Services, Inc., 1969—; pres., dir. Gates, McDonald & Co., 1969—. Mem. econ. life com. Nat. Council Chs.; mem. gen. bd. Columbus YMCA. Mem. Health Ins. Assn. Am. (membership and ethical standards com.), Inst. Life Ins. (environmental information system steering com.), Columbus Maennerchor. Republican. Methodist. Mason (32, Shriner). Clubs: Athletic, Scioto Country (Columbus). Home: 1631 Roxbury Rd Columbus OH 43212 Office: 246 N High St Columbus OH 43216

HUTCHINSON, JAMES GORDON, textile co. exec.; b. Dunkirk, N.Y., Jan. 7, 1910; s. Loren George and Agnes (Neal) H.; B.B.A., Coll. City N.Y., 1937; LL.D. (hon.), Davis and Elkins Coll., 1965; m. Ethel Erickson, Dec. 17, 1929 (dec. May 1963); children-Jay, Eric, Douglas; m. 2d, Irene Harkins, Nov. 30, 1968. Manager Price Waterhouse & Co., N.Y.C., 1935-51; auditor Lever Bros. Co., N.Y.C., 1951-54; comptroller Wheeling Steel Corp. (W.Va.). 1955-58, v.p. and comptroller, 1958-65; v.p. administrn. Rossville Yarn Processing Co. and affiliates, 1965—; dir. Oglebay Norton Corp., Trustee Linsly Military Inst. C.P.A., N.Y. Mem. Financial Execs. Inst., Nat. Assn. Accountants, Am. Inst. C.P.A.'s, N.Y. State Soc. C.P.A.'s. Home: Lyndhurst Dr Chattanooga TN 37405 Office: P O Box 40 Rossville GA 30741

HUTCHINSON, JAMES MELVIN, banker; b. Sioux City, Ia., Aug. 13, 1896; s. Thomas Clement and Katherine B. (Hart) H.; grad. high sch.; L.H.D., Marycrest Coll.; m. Seraphia M. Figge, Sept. 12, 1922; children—Joanne M. (Mrs. Thomas J. Coonan III), Barbara J. (Mrs. Robert T. Cassin). With Davenport Bank & Trust Co. (Ia.), 1933—, exec. v.p., 1948—, also dir.; dir. Ia. State Bank, Calmar, Ossian State Bank (Ia.). Mem. sponsoring com. ALCOA Sons and Daus. Scholarship Selection Com.; dir., past pres. Quad- City Devel. Group; mem. Davenport Airport Commn.; chmn. financial affairs com. Marycrest Coll., Davenport; active YMCA; mem. council adminstrn. Cath. Diocese Davenport; pres. adv. bd. Mercy Hosp., Davenport. Bd. dirs. Kahl Home for Aged, Davenport; trustee St. Ambrose Coll., St. Luke's Hosp. Decorated Knight of St. Gregory, Pope Pius XII; named B'nai B'rith Man of Year, Davenport. Mem. Davenport C. of C. (past pres.). K.C. Clubs: Rock Island Arsenal Golf; Union League (Chgo.); Davenport Outing, Davenport Exchange, Town, Davenport, Rod and Gun (Davenport), Home: 2532 E Locust St Davenport IA 52803

HUTCHINSON, MELVIN J., mfg. co. exec.; b. Pontiac, Mich., 1918. Chmn. bd., pres. DMH Co. div. Nat. Gypsum Co.; dir. Chem. Bank & Trust Co., Midland, Mich. Trustee Gratiot Community Hosp. Mason, Elk. Home: 203 Orchard St Alma MI 48801 Office: 1517 Virginia St St Louis MI 48880

HUTCHINSON, RAY CORYTON, novelist; b. Finchley, Middlesex. Eng., Jan. 23, 1907; s. Harry and Lucy Mabel (Coryton) H.; grad. Monkton Combe Sch.; M.A., Oriel Coll., Oxford U.; m. Margaret Owen Jones, Apr. 2, 1929; children—Ann Coryton, Jeremy Olpherts, Elspeth Owen, Piers Evelyn. Served as maj. Brit. Army, 1940- 45; historian Persia and Iraq Command. Fellow of Royal Soc. of Literature. Mem. Church of Eng. Author: The Answering Glory, 1932; The Unforgotten Prisoner, 1933; One Light Burning, 1935; Shining Scabbard, 1936; Testament, 1938; The Fire and the Wood, 1940; Interim, 1945; Elephant and Castle. 1949; Journey with Strangers, 1952; The Stepmother, 1955; March the ninth, 1957; The Inheritor, 1962; A Child Possessed, 1965; Johanna At Daybreak, 1969; Origins of Cathleen, 1971. Home: Dysart Blechingley Redhill Surrey RH1 4QT England

HUTCHINSON, WESLEY GILLIS, educator; b. Providence, Mar. 28, 1903; s. John W. and Harriet W. (Gould) H.; A.B. magna cum laude, Brown U., 1925, A.M., 1927; Ph.D., U. Pa., 1933. Instr. botany Brown U., 1925-28; instr. biology Franklin and Marshall Coll., 1928-34; asst. prof. botany U. Pa., 1934-44, asso. prof. microbiology, 1944-53, prof. microbiology, 1953—, dean Sch. Allied Med. Professions, 1950-69. Research asso. OSRD, 1942-45. Fellow A.A.A.S.; mem. Am. Soc. Microbiology, Sigma Xi, Phi Beta Kappa. Republican. Presbyn. Research on deterioration mil. equipment in tropics. Home: 4701 Pine St Philadelphia PA 19143

HUTCHINSON, WILLIAM NELSON LINDSAY, Jr., investment banker; b. San Francisco, Nov. 3, 1922; s. William Nelson Lindsay and Doris (Seymour) H.; B.S. in Engring., Stanford, 1946, M.B.A., 1948; m. Bona Comel di Socebran, Feb. 11, 1961; children—Cristiana, Isabella, William Nelson Lindsay III. With Crown Zellerbach Corp., 1948-52; sales engr. Mitchum, Jones & Templeton, Inc., 1952-67, chmn. exec. com., exec. v.p., dir., 1967—; pres., dir. William Hutchinson & Co., Inc., San Francisco, 1967—; dir. Darsie, Hutchinson & Pettigrew, Inc., Walnut Grove, Cal., Technicolor Inc., Los Angeles. Served to capt. AUS, 1943-46. Decorated Bronze Star medal; comdr. Crown of Italy. Mem. Investment Bankers Assn., Cal. Hist. Soc., Zeta Psi. Republican. Episcopalian. Clubs: Pacific Union; Bohemian; San Francisco Golf, Merchants Exchange, Olympic, San Francisco Bond; Stock Exchange Luncheon (N.Y.C.). Home: 2520 Divisadero St San Francisco CA 94115 Office: 44 Montgomery St San Francisco CA 94104

HUTCHINSON, WILLIAM THOMAS, historian, former educator; b. Freehold, N.J., Mar. 9, 1895; s. Thomas Combs and Anne (Thomas) H.; A.B., Rutgers U., 1916, Litt.D., 1941; A.M., Columbia, 1917; Ph.D., U. Chgo., 1927; m. Frances Runyon, Nov. 23, 1921; children—Anne (Mrs. Walter Sharp), Judith (Mrs. John K. Powell). Supercargo, U.S. Shipping Bd., 1919-21; instr. history Rutgers U. 1921-24; with U. Chgo., 1924-70, acting chmn. dept. history, 1942-43, chmn., 1943-50, Preston and Sterling Morton prof. Am. history, 1955-62, Preston and Sterling Morton prof. emeritus, 1962—; sec. Charles R. Walgreen Found. 1938- 45 (publs., 15 volumes "Walgreen Studies in Democratic Institutions". Mem. War Dept. Com. on History of the War, 1946-56. Served from pvt. to 1st lt. 5th Regt., 2d Div., USMC, AEF, 1917-19. Decorated Croix de Guerre with two citations, Purple Heart. Mem. Am., Miss. Valley (pres. 1958-59, bd. editors Rev. 1946-49) hist. assns., Phi Beta Kappa. Baptist. Club: Quadrangle. Author: Biographies of Cyrus H. McCormick and Frank O. Lowden. Editor: (with W.M.E. Rachal, others) Papers of James Madison, 7 vols., 1962-71. Home: 5716 Stony Island Av Chicago IL 60637

HUTCHISON, BRUCE, author, journalist; b. Prescott, Ont., Can., June 5, 1901; s. John and Constance Mary (Leslie) H.; ed. pub. schs.; m. Dorothy Kidd McDiarmid, Apr. 9, 1925; children-Joan Edith, Robert Bruce. With Vancouver Sun, 1938-43, Winnipeg Free Press, 1943-53; editor Victoria Times, 1951-63; editorial dir. Vancouver (B.C.) Sun, 1963-. Author: The Unknown Country, Canada and Her People 1942; The Hollow Men (novel), 1944; The Fraser, 1950; The Incredible Canadian (biography Mackenzie King, U. B.C. Pres.'s medal), 1952; The Struggle for the Border, 1956; Canada, Tomorrow's Giant, 1957; Mr. Prime Minister, 1964. Contbr. fiction to popular mags., also articles to many newspapers in U.S., Can. Recipient Gov.-Gen.'s award, 1943, 52, 57; Nat. Newspaper award for editorial writing, 1952, 58, 59; Commonwealth award Royal Soc. Arts, 1961; Service medal Order of Can., 1967. Home: 810 Rogers Av Victoria British Columbia Canada Office: The Sun Vancouver British Columbia Canada

HUTCHISON, CHARLES RICHARD, former army officer; b. Mineral Point, Wis., Feb. 25, 1903; s. Charles William and Bertha (Jackson) H.; student Lawrence Coll., 1921-23; B.S., U.S. Mil. Acad., 1927; grad. Indsl. Coll. Armed Forces, 1948-49; m. Esther G. Webb, June 24, 1931; children-Charles Richard, Joseph William. Commd. 2d lt. U.S. Army, 1927, advanced through grades to maj. gen., 1953; instr., asst. prof. econs. and govt. U.S. Mil. Acad., 1939-42; staff officer Gen. MacArthur's hdqrs. S.W. Pacific, 1944-48; comptroller U.S. Army Europe, 1949-54; dep. dir. budget Army Dept., Washington, 1954-59; dep. chief staff programs, comptroller U.S. Army Pacific, 1959-61; comdg. gen. U.S. Army Hawaii, 1961-63, ret., 1963; gen. mgr. Alexander Young Co., Honolulu, 1963—. Chmn. budget and allocations com. Aloha United Fund. Decorated Silver Star, Legion of Merit with oak leaf cluster, Bronze Star, D.S.M. Mem. Assn. U.S. Army, Alumni Assn. U.S. Mil. Acad., West Point Soc. Hawaii (pres.), Honolulu C. of C., Phi Kappa Tau. Author: Personal Finance and Management for the Army Officer, 1942. Home: 534 Ahina St Honolulu HI 96816 Office: Alexander Young Bldg Honolulu HI 96813

HUTCHISON, CLYDE ALLEN, Jr., educator; b. Alliance, O., May 5, 1913; s. Clyde A. and Bessie G. (Bicksler) H.; A.B., Cedarville Coll., 1933, D.Sc. (hon.), 1953; Ph.D., Ohio State U., 1937; m. Sarah Jane West, Dec. 29, 1937; children—Clyde Allen III, Sarah Jane, Robert W. NRC fellow in chemistry Columbia, 1937-38, research asso., 1938-39, Manhattan Project, SAM Labs., Columbia, 1943-45; asst. prof. U. Buffalo, 1939-45; Manhattan Project U. Va., 1941-43; Enrico Fermi Inst., U. Chgo., 1945—, dept. chemistry, 1948—, asst. prof., asso. prof., prof., 1954—, Carl William Eisendrath prof. dept. chemistry, 1963- 69, Carl William Eisendrath Distinguished Service prof. chemistry, 1969—, chmn. dept. chemistry, 1959-62, Cons. Argonne Nat. Lab. Guggenheim fellow Oxford U., 1955-56. Fellow Am. Phys. Soc. (mem. council 1967—), Am. Acad. Arts and Scis.; mem. Am. Chem. Soc., A.A.A.S., Nat. Acad. Scis., Sigma Xi, Phi Lambda Upsilon, Gamma Alpha. Editor Jour. Chem. Physics, 1953-59. Contbr. to Organic Structures by Physical Methods, 1954, Annual Review of Physical Chemistry, 1956, Internat. Symposium on the Triplet State, 1967. Contbr. articles to sci. jours. Office: Dept Chemistry U Chgo Chicago IL 60637

HUTCHISON, DALE HARTMAN, research exec.; b. Summerfield, Kan., May 15, 1915; s. Arthur Leslie and Hazel (Hartman) H.; B.S., Tarkio (Mo.) Coll., 1938; postgrad. Kan. U., 1939-40, Washington U., St. Louis, 1941-42, N.Y. U., 1943-44, Stanford, 1948-50; m. Charlotte Creger, Nov. 24, 1938; children—Thomas S., Mary Patricia, Teresa, Margaret. Asst. occupational analyst USES, 1940-43; dir. research Landing Aids Expt. Sta., Arcata, Cal., 1946-48; research asso. Stanford, 1948-51; with Stanford Research Inst., 1951-69, gen. mgr. phys. scis., 1962-65, asst. v.p. phys. and life scis., 1965-69; v.p. marketing Midwest Research Inst., 1969-71; asst. exec. dir. Stanford Research Inst., Irvine, 1970—. Mem. adv. council Bay Area Pollution Control Dist., 1955-62; adv. com. Cal. Dept. Pub. Health, 1958-61. Served to lt. USNR, 1943-46. Mem. Am. Chem. Soc., Research Soc. Am., Am. Meteorol. Soc., A.A.A.S., N.Y.C. Chemists Club, Air Pollution Control Assn. (v.p. 1960). 5322 Sierra Roja Irvine CA 92664 Office: 19722 Jamboree Blvd Irvine CA 92664

HUTCHISON, DORRIS JEANNETTE, educator, microbiologist; b. Carrsville, Ky., Oct. 31, 1918; d. John W. and Maud (Short) H.; B.S., Western Ky. State Coll., 1940; M.S., U. Ky., 1943; Ph.D., Rutgers U., 1949. Instr., Russell Sage Coll., 1942-44, Vassar Coll., 1944-46; staff Rutgers U., 1946-49, research asso., 1948-49; instr. Wellesley Coll., 1949-51; staff Sloan-Kettering Inst., N.Y.C., 1951-60, asso. mem., 1960-69, mem., 1969—, acting chief div. exptl. chemotherapy, 1965-66, div. chief drug resistance, 1967—; faculty Sloan Kettering Inst. div. Cornell U. Grad. Sch. Med. Coll., N.Y.C., 1952—, asso. prof. microbiology, 1958-70, prof. microbiology, 1970—. Faculty fellow Vassar Coll., 1946; USPHS fellow, 1951-53; Philippe Found. fellow, Paris, 1959. Fellow N.Y. Acad. Sci., Am. Acad. Microbiology (charter), N.Y. Acad. Medicine (asso.); mem. A.A.A.S., Am. Assn. Cancer Research, Harvey Soc., Genetics Soc. Am., Am. Inst. Nutrition, Am. Soc. for Microbiology (past pres. N.Y. br.), Soc. for Cryobiology, Am. Genetic Assn. Research, numerous publs. on antibiotics and chems. effective in treatment of Tb and leukemia, reports on mechanisms explaining how leukemic cells become resistant to treatment; search for more effective antileukemia drugs. Home: Southgate Bronxville NY 10708 Office: 410 E 68th St New York City NY 10021

HUTCHISON, JOHN ALEXANDER, educator; b. Cedar Grove, N.J., Mar. 2, 1912; s. Seeley and Fannie (Elwell) H.; B.S., Lafayette Coll., 1932; B.D., Union Seminary 1935: Ph.D., Columbia, 1941; student Univ. of Edinburgh, 1947-48. Univ. of Basel, 1948; m. Julia Kley, Nov. 28, 1936; children—John Stuart, Ralph. William, Helen, Ruth. Ordained to ministry of the Presbyterian Ch., 1935; asst. pastor, Brown Memorial Ch., Baltimore, 1935-37; pastor, Christ Ch., Bayonne, N.J., 1937-40; instr. of philosophy, Coll. of Wooster (Ohio). 1941-43, prof. of religion, 1943-47; prof. of religion, Williams Coll., 1947-55; prof. religion, Columbia U., 1955-60; Danforth prof. philosophy of religion, Claremont Grad. Sch., 1960—; Fund for Advancement Edn. fellowship 1952-53. Mem. Soc. on Religion in Higher Edn., Am. Philos. Assn., Am. Acad. Religion, Phi Beta Kappa. Author: We Are Not Divided, 1941; Ways of Faith (with J. A. Martin). 1953; Faith, Reason and Existence, 1955, The Two Cities, 1957; Paths of Faith, 1969. Editor: Christian Faith and Social Action, 1953; Language and Faith, 1963. Home: 473 Blaisdell Dr Claremont CA 91711

HUTCHISON, JOHN NELSON, fgn. service officer; b. Arlington, Ia., May 1, 1911; s. Orson Ray and Lulu Olive (Webber) H.; B.A., U. Ark., 1937; m. Sarabel Roberts, Dec. 24, 1937; children—Judith (Mrs.

Albert L. Connelly), Susan (Mrs. Austin Brink). Journalist, Cin. Post, 1937-38, Memphis Comml. Appeal, 1938-41, San Francisco News, 1946-48; with Fgn. Service, Paris, France, 1948-52; dir. press and publ. service USIA, 1953-54, 60-61; dep. pub. affairs officer, London, Eng., 1961-65, Wellington, New Zealand, 1968—; dir. USIS Regional Center, Manila, P.I., 1961-68. Pub. relations dir. United Bay Area Crusade, 1955-59; pub. information dir. A.R.C., Washington, 1959-60. Served to lt. col. AUS, 1941-46. Decorated Bronze Star. Mem. Wine and Food Soc. London, Pub. Relations Inst. New Zealand, Fgn. Service Assn. Democrat. Clubs: Savile (London); Wellesley (Wellington). Co-author: Wines of the World, 1967; through a Glass Brightly, 1971. Pub. Horizons mag., 1965-68. Home: 409 Sheldon St Petaluma CA 94952 Office: USIS IBM Center The Terrace Wellington New Zealand

HUTCHISON, JOSEPH CARSON, business exec.; b. Cross Hill, S.C., Sept. 17, 1894; s. Joseph Carson and Bessie (Cauthen) H.; A.B., Wofford Coll., Spartanburg, S.C., 1915; m. Annie Whitner, Oct. 7, 1919; children—Elise Whitner (Mrs. R. L. Cornell, Jr.), Helen (Mrs. T. E. Tucker). High school tchr., Sanford, Fla., 1915-17; clk. Sanford Truck Growers, Inc., 1919, asst. sec.- treas., 1919-20, gen. mgr., sales mgr., 1920-35; propr. J. C. Hutchison & Co., Sanford, Fla., and Savannah, N.Y., 1935—; chmn. bd. Chase & Co., Sanford, 1963-69, adv. dir., 1969—. Chmn. bd. Growers and Shippers League Fla., Orlando; chmn. exec. com. Fla. Fresh Product Exchange, Orlando; chmn. adv. com. Fla. Celery Marketing Order, Orlando; dir. Fla. Fruit and Vegetable Assn., Fla. Sweet Corn Exchange; pres. Zellwood (Fla.) Sweet Corn Exchange; dir. Sugar Cane Growers Coop. Fla. Served from pvt. to 2d lt., F.A., U.S. Army, 1917-19; commd. 1st lt. Fla. N.G., 1921, advanced through grades to brig. gen., 1940, comdr. 62nd Inf. Brig.; called to active duty 1940; asst. div. comdr., 31st Inf. Div., 1942-46, reverted to N.G. status, 1946; promoted to maj. gen., 1951; comdg. 48th Inf. Div., Fla. N.G.; ret. from mil. service as lt. gen. Fla. N.G., 1952. Decorated Silver Star, Legion of Merit, Bronze Star medal, Air medal, Florida Cross, Victory medal World Wars I and II, Nat. Defense medal, Asiatic-Pacific Theater and Philippine Liberation ribbons. Democrat. Mason, Elk, Kiwanian, Rotarian (hon.). Home: Box 906 Sanford FL 32771

HUTCHISON, PAUL PHELPS, lawyer; b. Winnipeg, Man., Can., July 29, 1895; s. WIlliam Watson and Maude (Phelps) H.; B.A., McGill U., 1916, B.C.L., 1921, D.C.L., 1956; LL.D., So. Meth. U., 1956; m. Mary Meredith Thorburn, Aug. 28, 1930; 1 dau., Mary Schmidt. Admitted to Que. bar, 1922; Queen's counsel, 1932; counsel McMaster, Meighen, Minnion, Patch & Cordeau, Montreal; dir. Merc. & Gen. Reins. Co. Can. Ltd., United N.Am. Holdings Ltd., Schering Corp. Ltd. Dir., past pres. Mental Hygiene Inst.; dir. Red Feather Services, 1968. Served with Black Watch (R.H.R.) of Can., 1915-46, col. comdt., 1939-45. Decorated Efficiency Decoration, King George V Jubilee medal, King George VI Coronation medal, Canadian Centennial medal. Mem. Canadian (council 1940—, pres. 1955-56), Am. (hon. life) bar assns., Law Soc. Eng. (hon. life), Alpha Delta Phi (internat. recorder 1922-28, pres. 1958-59). Author: Five Strenuous Years, 1921; The 73d Battalion Royal Highlanders of Canada, 1929; Canada's Black Watch, 1962. Contbr. articles to periodicals. Home: 34 Arlington Av Montreal Quebec Canada Office: 129 St James St W Montreal Quebec Canada

HUTCHISON, STANLEY PHILIP, lawyer, ins. co. exec.; b. Joliet, Ill., Nov. 22, 1923; s. Stuart Philip and Verna (Kinzer) H.; B.S., Northwestern U., 1947, LL.B., Kent Coll. Law, 1951; m. Helen Jane Rush, July 25, 1945; children—Norman, Elizabeth. Admitted to Ill. bar, 1951; legal asst. Wash. Nat. Ins. Co., Evanston, 1947-51, asst. counsel, 1951-55, asst. gen. counsel, 1955-58, asso. gen. counsel, 1958-60, gen. counsel, 1960-63, v.p., gen. counsel, dir., 1963-66, exec. v.p., gen. counsel, dir., 1966-67, exec. v.p., gen. counsel, sec., dir., 1968—, chmn. exec. com., 1970—; pres. Wash. Nat. Corp., 1970—; dir. Anchor Group Mut. Funds, Anchor Corp., Anchor Capital Fund, Inc., Anchor Growth Fund, Anchor Income Fund, Anchor Venture Fund, Inc., Fundamental Investors, Inc., Wash. Nat. Fund, Inc., Westminster Fund, Inc., Anchor Nat. Life Ins. Co., Wash. Nat. Trust Co. Served to lt. (j.g.) USNR, 1942-46. Mem. Ill., Evanston chambers commerce, Am., Ill. bar assns., Assn. Life Ins. Counsel. Home: 3001 Indian Wood Rd Wilmette IL 60091 Office: 1630 Chicago Av Evanston IL 60201

HUTCHISON, STUART NYE, Jr., lawyer; b. Norfolk, Va., Aug. 19, 1910; s. Stuart Nye and Mary Jane (Hall) H.; A.B., Lafayette Coll., 1932; LL.B., Harvard, 1935; m. Alberta McClure, Oct. 14, 1938; children—Barbara Ann (Mrs. James G. Groninger, Jr.), Stuart Nye III, Robert McClure. Admitted to Pa. bar, 1935; asso. firm Reed, Smith, Shaw & McClay, Pitts., 1935-44; partner firm Kirkpatrick, Lockhart, Johnson & Hutchison, Pitts., 1946—. Dir., sec. Thermal Transfer Corp., Salem Corp., Fortune Nat. Life Ins. Co.; dir. Oxford Electric Corp., Steel Publs., Inc., Fourth Allegheny Corp., Beaver-Advance Corp. Trustee Clan Donald Ednl. and Charitable Trust, West Nottingham Acad., Colora, Md. Served to lt. comdr. USNR, 1944-46. Mem. Am., Pa., Allegheny County bar assns., Phi Beta Kappa. Republican. Presbyn. Clubs: Duquesne, Yale-Harvard-Princeton, Allegheny (sec.), Oakmont Country (Pitts.); Yankanuck (pres. Sans Souci, Ont., Can.). Home: 6011 Wellesley Av Pittsburgh PA 15206 Office: Oliver Bldg Pittsburgh PA 15222

HUTCHISON, VICTOR HOBBS, educator, biologist; b. Blakely, Ga., June 15, 1931; s. Joseph Victor and Veva (Hobbs) H.; B.S., N. Ga. Coll., 1952; M.A., Duke, 1956, Ph.D., 1959; m. Theresa Dokos, Aug. 14, 1952; children—Victoria Ann, John Christopher, David Michael, Kenneth Hobbs. Instr., Duke, 1957-58, faculty fellow, So. Fellowship Fund fellow, 1958-59; mem. faculty U. R.I., 1959-70, prof. biology, 1968-70, dir. Inst. Environmental Biology, 1966-70; prof., chmn. dept. zoology U. Okla., Norman, 1970—. Research prof. Universidad de Los Andes, Bogota, Colombia, 1965-66; prin. investigator Nat. Geog. Soc.-U. R.I. Herpetological Expdn. to Colombia, 1964-65. Guggenheim Meml. fellow, 1965-66. Mem. A.A.A.S., Am. Inst. Biol. Sci., Am. Soc. Icthyologists and Herpetologists, Am. Soc. Mammalogists, Am. Soc. Zoologists, Am. Physiol. Soc., Ecol. Soc. Am., Herpetologists League, Assn. Latin Am. Herpetologists, Sigma Xi, Phi Sigma, Phi Kappa Phi. Author: (with George C. West) Laboratory Manual in Animal Biology, 1963, 2d edit., 1967; also articles. Taxonomic studies on amphibians and reptiles, zoogeography; research on animal-alga symbiosis, heat tolerances of lower vertebrates, effects of day-length on metabolism and temperature golerance of lower vertebrates, ecology of amphibians and reptiles; discovered that pythons are able to become facultative endotherms during brooding of eggs. Home: 2010 Crestmont St Norman OK 73069

HUTCHISON, WILLIAM ROBERT, educator; b. San Francisco, May 21, 1930; s. Ralph Cooper and Harriet (Thompson) H.; B.A., Hamilton Coll., 1951; B.A. (Fulbright scholar), Oxford U., 1953, M.A., 1957; Ph.D., Yale, 1956; M.A. (hon.), Harvard, 1968; m. Virginia Quay, Aug. 16, 1952; children—Joseph Cooper, Catherine Eaton, Margaret Sidney, Elizabeth Quay. Asst. in instrn., history dept. Yale, 1954-56; instr. history Hunter Coll., 1956-58; asso. prof. Am. studies Am. U., 1958-64, prof. history and Am. studies, 1964-68; Charles Warren prof. history of religion in Am., Harvard, 1968—. Vis. asso. prof. history U. Wis., 1963-64. Recipient Brewer prize Am. Soc. Ch. History, 1957. Guggenheim fellow, 1960-61; fellow Charles Warren Center for Studies in Am. history Harvard, 1966-67. Fellow Society for Religion in Higher Edn.; mem. Am. Hist. Assn., Orgn. Am. Historians, Am. Studies Assn., Am. Soc. Ch. History, Unitarian Hist. Soc., Phi Beta Kappa. Democrat. Mem. Soc. of Friends. Author: The Transcendentalist Ministers, 1959. Editor: American Protestant Thought, the Liberal Era, 1968. Contbr. articles to profl. Jours. Home: 1 Hunt Rd Lexington MA 02173 Office: 45 Francis Av Cambridge MA 02138

HUTCHSON, DAVID WILLIAM, oil co. exec.; b. Mineral Point, Wis., May 21. 1908; B.S., U.S. Mil. Acad., 1931; grad. AC Primary Flying Sch., Advanced Flying Sch., 1932, Tech. Sch., 1939: m. Jane Dalrymple, Feb. 20, 1937; 1 son David William; m. 2d, Jean D. Miller; children-William D., Adrian Jean. Commd. 2d lt. U.S. Army, 1931, advanced through grades to maj. gen. USAF, 1952; former gen. 308th Bomb Wing, 314th Composite Wing; dep. chief of staff operations 5th Air Force, 21st Air Div., Topeka, 1953, 5th Air Div., Rabat, French Morocco, 1953-54, Hdqrs. Tactical Air Command, Langley AFB. Va., comdr. 9th Air Force, Shaw AFB, S.C., ret. 1961: v.p. Cal.-Oak Oil & Gas Co., 1961—. Decorated D.F.C. with oak-leaf cluster, Air medal with oak-leaf cluster, D.S.M., Purple Heart, Silver Star, Legion of Merit (U.S.); Distinguished Service Order (Gt. Britain). Home: 1209 Glenwood Av Oklahoma City OK 73116

HUTH, DONALD EARL, fgn. corr.; b. Green Bay, Wis., May 28, 1915; s. Herman Albert and Ann (Klesges) H.; Ph.B., Marquette U.; m. Anne Marie Kelly, Sept. 24, 1938; children—Dennis, Kathleen Marie. Reporter, Milw. Sentinel, Milw. Jour., Waukesha (Wis.) Daily Freeman, Racine (Wis.) Jour.-Times, 1933-43; with A.P., 1943—, editor, Omaha, staff cable desk, N.Y.C., war corr., CBI Theater, corr., Calcutta, Bombay, New Delhi, 1945-48, world desk editor, chief bur., Manila, P.I., war corr., Korea, and chief bur. Manila, 1952-57, chief bur. Singapore, 1958-59, chief Southeast Asian services, from 1959, now exec. asst. world service div. Mem. publ. relations adv. com. Marquette U. Recipient Byline award for outstanding reporting in Korea, Marquette U., 1953. Mem. Fgn. Corrs. Assn. S.E. Asia (v.p. 1958-59). Clubs: Overseas Press of America: Overseas Press P.I. (v.p. 1952-55, pres. 1956-57); Tokyo Correspondents (sec. 1951-52). Contbr. chpt. on Nehru, Men Who Make Your World. Home: Tower 53 159 W 53d St New York City NY 10019 Office: 50 Rockefeller Plaza New York City NY 10020

HUTH, EDWARD ANDREW, sociologist; b. Tiffin, O., May 13, 1898; s. Edward Andrew and Mary Elizabeth (Flynn) H.; A.B. Heidelberg Coll., 1921; A.M., U. Notre Dame, 1928; Ph.D., Western Res. U., 1943; m. Margaret Mary Emmonds, Dec. 29, 1926 (dec. Dec. 1965); children—Mary Jo, William Edward. Supt. pub. schs., Risingsun, O., 1921-26; instr. history, sociology U. Notre Dame, 1926-29, asst. prof. history, polit. sci., 1929-32, asso. prof., 1932-37; asst. prof. sociology U. Dayton, 1939-42, asso. prof., 1942-50, prof., 1950—, chmn. dept., 1943-65. Guest prof. sociology U. San Francisco, summer 1948. U. Dayton rep. Family Life Bur., Nat. Cath. Welfare Conf.; pres. Nat. Cath. Conf. on Family Life, 1954-55; mem. com. on Americanism, Dayton Community Welfare Council. Bd. dirs. Dayton chpt. Nat. Conf. Christians and Jews, Social Health Assn. Dayton, Montgomery and Greene Counties, O., Dayton Civic Music Assn. Mem. Gem City (Dayton) Democratic Club; League Young Dem. Clubs of Ohio (hon.) Ohio Dem. Campaign Com., 1947-48; Dem. candidate for U.S. senator 1946. Scholar in sociology U. Chgo., 1924; Richard Butler scholar in history Columbia, 1925; fellow in history Fordham U., 1938, St. Louis U., 1942. Decorated Knight of St. Elizabeth (P.I.). Fellow Am. Sociol. Assn.; mem. Am. Legion, Ohio Valley, Am. Cath. (nat. dir. membership 1949, 2d v.p. 1950) sociol. socs., Nat. Conf. Christians and Jews (mem. commn. on ednl. orgns.), Nat. Cath. Rural Life Conf. (Des Moines), Nat. Cath. Ednl. Assn. (Wash.). Roman Catholic. Author: Pres. Ruthford B. Hayes: Civil Service Reformer, 1943. Contbr. articles to religious, sociol. jours. Editor: U. Dayton Survey Report (3 vols.), 1957. Home: 4207 Shroyer Rd Dayton OH 45429

HUTH, JOHN AUSTIN, former banker; b. Balt., Sept. 1, 1906; s. Frederick W. and Alma (Westendorf) H.; student Balt. City Coll., 1919-20, Johns Hopkins, 1926-29; Asso. Bus. Adminstrn., Balt. Coll. Commerce, 1939; m. Helen M. Melchior, July 30, 1929; children—Joan C. (Mrs. Raymond O. Eresman), Janice. With Merc.-Safe Deposit & Trust Co. (name formerly Merc. Trust & Deposit Co.), Balt., 1920-71, sr. v.p., 1965-71, sec., 1955-71. Democrat. Lutheran. Club: University (Balt.). Home: 605 Cliveden Rd Pikesville MD 21208

HUTNER, SEYMOUR HERBERT, microbiologist, protozoologist; b. Bklyn., Oct. 28, 1911; s. Julius and Fannie (Zuckerman) H.; B.S., Coll. City N.Y., 1932; Ph.D., Cornell, 1937; m. Reina Albagli, 1938 (dec. 1955); 1 son, Reed Albagli; m. 2d, Margarita Silva, Aug. 18, 1956. Research asso. dept. physics Mass. Inst. Tech., 1935-36; technician Labs. and Research Div., N.Y. State Health Dept., 1938-41; staff Haskins Labs., N.Y.C., 1941—, asso. research dir., 1965—; Haskins adj. prof. biology Pace Coll., 1970—. Vis. prof. Inst. Microbiology, U. Brazil, Rio de Janeiro, 1963-64, U. Ill., Urbana, 1967, U. Brazilia, 1970; adj. prof. Fordham U., N.Y.C., 1964-69; bus. mgr. Jour. Phycology, 1963-67. Fellow N.Y. Acad. Sci., Am. Acad. Microbiology; mem. Soc. Protozoologists (v.p., pres. 1961-62, chmn. com. spl. publs. 1963—), Soc. Gen. Microbiology, Am. Soc. Microbiology, Mycol. Soc. Am., Am. Soc. Tropical Medicine and Hygiene, Phycological Soc. Am., Soc. Indsl. Microbiology, Japanese Soc. Plant Physiology, Tissue Culture Assn. Editor: (with A. Lwoff) Biochemistry and Physiology of Protozoa, vol. 2, vol. 3, 1964; editorial bd. Jour. Protozoology, 1953—. Home: 142 West End Av New York City NY 10023 Office: Haskins Labs Pace Coll 41 Park Row New York City NY 10038

HUTSON, HAROLD HORTON, coll. pres.; b. Spring Hill, S.C., Jan. 14, 1914; s. Edward Palmer and Frances Jones (Horton) H.; A.B., Wofford Coll., Spartanburg, S.C., 1932; B.D., Duke U. (Duke Found. Scholarship), 1935; Ph.D., U. Chgo. (fellow Dept. N.T.), 1938; LL.D., Wofford Coll., 1955; L.H.D., Ohio Wesleyan U., 1967; m. Virginia Earle Hudson, June 2, 1942; children—Martha Frances, Mary Amanda, Mark William, Sara Jane, Prof. religion Birmingham-So. Coll., 1938-46; interim minister Pilgrim Congl. Ch., Birmingham, Ala., 1944-46; prof. and chmn. dept. religion Ohio Wesleyan U., 1946-52; pres. Greensboro (N.C.) Coll., 1952-64; provost, exec. v.p. Am. U., Washington, 1964-69; pres. Lycoming Coll., Williamsport, Pa., 1969—; vis. prof. Garrett Bibl. Inst., summer 1950; minister Jerome (Ohio) Methodist Ch., 1947-51, Waldo Meth. Ch., 1951-52. Program chmn. Birmingham Round Table, Nat. Conf. Christians and Jews, 1940-42; dean Ala. Meth. Student Movement, 1944-46. Mem. Am. Oriental Soc., Soc. Bibl. Lit. and Exegesis, Am. Acad. Religion, Religion on Coll. Campus (cons. Meth. bd. edn. 1956), Washington Inst. Fgn. Affairs, Phi Beta Kappa, Theta Phi, Pi Kappa Delta, Sigma Upsilon, Pi Gamma Mu, Theta Chi, Omicron Delta Kappa, Blue Key, Meth. Author: (with Donald W. Riddle) New Testament, Life and Literature, 1946; Survey of the New Testament, 1949. Contbr. Witness to the Campus, 1956; Hastings Dictionary of the Bible, rev. edit. 1959; articles to religious jours. Home: 325 Grampian Blvd Williamsport PA 17701

HUTSON, JEAN BLACKWELL, (Mrs. John O. Hutson), librarian; b. Summerfield, Fla., Sept. 7, 1914; d. Paul Douglass and Sarah Frances (Myers) Blackwell; student U. Mich., 1931-34; B.A., Barnard Coll., 1935; B.S., Columbia, 1936; m. John O. Hutson, June 3, 1950 (dec. 1957); 1 dau., Jean. Librarian, N.Y. Pub. Library, 1936—, br. librarian Woodstock Br., 1948, curator Schomburg Collection, 1948—; lectr. Coll. City N.Y., 1962—; asst. librarian U. Ghana, 1964-65; lectr. Tchrs. Coll., Columbia, 1969; adj. asso. prof. Coll. City N.Y., 1970. Vice pres. Harlem Cultural Council; sec. bd. dirs. Harlem Neighborhoods Assn. Mem. Jack and Jill Found. Recipient Distinguished Service award Caucus of Black Legislators N.Y. State, 1971. Mem. A.L.A., N.A.A.C.P., Nat. Urban League Guild, Am. Soc. African Culture, African Studies Assn., Black Acad. Arts and Letters, Delta Sigma Theta. Home: 2255 Fifth Av New York City NY 10037 Office: 103 W 135th St New York City NY 10030

HUTTENBACK, ROBERT ARTHUR, educator; b. Frankfurt, Germany, Mar. 8, 1928; s. Otto Henry and Dorothy (Marcuse) H.; B.A., U. Cal. at Los Angeles, 1951, Ph.D., 1959; postgrad. Sch. Oriental and African Studies, U. London (Eng.), 1956-57; m. Freda Braginsky, July 12, 1954; 1 dau., Madeleine Alexandra. Faculty, Cal. Inst. Tech., Pasadena, 1958—, asst. prof., 1960-63, asso. prof., 1963-66, prof. history, 1966—, master student houses, 1958-69, dean students, 1969—. Cons. Jet Propulsion Lab., Pasadena, 1966-68. Served to 1st lt. AUS, 1951-53. Mem. Assn. for Asian Studies, African Studies Assn. Author: British Relations with Sind, 1799-1843 An Anatomy of Imperialism, 1962; (with Leo Rose, Margaret Fisher) Himalayan Battleground-Sino-Indian Rivalry in Ladakh, 1963; The British Imperial Experience, 1966; Gandhi in South Africa, 1971. Home: 1661 Lombardy Rd Pasadena CA 91106

HUTTER, ROBERT VICTOR PAUL, medical educator; b. Yonkers, N.Y., May 25, 1929; s. Jack and Anna Hutter; B.A., Syracuse U., 1946; M.D., State U. N.Y. at Syracuse, 1950; M.A., Yale, 1969; m. Ruth Lauterbach, Aug. 7, 1955; children—Andrew, Edie, Randi. Intern Yale Med. Center, 1954-55, resident, 1955-56; resident Meml. Hosp. Cancer and Allied Diseases, N.Y.C., 1956-57, chief resident, 1957-58; practice medicine, specializing in pathology/oncology, 1958—; mem. staff Meml. Hosp. for Cancer and Allied Diseases, 1956-68; prof. pathology Yale Med. Sch., 1968-70; prof., chmn. dept. pathology Coll. Medicine and Dentistry N.J., Newark, 1970—, also Am. Cancer Soc. prof. oncology; mem. staff Maitland Med. Center N.J. Served with USNR, 1958-60. Diplomate Am. Bd. Pathology. Mem. Coll. Am. Pathologists, Phi Beta Kappa, Alpha Omega Alpha. Home: 30 Surrey Lane Livingston NJ 07039 Office: 100 Bergen St Newark NJ 07103

HUTTER, RUDOLF GUSTAV EMIL, educator; b. Berlin, Germany, Feb. 12, 1910; s. Georg and Marie (Hempt) H.; state exam. U. Berlin, 1936; Ph.D. in Physics, Stanford, 1944; m. Ruth S. Fraenkel, Nov. 17, 1939; 1 dau., Barbara S. Engr. Telefunken GmbH, Berlin, 1936-38; chief engr. Sta. KZIB, Manila, Philippines, 1938-40; research asso. Stanford, 1941-44; sr. engr.-asso. dir. research Sylvania Electric Products, Inc., N.Y., Cal., 1944-58, chief engr., 1958-64; prof. electrophysics Poly. Inst. Bklyn., 1964—; vis. McKay prof. U. Cal. at Berkeley, 1957-58; tech. adviser GTE Labs., Bayside, N.Y., 1964—. Fellow I.E.E.E.; mem. Research Soc. Am., Sigma Xi. Author: Beam and Wave Electronics in Microwave Tubes, 1960. Editor C. Sussking Electronics Handbook, 1962, Focusing of Charged Particles, 1967. Contbr. articles profl. jours. Home: 445 E 80th St New York City NY 10021

HUTTO, JAMES CECIL, journalist; b. Abbeville, Ala., Nov. 7, 1906; s. James B. and Ida (Bethune) H.; student N.Y. Mil Acad., Cornwall-on-the Hudson, 1923-24, Northwestern U., 1929-32; m. Rosa E. O'Neill, Nov. 23, 1933; children—Cecile (Mrs. David R. Hundley), James Cecil, Vicki (Mrs. Joseph G. Wilson). Reporter, polit. writer Birmingham (Ala.) Post, 1932-41; editorial writer Louisville Times, 1941—. Vol. worker Our Lady of Peace Hosp., Louisville, 1965—. Bd. dirs. Neighborhood House. Mem. Nat. Conf. Editorial Writers. Democrat. Roman Catholic. Home: 2836 Hoock Av Louisville KY 40205 Office: 525 W Broadway Louisville KY 40202

HUTTON, ANN HAWKES, state ofcl.; b. Phila., Feb. 16, 1909; d. Thomas G. and Katharine (Gallagher) Hawkes; B.S. in Edn., U. Pa., 1931, LL.B., 1934; postgrad. Temple U., 1940; m. Leon John H. Hutton, Sept. 23, 1939 (dec.); 1 dau., Katharine Ann (Mrs. Charles E. Tweedy III). Dir. advt. Wetherill Point Co., Phila., Memphis, 1936-38; dir. advt. Caravel Films, N.Y.C., 1938-39; dir. advt. Hutton Chevrolet Co., Riverside, N.J., 1949-70; mem. Washington Crossing Park Commn., 1939—, chmn., 1963—; dir. Bank of N.J.; mem. Fidelity Union Bancorp. Historian, authority, Emanuel Leutze painting Washington Crossing the Delaware; past chmn., now mem. Bucks County Hist.-Tourist Commn., Fallsington, Pa., 1960—; commr. Am. Revolution Bicentennial Commn., 1969—. Co-chmn. Citizens for Eisenhower, 1951; chmn. Citizens for Nixon, 1968; mem. State Republican Platform Com., 1970. Chmn. bd. Historic Fallsington, Washington Crossing Found.; bd. dirs., mem. adv. council Hist. Found. Pa.; bd. dirs. Bucks County Conservancy. Recipient award of merit D.A.R., 1955; Achievement award Commonwealth Pa. for research and furnishing historic Thompson-Neely House, 1955; citation Nat. Camp, Patriotic Order Sons Am., 1959; award Am. Legion Phila., 1960; Freedom Leadership award Freedoms Found. at Valley Forge (1st woman to receive this award), 1960; award Pa. Soc. D.A.R., 1960; award Freedoms Found. for drama The Decision, 1964; Good Citizenship medal Phila.-Continental chpt. S.A.R., 1967; Exceptional Citizenship award Patriotic Order Sons Am., 1968; named Distinguished Dau. Pa., 1958. Mem. Children Am. Revolution N.J. (hon., adv. state patriotic edn. bd.), Chi Omega, Pi Lambda Theta. Clubs: Bristol Travel; Lost Tree (North Palm Beach, Fla.); New Century (hon.), Union League (asso. Phila.). Author: George Washington Crossed Here, 1948; House of Decision, 1956; Portrait of Patriotism, 1959; The Pennsylvanian, 1962; (drama) The Decision, 1963. Author script for documentary film Washington Crossing the Delaware, 1966. Composer: 1776 Suite From the Decision, 1970. Home: 6900 N Radcliffe St Bristol PA 19007

HUTTON, BRIAN G., dir. films including The Wild Seed, The Pad, Sol Madrid, Where Eagles Dare, Kelly's Heroes. Address: care Universal Pictures Hollywood CA 90028 *

HUTTON, CLIFFORD EDWIN, educator; b. Dill City, Okla., Mar. 25, 1928; s. Clyde Edwin and Mamie Lee (Bright) H.; B.S., Okla. State U., 1952, M.S., 1953; Ph.D., U. Tex., 1961; postgrad. U. Cal. at Berkeley, 1962, U. Kan., 1963, Harvard, 1965; m. JoRetta Mae Walls, Sept. 22, 1951; children—Ronnie Edwin, Jimmy Glenn, Terry Joe. Teller, Home State Bank, Hobart, Okla., 1946-48; asst. prof. Oklahoma City U., 1953-55; asso. prof., prof. and asso. dean U. Tulsa, 1955-69; dean Coll. Bus. Adminstrn., N.Tex. State U., Denton, 1969—; cons. oil cos. and bus. firms; coordinator exec. devel. programs; faculty adviser several student orgns.; lectr. Mexican and U.S. businessmen. Baseball mgr. YMCA, 1962-69; chmn. Community Chest, 1968, Boy Scouts Am., 1961-71, supervisory com. Credit Union, 1961-71, P.T.A., 1965. Bd. dirs. Tex. Council Econ. Edn., Southridge Recreation Assn., County Tchrs. Credit Union. Recipient 3 Ford Found. grants, 1961-66, Gen. Electric Found. grant, 1960,

Scouting award, 1966, Outstanding Tchr. award, 1969. C.P.A., Okla. Mem. Financial Execs. Inst., Am. Inst. C.P.A.'s, Nat. Assn. Accountants, Beta Gamma Sigma, Phi Kappa Phi, Alpha Kappa Psi. Author: Controllership Function and Training, 1962. Contbr. articles profl. jours. Home: 1817 Woodbrook Dr Denton TX 76201

HUTTON, COLIN OSBORNE, educator; b. Dunedin, New Zealand, Jan. 10, 1910; s. John and Jessie Alexander (Holms) H.; M.S., U. Otago, 1934; Shirtcliffe fellow, external research student Emmanuel Coll., 1936-38; Ph.D., Cambridge, 1938, Sc.D., 1952; m. Mary Piggot, Dec. 26, 1940. Came to U.S., 1947. Acting lectr. geology U. Otago, 1934-36, sr. lectr., 1946-47; govt. mineralogist, petrologist, Wellington, New Zealand, 1938-46; hon. lectr. petrology Victoria U. Coll., 1943-46; asso. prof. Stanford, 1947-48, prof. mineralogy, 1948—. Guggenheim fellow, 1953-54. Recipient Hamilton award, 1937; Sir Julius Von Haast prize. 1934: NSF award research, 1961-63, 64-66, 68-7O. Fellow Geol. Soc. Am., Geol. Soc. London, Royal Soc. New Zealand, Mineral. Soc. Am., Cal. Acad. Scis.; mem. Mineral. Assn. Can., Mineral. Soc. Great Britain, Cambridge Natural History Soc., New Zealand Assn. Sci. Workers (hon. life), Sigma Xi. Contbr sci. articles to profl. jours. Former asso. editor Royal Soc. New Zealand. Home: No 1 Grove Court Portola Valley CA 94025 Office: Sch Earth Scis Stanford U Stanford CA 94305

HUTTON, EDWARD LUKE, corporate exec.; b. Bedford, Ind., May 5, 1919; s. Fred and Margaret (Drehoble) H.; B.S. with distinction, Ind. U., 1940, M.S. with distinction, 1941; m. Kathryn Jane Alexander, Dec. 22, 1942; children—Edward Alexander, Thomas Charles, Jane Clarke. Vice pres., dir. World Commerce Corp., N.Y.C., 1948-51; asst. v.p. W.R. Grace & Co., N.Y.C., 1951-53; cons. internat. trade, finance, 1953-54; v.p., dir. New York & Cuba Mail Steamship Co., N.Y.C., 1954-61, financial v.p., 1958-59; v.p. and group exec. W. R. Grace & Co., 1969-71; exec. v.p., gen. mgr. Dubois Chem. div. W. R. Grace & Co., 1964-68; pres. E. L. Hutton, Assos., Inc., 1960-70; pres. Chemed Corp., 1971—; dir. Hamilton Cosco, Dearborn Aqua-Serv, Inc., Dubois Chems. of Can., Ltd., Am. States Ins. Co., Am. States Life Ins. Co., Am. Economy, Figi's Inc., Veratex Corp., Elson T. Killam Assos., Inc., Sentinel Indemnity Co. Trustee Village Bronxville, 1965-68. Served from pvt. to 1st lt., AUS, 1943-46. Methodist. Clubs: Downtown Assn., University (N.Y.C.); Field (Bronxville, N.Y.) Home: 6680 Miralake Dr Cincinnati OH 45243 also Harris Rd East Orleans MA 02643 Office: 3 Hanover Sq New York City NY 10004 also 1100 DuBois Tower Cincinnati OH 45202

HUTTON, HUGH MCMILLEN, former editorial cartoonist; b. Lincoln, Neb., Dec. 11, 1897; s. Elmer S. and Eugenia (McMillen) H.; student U. Minn., 1919-21; m. Dorothy Wackerman, May 24, 1924; children—Elizabeth Jean, Robert Wackerman. With St. Paul Pioneer Press, 1925, United Features, N.Y.C., 1929, Phila. Pub. Ledger, 1933, Phila. Inquirer from 1934; exhibitor etchings, lithographs, cartoons. Mem. Phila. Art Alliance, Nat. Cartoonists Soc., Am. Assn. Editorial Cartoonists. Republican. Presbyn. Clubs: National Press (Washington); Philadelphia Sketch. Contbr. cartoons to various publs. Home: 42 Rosedale Rd Philadelphia PA 19151

HUTTON, JAMES, univ. prof.; b. Airth, Stirlingshire, Scotland, Nov. 30, 1902; s. John and Elizabeth (Arthur) H.; A.B., Cornell U., 1924, A.M., 1925, Ph.D., 1927; unmarried. Instr. Greek and Latin, Columbia, 1926-27; instr. classics. Cornell U. 1927-29, asst. prof., 1929-38, prof., 1938-61, Kappa Alpha prof., 1961—, chmn. dept., 1946-52; Guggenheim Meml. Foundation fellow, 1958-59. Mem. Com. on Renaissance Studies of Am. Council of Learned Socs., 1944-50. Mem. Am. Philol. Assn., Modern Lang. Assn. of Am., Am. Assn. U. Profs., Phi Beta Kappa, Phi Kappa Phi. Joint editor: Cornell Studies in Classical Philology. Author: The Greek Anthology in Italy, 1935; The Greek Anthology in France and in Latin Writers of The Netherlands, 1946, 2d edit., 1967. Contbr. articles to professional jours. Home: 123 Roberts Pl Ithaca NY 14850 Office: Goldwin Smith Hall Cornell Univ Ithaca NY 14850

HUTTON, JAMES FRANKLIN, food service exec.; b. Harrisburg, Pa., June 10, 1916; s. James N. and Mabel (Bowers) H.; B.A., Temple U., 1946; m. Shirley Roberts, Aug. 17, 1940; 1 dau., Jane. With Slater System, Inc., 1935-61, v.p. operations, 1942-46, exec. v.p., 1946-60, pres., 1960-61, sr. v.p., dir., mem. exec. com. parent co. ARA Services, Inc., 1961-65, exec. v.p., 1965—. Mem. exec. bd. Valley Forge council Boy Scouts Am.; mem. Phila. Crime Commn.; past pres. Cardiovascular Inst. Heart Research, Phila. Trustee Hahnemann Hosp., Harcum Jr. coll. Mem. English-Speaking Union, Nat., Pa. (pres. 1952-53), Phila. (pres. 1950-51) restaurant assns., Newcomen Soc., S.E. Pa. Heart Assn., Pa. Soc., Sigma Pi, Kappa Kappa Psi. Republican. Lutheran. Rotarian. Clubs: Union League, Overbrook Country, Porters Lake (Phila.). Home: 147 E Old Gulph Rd Wynnewood PA 19096 Office: Independence Sq W Philadelphia PA 19106

HUTTON, JAMES MORGAN III investment banker; b. Detroit, Aug. 18, 1927; s. James Morgan. Jr. and Marianne (Wurlitzer) H.; grad. Hill Sch., 1945, Dartmouth, 1950; m. Virginia Palfrey, Dec. 17, 1954; children—Marianne D., Sarah J., James P. Salesman, New Eng. Mut. Life Ins. Co., 1950-51; with W.E. Hutton & Co. N.Y.C., 1951—, partner, 1958-64, mng. partner, 1964-, also dir.; dir. Wurlitzer Co., Saxton Products Co. Served with USNR, 1945-46. Mem. Psi Upsilon. Clubs: Racquet and Tennis (N.Y.C.); Apawamis (Rye); Nantucket (Mass.) Yacht. Home: 101 Apawamis Av Rye NY 10580 Office: W E Hutton & Co 14 Wall St New York City NY 10005

HUTTON, ROBERT FRANKLIN, marine biologist, assn. exec.; b. Red Lion, Pa., July 18, 1921; s. Carl Stiles and Mary C. (Jones) H.; student Gettysburg Coll., summer 1947; B.S. cum laude, U. Miami (Fla.), 1949, M.S., 1951; Ph.D., U. London (Eng.), 1953; m. Wanda Lou Haviland; children—Suzanne Adair, Robert Franklin, Roberta Lou, Marilyn Diane. Research asst. U. Miami, 1949-50, research instr., 1951, asst. prof., 1954; biologist-in-charge, parasitologist Fla. Bd. Conservation Marine Lab., 1955-62; asst. dir., chief marine biologist Mass. Div. Marine Fisheries, 1963-65; exec. sec. Am. Fisheries Soc., Washington, 1965—. Mem. Nat. Conservation Awards Selections Com., 1965—, Atlantic States Marine Fisheries Commn., 1963-67, Gen. Thomas D. White Fish and Wildlife Conservation Award Selection Com., 1967, 68. Fulbright scholar, 1951-52, 52-53. Recipient Mass. Gov. Conservation award, 1965; new larval trematode, Cercaria huttoni, named for him, 1953; new trematode, Neostictodora huttoni, named for him, 1959. Fellow A.A.A.S., Internat. Acad. Fishery Scientists; mem. Am. Fisheries Soc., Natural Resources Council Am. (treas. 1966—), Am. Soc. Parasitologists, Helminthological Soc. Washington, Marine Biol. Assn. U.K. (life), Atlantic Fisheries Biologists, Outdoor Writers Assn. Am., New Eng. Fisheries Inst., Mass. Lobstermen's Assn., Fla. Acad Scis., Wildlife Soc., Sport Fishing Inst., Nat. Wildlife Fedn., Izaak Walton League, Mass. Inst. Biol. Scientists, Atlantic Estuarine Research Biologists, Beta Beta Beta. Contbr. articles to profl. jours. Home: 8105 Revatom Ct Dunn Loring VA 22027 Office: Washington Bldg Washington DC 20005

HUTTON, ROBERT JOHN, savs. and loan assn. exec.; b. Detroit, June 9, 1908; s. James and Nellie (McHugh) H.; A.B., U. Mich., 1929; J.D., Wayne State U., 1934; m. Dorothy E. Pendlebury, July 29, 1944; children—Judith Ann, Susan Beth, William James, Martha Nellie. With Standard Fed. Savs. & Loan Assn., Detroit, 1929—, treas., 1946—, pres., 1962—, also dir.; mem. adv. council Fed. Home Loan Bank Bd., 1964-68. Non-resident lectr. real estate U. Mich., 1956—. Mem. Com. Econ. Devel., Detroit Citizens Com. Equal Opportunity, Mich. Council Financial Advisers, Combined Episcopal Services Appeal Com. Mem. city council and mayor pro- tem, Grosse Pointe Park, Mich., 1965—, mem. City Plan Commn., 1964—. Trustee Greater Mich. Found. Served to lt. comdr. USNR, 1942-46. Recipient Layman of Year award Detroit Council Chs., 1963; Golden Door Knob award Central Bus. Dist. Assn., 1965; Hon. Dean award Am. Savs. and Loan Inst., 1966. Mem. Detroit Real Estate Bd. (dir.), Detroit Mortgage Bankers Assn. (pres. 1952), Mich Savs. and Loan League (pres. 1951, Community Service award 1968), Detroit Econ. Club, Phi Kappa Tau (alumni treas. 1955—). Republican. Episcopalian (sr. warden 1962-64). Mason, Elk. Clubs: Detroit, Detroit Grosse Pointe Yacht. Savoyard. Home: 1033 Devonshire Rd Grosse Pointe Park MI 48230 Office: 1500 N Woodward St Birmingham MI 48012

HUTTON, ROBERT WILLIAM, cement co. exec.; b. Olympia, Wash., Apr. 28, 1921; s. George W. and Elsie (Doragh) H.; B.A., U. Wash., 1943; M.B.A., Stanford, 1948; m. Charlotte Thompson, Feb. 4, 1944; children-Ann Christine, George Thompson. Credit analyst Seattle First Nat. Bank, 1948-51; controller, treas. Gaasland Constrn. Co., 1951-54; gen. mgr. Bellingham Builders Supply Co. (Wash.), 1954-64; with Lone Star Cement Corp., 1964—, sr. v.p., 1969—. Vice pres. Seattle Symphony, 1967-68; commnr. Whatcom County (Wash.) Pub. Utility. Served with AUS, 1943-46; PTO. Decorated Bronze Star. Episcopalian (vestryman 1958-65). Home: North Manursing Island Rye NY 10580 Office: 1 Greenwich Plaza Greenwich CT 06830

HUTTON, SIDNEY BUCHANAN, horticulturist; b. Brookeville, Md., Jan. 26, 1889; s. Ulric and Mary Brooke (Janney) H.; B.S., Earlham Coll., 1908; m. Laura Doan, Sept. 6, 1911 (dec. Jan. 1970); children—Sidney Buchanan, Robert D., Richard J. Drainage engr. U.S. Dept. Agr., 1908-09; dep. county surveyor, Chariton County, Mo., 1909; drainage engr., sec. Morgan Engring. Co., Memphis, 1910-16; accountant War Dept., Washington, 1916-19; devel., cultivation blueberries Jos. J. White, Inc., Whitesbog, N.J., 1919-26; cultivation blueberries, mgr. Blueberry Coop. Assn., New Lisbon, N.J., 1927-30; with Conard-Pyle Co., Star Rose Growers, West Grove, Pa., 1930—, v.p., 1937-51, pres., 1951-64, chmn. bd., 1964—; pres. All-Am. Rose Selections, Inc., 1953-55; dir. Nat. Bank & Trust Co. (Kennett Sq.). Pres., Avon-Grove Community Chest, West Grove, 1946-70, mem. bd. assistance, Chester County, Pa., 1948-56, chmn., 1955-56. Recipient Man of Year award Southeastern Chester County C. of C., 1971; Hall of Fame award Am. Assn. Nurserymen, 1971. Mem. Am. Rose Soc., Nat. Rose Soc. Eng., Royal Hort. Soc. Eng. Home: 147 W State St Kennett Square PA 19348 Office: Conard-Pyle Co West Grove PA 19390

HUTTON, WILLIAM art historian; b. N.Y.C., Oct. 2, 1926; s. George V. D. and Ruth (Shafer) H.; grad. Deerfield Acad., 1944; B.A., Williams Coll., 1950; M.A., Harvard, 1952; m. Marjorie Mary Matimoe, Dec. 29, 1956; children—William, Ruth K., Mary C., Eleanor A. Asst. curator Toledo Mus. Art, 1952-64; dir. Currier Gallery Art, Manchester, N.H. 1965-68. Served with AUS, 1945-46. Mem. Coll. Art Assn., Am. Assn. Museums. Episcopalian. Home: 4 York Av London SW 14 England

HUTZLER, ALBERT DAVID, Jr., merchant; b. Baltimore County, Md., Mar. 1, 1916; s. Albert David and Gretchen (Hochschild) H.; student Friends Sch.; A.B., Johns Hopkins, 1937; m. Bernice Levy, Sept. 22, 1937; children—Elizabeth Ann (Mrs. James P. Friedman), Albert David, III, James Levy. Trainee R.H. Macy & co., N.Y.C., 1937-38; with Hutzler Bros. Co., 1938—, pres., gen. mgr., 1954—; dir. Asso. Merchandising Corp., Central Savs. Bank Balt. Dir., past pres. Com. for Downtown, Inc.; exec. com. Greater Balt. Com., Inc. Bd. dirs. United Fund Central Md., Inc.; bd. dirs. Asso. Jewish Charities, pres., 1967-69; bd. dirs. Jewish Welfare Fund; mem. Gov.'s Com. to Promote Employment of Handicapped; trustee, mem. exec. com. Johns Hopkins; pres. Hutzler Fund, Inc. Mem. Retail Mchts. Assn. Balt. (dir., past pres.), Md. (dir.), Nat. (dir.) retail mchts. assns. Club: Center (gov.). Home: 17 Roland Mews Baltimore MD 21210 Office: Office Hutzler's Baltimore MD 21201

HUTZLER, JOEL GUTMAN DAVID, dept. store exec.; b. Balt., Dec. 23, 1892; s. David and Ella (Gutman) H.; A.B., Johns Hopkins, 1915; m. Carolyn H. Fuld, Oct. 22, 1929; children—Katherine A. (Mrs. Arthur L. Troutner), Betty Rose (Mrs. William Ives), Joel Gutman David, David A. With Hutzler Bros. Co., Balt., 1916—, sr. v.p., 1951-54, vice chmn. bd., 1954-65, chmn. bd., 1965—. Dir. Asso. Jewish Charities, 1931-49, 1st v.p., 1943-45; past dir. YM and YWHA, treas., 1934-36. Bd. dirs. A.R.C., Balt., 1948-53; trustee Commn. on Govtl. Efficiency and Economy, Inc., Balt., 1944-47, Hutzler Fund, Inc., 1944—. Served as ensign USNRF, 1918-19. Mem. Retail Mchts. Assn. Balt. (dir. 1925-46, pres. 1936-38), Howard Street Assn. (past v.p., dir.). Jewish religion. Clubs: Center, Johns Hopkins, Suburban of Baltimore County, (Balt.); Maryland Yacht (Anne Arundel County, Md.). Home: 11 Clovelly Rd Pikesville MD 21208 Office: Hutzler Bros Co 212 N Howard St Baltimore MD 21201

HUXLEY, ANDREW FIELDING, scientist, educator; b. Nov. 22, 1917; s. Leonard and Rosalind (Bruce) H.; student U. Coll. Sch., Westminster Sch.; M.A., Trinity Coll., Cambridge U.; M.D. (hon.), U. of Saar; D.Sc. (hon.), U. of Sheffield, Leicester U.; m. Jocelyn Richenda Gammell Pease, 1947; 1 son, 5 daus. Operational research Anti-Aircraft Command, 1940-42, for Admiralty, 1942-45; fellow Trinity Coll., Cambridge, 1941-60, dir. studies, 1952-60; demonstrator dept. physiology Cambridge U., 1946-50, asst. dir. research, 1951-59, reader exptl. biophysics, 1959-60; Herter lectr. Johns Hopkins, 1959; Jodrell prof. physiology U. Coll., London, 1960-69, Royal Soc. research prof., 1969—; Jesup lectr. Columbia, 1964; Forbes lectr., 1966; Croonian lectr. Royal Soc., 1967; Fullerian prof. Royal Inst., London, 1967—. Co-recipient Nobel prize for medicine, 1963. Hon. Fellow Trinity Coll., Cambridge. Fellow Royal Soc.; fgn. hon. mem. Am. Acad. Arts and Scis. Contbr. papers profl. jours. Address: Manor Field Grantchester Cambridge England

HUXLEY, ELSPETH JOSCELINE (Mrs. Gervas Huxley), author; b. July 23, 1907; d. Major Josceline and Eleanor Lillian (Grosvenor) Grant; student European Sch., Nairobi, Kenya; diploma in agr., Reading U., 1927; student Cornell U., 1927-28; m. Gervas Huxley, 1931; 1 son. Asst. pres officer Empire Marketing Bd., London, 1929-32; mem. gen. adv. council BBC, 1952-59. U.K. independent mem. Monckton Adv. Commn. on Central Africa, 1959; justice of the peace, Wiltshire. Author: White Man's Country, Lord Delamere and the Making of Kenya, vols., 1935; Red Strangers, 1939; (with Margery Perham) Race and Politics in Kenya, 1944; The Walled City, 1948; The Sorcerer's Apprentice, 1948; I Don't Mind If I Do, 1951; Four Guineas, A Thing of Love, 1954; The Red Rock Wilderness, 1957; The Flame Trees of Thika, 1959; A New Earth, 1960; On the Edge of the Rift, 1963; The Incident at the Merry Hippo, 1963; With Forks and Hope, 1964; Back Street New Worlds, 1964; A Man from Nowhere, 1965; Their Shining Eldorado, A Journey through Australia, 1967; Love Among the Daughters, 1968; also author articles, broadcasts on African affairs, short stories, criticism; contbr. Punch. Home: Woodfolds Oaksey nr Malmesbury Wiltshire England Office: care William Morrow & Co 425 Park Av S New York City NY 10022

HUXLEY, SIR JULIAN SORELL, author, biologist; b. Eng., June 22, 1887; s. Leonard Huxley; scholar Eton and Balliol Coll., Oxford U. (Newdigate Prize poetry 1908); m. Marie Juliette Baillot, 1919; 2 sons. Lectr. zoölogy Balliol Coll., 1910-12; research asso. (travelling in Germany), Rice Inst., Houston, 1912-13, asst. prof., 1913-16; fellow, sr. demonstrator zoölogy New Coll., Oxford U., 1919-25; mem. Oxford expdn. to Spitsbergen, 1921; prof. zoölogy King's Coll., London, 1925-27, hon. lectr., 1927-35; Fullerian prof. physiology Royal Inst., Eng., 1926-29; gen. supr. biol. films Gaumont Brit. Instructional, Ltd., 1933-36, Zoöl. Film Prodns., Ltd., 1937-42; sec. Zoöl. Soc. London, adv. editor Zoo mag., 1935-42; Beatty lectr. McGill U., Montreal, 1956. Mem. Commn. Higher Edn. W. Africa, 1944; mem. Com. Nat. Parks U.K., 1945-46; exec. sec. UN Ednl. and Cultural Orgn. Prep. Commn., 1946; dir. gen. UNESCO, 1947-48; v.p. Commn. Sci. and Cultural History Mankind, mem. Jordan expdn., 1963. Recipient Darwin medal Royal Soc., 1956; created knight, 1958. Former officer several profl. assns. Author or editor, some with others, over 40 books 1911—, including: The Individual in the Animal Kingdom, 1911; Religion without Revelation, rev. edit. 1957; Animal Biology (with J.B.S. Haldane), 1927; The Science of Life (with H.G. and G.P. Wells), 1929; The Elements of Experimental Embryology (with G.R. de Beer), 1934; Scientific Research and Social Needs, 1934; If I Were Dictator, 1934; T.H. Huxley's Diary on the Rattlesnake (editor), 1935; The Living Thoughts of Darwin (with J. Fisher), 1939; The Uniqueness of Man, 1941; Evolution, the Modern Synthesis, 2d edit., 1963; Evolutionary Ethics (Romanes lecture Oxford) 1943; Man In the Modern World, 1947; Evolution and Ethics, 1947; Evolution in Action (editor), 1953; The Evolutionary Process (editor), 1953; From an Antique Law rev. edit; 1966; The Kingdom of Beasts (with W. Suschitzky), 1956; Secrets of Life, 1957; Biological Aspects of Cancer, 1957; New Wine in New Bottles (essays), 1957; The Story of Evolution, 1959; The Humanist Frame (editor), 1961; Conservation of Wild Life in Central and East Africa, 1961; Essays of a Humanist, 1964; (with H. B. Kettlewell) Darwin and His World, 1965; Aldous Huxley, 1965; Memories, vol. I, 1970. Biol. editor Ency. Brit., 14th edit.; editorial bd. New Naturalist series, 1944—; editor (with others) Doubleday Pictorial Library of World History. Home: 31 Pond St Hampstead London NW 3 England

HUXTABLE, ADA LOUISE, architecture critic; b. N.Y.C.; d. Michael Louis and Leah (Rosenthal) Landman; A.B. magna cum laude Hunter Coll.; grad. student N.Y.U.; L.H.D., Smith Coll., Skidmore Coll.; D.F.A., Md. Inst.; m. L. Garth Huxtable. Asst. curator architecture and design The Museum of Modern Art, N.Y.C., 1946-50; Fulbright fellowship for advanced study in architecture and design, Italy, 1950, 52; free-lance writer, contbg. editor to Progressive Archtl. Art In American, 1950-63; Guggenheim fellow studies Am. arch., 1958; architecture critic N.Y. Times, N.Y.C., 1963—. Bd. dirs. Municipal Art Soc. N.Y. Recipient Pulitzer prize distinguished criticism, 1970; N.Y. Soc. Architects Strauss Meml. award, 1970; Am. Inst. Interior Designers Elsie de Wolfe award, 1969; Architecture Critics medal N.Y. chpt. A.I.A., 1969; Francis Jewett Mather award art criticism Coll. Art Assn., 1967; Newspaper Women's Club N.Y. Front Page award, 1965. Mem. Am. Soc. Archtl. Historians, Nat. Trust for Historic Preservation, Victorian Soc. Am. Author: Pier Luigi Nervi, 1960; Classic New York, 1964; Will They Ever Finish Bruckner Boulevard?, 1970. Office: NY Times 229 W 43d St New York City NY 10036

HUXTABLE, RICHARD SCOTT, corp. ofcl.; b. Cleve., Sept. 20, 1913; s. Harold Stafford and Mary Frances (Scott) H.; student U. Pa., 1931-33, Gen. Motors Inst., 1934-36; B.S. in Mech. Engring., Cleve. State U., 1940; m. Martha June Mix, Sept. 1, 1950; children—Richard C., Scott C. Asst. to gen. mgr. Cleve. diesel engine div. Gen. Motors Corp., 1934-47; exec. v.p., dir., gen. mgr. Fawick Airflex Co., Inc., 1947-52; pres. Fawick Corp., Cleve., 1952-54; v.p., dir. Fawick Flex-Grip Co., 1948-54; chmn. Cleve. Detroit Corp., 1954—; pres. Ray-Dor Mfg. Co., 1955-63, Ray-Dor Sales Corp., 1957-59, Howes Iron Works, 1957-59, Richfield Hills Corp., 1969—; exec. v.p. Nat. Mgmt., Inc., 1958-64. Mem. Newcomen Soc., Soc. Automotive Engrs., Soc. Naval Engrs., Navy League U.S. (past pres. Cleve. council), Am. Ordanance Assn., Better Bus. Bur. (past dir.), C. of C. (Man of Year award 1948), Sigma Alpha Epsilon. Republican. Mason (32, Shriner). Clubs: Westwood Country; Athletic (Cleve.). Home: Box 335 Richfield OH 44286 Office: 11350 Brookpark Rd Cleveland OH 44130

HUYGENS, REMMERT WILLIAM, architect; b. Haarlem, Holland, Apr. 19, 1932; s. Willem and Antoinette (Bruynzeel) H.; student Gymnazium, Alkmaar, 1951, Amsterdam HTS, Dept. Architecture, 1955. Came to U.S., 1956. With Marcel Breuer, architect, N.Y.C. until 1958; pvt. practice architecture, 1960—; partner Huygens and Tappe, Inc., architects and planners, Boston, 1962—; guest lectr. Brockton (Mass.) Art Center, 1970, 71, prin. works include Longy Concert Hall Library, Cambridge, Mass., Lynn Instn. Savs., Interfaith Religious Center, Columbia, Md., campus N.H. Coll., also residences in U.S., France, Switzerland and Holland. Recipient Progressive Architecture Design award, 1966; citation, 2 hon. mentions A.I.A., 1969, 1st honor award, 1970. Registered architect, Mass. Mem. A.I.A. (guest lectr. Ky. chpt. 1969, chmn. Ky. jury design awards 1969), Boston Soc. Architects, Nat. Council Archl. Registration Bds. Club: Boston Yacht (Marblehead, Mass.). Works published in U.S. and Europe. Home: 125 Old Connecticut Path Wayland MA 01778 Office: 462 Boylston St Boston MA 02116

HUYGHE, RENE LOUIS, historian, art critic; b. Arras, France, May 3, 1906; s. Louis and Marie (Delvoye) H.; M.A., Louvre Sch., Paris, France; 1 dau. by previous marriage, Claire-Helène; m. 2d. Lydie Bouthet, Oct. 9, 1950; 1 son, Francois-Bernard. Mission head Louvre, 1927, asst. curator, 1930-37, chief curator, 1937, now hon. chief curator paintings and drawings; prof., chmn., psychology plastic art dept. Coll. de France, 1951; prof. in residence Nat. Gallery, Washington, 1967-68; editor mag. Amour de l'Art, 1930—, Quadrige, 1945; organizer art expositions, confs., art films. Vice pres. Council Museums France; hon. chmn. Amis des Arts; pres., founder Internat. Assn. Art Films; pres. Amis du Musée pedagogique; v.p. Amis de Delacroix. Decorated comdr. Legion of Honor; comdr. Order Leopold; knight of Danebrog; Knight of Isabel the Catholic; Prix europeen Erasme La Haye, 1966. Mem. French Acad. Author: Histoire de L'Art Contemporain; Cezanne; Vermeer; Watteau; Gauguin; Van Gogh; Dialogue avec le visible; L'art et l'homme; L'art et l'Ame; Delacroix; Les puissances de l'Image.; Sens et destin de l'art; L'art at le monde moderne; Formes et Forces. Address: 3 rue Corneille Paris VI France

HUYLER, COULTER DUNHAM, Jr., former fgn. service officer; b. N.Y.C., Oct. 9, 1911; s. Coulter Dunham and Margaret (Porter) H.; grad. Kent (Conn.) Sch., 1930; B.A. magna cum laude, Princeton, 1934; m. Lola Anne McFadin, Sept. 7, 1946 (dec. Mar. 1957); children—Coulter Dunham, III, Anne, Margaret (dec.); m. 2d, Sarah Colquitt, Mar. 23, 1963. With J. Walter Thompson Advt. Co., N.Y.C.,

1934-41; joined Dept. of State, 1946, dir. USIS, The Netherlands, 1946-51, policy coordinator Office of Asst. Sec. State for Pub. Affairs, 1951-54, assigned information div. NATO Internat. Staff. 1954-56, U.S. Delegation to UN, N.Y.C., 1957-64; became dep. U.S. permanent rep. UNESCO, 1964. Observer 1st session All-India Nat. Congress. Trustee family enterprises, Served from pvt. to maj., Intelligence Overseas Service, U.S. Army, 1941-46. Decorated Bronze Star Medal (U.S.); 8th Army medal (Gt. Britain). Hon. mem. Minerva Societeit. Clubs: Cap and Gown (Princeton); University (N.Y.C.); Royal Bombay Yacht (Bombay, India); American Businessmen's (Paris, France); Round Hill (Greenwich, (Conn.). Home: Round Hill Greenwich CT 06830

HUYOT, ROBERT HENRY, hotel exec.; b. Eaubonne, France, Nov. 11, 1908; s. Jules and Marie (Petit) H.; A.B., U. Paris, 1926; LL.B., Paris Law Sch., 1935; postgrad. Paris Hotel Sch., 1928, Columbia, 1943, 48, N.Y. Sch. of Interior Design, 1957-58; m. Antje Schwecke, May 12, 1969; children—Marilise, Suzanne, Nicole, Giselle. Came to United States in 1936, naturalized, 1942. Student, cook, asst. mgr. Hotel Crillon Paris, 1928; asst. to mgr., grill room mgr. Queens Hotel, Cardiff, Wales, 1929; exec. asst. Hotel Esplanade, Berlin, 1930- 32; asst. to gen. mgr. Hotel Crillon, 1933-35; asst. mgr. Waldorf- Astoria, N.Y.C., 1936-40, mgr. Waldorf-Astoria Towers, 1940-43; resident mgr. Hotel Windsor, Montreal, 1944; pres., gen. mgr. Hotel Carlyle, N.Y.C., 1945-61; pres. Westchester Mgmt. Corp., Washington, 1950-58; v.p., gen. mgr., Summit Hotel, N.Y.C., 1961-62; pres., chief operating officer Inter-Continental Hotels Corp., N.Y.C., 1962-71, chmn. bd., 1971—; pres. Midtown Motor Inn, New Haven, 1962-65. Chmn. Nat. Culinary Exhbn., 1949-52; gen. chmn. Nat. Hotel Expn., 1953; past chmn. bd. N.Y.C. Hotel Assn.-Hotel Trades Council Health Center. Trustee, N.Y.C. Community Coll., 1955-63. Decorated Chevalier of Legion of Hon. (France), gold medal Sociéte é Culinaire Philanthropique. Recipient Hospitality Hall of Fame award, 1968; Silver medal City of Paris, 1970. Mem. Columbia Soc. Real Estate Appraisers, Am. (past chmn. residential hotels com.), N.Y.C. (chmn. legislative com.; pres. 1954-55) hotel assns., Art Students League, Am. Hotel-Motel Assn. (trustee Ednl. Inst. 1968—), Hotel Execs. Club (past pres.). Clubs: Gipsy Trail, Chevaliers du Tastevin (grand officier), Amis d'Escoffier, Lucullus Circle, Tipiere d'Or, Chaine Des Rotisseurs, Conseil Magistral. Home: 5 Meadow Dr Greenwich CT 06830 Office: 200 Park Av New York City NY 10017

HYAMS, JEROME SEYMOUR, motion picture and television exec.; b. N.Y.C., July 19, 1915; s. Saul and Mildred (Goldstein) H.; grad. N.Y.U., 1936; m. Sally Feldman, Feb. 17, 1936; children—Stephanie (Mrs. Stephen Geller), Gail, Nancy. Salesman, Guaranteed Pictures Co., Inc., N.Y.C., 1937-42; with OSS, Washington, 1942-46; v.p. charge sales Commonwealth Pictures Corp., N.Y.C., 1946-49; pres. Commonwealth Film & TV Corp., N.Y.C., 1949-52; founder Hygo TV Films, Inc., N.Y.C., 1952, pres., 1952-57; dir. syndication sales Screen Gems, Inc., N.Y.C., 1957-58, v.p. charge syndication, 1958-59, exec. v.p., gen. mgr., 1959-67, pres., 1967-69; dir. Columbia Pictures Corp., N.Y.C., 1962—; sr. exec. v.p. Columbia Pictures Industries, Inc., 1969—; dir. Prudential Bldg. Maintenance Co. Div. chmn. United Jewish Appeal Greater N.Y., 1964. Home: 5 Pond Park Rd Great Neck NY 11024 Office: 711 Fifth Av New York City NY 10022

HYAMS, JOE, writer; b. Cambridge, Mass., June 6, 1923; s. Joseph Irving and Charlotte (Strauss) H.; B.S., N.Y. U., 1948, M.A., 1949; m. Elke Sommer, Nov. 18, 1964. Editor, Reporter Publs., 1947-50; columnist N.Y. Herald Tribune, 1950-64. Mem. Author's Guild, Am. Newspaper Guild. Club: Overseas Press (N.Y.C.). Author: (with Walter Wagner) My Life With Cleopatra, 1963; (with Maj. Riddle) A Weekend Gamblers Handbook, 1963; (with Edith Head) How to Dress for Success, 1966; (with Peter Sellers) Seller's Market, 1964; Bogie, 1966; A Field of Buttercups, 1968; (with Thomas Murton) Accomplices to the Crime, 1969. Club: Savile (London). Address: 540 N Beverly Glen Blvd West Los Angeles CA 90024

HYATT, ABRAHAM, aero. engr.; b. Ukraine, July 15, 1910; s. Moshe and Raisie (Yablonsky) H.; B.S., Ga. Inst. Tech., 1933; student Washington U., 1940-42; m. Grace Holladay, Apr. 9, 1938; children—Linda (Mrs. Louis L. Lauve). Sherry V. Came to U.S., 1921, naturalized, 1927. Topographic engr. U.S. Geodetic Survey, 1935-36; engr. G.L. Martin Co., 1936-39; chief structural engr. McDonnell Aircraft Corp., 1939-44; head design research br. Bur. Aero., Navy Dept., 1946-48, asst. dir. research div., 1948-54, dir. research div., 1954-56, chief sci. and research analysis officer, 1956-58; asst. dir. for propulsion NASA, 1959-60; dep. dir. launch vehicle programs NASA, 1960, dir. plans and program evaluation, 1960-64; Hunsaker prof. aeros. and astronautics Mass. Inst. Tech., 1964-65; former exec. dir. corporate planning N. Am. Aviation, Inc., from 1965; cons. missile and space tech. Inst. Def. Analysis, Douglas Aircraft Co., IBM Corp., Adv. Panel Aerodynamics Dept. Def., 1956-60; mem. NACA com. on aerodynamics. 1957-58. spl. com. on space tech., 1958; mem. President's sci. adv. com. on high altitude detection, 1959—. Served to capt. USMRC, 1944-46; col. Res. Recipient award of merit Navy League, 1954, distinguished civilian service award U.S. Navy, 1955; decorated Commendation ribbon and metal pendant U.S. Navy. Fellow Am. Inst. Aeros. and Astronautics. Mem. B'nai B'rith. Home: 10301 Norton Rd Potomac MD 20854

HYATT, DAVID, assn. exec.; b. Cleve., May 1, 1916; s. Harry Cleve and Rose (Miller) H.; B.S., Northwestern U., 1939; Ed.D., Columbia, 1959; m. Lenore Wade, Dec. 12, 1944 (dec.); children—Caroline Wade, Ann Rose, Ellen Cleve; m. 2d, Lillian Laura Reiss, 1971. Performer on CBS, NBC Radio and TV, in Broadway play The French Touch, 1945-46; supr. English, Lenox Sch., N.Y.C., 1946-47; instr., dir. debate Manhattan Coll., 1947-48; asst. prof., dir. pub. relations Cornell U. Indsl. and Labor Relations Sch., 1948-50; mgr. pub. relations Hartford Accident & Indemnity Co., 1950-51; dir. pub. relations Inst. Internat. Edn., N.Y.C., 1951-52; mem. sales promotion staff Merrill, Lynch, Pierce, Fenner & Beane, N.Y.C., 1952-54; dir. pub. relations Nat. Conf. Christians and Jews, N.Y.C., 1954-59, v.p. pub. information, 1959-63, exec. v.p., 1965—; press attache Am. embassy, Pakistan, 1963-65. Mem. U.S. Commn. for UNESCO, 1967—, chmn. pub. liaison and information com., 1968—; mem. Pub. Policy Council, 1969—. Vice pres., trustee Cath. Interracial Council N.Y.C. Served with Brit. Army, 1941-43; to lt. USNR, 1943-45. Decorated Africa Star. Author: Introduction to Public Relations, 1950; Public Relations-A Handbook for Business, Labor and Community Leaders, 1963. Contbr. articles to profl. jours. Home: 6 Sunset Dr Scarsdale NY 10583 Office: 43 W 57th St New York City NY 10019

HYATT, DONALD BISHOP, TV and film producer-dir.; b. New Britain, Conn., Apr. 22, 1924; s. Isaac Robert and Emily (Cone) H.; grad. Taft Sch., 1943; B.A. summa cum laude, Dartmouth, 1950; m. Jeanne Hartnett, Mar. 14, 1959; children—Wendy, Christopher Robert. Dir. Plymouth (N.H.) Slopes Ski Sch. 1946-48; instr. skiing Dartmouth, 1946-50; dir. spl. projects NBC-TV, 1958—; exec. producer spl. projects programs including Wisdom series, 1958—, World of . . . series, 1961—; producer, dir. Project 20 programs, 1958—; producer dir., writer ski film Hanover Hickory, 1950. Pres., Linden Shore Dist., Branford, Conn. Recipient 94 nat. and internat. awards for Projects 20 and spl. projects programs. Served to 2d lt. USAAF, 1943-45. Mem. Nat. Acad. TV Arts and Scis. (bd. govs.), Dirs. Guild Am. Conglist. Clubs: Dutch Treat (N.Y.C.); Pine Orchard Yacht and Country (commodore). Author: (with Richard Hanser) Meet Mr. Lincoln, 1960; The Coming of Christ, 1963; The Law and The Prophets, 1971. Home: Linden Av Indian Neck Branford CT 06405 Office: NBC 30 Rockefeller Plaza New York City NY 10020

HYATT, JAMES PHILIP, educator, clergyman; b. Monticello, Ark., Feb. 16, 1909; s. Robert Lee and Mamie (Stanley) H.; A.B., Baylor U., 1929, LL.D., 1969; A.M., Brown U., 1930; B.D., Yale, 1933, Ph.D., 1938; postgrad. Am. Sch. of Oriental Research, Jerusalem (Two Brothers fellow of Yale), 1931-32, U. Marburg (Germany), summer 1932; D.D. (hon.), Christian Theol. Sem., 1967; L.H.D., Tex. Christian U., 1969; m. Elizabeth Bard, Sept. 12, 1932; children—James Lee, (dec.), Charles Sidney, David Philip. Ordained to ministry Bapt. Ch., 1929; pastor Hull Meml. Bapt. Ch., Cheshire, Conn., 1932-35; instr. Bibl. history Wellesley Coll., 1935-38, asst. prof., 1938-41; asso. prof. O.T., Vanderbilt U., Nashville, 1941-44, prof., 1944—, chmn. grad. dept. religion, 1944-64, acting dean Div. Sch., 1956-57, Harvie Branscomb Distinguished prof., 1969-70. Vis. prof. U. Chgo., winter 1944, Garrett Bibl. Inst., summer 1945, Union Theol. Sem., N.Y.C., summer 1950, Iliff Sch. Theology, summer 1958, Perkins Sch. Theology, summer 1961. Ford faculty fellow Hebrew Union Coll. 1952; mem. O.T. sect. Standard Bible Com. Fellow Soc. for Religion in Higher Edn.; mem. Am. Oriental Soc. (v.p. Middle West br. 1943-44), Am. Acad. Religion (v.p. 1941), Soc. Bibl. Lit. (pres. So. sect. 1949-50, pres. 1956), Brit. Soc. for O.T. Study (asso.), Phi Beta Kappa. Democrat. Mem. Disciples of Christ (minister 1946—). Author: Prophetic Religion, 1947; Introduction and Exegesis of Jeremiah, Interpreter's Bible, vol. V, 1956; Jeremiah: Prophet of Courage and Hope, 1958; The Heritage of Biblical Faith, 1964; Commentary on Exodus, 1971. Archeol. editor Jour. Bible and Religion, 1939-48; editor Jour. Bibl. Lit., 1948-49; The Bible in Modern Scholarship, 1965. Contbr. numerous articles to profl. jours. Home: 3614 Saratoga Dr Nashville TN 37205 ☆

HYATT, JOHN KENNETH, engr., brewery exec.; b. Bklyn., May 17, 1900; s. Thaddeus P. and Elizabeth (Mast) H.; B.S. in Engring., U.S. Naval Acad., 1924; J.D., Harvard, 1933; m. Elizabeth Dowdall, Aug. 25, 1928; children—John Kenneth, Elizabeth (Mrs. William J. O'Herin), Clifton M. Exec. asst. to v.p., mng. dir. Center Theatre, Rockefeller Center, Inc., N.Y.C., 1933- 41; asst. gen. mgr. Todd & Brown, Inc., Kingsbury Ordnance Plant (Ind.), 1941-43; chief engr., v.p. engring. Anheuser-Busch Inc., St. Louis, 1948—, ret. Chmn., St. Louis City Plan Commission, also St. Louis Air Pollution Control Board. Commissioned ensign, U.S. Navy, 1924, advanced through grades to lt., 1930; staff Office Sec. Navy, Under-Sec. Navy. also combat action U.S.S. Bennington, World War II; capt. Naval Adv. Council, comdt. 9th Naval Dist., also dir., Naval Res. Officers Sch., St. Louis. Mem. Navy League (past pres.), St. Louis, Mo. assns. commerce, Soc. Naval Architects and Marine Engrs. Home: 1 Lenox Pl St Louis MO 63108

HYATT, PAUL WINNIFORD, former judge; b. Coquille, Ore., June 26, 1901; s. Calvin Arthur and Mary (Winniford) H.; LL.B., U. Ida., 1927; m. Millie Margaret McCollum, Dec. 22, 1928; children—Rose Marie, Jerome, John Roderick. Admitted to Ida. bar, 1928; practiced in Orofino, Ida., 1928-34, Lewiston, Ida., 1934-47; pros. atty. Clearwater County, Ida., 1928- commr. Ida. State Bar, 1941-44, pres., 1943-44; justice Ida. Supreme Ct., 1947-49; pvt. practice law, Lewiston, 1949- 61; dist. judge 10th Jud. Dist. Ida., Grangeville, 1961-66, Lewiston, 1966-70. Mem. Am. Judicature Soc., Ida. State Bar, Am. Bar Assn., Phi Alpha Delta. Mason, Elk, Eagle, K.P. Home: 717 3d St Lewiston ID 83501

HYDE, BEAL BAKER, educator; b. Dallas, June 26, 1923; s. Mark Powell and Alice (Baker) H.; student Amherst Coll., 1941-43; A.B. cum laude, Harvard, 1948, Ph.D., 1952; m. Margaret Lynn Powe, Aug. 20, 1947; children-Margaret Lynn, Thomas Beal, Alice Robbins. Prof., chmn. dept. botany U. Vt., Burlington, 1965—. Trustee Cottonwood Gulch Fouund.; mem. corp. Marine Biol. Lab., Woods Hole. Served to 1st lt. USAAF, 1941-43. Mem. Am. Soc. Cell Biology, Bot. Soc. Am., Genetics Soc. Am., Am. Inst. Biol. Scis., A.A.A.S., Sigma Xi. Unitarian (pres. bd. trustees). Contbr. articles profl. jours. Home: 334 S Union St Burlington VT 05401

HYDE, DAYTON OGDEN, author; b. Marquette, Mich., Mar. 25, 1925; s. Frederick Walton and Rhoda (Williams) H.; B.A., U. Cal. at Berkeley, 1950; m. Gerda Isenberg, Sept. 23, 1950; children—Dayton, Virginia, Marsha, John, Taylor. Owner 6000- acre cattle ranch So. Ore., 1959—; lectr., conservationist, 1960, also radio and TV guest; articles and photographs appeared in nat. mags. and jours.; producer, star 1st Am. rodeos in So. Europe. Bd. dirs. Ore Wildlife Fedn., Internat. Wild Waterfowl Assn. Author: Sandy, 1968; Yamsi, 1971; Cranes in My Corral, 1971. Home: 1410 Pacific Terrace Klamath Falls OR 97601 Office: Yamsi Ranch Chiloquin OR 97624

HYDE, EDWIN, dept. store exec.; b. Charleston, S.C., June 15, 1905; s. Tristram Tupper and Minnie (Black) H.; student Furman U., Greenville, S.C., 192324; m. Camilla Price Alsop, Dec. 4, 1930; 1 dau., Camilla (Mrs. Carlton P. Moffatt, Jr.). Vice pres. The Bank of Va., Richmond, 1931-44; exec. v.p. Peoples Nat. Bank, Charlotteville, Va., 1944-46; v.p. Miller & Rhoads, Richmond, 1946-47, exec. v.p., 1947-53, pres., dir., 1953-68, chmn. dir. 1968—; vice chmn., chmn. finance com. Garfinckel, Brooks Bros., Miller & Rhoads, Inc., Washington, 1967—; pres. Sixth St. Enterprises; dir., mem. exec. com. Va. Indsl. Devel. Corp; dir. Central Va. Ednl. TV Corp., Shenandoah Life Ins. Co., United Va. Bank/State-Planters, Frederick Atkins, Inc. Mem. Adv. Council on the Va. Economy, Va. Industrialization Group, Citizens Adv. Com. of Community Improvement, merchants council N.Y. U., Adv. Council of Naval Affairs, Nat. Citizens Com. for Community Relations; corp. patron Va. Mus. Fine Arts; dir. United Givers Fund, Central Richmond Assn. Trustee, pres. Miller & Rhoads Found.; trustee Richmond Meml. Hosp., Richmond Forward, Am. Enterprise Inst. Pub. Policy Research; trustee, mem. finance com. retirement system A.R.C.; chmn. bd. dirs. Va. Found. for Independent Colls. Mem. Richmond C. of C. (mem. civic progress com.), Soc. Colonial Wars in Va., Sons of the Revolution, St. Cecelia Soc., Newcomen Soc. Episcopalian. Clubs: Commonwealth, Country of Virginia German (Richmond). Home: 209 Lock Lane Richmond VA 23226 Office: 517 E Broad St Richmond VA 23217

HYDE, FRANK TAYLOR, banker; b. Charleston, S.C., Dec. 15, 1914; s. Tristam Tupper and Mable (Taylor) H.; B.S., Hampden-Sydney Coll., 1938; postgrad. Stonier Grad. Sch. Banking, Rutgers U., 1953, U. Va., 1961; m. Katherine Allen Lorraine, Sept. 28, 1940; children—Janet Lorraine, Terry Taylor (Mrs. John K. Van Brunt, Jr.), Frank Taylor, William Bradford. Exec. v.p., chief credit officer, chmn. Richmond bd. Bank of Va.; dir. Automated Computer Systems, Gen. Med. Corp. Chmn. indsl. div. United Givers Fund, 1969-70; treas. Va. League for Planned Parenthood, 1964-65. Bd. dirs. Blue Cross-Blue Shield of Va.; chmn. found. com. St. Christophers Sch. Served to lt. comdr. USNR, 1941-45; PTO. Mem. Robert Morris Assos., S.A.R., Soc. Colonial Wars, Chi Phi, Omicron Delta Kappa. Presbyn. (elder). Clubs: Country of Va., Commonwealth (Richmond). Home: 113 Tempsford Lane Richmond VA 23226 Office: 800 E Main St Richmond VA 23219

HYDE, FRITZ CARLETON, Jr., metal products mfg. exec.; b. Greenwich, Conn., Oct 11, 1911; s. Fritz C. and Harriet (Baker) H.; B.A., Yale, 1929-33; m. Betty Clark Cornwall, Aug. 17, 1935; children—Fritz Carleton III, Andrew C., Lawrence D. Mgr. profl. summer stock, 1933; credit dept. Chase Nat. Bank, N.Y.C., 1933-34; credit mgr. Revere Copper & Brass, Inc., N.Y.C., 1935-37, salesman, 1937-40, asst. sales mgr., 1940-43, sales mgr., 1943-47, 55-57, mgr. N.Y. dist., 1957-59, asst. gen. sales mgr., 1959-61, v.p., gen. sales mgr., 1961-65, dir., 1961—, pres., 1965—; v.p. charge West Coast operations Goebel Brewing Co., Oakland, Cal., 1947-55. Chmn., Detroit Community Chest, March of Dimes, Oakland. Clubs: Burlingame (Cal.) Country; Detroit Athletic; Greenwich (Conn.), Country. Home: Midwood Rd Deer Park Greenwich CT 06830 Office: 605 3d Av New York City NY 10016

HYDE, GEORGE OSMOND, former govt. ofcl.; b. Downey, Ida., Dec. 17, 1898; s. George Tilton and Emma (Nibley) H.; spl. student Brigham Young U., 1920; J.D., George Washington U., 1926; m. Lona Stratford, July 8, 1924; childrenMarian S. (Mrs. Garn Anderson Brady), Lona Mae S. (Mrs. Vaughn Kent Lauritzen), Joanne S.(Mrs. Kenneth Latimer Kuttler), Edna Lou S. (Mrs. Donald Charles Harper-Smith), George Osmond, Adele S. Missionary, Ch. Jesus Christ Latter-day Saints, Gt. Britain, 1921-23; elevator condr. Ho. of Reps. Bldg., Washington, 1923; admitted to D.C. bar, 1926, Ida. Supreme Ct., U.S. Supreme Ct.; law clk., atty. Office Alien Property Custodian, Washington, 1923-29, atty., 1929-33; sr. atty., prin. atty. Solicitor's Office, U.S. Dept. Agr. Washington, 1934-44; spl. asst. to U.S. atty. gen., trial atty. war frauds sect., criminal div. Dept. Justice, 1944-47; assoc. prosecutor for U.S., mem. internat. prosecutors sect. SCAP maj. Japanese war criminals in Tokyo, Japan, 1945-46; chief counsel spl. com. to investigate food shortages Ho. of Reps., 1945; cons. market adminstr. N.Y. Met. Milk Marketing Area, 1947-53; hearing examiner U.S. Dept. Agr., 1953-56, chief hearing examiner, 1956-68. Served with Q.M.C., U.S. Army, 1918-19; AEF France. Home: 3944 Baltimore St Kensington MD 20795

HYDE, HAROLD ELDRED, coll. pres.; b. Hartwick, N.Y., July 22, 1911; s. Howard C. and Bertha (Eldred) H.; B.S. summa cum laude, Hartwick Coll., 1933; M.S., N.Y. State Coll. for Tchrs., 1939; Ed. D., N.Y. U., 1950; m. Mary Rita Oliver, Apr. 10, 1941; 1 dau., Mary Anne. Vice prin. Spencer (N.Y.) Central Sch., 1934-37; comml. tchr. Nyack (N.Y.) High Sch., 1937-39; asst. prin., guidance dir. Vestal (N.Y.) High Sch., 1939-44; dir. guidance and adult edn., Endicott, N.Y., 1944-48; chief div. ednl. research N.H. Dept. Edn., 1948-51; pres. Plymouth (N.H.) State Coll., 1951—. Mem. N.H. Coordinating Bd. Advanced Edn. and Accreditation. Trustee U. N.H., Sceva Speare Hosp., Plymouth. Mem. N.H. Ednl. Broadcasting Council (past pres.), New Eng. Tchr. Preparation Assn. (pres. 1953-54), N.H. Council Tchr. Edn., Am. Assn. State Colls. and Univs. (dir.), New Eng. Assn. Colls. and Secondary Schs. (commn. instns. higher edn.), Am. Assn. Colls. for Tchr. Edn. (state liaison officer), Kappa Delta Pi. Mason, Rotarian. Home: 10 School St Plymouth NH 03264

HYDE, HENRY VAN ZILE, assn. physician; b. Syracuse, N.Y., Mar. 3, 1906; s. Henry Neal and Madeleine (Van Zile) H.; grad. Deerfield Acad., 1925; B.A., Yale, 1929; M.D., Johns Hopkins, 1933; diploma Trudeau Sch. Tb, 1938; m. Ellen Sedgwick Tracy, June 24, 1933; children—Henry, Susan Sedgwick, Thomas Prentice. Pvt. practice internal medicine, Syracuse, 1936-41; dir. bur. pneumonia control N.Y. State Dept. Health, 1941; commd. sr. surgeon USPHS(R), 1941, med. dir. USPHS, 1950; regional med. officer Office Civilian Def., 1941-43, chief field casualty sect., med. div., 1943-44; dir. med. div. Middle East Supply Center, Cairo, Egypt, 1944-45; chief health div. UNRRA Balkan Mission, 1945, chief Middle East office UNRRA, 1945; asst. chief health services br., div. internat. labor, social and health affairs Dept. State, 1945-48, dir. div. health and sanitation Inst. Inter-Am. affairs, 1950-52, dir. health and sanitation staff Tech. Coop. Adminstrn., 1952-53; asst. chief div. internat. health USPHS, 1948-49, chief, 1953-58, asst. to surg. gen. for internat. health, 1958-62; dir. div. internat. med. edn. Assn. Am. Med. Colls., Evanston, Ill., 1962—. U.S. rep., exec. bd. WHO, 1948-52, 53-56, 57-59, chmn., 1954-55, v.p. U.S. citizens com.; bd. dirs. Nat. Health Council; tech. bd. Milbank Meml. Fund; vis. lectr. internat. health Sch. Pub. Health, Harvard, 1950-54, Johns Hopkins Sch. Pub. Health and Hygiene, 1950—; C.E.A. Winslow lectr. Yale, 1955; mem. USPHS Mission to USSR, 1957; U.S. del. 1st-14th, 20th World Health assemblies, 1948-61. Diplomate Am. Bd. Internal Medicine, Am. Bd. Preventive Medicine. Fellow Am. Pub. Health Assn.; mem. A.M.A., Am. Social Hygiene Assn., Soc. Internat. Devel., Assn. Am. Med. Colls., Am. Nat. Com. for Health Edn. Pub. (pres.), Phi Beta Kappa, Alpha Omega Alpha. Club: Cosmos (Washington). Contbr. numerous med. articles to profl. jours. Home: 5920 Bradley Blvd Bethesda MD 20014 Office: 1 Du Pont Circle NW Washington DC 20036

HYDE, HOWARD LINTON, lawyer, business exec.; b. Chillicothe, O., Dec. 15, 1900; s. Wilby G. and Helen (Frizell) H.; A.B., Ohio State U., 1922; LL.B., Harvard Law Sch., 1925; m. Katharine P. Litchfield, Oct. 1, 1927; children—Alan, Paul. Admitted to Ohio bar, 1925; asso., then partner Thompson, Hine & Flory, Cleve., 1925; v.p., gen. counsel Goodyear Tire and Rubber Co., Akron, O., and subsidiaries, 1939-60, exec. v.p. financial and legal affairs, 1960-64, vice chmn. bd., 1964-66. Vice chmn. Ohio Arts Council; trustee Cleve. Council World Affairs; overseer's vis. com. Harvard Law Sch., also asso. gen. counsel. Mem. Internat., Am., Ohio State, Cleve. bar assns., Phi Beta Kappa, Beta Theta Pi. Episcopalian. Clubs: University (N.Y.C.); Union, Kirtland Country, Tavern (Cleve.); Rolling Rock (Ligonier, Pa.); Mill Reef (Antigua); Wianno (Mass.). Home: 12411 Fairhill Rd Cleveland OH 44120 also 7421 Markell Rd Waitehill Willoughby OH 44094 Office: Nat City Bank Bldg Cleveland OH 44114

HYDE, JAMES NEVINS, lawyer; b. Chgo., Jan. 11, 1909; s. Charles Cheney and Mary (Tilton) H.; A.B., Yale, 1931; postgrad. Trinity Coll., Cambridge (Eng.) U., 1931-32; LL.B., Columbia, 1935; m. Margaret Wells, Nov. 30, 1935; children—Mary (Mrs. James H. Ottaway, Jr.), Margaret (Mrs. H. Denman Scott), James, Elizabeth, Andrea. Admitted to N.Y. bar, 1935; asso. firm Miller, Owen, Otis & Bailly, N.Y.C., 1935-40; appellate practice with Nathan L. Miller, 1940-42; asst. to gen. counsel U.S. Steel Corp., 1942, with law dept., 1946-48; adviser, interim com. affairs U.S. Mission to UN, 1948-53, adviser Security Council and Gen. Affairs, 1949, dep. U.S. rep. interim com. Gen. Assembly, 1951, adviser U.S. delegation 4th, 5th, 6th, 7th sessions Gen. Assembly; partner Gross & Hyde, N.Y.C., 1953-54, Hyde & de Vries, 1954-59; cons. internat. matters, 1959—. Lectr. internat. law; law faculty Salzburg Seminar in Am. Studies, 1966. Chmn. com. peaceful settlement disputes White House Conf. Internat. Cooperation, 1965; mem. curatorium Hague Acad. Internat. Law. Served from lt. (j.g.) to lt. comdr. USNR, World War II; PTO. Mem. Am. Soc. Internat. Law (pres. 1963-64, hon. v.p.), Council Fgn. Relations, Internat. Law Assn., Assn. Bar City N.Y. (chmn. fgn. law com. 1956-59). Contbr. articles to profl. jours. Bd. editors Am. Jour. Internat. Law, 1958—. Home: 200 E 66th St New York City NY 10021 Office: 30 Rockefeller Plaza New York City NY 10020

HYDE, JOSEPH REEVES, Jr., super market exec.; b. Memphis, Feb. 6, 1911; s. Joseph Reeves and Ruth (Sherman) H.; student Southwestern at Memphis U.; m. Susan Hightower, Nov. 14, 1933; children—Susan Hyde Boone, Joseph Reeves III. With Craddock &

Hyde Ins. Co., 1938; with Melone & Hyde, Inc., Memphis, 1938-70, pres., 1948-68, chmn. bd., 1968-70; pres. M & H Farms, Inc., 1961-70; now with DMC Food Stores; dir. First Nat. Bank, Memphis, Lincoln-Am. Life Ins. Co., Memphis. Bd. dirs. Memphis Univ. Sch. Republican. Presbyn. Clubs: Ocean (Delray Beach, Fla.); N.Y. Athletic (N.Y.C.); Memphis Country, University (Memphis); Belle Meade Country (Nashville). Home: 5455 Glenwild Rd Memphis TN 38117 Office: 1700 Dunn Av Memphis TN 38104

HYDE, LAURIN EBER, mgmt. cons.; b. Almont, N.D., Jan. 8, 1908; s. Eber Watson and Ida Augusta (Lebert) H.; A.B. magna cum laude, Fletcher Coll., 1930; M.A., U. Chgo., 1935; m. Marian Ward, 1939 (div. 1951); 1 son, Phillip Ward; m. 2d, Virginia Gabriel Parrott, Feb. 1955. Sr. social worker, supr. div. for Minors, Service Bur. for Men, Chgo., 1931-34; field instr., family casework and juvenile delinquency U. Chgo., 1934-36; asst. tech. adviser Social Security Bd., 1936-37, asso. tech. adviser, 1937-40, asst. regional pub. assistance rep., Denver, 1940-43, asst. chief field service sect. Bur. Pub. Assistance, Washington, 1943, regional pub. assistance rep.; Cleve. 1944-50; asso. prof. pub. social services and adminstrn. Columbia Univ. School Social Work, 1950-53; gen. dir. Nat. Travelers Aid Assn., 1953-58; pres. Laurin Hyde Assos., 1958—; lectr. social work adminstrn., Rutgers, 1958-59. Comdr. social work institutes Cornell U., 1947-48, 50, Western Res. U., summers 1950-51, Family Service Assn. Am., 1951, Columbia summers, 1963-65, Boston U., summer 1964; mem. bd. U.S. Civil Serv. Examiners, Cleve., 1947; examiner R.I. Civil Service Commn., 1951; cons. N.Y. State Civil Service Commn., 1951-52. Bd. govs. USO, 1953-58. Mem. Am. Assn. Social Workers (chmn. pub. welfare com., chmn. N.Y.C. chpt. 1952-53, nat. bd. 1950, treas. 1953-54), Nat. Social Welfare Assembly (dir. exec. com.), Am. Immigration Conf. (dir.), Am. Council Vol. Agencies for Fgn. Service (bd.), United Community Funds and Councils Am. (council planning execs., nat. budget com.), Am. Assn. Schs. Social Work (co-chmn. program. com.), Nat. Conf. Social Welfare (exec. com. 1955-57, nominating com. 1964-66) Council on Social Work Edn. (chmn. teaching materials in adminstrn.), Nat. Assn. Social Workers (v.p., nominating com. N.Y. chpt., steering com. council adminstrn., commn. on recruitment for profession), Am. Pub. Welfare Assn., Am. Soc. Pub. Adminstrn., Soc. Profl. Mgmt. Consultants (v.p., chmn. com. ethics; chmn. edn. com.), Inst. Mgmt. Consultants (founder, mem. nat. bd.), Nat. Commn. Social Work Careers, Internat. Conf. Social Work (U.S. del. 1961, 70), Am. Pub. Health Assn., Community Devel. Found., Pub. Health Assn. N.Y.C., Nat. Council on Aging. Nat. Council on Crime and Delinquency, N.Y. Citizens Union. Home: 50 Morningside Dr New York City NY 10025

HYDE, LAWRENCE HENRY, Jr., mfg. co. exec.; b. Cambridge, Mass., July 10, 1924; s. Lawrence Henry and Catherine I. (McMahon) H.; A.B., Harvard, 1946, M.B.A., 1947; m. Lois A. Crehan, May 31, 1947; children—Abigail Ellen, Lawrence Henry III. With Ford Motor Co., 1947-62, dir. internat. purchasing office, 1960-62; v.p., gen. mgr. consumer products div. Philco Corp., div. Ford Motor Co., 1962-64; dir. internat. operations Harris-Intertype Corp., 1965-69, group v.p. internat., 1969—. Served to ensign USNR, 1943-46. Office: 55 Public Sq Cleveland OH 44113

HYDE, MARY MORLEY CRAPO (Mrs. Donald F. Hyde), author; b. Detroit, July 8, 1912; d. Stanford Tappan and Emma Caroline (Morley) Crapo; A.B., Vassar Coll., 1934; M.A., Columbia, 1936, Ph.D., 1947; D.Litt., Beaver Coll., 1963, Douglass Coll., 1964; Litt.D., Brown U., 1968, U. Birmingham (Eng.), 1969; m. Donald Frizell Hyde, Sept. 16, 1939. Trustee, Pierpont Morgan Library, trustee, 1966—; bd. govs. Johnson House, London, 1963—; trustee Am. Shakespeare Festival Theatre and Acad., 1964—; mem. council Friends of Columbia U. Libraries, 1954—; mem. humanities vis. com. U. Chgo., 1956—; mem. English dept. and library adv. councils Princeton, 1965—; mem. English dept. and libraries vis. coms. Harvard, 1966—; trustee Yale Libraries Assos., 1970—, Friends of Winterthur, 1971—; mem. Council of Friends of Folger Shakespeare Library, 1970—. Mem. Shakespeare Assn. Am. (pres. 1956—), Johnson Soc. of Lichfield, Eng. (pres. 1957), Modern Lang. Assn., Bibliog. Soc. Am., The Johnsonians, Keats-Shelley Assn. Am. (dir. 1967—), Master Drawings Assn., N.Y. Hort. Soc., Phi Beta Kappa. Author: Playwriting for Elizabethans, 1949; Four Oaks Farm and Its Library, 1967. Editor: (with E. L. McAdam and Donald Hyde) Johnson's Diaries, Prayers and Annals, 1958. Mem. editorial com. Yale Works of Johnson, 1957, Private Papers of James Boswell, 1966—. Home: Four Oaks Farm R F D 3 Somerville NJ 08876 Office: 61 Broadway New York City NY 10006

HYDE, MELVIN WATSON, former coll. pres.; b. Hazel, S.D., Mar. 17, 1905; s. Orlow Miner and Anna Lucinda (Watson) H.; B.S., Dakota Wesleyan U., 1926; A.M., Columbia, 1930, Ph.D., 1932; LL.D., U. Evansville, 1968; m. Claudia Marie Bray, Aug. 28, 1929; children—James Stewart, Joanne Marie. Instr., Parker (S.D.) High Sch., Sioux Falls (S.D.) High Sch., 1926-29; head dept. edn. Dakota Wesleyan U., 1931-32, dean, 1932-36; dean, head dept. edn. Mt. Union Coll., Alliance, O., 1936-49; asst. pres. Drake U., Des Moines, 1949-55; pres. U. Evansville (Ind.), 1955-67, pres. emeritus, 1967—. Ednl. cons., 1967—. Mem. N.E.A., Phi Delta Kappa, Phi Kappa Phi, Pi Kappa Delta, Pi Gamma Mu, Sigma Tau Delta. Republican. Methodist. Rotarian. Home: 2960 Acacia Dr. Estes Park CO 80517.

HYDE, RANDOLPH WEATHERBY, steel co. exec.; b. Pitts., July 22, 1906; s. Roy S. and Ella (Reeves) H.; B.S., U. Pitts., 1936; grad. Advanced Mgmt. Program, Harvard, 1950; m. Elizabeth Robertson, Oct. 18, 1940 (dec); children—Robert R. Boyd (foster son), Heather R.; m. 2d, Rebekah Brown Taylor, Aug. 12, 1961. With U.S. Steel Corp., Pitts., 1922—, v.p., asst. treas., 1959-68, v.p., treas., 1968, adminstrv. v.p., treas., 1968—. Home: 950 Osage Rd Pittsburgh PA 15243 Office: 71 Broadway New York City NY 10006

HYDE, ROSEL HERSCHEL, ret. govt. ofcl.; b. Bannock County, Ida., Apr. 12, 1900; s. George T. and Emma (Nibley) H.; student Utah Agrl. Coll., 1920-21, George Washington U. 1924-29; LL.D., U. Utah, 1967; m. Mary Henderson, Sept. 3, 1924; children—Rosel Henderson, George Richard, William Henderson, Mary Lynn. Admitted to D.C. bar, 1928, U.S. Supreme Ct. bar, 1945; mem. staff Civil Service Commn., 1924-25; staff Office Public Bldgs. and Parks, 1925-28; asst. atty. Fed. Radio Commn. and successor, FCC, asso. atty., atty., atty. examiner, sr. atty., prin. atty., asst. gen. counsel, 1924-45, gen. counsel, 1945-46; became commr. FCC, 1946, vice chmn., 1953, chmn., 1953-54, 66-69, acting chmn., 1954. U.S. del. 3d Inter-Am. Telecommunications Conf., Rio de Janeiro, 1945; mem. council Adminstrv. Conf. U.S., 1968—. Mem. Fed. Bar Assn. Republican. Mem. Ch. of Jesus Christ of Latter-Day Saints. Home: 2709 McKinley St NW Washington DC 20015 Office: 1616 H St NW Washington DC 20015

HYDE, ROY EDWARD, former educator; b. Tangipahoa Parish, La., Apr. 30, 1902; s. Isaac Claiborne and Susan Nettie (Clark) H.; A.B., Northwestern La. Coll., 1927; M.A., La. State U., 1932, Ph.D., 1942; postgrad. Harvard, 1935-36; m. Elaine C. Lorio, July 25, 1933; children—Catherine (Mrs. Shappert), Susan (Mrs. Forbes), Carol (Mrs. Clark). Tchr., research La. State U., 1942-46; faculty Southeastern La. Coll., Hammond, 1932-69, prof. sociology, 1946-69, chmn. dept., 1946-58, dean div. liberal arts, 1952-67, emeritus, 1969—. Mem. Rural, So. sociol. socs., Am. Assn. U. Profs., Phi Kappa Phi, Pi Gamma Mu. Mason (K.T.), Kiwanian. Contbr. articles to profl. jours. Home: RFD 4 Box K16 Hammond LA 70401

HYDE, STUART WALLACE, educator, author; b. Fresno, Cal., Aug. 8, 1923; s. Henry Jacob and Anna (Stuckert) H.; student Fresno State Coll., 1941-42; B.A., U. Cal., Los Angeles, 1948; M.A., Stanford, 1951, Ph.D., 1953; m. Allie Caroline Bargum, June 17, 1949; children—Stuart Wallace, John Christian, Allison Elizabeth Ann. Instr. radio-television Stanford, 1953-55; asst. prof. telecommunications U. So. Cal., 1955-58; asso. prof. radio-television-film, dept. chmn. San Francisco State Coll., 1958-63, prof., 1963—, chmn. broadcast communication arts. Served to lt. (j.g.) USNR, 1943-46. Mem. Am. Council for Better Broadcasts, Assn. for Profl. Broadcasting Edn., Cal. Tchrs. Assn., Cal. State Employees Assn. Presbyn. (elder). Author: Television and Radio Announcing, 2d edit., 1971. Contbr. articles profl. jours. Home: 586 Chapman Dr Corte Madera CA 94925 Office: 1600 Holloway Av San Francisco CA 94132

HYDE, WALTER LEWIS, univ. ofcl.; b. Mpls., May 30, 1919; s. Walter Lloyd and Edith (Drake) H.; S.B., Harvard, 1941, A.M., 1943, Ph.D., 1949; m. Elizabeth Sanford, Aug. 14, 1941; children—Lee, Lewis, Benjamin, Elizabeth, Rebecca. With Polaroid Corp., 1943-46, Baird Assos., 1947-50, Office Naval Research, 1950-53; asst. dir. research Am. Optical Co., Southbridge, Mass., 1953-60, dir. devel., 1960-63, cons., 1963—; prof. optics U. Rochester, 1963-68, dir. Inst. Optics, 1965-68; provost Univ. Heights Center, N.Y. U., 1968—. Sec., treas. Internat. Commn. Optics, 1966-69; cons. Am. Inst. Physics. Sec., Fordham Rd. Area Devel. Corp., 1970—. Devel. Corp., 1970—. Trustee Nightingale-Banford Sch., 1970—. Mem. Am. Phys. Soc., Optical Soc. Am. (pres. 1970), Phys. Soc. (London, Eng.), Sigma Xi. Democrat. Unitarian. Home: 2195 Andrews Av Bronx NY 10453

HYDE, WILBUR TIMOTHY, Jr. chemist, educator; b. Chicago, 1928; B.S. in Physics, Yale, 1950; Ph.D. in Chemistry, Harvard, 1956; m. Sally Ann Jones, July 5, 1957; children--Kenneth J., Nancy A. Chemist, Acme Chem. Co., Blue Island, Ill., 1950-51; director of Reseach Lab., Indsl. Chemicals Corp., Cambridge, Mass., 1956-60; project coordinator environmental sect. Steinmetz Assos., Chgo., 1960-61; v.p. for reseach Bauer Bros. Chem. Co., Inc., Memphis, 1961-64; asst. prof. chemistry Washington U., St. Louis, 1964-66, asso. prof., 1966-70, prof., 1970--, head of chemistry dept., 1970-71. Vis. prof. So. Ill. U., summer 1967, U. of Ore., 1969. Scoutmaster, Boy Scouts America, University City, Mo., 1968-70. Bd. dirs. Rest Haven Home for Elderly, 1960-61; trustee of the Lutheran Hosp., 1965-71. Served from lt. to capt., AUS, 1951-53. Mem. Am. Chem. Soc., Sci. Research Soc. Am. (chpt. treas. 1967), Sigma Xi. Author: (with others) Basic Inorganic Chemistry, 1971. Contbr. articles to profl. jours., encys., also chpts. to books. Home: Fairfax Apts 7291 Windermere Dr University City MO 63105 Office: Dept Chemistry Washington University St Louis MO 63130

HYDEN, HOLGER, educator; b. Stockholm, Sweden, Jan. 31, 1917; s. Victor Hyden; M.D., Karolinska Inst., Stockholm, 1943; m. Barbro Rolfsdotter Steenhoff, Oct. 8, 1948; children—Dag, Charlotte, Eva. Asst. prof. Karolinska Inst., 1943-45; research fellow Nobel Inst. for Cell Research, Stockholm, 1945-49; head dept. histology U. Goteborg, 1949—, dir. Inst. Neurobioloogy, 1958—, v.p. univ., 1954-57, pres., 1957. Mem. Swedish Med. Research Council, Acad. Letters Goteborg, Internat. Brain Research Orgn. Contbr. articles to profl. jours. Home: 2 Prästgardsgatan Göteborg Sweden Office: 5 Medicinaregatan Göteborg Sweden

HYER, DAVID BURNS, Jr., former utilities exec.; b. Charleston, S.C., June 10, 1904; s. David Burns and Sally (Mazyck) H.; B.S., Ga. Inst. Tech., 1925; m. Selina Wilson, June 29, 1932; 1 son, David Burns III. Comml. mgr. Fla. Power Corp., St. Petersburg, Fla., 1950; exec. v.p. So. Colo. Power Co. div. Central Telephone & Utilities Corp., Pueblo, 1951, pres., dir., 1952-61, pres., 1961-69; exec. v.p., dir. Central Telephone & Utilities Corp., 1962-69; dir. Minnequa Bank of Pueblo, Ry. Bldg. & Loan Assn. Adv. bd. USAF Acad., 1957; bd. dirs. Pueblo Single Fund, 1953, Pueblo chpt. A.R.C., 1953; trustee Parkview Episcopal Hosp., 1959. Mem. Pueblo Engrs. Soc., Rocky Mountain Elec. League (past pres.), Greenhorns (past pres.), Pueblo C. of C. (v.p.). Episcopalian. Elk, Rotarian. Clubs: Pueblo Golf and country; Denver Country. Home: 1502 W 32nd St Pueblo CO 81003

HYER, FRANK PERRY, former engr., utility exec.; b. Rhinelander, Wis., Sept. 22, 1897; s. Frank S. and Hattie A. (Broché) H.; B.S., U. Wis., 1923; m. M. Lorena Bergquist, Sept. 15, 1930; children—Frank S., Jayne Allerton (Mrs. Wilbert T. Davidson, Jr.). Cadet course West Penn Power Co., Pitts., 1923, asst. to gen. supt., 1924; staff engr. A.C. Nielson Co., Chgo., 1925-27; asst. gen. mgr. Wis. Hydro Electric Co., Amery, 1928-33; asst. chief rates and research dept. Wis. Pub. Service Commn., Madison, 1934-40; cons. power br. TVA, 1939-43; operations and engrng. cons. Gen. Pub. Utilities Corp. and predecessor firms, N.Y.C., 1941-48; with Del. Power & Light Co., Wilmington, 1948-69, v.p. operations engrng. and constrn., 1953-59, pres., 1959-60, chmn., chief exec. officer, 1960-66, dir., 1958-66 (co. name changed to Delmarva Power & Light Co. 1966), chmn. bd., mem. exec. com., 1967-69. Served from pvt. to 1st lt., inf. U.S. Army, 1916-19; AEF in France. Recipient Del. Engr. of Year award, 1965; Silver Beaver award Boy Scouts Am., 1967; Distinguished Service citation U. Wis., 1967. Registered profl. engr., Pa. Mem. Del. Soc. Profl. Engrs. (pres. 1958-59), Del. C. of C. (legislative com. 1957), Del. Soc. Mayflower Descs. (gov. 1962-65), N.A.M., Edison Electric Inst., Am. Gas Assn., Eta Kappa Nu, Zeta Psi. Unitarian. Kiwanian. Clubs: University, Whist (Wilmington); Wilbur-by-the-Sea; Waupaca Country. Home: 3905 S Atlantic Av Daytona Beach FL 32019 also White Pine Lane Waupaca WI 54981

HYER, JULIEN CAPERS, lawyer; b. Greenville, S.C., Apr. 1, 1894; s. William C. and Mattie (Wagener) H.; A.B., Wofford Coll., Spartanburg, S.C., 1913; LL.B., Georgetown U., 1916; LL.D. (hon.), Baylor U., 1942; m. Agnes Bernhart, Dec. 25, 1919 (dec.); children—Agnes Ann, Martha, Jeanne; m. 2d, Norma Shoemaker, Feb. 12, 1970. Asst. in law library Supreme Ct. U. S., 1914-15; practiced law at Waco, Fort Worth, Tex.; mem. Tex. State Senate, 1929; civil dist. atty. Dallas County, 1950-56; judge Dallas County Ct. at Law, 1956-61, 44th dist. ct., 1961—. Served as capt. Trench Arty., 36th Div. U. S. Army, in France, 1918-19; recalled to active mil. service, Jan. 1941; served as col., judge adv. Judge Adv. Gen.'s Dept., 8th Service Command; judge adv. 4th U.S. Army; overseas as army judge adv., 15th U.S. Army (Germany), also with general bd. U.S.F.E.T. Awarded European ribbon, 2 battle stars, Legion of Merit with oak leaf cluster, Commendation medal. Member Am., Tex., Ft. Worth and Dallas bar assns., Mil. Order of World Wars, Veterans Adminstrn. (Dallas br.), V.F.W., Am. Legion, Pi Kappa Phi. Democrat. Methodist. Mason (K.T., Shriner), Lion (pres. Internat. Assn. Lions Clubs, 1931-32). A Author: The Land of Beginning Again, 1952, 2d edit., 1970; The Shepherd (syndicated feature verse collection), 1955; Texas Lions 1917-67; contbr. verse and articles to newspapers and mags. Home: 6211 W Northwest Hwy Dallas TX 75225

HYINK, BERNARD LYNN, coll. pres.; b. Hawarden, Ia., Apr. 5, 1913; s. Bernard John and Inez (Lynn) H.; A.B., U. Redlands, 1935; A.M., U. Cal. at Berkeley, 1936; Ph.D., U. So. Cal., 1943; m. June Rose Hinckley, Aug. 7, 1938; children—Shirley June, Barbara Jean. Asst. to pres. U. Redlands (Cal.), 1937-41, prof., 1943-48; asst. civil service examiner U.S. Civil Service Commn., Washington, 1942; edn. counselor Nat. Inst. Pub. Affairs, Washington, 1949; dean students U. So. Cal., Los Angeles, 1949-56, prof. polit. sci., 1957-60; prof. U. Tehran (Iran), 1956; v.p. acad. affairs, prof. Cal. State Coll., Fullerton, 1960-70; pres. Sacramento State Coll., 1970—. Cons. Ford Motor Co., Los Angeles C. of C., 1959-60. Mem. Cal. State Constl. Revision Commn., Cal. Fulbright Commn., 1967—. Mem. Am., Western (pres.) polit. sci. assns., Phi Beta Kappa, Pi Kappa Delta, Pi Sigma Alpha, Kappa Sigma Sigma. Author: Politics and Government in Cal., 7th ed., 1971; American and California Government Testing Manual, 1960; Government in Golden State, 1967. Contbr. articles profl. jours. Home: 878 Woodside Lane E Sacramento CA 95825

HYLAND, EDWARD WILLIAM, cement co. exec.; b. New Haven, July 21, 1925; s. David J. and Charlotte V. (Griffin) H.; B.A., Yale, 1949, LL.B., 1952; m. Melissa E. Twigg, Nov. 21, 1959; children—Paul, Charlotte, Sara, Thomas Hyland. Admitted to Conn. bar, 1952, N.Y. bar, 1953; with firm Brown, Wood, Fuller, Caldwell & Ivey, N.Y.C., 1952-58; atty. Lehigh Portland Cement Co., Allentown, Pa., 1959—, sec., counsel, 1960—. Mem. Am. Bar Assn., Am. Soc. Corporate Secs., Am. Arbitration Assn. Clubs: Livingston, Lehigh Country (Allentown). Home: 2802 Crest Av S Allentown PA 18104 Office: 718 Hamilton St Allentown PA 18101

HYLAND, FRANCES JEAN, actress; d. Thomas and Jessie (Worden) Hland; m. George Edward McCowan, Dec. 12, 1955; 1 son, Evan Max. Appeared on stage in London in Streetcar Named Desire, 1950, A Woman of No Importance, 1953; in N.Y.C. in Look Homeward Angel, 1958, Moby Dick, 1962; in Good Woman of Setzuan, Chgo.; in Measure for Measure, Merchant of Venice, Hamlet and Othello at Stratford Shakespearean Festival, Can. Address: 45 Woodlawn Av W Toronto 7 Ontario Canada

HYLAND, JOHN JOSEPH, Jr., ret. naval officer; b. Phila., Sept. 1, 1912; s. John Joseph and Josephine (Walker) H.; B.S., U.S. Naval Acad., 1934; grad. Nat. War Coll., 1954; m. Florence Day Whiting, Jan. 29, 1938; children—John Joseph 3d, Nancy, Pamela, Whiting. Commd. ensign U.S. Navy, 1934, advanced through grades to admiral in 1967; designated naval aviator, 1937; with Patrol Squadron 102, PTO, World War II; comdr. Carrier Air Group 10, PTO, 1944-45; test pilot Naval Air Test Center, Patuxent River, Md., 1946-49, 51-53; comdr. seaplane tender U.S.S. Onslow, 1956, attack carrier U.S.S. Saratoga, 1958-59, Atlantic Barrier Forces, 1959-60, Attack Carrier Div. 4, 1962-63; assigned strategic plans div. Office Chief Naval Operation, 1963-65, comdr. Seventh Fleet, 1965-67; commander-in-chief Pacific Fleet, 1967-70. Decorated D.S.M. with oak leaf cluster, Silver Star, D.F.C. with 20 oak leaf clusters, Air medal with 4 oak leaf clusters (U.S.); Bronze Cross (Netherlands). Home: 29 Makalapa Dr Honolulu HI 96818

HYLAND, WILLIAM FRANCIS, lawyer; b. Burlington, N.J., July 30, 1923; s. Theodore J. and Margaret M. (Gallagher) H.; B.S. in Econs., U. Pa., 1944, LL.B., 1949; m. Joan E. Sharp, Apr. 20, 1946; children—William Francis, Nancy E., Stephen J., Emma L., Margaret M., Thomas M. Admitted to N.J. bar, 1949, U.S. Supreme Ct. bar, 1960; mem. firm Hyland, Davis and Reberkenny, Cherry Hill, N.J.; mem. N.J. Gen. Assembly from Camden County, 1954-61, speaker of house, 1958; acting gov. N.J., 1958; pres. N.J. Bd. Pub. Utility Commrs., also mem. cabinet Gov. Meyner and Gov. Hughes, 1961-68; chmn. N.J. Atomic Energy Council, 1968-69; chmn. N.J. Commn. Investigation, 1969-71. Co-chmn. State Reapportionment Commn. Dir. Inter-Boro Savs. & Loan Assn., Laurel Springs, N.J. Chmn. Brazilian Mission Com., 1962-65. Del.-at-large N.J., Dem. Nat. Conv., 1964, del., 1968. Trustee Camden County United Fund; asso. trustee U. Pa. Served as officer USNR, 1943-46; ETO, PTO. Decorated knight Order of St. Gregory (Pope Paul VI), 1964; recipient Outstanding Young Man in Govt. N.J. award N.J. Jaycees, 1958; Distinguished Service award Camden County Jaycees, 1954. Mem. Camden County Bar Assn. (pres. 1959), Nat. Assn. R.R. and Utilities Commrs. (exec. com. 1965-68), Phi Kappa Psi. Home: 201 Horse Shoe Ct Cherry Hill NJ 08034 Office: 499 Cooper Landing Rd Cherry Hill NJ 08034

HYLE, JOHN F., banker; b. Hartford, 1915; grad. Princeton, 1936. Sec., asst. comptroller Mellon Nat. Bank and Trust Co., Pitts. Mem. Am. Soc. Corp. Secretaries. Mason. Home: 9135 Saginaw Dr Pittsburgh PA 15237 Office: Mellon Nat Bank and Trust Co Mellon Sq Pittsburgh PA 15230

HYMA, ALBERT, author, educator; b. Groningen, The Netherlands, Mar. 18, 1893; s. Abe and Dieuwke (Brouwer) H.; student Calvin Coll., Grand Rapids, Mich., 1913-14; A.B., U. Mich., 1915, A.M., 1916, Ph.D., 1922; studied in Europe, 1919-21; m. Vera Alberta Nodine, Aug. 20, 1927. Came to U.S., 1917, naturalized, 1927. Instr. German, Knox Coll., Galesburg, Ill., 1916-17; instr. history. U. N.D., 1922-23, asst. prof., 1923-24; with U. Mich., 1924-62, asst. prof. history, 1926-29, asso. prof. 1929-36, prof. 1936-62; prof. history Aquinas Coll., Grand Rapids, 1962-63; prof. history Christian Heritage Coll., San Diego, 1971—; mem. faculty Western Ky. U., Spring, Summer 1970. Dir. hist. research City Grand Rapids, 1962-63. Mem. Ref. Ch. in Am. Editor: (with J.F. Scott) Readings in Medieval History, 1933; editor, translator: The Imitation of Christ, 1927; The Golden Whip, 1947. Author many books on philosophy, theology and history, 1924-47; How We Become Good Citizens, 1949; Dynamic Citizenship, 1950; The Brethren of the Common Life, 1950; Renaissance to Reformation, 1951; A History of the Dutch in the Far East, 1953, Sir Henry Clinton and the American Revolution, 1957; Martin Luther and the Luther Film of 1953, 1958; New Light on Martin Luther, 1958; The Religious Views of Benjamin Franklin, 1958; (with Frank Woodford) Gabriel Richard-Frontier Ambassador, 1958; A Survey of Ancient Civilization, 1959; A Survey of Medieval Civilization, 1960; A Survey of Early Modern Civilization, 1960; Modern Civilization to 1870, 1961; Modern Civilization after 1870, 1961; The Christian Renaissance: A History of the Devotio Modern, 1965; The Youth of Erasmus, 1968. Contbr., editor articles various encys. Home: 2716 Madison Av San Diego CA 92116

HYMAN, AL, journalist. Editorial writer San Francisco Chronicle. Office: 901 Mission St San Francisco CA 94119*

HYMAN, ALBERT SALISBURY, cardiologist; b. Boston, Mass., Apr. 6, 1893; s. John Jacob and Caroline (Greenwood) H.; A.B., Harvard, 1915, M.D., 1918; Med. Sc.D., U. London, 1924; med. deg. cardiology U. Vienna, 1925; m. Lillian Edyth Levenson, Jan. 29, 1967. Resident physician Boston City Hosp., 1919-20; med. supt. Mt. Sinai Hosp., Phila., 1920-23; med. dir. Jewish Maternity Hosp., Phila., 1922-23; med. supt. Beth David Hosp., N.Y.C., 1923-24; cons. cardiologist VA, N.Y. City Hosp. div. Mt. Sinai Hosp., Manhattan Gen. Hosp. div. Beth Israel Hosp., Richmond Meml. Hosp. (S.I.), Hosp. for Aged (Bronx); cons. cardiologist Wolffe Clinic, Phila., U.S. Naval Hosp., St. Albans, N.Y., Valley Forge (Pa.) Heart Inst. and Hosp., Beth David Hosp., Jewish Meml. Hosp., N.Y.C. Hosp. at

Elmhurst, Long Beach Meml. Hosp.; attending physician N.Y. City Hosp.; dir. Daitz Cardiovascular Research Fund, N.Y. Dir. Witkin Found. for Study and Prevention Heart Disease, Cordiosonic Research Found. Examiner, Nat. Bd. Med. Examiners, 1948. Founders trustee Am. Coll. Cardiology; pres. Am. Coll. of Sports Medicine. Served from lt. comdr. to capt., USN, 1934-46; PT., and base hosps. Received Presidential Unit Citation (1st Marine Div.), Navy Commendation Ribbon. Diplomate Am. Bd. Internal Medicine. Fellow A. C. P.; mem. numerous nat., state, local profl. socs. and affiliated orgns., former pres. several. Clubs: Harvard (N.Y.C.); Rod and Gun, Outboard (Fairfield, Conn.). Medical editor Greenwood Collegiate Press. Author several books in field of cardiology, 1929—, latest being: Practical Cardiology, 1958; Acute Medical Syndromes, 1959. Co-author: Medical Care of the Athlete. Editor: The Medical Emergencies, 1957; Practical Cardiology, 1958; Functional Capacity of the Heart in Health and Disease, 1959. Editor: Ency. of Sports Medicine. Contbr. articles to sci. publs. Inventor artificial pacemaker for resuscitation of dying heart and other life-saving apparatus. Home: 12 E 86th St New York City NY 10028 Office: 450 E 63d St New York City NY 10021

HYMAN, ARTHUR, educator; b. Schwaebisch Hall, Germany, Apr. 10, 1921; s. Isac and Rosa (Weil) H; came to U.S., 1936; B.A., St. Johns Coll., Md., 1944; M.A., Harvard, 1947, Ph.D., 1953; M.H.L., Jewish Theol. Sem. Am., 1955; m. Ruth Salinger, Feb. 25, 1951; children—Jeremy Saul, Michael Samuel, Joseph Isaiah. Instr. coll. dept. Jewish Theol. Sem., N.Y., 1950-55; rabbi, 1955; lectr., asst. prof. Dropsie Coll. Phila., 1955-61, acting dean students, 1958-61; asso. prof. Yeshiva U., N.Y., 1961-67, prof., 1967—. Vis. prof. Hebrew U., Jerusalem, 1969-70; Ford Found. fellow, mem. exec. com. Am. Acad. Jewish Research, 1951-52. Am. Philos. Soc. grantee, 1964. Mem. Am. Philos. Assn., Assn. Am. Colls., Assn. Jewish Studies (dir. 1969—, chmn. conf. on Jewish philosophy 1967—), Mediaeval Acad. Am., World Union Jewish Studies, Societé Internationale pour l'Étude de la Philosophie Médiévale. Editor: (with J.J. Walsh) Philosophy in the Middle Ages, 1967; (with S. Lieberman et al) Harry A. Wolfson Jubilee Volume, 1965; editor Jewish philosophy div. Ency. Judaica, 1971; contbr. articles on medieval Jewsih and Islamic philosophy. Home: 845 West End Av New York City NY 10025

HYMAN, EDWARD LOUIS, corp. exec.; b. Buffalo, Dec. 2, 1894; s. Abraham and Rebecca (Bennett) H.; student pub. schs.; m. Grace Redans, Mar. 26, 1918; 1 dau., Jeanne (Mrs. William E. Blatz). Mgr., Victoria Theater, Buffalo, 1917; dir. picture div. Govt. Commn. on Tng. Camp Activities, 1918; mng. dir. Mark Strand Theatre, Bklyn., 1920-27; gen. mgr. Century Circuit Theatres, Bklyn., 1927-4O; asso. to pres. United Detroit Theatres, 1940 (joined Paramount Theatres); asso. to v.p. Paramount Theatres, N.Y.C., 1941-44, v.p., 1944-50; v.p. Am. Broadcasting- Paramount Theatres, Inc., N.Y.C., 1950-65; pres. 875 Fifth Av. Corp., 1965—. Counsellor, Small Bus. Adminstrn. Home: 875 Fifth Av New York City NY 10021

HYMAN, ELIOT, motion picture producer. A pioneer in recognizing profit potential in distbn. feature motion pictures to TV; founder Asso. Arts Prodn., Inc. (now United Artists Asso.), 1947; then pres. Seven Arts Prodn. Ltd.; became chmn. bd. Warner Bros.-Seven Arts, Ltd., 1967; co-producer, financier motion pictures including Lost Boundaries, Moulin Rouge, Moby Dick, The Misfits, By Love Possessed, Lolita, Whatever Happened to Baby Jane, Gigot.*

HYMAN, HAROLD MELVIN, educator, historian; b. N.Y.C., July 24, 1924; s. Abraham and Beatrice (Herman) H.; B.A., U. Cal. at Los Angeles, 1948; M.A., Columbia, 1950, Ph.D., 1952; m. Ferne B. Handelsman, Mar. 22, 1946; children—Lee, Ann Margaret, William. Asst. prof. history Earlham Coll., 1952-55; vis. asst. prof. U. Cal. at Los Angeles, 1955-56; asso. prof. Ariz. State U., 1956-57; prof. history U. Cal. at Los Angeles, 1957-63, U. Ill., 1963-68; William P. Hobby prof. history, chmn. dept. Rice U., Houston, 1968—. Cons. in history, 1966—. Mem. Tex. Bill of Rights Assn. Served with USMCR, 1941-45. Recipient Sidney Hillman award, 1960. Mem. Am. Hist. Assn. (Beveridge award 1954), Orgn. Am. Historians, Phi Beta Kappa. Author: Era of the Oath: Northern Loyalty Tests During the Civil War and Reconstruction, 1954; To Try Men's Souls: Loyalty Tests in American History, 1959; (with B.P. Thomas) Stanton: The Life and Times of Lincoln's Secretary of War, 1962; Soldiers and Spruce: Origins of the Loyal Legion of Loggers and Lumbermen: The Army's Labor Union of World War I, 1963; The Radical Republicans and Reconstruction, 1861-1870, 1966; New Frontiers of American Reconstruction, 1967; Heard 'Round the World: The Impact Abroad of the Civil War and Reconstruction, 1968. Editor: (with L.W. Levy) Freedom and Reform: Essays in Honor of Henry Steele Commager, 1967. Home: 4910 Braesvalley St Houston TX 77035

HYMAN, HARVEY EUGENE, lawyer; b. Lakewood, O., Feb. 28, 1917; s. Harvey G. and Bess (Sidle) H.; student Ohio U., 1935-37; LL.B., Ohio No. U., 1940; m. Juanita Marjorie Jacobs, Dec. 23, 1939; children-H. Douglas, Cara Lou (Mrs. Charles A. Strahley), David, Geoffrey. Admitted to Ohio bar, 1940, since practiced in Paulding; village solicitor various villages, 1942-70; county prosecuting atty., 1949-56; common pleas judge, 1956-59; sr. partner Hyman, McMaster & Cook, 1968—; spl. counsel atty. gen. Ohio; gen. counsel Herbert E. Orr, Inc.; dir., gen. counsel Nat. Bank of Paulding. County chmn. Nat. Polit. candidates, 1954-70. Mem. dist. exec. bd. Boy Scouts Am. Served with AUS, 1943-46, 51-52. Decorated Bronze Star medal with oak leaf cluster. Fellow Ohio Bar Assn. Found.; mem. Am., Ohio, Northwestern Ohio (past pres.), Paulding County (past pres.) bar assns., Prosecuting Attys. Assn., Judges Assn., Am. Judicature Soc., Municipal Attys. Assn. Republican. Presbyn. (elder). Mason (32, Shriner), Eagle, K.P., Odd Fellow. Home: 518 N Cherry St Paulding OH 45879 Office: 106 N Williams St Paulding OH 458799

HYMAN, HERBERT HIRAM, sociol. psychologist; b. N.Y.C., Mar. 3, 1918; s. David Elihu and Gisella (Mautner) H.; A.B. with honors, Columbia, 1939, A.M., 1940, Ph.D., 1942; m. Helen Raphael Kandel, Sept. 30, 1945; children—Lisa D., David K., Alex R. Social sci. analyst Dept. Agr., 1942; pub. opinion analyst OWI 1942-44; dir. field surveys, morale div. U.S. Strategic Bomb Survey, 1944-45; research asso. Nat. Opinion Research Center, 1947-57; asst. prof. Bklyn. Coll., 1946-47; vis. prof. U. Cal., 1950, U. Oslo (Norway), 1950-51, U. Ankara (Turkey), 1957-58; prof. Columbia, 1951-69, chmn. dept. sociology, 1965-68; fellow Center Advanced Studies, Wesleyan U., Middleton, Conn., 1968-69, prof. sociology 1969—. Program dir. Research Inst. Social Devel., UN, 1964-65. Recipient Fulbright award, Guggenheim award; spl. grantee Ford Found. Fellow Am. Psychol. Assn.; mem. Am. Assn. Pub. Opinion Research (past pres., Julian Woodward Meml. award), Sociol. Research Assn., Am. Sociol. Soc. (pres. methodology sect. 1962-63, social psychology sect. 1970-71), Soc. Psychol. Study Social Issues (exec. council), Sigma Xi. Author: Interviewing in Social Research, 1954; Survey Design and Analysis, 1955; Political Socialization, 1959; Applications of Methods of Evaluation, 1962; Readings in Reference Group Theory, 1968; Secondary Analysis of Sample Surveys, 1971. 38 Woodside Av Westport CT 06880 Office: Wesleyan Univ Middletown CT 06457

HYMAN, M. KENNETH, motion picture co. exec.; b. N.Y.C., Dec. 11, 1928; s. Eliot and Betty (Barbour) H.; grad. Columbia Prep. Sch., 1946; m. Caroline Godman, Mar. 1, 1964; children—Gregory James, Kate Elizabeth, Michael Anthony, Andrew Nicholas. Exec. v.p. Asso. Artists, also v.p. Seven Arts Prodns., 1954-57; prodn. exec. Anglo Am. Co. Prodns.-Seven Arts, 1957; with various motion picture companies, 1957-59; producer Gigot, 1961; exec. producer Whatever Happened to Baby Jane, 1962; Small World of Sammy Lee, 1963; producer The Hill, 1964; producer The Dirty Dozen, 1967; exec. v.p. worldwide prodn. Warner Bros.-Seven Arts, Inc. (now Seven Arts Feature Syndicate, Inc.), 1967—, also dir. Served with USMCR, 1949-51. Mailing Address: 144 Monovale Dr Beverly Hills CA 90210 Office: 6601 1st Av New York City NY

HYMAN, MILTON, dental educator; b. N.Y.C., Apr. 1, 1905; s. Abraham and Bella (Langer) H.; student Coll. City N.Y., 1923-26; D.D.S., N.Y.U., 1930; m. Elsie Reiter, June 20, 1937; children—Leonard S., Deborah S. Mem. faculty Coll. Dentistry, N.Y.U., 1930—, chmn. dept. oral diagnosis, 1943—, prof., 1952—, chmn. dept. oral diagnosis and roentgenology, 1954—, asst. dir. Dental Assts. Training Program, 1961-67, dir. Tumor Clinic, 1962—. Mem. senate N.Y.U., 1966-70 Fellow Am. Acad. Oral Medicine (pres. 1969), Am. Coll. Dentists; mem. Am. Dental Assn., Bronx County (dir. 1937-49, librarian, 1941-44, v.p. 1945, editor bull. 1937-40), 1st Dist. (dir. 1945-46, editor pathodontia sect. 1953, chmn. 1956) dental socs., A.A.A.S., Am. Assn. U. Profs., N.Y. Acad. Scis., Sci. Research Soc. Am., N.Y.U. Coll. Dentistry Alumni Assn., U.S. Power Squadron, Omicron Kappa Upsilon (pres. Omega chpt. 1959), Sigma Omega Psi (past pres. Alumni chpt.). Clubs: New York Univ.; Woodmere Bay Yacht. Asst. editor Dental Violet, N.Y.U., 1929, editor-in-chief, 1930, faculty adviser, 1931-70; staff writer N.Y. Jour. Dentistry, 1934-38. Contbr. articles textbooks, profl. jours. Home: 86-20 Eton St Jamaica NY 11432 Office: 57 W 57th St New York City NY 10019

HYMAN, RALPH ALAN, journalist; b. Rochester, N.Y., Sept. 8, 1928; s. Harold M. and Sade (Rubens) H.; B.A., U. Rochester, 1952; m. Norma Sheila Newman, June 19, 1955; 1 son, Daniel. Sports writer Rochester Times-Union, 1952-58, exec. sports editor, 1958—. Mem. sports com. A.P. Mng. Editors Report, 1964- 66, 68; co-chmn. N.Y. State A.P. Sports Report, 1966. Mem. Sigma Delta Chi. Home: 65 Beekman Pl Rochester NY 14620 Office: 55 Exchange St Rochester NY 14614

HYMES, DELL HATHAWAY, educator, anthropologist; b. Portland, Ore., June 7, 1927; s. Howard Hathaway and Dorothy (Bowman) H.; B.A., Reed Coll., 1950; M.A., Ind. U., 1953, Ph.D., 1955; postgrad. U. Cal. at Los Angeles, 1954-55; m. Virginia Margaret Dosch, Apr. 10, 1954; children—Alison Bowman, Kenneth Dell; stepchildren—Vicki (Mrs. David Unruh), Robert Paul. Instr., asst. prof. Harvard, 1955-60; asso. prof., prof. U. Cal., Berkeley, 1960-65; prof. anthropology U. Pa., Phila., 1965—, curator linguistic anthropology U. Mus., 1965—. Bd. dirs. Social Sci. Research Council, 1965-67, 69-70, 71-72. Served with AUS, 1945-47. Fellow Center Advanced Study Behavioral Scis., 1957-58, Clare Hall, Cambridge, Eng., 1968-69; Guggenheim fellow, 1969. Mem. Am. Anthropology Assn. (exec. bd. 1968-70), Am. Ethnol. Assn., Am. Folklore Soc. (2d v.p. 1971), Linguistic Soc. Am. (exec. bd. 1967-69), Linguistics Assn. Gt. Britain. Author: Language in Culture and Society, 1964: The Use of Computers in Anthropology, 1965; Studies in Southwestern Ethnolinguistics, 1967; Pidginization and Creolization of Languages, 1971. Asso. editor Am. Anthropologist, 1963-70, Internat. Jour. Am. Linguistics, 1963—, Daedalus, 1958—, Jour. History Behavioral Scis., 1966—; editor: Language in Society, 1972—. Home: 439 S 44th St Philadelphia PA 19104

HYMES, VIOLA HOFFMAN, community service cons.; b. Chgo., May 7, 1906; d. Aaron and Lena (Provol) Hoffman; B.S., U. Minn., 1926; m. Dr. Charles Hymes, Sept. 21, 1930; children—Alan, Richard. Tchr. secondary schs., East Chicago. Ind., 1928- 29; 1st nat. v.p. Nat. Council Jewish Women, also pres. Mpls. sect., 1938-42, nat. pres., 1959-63, hon. life v.p. nat., 1963—, hon. life pres. Mpls. sect.; sec. Internat. Council Jewish Women, 1951-54, edn. chmn., 1954-57, v.p. 1957-63; dir. urban affairs Mpls. Fedn. for Jewish Service, 1969—; bd. dirs. Am. Friends Hebrew U., Jewish Welfare Bd., 1959-63. Chmn. community services, past pres. Mpls. Citizens Com. Pub. Edn.; mem. Minneapolis Public School Bd.; dir. Minneapolis Board of Education, 1963-69; chmn. Minn. Governor's Commn. Status Women 1964-67; mem. Citizens Adv. Com. Status Women, Washington; chmn. edn. and tng. task force Econ. Opportunity Com., Mpls., 1964-69. Bd. dirs. Minn. Mental Health Assn., 1955-59, Hennenin County chpt. A.R.C., 1942-44, 63-65; trustee (KTCA, Twin City Ednl. TV Sta., 1955—, Hebrew U., Jerusalem; mem. Pres.'s Commn. Status of Women. Recipient Outstanding Achievement award U. Minn., 1961; Distinguished Serv. award City of Mpls., 1963; Minnesota Governor's citation of honor, 1968. Mem. League Wom. Voters, Citizens League Gtr. Mpls. (v.p. 1953-54), Am. Assn. U. Women (edn. chmn. Minn. 1952-53). Delta Sigma Rho, Pi Lambda Theta, Delta Phi Lambda, Delta Kappa Gamma (hon.). Home: 2044 Cedar Lake Blvd Minneapolis MN 55416

HYMON, MARY WATSON, (Mrs. George Jerome Hymon), librarian; b. Hagertown, Md., June 19, 1918; d. Ralph Wesley and Georgia (Reed) Watson; A.B., Ky. State Coll., 1940; B.S. in L.S., U. Denver, 1941, M.A., 1954; Ed.D., Ind. U., 1960; m. George Jerome Hymon, Jan. 2, 1949; 1 son, Nolan Jerome. Librarian, Bishop Coll., Marshall, Tex., 1941-43, 45-47, Ky. State Coll., 1943-45; now head librarian Grambling (La.) Coll. Cons. La. Library Resources Survey; mem. Library Devel. Com. La. Recipient leadership tng. award Fund for Adult Edn., 1957-58. Mem. A.L.A., La. Edn. Assn., Adult Edn. Assn., Am. Assn. U. Profs., Pi Lambda Theta. Home: PO Box 448 Grambling LA 71245 Office: Grambling Coll La Grambling LA 71245

HYNDMAN, DONALD E., bus. exec.; b. Denver, Colo., April 14, 1904; s. Archiebald and Alice (Miller) H.; B.S., in C.E., U. of Denver, 1922-26; student U. of Rochester (N.Y.), 1926-27, bus. adminstrn., Alexander Hamilton Inst., 1927-29; m. Genevieve C. Schelling, June 20, 1936; children—Martha Anne (Mrs. Neil Gray), Carla Alice, John Stuart. Began career as research chemical engr. at Eastman Kodak Co., 1926-29, photographic chem. engr., 1929-40, asst. engr. East Coast div. motion picture film dept., 1940-46, mgr., 1946-50, mgr. motion picture film dept., 1950, asst. v.p., mgr. motion picture product sales dept., 1962, asst. v.p., gen. mgr. motion picture and edn. markets div., 1965—. Mem. motion picture industry adv. com. W.P.B., 1942; cons. engr. and analyst, war activities com., Motion Picture Industry, 1942- 43; sub-com. adminstr., war com. on photography, Am. Standards Assn., 1943-46, mem. council 1947; mem. National Television System Com., 1950- 54. Mem. Thomas A. Edison Centennial Com., 1946-47. Fellow Soc. Motion Picture Engrs. (v.p. 1939-45; pres. 1945-46); mem. Rochester C. of C., British kinematograph Soc., Am. Soc. of Cinematographers, Armed Forces Communication Assn., Am. Photographic Soc. Radio and TV Execs., Acad. of Motion Picture Arts and Sci., also Phi Lambda Upsilon, Phi Beta Sigma, Eta Omega Delta. Republican. Presbyterian. Clubs: Phi Gamma Delta, Columbia (New York); National Sales Executives, Western Universities. Co-author: The Occurrence and Present Chemical Status of the Female Sex Hormone; Plastic Cellulose in Scientific Research; Automatic Silver Recovery from Hypo, and numerous publs. on motion picture engring. Home: 10 Creekside Lane Rochester NY 14618 Office: 343 State St Rochester NY 14608

HYNEK, JOSEF ALLEN, educator, astronomer; b. Chgo., May 1, 1910; s. Josef and Bertha (Waska) H.; B.S., U. Chgo., 1931, Ph.D., 1935; m. Martha Alexander, Dec. 25, 1932; m. 2d, Miriam Curtis, May 31, 1942; children—Scott, Roxane, Joel, Paul, Ross. Fellow Yerkes Obs., 1932-35; instr., asst. prof. Ohio State U., 1935-41, asso. prof., 1946-50, dir. McMillin Obs., 1946-53, asst. dean Grad. Sch., 1950-53, prof. astronomy, also astronomy, teaching and research Perkins Obs.; supr. tech. reports Applied Physics Lab., Johns Hopkins, 1942-45; formerly asso. dir. and in charge satellite optical tracking program Smithsonian Astrophys. Obs., Cambridge, Mass., research asso. Harvard Coll. Obs.; chmn. dept. astronomy, dir. Dearborn Obs., prof. Northwestern U., Evanston, Ill., 1960—, dir. Lindheimer Astron. Research Center, 1964—; sci. dir. USAF balloon astronomy prof. Stargazer. Mem. Internat. Astron. Union (past sec. U.S. nat. com.), Am. Astron. Soc. (past sec.), Astron. Soc. Pacific, Am. Mus. Natural History (corr.), Phi Beta Kappa, Sigma Xi. Author: Challenge of the Universe, 1962. Editor: Astrophysics, 1951. Address: Northwestern U Dept Astronomy Evanston IL 60201

HYNEMAN, CHARLES S., educator; b. Gibson County, Ind., May 5, 1900; s. Willis Smith and Hattie (Ford) H.; A.B., Ind. U., 1923, A.M., 1925; postgrad. U. Pa., 1925-26; Ph.D., U. Ill., 1929; L.H.D., Ohio No. U., 1960; LL.D., Wabash Coll., 1971; m. Frances Virginia Tourner, Aug. 31, 1926; children—Richard Frank, Ruth Anne, Elizabeth Harriet. High sch. tchr., univ. prof., 1923-41; prin. adminstrv. analyst U.S. Bur. Budget, 1942-43; chief tng. br. Mil. Govt. Div., Office Provost Marshal Gen., 1943-44; dir. Fgn. Broadcast Intelligence Service FCC, 1944-45, asst. to chmn. commn., exec. officer, 1945-47; prof. polit. sci. Northwestern U., 1947-56; prof. govt. Ind. U., Bloomington 1956-61, Distinguished Service prof. govt., 1961—. Mem. UN Monitoring Com., 1944-45, Social Sci. Research Council, 1944-47, NRC, 1963-65, Chgo. San. Dist. Civil Service Bd., 1952-56. Mem. Am. (pres. 1961-62), So., Midwest, polit. sci. assns., Midwest Conf. Polit. Scientists. Author: The First American Neutrality, 1935; Bureaucracy in a Democracy, 1950; The Study of Politics, 1959; The Supreme Court on Trial, 1963; Popular Government in America, 1968. Editor: (with George W. Carey) A Second Federalist, 1967. Contbr. articles to profl. jours. Address: 2320 Fritz Dr Bloomington IN 47401

HYNES, JAMES GORDON, educator; clergyman; b. Newburgh, N.Y., Oct. 1, 1907; s. James Louis and Elizabeth Lulu (Gordon) H.; B.Th., Gordon Coll., 193O; M.A., N.Y. U., 1934, Ph.D., 1937; B.D., Union Theol. Sem., N.Y.C., 1943; m. Ruth Marshall Sechler, Oct. 17, 1930; children—Marguerite Ruth, Joan Wright, James Gordon and Daniel Marshall (twins). Ordained to ministry Am. Bapt. Conv., 1930; asst. pastor Belmont St. Bapt. Ch., Watertown, Mass., 1928-30; pastor First Bapt. Ch., Freeport, N.Y., 1930-43, Auburn, N.Y., 1943-44; dir. Christian edn. Mich. Bapt. Conv., 1944-48; prof. religion U. Redlands, 1948—, Crawford prof. bibl., ethical and missionary instrn., 1951. Adnee Hall lectr. Berkeley Bapt. Div. Sch., 1959; tchr., dir., counselor youth camps, various states U.S. Mem. Am. Assn. U. Profs., Nat. Assn. Bibl. Instrs. (treas. Pacific Coast chpt. 1960), Cal. Tchrs. Assn., Phi Delta Kappa, Phi Alpha Chi. Home: 340 Summit Av Redlands CA 92373

HYNES, LEONARD, chem. co. exec.; b. Toronto, Ont., Can., July 3, 1911; B.A., U. Toronto, 1932, M.A., 1933; m. Jessie Grant, Oct. 1937; children—Katherine, James, Eleanor, Grant. With Canadian Industries, Ltd., Hamilton, Ont., Can., 1933—, chemist, various sales positions chem. div., mgmt. com. sec., asst. mgr. chem. div., mgr. paints and coated fabrics div., 1933-54, v.p. dir., 1954-62, pres., dir., 1962-70, chmn. bd., 1971; dir. Bank of Montreal, Pilkington Bros. (Can.) Ltd. Mem. Sci. Council Can., 1968-71; mem. Canadian council Conf. Bd., 1968-70, mem. corp., 1970-72. Pres., dir. St. Mary's Hosp., Montreal, 1960-62; trustee the Conf. Bd., N.Y.C., 1970—. Fellow Royal Soc. Arts, Chem. Inst. Can.; mem. Canadian Inst. Mining and Metallurgy, Canadian Chem. Producers Assn. (bd. dirs. 1967-71), Mfg. Chemists Assn. (bd. dirs. 1968-71), Montreal C. of C., N.Am. Yacht Racing Union (mem. exec. com. 1971), Canadian (chmn. exec. council 1960-61), Internat. (pres. Canadian council 1968-70, vice chmn. budget com. Paris 1969—) chambers commerce, Am. Mgmt. Assn., Soc. Chem. Industry. Club: Royal St. Lawrence Yacht (commodore 1965-66). Home: Rural Route 4 Picton Ontario Canada Office: 630 Dorchester Blvd W Montreal Quebec Canada

HYNES, SAMUEL, educator, author; b. Chgo., Aug. 29, 1924; s. Samuel Lynn and Margaret (Turner) H.; B.A., U. Minn., 1947, M.A., Columbia, 1948, Ph.D., 1956; m. Elizabeth Igleheart, July 28, 1944; children—Miranda, Joanna. Faculty, Swarthmore Coll., 1949-68, prof. English lit., 1965-68; prof. English, Northwestern U., Evanston, Ill., 1968—. Served to maj. USMCR, 1943-46, 52-53. Decorated Air medal, D.F.C. Fulbright fellow, 1953-54; Guggenheim fellow, 1959-60; Bollingen fellow, 1964-65; Am. Council Learned Socs. fellow, 1969. Mem. English Inst., Phi Beta Kappa. Author: The Pattern of Hardy's Poetry (Explicator award 1962), 1961; William Golding, 1964; The Edwardian Turn of Mind, 1968. Editor: Further Speculations by T.E. Hulme, 1955; The Author's Craft and Other Critical Writings of Arnold Bennett, 1968; Romance and Realism, 1970. Office: English Dept Northwestern U Evanston IL 60201

HYSLOP, RALPH DOUGLAS, educator, clergyman; b. Nampa, Ida., Dec. 12, 1913; s. Frederick Robert and Lilias (Morton) H.; B.A. with honors, U. Wis., 1935; B.D. summa cum laude (Rockefeller fellow 1937-38), Chgo. Theol. Sem., 1938, Ford Found. traveling fellow, 1938-40; Ph.D., U. Edinburgh (Scotland), 1947; student Union Theol. Sem., 1939-40; m. Elizabeth Garrison Curry, May 30, 1939; children—Elizabeth Anne, Helen Curry, Bruce Douglas, Stephen Garrison. Ordained to ministry Congl. Ch., 1938; asso., then acting minister Union Ch., Hinsdale, Ill., 1940-42; minister student life Congl. Christian Chs. U.S.A., 1942-47; asso. prof., then prof. hist. theology and history Christianity, Pacific Sch. Religion, 1947-55; prof. ecumenical studies, Union Theol. Sem., N.Y.C., 1955-69, prof. of ecumenical studies emeritus, 1969—; dir. program advanced religious studies, 1955-64. Mem. exec. com. Internat. Conglist. Council, 1946-50, del. observer Vatican Council II, 1965; bd. dirs. council Christian social action United Ch. Christ, 1957-63, vice chmn. missions council, 1958-60, mem. Commn. to Prepare Statement of Faith, 1957-59, mem. internat. relations com., publs. com., council for Christian social action United Ch. Christ; sec. dept. evangelism World Council Chs., 1953-54, sec. main theme commn., 1954, mem. Ecumenical Inst.; vis. prof. U. Utrecht (Netherlands), 1961; Fulbright scholar, Denmark, 1965-66. Mem. Am. Soc., Ch. History, Nat. Student Christian Fedn. (bd.), Soc. Religion Higher Edn., N.Am. Acad. Ecumenists (sec. treas. 1967—), Chi Alpha. Club: Commonwealth of California. Author: The Church is One, 1948; Marks of a Christian, 1949. Contbr.: Unity in Mid-Career, 1963; Ministers of Christ, 1963; Stewardship in Mission, 1964. Home: 1603 Altschul Av Menlo Park CA 94025

HYSON, CHARLES DAVID, econ. adminstr.; b. Hampstead, Md., Dec. 29, 1915; s. Harry Perry and Rose (Miller) H.; A.B., St. John's Coll., Annapolis, 1937; M.S., U. Md., 1939; M.A., Harvard, 1942, Ph.D., 1943; m. Winifred Chandler Prince, Sept. 7, 1946; children—David Prince, Pamela Chandler, Christopher Perry. Agrl. economist FCA, 1939-40; staff Surplus Marketing Adminstrn., Washington, 1940-41; resident tutor, then sr. tutor Harvard, 1942-49, research asso., 1943-44, resident cons. Grad. Sch. Pub. Adminstrn., 1943-49, instr. econs., 1946-48, asso. dir. marketing research program, 1948-49; regional economist, then chief prices and cost of living br. U.S. Bur. Labor Statistics, 1944-46; indsl. economist Fed. Res. Bank Boston, 1946-48; asst. econ. commr. ECA Mission to Norway, Oslo, 1949-50; trade specialist, staff spl. rep. in Europe, Paris, 1950, spl. asst. to chief of mission ECA, Mut. Security Agy., Lisbon, Portugal, 1950-52; dep. dir. U.S. Operations Mission to Portugal, Mut. Security Agy., FOA, ICA, 1952-55; spl. rep. to Portugal, ICA, 1955-57, chief Western Europe div., Washington, 1957-59, chief European Div., 1959-60; assigned to Nat. War Coll., 1960-61; counsellor of embassy for econ. affairs Am. embassy, Lisbon, 1955-57; dep. asst. dir. for exec. staffing AID, Washington, 1961-62; adviser for econ. affairs Office Material Resources, AID, 1962-63, spl. asst. for econs. and trade AID, 1963—. Dep. nat. coordinator, dep. exec. dir. Cabinet Com. Export Expansion, 1964; mem. White House Conf. on Internat. Cooperation, 1965. Decorated comdr. Order of Merit (Portugal). Mem. Am. Fgn. Service Assn., Royal Econ. Soc., Am. Acad. Polit. and Social Sci., Am. Econ. Assn., Am. Farm Econ. Assn., Sigma Alpha Epsilon. Clubs: Harvard, Internat. (Washington); Keene Valley (N.Y.) Country; Edgemoor (Md.). Contbr. articles econ. jours. Home: 7407 Honeywell Lane Bethesda MD 20014 Office: Dept of State Washington DC 20523

IACOCCA, LIDO ANTHONY, automotive mfr.; b. Allentown, Pa., Oct. 15, 1924; s. Nicola and Antoinette (Perrotto) I; B.S., Lehigh U., 1945; M.E., Princeton, 1946; m. Mary McCleary, Sept. 29, 1956; children—Kathryn Lisa, Lia Antoinette. With Ford Motor Co. Dearborn, Mich., 1946—, successively mem. field sales staff, various merchandising and tng. activities, asst. dirs. sales mgr., Phila., dist. sales mgr., Washington, 1946-56, truck marketing mgr. div. office, 1956-57, car marketing mgr., 1957-60, vehicle market mgr., 1960, v.p. Ford Motor Co., gen. mgr. Ford div., 1960-65, v.p. car and truck group, 1965-67, exec. v.p. of co., 1967-68, now pres. Ford N. Am. automobile operations. Wallace Meml. fellow Princeton. Mem. Tau Beta Pi. Club: Detroit Athletic. Home: 571 Edgemere Ct Bloomfield Hills MI 48013 Office: American Rd Dearborn MI 48121

IAKOVOS, ARCHBISHOP, (Demetrios A. Coucouzis), primate; b. Imvros, Turkey, July 29, 1911; s. Athanasios and Maria Coucouzes; grad. Theol. Sch. of Halki, Ecumenical Patriarchate, 1934; S.T.M., Harvard, 1945; D.D., Boston U., 1960, Bates Coll., 1970; L.H.D., Franklin and Marshall Coll., 1961; LL.D., Brown U., 1964; Seton Hall U., 1968; hon. degrees Holy Cross Fordham U., 1966; H.H.D., Suffolk U., 1967; D.S.T., Gen. Theol. Sem., 1967. Ordained deacon Greek Orthodox Ch., 1934, archdeacon Metropolitan Derkon, 1934-39; archdeacon Greek Archdiocese, prof. Archdiocese Theol. Sch., Pomfret, Conn., 1939; ordained priest, 1940; parish priest, Hartford, Conn., 1940-41; preacher Holy Trinity Cathedral, N.Y.C., 1941-42; parish priest, St. Louis, 1942; dean Cathedral of Annunciation, Boston, 1942-54; dean Holy Cross Orthodox Theol. Sch., Brookline, Mass., 1954, now pres.; bishop of Melita (Malta), 1954-56; rep. Ecumenical Patriarchate, World Council Chs., Geneva, 1955-59, also various other internat. confs.; elevated to Metropolitan, 1956; archbishop N. and S. Am., Holy Synod of Ecumenical Patriarchate, 1959—. Chmn. Standing Conf. Cannonical Bishops in the Americas; v.p. Religion in American Life. Pres. St. Basil's Acad., Garrison, N.Y. Mem. World Council Chs. (past co-pres.). Trustee Anatolia Coll., Salonika, Greece; pres. bd. trustees Hellenic Coll., Brookline, Mass. Mem. Am. Bible Soc. (bd. mgrs.). Author works in Greek, French, English, German. Address: 10 E 79th St New York City NY 10021

IAN, JANIS, singer. Address; 1540 Broadway New York City NY 10019

I'ANSON, LAWRENCE WARREN, state judge; b. Portsmouth, Va., Apr. 21, 1907; s. James Thornton and Emma (Warren) I'A.; A.B., Coll. William and Mary, 1928, LL.D., 1964; LL.B., U. Va., 1931; m. May Frances Tuttle, Aug. 5, 1933; children—Lawrence Warren, May Frances (Mrs. Peter McCrae Ramsey). Admitted to Va. bar, 1931; practiced in Portsmouth, 1931-41; commonwealth's atty., Portsmouth, 1938-41; judge Ct. of Hustings, 1941-58; judge Supreme Ct. Va., 1958—. Mem. jud. council, 1948-70; chmn. com. that prepared Handbook for Jurors used in all cts. of record in Va. Dir. First Fed. Savs. and Loan Assn. Portsmouth-Norfolk County (Va.). Mem. Council of Higher Edn. of Va., 1956-59. Pres. Beazley Found., Inc., Found. Boys Acad., Found. Boys Club, Inc.; trustee Eastern Va. Med. Sch. Found., Frederick Mil. Acad. Named First Citizen Portsmouth, 1946; William and Mary Alumni medallion; U. Va. Sesquicentennial award. Mem. Va. State Bar Assn. (chmn. jud. sect. 1949), Phi Beta Kappa, Pi Kappa Alpha, Omicron Delta Kappa, Order of Coif, Phi Alpha Delta. Democrat. Baptist. Mason (past dist. dept. Va.; Shriner), Kiwanian (past pres. Portsmouth). Home: 214 West Rd Portsmouth VA Office: Citizens Trust Bldg Portsmouth VA 23704 also Supreme Court Bldg Richmond VA 23219

IBBOTSON, JOSEPH SELWYN, former librarian; b. Clinton, N.Y., June 17, 1907; s. Joseph Darling and Hedwig (Tappe) I.; ed. Phillips Acad., Andover, Mass. A.B., Hamilton Coll., Clinton, N.Y., 1929; B.S., Columbia, 1930; Grad. Library Sch. U. Chicago, 1935-36; m. Anna C. Mills, May 19, 1930; children—David Mills, Carolyn Bond. Asst, N.Y. Pub. Library Reference Dept., 1930-31; librarian Colby College, Waterville, Me., 1931-35, Rosenberg Library, Galveston, Tex., 1936-47, Fort Worth Pub. Library, 1947-53, Tacoma (Wash.) Pub. Library, 1953-70. Mem. A.L.A., Wash., Pacific N.W. library assns. Home: Route 5 Box 5160 Gig Harbor WA 98335

IBBOTT, DOUGLAS M., ins. co. exec.; b. 1914; student Willamette U., So. Meth. U.; married. With Mut. of N.Y., 1933-36, Southland Life Ins. Co., 1938-40; with Southwestern Life Ins. Co., 1940—, chief underwriter, 1953-58, asst. sec., 1958-59, 2d v.p., 1959-69, v.p. underwriting, 1969—. Served with USNR, 1944-46. Office: Southwestern Life Bldg PO Box 2699 Dallas TX 75221*

IBELE, WARREN EDWARD, engring. educator; b. New Orleans, Aug. 17, 1924; s. Emile Frank and May Hilda (Labarthe) I.; B.S. in Mech. Engring., Tulane U., 1944; M.S., U. Minn., 1947, Ph.D., 1953; m. Mary Elizabeth Unumb, Sept. 3, 1947; childrenErik Warren, Gretchen Marie, Mark Adams, John Labarthe. Asst. project engr. Pratt & Whitney Aircraft Corp., 1955-57; faculty U. Minn., 1947-, prof. engring., 1959-, asso. dean Grad. Sch., 1967-. Visitor curriculum accreditation Engrs. Council Profl. Devel.; mem. sect. SABER, Navy Bd. Ednl. Requirements, 1966-69, Served with U.S. Navy, 1944-46. Decorated Naval Letter of Commendation with ribbon. Mem. Am. Soc. M.E., Am. Soc. Engring. Edn., Sigma Xi, Tau Beta Pi. Mem. Democratic Farm Labor Party. Conglist. Author: (with N.A. Hall) Engineering Thermodynamics, 1960; also numerous articles. Editor: Modern Developments in Heat Transfer, 1963. Home: 1729 Logan Av Minneapolis MN 55403

IBSEN, HENRI G., ins. exec.; b. Copenhagen, Denmark, Nov. 10, 1908; s. Mads and Agnes (Rasmussen) I.; student bus. colls., Denmark, Eng., France; m. Nell Priscott, June 6, 1940; 1 son, Max Emil. Came to U.S., 1947. Joined fgn. dept. Baltica Ins. Co., Ltd., Copenhagen, 1929, charge London (Eng.) office, 1939-47; student casualty, fire and marine ins. in Eng., France and Germany, 1935-38; dir. Constitution Ins. Corp. of N.Y., 1940—, pres., 1947-69, vice chmn., 1969—. Club: Drug and Chemical (N.Y.C.). Home: 315 Forest Dr Short Hills NJ 07078 Office: 110 William St New York City NY 10038

IBUKA, MASARU, electronics co. exec.; b. Nikko, Japan, Apr. 11, 1908; s. Tasuku and Sawa (Furuta) I.; B.S., Waseda U., Tokyo, Japan, 1933; m. Sekiko Maeda, Dec. 20, 1936; children—Shizuko, Taeko, Makoto. Research engr. Photo Chem. Lab., 1933-40; mng. dir. Japan Measuring Apparatus Co., Ltd., 1940- 45; organizer Sony Corp., and predecessor, 1945, pres., 1958—; chmn. Sony Shoji Co., Ltd., Sony Electron Tube Corp., Sony Chems. Corp. Chmn. Suginakai Found. Recipient Medal of Honor with blue ribbon (Japan). Mem. Japan Electronic Industries Assn. (council), Japan Sci. and Techniques Agy. (adv. councilor), Econ. Council Electronic Industries Assn. Japan (exec. dir.), Japan Com. Econ. Devel., Japan Electronic Devel. Assn. (bd. dirs.). Protestant. Home: 5 1-chome Shimomeguro Meguroku Tokyo Japan Office: 7-35 Kitashinagawa-6 Shinagawaku Tokyo Japan

ICE, HARRY TREESE, lawyer; b. Paulding, O., Oct. 17, 1904; s. Henry J. and Senna (Treese) I.; A.B., Butler U., 1926; LL.B., Harvard, 1929; LL.D., Ind. Central Coll., Indpls., 1966; m. Elizabeth McIntyre, July 9, 1932; 1 dau., Marabeth. Admitted to Ind. bar, 1929; asso, Ice, Miller, Donadio & Ryan Indpls., 1929—, partner, 1934—, Dir. Am. United Life Ins. Co., Fairbanks Broadcasting Co., Inc., Mchts. Nat. Bank & Trust Co., Union City Body Co. Bd. dirs. Greater Indpls. United Fund, YWCA, Indpls. Civic Progress Assn., Indpls. Hosp. Devel. Assn., Crossroads Rehab. Center, Central Ind. council Boy Scouts Am., Bd. Fundamental Edn.; trustee Butler U. Served to lt. comdr. USNR, 1943-45. Mem. Ind. (dir.), Indpls. (dir.) chambers commerce. Mem. Christian Ch. (trustee Found.). Home: 6370 Spring Mill Rd Indianapolis IN 46260 Office: 111 Monument Circle Indianapolis IN 46204

ICE, LEWIS MELVIN, librarian; b. Greencastle, Ind., Oct. 16, 1907; s. Lewis Hurlston and Mary Grace (Ely) I.; A.B., DePauw U., 1928; M.A., Columbia, 1931, B.S. in L.S., 1937; m. Dorothy R. Steiner, July 1, 1944; childrenGeoffrey Lewis, Curtis Wesley, Andrew Hilary. Tchr. pub. schs., Ind., N.Y., 1928-30; librarian Morristown (N.J.) Sch., 1936-39, asst. librarian charge book car service Ferguson Library, Stamford, Conn., 1939-41; tchr. Milton (Mass.) Acad., 1941-42; mem. profl. staff N.Y. Pub. Library, 1942-43, Coll. City N.Y., 1943-44; librarian Teaneck (N.J.) High Sch., 1944-46, Sampson Coll., Geneva, N.Y., 1946-49, U. Bridgeport, Conn., 1948—. Mem. Gov.'s Com. for State-Wide Library Devel; chmn. com. campus ministry Conn. Council Chs., 1962; adult program com. Bridgeport YMCA; council Sterling House, Stratford Community Center. Served with AUS, 1940-41. Mem. Am., Conn. (chmn. coll. and univ. sect. 1962, 69—) library assns., Phi Delta Kappa. Methodist (lay leader, trustee). Club: Torch (past pres.). Contbr. articles to profl. jours. Home: 490 Hilltop Dr Stratford CT 06497 Office: 303 University Av Bridgeport CT 06604

ICHIHASHI, TATSUHIKO, advt. exec.; b. Aichi Prefecture, Japan, Oct. 28, 1916; s. Masao and Nobu Ichihashi; grad. pharm. dept., Chiba U. (Japan), 1937; m. Keiko Nakazawa, Nov. 23, 1932; children—Yoshinori Uda, Hiromi Uda, Kazuhiko, Atsumi. Advt. mgr. Shionogi Pharm. Co., Ltd., Osaka, Japan, 1946-51; advt. dir. Readers Digest of Japan, Ltd., Osaka and Tokyo, 1951-60; mgmt. supr. Daiko Advt., Inc., Tokyo, 1960-63; pres., mng. dir. Grey-Daiko Advt., Inc., Tokyo, 1963—. Mem. Japan Advt. Assn. (dir. 1971—), Internat. Advt. Assn. (dir. Japan chpt. 1970—). Author: Product Manager, 1966; Advertising Changes the World, 1969. Home: 5 9 2 chome Hanegi Setagaya ku Tokyo Japan Office: 3 6 2 chome Ohtemachi Chiyoda ku Toyko Japan

ICHIKAWA, KON, Japanese film dir.; b. 1915; ed. Ichioka Comml. Sch., Dsaka, Japan. Films include: Poo-San, 1953, A Billionaire, 1954, The Heart, 1954, Punishment Room, 1955, The Burmese Harp, 1956, The Men of Tohoku, 1956, Conflagration, 1958, Fires on the Plain, 1959, The Key, 1959, Bonchi, 1960, Her Brother, 1960, The Sin, 1961, Being Two Isn't Easy, 1962, The Revenge of Yuki-No-Jo, 1963, Alone on the Pacific, 1963, Tokyo Olympiad, 1964. Address: care Ishihara Internat Prodns Kimuraya Bldg 24 Toranomon Shiba Minato-Ku Tokyo 105 Japan

ICHNIOWSKI, CASIMIR THADDEUS, educator, pharmacologist; b. Balt., Mar. 4, 1909; s. William and Marya (Tomaszkiewiez) I.; Ph.G., U. Md., B.S., 1930, M.S., 1932, Ph.D., 1936; m. Felice M. Wasell, Dec. 29, 1951; children—Thomas F., Michael J., Bernard E., Stephen P. Asst. toxicologist Chem. Warfare Service Edgewood, Md., 1936-38; pharmacologist Warner Inst. Therapeutic Research, N.Y.C., 1938-46, Wyeth, Inc., Phila., 1946-51; asst. dean, prof. pharmacology U. Md. Sch. Pharmacy, 1968—. Mem. Am. Pharm. Assn., A.A.A.S., Am. Acad. Pharm. Sci., Sigma Xi, Rho Chi, Phi Kappa Phi. Home: 625 Woodbine Av Towson MD 21204 Office: 636 W Lombard St Baltimore MD 21201

ICHORD, RICHARD HOWARD, congressman; b. Licking, Mo., June 27, 1926; s. Richard Howard and Minda (Curtis) I.; B.S., Mo. U., 1949; LL.B., 1952; m. Vera Rodgers, July 22, 1947; children—Richard Howard III, Pamela Lee. Instr. bus. law U. Mo., 1950, 51; admitted to Mo. bar, 1952; mem. firm Lay & Ichord, Houston, Mo., 1952-60; city atty., Houston, 1952; rep. Texas County, Mo. Ho. Reps., 1953, speaker pro tem, 1957-58, speaker, 1959-60; mem. 87th-92d Congresses 8th Dist. Mo. Served with Air Corps, USNR, 1944-46. Mem. V.F.W., Am. Legion, Houston C. of C. Democrat. Mason, Odd Fellow. Home: 505 Hawthorne St Houston MO 65483 Office: House Office Bldg Washington DC 20515

ICKES, WILLIAM KEITH, educator; b. Salt Lake City, Feb. 4, 1926; s. William B. and Anna Lucile (Christenson) I.; B.S., U. Utah, 1948, M.S., 1949; Ph.D., So. Ill. U., 1960; m. Shirley Doris Hallman, Aug. 27, 1946; children—William John, Bonnie Jean, Patricia Lynn, Joy Marie. Audiologist, Detroit Hearing Center, 1950-52, Mich. Assn. for Better Hearing, Lansing, 1952-54; exec. dir. Des Moines Hearing and Speech Center, 1954-62; dir. Speech and Hearing Clinic, prof. speech Tex. Tech. U., Lubbock, 1962-69, prof., chmn. dept. speech and theatre, 1969—. Dist. commr. So. Plains council Boy Scouts Am., 1964—. Bd. dirs., treas. Lubbock Theater Center; bd. dirs. Lubbock Family Service Agy. Served with USAAF, 1943-44. Mem. Am., Tex. (v.p. 1965) speech and hearing assns., Sigma Alpha Eta (pres. elect 1967, editor Keynotes 1964-67). Rotarian. Home: 4306 57th St Lubbock TX 79413

IDDINGS, ANDREW SHEETS, lawyer; b. Dayton, O., Oct. 18, 1880; s. Charles Dickens and Belle (Sheets) I; grad. Deaver Collegiate Inst., 1898; L.H.D. (hon.), U. of Dayton, 1957; LL.D., Miami U., Oxford, Ohio, 1964. Admitted to Ohio bar, 1903, since practiced in Dayton; founder, sec.- treas., gen. counsel Fyr-Fyter Co. of Dayton, 1916-47; dep. collector U.S. Internal Revenue, Dayton, 1898-1902; dep. clk. Supreme Ct. of O., 1902-06; chief dep. clk. cts., Dayton, 1906-09; U.S. commr. So. Dist. of O., 1924-26; sec., gen. atty. Dist Tb Hosp., Dayton, 1934-66; mem. firm Iddings, Jeffrey & Donnelly. Member Dayton City Plan Board, 1933- 47; mem. chmn. Dayton Met. Housing Authority, 1934—; v.p. Civic Music Assn. Dayton. Fellow Royal Geographical Soc. of London (life), Am. Bar Foundation; mem. Ohio State Bar Found. (an incorporator, sec.-treas. 1951-63), Montgomery County (past pres.), Ohio State (pres. 1941-42), Am., Internat. (charter patron) bar assns. Mason (33). Clubs: Lawyers, Engrs., Country (Dayton); Explorers (life) (N.Y.C.). Author: Andrew S. Iddings Explorer, 1967; also author law reports. Photographic reports of travels Am. and fgn. mags. Home: 218 Haver Rd Oakwood Dayton OH 45419 Office: 3d National Bldg Dayton OH 45402

IDE, CHANDLER, petroleum and shipping co. exec.; b. Mt. Vernon, N.Y., May 8, 1909; s. Herbert Chandler and Harriet (McDonald) I.; B.A. magna cum laude, Pomona Coll., 1930; m. Helen Evans, Oct. 13, 1934; children—Susan (Mrs. Dale Junta), Deborah (Mrs. Fredrick Palmer). With Standard Oil Co. of Cal., 1935-41; staff Office Petroleum Coordinator for War, Washington, 1941-42, Petroleum Adminstrn. for War, 1942-46, exec. asst. dep. adminstr., 1943-46; cons. Oil and Gas div. Dept. Interior, 1946, asso. dir., 1947; sec., treas. Am. Independent Oil Co., 1948-58, v.p., 1954-58; dir., sec., treas. Independent Tankships, Inc., 1948-57; dir., sec.-treas. Am. Independent Oil Co. of Iran, 1955-58, Am. Independent Oil Co. de Mexico S.A. de C.V., 1949-58; dir., sec., treas. Trunkline Gas Supply Co., 1948- 49; dir., v.p., sec.-treas. APL Assos., Inc., 1952-56; dir., mem. exec. com., v.p., sec.-treas. Natomas Co., San Francisco, 1956-66, pres., 1966—; chmn. bd., dir. Ind. Indonesian Am. Petroleum Co., 1970—; dir. v.p., sec.-treas. St. Mary's Square, Inc., San Francisco, 1960-69, pres., 1969—; dir., v.p., sec.-treas. Western Geothermal, Inc., San Francisco, 1961-68, pres., 1969—; v.p., dir. Natomas Co. of Peru, 1961—; v.p. Natomas Internat. Corp., 1967—; chmn. bd., dir. West Indies Oil Co., Ltd.; dir., chmn. Natomas Can. Ltd., 1968—; dir. Natomas Arabian Oil Co., Bank of California; Ind. Petroleum Supply Co., Am. Pres. Lines, Ltd. Bd. dirs. San Francisco Hearing and Speech Center, 1960-71, president, 1964-65; trustee World Affairs Council, 1971. Mem. No. Tennis Assn. (director 1953-56), Phi Beta Kappa. Clubs: Berkeley Tennis (pres. 1953-54); Claremont Country (Oakland, Cal.); Commonwealth (San Francisco). Home: 59 Plaza Berkeley CA 94705 Office: International Bldg San Francisco CA 94104

IDE, DONALD CHESTER, fgn. service officer; b. Seattle, Nov. 26, 1916; s. Clarence W. and Dora (McKay) I.B.A., U. Wash., 1940; m. Kathryn E. Kelly, May 16, 1942; childrenDonald W., Douglas C., Kathryn E. Asst. mgr. gen. mdse. dept. John P. Herber & Co., Inc., Seattle, 1946-55; tchr. extension course U. Wash., 1955; mem. sales dept. Great Western Chem. Co., Seattle, 1955-57; joined U.S. Fgn. Service, 1957; consul. Calcutta, India, 1957; 62; chief S. Asia sect. Dept. Commerce, 1962-65; comml. attache Am. embassy, Beirut, Lebanon, 1965-. Chmn. world trade div. Seattle C. of C., 1953; pres. World Trade Club Seattle, 1954; mem. Mercer Is. (Wash) Sch. Bd., 1954. Served as officer AUS, 1940-46; lt. col. Res. Mem. World Affairs Council Seattle, Pan Xenia. Clubs: Propellor (Beirut, Lebanon); Calcutta. Address: Am Embassy Beirut Lebanon

IDEMA, JAMES MEAD, editor; b. Grand Rapids, Mich., Mar. 29, 1920; s. Chester Frederic and Marion (Mead) I.; A.B., Dartmouth, 1942; m. Joyce Oelschlager, Aug. 26, 1967; children—James Mead, Marion M. City editor Grand Rapids Herald, 1945-55; life underwriter Aetna Life Ins. Co., Grand Rapids, 1955-60; reporter, copy editor Denver Post, 1960-62, editorial writer, 1962-64, editor of editorial page, 1965-71; exec. editor Newark (N.J.) News, 1971—. Served with USNR, 1942-45. Mem. Am. Soc. Newspaper Editors. Home: 33 Oakley Av Summit NJ 07901 Office: 207-221 Market St Newark NJ 07101

IDRIS, I, (Mohammed Idris as Sanusi) former King of Libya; b. 1890; m. Emira Fatima. As Emir of Cyrenaica, 1949, was chosen to be king of Libya, by constituent assembly, which decided the country's form of govt. should be a constitutional monarchy, 1950: monarchy proclaimed, 1951; deposed, 1969. Address: UAR*

IDZERDA, STANLEY JOHN, coll. pres.; b. N.Y.C., June 4, 1920; s. Hendrik and Therese (Miller) I.; B. Naval Sci., U. Notre Dame, 1946; A.B., Baldwin-Wallace Coll., 1947; A.M., Western Res. U., 1950, Ph.D., 1951; m. Geraldine Ann Waters, Oct. 26, 1945; childrenAnn, Geraldine, William, Christopher, Mary, James, Catherine. Asst. prof. history Western Mich. Coll., 1951-52: faculty Mich. State U., 1952-65, prof. history, 1958-65, dir. Honors Coll., 1957-65; adj. prof. history, dean undergrad. studies Wesleyan U, Middletown, Conn., 1965-68; now pres. Coll. St. Benedict, St. Joseph, Minn.: vis. lectr. history Yale Grad. Sch., 1966-67; distinguished vis. prof. No. Mich. U., 1967. Chmn. advanced placement com. Coll. Entrance Exam. Bd., 1965; regional asso. Am. Council Learned Socs., 1960-65. Mem. exec. com. Middletown Community Action Program, 1965—. Trustee Boston Coll., Macalester Coll., Mundelein Coll. Fellow Am. Council Learned Socs., 1950-51. Served with USNR, 1940-46. Decorated Purple Heart, Mem. Am., Am. Cath. hist. assns., Am. Soc. Aesthetics (trustee 1958-61), Soc. French Hist. Studies (pres. 1961-62), Soc. History Tech. Contbr. profl. jours. Home: Route 1 St Joseph MN 56374

IDZUMBUIR, THEODORE, diplomat Dem. Republic of Congo; b. Leverville, The Congo, Nov. 9, 1930; s. Antoine and Marie (Ngwolo) I.; student Bus. adminstrn. Lovanium- Kisantu Inst., 1950-54, Thomist philosophy Mayidi Sem., 1946-49; Licence degree polit. sci. internat. field, Univ. Inst. Internat. Studies, Geneva, Switzerland, 1961. Asst. psycho-technician charge personnel selection Office Congo Transp., 1954-58, gen. gov. attache, 1958-59; head Congolese delegation negotiations with Common Market, also pres. finance com., 1962; permanent rep. of the Congo to UN, 1962—, v.p. delegation XVII-XXIII gen. sessions; mem. Congolese delegation Addis-Ababa Conf. of Orgn. for African Unity, 1964, head Congolese delegation meeting of council of ministers, 1964, mem. delegation, 1966, chmn. 4th com., 24th session Gen. Assembly; leader good will mission to Tehad, 1964; head Congolese delegation 1st-3d session governing bd. UN Develop. Program, 1967. Decorated comdr. de l'Ordre Nat. du Leopard, 1966. Home: 215 E 68th St New York City NY 10021 Office: 400 E 51st St New York City NY 10022

IFFLAND, DON CHARLES, educator, chemist; b. Blissfield, Mich., Nov. 26, 1921; s. Fred C. and Letha (Lipp) I.; B.S., Adrian Coll., 1943; M.S., Purdue U., 1946, Ph.D., 1947; m. Mary Jane Sparks, Apr. 29, 1944; children—Diana, Charis. Asst. prof., asso. prof. W.Va. U., 1947-56; asso. prof., prof. Western Mich. U., Kalamazoo, 1956—, chmn. chemistry dept., 1968—. Mem. Am. Chem. Soc., Chem. Soc. (London), Am. Inst. Chemists, Sigma Xi. Contbr. articles profl. jours. Home: 3430 Northview Dr Kalamazoo MI 49001

IGL, RICHARD FRANKLIN, lawyer; b. Klamath Falls.., Ore., Feb. 15, 1923; s. Englebert Matthew and Rose Ann (Haas) I.; B.A., U. Ore., 1947, M.A. with honors, 1948; LL.B., Yale, 1950. Admitted to Cal. bar, 1951; law clk. to judge U.S. Ct. Apppeals, 1950-51; asso. firm O'Melveny & Myers, Los Angeles, 1951- 60, partner, 1960-63; pvt.

practice, Beverly Hills, Cal., 1964—; tchr. polit. sci. Yale, 1949-50; tchr. estate planning course U. Cal. at Los Angeles, 1963-64. Dir. Crobsy Investment Corp., Los Angeles. Served to capt. AUS, 1942-46. Mem. Cal., Los Angeles (trustee 1970-71), Beverly Hills (pres. 1969) bar assns., Phi Beta Kappa. Home: 9800 Yoakum Dr Beverly Hills CA 90210 Office: 9720 Wilshire Blvd Beverly Hills CA 90212

IGLEHART, JOSEPH ALEXANDER WILSON, investment banker; b. Balt., Nov. 15, 1891; s. Paul and May (Wilson) I.; C.E., Cornell U., 1914; m. Jane Margaret Cary Ulman, Dec. 29, 1917; children—Jane Margaret Cary (Mrs. Harold Purinton), Katharine Cary (Mrs. G. Ross French). Asso. with Brooks, Stokes & Co., Phila., 1914, partner 1920-25; owner Iglehart & Co., 1921-31; asso. with Field, Glore & Co., 1932-35; became partner W. E. Hutton & Co., 1935, now asso., chmn. finance com., dir. CBS; dir. City Stores Co., N.Y. Yankees, Nat. Wire Products Corp., N. Balt.; adv. dir. Nat. Gypsum Co., Buffalo. Trustee Cornell Plantations; pres. Boys Latin Sch., Balt. Served to maj. AUS. Clubs: Links, Maryland, Baltimore Country, Green Spring Valley Hunt, Elkridge, South River; Racquet and Tennis (N.Y.C). Home: RFD Lutherville MD 21093 Hotel Westbury New York City NY 10021 Office: 14 Wall St New York City NY 10005 ☆

IGLEHART, ROBERT LESLIE, educator; b. Balt., Feb. 2, 1912; s. Harry A. and Harriet (McDonnal) I.; student Md. Inst. Art, 1930-34, Johns Hopkins, 1935-36; B.S., Columbia, 1941; student New Sch. Social Research, 1949-50; m. Ruth Herscher, July 12, 1946; childrenAustin, Emily B. Comml. designer, N.Y.C., 1936-38; tchr. U. Wash., 1938-41, Columbia, 1941-42; tech. editor Personnel Research Center, Adj. Gen.'s Office, Washington, 1942-43; prof. edn., chmn. dept. art edn., N.Y. U., 1946-55; prof. art, chmn. dept. U. Mich., 1955-70. Cons. on art Tel-Aviv U., 1964, Chgo, Bd. Edn., 1965 Mem. study com. visual arts Mass. Inst. Tech., 1952-53; mem. adv. com. Graham Found., 1955; mem. council Coll. of Architecture, Cornell U., 1961. Chmn. com. on art Mich. Cultural Commn. Served AUS, 1943-46. Recipient medal for distinguished service to edn. in art Nat. Gallery Art, 1966. Fellow Royal Soc. Arts; mem. Nat. Com. Art Edn. (asst. chmn.), Midwest Coll. Art Assn., Nat., Mich. art edn. assns., N.E.A., Western Arts Assn., Inst. for Study of Art in Edn. (bd. govs.), Mich. Acad. Arts and Scis., Tau Sigma Delta. Contbr. profl. jours. Home: 117 Dixboro Rd Ann Arbor MI 48105

IGNATIEFF, GEORGE, Canadian ambassador, rep.; b. St. Petersburg, Russia, Dec. 16, 1913; s. Count Paul and Countess Natalie (Mestchersky) I.; B.A., Toronto U., 1936; Rhodes scholar Oxford, 1935; postgrad. Imperial Def. Coll., London, 1954; LL.D., Toronto and Brock univs., 1969, U. Guelph, 1970; m. Alison Grant, Nov. 17, 1945; children— Michael, Andrew. Third sec. Office High Commr. for Can., London, Eng., 1940, trans. to Ottawa, Can., 1944; adviser Canadian delegation AEC, N.Y.C., 1946-47; adviser Canadian delegation, 1st and 2d Gen. Assembly, UN, N.Y.C., 1946-47, prin. adviser Canadian Permanent Delegation, 1947—; alternate rep. Can. on Security Council, 1948; counsellor Canadian embassy, Washington, 1949; spl. asst. to under-sec. for external affairs; Canadian ambassador to Yugoslavia, 1957; dep. high commr. for Can. in U.K., 1958-60; asst. undersec. state for external affairs, 1960-62; ambassador, Canadian rep. NATO, 1962-66; Canadian ambassador, permanent rep. to UN, 1966-69; Canadian permanent rep. and ambassador to 18 Nation Disarmament Com., Geneva, 1969-70; permanent Canadian rep. to UN, Geneva, 1970—. Home: 15-17 Route de Collex Geneva Switzerland Office: 10A Av de Budé 1202 Geneva Switzerland

IGNATIUS, PAUL ROBERT, bus. exec.; b. Los Angeles, Nov. 11, 1920; s. H. B. and Elisa (Jamgochian) I.; A.B., U. So. Cal., 1942; M.B.A., Harvard, 1947; m. Nancy Sharpless Weiser, Dec. 20, 1947; children—David, Amy, Sarah, Alan. Instr. bus. adminstrn. Harvard Bus. Sch., 1947-50; v.p., dir. Harbridge House, Inc., mgmt. cons., Boston, 1950-61; asst. sec. army for installations and logistics, 1961-63, undersec., 1964; asst. sec. of def., 1964-67; sec. of navy, 1967-69; pres. The Washington Post, now exec. v.p. Served with USNR, 1943-46. Recipient Distinguished Civilian Service award Dept. Army, 1962; Civilian Pub. Service award Dept. Navy, 1969, Dept. Def., 1969. Mem. Phi Beta Kappa. Home: 3650 Fordham Rd Washington DC 20016 Office: 1515 L St NW Washington DC 20005

IGNATOW, DAVID, poet; b. Bklyn., Feb. 7, 1914; s. Max and Yetta (Reinbach) I.; ed. pub. schs., Bklyn: m. Rose Grauhart, July 20, 1940; children—David, Yaedi. Asso. editor Am. Scene mag., 1935-37; lit. arts editor N.Y. Analytic, 1937; editor Beloit (Wis.) Poetry Jour., 1949-59; poetry editor The Nation, 1962-63; guest editor Chelsea, N.Y., 1962, co-editor, 1968: instr. poetry workshop New Sch. Social Research, N.Y.C., 1964; vis. lectr. U. Ky., 1965-66; lectr. English, U. Kan., 1966—; vis. lectr. Vassar Coll., 1967-68; adj. prof. Southampton Coll. of L.I. U., 1967-68, Columbia U.; poet-in-residence York Coll. Recipient Nat. Inst. Arts and Letters award, 1964; Guggenheim fellow, 1965; Shelley Meml. award, 1966; Rockefeller Found. grant, 1968; Nat. Endowment for Arts award, 1970. Jewish religion. Author: Poems, 1948: The Gentle Weight Lifter, 1955; Say Pardon, 1962; Figures of the Human, 1964: Earth Hard, Selected Poems, 1968; Rescue the Dead, 1968; Poems: 1934-69, 1970. Co-editor: Chelsea (lit. semi-ann.). Address: 17th St and Gardiner Av East Hampton NY 11937

IGNICO, ROBERT VICTOR army officer: b. Boston, Mass., Oct. 14, 1895; s. Vincent and Mary Rose (Cavagnaro) I.; student Washington and Lee U., 1914-17; grad. U.S. Army Airship Sch., 1921, Air Corps Advanced Flying Sch., 1923, U.S. Army Indsl. Coll., 1932, Air Corps Tactical Sch., 1937; m. Arlene Davidson, June 23, 1917; children—Vivian Gertrude (Mrs. Louis B. Grossmith, Jr.), Vincent Anthony. Apptd. aviation cadet U.S. Army Air Forces, May 19, 1917, and advanced through grades to brig. gen., Sept. 1942. Decorated Victory medal, Asiatic-Pacific medal with Bronze Star. Am. Defense Ribbon with Bronze Star. Air Medal, Am. Theatre Medal, Legion of Merit Medal, Legion of Merit with 2 Oak Leaf Clusters. Commendation Ribbon, Asiatic Pacific with 2 Bronze Stars. Mem. Phi Kappa Sigma. K.C. Address: 540 Palmetto Rd Belleair FL 33540

IGO, GEORGE JEROME, educator, physicist; b. Greeley, Colo., Sept. 2, 1925; s. Henry Jerome and Ida (Danielsen) I.; A.B., Harvard, 1949; M.S., U. Cal. at Berkeley, 1951, Ph.D., 1953; m. Nancy Tebow, May 15, 1953; children—Saffron, Peter Alexander. Research asso. Sloane Physics Lab., Yale, 1953-54; research asso. exptl. physics Brookhaven Nat. Lab., Upton, L.I., N.Y., 1954-56; faculty Stanford, 1956-58, acting asst. prof., 1957-58; guest prof. U. Heidelberg Inst. for Theoretical Physics, also Max Planck Inst. for Nuclear Physics, Heidelberg, Germany, 1958-59; staff Lawrence Radiation Lab., U. Cal., Berkeley, 1959-63; dir. Cyclotron Inst., Tex. A. and M. U., 1963-64; vis. staff mem. Los Alamos Sci. Lab., 1964-68; prof. physics U. Cal. at Los Angeles, 1969—. Fulbright Travel fellow, Germany, 1958-59. Mem. Am. Phys. Soc. Contbr. articles profl. jours. Home: 209 Quadro Vecchio Pacific Palisades CA 90272 Office: Knudsen Hall U Cal Los Angeles CA 90024

IGOE, JAMES GERARD, librarian; b. Lackawanna, N.Y., Aug. 20, 1931; s. Gerard James and Olive Jesse (DuFrane) I.; A.B., Fordham U., 1955; Ph.L., 1956; M.L.S., Simmons Coll., 1961; m. Joan Marie Davis, Apr. 16, 1960; children—Beth Ann, Robert. Adult reference librarian Detroit Pub. Library, 1961-63, head service bur., 1963-64, asst. br. librarian, 1964-65; head reader services Mich. State Library, Lansing, 1965; library services program officer for Ind., Ill., Mich., Ohio, Wis. U.S. Office Edn., Chgo., 1968-69; state librarian Vt. Dept. Libraries, 1969—. Bd. dirs. Barre Town Sch., 1971—. Served with AUS, 1957-60. Mem. Am. (mem. council 1970-74), New Eng., Vt. library assns., Nat., Vt. edn. assns., Beta Phi Mu. Rotarian. Editor: Vermont Libraries, 1970—. Contbr. articles profl. jours. Home: Cobble Hill Rd Barre VT 05641 Office: Dept Libraries Montpelier VT 05602

IGOE, JOHN EDWARD, moving and storage co. exec.; b. Amsterdam, N.Y., Dec. 2O, 1919; s. John Bernard and Caroline (Dufel) I.; student Northwestern U.; grad. Bentley Coll., Boston, 1940; m. Zola Howard Wilson, Oct. 10, 1945; children-Kathleen Ann, Cynthia Mary, Nancy Wilson, John Howard, Jeffrey Robert. With Flintkote Co., 1940-69, asst. controller, 1962-66, controller, 1966-69; v.p. finance The Bekins Co., Los Angeles, 1969—. Served to capt. USAAF, 1942-45. Decorated Air medal with oak leaf cluster, D.F.C. with oak leaf cluster. Mem. Financial Execs. Inst., Cal. Taxpayers Assn. (dir.). Roman Catholic. Home: 1325 Ramona Rd Arcadia CA Office: 1335 S Figueroa St Los Angeles CA

IGUSA, JUN-ICHI, mathematician, educator: b. Japan, Jan. 30, 1924; s. Shiro and Rui (Fuku- shima) I.; Rigakushi, Tokyo Imperial U., 1945, Rigakuhakushi, 1953; m. Yoshie Yamamoto, Oct. 7, 1948; children—Kiyoshi, Takeru, Mitsuru. Came to U.S., 1953. Asst. prof. Kyoto (Japan) U., 1949-53: research asso. Harvard, 1953-55; faculty Johns Hopkins, 1955—, prof. math., 1961- -. Mem. Math. Soc. Japan, Am. Math. Soc. Home: 911 Breezewick Rd Towson MD 21204 Office: Johns Hopkins Univ Baltimore MD 21218

IHDE, AARON JOHN, educator; b. Neenah, Wis., Dec. 31, 1909; s. John Lewis and Ella (Haase) I.; B.S., U. Wis., 1931, M.S., 1939, Ph.D., 1941; m. Olive Jane Tipler, June 14, 1933; children—Gretchen (Mrs. Hendrik Serrie), John. Chemist, Blue Valley Creamery Co., Chgo., 1931-38; instr. chemistry Butler U., Indpls., 1941-42; mem. faculty U. Wis., Madison, 1942—, prof. chemistry, integrated liberal studies and history of sci., 1958—, chmn. dept. integrated liberal studies, 1963-70. Carnegie intern in gen. edn. Harvard, 1951-52; mem. Wis. Food Standards Adv. Com., 1955-68, chmn., 1964-65. Recipient Dexter award history of chemistry div. Am. Chem. Soc., 1968. Mem. History of Sci. Soc., A.A.A.S., Am. Chem. Soc., Wis. Acad. Scis., Arts and Letters (pres. 1963-64), Sigma Xi, Phi Lambda Upsilon. Democrat. Unitarian. Author: The Physical Universe, 1963; Development of Modern Chemistry, 1964; Selected Readings in the History of Chemistry, 1965. Home: 2626 Marshall Pkwy Madison WI 53713

IHDE, IRA CARLYLE, educator; b. Hoep, Kan., Aug. 27, 1904: s. Otto C. and Anna (Wuthnow) I.; A.B., McPherson (Kan.) Coll., 1928; M.A., U. Kan., 1932; Ph.D. (fellow 1948-49), U. N.M., 1950; postgrad. U. Tex., 1939-40; m. Martha Schaffner, Aug. 1, 1940; children—Daniel Carlyle, Charlotte Joey. Tchr. pub. schs., Kan., 1927-39; instr. history Parsons (Kan.) Coll., 1939-43; mem. faculty Eastern N.M. U., Portales, 1943—, prof. history, 1943—, chmn. dept., 1961—; grad. asst. history U. Kan., 1929-30; traveling history lectr. Omnibus Coll., summers 1932-37. Mem. Theodore Roosevelt Rough Riders Commn. N.M., 1949—; chmn. N.M. Records Commn., 1960-65. Recipient President's Faculty award superior teaching Eastern N.M. U., 1958. Mem. Orgn. Am. Historians, N.M. Hist. Soc., Am. Assn. U. Profs., Nat., N.M. edn. assns., Phi Alpha Theta, Phi Kappa Phi. Lion (pres. Portales 1946). Author: The Economic Status of the Southern Negro, 1932; Great Speakers of History, 1939; Our Greatest President, 1945; Washington Ellsworth Lindsey, 1951; W.E. Lindsey, A Progressive Frontiersman, 1952; International Relations, 1952; Presidential Elections in New Mexico, 1960. Home: 1311 S Av G Portales NM 88130

IHRKE, WALTER RUDOLPH, educator; b. Milw., May 21, 1908; s. Adolph W. and Emma (Eisfeld) I.; Mus.B., Wis. Conservatory Music, 1933; Mus.M., U. Mich., 1937; Ph.D., Eastman Sch. Music, 1947; m. Virginia Schaefer, Aug. 28, 1932; children—Jean (Mrs. Arthur Steele), Janet (Mrs. William King), Alice (Mrs. Richard Ward). Tchr., Mission House Coll., Plymouth, Wis., 1932-38, Stephens Coll., Columbia, Mo., 1938-43, Peabody Coll., Nashville, 1943-49; head music dept. U. Conn., 1949-65, prof. music, 1965—; composer, pianist. Mem. Am. Assn. U. Profs., Music Educators Nat. Conf., Conn. Music Educators Assn. Research in automated music tchg. Home: 25 Storrs Heights Rd Storrs CT 06268

IJAMS, CHARLES CARROLL, educator; b. Jackson, Tenn., Dec. 23, 1913; s. Charles Burgess and Edna (Carroll) I.; A.B., Union U., Jackson, Tenn., 1936; M.S., Vanderbilt U., 1937, Ph.D., 1941; m. Louise Perkinson, Sept. 8, 1947; children—Lola K., Carolyn. Chief chemist Gulf Ordnance Plant, Prairie, Miss., 1941-43; prof. chemistry Union U., 1947; prof. physics Memphis State U., 1947—, chmn. dept., 1957—; cons. tech. tng. command USN, 1958—, insts. sci. tchrs. NSF, 1960—. Served to capt. USNR, 1943-47. Recipient Alumni award Union U., 1969. Mem. Naval Res. Assn., Res. Officers Assn., Mil. Order World Wars. Presbyn. Home: 249 N Rose Rd Memphis TN 38117

IJAMS, MAITLAND TABB, social cons.; b. Lawrence, N.Y., Sept. 1, 1926; s. John Horton and Margaret Seton (Porter) I.; grad. St. Mark's Sch., 1944; A.B., Harvard, 1948; m. Blandina Elmendorf Babcock, June 15, 1963; children—Margaret Ditson, Maitland Tabb. With First Boston Corp., N.Y.C., 1950-56; partner W.C. Langley & Co., N.Y., 1956-69; chmn. Babcock & Ijams New York Without Tears, Inc., N.Y.C., 1969—. Served with USAAF, 1944-46. Mem. Investment Assn. N.Y. (past pres.), Bond Club N.Y. (past gov.). Mem. Ch. of Epiphany (vestry). Clubs: Links (N.Y.C.); Lawrence Beach (v.p. gov.) (Atlantic Beach, N.Y.); Adirondack League (Old Forge, N.Y.). Home: 550 Park Av New York City NY 10021 Office: 33 E 61st St New York City NY 10021

IKARD, FRANK NEVILLE, assn. exec.; b. Henrietta, Tex., Jan. 30, 1914; s. E.L. and Ena (Neville) I.; LL.B., U. Tex., 1937; m. Jean Hunter, Oct. 15, 1940; children—Frank Neville, William Forsythe. Admitted to Tex. bar, 1937; practiced law, Wichita Falls, 1937-48; judge 30th Jud. Dist. Ct. of Tex., 1948-51; mem. 82d-87th Congresses, 13th Texas, until 1961; exec. v.p. Am. Petroleum Inst., 1961-63, pres., 1963—; sr. v.p., dir. Leece- Neville Co., Clev. Mem. Natural Gas Adv. Council. Former mem. Dist. bd. govs. A.R.C. Board of regents U. of Texas, 1965—. Served as pvt. 1st class 110th Inf. Regt., 28th Div., 1944-45. Mem. Am. Legion, V.F.W., Am. Bar Assn., State Bar Tex., Am. Petroleum Inst. (pres.), Am. Soc. Assn. Execs., World Power Conf., Nat. Petroleum Council, Beta Theta Pi. Democrat. Episcopalian. Mason (Shriner), Rotarian. Home: 2005 Arthur St Wichita Falls TX 76309 Office: 1271 Av of the Americas New York City NY 10020

IKE, NOBUTAKA, educator; b. Seattle, June 6, 1916; s. Yasuji and Tsuya (Tanaka) I.; B.A., U. Wash., 1940, grad. student, 1940-41; Ph.D., Johns Hopkins, 1949; m. Tai Inui, Aug. 23, 1942; childrenLinda Y., Brian Y. Instr. Japanese U.S. Naval Tng. Sch., U. Colo., 1942-46; lectr., Charles Peck fellow Johns Hopkins, 1948-49; curator Japanese collections Hoover Instn., Stanford, 1949-58; faculty Stanford U., 1958—, prof. polit. sci., 1963—, exec. head of dept., 1963- 64; Rockefeller vis. prof. U. Philippines, 1968-69. Recipient Demobilization award Social Sci. Research Council, 1946-48; Ford fellow, 1953-55; Rockefeller fellow, 1964-65. Mem. Phi Beta Kappa, Pi Sigma Alpha. Author: The Beginnings of Political Democracy in Japan, 1950; Japanese Politics, 1957; Japan's Decision for War, 1966. Asso. editor Far Eastern Quar., 1950-55. Contbr. Major Governments of Asia, 2d edit., 1963. Home: 621 Alvarado Row Stanford CA 94305

IKEDA, MASUO, artist; b. 1934. Etcher and lithographer in pop-art style; exhibited one-man show Mus. Modern Art, N.Y., 1965; traveling show of prints in U.S., 1967. Recipient grand prize for graphics Venice Biennale, 1966. Address: 60 Grand St New York City NY 10013

IKELER, HAROLD EDWIN, Jr., banker; b. Lewisburg, Pa., Nov. 11, 1930; s. Harold Edwin and Geraldine (Lazarus) I.; B.A., U. Pa., 1952; m. Patricia A. Strine, June 28, 1952; children—R. Stephen, Thomas J., Robert A. Asst. examiner, examining officer Fed. Res. Bank Phila., 1955-64; v.p., auditor Girard Trust Bank, Phila., now v.p. Corr. bankers div. Served to lt. (j.g.) U.S. Navy, 1952-55. Mem. Nat. Assn. Bank Auditors and Controllers.

IKENBERRY, OLIVER SAMUEL, educator; b. Roanoke, Va., Jan. 6, 1908; s. Jacob and Edith (Stauffer) I.; A.B., McPherson Coll., 1929; A.M., Colo. State Coll. Edn., 1932, Ed.D., 1941; postgrad. Columbia, 1935-36; m. Margaret Moulton, June 11, 1933; children—Stanley, Betty, Jane. Sup. schs., Haswell, Colo., 1930-33; prin. Union High Sch., Lamar, Colo., 1933-37; prin. schs., Delta, Colo., 1937-41; extension instr. Colo. State Coll. Edn., 1933-36; Western State Coll. Colo., 1937-41; dean coll., prof. edn. Salem (W.Va.) Coll., 1941-47; prof. edn. W.Va. U., summers, 1946, 47; pres. Shepherd State Coll., Shepherdstown, W.Va., 1947-68, pres. emeritus, 1968—; with Inst. Edn., Oxford U., 1968-69; prof. edn. George Peabody Coll., Nashville, Tenn., 1969—. Adv. dir. Potomac Edison Co. of W.Va., 1952-68. Coordinator Civil Aeros. Adminstrn. War Service for Salem Coll., and Armed Services rep., 1941-44. Pres. W.Va. council of State Coll. and U. Presidents, 1954-56, Colo. Assn. Classroom Leaders Western Div., 1938, Colo. Assn. Secondary Sch. Prins., 1939-40, Coöp. Research Assn., Colo. State Coll., 1941, Assn. Higher Edn. W.Va., 1946; rep. Am. Assn. Colls. for Teacher Edn. to the Am. Council on Edn., 1956-59; mem. W.Va. White House Conf. on Edn., 1956-59, 66-69; mem. Gov.'s Adv. Com. on Mental Health, 1964-68; higher edn. cons. U.S. Office Edn., 1966-70; rep. to World Conf. on Orgns. Teaching Profession, Kingston, Jamaica, 1971. Recipient Citation of merit for distinguished service McPherson Coll., 1969; Ky. Col., 1967. Mem. Am. Assn. Higher Edn., N.E.A., Tenn. Edn. Assn., W.Va. Council State Coll. and Univ. Pres.'s (pres. 1954), Am. Assn. State Colls. and Univs. (state rep. 1966-68), W.Va. Acad. Sci., W.Va. Assn. Coll. Pres.'s (sec.), W.Va. Intercoll. Athletic Assn. (sec.-treas. 1952-55), C. of C., Phi Delta Kappa (v.p. 1971), Kappa Delta Pi. Presbyn Rotarian (pres. 1951). Clubs: University (Nashville); Freolac Discussion (Nashville). Author: Comparative Inequalities in Educational Finance, 1932; Economic Factors Affecting Education in an Agricultural Community, 1939; Leisure Activities in a Community, 1941; Health, Government, Education and Religion in a Community, 1941; articles ednl. jours. Editor: The Colorado Clearing.House Bull., 1938-40. Home: 120 Acklen Park Dr Nashville TN 37203

IKLE, FRANK WILLIAM, educator; b. Zurich, Switzerland, Jan. 18, 1921 (Parents Am. citizens); s. Martin W. and Helen (Prichystal) I.; B.A., U. Cal. at Berkeley, 1941, Ph.D., 1953; m. Maurine Barnes, May 4, 1944; childrenMartin, Maurice, Matthew. Instr., Reed Coll., 1950-54; Carnegie fellow Harvard, 1951-52; Fulbright prof. U. Philippines, 1955-56; asso. prof. Miami U., Oxford, O., 1957-63; prof. history, chmn. dept. U. N.M., 1963-. Served to lt. comdr. USNR, 1942-46. Mem. Am. Hist. Assn., Assn. Asian Studies, Assn. Am. U. Profs. Author: German-Japanese Relations, 1936-40, 1957; (with others) A History of Asia, 1963; also articles. Home: 508 Chamiso Lane NW Albuquerque NM 87107

ILER, FRANK ROBERTSON, apparel co. exec.; b. Hillsboro, N.C., Apr. 1, 1911; s. Henry Hammett and Ina (Gunter) I.; B.S., Clemson U., 1934; postgrad. U. Ia., 1942-43; m. Nan Smith, Sept. 16, 1939; children—Frank Robertson, William H., Henry B. Indsl. engr. div. Mills, LaGrange Ga., 1934-41; pres. Blue Bell Services; dir. Blue Bell, Inc., Greensboro, N.C., 1941—. Pres. Gen. Greene council Boy Scouts Am. Mem. Miss. Mfg. Assn. (pres.). Methodist. Rotarian. Home: 4005 Watauga Dr Greensboro NC 27420 Office: 335 N Church St Greensboro NC 27420

ILG, FRANCES L., educator; b. Oak Park, Ill., Oct. 11, 1902; d. Joseph and Lennore (Peterson) Ilg; A.B., Wellesley Coll., 1925; M.D., Cornell, 1929; 1 adopted dau., Tordis Kristin. Intern St. Mary's Hosp. for Children, N.Y.C., 1930, Bellevue Hosp., 1930-31, N.E. Hosp. Women and Children, Boston, 1931-32; vis. pediatrician Clinic of Child Development, Yale, 1932-33, research asst., 1933-36, asst. prof. child development, 1937- 50; child health work, Stockholm, 1936-37; dir. Gesell Inst. Child Development, New Haven, 1950-70. Author: (with Arnold Gesell, others) The First Five Years of Life, 1940; Infant and Child in the Culture of Today, 1943; The Child from Five to Ten, 1946; Youth: The Years from Ten to Sixteen, 1956; School Readiness. Home: 345 St Ronan St New Haven CT 06511

ILIESCU, NICHOLAE, educator; b. Romania, May 21, 1919; s. Marin and Iulia (Lupescu) I.; D.Letters, U. Padua (Italy), 1947; A.M., Harvard, 1956, Ph.D. in Romance Langs. and Lit., 1958; m. Esther Gheta, Apr. 26, 1953; children—Rodica P., Doina A. Came to U.S., 1952. Instr. Italian, Harvard, 1958-59, asst. prof., 1959-62, asso. prof. Romance langs. and lit., 1962-68, prof., 1968—. Recipient medaglia della cultura Italian Govt., 1964. Mem. Dante Soc. Am., Mediaeval Acad. Am., Renaissance Soc. Am., Modern Lang. Assn., Societas Academica Daco-Romana (Rome), Am. Assn. Tchrs. Italian. Author: Da Manzoni a Nievo-considerazioni sul romanzo italiano, 1959, Il 'canzoniere' petrarchesco e Sant'Agostino, 1962 (recipient Premio Della Cultura Pres. Council of Ministers Italy 1964). Contbr. articles to lit. jours. Home: Deerhaven Rd Lincoln MA 01773 Office: Boylston Hall Harvard U Cambridge MA 02138

ILIN, EPHRAIM, automobile co. exec.; b. Kharkow, Russia, Jan. 20, 1912; s. Joseph and Esther (Konikoff) I.; L.S.C., U. Liege (Belgium), 1932; m. Zfira Entin, Jan. 9, 1934; children—Arnon, Ram. Owner orange groves, Rechovoth, Israel, 1932-35; mng. dir. colonization and land settlement co., Tel- Aviv, 1933-35; owner, dir. Ilin-Abramovitz, Tel-Aviv, 1937-46; dir. Palbric Co., Tel-Aviv, 1946-49; owner, dir. E. Ilin Industries Ltd., Haifa, Israel, 1949—; chmn., dir. holding companies various affiliates. Bd. govs. Weizmann Inst. Sci., Rechovoth. Mem. Israel Belgium (chmn.), Israel, Am. chambers commerce. Home: 31 Horeb St Mount Carmel Haifa Israel Office: 2 Bank St Haifa Israel

ILLICH, IVAN, educator; b. Sept. 4, 1907, Founder, head Center Intercultural Documentation. Address: care CUDOC Cuernavaca Mexico also 166 E 61st St New York City NY 10021*

ILLICK, JOHN ROWLAND, educator; b. Nanchang, Kiangsi, China, Feb. 22, 1919 (parents Am. citizens); s. John Theron and Bernice (Rowland) I.; B.A., U. Syracuse, 1940, M.A., 1941; A.M., Harvard, 1943, Ph.D., 1954; m. Edith Alice Windels, June 19, 1943; children—Virginia Anne, Priscilla, Martha, John Rowland. Teaching asst. Harvard, 1942-44; faculty Middlebury (Vt.) Coll., 1946—, prof. geography, 1962—; asso. prof. Am. U. Beirut (Lebanon), 1958-60; prof. geography Coll. Petroleum and Minerals, Dhahran, Saudi Arabia, 1969-71; summer tchr. U. B.C., U. Man., Queens U., U. Mich., U. Vt., Syracuse U., Queens Coll. Chmn., Middlebury Planning Commn., 1964-66. Mem. Assn. Am. Geographers, Am. Geog. Soc., Sigma Xi. Contbr. articles to profl. jours. Home: 16 Springside Rd Middlebury VT 05753

ILLIG, CARL, lawyer; b. Houston, Sept. 10, 1909; s. Carl and Olive (Kirlicks) I.; B.A., Rice Inst., 1930; LL.B., U. Tex., 1933; grad. Advanced Mgmt. Program, Harvard, 1959; m. Lillian Elizabeth Horlock, Apr. 17, 1933; children—Elaine (Mrs. Franklin B. Davis), Carol (Mrs. Simcon T. Lake III), Dale. Admitted to Tex. bar, 1933; practiced in Galveston, Tex., 1933-34, Houston, 1967—; with Humble Oil & Refining Co., 1934-67, asso. gen. counsel, 1961-67, dir. Petroleum Casualty Co., 1961-66; partner Illig, Brill and Dewitt, 1969-70, Mem. Tex. Coordinating Water Com., 1960; mem. Gov. Tex. Statewide Water Com., 1961-62; mem. Nat. Budget and Consultation Com., 1960-63; chmn. budget com., trustee Houston-Harris County United Fund, 1957-58; chmn. Houston Community Council, 1960; mem. Tex. Water Devel. Bd., 1971—. Trustee Rocky Mountain Mineral Law Found., 1965-66; bd. govs. Rice U., 1970—; mem. Harvard Bus. Sch. Alumni Council, 1966-69. Mem. Am. (chmn. sect. mineral and natural resources law 1964-65, mem. ho. of dels. 1966-68), Tex. (chmn. sect. corp. banking and bus. law 1959-60), Houston bar assns., State Bar Tex., Am. Petroleum Inst., Mid- Continent Oil and Gas Assn., Houston Philos. Soc., Assn. Rice Alumni (pres. 1952-53), Houston C. of C. (chmn. water supply and conservation com. 1969-70), Phi Beta Kappa. Club: Houston Country. Home: 5327 Doliver Dr Houston TX 77027 Office: 626 Southwest Tower Houston TX 77002

ILLIG, JAMES MICHAEL, A.R.C. exec.; b. Erie, Pa., Mar. 6, 1913; s. William C. and Teresa A. (Messler) I.; B.S., U.S. Mil. Acad., 1936; M.B.A., Harvard, 1948; grad. Inf. Sch., 1939, Command and Gen. Staff Coll., 1943, Armed Forces Staff Coll., 1946, Indsl. Coll. Armed Forces, 1955; grad. Advanced Mgmt. Program. Harvard, 1961; m. Mary Elizabeth Moorhead, Sept. 1, 1936; children-Patricia Diane (Mrs. James A. Joy), Sally Louise (Mrs. Carl J. Santolli), Rosemary Elizabeth (Mrs. John R. Gilman). Commd. 2d lt. inf. U.S., Army, 1936, advanced through grades to brig. gen., 1961; air. Q.M. 391st Hdqrs. Anti-Submarine Command, 1941- 43; fiscal dir. Army Q.M. Corps, 1943-46; chief supply and procurement Hdqrs. European Command, 1948-51; chief programs and budget Army Gen. Staff (G-4), Dept. Army, 1951-55; chief staff U.S. Mil. Acad., 1955-57; comdg. officer U.S. Army Base Command, Hawaii, 1957-59; dir. financial operations Army Gen. Staff (logistics), Dept. Army, 1959-61; spl. asst. to dep. chief staff for logistics Army Gen. Staff, Dept. Army, 1961-62; comptroller Continental Army Command, Ft. Monroe, Va., 1961-65; ret. 1965; comptroller Am. Nat. Red Cross, 1965—. Decorated D.S.M., Legion of Merit with one oak leaf cluster, Medal for Humane Action, Berlin Airlift device. Mem. Assn. Grads. U.S. Mil. Acad., Harvard Alumni Assn., Am. Soc. Mil. Comptrollers, Def. Supply assn., Indsl. Coll. Armed Forces Alumni Assn., Army Athletic Assn., Assn. U.S. Army. Rotarian. Clubs: Army and Navy Country (Arlington, Va.); Washington Athletic, Harvard Business School (Washington). Home: 1428 Laburnum St Chesterbrook Woods McLean VA 22101 Office: Nat YHdqrs Am Nat Red Cross Washington DC 20006

ILMER, IRVING, violinist; b. Vienna, Austria, Sept. 13, 1919; s. Bernhard and Elizabeth (Smotricky) I.; came to U.S., 1921, naturalized, 1927; student applied music De Paul U., 1935-39; m. Jacobeth Kerr, Aug. 16, 1944 (div. June 1960); children—Steven, Paul. Violinist with Indpls. Symphony Orch., 1939- 42; mem. All-Am. Youth Orch. on S.Am. tour under Stowkowski, summer 1940; asst. concertmaster Grant Park Orch., Chgo., 1944-45; concertmaster San Antonio Symphony Orch., 1944-46; mem. Chgo. Symphony Orch., 1946-52; violist Fine Arts Quartet, 1952-63; artist-in- residence U. Wis., Milw., 1955-63, Community Music Center of N. Shore, Winnetka, Ill., 1960-63, Cleve. Inst. Music, 1961-63, Aspen (Colo.) Music Festival, 1962, 70; asso. prof. music Ind. U. School Music, mem. Berkshire String Quartet in residence, 1966-71; asso. prof. music U. Ky., Lexington, 1971—; appearances on ednl. TV, 1954—; violin and viola recitalist in Chgo., Ind. U., N.Y., Europe; recording artist for Concert-Disc Records, Everest, Vox, Coronet. Address: care Music Dept U Ky Lexington KY 40506

ILSLEY, JOHN P., judge; b. Sundance, Wyo., Dec. 3, 1913; A.B., U. S.D., 1936; LL.B., U. Wyo., 1939. Admitted to Wyo. bar, 1939, U.S. Dist. Ct. Wyo., 1941, U.S. Supreme Ct., 1957; practice of law, Gillette; mem. firm Ilsley & Lubnau; county and pros. atty., 1942-54; city atty., Gillette, 1950-54; dist. commr. 4th Jud. Dist. Wyo., 1952-54; judge 4th Jud. Dist., 1962-. Mem. Am. Bar Assn., Wyo. State Bar (pres. 1960-61). Rotarian (dist. gov. 1961-62). Address: 935 Pioneer Rd Sheridan WY 82801

ILUTOVICH, LEON, orgn. exec.; b. Odessa, Russia; s. Jacob and Leah (Plotycher) I.; ed. Law Sch., Warsaw (Poland) U. Exec. dir., nat. sec. Zionist Orgn. Am.; mem. actions com. World Zionist Orgn.; del. to Zionist congresses; exec. bd. World Union Gen. Zionists; bd. trustees United Israel Appeal; mem. nat. bd. Am. Zionist Fedn.; mem. Am. Conf. on Soviet Jewry, also Pres.'s Conf. of Major Am. Jewish Orgns. Mem. Jewish Book Council Am., Am. Arbitration Assn. (nat. panel), Hebrew Lang. and Culture Assn. Home: 900 West End Av New York City NY 10025 Office: 145 E 32d St New York City NY 10016

IMBER, MURRAY, educator; b. N.Y.C., Sept. 24, 1929; s. Sam and Lillian (Weitzenberg) I.; B.S. in Mech. Engring, U. Ill., 1953; M.S., Columbia, 1953, Sc.D., 1958; m. Elaine Burdette Jenkins, July 19, 1967. Faculty, Bklyn. Poly. Inst., 1958—, prof. mech. engring., 1965—, chmn. thermal engring. div., 1967; vis. prof. U. W.Va., 1962, U. Windsor (Ont.), 1970-72; cons. to industry, 1960—. Union Carbide Co. fellow, 1954-57. Mem. Am. Inst. Aeros. and Astronautics (council mem. met. sect. 1967—), Am. Soc. M.E., Am. Assn. U. Profs., Sigma Xi, Pi Tau Sigma. Heat transfer research on rocket motors, building walls, thermo-phys. properities visco-elastic materials, non-linear heat transfer. Home: 195 Willoughby Av Brooklyn NY 11205

IMBRIE, ANDREW WELSH, composer, educator; b. N.Y.C., Apr. 6, 1921; s. Andrew C. and Dorothy (Welsh) I.; A.B., Princeton, 1942; M.A., U. Cal. at Berkeley, 1947; m. Barbara Cushing, Jan. 31, 1953; children—Andrew, John. Instr. music U. Cal. at Berkeley, 1947, 49-51, asst. prof., 1951, asso. prof., 1957-60, prof., 1960—. Recipient Circle award N.Y. Music Critics, 1943-44; Alice M. Ditson fellow, Columbia, 1946-47; fellow Am. Acad. in Rome, 1947-49; grant Nat. Inst. Arts and Letters, 1950; Guggenheim fellow, 1953-54, 60-61; merit award Boston Symphony Orch., 1955; creative arts award Brandeis U., 1958; Naumberg award, 1960; grantee Nat. Found. on Arts and Humanities, composer in residence Am. Acad. Rome, 1967-68. Mem. Nat. Inst. Arts and Letters, Internat. Soc. Contemporary Music, Phi Beta Kappa. Compositions include four string quartets, trios, sonatas, songs, orchestral and choral works, Violin Concerto, Little Concerto for Piano 4-Hands and Ochestra, Ballad (orch.), Legend (orch.), Serenade (flute, viola and piano), Piano Sonata, Impromptu for Violin and Piano, Cello Sonata, Three Against Christmas (opera), Symphonies No 1, 2, 3, Chamber Symphony. Home: 2625 Rose St Berkeley CA 94708

IMBRIE, JOHN, geologist; b. Penn Yan, N.Y., July 4, 1925; s. Charles Kisselman and Margaret (Fleming) I.; student Coe Coll., 1942-43; B.A., Princeton, 1948; M.S., Yale, 1950, Ph.D., 1951; m. Barbara A. Zeller, Oct. 11, 1947; children—Katherine Palmer, John Zeller. Asst. prof. geology U. Kan., 1951-52; asst. prof. geology Columbia, 1952-54, asso. prof., 1955-60, former prof., exec. com. dept. geology; geologist Kan. Geol. Survey, 1952—; research asso. Am. Mus. Natural History, N.Y.C., 1953—; asst. dir. expdn. to study Great Bahama Bank, 1955-57; faculty fellow NSF, 1959, project dir., study evolution Paleozoic biofacies. Dir. Leonia Youth Mus., 1954-. Fellow Geol. Soc. Am.; mem. Soc. Econ. Mineralogists and Paleontologists (sec.-treas. 1959-60), Am. Assn. Petroleum Geologists, Paleontol. Soc., Soc. Systematic Zoologists, Phi Beta Kappa, Sigma Xi. Home: 111 Highwood Av Leonia NJ 07605 Office: Columbia University New York City NY 10027

IMHOFF, JOHN LEONARD, educator; b. Balt., Feb. 9, 1923; s. John and Elizabeth (Franz) I.; student Johns Hopkins, 1941; B.S., Duke, 1945; M.S., U. Minn., 1947; Ph.D., Okla. State, 1971; m. Lois Rebecca Johnson, Mar. 20, 1948; children—John Edwin, Karen Elizabeth, Carl Henning. Facilities design engr. Crosse & Blackwell, Ltd., Balt., 1940; head engring. metal treatment Rustless Iron & Steel Corp., Balt., 1941-43; asst. prof. indsl. engring. U. Minn., 1947-51; prof., head indsl. engring. U. Ark., Fayetteville, 1953—. Mgmt., engring. cons. Army Ordnance Mgmt. Tng. Div., 1949—; Ph.D. planning group So. Regional Edn. Bd., 1963—. Chmn. engring. sect. Boys Club Fund Raising Program, Fayetteville, 1964-65; dist. chmn., council mem. Boy Scouts Am. Served with USNR, 1943-46. Recipient Outstanding Educator award U. Ark., 1964. AEC fellow U. Cal. at Berkeley, 1958, Argonne Nat. Lab., 1959; NSF Sci. Faculty fellow Stanford, 1960-61. Registered profl. engr., Minn., Ark. Mem. Am. Inst. Indsl. Engrs. (past v.p., dir.), Am. Soc. Engring. Edn. (dir., past chmn. Mo.-Ark. sect.), A.A.A.S., Am. Statis. Assn., Nat. Soc. Profl. Engrs., Internat. Mgmt. Soc. for Educators, Indsl. Engring. Acad. Dept. Chmn. (chmn. nat. council), Phi Beta Kappa, Omicron Delta Kappa, Tau Beta Pi, Alpha Pi Mu (past nat. pres.). Methodist. Author: (with H.F. Dennett) Descriptive Geometry and Graphical Mathematics, 1962; (with O.W. Gatchell) Engineering Computations, 1964. Home: 224 Cleburn St Fayetteville AR 72701

IMHOFF, LAWRENCE EDWARD, govt. ofcl.; b. Elkville, Ill., July 25, 1908; s. Wiley B. and Laura E. (Castleton) I.; A.B., Oberlin Coll., 1930; student Manchester Coll., 1934-35; M.P.E., Purdue U., 1940; m. Maybelle B. Carroll, July 26, 1930; children-Larry C., Maren E. Engaged in investment banking, 1930-32, family bus., 1932-35, teaching, 1935-42; budget analyst Dept. Commerce, 1946-51; dir. minerals and fuels div., also staff asst. to asst. sec. mineral resources Dept. Interior, 1951-60; dep. dir. Office Budget and Mgmt., Dept. Commerce, 1960-62, dir. Office Budget and Finance, 1962-65, dep. asst. sec. commerce for adminstrn., 1965-. Served to capt. USAAF, World War II; PTO. Decorated Purple Heart, Bronze Star; recipient Meritorious Service award Dept. Interior, 1960; Exceptional Service award Dept. Commerce, 1965. Mem. Am. Soc. Pub. Adminstrn., Budget Officers Conf. (past chmn.). Conglist. Mason (32). Club: Kenwood Golf and Country (Bethesda, Md.). Home: 4540 Chesapeake St NW Washington DC 20016 Office: Dept of Commerce Washington DC 20230

IMIG, JACOB HENRY, accountant; b. Seward, Neb., Feb. 10, 1907; s. Jacob and Anna (Graff) I.; B.S.C., U. Neb., 1928; m. Gretchen Kirk, Oct. 15, 1933; children—John K., William G., Thomas J., Richard A. Staff accountant Ernst & Ernst, C.P.A.'s, Omaha, 1928-33; pvt. practice, Omaha, 1933-37; partner Irwin-Imig, Omaha, Haskins & Sells, C.P.A.'s, Omaha, 1956-71. Pres. Covered Wagon council Boy Scouts Am., 1960-61; v.p. Neb. Goodwill, 1965-66. Trustee Neb. Meth. Hosp., 1965—. C.P.A., Neb., Ia., N.Y., La. Mem. Am. Inst. C.P.A.'s (past mem. council), Neb. Soc. C.P.A.'s (past pres.), Am. Accounting Assn., Sigma Alpha Epsilon. Republican. Mem. United Ch. Christ. Rotarian. Home: 714 Ridgewood Av Omaha NB 68114 Office: Woodmen Tower Omaha NB 68102

IMIG, WARNER, univ. dean; b. Sioux City, Ia., Feb. 12, 1913; s. Louis H. and Ella (Sogge) I.; B.A., Yankton Coll., 1935; M.Music Edn., U. Colo., 1942; m. Norma Rapalee, Dec. 31, 1937; children—Gerry, Betsy, Lynn. Fellow, DePauw U., 1935-36; instr. Yankton Coll., 1936-37; faculty U. Colo., 1937—, asso. prof. music, 1947-52, dean Coll. Music, 1951—; lectr. music Stanford, 1950-51. Mem. Am. Choral Dirs. Assn. (dir., pres.), Music Tchrs. Nat. Assn. (nat. choral chmn.), Music Educators Nat. Conf. (pres. S.W. div.), Nat. Assn. Schs. Music (curriculum commn.), Pi Kappa Lambda, Phi Mu Alpha (province gov.). Author: American Play and Folk Songs, 1958; Play and Folk Songs of Other Lands, 1959. Co-author: Music in Our Life, 1959, Music in Our Times, 1959. Editorial asso. Jour. Research Music Edn. Home: 780 16th St Boulder CO 80302

IMIRIE, JOHN FREDERICK, Jr., hosp. adminstr.; b. Washington, Oct. 1, 1927; s. John Frederick and Ellen (Harkins) I.; B.S., U. Richmond, 1953; M.H.A., Columbia, 1955; m. Sallie Comley, Jan. 20, 1949; children—Bonnie, John, Alec, Leslie. Asst. adminstr. Shore Meml. Hosp., Ocean City, N.J., 1955-57; adminstr. Wooster (O.) Community Hosp., 1957-62; regional spl. rep. for med. services IBM Corp., Chgo., 1962-64; financial mgr. Georgetown U., 1964-66; adminstr. Georgetown U. Hosp., Washington, 1966-70; prof. hosp. adminstrn. Sch. Allied Health Professions, Va. Commonwealth U., Richmond, 1970—, v.p. for med. colls. of Va. hosps., 1970—; lectr. hosp. mgmt. IBM Corp., N.Y.C. Bd. dirs. Blue Cross of Va. Served with AUS, 1945-47, 50-52. Mem. Am., Md.-D.C.-Del. (trustee) hosp. assns., Am. Coll. Hosp. Adminstrs., Nat. League Nursing (mem. exec. com. Council Hosp. and Related Instl. Nursing Services), Central Va. Hosp. Council (dir.), Hosp. Council Washington (past pres.). Methodist. Home: 10400 Apache Rd Richmond VA 23235 Office: 1200 E Broad St Richmond VA 23219

IMIRIE, JOSEPH SCOTT, corp. exec.; b. Washington, July 11 1916 s. Austin S. and Augusta G. (Maddox) I.; B.S., Cath. U., 1938; m. Mildred F. Klinke, May 10, 1940; 1 son, Timothy D. Adminstrv. asst. Dept. of Interior, 1938-41; adminstr., orgn. planner War Dept., 1941-43; various positions, also dep. to under- sec. Dept. Air Force, 1946-51; asst. to pres. Carborundum Co., Niagara Falls, N.Y., 1952-54, gen. mgr. electro minerals div., 1955-63, v.p. 1956-61; asst. sec. USAF, 1961-63; sr v.p. profl. services, equipment group Litton Industries, Inc., Beverly Hills, Cal., 1963-67, sr v.p., 1967—. Maj., Air Transport Command, AUS, 1943-46. Clubs: Los Angeles Country; Congressional Country, Army and Navy (Washington); Duquesne (Pitts.). Home: 10433 Wilshire Blvd. Los Angeles CA 90024. Office: 360 N Crescent Dr Beverly Hills CA 90213

IMLAH, ALBERT HENRY, educator; b. New Westminster, B.C., Can., Jan. 30, 1901; s. John Mackie and Mary Ann (Richardson) I.; B.A., U. B.C., 1922; A.M., Clark U., 1923; Ph.D., Harvard, 1931; m. Helen Woodbridge, Apr. 2, 1925 (dec. Jan. 1954); children—Ann Gordon (Mrs. John H. Schneider), Janet Gay (Mrs. T. S. Collett); m. 2d, Miriam Beede, Apr. 4, 1955. Came to U.S., 1922, naturalized, 1938. Instr. history U. Maine, 1923-26; instr. history Tufts Coll., 1927-29, asst. prof., 1929-35, prof. history, 1935-56, prof. diplomatic history Fletcher Sch. Law and Diplomacy, Tufts U., 1944-70, Dickson prof. English and Am. history, 1956-70, prof. emeritus, 1970—, chmn. dept. history, 1956- 65; vis. lectr. history Harvard, 1949, vis. lectr. econs., 1958, vis. prof. econs., 1965-66. Mem. Am. Assn. U. Profs. (nat. council 1946-48, past chmn. com. econ. status of profession), Am. Hist. Assn., Econ. History Assn., Conf. Brit. Studies, Phi Beta Kappa. Author: Life of Lord Ellenborough, 1939; Economic Elements in the Pax Britannica, 1958. Author articles on Brit. diplomatic and econ. history, salaries in Am. colls. Home: 19 Sawyer Av Medford MA 02155

IMMEL, VINCENT CLARE, educator; b. Gibsonburg, O., Mar. 15, 1920; s. Joseph C. and Rosa F. (Bauer) I.; student U. Toledo, 1937-38; B.S., Bowling Green State U., 1941; J.D., U. Mich., 1948. Admitted to Ohio bar, 1949, U.S. Supreme Ct. bar, 1960, Mo. bar, 1962; with Ohio No. U., 1948-58, prof. law, 1957-58: with St. Louis U., 1958—, asso. prof. law, 1958-61, prof. law, 1961—, asst. dean Law Sch., 1959-62, dean Law Sch., 1962-69. Mem. exec. com. St. Louis Civil Liberties Com.; bd. dirs. Little Symphony Assn., Legal Aid Soc. City and County St. Louis, St. Louis Symphony Soc. Served to lt. AUS, 1942-46. Decorated Bronze Star. Mem. Am., Ohio, Mo. bar assns., Am. Judicature Soc., Bar Assn. St. Louis, Am. Law Inst., Phi Alpha Delta, Phi Kappa Theta, Kappa Mu Epsilon, Kappa Delta Pi, Pi Kappa Delta. K.C. Contbr. articles to legal jours. Home: 3733 Lindell Blvd St Louis MO 63108

IMMERWAHR, HENRY RUDOLPH, educator; b. Breslau, Germany, Feb. 28, 1916; s. Kurt and Johanna (Freund) I.; Dottore in Lettere, U. Florence (Italy), 1938; postgrad. (fellow) Am. Sch. Classical Studies, Athens, Greece, 1939-40; Ph.D., Yale, 1943; m. Sara Anderson, Mar. 4, 1944; 1 dau., Mary Elizabeth. Came to U.S., 1940, naturalized, 1943. Instr. classics Yale, 1947-52, asst. prof. 1952-57; asst. prof. U.N.C., Chapel Hill, 1957-59, asso. prof., 1959-63, prof., 1963—, Kenan prof., 1970-71; sr. fellow Center for Hellenic Studies, Washington, 1965—. Vis. prof. Am. Sch. Classical Studies, Athens, 1970-71, mem. mng. com., 1965—; mem. adv. bd. Greek, Roman and Byzantine Studies, 1968—. Served with AUS, 1943-45. Guggenheim Meml. Found. fellow, 1946-47; Morse fellow, Yale, 1955-56. Mem. Am. Philol. Assn., Soc. for Promotion of Hellenic Studies, Classical Assn. Midwest and South, Archaeol. Inst. Am., Am. Assn. U. Profs. Author: Form and Thought in Herodotus, 1966. Contbr. articles to profl. jours. Address: Classics Dept U NC Chapel Hill NC 27514

INBAL, ELLAHU, orch. condr.; b. Jerusalem, Feb. 16, 1936; student violin Jerusalem Acad. Music, conducting Conservatoire Nat. Sup. de Musique de Paris; pupil of Paul Ben-Haim, Sergiu Celibidache, Franco Ferrara. Guest condr., violin player Israeli orchs., 1956-60; European concert tours, 1963-68; several tours with Israeli Philharmonic Orch. to Australia, U.S.; musical dir. Radio Symphony Frankfurt. Am.-Israel Cultural Found. scholar, 1960- 63; 1st prize Guido Cantelli conducting competition, 1963. Address: care Finzi via Pietro Verri 10 Milan Italy

INBAU, FRED EDWARD, lawyer, educator; b. New Orleans, Mar. 27, 1909; s. Fred and Pauline (Boos) I.; B.S., Tulane U., 1930, LL.B., 1932; LL.M., Northwestern U., 1933; m. Ruth L. Major, Sept. 21, 1935 (div.); children—William Robert, Louise; m. 2d, Jane Hanchett Schoenewald, June 27, 1964. Practiced law since 1934; research asst. Sc. Crime Detection Lab., Northwestern U. Sch. Law, 1933-36; asst. prof. law, Northwestern U. Sch. Law, 1936-38; dir. Chgo. Police Sci. Crime Detection Lab., 1938-41; trial atty., firm of Lord, Bissell and Kadyk, 1941-45; prof. law Northwestern U., 1945—. Mem. Chgo. Crime Commn. Pres. Am. Acad. Forensic Scis., 1955-56, Ill. Acad. Criminology, 1951-52, Americans for Effective Law Enforcement. Republican. Author: Self-Incrimination, 1950; Cases and Comments on Criminal Justice, 3d edit., 1968; Criminal Interrogation and Confessions, 2d edit., 1967; Truth and Deception, 1966; Criminal Law for the Police, 1969; Criminal Law for the Layman, 1970; Medical Jurisprudence, 1971. Home: 40 E Oak St Chicago IL 60611

INCH, SCHUBERT S., former aluminum co. exec.; b. San Francisco, Feb. 22, 1908; s. Leonard P. and Helen (Schubert) I.; A.B., U. Cal., 1930; m. Ethel Woodward Glenn, June 18, 1934; children—Robert, Betsy. Project mgr. various constrn. projects affiliated Kaiser cos., 1934-46; v.p. Columbia Constrn. Co., 1941; v.p. Kaimer Aluminum & Chem. Sales, 1950—, Kaiser Industries Corp., 1962-70. Clubs: Yacht (Oakland); San Francisco Yacht; Seattle Yacht; Lahaina Yacht (Maui, Hawaii). Home: 6563 NE Windermere Rd Seattle WA 98105

INDIANA, ROBERT, artist; b. New Castle, Ind., Sept. 13, 1928; student John Herron Sch. Art, 1945-46, Munson-Williams- Proctor Inst., 1947-48, Skowhegan Sch. of Painting and Sculpture, summer 1953 (scholarship); B.F.A., Chgo. Art Inst., 1953; student U. Edinburgh (Scotland), 1953-54; A.F.D. (hon.), Franklin and Marshall Coll., 1970. Exhbns. include Mus. Modern Art, 1961, 63, Dallas Mus. Contemporary Arts, 1962, San Francisco Mus. Art, 1962, Art Inst. Chgo., 1963, Beaverbrook Art Gallery, Fredericton, New Brunswick, N.S., 1963, Tate Gallery, London, Eng., 1963-64, Washington Gallery Modern Art, 1963, Whitney Mus., 1963, Guggenheim Mus., 1963, Albright-Knox Art Gallery, Buffalo, 1963, Am. Cultural Center, Paris, France, 1963, Gemeente Mus., The Hague, Netherlands, 1964, U. Ill. at Champaign, 1965, Worcester (Mass.) Art Mus., 1965, White House Festival Arts, 1965, Stedelijk Mus., Amsterdam, Wurttembergischer Kunstverein, Stuttgart, U. St. Thomas, Houston, Smithsonian Instn., 6th Biennale San Marino, Carnegie Inst., Royal Dublin Soc., Documenta IV, Germany; one-man shows at Stable Gallery, N.Y.C., 1962, 64, 66, Rolf Nelson Gallery, Los Angeles, 1965, Stedelijk van Abbemuseum, Eindhoven, Holland, Mus. Haus Lange, Krefeld, Germany, Galerie Schmela, Dusseldorf, Germany, 1966, Wurttembergisher Kunstverein, Stuttgart, Germany, 1966, Inst. Contemporary Art U. Pa., 1968, McNay Inst., San Antonio, Herron Art Mus., Indpls., others; grantee Albert A. List Found. for inaugural poster N.Y. State Theatre, Lincoln Center, 1964; executed mural for N.Y. State Bldg., N.Y. World's Fair, 1964-65; rep. permanent collections Mus. Modern Art, Whitney Mus., Finch Coll., N.Y.C., Albright-Knox Gallery Art, Larry Aldrich Mus., Ridgefield, Conn., Balt. Mus. Art, Detroit Inst. Arts, Walker Art Center, Mpls., Rose Art Mus. of Brandeis U., Sheldon Meml. Art Gallery of U. Neb., Washington Gallery Modern Art, Stedelijk Mus., Amsterdam, Holland, Stedelijk van Abbemuseum, Eindhoven, Holland, Von der Heydt Mus., Wuppertal, Germany, Mus. Hans Lange, Krefeld, Germany, Art Gallery of Toronto, Carnegie Inst., Krannert Art Mus., U. Ill., Los Angeles County Mus., Mich. U. Mus. Art, Inst. Contemporary Art, U.Pa. Served with USAAF, 1946-49. Decorated

Medal of Merit; Brown Travelling fellow Art Inst. Chgo., 1953. Mem. Delta Phi Delta (pres. Zeta chpt. 1951-52). Address: 2 Spring St New York City NY 10012

INGALLS, DANIEL HENRY HOLMES, educator; b. N.Y.C., May 4, 1916; s. Fay and Rachel (Holmes) I.; A.B., Harvard, 1936, M.A., 1938; m. Phyllis Sarah Day, June 27, 1936; childrenSarah (Mrs. Gary Daughn), Rachel Holmes, Daniel Henry Holmes. Jr. fellow Soc. Fellows, 1938-42, 46-48; asst. prof. Sanskrit and Indian studies Harvard, 1948-52, asso. prof., 1952-56, Wales prof. Sanskrit, 1956—, editor Harvard Oriental Series, 1956—. Dir. Va. Hot Springs, Inc., 1946-57, pres., 1957-63, chmn. bd., 1963-. Trustee Harvard-Yenching Inst. Served to capt. AUS, 1944-46. Mem. Am. Oriental Soc. (past pres.), Am. Philos. Soc., Am. Acad. Scis. Author: An Introduction to Navva-Nyaya Logic, 1951; An Anthology of Sanskrit Court Poetry, 1965. Home: The Yard Hot Springs VA 24445.

INGALLS, GEORGE A., mfg. co. exec.; b. Bklyn., 1899; ed. Pace Inst., 1924; m. Ann C. Kane, 1935; children—Brian Edward, Andrea Marie. Vice pres., dir. Am. Machine & Foundry Co., until 1957, now dir. emeritus; exec. v.p. AMP, Inc., Harrisburg, Pa., 1957-62, pres., 1962-65, vice chmn. bd., 1965—, dir.; pres., dir. Am. Pamcor, Inc., Valley Forge, Pa., Pamcor, Inc., San Juan, P.R.; dir. Lukens Steel Co., Coatesville, Pa. Home: Whitney Lane Brookville Glen Head NY 11545 Office: 449 Eisenhower Blvd Harrisburg PA 17111

INGALLS, JAMES WARREN, Jr., educator, pharmacologist; b. Barre, Vt., July 31, 1919; s. James Warren and Velma (Melcher) I.; B.S., U. Me., 1942; M.S., N.Y.U., 1949, Ph.D., 1953; m. Flora Roberta Salvador, Dec. 26, 1944; childrenSusan Roberta, Patricia Joan, Victoria Ann. Grad. asst. zoology U. Me., 1942; grad. fellow biology N.Y.U., 1946-51; mem. faculty Bklyn. Coll. Pharmacy of L.I. U., 1951-, prof. pharmacology, chmn. dept. biol. scis., 1963-; adj. prof. pharmacology Grad. Sch., L.I. U., 1965-; vis. asst. prof. pathology Albert Einstein Coll. Medicine, 1958-67; vis. prof. pharmacology Columbia Coll. Pharmacy, 1965-66. Spl. cons. in pharmacology Air Reduction Co., 1966-. Served with AUS. 1943-45; PTO. Decorated Bronze Star; G. A. Pfeiffer Meml. postdoctoral research fellow L.I.U., 1955-57. Fellow N.Y. Acad. Sci. (life); mem. Am. Public Health Assn., N.Y. Zoological Soc. Am. Pharm. Assn., A.A.A.S. (life), Sigma Xi (life), Zeta Psi. Democrat. Mem. Universalist Ch. Contbr. prof. jours. Home: 34 Morse Av. Bloomfield NJ 07003. Office: 600 Lafayette Av Brooklyn NY 11216

INGARD, KARL UNO, educator; b. Gothenburg, Sweden, Feb. 24, 1921; s. Karl Oscar and Anna (Nilsson) I.; B.Sc., Chalmers Inst. Tech., Gothenburg, 1944, licentiate, 1948; Ph.D., Mass. Inst. Tech., 1950; m. Doris Charlotta Karlsson, Feb. 24, 1948; children—John, Sven, Marianne, Karl. Came to U.S., 1948, naturalized, 1964. Docent, dir., acoustics lab. Chalmers Inst. Tech., 1946-51; prof. physics Mass. Inst. Tech., 1951—. Served as engr. Signal Corps, Swedish Army, 1946-47. Recipient Gustaf Dalen medal, 1970, John Ericson medal, 1944, Biennial award Acoustical Soc. Am., 1954; Guggenheim fellow, 1960. Fellow Am. Phys. Soc., Acoustical Soc. Am.; mem. Am. Assn. Physics Tchrs., Sigma Xi. Author: (with Philip M. Morse) Theoretical Acoustics, 1968; (with William L. Kraushaar) Introduction to Mechanics, Matter, and Waves, 1960. Editor (with Herman Feshbach) In Honor of Philip M. Morse, 1969. Home: Tabor Hill Rd Lincoln MA 01773 Office: Dept Physics Mass Inst Tech Cambridge MA 02139

INGBAR, SIDNEY HAROLD, physician, educator; b.. Denver, Feb. 12, 1925; s. David Harry and Belle (Friedland) I., student U. Cal. at Los Angeles, 1941-43; M.D. magna cum laude (fellow), Harvard, 1947; m. Mary Lee Gimbel Mack, May 28, 1950; children-David Harry, Etic Edward, Jonathan Clarence. Practice medicine, specializing in endocrinology, Boston, 1949—; mem. faculty Harvard Med. Sch., 1955—; program dir. Harvard Clin. Research Center, Boston City Hosp., 1962—, physician-in-charge Out-patient Endocrine Clinic, 1963—; asso. dir. Thorndike Meml. Lab., 1963—; cons. Newton-Wellesley Hosp., 1957—, Mass. Soldiers Home, Chelsea, 1964—. Mem. Surgeon Gen. Adv. Com. Gen. Medicine, chmn. subcom. endocrinology and metabolism, 1963-70; mem. medicine test com. Nat. Bd. Med. Examiners, 1967-70. Recipient Maimonides award Boston Med. Soc., 1947. Diplomate Am. Bd. Internal Medicine. Mem. Assn. Am. Physicians, Am. Fedn. Clin. Research, Am. Soc. Clin. Investigation (councillor 1967-70), Am. Thyroid Assn (1st v.p.), Endocrine Soc. (Earnest Oppenheimer award 1965), Am. Physiol. Soc., Soc. Exptl. Biology and Medicine, Sigma Xi, Alpha Omega Alpha. Mem. editorial bd. Endocrinology, 1957-67, New Eng. Jour. Medicine, 1967-70, Jour. Clin. Investigation, 1968—. Contbr. articles profl. jours. Home: 41 Montvale Rd Newton Centre MA 02159 Office: 25 Shattuck St Boston MA

INGBRETSEN, EDWIN ANDREW, banker; b. N.Y.C., Oct. 4, 1922; s. Ole A. and Elly (Jensen) I.; B.B.A. cum laude, Pace Coll., 1953; m. Margaret Nicotra, June 12, 1949; children-David, Bruce. Auditor, Price Waterhouse & Co., N.Y.C., 1954-59; controller Fafnir Bearing Co., New Britain, Conn., 1959-64; v.p., gen. mgr. Wells Fargo Armored Service, N.Y.C., 1964-68; v.p., auditor Hartford Nat. Bannk & Trust Co. (Conn.), 1968—. Served with USAAF, 1942- 46. C.P.A., N.Y. Home: 149 Bellridge Rd Glastonbury CT 06033 Office: 799 Main St Hartford CT 06115

INGE, FREDERICK DOUGLASS, educator; b. Charlottesville, Va., May 30, 1896; s. George Pinkney and Kate Virginia (Ferguson) I.; B.S., U. Minn., 1924; M.S., Ia. State Coll., 1937, Ph.D., 1940; m. Lucille Elliott, Sept. 3, 1953. Asso. prof. biology So. U., 1929-36; prof. biology Fla. A. and M. Coll., 1937-44, Bennett Coll., 1944-45; prof. biology Hampton Inst., 1945—, chmn. dept. natural scis., 1957-61. Served as bn. supply sgt., 809th Inf., U.S. Army, World War I. Mem. N.Y. Acad. Sci., A.A.A.S., Am. Soc. Plant Physiologists, Bot. Soc. Am., Torrey Botany Club, Sigma Xi. Contbr. articles to profl. publs. Address: Hampton Inst Hampton VA 23368

INGE, WILLIAM, playwright; b. Independence, Kan., May 3, 1913; s. Luther Clayton and Maude Sarah (Gibson) I.; A.B., U. Kan., 1935; A.M., Peabody Tchrs. College, 1938. Staff Stephens Coll. for Women, 1938-43; newspaper drama, music critic St. Louis Star-Times, 1943-46; instr. English Washington U., 1946-49. Author plays: Farther Off from Heaven, 1947; Come Back, Little Sheba, 1950; Picnic, 1953 (winner Pulitzer prize, Drama Critics prize, and Donaldson award); Bus Stop, 1955; The Dark at the Top of the Stairs, 1957; A Loss of Roses, 1959; Natural Affection, 1963; Where's Daddy, 1966; author screenplay Splendor in the Grass (winner Acad. Award best original film script), 1961.

INGEBRETSEN, JAMES CHRISTOPHER, lawyer; b. Salt Lake City, Nov. 21, 1906; s. James and Mabel (Rohde) I.; A.B. magna cum laude, Stanford, 1930, J.D., 1932; m. Dorothy Hitchcock, Nov. 10, 1936; children—Dorothy Lee, Kaaren Elizabeth. Admitted to Calif. State bar, 1933, and practiced under own name, Los Angeles, 1933-34; partner firm Musick, Burrell and Ingebretsen, 1944-50; chief counsel Calif. Bldg. & Loan Commr., 1934-36; gen. counsel and Wash. rep. Los Angeles C. of C., 1939-42; gen. counsel and dir. govtl. affairs, U.S. C. of C., 1942-44. Mem. bd. Los Angeles Bd. Harbor Commrs., 1945-50, pres., 1949-50. Bd. dirs. San Pedro YMCA, 1955-57; trustee Blaisdell Inst., Found. for Spiritual Understanding, Jurupa Cultural Center, Philos. Research Soc.; pres. Found. for Social Research; past gov. Yokefellow Inst. Pres. Acad. Creative Education, Arts, Books, and Crafts, Inc. Mem. Los Angeles C. of C. (director, chmn. fed. affairs com. 1945-52), A.R.C. (dir., chmn. Coll. div. local chpt. 1949-52), Am. Cancer Soc. (past dir.), Cal. Heart Assn. (past dir. exec. com.), Nat. Assn. Congl. Christian Chs. (mem. exec. com. 1957-59), Phi Beta Kappa, Phi Beta Kappa Assos., Mont Pelerin Soc., Order Coif, Sigma Nu, Phi Delta Phi. Clubs: California Club; Palos Verdes Tennis, North Shore Yacht. Home: 32859 Seagate Dr Palos Verdes Peninsula CA 90274 Office: 43750 Castile Can PO Box 877 San Jacinto CA 92383

INGELFINGER, FRANZ JOSEPH, physician, educator; b. Dresden, Germany, Aug. 20, 1910; s. Joseph and Eleanor (Holden) I.; brought to U.S., 1922, naturalized, 1931; A.B., Yale, 1932; M.D., Harvard, 1936; D.Sc. (hon.), Marquette Sch. Medicine, 1970; m. Sarah Shurcliff, Aug. 23, 1941; children—Joseph Abbott, Alice. Intern Boston City Hosp., 1937; fellow Thorndike Meml. Lab., Resident Boston City Hosp., asst. medicine, Harvard, 1938; fellow gastroenterology, asst. medicine U. Pa. Hosp., 1939; instr. medicine Boston U., 1940-42, asst. prof., 1942-45, asso. prof., 1945-58, prof. of medicine, 1958-67, 1st Conrad Wesselhoeft prof. medicine, 1961-67, clin. prof. medicine, 1967—; dir. V and VI med. services Boston City Hosp., 1961-67; mem. staff R. D. Evans Meml. Hosp., Boston, 1944—; vis. physician, chief gastrointestinal clinic U. Hosp., 1943-67, mem. cons. staff, 1967—; dir. medical Foundation Inc., 1960-64; asso. staff gastroenterology New England Center Hosp.; cons. gastroenterology Robert B. Brigham Hosp., Boston VA Hosp., 1952—, Lemuel Shattuck Hosp., 1955—. Adv. com. on medicine Med. Research and Devel. Command, U.S. Army, 1963-67; nat. adv. council Nat. Inst. Arthritis and Metabolic Diseases, 1961-65; mem. commn. on enteric infections Armed Forces Epidemiological Bd., 1966—; spl. cons. NIH, 1966-69; nat. cons. to surgeon gen. USAF, 1967-70; cons. Medlars com. Nat. Library Medicine, 1967—; med. and sci. com. Mass. chpt. Arthritis Found., 1967-70, chmn. research com., 1968—, mem. exec. bd., 1969-70, trustee, 1969—; biomed. communications study sect. Pub. Health Service. Trustee Boston Med. Library, 1952-58, 64—; dir. Post-grad. Med. Inst., Boston, 1953-61. Friedenwald medal, Am. Gastroenterol. Assn., 1969. Diplomate (gastroenterol.) Am. Bd. Internal Med. (mem. subspecialty bd. gastroenterol. 1966-68). Fellow A.C.P.; mem. A.M.A., Am. Soc. Clin. Investigation, A.A.A.S., Am. Gastroenterological Assn. (v.p. 1959-61, pres. 1961-62), Assn. Am. Physicians, Am. Assn. for Study of Liver Diseases, Interurban Clinical Club, Am. Acad. of Arts and Sci. (councilor 1960-64, mem. Amory prize com. since 1963- -), Phi Beta Kappa, Alpha Omega Alpha, Beta Theta Pi, Nu Sigma Nu. Clubs: St. Botolph, Aesculapian (Boston). Editor: Gastroenterology sect., Year Book of Medicine, 1953-69. Contbr. articles, chpts. med. publs. Mem. editorial bd. New Eng. Jour. Med., 1961-67, editor, 1967—; mem. editorial bd. Disease-a-Month; chmn. editorial bd. Gastroenterology, 1964-68. Home: 28 Hubbard Park Cambridge MA 02138 Office: 10 Shattuck St Boston MA 02115

INGELS, E. G., glass container co. exec.; b. Edwardsville, Ill., Feb. 9, 1916; s. George W. and Florence (Kubicek) I.; student Ill. Coll., 1933-34, Washington U., St. Louis, 1940; grad. Stanford exec. mgmt. course, 1957; m. Beverly Martin, Aug. 3, 1935; children—Sandy (Mrs. Robert E. Frane), Jill (Mrs. Ferando Losada). With Owens Ill., Inc, 1936-68; pres., gen. mgr. Owens-Ill., S.A., Geneva, 1967-68; v.p. glass containers Indian Head Inc., 1968, exec. v.p. glass containers, 1968—. Trustee Glass Container Mfrs. Inst. Served with USNR, 1943. Club: Seaview Country (Absecon, N.J.). Home: 23 Templar Way Summit NJ 07901 Office: 111 W 40th St New York City NY 10018

INGELS, MARTY, actor; b. Bklyn., Mar. 9, 1936; s. Jacob and Minnie (Crown) Ingerman; ed. Erasmus High Sch., 1951-53, Forest Hills High Sch., 1953-55; m. Jean Maire Frassinelli, Aug. 3, 1960 (div. 1969). Star Dickens and Fenster series ABC-TV , 1964; co-star Pruitts of Southampton, 1968-69; films include Armored Command, 1962, Horizontal Lieutenant, 1965. Busy Body, 1967, Ladies Man, 1966, If It's Tuesday This Must Be Belgium, 1970, Wild and Wonderful, 1965, Guide for a Married Man, 1968; numerous TV appearances. Active various charity drives. Address: Penthouse 7364 Hollywood Blvd Hollywood CA 90046

INGER, ROBERT FREDERICK, zoologist; b. St. Louis, Sept. 10, 1920; s. Jacob and Anna (Bourd) I.; B.S., U. Chgo., 1942, Ph.D., 1954; m. Mary Lee Ballew, Apr. 19, 1946. Asst. curator fishes Field Mus. Natural History, 1949-54, curator reptiles, 1954—, also head sci. dept. Mem. Am. Soc. Ichthyologists and Herpetologists, Soc. Study Evolution, Soc. Systematic Zoology. Home: 18229 Riegel Rd Homewood IL 60430 Office: Field Mus Natural History Chicago IL 60605

INGERSOLL, ALFRED CAJORI, univ. dean; b. Madison, Wis., June 8, 1920; s. Leonard R. and Helen (Flint) I.; B.S. in Civil Engring., U. Wis., 1942, M.S. in Civil Engring., 1948, Ph.D., 1950; fluid mechanics symposium, U. Mich., summer 1947; m. Elizabeth R. McNamara, Feb. 22, 1946; 1 son, John Thomas. Mem. tech. staff lab. Linde Air Products Co., Tonawanda, N.Y., 1942-46; instr. civil engring. U. Wis., 1946-49, project asst. engring. expt. sta., 1949-50; from instr. to asso. prof. civil engring. Cal. Inst. Tech., 1950-60; guest prof. applied mechanics Bengal Engring. Coll., U. Calcutta (India), 1954-55; dean Sch. Engring., U. So. Cal., 1960-70; asso. dean continuing edn. Sch. Engring. and Applied Sci. U. Cal. at Los Angeles, 1970—; cons. U.S. Naval Ordnance Test Sta., 1958, Albert C. Martin & Assos., 1970. Dir., The Birtcher Corp., Los Angeles. Res. sr. san. engr. USPHS; chmn. com. on research and standards inventory Mayor's Council Environmental Mgmt., Los Angeles, 1970—; mem. Aerospace Tech. Applications Com., Los Angeles, 1970-71. Founding chmn. So. Cal. Engring. Socs. Com. Manpower Tng., 1970—. Diplomate Am. Acad. Environmental Engrs. Fellow Am. Soc. C.E. (pres. Los Angeles sect. 1970-71; mem. com. continuing edn. 1970—; Rudolph Hering medal for paper 1957, Daniel W. Mead prize student essay in ethics 1942, Edmund Friedman Profl. Recognition award, 1969); mem. Inst. Advancement Engring. (pres. 1970—), Am. Soc. Engring. Edn. (chmn. Pacific S.W. sect. 1961-62, v.p. West sections 1966-68, chmn. relations with industry div. 1964-65; chmn. com. on deans insts. Engring. Colls. Adminstrv. Council 1963-65; projects bd. 1970—), Am. Assn. U. Profs., Nat. (chmn. com. pub. relations, trustee ednl. found.), Cal. (pres. Los Angeles chpt. 1963-65, chmn. com. on profl. engrs. in edn. 1964-65, v.p. So. region 1965-66, nat. dir. 1968—) societies profl. engrs., Los Angeles Town Hall (chmn. met. transp. sect. 1962-65), Am. Inst. Aeros. and Astronautics (Los Angeles adv. council), Sigma Xi, Chi Epsilon (pres. 1956-58). Tau Beta Pi, Phi Kappa Phi, Pi Tau Sigma, Phi Eta Sigma. Club: Jonathan (Los Angeles). Author: (with R. L. Daugherty) Fluid Mechanics with Engineering Applications, 5th edit., 1954; (with L. R. Ingersoll and O. J. Zobel) Heat Conduction with Applications in Engineering and Geology, 1954. Home: 1098 Ravoli Dr Pacific Palisades CA 90272 Office: Univ Cal Los Angeles CA 90024

INGERSOLL, CHARLES EDWARD, corp. exec.; b. Phila., Mar. 3, 1922; s. R. Sturgis and Marion B. (Fowle) I.; grad. Millbrook Sch.; student Princeton, 1940; LL.B., U. Pa., 1949; m. 2d, Vivian Martin, June 6, 1964; children—Patricia (Mrs. Douglas Adams), Charles Jared II; stepchildren—Harriet (Mrs. Morton Saunders), Joan Martin (Mrs. Charles A. Hunt), Sydney Martin III. With Kan., Okla. & Gulf Railway Co., Midland Valley Railroad Co., and Okla. City-Ada-Atoka Railway Co., 1949-64, chmn. bd., 1954-64; admitted Pa. bar, 1950; pres. Muskogee Co., 1954-66; Sebastian County Coal & Mining Co., 1954-64; asst. v.p. staff, Pa. R.R. Co., 1965-66, asst. v.p. passenger service contracts, 1967-70, exec. rep., pub. affairs, 1970-71; exec. dir. Coll. Physicians Phila., 1971—; dir. Beneficial Mutual Savs. Bank, Provident Mutual Life Ins. Co. Vice pres. Mental Health Assn. Southeastern Pa. Bd. mem. Phila. Redevel. Authority, 1967-68, Phila., City Planning Commn. Trustee Phila. Coll. of Art; bd. mgrs. Children's Hosp., Home of Merciful Savior for Crippled Children. Served from pvt. to 1st lt., pilot, USAAF, World War II. Republican. Club: Philadelphia. Home: PO Box 139 Penllyn PA 19458 Office: 19 S 22d St Philadelphia PA 19103

INGERSOLL, CHARLES JARED, ret. ry. official, ins. exec.; b. Phila., Feb. 11, 1894; s. Charles Edward and Henrietta (Sturgis) I.; student St. Paul's Sch., Concord, N.H., 1908-13; C.E., Princeton, 1917; m. Marian Baird, Nov. 1, 1920 (dec. 1939); children—Anna Warren (Mrs. Brooke Roberts), Charles Jared (dec. W.W. II), Sally Wister (Mrs. Edward A. Fox), Gainor Baird (Mrs. John A. Miller); m. 2d, Agnes Clement Robinson, Jan. 25, 1942; step children—Ann Clement (Mrs. George Clay), Ellen Farr (Mrs. Langdon Clay). With Midland Valley R.R., 1920-54, chmn. bd., 1932-54; dir. Stock Ins. Co. of Green Tree; mgr. Mut. Assurance Co. Served as lt. (j.g.) USNRF, World War I; dist. chief Phila. Ordnance Dist., U.S. Army, World War II. Recipient Medal for Merit; Crozier gold medal Am. Ordnance Assn. Democrat. Clubs: Philadelphia; Penllyn (Pa.); Northeast Harbor (Me.) Fleet. Home: Fort Washington PA 19034 Office: Two Girard Plaza Philadelphia PA 19102

INGERSOLL, FRANK BOSTWICK, lawyer; b. Pitts., Nov. 22, 1893; s. Hartwell Bostwick and Susan Mary (Patterson) I.; LL.B., Cornell U., 1917; m. Melba R. Martin, Mar. 30, 1922. Admitted to Pa. bar, 1917, and since practiced in Pittsburgh; mem. firm Gordon & Smith, 1917-24, partner, 1924—, firm now Buchanan, Ingersoll, Rodewald, Kyle & Buerger. Dir. Union Nat. Bank, Pitts., McKinney Mfg. Co., J. B. Booth Co. Member board Eye and Ear Hosp. Mem. Am. Law Inst., Am. Judicature Soc., Assn. Bar of City of N.Y., Am., Pa. and Allegheny County bar assns., Cornell Law Assn. (past pres.), One Hundred Friends of Pitts. Art (exec. com.), Allegheny Co. Legal Aid Soc. (mem. bd.), Delta Chi. Republican. Mason. Clubs: Cornell of Western Pa., Duquesne, Fox Chapel Golf, Rolling Rock, University (Pittsburgh, Pa.); Cornell (N.Y.). Home: 4625 5th Av Pittsburgh PA 15213 Office: Oliver Bldg Pittsburgh PA 15222

INGERSOLL, JOHN E., govt. ofcl.; b. Westwood, Cal., Oct. 31, 1929; s. Edward E. and Elsie K. (Hutchison) I.; A.B. in Criminology, U. Cal. at Berkeley, 1956, grad. student, 1956-58; m. Ramona June Choins, Aug. 19, 1950; children—John Edward, Thomas Eugene, Susan Lynn, Linda Ann. Successively patrolman, investigator, supr., chief's aide, adminstrv. asst., dir. planning and research Oakland (Cal.) Police Dept., 1957-61; dir. field services Internat. Assn. Chiefs Police, 1961-66; chief police Charlotte, N.C., 1966-68; asst. dir. Office Law Enforcement Assistance, Dept. Justice, 1968. dir. Bur. Narcotics and Dangerous Drugs, 1968—; lectr. criminology U. Cal., also Oakland City Coll., 1957-59. Mem. policy com. Nat. Symposium on Law Enforcement Sci. and Tech., 1966- 68; mem. police sci. curriculum devel. com. Am. Assn. Jr. Colls., 1967; adviser President's Crime Commn. Law Enforcement, 1966-67; cons. Nat. Adv. Commn. Civil Disorder 1967—. Active local Boy Scouts Am., A.R.C., Travelers Aid Soc. Charter mem. vis. com. Sch. Criminal Justice, State U. N.Y. at Albany, 1966-69. Served with AUS, 1951-53. Recipient Silver medallion Nat. Conf. Christians and Jews, 1968. Mem. Internat. Assn. Chiefs Police (exec. com. 1969—), Lambda Alpha Epsilon (past nat. sec.- treas). Office; 1405 I St NW Washington DC 20537

INGERSOLL, JOHN JOSEPH, fgn. service officer: b. Phila., Jan. 11, 1920; s. Charles Eugene and Winifred Mary (O'Hara) I; A.B., Temple U., 1940; M.A., U. Mich., 1957; m. Betty Louise Dobson, Oct. 8, 1949; childrenLaura Anne, John Dobson. Joined U.S. Fgn. Service, 1946; vice consul, Aden, Arabia, 1946-48, Jidda, Saudi Arabia, 1948, Marseille, France, 1948-50, Tubabao, Philippines, 1950-51; consul, Amsterdam, Netherlands, 1951-52; 2d sec. embassy, Madrid, Spain, 1953-56; assigned State Dept., 1957-61: 1st sec. embassy, Buenos Aires, Argentina, 1961-64, London, Eng., 1964-. U.S. rep. Internat. Coffee Orgn., Internat. Rubber Study Group, Internat. Wool Study Group. Served with AUS, 1943-46; ETO. Address: American Embassy London England.

INGERSOLL, RALPH MCALLISTER, editor, pub.; b. New Haven, Dec. 8, 1900; s. Colin Macrae and Theresa (McAllister) I.; student Hotchkiss Sch., Lakeville, Conn., 1917-18; B.S., Yale, 1921; postgrad. Columbia, 1922; m. Mary Elizabeth Carden, 1925 (div. 1935); m. 2d, Elaine Brown Keiffer, Aug. 9, 1945 (dec. Apr. 1948); children—Ralph McAllister III, Ian Macrae; m. 3d, Mary Hill Doolittle, Nov. 25, 1948 (div. 1963); adopted son, Brooks; m. 4th, Thelma Bradford, 1964. Mining engr.; reporter New Yorker mag., 1925, mng. editor, 1925-30; asso. editor Fortune, 1930, mng. editor, 1930-35; v.p., gen. mgr. Time, Inc., pub. Time, Life, Fortune and Archtl. Forum, sponsoring radio and cinema prodns. "The March of Time", 1935-38; pub. Time mag., 1937-39; organizer, financier co. to publish PM (N.Y. daily evening newspaper); pres. R.J. Co., Inc., 1948-59, investments, principally newspapers, including Middletown (N.Y. Times Herald, Union Gazette, Port Jervis, N.Y.); pres. New Eng. Newspapers, Inc., pub. Pawtucket (R.I.) Times, 1957—; pres. Gen. Pubs., Inc., newspaper mgmt., 1959—; pres. dir. Mid Atlantic Newspapers, Inc., pub. Daily Jour., Elizabeth, N.J., 1959- -; pres., dir. Capitol City Pub. Co., Inc., pub., dir. Trentonian, Trenton, N.J., 1961—; pres., dir. Central States Pub. Co., pub. Del. County Daily Times, Chester, Pa., 1961—; pres., dir. Shenandoah Valley Pub. Corp. (pub. Shenandoah (Pa. Daily Herald), Riverdale (N.J.) Pub. Co. (pub. Riverdale Trends, biweekly), Milford Pub. Co., Inc. (pub. Milford (Conn.) Daily Citizen), Mid-Hudson Publs., Inc. (pub. Kingston (N.Y.) Daily Freeman), Peerless Publs., Inc. (pub. Pottstown (Pa.) Mercury), N.E. Pub., Inc. (pub. Fall River (Mass.) Herald), Acme Newspapers, Inc. (pub. Ardmore (Pa.) Main Line Times, Upper Darby (Pa.) News of Delaware County and Germantown (Pa.) Courier), Phoenix Publs. Inc. (pub. Daily Eagle), Claremont, N.H. Bd. dirs. Pub. Welfare Found., Washington; trustee Sculpture Center, N.Y.C. Served from pvt. Engr. Amphibian Command to lt. col. Gen. Staff Corps, AUS, 1943-45. Decorated Legion of Merit; officer Order of the Crown (Belgium). Episcopalian. Clubs: Racquet and Tennis, Brook (N.Y.C.); Mill Reef (Antigue, W.I.). Author: In and Under Mexico, 1924; Report on England, 1940; America Is Worth Fighting For, 1941; Action on All Fronts, 1941; The Battle is the Payoff, 1944; Top Secret, 1946; The Great Ones, 1948; Wine of Violence, 1951; Point of Departure, 1961. Home: Cornwall Bridge CT 06754

INGERSOLL, ROBERT STEPHEN, indsl. exec.; b. Galesburg, Ill., Jan. 28, 1914; s. Roy Claire and Lulu May (Hinchliff) I.; grad. Phillips Acad., 1933; B.S., Sheffield Sci. Sch., Yale, 1937; m. Coralyn Eleanor Reid, Sept. 17, 1938; childrenCoralyn Eleanor, Nancy, Joan (dec.), Gail, Elizabeth G. With Armco Steel Corp., 1937-39; with Ingersoll

Steel & Disc div. (later Ingersoll Products div.) Borg-Warner Corp., Chgo., 1939-41, 42-54, pres. Ingersoll Products div., 1950-54, adminstrv. v.p. Borg-Warner Corp., 1953-56, pres., 1956-61, chmn., 1961—, chief exec. officer, 1958—, also dir., with Central Research Lab., 1941-42; dir. 1st Nat. Bank Chgo., Marcor, Inc., Chgo., Burlington No. Inc. Trustee U. Chgo., Aspen Inst. Humanistic Studies. Cal. Inst. Tech., Smith Coll. Mem. Winnetka (Ill.) Sch. Bd., 1957-63. Mem. U.S. C. of C., Chgo. Assn. Commerce and Industry (dir.), Bus. Council, Phi Gamma Delta. Conglist. Clubs: Economic, Commercial (Chgo.): Indian Hill (Winnetka); Detroit Athletic: Yale (N.Y.C.): California (Los Angeles). Home: 10 Indian Hill Rd Winnetka IL 60093 Office: 200 S Michigan Av Chicago IL 60604

INGERSOLL, ROBERT STURGIS, lawyer; b. Phila., Dec. 16, 1891; s. Charles Edward and Henrietta A. (Sturgis) I.; Litt.B. Princeton, 1914; LL.B., U. Pa., 1921; LL.D., Temple U., 1954: L.H.D., St. Joseph's Coll.; D.F.A., Phila. Coll. Art; m. Marion B. Fowle, Oct. 31, 1914 (ded.); childrenRobert Sturgis, George Fowle (dec.), Phebe Warren, Charles Edward, Harry; m. 2d, Cornelia Shepard, Nov. 1, 1969. With editorial dept. J.B. Lippincott & Co., Phila., 1914-17; mem. law firm Ballard, Spahr, Andrews & Ingersoll, 1921—; dir. N. Penn. R.R., Phila. Park Nat. League Club. Trustee Phila. Mus. Art, Pa. Acad. Fine Arts, Fairmount Park Art Assn. Organizer, Phila. br. Com. to Defend Am. by Aiding the Allies; mem. Alien Enemy Hearing Bd. U.S. dist. Eastern Pa. Served as 1st lt., inf. U.S. Army, World War. Mem. Am., Pa. bar assns., Am. Philos. Soc. Democrat. Episcopalian. Clubs: Philadelphia, Franklin Inn, Midday, Rittenhouse, Print (ex-pres.) (Phila.); Ivy (Princeton, N.J.). Author: Open That Door, 1961; Henry McCarter, 1944. Home: Penllyn PO PA 19458 Office: Land Title Bldg Philadelphia PA 19110

INGERSOLL, TYRRELL MEYER, lawyer; b. Algona, Ia., Aug. 8, 1902; s. Charles Lawrence and Mathilda (Klamp) I.; A.B., U. Ia., 1925, J.D., 1928; m. Dorothy Denkmann, Apr. 11, 1936. Admitted to Ia. bar, 1928, since practiced in Cedar Rapids; partner firm Shuttleworth & Ingersoll, and predecessor, 1932—; chmn. adv. com. to Ia. Supreme Ct. on rules of practice and procedure. Dir. Diamond V Mills, Inc., Averill Wallace Welch Co., Ky. Midland Co. Inc. Bd. dirs. St. Lukes Meth. Hosp., Cedar Rapids Community Welfare Found., Linn County Humane Soc.; trustee Coe Coll. Fellow Am. Bar Found., Am. Coll. Probate Counsel; mem. Am., Ia. (pres. 1950-51), Linn County (past pres.) bar assns., Nat. Assn. Accountants, Phi Beta Kappa, Order of Coif, Alpha Sigma Phi, Phi Delta Phi. Mason (Shriner, 32), Elk, Rotarian (past pres.). Clubs: (edar Rapids Country, Pickwick, Embassy. Home: 2184 Linden Dr SE Cedar Rapids IA 52403 Office: Merchants Nat Bank Bldg Cedar Rapids IA 52401

INGERSON, FRED EARL, geologist, educator; b. Barstow, Tex., Oct. 28, 1906; s. Fred Percy and Mamie (Carson) I.; A.B., Simmons U., 1928, M.A., 1931, Sc.D. (hon.), 1942; Ph.D., Yale, 1934; postgrad. U. Innsbruck, 1934-35; m. Martha Anna Duncan, June 5, 1930; children—Mary (dec.), Fred Earl. Instr. Yale, 1932- 34; asst. phys. chemist, geophys. lab., Carnegie Instn. of Washington, 1935-39, phys. chemist, 1939-43, petrologist, 1943-47; ofcl. investigator contracts Office of Sci. Research and Devel., 1942-45; geologist, chief geochemistry and petrology br. U.S. Geol. Survey, Washington, 1947-57, geologist, 1957-58; prof. geology U. Texas, 1958—, asso. dean grad., sch., 1961-65; mem. Yale expdn. to Newfoundland, 1933; survey quartz, Brazil, 1945; mem. adv. bd. Geologische Rundschau, 1948-54; mem. div. geol. and geog. and div. chemistry and chem. tech. NRC, 1951-54; Lab. Tech. Petrofabric Analysis; spl. lectr. geology U. Mich., 1938. Recipient Day medal, Geol. Soc. Am., 1955; Distinguished Service medal, U.S. Dept. Interior, 1959. Fellow Am. Geophys. Union (charter), Geochem. Soc. of India (hon.), Commn. One Forming Fluids (hon.), Mineral. Society Am. (treas. 1941-58, translation editor 1959-67), Geol. Soc. Am. (council, 46,47-50); mem. Internat. Commn. on Geochemistry (sec. 1960-63, v.p. 1963-65), Internat. Assn. Geochemistry and Cosmochemistry (pres. 1965- -), Assn. Earth Sci. Editors (charter), Internat. Assn. Volcanology and Chemistry of Earth's Interior (exec. com. 1967-71), Mineral Soc. of London, Soc. Française de Minéralogie, Deutsche Mineralogische Gesellschaft, Soc. Geol. Mexicana, Am. Geol. Inst. (vis. scientist 1961; translation com. 1958—, chmn. 1958-61; internat. field inst. to Brazil 1966), Soc. Econ. Geologists, Geochem. Soc. (pres. 1955-57, translation com. 1958—, translation editor 1958-70), Geochem. Soc. of Japan, Geol. Soc. of Brazil, Mineral Assn. Can., Sigma Xi, Sigma Delta Pi, Kappa Delta Pi, Phi Kappa Phi. Club: Foreign Policy. Exec. editor of Geocheimica et Cosmochimica Acta, 1950-61, editorial adv. bd., 1961-66; editor-in-chief Internat. Series of Monographs on Earth Science, 1955—; chmn. bd. editors Internat. Geology Review, 1959-62; editorial bd. Mineralium Deposita. Author sci. articles. Home: 3402 Mount Bonnel Dr Austin TX 78731

INGHAM, CHARLES GREGORY, hosp. adminstr.; b. Sioux City, Ia., Aug. 9, 1913; s. Charles T. and Bertha E. (Starks) I.; student Wayne (Neb.) State Coll., 1930-33; M.D., U. Neb., 1937; m. Dorothy V. Ross, June 15, 1937; children-C. Thomas, Rodney R. Staff psychiatrist Norfolk Regional Center 1946-52, supt., 1952- 70, regional dir., 1970; faculty U. Neb. Coll. Medicine. Served with M.C., AUS, 1940-46. Certified Mental Hosp. Adminstr. Fellow Am. Psychiat. Assn.; mem. A.M.A. Republican. Methodist. Kiwanian. Address: Norfolk Regional Center Norfolk NB 68701

INGHAM, CHARLES S., architect; b. Pitts., Dec. 14, 1905; s. Charles T. and Cora (Rogers) I.; student Pa. Acad. Fine Arts, 1926; B.Arch., U. Pa., 1929; m. Helen Louise Reed, Nov. 30, 1940; 1 dau., Margaret Ann (Mrs. Paul L. Black). Partner Ingham, Boyd & Pratt, 1946-59, Ingham & McKinney, 1959-65, IKM Partnership, Pitts., 1965—. Dir. Action Housing; pres., dir. Chatham Village, Inc. Fellow A.I.A. (pres., dir. Pitts. chpt.); mem. Pa. Soc. Architects (pres., dir.). Episcopalian. (diocesan council). Home: 632 Pennridge Rd Pittsburgh PA 15211 Office: Empire Bldg Pittsburgh PA 15222

INGHRAM, MARK GORDON, physicist, educator; b. Livingston, Mont., Nov. 13, 1919; s. Mark Gordon and Luella Gallagher (McNay) I.; B.A., Olivet Coll., 1939; Ph.D., U. Chgo., 1947; m. Evelyn Mae Dyckman, May 12, 1946; children—Cheryl Ann, Mark Gordon. Physicist Manhattan Project, 1942-45; sr. physicist Argonne Nat. Lab., 1945-47; faculty U. Chgo., 1947—, successively instr., asst. prof., asso. prof., prof., Samuel K. Allison Distinguished Service prof. physics, 1969, chmn. dept. physics, 1959-70, acting dir. Inst. for Study of Metals, 1960-61, asso. dean div. of phys. scis., 1964-71. Member AEC com. for uranium isotopic standards, 1956-58; mem. com. on nuclear geophysics Nat. Acad. Sci., 1953-60; mem. adv. panel to Nat. Bur. Standards, 1960-63, mem. com. on exploration of moon and planets, 1958-61; mem. com. sci. and pub. policy Nat. Acad. Sci., 1966-69. Recipient J. Lawrence Smith medal Nat. Acad. Sci., 1957. Fellow Am. Phys. Soc.; mem. Nat. Acad. Scis., A.A.A.S. Asso. editor Jour. Chem. Physics. 1957-60; mem. editorial bd. The Review of Scientific Instruments, 1958- 61. Author articles in sci. jours. Home: 1534 E 59th St Chicago IL 60637

INGLE, DWIGHT JOYCE, physiologist; b. Kendrick, Ida., Sept. 4, 1907; s. David J. and Mattie (Self) I.; B.S., U. Ida., 1929, M.S., 1931, D.Sc. (hon.), 1962; Ph.D., U. Minn., 1941; m. Geneva McGarvey, Oct. 25, 1930; children—David, Ann, Jane. Mayo Found. fellow, 1934-38; George S. Cox med. research fellow U. Pa., 1938-41; Upjohn fellow Upjohn Research div., 1941-43, sr. research sci. Upjohn Co., 1943-53; prof. physiology Ben May Lab. U. Chgo., 1953—, chmn. dept. physiology, 1959-68. Chmn. adv. com. instl. research grants Am. Cancer Soc. Recipient Roche-Organon award Laurentian Hormone Conf., W. E. Upjohn prize; Outstanding Achievement award U. Minn., 1964; Modern Medicine Distinguished Achievement award, 1967. Fellow Am. Acad. Arts and Scis., N.Y. Diabetes Assn., A.A.A.S.; mem. Am. Physiol. Soc., Soc. Exptl. Biology and Medicine (pres. 1965- 67), Endocrine Soc. (pres. 1959-60; Koch award 1963), Nat. Acad. Scis., Sigma Xi (pres. Chgo. 1959- 60), Phi Beta Kappa, Alpha Omega Alpha. Clubs: Chgo. Literary (v.p. 1971-72); Quandrangle. Author: Physiological & Therapeutic Effects of Corticotropin (ACTH) and Cortisone, 1953; Principle of Research in Biology and Medicine, 1958; I Went to See the Elephant, 1962; also sci. papers. Founder, editor Perspectives in Biology and Medicine (Honor Award of AMWA, 1964, 68, 70). Home: 5514 Woodlawn Av Chicago IL 60637

INGLE, HAROLD EUGENE, publisher; b. Bondurant, Ia., Oct. 27, 1910; s. Otis Eldoris and Gracie Pearl (Collins) I.; B.S., Ia. State Univ., 1933; m. Norma Eveline Peterson, May 20, 1937; childrenHarold Norman, Richard Otis. Mgr. Ia. State Coll. Press, 1937-44, 1946-48; dir. Johns Hopkins Press, 1948-; sec., dir. Univ. Press Services, Inc., 1953-58, pres., 1958-60; dir. Franklin Pubs., Inc. Served as lt. USNR, 1944-46. Mem. Assn. Am. U. Presses (sec.-treas. 1953-55, pres. 1959-61, dir. 1967-68), Am. Book Pubs. Council (dir. 1960-63). Home: Gent Rd. Cockeysville MD 21030. Office: Johns Hopkins Press Baltimore MD 21218

INGLE, JOHN IDE, univ. dean; b. Colville, Wash., Jan. 19, 1919; s. John James and Jessie Valentine (Ide) I.; student Wash. State U., 1936-38; D.D.S., Northwestern U., 1942; M.S.D., U. Mich., 1948; m. Joyce Ledgerwood, July 11, 1940; children—John Geoffrey, Leslie, Schuyler Neal. Asst., Northwestern U., 1942-43; asst. prof. endodontics and periodontology Sch. Dentistry, U. Wash., 1948-51, asso. prof., 1951-59, prof., 1959-64, exec. officer dept., 1956-64; dean Sch. Dentistry, U. So. Cal., Los Angeles, 1964—; attending staff exec. com. Los Angeles County/U. So. Cal. Med. Center, 1964—. Cons. Nat. Bd. Dental Examiners, 1964—, endodontics, asst. surgeon gen. U.S. Army, 1969—; mem. adv. com. on dental health Office of Sec. Health, Edn. and Welfare, 1970—; mem. rev. com. on dental edn. NIH, 1970. Bd. dirs. Los Angeles United Way Crusade, 1967-69. Served with Dental Corps, AUS, 1943-46. Recipient Northwestern U. Alumni Merit award, 1966. Diplomate Am. Bd. Endodontics, Am. Bd. Periodontology. Fellow A.A.A.S., Internat., Am. colls. dentists; mem. Internat. Assn. for Dental Research, Am. Assn. Endodontists (past pres.), Am. Acad. Periodontology, Am. Dental Assn. and Constituents, Los Angeles Dental Soc. (sec.), Am. (cons. council on dental therapeutics), So. Cal. (del.) dental assns., Am. Assn. Dental Schs. Club: Cosmos (Washington). Author: (with others) Endodontics, 1965; (with A.L. Ogilvie) An Atlas of Pulpal and Periapical Biology, 1965. Home: 765 1/2 S Plymouth Blvd Los Angeles CA 9000591

INGLE, JOHN LINDSAY, savs. and loan assn. exec.; b. Glacier, B.C., Canada, July 5, 1920; brought to U.S., 1923; s. John L. and Gladys R. (Cooper) I.; student engring. U. Cal. at Los Angeles, 1938-41; m. Alice Pool, Oct. 7, 1944; children—Susan, Caroline, John Edward, Sallie Elizabeth. Tool engr. Douglas, N. Am., Luscombe Aircraft Cos., 1939-48; with Oak Cliff Savs. & Loan Assn., Dallas, 1948—, sucessively asst. sec., sec.-treas., v.p. and sec.-treas., sr. v.p., now pres., chief exec. officer; dir. Am. Bank & Trust Co. Trustee Dallas Mus. Fine Arts. Key holder Grad. Sch. Savs. and Loan. Mem. Dallas Citizens Council, Dallas C. of C. (former dir.). Democrat. Methodist. Club: Preston Trails Golf. Home: 4253 Armstrong Parkway Dallas TX 75205 Office: 325 W 12th St Dallas TX 75208

INGLES, EDWIN THOMAS, educator; b. Hillsboro, Ore., Feb. 21, 1907; s. Lemuel Reno and Mary Lavena (Furrow) I.; A.B., Pacific U., 1929; A.M., U. Ore., 1935, Ed.D., 1947; m. Carol Inderbitzin, Aug. 9, 1930; children—Nancy Carol, Edwin Theodore. Athletic coach, tchr. Condon (Ore.) High Sch., 1929-30; supt. schs., Lexington, Ore., 1930-33, Boardman, 1933-37; prof. edn. Pacific U., 1937-41, dir. admissions, 1937-39, comptroller, 1939-41, v.p., dean faculty, 1946-53, dir. summer sessions. 1947-53, coll. trustee, 1948-53; regional rep. Citizenship Edn. Project, Tchrs. Coll. Columbia, 1953-55; dean instrn. Modesto Jr. Coll., 1955-60, Coll. of Desert, Indio, Cal., 1960—. Mem. state bd. Community Chest, county chmn. Community Chest, 1948-50. Served to maj. USAAF, 1942-46; lt. col. Res., ret. Mem. Higher Commn. N.W. Assn. Secondary and Higher Sch., N.E.A., Nat. Soc. Coll. Tchrs. Edn., Am. Assn. Supervision and Curriculum Devel., Nat. Soc. for Study Edn., Forest Grove C. of C. (pres. 1949), Morrow County Ednl. Assn. (pres. 1936), Phi Delta Kappa, Gamma Sigma, Blue Key. Methodist. Mason, Kiwanian. Contbr. articles to ednl. jours. Home: 72-821 Pitahaya St Palm Desert CA 92260

INGLES, JAMES MAXWELL, govt. ofcl.; b. Clymer, Pa., July 8, 1918; s. Lloyd W. and Hope (Sickenberger) I.; B.S. in Civil Engring., U. Colo., 1940; m. Abbie Jean Stimbert, Sept. 1, 1953; children—Larry R. Crosson, Lon D. Crosson, Linda (Mrs. Richard Braunstein), Lee Ann Hope. Jr. engr. Colo. Fuel & Iron Corp., 1940-41, U.S. Govt., 1941-44; contractor, Colo., 1947-49; engr. City Los Angeles, 1949; with Bur. Reclamation, Dept. Interior, 1949—, regional dir. region 7, 1967—. Served with USNR, 1944-46. Registered profl. engr., Colo. Mem. U.S. Com. Internat. Commn. Irrigation and Drainage, Am. Soc. C.E., Denver Fed. Exec. Bd. Sigma Chi. Methodist. Rotarian, Elk. Home: 3232 Nelson St Wheatridge CO 80033 Office: Bldg 20 Denver Federal Center Denver CO 80225

INGLIS, DAVID RITTENHOUSE, educator; b. Detroit, Oct. 10, 1905; s. William and Carolyn Clay (Rittenhouse) I.; A.B., Amherst Coll., 1928, D.Sc. (honoris causa), 1963; D.Sc., Univ. of Mich., 1931; student U. Afloat, U. Heidelberg, Germany; m. Dorothy Rosalind Kerr, Mar. 26, 1934; 1 son, John Lockwood. Instr., Ohio State U., 1931-34, asst. prof., 1934; research asso. U. Leipsig, Fed. Inst. Tech., Zurich, 1932-33; asst. prof. U. Pitts., 1934-37, Princeton, 1937-38; asso. Johns Hopkins, 1938- 41, asso. prof., 1941-49; sr. physicist Argonne Nat. Lab., 1949-69; prof. physics U. Mass., 1969—; physicist OSRD, 1942, Ballistics Research Lab., Aberdeen Proving Ground, 1943; with theoretical div. Los Alamos Sci. Lab., 1943-46; vis. prof. U. Cal. at Berkeley, 1955-56; physicist European Orgn. Nuclear Research, Geneva, Switzerland, 1957-58; professorial lectr. U. Chgo., 1965-68. Fellow Am. Phys. Soc., Fedn. Am. Scientists (chmn. 1959-60), Phi Beta Kappa, Sigma Xi, Alpha Delta Phi. Author: Dynamic Principles of Mechanics, 1949; Nuclear Energy—Its Physics and Its Social Challenge, 1971. Editorial bd. Bull. Atomic Scientists. Contbr. articles profl. jours. Home: 15 Maplewood Dr Amherst MA 01002

INGLIS, JOHN, investment banker; b. N.Y.C., June 15, 1903; s. William Sloane and Sarah Louise (Meeks) I.; B.A., Columbia, 1924; m. Marcia M. Cahill, Aug. 12, 1926; childrenJohn, Marcia (Mrs. Russell D. Sayre); m. 2d, Marie Elizabeth Rossetti, Dec. 27, 1939; childrenPatricia Ann, William Rosetti. With Nat. City Co., 1924-33; head San Francisco municipal dept. Blyth & Co., Inc., 1933-41, head Pacific Coast municipal dept., 1941-64, joint mgr. nat. municipal dept., 1959-64, v.p., 1944-60, sr. v.p., 1960—, resident mgr. San Francisco office, 1962-68; dir. El Dorado Ins. Co., Eldorado Gen. Corp. Recipient distinguished service award Columbia Coll. Alumni Club, No. Cal. Clubs: Bohemian, Bond (past pres.; named Investment Banker of Year 1968), Municipal Bond (past pres.), Pacific Union, Merchants (San Francisco); Menlo Country (Redwood City, Cal.); Hillsborough (Cal.) Racquet. Home: 630 W Santa Inez St Hillsborough CA 94010 Office: Russ Bldg San Fransisco CA 94104

INGOLD, KEITH USHERWOOD, educator, chemist; b. Leeds, Eng., May 31, 1929; s. Christopher Kelk and Edith (Usherwood) I.; B.Sc. with honors in Chemistry, Univ. Coll., London, 1949; D.Phil., Oxford (Eng.) U., 1951; m. Carmen Cairine Hodgkin, Apr. 7, 1956; children—Christopher Frank, John Hilary, Diana Hilda. Postdoctoral fellow Nat. Research Council Can., 1951-53, research officer, 1955—; postdoctorate fellow U. B.C., 1953-55; vis. scientist Chevron Research Co., Richmond, Cal., 1966, Univ. Coll., London, 1969, 72. Fellow Royal Soc. Can.; mem. Chem. Inst. Can., Am. Chem. Soc. (award petroleum chemistry 1968), Chem. Soc. (London). Research papers in free radical chemistry. Home: Box 712 R R 5 Ottawa Ontario Canada Office: Nat Research Council Can Ottawa Ontario Canada

INGOLS, ROBERT SMALLEY, educator; b. Newark, Mar. 5, 1911; s. George A. and Nellie (Smalley) I.; B.Sc. in Biology, Bucknell U., 1931, D.Sc. (hon.), 1969; M.A. in Biochemistry, Columbia, 1934; Ph.D. in Sanitation, Rutgers U., 1939; m. Dorothy Ohlson, Nov. 4, 1939; children—Marcia R. (Mrs. H. Batchelor, Jr.), Cynthia A., George A. Research asst. Rutgers U., 1935-41; chemist sewage treatment plant, Hackensack, N.J., 1941-43; research fellow Fla. Citrus Commn., 1943-44; instr. Sch. Pub. Health, U. Mich., 1944-47; asso. prof. Ga. Inst. Tech., 1947-50, prof., 1950-57, prof., head dept. applied biology, 1957-60, prof., dir. Sch. Applied Biology, 1960-65, prof. Engring. Expt. Sta., 1965—. Chmn. Joint Com. on Uniformity of Methods for Water Exam.; mem. Nat. Tech. Adv. Com. Fed. Water Pollution Control Adminstrn. on Indsl. Water Supplies, 1967-68. Research participant Oak Ridge Inst. Nuclear Studies, 1950. Fulbright lectr. Instituto Politecnico di Milano, Italy, 1956-57. Fellow Am. Inst. Chemists; member A.A.A.S. (v.p. sect. C 1955), Am. Chem. Soc. (councillor 1955-58, chmn. water and wastes div. 1959; chmn. Ga. sect. 1967-68), Am. Water Works Assn., Water Pollution Control Fedn., Sigma Xi. Baptist. Club: Optimist. Home: 2973 Margaret Mitchell Ct Atlanta GA 30327

INGRAHAM, EDWARD CLARKE, Jr., fgn. service officer; b. Mineola, N.Y., Feb. 2, 1922; s. Edward Clarke and Dorothy Hathaway (Sutton) I.; B.A., Dartmouth, 1943; postgrad, Cornell U., 1957-58; m. Susan Hartman, Jan. 25, 1947; childrenJohn Edward, James William, Elizabeth Ann. Editorial asst. Moody's Investors Service, N.Y.C., 1946-47; joined U.S. Fgn. Service, 1947; vice consul, Cochabamba, Bolivia, 1947-48; 3d sec. embassy, La Paz, Bolivia, 1948-50; vice consul, Hong Kong, 1950-51, Perth, Australia, 1951-54; consul, Madras, India, 1954-56; 2d sec. embassy, Djakarta, Indonesia, 1958-60; officer charge Australia-New Zealand affairs State Dept., 1961-62, Indonesian affairs, 1962-65; assigned Nat. War Coll., 1965-66; chief of embassy polit. sect., Rangoon, Burma, 1966-69; dep. dir. research and analysis for E. Asia, State Dept., 1969—. Mem. U.S. delegation ANZUS council meeting, Canberra, Australia, 1962. Served with USAAF, 1943-45; ETO. Mem. Am. Fgn. Service Assn. Home: 7700 Scbago Rd Bethesda MD 20034 Office: INR/REA Dept State Washington DC 20520

INGRAHAM, H. GARDNER, lawyer; b. Bklyn., Apr. 22, 1912; s. Henry Andrews and Mary (Shotwell) I.; grad. Poly. Prep., 1929; B.A., Wesleyan U., 1933; LL.B., Yale, 1936; m. Barbara Lamb, Feb. 28, 1942; children—Michael Gardner, Henry Andrews II, Stevens Lamb, Robert Edward, Polly. Admitted to N.Y., D.C. bars; law sec. Hon. Thomas W. Swan, U.S. Circuit Ct. of Appeals, 1936-37; litigation atty. NLRB, 1937-39; atty. Office of Solicitor Gen., 1940-42; atty. U.S. rep. AEC, auspices Dept. State, 1946-47; partner firm Windels, Merritt & Ingraham, N.Y.C., 1964—. Dir. Pub. Service Co. of N.H. Trustee Wesleyan U. Served with USNR, 1942-46. Home: Locust Rd Northport NY 11768 Office: 40 Wall St New York City NY 10005

INGRAHAM, HOLLIS STEADMAN, physician; b. Brookline, Mass., Mar. 10, 1908; s. Alward and Grace (Steadman) I.; A.B., Harvard, 1930, M.D., 1933, M.P.H., 1935; D.Sc. (hon.), Union U.; m. Helena Johnson, June 1, 1931; children-Priscilla (Mrs. Albert Pultz), Irad Sylvia (Mrs. Harry Goetzman), Mark. Intern, USPHS Hosp., N.Y.C., 1933-34; Margaret Hague Maternity Hosp., Jersey City, 1940; epidemiologist N.Y. State Dept. Health, 1935-38, dist. state health officer, Kingston, N.Y., 1938-46, dir. epidemiology and communicable disease control, 1946-48, dep. commr., 1948-53, 1st dep. commr., 1953-63, commr. health, 1963—; prof. community health Albany Med. Coll.; adj. asso. prof. pub. health practice Columbia. Pres., bd. dirs. Health Research. Served as lt. comdr. USNR. 1942-46. Recipient medal U.S. Am. Typhus Commn., 1946. Diplomate Am. Bd. Preventive Medicine and Pub. Health. Mem. A.M.A., Am. Epidemiol. Soc., Am. Pub. Health Assn., N.Y. State Acad. Preventive Medicine. Clubs: University, Fort Orange. Contbr. articles to profl. jours. Home: 291 McCormack Rd Slingerlands NY 12159 Office: 84 Holland Av Albany NY 12208

INGRAHAM, JOE MCDONALD, U.S. circuit judge; b. Pawnee County, Okla., July 5, 1903; s. Millard F. and Emma (Patton) I.; LL.B., National U., 1927; m. Laura Munson, Oct. 29, 1954. Admitted to Okla. bar, 1927, D.C. bar, 1927, Tex. bar, 1928; practiced in Stroud, Okla., 1927-28, Ft. Worth, 1928-35, Houston, 1935- 54; judge U.S. Dist. Ct., So. Dist. of Tex., 1954-69, U.S. Ct. Appeals, Fifth Circuit, 1969—. Served as officer USAAF, 1942-46. Recipient Good Citizenship award Tex. Soc. S.A.R., 1958. Mem. Am., Houston bar assns., Tex. State Bar, Am. Judicature Soc., S.A.R. (pres. Tex. Soc. 1937-38), Am. Legion. Republican. Presbyn. Home: 1605 Banks St Houston TX 77006 Office: US Courthouse Houston TX 77002

INGRAHAM, MARY SHOTWELL (Mrs., Henry A. Ingraham), educator; b. Bklyn., Jan. 5, 1887; d. Henry Titus and Alice Wyman (Gardner) Shotwell: A.B., Vassar Coll., 1908; L.H.D., Wesleyan U., 1952, Columbia, 1961; m. Henry Andrews Ingraham, Oct. 28, 1908; children-Mary Alice (Mrs. Henry Bunting), Henry Gardner, Winifred Andrews (Mrs. Harold L. Warner, Jr), David. Mem. Dept. Edn., Bklyn. YWCA, 1908-15, chmn., 1915-22; pres. Bklyn. YWCA, 1922-39, v.p., 1939; pres. nat. bd. YWCA, 1940-46; vice chmn., dir. N.Y. Council Adult Edn., 1933-37; vice chmn. Bklyn. Council for Social Planning, 1933-38; mem. Bd. Higher Edn., N.Y.C., 1938-68, chmn. exec. com., 1944; v.p. United Service. Orgns., 1941-48; exec. com. Nat. Budget and Consultation Com., 1946-; bd. dirs. Nat. War Fund. Trustee Bklyn. Coll., 1938-68, chmn., 1943-52; mem. Nat. Inst. Social Scis., 1930-; mem. rep. council Vassar Coll.; mem. bd. dirs., exec. com. Community Chest, Council of U.S., 1946-52; v.p. Asso. Youth Serving Orgn., 1944-48. Chmn. Nat. Social Welfare Assembly, 1949-52, v.p., 1960- ; mem. Nat. Assembly for Social Policy and Devel.; mem. internat. com., pub. affairs com., mem. leadership devel. com. Nat. YWCA. Mem. Jr. League, Bklyn. Recipient Medal of Merit from Pres. of U.S., 1946. Republican. Mem. Society of Friends. Clubs:

Civitas. (Bklyn.); Brooklyn Heights Garden. Writer on edn. and social work. Home: 2 Montague Terrace Brooklyn NY 11201 also Northport Long Island NY 11768

INGRAHAM, MILLARD FILLMORE, lawyer; b. Enid, Okla., Feb. 20, 1934; s. James A. and Martha (Page) I.; A.B., Columbia, 1955; LL.B., Colo. U., 1958; m. Karen Burston, Mar. 9, 1968; children—Judith Ann, Jennifer. Admitted to Colo. bar, 1958, Alaska bar, 1962; practice in Colorado Springs, 1959-61, Fairbanks, 1961—; staff atty. Colo. Interstate Co., 1959-61; asso. Robert A. Parrish, 1961-64; partner Yeager & Ingraham, 1964-65, Ingraham & Niewohner, 1965—. Bd. dirs. Alaska Civil Liberties Union, 1968—, legal counsel, 1969—. Served with U.S. Army, 1958-59. Mem. Alaska (pres., bd. govs.), Tanana Valley (past pres.) bar assns., Alaska Acad. Trial Lawyers (bd. govs.), Am. Trial Lawyers Assn. Democrat. Home: 1533 Noble St Fairbanks AK 99701 Office: Nerland Bldg Fairbanks AK 99701

INGRAHAM, REX, dentist, educator; b. Fruitvale, Colo., Mar. 25, 1914; s. Eugene F. and Mary Della (Mace) I.; A.A., Mesa Coll., 1934; D.D.S., B.S., U. So. Cal., 1941; m. Lola Vanorsdel, June 1941 (dec.); children—Ronald R., Eric D.; m. 2d, Lucille Brokenshire, Oct. 1963. Faculty U. So. Cal. Sch. Dentistry, 1941—, prof., head dept. operative dentistry, 1945-69, Distinguished prof., 1966—, head dept. occlusion, 1969—; dir. human factors research dept. U. So. Cal. Dir. Jones Gold Foil Study Club; lectr. U.S., Alaska, S.Am., Hawaii, Europe, Australia, Africa. Active Boy Scouts Am. Club: Century. Author Manual on Operative Dentistry; Atlas of Gold Foil and Rubber Dam; Atlas of Cast Gold Procedures; Manual on Physiology of Occlusion. Contbr. articles to profl. jours. Home: 1612 Thompson Av Glendale CA 91201 Office: 1777 N Vine St Hollywood CA 90028

INGRAM, ALVIN JOHN, physician; b. Jackson, Tenn., Mar. 31, 1914; s. Alvin Hill and Margaret (Gallagher) I.; B.S., U. Tenn., 1939, M.D., 1939, M.S. in Orthopaedic Surgery, 1947; m. Catherine Davis, Feb. 7, 1943; children—Mildred, Cathy, Peggy. Intern Univ. Hosp., Ann Arbor, Mich., 1939-40, asst. resident surgery, 1940-41; fellow orthopaedic surgery Campbell Clinic, Memphis, 1941-42, 46-47, mem. staff, 1947—, dep. chief of staff, 1967-69, chief staff, 1970—; pvt. practice orthopaedic surgery, Memphis, 1947—; med. dir. Crippled Children's Hosp., 1948-61, chief staff, 1961—; med. dir. Les Passes Cerebral Palsy Treatment Center, 1953-56; med. adv. com. Memphis and W. Tenn. chpt. Nat. Found. Infantile Paralysis, 1947-57, chmn., 1947-55; med. adv. com. Shrine Sch. Crippled Children, 1947-56; med. adv. bd. Variety Club Convalescent Hosp., 1952-56; asso. prof. orthopaedic surgery U. Tenn. Coll. Medicine, 1960—; mem. staff Bapt. Meml. Hosp., exec. com. med. staff, 1969-70, chmn. orthopaedic dept., 1970—; mem. staff St. Joseph Hosp., LeBonheur Children's Hosp. (trustee 1968-71); cons. staff Meth. Hosp. Program chmn. 2d Tenn. Conf. Handicapped Children, 1958; chmn. med. div. United Fund Shelby County, 1961, mem. budget com., 1963-65; dir. at large Nat. Assn. Blue Shield Plans, 1965-70; mem. Gov. Tenn. Adv. Bd. Crippled Children's Service, 1961—, chmn., 1971. Bd. dirs. Front St. Theatre, Memphis, 1963-64. Served to maj., M.C., AUS, 1942-46. Diplomate Am. Bd. Orthopaedic Surgery. Mem. Am. Acad. Orthopaedic Surgeons (chmn. program com. 1954, 71), Am. Orthopaedic Assn. (chmn. program com.), Central Orthopaedic Club (charter mem.), Tennessee Clin. Orthopaedic Soc. (pres. 1963-64), Willis C. Campbell Club (pres. 1967), Internat. Soc. Orthopaedics and Traumatology, Am. Acad. Cerebral Palsy (chmn. program com. 1955, publs. com. 1957, exec. com. 1958, pres. 1958-59), A.C.S., Am. (ho. of dels. 1961-64, trustee 1964-70, sec. treas. 1968-70, sec. bd. trustees 1968-70), So., Tenn. med. assns., Memphis and Shelby County Med. soc. (pres. 1962, bd. censors, 1963-65, ho. of dels. 1965), Nat. Inst. Medicine Nat. Acad. Sci., U.S. C. of C. Methodist (ofcl. bd. 1952—, vice chmn. official bd. 1965, 66, 69, 70, chmn. 1971-72, gen. chmn. every mem. canvass 1955-57, 63, pres. men's club 1958, sec. stewardship 1964-65). Contbr. books. Home: 3876 Central Av Memphis TN 38111 Office: Campbell Clinic 869 Madison Av Memphis TN 38173

INGRAM, CHARLES CLARK, Jr., gas utility exec.; b. Henryetta, Okla., Dec. 10, 1916; s. Charles Clark and Winifred (Edwards) I.; B.S., U. Okla., 1940; m. Georgia Maxine Waterbury, Jan. 29, 1939; children—James Charles, Jack Roland. With Okla. Natural Gas Co., Tulsa, 1940—, v.p. land and geol., 1955-61; exec. v.p., 1961-66, pres., chmn. bd., 1966—; dir. Nat. Bank of Tulsa, Home Fed. Savs. & Loan Assn.; adv. dir. Rep. Nat. Bank. Bd. dirs. Downtown Tulsa Unltd., Inc., 1965-67, now adv. dir.; bd. dirs. Industries for Tulsa, Inc., 1966-68, Indian Nations council Boy Scouts Am., 1963-67, Tulsa Community Chest, 1967—; bd. dirs. Ark. Basin Devel. Assn., 1966-, Okla. v.p., 1967—; bd. dirs. City of Tulsa-Rogers County Port Authority, 1966-70, Tulsa bd. Nat. Conf. Christians and Jews, 1967—; exec. com. Okla. Med. Research Found., 1967—; mem. adv. bd. Okla. State U., 1963-66; trustee Oklahoma City U. Found., Inc., 1967-70, U. Tulsa, 1968—, Tulsa Psychiatric Found., 1963-70; bd. govs. Am. Citizenship Center, Oklahoma City, 1970—. Served from 2d lt. to maj., ordnance, AUS, 1941-46; PTO. Registered profl. engr., Okla. Mem. Am. Assn. Petroleum Geologists (asso.), A.I.M. (pres.'s council), Am. (dir. 1971—), So. (pres. 1967) gas assns., Am. Inst. Mining, Metall. and Petroleum Engrs., Am. Mgmt. Assn., Am. Petroleum Inst., Engrs. Soc. Tulsa, Am., Okla., Ind. petroleum assns., Oklahoma City, Okla. State, Tulsa chambers commerce Propeller Club US., Tulsa Geol. Soc., Ind. Natural Gas Assn. Am. (dir.), Mid-Continent Oil and Gas Assn. (dir.), Okla. Petroleum Council (dir.), N.A.M. (dir. 1971—), Newcomen Soc. N.Am. (Okla. com.), Sigma Tau, Sigma Gamma Epsilon. Mason. Clubs: Tulsa, Southern Hills Country (pres. bd. govs. 1971,), Cedar Ridge Country, Summit (Tulsa); Tower (Oklahoma City). Home: 3707 S Delaware Pl Tulsa OK 74105 Office: 624 S Boston Av Tulsa OK 74102

INGRAM, DEAN, banker; b. Non, Okla., Jan. 11, 1940; s. Milburn Cisney and Velma Viola (Russell) I.; B.S., Southwestern State Coll., 1962; certificate Am. Inst. Banking: 1 dau., Tammy Gay. Prodn. accountant Apco Oil Corp., Oklahoma City, 1962-63; auditor First Nat. Bank and Trust Co., Oklahoma City, 1963—. Mem. membership com. Oklahoma City YMCA, 1966-68. Mem. Bank Adminstrn. Inst. (dir. Oklahoma City). Home: 1437 NW 48th St Oklahoma City OK 73107 Office: 120 N Robinson St Oklahoma City OK 73125

INGRAM, EDGAR W., restaurant co. exec.; b. Wichita, Kan., 1910. Pres., dir. White Castle System, Inc., Columbus, O.; pres. Paperlynen Co., Porcelain Steel Bldgs. Co. Home: 330 Medick Way Worthington OH 43085 Office: 555 W Goodale St Columbus OH 43216*

INGRAM, ERSKINE BRONSON, marine transp. and constrn. co. exec.; b. St. Paul, Nov. 27, 1931; s. Orrin Henry and Hortense (Bigelow) I.; student Vanderbilt U., 1950; A.B., Princeton, 1953; m. Martha Robinson Rivers, Oct. 4, 1958: children—Orrin Henry II, John Rivers, David, Robin. With Ingram Oil & Refining Co., 1955-61, v.p., treas., 1958-61; v.p. Ingram Barge Co., also Gen. Properties Inc., 1958-61; merged to become Ingram Corp., 1962, pres., 1963—, also dir., dir. all subsidiaries; chmn. bd. Capitol Chevrolet Co. Nashville, 1970—; dir. Weyerhaeuser Co. Trustee, mem. exec. com. Vanderbilt U.; trustee Montgomery Bell Acad., Nashville. Clubs: Augusta (Ga.) Nat. Golf; Belle Meade Country, Cumberland (Nashville); White Bear Yacht (White Bear Lake, Minn.); Minnesota (St. Paul). Home: 120 Hillwood Dr Nashville TN 37205 Office: 4304 Harding Rd Nashville TN 37205

INGRAM, FREDERIC BIGELOW, marine transp. and constrn. exec.; b. St. Paul, Nov. 14, 1929; s. Orrin Henry and Hortense (Bigelow) I.; grad. Phillips Acad., Andover, Mass., 1947; student Princeton, 1951; m. Barbara Dobbins, Oct. 29, 1953; children—Frederic Bigelow, Eileen Bigelow, Philip Finley; m. 2d, Carole J. Goodman, Dec. 13, 1968. Asst. to pres. Ingram Oil & Refining Co., New Orleans, 1953-56, exec. v.p., 1956- 61; v.p. Ingram Barge Co., New Orleans, 1953-60, pres., 1960—; v.p. Ingram Corp., New Orleans, 1961-68, chmn. bd., 1968—; partner Ingram Brothers, New Orleans, 1962—; pres. Ingram-Armistead, New Orleans, 1962—, Ingram Contractors, Inc., 1964—; dir. Murphy Corp., Geophysics & Computer Service, Inc., La. & So. Life Ins. Co. Served to 1st lt. USAF, 1951-53. Clubs: White Bear Yacht (St. Paul); New Orleans Country, Metairie Country, Timberlane Country (New Orleans); Augusta (Ga.) Nat. Golf; Belle Meade Country (Nashville); Brook Hollow Golf (Dallas). Home: 620 Ursuline St New Orleans LA 70116 Office: Internat Trade Mart New Orleans LA 70130

INGRAM, GEORGE, Jr., bus. exec.; b. Montclair, N.J., Dec. 10, 1920; s. George and Frances Elizabeth (Watts) I.; B.S., Yale, 1942; M.S., Stevens Inst. Tech., 1948; m. Olive May Holtz, Feb. 15, 1947; children-Patricia (Mrs. S. K. Bone), George III, Sara, John. Indsl. engr. RCA, 1942-45; cons. mgmt. engr. Stevenson, Jordan & Harrison, Inc., N.Y.C., 1945-51; controller Riegel Paper Corp., 1951-57; controller Raytheon Co., Waltham, Mass., 1957-61, v.p., 1960-61, v.p. finance, 1961-63, sr. v.p., dir., 1963-68; sr. v.p U.S. Plywood-Champion Papers, Inc., N.Y.C., 1968-69, exec. v.p., 1969- dir., 1968—; dir. Microwave Assos., Inc., Burlington, Mass. Trustee Coll. Wooster (O.). Registered profl. indsl. engr., Pa. Mem. Financial Execs. Inst. (past pres. Boston; past chmn. nat. com. securities and exchanges regulation), Am. Soc. M.E., Am. Mgmt. Assn., Yale Engring. Assn., Phi Gamma Delta. Republican. Episcopalian. Clubs: Nantucket Yacht; Economic, Canadian, Wall Street (N.Y.C.). Home: 502 E 87th St New York City NY 10028 Office: US Plywood-Champion Papers Inc 777 3d Av New York City NY 10017

INGRAM, GEORGE MASON, III, govt. ofcl.; b. Nashville, Nov. 8, 1914; s. George Mason and Hattie (Wilson) I.; A.B. magna cum laude, Vanderbilt U., 1936; Rockefeller fellow, Harvard, 1936-37; Littauer fellow in pub. adminstrn., Harvard, 1938-39; m. Ashton Somerville, Feb. 24, 1940; children—Ashton (Mrs. W. Douglass) George, Elinor (Mrs. D. Boyce). Intern in pub. adminstrn., TVA 1937-38; budget and program planning officer, 1939-44; adminstrn. and budget officer Internat. Monetary Fund, 1946-48; chief internat. adminstrn. staff Office United Nat. Affairs, Dept. State, 1948- 50; chief div. internat. adminstrn. Office Internat. Adminstrn. and Conf., Bur. U.N. Affairs, Dept. State, 1950-52; dir. Office Internat. Adminstrn. and Conf., 1952-54; dir. adminstrn. U.S. Embassy, Vienna, 1954-56; exec. asst. to Sec. Gen. of Baghdad Pact, 1956-58; with Fgn. Service Inspection Corps, 1958-61; assigned Nat. War Coll., 1958-61; counselor, dep. chief of mission Am. Embassy, Helsinki, 1962-68; country dir. for Scandinavian affairs Dept. State, 1968—. Adviser U.S. del. to Conf. of FAD, U.N., 1948; 49, U.S. del. to 2d World Health Assembly, 1949; vis. lectr. U. Denver Inst. Internat. Adminstrn., 1950. Served as ensign, USNR, 1944-46. Mem. Phi Beta Kappa, Beta Theta Pi, Omicron Delta Kappa. Home: Nashville TN 37202 Office: Dept State Washington DC 20520

INGRAM, JAMES CARLTON, economist, educator; b. Roanoke, Ala., Jan. 11, 1922; s. John Henry and Isabelle (Shanks) I.; B.S., U. Ala., 1942; A.M., Stanford, 1947; Ph.D. (Social Sci. Research Council fellow), Cornell U., 1952; m. Alice Jane Graham, May 1, 1948; children—Deborah, Susan, Melissa. Research analyst Indsl. Indemnity Ins. Co., San Francisco, 1947-48; asst. prof., asso. prof., prof. econs. U. N.C., Chapel Hill, 1952—, dean Grad. Sch., 1966- 69; vis. mem. London Sch. Econs., 1963-64; vis. prof. Thammasat U., Bangkok, Thailand, 1969-71. Served with AUS, 1942-46. Ford Found. fellow, 1963-64. Mem. Am., So. (mem. exec. com.) econ. assns. Author: Economic Change in Thailand Since 1850, 1955; Regional Payments Mechanisms, 1962; International Economic Problems, 1966, 2d edit., 1970. Mng. editor So. Econ. Jour., 1961-65. Home: 1012 Highland Woods St Chapel Hill NC 27514

INGRAM, VERNON MARTIN, educator, biochemist; b. Breslau, Germany, May 19, 1924; B.S. in Pure Math., Chemistry, Zoology, U. London, 1943; B.S. in Chemistry 1st class, 1945, Ph.D., 1949, D.Sc., 1961. Mem. sci. staff Med. Research Council unit for molecular biology Cavendish Lab., Cambridge, Eng., 1952-58; faculty Mass. Inst. Tech., Cambridge, 1958—, prof. biochemistry, 1961—; Jesup lectr. Columbia, 1962; Harvey Soc. lectr., 1965. Fellow Royal Soc.; mem. Am. Chem. Soc., Genetical Soc., Chem. Soc., Biochem. Soc., Am. Soc. Biol. Chemists, Am. Acad. Arts and Scis. Research hemoglobin synthesis during devel., structure and function of s-RNA. Home: 45 Bellevue Av Cambridge MA 02138

INGRAM, WALTER ROBINSON, educator; b. Liverpool, Eng., Feb. 12, 1905; s. Walter and Elizabeth (Robinson) I.; A.B., Grinnell Coll., 1926; M.S., U. Ia., 1928, Ph.D., 1929; m. Lydia Margaret Bowen, Sept. 3, 1929; children—Walter Bowen, William Edmund. Came to U.S., 1909, naturalized, 1936. Instr. zoology Syracuse U., 1929-30; instr. neurology Med. Sch., Northwestern U., 1930-31, asso., 1931-32, asst. prof., 1932-36; asst. prof. anatomy Coll. Medicine, U. Ia., Iowa City, 1936-37, asso. prof., 1937-40, prof., 1940—, head dept., 1940-66, exec. com. Coll. Medicine, 1949-53. Commonwealth Fund fellow, 1958-59. Fellow Am. Electroencephalographic Soc. (hon.); mem. Royal Soc. Medicine (affiliate), Anat. Soc. Gt. Britain and Ireland, A.A.A.S., Am. Neurol. Assn., Am. Acad. Neurology, Am. Assn. Anatomists, Am. Physiol. Soc., Soc. Exptl. Biology and Medicine, Soc. for Neurosci., Phi Beta Kappa, Sigma Xi, Alpha Omega Alpha, Phi Beta Pi. Author: A Student's Introduction to Neurology, 1964; (with Fisher and Ranson) A Synopsis of Neuroanatomy: Diabetes Insipidus; papers on neuroanatomy and neurophysiology in sci. jours. Home: 333 Lexington Av Iowa City IA 52240

INGRAM, WILLIAM, ins. co. exec.; b. Kearny, N.J., Aug. 24, 1913; s. William and Agnes (Napier) I.; student Rutgers U.; m. Grace E. Whale, May 17, 1939; 1 dau., Janette Grace. With Prudential Ins. Co. Am., 1932—, sr. v.p., 1960-62, sr. v.p. charge Canadian operations, 1962-67, sr. v.p. charge Mid-Am. operations, 1967—. Home: 1179 Grandview Lane Lake Forest IL 60045 Office: Prudential Plaza Chicago IL 60601

INGRAM, WILLIAM AUSTIN, lawyer; b. Jeffersonville, Ind., July 6, 1924; s. William Austin and Marion (Lane) I.; student Stanford, 1947; LL.B., U. Louisville, 1950; m. Barbara Lender, Sept. 18, 1947; children—Mary Amanda, Claudia Franklin, Elizabeth Lane. Admitted to Cal. bar, 1951, Ct. Appeals and Dist. Ct. No. Dist. Cal., 1951; asso. firm Littler, Coakley, Lauritzen & Ferdon, San Francisco, 1951-55; dep. dist. atty., Santa Clara County, San Jose, Cal., 1955-57; asso., mem. firm Rankin, Oneal, Luckhardt, Center & Ingram, San Jose, 1957; partner Rankin, Oneal, Luckhardt, Center, Ingram & Bonney, San Jose; mem. nat. panel arbitrators Am. Arbitration Assn., 1963-67. Served with USMCR, 1943-46. Mem. State Bar Cal., Am., Santa Clara County (trustee 1967—) bar assns., Nat. Assn. R.R. Trial Counsel, Am. Bd. Trial Advocates, Santa Clara County Trial Lawyers Assn., Cal. Med.-Legal Assn. Republican. Episcopalian. Club: Bohemian (San Francisco). Home: 1975 Bryant St Palo Alto CA 94301

INGRAM, WILLIAM THOMAS, Jr., clergyman, sem. pres.; b. Pine Bluff, Ark., Mar. 24, 1913; s. William Thomas and Lillian (Johnston) I.; B.A., Tex. Christian U., 1934; M.A., So. Meth. U., 1935; B.D., Cumberland Presbyn. Theol. Sem., 1937; Ph.D., Vanderbilt U., 1956; m. Virginia Howell, Aug. 2, 1933; children—William Thomas III, John Howell. Ordained to ministry Presbyn. Ch., 1933; pastor First Cumberland Ch., Ft. Worth, 1933-34; pastor Cumberland Ch., McKenzie, Tenn., 1939-43, mem. bd. Christian edn., 1938-43, v.p. bd., 1940-43, mem. commn. on evangelism, 1947-50, dir. commn. on chaplains, 1947-54, moderator 127th Gen. Assembly, 1957-58; prof. missions and history of religions Bethel Coll., 1946-62; prof. missions and history religions Cumberland Presbyn. Theol. Sem., 1946-62, dean, 1962-64; pres. Memphis Theol. Sem., Memphis, 1964—. Served as maj. Chaplains' Corps, AUS, 1943-46; chaplain, col. Res. Mem. Alumni Assn. Div. Sch. Vanderbilt U. (past pres.), Soc. Bibl. Lit. and Exegesis, Am. Soc. Church History, Am. Soc. Christian Social Ethics, Am. Acad. Polit. and Social Sci. Rotarian (pres. 1958-59). Home: 210 N Avalon Memphis TN 38112 Office: 168 E Parkway S Memphis TN 38104

INGRAM, WILLIAM TRUITT, san. engr., educator; b. Cleve., June 16, 1908; s. Frank and Grace Lillian (Truitt) I.; B.A., Stanford, 1930; M.P.H., Johns Hopkins, 1942; m. Margaret B. Nelson, 1932; childrenBeryl (Mrs. Jon V. Nielsen), Judith (Mrs. John F. Nelson), John E., Diane F.: m. 2d, Filomena T. Lioy. Apr. 18, 1958. Office engr. Pacific Gas & Electric Co., San Francisco, 1930-32; recorder U.S. Coast and Geod. Survey, 1932-33; regional surveyor, supr. Fed. and State Mosquito Control, So. Cal. region, 1933-34; asst. county dir. Cal. Relief Adminstrn., 1934; san. engr. San Joaquin Local Health Dist., 1935-41; regional water works adviser Cal. Bur. San Engring., 1942; asst. regional san. engr. Office Civil Def., 9th region USPHS. 1942-44; camp san. engr. War Refugee Camps Middle East, Brit. Army, USPHS, UNRRA, 1943-44; chief engr. health div. UNRRA, Jugoslav Mission, 1944-46; engring, field asso. Am. Pub. Health Assn., 1947-49; asso. prof. pub. health engring. N.Y. U. Coll. Engring. 1949-54, adj. prof., 1954-; cons., 1947-; vis. prof. preventive med. div. Cornell Coll. Medicine, 1956—; lectr. Columbia Sch. Pub. Health, owner Wm. T. Ingram. cons. engr.; v.p. Newing Labs., Inc. Chmn. Engring. Found. Coordinating Com. Air Pollution Research, 1960-67; chmn. joint editorial bd. Revision Glossary Water and Wastewater Control Engring., 1962—. Recipient Kenneth Allen Meml. award. 1960. Diplomate Am. Acad. Env. Engrs. Fellow Am. Pub. Health Assn., A.A.A.S., Am. Soc. C.E. (chmn. research council air resource engring.); mem. Am. Soc. Engring. Edn., Am. Indsl. Hygiene Assn., Air Pollution Control Assn., Inter-Am. Assn. San. Engring., Conf. Municipal Pub. Health Engrs., Am. Water Works Assn., Sigma Xi. Author: The Proposed Sanitary Code- Part III, 1949. Contbr. to book, also articles to tech. jours. Home: 7 North Dr Whitestone NY 11357 Office: NYU Sch Engring and Sci Univ Heights Bronx NY 10453

INGRIM, WARD D., television ofcl.; b. Stockton, Cal., May 2, 1910; s. Elmer A. and Lottie (Haas) I.; B.S., U. Cal., 1931; m. Mary E. Torrey, Nov. 9, 1940; 1 dau., Mary Ann (Mrs. C.P. Telfer). Salesman radio sta. KJBS, San Francisco, 1931-35; salesman, comml. mgr., later asst. mgr. radio sta. KFRC, 1935-42; partner John Blair & Co., 1945-48; dir. advt., v.p. sales, exec. v.p. DLBS, Hollywood, Cal., 1948-54, gen. mgr., 1954-57; v.p., dir. Gen Teleradio Inc., 1951- 54; pres. treas., dir., San Francisco-Oakland TV, Inc., 1954-63; v.p. Cox Cablevision Corp., 1964-65; dir., chmn. finance com. Tele-Vue Systems, Inc., 1965-68; ltd. partner KMST-TV, 1969—. Bd. dirs. Oakland Better Bus. Bur., 1958-64, chmn. bd. dirs., 1961-63. Served from 2d lt. to maj. USAAF, 1942-45. Mem. TV Pioneers, Radio Pioneers. Clubs: San Francisco Golf, Orinda Country, Family; Rainier, Monterey Peninsula Country. Home: 3 Oak Arbor Rd Orinda CA 94563

INGRISCH, RUDOLPH, mfg. co. exec.; b. N.Y.C., Sept. 3, 1909; s. Martin G. and Clara (Machold) I.; A.B., Columbia, 1930, M.S., 1934; m. Gertrude T. Walsh, Sept. 10, 1938; 1 dau., Barbara A. (Mrs. Jeremy G. Freeman). Supervising sr. Price. Waterhouse & Co., C.P.A.'s N.Y.C, 1934-41; with Binney & Smith Inc., N.Y.C., 1941-71, exec. v.p., 1957-67, president, 1967-69, chmn. bd., chief exec. officer, 1969-71, chmn. exec. com., 1971, ret., 1971; chmn. Cosmic Crayon Co., Ltd., Eng., Delta Brush Mfg. Corp., P.R. Brush Corp., Binney & Smith Internat., Inc., Cal. Pacific Crayon Co., Inc.; pres. Can. Crayon Co., Ltd. Mem. Phi Delta Theta. Home: 162 Park St New Canaan CT 06840 Office: 380 Madison Av New York City NY 10017

INHORN, STANLEY LEE, educator; b. Phila., Aug. 1, 1928; s. Charles and Nan (Ostrow) Einhorn; B.S., Western Reserve U., 1949; M.D., Columbia, U., 1953; m. Shirley Gertrude Sherburne, Aug. 22, 1954; children—Lowell Frank, Marcia Claire, Roger Charles. Intern U. Wis. Hosp., Madison, 1953-54 resident, 1956-60; mem. faculty Med. Sch. U. Wis., Madison, 1959—, asso. prof. pathology and preventive medicine, 1969—; asst. dir. Wis. State Lab. Hygiene, Madison, 1960-66, dir., 1966—; cons. medicare div. Dept. Health, Edn. and Welfare, 1968-69, Center Disease Control, 1968-71, Am. Pub. Health Assn., 1967-71; violinist Madison Symphony Orch., 1967-71. Bd. dirs. Wis. Citizens for Family Planning, Am. Cancer Soc. Served with M.C., USNR, 1954-56. Diplomate Am. Bd. Pathology, Nat. Bd. Med. Examiners. Mem. Am. Soc. Clin. Pathologists, Am. Pub. Health Assn., Am. Soc. Cytology, and others. Research in cytogenetics of congenital anomalies and human abortion. Home: 210 Ozark Trail Madison WI 53705

INK, DWIGHT ALBERT, Jr., govt. ofcl.; b. Des Moines, Sept. 9, 1922; s. Dwight P. and Edna M. (Craun) I.; B.S., Ia. State U., 1947; M.A., U. Minn., 1950; m. Margaret L. Child, Aug. 31, 1947; children—Stephen D., Bruce C., Lawrence D., Barbara S., Lauri S. Budget and personnel officer, Fargo, N.D., 1948-50; municipal water studies Bur. Reclamation, Bismarck, N.D., 1950-51; with AEC, 1951—, spl. asst. to chmn., 1958-59, asst. gen. mgr., 1959—. Exec. dir. Fed. Reconstrn. Commn. for Alaska, 1964; chmn. White House Task Force on Edn., 1965-66; asst. sec. U.S. Dept. Housing and Urban Devel., 1966-68; asst. dir. Office Mgmt. and Budget, Exec. Office of Pres., 1968—. Chmn. S.C. Charter Com., 1954-55; cons. Little Hoover Commn., Minn., 1950. Recipient Fleming award, 1961, Career Service award Nat. Civil Service League, 1966. Mem. Delta Sigma Rho. Home: 11708 Farmland Dr Rockville MD 20852 Office: Exec Office of Pres Washington DC 20410

INKELES, ALEX, sociologist, educator; b. Bklyn., Mar. 4, 1920; s. Meyer and Ray (Gewer) K.; B.A., Cornell U., 1941, M.A., 1946; postgrad. Washington Sch. Psychiatry, 1946-46; Ph.D., Columbia, 1949; student Boston Psychoanalytic Inst., 1957-59; A.M. (hon.), Harvard, 1957; m. Bernadette Mary Kane, Jan. 31, 1942; 1 dau., Ann Elizabeth. Social sci. research analyst Dept. State and OSS, 1942- 46, cons. program evaluation br. Internat. Broadcasting Div., Dept. State, 1949-51; instr. dept. social relations Harvard, 1948, lectr., 1948-57, prof. sociology, 1957-71, dir. studies social relations Russian Research

Center, dir. studies on social aspects econ. devel. Center Internat. Affairs, 1963-71; Margaret Jacks prof. sociology and edn. Stanford U., 1971—; prof. honoris causa Faculdade de Ciencias Politicas e Economicas de Rio de Janeiro, 1969; cons., survey world communications facilities UNESCO, 1950. Mem. exec. com. behavioral sci. div. NRC, 1968—. Fellow Am. Acad. Arts and Scis.; mem. Am. (council 1961-64), Eastern (pres. 1961-62) sociol. socs., World, Am. assns. pub. opinion research, Inter-Am. Soc. Psychology, Soc. for Study Social Problems. Author: Public Opinion in Soviet Russia, 1950 (Kappa Tau Alpha award, 1950, Grant Squires prize Columbia, 1955); (with R. Bauer, C. Kluckhohn) How the Soviet System Works, 1956; (with R. Bauer) The Soviet Citizen, 1959; Soviet Society (edited with H.K. Geiger), 1961; What is Sociology, 1964; Reading on Modern Sociology, 1965; Social Change in Soviet Russia, 1968; also articles sociol., psychol. jours., nat. mags. Editor: Founds. Modern Sociology Series. Adv. editor in sociology to Little, Brown & Co. Home: 565 Arastradero Rd Palo Alto CA Office: Cubberly Hall Stanford CA 94305

INKER, MONROE L., lawyer; b. Boston, July 5, 1925; B.A., Bklyn. Coll., 1948; LL.B., Harvard, 1951, LL.M., 1953. Admitted to N.Y. bar, 1951, Mass. bar, 1953; now mem. firm Crane, Inker & Oteri, Boston; teaching fellow Harvard Law Sch., 1952-53; asst. prof. Northeastern U. Law Sch., 1953-55; lectr. Boston Coll. Law Sch., 1957—. Mem. Am., Middlesex, Boston (family law com. 1958, council 1961) bar assns. Author: Annual Survey of Massachusetts Law, 1957-63. Editor Mass. Bar Jour., 1963. Office: 20 Ashburton Pl Boston MA 02108*

INMAN, FRED WINSTON, educator; b. Mountain Home, Ark., Mar. 30, 1931; s. Fred Waldo and Mary Ruth (Smith) I.; A.B., U. Cal. at Berkeley, 1953, M.A., 1955, Ph.D., 1957; m. Betty Fern Waller, Dec. 19, 1955; children—Becky Ann, Fred Warren. Prof. physics, chmn. dept. Howard Payne Coll., Brownwood, Tex., 1957-64; faculty U. Pacific, 1964-67; prof. physics, chmn. dept. Mankato (Minn.) State Coll., 1967—. Cons. to govt., industry. Mem. Am. Phys. Soc., Am. Assn. Physics Tchrs., I.E.E.E., A.A.A.S., Sigma Xi. Home: Valley View Pl Mankato MN 56001

INMAN, MARK KEITH, educator; b. Argyle Shore, P.E.I., Can., Aug. 23, 1899; s. Peter and Emily (Matheson) I.; B.A., Acadia U., Wolfville, N.S., 1925; student Jesus Coll., Oxford (Eng.) U., 1926; M.A., Harvard, 1928, Ph.D., 1938; D.Litt. (hon.), Acadia U. 1966; m. Georgina Livingston, Sept. 10, 1932; children—Fay Ruth (Mrs. John H. Dirks), Heather Jean. Lectr. econs. Queen's U., Kingston, Ont., 1928; mem. faculty U. Western Ont., 1929—, prof. econs., chmn. dept., 1940-63, dean faculty arts and sci., 1963-65, v.p. arts and sci., 1965-68. Mem., past chmn. Bd. Arbitration and Conciliation; past pres. London Council Adult Edn.; chmn. regional com. Canadian Legion Ednl. Service, 1945-46; exec. com. Ont. Curriculum Inst., 1965; vice chmn. Ont. Univs. Council on Admissions, 1966. Bd. dirs. London Assn. Handicapped Adults, pres. 1954. Served with RAF, 1918. Mem. Am. Econ. Assn., Canadian Polit. Sci. Assn. Mem. Liberal Party. Baptist. Club: Sunningdale Country (London, Ont.). Author: (with H. A. Logan) A Social Approach to Economics, rev. edit., 1948; Economics in a Canadian Setting, 1959, rev. edit. (with F. R. Anton), 1965. Home: 1014 Colborne St London Ontario Canada

INMAN, VERNE THOMSON, physician, educator; b. San Jose, Cal., Nov. 6, 1905; s. Jesse Jay and Lois Elizabeth (Headen) I.; B.A. in Med. Scis., U. Cal. at Berkeley, 1928, M.A. in Anatomy, 1929, Ph.D. in Anatomy, 1934; M.D., U. Cal. at San Francisco, 1932; m. Irene Patricia Cootey, May 9, 1930; children—Robert Anthony, Verne Thomas, Richard Headen. Asst. instr. anatomy U. Cal. at Berkeley, 1928-29, instr. anatomy, 1932-36; intern, then resident U. Cal. Hosp., San Francisco, 1936-39; fellow orthopaedic surgery San Francisco Hosp., 1939-40; instr. anatomy U. Cal. Sch. Pharmacy, San Francisco, 1940-45; faculty dept. orthopaedic surgery U. Cal. Sch. Medicine, San Francisco, 1940—, prof., 1952—, chmn. dept., 1957-70; dir. biomechanics lab. U. Cal. at San Francisco and Berkeley, 1957—; acting chmn. dept. surgery U. Cal. Sch. Medicine, 1963- 64. Cons. adv. com. artificial limbs Nat. Acad. Scis.-NRC, 1952-56; cons. orthopaedic surgery to prosthetics research bd., 1956-59; mem. subcom. fundamental studies, com. prosthetics research and devel., 1966- -; mem. com. research-med. care, also com. research-clin. scis. Nat. Found., 1959—; ad hoc com. prosthetic aid to free world Internat. Inst. Welfare Cripples; mem. med. adv. com. Office Vocational Rehab., 1960—; com. rev. tng. grant applications Inst. Arthritis and Metabolic Diseases, 1963—; spl. research prosthetic and orthopedic design and studies human locomotion, med. problems related to lower-extremity amputation. Fulbright lectr. anatomy U. Assiut (UAR), 1964-65. Corr. fellow Brit. Orthopaedic Assn.; member Am., Western orthopedic assns., Orthopaedic Soc. (founder mem.), Am. Acad. Orthopaedic Surgeons, Orthopaedic Research and Edn. Found. (asso.), Am., Cal. med. assns., San Francisco City and County Med. Soc., Wilson Interurban Orthopaedic Club, Pan Am. Med. Assn. (life), Am. Orthopedic Foot Soc. (founder mem., v.p.), Phi Beta Kappa, Alpha Omega Alpha, Phi Sigma. Author articles in field. Asso. editor Jour. Bone and Joint Surgery, 1948-53. Home: 212 Edgewood St San Francisco CA 94117

INMAN, WILLIAM CHARLES, hosp. supt.; b. Denver, Oct. 28, 1899; s. Charles Thomas and Annie (Alber) I.; M.D., Tufts U., 1924; m. Dorothy Hathorne Brown, Mar. 13, 1925. Former supt. Grafton (Mass.) State Hosp. Home: 41 Hollywood St North Grafton MA 01519

INNERFIELD, IRVING, educator, research physician; b. Bklyn., June 15, 1912; s. Maurice and Frances (Schmetterling) I.; B.S., L.I. U., 1932; M.D., N.Y. Med. Coll., 1936; m. H. Jean Pozesky, Dec. 17, 1944; children—Ronald, Billie, Carla, Michael. Intern Queens Gen. Hosp., 1936-39; resident Columbia Coll. Phys. and Surg., 1939-42; pvt. practice internal medicine, Nyack, N.Y., 1945-50, N.Y.C., 1950-55; asst. prof. physiology N.Y. Med. Coll., 1949- 53; research asso. medicine Mt. Sinai Hosp., N.Y.C., 1953-56; research prof. biology L.I. U., 1956-60; asst. pathologist Harlem Hosp., N.Y.C., 1959-60; mem. faculty Fairleigh Dickinson U., 1960—, prof. biochemistry, 1960—, chmn. dept., 1962—. Trustee L.I. U. Served with USNR, World War II. Named Alumnus of Year, L.I. U., 1957. Fellow N.Y. Acad. Scis.; mem. Am. Fedn. Clin. Research, A.A.A.S., Am. Assn. U. Profs., A.M.A., Bergen County Med. Soc., Soc. Exptl. Biology and Medicine. Author: Enzymes in Clinical Medicine, 1960. Discoverer anti- inflammatory effect proteolytic enzymes, 1951; inventor intra-muscle and oral forms of proteolytic enzymes. Home: 20 Knickerbocker Rd Tenafly NJ 07670 Office: Dept Biochemistry Fairleigh Dickinson U Teaneck NJ 07666

INNESS-BROWN, VIRGINIA ROYALL, arts adviser, orgn. ofcl.; b. Medoud, Mass., May 4, 1901; d. John Allen Crosskeys and Agatha Caroline (Freeman) Royall; ed. pvt. schs.; m. Hugh Alwyn Iness-Brown, Mar. 26, 1921; childrenHugh Alwyn, Page Royall (Mrs. James B. Tharpe), Virginia (Mrs. Robert H. Conn), Constance Margaret (Mrs. Daniel J. Gore). Mem. ANTA, 1951-, pres. Greater N.Y. chpt., 1952- , mem. nat. bd. dirs., exec. com., 1953-, life mem., nat. v.p., 1963- 66, mem. finance council, since 1965—, vice chmn. Internat. Cultural Exchange of ANTA, 1954-63, vice chmn., coordinator performing arts program Salute to France, 1954-55, chmn. music adv. panel ANTA, 1954-63, acad./community music adv. panel, 1958-63, variety adv. panel, 1961-63, drama and dance adv. panels, 1954-57, drama adv. panel, 1962, 63, U.S. del. Internat. Theatre Inst. panel of ANTA, Warsaw, Poland, 1963, also mem. panel U.S. Centre. Mem. Informal Working Group on Arts and Humanities, 1961; mem. council Phoenix Theatre, N.Y.C., 1959-60; chmn. convocation Congress Hall, Berlin, 1957; sponsor Midtown Internat. Center, N.Y.C., 1963; mem. Nat. Council Arts and Govt., 1963-; spl. cons. to asst. sec. state for ednl. and cultural affairs, 1963-; U.S., specialist Bur. Cultural Affairs, State Dept., 1961, 63; mem. adv. com. arts Inst. Internat. Edn., N.Y.C., 1962-, trustee, 1964-; sponsor Arts Center, Columbia, 1962. Bd. dirs. Spencer-Chapin Adoption Service, N.Y.C., 1950-64, Agnes De Mille Lyric Theatre Dance Co; trustee Profl. Children's Sch., N.Y.C., 1955-64, hon. trustee, since 1964—, 1st v.p., 1957-59, treas., 1959-60, sec., 1961; trustee V. Beaumont Allen Found., 1954-64; v.p., 1962-64, mem. corp., 1954-64; mem. auxiliary bd. N.Y. Philharmonic Symphony Soc., 1944-50, exec., standing exec. com., 1945-50, chmn. jr. auxiliary bd., 1945-50, co-chmn. student ticket endowment fund, 1947-49; dir. bd. trustees Festival Found., N.Y.C. and Spoleto, Italy, 1961-, adv. bd., 1959-61, chmn. exec. com., 1964-66, mem. council Nat. Council Women of U. S., 1964—; mem. bd. advisers Clarion Concerts Soc., 1959-61, bd. dirs., 1961-64; mem. N.Y. friends com. Robert Coll., Istanbul, Turkey, 1960-64, devel. and planning com., 1960-61; bd. dirs., mem. exec. com. Manhattan div. Nat. Conf. Christians and Jews, 1959-63, bd. dirs. Manhattan div., 1963-, nat. rep. to conf. U.S. nat. orgns. on UN, 1964, nat. dir., 1966-, bd. govs., 1966-; exec. com. auxiliary bd., also mem. nat. com. Ballet Theatre Found., 1958-64; chmn. U.S. com. 1st World Festival Negro Arts, 1964-65, pres., 1965-, chmn. U.S. delegation, 1966; adv. bd. Empire State Music Festival, 1957-64, trustee 1960-64; bd. dirs. Acad. Instl. and Distbv. Services, Inc., 1965—, mem. exec. com., 1965—. Recipient Medaille de Versailles, 1955; Freedom Bell, Berlin, 1957; Handel award N.Y.C., 1959; citation for Achievement Congress Hall Berlin, 1959; Comdr.'s cross Legion of Merit, Fed. Republic Germany, 1961; Brotherhood award Nat. Conf. Christians and Jews, 1962; citation ANTA, 1962; comdr. l'Ordre National (Rep. of Senegal), 1966. Fellow Am. Geog. Soc.; mem. Am. Portuguese Cultural Soc. (founding mem., exec. v.p. 1961-), Nat. Inst. Social Scis. (life), Mus. Modern Art, Met. Mus. Art, R.I. Sch. Design, African-Am. Inst. (council 1966-). Little Orch. Soc. (pres. 1966), Inst. Advanced Studies in Theatre Arts. Episcopalian. (chmn. ways and means com. women's auxiliary, 1952-54). Address: 333 E 68th St New York City NY 10021

INNIS, DONALD QUAYLE, educator, geographer; b. Toronto, Can., Apr. 21, 1924; s. Harold Adams and Mary (Quayle) I.; B.A. with honors, U. Toronto, 1947; Ph.D., U. Cal. at Berkeley, 1959; m. Janet Marion Graham, 1949 (div. 1966); children—Mary Graham, John William; m. 2d, Winifred Norton Huggins, 1969. Came to U.S., 1963. Instr., U. Chgo., 1948-50, U. Western Ont., 1952-53; instr., then asst. prof. Queen's U., Kingston, Ont., 1953-63; mem. faculty State U. N.Y. at Geneseo, 1963—, prof. geography, chmn. dept., 1965—; research in Jamaica and India. Chmn. Kingston br. African Students Found., 1962-63. Mem. Canadian Assn. Geographers, Assn. Am. Geographers, Am. Geog. Soc. Author: Canada: A Geographic Study, 1966. Home: Valley View Apts Geneseo NY 14454

INNIS, ROBERT CECIL, research pilot; b. Red Bluff, Cal., Dec. 9, 1926; s. Cecil Robert and Violet May (McEwen) I.; student Coll. of Pacific, 1944-45; A.B., U. Cal., 1951; m. Joan Ann Powell, June 15, 1956; children—Robin Lynn, Robert Charles. Aero. research pilot NACA, Ames Aero. Lab., Moffett Field, Cal., 1953-58; aerospace research scientist and pilot NASA, Ames Research Center, Moffett Field, Cal., 1958—. Served with USNR, 1944-49, 52-53. Decorated Air medal (4); recipient Octave Chanute award Am. Inst. Aeros. and Astronautics, 1964. Asso. fellow Soc. Exptl. Test Pilots. Home: 317 Montclair Dr Santa Clara CA 95051 Office: NASA Ames Research Center Moffett Field CA 94035

INNIS, ROY EMILE ALFREDO, orgn. ofcl.; b. St. Croix, V.I., June 6, 1934; s. Alexander and Georgianna (Thomas) I.; student Coll. City N.Y., 1953-58; m. Doris Valdena Funnye, Feb. 13, 1965; children—Alexander, Cederic, Patricia, Corinne, Kimathi. Chem. technician Vick Chem. Co., 1961-63; research asst. cardiovascular research labs. Montefiore Hosp., 1963-67; mem. CORE, 1963—, edn. chmn. Harlem group, 1964-68, chmn., 1965-68, 2d nat. vice chmn., 1967-68, asso. nat. dir., 1968, nat. dir., 1968—; exec. dir. Harlem Commonwealth Council, 1967-68. Research fellow Met. Applied Research Center, 1967. Served with AUS, 1950-52. Home: 800 Riverside Dr New York City NY 10032 Office: 200 W 135th St New York City NY 10030

INNOCENTI, LUIGI, corp. exec.; b. Rome, Italy, Dec. 19, 1923; s. Ferdinando and Anita (Boccarini) I.; degree in Indsl. Engring., U. Rome. Dep. gen. mgr. Innocenti, Milan, Italy, 1951-58, vice chmn., 1958-66. chmn., 1966—. Home: 19 Via Senatol Milan Italy Office: 81 Via Pitteri Milan Italy

INONU, ISMET, Turkish govt. ofcl.; b. Izmir, Asia Minor, Sept. 24, 1884; s. Reshid and Djervriye; student Mil. High Sch. and Mil. Arty, Coll., Istanbul; m. Emine Mevhibe, Apr. 13, 1916; children—Omer, Erdal, Özden. Commd. capt., 1906, advanced through grades to gen., 1926; capt. 2d Army, 1906; mem. Gen. Staff, 2d Army Edirne, Eastern Thrace; mem. Expeditionary force against Arabian revolutionists, 1910; chief Gen. Staff, Army of Yemen, Arabia, 1912; dir. 1st sect. Great Gen. Staff, Istanbul, later mil. adviser to delegations to negotiate peace with Bulgaria at end of Balkan War, 1913; chief Gen. Staff, 2d Army, Eastern Thrace, 1915; comdr. 4th Army Corps against Russians on Eastern Front, World War, 1916; Comdr 20th Army Corps. later 3d Army Corps, Syria, 1917; undersec. to Ministry of War, Istanbul, 1918; comdr. Western Front, 1920-22 (won Battles of Inönü over Greece and given surname of Ionü by Kemal Ataturk); deputy from Edirne, Great Nat. Assembly; chief Great Gen. Staff, 1920; minister fgn. affairs, 1922; signed Treaty of Lausanne, July 24, 1923; ret., 1927; served as premier of Turkey, 1923-24, 25-37, 61-64, pres., 1938-50. Hon. prof. polit. sci. Ankara, faculty of law Higher Inst. Agr.; hon. pres. Turkish Ednl. Soc. Formerly v.p., now pres. Rep. Peoples Party, leader of party, 1939—. Awarded Medal of Independence 1922. Moslem. Author numerous published speeches. Home: Cankaya Ankara Turkey Office: C H P Genel Merkezi Ankara Turkey

INOUE, SHINYA, educator; b. London, Eng., Jan. 5, 1921; s. Kojiro and Hideko (Yano) I.; came to U.S., 1948; student Tokyo U., Rigakushi. Japan, 1944; M.A. Princeton, 1950. Ph.D. (Proctor fellow), 1951; m. Sylvia McCandless, July 28, 1952; children—Heather C. (Hill), Jonathan H., Christopher W., Stephen K., Theodore D. Instr., U. Wash., Sch. Medicine, Seattle, 1951- 53; asst. prof. Tokyo (Japan) Met. U., 1953-54; faculty U. Rochester, 1954-59. asso. prof., 1958-59; prof. chmn. dept. cytology Dartmouth Med. Sch., 1959-65, chmn. dept. anatomy, 1959-63, John La Porte Given prof. cytology, 1964-66; prof. biology U. Pa., Phila., 1966—. Cons. Am. Optical Co., 1954-60; instr. physiology Marine Biol. Lab., Woods Hole, Mass., 1962-66; mem. molecular biology panel NSF, 1961-65; mem. Woolridge study com. Office of Sci. and Tech., NIH, 1964, mem. biophys. scis. tng. com., 1965-69. Am. Cancer Soc. scholar in cancer research, 1955-58; Guggenheim fellow, 1971-72. Fellow A.A.A.S.; mem. Biophys. Soc. (mem. council 1968-71), Am. Soc. Cell Biology (mem. council 1970—), Soc. Gen. Physiologists (pres. 1969-70), Sigma Xi. Devel. rectified polarizing microscope; biophys. research on mitosis, living chromosomes, cell fine structure. Home: 2246 N 52d St Philadelphia PA 19131

INOUYE, DANIEL KEN, U.S. senator; b. Honolulu, Sept. 7, 1924; s. Hyotaro I. and Kame Imanaga; A.B., U. Hawaii, 1950; J.D., George Washington U., 1952; m. Margaret Shinobu Awamura, June 12, 1949; 1 son, Daniel Ken. Jr. asst. pub. prosecutor, Honolulu, 1953-54; practice of law, Honolulu, 1954—. Dir. Central Pacific Bank. Majority leader Territorial Ho. of Reps., 1954-58, Senate, 1958-59; mem. 86th-87th U.S. Congresses. Hawaii; mem. com. on agr.; mem. U.S. Senate from Hawaii, 1963—; asst. majority whip; mem. Senate Dem. Policy Com.; chmn. Dem. Senatorial Campaign com.; mem. senate com. on appropriations, chmn. subcom. on appropriations relating to D.C.; mem., chmn. various other coms. Successively precinct pres. of county committeeman, county com. sec., central committeeman Democratic Party of Hawaii. Active YMCA, Boy Scouts Am. Served from pvt. to capt., AUS, 1943-47. Decorated D.S.C., Bronze Star medal, Distinguished Unit citation with clusters; named 1 of 10 Outstanding Young Men of Yr. U.S. Jr. C. of C., 1960; recipient Alumnus of Yr. award George Washington U., 1961; Splendid Am. award Thomas A. Dooley Found., 1967; Golden Plate award Am. Acad. Achievement, 1968. Mem. D.A.V. (past comdr. Hawaii), Honolulu C. of C., Am. Legion. Methodist. Lion. Club: 442d Veterans (Hawaii). Author: Journey to Washington. Home: 2332 Coyne St Honolulu HI 96814 Office: Senate Office Bldg Washington DC 20510

INSKEEP, PATRICIA RUTH, life ins. co. exec.; b. Covington, Ky., Oct. 10, 1931; d. Norval Francis and Helen (Wilson) I.; student U. Ky., U. Cin. With Union Central Life Ins. Co., Cin., 1949—, sec., 1969—. Mem. Printing Industries Cin., Cin. Bus. and Profl. Women's Club, Altrusa Club Cin. Home: Harvard House 200 W Galbraith Rd Cincinnati OH 45215 Office: Union Central Life Ins Co Cincinnati OH 45240

INSKEEP, RICHARD GUY, educator; b. E. Liberty, O., Mar. 11, 1923; s. Guy Hamilton and Crete (Rily) I.; B.A., Miami U., Oxford, O., 1944; M.S., U. Ill., 1947, Ph.D., 1949; m. Margaret Anne Lynch, Dec. 28, 1951. Research fellow U. Minn., 1949-51; instr. Brown U., 1951-53; asst. prof., then asso. prof. U. Vt., 1953-61; asso. prof. U. Hawaii, 1961-65, prof. chemistry, 1965—, chmn. dept., 1962-71. Served with USNR, 1944-45. NSF sci. faculty of fellow Tech. U. Denmark, 1958-59. Mem. Am. Chem. Soc. (chmn. Hawaii 1963-64, nat. councillor 1968-71). Home: 1667 Kanalui St Honolulu HI 96816

INSLEY, WILL, artist; b. Indpls., Oct. 15, 1929; s. Francis Henry and Lois (Wishard) I.; B.A., Amherst Coll., 1951; B.Arch., Harvard, 1955. Exhbt. one man shows Amherst Coll., 1951, Stable Gallery, N.Y.C., 1965, 66, 67, 68, Oberlin (O.) Coll., 1967, Weatherspoon Gallery, U. N.C., 1967, Walker Art Center, Mpls., 1968, Albright-Knox Gallery, Buffalo, N.Y., 1968, Inst. Contemporary Art, U. Pa., 1969, John Gibson Comms., N.Y.C., 1969, Mus. Modern Art, N.Y.C., 1970; exhibited in group shows at Behn Moore Gallery, Cambridge, Mass., 1955, Daniels Gallery, N.Y.C., 1965, Tibor DeNagy Gallery, N.Y.C., 1965, Graham Gallery, N.Y.C., 1965, Inst. Contemporary Art, Chgo., 1965, Lyman Allyn Mus., New London, Conn., 1965, Kornblee Gallery, N.Y.C., 1965, Indiana Artists, Washington, 1965, Whitney Mus., N.Y.C., 1965, Grippi & Waddell Gallery, N.Y.C., 1966, Finch Coll., N.Y.C., 1966, 67, Park Pl. Gallery, N.Y.C., 1966, Riverside Mus., N.Y.C., 1966, Guggenheim Mus., N.Y.C., 1966, Eleanor Rigelhaupt Gallery, Boston, 1966, Kent (O.) Coll., 1967, U. Ill., 1967, Mus. Merchandise, Phila., 1967, Stadler Gallery, Paris, 1967, Richard Feigen Gallery, N.Y.C., 1967, Waddell Gallery, N.Y.C., 1967, Sixth Biennale, San Marino, Italy, 1967, Am. Watercolors, Washington, 1967, Weatherspoon Gallery, 1967, 68, Whitney Mus., N.Y.C., 1967, Aldrich Mus., Ridgefield, Conn., 1968, Des Moines Art Center, 1968, J.L. Hudson Gallery, Detroit, 1968, Univ. House, N.Y.C., 1968, Friedrich Gallery, Munich, Germany, 1968, New Delhi, India, 1968, U. P.R., 1968, Inst. Contemporary Art, 1969, John Gibson Commns., N.Y.C., 1969, 70, Ft. Worth Art Mus., 1969, Paula Cooper Gallery, N.Y.C., 1969, Leo Castelli Gallery, N.Y.C., 1969, Found Maeght, St. Paul de Vence, 1970, Winn Gallery, Austin, Tex., White Mus., Willard Gallery, N.Y.C., 1971, Internat. Art Fair, Berlin, 1971, others; artist in residence Oberlin Coll., 1966; lectr. dept. art U. N.C., 1967-68; vis. critic Cornell U., 1969; instr. Sch. Visual Arts, N.Y.C., 1969-71. Served with AUS, 1955-57. Recipient award Nat. Found. on Arts and Humanities, 1967; Guggenheim fellow, 1969—. Address: 2 Spring St New York City NY 10012

INTEMANN, HERMANN KOLLE, chem. co. exec.; b. Bklyn., May 31, 1908; s. Hermann A. and Clara (Kolle) I.; M.E., Stevens Inst. Tech., 1930; LL.D. (hon.), W.Va. Inst. Tech., 1960; m. Fannie Thranhardt, Jan. 20, 1950; children—Bruce, Christian Kolle; one stepdaughter, Helen Mix (Mrs. Bernard Bazydola); m. 2d, June Armstrong, July 28, 1969. With Halowax Corp., 1930-39, tech. rep., 1934-39; com. acquired by Union Carbide Corp., 1939, pres. div. Electro Metall. Co., 1957-60, dir. purchases parent co., 1960-63, v.p., 1963—. Mem. Am. Soc. M.E., Soc. Automotive Engrs., Am. Soc. Naval Engrs., Soc. Plastic Industry. Clubs: Duquesne (Pitts.); Chemists, N.Y. Yacht (N.Y.C.); Stamford Yacht. Home: Route 2 Box 233 Annapolis MD 21401 Office: 270 Park Av New York City NY 10017

INT-HOUT, DAN, Jr., paper co. exec.; b. Evanston, Ill., Mar. 5, 1917; s. Dan and Mary (Callahan) Int-H.; B.S., Ind. U., 1939; m. Nancy Goodman, Oct. 1, 1944; children—Dan III, Karen. Engaged in paper industry in Chgo., 1939-53; asst. to pres. Mich. Carton Co., Battle Creek, 1953-57, pres., 1957—; chmn. Litho Service Inc., dir. Grand Trunk & Western R.R. Co. Served to maj. USAAF, 1941-45; ETO. Decorated Air medal with 1 oak leaf cluster. Mem. Am. Paper Inst. (dir.), chmn. combination paperboard div.), Boxboard Research and Devel. Assn. (pres., trustee), Paperboard Packaging Council (dir.), Newcomen Soc., Phi Delta Theta. Clubs: Battle Creek Country; Canadian (N.Y.C.). Home: 90 Lynwood Dr Battle Creek MI 49017 Office: 79 E Fountain St Battle Creek MI 49014

INUMARU, TETSUZO, hotel exec.; b. Ishikawa Prefecture, Japan, June 8, 1887; grad. Hitotsubashi Higher Comml. Sch. Pres., gen. mgr. Imperial Hotel, Tokyo. Office: 1-chome Uchisaiwai cho Chiyoda-ku Tokyo Japan*

INZER, WILLIAM H., asso. justice Supreme Ct. Miss. Address: 312 E Northside Dr Jackson MS 63755 *

IOANES, RAYMOND ANDREW, govt. ofcl.; b. Cleve., July 18, 1918; s. Cornelius and Mary (Slovensky) I.; A.B., Kenyon Coll., 1940; student Nat. Inst. Pub. Affairs, 1940; m. Irma E. Blazo, July 6, 1941; children—Barbara, Joyce. With U.S. Dept. Agr., 1940-45, 48—, adminstr. Fgn. Agrl. Service, 1962—; with U.S. Mil. Govt. in Germany, 1945-48, dir. feeding German population, 1947-48. Recipient Superior Service award U.S. Dept. Agr., 1957, Distinguished Service award, 1962; award Nat. Civil Service League, 1969. Mem. Phi Beta Kappa. Home: 107 Poplar Dr Falls Church VA 22046 Office U S Dept Agr Washington DC 20250

IONESCO, EUGENE, playwright; b. Nov. 13, 1912; s. Eugene and Marie-Therese Ionesco; License es Lettres, Agrege de Lettres; m. Rodica Ionesco; 1 dau., Anne- Marie-Therese. Formerly lectr., critic, Bucharest; author various works written in French (trans. into 27 langs., performed in those langs.), the latest being The Chairs, Amedee, Victims of Duty, The New Tenant, Le Rhinocéros, The Killer, L'Impromptu de l'Alimat, the Picture, Le Piéton de l'air, Chemises de Nuit, Leroi se meurt, La Soif et la Faim, (ballet) Le Jeune Homme à Marien, also short stories. Decorated chevalier legion of Honor. Address: 14 rue de Rivoli Paris 4e France

IONESCU TULCEA, CASSIUS, educator, research mathematician; b. Bucarest, Rumania, Oct. 14, 1923; s. Ioan and Ana (Caselli) Ionesci T.; M.S., U. Bucarest, 1946; Ph.D., Yale, 1959. Came to U.S., 1957, naturalized, 1967. Mem. faculty, U. Bucarest, 1946-57, asso. prof., 1952-57; research asso. Yale, 1957-59, vis. lectr., 1959-61; asso. prof. U. Pa., 1961-64; prof. U. Ill., Urbana, 1964-66; Northwestern U., 1966—. Recipient Asachi prize Rumanian Acad., 1957; research grantee U.S. Army, 1961—. Mem. Sigma Xi. Author: Hilbert Spaces (in Rumanian), 1956; co-author: Probability Calculus (in Rumanian), 1956; Calculus, 1968; An Introduction to Calculus, 1969; Honors Calculus, 1970; Topics in the Theory of Liftings, 1969; Sets, 1971; Topology, 1971; also papers. Office: Math Dept Northwestern U Evanston IL 60201

IPOUSTEGUY, JEAN, sculptor; b. Surr-sur-Meuse, France, Jan. 6, 1920; studied with Robert Lesbounit. One-man show Gallerie Claude Bernard, Paris, 1962-64; exhibited in group shows in Salon de Mai, 1956, 57, 59-63, Salon jeune sculpture, Paris, 1959, St. Etienne Mus., 1960, Internat. Exhbn. Contemporary Painting and Sculpture, 1961, Albert Loeb Gallery, N.Y.C., 1962; represented in permanent collections Balt. Mus., CBS, Carnegie Inst., also pvt. collections. Address: Albert Loeb Gallery care Dir Public Relations 12 E 57th St 1 New York City NY 10022 *

IPPEN, ARTHUR THOMAS, educator; b. London, Eng. July 28, 1907; s. Peter Joseph and Augusta (Hechelmann) I.; diplom-ingenieur, Tech. Univ., Aachen, Germany, 1931; S.M., Cal. Inst. Tech.; 1935; Ph.D., 1936; Hon. Doctorate, U. Toulouse (France), 1962; Dr. Ing. honoris causa, Tech. U., Karlsruhe, Germany, 1967; D.Sc. honoris causa, U. Manchester (Eng.), 1968; m. Elizabeth Wagenplatz, Dec. 25, 1937 (dec.); children—Erich Peter, Karin Ann; m. 2d, Ruth M. Calvert, April 10, 1955. Came to U.S., 1932. Asst. geodesy, Aachen, 1932; research, teaching asst. hydraulics, Cal. Inst. Tech., 1933-36, research engr., instr., 1936- 38; instr., Lehigh U., 1938-39, asst., prof. civil engring., charge of hydraulic lab. 1939-45; asso. prof. hydraulics Mass. Inst. Tech., 1945-48, prof., 1948-65, Ford prof. engring., 1965-70, Inst. prof., dir. Ralph M. Parsons Lab. for Wmter Resources and Hydrodynamics, 1970—. Cons. to U.S. govt. and industry. dir. hydrodynamics lab., 1950-70, Registered prof. engr., Mass. Recipient Vincent Bendix Research award Am. Soc. Engring. Edn., 1963. Diplomate Am. Acad. Environmental Engrs. Fellow Am. Acad. Arts and Scis., Am. Soc. C.E., Am. Geophys. Union, Nat. Acad. Engring.; mem. Am. Soc. M. E., Boston Soc. Civil Engrs. (past pres.), Japan Soc. of Civil Engrs. (hon.), Am. Water Resources Assn., Am. Soc. for Engring. Edn., Internat. Assn. Hydraulic Research (past pres., hon. mem.), Sigma Xi, Tau Beta Pi, Chi Epsilon. Conglist. Author tech. articles. Home: 49 Pequossette Rd Belmont MA 02178 Office: RM Parsons Lab for Water Resources and Hydrodynamics Civil Engring Dept Mass Inst Tech Cambridge MA 02139 ☆

IPPOLITO, ANGELO, painter; b. S. Arsenio, Italy, Nov. 9, 1922 (parents Am. citizens); s. Arsenio and Margherita (Episcopo) I.; came to U.S., 1932, naturalized, 1932; student Ozenfant Sch. Fine Arts, N.Y.C., 1946-47, Bklyn. Mus. Sch., 1948, Inst. Meschini, Rome, Italy, 1949-50; m. Cynthia Hart Durfey, July 21, 1958; children—John Cooper, Michael Arsene. One-man exhbns. include Galleria della Rotonda, Bergamo, Italy, 1950, Tanager Gallery, N.Y.C., 1954, 62, Bertha Schaefer Gallery, N.Y.C., 1956, 58, Massillon (O.) Mus., 1960, Canton (O.) Mus., 1960, Cleve. Art Inst., 1960, U. Cal. at Berkeley, 1961, H.C.E. Gallery, Provincetown, Mass., 1961, Mich. State U., 1962, Grace Borgenicht Gallery, N.Y.C., 1963-64, 67, Arnot Art Gallery, Elmira, N.Y., 1965, Springfield (O.) Art Center, 1967, Besser Museum, Albion Coll., Western Mich. U., Grand Valley State Coll., Grand Rapids, Mich., 1971; two-man show Bolles Gallery, San Francisco, 1962; numerous group exhbns. throughout U.S. and Europe, 1950—; rep. permanent collections Whitney Mus., Munson-William-Proctor Inst., Utica, N.Y., Phillips Gallery, Washington, Massillon Gallery, Chrysler Mus., Provincetown, Sarah Lawrence Coll., Mich. State U., U. Mich., N.Y.U., Montreal Trust Co. (Can.), C.I.T. Bldg., N.Y.C., N.Y. Hilton Collection, Milw. Mus., New Am. Library, Joseph Hirshorn collection, U. Ky., Western Mich. U., Kalamazoo; tchr. Newark Sch. Fine and Indsl. Art, 1955, Cooper Union, 1956-59, 62-66, Sarah Lawrence Coll., 1957, U. Cal. at Berkeley, 1961-62, Stanford, summer 1961, Mich. State U., summers 1962-63, 65-66, full term, 1966-67, Queens Coll., 1963-64, Silver Mine (Conn.) Coll., 1963-64; artist in residence, Yale-Norfolk, Conn., 1957; Fulbright fellow, Florence, Italy, 1959, vis. critic Yale, 1961; artist in residence in museum Ford Found. grant Arnot Art Gallery, 1965, Besser Mus., Alpina, Mich., 1968. Served with AUS, 1943-45. Address: State U NY at Binghamton Binghamton NY 13901

IRBY, RICHARD LOGAN, mil. inst. pres.; b. Blackstone, Va., Feb. 26, 1918; s. William Logan and Emma (Gray) I.; B.S., Va. Mil. Inst., 1939; grad. Cav. Sch., 1941, Armor Sch., 1948, Command and Gen. Staff Coll., 1954, Army War Coll., 1961; M.A., George Washington U., 1961; m. Anne Short, Feb. 14, 1942; children—Richard Logan, Debra Anne, William Steed. Commd. 2d lt. U.S. Army, 1939, advanced through grades to maj. gen., 1965; asst. prof. mil. sci. and tactics, Va. Mil. Inst., 1948-50; br. chief G4, Gen. Hdqrs., Far East Command, 1950-51; comdg. officer 2d Bn., 5th Cav. Regt., Korea and Japan, 1951-52; comdg. officer 13th Tank Bn., 1st Armored Div., 1952-53, comdg. officer Combat Command A., 1953; instr. dept. II, Command and Gen. Staff Coll., 1954-57; dep. Tng. Div. G3, 7th U.S. Army, 1957-58, chief Tng. Div., 1958; comdg. officer Div. Trains, 3d Armored Div., 1958-59, comdg. officer Combat Command A, 1959-60; dep. Material Coordination Div., ODCSOPS, Dept. of Army, 1961-62, chief, 1962-63, asst. dir. Orgn. and Tng. Directorate, ODCSOPS and OACSFOR, 1963; planner U.S. Army Element, NATO mil. com. and standing group, 1963-64, asst. chief of staff, exec. officer to U.S. rep., 1964-65; dir. instrn. U.S. Army Armor Sch., 1965-66, dep. asst. comdt., dir. instrn., 1966-67; comdg. gen. Army Tng. Center, 1967; asst. div. comdr. 1st Cav. Div. (Airmobile), 1967-68, comdg. gen., 1968, asst. div. comdr., 1968-69; dep. comdg. gen. Army Tng. Center, Inf., Ft. Lewis, 1969; comdg. gen. Army Tng. Center, Inf., Ft. Polk, 1969-70; comdg. gen. Army Armor Center, comdt. Army Armor Sch., 1970-71; retired, 1971; supt. Va. Mil. Inst., 1971—. Tng. dir. Stonewall Jackson dist. Boys Scouts Am., 1949-50, council mem., Ft. Leavenworth, Kan., 1953-57, mem. Lincoln Trail dist., Ft. Knox, Ky., 1967, mem. exec. bd., mem. bd. counselors Old Ky. Home council, Ft. Knox, 1970—. Decorated D.S.M., Silver Star with oak leaf cluster, Legion of Merit with 3 oak leaf clusters, D.F.C., Bronze Star with V device and 2 oak leaf clusters, Air medal with V device and 54 oak leaf clusters, Joint Service Commendation medal, Army Commendation medal with 2 oak leaf clusters, Combat Inf. badge; Spl. Order of Yun Hui-Cloud and Banner with two clusters (Nationalist China); Nat. Order of Vietnam 5th Class, Gallantry Cross with palm, medal of Honor 1st Class, Mil. Merit Fourragere (Vietnam). Mem. Kappa Alpha. Democrat. Methodist. Address: Va Mil Inst Lexington VA

IREDELL, FRANCIS RAYMOND educator; b. Titusville, Pa., June 18, 1894; s. Charles Francis and Elizabeth (Hyde) I.; A.B., Pomona Coll., 1921; A.M., Harvard, 1922, Ph.D., 1937; postgrad. Commn, for Relief in Belgium (Belgian- Am.) fellow), U. Brussels, Belgium, 1924-25; m. Ruth Snyder, Aug. 3, 1926; children-Vernon Raymond, William Henry. Instr. philosophy Pomona Coll., 1925-29, asst. prof., 1929-38, asso. prof., 1939-43, prof. philosophy, Robert C. Denison Found. Pomona Coll., Claremont Grad. Sch., 1943-59, instr. Claremont (Cal.) Grad. Sch., 1936, sec. faculty Pomona Coll., 1944-48, dean faculty, 1948-59, emeritus, 1959—, head philosophy dept., 1938-54. USIA grantee serving as dir. Vietnamese-Am. Assn., Saigon, 1959-63; Fulbright coll. U. Ceylon, 1954-55; dir. seminar for Indian, Nepalese Coll. prins. in U.S. on State Dept. grants, 1964; vis. prof. philosophy Portland (Ore.) State Coll., 1965-66; vis. prof. Williamette U., Ore., 1967. Trustee pub. schs., Claremont, 1942-54. Served with Co. B, 316th Am. Tr., 91st div., U.S. Army, AEF 1917-1919. Recipient Distinguished Professorship award Pomona Coll., 1959; hon. certificate Confucian Studies Assn. Vietnam, 1960. Mem. Am. Philos. Assns. (exec. com. Pacific div. 1938-40, v.p. 1948), Cercle des Alumni de la Fond Universitaire, Belgium, Pacific Conf. on Teaching Philosophy (exec. com. 1951, pres. 1952), Phi Beta Kappa, Author: Viet-Nam, the Country and the People, 1966. Contbr. articles to profl. publs. Address: 1060 College Av Claremont CA 91711

IRELAND, CHARLES THOMAS, Jr., broadcasting co. exec.; b. Boston, Apr. 14, 1921; s. Charles Thomas and Margaret (Keough) I.; A.B. summa cum laude, Bowdoin Coll., 1942; LL.B., Yale, Admitted to Admitted N.Y. bar, asso. White and Case, N.Y.C., 1948-51; sec. N.Y.C. R.R., 1954-59; former sr. v.p. Internat. Tel. & Tel. Corp.; pres. CBS, N.Y., 1971—; dir. Levitt & Sons, Inc., Sheraton Corp. Am., Hartford Fire Ins. Co.; mem. Mid-Town adv. bd. Chem. Bank N.Y. Trust Co. Bd. overseers Bowdoin Coll.; former bd. dirs. Grand Central branch YMCA, N.Y.C. Served as captain USMC, 1942-46. Decorated Silver Star, Bronze Star, Purple Heart. Mem. A.I.M., Am. Bar Assn., Bar City of N.Y., Am. Mgmt. Assn., Phi Beta Kappa, Theta Delta Chi. Home: 55 Deepwood Dr Chappaqua NY 10514

IRELAND, GAIL LEONARD, lawyer; b. Denver, Nov. 21, 1895; s. Clarence Mead and Bertha (Strawn) I., student U. Colo., 1914-18; LL.B., Denver Law Sch., 1921; m. Eleanor Staats, Jan. 9,`1924; 1 son, Roger Gordon; m. 2d, Jewel Cawthon, Mar. 24, 1927; 1 dau., Collette. Began practice at Denver, 1921; clk. to chief justice Supreme Ct. Colo., 1921-23; mem. firm Wright & Ireland, 1928-33; pvt. practice, 1933-39; mem. in pvt. practice. firm Ireland & Ireland, 1939; atty. gen. Colo., 1941-45; now engaged in pvt. practice. Bd. mgrs. Council State Govts., 1941-42, v.p., mem. nat. exec. com., 1943; chmn. legal com. Colo. Centennial Commn.; Colo. chmn. Inter-state Cooperation Uniform Laws and Prevention of Crime. Mem. Colo. State Bd. Edn., Colo. State Bd. Equalization, Colo. Water Conservation Bd., 1941-45; Colo. water compact commr. Arkansas River, 1945-48; mem. Mo. River States Com., 1944-54. Chmn. trustees Salvation Army; trustee Voice of Youth. Served with U.S. Army, 1918-19, AEF, Mem. Am. Colo., Denver bar assns., Am. Legion (past post comdr., vice comdr. Dept. Colo., 1937-38, judge adv. dept. 1939-40), Phi Gamma Delta, Phi Delta Phi. Republican. Mason (32, Shriner), Kiwanian. Clubs: Petroleum, Law, Denver. Home: 855 Pennsylvania St Denver CO 80203 Office: Denver Club Bldg Denver CO 80202

IRELAND, HERBERT ORIN, educator, engr.; b. Buckley, Ill., June 12, 1919; s. Harvey Glenn and Anna Estella (Perkinson) I.; B.S., U. Ill., 1941, M.S., 1947, Ph.D., 1955; m. Mary Leota Austin, Mar. 1, 1941; children—Orin Lee, Marin Fae, Jeanne Lu. Research asst. to prof. civil engring. dept. U. Ill., Urbana, 1946—; cons. soil mechanics and found. engring., 1946—. Served from 2d lt. to maj., C.E., AUS, 1941-46. Registered structural and profl. engr., Ill. Fellow Am. Soc. C.E., Geol. Soc. Am.; mem. Am. Ry. Engring. Assn., Nat. Council Soil Mechanics and Found. Engring., Nat. Soc. Profl. Engrs., Sigma Xi. Methodist. Contbr. sect. to Structural Engineering Handbook, 1968; also articles profl. jours. Home: 609 S Prospect Av Champaign IL 61820 Office: Civil Engring Bldg Urbana IL 61801

IRELAND, JAMES DUANE, coal exec.; b. Duluth, Minn., Dec. 1, 1913; s. James Duane and Elizabeth Clark (Ring) I.; student St. Paul's Sch., 1928-31, Kent Sch., 1931-33, Cornell, 1933-36; m. Cornelia Wilmot Allen, Nov. 30, 1946; children— James Duane III, Lucy Elizabeth, Cornelia Seward, George Ring. With Hanna Coal Co., 1937-45; pres. Peters Creek Coal Co., Summersville, W.Va., 1947-60, chmn. bd. Peerless Eagle Coal Co., 1960—; pres., dir. Gauley Mountain Coal Co., 1957-70; chmn. bd. Bratenahl Devel. Corp., Cleve., 1959-70; dir. trustee 1st Union Realty Cleve., 1961—; dir., mem. exec. com. Cleve. Cliffs Iron Co., 1951—; dir. Reliable Spring Wire Forms Co., Soc. Nat. Bank, Soc. Corp. Trustee Western Reserve Hist. Soc., Cleve. Ins. of Music, Garden Ctr. of Cleve. (also treas.), Boy Scouts Am., Cleve. Council of World Affairs, Cleve. Symphony Orch., Hawken Sch., Cleve. Mus. Art (also mem. accessions com.), Cleve. Council Independent Schs., Central Sch. Practical Nursing, University Circle Devel. Found. (also exec. com.), Univ. Hosps., Cleve. Found.; trustee, exec. com. Holdon Arboretum; bd. govs. Case-Western Res. U.; trustee, treas. Greater Cleve. Asso. Found.; trustee, finance com., sec., mem. exec. com. Cleve. Inst. Art; pres. Elizabeth Ring Mather and William Gwinn Mather Fund; Mem. Psi Upsilon. Episcopalian (vestryman). Clubs: Union, Chagrin Valley Hunt, Tavern, Kirtland (Cleve.). Home: 2513 Malboro Rd Cleveland OH 44115 Office: Union Commerce Bldg Cleveland OH 44115 also Summersville WV 26651

IRELAND, LLOYD OWEN, mfg. co. exec:; b. De Kalb, Ill., Apr. 30, 1927; s. George II. and Edith (Nelson) I.; B.S., U. Ill., 1949; m. Frances Valentine, May 9, 1953; children—Paige, Pamela, Randolph. Comml. audit mgr. Arthur Andersen & Co., C.P.A., N.Y.C., 1939-63; controller Colgate-Palmolive Co., N.Y.C., 1963-68; v.p. finance, dir. VIA-TRON Computer Systems Corp., 1968-70; exec. v.p., dir. Kavic House, Inc., 1970-71; v.p., dir. FAIM Information Services, Inc., 1971—. Mem. bd. edn., Hillsdale, N.J., 1961-66. Served with AUS, 1945-47. C.P.A., N.Y. Mem. Am. Inst. C.P.A.'s, N.Y. State Soc. C.P.A.'s, Financial Execs. Inst. Home: 332 West Neck Rd Lloyd Harbor NY 11743 Office: 7600 Jericho Turnpike Woodbury NY 11797

IRELAND, RALPH LEONARD, dentist, educator; b. Rock Port, Mo., Aug. 3, 1901; s. Leonard Alvin and Clara Agusta (Broughton) I; D.D.S., U. Neb., 1927, B.S., 1929, M.S., 1944; m. Marion Ione Becker, June 27, 1935; 1 son, Robert Michael. Pvt. practice dentistry, Lincoln, Neb. 1929-36; faculty U. Neb. Coll. of Dentistry, 1936—, prof. pedodontics, 1939—, chmn. dept., 1939-58, dean Coll. Dentistry, 1958-68, dean emeritus, 1968-; dir. postgrad. and grad. courses coll. dentistry, 1948—. Cons., staff Children's Meml. Hosp. Omaha, 1949—; cons. VA Hosp., Omaha, Lincoln; spl. cons. USPHS, 1946-. Diplomate Am. Bd. Pedodontics (sec.- treas.). Fellow Am. Coll. Dentists; mem. Lincoln Dist., Am. (chmn. nat. bd. dental examiners 1964- 66), Neb. dental assns., Am. Assn. Dental Schs. (pres. 1966), Neb. Soc. Dentistry for Children (past pres.), Am. Acad. Pedodontics (past pres.), Internat. Assn. Dental Research, Sigma Xi, Omicron Kappa Upsilon, Sigma Chi, Xi Psi Phi. Republican. Episcopalian. Author: Dentistry for Children Lincoln State Dept. of Health, 1938, rev. edits. 1942, 48. Contbr. articles to profl. jours. Home: 3280 S 31st St Lincoln NB 68502 Office: Coll of Dentistry U Neb Lincoln NB 68508

IRELAND, ROBERT EBEL, ins. co. exec.; b. Hamilton, Ohio, Feb. 3, 1917; s. Otho T. and Helen (Ebel) I.; B.B.A., Miami U., 1938; m. Luella Gail Pratt, Sept. 15, 1940; children—Thomas R., Kathleen G., Sally J. (Mrs. James Robertson). With Philip Carey Mfg. Co., Lockland, O., 1938-40, Wright Aerospace Corp., 1940-45, Noma Electric Co. and RCA, 1946-55, Pillsbury Co., 1955-56, Barnitz Bank, Middletown, O., 1956-57; with Ohio Casualty Ins. Group, Hamilton, 1957—, controller, 1966—. Served with USNR, 1945-46. Mem. Adminstrv. Mgmt. Soc. (pres. Butler County chpt. 1961-62), Hamilton (pres. 1949-50), Ohio (v.p. 1951-52) Jaycees, Hamilton Assn. Trades and Industry (treas. 1953-54). Home: 967 Harrison Av Hamilton OH 45013 Office: 136 N 3d St Hamilton OH 45012

IRELAND, ROBERT ELLSWORTH, educator; b. Cin., Apr. 12, 1929; s. Ellsworth F. and Dorothy (Poysell) I.; B.A., Amherst Coll., 1951; M.S., U. Wis., 1953, Ph.D., 1954; m. Susan Lee Emerson, Nov. 4, 1966; children by previous marriage—Richard A., Mark A. From instr. to asso. prof. U. Mich., 1956-65; prof. organic chemistry Cal. Inst. Tech., 1965—; cons. Parke, Davis & Co., 1957—. Mem. fellowship panel NIH, 1965-69, mem. medicinal chemistry study sect., 1969—. Patron Foothill Family Service, 1965—. NSF postdoctoral fellow, 1955; Sloan Found. research fellow, 1962-66. Mem. Am., Swiss chem. socs., Chem. Soc. (London, Eng.). Author: Organic Synthesis, 1969, also research papers in field. Bd. editors Jour. Organic Chemistry, 1966—, Organic Syntheses. Home: 675 Elliott Dr Pasadena CA 91106

IRELAND, ROBERT LIVINGSTON, III, banker; b. Wilkes-Barre, Pa., Mar. 28, 1920, s. Robert Livingston and Margaret (Allen) I.; grad. Phillips Acad., Andover, Mass., 1938; A.B., Yale, 1942, LL.B., 1947; m. Jacqueline Mayhew, July 15, 1952; children—William Ellis (dec.), Thomas Ellis, Julia, Nancy and Robert Livingston. With N.Y. Trust Co., N.Y.C., 1948-59, v.p., 1952-59; v.p. Chem. Bank N.Y. Trust Co., 1959; partner Brown Bros. Harriman & Co., N.Y.C., 1960—; dir. Am. Security & Trust Co., Air Reduction Co., Inc., Hanna Mining Co.; Co.; trustee Dry Dock Savings Bank. Gen. Chmn. United Hosp. N.Y.C., 1967-68. Charter trustee Phillips Acad.; trustee Boys' Club Spence Sch., N.Y.C., John M. Archbold Meml. Hosp. Thomasville, Ga.; finance com. Maternity Center, N.Y.C. Mem. Assn. Res. City Bankers. Clubs: Downtown Assn., Links, Brook, Twenty Nine, Nat. Golf Links of Am.; Chicago; California (Los Angeles); Union (Cleve.); Metropolitan (Washington); Yale (N.Y.C.). Home: 71 E 71st St New York City NY 10021 Office: 59 Wall St New York City NY 10005

IRELAND, WILLARD ERNEST, librarian; b. Vancouver, B.C., Can., Jan. 4, 1914; s. Howard Arnold and Lenore Pearl (Haines) I.; B.A., U. B.C., 1933; M.A., U. Toronto, 1935; LL.D., Simon Fraser U., 1971; m. S. Grovena Anderson, Dec. 24, 1942; childrenRuth, Robert, Velma. High sch. tchr., B.C., 1936-38, 1939-40; apptd. provincial archivist B.C., 1940, provincial librarian and archivist, 1946—. Chmn. bd. govs. U. Victoria. Served with RCAF, 1942-45. Alexander MacKenzie research fellow U. Toronto, 1935-36. Mem. B.C., Pacific Northwest, Canadian library assns. (past pres.), B.C. (past pres.), Canadian hist. assns., A.L.A. Mem. United Church of Can. Editor B.C. Hist. Quar., 1947- -. Home: 184 St Charles St Victoria British Columbia Canada Office: Parliament Bldgs Victoria British Columbia Canada

IRELAND, WILLIAM COMER, bldg. materials co. exec.; b. Birmingham, Ala., Aug. 2, 1917; s. Clarance Eugene and Annette (Bickford) I.; student Vanderbilt U., 1936- 38; m. Anne Poole Leslie, June 29, 1940 (div. Nov. 1959); children—Leslie, William Comer; m. 2d, Dorothy Tidwell Tommie, Apr. 24, 1962. With Birmingham Slag Co., now div. Vulcan Materials Co., 1938—, pres., div. 1957—, dir. co., 1956—, v.p., mem. exec. com., 1966—. Trustee Ala. Sheriffs Boys Ranch. Mem. Nat. Slag Assn. (dir., mem. exec. com.), Nat. Skeet Shooting Assn., Phi Delta Theta. Presbyn. Kiwanian. Clubs: Downtown, The Club, Birmingham Country, Mountain Brook Country, Southern Skeet and Trap. Home: 4119 Old Leeds Lane Birmingham AL 35213 Office: PO Box 7497 Birmingham AL 35223

IRELL, LAWRENCE ELLIOTT, lawyer; b. Boston, Mar. 23, 1912; s. Hyman and Bessie (Shain) I.; B.A., U. Cal., 1932; LL.B., U. So. Cal., 1935; LL.M., Harvard, 1936; m. Elaine Smith, Mar. 26, 1939; childrenStephen Charles, Eugene Harvey, Lauren Catherine. Admitted to Cal. bar, 1935; partner Berger & Irell, Los Angeles, 1941-49, Irell & Manella, 1949—. Dir. Wyle Labs., Ponder & Best, Larwin Group, Inc. Lectr., Tex. Inst., U. So. Cal., 1950, 59, 61, 64, instr. income taxation trusts and estates, 1951-54. Bd. dirs. Jewish Centers Assn. Los Angeles, 1943—, pres., 1956-59; bd. dirs. Western states region Nat. Jewish Welfare Bd., pres., 1953-56; bd. dirs. Reiss-Davis Clinic for Child Guidance, v.p., 1955-58; bd. dirs. Met. Recreation and Youth Services Planning Council, 1950-68, pres., 1963-66; bd. dirs. Los Angeles Nillel Council, 1956-57; mem. nat. exec. council, vice chmn. exec. bd., chmn. finance com. So. Cal. chpt. Am. Jewish Com., 1970—; trustee Jewish Community Found. Los Angeles, 1964—, pres., 1967-69; bd. dirs. Jewish Fedn. Council Greater Los Angeles, 1963-66, 68—, vice chmn. community relations com., 1970—, v.p., 1965-67, 71—; bd. dirs. Council Jewish Fedns. and Welfare Funds, Inc., 1960—, nat. v.p., 1967-70, pres. Western region, 1966—; bd. dirs. Constl. Rights Found., 1969—, exec. com., 1970—; trustee Hope for Hearing Research Found., 1959—; trustee, exec. com., gen. counsel U. Cal. Los Angeles, 1967—; legal adv. com. Music Center Arts and Edn. Found., 1970—; steering com. Town Hall West, 1968—. Mem. Am., Los Angeles (trustee 1971—), Beverly Hills (gov. 1963-69, pres. 1969, chmn. taxation com.) bar assns., Harvard Law Sch. Assn. (nat. council 1964-65). Address: Gateway East Bldg Los Angeles CA 90067

IRENEY, METROPOLITAN, (John Bekish), bishop. b. S.W. Russia, Oct. 2, 1892; s. Dimitry and Agnia (Saltrukovich) Bekish; grad. Theol. Sem., Kholm, Rusia, 1914. Came to U.S., 1952, naturalized, 1957. Ordained priest Russian Orthodox Ch., 1916; asst. rector Cathedral of Lublin, Poland, 1916-19; mem. Polish consistory Diocese of Pinsk, 1935-47, also chmn. missionary com.; dean Counties of Sarna, Kqmen-Kashursk and Pinsk, 1938-44; displaced person, Germany, 1944-47; rector Russian Orthodox Ch., Charleroi, Belgium, 1947- 52, Holy Trinity Ch., McAdoo, Pa., 1952-53; bishop of Tokyo and Japan, 1953-60; archbishop of Boston and New Eng., 1960-65; archbishop of N.Y., Met. all Am. and Can., 1965—. Home: R F D 1 Syosett NY 11791 Office: 59 E 2d St New York City NY 10003

IRESON, WILLIAM GRANT, educator, author; b. N. Tazewell, Va., Dec. 23, 1915; s. Henry Frank and Hattie Grimm (Smith) I.; B.S. in Indsl. Engring., Va. Poly. Inst., 1937, M.S., 1943; m. Mamie Gillespie, Dec. 26, 1938; children—William Randall, Robert Grant. Indsl. engr. Wayne Mfg. Corp., Waynesboro, Va., 1937-41; from instr. to acting prof., acting head dept. indsl. engring. Va. Poly. Inst., 1941-48; prof. Ill. Inst. Tech., 1948-51; prof., chmn. dept. indsl. engring. Stanford, 1951—; cons. to govt. and industry. Recipient Air

Force scroll appreciation, 1958. Fellow Am. Inst. of Engrs., Am. Soc. Quality Control; mem. Am. Soc. M.E., Am. Soc. Engring. Edn., Soc. Internat. Devel. UN Assn., Inst. Mgmt. Sci., Tau Beta Pi, Phi Kappa Phi, Alpha Pi Mu. Episcopalian. Author or co-author; Principles of Engineering Economy, 5th edit., 1970; Factory Planning and Plant Layout, 1952; Handbook of Industrial Engineering and Management, rev. edit., 1971; also tech. papers. Editor: Reliability Handbook, 1966. Home: 735 Alvarado Ct Stanford CA 94305

IRETON, JOHN FRANCIS, lawyer; b. Balt., Dec. 9, 1905; s. John Francis and Blanche (Wolfe) I.; student Loyola Coll., Balt., 1923-25; LL.B., U. Md., 1929; m. Mary Frances O'Neill, Oct. 12, 1935; childrenMary Frances, John F., Thomas F., Peter Leo, Joseph P., Michael R. With Md. Casualty Co., Balt., 1925- 32; admitted to Md. bar, 1929; mem. law dept. City of Balt., 1932-40; practice law, 1930—, mem. firm Muecke, Mules & Ireton, Balt., 1940- -; now with C. Hammond Brown; asst. sec. Comm. Credit Co., 1948—; sec., dir. Calvert Fire Ins. Co., Phila., Cavalier Ins. Corp., Am. Health and Life Ins. Co., Eastern Ins. Co., Washington. Trustee St. Mary's Indsl. Sch., 1935-50. Fellow Am. Bar Found.; mem. Nat. Legal Aid Assn., Am. (chmn. sect. corp. banking bus. law 1952-53), Md., Balt. bar assns., Nat. Bankruptcy Conf. Am. Law Inst., Am. Judicature Soc. Md. Hist. Soc., Order of the Coif (hon. mem.), Delta Theta Phi. Democrat. Roman Catholic. Club: Merchants (Balt.). Home: 5011 Arabia Av Baltimore MD 21214 Office: 300 St Paul Pl Baltimore MD 21202

IRETON, JOHN FRANCIS, Jr., restaurant co. exec.; b. Balt., May 15, 1939; s. John Francis and Mary Frances (O'Neill) I.; B.A., Loyola Coll., Balt., 1962; m. Dorothy A. Minakowski, Nov. 23, 1961; children—Mary Catherine, Megan O'Neill, Amy O'Neill, Allison Brae. Sr. accountant Main Lafrentz & Co., C.P.A.'s, Balt., 1957-62; with Gino's Inc., King of Prussia, Pa., 1962—, exec. v.p., 1968—, also dir. Mem. Crime Commn. Phila. Mem. Financial Execs. Inst., Am. Mgmt. Assn. Roman Catholic. Club: Whitford Country (Exton, Pa.). Home: 424 Longwood Dr Exton PA 19341 Office: 215 W Church Rd King of Prussia PA 19406

IRIGARAY, PEDRO JOSE, hosp. supt.; b. Torreon Coah, Mexico, Apr. 28, 1932; s. Pedro and Maria Luisa (Gonzalez) I.; B.S., Centro U. Mexico, 1948; M.D., U. Nat. Autonoma de Mexico, 1955; m. Eleanor M. Durham, Feb. 21, 1959; childrenNedda Teresa, Marcos Federico. Came to U.S. 1957, naturalized, 1968. Psychiat. tng. Duke Med. Center, 1959-62; mem. staff John Umstead Hosp., Butner, N.C., 1962-, med. supt., 1968-; clin. asst. prof. psychiatry Duke Med. Center, 1968-. Mem. Am., So. med. assns., Am. Psychiat. Assn., N.C. Med. Soc. Home: 923 Lorain St Durham NC 27704 Office: John Umstead Hosp Butner NC 27509

IRION, ARTHUR LLOYD, psychologist, educator; b. Springfield Mo., May 14, 1918; s. Theophil William Henry and Edith Grace (Ham) I.; B.A., U. Mo., 1939; M.A., State U. Ia., 1941, Ph.D., 1947; m. Isabelle Virginia Cox, 1944; children-John, Millard, Janet. From instr. to asso. prof. U. Ill., 1947-51; prof., chmn. dept. psychology Tulane U., 1951-68; prof. U. Mo.-St. Louis, 1968—. Mem. Bd. La. Examiners of Psychologists, 1967-68. Served with AUS, 1942-46. Fellow Am. Psychol. Assn., A.A.A.S.; mem. Psychonomic Soc., Mo. Psychol. Assn., So. Soc. Philosophy and Psychology, Phi Beta Kappa, Sigma Xi. Author: (with John McGeoch) The Psychology of Human Learning, 1952; also numerous tech. articles and chpts. Cons. editor Jour. Exptl. Psychology, 1954-67; Perceptual and Motor Skills, Jour. Motor Behavior, Psychonomic Sci. Home: 8411 Knollwood Dr St Louis MO 63121

IRISH, EDWARD SIMMONS, sports promotion exec.; b. Lake George, N.Y., May 6, 1905; s. Clifford and Madeleine (Lancaster) I.; B.S. in Econs., Wharton Sch., U. Pa., 1928; 1 son, Ned. Sports writer Phila. Record, also N.Y. World Telegram, 1924-34; engaged in sports promotion, 1934-40; with Madison Sq. Garden Corp., N.Y.C., 1940-, acting pres., 1941-45, exec. v.p., 1945-60, pres., 1960-; pres. N.Y. Knickerbockers. Home: 30 Park Av New York City NY 10016 Office: 2 Penn Pl New York City NY 10001

IRISH, MARIAN DORIS, educator; b. Scranton, Pa., May 29, 1909; d. William Stitt and Martha Ann (Williams Irish); A.B., Barnard Coll., 1930; M.A., Bryn Mawr Coll., 1932; Ph.D., Yale, 1939. Research librarian in govt. and law Lafayette Coll., Easton, Pa., 1930-31; asso. prof. Fla. State Coll. for Women, 1933-40, prof., head div. polit. sci., 1940-47; prof., head dept. polit. sci. Fla. State U. 1947-63, prof. govt., 1963- 66, head dept. govt., 1959-63; Charles O. Lerche prof. internat. relations Sch. Internat. Relations, Am. U., Washington, 1966—; Ford Found. fellow Harvard, 1952-53; guest scholar Brookings Instn., 1963-64. Cons. Fla. Legislative Com. on Economy and Efficiency, 1945, Fla. Citizens Com. on Taxation, 1947, State Merit Council Fla., 1948. Mem. Am. (v.p., council), So. (pres.) polit. sci. assns., Am. Assn. U. Women, Exec. Council of Nat. Civil Service League, Phi Beta Kappa. Democrat. Author: The People Govern (with Laurence Paquin), 1953; The Politics of American Democracy (with James Prothro), 1959, rev. edit., 1962, 65, 68, 71; State and Local Government, 1960; Continuing Crisis in American Government, 1963; World Pressures and Am. Foreign Policy, 1964; Political Science: Advance of the Discipline, 1968; Readings in the Politics of American Democracy (with Robert Lineberry and James Prothro), 1969. Editor: Jour. of Politics, 1965-69. Contbr. articles and book reviews to polit. and ednl. jours. Home: 5903 Calla Dr McLean VA 22101 Office: Am U Washington DC 20016

IRISH, WILLIAN, (pseudonym) author, see Woolrich, Cornell.

IRONS, EDWARD PACE, rear adm., M.C., U.S. Navy; insp. gen. med. Bur. Medicine and Surgery, Navy Dept.; now comdg. officer Naval Aerospace Med. Center. Address: Pensacola FL 32502

IRONS, GEORGE VERNON, educator; b. Demopolis, Ala., Aug. 7, 1902; s. Andrew George and Belle (Allen) I.; A.B., U. Ala., 1924, M.A., 1925; postgrad. Emory U., 1929, U. N.C., 1928; Ph.D., Duke, 1936; postgrad. Ohio State U., 1952, Columbia, 1957; m. Irma Velma Wright, June 16, 1926; children—George Vernon, William Lee. Asst. prin. Perry County High Sch., Marion, Ala., 1925-27; master Darlington Sch. for Boys, Rome, Ga., 1927-31; asst. dept. history Duke, 1931-33; prof. history and polit. sci. Samford U., Birmingham, Ala., 1933-45, chmn. dept., 1945-67, chmn. div. social scis., 1962-67, prof. history, 1945-; participant Danforth Found. Seminar on Higher Edn., Bronxville, N.Y., 1957, Ford Found. Seminar in Polit. Sci., Berea, Ky., 1960. Mem. Jefferson County Jud. Commn., 1950-52; mem. Civil War Centennial Commn. Ala., 1961-65; mem. Home Service Council A.R.C., 1947-50; asso. dir. Freedoms Found. Seminar, Valley Forge, Pa., 1968, 70. Bd. dirs. Birmingham Council Parents and Tchrs. Served from capt. to lt. col., A.A.A., AUS., 1941-45. Recipient George Washington Honor medal Freedoms Found., 1962, Honor Certificate of award, 1963; Distinguished prof. award Samford bd. trustees, 1968. Mem. So., Ala. (past mem. exec. com., past mem. editorial bd.) Baptist hist. assns., John H. Forney Hist. Soc., Ala. Writers Conclave (past v.p.), Ala. Guidance Assn., Ala. Acad. Sci. (past v.p.), Res. Officers Assn., Phi Beta Kappa, Phi Alpha Theta. Omicron Delta Kappa, Pi Gamma Mu, Kappa Phi Kappa, Phi Sigma Kappa. Contbr. articles profl. jours., programs to Ala. Ednl. TV Network. Home: 316 Gran Av Birmingham AL 35209

IRONS, LESTER, lawyer; b. nr. Sullivan, Ind., May 14, 1908; s. Francis F. and Susie (McBride) I.; A.B., Ind. State U., 1929; J.D., U. Mich., 1935; m. Lucy M. Carmony, June 16, 1935; childrenDavid Lester, Martha Jane (Mrs. Kenneth McKenzie). Admitted to Mo. bar, 1936, Ind. bar, 1937, N.Y. bar, 1942; legal dept. Gen. Am. Life Ins. Co., St. Louis, 1935-38; gen. practice law, asso. firm Roberts & Warren, Evansville, Ind., 1938-40; mem. legal dept. Shell Oil Co., St. Louis, N.Y.C., 1940-46; partner Barnes, Hickam, Pantzer & Boyd, Indpls, 1946-. Dir. U.S. Corrugated- Fibre Box Co., So. Extract Co., Inc., Kokomo, Ind. Bd. dirs. United Fund Greater Indpls., 1962-70, also sec.; mem. nat. council Camp Central Coll. Recipient Luther Fire Girls, 1959; pres. Ind. Interch. Center Corp.; sec. bd. dirs. Edward F. Gallahue Found., 1955—; trustee Meth. Hosp.; sec., trustee Ind. Central Coll. Gulick Nat. Camp Fire award, 1961; selected Meth. Man of Year, Indpls. dist. Pres. Ch. Fedn. Greater Indpls., 1954. Mem. Am., Ind., Indpls. bar assns., Bar Assn. 7th Circuit, Order of Coif, Kappa Delta Pi. Republican. Kiwanian. Editor: U. Mich. Law Rev., 1934-35. Home: 804 Forest Blvd North Dr Indianapolis IN 46240 Office: Mchts Bank Bldg Indianapolis IN 46204

IRONS, ROBERT BRUCE, Jr., advt. exec.; b. Rapid City, S.D., Dec. 17, 1914; s. Robert Bruce and Frances (Lambert) I.; ed. pub. schs.; m. Mary Corning Winslow, Dec. 23, 1938; children—Emily (Mrs. Robert W. Rogers, Jr.), Robert Bruce III, Victoria. With Standard Oil Co., Ind., 1940-57, asst. div. Mgr., Grand Rapids, Mich., 1953-57; advt. exec. Standard Oil Co. Ind., Am. Oil Co., Chgo., 1957-62; dir. marketing Am. Internat. Oil Co. and overseas affiliates, 1962-64; pres. Fletcher Richard Co. Inc., and affiliates of Interpub. Group Cos., Inc., 1964-68, chmn. Communications Counselors Network, Inc., 1968-71; chmn. exec. com., dir. Ken Snyder Enterprises, 1971—; dir., mem. exec. com. Haniel-AMOCO, A.G., Basel, Switzerland, 1962-64; dir. AMOCO-Fina, S.A., Brussels. Belgium, 1962- 65. Chmn. finance com. Off The Street Boys Club, Chgo., 1960-62; pub. relations counselor, bd. edn. Wilmette (Ill.) Community Fund, 1958-59. Recipient Advt. award Freedom Found., 1960. Mem. Am. Assn. Advt. Agys. Republican. Episcopalian. Clubs: Players, Marco Polo (N.Y.C.); Ardsley Country; Ardsley Curling; Seaview Country Absecon, (N.J.). Home: 2 Ardsley Av E Ardsley-on-Hudson NY 10503 Office: 485 Lexington Av New York City NY 10017

IRRGANG, WILLIAM, mfg. exec.; b. Germany, Sept. 27, 1907; s. Theodor and Hedwig (Preyer) I.; E.E., State Tech. Sch., Cologne, Germany, 1928; Dr. Sc. (hon.) Lake Erie Coll., 1967; m. Mildred Klapka, Aug. 8, 1934; children—Rosemary, Dorothy Louise. Came to U.S., 1928, naturalized, 1933. With Lincoln Electric Co., Cleve., 1929—, successively supr., methods engr., plant engr., dir. plant engring., bd. dirs., exec. v.p. mfg., pres. and gen. mgr., 1954—; trustee Big 3 Industries, Houston. Trustee Lake Erie Coll., Euclid Gen. Hosp., Ednl. Research Council; exec. com. Case Assos. Mem. A.I.M., Am. welding Soc., Cleve. Engring. Soc., Nat. Elec. Mfrs. Assn. Baptist. Clubs: Fifty, University (Cleve.); Engineers (N.Y.C.). Home: 29555 Shaker Blvd Cleveland OH 44124 Office: 22801 St Clair Av Cleveland OH 44117

IRRMANN, ROBERT HENRY, educator; b. Chgo., Dec. 5, 1916; s. Henry Swissler and Lydia (Kringel) I.; B.A., Beloit (Wis.) Coll., 1939; M.A., Harvard, 1940; Ph.D., Ind. U., 1945. Faculty Denison U., 1945-48; faculty Beloit Coll., 1948—, prof. history, 1957—, coll. archivist, 1953—, chmn. dept., 1960—. Mem. regional com. X, Woodrow Wilson Nat. Fellowship Found., 1955-62; mem. bd. Danforth Assos., 1957-60; reader, interviewer Danforth Tchr. Grants, 1962-66. Faculty fellow Asso. Coll. of Midwest-Newberry Library Seminar in Humanities, 1966-67. Mem. Rock County Hist. Soc. (trustee), Am. Assn. U. Profs., Am. Hist. Assn., Mediaeval Acad. Am., Navy Records Soc., Soc. Nautical Research, State Hist. Soc. Wis. (mem. Old World Wis. com. 1971, curator 1971—), Phi Beta Kappa, Omicron Delta Kappa, Sigma Alpha Epsilon. Democrat. Episcopalian. Contbr. Essays in Modern European History, 1951. Home: 738 Park Av Beloit WI 53511

IRVIN, JOSEPH LOGAN, biochemist, educator; b. Jacksonville, Fla., Nov. 24, 1913; s. Joseph Logan and Eva (Hawkins) I.; B.S., U. S.C., 1934; Ph.D., U. Pa., 1938; m. Elinor Moore, Dec. 26, 1941. Instr. Wayne U. Coll. Medicine, 1938-41; instr. Johns Hopkins Sch. Medicine, 1941-43, asst. prof., 1943-50; asso. prof. biochemistry U. N.C., 1950-56, prof., chmn. dept., 1957—, Kenan prof., 1970—. Mem. Middle Atlantic Regional Heart Com., 1969—. Guggenheim fellow, 1956. Mem. Am. Chem. Soc., Am. Soc. Biol. Chemists, Soc. Exptl. Biology and Medicine, Am. Assn. Cancer Research, N.C. Heart Assn. (chmn. bd. dirs. 1967-69), Am. Heart Assn. (finance com. 1968—), Sigma Xi, Phi Beta Kappa. Mem. editorial bd. Biol. Bull., 1960-66. Home: Route 1 Chapel Hill NC 27514

IRVIN, REA, artist and art editor; b. San Francisco, Calif., Aug. 26, 1881; s. George C. and Mary Jane (Morse) I.; ed. Hopkins Art Inst., San Francisco; m. Dorothy Goodwin, June 12, 1916; children—Virginia, Barbara. Former artist and art editor of the New Yorker. Clubs: The Players (N.Y.C.); Dutch Treat. Home: Fredericksted 1031 St Croix VI 00840

IRVIN, ROBERT JOSEPH, paper co. exec.; b. Grand Island, Neb., Oct. 13, 1920; s. Ray J. and Beulah (Brown) I.; B.S. in Bus. Adminstrn., U. Neb., 1943; m. Nancy Story Irvin, Nov. 27, 1944; children—Catherine H., Robert C. Employment mgr. Inland Steel Co., East Chicago, Ind., 1950-53; dir. indsl. relations Kawneer Co., Niles, Mich., 1953-59; v.p. personnel and employee relations Inland Container Corp., 1959-69, v.p. staff services, 1969-71, v.p. staff and material services, 1971—; chmn. bd. Rexford Paper Co., 1971—. Mem. Bd. Child Guidance Clinic Marion County, 1963-71, pres., 1966-68; pres. Carmel Clay Ednl. Found., 1966-70; v.p. Carmel Clay Sch. Bldg. Corp., 1967—; mem. Greater Indpls. Progress Com., 1970—. Mem. bd. Salvation Army, Indpls., 1962—, Forward, Inc., 1967—. Served with inf. AUS, 1942-43. Mem. Am. Mgmt. Assn. (personnel planning council 1967—). Home: 4176 E 116th St Carmel IN 46032 Office: 120 E Market St Indianapolis IN 46206

IRVIN, WILLIAM DAVIS, ret. naval officer; b. Mt. Carmel, Pa., June 4, 1905; s. William R. and Gertrude (Davis) I.; B.S., U.S. Naval Acad., 1927; grad. U.S. Naval Postgrad. Sch., 1937; Nat. War Coll., 1950; m. Carolyn Vann, Nov. 26, 1930. Commd. ensign U.S. Navy, 1927; advanced through grades to rear adm., 1955; various submarine assignments including command U.S.S. Nautilus; comdg. officer U.S.S. Adirondak, 1952; 1st comdg. officer U.S.S. Northampton 1953; comdr. Cruiser Div. 2, 1956; comdr. Operational Test and Evaluation Force, 1958; dir. communications, electronics. Joint Staff, Joint Chiefs of Staff, 1957; 1st dir. Def. Communication Agy., 1960; comdr. Service Force, Pacific Fleet, 1963-65; comdr. M.S.T.S., Pacific, 1965-70. Decorated Navy Cross, D.S.M., Legion of Merit with two gold stars, Bronze Star. Home: 3011 Foxhall Rd N W Washington DC 20016

IRVIN, WILLIAM E., banker; b. Santa Rosa, Cal., June 25, 1906; s. James and Frances (Griffin) I.; m. Jessie Lois Deeble, Sept. 10, 1936; children—Ann Regina (Mrs. David R. Samuelsen), John Deeble. Nat. bank examiner, 1930-36; with Ida. First Nat. Bank, Boise, 1936—, exec. v.p., 1955-60, pres., 1960-70, chmn., 1970—; dir. Salt Lake City br. Fed. Res. Bd. Past chmn. 18th regional adv. bd. Comptroller Currency. Bd. dirs. Ida. Blue Cross; mem. adv. council Coll. Bus., Ida. State U. Mem. Am. (past exec. council), Ida., (past pres.) bankers assns., Ida. C. of C. Home: 4012 Edgemont Rd Boise ID 83704 Office: PO Box 7009 Boise ID 83707

IRVINE, ABRAHAM STEIN diversified mfg. co. exec.; b. Cin., May 21, 1910; grad. Phillips Acad., Andover, Mass., 1927; B.S., Princeton, 1931; postgrad. Mass. Inst. Tech., 1931-33; m. Jean R. Holland, June 16, 1935; children--Lois A., Andrew M., James. Salesman, Brown Mfg. Co., Boston, 1932-33; jr. engr. Ball Metals Co., Carson City, Nev., 1933-36, engr., 1936-37, sr. engr., 1937-40; project engr. Kingston Engring. Co., Los Angeles, 1940-43; with dept. engring. City of Denver, 1946-50, dep. head, 1950-52; 2d v.p. Johnson Mfg. Co., Kansas City, Kansas, 1952-54, v.p. for engring., 1954-57; v.p. research Consol. Industries, Inc., South Bend, Ind., 1957-60, exec. v.p., 1960-65, pres., 1965-70, chmn. bd., chief exec. officer, 1970--, also dir.; dir. ABC Chem. Co., 2d Nat. Bank, Country Food Storage Co., Providence Indsl. Corp. Pres., Dewey High Sch., Kansas City, Mo., 1953-54; fund chmn. local div. Salvation Army, 1959-60. Mem. South Bend Republican Com., 1964-68. Bd. dirs. Ind. council Boy Scouts Am., 1969-71; trustee Lovell Found. Served to lt., Corps Engrs., AUS, 1943-45. Decorated Bronze Star medal. Member N.A.M., South Bend C. of C. (v.p. 1963-65, dir. 1965-70), Am. Mgmt. Assn., Ind. Engrs. Soc. (program com. 1961-62), Princeton Alumni Assn. Episcopalian. Home: 6823 Broad Terrace Av South Bend IN 46505 Office: PO Box 1019 South Bend IN 46501

IRVINE, DONALD GREER, naval officer; b. Jesup, Ia., Dec. 5, 1910; s. Howard Clark and Lavinia (Greer) I.: student Parsons Coll., Fairfield, Ia., 1928-30; B.S., U.S. Naval Acad., 1934; grad. Armed Forces Staff Coll., 1950; m. Elizabeth Grace King, Mar. 6, 1937. Commd. ensign U.S. Navy, 1934, advanced through grades to rear adm., 1963; various assignments in ships, at submarine sch., also Navy Dept., 1934-42; surface tng. officer staff comdr. in chief 10th U.S. Fleet, 1942-44; assigned U.S.S. Pintado, 1944- 45; comdr. U.S.S. Piranha, 1945-46; assigned submarine decommissioning unit 19th U.S. Fleet, 1946; with fleet operational readiness div. Office Chief Naval Operations, 1946-49; chief staff officer, comdr. submarine devel. group 2, Atlantic Fleet, 1950-51; comdr. submarine div. 53, 1951- 52; head plans and policy rev. sect., staff comdr. Pacific Fleet, 1952- 54; comdr. submarine squadron 1, 1954-55, also comdr. submarines 7th U.S. Fleet; prof. naval sci. U. Tex., 1955-58; comdg. officer U.S.S. Passumpsic, 1958-59, U.S.S. Bremerton, 1959-60; chief navy sect. Mil. Assistance Adv. Group, Republic China, 1960-62; asst. chief naval personnel for edn. and tng., Navy Dept., 1962-65; comdr. cruiser destroyer flotilla 3, 1965—. Decorated Silver Star, Legion of Merit, Commendation ribbon, Order British Empire. Home: 15 Tally Ho Lane Alexandria VA 22307 Office: Bur Personnel Navy Dept Washington DC 20370

IRVINE, F. GERALD, lawyer; b. Salt Lake City, Aug. 3, 1901; s. James Alma and Ambia (Cantwell) I.; J.D., U. Utah, 1925; m. Bernice Irvine, July 13, 1929; children—Robert G., Mary Jane (Mrs. Smith). Admitted to Utah bar, U.S. Supreme Ct.; pvt. practice, 1926-29; pros. atty. Salt Lake City, 1929-32; corp. atty. Salt Lake City, atty. Utah League Municipalities, 1932-41; atty. Utah Power & Light Co., 1941-52, became gen. counsel, 1952, v.p., dir., 1964, spl. counsel, ret., 1968; engaged in pvt. practice law. Mem. Utah Liquor Control Commn. Mem. Am., Utah, Salt Lake County bar assns., Salt Lake City C. of C., Kappa Sigma, Delta Theta Phi. Mason (Shriner), Lion. Club: University. Home: 2365 Blaine Circle Salt Lake City UT 84108 Office: 1625 S 8th W Salt Lake City UT 84104

IRVINE, FRANCIS SPRAGUE, lawyer; b. Okmulgee, Okla., May 27, 1923; s. Francis Srague and Hazel (Beckett) I.; B.A., Okla. State U., 1947; LL.B., Okla. U., 1950; m. Betty Lee Sullivan, Sept. 3, 1949; children-Marilee, Robyn. Admitted to Okla. bar, 1950, since practiced in Oklahoma City; pvt. practice, 1950- 57; mem. firm Kerr, Conn & Davis, 1957-63; mng. partner Kerr, Davis, Irvine, Burbage & Foster, 1963—. Sec., dir. S.W. Factories, Inc. Served to 1st lt. AUS, 1943-46. Mem. Minerals Lawyers Group Oklahoma City, Oklahoma City Soc. Title Attys., Am., Okla., Oklahoma County bar assns., Oklahoma City C. of C. Christian Scientist (bd. dirs.). Club: Sertoma (Oklahoma City). Home: 1836 NW Terrace Oklahoma City OK 73118 Office: Kermac Bldg Oklahoma City OK 73102

IRVINE, GEORGE LYNN, mfg. exec.; b. Omaha, Neb., Oct. 6, 1907; s. Samuel Lynn and Grace (Carson) I.; B.S. in E.E., Ia. State Coll., 1930; m. Genevieve Jones, June 26, 1933; 1 son, Thomas Lynn. With Gen. Electric Co., 1930-71, mgr. apparatus agy. sales, 1941-49, mgr. agy. and distbr. div., 1949-53, regional v.p., 1953-71. Bd. dirs. Rehabilitation Inst. Chgo., Evanston Hosp. Mem. Chgo. Assn. Commerce and Industry (dir.), Chicago Council on Fgn. Relations, Ill. C. of C., Ill. Mfrs. Assn., Western Soc. Engrs., I.E.E.E., Newcomen Soc., Eta Kappa Nu, Tau Beta Pi, Sigma Nu. Presbyterian. Clubs: University, Chicago, Economic (Chicago) Glen View (Golf, Ill.); Royal Poinciana (Naples, Fla.). Home: 1003 Romona Rd Wilmette IL 60091 Office: 840 S Canal St Chicago IL 60680

IRVINE, JOHN WITHERS, Jr., chemist; b. Marshall, Mo., July 15, 1913; s. John Withers and Nadine (Young) I.; A.B., Mo. Valley Coll., 1934, Sc.D. (hon.), 1952; Ph.D., Mass. Inst. Tech., 1939; Sc.D., U. Ghent (Belgium), 1963; m. Fredna Tweedt, Aug. 14, 1941; children—Mary Jane, Kathryn, Janne Elizabeth. Instr. chemistry Mass. Inst. Tech., Cambridge, 1937-39, research asso. physics, 1939-43, asst. prof. chemistry, 1943-47, asso. prof., 1947-58, prof., 1958—, exec. officer dept. chemistry, 1966—, faculty resident Ashdown House, 1966—; sci. liaison officer Office of Naval Research, London, Eng., 1957-58; sr. chemist Clinton Labs. Monsanto Chem. Co., Oak Ridge, 1946. Mem. Am. Chem. Soc., Am. Acad. Arts and Sci., Sigma Xi, Sigma Nu. Contbr. articles to tech. jours. Home: 305 Memorial Dr Cambridge MA 02139

IRVINE, RALSTONE ROBERT, lawyer; b. Provo, Utah, Mar. 31, 1898; s. Robert R. and Dora (Davis) I.; A.B., Cornell U., 1923, LL.B., 1926; m. Mamie M. Miller, June 9, 1928; children—Dora Jean (Mrs. Herrick Jackson Young), Mary Ann (Mrs. H. Melvin Sartin), Barbara Lael. Admitted to D.C. bar, 1928, N.Y. bar, 1930, since practiced in N.Y.; spl. asst. to atty. gen. U.S. in enforcement anti-trust laws, 1926-29; mem. firm Donovan, Leisure, Newton & Irvine and predecessor firms. N.Y.C., Washington, 1934—; pres. Telluride Assn., Ithaca, N.Y., 1924-26; Mem. Cornell Law Assn. (past pres.), St. Andrew's Soc., Am., N.Y. State, Fed. bar assns., Bar Assn. City N.Y., Phi Beta Kappa, Delta Sigma Rho, Delta Theta Phi. Clubs: Downtown Association, University, Canadian, India House (N.Y.C.); St. Andrew's Golf (Hastings-on-Hudson, N.Y.); Venice (Fla.) Yacht; Cape Haze Golf (placida, Fla.). editor-in-chief Cornell Law Quar., 1926. Contbr. articles to periodicals. Home: 92 Popham Rd Scarsdale NY 10583 Office: 2 Wall St New York City NY 10005 also 17 Av Matignon Paris 8e France; also 1819 H St N W Washington DC 20006; also 16/17 Pall Mall London WI England

diversified mfg. co. exec.; b. Cin., May 21, 1910; grad. Phillips Acad., Andover, Mass., 1927; B.S., Princeton, 1931; postgrad. Mass. Inst. Tech., 1931-33; m. Jean R. Holland, June 16, 1935; children--Lois A., Andrew M., James.

Salesman, Brown Mfg. Co., Boston, 1932-33; jr. engr. Ball Metals Co., Carson City, Nev., 1933-36, engr., 1936-37, sr. engr., 1937-40; project engr. Kingston Engring. Co., Los Angeles, 1940-43; with dept. engring. City of Denver, 1946-50, dep. head, 1950-52; 2d v.p. Johnson Mfg. Co., Kansas City, Kansas, 1952-54, v.p. for engring., 1954-57; v.p. research Consol. Industries, Inc., South Bend, Ind., 1957-60, exec. v.p., 1960-65, pres., 1965-70, chmn. bd., chief exec. officer, 1970--, also dir.; dir. ABC Chem. Co., 2d Nat. Bank, Country Food Storage Co., Providence Indsl. Corp. Pres., Dewey High Sch., Kansas City, Mo., 1953-54; fund chmn. local div. Salvation Army, 1959-60. Mem. South Bend Republican Com., 1964-68. Bd. dirs. Ind. council Boy Scouts Am., 1969-71; trustee Lovell Found. Served to lt., Corps Engrs., AUS, 1943-45. Decorated Bronze Star medal. Member N.A.M., South Bend C. of C. (v.p. 1963-65, dir. 1965-70), Am. Mgmt. Assn., Ind. Engrs. Soc. (program com. 1961-62), Princeton Alumni Assn. Episcopalian. Home: 6823 Broad Terrace Av South Bend IN 46505 Office: PO Box 1019 South Bend IN 46501

IRVINE, WILLIAM LLOYD, coll. pres.; b. Framingham, Mass., Dec. 11, 1920; s. Vernard J. and Jeanette E. (Mayes) I.; A.B., U. Me., 1942, M.Ed., 1947; Ph.D., Cornell U., 1952; m. Martha Allen, Jan. 15, 1944; children—Elizabeth, Virginia, Margaret. Tchr., prin., coach Islesboro (Me.) High Sch., 1947-50; intern prof. ednl. adminstrn. Cornell U., 1952-53; adminstrv. asst. to supt. schs., Ithaca, N.Y., 1952-53, asst. supt. schs., 1953-56; rural supt. schs., Willimantic, Conn., 1956-57; asso. prof. edn. U. Vt., 1957-58; dean U. Me., Portland, 1958-61; coordinator inter-univ. program for univs. Buffalo, Cornell, Rochester and Syracuse, 1961-65; asso. prof. edn. Cornell U., 1961-66; formerly regional edn. officer Overseas Schs. Staff, Dept. State; pres. Vt. Coll., Montpelier, 1966—. Mem. N.E.A., Am. Assn. Sch. Adminstrs., Phi Kappa Phi. Presbyn. (elder). Rotarian. Home: 29 College St Montpelier VT 05602

IRVINE, WILLIAM MICHAEL, astrophysicist, educator; b. Los Angeles, Aug. 31, 1936; s. S. Rodman and Mary (Dailey) I.; B.A. summa cum laude, Pomona Coll., 1957; M.A., Harvard, 1958, Ph.D. (NSF fellow), 1961; m. Susan Wynn Ross, June 10, 1959; children—Douglas Ross, Kenneth Dwight, Peter Rodman. NATO fellow in astronomy Leiden (Holland) U., 1961-62; physicist Smithsonian Astrophys. Obs., Cambridge, Mass., 1962-66; research fellow Harvard Coll. Obs., Harvard, 1962-66, lectr., 1964-66, investigator, NASA grantee, 1964—; head astronomy program U. Mass., Amherst, head Four Coll. astronomy dept., asso. prof., 1966-69, prof., 1969—. Mem. Royal, Am. astron. socs., Am. Geophys. Union, Am. Phys. Soc., Optical Soc. Am., Phi Beta Kappa. Contbr. articles profl. jours. Home: 176 Heatherstone Rd Amherst MA 01002

IRVING, DONALD J., artist, educator; b. Arlington, Mass., May 3, 1933; ed., Mass. Coll. Art, 1955; student fine and indsl. arts edn., Columbia Tchrs. Coll., 1956, Ed.D., 1963; m. Jewel P. Irving; children—Kevin William, Todd Lawrence. Tchr. art White Plains (N.Y.) High Sch., 1958-60; instr. art U. State N.Y. at Oneonta, 1958-60; prof. art, dean Moore Coll. Art, Phila., 1963-67; chmn. art dept., dir. Peabody Mus. Art, George Peabody Coll. Tchrs., Nashville, 1967-69; dir. Sch. Art Inst., Chgo., 1969—; exhibited in group shows Va. Mus. Fine Arts, Richmond, 1958, Newark State Coll., Union, N.J., 1958, Emerson Mus., Syracuse, N.Y., 1960, Denver Art Mus., 1961, U. State N.Y. at Oneonta, 1961, Painters and Sculptors Soc. N.J., 1963, Nat. Arts Club, Knickerbocker Artists Ann., N.Y.C., 1963, Pa. Acad. Fine Arts, Phila., 1964, Main Line Center of Arts, Phila., 1965, Trio Show, Indiana (Pa.) State U. 1966, Camp Hill (Pa.) Gallery and Acad. Art, 1966, High Mus. Art, Atlanta, 1967, Peabody Mus., Nashville, 1968. Sec., Council on Urban Edn.; mem. U.S. delegation Conf. Nat. Soc. Edn. Through Art, Prague, Czechoslovakia, 1966; cons. ednl. TV series Art Now, WRCV-TV, Phila.; cons. ednl. series on architecuture Pa. Dept. Pub. Instrn. Mem. Phila. Council Profl. Craftsmen (dir. 1967-68), Nat. Art Edn. Assn. (officer Eastern region 1966-68), Eastern Arts Assn. (mem. council 1964-66, mgr. conv. 1959-64), Nat. Council Arts in Edn. (coordinator local arrangements 1965), Internat. Soc. Edn. Through Art, Am. Craftsmen's Council, Coll. Art Assn., Pa. State Edn. Assn. Phi Delta Kappa. Author: Sculpture Material and Process, 1970. Contbr. articles in field to profl. jours. Home: 1014 Superior St Oak Park IL Office: Art Inst Chicago IL

IRVING, FLORA MILLER, mus. ofcl.; b. N.Y.C., Sept. 21, 1928; d. George Macculloch and Flora (Whitney) Miller; student Barnard Coll., 1946-47; m. Michael Henry Irving, June 7, 1947; children—Michelle Mann, Duncan Duer, Macculloch Miller, Fiona. Vice pres. Whitney Mus. Am. Art, 1960—. Democrat. Conglist. Address: R R 1 N Wilton Rd New Canaan CT 06840

IRVING, FRANK DUNHAM, educator; b. Plainfield, N.J., July 30, 1923; s. Frank Dunham and Violet (Smith) I.; B.S., Rutgers U., 1948; M.F., U. Minn., 1950, Ph.D., 1960; m. Jeanne L'Heureux, July 5, 1948; children—June, Anne, Lynne. Dist. game mgr. Wis. Conservation Dept., Antigo, 1950-55; faculty U. Minn., St. Paul, 1955—, prof. forestry, 1966—. Served with USMCR, 1942-45. Mem. Soc. Am. Foresters, Wildlife Soc. Home: 1745 Tatum St St Paul MN 55113

IRVING, FREDERICK, fgn. service officer; b. Providence, May 2, 1921; s. Philip and Rebecca (Lerner) I.; A.B., Brown U., 1943; M.A., Fletcher Sch. Law and Diplomacy, 1946; grad. Nat. War Coll., 1960; m. Dorothy Jean Petrie, Apr. 5, 1946; children—Susan Jean, Richard Frederick, Barbara Jean. Exam. internat. econ. assistance programs, internat. div. U.S. Bur. of Budget, 1946-50; chief West European post mgmt. br., Bur. European Affairs, Dept. State, 1951-52; attache Am. Embassy, Vienna, Austria, 1952-54; dep. exec. dir. for German affairs, Dept. State, 1954-56, dep. exec. dir. for European affairs, 1956-58, dir. Office of Budget, 1958-59, spl. asst. to undersec. state, 1959; 1st sec., chief econs. sect. Am. Embassy, Wellington, New Zealand, 1960-62; exec. dir. Bur. Ednl. and Cultural Affairs, Dept. State, 1962-64, spl. asst. to dep. undersec. state for adminstrn., 1964-65, exec. dir. Bur. of European Affairs, 1965-57, counselor, dep. chief of mission Am. embassy, Vienna, Austria, 1967-68, dep. asst. sec. state for operations, 1968-69, dep. asst. sec. state for ednl. and cultural affairs. Served to lt. USAAF, 1943-45. Mem. Am. Fgn. Service Assn., English-speaking Union, Internat. Alumni Assn. Fletcher Sch. Law and Diplomacy, Am. Soc. Pub. Adminstrn., Am. Acad. Polit. and Social Sci. Unitarian. Clubs: Internat., Brown University (Washington). Home: 9622 Culver St Kensington MD 20795 Office: Dept State Washington DC 20520

IRVING, GEORGE W., Jr., ret. govt. ofcl.; b. Carlbou, Me., Nov. 20, 1910; s. George W. and Adelaide Louise (Butman) I.; B.S., George Washington U., 1933 M.A., 1935, Ph.D., 1939; m. Frances Catherine Connell; children—George W. III, Mary Constance. Lab. asst. U.S. Bur. Standards, 1927-28; lab. asst. Bur. Chemistry, Dept. Agr., 1928-35, head protein sect., oil and protein div. So. Regional Research Lab., New Orleans, 1942-44, head div. biologically active compounds Agrl. Research Center, Beltsville, Md., 1944-47, asst. chief Bur. Agrl. and Indsl. Chemistry, 1947-53, chief biol. scis. br. Agrl. Marketing Service, 1953-54, dep. adminstr. research, 1954-57, dep. adminstr. utilization research and devel., 1957-64, asso. adminstr. Agrl. Research Service, 1964-65, adminstr., 1965-71; research and teaching fellow biochemistry George Washington U. Med. Sch., 1936-38; research fellow Cornell U. Coll. Medicine, 1938-39; enzyme research Rockefeller Inst., N.Y.C., 1939-42. Recipient award sci. achievement Washington Acad. Scis., 1946; Distinguished Service award U.S. Dept. Agr., 1969. Fellow A.A.A.S. (v.p. 1962); mem. Am. Chem. Soc., Wash. Acad. Scis. (v.p. 1953, sec. 1962-64, pres.), Chem. Soc. Wash. (pres. 1957), Soc. Biol. Chemists, Inst. Food Technologists, Am. Inst. Chemists (honor scroll D.C. chpt. 1969), Sigma Xi, Alpha Chi Sigma, Tau Kappa Epsilon, Phi Eta Sigma. Club: Cosmos (Washington). Contbr. articles to profl. publs. Home: 4836 Langdrum Lane Chevy Chase MD 20015

IRVING, JACK HOWARD, planning exec.; b. Cleve., Dec. 31, 1920; s. William M. and Lottie (Green) I.; B.S., Cal. Inst. Tech., 1942; M.A., Princeton 1948, Ph.D. in Physics, 1965; m. Florence Friedman, Feb. 1, 1948; children—Paul Howard, Karen Joy, Michael William. Staff radiation lab. Mass. Inst. Tech., 1942-45; asst., teaching asst. physics Princeton, 1946-48; fellow chemistry Cal. Inst. Tech., 1948-49; sr. mem. tech. staff, head systems planning and analysis dept. research and devel. labs., Hughes Aircraft Co., 1949-54; head spl. devices dept. Ramo-Wooldridge Corp., 1954-55, head intelligence systems dept., 1955-56, spl. asst. to exec. v.p., 1956-57, spl. asst. to pres. space tech. labs., 1957-58; corp. staff sci. Thompson Ramo-Wooldridge, Inc., 1958-60; asst. dir. Advanced Systems Planning div. Space Tech. Labs., Inc., 1960; v.p., gen. mgr. systems research and planning div. Aerospace Corp., El Segundo, Cal., 1960-63, v.p. corporate planning, 1965—; aerospace vis. fellow Princeton, 1963-65. Dir. study fire control systems, Minuteman ballistic missile, communication satellite. Asso. fellow Am. Inst. Aeros. and Astronautics; mem. Am. Physical Soc., Am. Acad. Engring. (mem. com. on interplay of engineering with biology and medicine), Sigma Xi. Contbr. articles tech. publs. Home: 13202 Jonesboro Pl Los Angeles CA 90049 Office: 2350 El Segundo Blvd El Segundo CA 90245

IRVING, JULES, theater dir.; b. Bronx, Apr. 13, 1925; s. Jacob and Ida (Emanuel) Israel; B.A. in English Lit., N.Y.U., 1947; M.A. in Theater and Drama, Stanford, 1949; m. Priscilla Pointer, Dec. 28, 1947; children—Davie, Katie, Amy. Co-founder, Mem. Actor's Workshop, San Francisco, 1952-65; dir. The Repertory Theater of Lincoln Center, N.Y.C., 1965—; prof. drama San Francisco State Coll., 1949-62; chief instr. Fordham U., 1970-71. Served with inf. AUS, 1943-46; ETO. Mem. Theatre Communications Group (exec. com. 1960—), Orgn. Legitimate Theatres (pres.), Soc. Stage Dirs. and Choreographers (past mem. exec. bd.). Home: 160 West End Av New York City NY 10023 Office: 150 West 65th St New York City NY 10023

IRVING, K. C., oil co. exec.; b. Buctourche, N.B., Can., Mar. 14, 1899; s. James D. and Mary E. (Gifford) I.; student Dalhousie U., Acadia U.; LL.D., U. N.B., 1954; m. Harriet L. MacNarin, Feb. 4, 1927; children—Jam es K., Arthur L., John E. Pres. Irving Oil Co., Ltd., 1929—; also pres. Irving Pulp & Paper, Ltd., K.C. Irving, Ltd. Home: 197 Mount Pleasant Av St John New Brunswick Canada Office: Golden Bell Bldg St John New Brunswick Canada

IRVING, LAURENCE, biologist; b. Boston, May 3, 1895; s. Wm. Nathaniel and Esther (Messenger) I.; prep. edn., Roxbury Latin School; A.B., Bowdoin Coll., 1916, Charles Carroll Everett grad. scholar, 1916-17, Sc.D. (hon.), 1959; A.M., Harvard U., 1917; Ph.D., Stanford, 1924; M.D. (hon.), U. Oslo, 1956; D.Sc. (hon.), U. of Alaska, 1968; m. Florence A. Binsley; children—Susan, William Nathaniel, Laurence, Alan. Instr. Wm. Warren Sch., Menlo, Cal., 1921-23, Stanford, 1924-27; NRC fellow U. of Frankfurt-am-Main, 1925-27; asso. prof. physiology U. Toronto, 1927-31, prof. exptl. biology, 1931-37; prof. biology Swarthmore Coll., 1937-49, chmn. dept. zoology, dir. Edward Martin Biol. Lab., 1937-49; lectr. physiology, U. Pa., 1937-49; chief physiology sect. Arctic Health Research Center, USPHS, Anchorage, 1949-62; prof. zoophysiology Lab. of Zoophysiology, U. Alaska, 1962—, dir. Inst. Arctic Biology, 1962-66, adv. sci. dir., 1966—. Mem. corp. Marine Biol. Lab. Served as lt., 165th Inf. with A.E.F. and Army of Occupation, 1917-19. Commd. major, lt. col., USAAF, 1943; chief, physiological test sect. Army Air Force Proving Ground Command, Eglin Field, Fla., 1943-45; chief, physiol. branch, Aero Med. Lab., Wright Field, 1945-46; sci. dir. Arctic Research Lab., Pt. Barrow, Alaska, 1948; George Cyril Graves lectr. in physiology, U. Ind., 1948-49; hon. research asso. Woods Hole Oceanographic Inst., 1956-68, Smithsonian Instn., 1958-69. Chmn. 2d, 3d, and 22d Alaskan Science Conf. Fellow Arctic Inst. N. Am. (gov. 1964-70), A.A.A.S. (pres. Alaska div.), Am., Can. (hon.) physiol. socs., Am. Soc. Zoologists, Am. Soc. Naturalists, Phila. Physiol. Soc. (v.p. 1940-42, pres. 1942); mem. Norwegian Acad. Sci. and Letters, Delta Kappa Epsilon, Phi Beta Kappa, Sigma Xi. Chmn. Panel Expeditionary Physiology, Joint Research and Devel. Bd., 1947; leader expdn. for physiol. research Office of Naval Research and Swarthmore Coll., Point Barrow, Alaska, 1947-49. Unitarian. Writer of articles. Clubs: Explorers, Cosmos. Research physiology. Home: PO Box 5070 College AK 99504 Office: Inst Arctic Biology Lab of Zoophysiology U Alaska College AK 99701 ☆

IRVING, MICHAEL HENRY, architect; b. N.Y.C., Aug. 2, 1923, s. E. duPont and Carolyn (Mann) I.; grad. St. Paul's Sch., Concord, N.H., 1941; B.A., Harvard, 1945; B Arch., Columbia, 1953; m. Flora Miller, June 7, 1947; children—Michelle Mann, Duncan Duer, Macculloch Miller, Fiona. With archtl. firms Harrison & Abramovitz, N.Y.C., 1953-54, Sherwood, Mills & Smith, Stamford, Conn., 1954-60; pvt. practice, Westport, Conn., 1961-63, N.Y.C., 1964-69, New Canaan, Conn., 1969—. Dir. Whitney Industries, Inc., N.Y.C. Trustee Whitney Mus. Am. Art, New Canaan County Sch., Silvermine Coll. Art. Served with USNR, 1943-46. Mem. A.I.A., Archtl. League N.Y., Am. Arbitration Assn. Home: N Wilton Rd New Canaan CT 06840 Office: 88 Main St New Canaan CT 06840

IRVING, ROBERT AUGUSTINE, condr., pianist; b. Winchester, Eng., Aug. 28, 1913; s. Robert Graham and Oriane (Tyndale) I.; scholar Winchester (Eng.) Coll., 1926-32, Royal Coll. Music, 1934-36; B.A. (scholar), New Coll., Oxford (Eng.) U., 1935. Came to U.S., 1958. Prof. piano Winchester Coll., 1936-40; asso. condr. BBC Scottish Orch., 1945-48; mus. dir. Royal Ballet Eng., 1949-58, N.Y.C. Ballet, 1958—; vis. condr. numerous orchs., U.S. and Eng., 1951—; rec. artist for HMV, RCA Victor, EMI, Capitol, Angel, Kapp records. Served with Royal Arty., 1940-41, RAF, 1941-45. Decorated D.F.C. with bar. Composer; As You Like It (with K. Hepburn), 1949; also scores for films. Home: 160 West End Av New York City NY 10023 Office: New York City Ballet NY State Theatre Lincoln Center New York City NY 10023

IRVING, ROBERT SHIPPEN, mortgage banker; b. Phila., June 15, 1909; s. Robert Archibald and Bertha (Shippen); grad. Phillips Exeter Acad., 1926; A.B., Williams Coll., 1930; m. Ruth Winchester, May 27, 1933; children—Robert Winchester, Kathleen Winslow (Mrs. Paul B. Repetto), Nancy Shippen. Underwriting supr. FHA, Washington, 1934-40; exec. v.p. W.A. Clarke Mortgage Co., Phila., 1940-61; v.p. 1st Pa. Banking & Trust Co., Phila., 1961-68, sr. v.p., 1968-70; v.p. finance, treas. Nat. Corp. for Housing Partnerships, Washington, 1970—; dir. Colonial Surety Co., Baederwood Center, Inc.; lectr. Northwestern U., 1963-66; instr. Phila. Bd. Realtors Sch., 1958-62. Mem. Phila. Mortgage Bankers Assn. (pres. 1961-62), Beta Theta Pi. Episcopalian. Clubs: Little Egg Harbor Yacht (Beach Haven, N.J.); Corinthian Yacht (Phila.); Merion Golf (Ardmore, Pa.); University (Washington); Miles River Yacht (St. Michaels, Md.); Talbot Country (Easton, Md.). Home: 3003 Van Ness St Washington DC 20008 Office: 1133 15th St NW Washington DC 20005

IRWANE, SHELDON JOHN, Jr. mfg. exec.; b. Lima, O., Apr. 1, 1932; B.S., U. San Francisco, 1954; M.S., Stanford University, 1956; m. Rosemarie Lois Brown, May 15, 1955; 1 son, Anthony Robinson. Sales rep. Ames-Brockton Fabricated Products, Akron, O., 1956-58, sales mgr. Coshocton, Ohio, 1959-61, gen. manager plant, 1961-68, v.p. sales, 1968--. Instr. bus. Coshocton Jr. College, 1968-69. Named Man of Year, Coshocton Junior Chamber of Commerce, 1968. Mem. Coshocton C. of C. (vice president 1967-68, pres. 1969-70), English Speaking Union, Coshocton Sertoma Club, Nat. Assn. Mfrs., Sales Executives Institute, Phi Beta Kappa, Sigma Chi, Phi Mu. Democrat. Mem. Christian Ch. (lay leader). Mason (32, Shriner). Clubs: Coshocton Country, Coshocton City, Running Deer Country. Home: 2d Av Coshocton OH Office: 3d Av Coshocton OH

IRWIN, CLIFFORD HOWARD, advt. exec.; b. Chgo., Aug. 6, 1923; s. Charles R. and Elizabeth (Hanson) I.; student U. Ill., 1946, Northwestern U., 1945, 47, 48; m. Wilma M. Nystrom, May 2, 1947; children—Laurie C., Sharon L. Asst. comptroller Dancer-Fitzgerald-Sample, Inc., Chgo., 1947-52; sec., v.p., asst. treas. Leo Burnett Co., Inc., Chgo., 1952—. Treas. Leo Burnett Found., Inc. Mem. Am. Assn. Advt. Agys. Home: 512 Brookwood Terrace #3 Olympia Fields IL 60461 Office: Prudential Plaza Chicago IL 60601

IRWIN, DONALD, Jr., wholesale grocery co. exec.; b. Phila., Apr. 1, 1916; s. Donald and Jessie (Dittrich) I.; ed. pvt. and pub. schs.; m. Gladys E. Hershey, Apr. 20, 1938; children—Donald III, Susan, Janet, Andrew, Sally. With L.H. Parke Co., Phila., 1935-64, pres., 1949-64; pres. J.E. Dyer Co., Washington, 1955-64, chmn. bd., 1957; pres. George S. Daugherty Co., Pitts., 1956-64, Phillips-Lewis Co., Richmond, Va., 1960-64, WGY Foods Co., Albany, N.Y., 1961-64, pres. Monarch Finer Foods div. Consol. Foods Corp., Chgo., 1962-64, v.p. corp., 1962-64; exec. v.p. United Cerebral of Greater Chgo., 1964-65; investment banker Shearson-Hammill, 1965-67; pres. Palomar Foods Co., San Diego, 1967—; dir., exec. com. C.O.D.E. Inc., Pitts. Pres. Instl. Wholesale Grocers Nat. Trade Assn., 1959-60, chmn. exec. com., 1961-62; mem. adv. bd. OPS, 1952-53; mem. food distbn. research adv. com. Dept. Agr., 1962—. Pres., United Cerebral Palsy Found., San Diego, 1969-70. Served with AUS, 1942-44. Mem. Phila. Restaurant. Clubs: Kona Kai (San Diego); Union League (Phila.). Editorial adv. bd. Instnl. Distbn. mag. Home: El Secreto Rancho Santa Fe CA 92067 Office: 2191 Main St San Diego CA 92113

IRWIN, DONALD J., former congressman; b. Argentina, July 7, 1926 (parents Am. citizens); grad. Yale Coll., 1951, LL.B., Yale, 1954; m. Mary Stapleton; children—Patrick, Marion, Lucile, Stephen. Admitted to Conn. bar, 1954; mem. 86th Congress, 4th Conn. Dist.; gen. counsel USIA, Washington, 1961; treas. State of Conn., 1961-62; mem. 89th-90th Congress, 4th Dist. Conn. Mem. Norwalk Bd. Edn.; mem. Rowayton Vol. Hose Co. Past vice chmn. Norwalk Dem. Town Com. Recipient distinguished service award U.S. Jr. C. of C. Democrat. K.C. Home: 3 Topsail Rd Rowayton CT 06853

IRWIN, FRANCIS WILLIAM, psychologist, educator, cons.; b. Phila., Feb. 11, 1905; s. Francis Baker and Caroline Eva (Smith) I.; A.B., U. Pa., 1926, M.A., 1928, Ph.D., 1931; m. Emma Talbott Embry, Aug. 17, 1930. Asst. instr., instr. psychology U. Pa., 1926-39. asst. prof., 1939-45, asso. prof., 1945-52, prof., 1952—, acting chmn. dept. psychology, 1957-58; Social Sci. Research Council fellow U. Cal., U. Ia., 1940-41; research cons. mil. research Franklin Inst., 1941-45; cons. Elmo Roper, N.Y.C., 1951-52, Vineland Tng. Sch., 1949-55; vis. prof. psychology U. Cal. at Berkeley, 1956-57. Mem. tech. adv. com. research on mental health State N.J., 1954-57. Mem. Am. (chmn. publs. bd. 1962-64), Eastern psychol. assns., Psychonomic Soc., Civil Liberties Union, Soc. Exptl. Psychologists, Am. Assn. U. Profs., A.A.A.S., Sigma Xi. Club: Art Alliance (Phila.). Author: Intentional Behavior and Motivation: A Cognitive Theory, 1971. Acting editor Jour. Exptl. Psychology, 1942-47, editor, 1947-51. Contbr. profl. jours. Home: 2215 Delancey Pl Philadelphia PA 19103

IRWIN, GLENN WARD, Jr., univ. dean; b. Roachdale, Ind., July 18, 1920; s. Glenn Ward and Elsie (Browning) I.; B.S., Ind. U., 1942, M.D., 1944; m. Marianna Ashby, Nov. 2, 1922; children—Ann Graybill, William Browning, Elizabeth Ashby. Intern Meth. Hosp., 1944, resident medicine, Ind. U. Med. Center, 1945-46, 48-50; faculty Ind. U. Sch. Medicine, 1950—, prof. medicine, 1961—, dean Sch. Medicine 1965—. Mem. Gov. Ind. Med. Adv. Bd., 1961; chmn. Ind. Med. Edn. Bd., 1967—. Served to capt., M.C., AUS, 1946-48. Mem. A.M.A., Am. Thyroid Assn., Am., Indpls. (pres. 1959) Diabetes Assns., A.C.P. (bd. govs. Ind. 1963-69), Marion County Med. Soc. (bd. dirs. 1964), Sigma Xi. Alpha Omega Alpha. Home: 8025 N Illinois St Indianapolis, IN 46260.

IRWIN, HALE S., Jr., golfer; b. Joplin, Mo., June 3, 1945; s. Hale S. and Mabel M. (Philipps) I.; B.S. in Marketing, U. Colo., 1968; m. Sally Jean Stahlhuth, Sept. 14, 1968. Touring prof. golfer, 1968—. Mem. Phi Gamma Delta. Republican. Presbyn. Home: 4360 Darley Av Boulder CO 80303 Office: c/o Jack Mills P O Box 187 Boulder CO 80302

IRWIN, JAMES BENSON, astronaut; b. Pitts., Mar. 17, 1930; s. James and Elsie (Strebell) I.; B.S., U.S. Naval Acad., 1951; M.S. in Aero. Engring., U. Mich., 1957; m. Mary Ellen Monroe, Sept. 4, 1959; children-Joy Carmel, Jill Cherie, James Benson, Jan Caron. Commd. 1st lt. USAF, 1951, advanced through grades to lt. col., 1964; project officer Wright Patterson AFB, 1957-60; test dir. ASG-18/AIM-47 armament system, Edwards AFB, Cal., 1961-63; test pilot F-12 Test Force, Edwards AFB, 1963-65; br. chief Advanced Systems Hdqrs. Air Def. Command, Colorado Springs, Colo., 1965-66; astronaut NASA, 1966—. Home: 18410 Kingstown Ct Houston TX 77058 Office: Manned Space Center NASA Houston TX 77058

IRWIN, JAMES WESLEY, mgmt. cons.; b. Portage, Wis., July 4, 1902; s. Paul Fisher and Maybel (Robertson) I; student U. Wis., m. Mary Fawcett Bridgman, 1924 (dec.); children—James W., Carolyn Elizabeth; m. 2d, Loretta Moushey, 1948; step-children—William, Michael (dec.). Reporter to mng. editor Wis. State Jour., 1921-25; city editor Chgo. Herald and Examiner, 1926-28; supervising, mng. editor, asst. to pub. Denver Post. 1928-30; dir. pub. relations Frigidaire Corp., 1930-32; dir. pub. and employee relations Dayton Divs. Gen. Motors Corp., 1932-38; exec. asst. to pres., chmn. in charge labor relations, pub. relations, stockholder relations, advt. and promotion Monsanto Chem. Co., St. Louis, 1938-44; sr. partner James W. Irwin & Assos., 1944—; asst. to pres., mem. policy com. Ford Motor Co., 1947. Labor, pub. relations cons. Navy Dept., Army Air Forces, 1941-46. With others, developed, executed prodn. incentive program, symbolized by Army- Navy "E." Trustee Am. Council on Pub. Relations. Named One of All Time Gts. Pub. Relations, U. Mich. Poll, 1970. Mem. Pub. Relation Soc. Am. (founder, dir.), Nat. Assn. Pub. Relations

Counsellors (dir.), Chgo. Press Vets. Assn., Sigma Delta Chi (chmn. internat. expansion 1961-65), Theta Nu Epsilon, Lambda Chi Alpha. Republican. Clubs: Headline, Union League (Chgo.); National Press (Washington); Union League (N.Y.C.); Detroit. Contbg. editor mgmt. problems Am. Chem. Soc. publs., Harvard Bus. Rev. Contbr. articles to profl. jours. Home: 332 Sunset Ridge Rd Northfield, IL 60093

IRWIN, JOHN NICHOL II, govt. ofcl., lawyer; b. Keokuk, Ia., Dec. 31, 1913; s. John R. and Florence V. (Johnstone) I.; grad. Lawrenceville Sch., 1933; A.B., Princeton, 1937; B.A. in Jurisprudence, Balliol Coll., Oxford U., Eng., 1939. M.A., 1944; LL.B., Fordham U., 1941; LL.D., Parsons Coll., 1960; LL.D., Union Coll., Schenectady, N.Y., 1963; m. Jane Watson, June 2, 1949 (dec. Dec. 1970); children—Jane, John. Admitted to N.Y. bar. 1946; asso. Davis, Polk, Wardell, Sunderland and Kiendl, N.Y.C., 1946-50; partner Patterson, Belknap & Webb, 1950-57, 61-70; dep. asst. sec. def. for internat. security affairs Dept. Def., 1957-58; asst. sec. def. for internat. security affairs, 1958-61; under sec. of state, 1970—. Trustee Lawrenceville Sch., John Simon Guggenheim Meml. Found., N.Y. Hist. Soc., N.Y. Zool. Soc., Met. Mus. Art, Princeton U. Served from 1st lt. to col., AUS, 1941-46; adviser Joint Philippine-Am. Finance Commn., 1947. Decorated Legion of Merit; medal of Freedom, 1961; comdr. Philippine Legion of Honor. Mem. Bar Assn. City N.Y., Am., Fed., N.Y. State bar assns., Council Fgn. Relations, Pilgrims of U.S., Newcomen Soc. Presbyn (elder). Clubs: Country (New Canaan, Conn.); 1925 F Street, Metropolitan, Chevy Chase, City Tavern Association (Washington); Downtown, Economic, Princeton, River, University (N.Y.C.); Century Assn., Links. Home: 2510 Virginia Av NW Washington DC 20037 Office: Dept State Washington DC 20520

IRWIN, JOHN VALEUR, educator, speech pathologist; b. Muskogee, Okla., July 17, 1915; s. John W. and Margaret (Vogel) I.; B.A., Ohio Wesleyan U., 1937; M.A., Ohio State U., 1940; Ph.D., U. Wis., 1947; m. Phyllis Stacy, Jan. 15, 1944; children—John O., Nancy A. Asst. prof., then asso. prof. U. Minn., 1947-50; prof. speech, dir. Speech and Hearing Clinics, U. Wis., 1950-66; Roy A. Roberts prof. speech pathology and audiology U. Kan., 1966-70; Pope M. Farrington prof. Memphis State U., 1970—. Mem. Nat. Adv. Com. Handicapped, 1967-69, Nat. Adv. Com. Dyslexia and Related Reading Problems, 1968-69; chmn. program project com. Nat. Inst. Dental Research; mem. task force on speech lang. and hearing perinatal research br. NIH, 1970—. Served to capt. USAAF, 1942-46. Fellow Am. Speech and Hearing Assn. (exec. v.p., 1963-66, pres. 1968), Nat. Assn. Hearing Speech Agys. (bd. dirs. 1967-69), Phi Beta Kappa, Delta Sigma Rho, Omicron Delta Kappa, Kappa Sigma. Co-author: Voice and Articulation, 1958; The Psychology of Communication, 1963; Modern Speech, 1966. Home: 4870 Briarcliff Av Memphis TN 38117

IRWIN, JOSEPH JAMES, educator; b. Clinton, Ia., Oct. 29, 1908; s. Joseph Glen and Elizabeth Margaret (Paul) I.; B.A., Grinnell Coll., 1931; M.A., State U. Ia., 1934, Ph.D., 1942; m. Laurentia Mae Donhowe, Dec. 25, 1937; children—Joseph Paul, Martha Elizabeth, James Donhowe. Tchr. English, speech and journalism Buena Vista Coll., Storm Lake, Ia., 1934-36; faculty Albion (Mich.) Coll., 1937—, prof. English, 1947—, chmn. dept., 1949-71, chmn. div. lang., lit. and speech, 1952-59; dean Bay View (Mich.) Summer Coll. Liberal Arts, 1947-63, prof. English program liberal arts edn. for adults Mich. State U., 1957-60. Trustee Bay View Assn., 1947-53. Mem. Am. Assn. U. Profs. (council 1948-52), Mich. Coll. English Assn. (pres. 1949-50), Modern Lang. Assn., Nat. Council Tchrs. English, Nat. Collegiate Players, Theta Alpha Phi, Alpha Phi Gamma. Rotarian. Contbr. articles to profl. publs. Home: 416 E Erie St Albion MI 49224

IRWIN, LEO HOWARD U.S. judge; b. Stratford, N.C., Aug. 1, 1917; s. W. Carl and Mallie (Wilson) I.; student U. N.C., 1935-38; A.B., George Washington U., 1940; LL.B., Georgetown U., 1947; m. Doris Mickelson; children—Sandra Lee, Lisa Ann, Patrice Camille, Leo Howard, Lori Denice. Admitted to N.C., D.C. bars, 1947, U.S. Supreme Ct. bar; with various govt. agys., 1938-42, atty. Gen. Counsel's Office, CAB, 1947-48; mem. profl. staff, minority counsel com. ways and means Ho. of Reps., 1949-55, chief counsel, 1955-68; judge U.S. Tax Ct., Washington, 1968—. Guest, German Govt. on econ. study tour, 1964, Swedish and Danish govts., 1964; adj. prof. Georgetown U. Law Center Grad. Sch., evenings 1962-63. Active local Boy Scouts Am. Served as officer USNR, 1942-46. Mem. Fed. Bar Assn. Home: 5508 24th Av SE Washington DC 20031 Office: US Tax Ct Washington DC 20044

IRWIN, MALCOLM ROBERT, biologist; b. Artesian, S.D., Mar. 2, 1897; s. Joseph Speer and Mary T. (McCollum) I.; B.S., Ia. State Coll., 1920; M.S., 1925, Ph.D., 1928; m. Margaret House, July 5, 1929; children—Joe Robert, Harriet Anne. Teacher, Am. Farm Sch., Saloniki, Greece, 1921-24; instr. genetics Ia. State Coll., 1927-28; Fellow NRC, Bussey Instn., Harvard, 1928-29, Rockefeller Inst. Med. Research, 1929-30; coop. agt. U.S. Dept. Agr., 1930-56; asst. prof. genetics U. Wis., 1930-36, asso. prof., 1936-39, prof., 1939-67, prof. emeritus, 1967—, chmn. dept., 1951-65. Served as 2d lt. inf., U.S. Army, 1918. Recipient Elliot medal for 1938 by Nat. Acad. Scis.; Alumni award Ia. State U., 1962; Von Nathusius medal Deutsche Gesellschaft für ZEhtungskunde, 1965. Mem. village bd. Shorewood Hills, 1941-42. Mem. Nat. Acad. Scis., Genetics Soc. Am. (sec.-treas. 1947-49, pres. 1951), Am. Soc. Zoologists, Am. Soc. Naturalists (treas. 1942-44), Am. Assn. Immunologists, Soc. for Exptl. Biology and Medicine, A.A.A.S., Am. Soc. Animal Sci. (recipient Morrison award 1962), Internat. Union Biol. Scis. (U.S. nat. com. 1966-71), Soc. for Study Evolution, Sigma Xi, Phi Kappa Phi; fgr. mem. Swedish Royal Acad. Agr. Clubs: University, Blackhawk Country. Contbr. numerous articles to biol. jours. Home: 4720 Regent St Madison WI 53705

IRWIN, RALPH ALEXANDER, educator; b. San Francisco, Jan. 24, 1905; s. Ralph Bert and Sadie (Lyons) I.; B.S., Kan. State Coll., 1928, M.S., 1929; Ph.D., Ohio State U., 1938; m. Elsie Dora Eustace, June 1, 1929; children—Elsie Ruth, Barbara Jean. Prof. U. Nev., 1929-, chmn. dept. psychology, 1948-56, dean Coll. Arts and Sci., 1955-68, acting exec. v.p., 1964-65, adminstrv. v.p., 1968-; prof. summer session Wash. State Coll., 1939, U. Mo., 1944, San Jose (Cal.) State Coll., 1945; test technician Neb. State Merit Bd., 1937-54, acting supr., 1945-46. Bd. dirs. Council of Colls. Arts and Scis., State Univs. and Land Grant Colls., 1965-68. Mem. commn. on arts and scis. Nat. Assn. State Univs. and Land Grant Colls., 1967-70. Mem. Am. Assn. U. Profs., Phi Kappa Phi. Baptist. Mason (33) Home: 1160 Dennison Dr Reno NV 89502

IRWIN, RICHARD ARNOLD, paper mfr.; b. Tara, Ont., Apr. 5, 1909; s. Alexander J. and Amelia (Hassard) I.; B.A.Sc., U. Toronto, 1931; m. Catherine Janet Moffat, Sept. 4, 1937; children—Richard, Judith, Catherine, Elizabeth. Chemist Ont. Dept. Health, 1931-33, Nat. Carbon Co., 1933-34; estimator Somerville, Ltd., 1934-36, Toronto sales mgr., 1936-39, Montreal sales mgr., 1939-41, mgr. war products div., 1941-44, dir. sales, 1944-45, gen. mgr., 1945-48, v.p., gen. mgr., 1948-53, pres., gen. mgr., 1953-57; pres. Eddy Paper Co., Ltd., Hull, Que., 1954-56; pres., mng. dir. The E. B. Eddy Co., 1954-56; v.p. Bathurst Power and Paper Co., Ltd. (co. name changed to Bathurst Paper, Ltd. 1965), Montreal, 1957-59, dir., 1958, pres., 1959—; pres., chief exec. officer, dir. Consol. Paper Corp., Ltd.; chmn. bd. Bathurst Containers, Ltd., Bathurst Paper Sales (U.K.) Ltd.; pres. dir. Bathurst Paper Sales, Ltd., Bathurst Containers (Maritimes), Ltd.; dir. Rolland Paper Co., Ltd., Maritime Paper Products Ltd., Stand-Modern Tool Co. Ltd. Bd. govs. Royal Victoria Hosp., Montreal; dir. met. bd. YMCA. Mem. Canadian Paper Box Mfrs. Assn. (pres. 1953-54), Canadian Pulp and Paper Assn. (chmn. exec. bd. 1964-65), Phi Delta Theta. Clubs: St. James; London Hunt and Country, London; National (Toronto); Mount Royal, Engineers (Montreal); Seigniory (Montebello). Home: 3555 Cote des Neiges Rd Quebec Canada Office: 800 Dorchester Blvd W Montreal 101 Quebec Canada

IRWIN, RICHARD DORSEY, publisher; b. St. Joseph, Mo., Nov. 2, 1905; s. William Herbert and Ida Ferrell (Dorsey) I.; student U. Ill., 1924-27; LL.D. (hon.), Ball State U., 1970; m. Anne Marie Thompson, Feb. 2, 1927; children—Jacqueline Marie (Mrs. Charles E. Pipher), Richard Dorsey. Mgr. coll. dept. A.W. Shaw Co., 1928, McGraw-Hill Book Co., 1928-32; chmn. bd. dirs. Richard D. Irwin, Inc., Homewood, Ill., 1933—; chmn. bd. Dorsey Press, Irwin-Dorsey Ltd. of Can., Learning Systems Co., Bus. Publs., Inc.; pres. Dow Jones-Irwin, Inc.; chmn. bd. 1st Nat. Bank of Harvey. Cons. O.P.A., 1943. Mem. Dist. 161 Sch. Bd., Flossmoor, Ill., 1948-54. Chmn. bd. Richard D. Irwin Found.; trustee U. Ill. Found., Glenwood Sch. for Boys. Mem. Am. Assn. Collegiate Schs. of Bus., Am. Accounting Assn., Am., Midwest, So. econ. assns., Am. Marketing Assn., Midwest Bus. Adminstrn. Assn., Am. Bus. Law Assn., Profl. Golfers Assn. (nat. adv. com.), Alpha Kappa Psi, Omicron Delta Epsilon, Beta Gamma Sigma. Clubs: Olympia Fields (Ill.) Country; Flossmoor Country; Chgo. Athletic Assn. Home: 1230 Braeburn Rd Flossmoor IL 60422 Office: 1818 Ridge Rd Homewood IL 60430

IRWIN, ROBERT JAMES ARMSTRONG, Jr., bankholding co. exec.; b. Buffalo, June 27, 1927; s. Robert J.A. and Dorothy (McLean) I.; B.A., Colgate U., 1949; postgrad. U. Buffalo, 1949-50, Babson Inst. Finance, Wellesley, Mass., 1952-53; m. Donna Henwood, Sept. 10, 1966; children—William Baird, Elaine Mitchell, Elizabeth Flora, Robert J.A. IV, Ronald Henwood, Derrick Millet. Exec. trainee Mfrs. & Traders Trust Co., Buffalo, 1950-52; registered rep. Doolittle & Co., Buffalo, 1953-58; with Marine Trust Co. Western N.Y., Buffalo, 1958-66, investment mgmt. officer, 1959-61, v.p. in charge investment mgmt. dept., 1961-66; v.p. Marine Midland Banks, Inc., N.Y.C., 1966-69, sr. v.p., 1969—; exec. v.p. Dreyfus-Marine Midland Mgmt. Corp., 1970—; dir. Colonial Penn Group, Inc. Bd. dirs. Boys Club Buffalo, Inc., 1953—, v.p., 1964-65; bd. dirs. Kleinwort Benson Internat. Fund; trustee Baird Found., 1965—. Mem. N.Y. C. of C., Buffalo Fine Arts Acad. (life), Beta Theta Pi. Clubs: Saturn, Canoe (Buffalo); Royal Canadian Yacht (Toronto); City Mid-Day, Metropolitan Opera, University (N.Y.C.). Home: Easton Rd Weston PO Fairfield CT 06430 Office: 241 Main St Buffalo NY 14203 also 250 Park Av New York City NY 10017

IRWIN, THEODORE writer; b. N.Y.C., Sept. 17, 1907; s. Ira S. and Rebecca (Arlow) I.; B.S., N.Y. U., 1928; m. Rita Reisman, June 13, 1931 (dec. Mar. 1962); children—Jed, Kenneth; m. 2d, Helen Ross, Apr. 12, 1964. Newspaper reporter, feature writer, 1928-31; free lance mag. writer, novelist, 1931-39; mng. editor Cue Mag., 1939-41; asso. editor Look Mag., 1941-45; edit. dir. Farrell Pub. Co., 1945-52; editor Real Mag., 1952-54; pres. Editorial Services, 1954-56; Mem. Soc. Mag. Writers (pres. 1970), Nat. Assn. Sci. Writers. Author: Collusion, 1932; Strange Passage, 1935; Accident of Birth, 1937; Holland: Fantastic Land Below the Sea, 1961; Modern Birth Control, 1961; Better Health After Fifty, 1964; What Executives Should Know About Tension, 1965; Instant Shrink, 1971. Contbr. to nat. mag. Home: 250 E 73d St New York City NY 10021

IRWIN, THEODORE HAYWARD II, investment co. exec., b. Buffalo, July 3, 1932; s. Dudley M. and Margaret (Smith) I.; B.A., Williams Coll., 1954; m. Miriam Cartwright Eustis, Apr. 16, 1955; children-Catherine Cartwright, Lisa Lucille, Marcelle Miriam, Theodore Hayward, James Wickham. Gen. partner L.A. Mathey & Co., N.Y.C., 1957-64; with Spencer Trask & Co., Inc., and predecessor, N.Y.C., 1964—, v.p., treas., dir., 1969—; dir. Am. Stock Exchange Clearing Corp., 1962—. Mem. nominating com. N.Y. Stock Exchange, 1970, mem. arbitration com., 1970—. Mem. United Fund N. Essex, N.J., 1958—; chmn. of apartments, Montclair, N.J., 1960, chmn. Upper Montclair Residential, 1963. Served as 1st lt. USAF, 1955-57. Home: 224 Fells Rd Essex Fells NJ 07021 Office: 60 Broad St New York NY 10004

IRWIN, WALTER WAYNE, air force officer; b. Everett, Wash., Aug. 27, 1923; s. John Harvey and Stella Mildred (Barron) I.; m. Christine Ann Stevens, Dec. 4, 1954; children—Michael, Steven, Christine, Mark. With USAC, 1942-45, USAF, 1951—, maj., 1959—; combat missions ETO, 1944-45; jet pilot, 1952—; civilian pilot, 1945-51. Decorated D.F.C., Air medal with clusters; recipient Thompson Trophy, 1958; co-recipient Collier Trophy, 1959. Established world straightaway speed record, 1958. Home: 3620 Zuni St Glendale AZ 98530

IRWIN, WAYNE, ret. assn. exec.; b. DeSoto, Ia., Nov. 15, 1904; s. Rolla Curtis and Mary Elizabeth (Culver) I.; B.C.S., Drake U., 1929; m. Inez Elizabeth Erwin, Mar. 23, 1930. With U.S. Gypsum Co., 1929-53, controller, 1943, sec., 1951, treas., 1952; v.p., comptroller Pullman Co., 1953-59; v.p., dept. finance and accounting Assn. Am. Railroads, Washington, 1959-69, (v.p., spl. asst. to pres., 1969; dir. Merchandise Nat. Bank Chgo. Mem. Financial Execs. Inst., Delta Sigma Pi. Club: Executive (Chgo.). Home: 5001 Loughboro Rd NW Washington DC 20016

IRWIN, WILLIAM PRYOR, educator; b. Cleve., May 6, 1924; s. John Preston and Josephine (Saxer) I.; A.B., Hiram Coll., 1947; A.M., Case-Western U., 1950; Ph.D., U. Cal. at Berkeley, 1955; postgrad. Yale, U. Chgo.; m. Bobbie Jo Shaeffer, Sept. 7, 1947; children—Rebecca Jo, William Pryor III, Elizabeth Jo. Asst. prof. polit. sci. Heidelberg Coll., 1950-52; asst., then asso. prof. polit. sci. Colo. State U., 1955-61; asso. dir. Nat. Center for Edn. in Politics, N.Y.C., 1961-62; prof., Case- Western U., 1962—, former chmn. dept. polit. sci. Planner Colo. Survival Plan Commn., 1956-58. Rocky Mountain regional coordinator Humphrey for Pres. Com., 1960; Congl. adminstrv. asst., 1960-61; polit. and campaign pub. relations cons. Served to lt. (j.g.) USNR, 1943-46. Mem. Am. Assn. U. Profs., Am., Western polit. sci. assns., Pi Sigma Alpha, Pi Kappa Delta. Democrat. Home: 2528 Derbyshire Rd Cleveland Heights OH 44106 Office: Case-Western U Cleveland OH 44106

IRZYK, ALBIN FELIX, army officer; b. Salem, Mass., Jan. 2, 1917; s. Felix and Sophia (Mroczka) I.; A.B., U. Mass., 1940; M.A., Am. U., 1966; grad. Armor Sch., 1949, Command and Gen. Staff Coll., 1950, Nat. War Coll., 1958; m. Laura Evelyn Abbott, May 14, 1946; children—Elizabeth Jane, Albin Felix, Laura Evelyn. Commd. 2d lt. U.S. Army, 1940, advanced through grades to brig. gen., 1963; assigned 3d U.S. Cav., 1940-42; tank battalion comdr., chief staff 4th Armored Div., Europe, 1942-45; mem. staff, faculty Armor Sch., Ft. Knox, Ky., 1947-49, 51-54; staff officer to comdr.-in-chief Pacific, Hawaii, 1954-57; chief Office Internat. Affairs, Dept. Army Gen. Staff, 1958-61; regtl. comdr. 14th Armored Cav., Fulda, Germany, 1961-62; asst. chief staff plans, operations and tng. Hdqrs, 7th U.S. Army, Stuttgart, Germany, also Allied Land Forces, Central Europe, Fontainebleau, France, 1962-65; asst. comdt. U.S. Army Armor Sch., Ft. Knox, 1965-67; comdg. gen. U.S. Army Hdqrs. Area Command, Saigon, Vietnam, 1967-68; asst. div. comdr. 4th Inf. Div., Vietnam, 1968-69; comdg. gen., Ft. Devens, Mass., 1970—. Active Boy Scouts Am., Girl Scouts. Decorated D.S.C., D.S.M., Silver Star with oak leaf cluster, Legion of Merit, Purple Heart with oak leaf cluster, Air medal with 10 oak leaf clusters; Croix de Guerre (France); Czech War Cross; Chuong My medal (Korea); recipient silver anniversary All American award Sports Illus. mag., 1964, Sir Thomas More award Nat. Council Cath. Men, 1965. Mem. 4th Armored Div. Assn. (pres. 1948-49), European Council Cath. Men (pres. 1964-65), Legion of Valor, Hon. Order Ky. Cols. Contbr. articles profl. jours. Home: 700 McDaniel Av Greenville SC 29605 Office: 1 Buena Vista Fort Devens MA 91433

ISAAC, CHARLES MARTIN, business exec., distbn. authority; b. Phila., Jan. 11, 1896; s. M.J. and Violet (Francis) Behr; legally adopted s. William J. and Mary (Griffiths) I.; A.B., George Washington U., m. Gula Louise Welsh, Mar. 1, 1920; 1 dau., Marijean. Engaged in retail bus., 1922-34; pres., exec. mgr. Canton (O.) Retail Mchts. Bd., 1934-42; exec. asst. to pres. Am. Retail Fedn., Washington, 1942-44; mgr. domestic distbn. dept. C. of C. U.S., 1944-51; exec. v.p. Retail Jewelers of Am., N.Y.C., 1951-60; pres. Behr Enterprises, Inc. 1960-69; asso. Joseph T. Roy Realty, Inc., Ft. Lauderdale, Fla., 1969—. Lectr. distbn. Northwestern U., 1943, Yale, 1946, U. Pa., 1946, N.Y. U., 1958. Mem. Nat. Distbn. Council, 1944-52; chmn. advancement com. McKinley chpt. Boy Scouts Am., (canton). Bd. dirs. C. of C., A.R.C., Travelers Aid Soc., Community Fund. Served as mem. staff insp. gen. SOS, AEF, World War I. Decorated Purple Heart. Recipient certificate of Merit; John N. van der Vries award Northwestern U.; award Am. Trade Assn. Execs. Mem. Artus, Sigma Chi, Alpha Kappa Psi. Republican. Presbyn. (ruling elder). Rotarian, Mason (32). Clubs: University (Washington, N.Y.C.). Contbr. trade jours. Address: 3201 NE 19 Av Fort Lauderdale, FL 33306.

ISAAC, SOL MORTON, lawyer; b. Columbus, O., Dec. 5, 1911; s. Arthur J. and Bella (Loewenstein) I.; B.A., Yale, 1933; LL.B., Harvard, 1936; m. Dorothy Durlacher, Dec. 18, 1936; children—Beatrice, Frederick Morton, Thomas Durlacher. Admitted to Ohio bar, 1936; asso. James M. Butler, 1936-40, Butler & Isaac, 1940-47; partner Isaac, Postlewaite, O'Brian and Oman, and predecessor, Columbus, 1950—. Sec., dir. Diamond Milk Products, Inc., 1959-70; chmn. bd. Sunday Creek Coal Co., 1970-71. Bd. dirs. United Community Council Columbus and Franklin County, 1958—, pres., 1969-70; chmn. Gov.'s Survey Com. Mental Health, 1956-57; mem. Ohio Commn. Children and Youth, 1961-62; mem. council on intercultural edn. Columbus Sch. Bd., 1966-68; bd. Ohio Citizens Council for Health and Welfare (pres. 1956-59). Pres. Family Service Assn. Am., 1953-54; v.p. Nat. Social Welfare Assembly, 1958-60; bd. dirs. Nat. Legal Aid and Defender Assn., 1958-60; co-chmn. Nat. Conf. Lawyers and Social Workers, 1961-67; dir. Columbus Acad., 1947-65, v.p., 1948-59; bd. dirs., exec. com. Riverside Meth. Hosp. Served from lt. (j.g.) to lt., USNR, 1943-45. Fellow Am. Bar Found., Am. Coll. Probate Counsel; mem. Am. (chmn. sect. family law 1960-61); Ohio, Columbus (pres. 1952-53, Community Service award 1969), bar assns., Nat. Conf. Social Welfare (pres. 1964-65). Home: 222 Ashbourne Rd Columbus OH 43209 Office: 88 E Broad St Columbus OH 43215

ISAACMAN, DANIEL, coll. adminstr.; b. Phila., Oct. 8, 1924; s. Reuben and Esther (Handelman) I.; B.A., U. Pa., 1948, M.S. in Edn., 1951; Ed. D., Dropsie U., 1970; m. Clara Heller, July 24, 1945; 1 son, Yonatan. Tchr., United Hebrew Schs., Phila., 1947-49, prin., 1949-51; mem. faculty Gratz Coll., Phila., 1951—, asso. prof. history and edn., 1959—, v.p., 1970—; ednl. cons., 1958—. Dir. Camp Galil, Pa. Chmn. schs. and tchrs. div. Allied Jewish Appeal, Fedn. Jewish Agencies, Phila., 1960-70, vice chmn. trade council, , 1970, exec. com. Nat. Conf. Jewish Communal Services, 1969-70. Trustee Am. Zionist Youth Found., 1966-70. Served with AUS, 1943-45. Mem. Nat. Council Jewish Edn. (pres. 1969-71). Democrat. Home: 9211 Pine Rd Philadelphia PA 19111

ISAACS, GERALD WILLIAM, agrl. engr., educator; b. Crawfordsville, Ind., Sept. 3, 1927; s. William Paul and Verna (Johnson) I.; B.S., Purdue U., 1947, M.S., 1949; Ph.D., Mich. State U., 1954; m. Phyllis Joyce Seaton, Aug. 22, 1948; children—Joyce Irene (dec.), David Gerald, Donald Phillip, Joseph Lee (dec.), Susan Verna, Linda Kay. Instr., Purdue U., Lafayette, Ind., 1948- 52, asst. prof., 1954-57, asso. prof., 1957-60, prof., 1960-64, head agrl. engring. dept. 1964—; grad. research asst. Mich. State U., 1952- 54; cons. Butler Mfg. Co., Clayton-Lambert Mfg. Co., Inter Am. Devel. Bank, U.S. Adminstrn. for Internat. Devel. Served with USNR, 1945-46. Registered profl. engr., Ind. Mem. Am. Soc. Agrl. Engrs. Found., Sigma Xi, Pi Mu Epsilon, Alpha Epsilon, Phi Tau Sigma, Tau Beta Pi. Lutheran. Rotarian. Contbr. articles profl. jours. Home: RR 9 Box 309A West Lafayette IN 47906 Office: Agrl Engring Dept Purdue U Lafayette IN 47907

ISAACS, HAROLD ROBERT, writer; b. N.Y.C., Sept. 13, 1910; s. Robert and Sophie (Berlin) I.; A.B., Columbia, 1930; m. Viola Robinson, Sept. 14, 1932; children—Arnold R., Deborah S. Reporter, N.Y. Times, also Honolulu Advt., Shanghai Evening Post and China Press, 1928-31; with Agence Havas, Shanghai and N.Y.C., 1931-40, CBS, N.Y.C. and Washington, 1940-43; war corr., CBI, asso. editor Newsweek mag., Washington, also China, S.E. Asia and N.Y.C., 1943-50; research asso. Center Internat. Studies, Mass. Inst. Tech. Cambridge, 1953-65, prof. polit. sci., 1965—. Guggenheim fellow, 1950. Mem. Assn. Asian Studies, African Studies Assn., Assn. Pub. Opinion Research. Author: The Tragedy of the Chinese Revolution, 1938; No Peace for Asia, 1947; Two-Thirds of the World, 1950; Scratches on Our Minds, American Images of China and India, 1958; Emergent Americans, a Report on Crossroads Africa, 1961; The New World of Negro Americans (Anisfield-Wolf award 1964), 1963; India's Ex- Untouchables, 1965; American Jews in Israel, 1967. Home: 96 Farlow Rd Newton MA 02158 Office: Center Internat Studies Mass Inst Tech Cambridge MA 02139

ISAACS, KENNETH L., banker; b. Scranton, Pa., June 18, 1904; s. Albert George and Anna Carpenter (Richards) I.; M.E., Lehigh U., 1925, LL.D., 1965; M.B.A., Harvard, 1927; m. Elizabeth Tudor Thacher, Feb. 1, 1939 (div. Sept. 1947); m. 2d, Helen Coolidge Adams, Mar. 10, 1949; children—Kenneth C.A., Anne Carpenter Richards. Buying dept. Nat. City Co., 1927- 30; private investment work 1930-32; asst. to comptroller Cornell U. specializing on endowment fund investments 1932-36; with Mass. Investors Trust, 1936-69; formerly chmn., mem. investment mgmt. com. Mass. Investors Trust, Investors Growth Stock Fund, Inc.; partner Mass. Financial Services; trustee Suffolk-Franklin Savs. Bank; dir. So. Pacific Co., Phelps Dodge Corp., Boston Common Stock Fund Inc., Fiduciary Exchange Fund. Capital Exchange Fund, Exchange Fund of Boston, Inc., Gen. Pub. Utilities Corp. Trustee, mem. corp. Children's Hosp., Boston; trustee Lehigh University. Clubs: Somerset (Boston); Brook, River, Harvard, Recess, Knickerbocker (N.Y.C.). Republican. Episcopalian. Home: North Brook Farm Walpole MA 02081 Office: 200 Berkeley St Boston MA 02116

ISAACS, NORMAN ELLIS, editor, educator; b. Manchester, Eng., Mar. 28, 1908; s. Rufus and Esther (Simon) I.; brought to Canada, 1911, to U.S., 1922; student Montreal, Indpls. pub. schs.; m. Dorothy Ritz, Mar. 21, 1932; children—Roberta (Mrs. John F. Matthews III), Stephen. With Indpls. Star, 1925; with Indpls. Times, 1926-43, mng. editor, 1936-43; editorial dir. Indpls. News, 1943-45; mng. editor St. Louis Star-Times, 1945-51; mng. editor Louisville Times 1951-61; v.p., exec. editor Courier-Jour. and Louisville Times, 1962-71; prof., editor in residence Columbia, 1971—; cons. Acad. for Ednl. Devel., Louisville newspapers, Paddock Publs., other newspapers; dir. Courier-Jour. and Louisville Times Co., Roper Orgn. Former mem. journalism fellowship bd. Stanford, selection com. Harvard Nieman Fellowship, adv. bd. Pulitzer Prize, Edward Murrow fellowship com. Council Fgn. Relations; chmn. U. Cal. Commn. Campus Press, 1970; mem. task force on govt. and press 20th Century Fund, 1971. Pub. affairs mission Dept. State to India, 1958, to Yugoslavia, 1959. Pres. Louisville Philharmonic, 1956-66. Louisville Fund, 1958-59. Recipient William A. White award, So. Methodist U. medal, 1955. Mem. Internat. Press. Inst., Am. Soc. Newspaper Editors (dir., chmn. com. editorial future), Council Fgn. Relations, Nat. Probation and Parole Assn. (dir.), Asso. Press Mng. Editors Assn. (pres. 1953), Sigma Delta Chi (chmn. com. to review press 1954). 1951, nat. chmn. Ethics com., 1955-56). Home: 45 E 89th St New York City NY 10028 Office: Grad Sch Journalism Columbia U New York City NY 10027

ISAACS, REGINALD RODERIC, educator; b. Winnipeg, Can., July 20, 1911; s. Mark and Sophia (Rau) I.; came to U.S., 1922, naturalized, 1944; B. Arch., U. Minn., 1935; M. Arch., Harvard, 1939; student U. Chgo., 1947-50; m. Charlotte Aldes, Mar. 24, 1937; children—Merry Aldes, Mark Aldes, Henry Aldes. Architect housing, city planner, Washington, D.C., Mpls., Chgo., Phila., other cities, 1926-40; city planner Chgo. Plan Commn., Syracuse Plan Commn.; various fed. agys., 1940-45; dir. planning staff Michael Reese Hosp., Chgo., 1945-53; cons. South Side Planning Bd., Chgo., 1946-53; Charles Dyer Norton prof. regional planning, Harvard, 1953—, chmn. dept. city and regional planning, 1953-64; exhbns. Mus. Modern Art, 1947, Chgo. Art Inst., 1936, 7th Pan-Am. Congress Architects, Havana 1950: cons. to P.R. Govt., 1956—, UN, 1960-62, V.I. Gov., 1961—, Gulf Regional Planning Comm., 1966—, Ford Found.; specialist U.S. State Dept., 1959; chmn. cons. Am. Council to Improve Our Neighborhoods, 1954-55; dir. metropolitan area planning study Met. Housing and Planning Council of Chgo., 1955-56. Mem. bd. overseers com. to visit Harvard Grad. Sch. Design, 1951-53. Licensed architect, Nat. Council Archtl. Registration Bds., D.C., Ill., Mass., P.R. Author: Capital Requirements for Urban Development and Renewal (with John Dyckman), 1960. Contbr. articles profl. publs. Address: 11 Shady Hill Sq Cambridge MA 02138

ISAACSON, BERNARD BENJAMIN, accountant; b. Bklyn., July 12, 1917; s. Harry and Celia (Solomon) I.; student Rider Coll., U. Pa.; m. Cecilia Laub, Dec. 22, 1940; children—Barbara Ruth, Dana. With Park Lane Handbags, 1935-37; clk. S. Leopold, C.P.A., 1937-39, Puder & Puder, C.P.A.'s, 1939-40; accountant N.Am. Ins. Co., 1940-42; auditor Bellanca Aircraft, 1943-45; partner Isaacson, Stolper & Co., C.P.A.'s, Wilmington, Del., 1945-70; v.p., treas. Commonwealth Trust Co., 1958—; partner J.K. Lasser & Co., 1970—. Mem. Del. Hwy. Commn., 1969-71; mem. Gov. Del. Com. Revision Penal System Del., 1954-56, Gov. Del. Com. State Indsl. 1955—, Gov. Del. Com. State Sch. Health Adv. Bd., 1955-57, Mayor's Com. Revenue, 1966-69; mem. execs. coms. United Community Fund No. Del., 1966-68, Delmarva council Boy Scouts Am.; treas. Better Bus. Bur. Wilmington, 1969-71. Chmn. bd. Alma Moore Coll. Served as accountant USAAF, 1942-43. Recipient 1st Distinguished Alumnus award Rider Coll., 1965. C.P.A., N.J., Del., N.Y., La. Mem. Del. Accountants Assn. (pres. 1946-47), Am. Inst. C.P.A.'s (v.p.), Am. Inst. Accountants (council 1953-56, 60-68), Del. (pres.), N.Y. socs. C.P.A.'s, Nat. Conf. Christians and Jews, Jewish Fedn. Del. Mason (Shriner), Elk, Kiwanian. Club: Brandywine Country (dir., pres. 1968-70 Wilmington). Author: Guides to Successful Accounting Practice. Editor: Practitioners Forum Jour. Accountancy. Contbr. articles to profl. jours. Home: 400 Hawthorne Dr Wilmington DE 19802 Office: 3411 Silverside Rd Wilmington DE 19899

ISAACSON, LOUIS, union ofcl. Pres., Internat. Union of Dolls, Toys, Playthings, Novelties and Allied Products U.S. and Can. Office: 132 W 43d St New York City NY 10036*

ISAACSON, LOUIS GUNSEN, lawyer; b. Denver, Feb. 26, 1910; s. Sam and Bertha (Rosenfeld) I.; Ph.B., U. Chgo., 1930, J.D., 1932; m. Henriette F. Freund, June 14, 1933; children—Ellen (Mrs. Sheldon Friedman), Linda (Mrs. Kenneth Heller). Admitted to Colo. bar, 1932, since practiced in Denver, partner firm Isaacson, Rosenbaum, Goldberg and Miller, 1961—. Dir. Navajo Freight Lines, Inc. Chmn. Denver exec. com. Anti-Defamation League of B'nai B'rith, 1966—. Pres., Rose Meml. Hosp., Denver, 1970—. Mem. Am., Colo., Denver (pres. 1954) bar assns. Home: 790 Washington St Denver CO 80203 Office: 1700 Broadway Denver CO 80202

ISAACSON, WALTER FRANCIS, stock broker; b. Bayonne, N.J., Dec. 11, 1925; s. Harold B. and Rose (Pisani) I.; B.S., Seton Hall U., 1950; m. Constance Bakker, June 23, 1956. Sr. auditor R.G. Rankin and Co., C.P.A.'s, N.Y.C., 1952-55; v.p., controller Bache and Co., 1955-66; exec. v.p., treas. Hayden, Stone, Inc., N.Y.C., 1966-70; v.p. Klemwort Benson Inc., 1970—. Past pres. accounting div. Assn. Stock Exchange Firms, 1965-66. Served with AUS, 1944-47. Mem. Am. Inst. C.P.A.'s, Financial Execs. Inst. Home: 436 Roanoke Rd Westfield NJ 07090 Office: 160 Wall St New York City NY 10005

ISAACSON, WILLIAM JOSEPH, lawyer; b. Gallitzin, Pa., Jan. 10, 1913; s. Louis and Anna (Kaufmam) I.; A.B. with distinction, U. Mich. 1935. J.D., 1937; m. Bernice N. Kavinoky, Feb. 9, 1936 (dec. Feb. 1965); 1 son, Stephen S.; m. 2d, Inge R. Ryfordt, Apr. 1966; 1 son, Stig Birger. Admitted to Mich. bar, 1937, N.Y. bar, 1948; practiced law, Detroit, 1937-39; atty., trial examiner, regional dir. NLRB, 1939-48; gen. counsel Amalgamated Clothing Workers Am., N.Y.C., 1948-58; vis. prof. Cornell U., 1958; pvt. practice law, N.Y.C., 1958-59; dep. indsl. commr. N.Y., 1959-60; partner Kaye, Scholer, Fierman, Hays and Handler, 1960—. Chmn., N.Y. State Grievance Appeals Bd., 1965-69. Vice pres. Lenox Hill Neighborhood House, 1967—. Mem. Am. (chmn. labor relations law com. 1958-59), N.Y. bar assns., Am. Law Inst., Assn. Bar City N.Y. (chmn. com. labor and social security legislation 1963-66, post admissions legal edn. com.), Am. Arbitration Assn. Author articles to profl. publs. Home: 860 UN Plaza New York City NY 10017 Office: 425 Park Av New York City NY 10022

ISAAK, NICHOLAS, architect; b. Dardhe, Albania, Sept. 22, 1913; s. Charles and Olympia (Stephany) I.; student Sanborn Sem., 1932, St. Anselms Coll., 1933; B.S., U. N.H., 1936; m. Barbara Pineo, July 6, 1940; children—Marcia, Nicholas, Carolyn. Draftsman, supervising architects office U. N.H., 1937-40; designer Lockwood Greene Engrs., 1941-42; practicing architect Koehler & Isaak, Manchester, N.H., 1946—; designed St. Anselms Coll. bldgs., Pease AFB bldgs., dormitory at U. N.H., bldgs. at Keene Tchrs. Coll., Cts., P.O. bldgs., Concord, N.H., Chancery Bldg., Manchester, Fed. office bldgs., P.O., Concord and Portsmouth, others. Water color exhibit Currier Gallery Art, 1946. Mem. City Planning Commn., Manchester; vice chmn. So. N.H. Planning Commn. Served as lt. (j.g.) USNR, 1943-46. Mem. A.I.A. (pres. N.H. chpt.; Design award N.H. chpt. 1965, 68, 70), N.H. Art Assn., Soc. Archtl. Historians. Home: 228 Oak St Manchester NH 03104 Office: 1880 Elm St Manchester NH 03104

ISAKOFF, JACK FEIN, educator; b. N.Y.C., Sept. 23, 1910; s. Abram and Anna (Mordis) I.; A.B., Western Res. U., 1931; M.A., Ohio State U., 1932; Ph.D., U. Ill., 1937; LL.B., Lincoln Coll. Law, 1948; m. Shirley Klein, Sept. 3, 1933; 1 dau., Barbara Ann (Mrs. Allan Peskin). Mem. polit. sci. faculty U. Ill., 1934-38, vis. prof., 1957-58; asst. dir. research Ill. Legislative Council, 1938-39, dir. research, 1939-60, cons., 1960—; admitted to Ill. bar. 1948; dir. research Ill. Commn. to Study State Govt., 1949-51; prof. polit. sci., chmn. dept. Western Res. U., 1960-62; prof. govt. So. Ill. U., 1962—; asst. atty. gen. Ill., 1961. Govt. operations cons. U.S. Bur. Census, 1948, Conn. Commn. on State Govt. Orgn., 1949, Ill. Commn. on Muncipal Revenue, 1951-53, Chgo. Home Rule Commn., 1954, Ohio Legislative Service Commn., 1956; mem. Ill. Commn. on Intergovtl. Cooperation, 1949-60, sec., 1953-60; staff dir. Ill. Council Econ. Advisers, 1962-63; v.p. Nat. Legislative Conf., 1958-59, pres., 1959-60; 3d v.p. Council State Govt., 1960. Adv. com. state and local govts. U.S. Census Bur., 1964-66; chmn. Ill. Commn. on State Govt., 1965-67; mem. Ill. Commn. on Orgn. Gen Assembly, 1965-69; staff counsel 6th Ill. Constl. Conv., 1970. Served to staff sgt. USAAF, 1943-45. Recipient award for distinguished pub. service Springfield-Urbana (Ill.) chpt. Am. Soc. Pub. Adminstrn., 1958; research honor award Citizens of Greater Chgo., 1958. Mem. Am. Polit. Sci. Assn., Am. Soc. Pub. Adminstrn., Am. Assn. U. Profs., Nat. Municipal League. Author: The Public Works Administration, 1939. Home: 1604 Briarwood Dr Carbondale IL 62901

ISARD, WALTER, educator; b. Phila., Apr. 19, 1919; A.B., Temple U., 1939; M.A., Harvard, 1941, Ph.D., 1943; postgrad. U. Chgo., 1941-42; m. Caroline Berliner, July, 1943; children—Peter, Susan, Toni, Michael, Scott A., Roberta J., Anni K., Arthur. Lectr., research asso. Harvard, 1949-53, vis. prof., 1965—; asso. prof. regional econs. Mass. Inst. Tech., 1953-56, asso. dir. sect. urban and regional studies, 1953-55, dir., 1955-56; prof. econs. U. Pa., Phila., 1956—, past chmn. dept. regional sci. Vis. prof. regional sci. Yale, 1960-61; pres. Regional Sci. Research Inst., 1957—; exec. sec. Peace Research Soc. (Internat.), 1955; cons. Resources for Future. Fellow World Acad. Art and Sci.; mem. Regional Sci. Assn. (pres.), Am. Econ. Assn., Am. Sociol. Soc., Econometric Soc., Assn. Am. Geographers. AUthor: Atomic Power, An Economic and Social Analysis, 1952; Location and Space-Economy, 1956; Municipal Costs and Revenues, 1957; Methods of Regional Analysis, 1960; General Theory, 1969. Editor: Jour. Regional Sci., Regional Sci. Studies series. Home: 3218 Garrett Rd Drexel Hill PA 19026 Office: McNeil Bldg U Pa Philadelphia PA 19104

ISBELL, HARRIS, physician; b. Horatio, Ark., June 7, 1910; s. Francis T. and Celeste (Matthews) I.; M.D., Tulane U., 1934; m. Laverne McMillan, 1937 (dec.); children—Ann, Elizabeth. Intern Charity Hosp., New Orleans, 1934-35; with USPHS, 1935—; research in addiction USPHS Hosp., Lexington, Ky., 1944—; dir. Addiction Research Center, Nat. Inst. Mental Health, Lexington, 1945-63; lectr. U. Cin., U. Louisville, U. Ill.; prof. medicine and pharmacology U. Ky. Mem. panel of experts on drug dependence WHO. Recipient meritorious service award USPHS, 1962. Fellow A.C.P.; mem. Am. Coll. Neuropsychpharmacology, Internat. Brain Research Orgn., Soc. Parm. and Exptl. Therapeutics, Collegium Internationale Psychopharmacologium, Sigma Xi. Home: Lawn-Mark Farm Paris Pike Lexington KY 40501

ISBELL, HORACE SMITH, chemist; b. Denver, Nov. 13, 1898; s. Harvey G. and Mary E. (White) I.; B.S., U. Denver, 1920, M.S., 1923; Ph.D. (USPHS fellow), U. Md., 1926; m. May Davidson, June 26, 1930. Asst. chemist Am. Smelting & Refining Co., Pueblo, Colo., 1920-21, Bur. Animal Industry, Dept. Agr., Washington, 1923-25; research chemist, chief organic chemistry sect. Nat. Bur. Standards, Washington, 1927-68; senior research scientist Am. U. Wash., 1968—. Recipient meritorious award Dept. Commerce, 1950; Distinguished Alumni award U. Denver, 1953. Mem. Washington, N.Y. acads. sci., Am. Chem. Soc. (Hillebrand award Washington sect. 1951, Hudson Honor award div. carbohydrate chemistry 1954; councilor 1946, 63-66, chmn. div. carbohydrate chemistry 1938, chmn. Washington sect. 1945),Sigma Xi, Phi Lambda Upsilon, Alpha Chi Sigma. Club: Cosmos (Washington). Patentee and researcher field of sugars, sugar derivatives, tritium-labeled carbohydrates. Home: 4704 Blagden Av Washington DC 20011 Office: Chemistry Dept American Univ Washington DC 20016

ISBELL, JOHN ROLFE, educator, mathematician; b. Portland, Ore., Oct. 27, 1930; s. Henry Wyatt and Dana (Martin) I.; B.S., U. Chgo., 1951; Ph.D., Princeton, 1954; m. Joan Gilbreath, Aug. 1, 1960; children—Margaret, John Claiborne, Brecht. NSF fellow Inst. Advanced Study, Princeton, 1956-57; faculty U. Wash., 1957-65, prof. math., 1962-65; prof. Case Western Res. U., 1965-69; prof. State U. N.Y., Buffalo, 1969—. Served with AUS, 1954-56. Mem. Am. Math. Soc., Am. Assn. U. Profs. Author: Uniform Spaces, 1964; also numerous articles. Office: 4246 Ridge Lea Rd Amherst NY 14226

ISBELL, MARION WILLIAM restaurant and hotel exec.; b. nr. Memphis, Aug. 12, 1905; s. Howard James and Mary (Mayfield) I.; student pub. schs.; m. Ingrid Ludica Helsing, Oct. 2, 1927; children—Marion William, Mary Elaine, Robert James. Owner, pres., dir. Isbell's, chain of restaurants, Chgo., 1943-46; pres. Ramada Inns, Inc., 1962-70, chmn. bd., 1962—. Chief instl. users br. OPA, 1943-45, dir. Chgo. Met. Area, 1943-45; active A.R.C., Chgo. Community Fund. Mem. Nat. (past pres., dir.), Chgo (past pres., dir.) restaurant assns. Club: Executives (Chgo.). Office: Ramada Inns 3838 E Van Buren St Phoenix AZ 85008

ISBELL, MARION WILLIAM, Jr. motel chain exec.; b. Chgo., July 8, 1935; s. Marion William and Ingrid (Helsing) I.; B.A., U. Notre Dame, 1958; m. Susan K. Greenleaf, May 19, 1962; children—Marion William III, Madeline B. Andrew G., John Bardon. Various positions Isbell's Restaurant, Chgo., summers 1950-58; pres. Ramada Inns, Inc., Phoenix, 1962—. Served to lt. (j.g.) USNR, Phoenix br.). Home: 5306 N Wilkinson Rd Paradise Valley AZ 85253 Office: 3838 E Van Buren St Phoenix AZ 85008

ISBELL, N. PAUL, physician and surgeon; b. Denver, Sept. 9, 1904; s. Harvey Gilbert and Mary Elnora (White) I.; A.B., U. Denver, 1926; M.D., U. Colo., 1930; m. Stella Dee Hopkins, Aug. 19, 1939; children—Albert Russell Burgess, Rachel Mae Burgess Gillespie, Michael Paul. Intern Charity Hosp., New Orleans, 1930-32; fellow pathology Harvard, 1946-47; pvt. practice obstetrics and gynecology, Denver, 1932-42, 47—; chief Denver Gen. div. U. Colo. dept. obstetrics and gynecologists, 1952-62; clin. prof. gynecology U. Colo. Med. Sch., 1957—. Pres. Colo. div. Am. Cancer Soc., 1967; chmn. cancer com. Colo.-Wyo. Regional Med. Program, 1967-69; mem. Colo. Health Planning Council, 1967-69. Served with USAAF, 1942-46. Recipient Alumni award U. Colo. Sch. Medicine, 1962. Diplomate Am. Bd. Obstetrics and Gynecology. Fellow A.C.S., Internat. Coll. Surgeons; mem. Am. Soc. Cytology (pres. 1969), Am. Coll. Obstetrics and Gynecology (chmn. Colo. sect. 1968-70), Central Assn. Obstetrics and Gynecology, N.Y. Acad. Sci. Mason (33 hon.). Home: 2945 E Kentucky Av Denver CO 80209 Office: 1801 Williams St Denver CO 80218

ISBELL, ROBERT, banker; b. Anderson, S.C., Nov. 26, 1923; s. Henry Pope and Aileen Annette (Dixon) I.; A.B. in Journalism, U. S.C., 1948; grad. Sch. Financial Pub. Relations, Northwestern U., 1965; m. Frances Griffin, Apr. 19, 1953; children—Lyn, Andrea, Glen. News editor Elkin (N.C.) Tribune, 1948-50; mng. editor Florence (S.C.) Morning News, 1950-53; pub. relations counsel Tobias & Co., Charleston, S.C., 1954-62; v.p. Bankers Trust of S.C., Columbia, 1963-68; sr. v.p., adminstr. marketing S.C. Nat. Bank, Columbia, 1969—; mem. faculty Sch. Banking of South, La. State U., summers, 1971—. Pres. Watauga (N.C.) Crippled Children's drive, 1955, Carolina Carillon, 1968. Served with AUS, 1943-46; PTO. Recipient Silver medal Am. Advt. Fedn., 1966, Laurel award (White's Dept. Store, Columbia, 1969. Mem. Am. Advt. Fedn. (S.C. gov. 1966-67), Columbia Advt. Council (pres. 1966), Pub. Relations Soc. Am. (dir. S.C. chpt. 1969—). Episcopalian. Clubs: Forest Lake Country, Palmetto (Columbia). Home: 3011 Petigru St Columbia SC 29204 Office: 1241 Main St Columbia SC 29202

ISBIN, HERBERT STANFORD, educator; b. Seattle, Dec. 9, 1919; s. Isadore and Rose (Metzger) I.; B.S., U. Wash., 1940, M.S., 1941; postgrad. U. Minn., 1941-43; Sc.D., Mass. Inst. Tech., 1947; m. Katherine Brudnoy, June 15, 1948; children—Ira Michael, Neil Walter, Sharon Gail, Rena Ann. Chem. engr. Md. Research Labs., 1943-45; chem. engr. Gen. Electric Hanford Works, Richland, Wash., 1947-50; prof. dept. chem. engring. U. Minn., Mpls., 1950—; mem. adv. com. on reactor safeguards AEC. Mem. Am. Inst. Chem. Engrs. (past chmn. nuclear engring. div.). Author: Introductory Nuclear Reactor Theory, 1963. Contbr. articles to profl. jours. Home: 2815 Monterey Pkwy Minneapolis MN 55416

ISBRANDT, RALPH H., ret. automobile mfg. co. exec.; b. Milw., Apr. 9, 1905; s. Herman and Fredericka (Roeming) I.; ed. pub. schs., Milw., also extension courses; m. Loraine D. Dauer, Aug. 28, 1926; children—Loraine (Mrs. Arthur F. Eliason), Donald R. Automotive engr. Buick Motor div. Gen. Motors Corp., 1926-29, Nash-Kelvinator Corp., 1929-36, Firestone Tire & Rubber Co., 1936-43; v.p. Firestone Aircraft Co., 1943-47; chief engr. Kaiser Frazier Corp., 1947-53; with Am. Motors Corp., 1953-70, dir. engring, and research, 1956-61, v.p. engring. and research, 1961-68, v.p. product staff, 1968-70; cons., 1970—. Mem. Nat. Motor Vehicle Safety Adv. Council, Dept. of Transp. Mem. Soc. Automotive Engrs. (pres. 1967), Automobile Mfrs. Assn., Am. Ordnance Assn. Lutheran. Club: Western Golf and Country (Detroit). Home: Seville House 299 N Riverside Dr Pompano Beach FL 33062

ISBRANDTSEN, WALDEMAR MIRUS, shipping co. exec.; b. Bklyn., Nov. 8, 1916; s. Hans Jeppesen and Gertrude Eugenie (Mirus) I.; student Dartmouth, 1935-37, 39; grad. U.S. Merchant Marine Acad., 1944; m. Evelyn Elizabeth Kelley, Mar. 25, 1944; children—Lynne Mirus, Dirk Hans, Carl Walter, Jeffrey A., J. Michelle; m. 2d, Norma Harriet Weaver. Longshoreman, S. Scottnex & Co., 1934-35; steamship apprentice H. Hogarth & Son Ltd., Glasgow, Scotland and London, Eng., 1937-38; with Isbrandtsen Miller Co., Inc., N.Y.C., 1939-41; at sea with Army Transp. Service, also United Fruit Co., 1942-43, Moore-McCormack Steamship Co. and Trinidad Corp., 1944-47; with Isbrandtsen Sons & Co., 1947-51; owners operations rep., Pacific Far East Line, Philippines, 1949-51; with Isbrandtsen Co., Inc., (became Am. Export Isbrandtsen Lines Inc., 1964), 1951—, v.p. export despatch div., 1964-65, v.p. research and devel., 1965—, also dir., v.p., dir. subsidiaries; founding dir. Walter Isbrandtsen & Assos. Ltd. Past pres., dir. Bulk Packaging and Containerization Inst.; past del. N. Am. to Internat. Container Bur., Paris, France. Bd. dirs. Talbor Perkins Adoption Service, Bklyn. Recipient Presdl. Commendation for Service at Sea, 1946; named Transp. Man of Year, 1962. Mem. Nat. Def. Transp. Assn., Transp. Research Forum, Am. Mgmt. Assn., C. of C. State N.Y., Alumni Assn. U.S. Merchant Marine Acad. (Bus. Man of Year award 1960), Internat. Longshoreman's Assn., Phi Tau. Patentee self loading, self discharging granular and liquid bulk cargo lighter. Home: care Bruck 25 Central Park W New York City NY 10023 Office: 26 Broadway New York City NY 10004

ISELIN, JOHN JAY, journalist; b. Greenville, S.C., Dec. 8, 1933; s. William Jay and Fannie Harrington (Humphreys) I.; grad. St. Mark's Sch., 1952; A.B., Harvard, 1956; B.A., Corpus Christi Coll., Cambridge (Eng.) U., 1958, M.A., 1963; Ph.D., Harvard, 1965; m. Josephine Lea Barnes, Sept. 8, 1956; children—William Jay II, Benjamin Barnes, Josephine Lea, Fannie, Alison. Research fellow Brookings Instn., 1960-61; sr. writer Congl. Quar., 1961; corr.-editor Newsweek mag., 1962-69, sr. editor nat. affairs, 1965- 69; v.p., pub. Harper & Row, Pubs., Inc., 1969-71; v.p. Ednl. Broadcasting Corp., gen. mgr. Channel 13, WNET, N.Y.C., 1971—. Bd. overseers Harvard. Clubs: Metropolitan, Federal City (Washington). Home: 159 E 61st St New York City NY 10022 Office: 304 W 58th St New York City NY 10019

ISENBERGH, MAX, lawyer, educator, musician; b. Albany, N.Y., Aug. 28, 1913; s. David William and Tess (Solomon) I.; A.B., Cornell U., 1934; J.D., Harvard, 1938, LL.M., 1939, A.M., 1942; m. Pearl Evans, Aug. 10, 1939; children—Tess, David William, Joseph. Admitted to N.Y. bar, 1938; U.S. Supreme Ct. bar, 1945, D.C. bar, 1950; fellow Harvard Law School, 1938-39; tutor U. Chgo. Law Sch., 1939-40; various govt. positions, 1940-48; legal sec. to U.S. Supreme Ct. Justice Hugo Black, 1941-42; special asst. to atty. gen. U.S., 1944-48; counsel European operations Am. Jewish Com., 1948-50; legal adviser Point Four Program, State Dept., 1950-51; gen. counsel Pres.'s Materials Policy Commn., 1951-52; dep. gen. counsel AEC, cons. internat. affairs, 1952-56; spl. asst. for atomic energy Am. embassy, Paris, 1956-61; dep. asst. sec. of state for edn. and cultural affairs, 1961-62; chmn. U.S. delegation to UNESCO Conf. on Protection Cultural Property, 1962; counsel to chmn. Communications Satellite Corp., 1962-63; prof. George Washington U. Law Sch., 1963-65, U. Md. Law Sch., 1970—; vis. prof. U. Va. Law Sch., 1956- 66, 68, 69, Yale Law Sch., 1966-67, Am. U. Law Sch., 1969-70; cons. Peace Corps, 1966—; prof. law Salzburg (Austria) Seminar Am. Studies, summer 1965; cons. Internat. Atomic Energy Agy., Vienna, Austria, also European Nuclear Energy Agy., Paris. Participated as delegate, adviser, ofcl. observer numerous internat. confs. Exec. com. 3d Inter-Am. Music Festival; bd. dirs. Washington Chamber Orch.; bd. dirs. Philip M. Stern Family Fund; media review panel Nat. Cultural Center. Recipient Rockefeller Pub. Service award, 1954. Member Cercle Culturel de Royaumont, Asnieres (S. et O.) France, Friends of Washington Chamber Orch. (pres.), Am. Fedn. Musicians, Phi Beta Kappa, Pi Lambda Phi (past pres. chpt.). Club: Cosmos (Washington). Editor Harvard Law Review, 1937-38. Author articles, book reviews. Active musical circles Washington and Paris, occasionally playing clarinet in pub. performances; concerts in U.S. Europe. Home: 2216 Massachusetts Av NW Washington DC 20008 Office: 500 W Baltimore St Baltimore MD 21201

ISENBURGER, ERIC, artist; b. Frankfurt on Main, Germany, May 27, 1902; s. Sally R. and Olga (Neurmond) I.; student Art Sch., Frankfurt on Main; m. Jula Elenbogen, Dec. 10, 1927. Came to U.S.,

1941, naturalized, 1949. One-man shows Gallery Gurlitt, Berlin, Germany, 1933. Gallery Modern, Stockholm, Sweden, 1934-38, Gallery Wolfgang Gurlitt, Munich, Germany, 1962, Knoedler Galleries, N.Y.C., 1941, 43, 45, 47, 48, 50, 53, 55, Balt. Mus., 1943, DeYoung Meml. Mus., San Francisco, 1945, Springfield (Mass.) Mus., 1945, Colorado Springs Fine Arts Center, 1945, John Herron Art Inst., Indpls., 1946, others; represented in permanent collections Wadsworth Atheneum, Hartford, Conn., Mus. Tel-Aviv, Israel, Ency. Britannica, Pa. Acad. Fine Arts, also colls. Mus. Modern Art, Pa. Acad. Fine Arts, Corcoran Gallery Art, Bezalel Mus. of Jerusalem, John Herron Art Inst., Indpls., M.H. de Young Mus., San Francisco, Am. Acad. Arts and Letters, N.A.D., others. Recipient prize N.A.D., 1945, Edwin Palmer Meml. prize 1957, Henry Ward Ranger Fund purchase, 1957; 3rd prize Carnegie Inst., 1947; Medal of Honor, Pepsi Cola Art competition, 1948; 1st prize and Corcoran gold medal Corcoran Gallery Art, 1949; Thomas Proctor Prize N.A.D., 1963; Salmagundi Club prize N.A.A.D., 1966; Edwin Palmer Meml. prize N.A.D., 1970. Mem. N.A.D. (council 1964—), Audubon Artists (award 1969, Jane Peterson medal and prize 1971); Home: 140 E 56th St New York City NY 10022

ISENBURGER, HERBERT RUDOLF indsl. radiologist; b. Frankfurt a/Main, Germany, July 22, 1900; student schs. of Frankfurt on Main and Berlin, Germany; m. Anne Landsman, July 11, 1930. Came to U.S., 1925, naturalized, 1932. Asso. Dr. Ancel St. John, 1927; pres. St. John X-Ray Service., 1933; owner St. John X-Ray Lab., Califon, N.J., 1946—. Mem. gov's adv. com. on radiation protection, 1954-56. Mem. Am. Soc. M.E. (rep. on ANSI com. equipment for non-med. radiation applications), Am. Soc. Testing Materials, Am. Soc. for Metals, Soc. for Nondestructive Testing. Author: Industrial Radiology (with Ancel St. John), 1943; also bibliographies on indsl. radiology, X-Ray stress analysis and filmbadge monitoring. Contbr. to Ency. Chem. Tech. Pioneer in field of indsl. radiology; expert in X-ray diffraction and X-ray stress analysis: developed film monitoring for civil def.; 3 X-ray machines accepted by Smithsonian Instn. Address: Califon NJ 07830

ISERN, MILTON ALVIN, banker; b. Ellinwood, Kan., June 22, 1901; s. Edward Dietrich and Lydia (Mellies) I.; LL.B., U. Kan., 1923; m. Helen Lucile Weber, Apr. 18, 1905; children-Carolyn (Mrs. Dean Wells), Alan. With Peoples State Bank, Ellinwood, 1924—, pres., 1948-70, chmn. bd., 1970—; ind. oil producer, 1930—; dir. Kan. State Network. Mem. Bd. Edn., Ellinwood Sch. Dist., 1950-58. Mayor, Ellinwood, 1935-38. Bd. dirs. Lutheran Ch.-Mo. Synod, 1967—, Lutheran Social Service, Greater U. Kan. Fund. Named Kan. Oil Man of Year, 1959. Mem. Kan. C. of C. Home: 512 W 3d St Ellinwood KS 67526 Office: Box 546 Ellinwood KS 67526

ISHAK, YUSOFFBIN, pres. of Singapore; b. Aug. 12, 1910; ed. Raffles Inst., Singapore. Mem. staff Warta Malaya, 1932-39; founder Malay paper Utusan Melayu, 1939, mng. dir., editor, 1946-59; chmn. Pub. Service Commn., 1959; head of state of Singapore, 1959-65; 1st pres. Republic of Singapore after independence, 1965—. Address: The Istana Singapore*

ISHAM, JAMES LIVINGSTON, advt. exec.; b. St. Louis, Apr. 28, 1920; s. Emmett Louis and Delphine (Lanning) I.; B. Journalism, U. Mo., 1942; m. Mary Josephine Dobbine, Mar. 6, 1943: children—Randolph D., John L., William P. Copy writer K. E. Shepard Agy., Chgo., 1946; writer Donald L. Campbell Assos., pub. relations. Chgo., 1946-47; copy writer Aubrey, Moore & Wallace Agy., Chgo., 1947-48; with Needham, Harper & Steers. Inc., Chgo., 1948—, dir. creative services, 1959-62, v.p., 1954-60, exec. v.p., 1960-67; pres., 1967—, also dir., chmn. plans bd. Served to lt. (s.g.) USNR, 1942-46. Club: University, MidAm. (Chgo.). Home: 921 Private Rd Winnetka IL 60093 Office: Needham Harper & Steers Inc 401 N Michigan Av Chicago IL 60610

ISHERWOOD, CHRISTOPHER author; B. High Lane, Chesire, Eng., Aug. 26, 1904; s. Francis Edward and Kathleen (Machell-Smith) I.; student Repton Sch., 1919-22, Corpus Christi Coll., Cambridge, 1924-25; unmarried. Came to U.S., 1939, naturalized, 1946. Sec. to Music Soc. String Quartet. London, 1926-27; med. student U. London, 1927-28; pvt. tchr. English, Berlin, 1928-33; travelled in Europe and China, 1934-38; scenario-writer for M.G.M., Warner Bros. and other motion picture studios intermittently, 1939—; free-lance writer 1926—; guest prof. Modern English lit. at Los Angeles State Coll. and U. Cal. at Santa Barbara, 1959-60; Regents prof. U. Cal. at Los Angeles, 1965, U. Cal. at Riverside, 1966. Worked with Am. Friends Service Com. on refugee relief project, Haverford, Pa., 1941-42; editor Vedanta and the West (mag.), Hollywood, 1943-44. Recipient N.Y. Drama Critics Circle award, best musical, Cabaret (based on his stories), 1966-67. Mem. Am. Civil Liberties Union, Wider Quaker Fellowship, Screenwriters Guild, Nat. Inst. Arts and Letters. Vedantist. Author books including: Prater Violet, 1945; and the World in the Evening (novel), 1954; co-author plays with W.H. Avden including: On the Frontier, 1938; translator; The Intimate Journals of Charles Baudelaire, 1947; The Bhagavad-Gita (with Swami Prabhavananda), 1944; The CrestJewel of Discrimination (with Swami Prabhavananda), 1947; How to Know God (with Swami Prabhavananda), 1953; (travel) The Condor and the Cows, 1949; Stage play, I Am A Camera (adapted by John van Druten from stories) (critics award, 1951); Down There On A Visit, 1962; A Single Man, 1964; Ramakrishna and His Disciples; Exhumations, 1966; A Meeting by the River, 1967; Kathleen and Frank, 1971. Editor Vendanta for the Western World with introduction, and several contbns., 1945. Home: 145 Adelaide Dr Santa Monica CA 90402

ISHINO, IWAO, educator; b. San Diego, Cal., Mar. 10, 1921; s. Tomota and Tei (Yoshizuka) I.; Ph.D., Harvard, 1954; m. Mary Tomiko Kobayashi, June 18, 1944; children—Marilyn (Mrs. William G. Tanner), Catherine, Ellen, Tomi. Asst. prof. sociology and anthropology Ohio State U., 1951-56; prof. anthopology Mich. State U., 1956—; Fulbright lectr. U. Tokyo, 1958-59; vis. prof. U. Ryukyus, Okinawa, 1963-65. Served with AUS, 1946-47. Mem. Am. Anthropol. Assn., A.A.A.S., Soc. Applied Anthropology. Author: (with John Bennett) Paternalism in the Japanese Economy, 1963; (with Dynes, Clarke & Dinitz) Social Problems: Dissensus and Deviation in an Industrial Society, 1964. Home: 1736 Ann St East Lansing MI 48823

ISIDORE, ANTHONY, advt. exec.; b. Rochester, N.Y., June 13, 1933; s. Violante and Agnes (Taverrite) I.; B.A. in English Lit., Rutgers U., 1955; m. Nancy Ruth Meyer, Dec. 30, 1956; children—Christopher Allen, Adam Philip. Copywriter, Rumrill Co., Rochester, 1957-59; with Young & Rubicam, Inc., N.Y.C., 1959—, sr. v.p., 1969—. Trustee Inst. Advanced Advt. Studies. Served with AUS, 1956-57. Recipient Gold Key award N.Y. Copy Club, 1969 (3), 70 (2), Clio award Am. TV and Radio Festival, 1966, 67, 68 (5), 69 (3), Andy award Ad Writers N.Y., 1967, 68 (3), 69 (2), award Internat. Broadcast Assn., 1967, 68 (3), 69. Home: 16 Kipp St Chappaqua NY 10514 Office: 285 Madison Av New York City NY 10017

ISLEIB, HORACE F., banker; b. Wilkinsburg, Pa., Nov. 11, 1909; s. Albert Henry and Florence Eleanor (Oatman) I.; grad. N.Y. Mil. Acad.; B.S., Yale, 1933; m. Anna Theodora Elmendorf, June 29, 1934; children-Elizabeth Lawrence, Jonathan Bartlett, Lawrence Bartlett. Security Analyst Dubosque & Co., N.Y.C., 1933-34. Granberry Marache & Lord, 1934-42; with Yale, 1942-58, successively asst. to treas., asst. sec., 1946-58, asst. treas., asso. treas., 1962-58, investment officer, 1954-58; trustee,treas. Sheffield Sci. Sch., 1954-58; gen. partner Jesup & Lamont, N.Y.C., 1958-68; exec. v.p. Conn. Savs. Bank, New Haven, 1969—, also dir. Trustee Yale-In- China Assn., Inc.; dir. Flexible Tubing Corp. (Guilford, Conn.), C. S. Mersick & Co., Human Relations Area Files, Inc., Tropical Gas Co., (Miami, Fla.), Kaneb Pipe Line Co., Augusta Pipe Line Co. (Houston). Trustee New Haven Orphan Asylum, Family Service of New Haven, Bethany Library Assn.; dir., treas. Bethany Pub. Health Nursing Agy., Inc.; dir. internat. research on Communist Techniques, Inc.; mem. Town Bd. Finance. Bethany. Mem. Mory's Assn. New Haven, Chi Phi. Republican. Episcopalian. Clubs: N.Y. Yacht, Yale (N.Y.C.); Faculty, Graduates, Kiwanis (New Haven) Am. Yacht (Rye, N.Y.); Essex (Conn.) Yacht. Home: Lyme Ct New Haven CT 06371 Office: 47 Church St New Haven CT 06501

ISMAIL, ABDUL MALEK, diplomat of Yemen; b. Aden, Yemen, Nov. 26, 1937; s. Ismail Mohamed and Aisha (Naser) Hussain; student Tech. Inst. Aden, 1953-56, Secondary Sch., Cairo, 1956-60, Cairo U., 1960-61; m. Hana Alazab, Sept. 25, 1963; children—Khaled, Alia, Nahla. Chmn. Petroleum Workers Union, Aden, 1962-64; v.p. Arab Fedn. Petroleum Workers, Cairo, 1962-65; minister of labour and social affairs, 1967-68, minister of economy, 1968-69; dir.-gen. Office of the Prime Minister, 1969-70; ambassador, permanent rep. People's Democracy of Yemen to UN, 1970—. Mem. steering com. Arab Nationalist Movement, 1956-63; mem. high comd. Nat. Liberation Front, Aden, 1963-68. Decorated 1st Class medal UAR. Mem. Aden Sports Assn. (adminstrv. com.). Home: 340 Overlook Rd New Rochelle NY 10804 Office: 211 E 43d St New York City NY 10017

ISMAIL, BIN MOHAMED ALI, Malaysian banker; b. Port Swettenham, Malaya, Sept. 16, 1918; s. Mohamed Ali bin Taib and Khatijah; B.A., Trinity Hall, Cambridge U., Eng., 1941, M.A., 1945; Barrister-at-Law, Middle Temple, Inn of Court, London, Eng., 1943; m. Maimunah, Mar. 12, 1949; children—Iskander, Ahmad Kamal. Radio news broadcaster, commentator Malay sect. BBC, London, 1944-46; lectr. Malay, Sch. Oriental Studies, U. London, Eng., 1944-45; with Malayan Civil Service, 1946-68; asst. state sec. Govt. State of Selangor Malaya, 1948-50; asst. econ. sec. treasury Fedn. of Malaya, 1950-53; econ. officer, Penang, 1954-55; controller trade div. Ministry Commerce and Industry, 1955-57; minister Fedn. of Malaya Embassy, Washington, 1957-59; exec. dir. Internat. Bank Reconstrn. and Devel., rep. Fedn. Malaya, Ghana, Indonesia, Libya, Morocco, Tunisia, 1958-60; dir. Internat. Financial Corp., 1958-60; econ. minister Fedn. Malaya Embassy, 1959-60; dep. gov. Central Bank of Malaysia, 1960-62, gov., 1962—; chmn. Malaysian Indsl. Devel. Finance Ltd., 1969—; adviser Nat. Corp., 1970—. Mem. Nat. Devel. Planning Com. Rep., UN Econ. Commn. Asia and Far East, Lahore, 1951, Rangoon, 1952, Bandung, 1953, Bangkok, 1957, UN Gen. Assembly, 1957; Commonwealth Finance Ministers Conf., Mont Tremblanc, Que., 1957, Commonwealth Trade and Econ. Conf., Montreal, 1958. Mem. council U. Malaya. Mem. Malaysian Inst. Mgmt. (pres. 1966-68), Asian Inst. Mgmt. (gov. 1971—). Club: Royal Selangor Golf (pres. 1964). Home: 23 Jalan Natesa Kuala Lumpur Malaysia Office: Central Bank of Malaysia Kuala Lumpur Malaysia

ISNOR, GORDON BENJAMIN, Canadian politician; b. Dartmouth, N.S., May 10, 1885; s. William Henry and Annie M. (Hubley) I.; ed. pub. schs., Maritime Bus. Coll.; m. Mary E. Ormond, Sept. 3, 1907; 1 son, W. Roy. Pres. Gordon B. Isnor, Ltd., Halifax, N.S., 1906—, Isnor Investment Co., Ltd., Halifax, 1906—; dir. N.S. Light & Power Co., Ltd., Can. Permanent Trust Co. (Toronto). Alderman City of Halifax, 1914-15; mem. N.S. Legislature, 1928-34; elected Canadian House of Commons, 1935-49; apptd. life mem. Senate, 1950—. Served to lt., Canadian Army, 1915-18. Mason (Shriner), K.P. Clubs: Progressive Service, Halifax, Mayflower Curling, Weagwoltic Boating, Armdale Yacht, Port of Halifax (Halifax). Home: 2094 Robie St Halifax Nova Scotia Canada Office: 2169 Gottingen St Halifax Nova Scotia Canada

ISONG, CLEMENT NYONG, banker; b. Ikot Osong, Nigeria, Apr. 20, 1920; s. Nathaniel Udo and Obot (Udo Udom) I.; tchrs. certificate, Methodist Coll., Uzuakoli, 1940, Univ. Coll., Ibadan, 1948; B.A., Ia., Wesleyan Coll., 1954; M.A. Harvard 1955, Ph.D., 1957; m. Une Akpaete, Dec. 1957; children—Ekaete, Clement, Umo, Eno, Inyang. Tchr., Meth. Central Sch., Oyubia, Oron, Nigeria, 1940; headmaster Meth. Sch., Ukpuj, Ikot Ekpene, 1941-45; master Oron (Nigeria) Boys' High Sch., 1946-51; asst. economist Fed. Reservice Bank, N.Y.C., 1957; lectr. Univ. Coll., Ibadan, Nigeria, 1958; sec. Central Bank Nigeria, Lagos, 1959-61, dir. research, 1961-62; adviser African dept. Internat. Monetary Fund, Washington, 1962-67; gov. Central Bank Nigeria, Lagos, 1967—, chmn. bd. dir., 1967—; alternate gov. Nigeria, Internat. Monetary Fund, 1967—. Chmn. Nat. Wages Adv. Com. Council, Fed. Ministry Labour, 1967—. Nat. trustee Boy Scouts Nigeria. Club: Island. Home: 6 Queen's Dr Ikoyo Lagos Nigeria Office: Tinubu Sq PMB 12194 Lagos Nigeria

ISRAEL, ADRIAN CREMIEUX, investment banker; b. N.Y.C., Nov. 6, 1915; s. Aldolph Cremieux and Babette (Bloch) I.; grad. Phillips Acad., Andover, Mass., 1932; B.S., Yale, 1936; m. Helene Levison, July 24, 1953 (dec.); children by previous marriage—Ellen I. Rosen, Andrew C., Thomas C. With A.C. Israel Commodity Co., Inc., N.Y.C., 1936—, pres., 1945-65, chmn. bd., 1965—; limited partner Bache & Co., N.Y.C., 1945-64, gen. partner, chmn. exec. com., 1964-65; pres., dir. Bache & Co. Inc., N.Y.C., 1965-66, Adrian & James, Inc., Stamford, Conn., 1936—; chmn. bd. Lane Drug Co., Inc., Cleve., 1956—, Ingleside Industries, Inc., 1965—, Havenfield Corp., 1967—, Health Mart, Inc., 1968—, Reed Drug Co., Lee Drug Co. of Ga., 1970—, A.C. Israel Woodhouse & Co., London, 1970—. Mem. N.Y. Coffee and Sugar Exchange, N.Y., Coffee and Sugar Clearing Assn., N.Y. Cocoa Exchange, N.Y., Cocoa Clearing Exchange, Commodity Exchange, Commodity Exchange Rubber Clearing Assn., N.Y. Produce Exchange, Commodity Exchange Metal Clearing Assn., Inc.; allied mem. N.Y., Nat., Am., Pacific Coast stock exchanges. Cons. WPB, also War Food Adminstrn., 1942-46. Pres. A. Cremieux Israel Found., 1946—; mem. Yale Devel. Bd., 1965—, Trustee Monefiore Hosp., N.Y.C., bd. incorporators Stamford Hosp. Clubs: Wall Street, Yale, Bond (N.Y.C.); Century Country (Purchase, N.Y.); Stanwich (Greenwich, Conn.); Bermuda Dunes (Cal.) Country; Mid-Ocean (Bermuda). Home: 247 Ingleside Rd Stamford CT 06903 Office: 110 Wall St New York City NY 10005

ISRAEL, DORMAN DANIEL, engring., mgmt. cons.; b. Newport, Ky., July 21, 1900; s. Charles L. and Emma (Linz) I.; E.E., U. Cin., 1923; m. Frances Julia Murr, April 3, 1924; 1 dau., Betty Murr (Mrs. Edgard Schwab). Radio design engr. Crosley Radio Corp., Cin. 1921-23, chief redio engr., 1932-36; chief engr. Emerson Radio and Phonograph Corp., N.Y., 1936-42, v.p. in charge engring., 1942-44, dir., 1943-66, v.p. in charge engring. and prodn., 1944-47, exec., v.p., 1947-64, chmn. exec. com., 1951-59, vice chmn. bd., 1964-66; sr. v.p. engring. Emerson TV and Radio Co. div. Nat. Union Electric Corp., 1966-67; pres., treas. Dorman D. Israel & Assos., Inc., 1968—; chmn. Granco Products, Inc., 1961-63; pres., dir. Plastimold Corp., 1946-56, Radio Speakers Inc., 1946-50; with radio and TV mfr. Internat. Exec. Service Corps., Tehran and Hamadan, Iran, 1970-71. Instr. radio engring. evening coll. U. Cin. 1928-31. Chmn. joint tech. adv. com. Radio Electronics TV Mfrs. Assn. and Inst. Radio Engrs., 1955, 56, 64-67. Mem. OCSigO adv. com. Electronic Aids Army Aviation, 1952-53, tech. adv. panel on Electronics, Dept. Def. 1955-57; mem. FCC gen. industry adv. com. N.Y. UHF-TV project. Fellow I.E.E.E. (life); mem. Radio Electronic Mfrs. Assn. (chmn. receivers sect. 1939-50, chmn. gen. standards com. 1950-57). Recipient awards from War Dept., Navy Bur. of Ships and Bur. of Aeros., OSRD and OSS; Spl. award Radio and Electronic Mfrs. Assn., and Inst. Radio Engrs. Profl. Group on Broadcast and TV Receivers, 1957, 67; Distinguished Alumnus award, U. Cin., 1969. Pres. Temple Israel, New Rochelle, 1950-51, trustee, 1942-52, hon. bd. mem. 1952—. Mason. Club: Quaker Ridge Golf. Contbr. numerous papers to tech. publs. Home and Office: 605 Harrison Av Harrison NY 10528 ☆

ISRAEL, LARRY HERBERT, broadcasting co. exec.; b. McKeesport, Pa., Nov. 4, 1919; s. Nathan and Sophia (Eliashof) I.; B.J., U. Mo., 1948; m. Audrey Westerman, Oct. 14, 1951; children—Susan, Howard. Vice pres., gen. mgr. sta. WENS-TV, Pitts., also gen. mgr. KMGM, Mpls., 1953-57; gen. mgr. sta. WJZ-TV, Balt., 1957-59; v.p., gen. mgr. Television Advt. Reps., 1959-61, pres., 1961-63, also dir.; exec. v.p. Westinghouse Broadcasting Co., 1963-66; pres. Westinghouse Broadcasting Sta. Group, 1966-68; chmn. bd., chief exec. officer Post-Newsweek Stas., Inc., 1968—; v.p., dir. Washington Post Co., 1968—. Mem. Newcomen Soc., Mo. Soc. N.Y., Kappa Tau Alpha, Sigma Delta Chi. Home: 22 Stanmore Ct Potomac MD 20854 Office: Broadcast House 40th and Brandywine Sts N W Washington DC 20016

ISRAEL, ROBERT HENRY, psychiatrist; b. Wapello County, Ia., Oct. 1, 1900; s. Lon H. and Mabel (Rock) I.; M.D., U. Ore., 1923; m. Helen Marie Webber, Aug. 4, 1927; children—Leslie Jean (Mrs. Edward Schrag, Jr.), Anne Marie (Mrs. Owen Roth.), John Robert. Mem. staff Warren (Pa.) State Hosp., 1926-70, supt., 1935-70. Life fellow Am. Psychiat. Assn.; mem. A.M.A., Pa. Psychiat. Assn. (past pres.). Address: 20 4th Av Warren PA 16365

ISRAEL, S. LEON, physician, educator; b. Phila., Jan. 29, 1906; s. Emanuel and Rebecca (Cohen) I.; A.B., U. Pa., 1926, M.D., 1930; m. Esther Seitchik, Dec. 22, 1929; 1 son, Robert. Intern Mt. Sinai Hosp., Phila., 1930-31, chief resident, 1931-33; postgrad. univs. Vienna and Budapest, 1933-35; faculty Sch. Medicine and Grad. Sch. Medicine, U. Pa., 1935-71, prof. obstetrics and gynecology schs. medicine, 1960-71, emeritus, 1971—, former dir. div. obstetrics and gynecology Pa. Hosp.; prof. obsetrics and gynecology Coll. Medicine, U. Fla., 1971—. Fulbright lectr. Australia and New Zealand, 1960. Diplomate Am. Bd. Obstetrics and Gynecology (dir. 1961-68). Fellow Am. Gynecol. Soc.; mem. Am. Assn. Obstetricians and Gynecologists, Am. Coll. Obstetricians and Gynecologists, A.C.S., Am. Fertility Soc., Alpha Omega Alpha. Author: Menstrual Disorders and Sterility, 5th edit., 1967. Editor Obstetrics and Gynecology, 1966—. Address: J Hillis Miller Health Center Gainesville GA 32601

ISRAEL, SAM, Jr., coffee importer; b. New Orleans, July 7, 1910; s. Samuel and Edna (Shwartz) I.; student Tulane U., 1927-28; m. Merryl Silverstein, Dec. 1, 1931; 1 son, Lawrence Joseph. With Leon Israel & Bros., Inc., green coffee importers, New Orleans, 1928—, pres., 1946—; dir. Times- Picayune Pub. Co., Hibernia Nat. Bank New Orleans, also dir. Delta Capital Corp. Mem. Bd. Liquidation City Debt New Orleans; former pres. Bd. Comms. Port of New Orleans; mem. study assessment group Mayor New Orleans, Miss. Valley World Trade Council, Council Lower Miss. River Port Interests, Bur. Govt. Research, Council Better La., Met. New Orleans Crime Commn. Bd. dir. Internat. Trade Mart; bd. adminstrs. ednl. fund Tulane U. Served to lt. col. Transp. Corps, AUS, 1942-45; ETO. Decorated Bronze Star with oak leaf cluster; French Medal Merit. Mem. Nat. Coffee Assn. (chmn. fgn. affairs com.), N.Y. Coffee and Sugar Exchange, New Orleans Bd. Trade, Mil. Order World Wars, Confererie de la Chaine des Rotisseurs, Confrerie des Chevaliers du Tastevin, Fgn. Relations Assn. New Orleans. Jewish religion. Clubs: Internat. House (dir., exec. com., chmn. nominating com.), Timberlane Country, Lakewood Country (New Orleans). Home: 1331 1st St New Orleans LA 70130

ISRAEL, W.W., mfg. co. exec. Sr. v.p. Chamberlain Mfg. Corp. Office: 845 Larch Av Elmhurst IL 60126*

ISRAELI, NATHAN, psychologist; b. Williamsport, Pa., Aug. 19, 1906; s. Phineas and Sophia (Kaplan) I.; B.S. (Tremain scholar 1925), Coll. City N.Y., 1926; student Harvard, 1926; M.A., Columbia, 1927, Ph.D., 1930; M.Social Sci., New Sch. Social Research, 1941; m. Doris Solomon, June 28, 1940; children—Miriam Stella, Beulah Rachel (dec.), Phineas Robert. Reader philosophy and psychology Coll. City N.Y., 1928-30; asst. prof. psychology U. Me., 1930-31; gen. sci. tchr. James Madison High Sch., Bklyn., 1931-32, Thomas Jefferson High Sch., Bklyn., 1934; research Inst. Human Relations, Yale, also Worchester (Mass.) State Hosp., 1932; Bethlem Royal, Maudsley hosps. in Great Britain, 1932-33, high schs. in Scotland, 1933; social investigator Dept. Welfare, N.Y.C., 1939-41; personnel worker, state tech. adv. service Social Security Bd., 1941; with ordnance dept. War Dept., 1942-43; with standards and spl. studies sect., personnel classification div. U.S. Civil Service Commn., 1943-48; mem. faculty L.I. U., 1948—, prof. psychology, 1956—, faculty research grantee, 1958-67; cons. psychologist, 1948—. Postdoctoral fellow Social Sci. Research Council, 1932-33; scholar New Sch. Social Research, 1937; research grantee James M. Cattell Fund, 1961. Fellow A.A.A.S., Am. Psychol. Assn.; mem. Am. Assn. U. Profs., Sigma Xi. Author: Illusions in the Perception of Short Time Intervals, 1930; Outlook Upon the Future of British Unemployed Mental Patients and Others, 1935; Abnormal Personality and Time, 1936; Contbr. articles to profl. jours. Home: 1165 E 54th St Brooklyn NY 11234

ISSAWI, CHARLES PHILIP, educator, economist; b. Cairo, Egypt, Mar. 15, 1916; s. Elias and Alexandra (Abouchar) I.; B.A., Magdalen Coll., Oxford (Eng.) U., 1937, M.A., 1944; m. Janina M. Haftke, July 20, 1946. Came to U.S., 1947, naturalized, 1957. With Egyptian Ministry Finance, 1937-38; chief research Nat. Bank Egypt, 1938-43; adj. prof. Am. U., Beirut, Lebanon, 1943-47; mem. Middle East unit, econ. dept. UN Secretariat, 1948-55; faculty Columbia, 1955—, prof. econs., 1961—, dir. Near and Middle East Inst., 1962-64. Cons. FAO, 1955, UN, 1956, 70. Guggenheim fellow, 1961, 68; Social Sci. Research Council fellow, 1962. Fellow Middle East Inst. (bd. editors jour. 1958-); mem. Soc. Internat. Devel., Council Fgn. Relations, Am. Econ. Assn., Middle East Studies Assn. (v.p. 1968-69, bd. editors jour. 1970—), Econ. History Assn. Author: Egypt: an Economic and Social Analysis, 1947; An Arab Philosophy of History, 1950; Mushkilat Qaumiyya, 1959; Egypt in Revolution, 1963; co-author: The Economics of Middle Eastern Oil, 1962; The Economic History of Iran, 1971. Editor: The Economic History of the Middle East, 1800-1914, 1966. Home: 404 Riverside Dr New York City NY 10025

ISSELBACHER, KURT JULIUS, educator, physician; b. Wirges, Germany, Sept. 12, 1925; s. Albert and Flori (Strauss) I.; came to U.S., 1936, naturalized, 1945; A.B., Harvard, 1946, M.D. cum laude, 1950; m. Rhoda Solin, June 22, 1955; children—Lisa, Karen, Jody, Eric. Intern, then resident Mass. Gen. Hosp., Boston, 1950-53; investigator NIH, 1953-56; chief gastrointestinal unit Mass. Gen. Hosp., 1957, chmn. com. research, 1967; prof. medicine Harvard Med. Sch., 1966—, chmn. exec. com. depts. medicine, 1968—. Fellow Am. Acad. Arts and Scis., A.C.P. Co-editor; (Harrison) Principles of Internal Medicine, 1967. Discovered cause of galactosemia as 1st definitely proven disease due to hereditary enzyme defect; elucidated mechanism of intestinal fat absorption and causes of fatty liver; described disturbance of amino acid and lipid metabolism (isovaleric acidemia). Home: 2O Nobsoot Rd Newton Center MA 02159 Office: Mass Gen Hosp Boston MA 02114

ISSENMANN, CLARENCE GEORGE, bishop; b. Hamilton, O., May 30, 1907; s. Innocent J. and Millie (Stricker) I.; A.B., St. Gregory Sem., Cin., 1929; S.T.D., U. Fribourg, Switzerland, 1934; Ph.L., The Angelicum, Rome, Italy, 1935; Dr. Journalism, Register Coll. of Journalism, Denver 1938. Ordained priest Roman Catholic Ch., 1932; papal chamberlain, 1943, domestic prelate, 1945, protonotary apostolic, 1949; sec. to Archbishop Cin., 1938, asso. editor Cath. Telegraph Register, Cin., 1938-42; prof. moral theology Mt. St. Mary Sem., Norwood, O., 1942-45; pastor St. Susanna Ch., Mason, O., 1941-42, St. Louis Ch., Cin., 1946-56, Old Cathedral of St. Peter in Chains, 1956-58; chancellor Archdiocese Cin., 1945-48, vicar gen., 1947-57; titular bishop of Phytea, aux. archbishop of Cin., 1954-57; bishop of Columbus (O.), 1957-64; co-adj. bishop, apostolic adminstr. Cleve. Diocese, 1964-66; bishop of Cleve., 1966—. Address: Chancery Bldg 1027 Superior Cleveland OH 44114

ISSERMAN, FERDINAND MYRON, rabbi; b. Antwerp, Belgium, Mar. 4, 1898; s. Alexander and Betti (Brodheim) I.; A.B., U. Cin., 1910; Rabbi, Hebrew Union Coll., 1922, D.H.L., 1950; A.M., U. of Pa., 1924; postgrad. U. Toronto, 1926-27, U. of Chicago, 1928, LL.D., Douglass U., 1941; D.D., Central Coll., 1945; m. Ruth V. S. Frankenstein, June 6, 1923; children—Irma (Mrs. Stanley Gertz), Ferdinand Myron. Came to U.S., 1906, naturalized, 1918. Asst. rabbi Rodef Shalom Congregation, Phila., 1922- 25; rabbi Holy Blossom Congregation, Toronto, Can. 1925-29, Temple Israel, St. Louis, 1929-66, sr. rabbi, 1963-66. Jewish chaplain, asst. prof. religion U. Seven Seas, 1964-65. Chmn., guest rabbi Jewish Community, Hong Kong, 1963-64; co-founder Social Justice Commn., St. Louis, Mo., 1930-35. Mem. Mo. Library Commn. Field dir. A.R.C. in Tunisian campaign; attached to Am. Red Cross Hdgrs. in N. Arfica. hon. chmn. Rosalie Tilles Non-Sectarian Fund; chmn. Jewish Welfare Fund Campaign, St. Louis, 1939; past nat. chmn. combined campaign for support of Hebrew Union Coll.-Jewish Inst. Religion, Union Am. Hebrew Congregations; chmn. Commn. on Social Justice and Internat. Peace of World Union for Prog. Judaism; co-chmn. St. Louis Seminar of Jews and Christians, 1930-34. Pres. Jewish Student Foundn., 1930-48. Chmn. Justice and Peach Commn., 1941-46, Central Conf. of Am. Rabbis; chmn. Am. Inst. on Judaism and a Just and Enduring Peace; mem. governing bd. World Union for Progressive Judaism; past chmn. Am. Bd. World Union Progressive Judaism; Mem. bd. Indsl. Aid for the Blind of the State of Mo., Urban League, St. Louis; hon. pres. Hillel adv. council U. of Mo.; pres. St. Louis Rabbinical Assn., 1946, 53-54, 60-61; chmn. Inst. on Judaism and Race Relations, 1945; vice chmn. Nat. Conf. Religion and Race, 1963. Bd. dirs. Bible Coll., U. Mo.; former Trustee Hebrew Union Coll. Recipient citations Met. Ch. Fedn., 1955, St. John's Meth. Ch., 2d Bapt. Ch. 2d Unitarian Ch.; honored by resolution of Mo. Ho. of Reps. Served in U.S. Army during World War. Mem. Sigma Alpha Mu. Mason (32). Author books including: The Jewish Jesus and the Christian Christ, This is Judaism, Rebels and Saints; A Rabbi with the American Red Cross, 1958; Sentenced to Death the Jews in Nazi Germany, 1961; David Friedländer; A Reform Jewish Pioneer. Home: 82 Arundel P1 Clayton MO 63105 Office: 10675 Ladve St Louis MO 63124 ☆

ISTOMIN, EUGENE, concert pianist; b. N.Y.C., Nov. 26, 1925 s. George T. and Assia (Chavin) I.; grad. Profl. Children's Sch.; studied with Kyriena Siloti, Rudolf Serkin; student Mannes Sch., 1935-38, Curtis Inst. Music, 1939-43, Appeared major orchestras U.S. and abroad; currently on six- continent world tour; collaborator Pablo Casals, having appeared annually at Casals Festivals, 1950—; mem. Istomin, Stern, Rose trio; recordings Columbia Masterworks. Winner Phila. Youth Contest and Leventritt award, 1943. Home: 225 W 71st St New York City NY 10023 Office: care Hurok Attractions 730 Fifth Av New York City NY 10019

ITKIN, BELLA, educator; b. Moscow, USSR, Feb. 17, 1920; d. David B. and Leno Itkin; brought to U.S., 1932, naturalized, 1942; B.F.A., Goodman Theatre, 1941, M.F.A., 1943; Ph.D., Case-Western U., 1954; m. Frank John Runrath, July 29, 1969. Tchr. Goodman Theatre, Chgo., 1944—, head Evening Sch., 1954—, head Children's Theatre, 1959-65, dir., producer Children's Theatre, 1965—; lectr. on theatre, 1944—; vis. prof. U. Kan., 1960. Mem. ANTA, Am. Assn. U. Profs., Am. Edn. Theatre Assn. Home: 1130 S Michigan Av Chicago IL 60605 Office: Goodman Theatre Columbus Dr and Monroe St Chicago IL 60603

ITO, SUSUMU, educator; b. Stockton, Cal., July 27, 1919; s. Sohei and Hisayo (Watanabe) I.; B.S., Fenn Coll., 1949; M.S., Western Res. U., 1951, Ph.D., 1954; M.A. (hon.), Harvard, 1968; m. Minnie Tsuji, May 30, 1958; children—Linda, Daniel, Celia, Bruce. Post-doctoral fellow Western Res. U., 1955-56; fellow Max Plank Inst., Wilhelmshaven, Germany, 1956; instr. Cornell U. Med. Sch., 1957-59; Harvard Med. Sch., 1960-63, asst. prof., 1963-66, asso. prof., 1966-68, prof. anatomy, 1968—. Served to 1st lt. AUS, 1941-46. Decorated Bronze Star medal. Mem. Am. Assn. Anatomists, Am. Soc. Cell Biologists, N.Y. Acad. Sci., Electron Microscope Soc. Am., Soc. Study Reproduction, Am. Soc. Gastroenterology. Home: 16 Stearns St Wellesley MA 02181 Office: 25 Shattuck St Boston MA 02115

ITSCHNER, EMERSON CHARLES, ret. army officer; b. Chgo., July 1, 1903; s. Charles and Lucrecia (Burns) I.; B.S., U.S. Mil. Acad., 1924; C.E., Cornell U., 1926; E.D., Drexel Inst., 1958, Mo. Sch. of Mines, 1959; m. Eleanor Corey, Jan. 30, 1932; children—Ann, Gail, Carol. Commd. 2d. lt. U.S. Army, 1924, advanced through grades to lt. gen., 1959; mem. Alaska Road Commn., 1927-29; prof. mil. sci. and tactics Mo. Sch. Mines, 1932-36; chief Air Force constrn. sect. Office Chief Engrs., 1941-42; engr. advance sect. Europe, 1944-45; dist. engr., Seattle, 1949-50; engr. I. Corps, Korea, 1950-51; div. engr. North Pacific div. Portland, Ore., 1952-53; asst. chief engrs. for civil works, 1953-56, chief engrs., 1956-61, ret. 1961; chief tech. advisor Water and Power Devel. Agy., Lahore, Pakistan, 1961-64; vice pres. Portland Gen. Elec. Co. (Ore.), 1964-71, cons., 1971—. Mem. Permanent Internat. Nav. Congress, U.S. Com. on Large Dams. Decorated D.S.M., Fellow Am. Soc. C.E.; mem. Soc. Am. Mil. Engrs., Mil. Order World Wars, Nat. Soc. Profl. Engrs., Am. Nuclear Soc., Chi Epsilon. Address: 4435 S W Carl Pl Portland OR 97201

ITTELSON, WILLIAM HOWARD, psychologist; b. N.Y.C., May 4, 1920; s. Ralph B. and Julia (San) I.; B.A., Columbia, 1941, B.S. in Elec. Engring., 1942; M.S., Princeton, 1948, Ph.D. in Psychology, 1950; m. Martha Lane, Feb 16, 1946; 1 son, Lane. Staff, Naval Research Lab., 1942-43; instr. elec. engring. Princeton, 1947-48, instr. psychology, 1950-52, asst. prof., 1952-55; asso. prof. psychology Bklyn. Coll., 1955-61, prof., chmn. dept., 1961-68; acting exec. officer grad. program psychology City U. N.Y., 1963, prof. psychology, grad. div. 1968—; cons. VA, 1952-68; Fulbright lectr., Japan, 1961-62. Served to lt. USNR, 1943-46. Author: The Ames Demonstrations in Perception, 1952; Visual Space Perception, 1960; (with S.B. Kutash) Perceptual Changes in Psychopathology, 1961; (with H. Proshansky and L. Rivlin) Environmental Psychology, 1970. Home: 1585 Westervelt Av Baldwin NY 11510 Office: 33W 42d St New York City NY 10036

ITTLESON, HENRY, Jr., banker; b. St. Louis, Oct. 25, 1900; s. Henry and Blanche (Frank) I.; student Worcester (Mass.) Acad., 1914-17; Colgate Univ., 1919-21, U. Mich., 1921-22; m. Nancy Strauss, Jan. 4, 1936; children—Henry Anthony, Pamela Lee. Chmn. bd. C.I.T. Financial Corp., N.Y.C., 1962-68, hon. chmn. bd., 1968—, also dir.; dir. Nat. Bank N. Am. Served as lt. col. USAAF, 1942-45. Clubs: Westchester (N.Y.) Country; Turf and Field (Belmont Park, N.Y.); Tamarisk Country, O'Donnell Golf (Palm Springs, Cal.). Home: Hotel Pierre New York City NY 10021 Office: 660 Madison Av New York City NY 10021

ITURBI, JOSE, pianist, orchestra conductor, composer; b. Valencia, Spain, Nov. 28, 1895; s. Ricardo and Teresa (Baguena) I.; educated at Escuela de Música de Maria Jordan, Valencia, Spain, 1900-05; Conservatorio de Musica, Valencia (with Jose Bellver), 1903-05; Conservatoire de Musique, Paris, France; m. Maria Giner, June 8, 1916 (dec.); 1 dau., Maria (dec.). Has given piano concerts in all prin. cities of Europe, N. and S. America, Africa and East Indies, U.S. debut Oct. 1929; has conducted N.Y. Philharmonic-Symphony and symphony orchs. of Phila., Los Angeles, San Francisco, Detroit, Chgo., St. Louis, Cin., London, Madrid, Buenos Aires, Mexico City, etc.; also BBC Orch.; condr. Ford Sunday Evening Hour Orch. on radio; musical dir. Rochester (N.Y.) Philharmonic Orchestra, 1935-44; musical and artistic dir. of the Valencia Symphony Orchs. in Valencia, Spain 1956—; mus. dir., condr. Bridgeport Symphony Orch., 1967—. Composer Fantasy for piano and orch., Soliloquy for orch., Spanish Dance, Cradle Song, for piano. Decorated Legion d'Honneur (France), Alphonso el Sabio, Spain. St. Georges (Greece). Maj. and Nat. Music Dir., Civil Air Patrol. Mem. Real Academia de Bellas Artes de San Fernando (Madrid), Real Academia de Bellas Artes de San Carlos (Valencia, Spain). Home: 915 N Bedford Dr Beverly Hills CA 90210

IVAN, THOMAS NATHANIEL, profl. hockey team exec.; b. Toronto, Ont., Can., Jan. 31, 1911; s. Nickolas T. and Vera (Paul) I.; ed. pub. schs.; m. Dorothy L. Gardner. Came to U.S., 1945, naturalized, 1957. Gen. mgr. Chgo. Blackhawk Hockey Team, Inc., 1955—. Clubs: Ak-Sar-Ben (Omaha); Detroit Golf; North Shore Country (Glenview, Ill.); Lake Shore, Tavern (Chgo.). Home: 557 N King Muir Rd Lake Forest IL 60045 Office: Chgo Blackhawks Hockey Team Inc Madison Wood Warren and Wolcott Sts Chicago IL 60612

IVANS, WILLIAM STANLEY, electronics co. exec.; b. New Rochelle, N.Y., June 17, 1920 s. William S. and Marion (Schultz) I.; B.S. in Elec. Engring., Pa. State U., 1942; m. Rebecca Peck Llewellyn, May 18, 1962; children—Dennis Llewellyn, Denise Louise; stepchildrenVirginia Kay Liebner, Joan Renee Liebner. With Convair div. Gen. Dynamics Corp., San Diego, 1946-57; chief electronics engr., 1954-57; v.p. engring. Cohu Electronics, Inc., San Diego, 1957-65, pres., 1965—, chief exec. officer, 1968—, also dir.; dir. Meteorology Research, Inc. U.S. rep. gliding com. Fedn. Aero Internat., 1960-65, 66—. Recipient Lilienthal medal, 1950. Served as officer USAAF, 1942-46; ETO. Mem. Soaring Soc. Am. (pres. 1963-64), Western Electronic Mfrs. Assn. (bd. dirs. 1960-61), Nat. Aero. Assn. (bd. dirs. 1963-64, v.p. 1965—). Home: 807 La Jolla Rancho Rd La Jolla CA 92037 Office: 5725 Kearny Villa Rd San Diego CA 92123

IVASH, EUGENE VASILY, educator; b. Windsor, Ont., Can., July 24, 1925; s. Vasily Alexander and Sophie (Maschtaller) I.; B.S. in Engring. Physics, U. Mich., 1945, M.S., 1947, Ph.D., 1952; m. Edna A. Russell, Sept. 6, 1953; children—Carol, Catherine, Thomas. Mem. faculty U. Tex., Austin, 1958—, prof. physics, 1966—; tech. adviser Chalalonghorn U., Bangkok, Thailand, 1958-59; vis. lectr. U. Cambridge (Eng.), 1959; cons. U. Baruoda, India, 1968, NSF, 1968, Oak Ridge Nat. Lab., 1957-58, Gen. Atomic Co., LaJolla, Cal., 1963; research physicist Accelerator Lab., U. Tex., 1952-67, Center Nuclear Studies, 1967—. Mem. regional exec. com. Am. Friends Service Com., 1965-69. Served with USNR, 1944-46. Mem. Am. Phys. Soc., Assn. Physics Tchrs. Mem. Soc. of Friends (clk.). Contbr. profl. jours. Home: 4701 Shadow Lane Austin TX 78731

IVERSEN, JOHN DONALD, machine co. exec.; b. Pitts., Jan. 21, 1913; s. Lorenz and Gertrude (Adelsperger) I.; student Ohio State U., 1931, Washington and Jefferson Coll., 1932-35; m. Lillian Helenae Starzynski, Oct. 3, 1935; children—John Lorenz (dec.), Joan Goswell. With Mesta Machine Co., Pitts., 1935—, gen. mgr. navy plant, 1943-52, gen. supt., 1952-54, v.p. operations, 1954-64, pres., 1964—, also dir.; dir. Union Nat. Bank. Vice pres., dir. Central Blood Bank Pitts. Mem. Am. Iron and Steel Inst. Clubs: Pittsburgh Field, Athletic Assn., Duquesne, Laurel Vally Country. Home: 50 Woodland Rd Pittsburgh PA 15232 Office: PO Box 1466 Pittsburgh PA 15230

IVERSON, FRANCIS KENNETH, metals co. exec.; b. Downers Grove, Ill., Sept. 18, 1925; s. Norris Byron and Pearl Irene (Kelsey) I.; student Northwestern U., 1943-44; B.S., Cornell U., 1946; M.S., Purdue U., 1947; m. Martha Virginia Miller, Oct. 24, 1945; children—Claudia (Mrs. Wesley Watts Sturges), Marc Miller, Research physicist Internat. Harvester, Chgo., 1947-52; tech. dir. Illium Corp., Freeport, Ill., 1952-54; dir. marketing Cannon-Muskegon Corp. (Mich.), 1954-61; exec. v.p. Coast Metals, Little Ferry, N.J., 1961-62; v.p. Nuclear Corp. Am., Charlotte, N.C., 1962-65, pres., dir., 1965—. Served to lt. (j.g.) USNR, 1943-46. Mem. Steel Joist Inst. (dir.), Am. Soc. Metals, Am. Inst. Mining and Metall. Engrs., Am. Foundrymens Soc., Electron Microscope Soc. Am. Clubs: Carmel Country, Old Providence Racket (Charlotte). Contbr. articles to profl. jours. Home: 2410 Thornridge Rd Charlotte NC 28211 Office: 4425 Randolph Rd Charlotte NC 28211

IVERSON, MARVIN ALVIN, educator, psychologist; b. Waseca, Minn., Feb. 26, 1924; s. O.T. and Frieda (Ristau) I.; B.S. with high distinction, U. Minn., 1944, A.M., 1947; M.A., U. Pa., 1950, Ph.D., 1953; m. Mary E. Reuder, July 11, 1953; children—Carol, Kent. Research psychologist Am. Insts. for Research, Washington, 1952-54; asst. prof. psychology Adelphi U., Garden City, N.Y., 1954-59, asso. prof. 1959-65, prof., 1965—, chmn. dept., 1966—. Mem. N.Y. State Psychology Adv. Council, 1968-71. Fellow Am. Psychol. Assn. (covention bd. 1969-70), A.A.A.S. (council reps. 1964—), N.Y. Acad. Scis. (chmn. sect. psychology, 1968-70), Sigma Xi; mem. Eastern Psychol. Assn. exec. sec. 1961-67, (historian 1968-73), N.Y. State Psychol. Assn. (pres. div. social psychology 1968), Am. Assn. U. Profs., Am. Statis. Assn., Biometric Soc., Psychonomic Soc. Author: (monograph with M.E. Reuder) Ego Involvement as an Experimental Variable, 1956. Contbr. articles profl. jours. Home: 154 Charles St East Williston NY 11596 Office: Adelphi University Garden City NY 11530

IVERSON, ROBERT LESTER, textbook co. exec.; b. Oak Park, Ill., Jan. 2, 1936; s. Edward Webster and Elvira (Grashorn) I.; B.S. magna cum laude, Williams Coll., 1958; M.B.A., with honors, U. Mich., 1960; m. Michelle Ann Follett, Aug. 9, 1958; children—Heather, Robert Michael, Wendy Michelle. Mgr. trade dept. Follett's Mich. Book Store, Ann Arbor, 1958-60; asst. mgr. Follett's Book Inc., Chgo., 1960-63; mgr. mdse. and systems Follett Retail Stores, Chgo., 1963-68; treas. Follett Corp., Chgo., 1968—, also dir. Mem. budget com. Oak Park River Forest Community Chest, 1969, 70. Mem. Nat. Assn. Accountants, Am. Mgmt. Assn., 100 Thousand Miler Club, Phi Beta Kappa, Phi Kappa Phi, Beta Gamma Sigma. Clubs: River Forest Tennis. Home: 558 Keystone St River Forest IL 60305 Office: 1000 W Washington Blvd Chicago IL 60307

IVES, ALMON BINGHAM, educator; b. Bloomington, Ill., July 12, 1909; s. Charles Bingham and Ethyln Mae (Bishop) I.; A.B., Ill. Wesleyan U., 1931; B.Ed., Ill. State Normal U., 1932; M.A., Northwestern U., 1936; postgrad U. Wis., 1940; M.A. (hon.), Dartmouth, 1950; m. Mary Elizabeth Abraham, June 1, 1936; children—Almon W., Mary M., Daniel M., Ellen A. Tchr., Divernon, Ill., 1933-34, Casey, Ill., 1936-37; asst. prof. speech, dir. drama Stout Inst., Menomonie, Wis., 1937-38; instr. speech Dartmouth 1939, asst. prof. speech. cons. in radio, 1946-50, prof. speech, 1950-54, chmn. speech, 1954—, acting dean, 1962-63, chmn. television com., 1951-56 dir. general reading program, 1963-65; committeeman Eastern Radio Network; fellow in radio NBC, 1942; radio information specialist for Occupation Forces in Japan, 1951; lectr. World Radio Aoyama U., Tokyo, 1951, Pub. Service Programs Japan Broadcasting Corp., Tokyo, Osaka, Nagoya, Sendai, Sapporo, 1951; dir. speech, reading clinic Ind. State U., 1940; dir. radio U. Vt., summers, 1948-49; tchr. speech, oral reading Harvard, summers, 1956-58; mem. summer faculty Queens Coll., 1966, Georgetown U., 1968, Dartmouth Alumni Coll., 1964, 68-69; lectr. Lebanon Coll.; cons. in speech Amos Tuck Sch. Bus. Adminstrn., 1967-69. Mem. N.H. Commn. Ednl. TV, N.H. Citizens Com. Better Schs.; chmn. Hanover Sch. Bd.; moderator Hanover Sch. Dist. Mem. Howe Library Corp. Candidate for General Ct., 1950. Served as lt. USNR, 1943-46. Mem. Am. Assn. U. Profs., Speech Assn. Am. (legislative assembly), Eastern States (mem. exec. com.), New Eng. speech assns., Assn. Asian Studies, Japan Soc. N.Y., Sigma Chi. Ch. of Christ (deacon). Author: Play Ready Room (with James B. Dawson), 1946. Editor recordings of Am. Folk Songs. Home: 17 E Wheelock St Hanover NH 03755

IVES, BURL, (Icle Ivanhoe), singer, actor; b. Hunt, Ill., June 14, 1909; s. Frank and Cordella (White) I.; student Eastern Ill. State Tchrs. Coll., 1927-30, N.Y. U., 1937-38; m. Dorothy Koster, Apr. 1971; 1 son, Alexander. Travelled throughout 46 states as troubadour, collecting and singing Am. folk songs, memorizing about 500 of them; with CBS 1940-42; made Columbia concerts annual country-wide concert tour as solo concert artist presenting folksongs and ballads; appears on radio and TV; makes theatrical appearances, tours and stars in own co. every summer, also world tours. Participated in film productions including: So Dear to My Heart, Sierra, East of Eden, The Power and the Prize, Cat on a Hot Tin Roof, Let No Man Write My Epitaph, Our Man in Havana, The Big Country (Acad. award), Those Fantastic Flying Fools, and numerous other motion pictures; appeared in musical productions including: This Is the Army, Knickerbocker Holiday, Showboat; plays including Cat on a Hot Tin Roof. Records for Columbia and Decca; hist. song series Ency. Britannica, Recipient Motion Picture Acad. award for The Big Country. Mem. Am. Fedn. TV and Radio Artists, Writers Guild, Am. Fedn. Musicians, Screen Actors Guild. Democrat. Author: (autobiography) Wayfaring Stranger, 1948; Burl Ives Song Book, 1953; Sailing on a Very Fine Day, 1955, Tales of America, 1954, Burl Ives' Book of Seas Songs, Burl Ives Book of Irish Song; Song in America, 1961; A Wayfaring Stranger's Notebook: Albad, The Oaf, 1966. Mailing Address:

IVES, CHARLES POMEROY, 2d, newspaper man; b. Guilford, Conn., May 29, 1903; s. Paul Pomeroy and Blanche Garfield (Hammond) I.; A.B. cum laude, Brown U., 1925; M.A., Yale, 1938; m. Pearl Blatchley Putney, Sept. 3, 1921; children—Irene P. (Mrs. H.T. Wagner, dec.), Paul Pomeroy II, Cornelia Merriman. With New Haven Union, 1925-27, Bridgeport Telegram, 1927; reporter New Haven Jour.-Courier, 1927-28, asso. editor, 1929-32, editor, 1932-39; mng. editor Eugenics Mag., 1928-31; with Balt. Sun, 1939—, now asso. editor. Vis. lectr. polit. sci. Goucher Coll., 1952-56, 65-66. Mem. Phi Beta Kappa, Kappa Sigma, Episcopalian. Clubs: 14 West Hamilton Street, Graduates (New Haven). Book rev. editor Studies in Burke and His Time; editorial adviser Modern Age. Home: 10 Dunkirk Rd Baltimore MD 21212 Office: The Sun Baltimore MD 21202

IVES, DERMOD, lawyer; b. London, Eng., Jan. 23, 1904; s. Robert Franklin and Mildred (Card) I.; brought to U.S., 1909, naturalized, 1928; B.A., Columbia, 1925, LL.B., 1928, M.A. in Internat. Law, 1928; m. Kathleen Christy, May 17, 1928; children—Patricia (Mrs. Endicott Perry), Dermod. Admitted to N.Y. bar, 1928, since practiced in N.Y.C.; partner firm Davies, Hardy, Ives & Lawther, and predecessors, 1938—. Dir. R.B. Davis Investment Co., Davis Jephson Finance Co. Chief counsel N.Y. Commn. to Revise Laws Estates, 1961-67. Vice chancellor L.I. Diocese Episcopal Ch., 1954-70, chancellor, 1971—, adv. eccles. ct., 1958-62, standing com., 1962—. Trustee Oxhollow Found., Anne B. Lichtenstein Found., Am. Church Bldg. Fund Commn. Mem. Am., N.Y. State, Nassau County (pres. 1960-61) bar assns., Assn. Bar City N.Y. Clubs: Stanwich (Greenwich, Conn.); Cherry Valley (Garden City, N.Y.); University Glee, University, Downtown Athletic, Atlantic Beach (N.Y.C.). Home: 884 North St Greenwich CT 06830 Office: 2 Broadway New York City NY 10004

IVES, GEORGE SKINNER, govt. ofcl.; b. Bklyn., Jan. 10, 1922; s. Irving McNeil and Elizabeth (Skinner) I.; student Taft Sch., 1940; A.B., Dartmouth, 1943; LL.B., Cornell U., 1949; m. Barbara K. Turner, Aug. 14, 1948; children-Elizabeth Turner, Nancy McNeil. Admitted to D.C. bar, 1959, N.Y. bar, 1949; practice in Washington, 1959-69, N.Y.C., 1950-53; legal asst. to chmn. NLRB, 1949-50; asso. atty. Simpson, Thatcher & Bartlett, 1950-53; adminstrv. asst., legal counsel U.S. Senator Irving M. Ives, N.Y., 1953-58; pvt. practice law, labor arbitrator, Washington, 1959-69; chmn. Nat. Mediation Bd., 1970—. Served to lt. USNR, 1943-46. Mem. Am., N.Y., D.C. bar assns., Nat. Acad. Arbitrators, Am. Arbitration Assn. Home: 5969 Searl Terrace Washington DC 20016 Office: Nat Mediation Bd Washington DC 20572

IVES, HIRAM DUDLEY, ret. army officer; b. Balt., Nov. 11, 1905; s. James Lawrence and Mary Orilla (Dudley) I.; student Cornell U., 1924-26, Johns Hopkins, 1926-28; grad. Command and Gen. Staff Sch., 1944, Army War Coll., 1951; m. Anne Bartlett Mason (div. 1944); m. 2d, Constance Elizabeth Morley, June 14, 1944; children—Hiram Dudley, Mary Elizabeth (dec.), Stewart Morley. Served to capt. Md. N.G., 1928-40; commd. capt. U.S. Army, 1946, advanced through grades to maj. gen., 1960; assigned inf. units 3d Army, Western Europe, 1944-47; mem. War Dept. Gen. Staff, 1948-50, 51-53; G-3, U.S. Forces, Trieste, 1953-54, 7th Army, Germany, 1954-55; asst. div. comdt. 5th Inf. Div., Germany, 1955-56; chief Ill. Mil. Dist., 1956-58; sr. adviser Korean Army Tng. Command, also 2d Republic of Korea Army, 1958-59; chief staff 3d Army, Ft. McPherson, Ga., 1959-60; comdg. gen., Ft. Jackson, S.C.,

1960-61; dep. insp. gen. Dept. Army, Washington, 1961-63, insp. gen. Dept. of Army, 1963-65; became cons. Research Analysis Corp., McLean, Va., 1965, now ret. Decorated Silver Star with cluster, Bronze Star with cluster, D.S.M., Distinguished Unit citation. Mem. Phi Gamma Delta. Episcopalian. Home: MacKey's Choice Farm Ladiesburg MD 21759

IVES, JOHN HARRISON, realtor, ins. broker; b. Milford, Conn., May 9, 1909; s. John W. and Agnes (Cochrane) I.; student pub. schs.; m. Marjorie Sillman, Jan 21, 1939; children—John Harrison II, Robert S., Frederick W.; m. 2d, Lillian A. Hanson, Aug. 12, 1960. With First Nat. Bank & Trust Co. of Bridgeport, 1925-35, mgr. real estate and mortgage dept., 1932-35; owner John H. Ives Ins. Agy., 1935-47; with Staples, Inc., 1937-47; pres., treas., dir. Ives-Staples Co., 1947-52; pres., treas., dir. Ives-Hanson Co., 1952-59, sr. partner, 1960-69; owner John H. Ives Real Estate Agy., Bridgeport, Conn., 1970—; mgr. Arcade Hotel, 1937—; propr. Goshen Gen. Store (Conn.), 1959-60. Past pres. Fairfield (Conn.) Little League Baseball; mem. br. bd. mgrs., chmn. residence Bridgeport YMCA. Ofcl., Congl. Christian Ch.; past pres. Am. Missionary Assn.; past dir., mem. exec. com., past chmn. div. ch. extension and evangelism, past chmn. budget com. bd. Home Missions; past pres. Bd. Ministerial Relief, Ch. Bldg. Soc., Edn. Soc., Home Missionary Soc., Pub. Soc., Sunday Sch. Extension Soc.; past chmn., mem. adv. com. Missions Council, chmn. office communication; past mem. bd. mgrs. Pilgrim Press; mem. benevolence planning com. United Ch. of Christ. Mem. bd. assos. Chgo. Theol. Sem., U. Bridgeport; chmn. bd. trustees Milford Acad., 1964-70. Recipient citation for leadership Nat. Council Chs. (mem. gen. bd., past chmn. dept. racial and cultural relations, broadcasting and film commn.). Mem. Nat. Geog. Soc., Goshen (Conn.) Hist. Soc. (dir.). Mason, Rotarian. Home: 985 Fairfield Av Bridgeport CT 06603 Office: 19 PO Arcade Bridgeport CT 06603

IVES, PHILIP, architect; b. N.Y.C., Aug. 8, 1904; s. Kenneth and Edith (Appleton) I.; student Taft Sch., Watertown, Conn., 1922-23, Yale, 1927; m. Sarah Holter, Nov. 10, 1928; children—Elizabeth (Mrs. David C. Clark), Sarah (Mrs. David W. Scully), Philip Appleton. Jr. designer, asso. Ewing & Allen and Lee Hill French, Jr., 1927-32; practice architecture under firm name of Philip Ives Assos., N.Y.C., 1932—, interim name Ives, Turano & Gardner, 1956-62; sr. project planner FPHA, World War II. Fellow A.I.A.; mem. Archtl. League N.Y., Century Assn., Psi Upsilon. Republican. Episcopalian. Club: Field (past pres.) (Greenwich, Conn.). Important works include St. Barabas Ch. (award Ch. Archtl. Guild Am.), Corporate Research Lab., Sterling Forest, N.Y. (certificate of merit N.Y. State Assn. Architects), Quarry Knolls Housing, Greenwich (Honor award for design excellence Fed. Housing and Home Finance Agy.), (cons. architect) Pan Am. World Airways Terminal at Kennedy Airport (Gold medal Archtl. League N.Y.), Chapel of St. Jude, Georgetown, Washington (Honor award Guild for Religious Architecture), First Presbyn. Ch., New Canaan, Conn. Home: Parsonage Rd Greenwich CT 06830 Office: 65 E 55th St New York City NY 10022

IVES, STEPHEN BRADSHAW, Jr., lawyer; b. N.Y.C., Oct. 6, 1924; s. Stephen Bradshaw and Ellen Gardiner (Atwood) I.; A.B., Harvard, 1948; LL.B., Yale, 1951; m. Margaret Hallowell Crocker, Aug. 3, 1946; children—Catherine C., Stephen Bradshaw III, David A., Margaret H., Joshua K. (dec.). Admitted to R.I. bar, 1952, D.C. bar, 1970; practice in Providence, 1952-61; asso. Hinckley, Allen, Salisbury & Parsons, 1952-57, partner, 1957-61; exec. asst. to adminstr. AID, Washington, 1961-62, dir. Office Korea Affairs, 1962-64, dir. Office East Asian Affairs, 1964-66, asso. asst. adminstr. Far East, 1966-67, dep. asst. adminstr. East Asia, 1967-68, gen. counsel, 1968-70; partner Wald, Harkrader, Nicholson and Ross, Washington, 1970—. Mem. R.I. Mechanics Lien Law Commn., R.I. Commn. Interstate Coop. Vice chmn. R.I. Vols. for Stevenson, 1956, R.I. chpt. Ams. for Democratic Action, 1958-60; treas. Pell for Senator Com., 1960, People for Pell Com., 1960. Bd. dirs. Providence Community Fund, Childrens Friend and Service R.I. Served to 1st lt. AUS, 1943-46. Decorated Bronze Star. Mem. Am., R.I. (past mem. exec. com.) bar assns., Am. Arbitration Assn. (panel), Order of Coif, Phi Beta Kappa. Home: 3025 Newark St N W Washington DC 20008 Office: 1320 19th St N W Washington DC 20036

IVEY, JAMES BURNETT, polit. cartoonist; b. Chattanooga, Apr. 19, 1925; s. Bernard Steele and Alise (Buford) I.; A.A., George Washington U., 1948; student U. Louisville, 1943, Nat. Art Sch., Washington, 1948-50; m. Ellen Shea, Aug. 29, 1947 (div. Jan. 1957); m. 2d, Evelyn Rogers, Jan. 12, 1957; children—Susan Ellen, Donald James. Polit. cartoonist Washington Star, 1950-53, St. Petersburg (Fla.) Times, 1953-59, San Francisco Examiner, 1959-66; free-lance polit. cartoonist, 1966-69; with Orlando Sentinel-Star, 1970—. Curator, Cartoon Mus., 1967-68. Bd. dirs. San Francisco Acad. Comic Art. Served with USNR, 1943-46. Reid fellow, 1959. Mem. Nat. Cartoonists Soc., Assn. Am. Editorial Cartoonists. Contbr. articles newspapers, jours. Address: 561 Obispo Av Orlando FL 32807

IVEY, JOHN COURTNEY, lawyer; b. Dillon, S.C., Aug. 12, 1903; s. William Stinceon and Mary Frances (LeGett) I.; student U.S. Naval Acad., 1921-24; B.S., Yale, 1928, LL.B., 1929; m. Elizabeth Dorsey Bruen, June 26, 1937; children—Elizabeth Dorsey, Mary Stinceon, Courtney Bruen. Admitted to N.Y. bar, 1932; practice in N.Y.C., 1928-; partner Brown, Wood, Fuller, Caldwell & Ivey, 1942—. Mem. Am., N.Y. State bar assns., Bar Assn. City N.Y., Phi Delta Phi. Clubs: Down Town Assn. (N.Y.C.); Delray Beach Golf and Country, Ocean (Delray Beach, Fla.); St. Andrew's Golf (Hastings-on-Hudson, N.Y.); Bronxville Field. Home: 17 Locust Lane Bronxville NY 10708 Office: 70 Pine St New York City NY 10005

IVEY, JOHN ELI, Jr., sociologist, coll. dean; b. Raleigh, N.C., Jan. 21, 1919; s. John Eli and Vera (House) I.; B.S., Ala. Poly Inst., 1940; Ph.D., U. N.C., 1944; LL.D., U. Chattanooga; m. Melville Corbett, July 25, 1942; children—Melville Elizabeth, Howard William, Lela. Instr. sociology U. N.C., 1941-43, asso. prof., 1946-48, prof. dept. city and regional planning, 1948; chief div. research interpretation Inst. Research Social Sci., 1946-48, prof. sociology, research prof., 1948; dir. Regional Council Edn., 1948-49; dir. Bd. Control., So. Regional Edn., 1949-57; became exec. v.p. N.Y.U., 1957; now dean Coll. Edn., also prof. sociology Michigan State U., 1962—. Chmn. of Council for Study Fla. Higher Edn., 1954-57; chmn. council reorgn. Atlanta Sch. System, 1955; specialist edn. evaluation TVA, 1944-45; reorgn. N.C. Planning Bd., 1944, Fla. Survey Edn., 1946-47; cons. Atlanta City Sch. Bd., 1946—, N.C. Ednl. Survey, 1947-48; mem. Columbia U. Research Team on Study P.R. Pub. Sch. System, 1948-50. Exec. sec. com. on So. regional studies and edn. Am. Council Edn., 1943-48, sec., mem. exec. com., 1949-52; chmn. conf. in resources-use edn., So. States Work Conf., 1946-48; mem. bd. advisers Films, Inc., 1947-50; pres. Midwest Program on Airborne TTV Instrn., Inc., 1958-63, chmn. bd., 1963—; chmn. bd. consultants Ga. Survey of Public Education, 1963—. Recipient Freedoms Found. medal, 1951; Eisenhower exchange fellow world travel, 1956. Mem. N.E.A., Soc. Pub. Adminstrn., Am. Acad. Polit. and Social Sci., A.A.A.S., Am., Rural sociol. socs., Am. Anthrop. Assn., Phi Beta Kappa, Alpha Kappa Delta, Omicron Delta Kappa, Delta Sigma Pi. Author: Channeling Research into Education, 1944; (with N.J. Demerath, Woodrow W. Breland) Building Atlanta's Future, 1948; (with Rupert B. Vance, Marjorie Bond) Exploring the South, 1949; (with Breland, Demerath) Community Resources, 1951; also articles profl. jours. Editor: Using Regional Resources, 1945; Scientists Look at Resources. Mem. bd. editors Social Forces, 1946-48. Home: 345 Whitehills Dr East Lansing MI 48823

IVEY, RICHARD MACAULAY, lawyer; b. London, Ont., Can., Oct. 26, 1925; s. Richard Green and Jean (Macaulay) I.; B.A., U. Western Ont., 1947; B.A., Osgoode Hall, 1950; m. Beryl Marcia Nurse, Aug. 6, 1949;children-Richard William, Jennifer Louise, Rosamond Ann, Susanne Elizabeth. Called to bar, 1950, created Queen's counsel, 1963; asso. Ivey, Livermore & Dowler, London, Ont., 1950-60, partner, 1960-64; partenr Ivey & Dowler, London, 1964—. Pres. Allpak Products, Ltd., London 1967—; v.p., dir. No. Life Assurance Co. Can., London 1967—; v.p., dir. No. Life Assurance Co. Can., London, 1960—; dir. F.W. Woolworth Co. Ltd., Bank of Montreal, Canadian Scudder Investment Fund Ltd., Scudder N.Am. Fund Ltd., Scudder Internat. Investments Ltd., IWC Industries Ltd., Livingston Industries Ltd., Jespersen-Kay Systems Ltd., S.F. Lawrason and Co. Ltd., Ellis-Don Ltd. Bd. govs. U. Western Ont.; chmn. bd. St. Joseph's Hosp., London. Clubs: London Hunt and Country, London; Toronto. Home: 990 Wellington St London 11 Ont Can Office: 291 Dundas St London 14 Ont Can

IVIE, ROBERT S., lawyer; b. Tacoma, Nov. 22, 1918; B.A., U. Ia., 1940; LL.B., Harvard, 1947. Admitted to N.Y. bar, 1947, Wash. bar, 1949; partner firm Riddell, Williams, Voorhees, Ivie & Bullitt, Seattle. Mem. Am., Wash. State, Seattle-King County bar assns., Phi Beta Kappa. Office: 4310 Seattle First Nat Bank Bldg Seattle WA 98104*

IVINS, GEORGE HARVEY, ret. educator; b. Havre de Grace, Md., Dec. 15, 1902; s. Samuel Irvin and Mary Jane (Maslin) I.; A.B., Swarthmore Coll., 1926; A.M., Columbia; student Spl. Service Sch., Ft. Meade, Md., 1942; m. Mildred Mead, June 15, 1939; 1 son, George Anthony. Tchr. Central High Sch., San Juan, P.R., 1926-27; master Sch. for Boys, Palm Beach, Fla., 1927-28; prin. high sch., St. Thomas, V.I., 1928-29; asso. prof. Eastern Ill. Tchrs. Coll., 1930-31; commr. edn., V.I., 1931-35; asso. dir. Oak Lane Country Day Sch., Phila., 1935-37, headmaster, 1937-42; cons. VA guidance Western Ill. Coll., 1946-47; vis. prof. U. N.C., 1947-48; research Gen. Staff and Command Coll., 1948; asso. prof. edn. Roosevelt U., Chgo., 1949-53, prof. edn., 1953-70, prof. emeritus, 1970—, acting chmn. dept. edn., 1952-54, chmn., 1954-70, Maud Scott Distinguished prof. fundamental edn., 1962. Adviser Economy League, Phila., radio sta. WCAU, 1940; curriculum council Chgo. Bd. Edn.; edn. adv. com. Anti-Defamation League; mem. Chgo. Commn. on Human Relations. Served as lt. col. Gen. Staff Corps, AUS, 1942-46. Mem. N.E.A., Delta Upsilon, others. Contbr. articles to profl. publs. Home: 1129 E 12th St Casa Grande AZ 85222

IVINS, JAMES ELBERT, lawyer, exec. cons.; b. Chgo., Oct. 8, 1912; s. Donald A. and Veronica (McMahon) I.; Ph.B., U. Wis., 1935, J.D., 1938; m. Margaret Milne, Sept. 7, 1940; children—Sara, Mary, Andrew. Admitted to Wis. bar, 1938, Mo. bar, 1941, Ill. bar, 1946, Tex. bar, 1950, Md. bar, 1969; atty. SEC, Chgo., St. Louis, 1939-42; asso. Pam, Hurd & Reichman, Chgo., 1945-49; atty. Tenn. Gas Transmission Co. (now Tenneco, Inc.), Houston, 1949—, corporate sec., 1952-58, sr. atty., sec., 1958-60, v.p., sr. atty., 1960- 65, v.p., gen. counsel, 1965-68; pres., dir. Tenneco Corp. 1968—; sec., dir. Deepsea Ventures, Inc.; dir. Market Research Corp. Am. Bd. govs. State Auto Ins. Assn. Served with USCGR, 1942-45; PTO. Mem. Kappa Sigma (nat. pres. 1959-61). Club: New York Yacht. Home: RFD 5 Easton MD 21601 Office: Tenneco Corp Wilmington DE 19899

IVISON, MAYNARD C. broker; b. Cleve., Sept. 21, 1895; s. William Crane and Celia Mae (Cady) I.; A.B., Yale 1918; m. Alice R. Thayer, Dec. 4, 1919; children—Audrey (Mrs. Audrey Pattinson), Maynard Thayer. With Anglo-Am. Comml. Corp., 1919-20, Fgn. Commerce Corp. Am., 1920-21, G.M.P. Murphy & Co., 1921-23; with Mechanics & Metals Nat. Bank, 1923-26, mgr. bond dept., 1925-26; with Chisholm & Chapman (mem. N.Y. Stock Exchange), 1926-27, Chase Nat. Bank, 1927-29; partner Abbott, Hoppin & Co. (mem. N.Y. Stock Exchange), 1929-34, Abbott, Proctor & Paine 1934-70; ltd. partner Paine Webber Jackson & Curtis, N.Y.C., 1970—. Mem. bd. govs. N.Y. Stock Exchange, 1954-57. Served as 1st lt. 303d F.A., U.S. Army, 1917-19, Mem. Assn. Stock Exchange Firms (bd. govs. 1947-53, v.p. 1950-52). Clubs: Union, Racquet and Tennis (N.Y.C.); Rockaway Hunting (Cedarburst, L.I., bd. govs. 1950-53); Lawrence Beach (Atlantic Beach, L.I., bd. govs. 1927-56, pres. 1930-33). Home: 161 E 79th St New York City NY 10021 Office: 425 Park Av New York City NY 10022

IVORY, JAMES dir. Shakespere Wallah, The Guru. Address: care 20th Century Fox 444 W 56th St New York City NY 10019*

IVY, ANDREW CONWAY, physiologist; b. Farmington, Mo., Feb. 25, 1893; s. Henry McPherson and Cynthia (Smith) I.; A.B., B.Pd., State Normal Sch., Cape Girardeau. Mo., 1913; B.S., U. Chgo., 1916, M.S., 1917, Ph.D., 1918, M.D., Rush Med. Coll., 1922; D.Sc. (hon.) U. Neb., 1947, Grinell (Ia.) Coll., 1947, Boston U., 1948; LL.D., (hon.) Loyola U., 1950; D.Sc., Hastings (Neb.) Coll., 1951, Cole Coll., Ia., 1957; m. Emma Kohman, Dec. 24, 1919; children—John Henry, William Harvey, Andrew Conway, Horace Kohman, Robert Emerson. Instr. in physiology, U. Chgo., 1917, asso. prof., 1922-25; asso. prof. physiology Loyola, 1919-22; intern Mercy and Augustana hosps., Chgo., 1920-22; head div. physiology and pharmacology, Northwestern U. Med. Sch., 1925-46; v.p. charge Chgo. profl. Colls., U. Ill., 1946-53; distinguished prof. physiol., head dept. clin. sci., 1946-61, distinguished prof. emeritus, 1961—; prof. emeritus biochemistry, dir. lab. med. research Roosevelt U., Chgo., 1962—; sci. dir. Naval Med. Research Inst., 1942-43; cons. Q.M. AUS, 1943-44; mem. Nat. Adv. Cancer Council, 1944-51, exec. dir., 1947-51. Dep. dir. Chgo. Med. Civil Defense 1950—. Mem. Com. Aviation Med. N.R. Council, 1941; co-founder Space Med. Soc., 1945; cons. Sec. War on War Crimes, 1946-47; mem. Internat. and Nat. Commn. Prevent Alcoholism; pres. Partal House, Rehab. Alcoholics, 1951. Dir. Ivy Cancer Research Found. Served as 2d lt., M.N.G., 1912-13; student officer, M.O.T.C., AUS, 1917-18: Mem. bd. mgrs. YMCA 1955—. Recipient Pope Leo XIII award, Hoover award. Fellow A.C.P., Gorgas Med. Soc. (hon.); mem. A.M.A. (chmn. sect. physiology and pathology 1931), Ill. Chgo. med. socs., Soc. Internal Medicine (pres. 1941-42), Am. Assn. U. Profs. (council 1929-31), Am. Gastro-Enterol. Assn. (pres. 1940-41; D.S.M.; mem. editorial bd.), Harvey Soc. (hon.), Am. Physiol. Soc. (sec. 1935-39; pres. 1939-41; mem. editorial bd.), Soc. Exptl. Biology (mem. editorial bd.), Des Moines Acad. Med. (hon.), Chgo. Inst. Med. (pres. 1943), Am. Inst. Nutrition, Ill. Acad. Sci., Assn. Study Internal Secretions, Commn. Chronic Illness (exec. com.), Alpha Omega Alpha, Phi Beta Kappa (hon.), Sigma Xi, Alpha Kappa Kappa, A.A.A.S. Methodist. Mason. Clubs: Commercial, Executive (Chgo.). Author: Nuremburg Code; Peptic Ulcer; Observations on Krebiozen in Management of Cancer Patients, 1956, 1550 sci. articles. Co-founder, mng. editor Gastroenterology 1942-52. Address: 178 W Randolph Chicago IL 60601

IWASA, YOSHIZANE, banker; b. Tokyo, Japan, Feb. 6, 1906; s. Teizo and Nami Iwasa; m. Michi Iwasa, Apr. 16, 1928; children—Kaizo, Taizo, Kiyoko (Mrs. Mitsuo Ohashi). With Yasuda Bank, Tokyo, 1928—, dep. chmn. 1957-63, chmn. bd., pres., 1963—, also dir. Vice chmn. Fedn. Econ. Orgn. Trustee Japan Com. Econ. Devel. Recipient medal of honour with blue ribbon for pub. service. Home: 5-2-4 Minami Aoyama Minato-ku Tokyo Japan Office: 5-5 Otemachi 1-chome Chiyoda-ku Tokyo Japan

IWASAKI, IWAO, educator; b. Tokyo, Japan, Feb. 6, 1929; s. Kuramatsu and Ichiko (Ishihara) I.; student U. Tokyo, 1948-50; B.S., U. Minn., 1951, M.S., 1953; Sc.D., Mass. Inst. Tech., 1957; D.Eng., Tohoku U., 1961. Came to U.S., 1950. Asst. prof. U. Minn., Mpls., 1957-59, asso. prof., 1963-66, prof., 1966—; research engr. Fuji Iron & Steel Co., Tokyo, 1959-63. Mem. Am. Inst. Mining, Metall. Engrs., Am. Chem. Soc., Mining Inst. Japan, Iron and Steel Inst. Japan, Electrochem. Soc. Japan, Sigma Xi, Tau Beta Pi. Contbr. articles profl. jours. Home: 48 Groveland Terrace Minneapolis MN 55403

IWASAWA, KENKICHI, mathematician; b. Kiryu, Japan, Sept. 11, 1917; s. Zensuke and Katsu (Anzai) I.; Dr. Sci., U. Tokyo (Japan), 1945; m. Aiko Kaneko, Mar. 30, 1941; children—Kazuko (Mrs. Yasutaka Ihara), Takashi, Mariko. Came to U.S., 1950. Asst. prof. U. Tokyo, 1949-52; asst. prof., asso. prof. then prof. Mass. Inst. Tech., 1952-67; prof. math. Princeton, 1967—.' Mem. Am. Math. Soc. (Cole prize 1962). Home: 12 Newlin Rd Princeton NJ 08540

IYALLA, JOSEPH T.F., Nigerian ambassador to U.S. Address: 1333 16th St N W Washington DC 20036.*

IZARD, CARROLL ELLIS, educator; b. Georgetown, Miss., Oct. 8, 1923; s. Willis Lee and Willie (Cliburn) I.; B.A., Miss. Coll., 1943; B.D., Yale, 1945; M.A., Syracuse U., 1951, Ph.D., 1952; m. Barbara Sinquefield, Dec. 25, 1944; children—Carroll Ellis, Camille Sinquefield, Ellen Ashley. Research asso. Tulane U., 1952-54; research asso. Research Assos., Inc., Phila., 1954-55; specialist, individual devel. and human relations Gen. Electric Co., Lynn, Mass., 1955-56; asst. prof. psychology Vanderbilt U., Nashville, 1956-61, asso. prof., 1961-64, prof., 1964—, dir. Counseling Center, 1956—, dir. clin. tng. program, 1962-67. Cons., Tenn. Dept. Edn., VA; mem. Tenn. Bd. Examiners in Psychology, 1962-66. Bd. dirs., exec. com. Center for Community Studies, Peabody Coll., Nashville. Served to lt. (j.g.) USNR, 1944-46. Diplomate, Am. Bd. Examiners in Profl. Psychology. Mem. Tenn. (past pres.), Am. psychol. assns., Sigma Xi. Author: The Face of Emotion (Elliot Meml. award Century Psychology Series 1969). Editor: (with S.S. Tomkins) Affect, Cognition and Personality, 1965. Contbr. articles profl. jours. Home: 1701 Graybar Lane Nashville TN 37215

IZENOUR, FRANK MILTON, army officer; b. New Brighton, Pa., Oct. 6, 1913; s. Charles S. and Wilhelmina (Freesman) I.; student Ashland (O.) Coll., 1932-33; B.S., U.S. Mil. Acad., 1938; postgrad. Command and Gen. Staff Coll., 1947, Armed Forces Staff Coll., 1950, Army War Coll., 1953; m. Billie W. Boettcher, Dec. 10, 1938; children—Janet R., Frank Milton, Jo Ann, Jennifer. Commd. 2d. lt. U.S. Army, 1938, advanced through grades to maj. gen., 1966; chief mil. personnel mgmt. div. Officer Asst. Chief Staff Personnel, Dept. Army, Washington, 1955, dept. G-3 Army Forces Far East 8th U.S. Army, Seoul, Korea, 1955, G-3, 1955-56; comdg. officer 17th Inf., Camp Kaiser, Korea, 1956-57; dir. command and staff dept. Inf. Sch., Ft. Benning, Ga., 1957-59, dep., asst. comdt., dir. instrn., 1959-60; liaison officer U.S. Comdr. in Chief Europe, Bonn. Germany, 1960-62; a.d.c. 4th Armored Div. USAREUR, 1962-64; dir. manpower Office Dept. Chief of Staff for Personnel, Dept. Army, 1964-66, dir. procurement and distbn. ODCSPER, 1966-67; comdg. gen. 2d Inf. Div., 1967- 68; comdg. gen. U.S. Army Test and Evaluation Command, Aberdeen Proving Ground, M.D., 1968—. Decorated D.S.M. with oak leaf cluster; Silver Star medal, Legion of Merit, Bronze Star medal, Purple Heart with oak leaf cluster; French Croix de Guerre with bronze star; Italian Mil. Valor Cross; Order Nat. Security Merit (Korean). Address: Quarters 1 Aberdeen Proving Ground MD 21005

IZENOUR, GEORGE CHARLES, educator; b. New Brighton, Pa. July 24, 1912; s. Charles S. and Wilhelmina (Freseman) I.; A.B., Wittenberg Coll., 1934, M.A., 1936, D.F.A. (hon.). 1960; M.A., (hon.), Yale, 1961; m. Hildegard Hilt, Sept. 7, 1937; 1 son, Steven. Lighting dir. fed. theatres in Cal., 1938-39; with OSRD, 1943-46; mem. faculty Yale, 1946—, prof. theatre design and tech., 1960—, dir. electromech. lab. Sch. Drama, 1946—; pvt. practice as theatrical cons., 1958—. Fellow Rockefeller Found., 1939-43, 46-47; Ford Found. fellow, 1960-61; Guggenheim fellow, 1971-72. Recipient Rodgers and Hammerstein award theatre design, 1960. Mem. A.A.A.S., ANTA, I.E.E.E., Conn. Acad. Arts and Scis. Inventor lighting systems, rigging, lighting and computer controls for theatre and TV. Home: 10 Alston Av New Haven CT 06515

IZUTSU, SATORU, govt. health adminstr.; b. Hawaii, Sept. 7, 1928; s. Ryozo and Iseno (Yamashita) I.; B.A., U. Hawaii, 1950; profl. certificiate, Columbia, 1952, M.A., 1955; Ph.D., Western Res. U., 1963. Tng. adminstr. Waimano Tng. Sch. and Hosp., Hawaii Dept. Health, 1961-64; planner Comprehensive Plan Mental Retardation, Honolulu Dept. Health, 1964-65; exec. officer Waimano Tng. Sch. and Hosp., 1965-68; chief operations and planning Regional Med. Program Hawaii, Guan, Samoa and Trust Terr., 1969—. Vice chmn. Commn. Certification Psychologists Hawaii, 1968—. Bd. dirs. Goodwill Industries Hawaii. Served to 1st lt. AUS, 1952-53. Mem. Am. Psychol. Assn., Am. Personnel and Guidance Assn., Am. Occupational Therapy Assn., Am. Assn. Mental Deficiency. Home: 1350 Ala Moana Blvd Honolulu HI 96813 Office: 1301 Punchbowl St Honolulu HI 96813

IZZARD, WESLEY SHERMAN, editor; b. Chgo., Apr. 19, 1900; s. Arthur John and Cora May (Sherman) I.; A.B., U. Ill., 1923; m. Helen Elizabeth Easterday, Feb. 3, 1922; children—Wesley Robert, Marilyn Ann. Reporter, Kansas City Jour., 1919, copy desk chief, 1923-24; mng. editor Amarillo (Tex.) Globe, 1924-26, mng. editor Amarillo Globe and Daily News (combined), 1926-35; prodn. mgr. Radio Sta. KGNC, Amarillo, 1935-38; editor-in-chief Globe-News, 1943-51; editor, pub. Daily News, 1951—; sec., Plains Radio Broadcasting Co., Amarillo, 1937—; news commentator radio sta. KGNC, 1935-61, gen. mgr. KGNC radio and TV sta., 1954-66. Mem. Am. Soc. Newspaper Editors, Delta Alpha Epsilon, Sigma Delta Chi. Home: 2605 Hughes St Amarillo TX 79109 Office: Globe-News Pub Co Amarillo TX 79101

JAAKSON, ERNST diplomat of Estonia; b. Riga, Latvia, Aug. 11, 1905; s. Jaan and Marie (Jaakson) J.; student U. Latvia, 1925-26, U. Tartu (Estonia) 1928-29, Columbia, 1932-34; m. Claire Langenbacher, June 22, 1934. Assigned legation, Riga, 1919-26, Ministry Fgn. Affairs, Tallinn, 1928-29; sec. consulate San Francisco, 1929-32, N.Y.C., 1932—; consul gen., N.Y.C., also charge legation Washington, 1965—. Served with Estonian Army, 1926-28. Decorated White Cross (Estonia). Home: 9OO Palmer Rd Bronxville NY 10708 Office: 9 Rockefeller Plaza New York City NY 10020

JABARA, FRANCIS DWIGHT, educator; b. Cambridge, Kan., Oct. 13, 1924; s. Farris George and Helen (Hourany) J.; B.S., Okla. State U., 1948; M.B.A., Northwestern U., 1949, C.P.A., 1956; m. Geri Ablah, Dec. 30, 1956; children—Leesa, Lori, Harvey F.G. Faculty

Wichita (Kan.) State U., 1949—, asso. prof. accounting, 1954-59, prof., 1959-, head dept., 1962-64, dean Coll. Bus. Adminstrn., 1964-71, Wichita Soc. Accountants prof. bus., 1971—. Dir. Gates Lear Jet Industries, Kan. Beef Industries, Union Nat. Bank. Mem. Gov. Kan. Adv. Bd. to Bd. Accountancy, 1962—. Trustee Wichita YMCA. Mem. Am. Inst. C.P.A.'s, Kan. Soc. C.P.A.'s, Wichita C. of C., Wichita Sales and Marketing Execs., Alpha Kappa Psi, Beta Alpha Psi, Phi Kappa Phi, Alpha Tau Omega. Republican. Mem. Greek Orthodox Ch. Rotarian. Home: 6110 E 11th St Wichita KS 67208

JACHE, ALBERT WILLIAM, chemist, educator; b. Manchester, N.H., Nov. 5, 1924; s. William Frederick and Esther (Ruemely) J.; B.S., U. N.H., 1948, M.S., 1950; Ph.D., U.Wash., 1952; m. Luch Ellen Hauslein, June 14, 1948; children-Ann Gail, Ellen Ruth, Philip William, Heidi Verena. Sr. chemist Air Reduction Co., Murray Hill, N.J., 1952-53; research asso. physics dept. Duke, 1953-55; asst. prof. chemistry dept. Tex. A. and M. U., College Station, 1955-58, asso. prof., 1958-61; asso. research dir. Ozark Mahoning Co., Tulsa, 1961-64, cons., 1960-61; sr. research asso. Olin Mathieson Chem. Corp., New Haven, 1964-65, sect. mgr., 1965-67, cons., 1967—; prof., chmn. chem. dept. Marquette U., Milw., 1967—; lectr. U. Tulsa, 1963—, New Haven Coll., 1967. BD. dirs. Milw. Sci. Ednl. Trust. Served with AUS, 1943-46. Mem. Research Soc. Am., N.Y. Acad. Sci., A.A.A.S., Am. Chem. Soc. (sect. chmn.), Sigma Xi. Home: 1616 Martha Washington Dr Wauwatosa WI 53213 Office: 535 N 14th St Milwaukee WI 53233

JACK, GLENN ROBERT, lawyer; b. Mount Angel, Ore., Sept. 16, 1895; s. Joel Lincoln and Ida E. (Simmons) J.; A.B., Pacific U., 1919; LL.B., Northwestern Coll. Law, Portland, 1923; m. Vanessa Chisholm, Jan. 22, 1922; children—Patricia (Mrs. James Skene), Norma (Mrs. Phillip Sabag), Alan R. Admitted to Ore. bar, 1923; practiced law, Oregon City, 1924—; mem. firm Butler & Jack, 1924-47, Butler, Jack, Beckett & Holman, 1947-50, Butler, Jack & Beckett, 1950-55, now Jack, Goodwin & Anicker. Trustee Pacific U. Served with USN, World War I. Fellow Am. Coll. Trial Lawyers, Am. Bar Assn. (mem. ho. dels.; bd. govs. 1968—), Am. Bar Found.; mem. Ore. (gov., pres.), Cal., bar assns., Am. Judicature Soc., Nat. Conf. Bar Presidents (chmn. 1957-58), Western Bar Conf. (chmn. 1960-61), Delta Theta Phi. Home: 5495 Grove St West Linn OR 97068 Office: Smith Bldg Oregon City OR 97045

JACK, HAROLD HARRY, labour union exec.; b. De Yarmonsville, O., Apr. 19, 1921; s. Harry Donald and Ruth (De Yarmon) J.; B.C.S., Benjamin Franklin U., Washington, 1950; m. Marjorie Engstrom, March 17, 1945; children—Daria (Mrs. William H. Hunley, Jr.), Sandra (Mrs. Randall Crittenden), Patricia. Bookkeeper, CIO, 1947-52, controller, 1952-55; controller AFL-CIO, 1955—. Sec.-treas. Human Resources Devel. Inst., 1968—. Served with USNR, 1942-45. Mem. Office Employees Internat. Union, Benjamin Franklin U. Alumni Assn. Democrat. Methodist. Club: Manor Golf and Country (Rockville, Md.). Home: 4925 Bel Pre Rd Rockville MD 20853 Office: 815 16th St NW Washington DC 20006

JACK, HOMER A., clergyman, assn. exec.; b. Rochester, N.Y., May 19, 1916; s. Alexander and Cecelia (Davis) J.; B.S., Cornell U., 1936, M.S., 1937, Ph.D., 1940; B.D., Meadville Theol. Sch. 1945; m. Esther Rhys Williams, Nov. 23, 1939; children—Alexander, Lucy. Ordained to ministry Unitarian Ch.; minister, Lawrence, Kan., 1943-44, Evanston, Ill., 1948-59; asso. dir. Am. Com. on Africa, 1959-60; exec. dir. Nat. Com. for Sane Nuclear Policy, 1960-64; dir. div. social responsibility Unitarian Universalist Assn., Boston, 1964-70; sec.-gen. World Conf. Religion for Peace, 1970—. Exec. sec. Chgo. Council Against Racial and Religious Discrimination, 1943-48. Recipient Thomas H. Wright award City of Chgo.; citations North Shore Citizens Com., Chgo. Defender. Mem. Unitarian Fellowship for Social Justice (chmn. 1946-48), Liberal Religious Peace Fellowship (chmn. 1958-59), Am. Civil Liberties Union (vice chmn. Ill. div. 1947-59), Unitarian Ministers Assn., Fellowship of Reconciliation. Author: Biological Field Stations of the World, 1945; The Wit and Wisdom of Gandhi, 1951; Albert Schweitzer Festschrift, 1955; The Gandhi Reader., 1956; Religion and Peace, 1966; World Religions and World Peace, 1969. Contbr. articles to mags., newspapers, anthologies. Home: 34 Cedar Lane Way Boston MA 02108 Office: 777 UN Plaza New York City NY 10017

JACKEL, WILLIAM JOHN, mfg. co. exec.; b. McKeesport, Pa., Nov. 19, 1910; s. William Theodore and Clara Elizabeth (Miller) J.; B.S. in Metall. Engring., Lehigh U., 1932; m. Dorothy Lundgren, Apr. 30, 1938; children—Christine, John, William. Engr., U.S. Steel Corp., 1933-36, Standard Oil Co. Cal., 1936-40; asst. dir. metall. research A. O. Smith Corp., 1940-45, mgr. pressure equipment sales, 1945-48; with ACF Industries, Inc., 1948—, pres. Albuquerque div., 1956-60, v.p. corp., gen. mgr. Albuquerque div., 1960-68, v.p., div. gen. mgr., 1968—. Mem. Am. Ordnance Assn., Am. Soc. Metals, Am. Welding Soc., Beta Theta Pi. Clubs: Albuquerque Country. Home: 160 E 65th St New York City NY 10021 Office: 750 3d Av New York City NY 10017

JACKENDOFF, NATHANIEL, educator; b. N.Y.C., Feb. 24, 1919; s. Harry and Bella (Brainin) J.; B.S.S., Coll. City N.Y., 1938; M.A., U. Ill., 1939, Ph.D., 1948; m. Elaine Muriel Flanders, Apr. 4, 1943; children—Ray Saul, Harry Alan, Samuel Jay. Asst. prof. econs. Washington and Jefferson Coll., 1948-50; asst. prof. to prof. finance, chmn. dept. Temple U., 1950—. Dir. Small Bus. Adminstrn. Research Project, 1959-60; econ. cons. U.S. Naval War Coll., Newport, R.I., 1962. Served to tech. sgt., USAAF, 1943-45. Fulbright research scholar, Spain, 1969. Mem. Am. Econ. Assn., Am. Finance Assn., Am. Assn. Univ. Profs. Jewish religion. Author: The Use of Financial Ratios by Small Business, 1961; A Study of Published Industry Financial and Operating Ratios, 1962; Money, Flow of Funds and Economic Policy, 1968. Home: 2217 Panama St Philadelphia PA 19103

JACKETT, WILBUR ROY, jurist; b. Tompkins, Sask., Can., June 27, 1912; s. William Henry and Frances Victoria (Sweet) J.; B.A., U. Sask., 1931, LL.B., 1933; B.A. in Jurisprudence (Rhodes scholar) Oxford (Eng.) U., 1936, B.C.L., 1937, M.A., 1949; m. Kathleen Robertson, Sept. 5, 1939. Admitted to Sask. bar, 1938, Ont. bar, 1952, Que. bar, 1960, B.C., 1964; Queen's counsel, 1949; asso. with G.H. Yule, Saskatoon, 1937-38; with Canadian Dept. Justice, 1939-60, dep. minister justice, dep. atty. gen. Can., 1957-60; gen. counsel C.P. Ry., 1960-64; pres. Exchequer Ct. of Can., 1964-71; chief justice Fed. Ct. Can., 1971—. Hon. lectr. Osgoode Hall Law Sch., Toronto, 1954. Clubs: Rideau, Cerle Universitaire (Ottawa). Contbr. legal articles to profl. jours. Home: Tiffany Apts 150 Driveway Ottawa Ontario Canada Office: Supreme and Exchequer Ct Bldg Ottawa Ontario Canada

JACKMAN, ALBERT HAVENS, educator; b. Rosedale, Kan., Feb. 15, 1908; s. Samuel Edwin and Lou (Havens) J.; grad. Lawrenceville Sch., 1927; B.S., Princeton, 1931; Ph.D., Clark U., 1953; postgrad. Army Command and Gen. Staff Coll., 1950- 51; m. Janet Bubier, Dec. 14, 1946; children—Jean Alice, Samuel Bubier. Spl. agt. Northwestern Mut. Life Ins. Co., Washington, 1931-41; commd. capt. U.S. Army, 1941, advanced through grades to col., 1954; ret., 1962; asst. prof. dept. geography Western Mich. U., Kalamazoo, 1962-63, asso. prof., 1963-64, prof., head dept., 1964—. Cons. Arctic Inst. N.Am., 1967—; dir. Leidigh & Havens Lumber Co., Kansas City, Mo. Bd. dirs. Nature Center Kalamazoo. Decorated Bronze Star medal with V. Mem. A.A.A.S., Assn. Am. Geographers, Arctic Inst. N.Am., Am., Nat. geog. socs., Am. Assn. U. Profs., Mich. Acad. Sci., Arts and Letters, Nat. Council Geog. Edn., 10th Mountain Div. Assn. (Rocky Mountain chpt.). Episcopalian. Rotarian. Clubs: American Alpine (N.Y.C.); Potomac Appalachian Trail (Washington); Kalamazoo Country, Kalamazoo Ski. Home: 1405 Meadowbrook Lane Kalamazoo MI 49008

JACKMAN, HENRY RUTHERFORD, investment exec.; b. Toronto, Can., Nov. 5, 1900; s. Henry B. and Sarah Ann (Rutherford) J.; student Osgoode Hall Law Sch.; LL.B., U. Toronto, 1924; grad. Sch. Bus. Adminstrn., Harvard; m. Mary Coyne, Apr. 26, 1930; children—Henry, Eric, Edward, Nancy Ruth. With Dominion Securities Corp., 1928-31; spl. lectr. investment banking U. Toronto, Extension Div., 1931-33; pres. Rosedale Riding Conservative Assn., 1936-38; pres. Dominion & Anglo Invrstment Corp., Ltd., Electra Investments (Can.) Ltd.; dir. E-L Financial Corp., Ltd.; hon. chmn. Empire Life Ins. Co.; chmn. of Canadian & Fgn. Securities Co., Ltd.; dir. of Dominion of Can. Gen. Ins. Co., Casualty Co. of Can., Algoma Central Railway Co., Bank of Nova Scotia, United Accumulative Fund, Ltd., also dir. United Funds Can. Internat., Ltd., Canadian Internat. Investment Trust, Ltd. Toronto-Rosedale, mem. House of Commons, 1940-48; sec., exec. com. Empire Parliamentary Conf., Ottawa, 1943. Vice chmn. Canadian com. Atlantic Congress London, 1959; chmn. Canadian Red Cross Pension Fund; nat. exec. com. Canadian Inst. Internat. Affairs. Served as second 2d lt. Royal Air Force, 1918. Mem. of Military and Hospitaller Order St. Lazarus of Jerusalem (referendary), Venerable Order St. John of Jerusalem, Commonwealth Parliamentary Assn. Conservative. United Church of Can. (mem. treasury bd.). Mason. Clubs: Toronto: National; Albany; Badminton and Racquet; Eglinton Hunt, Toronto Hunt, Harvard U. Asss. in Can., Inc. (pres.). Home: 35 Rosedale Rd Toronto 5 Ontario Canada Office: 44 King St West Toronto Ontario Canada

JACKMAN, LLOYD MILES, educator; b. Goolwa, South Australia, Apr. 1, 1926; s. Charles Stuart and Florence Olive (Green) J.; B.Sc., U. Adelaide (Australia, 1945, B.Sc. with honors, 1946, M.Sc., 1948, Ph.D., 1951; m. Marie Alma Sandow, 1950; children—Richard Miles, Donald Charles, Andrew Thorpe. Came to U.S., 1967. Asst. lectr. organic chemistry Imperial Coll., London, Eng., 1952, lectr., 1953; reader U. London, 1961-62; prof., head dept. organic chemistry U. Melbourne (Australia), 1962-67; prof. chemistry Pa. State U., 1967—; cons. in field. Beit fellow U. London, 1951-52; NSF sr. fgn. fellow, 1965. Fellow Chem. Soc. London, Am. Chem. Soc., Royal Australian Chem. Inst.; mem. Phi Lambda Upsilon. Author: Applications of NMR in Organic Chemistry. Home: 710 Glenn Rd State College PA 16801 Office: 212 Whitmore Lab University Park PA 16802

JACKMAN, RAYMOND JOSEPH, surgeon, author; b. Emmetsburg, Ia., May 16, 1906; s. Joseph and Mary (Jennings) J.; student Ia. State Coll., 1924-25; M.D., U. Ia., 1930; m. Lois Hovenden, Jan. 18, 1934; children—Colette, Roger, Steven. Intern St. Mary's Hosp., Kansas City, Mo., 1930-31; pvt. practice medicine, Laurens, Ia., 1931-35; fellow Mayo Found. Grad. Sch., U. Minn., 1935-37; head dept. protology Mayo Clinic, Rochester, Minn., 1953—; asso. prof. U Minn., prof. proctology grad. sch. medicine U. Minn. Mayo Found. Past pres. Minn. State Bd. Health. Diplomate Am. Bd. Proctology. Mem. Am. Proctologic Soc. (past pres.), Am., Minn. (ho. dels., pres. 1971) med. assns., Olmstead County Med. Soc. (pres.), Sigma Xi. Author: Lesions of the Lower Bowel, 1959; Tumors of the Large Bowel, 1968; also numerous publs. on colon and rectal diseases. Home: 913 9th Av SW Rochester MN 55901 Office: 200 1st St SW Rochester MN 55901

JACKMAN, WILLIAM, assn. exec.; b. Manchester, Eng., Nov. 9, 1893; s. Thomas and Mary Ann (Schucker) J.; Mech. Engr., Elec. Engr., U. Manchester, 1912; m. Mary Ann Benson, Jan. 23, 1923; 1 son, Roy Parker. Came to U.S., 1922, naturalized, 1953. Vice pres. Investors Fairplay League, N.Y.C., 1945-48; v.p. Investors League, N.Y.C., 1950, dir., 1945—, pres., 1950—. Served with British Army, 1914-18. Mem. Newcomen Soc. N. Am. Protestant Episcopalian (vestry). Club: Capitol Hill (Washington). Author: How Your Laws Are Made, 1959. Home: 40 Washington St East Orange NJ 07017 Office: Investors League Inc 1 The Crescent Montclair NJ 07042

JACKSON, AL, mem. Booker T and the M. G's rock group. Address: care BEA 200 W 57th St New York City NY 10019*

JACKSON, ALLEN KEITH, coll. pres.; b. Rocky Ford, Colo., July 22, 1932; s. Monford L. and Leliah Jean (Hipp) J.; B.A., U. Denver, 1954; Fulbright fellow Cambridge (Eng.) U., 1955; Th.M. (Elizabeth Iliff Warren fellow), Iliff Sch. Theology, 1958; Ph.D. (Honor fellow), Emory U., 1960; m. Barbara May Hollard, June 13, 1954; childrenCary Vincent, Deborah Kay and Edward Keith (twins), Frederick James. Meth. student minister, Erie, Colo., 1955-58; ordained elder Meth. Ch., 1958; instr. sociology Emory U., 1958-60; chaplain, asst. prof. religion and sociology Morningside Coll., Sioux City, Ia., 1960-62, dean coll., 1962-67; pres. Huntingdon Coll., Montgomery, Ala., 1968-. Mem. Community Council; pres. Council Ch.-related Colls.; adv. bd. St. Margaret's Hosp., Mem. Ala. Assn. Ind. Colls. and Univs. (pres. 1969-71), UN Assn. (past pres. Sioux City chpt.), Phi Beta Kappa, Omicron Delta Kappa, Beta Theta Pi. Rotarian. Contbr. articles to profl. jours. Home: 1393 Woodley Rd Montgomery AL 36106

JACKSON, AMOS WADE, former state justice; b. Versailles, Ind., June 25, 1904; s. Rowland II Georgia W. (Frohliger) J.; A.B., Hanover (Ind.) Coll., 1926; m. Lola M. Raper, Aug. 20, 1927; children—Jeannette (dec.), Ann Louise (Mrs. Richard B. Stanley). Admitted to Ind. bar, 1925, practiced in Versailles until 1959; pros. atty. Ripley County, 1937-40; asso. atty. C.E., War Dept., 1942-43; asso. justice Ind. Supreme Ct., 1959-71. Pres., Jackson Abstracts, Inc. Mem. Hoosier Hills council Boy Scouts Am., 1928-29. Named Ky. col. Mem. Ind. Judges Assn., Am. Judicature Soc., Ind. Fedn. Art Clubs, Am., Ind., Ripley County, Indpls. bar assns., Southeastern Ind. Park Assn., Lambda Chi Alpha, Phi Alpha Delta, Baptist. Mason (Shriner). Address: Versailles IN 47042

JACKSON, ANDREW MCBURNEY, Jr., ret. naval officer; b. Holly Springs, Miss., Mar. 12, 1907, s. Andrew McBurney and Alice (Quiggins) J.; student La. State U., 1923-26; B.S., U.S. Naval Acad., 1930, postgrad. Postgrad. Sch., 1936-38; M.S., Cal. Inst. Tech., 1939; m. Bertha Latane Lewis, Dec. 10, 1934; 1 dau., Helen Lewis (Mrs. J. Beverly Young, Jr.). Commd. ensign USN 1930, advanced through grades to vice adm., 1964; naval aviator, 1932; served in cruisers, aircraft carriers, patrol squadrons prior to World War II; comdr. Carrier Air Group 8 in U.S.S. Intrepid, U.S.S. Bunker Hill, World War II; chief staff Carrier Task Force, Korean War; comdr. carrier U.S.S. Ticonderoga, 1955-56, Carrier Div. 3, 1959, Middle East Force, 1961; chief staff Naval War Coll., 1961-63; asst. chief naval operations plans and policy, 1963, dep. chief, 1963-67; vice chmn. U.S. delegation UN Mil. Staff Com., comdr. Eastern Sea Frontier, 1967-69. Decorated D.S.M. with star, Legion of Merit with 2 stars, D.F.C. Mem. Kappa Alpha. Address: 213 Providence Rd Annapolis MD 21401

JACKSON, ARNOLD WILLIAM, banker; b. Foxburg, Pa., June 9, 1920; s. William Arnold and Beulah Mae (Moyer) J.; grad. Richland Twp. High Sch., St. Petersburg, Pa., 1938; m. Glenna Maxine Levy, Oct. 1, 1944; 1 son, Phillip Keith. Bookkeeper Foxburg Bank, 1943-50; asst. cashier First Nat. Bank, Rimersburg, Pa., 1950-54; asst. v.p. First Seneca Bank & Trust Co., Oil City, a.-Rimersburg, 1954-67, treas., mgr. Oil City Office, 1967-71, v.p., sr. loan officer, 1971—; pres., dir. Intercounty Credit Bur., 1967—. Club: Oil City. Home: 1014 Grandview Rd Oil City PA 16301 Office: First Seneca Bank and Trust Co 248 Seneca St Oil City PA 16301

JACKSON, BAGS, see Jackson, Milton,

JACKSON, BARRY WENDELL, lawyer; b. Long Beach, N.J., Jan. 27, 1930; s. Rodney H. and Marion (Englebright) J.; A.B., Stanford, 1952, LL.B., 1958; m. Susan B. Shields, June 4, 1955; children-Stacy Ann, Sydney Elise, Leslie Barry, Morgan Susan, Bruce Edward. Admitted to Alaska bar, 1959; law clk. U.S. Dist. Ct., Fairbanks, 1958; city atty., Fairbanks, 1959-63; partner firm Jackson & Fenton, Fairbanks, 1963-69; pvt. practice, Fairbanks, 1970—. Mem. exec. bd. Episcopalian Missionary Dist. Alaska, 1967-68. Mem. Alaska Ho. of Reps., 1965-66, 69-70. Bd. dirs. United Good Neighbors Tanana Valley. Served to 1st lt. USMCR, 1952-55; maj. Res. Recipient Rotary Club award for service in fostering Japanese-Am. relations, 1954. Mem. Am., Alaska, Tanana Valley bar assns., Alaska Acad. Trial Lwyers, Am. Judicature Soc., Nat. Assn. Tax Attys, Am. Civil Liberties Union, N.A.A.C.P., Alaska Conservation Soc., Marine Corps Res. Officers Assn., Assn. U.S. Navy, Marine Corps League, Am. Legion, Am. Trial Lawyers Assn., Acad. Polit. Sci., Alaska Miners Assn., Assn. Am. Indian Affairs, Delta Theta Phi. Democrat. Episcopalian. Elk, Kiwanian. Home: 1140 Sunset Dr Fairbanks AK 99701 Office: P O Box 348 527 4th Av Fairbanks AK 99707

JACKSON, BLYDEN, educator; b. Paducah, Ky., Oct. 12, 1910; s. George Washington and Julia Estelle (Reid) J.; A.B., Wilberforce U., 1930; A.M., U. Mich., 1938, Ph.D. (Rosenwald fellow 1947-49), 1952; m. Roberta Bowles, Aug. 2, 1958. Tchr. English, pub. schs., Louisville, 1934-45; asst., then asso. prof. English, Fisk U., 1945-54; prof. English, head dept. Southern U., 1954-62, dean Grad. Sch., 1962-69; prof. English, U. N.C., 1969—. spl. research criticism Negro lit. Mem. Coll. Lang Assn. (pres. 1957-59), Modern Lang. Assn., Nat. Council Tchrs. English, Coll. English Assn., Speech Assn. Am., La. Edn. Assn., Alpha Phi Alpha. Author articles profl. jours. Asso. editor CLA Bull., 1159—. Home: 102 Laurel Hill Rd Chapel Hill NC 27514

JACKSON, CARROLL S., banker; b. Balt., 1925; grad. Princeton, 1948. Sr. v.p. First Nat. Bank Md., Balt. Home: 921 Bellemore Rd Baltimore MD 21210 Office: Light & Redwoods Sts Baltimore MD 21203*

JACKSON, CHARLES P., utility exec.; b. Birmingham, Ala., 1912; ed. U. Fla., 1934, U. Ala., 1940. Treas., v.p. Ala. Power Co. Home: 2945 Balmoral Rd, Birmingham AL 35223 Office: 600 N 18th St Birmingham AL 35203 *

JACKSON, CLARENCE A., ins. exec.; b. Columbus, O., June 29, 1891; s. Charles and Isa (Frampton) J.; student Wabash Coll., 1915, LL.D., 1965; m. Edith Gronendyke, Oct. 28, 1916; children—Ann, Robert Gronendyke. Sales mgr. Hoosier Mfg. Co., 1928-32; partner Smith-Jackson Co., wholesalers, 1918-33; organizer, dir. Ind. State Gross Income Tax Div., 1933-39, Ind. State Employment Security Div., 1936-39; spl. asst. adminstr. Fed. Security Agy., 1939- 40; exec, v.p. Ind. C. of C., 1939-52; pres. Am. United Life Ins. Co., Indpls., 1952-62, chmn. bd. dirs., 1957—. Vice chmn. Ind. Com. Econ. Devel., 1943-48; chmn. Ind. Bd. Tax Commrs. 1968-69; vice chmn. Ind. War History Commn. Chmn. devel. bd. Wabash Coll., 1960-64. Mem. Nat. Fedn. Tax Adminstrs. (founder), Am. Legion (state comdr. 1926, pres. res. finance com. Ind.), Council State C. of C. (past pres.), Sigma Chi, Beta Gamma Sigma. Methodist. Mason, Elk. Clubs: Athletic, Columbia, Press (Indpls.). Home: 4202 Central Av Indianapolis IN 46205 Office: PO Box 368 Indianapolis IN 46206

JACKSON, CLARENCE EVERT, educator, engr.; b. Graceville Minn., Sept. 4, 1906; s. Caleb Adin and Anna Emily (Johnson) J.; B.A. with honors, Carleton Coll., 1927; postgrad George Washington U., 1932; m. Anne Grace Scott, June 25, 1936; children—Sue Anne (Mrs. Ronald J. Sloan), William Evert, Jane Scott. Sci. instr., Hot Springs, S.D., 1927-30; jr. metallurgist Nat. Bur. Standards, Washington, 1930-37; asst. metallurgist U.S. Naval Gun Factory, Washington, 1937-38; head welding sect. Naval Research Lab., Washington, 1938-46; research metallurgist, head welding sect. metals research lab. Union Carbide Corp., Niagara Falls, N.Y., 1946-57, asso. mgr., electric welding devel. Newark Labs., Linde Co. div. 1957-64; asso. prof. welding engring. Ohio State U., Columbus, 1964—. Guest lectr. Australian Welding Inst., Sydney; del. Internat. Inst. Welding 1960—; conferee 1st and 2d World Metall. Congresses, Am. Soc. Metals; C.A. Adams lectr. sci. arc welding Am. Welding Soc. Recipient Distinguished Civilian Service award Sec. Navy; MacQuigg Outstanding Tchr. award, 1971. Registered profl. engr., Ohio. Fellow Brit. Instn. Metallurgists, Brit. Inst. Welding (hon.); mem. Am. Welding Soc. (nat. pres., 1963-64, S.W. Miller gold medal, life), Am. Soc. Metals, Am. Inst. Mining and Metall. Engrs., Am. Soc. Engring. Edn., French Soc. Welding Tau Beta Pi. Presbyn. (elder). Editor; Arc Welding, 1958. Contbg. author: Modern Materials, 1960; Ency. Americana, 1962. Contbr. numerous tech. papers to profl. lit. Home: 866 Mission Hills Lane Worthington OH 43085 Office: 190 W 19th Av Columbus OH 43210

JACKSON, CORNWELL, TV producer; b. St. Louis, Jan. 17, 1902; s. George Martin and Anne (Costello) J.; m. Gail Patrick, July 25, 1947 (div. Jan. 1970); children—Jennifer S., Thomas Cornwell. Clk. Kingsbaker Bros. Co., Los Angeles, 1920-24; salesman Barstow & Co., Norwich, Conn., 1924-26; sec. treas. Standard Home Utilities, N.Y.C., 1926-29; sec. to Rupert Hughes, 1929-35; mgr. lit. and radio dept. Berg-Allenberg Agy., Beverly Hills, Cal., 1935-42; dep. chief domestic radio bur. OWI, 1942-45; v.p., mgr. J. Walter Thompson Co., 1945-59; co-owner and television prod. Paisano Prodns. Spl. cons. Fed. Civil Def., 1954-60, Treasury Dept., 1943-60. Dir. So. Cal. Symphony Assn.; trustee Freedoms Found., chief protocol So. Cal., 1969. Club: Los Angeles Tennis (pres. 1944-45, 47, 49-69, pres. emeritus 1969—). Home: 3496 Berry Dr Studio City CA 91604

JACKSON, DANIEL FRANCIS, educator; b. Pitts., June 11, 1925; s. Daniel F. and Edna (Marzolf) J.; B.S., U. Pitts., 1949, M.S., 1950; Ph.D., State U. N.Y. Coll. Forestry at Syracuse U., 1957; m. Bettina B. Bush, Dec. 15, 1951. Lectr., U. Pitts., 1949-51; asst. prof. Coll. Steubenville (O.), 1952-55; asst. prof., then asso. prof. Western Mich. U., 1955-59; asso. prof. U. Louisville, 1959-63; prof. civil engring. Syracuse U., 1963-; dir. C.C. Adams Center Ecol. Study, 1955-59; asso. dir. Potamological Inst., 1960- 63; dir. 1st NATO sponsored Advanced Study Inst., U.S., summer 1962. Pres. Ky. Soc. Natural History, 1961-63. Bd. dirs. Mich. Conservation Clubs, 1955-57. Served with AUS, 1943-46; ETO. Recipient Rotary Internat. award as outstanding tchr. in Ky., 1962; Outstanding Community Leader award for environmental improvement Onondaga County, 1969. Mem. Internat. Limnological Soc., Freshwater Assn. Brit. Empire, Ecol. Soc. Am., Brit. Ecol. Soc., Limnology and Oceanography Soc.,

Sigma Xi (treas. Louisville 1962-63), Phi Sigma Nu Sigma Nu, Beta Beta Beta. Author: Algae and Man, 1963; Some Aquatiac Resources of Onondaga County, 1964; Algae, Man, and Environment, 1968; filmstrip sets Environmental Pollution, 1969, Man in the Biosphere, 1971. Home: 1200 Comstock St Syracuse NY 13210

JACKSON, DAVID MUNRO, govt. ofcl.; b. Canton, Ill., Sept. 5, 1925; s. William Clifford and Margaret Gertrude (Munro) J.; A.B. with highest honors in History, U. Ill., 1948, A.M., 1949; Ph.D., U. Chgo., 1956; m. Betty Ann Small, June 13, 1948; children—Clifford, Thomas. Tchr., Reed Jr. High Sch., Springfield, Mo., 1948-50; prin. Taylorville (Ill.) Jr. High Sch., 1950-53; research asst. Midwest Adminstrn. Center, U. Chgo., 1953-54; head, lower and middle schs. North Shore Country Day Sch., Winnetka, Ill., 1954-57; prin. U. Ill. High Sch., Urbana, 1957-64; asst. prof. U. Ill., 1957-59, asso. prof., 1959-62, prof. edn., 1962-66, asso. dean Coll. Edn., 1964-66; exec. dir. Coop. Ednl. Research Lab., Inc., Northfield, Ill., 1966-69; prof., dir. devel. Coll. Edn., U. Ill., Chgo., 1969-71; asso. supt. pub. instrn. Ill., Springfield, 1971—; cons. to minister edn. Republic of Korea, 1970. Mem. Ill. Adv. Council on Edn. Gifted, 1967-71, chmn., 1968-69. Bd. trustees Wesley Found., U. Ill. Served with USNR, 1943-45. Recipient Karl J. Holzinger prize U. Chgo., 1957. Mem. U. Chgo. Alumni Assn. (nat. council), Phi Beta Kappa, Alpha Kappa Lambda. Editor: Illinois Evaluates Its Special Program for the Gifted (with others) 1963-71; Report to the Congress of the United States on the Education of Gifted and Talented Youth, 1971. Home: 3112 Stonehill Dr Springfield IL 62704 Office: State Office Bldg Springfield IL 62706

JACKSON, MRS. DONALD ELDREDGE, Jr., (Mary Hilliard Jackson), mem. Republican Nat. Com.; b. St. Paul; d. Thomas J. and Marianna L. (Talbott) Hilliard; student Sarah Lawrence Coll.; m. Donald Eldredge Jackson, Jr., July 4, 1938; children—Donald Eldredge III, Marianna II, Holiday. Mem. Rep. Nat. Com., 1960-69. Mem. exec. com. Pres.'s Adv. Com. on Arts, 1970—. Address: 99 President Av Providence RI 02906

JACKSON, DONALD LESTER, govt. ofcl.; b. Ipswich S.D., Jan. 23, 1910; s. Cyrus Lester and Betina Lacobe (Ames) J.; ed. pub. schs., Ipswich Tribune; m. Shirley Jessica Connell, Jan. 9, 1932; 1 son, Donald Cyrus. Began as newspaper reporter and editor, Santa Monica (Cal.) Press and Santa Monica Topics, 1938-40; became dir. publicity, City of Santa Monica, 1940; mem. 80th-86th Congresses, 16th Cal. Dis.; Congl. adv. 9th Conf. Am. States, Bogota, Colmbia, 1948; chmn. Commn. on Investigation in Greece, 1947; mem. House Com. Fgn. Affairs, chmn. subcom. on W. Hemisphere, com. on Jn.-Am. activities; commr. ICC, 1969—. Served with USMC, Nicaraguan expdn. as pvt., 1927-31; capt. overseas 2d Marine div. combat at Tarawa and Saipan- Tinian, 1942-45. Recipient Unit Presdl. citation. Republican. Conglist. Mem. Res. Officers Assn., Marine Corps League, Optimist Internat., Am. Legion, Elkk. Home: Pacific Palisades CA Office: 2800 Wisconsin Av NW Washington DC 20007

JACKSON, DONALD R., chem. co. exec.; b. 1918; m.; A.B.A., Balt. Coll. Commerce. With U.S. Rubber Co., 1946-48, Montgomery Ward & Co., 1948-57; with Olin Corp., 1957-, asst. comptroller, 1957, 1st asst. treas., 1959-66, treas., 1966-. Address: 120 Long Ridge Rd Stamford CT 06904

JACKSON, EDITH BANFIELD, physician; b. Colorado Springs, Colo., Jan. 2, 1895; d. William and Helen Fiske (Banfield) Jackson; A.B., Vassar, 1916; M.D., Johns Hopkins, 1921; grad. student Inst. Psychoanalysis, Vienna, 1930-36. Interne U. Ia. Hosp., 1921-22; interne pediatrics Bellevue Hosp., N.Y. City, 1922- 23; asst. physician U.S. Children's Bur., New Haven, 1923-28; asst. physician St. Elizabeth Hosp., Washington, 1928-29; asst. in pediatrics Yale Sch. of Medicine, 1924-25, instr., 1925-27, clin. instr., 1927-29, clin. instr. psychiatry and mental hygiene, 1936-39, asst. clin. prof., 1939-41, asst. clin. prof. pediatrics (psychiatry), 1941-45, asso. clin. prof., 1945-49, clin. prof. pediatrics and psychiatry, 1949-59, emeritus 1959; vis. prof. pediatrics and psychiatry U. Colo., 1960-; attending pediatrician (psychiatric cons.) Grace-New Haven Community Hosp. (unit service), 1936-59, dir. rooming-in project, 1946-53; dir. Sigmund Freud Archives, Inc. Recipient Agnes McGavin award for preventive psychiatry Am. Psychiat. Assn., 1964. Fellow Am. Psychiat. Assn., Am. Acad. Child Psychiatry; mem. Denver Psychoanalytic Soc., Am. Acad. of Pediatrics (hon. asso. mem.; C. Anderson Aldrioh award in child devel. 1968), Am. Com. on Maternal Welfare, W. New Eng. Psychoanalytic Soc., Am. Orthopsychiat. Assn., World Federation Mental Health (asso.), Am. Psychoanalytic Assn., Am. Psychosomatic Soc., Am. Pediatric Soc. Editor (with Genevieve Trainham); Family Centered Maternity and Infant Care, supplement to Problems of Infancy and Childhood Trans., 4th Conf., 1950, of Josiah Macy, Jr., Found. Contbr. articles on care of child in hospital, clinic aspects of learning and discipline, rooming- in, etc. Home: 38O Albion St Denver CO 80220 Office: 4200 E 9th Av Denver CO 80220

JACKSON, EDWARD N., lawyer; b. San Francisco, Feb. 15, 1902; s. Abraham and Annie (Harris) J.; A.B., U. Cal. at Berkeley, 1923; student Hastings Coll. Law; m. Clarice Cohen, Dec. 6, 1928; 1 dau., Paula (Mrs. Richard E. Silverman). Admitted to Cal. bar, 1927, Supreme Ct. U.S., 1949; pvt. practice comml. law, San Francisco. Mem. Am. Bar Assn., Am. Judicature Soc., Comml. Law League Am., Lawyers Club San Francisco (pres. 1962-63), San Francisco Bar Assn. Hasting Coll. Law Alumni Assn. (pres. 1964). Home: 44 Lupine Av San Francisco CA 94118 Office: 1255 Post St San Francisco CA 94109

JACKSON, EDWIN GEORGE, librarian; b. Detroit, Feb. 28, 1911; s. Hiram and Louise S. (Leakey) J.; A.B., U. Mich., 1933; A.B. in L.S., Columbia, 1938; m. Archer Woodward Sims, Sept. 19, 1938; children—David Archer, Bruce Edwin, Anne Elizabeth. With N.Y. Pub. Library, 1937-41; corp. trust adminstr., chief job analyst Bank of Manhattan Co., 1942-50; asst. librarian Akron (O.) Pub. Library, 1951-57; dir. Free Pub. Library, Trenton, N.J., 1957-61; librarian Hartford (Conn.) Pub. Library, 1961-. Chmn. Gov. Conn. Com. Library Improvement, 1963-65; working com. Conn. State Library Research Advisory Committee. Mem. of Am. (mem. of council 1967-71), Conn. (pres. 1964-65), New Eng. Library assns., Capitol Region Library Council (treas. 1970—). Clubs: Rotary (Hartford). Home: 30 Fairlee Rd West Hartford CT 06107 Office: 500 Main St Hartford CT 06103

JACKSON, ELMER MARTIN, Jr., publishing exec.; b. Hagerstown, Md., Mar. 9, 1906; s. Elmer Martin and Blanche Beatrice (Bower) J.; A.B., St. John's Coll., Annapolis, Md., 1926; m. Mary W. A. Conard, Aug. 27, 1929; childrenElmer Martin III, Allen Conard, Pamela Conard. Reporter, sports editor, city editor Hagerstown and Annapolis, 1920-30; editor Evening Capital and Md. Gazette, Annapolis, 1933-41; v.p., editor and general mgr. Evening Capital and Md. Gazette Newspapers, 1947-69; pres., pub. Anne Arundel Times, 1969—; owner-pub. Worcester Democrat, Pocomoke City, Md.; gen. mgr., editor Capital-Gazette News, also County News, 1961-69; pres. Carroll County Times, Westminster, Md.; also dir. Md. Nat. Bank. Served as comdr. USNR, 1941-47. Past pres. dist. and state press assns.; mem. evaluating commn. Instns. Higher Learning. Mem. bd. Fed. Council State Govt., Chgo. Alderman, Annapolis, 1932-36; delegate Md. Legislature, 1937-41. Pres., Anne Arundel Pub. Library Assn., 1945—, Fine Arts Festival Found.; chmn. Anne Arundel County Econ. Devel. Commn., State Capital Planning Commn.; pres. Md. Gov.'s Prayer Breakfast Soc., 1967. Named hon. adm. U.S. Naval Acad., 1965; recipient Man of Year award Anne Arundel County, 1965. Mem. Am. Soc. Newspaper Editors, Newcomen Soc. Md., Hist. Soc., Polit. Sci. Club, Sigma Delta Chi. Democrat. Episcopalian. Elk. Clubs: Annapolis Athletic (past pres.), Annapolitan (sec.-treas.), Thirteen, Annapolis Yacht, Annapolis Roads Golf and Beach, Naval Academy Officers, Naval Academy Golf, Naval Academy Beach, Young Democratic of Anne Arundel County (past pres.); Army-Navy (Washington); University; So. Md. Soc.; Propeller. Author: The Rat Tat, 1927; Annapolis, Three Centuries of Glamour, 1938; (nature study) The Baltimore Oriole; Maryland Symbols, 1964. Home: 8 Norwood Rd Wardour Annapolis MD Office: Anne Arundel Times Bldg 208-10 West St Annapolis MD 21401

JACKSON, ELMORE, assn. exec.; b. Marengo, O., Apr. 9, 1910; s. John Wesley and Cora (Osborn) J.; B.A., Pacific Coll., Newberg, Ore., 1931; B.D., Yale, 1934, (Tew prize), Univ. fellow in Govt., 1935-36; m. Elisabeth Averill, Dec. 26, 1934; children—Karen J. Williams, Gail Elisabeth. Asst. sec. social- indsl. sect. Am. Friends Service Com., 1936-40, personnel dir., 1941-46, asst. exec. sec., 1946-48; cons. Palestine refugees UN, 1948; dir. Quaker Program UN, 1948-52, 53-57, 58-61, personal asst. UN Rep. India, Pakistan, 1952, personal asst., polit. officer, 1952-53, cons., 1953-54, spl. adviser, 1958; dir. Project Survey of Middle East, Am. Friends Service Com., 1957-58; lectr. internat. relations Haverford Coll., 1951-53; spl. asst. policy planning to asst. sec. state internat. orgn. affairs Dept. State, 1961-64, spl. asst. to asst. sec. state for internat. orgn. affairs, 1964-66; v.p. policy studies UN Assn. U.S.A., 1966—, bd. editors internat. orgn. Mem. Council Fgn. Relations; adviser U.S. delegation 16th-18th UN Gen. Assemblies. Mem. corp. Haverford Coll. Mem. Am. Polit. Sci. Assn., Am. Soc. Internat. Law. Clubs: Yale, International (Washington). Author: Meeting of Minds, 1952. Contbr. articles to profl. jours. Home: 415 E 52d St New York City NY 10017

JACKSON, ELSWORTH EUGENE, banker; b. Tacoma, Jan. 26, 1927; s. Louie E. and Rose (Hymm) J.; grad. high sch.; m. Ellen Lee King, Feb. 14, 1947; children—Gary Eugene, Gail Yvonne, Gregory Bruce. Comml. and note teller Bank of Am., San Francisco, 1947-50; cashier Pacific Nat. Bank of Wash., Tacoma, 1950—, v.p., 1961—. Mem. Tacoma Athletic Commn., 1963—; vice chmn. Tacoma City Bd. Adjustments, 1964. Mem. Wash. Bank Assn., Assn. Bank Audit, Control and Operation, Financial Execs. Inst., Tacoma C. of C. Clubs: Lions (pres.); Fircrest Golf and Country; Tacoma Country. Home: 6827 N 11th St Tacoma WA 98406 Office: 1123 Pacific Av Tacoma WA 98401

JACKSON, ERNEST A., educator; b. Saugus, Mass., Mar. 4, 1925; s. Ernest and Christina (McLaughlin) J.; B.A., Boston U., 1948; M.A., Yale, 1952; certificate U. Paris (France), 1951; Ph.D., U. Mich., 1962; m. Jean F. Phillips, June 15, 1956. Prof., chmn. dept. European Langs., U. Hawaii, Honolulu, 1961-66, chmn. French grad. div., 1967-70, chmn. French div., 1970—; vis. prof. Brazzaville, Congo, 1965. Cons. Hawaii Dept. Edn. Bd. dirs. Alliance Francaise of Honolulu. Served with AUS, 1943-46. Mem. Am. Assn. U. Profs., Modern Lang. Assn., Am. Assn. Tchrs. French. Author: The Critical Reception of Gustav Flaubert in the United States, 1966; also articles on the novel and criticism. Home: 2575 Kuhio Av Honolulu HI 96815

JACKSON, EUGENE BERNARD, librarian; b. Frankfort, Ind., June 18, 1915; s. John Herman and Goldie Belle (Michael) J.: B.S. with distinction, Purdue U., 1937; B.S. in L.S. with honors, U. Ill., 1938, M.A., 1942; m. Ruth Lillian Whitlock, Aug. 6, 1941. Asst. engring; library U. Ill., 1938-40; asst. charge newspaper div. U. Ill. Library, 1940-41; documents librarian U. Ala., 1941-42; with tech. dept. Detroit Pub. Library, 1942-46; chief reference library, Wright Field, O., chief library sect. Central Air Documents Office, Dayton, O., 1946-49; chief research information sect. Research and Devel. Command, Q.M.C., Washington, 1949-50; chief div. aero. intelligence NACA, 1950-52, chief div. research information, 1952-56; head library dept. research labs. Gen. Motors Corp., Warren, Mich. 1956-65, chmn. corp. com. tech. lit., 1959-65; dir. information retrieval and library services IBM Corp., Armonk, New York, 1965-71; prof. library sci. Grad. Sch. Library Sci., library cons. in automation U. Tex., Austin, 1971—; v.p. Engring. Index, Inc., 1967-68, pres., 1968—, also dir.; Vis. summer lectr. U. Mich., 1965, U. Ill., 1968; mem. task force United Engring. Information System, 1966. U.S. mem. documentation com., adv. group aero. research and devel. NATO, Paris, France, 1953-61, chmn., 1955-56, dep. chmn., chmn. elect. 1960-61; McBee lectr. Boston Coll., 1956; ofcl. U.S. del. gen. assemblies Fedn. International de Documentation, Tokyo, 1967, The Hague, 1968, Buenos Aires, 1970, chmn. U.S. nat. com., 1970—. Mem. tech. adv. com. Macomb County (Mich.) Planning Commn. Served with AUS, 1943-46. Mem. Spl. Libraries Assn. (pres. 1962-63), A.L.A., Am. Soc. Info. Scis., Am. Inst. Aeros. and Astronautics (sec. Mich. 1964-65). Protestant Episcopalian. Contbr. articles to profl. jours. Home: 8512 Silver Ridge Dr Austin TX 78759

JACKSON, EVERETT GEE, painter, illustrator; b. Mexia, Tex., Oct. 8, 1900; s. W.B. and Fanny (Eubank) J.; student Tex. A. and M. Coll., 1919-21, Art. Inst. Chgo., 1921-23; A.B., San Diego State Coll., 1929; A.M., U. So. Cal., 1934; m. Eileen Dwyer, July 21, 1926; 1 dau., Jerry Gee (Mrs. Thomas Williamson). Faculty, Sul Ross State Tchrs. Coll., Alpine, Tex., 1929; prof. art San Diego State Coll., 1930-63; tchr. U. Costa Rica, 1962; painter, illustrator, 1926—, nat. exhbns. Adv. bd. to pres. San Diego State Coll. Mem. Am. Assn. U. Profs., Fine Arts Soc. San Diego (trustee; chmn. Latin- Am. arts com.). Illustrator: Miller, Mexico Around Me, 1937; Louis Untermeyer, Paul Bunyan, 1945; Ugly Duckling; Popol Uuh, 1954; Conquest of Peru, 1956; American Chimney Sweeps, 1958; Ramona, Helen Hunt Jackson, 1960; Estudio de Evaluation de la Academia de Bellas Antes, Universidad de Costa Rica, 1963; American Indian Legends, 1971. Home: 1234 Franciscan Way San Diego CA 92116

JACKSON, FELIX, writer and producer; b. Hamburg, Germany, June 5, 1902; s. Siegfried and Fanny (Bloemendal) Joachimson; student U. Freiburg (Germany), 1920-23; m. Ilka Windish, Aug. 6, 1955; 1 son, Lawrence Felix. Came to U.S., 1937, naturalized, 1940. Reporter, city-editor, drama and music critic, Berlin, 1923-27; asst. theatre mgr., Berlin, 1927-30; freelance writer and playwright, Berlin, 1930-33, Vienna and Budapest, 1933-37; writer for motion pictures, Hollywood, Cal., 1937-39; writer, producer Universal Pictures, Hollywood, 1939-47; writer, producer Young & Rubicam, advt., N.Y.C., 1947-48, exec. producer for TV, 1948-52; producer Studio One, CBS, N.Y.C., 1953-57; producer Nat. Telefilm Assos., Hollywood, also BBC, London, Eng., 1958-60; v.p. West Coast programming NBC, 1960-63, v.p. prodns., TV network, 1963-65; free-lance author and producer, 1965—. Mem. Acad. Motion Picture Arts and Scis., Acad. TV Arts and Scis. Author: So Help Me God, 1955; Maestro, 1957 (trans. Swedish and Polish). Home: 4149 Murietta Av Sherman Oaks CA 91403

JACKSON, FLOYD LOUIS, judge; b. Alvord, Tex., Apr. 13, 1902; s. John Washington and Laura May (Parson) J.; LL.B., U. Okla., 1927; m. Geneva Morrison, Sept. 7, 1931. Admitted to Okla. bar, 1927; practicing atty., 1927-42; dist. judge, Cotton and Comanche counties, Okla., 1947-54; justice Okla. Supreme Ct., 1955—, vice chief justice, 1966, chief justice, 1967-69; justice Oklahoma Supreme Court, since 1969—. Served with AUS, 1942-46; lt. col. ret. Named to Okla. Hall of Fame, 1968. Home: Lawton OK 73501 Office: State Capitol Bldg Oklahoma City OK 73105

JACKSON, FRANCIS CHARLES, physician, surgeon; b. Rutherford, N.J., Sept. 2, 1917; s. Frank Emil and Margaret Charlotte (Kuhn) J.; B.A., Yale, 1939; M.D., U. Va., 1943; m. Joan Gloria Mortenson, Sept. 1, 1949; children—Geoffrey P., Bradford M., Gregory C., Donna E. Intern, N.Y. Hosp.-Cornell Med. Center, 1944, asst. resident surgery, 1945, asst. resident surgery to 1st asst. chief surgeon, 1947-49, chief resident surgeon, 1950; practice medicine, specializing in gen. and vascular surgery, Pitts., 1952-70; cons., chief surgeon Arabian Am. Oil Co., Dhahran, Saudi Arabia, 1951; asst. chief surg. service VA Center, Togus, Me., 1952; chief surg. service, dir. Gen. Surg. Residency Program, VA Hosp., Pitts., 1952-70; dir. surg. service VA, Washington, 1970—; mem. cons. staff Presbyn.-Univ. Hosp., Pitts., 1959-70; asst. in surgery Sch. Medicine Cornell U., 1946-49, asst. in anatomy, 1946, instr. surgery, 1950; asst. prof. surgery Sch. Medicine U. Pitts., 1953-60, asso. prof. surgery, 1961- 65, prof. surgery, 1965-70, sec. exec. com. dept. surgery, 1964-70, also MEND coordinator, 1967-68; clin. prof. surgery Georgetown U. Sch. Medicine, also George Washington U. Sch. Medicine, 1970—. Chairman local com. Vet. Adminstrn. Adj. Cancer Chemotherapy Study, 1957-70; chmn. exec. com. Operation Prep. Pitts. Annual Med-Civil Defense Disaster Drill, 1958-60; mem. ad hoc com. disaster med. surveys, div. med., vice chmn. com. emergency med. services Nat. Acad. Scis.-NRC, 1964—; mem. surgery adv. com. Food and Drug Adminstrn.; mem. panel on physicians asst. Civil Service Commn.; cons. on emergency and disaster services USPHS. Served to lt. (j.g.) USNR, 1945-46, to lt. comdr., M.C., 1953-55. Recipient Pfizer award of merit U.S. Civil Defense Council, Mpls., 1960, Key to City Louisville, 1964; Billings Gold Medal award A.M.A., 1966. Diplomate Am. Bd. Surgery, Nat. Bd. Med. Examiners. Fellow A.C.S. (past chmn. residents program com. Southwestern Pa. chpt.; chmn. subcom. disaster, surgery and communications of trauma com.; mem. trauma com.; exec. com.; president Southwestern Pa. chapter 1970, gov. 1970—); mem. A.M.A. (chmn. com. disaster med. care, mem. Council Nat. Security), Pa. (chmn. commn. on emergency med. services), Allegheny County med. socs., Soc. Biol. Research U. Pitts. Sch. Medicine, Pitts. Surg. Soc., Am. Assn. Surgery of Trauma, Central Surg. Assn., Soc. For Surgery Alimentary Tract, Aerospace Med. Assn., Assn. Mil. Surgeons U.S. (Stitt award 1968), Pitts. Acad. Medicine, Pan Pacific Surg. Assn., Pitts. Surg. Soc., D.C. Med. Soc., Am. Surg. Assn. Author: Role of Medicine in Emergency Preparedness, 1968; also articles in surg. jours. Home: 310 Chesapeake Dr Riverside Manor Great Falls VA 22066 Office: VA Dept Medicine and Surgery Washington DC 20420

JACKSON, FREDERICK HERBERT, ednl. adminstr.; b. New Haven, May 16, 1919; s. Fred and Mary (Butler) J.; A.B., Brown U., 1941, LL.D., 1968; A.M., U. Pa., 1948, Ph.D., 1950; m. Eleanor Stearns Whittemore, May 2, 1942; children—Isabel S., David L. Instr., Marietta Coll., 1948-49, asst. prof., 1949-50; instr. U. Ill., 1950-52, asst. prof., 1952-55; exec. asst. Carnegie Corp., N.Y.C., 1955-57, exec. asso., 1957-64; asst. exec. v.p. N.Y.U., 1964-66, v.p. humanities and social scis., 1966-67; pres. Clark U., Worcester, Mass., 1967-7O; dir. com. on Instl. Cooperation Council of Ten. and U. Chgo., 1970—. Dir. Guaranty Bank & Trust Co., 1967-70, Paul Revere Variable Annuity Ins. Co. Mem. Representative Town Meeting, Westport, Conn., 1957-59, 61-67. Trustee U. Bridgeport, 1961—; bd. dirs. Worcester Art Mus., 1968-70. Served to 1st lt. USAAF, 1942-46. Mem. Am. Hist. Assn., Am. Assn. U. Profs., Am. Antiguarian Soc., Phi Beta Kappa. Author: Simeon Eben Baldwin, American Social Scientist, 1955. Home: 1260 21st St Wilmette IL 60091 Office: 1603 Orrington Av Evanston IL 60201

JACKSON, GABRIEL, educator, historian; b. Mt. Vernon, N.Y., Mar. 10, 1921; s. Walter and Julia (Goldberg) J.; A.B., Harvard, 1942; M.A., Stanford, 1950; Ph.D., U. Toulouse (France), 1952; m. Elizabeth Kerr Riddle, Dec. 23, 1948, (div. 1970); children—Katharine, Rachel; m. 2d, Dorothy Dickson Jones. Tchr. English and Spanish, Putney Sch., 1946-49; instr. history Goddard Coll., 1952-55; instr., asst. prof. history Wellesley Coll., 1955-60; asso. prof. history Knox Coll., 1962-65; prof. U. Cal. at San Diego, 1965—, chmn. dept. history, 1965-67, 70-71, chmn. faculty senate, 1969-71; cons. Hispanic Found. of Library of Congress, 1958—, Wesleyan U. Press, 1958—, Ency. Americana, 1960, Ind. U. Press, 1965—. Mem. Ill. Freedom of Residence Com., 1962-65. Served with AUS, 1942-45. Fulbright fellow, 1950-51; Social Sci. Research Council fellow, 1960-62; Am. Council Learned Socs. fellow, 1967-68. Mem. Am. Hist. Assn., Am. Assn. U. Profs., Am. Civil Liberties Union, N.A.A.C.P. Author: The Spanish Republic and the Civil War, 1965; Historian's Quest, 1969; The Making of Medieval Spain, 1976. Contbr. articles profl. jours. Home: 5959 Waverly Av La Jolla CA 92037

JACKSON, GAIL PATRICK, TV producer; b. Birmingham, Ala., June 20; d. Lawrence C. and La Valle (Smith) Fitzpatrick; A.B. with honors, Howard Coll. (now Samford U.), 1932; m. Cornwell Jackson, July 25, 1947 (div. 1970); children—Jennifer Stanley, Thomas Cornwell. Film actress, 1932-47; motion pictures include My Man Godfrey, Stage Door, My Favorite Wife, Up in Mabel's Room, Claudia and David; propr. Gail Patrick's Enchanted Cottage, children's shop, Beverly Hills, Cal., 1945-54, Gail Patrick's Enchanted Weavers, Beverly Hills, 1950-51; exec. producer Perry Mason Show, Paisano Prodns., Hollywood, Cal., 1957-66; pres. Paisano Prodns., Inc., 1966—. Treas., Los Angeles County chpt. Freedoms Found. at Valley Forge, 1967-68; 1st v.p. The Muses, Mus. Sci. and Industry, Los Angeles, 1967-68; co-chmn. Mayor's Celebrity Com., Los Angeles, 1966—; nat. hon. chmn. Christmas Seal Campaign, 1970, Nat. Tb and Respiratory Disease Assn. Regent Immaculate Heart Coll., Los Angeles, 1968—; bd. dirs. Film Industries, Workshop, 1966-68. Named Bus. Woman of Year, Woodbury Bus. Coll., Los Angeles, 1950, Los Angeles Times, 1961, Businesswomen of Year, Nat. Assn. Accountants, 1962; recipient Muses award, 1966; Justica award Nat. Assn. Women Lawyers, 1960. Trustee Columbia Coll., 1963. Mem. Acad. TV Arts and Scis. (nat. trustee, bd. govs. 1959-63, chpt. pres. 1960-62, nat. v.p. 1960-62), Delta Zeta (v.p. found 1961-62, dir. 1961-65), Zeta Phi Eta. Home: 2003 LaBrea Terrace Hollywood CA 90046

JACKSON, GEOFFREY HOLT SEYMOUR, British diplomat; b. Little Hulton, Eng., Mar. 4, 1915; s. Samuel Seymour and Marie Cecile Dudley (Ryder) J.; B.A., Emmanuel Coll., Cambridge U., 1936, also M.A., Cambridge U.; m. Patricia Mary Evelyn Delany, Dec. 6, 1939; 1 son, Anthony Bernard Seymour. Joined British Fgn. Service, 1937; assigned successively Beirut, Cairo, Bagdad and Basra, 1937-56; 1st sec., Bogota, Colombia, 1946-50; with Am. dept. Fgn. Office, 1950-54; 1st sec., Berne, Switzerland, 1954-56; ambassador to Tegucigapda, Honduras, 1956-60; consul gen., Seattle, 1960-64; senior Brit. trade commr. to Ontario, Can., 1964-69; ambassador to Montevideo, Uruguay, 1969—; attached to U.K. delegation to UN, 1949, 53, 56, 59, 61, Econ. Commn. Latin Am. delegation, 1952.

Decorated comdr. Order St. Michael and St. George. Clubs: Lansdowne, Canning (London). Address: British Embassy Cerrito 420 Piso 7 Montevideo Uruguay

JACKSON, GEORGE GEE, educator, physician; b. Provo, Utah, Oct. 5, 1920; s. Elvon L. and Adelia (Gee) J.; A.B., Brigham Young U., 1942; M.D., U. Utah, 1945; m. Amy Smith Cox, Sept. 4, 1943; children—Janet (Mrs. Bruce J. Hendricks), Sandra, Christopher G., Amy Adelia, John Gee. Intern Boston City Hosp., 1945-46, asst. resident, 1948-49, resident medicine, 1949-50, asst., 1950-51; concurrently teaching fellow medicine Harvard, 1948-49, research fellow, 1949-50, Milton fellow in medicine, 1950-51; asst. prof. medicine and preventive medicine U. Ill. Coll. Medicine, 1951-52; attending physician U. Ill. Hosp., Chgo., 1951—, mem. grad. faculty microbiology, 1951—, prof. medicine, 1959—. Spl. fellow Tropeninstitut, Hamburg, Germany, 1968-69; dep. dir. commn. acute respiratory diseases Armed Forces Epidemiol. Bd., 1970-71, now asso. mem. commn. influenza; mem. med. examining com. Ill. Dept. Registration and Edn., 1961-67; cons. infectious diseases Westside VA Hosp. Served as lt. (j.g.), MC, USNR, 1946-48. Fellow A.C.P.; A.A.A.S., Am. Assn. Immunologists, Am. Epidemiol. Soc., Assn. Am. Physicians, Central Soc. Clin. Research, Infectious Disease Soc. Am. (sec.-treas. 1968—), Sigma Xi, Alpha Omega Alpha. Editorial bd. Jour. Lab. and Clin. Medicine, 1965—, Proceedings Soc. Exptl. Biology and Medicine, 1970—. Contbr. articles profl. jours. Home: 315 N Lincoln St Hinsdale IL 60521 Office: Univ Illinois Hosp 840 S Wood St Chicago IL 60612

JACKSON, GEORGE WOODROW, psychiatrist; b. White House, Tenn., Feb. 3, 1914; s. Alfred Thomas and Myra (Barry) J.; M.D., U. Tenn., 1937; m. Ruth Gray, June 12, 1934; children—George Barry, William Thomas, Robert Graylon. Intern, USPHS Hosp., New Orleans, Wallace Sanitarium, Memphis, 1937-38; resident psychiatry Western State Hosp., Bolivar, Tenn., 1940-42, asst. supt., 1942; clin. dir., supt. Ark. State Hosp., Little Rock, 1946-51, supt., 1961—. Med. dir. Bd. Tex. State Hosps. and Spl. Schs., 1951-53; dir. instns. Kan. Dept. Social Welfare, Topeka, 1953-61. Bd. dirs. A.R.C. Served with M.C., AUS, 1942-46. Diplomate Am. Bd. Psychiatry and Neurology. Fellow Am. Psychiat. Assn. (com. on certification mental hosp. adminstrs.); mem. Ark., Pulaski County med. socs., Mid-Continent Psychiat. Assn., Nat. Assn. State Mental Health Program Dirs. Address: 4313 W Markham St Little Rock AR 72201

JACKSON, GERALD AUDRON, paper co. exec.; b. Lexington, Tex., Jan. 3, 1916; s. Miles and Mary Ellen (Cameron) J.; m. Mary E. Byrne, Feb. 1, 1946; children—Elizabeth Byrne (Mrs. Fritz L. Connally), Joe Patrick. With shipbuilding div. U.S. Steel Co., 1940-44, Levingston Shipbuilding Co., Orange, Tex., 1944-45; asst. gen. mgr. Austin Transit Co. (Tex.), 1945-49; with Champion Papers Inc., Hamilton, O., 1949-67, dir. adminstrv. services, 1959-62, v.p. of materials planning services, 1962-67, formerly v.p. spl. relations and v.p., dir. materials services, Chgo.; v.p. materials services U.S. Plywood-Champion Papers Inc., N.Y.C., 1967-69, pres. Alaska div., 1969—. Vice president, dir. Pasadena (Tex.) Rodeo and Livestock Assn., 1955-58; chmn. Gov. Tex. Com. Alcoholism, 1957; mem. Water Pollution Control Adv. Bd., Dept. Interior, 1964-67, Nat. Adv. Com. Alocholism, Dept. Health, Education and Welfare, 1966-69. Bd. directors Nat. Council on Alcoholism, 1968-70. Member of the National Assn. Purchasing Agts. (dir. Houston 1956), Ohio, Ill. chambers commerce. Mason (Shriner). Clubs: International (Chgo.), International (Washington), Headliners (Austin). Co-author purchasing manual of Nat. Assn. Purchasing Agts., 1956. Home: Route 1 Box 247 Lexington TX 78947 Office: 777 3d Av New York City NY 10017

JACKSON, GLENN L., utility exec.; b. Albany, Ore., Apr. 27, 1902; s. W.L. and Minnie (Perry) J.; B.S., Ore State Coll., 1925; m. Helen Simpson, July 15, 1927; 1 dau., Cynthia Lee. Salesman to v.p. Mountain States Power Co., Medford, 1925-28; with Cal. Ore. Power Co. (now Pacific Power & Light), 1929—, v.p., 1931—, dir., 1936—, now chmn. and dir.; pres. Democrat Herald Pub. Co., pres., dir. Golf Holding Company; dir. Standard Ins. Co., U.S. Nat. Bank of Portland. Chmn., Ore. State Hwy. Commn.; dir. Rogue Valley Meml. Hosp. Mem. Ore. State Coll. Served as col. USAAF WW II. Decorated Bronze Star, Legion of Merit, Order Brit. Empire (hon. officer), Crown of Italy (comdr.). Clubs: University, Rogue Valley Country (Medford); Arlington (Portland, Ore.); Army and Navy (Washington). Home: 117 Greenway Circle Medford OR 97501 Office: 920 S W Sixth Av Portland OR 97204

JACKSON, HARRY ANDREW, former petroleum co. exec.; b. Eureka, Nev., May 29, 1900; s. Harry Andrew and Ina Elizabeth (Ford) J.; grad. univ., 1921; m. Marion Jordan, Aug. 23, 1924; children—Lorraine, Harry Andrew III. With Tidewater Oil Co., 1922-56; pres. Am. Petrofina, Inc., N.Y.C., 1956-68, chmn. bd., 1968—, also dir.; chmn. Am. Petrofina Co. of Tex.; chmn., dir. Am. Petrofina of Venezuela, Am. Petrofina Exploration Co., Am. Petrofina Holding Co.; dir. Am. Petrofina Pipeline Co., Dallas, Wilmington Trust Co. (Del.). Clubs: Links (N.Y.C.); Bohemian, Pacific Union (San Francisco); Wilmington (Del.). Home: 331 N Braddock St Winchester VA 22601

JACKSON, HAZEL BRILL, sculptor; b. Phila.; d. William Henry and Lizabeth Lee (Stone) Jackson; student Friends Select Sch., Phila., Boston Mus. Sch. Fine Arts, Scuola Rosatti, Florence, Italy, with Angelo Zanelli, Rome, Italy. Exhibited Nat. Mus. Modern Art, Rome, Trieste and Florence, Royal Acad. Scotland, Nat. Acad. N.Y.C., Guild Boston Artists; represented museums, pvt. collections, including Brookgreen Garden, S.C., Newburgh Pub. Library, bronzes at Wellesley, Vassar, Dartmouth colls., Springfield (Mass.) Art Mus. Recipient Ellen Spayer Meml. award Nat. Acad., 1945, 48, 60, 65; Allied Artists prize Smithsonian Instn., 1963; other awards. Fellow Nat. Sculpture Soc.; mem. N.A.D. (Young Meml. prize 1965), Guild Boston Artists, Soc. Animal Artists, Am. Artists Profl. League. Clubs: American Alpine, Italian Alpine. Home: Old Balmville Rd Newburgh NY 12550

JACKSON, HENRY A., utilities co. exec.; b. Merrimac, Mass., 1914; grad. Pa. State U., 1937. Sec., gen. counsel, dir. Peoples Natural Gas Co., Pitts. Home: 27 Brucewood Dr Pittsburgh PA 15228 Office: Two Gateway Center Pittsburgh PA 15222*

JACKSON, HENRY MARTIN, U.S. senator; b. Everett, Wash., May 31, 1912; s. Peter and Marie (Anderson) J.; LL.B., U. Wash., 1935; m. Helen E. Hardin, Dec. 16, 1961; children—Anna Marie, Peter Hardin. Admitted to Wash. bar, 1935; asso. with Black & Rucker; pros. atty. Snohomish Co., 1938-40, mem. 77th-82 Congresses, Wash. 2d Dist.; U.S. senator from Wash., 1953—, chmn. com. on interior and insular affairs Author NATO sci. fellowship program. Chmn., Democratic Nat. Com., 1960-61. Mem. Wash. Bar Assn., Phi Delta Phi, Delta Chi. Presbyn. Home: Everett WA 98201

JACKSON, HERBERT COOPER, former corp. exec.; b. Cleve., Mar. 27, 1894; s. Charles Edmund and Mary Mulvina (Cooper) J.; B.A., Yale, 1916; m. Norma Jean Witt, May 19, 1917; children—Jean (Mrs. James T. Shilcock), Dawn (Mrs. J.S. Hassett). With Pickands Mather & Co., Cleve., 1916-, partner, 1942-55, mng. partner, 1955-60 (became a corp.), exec. v.p., 1960-62, dir. until 1965; admitted to D.C. bar, 1941; owner operator amateur radio stas W8ERC, W8EXM. Chmn., Cleve. Yale Scholarship Com., chmn. exec. com. Christian Residences Found. Trustee, mem. corp. U. Hosps, 1955—; trustee Blue Cross No. Ohio. Mem. Am. Mining Congress (past pres., dir.). Am. Iron Ore Assn. (hon. dir.), Am. Iron and Steel Inst., Am. Inst. Mining and Metall. Engrs. N.A.M. (conservation and mgmt. natural resources com.), Beta Theta Pi. Clubs: Union (Cleve.); Shaker Heights (O.) Country. Home: 16608 Aldersyde Dr Shaker Heights OH 44120 Office: Union Commerce Bldg Cleveland OH 44115

JACKSON, HEZEKIAH, coll. dean; b. Greensburg, La., Feb. 8, 1917; s. Harvey and Dicy (Lewis) J.; B.S., So. U., 1941; M.S., Mich. State U., 1947, Ph.D., 1952; m. Adele Martin, May 26, 1949; children—Reginald Jerome, Raymond Eugene, Ronald Keith. Prof. horticulture, head dept. So. U., Baton Rouge, 1947-56, dir. div. agr., 1956-58, dean Coll. Agr., 1958-. Mem. nat. adv. com. Hort. Crops Research; mem. La. State adv. com. Agrl. Stblzn. Conservation Service. Active local YMCA, United Givers Fund, Blundon Orphange. Served to capt., inf. AUS, 1941- 45. Mem. Am. Soc. Hort. Sci., Am. Soc. Plant Physiologist, Bot. Soc. Am., Phi Beta Sigma. Republican. Methodist (chmn. stewardship and finance commn.). Mason (32). Club: Frontiers Internat. (Baton Rouge). Home: 2066 79th Av Baton Rouge LA 70807

JACKSON, HOYT MILTON, educator; b. Ennis, Tex., Feb. 19, 1923; s. Robert Milton and Mary (Preddy) J.; A.B., Chico State Coll., 1948; M.A., U. Cal. at Berkeley, 1950; Ph.D., U. Neb., 1955; m. Louise Ann Dalton, June 17, 1951; children—Catharine, William, Joan, Patrick. Asst. prof. polit. sci. Chico (Cal.) State Coll., 1955-61; mem. faculty State U. Coll., Oneonta, N.Y., 1961—, prof. polit. sci., 1965—. Mem. Butte County (Cal.) Democratic Central Com., 1956-60; chmn. Liberal party, Otsego Co., N.Y., 1962-68. Served with AUS, 1943-46. Mem. Am. Polit. Sci. Assn. Home: 50 Elm St Oneonta NY 13820

JACKSON, J. H., clergyman; b. Rudvard, Miss.; s. Henry and Emily (Johnson) J.; A.B., Jackson Coll., 1927, D.D.; B.D., Colgate Rochester Div. Sch., 1932; M.A., Creighton U., 1933; D.D., Central State Coll., Wilberforce, O., 1954; LL.D., Bishop Coll., Marshall, Tex., 1956; m. Maude T. Alexander; 1 dau., Kenny. Ordained to ministry Bapt. Ch.; pastor Olivet Bapt. Ch., Chgo., 1941—. Pres. Nat. Bapt. Conv., Inc., 1953—. Mem. Nat. Council Chs. (gen. bd.). Home: 4937 Kimbark Av Chicago IL 60615 Office: 405 E 31st St Chicago IL 60616

JACKSON, J. HARRY, metals co. exec.; b. Troy, N.Y., Apr. 19, 1915; s. Myron J. and Irene (Yates) J.; Chem. Engr., Rensselaer Poly Inst., 1936; m. Marian Anderson, Oct. 12, 1940; children—Elizabeth I., Anne V. (Mrs. John E. Hohmann), John H. Welding and metall. engr. Caterpillar Tractor Co., 1936-41; sect. editor Chem. Abstracts, Columbus, O., 1950-59; mgr. metall. research Battelle Meml. Inst., Columbus, 1941-61; gen. dir. metall. research div. Reynolds Metals Co., 1961—; exec. v.p. Reynolds Research Corp., 1966—; cons. to industry and govt., 1947—. Mem. metals adv. bd. Nat. Acad. Scis., 1959—; chmn. com. composites Dept. Def., 1963—. Engring. Found., 1963—. Fellow Am. Inst. Mining, Metall. and Petroleum Engrs. (chmn. titanium com. 1955-58; bd. dirs. 1965—, pres. elect Metal Soc., 1966-67, pres. 1967-68, bd. dirs. 1965—); mem. Am. Soc. Metals (pres. Columbus, 1956, nat. trustee 1963-64), Am. Soc. Testing and Materials, Am. Ordnance Assn., Am. Foundry Soc., Am. Soc. M.E., Am. Inst. Aero. and Astronautics, Engrs. Club Richmond, Sigma Xi. Author, patentee in field. Home: 8201 Diane Lane Richmond VA 23227 Office: Reynolds Metals Co 4th and Canal Sts Richmond VA 23219

JACKSON, JACQUELINE DOUGAN, educator, author; b. Beloit, Wis., May 3, 1928; d. Ronald Arthur and Vera Arlouine (Wardner) Dougan; B.A., Beloit Coll., 1950; M.A., U. Mich., 1951; m. Robert Sumner Jackson, June 17, 1950; children—Damaris Lee, Megan Trever, Gillian Patricia, Jacqueline Elspeth. Instr. English, Kent (O.) State U., 1964-68; asso. prof. lit. Sangamon State U., Springfield, Ill., 1970—; writer, presenter radio show The Author is You, U. Wis. WHA Sch. of Air, 1969—. Mem. Modern Lang. Assn., Children's Reading Round Table, Phi Beta Kappa. Episcopalian. Author: Julie's Secret Sloth, 1953; The Taste of Spruce Gum (Dorothy Canfield Fisher award 1967), 1966; Missing Melinda, 1967; Chicken Ten Thousand, 1968; Spring Song, 1969; The Orchestra Mice, 1970; author-illustrator: The Paleface Redskins, 1958; The Ghost Boat, 1969; illustrator: Knock and Enter (Chad Walsh), 1953. Home: 816 N 5th St Springfield IL 62702

JACKSON, JAMES HARVEY, educator, clergyman; b. Stroll, S.D., June 24, 1920; s. George William and Margaret (Judy) J.; A.B., Pasadena Coll., 1941, M.A., 1943; M.A., U. So. Cal., 1955, Ph.D.; 1957; m. Alida Scharn, June 30, 1944; children—James Harvey, Gerald Wesley. Ordained to ministry Ch. of Nazarene, 1944; pastor in Oakland and Merced, Cal., 1943-49; prof. speech Pasadena Coll., 1949-, dean students, 1960-, chmn. div. letters, 1958-62. Active local Boy Scouts Am., YMCA. Grantee Danforth Found., 1955-56. Mem. Speech Assn. Am., Western Speech Assn. (bus. mgr. Western Speech 1952-55), So. Cal. Collegiate Forensic Assn. (pres. 1958- 59), Coll. Student Personnel Inst., Phi Delta Lambda (pres. 1964-68), Kappa Phi Kappa, Pi Kappa Delta. Republican. Author: I Believe, 1949; Too Young to Love, 1968. Rotarian (pres. Altadena 1967-68)†

JACKSON, JAMES SNOWDEN, editor; b. Akron, O., Feb. 3, 1905; s. George C. and Ethel S. (Snowden) J.; A.B., Middlebury Coll., 1926; m. Margot Younger, Oct. 18, 1936; children—Muriel Ethel (Mrs. Richard R. Lewellen), Susan (Mrs. Miles D. Wolpin), John Younger. Reporter, Hartford (Conn.) Courant, 1926-27; life ins. salesman, 1928-32; printer, 1932-33; reporter Akron Beacon Jour., 1933-40, editorial writer, 1940—, asso. editor, 1944—. mem. Bath- Richfield (O.) Bd. Edn., 1958-65, pres., 1964-65. Bd. dirs. Family Service Soc., Akron 1946—, pres., 1955-57; dirs. Akron Community Service Center, Urban League, 1946-51. Recipient Ann. Brotherhood award Akron Coll. Chs., 1969. Mem. Am. Soc. Newspaper Editors. Club: Nat. Press, Torch. Home: 2574 Ira Rd Akron OH 44313 Office: Beacon Jour Akron OH 44309

JACKSON, JAMES WYLY, Jr., educator; b. Tallahassee, Feb. 6, 1924; s. James Wyly and Alice (Stewart) J.; A.B., Davidson Coll., 1947; student U. S.C., 1953-55; m. Blanche DeWeen Gibbs, Dec. 23, 1947; children—Lynne Stewart, James Wyly III, Leslie Gibbs, Thomas Ross. Sports writer, sports editor Columbia (S.C.) Record, 1947; clk. Office of Gov. S.C., 1947; sports dir. sta. WKIX, Columbia, 1948; dir. pub. relations Coll. William and Mary, 1949- 51; asst. dir. pub. relations Rollins Coll., 1953; promotion mgr., sports dir., staff announcer sta. WIS-TV, Columbia, 1953-55; mng. dir. Carolina Carillon, 1954; asso. dir. alumni and pub. relations Davidson Coll., 1955-57; asst. to pres., dir. devel., v.p. Mary Baldwin Coll., 1957-60; dir. Assos. Program, Washington U., 1961; exec. v.p. Am. Coll. Pub. Relations Assn., 1961-63; dir. Cal. Inst. Arts, Los Angeles, 1965- 67; exec. dir. Fedn. World Health Founds., Geneva, Switzerland, 1967-70; pres. Corp. for Ednl. Planning, Columbia, S.C., 1970—. Cons. LaVerne Coll. Mem. ednl. fundraising com. America Alumni Council, 1958-59. Mem. bd. dirs. Staunton chpt. Am. Cancer Soc., Crusade chmn., 1958; bd. corporators Kings Daughters Hosp., Staunton, Va., 1960. Served as 1st lt. USAAF, 1943-45; capt. USAF, 1951-52; maj. Res. Mem. Omicron Delta Kappa, Sigma Upsilon, Kappa Alpha. Republican. Presbyn. Home: 3024 Kershaw St Columbia SC Office: 106 Lancer Dr Columbia SC 29210

JACKSON, JAY MARION, airline exec.; b. Kansas City, Mo., Oct. 3, 1911; s. Merrill Marion and Vera (Long) J.; student Antioch Coll., 1929-30, Kansas City (Mo.) Jr. Coll., 1930-31; LL.B., Kansas City (Mo.) Sch. Law, 1936; m. Emily May Tandy, Feb. 17, 1940; children—Jay Marion III Roger Tandy, Thomas Frank. Admitted to Mo. bar, 1936; claims atty. Hardware Mut. Casualty Co., 1937- 38; asst. to resident atty. Transcontinental & Western Air, Inc., 1939- 44; legal counsel Braniff Airways, Inc., 1944-, sec., 1961-, dir., 1962-64. Mem. Am. Bar Assn., Am. Soc. Corp. Secs. (v.p., dir. 1966- 67), Phi Alpha Delta. Home: 4445 Fairfax Av Dallas TX 75205 Office: Braniff Airways Inc Exchange Park Dallas TX 75235

JACKSON, JOE CLARENCE, coll. ofcl.; b. Gene Autry, Okla., Apr. 24, 1911; s. Walter W. and Bessie F. (Crider) J.; B.S., U. Okla., 1934, Ed. M. 1940, Ed.D., 1950; m. Enid Louise Renois, May 5, 1934; 1 son, Victor Lee. Tchr., Okla. high schs. , 1934-48; instr. history, dean Bristow (Okla.) Jr. Coll., 1937-48; prof. history and govt. Central State U., Edmond, Okla., 1948-51, dean, 1951-69, acad. v.p., 1969—, also mem. bd. coll. scholarship found. Mem. Spl. Okla. Com. to Evaluate Ednl. TV, 1958; ofcl. visitor Nat. Coll. Accrediting Agys., 1952-55. Mem., pres. Edmond Community Achievement Council, 1958, com. to select nominees Cowboy Hall of Fame, 1958-68; adv. com. Okla. Regents for Higher Edn. Mem. Nat., Okla. edn. assns., Okla. Sch. Adminstrs. Assn., Okla. Hist. Soc., Edmond C. of C., U. Okla. Alumni Assn. (life), Okla. Sch. Safety Council, Okla. Council Tchr. Edn., Okla. Assn. Coll. Deans (pres. 1962), Okla. Assn. History Tchrs. (past pres.), Phi Beta Sigma, Phi Delta Kappa. Democrat. Methodist (ofcl. bd.). Mason (Shriner), Rotarian (dist. gov. 1962). Contbr. articles to profl. jours. Home: 319 13th St Edmond OK 73034

JACKSON, JOHN ALBERT lawyer, corp. exec.; b. Kent, O., 1922; B.A., Yale, 1943, LL.B., 1944; m. Mae Reed, May 2, 1949; 1 son. Admitted to Massachusetts bar, 1944; practi ced in Boston, 1947--. Home: 23 Beacon St Boston MA 02107

JACKSON, JOHN DAVID, educator, theoretical physicist; b. London, Ont., Can., Jan. 19, 1925; s. Walter David and Lillian Margaret (Ferguson) J.; B.S. honors, U. Western Ont. 1946; Ph.D., Mass. Inst. Tech., 1949; m. (Marilyn) Barbara Cook, June 26, 1949; children—Ian David, Nancy Christine, Maureen Barbara, Mark Walter. Asst. prof. math. McGill U., Montreal, Que., Can., 1950-55, asso. prof., 1955-56; Guggenheim fellow Princeton, 1956-57; asso. prof. physics, U. Ill., Urbana, 1957-58, prof., 1958-67; prof. physics U. Cal. at Berkeley, 1967—. Ford Found. fellow European Centre for Nuclear Research, Geneva, Switzerland, 1963-64; vis. fellow Clare Hall, Cambridge (Eng.) U., 1970. Fellow Am. Phys. Soc.; mem. Am. Assn. U. Profs., Am. Civil Liberties Union. Author: Physics of Elementary Particles, 1958; Classical Electrodynamics, 1962; Mathematics for Quantum Mechanics, 1962. Asso. editor: Reviews of Modern Physics, 1968—. Contbr. articles to jours., research books in field. Office: Dept Physics U Calif Berkeley CA 94720

JACKSON, JOHN ELLETT, lawyer; b. Palestine, Tex., Aug. 3, 1892; s. Alexander Ellett and Abby Frederick (Watts) J.; LL.B., Georgetown U. 1916; m. Mary Louise Allen, Dec. 29, 1917; children—Mary Allen (Mrs. H. Robert Corder), John E. Jr. Admitted to Tex. bar, 1914, La. bar 1920, to U. S. Supreme Court bar, 1928; pvt. practice law, New Orleans 1921—. Republican candidate for lt. gov. of La., 1928; chmn. Rep. State Central Com., La. 1929-34; Rep. nat. committeeman for La., 1934-52, mem. exec. com., 1951-52, sub-com. on South, 1950-52; del. Rep. Nat. Convs., 1932, 36, 40, 44, 48. Trustee Robert A. Taft Meml. Found., Inc. Decorated hon. officer and comdr. Order British Empire. Mem. Am. Bar Assn., La. Bar Assn., New Orleans Bar Assn. (pres. 1936-37). Republican. Presbyterian. Mason (K.T. Shriner). Clubs: Pickwick, New Orleans Country Stratford (New Orleans). Home: Andrew Jackson Apts 1550 2d St New Orleans LA 70130 Office: Nat Bank of Commerce Bldg New Orleans LA 70112

JACKSON, JOHN GILLESPIE, Jr., lawyer; b. N.Y.C., Nov. 1, 1909; s. John Gillespie and Grace J. (Bunce) J.; A.B., Princeton U., 1932; LL.B., Columbia, 1935; m. George-Anne Collin, Aug. 4, 1950; children—Marian Q. (Mrs. William A. Davidson), John Gillespie III. With Dept. Justice, Washington, 1935-37; admitted to N.Y. bar; practiced in N.Y.C., 1937-70; partner Jackson, Nash. Brophy, Barringer & Brooks, 1937—. Mayor, Inc. Village Mill Neck, 1964-70. Bd. dirs. Home For Old Men and Aged Couples. Served to maj. USAAF, 1942-45. Republican. Episcopalian. Home: Feeks Lane Locust Valley NY 11560 Office: 330 Madison Av New York City NY 10017

JACKSON, JOHN HOWARD, educator; b. Kansas City, Mo., Apr. 6, 1932; s. Howard Clifford and Lucile (Deischer) J.; A.B., Princeton, 1954; J.D., U. Mich., 1959; m. Joan Leland, Dec. 16, 1962; children—Jeanette, Lee Ann. Admitted to Wis. bar, 1959, Mo. bar, 1959, Cal. bar, 1964, Mich. bar, 1970; practice in Milw., 1959-61; asso. prof., prof. law U. Cal., 1961-66; prof. law U. Mich., 1966-. Ford Found. cons. legal edn., vis. prof. U. Delhi (India), 1968-69; cons. U.S. Treasury Dept., U.S. Office Spl. Trade Reps. Served with M.I., AUS 1954-56. Mem. Am. Bar Assn., Am. Soc. Internat. Law, Phi Beta Kappa, Order of Coif. Author: World Trade and the Law of Gatt, 1969. Contbr. articles to profl. jours. Bd. editors Jour. Law and Policy in Internat. Bus., Jour. World Trade Law. Home: 1 Heatheridge St Ann Arbor MI 48104

JACKSON, JOHN MATHEWS, food technologist; b. Chgo., July 9, 1908; s. William Hayden and Adeline (Mathews) J.; B.S., U. Chgo., 1929, Ph.D., 1932; m. Elizabeth Burd, Jan. 31, 1931; children—Frances (Mrs. Harry A. Skevington), William, Lynette (Mrs. Thomas G. Colmey), Margaret (Mrs. Curtis C. Haan), Martha A. (Mrs. William J. Fisher III), Barbara J., Robert M. (dec.). With Am. Can. Co., 1932-63, asst. mgr. Pacific div. lab., 1949-51, mgr. research div. lab., Maywood, Ill., 1952-55, research div. lab., Barrington, Ill., 1955-57, sect. mgr., 1957-63; dir. research Green Giant Co., Le Sueur, Minn., 1963-67, dir. tech. relations and packaging research, 1967—. Mem. Inst. Food Technologists, 1940—. pres., 1962- 63; pres. research and devel. assos. Q.M. Food and Container Inst., 1962-63; mem. subcom. radiation preservation foods NRC, 1955-57. Trustee Village of Barrington, 1961-63. Mem. Am. Chem. Soc., Nat. Canners Assn. (com. sci. research 1965—). Mason. Home: 260 Elmwood St Le Sueur MN 56058 Office: Green Giant Co Le Sueur MN 56058

JACKSON, JOHN NELSON, lawyer; b. Brownwood, Tex., Apr. 28, 1905; s. Charles Young and Kate Venable (Wood) J.; student Howard Payne Coll., 1922-24; LL.B. with highest honors, U. Tex., 1927; m. Sallie Bell Gaston, May 17, 1935; children—Gertrude Gaston (Mrs. Robert Bush Smither, Jr.), Sallie Bell Flippen (Mrs. Nowell E. Loop). Admitted to Tex. State bar, 1927; practiced law in Ft. Worth, 1927-30, asso., later mem. firm. Coke & Coke, Dallas, 1930-. Mem. World Peace Through Law Center. Fellow Am. Bar Found., Am. Coll. Probate Counsel, Southwestern Legal Found. (trustee; past chmn. research fellows); mem. Am., Dallas (pres. 1959) bar assns., State Bar

Tex. (chmn. sect. corp. banking and bus. law 1965), Am. Soc. Internat. Law, Am. Judicature Soc., Mexican Ada. Internat. Law, Am. Law Inst., Chancellors, Order of Coif, Phi Gamma Delta, Phi Delta Phi, Pi Kappa Delta. Episcopalian. Mason. Clubs: Northwood City, Idlewild, Petroleum (Dallas). Home: 7408 Greenbrier Dr Dallas TX 75225 Office: First Nat Bank Bldg Dallas TX 75202

JACKSON, JOHN TILLSON, corp. exec.; b. Milw., May 13, 1921; s. John F. and Elizabeth (Tillson) J.; B.S. in Adminstrv. Engring., Cornell U., 1942; m. Suzanne Bartley, Apr. 1953; children—Suzanne, Jennifer, John Tillson. Jr. engr. George S. Armstrong & Co., Inc., 1946-48, sr. engr. 1948-49, v.p., 1949, dir., 1951; asst. to pres. Fed. Telecommunication Labs., 1953-55; asst. to pres. Internat. Tel. & Tel. Corp., N.Y.C., 1956-57, asst. v.p., 1957-58, v.p., 1959-60; v.p. Remington Office Equipment div. Sperry Rand Corp., 1960-66; v.p. Gen. Waterworks Corp., 1966-68; v.p. Internat. Utilities Corp., 1968-69, sr. v.p., 1969—. Served from 2d lt. to maj. AUS, 1942-46. Mem. Am. Soc. M.E., Zeta Psi. Home: 155 Rose Lane Haverford PA 19041 Office: 1500 Walnut St Philadelphia PA 19102

JACKSON, JOSEPH GRAY, patent lawyer; b. Washington, May 4, 1904; s. William Steell and Vanette (Bogan) J.; Chem. Engr., Lehigh U., 1926; LL.B., U. Pa., 1929; m. Miriam Howarth, May 28, 1932; 1 son, Joseph Gray (dec.). Amitted to Pa. bar, 1929, since practiced in Phila.; partner firm William Steell Jackson and Sons, 1929-42, 45-66; partner firm Jackson, Jackson & Chovanes, 1967-; metallurgist, asst. chief engr. Office Chief Ordnance, indsl. service, arty. div., 1942-45; instr. bus. law Ursinus Coll., 1958-70. Bd. mgrs. Franklin Inst., Phila., 1959—, chmn. sci. and arts com., 1957-58; mem., former chmn. bd. mgrs. Spring Garden Inst., Phila. Registered profl. engr., Pa. Mem. Am. (chmn. patent, trademark and copyright sect. 1961-62), Pa., Phila. bar assns., Am., Phila. (past pres., sec.) patent law assns., Am. Soc. Testing Materials, Am. Soc. Metals (nat. treas. 1961-63, past chmn. Phila. chpt.), Nat. Soc. Profl. Engrs., Phi Beta Kappa, Tau Beta Pi, Scabbord and Blade. Clubs: Phila. Engineers (past pres., treas.). Author chpts. in books, also articles in field. Home: 153 Upland Terrace Bala Cynwyd PA 19004 Office: 117 S 17th St Philadelphia PA 19103

JACKSON, JULIAN ELLIS, corp. pres.; b. Perry, Fla., Oct. 24, 1913; s. Eddie H. and Eva M. (Reid) J.; grad. Andrew Jackson High Sch., Jacksonville, Fla., 1931; m. Laurana H. Filson, Oct. 6, 1956; children—Julian Ellis, Eddie King, Robert Allen, Victor Pharis, Julian Ellis IV, Lester Mitchell. With Great Atlantic & Pacific Stores, 1931-43; pres. Jax Meat Co., 1943-58, Jackson's Minit Markets, Inc., 1958-69, Julian Jackson Investment Co., 1955—; co-owner Jackson-Cowart Realty Co., 1955-71; dir. Fla. Nat. Bank, Jacksonville, Fla. Nat. Bank, Arlington. Past pres. United Cerebral Palsy, Jacksonville; chmn. Jacksonville Boxing Commn., 1952—; pres. Gator Bowl Assn., 1957, Fla. Baseball League, 1958-60. Bd. dirs. Palmdale Med. Center. Named Super Market Man of Year, 1960. Mem. Fla. Ind. Super Market Assn. (pres. 1950-59), Fraternal Order Police. Mason (Shriner). Clubs: River, University, Sportsman (Jacksonville). Home: 1005 Rio St Johns Dr Jacksonville FL 32211 Office: 5165 Beach Blvd Jacksonville FL 32207

JACKSON, JULIUS LEON, physicist, educator; b. N.Y.C., Nov. 9, 1924; s. Hyman and Rose (Margolis) J.; B.A., Bklyn. Coll., 1945; M.A., Princeton, 1947; Ph.D., N.Y.U., 1950; m. Charlotte Alpert, June 27, 1947 (dec. Dec. 1959); m. 2d, Raya Shveiger, Dec. 20, 1960; children—Meyer Benjamin, Mark N., Irene J., Morris M. Vis. asst. prof. physics State U. Ia., 1950; physicist Applied Physics Lab., Johns Hopkins, 1951-54, Office Naval Research, Washington, 1954-56, Nat. Bur. Standards, Washington, 1956-65; prof. physics Howard U., 1965-69; prof., chmn. dept. chem. engring. and material scis. Wayne State U., 1969—. Cons. Nat. Bur. Standards, NIH, United Aircraft Research Lab., Inst. Def. Analyses, Lawrence Radiation Lab.; Fulbright Research prof. physics U. Leiden (Netherlands), 1963- 64; guest scientist Weizmann Inst. Sci., Israel, 1961, 64, 66, 68; participant confs. and insts. Fellow Am. Phys. Soc., Washington Acad. Scis.; mem. Washington Philos. Soc. Contbr. articles profl. jours. Home: 25925 York Rd Huntington Woods MI 48070 Office: 5050 Anthony Wayne Dr Detroit MI 48202

JACKSON, KATHERINE GAUSS, mag. editor; b. Bethlehem, Pa., May 20, 1904; d. Christian and Alice (Hussey) Gauss; A.B., Smith Coll., 1924; m. Andrew Jackson, May 30, 1930; childrenAndrew (dec.), Stuart Agar. Asst. to publicity dir. Princeton, 1924-27; asst. editor Charm mag., 1927-32; asst. editor Scribner's mag., 1932-38; sr. editor charge fiction and book revs. Harper's mag., 1938-69; cons. Harper's Mag. Press, 1969—. Bd. dirs. Freedom House, N.Y.C., 1940-63, asst. treas., 1963-. Editor : (with Hiram Haydn) The Papers of Christian Gauss, 1957. Home: 17 E 97th St New York City NY 10029 Office: 2 Park Av New York City NY 10016

JACKSON, KERN CHANDLER, educator; b. Kansas City, Mo., Oct. 13, 1920; s. Chandler Cheshire and Maude Kern J.; B.S. in Geology, Mich. Technol. U., 1946, M.S. in Geology, 1950; Ph.D., U. Wis., 1951; m. Barbara Ann Garvey, Mar. 29, 1970; children by previous marriage—Kern Chandler II, Ross Dillon, Bruce Rogers, Paul Dana. Instr. U. Me., 1950-51, asst. prof., 1951-52; asst. prof. geology U. Ark., 1952-55, asso. prof., 1955-61, prof., 1961—, chmn. dept., 1954-59; cons. Humble Oil & Refining Co., Houston, 1954-59; geologist Ark. Geol. Commn., summers 1960-70. Served to lt. USNR, 1940-46. Decorated Purple Heart. Fellow Geol. Soc. Am. (mgmt. bd. S. Central sect. 1968, 71); mem. Mineral. Soc. Am., Am. Assn. Petroleum Geologists, A.A.A.S., Sigma Xi. Author: Textbook of Lithology, 1970. Home: 235 Baxter St Fayetteville AR 72701

JACKSON, LEE, artist; b. N.Y.C., Feb. 2, 1909; s. Harry and Charlotte (Tallis) J.; student Art Students League, with John Sloan, George Luks; m. Adele Grapes, Apr. 11, 1950. Faculty, Sch. for Art Studies, 1947-48, Coll. City N.Y., 1948-54; one man show Babcock Galleries, 1941, 43, 58; works exhibited Met. Mus. Art, Whitney Mus. Am. Art, Art. Inst. Chgo., U. Ill., Corcoran Galleries of Art, Va. Mus. Fine Art, Pa. Acad. Art, N.A.D., Mus. City N.Y., Butler Art Inst., Audubon Artists, Nat. Art Mus. Sport, Madison Sq. Garden, 1968, others; rep. permanent collections Met. Mus. Art, N.Y.C., Corcoran Galleries Art, Washington, Los Angeles County Mus. Art, Athens (Ga.) Mus., Walker Art Center, Mpls., Norfolk (Va.) Art Mus., Syracuse U., others. Guggenheim fellow in painting, 1941. Recipient ann. purchase prize Neg. Art Assn., 1946; spl. invitation prize Salmagundi Club, 1950; Thomas G. Clarke prize N.A.D., 1951; Grumbacher prize, 1956; prize for painting in oil N.A.D., 1961. Mem. Art Student's League, Audubon Artists Am., Grumbacher purchase prize 1964; Artists Equity Assn., Am. Water Color Soc., Nat. Soc. Painters in Casein. Sudler and Hennessey prize 1955. Home: Strongs Lane Water Mill NY 11976

JACKSON, LEWIS ALBERT, ednl. adminstr.; b. Angola, Ind., Dec. 29, 1912; s. Albert and Cora (Beverly) J.; B.S., Marion (Ind.) Coll., 1939; M.A. Miami U., Oxford,O., 1948; Ph.D., Ohio State U., 1950; m. Violet Burden, Sept. 17, 1938; children—Joyce Harlene, Robert Lewis. Tchr., Grant County (Ind.) Pub. Schs., 1936-40; contractor-flight instr. Chgo. Sch. Aeros., 1940; dir. tng. div. aeros. Tuskegee Inst., 1940-46; tchr. Gary (Ind.) Pub. Schs., 1964; faculty Central State U., Wilberforce, O., 1946-66, 67—, prof. edn., dir. student personnel, 1950-57, dean coll., 1957-60, v.p., dean adminstrn., 1961-66, acting pres., 1965-66, chmn. dept. ednl. adminstrn. and guidance, 1967-69, dir. grad. studies, 1969-70, pres. univ., 1970—; asso. prof. dept. aviation Ohio State U., 1966-67. Mem. tech. edn. com. Ohio Bd. Regents, cons. to evaluate programs, summer 1968; chmn. aviation com. Dayton-Miami Valley Consortium Colls. and Univs., 1968; mem. home econs. com. Ohio Dept. Vocational Edn.; sch. survey team Lincoln Heights Sch. Dist., 1961. Mem. Conf. Deans Edn. State Univs. Ohio (sec. 1959, chmn. 1960), N.E.A., Am. Indsl. Arts Assn., Ohio Ednl. Assn., Am. Assn. U. Profs. Beta Kappa Chi, Phi Delta Kappa. Editor sect. in Jour. Human Relations, 1952-57. Home: PO Box 532 Wilberforce OH 45384

JACKSON, MAHALIA, singer; b. New Orleans, Oct. 26, 1911; d. John Andrew and Charity (Clark) J.; student pub. schs., New Orleans; m. Isaac Hackenhull, 1936. Address: 5201 S Cornell Av Chicago IL 60615

JACKSON, MARION LEROY, educator; b. Reynolds, Neb., Nov. 30, 1914; s. Cleve L. and Belle Josephine (Hanson) J.; B.S., U. Neb., 1936, M.S., 1937; Ph.D., U. Wis., 1939; m. Chrystie Marie Bertramson, Sept. 2, 1937; children—Marjorie Lee, Virginia Lynn (Mrs. Bruce P. Conlon), Stanley Bertram, Douglas Mark. Land classification aide Dept. Agr., Lincoln, Neb., 1936-37; grad. research asst. U. Wis., Madison, 1937-39, postdoctoral fellow 1939-41, instr., 1941-42, asst. prof., 1942-45, asso. prof., 1946-50, prof., 1950- -; chemist Purdue U., 1945-46. Lectr. U.S., Canadian govts., numerous univs. Troop chmn. Four Lakes council Boy Scouts Am., 1965, scoutmaster, 1966. Recipient Soil Sci. Achievement award, 1958. Fellow Am. Soc. Agronomy, A.A.A.S., Mineral Soc. Am.; mem. Soil Sci. Soc. Am. (past pres.), Clay Minerals Soc. (past pres.), Internat. Soc. Soil Sci., Mineral Soc. London, Phi Beta Kappa, Sigma Xi, Phi Lambda Upsilon, Alpha Zeta, Gamma, Sigma Delta, Pi Mu Epsilon. Author: Soil Chemical Analysis, 1958; Soil Chemical Analysis-Advanced Course, 1968. Contbr. articles to profl. jours. Home: 563 Park Lane Madison WI 53711

JACKSON, MAYNARD, vice mayor; b. 1938; A.B., Morehouse Coll.; LL.B., N.C. Coll., Dunham. Admitted to bar, 1965; vice mayor of Atlanta, 1969—. Address: 68 Mitchell St S W Atlanta GA.*

JACKSON, MELBOURNE LESLIE, chem. engr., educator; b. Wisdom, Mont., Sept. 27, 1915: s. James R. and Adaleine (Mallon) J.; B.S., Mont. State Coll., 1941; student Inst. Paper Chemistry, Appleton, Wis., 1941-42; Ph.D., U. Minn., 1948; m. Elizabeth C. Ford, Apr. 2, 1944; childrenGary Leslie, Linda Mary, Laurie Elizabeth, Nancy Ruth. Instr. chem. engring. Mont. State Coll., 1942-44, U. Minn., 1944-48; asst. prof. U. Colo., 1948-50; head process development br. U.S. Naval Ordnance Test Sta., China Lake, Cal., 1950- 53; prof., head chem. engring. U. Ida., 1953-65, dean of the Graduate School, since 1965-; cons. FMC Corp., J.R. Simplot Company. Chairman Ida. Air Pollution Commn. ; cons. Ida. Potato Processors Com. Chmn. bd. trustees Moscow Sch. Bd. Registered profl. engr., Ida., Minn., Wash. Mem. Am. Inst. Chem. Engrs., Am. Chem. Soc., Am. Soc. Engring. Edn., Sigma Xi. Author papers in field. Home: 1422 Alpowa St Moscow IA 52760

JACKSON, MILES MERRILL, Jr., educator; b. Richmond, Va., Apr. 28, 1929; s. Miles Merrill and Thelma Eugertha (Manming) J.; student U. N.M., 1949-50; B.A. in English, Va. Union U., 1955; M.S. in L.S., Drexel U., 1956; postgrad. Ind. U., 1961, 64; m. Bernice Olivia Roane, Jan. 7, 1954; children—Miles Merrill III, Marsha, Muriel, Melia. Br. librarian Free Library Phila., 1955-58; acting librarian C.P. Huntington Meml. Library, Hampton (Va.) Inst., 1958-59, librarian, 1959- 63, asst. prof. library sci., 1958-62; territorial librarian Am. Samoa, 1962-64; chief librarian Trevor Arnett Library, Atlanta U., 1964-69, also lectr. Sch. Library Sco.; asso. prof. State U. N.Y., Genesco; 1969—. Fulbright lectr. U. Tehran, Iran, 1968, 69. Mem. bds. We Shall Overcome Fund, Martin L. King Jr. Meml. Library. Served with USNR, 1945-48. Research grantee Am. Philos. Soc., 1966. Mem. A.L.A., Charles Sumner Lit. Soc. (pres. 1961-62), Coll. Lang. Assn. (hon. mention poetry, 1954, 2d prize award short story 1955), Democrat Editor: A Bibliography of Materials on Negro History and Culture for Young People, 1968; Comparative and International Librarianship, 1970. Contbr. articles to profl. jours. Book reviewer Library Jour. Home: PO Box 9980 Rochester NY 14623 Office: Sch Library Sci State U NY Genesco NY 14454

JACKSON, MILTON, (Bags Jackson), jazz musician; b. Detroit, Jan. 1, 1923; studied music Mich. State U. With Dizzie Gillespie, N.Y.C., 1945, piano and vibraharp, 1950-52; with Howard McGhee, Tadd Dameron, Thelonious Monk; with Woody Herman Band, 1949-50, Modern Jazz Quartet, 1953—; faculty Sch. of Jazz, Lenox, Mass., 1957; on tour Europe, 1957-58, concert Town Hall, N.Y.C., 1958. Recipient new star award Esquire mag., 1947, critics poll award Down Beat mag., 1954. Recordings include Plenty, Plenty Soul Ballads in Blues, Jacksonville, Opus de Jazz, New Sounds in Modern Music, Modern Jazz Quartet. Address: 192-12 105th Av Hollis NY 11423*

JACKSON, N. BAXTER, banker; b. Nashville, Dec. 3, 1890; s. Robert Fenner and Mannie (Baxter) J.; B.S., Vanderbilt U. 1911; m. 2d, Mrs. Judith Blank, Nov. 21, 1945. Clerk First Nat. Bank Nashville, 1911-14; cashier Cumberland Valley Nat. Bank, Nashville, 1914-17; v.p. Am. Nat. Bank, Nashville, 1919-20; with Chem. Nat. Bank, N.Y.C., Chem. Bank & Trust Company, 1920—, chmn. bd. Chem. Corn Exchange Bank to 1956, chmn. exec. com., 1956—, hon. chmn. internat. adv. bd. Chem. Bank, 1966—; dir. Home Life Ins. Co., Warner-Lambert Pharm. Co. Bd. dir. Beekman- Downtown Hosp., trustee Vanderbilt U., Roosevelt Hosp. Served to maj. 114th F.A., U.S. Army, 1917-19. Decorated Medal of Merit (U.S.) given with diploma by Gen. Pershing (citations and battle stars included); Black Star, Legion of Honor. Mem. S.A.R., Phi Delta Theta. Roman Catholic. Clubs: Mount Royal (Montreal, Que., Can.); Brook, Downtown Association, Recess, University, Manhattan, Merchants, Links (N.Y.C.); Rolling Rock (Ligionier, Pa.); Connequot River. Home: 19 E 72d St New York City NY 10021 Office: 20 Pine St New York City NY 10005

JACKSON, NELSON A., hosp. dir.; b. Port Huron, Mich., Feb. 17, 1919; s. John Welington and Mary (Wright) J.; B.S., Wayne State U., 1933; M.S. in Hosp. Adminstrn., Northwestern U., 1958; m. Isabelle Barton, May 5, 1937; children—John, Nelson, Mary Lynn. Pub. accountant John Ver Kortern, Washington, 1935-37, Ernst & Ernst, Detroit, 1932-39; with Controllers Office, City Detroit, 1939-43, Exec. Office of President, 1944-45; with VA, 1946—, adminstrn. hosp., Ft. Lyon, Colo., 1968—; instr. U. Ill., 1954-56. Served with USNR, World War II. Mem. Am. Coll. Hosp. Adminstrs.; mem. Area Six Health Assn. (bd. dirs., chmn. chronic care com.), Am. Legion. Rotarian, Elk, Mason. Address: Box 188 VA Hosp Fort Lynn CO 81038

JACKSON, NYLE M., govt. ofcl.; b. Bradleyville, Mo., Mar. 27, 1914; s. James Richard and Emma (Huntsman) J.; B.A., Westminster Coll., 1935; m. Elaine Hutcheson, Sept. 4, 1938. Advt. mgr. for daily and weekly newspapers, Seymour, Ind., 1938-41; exec. sec. Rep. Earl Wilson of Ind., 1941-53; adminstrv. asst. Sen. William E. Jenner of Ind., 1953-59; spl. staff mem. for Sen. Homer E. Capehart of Ind., 1959; legislative asst. to Sen. Thruston B. Morton, chmn. Republican Nat. Com., 1959; exec. asst. to postmaster gen., 1959-61, asst. to exec. asst., 1961-63; asst. dir. customer relations div. P.O. Dept. Washington, 1963-68, exec. asst. to asst. postmaster gen., 1969; asst. to dep. counsel to Pres., White House Staff, 1969-70; mng. dir. ICC, Washington, 1970—. Del.-observer Intergovtl. Commn. European Migration, 1957. Asst. sgt.-at-arms Rep. Nat. Conv., 1956. Served to lt. USNR, World War II. Mem. Am. Legion,V.F.W., Congl. Secs. Club, Orgn. Cabinet Assts., Senate Assts. Group, Mil. Order of Carabao. Club: Capitol Hill (Washington). Baptist. Home: 4429 35th St NW Washington, DC 20008 Office: ICC Washington DC 20423

JACKSON, PERCIVAL WILLIAM, naval officer; b. Middlebury, Vt., Sept. 16, 1914; s. Dane Dutton and Elizabeth (Caswell) J.; B.S., Syracuse U., 1936; m. Virginia Ohm, Mar. 22, 1941; children—Pamela (Mrs. Robert Everton), Peter William, Susan Virginia. Enlisted USN, 1936; commd. aviation cadet, 1936, advanced through grades to rear adm., 1966; comdr. Carrier Div. 14, 1966-67; comdg. officer U.S.S. Orca, 1959-60, U.S.S. Kearsarge, 1960-61, J-I OJCS, Pentagon, 1968-70; now dep. comdt. Nat. War Coll., Washington. Decorated Navy Cross, Silver Star medal, Legion of Merit, D.F.C. Mem. Kappa Sigma. Home: Qtrs 14 Ft McNair Washington DC 20024 Office: Nat War Coll Washington DC 20315

JACKSON, PHILIP WESLEY, educator; b. Vineland, N.J., Dec. 2, 1928; s. Raymond and Estelle (Sword) J.; B.S., N.J. State Coll., Glassboro, 1951; M.Ed., Temple U., 1952; Ph.D., Columbia, 1954; m. Josephine Dandrea, May 1, 1948; children—Nancy, David, Steven. Instr., Columbia Tchrs. Coll., summer 1954, Wayne U., 1954-55; faculty U. Chgo., 1955—, prof. edn., 1963- -; dir. Lab. Schs., 1970—. Cons. U.S. Office Edn., NSF.; Simon vis. prof. U. Manchester, Eng., 1968-69. Served with USNR, 1947-48. Recipient Distinguished Alumnus award Glassboro State Coll., 1970. Fellow Center Advanced Study Behavioral Scis., 1962-63. Author: (with J.W. Getzels) Creativity and Intelligence, 1962; Life in Classrooms, 1968; The Teacher and the Machine, 1968. Contbr. articles to profl. jours., monographs. Home: 1357 E 56th St Chicago IL 60637

JACKSON, RALPH FREDERICK, Jr., air force officer; b. Kansas City, Mo., Mar. 18, 1923; s. Ralph and Helen (Ryan) J.; B.A., U. Pitts., 1956, M.A., 1959; m. Dorthy Lee Donaldson, Feb. 20, 1946; children—Susan (Mrs. Richard Hulse), Janet Lee. Commd. 2d lt. USAAF, 1943, advanced through grades to col. USAF, 1967; successively instr., asst. prof., asso. prof. geography USAF Acad., 1959-64; prof., head dept. aerospace studies Utah State U., Logan, 1969—. Decorated Legion of Merit, D.F.C., Air medal with 1 silver, 4 bronze oak leaf clusters. Home: 1719 E 1400 N Logan UT 84321

JACKSON, REGGIE, baseball player; ed. U. Ariz. Outfielder, Oakland (Cal.) Athletics baseball team. Office: care Dir Pub Relations Oakland Athletics Baseball Team Oakland-Alameda County Coliseum Oakland CA 94621*

JACKSON, RICHARD, lawyer; b. Medford, Mass., Dec. 28, 1910; s. Henry Clinton, Jr. and Clara Wild (Goodwin) J.; grad. Phillips Andover Acad., 1929; A.B., Dartmouth, 1933; LL.B., Columbia, 1938; m. Helen Pfeiffer, Sept. 16, 1939; children—Deborah, Faith. Instr. Latin, Phillips Acad., Andover, Mass., 1933-35; admitted to N.Y. bar, 1938, Mass. bar, 1946, R.I. bar, 1963; asso. law firm Simpson, Thacher & Bartlett, N.Y.C., 1938-43; law staff R & M. R.R., Boston, 1946-57, gen. counsel, 1954-57; asst. sec. personnel and res. forces Navy Dept., 1957-61; v.p., gen. counsel Fram Corp., East Providence, 1961-66; v.p. law Erie-Lackawanna R.R., Cleve., 1966—. Served as lt. comdr. USNR, 1943-46. Mem. Am. Bar Assn., U.S. (nat. def. com.), Greater Providence (chmn. nat. legislation com.) chambers commerce. Home: 13805 Shaker Blvd Cleveland OH 44120 Office: Midland Bldg Cleveland OH 44115

JACKSON, RICHARD MONTGOMERY, airline exec.; b. Jacksonville, Fla., Dec. 9, 1920; s. William Kenneth and Katharine (Mitchell) J.; B.Sc., Harvard, 1942; m. Martha Eustis Turner, Sept. 12, 1942; children—Richard Montgomery, Susanne, William Mitchell. With Am. Airlines, Inc., 1945-58; asso. L.S. Rockefeller, 1958- 60; with Seaboard World Airlines, Inc., Jamaica, N.Y., 1960-, pres., chmn. bd., 1960—; dir. Hempstead Bank, Vernors Inc. Trustee Village Lloyd Harbor, N.Y., 1960-68; pres. Lloyd Harbor Sch. Bd., 1957-58; bd. govs. Huntington (N.Y.) Hosp. Served to lt. USNR, World War II. Internat. Air Transport Assn. (exec. com. 1970—), Clubs: Cold Spring Harbor Beach (N.Y.); Island (Hobe Sound, Fla.). Wings (N.Y.C.); Aero, National Aviation (Washington). Home: 273 Southdown Rd Lloyd Harbor Huntington NY 11743 Office: John F Kennedy Internat Airport Jamaica NY 11430

JACKSON, RICHARD SEYMOUR, newspaperman; b. New Haven, Aug. 30, 1910; s. John Day and Rose Marie (Herrick) J.; grad. Taft Sch., 1929; B.A., Yale, 1934; m. Helene Danforth Coler, Oct. 10, 1942 (div. Mar. 1954); children-Helene Danforth, Rosemary Herrick, (Mrs. Joseph P. Wells); m. 2d, Jean W. Washburn, Nov. 15, 1956. Reporter, legislative corr. New Haven Register, 1934-37, asst. to pub., 1937-52, asst. pub., 1953-60, asso. ed., 1958-60, editor, co-pub., 1960—; pres. Asso. Dailies of Conn. 1942-45; pub. New Haven Journal Courier, 1951-52; dir. Carrington Pub. Co., New Haven, 1947-64; v.p., sec. dir. Register Pub. Co., 1956-60, sr. v.p., 1960, pres., dir., 1960—. Mem. Mayor's Human Rights Com., 1963-64; mem. Clean Water Task Force, 168, Environmental Policy Com., 1970. Trustee Hosp. St. Raphael, New Javen; bd. dirs. Gaylord Hosp., Wallingford, Conn.; bd. advisors Conn. Found Ind. Schs. Fellow Pierson Coll., Yale. Fellow Am. Geog. Soc.; mem. Am. Soc. Newspaper Editors, Soc. Colonial Wars, Internat. Press Inst., Soc. Cincinatti, Inter Am. Press Assn., Newcomen Soc., Sigma Delta Chi, Chi Psi. Episcopalian. Clubs: Laurel; Devon Yacht (bd. govs.); Maidstone (East Hampton, L.I.); Yale (N.Y.); Graduates, Mory's, New Haven Lawn, Faculty (New Haven). Home: 1180 Ridge Rd North Haven CT 06473 Office: 367 Orange St New Haven CT 06503

JACKSON, ROBERT CECIL, textile assn. exec.; b. Rosedale, Miss., Mar. 2, 1911 s. Oscar Cecil and Geneva (Combs) J.; student U. Miss., 1929-30; LL.D., Clemson Coll., 1962; m. Fan Minor Ames, Dec. 20, 1934; 1 dau., Ann Valentine (Mrs. Ronald Hale Post). Agrl. work, cotton prodn., marketing, Macon, Miss., 1932-39; div. dir. Nat. Cotton Council Am., Memphis, 1939-44; Washington rep., 1946-49; asst. to v.p. Coker Pedigreed Seed Co., Hartsville, S.C., 1944-46; exec. v.p. Am. Textile Mfrs. Inst., Inc., Charlotte, N.C., Washington, N.Y.C., 1949—. Chmn., Am. unit Anglo-Am. Textile Mission, Japan, 1950; mem. U.S. delegation 1st Internat. Textile Conf., Buxton, Eng., 1952; rep. textile industry Rusk-Van Fleet Mission to Korea, Am.-Korean Found., 1953; mem. Am. delegation Internat. Fedn. Cotton and Allied Textile Industries, 1955—; mem. mgmt.-labor textile adv. com. U.S. Govt., 1962—. Served with U.S. Army, spl. textile industry assignment, Germany, Italy, 1945. Named Textile Man of Year, N.Y. Bd. Trade, 1962; recipient Silver medal award No. Textile Assn., 1970. Mem. Phi Psi. Baptist. Clubs: National Press, Jefferson Island (Washington); International; Belle Haven Country (Alexandria, Va.). Home: 1717 Belle Haven Rd Alexandria VA 22307 Office: 1150 17th St NW Washington DC 20036

JACKSON, ROBERT CHARLES, aero. co. exec.; b. Racine, Wis., Feb. 26, 1908; s. Robert Charles, Sr., and Gertrude (Carson) J.; A.B. in Econs., Stanford, 1929, C.P.A., 1934, M.B.A., 1931; m. Elizabeth Jane Burdell, Nov. 24, 1937; children—Bruce B., Robert D., Mark B. With Lybrand, Ross Bros. & Montgomery, pub. accountants, 1931-34, security First Nat. Bank of Los Angeles, 1934-36; v.p. West Shore Co., investment holding co., 1936-60; dir. Ryan Aero. Co., 1957-69, exec. com., 1958-69, exec. v.p., vice chmn., 1959-61, pres., 1961-69, now chmn. and chief exec. officer, 1969—; chmn. bd. Continental Motors Corp., 1965-70, Jackson Investment Co., 1946—, Emtor, Inc., 1953-69, Wis. Motors, 1967-69; gen. partner Carter Investment Co., Carter Co.; dir. Security Pacific Nat. Bank, Los Angeles. Dir. San Diego Mgmt. Council for Merit Employment, 1967-68; mem. steering com. Urban Coalition, San Diego, 1968-70. Trustee U. Redlands. Served to lt. col. AUS, 1942-46. Decorated Bronze Star medal. Mem. Def. Orientation Conf. Assn., Soc. Automotive Engineers, also Air Force Association, Army Aviation Assn., Nat. Mgmt. Assn., Navy League U.S., Aerospace Industries Assn. Am., San Diego C. of C. (dir. 1965-69). Clubs: California, Los Angeles Country, San Diego Country, Cuyamaca, San Diego Yacht, Burning Tree (Bethesda, Md.). Home: 4310 Arista St San Diego CA 92103 Office: Ryan Aero Co Lindberg Field San Diego CA 92112

JACKSON, ROBERT HILL, news photographer; b. Dallas, Apr. 8, 1934; s. William C. H. and Anna (Bridges) J.; student So. Methodist U., 1956; m. Margaret Ann Looney, Feb. 3, 1962; children—Carol Lynn, Anne E., Kelly. Staff photographer Dallas Times Herald, 1960—. Served with AUS, 1958-59. Recipient (all for picture of Jack Ruby shooting Harvey L. Oswald) Best Spot News Picture of Year award Dallas Press Club, Best News Picture of Year award Tex. Headliners Club, Sweepstakes award and Best Spot News Picture award A.P., Nat. Best News Picture of Year award Sigma Delta Chi, Pulitzer prize for News Photography, 1st place in news photography Nat. Press Photographers Assn., Pictures of Year, 1964. Mem. Nat. Press Photographers Assn., Delta Chi Alumni Assn., Sports Car Club Am., Porsche Club Am. Home: 6240 Town Hill Lane Dallas TX 75214 Office: Dallas Times Herald Herald Sq Dallas TX 75202

JACKSON, ROBERT LAWRENCE, physician, educator; b. Clare, Mich., Nov. 30, 1909; s. Lawrence W. and Josephine L. (Cour) J.; B.S., U. Notre Dame, 1930; M.D., U. Mich., 1934; m. Sara Elizabeth Soisson, Sept. 6, 1937; childrenAnn, Mary, Sara, Kathryn, Margaret, Martha, Robert. Intern U. Ia., 1934-35, resident, 1935-37, instr., 1937-41, asso., 1941-43, asst. prof., 1943-46, asso. prof., 1946-51, prof. pediatrics, 1951-54; resident U. Rochester, 1936- 37; prof., chmn. dept. pediatrics U. Mo., Columbia, 1954—. Guest lectr. Internat. Pediatric Congress, Zurich, Switzerland, 1950, Pan Am. Pediatric Congress, Sao Paulo, Brazil, 1954; vis. prof. pediatrics Am. U. Beirut, 1962-63; mem. NRC cons. NIH. Mem. Am. Council Rheumatic Fever, Am. Diabetes Assn., A.M.A., Am. Pediatric Soc., Soc. Pediatric Research, Am. Acad. Pediatrics, Central Soc. Clin. Research. Am. Inst. Nutrition, Sigma Xi, Alpha Omega Alpha. Home: 1103 Stewart Rd Columbia MO 65201

JACKSON, ROBERT MANSON, editor; b. Alamogordo, N.M., Jan. 21, 1907; s. Robert Mallory and Margaret (Manson) J.; B.J., U. Mo., 1928; m. Helen Dowty, Nov. 17, 1936; 1 son, Robert Manson III. Mem. staff San Angelo (Tex.) Standard- Times, 1928-31; clk. R.E. Thomason, M.C., 1931-33; asst. librarian U.S. Senate, 1933-34; sec. to Senator Tom Connally, 1934-38; staff writer Wash. Bur. A.P., 1938-41; mng.editor Corpus Christi (Tex.) Times, 1941-45, editor Caller-Times, 1945-. Recipient Honor award distinguished service in journalism U. Mo., 1966. Member Am. Soc. of Newspaper Editors. Presbyn. Club: National Press (Washington). Home: 314 Laurel Dr Corpus Christi TX 78404 Office: Box 9136 Corpus Christi TX 78408

JACKSON, ROBERT TILDEN, life ins. co. exec.; b. Barre, Vt., Sept. 18, 1917; s. Henry Hollister and Carrie Carlton (Bemis) J.; B.A., Yale, 1939; LL.B., U. Conn., 1952; m. Edna Florence Otka, Sept. 21, 1946; children-Sherry Ann, Patricia Carrie, Henry Hollister. With Phoenix Mut. Life Ins. Co., Hartford, Conn., 1939—, v.p., actuary 1960-68, exec. v.p., 1968—; admitted to Conn. bar, 1952. Served to maj. USAAF, 1942-46. Fellow Soc. Actuaries. Home: 35 Waterside Lane Hartford CT 06107 Office: 1 American Row Hartford CT 06115

JACKSON, ROY GRAHAM, architect; b. Sherman, Tex., July 1, 1913; s. Watt J. and Lilly Thompson (Graham) J.; B.S. in Architecture, Rice U., 1935; m. Violet Stephen Lawrence, May 1, 1971. With R. Graham Jackson, architect, 1936-45; partner Jackson & Dill, architects, Houston, 1946-53, Wirtz, Calhoun, Tungate & Jackson, architects, Houston, 1953-65, Calhoun, Tungate & Jackson, architects, Houston, 1965—; asst. prof. architecture U. Houston, part time 1947-51; vis. lectr., critic Rice U., 1963-67. Mem. Houston Symphony Soc. Fellow Constrn. Specifications Inst. (pres. Houston chpt. 1958-59), A.I.A. (pres. Houston chpt. 1959; mem. adminstrv. office practice com. 1951-53, 67-71); mem. Houston C. of C. (edn. com. 1950-53). Baptist (deacon). Club: Houston. Archtl. works include design Manned Spacecraft Center, NASA, Houston; Willford Hall Hosp., Lackland AFB, Tex.; Ryon Engring. Bldg., Rice U., Houston; Hankammer Sch. Bus., Baylor U. Home: 716 Chimney Rock Houston TX 77027 Office: 2506 Richton St Houston TX 77006

JACKSON, SAMUEL CHARLES, govt. ofcl.; b. Kansas City, Kan., May 8, 1929; s. James C. and Mattie (Webber) J.; A.B., Washburn U., 1951, LL.B., 1954, J.D., 1970; m. Judith M. Bradford, Jan. 27, 1952; children—Marcia Lyn, Brenda Sue. Admitted to Kan. bar, 1954; pvt. practice, Topeka, 1957-65; dep. gen. counsel Kan. Dept. Social Welfare, 1963-65; commr. Equal Employment Opportunity Commn., Washington, 1965-68; v.p. Am. Arbitration Assn. Center Dispute Seattlement, Washington, 1968; asst. sec. met. devel. Dept. Housing and Urban Devel., 1969—. Precinct committeeman Shawnee County Republican Com., 1960, 63. Served with USAF, 1954-57. Mem. Nat., Am., Fed. Topeka bar assns., Kappa Alpha Psi. Republican. Home: 1855 Upshur St NW Washington DC 20011 Office: 451 7th St SW Washington DC 20410

JACKSON, STANLEY BARTLETT, educator; b. Wiscasset, Me., Aug. 11, 1913; s. Frank Ward and Marian Edna (Files) J.; A.B., Bates Coll., 1933; A.M., Harvard, 1934, Ph.D., 1937; m. Edith Elizabeth Pearson, Sept. 4, 1937; chiildren—Marian (Mrs. Robert P. Rogers), Nancy (Mrs. John O. Thayer), Robert. Grad. asst. mathematics Harvard, 1936-37; instr. mathematics U. Wis., 1937-41; asst. prof. mathematics U. Md., 1941-46, asso. prof., 1946-48, prof., 1948—, head dept., 1954-58. NSF faculty fellow, 1959-60. Mem. Am. Math. Soc., A.A.A.S., Nat. Council Tchrs. of Mathematics, Math. Assn. Am. (regional gov.), Phi Beta Kappa, Sigma Xi. Author: (with H.L. Garstens) Mathematics for Elementary School Teachers, 1967. Home: 1002 Heather Av Takoma Park MD 20012 Office: Univ Maryland College Park MD 20742

JACKSON, STEPHEN SAMUEL, former govt. ofcl.; b. Springfield, Mass., Jan. 10, 1899; s. Samuel Stephen and Catherine (Fitzgerald) J.; A.B., Holy Cross Coll., 1921; LL.B., Harvard, 1927; LL.D. (hon.). Catholic U., 1961; m. Ruth Linson, Sept. 7, 1929; children—Martha Ann (Mrs. James O. Sanfellino), Stephen Samuel. Admitted to N.Y. bar, 1928; referee Workmen's Compensation Bur., N.Y. State, 1929-34; justice Domestic Relations Ct., N.Y.C., 1934-44; instr. Fordham Sch. Social Service, 1929-34; instr. Sch. Social Service Catholic U., 1949-69; pvt. practice law Jackson & Pavarini, N.Y.C., 1944- 48; acting dir. Motion Picture Prodn. Code, Hollywood, Cal., 1948-49; atty. adviser, asst. gen. counsel Office Sec. Def., 1950-56, spl. asst. to asst. sec. def. (manpower), ret., 1969. Active U.S.O.; established, directed Bur. Prevention Juvenile Delinquency, N.Y.C., 1941-44. Trustee Shrine Immaculate Conception. Mem. Internat. Platform Assn. Home: 3311 S Leisure World Blvd Silver Spring MD 20906

JACKSON, THADDEUS RICE, former mfg. co. exec.; b. Akron, O., May 27, 1907; s. George C. and Ethel (Snowden) J.; B.S., Middlebury Coll., 1929; m. Janice E. Alwill, Sept. 16, 1933; children—George Arthur, Thad Alwill, Thomas Snowden. Mng. accountant Price Waterhouse & Co., C.P.A.'s, Boston, 1929-59; controller Blair & Co., N.Y.C., 1959-60; with Draper Corp., Hopedale, Mass., 1960-70, treas., 1964-70, ret., 1970; dir. Milford Nat. Bank & Trust Co. (Mass.). C.P.A., Mass. Mem. Am. Inst. C.P.A.'s Home: 9 Park St Hopedale MA 01747 Office: 25 Hope St Hopedale MA 01747

JACKSON, THOMAS SEARING, lawyer; b. Washington, Dec. 1, 1909; s. Thomas and Jeannette (Hutchins) J.; A.B., George Washington U., 1933, LL.B., 1935; m. Elizabeth Jacobs, Nov. 29, 1933; children—Thomas Penfield, Jeffrey Andrew. With Dept. Commerce, U.S. Forest Service, 1927-35; admitted to D.C. bar, 1935, Md. bar, 1941, U.S. Supreme Ct. bar, 1949; asso. Brandenburg & Brandenburg, Washington, 1935-57; partner Jackson, Gray & Laskey, and predecessors, Washington, 1957—. Gen. counsel Restaurant Assn. Met. Washington Am. Land Title Assn., Dist.-Realty Title Ins. Corp.; dir., gen. counsel Liberty Savs. Assn. Past pres. Bd. Edn. Montgomery County, Md. Served to lt. comdr. USNR, 1943-45. Fellow Am. Coll. Trial Lawyers (bd. regents 1964-68. pres. found.), Am. Bar Found.; mem. Internat. Assn. Ins. Counsel, Am. Bar Assn., Am. Judicature Soc. (dir.), Bar Assn. D.C. (pres. 1962-63). Clubs: Rehoboth Beach (Del.); University, Barristers, Lawyers, City Tavern, Chevy Chase (Washington). Home: 4545 MacArthur Blvd NW Washington DC 20007 Office: 1828 L St NW Washington DC 20036

JACKSON, THOMAS WOODROW, engr.; b. Chgo., Apr. 3, 1917; s. Thomas and Elizabeth (Slivka) J.; B.S. in Mech. Engring., U. Ill., 1941; M.S., U. Cal., 1946; Ph.D. (XR fellow), Purdue U., 1949; m. Dymitrea Alice Templeman, Feb. 7, 1943; children—Anita Louise, Elizabeth Ann. Instr., designing engr. Standard Oil Co. (Ind.), 1941-42; aero. research scientist Lewis Flight Propulsion Lab., NACA, 1949-51; air force office (lt. col.) civilian Aircraft Nuclear Propulsion Program, 1951-54; chief mech. scis. div. Engring. Expt. Sta., Ga. Inst. Tech., 1954-67, prof. 1954—, asso. dean engring. (research), 1965-67, acting dean grad. div., 1966-67; dir. Skidaway Inst. Oceanography, Univ. System Ga., 1967-70; tech. dir. Pres.'s Nat. Indsl. Pollution Control Council, Dept. Commerce, 1970—. Served from aviation cadet to lt. col. USAAF, 1942-46; now col. Res. Mem. Am. Soc. M.E., Marine Tech. Soc., Sigma Xi, Phi Kappa Phi, Tau Beta Pi, Pi Tau Signa, Sigma Pi Sigma. Co-author: Research and Development Management, 1966. Home: 2000 S Eads St Arlington VA 22202

JACKSON, TIMOTHY EDWARD, utilities exec.; b. Hutchinson, Kan., July 6, 1941; s. Sam L. and J.V. (Morgan) J.; B.A., Northwestern U., 1963; M.B.A., U. Chgo., 1968; m. June Ruddy, Aug. 13, 1966; 1 dau,, Jennifer. Plant service chemist E.I. duPont de Nemours & Co., Chgo., 1965-67; systems engr. IBM Corp., Chgo., 1967-68; sr. systems analyst Lone Star Gas Co., Dallas, 1968-69, asst. to sr. v.p. financial matters, 1969-70, treas., 1970—. Served to lt. (j.g.) USNR, 1963-65. Mem. Am. Gas Assn., Financial Execs. Inst. Home: 15741 Daleport Circle Dallas TX 75240 Office: 301 S Harwood St Dallas TX 75201

JACKSON, WILL WOODWARD, former ins. co. exec.; b. Waynesboro, Tenn., Apr. 20, 1890; s. George Washington and Martha Mollie (Craig) J.; A.B., Southwestern U., Georgetown, Tex., 1916, Litt.D., 1940; M.A., U. Tex., 1928; postgrad. Yale, 1929-30; m. Ruth Goddard, Aug. 20, 1919; children—Leila Craig, Will Woodward. Supt. pub. schs., Normangee, Tex., 1916-17; sec. Student YMCA of Ark., 1919-21; pres. Wesleyan Inst., San Antonio, 1921-29; Westmoreland Coll., 1930-36, U. San Antonio, 1936-42; v.p., dir. pub. relations Trinity U., 1942-46; v.p. Am. Hosp. Life Ins. Co., San Antonio, 1946-60. Regional exec. USO, 1942-46; mem. Air Force Community Council; mem. exec. com. jurisdictional conf. Meth. Ch., lay del. world-wide confs.; pres. Community Welfare Council, San Antonio, 1964-66; mem. Tex. State Bd. Edn., 1950-69, chmn. 1959-69; bd. govs. St. Mary's U.; mem. bd. devel. So. Meth. U. Chmn. bd. dirs. San Antonio Heart Assn., 1954-61, Tex. Heart Assn., 1961; bd. dirs. YMCA, Nat. Travelers Aid Assn., A.R.C., Tex Council Econ. Edn., S.W. Ednl. Research Lab. Served with F.A., U.S. Army, 1917-19. Recipient Distinguished Alumnus award Southwestern U., 1961; Ann. Conf. award Christians and Jews for contbn. to human relations, 1962. Mem. San Antonio Council Chs. (pres.), C. of C. (dir.), Am. Sociol. Soc., Am. Acad. Polit. and Social Scis., Alpha Chi. Methodist. Mason, Rotarian (dist. gov. 1943). Home: 2136 W Summit St San Antonio TX 78201

JACKSON, WILLIAM CALHOUN DECKER, Jr., investment banker; b. Celeste, Tex., Mar. 20, 1907; s. William Calhoun and Lydia Zora (Vernon) J.; student Burleson Coll., 1923-24; Registered pharmacist, Danforth Sch. Pharmacy, 1928; m. Sally Carolyn Harrington, May 28, 1928. Mem. comml. banking dept. First Nat. Bank, Plano, Tex., 1929-30; dir., chmn. bd. First Southwest Co., 1946—. pres., dir. Antelope Oil Corp., 1950—, Provident Oil Co., 1954—. Chmn. bd. Municipal Adv. Council, Tex., 1956-57. Served as lt. comdr. USNR, 1945. Mem. Investment Bankers Assn. Am. (gov. 1954- 55, v.p. 1955-57, pres. 1957-58). Clubs: Dallas, Dallas Country, Athletic. Northwood, City, Chaparral (Dallas). Home: 5122 Shadywood Lane Dallas TX 75209 Office: Mercantile Bank Bldg Dallas TX 75201

JACKSON, WILLIAM KENNETH, architect; b. Lakeland, Fla., May 13, 1913; s. Alfred Montgomery and Margaret (Nelson) J.; B.S. in Architecture, U. Fla., 1936; certificate of design, AA Sch. Architecture, London, 1945; m. Kathryn J. Jackson, Sept. 28, 1969; children—William Kenneth, James M. Partner Kemp, Bunch & Jackson, Architects, Inc. and predecessor firm, Jacksonville, Fla., 1946—. Chmn. Jacksonville Area Planning Bd., 1962—; mem. Com. of 100, 1953—, Mayor's Com. on Water Pollution, 1970—. Bd. dirs. Boys' Club Jacksonville. Served with C.E., AUS, 1942-45; ETO. Decorated Bronze Star. Mem. A.I.A., Am. Soc. Planning Ofcls., Jacksonville C. of C. (bd. govs. 1971—). Home: 4834 Malpas Lane Jacksonville FL 32210 Office: Seaboard Coast Line Bldg Jacksonville FL 32202

JACKSON, WILLIAM MACLEOD, mfg. co. exec.; b. New Rochelle, N.Y., Apr. 18, 1926; s. William and Florence (MacLeod) J.; student Deerfield Acad., 1941-43, Mass. Inst. Tech., 1943-45; B.S., Princeton, 1947; m. Mary Stuart Otto, June 12, 1948; children—Stuart MacLeod, Frederick Elliott, Allen Proctor, Susan Elizabeth. With Bonney Forge div. Bonney Forge & Foundry, Inc., Allentown, Pa., 1948-69, v.p., 1958-66, pres., 1966-69, also dir.; pres. Bonney Forge & Foundry div. Gulf & Western Indsl. Products Co., Allentown, 1969—; chmn. bd., dir. Bonney Forge Internat., Ltd., Barr Thompson & Co., Scotland, Bonney Forge Italia, Milan; dir. Francis Caird, Ltd., London, Mosser Industries Inc., Allentown, Bonney Forge Australia Pty., Ltd., Sydney. Pres. Friends of Allentown Pub. Library, also mem. bd. dirs. Served with USNR, 1944-46. Mem. Am. Soc. M.E., Phi Gamma Delta. Presbyn. (trustee). Clubs: Princeton (N.Y.C.); Lehigh Country (bd. govs. 1967-70), Livingston (Allentown). Home: 910 N 27th St Allentown PA 18104 Office: Bonney Forge & Foundry P O Box 1755 Allentown PA 18105

JACKSON, WILLIAM NICHOLS, educator; b. Lyerly, Ga., Dec. 27, 1912; s. William F. and Lavinia (Nichols) J.; B.S., Morehouse Coll., Atlanta, 1933; M.S., Atlanta U., 1938; Ph.D., Ohio State U. 1952; m. Dorwatha C. Watkins, Dec. 22, 1940; childrenGerald W., William N., Bernell R. Tchr. math. and sci., pub. schs. in Chattanooga, Atlanta and Covington, Ky., 1933-54; staff mem. secondary sch. study Assn. Negro Colls. and Schs., 1942-45; mem. faculty Tenn. A. and I. State U., 1954-, dean faculty, 1963-; guest prof. edn. Savanah State Coll., 1949, Tex. So. U., 1952-54; dir. sci. and math. edn. workshops Alcorn Coll., 1944, Atlanta U., 1945-47. Tex. So. U., 1952-53. Fellow Gen. Edn. Bd., 1947-48. Mem. Nat. Council Tchrs. Math., Nat. Sci. Tchrs. Assn., So. Conf. Acad. Deans, Kappa Delta Pi, Phi Delta Kappa, Beta Kappa Chi, Alpha Phi Alpha, Sigma Pi Phi. Baptist. Contbr. profl. jours. Home: 4140 W Hamilton Rd Nashville TN 37218

JACKSON, WILLIAM PHILIP, Jr., cement co. exec.; b. Oakland, Cal., Feb. 10, 1914; s. William Philip and Marie A. (Southard) J.; B.A., U. Cal. at Berkeley, 1936; m. L. Jayne Gilbert, Feb. 21, 1941; 1 dau., Nancy Jayne. With Kaiser Paving Co., 1931; technician, salesman Henry J. Kaiser Co., 1936-42; operations mgr. Glacier Sand & Gravel Co., 1946-55, v.p., gen. mgr., 1955—; v.p. Kaiser Cement & Gypsum Corp., 1961—; dir Pacific Gypsum Co. Served to lt. (s.g.) USNR, 1942-45; PTO. Decorated Commendation ribbon. Mem. Am. Concrete Inst. Clubs: Rainier, Washington Athletic (Seattle). Home: 5537 NE Penrith Rd Seattle WA 98105 Office: 5975 E Marginal Way S Seattle WA 98134

JACKSON, WILLIAM RICHARD, steel co. exec.; b. Des Moines, May 25, 1908; s. William H. and Minnine (Long) J.; student Ohio Wesleyan U., 1925-27; B.S. in Bus. Adminstrn., Mass. Inst. Tech., 1930; m. Lucilla Scribner, June 4, 1932; children—William Richard, Mary (Mrs. A. P. Denmark); Polly (Mrs. G.B. Townsend). With Am. Bridge div. U.S. Steel Corp., 1930-36; with Pitts.- Des Moines Steel Co., 1936—, sec.-treas., 1943-59, pres., 1959-71, chmn. bd., 1971—, also dir.; pres., dir. Des Moines Steel Co., 1964—; v.p., dir. Des Moines Bridge & Iron Works, 1943—; trustee Dollar Savs. Bank, Pitts. Vice pres., bd. dirs. Allegheny council Boy Scouts of Am., 1961—, exec. bd. nat. council, 1964—; bd. dirs. Pitts. Theol. Sem. Councilman, Borough Sewickley Heights, Pa., 1958—. Mem. Am. Inst. Steel Constrn. (exec. com., dir.; treas.), Steel Plate Fabricators Assn. (dir.). Presbyn. (elder). Clubs: Duquesne (Pitts.); Allegheny Country, Edgeworth (Sewickley). Home: Country Club Rd RD 1 Sewickley PA 15143 Office: Pitts-Des Moines Steel Co Neville Island PA 15225

JACKSON, WILLIAM THOMAS HOBDELL, educator; b. Sheffield, Eng., Apr. 2, 1915; s. William A. and Harriet (Williams) J.; B.A., Sheffield U., 1935, M.A., 1938; Ph.D., U. Wash., 1951; m. Erika Anna M. Noltemeyer, Aug. 23, 1945; childrenThomas C.H., Inge A.M., Christopher M.P. Came to U.S., 1948, naturalized, 1957. Instr., U. Wash., 1948-50; asst. prof. Coe Coll., 1950-52; asst. prof. medieval lit. Columbia, 1952-55, asso. prof., 1955-58, prof., 1958-, chmn. German dept., 1961-67. Vis. prof. U. Chgo., 1955, Rutgers State U., 1962-70, Duke, 1965, Yale, 1966; vis. lectr. Princeton, 1957; Phi Beta Kappa vis. scholar, 1965-66. Served with Brit. Army, 1940-46. Guggenheim fellow, 1958-59, 67-68; grantee Am. Council Learned Socs. Mem. Medieval Acad. Am. (mem. council 1968—), Modern Lang. Assn. Am. (exec. council), Dante Soc., Renaissance Soc., Modern Humanities Research Assn. Author: The Literature of the Middle Ages, 1960; Essential Erasmus, 1964; Medieval Literature: A History and a Guide, 1965; (with P. Demetz) Anthology of German Literature to 1750, 1968; The Anatomy of Love-A Study of the Tristan of Gottfried von Strassburg, 1970. Contbr. articles on medieval lit. to profl. jours. Editor: Germanic Rev., 1955- 66, Columbia Records of Civilization Series, 1962—. Home: 9O Morningside Dr New York City NY 10027

JACKSON, WILLIAM TURRENTINE, educator; b. Ruston, La., Apr. 5, 1915; s. Brice H. and Luther (Turrentine) J.; A.B., Tex. Western Coll., 1935; A.M., U. Tex., 1936, Ph.D., 1940; m. Barbara Kone, Nov. 28, 1942. Instr. history U. Cal. at Los Angeles, 1940-41; instr. history Ia. State U., Ames, 1941-42, asst. prof., 1944-46, asso. prof., 1946-48; asst. prof. Am. history U. Chgo., 1948-51; dir. Am. civilization program, asst. prof. Am. history U. Cal. at Davis, 1951-53, asso. prof. history, 1953-56, prof., 1956—, chmn. dept., 1959-60; Fulbright research fellow Scotland, 1949-50; Rockefeller Found. fellow Huntington Library, 1953; research grant Am. Philos. Soc., 1955, Social Sci. Research Council grantee, 1956; grantee Am. Hist. Research Center, 1955-56; Guggenheim fellow, 1957-58, 65; Pub. program grant Nat. Endowment for Humanities, 1969-70; vis. prof. Mont. State U., 1941, univs. Mich., 1944, Wyo., 1945, Minn., 1946, Tex., 1947, So. Cal., 1953, 56, Colo., 1961, San Francisco State Coll., 1962, Wyo., 1963, Yale and R.I., 1964, NDEA History Inst., Chadron (Neb.) State Coll., 1965; La. State U., 1967, U. Ariz., 1968, U. Alta., 1969, U. Nev., 1970, U. Hawaii, 1970. Cons. hist. sect. Cal. Div. Beaches and Parks, Wells Fargo Bank; mem. Cal. Gov.'s History Commn.; com. preservation hist. sites Nat. Park Service, 1960-68, Pelzer award com., 1968—; com. preservation hist. sites Orgn. Am. Historians; adv. com. Sacramento Landmarks Comn.; nominating com. Western History Assn., 1967-69. Bd. dirs. Cal. Heritage Council. Served to ensign USNR, 1942-44. Mem. Am. Hist. Assn., Orgn. Am. Historians, Am. Assn. U. Profs., Phi Alpha Theta, Pi Sigma Alpha, Theta Xi. Democrat. Methodist. Author: Wagon Roads West, 1942, 1965 (awards from Pacific Coast br. Am. Hist. Assn., Nat. Inst. Graphic Arts, N.Y.C.); When Grass Was King, 1956 (recipient merit award Am. Assn. State and Local History, 1957); Treasure Hill, 1963 (merit award Am. Assn. State and Local History); Twenty Years on the Pacific Slope, 1965; The Enterprising Scot, 1968; Gold Rush Diary of a German Sailor, 1970; also numerous hist. monographs and articles. Bd. editors Pacific Hist. Rev., 1961-64, 67-70, So. Cal. Quar., 1962—, Arizona and the West, 1968—. Club: Commonwealth. Home: 702 Miller Dr Davis CA 95616

JACKSON, WILLIAM WARD, chem. co. exec.; b. Irvington, N.J., Apr. 19, 1913; s. William Henry and Edwina (Ward) J.; B.S. in Chem. Engring., Newark Coll. Engring., 1936; m. Rae M. Applegate, Jan. 1, 1943; 1 dau., Hollace D. Prodn., sales positions Celanese Corp. Am. and affiliates, 1932-51; gen. mgr. indsl. chems. dept. Comml. Solvents Corp., N.Y.C., 1951-53, v.p. petrochem. div., 1953-54, v.p. marketing, 1954—, also dir.; dir., mem. exec. com. N.W. Nitro Chem. Corp., Medicine Hat, Alta. Mem. Aircraft Prodn. Bd., 1942-43; asst. to vice chmn. WPB, 1943-44; aircraft cons. WPB, 1943-44. Chmn. bd. Millburn-Short Hills chpt. A.R.C., 1956-59, dir., 1954-6O; bd. dirs. Animal Health Inst. Recipient Certificate of Achievement, U.S. Army, Certificate of Service, Dept. Commerce. Fellow Am. Inst. Chemists; mem. Am. Inst. Chem. Engrs., Mfg. Chemists Assn., Pharm. Mfg. Assn., Am. Chem. Soc., Soc. Chem. Industry, Fertilizer Inst. Sales Exec. Club, Newcomen Cos., Drug Chem. and Allied Trade Assn. (past pres., treas., dir., chmn. adv. council, exec. com.),

Am. Ordnance Assn. (dir.), N.Y. Bd. Trade (past dir., exec. com.), Armed Forces Chem. Assn. (past nat. dir., exec. com., v.p., past pres.). Clubs: Short Hills; Union League, Racquet and Tennis, Canadian (N.Y.C.). Patentee in field. Home: 2 Brooklawn Short Hills NJ 07078 Office: 245 Park Av New York City NY 10017

JACKSON, WILLIS CARL, univ. librarian; b. Beverly, Mass., May 20, 1923; s. Willis Carl and Olive (McAllister) J.; A.B., Fla. State U., 1951, M.A., 1952; m. Mary Elisabeth Lett, Aug. 13, 1948; 1 dau., Carla. Asst. order librarian U. Tenn., 1952-54; head order dept., head acquistions State U. Ia. Library, 1954-57; chief acquistions librarian U. Minn., 1957-63; asso. dir. libraries U. Colo., 1963-65; dir. libraries Pa. State U., 1966—. Cons. lectr. in field, 1956—. Mem. Benner Twp. (Pa.) Gen. Authority, 1966—. Served with AUS, 1942-45. Mem. Am. (pres., resources and tech. services div. 1970-71), Pa., Colo., Mountain-Plains library assns., Am. Aviation Hist. Soc., Soc. World War II Aero. Historians, Air Power History Found., OX-5 Club, Beta Phi Mu. Democrat. Methodist. Elk. Contbr. articles to profl. jours. Home: 564 Rock Rd State College PA 16801 Office: Pattee Library University Park PA 16802

JACOB, EMERSON DONALD, librarian; b. Canton, O., Mar. 17, 1914; s. John and Cora Louise (Kneuss) J.; A.B., Mt. Union Coll., 1939; B.S. in L.S., Western Res. U., 1942, Ph.D., 1961; M.A., Columbia, 1952; student U. Mich., 1956; m. Doris Geiger, Sept. 29, 1940; 1 dau., Patricia Lou. Asst. librarian Mt. Union Coll., 1943-45; order librarian U. Md., 1945-48; acquisitions librarian Mich. State U., 1948-58; librarian Baldwin Wallace Coll., 1959- 64, Cal. State Poly. Coll., 1964-65, N.Y. State U. Coll. at Fredonia, 1965-68, Rutgers U. at Newark, since 1968—. Member librarians commn. Cleve. Commn. Higher Edn.; trustee Western N.Y. Library Resources Council. Mem. A.L.A., Am. Hist. Assn. Democrat. Episcopalian. Home: 2202 Rudy Rd Harrisburg PA 17104

JACOB, FRANCOIS, geneticist; b. 1920; M.D., D.Sc. (hon.), U. Chgo., 1965. Mem. staff Pasteur Inst., 1950—, now chief service genetic microbiology; now also prof. cellular genetics Coll. de France. Served with Free French Forces, 1940-45. Co-recipient Nobel prize medicine and physiology, 1965. Fgn. mem. Nat. Acad. Scis., Acad. Arts and Scis., Am. Philos. Soc. Address: care Pasteur Inst Paris France

JACOB, HARRY MYLES, mining co. exec.; b. Bloomfield, N.J., Mar. 19, 1913; s. Henry Martin and Edith (Myles) J.; B.C.S., N.Y.U., 1936; m. Elsie Mary Medlicott, June 12, 1937; children—Reid M., Jere V. With Pogson, Peloubet & Co., C.P.A.'s, 1930-36; with Inspiration Consolidated Copper Co., N.Y.C., 1936—, successively asst. sec. and treas., sec. and treas., v.p. and sec., 1936-57, dir., 1953—, exec. v. p., 1958-59, pres., 1960—; dir. Sperry Rand Corp. Member Am. Inst. of Mining. Metallurgical and Petroleum Engineers, Mining and Metallurgical Society of America, Mining Club of N.Y. Clubs: (love Valley Rod and Gun; Economic, Downtown. Harbor View (N.Y.C.). Home: Box 140 R D 5 Flemington NJ 08822 Office: 25 Broadway New York City NY 10004

JACOB, HENRY GEORGE, educator, mathmatician; b. New Haven, June 11, 1922; s. Henry George and Catherine (Blockhaus) J.; B.E., Yale, 1943, M.E., 1947, Ph.D., 1953; m. Gretchen Mary Asman, Feb. 26, 1944; children—Paula Louise (Mrs. James Reddam), Philip Henry, Victoria Elaine. Mem. faculty La. State U., 1953-62; prof. math. U. Mass. at Amherst, 1962—; vis. prof. Johns Hopkins, 1956-57, 69-70. Served to lt. (j.g.), USNR, 1943-46. Mem. Math. Assn. Am., Am. Assn. U. Profs., Am. Math. Soc. Author: (with Duane Bailey) Linear Algebra, 1971. Home: 51 Butterfield Terrace Amherst MA 01002

JACOB, PHILIP ERNEST, educator; b. Istanbul, Turkey, July 12, 1914; s. Ernest Otto and Sarah Orilla (Conrad) J.; B.A., Yale, 1935; M.A., U. Pa., 1939; Ph.D., Princeton, 1941; m. Betty Muther, Dec. 24, 1935; children—Sarah Elizabeth, Albert Kirk, Stephen Philip. Sec. Am. Friends Service Com., Phila., 1936-38, 1941-45; teacher polit. sci. Princeton, 1939-40, research radio propaganda Princeton Listening Center, 1940-41; faculty internat. law and orgn., prof. polit. sci. U. Pa., 1945-71, dir. summer sch., also college collateral courses, 1950-57, director Internat. Studies Values in Politics; prof. polit. sci. U. Hawaii, 1970—; lectr. polit. sci. Swarthmore Coll., 1946- 55. Co-director Ford Foundation Grant Research on Social Values and Public Policy, 1960-65. Recipient Franklin D. Roosevelt Found. award, 1953. Fellow National Council on Religion in Higher Edn.; mem. Am. Polit. Sci. Assn., Am. Soc. Internat. Law, Am. Assn. of University Profs., Phi Beta Kappa. Mem. Soc. Friends. Author: Propaganda by Short Wave (with Childs, Whitton), 1942; Conscription of Conscience (with M. Sibley), 1952; Changing Values in College, 1957; (with J. Flink) Values and Their Function in Decision-Making, 1962; (with others) The Integration of Political Communities, 1964; (with A. Atherton) The Dynamics of International Organization, 1965; (with others) Values and the Active Community, 1971. Address: Polit Sci Dept U Hawaii Honolulu HI 96822

JACOB, RICHARD JOSEPH, rubber and plastic mfg co. exec.; b. Detroit, July 25, 1919; s. Ben B. and Nettie (Byron) J.; student Butler U., 1938-39, Miami U. 1940-41; m. Louise Marks, Apr. 2, 1949; children-Patricia Josephine, Arnold Marks. Exec. with Mfg. Engring. Co., Detroit, 1945-46; exec. v.p., pres. Cadillac Plastics & Chem. Co., Detroit, 1945-65, dir., 1945—i exec. v.p. Dayco Corp., Dayton, O., 1965-68, pres., 1968—, also dir.; dir. Elder-Beerman Stores Corp., Dayton, Tech. Inc., Dayton, Mich. Bank, Detroit; adviser Wayne State U. Press. chmn., Christmas Seal campaign, Detroit; capt. United Found. dr., Detroit; Bd. life mem. Brandeis U. dirs. Tb Health Soc., Detroit; trustee Barney Children's Med. Center, Automotive Presidents Council. Mem. Dayton Area C. of C. (Wright State Com.), Soc. Plastics Industry, Soc. Plastic Engrs., Detroit Hist. Soc. Club: Standard-City (past pres., dir. Detroit). Home: 3688 Wales Dr Dayton OH 45405 Office: Dayco Corp Dayton OH 45401

JACOB, STANLEY WALLACE, surgeon, educator; b. Phila., 1924; s. Abraham and Belle (Shulman) J.; M.D. cum laude, Ohio State U., 1948; m. Marilyn Peters, 1 son, Stephen; m. 2d, Beverly Swarts; children—Jeffrey, Darren, Robert. Intern, Beth Israel Hosp., Boston, 1948-49, resident surgery, 1949-52, 54-56; chief resident Harvard Med. Sch. Surg. Service, 1956-57; asso. vis. surgeon Boston City Hosp., 1958-59; Kemper Found. research scholar A.C.S., 1957- 60; instr. surgery Harvard Med. Sch., 1958-59; asst. prof. surgery U. Ore. Med. Sch., 1959-66, asso. prof., 1966—. Served to capt. M.C., AUS, 1952-54; now col. Res. Recipient Gov.'s award Outstanding N.W. Scientist, 1965. Markle scholar med. scis., 1960. Diplomate Am. Bd. Surgery. Mem. Phi Beta Kappa, Sigma Xi, Alpha Omega Alpha. Author: Structure and Function in Man, 1965; Dimethyl Sulfoxide Basic Concepts, 1971. Co-discoverer therapeutic usefulness of dimethyl sulfoxide. Home: 19117 S W Old River Dr West Linn OR 97068 Office: 3181 S W Sam Jackson Park Rd Portland OR 97201

JACOBAEUS, ANTON CHRISTIAN, telephone co. exec.; b. Stockholm, Sweden, June 15, 1911; s. Hans Christian and Anna (Carlquist) J.; M. Elec. Engring., Royal Tech. Inst. Tech., Stockholm, 1933, Dr. Elec. Engring., 1950; m. Eva Britta Widforss, June 6, 1947; 1 dau., Eva Antonia. Project and sales engr. signalling div. Telefonaktiebolaget L.M. Ericsson, Stockholm, 1935-37, project and sales engr. switching div., 1937-42, asst. to head switching div., 1942-50, head research dept., 1950-53, v.p., chief tech. officer, 1953-63, exec. v.p., 1963—. Mem. presidium Internat. Teletraffic Congresses on Application of Probability to Telecommunications, 1955—. Recipient Polhem award Svenska Teknologföreningen, 1955. Fellow I.E.E.E.; mem. Swedish Acad. Engring. Scis. (chmn. elec. engring. br. 1965-66; vice chmn. 1967-69), Swedish Assn. Engrs. and Architects. Contbr. articles profl. jours. Patentee in field. Home: 43 Bastugatan Stockholm S-117 25 Sweden Office: LM Ericcson Telephone Co Stockholm S-126 11 Sweden

JACOBANSKY, ANN MADELINE, nurse educator; b. McKeesport, Pa., Jan. 7, 1913; d. Adolph and Anna (Timks) Jacobansky; R.N. Shadyside Hosp. Sch. Nursing. Pitts, 1934; B.S., U. Pitts., 1949, M Ed., 1953. Nurse Shadyside Hosp., Pitts., 1934-43, 46-48; instr., ednl. dir. Presbyn. Hosp., 1950-53; dir. undergrad. instrn. Duke, 1953-54, dean Sch. Nursing, 1955-67, 70—, prof. nursing, 1955—. Served as lt. Nurse Corps, AUS, 1943-45. Mem. Am., N.C. (chmn. EACT sect, 1958-60) nurse assns., Nat. League Nursing, Am. Assn. U. Profs., Am. Assn. for Higher Edn., Sigma Theta Tau. Club: Altrusa (pres. 1961-62 Durham). Home: 1200 Leon Durham NC 27705

JACOBI, EILEEN M., assn. exec.; b. Ireland, May 7, 1918; d. Patrick and Marion (Mahon) Ahern; came to U.S., 1930, naturalized, 1941; diploma nursing Cumberland Hosp., 1940; B.S., Adelphi Coll., 1954, M.A., 1956; Ed. D., Columbia Tchrs. Coll., 1968; m. A. Francis Jacobi, Aug. 2, 1941; children—Francis, Virginia. Charge nurse Queens Gen. Hosp., Jamaica, N.Y., 1941-43; pvt. duty nursing, N.Y. area, 1943- 50; supervising nurse Creedmoor Inst. Psychobiol. Studies, Queens Village, N.Y., 1950-56; asst. prof. nursing Adelphi Coll., 1956-60, asso. prof., dean Sch. Nursing, 1960-66, prof., dean, 1960- 68; asso. exec. dir. Am. Nurses Assn., 1969-70, exec. dir., 1970—. Mem. survey team for survey med. and nursing edn. in Iran, ICA, 1961. Mem. Am. Nurses Assn., Nat. League Nursing, Am. Pub. Health Assn., L.I. Regional Hosp. Rev. and Planning Council, Am. Heart Assn., Kappa Delta Pi, Pi Lambda Theta, Sigma Theta Tau. Home: 39 Euston Rd Garden City Long Island NY 11530

JACOBI, HERBERT JOHN, lawyer; b. N.Y.C., July 27, 11907; s. Herman August and Magdelen (Schutz) J.; A.B., Columbia, 1927, J.D., 1930; m. Carolyn M. Reinisch, July 29, 1933; children-Barbara, Herbert John, David. Admitted to N.Y. bar, 1930; asso. Cravath, de Gersdorff, Swaine & Wood, N.Y.C., 1930-38; v.p. Carter Coal Co., N.Y.C., 1938-41; partner firm Wickes, Riddell, Bloomer, Jacobi & McGuire, N.Y.C., 1941—. Trustee Mary Flagler Cary Charitable Trust. MEm. Am., N.Y. State bar assns., Bar of City of N.Y., N.Y. County Bar Assn., Phi Delta PHi. Home: 2 Cowdin Lane Mount Kisco NY 10549 also 2545 Lantern Lane Naples FL 33940 Office: 59 Maiden Lane New York City NY 10038

JACOBI, JOHN EDWARD, educator; b. Mansfield, O., Feb. 4, 1907; s. Edward Walter and Josephine (Munhall) J.; B.A., Lehigh U., 1929; Ph.D., N.Y. U., 1933; m. Carrie Anna Baumann, Dec. 29, 1933; children—John Edward, Susan Jane (Mrs. Kenneth Howard Sherman). Prof. sociology, dean Tusculum Coll., Greeneville, Tenn., 1941- 46; prof. sociology Albright Coll., Reading, Pa., 1946-48, Lehigh U., Bethlehem, Pa., 1948-62; lectr. Boston Coll., 1965-68; prof. sociology State U. Coll., Oneonta, N.Y., 1968—, head dept., 1970—; vis. prof. N.Y.U., summers 1946, 48, 49; dir. local area research and demonstration project Mass. Com. Children and Youth, 1962-68; co-dir. inter-disciplinary research team Lehigh U., 1957-60. Mem. nat. youth program com. YMCA, 1959-65. Rockefeller fellow, 1930-33. Mem. Am. Sociol. Assn. Eastern Sociol. Soc., Pi Gamma Mu, Beta Gamma Sigma, Lambda Chi Alpha. Author: Meeting the Needs of Children and Youth in a Regional Area, 1968; Meeting the Needs of Children and Youth in an Urban Community, 1968; Meeting the Needs of Children and Youth in Massachusetts Communities, 1968. Co-editor: An Introduction to the Social Sciences 1954. Home: Box 219 West Oneonta NY 13861

JACOBI, LEE, advt. exec.; b. San Francisco, Nov. 11, 1912; s. John Thomas and Beulah (Lee) J.; B.A., U. Wash., 1936; m. Joanne E. Wood, May 27, 1939; childrenJohn W., Joanne Lee (Mrs. Richard C. Swanson). Pub. relations dir. Seattle C. of C., 1938-42; dir. visual tng. Todd Pacific Shipyards, Seattle, 1942-44; exec. v.p., gen. mgr.Cole Weber, Inc., Seattle, 1945—. Pub. relations chmn. Wash. Artificial Kidney Center, 1966-67; mem. Nat. Educators Com., 1966-; chmn. Seattle Community Publicity Council, 1967-; mem. Citizens Com. to Reform Cts., 1967, Com. to Reorganize State Govt., 1967. Bd. dirs. Seattle Area Indsl. Council. Named Man of Year, Sigma Nu, 1963. Mem. Am. Assn. Advt. Agys. (gov.), Sigma Delta Chi, Sigma Nu, Episcopalian. Clubs: Washington Athletic, Ranier, Alumni Big W (Seattle); Tacoma. Home: 8748 Sand Point Way NE Seattle WA 98115 Office: 3100 S 176th St Seattle WA 98188

JACOBI, LOU actor; b. Toronto, Ont., Can., Dec. 28, 1913; s. Joseph and Fay Jacobi; student Jarvis Collegiate Sch., Toronto; m. Ruth Ludwin, July 15, 1957. Drama dir. Toronto Y.M.H.A., 1940; theatrical appearances include The Rabbi and the Priest, 1924, Spring Thaw, 1949, Remains to be Seen, 1952, Pal Joey, 1954, The World of Shalom Aleichem, 1955, Into Thin Air, 1955, The Diary of Ann Frank, 1955, The Tenth Man, 1959, Come Blow Your Horn, 1961, Fade In—Fade Out, 1964, Don't Drink the Water, 1966; motion picture appearances include A Kid for 2 Farthings, 1956. The Diary of Anne Frank, 1959, Song Without End. 1960, Irma La Douce, 1963; numerous radio and TV appearances, 1954-†

JACOBI, PETER PAUL, educator; b. Berlin, Germany, Mar. 15, 1930; s. Paul A. and Liesbeth (Kron) J.; came to U.S., 1938, naturalized, 1944; B.S., Northwestern U. Medill Sch. Journalism, 1952, M.S., 1953; m. Harriet Ackley, Dec. 8, 1956; children—Keith Peter, John Wyn. Faculty journalism Northwestern U., 1955—, profl. lectr., 1955-63, asst. prof., 1963-66, asso. prof., 1966-69, prof. journalism, 1969—, asso. dean, 1966—. Editor, Chgo. Lyric Opera News, 1958-61, Music Mag., Mus. Courier, Chgo., 1961-62; news assignment editor, newscaster, theatre-music reporter NBC, Chgo., 1955-61; radio commentator music and opera, 1958-65; theatre, film critic WMAQ-TV, Chgo., Hollister Newspapers of Suburban Chgo., 1964—. Mem. adv. com. Ill. Arts Council. Trustee Roycemore School, Evanston, Ill. Mem. Assn. for Edn. in Journalism, Sigma Delta Chi, Alpha Delta Phi. Contbr. articles on arts to Saturday Rev., Christian Sci. Monitor, N.Y. Times, others. Home: 2712 Broadway Evanston IL 60201

JACOBS, ALAN JOSEPH, advt. and pub. relations exec.; b. Omaha, Nov. 6, 1922; s. Joseph and Tillie (Greenblatt) J.; B.A., U. Neb., 1950; M.B.A., U. Chgo., 1957; m. Phyllis J. Leaf. Aug. 28, 1949; childrenPeggy, Joanne, Peter, David, Parttime reporter Omaha World-Herald, 1937-42; exec. v.p., chmn. exec. com. Bozell & Jacobs, Inc., Chgo., 1946—; v.p., dir. Leaf Brands Inc., Chgo.; dir. Kabaya-Leaf, Inc., Okayama, Japan. Dir. Better Govt. Assn. Chgo., 1966. Mem. bd. Ill. Voters Assn., 1960—. Served to 1st lt. F.A., AUS, 1943-46; CBI. Recipient Quill and Scroll Writing award, 1940; recognition certificate for contbns. Ill. Const. Reform, 1962, 69-70. Mem. Pub. Relations Soc. Am., Publicity Club Chgo., Am. Jewish Com., Am. Acad. Polit. Sci., U. Chgo. Grad. Sch. Bus. Execs. Club (pres. 1966-67), Zeta Beta Tau. Club: North Shore Yacht (Highland Park). Contbr. articles to profl. jours., to books. Home: 425 Cedar Av Highland Park IL 60035 Office: 120 S Riverside Plaza Chicago IL 60606

JACOBS, ALAN MARTIN, educator; b. N.Y.C., Nov. 14, 1932; s. Samuel J. and Amelia M. (Ziegler) J.; B.Engring. Physics (John McMullen scholar LeVerne Noyes scholar, Clevite scholar), Cornell U., 1955; postgrad. Oak Ridge Sch. Reactor Tech., 1955-56; M.S. in Physics, Pa. State U., 1958, Ph.D., 1963; m. Evelyn Lee Banner, Aug. 7, 1955; children—Frederick Ethen, Heidi Joelle. Research asso. nuclear reactor facility Pa. State U., 1956-63, mem. faculty, 1963—, prof. nuclear engring., 1968—. Cons. to industry. NSF sci. faculty fellow, 1960-61. Mem. Am. Nuclear Soc., Sigma Xi, Tau Beta Pi, Pi Mu Epsilon. Co-author: Basic Principles of Nuclear Science and Reactors, 1960. Home: 1238 S Garner St State College PA 16801 Office: Sackett Bldg University Park PA 16802

JACOBS, ALGER JAY, banker; b. Elko, Nev., Oct. 3, 1908; s. Seymour and Rosa (Alexander) J.; A.B., U. Nev., 1929; M.A., U. Cal. at Berkeley, 1931; m. Leonore Lazarus, Feb. 19, 1933; children—Barbara (Mrs. Edwin Miller), Janet (Mrs. Ernest Michels), Donald A. With Crocker Nat. Bank and predecessors, San Francisco, 1931—, asst. v.p., 1948-51, v.p., 1951-64, sr. v.p., 1964-70, exec. v.p., 1970—. Mem. Investment Bankers Assn. Am. (exec. com. Cal. group 1955-61, chmn. Cal. group 1958-59, gov. 1959- 62, govtl. securities com. 1964-68), San Francisco C. of C. Mason. Clubs: Bond (past pres.), Municipal Bond (past pres.), Merchants Exchange, Stock Exchange (San Francisco). Home: 125 30th Av San Francisco CA 94121 Office: 1 Montgomery St San Francisco CA 94104

JACOBS, ALMA SMITH, librarian; b. Lewistown, Mont., Nov. 21, 1916; d. Martin Luther and Emma Louise (Riley) Smith; B.A., Talladega Coll., 1938; B.S. in L.S., Columbia, 1942; Litt. D., Mont. State Coll., 1962; L.H.D., Mt. Holyoke Coll., 1968; m. Marcus Jacobs, July 18, 1945. Catalog librarian Great Falls (Mont.) Pub. Library, 1946-54, librarian, 1954—. Mem. Mont. adv. com. U.S. Civil Rights Commn. Mem. Am. (exec. bd. 1964- 68), Pacific N.W. (pres. 1957), Mont. (pres. 1960) library assns., Delta Kappa Gamma. Home: 616 8th Av S Great Falls Mt 59401 Office: Great Falls Pub Library Great Falls MT 59401

JACOBS, ANDREW, Jr., congressman; b. Indpls., Feb. 24, 1932; s. Andrew and Joyce Taylor (Wellborn) J.; B.S., Ind. U., 1955, LL.B., 1958. Admitted to Ind. bar, practiced in Indpls.; mem. firm Jacobs & Kelley, 1958—; mem. 89th to 91st Congresses, 11th Dist. Ind. Mem. Ind. Ho. of Reps., 1958-60. Served with USMCR, 1950-52. Mem. Indpls. Bar Assn., Am. Legion. Democrat. Roman Catholic. Home: 407 N Pennsylvania Indianapolis IN 46204 Office: House Office Bldg Washington DC 20515

JACOBS, ARTHUR P., film producer; b. Los Angeles, Mar. 7, 1922; s. Arthur P. and Natalie (Ankle) J.; student U. So. Cal., 1942. Messenger, MGM Studios, 1943-44, apprentice publicity dept., 1944-45; publicist Warner Bros. Studios, 1946; opened own pub. relations office, 1947; formed Arthur P. Jacobs Co., Inc., representing entertainment and indsl. accounts, Beverly Hills, Cal., 1956, pres., 1956—; pres. APJAC Prodns., Inc., 1963—; films include What A Way to Go!, Doctor Dolittle, Planet of the Apes, Goodbye, Mr. Chips, The Chairman, Beneath the Planet of the Apes, Escape from the Planet of the Apes, Play it Again, Sam. Mem. Acad. Motion and Scis., Acad. TV Arts and Scis. Office: APJAC Prodns 20th Century Fox 10201 W Pico Blvd Los Angeles CA 90035

JACOBS, ARTHUR THEODORE, sem. exec.; b. Chgo., Aug. 19, 1912; s. Morris and Laura (Abraham) J.; B.A., U. Wis., 1934, M.A., 1935; Ph.D., U. Mich., 1951; m. Marcia Fox, Oct. 23, 1937; children—John, Jeffrey. Asst. chief statistician Pub. Welfare Dept., Indsl. Commn. Wis., Madison, 1935-38; research economist Social Sci. Research Council, Washington, instr. econs. U. Mich., 1939-40; economist Bur. Budget, USES, War Manpower Commn., 1940-44; mgmt. cons. Labor Relations Asso., Inc., Chgo., 1944-45; dir. execs. labor service, editor Execs.' Labor Letter, Nat. Foremen's Inst., Inc., N.Y.C., New London, Conn., 1945-48; asso. exec. dir. N.Y. Assn. New Ams., N.Y.C., 1948-52; mgmt. cons. Fedn. Jewish Philanthropies N.Y., 1952-53; exec. dir. Hebrew Immigrant Aid Soc., 1953-55; dir. adminstrn., adminstrv. sec. Union Am. Hebrew Congregations, N.Y.C., 1955-65; exec. v.p. Jewish Theol. Sem. Am., 1965-. Labor arbitrator N.Y. State Bd. Mediation, Am. Arbitration Assn., N.Y. State Pub. Employment Relations Bd., Fed. Mediation and Conciliation Service; sec. Temple Service Agy. Bd. dirs. Am. Immigration Conf.; bd. dirs., asst. sec. Rabbinical Pension Bd. Mem. Am. Econ. Assn., Nat. Conf. Jewish Communal Service, Assn. Jewish Book Pubs. (founder, 1st pres. 1962-65), Am. Civil Liberties Union (labor com.), Ams. for Dem. Action (dir.). Home: Tamarac Trail Harrison NY 10528 Office: 3080 Broadway New York City NY 10027

JACOBS, BRADFORD MCELDERRY, newspaper editor; b. Balt., Sept. 30, 1920; s. Joseph Streett and Sarah Hopkins (McElderry) J.; B.A., Princeton, 1942; m. Molly Carter Bruce, May 10, 1952; children—Molly Bruce, Sarah Hopkins, Ann McElderry. With Balt. Sunpapers, 1946—, beginning as reporter, successively editorial writer, 1953-54, chief London (Eng.) bur., 1954-56, Washington corr., 1956-57, editorial writer, 1957-68, polit. columnist, 1962-68, editor The Evening Sun, 1968—. Served with AUS, 1942-46; ETO. Decorated Bronze Star; Croix de Guerre (France). Democrat. Clubs: Elkridge, Green Spring Valley Hunt (Balt.). Home: Stevenson P O Baltimore County MD 21153 Office: Balt Sun Calvert and Center Sts Baltimore MD 21203

JACOBS, BURLEIGH EDMUND, Jr., foundry exec.; b. Milw., Feb. 3, 1920; s. Burleigh Edmund and Ora (Harmon) J.; B.A., U. Wis., 1942; m. Janet Eloise Grede, Nov. 1, 1942; children—Mary (Mrs. Merrill York), Bruce, Scott, William. Joined Grede Foundries, Inc., Milw., 1945, successively works mgr. Iron Mountain Foundry, 1947-50, works mgr. Milw. Steel Foundry, 1948-51, asst. sales mgr., 1955-59, asst. v.p., 1959-60, pres., 1960—; dir. Marshall & Ilsley Bank, Milw., Milsco Mfg. Co., Milw., Sta-Rite Industries, Inc., Delavan, Wis. Pres. Met. Milw. YMCA, 1968-70; mem. Greater Milw. Com., 1969—. Bd. dirs. Jr. Achievement, 1968-71, Better Bus. Bur. Served with USNR, 1942-45. Recipient Frederick A. Lorenz Meml. medal Steel Founders' Soc. Am., 1970. Mem. Steel Founders' Soc. Am. (pres. 1966-69), Am. Foundrymen's Soc. (v.p. 1971-72). Conglist. (moderator 1962-64). Club: Bluemound Country (Wauwatosa, Wis.). Home: 1040 Madera Circle Elm Grove WI 53122 Office: 1320 S First St Milwaukee WI 53204

JACOBS, CARL BEARSE, steel co. exec.; b. Bethlehem, Pa., Apr. 10, 1918; s. Myrl Lamont and Hermia Grace Jacobs; grad. Phillips Acad., 1937; B.A. in Polit. Sci., Princeton, 1941; m. Ann Faulkner, May 12, 1942; children—Carl Bearse, Katherine Grace, Nancy Faulkner. With Inland Steel Co., Chgo., 1941—, v.p. raw materials, 1959—; pres., dir. Caland Ore Co., Ltd., Chgo.; pres., dir. Jackson County Iron Co., Chgo.; dir. Hurlbut Calcium & Chem. Co., Green

Bay, Wis., Butler Bros., Empire Mining Co., Cleve., Bishop Coal Co., Pitts. Served as lt. USNR, 1942-45. Mem. Am. Mining Congress, Lake Charles Assos. (dir.), Am. Iron Ore Assn. (dir.), Am. Inst. Mining, Metall. and Petroleum Engrs., Am. Iron and Steel Inst., Bituminous Coal Operators Assn. (dir.), Ill. Coal Operators Assn. (dir.). Home: 632 Chatham Rd Glenview IL 60025 Office: 30 W Monroe St Chicago IL 60603

JACOBS, CARL NICHOLAS ins. exec.; b. Stevens Point, Wis., June 30, 1895; s. Peter James and Josephine (Krembs) J.; student pub. schs. Stevens Point; LL.D., St. Anselm's Coll., 1958; m. Ella Meyer, Nov. 18, 1920; children—James Peter, Robert Carl. Asst. cashier Soo Line R.R., Stevens Point, 1913-14; clk. Hardware Mut. Casualty Co., 1914-18, asst. sec., 1918-27, sec.-treas., 1927-29, v.p., 1929-30, pres., 1930-60, chmn., 1960-66, hon. chmn., 1966-68; chmn. Hardware Dealers Mut. Fire Ins. Co., 1937-45, pres., 1945-60, chmn., 1960-66, hon. chmn., 1966-68; dir. Dairy State Markets, Stevens Point, 1958-60; past pres., past dir. Am. Mut. Ins. Alliance, Nat. Assn. Automotive Mut. Ins. Cos., Nat. Assn. Mut. Casualty Cos.; trustee Am. Inst. for Property and Liability Underwriters, Inc., Phila., 1959-70, chmn. bd., 1964-66; chmn. Ins. Inst. Am., Bryn Mawr, Pa., 1965-66. Dir. C. of C. of U.S., 1941-55, v.p., 1951-54, treas., 1954. Trustee Northwestern Mut. Life Ins. Co., 1946-58. Bd. dirs. St. Norbert Coll., DePere, Wis.; trustee Inter-Am. Council Commerce and Prodn., N.Y., 1951-58, Am. Enterprise Inst., Washington. Recipient Nat. Office Mgmt. Assn. award, 1956. Mem. Casualty Actuarial Soc., Newcomen Soc. Roman Catholic. Elk, K.C., Knight of Malta. Clubs: Rotary (Stevens Point); Union League (Chgo.), Sera; Marco Polo (N.Y.C.). Home: 1909 Plover St Stevens Point WI 54481 Office: 1421 Strongs Av Stevens Point WI 54481

JACOBS, CLYDE EDWARD, educator, author; b. Herington, Kan., Jan. 19, 1925; s. Harry Charles and Jessie Irene (Tarbill) J.; A.B., U. Kan., 1946; postgrad. Inst. des Sciences Politiques, Paris, France, 1946-47; M.A., U. Mich., 1948, Ph.D., 1952. Faculty, U. Cal. at Davis, 1952—, asso. prof. polit. sci., 1960-63, prof., 1963—, chmn. dept., 1960-66, acting dir. Inst. Govt. Affairs, 1961-62. Mem. Davis Planning Commn., 1960-62, Yolo County Water Resources Bd., 1962-64; chmn. Davis Personnel Bd., 1966—. Councilman, City of Davis, 1960-64. Mem. Am., Western polit. sci. assns., Phi Beta Kappa. Beta Theta Pi, Pi Sigma Alpha, Phi Kappa Phi, Delta Sigma Rho. Republican. Roman Catholic. Clubs: Commonwealth (San Francisco). Author: Law Writers and the Courts, 1954; Justice Frankfurter and Civil Liberties, 1961. Co-author: California Government, 1966, 70; The Selective Service Act, 1967. Contbr. articles to profl. jours. Home: 1005 Cornell Dr Davis CA 95616

JACOBS, DAVID, sculptor; b. Niagara Falls, N.Y., Mar. 1, 1932; s. John B. and Adell (Pruitt) J.; student So. Cal. Coll., 1949-51; A.A., Orange Coast Coll., 1953; A.B., Los Angeles State Coll., 1955, M.A., 1957; m. Joan Berlingeri, 1969; children—Christine Ann, Kathryn Lee, David Theodore, Jr. Tchr., W.F. Dexter Sch., Whittier, Cal., 1955-56; supr. crafts Ohio Union, Ohio State U., 1957-61; instr. Ohio State U. Sch. Art, 1961-62; instr. art dept. Hofstra U., 1962-66, asst. prof., 1966; instr. sculpture Jewish Center, Columbus, O., 1959, Huntington (N.Y.) Twp. Art League, 1963-64, Marcusson Sch., Port Washington, N.Y., 1963-64; exhibited in one man shows at Los Angeles State Coll., 1957, Otterbein Coll. (O.), 1958, Ohio State U., 1959, Barone Gallery, N.Y.C., 1961, Kornblee Gallery, N.Y.C., 1963-65, Emily Lowe Gallery, Hempstead, N.Y., 1964-67, Witte Mus., 1969, Colgate U., 1970, San Jose State Coll., 1970, Albion Coll., 1970, Cornell U., 1971; works performing soft and hard, moving, sound sculpture Wah Chang-Box Works Assyrian Air Fair, 1967; rep. permanent collections Assyrian embassy, Va. Mus., Otterbein Coll., Guggenheim Mus., Ohio State U., Hofstra U., Raycom Industries; designer set decoration for A Farce, T. Griffith Prodns., Hollywood, Cal., 1955; producer Three Artists WOSU-TV, Columbus, 1958; designer props Naked City, N.Y.C., 1963. Contbr. revs., reprodns. to periodicals. Address: 51 8th Av Sea Cliff NY 11579 also 63 Herb Hill Rd Glen Cove NY 11542

JACOBS, DONALD P., educator; b. Chgo., June 22, 1927; s. David and Bertha (Nevod) J.; B.A., Roosevelt Coll., 1949; M.A., Columbia, 1951, Ph.D., 1956; m. Mary Stanton Elliott, June 8, 1952; children—Elizabeth, Ann, David. Mem. research staff Nat. Bur. Econ. Research, 1952-57; instr. Coll. City N.Y., 1955-57; mem. faculty to Morrison prof. finance, chmn. dept. Northwestern U. Inst. Mgmt., 1957—, Inst. Internat. Mgmt., Burgenstock, Switzerland, 1965, 66, 69. Dir. Pelika Mfg. Co., Benefit Trust Life Ins. Co. Co-dir. financial studies Presdl. Commn. Financial Structure and Regulation, 1970-71; sr. economist banking and currency com. U.S. Ho. of Reps., 1963-64; dir. Conf. Savs. and Residential Financing, 1967—. Served with USNR, 1945-46. Ford Found. fellow, 1959-60, 63-64. Mem. Am. Econ. Assn., Am. Statis. Assn., Am. Finance Assn., Econometrics Soc., Inst. Mgmt. Sci. Editor proc. Conf. Savs. and Residential Financing, 1967, 68, 69. Contbr. articles profl. jours. Home: 830 Milburn St Evanston IL 60201

JACOBS, HELEN HULL, writer; b. Globe, Ariz., Aug. 6, 1908; d. Roland Herbert and Eula (Hull) Jacobs; student U. Cal. at Berkeley, 1926-29, William and Mary Coll., 1942. Nat. jr. tennis champion, 1924-25; champion U.S. women's singles and doubles, 1932, singles champion, 1933, champion U.S. singles, doubles and mixed doubles, 1934; champion U.S. singles, doubles, 1935 (1st to win single championship 4 times successively); 6 times Wimbledon finalist; Wimbledon singles champion, 1936; mem. Am. Wightman Cup team for 13 successive years; designer sports clothes, N.Y.C. Served as lt. USNR (W.R.), 1943- 46, to comdr., 1952-54. Recipient Tennis Immortal award Tennis Writers Assn. Am., 1968, Tennis Hall of Fame. Hom. mem. All Eng. Lawn Tennis and Cricket Club, Eugene Field Soc., English Speaking Union (London), Nat. Geog. Soc., Mark Twain Soc.; mem. Kappa Alpha Theta. Republican. Episcopalian. Clubs: Women's Athletic, San Francisco Press, California Writers, Berkeley Tennis; Women's Athletic (Oakland, Cal.); Nice (France) Tennis. Author books including: Beyond the Game (autobiography), 1936; Storm Against the Wind, 1944; Laurel for Judy; Gallery of Champions, 1949; Center Court, 1950; Judy, Tennis Ace, 1951; Proudly She Serves, 1953; Famous American Women Athletes, 1964; Better Physical Fitness for Girls, 1964; The Young Sportsman's Guide to Tennis, 1965; Courage To Conquer, 1967. Contbr. articles to mags. Home: Ocean Av East Hampton NY 11937

JACOBS, HOWARD MILTON, hotel exec.; b. N.Y.C., June 28, 1911; s. Herman and Hannah (Reisner) J.; ed. pub. schs.; m. Lillian Lotenberg, Feb. 15, 1934; children—Rose Joan (Mrs. Marvin Tabb), Stephen John. With N.Y. Jour., 1927-31, N.Y. Am., 1931-36, N.Y. Jour.-Am., 1936-38; exec. sports editor Washington Times-Herald, 1938-48; dir. sales Willard Hotel, Washington, 1953-66; gen. mgr. Gramercy Inn, Washington, 1966-67; gen. mgr. Lord Baltimore Hotel, Balt., 1967-70, also v.p., treas. Mem. Banquet Mgrs. Am., Md. Hotel Assn. (bd. dirs.), Hotel Sales Mgrs., Advt. Club Balt. Club: Skal (Balt.). Home: Lord Baltimore Hotel Baltimore and Hanovers Sts Baltimore MD 21203

JACOBS, JAMES ALBERT, educator; b. Sioux City, Ia., Apr. 10, 1913; s. James Ernest and Grace (Gillespie) J.; A.B., State U. Ia., 1937, M.S., 1940, Ph.D., 1941; m. Phyllis Margaret Moorcroft. Asst. prof. physics, dir. electronics, physics, State U. Iowa, 1942-45, then prof. physics; now prof. physics, head dept. Va. Polytech. Inst. Mem. Am. Phys. Soc., Am. Assn. U. Profs., Am. Assn. Physics Tchrs., Ia. Acad. Scis., Phi Beta Kappa, Sigma Xi. Address: Physics Dept Virginia Polytech Inst Blacksburg VA 24060

JACOBS, JAMES PETER, former ins. exec.; b. Stevens Point, Wis., June 20, 1922; s. Carl N. and Ella (Meyer) J.; student Northwestern Mil. and Naval Acad., U. Pa., 1940-42; M.B.A., Harvard, 1947; m. Marjorie Ann Hester, Apr. 30, 1949; children—Peter J., John R., Richard W., Ann, Carl, Erich, Kurt. Began career as trainee at the A. O. Smith Corporation, Milw., 1947-49; various positions Hardware Mut. Cos., 1949—, mgr. Milw. br., 1953-54, Wis. dist. mgr., 1954-56, former pres. Hardware Mut. Casualty Co., Hardware Dealers Mut. Fire Ins. Co., Sentry Life Ins. Co., 1960-66, chmn. bd. 1966—. Home: Ephraim WI 54211

JACOBS, JAMES VINCENT, banker; b. Los Angeles, Mar. 4, 1921; s. James Daniel and Dorothy V. (Vincent) J.; M.B.A., Harvard, 1942; m. Marjorie Cox, Aug. 2, 1952; children—Joseph, Catherine, Barbara. Mgmt. cons. Robert Heller & Assos., Cleve., 1952-64; v.p. Bank N.Y., N.Y.C., 1964-70; exec. v.p., dir. Ariz. Bank, Phoenix, 1970—. Served to lt. USNR, 1942-46. Mem. Phoenix C. of C. Clubs: Arizona Country, Arizona (Phoenix). Home: 5817 N 38th Pl Paradise Valley AZ 85253 Office: PO Box 2511 Phoenix AZ 85002

JACOBS, JANE, author; b. Scranton, Pa., May 4, 1916; d. John Decker and Bess Mary (Robison) Butzner; m. Robert Hyde Jacobs. Jr., May 27, 1944; children—James Kedzie, Edward Decker, Mary Hyde. Asso. editor Archtl. Forum mag., 1952-62. Author: Downtown is for People in The Exploding Metropolis, 1959; The Death and Life of Great American Cities, 1961; The Economy of Cities, 1969. Address: care Random House 201 E 50th St New York City NY 10022

JACOBS, JOHN CLAYTON, corp. exec., lawyer; b. Guymon, Okla., June 27, 1917; s. John Clayton and Patience (Goodlander) J.; B.S., Ga. Inst. Tech., 1939; LL.B., Yale, 1948; m. Elinor Margaret Blanchard, June 20, 1942; children—Ann Clayton, Elizabeth Pelham. Admitted to Tex. bar, 1949; process engr. Standard Oil Co. La., 1939-44; supervisory engr. Creole Petroleum Corp., 1944-46; with firm Heldt & O'Boyle, Dallas, 1948-51; pvt. practice, Dallas, 1951-53; exec. v.p., dir. Wilcox Trend Gathering System, Inc., Dallas, 1953- v.p. Tex. Eastern Transmission Corp., Houston, 1955-66, sr. v.p., 1966—. Mem. Am. Inst. Chem. Engrs., Am. Inst. Mining, Metall. and Petroleum Engrs., Am. Bar Assn., Am. Gas Assn. (chmn. natural gas reserves com.), Colegio de Ingenieros de Venezuela. Inst. Petroleum Engrs., Inst. Gas Engrs., Beta Theta Pi, Omicron Delta Kappa, Phi Kappa Phi. Episcopalian. Clubs: Ramada, Petroleum (Houston); Bankers (Mexico City); Hurlingham (London, Eng.). Author: (with Leeston and Crichton) The Dynamic Natural Gas Industry, 1963. Home: 4627 Banning St Houston TX 77027 Office: PO Box 2521 Houston TX 77001

JACOBS, JOHN EDWARD, educator; b. Kansas City, Mo., June 15, 1920; s. Charles Hawley and Lucille Hartman (Boetjer) J.; B.S. in Elec. Engring., Northwestern Tech. Inst., 1947, M.S., 1948, Ph.D., 1950; m. Elizabeth Anne Brazell, Feb. 23, 1945; children—Patricia, Robert, William, Thomas, Marie, Stephen. Mgr. advance devel. X-ray dept. Gen. Electric Co., Milw., 1950-58, engring. scientist research labs., Schenectady, 1958-60; prof. elec. engring. Northwestern U., Evanston, Ill., 1960—, Walter P. Murphy prof. elec. engring. and engring. scis., 1969—. Exec. dir. Bio-med. Engring. Center; pres. Biomed. Engrs. Resource Corp., 1968—; cons. to industry and govt., 1961—. Spl. adviser Nat. Inst. Gen. Med. Scis. of Dept. Health, Edn. and Welfare, 1966—. Mem. research com. Chgo. Heart Assn., 1962-65. Served to lt. (j.g.) USNR, 1942-46. Mem. I.R.E. (chmn. Milw. sect. 1957-58; asso. editor bio-med. trans. 1960-65), Bio-Med. Engring. Soc. (founder 1968, treas. 1968—), Nat. Acad. Engring. Patentee in field. Home: 631 Milburn St Evanston IL 60201

JACOBS, JOHN ELMER, steel co. exec.; b. Swissvale, Pa., Mar. 11, 1906; s. David E. and Bertha (Keubert) J.; B.S. in Metallurgy, Carnegie Inst. Tech., 1928, M.S. in Metallurgy, 1929; m. Jeanne King, Nov. 23, 1932; 1 dau., Johanna (Mrs. Perry Newport). Staff metall. adv. bd. U.S. Bur. Mines, 1929-31; research metallurgist Heppenstall Co., Pitts., 1931-34; metallurgist Lukens Steel Co., Coatesville, Pa., 1934-35; with Bethlehem Steel Co., 1935—, asst. v.p. steel operations, 1958-60, v.p. steel operations, 1960-70, sr. v.p., 1970—, also dir. Mem. Am. Iron and Steel Inst., Am. Soc. Metals, Assn. Iron and Steel Engrs., Am. Inst. Metall. Engrs., Navy League, Pa. Soc., Sigma Nu, Theta Tau. Clubs: Wanakah Country (Hamburg, N.Y.); Bethlehem, Saucon Valley Country (Bethlehem). Home: Saucon Valley Rd Bethlehem PA 18015 Office: Bethlehem Steel Co Bethlehem PA 18016

JACOBS, JOHN ROLAND, former fgn. service officer; b. Pleasant Grove, Utah, Feb. 23, 1911; s. Hugh West and Kate (Halliday) J.; student Brigham Young U., 1929-30, U. Grenoble, France, 1932-33, U. Poitier, France, 1933-34; B.A. with honors, U. Utah, 1937, M.A., 1938; postgrad. Stanford, 1939-42; m. Janine Cleyet-Marrel, June 23, 1934; children—Denis Georges, Michel Roland. Missionary, Ch. Jesus Christ of Latter Day Saints, France, 1930-32; instr. Stanford, 1942-45; vice consul, Antwerp, Belgium, 1945-50; vice consul, Le Havre, 1950, consul, 1951; consul, Marseille, 1951-55; chief Western Europe br., div. biographic information Dept. State, 1955- 58, asst. chief div. intelligence collection and distbn., 1958-59; consul. Tananarive, Madagascar, 1959-60, counselor of embassy, dep. chief of mission, 1960-63, dep. dir. Office African Programs, Bur. Ednl. and Cultural Affairs, Dept. State, Washington, 1963-64, dir. Office African Programs, Bur. Ednl. and Cultural Affairs, 1964-70. Mem. Am. Fgn. Service Assn., Diplomatic and Consular Officers Ret. Lion. Club: Internat. (Washington). Home: 3024 Arizona Av Washington DC 20016

JACOBS, JOSEPH MAURICE, lawyer; b. Rochester, N.Y., Nov. 7, 1907; s. Hyman and Leah (Abrams) J.; B.A. cum laude, Syracuse U., 1928; J.D., John Marshall Coll. Law, 1931; m. Esther Goodman, Nov. 8, 1931; children—Helene Barbara, Mark Donald. Admitted to Ill. bar, 1931, U.S. Supreme Ct., bar; partner Jacobs, Gore, Burns & Sugarman, Chgo., 1960—; gen. counsel Amalgamated Meat Cutters and Butcher Workmen N.Am., Upholsters Internat. Union, Phila., Am. Fedn. Grain Millers, Mpls.; Midwest counsel numerous other unions. Lectr. labor law problems Northwestern U., Loyola U., Chgo., U. Chgo., Roosevelt U. Chmn. bd. dirs. Ill. Labor History Soc. Ky. col.; col. a.d.c. to Gov. N.M. Hon. fellow Truman Library Inst. Fellow Am. Coll. Trial Lawyers; mem. Am., Ill., Chgo. bar assns., Am. Judicature Soc., Decalogue Soc. Lawyers, Indsl. Lawyers Research Assn., Soc. Commerce Commn. Attys., Fed. Immigration Service Attys., Franklin D. Roosevelt Collectors Assn., Nat. Assn. Manuscript Collectors, Am. Polit. Items Collectors Assn., Brandeis U. Bibliophiles, Workmen Circle, Am. Trade Union Council, Jewish Nat. Workers Alliance, Ill. Alumni Assn., U. Ill. Found. Mem. B'nai B'rith. Clubs: Presidents of U. Ill. (Chgo.). Home: 2800 Lake Shore Dr Chicago IL Office: 201 N Wells St Chicago IL 60606

JACOBS, KLAUS KARL EWALD, banker; b. Munich, Germany, Mar. 9, 1934; s. Hermann and Therese (Hinlein) J.; ed. Comml. Coll., Munich, 1952-54; m. Karin Heik, Oct. 28, 1961. Came to U.S., 1968. With Deutsche Bank A.G., Germany, 1955-68; exec. asst. to chmn., 1957-64, mgr., 1964-68; exec. v.p., dir. asst. to chmn., 1957-64, mgr., 1964-68; exec. v.p., dir. European-Am. Banking Corp., European Am. Bank & Trust Co., N.Y.C., 1968—; pres. European-Am. Finance (Bermuda) Ltd. Home: 1968—; pres. European-Am. Finance (Bermuda) Ltd. Home: 1035 Fifth Av New York NY 10028 Office: 52 Wall St New York NY 10005 Av New York NY 10028

JACOBS, LEON, medical scientist; b. Bklyn. Mar. 26, 1915; s. Samuel and Evelyn (Rosenthal) J.; B.A., Bklyn. Coll., 1935; M.A., George Washington U., 1938, Ph.D., 1947; m. Eva. Eisenberg, Nov. 26, 1946; children—Jonathan H., Alice E., Abby M. Scientist div. zoology NIH, 1937-43, sci. Tropical Disease lab., 1946-59, chief Parasitic Diseases lab., 1959-64, acting scientific dir. Nat. Inst. Allergy and Infectious Diseases, 1964-65; sci. dir. div. biologics standards NIH, 1966-67; dep. asst. sec. for sci. Dept. Health, Edn. and Welfare, 1967-69; asst. dir. NIH, 1969—. Cons. to com. on uveitis American Acad. Ophthalmology and Otolaryngology, 1957-63. Mem. grad. council George Washington U., 1956—. Fulbright research scholar to New Zealand, 1960; Guggenheim fellow, 1960-61; recipient Arthur S. Flemming award U.S. Jr. C. of C., Washington, 1954; award biol. sci. Washington Acad. Scis., 1954; Alumnus award Bklyn. Coll., 1955; Barnett Cohen award Md. br. Soc. Bacteriologists, 1956; Dist. Alumnus award. Geo. Wash. U. 1967. Mem. A.A.A.S., Am. Soc. Parasitologists (mem. council 1963—; Henry B. Ward medal 1963), Am. Soc. Tropical Medicine and Hygiene, Am. Assn. Immunologists, Helminthological Soc. Washington (pres. 1951), Conf. Biol. Editors. Editor Tropical Medicine and Hygiene News, 1950-55, Jour. Parasitology, 1956-58. Home: 3705 Morrison St NW Washington DC 20015 Office: NIH Bethesda MD 20014

JACOBS, MORRIS ELIAS, advt. exec.; b. Omaha, Aug. 7, 1896; s. Nathaniel Elias and Gertrude (Shafton) J.; student U. Mo., 1914-16; LL.D., Creighton U., 1954, St. Joseph's Coll., 1960; m. Rae Sara Iseman, Sept. 15, 1927; 1 dau., Susie. Reporter, Des Moines Register-Tribune, 1917-18; reporter, feature writer Omaha Daily Bee, Omaha Daily News, 1918-20; owner Bozell & Jacobs Advt. and Pub. Relations Agy., Omaha, 1922; dir. Omaha Downtown Parking Assn. Mem. exec. com. Omaha Indsl. Found., 1953—; pres. State Bd. Edn., 1955-57; active Boy Scouts of Am.; chmn. Nat. Planning Com. for Coop. Electric Refrigeration Bur., 1931-33; mem. exec. com. Pub. Utilities Advt. Assn., 1932-36; co-chmn. initial gifts com. Jewish Philanthropies, 1939; mem., vice chmn. midwest region Am.-Jewish Joint Distbn. Com., 1940; mem. bd. electors Hall of Fame of Omaha U.; chmn. Jewish Philanthropies campaign for war relief and refugees, 1940; pres. W. Central States regional conf. Jewish Fedns. and Welfare Funds, 1941; del. Am. Jewish Conf., 1943; mem. nat. exec. com. Am. Jewish Com.; chmn. Com. of '52 Found. Bd. dirs. Children's Meml. Hosp.; Omaha Symphony Orch. Found.; nat. bd. dirs. United Service Orgn.; trustee Clarkson Hosp.; bd. dirs. Omaha YMCA, Nat. Conf. Christians and Jews; bd. regents Creighton U.; trustee St. Joseph Coll.; chmn. 1954 Omaha Centennial Celebration, selected King Ak-Sar-Ben LX, 1954; nat. chmn. U. Mo. Sch. Journalism 50 year commemoration. Recipient B'nai B'rith Americanism citation, 1953; Beth Israel Synaby Neb. Wesleyan U., 1957. Mem. Am. Legion (life); Alpha Delta Sigma, Delta Sigma Chi, Zeta Beta Tau (asso.). Republican. Jewish religion (pres. temple 1940-41). Home: Regency House 2323 N Central Av Phoenix AZ 85004 Office: Kiewit Plaza Omaha NB 68131

JACOBS, NATHAN L., judge; b. Feb. 28, 1905; B.S., U. Pa., 1925; LL.B. magna cum laude, Harvard, 1928, S.J.D., 1931. Admitted to N.J. bar, 1928; law practice with Arthur T. Vanderbilt, 1928-34; mem. Frazer, Stoffer & Jacobs, Newark, 1934-48; chief dep. commr., counsel to D. Frederick Burnett, N.J. State commr. alcoholic beverage control, 1934-39; state atty., dist. enforcement attorney O.P.A., Newark, 1942-45; prof. adminstrv. law Rutgers U., 1929-48; chmn. state arbitration board Bell Telephone Co.-Telephone Workers Union of N.J., 1947; sr. judge Appellate Div., N.J. Superior Court, 1948-52; asso. justice N.J. Supreme Ct., 1948, since 52. Del., vice chmn. jud. com. N.J. Constl. Conv., 1947. Chmn. adv. council Inst. Management and Labor Relations, Rutgers U., 1947-48. Recipient Sears prize, 1927; Judah P. Benjamin fellowship, 1930-31. Mem. Am., N.J. State, Essex Co. bar assns. Address: 284 W Hobart Gap Rd Livingston NJ 07039

JACOBS, PAUL, author; b. N.Y.C., Aug. 24, 1918; s. Julius and Tecla (Schmidt) J.; student Coll. City N.Y., U. Minn.; m. Ruth Rosenfield, Jan. 1, 1939. Organizer, Internat. Ladies Garment Workers Union, 1941-43; race relations specialist Am. Jewish Com., 1946-48; internat. rep. Oil Workers Internat. Union, 1948-51; author, 1955—; mem. staff Center Study Democratic Instns., Santa Barbara, Cal., 1956-69; research staff Center Study Law and Soc., U. Cal. at Berkeley, 1964—; assoc. fellow Inst. for Policy studies, Washington, 1970—. Served with USAAF, 1943-46. Recipient award for pub. service to journalism Sigma Delta Chi, 1958. Mem. Indsl. Relations Research Assn., Soc. Mag. Writers, Congress Racial Equality, N.A.A.C.P. Author: (with F. Pinner, P. Seiznick) Old Age and Political Behavior, 1959; (with M. Harrington) Labor in a Free Society, 1959; The State of the Unions, 1963; Is Curly Jewish, 1965; (with S. Landau) The New Radicals, 1966; Prelude to Riot, 1968; Between the Rock and the Hard Place, 1970; (with Saul Landau, Eve Pell) To Serve the Devil, 1970; The Red, Black and Brown Experience in America, 1971. Contbr. articles to profl. jours. Address: 2500 Filbert St San Francisco CA 94123

JACOBS, PAUL M., food co. exec.; b. Boston, Apr. 30, 1916; s. Joseph B. and Rita (May) J.; B.A., Williams Coll., 1937; student Harvard Law Sch.; m. Emilie Kallmoor, Nov. 29, 1939; children-Susan (Mrs. Richard P. Kotz), Eleanor L., Katherine M. Pres. N. Atlantic Packing Co., 1942-53; with Gorton Corp., Gloucester, Mass., 1953-70, chmn., 1969-70; v.p. H.P. Hood Co., Boston, 1970—. Bd. dirs. Mass. Merchants Assn.; mem. com. Mass. Fisheries Adv. Commn., 1966—; mem. advt. com. State Dept. Mem. town meeting, Belmont, Mass. Bd. dirs. Mass. Blue Cross; chmn. Belmont United Fund, 1951-52; pres. Buckingham Sch., Cambridge, Mass., 1966-69, trustee, 1960—. Mem. Nat. Fisheries Inst. (pres. 1968-69, chmn. 1969- 70). Club: Eastern Point Yacht (commodore) (Gloucester). Home: 15 Pinehurst Rd Belmont MA 02178 Office: 327 Main St Gloucester MA 01930

JACOBS, ROBERT, educator; b. Murphysboro, Ill., July 17, 1913; s. Arthur Clarence and Zylphia May (Porter) J.; B.Ed., So. Ill. U., 1935; M.A., U. Ill., 1939; Ed.D., Wayne State U., 1949; m. Oma Lee Corgan, Aug. 13, 1939; children—Robert Corgan, Janice Lee (Mrs. Royce Fichte), Lawrence James, Linda May. Pub. Sch. tchr., adminstr., Wood River, Ill., 1935-42; personnel staff Ford Motor Co., 1945-46; asst. instr. Wayne U., 1946-47; asst. dir. Ednl. Records Bur., N.Y.C., 1947-51; dir. counseling, prof. edn. Tex. A. and M. Coll., 1951-54; ednl. measurements adviser, dep. chief edn. div. U.S. Operations Mission to Ethiopia, FOA, 1954-56; regional edn. adviser S.E. Asia, U.S. Operations Mission, Thailand, 1956-58; chief Far East program div. Office Edn., ICA, 1958-61; chief edn. div. Office Ednl.

and Social Devel. Aid, 1961-62; prof. edn., dean internat. service div. So. Ill. U., Carbondale, 1962-67; regional edn. adviser Office Regional Devel. Affairs, Am. embassy, Bangkok, Thailand, 1967—; vis. prof., extension lectr. U. Ark., U. Ala., Rutgers U., U. Addis Ababa, George Washington U.; numerous surveys and evaluations edn. programs abroad, including Korea, Cambodia, Syria, Nigeria, India, Congo, Chile, Colombia; mem. internat. adv. com. Ednl. Records Bur. Served with AUS, 1942-45. Recipient of meritorious service citation ICA, AID. Fellow Am. Psychol. Assn.; mem. N.E.A., Nat. Vocational Guidance Assn., Am. Personnel and Guidance Assn., A.A.A.S., Am. Ednl. Research Assn., Nat. Soc. Study Edn., Fgn. Service Assn., Nat. Platform Assn., N.Y. Acad. Scis., Phi Delta Kappa. Methodist. Home: Heritage Hills R R 1 Carbondale IL 62901 Office: Am Embassy APO San Francisco CA 96346

JACOBS, ROBERT, steel co. exec.; b. Phila., Aug. 6 1918; s. Sidney and Helen (Mellor) J.; B.S., U. Pitts., 1939; m. Louise Tice, Apr. 12, 1945; children—Michael, Stephen, Judy. Vice pres. finance Interlake, Inc., 1963—. Served with USAAF, 1941-45. Home: 902 S Bruner St Hinsdale IL 60521 Office: 310 S Michigan Av Chicago IL 60604

JACOBS, ROBERT ALLAN, architect; b. N.Y.C., Sept. 16, 1905; s. Harry Allan and Elsie (Wolf) J.; student Choate and Horace Mann Schs., 1920-23; A.B., Amherst, 1927, M.A. (hon.), 1957; B.Arch., Columbia Archtl. School, 1935; m. Frances Cullman, June 3, 1934 (div. June 1956); children—Frances, Barbara, Robert Allan; m. 2d, Ellen D. Dribben, Sept. 1, 1958 (div. Feb. 1963); m. 3d, Lili Finletter Bright, Mar. 1963 (div. Mar. 1964); m. 4th, Margot Helland Koehler, Dec. 10, 1966. Engaged in bus., 1927-30; with office LeCorbusier, Paris, 1934-35; lectr. tour in U.S. with LeCorbusier, 1935; designer, draftsman Harrison & Fouilhoux, 1935-38; partner Kahn & Jacobs, 1940—. Mem. exec. com. Manhattan council Boy Scouts Am. Trustee Nat. Inst. Archtl. Edn. Fellow A.I.A.; mem. Internat. Union Architects (rep. to U.N. 1950), Nat. Council Architects (registration bd.), Archtl. League N.Y. (pres. 1962-64), N.Y. Bldg. Congress (past v.p., mem. bd. govs.), Municipal Arts Soc. Clubs: University, Sky, Dutchess Valley Rod and Gun, Quaker Hill. Home: 1065 Lexington Av New York City NY 10021 Office: Two Park Av New York City NY 10016

JACOBS, SIDNEY R., publisher; b. N.Y.C., Dec. 2, 1909; s. Philip and Fannie (Roseman) J.; student N.Y. U., 1925-29; m. Joan Freund, Dec. 7, 1935. With Alfred A. Knopf, Inc., N.Y.C., 1928-, prodn. mgr., 1933-57, dir., 1955—, v.p. prodn., 1957—, asst. to chmn. bd., pres., 1957-60; dir. prodn. Random House, Inc., 1960—, v.p. prodn., 1966—. Served with AUS, 1943-45. Decorated Bronze Star medal. Mem. Am. Inst. Graphic Arts (pres. 1957-58, past v.p., dir.). Club: Public Lunch (sec.-treas. 1969-70). Home: 235 E 57th St New York City NY 10022 Office: 201 E 50th St New York City NY 10022

JACOBS, SOPHIA YARNELL, civic worker; b. Haverford, Pa., June 23, 1902; d. Charlton and Anna Brinton (Coxe) Yarnall; student Bryn Mawr Coll., 1919-21; m. Reginald Robert Jacobs. Oct. 14, 1921 (div.); children—Denholm Muir, Charlton Yarnall (Mrs. Stowe Catlin Phelps). Free lance writer women's mags., including Good Housekeeping, Parents, 1930—; promotion mgr. Phila. Orch., 1942-45. Former bd. dirs. Am. Symphony Orch.; former mem. Urban League Greater N.Y. (pres. 1956-60, chmn. bd. 1960-64, dir.), Rachel Carson Trust for Living Environment (dir.), Am. Civil Liberties Union, Planned Communities, Nat. Council Women U.S. (pres. 1959-64, hon. pres. 1964-69). Clubs: Acorn (Phila.); Cosmopolitan, Women's City (N.Y.C.). Home: 11 E 73d St New York City NY 10021

JACOBS, STEPHEN W., educator, architect; b. Woodmere, N.Y., May 12, 1919; s. E. Louis and Grace Aguilar (Blitz) J.; grad. Woodmere Acad., 1936; A.B., Harvard, 1940, M.Arch., 1947; M.F.A., Princeton, 1952, Ph.D., 1966; m. Helen Ogden Olcott, Jan 19, 1952; children—Katharine Lawrence, David Keller. Asst. prof. architecture Miami U., Oxford, O., 1947-48; instr., preceptor Princeton, 1948-52; asst. prof. fine arts Middlebury Coll., 1952-55; lectr., asst. prof. U. Cal., 1955-60; asso. prof. to prof. architecture Cornell U., 1960—. Asso. dir. Cornell-Harvard Archaeol. Exploration of Sardis, Turkey, 1970—; field rep. history of architecture and urban devel. Cornell U. Grad. Sch., 1970—; group leader Expt. in Internat. Living, France, 1949-51, Sweden, 1950, Denmark, 1953. Pres. Historic Ithaca and Tompkins County, 1968—. Served with USAAF, 1942-45; ETO. Mem. A.I.A., Am. Inst. Archaeology, Assn. Collegiate Schs. of Architecture, Soc. Archtl. Historians (pres. Central N.Y. 1962-65), Coll. Art Assn. Home: 303 Highgate Rd Ithaca NY 14850

JACOBS, SYDNEY, physician; b. New Orleans, Nov. 23, 1907; s. Wolf Nathan and Hannah (Abramson) J.; B.S., Tulane U., 1928, M.D., 1930; postgrad. Trudeau Sch. Tb, Saranac Lake, N.Y., 1937; m. Sadie Frumin, June 12, 1938 (dec.); children—Alan Norman, Jerome Mark, Myron Hillel, Joel Frumin; m. 2d, Bernice Loeffelholz, Mar. 22, 1970. Intern, Touro Infirmary, New Orleans, 1930-31, sr. physician, chief dept. medicine, 1952-56; med. resident Gen. Hosp., Syracuse, N.Y., 1931-32; pvt. practice internal medicine, New Orleans, 1932—; with Tulane U., 1932—, asso. prof. clin. medicine, 1954-60, prof., 1960—; chief dept. medicine Touro Infirmary, 1967—; sr. cons. medicine Jewish Children's Home, Meth. Home Hosp., Municipal Boys' Home; cons. Chest Clinic VA, sr. vis. physician Charity Hosp.; cons. chest diseases USPHS, New Orleans. Diplomate Am. Bd. Internal Medicine, subsplty. pulmonary diseases. Fellow A.C.P.; mem. Nat. (dir., v.p. 1953-54, pres. 1966), La. (pres. 1947-51) Tb assns., So. (pres. 1954-55), La. (pres. 1953-54) thoracic socs., Am. Coll. Chest Physicians, Am. Heart Assn., Internat. Union Against Tb (councillor 1967), Nat. Rehab. Assn., Alpha Omega Alpha. Contbr. numerous papers to sci. lit. Home: 3704 Octavia St New Orleans LA 70125 Office: Touro Infirmary 1400 Foucher St New Orleans LA 70115

JACOBS, THOMAS LLOYD, educator; b. Forest City, Ia., Aug. 18, 1908; s. Richard Raymond and Helen (Lloyd) J.; A.B., Cornell Coll., Mt. Vernon, Ia., 1930; Ph.D. in Organic Chemistry, Cornell U., 1935; m. Ruth Fielden, Oct. 4, 1934; children—Antoinette (Mrs. David Kayser), Richard, William. Instr., Harvard, 1935-39; faculty U. Cal., Los Angeles, 1939—, prof. chemistry, 1951—. Spl. research organic chemistry acetylenes and allenes, synthesis compounds for testing as antimalarials, stereochemistry; cons. to industry, 1956—. Civilian with OSRD, 1943-46. Guggenheim fellow, 1946-47, Mem. Am. Chem. Soc., Chem. Soc. (London), Phi Beta Kappa, Sigma Xi, Phi Kappa Phi, Phi Lambda Upsilon, Alpha Chi Sigma. Home: 10707 Wellworth Av Los Angeles CA 90024

JACOBS, WALTER B., business exec.; b. Shreveport, 1895; grad. Notre Dame, 1917. Chmn. bd., chief exec. officer First Nat. Bank, Shreveport, dir. Kilgore (Tex.) Nat. Bank, La. Fire Ins. Co., Baton Rouge, Shreveport Rys. Co., Inc. Dir. La. State Fair Assn. Home: 5935 E Ridge Dr Shreveport LA 71109

JACOBS, WALTER L., former financier; b. Chgo., June 15, 1896; s. Leon and Anna J.; student pub. schs.; m. Jeannette A. Rothschild, Apr. 24, 1918 (dec. Sept. 1964); 1 son, Walter A. (killed in action World War II); m. 2d, Mildred Michele, Nov. 2, 1964; 1 son, Richard. Salesman, Ford Motor Co., 1916; automobile retail bus., 1917; automobile rental bus. under name Rent-A-Car, Inc., 1918, pres., chief exec. of co. until corp. sold to Gen. Motors, 1926; pres., mgr. Hertz Corp. (for Gen. Motors), until 1960, cons., 1960—; dir. Amalgamated Trust & Savs. Bank, Chgo. Recipient Horatio Alger Award, 1960. Clubs: Standard (Chgo.); Westview Country (Miami, Fla.). Home: 9424 W Broadview Dr Miami Beach FL 33154

JACOBS, WALTER WILLIAM, educator; b. Newark, Sept. 26, 1914; s. Harry Simon and Beatrice (Kaplan) J.; B.S., Coll. City N.Y., 1934; A.M., George Washington U., 1940, Ph.D., 1951; m. Irene Ostreicher, Mar. 30, 1941. Analyst, War Dept., 1945-47, chief prodn. and marketing sect. Dept. Commerce, 1947-51; dept. chief computation div. Hdqrs. USAF, 1951-57, Office Research, Nat. Security Agy., 1957-65; comdt. Nat. Cryptologic Sch., 1966-69; chmn. dept. math. Am. U., 1969—. Served with AUS, 1943-46. Decorated Legion of Merit. Mem. Math. Assn. Am., Assn. Computing Machinery, Sigma Xi, Phi Kappa Phi. Author: (with Alain C. White) Variation Play, 1943. Home: 3003 Van Ness St Washington DC 20008

JACOBS, WILBUR RIPLEY, historian, educator; b. Chgo., June 30, 1918; s. Walter R. and Nona I. (Deutsch) J.; B.A., U. Cal. at Los Angeles, 1940, M.A., 1941, Ph.D., 1947; postgrad. (John Martin Vincent scholar) Johns Hopkins, 1946; m. Josephine Elizabeth Kingsbury, Aug. 19, 1951; children—Shirley Elizabeth, Catherine Elaine. Jr. instr. Johns Hopkins, 1946; instr. history Stanford, 1947-49; instr. Am. history U. Cal. at Santa Barbara, 1949-51, asst. prof., 1951-55, asso. prof., 1955-60, prof., 1960—; dean men, 1950-51, research lectr., 1956, chmn. dept. history, 1959-63; acad. asst. to pres. U. Cal. at Berkeley, 1964-65; mem. editorial bd. history panel U. Cal. Press, 1965-68; vis. prof. Ind. U., U. Colo., summers, U. Cal. at Los Angeles, 1964, Claremont Grad. Sch., 1968; William L. Clements library lectr. U. Mich., 1967; U.S. State Dept. del. Cultural Exchange Program Yugoslavia, 1965; Fulbright vis. prof. Australian Nat. U., 1969; Lectr. U. Papua, New Guinea, 1969, Melboure W., 1969. Served with USAAF, 1941-45. Research grantee Rockefeller Found., 1949, Am. Philos. Soc., 1956, 69, Huntington Library, 1960, 64, 70, Ford Found., 1962. Mem. Am. Hist. Assn. (council mem. Pacific Coast br., Pacific Coast prize 1947, mem. Bzveridge and Dunning prize com. 1969—), Orgn. Am. Historians, Am. Studies Assn., Conf. on Early History, History Guild So. Cal. (mem. council Conf. for Peace Research in History, 1966). Author: Wilderness Politics and Indian Gifts, 1966; The Historical World of Frederick Jackson Turner, 1968; also articles in Ency. Britannica and other reference works, scholarly jours., mags., newspapers. Co-author: Turner, Bolton and Webb, 1965. Editor: Letters of Francis Parkman, 2 vols., 1960; America's Great Frontiers and Sections, Frederick Jackson Turner's Unpublished Writings, 1969; The Appalachian Indian Frontier, 1967; The Paxton Riots and the Frontier Theory, 1967. Research on early Am. history, Am. Indian frontier, historiography. Mem. editorial bd. Pacific Hist. Rev., 1966-70, American West mag., 1969—, Western Hist. Quar., 1969—, Am. History and Life, 1969—. Office: Dept History U Cal Santa Barbara CA 93106

JACOBS, WILLIAM KETCHUM, Jr., investment co. exec.; b. Bklyn., Mar. 17, 1908; s. William K. and Frances (Halper) J.; student pub. schs., extension courses Columbia; m. Edna Grace Link, Oct. 17, 1929. With H. Hentz & Co., investment bankers, N.Y.C., 1924-32; engaged in pvt. practice as financial counsel, cons., 1932-57; pres., dir. Abacus Fund, Inc., registered investment co., 1957—, now chmn. bd.; dir. Govt. Employees Ins. Co., Criterion Ins. Co., Govt. Employees Corp., Govt. Employees Life Ins. Co., Govt. Employees Financial Corp.; adv. dir. Worldwide Spl. Fund, N.Y., Curacao, N.W.I.; dir. Worldwide Fund, Ltd., Bermuda. Executor, trustee numerous estates and trust funds; pres., dir. Tebil Found. Inc., N.Y.C. Mem. N.Y. Soc. Security Analysts, Tax Inst. Home: 895 Park Av New York City NY 10021 Office: 654 Madison Av New York City NY 10021

JACOBS, WILLIAM MORTON, pub. utility exec.; b. Pasadena, Cal., Nov. 18, 1907; s. Guy R. and Lulu (Morton) J.; B.S. in Mech. Engring., Cal. Inst. Tech., 1928; m. Frances Scoville, Nov. 1, 1930; children—Janice, Carol, William. Design engr. Collins-Western Corp., Los Angeles, 1928-30; with So. Cal. Gas Co., 1930-56, v.p., asst. gen. mgr., dir., 1953-56; v.p. Pacific Lighting Corp., San Francisco, 1956-65; pres. Pacific Lighting Service & Supply Co., Los Angeles, 1961-67; pres., dir. So. Cal. Gas Co., 1967—, chief exec. officer, 1968—. Mem. Am. (past pres.), Pacific Coast (past pres.) gas assns., Cal. Inst. Tech. Alumni Assn. (past pres.). Mason. Clubs: California (Los Angeles); Annandale Golf (Pasadena); Family (San Francisco). Address: 810 S Flower St Los Angeles CA 90017

JACOBS, WILLIAM PAUL, educator, scientist; b. Boston, May 25, 1919; s. Vincent H. and Elizabeth (Kennedy) J.; A.B., Harvard, 1942, Ph.D., 1946; m. Jane Shaw, Mar. 12, 1949; children—Mark, Anne. Research asso. biology Harvard, 1946-47; jr. prize fellow Harvard Soc. Fellows, 1947-48; faculty Princeton, 1948—, prof. biology, 1962—, W.L. Schultz prof. biology, 1969. Mem. com. innovation lab. study Biol. Scis. Curriculum Study, 1959-64. Served with M.C., AUS, 1942-44. Recipient Morrison prize N.Y. Acad. Scis., 1951. Lalor fellow, 1950-51; NSF sr. postdoctoral fellow, 1957; NSF Sci. Faculty fellow, 1962; Guggenheim fellow, 1967. Mem. Soc. Study Devel. and Growth (pres. 1960-61), Bot. Soc. Am., Am., Japanese socs. plant physiologists, Internat. Soc. Plant Morphologists, Internat. Phycological Soc., Soc. Exptl. Biology (Brit.). Author: (with C.E. LaMotte) Regulation in Plants by Hormones, 1964. Contbr. articles to sci. publs. Home: 72 The Western Way Princeton NJ 08540

JACOBS, WOODROW COOPER, meteorologist, oceanographer; b. Pasadena, Cal., Sept. 11, 1908 s. William Rozel and Mabelle (Cooper) J.; A.B., U. Cal. at Los Angeles, 1930, Ph.D., 1948; M.S., U. So. Cal., 1934; m. Dorothy Cecelia Quinn, June 15, 1933; 1 dau., Marilyn Rozel (Mrs. Wilbur M. Ott). With U.S. Weather Bur., San Diego, 1931-36, forecaster fruit-frost service, Pomona, Cal., 1936-41; research asso. Scripps Instn. Oceanography, also Carnegie Inst., 1937; chief civilian meteorologist Hdqrs. USAAF, 1941-46; head climatological branch U.S. Weather Bur., Washington, 1946-48; dir. climatology USAF Air Weather Service Washington, 1948-60; physical science specialist Library of Congress, 1960-61; dir. National Oceanographic Data Center, 1961-67, World Data Center A, Oceanography, 1962-67; dir. environmental data service Environmental Sci. Service Administration, Silver Spring, Md., 1967—; vis. lecturer Mass. Inst. Tech., 1950, U. Chgo., 1956; lectr. meteorology and oceanography Dept. Agr. Grad. Sch., 1942-58. USAF mem. two panels Research and Devel. Bd., Dept. Def., 1948-52; com. climatology joint meteorol. com. Joint Chiefs Staff, 1948-62; U.S. del. Internat. Meteorol. Orgn., Toronto Can., 1947, pres. subcom. agrl. forecasts, 1947-50; mem. commn. climatology World Meteorol. Orgn., 1950-60, chmn. internat. com. exchange data, 1953-60; U.S. del. of Nat. Acad. Scis. to assembly Internat. Union Geodesy and Geophysics, Brussels, 1951, Rome, 1954, Toronto, 1957, Lucerne, 1967; mem. coms. NRC-National Sci. Foundation, 1948—; chmn. interagency atmospheric scis. oceanography com. on air-sea research, 1963-64; adv. com. on oceanography Smithsonian Instn., 1962—; working group Intergovtl. Oceanographic Commn., UNESCO, 1962-67; panel mem. Interagey Com. on Oceanography, 1961-67; adv. council Oceanic Research Inst. of San Diego, 1964—; adv. panel on sea-air interaction program Dept. Commerce, 1964—; chmn. working group on air-sea inter actions World Meteorol. Orgn., UN, 1964—; U.S. del. 2d Oceanographic Congress, Moscow, 1966; U.S. mem. Intergovernmental Oceanographic Commn. Committee on Ocean Stations, Paris, 1966. Mem. board of advisors Am. Institute Crop Ecology, 1948-56. Recipient Certificate of Appreciation, USAAF, 1946. Fellow Am. Geophys. Union (exec. com. 1947-61, council 1961, sec. sect. meteorology 1947—, chmn. com. geophys. data), Washington Acad. Sci.; mem. Internat. Platform Assn., Am. (council 1961—, chmn. bd. certified cons. meteorologists 1960-62), Royal meteorol. socs., Maryland, New York acads. scis., Marine Tech. Soc., Oceanographical Soc. Japan, Am. Soc. Limnology and Oceanography, Sigma Xi, Alpha Tau Omega, Alpha Kappa Psi. Blue Key. Methodist. Club: Oakcrest Country (Wash.). Author: Energy Exchange Between Sea and Atmosphere, 1951; Meteorological Satellites, 1962; co-author Arctic Meteorology, 1956; also numerous articles in field. Editor: English edit. Transactions Marine Hydrol. Inst. Acad. Sci. U.S.S.R. for scripta technica. Inc., 1962—; adv. bd. Meteorol. and Geoastrophys. Abstracts, 1963—. Home: 6300 Bradley Blvd Bethesda MD 20034 Office: Environmental Sci Service Adminstrn Bethesda MD 20910

JACOBSEN, ARNE, architect; b. Denmark, Feb. 11, 1902; ed. Royal Danish Acad.; Dr.Litt., Oxford, 1966; LL.D., Strathclyde, 1968. Prof., Royal Acad. Copenhagen, 1956-65. Prin. works include villas, town halls, comml. structures, furniture, textiles, banks, Royal Hotel, Copenhagen, Denmark, St. Catherine's Coll., Oxford (Eng.) U., Nat. Bank of Denmark, HEW Electricity Bldg., Hamburg, Germany, indsl. factories for Novo Industri A/S. Recipient Silver medal World Exhbn., Paris, 1925, Gold medal Royal Danish Acad., 1928; Eckersberg medal, 1936; Prize of Honour, Sao Paulo, Brazil, 1954; C.F. Hansen medal, 1956; Grand Prix, Architecture d'aujourd'hui, 1960; Medal of Honour, Akademisk Arkitektforening, 1962; Fritz-Schumacher prize, Hamburg, 1963; Prince Eugen medal Sweden, 1962; Gold medal pio manzu, San Marino, 1969; plaque Akademie der Künste, Hamburg, 1969; Wood prize, Copenhagen, 1970; Gold medal Acad. d' Architecture, Paris, 1971. Fellow A.I.A.; mem. Royal Inst. Brit. Architects (hon. corr., Bronze medal. 1962-64), Akademie der Künste (Berlin), Académia Nazionale di San Luca (Rome), Academie Serbe des Sciences et des Arts (Belgrade, Yugoslavia). Address: Strandvejen 413 2930 Klampenborg Denmark

JACOBSEN, ARTHUR, dept. store exec.; b. S.I., N.Y., Sept. 21, 1921; s. Alf and Jenny S. (Smith) J.; student N.Y.U., 1939-42; B.A., Princeton, 1948; m. Elizabeth B. Sayford, May 12, 1951; children—Martha, Bruce. Asst. cashier First National City Bank N.Y., 1939-55; with J. C. Penney Co., N.Y.C., 1955—, treas., 1957-69, v.p., dir. consumer financial servs., 1969—; pres. J.C. Penney Credit Corp., 1964-69, J. C. Penney Life Ins. Co., 1967—; mem. W. Side adv. bd. Chem. Bank N.Y. Trust Co. Mem. council financial execs. Nat. Indsl. Conf. Bd. Mem. Phi Beta Kappa. Home: 77 Midwood Terrace Madison NJ 07940 Office: 1301 Av of Americas New York City NY 10019

JACOBSEN, BERNE SELVIG, newspaperman; b. Portland, Ore., Oct. 31, 1906; s. Roy Bernhardt and Sophia (Romtvedt) J.; B.A. in Journalism, U. Wash., 1932; m. Virginia Friese, Aug. 31, 1932; 1 son, Keith (dec.). Reporter, Seattle Star, 1929, Denver Post, 1929. Seattle Post-Intelligencer, 1930-31; news editor China Press, Shanghai, 1932; mem. staff Seattle Post- Intelligencer, 1933-66, editor, 1965-66; engaged in writing, travel, 1967—. Asso. journalism U. Wash., part-time 1943-47. Mem. Wash. Tourist Commn., 1960-65. Mem. Am. Soc. Newspaper Editors, A.P. Mng. Editors Assn., Sigma Delta Chi. Author: Your Newspaper, 1961. Address: 4103 Lake Washington Blvd S Seattle WA 98118

JACOBSEN, BOARDWELL LOWELL, tobacco exec.; b. Chgo., Dec. 15, 1912; s. Boardwell Luther and Josephine (Nielsen) J.; B.S., North Central Coll., 1934; m. Eunice M. Fry, June 12, 1937; children—Ronald L., Kenneth A. With Spiegel, Inc., 1935-43; dir. personnel RCA, 1943-53; v.p. personnel and labor relations NBC, N.Y.C., 1953-61; v.p. indsl. relations Pepsi-Cola Co., 1961-63; v.p. personnel P. Lorillard Co., 1963-70; cons. Golightly Internat., 1970—. Trustee North Central Coll., Sanger Research Bur., N.Y. Mem. Am. Mgmt. Assn., N.A.M., Ind. Personnel Assn. (pres. 1950), Ind. Jr. C. of C. (pres. 1948). Club: Burning Tree Country. Home: West Lane Revonah Woods Stamford CT 06905 Office: Rockefeller Plaza New York City NY 10020

JACOBSEN, ECKHART ADELBERT, educator; b. Rochester, N.Y., Feb. 12, 1915; s. Edmond and Margaret (Matzmor) J.; student N.Y. State Coll., Oswego, 1937; M.S. in Edn., Cornell U., 1946; Ph.D., U. Conn., 1957; m. Najla Bloomquist, Aug. 19, 1939; children—Karen (Mrs. Earle Wood, Jr.), Hart, Peter, Holly. Tchr. indsl. arts jr.-sr. high sch., Hillsdale, N.Y., 1937-40; tchr., supr. Elmira (N.Y.) Schs., 1940-46, instr., supr. vocational edn. for nat. def., 1941-44; asst. prof. tchr. edn. and indsl. arts Mass. State Coll., Fitchburg, 1946-57; asso. prof. tchr. edn. and indsl. edn. U. Md., 1957-61; prof. indsl. edn., prof., head dept. industry and tech. No. Ill. U., DeKalb, 1961—. Ednl. and tng. cons. to sch. bd., bus. and industry, state edn. depts.; curriculum adviser indsl. and tech. edn., higher edn., teaching methods, adminstrn. Faculty adviser higher edn., mem. bd. Luth. Student Found. Mem. A.A.A.S., Am. Soc. Engring. Edn., Am. Council Indsl. Arts Tchr. Edn., Am. Indsl. Arts. Assn., N.E.A., Assn. Supervision and Curriculum Devel., Am. Vocational Assn., Nat. Assn. Indsl. Educators, Nat. Assn. Higher Edn. Author: Study of Technical Needs of Industry and Implications for Higher Education, 1965; also bulls. Contbr. articles to profl. jours. Home: Rural Route 2 Sycamore IL 60178 Office: Dept Industry and Tech No Ill U DeKalb IL 60115

JACOBSEN, EINAR A., mfg. exec.; b. Racine, Wis., Jan. 21, 1906; s. Knud F. and Ellen S. (Hansen) B.S. in Mech. Engring., U. Wis., 1928; m. Elsa M. Paur, July 20, 1929; children—Mary C. Wellman, Lois J. Medgyesy. With Jacobsen Mfg. Co., Racine, 1928—, pres., dir., 1958—; dir. Racine Savs. & Loan Assn., Allegheny Ludlum Industries. Mem. Racine Mfg. Assn. (dir., past pres.). Club: Somerset (Racine). Home: 2400 Washington Av Racine WI 53405 Office: 1721 Packard Av Racine WI 53403

JACOBSEN, HUGH NEWELL, architect; b. Grand Rapids, Mich., Mar. 11, 1929; s. John E. and Lucy (Newell) J.; B.Arch., Yale, 1955; B.A., U. Md., 1951; certificate Archtl. Assn., Sch. Architecture, London, 1954; m. Robin Kearney, Dec. 27, 1952; children—John E., Matthew C., Simon T. With Philip Johnson, New Canaan, Conn., 1955, Paul Schweikher, New Haven, 1955, Keyes, Lethbridge & Condon, Washington, 1957-58; pvt. archtl. practice, Washington, 1958—. Mem. Com. 100 Fed. City, Washington Planning and Housing Assn. Class sec. Yale Sch. Architecture, mem. commn. alumni affairs. Trustee Washington Theatre Club, Georgetown Planning Council; bd. govs., exec. com. Corcoran Gallery Art, 1969—. Served to 1st lt. USAF, 1955-57. Recipient Archtl. Record award house design, 1964-71; award A.I.A. Potomac Valley chpt., 1962, 65, 66, 69; A.I.A. award homes for better living, 1965-68, 68, (3), 69; award A.I.A. N.Y. chpt., 1964 (2) 67; award of merit Washington Bd. Trade, 1962, 64, 66 (3), 69 (2); Honor award A.I.A., 1969; award No. Va. sect. A.I.A., 1969; Masonry Inst., 1961; others.

Mem. A.I.A. (exec. com. Washington met. chpt. 1964-67). Club: Cosmos (Washington) Home: 1352 28th St NW Washington DC 20007 Office: 1427 27th St NW Washington DC 20007

JACOBSEN, JAMES CONRAD, steel co. exec.; b. Highland Park, Ill., May 3, 1935; s. Harry Jacobsen and Grace (Niebuhr) J.; B.A., Lake Forest Coll., 1957; M.S., U. Ill., 1962; m. Dorothy Barrett, July 18, 1959; children—Jenifer Ann, Pamela Beth, Roger, Scott. With Price Waterhouse & Co., Chgo., 1959-66, sr. accountant, 1961-66; controller Continental Steel Corp., Kokomo, Ind., 1966-70, v.p., treas., 1971—; sec., dir. Stevens Spring Co., Elwood, Ind. 1970—; lectr. bus. Ind. U., Kokoamo, 1967—. Chmn. audit com. United Fund, 1968, 69-70. Treas., bd. dirs. Howard-Tipton chpt. A.R.C. C.P.A., Ill. Mem. Am. Inst. C.P.A.'s, Ill. Soc. C.P.A.'s, Nat. Assn. Accountants (v.p., dir. Kokimo area chpt. 1970-71), Am. Accounting Assn., Am. Iron and Steel Inst., Kokomo Area C. of C. Home: 1732 W Walnut Av Kokomo IN 46901 Office: 1109 S Main St Kokomo IN 46901

JACOBSEN, OSCAR THORKILD, former mfg. exec.; b. Racine, Wis., Dec. 30, 1895; s. Knud Ferdinand and Ellen Sophia (Hansen) J.; student U. Minn., 1916-17; m. LaDora Ruth Vaughan; children—Ellen Jean (Mrs. George Holcomb), John Knud. Pres. Jacobsen Mfg. Co., Racine, Wis., 1929-58, chmn., 1959—. Chmn. campaign Racine chpt. A.R.C., 1958; active cancer, community chest campaigns. Bd. dirs. Racine YMCA. Served with USMC, 1917-18; AEF; lt. col. Wis. N.G. Decorated knight of Dannebrog (Denmark). Home: 5333 Wind Point Rd Racine WI 53402

JACOBSEN, THORKILD orientalist; b. Copenhagen, Denmark, June 7, 1904; s. Christian Lauritz and Gerda Marie (Jensen) J.; A.M., U. Copenhagen, 1927, Dr. Phil., 1939; Ph.D., U. Chgo., 1929; M.A. (hon.), Harvard, 1963; m. Rigmor Schroll, Sept. 16, 1927 (dec.); m. 2d, Joanne Switzer, Aug. 11, 1949 (dec.); m. 3d, Katryna Hadley, June 21, 1966; stepchildren—Dana Perrone, Pamela Hadley, Caroline Hadley, Katryna Hadley. Field Assyriologist, Iraq expdn. Oriental Inst., U. Chgo., 1929-37, research asso., instr. Univ. 1937, asst. prof., 1942, asso. prof., 1944, prof., 1946; chmn., dept. Oriental langs. and civilizations, 1946-48, dir. Oriental Inst., 1946-48, dean. div. humanities, 1948-51; vis. prof. Assyriology, Harvard, 1962-63, prof. Assyriology, 1963-66, Peabody fellow archaeology, 1970; Am. Council Learned Socs. lectr. history of religion, 1966-67; mem. Columbia Seminar on archaeology, Eastern Mediterranean, 1966; dir. Diyala Basin Archaeol. project, 1957—. Guggenheim fellow, 1969. Mem. Am. Acad. Arts and Scis., Royal Danish Acad. Scis., Am. Philos. Soc., German Archaeol. Inst. (corr.). Asso. editor Jour. Cuneiform Studies, 1946; cons. editor Jour. Nr. Eastern Studies, 1949-62. Home: 36 Winslow St Cambridge MA 02138 Office: Dept Near Eastern Langs and Lit 6 Divinity Av Cambridge MA 02138

JACOBSEN, T.L., hosp. adminstr. Exec. dir. Lutheran Gen. Hosp., Park Ridge, Ill., also Deaconess Hosp., Chgo. Office: 1775 Dempster St Park Ridge IL 60068*

JACOBSMEYER, VINCENT PAUL, physicist, educator; b. St. Louis, July 7, 1906; s. Bernard Frank and Clara (Richter) J.; A.B., Gonzaga U., Spokane, Wash., 1931; M.A., St. Louis U., 1933, M.S., 1935, Ph.D., 1945; S.T.L., St. Mary's Coll. (Kan.), 1940. Instr., Marquette U. High Sch., 1935-36; ordained priest Roman Catholic Ch., 1939; instr. St. Louis U., 1944-48, asst. prof., 1948-54, asso. prof., 1954-63, prof. physics, 1963—. Mem. Am. Phys. Soc., Am. Assn. Physics Tchrs., Albertus Magnus Guild, Sigma Xi. Home: 221 N Grand Blvd St Louis MO 63103

JACOBSON, ALBERT HILLMAN, ins. broker; b. Chgo., Apr. 17, 1907; s. Harry E. and Ida (Klink) J.; student Northwestern U., John Marshall Law Sch., Central YMCA Coll., Chgo.; m. Bette Wolf, June 30, 1935. Ins. broker, 1932—. 50 year vet. Boy Scouts Am.; pres. Greater Chgo. council United Synagogues Am., 1966-68, now chmn. youth commn.; vice chmn. adminstrv. com. Zionist Orgn. Chgo., 1967—, v.p. North dist., 1966, treas., 1969-70. Served with AUS, World War II. Mem. Chgo. Council Conservative Men's Clubs (past pres.), Nat. Fedn. Jewish Men's Clubs (nat. pres. 1952-54, hon. pres. midwest region), Am. Legion (past post comdr.), Alpha Gamma Pi (past chpt. chancellor). Jewish religion (past pres. congregation). Lion (1st v.p. Roger Park 1967-68), Mason (Shriner); mem. B'nai B'rith (past pres.). Club: Star Craft Illinois, North Shore Shrine. Home: 7415 N Ridge Av Chicago IL 60645 Office: 2716 W Devon Av Chicago IL 60645

JACOBSON, ALFRED THURL, petroleum co. exec.; b. Delta, Utah, Nov. 12, 1919; s. Joseph Alfred and Ella Adelia (Robison) J.; A.B. in Geology, U. Utah, 1940, M.A., 1941; m. Virginia Lorraine LaCom, Apr. 7, 1942; children—Wendy Jean (Mrs. Higginbotham), Deborah Ann (Mrs. Wasden), Alfred Thurl. With Amerada Petroleum Corp., N.Y.C., 1946—, mgr. fgn. operations, 1960-61, v.p., 1961-62, sr. v.p., 1962-63, exec. v.p., 1963-67, pres., chief exec. officer, 1967-69, also dir.; pres. Amerada Hess Corp., 1969—, also dir. Mem. nat. adv. council U. Utah. Trustee Tulsa U. Served with F.A., AUS, 1941-46; ETO. Decorated Croix de Guerre (France). Mem. Am. Inst. Mining and Metall. Engrs., Am. Petroleum Inst., Am. Assn. Petroleum Geologists, Phi Beta Kappa, Phi Kappa Phi. Mem. Ch. of Jesus Christ of Latter-Day Saints. Home: 358 Oxford Dr Short Hills NJ 07078 Office: 51 W 51st St New York City NY 10019

JACOBSON, ALMA FRANK, telephone exec.; b. Omaha, Neb., Apr. 27, 1905; s. Alma Frank and Vilate (Angel) J.; student U. Neb., 1922-25; L.H.D. (hon.), Midland Coll., 1960, Hastings Coll., 1968; LL.D. (hon.), Creighton U., 1963; m Ruth Saalfeld, Nov. 14, 1925; children—Allen, Mary (Mrs. James F. Johnson). Clk. Northwestern Bell Telephone Co., Omaha, 1922-28, various positions in Minn., 1928-38, dist. mgr., Sioux Falls, S.D., 1938-39, Mpls., 1939-43, comml. operations supvr., gen. hdqrs., Omaha, 1943-48, v.p., gen. mgr., Neb.-S.D., 1948, v.p., operations, dir., 1949-51, pres., director, 1955-70; v.p., operations, dir., Ill. Bell Telephone Co., 1951-52; dir. operations long lines dept., Am. Tel. & Tel. Co., 1952-53; asst. v.p. operations, engring. dept., 1953; cons. Bazell and Jacobs, advt., Omaha; communications cons. Govt. of Italy, Rome; dir. U.S. Nat. Bank, Neb. Savs. & Loan Assn., Omaha, Northwest Bancorporation, Mpls., Central Nat. Ins. Group of Omaha. B'nai B'rith Americanism citation for meritorious service, 1958; Knight St. Gregory, Civil Class, Pope Paul VI. Trustee, U. Nebraska Found., Omaha Indsl. Found.; dir. Meyer Therapy Center, Inc., Omaha, 1959-65; chmn. bd. dirs. Creighton U.; trustee Joslyn Center of Soc. Liberal Arts, Omaha; bd. govs. Knights of Ak-Sar-Ben, Omaha; bd. dirs. Father Flanagan's Boys' Home (Boys Town), Omaha; chmn. bd. dirs. Girls Town, Omaha. Mem. C. of C. (pres. 1961-62), Telephone Pioneers of Am. (pres. 1966-67), Alpha Kappa Psi, Beta Gamma Sigma, Alpha Sigma Nu. Mason (Shriner). Clubs: Omaha, Omaha Country; Minneapolis (Mpls.). Home: 6485 Cuming St Omaha NB 68132 Office: 100 S 19th St Omaha NB 68102

JACOBSON, BERNARD, music critic; b. London, Eng., 1936; grad. (scholar in classics) Corpus Christi Coll., Oxford (England) U., 1960; m. Bonnie Brodsky, August 1968. Former Dutch mus. correspondent London Times, music critic for London Times, Manchester Guardian, also mags. Opera, Opera News; former N.Y. corr. for Brit. publs. Music and Musicians, The Musical Times, repertoire adviser Mercury and Philips records, program annotator Little Orchs. Soc. of N.Y.; contbg. editor High Fidelity mag.; mus. adviser Nonesuch Records; now music critic Chgo. Daily News; contbg. editor Stereo Rev. Mem. music adv. panel Ill. Arts Council. Address: care Chgo Daily News 401 N Wabash Av Chicago IL 60610

JACOBSON, CARL A., oil and gas producer; b. East Chicago, Ind., Feb. 13, 1917; s. Gustav H. and Nelle K. (Holmes) J.; B.A., Ind. U., 1940; m. Betsy V. Johnson, Sept. 1, 1940; children—Ann D'Andrea, JoBeth, Ross. With Philgas div. Phillips Petroleum Co., Indpls., 1940-51; with Protane Corp., Erie, Pa., 1951-53; exec. v.p., dir. Nat. Propane Corp., Miami Springs, Fla., 1953—; exec. v.p., dir. Southeastern Pub. Service Co., Miami Springs, 1969—; dir. DWG Corp., N.Y.C. Served with USAAF, 1943-45. Decorated Air medal with 2 oak leaf clusters, D.F.C. Home 135 Solano Prado Coral Gables FL 33156 Office: PO Box 600 Miami Springs FL 33166

JACOBSON, CHARLES LINTNER, auto sales exec.; b. Paw Paw, Ill., May 29, 1896; s. Henry Lorenzo and Florence Carolina (Lintner) J.; student Western Mich. U., 1911-14; m. Marjorie Trumbower, June 20, 1937; children—Eleanor, Carolyn. With Ford Motor Co., 1914-19, Wills-St. Clair Co., Marysville, Mich., 1919-25; with Chrysler Corp., from 1925, successively regional mgr., Mpls., br. mgr., Phila., dir. sales and mgr. retail br., Detroit, pres. br., Pitts., in charge retail sales branches, gen. sales mgr. Chrysler sales div., v.p. Chrysler sales div., asst. to gen. mgr. in charge subsidiary activities Chrysler Corp., 1925-49, pres. Chrysler Motor Parts Corp., 1949-54, in charge sales activities and v.p. Chrysler Corp., 1954-56, v.p. dealer relations, dir., 1956-61. Trustee, Grace Hosp., Detroit. Mem. Automobile Mfrs. Assn. (dir. Detroit), Am. Ordnance Assn. (pres. Mich. post), Newcomen Soc. Presbyn. (trustee). Mason. Clubs: Detroit Athletic, Grosse Pointe Yacht, Players. Home: 70 S Deeplands Rd Grosse Pointe Shores MI 48236

JACOBSON, CHARLOTTE STONE, organization exec.; b. Apr. 27, 1914; d. Jonas and Lena (Alexander) Stone; ed. pub. schs., N.Y.C.; m. Mortimer Jacobson, May 31, 1936 (div.). Mem. Hadassah, 1939—, nat. pres., 1964-68; mem. Jewish Agency, 1968—; mem. actions com. World Zionist Orgn., 1956—; mem. exec. com. Am. Zionist Council, 1956—. Chmn. bd. Bronx chpt. A.R.C., 1951-52, Bronx chpt. Am. Cancer Soc., 1962-63. Mem. League Women Voters. Home: 200 E 205th St New York City NY 10458 Office: 65 E 52d St New York City NY 10022

JACOBSON, DAN, writer; b. Johannesburg, South Africa, Mar. 7, 1929; s. Hyman Michael and Liebe (Melamed) J.; B.A., U. Witwatersrand, Johannesburg, 1949; m. Margaret Pye, Feb. 13, 1954; children—Simon Orde, Matthew, Jessica. Journalist and tchr., 1950-54; profl. writer, 1954—; fellow creative writing Stanford, 1956-57; vis. prof. English lit. Syracuse U., 1965-66. Recipient John Llewelyn Rhys award Nat. Book League, 1958; W. Somerset Maugham award Soc. Authors, 1964. Author: The Trap, 1955; A Dance in the Sun, 1956; Price of Diamonds, 1957; The Zulu and the Zeide, 1959; Evidence of Love, 1960; No Further West, 1961; The Beginners, 1966; Through The Wilderness, 1968; The Rape of Tamar, 1970. Contbr. Commentary, New Yorker, Atlantic Monthly, New Statesman, others. Address: care Russell & Volkening Inc 551 Fifth Av New York City NY 10017

JACOBSON, DAVID, rabbi; b. Cin. Dec. 2, 1909; s. Abraham and Rebecca (Sereinsky) J.; A.B., U. Cin., 1931; Rabbi, Hebrew Union Coll., 1934, D.D., 1959; Ph.D., St. Catherine's Coll., U. Cambridge (Eng.), 1936; LL.D., Our Lady of Lake Coll., 1964; m. Helen Gugenheim, Nov. 6, 1938; children—Elizabeth Anne, Dorothy Jean (Mrs. Sam Miller). Instr. Hebrew Union Coll., 1933-34; rabbi West Central Liberal Congregation, London, Eng., 1934-36, Indpls. Hebrew Congregation, 1936-38, Temple Beth-El, San Antonio, 1938—. Chancellor Kallah of Tex. Rabbis, 1969—. Pres., San Antonio Soc. Crippled Children and Adults, 1963-66, Goodwill Industries San Antonio, 1956-60, Bexar County chpt. Nat. Tb Assn., 1955-57, Community Welfare Council San Antonio, 1951-53, San Antonio Area Found., 1965—, Research and Planning Council San Antonio, 1966-67, Tex. Social Welfare Assn., 1967-69, San Antonio Manpower Devel. Council, 1968—; commr. Housing Authority San Antonio, 1954-58; v.p. Keystone Sch. Adv. Bd., 1969—. Bd. dirs. Our Lady of Lake Coll., 1966—, also chmn. adv. bd. Worden Sch. Social Service of coll., 1958-67; founder U. Ind. Hillel Found., 1938; San Antonio Vis. Nurses Assn., 1952; founder Community Welfare Council San Antonio, 1944, pres., 1951-53; bd. dirs. S.W. Tex. Meth. Hosp., 1956—, San Antonio Med. Found., 1962—, Luth. Hosp., San Antonio, 1967—, Cath. Youth Orgn. San Antonio, 1965—, Alamo council Boy Scouts Am., 1950—, Children's Hosp. Found., 1964—, Keystone Sch., San Antonio, 1960—, Tex. Council Higher Edn., 1969—, Nat. Jewish Welfare Bd., 1964—, Alamo chpt. Assn. U.S. Army, 1964—, Hemis Fair 1968; life mem. bd. Tex. United Community Services, 1970—; mem. nat. bd. Goodwill Industries Am., 1965—, chmn. pub. relations com., 1968—; bd. overseers Hebrew Union Coll.-Jewish Inst. Religion, 1966—, bd. govs., 1966-68; mem. nat. bd. Nat. Conf. Social Welfare, 1967-69, Nat. Assn. Doctors in U.S., 1960—, Florence G. Heller-Jewish Welfare Bd. Research Center, 1966—; nat. council U.S.O., 1968—. Served as chaplain with USNR, 1944-46. Recipient Silver Beaver award Boy Scouts Am., 1958; Aristotle-Aquinas award Cath. Coll. Found. S.A., 1959; Golden Deeds award Exchange Club San Antonio, 1959; named outstanding Jew, Nat. Conf. Christians and Jews, 1961; Keystone award Boys Club Am., 1962, Lifetime Achievement award B'nai B'rith, 1964. Mem. Central Conf. Am. Rabbis (pres. S.W. region 1969-70, chmn. com. on Judaism and health, 1967—), Soc. Bibl. Lit., San Antonio Ministers Assn., Nat. Assn. Statewide Health and Welfare (dir. 1969—), Am. Social Health Assn. (dir. 1969—), Tex. Congress Parents and Tchrs. (hon. life), Sigma Alpha Mu, Pi Tau Pi. Rotarian. Clubs: Torch (past pres.), Argyle (San Antonio). Author: Social Background of the Old Testament, 1942; The Synagogue Through the Ages, 1958. Contbr. articles to profl. and gen. publs.; also contbr. to Universal Jewish Ency., 1939-43. Home: 207 Beechwood Lane San Antonio TX 78216 Office: 211 Belknap Pl San Antonio TX 78212

JACOBSON, DOROTHY HOUSTON, govt. ofcl.; b. Herman, Minn., Nov. 13, 1907; d. George Franklin and Christine (Dalager) Houston; student State Tchrs. Coll. St. Cloud. Minn., 1922-24; B.S., M.A., U. Minn., 1928, Clara Ueland fellow, 1932-34; m. George William Jacobson, Mar. 15, 1937. Tchr. pub. schs., Hallock, Minn., 1924-26, Univ. High Sch., U. Minn., 1928-30, Lincoln Sch. of Columbia Tchrs. Coll., 1930-32; with Minn. Dept. Edn., 1934-36, 37-41; program sec. Nat. League Women Voters, Washington, 1936-37; asst. prof. polit. sci. Macalester Coll., 1945-55; adminstrv. asst. to gov. Minn., 1955-61; spl. asst. to sec. U.S. Dept. Agr., Washington, 1961-64, asst. sec. agr. for internat. affairs, 1964-69; exec. dir. Population Crisis Com., 1969-70, Am. Freedom from Hunger Found., 1970. Chmn., Democratic Farm Labor party of Minn., 1949-56. Mem. Am. Polit. Sci. Assn., Am. Soc. Pub. Adminstrn., Phi Beta Kappa. Democrat. Unitarian. Home: 3438 Blair Rd Falls Church VA 22041

JACOBSON, EDMUND, physician; b. Chgo., Apr. 22, 1888; s. Morris and Fannie (Blum) J.; B.S., Northwestern U., 1907; A.M., Harvard, 1909, Ph.D., 1910; fellow Cornell U., 1911; M.D., U. Chgo., 1915; LL.D., George Williams Coll., 1962; m. Elizabeth Ruth Silberman, Dec. 16, 1926; children—Ruth Frances, Edmund, Nancy Elizabeth. Practice internal medicine, 1917—; research asso. U. Chgo., 1926-30, asst. prof. physiology, 1930-36, dir. Lab. for Clin. Physiology, 1936—; condr. investigations. Bd. dirs. Found. Sci. Relaxation. Fellow Internat. Coll. Angiology, A.A.A.S., A.C.P., St. Louis Med. Soc. (hon.); mem. A.M.A., Ill., Chgo. med. socs., Am. Physiol. Assn., Phi Beta Kappa, Sigma Xi. Club: Quadrangle (U. Chgo.). Author books including: Progressive Relaxation, 1929, rev. edit., 1938; You Must Relax, 1934, rev. edit., 1957; The Peace We Americans Need, 1944; How to Relax and Have Your Baby, 1959; Tension Control for Businessmen, 1963; Anxiety and Tension Control, 1963; Tension in Medicine, 1967; Biology of Emotions, 1966; Modern Treatment of Tense Patients, 1969. Contbr. articles to med. jours. Home: 5532 S Shore Dr Chicago IL 60637 Office: 55 E Washington St Chicago IL 60602 and Hotel Commodore New York City NY 10017*

JACOBSON, EDWARD WILLIAM, airline exec.; b. Wilkinsburg, Pa., Oct. 11, 1915; s. Edward B. and Vira (Wolfe) J.; B.A., Oberlin Coll., 1938; grad. student U. Chgo., 1943-45; m. Helen Deborah White, Sept. 4, 1942; children—Edward William, Robert White, Deborah Ann. With Trans World Airlines, Inc., 1940-65, system dir. operational control, 1958-59, system dir. transp. planning and control, 1959-62, regional v.p. transp. central, 1962-65; v.p., exec. asst. to pres. Eastern Airlines, N.Y.C., 1965—. Mem. Am. Assn. Geographers, Newcomen Soc., Ky. Colonels. Republican. Presbyn. Mason. Clubs: Wings (N.Y.C.); Skytop (Pa.); Homestead Country (Prairie Village, Kan.). Home: 73 Park Av Bronxville NY 10708 Office: Eastern Airlines Inc 10 Rockefeller Plaza New York City NY 10020

JACOBSON, EUGENE DONALD, educator, physiologist; b. Bridgeport, Conn., Feb. 19, 1930; s. Morris David and Mary (Mendelsohn) J.; student Ohio Wesleyan U., 1947-48; B.A., Wesleyan U., Middletown, Conn., 1951; M.D., U. Vt., 1955; M.S., State U. N.Y., 1960; m. Joyce Elma Bravender, Dec. 19, 1953, (dec. Apr. 1971); children—Laura Ellen, Susan Ruth, Morris David, Daniel Frederick, Miriam Louise; m. 2d, Linda L. Shanbour, June 18, 1971. Mem. faculty dept. physiology Sch. Medicine, U. Cal. at Los Angeles, 1964-71, asso. prof., 1965-66; prof., chmn. dept. physiology U. Okla. Med. Center, 1966-71; prof. dir. program physiology U. Tex. Med. Sch. at Houston, 1971—. Mem. Am. Physiol. Soc., Western Soc. for Clin. Research, Am. Soc. Clin. Investigation, Soc. Exptl. Biology and Medicine, Am. Gastroent. Assn. Research and numerous publs. on gastrointestinal tract. Office: Dept Physiology U Tex Med Sch Houston TX 77025

JACOBSON, EUGENE WILLIAM, mech. engr.; b. Waterloo, Neb., Jan. 23, 1905; s. William Herman and Mary Ellen (Bryant) J.; student U. Omaha, 1922-23; B.S., U. Neb., 1928, M.E., 1938; postgrad. Carnegie Inst. Tech., U. Pitts., Rutgers U., Mass. Inst. Tech.; m. Miriam Isabel Stewart, June 30, 1931; children—Betty Jean (Mrs. James Myron Lord), William Stewart, Mary Ellen (Mrs. Thomas Labiosa). Designer, erection foreman, master mechanic heavy marine and material handling equipment Dravo Contracting Co., Pitts., 1928-32; research engr. measurement of liquid hydrocarbons, design engr. spl. machines and equipment Gulf Research & Devel. Co., Pitts., 1933-39, chief design engr. lab. bldgs., facilities and spl. equipment for petroleum research, 1939-61, dir. plant engring. services, 1961-63, mgr. plant engring. and maintenance, 1966-69, tech. cons., 1969-70; cons. mech. engr., 1970—. Chmn., Oakmont Joint Boro-Authority Sewage Com.; cons. engr., dir., 2d vice chmn. Municipal Authority Borough of Oakmont, Pa., 1950—; cons. War Dept., 1942. Mem. Mendelssohn Choir of Pitts., 1950—, v.p., 1970-71. Recipient award Lincoln Arc Welding Found., 1942; certificate of appreciation Am. Petroleum Inst., 1959. Registered profl. engr., Pa. Mem. Soc. Automotive Engrs., Am. Soc. M.E. (sec. research com. fluid meters 1941-63, chmn. constn. and by-laws com. 1967-68), Am. Petroleum Inst. (sec. joint com. p.d. meters 1941-57). Patentee spl. fields of flow measurement, vehicles for difficult terrain, pressure vessels for high-temperature. Address: 800 12th St Oakmont PA 15139

JACOBSON, GAYNOR I., assn. exec.; b. Buffalo, May 17, 1912; s. Morris and Rose (Fleishman) J.; B.A., U. Buffalo, 1937, M.S.W., 1941; m. Florence Stulberg, Feb. 22, 1937; children—Margot (Mrs. Harold Gotoff), Helen (Mrs. Barry Goldstein). Exec. sec. Jewish Community Council, Rochester, N.Y., 1937-40; exec. dir. Jewish Family and Child Care, Rochester, 1938-44, Jewish Child Care Assn., Phila., 1950-51, Am. Technion Soc., 1951-53; country dir. Am. Joint Distbn. Com., Italy, 1944-45, Greece, 1945-46, Czechoslovakia, 1946-47, Hungary, 1947-50; dir. European and North African operations United HIAS Service, 1953-54, 61-66, dir. Latin Am. operations, 1955-61, exec. dir., 1966-68, exec. v.p., 1968—. Vice chmn. Am. Council Vol. Agys. for Fgn. Service, vice chmn. migration and refugee problems com.; mem. exec. com. Am. Immigration and Citizenship Conf.; dir. Jewish Occupational Council, Bur. for Careers in Jewish Service; rep. Internat. Council on Jewish Social and Welfare Services; mem. Nat. Com. Plastics Arts Brazil. Mem. Nat. Assn. Social Workers, Nat. Assn. Jewish Family and Children's Health Services. Sculpture exhibited various galleries in U.S. and Brazil. Home: 340 E 64th St New York City NY 10021 Office: 200 Park Av S New York City NY 10003

JACOBSON, HARALD WILLIAM, fgn. service officer; b. Aalesund, Norway, Sept. 24, 1910 (parents U.S. citizens); s. Isaac W. and Anna (Lassesen) J.; B.S., Northwestern U., 1933; M.A., U. Chgo., 1935, Ph.D., 1938. Instr., North Park Jr. Coll., Chgo., 1939-42; with U.S. Govt., 1946-51; joined Dept. State, 1951; fgn. service officer, 1957—; consul, Hong Kong, 1957-61, Macau, 1960-61, 1st sec., polit. officer, New Delhi, India, 1962-65; dir. Office Asian Communist Affairs, Dept. State, Washington, 1965-68; dep. prin. officer Am. Consulate Gen., Hong Kong, 1968—. Macau, 1968-. Mem. Am. Oriental Soc., Fgn. Service Assn. Home: 1 Peak Rd Hong Kong

JACOBSON, HAROLD GORDON, physician; b. Cin., Oct. 12, 1912; s. Samuel and Regina (Dittman) J.; B.S., U. Cin., 1934, M.B., 1936, M.D., 1937; m. Ruth Enenstein, Aug. 10, 1941; children—Richard, Arthur. Intern Los Angeles County Gen. Hosp., 1936-38; fellow pathology Longview Hosp., Cin., 1938; resident Mt. Sinai Hosp., N.Y.C., 1939-41, Asso. Hosps. U. Tex., 1941-42; asst. radiology U. Tex., 1941-42; asso. Radiol. New Haven (Conn.) Hosp., also instr. Yale, 1952; asst. chief, asso. radiologist VA Hosp., Bronx, N.Y., 1946-50, chief radiology service, 1950-53, cons., 1958-; asst. clin. prof. N.Y.U., 1952-53, clin. prof., 1953-59, prof. clin. radiology, 1959-64; prof. radiology Albert Einstein Coll. Medicine, 1964. Dir. dept. roentgenology Hosp. for Special Surgery, N.Y.C., 1953-55; chief div. diagnostic radiology Montefiore Hosp., N.Y.C., 1955—. Vis. prof., lectr. U.S.A., Israel, Brazil, Finland, Eng. Served to maj. M.C, AUS, 1942-46. Diplomate Am. Bd. Radiology (trustee 1971—). Fellow Am. Coll. Radiology (councilor 1960—, also mem. bd. chancellors, chmn. com. on radiol. coding 1967—, mem. commn. on credentials, 1968—); mem. N.Y. Roentgen. Soc. (pres. 1959-60, historian 1967—), A.M.A., N.Y. State, N.Y. med. socs., Radiol. Soc. N. Am. (pres. 1966-67, mem. bd. censors 1968—), Am. Roentgen Ray Soc., Alpha Omega Alpha. Author: (with Clarence Schein, William Z. Stern) The Common Bile Duct, 1967; Neuroradiology Workshop,

Vol. III, 1968; (with Ronald O. Murray) Radiology of Skeletal Disorders: Exercises in Diagnosis, 1971; also other books, numerous articles in profl. jours. Home: 3240 Henry Hudson Pkwy New York City NY 10463

JACOBSON, HERBERT LAURENCE, UN ofcl.; b. N.Y.C., Apr. 7, 1915; s. Benjamin Paul and Katherine (Laurence) J.; B.A. with honours, Columbia, 1936; LL.D., Waterloo U., Ont., Can., 1969; m. Fiora Ravasini-Osti, May 29, 1949; children-Jesse, Julian. Editor in chief World News mag., 1937-40; head radio dept. MCA, 1940-41; dir. gen. radio network Free Territory Trieste, 1946-52; with U.S. High Commn., Germany, 1953-55, U.S. embassy, Rome, Italy, 1955-57; fgn. bus. mgr. Mondadori Publs., Milan, Italy, 1957-58; export mgr. Squibb of Italy, Rome, 1959-60; regional dir. So. Europe, Cotton Council Internat., 1960-64; dir. Internat. Trade Center, UNCTAD/GATT, Geneva, Switzerland, 1964—. Mem. adv. bd. internat. bus. programmes Waterloo Luth. U. Served with AUS, 1941-46. Recipient Nashville Mayor's key, 1957. Mem. Phi Beta Kappa. Contbr. articles to various publs. Home: 10 Chemin de Tavernay Geneva Switzerland Office: Internat Trade Centre UNCTAD/GATT Villa le Bocage Palais des Nations CH-1211 Geneva 10 Switzerland

JACOBSON, HOWARD HAHN, lawyer; b. Toledo, Apr. 1, 1902; s. Louis and Cora (Hahn) J.; B.S., Harvard, 1924, J.D., 1927; m. Betty Frankel, May 19, 1970; 1 dau., Louise I. Admitted to Ohio bar, 1927, N.Y. bar, 1948; practice in Toledo, 1927—; pvt. practice, 1927-42; counsel Doehler-Jarvis Corp. and Doehler-Jarvis div. Nat. Lead Co., 1946—. Served from 1st lt. to maj., USAAF, 1942-46. Mem. Am., Ohio Toledo (mem. exec. com.) bar assns. Jewish relgion (trustee congregation). Mason (32, Shriner). Home: 2914 Pembroke Rd Toledo OH 43606 Office: 1945 Smead Av Toledo OH 43601

JACOBSON, IRVING, actor, producer; b. Cin., 1905; s. Joseph and Betty J.; ed. pub. schs., N.Y.C.; m. Mae Schoenfeld, 1929; 1 son. With Yiddish Theater, N.Y.C., 1920's—; nightclub performer, London, Eng., 1951-52; actor in plays including Abi Gezunt, 1949, It's a Funny World, 1956, Man of La Mancha, 1965-68 (all N.Y.C.); actor and producer Mazeltov, Molly, 1950, Don't Worry, 1951. Girl of My Dreams (also co-dir.), 1952, Wish Me Luck, 1954, Go Fight City Hall, 1961 (all N.Y.C.). Mem. Actors' Equity Assn., Hebrew Actors' Union, Screen Actors Guild. Address: 420 E 23d St New York City NY 10010

JACOBSON, JAMES A., banker; b. Manfred, N.D., Feb. 1, 1908; s. Rasmus and Margret (Nordtorp) J.; A.B., St. Olaf Coll., Northfield, Minn., 1929, LL.D., 1960; M.B.A., Harvard, 1931; m. Norma Ayres, June 18, 1936. With Chase Manhattan Bank, and predecessors, N.Y.C., 1931-42, 46—, now sr. v.p., exec. asst. to chmn. WPB, 1942-46; treas., dir., mem. exec., finance and patent coms. Research Corp.; dir. Research-Cottrell, Inc. Mem. U.S. C. of C., Am. Friends Vietnam (dir., exec. comm.), Asia Soc. (trustee), Japan Soc., China Soc., Am. Philippine Sci. Fedn. (dir., exec. com., chmn. program com.), Newcomen Soc. N. Am., Circumnavigators, Nat. Geog. Soc., Acad. Polit. Sci. Clubs: Union League (N.Y.C.); Rock Springs (West Orange, N.J.). Home: 257 Irving Av South Orange NJ 07079 Office: 1 Chase Manhattan Plaza New York City NY 10005

JACOBSON, JAMES M., publisher; b. New Rochelle, N.Y., Aug. 25, 1915; s. Alex and Rosa (Worth) J.; B.S., N.Y.U., 1936; M.B.A., Harvard, 1939; m. Helen Ostron, May 31, 1951 (div. 1966); children—Seniel, James; m. 2d, Joanne Fox Hellman, 1966. Executive tng. program Macy's, 1939-40; formerly exec. v.p., dir. Pocket Books, Inc. (now Simon & Schuster, Inc.), N.Y.C.; past chmn. bd. Golden Press, Inc. lt., USNR, 1942-46. Clubs: Harvard University Graduate Business School; New Rochelle Tennis. Nat. U.S. Table Tennis Champion, 1933, N.Y. State Inter-College Tennis Doubles Champion, 1936. Home: 25 Ocean Av Larchmont NY 10538 Office: 4 W 58th St New York City NY 10019

JACOBSON, JOEL ROSS, labor union ofcl., univ. trustee; b. Newark, July 30, 1918; s. Herman and Gussie (Ross) J.; B.S., N.Y.U., 1941; Litt. D. (hon.), Montclair (N.J.) State Coll., 1959; children—Howard Michael, Monica. Began as exec. sec. Essex-W. Hudson (N.J.) CIO Council, 1949-54; exec. v.p. N.J. CIO Council, 1954-60 pres., 1960-61; 1st exec. v.p. N.J. AFL-CIO, 1961-68; pres. N.J. Indsl. Union Council, until 1968; dir. community affairs Region 9, U.A.W., Cranford, N.J., since 1968—. Delegate to the Whie House Conf. Edn., 1955; mem. N.J. adv. com. to U.S. Civil Rights Commn., 1960—; mem. N.J. Health Planning Council, 1969—. Vice chmn. New Democratic Coalition, 1968-69. Bd. govs. Rutgers U., 1959—. Served to 2d lt. AUS, World War II. Decorated Bronze Arrowhead. Home: 2 Kendall Av South Orange NJ 07079 Office: 16 Commerce Dr Cranford NJ 07016

JACOBSON, LEON ORRIS, physician, educator; b. Sims, N.D., Dec. 16, 1911; s. John and R. Patrine (Johnson) J.; B.S., N.D. State Coll., 1935; M.D., U. Chgo., 1939; m. Elizabeth Benton, Mar. 18,1938; children—Eric Paul, Judith Ann. Intern, U. Chgo., 1939-40, asst. resident medicine, 1940-41, asst. in medicine, 1941-42, instr., 1942-45, asst. prof., 1945-48, asso. dean, div. biol. scis., 1945-51, asso. prof., 1948-51, prof. medicine, 1951—, chmn. dept. medicine, 1961-65, dean div. biol. scis., 1965—, head hematology sect. U. Chgo. Clinics, 1951-62, mem. Inst. Radiobiology and Biophysics, 1949-54; asso. dir. health Plutonium project Manhattan Dist., 1943-45, dir. health, 1945-46; dir. Argonne Cancer Research Hosp., U. Chgo., 1951-67. Dir. Packard Instrument Co., Inc. U.S. rep. 1st and 2d UN Conf. on Peaceful Uses Atomic Energy, Geneva, 1955, 58; U.S. rep. WHO conf. Research Radiation Injury, Geneva, 1959; cons. biology div. Argonne Nat. Lab., mem. adv. com. on isotope distbn. AEC, 1952-56; mem. nat. adv. com. on radiation USPHS, 1961, mem. com. radiation studies, cons. hematology study sect. USPHS; mem. com. cancer diagnosis and therapy NRC, 1949-55; mem. bd. sci. counselor Nat. Cancer Inst., 1963—; lectr. Internat. Soc. Hematology and Internat. Congress Radiology, Eng., France, Norway, Sweden, 1950, 5th Internat. Cancer Congress, Paris, 1950, Internat. Soc. Hematology, Argentina, 1952, Paris, 1954, others. Recipient Janeway medal, 1953; Robert Roesler de Villers award Leukemia Soc., Borden award med. scis. Assn. Am. Med. Colls., 1962, Modern Med. and Am. Nuclear Soc. awards, 1963; Kennecott lectr., 1963. Mem. A.C.P. (master), Am. Soc. Clin. Investigation, Assn. Am. Physicians, Soc. Exptl. Biology and Medicine, Central Soc. Clin. Research, Am. Assn. Cancer Research, Internat. Soc. Hematology, A.M.A., Nat. Acad. Sci., Central Clin. Research Club, A.A.A.S., Radiation Research Soc., Am. Soc. Exptl. Pathology, Sigma Xi, Theta Chi, Nu Sigma Nu, Blue Key, Alpha Omega Alpha. Author book on erythropoietin. Contbr. chpts. on specialized items to various med. books, articles to med. jours. Home: 5811 Dorchester Av Chicago IL 60637 Office: 950 E 59th St Chicago IL 60637

JACOBSON, MELVIN JOSEPH, mathematician, educator; b. Providence, Nov. 25, 1928; s. Charles and Rose (Chusmir) J.; A.B., Brown U., 1950; M.S., Carnegie Inst. Tech., 1952, Ph.D., 1954; m. Dorothy Troup, June 8, 1952; children—Deborah Lynn, Donald Bruce. Instr., Carnegie Inst. Tech., 1953-54; mem. tech. staff Bell Telephone Labs., Whippany, N.J., 1954-56; asst. prof. math. Rensselaer Poly. Inst., Troy, N.Y., 1956-58, asso. prof., 1958-63, prof., 1963—, prin. investigator Office Naval Research Contract, 1957—, prin. investigator NSF grant, 1962-67; vis. prof. Rosenstiel Sch. and Atmospheric Marine Scis., U. of Miami (Fla.), 1963-64, adj. prof., 1969—. Cons. to industry. Mem. of the Am. Assn. U. Profs., Am. Math. Soc., Math. Assn. Am., Acoustical Soc. Am., Sigma Xi, Phi Kappa Phi, Pi Mu Epsilon. Contbr. articles to numerous publs. Home: 1 Lisa Lane Troy NY 12180

JACOBSON, NATHAN, mathematician, educator; b. Warsaw, Poland, Sept. 8, 1910; s. Charles and Pauline Ida (Rosenberg) J.; brought to U.S., 1917, naturalized, 1921; A.B., U. of Ala., 1930; Ph.D., Princeton, 1934, Procter fellow, 1934-35; Nat. Research fellow U. of Chicago, 1936-37; m. Florence Dorfman, Aug. 25, 1942; children—Michael Sidney, Pauline Ida. Asst. in mathematics Inst. for Advanced Study, Princeton, 1933-34; lectr. Bryn Mawr Coll., 1935-36; instr. U. of N.C., 1937-38, asst. prof., 1938-40, asso. prof., 1941-42; vis. asso. prof. Johns Hopkins, 1940-41, asso. prof., 1943-47; asso. ground sch. instr. Navy Pre-Flight Sch., 1942-43; asso. prof. Yale, 1947-48, prof. since 1949, now Henry Ford II prof. of math., 1964—; vis. prof. U. Chgo., summer 1947, fall, 1964, Tokyo U., spring 1965, Tata Inst. Fundamental Research, spring 1969, U. Rome, Weizmann Inst. and Hebrew U., spring 1971; Fulbright research grant for France, 1951-52, Guggenheim Meml. fellow, 1951-52. Mem. Am. Acad. of Arts and Scis., Am. (coun. 1943-48, editor bull, 1948-54, v.p., 1956-58, trustee, pres. 1971—), French, Japan math. socs., Nat. Acad. Scis., Phi Beta Kappa, Sigma Xi. Author: Theory of Rings, 1943; Lectures in Abstract Algebra, 3 vols., 1953-64; Structure of Rings, 1956; Lie Algebras, 1962; Structure and Representations of Jordan Algebras, 1968. Home: 2 Prospect Ct Hamden CT 06514

JACOBSON, NORMAN LEONARD, educator; b. Eau Claire, Wis., Sept. 11, 1918; s. Frank R. and Elma E. (Baker) J.; B.S., U. Wis., 1940; M.S., Ia. State U., 1941, Ph.D., 1947; m. Gertrude A. Neff, Aug. 24, 1943; children—Gary, Judy. Faculty, Ia. State U., 1947—, prof. animal and dairy sci., 1953—, Charles F. Curtiss distinguished prof. agr., 1963—. Mem. subcom. feed additives NRC-Nat. Acad. Scis., 1952—, subcom. dairy cattle nutrition, 1961—, subcom. on standards for large lab. animals, 1971—. Served to lt. USNR, 1942-46. Recipient award dairy nutrition Am. Feed Mfrs. Assn., 1955, Borden award dairy prodn. Borden Found., 1960; Distinguished Nutritionist award Distillers Feed Research Council, 1964; award merit for distinguished service to agr. Ia. State U. chpt. Gamma Sigma Delta, 1970, Faculty citation Ia. State U., 1971. Moorman travel fellow, 1966. Fellow A.A.A.S.; mem. Am. Dairy Sci. Assn. (gen. chmn. program com. 1960, v.p. 1971), Am. Inst. Nutrition, Am. Soc. Animal Sci. (Morrison award animal prodn. 1970), Sigma Xi, Phi Kappa Phi, Alpha Zeta. Presbyn. (elder). Contbr. articles to profl. jours. Home: 339 Hickory Dr Ames IA 50010

JACOBSON, PAUL B., univ. dean; b. Albany, Wis., June 30, 1901; s. Harry and Anna (Paulson) J.; A.B., Luther Coll., Decorah, Ia., 1922; A.M., U. Ia., 1928, Ph.D., 1931; m. Lorinda Larson, Aug. 10, 1927; 1 dau., Karen. High sch. tchr., Elmore and Glencoe, Minn., 1922-26; high sch. prin., Little Falls and Milaca, Minn., 1926-30, Austin, Minn., 1931-35; dir. secondary edn., Hibbing, Minn., 1935-36; asst. prof., high sch. prin. U. Chgo., 1936-44; supt. schs., Davenport, Ia., 1944-47; prof. edn., dean Sch. Edn., U. Ore., Eugene, 1947. Vis. prof. Tchrs. Coll. Columbia, 1945. Mem. Am. Assn. Adminstrs., Nat. Soc. Study Edn., Nat. Assn. Secondary Sch. Prins., Am. Ednl. Research Assn. Author books including: (with H.R. Douglass, editor) The High School Curriculum, 1962; (with commn. mems. Am. Assn. Sch. Adminstrs.) The Expanding Role of Education, 1948; (with others) The American Secondary Schools, 1952; (with others) The American School Superintendency, 1952; (with Reaves, Loysdon) The Effective School Principal, 1964; (with others) The Economic Returns to Education, 1965. Contbr. articles to ednl. publs. Home: 1234 E 21st Av Eugene OR 97403

JACOBSON, ROGER EMERY, hotel exec.; b. Baileys Harbor, Wis., Aug. 30, 1919; s. David C. and Jennie (Eatough) J.; Ph.B., U. Wis., 1942; m. Estelle Bokyo, June 21, 1952; 1 dau., Cynthia Joy. With Pick Hotels, 1952—, mgr. Pick Roosevelt Hotel, Pitts., 1961—. Mem. Am., Pa., Pitts. (pres. 1965-66) hotel assns., Pitts. C. of C. Lutheran (trustee). Rotarian. Moose, Eagle. Home: 607 Penn St Pittsburgh PA 15222

JACOBSON, SAMUEL DAVID, hosp. adminstr.; b. Detroit, 1913; M.D., Wayne U., 1937, M.Sc. in Internal Medicine, 1941. Intern Wayne County Gen. Hosp., Eloise, Mich., 1937-38, resident internal medicine, 1938-40, research fellow medicine, 1940-44, jr. attending medicine, physician in chief, now gen. supt. Wayne County Gen. Hosp. and Infirmary; asso. prof. Wayne U.; jr. attending med. staff Detroit Receiving Hosp. Diplomate Am. Bd. Internal Medicine, 1946. Fellow A.C.P.; mem. A.M.A., Central Soc. Clin. Research, Am. Fedn. Clin. Research. Address: Wayne County Gen Hosp and Infirmary Eloise MI 48132*

JACOBSON, SAUL P., mfr. med. recreational equipment; b. Los Angeles, Nov. 2, 1916; s. Alexander and Rosa (Breamer) J; B.S., Mass. Inst. Tech., 1938; children—Paul, Stephen; m. 2d, Karin Belling, 1969. Mech. engr. Bennis & Call Co., Springfield, Mass., 1938-39; indsl. engr., prodn. mgr. Sears, Roebuck & Co., Louisville, 1939-42; asst. chief mfg. engr. Fairchild Aircraft Co., Hagerstown, Md., 1942-43; with Brunswick Corp., Muskegon, Mich., Chgo., 1943—, corporate officer and dir., 1951—, pres. Bowling div., 1959-61, variously group v.p. bowling, sporting goods and boating Internat. Def. Products div., 1961-65, sr. v.p. bus. devel. and tech., 1965—; dir. Glenside Housing Corp., Muskegon, Am. Store Equipment Co., Muskegon. Adv. com. Mich. State U. Grad. Sch. Service Industries. Recipient Distinguished Service award U.S. Jr. C. of C., 1951. Mem. Am. Mgmt. Assn., Soc. Plastics Industry, Chgo. Assn. Commerce, Muskegon C. of C. Mason (Shriner). Clubs: Muskegon Country, Century; Standard, Executive (Chgo.). Home: 931 Sunset Rd Winnetka IL 60093 Office: 69 W Washington St Chicago IL 60602

JACOBSTEIN, JOSEPH MYRON, educator, librarian; b. Detroit, Jan. 27, 1920; s. Benjamin and Etta (Roberts) J.; B.A., Wayne State U., 1946; M.S., Columbia, 1950; LL.B., Chgo.-Kent Coll. Law, 1953; m. Belle Lottman, Sept. 29, 1949; children—Ellen R. Bennett M. Cataloger, U. Chgo. Library, 1950-51; librarian Cowles Commn. for Research in Econs., 1951-53; asst. law librarian U. Ill., 1953-55; asst. law librarian Columbia, 1955-59; law librarian, prof. law U. Colo., Boulder, 1959-63; law librarian, prof. law Stanford, 1963—. Served with USAAF, 1942-45. Mem. Am. Assn. Law Libraries, Am. Soc. Information Sci., Am. Soc. Internat. Law. Editor: Law Books in Print, 3 vols., 1957-60, 2 vols., 1966. Home: 882 Cedro Way Stanford CA 94305

JACOBUS, JOHN M., Jr., educator, author; b. Poughkeepsie, N.Y., Sept. 15, 1927; s. John M. and Louise (Rayland) J.; A.B., Hamilton Coll., 1952; M.A., Yale, 1954, Ph.D., 1956; m. Marion Langdon Townsend, Nov. 12, 1951; children—Jacqueline. Mem. faculty Princeton, 1956-60, U. Cal. at Berkeley, 1960-63, Ind. U., 1963-69; mem. faculty Dartmouth, 1969—, prof. art and archtl. history, 1956—. Author: Philip Johnson, 1962; Twentieth Century Architecture, The Middle Years, 1967. Home: 16 School St Hanover NH 03755

JACOBY, ALEXANDER ROBB, educator; b. St. Louis, Oct. 8, 1922; s. Leslie K. and Estelle (Robb) J.; S.B., U. Chgo., 1941, S.M., 1942, Ph.D., 1946; m. Carol Fitz-Hugh, Apr. 6, 1945; children—Thomas Erling, Melissa Ann, Mary Nell. Asst. prof. math. U. Miami (Fla.), 1947-49; asst. prof. Rutgers U., 1949-55, asso. prof., 1955-57; mathematician Gen. Electric Corp., 1957-61; asso. prof. U. N.H., 1961-64, prof., 1964—. Mem. Am. Math. Soc., Assn. for Symbolic Logic, Phi Beta Kappa, Sigma Xi. Home: Bagdad Rd Durham NH 03824

JACOBY, GEORGE ALONZO, former personnel exec.; b. Pleasureville, Ky., May 13, 1904; s. George Alonzo and Sarah (Hieatt) J.; A.B., Georgetown (Ky.) Coll., 1924, LL.D., 1958; M.S., Columbia, 1927; m. Ruth Burtner, Oct. 6, 1928; children—George Alonzo, John Burtner. With Irving Trust Co., N.Y.C., 1925-40, asst. sec., 1929-37, asst. v.p., 1937-40; asst. personnel dir. Buick Motor div. Gen. Motors Corp., Flint. Mich., 1941-45, mem. labor relations staff Gen. Motors Corp., Detroit, 1945-46, dir. personnel services, 1946-56, dir. personnel relations, 1956-69. Pres., Mich. Safety Conf., 1954; dir. Nat. Safety Council, 1947-66; mem. Mich. Employment Security Adv. Council, 1947-60, Fed. Adv. Council Employment Security, 1952-54; exec. dir. Gen. Motors Com. Ednl. Grants and Scholarships, 1955-69. Regent Gen. Motors Inst., 1957-69; trustee Alma Coll., 1956-70; bd. govs. Inst. Indsl. Health, U. Mich., 1957-69. Recipient achievement award Georgetown Coll., 1953. Mem. Pi Kappa Alpha, Alpha Kappa Psi, Beta Gamma Sigma. Presbyn. Clubs: Orchard Lake Country, Recess (Detroit); Columbia University (N.Y.C.). Home: 245 Puritan Rd Birmingham MI 48009

JACOBY, JAY JOSHUA, physician, educator; b. N.Y.C., Dec. 12, 1917; s. Harry and Rose (Berlin) J.; B.S., U. Minn., 1939; M.B., 1941, M.D., 1942; Ph.D., U. Chgo., 1947; m. Helene Kurshan, Nov. 8, 1942; children—Jane Alice, Carolyn Sue, Elizabeth Ann. Intern, Kings County Hosp., N.Y.C., 1941-42; research asso. U. Chgo., 1946-47; faculty Ohio State U. Med. Sch., 1947-59, prof. anesthesiology, 1947-59, chmn. dept., 1947-59; prof. anesthesiology, head dept. Marquette U. Med. Sch., 1959-65, Jefferson Med. Coll., Phila., 1965—. Pres., Ohio Soc. Anesthesiologists, 1952; chmn. sect. anesthesiology Ohio Med. Assn., 1954; cons. USN, 1960-65, U.S. Army, 1965—. Served to capt. AUS, 1942-46; Arctic, ETO. Recipient Outstanding Tchr. awards Ohio State U. Med. Sch., 1954, Marquette U. Med. Sch., 1960, Jefferson Med. Coll., 1966. Diplomate Am. Bd. Anesthesiologists. Fellow Am. (bd. govs. 1963-69), Internat. colls. anesthesiologists; mem. Am., Internat. socs. anesthesiologists, Assn. U. Anesthetists, A.M.A., Pa. Med. Soc., Pa. Soc. Anesthesiologists, Sigma Xi, Alpha Omega Alpha. Spl. research safety anesthesia, transtracheal resuscitation technique. Home: 20 Conshohocken State Rd Bala Cynwyd PA 19004 Office: 1025 Walnut St Philadelphia PA 19107

JACOBY, NEIL HERMAN, educator; b. Dundurn, Sask., Can., Sept. 19, 1909; s. Herman Reynold and Christina (MacMillan) J.; came to U.S., 1930; naturalized, 1937; B.A., U. Sask., 1930, LL.D., 1950; Ph.D., U. Chgo., 1938; m. Clair Gruhn, Dec. 23, 1933; children—Neil Herman, Christina. Supr. legal and research divs. State Dept of Finance, 1933-36; chmn. Sask. Taxation Commn., 1936; mgr. research dept. Lawrence Stern & Co., Chgo., 1937; asst. prof. finance U. Chgo., 1938-40, asso. prof., 1940-42, prof., sec., 1942-48, v.p., 1945-48; prof. bus. and econ. policy. dean. U. Cal. Grad. Sch. Bus. Adminstrn., Los Angeles, 1948-68, prof. bus. econs. and policy, 1968—. Cons. Rand Corp., 1951-61. Chmn., Ill. Emergency Relief Commn., 1940-41; mem. research adv. bd. Com. for Econ. Devel., 1942-48, mem. research staff Nat. Bur. Econ. Research, 1940-45; mem. Pres.'s Council Econ. Advisors, 1953-55; U.S. rep. Econ. and Social Council UN, 1957—; dir. Occidental Petroleum Corp., 1959—; head U.S. Aid Evaluation Mission to Taiwan, 1965; chmn. Pres.'s Task Force on Econ. Growth, 1969. Mem. Am. Econ. Assn., Royal Econ. Soc., Nat. Tax Assn., Beta Gamma Sigma, Pi Gamma Mu. Club: Cosmos (Washington). Author books including: Business Finance and Banking (with R.J. Saulnier). 1946; Can Prosperity Be Sustained, 1956; U.S. Aid to Taiwan, 1966; European Economics: East and West, 1967. Address: Grad Sch Bus Adminstrn U Cal Los Angeles CA 90024

JACOBY, OSWALD, actuary, writer; b. Bklyn., Dec. 8, 1902; s. Oswald N. and Edith (Sondheim) J.; student Columbia; m. Mary Zita McHale, Apr. 25, 1932; children—James O., Jon P. With Met. Life Ins. Co., 1922-28; cons. actuary, Dallas, 1937—; writer syndicated newspaper column on bridge, 1946—. Served with U.S. Army, World War I; lt. USNR, World War II; comdr., Korean War; mem. original staff Pan Mun Jom armistice talks. Selected as No. 1 bridge player in Am., by Shepard Barclay, 1936-40, 62—; recipient McKenney trophy as Am.'s bridge player of yr., 1959, 61, 62, 63. Fellow Soc. Actuaries; mem. Am. Contract Bridge League (hon.), Phi Kappa Sigma. Clubs: Arizona (Phoenix); Regency, Whist, Bridge Whist, Cavendish (N.Y.C.); Dallas Country, Fort Worth. Author: Oswald Jacoby on Poker, 1940; How To Figure the Odds, 1946; Gin Rummy, 1946; How To Win at Canasta, 1949; Oswald Jacoby's Complete Canasta, 1950; Winning Poker, 1950; What's New in Bridge, 1953; (with William H. Benson) Mathematics for Pleasure, 1962; Oswald Jacoby on Gambling, 1963. Home: 4246 Woodfin Dr Dallas TX 75220

JACOBY, ROBERT BIRD, lawyer; b. Marion, O., July 2, 1906; s. John Wilbur and Edna Leora (Bird) J.; A.B., Ohio Wesleyan U., 1928; LL.B., Harvard, 1931; m. Alice Helen Matthias, June 25, 1938; children—Robert Matthias, Richard Matthias. Admitted to Ohio bar, 1932, U.S. Dist. Court for D.C., 1944, U.S. Supreme Ct., 1945; practiced law firm Jacoby and Jacoby, Marion, O., 1932; asso. firm Taft, Stettinius and Hollister, Cin., 1933-40; counsel Fed. Home Loan Bank of Cin., 1933-40; asso. gen. counsel Fed. Savs. and Loan Ins. Corp., Washington, 1941-46; dep. gov. Fed. Home Loan Bank System, 1946-47, became acting gov., Dec. 1947; with office chief counsel Bur. Internal Revenue, 1948—. Lectr. Am. Savs. and Loan Inst., 1937-40. Mem. Ohio State, Am., Fed. bar assns., Phi Gamma Delta. Democrat. Methodist. Mason. Club: Harvard (Washington). Co-author: Cyclopedia of Federal Savings and Loan Associations, 1939. Contbr. articles to savs. and loan pubs. Home: Cincinnati OH also 3806 47th St NW Washington DC 20016 Office: Internal Revenue Bldg Washington DC 20225

JACOBY, ROBERT EAKIN, Jr., advt. exec.; b. Union City, N.J., Mar. 26, 1928; s. Robert E. and Anna M. (Bach) J.; A.B. in Econs. cum laude, Princeton, 1951; m. Monica Ann Flynn, Oct. 23, 1954; children—Debra Jean, Cynthia Marie, Patricia Ann, Laura Jayne. Econ. analyst Shell Oil Co., N.Y.C., 1951-52; v.p., account supr. Compton Advt. Agy., N.Y.C., 1952-62; sr. v.p., dir. Needham, Harper & Steers Advt., N.Y.C., 1963-65; v.p., account group head Ted Bates & Co., N.Y.C., 1962-63, pres., 1965—. Served with U.S. Army, 1946-47; Japan. Mem. Sales Execs. Club N.Y., Assn. Am. Advt. Agencies, Phi Beta Kappa. Home: 1 Saddle Ridge Rd Ho-Ho-Kus NJ 07423 Office: Ted Bates & Co 666 Fifth Av New York City NY

JACOMET, ANDRE ALEXANDER, metals co. exec.; b. Limoges, France, 1917; diplome d'Etudes superieures de Droit pub. etd'Economie Politique, U. Paris, 1938, Licencie es Lettres, 1937, diplome de l'Ecole Nationale des Scis. Politiques, 1939; m. Helene Cathala, Dec. 1, 1942; children—Thierry, Fabrice, Christine (Mrs.

Antoine Bastin), Lionel. Registered with Paris Ct. of Appeal as lawyer, 1938; jr. mem. Conseil d'Etat, 1946-52; maitre des Requetes, 1952; legal counselor to French High Commr. in Germany, 1949-52; adviser to sec. state for Air Force, 1956-58; adviser to minister Constrn., 1958; sec. charge adminstrv. affairs in Algeria, 1958-60; with Compagnie Pechiney, 1961—, head Australian operations, 1963, Australian and Am. operations, 1964-67, v.p., 1966, charge operations in N. and S.Am., Pacific and Spain, 1967-69; pres., dir. Howmet Corp., Greenwich, Conn., since 1970—; dir. Pechiney Enterprises, Inc., N.Y.C. Decorated knight Legion of Honor (France). Home: 455 E 51st St New York City NY 10022 Office: Howmet Center Greenwich CT 06830

JACOPETTI, GUALTIERO, producer-dir., journalist; b. Barga, Italy, Sept. 4, 1919; s. Francesco and Teresa (Nardini) J.; D.Polit. Sci., U. Pavia (Italy), 1948. Journalist, Coriere Della Sera, Milan, Italy, 1947-50; mng. editor La Settimama Incom, Rome, Italy, 1950-53; editor in chief Cronache, Rome, 1953-55, Europeo Ciack Rome, 1955-62; now contbr. various Italian, fgn. publs.; writer, producer, dir. Mondo Cane (Golden Globe award best fgn. picture), 1962, Women of the World, 1963, Africa Addio (David di Donatello award Italian Republic), 1965. Served as Italian liaison officer with 5th Am. Army, 1944-45. Mem. Nat. Order Journalists, Nat. Order Authors. Author: (plays) La storia Degli Altri, 1940, Conquistatemi Quella Signora, 1951. Home: 9 Via Monte Delle Gioie Rome Italy Office: 9 Viale Castrense Rome Italy

JACOX, HAROLD WILLIAM, physician; b. Detroit, Aug. 31, 1904; s. William Garrett and Cora (McGraw) J.; B.S., U. Mich., 1926, M.D., 1928; m. A. Lois Kimball, 1928; children—Judith (Mrs. Norman B. Peachey), Elizabeth Kimball (Mrs. James C. Warner). Intern, Naval Hosp., Chelsea, Mass., 1928-29; instr. radiology U. Mich., 1930-31, asst. prof., 1931-36; dir. radiation, phys. therapy depts. Western Pa. Hosp., Pitts., 1936-47; prof. emeritus radiology Columbia, 1947—; cons. physician radiology Presbyn. Hosp., N.Y.C., 1947-69; cons. radiology Surg. Gen. U.S. Army, VA. Diplomate Am. Bd. Radiology. Mem. Am. Radium Soc., Am. (past v.p.), N.Y. (past pres.) roentgen ray socs., Radiol. Soc. N.Am. (past v.p.), Pa. Radiol. Soc., Flint (Mich.) Acad. Surgery, Pitts. Acad. Medicine, Phi Beta Pi, Alpha Omega Alpha, Phi Kappa Phi. Presbyn. Home: 77 Glenwood Rd Tenafly NJ 07670 Office: Grasslands Hosp Valhalla NY 10595

JACQUEMARD, SIMONNE, author; b. May 6, 1924; ed. Les Oiseaux, U. Paris (France), Tchr. music, Latin, French; author, 1951—. Recipient Prix Renaudot, 1962. Author: Les Fascines, 1951; Sable, 1952; La Lecon des Ténèbres, 1954; Judith Albarès, 1958; Planant sur les Airs, 1960; Compagnons Insolites, 1961; Le Veilleur de Nuit, 1962; L'Oiseau, 1963; L'Orangerie, 1963; Les Derniers Rapaces, 1965; Dérive au Zénith, 1965; Exploration d'un corps, 1965; (with Lucette Descave) studies on music, bird life, observation of wild animals. Collaborator Laffont-Bompiani Dictionaries; contbr. Figaro Littéraire, La Table Ronde. Address: 35 rue de la Harpe Paris 5e France*

JACQUES, MAURICE, lawyer; b. Quebec City, Que., Can., Oct. 13, 1924; B.A., U. Ottawa (Can.), 1952; LL.L., Laval U. (Can.), 1955; postgrad. London Sch. Econs. (Eng.). Admitted to Que. bar, 1955; counsel to Royal Commn. on Pilotage, 1963—; partner firm Flynn, Rivard, Jacques, Cimon, Lessard & LeMay, Quebec City. Lectr. municipal law Laval U., 1966-68. Mem. Canadian, Que. bar assns. Office: 2 Av Chauveau Quebec City 4 Quebec Canada*

JACQUET, JEAN BAPTISTE ILLINOIS, musician; b. Broussard, La., Oct. 31, 1922; s. Gilbert and Maggie (Trayhan) J.; student City Coll. Los Angeles, 1940; m. Barbara Potts, Sept. 9, 1948; children—Michael Lane, Pamela Baptiste. Recorded Flying Home on tenor sax; soloist with Lionel Hampton, 1940-42, Cab Calloway, 1943; creator jazz at Philharmonic Blues Pt. II, 1944, 45; recorded The King with Count Basie, 1946; formed own band Illinois Jacquet and His Orch., 1947; frequent appearances at Newport, Monterey, Tex. Longhorn Jazz Festivals; pres. Gilbert Music Pub. Co., 1947—. Roman Catholic. Composer: You Left Me All Alone, 1936; Bottoms Up, 1945; Robbins Nest, 1947; Illinois Jacquet Flies Again, 1966. Address: 112-44 179th St St Albans NY 11412

JAECK, GORDON SLOAN, correctional and child welfare adminstr., educator; b. Beaver Dam, Wis., Aug. 15, 1916; s. Otto Richard and Mabel (Sloan) J.; B.A., Macalester Coll., St. Paul, 1937; M.A., U. Minn., 1946; postgrad. George Williams Coll., Chgo., 1947-48, U. Cal. at Berkeley, summer 1955; m. Dorothea Gies, Nov. 30, 1939; children—Juliana (Mrs. Dennis L. Hunter), Lucinda Ann, David Gordon, Elisabeth Ann. Caseworker, camp dir. Big Bros., Inc., Mpls., 1937-41; dir. social services Hennepin County Juvenile Ct., Mpls., 1939-46; supr. probation and parole services Minn. Youth Conservation Commn., St. Paul, 1946-49; chmn., dir. Minn. Bd. Probation and Parole, 1949-55; chmn. dept. sociology and anthropology, Wheaton (Ill.) Coll., 1955-69; research cons. div. criminologist Ill. Dept. Pub. Safety, 1965-69; exec. dir. Camelback Girls' Residence, Phoenix, 1969—; spl. cons. Pres.'s Commn. Law Enforcement and Adminstrn. Justice, 1966; cons. Marquette County (Mich.) Family Project, 1967-68. Chmn. profl. adv. com. John Howard Assn., Chgo., 1968—; dir. Action for Appalachian Youth, Charleston, W.Va., 1964-65. Served to lt. USNR, 1942-46. Mem. Nat. Assn. Social Workers, Acad. Certified Social Workers, Nat. Council Crime and Delinquency, Am. Soc. Criminology, Ill. Acad. Criminology. Am. Correctional Assn. Home: 5039 N 38th Pl Phoenix AZ 85018 Office: 3324 E Camelback Rd Phoenix AZ 85018

JAECKLE, EDWIN F. lawyer; b. Buffalo, Oct. 27, 1894; s. Jacob and Mary (Marx) J.; LL.B., U. Buffalo, 1915; LL.D., Canisius Coll., 1960, Rosary Hill Coll., 1969; m. Grace Drechsel, Aug. 19, 1920. Admitted to N.Y. bar, 1916; practiced in Buffalo, 1916—; mem. firm. Jaeckle, Fleischmann & Mugel, Buffalo; sec., gen. counsel, dir. Mchts. Mut. Ins. Co.; dir., gen. counsel Liberty Bank & Trust Co., Erie & Niagara Ins. Assn.; dir. Monroe Abstract & Title Co., Niagara Mohawk Power Corp., Buffalo Evening News Inc., Niagara Frontier Transit System, Inc. Mem. N.Y. State Reapportionment Commn., 1966, N.Y. State Law Revision Commn., 1949-56. Chmn., Erie County Republican Com., 1935-48, N.Y. Rep. State Com., 1940-44. Bd. regents Canisius Coll.; trustee State U. N.Y., 1962-65. Recipient Chancellor's medal State U. N.Y. at Buffalo, 1966. Mem. C. of C., Am., N.Y. State, Erie County bar assns. Home: 33 Gates Circle Buffalo NY 14209 Office: Liberty Bank Bldg Buffalo NY 14202

JAEDICKE, ROBERT K., ednl. adminstr. Prof. accounting, asso. dean Grad. Sch. Stanford. Office: Grad Sch Bus Stanford U Stanford CA 94305*

JAEGER, JACOB JOSEPH, machinery mfg. exec.; b. Phila., Nov. 23, 1909; s. Jacob Ferdinand and Katherine (Fink) J.; B.S. in Elec. Engring., Drexel Inst. Tech., 1933; S.M., Mass. Inst. Tech., 1934; m. Dorothy Mason, July 2, 1938; children—Paul, Ann, Mark. Research asst. Mass. Inst. Tech., Cambridge, 1934-39; research engr. Pratt & Whitney Co., Inc., 1940-49, asst. mgr. machinery engring., 1949-54, chief engr. machinery div., 1954-59, v.p., 1955-59, exec. v.p., 1959, pres., 1959-61, also dir.; pres. Potter & Johnston Co., West Hartford, Conn., 1959-61; v.p. engring. Massey- Ferguson, Ltd., Toronto, Ontario, Can., 1961-67, v.p. research and devel., from 1967. Recipient engring. citation Am. Soc. Tool Engrs., 1959. Mem. I.E.E.E., Am. Soc. Tool Engrs., Am. Soc. Agrl. Engrs., Soc. Automotive Engrs., Sigma Xi, Eta Kappa Nu, Tau Beta Pi. Home: The Green Lane RFD 1 King Ontario Canada

JAEGER, LEONARD HENRY, former pub. utility exec.; b. Bklyn., Oct. 6, 1905; s. Leonard and Marie (Ziegler) J.; grad. Pace Coll., 1926; postgrad. N.Y. U., evenings 1925-30; m. Mary Elizabeth Fallon, Dec. 15, 1951. Accountant, Southeastern Power & Light Co., 1926-30; with Commonwealth & So. Corp., 1930-42, 46-49, asst. comptroller, 1948-49; treas. So. Co., Atlanta, 1949-70, v.p. finance, 1957, also dir. to 1970, adv. dir., 1970—; exec. v.p. Services, Inc., 1963-67, dir., vice chmn. board, 1967-70, adv. dir., 1970—. Served to capt. AUS, 1942-45. Mem. Atlanta C. of C., Financial Execs. Inst., N.Y., Atlanta socs. security analysts, Pace Alumni Assn., Edison Electric Inst. (mem., past chmn. investor relations com.). Republican. Lutheran. Club: Highlands Country (N.C.). Home: 98 Interlochen Dr Atlanta GA 30342 also Sarasota FL

JAEKE, HAROLD THEODORE, meat co. exec.; b. Janesville, Wis., May 25, 1906; s. Hans G. and Meta (Henrich) J.; A.B., Augustana Coll., 1930; m. Violet May Renfro, May 30, 1931; children—Richard, Sally (Mrs. Donald Punswick), Marlene (Mrs. Allen Kuhl). Indsl. engr. Deere & Co., 1923-30; engr. Ill. Bell Telephone Co., 1930-37; indsl. engr. Johns Manville Co., 1935-37; with Oscar Mayer & Co., Madison, Wis., 1937—, v.p. engring. and research, 1947-66, exec. v.p., 1966—, also dir.; dir. Security State Bank, Madison. Mem. Am. Meat Inst., Am. Mgmt. Assn. Home: 50 East Rd Delray Beach FL 33444 Office: 910 Mayer Av Madison WI 53705

JAENKE, EDWIN AUGUST, agrl. economist; b. St. Louis, Sept. 14, 1930; s. Edwin A. and Flora E. (Schneider) J.; A.A., Blackburn U., 1950; B.S., U. Ill, 1952; M.S., U. Mo., 1957; m. Claire L. Schmidt, Oct., 1952; children—Janet, Dale, Karen, Paul. Research instr. agrl. econs. dept. U. Mo. Coll. Agr., 1955-57; agrl. adviser, asst. to Sen. Stuart Symington, 1957-61; asso. adminstr. Agrl. Stblzn. and Conservation Service, Dept. Agr., 1961-69; v.p. CCC, 1961-69; gov. FCA, Washington 1969—. Staff economist Senate Spl. Investigating Com., 1959-60. Served to lt. (j.g.) USNR, 1952-55. Recipient Arthur Fleming award Jr. C. of C., 1966. Mem. Am. Farm Econ. Assn., N.E.A., Alpha Gamma Rho, Gamma Sigma Delta. Contbr. tech. papers, treatises to lit. Home: 2016 Rhode Island Av McLean VA 22101 Office: Farm Credit Adminstrn Washington DC 20250

JAENKE, RUSSELL CHESTER, publishing co. exec.; b. Cleve., Aug. 29, 1904: s. Otto E. and Bertha (Flickinger) J.; B.S., Ohio State U., 1926; m. Janet V. Watt, Nov. 5, 1929; children—Don, Lynn. With Penton Pub. Co., Cleve., 1926—, exec. v.p., 1954-58, pres., 1958-69, chmn., chief exec. officer, 1969—, also dir.; dir. Rex Chainbelt Co. Trustee Southwest Gen. Hosp.; bd. dirs. Nat. Bus. Publs., 1954-59, chmn., 1957-58. Home: 20660 Stratford Av Rocky River OH 44116 Office: 1213 W 3d St Cleveland OH 44113

JAESCHKE, WALTER HEURY, educator, physician; b. Milw., Nov. 25, 1909; s. Alfred Paul and Clara (Buchholz) J.; B.S. in Med. Sci., U. Wis., 1932, M.D., 1934; m. Inga Caroline Walhus, Sept. 3, 1938; 1 son, John Alfred. Intern Med. Coll. VA Hosp. Div., 1934-35; resident Wis. Gen. Hosp., Madison, 1935-38, instr. clin. pathology, 1939-41; practice medicine, specializing in pathology, 1938—; mem. faculty Med. Center, U. Wis., Madison, 1942—, prof., 1950—, prof. surg. pathology and pathology, 1966—, also dir. lab. surg. pathology, consulting pathologist hosp. clin. labs., 1958—; cons. Wis. Lab. Hygiene, 1958—; mem. staff Univ. Hosps., Madison. Leader Madison council Boy Scouts Am., 1949-63. Recipient Basic Sci. Tchr. Yr. award Med. Sch. U. Wis., 1950, 56, also Clinician Yr. award, 1966. Mem. Dane Co. Med. Soc., Med. Soc. Wis., A.M.A., Wis. Soc. Pathologists (past pres.), Am. Soc. Clin. Pathologists, Alpha Kappa Kappa, Alpha Omega Alpha, Alpha Delta Theta (hon. faculty mem.). Contbr. profl. jours. Home: 2313 Kendall Av Madison WI 53705

JAFFE, BERNARD FREDERICK VICTOR, elec. mfg. exec.; b. Posen, Germany, July 16, 1890; s. Maurice and Félicie (Schaps) J.; Dr. Law, U. Rostock, 1914; m. Garda Platen- Hällermund, May 7, 1931; 1 son, Bernard W. Naturalized Brit. citizen, 1945. Regular and res. service Royal Saxon Army, 1908-18; mem. German Peace Delegation, Versailles, 1919; engaged in bus., 1924—; with Internat. Tel. & Tel. Corp., N.Y.C., 1928—; v.p., dir. subsidiary Internat. Standard Electric Corp., 1928-62; chmn. subsidiary Standard Elektrik Lorenz A.G., Stuttgart: vice chmn. Hanseatische Industrie Beteiligung GmbH, Bremen, Germany, Home: 13 Flurweg Bottmingen Switzerland Office: care Standard Elektrik Lorenz AG Hirth-Strasse 42 Stuttgart-Zuffenhausen Germany

JAFFE, DAVID LAWRENCE, govt. ofcl.; b. Bklyn., July 6, 1913; s. Harry and Dora (Botwinick) J.; B.S. in Engring., Coll. City N.Y., 1935; M.S. in Elec. Engring., Columbia, 1936, Ph.D. (S.W. Bridgham fellow 1937-39), 1940; m. Sylvia Ann Finkelstein, Aug. 25, 1940; children—Robert Franklin, Peter Allen, Gilbert Roy, Donald Benton. Asst. elec. engring. City Coll. N.Y., 1935-37; research problems frequency modulation Columbia, 1937-39; with CBS, 1939-42, supr. maintenance video facilities Grand Central Terminal, 1940-42; with Raytheon Mfg. Corp., 1942-44; chief research engr. Templeton Radio Corp., New London, Conn., 1944-45; co-founder Polarad Electronics Corp., Long Island City, 1945, pres., chmn. bd. 1950-69; cons. electronics industry, 1969-71; dep. dir. Nat. Maritime Research Center, Office Research and Devel., Maritime Adminstrn., U.S. Dept. Commerce, Kings Point, N.Y., 1971—. Mem. engring. council Columbia; mem. industry adv. council Dept. Def. Bd. dirs. Armstrong Meml. Found. Fellow Radio Club Am., I.E.E.E.; mem. Am. Assn. U. Profs., Sigma Xi. Clubs: Columbia (N.Y.C.); Officers Patentee microwave components and systems, radio, locating devices, microwave instruments and electromech. devices. Home: 33 Nassau Dr Great Neck NY 11021 ‡

JAFFE, HANS H., chemist, educator; b. Marburg, Germany, Apr. 17, 1919; s. Gunther and Hedwig (Schlesinger) J.; came to U.S., 1940, naturalized, 1946; B.S., State U. Ia., 1941; M.S. Purdue U., 1943; Ph.D., U. N.C., 1952; m. Martha Ledbetter, Mar. 1946 (div. Jan. 1959); children—Charles, Charlotte, John. Phys. chemist U.S. Health Service, Balt., Chapel Hill, N.C., 1946-54; asst. prof. U. Cin., 1954-59, asso. prof., 1959-61. prof., 1961—, head dept. chemistry, 1966-71. Served with AUS, 1943-46. Mem. Am. Chem. Soc. (Eminent Chemist Cin. sect. 1961), Am. Phys. Soc., A.A.A.S., Sigma Xi (1st Ann. Distinguished Research award U. Cin. chpt. 1961), Phi Lambda Upsilon. Author: Theory and Applications of Ultraviolet Spectroscopy, 1962; Symmetry in Chemistry, 1965; The Importance of Antibonding Orbitals, 1967; Symmetry Orbitals and Spectra, 1971. Contbr. articles to profl. jours. Home: 2069 Faywood Av Cincinnati OH 45238

JAFFE, LEO, motion picture exec.; b. N.Y.C., Apr. 23, 1909; B.C.S., N.Y.U., 1931. Pres. Columbia Pictures Industries, Inc., 1967—, Columbia Pictures Internat. Corp. Past Industry chmn. United Jewish Appeal, Federated Charities. Bd. dirs. Will Rogers Meml. Hosp.; bd. dirs., mem. exec. com. Nat. Found. March of Dimes; trustee Beth Abraham Hosp. Commandatore Italian Republic; Grande Ufficiale-Italy, N.Y.C. medal honor. Fellow Brandeis U., N.Y.U. Sch. Commerce and Finance. Mem. Motion Picture Pioneers (dir.), Motion Picture Assn. Am. (dir.), Delta Mu Delta, Alpha Phi Sigma. Clubs: Hampshire Country (dir.); Friars (N.Y.C.). Home: 985 Fifth Av New York City NY 10028 Office: 711 Fifth Av New York City NY 10022

JAFFE, LEONARD, govt. ofcl.; b. Cleve., Feb. 1, 1926; s. Isidore and Anne (Spier) J.; B.E.E., Ohio State U., 1948; postgrad. Case Inst. Tech., 1960; m. Elaine June Michael, Oct. 23, 1949; children—Barbara Lynn (dec.), Ronald Howard, Norman David. With NASA, and predecessor, 1948—, dir. communications and nav. satellite programs Office Space Sci. and Applications, 1963-66, dir. space applications, 1966-69, dep. asso. adminstr. space sci. and applications, 1969—. Served with USNR, 1944-46. Recipient Arthur S. Flemming award U.S. Jr. C. of C., 1964: Exceptional Service award NASA, 1964. Registered profl. engr. Ohio, Fellow I.E.E.E. (Behn Internat. Communication award 1967), Am. Astronautical Soc.; mem. Ohio Soc. Profl. Engrs., Tau Beta Pi, Eta Kappa Nu. Contbr. numerous reports in field. Home: 418 Sisson Ct Silver Spring MD 20902 Office: NASA 4th and Maryland St SW Washington DC 20546

JAFFE, LOUIS LEVENTHAL, educator; b. Seattle, Dec. 18, 1905; s. Aaron Louis and Rachel Harriet (Leventhal) J.; A.B., Johns Hopkins, 1925; LL.B., Harvard, 1928, S.J.D., 1932; m. Mildred Dunbar Miles, June 6, 1938; children—Deborah, Henry Miles. Admitted to Cal. bar, 1928, N.Y., 1942; law clk. Justice Brandeis, 1933-34; legal staff A.A.A., 1934-35, N.L.R.B., 1935-36; prof. law U. Buffalo, 1936-48, dean law sch., 1948-5O; Byrne prof. adminstrv. law Harvard, 1950—. Pub. mem. ship-bldg. commn. War Labor Bd., 1944-45. Dir. Syndics Harvard Press. Mem. Nat. Acad. Abritrators, Am. Acad. Arts and Sciences. Club: St. Botolph's. Author of: Judicial Aspects of Foreign Relations, 1933; Cases and Materials on Adminstrative Law, 3d edit., 1969; Judicial Control of Adminstrative Action, 1965; English and American Judges as Lawmakers, 1970. Contbr. articles law reviews. Home: 164 Brattle St Cambridge MA 02138

JAFFE, PAUL LAWRENCE, lawyer; b. Phila., June 24, 1928; s. Albert L. and Elsie (Pelser) J.; B.A., Dickinson Coll., 1947; LL.B., U. Pa., 1950; m. Joan Helene Feldgoise, Mar. 13, 1955; children—Marc David, Richard Alan, Peter Edward. Admitted to Pa. bar, since practiced in Phila.; sr. partner firm Mesirov, Gelman, Jaffe and Levin, and predecessor, 1959—. Dir. Eanco, Inc. Trustee Fedn. Jewish Agencies Phila., Moss Rehab. Hosp., Am. Jewish Com. Mem. Am., Pa., Phila. bar assns. Jewish religion (sec. congregation 1967—). Clubs: Locust, Midday, Lawyers, Philmont Country (Phila.). Home: 1222 Gordon Rd Jenkintown PA 19046 Office: 123 S Broad St Philadelphia PA 19109

JAFFE, RAYMOND, educator; b. Chgo., Jan. 22, 1916; s. Herman and Sadie (Rudnick) J.; A.B., U. Chgo., 1938; certificate d'Etudies francaises, also diplome de Litterature francaise en francais, U. Besancon (France), 1945; M.A., U. Cal. at Berkeley, 1951, Ph.D., 1953; m. Ruth Golden, Sept. 20, 1941; children—Joel, Carla, Lisa. Teaching asst. philosophy U. Cal. at Berkeley, 1949-50, lectr. philosophy, spring 1954; lectr. philosophy medicine U. Cal. Med. Sch., San Francisco, spring 1954; mem. faculty Wells Coll., Aurora, N.Y., 1954—, prof. philogophy, chmn. dept., 1958—; lectr. medicine U. Cal. Med. Sch., 1963-64; vis. prof. philosophy U. Cal. at Berkeley, spring 1964, vis. prof. exptl. collegiate program, 1967-69. Served to maj. AUS, 1942-46. Grantee Columbia Found., 1950-51; advanced grad. fellow Am. Council Learned Socs., 1952-53. Mem. Am. Assn. U. Profs., Am. Philos. Assn., Am. Civil Liberties Uniøn, Internat. League Rights of Man. Author: The Pragmatic Conception of Justice, 1960; also articles. Office: Experimental College Univ of Cal Berkeley CA 94720

JAFFE, SAM, actor; b. N.Y.C., Mar. 10, 1891; s. Bernard and Ada (Steinberg) J.; B.S., Coll. City N.Y., 1912; m. Lillian Taiz, 1936 (dec. 1941); m. 2d, Bettye Louise Ackerman, June 7, 1956. Dean math. Bronx Cultural Inst., 1915-16; tour Washington Sq. Players Theatre, N.Y.C., 1917-18; plays include The Jazz Singer, 1927, Grand Hotel, 1930, The Eternal Road, 1937, A Doll's House, 1938, The Gentle People, 1939; films include The Scarlet Empress, 1933, Lost Horizon, Gunga Din, The Day The Earth Stood Still, Asphalt Jungle, Ben Hur; TV appearances include Ben Casey series, 1961-65, Playhouse 90, Hitchcock Presents, Naked City, Bonanza, Daniel Boone, Alias Smith and Jones. Served with U.S. Army, 1919. Recipient Venice Internat. award, 1950; named Best Male Performance of Year, 1950; Edgar Allen Poe award, 1950; Acad. award nomination, 1950, Emmy award nomination, 1961-62, Townsend Harris award, 1962, James K. Hacket award, 1971. Co-founder, curator theatre sect. N.Y. Pub. Library, Equity Library Theatre, 1948. Home: 302 N Alpine Dr Beverly Hills CA 90210 Office: care CMA 8899 Beverly Blvd Los Angeles CA 90048

JAFFE, SAM, ind. producer; b. N.Y.C., May 21, 1901. Studio mgr., then prodn. mgr. Mayer-Schulberg, 1920-22; prodn. mgr., exec. mgr. Paramount Studios, 1923-29; prodn. mgr., asst. to David Selznick, RKO Radio, 1930-32; asst. to Sam Briskin, Columbia, 1933; partner Schulberg-Feldman-Jaffe, talent agy., Hollywood, Cal., 1934; organized Sam Jaffe, Inc., Sam Jaffe, Ltd., 1935; head Jaffe Agy., Beverly Hills, Cal., merged Famous Artists to become Famous Artists Assos., Beverly Hills, later Sullivans, Damon and Pythias; co-producer Born Free; now ind. producer. Address: London England

JAFFE, SIGMUND, educator, chemist; b. New Haven, Mar. 1, 1921; s. Morris and Rose (Blosveren) J.; A.B. with high distinction in Chemistry, Wesleyan U., Middletown, Conn., 1949; Ph.D., Ia. State U., 1953; m. Elaine Leventhal, Aug. 25, 1946; children—Matthew Lee, Paul Jonathan. Research in rare earths Ames (Ia.) Lab., 1949-53, in carbides, metal and high temperature inorganic reactions, research labs. Air Reduction Corp., 1953-58; prof. chemistry Cal. State Coll. at Los Angeles, 1958—. chmn. dept., 1958-64. Research solid propellant fuel systems, 1958-60, photochemistry and gas phase kinetics, Jet Propulsion Lab., Pasadena, Cal., 1960-64. NIH fellow Wiezmann Inst. Sci., Israel, 1964-65. Served with USNR, 1942-46. Mem. Am. Chem. Soc., Phi Beta Kappa, Sigma Xi, Phi Lambda Upsilon. Contbr. articles to profl. jours. Office: Dept Chemistry Cal State Coll Los Angeles CA 90032

JAFFE, THEODORE, govt. ofcl.; b. Providence, Aug. 24, 1910; s. David and Ette (Cipkin) J.; Ph.B., Brown U., 1932; LL.B., Harvard, 1935. Admitted to Mass. bar, 1935, R.I. bar, 1936, D.C. bar, 1948; practiced in Providence, 1935—; mem. firm Higgins, Cavanaugh & Cooney. Commr. U.S. Fgn. Claims Settlement Commn. U.S., 1961—. Served with AUS, 1942-45. Mem. Am., R.I. bar assns., Bar Assn. D.C. Home: 2727 29th St N W Washington DC 20008 Office: 1111 20th St NW Washington DC 20579

JAFFE, WILLIAM, educator, economist; b. N.Y.C., June 16, 1898; s. Morris and Mary (Pomerantz) J.; B.A. summa cum laude, Coll. City N.Y., 1918; M.A., Columbia, 1919; Docteur en Droit Faculte de Droit, U. Paris (France), 1924; m. Grace Mary Spurway, Jan. 22, 1922; children—Ghita Elizabeth (Mrs. Oliver Hardimon), David Spurway, Peter Langdon; m. 2d, Olive Caroline Weaver, Oct. 4, 1948.

Research asst. U.S. Govt. Inquiry, 1918; tutor Coll. City N.Y., 1924-25; asso. Social Sci. Research Council, Columbia, 1926-28; mem. faculty Northwestern U., 1928—, prof. econs., 1956-66, now prof. emeritus; prin. investigator NSF grant, 1965-71; vis. prof. econs. Harvard, 1967-69; vis. prof. U. Algiers (Algeria), 1956; Fulbright lectr. U. Genoa (Italy), 1956-57; vis. prof. U. Cal. at Riverside, 1965; vis. prof. U. B.C., 1969-70; prof. econs. York U., Downsview, Ont., Can., 1970—. Social Science Research Council fellow, 1925-26; Fulbright grantee, France, 1951-53; Guggenheim fellow, Switzerland, 1958-59; Ford Faculty Research fellow 1963-64. Fellow A.A.A.S., Econometric Soc.; mem. Am. Econ. Assn., Royal Econ. Soc., Phi Beta Kappa; fgn. mem. Royal Netherlands Acad. of Sci. and Letters. Author: Les Theories économiques et sociales de Thorstein Veblen, 1924; (with W.F. Ogburn) The Economic Development of Post-War France, 1929; (translation) Leon Walras: Elements of Pure Economics, 1954; Histoire des Doctrines Walrasiennes, 1956. Editor: Correspondence of Leon Walras and Related Papers, 1965; mem. adv. editorial bd. History of Political Economy. Home: 10 Pratt Circle Unionville Ontario Canada Office: Dept of Economics York University Downsview Ontario Canada

JAFFEE, ROBERT ISAAC, research metallurgist; b. Chgo., July 11, 1917; s. Louis Robert and Sadie (Braidman) J.; B.S., Ill. Inst. Tech., 1939; S.M., Harvard, 1940; Ph.D., U. Md., 1943; m. Edna Elspeth Winram, June 2, 1945; children— William Louis, Michael David. Lectr. U. Md., 1942; metallurgist Leeds & Northrup, Phila., 1943, U. Cal., 1944; with Battelle Meml. Inst., Columbus, O., 1944—, asso. mgr., 1960-64, sr. fellow, 1964—. Mem. Nat. Material Adv. Bd., 1970-73, Acta Metall. Bd. Govs., 1969-72; cons. PSAC, 1966; chmn. NASA Adv. Com. Materials, 1966-71; mem. NATO-AGARD Structure and Materials Panel, 1961-63, 69—. Fellow Inst. Metallurgy (London), Am. Soc. Metals; mem. Nat. Acad. Engring., Am. Inst. Metall. Engrs., Am. Phys. Soc., A.A.A.S., Harvard Soc. Sci. and Engring., Sigma Xi, Tau Beta Pi, Phi Lambda Upsilon. Club: Brookside Golf and Country (Columbus). Author: The Science, Technology and Application of Titanium, 1970; Refractory Metals and Alloys III, Applied Aspects, 1966; Refractory Metals and Alloys IV, Research and Development, 1967; Phase Stability in Metals and Alloys, 1967; Dislocation Dynamics, 1968; Molecular Processes on Solid Surfaces, 1970; Critical Phenomena in Alloys, Magnets and Superconductors, 1971; also articles. Patentee in field. Research non-ferrous phys. metallurgy, particularly titanium and refractory metals. Home: 5263 Rush Av Columbus OH 43214 Office: 505 King Av Columbus OH 43201

JAFFIN, CHARLES LEONARD, lawyer; b. Bklyn., Feb. 27, 1928; s. Joseph M. and Rhoda (Abeloff) J.; A.B., Princeton, 1948; LL.B., Columbia, 1951; m. Rosanna G. Webster, June 12, 1952; children—David W., Jonathan H., Rhoda E., Lora W., Katherine G. Admitted to N.Y. bar, 1951, since practiced in N.Y.C.; partner firm Battle, Fowler, Stokes & Kheel, 1960—. Dir. Sterling Extruder Corp., Pamarco, Inc., Kepner-Tregoe, Inc., Westours, Inc. Home: 522 Rosedale Rd Princeton NJ 08540 Office: 280 Park Av New York City NY 10017

JAFFRAY, JAMES FREEMAN, banker; b. Mpls., Sept. 1, 1919; s. Clive Palmer and Mary Vigelius (Freeman) J.; A.B., Yale, 1941; m. Margaret Sterling Lambie, May 25, 1946; children—James Freeman, Lucy, Kate. With First Nat. City Bank, N.Y.C., 1947—, v.p., 1952-63, sr. v.p., 1963—; dir. Albany Ins. Co. Bd. dirs., treas. Met. Opera Assn. Served to maj., armored service, AUS, 1941-46; ETO. Episcopalian. Clubs: Manursing Island (Rye, N.Y.); River (N.Y.C.); Minneapolis. Home: 30 Grace Church St Rye NY 10580 Office: 399 Park Av New York City NY 10022

JAGANNATHAN, SARUKKAI, diplomat of India; b. Srirangam, India, May 18, 1914; s. Acharya Srinivasa and Lakshmi Aiyangar; B.S. with honors, U. Madras (India), 1933; reader econs., law and history U. London, 1934-36; m. Padma Aiyanger, Aug. 20, 1934; children-Murli, Mukund. Joined Indian Civil service, 1935; dep. sec. Ministry of Finance, 1948-60; financial commr. Indian Rys., also mem. Atomic Energy Commn. India, 1966-68; permanent sec. Ministry Finance, also alternate gov. World Bank, 1966-68; exec. dir. for India, World Bank, also ambassador (econ.) Indian embassy, Washington, 1968-70; gov. Res. Bank India, 1970—. Office: Reserve Bank India Bombay India

JAGELS, CHARLES HENRY, ret. dept. store exec.; b. N.Y.C., Mar. 30, 1902; s. Charles and Margarethe (Grube) J.; B.A., Lehigh U., 1922; m. Helen LaVake, Nov. 19, 1923; children—Joan (Mrs. Lester Hardwick), Nancy. Executive v.p. of R.H. Macy & Co., Inc., N.Y.C., 1937-40; pres. Davison-Paxon Co., Atlanta (div. R.H. Macy & Co., Inc.), 1940, chmn. bd., 1958-60; pres. Lansburgh's, Washington, 1960-65. Pres., Atlanta Arts Alliance, Inc., 1965-70. Home: 480 Valley Rd N W Atlanta GA 30305

JAGGER, DEAN, actor; b. Columbus Grove, O., Nov. 7, 1905; s. Albert and Lily (Mayberry) J.; student Wabash Coll., 1923-24; Lyceum Arts Cons., Chicago, 1925; m. Gloria Joan Ling, Jan. 25, 1947; 1 dau., Diane Marion. Appeared in plays: Tobacco Road, 1933, They Shall Not Die, 1934, Missouri Legend, 1938; pictures: Brigham Young, 1940, Western Union, 1941, Yank in London, 1944; Sister Kenney, 1945, Pursued, 1947, 12 O'Clock High, 1949; My Son John, 1951; It Grows on Trees, 1952, The Robe, Executive Suite, White Christmas; Bad Day at Black Rock, 1954; Threshold of Space, The Three Brave Men, 1955; The Great Man, 1956: The Nun Story, 1959; Elmer Gantry, 1960; Jumbo, 1962; Fury at Fire Creek, 1967; The Evil Gun, 1967; TV series Mr. Novak, 1963-65. Recipient Asso. Press poll. Look Achievement award, Acad. Award, for performance in 12 O'clock High, 1949; Laurel award, 1952. Mem. Lambda Chi. Club: N.Y. Athletic. Office: care Hodge & Co 205 S Beverly Dr Beverly Hills CA 90212

JAGGER, MICK, leader Rolling Stones. Address: London Records 539 W 25th St New York City NY 10001

JAGOW, ELMER, coll. pres.; b. West Bend, Wis., Apr. 25, 1922; s. Bernard and Florence (Kurth) J.; B.S. in Edn., Concordia Tchrs. Coll., 1944; M.B.A., Northwestern, 1955; L.H.D. (hon.), Christian Theol. Sem., 1968; m. Ellen Knief, Oct. 7, 1944; children—Kathryn (Mrs. William Mohrman), Allyson (Mrs. William Weir). Asst. bus. mgr. Concordia Tchrs. Coll., River Forest, Ill., 1944-46; bus. mgr., 1946-56; mem. adminstrn. Knox Coll., Galesburg, Ill., 1956-66, treas., bus. mgr., 1961-64, v.p. finance, treas., 1964-66; pres. Hiram (Ohio) Coll., 1966—. Mem. adv. com. Inst. Coll. and Univ. Adminstrs., 1969—. Trustee Christian Theol. Sem., Indpls. Mem. Am. Council Edn. (commn. on colls.), N. Central Assn. Colls., Assn. Am. Colls. (commn. on coll. adminstrn.), Am. Mgmt. Assn. (pres.'s assn.), Ohio Coll. Assn. Clubs: Union, Playhouse (Cleve.). Home: 11861 Garfield St Hiram OH 44234

JAHN, EDWIN CORNELIUS, coll. dean; b. Oneonta, N.Y., Sept. 6, 1902; s. Cornelius and Nellie Louise (Yager) J.; B.S. cum laude, N.Y. State Coll. Forestry, 1925, M.S., 1926; Ph.D., McGill U., 1929; m. Helen Louise Schumann, Jan. 29, 1927 (dec. Jan. 1969); children—Elena Louise (Mrs. Garrett C. Clough), Carl Gordel; m. 2d, Jesse Beatrice Silverman, Feb. 20, 1970. Asst., N.Y. State Coll. Forestry, Syracuse U., 1925-26; fellow Am. Scandinavian Found., Sweden, 1929-30; asso. prof., then prof. forestry U. Ida., 1930-38; prof. forest chemistry State U. N.Y. Coll. Forestry, Syracuse U., 1938—, dir. research, 1949-52, asso. dean phys. scis. and research, 1952-66, exec. dean, 1966-67, dean, 1967-69; technical attaché of the State Dept. to Sweden, 1943-44; sr. econ. analyst depts. Commerce and State to Sweden, Finland, Norway and Denmark, 1945-46; guest lectr. Polish Acad. Sciences, 1963. Collaborator Dept. Agr. to Sweden, Finland and Great Britain, 1943-44; mem. wood chemistry com. FAO, UN, 1947-65; adviser to Royal Tech. U., Stockholm, 1954. Pres., trustee Monhegan Assos., Inc. (Me.) (conservation wild lands and historic features Monhegan Island), 1961-65. Fellow T.A.P.P.I. (chmn. plastics com. 1944-52, div. medals for research and devel., paper synthetics 1970), Soc. Am. Foresters; mem. Am. Chem. Soc. (councillor 1954; chmn. Wash.-Ida. Border sect. 1933, Syracuse sect. 1941), Finnish Forestry Soc., The Swedish Assn. of Pulp and Paper Engrs., N.Y. Acad. of Scis., Forest Products Research Soc., Sigma Xi, Phi Lambda Upsilon. Co-author, co-editor: Wood Chemistry, 2 vols., 1952. Editorial bd. TAPPI, 1949-53; editorial; adv. bd. Modern Materials: Advances in Development and Application, 1958-70. Author: articles, chpts. in books. Home: 546 Fayette Blvd Syracuse NY 13224

JAHN, JOHN RUSSELL, educator; b. Spirit Lake, Ia., Dec. 2, 1926; s. John Randolph and Bionda (Reimers) J.; student State U. Ia., 1947-49; M.S., S.D. State U., 1960, Ph.D., 1963; m. Delores F. Bessler, Aug. 13, 1950; children—Jon R., Debra L., Dona R. Dairy Farmer, Spirit Lake, 1950-59; mem. faculty dept. agrl. sci. Wis. State U., Platteville, 1962—, asso. prof. animal sci., 1964-66, prof., chmn. dept., 1966—; mem. Wis. Meat Inspection Bd., 1969—. Served with USAAF, 1945-47. Mem. Wis. Beef Improvement Assn., Am. Soc. Animal Sci., Republican. Conglist. (elder). Home: Rte 1 Platteville WI 53818

JAHN, ROBERT GEORGE, educator; b. Kearny, N.J., Apr. 1, 1930; s. George E. and Minnie (Holroyd) J.; B.S. in Mech. Engring. with highest honors, Princeton, 1951, M.A. in Physics, 1953, Ph.D., 1955; m. Catherine Seibert, June 20, 1953; children—Eric George, Jill Ellen, Nina Marie, Dawn Anne. Teaching asst. Princeton, 1953-55; instr. Lehigh U., Bethlehem, Pa., 1955-56, asst. prof., 1956-58; asst. prof. jet propulsion Cal. Inst. Tech., Pasadena, 1958-62; asst. prof. aero. engring. Princeton, 1962-64, asso. prof., 1964-67, prof. aerospace scis., 1967—, dir. grad. studies aerospace and mech. scis. dept., 1968-71, dean. engring. and applied sci., 1971—, exec. com. council univ. community, 1969—. Cons. editor Am. Scientist, 1966-70; mem. research adv. com. on fluid mechanics NASA, 1965-68, mem. research and tech. adv. subcom. on electrophysics, 1968—; Recipient Shuichi Kusaka Meml. prize in physics, 1951, Curtis W. McGraw Research award Am. Soc. for Engring. Edn., 1969. Fellow Am. Phys. Soc.; asso. fellow Am. Inst. Aeros. and Astronautics (lectr. electric propulsion Ednl. Programs, 1971—, electric propulsion tech. com. 1963-67, 71—); mem. Phi Beta Kappa, Sigma Xi. Author: Physics of Electric Propulsion, 1968; also contbr. articles in field. Home: 60 Monroe Lane Princeton NJ 08540

JAHN, THEODORE LOUIS, educator; b. New Orleans, Dec. 17, 1905; s. Edward Charles and Aline (Blair) J.; A.B. with distinction, Rice Inst., 1927; M.S., N.Y.U., 1929, Ph.D., 1931; m. Frances Floed, July 18, 1931. Nat. Research fellow in zoology Yale, 1931-33 instr., 1933-34; research asso. State U. Ia., 1934-36, asso. zoology, 1936-37, asst. prof., 1937-41, asso. prof., 1941-48; prof. zoology U. Cal. at Los Angeles, 1948-, chmn. dept., 1949-58. Mem. adv. panel gen. biology Am. Inst. Biol. Scis., Office of Naval Research, 1950-52; panel mem. NIH, 1960-64, NSF, 1961-64; mem. com. internat. exchange persons Conf. Bd. Asso. Research Councils, 1960-63; adv. panel behavioral biology Am. Inst. Biol. Scis.- NASA, 1965-67; bd. dirs. council on biol. scis. information Nat. Acad. Scis., 1969—, pres., 1970—; bd. dirs. Com. on Advanced Sci. Tng., Los Angeles, 1968-70, v.p. bd. dirs., 1969-70; mem. Council Biol. Editors. Recipient Distinguished Alumni award N.Y.U., 1968; Award of Merit, Com. on Advanced Sci. Tng., 1967; named to Wisdom Soc. Hall of Fame. Mem. A.A.A.S. (exec. com. Pacific div. 1961-66, pres. Pacific div. 1969-70, mem. nat. council 1969), Am. Micros. Soc. (pres. 1954-55), Am. Soc. Cell Biology, Soc. Gen. Physiologists, Soc. Protozoologists (sec. 1947-49, v.p. 1949-50, pres. 1952-53, mem. exec. com. 1953, 56), Soc. Systematic Zoologists, Ia. Acad. Sci., Western Soc. Naturalists, N.Y. Acad. Sci., Am. Soc. Zoologists (Treas. 1953-56, chmn. div. comparative physiology 1964-65), Zool. Soc. Los Angeles, Biophys. Soc. Am. Soc. Microbiology, Am. Physiol. Soc., NRC, Soc. Exptl. Biology and Medicine, Phycological Soc. Internat. Assn. Microbiol. Socs. (documentation com. sect. on cultural collections), Am. Soc. Naturalists, Optical Soc. Am., Sigma Xi. Author: How to Know the Protozoa (with Frances Jahn); 1949; articles sci. jours. Editorial Com. Annual Review of Microbiology, 1958-63. Contbr. Protozoa in Biological Research, 1941; Comparative Animal Physiology, 1950; Research in Protozoology, 1967: Primitive Motle Systems in Cell Biology, 1964; Infectious Blood Diseases in Man and Animals, 1968; The Biology of Euglena, 1968. Editorial bd. Jour. Protozoology, 1960-63, Am. Midland Naturalist; trustee Biol. Abstracts, 1963-68, pres. bd. trustees, 1966-67. Home: 10241 Chrysanthemum Lane Los Angeles CA 90024

JAHNCKE, ERNEST LEE, Jr., assn. exec.; b. New Orleans, Aug. 8, 1912; s. Ernest Lee and Cora (Stanton) J.; B.S., U.S. Naval Acad., 1933; m. Cornelia Redington Dickerman, Jan. 20, 1940; children—Leila Dickerman, Ernest Lee, Carter Dickerman, Redington Townsend. With NBC, 1937-41, dir. standards and practices, N.Y.C., 1960, v.p. standards and practices, 1961-70; with ABC, 45-57; v.p in charge radio network, 1950-52, v.p., asst. to pres., 1952-57; v.p., asst. to bd. chmn. Edward Petry & Co., 1957-59; Eastern dir. Am. Humane Assn., N.Y.C., 1970—. Served in USN, 1933-37; to comdr. USNR, 1941-45. Mem. Am. Arbitration Assn., S.A.R., Newcomen Soc., Sigma Alpha Epsilon. Clubs: University, Round Hill (Greewich, Conn.); Army-Navy, Chevy Chase (Washington). Home: 93 Clapboard Ridge Rd Greenwich CT 06830 Office: 485 Lexington Av New York City NY 10017

JAHNCKE, HERBERT GRANT, business exec.; b. New Orleans, Jan. 18, 1910; s. Walter F. and Emily (Grant) J.; B.S., Washington and Lee U., 1930; student Harvard Law Sch., 1931; m. Margaret Henriques, Apr. 30, 1934; children—Walter F., Robert H., Herbert Grant. With Jahncke Service, Inc., New Orleans, 1931—, now chmn.; dir. Nat. Am. Bank, New Orleans. Pres. New Orleans Pkwy. and Park Commn., 1956, 65-68, 71, treas., 1958-64; pres. City Park Improvement Assn., 1959, dir., 1954—; campaign chmn. Cultural Attractions Fund Greater New Orleans, 1966; div. chmn. large donors Meth. Hosp. Bldg. Fund. Chmn. of United Fund Greater New Orleans, 1955. New Orleans dist. capital expansion fund dr., Episcopal Diocese La., 1958, chmn. Tb. Assn. Greater New Orleans, 1959- 64, pres., 1965-67; dir. Isaac Delgado Museum, pres., 1960; mem. board of directors Dixie Homestead Assn. vice chmn. New Orleans chapter A.R.C. Served as lt. (j.g.). Supply Corps, USNR, 1944-45. Decorated Order of St. Olaf (Norway); named Rex, King of Carnival, New Orleans, 1966. Mem. Newcomen Soc. N.Am., N.Am. (dir. 1961-64), Construction Industry Assn. (mem. bd. dirs. 1950-51, pres. 1950), Nat. Ready Mixed Concrete Assn. (pres. 1953), Phi Beta Kappa, Beta Gamma Sigma. Mason (32). Clubs: International House, New Orleans Country, Boston (New Orleans); Stratford; Pickwick; Rotary. Home: 3 Bamboo Rd New Orleans LA 70124 Office: 814 Howard Av New Orleans LA 70150

JAHNKE, JOHN CURTIS, psychologist; b. Barrington, Ill., June 13, 1929; s. C. Curtis and Doris (Goff) J.; A.B., U. Ill., 1951; A.M., Northwestern U., 1954, Ph.D., 1955; m. Melissa Phyllis Bergmann, Mar. 29, 1958; children-John Curtis, Sander Alan. Instr. Ind. U. at Jefferson, 1955-57; instr. Miami U., Oxford, O., 1957-58, asst. prof. psychology, 1958-63, asso. prof., 1963- 68, prof., 1968—, chmn. dept. psychology, 1969—; spl. research fellow U. Mich., 1967-68. Mem. Am., Midwestern psychol. assns., Psychonomic Soc., A.A.A.S., Sigma Xi, Psi Chi. Asso. editor Jour. Motor Behavior, Soc., A.A.A.S., Sigma Xi, Psi Chi. Asso. editor Jour. Motor Behavior, 1968—. Contbr. articles to profl. jours.‡

JAHNKE, KARL DODD, electric co. exec.; b. Beloit, Wis., Dec. 14, 1915; s. Charles B. and Gladys (Dodd) J.; B.S., U. Ill., 1938; C.P.A., 1948; m. Elizabeth Ann Mosiman, Jan. 30, 1944; children—Jill Susan (Mrs. Robert W. Paris), Richard Charles. With Internat. Harvester Co., 1938-41; auditor Ernst & Ernst, C.P.A.'s Chgo. and Canton, O., 1941-42, 46-52; sec.-treas. Dodge Mfg. Co., 1956-68; controller Reliance Electric Co., 1968—. Officer, South Bend (Ind.) C. of C., 1960-68; pres. South Bend Civic Planning Assn., 1959, bd. dirs., 1955-65; pres. South Bend United Fund, 1967, bd. dirs., 1956-66; treas., dir. Dodge Found., 1956-68. Served with AUS, 1942-46. Mem. Am. Inst. C.P.A.'s, Financial Execs. Inst. (bd. dirs.), Theta Delta Chi. Kiwanian. Home: 14661 Hillbrook Lane N Chagrin Falls OH 44022 Office: 24701 Euclid Av Cleveland OH 44117

JAHNS, RICHARD HENRY, geologist; b. Los Angeles, Mar. 10, 1915; s. Alfred H. and Cecelia (Schnackenbeck) J.; B.S., Cal. Inst. Tech., 1935, Ph.D., 1943; M.S., Northwestern U., 1937; m. Frances M. Hodapp, Sept. 5, 1936; children—Alfred, Jeannette. Teaching fellow Northwestern U., 1935-37, Cal. Inst. Tech., 1937-39, asst. prof. geology, 1946, asso. prof., 1946-49, prof., 1949-60; prof. geology Pa. State U., 1960-65, chmn. div. earth scis., 1960-62, dean Coll. Mineral Industries, 1962-65; prof. geology, dean Sch. Earth Scis. Stanford, 1965—; jr. geologist U.S. Geol. Survey, Washington, 1937-40, asst. geologist, 1940-42, asso. geologist, 1942-44, geologist, 1944-48, sr. geologist, 1949-65, cons., 1967—; nat. lectr. Sigma Xi, 1965. Mem. Cal. State Mining and Geology Bd., 1965—, Gov.'s Sci. Adv. Bd. Cal. Recipient Distinguished Alumnus award Cal. Inst. Tech., 1970. Mem. A.A.A.S., Am. Assn. Petrol. Geol., Am. Geophys. Union, Am. Inst. Mining and Metall. Engrs., Geol. Soc. Am. (pres. 1970-71), Geol. Soc. Washington, Am. Assn. U. Profs., Mineral. Soc. Am., Soc. Econ. Geologists, Soc. Vertebrate Paleontologists, Geochem. Soc., Am. Inst. Profl. Geologists, Assn. Engring. Geologists, Nat. Assn. Geology Tchrs. Author: Hand Specimen Petrology. Editor: Geology of Southern California; asst. editor Economic Geology, Am. Minerologist and Engring. Geology. Contbr. numerous articles and reports on econ., glacial and structural geology, and petrology to sci. publs. Home: 2312 Branner Dr Menlo Park CA 94025 Office: Stanford U Stanford CA 94305

JAHODA, FRITZ, educator, musician; b. Vienna, Austria, May 23, 1909; s. Karl and Betty (Probst) J.; student U. Vienna, 1928-30; m. Hedwig Kramer, Oct. 26, 1935 (dec. 1961); 1 dau., Eleanor (Mrs. Paul Horwitz). Came to U.S., 1939, naturalized, 1945. Free-lance pianist and chamber music player, 1928—; opera condr., Dusseldorf, Germany, 1930-33, Graz, Austria, 1934-38; faculty Converse (S.C.) Coll., 1939-40, Sarah Lawrence Coll., 1940- 46; prof. City Coll., City U. N.Y., 1946—, chmn. music dept., 1964-69; mem. N.Y. Trio, 1951-61; guest condr. State Opera Vienna, 1947, Radio Orch. Vienna, 1958. Home: 3530 Henry Hudson Pkwy New York City NY 10463

JAICKS, FREDERICK G., steel co. exec.; b. Chgo., 1918; ed. Cornell U., 1940. Pres., dir. Inland Steel Co., 1966-71, chmn., chief exec. officer, 1971—. Home: 81 Graymoor Lane Olympia Fields IL 60461 Office: 30 W Monroe St Chicago IL 60603*

JAINSEN, WILSON CARL, ins. exec.; b. Hartford, Conn., May 14, 1899; s. Carl W. and Julia (Goodrich) J.; student Wesleyan U.; Ph.B., Brown U., 1922; m. Ann Morgan, Sept. 21, 1953. With Hartford Accident & Indemnity Co., 1922—, adjuster, v.p., 1922-53, pres., dir., 1953—; pres. Greater Hartford Corp.; dir. Conn. Gen. Life Ins. Co., United Bank & Trust, Soc. for Savs., Hartford Gas Co. Former pres. Govtl. Research Inst.; chmn. Conn. Pub. Expenditure Council. Served with USN, World War I. Mem. Conn. C. of C. (v.p.). Am. Arbitration Assn. (dir.). Home: 779 Prospect Av West Hartford CT 06105 Office: 690 Asylum St Hartford CT

JAKLITSCH, JOSEPH JOHN, Jr., mag. editor; b. Bklyn., Mar. 28, 1919; s. Joseph John and Josefa (Stonitsch) J.; B.S., Pratt Inst., 1940; m. Eleanor Mulligan, May 29, 1948; children—Gary, Diane. With planning dept. Brewster Aero. Corp., N.Y.C., 1940-41; test engr. ordnance dept., U.S. Army, 1941-44, editor, 1944-45; tech. editor Am. Soc. M.E., N.Y.C., 1945-50, asso. editor, 1950-55, acting editor, 1956, editor, Mech. Engring. mag., also trans. Am. Soc. M.E., 1957—; editorial adv. com. Engrs. Joint Council; cons. editor Crowell-Collier Ednl. Corp.; spl. cons. Barnhart World Book Dictionary; contbg. editor Am. Year Book, 1946-50, Collier's Year Book, 1951-59; asso. editor Applied Mechanics Revs., 1948-56; information com. Engrs. Council Profl. Devel. Adv. council Pratt Inst. Sch. Engring. Fellow Am. Soc. M.E., (Outstanding Leadership in Engring. award 1968); mem. N.Y. Bus. Press Editors. Clubs: Tamarack Assn. (N.J.); Walkill Country (Franklin, N.J.). Home: 158-14 Oak Av Kissena Park Flushing NY 11358 Office: 345 E 47th St New York City NY 10017

JAKOBSEN, JAKOB KNUDSEN, mech. engr.; b. Bording Sogn, Denmark, Aug. 7, 1912; s. Laust Peder and Inger Marie (Kristensen) J.; M.S. in Mech. Engring., Royal Tech. U. Denmark, 1941; m. Eva Koch, Nov. 19, 1941; children—Marianne Gyrithe (Mrs. Earl C. Green), Peter Laust (dec. 1969), Claus Michael, Suzanne Elizabeth, Niels-Olaf Sejten, Lars Jakob. Came to U.S., 1952, naturalized, 1958. Mech. engr. Brown Boveri et Cie, steam and gas turbines, Switzerland, 1941-43; project engr. Pub. Power Utilities of Copenhagen (Denmark), 1943-45; mech. engr. Burmeister & Wain, diesel engine and shipbuilders, Copenhagen, 1945-52; gas turbine engr. Clark Bros. Co., Olean, N.Y., 1952-55; staff engr. automotive research Chrysler Corp., Detroit, 1955-60; sr. tech. specialist for research Rocketdyne, Canoga Park, Cal., 1960—; asst. prof. machine design Royal Tech. U. Denmark, 1941. Registered profl. engr., Mich., Cal. Mem. Am. Soc. Testing and Materials (com. for erosion by cavitation and impingement 1964—), Am. Soc. M.E. (recipient Melville gold medal 1964), Soc. Automotive Engrs., Am. Inst. Aeros. and Astronautics, Nat. Soc. Profl. Engrs., Danish Inst. Civil Engrs. Republican. Lutheran. Author: Rocket Engine Turbopump Inducers, NASA monograph, 1971. Contbr. articles profl. jours. Patentee compressor design, diesel engine turbosupercharger, pump diffusor, Denmark and U.S. Home: 10531 Etiwanda Av Northridge CA 91324 Office: Rocketdyne 6633 Canoga Av Canoga Park CA 91304

JAKOBSON, MARK JOHN, physicist, educator; b. Carlyle, Mont., May 4, 1923; s. Hans M. and Bessie Mae (Fessenden) J.; B.A., U. Mont., 1944; M.A., 1947; Ph.D. (Whiting fellow), U. Cal. at Berkeley, 1951; m. Marguerite Elizabeth Thomsen, Aug. 17, 1945;

children—Kristin Marie, Sandra Lynne (Mrs. William Bardewyck). Physicist, Lawrence Radiation Lab., 1951-52; instr. U. Wash., 1952-53; prof. U. Mont., Missoula, 1953—, chmn. physics and astronomy dept., 1969—; mem. vis. staff Los Alamos Sci. Lab., 1963—. Bd. dirs. Lutheran Found. Mont. Served to lt. (j.g.) USNR, 1944-46. Mem. Am. Phys. Soc., Phi Beta Kappa, Sigma Xi, Pi Mu Epsilon. Democrat. Lutheran. Home: Route 3 Pattee Canyon Missoula MT 59801

JAKOBSON, MAX, Finnish diplomat; b. Viipuri, Finland, Sept. 30, 1923; s. Jonas and Helmi (Virtanen) J.; m. Marilyn Z. Medney, Apr. 14, 1954; children—Ralph Daniel, Linda Deborah, David Robert. Reporter, Finnish News Agy., 1941-42, U.P.I., Helsinki, 1944-45, BBC, London, Eng., 1946-48; London corr. for Helsinki newspaper UUSI SUOMI, 1948-53; press attache Finnish embassy, Washington, 1953-58; head press bur. Finnish Ministry Fgn. Affairs, 1958-61, dir. polit. affairs, 1961-65; permanent rep. Finland to UN, 1965—. Served to lt. Finnish Army, 1942-44. Decorated Commemorative medal War 1941-44; comdr. Order Lion (Finland); comdr. 1st class Order N. Star (Sweden); comdr. Order Olaf (Norway); comdr. 1st class Polonia Restituta (Poland). Author: Diplomacy of the Winter War, 1960; Finnish Neutrality, 1969. Home: 165 Boulevard Pelham NY 10803 Office: 866 UN Plaza New York City NY 10017

JAKOBSON, ROMAN, linguist, literary historian; b. Moscow, Russia, Oct. 11, 1896; s. Osip and Anna (Volpert) J.; A.B. with silver medal, Lazarev Inst. Oriental Langs., Moscow, 1914; Diploma first degree, Moscow U. (Buslaev prize for study lang. North Russian Oral Epos 1916), 1918; Ph.D., Prague U., 1930; A.M., Harvard, 1949; D.Litt., U. Cambridge, 1950, U. Chgo., U. Oslo, 1961, U. Uppsala, U. Mich., 1963, U. Grenoble, U. Nice, 1966, U. Rome, 1967, Yale, 1967, Charles U., Prague, U. Brno, 1968, Ohio State U., 1970; D.Sc., U. N.M., 1966, Clark U., 1969; m. Krystyna Pomorska, Sept. 28, 1962. Came to U.S., 1941. Research asso. Moscow U., 1918-20; prof. gen. linguistics and Czechoslovak studies Ecole Libre des Hautes Etudes, N.Y.C., 1942-46; vis. prof. linguistics Columbia, 1943-46, T.G. Masaryk prof. Czechoslovak studies, 1946-49; S.H. Cross prof. Slavic lang. and lits. Harvard, 1949—, also gen. linguistics, 1960—; Inst. prof. Mass. Inst. Tech., 1957—. Decorated Chevalier de la Légion d'Honneur; recipient award Am. Council Learned Socs., 1960. Mem. Royal Netherlands, Polish, Norwegian, Danish, Serbian, Irish acads. sci., Bohemian Royal Soc. Sci., Finno-Ugric Soc. (hon.), Am. Acad. Arts and Sci., Philol. Soc. (London), Mediaeval Acad., Acad. Aphasia (hon.), Tokyo Inst. for Advanced Studies Lang. (hon.), Am. Anthrop. Assn., Soc. de Ling. de Paris, Linguistic Soc. Am. (pres. 1956), Internat. Com. Slavists (v.p.), Cercle Ling. de Copenhague (hon.), Moscow (founder, chmn., 1915-20), Prague (cofounder, v.p., 1927-38), linguistic circles, Linguistic Circle N.Y. (co-founder, v.p. 1943-49), Acoustic Soc. Am., Internat. Phonetic Assn. (hon.), Slovak Acad. Sci. (Golden medal 1968). Author books including: Kindersprache, Aphasie und allgem Lautgesetze, 1941,7O; Preliminaries to Speech Analysis (with G. Fant and M. Halle), 1952; Fundamentals of Language, 1956,71; Selected Writings I, 1962, II, 1971, IV, 1968; Essais de linguistique générale, 1963; Saggi di linguistica generale, 1966; Fonemae Fonologia, 1967; Child Language, Aphasiaand Phonological Universals, 1968; Lingüistica, Poética, Cinema, 1970; Language enfantin et aphasie, 1969; (with L.L. Hammerich) Low German Manual of Spoken Russian-16O7, I, 1961, II, 1970; (with L.G. Jones) Shakespeare's Verbal Art, 1970; Studies on Child Language and Aphasia, 1971. Bibliography of Publications, 1967. Address: Boylston Hall 301 Harvard U Cambridge MA 02138 ☆

JAKOWATZ, CHARLES V., univ. dean; b. Kansas City, Kan., Feb. 6, 1920; s. Louis and Pauline (Steinmetz) J.; B.S. in Elec. Engring., Kan. State Coll., 1944, M.S. in Elec. Engring., 1947; Ph.D., U. Ill., 1953; m. Robert Townley, June 27, 1947; children—Judy, Charles V. Asst. prof. elec. engring. U. Ill., 1948- 53; communications engr. research lab. Gen. Electric Co., 1953-63, liaison scientist, 1963-65; dean Sch. Engring., Wichita State U., 1965—; adj. prof. Rensselaer Poly. Inst., 1956-65, Bd. dirs. Midwest Med. Research Inst. Served to lt. (j.g.) USNR, 1944-45. Registered profl. engr., Kan. Mem. I.E.E.E., Math. Assn. Am., Am. Soc. Engring. Edn., Sigma Xi, Tau Beta Pi, Phi Kappa Phi, Eta Kappa Nu, Phi Mu Epsilon, Sigma Tau. Contbr. articles to prof. jours. Patentee in field. Home: 533 N Broadmoor Av Wichita KS 67206

JAKSTAS, ALFRED JOHN, museum conservator; b. Boston, Oct. 30, 1916; s. Walter John and Julia (Barkevich) J.; A.B., Harvard, 1938; m. Valerie Jevaraus, Oct. 11, 1942; children Janet, Julianne. Teaching fellow Harvard, 1943-44; conservator Isabella Stewart Gardner Mus., 1943-61; conservator paintings Art Inst. Chgo., 1961-. Cons. conservation Currier Gallery Art, Mus. Art, R.I. Sch. Design, Wadsworth Atheneum, Springfield Mus. Fine Arts, Notre Dame Gallery, various colls. Fellow Internat. Inst. Conservation Mus. Objects. Home: 1287 Scott Av Winnetka IL 60093 Office: Art Inst Chgo Chicago IL 60603

JALKUT, LEE DAVID, retail co. exec.; b. N.Y.C., Apr. 2, 1905; s. Benjamin and Besse (Sachs) J.; B.S., Franklin and Marshall Coll., 1926; m. Jane Scott, Mar. 10, 1945 (dec. Aug. 1, 1955); children—Susan Ann, Michael Lee; m. 2d, Marguerite DeHaven, Apr. 5, 1957. Buyer, R.H. Macy & Co., N.Y.C., 1926-32; mdse. man Gimbel Bros., 1932-34; group mdse. mgr. Montgomery Ward & Co., Chgo., 1934-45; v.p. Dearborn Co., furniture mfr., Chgo. and Wis., 1945-52, Munising Wood Products Co., Inc., Chgo. and Mich., 1946-52, Freeman Co., furniture distbr., Chgo., 1945-52; v.p. Fedway Stores, div. Federated Dept. Stores, 1952-54; pres. Jalkut Assos., 1954-57, Ben Franklin Stores, 1957-66; exec. v.p. City Products Corp., Des Plaines, Ill., 1967-70, also dir.; ret., 1970. Trustee Franklin and Marshall Coll., Lancaster, Pa. Club: Northmoor Country. Home: 1030 Cherry Tree Lane Glencoe IL 60022

JALONICK, GEORGE WASHINGTON, III, business exec.; b. Dallas, Oct. 10, 1913; s. George Washington, Jr. and Charlotte Katherine (Johnston) J.; student U. Tex., 1932-34; m. Dorothy Elizabeth Cockrell, Nov. 22, 1938; children—George Washington, IV, Dorothy Aurelia, Sally Ann. With Southwest Airmotive Co., 1941—, v.p., 1941-58, exec. v.p., dir., pres., now chmn. bd., chmn. exec. com., also bd. dirs. Dist. coordinator aviation for civil def.; mem. Dallas Planning Council, Dallas Crime Commn. (dir.), Tex. Aviation Adv. Council and Aviation Council of Texas, Aviation Legislative Com.; mem. adv. bd. Aviation Distributors and Mfrs. Assn. (past pres.); mem. Highland Park Bd. of Edn.; bd. dirs. Dallas Soc. for Prevention Cruelty to Animals. Mem. Tex. Police Assn., Dallas Wholesalers and Mfrs. Assn. (dir.), Tex. Pvt. Flyers Assn., Kappa Alpha. Clubs: Dallas Country; Northwood, Terpsichorian; Wings (N.Y.C.); Dallas; Imperial; Headliners (Austin, Tex.). Home: 3509 Euclid Highland Park Dallas TX 75205 Office: Love Field Dallas TX 75219

JAMAL, AHMAD, pianist; b. Pitts., July 2, 1930; s. Robert S. and Lottie (Wilson) Jones; ed. pub. schs., Pitts.; div. Pianist, 1933—; featured pianist George Hudson's band, Club Harlem, Atlantic City, on tour, 1948; formed own group Three Strings, 1951, appeared Blue Note, Chgo., The Embers, N.Y.C., 1952; participated Duke Ellington concert Carnegie Hall, 1952; numerous radio, TV appearances; recordings include Argo Albums, But Not for Me, 1958; organized export-import div. Ahmad Jamal Enterprises, Inc., pres., 1959—; formed Mazzan Music Corp., 1960; pres. Hema Music Pubs., 1962—; operator Alhambra, restaurant-night club, Chgo. Pres. Ahmad Jamal Found.; mem. Internat. Soc. Propagation Islamic Culture. Recipient Man of Year award Pitts. Jr. C. of C., 1960. Composer: New Rhumba, 1948; Seleritus, 1951; Concert Miniature, 1953; Forever Spring, 1953.‡

JAMAL, MOHAMED AHMED, diplomat of Sudan; b. Wadi Halfa, Sudan, 1917; s. Mohamed Ahmed and Fatima (Raya) J.; grad. Gordon Coll., Khartoum, 1937; B.A., Univ. Coll., Exeter, Devon, Eng., 1946; B.Litt., Baliol Coll., Oxford, 1954; m. Fatima Hassan, 1937; 7 children. Tchr., Sundanese high schs., 1938-44; with Sudanese Ministry of Edn., 1947-50; dean students Khartoum U., 1949; ambassador of Sudan to Iraq, 1956-59, to Ethiopia, 1959-64, to United Kingdom, 1965-67; undersec. (polit. affairs) Ministry Fgn. Affairs, Khartoum, 1967; permanent rep. of Sudan to the UN, 1964-66; undersec. polit. affairs Ministry Fgn. Affairs, Khartoum, 1967-69. Formerly sec. Cultural Center, Khartoum. Decorated by King of Iraq, King of Jordan, Emperor of Ethiopia, Pres. of Syria. Author of works in Arabic and English, latest being Intellectual Origins of Egyptian Nationalism, 1960. Contbr. articles on African affairs to periodicals. Translator: The Federalist Papers, also Africa Rediscovered (into Arabic). Adviser, HIWAR mag., Beirut; editorial bd. Modern Jour. African History. Home: PO Box 83 Khartoum Sudan

JAMBOR, AGI, educator, pianist; b. Budapest, Hungary, Feb. 4, 1909; d. William and Olga (Riesz) Jambor; student piano with Olga Jambor, Paula Braun and Edwin Fischer; student composition with Zoltan Kodaly and Leo Weiner; student musicology with Curt Sachs; Master's Degree, Royal Acad. Music, Budapest; m. Imre Patai, Jan. 3, 1933 (dec. Jan. 1949); 1 son, Peter Thomas Gabriel (dec.); m. 2d, Claude Rains, Oct. 7, 1959 (div. 1960). Came to U.S., 1947, naturalized, 1953. Concertized throughout Europe and U.S.; tchr. Am. U., 1947-48, Phila. Mus. Acad., 1948-53, Peabody Conservatory Music, 1953-57, Goucher Coll., 1956-57; vis. lectr. Bryn Mawr Coll., 1957, prof., 1958-; hon. curator mus. instrument collection U. Mus. of Pa.; many radio and TV appearances; recording artist for Capitol Records; founder Childrens Music Club, Gotheborg, Sweden, also Oak Ridge Sch. Music. Mem. bd. Women's Med. Coll. Hosp. Recipient Brahms prize, Berlin, Germany, 1928; Internat. Chopin prize, Warsaw, Polan, 1937; grantee Am. Philos. Soc., 1959, 60; Szent-Gyorgyi certificate for underground work against Nazis. Mem. Am., Internat. musicol. socs., Am., Internat. ethnomusicol. socs., Musicians Union, Mu Phi Epsilon. Home: 103 Pine Tree Rd Radnor PA 19087 Office: Bryn Mawr Coll Bryn Mawr PA 19010

JAMES, ALBERT WILLIAM, lawyer; b. Cobden, Ill., June 12, 1902; s. Albert W. and Alice (Broadway) J.; LL.B., Dickinson Law Sch., 1927; m. Madalin Winthrop, July 12, 1929; children—Albert W., Hugh Winthrop, Jay Paul. Clerk du Pont Co., 1920-22; atty. Fidelity & Deposit Co. of Md., 1927-29; admitted to Del. bar, 1929; instr. law Goldey Coll., 1929-33, 52-60; asso. firm Hering & Morris, 1929-36; mem. firm Morris, James, Hitchens & Williams, 1936—; pres. City Council of Wilmington, 1935-40; dep. atty. gen. Del. in charge of taxes, 1939-41; mayor of Wilmington, 1941- 45; atty. gen., Del., 1947-51 Mem. Wilmington Community Concert Assn., Am. Bar Assn., Phi Kappa Psi. Republican. Clubs: Kiwanis, Whist, University, Torch (pres., 1941-42), Wilmington Country. Home: Plaza Apts Wilmington DE 19806 Office: Market Tower Bldg Wilmington DE 19801

JAMES, ALLIX BLEDSOE, univ. pres.; b. Marshall, Tex., Dec. 17, 1922; s. Samuel Horace and Tannie Etta (Judkins) J.; A.B., Va. Union U., 1944, B.D., 1946; Th.M., Union Theol. Sem. Va., 1949, Th.D., 1957; postgrad. Boston U., summer 1951, Pa. Sem. Va., 1949, Th.D., 1957; postgrad. Boston U., summer 1951, Pa. State U., summer 1957; m. Sue Nickens, Feb. 14, 1945; children-Alvan Bosworth, Portia Veann. Ordained to ministry Bapt. Ch., 1942; moderator No. Neck Bapt. Assn., 1950-52; minister Union Zion Bapt. Ch., Gloucester, Va., 1944-53; minister Mt. Zion Bapt. Ch., Downings, Va., 1945-57; minister Third Union Bapt. Ch., King William, Va., 1953-70; dean students Va. Union U., Richmond, 1950-57, dean Sch. Theology, dean students Va. Union U., Richmond, 1950-57, dean Sch. Theology, 1957-70, v.p., 1960-70, pres., 1970—. Chmn. Richmond City Planning Commn., 1969- -; mem. Mayor's Commn. on Human Relations, 1963-65; pres. Norrell Sch. P.T.A., 1963-65; co-chmn. Northside Community Assn., 1964-68. Bd. dirs. Va. Inst. Pastoral Care, Task Force for Renewal Urban Strategy and Tng., Better Richmond, Inc., Am. Council on Edn., Fund for Theol. Edn.; mem. adv. bd. Inst. for Bus. and Community Devel. Fund for Theol. Edn.; mem. adv. bd. Inst. for Bus. and Community Devel. U. Richmond; mem. exec. bd. Bapt. Gen. Conv. Va.; bd. fellows Interpreters House, Lake Janaluska, N.C. Mem. Clergy Assn. Richmond Area (pres.), Am. Assn. Theol. Schs. (pres.), Am. Bapt. Conv. (pres. council on theol. edn.), Bapt. Gen. Conv. Va. (mem. exec. bd.), Soc. for Advancement Continuing Edn. for Ministers (mem. exec. bd.), Alpha Phi Alpha. Contbg. editor: The Continuing Quest, 1970. Home: 1200 W Graham Rd Richmond VA 23220 Office: 1500 N Lombardy St Richmond VA 23220

JAMES, ARTHUR FREDERICK, lawyer; b. Toledo, Feb. 7, 1932; s. Harold Arthur and Alice (McCann) J.; B.A., Columbia, 1954, LL.B., 1956; m. Anna Hewlett, Feb. 9, 1957; children-Cerl Elaine Amelia McCann. Admitted to Ohio bar, 1956, also U.S. Supreme Ct.; practice in Toledo, 1960—; asso. firm Doyle, Lewis & Warner, 1960-63, partner, 1963—. Dir. Maumee Metal Treating Co. (O.), 1964—, Metal Forming and Coining Corp., Maumee, 1965—, Canadian Cold Forging & Coing Corp., Ltd., Windsor, Can., 1965—. Mem. Lucas County Republican Central Com., 1961—, pres. workshops, 1964-65. Served to capt. USMCR, 1956-60. Mem. Toledo Bar Assn., (exec. com.), Toastmasters Internat. (gov. Toledo area 1964-65). Home: 4562 Penridge Rd Toledo OH 43615 Office: Nat Bank Bldg Toledo OH 43604

JAMES, BENJAMIN DAVID, coll. dean; b. Plymouth, Pa., Aug. 10, 1912; s. David John and Jeanette (King) J.; A.B., Dickinson Coll., 1934; M.A., Bucknell U., 1936; Ph.D., U. Pa., 1962; m. Grace Davis Picton, Jan. 12, 1937; children—Benjamin David, J. Wesley. Tchr., coach Plymouth (Pa.) High Sch., 1934-41; instr. edn. and psychology, head football and track coach Dickinson Coll., Carlisle, Pa., 1941- 44, prof. edn., chmn. dept. edn. and psychology, dean admissions, 1944-63, R.V.C. Watkins prof. psychology, 1957—, dir. summer session, dean students, 1963-68, prof. psychology and edn., dean tchr. edn., 1968—, also prof. edn. Cons. to industry. Chmn. classified sect. United Fund; chmn. Pa. Adv. Com. for Econ. Security, 1968—; mem. adv. com. to Harrisburg Community Coll. Past chmn. Cumberland County Child Welfare Adv. Com. Trustee Kiskiminetas Springs Prep. Sch., Methodist Home for Children. Served to lt. USNR, 1944-46. Mem. Pa. Admissions Assn. (v.p.), Nat. Assn. Coll. Admissions Counselors (Pa. officer), Kappa Phi Kappa, Omicron Delta Kappa, Phi Kappa Psi. Rotarian (past pres.). Author: Graduate Study in the Liberal Arts College, 1962. Home: 355 Graham St Carlisle PA 17013

JAMES, BYRON ELFED, mfg. co. exec.; b. Nanticoke, Pa., Aug. 7, 1909; s. William Lewis and Mary (Davis) J.; B.S. in Gen. Engring., Mass. Inst. Tech., 1932; m. Anna Mae Rees, June 20, 1936; children—Barry Rees, Sally Ann (Mrs. Steven R. Jones), Daniel William. Chief devel. engr. York Corp. (Pa.), 1937-47, chief comml. engr., 1952-53; gen. mgr. Morrison (Ill.) plant Liquid Carbonic Corp., 1947-49; chief engr. McQuay, Inc., Mpls., 1949-52, v.p. engring., 1953-56, exec. v.p., 1956-57, pres., dir., 1957-69, chmn., chief exec. officer, 1969—; dir. N.W. Nat. Bank of Mpls., Waters Instruments, Inc., Rochester, Minn., Tonka Corp., Hopkins, Minn. Mayor, Minnetonka Beach 1958. Bd. dirs. Air Conditioning and Refrigerating Inst. Registered profl. engr., Minn., Pa. Mem. Am. Soc. Heating, Referigerating and Air Conditioning Engrs., Tau Beta Pi. Republican. Episcopalian. Mason (Shriner). Clubs: Minneapolis, Minikahda Country; Lafayette Country (Minnetonka Beach, Minn.). Home: 2603 Arcola Lane Wayzata MN 55391 Office: PO Box 1551 Minneapolis MN 55440

JAMES, CHARLES D., ins. exec.; b. Milw., Apr. 23, 1905; s. Alfred Farragut and Kathryn Helen (Durand) J.; student Phillips Andover Acad., 1922-23; A.B., Princeton, 1927; m. Grace E. Velie, Sept. 15, 1928; childrenAlfred, Charles Velie, David Farragut, Douglas Craig. Ins. accountant, 1927; chmn. bd. Northwestern Nat, Ins. Co., Northwestern Nat. Casualty Co., NN Corp., Milw.; dir. Marine Corp., Marine Nat. Exchange Bank (both Milw.). Pres., Layton Art Gallery. Trustee Milw. Art Center. Clubs: Town, Milwaukee, University, Country (Milw.). Home: 921 E Wye Lane Milwaukee WI 53217 Office: P O Box 2070 Milwaukee WI 53101

JAMES, CHARLES FRANKLIN, Jr., educator; b. Des Arc, Mo., July 16, 1931; s. Charles Franklin and Beulah Frances (Kyte) J.; B.S., Purdue U., 1958, M.S., 1960, Ph.D., 1963. Sr. indsl. engr. McDonnel Aircraft Co., 1963; asst. prof. U. R.I., 1963-66; asso. prof. U. Mass. at Amherst, 1966-67; prof., chmn. dept. indsl. engring. U. R.I., 1967—; cons. in field; arbitrator Am. Arbitration Assn. Served with USAF, 1951-55. Mem. Am. Inst. Indsl. Engrs., Am. Soc. Engring. Edn., Operations Research Soc. Am, Author articles in field. Home: RR 1 Box 245 B Saunderstown RI 02874 Office: Dept Indsl Engring Univ Rhode Island Kingston RI 02881

JAMES, CLIFFORD CYRIL, educator, mgmt. adviser; b. Timsbury, Somerset, Eng., Dec. 9, 1900; s. George Thomas and Dora Elizabeth (Maggs) J.; ed. in Eng., Can., U.S.; m. Mae Laura Coleman, Dec. 27, 1941. Came to U.S., 1923, naturalized, 1942. Writer mags. and newspapers, also advt. exec., Can. and Cal., 1920-25; internat. dir. Round Table Internat., 1925-29; advt. and pub. relations exec. and cons., N.Y.C. and Phila., 1929-40; mng. editor Economic Forum, 1932-40; organizer, dir. engring., sci. and mgmt. war tng. program, also U.S. pilot tng. program, U. Balt., 1940-45, founder, 1945, dean Sch. Bus., 1945-69, now dean emeritus; mgmt. and marketing adviser. 1940—; mgmt. devel. adv. Md. Comptroller's Office, 1970—. Dir. Addison Clarke & Brother, Chmn. pub. relations Community-Red Cross United Appeal, Balt., 1958-60; chmn. membership com. Balt. Assn. Commerce, 1959-61, mem. edn. com., chmn. edn.-bus. coordinating council, 1954—; dir. Advt. Club Balt., 1961—. Mem. Md. adv. council Small Bus. Adminstrn., 1964—; mem. export expansion council U.S. Dept. Commerce, 1969—; com. mem. Md. Council for Higher Edn., 1964—. Fellow Soc. Advancement Mgmt. (Outstanding Mgmt. award 1956); mem. C. of C. of Met. Balt., Traffic Club Balt., Sales and Marketing Execs. Internat. Author syndicated articles Management Guideposts, 1952—. Home: Ambassador Apts Canterbury Rd and 39th St Baltimore MD 21218

JAMES, BROTHER CYPRIAN, (Nicholas William Walton), educator; b. Bklyn., July 1, 1909; s. James John and Catherine (Greevy) Walton; B.A., Manhattan Coll., 1932, M.A., 1936; M.S., Fordham U., 1939, Ph.D., 1944. Faculty St. Thomas Apostle Sch., N.Y.C., 1929-32, St. James High Sch., Bklyn., 1932-33, Bishop Laughlin High Sch., 1932-34, Hillside Sch., Troy, N.Y., 1934-35, St. Joseph's High Sch., Manchester, N.H., 1935-36; instr. genetics, embryology, bacteriology Manhattan Coll., 1936- 39, asst. prof., 1939-44, asso. prof., 1944-47, prof., head dept. biology since 1947. Mem. A.A.A.S., Entomol. Soc. Am., Am. Genetic Assn., N.Y. Acad. Sci., Assn. Am. Med. Colls., Sigma Xi. Office: Manhattan College Bronx NY 10471

JAMES, DOUGLAS, savs. and loan exec.; b. Bklyn., Aug. 14, 1907; s. Warner and Mary Douglas (Rutherford) J.; grad. Phillips Acad., 1925; B.S., Princeton, 1929, M.A., 1931; postgrad. Am. Sch. Oriental Research, Jerusalem, 1929-30; m. Elizabeth Ranken MacLenathen, Sept. 7, 1940; children—Elizabeth S. (Mrs. Peter Roy Faber), Douglas L., Virginia R., Althea M. Vice consul U.S. Fgn. Service, Egypt, Italy, 1932-35; instr. Bklyn. Coll., 1935-39; with Towns & James, Inc., Bklyn., 1940-68; with Equitable Fed. Savs. & Loan Assn., Bklyn., 1957—, pres., 1969—. Bd. dirs. Berkeley Inst., 1959—, treas., 1962—; bd. dirs. Brotherhood-in-Action, 1970—, treas., 1971—; bd. dirs. Navy Yard Boys' Club. Mem. Downtown Bklyn. Assn. (dir.), Bklyn. Bd. Realtors (dir.). Conglist. (trustee). Mason. Clubs: Brooklyn; Norfolk (Conn.) County. Home: 490 Argyle Rd Brooklyn NY 11218 Office: 356 Fulton St Brooklyn NY 11201

JAMES, EARL DANIEL, mayor of Montgomery, Ala.; b. Florala, Ala., Aug. 10, 1914; s. Walter Home and Atha (Daniel) J.; B.S., Ala. Poly. Inst.; m. Dorothy Goggans; children—Walter Thomas, Kathleen Sue. Former tchr., athletic instr. Montgomery (Ala.) pub. schs., also former athletic dir.; former asso. city commr. City of Montgomery, now mayor. Served with USAAF, World War II. Mem. Phi Delta Kappa. Methodist. Club: Optimist. Home: 26 Oak Forest Dr Montgomery AL 36109 Office: Office of the Mayor Montgomery AL 36104*

JAMES, EDWARD WASHINGTON, coll. dean; b. nr. Piave, Miss., Dec. 2, 1916; s. Edward Washington and Emma (Henderson) J.; B.S., Miss. State Coll., 1938; M.A., Miss. So. Coll., 1949; Ed.D., U. Tex., 1953; m. Mexie Bradshaw, Dec. 18, 1937; children—Barbara Faye (Mrs. James Baxter Elliott), Charlotte Ann (Mrs. Keith Dotson), Edward Washington Ill. Vocational agr. tchr., high sch., Becker, Miss., 1938-41, Ruffin, N.C., 1941-43, Richton, Miss., 1944; supt. Sand Hill Spl. Schs., Richton, 1945-49; supt. high sch., Tylertown, Miss., 1949-51; instr. U. Tex., 1951-53; prof. edn. East Central State Coll., Ada, Okla., 1953-54, dean instrn., 1954-69, dean of Coll., 1970—. Dir. Okla. State Bank, Ada; mem. Okla. Commn. on Tchr. Edn. and Certification, 1957—, v.p., 1958-59, pres., 1959. Mem. Ada City Council, 1962-65. Mem. adv. bd. Salvation Armn; drive chmn. Pontotoc County chpt. A.R.C.; mem. Ada Safety Council, Ada Health Council. Mem. Miss. Sch. Adminstrs. Assn. (pres. 1948), Coll. Tchrs. Assn. Okla. (pres. 1956), Okla. Coll. Deans Assn. (pres. 1956), Okla. Council Edn. (v.p. 1955), Okla. Edn. Assn., Nat. Coll. Assn., Ada C. of C., Alpha Tau Alpha, Phi Delta Kappa, Phi Kappa Tau. Baptist (deacon). Kiwanian (pres. 1956, lt. gov. Tex.-Okla. dist. 1957). Home: 400 S Highland St Ada OK 74820

JAMES, ERIC, coll. dean; b. Jamaica, B.W.I., Aug. 6, 1910; s. Daniel Emanuel and Ella (Henry) J.; came to U.S., 1928, naturalized, 1928; B.A., McGill U., 1941; M.A., N.Y.U., 1948, Ph.D., 1956; m. Beryl Theodore Clarke, Apr. 6, 1958; 1 dau., Terri. Sr. lectr. pub. adminstrn. U. W. I., Jamaica, 1949-52; adviser labor relations to Jamaica, also mem. Jamaica Planning Bd., 1952-56; instr. govt. Bklyn., also lectr. pub. adminstrn. N.Y.U., 1956-59; UN sr. adviser in adminstrn. to Republic of Sudan, 1959-63; asso. prof. internat. affairs U. Pitts., 1963-64; dean Manhattan Community Coll., City U. N.Y., 1964-67, 71—; asso. dir. U.S. AID Mission to Liberia, Dept. of State, 1967-69, dep. dir., 1969-71. Bd. dirs. N.Y.C. Econ. Council, 1964—; adv. council Internat. Study and Research Inst., 1964—. Served to 2d lt. USAAF, 1942-44. Fellow Am. Sociol. Assn.; mem. Am. Acad. Pub. Adminstrn. and Social Sci., Am. Polit. Sci. Assn., Soc. Internat. Devel., Soc. Applied Anthropology, British Inst. Pub. Adminstrn., Soc. Pub. Adminstrn. Home: 14 Sevenoake Rd Melville NY 11746 Office: Manhattan Community College 134 W 51st St New York City NY 10020

JAMES, ERNEST KELLY, lawyer; b. Maple Hill, N.C., June 29, 1895; s. Gibson and Annabelle (Murray) J.; A.B., Maryville (Tenn.) Coll., 1920; J.D., U. Chgo., 1923; m. Mary Summers, July 6, 1929. Admitted to W.Va. bar, 1923; practice of law, specializing pub. utility law and taxation, 1923—; mem. firm McClintic, James, Wise & Robinson. Mem. W. Va. Legislature, 1934-36; state tax commr. W.Va., 1937-41. Served as lt. A.S., U.S. Army, 1917-19. Mem. W.Va. Ry. Assn. (chmn. exec. com.), W.Va. C. of C. (pres. 1947-52, dir.), Am., W.Va. (pres. 1952-53), Charleston bar assns., Am. Judicature Soc., Phi Alpha Delta. Democrat. Presbyn. Mason. Clubs: Edgewood Country. Home: 1213 Upper Ridge Road Charleston WV 25314 Office: Charleston National Bank Bldg Charleston WV 25323

JAMES, ETTA, (Jamisetta Hawkins), singer; b. Los Angeles, 1941. Formerly mem. choir of St. Paul Baptist Ch., Los Angeles, then mem. girl trio, The Peaches; auditioned with bandleader Johnny Otis, 1955; recording artist for Cadet Records (formerly Argo). Named among best vocal groups in Cashbox mag. annual, 1965, also one of best female vocalists. Address: care Cadet Records 2120 S Michigan Av Chicago IL 60616

JAMES, EVAN EDSON, lawyer; b. Chgo., Feb. 19, 1918; s. Grover R. and Pearl (Gregory) J.; A.B., Western Res. U., 1940; J.D., U. Buffalo, 1948; m. M. Elizabeth Haag, Oct. 16, 1944; childrenJoanne (Mrs. Michael Finberg), Evan E., Lewis G., Garrick D. Admitted to N.Y. bar, 1948, since practiced in Buffalo; sr. partner firm Lipsitz, Green, Fahringer, Roll, Schuller & James, 1965—. Chmn., Amherst (N.Y.) Republican Com., 1958-63; mem. exec. com. Erie County Rep. Com., 1963-69; mem. N.Y. State Rep. Com., 1963-69. Served to capt. AUS, 1941-47. Mem. N.Y. State, Erie County (bd. dirs. 1961-64) bar assns., N.Y. State Trial Lawyers Assn., Am. Judicature Soc., Am. Field Service (dist. rep.), State U. N.Y. at Buffalo Alumni Assn. (bd. dirs. 1967-70). Home: 259 Washington Hwy Amherst NY 14226 Office: 1 Niagara Sq Buffalo NY 14202

JAMES, FLEMING, Jr., educator; b. Shanghai, China, Mar. 26, 1904 (parents Am. citizens); s. Fleming and Rebecca (Godwin) J.; A.B., Yale, 1925, LL.B., 1928; LL.D., U. Lund (Sweden), 1968, U. Chgo., 1968; m. Harriet Fairchild, June 26, 1930; children—Fleming, Sarah; m. 2d, Ruth Kaubisch, Nov. 23, 1948. Admitted to Conn. bar, 1928; law clk. Watrous, Hewitt, Sheldon & Gumbart, New Haven, 1928-29; mem. law dept. N.Y., N.H. & H. R.R. Co., 1929-33; asso. prof. Yale, 1933-38, prof. law, 1938-41, Lafayette S. Foster prof. law, 1941-68, Sterling prof. law, 1968—; acting dean U. Utah Sch. Law, 1939-40. Dir. litigation div. O.P.A. (nat. office), 1943-45; vis. prof. law Harvard, 1957- 58, univs. Stockholm, Uppsala, Lund (Sweden), 1968. Mem. North Haven Bd. Edn., 1938-42, Zoning Commn., 1936-39, Town Plan Commn., 1946- 47; chmn. Conn. Bd. Labour Relations, 1955—. Democratic candidate for state senator, 1938, 50; town chmn., North Haven, 1946-48. Mem. Am., Conn., New Haven County bar assns., Phi Beta Kappa, Phi Delta Phi. Club: Corbey Court (Yale Law Sch.). Co-author: Cases on Trials Judgments and Appeals, 1936; Cases and Materials on Torts, 1942; Law of Torts, 1956; author Civil Procedure, 1964. Adviser: Reporter, Torts Restatement. Contbr. articles on torts and civil procedure to profl. jours. Home: 117 State St North Haven CT 06473

JAMES, FLOYD BENJAMINE, constrn. co. exec.; b. Gibsland, La., Jan. 24, 1907; s. Thomas L. and Maggie (Hodges) J.; B.A., U. Tenn., 1927; m. Kathryn Ayres, June 12, 1928; childrenRenna (Mrs. L.O. Burkhalter), Floyd Benjamine, John, Tom. Sec., treas. Ruston (La.) Drilling Co., 1927-33; sec.-treas. T.L. James & Co., Ruston, 1933-44, pres., 1944-68, chmn. bd., 1968-; dir. Central La. Electric Co. Trustee So. Meth. U., La. Meth. Children's Home, Ruston Hosp., Lincoln Hosp., Nat. council Boy Scouts Am. Recipient Silver Beaver, Boy Scouts Am., 1955, Silver Antelope, 1961. Mem. Ind. Petroleum Assn., Phi Kappa Phi, Sigma Chi. Methodist. Kiwanian. Home: 1500 N Trenton St Ruston LA 71270 Office: PO Box O Ruston LA 71270

JAMES, FORREST DONALD, coll. pres.; b. Oklahoma City, Sept. 14, 1927; s. Forrest and Dorothy (Donaldson) J.; A.B. magna cum laude, Oklahoma City U., 1951; S.T.B., Boston U., 1954, Ph.D. (Lucinda Bidwell Beebee fellow), 1959; postgrad. (Rotary Found. fellow) U. Zurich (Switzerland), 1956-57; m. Janet Petree, June 29, 1951; children—Kevin, Kurt. From instr. to asso. prof. Miami U., Oxford, O., 1958-65, asst. dean arts and scis., 1961-64, acting dean arts and scis., 1964-65; v.p. acad. affairs U. R.I., Kingston, 1965-67, acting pres., 1967-68; pres. Central Conn. State Coll., New Britain, 1968—. Corporator, Savs. Bank New Britain, New Britain Gen. Hosp.; trustee New Britain Bank and Trust. Served with USNR, 1945-48. Mem. Am. Assn. for Higher Edn., Soc. Biblical Lit. and Exegesis, Am. Schs. Oriental Research, Am. Acad. Religion, Phi Mu Alpha Sinfonia. Rotarian. Home: 10 Highwood Circle Avon CT 06001 Office: 1615 Stanley St New Britain CT 06050

JAMES, FRANK CYRIL, univ. pres., economist, historian; b. London, Eng., Oct. 8, 1903; s. Frank and Mary Lucy (Brown) J.; student Grocers' Company's Sch., London, 1910-20; B. Commerce, London Sch. of Economics, 1923; A.M., U. of PA., 1924, Ph.D., 1926; hon. D.C.L., Bishops, U. Kansas City; LL.D., U. Brit. Columbia, 1956, Princeton, Queens U., Syracuse U., Ursinus Coll., Cambridge Univ., Glasgow 1953, Rochester, 1954; Toronto U.; New York U.; U. of Saskatchewan, U. of Manitoba, U. of London, U. of Punjab, Lahore, McMaster U., U. of N.B., Northwestern U., 1958, U. of Alberta, 1958, U. Ottawa, 1959; D.Sc., Memorial Univ. of Newfoundland, 1961, Clarkson Coll., U. Punjab (Pakistan), 1962; D.Sc. in economics, Laval U., U. of Pa. Chon.). 1957; Docteur de l'Université de Montréal; m. Irene L.V. Leeper, Aug. 19, 1926. Lived in U.S., 1923-39. Clerk in Barclay's Bank, London, 1921-23; instr. in finance and trans., U. of Pa., 1924-27, asst. prof. of finance, 1927-33, asso. prof., 1933-35, prof., 1935-39, chmn. graduate faculty in social science, 1936-37, prof. of finance and economic history, 1938-39; prof. of polit. economy, McGill Univ., 1939-63, dir. Sch. of Commerce, Sept.-Dec. 1939, principal and vice-chancellor 1939-63, principal emeritus, 1963—. Vice chmn. Commn. Econ. Devel. Quebec, 1960-64. Pres. Internat. Assn. Univs., 1960-66. Chmn. exec. com. Oxford Com. Famine Relief, Eng. Has served in a variety of positions in business, primarily in econ. field; has been adv. to numerous organizations and socs. Decorated Chevalier de la Legion d'Honneur. Fellow Royal Econ. Soc. (London). Royal Soc. (Can.). Member several professional assns. Clubs: Atheneum (London); University, McGill Faculty, Royal Montreal Curling (Montreal); University (N.Y.). Author several books 1926—, including: The Economic Doctrines of John Maynard Keynes (with others), 1938; Economic Problems in a Changing World (with others), 1939; On Understanding Russia, 1960; The Growth of Chicago Banks, 1969. Address: Pipers Croft Devonshire Av Amersham Bucks England ☆

JAMES, GEORGE, physician; b. N.Y.C., Nov. 15, 1915; s. Victor and Lillian (Gilman) J.; A.B., Columbia, 1937; M.D. cum laude, Yale, 1941; M.P.H., Johns Hopkins, 1945; H.L.D., Adelphi U., 1970; m. Beatrice Lucille Kerner, Dec. 16, 1939; 1 dau., Barbara. Intern pediatrics New Haven Hosp., also asst. pediatrics Yale Sch. Medicine, 1941-42; dir. Obion Lake (Tenn.) Health Dist., 1942-44; mem. staff N.Y. State Dept. Health, 1945-55, regional health dir. liaison with N.Y.C., 1951-52, asst. commr. program devel. and evaluation, also liaison with N.Y.C., 1952-55; lab. asst. biostatistics Johns Hopkins Sch. Hygiene and Pub. Health, 1946; asst. clin. prof. pub. health practice Yale Sch. Medicine, 1947-52; mem. faculty Albany Med. Coll., Union U., 1949-55, asso. prof. preventive medicine and pub. health, 1954-55; dir. health Akron (O.) City Dept. Health, 1955-56; mem. staff N.Y.C. Dept. Health, 1956-65, 1st dep. commr., 1959-62, commr. health, chmn. bd. health, 1962-65; adj. asso. prof., then adj. prof. Columbia Sch. Adminstrv. Medicine and Pub. Health, 1956-65; pres. Mt. Sinai Med. Center, Mt. Sinai Sch. Medicine, Mt. Sinai Hosp., 1968—; prof. dept. community medicine, dean Mt. Sinai Sch. Medicine, City U. N.Y., 1965—; professorial lectr. preventive medicine St. John's Sch. Edn., 1957-63; vis. lectr. Harvard Sch. Pub. Health, 1962-63. Pres. N.Y. State Conf. County, City and Dist. Health Officers, 1961-62; exec. com. Health Research Council N.Y.C., 1962—; mem. Hosp. Rev. and Planning Council So. N.Y. and N.Y. State, 1962-65; mem. President's Task Force on Health, 1964-65; bd. mgrs. State Communities Aid Assn., 1966—; subcom. edn. and supply, Nat. Adv. Com. Med. Manpower, 1966-67; mem. N.Y.C. Community Mental Health Bd., 1962-65, Greater N.Y. Safety Council, 1966-70; Nat. Council Alcolholism, 1967-70, N.Y. Blood Center; cons. N.Y. State Joint Legislative Com. Problems Pub. Health and Medicare, 1966-69, ad hoc com. narcotic addiction President's Office Sci. and Tech., 1962-63, White House Conf. Narcotic Addiction, 1963; Wooldridge com. evaluation program NIH, 1964-65, chmn. study sect. regional med. programs, 1966-69, vice chmn. regional med. programs, 1969—; chmn. nat. conf. pub. health training USPHS, 1967; Lasker Journalism Award Com., 1964-66; Lasker Med. Research Award Com., 1967—; cons. USPHS, WHO; Sheckman lectr. Soc. Pub. Health Edn., 1962; Crocker lectr. Roosevelt Hosp., N.Y.C., 1964; Harold Jacobziner lectr. N.Y.U., 1971; sec. Health, Edn. and Welfare's Rev. Com. Prescription Drugs, 1969. Pres. bd. trustees Med. Library Center; trustee Case Western Res. U., 1969—, Continental Research Inst., 1970—. Recipient Campbell Gold medal Yale Sch. Medicine, 1941; Bronfman award Am. Pub. Health Assn., 1965; Meritorious Service award Nat. Found. Neuromuscular Diseases, 1966; Hermann M. Biggs Meml. award, N.Y. State Pub. Health Assn. Diplomate Nat. Bd. of Medical Examiners, Am. Bd. Preventive Medicine and Pub. Health. Fellow Royal Soc. Health, A.M.A., Am. Pub. Health Assn., N.Y. Acad. Sci.; mem. N.Y. Acad. Medicine (anniversary discourse 1964), N.Y.C. Pub. Health Assn. (pres. 1961-62), N.Y. Diabetes Assn. (dir. 1964-67), Am. Hosp. Assn., N.Y. State Acad. Preventive Medicine (exec. bd. 1956-62, pres. 1960- 61), N.Y. State, N.Y. County med. socs., Hosp. Soc. N.Y., A.A.A.S., Am. Coll. Preventive Medicine (v.p. 1964), Asso. Hosp. Service N.Y. (dir. 1965—), Am. Thoracic Soc., Am. Assn. Pub. Health Physicians, Harvey Soc., Nat. Health Council (pres. 1965-66), Assn. Tchrs. Preventive Medicine, Internat. Health Adv. Council, Am. Health Fedn. (trustee 1969, chmn. sci. com. 1968), Phi Beta Kappa, Alpha Omega Alpha. Clubs: Columbia, Yale (N.Y.C.). Presbyn. Author numerous articles in field. Editorial bd. Med. Opinion & Review, Inc., 1965-71. Home: 45 E 89th St New York City NY 10028 also 155 Peninsula Dr Babylon NY 11702 Office: Fifth Av and 100th St New York City NY 10029

JAMES, GEORGE FRANCIS, lawyer, univ. dean; b. Mpls., June 12, 1909; s. George Francis and Pauline (Sholes) J.; Ph.B., U. Chgo., 1930, J.D., 1932; LL.M., Columbia, 1934; m. Mary Ella Bickell, Sept. 1, 1934; children—George Francis (dec.), Suzanne, Victoria Ten Eyck. Admitted to Ill. bar, 1932, practiced in Chgo., 1932-42; asso. prof., asst. dean Law Sch., U. Chgo., 1939-42; chief price adjustment sec. Chgo. Ordnance Dist., War Dept., 1943-44; tax atty. Standard-Vacuum Oil Co., N.Y.C., 1944- 49, treas., 1949-51, dir. 1951-57; chmn. bd. Vacuum Oil Co. (Australia), 1957-58; asst. to v.p. finance Mobil Oil Corp., N.Y.C., 1958- 59, sr. v.p. finance, 1959-69, also dir.; dean Grad. Sch. Bus., Columbia, 1969—; dir. Equitable Life Assurance Soc., Huyck Corp., Edie Spl. Growth Fund, F.W. Woolworth Co. Trustee Com. on Econ. Devel. Mem. Council Fgn. Relations, Phi Beta Kappa, Delta Upsilon, Phi Delta Phi. Republican. Episcopalian. Clubs: Union League (N.Y.C.); Golf (Scarsdale, N.Y.). Home: 870 UN Plaza New York City NY 10027

JAMES, GEORGE WILLIAM, constrn. co. exec.; b. Dubach, La., Mar. 11, 1909; s. Thomas Lewis and Margaret D. (Hodges) J.; student U. Tenn., 1925-27; A.B., Centenary Coll., 1929; postgrad. Harvard Grad. Sch. Bus. Adminstrn., 1929; m. Sarah Bond, Sept. 26, 1930; children—George William, Thomas Dawson, Robert Bond. Pres., T.L. James & Co., Inc., Ruston, La., 1930—; pres., dir. Prestressed Concrete Products Co., Inc., Mandeville, La.; dir. First Nat. Bank, Ruston, La. Ark. Ry. Co. Trustee Centenary Coll., Fellowship Christian Athletics Found. Mem. Asso. Gen. Contractors Am., Sigma Chi. Methodist. Home: 914 N Vienna St Ruston LA 71270 Office: PO Box O Ruston LA 71270

JAMES, HAL, theatrical producer; b. Chgo.; ed. U. Chgo. Played title role in Andrew Jackson at U. Chgo.; played stage mgr. in world premier Happy Journey from Trenton to Camden; later spent 2 years on Broadway, 3 summers with Mohawk Drama Festival; then became writer, dir., producer on radio and TV, asso. with programs including Cities Service Band of Am., Milton Berle Show, Against the Storm, Playwrights Theatre; producer stage play Man of La Mancha; co-producer Hallelujah, Baby (Tony award for best musical 1968).

JAMES, HAROLD ARTHUR, lawyer; b. Youngstown, O., Oct. 4, 1903; s. Arthur and Webster Minnie (Williams) J.; Ph.B., Denison U., 1926; LL.B., Ohio State U., 1929; m. Alice Beaver McCann, Nov. 7, 1929; children—Franklin D., Arthur F., Douglas H. Admitted to Ohio bar, 1929; practiced in Toledo, 1929—; partner firm Doyle, Lewis & Warner, 1937—. Chmn. cts. com. Toledo Bar Assn.-Reorgn. Ct. Rules, 1952-53. Pres., dir. Jesse James Enterprises, Inc.; dir. Lamson Brothers Co., Nazar Rubber Co., Jobst Inst., Inc. Commr., Nat. Commn. Community Health Services, 1963-67. Trustee, v.p. Toledo YMCA, 1950—, pres., 1965-69; mem. Nat. council YMCA, 1968—; mem. board directors Greater Toledo Community Chest, 1954-62; bd. dirs. Toledo Council Social Agencies, 1952-62, pres., 1958-59; trustee Greater Toledo Area C. of C., 1959-60, Ohio Baptist Conv. Endowment Fund, 1954—, Ohio Council Chs. Found., 1961-69; bd. dirs., treas. Hosp. Planning Assn. Toledo, 1960-68; bd. dirs. Ohio Citizens Council Health and Welfare, 1957—, pres., 1961-63; chmn. Community Planning Adv. Council, 1961-67; bd. dirs. United Community Funds and Councils Am., 1961-69, v.p., 1963—. Recipient Distinguished Service award Toledo Council Social Agencies, 1963; alumni citation Denison U., 1966. Member of Am., Ohio, Toledo bar assns., Ohio Soc. N.Y., Kappa Sigma, Phi Delta Phi. Republican. Baptist. Club: Toledo. Home: 4922 Courville Rd Toledo OH 43523 Office: Nat Bank Bldg Toledo OH 43604

JAMES, HAROLD LLOYD, geologist; b. Nanaimo, B.C., Can., June 11, 1912; s. Evan and Blodwen (Davies) J.; came to U.S., 1923, naturalized, 1933; student Western Wash. Coll., 1933; B.S., Wash. State U., 1938; student U. Wash., 1938- 40; Ph.D., Princeton, 1945; m. Ruth Graybeal, Feb. 13, 1936; childrenDavid E., Robert C.L., Hugh L., Herbert T. Field asst. U.S. Geol. Survey, 1939-40, geologist, 1941-61, 64-65, chief geologist, 1965- -; vis. lectr. Northwestern U., 1952-53; prof. geology U. Minn., 1961-64. Mem. Nat. Acad. Scis., Mineral. Soc. Am. (council 1964-), Soc. Econ. Geologists (council 1962-65, pres. 1970), Geol. Soc. Am. (council 1959-62), Geochem. Soc., Am. Geophys. Union, Phi Beta Kappa, Sigma Xi, Phi Kappa Phi. Home: 1001 Wilson Blvd Arlington VA 22209 Office: U S Geol Survey DC 20242

JAMES, HARRY HAAG, dance band leader; b. Albany, Ga., Mar. 15, 1916; s. Everette Robert and Maybelle (Stewart) J.; ed. grade and high school, Beaumont, Tex.; m. Louise Tobin, May 4, 1935; childrenHarry Jefferey, Timothy Ray; m. 2d Elizabeth Grable, July 5, 1943 (div. 1965); children—Victoria Victoria Elizabeth, and Jessica; m. 3d, Joan Boyd. His parents were circus people and the early years were spent with the circus; his father taught him to play the trumpet and at age 14 he played in local dance bands, Beaumont; traveled with Joes Gale's orchestra at age 15; played with Ben Pollock's orchestra, 1935-36, with Benny Goodman's orchestra, 1937-39; organized his own orchestra, Jan. 1939, later adding a string quartet to usual instrumentation; made recording of "You Made Me Love You," spring 1941 (has sold over a million copies); went to Hollywood for motion pictures, spring 1942; played on Coca Cola Spotlight Saturday Show, 7 times, 1942; returned to N.Y. City and played at Hotel Astor and again on Spotlight Show; now appearing TV, clubs in various cities. Numerous motion pictures. Received No. 1 rating for swing bands from Radio Daily Poll, 1942. Address: 1009 N Beverly Dr Beverly Hills CA 90210 ☆

JAMES, HELEN SOYARS, constrn. co. exec.; b. Nashville, Nov. 20, 1904; d. William Witcher and Laura (Temple) Soyars; student U. Tenn., 1923-25; m. Thomas Lewis James, Jr., Oct. 25, 1925; children—Jacqueline (Mrs. Hamp H. Hanks), Laura (Mrs. Alex T. Hunt, Jr.). With T.L. James & Co., Inc., Ruston, La., 1934—, treas., 1960, also dir. Active local Girls Scouts, Ruston Symphony, La. Found., Women's Soc. Christian Service, Garden Club, Little Theatre, P.T.A., Hosp. Aux. Mem. Sigma Kappa. Methodist. Address: TL James & Co Inc Florida and Bonner Sts Ruston LA 71270

JAMES, HENRY THOMAS, found. exec.; b. Ferryville, Wis., May 19, 1915; s. Harry T. and Alice (Morgan(J.; B.S., Wis. State U., 1938; Ph.M., U. Wis., 1939; Ph.D., U. Chgo., 1958; m. Vienna Lewis, June 6, 1939; children—Angelyn Alice (Mrs. Richard J. Grillo), Henry Thomas, Jennifer Lewis, Mary Ellen, Elizabeth Elinor, Arthur Earl. High sch. tchr., Barron, Wis. 1939- 42; supervising prin., Woodville, Wis., 1942-43; counselor U. Wis., Madison, 1946; supt. schs., Augusta, Wis., 1946-49, Whitewater, Wis., 1949-50; asst. supt. pub. instrn. Wis., 1950-54; lectr. U. Mich., 1954; asso. dir. Midwest Adminstrn. Center, asst. prof., asso. prof., dir. field services U. Chgo., Sch. Edn., 1954-58; prof. Stanford Sch. Edn., 1958-70, dean, 1966-70; pres. Spencer Found., Chgo., 1970—. Cons. in field, 1954—; dir. studies sch. bds. and state sch. finance systems 1954-; adviser subcom. efficiency and innovation in edn. Com. Econ. Devel. Served to lt. USNR, 1943-46. Mem. Am. Ednl. Research Assn. (chmn. nominating com. 1964-65; cons. editor jour. 1964- -, program chmn. 1968), Am. Assn. Sch. Adminstrs., Nat. Acad. Edn., Univ. Council Ednl. Adminstrn. Presbyn. Club: Quadrangle (Chgo.). Sr. author: School Revenues Systems in Five States, 1961; Wealth, Expenditures and Decision-Making for Education, 1963; Determinants of Educational Expenditures in Large Cities of the United States, 1966; The New Cult of Efficiency in Education, 1969. Editor: Boardmanship, 1961. Contbr. articles to profl. jours. Home: 175 E Delaware Pl Chicago IL 60611

JAMES, HERBERT ISIDOR, chemist; b. St. Thomas, V.I., Mar. 30, 1933; s. Henry O. and Frances (Smith) J.; B.S., Hampton Inst., 1955; M.A., Clark U., 1958, Ph.D., 1965; m. Christine M. Stolz, Nov. 29, 1962; children—Herbert Isidor, Robyn. Instr. math. and sci. Hampton Inst., 1958-61; instr. math. and sci. Exptl. Coll. of V.I., 1960-61; instr. math. Charlotte Amalie (V.I.) High Sch., 1960-61; research scientist Electric Storage Battery, Inc., Yardley, Pa., 1965—; stock broker, financial planner, life ins. broker. Commnr. Episcopal Restitution Fund. Commn. Recipient VIPAC award, 1965. Mem. Am. Chem. Soc., Electrochemical Soc., A.A.A.S., Instrument Soc. Am., Beta Kappa Chi, Alpha Kappa Mu. Contbr. articles profl. jours. Patentee in field. Home: 8 Harp Rd Levittown PA 19056 Office: 19 W College Av Yardley PA 19067

JAMES, HERMAN BROOKS, educator; b. nr. Oakboro, N.C., Aug. 27, 1912; s. Martin L. and Carrie Ellen (Brooks) J.; B.S., N.C. State Coll., 1932, M.S., 1940; Ph.D., Duke, 1949; m. Verna Lee Greene, May 31, 1941; children—David Brooks, Sarah Ellen. Tchr. vocational agr., Knightdale, N.C., 1933; county agt., Montgomery County, N.C., 1934-38; farm mgmt. specialist N.C. Agr. Extension Service, Raleigh, N.C., 1939-42; agrl. economist Appalachian and S.E. regions U.S. Dept. Agr., 1943-44, Dept. Agr. adv. com. on agrl. econs., Raleigh, 1954—; in charge farm mgmt. extension dept. N.C. State Coll., 1945-46; charge teaching and farm mgmt. research, dept. agrl. econs. as prof. agrl. econs., 1947-49; head dept. agr. econs., N.C. State U., 1949-57, dir. instrn. Sch. Agr., 1958-60, prof., dean agr., 1960-70; v.p. in charge research and pub. service programs Consol. U. N.C., 1970—. Asst. adminstr. Office War on Hunger, AID, 1968; AID cons. Peru, 1962, Nicaragua, 1964, Laos, 1965, Africa, 1966; mem. Nat. Agr. Research Adv. Com., 1965-69; adv. com. Kellogg Found., 1963-67; chmn. com. agrl. econs. Social Sci. Research Council, 1954-56; mem. adv. bd. Nat. Agrl. Extension Center for Advanced Study, 1961-66; chmn. deans agr. Nat. Assn. State Univs. and Land Grant Colls., 1968. Mem. Am., So. econ. assns., Am. Agr. Econ. Assn. (pres. 1956-57), Nat. Acad. Scis. (agrl. bd. 1956-57), So. Farm Mgmt. Research Com. (chmn. 1949-51), Grange, Farm Bur., Alpha Zeta, Phi Kappa Phi, Kappa Phi Kappa. Author numerous expt. sta. bulls., circulars. Contbr. articles to profl. jours. Home: 1323 Lutz Av Raleigh NC 27607

JAMES, HOWARD ANTHONY, journalist, author; b. Iowa City, May 28, 1935; s. Howard Anthony and Catherine (Richey) J.; B.A., Mich. State U., 1958; m. Dorothy Spear Fontaine, Aug. 25, 1956; children—Paul Cooper, Heidi Sue. Radio and TV news reporter, 1955-60, pub. weekly newspaper, Mich., 1959; reporter Chgo. Tribune, 1960-63; city-state editor Morning Democrat, Davenport, Ia., 1963-64; pub. relations dir. Chgo. met. dist. Montgomery Ward & Co., 1964; with Christian Sci. Monitor, 1964-, Midwestern news bur. chief, 1965—; mem. editorial adv. bd. Am. Judicature Soc., 1968—. Mem. law and govt. task force Urban Coalition, 1969—. Recipient Silver Gavel award Am. Bar Assn., 1968, Pub. Service award Am. Trial Lawyers' Assn., 1968, Pub. Service award Am. Trial

Lawyers' Assn., 1968. Author: Crisis in the Courts (Pulitzer prize nat. reporting 1968, Sidney Hillman Found. award 1968), 1968. Home: Wheaton IL 60187 Office: 332 N Michigan Av Chicago IL 60601

JAMES, HUBERT MAXWELL, physicist; b. Clarksburg, W.Va., Mar. 10, 1908; s. Ernest Wilbur and Edna Virginia (Maxwell) J.; A.B., Randolph-Macon Coll., 1928, D.Sc., 1955; A.M., Harvard, 1930, Ph.D., 1934; D.Sc., Otterbein Coll., 1971; m. Madeline Roxane Fitzpatrick, Aug. 29, 1932; 1 dau., Martha Virginia. Asst. prof. physics Purdue U., West Lafayette, Ind., 1936-38, asso. prof., 1938-44, prof., 1944—, acting head dept. physics, 1958-59, head, 1959-66; on leave for research as Guggenheim Meml. Found. fellow, Oslo, Norway, 1939-40; on leave to work on radar problems Mass. Inst. Tech. Radiation Lab., 1941-46; tech. editor Radiation Lab. Series. Fellow Am. Phys. Soc. (chmn. high-polymer div. 1948); mem. Am. Assn. Physics Tchrs., Am. Assn. U. Profs., Phi Beta Kappa, Sigma Xi, Chi Beta Phi, Sigma Pi Sigma, Kappa Alpha. Methodist. Co-author: Advances in Colloid Science, Vol. II, 1946. Editor and co-author: Theory of Servomechanism, 1947. Contbr. articles profl. jours. Home: 316 Forest Hill Dr West Lafayette IN 47906

JAMES, JAMES CHARLES, lawyer; b. Aurora, Ill., Feb. 21, 1882; s. George Albert and Mary (Rooney) J.; A.B., U. of Wis., 1904; student George Washington U. Law Sch.; m. Julia Brady Haring, July 11, 1910; childrenMarion, Martha, James Charles, Jr. Admitted to Ill. bar, 1905, Supreme Court U.S., 1926; practiced law at Aurora, Ill., 1905-17; asst. state's attorney Kane County, Ill., 1907-10; mem. firm of Alschuler, Putnam & James, Aurora, 1910-17; local atty. C.,B.& Q. R.R. Co., 1914-17; asst. to Ill. dist. atty., same road, Chicago, 1917-19, gen. atty., 1919-24, gen. solicitor, 1924-38, gen. counsel, 1938-49, v.p. and dir., 1939- 49, mem. exec. com., 1941, exec. v.p., gen. counsel 1949-52, ret., 1952, dir. mem. exec. com., 1962-. Dir. Aurora Found. Mem. adv. bd. St. Joseph Mercy Hosp. Mem. Phi Kappa Psi. Republican. Club: Chicago. Home: 909 Downer Pl Aurora IL 60506 Office: 547 W Jackson Blvd Chicago IL 60606

JAMES, JOHN WILLIAM, research exec.; b. Brookville, Ind., Jan. 12, 1907; s. Charles M. and Mary Louisa (Fieber) J.; B.S., Ore. State Coll., 1928; M.S., U. Wis., 1934; m. Helen Penn Hill, Aug. 27, 1938; children—Virginia, Kathryn. Cons. engr., Portland, Ore., 1928-32; research fellow U. Wis., 1932-34; engr. Gen. Electric Co., Schenectady, 1934-35; tech. sec. Am. Soc. Heating and Air Conditioning Engrs., N.Y.C., 1935-43, tech. editor A.S.H.A.E. Guide, 1936-43; instr. Poly. Inst. Bklyn., 1936-39; research engr. Iron Fireman Mfg. Co., Cleve., 1943-48; v.p. research McDonnell & Miller, Inc., Chgo., 1948—, Profl. engr., Ore., O., Ill. Fellow Am. Soc. Heating, Air Conditioning Engrs. (nat. 2d v.p. 1954, 1st v.p. 1955, pres., 1956); mem. Am. Soc. M.E. (boiler and pressure vessel com.), Instrument Soc. Am., A.A.A.S., Am. Soc. San. Engrs., N.A.M., Western Soc., Engrs., The Engrs. Club N.Y.C., Gas Appliance Engrs. Soc., Instn. Heating and Ventilating Engrs., London, Sigma Xi, Pi Tau Sigma, Phi Sigma Kappa. Author: Heating and Air Conditioning (with Allen, Walker), 1946. Asso. editor: Handbook of Oil Burning, 1951. Contbr. Kent's Mech. Engrs. Handbook, 12th edit., 1950. Home: 2320 Greenwood Av Wilmette IL 60091 Office: 3500 N Spaulding Av Chicago IL 60618

JAMES, JOYCE BAILEY, account exec., former army officer; b. Bay Village, Ark., Aug. 14, 1917; s. Garland and Belle (Curtner) J.; grad. Command and Gen. Staff Coll., 1955, Army War Coll., 1965; m. Patricia June High, Mar. 14, 1939; children—Constance, Corinne. Enlisted in U.S. Army, 1935, commd. 2d lt., 1942, advanced through grades to brig. gen., 1966; mem. staff and faculty Officer Candidate Sch., 1942-44; comdg. officer signal bn., New Guinea and Phillipines, 1944-47; exec. officer Alaska Communication System, 1947- 50; operations officer Long Lines Signal Group, Korea, 1950-52; signal officer U.S. Army Pacific, 1952-54; chief combat devels. U.S. Army Signal Corps, 1955-59; comdg. officer U.S. Army Middle East Regional Command, Asmara, Ethiopia, 1959-63; dep. comdg. gen. U.S. Army Strategic Communications Command, 1965-67; dep. chief staff communications and electronics N.Am. Air Def. Command, Colorado Springs, Colo., 1967-71; prin. account exec. Raytheon Data Systems Co., Washington, 1971—. Decorated Army Commendation medal, Legion of Merit with oak leaf cluster, D.S.M. Mem. Assn. U.S. Army, Armed Forces Communications and Electronics Assn. (bd. govs. Pikes Peak chpt. 1967-68), Old Crows Assn. (pres. Pikes Peak roost 1968-69). Democrat. Episcopalian. Mason (32, Shriner); mem. Order Eastern Star. Home: 301 N Beauregard St Apt 604 Alexandria VA 22312 Office: Raytheon Data Systems Co Washington DC

JAMES, L. ELDON, lawyer; b. Dendron, Surry County, Va., Jan. 1, 1913; s. Leonard Wallace and Lillian (Noyes) J.; B.S., William and Mary Coll., 1934, student Marshall Wythe Sch. Law, 1933-35; LL.B., George Washington U., 1937; m. Aurelia Mitchell, Feb. 17, 1939; children—Aurelia Quinby (Mrs. Charles R. Amory, Jr.), Nancy Noyes (Mrs. John Martin Buhl, Jr.), Sally Leonard, Leonard Eldon. Admitted to Va. bar, 1935; legal and legislative asst. U.S. Employment Service, Dept. Labor, 1937-39; personnel classifications Social Security Bd., 1939-41; chief personnel classification Bur. Ships, Navy Dept. 1941-44, dir. personnel, 1947-50; partner firm James, Richardson & James, Hampton, Va., 1950—. Past pres. Peninsula Health Fund; past vice chmn. citizens adv. com. Hampton Salvation Army. Bd. dirs. Tidewater chpt. Cystic Fibrosis Found., Peninsula United Fund, Dixie Hosp., Hampton; bd. dirs., past pres. Am. Legion Child Welfare Found. Served to lt. USNR, 1944-46. Mem. Va. State Bar (council), Am., Va. bar assns., Va. Trial Lawyers Assn., Peninsula C. of C. (bd. dirs.), Am. Legion (nat. comdr. 1965-66), Sigma Phi Epsilon. Lion (past pres., mem. bd. Hampton). Home: 9 Terrace Rd Hampton VA 23361 Office: P O Box 38 Hampton VA 23369

JAMES, LEONARD GAGE, lawyer; b. St. Louis, June 4, 1912; s. Charles Couch and Blanche (Mantler) J.; grad. Phillips Exeter Acad., 1931; A.B., Yale, 1935; LL.B., Harvard, 1938; m. Marjorie Haines, Apr. 22, 1939 (dec. Oct. 11, 1968). m. 2d, Fritze Winkler, Jan. 17, 1970. Admitted to N.Y. bar, 1939, Cal. bar, 1948, Japanese bar, 1942, U.S. Supreme Ct. bar, 1968, D.C. bar, 1968; practiced in San Francisco, 1947—; sr. partner firm Graham and James, 1950—; Am. counsel and adv. for European, Scandinavian, U.K. and Far East shipping concerns and govts. on internat. trade and shipping matters. Asst. gen. counsel Navy Dept., 1943-45; spl. adviser War Shipping Adminstrn., 1945-46; U.S. rep. Com. European Shipowners, 1958—; U.S. atty. Pacific Coast European Conf., Latin Am. and Far Eastern confs. on internat. shipping, 1950—. Dir. P & O Orient Lines, Interocean S.S. Corp., Marine Chartering Co., Inc. Mem. World Peace Through Law Center. Mem. Am. Judicature Soc., Am. Fed. Inter-Am. bar assns., Am.- Netherlands (dir.), Swedish-Am., Brit.-Am. chambers commerce, Cal. Marine Parks and Harbors Assn. (past pres., dir.), World Affairs Council, Alpha Sigma Phi. Clubs: Commonwealth, World Trade, Yacht, Propeller, Harvard, Yale (San Francisco). Contbr. to shipping and legal jours. Home: 70 San Carlos Av Sausalito CA 94965 Office: 310 Sansome St San Francisco CA 94104

JAMES, LEONARD STANLEY, educator, pediatrician; b. New Zealand, Nov. 2, 1924; s. Leonard Arnold and Constance (Kempthorne) J.; M.B., Ch.B., Otago U., 1948. Came to U.S., 1953. Intern. then resident Auckland (N.Z.) Hosp., 1949-50; gen. practice, 1951-52; resident Hosp. Sick Children, Toronto, Can., 1952-53; chief resident pediatrics Bellevue Hosp. N.Y.C., 1953-54; research tng. N.Y. State U. and Coll. Phys. and Surg., Columbia, 1954-55; mem. faculty Columbia Coll. Phys. and Surg., 1955-, prof. pediatrics, 1967-. Recipient E. Mead Johnson award, 1965; Arthur Parmelee Meml. lectr. Los Angeles Pediatric Soc., 1962; Windemere lectr. Brit. Pediatric Assn., 1966; Rackford Meml. lectr. Children Hosp. Cin. Mem. Am. Soc. Pediatric Research, Am. Pediatric Soc., Am. Acad. Pediatrics. Home: 20 E 23d St New York City NY 10010

JAMES, LOUIS G., b. Ft. Worth, 1905. Exec. v.p. finance and accounting, also dir. Lone Star Producing Co., now pres.; vice chmn., former pres., exec. v.p. finance and accounting Lone Star Gas Co.; exec. v.p. finance and accounting. dir. Lone Star Gathering Co., now pres. Home: 6715 Stichter St Dallas TX 75230 Office: 301 S Harwood St Dallas TX 75201*

JAMES, OLIVER BURR, banker; b. N.Y.C., Feb. 11, 1925; s. Oliver Burr and Angeline Jackson (Krech) J.; grad. Groton Sch., 1942; B.A., Yale, 1947; J.D., Columbia, 1950; m. Norma Elaine McNeill, Feb. 14, 1955; children—Patricia (Mrs. Stephen Yetter), Oliver Burr. Admitted to N.Y. bar, 1950; law asso. firm Sullivan & Cromwell, N.Y.C., 1950; with San Diego Trust & Savs. Bank, 1956—, exec. v.p., trust officer, 1957—; dir. Brit. Motor Sales San Diego. Pres. San Diego Symphony, 1964, San Diego Mus. Assn., 1967-68; treas. San Diego Children's Hosp., 1971. Mem. Mayor's Com. on Municipal Finance, 1966—; city commr., San Diego, 1959-64. Bd. dirs. United Community Services. Served from ensign to comdr., USNR, 1943-46, 51-56. Mem. Chi Psi, Phi Delta Phi. Republican. Episcopalian. Clubs: San Diego Yacht, University (San Diego); La Jolla Country, La Jolla Beach. Home: 1504 Buckingham Dr La Jolla CA 92037 Office: 540 Broadway San Diego CA 92101

JAMES, OLLIE MURRAY, newspaperman; b. Kuttawa, Ky., Oct. 16, 1908; s. Edgar Harrison and Mary (Campbell) J.; student U. Louisville, U. Ky.; m. Elizabeth Hazelrigg Hall, Dec. 31, 1931. Reporter, polit. writer, legislative corr. Lexington (Ky.) Herald, 1928-34; reporter, Washington corr., asso. editor Louisville Herald-Post, 1934-36; editorial writer, asst. mng. editor Cin. Enquirer, 1936-44, chief editorial writer, 1944—; editor Union Central Advocate, nat. policyholders' publ. Union Central Life Ins. Co.; writer column Innocent Bystander; speaker, master ceremonies various radio and TV shows. Trustee voting trust Cin. Enquirer, Inc. Recipient Ohio Gov.'s award for advancement of prestige of Ohio, 1970. Mem. Nat. Conf. Editorial Writers, Sigma Nu, Sigma Delta Chi. Author: Splendid Century. Contbr. articles to mags. Home: 1885 Dixie Hwy Fort Mitchell Covington KY 41017 Office: 617 Vine St Cincinnati OH 65202

JAMES, PHILIP, (Frederick Wright), composer, conductor; b. Jersey City, May 17, 1890 s. Philip William and Ernestine (Wildhagen) J.; ed. Coll. City N.Y.; Mus.D., N.Y. Coll. Music, 1946; m. Millicent Eady, Sept. 7, 1916 (dec. July 1945); m. 2d, Helga Boyer, Feb. 3, 1952; children—Vivian, Philip. Mus. dir. operettes for Victor Herbert and prodns. Winthrop Ames, N.Y.C., 1911-16; condr. Bklyn. Orchestral Soc., N.J. Symphony Orch.; prof. music, head music dept., N.Y. U., now prof. emeritus; instr. music, Columbia v.p. Llangollen Internat. Mus. Eisteddfod, North Wales; condr. Bamberger Symphony Orch., Radio Sta. WOR; Guest condr. Nat. Symphony Orch., Washington, N.Y. Orch., NBC Orch., Phila. Orch., CBS, N.Y. Philharmonic-Symphony Orch., Bronx Symphony Orch. Served as 2d lt., inf., U.S. Army, later bandmaster and comdg. officer A.E.F. Hdgrs. Band, World War. Recipient 1st prize ($5000) NBC for suite for orch.; hon. mention for overture Bret Harte Philharmonic Symphony Soc. N.Y., 1937; Juilliard Found. Publ. award, 1937; 1st prize Women's Symphony Orch. N.Y., 1938; award of merit for outstanding service to Am. music Nat. Assn. Am. Composers and Conductors, 1970.hon. fellow Trinity Coll., London, Eng., 1938; Mem. Nat. Inst. of Arts and Letters, Soc. Publ. Am. Music (chmn. bd), Am. Musicol. Soc., MacDowell Allied Mems. (pres. 1953), Edw. MacDowell Assn. (v.p.), A.S.C.A.P., Phi Beta Kappa, Mu Sigma. Episcopalian. Club: Century Assn. (N.Y.C.). Composer two symphonies, five suites, seven concert overtures, choral works, chamber music and songs. Home: 29 Oak Tree Lane Manhasset NY 11030

JAMES, POE, screenwriter; b. Dobbs Ferry, N.Y., Oct. 4, 1921; s. James and Peggy (Bobbit) P.; student St. John's Coll.; children-Lorna, Adam, Jonathan. Engaged in motion picture industry, 1941—; pres. James Poe Co., Inc., 1967- -; credits include Around the World in 80 Days, Cat on a Hot Tin Roof, Attacks!, Big Knife, Hot Spell, Summer and Smoke, Toys in the Attic, The Bedford Incident, Lilies of the Field, They Shoot Horses, Don't They?. Mem. bd. Nat. Council Arts and Govt., 1965—. Served as aviator USNR, World War II; ETO. Recipient award Am. Acad. Motion Picture Arts and Scis., 1957, 3 nominations; award Screen Writers Guild, 1957, 63, Writers Guild Am. West, 1957, 63, 69; Laurel award, 1971. Mem. Writers Guild Am. West (pres. screen br. 1965-67), Acad. Motion Picture Arts and Scis., Screen Dirs. Guild, Film Editors Guild. Address: 760 N La Cienga Blvd Los Angeles CA 90069

JAMES, PRESTON EVERETT, ret. educator; b. Brookline, Mass., Feb. 14, 1899; s. Frank Everett and Gertrude (Woodworth) J.; A.B., Harvard, 1920, A.M., 1921; Ph.D., Clark U., 1923, LL.D., 1968; Sc.D., Eastern Mich. U., 1967; m. Dorothy Tenney Upham, Apr. 3, 1922 (div.); m. 2d, Eileen Woodbury Bowles, July 23, 1943; 1 son, Everett Woodbury. Teaching asst. geography Harvard U. 1919-21, Radcliffe Coll. 1920; instr. Clark U. 1921-23; instr. U. Mich., 1923-24, asst. prof., 1924-28, asso. prof., 1928-34, prof. geography, 1934-45; prof. geography Syracuse U., 1945-70, chmn. dept., 1951-68, Frank Smalley prof. geography, 1961-64, Maxwell prof. geography, 1964-70, Maxwell prof. emeritus, 1970—; geog. cons. Conselho Nacional de Geografia (Brazil), 1949- 50; chief Latin-Am. div. O.S.S., 1941-43, Europe-Africa div., 1943- 45; Fulbright prof. U. Edinburgh, 1957; vis. prof. U. P.R., 1971. Mem. NRC 1937-40, vice chmn. div. geology and geography, 1939-40; U.S. mem. Commn. on Geog., Pan-Am. Inst. Geog. and Hist., 1949- 57; mem. U.S. Exchange Mission to Soviet Union, 1963; chief U.S. del. 1st consultation in geog., Rio de Janeiro, 1949, chmn. 3d consultation, Washington, 1952, chief U.S. del. 4th consultation, Mexico, 1954; chief U.S. delegation, meeting commn. Rio de Janeiro, 1956; mem. U.S. delegation to 18th Internat. Geog. Congress, Rio de Janeiro, 1956, 20th, London, 1964, 21st, New Delhi, India, 1968. Mem. com. on geo- physics and geography Research and Devel. Bd., 1948-53. Served in O.T.S., U.S. Army, Camp Lee, Va., 1918; M.I. Res. 1923-57; in active service, U.S. Army, Aug. 1942-Nov. 1945, ret. col., 1957. Recipient Distinguished Writing award Nat. Council Geog. Edn., 1963, Distinguished Service award, 1964; George Morgan Ward medal Rollins Coll., 1964; Pan Am. medal Pan Am. Inst. Geography and History, 1965; Livingstone Centenary medal Am. Geog. Soc., 1966. Mem. Am. Geophys. Union, Assn. Am. Geographers (pres. 1951; hon. pres. 1966), Am. Geog. Soc. N.Y., Am. Meteorol. Society, A.A.A.S., Nat. Council Geog. Edn., Nat. Council for Social Studies, Council for Latin Am. Affairs (pres. 1957), Phi Kappa Phi, Sigma Xi. Unitarian. Clubs: Onandaga Country; Skaneateles COuntry; Cosmos (Washington); University, Rotary (Syracuse, N.Y.). Author: An Outline of Geography, 1935; Latin America, 1942, rev. edits., 1950, 59, 69; A Geography of Man, 1949, rev. edits., 1959, 66; series grade- School geographies (with Gertrude Whipple), 1947-71; (with Nelda Davis) The Wide World A Geography, 1959, rev. edit., 1967; One World Divided, 1964, rev. edit., 1972; An Introduction to Latin America, 1964; All Possible Worlds; A history of Geographical Ideas, 1971; Editor: American Geography, Inventory and Prospect (with C.F. Jones), 1954; New Viewpoints in Geography (Yearbook of the Nat. Council for Social Studies), 1959; also Brazil-Geography in Handbook of Latin Am. Studies, 1935-59; Geography as a Professional Field (with Lorrin Kennamer), 1966, 69. Contbr. to mags. Home: 220 Standish Dr Syracuse NY 13224 ☆

JAMES, RALPH KIRK, ret. naval officer, marine cons.; b. Chgo., May 21, 1906; s. Charles B. and Mary E. (Kirk) J.; student Armour Inst. Tech., 1923-24; B.S., U.S. Naval Acad., 1928; M.S. in Naval Architecture, Mass. Inst. Tech., 1933; student U.S. Naval War Coll., 1948-49; m. Virginia A. Cooper, June 1, 1929; children—Patricia Ann (Mrs. John K. Withers), Richard K. Commd. ensign U.S. Navy, 1928, advanced through grades to rear adm., 1956; trans. Constrn. Corps, 1930; various ship and shore activities, 1930-42; mem. Glassford Mission to French West Africa, 1942-43; officer-in-charge battle damage repair Espiritu Santo and Manus, 1943-45; comdg. officer Ships Parts Control Center, Mechanicsburg, Pa., 1945-48; later shipbuilding and repair supt. Mare Island Naval Shipyard, Vallejo, Cal.; comdg. officer Shipbuilding Scheduling Activity, Phila., 1951-53; comptroller Bur. Ships, 1953-55; comdr. Long Beach Naval Shipyard, Cal., 1955-58; chief Bur. Ships, 1959- 63, exec. dir. Com. Am. S.S. Lines, 1963-69; marine cons., 1969—. Mem. Anti-Submarine Conf. Adv. Group, Nat. Indsl. Conf. Bd.; USN rep. Internat. Conf. Naval Architects and Marine Engrs., London, 1951; mem. travel adv. com. U.S. Dept. Commerce. Decorated knight Royal Order of Sword (King of Sweden); Legion of Merit, Bronze Star, Navy Commendation (twice), D.S.M.; grand officer Order Orange Nassau; recipient James medal N.E. Coast Inst. Engrs. and Shipbuilders, 1951; Distinguished Service medal from Pres. U.S., 1963; Vice Adm. Jerry Land medal for outstanding contbn. to maritime field Soc. Naval Architects and Marine Engrs., 1969. Mem. Soc. Naval Architects and Marine Engrs. (pres., 1963-65), Am. Soc. Naval Engrs. (pres. 1962-63), Mil. Order World Wars, Naval Order U.S. (S.W. commandery 1956—). Clubs: Propeller U.S.; Cosmos, Army-Navy (Washington); Pacific Coast, Long Beach, Rotary (Long Beach, Cal.); N.Y. Yacht (N.Y.C.); India House; Yacht (Annapolis, Md.). Home: 227 Providence Rd Annapolis MD 21401 Office: 1000 Conn Av NW Washington DC 20006

JAMES, REMBERT FAULKNER, newspaperman; b. Waxahachie, Tex., Oct. 14, 1905; s. Benjamin Franklin and Mae (Faulkner) J.; student U. So. Cal., 1922-24, U. Cal. at Los Angeles, 1927, at Berkeley, 1942; m. Catherine Moore Hodges, Aug. 11, 1934. Reporter, Santa Monica (Cal.) Outlook, 1926; mng. editor Culver City (Cal.) Star-News, 1928-35; with A.P., bureaus in Los Angeles, San Francisco, Moscow USSR, and Paris, France, 1936-48; gen. mgr., editor Copley News Service, San Diego, Cal., 1960-68, v.p. and editor, 1968-70. Mem. Sigma Delta Chi. Republican. Episcopalian. Clubs: Nat. Press (Washington); Overseas Press, Circumnavigators (N.Y.C.); Cuyamaca (San Diego). Home: 5578 Calumet Av La Jolla CA 92037 Office: Charter Oil Bldg 110 W C St San Diego CA 92101

JAMES, ROBERT CLARKE, educator, mathematician; b. Bloomington, Ind., July 30, 1918; s. Glenn and Inez (Clarke) Jr.; B.A., U. Cal. at Los Angeles, 1940; Ph.D., Cal. Inst. Tech., 1947; m. Edith Maria Peterson, Oct. 28, 1945; children—Judith Marie (Mrs. Joseph Grouns), Linda Inez (Mrs. Gerald Anooshian), David Vernon, Robert Glenn. Benjamin Pierce instr. math. Harvard, 1946-47; instr. math. U. Cal. at Berkeley, 1947-49, asst. prof., 1949-51; asso. prof. math. Haverford (Pa.) Coll., 1951-57; prof. math., chmn. dept. Harvey Mudd Coll., Claremont, Cal., 1957-67; prof. math. State U. N.Y., Albany, 1967-68; prof. math., chmn. dept. Claremont (Cal.) Grad. Sch., 1968—. Mem. Am. Math. Soc., Math. Assn. Am., Soc. Indsl. and Applied Math., A.A.A.S., Fedn. Am. Scientists, Soc. Social Responsibility in Sci. Mem. Soc. of Friends. Author: Mathematics Dictionary, 1942, rev. 1949, 59, 68; University Mathematics, 1963; Advanced Calculus, 1966. Contbr. articles to profl. jours. Home: 1121 Oxford Av Claremont CA 91711

JAMES, ROBERT LEO, advt. exec.; b. N.Y.C., Sept. 23; s. Leo Francis and Mildred Virginia (Schaffa) J.; A.B., Colgate U., 1958; M.B.A., Columbia, 1961; m. Anne Krapp, Feb. 2, 1968; chilildren—Robert Leo, Victoria, Jeffrey. Field researcher Farm Jour., Inc., Cleve., 1956-57; salesman Procter and Gamble Co., Schenectady, 1958-59, office head sales mgr., Syracuse, N.Y., 1959-60; product mgr. household products, brand marketing and new product devel. Colgate Palmolive Co., N.Y.C., 1961-64; account exec. Ogilvy and Mather, Inc., N.Y.C., 1964, account supr, 1965-66, v.p., account supr., 1967-69; sr. v.p., mgmt. service dir. Marschalk Co., Inc., N.Y.C., 1968, dir., 1969—, exec. v.p., 1970—, operating officer, 1971—; dir. Comprehensive Resources Corp., Tax-Shelter Newsletter; adj. asso. prof. marketing Fordham U., 1968-69. Mem. Am. Mgmt. Assn., Am. Marketing Assn., Greenwich Power Squadron, Delta Kappa Epsilon. Clubs: Millbrook (Greenwich); Yale (N.Y.C.). Home: 68 W Brother Dr Greenwich CT 06830 Office: 1345 Av Americas New York City NY 10019

JAMES, ROY ELIAS, lawyer, AID ofcl.; b. Weissport, Pa., May 13, 1909; s. Reese and Wara (Messinger) J.; student Pa. State Coll. 1927-29; student Sch. Fgn. Service, Georgetown U., 1930-31; J.D., George Washington U., 1938; student U.S. Navy Sch. Mil. Govt. and Adminstrn., Columbia, 1944, Industrial Coll. of Armed Forces, 1954-55, 60-61; m. Virginia Epperson, June 30, 1937; children—Reese Epperson, Eileen Virginia (Mrs. W. B. Ward). Admitted to D.C. bar, 1939, U.S. Supreme Ct. bar, 1951, U.S. Ct. Mil. Appeals, 1955; partner firm Olson & James, 1965-66; instr. U.S. Navy Sch. Mil. Govt., Princeton, 1944; asso. justice Guam Ct. Appeals, 1945; adviser to U.S. delegation UN Gen. Assembly ad hoc com. on transmission of information on self-governing territories, 1947; adviser U.S. delegation South Seas Conf., Canberra, Australia, 1947; atty. Washington office Hawaii Statehood Commn., 1950; staff dir. com. on labor and pub. welfare U.S. Senate 1953; dir. labor activities Republican Nat. Com., 1956; dep. dir. U.S. Mut. Security Mission to China, 1959-61; now AID rep., attache, AID, Colombo, Ceylon. Vis. lectr. Lafayette Coll., Easton, Pa.; prof. Am. govt. Nat. Cheng Chi U., Taipei, Taiwan, 1959-60; chmn. bd. dirs. Taipei Am. Sch., 1960. Candidate for Congress from 20th Dist. Pa., 1948; dir. voter registration Republican Nat. Com., 1964. Capt. USNR (ret.). Mem. Fed. Bar Assn., Bar Assn. D.C., Am. Polit. Sci. Assn., Am. Assn. U. Profs., Am. Legion, Pi Chiao Law Soc. Free China. Clubs: National Lawyers; National Press. Author various articles on mil. govt. and Pacific affairs. Home: 7702 Meadow Lane Chevy Chase MD 20015 Office: Dept of State (Ceylon) (ID) Washington DC 20521

JAMES, SIDNEY LORRAINE, TV exec.; b. St. Louis, Aug. 6, 1906; s. William Henry and Katherine (Wiese) J.; student Washington U., St. Louis; m. Agnes McCarthy, Oct. 21, 1932; children—Christopher, Timothy, Mary, Sidney. Mem. editorial staff St. Louis Post-Dispatch, 1928-36; nat. affairs writer Time mag., 1936-38; chief Time, Inc., Chgo., 1938-41, chief Western editorial operations, 1941-46; asst. mng. editor Life mag., 1946-54; mng. editor Sports Illustrated, N.Y.C., 1954-60, pub., 1960-65; v.p. corp. mgmt. Time, Inc., N.Y.C.,

1965-67, v.p., Washington, 1967-70; chmn. bd. Greater Washington Ednl. Television Assn., (WETA), Inc. Mem. President's Adv. Com. Youth Fitness; lay trustee Trinity Coll. Mem. Def. Orientation Assn. Clubs: American Yacht, Apawamis (Rye, N.Y.); New York Racquet and Tennis; Burning Tree; 1925 F Street, The International (Washington). Home: 2101 Connecticut Av N W Washington DC 20008 Office: 2600 4th St N W Washington DC 20001

JAMES, WALTER DELOS, motor carrier exec.; b. Oregon, Ill., Nov. 9, 1916; s. Delos Lawrence and Edna (Walter) J.; A.B., Duke, 1939; postgrad. Babson Inst., 1940; m. Jacqueline Mae Ostgard, May 4, 1962; children—Janie Burke (Mrs. R.C. Davis), Judith Ellen, Justin Delos, Joyce Maureen. With Julius Garfinckel & Co., Washington, 1933-35; with Roadway Express, Inc., 1940-57, terminal mgr., Atlanta, 1944-46, So. dist. mgr., 1946-52, asst. to v.p., Akron, O., 1952, v.p. sales and traffic, Akron, 1953-57; exec. v.p. So. Cal. Freight Lines, Los Angeles, 1957-60; exec. v.p. ONC Motor Freight System and So. Cal. Freight Lines, Palo Alto, Cal., 1960-65, pres., 1966-69, vice chmn. bd., 1970—. Mem. Cal. (bd. dirs. 1967-70), Am. (planning com. Customer Relations Council 1948-52, bd. govs. Regular Common Carrier Conf. 1969—) trucking assns., San Francisco C. of C. Presbyn. Home: 250 Camino Al Lago Atherton CA 94025 Office: 2800 W Bayshore Rd Palo Alto CA 94303

JAMES, WILBUR ALBERT, wholesale food co. exec.; b. New Engle, Pa., June 3, 1923; s. Martin L. and Sarah (Todd) J.; diploma Robert Morris Coll., 1949; m. Virginia Jones, Feb. 26, 1947; children—Linda Carol (Mrs. James Fetchen), Keith James, Virginia L. With Miss. Glass Co., Floreffe, Pa., 1941-43; auditor Pitts. Coal Co., Library, Pa., 1950-54; with Fox Grocery Co., Belle Vernon, Pa., 1954—, dir. finance, 1958—, sec.-treas., 1961—; dir. Follow Co., Green Thumb Produce Co. Chmn. New Eagle (Pa.) Sch. Dist. Authority, 1964; pres. Mon Valley United Fund, 1971—; active Boy Scouts Am., Boys Club. Trustee Fox Ednl. Found., Served with USAAF, 1943-46; ETO. Decorated Purple Heart. Mem. New Eagle Sportsmen Assn. (v.p. 1949-50). Baptist (chmn. bd. trustees 1955—). Home: RD 2 Finleyville PA 15332 Office: Box 29 Belle Vernon PA 15012

JAMES, WILLIAM THOMAS, ret. educator; b. Greer, S.C., June 9, 1903; s. Walter Ennis and Martha (Smith) J.; B.S., Furman U., 1924; Ph.D., Cornell U., 1929; m. Muriel Leslie Phillips, Apr. 19, 1935; children—Muriel Leslie, Martha Margaret. Instr. math. and physics Greer High Sch., 1924-26; asst. prof. psychology Miss. State Coll. for Women, 1929-31; research asso. Cornell U. Med. Coll., 1931-39, research asso. Behavior Lab., 1939-42; asst. prof. psychology U. Colo., 1942-46; prof. psychology U. Ga., Athens, 1946-70, head dept., 1959-62. Vis. prof. Fla. State U., summer 1949; researcher on animal behaviour Jackson Meml. Lab., Bar Harbor, Me., summers 1947, 48. Mem. Am., Ga. psychol. assns., A.A.A.S., Ga. Acad. Sci., So. Soc. Philosophy and Psychology, Ecol. Soc. Am., Sigma Xi, Phi Delta Kappa, Psi Chi (v.p. southeastern div. 1960-63), Phi Kappa Phi. Democrat. Contbr. articles to profl. and tech. jours. Home: 355 Springdale Av Athens GA 30601

JAMES, WINFIELD HENRY, newspaper exec.; b. Hampton, Va., Oct. 24, 1918; s. W.S. and Lucy (Heath) J.; B.S., Mass. Inst. Tech., 1940; m. Marian Theo Perry, June 10, 1944; children-Scott, Ellen, Carol, Brian. With N.Y. News Inc., pubs. N.Y. Daily and Sunday News, N.Y.C., 1940—, acting circulation dir., 1962-63, exec. asst. to pub., 1962-65, exec. v.p., 1965-70, pres., 1970—; v.p., dir. Tribune Co., Chgo., 1968—; dir. Met. Sunday Newspapers, Inc. Mem. Planning Bd., Mamaroneck, N.Y., 1965-69; mem. com. 2d Regional Plan N.Y. Met. Region, 1966-68. Bd. dirs. N.Y. Conv. and visitors Bur. Served to capt. ordnance dept. AUS, 1942-46. Mem. Am. Newspaper Pubs. Assn. (dir. Research Inst., dir. Bur. Advt.). Clubs: Winged Foot Golf (Mamaroneck); Board Room (N.Y.C.); Larchmont (N.Y.) Yacht. Home: 43 Eton Rd Larchmont NY 10538 Office: 220 E 42d St New York City NY 10017

JAMES, WRIGHT ELWOOD, lawyer; b. Compton, Cal., Jan. 16, 1900; s. Edward M. and Lillie (Edwards) J.; student Ore. State Coll., 1919-20; A.B., Stanford, 1924, LL.B., 1934; m. Josephine Rush, Sept. 28, 1927; 1 son, William E. Geologist, Gen. Petroleum Corp., 1924-31; admitted to Cal. bar, 1934, since practiced in Bakersfield; partner firm Conron, Heard & James, 1950- -. Vice pres., gen. counsel Norris Oil Co.; sec. Layinac Corp. Mem. Cal. Legislature, 1947-48; chmn. Kern County Republican Central Com., 1957- 58. Served to lt. comdr. USNR, 1942-45. Mem. Am. Assn. Petroleum Geologists, Internat., Am. bar assns., State Bar Cal., Res. Officers Assn., Am. Assn. Ry. Trial Lawyers, Phi Gamma Delta. Clubs: Los Angeles Country, Los Angeles Athletic; Stockdale (Cal.) Country. Home: 2418 Spruce St Bakersfield CA 93301 Office: Haberfelde Bldg Bakersfield CA 93301

JAMESON, MARGARET STORM, (Mrs. Guy Chapman), author; b. Whitby, Yorkshire, Eng., 1897; student pvt. schs., M.A., Leeds (Eng.) U.; D.Litt. (hon.); m. Guy Patterson Chapman; 1 son. Author: Happy Highways, 1920; Modern Drama in Europe, 1920; The Lovely Ship, 1927; Farewell to Youth, 1928; The Voyage Home, 1930; A Richer Dust, 1931; That Was Yesterday, 1932; Women Against Men, 1933; The Day Off. 1933; No Time Like the Present (autobiography) 1933; Company Parade, 1934; Love in Winter, 1935; In the Second Year, 1936; None Turn Back, 1936; Captain's Wife, 1939; Europe to Let, 1940; Cousine Honoré, 1941; The Fort, 1941; The End of This War, 1941; Then We Shall Hear Singing, 1942; Cloudless May, 1943; The Journal of Mary Hervey Russell, 1945; The Other Side, 1946; Before the Crossing, 1947; Black Laurel, 1948; The Moment of Truth, 1949; The Writer's Situation, 1950; The Green Man, 1953; The Hidden River, 1955; The Intruder, 1956; A Cup of Tea for Mr. Thorgill, 1957; One Ulysses Too Many; Last Score, 1961; The Road from the Monument, 1962; The Blind Heart, 1964; The Early Life of Stephen Hind, 1966; The White Crow, 1968; Journey from the North (autobiography), 1971; Parthian Words, 1971. Address: care Macmillan & Co St Martin's St W C 2 London England

JAMESON, MICHAEL HAMILTON, educator; b. London, Eng., Oct. 15, 1924; s. Raymond Deloy and Rose (Perel) J.; A.B., U. Chgo., 1942, Ph.D., 1949; m. Virginia Broyles, June 8, 1946; childrenNicholas Andrew, Anthony David, John Timothy, David Richmond. Asst. prof. classical langs. and archaeology U. Mo., 1950-53; mem. faculty U. Pa., 1954-, prof. classical studies, 1962-, dean Grad. Sch. Arts and Scis., 1966-68, research asso. classical archaeology Univ. Mus., dir. Argolid Exploration Project, 1960-, dir. Center Ancient History, 1968-. Served to lt. USNR, 1943-46. Recipient citation teaching and research Pa. Dept. Pub. Instrn., 1963; fellow Am. Council Learned Socs., 1958; Guggenheim fellow, 1965. Mem. Am. Philol. Assn., Archaeol. Inst. Am., Am. Acad. Arts and Scis., Am. Acad. in Rome (sr. fellow classics 1958-59). Contbr. profl. jours. Home: 151 W Tulpehocken St Philadelphia PA 19144

JAMESON, MINOR STORY, Jr., trade assn. exec.; b. Worcester, Mass., Jan. 13, 1911; s. Minor Story and Josephine Eunice (Bingham) J.; B.S. in Bus. and Engring. Adminstrn., Mass. Inst. Tech., 1934; m. Rita Anne Donnelly, Feb. 14, 1941; 1 son, Minor Story 11. With econ. div. FTC, 1935-37; with Ind. Petroleum Assn. Am., Washington, 1937—, asst. to pres., 1950-58, exec. v.p., 1958—. Cons. com. energy supplies and resources policy, President's Cabinet, 1954, Interior Dept., 1951-52, 56-57, OCDM, 1958-60; mem. Mil. Petroleum Ad. Bd., 1954-59. Served to capt. AUS, 1942-45. Mem. Am. Inst. Mining and Metall. Engrs. (nat. engrs. com. on Engrs. Joint Council 1951—). Kappa Sigma. Roman Catholic. Author articles. Home: 13932 Esworthy Rd Germantown MD 20767 Office: 1101 16th St Washington DC 20036

JAMESON, PAUL C., corp. exec.; b. Concord, N.H., 1906; ed. Dartmouth, 1929. Exec. v.p., sec. Nat. Distillers & Chem. Corp.; sec., treas., dir. Nat. Petro Chems. Corp., Sunny Brook Distillery Co., Old Crow Distillery Co., Old Grand- Dad Distillery Co., Old Taylor Distillery Co.; sec., treas. John de Kuyper & Son, Inc. Home: 70 Harrison St Verona NJ 07044 Office: 99 Park Av New York City NY 10016*

JAMESON, WILLIAM JAMES, judge; b. Butte, Mont., Aug. 8, 1898; s. William J. and Annie J. (Roberts) J.; A.B., Mont. U., 1919, LL.B., 1922, LL.D., 1952; LL.D., U. Man. (Can.), 1954; Doctor of Laws, McGeorge Coll. Law, 1965; LL.D., Rocky Mountain Coll., 1969; m. Mildred Lore, July 28, 1923; children—Mary -Mary Lucille (Mrs. Walker Honaker), William James, Jr. Admitted to Mont. bar, 1922; asso. firm Johnston, Coleman and Johnston, Billings, 1922-29; mem. firm Johnston, Coleman & Jameson, 1929-40, Coleman, Jameson & Lamey, 1940-57; judge U.S. Dist. Ct. for Mont., 1957—. Mem. Mont. Ho. of Reps., 1927-30. Mem. bd. sch. trustees, Billings, 1930- 32; chmn. Yellowstone County chpt. A.R.C., 1931-45. Mem. S.A.T.C. Fellow Am. Bar Found.; mem. Am. Bar Assn. (bd. govs. 1943-46, assembly del. 1946-53, pres. 1953-54, pres. endowment 1961-63, chmn. spl. com. on adminstrn. criminal justice 1969—), Mont. Bar Assn. (pres. 1936- 37), Am. Law Inst. (mem. council 1956—), Am. Judicature Soc. (pres. 1956-58), Conf. of Commn. Uniform State Laws (exec. com. 1946-48), Am. Legion, Phi Delta Phi. Republican. Methodist. Mason, Lion (dist. gov. 1941-42). Home: 327 North Rim Terrace Billings MT 59101 Office: Fed Bldg-U S Courthouse Billings MT 59101

JAMIESON, CAMPBELL DONALD, Canadian minister transport; b. St. John's, Nfld., Can., Apr. 30, 1921; s. Charles and Isabelle (Bennett) J.; ed. Prince Wales Coll.; m. Barbara Elizabeth Oakley, Dec. 20, 1946; children—Donna, Healther, Roger, Deborah. Began career with Dept. Rural Reconstruction; joined Crosbie & Co. Ltd. fishery; sales mgr. Coca-Cola, Nfld.; with Canadian Naval Spl. Services and USO Camp Shows, regular broadcasts, 1941-46; began news broadcasting nightly, 1946; attaché Parliamentary Press Gallery, Ottawa, 1948; former pres. Nfld. Broadcasting Co. Ltd.; formerly dir. broadcast news, past chmn. affiliates sect. network advt. com. Canadian Broadcasting Corp.; mem. Troika Com. Broadcasting Fed. Govt. Can., 1963; M.P., 1966, formerly minister def. prodn., minister transp., 1968—. Adviser, Bd. Broadcast Govs., mem. cons. com. pvt. broadcasting. Chmn. financial campaign Canadian Cancer Soc.; chmn. program com. Nfld. Come Home Year, 1966. Former bd. dirs. Canadian Centennial Council, Nat. Theatre Sch., Montreal, Que., Neptune Theatre Found., Halifax, N.S. Mem. Privy Council. Mem. Canadian Assn. Broadcasters (pres., 1961-64). Liberal. Presbyn. Author: The Troubled Air, 1966. Home: 4 Winter Pl St Johns Nfld Canada Office: MacDonald Bldg Ottawa Ontario Canada

JAMIESON, EDWARD LEO, magazine editor; b. Boston, Sept. 18, 1929; s. Leo and Estelle (Mullen) J.; A.B., Boston U., 1951; m. Ann Booth, Sept. 1955-58, 1961. Reporter, Medford (Mass.) Daily Mercury, 1951-54; contbg. editor Time mag., 1955- asso. editor, 1958-63, sr. editor, 1963-69, asst. mng. editor, 1969—. Home: 185 E 85th St New York City NY 10028 Office: Time Mag Rockefeller Center New York City NY 10020

JAMIESON, JOHN CALHOUN, geophysicist, educator; b. St. Joseph, Mo., Jan. 5, 1924; s. William Thomas and Glessie (McPike) J.; B.S., U. Chgo., 1947, M.S., 1951, Ph.D., 1952; m. Ruth Virginia Lamb, Mar. 26, 1949; children-William Thomas, Virginia Anne, John Booth. Mem. faculty U. Chgo., 1953—, prof. geophysics, 1965—; with Cal. Research Corp., summer 1953, Stanford Research Inst., summers 1959-63, U.S. Geol. Survey, 1958—; cons. Los Alamos Sci. Lab., 1964—. NSF fellow, 1953. Mem. Am. Geophys. Union, A.A.A.S., Geochem. Soc., Sigma Xi. Contbr. articles profl. jours. Address: Dept Geophys Scis U Chgo 5734 Ellis Av Chicago IL 60637

JAMIESON, JOHN KENNETH, oil co. exec.; b. Medicine Hat, Can., Aug. 28, 1910; s. John Locke and Kate (Herron) J.; S.B., Mass. Inst. Tech., 1931; m. Ethel May Burns, Dec. 23, 1937; children—John Burns, Anne Frances. Came to U.S., 1959, naturalized, 1964. Vice pres., dir. Imperial Oil, Ltd., Toronto, Can., 1948-58; pres. Internat. Petroleum Co., Ltd., 1959-61; v.p., dir. Humble Oil & Refining Co., Houston, 1961-62, exec. v.p., dir. 1962-63, pres., 1963-64; exec. v.p. Standard Oil Co. (N.J.), 1964-65, pres., dir., 1965-69, chmn., chief exec. officer, 1969—; dir. Chase Manhattan Bank, Internat. Nickel Co. Can., Ltd. Mem. Mass. Inst. Tech. Corp. Mem. Lambda Chi Alpha. Clubs: Rosedale Golf (Toronto); Winged Foot Golf (Mamaroneck, N.Y.); Blind Brook Golf (Port Chester, N.Y.); Houston Country. Home: 1310 E Flagler Dr Mamaroneck NY 10543 Office: 30 Rockefeller Plaza New York City NY 10020

JAMIESON, ROBERT ARTHUR, savs. and loan exec.; b. Nairn, Scotland, Dec. 20, 1908; s. Alexander Lawrence and Jean Fleming (Smith) J.; came to U.S., 1924, naturalized 1928; A.B., Knox Coll., 1932; M.A., U. Ill., 1940; grad. student U. Colo.; m. Evelyn C. McNeil, Dec. 24, 1934; children—Richard, Robert, Kathleen. Athletic dir., social sci. tchr. Sparta Twp. High Sch., Wataga, Ill., 1933-35; supt. schs., Varna, Ill., 1935-41; staff Fed. Security Agy., 1941-43; employment mgr. R.G. LeTourneau, Inc., Peoria, Ill., 1943-48; asst. to pres. Bradley U., 1948-50, became dean Coll. Commerce, 1950; arbitrator labor disputes, 1948—; v.p. Irions' Concrete Products Co., 1954-65; v.p. Security Savs. & Loan Assn., Peoria, 1966-67, pres., 1967—; dir. Bank for Savs. & Loans, Roosevelt Nat. Life Ins. Co. Pres., Ill. Tb Assn., 1971, Ill. Assn. Sch. Boards, 1969-70, Crippled Childrens Center, 1971. Mem. Peoria Bd. Edn., 1955-70. Recipient Knox Coll. Alumni Distinguished Service award, 1954. Mem. Tau Kappa Epsilon, Alpha Kappa Psi, Phi Delta Kappa, Omicron Delta Kappa. Clubs: Creve Coeur, Rotary. Author articles on personnel, labor relations, sch. bd. practices. Home: 223 W Hollyridge Circle Peoria IL 61614 Office: 200 N E Adams St Peoria IL 61602

JAMIESON, ROBERT GORDON, corp. exec.; b. Honolulu, June 18, 1920; s. William and Margaret (Quinan) J.; A.B., Honolulu, 1941; grad. Advanced Mgmt. Program, Harvard, 1956; m. Virginia Dargel Leithead, Aug. 15, 1953; 1 stepson, Thomas William Leithead. Asst. auditor Alexander & Baldwin, Honolulu, 1941-50, adminstrv. asst., 1950-60, asst. treas., 1960-61, treas., 1961-69, asst. treas., asst. sec., 1969-70, v.p., treas., 1970—, also officer, dir. various subsidiaries. Served to lt. USNR, 1942-46. Mem. Nat. Assn. Accountants, Financial Execs. Inst., Chi Psi. Republican. Club: Oahu Country (Honolulu). Home: 4809 Kolohala St Honolulu HI 96816 Office: 822 Bishop St Honolulu HI 96801

JAMISON, EDWARD ALDEN, educator; b. Pontiac, Ill., July 10, 1909; s. Edward Austin and Cora Elizabeth (Reed) J.; B.S., Northwestern U., 1931; A.M., Tufts Coll., 1933; student Fletcher Sch. Law and Diplomacy, 1933-34; Ph.D., Harvard, 1943; attended Nat. War Coll., Washington, 1955-56; m. Helen Barry, June 23, 1937; children—David Campbell, Alice Reed. Instr. history and govt. Earlham Coll., 1934-36; part time instr. history Tufts Coll. and other schs. in Boston area, 1936-41; instr. history Williams Coll., 1941- 45; fgn. affairs specialist Central Secretariat, Dept. State, Washington, 1945-46; spl. asst. Div. Spl. Inter-Am. Affairs, 1947-49, asst. chief, 1949; officer-in-charge inter-Am. security affairs Office Regional Am. Affairs, 1950-52, dep. dir., 1952-55; fgn. service officer, sec. Diplomatic Service, consul of U.S.A., 1955-56; counselor of embassy, Jose, Costa Rica, 1956-59; counselor of embassy, dep. chief of mission Guatemala, 1959-60; dir. Office Inter-Am. Regional Polit. Affairs, Dept. State, 1960-63; dir. politico-mil. affairs Supreme Allied Command, Atlantic, NATO, 1963-65; with Fgn. Service Inspection Corps., 1965-67; consul gen., Monterrey, Mexico, 1967-69; prof. history, dir. internat. studies Wis. State U. Advisor to U.S. delegations various confs., 1948- -. Mem. Phi Beta Kappa, Sigma Alpha Epsilon. Address: 600 Graham Av Eau Clair WI 54701

JAMISON, FRANK STOVER, educator; b. Bellwood, Pa., Feb. 12, 1903; s. Isaac McCarty and Mary Elizabeth (Stover) J.; B.S., Pa. State Coll., 1924; M.S., Ia. State Coll., 1925; Ph.D., Cornell U., 1934; m. Ellen Elizabeth Van Arnam, Apr. 1, 1933. Research fellow Ia. State Coll., 1924-25; instr. horticulture Tex. A. and M. Coll., 1925-28, asst. prof., 1928-30; research instr. Cornell U., 1930-34; horticulturist Fla. Agrl. Expt. Sta., 1934-68, extension vegetable crops specialist, 1948-68, head dept. vegetable crops U. Fla., 1956-68, prof. emeritus, 1968—; cons. AID, Jamaica, 1968, Costa Rica, 1969; cons. FAO, Singapore, 1971; pres. D.A.C. Agri-Bus. Cons. Service; asst. econ. commr. Dept. State, Paris, France, 1952-53. Recipient Distinguished Service award Fla. Seedmen's Assn., 1951, Award of Merit, 1954; named hon. state farmer Future Farmers Am., 1959; Research award Fla. Fruit and Vegetable Assn., 1960; named Seedsman of 1966, So. Seedsmen Assn. Fellow A.A.A.S. (council), Am. Soc. for Hort. Sci. (pres. 1961-62, chmn. bd. 1962-63); mem. Am. Inst. of Biological Sci., Florida Hort. Soc. (hon.; v.p. 1941, asst. sec. 1942-51), Fla. Soil Sci. and Corp Soc., Sigma Xi, Gamma Sigma Delta, Epsilon Sigma Phi, Alpha Gamma Rho. Presbyn. Kiwanian. Home: 709 N W 22d St Gainesville FL 32601

JAMISON, OLIVER MORTON, lawyer; b. Portland, Ore., Aug. 1, 1916; s. Homer B. and Jean (Allison) J.; A.B., Stanford, 1938, LL.B., 1941; m. Margaret Ratcliffe, July 18, 1941; children—Stephen, -Stephen, Thomas, Daniel. Admitted to Cal. bar, 1941, since practiced in Fresno; partner firm Thomas, Snell, Jamison, Russell, Williamson & Asperger, 1941—. Lectr. taxation Cal. Bar Continuing Edn. Program, 1948, 51, 54, 64, Am. Law Inst., 1949, 50, 53, U. So. Cal. Inst. Fed. Taxation, 1961. Served to capt. AUS, 1942-46. Mem. Am., Fresno County bar assns., Fresno County and City C. of C. (pres. 1960), State Bar Cal., Am. Law Inst., Am. Judicature Soc., Order of Coif, Phi Alpha Delta. Home: 4950 Sunset Dr Fresno CA 93721 Office: Del Webb Center Fresno CA 93721

JAMISON, PHILIP DUANE, Jr., artist; b. Phila., July 3, 1925; s. Philip Duane and Daisy (McCadden) J.; student Phila. Mus. Sch. Art, 1946-50; m. Jane B. Gray, Oct. 11, 1950; children—Philip Duane III, Terry Jane, Linda B. One man shows Hirschl & Adler Galleries, N.Y.C., 1959, 63, 65, 67, 69, 71, Sessler Gallery, Phila., 1963, Duke U., 1969; represented in permanent collections Pa. Acad. Fine Arts, N.A.D., Wilmington (Del.) Soc. Fine Arts, U. Del., others. Recipient Dawson medal Pa. Acad. Fine Arts, 1959, Dana medal, 1961; first award Nat. Arts Club, N.Y.C., 1961; Lena A. Mason prize N.A.D., 1962; William Church Osborn prize Am. Watercolor Soc., 1961; Medal of Honor, Knickerbocker Artists, N.Y.C., 1961; Bainbridge award Allied Artists Am., 1958, 60; first prize Wilmington Soc. Fine Arts, 1957, 59, 61; M.W. Zimmerman Meml. prize Phila. Watercolor Club, 1963; Gold medal honor Allied Artists Am., 1964; Childe Hassam Fund purchase prize Am. Acad. Arts and Letters, 1965; Lily Saportas award Am. Watercolor Soc., 1965, C.F.S. award, 1966; N.A.D. prize, 1967; Thornton Oakley Meml. prize Phila. Watercolor Club, 1967; Samuel Finley Breese Morse medal N.A.D., 1969; Edgar A. Whitney award Am. Watercolor Soc., 1971. Served with USNR, 1943-46. N.A. Mem. Am. Watercolor Soc., Phila. Water Color Club. Home: 705 W Union St Chester PA 19013 Studio: 104 Price St West Chester PA 19380

JAMISON, W. GRAHAM, constrn. co. exec.; b. Ireland, 1909; grad. U. Pa., 1944. Sr. v.p., asst. sec., dir. Catalytic Constrn. Co., Phila.; v.p., treas., sec. dir. Catalytic Constrn. Can., Ltd.; v.p., comptroller, asst. sec., dir. Catalytic Caribe, Inc., Ind. Constrn. Corp.; v.p., treas., comptroller, asst. sec., dir. Catalytic Ind. Maintenance Co., Inc., Catalytic Internat., Inc., Catalytic Belgium, Inc. Office: 1528 Walnut St Philadelphia PA 19102*

JAMOUNEAU, WALTER COREY, aircraft co. exec.; b. Irvington, N.J., Sept. 21, 1912; s. Walter H. and E. Prudence (Corey) J.; B.S. in Mech. Engring., Rutgers U., 1932; m. Helen E. Hoey, June 22, 1934; children—W. Jeffry, William C. With Piper Aircraft Corp., and predecessor, 1933—, chief engr., 1936—, sec., 1947-69, asst. sec., 1969—, v.p. engring., 1969—, also dir. Chmn., Lock Haven United Fund drive, 1961; mem. Lockhaven Sch. Bd., 1961—. Chmn. finance com. Clinton County Republican Com., 1962—. Trustee Lock Haven State Coll.; mem. adv. bd. Lock Haven Salvation Army; trustee Piper Found. Mem. Soc. Automotive Engrs., Inst. Aerospace Scis., Rutgers Engring. Soc., Lambda Chi Alpha, Tau Beta Pi. Home: 309 Susquehanna Av Lock Haven PA 17745 Office: 820 E Bald Eagle St Lock Haven PA 17745

JAMRICH, JOHN XAVIER, univ. pres.; b. Muskegon Heights, Mich., June 12, 1920; s. John and Mary (Mudry) J.; student Milw. State Tchrs. Coll., 1939-40, Ripon Coll., 1940-42; B.S., U. Chgo., 1942-43; M.S., Marquette U., 1946-48; Ph.D., Northwestern U., 1951; L.H.D. (hon.), No. Mich. U., 1968; m. June Ann Hrupka, June 26, 1944; children—June Ann, Marna Mary, Barbara Sue. Instr. math. Marquette U., 1946-48; asst. instr. math. U. Wis., 1948-49; asst. dean men Northwestern U., 1949-51; dean students Coe Coll., Cedar Rapids, Ia., 1951-55; dean faculty, prof. math. Doane Coll., Crete, Neb., 1955-57; asst. dir. Legislative Survey Higher Edn. in Mich., 1957- 58; prof. higher edn., dir. Center Study Higher Edn., Mich. State U., 1957-63, asso. dean Coll. Edn., prof. higher edn., 1963-68; pres. No. Mich. U., 1968-; cons.-examiner N. Central Assn. Colls. and Secondary Schs., 1957—; cons. in field, 1959—; Ford Found. cons. for devel. U. Nigeria, 1964; cons. higher edn. Govt. of Thailand, 1967; cons. and Ishpeming R.R. Bd. dirs. St. Luke's Hosp., Marquette, Mich., Bay Cliff Health Camp, Marquette. Served to capt. USAAF, 1942-46. Author numerous articles in field; co-author several books. Home: 537 W Kaye Av Marquette MI 49855

JANASKE, PAUL CARLYLE, information scientist; b. Shamokin, Pa., July 28, 1920; s. Michael Edward and Pearl Anna (Paul) J.; B.S., Dickinson Coll., 1942; M.S. in L.S., Columbia, 1949; m. Virginia May Lightner, Nov. 4, 1945; chilren—Paul Carlyle, Stephen Charles. Head service dept., instr. Sch. Library Sci., Kent State U. Library, 1949-51; with U.S. Govt., 1951-60; asst. dir. biol. scis. communication project Am. Inst. Biol. Scis., 1961- 63; exec. dir. Am. Documentation Inst., 1963-64, Fed. Clearinghouse for Sci. and Tech. Information, 1964-67, div. library programs, research and planning devel. br. U.S. Office

Edn., Washington, 1967—; lectr. dept. library sci. Cath. U. Am. 1966—. Served with USNR, 1942-46. Mem. Phi Kappa Sigma. Methodist. Editor: Information Handling and Science Information, 1962; Automation and Scientific Communication, 1963. Home: 4508 N Dittmar Rd Arlington VA 22207 Office: 7th and D Sts S W Washington DC 20202

JANDL, HENRY ANTHONY, educator; b. Spokane, July, 17, 1910; s. Paul and Marie (Zitterbart) J.; student Fontainebleau (France) Sch. Fine Arts, 1933; B.Arch., M.Arch., Carnegie Inst. Tech., 1935; M.F.A. in Architecture, Princeton 1937; postgrad. Ecole des Beaux Arts, Paris, 1937-39; m. Gertrude Ward, June 4,1940; children—Margaret M., H. Ward. Faculty, Princeton, 1940-43, 45—, prof. architecture, 1957—, acting dir. Sch. Architecture, 1964, exec. officer Sch. Architecture and Urban Planning, 1968—; plant engr. Corning Glass Works (N.Y.), 1943-45; pvt. practice architecture, 1943—. Vis. critic U. Va., 1957; cons. architect; cons. on phys. facilities to comdg. gen. Ft. Monmouth, N.J., 1966-67. Mem., vice chmn. bd. Environmental Design Rev. for Princeton Twp. John Stewardson fellow, 1933; Whitney Warren fellow, 1937. Recipient Princeton prize, 1935; honor award for design of Princeton Borough Hall, N.J. chpt. A.I.A., 1966. Fellow A.I.A. (pres. Capitol chpt. N.J. 1961); mem. Assn. Collegiate Sch. Architecture, Am. Assn. U. Profs., Assn. Princeton Grad. Alumni, Nat. Inst. Archtl. Edn., Bldg Research Inst., Constrn. Specifications Inst., Alpha Rho Chi (medal for excellence 1935), Phi Kappa Phi, Tau Sigma Delta. Republican. Home: 30 Russel Rd Princeton NJ 08540

JANDL, JAMES HARRIMAN, physician; b. Racine, Wis., 1925; M.D., Harvard, 1949. Successively intern, asst. resident, research fellow, research asso., asst. physician, asso. physician Thorndike Meml. Lab., asst. physician, asso. physician, physician Boston City Hosp., 1961-; mem. faculty Harvard Med. Sch., 1952-, asso. prof. medicine, 1964-68, prof. medicine, 1968—, George R. Minot prof. medicine, 1968—. Served with USNR, 1950-52. Diplomate Am. Bd. Internal Medicine. Mem. Am. Fedn. Clin. Research, Am. Soc. Clin. Investigation, Am. Assn. Physicians. Address: 104 Plain Rd Wayland MA 01778

JANE, JOHN ANTHONY, neurol. surgeon, educator; b. Chgo., Sept. 21, 1931; s. Kamil Schulhof and Serrita Jane; B.A. cum laude, U. Chgo., 1951, M.D., 1956, Ph.D., 1967; postgrad. Montreal Neurol. Inst., 1956-60; m. Noella Fortier, Dec. 17, 1960; children—Jane Serrita, Jennie Elizabeth, Katherine Colette, John Anthony. Intern Royal Victoria Hosp., 1956-57, Montreal Neurol. Inst., 1957-61, Atkinson Morley's Hosp., 1961-62, Ill. Neuropsychiat. Inst., 1963-65; sr. instr. neurosurgery Case Western Res., Cleve., 1965-66, asst. prof., 1967-68, asso. prof., 1968-68; prof., chmn. dept. neurosurgery Med. Sch. U. Va., Charlottesville, 1969—. Fellow Royal Coll. Surgeons (Can.), A.C.S.; mem. Am. Assn. Anatomists, Am. Physiol. Soc., Am. Assn. Neurol. Surgeons, Research Soc. of Neurol. Surgeons, Soc. U. Surgeons. Author: The Cytology of Tumors of the Nervous System, 1969. Contbr. articles profl. jours. Home: 1902 Blue Ridge Rd Charlottesville VA 22901

JANES, JOHN VALLE, chem. co. exec.; b. St. Louis, Oct. 31, 1898; s. John M. and Catherine (Valle) J.; student Mass. Inst. Tech., 1923; m. Genevieve Barnickel, May 23, 1927; children—John Valle, Genevieve Brown, William B., Michael V. Vice pres., treas. Gross & Janes Co., St. Louis, 1924—, Petrolite Corp., St. Louis, 1930—; pres. Wm. S. Barnickel & Co.; trustee Barnickel Co. Life dir. Boys Club St. Louis; pres. Father Tim Dempsey Charities. Served with U.S. Army, World War I. Decorated Verdun medal, Croix de Guerre (France). Clubs: Metropolitan (N.Y.C.); Petroleum (Dallas and Houston); California (Los Angeles). Home: 5 Apple Tree Lane St Louis MO 63105 Office: 506 Olive St St Louis MO 63101

JANES, JOSEPH MOWAT, physician. Prof. orthopedic surgery Mayo Found. Diplomate Am. Bd. Orthopedic Surgery. Home: 1809 7th St S W Rochester MN 55901 Office: 200 1st St S W Rochester MN 55901

JANEWAY, CHARLES ALDERSON, physician, educator; b. N.Y.C., May 26, 1909; s. Theodore C. and Eleanor C. (Alderson) J.; A.B., Yale, 1930; postgrad. Cornell U. Med. Coll., 1931-32; M.D., Johns Hopkins, 1934; M.A. (hon.), Harvard, 1946; M.D., U. Uppsala (Sweden), 1964; Dr. honoris causa, U. Reims (France), 1969; m. Elizabeth Bradley, July 9, 1932; children—Anne Alderson, Elizabeth (Mrs. Ronald Gold.), Charles A., Barbara Bradley. Hosp. tng. Boston City Hosp. and Johns Hopkins Hosp., 1935-37; mem. dept. bacteriology and immunology Harvard Med. School, 1938-39, dept. medicine, 1940-42, dept. pediatrics, 1943—, Thomas Morgan Rotch prof. pediatrics, 1946—; physician-in-chief Children's Hosp. Med. Center, 1946—; chmn. com. on blood and blood derivatives NRC, 1948- 51; chmn. com. on blood and blood derivatives, vice chmn. exec. com., adv. bd. on health services, A.R.C., 1946-50; mem. med. adv. council Iran Found., 1955-64, pres., 1958-65, chmn. med. adv. council 1965—; pres. Protein Found., 1955-60, sci. dir., 1960-68, bd. dirs., 1955—; chmn. med. adv. bd. Nat. Found. Muscular Dystrophy, 1954-60; chmn. med. adv. bd. Nat. Found. Neuromuscular Disease, 1960-68, hon. chmn., 1968—; mem. exec. bd. Internat. Pediatric Assn., 1956-62, chmn. exec. com., 1963-68; mem. adminstrv. bd. Internat. Children's Center, Paris, 1967—; mem. Nat. Adv. Allergy and Infectious Diseases Council, NIH, 1970—. Recipient Peter Bent Brigham medal, 1963; Rosen von Rosenheim medal Swedish Paediatric Assn., 1964; Alan Gregg travel fellow China Med. Bd., N.Y., 1965-66. Mem. Brit. Paediatric Assn. (hon.), Soc. de Pediatrie de France (corr.), Finnish Paediatric Assn. (hon.), Korean Acad. Pediatrics (hon.), Assn. de Professores de Pediatria de Mexico (hon.), Canadian Pediatric Assn., Mass. Med. Assn., New Eng. Pediatric Soc., Am. Acad. Pediatrics, Am. Acad. Arts and Scis., Am. Soc. for Clin. Investigation (v.p. 1953), Soc. for Pediatric Research (pres. 1955), Am. Pediatric Soc. (Pres. 1971), Assn. Am. Physicians, Philippine Prediatric Soc. (hon.). Contbr. sci. articles and jours. Editorial bd. Pediatrics, 1954- 60. Home: 445 Concord Rd Weston MA 02193 Office: 300 Longwood Av Boston MA 02115

JANEWAY, EDWARD G., senator, mem. Rep. Nat. Com.; b. New Rochelle, N.Y., Aug. 25, 1901; s. Theodore Caldwell and Eleanor (Alderson) J.; grad. Yale, 1922; m. Elinor White, May 23, 1925; 6 children. Investment offices, 1927-41; partner Stanley, Janeway & Howe (mem. N.Y. Stock Exchange), 1936-41; operator Middletown Farm, South Londonderry, 1945—; chief conservation tin and lead div. W.P.B., Washington, 1941-42; mem. Vermont Little Hoover Commn., 1958-59; mem. Vt. senate, 1959—, pres. pro-tempore, 1968—. Mem. Vermont Ho. Reps., 1950-56; mem. Rep. Nat. Com., 1952—; vice chmn. Legislative Council, 1966; town moderator, 1955—. Dir. The Stratton Corp., 1960—, Catamount Nat. Bank. Trustee Conservation Soc. Southern Vt., 1967—, Experiment in Internat. Living, Grace Cottage Hosp. Served as lt. comdr., USNR, 1942-47. Decorated Bronze Star, Croix de Guerre (France). Conglist. Home: Middletown Farm Londonderry VT 05148 Office: Box 117 South Londonderry VT 05155

JANEWAY, ELIOT, economist; b. N.Y.C., Jan. 1, 1913; s. Meyer Joseph and Fanny (Siff) J.; ed. Cornell, 1932; grad. student London Sch. Econs.; m. Elizabeth Hall, Oct. 29, 1938; children—Michael Charles, William Hall. Bus. editor Time mag., N.Y.C.; adviser to editor-in-chief Time, Inc.; bus. trends cons. Newsweek mag.; econ. adviser numerous industries; syndicated columnist Chgo. Tribune-N.Y. News Syndicate; pub. Janeway Service; pres., dir. Janeway Pub. & Research Corp.; econ. adviser Prudential Funds, Inc.; dir. Nat. Bank of Washington; dir., mem. exec. com. Realty Equities Corp. N.Y. Author: The Struggle for Survival, 1951, reissue, 1968; The Economics of Crisis, 1968; What Shall I Do With My Money?, 1970. Syndicated columnist. Address: 15 E 80th St New York City NY 10021

JANEWAY, ELIZABETH HALL, author; b. Bklyn., Oct. 7, 1913; d. Charles H. and Jeannette F. (Searle) Hall; student Swarthmore Coll.; A.B., Barnard Coll., 1935; m. Eliot Janeway; children—Michael, William. Author: The Walsh Girls, 1943; Dairy Kenyon, 1945; The Question of Gregory, 1949; The Vikings, 1951; Leaving Home, 1953; Early Days of the Automobile, 1956; The Third Choice, 1959; Angry Kate, 1963; Accident, 1964; Ivanov Seven, 1967; Man's World, Woman's Place, 1971; also short stories and critical writing in periodicals and newspapers. Trustee, Barnard Coll. Mem. Authors Guild (council), Authors League Am. (council), P.E.N. (exec. bd.), Nat. Book Com. Home: 15 E 80th St New York City NY 10021

JANEWAY, RAY CURTIS, librarian; b. Siloam Springs, Ark., Mar. 14, 1916; s. Charles Newton and Blanche (Moore) J.; A.B., U. Kan., 1938; B.L.S., U. Ill., 1941, M.S., 1944; m. Bonnie Ethel Fenstemaker, July 22, 1935; children—Gerald Ray, Bonnie Joyce (dec.). Library asst. U. Kan., 1938-40, asst. dir. libraries, 1946-49; library asst. U. Ill., 1941-44; librarian Bradley U., 1944-46, Tex Tech. U., 1949—. Summer tchr. Grad. Library Sch., U. Tex., Austin. Mem. Tex. (pres. 1959-60), S.W. library assns., Tex. Assn. Coll. Tchrs. (pres. 1968-69). Rotarian. Home: 3207 45th St Lubbock TX 79413

JANIGRO, ANTONIO, cellist, condr.; b. Milan, Italy, Jan. 21, 1918; s. Nicola and Maria (Cavo) J.; student Gilberto Crepax at Milan Conservatory, 1929-34, Diran Alexanian at Ecole Normale de Musique, Paris, France, 1934-38, Licence de Concert, 1935; m. Neda Cihlar, May 24, 1953; children—Nicole, Damir. Concert cellist, 1933—; concert tours throughout Europe, USSR, U.S.A., Central and S.Am., Japan, Indonesia, Israel; soloist with orchs. chamber music groups, throughout world; in charge advanced cello class Zagreb (Yugoslavia) Conservatory, 1939-53; condr. Zagreb Radio-TV Orch., 1954-64; founder, condr., soloist Zagreb Soloists, 1954-67; guest condr. symphony orchs. throughout world, 1954—; participant numerous internat. festivals, 1938—; condr. Angelicum Orch., Milan, 1965-67; permanent condr. Chamber Orch. of Saar, 1968—; charge advanced cello class Robert Schumann Conservatory, Dusseldorf, Germany, 1965—; rec. artist for RCA-Victor, Vanguard-Amadeo, Westminster records. Prize winner 6 nat. and internat. competitions; named cavaliere Al Merito Della Repubblica Italiana, 1966; named cavaliere Pres. Tito of Yugoslavia, 1962, 65; grand knight of Mark Twain, 1970. Address: 11 Piazza-Erculea Milan Italy

JANIS, ALLEN IRA, educator, physicist; b. Chgo., Sept. 11, 1930; s. David M. and Rosa (Ginsburg) J.; B.S., Northwestern U., 1951; postgrad. Cornell U., 1951-53; Ph.D., Syracuse U., 1957; m. Phyllis Meyer, Sept. 6, 1953; children—Stuart, Wynne. Faculty, U. Pitts., 1957—, asso. prof. physics, 1963-68, prof., 1968—, sr. research asso. Philos. Sci. Center, 1967—. Mem. Fedn. Am. Scientists (sec. 1964-65), Am. Phys. Soc., Am. Assn. Physics Tchrs., A.A.A.S., Am. Assn. U. Profs., Philosophy of Sci. Assn. Home: 425 Garden City Dr Monroeville PA 15146 Office: Dept Physics Univ Pitts Pittsburgh PA 15213

JANIS, BYRON, concert pianist; b. McKeeport, Pa., Mar. 24, 1928; s. Samuel and Hattie (Horelick) Yanks; pvt. student of Adele Marcus and Vladimir Horowitz; m. June Dickson-Wright. Nov. 30, 1953 (div. Aug. 1965); 1 son, Stefan, m. 2d, Maria Cooper, Apr. 11, 1966. Debut, Carnegie Hall, N.Y.C., 1948; European debut Concertgebouw Orch., Amsterdam, 1952; rep. U.S. at Brussels World Fair, 1958; tours N. and S.A., 1947—, USSR, 1960, 62; soloist major Am. orchs., 1948—; rec. artist Mercury, R.C.A Victor. Decorated chevalier Dans L'ordre Des Artes et Lettres (France). Address: care Hurok Attractions 730 Fifth Av New York City NY 10019

JANIS, IRVING LESTER, educator, psychologist; b. Buffalo, May 26, 1918; s. M. Martin and Etta (Goldstein) J.; B.S., U. Chgo., 1939; Ph.D. in Psychology, Columbia, 1948; m. Marjorie Graham, Sept. 5, 1939; children—Cathy Wheeler, Charlotte Janis. Research asst., exptl. div. study war time communications Library of Congress, 1941; sr. social sci. analyst, spl. war policies unit Dept. Justice, 1941-43; research asso., spl. com. Social Sci. Research Council, 1945-46, research fellow, 1946-47; mem. faculty Yale, 1947—, prof. psychology, 1960—; research cons. RAND Corp., 1948—. Mem. panel social psychol. research NSF, 1965-66; mem. com. disaster studies NRC-Nat. Acad. Scis., 1953-57; member Surgeon Gen.'s Sci. Adv. Com. on TV and Social Behavior, 1969—. Served with AUS, 1943-45. Recipient Hofheimer prize Am. Psychiat. Assn., 1959; Socio-Psychol. prize A.A.A.S., 1967; Fulbright Research fellow, 1957-58; Sr. Faculty fellow Yale, 1961- 62, 69 70; Faculty Research fellow Social Sci. Research Council, 1961-62, 66-67. 67. Mem. Am. Psychol. Assn. (rep. on council A.A.A.S. 1965-70), A.A.A.S. (judge sociol-psychol. prize 1963-64). Author: Air War and Emotional Stress, 1951; (with Hovland and Kelley) Communications and Persuasion, 1953; Psychological Stress, 1958; (with others) Personality and Persuasibility, 1959; (with Mahl, Kagan and Holt) Stress and Frustration, 1971; articles, chpts. in books. Contbg. editor Jour. Abnormal and Social Psychology, 1955-65; mem. editorial bd. Jour. Exptl. Social Psychology, 1966—. Home: 1205 Race Brook Rd Woodbridge CT 06525 Office: Dept Psychology Yale Univ 333 Cedar St New Haven CT 06510

JANIS, SIDNEY, art dealer, author; b. Buffalo, July 8, 1896; s. Isaac and Celia (Cohn) J.; student pub., tech. and aero. schs.; m. Harriet Grossman, Sept. 2, 1925; children—Conrad, Carroll. Engaged in mfg., 1924-39; collector modern art, 1925—; owner Janis Gallery, N.Y.C., 1948—. Mem. adv. com. Mus. Modern Art, N.Y.C., 1933-48. Author: They Taught Themselves, 1940; Abstract and Surrealist Art in America, 1942; (with Mrs. Janis) Picasso: Recent Years, 1946; also articles in art jours., 1941-71. Donated Sidney and Harriet Janis collection 20th Century Art to Mus. Modern Art, N.Y.C. Address: 6 W 57th St New York City NY 10019

JANKE, OTTO M., hosp. adminstr.; b. Freystadt, Germany, Aug. 11, 1925; s. Martin and Alice (Gehring) J.; came to U.S., 1925, naturalized, 1933; student Bethel Coll., 1947-49; B.A., Hamline U., 1952; M.H.A., U. Minn., 1954; J.D., William Mitchell Coll. Law, 1963; m. Inez I. Leverude, June 24, 1950; children—Cheryl Ann, Cynthia Rae, Paul G., Mark D., David T. With Asbury Hosp., Mpls., 1947; with St. Barnabas Hosp., Mpls., 1947-52, chief admitting officer, 1950-52; purchasing agt. Abbott Hosp., Mpls., 1952-54, adminstrv. resident, 1954; with St. Paul-Ramsey (Ancker) Hosp. and Med. Center, St. Paul, 1954—, exec. dir., supt., 1968; adminstr. St. Paul-Ramsey Hosp. Community Mental Health Center, 1968—. Mem. Mayor's Task Force on Central Data Processing for City St. Paul and County Ramsey, 1966—; mem. State Civil Service. Oral Interview Bd., 1961—, Inter Gov. Council, 1969—; faculty dept. econs. and bus. adminstrn. Bethel Coll., 1968—, Xavier U., Cin., 1968—; faculty Sch. Pub. Health, U. Minn., 1960—, Sch. Hosp. Adminstrn., 1955—. Bd. dirs. Minn. Soc. for Prevention Blindness, Intergovtl. Policy and Planning Bd. Served with USAAF, 1944-47. Mem. Am. Hosp. Assn., Met. Hosp. Planning Council, Am. Assn. Med. Colls., Nat. League Nursing, Am. Assn. Med. Adminstrs. (charter). Rotarian. Home: 1835 Simpson St St Paul MN 55112 Office: 640 Jackson St St Paul MN 55101

JANNARONE, JOHN ROBERT, army officer, educator; b. Newark, July 3, 1914; s. Charles and Concetta (Caruso) J.; student Montclair State Coll., 1932-34; B.S., U.S. Mil. Acad., 1938; M.S., Cal. Inst. Tech., 1951; C.E., Columbia, 1962; m. Anna May Miller, Nov. 22, 1941; children—Jack Miller, Robert Neil, Richard Thomas, Dorothy Ann, Nancy May. Commd. 2d lt. C.E., U.S. Army, 1938, advanced through grades to brig. gen., 1965; comdg. officer 293d Engr. Combat Bn., 1943; asst. engr. 8th Army, 1944- 45; spl. asst. to comdg. gen. Manhattan Project, 1945-47; dep. dist. engr., Los Angeles, 1951-53; charge C.E. Ark.-White-Red River Basins Planning Office, 1952-55; chief program rev. and analysis sect. Office Chief Staff, U.S. Army, 1956-57; asst. prof. physics U.S. Mil. Acad., 1947-50, prof., 1957-65, dean acad. bd., 1965—. Decorated Legion of Merit, Bronze Star. Fellow Am. Soc. C.E.; mem. Am. Soc. Engring. Edn., Soc. Am. Mil. Engrs., Am. Assn. Physics Tchrs., A.A.A.S. Home: 102 Washington Rd West Point NY 10996

JANNEY, FREDERICK EMERY, naval officer; b. Brookline, Mass., Oct. 27, 1914; s. Laurence A. and Marion (Robbins) J.; grad. Lawrenceville Sch., 1933; B.S., U.S. Naval Acad., 1937; postgrad. Nat. War Coll., 1955-56; m. Ethel Wanner, June 3, 1939; 1 dau., Carol (Mrs. Denis R. Regan). Commd. ensign USN, 1937, advanced through grades to rear adm., 1965; comdr. U.S.S. Topeka, 1960- 61; comdr. Mobile Logistic Support Force, U.S. 7th Fleet, 1965-67; dir. shore installations div. Office Chief Naval Operations, Navy Dept., Washington, 1967-69; dep. chief of staff Comdr. in Chief Pacific, 1969—. Decorated Silver Star medal with gold star, Bronze Star medal with combat V, Legion of Merit, Navy Commendation medal; Navy D.S.M. (Vietnam). Fellow Center for Internat. Affairs, Harvard, 1963-64. Club: Chevy Chase. Home: 5203 Abingdon Rd Washington DC 20016 Office: Hdqrs Comdr in Chief Pacific FPO San Francisco CA 96610

JANNEY, STUART SYMINGTON, Jr., lawyer, b. Baltimore County, Md., May 31, 1907 s. Stuart Symington and Frances Moale (Spencer) J.; A.B., Princeton, 1929; LL.B., Harvard, 1932; m. Barbara Phipps, May 26, 1936; children—Sheila (Mrs. Rufus M. G. Williams), Barbara (Mrs. William C. Trimble, Jr.), Stuart Symington, Sarah. Admitted to Md. bar, 1932; partner in the firm of Venable, Baetjer & Howard, Balt., 1939-58; atty. WPB, 1942. Dir. Merc.-Safe Deposit Trust Co. Balt., Bessemer Securities Corp. Chmn. Md. Racing Comm., 1947-49. Trustee Johns Hopkins Hosp., Johns Hopkins. Served as capt. USMCR, 1942-45. Clubs: Maryland (past pres.); Green Spring Valley Hunt (past pres.);The Brook (N.Y.C.); The Jockey. Home: Glyndn P O MD 21071

JANOFSKY, LEONARD S., lawyer; b. Los Angeles, Oct. 13, 1909; s. E. and Ida (Schwartz) J.; B.A., Occidental Coll., 1931; LL.B., Harvard, 1934; m. Nancy Nielson, Dec. 29, 1948; children—Annelies Irene, John Stephen. Admitted to Cal. bar, 1934, since practiced in Los Angeles; sr. regional atty. NLRB, 21st Region Ariz. and So. Cal., 1935-36 spl. trial counsel eminent domain proceedings Housing Authority City Los Angeles, 1950-54; partner firm Paul, Hastings, Janofsky & Walker, 1951—. Alumni trustee Occidental Coll.; mem. overseers com. to visit Harvard Law Sch. Served to lt. comdr. USNR, 1942-45. Fellow Am. Bar Found.; mem. Am. (mem. council sect. labor relations law), Cal. (com. chmn.), Los Angeles County (pres., trustee) bar assns., Phi Beta Kappa. Club: Chancery (Los Angeles). Contbr. articles profl. jours. Home: 661 Thayer Av Los Angeles CA 90024 Office: 510 S Spring St Los Angeles CA 90013

JANOS, A.G., applicance mfg. co. exec. Pres., Franklin Appliance div. Studebaker Corp., Mpls. Office: 65 22d Av NE Minneapolis MN 55418*

JANOS, JOHN WILLIAM, chem. co. exec.; b. North Tarrytown, N.Y., Nov. 29, 1924; s. Leonard William and Mary (Kopel) J.; B.B.A., Iona Coll., 1956; m. Catherine Reilly, Aug. 10, 1946; 1 son, Jeffrey. Clk.-cost accountant Sonotone Corp., Elmsford, N.Y., 1946-57; cost accountant, staff accountant, asst. comptroller, comptroller Reichhold Chem., Inc., White Plains, N.Y., 1957—. Trustee Reichhold Chems., Inc. Profit Sharing Stock Purchase Plan, Cooke Color & Chem. Co. Employees Profit Sharing Plan. Served with USNR 1943-46. Mem. Nat. Assn. Accountants. Home: Pines Bridge Rd Ossining NY 10562 Office: 525 N Broadway White Plains NY 10602

JANOSIK, EDWARD GABRIEL, educator; b. Youngstown, O., Jan. 16, 1918; s. Gabriel John and Katrina (Javorsky) J.; B.S. in Edn., S.E. Mo. State Coll., 1939; postgrad. U. Mich., summers 1939, 40; M.A., U. Pa., 1947, Ph.D., 1951; m. Ellen Martin Hastings, Aug. 10, 1943; children—Susanne (Mrs. Charles McNally), Claire Louise. Asst. prof. Washington Coll., Chestertown, Md., 1947-49; from instr. to asso. prof. U. Pa., 1951-67; prof., chmn. dept. polit. sci. State U. N.Y. at Geneseo, 1967—; vis. lectr. Haverford Coll., 1949-50, 57, Franklin and Marshall Coll., 1950- 51. Democratic candidate for Pa. Gen. Assembly, 1958; alternate del.-at- large Dem. Nat. Conv., 1960. Served to maj. AUS, 1940-46. Decorated Purple Heart. Mem. Am. Polit. Sci. Assn., Am. Assn. U. Profs. Author: (with Edward Cooke) Pennsylvania Politics, 2d edit., 1964; (with Garold Thumm) Parties and the Governmental System, 1967; Constituency Labour Parties in Britain, 1968. Home: 11 Elm St Geneseo NY 14454

JANOVY, DAVID LEE, educator; b. Seward, Neb., Nov. 10, 1934; s. Joseph F. and L. Gretchen (Hoagland) J.; B.A. in Edn., Neb. State Coll., 1956; M.A., U. Neb., 1962, Ph.D., 1967; m. Darlene Joan Murphy, Dec. 23, 1956; children—Lisa, Jennifer. From asst. to asso. prof. Ill. State U., 1964-68; faculty Mankato (Minn.) State Coll., 1968—, prof. sociology, dept. chmn., 1968—. Mem. budget div. Mankato United Fund. Served to 1st lt. USMCR, 1956-60. NSF grad. fellow, 1963-64; Fulbright-Hayes advanced research grantee, 1967; postdoctoral fellow Midwest Council Social Research in Aging, 1966-68. Mem. Am. Sociol. Assn., Midwest Sociol. Soc., Midwest Council Social Research in Aging, Omicron Delta Kappa. Mason. Home: 106 Westwood Dr Mankato MN 56001

JANOW, SEYMOUR JUDSON, govt. ofcl.; b. N.Y.C., Jan. 22, 1913; s. Henry and Elizabeth (Palestine) J.; A.B., U. Cal. at Los Angeles, 1934, grad student at Berkeley, 1937-39; m. Selma Y. Goldstein, Mar. 13, 1938; children—Amity Marle, Merit Elizabeth. Charge surveys populations movements 5 Western states Dept. Agr., 1940-41; with enemy br. Rd. Econ. Warfare, also Fgn. Econ. Adminstrn., 1942; with operations analysis sect. USAAF, 1943; personal cons. Gen. Claire Chennault, 1943-45; adviser Export-Import Bank, Washington, 1946; with fgn. trade div. SCAP, 1946-48; v.p. pvt. engring. orgns. in Far East, 1949-61; adminstr. Far East region AID, 1962-63; pres. U.S. Consultants, Inc. 1966—: v.p. U.S. Consultants, Overseas, Inc., 1952—. Mem. Am. C. of C. Tokyo,

Operations Research Soc. Am. (charter), Am. Soc. Testing Materials. Clubs: Correspondents, American (Tokyo). Home: 1327 33d St NW Washington DC 20007

JANOWITZ, MORRIS, education; b. Paterson, N.J., Oct. 22, 1919; s. Samuel Louis and Rose (Myers) J.; A.B., N.Y. U., 1941; Ph.D. in Sociology, U. Chgo., 1948; m. Gayle Arlene Shulenberger. Dec. 22, 1951; children—Rebecca, Naomi. Research asst. Library of Congress, 1941; sr. propaganda analyst Dept. Justice, 1941-43; instr. then asst. prof. The Coll., U. Chgo., 1947-51; from asst. prof. to prof sociology U. Mich., 1951-61; vis. prof. Grad. Sch. Bus., U. Chgo., 1961, prof. sociology, dir. Center Social Orgn. Studies, chmn. dept. sociology, 1967. Cons. to govt., pvt. agys.; mem. social sci. adv. bd. U.S. Arms Control and Disarmament Bd.; chmn. Inter-U. Seminar on Armed Forces and Soc. Served to 2d lt. AUS, 1943-46. Decorated Purple Heart; Fulbright research prof. U. Frankfurt (Germany) 1954-55; fellow Center Advanced Study Behavioral Sciences, 1958-59. Fellow Am. Acad. Arts and Scis.; mem. Am. Sociol. Assn. (v.p. 1970-71), Am. Polit. Sci. Assn., Internat. Sociol. Assn. (research council), Phi Beta Kappa. Democrat. Author: The Professional Soldier, 1950; Social Change and Prejudice, 1964; Political Conflict, 1970. Editor: Heritage Sociology Series, U. Chgo., 1964—; editorial bd. Am. Jour. Sociology, 1962—. Home: 1357 E 55th Pl Chicago IL 60637

JANOWSKI, THADDEUS MARIAM, architect, city planner; b. Cracow, Poland, Aug. 16, 1923; s. Stanislaw F. and Maria (Kijak) J.; M.C.P. in Architecture, Poly. Acad., Cracow, 1949; M.Arch., U. Ill., 1962; m. Zofia K. Owinski, Apr. 19, 1949; 1 dau., Barbara Margaret. Chief architect Miastoprojekt Cracow, 1949-58, So. Poland K.U.A. Warsaw, 1958-60; lectr. Poly Acad. Cracow, 1947-50, 58-60; instr. U. Ill., 1960-62; asso. prof. U. Man., 1962-65; asso. prof. Ia. State U., Ames, 1965—; numerous exhbns, in U.S., 1961—; built over 57,000,000 cubic feet constrn. Winner numerous prizes nat. or internat. competitions including prize Polish Embassy bldg., Peking, China, 1955, 1st prize Polish Pavillion, Brussels, Belgium, 1956, 1st prize astronomy obs. and planetarium, Warsaw, 1956, award exptl. bdlg., Moscow, 1959, 1st prize sch. bldgs., Poland, 1960, prize Red Rock Hill Devel., San Francisco, 1961, 2d prize campus, Dublin, Ireland, 1964, 2d and 3d prizes fall out shelters Office Civil Def., 1964, 2d prize, 1966; commns., include Ch. of Three Crosses, Chgo., 1967, Interstate Farms Devel., Des Moines, 1967. Mem. Assn. Polish Architects, Assn. Painters, Sculptors and Artists in Poland, Assn. Scientists Hist. Armament, Canadian Assn. U. Tchrs., Nat. Rifle Assn. Co-author: Sacred Art in Poland, 1955; The Urban Scale, 1968. Patentee in field. Address: 2122 McCarthy Rd Ames IA 50010

JANSEN, GUENTER ALFRED, librarian; b. Phila., Sept. 19, 1930; s. Alfred Gaston and Ella (Gieseler) J.; A.B., U. Pa., 1955; M.S., Drexel U., 1956; m. Helen Frenzel, June 16, 1956 (dec. May 1962); children—Werner Paul, Peter Gregory, Christopher Eric; m. 2d Herge Meykranz, June 14, 1963; 1 son, Wilhelm Georg. With Free Library, Phila., 1956; intern, cataloger Library of Congress, Washington, 1956-58; head extension dept. Cedar Rapids (Ia.) Pub. Library, 1958-60; asst. dir., dir. Mobile (Ala.) Pub. Library, 1960-65; city librarian, New Orleans, 1965-67; dir. Suffolk Coop. Library System, Suffolk County, L.I., N.Y., 1967—; lectr. tours Germany, 1965, 70; pub library bldg. cons. Life master, regional tournament dir. Am. Contract Bridge League, 1963—. Founder, pres. Mobile Chamber Music Soc. Served with AUS, 1952-54. Mem. A.L.A. Home: 2 Livingston Rd Bellport NY 11713 Office: P O Box 187 Bellport NY 11713

JANSEN, MARIUS BERTHUS, educator, historian; b. Vleuten, The Netherlands, Apr. 11, 1922; s. Berthus and Gerarda Christina (Holscher) J.; came to U.S., 1923, naturalized, 1937; A.B., Princeton, 1943; M.A., Harvard, 1948, Ph.D., 1950; m. Margaret Jean Hamilton, July 30, 1948; 1 dau., Maria Christine. Faculty U. Wash., 1950-59, prof. history, 1958-59; prof. history Princeton, 1959—, dir. E. Asian studies program, 1962-68, chmn. East Asian studies dept. 1969—. Bd. dirs. Far Eastern Assn., 1954-57; exec. asso. Internat. House Japan, 1960-61. Served with AUS, 1943-46. Mem. Assn. Asian Studies. Author: The Japanese Sun Yat-sen, 1954; Sakamoto Ryoma and the Meiji Restoration, 1961. Editor: (with Harold C. Hinton) Major Topics on China and Japan: A Handbook for Teachers, 1957; Changing Japanese Attitudes Toward Modernization, 1965; (with J.W. Hall) Studies in the Institutional History of Early Modern Japan, 1968. Home: 222 Mount Lucas Rd Princeton NJ 08540

JANSEN, VERNOL R., Jr., lawyer; b. Mobile, Ala., May 30, 1923; A.B., U. Ala., 1943, J.D., 1948. Admitted to Ala. bar, 1949, U.S. Supreme Ct. bar, 1959; dep. state prosecutor, 1950-54; judge Mobile (Ala.) Criminal Ct., 1954-56; U.S. atty. So. Dist. Ala., 1961-69. Served with USAIR, 1943-46. Mem. Am., Fed., Mobile County bar assns., Ala. State Bar, Phi Alpha Delta. Address: 302 Wingfield Dr Mobile AL 36607*

JANSON, HORST WOLDEMAR, educator; b. St. Petersburg, Russia, Oct. 4, 1913; s. Friedrich and Helene (Porsch) J.; ed. schs. of Hamburg, Germany; M.A., Harvard, 1938, Ph.D., 1942; m. Dora Jane Heineberg, Aug. 14, 1941; children—Anthony Frederick, Peter, Josephine, Charles. Asst. in fine arts Harvard, 1936-38; lectr. Worcester Art Mus., 1936-38; instr., State U. Ia., 1938-41; asso. prof., curator of art coll. Washington U., St. Louis, 1941-48; Guggenheim fellow, 1948-49, 55-56; prof. arts Washington Sq. Coll., N.Y. U., 1949—, chmn. dept. of fine arts, 1949—; vis. prof. Harvard, 1967. Mem. Coll. Art Assn. (editor-in-chief Art Bull. 1962-65, pres. 1970-72), Am. Studies Assn. Author: Apes and Ape Lore in the Middle Ages and the Renaissance; The Story of Painting for Young People; The Sculpture of Donatello; The Picture History of Painting; Key Monuments of the History of Art; History of Art. Cons. editor Time-Life Library of Art. Contbr. articles in fine arts publs. Home: 29 Washington Sq W New York City NY 10011

JANSON, LEIF, shipping co. exec.; b. Gothenburg, Sweden, Oct. 20, 1908; s. Sven Gustaf and Jenny Sofia (Werner) J.; student Gothenburg Inst. Commerce, 1925-28, Columbia, 1929-31; m. Barbara Brostrom, Oct. 1, 1942; children—Kitty (Mrs. Dag Victor), Ivar, Beata, Susanne, Martin. Apprentice, Swedish Orient Line, Hamburg, 1929; charterer Swedish Am.-Mexico Line, N.Y.C., 1930-32; mgr. Axel Johnson Group, 1932-50; dep. pres. Swedish Am. Line, Gothenburg, 1950-70, pres., 1970—, also dir.; pres., dir. Swedish Atlantic Line, 1967—; chmn. Eriksbergs Mek Verkstads A.B.; dep. chmn. Tirfing Steamship Co.; dep. chmn. working com. ABA (Swedish Airlines); mem. council reps. SAS (Scandinavian Airlines System); chmn. exec. com. Brostrom Group; dir. Atlantic Container Line Ltd., Swedish Orient Line, Swedish East Asia Co., Brostrom Trading Co., Timex, Posteritas Pension Fund, Gothenburg Towage & Salvage Co., Brostrom Tender Service, Leffler Group, Automobilfirma Ragnar Janson AB, Farg AB Internat., Marieholms Industri AB, Lindholmen Motor AB, Analytical Inst. for Maritime Services, Swedish Lloyd, Skandiakoncernens Zonrad (Western Zone), Gen. Swedish Shipping Assn., Acad. Tech. Sci., Swedish Shipping and Navy League, Swedish Shipowners Assn. (Western Zone), SILA (Svensk Interkontinental Lufttrafik AB. Decorated knight and comdr. Order of Vasa. Home: 6 Hogasplatsen Gothenburg S-412 56 Sweden Office: 6 Packhusplatsen Gothenburg S-411 13 Sweden

JANSS, WILLIAM CLUFF, recreation and resort devel. exec.; b. Los Angeles, June 9, 1918 s. Edwin and Florence (Cluff) J.; B.A., Stanford, 1940; m. Anne Searls, Dec. 30, 1940; children—Suzanne (Mrs. James Ferguson), Mary, William Cluff. Dir. for winter sports Yosemite Co., 1946; pres. Janss Cattle Industries, Thermal, Cal., 1950-64; chmn. bd. dir. Janss Inv. Co., Thousand Oak, Cal., 1956—; chmn., chief operating officer Sun Valley Co. (Ida.), 1968—; dir. Yosemite Park & Curry Co., Nat. Ski Area Operators Assn., Aspen Ski Corp., Head Ski Corp Mem. U.S. Olympic Ski Team, 1940. Trustee Aspen Inst; bd. dirs. Internat. Design Conf.; mem. bd. athletic control Stanford. Served USAAF, 1943-45. Home: Sun Valley ID 83353

JANSSEN, DAVID, actor; b. Naponee, Neb., Mar. 27, 1930; s. Harold Meyer and Berniece Graf; Berniece Graf; ed. high sch. Began acting career at age 9; under contract Universal Pictures, 1951-56; recent movies include Hell to Eternity, My Six Loves, The Green Berets, Shoes of the Fisherman, Where It's At, Marooned, Generation, Macho Callahan; guest Generation, Macho Callahan; guest star various TV shows; role Richard Diamond, TV series, 1957-60; title role The Fugitive, ABC-TV series, 1963-67. Served with AUS, 1952-54. 1952-54. Recipient TV Guide award, TV-Radio Mirror award, 1964; selected Man of Year on TV, Radio-TV, Daily, 1964; Emmy nomination Nat. Acad. TV Arts and Scis., 1964, 66; Spl. Editor's award Photoplay Mag., 1965; recipient Golden Globe, Hollywood Fgn. Press. Assn., 1965; Gold Camera award as as most popular star in S.Am., Ecran mag., Santiago, Chile, 1966. Mem. A.F.T.R.A., Acad. Motion Picture Arts and Scis., Acad. Television Arts and Scis., Artists Equity Assn. Clubs: Friars; Tamarisk and Canyon Country (Palm Springs, Cal.); Beverly Hills (Cal.). Address: 9255 Sunset Blvd Hollywood CA 90069

JANSSEN, WERNER, symphony conductor; b. N.Y.C., June 1, 1900; B.A., Dartmouth, 1921, Mus. D., 1935; music degree U. Cal.; m. Ann Harding (div. Feb. 1963). Conducted 1st concert Royal Symphony Orch. at Acad. Rome, 1931; guest condr. Budapest Philharmonic Orch., Berlin, Vienna, Helsingfors, Copenhagen, Turin, Milan, Riga; made Am. debut with N.Y. Philharmonic-Symphony Orch., 1934; also condr. maj. U.S. orchs.; condr. Balt. Symphony Orch., 1938; now guest condr. in Europe. Fellow Juilliard Found., Am. Acad. Rome, 1930. Compositions include: (for theatre) symphonic score for The General Died at Dawn, 1936; (for orch.) New Year's Eve in New York, 1930, Louisiana Symphony, 1932, Dixie Fugue, 1932, Foster Suite, 1937; (chamber music) Kaleidoscope for string quartet, 1932, Fantasy, for string quartet, 1934, String Quarter No. 1, 1934, String Quartet No. 2, 1935, Obsequies of a Saxophone, for six wind instruments, snare drums, 1930; (for piano) An Old Love Song, Ragamuffin. Address: Am Express Co Frankfurt am Main West Germany*

JANSSON, KARL OSCAR, r.r. ofcl.; b. St. Louis, Jan. 22, 1906; s. Karl Gustaf and Wilhelmina (Anderson) J.; certificate accounting Washington U., St. Louis, 1932; m. Frances Augsberger, Aug. 5, 1929 (dec.); m. 2d, Helen Grindle Baker, Nov. 26, 1969. With M.-K.-T. R.R., 1926—, treas., 1956-67, asst. sec., 1958-67, sec., treas., 1967—; sec., treas. Katy Transp. Co., Beaver Meade & Englewood R.R. Co., San Antonio Belt & Terminal Ry. Co., Co- ordinated Transp. Co., Southwestern States Mgmt. Co., M-K-T Industries, Inc.; sec., treas., dir. Donland Devel. Co.; dir. Trailer Trains Co. Mem. Western Treasurers Group, Adv. Com. Assn. Am. Railroads, Newcomen Soc. N.Am. Republican. Presbyn. Home: 5622 Del Roy Dr Dallas TX 75230 Office: 701 Commerce St Dallas TX 75202

JANTZ, HAROLD EDWARD STEIN, educator; b. Elyria, O., Aug. 26, 1907; s. Emil and Anna (Stein) J.; A.B., Oberlin (Ohio) Coll., 1929, Litt.D., 1960; M.A., U. Wis., 1930, Ph.D., 1933; student Univs. of Munich and Bonn. 1930-31; m. Eleanore M. Whitmore, June 7, 1935. Teaching asst. U. Wis., 1931-33, asst. prof. German and comparative literature Antioch Coll., 1933-34, Clark U., 1934-42; asst. prof. Princeton, 1942-46 asso. prof., 1946-47; prof. German Northwestern U., Evanston, Ill., 1947-56, Johns Hopkins, Baltimore, 1956—; guest prof. for Am. studies U. Hamburg, 1953-54; guest prof. U. Vienna, 1948, 54, U. Pa., 1970; lectr. series various univs.; vis. expert Am. lit. and cultural relations U.S. Allied Commn. in Austria, summer 1948; U.S. specialist Dept. of State, Edn. Exchange Program, Vienna, 1954. Mem. Nat. Fulbright Com. for Austria, 1962—, chmn., 1964-65. Served with Army Specialists Training Program, 1943-46. Recipient Gold medal Goethe Inst.; Guggenheim Meml. Found. fellow, 1942-43, 47. Mem. Modern Lang. Assn. Am. (exec. council, chmn. various sects. and groups), Am. Antiquarian Soc., Mass. Hist. Soc., Phi Beta Kappa. Guggenheim Memorial Found. fellow, 1942-43 and 1947. Author books including: The First Century of New England Verse, 1944, 62; Geothe's Faust as a Renaissance Man, 1951; America in German Thought and Literature, 1955, 62; The Sooth Sayings of Bakis: Goethe's Tragi-Comic Observations on Life, Time and History, 1966; The Mothers in Faust: The Myth of Time and Creativity, 1969; also articles and papers. Home: 101 E Highfield Rd Baltimore MD 21218

JANTZEN, ALICE CATHERINE, occupational therapist; b. Brookline, Mass., Aug. 17, 1918; d. Francis T. and Alice M. (Doyle) Jantzen; A.B., Wellesley Coll., 1939; diploma Boston Sch. Occupational Therapy, 1952; M.S. in Edn., U. Pa., 1957; Ph.D., Boston Coll., 1971. Occupational therapist N.Y. State Rehab. Hosp., 1952-54; asst. prof. Western Mich. U., 1954-55; teaching fellow, instr. U. Pa., 1955-58; prof., chmn. dept. occupational therapy, dir. occupational therapy service U. Fla., 1958—. Pres., Am. Occupational Therapy Found., 1965-66. Served with USNR, 1943-46. Mem. Am. (chmn. com. grad. study 1962-64, bd. mgmt. 1962-64, v.p. 1964-66, exec. bd. 1964-66), Fla. (pres. 1971—, mem. exec. bd. del. to Am. Occupational Therapy Assn. 1971—) occupational therapy assns., Am. Personnel and Guidance Assn. Club: Altrusa. Author articles. Home: 3201 S W 5th Ct Gainesville FL 32601 Office: Box 212 J Hillis Miller Health Center U Fla Gainesville FL 32601

JANTZEN, JOHN MARC, univ. adminstr.; b. Hillsboro, Kan., July 30, 1908; s. John D. and Louise (Janzen) J.; A.B., Bethel Coll., Newton, Kan., 1934; A.M., U. Kan., 1937, Ph.D., 1940; m. Ruth Patton, June 9, 1935; children—John Marc, Myron Patton, Karen Louise. Elementary Sch. tchr. Marion County, Kan., 1927-30, Hillsboro, 1930-31; high sch. tchr., Hillsboro, 1934-36; instr. sch. edn. U. Kan., 1936-40; asst. prof. Sch. Edn., U. of Pacific, Stockton, Cal., 1940-42, asso. prof., 1942-44, prof., dean sch. edn., 1944—, dir. summer sessions, 1940—. Past chmn. commn. equal opportunities in edn., Cal. Dept. Edn.; mem. Nat. Council for Accreditation Tchr. Edn. Mem. Am. Edn. Research Assn., Cal. Edn. Research Assn. (past pres.), Cal. Council for Edn. Tchrs., Cal. Tchrs. Assn. (past chmn. commn. on tchr. edn.), N.E.A., Phi Delta Kappa. Methodist. Rotarian. Home: 117 W Euclid St Stockton CA 95204

JANTZEN, WILLIAM J., banker; b. N.Y.C., 1909. Pres., dir. Sterling Nat. Bank & Trust Co. N.Y.; dir. Standard Prudential Corp., Health Information Systems, Inc., N.Y. Credit and Financial Mgmt. Assn., Inc., Damon Creations, Inc. Chmn. bd. govs. Credit Men's Frat. Inc.; chmn. bd. trustees N.Y. Inst. Credit, Inc. Home: 1241 E 26th St Brooklyn NY 11210 Office: 1410 Broadway New York City NY 10018

JANUARY, LEWIS EDWARD, physician, educator; b. Haswell, Colo., Nov. 14, 1910; s. Frank Puleng and Estella (Miller) J.; B.A., Colo. Coll., 1933, D.Sc. (hon.), 1966; M.D., U. Colo., 1937; m. Virginia Eloise Taylor, Sept 13, 1941; children—Alan Frank, Craig Taylor. Successively intern, resident internal medicine, asst. physician U. Ia. Hosps., 1937-42; mem. faculty U. Ia. Coll. Medicine, 1946—, prof. medicine, 1953—; mem. attending staff U. Ia. Hosps., VA hosps., Iowa City, Des Moines; chief cardiology U. Ia. Hosp., VA Hosp., Iowa City. Mem. Inter-Soc. Commn. for Heart Disease Resources, 1968-71. Bd. dirs. Community Health, 1966-67. Served to lt. col., M.C., AUS, 1942-46. Recipient Honors Achievement award Angiology Research Found., 1965; Gold Heart award Am. Heart Assn., 1969; Silver and Gold award U. Colo. Sch. Medicine, 1971. Diplomate Am. Bd. Internal Medicine. Fellow A.C.P., Am. Coll. Cardiology, Council Clin. Cardiology (chmn. 1961-63); mem. A.M.A., Am. Clin. and Climatol. Assn., Am. Fedn. Clin. Research Am. (bd. dirs. 1955—, pres. 1966-67), Ia. (dir. 1948-52, heart fund chmn. 1963, pres. 1952-53) heart assns., Assn. U. Cardiologists, Am. Soc. Internal Medicine, Am. Assn. U. Profs., Central Soc. Clin. Research (council 1951-54), Central Clin. Research Club (pres. (1954), Ia. Clin. Med. Soc., Pan Am. Med. Soc. (life), Internat. Cardiology Fedn. (v.p. 1970—), Sigma Xi, Phi Delta Theta, Nu Sigma Nu, Alpha Omega Alpha. Club: University Athletic (pres. 1961-64) (Iowa City). Author: articles in field. Editorial bd. Circulation, 1969—. Home: 425 Lexington Av Iowa City IA 52240

JANURA, ARTHUR L., supt. Cook County Forest Preserve Dist., Harlem Av River Forest IL 60305

JANZEN, ASSAR GOTRIK, educator; b. Gôteborg, Sweden, Aug. 22, 1904; s. Anders and Agnes Sofia (Ekeblad) J.; B.A., U. Gothenburg, Sweden, 1929, Ph.D., 1936; m. Saimi Margareta Johansson, Sept. 10, 1936; 1 son, Hans Erik. Came to U.S., 1946, naturalized, 1959. Asst. inst. for research in place names, dialects U. Gothenburg, 1929-42, docent U. Gothenburg, 1936-41, research fellow, 1937-38, prof., 1945; faculty Filip Holmguists Handels Inst., Gothenburg, 1930-32; docent U. Lund, Sweden, 1941-46, research fellow, 1942-46; staff Svenska Akademien Lund, Sweden, 1942-45; vis. prof. Scandinavian langs. and lit. U. Cal., 1946-49, prof., 1949-, chmn. Scandinavian dept., 1951-59. Decorated Knight of Royal Order of the North Star, (Sweden). Mem. Am. Scandinavian Found. Mem. Modern Lang. Assn. Am., Am. Name Soc., Soc. Advancement Scandinavian Study (pres.), Royal Gustaf Adolf Acad. (Stockholm), Royal Soc. Humanities (Uppsala, Sweden), Modern Lang. Tchrs. Assn., Vetenskaps Societeten Lund, Royal Soc. Letters and Sci. (Gothenburg). Author books published in Sweden. Contbr. articles Scandinavian, German, U.S. publs. Home: 810 Euclid Av Berkeley CA 94708

JAQUES, GUY EDWARD, Jr., savs. and loan exec.; b. Portland, Ore., Apr. 30, 1927; s. Guy Edward and Evalyn Ilene (Bailey) J.; B.A., U. Wash., 1950; m. Anna R. Makus, Mar. 19, 1950; children—Mark E., Neil G., Nanette I. Pres., Portland Fed. Savs. & Loan Assn., 1950—; chmn. Green Tree Devel. Co., Mountain Devel. Corp.; dir. Security Mortgage Ins. Co., Excel Mortgage Ins. Co. Mem. exec. council Columbia Pacific council Boy Scouts Am. Served with USNR, World War II. Mem. Ore. Savs. and Loan Leagues (past pres.), Pacific NW Conf. Savs. and Loans (past pres.), Alpha Tau Omega. Republican. Clubs: Multnomah Athletic, Arlington (Portland); Oswego Lake (Ore.) Country. Home: 303 Iron Mountain Blvd Lake Oswego OR 97034 Office: 444 SW Fifth Av Portland OR 97204

JAQUETTE, JOHN JOSEPH, utility exec.; b. Phila., Aug. 30, 1918; s. William Alderman and Henrietta (Stratton) J.: B.S., Haverford Coll., 1939; M.B.A., Harvard, 1941; m. Margaret Laura Leaf, Sept. 7, 1940; children—David L., Stratton C., Peter B. Prodn. planner Armstrong Cork Co., Pa., 1941-42; customer ser. mgr. Sears, Roebuck & Co., Honolulu, 1946-48; mng. dir. Cardinal Services, Ltd., Honolulu, 1948-49; with Hawaiian Telephone Co., Honolulu, 1949-70, financial v.p., 1965-70, exec. v.p., 1962-65; sr. v.p. finance United Utilities, Inc., Kansas City, Mo., 1970—; dir. N. Electric Co., United Bus. Communications, Inc., Rixon Electronics, Inc., GDI, Inc., United Telephone Co. Pa., Jefferson-Carolina Corp. Mem. Hawaii Manpower and Full Employment Commn., 1965-70; lectr. pub. utility econs. U. Hawaii, 1956-57; bd. dirs. Hawaii Joint Council Econ. Edn. Del., com. chmn. Hawaii Constl. Conv., 1968. Served from ensign to lt., USNR, 1942-46. Mem. C. of C. Hawaii (dir. 1966-70), Financial Execs. Inst. (pres. 1967-68), Nat. Assn. Accountants (pres. Hawaii 1961-62), Phi Beta Kappa. Clubs: Pacific (sec. 1969-70, bd. govs. 1969-70) (Honolulu); Oahu (Hawaii) Country (bd. dirs. 1967-69); Indian Hills Country (Shawnee Mission). Contbr. articles profl. jours. Home: 2411 W 69th Terrace Shawnee Mission KS 66208 Office: 2330 Johnson Dr Shawnee Mission KS 66205

JARDINE, JOHN EARLE, Jr., investment exec.; b. Pasadena, Cal., July 31, 1899; s. John Earle and Mary Chater (Peck) J.; student U. Cal. at Berkeley; m. Laura Blair Snyder, Oct. 21, 1922 (dec. Sept. 1966); children—John Earle III, Lauris Earle (Mrs. James Albert Philips III); m. 2d, Alice Ayer Ellis, May 15, 1967. With William R. Staats and Co., Los Angeles, 1922—, gen. partner charge syndicate buying, 1951—, sr. v.p., sec.; sr. v.p., dir. Glore Forgan, Wm. R. Staats; now v.p. du Part Glore Forgan, Inc. Past chmn. Los Angeles chpt. A.R.C., chmn. fund campaign, 1955, exec. com., dir. Los Angeles chpt., vice chmn. nat. conv., St. Louis, 1956. Bd. dirs. So. Cal. Area Bldg. Fund, AID-United Givers; treas., bd. dirs. Braille Inst. of Am., Inc.; pres., bd. dirs. San Gabriel Cemetary Assn.; bd. govs. Am. Nat. Red Cross. Served as 2d lt. U.S. Army, World War I; as lt. col. AUS, World War II. Mem. Soc. Colonial Wars (gov. for Cal.) S.R., Investment Bankers Assn. Am. (past v.p., past gov.), Assn. Stock Exchange Firms (past gov.), Los Angeles C. of C. (past dir., v.p.), Phi Delta Theta. Clubs: Bond (pres. 1948-49), Municipal Bond (past pres.) (Los Angeles); California; Stock Exchange (dir., past pres.); Valley Hunt. Home: 766 Linda Vista Av Pasadena CA 91103 Office: 833 Wilshire Blvd Los Angeles CA 90017

JAREM, JOHN, elec. engr., educator; b. Yarembina, Czechoslovakia, July 4, 1921; s. John and Anna (Kmec) Jarembinsky; came to U.S., 1929, naturalized, 1942; B.Elec. Engring., Bklyn. Poly. Inst., 1947, M.Elec. Engring., 1951; M.Systems Engring., U. Pa., 1956, Ph.D., 1961 m. Sarah Mildred Simmons, June 4, 1944; children—John Michael, Robert Stephen, James Peter, Edward Shannon. Asst. prof. elec. engring. U.S. Naval Postgrad. Sch., Monterey, Cal., 1947-51; engring. and math. specialist Lockheed Aircraft Corp., Burbank, Cal., 1951-54; systems engr. RCA, 1954-64; prof. elec. engring., head dept. Drexel Inst. Tech., 1964—; cons. in field, 1962—. Served with USAAF, 1942-46. Sr. mem. I.E.E.E.; mem. Am. Phys. Soc., Eta Kappa Nu, Tau Beta Pi, Sigma Pi Sigma. Research in plasma physics, electromagnetic scattering theory, def. analysis. Home: 7 W Close St Morrestown NJ 08057 Office: Drexel U 32d and Chestnut Sts Philadelphia PA 19104

JARMAN, BURNICE HERMAN, educator; b. Snow Hill, Md., June 3, 1905; s. William Barton and Edith Amelia (Purnell) J.; B.S., West Chester State Coll., Pa., 1928; A.M., George Washington U., 1932, Ed. D., 1938; Litt. D. (hon.), Ewha U., Seoul, Korea, 1961; m. Naomi Virginia Crain, June 22, 1935; children—Richard Crain, Patricia Crain. Master, The Episcopal Acad., 1928-30, St. Albans

Sch., Washington, 1930-39; dir. instrn., Arlington, Va., 1941-45; asst. prof. edn. George Washington U., 1939-43, asso. prof., 1943-47, prof. edn., 1947-63, registrar and sec. faculties, 1945-50, asst. to pres., 1950-51, dean summer sessions, 1951-60; pres. Pikeville (Ky.) Coll., 1963-65. Recipient citations Korean Ministry of Edn., 1961, Seoul Nat. U., 1961, U.S. Army Mgmt. Sch., 1960, Govt. Services, Inc., 1963; Distinguished Service award West Chester State Coll. Alumni Assn., 1967; named Ky. Col., 1963. Mem. Gate and Key, Phi Delta Kappa, Pi Gamma Mu, Omicron Delta Kappa, Phi Alpha Theta. Presbyn. (elder). Pub. speaker, author articles on edn., pub. affairs. Address: RFD 1 Middletown VA 22645

JARMAN, FRANKLIN MAXEY, apparel co. exec.; b. Nashville, Nov. 10, 1931; s. Walton Maxey and Sarah (Anderson) M.; B.S., Mass. Inst Tech., 1953. With Third Nat. Bank, Nashville, 1953; with Genesco, Inc., 1957—, treas., 1962-64, financial v.p., 1963-66, exec. v.p., now chmn., also dir.; dir. First Am. Nat. Bank, 721 corp.; pres. Beacon Aircraft Inc., 1963—; v.p. S. H. Kress Co., 1963—. Trustee Christian Mission Found. Served to lt. (s.g.) USNR, 1953-58; capt. USAF Res. Mem. Sigma Alpha Epsilon. Club: Belle Meade Country (Nashville). Home: 601 Bowling Av Nashville TN Office: 111 7th Av N Nashville TN 37202

JARMAN, JOHN, congressman; b. Sallisaw, Okla., July 17, 1915; s. John H. and Lou Neal (Jones) J.; student Westminister Presbyn. Coll., Fulton, Mo., 1932-34; A.B., Yale, 1937; LL.B., Harvard, 1941; m. Ruth Virginia Bewley, Feb. 25, 1942 (dec. 1964); children—Jay, Susan, Steve; m. Marylin Grant, Feb. 10, 1968. Admitted to Okla. bar, 1941, since practiced in Oklahoma City. Mem. Okla. Ho. of Reps., 1947, Okla. Senate, 1949; mem. 82d-92d congresses from 5th Dist. of Okla. Served to master sgt. AUS, 1942-45. Democrat. Home: 1805 Huntington St Oklahoma City OK 73116 Office: Rayburn Bldg Washington DC 20525

JARMAN, JOSEPH, musician; b. Pine Bluff, Ark., Sept. 14, 1937; s. Joseph and Eva (Robinson) J.; student Chgo. City Jr. Coll., 1958-59, Chgo. Tchrs. Coll., 1958-59, Mil. Inst. Tech., 1959-60, U. Ariz., 1960-61, Am. Conservatory Music, 1966. Appeared at Harper Theatre, Chgo., 1965; neo- music theatre concert, Chgo., 1966; selected to Detroit Jazz Conf. Wayne State U., 1967; environmental music concert U. Chgo., 1967; tchr. Goodman Sch. Music, 1964; lectr. U. Chgo., 1966; pvt. tchr., 1966—. Served with AUS, 1955-58. Mem. Assn. Advancement Creative Musicians (dir.). Composer: Tribute to the Hard Core, 1965; Non- Cognitive Aspects of the City, 1966; Hollows Ecliptic, 1967.‡

JARMAN, WALTON MAXEY, business exec.; b. Nashville, May 10, 1904; s. J.F. and Eugenia (Maxey) J.; ed. Mass. Inst. Tech.; LL.D., Stetson U.; m. Sarah Anderson, Oct. 10, 1928; children—Franklin, Anne, Eugenia. Sec.-treas. Jarman Shoe Co., 1925-32, pres., 1932-33; pres. Gen. Shoe. Corp. (became GENESCO, Inc. 1959), 1933-47, chmn., 1947-69, now chmn. finance com.; dir. Bonwit Teller Co., S.H. Kress & Co., Nashville City Bank & Trust Co., H & M Rayne, Ltd. (London); trustee Mut. Life Ins. Co. N.Y., Greenfield Real Estate Investment Trust. Mem. Tenn. Tax Commn., 1949; chmn. Gov's Study on Cost Control. Pres. Billy Graham Evangelistic Trust; trustee Moody Bible Inst., Nat. Jewish Hosp., Denver; dir. Freedoms Found., Renfret Growth Fund; v.p. So. Bapt. Conv., 1950. Mem. Nat. Boot and Shoe Mfrs. Assn. (dir.), Dirs. Inst. (Eng.), Am. Bible Soc. (v.p.), Pi Delta Epsilon, Theta Delta Chi, Theta Tau, Eta Mu Pi, Beta Gamma Sigma. Republican. Baptist. Clubs: Bellemeade Country; Fifth Avenue (N.Y.C.); Everglades, Bath and Tennis (Palm Beach). Dir. Christianity Today mag. Author: A Businessman Looks at the Bible; O Taste and See. Home: 3610 Woodlawn Dr Nashville TN 37215 Office: 111 7th Av N Nashville TN 37202

JARMAN, WILLIAM JACKSON, clergyman; b. Kansas City, Mo., Jan. 18, 1916; s. Eugene Oswald and Alpha Ellen (Bratten) J.; A.B. with distinction in English, U. Mo., 1937, grad. student, 1940-41; B.D., Union Theol. Sem., N.Y.C., 1940; D.D., Culver-Stockton Coll., 1959; m. Mary Mona Love, May, 1, 1946; children—William Jackson, Mona, Mary. Ordained to ministry Christian Ch., 1933; pastor in Paris, Mo., 1941-42, Mexico, Mo., 1946-48, Univ. Pl. Ch., Champaign, Ill., 1948-65, Park Av. Christian Ch., N.Y.C., 1965—; lectr. Union Theol. Sem., N.Y., 1966—; pres. Ill. Disciples Found., Champaign, 1948-66. Pres., Council Christian Unity, 1957-64; mem. gen. bd. Nat. Council Chs., 1957—; bd. higher edn. Disciples of Christ, 1948-65, commn. ministry Ill. Disciples, 1948-65, mem. exec. com. Consultation on Ch. Union, 1966—. Exec. com. Champaign County Mental Health Clinic, 1956-65. Pres. bd. trustees Disciples Div. House of U. Chgo., 1960-66; trustee Christian Theol. Sem., Indpls., 1966—; chmn. Unity Commn. of Christian Chs. Served to lt. comdr. chaplain USNR, 1942-46. Mem. Acad. Religion and Mental Health. Author: Manual for Burial of the Dead at Sea, 1942; Looking Toward Marriage, 1960. Home: 505 Queen Anne Rd Teaneck NJ 07666 Office: 1010 Park Av New York City NY 10028

JARNAGIN, RICHARD CALVIN, educator; b. Dallas, Aug. 26, 1930; s. Calvin Elgin and Dorothy Edris (Brown) J.; student North Tex. Agrl. Coll., 1947-49; B.S., So. Meth. U., 1952; Ph.D., Yale, 1958; m. Patsy Sue Hatchel, June 20, 1952; children—Kurt Randall, Forest Neal. Mem. staff chemistry dept. U.N.C., 1958—, prof., 1967—. Served with USAF, 1953-55. Guggenheim fellow, 1967-68. Mem. Am. Chem. Soc., Am. Phys. Soc., Sigma Xi. Home: 609 Caswell Rd Chapel Hill NC 27514

JARNSTEDT, BO GUNNAR, Swedish diplomat; b. Eksjö, Sweden, Sept. 2, 1911; s. Justus Sigfrid and Elsa Valborg Andre (Engström) J.; degree in law Upsala, 1934, in arts, 1938; degree in bus. adminstrn., U. Stockholm, 1937; degree in pub. adminstrn., U. Wellington (New Zealand), 1955; m. Margareta Lundgren, May 18, 1939; children—Margareta, Bo Bosson. Asst. mil. attache, Berlin, Germany; 1940; joined Swedish Fgn. Service, 1940; attache Swedish Fgn. Office, 1940-41; assigned Finland and Can., 1941-48, Stockholm, 1948-52; charge d'affaires, Wellington, 1953-57; dep. and acting Swedish mem. Neutral Nations Supervisory Commn., Korea, 1954-55; counsellor of embassy New Delhi, India, 1957-59; consul gen. of Sweden in Chgo., 1959-62, 64—; ambassador of Sweden to Liberia, Ghana, Ivory Coast, Sierra Leone, Guinea, 1962-64. Decorated Grand Cross Order Liberian Redemption (Liberia); comdr. Order North Star (Sweden); officer Order Dannebrog (Denmark); Order White Rose (Finland); Order Phenix (Greece); Order Orange-Nassau (Netherlands). Club: Tavern (Chgo.) Home: 199 E Lake Shore Dr Chicago IL 60601 Office: 333 N Michigan Av Chicago IL 60601

JAROFF, SERGEY, conductor; b. Moscow, Russia, Mar. 20, 1896; student Acad. Ch. Singing, also Imperial Synod. An officer of the Cossacks; after revolution left Russia and founded Don Cossack Chorus; extensive conducting tours of Europe and U.S. Address: care Allied Arts Corp 200 N Wacker Dr Chicago 60606*

JAROS, ROBERT VICTOR, ret. pharm. co. exec.; b. Chgo. Feb. 2, 1905; s. Ferdinand W. and Clara C. (Kuehne) J.; A.B., U. Mich., 1927; grad. Advanced Mgmt. Program, Harvard 1949; m. Marion G. Hopwood, Apr. 30, 1960; stepchildren—Howard D. Jones, Ann L. Jones; 1 adopted son, Richard R. With No. Trust Co., 1927-29, Am. Express Co., 1929; with Abbott Labs., North Chicago, Ill., 1930-70, treas., 1957-70, v.p., 1961-70. Mem. Pharm. Mfrs. Assn., Phi Beta Kappa, Phi Kappa Phi, Alpha Kappa Psi. Home: 33 S Sheridan Rd Lake Forest IL 60045

JARRARD, CHARLES FARNHAM, Jr., structural steel co. exec.; b. Oak Park, Ill., Apr. 8, 1933; s. Charles Farnham and Margaret (Burkhardt) J.; student U. Wis., 1951-53; B.A., Lawrence U., 1958; m. Holly Piper, Aug. 31, 1957; children—Charles F. III, Jeffrey David, David Stuart. Foreman, supt., plant mgr. Allied Structural Steel Co., Hammond, Ind., 1957-61, v.p., 1962-69, pres., 1969—; dir. Am. Inst. Steel, Lawndale Trust & Savs. Bank, Chgo. Mem. exec. council Calumet council Boy Scouts Am., 1969—. Bd. dirs. Hammond YMCA. Served with AUS, 1953-55. Mem. Central (dir.), Ind. (past pres.) fabricators assns., Am. Welding Soc., Quality Criteria Inspection Standards Assn. Home: 20521 Greenwood Dr Olympia Fields IL Office: 1435 165th St Hammond IN 46320

JARRARD, JAMES RICHARD, producer; b. Waycross, Ga., Aug. 14, 1939; s. Verlie D. and Nelle (Lloyd) Armstrong; B.S., U. Ill., 1961; m. Donna DiMartino, May 5, 1967; 1 son, Josh Cameron. Free lance arranger, producer, song writer, studio musician; mem. various groups including Greenwood County Singers, others, 1961-66; artists and repertoire producer RCA Victor, Hollywood, Cal., 1966—; producer Jefferson Airplane, Surrealistic Pillow, 1967, Jose Feliciano, Feliciano, 1968, Nilsson, Pandemonium Shadow Show, 1967, Aerial Ballet, 1968, Glen Yarbrough, 1968, John Hartford, 1969, Jose Feliciano 10 to 23, 1969, Alive- Alive-O, 1969, Fireworks, 1970. Mem. A.S.C.A.P., Nat. Acad. Recording Arts and Scis. (bd. govs. 1969—), Phi Gamma Delta. Methodist. Office: care Marchat & Kronfeld 1501 Broadway New York City NY 10036

JARRARD, JERALD OSBORNE, airline catering services exec.; b. Mt. Washington, Mo., Oct. 12, 1917; s. Frank Lewis and Mary Minerva (Osborne) J.; student Kansas City (Mo.) Jr. Coll., 1935-36, 38-39; LL.B. magna cum laude, U. Mo., 1947; m. Marjorie M. McInteer, Dec. 23, 1938; children—Louise Louise (Mrs. John F. Lloyd), Jerry Michael, Janeece Rene. Admitted to Mo. bar, 1947; with Trans World Airlines, 1942-60, dir. labor relations, 1957-60; v.p. indsl. relations Eastern Airlines, 1960-63; v.p. personnel Am. Airlines, Inc., 1963, regional v.p. sales and services, N.Y., 1964-66, system v.p. sales and services, 1966-68; pres. In-Flite Services div. Marriott Corp., Washington, 1968-. Mem. Mo. Integrated Bar, I.E.E.E., Am. Soc. Travel Agts., Newcomen Soc. N. Am., Nat. Restaurant Assn., Nat. Rifle Assn., Sales Execs. Club, Phi Delta Phi. Methodist. Clubs: Burning Tree Country (Greenwich, Conn.): Pinnacle, Wings (N.Y.C.); Congressional (Washington.). Editor U. Mo. Law Rev., 1944-46. Home: 9629 Weathered Oak Ct Bethesda MD 20034 Office: Marriott Corp 5161 River Rd Washington DC 20016

JARRE, MAURICE, composer, orch. leader; b. Lyon, France, Sept. 13, 1924; s. Andre and Gabrielle (Boullu) J.; bachelor's degree, Ampere Acad., Lyon; student Nat. Conservatory Music, Paris. Composer background music Theatre Nat. Popilaire, Paris, 1951-62, mus dir., 1951-63; sound and lighting for Chateau du Chambord; composer music for radio and TV, also motion pictures; full-length films include La Tete contre les murs, 1958; Les Etoiles du Midi; Crack in the Mirror, 1959; Therese Desqueyroux, 1962; Longest Day; Sundays and Cybele; Mourir a Madrid; Lawrence of Abrabia, 1963; le Jourle plus long, les Animaux, Index, le Train, Week-end à Zuydcoote, le Docteur Jivago (Acad. award 1965) all 1965; Paris brule-t-il?, Grand Prix, la Nuit des generaux, all 1967; Pancho Villa, 1968, others; symphonic compositions include Passacaille a la memorire d'Arthur Honegger, 1955; for violin and orch. Mobiles, 1961, Cantate pour une demente, 1963; for baletts Masque de femme, 1951, Facheuse rencontre, 1959, Maldorei, 1962. Decorated chevalier des Arts et Lettres; recipient Italian Broadcasting prize, 1955, Italian TV award, 1962, Harriet Cohen Internat. Music award for film music, 1962, Grand prize for records l'Academie Charles Cros, 1957, Acad. Motion Picture Arts and Scis. award for Lawrence of Arabia, 1963. Address: 37 rue Marbeuf Paris 8 France

JARRELL, JAMES HOYT, life ins. exec.; b. Milltown, Ala., Nov. 26, 1902; s. James Robert and Cora (Northen) J.; A.B., Howard Coll., 1924. Pres., Old Republic Life Ins. Co., Chgo., 1943-68, chmn. bd., 1968—; chmn. bd. Old Republic Ins. Co., Greensberg, Pa., 1955, Old Republic Internat. Corp., Chgo., 1969, Motorists Beneficial Ins. Co., Chgo., Old Republic Life Ins. Co. of N.Y., Old Republic Assurance Co., Phoenix. Served with USNR, 1941-44; lt. comdr. res. Mem. Sigma Nu. Home: 1500 N Lake Shore Dr Chicago IL 60610

JARRELL, JOHN WILLIAMS, newspaper corr.; b. Holton, Kan., July 13, 1908; s. John Frank and Myra (Williams) J.; student, Washburn Coll., Topeka, Kan., 1926-30; m. Lois Stephens, Sept. 12, 1940; 1 stepson, Andrew. Reporter, Topeka Daily Captial, 1930, Topeka State Jour., 1931-35, rejoined 1938, city editor, 1940-41; reporter, Shanghai (China) Evening Post-Mercury, 1935, Kansas City Star, Salt Lake Telegram, 1938; spl. rep. Santa Fe R.R. pub. relations dept., Chgo., 1936-37; Internat. News Service Staff, N.Y., 1941; war corr. Africa, Asia, Europe, 1942-44; joined Omaha World- Herald, 1944, chief Washington Bur., 1946—. Recipient medal of Freedom, USAF; medal of France's Liberation Paris, 1949. Mem. White House Corrs. Assn., Overseas Writers, Sigma Delta Chi, Phi Delta Theta. Clubs: National Press; Gridiron. Home: 4301 Massachusetts Av NW Washington DC 20016 Office: Nat Press Bldg Washington DC 20004

JARRETT, EDWIN BOSLEY, Sr., physician; b. Jarrettsville, Md., Aug. 18, 1896; s. William Hope and Mary Virginia (Streett) J.; A.B., Johns Hopkins, 1918, M.D., 1922; m. Dorothy Duncan, June 28, 1930; children—Edwin Bosley, William Hope II, John Duncan. Intern Union Meml. Hosp., Balt., 1922-23, Johns Hopkins Hosp., 1923-24; asst. resident physician Union Meml. Hosp., 1924-25, resident physician, 1925-26; pvt. practioe internal medicine, Balt., 1926—; attending physician Ch. Home and Hosp., Greater Balt. Med. Center, Union Meml. Hosp., Good Samaritan Hosp., Johns Hopkins Hosp. Mem. Joint com. trustees John Hopkins U. and Johns Hopkins Hosp., 1966-68; alumni trustee Johns Hopkins, 1957-63, life trustee, 1964—. Served with U.S. Army, 1918. Recipient Distinguished Alumnus award Johns Hopkins, 1967. Fellow A.C.P.; mem. Balt. City Med. Soc., Med. and Chirurgical Faculty Md., A.M.A., Johns Hopkins Roll Call (chmn. 1956-58), Johns Hopkins Alumni Assn. (pres. 1953-55), Delta Upsilon, Nu Sigma Nu, Omicron Delta Kappa. Club: Johns Hopkins Faculty (pres. 1958-68). Democrat. Methodist. Home: 213 Ridgewood Rd Baltimore MD 21210 Office: 11 E Chase St Baltimore MD 21202

JARRETT, JAMES LOUIS, coll. dean; b. Little Rock, Oct. 7, 1917; s. James Louis and Pauline May (Williams) J.; B.S., U. Utah, 1939, M.S., 1940; Ph.D., U. Mich., 1948; children by previous marriage—Dennis, Brent, Julie; m. Marjorie Ellen Clegg, Jan. 4, 1956; children—Devin, Timothy, Gregory, Malcolm. Tchr., English and speech Murray (Utah) High Sch., 1939-40; from instr. to prof. philosophy U. Utah, 1942-55; regional dir. Great Books Found., 1955-57, nat. pres., 1958-59; lectr. philosophy U. Mich., 1957-58; pres. Western Wash. State Coll., 1959-64; prof., asso. dean edn. U. Cal. at Berkeley, 1964—; exec. dir Hazen Found.'s Com. on Undergrad. Teaching, 1966-67; vis. prof. philosophy Colo. Coll., 1969-70. Mem. research adv. com. U.S. Office Edn., 1961-64. Served with AUS, 1944-46. Mem. Am. Philos. Assn. (pres. Pacific div. 1967). Author: (with Robert T. Harris) Language and Informal Logic, 1956; Quest for Beauty, 1957. Editor: (with Sterling McMurrin) Contemporary Philosophy, 1954; Philosophy For The Study of Education, 1969; The Educational Theories of the Sophists, 1970. Home: 534 The Arlington Berkeley CA 94707

JARRETT, KEITH, pianist, composer; b. Allentown Pa., May 8, 1945. Two hour solo concert of own compositions, 1962; scholar Berklee Sch.; leader own trio, appeared on TV; joined Art Blakey, 1965; European tour with Charles Lloyd, 1966; recording artist for Limelight records. Address: 635 E 11th St New York City NY 10009 *

JARRETT, THOMAS DUNBAR, univ. pres.; b. Union City, Tenn., Aug. 30, 1912; s. William Robert and Annie Sybil (Thomas) J.; A.B., Knoxville Coll., 1933; A.M., Fisk U., 1937; Ph.D., U. Chgo., 1947; m. Annabelle Madeline Gunter, Aug. 22, 1939; 1 dau., Paula Lynn. Tchr., Central High Sch., Paris, Tenn., 1933-37; asst. prof. English, Knoxville, Coll., 1937-40; asso. prof. English, Louisville Municipal Coll., 1941-43; prof. English, Atlanta U., 1955-67, acting dean Sch. Art and Scis., 1957-61, dean Grad. Sch., 1961-67; pres. Atlanta U., 1968—. Ford Found. fellowship lectr., Eng., 1953; mem. Mayor's Com. on Adult Edn., Atlanta, 1962-64; cons. Dept. Health, Edn. and Welfare Prospective Tchrs. Fellowship Program, 1966-68; adv. com. Nat. Def. Lang. Devel. Program, 1966-68; Ga. Sci. and Tech. Commn., 1969—. Served to lt. inf. AUS, 1943-46. Fellow Gen. Edn. Bd., 1939-40; Carnegie grantee for research, 1951-52. Mem. Nat. Council Tchrs. English (dir. 1963—, chmn. nominating com. 1962, commn. on English 1968—), Nat. Assn. of Deans and Registrars (pres. 1968-69), Coll. Lang. Assn., Council Grad. Schs., U.S., Kappa Boule, SIgma Pi Phi, Alpha Phi Alpha, Editor, Lang. and Lit., 1959-64. Book and poetry editor Phylon, 1948-67. Contbr., editor English Jour., monthly, 1959-64. Contbr. numerous articles profl. publs. Home: 691 Beckwith St SW Atlanta GA 30314

JARVIE, LAWRENCE LEE, orgn. exec.; b. Renfrew, Scotland, Jan. 5, 1906; s. William Lee and Sarah (Smith) J.; B.S., Ohio U., 1928; A.M., Ohio State U., 1933, Ph.D., 1936; m. Helen Elizabeth Williams, Aug. 20, 1927; 1 son, Charles Lawrence. Came to U.S., 1912, naturalized, 1919. Headmaster Valley Ranch Sch., Valley Wyo., 1928-33; asst. prof. George Washington U., 1935-37; dir. research Rochester Inst. Tech., 1937-42; asso. commr. edn. State of N.Y., 1946-49; exec. dean State U. of N.Y. 1949-60; pres. N.Y.C. Community Coll., 1960-62; gen. sept. community edn., Flint, Mich., 1962-66; pres. Fashion Inst. Tech., N.Y.C., 1966-71; cons. ednl. and training programs; pres. Council Higher Ednl. Instns. N.Y.C., 1969—. Chief training Command and Gen. Staff Sch., 1942-45; cons. War Dept., 1943-45; dir. Warton Am. Tech. Sch., E.T.O., 1945; lt. col. O.R.C. Mem. Albany Army Adv. Bd. Mem. Am. Assn. Sch. Adminstrs, Am. Ednl. Research Assn., Am. Soc. Engring. Edn., Middle States Assn. Colls. and Secondary Schs. (exec. com.), Nat. Commn. on Accrediting (dir.), St. Andrew's Soc. (Albany). Phi Delta Kappa, Phi Kappa Tau. Presbyn. Author books. Contbr. to profl., lay mags. Home: 9 Garrison Rd Falmouth MA

JARVIS, ALAN HEPBURN, museum dir.; b. Brantford, Ont., Can., July 26, 1915; s. Charles A. and Janet (Mackay) J.; B.A., U. Toronto, 1938; postgrad. Univ. Coll., Oxford U., 1939, N.Y. U., 1941; m. Elizabeth D. Kingsmill, July 23, 1955. With Ministry Aircraft Prodn., Eng., 1941-45; spl. sec. to Sir Stafford Cripps, 1945-57; dir. pub. relations Council Indsl. Design., London, 1947-50; exec. dir. Pilgrim Pictures, Ltd., London, 1950-55; head Oxford House, London, 1955; dir. Nat. Gallery of Can., Ottawa, 1955-60; nat. dir. Canadian Conf. of the Arts, Toronto, 1960—. Mem. Canadian Housing' Design Council, Canadian Inst. Design (hon.). Author (with Sir Gordon Russell) How to Buy Furniture, 1952. Editor: The Things We See, 1946; Democracy Alive, The Collected Speeches of Sir Stafford Cripps, 1946; The Gallery of Canadian Art. Office: 88 Richmond St W Toronto Ontario Canada

JARVIS, DONALD EDWARD, architect; b. Ft. Worth, Apr. 2, 1928; s. William Ed and Mattie (Shelton) J.; B.Arch., Tex. A. and M. U., 1950; M.Arch., Mass. Inst. Tech., 1952; m. Barbara Sterling, Sept. 19, 1929; children—Mark, Kirk, Laura Lee, Clay. With Wiltshire & Fisher, Dallas, 1950-51, Dahl, Dallas, 1952-55; partner Fisher & Jarvis, 1955-62; partner Jarvis, Putty & Jarvis, Dallas, 1962—. Bd. dirs. Juliet Fowler Homes, 1965-70; trustee Dallas Library, 1968-70. Recipient First Honor award for library design A.I.A., 1963. Fellow A.I.A. (pres. Dallas chpt. 1970); mem. Oak Cliff C. of C. (dir. 1968—). Important works include Library and Auditoriums Tex. A. and M. U., Library, Richardson, Tex., Lakewood Tower Office Bldg., Dallas, Duncanville (Tex.) High Sch. Mailing Address: ‡

JARVIS, HERBERT WOODHULL, Jr., mfg. co. exec.; b. Greenwich, Conn., Mar. 9, 1925; s. Herbert Woodhull and Harriet (Belmer) J.; B.S., Yale, 1947; postgrad. Boston U., 1948-54; m. June Reid, Jan. 2, 1947; children—Laurian, Averill Rand, Leslie Suzanne. With USM Corp., 1947—, mgr. gen. industry group, 1962-63, v.p., asst. to pres., 1963-68, pres., 1968—, also dir., mem. exec. com.; dir. S.A. Felton and Son Co., Inc., USM Precision Products, Inc., Truelove and Maclean, Inc., Nylok-Detroit Corp.; trustee Suffolk Franklin Savs. Bank. Bd. govs. Mass. Safety Council. Mem. N.A.M. (dir.), New Eng. Footwear Assn. (dir.), Greater Boston C. of C. (dir.). Conglist. (trustee). Clubs: Fort Hill; Cohasset Golf, Hingham Yacht, Cohasset Tennis and Squash. Home: 63 Lincoln St Hingham MA 02043 Office: 140 Federal St Boston MA 02110

JARVIS, JOHN ASA, coll. adminstr., b. Janesville, Wis., June 14, 1908; s. John and Harriet (Anderson) J.; B.S. in Mech. Engring., U. Wis., 1931; B.S. in vocational Edn., Stout State Coll., Menomonie, Wis., 1936; M.Ed., Wayne State U., 1941; Ph.D., U. Minn., 1953; m. Kathryn Marie Mulligan, June 23, 1937; children—Kay Ann, Thomas John. With accounting dept. Chevrolet Motor Co., 1933-35; tchr. pub. schs., Flint, Mich., 1936-42; tchr.-trainer Armored Force Sch., Ft. Knox, Ky., 1942; mem. faculty Stout State U., 1946—, prof. indsl. edn., 1953—, dean instrn., 1964- 66, v. p. acad. affairs, 1966—; cons. text book seminar Franklin Book Program, Indonesia, 1970. Bd. dirs. Menomonie Devel. Corp., pres., 1962—. Mem. Gov.'s Ednl. Adv. Com. Served to lt. comdr. USNR, 1942-46. Resistered profl. engr., Wis. Mem. Am. Vocational Assn. (pres., bd. dirs. 1959-65), Menomonie Co. of C. (pres. 1960), Am. Legion, Phi Delta Kappa, Iota Lambda Sigma. Mason, Rotarian (pres. Menomonie 1959). Mem. editorial adv. bd. Am. Tech. Soc., School Shop mag. Contbr. to profl. jours.; notes Mathematics Textbook. Home: 1414 Wilson Av Menomonie WI 54751

JARVIS, JOSEPH BOYER, univ. adminstr.; b. Springville, Utah, June 1, 1923; s. Joseph Smith and Mildred (Boyer) J.; student Harvard, 1942; B.A., U. Ariz., 1947; M.A., Ariz. State U., 1950; Ph.D., Northwestern U., 1958; m. Patricia Ann Potts, Dec. 17, 1955; children-Seth N., Nathan Y., Mary Beth. Instr. speech U. Ariz., 1950-52 Dartmouth, 1954-55; asst. prof. U. Utah, 1956- 63, asso. prof. 1963-68, prof. speech, 1968—, asst. dean Coll. Letters and Sci., 1958-60, asso. program dir. sta. KUED-TV, 1957-60, asst. to pres., 1962-64, dean summer sch., 1962-67, dean admissions and registration, 1965—, asso. v.p. acad. affairs, 1967—. Spl. asst. to U.S.

Commr. Edn., Washington, 1961-62. Mem. Speech Communication Assn. Western Speech Assn. Home: 2357 Blaine Av Salt Lake City UT 84108

JARVIS, LUCY HOWARD, TV producer; b. N.Y.C.; d. Herman M. and Sophie (Kirsch) Howard; B.S., Cornell U., 1938; M.S., Columbia Tchrs. Coll., 1941; postgrad. New Sch. Social Research, 1942; m. Serge Jarvis, July 18, 1940; children—Barbara Ann, Peter Leslie. Dietitian, N.Y. Hosp., 1938-39; copywriter, spl. campaign dir. Beechnut Foods Co., 1939-40; asso. food editor McCall's mag., 1940-43; nat. v.p. Women's Am. Orgn. Rehab. through Tng., 1944-51; 51; asso. to producer Talent Assos., N.Y.C., 1955-56; women's TV editor Pathe News, 1956-57; co-producer radio show Capitol Close-Up, WOR Mut. Broadcasting Co., 1957-60; TV producer news and pub. affairs NBC, 1960—; prodns. include the Nations Future, 1960-62; White Paper, 1962; The Kremlin, 1963; The Louvre, 1964-65; Who Shall Live?, 1965-66; Hello Dolly 'Round the World, 1966, Bravo Picasso, 1967; Kruschev in Exile: His Opinions and Revelations, 1967; An Exclusive Conservation with Dr. Christian Barnard, 1967; Dr. Barnard's Heart Transplant Operations, 1968; Vietnam and After, 1969; Cry Help!, 1970; Trip to Nowhere, 1970; Scotland Yard, 1971; also lectr. Vol. instr. A.R.C., 1943-45. Named Producer of Year, Radio and TV Daily, 1964; decorated chevalier Order Arts and Letters (France); recipient Internat. Guardianship award Orgn. Rehab. Through Tng., 1951, Bronze medal Pan Am. Soc., 1953, golden award McCall's mag., 1963, Peabody award, 1965, Emmy award, 1965, Thomas Alva Edison award, 1964, A Film Festival award, 1965, Med. Journalism award A.M.A., 1966, Ohio State U. Journalism award, 1966, 71, Christopher award, 1971. Mem. Cornell Alumni Assn. (centennial campaign 1964-65), Women's Nat. Press Club, Am. Women Radio and TV (Golden Mike award 1967), Nat. Acad. TV Arts and Scis., Nat. Endowment Arts, Sigma Delta Tau. Club: Overseas Press. Author: Pocket Book Cook-Book, 1942; Enjoyment of Wines, 1957. Home: 116 Central Park S New York City NY 10019 Office: 30 Rockefeller Plaza New York CIty NY 10020

JASKOT, WOJCIEEH, consul. gen. of Poland in Chgo. Address: 1525 N Astor St Chicago IL*

JASLOW, ROBERT IRWIN, physician, hosp. adminstr.; b. Reading, Pa., Apr. 27, 1923; s. Paul and Frances (Miller) J.; B.A., Lehigh U., 1943; M.D., Jefferson Med. Coll. Phila., 1947; m. Edith Kay Supak, May 18, 1946; children—Ann Sharon, Alan Philip, Paula Sue. Intern, Jewish Hosp., Phila., 1947-48; resident Willard Parker Hosp. for Contagious Diseases, N.Y.C., 1948; resident pediatrics Jewish Hosp., Bklyn., 1949-50; practice medicine, specializing in pediatrics, Chambersburg, Pa., 1953-60; adminstr. medicine, Northville, Mich., 1960-65, Washington, 1965-71, White Plains, N.Y., 1971—; clin. dir. Pennhurst State Sch. Annex No. 1 South Mountain, Pa., 1955-59; psychiat. clin. dir. Plymouth State Home and Tng. Sch., 1960-61, acting med. supt., 1961, med. supt., 1961-65; asso. pediatrician Children's Hosp., Detroit, 1964-65; chief Mental Retardation br. USPHS, Washington, 1965-67, dir. div. mental retardation Dept. Health, Edn. and Welfare, 1967-71; dir. Westchesster (N.Y.) State Sch., 1971—; instr. pediatrics Sch. Medicine, Wayne State U., 1961-64, clin. asst. prof., 1964-65; asso. prof. clin. pediatrics Georgetown U., 1966-70, prof. clin. pediatrics, 1970-71; faculty Sch. Edn. U. Mich., summer 1963, lectr. maternal and child health Sch. Pub. Health 1963-70; cons. Nat. Inst. Child Health and Human Devel. Dept. Health, Edn. and Welfare, 1963-65. Served to capt. AUS, 1951-53. Diplomate Am. Bd. Pediatrics. Fellow Am. Acad. Pediatrics (past chmn. juvenile delinquency com. Mich. chpt.), Am. Assn. Mental Deficiency, Am. Pub. Health Assn.; mem. Soc. For Research Child Devel., N.Y. Acad. Scis. Contbr. articles to profl. jours. Home: 379 Quaker Rd Chappaqua NY 10514 Office: 202 Mamaroneck Av White Plains NY 10601

JASON, ROBERT STEWART, physician, educator; b. Santurce, P.R., Nov. 29, 1901; s. Howard Talbot and Lena Belle (Wright) J.; A.B., Lincoln U., 1924, hon. D.Sc., 1948; M.D., Howard U., 1928; Ph.D., U. Chgo., 1932; D.Sc., N.J. Coll. Medicine and Dentistry, 1969; m. Elizabeth Gaddis, Sept. 25, 1929; children—Jeanne Elizabeth (Mrs. Benjamin H. Wright), Robert Steward. Intern, Freedmen's Hosp., Washington, 1928-29; asst. prof. Howard U., Washington, 1931-35, acting head dept. pathology, 1934-35, asso. prof., 1935-37, head dept. pathology, 1935-58, prof., 1937-70, vice dean, 1946-53, dean, 1955-65, coordinator for design and planning new hosp. and med. center, 1965-70; vis. pathologist at Freedmen's Hosp., 1931-37, pathologist, 1937-70; cons. pathology NIH, 1955-70; med. edn. cons. to Vietnam for ICA, 1958, 61. Exec. com. D.C. div., nat. dir.-at-large Am. Cancer Soc.; med. adv. com. VA Hosp., Tuskegee, Ala.; mem. Nat. Adv. Council on Edn. for Health Professions, 1964-68; mem. D.C. Pub. Health Adv. Council, 1962-69, chmn., 1968-69; mem., chmn. D.C. Health Planning Adv. Com., 1969-70; mem. com. on pathology Nat. Acad. Scis.-NRC; mem. adv. com. internat. health AID-Dept. State. Sec., YMCA Camp Las Casas, P.R., 1918. Recipient Nat. Ann. Divisional award and medal Am. Cancer Soc., 1967; Distinguished Service award Nat. Med. Assn., 1969; Profl. Achievement award U. Chgo. Alumni Assn., 1970; award for distinguished achievement in medicine and pub. service Howard U. Alumni, 1971. Fellow Coll. Am. Pathologists; mem. Am. Assn. Pathologists and Bacteriologists, Internat. Acad. Pathology, Nat. Med. Assn., (chmn. jud. council), Am. Acad. Forensic Scis., Nat. Assn. Med. Examiners, Assn. Former Interns and Residents Freedmen's Hosp., A.M.A., A.A.A.S., Dist. Med. Soc., Washington Soc. Pathologist's, Assn. Am. Med. Colls., Alpha Omega Alpha, Kappa Pi, Alpha Phi Alpha. Presbyn. Contbr. articles to profl. jours. Home: 3421 Park Blvd San Diego CA 92103

JASPAR, JAY CHARLES, ret. r.r. exec.; b. London, Eng., May 5, 1905; s. Harry and Phyllis (Welch) J.; student pub. schs., Ore., Cal., also Margate Coll. (Eng.), 1919-20; brought to U.S., 1909, naturalized, 1934; m. Helen Marie LeBeuf, June 28, 1924; children—Robert Charles, Laura Anne. With S.P. Co., 1922-70, various positions operating and accounting depts., 1922-47, asst. to gen. auditor, 1947, exec. asst. to pres., 1948-61, sec., 1961-70. Mem. Am. Soc. Corporate Secs. Club: Contra Costa Country (Concord, Cal.). Home: 10 Frances Way Walnut Creek CA 94596

JASPER, DAVID WESTWATER, lawyer; b. Columbus, O., Aug. 31, 1916; s. David W. and Charlotte (Evans) J.; A.B., Kenyon Coll., 1938; J.D., Northwestern U., 1941; m. Eleanor Frances Osborn, Aug. 2, 1941; children—Sara C., Mary H., David W., Kenneth O., Jasper. Gen. atty. Carrier Corp., Syracuse, N.Y., 1953-59, v.p., gen. counsel, 1959-70, v.p. legal and tax adminstrn., 1970—; dir. Manco Mfg. Co., Bradley, Ill., Carrier Distbn. Credit Corp., Carrier Overseas Corp., Dempster Bros., Inc., Knoxville, Tenn., Blomarine Research Corp., Marathon, Fla.; trustee Onondaga County Savs. Bank. Mem. adv. council N.Y. State Health Planning Commn., 1970. Pres., Republican Citizens com. Onodaga County, 1964. Trustee Kenyon Coll.; bd. dirs. Carrier Found., Community Health Information and Planning Service, Inc., Syracuse, N.Y. Mem. Am., N.Y. State bar assns., Phi Beta Kappa, Beta Theta Phi, Phi Alpha Delta. Clubs: University, Century, Sedgwick Farms Tennis. Home: 309 Sedgwick Dr Syracuse NY 13203 Office: Carrier Pkwy Syracuse NY 13201

JASPER, PAUL G., lawyer; b. Fort Wayne, Dec. 15, 1908; s. George W. and Anna (Stammer) J.; LL.B., Ind. U., 1932; m. Mary Esther Tucker, Sept. 12, 1931; children—Paul Tucker, Mary Jamia. Admitted to Ind. bar, 1932; practiced in Fort Wayne as asso. Peters, Leas & Murphy, 1932, mem. firm, 1932-38; mem. firm Peters, Campbell & Jasper, 1938-42; practiced individually, 1946-48; judge Supreme Ct. of Ind., 1949-53; became gen. counsel Public Service Indiana, 1953, now v.p., spl. counsel. Mem. Ind. State Police Bd., 1957—, pres. Served as capt. AUS, 1942-46; 98th Inf. Div. Central Pacific. Mem. Am., Ind., Allen County bar assns., Am. Legion (judge advocate Ind. dept. 1959), V.F.W., Delta Chi, Delta Theta Phi. Democrat. Methodist. Mason (33), Elk (pres. Ind. Elks State Assn., 1946-47), Turner, Rotarian. Clubs: Indpls., Athletic, Highland Golf and Country (sec., dir., pres. 1969-70). Home: 5953 Washington Blvd Indianapolis IN 46220 Office: 1000 E Main St Plainfield IN 46220

JASPERS, KARL, philosopher, psychiatrist; b. Oldenburg. Germany Feb. 23, 1883; s. Karl and Henriette (Tantzen) J.; ed. univs. Heidelberg. Munich, Berlin Göttingen: M.D., 1909; Dr. es lettres h.c., U. Paris, U. Lausanne, U. Geneva; M.D. h.c., U. Basel; Dr. phil. h.c., U. Heidelberg; m. Gertrud Mayer, 1910. Asst. at Psychiat. Clinic. Heidelberg, 1910; lectr. in philosophy U. Heidelberg. 1913-16, asst. prof., 1916-21 prof., 1921-48, dismissed by Nazi govt., 1937. reinstated, 1945; prof. philosophy U. Basel (Switzerland), 1949-61, emeritus, 1961-; leader in existential thought. Recipient Goethe Prize, Frankfurt, 1947; Peace prize Deutsches Buchhandel, Frankfurt, 1948. Hon. mem. Netherlands Soc. for Psychiatry and Neurology, Soc. German Neurologists and Psychiatrists, Royal Medico- Psychol. Assn. (Eng.); corr. mem. Acad. Scis., Heidelberg. Author: General Psycholpathology, 1913; Man in the Modern Age, 1931; Philosophie, 3 vols. 1932; Max Weber, 1932; Reason and Existence, 1935; Nietzche, 1936; Descartes, 1937; Existenzphilosophie, 1938; Nietzsche and Christianity, 1946; The Question of German Guilt (English transl. 1947) On the Origin and Goal of History, 1950; Reason and Anti-reason in Our Time, 1950; Way to Wisdom, 1950; Tragedy is Not Enough, 1952; Leonardo, 1953; Entmythologisierung. 1954; The Great Philosophers, 1957; Philosophy and the World, 1958; The Future of Mankind, 1958; Der philosophische Glaube angesichts der Offenbarung, 1962; Nicolaus Cusanus, 1964; Wohin Treibt die Bundesrepublik?, 1966.*

JASPERSEN, J. WILLIAM, automotive parts distbg. co. exec.; b. St. Mary's, O., Oct. 2, 1917; s. William and Margaret (Puck) J.; student Toledo U., 1939-42; m. Mary Jane Balog, May 29, 1947; children—Barbara Jane, Diane Mae, William Stephen. Dist. mgr. Walker Mfg. Co., Racine, Wis., 1948-54, sales mgr., 1954-56, v.p. sales, 1956-62; v.p. Gen. Automotive Parts Corp., Dallas, 1962-69, exec. v.p., 1970—, also dir. Home: 11141 Lamplighter St Dallas TX 75229 Office: 4600 Harry Hines Blvd Dallas TX 75207

JASTROW, ROBERT, physicist; b. N.Y.C., Sept. 7 1925; s. Abraham and Marie (Greenfield) J.; A.B., Columbia, 1944, M.A., 1945, Ph.D., 1948; post-doctoral fellow Leiden U., 1948-49, Princeton Inst. Advanced Study, 1949-50, 53, U. Cal. at Berkeley, 1950-53. Asst. prof. Yale, 1953-54; cons. nuclear physics U.S. Naval Research Lab., Washington, 1958-62; head theoretical div. Goddard Space Flight Center NASA, 1958-61, chmn. lunar exploration com., 1959-60, mem. com., 1960-62, dir. Goddard Inst. Space Studies, 1961—; adj. prof. geophysics Columbia, 1961—, dir. Summer Inst. Space Physics, 1962-70. Recipient Medal of Excellence, Columbia, 1962, Grad. Faculties Alumni award, 1967; Arthur S. Flemming award, 1965; medal for exceptional scientific achievement NASA, 1968. Fellow Am. Geophys. Union, A.A.A.S.; mem. Am. Phys. Soc., Internat. Acad. Astronautics, Council Fgn. Relations. Clubs: Cosmos, Explorers. Author: Red Giants and White Dwarfs; The Evolution of Stars, Planets and Life, 1967; Astronomy: Fundamentals and Frontiers. Editor: Exploration of Space, 1967; co-editor Jour. Atmospheric Scis., 1962—; the Origin of the Solar System, 1963; The Venus Atmosphere, 1969. Home: 22 Riverside Dr New York City NY 10023 Office: 2880 Broadway New York City NY 10025

JASTRZEBSKI, ZBIGNIEW DAMAZY, educator, b. Warsaw, Poland Sept. 15, 1910; s. Toefil and Apolonia (Niesiobedzka)J.; Dipl. Ing., Tech. U. of Warsaw, 1935, D.Sc., 1961; m. Irena Siedlecka, Apr. 17, 1948; children—Christopher Z., George W. Came to U.S., 1953, naturalized 1958. Sr. asst. lectr. research engr. Road Research Inst., Warsaw Polytech., 1935-39; dir. research labs., Kabul, Afganistan, 1939-43; prof., head dept. chemistry and chem. engring. Polish U. Coll., also vice prin., London, Eng., 1946-53; prof. chem. engring. Lafayette Coll., Easton, Pa., 1953-. head dept 1961-. Recipient Jones outstanding teachers award Lafayette Coll., 1958. Served with Polish Forces under Brit. Command, 1943-36. Mem. A. Inst. Chem. Engrs., Am. Soc. Engring. Edn., Nat. Assn. Corrosion Engrs., Am. Assn. U. Profs., Instn. Chem. Engrs. Gt. Britain. Author: Nature and Properties of Engineering Materials, 1959. Home: 1501 Paul Eaton Rd Easton PA 18042

JASWON, MAURICE AARON, educator; b. Dublin, Ireland, June 19, 1922; s. Tobias and Fanny (Cohen) J.; student Wesley Coll., Dublin, 1934-40; B.Sc., Trinity Coll., Dublin, 1940-44; Ph.D., Birmingham (Eng.) U., 1949; m. Rachel Miller, Aug. 24, 1948; children—Mervyn S., David I. (dec.), Jeremy D. Came to U.S., 1963. Lecturer mathematics Imperial Coll., London, 1949-57, reader math., 1957-65; vis. prof. engring. Brown U., 1963-64; prof. engring. mechanics, chmn. dept. U. Ky., 1965-67; prof. math., head dept. City Univ., London, 1967—. Fellow Inst. Math. and Applications; mem. A.A.A.S. Author: Theory of Cohesion, 1954; Studies in Crystal Physics, 1959; Mathematical Crystallography, 1965; also articles. Address: Dept Math City Univ London EC 1 England

JASZI, ANDREW OSCAR, educator; b. Budapest, Hungary, Mar. 1, 1917; s. Oscar and Amalia (Moskovics) J.; came to U.S., 1935, naturalized, 1942; B.A., Oberlin (O.) Coll., 1938; M.A., Harvard, 1939, Ph.D., 1947; m. Jean Yourd, Sept. 2, 1944; children—Paul Oscar, Elizabeth Anne. Instr. German, Harvard, 1947-48; faculty U. Cal. at Berkeley, 1948—, now prof. German. Served with AUS, 1942-46. Guggenheim fellow, 1966. Mem. Modern Lang. Assn., Am. Civil Liberties Union, Phi Beta Kappa. Contbr. articles to profl. jours. Home: 371 60th St Oakland CA 94618

JASZI, GEORGE, govt. ofcl., economist; b. Hungary, Sept. 23, 1915; s. Oscar and Amalia Moscovitz, J.; came to U.S., 1931, naturalized 1931; student Oberlin Coll., 1931-33; B.Sc. in Econs., London (Eng.) Sch. Econs., 1933-36; Ph.D., Harvard, 1946; m. Helen R. Heinemann, Feb. 23, 1943; children—Peter Andrew, Daniel George. With div. research and statistics Fed. Res. Bd., 1936-38, 40-42, nat. income div. Office Bus. Econs., 1951-59, asst. dir. Office Bus. Econs., 1959-63, dir., 1963—; lectr., professorial lectr. George Washington U., 1950-56; vis. prof. Stanford, 1957; adj. prof. Am. U., 1959-63; professorial lectr. Georgetown U., 1963—. Cons., League Nations, 1945, UN, 1952, 64, 66, Central Bank of Colombia, 1955; mem. exec. com. Conf. Research in Income and Wealth, 1949-52, 55-58, 59-62, chmn., 1956-57. Recipient Career Service award Nat. Civil Service award Nat. Civil Service League, 1965. Fellow Am. Statis. Assn.; mem. Am. Econs. Assn. Contbg. author: A Critique of the U.S. Income and Products Accounts, 1958. Contbr. profl. jours., Ency. Brit. Home: 4910 Cumberland Ac Chevy Chase MD 20015 Office: Office Bus Econs Dept Commerce Washington DC 20230

JATRAS, STEPHEN JAMES, electronics co. exec.; b. Mckeesport, Pa., Apr. 7, 1926; s. Andrew and Verna (Filakowski) J.; B.S. in Elec. Engring., Carnegie Inst. Tech., 1947; S.M., Mass. Inst. Tech., 1952; Sloan fellow Stanford Grad. Sch. Bus, 1958; m. Frankie Jean McKinney, July 3, 1952; children—Stephanie Ann, Andrew Anthony, Christopher Dale, Cindy Lou, Shawn James, Todd Charles. Dial systems engr. Stromberg Carlson Co., Rochester N.Y., 1947-48; instr. elec. engring. U. Mass., 1948-50; research engr. Mass. Inst. Tech., 1950-52; v.p. chief engr. Midwestern Instruments Co., Tulsa, 1952-56; v.p., gen. mgr. Lockhead Electronics div. Lockhead Aircraft Cor., 1956-65; pres. Telex Corp., Tulsa, 1965-; dir. D.G., O'Brien Inc. Mem. adv. bd. Tulsa YMCA. Served with AUS, 1944-46. Mem. I.E.E.E., Sigma XI. Home: 2604 E 38th St Tulsa OK 74105 Office: Box 1526 Tulsa OK 74101

JAUCHEM, CLARENCE RALPH, govt. ofcl.; b. Akron O., Nov. 22, 1916; s. Edward B. and Mina (Rutteman) J.; B.S. in Bus Administrn., U. Akron, 1941; grad. auditing Ohio State U., 1945-46; m. Roberta M. Ohl, Jan 9, 1942; children—Philip, James. Cons. to sec. treasury Commonwealth P.R., 1955; asst. dir., policy staff comptroller gen. U.S., 1958; mem. profl. staff U.S. Congress, 1958-60; treas., dir. finance Pan Am. Union, 1961-64; dir. budget and finance systems staff, spl. asst. State Dept., 1964-65; dir. financial systems div. P.O. Dept., Washington, 1965-70; asst. controller for accounting U.S. Postal Service, Washington, 1970—. Bd. dirs. Pan Am. Devel. Found. C.P.A., N.C. Mem. Fed. Govt. Accountants Assn. (dir.). Methodist (asso. dist. lay leader Va. conf.). Home: 7112 Capital View Dr Mclean VA 22101 Office: PO Dept Washington DC 20260

JAUS, WILLIAM CURRIE, cosmetic co. exec.; b. Camden, N.J., Oct. 20, 1920; s. William R. and Estella (Feuerstein) J.; B.S., Drexel U., 1943; m. Barbara Alene Sharpe, Aug. 4, 1946; children—Ava, Amy, William. Sales mgr. Eastern region Kraftco, Phila., 1946-63; pres. Alderny-Puritan Dairy, Newark, 1963-67; pres. foods div. Dolly Madison Industries, Phila., 1967-69; pres. chief exec. officer Bishop Industires, Inc., Union, N.J., 1969—; dir. Surfset, Inc. Vice chmn. Commn. on Efficiency and Economy State of N.J., 1966-69. Bd. dirs. Conf. Christians and Jews. Served to lt. col., inf., U.S. Army, 1943-46. Decorated Bronze Star medal. Mem. Pi Kappa Phi. Clubs: Ft. Monmouth Country; Shrewsbury River Yacht (rear commodore) (Fair Haven, N.J.). Home: 15 Sheraton Lane Rumson NJ 07760 Office: 2345 Vauxhall Rd Union NJ 07083

JAVAN, ALI, educator, physicist; b. Teheran, Iran, Dec. 27, 1926; s. Moosa and Jamileh (Azarbaghi) J.; came to U.S., 1948, naturalized, 1963; student Teheran U., 1947-48; Ph.D., Columbia, 1954; m. Marjorie Browning, July 12, 1962; children—Maia Azar, Lila Hamideh. Mem. research staff Bell Telephone Labs., Murray Hill, N.J., 1958-61; mem. faculty Mass. Inst. Tech., 1960—, prof. physics, 1964; cons. to industry and govt., 1960—, Recipient John and Fanny Hertz Found. award, 1964; Ballantine medal Franklin Inst., 1962; Guggenheim fellow, 1967. Fellow Am. Phys. Soc.; mem. Am. Acad. Arts and Scis., Sigma Xi. Inventor first gas laser, 1960; spl. research fundamental quantum electronics. Home: 69 River St. Boston MA 02108 Office: Mass Inst Tech Cambridge MA 02139

JAVERT, CARL THEODORE, physician, surgeon; b. Depew, N.Y., Nov. 12, 1907; s. Eric Gustav and Selma (Asplund) J.; M.D., U. Buffalo, 1932; m. Nancy Viscariello, June 4, 1954; children—Yvonne Marshall, Carl Tyrrell. Asso. prof. obstetrics, gnyecology Cornell U., N.Y.C., 1946-56; clin. prof. Coll. Physicians and Surgeons Columbia, 1956—; pathologist N.Y. Lying-in Hosp., 1947-56; dir. obstetrics gynecology Womans Hosp., N.Y.C., 1956-63; practice medicine, specializing in obstetrics and gynecology, N.Y.C., 1940—. Pres., Well Born Found., N.Y.C., 1958—. Served with AUS, 1942-46. Decorated Soldiers medal. Fellow A.C.S.; mem. Coll. Obstetricians and Gynecologists (a founder), N.Y. Obstet. Soc. (past pres.), N.Y. Gynecol. Soc. (founder, past pres.). Author: Spontaneous and Habitual Abortion, 1957. Contbr. numerous articles to profl. jours. Research on X-ray pelvimetry, endometriosis theory benign metastasis, cancer ovary, cervix and endometrium, habitual abortion, erythoblastosis, Rh and HR factor, marriage contract, therapeutic abortion. Home: 20 Stellar Pl Pelham Manor New York CIty NY 10803 Office: 580 Park Av New York City NY 10021

JAVID, HUSHANG, educator, surgeon; b. Tehran, Iran, Aug. 10, 1921; s. Hossein and Ruh (Nafas) J.; came to U.S., 1944, naturalized, 1956; M.D., U. Ill., 1946, M.S. in Surgery, 1948, Ph.D. in Surgery, 1954. m. Doloris Patricia Higgins, June 15, 1951; children—Leighton, Linette, Liana, Laurel. Intern. U. Ill. Research and Ednl. Hosp., Chgo., 1946-47, resident surgery, 1947-53; pvt. practice medicine specializing in cardiovascular surgery, Chgo., 1953—; prof. surgery U.. Ill. Med. Sch., 1966—, Rush Med. Sch.; attending vascular surgeon Presbyn.-St Luke's, Hines VA, Westside VA hosps.; cons. surgery MacNeal Meml. Hosp., Berwyn, Ill. Served to maj., M.C., AUS, 1955-57. Recipient Joseph A. Capps prize Inst. Medicine Chgo., 1948, Nelson M. Percy award Chgo. Surg. Soc., 1954. Diplomate Am. Bd. Surgery, Am. Bd. Thoracic Surgery. Fellow A.C.S.; mem. A.M.A., Internat. Cardiovascular Soc., Am. Fedn. Clin. Research, Western Central Surg. Assn., Soc. Vascular Surgery. Contbr. med. jours. Home: 27 Royal-Vale Dr Oak Brook IL 60512 Office: 1725 W Harrison St Chicago IL 60612

JAVID, MANUCHER J., neurosurgeon, educator; b. Tehran, Iran, Jan. 12, 1922; s. Asdolah and Touba (Ahdiyeh) J.; came to U.S., 1944, naturalized, 1957; M.D., U. Ill., 1946; m. Lida Emma Fabbri, Oct. 19, 1951; children—Roxane, Daria, Jeffrey, Claudia. Intern Augustana Hosp., Chgo., 1946-47, resident gen. surgery, 1947-48, resident neurosurgery, 1948-49; asst. in neuropathology Ill. Neuropsychiat. Inst., Chgo., 1948-49; fellow in neurosurgery Lahey Clinic, Boston, 1949; resident neurosurgery New Eng. Med. Center, Boston, 1950; clin. research fellow neurosurgery Mass. Gen. Hosp., Boston, 1950, asst. resident, 1951, sr. resident neurosurgery, 1952; teaching fellow in surgery Harvard, 1952; instr. Med. Sch. U. Wis., Madison, 1953-54, asst. prof., 1954-57, asso. prof., 1957-62, prof. neurosurgery, 1962, chmn. div. neurosurgery, 1963—. Diplomate Am. Bd. Neurosurgery. Mem. A.M.A., A.C.S., Am. Assn. Neurol. Surgeons, A.A.A.S., Am. Assn. Med. Colls., Am. Assn. U. Profs., Pan Am. Med. Assn., Milw. Neuropsychiat. Soc., Central Neurosurg. Soc. (pres. 1964), Sigma Xi, Phi Beta Pi. Mem. Baha'i Faith. Rotarian. Contbr. articles profl. jours. Introduced clin. use of urea for reduction intracranial and intraocular pressure. Home: 4750 Lafayette Dr Madison WI 53705

JAVITS, BENJAMIN ABRAHAM, lawyer, economist; b. N.Y.C., Oct. 21, 1894; s. Morris and Ida (Littman) J.; student Coll. City N.Y., 1909-11; LL.B., Fordham U., 1918; m. Lily Birnbaum, Feb. 12, 1926; children—Joan Ellen, Eric M. Various positions selling, mgmt., indsl. reorgn. also bus. counseling, 1911-22; admitted to N.Y. bar, 1922, practiced in N.Y.C. and Washington, 1922-69; counsel, mem. firm Javits & Javits, domestic and fgn. corp. practice, corporate reorgn., trade assn. law, anti-trust law, N.Y.C. and Washington, ret., 1969. Sponsored movement to amend anti-trust laws, 1926; organized nat. conf. for nat. econ. planning, Washington, 1929; filed petition in bankruptcy for Am. creditors of Kreuger and Toll affairs, 1932; assisted drafting Nat. Indsl. Recovery Act, 1933; pres., founder United Shareowners Am., Inc., 1950; co-founder Investors League, Inc. Pres. Shareowners Ednl. Found., Inc.; pres. Fair Return League, Inc., ednl. found. Republican. Mason. Clubs: Palm Beach Country; Noyak Golf, Overseas Press, City Athletic. Author: Make Everybody RichIndustry's New Goal, 1929; Business and the Public Interest-Trade Associations, The Anti- Trust Laws and industrial Planning, 1932; The Commonwealth of Industry, The Separation of Industry and the State, 1936; Peace by Investment, 1950; How the Republicans Can Win in 1952, 1952; The Manifesto of Freedom for Mankind, 1962; Ownerism: A Better World for All Through Democratic Ownership, 1969; also pamphlets, articles. Home: 980 Fifth Av New York City NY 10021 also 230 Palmo Way Palm Beach FL 33480

JAVITS, JACOB KOPPEL, U.S. senator; b. N.Y.C., May 18, 1904; s. Morris and Ida (Littman) J.; LL.B., N.Y. U., 1926; 21 hon. degrees; m. Marion Ann Borris, Nov. 30, 1947; children—Joy D., Joshua M., Carla. Admitted to bar of N.Y. State, 1927; and since practiced in N.Y. as trial lawyer, special asst. to chief of Chem. Warfare Service, AUS, Washington, 1941-42; mem. 80th- 83d, 85th Congresses, 21st N.Y. Dist.; atty gen. New York, 1955-57; U.S. senator from N.Y., 1957—, mem. fgn. relations com., govt. operations com., select com. on small businesses, select com. on equal ednl. opportunity, joint econ. com. of Congress and Senate Labor and Pub. Welfare Com.; mem. firm Javits, Trubin, Sillcocks, and Edelman, N.Y.C., 1958—. Chmn. No. Atlantic Assembly's Polit. Com., Parliamentarian's Com. for Less Developed Nations; U.S. del. to 25th anniversary UN Gen. Assembly, 1970. Commd. maj. U.S. Army, 1942; asst. to chief of operations in C.W.S.; served in U.S. ETO and PTO, 1942-45; disch. as lt. col.; col. chem. warfare N.Y.N.G., A.U.S. Decorated Legion of Merit, Commendation ribbon. Mem. Am. Legion, V.F.W., Amvets, Jewish War Veterans, Am. Veterans Com. Republican. Jewish religion. Clubs: City Athletic, National Republican (N.Y.); Capitol Hill, Army and Navy (Washington). Author: A Proposal to Amend the Anti-Trust Laws, 1939; Discrimination U.S.A., 1960; Order of Battle, A Republican's Call to Reason, 1964; series of articles on polit. philosophy for Rep. party, 1946. Lectr. on econ. and polit. subjects. Home: 911 Park Av New York City NY 10028 Office: 110 E 45th St New York City NY 10017

JAWARA, DAWDA KAIRABA, pres. Gambia; b. Barajally, Gambia, May 16, 1924; s. Almany and Mama (Fatty) J.; diploma tropical vet. medicine, U. Edinburgh (Scotland), 1957. Vet. officer, Gambia, 1954-57, prin. vet. officer, 1957-60; leader People's Progressive Party, 1960; minister edn., 1960-61; premier, 1962-63; prime minister, 1963-70; pres. Republic Gambia, 1970—. Recipient decorations from Senegal, Mauritania, Lebanon, Liberia, China, Nigeria; created knight bachelor, 1966; Collar of Order of Nile, 1971. Mem. Royal Coll. Vet. Surgeons. Home: 1 Marina Bathurst Gambia Office: Prime Minister's Office Bathurst Gambia

JAWETZ, ERNEST, educator, physician; b. Vienna, Austria, June 9, 1916; s. Karl and Angela (Goldhammer) J.; came to U.S., 1939, naturalized, 1944; student U. Vienna, 1934-38; M.S., U. N.H., 1940; Ph.D., U. Cal. at San Francisco, 1942; M.D., Stanford, 1945; m. Mary Jean Morse, Oct. 29, 1954; children—Katherine, Steven, Michael, Ann. Intern Stanford Lane Hosp., San Francisco, 1945-46; sr. asst. surgeon USPHS, 1946-48; mem. faculty U. Cal. Med. Center, San Francisco, 1948—, prof. microbiology and medicine, lectr. pediatrics, 1953—, chmn. dept. microbiology, 1962—; cons. VA, 1952—; A. Wright lectr., London, Eng., 1952; McArthur lectr., Edinburgh, Scotland, 1952; Univ. lectr. U. London, 1962; spl. research infectious diseases, chemotherapy, virology, immunology. Served with AUS, 1943-46. Fellow N.Y. Acad. Scis.; mem. Am. Fedn. Clin. Research (chmn. Western sect. 1952), Western Soc. Clin. Research (pres. 1961), Am. Soc. Clin. Investigation, Western Assn. Physicians. Author: Review of Medical Microbiology, 9th edit., 1970; also numerous articles. Mem. editorial bds. med. jours. Home: 19 Cushing Dr Mill Valley CA 94941 Office: Univ California Med Center San Francisco CA 94122

JAWOROWSKI, JAN WLODZIMIERZ, educator; b. Augustow, Poland, Mar. 2, 1928; s. Jan and Helena (Heybowicz) J.; M.S., U. Warsaw, 1952; Ph.D. in Math., Math. Inst. Polish Acad. Scis., Warsaw, 1955. Asst., U. Warsaw, 1950-52, adj., docent, 1955-63; extraordinary prof. Inst. Math., Polish Acad. Scis., 1963-64; asso. prof. math. Cornell U., Ithaca, N.Y., 1964-65; prof. math. Ind. U., Bloomington, 1965—. Mem. Inst. for Advanced Study, Princeton, N.J., 1960-61. Home: 106 S Overhill Dr Bloomington IN 47401

JAWORSKI, LEON, lawyer; b. Waco, Tex., Sept. 19, 1905; s. Rev. Joseph and Marie (Mira) J.; LL.B., Baylor U., 1925, LL.D., 1960; LL.M., George Washington U., 1926; m. Jeannette Adam, May 23, 1931; children—Joanie, Claire, Joseph III. Admitted to Tex. bar, 1925; asso. firm Fulbright, Crooker, Freeman & Bates, Houston, also Washington, 1931-34, partner, 1934-51; sr. partner firm Fullbright, Crooker, Freeman, Bates & Jaworski, Houston, 1951—; spl. asst. U.S. atty. gen., 1962-65; spl. counsel atty. gen. Tex., 1963-65; dir., chmn. exec. com. Bank of Southwest, Anderson Clayton & Co., Gulf Pub. Co., Intercontinental Nat. Bank (all Houston), Coastal States Gas Producing Co., Benjamin Franklin Savs. Assn. Mem. Pres.'s Commn. on Law Enforcement and Adminstrn. of Justice; U.S. mem. Permanent (Internat.) of Arbitration, The Hague; chmn. gov.'s Com. on Pub. Sch. Edn.; mem. Commn. on Marine Sci., Engrng. and Resources, Pres.'s Commn. on Causes and Prevention of Violence. Bd. dirs. A.R.C., chpt. chmn., 1954-55; trustee United Fund, 1958—; trustee, mem. exec. com. Southwestern Legal Found. (chmn. trustees); trustee Texas Med. Center, Baylor Coll. Medicine; pres. Baylor Med. Found., M.D. Anderson Found. Served as col. AUS, 1942-46, chief war crimes trial sect. judge Adv. Gen. Dept.; ETO. Fellow Am. Coll. of Trial Lawyers (regent 1958-66, also pres. 1961-62), Am. Bar Foundation; mem. State Bar Tex. (pres. 1962-63), Am. Law Inst., Am. (pres. 1971-72), Houston (pres. 1949) bar assns., Tex. Civil Jud. Council (pres. 1950-52), C. of C. (pres. 1960), Phi Delta Phi, Order of Coif. Presbyn. Rotarian (pres. 1955-56). Clubs: Houston, Houston Country; Coronado, Headliners; Warwick. Author: After Fifteen Years, 1961. Home: 3665 Ella Lee Lane Houston TX 77027 Office: Bank of Southwest Bldg Travis and Walker Houston TX 77002

JAY, BURTON DEAN, ins. actuary; b. Sparta, Ill., Jan. 16, 1937; s. Everett Russell and Bertha (Halemeyer) J.; B.A. In Math., Ripon Coll., 1959; m. Eva May Eudy, Aug. 10, 1958; children—Cynthia Ann, Sylvia Ruth, Jon Russell. Actuarial student Northwestern Nat. Life Ins. Co., Mpls., summers 1953-55; v.p., chief actuary United Benefit Life Ins. Co., Omaha, 1962—. Served to 1st lt. AUS, 1959-62. Fellow Soc. Actuaries (chmn. part VI com. 1969—); mem. Omaha Jr. C. of C. (bd. dirs. 1967), Am. Acad. Actuaries. Methodist (adminstrv. bd.). Home: 3056 Armbrust Dr Omaha NB 68124 Office: United Benefit Life Ins Co 30th and Dodge St Omaha NB 68131

JAY, DOUGLAS PATRICK THOMAS, Brit. mem. Parliament; b. London, Eng., Mar. 23, 1907; s. Edward Aubrey Hastings Jay; student Winchester Coll.; Litterae Humaniores First Class, New Coll., Oxford U.; m. Margaret Christian Garnett, Sept. 30, 1933; children—Peter, Martin, Catherine and Helen (twins). Fellow All Souls' Coll., Oxford U., 1930-37, 68—; staff The Times, 1929-33, The Economist, 1933-37; city editor Daily Herald, 1937-41; mem. Parliament for North Battersea, 1946—; asst. sec. Ministry of Supply, 1941-43, prin. asst. sec. Bd. of Trade, 1943-45, personal asst. to prime minister, 1945-46, econ. sec. to Treasury, 1947-50, financial sec., 1950-51; Prilby councillor, 1951—; pres. Brit. Bd. of Trade, London, 1964-67; dir. Courtaulds Ltd., 1967-70. Chmn. Common Market Safeguards Campaign; chmn. London Motorway Action Group. Author: The Socialist Case, 1937; Who is to Pay for the War and the Peace, 1941; Socialism in the New Society, 1962; After the Common Market, 1968. Office: House of Commons London SW 1 England

JAY, ERIC GEORGE, educator; b. Colchester, Eng., Mar. 1, 1907; s. Henry and Maude (Lucking) J.; B.A., Leeds (Eng.) U., 1929, M.A., 1930; B.D., London (Eng.) U., 1937, M.Th., 1940, Ph.D., 1951; D.D. (hon.), Montreal Diocesan Theol. Coll., 1965; m. Margaret Webb, July 22, 1937; children—Christine (Mrs. Oskar Sykora), Susan (Mrs. Phillip Andersen), Peter. Ordained to ministry Anglican Ch., 1931; asst. curate St. Augustine's Ch., Stockport, Cheshire, Eng., 1931-34; lectr. theology King's Coll., London, 1934-47; dean of Nassau, Bahamas, 1948-51; sr. chaplain to Archbishop of Canterbury, 1951-58; prin. Montreal Diocesan Theol. Coll., 1958-63; prof. hist. theology McGill U., 1958—, dean faculty div., 1963- 70; canon Christ Ch., Montreal, 1960—. Served as chaplain Royal Air Force, 1940-45. Fellow King's Coll., 1949. Mem. Canadian Theol. Soc. (pres. 1965). Author: The Existence of God, 1946; Origen's Treatise on Prayer, 1954; Friendship with God, 1958; New Testament Greek, An Introductory Grammar, 1958; Son of Man, Son of God, 1965. Home: 570 Milton St Montreal 130 Quebec Canada

JAY, GEORGE EDGAR, Jr., scientist; b. Windham, Mont., Sept. 8, 1914; s. George E. and Josephine Helen (Bixenman) J.; B.A., U. Ia., 1936, M.S., 1938; Ph.D. with distinction, Mich. State U., 1949; m. Phyllis Jeanne Ruhland, Mar. 21, 1947; children—Holly Elizabeth, Christopher Lewis. Instr. biology Basic Coll., Mich. State U., 1946-47; research asso. R.B. Jackson Meml. Lab., Bar Harbor, Me., 1947-50; animal geneticist NIH, USPHS, 1950-51, sr. scientist, 1951-60, scientist dir. Nat. Cancer Inst., 1966—; dir. dept. lab. animals Microbiol. Assos., Inc., Bethesda, Md., 1960-66. Cons. USPHS; asso. NIH. Mem. bd. Inst. Animal Resource NRC, Nat. Acad. Scis.; chmn. exec. com. Internat. Com. on Lab. Animals; mem. com. on animal models and genetic stock NRC; mem. grants com. Md. div. Am. Cancer Soc. Served to lt. USAAF, 1942-46. Mem. Am. Soc. Human Genetics, Genetics Soc. Am., Am. Genetics Assn., Washington Acad. Sci. Home: 12400 Greenhill Dr Silver Spring MD 20904 Office: Nat Cancer Inst NIH Bethesda MD 20014

JAY, HERBERT LLOYD, advt. exec.; b. N.Y.C., May 11, 1924; s. Louis Maurice and Bess (Schottenfeld) J.; student Cornell U., 1942, 45, 46; m. Charlotte E. Masia, July 31, 1949; children—Adam Reid, Amy Louise. Advt. mgr. Alexander Smith Inc., 1950-53; v.p., asst. to pres. Aldon Rug Mills. Inc., 1953-56; v.p. marketing Spectrum Fabrics Inc., N.Y.C., 1956-57; dir. advt. Mohasco Industries Inc., Amsterdam, N.Y., 1957-67; pres. Harold J. Siesel Co. Inc., N.Y.C., 1967-71; formed Herbert L. Jay Assos., Inc., 1971—. U.S. delegate 1st Internat. Econ. Conf., Jerusalem, 1968. Active sch. coms. Dobbs Ferry and Irvington, N.Y., also local Boy Scouts Am. Served with AUS, 1943-44. Mem. N.Y. Sales Promotion Execs. Club (charter), Advt. Club N.Y.C., Cornell Book and Bowl Soc. Home: 248 Harriman Rd Irvington-on-Hudson NY 10533 Office: 845 3rd Av New York City NY 10022

JAY, NELSON DEAN, ret. banker; b. Elmwood, Ill., Mar. 7, 1883; s. Fred Dean and Elizabeth (Buchanan) J.; A.B., Knox Coll., Galesburg, Ill., 1905, LL.D., 1960; m. Anne Augustine, June 23, 1910; children—Nelson D., George A. (dec.), Robert Dean. With Milw. Trust Co., 1907-10, mgr. bond dept., 1910; v.p. First Nat. Bank, Milw., 1911-15; mgr. bond dept. Guaranty Trust Co., N.Y.C., 1915-16, v.p., 1916-20; partner Morgan and Cie, Paris, France, 1920-45; chmn. Morgan & Cie, Inc., Paris, France, until 1955; mem. dirs. adv. com. Morgan Guaranty Trust Co. Chmn. administrv. com. A.R.C., 1943-44; chmn. bd. Am. Hosp. Paris, 1937-57; trustee of Knox Coll. Served from capt. to lt. col., U.S. Army, World War I; asst. gen. purchasing agt. AEF. Decorated D.S.M. (U.S.); Order of Honor with Star (Austria); comdr. Legion d'Honneur (France); officer d l'Ordre de Léopold (Belgium). Clubs: Knickerbocker, Century (N.Y.C.). Address: 55 E 72d St New York City NY 10021 also Box 1306 Ridge Rd Laurel Hollow Syosset NY 11791

JAYARATNE, MERENNA FRANCIS DE SILVA, former ambassador of Ceylon; b. Ambalangeda, Ceylon, July 12, 1904; s. Muhunduram Sirineris de Silva; student St. Thomas Coll., Colombo, also U. Ceylon; B.A., U. London (Eng.); m. Lela Abeyagunaratne, Oct. 18, 1935; children—Prithie, Bhatiya, Ajit, Srinika, Panchal. Joined Ceylon Civil Service, 1927; dir. commerce, also dir. Tourist Bur. Ceylon, 1948- 49; acting dir. edn., 1949-51; permanent sec. Ministry Commerce and Trade, 1953-57; permanent sec. Ministry Transp. and Power, 1953-57, 59- 60; permanent sec. Ministry Def. And External Affairs, 1960, then adv. prime minister Ceylon; former ambassador of Ceylon to U.S.; del. Commonwealth Prime Ministers Conf., 1961, UN Gen. Assembly, 1961; dep. chmn. Ceylon delegation UN Gen. Assembly, 1963. Chmn bd. dirs. Port Cargo Corp., Ceylon, 1958, Air Ceylon Corp., 1962. Vice pres. Washington Friends of Buddhism. Mem. Asia Soc. Am. Clubs: Orient, Tamil Sports (Colombo). Home: 2503 13th St NW Washington DC 20008

JAYE, MERI, designer ships interiors; b. Buenos Aires; student architecture and design, U. Mexico, also Ecole des Beaux Arts, Paris, France; widow. Propr., Meri Jaye and Assos., maritime interior designers. Address: Meri Jaye and Assos Pier 39 San Francisco CA 94133

JAYNE, BENJAMIN WAITE, lawyer; b. Detroit, Dec. 4, 1915; s. Ira Waite and Jean (Bilton) J.; A.B., Wayne U., 1937; postgrad. Duke, 1936; LL.B., U. Mich., 1939; m. Shirley Margaret Seiloff, Oct. 14, 1944; children—Bradford Waite, Deborah Margaret. Admitted to Mich. bar, 1939; enforcement atty. OPA, 1939-42; practice in Detroit, 1942—; partner firm Dahlberg, Mallender & Gawne, 1944—; co-counsel Am. Football League, 1959—; counsel Buffalo Bills Profl. Football Team, 1959—. Mem. Am., Detroit (dir. 1952) bar assns. Home: 278 Woodberry Dr Bloomfield Hills MI 48012 Office: 1400 N Woodward Birmingham MI 48012

JAYNES, LAWRENCE C. corp. exec.; b. Coalton O., Aug 10, 1891; s. William M. and Mary Margaret (McMonigle) J.; grad. Inf. Sch., 1928, Command and Gen. Staff Sch., 1935, Army War Coll., 1939; m. Georgia Rose Joyner, July 19, 1926 (dec.); 1 dau., Margaret Gail; m. 2d, Frances Lacy Adams, Jan. 15, 1966. Commd. 1st lt. Ordnance, O.R.C. 1918 active duty, 1918; pvt. sgt. comdg. 2d lt. Tank Corps, 1918; commd. 1st lt. inf. U.S. Army, 1920, advanced through grades to brig. gen., 1942, maj. gen., 1943; comdg. gen., combat command A 13th Armored Div., 1942-44, comdg. gen. replacement and tng. command, MTO, 1944-45; theater inspector gen., 1945, dep. theater comdr., 1945-47, chief of staff. 1946-47; dep. chief of staff Allied Force Hdgrs., 1946-47, chief of staff, 1947; comdg. gen. MTO, 1947; comdg. gen., N.Y.-N.J.-Del. Mil. Dist., 1947-1950; spl. asst. to chief of staff U.S.A. for civilian component affairs, 1950-53, ret.; pres. Nat. Trailways Bus System & Trailways Travel Bur. Corp., 1954—, chmn. bd., 1955—. Mem. Travel Adv. Com. Dept. Commerce. Decorated D.S.M., Legion of Merit with oak leaf cluster, Bronze Star, Victory Cross; Occupation medal (Italy); Companion of the Most Honorable Order of the Bath (Gt. Britain); officer Legion of Honor, Croix de Guerre, Legionaire, first class. hon. (France); Medal of War (Brazil.); The Cross of the Grand Officers in the Order of St. Maurice and St. Lazarus, The Cross of the Grand Officers in Order Crown of Italy, Order of the Crown of Italy, Commander's Degree, Cross of War (Italy). Life mem. Nat. Def. Transp. Assn., Res. Officers Assn. U.S., Assn. U.S. Army, Nat. Assn. Travel Orgns., Am. Soc. Travel Agts., Ohio Soc. N.Y., U.S. C. of C., Washington Bd. Trade. Methodist. Mason (32), Rotarian. Home: 5000 Brookeway Dr Washington DC 20016

JAYSON, LESTER SAMUEL, govt. ofcl., lawyer; b. N.Y.C., Oct. 25, 1915; s. Morris and Mary (Gardner) J.; B.S.S. with spl. honors in History and Govt., Coll. City N.Y., 1936; J.D. (bd. student advisers), Harvard, 1939; m. Evelyn Sylvia Lederer, Feb. 6, 1943; children—Diane Frankie, Jill Karen. Admitted to N.Y. bar, 1940, also U.S. Supreme Ct.; with firm Oseas and Pepper, N.Y.C., 1939-40, Marshall, Bratter & Seligson, N.Y.C., 1940-42; spl. asst. to atty. gen. U.S., 1942-50; trial atty. Dept. Justice, 1951-56, cheif torts sect. civil div., 1957-60; sr. specialist Am. pub. law, chief Am. law div. Congl. Research Service, Library of Congress, 1960-62, dep. dir. service, 1962-66, dir., 1966-. Vice chmn. Interdeptl. Fed. Tort Claims Com., 1958-60; rep. Justice Dept. to legal div., air coordinating com. Internat. Civil Aviation Orgn., 1959-60; mem. com. exec. privilege Justice Dept., 1956-60. Mem. Am., Fed. (chmn., then vice chmn. fed. tort claims com. 1963-66, 70—, chmn. 1967-68, mem. nat. council 1967—) bar assns., Am. Friends of Wilton Park, Pi Sigma Alpha (hon.). Clubs: Cosmos, Harvard, (Washington). Author: Handling Federal Tort Claims; Judicial and Administrative Remedies, 1964, 68, 7O; also articles. Supervising editor; The Constitution of the United States of AmericaAnalysis and Interpretation, 1964. Home: 7512 Newmarket Dr Bethesda MD 20034 Office: Library of Congress Washington DC 20540

JEAKINS, DOROTHY, designer costumes for motion picture films, including Joan of Arc, Samson and Delilah, Greatest Show on Earth, also for Broadway plays; created costumes for Sound of Music. Recipient six Acad. Award nominations, two Oscars for costume design. Address: care Twentieth Century Fox Film Corp 1417 N Western Los Angeles CA 90027*

JEAN, SISTER ANNE, hosp. adminstr.; b. Montclair, N.J., Dec. 13, 1910; d. Timothy Joseph and Anne (Sharkey) Regan; A.B., Coll. of St. Elizabeth, 1953. Bus. mgr. St. Joseph's Hosp., Paterson, N.J., 1936-42, asst. adminstr., 1942-53, adminstr., 1953—. Mem. arbitration bd. Province of N.J.; mem. Synod Cath. Diocese of Paterson. Mem. Mayor's Com. on Health, 1960—. Pres. Mental Health Council; past pres. N.J. Conf. Cath. Hosps.; v.p. Community Home Care Greater Paterson; sec., bd. dirs. Health Edn. Advancement League; bd. dirs. N.J. League Nursing, Community Health Services Council, Passaic Valley Health Facilities Planning Council; trustee St. Mary's Hosp., Passaic, St. Vincent's Hosp., Montclair, Holy Name Hosp., Teaneck, N.J., St. Joseph's Hosp. Fellow Am. Coll. Hosp. Adminstrs. Home: 703 Main St Paterson NJ 07503 Office: St Joseph's Hosp Paterson NJ 07503

JEAN, GRAND-DUKE OF LUXEMBOURG, b. Berg Castle, Luxembourg, Jan. 5, 1921; s. Felix, Prince of Bourbon- Parma and Prince of Luxembourg, and Charlotte, Grand-Duchess of Luxembourg, educated Luxembourg and Ampleforth Coll. (Gt. Brit.), Laval U. (Que., Can.), 1940-42; Dr. Hon., U. Strasbourg (France), 1957; m. Princess Josephine-Charlotte of Belgium, Apr. 9, 1953; children —Marie Astrid, Henri, Jean, Margaretha, Guillaume. Mem. Luxembourg Council of State, 1951-61; lt.-rep. of Grand Duchess, 1961-64; Grand Duke of Luxembourg, 1964-. Chief scout of Luxembourg, 1945-; mem. Internat. Olympic Com., 1946-. Served as capt., Irish Guards, Brit. Army, 1942- 45; co. Luxembourg Army, 1945-, gen. 1964. Decorated Croix de Guerre (Luxembourg, France, Belgium and Netherlands); Silver Star (U.S.). Home: Chateau de Berg Colmar-Berg Luxembourg Office: Grand Ducal Palace Luxembourg

JEANES, ALLENE ROSALIND, chemist; b. Waco, Tex., July 19, 1906; d. Lonnie E. and Viola (Herring) Jeanes; B.A., Baylor U., 1928; M.A., U. Cal. at Berkeley, 1929; Ph.D. in Organic Chemistry, U. Ill., 1938. Instr. math. and physics high sch., 1930; head sci. dept. Athens (Ala.) Coll., 1930-35; instr. chemistry U. Ill., 1936-37, Chem. Found. fellow, 1937-38; Corn Industries Research Found. fellow NIH, USPHS, 1938-40; research chemist starch and dextrose div. No. Regional Research Lab., U.S. Dept. Agr., Peoria, Ill., 1941—. Recipient Distinguished Service award, U.S. Dept. Agr., 1953; Fed. Woman's award U.S. Civil Service Comm., 1962. Mem. Am. Chem. Soc. (Garvan award 1956), Sigma Xi, Iota Sigma Pi. Home: 5021 N University St Peoria IL 61614 Office: 1815 N University St Peoria IL 61604

JEAN-LOUIS, designer; b. Paris, France, Oct. 5, 1907; s. Louis and Mathilde (Rebellard) Berthault; m. Marcelle Martin, 1954 (dec.); m. 2d Maggy Fisher, Nov. 26, 1955. Came to U.S., 1936, naturalized, 1943. Fashion designer Hattie Carnegie, 1936-43; head designer Columbia Pictures, Inc., 1943-60; free-lance designs Universal Pictures; pres. Jean-Louis, Inc., Thaddeus Prodns. Recipient Academy Award for best costume design; Internat. Silk Award, 1960. Mem. Mary and Joseph League (founder, co-pres. 1958). Club: New York Athletic. Home: 22012 Pacific Coast Hwy Malibu CA 90265 also 1540 S Ocean Blvd Manalpan FL 33101 Office: 2020 Stoner Av W Los Angeles CA 90025

JEANLOZ, ROGER WILLIAM, biochemist, educator; b. Berne, Switzerland, Nov. 3, 1917; s. William M. and Rose (Poisat) J.; Baccalaureate, Coll. Geneva (Switzerland), 1936; Chem.E., U. Geneva, 1941, D.Sc., 1943; A.M. (hon.), Harvard, 1961; m. Dorothea A.H. de Passavant, Dec. 20, 1945; children—Claude-André, Raymond François, Danielle Renée, Sylvie Anne. Came to U.S., 1947, naturalized, 1953. Research asso. U. Geneva, 1943-45, U. Basel, 1945-46; asst. U. Montreal, 1946-47; sr. research fellow NIH, 1947-48; sr. scientist Worcester Found. Exptl. Biology, 1948-51; asso. biochemist Mass. Gen. Hosp., Boston, 1951-61, biochemist, 1961—; research asso. Harvard Med. Sch., 1951-57, asso. organic chemistry, 1957-60, asst. prof. biol. chemistry, 1960-61, asso. prof., 1961-69, prof., 1969—. Mem. study sect. physiol. chemistry div. research grants NIH 1964-68, 69-70. Recipient medal Societe de Chimie Biologique de France, 1960, U. Liege 1964. Mem. Am. Soc. Biol. Chemists, Am., Swiss chem. socs., Chem. Soc. (London), Am. Rheumatism Assn. Author: (with Balazs) The Amino Sugars, 4 vols., 1965. Contbr. articles profl. jours. Home: 42 Ruthven Rd Newton MA 02158 Office: Mass Gen Hosp Fruit St Boston MA 02114

JEBB, SIR GLADWYN, see Gladwyn, Lord

JEBSEN, ROBERT HARRY, med. educator; b. Bklyn., Sept. 5, 1931; s. Henry O. and Frieda P. (Stockfish) J.; B.A., Bklyn. Coll., 1953; M.D., N.Y. State U. Downstate, 1956; M.Med. Sci., Ohio State

U., 1960; m. Joan H. Dannevig, Mar. 25, 1951; children—Eric, James, Lawrence. Intern, Harrisburg (Pa.) Hosp., 1956-57; resident Ohio State U., 1957-60; dir. dept. phys. medicine and rehab. St. Luke's Hosp., Cedar Rapids, Ia., 1962-63; asst. prof., asso. prof. phys. medicine and rehab. U. Wash. Sch. Medicine, 1963-68; prof., dir. dept. phys. medicine and rehab. U. Cin. Coll. Medicine, 1968—. Served to capt. M.C., USAF, 1960-62. Nat. Found. Infantile Paralysis grantee, 1957-60. Mem. Am. Acad. Phys. Medicine and Rehab., Am. Congress Rehab. Medicine, Am. Assn. Electromyography and Electrodiagnosis (sec. treas. 1968-71), Am. Rheumatism Assn., Assn. Acad. Physiatrists, Cin. Rheumatism Soc. (sec.-treas. 1970-71). Home: 5983 Ropes Dr Cincinnati OH 45244

JEFFAY, HENRY, educator; b. Bklyn., Feb. 9, 1927; s. Alexander and Dora (Soloman) J.; B.S., U. Wis., 1948, M.S., 1949, Ph.D., 1953; m. Ana Idalia Muniz, Feb. 9, 1957; children-Randall, Kevin, Jason, Stefanie. Instr. U. P.R. Sch. Medicine, 1955; research asso. U. Ill. Coll. Medicine, 1955, asst. prof. biochemistry, 1956, asso. prof., 1961-67, prof., 1967—, asst. dean, 1970—; cons. West Side VA Hosp., Chgo., Norwegian Am. Hosp., Chgo; dir. med. edn. Roosevelt Meml. Hosp., Chgo. Trustee Glen Ellyn (Ill.) Pub. Library, 1970-76. Served with AUS, 1945-46. Recipient research award Chgo. Dental Soc., 1959. Mem. Am. Soc. Biol. Chemists, A.A.A.S., Internat. Assn. Dental Research. Contbr. articles profl. jours. Home: 354 Hawthorn St Glen Ellyn IL 60137 Office: 1853 W Polk St Chicago IL 60612

JEFFE, EPHRAIM F., elec. engr.; b. St. Louis, Feb. 22, 1897; s. Maurice J. and Frieda Frances Jeffe; E.E., Polytechnic Inst. Bklyn., 1916, married. Elec. engr. Bklyn. Edison Co., Inc., 1916-17; pres. Nat. Electric Service Corp., 1923-32; asst. v.p. Consol. Edison Co., Inc., 1932-35; v.p. Consol Edison System Cos., 1935-42; pres., dir. Kings Co. Lighting Co., N.Y. & Richmond Gas Co., 1951-57; pres., chief exec. officer Michigan Gas Utilities Co., 1959-; pres.,chmn. bd., dir. No. Utilities, Inc.; pres. Pa. Utilities Investment Corp., Inc.; mem. bd. dirs. Commonwealth Financial Corp., also dir. Newport Gas Co. (Rhode Island), Knapp-Monarch Co. Mem. N.Y.C. Transit Authority, 1953- . Served to maj., Signal Corps. U.S. Army, 1917-20; served with U.S. Army, World War II, disch. as brig. gen., 1956. Pres. dir. N.Y. Eye and Ear Infirmary, 1948-52; dir. Roosevelt Hosp; Greater N.Y. Red Cross Campaign chmn. 1949, 50; dir. N.Y. chapt. A.R.C. Mem. Army Adv. Com. Dir. N.Y. Women's League for Animals (Ellin Prince Speyer Hosp. for Animals), 1948-. Mem. Tau Beta Pi. Home: 680 S County Rd Palm Beach FL 33480

JEFFE, HULDAH CHERRY, artists; b. Dallas; D. Max Milion and Getrude (Morgan) Cherry; grad. Miss Hockaday Sch., Dallas; studied art in Italy, France; student Grand Central Sch. Arts, N.Y.C.; pupil Robert Brackman; m. Gen. Ephraim Franklin Jeffe, Dec. 29, 1945. Designed series of covers for Brides Mag., 1945-46; paintings reproduced in Mademoiselle, Vogue, Harper's Bazaar, Town and Country; prints works reproduced annually by N.Y. Graphic Soc.; paintings reproduced by Hallmark on greeting cards; represented in permanent collections Ga. Mus. Art, Columbia Mus. Fine Arts, Norfolk Museum Art, Sheldon Swope Mus. Art; new designs of Huldah Girls for ceramic figurines by Hummelwerks, Bavaria, West Germany, W. Gaebel Co., West Germany. Awarded hon. mention Salon des Artistes Francais, Paris, France, 1948. Address: 680 S County Rd Palm Beach FL 33480

JEFFERIES, JOHN TREVOR, astrophysicist, educator, b. Kellerberrin, Western Australla, Apr. 2, 1925; s. John and Vera (Healy) J.; B.Sc., U. Western Australia, 1947, D.Sc., 1961; M.A., Cambridge U., 1949; m. Charmian Candy, Sept. 10, 1949; children—Stephen R., Helen C., Trevor R. Research officer Commonwealth Sci. and Indsl. Research Orgn., Sydney, Australia, 1949-60; cons. to dir. Nat. Bur. Standards, Boulder, Colo., 1960-62; fellow Joint Inst. Lab. Astrophysics, Boulder, 1962-64; prof. physics and astronomy, dir. Inst. Astronomy, U. Hawaii, 1964—. Guggenheim fellow, 1970. Fellow Royal Astron. Soc.; non-resident fellow Joint Inst. Lab. Astrophysics; mem. Internat. Astron. Union (pres. commn. X 1970—), Am. Astron. Soc. Author: Spectral Line Formation, 1967. Contbr. articles profl. jours. Home: 2872 Pacific Heights Rd Honolulu HI 96813

JEFFERS, DEAN W., ins. co. exec.; b. Woodsfield, O., Sept. 7, 1916; grad. Ohio U., 1936; m. Ruth Workman. With Nationwide Mut. Ins. Co., 1940—, pres., gen. mgr., 1969—; v.p. Nationwide Life Ins. Co. Served with USMCR, 1943. Home: 2600 Clairmont Ct Columbus OH 43220 Office: 246 N High St Colujbus OH 43216

JEFFERS, JOHN LEROY, lawyer; b. Ferris, Tex., Oct. 15, 1909; s. Theodore Franklin and Cynthia (Ewing) J.; LL.B with highest honors, U. Tex., 1932; m. Nell Elise Walker, Feb. 8, 1935; children—John Leroy, Mary Nell (Mrs. H. Malcolm Lovett, Jr.). Admitted to Tex. bar, 1932; practice in San Antonio, 1932-42; asst. criminal dist. atty., San Antonio 1935-39; mem. firm Vinson, Elkins, Searls & Connally, Houston, 1942—; part time mem. faculty St. Mary's U. Sch. Law, San Antonio, S. Tex. Sch. Law, Houston; lectr. Southwestern Legal Found, 1966—. Del.-at-large Democratic Nat. Conv. 1952. Bd. regents U. Tex., 1953-59, chmn., 1957-59; trustee Houston Legal Found., S. Tex. Sch. Law, Tex. Bill of Rights Found., Univ. Cancer Found., U. Tex. Law Sch. Found., Episcopal Theol. Sem. Southwest. Recipient Outstanding Achievement award U. Tex., 1969. Fellow Am. Coll. Trial Lawyers, Am. Bar Found.; Mem. Am. (ho. dels. 1966-67, chmn. anti-trust sect. 1970-71),, Houston (pres. 1968-69) bar assns., State Bar Tex., Order of Coif, Delta Theta Pi. Author articles. Home: 674 Piney Point Rd Houston TX 77024 Office: First City Nat Bank Bldg Houston TX 77002

JEFFERS, LEWIS FRANCIS, mfg. co. exec.; b. Calera, Ala., Aug. 28, 1899; s. Henry Lewis and Sarah (Francis) J.; grad Marion Mil. Inst., 1917; m. Mimi Bell Haynes, Sept. 26, 1923; children—Bell (Mrs. Henry Fowlkes), Jane (Mrs. Willis Hagan). Pres., Trustees Loan & Guaranty Co., Birmingham, Ala., 1920-50; with Hayes Internat. Corp., Birmingham, 1951—, pres., 1954-65, chmn. bd., 1965—; dir. City Investing Co., N.Y.C., Rheem Mfg. Co., N.Y.C. Chmn., Ala. Export Council, 1962-66; mem. exec. bd. Nat. Export Council, 1964—. Bd. dirs. Birmingham Community Chest, 1950—; trustee Samford U., 1957-71, Crippled Children's Hosp., Birmingham, 1958—, Southside Bapt. Ch., Birmingham; bd. advisers Ala. chpt. AIESEC, U. Ala. Served with U.S. Army, 1917-19; AEF in France. Named Golden Knight Mgmt., Nat. Mgmt. Club, 1957. Mem. Ala. (dir. 1960-66), Birmingham Area chambers commerce, Air Force Assn. (past pres. Birmingham chpt.), Army Aviation Assn., Assn. of U.S.A., N.A.M., Newcomen Soc. N.Am., Am. Ordnance Assn. (past pres. Birmingham chpt.), Beta Gamma Sigma (hon.). Rotarian (pres. 1957-58). Clubs: Birmingham Country, Mountain Brook Country, Relay House, The Club (Birmingham). Home: 2920 Pumphouse Rd Birmingham AL 35243 Office: Hayes Internat Corp Birmingham AL 35201

JEFFERS, WILLIAM ARMAND, investment banker; b. San Antonio, Feb. 17, 1910; s. S.L. and Frances (Schreiner) J.; B.B.A., U. Tex., 1929; M.B.A., U. Pa., 1930; m. Alice B. Combs, Nov. 13, 1937; children—Anne (Mrs. James M. Dunnam), William Armand. Supr., White's Mines, Uvalde, Tex., 1930-31; office mgr. Universal Credit Co., San Antonio, Houston, El Paso, Detroit, 1931-42; chmn. bd. Dittmar & Co., Inc., San Antonio, 1945-71; mgr. municipal dept. Domincik & Dominick, San Antonio, 1971—. Served to maj. finance dept. AUS, 1942-45. Home: 3225 Howard St San Antonio TX 78212 Office: 214 Soledad San Antonio TX 78205

JEFFERSON, HOWARD B., former univ. pres.; b. Norwalk, O., Sept. 28, 1901; s. George E. and Isabella Ann (Bonar) J.; B.A., Denison U., 1923; Ph.D., Yale, 1929; LL.D., Denison U., 1948, Hillsdale Coll., 1952, Northwestern U., 1958, Emerson Coll., 1968; L.H.D., Colgate U., 1951, Assumption Coll., 1956, Clark U., 1967; Litt.D. (hon.), Coll. Holy Cross, 1962; m. Genevieve Ruth Rowe, June 19, 1926; children—David R., William H. Dir. athletics, Hillsdale Coll., 1923-25; asst. prof. philosophy Colgate U., 1929-30, asso. prof., 1930-35, prof., 1935-46, dir. Sch. Philosophy and Religion, 1945-46, acting dir. of admissions, 1943-45; pres. Clark U., Worcester, Mass., 1946-67; vis. prof. theology U. of Chgo., 1937. Trustee Worcester County Instn. for Savs. Bd. dirs. Worcester Free Pub. Library; trustee Leicester Jr. Coll., Emerson Coll.; asso., trustee Coll. Holy Cross; trustee Bancroft Sch., Old Sturbridge Village. Fellow Am. Acad. Arts and Scis.; mem. Am. Philos. Assn. (sec., treas. Eastern div. 1943-45), Nat. Council on Religion in Higher Edn. (pres. 1956-60), Am. Antiquarian Soc., Phi Beta Kappa, Beta Theta Pi. Baptist. Rotarian. Clubs: Worcester; Tatnuck Country. Author: The God of Ethical Religion, 1933; Experience and the Christian Faith, 1942. Co-author: Experience, Reason and Faith, 1940; The American Idea, 1942; The Vitality of the Christian Tradition, 1944; The Teaching of Religion in American Higher Education, 1951. Contbr. to Jour. of Religion and other religious and philos. jours. Home: 53 Elm St Worcester MA 01609

JEFFERSON, THOMAS BRADLEY, mech. engr., educator; b. Urich, Mo., Nov. 25, 1924; s. Thomas Ulmont and Mary (Bradley) J.; B.S. in Mech. Engring., Kan. State U., 1949; M.S. in Mech. Engring., U. Neb., 1950; Ph.D., Purdue U., 1955; m. Carolyn Chelf, Dec. 20, 1946; children—Thomas Calvin, Richard Kent, Terry Anne. Instr. mech. engring. U. Neb., 1949-52; instr. mech. engring. Purdue U., 1952-55, asst. prof., 1955-58; prof. mech. engring., head dept. mech. engring. U. Ark., 1958-68, asso. dean engring., 1968-69; dean Sch. Engring. and Tech., So. Ill. U., Carbondale, 1969—. Ednl. cons. Allison div. Gen. Motors Co., 1956-57; summer faculty participant Boeing Co., Wichita, Kan., 1957; sr. engr., design engr. 1, Martin Co., Denver, summers 1958-64, 66-67. Served as pilot USAAF, 1943-46. Registered profl. engr., Ark., Ind., Ill. Mem. Am. Soc. M.E., Am. Soc. Engring. Edn., Nat. Soc. Profl. Engrs., Sigma Xi, Tau Beta Pi, Pi Tau Sigma, Sigma Tau, Omicron Delta Kappa, Phi Kappa Phi. Presbyn. (elder). Rotarian. Home: 901 S Glenview Carbondale IL 62901

JEFFERY, EDWIN T., business exec.; b. Cleve., 1908; grad. Fenn Coll. Chmn., chief exec. officer W.S. Tyler, Inc., Cleve.; dir. Soc. Nat. Bank Cleve., Soc. Corp., Cleve. Indians, Inc., Combustion Engr., Inc. Trustee St. Vincent Charity Hosp., John Carroll U., Am. Cancer Soc. Home: 21200 Almar Dr Cleveland OH 44122 Office: 3615 Superior Av Cleveland OH 44114•

JEFFERY, GEOFFREY MARRON, med. parasitologist; b. Dundee, N.Y., May 13, 1919; s. Joseph Ewart and Augusta (Knapp) J.; A.B., Hobart Coll., 1940; M.A., Syracuse U., 1942; Sc.D., Johns Hopkins, 1944; M.P.H., Yale, 1961; m. Jane Wicker, Aug. 16, 1941; children—Janet A., Thomas W., Sarah V., Susan E. Biol. aide health and safety dept. TVA, 1944; commd. officer USPHS, 1944, scientist dir., 1960; tech. aid, cons. malaria control in war areas TVA, 1944-45; assigned div. lab. services Communicable Disease Center, 1945-46; charge br. lab. Communicable Disease Center, Sch. Tropical Medicine, San Juan, P.R., 1946-47; asst. prof. biology U. Bridgeport (Conn.), 1947-48; charge Malaria Research Lab., NIH, Milledgeville, Ga., 1948-54; mem. staff Lab. Tropical Diseases-Lab. Parasite Chemotherapy, NIAID, NIH, Columbia, S.C., 1948-63, head sect. epidemiology, 1961-63; asst. chief Laboratory Parasite Chemotherapy, NIAID, NIH, Bethesda, 1963-66, acting chief Laboratory Parasite Chemotherapy, 1966, chief, 1967-69; chief Central Am. Malaria Research Sta. CDC, San Salvador, El Salvador, C.Am., 1969—. Member expert adv. panel on malaria WHO, 1963—; asso. mem. commn. malaria Armed Forces Epidemiol. Bd., 1965-69, mem., 1969—. Del. Internat. Congress Tropical Medicine and Malaria, Lisbon, 1958, Rio de Janeiro, 1963, Teheran, Iran, 1968, Internat. Congress Parasitology, Rome, Italy, 1964, Internat. Conf. on Protozoology, London, 1965; mem. scientific group on chemotherapy of malaria WHO, Geneva, 1967, mem. scientific group on parasitology, Teheran, 1968. Recipient Pub. Health Service Commendation medal, 1966. Fellow Royal Soc. Tropical Medicine; mem. Am. Soc. Tropical Medicine and Hygiene (sec.-treas. 1961-67, v.p. 1971; Bailey K. Ashford Award 1959), A.A.A.S., Am. Soc. Parasitologists, Assn. Southeastern Biologists (editor bull. 1959-60, exec. com. 1962-66), Tropical Medicine Assn. Washington, S.C. Acad. Sci. (council 1960, 62; Jefferson award 1952, 56, 60), Commd. Officers Assn. USPHS, Am. Mosquito Control Assn., Sigma Xi, Kappa Sigma. Presbyn. Contbr. numerous articles sci. jours. tropical medicine and parasitology. Home: care of US embassy San Salvador El Salvador Central America

JEFFERY, JOSEPH, lawyer; b. London, Ont., Can., Sept. 1, 1907; s. James Edgar and Gertrude (Dumaresq) J.; grad. Osgoode Hall Law Sch., 1927-30; grad. Ins. Inst., 1936; m. Nora Alicia Morris, Oct. 19, 1949; children—Elizabeth, Joseph, John, Alicia, Jennifer, Deborah. Admitted to bar, 1930, since practiced in London, Ont.; created Queen's counsel, 1956; mem. firm Jeffery & Jeffery, 1930—, partner, 1958—; with London Life Ins. Co., 1930—, pres., 1953—, chmn. bd.; pres. Covent Garden Bldg., Inc.; pres., dir. London Hunt Kennels, Ltd., Two Hundred Queens Av., Ltd.; v.p., dir. London Winery, Ltd., Forest City Investment Ltd., London Realty Mgmt. & Rentals, Ltd.; sec., dir. Thames Valley Investments, Ltd., London Broadcasters Ltd.; dir., mem. exec. com. Toronto-Dominion Bank; dir. Rediffusion, Inc., Boug Realty, Ltd., Hiram Walker-Gooderham & Worts, Ltd., Dunwell Holdings, Ltd., Orchard Park (London) Devel. Co. Ltd., Canadian Enterprise Devel. Corp., Ltd. Mem. Canadian bus. and industry adv. com. OECD. Trustee YMCA, YWCA; chmn. bd. govs. U. Western Ont.; past pres. London United Services Inst.; adv. bd. London Little Theatre; mem. bd. mgmt., past pres., life mem. Victorian Order of Nurses for Can. Served as capt. Royal Canadian Navy; sec. Naval Intelligence Dept., later mem., sec. naval bd. Decorated Order Brit. Empire. Mem. John Howard Soc. of London and Middlesex (v.p.), Internat. (v.p. Candian council member exec. com. Canadian sect.), Canadian (pres. 1960-61, mem. adv. com., mem. bd. dirs.), London (past pres.) C.'s of C., Ontario C. of C. Execs. (hon. pres.), Fedn. Commonwealth Chambers of Commerce (chmn.), Canada-Israel Chamber of Commerce and Industry (dir.), Can. Inst. Internat. Affairs, UN Assn. (past pres. London br.), Can. Bar Assn. (past v.p.), Can. Legion (past pres. Vimy br.), Canadian Council Christians and Jews (dir., exec. com.; Human Relations award 1956), I.E.E.E., Canadian Inst. Internat. Affairs, Canadian Tourist Assn. (adv. council), Newcomen Soc. N. Am., Law Soc. Upper Can. Liberal. Anglican Ch. Mason. Clubs: London Hunt and Country Limited (joint master of foxhounds), Baconian (London); Royal Canadian Yacht (Toronto); Caledon (Ont.) Mountain Trout; Jovial Fish and Game (Que.); London Press; Sarnia Yacht; Detroit Yacht; Great Lakes Cruising; London; Granite; St. Denis; Sarnia Golf and Curling Ltd.; Royal Canadian Naval Sailing Assn.; Fanshawe Yacht. Home: Black Acre Pl Route 3 London Ontario Canada Office: care Jeffery & Jeffery P O Box 2095 London 12 Ontario Canada

JEFFERY, WALTER JAMES, ins. exec.; b. Laurium, Mich., Nov. 16, 1907; s. Joseph C. and Elizabeth (Hodges) J.; LL.B., John Marshall Law Sch., 1934; 1 son, David J. With U.S. Fidelity and Guaranty Co., Balt., 1929—, resident sec., Chgo., 1943-52, v.p., N.Y.C., 1952-55, exec. v.p., 1955-60, sr. exec. v.p., 1960-63, pres., 1963-65, chmn. bd., pres., 1965—, also dir.; chmn., pres., dir. Fidelity & Guaranty Ins. Underwriters, Inc., Fidelity & Guaranty Life Ins. Co., Fidelity Ins. Co. Can., Del Mar Co.; dir. Balt. Gas & Electric Co., Merc.-Safe Deposit & Trust Co., Savs. Bank of Balt. Trustee Johns Hopkins Hosp., Balt., Walters Art Gallery. Served with USCGR, 1943-45. Mem. Ill. Bar Assn. Home: 1311 Aintree Rd Towson MD 21204 Office: U S Fidelity & Guaranty Co Redwood and Calvert Sts Baltimore MD 21203

JEFFORD, BARBARA, Mary, actress; b. Plymstock, Eng., July 26, 1930; d. Percival Francis and Elizabeth Mary Ellen (Laity) Jefford; student Hartly-Hodder Studio, Bristol, Eng., 1946-47; diploma speech and drama (Bancroft Gold medal 1949), Royal Acad. Dramatic Art, London, 1947-49; m. John Turner, May 13, 1967. Began career as mem. Shakespeare meml. Theatre, Stratford- on-Avon, 1950-51, 53-54, Old Vic Theatre Co., London, 1956-62; toured Australia, New Zealand, 1953, Yugoslavia, Austria, Holland, Norway, Greece, Egypt; first Am. appearance in Tiger of the Gates, 1955; toured U.S. with Old Vic Theatre Co., 1958, 62, also Russia, Poland, Czechoslovakia, Finland, Germany, France; appearance in Six Characters in Search of an Author, London, 1963; toured S.Am. and Europe with Shakespeare, 1964; appeared in Ride a Cock Horse, London, 1965; with Oxford Playhouse Co., 1965-66, 67, Nottingham Playhouse, 1966, Royal Shakespeare Co., 1967—; appeared in films Ulysses, 1966, Shoes of the Fisherman, 1968; also various television appearances, radio plays, poetry recitals; also S.Am., India, Far East tours. Decorated Order Brit. Empire. Address: 46 Devonshire Close London W1 England

JEFFORDS, JAMES MERRILL, state govt. ofcl.; b. Rutland, Vt., May 11, 1934; s. Olin Merrill and Marion (Hausman) J.; B.S., Yale, 1956; LL.B., Harvard, 1962; m. Elizabeth Daley, Aug. 26, 1961; children—Leonard Olin, Laura Louise. Admitted to Vt. bar, 1962; law clk. Judge Ernest Gibson, Vt. Dist., 1962; partner Bishop, Crowley & Jeffords, Rutland, 1963-66, Kinney, Carbine & Jeffords, Rutland, 1967-68; atty. gen. State of Vt., 1969—. Town agt., Shrewsbury, 1964-68; zoning adminstr., Shrewsbury, 1966-68; mem. Judicial Selection Bd., 1967-68; chmn. Hwy. Dept. Investigating Com., 1968. Mem. Vt. Senate, 1967-68. Served with USNR, 1956-59. Mem. Am., Vt., Rutland County bar assns. Republican. Conglist. (trustee). Lion, Elk. Home: 5 Heaton St Montpelier VT 05602 Office: Atty Gen State of Vt Montpelier VT 05602

JEFFORDS, LAWRENCE, Suggs, railroad officer; b. Florence, S.C., July 2, 1892; s. William Quinn and Sarah Margaret (Suggs) J.; ed. Clemson (S.C.) Coll.; m. Mary Howell, Sept. 27, 1922 (dec. Nov. 1962); m. 2d, Fannie Mae Weatherford Baker, July 2, 1964. Entered business with Atlantic Coast Line R.R. Co., 1910, successively rodman, transitman, resident engr., asst. div. engr., roadmaster, asst. engr. maintenance of way; transf. to Charleston and Western Carolina Ry. Co., Augusta, Ga., 1921, successively engr. maintenance of way, supt. and gen. supt.; returned to Atlantic Coast Line R.R. Co., 1944, chief of personnel, chief engr., 1945, gen. mgr., 1947, v.p. and gen. mgr., 1947, v.p. operations, 1950- 62; v.p., gen. mgr., dir. C.N. & L. R.R., 1960—. Episcopalian. Club: River (Jackson, Fla.). Home: 7063 Salamanca Av Jacksonville FL 32217 ☆

JEFFREY, BALFOUR SILLIMAN, utilities exec.; b. Chgo., Apr. 12, 1906; s. Alexander B. and Alice (Silliman) J.; A.B., U. Kan., 1928; LL.B., Harvard, 1932; m. Margaret Smith, July 7, 1933; 1 dau., Ann. Admitted to Kan. bar, 1932; practiced in Topeka, 1933-53; lectr. Washburn Coll. Law, Topeka, 1933-53; asst. pres. Kansas Power & Light Co., Topeka, 1953-56, pres., 1956—, also dir. Treas., trustee Kansas 4-H Found.; trustee U. Kan. Endowment Assn., Stormont Hosp. Recipient citation for contbn. to bus. Who's Who in Midwest; Outstanding Service citation U. Kan.; Distinguished Citizen award Washburn U., 1967. Served as maj. AUS, 1943-46, Mem. Kan., Am. bar assns., Nat. Alumni Assn. U. Kan. (pres. 1964-65), A.I.M. (pres.'s council, Marquis award 1969), Phi Delta Theta, Phi Delta Phi, Alpha Kappa Psi, Beta Gamma Sigma. Episcopalian. Rotarian. Home: 3141 W 15th St Topeka KS 66604 Office: 818 Kansas Av Topeka KS 66608

JEFFREY, FRED PAINTER, coll. dean; b. Trauger, Pa., Feb. 19, 1911; s. William and Lillie Mae (Bailey) J.; B.S., Pa. State U., 1932; M.S., U. Mass., 1934; m. Millicent Olive McKie, June 26, 1937; children—Robert McKie, Judith Barbara, Roy Frederick. Tchr., research in poultry genetics Rutgers U., 1935-44; head poultry dept. U. Mass., 1944-54, asso. dean Coll. Agr., dir. Stockbridge Sch. Agr., 1954-. Mem. Amherst Sch. Com., 1956-61; chmn. Amherst Community Chest, 1957. Mem. Poultry Sci. Assn. (dir. 1952- 54), Am. Genetic Soc., A.A.A.S., Am. Eugenics Soc., Population Reference, Amherst Philos. Soc., Sigma Xi, Phi Kappa Phi, Alpha Zeta (nat. high council 1962-67). Mem. United Ch. Christ. Author: (with D. R. Marble) Commercial Poultry Production, 1955. Home: 97 Pine St North Amherst MA 01002 Office: Univ Massachusetts Amherst MA 01002

JEFFREY, GEORGE ALAN, scientist; b. Cardiff, Eng., July 28, 1915; s. George F. and Beatrice (Hand) J.; B.Sc., U. Birmingham (Eng.), 1936, Ph.D., 1939, D.Sc., 1953; m. Maureen Ward, Sept. 5, 1942; children—Susan M., Paul D. Came to U.S., 1953, naturalized, 1962. Crystallographer, Brit. Rubber Producers Assn., 1939-45; lectr. U. Leeds (Eng.), 1945-53; prof. chemistry and physics, dir. crystallography lab. U. Pitts. 1953—, prof. crystallograpy, 1965—, chmn. dept. crystallography, 1969—. Sec., U.S. Nat. Com. Crystallography, 1956-58, chmn., 1965-66. Mem. Am. Crystallographic Soc. (pres. 1963), Am. Inst. Physics (bd. govs. 1969—). Home: 200 Mary Ann Dr Glenshaw PA 15116

JEFFREY, MILDRED, labor rep.; b. Alton, Ia., Dec. 29, 1911; d. Bert David and Bertha (Merritt) McWilliams; B.A., U. Minn., 1932; grad. student social economy, Bryn Mawr Coll., 1934; m. Homer Jeffrey, Nov. 27, 1936 (div. 1965); children—Sharon Rose, Daniel. Investigator, NRA, 1935-36; ednl. dir. Pa. joint bd. shirt workers Amalgamated Clothing Workers Am., 1936; asso. editor Sheboygan (Wis.) Times, 1937; gen. rep. Amalgamated Clothing Workers Am., 1938-39; labor specialist WPB, 1941-43; dir. women's bur. Internat. Union United Automobile, Aircraft and Agrl. Implement Workers Am., 1944-49, dir. radio dept., 1949-50, dir. community relations dept., 1951—. Mgr. sta. WDETFM, Detroit, 1950-51. Mem. Citizens Adv. Commn. Sch. Needs, 1957-59; mem. Detroit Library Commn., 1959—, pres., 1969; mem. Detroit Parks, Recreation Commn.; del. White House Conf. Children and Youth, 1950, 60; sec. Met. Detroit Religion and Labor Conf., 1954-59; vice chmn. Nat. Com. Employment Youth, 1959—, Mich. Consumers Assn., 1959—; chmn. adult edn. study United Community Services, 1958-60. Chmn. platform com., Mich. Dem. Party, 1955-60, mem. nat. platform com., 1956-60; alternate nat. committeewoman Mich. Dem. Party, 1957—, nat. committeewoman, 1961- -; mem. exec. com. Democratic Nat. Com., 1969. Recipient award for Distinguished Community Service, Workmen's Circle, 1955, Outstanding Layman of Year award Detroit Council Chs., 1960, award St. Cyprian's P.E. Ch. of Diocese Mich., 1959. Home: 10045 Grandville St Detroit MI 48228 Office: 8000 E Jefferson St Detroit MI 48214

JEFFREY, RICHARD CARL, educator; b. Boston, Aug. 5, 1926; s. Mark M. and Jane (Markovitz) J.; student Boston U., 1943-44; M.A., U. Chgo., 1951; Ph.D., Princeton, 1957; m. Edith Kelman, Jan. 2, 1955; children—Daniel, Pamela. Logical designer computers Mass. Inst. Tech. Digital Computer Lab. also Lincoln Lab., 1952-55; asst. prof. elec. engring. Mass. Inst. Tech., 1958-59; asst. prof. philosophy Stanford, 1959-63; vis. mem. Inst. for Advanced Study, 1963; asso. prof. philosophy Coll. City N.Y., 1964-67; prof. philosophy U. Pa., 1967—. Served with USNR, 1944-46. Mem. Am. Philos. Assn., Assn. for Symbolic Logic, Philosophy of Sci. Assn. (govg. bd. 1969-71). Author: The Logic of Decision, 1965; Formal Logic: Its Scope & Limits, 1967. Home: 55 Patton Av Princeton NJ 08540 Office: Dept Philosophy U Pa Philadelphia PA 19104

JEFFREY, THOMAS STANLEY, Jr., air force officer; b. Arvonia, Va., Feb. 5, 1917; s. Thomas Stanley and Eleanor (Morgan) J.; B.S. in Elec. Engring., Va. Mil. Inst., 1938; grad. Air War Coll., 1954, Indsl. Coll. Armed Forces, 1960; m. Helen Lucille Stewart, Apr. 13, 1940; children—Thomas Stanley III, Ann Morgan. Commd. 2d lt. USAAF, 1939, advanced through grades to maj. gen. USAF, 1967; served in P.R., Panama, Guatemala, Eng., France and Germany, 1939-46; served with Air Tng. Command, SAC, Air Research and Devel. Command, Armed Forces Spl. Weapons Project, 1946-57; dir. operations atomic test, Eniwetok, 1959; comdr. activation Atlas and Minuteman complexes, Washington and N.D., 1960-64; vice comdr. aero. systems div., Wright Field, O., 1964-66; dir. aircraft and missiles, OASD, 1966-67, dir. prodn. and programming Hdqrs. USAF, 1967-70. Decorated D.S.M., Silver Star, Legion of Merit with 2 oak leaf clusters, D.F.C., with 4 oak leaf clusters, Bronze Star, Air medal with 5 oak leaf clusters, Commendation medal with oak leaf cluster; Polish Cross Valor; Croix de Guerre (France). Registered profl. engr., N.D. Mem. Am. Ordnance Assn., Air Force Assn., Air Force Hist. Found., Order Daedalians. Home: Arvonia VA 23004

JEFFREY, WALTER LESLIE, corp. exec.; b. Evansville, Ind. Nov. 7, 1908; s.Leslie L. and Dora Ann (McCarty) J.; B.S., Evansville Coll., 1929; M.B.A., U. Dayton (Ohio), 1964; m. Jane Rundell, Oct. 8, 1934; children—Judith Ann, Nancy Jean. Advt. dept. Kelvinator div. Am Motors Corp., Detroit, 1929-39, advt. mgr., 1939-41, sales mgr., 1941-55, v.p. sales, 1955, v.p., gen. mgr., 1956-59; v.p. Am. Motors Corp., 1955-59; sr. economist Stanford Research Inst., Menlo Park, 1960-61; pres. E.F. MacDonald Stamp Co., 1962-67; vice chmn., dir. E.F. MacDonald Co.; dir. Belton Corp., Brecks of Boston, Am. Loan & Finance Co., Shopping Bag Food Stores. Mem. Sigma Alpha Epsilon. Mason. Clubs: Detroit Athletic; Dayton Country. Co-author: Tribulations of Hawkeye. Home: 2230 S Patterson Blvd Kettering OH 45409 Office: 115 S Ludlow St Dayton OH 45401

JEFFRIES, ALLERTON HUBBELL, printing exec.; b. Los Angeles, Aug. 28, 1905; s. Willaim Parrish and Lora (Hubbell) J.; U. Calif., 1926; m. Louise Little. July 19, 1933; children—Jerome Allerton, Thomas Little, Judy Jane; m. 2d, Tholen Daniels, Feb. 14, 1964. Formerly with Jeffries Banknote Co., Los Angeles, salesman, 1926-32, v.p., 1932-40, pres., 1940-66, chmn. bd., also dir.; dir. Title Ins. & Trust Co. Pres. Welfare Fedn. Los Angeles. Mem. Los Angeles C. of C. (dir.), Merchants and Mfrs. Assn. (dir.), Printing Industry of Am. (past pres.), Printing Industry Assn. of Los Angeles (past pres.). Mason (Shriner). Clubs: Jonathan, Balboa Bay; Newport Harbor Yacht, California. Home: 921 S Riverside Dr Palm Springs CA 92262 Office: 1330 W Pico Blvd Los Angeles CA 90015

JEFFRIES, CARSON DUNNING, educator, physicist; b. Lake Charles, La., Mar. 20, 1922; s. Charles William and Yancey (Dunning) J.; B.S., La. State U., 1943; Ph.D., Stanford, 1951; m. Elizabeth Dyer, Sept. 15, 1945; children—Andrew, Patricia. Research asso. Radio Research Lab., Harvard, 1943-45; research asst. Stanford, 1946-50; instr. Physikalisches Institut der Universitat, Zurich, Switzerland, 1951; mem. faculty U. Cal. at Berkeley, 1952—, prof., 1963—, dir. AEC, Office Naval Research projects in solid state physics, 1953—. Sr. Postdoctoral fellow NSF, Oxford (Eng.) U., 1958, Harvard, 1965-66; Fulbright prof., France, 1959. Mem. Am. Phys. Soc. Author: Dynamic Nuclear Orientation, 1963. Contbr. articles profl. jours. Profl. sculptor. Office: Le Conte Hall U Cal Berkeley CA 94720

JEFFRIES, LIONEL, actor; b. Forest Hill, London, Eng. Entered motion pictures, 1952; movies include The Nun's Story, Two-Way Stretch, The Trials of Oscar Wilde, Fanny, The Notorious Landlady, The Wrong Arm of the Law, First Men on the Moon, Call Me Bwana, The Truth About Spring, You Must Be Joking, The Crimson Blade, Camelot, Chitty Chitty, Bang Bang; writer, dir. The Railway Children. Address: 67 Brook St London WI England

JEFFRIES, ROBERT JOSEPH, educator; b. Norwalk, Conn., Jan. 6, 1923; s. Charles William and Christine (Jacobsen) J.; B.S., U. Conn., 1944, M.S., 1946; D.Eng., Johns Hopkins, 1948; m. Anna Darling Cumming, Oct. 13, 1945; children—Christine Darling, Bruce Cumming. Engr., NACA, 1944-46; instr. Johns Hopkins, 1946-48; research asso. N.C. State Coll., 1948-49; asso. prof. Mich. State U., 1949-54; tech. planning adviser Schlumberger Instrument Co., 1954-55; asst. to pres. Daystrom, Inc., 1955-57; pres., founder Data-Control System, Inc., 1957-66, chmn. bd., 1966-68; prof. U. Bridgeport (Conn.), 1968—; founder, mem. bd. dirs. Ednl. & Tech. Consultants, Inc., 1953—. Vice pres., founder Found. Instrumentation Edn. and Research, 1958—; bd. dirs. Van Dyck Corp., Life Energies Research, Inc. Trustee U. Bridgeport. Mem. Instrument Soc. Am. (pres. 1957-58), NRC, Assn. for Research and Enlightenment (trustee), Conn. Commn. for Higher Edn., U. Conn. Engring. Alumni Assn. (pres. 1969-71), Sigma Xi, Tau Beta Pi, Eta Kappa Nu. Clubs: University (N.Y.C.); Cedar Point Yacht (Westport, Conn.); Bird Key Yacht (Sarasota, Fla.). Editor Jour. Instrument Soc. Am., 1953-54. Author tech. papers. Home: 53 Agawam Av Owenoke Park Westport CT 06880 Office: Waldemere Hall U Bridgeport Bridgeport CT 06602

JEGHERS, HAROLD JOSEPH, physician; b. Jersey City, Sept. 26, 1904; s. Albert and Matilda (Gerckens) J.; B.S., Rensselaer Poly. Inst., 1928; M.D., Western Res. U., 1932; m. Isabel Wile, June 21, 1935; children—Harold, Dee, Sanderson, Theodore. Intern Boston City Hosp., 1933-34, resident, 1935- 37, physician-in-chief 5th Med. Service, 1943-46, now cons. physician; instr. to asso. prof. medicine Boston U. Sch. Medicine, 1935-46; prof. and dir. dept. medicine Georgetown U. Sch. Medicine, 1946-56; prof., dir. dept. medicine N.J. Coll. Medicine and Dentistry, Jersey City, 1956-66, emeritus, 1966-; med. dir. St. Vincent Hosp., Worcester, Mass., 1966—; prof. Tufts, 1966—; dir. med. ward service Jersey City Med. Center, 1956-66; dir. Tufts med. service Boston City Hosp., 1969-71; cons. internal medicine Georgetown U. Hosp. Rep. from A.C.P. to div. med. scis. NRC, 1950-53. Recipient Laetare award Guild of St. Luke, Boston, 1958. Fellow A.C.P., Am. Soc. for Clin. Investigation; mem. A.M.A., Am. Fedn. for Clin. Research, So. Soc. for Clin. Research (v.p. 1948-49), Assn. Am. Physicians, Mass. Med. Soc., Sigma Xi. Author articles and sects. in books. Home: 10 Orchard Rd Shrewsbury, MA 01545. Office: 25 Winthrop St Worcester MA 01604

JEKELI, WALTER, educator; b. Wiesbaden, Germany, Feb. 23, 1925; s. Julius Michael and Gertrud (Kuhn) J.; M.A. Staatsexamen U. Marburg, 1955, Ph.D., 1955, Staatsexamen II, 1957; m. Eva Ingeborg Kuhn, Apr. 15, 1952; children—Christoph, Klaus. Came to U.S. 1962. Instr. U. Marburg, 1953-55; tchr. Gymnasium, Marburg/Kassel, Germany, 1955-62; asst. prof. physics Clarkson Coll. Tech., Potsdam, N.Y., 1962-64, asso. prof., 1964-66; prof. physics State U. Coll. at Potsdam, 1966—, chmn. dept., 1967—. Mem. Am., German phys. socs., Am. Assn. Physics Tchrs. Research theoretical physics, solid state and microwave spectroscopy. Home: 51 Pierrepont Av Potsdam NY 13676

JELINEK, HANS, artist, educator; b. Vienna, Austria, Aug. 21, 1910; s. Hermann and Paula (Stwertka) J.; grad. U. Vienna, 1933, Vienna Kunstgewerbeschule, 1933; M.A., Columbia; m. Trudy Stwertka. Came to U.S., 1938, naturalized, 1943. Mem. art faculty New Sch. Social Research, 1945—; asst. prof. art Coll. City N.Y., 1948-58, asso. prof., 1958-66, prof., 1966—; represented permanent collections Met. Mus., Library of Congress, Cooper Union, Dartmouth, N.Y. Pub. Library, Nelson A. Rockefeller collection, many others; work exhibited throughout U.S.; one man shows Va. Mus. Art, Smithsonian Inst., others. Awarded 1st prize Artists for Victory, Nat. Graphic Art Exhbn.; Pennell prize Library Congress 3rd nat. print exhbn.; Tiffany award, others. Address: care City Coll Eisner Hall 133d St and Convent Av New York City NY 10031

JELINEK, JOHN PETER, educator; b. Omaha, May 16, 1916; s. Vaclav Francis and Frances (Holy) J.; A.B., St. Louis U., 1939, M.A., 1943, S.T.L., 1949; Ph.D., Gregorian U., Rome, Italy, 1951. Joined Soc. of Jesus, 1934, ordained priest Roman Cath. Ch., 1947; instr. Latin and English, Campion High Sch., Prairie du Chien, Wis., 1942-45; instr. philosophy Regis Coll., Denver, 1951-52; instr. philosophy St. Louis U., 1952-55, asst. prof., 1955-59; mem. faculty Creighton U., 1959—, prof. philosophy, 1962—, chmn. dept. philosophy, 1962-67; summer vis. lectr. Rockhurst Coll., Kansas City, Mo., 1948, 52, Regis Coll., 1954. Mem. Am. Cath. Philos. Assn., Mountain-Plains Philos. Conf. Contbr. profl. jours. Address: Creighton Univ Omaha NB 68131

JELINEK, VLADMIR, conductor, pianist, composer; b. Nove Straseci, Czechoslovakia, Aug. 16, 1923; s. Antonin and Julie (Kurzweilova) J.; student piano and composition Prague Conservatory; grad. Prague Acad. Music, 1951; m. Sona Pecmanova, Sept. 13, 1957; children by previous marriage—Vladimira and Marcela (twins). Came to Can., 1965. Conductor, Czechoslovakia Nat. Ballet, 1950-65; tours of Europe and China, 1952-64; music dir. Grandes Ballets Canadiens, Montreal, 1965-: tours of U.S., 1966-68; conducted Carmina Burana at L.I. Festival, 1967; volin-piano recitals with wife, 1965—, conducted first Canadian performance of whole Orff trilogy Europe performing Triomfi, London, Paris, Brussels, Geneva, Zurich, 1969; conducted first performance in N. Am. of Stravinsky's Symphony of Psaulmes as a ballet danced in St. Joseph's Oratory, Montreal, 1970, Composer ballets, also songs. Home: 178 Trenton St Montreal Quebec Quebec Canada Office: 5415 Queen Mary Rd Montreal Quebec Canada

JELKS, JOSEPH WILLIAM, Jr., textile co. exec.; b. Southport, N.C., Mar. 27, 1916; s. Joseph William and Josie (Garrett) J.; B.S. in Math. and Sci., Wake Forest Coll., 1936; m. Ann Elizabeth Ray, Aug. 15, 1936; children—Peggy (Mrs. Charles R. Duncan, Jr.), Joseph William III. Indsl. relations mgr. Winnsboro Mills, U.S. Rubber Co., 1939-51; personnel dir. Ware Shoals div. Riegel Textile Corp., 1951-57; v.p., dir. indsl. relations J.P. Stevens & Co., Inc., 1957—. Tchr. personnel adminstrn. and indsl. safety U. S.C. Extension, 1947-50; tchr. indsl. engring. Methods Engring. Council Pitts., 1954-56. Dir. So. Indsl. Relations Conf., 1963—. Chmn. Fairfield County chpt. A.R.C., 1948, Fairfield County chpt. Nat. Found., 1950. Dir.-at-large S.C. Tb Assn. Bd. dirs. Unemployment Benefit Advisors; adv. bd. Liberty Mut. Ins. Co. Hon. life mem. So. Conf. Football Ofcls. Assn.; mem. Southeastern Personnel Assn. (dir., past chmn.), S.C. Textile Mfrs. Assn. (chmn. safety com., past chmn., dir. personnel div.), Wake Forest Coll. Alumni Council, Soc. Advancement Mgmt., Am. Textile Mfrs. Inst., S.C. Accident Prevention Conf., S.C. (v.p.), Greater Greenville chambers commerce, Am. Soc. Personnel Adminstrn. Episcopalian. Clubs: Greenville Country, City, Poinsett (Greenville). Home: 34 Sirrine Dr Greenville SC 29605 Office: Daniel Bldg Greenville SC 29601

JELLIFFE, CHARLES GORDON, banker; b. Mansfield, O., Nov. 28, 1914; s. Charles Mitchell and Florence (Findley) J.; B.Sc., Ohio State U., 1937; m. Carolyn V. Wolf, Oct. 3, 1942; children—Charles Martin, Joyce Findley, John Bour, Jannell W. Salesman, Hawley Huller & Co., investment securities, Cleve., 1937- 40; with Columbus Coated Fabrics Corp. (O.), 1940-64, pres., chmn. bd., 1961-64; former vice chmn. bd., now pres. City Nat. Bank & Trust Co., Columbus, 1964—, also dir.; sec., treas., dir. First Banc Corp. of Ohio, Inc., Columbus; dir. Lumbermand Mut. Ins. Co., Mansfield, O, Edmont, Inc., Coshocton, O., Republic Franklin Life Ins. Co., Tracy Wells Co., Brun Sensors Inc. Bd. dirs. Columbus Downtown Area Commn., 1966-, Devel. Com. Greater Columbus, 1962—. Pres., trustee Gladden Community House, Columbus, 1955-63; trustee Columbus United Community Council, 1964—, Columbus Gallery Fine Arts, 1963-, Defiance (O.) Coll., 1961-. Served to maj. AUS, 1941- 46. Mem. Columbus Area C. of C. (dir., treas.), Ohio State U. Alumni Assn. (pres.), Conglist. (chmn. trustees). Clubs: Columbus (v.p., dir.), the Golf, Columbus Athletic, Scioto Country (Columbus); Pinnacle (N.Y.C.). Home: 2405 Onandaga Dr Columbus OH 43221 Office: 100 E Broad St Columbus OH 43215

JELLIFFE, RUSSELL WESLEY, social adminstr.; b. Mansfield, O., Nov. 19, 1891; s. Charles Wesley and Margaret (Ward) J.; A.B., Oberlin Coll., 1914, LL.D., 1944; A.M., U. Chgo., 1915; H.H.D., Western Res. U., 1951; L.H.D., Cleve. State U., 1966; m. Rowena Woodham, May 28, 1915; 1 son, Roger Woodham. Founder, exec. dir. (with Mrs. Jeliffe), Karamu House cultural- ednl. inst. 1915-63, Karamu Found. 1963—; del. 2d Pan- African Congress, Paris, France, 1921; active in establishing Cleve. Urban League, 1916, Cleve. Met. Housing Authority, 1933, Cleve. Community Relations Bd. on Race Relations, 1945; pres. group work council Welfare Fedn. Cleve., 1938-40; foreman Cuyahoga County Grand Jury, 1960. Civic cons.; dir. Arts and Edn. Survey Boston, 1963, Cultural-Ednl. Survey St. Louis, 1967, Arts Survey Indpls., 1967, Arts and Cultural Survey Canton, O., 1968. Trustee Cleve. Council on Human Relations, 1960-65; trustee Oberlin Coll., 1960-67, now hon. life trustee; trustee Cleve. Civil Liberties Union, 1963—; hon. life trustee Karamu House, 1963—; mem. Cleve. Selective Service Bd. 20, 1960-68, Nat. Council Arts in Edn., 1960-63; life fellow Cleve. Mus. Art. Recipient (with Mrs. Jelliffe) Charles Eisenman Civic award Jewish Welfare Assn., 1941, Human Race Relations award Nat. Council Christians and Jews, 1944, Lane Bryant award, 1958; one of 10 outstanding citizens Cleve. award, Cleve. Press, 1950, 58; Cleve. Distinctive Service award United Appeal of Cleve., 1961; Distinguished Service award Nat. Fedn. Settlements, 1963; numerous others. Mem. N.A.A.C.P. (exec. com. Cleve. br. 1926-), Great Lakes Shakespeare Assn. (1st v.p. 1962, trustee 1962—), Grand Jury Assn. (trustee 1960-), Jury Foremen's Council (trustee 1965-), United World Federalists (trustee 1962), Oberlin Coll. Alumni Assn. (trustee 1958- 60), Citizens League Cleve. Club: Men's City (Cleve.) Home: 12427 Fairhill Rd Cleveland OH 44120. Office: 12427 Fairhill Rd Cleveland OH 44120

JELLINGHAUS, CARL FREDERIC, newspaper editor; b. N.Y.C., Feb. 15, 1917; s. C. Frederic and Marguerite (de Langeais) J.; grad. Hill Sch., Pottstown, Pa., 1934; B.A., Yale, 1938; m. Phyllis Howard, July 6, 1946; children-Carl Frederic, Adrian, Lisa H. Salesman, E.L. Hildreth & Co., Brattleboro, Vt., 1939-40; with Western Printing and Lithographing Co., 1940-41; with Bergen Eve. Record Corp. Hackensack, N.J., 1947—, mng. editor, 1969—. Mem. A.P. Mng. Editors Assn., Sigma Delta Chi. Home: 10 Beechwood Rd Ho Ho Kus NJ 07423 Office: 150 River St Hackensack NJ 07602

JEMISON, GEORGE M., forester; b. Spokane, July 11, 1908; s. George Homer and Margaret (Meredith) J.; B.S. in Forestry, U. Ida., 1931, D.Sc. (hon.), 1967; M.F., Yale, 1936; Ph.D., Duke; 1942; m. Beatrice Gibbs, Dec. 30, 1931; children—Meredith (Mrs. Allan Paramore), Carol (Mrs. R.H. Reynolds). With Forest Service, Dept. Agr., 1931-69, asso. dep. chief research, 1957-66, dep. chief, 1967-69, ret.; prof. forestry Ore. State U., 1969—. Pres., Internat. Union Forestry Research Orgn., 1968-71. Recipient Distinguished Service award Dept. Agr., 1967. Fellow Soc. Am. Foresters; mem. Phi Beta Kappa, Sigma Xi. Mason, Elk. Home: 3920 N W Elizabeth Pl Corvallis OR 97330

JEN, FRANK CHIFENG, educator; b. Shanghai, China, May 15, 1931; s. Seybold E. and Susan (Lin) J.; came to U.S., 1957; B.S., N. Central Coll., 1959; M.B.A., U. Wis., 1960, Ph.D., 1963; m. Daisy Chi, Aug. 26, 1962; children—Amy K., Wendy K., Edward K. Asst. prof. finance State U.N.Y. at Buffalo, 1964-66, asso. prof., 1966-68, prof., 1968—, chmn. dept. finance, 1967-70, chmn. dept. operating analysis, 1970—. Mem. Inst. Mgmt. Scis., Am. Finance Assn., Am. Econ. Assn., Econometric Soc., Pi Gamma Mu, Beta Gamma Sigma. Asso. editor finance dept. Management Science, 1970—, Jour. Financial and Quantitative Analysis, 1970—. Home: 40 Ranch Trail Williamsville NY 14221 Office: Sch Mgmt State U NY at Buffalo NY 14214

JENCKES, ERNEST ASHLEY, lawyer; b. Providence, Aug. 20, 1898; s. Robert A. and Jessie (Ashley) J.; A.B., Brown U., 1920; LL.B. (bd. editors Rev. 1922-23), Harvard, 1923; m. Dorothy B. Hotchkiss, Oct. 1, 1927; 1 son, Henry W. Admitted to R.I. bar, 1923, since practiced in Providence; mem. firm Swan, Keeney and Jenckes, 1936—. Mem. Estate Planning Council R.I., 1960—; mem. local SSS bd., 1942-68. Pres., Bethany Home of R.I., 1932-64; head agt. 1923 class fund Brown U., 1960—. Mem. Am., R.I. bar assns., Providence, Barrington players assns. Conglist. Mason. Clubs: Turks Head (past pres.), University, Art (Providence); Dunes (Narragansett, R.I.); Barrington Yacht; Rhode Island Country. Home: 114 Governor Bradford Dr Barrington RI 02806 Office: Turks Head Bldg Providence RI 02903

JENCKES, LESLIE CLIFFORD, economist; b. Beloit, Wis., Feb. 11, 1917; s. Joseph Martin and Tena (Gilbertson) J.; B.A., Temple U., 1964; m. Ruth Holliday, Nov. 11, 1944; 1 son, Charles Holliday. Engr. tech. service Sun Oil Co., Phila., 1945-51, tech. econs., 1952-60, engring. econs., 1961-70, planning and econs., 1971—. Served with C.E., AUS, 1941-42. Mem. Am. Assn. Cost Engrs. (chmn. operating cost com. 1963-66, dir. cost information 1968-69, dir. publs. 1970, treas. 1971). Home: 330 Timber Jump Lane Media PA 19063 Office: 1608 Walnut St Philadelphia PA 19103

JENCKS, FRANCIS HAYNES, architect; b. Balt., Nov. 16, 1902; s. Francis Mankin and Elizabeth (Platt) J.; B.A., Harvard, 1924; B.Arch., Columbia, 1927; m. Elizabeth P. Pleasants, Dec. 14, 1932; children—Christopher, Stephen, Helen (Mrs. J. Luke Featherstone). Partner firm Wrenn, Lewis, Westenhaver & Jencks, Balt., 1929-34, firm Wrenn, Lewis & Jencks, Balt., 1934—. Bd. dirs. Citizens Planning and Housing Assn.; trustee Balt. Mus. Art, 1930-69, Peale Mus., 1930—. Served to lt. comdr. USNR, 1942-46. Fellow A.I.A.; mem. Md. Soc. Architects (bd. dirs. 1970—). Home: 530 Greenwood Rd Towson MD 21204 Office: 113 W Mulberry St Baltimore MD 21201

JENCKS, RICHARD WILLIAM, broadcasting co. exec.; b. Oakland, Cal., Apr. 18, 1921; s. Frederick Marshall and Antia (de Laguna) J.; student U. Cal. at Berkeley, 1938-41; A.B., Stanford, 1946, LL.B., 1948; m. Mary Barrett Wells, 1942 (div. 1955); children—Michael Reynolds, Nancy de Laguna; m. 2d, Joan Workman, 1955 (div. 1964); m. 3d, Mary Barrett Wells, Feb. 28, 1966. Asst. to gen. counsel Nat. Assn. Broadcasters, 1948-50; atty. CBS 1950-59, West coast resident counsel, 1953-59; pres. Alliance TV Film Producers. Inc., Hollywood, Cal., 1959-65; v.p. Assn. Motion Picture and TV producers, Hollywood, 1963-65; dep. gen. counsel CBS, 1965-68, gen. counsel, 1967- 68, exec. v.p. CBS TV Network div., 1968-. Mem. city council, Pasadena, Cal. 1963-65. Served to lt. comdr. USNR, 1941-45. Mem. Am., Fed. Communications bar assns. Home: 324 Riverside Av Riverside CT 06878 Office: 51 W 52d St New York City NY 10019

JENCKS, WILLIAM PLATT, educator, biochemist; b. Bar Harbor, Me., Aug. 15, 1927; s. Gardner and Elinor (Melcher) J.; grad. St. Paul's Sch., Balt., 1944; student Harvard, 1944-47, M.D., 1951; m. Miriam Ehrlich, June 3, 1950; children—Helen Esther, David Alan. Intern, Peter Bent Brigham Hosp., Boston, 1951-52; postdoctoral fellow Mass. Gen. Hosp., Boston, 1952- 53, 55-56; postdoctoral fellow chemistry Harvard, 1956-57; mem. faculty Brandeis U., 1957—, prof. bio-chemistry, 1963—. Served as 1st lt., M.C., AUS, 1953-55. Mem. Am. Chem. Soc. (award biol. chemistry 1962), Am. Soc. Biol. Chemists, Am. Acad. Arts and Scis., A.A.A.S., Nat. Acad. Scis., Alpha Omega Alpha. Home: 11 Revere St Lexington MA 02173 Office: Grad Dept Biochemistry Brandeis Univ Waltham MA 02154

JENDEN, DONALD JAMES, educator, pharmacologist; b. Horsham, Sussex, Eng., Sept. 1, 1926; s. William Herbert and Kathleen Mary (Harris) J.; B.Sc. in Physiology with 1st class honours (scholar 1944), Westminster Med. Sch., U. London, 1947; M.B., B.S. (Univ. gold medal 1950), U. London, 1950; m. Jean Ickeringill, Nov. 18, 1950; children—Particia Mary, Peter D., Beverly J. Came to U.S., 1950, naturalized, 1958. Demonstrator physiology and pharmacology U. London, 1947-50; lectr. pharmacology, then asst. prof. pharmacology U. Cal. at San Francisco, 1950-53; mem. faculty U. Cal. at Los Angeles, 1953—, prof. pharmacology, 1960-68, prof. pharmacology and biomath., 1968—, chmn. dept. pharmacology, 1968—; hon. research asso. Univ. Coll., London. 1961-62. Cons. neuro- pharmacology VA Hosp., Long Beach, Cal. Served to lt. M.C., USNR, 1954-56, Mem. Am. Soc. Exptl. Pharmacology and Therapeutics, Am. Physiol. Soc., A.A.A.S., Physiol. Soc. (London), British Med. Assn. Author articles in field. Home: 3814 S Castlerock Rd Malibu CA 90265 Office: Sch Medicine Center Health Scis Univ California Los Angeles CA 90024

JENKIN, NOEL, research exec.; b. New Zealand, May 15, 1918; s. Stanley W. and Dora (Ladley) J.; B.A., Cambridge Coll., U. New Zealand, 1951, M.A. with 1st class honours, 1953; Ph.D. in Social Psychology, Harvard, 1957; m. Betty I. Blackburn, May 11, 1953; children-Melanie C., Anthony D.M. Came to U.S., 1953, naturalized, 1966. Lectr., Victoria U., Wellington, New Zealand, 1953; research asst. Harvard Psychol. Clinic, 1953-54, research asst. Lab. Social Relations, 1954-55; asst. prof. U. N.B., 1955-56; co- dir. Ability Structure Project, Tng. Sch., Vineland, N.J., 1956-58; lectr. U. Sydney, 1958-59; dir. research Inst. Juvenile Research, Chgo., 1960—; acting div. dir. research Ill. Dept. Mental Health, 1967-69; mem. faculty U. Ill., 1961—, prof. psychology dept. psychiatry Abraham Lincoln Coll. Medicine, 1967—. Fellow Am. Psychol. Assn., A.A.A.S. Author articles in field. Home: 326 S Elmwood Av Oak Park IL 60302 Office: 232 E Ohio St Chicago IL 60611

JENKIN, THOMAS PAUL, educator; b. Elcho, Wis., June 3, 1915; s. Thomas Vincent and Bessie Caren (Due) J.; B.A., Lawrence Coll., 1937; M.A., U. Mich., 1939, Ph.D., 1943; m. Mary Ethel Fulton, Dec. 26, 1938. Teaching fellow U. Mich., 1940-42; instr. U. Cal. at Los Angeles, 1942-45, asst. prof., 1945-50, asso. prof., 1950-56. prof., 1956-63, chmn. dept. polit sci., 1952-56; prof., dean Coll. of Letters and Sci., U. Cal. at Riverside, 1963-65, former vice chancellor. Recipient Rockefeller Foundation research grant, 1956-57. Served as lt. medical adminstrv. corps. U.S. Army, 1943-46. Mem. American (past nat. council member), Western, So. polit. sci. assns., Am. Assn. U. Profs., Phi Beta Kappa, Phi Kappa Phi, Pi Sigma Alpha. Club: The Commonwealth of California. Author: Reactions of Major Groups to Positive Government in the United States, 1930-1940. 1945; (with J. K. Pollock, L. H. Laing. S. J. Eldersveld, R. M. Scammon) British Election Studies, 1951; The Study of Political Theory. Contbr. profl. jours. Home: 5190 Stonewood Dr Riverside CA 92506

JENKINS, ALFRED LE SESNE, fgn. service officer; b. Manchester, Ga., Sept. 14, 1916; s. Charles Rush and Beulah (Hall) J.; A.B. with honors, Emory U., 1938; M.Ed., Duke, 1946; student U. Chgo., Nat. War Coll.; m. Martha Elizabeth Lippiatt, Oct. 14, 1945; children—Sara Gere, Stephen Lippiatt. Sch. prin., Appling County, Ga., 1940-41; supt. schs., Naylor, Ga., 1941-42; fgn. service officer, 1946—; vice consul, Peiping, 1946, Tientsin, 1948, Hong Kong, 1949; 2d sec., consul, Taipei, 1950; internat. relations officer Dept. State, 1952, officer-in-charge Chinese polit. affairs, 1953-55; counselor Embassy, dep. chief of mission, Jidda, Saudi Arabia, 1955; dep. dir. Office of S.E. Asian Affairs, Dept. State, 1958, regional planning adviser Far Eastern affairs, 1959; counselor of embassy, dep. chief mission Am. embassy, Stockholm, Sweden, 1961-65; sr. fgn. service insp. Dept. State, 1965-66, 69-70; dir. Office of Asian Communist Affairs, Dept. State, 1970—; staff Nat. Security Council, 1966-69. Mem Am. Acad. Polit. and Social Sci., Am. Oriental Soc., Phi Beta Kappa, Omicron Delta Kappa, Chi Phi. Club: Metropolitan (Washington). Home: 2704 O St NW Washington DC 20007 Office: Dept of State Washington DC 20520

JENKINS, DALE WILSON, govt. ofcl.; b. Wapakoneta, O., June 17, 1918; s. Roy William and Estella Grace (Young) J.; B.Sc., Ohio State U., 1938, M.A. (fellow), 1939, Ph.D., 1947; postgrad. (fellow) U. Chgo., 1939-40, U. Ill., 1940-41, U. Minn., 1941-42; grad. Army Malaria Sch., 1944; m. Stella Elizabeth Bowen, Jan. 18, 1942; children—Nancy, Paul, Kenneth, Rebecca, Elizabeth. Ecologist, Soil Conservation Service, summers 1936, 41; grad. instr. Ohio State U., U. Chgo., U. Ill., U. Minn., 1938-42; research student, scholar Marine Biol. Lab., Mass., 1939, Stone Biol. Lab., Ohio, 1938-39; agrl. specialist Bd. Econ. Warfare, Fgn. Econ. Adminstrn., 1943-44; entomologist, chief animal ecol. br., med. div. Army Chem. Center, 1946-42, chief entomol. br., dep. chief Allied Scis. div., 1953-56; chief entomology div., Ft. Detrick, Md., 1957-62; chief environmental biology NASA, Washington, 1962-66, asst. dir. biosci. programs, 1966-69; dir. ecology program Smithsonian Instn., Washington, 1970—; lectr. med. entomology and pathobiology Sch. Pub. Health, Johns Hopkins, 1950—. Mem. Armed Forces Pest Control Bd., 1953-62; chmn. Inst. Lab. Animal Resources, NRC, 1955-60; mem., cons. Internat. Com. Lab. Animals, Internat. Union Biol. Sci., Paris, 1956-60; head Am. regional office Internat. Com. Lab. Animals, 1958-61. Del. Internat. Conf. on Peaceful Uses of Atomic Energy, Geneva, 1953; adviser UNESCO on Peaceful Uses Atomic Energy, Paris, 1957; adviser on UNESCO to NRC, 1957-59; cons. space biology USAF, 1959-62; cons. Internat. Atomic Energy Agy., WHO; Nat. Acad. Sci.-NRC del. Internat. Congress Entomology, Montreal, 1956; chmn. med. entomology sect. Internat. Congress Entomology, Vienna, Austria, 1960; insect ecology cons. U.S. Dept. Agr., Alaska, 1947; cons., mem. mission to Venezuela, FAO, UN, 1948; entomol. cons. USPHS, 1948; entomol. collaborator No. Insect Survey. Canadian Def. Research Bd., 1949-50. Served to lt. col., entomologist AUS, 1942-65. Fellow A.A.A.S.; mem. Washington Acad. Sci., Ecol. Soc. Am. (v.p., chmn. med. entomol. sect. 1953), Ecol. Soc. Am., Am. Soc. Tropical Medicine and Hygiene, Am. Mosquito Control Assn., Animal Care Panel, Entomol. Soc. Washington, Soc. Tropical Biology, Sigma Xi, Phi Sigma. Author books; contbr. articles to profl. jours. Home: 700 7th St NW Washington DC 20024 Office: NASA Hdqrs Washington 25 DC

JENKINS, DANIEL EDWARDS, Jr., educator, physician; b. Omaha, July 19, 1916; s. Daniel Edwards and Anne (Finley) J.; student Hampden-Sydney Coll., 1934; B.A., U. Tex., 1936, M.D., 1940; m. Dora Solis, Aug. 1, 1942; children—Daniel Edwards III, Mark Shering, Tessa Ann. Intern, then resident U. Mich. Hosp., 1940-44; asst. prof. medicine U. Coll. Medicine, 1947-, prof. internal medicine, 1956—, chief sect. pulmonary diseases, 1947—; part-time pvt. practice, 1947—; chief pulmonary disease service Harris County Hosp. Dist., 1947—; cons. VA, 1949-65. Recipient So. Conf. award So. Tb Conf., 1967. Fellow A.C.P., Am. Coll. Chest Physicians; mem. A.M.A., Am. Thoracic Soc. (pres. 1958-59), Am. Fedn. Clin. Research, Am. Clin. and Climatol. Assn., Nat. (pres. 1967-68, bd. dirs. 1958—). Tex. (pres. 1966-67) Tb and respiratory disease assns., Am. Coll. Chest Physicians (pres. So. chpt. 1958), Alpha Omega Alpha, Alpha Kappa Kappa. Author articles in field. Home: 3550 Sun Valley Dr Houston, TX 77025.

JENKINS, DANIEL HENRY, lawyer; b. Scranton, Pa., Sept. 5, 1899; s. Daniel Henry and Margaret Silvanus (Roberts) J.; A.B., Pa. State U., 1923; A.M., Dickinson Coll., 1926; J.D., Dickinson School of Law, Carlisle, Pa., 1926; m. Margaret Watkins, Dec. 31, 1936; children—Arthur V., David Silvanus, Gwyneth Silvanus Hughes, Dana Watkins Fuller, Daniel Henry III. Admitted to Pa. bar, 1927, U.S. Supreme Ct., 1944, also ICC and Treasury Dept.; asst. city solicitor, Scranton, 1942; mem. firm Jenkins and Ligi, Scranton, 1947—; prin. examiner Pa. Pub. Utility Commn., 1947-58; U.S. atty. Middle Dist. Pa., 1958-62; counsel, dir. Abington Hills Cemetery Assn., Scranton Casket Co. Vice chmn. local Boy Scouts Am. Served with U.S. Navy, 1918. Mem. Am., Pa., Lackawanna (v.p., dir.) bar assns., St. David's Soc. (past pres.), Cambrian Soc. (past pres.), Sigma Chi (past consul), Gamma Eta Gamma. Episcopalian (vestry, exec. com. diocese Bethlehem. Pa). Mason (32, K.T., Shriner), Rotarian (past pres. Scranton). Home: 1930 N Main Av Scranton PA 18508 Office: Jenkins Ligi & Dunn Mears Bldg Scranton PA 18503

JENKINS, EDWARD C., educator; b. Phila., Jan. 28, 1904; s. Charles Francis and Maria G. (Cope) J.; A.B., Swarthmore Coll., 1927; M.A., U. Chgo., 1929; m. June F. Blaisdell, Dec. 28, 1927 (dec. 1942); children—Nancy (Mrs. Walter Burdsall), Charmarie (Mrs. Robert Webb); m. 2d, Betty Karge, Sept. 25, 1943; one dau., Susan Hayhurst. With Bauer & Black div. of Kendell Co., Chgo., 1929-32; sec., treas. Buck Hill Falls (Pa.) Co., 1932-55, Buck Hill Water Co., 1940-55; pres., gen. mgr. Pocono Lodges, Inc., operators The Skyline Inn, Mt. Pocono, 1955-67, dir., 1951-67; dir. Pocono Mts. Vacation Bur., pres., 1932-51; dir. Am. Youth Hostels, Inc., 1951-58, pres., 1953-55, chmn. bd., 1956-58. Asst. prof. Sch. Hotel Adminstrn. Delhi Agr. and Tech. Coll. State U. N.Y. Trustee Gen. Hosp. Monroe County 1941-67; dir. Top of the Poconos Assn., 1962-67, Racing, Inc. Mem. Pa. Hist. Soc., Pa. Hotel and Motor Inn Assn., Welsh Soc. Pa., Ye Hosts, Phi Delta Theta, Pi Delta Epsilon. Mason (32), Kiwanian. Home: 6 Franklins St Delhi NY

JENKINS, ELIZABETH, author; ed. Newham Coll., Cambridge (Eng.) U. Author: Lady Caroline Lamb: a Biography, 1932; Portrait of an Actor, 1933; Harriet (Femina Vie Heureuse prize), 1934; The Phoenix Nest, 1936; Jane Austen-a biography, 1938; Robert and Helen, 1944; Young Enthusiasts, 1946; Henry Fielding (English Novelists series), 1947; Six Criminal Women, 1939; The Tortoise and the Hare, 1954; Ten Fascinating Women, 1955; (biography) Elizabeth the Great, 1958; Elizabeth and Leicester, 1961; Brightness, 1964; Henry Fielding, 1966; Honey, 1968. Address: 8 Downshire Hill Hampstead NW 3 England

JENKINS, ELLA L., folk singer; b. St. Louis, Aug. 6, 1924; B.A., San Francisco State Coll. Dir. teenage program YWCA Chgo., 1952-56; folk singer, 1956—; formerly hostess folk music TV show Meetin House, also other TV appearances; conductor workshops in Austria, Montreal and Toronto; worked with children in Switzerland; numerous recordings. Mem. A.S.C.A.P., Internat. Platform Assn., Am. Fedn. Musicians, Music Educators Nat. Conf. Author: This is Rhythm; The Ella Jenkins Song Book for Children. Author, arranger, singer film series Themetoshow. Address: care Folkway Records 701 7th Av New York City NY 10036

JENKINS, EMERSON DANIEL, educator; b. Utica, N.Y., Jan. 13, 1909; s. John Addison and Cora Mabel (Edwards) J.; A.B., Colgate U., 1931; M.A., Ohio State U., 1932, Ph.D., 1935. Instr. math. U. Ky., Lexington, 1935-37; asso. prof. Eastern Ky. State U., Richmond, 1937-47; asso. prof. Kent (O.) State U., 1947-52, prof., 1952—. Served to lt. USNR, 1943-46. Mem. Am. Math. Soc., Math. Assn. Am., Am. Assn. U. Profs., Sigma Xi, Phi Beta Kappa. Home: 1538 Vine St Kent OH 44240

JENKINS, ERBY LEE, lawyer; b. Raccoon Valley, Tenn., Sept. 19, 1907; s. Marion Lockwood and Bertha Alma (Smith) J.; student Racoon Valley Acad., U. Tenn.; LL.B., Cumberland U., 1931; m. Nell Hubbs, Apr. 26, 1929; 1 son, Ray Lee. Admitted to Tenn. bar, 1931; since practiced in Knoxville; mem. firm Jenkins & Jenkins. Chmn. Knox County Rep. Exec. Com., 1942-48, 50-58; mem. Tenn. Rep. Exec. Com., 1956—, chmn., 1962—. Trustee Cumberland Coll. of Tenn. Recipient Presdl. Award Spl. merit, Tenn. Bar Assn., 1966. Fellow Am. Bar Found., Am. Coll. Trial Lawyers (mem. bd. regents; sec. 1968-69), The Internat. Acad. Trial Lawyers; mem. Am. (state delegate), Tenn. (pres. 1959-60), Internat. bar assns., Phi Delta Phi. Home: 4608 Tazewell Pike Knoxville TN 37918 Office: Bank of Knoxville Bldg Knoxville TN 37902

JENKINS, FARISH ALSTON, marketing exec.; b. Hannibal, Mo., July 4, 1914; s. Henry Edgar and Ida (Farish) J.; A.B., Princeton, 1938; grad. Advanced Mgmt. Program, Harvard, 1957; m. Judith Black, July 9, 1938 (div.); children—Fariah A., Henry Edgar II, Andrews D.; m. 2d, Muriel Geril LeMaire, May 18, 1963. With MacCann-Erickson, Inc., N.Y.C., 1940—, v.p., 1953-60, sr. v.p., 1960-62, exec. v.p., 1962-64; v.p. communications Nat. Biscuit Co., N.Y.C., 1964-69, sr. v.p. corporate marketing, 1969—. Dir., Nat. Better Bus. Bur. Served from 2d lt. to lt. col., AUS, 1940-45. Clubs: Links, Twenty-Nine (N.Y.C.); Apawamis (gov., pres.) (Rye). Home: Sunset Lane Rye NY 10580 Office: 425 Park Av New York City NY 10022

JENKINS, FERGUSON, baseball player. Pitcher, Chgo. Cubs baseball team. Address: care Pub Relations dir Chgo Cubs Baseball Team Wrigley Field N Clark and Addison Sts Chicago IL 60613*

JENKINS, FRANCES BRIGGS, educator; b. San Diego; B.S., U. Ill., 1926; M.S., Tulane U., 1928; Ph.D., U. Ill. at Urbana, 1937; B.L.S., U. Cal., 1947; postgrad. Columbia, summer 1951. Asst. biochemistry Agr. Expt. Sta. U. Tenn., 1928-29; instr. dept. biochemistry U. Ill. Coll. Medicine, 1929-41; supr. correction sect. Communications Div. 11th Naval Dist., San Diego, 1942-44; head br. libraries U. Cal., 1947-51; prof. library sci. Grad. Sch. Library Sci. U. Ill. at Urbana, 1951—. Mem. adv. com. for Manpower and Tng. NLM, 1966-68. Served to lt. USNR, 1944-46. Recipient Isadore Gilbert Mudge citation, 1966. Mem. A.L.A. (council 1954-57, 62—, exec. bd. 1965—), A.A.A.S., Am. Chem. Soc., Am. Acad. Library Sci., Med., Ill. library assns., Sigma Xi, Beta Phi Mu, Sigma Delta Epsilon. Author: Science Reference Sources, 5th edit., 1969. Editor: Collecting Sci. Lit. for Gen. Reading, 1960; co-editor: Bibliography: Current State and Future Trends, 1967. Editorial staff ACRL Monographs, 1952-60. Publ. bd. Library Trends, 1955—. Address: Grad Sch Library Sci U Ill Urbana IL 61803*

JENKINS, GEOFFREY, author; b. Port Elizabeth, S. Africa, June 16, 1920; s. Ernest Henry and Daisy Agnes (Gardiner) J.; grad. Potchefstroom Boys High Sch., Transvaal, S. Africa, 1937; m. Evelyn Mary Palmer, Mar. 17, 1950; 1 son, David. Reporter, Rhodesia Herald, 1940, sub-editor, 1941-45, chief sub- editor, 1946; sub-editor Daily Graphic, London, Eng., also Sunday Times, Sunday Graphics, Empire News, Sunday Dispatch and Manchester Eve. News, 1946-47; picture feature writer Kemsley Newspapers, London, 1947-48; editor Umtali Advertiser, Rhodesia, 1949; rep. The Star in Pretoria, 1950-62; broadcaster BBC, 1947-48. Recipient Lord Kemsley's Commonwealth scholarship for journalists, 1947. Mem. Am. Authors Guild, British and Am. Screenwriters Guild. Author: (books) A Century of History, 1937, A Twist of Sand, 1959, The Watering-Place of Good Peace, 1960; A Grue of Ice, 1962; The River of Diamonds, 1964; Hunter-Killer, 1966; (motion picture scripts) A Twist of Sand, 1964, The Rivers of Diamonds, 1964, The Fifth Paw of the Lion, 1964. Address: 108 Albert St Waterkloof Pretoria South Africa

JENKINS, GEORGE POLLOCK, ins. co. exec.; b. Clarksburg, W.Va., Feb. 24, 1915; s. Roy N. and Gertrude S. (Pollock) J.; grad. Blair Acad., 1932; A.B., Princeton, 1936; M.B.A., Harvard, 1938; m. Marian E. O'Brien, Apr. 10, 1945; children—James P., Robert N., Richard G. With Metropolitan Life Ins. Co., N.Y.C., 1938—, v.p., 1956-62, financial v.p., 1962-65, chmn. finance com., 1965—, vice chmn., 1969—; dir. St. Regis Paper Co., First Nat. City Bank, Am. Broadcasting Cos., Inc., Bethlehem Steel Corp. Trustee Blair Acad., Blairstown, N.J. Served to capt. AUS, 1942-46. Mem. Phi Beta Kappa. Home: 485 Ridgewood Av Glen Ridge NJ 07028 Office: 1 Madison Av New York City NY 10010

JENKINS, HARRY EARLE, coll. pres.; b. Pittsburg, Kan., Aug. 23, 1899; s. Charles Benton and Minnie (Wade) J.; B.S., Kan. State Coll., 1924; M.S., U. Mo., 1939; Ph.D., U. Tex., 1942; m. Iva Alice Willey, July 30, 1920; 1 son, Harry Earle. Supt. schs. Kan., 1929-34; asst. supt. schs., dean Tyler (Tex.) Jr. Coll., 1934-46; pres. Tyler Jr. Coll., 1946—. Mem. financial aid com. Dept. Health, Edn. and Welfare, HEW, 1957-61; adv. com. VA, 1959-63. Recipient T.B. Butler Outstanding Citizen award Tyler C. of C., 1960. Mem. So. Assn. Colls. and Schs. (past pres.), Tex. Assn. Colls. and Univs. (past pres.), Tex. Assn. Jr. Colls. (past pres.), Am. Assn. Jr. Colls. (past bd. dirs.). Methodist (chmn. bd stewards 1964-65). Mason (33, Shriner, K.T.), Kiwanian. Home: 1611 S Wall St Tyler TX 75701

JENKINS, HARRY MACK, plastics co. exec.; b. Oshkosh, Wis., July 15, 1912; s. Harry C. and Clara (Mack) J.; B.E., Wis. State Coll., Oshkosh, 1935; m. Jeanette M. Sebald, Nov. 21, 1942; children—Harry Mack, Susan Mary, Sarah Ann. Tchr. sr. high sch., Oshkosh, 1936-40; with Gen. Am. Transp. Co., Chgo., 1945-68, gen. mgr. plastics div., 1954-65, corp. v.p., 1965-68; v.p. Molded Plastic Products div. U.S.S. Chems. div. U.S. Steel Corp., 1968—. Served to lt. comdr. USNR, World War II. Decorated individual Commendation ribbon. Mem. Soc. Plastics Industry (pres. 1965—). Home: 622 S Bristol Lane Arlington Heights IL 60005 Office: 120 S Riverside Plaza Chicago IL 60680

JENKINS, HOWARD, Jr., govt. ofcl.; b. Denver, June 16, 1915; s. Howard and Nellie Louise (Poague) J.; A.B., U. Denver, 1936, LL.B., 1941; grad. law student, N.Y. U., 1955-56; m. Alice Elaine Brown, June 24, 1940; children—Judith Elaine, Howard III, Lawrence Coleman. Admitted to Colo. bar, 1941, D.C. bar, 1948; enforcement officer OPA, Denver, 1942-43; acting regional atty. WLB, Denver, 1943-45; chief regional enforcement officer Nat. Wage Stblzn. Bd., Denver, 1945-46, cons. to gen. counsel, Washington, 1946- 47; prof. law Howard U., 1946-56; atty. Office Solicitor Labor, Dept. Labor, 1956-57, spl. asst. to solicitor labor, 1957-59, dir. Office Regulations, Bur. Labor-Mgmt. Reports, 1959-62, asst. commr. bur., 1962-63; mem. NLRB, 1963—. Home: 1333 Tuckerman St NW Washington DC 20011 Office: 1717 Pennsylvania Av Washington DC 20006

JENKINS, IREDELL, educator; b. Blue Ridge Summit, Md., Aug. 12, 1909; s. James Iredell and Mary (Dobie) J.; B.A., U. Va., 1933, M.A., 1934, Ph.D., 1937; student U. Paris (France), 1935-36; m. Isabel Lawson Cook, Dec. 27, 1934; children—Anne (Mrs. William F. Bridgers) Armistead Dobie. From instr. to asso. prof. philosophy Tulane U., 1937-46; asst. philosophy Yale, 1946-49; prof. philosophy, chmn. dept. U. Ala., 1949—; vis. prof. Northwestern U., 1964-65. Research grantee Rockefeller Found., 1957-58, Am. Council Learned Socs., 1952-53, U. Chgo., 1959-60. Mem. Am. Philos. Assn., Metaphys. Soc. Am., Internat. Assn. Philosophy Law and Social Philosophy, (pres. Am. sect.), Am. Soc. Aesthetics, also mem. Phi Beta Kappa. Author: Art and The Human Enterprise, 1958; also numerous articles. Mem. editorial bd. Natural Law Forum, So. Jour. Philosophy, Law and Soc. Rev. Home: 90 Brookhaven Tuscaloosa, AL 35401. Office: Box 6287 University AL 35486

JENKINS, JAMES ALLISTER, educator; b. Toronto, Ont., Can., Sept. 23, 1923; s. James Thomas and Maude (Zuern) J.; B.A., U. Toronto, 1944, M.A., 1945, postgrad., 1946; Ph.D., Harvard, 1948. Came to U.S., 1950, naturalized, 1956. Postdoctoral fellow Harvard U., 1948-49, Inst. for Advanced Study, 1949-50; asst. prof. math. Johns Hopkins U., 1950-54; asso. prof. U. Notre Dame, 1954-56, prof., 1956-59; prof. Washington U., St. Louis, 1959—. Mem. Am., French, German math. socs. Author: Univalent Functions and Conformal Mapping, 1965. Contbr. profl. jours. Home: 526 Purdue Av St Louis MO 63130

JENKINS, JAMES HOPKINS HARRISON, banker, assn. ofcl.; b. Mt. Vernon, N.Y., Jan. 21, 1904; s. Thomas Angus and Sarah Harrison (Bennett) J.; B.S. in Econs., Dartmouth, 1926; student Am. Inst. Banking, 1931; m. Jean Walbridge Montignani, Feb. 19, 1931; children—Deborah Ann (Mrs. W. S. Hoyt II), Lynn Walbridge (Mrs. Eric Brown); m. 2d, Eleanor Davidson Worley, Dec. 8, 1961. With Harris, Forbes & Co., 1927-31, F. S. Moseley & Co., 1932-39, Hanover Bank & Trust Co., N.Y.C., 1944; with Bankers Trust Co., N.Y.C., 1945-69, v.p., 1948-69; dir., mem. exec. com. Rochdale Ins. Co.; dir., treas. Saunders Asso. Inc.; dir. Worley Pub. Co. Treas., bd. dirs. Am. Soc. Prevention Cruelty to Animals, 1957-64, pres., 1964-70; hon. v.p. Am. Humane Soc., 1964-71; bd. dirs. N.Y. State Humane Assn. Mem. Accountants Club of Am., Phi Kappa Psi. Clubs: Union League, Dartmouth (N.Y.C.); Fairfield (Conn.) Country. Home: Jericho Hill Mountain Rd West Redding CT 06896 also 30 Sutton Pl New York City NY 10022

JENKINS, JOHN ANDREW, lawyer orgn. ofcl.; b. Geneva, Ala., Mar. 6, 1909; s. John Andrew and Daisy (Carr) J.; ed. Birmingham So. Coll., Washington and Lee U.; m. Louise Shinpock, June 4, 1938; children—James Rogers, Bonham L., Jennie K. Admitted to Ala. bar, 1932; practiced in Birmingham, 1932-70; city atty. Vestavia Hills, Ala., 1932-70; judge, Trussville, Ala., 1950. Instr., Birmingham Law Sch., 1955-61; arbitrator Fed. Mediation and Conciliation Commn., 1955-70. Dir. sec. South Motel Properties Co., Inc., Am. Educators Ins. Co. Past pres. Ala. Anti-Tb Assn.; pres. Clean Air Com.; vice chmn. Ala. Anti Pollution Commn. Served to capt. F.A., AUS, World War II. Mem. Am., Ala., Birmingham bar assns., V.F.W. (nat. comdr. 1964-65), Am. Legion, Marion Mil. Inst. Alumni Assn. (past pres.). Home: 2201 Great Rock Rd Vestavia Hills Birmingham AL 35216 Office: Frank Nelson Bldg Birmingham AL 35203 Died Aug. 18, 1970

JENKINS, JOSEPH ALTON, lawyer; b. Salt Lake City, Jan. 30, 1919; s. Joseph and Bessie (Iverson) J.; B.A. in Econs., U. Utah, 1939; J.D., Georgetown U., 1944; m. Betty Everett, Jan. 3, 1940 (div. Mar. 1948); 1 dau., Josephine M.; m. 2d, Antoinette D'Hooge, Sept. 28, 1948. Export, import broker on articles moving from U.S. to Belgium; admitted to N.Y. bar, 1947, Tex., bar 1952, also D.C. bar, 1957, New atty. NLRB, Ft. Worth, 1948-51; chief enforcement and litigation br., region 10, Nat. Wage Stblzn. Bd., 1951- 53; partner Rawlings, Savers. Scurlock & Edison, Ft. Worth, 1953-57; mem. NLRB, Washington, 1957-61, director regional office, Albuquerque, 1961-63; pvt. practice law as firm Joseph Alton Jenkins Law Offices, Inc., Dallas, 1964—. Mem. panel arbitrators Fed. Mediation and Counciliation Service and Am. Arbitration Assn. Served from ensign to lt. comdr., USNR, 1942-46. Cited by City of Antwerp, Belgium. Mem. Internat. Platform Assn., Am., Fed., Tex., Dallas, N.M. bar assns., Bar Assn. D.C., Am. Judicature Soc., Reserve Officers of Naval Reserve, Fort Worth-Tarrant County Res. Officers Assn. (past pres.), Nat. Lawyer's Club, S.W. Legal Found., Indsl. Relations Research Assn., Phi Beta Kappa, Phi Kappa Phi, Tau Kappa Alpha, Delta Theta Phi. Club: Cosmos. Author: Treatise on Labor Law (4 vols.), 1968; also articles profl. publs. Home: 413 Little John Sherwood Forest Irving TX 75060 Office: Praetorian Bldg Dallas TX 75201

JENKINS, LEO WARREN, univ. pres.; b. Succasunna, N.J., May 28, 1913; s. Warren Maylon and Cecila (McPeek) J.; B.S., Rutgers U., 1935; M.A., Columbia, 1937; postgrad. Duke, summer 1937; Ed.D., N.Y. U., 1941; m. Lillian Olga Jacobsen, Oct. 11, 1942; children—James, Jeffrey, Patricia, Sallie, Jack, Suzanne. Tchr. English and social studies Pleasantville (N.J.) High Sch., 1935-37;

tchr. history, dean boys Somerville (N.J.) High Sch., 1937-41; supr. practice tchrs., faculty mem. Montclair (N.J.) State Tchrs. Coll., 1945-46; asst. higher edn. N.J. State Dept. Edn., Trenton, 1946-47; dean instrn., dir. summer sch. E. Carolina Coll., Greenville, N.C., 1947-55, v.p., 1955-60, pres., 1960—. Dir. Wachovia Bank & Trust Co., Carolina Tel. & Tel. Member AEC; mem. Governor's Com. for Pub. Schs.; mem. N.C. State Adv. Com. Ednl. Adminstrn.; cons. N.C. Edn. Commn.; advisor to dir., div. spl. edn. N.C. Dept. Edn. Resource-Use Edn. Commn.; ednl. chmn. N.C. Congress Parents and Tchrs.; mem. N.C. Sch. Survey Panel; chmn. Pitt Co. Polio Campaign, 1950; mem. Nat. Commn. on Accrediting. Bd. dirs. N.C. League for Crippled Children. Served as capt. USMCR, Guadalcanal, Guam, Iwo Jima, 1942-46. Decorated Bronze Star medal (2), Presidential Unit citation. Mem. N.E.A. (dept. higher edn.), Am. Assn. Sch. Adminstrs., N.C. Edn. Assn., Am. Legion. Methodist (steward). Kiwanian (dir.). Home: 605 E 5th St Greenville NC 27834

JENKINS, MARTIN DAVID, govt. ofcl.; b. Terre Haute, Ind., Sept. 11, 1904; s. David and Josephine (Miller) J.; B.S., Howard U., 1925; A.B., Indiana State Coll., 1930; M.S., Northwestern U., 1933, Ph.D., 1935; m. P. Elizabeth Lacy, Sept. 6, 1927. Inst. Va. State Coll. 1930-32; prof. edn. and registrar Agrl. and Tech. Coll. of N.C., Greensboro, N.C., 1935-37; dean instrn. Cheyney State Teachers Coll., Pa., 1937-38; prof. edn. Howard U., 1938-48; sr. specialist higher edn. U.S. Office Edn., 1940-42; pres. Morgan State Coll., Baltimore, 1948-70; now dir. Office Urban Affairs Am. Council on Edn., Washington; cons. on coll. orgn. and adminstrn. Staff mem. U.S. Office of Edn. Nat. Survey Higher Edn. of Negros, 1940-42, Survey of Delaware Pub. Schs., 1946, Survey of Higher Edn. in Md., 1946. Trustee Nat. Urban League, Inst. for Services to Edn. Dept. Housing and Urban Devel.; adv. bd. Urban Studies Fellowship. Awarded Selective Service Medal. Diplomate Am. Bd. Examiners in Profl. Psychology (counseling and guidance). Mem. N.E.A., Kappa Alpha Psi. Baptist. Author: National Survey Higher Education of Negroes (co-author Vols. II and III); co- author; Black and White of Rejections for Military Service, 1944; The Morgan State College Program—An Adventure in Higher Education, 1964; numerous articles in ednl. and psychol. jours. on superior Negro children and adults, higher edn. of Negroes, and on urban affairs. Address: Office Urban Affairs Am Council on Edn 1 Dupont Circle Washington DC 20036

JENKINS, PAUL, painter; b. Kansas City, Mo., July 12, 1923; s. William Burris and Nadyne (Fellers) J.; student Art Students League, N.Y.C., 1948-52; m. Alice Baber, June 1964; 1 dau. by previous marriage, Hilarie Paula. Exhbns. include Martha Jackson Gallery, N.Y.C., Daniel Gervis Gallery, Paul Facchetti Gallery, Paris, France, Arthur Tooth Gallery, London, Eng., Tokyo (Japan) Gallery; rep. permanent collections Mus. Modern Art, Whitney Mus., Guggenheim Mus., Corcoran Gallery, Tate Gallery, London, Musee D'Art Moderne, Paris, Stedelijk Mus., Amsterdam, Netherlands, Mus. Western Art, Tokyo. Served with USNR, 1943-45. Recipient Silver medal Corcoran Gallery Art, 1967. Author: (play) Strike the Puma, 1966; also articles. Producer: (film) The Ivory Knife (award Venice Biennale 1966), 1965. Address: 31 E 72d St New York City NY 10021

JENKINS, RAY HOWARD, lawyer; b. Unaka, N.C., Mar. 18, 1897; s. Columbus Sheridan and Amanda (Nicholson) J.; LL.B., U. Tenn., 1920; m. Evalyn Lavinia Nash, Nov. 20, 1926 (deceased); 1 dau., Eva Lois (Mrs. Alexander Marion Cuningham, Jr.); m. Eva Crouch Tedder, Dec. 15, 1963. Admitted to Tenn. bar, 1919; practice in Knoxville, 1920-; spl. counsel Senate Permanent Sub- Com. on Investigations in Army-McCarthy Hearings, 1954. Rep. presidl. campaign mgr., 1940. Mem. Tenn. Bar Assn., Tenn. Soc. S.R., Am. Legion, Order of Coif, Am. Coll. of Trial Lawyers, Phi Kappa Phi, Phi Delta Phi, Tau Kappa Alpha. Episcopalian. Clubs: Cherokee Country, City (Knoxville). Home: 3926 Kenilworth Dr SW Knoxville TN 37919 Office: Bank of Knoxville Bldg Knoxville TN 37902

JENKINS, RAYMOND TAYLOR, ret. air force med. officer; b. Kinston, N.C., July 5, 1908; s. John Franklin and Pennie (Jenkins) J.; student U. N.C., 1928-31; M.D., Duke, 1935; grad. U.S. Army Med. Field Service Sch., 1939, Sch. Aviation Medicine, 1940, Command and Staff Sch., 1942, Air War Coll., 1953; m. Blanche Evelyn Brickle, June 10, 1939; children—Pennie M. (Mrs. George B. Harrison), Betty B. Intern Duke Hosp., 1935-36; resident N.C. Tb Sanitorium, 1936-38; commd. 1st lt., M.C. U.S. Army, 1939, advanced through grades to maj. gen. USAF, 1964; comdr. USAAF Begional Hosp., 1941-43; dep. Surgeon Hdqrs. 5th Air Force, 1944-45; dir. plans and hosp. office Surgeon Gen., Hdqrs. USAF, 1958-64; surgeon gen. USAF Europe, 1965-69. Pres. N. Atlantic council Girl Scouts, Europe, 1965-67. Decorated D.S.M., Legion of Merit with 2 oak leaf clusters, Commendation medal, numerous unit and area ribbons. Diplomate Nat. Bd. Med. Examiners, Am. Bd. Preventive Medicine (aviation medicine). Fellow Am. Coll. Preventive Medicine; mem. A.M.A., Aerospace Med. Assn., Am. Pub. Health Assn., Assn Mill. Surgeons, Soc. USAF Flight Surgeons, Sojourners. Presbyn. Mason (32, Shriner, Jester). Home: Lehigh Acres FL 33936 Office: 710 East Lake Dr Lehigh Acres FL 33936

JENKINS, READ, retailer; b. Detroit, Apr. 9, 1908; s. Isaac Gray and Sarah Maude (Read) J.; m. Winona E. Pratt, Aug. 16, 1932 (dec. Aug. 1967); m. 2d, Dorothy M. Hubert, July 27, 1968; children—Robert Read, Nancy Gray, Barbara Francis. With J.L. Hudson Co., 1930—, v.p., dir., 1951-56, exec. v.p., dir., 1956-61, sr. v.p., dir., 1961—; v.p., dir. Shopping Centers, Inc., Vernier Properties, Inc., Miller Fur Co. Mem. exec. bd. Region 7, past pres. Detroit council Boy Scouts Am.; past pres. Presbyn. Village Home for Aged; past pres., trustee Bloomfield Country Day Sch.; past mem. adv. bd. Greater Detroit Salvation Army. Mem. Am. Retail Fedn. (past chmn. bd. trustees), Nat. Retail Mchts. Assn., Detroit Bd. Commerce (nat. affairs council), Am. Mgmt. Assn., Detroit Hist. Soc. (past trustee). Presbyn. Clubs: Detroit Athletic, Rotary (dir., pres.) (Detroit); Bloomfield Hills Country, Skyline Country (Bloomfield Hills). Home: 1003 Stratford Lane Bloomfield Hills MI 48013 Office: 1206 Woodward Av Detroit MI 48226

JENKINS, ROBERT MERLE, govt. ofcl.; b. Kansas City, Mo., June 18, 1923; s. Raymond and Ethelyn F. (Fidler) J.; B.S., U. Okla., 1948, M.S., 1949; m. Caddie L. Beecher, May 26, 1956; children—Patricia, Carol, Suzanne, Gayle. With Okla. Game and Fish Dept., mem. staff U. Okla., dir. Okla. Fishery Research Lab., 1949-57; asst. exec. v.p. Sporting Fishing Inst., Washington, 1958-63; dir. nat. reservoir research program U.S. Bur. Sport Fisheries and Wildlife, 1963—. Fishery adviser UNFAO. Bd. dirs. Sport Fishery Research Found. Served with USNR, 1942-46, 50-52. Fellow Okla. Acad. Sci.; mem. Am. Fisheries Soc. (pres. 1970-71), Am. Soc. Limnology and Oceanology, Internat. Soc. Limnology, Ark. Acad. Sci., Am. Water Resources Assn., Sigma Xi. Mem. Disciples of Christ Ch. Editor: Reservoir Fishery Resources Symposium, 1968; co-editor SFI Bull., 1959-62. Contbr. papers to sci. lit. Home: 1223 Viewpoint St Fayetteville AR 72701 Office: 113 South East St Fayetteville AR 72701

JENKINS, ROBERT O., dairy co. exec.; b. Lafayette, Tenn., June 7, 1902; s. W.F. and Hattie Jenkins; B.S.C. in Accounting Bowling Green U.; m. Pauline Conner, June 11, 1922; children—William H., Jemima (Mrs. Glen Mihorn), Roberta (Mrs. C. H. Slagle), R. David. With Pet, Inc., 1928—, gen. mgr. Pet Dairy, Johnson City, Tenn., 1956-61, pres. dairy div., Johnson City, 1961-69, past v.p. parent co., now adv. dir.; dir. First Peoples Bank, Johnson City. Bd. dirs. N.C. Dairy Found. Mem. Internat. Assn. Ice Cream Mfrs. (dir.), Nat. Dairy Council (dir.), Tenn. Dairy Products Assn. (dir.). Baptist. Clubs: Johnson City, Country; Cyprus Country (Ft. Myers Fla.). Home: 301 Marshall Ct Johnson City TN 37601 Office: PO Box 1100 Johnson City TN 37601

JENKINS, ROY HARRIS, Brit. polit. worker; b. Abersychan, Wales, Nov. 11, 1920; s. Arthur and Hattie (Harris) J.; B.A. with 1st class honours, Balliol Coll., Oxford (Eng.) U., 1941; m. Jennifer Morris, Jan. 20, 1945; children—Charles, Cynthia, Edward. Mem. Parliament for Central Southwark Constituency, 1948-50, Stectford Div. of Birmingham, 1950—, minister aviation, 1964-65, home sec., 1965-67; chancellor of the exchequer, 1967-70; dep. leader Brit. Labour Party, 1970—. Club: Brooks's (London). Author: Mr. Attlee; An Interim Biography, 1948; Pursuit of Progress, 1953; Mr. Balfour's Poodle, 1954; Sir Charles Dilke: A Victorian Tragedy, 1958; The Labour Case, 1959; Asquith, 1964; Essays and Speeches, 1967. Editor: Purpose and Policy, A Vol. of the Prime Minister's Speeches, 1947. Home: 33 Ladbroke Sq London W 11 England Office: House Commons London SW 1 England

JENKINS, SIDNEY BERNARD, physician; b. York, S.C., Dec. 29, 1926; s. Amos Rickett and Jessie (Lowry) J.; A.B., Temple U., 1947; M.D., Howard U., 1951; m. Barbara Jeanne Stewart, Sept. 22, 1951; children—Kevin, Judith, Sharolyn, Marc, Kayla. Resident psychiatry VA Hosp., Lyons, N.J., 1952-53, Wayne County Gen. Hosp., Eloise, Mich., 1953-55; mem. staff Wayne County Gen. Hosp., 1955—, dir. psychiat. div., 1963—; instr. psychiatry Wayne State U. Med. Sch., 1958—. Served to capt., M.C., AUS, 1956-58. Diplomate Am. Bd. Neurology and Psychiatry. Fellow Am. Psychiat. Assn.; mem. Am., Nat. med. assns., Mich. Assn. Neuropsychiatry Hosp. and Clinic Physicians (pres.), N.A.A.C.P. (life), Alpha Phi Alpha. Methodist. Contbr. profl. jours. Mailing address: Office: 2617 W Grand Blvd Detroit MI 48208

JENKINS, THOMAS F., banker; b. Vanndale, Ark., Feb. 22, 1923; s. William Nathaniel and Bird (Hare) J.; student U. Ark., 1946-48, So. Law U., 1948-49, U. Wis., 1966-68; grad. Nat. Assn. Bank, Auditors and Comptrollers Sch., 1969; m. Dorothy Elizabeth Goodrum, July 4, 1948; children—Thomas F., Peggy Jean, John Barry, Tiffany Elizabeth. With Union Planters Nat. Bank, Memphis, Tenn., 1948—, asst. auditor, 1964-68, auditor, 1968—. Troop chmn. Chickasaw council Boy Scouts Am., 1967. Served with USAAF, World War II. Decorated Bronze Star medal, Air medal with three oak leaf clusters; Purple Heart medal. Mem. Nat. Accountants Assn., Bank Adminstrn. Inst. (pres. Mid South chpt. 1967), Pi Kappa Alpha. Presbyn. (chmn. bd. deacons 1960, pres. Men's fellowship 1961, chmn. finance com. 1966). Home: 3068 Emerald Av Memphis TN 38118 Office: 67 Madison Av Memphis TN 38101

JENKINS, THOMAS LLEWELLYN, educator, physicist; b. Cambridge, Mass., July 16, 1927; s. Francis A. and Henrietta (Smith) J.; B.A., Pomona Coll., 1950; Ph.D., Cornell U., 1956; m. Glen Pierce, July 8, 1951; children—Gale F., Phillip P., Matthew A., Sarah B. Physicist, Lawrence Radiation Lab., Livermore, Cal., 1955-60; faculty Case Western Res. U., Cleve., 1960—, prof. physics, 1968—. Mem. Am. Phys. Soc. A.A.A.S., Phi Beta Kappa, Sigma Xi. Home: 869 Belwood Dr Highland Heights OH 44143 Office: Physics Dept Case Western Res Univ Cleveland OH 44106

JENKINS, THOMAS MILLER, coll. pres.; b. Hot Springs, Va. Apr. 23, 1925; s. Beaufort Z. and Pauline (Beale) J.; B.A. summa cum laude, W. Va. State Coll., 1946; LL.B. cum laude Boston U., 1950; m. Evelyn Mildred Kyes, Sept. 15, 1950; 1 son, Thomas Miller III. Admitted to Mass. bar, 1950. Tex. bar, 1951; dep. research dir. Mass. Re-Codification Commn., Boston, 1949-51; law librarian, asst. prof. law Tex. So. U., 1951-53; dean, prof. law Fla. A. and M. U., 1953-65; pres. Albany (Ga.) State Coll., 1965—. Faculty adviser Fla. Bar com. municipal law, traffic cts. and safety, memls., also Communist tactics strategy and objectives, 1958-65; mem. com. legal edn. and admissions to bar Fla. Supreme Ct., 1958-65; mem. Ga. Adult Edn. Council 1967—, Ga. Assn. Coll., 1966—; exec. com. Nat. Bar Assn., 1959—, world peace through law com., 1961—; spl. cons. wage and hour pub. contracts div. Dept. Labor, 1963—. Sec. trustee Fla. A. and M. Hosp., 1963-65; bd. dirs. legal edn. Southwest Bar Assn., 1958-65, United Fund Dougherty County, 1968—, Ga. Planning Commn., 1968—; v.p., bd. dirs. Albany Urban League, 1968—; v.p. Chehaw council Boy Scouts Am., 1968—. Recipient citations Kappa Alpha Psi, Tallahassee Bus. League, Chehaw council Boy Scouts Am., Southwest Bar Assn., English High Sch., Boston, W.Va. State Coll., Boston U.; recipient plaque Nat. Assn. Colored Women's Clubs, 1966, Albany Ministers Wives, 1967. Contbr. profl. jours. Home: 129 Peyton Pl S W Atlanta GA 30311.

JENKINS, THOMAS SCHUYLER, coll. pres.; b. Oakes, N.D., Aug. 16, 1908; s. Clarence P. and Bessie (Craven) J.; B.S., State Normal and Indsl. Coll., Ellendale, N.D., 1931; M.S., State U. Ia., 1934; Ed.D., U. Ore., 1952; student Stout Inst., George Peabody Coll., U. Ia.; m. Marjorie Havreberg, Sept. 11, 1950. High sch. tchr., Redfield, S.D., 1930-33; instr. State Tchrs. Coll., Minot, N.D., 1934-37, registrar, 1937-42, 45-48, dean pub. relations, 1949-50, dir. admissions and field services, 1951-54; pres. State Normal and Indsl. Coll., Ellendale, 1954-59, Mayville (N.D.) State Coll., 1959—; instr. Naval Vocational Sch., Chgo., 1942-43. Mem. Nat., N.D. edn. assn., Greater N.D. Assn., Phi Delta Kappa, Kappa Delta Pi, Phi Sigma Pi. Presbyn. Mason, Elk. Club: Mayville Civic. Home: 329 3d St NE Mayville ND 58257

JENKINS, WARREN GARD, educator; . Okeana, O., Dec. 12, 1904; s. John Elimus and Anna Belle (Phipps) J.; A.B., Miami U., Oxford, O., 1929; M.A., U. Wis., 1932, Ph. D., 1941; m. Marion Gertrude Borne, May 30, 1931; children—Richard Bourne, Barbara Ann. Mem. faculty Wis. State Univ., Stevens Point, 1935—, dean letters and sci., 1950-70. Bd. curators Wis. Hist. Soc., 1955-57. Mem. Am., Miss. Valley hist. assns., Nat., Wis. edn. assns., Am. Radio Relay League. Episcopalian. Home: 811 Green Av Stevens Point WI 54481

JENKINS, WILLIAM ATWELL, univ. dean; b. Soranton, Pa., Nov. 18, 1922; s. William A. and Thelma (Atwell) J.; B.S. in Edn., N.Y.U., 1948; M.S., U. Ill., 1949, Ph.D., 1954; m. Gloria Hyam, Mar. 12, 1944; children—William Arthur II, Darcy Ann. Mem. faculty U. Milw.-Wis., 1953-70, asso. dean, dir. tchr. edn. and grad. studies, 1963-70; vis. prof. edn. U. Hawaii, summer 1969; dean Sch. Edn., Portland State U., 1970—; cons. in field. Served to 1st lt., C.E., AUS, 1943-46. Mem. Nat. Council Tchrs. English (pres. 1968-69), Nat. Conf. Research and English, Edn. Writers Assn., Wis., Ore. council tchrs. English, Phi Kappa Phi, Phi Delta Kappa, Kappa Delta Phi. Co-author numerous texts, articles. Home: 14420 SW 114th Av Tigard OR 97223 Office: PO Box 751 Portland OR 97207

JENKINS, WILLIAM MARSHALL, Jr., coll. dean; b. Guthrie, Ky., Sept. 12, 1918; s. William Marshall and Eddie (Rust) J., B.A., The Citadel, 1941; M.A., U. Ky., 1957, Ph.D., 1960; m. Jane Lee McLean, Sept. 3, 1946 (dec.); 1 dau., Jeannette; m. 2d, Elizabeth Hancock, Dec. 26, 1970. Engaged in retail business, Guthrie, 1946-55; asst. coordinator U. Ky.-Indonesian Project, 1956-59; asst., prof. history and polit. sci. Western Ky. State U., 1959-61, head dept. bus. and govt., 1961-64, dean Bowling Green Coll. Commerce of univ., 1964—. Adviser to mayor of Bowling Green, 1966. Served with AUS, 1941-46. Mem. Am., So. polit. sci assns., Ky. Planning Assn., Ky. Edn. Assn., Frat. Order Police (hon. life), Phi Alpha Theta, Pi Sigma Alpha, Delta Sigma Pi, Pi Sigma Epsilon. Mem. Disciples of Christ Ch. Collaborator, author: (with P. P. Karan) Nepal, A Physical and Cultural Geography, 1960, The Himalayan Kingdoms, 1963; also articles. Home: 1723 Karen Circle Bowling Green KY 42101

JENKINS, WILLIAM MAXWELL, banker; b. Sultan, Wash., Apr. 19, 1919; s. Warren Maxwell and Louise (Black) J.; A.B., U. Wash., 1941; M.B.A., Harvard, 1943; m. Elisabeth Cordua Taber, Oct. 11, 1946; children—Elixabeth Cordua, Ann Hathaway, William Morris, Karen Louise, Peter Taber, David Maxwell, Barbara Fessenden. Asst. cashier, asst. v.p., asst. mgr. Met. br. Seattle-First Nat. Bank, 1945-53, exec. v.p., mgr. Everett div., 1961-62, chmn. bd., chief exec. officer, 1962—, also dir.; v.p. to exec. v.p. First Nat. Bank of Everett, 1953-57, pres., 1957-61; chmn. Everett Trust & Savs. Bank, 1956-61; dir. Gen. Am. Corp., Everett Improvement Co., Rainier Nat. Park Co. (Tacoma), Western Gear Corp. (Lynwood, Cal.), Scott Paper Co. Trustee Com. Econ. Devel.; pres. Everett YMCA, 1960, 61; dir. Pacific Coast Banking Sch., 1954, 55; trustee Found. for Comml. Banks; regent Seattle U.; mem. men's adv. bd. Children's Orthopedic Hosp., Seattle. Served to lt. (j.g.) USNR, 1943-45. Mem. Assn. Reserve City Bankers (dir. 1966-68), Washington Bankers Assn. Republican. Presbyn. Clubs: Cascade, Everett Yacht (Everett, Wash.); Seattle Tennis, Harbor, Rainier, University, Seattle Golf (Seattle). Home: 3008 Webster Point Rd NE Seattle WA 98105 Office: Seattle-First Nat Bank Box 3586 Seattle WA 98124

JENKS, BRUCE NORTON, cosmetics and toiletries co. exec.; b. Wheaton, Ill., Nov. 1, 1928; s. Herman H. and Lois (Lyman) J.; B.A., Carleton Coll., 1950; M.B.A., Northwestern U., 1958; m. Susan Wiegman, Mar. 28, 1951; children—Andrew, Sarah, Peter, Paul. Statis. clk. Peoples Gas Co., 1950-55; systems analyst Continental Assurance Co., 1955-57; systems cons. Arthur Andersen & Co., 1957-60 (all Chgo.); asst. controller Cook Electric Co., Morton Grove, Ill., 1960-63; asst. to controller Chem. Coatings Div., Mobil Chem. Co., Planfield, N.J., 1963-66; controller Shulton, Inc., Clifton, N.J., 1966—; guest lectr. profl. accounting program Rutgers U. Grad. Sch. Bus., Newark, 1969-70. Served with AUS, 1950-52. Mem. Financial Execs. Inst. Episcopalian (vestryman). Club: Monmouth Boat (Red Bank, N.J.). Home: 56 W River Rd Rumson NJ 07760 Office: Shulton Inc Route 46 Clifton NJ 07015

JENKS, CLARENCE WILFRED, internat. labour ofcl.; b. Bootle, Liverpool, Eng., Mar. 7, 1909; s. Richard and Alice Sophia (Craig) J.; scholar Gonville and Caius Coll., Cambridge U., 1927-31, B.A., 1931, M.A., 1936, LL.D., 1953; LL.D., Edinburgh, 1967, Delhi U., 1970; m. Jane Louise Broverman, Oct. 19, 1949; children—Craig B., Bruce F. E. Mem. legal sect. Internat. Labour Office, Geneva, Switzerland, 1931-40, legal adviser, 1940-48, asst. dir.-gen., 1948-64, deputy dir. gen., 1964-67, prin. dep. dir.-gen., 1967-70, dir. gen., 1970—; prof. The Hague Acad. Internat. Law, 1939, 50, 55, 66; Storrs lectr. jurisprudence Yale Law Sch., 1965; adviser Venezuelan Govt. on labour legislation, 1938. Mem. Internat. Labour Office dels. at U.N. Conf. on Internat. Organization, San Francisco, 1945, U.N. Monetary and Financial Conf., Bretton Woods, 1944, The Inter-Am. War and Peace Conf., Chapultepec, Mexico City, 1945, Intergovtl. Copyright Conf., 1952, Internat. Conf. on Peaceful Uses of Atomic Energy, 1955, 58, Conf. on Statute of Internat. Atomic Energy Agy., 1956, U.N. Conf. on Law of the Sea, 1958, 60, Gen. Assembly and Econ. and Social Council of U.N., other internat. confs. and coms.; adviser to Constitutional Com. of U.N. Interim Commn. on Food and Agr., 1944, to Am. Law Inst. on essential human rights project, 1942-44; mem. Inst. of Internat. Law. Called to Bar by Gray's Inn, in 1936. Awarded Cecil Peace prize, 1928; Ann. award Am. Soc. Internat. Law, 1959; World Legal Scholarship award, World Peace Through Law Center, 1967. Pres. Cambridge Union Soc., 1930. Mem. Internat. Acad. of Astronautics (corr.), Internat. Acad. Comparative Law. Clubs: Cosmos (Washington); Athenaeum, Reform (London). Author: The Headquarters of International Institutions, 1945; The International Protection of Trade Union Freedom, 1957; The Common Law of Mankind, 1958; Human Rights and International Labour Standards, 1960; International Immunities, 1961; The Proper Law of International Organizations, 1962; Law, Freedom and Welfare, 1963; The Prospects of International Adjudication, 1964; Space Law 1965; Law in the World Community, 1967; The World Beyond the Charter, 1969; A New World of Law?, 1969. Editor of: The International Labour Code, 1939, 52; Constitutional Provisions concerning Social and Economic Policy, 1944. Contributor legal journals. Home: 3 Contamines Geneva Switzerland Office: International Labour Office Geneva Switzerland

JENKS, DOWNING BLAND, railroad exec.; b. Portland, Ore., Aug. 16, 1915; s. Charles O. and Della (Downing) J.; B.S., Yale, 1937; m. Louise Sweeney, Nov. 30, 1940; children—Downing Bland, Nancy Randolph. Chainman, Spokane Portland & Seattle Ry., Portland, 1934-35; asst., engr. corps N.Y. div. Pa. R.R., 1937-38; roadmaster, div. engr., trainmaster various divs. G.N. Ry., 1938-47, div. supt., Spokane, Wash., 1947-48; gen. mgr. C.&E.I. R.R., Chgo., 1948-49, v.p., gen. mgr., 1949-50, asst. v.p. operations Rock Island Lines, Chgo., 1950-51, v.p. operations, 1951-53, exec. v.p., dir., 1953-56, pres., 1956-61; dir., pres. M.P.R.R., St. Louis, 1961—; chmn. bd. dirs. Tex. & Pacific R.R., 1968—, C. & E.I. R.R., Mo. Pacific Trunk Lines, 1969—; pres. Miss. River Corp., 1969—; dir. Bankers Life Co., 1st Nat. Bank (St. Louis), Insco Corp., 1st Union, Inc. Mem. adv. com. Transp. Center. Trustee Northwestern U. Served from 1st lt. to lt. col. AUS, 1942-45; ETO. Mem. Assn. Am. R.R.'s (dir.), Tau Beta Pi. Home: 8 Greenbriar St Louis MO 63124 Office: Mo Pacific Bldg St Louis MO 63103 also 9900 Clayton Rd St Louis MO 63124

JENKS, GEORGE FRANCIS, newspaper editor; b. Detroit, Oct. 19, 1908; s. Frank H. and Julia (Pennington) J.; A.B., Colo. Coll., 1929; m. Louise McMahon, July 19, 1937; children—Judith P., George M., Frank M., Ann B. Staff, Wood County News, Bowling Green, O., 1930-32; successively reporter, legislative corr., asst. to publisher Toledo Blade, 1933-38, chief Washington bur., 1958-69, nat. affairs editor, Toledo, 1969—. Mem. Sigma Delta Chi. Clubs: Nat. Press (Washington); Press of Ohio. Home: 3023 Redington Woods Rd Toledo OH 43615

JENKS, GEORGE MERRITT, librarian; b. Purcell, Okla., Aug. 1, 1929; s. Darrell C. and Muriel Helena (Denison) J.; B.A., U. Okla., 1949, M.A., 1951, M.L.S., 1959; postgrad. U. Cal. at Los Angeles, 1954-56; m. Zoya Elaine Hochstein, Mar. 2, 1957; children—Darrell Allan, Mark Denison, Andrew Leslie. Reports officer CIA, Washington, 1956-57; instr. fgn. langs. N.M. State U. at Las Cruces, 1957-58; librarian Queens Borough Pub. Library, Jamaica, N.Y., 1959-60; cataloger, head acquisitions librarian San Fernando Valley State Coll., Northridge, Cal., 1960-63; asst. and acting librarian U. Tasmania, Hobart, 1963-66; chief tech. services, asso. librarian, univ. librarian, Bucknell U., Lewisburg, Pa., 1966—. Lectr. library sci.

Immaculate Heart Coll., Los Angeles, 1961-62; lectr. in librarianship Hobart Tech. Coll., Tasmania, 1965; mem. Australian Adv. Council on Bibliograph. Services, 1965-66. Served with USMC, 1951-53. Decorated Purple Heart. Grantee Library Systems Inst.,, Rennselaer Poly. Inst., 1968. Asso. Library Assn. Australia; (pres. Tasmanian br. 1965); mem. Penn. (pres. West Br. chpt. 1969-71), Am. library assns., Am. Civil Liberties Union Pa. (sec. N. Central chpt. 1969-71), Sigma Delta Pi, Beta Phi Mu. Democrat. Editor Library Opinion, 1964. Home: 202 N 2nd St Lewisburg PA 17837

JENKS, HOMER, (Simeon), editor; b. Waltham, Mass. Nov. 13, 1949; s. Willard Irving and Iva Mae (Shepardson) J.; student Boston U., 1932-35; m. Beryl Louise Clinton, Sept. 21, 1940 (dec. 1966); m. 2d, Moira Catherine O'Connor, Aug. 19, 1968; 1 dau., Jacqueline Moira. City editor Quincy (Mass.) Evening News, 1931-35; staff corr. United Press, Boston, N.Y.C., London, 1935-52; asso. editor Collier's, 1952-56, Newsweek, 1956-57; exec. news editor Boston Traveler, 1957-62, mng. editor, 1962-64; editor Sunday Herald Traveler, 1964—. Mem. Am. Soc. Newspaper Editors. Home: 30 Greenfield Lane Scituate MA 02066 Office: 300 Harrison Av Boston MA 02106

JENKS, LIVINGSTON, lawyer; b. San Francisco, Aug. 3, 1901; s. Livingston and May Evelyn (Harley) J.; A.B., U. Cal. at Berkeley, 1921; A.M., Columbia, 1922, postgrad. Law Sch., 1922-24; m. Kathrine McLane, Feb. 11, 1933; children—Livingston, Mary Harley, Alan. Admitted to N.Y. bar, 1924, Hawaii bar, 1929; asso. firm Cotton & Franklin, N.Y.C., 1924-29; asso. firm Prosser, Anderson & Marx, Honolulu, 1929-32; partner firms Prosser, Anderson, Marx, & Wren, Honolulu, 1933-36, Anderson, Marx, Wrenn Jenks, 1937-40, Anderson Wrenn Jenks, now Jenks, Kidwell, Goodsill & Anderson. Dir. Dole Corp., 1940—. Mem. Am. Bar Assn. Home: 37 Kawananakoa Pl Honolulu HI 96817 Office: Bank of Hawaii Bldg Honolulu HI 96813

JENKS, MAJOR B., coll. adminstr.; b. N. Adams, Mass., May 14, 1910; s. Floyd B. and Lucile (Major) J.; B.S., U. Vt., 1930, A.M., 1932; Ph.D., Cornell U., 1936; m. Ruth Acklin, Aug. 1, 1936; children—Barbara, Carolyn, Carl. Asst. prof. history and polit. sci. Fenn Coll., 1935-37, asso. prof., 1937-42, prof., 1942-65, dean Sch. Arts and Scis., 1944-65; prof. history, dean Coll. Arts and Scis., Cleve. State U., 1965-68, asst. acad. v.p., 1968-69, exec. asst. to the pres., 1969—. Mem. Am. Hist. Assn., Orgn. Am. Historians, Phi Beta Kappa. Presbyn. (elder). Home: 3165 Coleridge Rd Cleveland Heights OH 44118 Office: Cleve State U Cleveland OH 44115

JENKS, MORTON, financier; b. N.Y.C., 1907; s. John Story and Isabella F. G. (Morton) J.; student St. Georges School; D.Sc. (hon.), Pa. Mill. Coll., 1951; m. Margaret D. Mathews, 1945; children—Constance M., John S., Margaret, Elizabeth. With Janney & Co., 1928-31; mgr. Phila. Jenks, Gwynne & Co., 1932-35; partner Bioren & Co., 1935-40; sr. partner Jenks, Kirkland & Co., 1940-57; partner Hallowell, Sulzberger, Jenks & Co., 1957—; dir. Hyper-Humus. Mem. Phila. Stock Exchange. Mem. First Troop Phila. City Cav., 1928-36. Trustee Hahnemann Med. Coll. and Hosp., Phila. Mus. Art; trustee, former pres. Skin and Cancer Hosp. Phila.; pres., trustee Kirkbride Fund; trustee PMC Colls., Harcum Jr. Coll. Served as capt. Med. Adminstrv. Corps., 1942-45. Mem. Numis. and Antiguarian Soc., Welcome Soc. (treas.), Colonial Soc. Pa., Soc. Colonial Wars, S.R., Loyal Legion, Fgn. Wars. Clubs: Philadelphia, Racquet, Penn (Phila.); Brook, River (N.Y.C.); Rumson (N.J.) Country. Home: Seminole and Chestnut Hill Avs Philadelphia PA 19118 Office: Phila Nat Bank Bldg Philadelphia PA 19107

JENKS, THOMAS ELIJAH, lawyer; b. Bronxville, N.Y., Apr. 5, 1910; s. Elijah and Anna (Robeson) J.; A.B., Williams Coll., 1931; LL. B., Columbia, 1934; m. Janet Shares, Sept. 19, 1936; children—Linda Ann (Mrs. Nils Swanson), Susan Shares. Admitted to N.Y. bar, 1934, D.C. bar, 1936; with Office Spl. Adviser Fgn. Trade, 1934-35; sec., asst. gen. counsel Export-Import Bank, 1935- 36; with firm Alvord & Alvord, Washington, 1936-41, partner, 1942-50; partner firm Lee, Toomey & Kent, Washington, 1950—. Treas., dir. Nat. Children's Rehab. Center; v.p., dir. Epilepsy Found.; hon. trustee Miss Hall's Sch., Pittsfield, Mass. Mem. Am., Inter-Am., D.C. bar assns., Internat. Fiscal Assn. (exec. council U.S. br.), Soc. Alumni Williams Coll. (exec. com.), Tax Inst. Am., Phi Beta Kappa. Republican. Clubs: Chevy Chase (Md.); Nat. Lawyers (Washington); Congressional Country (Md.). Contbr. legal jours. Home: 5044 Millwood Lane NW Washington DC 20016. Office: 1200 18th St N W Washington DC 20036

JENKS, WILLIAM ALEXANDER, historian, educator; b. Jacksonville, Fla., Jan. 20, 1918; s. Thomas William and Marjorie (Garvie) J.; B.A., Washington and Lee U., 1939; M.A., Columbia, 1940, Ph.D., 1949; m. Dorothy Jane Irving, Dec. 26, 1949; children—Margaret Elaine, Thomas William II. Faculty, Washington and Lee U., Lexington, Va., 1946—, asso. prof., 1951-56, prof., 1956—, William R. Kenan, Jr. prof. history, 1971—; vis. asst. prof. U. Va., 1950-52; vis. prof. Duke, summer 1963, U. Md., summer 1966, Va. Mil. Inst., spring 1967, Va. Poly. Inst., summer 1968. Served with OSS, AUS, 1942-45. Faculty fellow Fund for Advancement Edn., 1954-55; recipient Fulbright research award, Austria, 1955; Social Sci. Research Council faculty fellow, 1961-62; fellow Am. Council Learned Socs., 1967-68. Mem. Am. Hist. Assn., Phi Beta Kappa, Omicron Delta Kappa, Sigma Nu. Democrat. Presbyn. Author: The Austrian Electoral Reform of 1907, 1950; Vienna and the Young Hitler, 1960; Austria under the Iron Ring, 1879-1893, 1965. Home: 617 Marshall St Lexington VA 24450

JENKS, WILLIAM FURNESS, geologist, educator; b. Phila., June 28, 1909; s. Horace Howard and Eloise Comstock (North) J.; grad. The Hill Sch., 1928; A.B. cum laude, Harvard, 1932, Ph.D., 1936; M.A., U. Wis., 1933; m. Elizabeth Pratt, June 10, 1935; children—Barbara Eloise, Margaret Carolyn, Helen Carnan. Jr. geologist Texas Co., Denver, 1936-38; asst. geologist Cerro de Pasco Corp., Peru, 1938-40, geologist, 1940-45; Dept State vis. prof. U. Arequipa, Peru, 1945-46; asst. prof. geology U. Rochester, 1946-49, asso. prof., 1949-55; prof. geology U. Cin., 1955—, head dept. geology dir. U. Mus., 1955-68; Fulbright lectr. U. Tokyo, 1962-63, cons. mining geologist. Fellow. Geol. Soc. Am., Ohio Acad. Scis., A.A.A.S.; mem. Am. Assn. Petroleum Geologists, Am. Geophys. Union, Soc. Econ. Geologists, Socieded Geologica del Peru, Ohio Acad. Scis., Rochester Assn. UN (dir. 1950-55, v.p. 1952-54), Am. Civil Liberties Union, Sigma Xi. Club: Harvard of Cincinnati. Editor: Handbook of South American Geology, 1956. Home: 4049 Clifton Av Cincinnati OH 45220

JENNER, ALBERT ERNEST, Jr., lawyer; b. Chgo., June 20, 1907; s. Albert E. and Elizabeth (Owens) J.; LL.B., U. Ill., 1930; m. Nadine Newbill, Mar. 19, 1932; 1 dau., Cynthia Lee. Admitted to Ill. bar, 1930; since practiced in Chgo.; sr. partner firm Jenner & Block. Spl. asst. atty gen. Ill., 1956-65; counsel Ill. Budgetary Commn., 1956-57; prof. law Northwestern U., 1952-53;chmn. U.S. Supreme Ct. Adv. Com. on Fed. Rules of Evidence, 1965—. Chmn. Ill. Commn. on Uniform State Laws, 1952-69; pres. nat. conf. on Uniform State Laws, 1969—; mem. adv. com. federal rules of civil procedure U.S. Supreme Court, 1960-70; mem. Nat. Conf. Bar Assn. Presidents of U.S., pres. 1952-53; mem. U.S. Loyalty Review Bd., 1952-53; mem. council U. Ill. Law Forum, 1948-51; sr. counsel Presdl. Commn. to Investigate the Assassination of President Kennedy, 1963-64. Dir. Gen. Dynamics Corp., Walter E. Heller Internat., United of Am. Bank, Law mem. Ill. Bd. Examiners Accountancy, 1948-51; mem. Pres.'s Nat. Commn. on Causes and Prevention of Violence, 1968-69. Recipient Distinguished Service award for outstanding pub. service Chgo. and Ill. Jaycees, 1939. Fellow Am. Coll. Trial Lawyers (bd. regents, pres. 1958-59); mem. Ill. Soc. Trial Lawyers, Am. (mem. ho. of dels. 1948—, chmn. standing com. on fed. judiciary (1965-69) Ill. (pres. 1949-50), Chgo. (sec. 1947-49) bar assns., Am. Judicature Soc. (pres. 1958), Am. Inst. Jud. Adminstrn., Bar Assn. U.S. Ct. Appeals 7th Circuit (bd. govs. 1955-60), Am. Law Inst., Order of Coif, Alpha Chi Rho, Phi Delta Phi. Republican. Clubs: Tavern, Skokie Country, Law, Legal, Chicago, Author and co-author: Illinois Civil Practice Act Annotated; Outline of Illinois Supreme Court and Appellate Court Procedure, 1935; Smith-Hurd Ill. Annotated Statutes, 3d edit. 1955; Volumes five on Pleading and Practice. Mem. permanent editorial bd. Uniform Commercial Code, 1961—. Contbr. law revs. and legal publs. on various phases of practice, pleading procedure and other legal subjects. Home: 119 Tudor Pl Kenilworth IL 60043 Office: 135 S LaSalle St Chicago IL 60603

JENNER, WILLIAM ELLIOTT, educator, mathematician; b. Goderich, Ont., Can., Sept. 9, 1924; s. Harvey Easton and Ella Lasca (Elliott) J.; B.A., Queen's U., 1947; M.A., U. Toronto, 1948; Ph.D., U. Mich., 1952; m. Mildred Helen McLeroy, Dec. 22, 1956; children—Christopher Owen, Stephen Andrew, Thomas Alban. Came to U.S., 1949. Lectr., U. B.C., 1948-49; instr., then asst. prof. Northwestern U., 1951-57; asso. prof. Bucknell U., 1957-62; mem. faculty U. N.C., 1962—, now prof. math. Mem. Am. Math. Soc., Soc. Math. de France, Indian Math. Soc., Canadian Math. Congress, Math. Assn. Am., Am. Assn. U. Profs. Home: 809 Shadylawn Rd Chapel Hill NC 27514

JENNESS, ARTHUR, (Freeman), psychologist; b. Rosario, Argentina, Jan. 6, 1901; s. James Freeman and Beulah (Steele) J.; B.A., Northwestern U., 1923, M.A., 1927; Ph.D., Syracuse U., 1930; m. Margaret Babcock, June 14, 1930; 1 son, David. Asst. employment mgr. R.R. Donnelley & Sons Co., Chgo., 1923; exec. finance campaign Northwestern U., 1924; asst. sec. U.S. Govt. Clubhouse, Cristobal, C.Z., 1925-26; fellow, instr. psychology Syracuse U., 1927-30; instr., counselor to prof., chmn. dept. psychology U. Neb., 1930-46; prof. Williams Coll., 1946-66, prof. emeritus, 1966—, chmn. dept., 1946-62; prof. psychology N.C. Wesleyan Coll., 1966-68, chmn. dept. psychology, 1967-68; vis. prof. psychology Ft. Lewis Coll., 1968-69; vis. Lectr. Harvard, Radcliffe Coll., 1937-39. Served as 1st lt. USAAF, 1943-44. Diplomate Am. Bd. Profl. Psychology, Am. Bd. Examiners Psychol. Hypnosis. Certified psychologist, Mass.; licensed psychologist, N.C. Fellow Am. Psychol. Assn., A.A.A.S.; mem. Psychonomic Soc., Am. Assn. U. Profs., Eastern Psychol. Assn., Sigma Xi, Alpha Delta Phi. Unitarian. Club: Williams (N.Y.C.). Asso. editor Jour. Abnormal and Social Psychology, 1950-55. Contbr. to profl. jours. tech. books, mags. Home: 550 Marion Av Palo Alto CA 94301

JENNESS, ROBERT, educator, biochemist; b. Rochester, N.H., Sept. 21, 1917; s. Myron I. and Ruth (Libby) J.; B.S., U. N.H., 1938; M.S., U. Vt., 1940; Ph.D., U. Minn., 1944; m. Katherine Ward, Aug. 30, 1940; children—Douglas F., Malcolm I., David R. With Vt. Agrl. Expt. Sta., 1938-40; mem. faculty U. Minn., 1940—, prof. biochemistry, 1953—. Fulbright scholar, Netherlands, 1961-62. Fellow A.A.A.S.; mem. Am. Chem. Soc. (Borden award in dairy chemistry 1953), Am. Soc. Biol. Chemists, Am. Dairy Sci. Assn., Am. Soc. Mammalogists, Sigma Xi, Phi Kappa Phi, Phi Lambda Upsilon, Alpha Zeta. Author: (with Patton) Principles of Dairy Chemistry, 1959; also numerous articles. Research on structure and properties milk proteins in relations to species and genetic variation, immunology denaturation, indsl. utilization. Home: 942 Oak Ridge Av St Paul MN 55112

JENNETTE, MARSHALL COX, r.r. exec.; b. Goldsboro, N.C., June 19, 1909; s. Ezra W. and Annie Eliza (Cox) J.; B.S. in Civil Engring., N.C. State Coll., 1932; m. Ruth A. Munden, Sept. 23, 1934; children—Marshall E. and Ruth Anne (twins), Dorothy Lou. Engring. dept. S.A.L. Ry., 1932-46; spl. rep. office of pres. Norfolk So. Ry Co., 1946-47, chief engr., 1947-55, asst. v.p., 1956, v.p. operations, 1956-62; chief engr. Jacksonville Terminal Co., 1962, pres., gen. mgr., 1962-66; gen. supt.-terminals Atlantic Coast Line R.R., Jacksonville, Fla., 1967—, Seaboard Coast Line R.R., Jacksonville, 1967—; with York Bldg., Co., Raleigh, N.C., 1955-56. Registered profl. engr., N.C. Mem. Assn. R.R. Supts., N.C. Soc. Engrs., Nat. Def. Transp. Assn. Home: 2331 Ironwood Dr Jacksonville FL 32216 Office: 500 Water St Jacksonville FL 32202

JENNEWEIN, CARL PAUL, sculptor; b. Stuttgart, Germany, Dec. 2, 1890; s. Louis and Emilie (Weber) J.; art edn. Art Students League, N.Y.C.; Prix de Rome scholar Am. Acad. in Rome, 1912-21; m. Gina Pirra, Jan. 27, 1918; children—Paul Romano, Emilia Pirra, Alessandro Louis, James Joseph, Peter Gino. Came to U.S., 1907, naturalized, 1915. Prin. works: Sculpture for Phila. Mus. Art, many public bldgs. and memorials, portraits and medals, including work for House Office Bldg., Washington; statue and frieze Washington Meml. Valley Forge Tower; two panels for White House, Washington; also executed many bronzes including, four pylons, N.Y. World's Fair, and several others, bronzes on permanent exhbn. at Met. Mus. Art, N.Y.C., Balt. Mus. Art, Corcoran Art Galleries, Washington, Cin. Mus. Art, Detroit Mus. Art; represented in Bklyn. Mus. Art, Newark Mus. Art, Houston Mus. of Art, Hartford Mus. of Art, Pa. Acad. Fine Arts, Brookgreen Gardens, Georgeton, S.C., others. Awarded several medals and prizes including Saltus medal N.A.D., 1942; Sanford Saltus award, 1949; Elizabeth N. Watrous Gold medal, N.A.D., 1960; Golden Plate award Am. Acad. Achievement, 1966; Medal of Honor, Nat. Sculpture Soc., 1967; Benjamin West Clinedinst Meml. medal, 1967; 50th Anniversary medal Am. Legion; Hall of Fame medal James Monroe, Outstanding Aerospace Rescue, Recovering award Albert P. Loening trophy, 1968; Gold medal Am. Artists Profl. League, 1968; Gold medal 75th Ann. Exhbn. Nat. Sculpture Soc., 1968. A.N.A. Numismatic Art award, 1970. Mem. N.G., N.Y., 1915-16; served with A.R.C., Italy, World War. A.N.A., 1930, N.A., 1933. Fellow Am. Acad. in Rome, Nat. Sculpture Soc. (pres. 1960-63), Am. Numismatic Soc.; mem. N.A.D. (past v.p.), Beaux Arts Inst. Architects, A.I.A., Nat. Inst. of Arts and Letters Alumni Assn. Club: Century Assn. (N.Y.). Home: 11 Serpentine Trail Larchmont NY 10538 Studio: 538 Van Nest Av Bronx 60 NY ☆

JENNEY, JOHN KING, ret. business exec.; b. Syracuse, N.Y., Sept. 8, 1904; s. Alexander D. and Caroline (King) J.; B.S., Princeton, 1925; m. Anne West, Nov. 11, 1938; children—Marshall W., John King. With E. I. du Pont de Nemours & Co., Inc., 1925-67, dir. fgn. relations, 1954-58, asst. gen. mgr. internat. dept., 1958-67. Vice chmn. U.S. Inter-Am. Council, 1960-64; bd. dirs. Nat. Fgn. Trade Council, 1954-67, Council on Fgn. Relations. Trustee Tower Hill Sch., Wilmington, 1945-68; bd. dirs. Wilmington Gen. Hosp, 1945-54; adv. com. history dept. Princeton; pres. Wilmington Fine Arts Soc. Episcopalian (vestry). Clubs: Wilmington, Wilmington Country, Vicmead Hunt, University of N.Y. Home: Montchanin DE 19710 Office: Beneficial Bldg 1300 Market St Wilmington DE 19801

JENNEY, MELVIN RICHARD, lawyer; b. Boston, Aug. 23, 1900; s. Frederic H. and Mabel (Tukey) J.; S.B., Mass. Inst. Tech., 1921; postgrad. Suffolk Law Sch., Boston; m. Anne D'Orsay, Sept. 16, 1927; children—Richard F., Robert M., Louise (Mrs. James Rouvalis). Admitted to Mass. bar, 1926, since practiced in Boston; mem. firm Keaway, Jenney & Hildreth, 1947—. Mem. Melrose (Mass.) Bd. Appeal, 1947—. Served with USNRF, 1918. Mem. Am., Mass., Boston bar assns., Boston Patent Law Assn. (pres. 1952-53). Republican. Methodist. Mason. Home: 9 Meadowview Rd Melrose MA 02176 Office: 24 School St Boston MA 02108

JENNEY, RAY FREEMAN, clergyman; b. Meriden, N.H., Apr. 21, 1891; s. Frank Ezekiel and Louis A. (Cutting) J.; grad. Kimball Union Acad., Meriden, 1909; B.P.E., Springfield Coll., 1914, H.D., 1958; A.B., Miliken U., 1915, LL.D., 1942; B.D., Union Theol. Sem., 1920; M.A., Columbia, 1921, postgrad., 1921-22, 42; D.D., Knox Coll., 1925; m. Edna Belle Orr, June 18, 1917; children—Lois Virginia (Mrs. W.E. Gregg, Jr.), Eleanor (Mrs. Lyman Anson) (dec.), Dorothy Orr (Mrs. Paul Douglas McKown). Ordained to ministry Presbyn. Ch., 1917; pastor Faith Ch., N.Y.C., 1919-22, First Ch., Galesburg, Ill., 1922-1926, Park Central Ch., Syracuse, N.Y., 1929-42, emeritus; minister Bryn Mawr Community Ch., Chgo., 1942-59, emeritus; interim minister 1st Presbyn. Ch., Libertyville, Ill., 1959-60, Old First Ch., Newark, 1960-61, North Av. Ch., New Rochelle, N.Y., 1961-62, Reformed Ch., Bronxville, N.Y., 1962-63, 1st Presbyn. Ch., Utica, N.Y., 1963, Glen Ridge (N.J.) Congl. Ch., 1965, Westminister Presbyn. Ch., Bloomfield, 1966, First Bapt. Ch., Montclair, 1967-68, 1st Presbyn. Ch., Tenafly, N.J., 1968; gen. dir. Christian Assn. (united ch. work), U. Pa., 1926-29; Vice moderator Gen. Assembly of Presbyn. Ch. of U.S.A., 1940-41. Hon. trustee Lincoln Coll; former trustee Knox Coll., Union theol. Sem.; trustee Kimball Union Acad., Meriden, N.H.; mem. Am. Seminar in Europe and Russia, 1933; world-wide speaking engagements, 1964; exchange preacher Gr. Britain, summer 1936,37. Pres. Ch. Fedn. of Greater Chgo., 1946-48. Served as chaplain, 1st lt., 59th Inf., 4th Div., A.E.F., World War I; wounded in action. Decorated Purple Heart; recipient Presdl. Citation. Mem. Phi Sigma Kappa, Pi Gamma Mu, Sigma Chi Circle New York. Club: Skaneateles (N.Y.) Country. Author: Speaking Boldly; I am a Protestant; Bible Primer; also articles and sermons. Mason (32). Home: 160 Gordonhurst Av Upper Montclair NJ 07043 also East Lake Rd Skaneateles NY 13152

JENNEY, ROBERT M., mfg. co. exec.; b. Boston, 1918; grad. Harvard, 1941. Pres., dir. Jenney Mfg. Co., Boston; dir. Nat. Shawmut Bank of Boston, Combustion Engring., Inc., N.Y.C., CBK Industries, Inc., Kansas City, Shawmut Assn., Inc., Boston, Nat. Tank Co., Tulsa. Vice chmn. Greater Boston Stadium Authority. Pres. New Eng. Heritage Trail Found.; overseer Old Sturbridge Village. Mem. Greater Boston C. of C. (v.p., dir.). Home: 209 Newton St Brookline MA 02146 Office: P O Box 100 Chestnut Hill MA 02167

JENNEY, WARREN, paper co. exec.; b. Belmont, Mass., June 26, 1904; s. Charles and Blanche (Howe) J.; A.B., Harvard, 1926; m. Mary Thomas, Dec. 26, 1930; children—Nancy Cate (Mrs. Frank Seabury III), Mary Howe (Mrs. Charles A. Stewart). With S. D. Warren Co., 1927—, head book pub. sales, Boston, 1948-62, dir., 1961—, sec., 1962—. Served to lt. comdr., Supply Corps, USNR. Clubs: Harvard (N.Y.C.), Concord Country. Home: Monument St Concord MA 01742 Office: 225 Franklin St Boston MA 02101

JENNINGS, ALSTON, lawyer; b. West Helena, Ark., Oct. 30, 1917; s. Earp Franklin and Irma (Alston) J.; A.B., Columbia, 1938; J.D., Northwestern U., 1941; m. Dorothy Bulie Jones, June 12, 1943; children—Alston, Eugene Franklin, Ann Bulle. Admitted to Ark. bar, 1941; since practiced in Little Rock, 1947—; spl. agt. intelligence unit Treasury Dept., 1946; asso. firm Wright, Harrison, Lindsey & Upton, 1949-51, mem. firm, 1951-60; mem. firms Wright, Lindsey, Jennings, Lester & Shults, 1960-65, Wright, Lindsay and Jennings, 1965—. Bd. dirs. Community Chest Greater Little Rock; mem. adv. bd. Salvation Army Pulaski County. Served to lt. USNR, 1941- 45. Mem. Am., Ark., Pulaski County (past pres.) bar assns., Internat. Assn. Ins. Counsel (pres.-elect 1970-71), Am. Coll. Trial Lawyers. Home: 5300 Sherwood Little Rock AR 72207 Office: 2200 Worthen Bank Bldg Little Rock AR 72201

JENNINGS, BURGESS HILL, educator, mech. engr.; b. Balt. Sept. 12, 1903; s. Henry Hill and Martha Whitfield (Burgess) J.; B.E., Johns Hopkins, 1925; M.S., Lehigh U., 1928, A.M., 1935; m. Etta M. Crout, Nov. 7, 1925; 1 son, Robert Burgess. Test engr., Consol. Gas & Electric Co., Balt., 1925; mem. faculty Lehigh U., 1926-40; prof. dept. mech. engring. Northwestern U., 1940—, chmn. dept., 1943-57, asso. dean, 1962-70; research investigator U.S. OSRD, 1942-45; dir. research labs. Am. Soc. Heating, Refrigerating and Air Conditioning Engrs., Cleve., 1957-60; cons. and gen. research and writing relating to refrigeration, air conditioning and power prodn., 1930—. Recipient Richards Meml. Award in Mech. Engring., 1950; Merit award Chgo. Tech. Socs. Council, 1963. Fellow Am. Soc. M.E., Am. Soc. Heating, Refrigerating and Air Conditioning Engrs. (pres. 1948-49); mem. Am. Soc. Lubricating Engrs. (past v.p.), Am. Soc. Engring. Edn., Internat. Inst. Refrigeration (v.p. 1958-67), Sigma Xi, Pi Tau Sigma (pres. 1948-50), Tau Beta Pi, Pi Tau Sigma. Clubs: Michigan Shores (Wilmette, Ill.); University (Evanston, Ill.). Author of books and articles on engring., heating, air conditioning; Toxic Gases and Dusts in Industry, 1957; Heating and Air Conditioning, 1956; Environmental Engineering, 1970; co-author: Gas Turbine Analysis and Practice, 1953; Air Conditioning and Refrigeration, 1958. Home: 1500 Sheridan Rd Wilmette IL 60091

JENNINGS, CLARENCE A., Jr., cement co. exec.; b. Fort Worth, 1923; B.S., U. So. Cal., 1947; married. Accountant, C.H. Wright Co., 1948-49; gen. mgr. M.H. Cass Co., 1949-50; controller So. Cal. Petro Corp., 195-57; mgr. finance and planning Tidewater Oil Co., 1958-62; controller Am. Cement Corp., Los Angeles, 1962-69, v.p., controller, 1969-70, v.p. investments, 1970—. Served with USMCR, World War II. C.P.A., Cal. Home: 3016 Shakespeare Dr Pasadena CA 91109 Office: 2404 Wilshire Blvd Los Angeles CA 90057*

JENNINGS, DAVID HENRY, historian, educator; b. Utica, N.Y., Feb. 24, 1918; s. James and Annie (Baker) J.; A.B., Bates Coll., Lewiston, Maine, 1941; M.A., Syracuse U., 1946; Ph.D., Ohio State U., 1958; m. Olive Van Eenwyk, Mar. 16, 1946; children—Shirley Ann., Richard James. History tchr. Pembroke (N.H.) Acad., 1941-44, Wilbraham (Mass.) Acad., 1944-46; mem. faculty Ohio Wesleyan U., 1946—, chmn. dept., 1960-66, Britton prof. history, 1960- -. Mem. Am., Miss. Valley hist. assns., Ohio Acad. History, Delta Sigma Rho, Omicron Delta Kappa, Phi Alpha Theta, Phi Kappa Tau. Co-author: Values and Policy in American Society, 1954; Goals of American Foreign Policy, 1955. Co-editor: Readings in Social Policy, 1954. Home: 42 Westgate Dr Delaware OH 43015

JENNINGS, DONN O., paperboard co. exec.; b. B.C., Can., Feb. 20, 1917; s. Roy L. and Hazel (Steele) J.; M.E., U. Cin.; m. Betty V., 1937; children—Mrs. Brown, James Craig, Susan Beth. Formerly v.p. Container Corp. Am., Chgo., now sr. v.p. Home: PO Box 932 RR 1 St Charles IL 60174 Office: 38 S Dearborn St Chicago IL 60603

JENNINGS, EDWARD MORTON, Jr., banker; b. Winthrop, Mass., Nov. 24, 1906; s. Edward Morton and Grace W. (Waite) J.: grad. Philips Acad., Andover, Mass., 1924; B.S., Dartmouth, 1928, M.C.S., Amos Tuck Sch. Bus. Adminstrn., 1929; grad. Stonier Grad. Sch. Banking, 1944; m. Mary L. Sabine, July 14, 1934; children—Edward Morton III, Charles Sabine. With First Nat. Bank Boston, 1929—, v.p., 1948-65, sr. v.p., 1965—; dir. Morse Shoe, Inc., Howes Leather Co., Inc., H.A. Johnson Co., Mass. Mut. Corporate Investors, Inc. Trustee Boston Symphony Orch. Author: Bank Loans to Shoe Manufacturers, 1944. Home: 14 Jefferson Rd Chestnut Hill MA 02167 Office: 100 Federal St Boston MA 02110

JENNINGS, EDWARD QUENTIN, bishop; b. St. John, N.B., Can., Oct. 4, 1896; s. Patrick Lewis and Elizabeth (Wallace) J.; B.A., St. Francis Xavier U., Antigonish, N.S., 1922; student Holy Heart Sem., Halifax, N.S., 1922- 25; acad. teaching certificate Calgary Normal Sch., 1926. Ordained priest Roman Catholic Ch., 1925; consecrated bishop, June 11, 1941; aux. to arch-bishop of Vancouver, 1941-46; apptd. bishop of Kamloops, B.C., 1946, Ft. William, Ont., 1952-69; apptd. titular bishop of Assidona, 1969. Address: 1306 Ridgeway St P O Box 113 Thunder Bay F Ontario Canada

JENNINGS, ELEANOR ELIZABETH Mrs. Alvin R. Jennings; b. Blue Ridge, Ga., Feb. 23, 1905; d. William Thomas and Isabel (Jordan) Foster; student Sullins Coll., 1923-24; m. Robert H. Montgomery, July 26, 1934 (dec. May 1953); m. 2d Alvin R. Jennings, Feb. 23, 1956. Co-founder, 1st pres. Fairchild Tropical Garden, Coral Gables, Fla., 1938; pres. Montgomery Found., Miami. Recipient Achievement medal Garden Club Am., 1964. Home: 11901 Old Cutler Rd Miami FL 33156 also Laurel Park Hendersonville NC 28739

JENNINGS, FARNSWORTH LEROY, chem. co. exec.; b. Clarkston, Wash., Sept. 25, 1906; s. Leroy Garfield and Helen Emma (Wing) J.; B.A., U. Ida., 1928; B.A. in Jurisprudence (Rhodes scholar 1929-32), Oxford (Eng.) U., 1931, B.C.L., 1932, D.S. in Jurisprudence (Sterling fellow 1932-33), Yale, 1933; m. Jeanne Marie Lebegue, July 16, 1932; 1 son, Nicholas L. Clk. to U.S. judge, 1933-34; admitted to N.Y. bar, 1936; with firm Chadbourne, Stanchfield and Levy, N.Y.C., 1934-35; with Union Carbide Corp., 1935—, v.p., 1963—, also dir. affiliated cos. Recipient Proximus Vinearian Law prize Oxford U., 1933. Mem. Assn. Rhodes Scholars, Phi Beta Kappa, Tau Kappa Epsilion, Delta Sigma Rho. Club: Marco Polo (N.Y.C.). Author articles law revs. Home: Winfield Av Harrison NY 10528 Office: 270 Park Av New York City NY 10017

JENNINGS, FRANK GERARD, editor, educator; b. Bklyn., May 23, 1915; s. Gerard Thomas and Martha (Hirsch) J.; B.S., N.Y. U., 1949, M.A., 1950; m. Gloria Miehling, Mar. 22, 1941. Tchr. composition, lit. and allied courses N.Y. U., U. Denver, Walter Harvey Jr. Coll. (N.Y.C.), Yeshiva U., Columbia Tchrs. Coll., Dillard U., pub. high schs.; participant ednl. confs., book award juror; reading specialist; exec. dir. Library Club Am., 1956-65; editor-at-large Sat. Rev., 1959—; asso. Lang. Arts Inst., Columbia, 1956-57; cons. Horace Mann-Lincoln Inst. for Sch. Experimentation, Columbia Tchrs. Coll., 1957-58, dir. coll. relations Tchrs. Coll., 1969-70, sec. coll., 1970—; editor Tchrs. Coll. Record, 1970—; editorial cons. Harcourt, Brace & Co., 1957-64; sr. editor Harvard Classics, 1960-62; ednl. editor Crowell Collier Ednl. Corp., 1960-62; ednl. cons. New World Found., 1963-69. Cons. fed., state edn. agys. Mem. Com. on Study History C, Amherst Project. Bd. dirs. Found. Am. Served with USAAF, 1942-45. Mem. Nat. Acad. Edn. (sec. com. on reading), Internat. Reading Assn. (pres. Manhattan chpt. 1960-61), Phi Delta Kappa, Kappa Delta Pi. Author: This is Reading, 1965, also textbooks. Contbr. articles to numerous mags., profl. jours. Home: 101 W 12th St New York City NY 10011 Office: Tchrs Coll Columbia U New York City NY 10027

JENNINGS, FRANK LAMONT, educator, pathologist; b. Mpls., Apr. 25, 1921; s. Frank L. and Helen (Germond) J.; A.B., Ind. U., 1942, M.D., 1947; m. Beverly K. Carlson, Dec. 15, 1948; children—Frank Lamont III, Kathryn Eleanor, Paul Ernest, Mark Oliver. Fellow U. Chgo. Hosps., 1947-51, intern, 1951-52; instr., then asst. prof. U. Chgo. Clinics, 1954-60; mem. faculty U. Tex. Med. Br., Galveston, 1960—, prof. pathology, chmn. dept., 1963—. Sec. Gulf Coast Waste Disposal Authority, 1970—. Bd. dirs. Tex. div. Am. Cancer Soc. Served with M.C., AUS, 1955-57. Mem. Am. Soc. Clin. Pathologists, Coll. Am. Pathology, Am. Assn. Pathologic Bacteriologists, Internat. Acad. Pathology, Am. Soc. Exptl. Pathology, Am. Assn. Cancer Edn., Radiation Research Soc. Home: 1904 Evergreen St LaMarque TX 77568 Office: Univ Tex Med Br Galveston TX 77550

JENNINGS, HELEN HALL, psychologist, sociometrist; b. Buffalo, N.Y., July 31, 1905 d. Alvin Henry and Mertha (Hall) Jennings; B.L., Rutgers U., 1927; M.A., Columbia Univ., 1931, Ph.D., 1942. Research collaborator with J.L. Morena, M.D., in developing sociometric methods for study inter-personal structures of groups, 1929-39; research work and teaching 1939-44; psychologist, Office of Scientific Research and Development dept. of psychology, Stanford U., 1945; specialist group relations, Am. Council on Edn. project Intergroup Edn. in Cooperating Schs., 1946-48; com., Am. Sociometric Assn, 1945—; managing editor, Sociometry: A Journal of Inter-Personal Relations, Jan. 1942-50; instr. Intergroup Workshop U. Chgo., 1946-48, La. State U., 1949. U. Vt., 1949; cons. group dynamics Center for Human Relations Studies, N.Y.U. 1950-54; asso. prof. edn. Brooklyn Coll., 1951-61, prof. edn. 1961—; co-founder, co-dir. Moreno Found., 1964—; cons. psychologist George W. Henry Found., 1956-59. Fellow Am. Soc. Group Psychotherapy and Psychodrama (pres., 1954), Am. psychol. assn.; mem. N.Y. Psychol. Assn., Sociometric Inst., Am. Sociological Soc., Sigma Xi. Collaborator: on J.L. Moreno's Who Shall Survive? A New Approach to the Problem of Human Interrelations, relations, 1934. Author Sociometric Studies, 1934; A Sociometric Study of Emotional and Social Expansiveness (in child behavior and development), 1943; Leadership and Isolation, 1943 (second edition, 1950); Sociometry of Leadership, 1947; Sociometry in Group Relations, 1948 (rev. 1959), Trans. abroad in several langs. Editor (with others) Sociometry Reader, 1960; (with Sherif and Wilson) Group Relations at the Crossroads. Contributor to Sociometric Review, Sociometry, Am. Sociological Rev., Ency. of Psychology, other profl. publs. Address: 470 West End Av New York City NY 10024

JENNINGS, IRVING ANTHONY, lawyer; b. Taylor, Ariz., May 21, 1896; s. Cyrus Morgan and Hannah Jane (Hansen) J.; student U. Ariz.; law studies, U. Mich.; m. Emogene Mercer, Mar. 8, 1924; children—Irving Anthony, Roderic Mercer, Terry Marshall, Judith Ann. Admitted to Ariz. bar, 1921, since practiced in Phoenix; mem. firm Jennings, Strouss & Salmon; city atty., Phoenix, 1936-39. Mem. Am., Maricopa County bar assns., State Bar Ariz. Home: 6502 N Central Phoenix AZ 85013 Office: Ariz Title Bldg Phoenix AZ 85003

JENNINGS, IRWIN LYNN, banker; b. Zanesville, O., Oct. 23, 1906; s. Irwin G. and Charlotte (Lynn) J.; student Columbia, 1923-24; A.B., Marietta Coll., 1926; m. Charlotte Schoenemann, Nov. 28, 1934; children—Kenneth, George, Donald. Bank examiner Office Comptroller of Currency, 1927-65; sr. v.p. Fed. Res. Bank San Francisco, 1968—. Mem. Joe Jefferson Players, Ridgewood, N.J. Recipient Silver Beaver award Boy Scouts Am. Mem. Phi Beta Kappa, Delta Upsilon. Mem. Reformed Ch. Am. Home: 155 Jackson St San Francisco CA 94111 Office: 400 Sansome St San Francisco CA 94120

JENNINGS, JEROME, business exec.; b. N.Y.C., July 29, 1900; s. Abraham and Lena (Smith) J.; student Columbia, 1923. Chmn. bd. La Primadora-Optimo Cigar Co., 1953—, First Nat. Bank, Fair Haven, Vt., 1955—, Chamberlin Co. of Am., 1956—, Northfield Nat. Bank, Vt., 1958—, LaSalle Wines & Champagne, Inc., Universal Cigar Corp., Lehigh Valley Plumbing Supply Co., Allentown, Pa.; dir. Sioux Falls Paint and Glass Co. (S.D.), Forman, Ford and Co. of Iowa, Des Moines, Ia. Clubs: Columbia U., City Athletic, Harmonie, Bankers, Lambs (N.Y.C.); Quaker Ridge Golf (Scarsdale, N.Y.); Inwood Country (Far Rockaway, L.I.); Inwood Beach (Atlantic Beach, L.I.); Standard (Chgo). Home: 530 Park Av New York City NY 10021 Office: 660 Madison Av New York City NY 10021

JENNINGS, JESSE DAVID, educator, anthropologist; b. Oklahoma City, July 7, 1909; s. Daniel Wellman and Grace (Cruce) J.; B.A., Montezuma Coll., 1929; Ph.D., U. Chgo., 1943; m. Jane Noyes Chase, Sept. 7, 1935; children—Jesse David, Herbert Lee. Anthropologist, Nat. Park Service, 1937-42, 45-48; mem. faculty U. Utah, 1948—, prof. anthropology, 1949- -, Distinguished Research Prof., 1970—. Mem. anthropology- psychology div. Nat. Acad. Sci.-NRC, 1954-56; vis. prof. anthropology Northwestern U., 1960, U. Minn., 1961, U. Hawaii 1965, 67-68; lectr. summer inst. anthropology U. Colo., 1961, Fairmont Coll., 1962; lectr. semi-centennial symposium Am. archeology Rice U., 1962; Reynolds lectr. U. Utah, 1962; dir. Glen Canyon Archeol. Salvage Project, 1957-66, Utah Mus. Natural History, 1965—; cons. instl. studies NSF, 1964-66. Served to comdr. USNR, 1942-45. Recipient Viking medal in archaeology Wenner Gren Found. Anthrop. Research, 1958. Mem. Soc. Am. Archaeology (pres. 1959-68; editor bull. 1950-54), Am. Anthrop. Assn. (exec. bd. 1953-56), A.A.A.S. (nat. v.p., chmn. sect. H 1961, 69), Sigma Xi, Phi Kappa Phi. Author: (with A.V. Kidder and E. M. Shook) Excavations at Kaminal Juyu, Guatemala, 1946; (with E. A. Hoebel) Readings in Anthropology, 3d edit., 1972; The Archeology of the Plains: An Assessment, 1956; Danger Cave, 1957; also numerous articles, reports, papers. Editor: (with Edward Norbeck) Prehistoric Man in the New World, 1964; (with Robert F. Spencer) Native Americans, 1965; Prehistory of North America, 1968. Home: 2802 South 2950 East Salt Lake City UT 84109

JENNINGS, JESSE LEE, lawyer; b. Dayton, O., Sept. 28, 1922; s. Fred S. and Elizabeth (Gilbert) J.; B.A., LL.B., Ohio State U., 1951; m. Belvia Crisp, Oct. 15, 1966; stepchildren-Michael, Ronald, Kevin. Admitted to Ohio bar, 1951, since practiced in Dayton; mem. firm Talbot, Jennings & Ducker and predecessor firms, 1951—. Pres. Young Republicans of Montgomery County, 1956. Served with AUS, 1942-43. Mem. Am., Ohio, Dayton bar assns. Mem. editorial bd. Ohio State Law Jour., 1950-51. Home: 5441 Colborne Dr Dayton OH 45430 Office: Harries Bldg Dayton OH 45402

JENNINGS, JOHN EDWARD, Jr., author; b. Bklyn., Dec. 30, 1906; s. John Edward (M.D.) and Florence (Thistle) J.: ed. Brown Sch., N.Y.C., 1924, Colo. Sch. of Mines, 1925, Columbia, 1925-26; m. Virginia Lee Storey, June 20, 1931 (div. 1959); m. 2d, Elise Durrin Dunlap, Jan. 9, 1960; 1 son, John Edward, III. Writer, 1932—, books include: Out American Tropics, 1938; Next to Valour, 1939; Call the New World, 1941; Gentleman Ranker, 1942; Wheel of Fortune (serialized in Liberty Mag., July-Aug.), 1943; The Shadow and the Glory, 1943; The Salem Frigate, 1946; Boston, Cradle of Liberty, 1630-1776, 1947; River To the West, 1948; The Sea Eagles, 1950; The Pepper Tree, 1950; The Strange Brigade, 1952; Clipper Ship Days, 1953; Rogue's Yarn, 1953; Banners Against the Wind, 1954; Chronicle of the Calypso, Clipper, 1955; The Wind in His Fists, 1956; Blood on the Moon, 1957; The Tall Ships, 1958; The Golden Eagle, 1959; The Raider, 1963; Tattered Ensign, 1966. Contbr. short stories to Sat. Eve. Post, Cosmopolitan, others. Served from lt. (j.g.) to lt. USNR, 1942-44; officer in charge Naval Aviation History Unit, 1944; lt. comdr., 1948. Democrat. Episcopalian. Address: PO Box U Pipestave Hollow Rd Miller Place NY 11764

JENNINGS, JOHN MELVILLE, hist. soc. dir.; b. Toano, Va., Oct. 22, 1918; s. John Melville and Grace Armistead (Davis) J.; B.A., Coll. William and Mary, 1938, LL.D., 1968; M.A., Am. U., 1948. Curator manuscripts and rare books Coll. William and Mary, 1939-43, 46-47; librarian Va. Hist. Soc., Richmond, 1948-51, dir., 1953—. Vice chmn. Va. Historic Landmarks Commn.; adv. bd. Assn. Preservation Va. Antiquities; cons. Robert E. Lee Meml. Found.; mem. publs. adv. com. Winterthru Mus.; mem. adv. bd. Nat. Cathedral Rare Book Library. Served with USNR, 1944-46, 51-53. Fellow Soc. Am. Archivists; mem. Bibliog. Soc. Am., Am. Hist. Assn., Mass. Hist. Soc., Am. Antiquarian Soc. Home: 204 N Granby St Richmond VA 23220 Office: P O Box 1194 Richmond VA 23209*

JENNINGS, JOSEPH ASHBY, banker; b. Richmond, Va., Aug. 12, 1920; s. Joseph Ashby and Leone (Bishop) J.; B.S., U. Richmond, 1949; grad. certificate, Stonier Grad. Sch. Banking, Rutgers U., 1952; m. Anne Barrow Hatcher, Oct. 19, 1960; children-Joseph Ashby III, Ashby Anne. With United Va. Bank/State Planters, Richmond, 1951—, v.p., 1956-66, sr. v.p., 1966-67, exec. v.p., 1967—; dir. Life Ins. Co. Va., Titmus Optical Co., Commonwealth Natural Gas Corp. Trustee U. Richmond. Served with USAAF, 1942-46. Mem. Financial Analysts Fedn. (past exec. v.p.,) dir.), Va., Richmond chambers commerce, Phi Beta Kappa, Omicron Delta Kappa, Phi Delta Theta. Presbyn. Home: 310 Charmian Rd Richmond VA 23226 Office: 900 E Main St Richmond VA 23219

JENNINGS, LEE BYRON, educator; b. Williard, O., May 3, 1927; s. Lee and Grace (Kime) J.; B.A. in German, Ohio State U., 1949; M.A., U. Ill., 1951, Ph.D., 1955. Teaching asst. U. Ill., Champaign-Urbana, 1949-52; instr. U. Colo., Boulder, 1956, Harvard, 1956-57; from instr. to asst. prof. U. Cal., 1957-62; asso. prof. U. Tex., Austin, 1962-68; prof. German, U. Ill. at Chgo., Circle, 1968—; vis. prof. U. Marburg, West Germany, summer 1965, U. Cal. at Berkeley, summer 1961, summer 1969. Fulbright research grantee, West Germany, 1954-55; Alexander von Humboldt Found. research fellow, 1965-67. Mem. Modern Lang. Assn., Am. Assn. Tchrs. of German (pres. Tex. chpt. 1964), Phi Beta Kappa. Author: The Ludicrous Demon: Aspects of the Grotesque in German Post-Romantic Prose, 1963. Contbr. articles to profl. jours. Home: 708 N Kenilworth Av Oak Park IL 60302 Office: Dept German U Ill at Chgo Circle Box 4348 Chicago IL 60680*

JENNINGS, LEWELLYN A., banker; b. Birch Tree, Mo., Dec. 1, 1906; s. Horace and Laura (Bodle) J.; student pub. schs. Silver Creek, N.Y.; m. Virginia Lee Cambell, June 28, 1941. With Silver Creek (N.Y.) Nat. Bank, 1924-29; asst. nat. bank examiner Office Comptroller of Currency, 2d Fed. Res. Dist., N.Y.C., 1929-35, nat. bank examiner, N.Y., N.J., Conn., 1935-37, examiner fgn. brs. nat. banks, Europe, S.A. and Caribbean area, 1937-39, asst. chief nat. bank examiner, Washington, 1941-50, 3d dept. comptroller, 1950-51, 2d dep. comptroller, 1951-52, 1st dep. comptroller of currency, 1952-60; on loan to Govt. of Haiti to make surveys and exams. of Central Bank, Republic of Haiti, part-time, 1938, 41, Guam and Samoa, for U.S. Navy Dept., 1948; sr. v.p., exec. com. Republic Nat. Bank Dallas 1960-61, exec. v.p. for adminstrn., 1961-63; chmn. bd., chief exec. officer Riggs Nat. Bank, Washington, 1963—; dir. Met. Life Ins. Co., Potamac Electric Co., Chesapeake and Potamac Telephone Co., Garfinckel, Brooks Bros., Miller & Rhodes Co. Bd. dirs. George Washington U., D.C. chpt. A.R.C.; chmn. bd. regents Georgetown U. Served to capt. AUS, 1942-46, mil. govt. officer, ETO, 1944-46. Decorated Legion of Merit. Mem. Assn. Res. City Bankers D.C. Bankers Assn. (vice chmn. law and legislative com.), Nat. Civil Service League (dir.), Transp. Assn. Am. (dir.), Washington Inst. Fgn. Affairs, Met. Washington Bd. Trade (dir.), Fed. City Council (chmn.). Mason. Clubs: Congressional Country, Alfalfa, Burning Tree, Metropolitan, Internat. (Washington). Home: 16 Farmington Ct Chevy Chase MD 20015 Office: Riggs Nat Bank Washington DC

JENNINGS, MANSON VAN BUREN, coll pres.; b. Trenton, N.J., Oct. 24, 1916; s. Harold Manson and Mabel (Tuthill) J.; A.B., Harvard, 1938; M.A., Columbia, 1939, Ph.D., 1949; m. Deborah Hunt, Sept. 14, 1946; children—Susan Briggs, David Tuthill. Instr., Horace Mann Sch. Tchrs. Coll., Columbia, 1939-41, instr. social studies dept., 1946-49, asst. prof., 1949-54, asso. prof., 1954-58, prof. history, 1958-61; dean Cortland Coll., State U. N.Y., 1961-65; dean Adelphi U. Grad. School of Arts and Scis., Garden City, N.Y., 1965-71; pres. So. Conn. State Coll., New Haven, 1971—. Ednl. cons. Current Affairs Films, 1956—; social studies cons. Charles Scribner's Sons, 1960-62. Served from pvt. to 1st lt., AUS, 1941-45. Mem. Nat. Council Social Studies (monthly contbr. Social Edn. 1952-59), Am. Assn. U. Profs. Author: Development of the Modern Problems Course in the Senior High School, 1949. Contbr. articles to profl. jours. Home: 30 Prospect Ct Woodbridge CT 06525 Office: 501 Crescent St New Haven CT 06515

JENNINGS, PAUL, labor union ofcl.; b. Bklyn., Mar. 19, 1918; ed. RCA Inst., Crown Heights Labor Sch.; m. Dorothy; children—Paul, Eileen. Electronic technician Sperry-Gryo, Bklyn.; successively mem. union organizing com., shop steward, grievance and shop chmn., acting pres. local union Internat. Union Elec. Radio and Machine Workers, AFL-CIO, later mem. exec. bd., treas., local pres., from 1948, exec sec. Dist. 4, from 1949, later exec. sec. Dist. 3, now internat. pres., also v.p. AFL-CIO. Vice pres. non-proliferation, nuclear reactor safety. Mem. adv. com. AEC, 1956-62, mem. adv. com. reactor safeguards, 1962- N.Y.C. CIO Council, also chmn. merger com.; v.p. N.Y. State CIO Council, also co-chmn. merger com.; mem. exec. bd. N.Y. Central Labor Council; chmn. Internat. Fedn. Elec. and Electronics Co. Council Com.; chmn. Elec. and Electronics Industry Co. Council, Internat. Metalworkers Fedn., 1968. Mem. N.Y.C. Mayor's Com. on Exploitation; labor del. Orgn. Econ. Cooperation and Devel.; mem. council Hofstra U.; mem. AFL-CIO Civil Rights Com. Trustee U. State N.Y., Urban League. Address: 1126 16th St NW Washington DC 20036

JENNINGS, PETER, newscaster. Address: care ABC-TV Network 7 W 66th St New York City NY 10023 *

JENNINGS, RICHARD WORMINGTON, educator; b. Bois D' Arc, Mo., Oct. 19, 1907; s. William Thomas and Hattie (Wormington) J.; A.B., Park Coll., Parkville, Mo., 1927; M.A., U. Pa., 1934; J.D., U. Cal. at Berkeley, 1939; m. Elizabeth Robison, Aug. 10, 1935; children—Susan Elizabeth, Margaret Anne, William Thomas. Tchr. high sch., Pinckneyville, Ill., 1927-30, Camden, N.J., 1930-33; admitted to Cal. bar, 1939; asso. firm Jesse H. Steinhart, San Francisco, 1939-45, mem. firm, 1945-47; atty. OPA, 1942; lectr. law U. Cal. at Berkeley, 1940-42, prof., 1947—, James W. and Isabel Coffroth prof., 1955—; Fulbright lectr. U. Tokyo, Japan, 1961. Cons. Securities and Exchange Commn., 1962. Pres. Internat. Inst. San Francisco, 1949-51. Mem. Am., Cal., San Francisco bar assns., Am. Law Inst., Am. Bar Found. Presbyn. Author: (with Harold Marsh, Jr.) Securities Regulation- Cases and Materials, 1963, 2d edit., 1968; (with Norman D. Lattin and Richard M. Buxbaum) Corporations-Cases and Materials, 1959, 4th edit., 1968. Home: 425 Vassar Av Berkeley CA 94708

JENNINGS, ROBERT BURGESS, med. educator; b. Balt., Dec. 14, 1926; s. Burgess Hill and Etta (Crout) J.; B.S., Northwestern U., 1947, M.S., B.M., 1949, M.D., 1950; m. Linda Lee Sheffield, June 28, 1952; children—Carol L., Mary G., John B., Anne E., James R. Intern, Passavant Meml. Hosp., Chgo., 1949-50, resident pathology, 1950-51; mem. faculty Northwestern U. Med. Sch., 1953—, prof. pathology, 1963—, Magerstadt prof. and chmn. pathology dept., 1969—; vis. scientist Middlesex Hosp. Med. Sch., London, Eng., 1961-62; cons. Baxter Labs. Morton Grove, Ill., VA Research Hosp., Chgo.; mem. attending staff Passavant Meml. and Wesley Meml. hosps., Chgo., 1969. Mem. pathology A study sect. USPHS, 1960-65. Served as lt. (j.g.) USNR, 1951-53. Markle scholar med. scis., 1958-63. Diplomate Am. Bd. Pathology in pathologic anatomy, 1954, in clin. pathology, 1955. Mem. Am. Soc. Exptl. Pathology, Am. Assn. Pathologists and Bacteriologists, A.M.A., Ill., Chgo. med. socs., Soc. Exptl. Biology and Medicine, Am. Soc. Cell Biology, Internat. Acad. Pathology, Alpha Omega Alpha, Alpha Delta Phi, Nu Sigma Nu. Author research papers. Editorial bd. Lab. Investigation, 1967—, Archives of Pathology, 1970—. Home: 901 Chestnut Av Wilmette IL 60091 Office: 303 E Chicago Av Chicago IL 60611

JENNINGS, ROBERT BURTON, carpet co. exec.; b. Bridgeport, Conn., July 31, 1923; s. Lorin Hull and Ethel (Burton) J.; B.A., Trinity Coll., Hartford, Conn., 1947; m. Shirley Elsa Narvesen, Aug. 30, 1947; children—Robert S., Jeffrey, Christopher, Peter. With James Lees & Sons Co., 1947-59, dir. products, 1956-59; with Bigelow-Sanford, Inc., 1959—, pres., chief exec. officer, dir., 1968—; chmn. bd., chief exec. officer Bigelow-Can. Ltd., Ste. Agathe-Des-Monts, Can.; dir. Bigelow-Sanford, S.A., Oconee Realty Corp., Imbrex, Ltd., Montreal, Can., Gunlocke Co., Inc., Wayland, N.Y., Lea Industries, Inc., Richmond, Va., Bigelow- Sanford, A.G., Chur, Switzerland; asso. dir. State Nat. Bank Conn. Chmn. N.Y.C. div. floor covering industry Am. Cancer Soc., 1967-68. Bd. govs. Darien YMCA; vice chmn. bd. Carpet and Rug Inst., Dalton, Ga. Served with USNR, World War II. Mem. Trinity Coll. Alumni Assn. (pres. Fairfield County 1968-69), A.I.M. (president's council), Advt. Club N.Y.C., Marketing Execs. Club N.Y., Newcomen Soc. N.Am. Clubs: Union League (N.Y.C.); Wee Burn Country (dir.); Tokeneke (Darien); Economic, Empire State. Home: 17 Contentment Island Rd Darien CT 06820 Office: 140 Madison Av New York City NY 10016

JENNINGS, ROBERT MAURICE, journalist; b. Nashville, Nov. 1, 1924; s. Robert Maurice and Ethel (McHughes) J.; B.A., U. Mo., 1948, B.J., 1949; m. Betty Ann Prall, May 14, 1956; 1 dau., Elizabeth McHughes. Staff writer Comml. Appeal, Memphis, 1958—. Served with AUS, 1943-46. Decorated Silver Star. Mem. Phi Beta Kappa. Home: 918 East Dr Memphis TN 38108 Office: 495 Union Av Memphis TN 38101

JENNINGS, ROBERT W., exec. engr.; b. Logan, Utah, Mar. 23, 1911; s. David Stout and Harriet (Webb) J.; B.S. in C.E., Utah State Agrl. Coll., 1933, grad. study, 1941- 42; postgrad. Colo. U., 1937-38, Brigham Young U., 1945-46; m. Elva Simonsen, Mar. 18, 1933; children—Robert W., Paul C. Various engring., surveying positions, 1928-35; with U.S. Bur. Reclamation, 1935-68, beginning as jr. and asso. engr., successively project field engr. Provo River Project, constrn. engr. Paonia project, area engr., Grand Junction, Colo., dist. mgr. constrn. and project planning, Juneau, Alaska, 1953- 54, regional dir. constrn. and project planning, Amarillo, Tex., 1954- 59, project mgr., Grand Junction, 1959-68; dir. engring. Harza Engring. Co. Internat., Lahore, West Pakistan, 1968-70. Served as lt., 9th Naval Constrn. Bn., USNR, 1943-45. Recipient Meritorious Service award U.S. Dept. Interior. Registered profl. engr. Fellow Am. Soc. C.E. (past pres. Western Slope br.); mem. Pi Kappa Alpha. Rotarian. Home: 213 Easter Hill Dr Grand Junction CO 81501

JENNINGS, THEODORE MCKINLEY, Jr., educator; b. Laurel, Miss., Oct. 15, 1929; s. Theodore McKinley and Lizella Julia (Scott) J.; B.A., Fisk U., 1952, M.A., 1954; Ph.D., Ind. U., 1967; m. Beatrice Christine Moore, Aug. 25, 1960. Faculty, Ark. Bapt. Coll., 1956-58; faculty Grambling (La.) Coll., 1963—, prof. music, chmn. dept., 1968—, coordinator humanities teaching team, 1967-68, 70-71. Cons. Ford Found., 1970-71. Served with AUS, 1954-56. Mem. Music Educators Nat. Conf., Music Tchrs. Nat. Assn., La. Music Tchrs. Assn., La. Music Educators Assn., Pi Kappa Lambda, Phi Mu Alpha, Alpha Phi Alpha. Home: PO Box 357 Grambling LA 71245

JENNINGS, W. CROFT, lawyer; b. Bishopville, S.C., Nov 8, 1906; s. Larkin Hamilton (M.D.) and Maria Anne Lenud (Croft) J.: B.S., U.S. Naval Acad., 1927; student Harvard Law Sch., 1929-30; J.D., U. Mich., 1932; m. Elizabeth Bethune Brandon, Feb. 14, 1928; children—Anne M., W. Croft. Admitted to S.C. bar; asso. Bulkley, Ledyard, Dickinson & Wright, Detroit, 1932- 34; spl. asst. U.S. Atty. Gen., 1934-41; partner Roberts & Jennings, Columbia, S.C., 1946-56, Roberts, Jennings, Thomas & Lumpkin, 1956-62, Roberts, Jennings & Thomas, 1963—; spl. lectr. fed. taxation U.S.C. Law Sch., 1946-54. Vice pres., dir. Palmetto Radio Corp. (WKNOK-AM-FM-TV); mem. adv. group to U.S. Commr. Internal Revenue. Active local chpt. A.R.C., nat. bd. govs., 1954-60, vice chmn., 1959-60; bd. dirs. Joint Blood Council, Inc., 1958-62, Columbia Music Festival Assn., 1949-51; bd. dirs. Columbia Art Assn., 1964-67, pres., 1967-69; commr. Columbia Art Commn., 1970—. Chancellor, Episcopal Diocese Upper S.C., 1950—; dep. Triennial Conv., P.E. Ch., 1958, 61 64, 67, 69, 70. Served as ensign USN, 1927-29, from lt. to capt. USNR, 1941-46; comdr. USNR Battalion, Columbia, 1946-49; rear adm., ret. 1953. Decorated Legion of Merit, other combat decorations. Mem. Am., S.C., Richland County bar assns., Am. Judicature Soc., Am. Law Inst., Phi Delta Phi. Episcopalian. Clubs: Pine Tree Hunt, Forest Lake, Palmetto (Columbia); Army Navy (Washington). Home: 550 Spring Lake Rd Columbia SC 29206 Office: Barringer Bldg Columbia SC 29201

JENNINGS, WILLIAM HAROLD, lawyer; b. San Diego, Jan. 20, 1899; s. Frederick Merrick and Ida (Orrell) J.; student U. Cal. at Berkeley, 1921; J.D., Los Angeles Coll. Law, 1930; m. Margaret Mary Donahue, Sept. 14, 1945; 1 son by previous marriage, Bill H. Admitted to Cal. bar, 1930; with Cal. Legislative Counsel Bur., 1930-31; gen. practice, La Mesa, 1931—; mem. firm Higgs, Jennings, Fletcher & Mack, 1966—; city atty. La Mesa, 1934-52, El Cajon, 1937-38; gen. counsel Helix Irrigation Dist., 1936-69; legal cons. Internat. Boundary and Water Commn. U.S. and Mexico, 1952—; tech. cons. Colorado River Bd., 1946—; gen. counsel San Diego County Water Authority, 1944—. Mem. Cal. Water Commn., 1958—, chmn., 1961, vice chmn., 1962-69; mem. Cal. adv. com. Western States Water Planning, 1966-69; mem. exec. com. legal coms. Cal. Irrigation Dists. Assn., 1938-69. Served with USNRF, 1918. Mem. Sigma Chi. Rotarian (pres. La Mesa 1935-36). Home: 8540 Tio Diego Pl La Mesa CA 92041 Office: Hewe Tower 707 Broadway San Diego CA 92112

JENNINGS, WILLIAM MITCHELL, lawyer; b. N.Y.C., Dec. 14, 1920; s. Harry B. and Nettie I. (Mitchell) J.; grad. Hotchkiss Sch., 1937; A.B., Princeton, 1941; J.D., Yale, 1943; m. Elizabeth Hite, Oct. 16, 1943; children—William Mitchell, Jeffrey H., Eunice M., Elizabeth B., Priscilla H. Law clk. to judge U.S. Circuit Ct. Appeals for 2d circuit, N.Y.C., 1943-44; admitted to N.Y. bar, 1945; since practiced in N.Y.C., 1944—; asso. firm Simpson Thacher & Bartlett, 1944-51, partner, 1952—. Pres., dir. N.Y. Rangers, Inc.; vice chmn., dir. Teleprompter Corp.; chmn. finance com., dir. Madison Sq. Garden Corp.; dir. Suburban Propane Gas Corp., Lee Nat. Corp., Warnaco Inc. Gen. chmn. Thunderbird Golf Classic, 1963-65, Westchester Golf Classic, 1967-71. Chmn. bd. govs. Nat. Hockey League, 1968-70, now chmn. finance com., gov.; chmn., trustee United Hosp., Port Chester, N.Y.; bd. dirs. Roosevelt Raceways, Inc., Chgo. Thoroughbred Enterprises, Inc.; trustee Cameron-Brown Investment Group. Mem. N.Y. State, N.Y.C. bar assns., Princeton-Westchester Alumni Assn. (sec., dir.). Clubs: Apawamis, Manursing Island (Rye, N.Y.); Country of North Carolina (Pinehurst); Links, Downtown Assn., Madison Square Garden (N.Y.C.); Blind Brook (Port Chester, N.Y.). Home: Byram Shore Rd Byram CT 10573 Office: 350 Park Av New York City NY 10022

JENNISON, MARSHALL WALKER, bacteriologist; b. Portland, Me., May 27, 1905; s. William Walker and Harriet (Marshall) J.; B.S., Mass. Inst. Tech., 1927, Ph.D., 1932; m. Cynthia M. Lamb, Aug. 15, 1929 (dec.); children—Cynthia M., Margaret W.; m. 2d, Margaret Kerfoot, Jan. 3, 1952. Asst. in biology Mass. Inst. Tech., 1927-30, instr., 1930-35, asst. prof. san. biology, 1935-41, asso. prof. bacteriology, 1941-46; prof. bacteriology Syracuse U., 1946- 71, chmn. dept. bacteriology and botany, 1956-69; vis. lectr. Harvard Sch. Pub. Health, 1945. Fellow Am. Pub. Health Assn., A.A.A.S., Am. Acad. Microbiology; mem. Am. Inst. Biol. Scis., Am. Soc. Microbiology (chmn. com. bacteriological technic 1948-53), Mycol. Soc. Am., Soc. Indsl. Microbiology, Sigma Xi, Kappa Sigma. Editorial bd. Jour. Bacteriology, 1931-51. Contbr. to sci. jours. in field. Home: 307 Standish Dr Syracuse NY 13224

JENNISON, WALTER CHARLES, bldg. materials co. exec.; b. Los Angeles, Aug. 20, 1917; s. George Edward and Hazel (Fitzgerald) J.; student U. So. Cal., 1934-37; m. Catherine Schaub, Sept. 16, 1939; children-Gary, Terry (Mrs. Larry Schilling), Robert, Nanci, Mary. Passenger agt. S.P. R.R., 1936-46; owner textile co., Glendale, Cal., 1946-50; sales mgr. Davidson Plywood & Lumber Co., Los Angeles, 1950-60; v.p. Pacific Wood Products, Los Angeles, 1960-65; exec. v.p. Evans Products Co., Santa Ana, Cal., 1965- -. Served with AUS, 1944-46. Mem. Imported Hardwood Products Assn. Fgn. Trade Assn. So. Cal. Lion (past pres.). Clubs: Los Angeles Athletic, Jonathan (Los Angeles); Irvine Country (Newport Beach, Cal.). Home: 4533 Roxbury Rd Corona Del Mar CA 92625 Office: 2333 N Broadway Santa Ana CA 92711

JENRETTE, RICHARD HAMPTON, investment counsel; b. Raleigh, N.C., Apr. 5, 1929; s. Joseph M. and Emma (Love) J.; A.B., U. N.C., 1951; M.B.A., 1957. With Brown Bros., Harriman & Co., N.Y.C., 1957-59; pres. Donaldson, Lufkin & Jenrette, Inc., N.Y.C., 1959—; dir. Roses Stores, Inc. Served to 2d lt. AUS, 1953-55. Mem. N.Y. Soc. Security Analysts, U. N.C. Alumni Assn. N.Y. (bd. dirs.), N.C. Soc. (bd. govs., bd. dirs.), Chi Psi (chmn. ednl. trust). Clubs: Harvard, Downtown Athletic, City Midday, Brook (N.Y.C.). Home: 152 E 38th St New York City NY also 9 E Battery St Charleston SC Office: 140 Broadway New York City NY 10004

JENSEN, ADOLPH LADRU, educator; b. Ephriam, Utah, Apr. 14, 1896; s. Adolph Willard and Elizabeth (James) J.; A.B., Brigham Young U., 1917; student U. Chgo., summer 1919, Utah Agrl. Coll., 1920; A.M., U. Cal., 1924, J.D., 1925; m. Loila Dudley Merrill, June 30, 1922; children—Ora Lou (Mrs. Jerry Whitney), Julia Merle (Mrs. Robert Vanderpool), Janeth Clair (Mrs. Burtis R. Evans). With U.S. Biol. Survey on the Uintah Nat. Forest survey, summer 1917; admitted to Cal. bar, U.S. Dist. Ct., No. Dist. Cal., 1925; asso. firm Koford & Woolsey, Oakland, 1925- 26; gen. counsel Farmers Grain Coop., Ogden, 1947-64; personnel dir. Salt Lake Delta Freight Lines, 1942-45. Asso. prof. law U. Utah, 1926-32, prof., 1932—. Cons. on legal edn. Am. Inst. Cooperation, Washington, 1945-50. Draftsman for Utah Bar Com. on Criminal Procedure to intergrate the model code of criminal procedure into the criminal procedure code of Utah. 1931-35. Served as cpl. to adj., 316th ammunition trains, 91st div., U.S. Army. 1917-18. Fellow Utah Acad. Arts, Sci. and Letters; mem. Am. (chmn. com. on classification and termlnol. on co-op. corp. law Jan. 1947-52), Cal., Utah, Salt Lake County bar assns., English Speaking Union, Salt Lake Legal Aid Soc. (mem. bd. dirs. 1926-71, pres. 1957-58), U. Utah Employees Credit Union (pres. 1956—), Am. Assn. U. Profs. (dir. nat. council 1942-44), Order of Coif (pres. Utah chpt. 1957-58), Phi Kappa Phi, Alpha Phi Zeta, Delta Theta Phi. Clubs: Aztec, Ensign. Author: Cooperative Corporate Association Law. 1950; (monograph) The Indeterminate Sentence, Probation and Parole in Utah (with George Thomas), 1931. Contbr. articles on legal topics, also book revs. Home: 1536 Harvard Av Salt Lake City UT 84105 ☆

JENSEN, ADOLPH ROBERT, educator; b. Elmhurst, Ill., Apr. 14, 1915; s. Adolph George William and Marie (Diener) J.; B.S., Wheaton (Ill.) Coll., 1937; M.S., U. Ill., 1940, Ph.D., 1942; postgrad. Ohio U., summer 1959, Rensselaer Poly. Inst., summer 1962, Purdue U., summer 1970, Duke, summer 1971; m. Nelle B. Willams, Sept. 5, 1950; children—Robert, Margaret. Head analytical chemistry sect. Lewis Flight Propulsion Lab., NASA, Cleve., 1942-46; prof. chemistry Baldwin-Wallace Coll., Berea, O., 1946—, chmn. dept. chemistry, 1956-71; vis. scientist Ohio Acad. Sci., 1960-64. Fellow A.A.A.S.; mem. Am. Chem. Soc., Ohio Acad. Sci. (v.p. chemistry sect. 1969-70), Am. Assn. U. Profs., Lutheran Acad. Scholarship, Sigma Xi, Phi Lambda Upsilon, Sigma Pi Sigma. Home: 25527 Butternut Ridge North Olmsted OH 44070 Office: Wilker Hall Baldwin-Wallace Coll Berea OH 44017

JENSEN, ALFRED JULIUS, artist; b. Guatemala City, Guatemala, Dec. 11, 1903; s. Peter and Anna (Shipke) J.; studied at Horsholn, Denmark, 1910-19, with Hans Hofmann, 1927-28; student Ecole Scandinave, Paris, France, 1929-34, Fine Arts Mus., San Diego, 1925-26; m. Regina Bogat, Nov. 12, 1963; children—Anna Bogat, Peter Bogat. Came to U.S., 1934. One-man shows Tanager Gallery, 1955, Bertha Schaefer Gallery, 1957, Martha Jackson Gallery, 1959, 61, Solomon R. Guggenheim Mus., 1961, Graham Gallery, 1962, 64, 65, Fairleigh-Dickinson U., 1963, Kornfeld and Klipstein, Berne, Switzerland 1963, Kunsthalle, Basel, Switzerland, 1964, Rolf Nelson Gallery, Los Angeles, 1964, Stedelijk Mus., Amsterdam, 1964, Royal Marks Gallery, 1966, Galerie Ziegler, Zurich, Switzerland, 1966, Cordier and Ekstrom, 1967, 69; exhibited numerous group shows, 1954- -, including Inst. Contemporary Art, Boston, 1960, St. Louis City Art Mus., 1960, Art Inst. Chgo., 1961, Guggenheim Mus., 1961, Corcoran Gallery Art, Washington 1962, Whitney Mus. Am. Art, 1962, 63, 66, 71, San Francisco Mus. Art, 1963, Nat. Gallery Art, Washington, 1963, Los Angeles County Mus., 1964, Venice Biennale, 1964, Brown U., 1965; permanent collections Mus. Modern Art, N.Y.C., Rose Art Mus., Brandeis, Dayton Art Mus., Whitney Mus. Am. Art, N.Y.C., Chase Manhattan Bank, N.Y.C., Time, Inc., N.Y.C., Am. Rep. Ins. Co., Des Moines, Galerie Beyeler, Basel, Hayes Galleries, N.Y.C., also numerous pvt. collections. Ford Found. grantee, summer 1965. Home: 52 Division St New York City NY 10002 Office: 284 E 10th St New York City NY 10009

JENSEN, ARTHUR ROBERT, educator; b. San Diego, Aug. 24, 1923; s. Arthur Alfred and Linda (Schachtmayer) J.; B.A., U. Cal. at Berkeley, 1945; Ph.D., Columbia, 1956; m. Barbara Jane DeLarme, May 6, 1960; 1 dau., Roberta Ann. Asst. med. psychology U. Md., 1955-56; research fellow Inst. Psychiatry, U. London, 1956-58; prof. ednl. psychology U. Cal. at Berkeley, 1958—. Guggenheim fellow, 1964-65; fellow Center Advanced Study Behavioral Scis., 1966-67. Mem. Am. Psychol. Assn., Am. Ednl. Research Assn. (v.p. 1968-70), Psychonomic Soc., A.A.A.S., Sigma Xi. Contbr. profl. jours., books. Home: 30 Canyon View Dr Orinde CA 94563

JENSEN, BRYANT I., corp. exec.; b. Mason City Ia., May 2, 1927; s. I.C. and Norma (Bryant) J.; B.S., U. Ia., 1950, M.A., 1951; m. Lucy Johnson, June 10, 1955; children—Natalie M., Phebe C. Mem. audit staff Arthur Andersen & Co., C.P.A.'s. N.Y.C., 1951-57, audit mgr., 1957-66; controller Bell Intercontinental Corp. and affiliates, 1967—. Served with AUS, 1945-47. C.P.A., 1953. Mem. Am. Inst. C.P.A.'s N.Y., Ia. socs. C.P.A.'s Am. Mgmt. Assn. Home: 2 Peter Cooper Rd New York City NY 10010 Office: 26 Broadway New York City NY 10004

JENSEN, CECIL LEON, cartoonist; b. Ogden, Utah, Jan. 17, 1902; s. Arthur Lorenzo and Lucy Mary (Rose) J.; ed. high sch., Ogden; student Chgo. Acad. Fine Arts; m. Margaret Buchmiller, May 3, 1924; children—Patricia (Mrs. Frank Benson), Barbara (Mrs. Norman Nuckolis); m. 2d, Mary Lou Allegretti, Oct. 10, 1969. Circulation dist. mgr. Ogden Standard-Examiner, 1919; comic artist Bell Syndicate, 1921; cartoonist Salt Lake Telegram, 1922; editorial cartoonist Los Angeles Daily News, 1924-28; cartoonist Chgo. Daily News, 1928—, also editor. Creator of comic strip Little Debbie, syndicated by Des Moines Register and Tribune, 1946. Recipient Sigma Delta Chi award for editorial cartooning, 1952. Home: 1188 Royal Glen Dr Glen Ellyn IL 60137 Office: 401 N Wabash Av Chicago IL 60611

JENSEN, CHARLES J., real estate co. exec.; b. Hackettstown, N.J., 1909; ed. Rider Coll., 1932, Temple U., 1940. Former pres., gen. mgr. Vikon Tile Corp.; now partner real estate operating project, Washington, N.J. Mason. Home: Kinnaman Av Washington NJ 07882.

JENSEN, DE LAMAR, educator, historian; b. Roseworth, Ida., Apr. 22, 1925; s. Jacob A. and Johanna (Petersen) J.; B.A., Brigham Young U., 1952; M.A., Columbia, 1953, Ph.D., 1957; m. Mary White, May 18, 1951; children—Jonna Lu, Marde, Bradford, Emily, Christine. Instr., N.Y.U., 1954-57; mem. faculty Brigham Young U., 1957—, prof. history, 1965—, chmn. dept., 1967—; vis. prof. Tulane U., 1966, Utah State U., 1967. Served with USAAF, 1943-46. Grantee Inst. Internat. Edn., 1956, Nat. Endowment for Humanities, 1970-71; Rockefeller fellow, 1964-65; recipient Karl G. Maeser award, 1970. Mem. Am. Hist. Assn., Renaissance Soc. Am., Am. Soc. Reformation Research, Historians of Early Modern Europe (co-founder, dir.). Author: Machiavelli, 1960; Diplomacy and Dogmatism, 1964; The Expansion of Europe, 1967; also articles. Contbg. editor Found. for Reformation Research Newsletter. Home: 1079 Briar Av Provo UT 84601

JENSEN, DICK LEROY, food co. exec., lawyer; b. Audubon, Ia., Oct. 25, 1930; s. A.B., Bernice (Fancher) J.; LL.B., U. Ia., 1954; m. Nancy Wilson, June 30, 1956; children—Charles F., Sarah R. Admitted to Ia. bar, 1954; practice in Audubon, Ia., 1958-60; gen. counsel, sec. Walnut Grove Products, Co., Atlantic, Ia., 1960-64; legal staff W.R. Grace & Co., Atlantic, 1964-66; gen. counsel, v.p., sec. Spencer Foods, Inc. (Ia.), 1966—, dir., 1968—. Pres. S.W. Ia. Mental Health Inst., 1964-66. Served to lt. USNR, 1955-58. Mem. Sigma Nu. Phi Delta Phi. Republican. Presbyn. Mason. Notes and legis. editor Ia. Law Rev., 1953-54. Home: 916 W 10th St Spencer IA 51301 Office: Spencer Foods Inc Hwy 71 N Spencer IA 51301

JENSEN, DONALD C., food co. exec. Cost clk. Square D Switch Co., 1934-39; cost accountant Evans Products Co., 1939-42; supr. field auditor Ordnance Div., U.S. Army, 1942-44; accounts payable supr. Fruehauf Trailer Co., 1944-48; chief accountant Jervis B. Webb Co., 1948-50; budget accountant Gerber Products Co., 1950-54, asst. to v.p. finance, 1954-60, asst. treas., 1960-70, treas., 1970—. Address: State St Fremont MI 49412*

JENSEN, EDWIN CHRISTIAN, law librarian; b. Waupaca, Wis., Aug. 5, 1903; s. Nels Christian and Petrea (Christiansen) J.; student Wis. State Tchrs. Coll.; LL.B., U. Wis., 1934; m. Dora E. Doolittle, June 6, 1926 (dec. Nov. 1949); 1 son, Wade; m. 2d, Agnes M. Grube, Feb. 21, 1951. Admitted to Wis. bar, 1934; practiced in Sparta, 1934-35; asst. law librarian Wis. Supreme Ct. Library, 1936-57, librarian, 1957-68. Mem. Wis., Dane County bar assns. Home: 4800 Winnequah Rd Madison WI 53716

JENSEN, ELLIS EGBERT, ret. corp. exec.; b. Janesville, Wis., Oct. 27, 1907; s. J.K. and Anna (Nygaard) J.; A.B., St. Olaf Coll., 1928; B.D., Northwestern Theol. Sem., 1931; exchange fellow U. Berlin, 1931-32; Ph.D., U. Chgo., 1937- 39; m. Marion Gottschalk, May 11, 1935; 1 dau., Barbara (Mrs. James Bilderback). Wis. dir. Nat. Conf. Christians and Jews, 1939-41; indsl. relations research dir. Allis-Chalmers Mfg. Co., 1941-45; treas. Janesville Sand & Gravel Co. (Wis.), 1945-54, pres., 1954-66, chmn. bd., 1966-70. Regent, U. Wis., 1955-64; trustee Milton Coll., 1969-70. Mem. Phi Kappa Phi. Home: Webster Rd Temple NH 03084

JENSEN, ELWOOD VERNON, biochemist; b. Fargo, N.D., Jan. 13, 1920; s. Eli A. and Vera (Morris) J.; A.B., Wittenberg U., 1940, D.Sc. (hon.), 1963; Ph.D., U. Chgo., 1944; m. Mary Welmoth Collette, June 17, 1941; children—Karen Collette, Thomas Eli. Faculty, U. Chgo., 1943—, asso. prof. biochemistry Ben May Lab. Cancer Research, 1954-60, prof., 1960-63, Am. Cancer Soc. research prof. physiology, 1963-69, dir. Ben May Lab., 1969—, prof. physiology, 1969—. Vis. prof. Max-Planck-Inst. für Biochemie, Munich, Germany, 1958; cons. Upjohn Co., 1955-65, USPHS, 1956-66, Vitamins, Inc., 1966—. Chmn. endocrinology panel Cancer Chemotherapy Nat. Service Center, 1960-62; mem. chemotherapy rev. bd. Nat. Cancer Inst., 1960-62, bd. sci. counselors, 1969—; adv. bd. Ill. Clin. Chemistry and Blood Bank, 1966-68; mem. oviduct panel Center for Population Research, 1968—; mem. adv. com. pathogenesis of cancer Am. Cancer Soc., 1968-71. Guggenheim fellow, 1946-47. Recipient D.R. Edwards medal, 1970. Mem. Am. Soc. Biol. Chemists, Am. Chem. Soc., Am. Assn. Cancer Research, Endocrine Soc., A.A.A.S., Soc. Study Reprodn. Club: Chicago Literary. Editorial bd. Perspectives in Biology and Medicine, 1966—; editorial adv. bd. Biochemistry, 1969—, Jour. Steroid Biochemistry, 1970—. Contbr. articles to profl. jours. Home: 5650 Dorchester Av Chicago IL 60637

JENSEN, ERIC FINN, lawyer, mfg. co. exec.; b. N.Y.C., Oct. 17, 1927; s. Olaf and Sigrid (Anderson) J.; B.S., Cornell, 1951; LL.B., Bklyn Law Sch., 1956; grad. Advanced Mgmt. Program Harvard, 1968; m. Janet Sterling Clark, Aug. 26, 1950; children—Mari Nelms, Deborah Bowne, Eric David. Admitted to N.Y. bar 1956, since practiced in N.Y.C.; arbitration atty. Bethlehem Steel Corp., 1951-61; mgr. labor relations ACF Industries, Inc., N.Y.C., 1961- 64, dir. indsl. relations, 1964-65, v.p. indsl. relations, 1965—. Chmn. adv. council Cornell Sch. Indsl. and Labor Relations. Served with AUS, 1946-47. Mem. Am. Bar Assn., Indsl. Relations Soc. (dir., past pres.), N.Y. Indsl. Relations Assn., Bklyn. Law Sch. Rev. Assn. Clubs: Cornell (N.Y.C.); Knollwood Country (White Plains). Home: 15 Winslow Rd White Plains NY 10606 Office: 750 3d Av New York City NY 10017

JENSEN, ERLING N., educator; b. Des Moines, Sept. 3, 1908; s. J.L. and Efra (Nielsen) J.; A.B., Drake U., 1932; LL.D., 1969 A.M. (Lydia Roberts fellow 1932-33), Columbia, 1933; Ph.D., Ia. State U., 1947; Litt.D., Lafayette Coll., 1962; LL.D., Lehigh U., 1969, Muhlenberg Coll., 1969; m. Ruth McElhinney, Aug. 9, 1936; children—Richard Erling, Carl Harold, Edward Erik, David Paul. Sci. tchr., high sch. prin., Goldfield, Ia., 1934-35; prof. sci. Grand View Coll., 1935-43; prof. physics, sr. physicist Ia. State U., Ames Lab. of AEC, 1943-61; pres. Muhlenberg Coll., 1961-69, pres. emeritus, 1969—; prof. physics Iowa State U., Ames, 1969—. Mem. Allentown Charter Commn. Study, 1966-67; mem. liason com. from pvt. colls. and univs. to Council of Higher Edn. in Pa., 1967-69. Dir. Indsl. Devel. Corp., Allentown, Pa., 1964-69, Muhlenberg Med. Center, Allentown 1962-69. Dir. Grand View Coll., Grand View Sem., 1949-62, chmn. bd., 1952-62; bd. dirs. United Fund, 1964-69. Councillor, Nat. Lutheran, 1963-66, mem. exec. com.; exec. com. Commn. on Ind. Colls. and Univs. in Pa., 1965-69; del. to the 4th Assembly Lutheran World Fedn., Helsinki, Finland, 1963; chmn. nat. conv. Am. Luth. Ch., 1943-62; del. nat. conv. Luth. Ch. Am., 1964, 66, 68; rep. Luth. Council U.S.A., 1966-70, mem. exec. com., 1969-70; mem. steering com. Council on Mission, Luth. Ch. in Am. Colls., 1968-69. Recipient Alumni Distinguished Service award Drake U., 1965, Double D award for letter winners Drake U., 1968, Distinguished Service award Allentown-Lehigh County C. of C., 1969. Fellow Am. Phys. Soc.; mem. Am. Assn. Physics Tchrs., Allentown-Lehigh County C. of C. (gov. 1965-68), Am. Fedn. Scientists, Phi Beta Kappa, Sigma Xi, Kappa Phi Kappa, Phi Kappa Phi, Pi Mu Epsilon. Sr. author: College Physics Lab. Manual. Home: 2522 Pierce St Ames IA 50010

JENSEN, FREDERICK RICHARD, educator; b. Yerington, Nev., Dec. 8, 1925; s. John Arendt, Jr., and Wilhemina (Springmeyer) J.; B.S., U. Nev., 1951, M.S., 1952; Ph.D., Purdue U., 1955; m. Patricia Ann Powell, Oct. 2, 1948 (dec.); children—Rick Edmund, Rory Daniel, Rebecca Ann. From instr. to prof. chemistry U. Cal. at Berkeley, 1955—; chem. cons. organic chemistry, organometallic chemistry, free radical chemistry. Served with USNR, 1944-45. Guggenheim fellow, 1968-69. Mem. Am. Chem. Soc., Cooper Ornithol. Soc., Am. Rifle Assn. (life), Phi Beta Kappa, Sigma Xi, Phi Lambda Upsilon. Author: (with Bruce Rickborn) Electrophilic Substitution of Organomercurials, 1968. Contbr. articles profl. jours. Patentee on preparation of aziridines. Home: 25 Camino del Diablo Orinda CA 94563 Office: Univ California Berkeley CA 94720

JENSEN, GEORGE AARON, banker; b. New Haven, May 17, 1934; s. Joseph John and Mary Florence (Conniff) J.; B.A., Yale, 1957; m. Cynthia Lee Michaels, Sept. 23, 1961; children—Kristin, Karin, Erik. With Colonial Bank & Trust Co., Waterbury, Conn., 1962—, asst. trust officer, 1962-66, v.p. trust, 1966-68, v.p., sr. trust officer, asst. head, trust, 1968-69, sr. v.p., head, trust group, 1969, sr. v.p., treas., head, corporate banking, 1970—. Bd. dirs. Family Service Assn. Waterbury, 1968—, Mattatuck Hist. Soc., 1966—, Cheshire Community Theater, 1967—, Am. Field Service, 1971—; trustee Williams Sch. Banking, 1971—. Mem. Am. Inst. Banking, Conn. Bankers Assn. Episcopalian (vestryman, chmn. stewardship). Home: 195 Wildwood Dr Cheshire CT 06410 Office: 81 W Main St Waterbury CT 06720

JENSEN, GEORGE ALBERT, lawyer; b. St. Louis, June 27, 1929; s. Albert P. and Mary E. (Baker) J.; A.B., Washington U., 1952, J.D., 1954; m. Martha Jean Collins, Sept. 10, 1949; children-Nancy, Georgia, Peter. Admitted to Mo. bar, 1954, since practiced in St. Louis; mem. Peper, Martin, Jensen, Maichel & Hetlage and predecessor firms, 1954—, partner, 1958—. Dir., gen. counsel Mound City Trust Co., Valley Bank of Florissant; dir., mem. exec. com. Nat. Aviation Underwriters, Inc., Nat. Gen. Ins. Co.; dir. A.G. Edwards & Sons, Inc. Pres., bd. dirs. Urban League St. Louis. Served with U.S. Army, 1946-48. Mem. Mo. Bar (chmn. corp. law and bus. orgns. com.), Bar Assn. Met. St. Louis (chmn. securities law com.) Am. Bar Assn., Order of Coif, Phi Beta Kappa, Phi Delta Phi. Conglist. (deacon, trustee, moderator). Clubs: Noonday, University (St. Louis). Contbr. articles profl. jours. Home: 6326 Pershing St St Louis MO 63130 Office: 407 N 8th St St Louis MO 63101

JENSEN, GLENN S., educator; B.A., Yankton Coll., 1936; M.A., U. S.D., 1947; D.Ed., U. Colo., 1951. Now prof. adult edn., head dept. adult edn. and instrnl. services U. Wyo. Pres. Adult Edn. Assn. U.S., 1969. Address: care Univ Wyoming Laramie WY 80270*

JENSEN, HARRY ARTHUR, mfg. co. exec.; b. Council Bluffs, Ia., July 17, 1918; s. Arthur J. and Bess (Crowl) J.; A.B., Grinnell Coll., 1940; m. Lydia Cole, July 30, 1941; children—Stephen, Kristie, Eric. With Armstrong Cork Co., Lancaster, Pa., 1940—, successively floor div. sales tng., salesman, Dallas, resident salesman floor div., Omaha, salesman floor div., Chgo., asst. dist. mgr., dist. mgr., Lancaster, marketing mgr., 1940-61, gen. sales mgr. floor div., 1961-62, v.p., gen. mgr. floor and indsl. operations, 1962-69, exec. v.p., 1968—, also dir. Served as lt. (j.g.) USNR, 1943-46. Mem. Lancaster C. of C. (dir.). Republican. Presbyn. Clubs: Lancaster Country, Hamilton (Lancaster). Home: 1524 Quarry Lane Lancaster PA 17603 Office: Armstrong Cork Co Lancaster PA 17604

JENSEN, HENRY EDWARD, indsl. battery co. exec.; b. Phila., Oct. 6, 1912; s. Aksel Leonard and Hilda (Andersen) J.; E.E., Drexel Inst. Tech., 1936; m. Ruth Naomi Friel, Sept. 4, 1937; children—Nils Henry, Barbara L. (Mrs. John Broadbent, Jr.), Paul Edward. Lab. supr. Philco Corp., 1936-42; supr. spl. projects Bur. Ships, Navy Dept., 1942-50; v.p. engring. C & D Batteries Inc., Conshohocken, Pa., 1950-59, also dir.; v.p. C & D batteries div. ELTRA Corp., 1959—. Mem. I.E.E.E. Author, patentee in field. Home: 4126 Presidential Dr Lafayette Hill PA 19444 Office: C & D Batteries Div ELTRA Corp Conshohocken PA 19428

JENSEN, HOWARD FRANCIS, steel co. exec.; b. Breckenridge, Tex., Oct. 31, 1921; s. Soren C. and Eula Nora (Shepherd) J.; student A. and M. Coll. Tex., 1938-40; LL.B. U. Tex., 1943; m. Marjorie Elizabeth Harris, June 28, 1942; children—Gregory Eric, Margaret Elizabeth, David Alan. Admitted to Tex. bar, 1943; law clk. Supreme Ct. of Tex., 1943-44; partner Burford, Ryburn & Ford, Dallas, 1945-59; v.p., gen. counsel, sec. Lone Star Steel Co., Dallas, 1960—. Employer, adviser U.S. delegation Internat. Labor Conf., 1966-67. Mem. park bd., Dallas, 1956-59. Mem. Am., Dallas bar assns., State Bar Tex., Am. Judicature Soc. Methodist. Clubs: Dallas Athletic, Chaparral, Lancers, (Dallas); Headliners (Austin). Home: 1021 Forest Grove Dallas TX 75218 Office: P O Box 12226 Dallas TX 75225

JENSEN, IVAN RAYMOND, educator; b. Mpls., May 28, 1920; s. Jacob and Elvera (Anderson) J.; B.S. in Civil Engring., U. Minn., 1942, M.S., 1946; m. Mildred Blanche Skiba, Jan. 1, 1944; children—Ronald Ivan, Roger Alan, Russell Lee, Rodney David. Jr. constrn. engr. E.I. DuPont de Nemours & Co., St. Paul, 1942; structural engr. Consol. Vultee Aircraft Corp., Fort Worth, Tex., 1943-46; teaching asst. U. Minn., Mpls., 1946; instr. civil engring. Ia. State U., Ames, 1946-47; asso. prof. U. N.D., Grand Forks, 1947-52, prof., head dept., 1952—; pres., owner Western Testing Lab., Grand Forks, 1950—; dir. Nat. Ins. Co. Am., Minot, N.D.; pvt. practice consulting structural engring., 1948—. Bd. dirs. N.D. Hwy. Research Bd., 1963—, N.D. Profl. Adv. Service, Office Civil Def., 1970—, Salvation Army, Grand Forks, 1963—. Registered profl. engr., Minn., N.D. Mem. Am. Soc. C.E., Am. Soc. E.E., Nat., N.D. socs. profl. engrs., Am. Concrete Inst., Sigma Tau, Lutheran. Lion, Elk. Author: Problems in Airplane Structures, 1948. Home: 3600 Belmont Rd Grand Forks ND 58201

JENSEN, J. HANS D., physicist; b. Hamburg, Germany, 1907. Staff, U. Hamburg, 1937-41, Inst. Tech., Hanover, 1941-49; prof. theoretical physics Heidelberg U., 1949- -; with Maria Goeppert-Mayer, developed theory on nuclear shell structure. Recipient Nobel prize for physics, 1963. Mem. German Acad. Sci. (Heidelberg), Max Planck Inst. Editor: (with Otto Haxel) Zeitschrift für Physik, 1955—. Address: Heidelberg U Philosophenweg 16 Heidelberg Germany

JENSEN, JAMES HERBERT, agriculturist; b. Madison, Neb., June 16, 1906; s. Jens and Eda (Hansen) J.; B.Sc., U. Neb., 1928, A.M., 1930; postgrad. Columbia, 1931-32; Ph.D., U. of Wis. 1935; D.Sc., N.C. State U. Raleigh, 1966, LL.D., U. Neb., 1966; m. Lucille Christopher, Nov. 2, 1931; children—James Michael, Karen (Mrs. J.A. Bailey), Stephen, Roger. Asst. pathologist Tropical Plant Research Found., Baragua, Cuba, 1930-31; plant pathologist P.R. Agrl. Expt. Sta., 1935-37; asst. prof. plant pathology U. Neb., 1937-45; plant pathologist, N.C. Agrl. Expt. Sta., 1945-48; chief biology br., div. biology and medicine, A.E.C., Washington, 1948-49; chmn. sub-com. Nat. Com. Radiation Protection, 1949-57; prof. and head plant pathology, faculty N.C. State Coll. A. and E., 1949-53, Reynolds prof., 1951-53; provost, and prof. botany Ia. State U., 1953-61; president Oregon State U., Corvallis, 1961-69, prof. botany and plant pathology on leave, 1969—; agr. project leader Rockefeller Found., Bangkok, Thailand, 1969—; acting vice rector planning and devel. Kasetsart U. Mem. exec. com. Assn. State Univs. and Land-Grant Colls., 1962-64, pres., 1966-67, chmn., 1967-68; mem. Nat. Commn. on Accrediting, 1964-69; agrl. research planning com. U.S. Dept. Agr., 1964-66; chmn. pesticides resideus com. Nat. Acad. of Sci., 1964-65, chmn. persistent pesticides com., 1967- 68; pres. Associated Midwest Univs., 1958-59, dir., 1959-65; mem. research adv. com. Boyce Thompson Inst., 1960-69; mem. policy adv. bd. Argonne Nat. Lab., 1961-67. Fellow A.A.A.S., Am. Phytopathol. Soc. (pres. 1954- 55); mem. Sigma Xi, Phi Kappa Phi. Club: Cosmos. Author: Refugee Settlement in the Dominican Republic, 1942; also articles on plant viruses and diseases of tropical plants, profl. publs. Home: GPO Box 2453 Bangkok Thailand ☆

JENSEN, JAMES ROBERT, educator, dentist; b. Mpls., Mar. 17, 1922; s. Ernest William and Edith Ann (Norstedt) J.; B.A., U. Minn., 1944, D.D.S., 1946, M.S., 1950; m. Alvern Halverson, Mar. 24, 1945; children—Thomas, Mark, James, Elizabeth. Teaching asst. U. Minn., 1948-50, asst. prof., 1950-53, asso. prof., 1953-57, prof., chmn. dept. endodontics, 1957-69, asst. dean acad. affairs, prof., chmn. dept., 1969—; part time practice specializing endodontics; cons. operative dentistry VA Hosps., St. Cloud, Minn. and Mpls.; team leader operative dentistry and endodontics Project Vietnam of AID; cons. dental health WHO and Pan Am. Health Orgn.; mem. staff Hennepin County Gen. Hosp., Univ. Hosp. of U. Minn. Served as capt. Dental Corps, AUS, 1946-48; res. dental surgeon USPHS. Diplomate Am. Bd. Endodontists. Fellow Am. Coll. Dentists; mem. Am., Minn. dental assns., Mpls. Dist. Dental Soc., Internat. Assn. Dental Research, Dental Materials Group, Internat. Assn. Dental Research, Minn. Acad. Restorative Dentistry, Assn. Res. Officers and Res. Dental Surgeons, Am. Assn. Endodontists, Fedn. Dentaire Internationale, Am. Pub. Health Assn., Am. Assn. Dental Schs. Contbr. articles profl. jours. Home: 2167 N Rosewood Lane St Paul MN 55113 Office: Owre Hall Univ Minnesota Minneapolis MN 55455

JENSEN, JAY WALBOURNE, educator; b. Sheffield, Ill., June 13, 1917; s. Theodore Carl and Gertrude (Walbourne) J.; student U. Wis., 1938; A.B., Emory U., 1948; M.S., Ph.D., U. Ill., 1957; m. Jessie Eleanor Neale, Feb. 19, 1943; children—Jan Neale, Julie Anne. Reporter, editor Sheffield (Ill.) Times, 1936-39; news editor Woodland (Cal.) Record, 1939; asso. editor Flodin Pub. Co., 1940; publicist Conron Assos., 1940-41; promotional rep. Macmillan Pub. Co., 1949-50; now head dept. journalism Coll. Communications, U. Ill. Cons., Dept. Def., 1951; staff cons. Nat. Com. on Violence, 1970. Served as maj. M.I., AUS, 1942-46, staff officer Inf. Div., 1942-45; writer, editor Gen. Hdqrs. Armed Forces Pacific, 1945, now maj. res., ret. Ford Found. fellow, 1953-54. Mem. Am. Assn. U. Profs., Am. Civil Liberties Union, Assn. for Edn. Journalism, Am. Hist. Assn., Am. Polit. Sci. Assn., Am. Sociol. Assn., Nat. Conf. Editorial Writers, Phi Beta Kappa, Phi Kappa Phi, Sigma Delta Chi, Delta Tau Delta, Kappa Tau Alpha. Author: Mass Media and Modern Society. Contbr. articles profl. jours. Home: 2027 Burlison Dr Urbana IL 61801

JENSEN, JOHANNES EMIL NODAGER, govt. ofcl.; b. Fredsville, Ia., Apr. 14, 1913; s. Rasmus M.J. and Marie (Nielsen) J.; B.S., U. Mich., 1935; postgrad. Wayne State U., 1956-57; m. Helene B. Kipf, June 29, 1940; children-Shirley (Mrs. Charles E. Bauer), Janet (Mrs. Victor Henrich), Eric Walter. Designer, Mich. State Hwy. Dept., Lansing, 1935-39; project supt. Austin Co., Detroit, 1939- 41; pres. Wm. Esslinger Co., Detroit, 1946-52; partner Prince & Jensen, contractors, Detroit, 1952-57; asso. partner Eero Saarinen & Assos., architects, Detroit, 1957-63; asso. dir. Nat. Park Service, Washington, 1963—. Served to lt. USNR, 1943-46. Decorated Bronze Star Medal; recipient Meritorious Service award for pub. service Dept. Interior, 1969. Mem. Am. Soc. C.E., Nat. Soc. Profl. Engrs. Home: 7705 Elba Rd Alexandria VA 22306 Office: Interior Bldg Washington DC 20240

JENSEN, JOHN GRANVILLE, educator; b. Portland, Ore., Dec. 18, 1911; s. Jens Gundersen and Lucy (Parsons) J.; B.S., Western Wash. Coll.; M.A., Clark U., 1942, Ph.D., 1946; m. Eva Phyllis Watson, Nov. 10, 1934 (dec. 1968); children—Robert, Barbara Louise (Mrs. Gary F. Jones). Faculty, Ore. State U., 1946—, prof. geography, 1947—, chmn. dept. natural resources, 1951-64. Adviser resources devel. Nat. Park Service; cons. map editor Denoyer Geppert Co., Chgo.; del. Internat. Geog. Union Congress, India, 1968. Mem. Pacific Coast Council Latin Am. Studies (sec.-treas.), Assn. Am. Geographers, Nat. Council Geog. Edn., Ore. Acad. Sci., A.A.A.S. Methodist. Co-author: Geography of Commodity Production, 1958; Case Studies in World Geography, 1961; Conservation in the United States, 1962, rev. edit., 1969. Contbr. World Political Geography, 1957, Atlas of the Pacific Northwest, 3d edit., 1962. Grolier Ency. Home: 1131 SW Sunset Dr Corvallis OR 97330

JENSEN, LEONA SCHROEDER, mem. Republican Nat. Com.; b. Huron, S.D., Dec. 31, 1919; d. William Frederick and Ella Sophia (Vetterman) Schroeder; grad. Huron Bus. Coll., 1940; m. William Robert Jensen, Sept. 21, 1947; 1 dau., Barbara J. (Mrs. J.B. Ahrens). Republican precinct committeewoman, Cheyenne, Wyo., 1947-52; vice chmn. Laramie County (Wyo.) Rep. Com., 1951-54; mem. Wyo. Rep. Com., 1954-57, vice chairwoman, 1957-60; mem. Rep. Nat. Com. for Wyo., 1960-68; sec. Rep. Western Conf., 1963-64. Past chmn. finance, area dir. Wyo. Girl Scouts; pres. Cheyenne Little Theatre, 1962-64; treas. Jaskson Hole Art Assn., 1970-71. Home: Box 30 Teton Village Jackson Hole WY 83025

JENSEN, LLOYD THORVALD, sugar co. exec.; b. Longmont, Colo., May 26, 1910; s. William and Marie Martha (Iverson) J.; B.S. in Chem. Engring., U. Colo., 1932; m. Cleo Bea Simmons, Oct. 24, 1932; children—William C., Kirstin Lou (Mrs. Edward O'Keefe), Phillip Gary. Chemist Great Western Sugar Co., Dnever, 1932-35, foreman, 1936-41, supt., dist. supt., 1942-57, v.p. operations, 1957, now pres., dir.; chemist Amalgamated Sugar Co., 1935-36; with Smith Hinchman & Grylls, Architects and Engrs., 1941-42; became gen. supt. No. Ohio Sugar Co., 1957, then sr. v.p. operations, now pres., dir.; pres. Big Horn Limestone Co., Warren, Mont., 1957-; dir. subsidiary Great Western Ry. Co. Mem. Nat. Tech. Task Com. on Indsl. Wastes. Bd. dirs. Beet Sugar Devel. found. Mem. Sugar Industry Technicians, Am. Soc. Sugar Beet Technologists, Denver C. of C., Alpha Chi Sigma, Kappa Sigma. Presbyn. Mason. Club: Valley Country. Home: 3974 S Ivy Way Denver CO 80220 Office: 1530 16th St Denver CO 80217

JENSEN, MERRILL MONROE, educator, historian; b. Elkhorn, Ia., July 16, 1905; s. John Martin and Julia (Seymour) J.; B.A., U. Wash., 1929, M.A., 1931; Ph.D., U. Wis., 1934; m. Genevieve Margaret Privet, Dec. 24, 1929; 1 dau., Julanne (Mrs. David G. Pease). From instr. to asso. prof. history U. Wash., 1935-44; mem. faculty U. Wis., 1944—, prof. history, 1946—, Vilas Research prof. of history, 1964—, chmn. dept., 1961-64; Harmsworth prof. history U. Oxford (Eng.), 1949-50; vis. prof. U. Tokyo (Japan), 1955, U. Ghent (Belgium), 1960; historian USAAF, 1944. Mem. Am. Hist. Assn., Orgn. of Am. Historians (pres. 1969-70), Mass. Hist. Soc. (corr.), Brit. Am. Studies Assn. Author: The Articles of Confederation, 3d edit., 1959; The New Nation: A History of the U.S. During the Confederation, 1950; American Colonial Documents to 1776, 1955; The Making of the American Constitution, 1964; Tracts of the American Revolution, 1967; The Founding of a Nation; A History of the American Revolution 1763-1776, 1968. Editor: Regionalism in America, 1951; Pacific Northwest Quar., 1935-42. Home: 2810 Ridge Rd Madison WI 53705

JENSEN, OLIVER ORMEROD, editor, writer; b. Ithaca, N.Y., Apr. 16, 1914; s. Gerard E. and Dorothea H. (Ormerod) J.; grad. Phillips Andover Acad., 1932; B.A., Yale, 1936; m. Mrs. Alison Pfeiffer Hargrove, Feb. 21, 1970; stepchildren—Christopher, Stephen, Penelope. With J. Walter Thompson Co., 1937-38; asst. mng. editor Judge mag., 1938-39; with Benton & Bowles, 1939-40; writer Life mag., 1940-50, articles editor, mem. bd. editors, 1946-50; a founder Thorndike, Jensen & Parton, Inc., publishers, 1950, v.p. 1950- 57; a founder Am. Heritage mag., 1954, managing editor, 1954- 59, editor, 1959—; editorial bd. Horizon Magazine, 1958—; v.p., dir. Am. Heritage Pub. Co.; pres. Conn. Valley R.R. Co., Essex, Conn., 1971—. Mem. Andover Alumni Council, 1962-65. Trustee Empire State Ry. Mus. Served from ensign to lt. USNR, 1942-45. Recipient James Gordon Bennett prize Yale, 1936. Mem. Am. Scenic and Historic Preservation Soc. (trustee), Am. Assn. State and Local History (mem. council), Soc. Am. Historians, Phi Beta Kappa. Episcopalian. Clubs: Grolier, Yale, P.E.N., Century (N.Y.C.). Author: Carrier War, 1945; The Revolt of American Women, 1952, reissued, 1971; America and Russia, 1962. Co-author: American Album, 1968. Address: care Am Heritage 551 Fifth Av New York City NY 10017

JENSEN, ROBERT ARTHUR, lawyer; b. Cin., Mar. 24, 1934; s. Carroll Miller and Phyllis (Walters) J.; B.A., Oberlin Coll., 1956; J.D., U. Chgo., 1962; m. Helen Porter Bishop, Apr. 6, 1957; children—Anne, Sara. Admitted to Minn. bar, 1962, Ariz. bar, 1966; asso. firm Dorsey, Owen, Marquart, Windhorst & West, Mpls., 1962-65; practice in Phoenix, 1965—; partner firm Moeller, Hover, Jensen & Henry, 1970—. Bd. dirs. Phoenix Family Service. Served with USAF, 1956-59. Home: 902 W Royal Palm Rd Phoenix AZ 85021 Office: 234 N Central Av Phoenix AZ 85004

JENSEN, ROBERT EUGENE, educator; B.S., U. Denver, 1960, M.B.A., 1961; Ph.D., Stanford, 1966. Now Nicholas M. Salgo prof. business adminstrn. U. Me. Address: care Dept Business Adminstrn U Maine Orono ME 04473*

JENSEN, ROBERT TRYGVE, lawyer; b. Chgo., Sept. 16, 1922; s. James T. and Else (Uhlich) J.; student U. N.C., 1943; LL.B., Northwestern U., 1949, B.S., 1949; LL.M., U. So. Cal., 1955; m. Marjorie Rae Montgomery, Oct. 3, 1959; children—Robert Trygve, James Thomas, John Michael. Admitted to Cal. bar, 1950; asst. counsel Douglas Aircraft Co., Inc., 1950-52, 58-60, counsel El Segundo div., 1952-58; gen. counsel Aerospace Corp., El Segundo, 1960—, asst. sec., 1961-67, sec., 1967—. Served with AUS, 1942-46; PTO. Mem. Am., Beverly Hills bar assns., Am. Arbitration Assn. (nat. panel arbitrator), Am. Soc. Internat. Law, Alpha Delta Phi, Phi Delta Phi. Home: 1865 Marcheeta Pl Los Angeles CA 90069 Office: 2350 E El Segundo Blvd El Segundo CA 90245

JENSEN, RUE L., univ. adminstr.; b. Vermillion, Utah, Oct. 24, 1911; s. James Louis and Ella (Casto) J.; B.S., Utah State U., 1937, M.S., 1939; D.V.M., Colo. State U., 1942; Ph.D., U. Minn., 1953; V.Sc.D. (hon.), Kasetsart U., Thailand, 1965; m. Millie Domgaard, May 19, 1942; children—Louis, Mary Ann. Instr., La. State U., 1942-43; mem. faculty Colo. State U., 1943—, successively asst. prof. pathology Coll. Vet. Medicine, asst. pathologist Expt. Sta., 1943-48, prof. pathology, also pathologist, 1948- -, dean Coll. Vet. Medicine, chief animal disease sect. Expt. Sta., 1957- 66, dir. Exptl. Sta., 1966-69, v.p. for research, 1966—. Mem. delegation vet. sci. from U.S. Dept. Agr. to USSR, 1958; cons. Dept. Agr., A.I.D. at U. Tehran, 1962, at Kasetsart U., Thailand, 1964. Active Boy Scouts Am. Pres., Colo. State U. Research Found., 1955. Ralston Research fellow, 1950. Diplomate Am. Coll. Vet. Pathologists. Fellow A.A.A.S.; mem. Internat. Acad. Pathologists, Am. Vet. Med. Assn., Sigma Xi, Phi Kappa Phi. Home: 1712 W Vine Dr Fort Collins CO 80521

JENSEN, VERNON HORTIN, educator; b. Salt Lake City, July 10, 1907; s. Joseph E. and Grace E. (Hortin) J.; student U. Utah, 1926-27; B.S. Brigham Young U., 1933; Ph.D., U. Cal. at Berkeley, 1939; m. Esther Chapman, June 3, 1931; children—Karen (Mrs. Melvin G. Harvey), Vernon H., Margaret (Mrs. Manning Gasch, Jr.), Linda (Mrs. Kenneth Hamlet). Mem. faculty dept. econs. U. Colo., 1937-46; faculty Cornell U., 1946—, now prof. indsl. and labor relations N.Y. State Sch. Indsl. and Labor Relations, asso. dean, 1965-71; Montague Burton prof. indsl. relations U. Leeds, Eng., 1959-60; Guggenheim fellow, 1959-60. Cons., Nat. Def. Mediation Bd., summer 1941; arbitrator, panel mem. Nat. War Labor Bd., 1942; wage stblzn. dir., regional pub. mem. WBS, 1942-44; mem. Presdl. R.R. Marine Workers Commn., 1962; chmn. adv. council Employer, Union Improper Practice Act, N.Y. Mem. Am. Econ. Assn., Indsl. Relations Research Assn., Nat. Acad. Arbitrators. Mem. Ch. of Jesus Christ of Latter-Day Saints. Author: Lumber and Labor, 1945; Heritage of Conflict-Labor Relations in the Nonferrous Metals Industry Up to 1930, 1950; Hiring of Dock Workers in the Ports of New York, Liverpool, London and Marseilles, 1964; others. Home: 326 Fall Creek Dr Ithaca NY 14850

JENSEN, WALTER AUGUST, retired army officer, investment co. exec.; b. Boston, Nov. 7, 1910; s. August Christian and Nellie (Hansen) J.; student Oahu Coll., 1925-27; B.S., U.S. Mil. Acad., 1933; grad. Command and Gen. Staff Coll., 1944, Nat. War Coll., 1954; m. Charlotte Genevieve Lysaker, Sept. 14, 1947; children—Karen Jean, Kristine Ann. Commd. 2d lt. U.S. Army, 1933, advanced through grades to maj. gen., 1963; comdr. 20th Armored group, Leyte and Okinawa, 1944-45; dep. chief staff U.S. Army Group, Greece, 1948-50; comdg. gen. Ft. Irwin, Cal., 1956-58; dep. chief staff 8th Army, Korea, 1958-59; asst. comdt. U.S. Armor Sch., Ft. Knox, Ky., 1959- 61; chief staff 4th U.S. Army, Ft. Sam Houston, Tex., 1961-63; comdr. XI U.S. Army Corps, St. Louis, 1963-64, XIV U.S. Army Corps, Mpls., 1964- 66, ret., 1967; armed forces sales service mgr. Investors Diversified Services, Mpls., 1967—; v.p. IDS Oil Programs, Inc., 1970—. Vice chmn. Mpls. area chpt. A.R.C. Decorated D.S.M., Legion of Merit, Bronze Star; Distinguished Service medal (Greece); Order Mil. Merit Ulchi (Korea). Mem. Assn. U.S. Army (vice chmn. bd. Twin Cities chpt.), Ret. Officers Assn., Pearl Harbor Survivors Assn. (life), West Point Soc., Res. Officers Assn., Army Athletic Assn., U.S. Army Armor Assn. Clubs: Minnetonka Racquet; Bath and Tennis (St. Louis); University (Mpls.). Home: 16115 5th Av N Wayzata MN 55391 Office: Investors Diversified Services 8th and Marquette Minneapolis MN 55402

JENSEN, WILLIAM AUGUST, botanist, educator; b. Chgo., Aug. 22, 1927; s. William McKinley and Gertrude (Hild) J.; Ph.B., U. Chgo., 1948, M.S., 1950, Ph.D., 1953; m. Joan Nancy Sell, June 20, 1948; children—Scott William, Christina Cathrine. NIH fellow Carlsberg Lab., Copenhagen, Denmark, 1952-53, Cal. Inst. Tech., Pasadena, Cal., 1953-55; NSF fellow U. Brussels (Belgium), 1955-56; asst. prof. dept. biology U. Va., Charlottesville, 1956-57; faculty dept. botany U. Cal. at Berkeley, 1957—, prof., 1963—, chmn. dept. botany, 1971—, asso. dean Coll. Letters and Sci., 1963-66. Recipient Distinguished Teaching award U. Cal. at Berkeley, 1960, N.Y. Bot. Garden award for bot. research, 1964. Mem. Soc. for Study Devel. and Growth (past sec.), Bot. Soc. Am. (program dir. 1963-67), A.A.A.S., Am. Inst. Biol. Scis., Am. Soc. Plant Physiologists, Soc. for Developmental Biology, Am. Soc. Cell Biology, Histochem. Soc. Author: Botanical Histochemistry, 1962; The Plant Cell, 1964, 71; (with R. Park) Cell Utrastructure, 1967; (with F. Salisbury) Botany, 1972. Contbr. articles to profl. jours. Devel. bot. histochem. procedures and application of these procedures to problems of early cell devel. in plants especially root tips and embryos; research on distbn. nucleic acids in plant tissues especially embryos, cell wall devel. Home: 280 Los Altos Dr Kensington CA 94708

JENSIK, ROBERT JOSEPH, surgeon; b. Chgo., Sept. 15, 1915; s. William Paul and Marie (Eck) J.; student Morton Jr., Coll., 1932-34; B.S., U. Ill., 1936, M.S., 1938, M.D., 1939; m. Florence M. Hassebrook, Oct. 25, 1941; children—Stephen Carl, Robert Ross. Intern, Milw. Gen. Hosp., 1938-39; resident, fellow surgery, pathology, tb U. Ill., 1939-43, clin. prof. surgery, 1965—; practice medicine, specializing in thoracic surgery, Chgo., 1944—; mem. staff Rockford (Ill.) Sanitarium, 1941-42, St. Joseph's Hosp., Chgo.,

1948—; attending surgeon Presbyn-St. Luke's Hosp., 1957—; cons. thoracic surgeon Sunny Hill Sanatorium, Joliet, Ill., West Side VA Hosp., Chgo. Bd. dirs. Tb. Inst. Chgo. and Cook County. Mem. Sigma Xi, Alpha Omega Alpha, Phi Chi. Club: Medinah (Ill.) Country. Home: 9 Royal Vale Dr Oak Brook IL 60521 Office: 1725 W Harrison St Chicago IL 60612

JENSON, LLOYD G., physician. Adminstr. Hastings Regional Center, Ingleside, Neb. Office: Hastings Regional Center Ingleside NB 68953*

JENSON, PAUL GERHARD, coll. dean; b. Milan, Minn., June 27, 1925; s. Canute T. and Emma (Rohne) J.; B.A., Luther Coll., 1948; M.A., U. Minn., 1951, Ph.D., 1955; m. Elizabeth Ann Dybdal, Aug. 24, 1947; children—Thomas Dybdal, John Jacob, Paula Gay, Brian Dean, Richard Asle. Research asst., teaching asst., jr. student personnel worker U. Minn., 1950-53, research asso. Bur. Instl. Research, 1961-62; instr., prof., chmn. dept. psychology Macalester Coll., St. Paul, 1953-64; asso. leadership tng. project N. Central Assn. Colls. and Secondary Schs., 1957-58, cons., examiner, 1958—, coordinator, dir., dir. workshops in higher edn. com. liberal arts edn., 1959-64; v.p. acad. affairs Temple Buell Coll., Denver, 1964-71; dean faculty, prof. psychology Colby Coll., Waterville, Me., 1971—. Served with USAAF, 1943-46. Research grantee U.S. Office Edn., 1964. Mem. Am. Psychol. Assn., A.A.A.S., Am. Civil Liberties Union, Am. Assn. U. Profs. Home: Washington St Waterville ME 04901

JENSON, THEODORE JOEL, educator; b. New Richmond, Wis., Oct. 9, 1905; s. John Gabriel and Tilla (Johnson) J.; diploma Wis. State Coll., River Falls, 1926; Ph.B., U. Chgo., 1928; M.S., U. Wis., 1930, Ph.D., 1952; m. Gertrude Beatrice Eberdt, June 7, 1930; children—Jon Eberdt, Karen Ann (Mrs. Daniel M. Voecks). Student sec. YMCA, 1928-30; supervising prin. schs., Wis., 1930-34; supt. schs., Delavan, Wis., 1934-40, Fond du Lac, 1940-46, Shorewood, Wis., 1946-57; instr. Wis. State Coll., Milw., summers 1953- 54; cons., adviser Internat. Edn. Service, Hesse, Germany, 1594; lectr. U. Wis., 1954, instr., summer 1955; prof. edn. Ohio State U., 1957-62, chmn. dept., 1962-65; prof., dean Coll. Edn. Bowling Green State U., 1965—, also dir. Anderson Center for Personal Devel.; prof. U. So. Cal., summer 1961. Del. White House Conf. on Edn. Active Boy Scouts Am. Mem. Am. Assn. Sch. Adminstrs., Am. Ednl. Research Assn., N.E.A., Nat. Soc. Study Edn., Ohio Sch. Adminstrs., Wis. Sch. Adminstrs. (past pres.), Classroom Tchrs. Assn., Nat. Conf. Christians and Jews, Ohio, Wis. edn. assns., Am. Acad. Polit. and Social Sci., Columbus Schoolmasters Club, Ohio Council Advancement Ednl. Adminstrn. (chmn.), Kappa Delta Pi, Phi Kappa Phi, Phi Delta Kappa. Rotarian. Club: Conservation (Fond du Lac, Wis.). Co-author: Educational Administration: The Secondary School, 1961; Elementary School Administration, 1963; Practice and Theory in Educational Administration, 1963; also articles. Home: 1024 Lyn Rd Bowling Green OH 43402

JENZANO, ANTHONY FRANCIS, planetarium dir.; b. Phila., May 20, 1919; s. Joseph and Theresa (Monzo) J.; grad. Marine Elec. Sch., Phila., 1942, USN Gun Fire Control Sch., 1943, USN Advanced Gun Fire Control Sch., 1943; student, Capitol Radio Engring. Inst., 1948-51; m. Myrtle E. Packer, Nov. 12, 1941; children—Anthony Francis, Carol. Head technician Fels Planetarium, Phila., 1946-49; chief technician Morehead Planetarium, U. N.C., 1949-51, mgr. planetarium, art galleries and sci. exhibit areas, 1951-60, planetarium dir., 1960—; engaged in complete dismantlement and reassembly Fels Zeiss Planetarium instrument, 1948, Morehead Zeiss Planetarium instrument, 1949, Model VI, 1969. U.S. adviser to architect and contractors for London (Eng.) Planetarium, 1956-57; cons. Buhl Planetarium console, 1957, Atlanta Planetarium, 1968. Dir. Celestial Tng. Program for U.S. Mercury and Gemini, also Apollo Astronauts, 1960—; state dir. N.C. Sci. Fairs, 1961-63. Instnl. rep. Boy Scouts Am. Served with USNR, 1943-45. Mem. Am. Assn. Museums, U.S. Maj. Planetarium Ofcls. Group, N.C. Acad. Scis., Am. Astron. Soc. (asso.). Home: 37 Oakwood Dr Chapel Hill NC 27514 Office: Morehead Planetarium Chapel Hill NC 27514

JEPPESEN, CHARLES RULON, educator; b. Logan, Utah, July 22, 1902; s. Charles R. and Matilda (Jensen) J.; B.A., Brigham Young U., 1928; M.A., U. Cal. at Berkeley, 1930, Ph.D., 1932; Johnston scholar Johns Hopkins U., 1935-36; m. Thelma Hoover, June 25, 1942; children—C. Rulon, Alva Sylvia. Instr. physics U. Cal. at Berkeley, 1932-34, 36-39; lectr. U. B.C., 1939-40; instr. Mont. State U., 1940-41, asso. prof. physics, 1943-46, prof., 1946—, chmn. dept., 1954—; asst. physicist Western Regional Research Lab., Bur. Agrl. Chemistry and Engring., Dept. Agr., 1941-42, asso. physicist, 1942-43. Fellow Am. Phys. Soc.; mem. Am. Assn. U. Profs., Sigma Xi. Author tech. articles. Home: 238 E Sussex Av Missoula MT 59801

JEPPESEN, MYRON ALTON, educator; b. Logan, Utah, Oct. 28, 1905; s. Charles R. and Matilda (Jensen) J.; B.S., U. Ida., 1930; M.S., Pa. State U., 1932, Ph.D., 1936; m. Madeleine Caron, June 25, 1939; children—Martha (Mrs. Peter Meyer), Matilda (Mrs. Dexter Morse), Mary (Mrs. Peter Hepburn), Laura. Mem. faculty Bowdoin Coll., 1936—; prof. physics, 1948—, chmn. dept., 1964- -; lectr., vis. prof. Stanford, 1947-49; research fellow physics U. Cal. at Berkeley, 1956-57; cons. in field, 1954—. Asso. program dir. grad. fellowships NSF, 1963-64. Guggenheim fellow, 1956-57. Fellow A.A.A.S., Am. Optical Soc.; mem. Am. Inst. Physics, Am. Assn. Physics Tchrs. Author articles optics, spectroscopy, solid state physics. Home: 10 Harpswell Pl Brunswick ME 04011

JEPPESEN, SYLVAN A., U.S. atty.; b. Moore, Ida., Oct. 9, 1922; s. Charles R. and Matilda (Jensen) J.; B.A., U. Ida., 1947, LL.B., 1949; m. Hilma Irene Sweet, Nov. 29, 1957. Admitted to Ida. bar, 1949; partner firm Hall & Jeppesen, Jerome, 1949-52; asst. U.S. atty. Dist. Ida., 1952-53; partner firm Jeppesen & Jeppesen, Boise, 1953-61; spl. prosecuting atty. Owyhee County, Ida., 1957-58; atty. Ida. Ho. Reps., 1959; U.S. atty. Dist. Ida., 1961—. Mem. Am., Ida. bar assns., Phi Alpha Delta. Elk. Home: 1418 Wilcomb St Boise ID 83705 Office: Federal Bldg Boise ID 83702

JEPPSON, JOHN, 2d, abrasives exec.; b. Worcester, Mass., Dec. 10, 1916; s. George Nathaniel and Selma U. (Swanstrom) J.; grad. Deerfield Acad., 1934; A.B., Amherst Coll., 1938; M.B.A., Harvard, 1940; D.Sc. (hon.), Amherst Coll., 1963; LL.D., Clark U., 1968; m. Julie Armstrong (div. Feb. 1946); children—John III, Julie; m. 2d, Marianne Jenner Shellabarger, Jan. 15, 1947; children—Eric Shellabarger, Ingrid Georgia. With Norton Co., 1940—, plant operations analyst, 1940-41, specialized work, prodn. dept., abrasive div., 1945, mem. and sec. new devel. com. 1945—, asst. sec. of co. and foreman small wheel dept., 1947-48, dir., 1948—, supt. plant 7, 1948-50, works mgr., abrasive div. and sec. of co., 1950-53, v.p. prodn., 1953, v.p. mfg. abrasive div. 1954-56, v.p., gen. mgr., dir. mfg., 1956-61, became exec. v.p., 1961, pres., chief exec. officer, 1967-71, chmn. bd., 1971—, also dir.; chmn. bd. Guaranty Bank and Trust Co.; dir. Crompton & Knowles Corp., New England High Carbon Wire Co., Foxboro Co., New Eng. Mchts. Nat. Bank, Boston, Kennecott Copper Corp., N.Y.C. Bd. dirs. Machinery and Allied Products Inst., Washington, Asso. Industries Mass.; trustee Clark U. Worcester Art Mus., Council Americas; bd. govs. Am. Swedish Hist. Found., Phila. Mem. tech. sect. machine tool div., W.P.B. also mem. Brit. Am. allocation com., 1941-42. Served to lt. USNR, 1942-45. Mem. Am. Ceramic Soc., Swedish Charitable Assn. (dir.), Worcester County Musical Assn. (dir., v.p.), Swedish C. of C. of U.S. (dir.), N.A.M. (dir.), Worcester Hort. Soc., Worcester Fire Soc., Amherst Alumni Assn., Harvard Bus. Sch. Club, Am. Antiquarian Soc. (mem. council). Lutheran (trustee). Clubs: Worcester; Tatnuck Country; Midas; Commercial (Boston); Merchants. Home: 7 Old Colony Rd Worcester MA 01609 Office: The Norton Co Worcester MA 01606

JEPSEN, GLENN LOWELL, educator, geologist; b. Lead, S.D., Mar. 4, 1903; s. Victor Theodore and Kittie Elizabeth (Gallup) J.; student U. Mich., 1922-23, S.D. State Sch. Mines and Tech., Rapid City, 1923-25; B.S., Princeton, 1927, Ph.D., 1930; m. Janet E. Mayo, June 14, 1934 (div. Dec. 1953); one dau., Katherine Alice. Instr. English, S.D. State Sch. Mines and Tech., 1924-25; instr. geology Princeton, 1930-34, asst. prof. geology, 1934- 40, asso. prof., 1940-46, Sinclair prof. vertebrate paleontology, 1946—, dir. Princeton Scott Fund Expdns., curator vertebrate paleontology, 1935—, dir. Princeton Natural History Mus. Recipient Addison Emery Verrill medal Yale, 1962. Mem. A.A.A.S., Am. Soc. Mammologists, Geol. Soc. Am. (councilor 1951-54), Paleontol. Soc. Am. (v.p. 1955-56), Soc. Vertebrate Paleontology (pres. 1944-45), Am. Philos. Soc., Am. Assn. U. Profs., Geol. Soc. N.J. (pres. 1959-61), Phi Beta Kappa, Sigma Xi. Home: 144 Patton Av Princeton NJ 08540

JEPSEN, ROGER W., lt. gov. Iowa; b. Cedar Falls, Ia., Dec. 23, 1928; s. Ernest E. and Esther Jepsen; B.S. in Psychology, Ariz. State U., 1950, also M.A. in Counseling and Guidance; m. Dee Ann Delaney; children—Jeffrey, Ann Marie, Craig, Linda, Deborah, Coy. Br. mgr. Conn. Gen. Life Ins. Co.; formerly mem. Ia. Senate from 15th Senatorial Dist.; now lt. gov. Ia. Chmn. bd. JPD, Inc. Past chmn. Scott County Young Republicans and chmn. Republican party Davenport. Served with AUS, 1946-47. Mem. Izaac Walton League, Scott County Retarded Children's Assn., Farm Bur., Dad's Assn. U. Ia., Nat. Assn. Life Underwriters, Gen. Agts. and Mgrs. Assn., Res. Officers Assn. (nat. v.p. 1958-59), Lt. Govs. of U.S.A. (nat. vice chmn. 1970-71, nat. chmn. 1971-72). Lutheran. Mason (Shriner). Address: State Capitol Building Des Moines IA 50319

JEREMIAH, ROBERT A., utilities exec.; b. N.Y.C., Mar. 25, 1918; B.B.A., Manhattan Coll., 1941; m. Anne D. Jeremiah; 1 son. Controller L.I. Lighting Co., Mineola, N.Y., 1965—.

JERGE, CHARLES, educator; b. Buffalo, Mar. 21, 1929; s. Charles J. and May (Conely) J.; B.S., State U. N.Y., 1951; D.D.S., U. Pa., 1958, Ph.D., 1961; m. Janet Mehler, June 1, 1957; children-Carolyn, Susan, Ann, Gail. Asso. prof. Sch. Dental Medicine, U. Conn., Hartford, 1963-67, prof. dental medicine, 1967—, asso. dean Sch. Dental Medicine, 1967-68, dean, 1969- -. Mem. Nat. Acad. Scis.-NRC Council on Naval Med. Research, 1969. Served with U.S. Army, 1952-54. Recipient Alpha Omega award U. Pa., 1958, Edward H. Hatton award Internat. Assn. Dental Research, 1961, Pa. Plan Scholar 1958-61. Mem. Internat. Assn. Dental Research. Contbr. articles profl. jours. Home: 150 Reverknolls St Avon CT 06001 Office: U Conn Heatlh Center Sch Dental Medicine Hartford Plaza Hartford CT 06105

JERICHO, JACK FRAKER, assn. exec.; b. LaHarpe, Ill., Nov. 8, 1912; s. Warren B. and Mary M.F. (Fraker) J.; student Northwestern U., 1930-32; student Gary Coll., 1937-39; m. Josephine M. Bennett, Mar. 20, 1943. Indsl. engr. Bear Brand Hosiery Co., Kankakee, Ill., 1932-37; mgr. indsl. engring. Carnegie Ill. Steel Co., Gary, Ind., 1937-42, Graver Tank & Mfg. Co., East Chicago, Ind., 1942-47, United Air Lines, Denver, 1947-57; supt. work analysis United Air Lines, Chgo., 1957-63; exec. dir. Am. Inst. Indsl. Engrs., N.Y.C., 1963—; trustee Am. Inst. Indsl. Engrs. Pension Trust. Recipient Merit award United Air Lines, 1963, Distinguished Service award Am. Inst. Indsl. Engrs., 1963, Silver Dollar award City Denver, 1959. Fellow Am. Inst. Indsl. Engrs.; mem. Am. Soc. Assn. Execs., Am. Soc. Engring. Edn., Am. Mgmt. Assn., Alpha Pi Mu. Home: 14 Ox Ridge Rd Elmsford NY 10523 Office: 345 E 47th St New York City NY 10017

JERISON, MEYER, educator; b. Bialystok, Poland, Nov. 28, 1922; s. Elia Israel and Esther (Rasky) J.; came to U.S., 1929, naturalized, 1933; B.S., Coll. City N.Y., 1943; M.S., Brown U., 1947; Ph.D., U. Mich., 1950; m. Miriam Schwartz, Aug. 5, 1945; children—Michael, David. Physicist, NACA, 1944-46; lectr. Case Inst. Tech., 1945-46; research asso. U. Ill. at Urbana, 1949-51; research engr. Lockheed Aircraft Corp., 1952; asst. prof. Purdue U., 1951-56, asso. prof., 1956-60, prof., 1960—, chmn. div. math. scis., 1969—. Mem. Am. Math. Soc., Am. Assn. U. Profs., Math. Assn. Am. (com. on undergrad. program in math. 1968-71), Phi Beta Kappa, Sigma Xi. Author: Rings of Continuous Functions (with Leonard Gillman), 1960. Home: 147 Pathway Lane West Lafayette IN 47906

JERNEGAN, JOHN DURNFORD, govt. ofcl.; b. Los Angeles, June 12, 1911; s. Edward Skinner and Ida Latham (Hollingsworth) J.; A.B. with great distinction, Stanford 1933, A.M., 1935; postgrad. Georgetown U., 1933-34; m. Mary Margaret Brownrig, June 5, 1948; children—Jeffrey, Joan, John B., Jeremy. Sports writer, Oakland (Cal.) Tribune, 1936; U.S. fgn. service officer, 1936; several fgn. service positions, 1936-41; desk officer Near Eastern div. Dept. State, 1941-43, asst. chief, 1946-47, chief div. Greek, Turkish and Iranian affairs, 1947-49; dir. Office Greek, Turkish and Iranian affairs, 1949-50; Am. consul gen., Tunis, Tunisia, 1950-52; dep. asst. sec. state Bur. Near Eastern, South Asian and African Affairs, 1952-55; 3d then 2d sec. Am. embassy, Tehran, Iran, 1943- 46; accompanied sec. of state to Moscow Conf. Fgn. Ministers, 1943; mem. staff sec. of state, 2d Conf. of Fgn. Ministers, Moscow, 1945; minister-counselor Am. Embassy, Rome, Italy, 1955-58; ambassador to Iraq, 1958-62; named career minister, 1962; State Dept. adviser to comdr. Air U., 1962-63, dep. asst. sec. state for Near Eastern and S. Asian affairs, 1963-65; ambassador to Algeria, 1965-67; diplomat-in-residence Emory U., Atlanta, 1967-68; polit. adviser, comdr. in chief Atlantic and supreme allied comdr. Atlantic, 1968—. Address: 1211 Langley Rd Norfolk VA 23507

JERNEGAN, PAUL FRANK, architect; b. Mishawaka, Ind., Apr. 17, 1908; s. Ralph Hartwell and Estella (Frank) J.; B.S., U. Mich., 1929, M.S., 1931; postgrad. U. Chgo., 1958; m. Imogene Lucille Crooks, July 31, 1943. Draftsman, designer W.W. Schneider, South Bend, Ind., 1927-32; founder, dir. Paulon Art Centre and Sch., South Bend, 1933-34; owner, prin. Paul Frank Jernegan Architect, Mishawaka and Chgo., 1941—; archtl. design critic U. Notre Dame, 1947; organizer, first chmn. Lake Mich. Region Planning Council, 1960-62, dir., 1960—; mem. Mishawaka Bd. Zoning Appeals, 1941-42; chmn. planning com. Mishawaka C. of C., 1954-55. Served with AUS, 1942-46. Fellow A.I.A. (pres. N. Ind. chpt. 1962-63, chmn. Ind. civic design com. 1954-61); mem. St. Joe Valley Architects (pres. 1953-54), Soc. Am. Mil. Engrs., Soc. Archtl. Historians, Mich. Ind. socs. architects, Nat. Trust Hist. Preservation, Mishawaka C. of C., Tau Sigma Delta, Lambda Chi Alpha. Research on housing bldg. techniques and systems, structure, air support, metro-urban design. Home: 316 Niles Av Mishawaka IN 46544 Office: 223 Lincolnway E Mishawaka IN 46544

JERNIGAN, JAMES COFFEY, univ. pres.; b. nr. Van Alstyne, Tex., Dec. 20, 1914; s. Austin Wallace and Blanche (Coffey) J.; B.S., N. Tex. State Tchrs. Coll., 1937, M.S., 1939; postgrad. U. Tex., summers 1941-42; Ph.D., U. Chgo., 1949; m. Frances Williams, June 28, 1940; children—James William, Laura Frances. Tchr., Rosamond Chapel Sch., 1934-36; tchr., prin. Whitewright (Tex.) Pub. Schs., 1939-41; dep. state supt. Tex. State Dept. Edn., 1941-42; dean student life Tex. A. and I. U., Kingsville, 1946-47, dir. student personnel, 1949-50, dean coll., 1950- 62, pres., 1962—. Condr. guidance workshop So. Meth. U., summer 1950. Served to capt., inf. AUS, 1942-46; ETO. Mem. N.E.A., Tex. State Tchrs. Assn., Tex. Assn. Colls and Univs. (pres. 1962-63). Mem. First Christian Ch. (elder). Kiwanian (past pres.). Home: President's Home Kingsville TX 78363

JEROME, JERROLD VINCENT, corp. exec.; b. Seattle, Sept. 13, 1929; s. Vincent Barnes and Mary (McNamara) J.; B.S., Linfield Coll., 1952; M.B.A., Stanford, 1959; m. Elaine Joy Bilsland, Sept. 14, 1962. Cost analyst Pan Am. Airways, San Francisco, 1959; financial planning analyst and accountant Ampex Corp., Redwood City, Cal., 1960-61; accounting supr. electron tube div. Litton Industries, San Carlos, Cal., 1961-62; treas., controller Teledyne, Inc., Los Angeles, 1962—. Served to lt. USNR, 1952-57. Mem. Financial Execs. Inst., Stanford Bus. Sch. Assn., Theta Chi (past chpt. pres.), Pi Gamma Mu (past chpt. pres.). Club: Jack Kramer Tennis (Rollings Hills). Home: 44 Cayuse Lane Rolling Hills CA 90274 Office: 1901 Av of the Stars Los Angeles CA 90067

JEROME, WILLIAM TRAVERS, III, coll. adminstr.; b. N.Y.C., July 29, 1919; s. William Travers and Hope (Colgate) J.; B.A., Colgate U., 1941; postgrad. Yale Law Sch.; M.B.A., Harvard, 1946, D.C.S., 1952; LL.D., Middlebury Coll., 1963; H.H.D., Toledo U., 1969; Dr. Pub. Service (hon.), Bowling Green State U., 1970; m. Jean C. Bewkes, May 15, 1943; children—Jennie Hall (Mrs. Robert Farnsworth), William Travers IV, Lawrence, Kate. Asst. to pres. Middlebury Coll., 1946-50; instr., research asso. Harvard Bus. Sch., 1950-53; dir. Army Comptrollership Sch., asso. prof. Coll. Bus. Adminstrn., Syracuse U., 1953-58; dean, prof. bus. adminstrn., 1958-63; pres. Bowling Green (O.) State U., 1963-70; v.p. for academic affairs, cons. Fla. Internat. U., Miami, 1970—. Served with AUS, World War II. Mem. Am. Accounting Assn., Financial Execs. Inst., Phi Beta Kappa, Delta Kappa Epsilon, Beta Gamma Sigma, Phi Kappa Phi. Author: Executive Controls-The Catalyst, 1961. Contbr. articles on mgmt. control to profl. jours. Home: 4525 Anderson Rd Coral Gables FL 33146

JERRARD, RICHARD PATTERSON, educator; b. Evanston, Ill., July 23, 1925; s. Leigh Patterson and Lillian (Taylor) J.; B.S., U. Wis., 1949, M.S., 1950; Ph.D., U. Mich., 1957; m. Margot Leon Poritsky, June 23, 1951; children—Laura, Leigh, Robert. Devel. engr. Gen. Electric Co., Schenectady, 1950-54; instr. U. Mich., 1956-57; mathematician Bell Telephone Labs., Whippany, N.J., 1957-58; from asst. prof. to prof. math. U. Ill., Urbana, 1958—. Fellow U. Warwick (Eng.), 1965-66. Served with USAAF, 1943-45. Prin. investigator for NSF grants for research in differential geometry, 1964-70. Mem. Am. Math. Soc., Math. Assn. Am., Sigma Xi. Home: 507 W Indiana St Urbana IL 61801

JERSEY, WILLIAM CLIFFORD, Jr., film maker; b. Jamaica, N.Y., June 9, 1927; s. William Clifford and Alice (Loetzer) J.; B.A., Wheaton Coll., 1951; M.A. magna cum laude, U. So. Cal., 1954; m. Gwen Brown, Aug. 28, 1971; children (by previous marriage)—Beth Anne, Todd, Brian, Colin. Artist for ceramic designer, 1946; dir. indsl., religious films Valley Forge Films, 1952-54; lectr. Columbia, N.Y. U., U. So. Cal.; free lance film documentary writer, producer, dir. for comml. cinema, TV, ednl. TV, 1957—; films include Black Cat, 1957, Behind the Spaceman, 1966, My Name Is Children, 1966, Goodbye and Good Luck (co-producer), 1966, A Time for Burning, 1965, Riddle (co-film maker), 1965, A Simple Cup of Tea, 1965, Manhattan Battleground, 1964, Incident on Wilson Street, 1964, Captive, 1964, City of Necessity (co-dir.), 1964, Cowboy, 1970, Sea Venture, 1971, Newborn, 1971, Prisoner-at-Large, 1962; art dir. motion picture features Manhunt in Jungle, 1963, Blob, 1962, 4-D Man, 1964. Chmn. Ridgewood (N.J.) Fair Housing Com., 1964. Served with USNR, 1945. Recipient awards for following films: A Time for Burning (Acad. award Acad. Motion Picture Arts and Scis. 1966, CINE Golden Eagle award 1966, Catholic Audio Visual Educators Assn. award 1966, Sidney Hillman Found. award 1966); Behind the Spaceman (CINE Golden Eagle award 1966, internat. awards Cracow, Poland, Edinburgh, Scotland, Locarno, Switzerland 1966), Captive (Blue Ribbon Ednl. Film Library Assn. 1964, CINE Golden Eagle 1964), Incident on Wilson Street (award Protestant Council City N.Y. 1964), Manhattan Battleground (Emmy nomination Nat. Acad. TV Arts and Scis. 1963), City of Necessity (San Francisco Golden Gate award 1963). Mem. Writers Guild Am., Dirs. Guild Am. Presbyn. (elder). Home: Lakeside Dr Ridgefield CT Office: 630 9th Av New York City NY 10036

JERSKEY, RALPH M., business exec.; b. N.Y.C., 1913; grad. Coll. City N.Y., 1934; LL.B., U. Ba., 1937; married. Mem. firm Townsend & Lewis, 1937-53; gen. counsel, sec. Congoleum Industries, Inc. subs. Bath Industries, Inc., Kearny, N.J., 1953—; sec., dir. Loomweve Corp., Lewis Carpet Mills, Inc., Kinder Mfg. Co. Office: 195 Belgrove Dr Kearny NJ 07032*

JERTBERG, GILBERT H., judge; b. Springfield, Mo.; s. Henry and Augusta (Swanson) J.; A.B., Stanford, 1920, J.D., 1922; m. Henrietta Burns; 1 dau., Joan (Mrs. T. N. Russell). Gen. practice law, Fresno, Cal., 1922-55; U.S. dist. judge So. Dist. Cal., 1955-58; judge U.S. Ct. of Appeals, 9th Circuit, Fresno, 1958—. Mem. Cal. Bd. Edn., 1943-54. Bd. govs. Fresno State Coll. Found. Mem. Fresno County C. of C. (pres. 1939), Fresno County (pres. 1940), Am. bar assns., Stanford Alumni Assn. (pres. 1941), Am. Legion, Phi Beta Kappa, Theta Chi, Phi Alpha Delta. Elk. Home: 3917 N Wilson St Fresno CA 93704 Office: U S Court House Fresno CA 93721

JERVEY, HAROLD EDWARD, Jr., physician; b. Charleston, S.C., Dec. 3, 1920; s. Harold Edward and Stella (White) J.; B.S., U. S.C., 1941; M.D., Med. Coll. S.C., 1949; m. Lillian Pearce Hair, July 13, 1946; children—Nancy, Harold Edward III, Margaret Pearce, Harriet Beacham, Helen White, Charles Stewart, Lillian Pearce. Intern Greenville (S.C.) Gen. Hosp., 1949-50, Baptist Gen. Hosp., Columbia, S.C., 1951-54; gen. practice, Columbia, 1951—; mem. staff Columbia, Bapt. and Providence hosps. Mem. S.C. Bd. Med. Examiners, 1953—, sec., 1955-58; pres. Fedn. State Med. Bds., 1960, sec., editor bull., 1961; treas., 1962—; mem. Adv. Bd. Med. Specialists, 1959-69. Served to lt. comdr. USNR, 1941-45. Decorated Bronze Star. Mem. Am. Acad. Gen. Practice (S.C. del. 1956-60), A.M.A., Columbia C. of C., Soc. Cincinnati, Kappa Sigma. Episcopalian. Clubs: Sertoma Internat.; Carolina Yacht (Charleston); Columbia Sailing, Forest Lake Country (Columbia). Home: 798 Kawana Rd Columbia SC 29205 Office: 1515 Bull St Columbia SC 29201

JESCHKE, REUBEN PETER, clergyman; b. Russia, July 20, 1911; s. Reinhold and Alvina (Arndt) J.; came to U.S., 1928, naturalized, 1940; B.A., Wesleyan U., Middletown, Conn., 1934; B.D., Hartford (Conn.) Theol. Sem., 1935, S.T.M., 1937; Ph.D., Columbia, 1951; D.D., No. Baptist Theol. Sem., 1966; L.H.D., Sioux Falls Coll., 1971;

m. Sabina Jacopian, Aug. 10, 1935; children—Paul, Thomas. Ordained to ministry Baptist Ch., 1933; pastor in Conn., 1934- 37, in Ohio, 1937-46; prof. practical theology N.A. Bapt. Sem., Sioux Falls, S.D., 1947-52; dean Sioux Falls (S.D.) Coll., 1952-53, pres., 1953-70; minister First Bapt. Ch., Branford, Conn., 1970—. Recipient Freedoms Found. award, 1952. Rotarian. Author: Dreams of the Pioneers, 1957. Home: 54 Riverside Dr Branford CT

JESINA, CARL LEE, retail drug store exec.; b. Cedar Rapids, Ia., Aug. 29, 1929; s. Frank and Faye A. (Sheldon) J.; B.A., U. Ia., 1952, B.S. in Pharmacy, 1955; J.D., Georgetown U., 1960; m. Joan Atkinson, Dec. 27, 1957; children—Jenny Lee, Kenneth Frank. With Peoples Drug Stores Inc., 1957- -, asst. sec., 1964, sec., 1965-70, exec. v.p., 1970; v.p. Super X div. Kroger Co., Cin., 1971—. Admitted to Md. bar, 1961, also U.S. Supreme Ct. Mem. com. to reduce crime Met. Washington Bd. Trade, 1967—. Bd. dirs. D.C. Soc. Crippled Children, Met. Washington Police Boys Club. Mem. Am., Md. bar assns., D.C. (exec. com.), Md., Va., Ia., Ohio pharm. assns. Republican. Methodist. Office: 222 E Central Pkwy Cincinnati OH 45201

JESKE, HOWARD LEIGH, life ins. co. exec.; b. York, Neb., Sept. 25, 1917; s. Charles W. and Sina (Hanna) J.; A.B., Cornell Coll., Mt. Vernon, Ia., 1940; LL.B., McGeorge Coll. Law, Sacramento, 1951; m. Bettyclaire Barton, Nov. 23, 1943; children—Vaughn C., Craig B., Lynn Ellen, Laurel Claire. With Carnegie-Ill. Steel Corp., 1940-41; accountant Spreckles Sugar Co., Sacramento, 1946-51; admitted to Cal. bar, 1951; practice law, Sacramento, 1952-53; with Cal.-Western States Life Ins. Co., Sacramento, 1954—, v.p., gen. counsel, sec., 1968—; sec. treas. Cal.-Western Securities Co. Served to capt. USAAF, 1942-45. Mem. Am., Cal., Sacramento bar assns. Republican. Club: Sutter (Sacramento). Home: 3421 E Curtis Park Dr Sacramento CA 95818 Office: 2020 L St Sacramento CA 95814

JESKEY, HAROLD ALFRED, educator; b. St. Louis, Aug. 18, 1912; s. Alfred Thomas and Kathryn W. (Schaum) J.; B.S., St. Louis Coll. Pharmacy, 1933; B.A., Washington U., St. Louis, 1937; Ph.D., U. Wis., 1942; m. Margaret Schlichting, June 16, 1939; children—Judith Jean (Mrs. Richard Watson), Janet Susan. Chemist James F. Ballard, Inc., St. Louis, 1933-35; instr. St. Louis Coll. Pharmacy 1935-38; teaching fellow U. Wis., 1938-41; instr. chemistry, then asst. prof. U. Tenn., 1941-44; mem. faculty So. Meth. U., Dallas, 1945—, prof., 1957—, chmn. dept. chemistry, 1962—; prof. biochemistry U. Tex. Southwestern Med. Sch., 1965—; cons. in field. Pres. S.W. Athletic Conf., 1971-72. Mem. Am. Chem. Soc. (nat. council 1948-57), A.A.A.S., Sigma Xi, Alpha Tau Omega, Phi Chi, Phi Lambda Upsilon. Author: Introductory Organic Chemistry, 1956. Contbr. articles profl. jours. Home: 2929 Fondren Dr Dallas TX 75205

JESSEL, GEORGE, actor; b. N.Y. City, Apr. 3, 1898; s. Joseph Aaron and Charlotte (Schwartz) J.; m. 1st, Florence Courtney; m. 2d, Norma Talmadge; m. 3d, Lois Andrews; 1 dau., Jerilynn. Began career as nickelodean singer and bat boy for N.Y. Giants; 1st singing partner of Walter Winchell; teamed with Eddie Cantor in Gus Edward's Vaudeville Acts, 1910; 1st Broadway appearance in Shubert Gaieties of 1918; appeared in dramas, The Jazz Singer, The War Song, Joseph and His Brethren, The War Song (co-author: with Fannie Brice in musical, Sweet and Low; again teamed with Eddie Cantor for 2-year tour beginning at N.Y. Palace theatre; wrote and appeared in musical plays, High Kickers, Show Time; joined 20th Century Fox as producer and author, 1943-63; prod. several well known stage prodns.; active City of Hope, Govt. of Israel, numerous other ogrns.; chmn. bd. Israel Hotel Co., Inc. Nat. Vaudeville Artists (pres.). Clubs: Friars of Cal. (abbot); Jewish Theatrical of Am. (v.p.). Author: So Help Me (autobiography), 1943, Hello Momma, 1946; Elegy in Manhattan, 1961; This Way, Miss; Jessel Anyone; You Too Can Make A Speech. Address: Hillcrest Country Club Los Angeles CA 90016 ☆

JESSER, EDWARD A., Jr., banker; b. N.Y.C.; Nov. 6, 1916; s. Edward A. and Vera (Benn) J.; A.B., Lafayette Coll., 1939; postgrad. N.Y. U., Rutgers U., Stanford; m. Ruth Anderson, June 21, 1940; children—Wynne M., Richard A. III, Leigh Benn. Trainee, Nat. City Bank of N.Y., 1939-46, asst. cashier, 1946-49, asst. v.p., 1949-54, v.p. charge Western div., 1954-60; pres., chief exec. officer Peoples Trust Co. N.J., Bergen County, 1960—, chmn. bd., 1970—; dir. Reinhold-Chapman, Inc. Chmn. exec. com. Better Bus. Bur. Bergen, Passaic and Rockland Countries. Pres. N. Bergen County council Boy Scouts Am. Former commr. Village Ridgewood. Bd. dirs. Regional Plan Assn.; bd. fellows Fairleigh Dickinson U. Decorated Couronne de Chenne, Croix de Guerre (Luxemburg). Mem. Bergen County C. of C. (v.p.). Clubs: Economic (N.Y.C.); Ridgewood Country; Arcola Country. Home: 224 Glenwood Rd Ridgewood NJ 07450 Office: 210 Main St Hackensack NJ 07601

JESSERAMSING, CHITMANSING, diplomat; b. Mauritius, Aug. 25, 1933; s. Jeewoonarain and Banita (Bindah) J.; B.A. with honors U. New Delhi, 1957, M.A., 1959; diploma in diplomatic studies Oxford U. (Eng.) and Canberra (Australia) U., 1967; m. Usha Seereeram, Sept. 21, 1958; children—Devindra, Janita, Anjali. Prin., Islamic Cultural Coll., Mauritius, 1954-55, 61-62, 1954-55; edn. officer Royal Coll., Curepipe, 1962-66; officer Govt. Tourist Office, Mauritius, 1967-68; 1st sec. Mauritius embassy, Washington, UN, and High Commn. in Can., 1968—. Mem. Royal Coll. Philos. Soc. (founder, pres. 1962-66), Extra/Sensory Perception at Oxford. Club: Harold Macmillan (Oxford). Home: 122 Grafton St Chevy Chase MD 20015 Office: 2308 Wyoming Av NW Washington DC 20008

JESSUP, CLAUDE AMBROSE, bus transp. co. exec.; b. Camelia, Va., Nov. 19, 1904; s. Samuel Ambrose and Fanny Elizabeth (Hatcher) J.; ed. pub. schs., Charlottesville, Va.; m. Mamie Virginia Atkinson, June 19, 1930; 1 dau., Claudia Jane. Engaged in bus transp. bus., 1926—; chmn. bd. Continental Trailways, Inc., Charlottesville, 1968—, chmn. bd. Va. Mutual Insurance Co., Richmond, 1963—, Alderman 250 Corp., 1964—; vice chmn. bd. City Laundry, Inc., 1966—; pres. Va. Peaks Otter Co., 1958-71, chmn. bd., 1971—; pres. Autocase Corp., Richmond, Va., 1964—, Natural Bridge Va., Inc., 1966—, Riverview Cemetery Co., Charlottesville, 1969—; exec. com., dir. Va. Nat. Bank, Norfolk, Allied Capital Corp., Washington; dir. Jefferson Cable Corp., Charlottesville, Go Pub. Co., Washington, Jackson Park Realty Co.; chmn. bd. The Boar's Head Inn; dir., chmn. finance com. Universal Minerals & Metal, Inc., McAlester, Okla. Mem. bd. Va. Dept. Conservation and Econ. Devel.; past pres. Charlottesville 200th Anniversary Commn.; past dir. Nat. Safety Council, Chgo., Charlottesville-Albemarle YMCA; former mem. finance Com. Econ. Devel.; past mem. travel adv. com. U.S. Travel Service; bus. industry rep. Transp. Council, Dept. Commerce, 1952-61. Treas. Va. Democratic Com., 1964-65. Devel. com. U. Va. Grad. Sch. Bus. Adminstrn., 1966-67. Mem. Nat. Assn. Motor Bus Owners (v.p.), Newcomen Soc. of N.Am., Virginia C. of C. (dir.), Beta Gamma Sigma (hon.). Presbyn. Mason (Shriner). Clubs: Farmington Country, Red Land, Piedmont Shriner, Boar's Head (Charlottesville); James River (Lynchburg, Va.); University (Washington). Home: 10 Ivy Lane Farmington Charlottesville VA 22901 Office: 114 4th St S E Charlottesville VA 22902

JESSUP, JOE LEE, educator, management cons.; b. Cordele, Ga., June 23, 1913; s. Horace Andrew and Elizabeth (Wilson) J.; B.S., U. Ala., 1936; M.B.A., Harvard Grad. Sch. Bus. Adminstrn., 1941; LL.D., Chung-Ang U., Seoul, Korea, 1964; m. Genevieve Quirk Galloway, Aug. 29, 1946; 1 dau., Gail Elizabeth. Sales rep. Proctor & Gambee, 1937-40; liason officer bur. pub. relations, U.S. War Dept., 1941; spl. asst. and exec. asst. Far Eastern div. and office exports, Bd. Econ. Warfare, 1942-43; exec. officer office departmental adminstrn., Dept. of State, 1946; exec. sec. adminstr's adv. council, War Assets Adminstrn., 1946-48; v.p. sales Airken, Capitol & Service Co., 1948-49; asso. prof. bus. adminstrn. George Washington U., 1949, prof., 1952, asst. dean Sch. Gov., 1951-60; mng. dir. Jessup and Co., Washington, 1957—; dir. Hunter Assos. Labs., Inc., Fairfax, Va., 1964-70, Giant Food Dept. Stores, Washington. Coordinator air force resources mgmt. program, 1951-57. Del. in edn. 10th Internat. Mgmt. Conf., Sao Paulo, Brazil, 1954, 11th Conf., Paris, France, 1957, 12th Conf., Sydney and Melbourne, Australia, 1960, 13th Conf., Rotterdam, Netherland, 1966, 14th Conf., Tokyo, Japan, 1969. Served from 2d lt. to lt. col., AUS, 1941-46. Dec. Bronze Star Recipient certificate of appreciation sec. of Air Force, 1957. Mem. Academy of Mgmt., Am. Mgmt. Assn., Am. Marketing Assn., Soc. Advancement Mgmt., Alpha Kappa Psi. Clubs: Harvard (N.Y.C.); Army and Navy, Congressional Country, Internat. (Washington). Home: 8539 W Howell Rd Bethesda MD 20014 Office: 1026 17th St N W Washington DC 20036

JESSUP, JOHN KNOX, editor; b. Rochester, N.Y., Mar. 5, 1907; s. John Colgate and Louise (Foote) J.; student Taft Sch., 1922-24; A.B., Yale, 1928; m. Margaret Tarbox, Sept. 23, 1932; 1 son, John Knox; m. 2d, Eunice Clark Rodman, Sept. 11, 1937; children—Nathaniel Foote, Amos Huntington, Rebecca Phelps, Maria Forward. Asst. in English, Yale, 1928-29; asst. editor Yale Alumni Weekly, 1928-30; with J. Walter Thompson, advt., 1930-35; with Time, Inc., 1935-69, chief editorial writer Life mag., 1951-69; editorial broadcaster CBS Radio, 1971. Trustee New Eng. Inst. for Med. Research. Mem. Council on Fgn. Relations, Sigma Delta Chi. Clubs: Yale, Century Association (N.Y.C.). Editor: The Ideas of Henry Luce, 1969. Home: 122 Rdigefield Rd Wilton CT 06897

JESSUP, PHILIP C., former judge; b. N.Y.C., Jan. 5, 1897; s. Henry Wynans and Mary Hay (Stotesbury) J.; A.B., Hamilton Coll., 1919, LL.D., 1937; LL.B., Yale, 1924, LL.D., 1964; A.M., Columbia, 1924, Ph.D., 1927; LL.D., Western Res. U., 1941, Rutgers U., 1950, Seoul Nat. U., 1950, Middlebury Coll., 1950, Brown U., 1949, St. Lawrence U., 1966, U. Mich., 1966, Johns Hopkins, 1970, Brandeis U., 1971; L.C.D., Colgate U., 1950, Union Coll., 1951, Litt.D., U. Hanoi, 1950; J.D., Oslo U., 1946; Dr.hon.causa, U. Paris, 1948; m. Lois Walcott Kellogg, July 23, 1921; 1 son, Philip C. Admitted to D.C. bar, 1925, N.Y. bar, 1927; mem. Parker & Duryea, 1927-43; lectr. internat. law Columbia, 1925-27, asst. prof., 1927-29, asso. prof., 1929-35, prof., 1934-46, Hamilton Fish prof. internat. law and diplomacy, 1946-61, Jacob Blaustein lectr., 1970; judge Internat. Ct. of Justice, 1961-70; Whitney H. Shepardson sr. research fellow in residence Council on Fgn. Relations, 1970-71. Vis. prof. Harvard Law Sch., 1938-39; Storrs lectr. Yale Law Sch., 1956; Cooley lectr. Mich U. Law Sch., 1958; Sibley lectr. U. Ga. Sch. of Law, 1970; Legal adviser to fed. govt. officers, 1924-53, at internat. confs., embassies and to U.S. dels. at UN; U.S. Rep. to UN Gen. Assembly, 1948-52; apptd. ambassador at large, 1949, resigned 1953. Chmn. Chile-Norway Permanent Councilliation Commn. Hon. mem. governing council Internat. Inst. for Unification of Pvt. Law, 1967—. Served with A.E.F., World War I. Decorated Hungarian Cross of Merit, Class II; Oficial Ordem Nacional do Cruzeiro do Sul (Brazil); grand officer Nat. Order Cedars (Lebanon), 1956; recipient Hudson Gold medal Am. Soc. Internat. Law; Fowler Harper fellow Yale Law School, 1966. Mem. Am. Philos. Soc., Am. Acad. Arts and Scis., Institut de droit internat., Am. Soc. Internat. Law (hon. pres. 1969—), Internat. Law Assn. (hon. pres. Am. br. 1970—), Conn. Bar Assn. (Distinguished Pub. Service award 1970), other assns. Clubs: Century (N.Y.C.); Cosmos (Washington). Author several books in field 1927—, including Elihu Root, 2 vols., 1938; A Modern Law of Nations, 1948; Transnational Law, 1956; The Use of International Law, 1959; (with H. H. Taubenfeld) Controls for Outer Space & The Antarctic Analogy, 1959; The Price of International Justice, 1971. Supervising editor Columbia U. Studies in History, Economics and Public Law, 1929-33; hon. mem. bd. editors Am. Jour. Internat. Law; former mem. bd. editors World Politics, Internat. Orgn. Home: Norfolk CT 06058

JESTER, ROBERTS CHARLES, Jr., engring. services co. exec.; b. Atlanta, July 12, 1917; s. Roberts Charles and Lynwood (Waters) J.; B.S., U. Ga., 1940; grad. Harvard, Advanced Mgmt. Program, 1957; m. Ann Nell Padgett, Dec. 31, 1936; children—Rita (Mrs. Charles B. Jones, Jr.), Carol (Mrs. John M. Sisk, Jr.), Janelle (Mrs. Michael C. Patty). Chief clk. Ga. R.R., 1936-40; project mgr. Mich. Design & Engring. Co., 1941-42; partner Allstate & Engring. Co., Dayton, O., 1943-45, pres., 1945— to date pres. chief executive officer Allstates Design & Devel. Co. Inc., Trenton, N.J., 1954—to date; dir. N.J. Nat. Bank. Bd. dirs., v.p. Greater Trenton Symphony Assn.; bd. dirs. George Washington council Boy Scouts Am.; bd. govs. Hamilton Hosp.; mem. lay adv. bd. St. Francis Hosp. Mem. Greater Trenton C. of C. (bd. dirs.), Trenton Coalition, Metro 49'ers. Republican. Presbyn. Mason (Shriner, Jester). Clubs: Engineers, Trenton Country (past pres.); Key Biscayne (Fla.) Yacht; Metropolitan (N.Y.C.); Pittsburgh Athletic. Home: 119 Windsor Rd Yardley PA 19067 Office: 25 N Warren St Trenton NJ 08608

JESTER, DOROTHY MARGARET, fgn. service officer; b. Mesa, Ariz., July 4, 1914; d. John H. and Carmelita (Spilsbury) Jester; A.A., Pasadena Jr. Coll., 1934; B.A., Stanford, 1936, M.A., 1940. Tchr., Cal. high schs., 1937-41, Am. Sch., Quito, Ecuador, 1941-42; sec., adminstrv. asst. Pan Am. San. Bur., Lima, Peru, 1942-45; fgn. service clk., Munich, Germany, 1946-48; mem. U.S. Fgn. Service, 1948—; assigned Mexico City, 1948-51, Mexicali, 1951-54, Managua, 1954-55, Bonn, 1956-58; with Office Internat. Resources. Dept. State, 1958-62; 1st sec., econ. officer, Santiago, Chile, 1963-64, Santo Domingo, Dominican Republic, 1964-65; 1st sec., dep. chief econ. sect. Am. embassy, Mexico City, Mexico, 1966-70, counselor for econ. affairs, 1970—. Mem. Phi Beta Kappa. Home: Box 146 Flagstaff AZ 86001 Office: Am Embassy Mexico City Mexico

JESTIN, HEIMWARTH B., coll. adminstr.; b. Montreal, Que., Can., Sept. 24, 1918; s. Emil Ernst and Rosa (Ege) J.; B.S., Central Conn. State Coll., 1947; M.A., Yale, 1949, Ph.D., 1954; m. Catherine M. Townshend, Oct. 14, 1944; children—Loftus, Jennifer, Carolyn. Head English dept., tchr. history Thomaston (Conn.) High Sch., 1947-50; prin. Canton High Sch., Collinsville, Conn., 1951-53; supt. schs., Canton, Conn., 1953-62; prof. philosophy and edn. Central Conn. State Coll., 1956-65, dean coll., 1965-67, v.p. acad. affairs, 1967—; prof. U. Hartford, 1961-63. Trustee Roaring Brook Nature Center; bd. mgrs., life mem. Conn. P.T.A. Served with AUS, 1941- 46. Decorated Order Brit. Empire. Mem. Am. Assn. Sch. Adminstrs., Conn. Council Sch. Coll. Relations. Author: Critical Experiences During the Early Years of Superintendency, 1955; The Canton Evaluation Plan, 1960; Role of the Superintendent of Schools in Connecticut, 1967; Ecology Holds Key to Man's Destiny, 1969; Well-Educated Barbarians?, 1970. Co-editor The Connecticut Study of the Role of the Public School, 1960. Home: 180 Garden St Farmington CT 06032 Office: 1615 Stanley St New Britain CT 06050

JETER, RAPHAEL GARLAND, corp. exec.; b. Conway, Ark., Mar. 13, 1909; s. George Wesley and Ella (Cook) J.; student U. Akron, 1927-29; LL.B., Ohio State U., 1932; m. Helen T. Robinson, Nov. 27, 1953; children—Judith, Joan, Anne Robinson. Admitted to Ohio bar, 1932; asso. R.H. Nesbitt, 1932-40; counsel Ohio Edison Co., Akron Transp. Co., Erie R.R. Co., Med. Protective Co., 1932- 48; partner Slabaugh, Guinther, Jeter & Pflueger, 1945-48; gen. counsel B.F. Goodrich Co., 1948—, sec., 1950—, v.p., 1957—. Home: 500 Hampshire Rd Akron OH 44313 Office: 500 S Main St Akron OH 44311

JETER, WAYBURN STEWART, educator, microbiologist; b. Cooper, Tex., Feb. 16, 1926; s. Joseph Plato and Beulah (Stewart) J.; B.S., U. Okla., 1948, M.S., 1949; Ph.D., U. Wis., 1950; m. Margaret Ann McDonald, May 30, 1947; children—Randall Mark, Monette Ann, Marcus Kent. Mem. faculty U. Ia., 1950-63, asso. prof., 1958-63; prof. microbiology U. Ariz., Tucson, 1963—, head dept. microbiology and med. tech., 1967—. Diplomate Am. Bd. Microbiology. Mem. Am. Acad. Microbiology, Am. Assn. Immunologists, A.A.A.S., Am. Soc. Microbiology, Reticuloendothelial Soc., Soc. Explt. Biology and Medicine, Sigma Xi. Contbr. articles profl. jours. Home: 4834 E Glenn St Tucson AZ 85712

JETT, THOMAS SUTTON, govt. ofcl.; b. Fleeton, Va., July 20, 1910; s. Joseph Clarence and Mable (Marsh) J.; B.S., William and Mary Coll., 1932; postgrad. Johns Hopkins, 1936-37; m. Martha Louise Thornburg, Aug. 19, 1939; children—Frances Ann, Carol Louise. With Nat. Park Service, Dept. Interior, 1933—, asso. supt. Nat. Capital Parks, 1958-61, supt., 1961- 62, regional dir. Nat. Capital Region, 1962-68, spl. asst. to asso. dir. of the service, 1968-71, spl. asst. to dir. service, 1971—. Dir. White House Historical Assn.; bd. dirs. Christmas Pagent of Peace, President's Cup Regatta Assn.; mem. D.C. Commrs. Com. Recreation Distinguished Guests, Nat. Cherry Blossom Festival Com., Nat. Ind. Day Celebration Com. Served to lt. (s.g.) USNR, World War II. Distinguished Service award Dept. Interior, 1963. Fellow Am. Inst. Park Execs.; mem. Am. Planning and civic Assn., Washington Bd. Trade, Woodlawn Plantation Com., Nat. Trust Historic Preservation, Interstate Commn. Potomac River Basin-Recreation Com. Club: Nat. Press (Washington.) Home: 121 Hilltop Rd Silver Spring MD 20910 Office: Dept Interior Bldg Nat Park Service 18th and C Sts Washington DC 20240

JETTE, ELLERTON MARCEL, fabric mfg. co. exec.; b. Plainfield, Conn., Dec. 8, 1899; s. Joseph Zoel and Nellie (Williams) J.; student Boston U., 1917; LL.D., Colby Coll., 1956; m. Edith Kemper, Aug. 14, 1945. Salesman, Brown Durrell Co., Boston, 1917-24; fabric buyer Buffalo Short Co., 1924-32; pres. C.F. Hathaway Co., Waterville, Me., 1932-60, chmn. bd., 1960—. Mem. adv. council Me. Dept. Econ. Devel., 1964-66. Pres., Goodwill Home Assn., Binkley, Me., 1960-66; commr. arts and humanities Me., 1961-68. Trustee Thayer Hosp., 1946—, Colby Coll., 1950—. Served with U.S. Army, 1917- 18. Clubs: Union (Boston); Tarriten (Bangor, Me.). Home: Sebee ME 04481 Office: C F Hawathaw Co Waterville ME 04901

JETTER, WILLIAM F., Jr., food co. exec.; b. 1925; A.B., Princeton, 1949; LL.B., Harvard, 1953; m. Labor relations rep. Sunshine Biscuits, Inc., 1953-66, asst. sec. employee benefits adminstrn., 1966-68, personnel relations dir., 1968-69, sec., personnel relations dir., 1969—. Address: 245 Park Av New York City NY 10017*

JEUCK, JOHN EDWARD, educator; b. Chgo., Oct. 17, 1916; s. John S. and Lila E. (Burke) J.; A.B., U. Chgo., 1937, M.B.A., 1938, Ph.D., 1949; M.A. (hon.), Harvard. Instr. marketing, dir. placement, sch. bus. Miami U., 1940-41; instr. marketing, sch. bus. U. Chgo., 1946-47, asst. prof., 1947-50, asso. prof. marketing, asso. dir. exec. program, 1950-52, prof. marketing, dean sch. bus., dir. exec. program, 1952-56; prof. bus. adminstrn. Harvard Grad. Sch Bus. Adminstrn., 1955-58; cons. in mgmt. edn. European Productivity Agy., 1956-57; bus. cons., 1950—; bd. editors Jour. Marketing, 1951-61; Robert Law prof. bus. adminstrn. U. Chgo., 1958—. Served as lt. USNR, 1942-46. Mem. Am. Econ. Assn., Bus. Hist. Soc., Am. Marketing Assn. (nat. award 1951), Beta Gamma Sigma, Phi Kappa Psi. Republican. Roman Catholic. Clubs: Quadrangle, University, Economic, Tavern (Chgo.). Author: Catalogues and Counters, A History of Sears, Roebuck and Company (with Boris Emmet), 1950. Co-editor: Readings in Market Organization and Price Policy, 1952. Contbr. articles profl. jours. Home: 5807 Dorchester Av Chicago IL 60637

JEWELL, ALAN JAMES, food co. exec.; b. Dover, N.J., Apr. 20, 1935; s. James P. and Gladys (Gardner) J.; M.S. in Indsl. Engring., Ohio State U., 1958; M.B.A., U. Cal. at Los Angeles. With Carnation Co., 1958—, treas., 1969—. Home: 105 S Mansfield St Los Angeless CA 90036 Office: 5045 Wilshire Blvd Los Angeles CA 90036

JEWELL, GILBERT, union ofcl. Sec.-Treas. Internat. Union Allied Indsl. Workers Am. AFL-CIO. Office: 3520 W Oklahoma Av Milwaukee WI 53215*

JEWELL, WILLIAM MACINTYRE, educator, artist; b. Lawrence, Mass., Dec. 9, 1904; s. Ernest C. and Elizabeth Galbraith (MacIntyre) J.; A.B., Harvard, 1927, student archtl. sch., 1927-29; m. Barbara Dailey, Sept. 6, 1939; children—Thomas N., Lydia R. Designer Boston archtl. firms, 1929-31; designer residences, Mass., N.H.; 1st one man show paintings Doll & Richards Gallery, Boston, 1934, other local, nat. groups shows, 1934—; instr. Boston U., 1934-46, asst. prof., 1946-50, asso. prof., 1950-54, prof. fine arts, 1955-70, prof. emeritus, 1970—, chmn. dept., 1955-68; faculty Harvard U. Extension, 1958—; rep. permanent collections Fogg Mus. Art, Farnsworth Mus., Rockland, Me., Boston U. Mus., other pvt. collections; portraits at Me. State House, Augusta, Putnam Lodge, Pomfret, Conn., others. Auditor, Boston Soc. Water Color Painters. Trustee Boston Arts Festival. Recipient Mitton gold medal and cash award, N.E. Artists, 1941, 46, 47, 62; grant-in-aid Am. Council Learned Socs., 1960; award spring exhbn. Boston Water Color Soc., 1960. Fellow Am. Acad. Arts and Sci.; mem Pierian Sodality, Harvard Glee Club Alumni Assn., Guild Boston Artists, Am. Water Color Soc., Colonial Soc. of Mass., Medieval Acad. (asst. editor Speculum 1956-62), Am. Assn. U. Profs., Coll. Art Assn., Harvard Grad. Sch. Design Assos., Copley Soc., Phi Beta Kappa (hon.). Club: St Botolph. Home: 37 Dana St Cambridge MA 02138 Office: 725 Commonwealth Av Boston MA 02215

JEWELL, WILLIAM SYLVESTER, educator; b. Detroit, July 2, 1932; s. Loyd Vernon and Marion (Sylvester) J.; B.Engring. Physics, Cornell U., 1954; M.S. in Elec. Engring., Mass. Inst. Tech., 1955, Sc.D., 1958; m. Elizabeth Gordon Wilson, July 7, 1956; children—Sarah, Thomas, Miriam, William Timothy. Asso. dir. mgmt. scis. div. Broadview Research Corp., Burlingame, Cal., 1958-60; asst. prof. dept. indsl. engring. and operations research U. Cal. at Berkeley, 1960-63, asso. prof., 1963-67, prof., 1967—, chmn. dept., 1967-69; v.p., chmn. Teknekron, Inc., Berkeley, 1968—. Cons. operations research problems, 1960—. Fulbright research scholar, France, 1966. Mem. Operations Research Soc. Am., Inst. Mgmt. Scis., Soc. Indsl. and Applied Math., Assn. for Computer Machinery,

Mensa, Sigma Xi, Triangle. Contbr. articles profl. jours. Home: 67 Loma Vista Orinda CA 94563 Office: U Cal Dept Indsl Engring and Operation Research Berkeley CA 94720

JEWETT, FRANK BALDWIN, Jr., mech. engr.; b. N.Y.C. Apr. 4, 1917; s. Frank B. and Fannie (Frisble) J.: B.S., Cal. Inst. Tech., 1938; M.B.A. magna cum laude, Harvard, 1940; m. Edar von L. Fleming, Sept. 5, 1942; children—Frank Baldwin, Robert F., Rebecca L., Edar F. Research asst. Harvard Bus. Sch., 1940-41; with Nat. Research Corp., 1941-47, v.p., mgr. vacuum engring. div., 1944-47; with Gen. Mills, Inc., 1947-55, dir. devel. and bus. adminstrn. research labs., also dir. aero. research labs., 1947-52, mng. dir. engring. research and devel. Mech. div., 1952-55; v.p., dir. Vitro Corp. Am., N.Y.C., 1956-58, exec. v.p., 1959, pres. dir., 1959-69; pres. Tech. Audit Assos., Inc., 1969—. Mem. sch. bd., Edina, Minn., 1953-55. Trustee Tabor Acad., Marion, Mass., Rockford Coll., Ill.; mem. corp. Woods Hole Oceanographic Instn.; dir. Silver Anniversary All Am. Found., Inc. Recipient certificate merit Crusade for Freedom, 1951. Registered profl. engr., Minn. Mem. Am. Soc. M.E., Am. Ordnance Assn., Newcomen Soc., So. Mass. Yacht Racing Assn. Clubs: Union League (N.Y.C.); Vineyard Haven Yacht (exec. com.) (Mass.); Norwalk (Conn.) Yacht, N.Y. Yacht. Home: 589 Oenoke Ridge New Canaan CT 06840

JEWETT, GEORGE FREDERICK, Jr., forest products exec.; b. Spokane, Wash., Apr. 10, 1927; s. George Frederick and Mary Pelton (Cooper) J.; B.A., Dartmouth, 1950; M.B.A., Harvard, 1952; m. Lucille Winifred McIntyre, July 11, 1953; children—Mary Elizabeth, George Frederick III. Asst. sec., asst. treas. Potlatch Forests, Inc., 1955-62, v.p. adminstrn., 1962-68, corporate v.p. adminstrn., 1968—, dir., 1957—. Chmn. San Francisco Com. of Asian Art and Culture. Trustee Pacific Med. Center, San Francisco, Asia Found.; chmn. Asian Art Found. San Francisco; rep. to nat. council Boy Scouts Am. Mem. Forest Products Research Soc., Met. Opera Assn. Clubs: St. Francis Yacht, Marin Yacht, New York Yacht. Home: Skyland Way Ross CA 94957 Office: P O Box 3591 San Francisco CA 94119

JEWETT, HUGH JUDGE, surgeon; b. Balt., Sept. 26, 1903; s. Hugh Judge, Jr. and Anne Van Lent (Ingraham) J.; student St. Paul's Sch., Concord, N.H., 1917-22; A.B., Johns Hopkins, 1926, M.D., 1930; m. Rosalind Huidekoper, Nov. 22, 1941 (div. Sept. 1971); 1 dau., Rosalind Nelson. Intern, Johns Hopkins Hosp., 1930-31, resident urologist, 1935-36; prof. urology, sch. medicine Johns Hopkins, 1966—; urologist Johns Hopkins Hosp., Ch. Home and Hosp., Balt. City Hosp.; cons. staff Walter Reed Army Hosp., Washington, 1948-59; chmn. registry genito- urinary pathology Armed Forces Inst. Pathology, 1958-64. Trustee Am. Urol. Research Found., 1952; pres. Md. Med. Service, Inc. (Blue Shield), 1950-54; councilor Med. and Chirurg. Faculty State Md., 1953-55. Served as lt. M.C., USNR, 1942. Recipient Barringer medal Am. Assn. Genito-Urinary Surgeons, 1962. Diplomate Am. Bd. Urology, Inc. (bd. govs. 1959-66). Fellow A.C.S. (gov. 1958-64); mem. Am. Urol. Assn. (pres. 1965-66; pres. of mid-Atlantic sect. 1956-57; recipient Ramon Guiteras award 1963), Clin. Soc. Genito-Urinary Surgeons (pres. 1968-69), Am. Assn. of Genito-Urinary Surgeons (pres. 1970-71), Soc. Univ. Urologists, Internat. Soc. Urology, Sociedad Venezolana de Urologia, Phi Beta Kappa, Alpha Delta Phi. Episcopalian. Clubs: Elkridge, L'Hirondelle, Hamilton Street, Johns Hopkins Faculty (Balt.). Author chpts. med. books. Editor-in-chief of Urological Surgery, Jour. of Urology; editorial bd. Rev. Surgery, Md. Med. Jour., 1952-60. Home: 3900 N Charles St Baltimore MD 21218 Office: 1201 N Calvert St Baltimore MD 21202

JEWETT, ROBERT HOMER, aero. engr.; b. Rice Lake, Wis, Apr. 21, 1910; s. Herman H. and Edna (Whiting) J.; B.S., U. Minn., 1931; m. Marjorie J. Fjerstad, Jan. 7, 1940; children—John Robert, Donald Scht, Charles W. Engr., Glen L. Martin Co., Balt., 1935; staff Dept. of War, Wright Field, Dayton, O., 1935-37; chief engr. Boeing Airplane Co., Seattle, 1937—, v.p., 1960—, asst. gen. mgr. aero space div., 1961-65, gen. mgr. missile and information systems, 1966—; tech. cons. Research and Devel. Ed., Dept. Def., also cons. Tech. Adv. Panel on Aero., 1956—. Recipient outstanding achievement award for graduates U. Minn., 1955. Registered profl. engr., Wash. State. Fellow Am. Inst. Aeros. and Astronautics. Home: 12461 N E Bellevue Redmond Rd Bellevue WA 98004 Office: 7755 E Marginal WaV Seattle WA 98108

JEWISON, NORMAN F., producer-dir.; b. Can.; student Malvern Collegiate Inst., Toronto, Ont., Can., 1940-44; B.A., Victoria Coll., U. Toronto, 1950. Dir. Belafonte, Danny Kaye, Jackie Gleason, Andy Williams TV shows, 1960; producer-dir. Judy Garland spls.; pictures directed include; 40 Pounds of Trouble, The Thrill of It All, Send Me No Flowers, Art of Love, The Cincinnati Kid, In the Heat of The Night (Acad. award 1967); producer, dir. The Russians Are Coming, The Russians Are Coming, Thomas Crown Affair, Gaily Gaily, Fiddler on the Roof; producer The Landlord. Address: care United Artists Corp 729 7th Av New York City NY 10019

JEWITT, DAVID WILLARD PENNOCK, banker; b. Cleve., Feb. 22, 1921; s. Homer Moore and Helen Katherine (Pennock) J.; B.A., Amherst Coll., 1943; Amherst Meml. fellow Harvard, 1946-47; m. Margaret Van Pelt Cool, Apr. 13, 1957; children—Andrea, Joel. With Irving Trust Co., N.Y.C., 1947-51, Chem. Corn Exchange Bank, N.Y.C., 1951-59; with Conn. Nat. Bank, Bridgeport, 1959—, sr. v.p., 1969—; dir. Conn. Devel. Credit Corp., Meriden, Edgcomb-Milford, Inc. Trustee Am. Seamen's Friend Soc., N.Y.C., 1949—, treas. 1950—; trustee Fairfield U. (recipient medal of Merit 1968). Served to lt. USNR, 1943-46. Decorated comdr. Order Ruben Dario (Nicaragua). Mem. Theodore Gordon Flyfishers, Nat. Beagle Club, The Pilgrims, Ex-Mems. Assn. Squadron A, Soc. Colonial Wars, Beta Theta Pi. Episcopalian. Clubs: Fairfield Beach; Algonquin (Bridgeport); Graduate (New Haven); Army and Navy (Washington); Royal Bermuda Yacht; Royal Swedish Yacht (Stockholm). Home: 1498 Bronson Rd Fairfield CT 06430 Office: 888 Main St Bridgeport CT 06602

JEWSON, RUTH HATHAWAY, (Mrs. Vance Jewson), assn. exec.; b. Ellendale, N.D., Mar. 3, 1914; d. Floyd C. and Mabel (Hay) Hathaway; M.S., U. Minn., 1971; m. W. Vance Jewson, Mar. 19, 1938; children—Douglas, Meredith, Roberta, Dwight. Tchr., Avon-Grove Consol. High Sch., West Grove, Pa., 1935-37, Hudson (Wis.) High Sch., 1937-38, U. High Sch., Mpls., 1939-40; research asst. U. Minn., 1938-39; tchr. adult edn. Mpls. Pub. Schs., 1951—; exec. officer Nat. Council Family Relations, 1956—. Mem. bd., sec. Minn. Council on Family Relations; standards and personnel com. Mpls. YWCA; bd. dirs. Christian Children's Fund; mem. bd. U. Minn. YWCA; past mem. bd. Pillsbury Citizens Service Neighborhood House; past co-chmn. strengthening family life com. Gov.'s Council Children and Youth. Mem. Am. (resolutions com.), Minn. (past v.p. and past sec.) home econs. assns., U. Minn. Coll. Agr., Forestry and Home Economics Alumni Assn. (bd. dirs. 1965-69), Twin City Home Economists in Homemaking (past pres.), Groves Conf., Mortar Bd., Phi Upsilon Omicron, Omicron Nu, Gamma Sigma Delta. Methodist. Home: 205 W Rustic Lodge Av Minneapolis MN 55409 Office: 1219 University Av S E Minneapolis MN 55414

JEX, RUSSELL BECK, consumer credit co. exec.; b. Burley, Ida., Dec. 12, 1919; s. Alex J. and La Rue (Beck) J.; B.A., U. Utah, 1940; student Harvard Grad. Bus. Sch., 1940-41; m. Mary Beckstead, Nov. 7, 1949 (div.); children—Sharie Lyn Hilton (stepdau.), Debra LaRue. With Peoples Finance & Thrift Co., Salt Lake City, 1955—, sec.-treas., 1951-64, pres., treas., 1964—, also dir.; sec., dir. Peoples Finance & Thrift Co. Utah, 1962-64, pres., treas., 1964—; pres. Peoples Finance & Thrift Co., South Ogden, also Ogden. Trust., past chmn. bd. Nat. Installment Bnkg. Sch., U. Colo. Served to capt. AUS, 1942-45. Mem. Utah Consumer Finance Assn. (dir., past pres.), Am. Indsl. Bankers Assn. (pres. 1961-62, chmn. bd. 1962-64, Utah dir.), Salt Lake City Jr. C. of C. (past dir.), Salt Lake C. of C. (adv. council) Rotarian.*

JHA, LAKSHMI KANT, Indian ambassador to U.S.; b. Nov. 22, 1913; ed. Hindu U. (Banaras); B.A., Trinity Coll., Cambridge (Eng.) U. Dep. sec. supply dept. Govt. India, 1942-46; chief controller imports and exports, 1947-50; joint sec. Ministry Commerce and Industry, 1950-56, additional sec., 1957-60; sec. Ministry Heavy Industries, 1956-57; sec. dept. econ. affairs Union Finance Ministry, 1960-64; sec. to prime minister, 1964-67; gov. Res. Bank India, 1967-69; ambassador to U.S., Washington, 1969—. Chmn. contracting parties to GATT, 1957-58; chmn. UN interim com. for coordination internat. commodity arrangements, 1959-61. Author: India's Foreign Trade. Address: Indian Embassy 2107 Massachusetts Av NW Washington DC 20008*

JHUNG, FINIS, ballet dancer; b. May 28, 1937; grad. U. Utah. Prin. dancer Harkness Ballet, 1964—. Address: 4 E 75th St New York City NY 10021

JILLANA, ballerina; b. Hackensack, N.J., Oct. 11, 1939; d. W.M. and M.K. (Knoblauch) Zimmermann; student Profl. Sch. N.Y., 1953. Ballerina, N.Y.C. Ballet, 1953-66, ret.; tchr., 1966—. Appeared With Am. Ballet Theatre, 1957-58, on Broadway in Destry Rides Again, 1958-59, with Los Angeles Civic Light Opera Co., 1956, also on numerous TV shows.

JIMENEZ, JORGE JAIME, cons. engr.; b. Rio Piedras, P.R., Oct. 4, 1908; s. Juan Jose and Mila (Lopez) J.; B.C.E., U. Mich., 1933; grad. Command and Gen. Staff Sch., 1944; m. Bernice Brackel, Apr. 7, 1933; children—James John, Mila Louise, Mark Courtney, Jr. engr., supt. San Juan Municipal Water Works, 1934-36; constrn. supt. P. R. Re-constrn. Adminstrn., 1936-39; asst. dir. operations Works Project Adminstrn. for P.R., 1939-40; dir. Isabela Irrigation Service, 1946-47; commr. interior, P.R., 1947-52; cons. engr., 1952—. Served with the Q.M.C., AUS, 1940-46, now col. Quartermaster Corps Reserve ret. Major Boston Sch. Cadets, City of Boston, 1928—. Awarded Franklin Medal, Cumston's prize, Boston English High Sch., 1928; Distinguished visitor, Mexico City, Mexico, 1949. Fellow Am. Soc. C.E.; mem. Colegio de Ingenieros de P.R., Sociedad de Ingenieros de P.R., Am. Rd. Builders Assn. (hon.), Latin Am. Soc. (pres. U. Mich. 1933), Assn. U.S. Army (pres. Antillies chpt. 1961), Res. Officers Assn. (past pres. P.R. dept.), Scabbard and Blade, Phi Kappa Phi, Phi Eta Sigma. Rotarian (pres. San Juan 1961-62). Home: No 5 Jaguas St Milaville Rio Piedras PR 00926 Office: GPO Box 2288 San Juan PR 00936

JIMENEZ, JOSEPH GUSTAVE, oil co. exec.; b. New Orleans, Feb. 20, 1904; s. Alfonso L. and Edmee (Andry) J.; B.A., U. So. Cal., 1927; postgrad. Harvard, 1927-28, 1929- 30; m. Margaret Jane Clarke, Sept. 3, 1928. With Tidewater Oil Co., 1930- 66, successively various sales positions, 1930-46, asst. dist. marketing mgr., 1946-54, asst. div. marketing mgr., 1954-56, div. marketing mgr., 1956-58, v.p., gen. mgr., 1958-66; v.p. CORCO, Inc., subsidiary Commonwealth Oil Refinery Co., Inc., 1966-69, cons., 1969—. Mem. Am. Petroleum Inst., Delta Chi. Clubs: Greenwich (Conn.) Country; Wilmington (Del.); Pinnacle (N.Y.C.). Address: 49 Hunting Ridge Rd Greenwich CT 06830

JIMENEZ, PRIVADO GARCIA, Philippine diplomat; b. Binan, Philippines, Aug. 21 1918; s. Jose and Tomasa (Garcia) J.; A.A., Far Eastern U., Manila, 1941; m. Imelda Yatco, Jan. 3, 1945; children—Maria Rosario, Edmundo, Emmanuel, Maria Lourdes. Admitted to Phillipine bar, 1941; register of deeds, Laguna, Phillipines, 1945-46; joined Dept. Fgn. Affairs, 1946; Philippine participant UN internship program 1949; chief div. UN. affairs Dept. Fgn. Affairs, 1950-56, counselor on coordination and rev., 1957-61; chief mission, 1959—; mem. UNESCO Nat. Commn. of Philippines, 1957-61; acting insp.-gen. fgn. service , 1960-61; dep. permanent rep. Philippines to UN, 1962—, A.E. and P., 1963—; professorial lectr. internat. law and polit. law Far Eastern U., 1949-61. Philippine rep. 2d regional conf. UNESCO Nat. Commns., Bangkok, 1951; alternate rep. Security Council, 1963, UNICEF Exec. Bd., 1963-65. Gen. Assembly UN, 1954, 62, 63, 64; Philippine rep. Spl. Com. on Apartheid, 1963—. Home: 150 E 77th St New York City NY 10021 Office: Philippine Mission to UN 13 E 66th St New York City NY 10021

JINKS, ROBERT LARRY, newspaper editor; b. Mt. Pleasant, Tex., Jan. 26, 1929; s. Leon Carlton and Mary (Cunningham) J.; B.J., U. Mo., 1950; M.S., Columbia, 1956; children—Laura Beth, Daniel Carlton; m. 2d, Ann Claire Van Raesteyn, May 8, 1971. News editor Muskogee (Okla.) Times-Democrat., 1950-51; reporter Greensboro (N.C.) Daily News, 1953-55; reporter, city editor Charlotte (N.C) Observer, 1950-60; mem. staff Miami (Fla). Herald, 1960—, mng. editor, 1966—. Sec. Dade County chpt. A.R.C. Served with AUS, 1951-53. Named to 50th anniversary honors list Columbia Grad. Sch. Journalism, 1963. Unitarian. Home: 14530 SW 64th Ct Miami FL 33158 Office: 1 Herald Plaza Miami FL 33101

JOACHIM, HAROLD, museum ofcl.; b. Göttingen, Germany, Jan. 5, 1909; s. Johannes and Else (Gensel) J.; Ph.D., U. Leipzig, Germany, 1935. Came to U.S., 1938, naturalized, 1944. Asst. dept. printing and graphic arts Harvard Library, 1940-41; research asst., later asst. curator dept. prints and drawings Chgo. Art Inst., 1946-56, curator prints, drawings, 1958— curator prints Mpls. Inst. Arts. 1956-58. Served with AUS, 1941-45. Contbr. articles Art Inst. Chgo. Quar., Mpls. Inst. Arts Bull. Office: Art Inst of Chgo Chicago IL 60603

JOANIS, JOHN WESTON, ins. co. exec. b. Hopewell, Va., June 13, 1918; s. Edmund W. and Emma Elvira (Westen) J.; LL.B., U. Wis., 1942; grad. Advanced Mgmt. Program, Harvard, 1950; m. Marian g. Sinrud, Aug. 16, 1945; children—Susan Kay, Mary Ellen, William John. Admitted to Wis. bar, 1943; pvt. practice, Oshkosh, 1945-47; with Hardware Mut. Casulty Company (now Sentry Ins. a Mutual Co.), Stevens Point, Wis., 1947—, v.p., gen. counsel, 1956-62, exec. v.p., 1962-66, pres., chief exec. officer, 1966—, also dir.; chmn. bd., dir. Sentry Life Ins. Co. N.Y., 1966—; pres., dir. Sentry Corp., 1967—; dir. Sentry Plan, Inc., Sentry Found., Inc., Am. Mut. Ins. Alliance, 1st Nat. Bank Stevens Point, Dairyland Ins. Co., Cloverleaf Ins. Co. (London), Manor Ins. Co. (Bermuda), Dairyland Services, Inc., Sentry Investment Mgmt., Inc., Sentry Ins. Mgmt., Ltd., Manor Ins., Ltd. (Australia), Manor Holdings, Ltd., Comml. Life Assurance Ltd. Served to capt. USAAF, 1942-45. Mem. Am., Wis. bar assns., Internat. Assn. Ins. Counsel, Phi Delta Phi Clubs: Rotary, Elks (Stevens Point); Madison (Wis.); Milwaukee Athletic; Union League (Chgo.). Home: 709 Ridge Rd Stevens Point WI 54481 Office: 1421 Strongs Av Stevens Point WI 54481

JOANNING, HAROLD T., life ins. co. exec.; b. Alton, Ia., May 30, 1927; A.B., Claremont Men's Coll., 1954. With Pacific Mut. Life Ins. Co., 1944—, asst. v.p. adminstrn., 1964-65, treas., 1965—, v.p., 1970—. Mem. United Way. Office: Pacific Mut Bldg Los Angeles CA 90054

JOBE, LARRY ALTON, govt. ofcl.; b. Knox City, Tex., Jan. 12, 1940; s. Lloyd Alton and Georgia (Swift); B.B.A., N. Tex. State U., 1961, postgrad., 1961-65; m. Adrienne Sue Edwards, Sept. 1, 1960; children—Lorrie Aileen, Lezlie Amee, Lowell Alton, Lloyd Alan, Leland Austin. Joined Alexander Grant & Co., Dallas, 1961, mgr., 1967-69, partner, 1968-69; asst. sec. commerce, Washington, 1969—. Mem. accounting adv. bd. N. Tex. State U., U. Tex. Recipient Excellence in Accounting award Haskins & Sells Found., 1960, U.S. Interagency Audit Tng. Program award, 1970. C.P.A., Tex., Ill., Ia., D.C. Mem. Am. Inst. C.P.A.'s Tex., Ill., D.C. socs. C.P.A.'s, Nat. Accounting Assn., Am. Soc. Pub. Adminstrn., Fed. Govt. Accountants Assn., Blue Key, Phi Eta Sigma, Alpha Chi, Alpha Lambda Pi, Beta Alpha Psi. Home: 2762 N Quebec St Arlington VA 22207 Office: Dept Commerce Washington DC 20230

JOBE, MORRIS BUTLER, aerospace co. exec.; b. Princeton, Ia., Jan. 29, 1916; s. William H. and Irene (Butler) J.; B.A. in Edn., U. Akron, 1938; certificate Northwestern Inst. Mgmt., 1957; m. Maxine Gerber, Nov. 13, 1942; children—Barbara (Mrs. David Sink), Kathryn. With Goodyear Aerospace Corp., 1938—, pres., chief exec. officer, 1968—. Mem. Nat. Security Indsl. Assn. (trustee, exec. com.), Aerospace Industries Assn. (bd. govs.), Am. Inst. Aero. and Astronautics, Am. Ordnance Assn., (bd. dirs. Cleve,), Phi Kappa Tau. Trustee Mt. Union Coll., 1968—. Mason (32). Clubs: City Portage Country (Akron); Phoenix Country; Wigwam Country (Litchfield Park, Ariz.). Home: 2329 Lancaster Rd Akron OH 44313 Office: 1210 Massillon Rd Akron OH 44315

JOBIN, PIERRE, medical educator; b. Quebec City, Can., Sept. 8, 1907; s. Albert and Julie-Anna (Delage) J.; B.A., Laval U., 1927, M.D., 1932; m. Blanche C. De Lery, Feb. 6, 1970; 1 son, Pierre G. Intern Hotel Dieu Hosp., Quebec, 1932-33, resident, 1933-34; surgeon, Lyon and Paris, France, 1937-41; head dept. anatomy Laval U., Quebec, 1941-70, dir. continuing med. edn., 1970—. Clubs: Richelieu, Royal Quebec Golf (Quebec). Home: 610 Chemin St Louis Quebec 6 Quebec Canada

JOBIN, RAOUL, opera singer; b. Quebec City, Canada, Apr. 8, 1906; s. Raoul and Amanda (Bedard) J.; ed. in Canada; m. Therese Drouin, Apr. 22, 1930; children—Claudette, Andre, France. Debut with Paris Grand Opera, 1930; mem. Paris Grand Opera, 1930-40, 47-55; Paris Opéra Comique, 1936-40, 1947-55; sang in concerts and opera, Belgium, Holland, Switzerland, Spain, France, Canada, U.S., Italy, Egypt; debut with Met. Opera, N.Y. City, in Manon, Feb. 19, 1940; mem. Met. Opera, 1940-50, 56, Buenos Aires (Teatro Colon), 1941-43, 45, 48, 54; Rio de Janeiro (Municipal) 1939, 41-43; Mexico (Opera Nacional), 1944-48; tchr. Conservatoire de Musique et D'Art Dramatique, Que., 1948-61, dir. Conservatoire, 1961-70; cultural adviser Delegation Générale du Quebec in Paris, 1970—. Address: 66 rue Pergolése Paris 16 éme France

JOBSON, ALFRED PEARS, former ins. exec.; b. W. Hartlepool, Eng., Apr. 27, 1902; s. Hugh George and Agnes Anne (Simpson) J.; ed. pub. and pvt. schs., Eng.; m. Katharine Bleecker, Sept. 23, 1939. Came to U.S., 1911, naturalized, 1943. With Lukis Stewart & Co., Montreal, Can., 1920-21; began with Marsh & McLennan, Inc., N.Y.C., 1921, became sr. v.p., 1959, also dir.; dir. Salisbury, Brokerage, Inc., Cedarpine Found., 1080 Apartment Corp. Clubs: N.Y. Yacht, Metropolitan, India House (N.Y.C.); Nat. Golf Links Am. (Southampton, L.I.); Quoque Field (L.I.); Upland Farm Gun (Remsenburg L.I.); American London, Eng.). Home: 1080 Fifth Av New York City NY 10028

JOCHIM, EDWARD WILLIAM, former corp. exec.; b. Chgo., Sept. 17, 1906; s. A.H. and Mary (Hanafen) J.; student U. Ill., 1925-29; B.S., Ill. Inst. Tech., 1931; m. Esther D. Barkman, Aug. 13, 1938; children—Edward William, William Edward. With U.S. Gypsum Co., 1928-32, Mills Industries, 1933-39; asst. works mgr. Nat. Metal Trades Assn., 1939-40; with Johnson & Johnson 1940-71, former v.p. charge Wilmington (Ill.) plant and Sunnyvale (Cal.) plant Personal Products Corp. div., also dir. parent co., ret., 1971; dir. Flick- Reedy Corp. Mem. Will County Com. to Aid Non-Pub. High Schs. Chmn. bd. trustees Ill. Benedictine Coll. Mem. pres.'s council Coll. St. Francis, Joliet; lay adv. board St. Joseph Hosp., Joliet, mem. businessmen's council Lewis Coll. Mem. edn. com. Taxpayers Fedn. Ill. Registered profl. engr., Ill. Mem. Am. Arbitration Assn., Soc. Advancement Mgmt. (nat. pres. 1952-53), Am. Mgmt. Assn., Ill., Will-Grundy County (past pres.) mfrs. assns. Clubs: Joliet Country; Union League (Chgo.). Home: 1010 Western Av Joliet IL 60435

JOCHUM, EUGEN, conductor; b. Babenhausen, Germany, Nov. 1, 1902; s. Ludwig and Judith (Seitz) J.; student Augsburg (Germany) Conservatory, 1922; M.A., Hochschule für Musik, Munich, Germany, 1925; m. Maria Montz, Dec. 3, 1927; children—Veronica von Moltke, Romana. Asst. conductor Mönchengladbach, 1925-26, Kiel Opera, 1926-29, Mannheim Nat Theatre 1929-30, Duisberg, 1930-32; chief conductor Berlin Opera and Radio, 1932-34; Hamburg State Opera and Philharmocic Orch., 1934-49, Bavarian Radio Orch., 1949-59; guest conductor 1959—, including Amsterdam Concertgebouw, Berlin Philharmonic, West Berlin Opera, Lyric Opera, Chgo., also capitals of Europe, numerous festivals, U.S. orchestras. Named Bayerische Verdienstorden, 1959; decorated commendatore Di San Cregorio Magno (Vatican), 1963; recipient Brahms plague, 1935, Brucker medal, 1938. Address: Brunhildenstrasse 2 Munich 19 Germany

JOCKERS, HAROLD WILLIAM, dept. store exec.; b. N.Y.C., July 31, 1906; S. Harry M. and Charlotte (Johnson) J.; B.C.S., N.Y.U., 1926; m. Helen Dietz, Mar. 16, 1929; children—Carol (Mrs. Robert M. Amick), Helen (Mrs. J.E. Bradley, Jr.). Pres. McCreery & Co., Pittsburg, 1936-39, McDougall Southwick Co., Seattle, 1939-41; pres., dir. Merc. Stores Co., Inc., N.Y.C., 1941-60; became chmn. bd. and chief exec. officer, 1960, now chmn. bd. dir. Clubs: Union League (N.Y.C.); Woodway Country (Stamford, Conn.); Tokeneke (Darien, Conn.). Home: Pembroke Rd Darien CT 06820 Office: 128 W 31st St New York City NY 10001

JODOIN, CLAUDE, labor union ofcl.; b. Westmount, Que., Can., May 25, 1913; s. Henri and Beatrice (Crepeau) J.: student Ste. Marie Coll., Jean de Brebeuf Coll., (both Montreal); m. Lily Cooke, Feb. 14, 1948. Organizer Internat. Ladies' Garment Workers' Union, 1937-40, asst. mgr. Montreal joint bd. Dressmakers' Union, 1940, gen. mgr., 1947; v.p. Montreal Traders and Labor Council, 1940-42, pres., 1947-54; v.p. Trades and Labor Congress of Can., 1949-54, chmn. nat. union-label com., 1952-54, pres., 1954-66; pres. Canadian Labour Congress, 1956-68; exec. bd. Internat. Labor Ofc. Councillor Montreal City Council, 1940-42, 47-54; mem. Que. Legislature for Montreal-St. James, 1942-44. Mem. exec. bd. ICFTU, 1940—; mem.

Econ. Council Can., Canadian Trade Com., Can.-Am Com.; labor adviser Canadian World Exhbn; mem. Nat. Conf. on Contennial. Mem. exec. com. Canadian Red Cross. Home: 200 Somerset St W Ottawa Ontario Canada Office: 100 Argyle Av Ottawa Ontario Canada

JOEL, HARRY J., mining exec.; b. Sept. 4, 1894; s. Jack Barnato Joel; ed. Malvern Coll., Eng. Hon. pres. Johannesburg Consol. Investment Co.; dir. De Beers Cons. Mines, Ltd., and other cos. Served with 15th Hussars, World War I. Clubs: Buck's Jockey (Newmarket). Address: Childwick Bury St Albans Herts England

JOELSON, CHARLES S., judge; b. Paterson, N.J., Jan. 27, 1916; s. Harry and Jennie (Ellenstein) J.; B.A., Cornell U. 1937, LL.B., 1939; 1 dau., Susan. Admitted to N.J. bar, 1939, and practiced in Paterson, until 1961; city counsel, 1950-53; dep. atty. gen. N.J., 1954- 56; prosecutor Passaic County, 1956-58; dir. criminal investigation N.J., 1958-60; mem. 87th-91st congresses 8th Dist. N.J., mem. appropriations com.; judge N.J. Superior Ct., 1969—. Served to ensign USNR, 1942-44. Mem. N.J. Bar Assn. Democrat. Home: 599 Broadway Paterson NJ 07514 Office: Passaic County Courthouse Paterson NJ 07514

JOFFE, JOSEPH, educator; b. Moscow, Russia, Oct. 14, 1909; s. Lew Moses and Sophie (Joffe) J.; came to U.S., 1921, naturalized, 1926; A.B., Columbia, 1929, B.S. in chem. Engring., 1930, M.A. in Physics, 1931, Ph.D. in Phys. Chemistry, 1933; m. Bertha Pashkovsky, June 20, 1931; children— Robert, Paul, Richard. Asst. physics dept. Columbia, 1931, Univ. fellow chemistry, 1931-1932; instr. to prof. Newark Coll. Engring., 1932-65, Distinguished prof. chem. engring, 1965—, acting chmn. dept. indsl. chem. engring., 1946-48, charge sponsored research, 1951-61, chmn. dept. chem. engring., 1963—; chem. engr. Esso Research & Engring. Co., summer 1948—. Mem. Am. Inst. Chem. Engrs., Am. Chem. Soc., Am. Soc. Engring. Edn., Phi Beta Kappa, Sigma Xi, Tau Beta Pi, Phi Lambda Upsilon. Contbr. profl. jours Home: 77 Parker Av Maplewood NJ 07040

JOFFREY, ROBERT ANVER BEY KHAN, ballet dir.; b. Seattle, Dec. 24, 1930; s. Dolha and Marie (Galetti) J.; student Mary Ann Wells Sch. of Dance, Seattle, 1944-48, Cornish Sch. Music, Seattle, 1945-48, Sch. Am. Ballet, 1948; student modern dance with May O'Donnell, Gertrude Shurr, 1949-52. Mem. faculty High Sch. Performing Arts, N.Y.C., 1950-55; founder ballet sch. Am. Ballet Center, 1953, dir. faculty, 1953-65; resident choreographer N.Y. city Center Opera, 1955-61; founder 1956, since dir. Robert Joffrey Ballet Co.; company on tour Near East for State Dept., 1962-63, toured Russia 1963, performed at White House, 1963, 65, ann. U.S. tours, 1956-64; organizer dance dept. Chautauqua, N.Y., 1959; choreographer NBC-TV Opera, 1955, 57, 58; creator ballets; Persephone, Scaramouche, Umpateedle, Pas des Deesses, Bal Masque, Pierot Lunaire, Harpsichord Concerto, Gamelon. Pres. Ballet Am. Found.; bd. dirs. Found. Am. Dance. Recipient ann. award Nat. Acad. Dance Masters, Chgo., 1962; Dance mag. award, 1964; Dance Masters of Am. award, 1965; Ford Found. grant Robert Joffrey Ballet, 1964. Office: 434 6th Av New York City NY 10009 also 23 W 16th St New York City NY 10011

JOHANN, ROBERT OLIVER, educator; b. Bronx, N.Y., Apr. 7, 1924; s. Philip A. and Olive (Kelley) J.; A.B., St. Louis U., 1947, M.A., 1948; Ph.D., Louvain U., 1953; S.T.L., Woodstock Coll., 1955; m. Claire J. Klingel, June 27, 1970. Mem. Soc. of Jesus, 1942-69; ordained priest Roman Catholic Ch., 1954; mem. faculty Fordham U., 1956—, prof., 1968—; vis. asso. prof. philosophy Yale, 1963-64; lectr. Christian ethics Union Theol. Sem., 1966; Luther A. Weigle vis. prof. Yale Div. Sch., 1968. Mem. Am. Theol. Soc., Am. Cath. Philos. Assn., Metaphys. Soc. Am. (councillor 1962-66), Am. Philos. Assn. Author: The Meaning of Love, 1955; The Pragmatic Meaning of God, 1966; Building the Human, 1968. Home: 2465 Palisade Av Bronx NY 10463

JOHANNESON, HELGL, atty. gen. N.D.; b. Gardar, N.D., June 21, 1906; s. Benedict and Hildur (Gudjonson) J.; student U. N.D., 1924-25; LL.B., St. Paul Coll. Law, 1930; m. Ann Katherine Prokosch, Nov. 27, 1930; children—Carole (Mrs.Harry Miller), Kent, Jeanne (Mrs. Gordon Cummings) Robert Jay. Admitted to N.D. bar, 1930; states atty. Pembina County, N.D., 1932-36; asst. atty. gen. N.D., 1951-52, 1st asst. atty. gen., 1952-60, atty. gen., 1960—. Mem. Newfolden (Minn.) Sch. Bd., 1946-48; bd. dirs. Marshall County (Minn.) Locker Assn., 1946-50. Bd. dirs. Boy Scout Club, Newfolden, 1943-48. Mem. Am., N.D. bar assns. Republican. Catholic. Club: Newfolden Commercial (pres. 1944-50). Home: 1616 Av E East Bismarck ND 58501 Office: State Capitol Bldg Bismarck ND 58501

JOHANNESSON, ERIC O., educator. Prof., chmn. dept. Scandinavian lit. U. Cal. at Berkeley. Office: 1305 Dunnelle Hall U Cal Berkeley CA 94720*

JOHANNSEN, ALICE E., museologist; b. Havana, Cuba, Apr. 19, 1911, d. Herman Smith and Alice (Robinson) Johannsen; B.Sc. in Geology, McGill U., Montreal, Can., 1934; student Newark Mus. 1934-35, Nat. Gallery Can., 1935-36. Sec., travelling lectr. Fine Arts Com. Man., Can., 1936-39; sec. demonstrator zoology McGill U., 1939-42, mem. staff univ. museums, 1942- -, dir., 1951-67, coordinating dir. McGill U. Museums, 1968—; dir. Redpath Mus., 1968—. Chmn. Canadian nat. com. Internat. Council on Museums, 1968—. Mem. Canadian Museums Assn. (council 1955- 59, pres. 1959-61), Province Que. Museums Assn. (a founder, pres. 1958- 61), Am. Assn. Museums (chmn. coll. and univ. sect. 1957, pres. N.E. conf. 1957, (Council 1961—), Canadian Handicrafts Guild, Canadian Field Naturalists Soc., British Museums Assn., Am. Nature Study Soc., Sigma Xi, Delta Gamma. Address: Redpath Mus McGill U Montreal 110 Quebec Canada

JOHANNSEN, GRANT, pianist; b. Salt Lake City, 1921; student of Robert Casadesus, Egon Petri, Roger Sessions, Nadia Boulanger; H.H.D., U. Utah, 1966; m. Helen Taylor (dec. Oct. 1950); 1 son, David; m. 2d, Zara Nelsova, 1963. Debut Times Hall, N.Y.C. 1944; first European tour, 1949, S.Am. tour, 1952, Australia, 1960, USSR, 1963, 65; appearance with numerous orchestras throughout U.S., also festivals including Aix-en-Provence, France, Amsterdam, The Netherlands, also Brevard, N.C., Prague, Bergen, Aspen, Tanglewood; performed maj. capital cities of Europe, 1964, 66; radio and TV include Bell Telephone Hour, Standard Hour, also Piano Playhouse; recording artist for Concert Hall, Vox, Capitol, His Master's Voice. Recipient 1st prize Ostend (Belgium) Internat. Piano Festival, 1949; laurel wreath from King Olaf V of Norway. Address: care Columbia Artists Mgmt Inc 165 W 57th St New York City NY 10019

JOHANNSEN, ROBERT WALTER, educator; b. Portland, Ore., Aug. 22, 1925; s. Walter George and Hedwig Bertha (Flemming) J.; B.A., Reed Coll., 1948; M.A., U. Wash., 1949, Ph.D., 1953; m. Lois Adele Calderwood, Mar. 19, 1949; children—Nancy Louise, Robert Douglas. Instr. history U. Wash., 1953-54; asst. prof., then asso. prof. U. Kan., 1954-59; mem. faculty U. Ill., 1959—, prof. history, 1962—, chmn. dept., 1963-67, Center for Advanced Study, 1968- 69; vis. lectr. U. Wis., 1957; vis. asso. prof. U. Ore., summer 1960, Duke, Summer 1962. vis. Coe. prof. Stanford, summer 1970. Served with F.A., AUS, 1944-46. Recipient Award of Merit, Am. Assn. State and Local History, 1962; Guggenheim fellow, 1967-68. Mem. Am. (recipient Koontz prize Pacific Coast br. 1953), So., Western Hist. assns., Ill. Hist. Soc., Orgn. Am. Historians (Pelzer prize 1952), Am. Assn. U. Profs., Am. Studies Assn. Author: Frontier Politics and the Sectional Conflict, 1955; The Union in Crisis, 1965; Democracy on Trial, 1966; also articles. Editor: (with H. V. Jaffa) In the Name of the People, 1959; The Letters of Stephen A. Douglas, 1961. Home: 1019 W Union St Champaign IL 61820

JOHANOS, DONALD, orch. conductor; b. Cedar Rapids, Ia., Feb. 10, 1928; s. Gregory Hedges and Doris (Nelson) J.; Mus.B., Eastman Sch. Music, 1950, Mus.M., 1952; D.F.A. (hon.), Coe Coll., 1962; m. Thelma Trimble, Aug. 27, 1950; children—Jennifer Claire, Thea Christine, Gregory Bruce (dec.), Andrew Mark, Eve Marie. Mus. dir. Altoona (Pa.) Symphony, 1953-56, Johnstown (Pa.) Symphony, 1955-56; asso. cond. Dallas Symphony Orch., 1957-61, resident cond., 1961-62, mus. dir., 1962—; guest condr. Phila. Orch., Amsterdam Concertgebouw Orch., Pitts. Symphony, Rochester Philharmonic, New Orleans Philharmonic, Denver Symphony, Vancouver Symphony, Netherlands Radio Philharmonic, Swiss Radio Orch., Mpls. Symphony; tchr. Pa. State U., 1953-55, So. Methodist U., 1958-62, Hockaday Sch., 1962-65. Advanced study grantee Am. Symphony Orch. League and Rockefeller Found., 1955-58. Mem. Am. Fedn. Musicians Internat. Congress of Strings (dir.). Office: Dallas Symphony Orchestra P O Box 8472 Dallas TX 75205

JOHANSEN, ERLING, educator; b. Overhalla, Norway, Apr. 8, 1923; s. Trygve Vilmar and Jenny M. (Gansmo) J.; Artium. Orkdal Langsygymnsa Orkdal, Norway, 1943; D.M.D., Tufts Coll., 1949, Ph.D., U. Rochester, 1955; m. Inger M. Nordback, July 4, 1952; children—Erling T., Erik B., Steven. Naturalized, 1963. Student instr. oral pathology Tufts Coll. Dental Sch., Boston, 1948-49; instr. oral histology Eastman Sch. Dental Hygiene, Rochester, N.Y., 1952-64; asst. prof. dental research Univ. Rochester, 1955-58, asso. prof., 1958-61, prof., chmn. dept. dentistry. dental research Sch. Medicine and Dentistry, 1955—, Margaret and Cy Weicher prof. dental research, 1966—; hon. guest prof. Kanawoga (Japan) Dental Sch., 1969; lectr., Japan, Korea, Taiwan, Philippines, Thailand, India, Iran. Eastman fellow, dental research, 1952 fellow, dental research, 1950-52, 53-54, Squibb 1952-53, U. Rochester sr. fellow dental research, 1954-55; spl. cons. Nat. Inst. Dental Research, 1959-64; mem. clin. fellowship review panel USPHS, 1960-64, anat., path. fellowship com., 1968-70. Bd. dirs. Assn. Instns. for Advanced Study in Dentistry, 1967—. Fellow A.A.A.S. (counselor dental sect. 1963-67, Internat. (traveling scholar), Am. colls. dentists; mem. Am. Assn. Dental Sci. (com. on advanced edn. 1968-70, v.p. advanced edn. programs 1970-73), Internat. Assn. Dental Research (counselor 1958-61), Am. Pub. Health Assn., Am. Dental Assn. (mem. fellowship panel coll. student fellowship program 1964-69), Dental Soc. Norway, Korean Dental Soc. (hon.), N.Y. Soc. Med. Research, Robert R. Andrews Honor Soc., Fedn. Dentaire Internat., Sigma Xi, Omicron Kappa Upsilon. Co- editor: Proc. 25th Year celebration U. Rochester Dental Research Fellowship Program, 1955. Asso. editor Dental Clinics of North America, 1962. Adv. editorial bd. Jour. Dental Research, 1961-65, asso. editor, 1971—. Author articles in field. Home: 27 Cricket Hill Dr Pittsford NY 14534 Office: 260 Crittenden Blvd Rochester NY 14620

JOHANSEN, JOHN MACLANE, architect; b. N.Y.C., June 29, 1916; s. John Christen and Jean (MacLane) J.; grad. Choate Sch., 1935; B.S. cum laude, Harvard, 1939, B. Arch., 1942; B.F.A. (hon.), Maryland Inst.; m. Mary Lee Longcope, Feb. 2, 1946; children—Deborah, Christen; m. 2d, Mary Ellen Goode, Aug. 21, 1955. Propr. archtl. offices, N.Y.C., 1962—, New Canaan, Conn., 1949; formerly tchr. Pratt Inst., Harvard, Mass. Inst. Tech., Yale, Carnegie Inst. Tech., R.I. Sch. Design, now prof. arch. Columbia: lectr. numerous univs. and socs. throughout U.S. and Can., 1952-63; prin. works include U.S. Exhb. Pavillion, Internat. Trade Fair, Yugoslavia, 1956, Taylor residence, Westport, Conn., 1962, Clowes Meml. Hall, Butler U., Indpls., 1963, U.S. Embassy, Dublin, Ireland, 1964, Dixwell Redevel. Project, New Haven, 1964. Orlando (Fla.) Pub. Library, numerous others. Recipient Arnold W. Brunner Meml. prize in architecture Nat. Inst. Arts and Letters, 1968. Fellow A.I.A.; mem. Conn. Soc. Architects. Archtl. League N.Y. (pres. 1968-70). Soc. Archtl. Historians. U.S. Inst. Theatre Technicians. Author articles. Home: PO Box 306 Canaan CT 06840 also New York City NY 10001 Office: 401 E 37th St New York City NY 10016

JOHANSEN, WALDEMAR WLLHELM ANTON, educator; b. Berlin, Germany, Oct. 18, 1904; s. Anton and Minna (Gabriel) J.; student Gymanasium Osnabruck, Germany, 1919-21; Acad. Fine Arts, Munich, Germany, 1922-23; student (scholar 1927) Art Inst.Chgo. 1927-30; Alfred U., 1931, U. So. Cal., 1932; A.B., A.M., Stanford, 1933: m. Juantia Zerbe. Came to U.S., 1923, naturalized, 1930. Free-lance designer, advt. designer, art instr., theatre designer, technician. U.S., 1923-36: head art dept. Santa Monica Jr. Coll., 1936-Jan. 1937; art and tech. dir. Meml. Hall, Stanford, 1937-42; program dir. Montalvo Found. of San Francisco Art Assn., 1946; chmn. art dept. U. of Cal., Santa Barbara Coll., 1947; became chmn. art dept. and prof. art, San Francisco State Coll., 1948, now prof. indsl. arts: cons. and designer, product styling and advt. in San Francisco, 1947—; cons., designer numerous theater groups; exhibited in group shows; participant in pub. art activities; art dir. San Francisco Opera Assn.; cons. U.S. Aid, Liberia, West Africa. Mem. Pacific Arts Assn. (pres. 1952-54), Delta Phi Delta. Phi Delta Kappa. Club Bohemian. Address: San Francisco State College San Francisco CA 94132

JOHANSON, PERRY BERTIL, architect; b. Greeley, Colo., May 9, 1910; s. Erik and Martina (Pehrson) J.; B.Arch. (traveling scholar 1931), U. Wash., 1934; m. Jean Louise Peterson, Apr. 4, 1936; two children—Peter Erik, Kristina Therese (Mrs. Bruce Peters). Partner, Smith-Caroll & Johanson, Seattle, 1935-50, Naramore-Bain-Brady & Johanson, Seattle, 1943—; works include VA Hosp., Seattle, U. Wash. Health Sci. Bldg., Swedish Hosp., Seattle, IBM Bldg., Seattle, Seattle First Nat. Bank Bldg. Mem. of plan commn. King County, 1951-63, chmn., 1953-54, vice chmn., 1956-57; pres. Nat. Archtl. Accrediting Bd., 1955-57. Trustee Wash. Children's Home, pres., 1957-59. Fellow A.I.A. (pres. Wash. 1950-51). Home: 5261 148th Av SE Bellevue WA 98006 Office: 904 7th Av Seattle WA 98104

JOHN, DEWITT, ch. exec.; b. Safford, Ariz., Aug. 1, 1915; s. Franklin Howard and Frances (DeWitt) J.; B.A., Principia Coll., Ill., 1936; M.A., U. Chgo., 1937; M.S., Columbia, 1938; m. Morley Marshall, Feb. 14, 1942; children—DeWitt, Jennifer. Editorial page writer St. Petersburg (Fla.) Times, 1938-39; mem. staff Christian Sci. Monitor, Boston, 1939-42, editor, 1964- 70, mgr. Christian Sci. coms. on publ., 1962-64, ch. dir., 1970—. Served with USNR, 1942- 45. Decorated Bronze Star medal. Author: The Christian Science Way of Life, 1962. Home: Old Concord Rd Lincoln MA 01773 Office: Christian Sci Center Boston MA 02115

JOHN, EDWARD CLARENCE, clergyman; b. New Castle, Pa., Mar. 30, 1905; s. Daniel and Catherine Edna (Velker) J.; student Westminster Coll., 1924-25; B.S. in Edn., State Tchrs. Coll., 1948; M.A., Mich. State U., 1959; m. Isabelle Johnston Gass, Jan. 15, 1926; children—Edward Clarence, Janet (Mrs. Douglas E. Tullar), Shirley (Mrs. James Johnson). Ordained to ministry Meth. Ch., 1935; pastor Free Meth. Ch., 1933-39; dist. supt. Free Meth. Chs. W.Va., 1939-43; pastor Free Meth. Chs. S.W. Pa., 1943-44, dist. supt., 1944-48; Asia area sec. gen. missionary bd. Free Meth. Ch., 1949-50; reorganized Free Meth. Ch., Japan, 1949-50, established Osaka Christian Coll., Osaka, Japan, v.p. coll. charge tchr. edn., 1949-50, Asia area sec., 1955; pastor Free Meth. Chs. Mich., 1956-58, supt., 1959-60; bishop Free Meth. Ch. N.Am., Winona Lake, Ind., 1961—, chmn. dept. social ministry, 1969—. Chmn. Commn. Christian Edn., 1961-64; chmn. Commn. Evangelistic Outreach and Ch. Extension, 1964-69, chmn. adminstrv. commn., 1969—. Mem. Pres.' White Ho. Conf. on Aging, 1971. Pres. bd. dirs. Free Meth. Pub. House, Winona Lake. Mem. Christian Holiness Assn. (dir. 1961—), Wesleyan Theol. Soc., Pi Gamma Mu, Phi Sigma Pi. Home: Route 1 Box 323C Hubbard Lake MI 49747 Office: Bd Bishops 900 College Av Winona Lake IN 46590

JOHN, ELTON, (Reginald Kenneth Dwight), musician; b. Pinner, Middlesex, Eng., Mar. 25, 1947; s. Stanley and Sheila Eileen (Farebrother) Dwight; student Royal Acad. Music, London, 1959-64. Singer, songwriter, musician; toured America four times, 1970-71. Recipient gold discs for all four albums composed and performed, 1971. Composer, performer: Empty Sky, 1965; Elton John, 1970; Tumblewood Connection, 1971; Friends, 1971; 11.17.70, 1971; Madman Across the Water, 1971 (all albums); Your Song, 1970 (single record). Office: James House 71-75 New Oxford St London WC 1 England

JOHN, ERNEST FALCON, air force officer; b. Douglas, Ariz., Aug. 10, 1921; s. Ernest and Jeannette (Markus) J.; B.A., Brown U., 1942; M.A., Georgetown U., 1949; grad. Air War Coll., 1958-599; m. Marion Louise Whetham, July 21, 1945; children-William Thomas, Douglas Falcon Commd. 2d lt. USAAF, 1943, advanced through grades to brig. gen. USAF, 1969; vice-comdr. USAF Security Service, 1969—. Decorated Legion of Merit with oak leaf cluster, D.F.C., Air medal with four oak leaf clusters, Joint Service, Army, Air Force commendation medals. Mem. Georgetown. GOold Keyy Soc., Air Force Assn., Delta Tau Delta. Home: 1753 Chennault St Sann Antonio TX 78241 Office: Hdqrs USAF Security Service San Antonio TX 78241

JOHN, ERROL, playwright; b. Trinidad. Author; (off Broadway) Moon on a Rainbow Shawl. Address: care Grove Press 80 University Pl New York City NY 10003

JOHN, ERWIN ROY, educator, psychologist; b. Brownsville, Pa., Aug. 14, 1924; s. Seigfried and Josephine (Kroh) J.; student City Coll. N.Y., 1944; B.S., U. Chgo., 1948, Ph.D., 1954; m. Miriam Garfin; children—Sarah A., Sheila P., Steven S., Martha S., Michael S., David J. Sr. research technician Argonne Nat. Lab., 1946-51; from research fellow to research asso. U. Chgo., 1951-56; asso. research physiologist U. Cal. at Los Angeles, 1956- 58; asso. prof. U. Rochester, 1959-60, prof., dir. center brain research, 1961-64; prof., dir. brain research lab. N.Y. Med. Coll., 1964—. Served with AUS, 1943-46. Mem. Am. Psychol. Assn., A.A.A.S., Am. Physiol. Soc. Home: 3135 Netherland Av Riverdale NY 10463 Office: NY Med Coll Fifth Av and 106th St New York City NY 10029

JOHN, FRITZ, educator, mathematician; b. Berlin, Germany, June 14, 1910; s. Hermann and Hedwig (Buergel) Jacobsohn; Ph.D., Goettingen (Germany) U., 1933; student Cambridge (Eng.) U., 1934-35; m. Charlotte Woellmer; children—Thomas Franklin, Charles Frederic. Came to U.S., 1935, naturalized, 1941. Asst., then asso. prof. U. Ky., 1935-42; mathematician Aberdeen Proving Grounds, 1942-45; prof. math. N.Y. U., 1946—; dir. Research Inst. Numerical Analysis, Nat. Bur. Standards, 1950-51; spl. research applied math., math. analysis. Rockefeller fellow, 1935, 42; Fulbright lectr. Goettingen U., 1935; Guggenheim travel grantee, 1963. Benjamin Franklin fellow Royal Soc. Arts. Mem. Nat. Acad. Scis., Am. Math. Soc., A.A.A.S., Math. Assn. Am., Sigma Xi. Author: Plane Waves and Spherical Means, 1955; (with L. Bers and M. S. Checter) Partial Differential Equations, 1964; (with R. Courant) Introduction to Calculus and Analysis, 1965. Office: New York Univ 251 Mercer St Courant Inst New York City NY 10012

JOHN, JOHN PICE, (Mr. John), couturier-milliner; b. Florence, Italy, Mar. 14, 1906; s. Henry Pico and Rose (Laurel) J.; student U. Lucerne, Switzerland, 1924, Sorbonne, Paris, 1925-26; student art L'Ecole des Beaux Arts, Paris, Fashion designer various couture houses, France; apprentice to Madame Laurel, N.Y.C.; designer fabrics Pine Tree Silk Mills, Phila.; opened N.Y. salon, Mr. John, 1927, partnership with Peter Brandon as Mr. John, Inc., N.Y.C., 1948—; designer custom-made hats, accessories, dresses, perfumes, furs for women, also cravats, shirts, accessories for men; lectr. on fashion various univs. and colls. Exhibitor collection authentic original hats 18th, 19th, early 20th Century; oil paintings exhibited galleries in N.Y.C., Kansas City, Los Angeles, Paris. Recipient Am. Fashion Critics award, Nieman-Marcus award, Millinery Inst. Am. Oscar, 2d time, 1958, also award Internat. Center Arts and Costume, Palazzo Grassi, Venice, Designer Sportswear award, 1958. Mem. New York Mus. Art, N.Y. Mus. Modern Art, N.Y. Mus. Natural History, N.Y. Zool. Soc. Republican. Methodist. Address: 24 W 57th St New York City NY 10019

JOHN, RALPH CANDLER, coll. pres., clergyman; b. Prince Frederick, Md., Feb. 18 1919; s. Byron Wilson and Gladys Bennett (Thomas) J.; B.A., Berea Coll., 1941; student Duke, 1941-43; S.T.B., Boston U., 1943, S.T.M., 1944; Ph.D., Am. U., 1950; L.H.D., Ia. Wesleyan U., 1968; m. Dorothy Corinne Prince, Aug. 17, 1943; children—Douglass Prince, Byron Wilson II, Alan Randall. Ordained to ministry Methodist Ch., 1941; asso. minister Foundry Meth. Ch., Washington, 1945-49; chmn. dept. philosophy and religion Am. U., 1949-51, dean students, 1955-58, dean Coll. Arts and Scis., 1958-63, hon. lifetime prof. philosophy, 1963—; pres. Simpson Coll., Indianola, Ia., 1963—. Dir. mut. funds Bankers Life Co. Chmn. adv. com. Washington Internat. Center, 1959-63; mem. adv. com. Nat. Sch. and Scholarship Com. for Negro Students; mem. commn. on higher edn. Assn. Am. Colls. Trustee Randolph-Macon Acad., 1959- -. Del., World Meth. Conf., London, 1966. Served to capt. AUS 1951-53; maj. Res. Recipient Alumni Recognition award Am. U., 1968, Distinguished Alumnus award Boston U., 1969. Mem. Am. Council on Edn. (commn. on edn. and internat. affairs, 1959-63), Am. Philos. Assn., Am. Acad. Religion, Am. Acad. Polit. and Social Sci., Central States Coll. Assn., Newcomen Soc. N.Am., Ia. Assn. Pvt. Colls. and Univs. (dir., chmn. 1969—), Phi Kappa Phi. Omicron Delta Kappa, Pi Gamma Mu, Pi Sigma Alpha. Clubs: University (N.Y.); University (Chgo.); Des Moines; Prairie. Home: 300 W Girard Av Indianola IA 50125

JOHNPOLL, ALEXANDER CECIL, fgn. service officer; b. N.Y.C., Apr. 18, 1917; s. J. Joseph and Ray (Elkins) J.; student Juilliard Sch., 1935-36; B.A., U.N.M., 1941; student Nat. War Coll., 1960-61; m. Karen Sorensen, Sept. 1, 1962. Joined U.S. Fgn. Service, 1947; posts include Sydney, Australia, 1947-49, Belgrade, Yugoslavia, 1949-51, Vienna, Austria, 1952-57, Dept. State, 1957-61, 66-69; consul gen., Hamburg, Germany, 1969—. Served with AUS, 1946; ETO. Rotarian.

Clubs: Anglo-German (Hamburg); Kenwood Golf and Country (Washington). Address: Am Consulate Gen Alsterufer 27 2 Hamburg -36 Federal Republic Germany

JOHNS, DALE MARTIN, journalist; b. Iowa Falls, Ia., Dec. 1, 1913; s. Lincoln Eugene and Veva (Martin) J.; B.A., U. Neb., 1939; m. Ruth Dobson, June 6, 1939; children—Stephen, Michael, Martha. Reporter, bur. mgr. United Press, 1939-43; with U.P.I., 1946—, Northeastern div. mgr., 1954-62, central div. mgr., Chgo., 1962-69, N. Am. bus. mgr., 1969—. Served to lt. (j.g.) USNR, 1943-46. Mem. Chgo. Press Vets. Assn., Sigma Delta Chi (pres. New Eng. chpt. 1957-58), Kappa Tau Alpha (hon.). Episcopalian (vestry 1952-54). Clubs: Deadline of New York; Chicago Press; Shenorock Shores. Home: 118 Lockwood Rd Riverside CT 06878 Office: 220 E 42d St New York City NY 10017

JOHNS, FRANK JOSEPH, retail mcht.; b. Moline, Kan., Nov. 28, 1902; s. Joseph Marion and Henrietta (Dawson) J.; student U. Kan., 1918-19, U. Denver, 1920-22; m. Maude E. Butell, Nov. 28, 1924; children—Joseph Butell. Robert Frank. With Denver Dry Goods Co., 1936—, gen. mgr., 1944—, pres., 1948—, now chmn. bd.; dir. Scruggs, Vandervoort, Barney, Inc., St. Louis. Frederick Atkins. Denver U.S. Nat. Bank, Silver State Savs. & Loan Assn. Exec. com. Denver Area council Boy Scouts Am., Nat. Western Stock Show: chmn., past campaign mgr. Mile High United Fund; dir. Mountain States Employers Council, Colo. Pub. Expenditures Council. Dir. Goodwill Industries, Denver Symphony Soc.; trustee U. Denver. Dever Mus. Natural History: adv. council Children's Hosp. Arapahoe Nat. Forest. Recipient Alumni Award U. Denver, 1952., Evans award, 1958; named Colo. Businessman of Year, U. Colo., 1956. Mem. Rocky Mountain Gourmet, Nat. (past v.p.), Denver (dir.) retail mchts. assns., Denver C. of C. (past pres.). Clubs: Denver, Tower, Mile High (Denver). Home: 3853 S Hudson St Denver CO 80237 Office: Denver Dry Goods Co 16th and California Sts Denver CO 80201

JOHNS, JASPER, artist; b. Augusta, Ga. May 15, 1930; s. Jasper and Jean (Riley) J.; student U. S.C., 1947-48. One man exhbns. include Leo Castelli Gallery, N.Y.C., 1958, 60, 61, 63, 66, 68 Minami Gallery, Tokyo, Japan, 1965, Galerie Rive Droite, Paris, France, 1959, 61, Galleria D'Arte Del Naviglio, Milan, Italy, 1959, Ileana Sonnabend, Paris, 1963, Columbia (S.C.) Mus. Art, 1960, Jewish Mus., N.Y.C., 1964, White-chapel Gallery, London, Eng., 1964, Pasadena (Cal.) Mus., 1965; rep. permanent collections Mus. Modern Art, Albright-Knox Art Gallery, Buffalo, Tate Gallery, London, Moderna Museet, Stockholm, Sweden, Stedelijik Mus., Amsterdam, Holland, Whitney Mus., N.Y.C. Recipient 1st prize Print Biennale, Ljubljana, Yugoslavia, prize IX Sao Paulo (Brazil) Bienal. Address: care Leo Castelli Gallery 4 E 77th St New York City NY 10003

JOHNS, JAY WINSTON, business exec.; b. Uniontown, Pa., July 14, 1888. Former pres., Atlas Fuel Corp., Pittsburgh, Pa.; dir. Va. Electric & Power Co., Charlottesville, Va. Pres., dir. Stonewall Jackson Meml., Lexington, Va.; bd. visitors Va. Mil. Inst. Trustee Va. Mus. Fine Arts, Richmond. Clubs: Metropolitan (N.Y.C.); Collonnade; Commonwealth (Richmond). Home: Ash Lawn Charlottesville VA 22902 Office: Pittsburgh PA 19144

JOHNS, JESS M., advt. exec.; b. Pitts., Oct. 15, 1923; s. John F. and Jane (Morrow) J.; grad. Shadyside Acad., Pitts., 1942; B.A. in Econs., Yale, 1945; postgrad. Columbia Law Sch., 1947; m. Dorothy Jean Doyle, June 20, 1945 (div.); children—Melinda Morrow, Dale Michele; m. 2d, Ruth Marilyn Brand, June 7, 1970. With Gulf Refining Co., O., 1948- 49; pres., partner Eisaman, John & Laws Advt. & Pub. Relations, Inc., Los Angeles, 1949—. Chmn. Hollywood (Cal.) Community Chest, 1961-62; mem. Los Angeles Dist. Atty. adv. Council. 1965-66: mem. Burbank (Cal.) Park and Recreation Bd., 1965-66, Burbank Sister City Com., 1965-66; regional rep. fund dr. Yale Alumni, 1964-65. Served to 1st. lt. USAAF, 1943-45; ETO, PTO. Decorated Phillipine Liberation medal, Air medal, Mem. Am. Assn. Advt. Agys. (bd. govs. 1971-72), Advt. Assn. of West, Swoed and Gate, Phi Gamma Delta. Club: Milline. Home: 1060 Laurel Way Beverly Hills CA 90210 Office: 6290 Sunset Blvd Hollywood CA 90028

JOHNS, LUCY ISABELLE, nursing exec.; b. Lawrence County, Pa., July 18, 1910; d. Jay Sharp and Mabel (Walker) Johns; R.N., Jameson Meml. Sch. Nursing, New Castle, Pa., 1932; B.S. in Nursing Edn. with high honor, U. Pitts., 1950. Head nurse Cook County Hosp., Chgo., 1935-36; supr. obstetrics Henrotin Hosp., Chgo., 1936-38; head nurse Union Meml. Hosp., Balt., 1938-41, Wesley Meml. Hosp., Chgo., 1946-48; mem. nursing staff A.R.C., 1950—, dir. nursing services Eastern area, 1960-64, nat. dir. nursing services, 1964- -. Served to capt., Nurse Corps, AUS, 1941-46; ETO. Mem. Am. Nurses Assn., Nat. League Nursing, Am. Pub. Health Assn., Sigma Theta Tau. Home: 6304 Golf Course Sq Alexandria VA 22307 Office: Am Nat Red Cross Washington DC 20006

JOHNS, MARTIN WESLEY, educator, physicist; b. Chengtu, China, Mar. 23, 1913; s. Alfred and Myrtle (Madge) J.; B.A., McMaster U., Ont., Can., 1932, M.A., 1934; Ph.D., U. Toronto (Ont.), 1938; m. Margaret Hilborn, July 15, 1939; children—Robert, Beth, Kenneth, Kathryn. Prof. physics Brandon Coll., 1937-46; research physicist Atomic Energy Can., Chalk River, Ont., 1946-47; faculty McMaster U., Hamilton, Ont., 1947—, prof., 1953—, chmn. dept. physics, 1961—; vis. prof. Clarendon Lab., Oxford, Eng., 1959-60, Chalk River Nuclear Lab., 1967-68. Fellow Royal Soc. Can.; mem. Canadian Assn. Physicists, Am. Phys. Soc. Research, publs. on decay mechanisms of radioactive nuclei using techniques of beta and gamma ray spectroscopy and particle accelerators. Home: 116 Sterling St Hamilton Ontario Canada

JOHNS, MERRILL BLAINE, Jr., investment exec., state ofcl.; b. Chgo., Apr. 9, 1916; s. Merrill and Ellen (Davis) J.; student Cornell U., 1933, U. Chgo., 1935; m. Claire Golden, Dec. 26, 1940; children—Gail, Jennifer. Rep. Leo Burnett, Inc., 1937-40, Time mag., 1940-46; owner Santa Fe Real Estate Investment Co. (N.M.), 1946—; v.p. U.S. Uranium Corp., 1952-55; owner State Line Ranch (Wyo and Colo.), Cowdrey, Colo.; treas. State of N.M., 1968—; dir. Storer Broadcasting Co., Guadalupe Resources, Inc.; pres. Strata Corp., 1968-70; chmn. bd., dir. Santa Fe Cablevision Co.; Mem. N.M. State Investment Council, 1968, Pub. Employees Retirement Assn., 1968, N.M. Ednl. Retirement Bd., 1968, N.M. State Bd. Finance, 1953-55, 57-59, 70—. Mem. exec. bd. Santa Fe County chpt. A.R.C., 1952-56, state rep. 1952-54. Mem. N.M. Republican Finance Com., 1954- -; chmn. N.M. Rep. State Central Com., 1966-68; mem. Rep. Nat. Com., 1954- 56, 66-68, chmn. state central com., 1954-56; mem. N.M. Ho. Reps., 1954-56. Served as maj. Adj. Gen. Dept., AUS, 1941-46. Mem. Am. Nat. Cattlemen's Assn., Colo. Cattlemen's Assn., Wyo. Stock Growers Assn., Am. Quarter Horse Assn., Psi Upsilon. Clubs: Denver (Denver); Old Baldy (Saratoga); Kiva (Santa Fe); Foundation (Chgo.); El Paso (Colorado Springs). Home: 409 Hillside Santa Fe NM 87501 Office: P O Box 2425 Santa Fe NM 87501

JOHNS, RALPH STANLEY, certified pub. accountant; b. Oak Park, Ill., July 8, 1904; s. Albert Frederick and Gertrude Martha (Bartusch) J.; B.S. with high honors, U. Ill., 1925, M.S., 1926; m. Elizabeth Louise Florin, Sept. 2, 1933; children—Gordon Malcolm, Barbara Marilyn. Asso., Haskins & Sells, C.P.A.'s N.Y.C., 1926—, partner, 1943—, sr. resident partner, Chgo., 1951-69; pres. Assn. of C.P.A. Examiners, 1958-59. Mem. Haskins and Sells Found. Mem. Am. Inst. Accountants, Am. Accounting Assn., Ill., N.J., N.Y. State socs. C.P.A.'s, U. Ill. Alumni Assn. (pres. 1969-71). Baptist. Clubs: Chicago, Union League (Chicago); Westmoreland. Author: Auditing (with Bell), 1952; Accountants' Working Papers (with Palmer and Bell), 1950. Home: 111 N Pompano Beach Blvd Pompano Beach FL 33062 Office: Board of Trade Bldg Chicago IL 60604

JOHNS, RICHARD JAMES, physician; b. Pendleton, Ore., Aug. 19, 1925; s. James Shanard and Pearl (McKenna) J.; B.S., U. Ore., 1947; M.D., Johns Hopkins, 1948; m. Carol Greacen Johnson, June 27, 1953; children—James Ashmore, Richard Clark, Robert Shanard. Intern, Johns Hopkins Hosp., 1948-49, asst. resident, 1951-53, resident, 1955-56, physician, 1956—; asst. in medicine Johns Hopkins U., 1951-53, fellow in medicine, 1953-55, instr., 1955-57, asst. prof., 1957-61, asso. prof., 1961-66, asst. dean admissions, 1962-66, prof. medicine, 1966—, dir. subdept. biomed. engring., 1966-70, prof., dir. dept. biomed. engring., 1970—, mem. adv. bd. and prin. profl. staff Applied Physics Lab., 1967—. Sec., vice chmn., chmn. med. bd. Myasthenia Gravis Found. Served from 1st lt. to capt. M.C., AUS, 1949-51. Diplomate Am. Bd. Internal Medicine. Fellow A.C.P.; mem. Am. Clin. and Climatological Assn., Am. Soc. Clin. Investigation, Assn. Am. Physicians, Biomed. Engring. Soc., I.E.E.E., Instrument Soc. Am., Johns Hopkins Med. Soc. (pres. 1968-69), Sigma Xi, Alpha Omega Alpha, Phi Kappa Psi, Nu Sigma Nu. Clubs: Peripatetic; Johns Hopkins (v.p. 1969-70). Home: 203 E Highfield Rd Baltimore MD 21218 Office: Johns Hopkins Med Sch Baltimore MD 21205

JOHNS, ROBERT, business exec.; b. Mt. Vernon, O., May 12, 1921; s. William A. and Jane (Weekly) J.; student Westminster Coll., New Wilmington, Pa., 1938-40; B.S., Ohio State U., 1942; Ph.D., Stanford, 1949; postgrad. Harvard, 1963; m. Virginia Ann Wolfe, Sept. 28, 1945; children—Charles Michael, Rebecca Lynn, Thomas Frederick, Kathryn Louise. Tchr. high schs., Titusville, Pa., 1946; asst. dean students U. Omaha, 1946-47; asst. chief counselor men Stanford, 1947-48; adminstrv. asst. to pres., asst. prof. edn. Purdue U., 1949-52, exec. asst. to pres., asso. prof., 1952-53; dir. U.S. Armed Forces Inst., 1953-58; dir. Ill. Commn. Higher Edn., 1958-61; exec. v.p. U. Miami (Fla.), 1960-63; pres. U. Mont., Missoula, 1963-66; pres. Sacramento State Coll., 1966-69; chmn. bd. Servomation Mathias, Inc., Townson, Md., 1969—; cons. finance and mgmt., 1956—. Mem. higher commn. N.W. Assn. Secondary and Higher Schs.; mem. N. Central Assn. Commn. TV Edn.: Mont. commr. Western Interstate Commn. Higher Edn. Dir. Walter L. Darling Corp., Chgo., Western Mont. Nat. Bank, Missoula; cons. Western Broadcasting Co. Mem. adv. council Mont. Planning Bd.; bd. dirs. St. Patrick's Hosp., Missoula; mem. Nat. council Boy Scouts Am.; bd. reference Am. Heritage Program; incorporator, founder, bd. dirs. Miami Internat. Research Found. Served with USNR, 1942-45. Mem. Miami-Dade C. of C. (dir.), Sigma Chi, Phi Kappa Phi, Phi Delta Kappa, Phi Eta Sigma. Methodist. Rotarian. Clubs: Union League (Chgo.); Montana (Helena); Riviera Country (Coral Gables, Fla.); Cuyamaca (San Diego); Center, Hunt Valley Country (Balt.). Home: 2430 Chetwood Circle Timonium MD 21093

JOHNS, ROE LYELL, ednl. adminstr.; b. Jefferson County, Mo., Dec. 11, 1900; s. Edwin Caleb and Minnie Deliah (Couch) J.; B.S., S.E. Mo. State Tchrs. Coll., 1923; M.A., Columbia, 1927, Ph.D., 1928; m. Gladys Liston, May 24, 1929. Tchr. rural schs. Wayne and Jefferson Counties, Mo., 1918-20; supt. schs., Hunter, Mo., 1921-22, Bloomfield, 1923-26; prof. school adminstrn., Ala. Poly. Inst., Auburn, 1928-35; directed research projects for TVA, 1933; dir. adminstrn. and finance Ala. State Dept. Edn., 1934-43; prof. ednl. adminstrn., dir. nat. ednl. finance project Coll. Edn., U. Fla., 1968-72. Cons., State Dept. Edn. of Fla., and others; exec. sec. So. States Work Conf. Cons. to Com. White House Conf. on Edn., 1955. Served to capt. AUS, 1943-45. Mem. N.E.A., Am. Assn. Sch. Adminstrs., Am. Ednl. Research Assn., Fla. Edn. Assn., Phi Delta Kappa, Kappa Delta Pi, Phi Kappa Phi. Cons. numerous state and local surveys sch. financing. Author (with others) Problems and Issues in Public School Finance, 1952; Educational Administration, 1959; Fianancing the Public Schools, 1960; Educational Organization and Administration, 1967; Economics and Finance of Education, 1969. Home: 2215 2d Av N W Gainesville FL 32601

JOHNS, RUSSELL CARL, publisher; b. Newark, Apr. 23, 1907; s. James Benjamin and Anna (Bothe) J.; student Rutgers U., 1924-25, Columbia, 1926; m. Esther Weller, Oct. 10, 1936. Asst. pub. Aero Digest, N.Y., 1927-43; v.p., dir., gen. mgr. Air Review Pub. Co., Dallas, 1946-1948; publ. sec. Gen. Pub. Co., Inc., Chgo., 1948-56. Motel Pub. Corp., 1955-56; pub., v.p. Peacock Bus. Press. Inc., Park Ridge, Ill., 1957—, also pub. Served office chief of staff USAAF, World War II. Home: 1431 South Prospect Park Ridge IL 60068 Office: 200 S Prospect Park Ridge IL 60068

JOHNS, THOMAS RICHARDS II, educator, physician; b. Fairmont, W.Va., Aug. 25, 1924; s. John Rosslyn and Genevieve (Carpenter) J.; A.B., W.Va. U., 1945; M.D., Harvard, 1948; m. Virginia Johnson, Aug. 3, 1946; children-Anne Elizabeth, Rebecca Longridge, Thomas Richards III. Intern Faulkner Hosp., Boston, 1948-49; resident neurology Jefferson Hosp., Phila., 1949-51; asst. resident, then chief resident Neurol. Inst., Columbia-Presbyn. Med. Center, N.Y.C., 1953-55; asst. neurology Columbia Coll. Phys. and Surg., 1955; mem. faculty U. Va. Sch. Medicine, 1956—, prof. neurology, 1964—, chmn. dept., 1966—; research asso. Inst. Pharmacology, U. Lund (Sweden), 1960. Mem. med. adv. bd. Nat. Multiple Sclerosis Soc., Myasthenia Gravis Found.; sec. adv. com. epilepsy Dept. Health, Edn. and Welfare, 1966-70; mem. med. research study sect., med. adv. bd. Soc. Rehab. Service, 1963-70, chmn., 1965-68; mem. tng. com. Nat. Inst. Neurol. Diseases, 1969—. Served with USNR, 1951-53. Fellow Am. Acad. Neurology; mem. A.M.A. (chmn. sect. nervous and mental disease 1966), Assn. U. Profs. Neurology (pres. 1970-71), Assn. Research Nervous and Mental Diseases, A.A.A.S., Am. Assn. U. Profs., Phi Beta Kappa, Alpha Epsilon Delta, Alpha Omega Alpha. Home: 2014 Hessian Rd Charlottesville VA 22903

JOHNS, WALTER HUGH, educator; b. Exeter, Ont., Can., Nov. 10, 1908; s. William Charles and Martha (Hern) J.; B.A., U. Western Ont., 1930, LL.D., 1959; Ph.D., Cornell U., 1934; D.ès L. (hon.), Laval U., 1964; LL.D., U. Sask., Waterloo Luth. U., 1968, U. Alta., 1970; m. Helen Elizabeth Merritt, Jan. 9, 1937; children—Barbara Ann, Mary Elinor. Prof., Waterloo Coll., Ont., Can., 1934-38; lectr. classics U. Alta., Edmonton, 1938-45, asst. to dean arts and scis., 1945-47, asst. to pres. 1947-52, dean faculty arts and sci., 1952-57, v.p., 1957-59, pres., 1959-69, prof. classics, 1969—. Pres., Assn. Univs. and Colls. Can., 1965-66. Mem. Am. Philol. Assn., Classical Assn. Can. Home: 103 Fairway Dr Edmonton Alberta Canada

JOHNS, WILLIAM DAVIS, Jr., educator, scientist; b. Waynesburg, Pa., Nov. 2, 1925; s. William Davis and Beatrice (VanKirk) J.; B.A., Coll. Wooster, 1947; M.A., U. Ill., 1951, Ph.D., 1952; m. Marianna Paull, Aug. 28, 1948; children—Sydney Ann, Susan Helen, David William, Amy Matilda. Spl. research asst. petrology Engring. Expt. Sta., U. Ill., 1949-52; research asst., then asst. prof. geology U. Ill., 1952-55; mem. faculty Washington U., St. Louis, 1955-69, prof. earth scis., 1964-69, chmn. dept., 1962-69; now with dept. geology U. Mo., Columbia. Fulbright fellow U. Goettingen (Germany), 1959-60, U. Heidelberg (Germany), 1968-69. Fellow Geol. Soc. Am., Mineral. Soc. Am.; mem. Mineral. Soc. Great Britain and Ireland, Mineral. Soc. Can., Deutsches Mineralogisches Gesellschaft, Geochem. Soc., Phi Beta Kappa. Presbyn. (elder). Home: 2200 Yuma Dr Columbia MO 65201 Office: Dept Geology U Mo Columbia MO 65201

JOHNSEN, HARVEY M., judge; b. Hastings, Neb., July 16, 1895; s. Peter C. and Mary (Jensen) J.; A.B., U. of Neb., 1921, LL.B., 1919, LL.D. (hon.), 1951; LL.D. (hon.), Creighton U., 1960; m. Helene M. Miles, Oct. 5, 1949 (dec. 1957). Admitted to Neb. bar, 1919; asso. with Montgomery, Hall, & Young Omaha, 1920-25; partner Montgomery, Hall, Young & Johnsen, Omaha, 1926-31; mem. faculty Creighton Law Sch., Omaha, 1922-26; gen. counsel Farm Credit Adminstrn., Omaha, 1931-33; partner Johnsen, Gross & Crawford, Omaha, 1934-38; asso. justice Supreme Court of Neb., 1939-40; judge U.S. Circuit Court of Appeals, 8th Circuit, 1940—, chief judge, 1959-65. Mem. Am., Neb. State (pres. 1938) bar assns., Am. Judicature, Soc. Am. Law Inst., Rotary, Order of Coif, Phi Beta Kappa, Phi Delta Phi. Democrat. Episcopalian. Home: 3870 Harney St Omaha NB 68131 Office: U S Court of Appeals Omaha NB 68102

JOHNSEN, JACK CARLYLE, stock exchange exec.; b. Mobridge, S.D., Sept. 16, 1917; s. Harry T. and Irene (Ewing) J.; m. Frances Bourshon, Dec. 20, 1952; children—Jane, Nancy. With San Francisco Stock Exchange 1946-47; with Parish & Maxwell, San Francisco 1947-67, gen. partner, 1952-67; with Schwobacher & Co., San Francisco, 1967-70; with Edelstein Campbell, San Francisco, 1970—; bd. govs. Pacific Coast Stock Exchange, 1954—, stock specialist San Francisco div., 1956—. Served with USAAF, 1941- 45. Home: 40 Van Gordon Pl Danville CA 94526 Office: 301 Pine St San Francisco CA 94104

JOHNSEN, JOHN HERBERT, educator, geologist; b. S.I., N.Y., Aug. 19, 1923; s. John Hansen and Sigrid (Rueness) J.; A.B., Syracuse U., 1947, M.S., 1948; Ph.D., Lehigh U., 1957; m. Catherine Priscilla Brush, June 25, 1948; children—John Frederick, Catherine Sigrid and Cynthia Ellenor (twins). Geol. asst. Syracuse U., 1946-48; mining geologist N.J. Zinc Co., 1948-49; faculty Vassar Coll., 1951—, prof. geology, chmn. dept., 1964—, dir. summer inst. geology, 1961-64, 66-70; research geologist N.Y. State Geol. Survey summers 1950-52, 54-58. Vis. prof. sci. camp U. Wyo., 1953; engring. geologist Bur. Phys. Research, N.Y. State Dept. Pub. Works, summer 1959; vis. prof. State U. Coll., New Paltz, N.Y., summer 1960, spring 1964, 65; geol. cons. Hudson River Valley Commn., 1965, Office Planning Coordination, 1966. Mem. radiol. team Dutchess County Civil Def., 1956—; mem. Central N.Y. Region Planning and Devel. Bd., 1969-70. Bd. dirs., exec. com. Dutchess County chpt. A.R.C., chmn., 1964-67. Served to 1st lt. USAAF, 1942-46. Decorated Air medal with four clusters. N.J. Zinc research fellow, 1949-51. Fellow Geol. Soc. Am.; mem. Paleontol. Soc., Soc. Econ. Paleontologists and Mineralogists, Am. Geophys. Union, Assn. Geology Tchrs., N.Y. State Geol. Assn., A.A.A.S., Am. Assn. Profl. Geologists, Sigma Xi. Home: 46 Thornwood Dr Poughkeepsie NY 12603

JOHNSEN, MAURICE CARL, Jr., advt. agy. exec.; b. Chgo., Apr. 25, 1920; s. Maurice Carl and Jeanne (Norr) J.; student U. Ill., 1939-42; m. Lenore Elizabeth Russell, May 3, 1947; children—Maurice Carl III, Craig R., Laurence S. Buyer, Montgomery Ward & Co., Chgo., 1948-49; v.p., merchandising mgr. Affiliated Retailers, Inc., N.Y.C., 1950-52; partner Ransford- Johnson & Co., Inc., N.Y.C., 1953-54; marketing exec. Young & Rubicam, N.Y.C., 1954-56; McCann-Erickson, N.Y.C., 1956-61; pres. McCann Erickson- Hakuhodo, Tokyo, Japan, 1961-64; exec. v.p. McCann-Erickson, Inc., Chgo., 1964-69; chmn., chief exec. officer Pritchard Wood Assos., 1969- -. Served to 1st lt. F.A., AUS, 1942-45. Decorated Purple Heart, Air medal. Mem. Am. Assn. Advt. Agys. (chmn. Chgo. council), U.S. Spain C. of C. of Midwest (pres.), Tau Kappa Epsilon. Republican. Clubs: Sunset Ridge Country (Winnetka); Tavern, Executives, Chicago Athletic Association University, Mid-America. (Chgo.). Home: 11 Kent Rd Winnetka IL 60093

JOHNSEN, RUSSELL HAROLD, educator, chemist; b. Chgo., Aug. 5, 1922; s. Harold Gunnar and Irene (Gaul) J.; B.S., U. Chgo., 1947; Ph.D., U. Wis., 1951; m. Dorothy Ruth Pehta, Jan. 20, 1948; children—Peter B., Margaret A. Research chemist Ninol Labs., Chgo., 1947-48; teaching asst. U. Wis., 1948-51; mem. faculty Fla. State U., Tallahassee, 1951—, prof. chemistry, 1961—, chmn. dept. phys. sci., 1951-65, sr. scientist Electron Van de Graaf program, 1958—; cons. editor W. A. Benjamin, Inc., N.Y.C., 1961-68. Bd. govs. Center Research Instruction in Coll. Sci. and Math., 1966-71. Fellow A.A.A.S.; mem. Am. Chem. Soc., Am. Phys. Soc., Chem. Soc. (London), Radiation Research Soc. (councilor 1970-71), Faraday Soc., Am. Assn. U. Profs., Am. Soc. Mass Spectrometry, Sigma Xi. Author: (with E.M. Grunwald) Atoms, Molecules and Chemical Change, 3d edit., 1971; (with G.R. Choppin) Introductory Chemistry, 1972. Research, publs. on chem. effects of ionizing radiation, with emphasis on primary reaction steps, reaction mechanisms of gaseous hydrocarbons and condensed phase alcohols. Bd. editors Jour. Radiation Research Soc. Home: 1425 Devil's Dip Tallahassee FL 32303

JOHNSON, A. DEXTER, photo. equipment co. exec.; b. Manchester, Conn., Sept. 17, 1907; s. Aaron and Christine (Magnell) J.; grad. Worcester Acad., 1926; Ph.B., Brown U., 1930; m. Lois G. Stoller, July 15, 1957; children—Robert D., Dexter A. With Eastmen Kodak Co., 1934—, advt. mgr., 1959-64, asst. v.p., 1960—, dir. advt., 1964—; dir. Eastman Savs. & Loan Assn. Mem. advt. mgmt. devel. com. Assn. Nat. Advertisers, 1962—, dir., 1968—; dir. Rochester Advt. Council, 1959-61; pub. relations dir. new campus fund Rochester Inst. Tech., 1964-68, trustee, 1965—; dir. Audit Bur. of Circulations, 1968—; bd. Point-of-Purchase Inst., 1956-60; trustee Harley Sch., Rochester, 1953-54. Clubs: Genese Valley (Rochester); Brown Univ (N.Y.C.). Home: 4052 East Av Rochester NY 14618 Office: Eastman Kodak Co Rochester NY 14650

JOHNSON, ADGER SMYTH, former mfg. exec.; b. Charleston, S.C., Dec. 27, 1907; s. John Samuel Adolphous and Margaret Milliken Adger (Smyth) J.; B.S. in Chem. Engring., Va. Polytech. Inst., 1928; D.Sc. (hon.), Clarkson Coll. Tech.. 1952; m. Elizabeth Hitchcock Jenkins, June 12, 1931; children—Robert Neal, Michael Smyth, Katharine Hitchcock. With Nat. Carbon Co., div. Union Carbide Corp., 1928-51, pres. div. 1951-59, v.p. corp., 1959-66, exec. v.p., 1966-70, ret. Club: Union League. Home: 275 Engle St Englewood NJ 07631 also High Knob P O Box 71 Blacksburg VA 24060

JOHNSON, ALAN ARTHUR, educator, physicist; b. Beckenham, Eng., Aug. 18, 1930; s. Frederick W. and Dorothy (Tew) J.; B.Sc. with spl. honours in Physics, Reading (Eng.) U., 1952; M.A. in Physics, U. Toronto, 1954; Ph. D. in Metal Physics, U. London (Eng.); diplomate Imperial Coll., London, 1960; m. Elizabeth Ann Banks, June 22, 1958; children—Stephen Graham, Michael Andrew, David Nicholas, Brian Phillip, Susan Christine. Came to U.S., 1962. Sci. officer Royal Naval Sci. Service, Eng., 1954-56; lectr. metallurgy Imperial Coll. Sci. and Tech., U. London, 1960-62; dir. research Materials Research Corp.,

Orangeburg, N.Y., 1963-65; prof. phys. metallurgy Bklyn. Poly. Inst., 1965-71, head dept. phys. and engring., metallurgy, 1967-71; prof. materials sci., chmn. dept., Wash. State U., 1971—; cons. to govt. and industry, 1960—. Mem. Am. Soc. Engring Edn., Am. Assn. U. Profs., Am. Inst. Mining and Metall. Engrs., Marine Tech. Soc., Internat. Assn. Dental Research, Sigma Xi. Editor: Water Pollution in the Greater New York Area, 1971. Contbr. profl. jours. Editor in chief Internat. Jour. Ocean Engring., 1968—. Home: 604 Dawnview St Pullman WA 99163

JOHNSON, ALBERT PEMBERTON, personnel psychologist; b. Annapolis, Md., May 27, 1911; s. Albert Sidney and Virginia Ann (Parlette) J.; B.M.E. cum laude, Johns Hopkins, 1932; M.S., Stevens Inst. Tech., 1934; Ph.D., Purdue U., 1942; m. Roberta Davis Connolley, Jan. 31, 1942; 1 dau., Judith Ann. Research asst. aptitude testing Human Engring. Lab. 1934-36; asst. dir. personnel Vick Chem. Co., 1936-38; asst. to and asst. dir. personnel Purdue U., 1938-42, coordinator personnel guidance, 1946-49; project dir. Ednl. Testing Service, 1949-55; counselor Newark (N.J.) Coll. Engring., 1955- -, asst. dir. counseling center, 1956-60, dir., 1960—; chmn. selection, guidance, placement com. of engineering coll. adminstv. council Am. Soc. Engring. Edn., 1958-60, chmn. guidance com., 1960-61. Sec. com. engring. schs. Engrs. Council for Profl. Development, 1939-41, mem. guidance com., 1961-71. Served from 1st lt. to maj. USAAF, 1942-46, research in selection, tng., evaluation air crew personnel; maj. USAF Res. Diplomate in counseling Am. Bd. of Exam. in profl. Profl. Psychology. Fellow Am. Psychol. Assn., Am. Soc. M.E. A.A.A.S.; mem. Am. Edn. Research Assn., Am. Soc. Engring. Edn., Am., N.J. personnel and guidance assns., Nat. Vocational Guidance Assn., N.J., N.Y. acads. sci., Scabbard and Blade, Sigma Phi Epsilon, Tau Beta Pi, Pi Tau Sigma. Mem. United Ch. of Christ. Author: Psychological Research in Bombardier Training (with E. H. Kemp), 1947; The Law School Admission Test and Suggestions for its Use (with M. A. Olsen and J. A. Winterbottom), 1955; Toward Cooperation in Career Guidance in Science (with others), 1965; Manual for Engineers Serving As Career Advisers (with Larry Dwon and others), 1968. Contbr. profl. jours. Address: Newark Coll Engring Newark NJ 07102

JOHNSON, ALBERT WALTER, congressman; b. Smethport, Pa., Apr. 17, 1906; s. John Aaron and Edla (Ostrom) J.; student U. Pa., 1926-27; LL.B., Stetson U., 1938; m. Virginia Balsley, June 23, 1926; children—Richmond, David, Ronald, Karen. Admitted to Fla. bar, 1938, Pa. bar, 1939; dir., counsel Smethport Nat. Bank, 1942-62; mem. Pa. Ho. of Reps. from McKean County, 1946-62, majority whip, 1951, minority whip, 1955, minority leader, 1959, 61, majority leader, 1953, 57, 63; mem. 88th-92d congresses from 23d Dist. Pa. Chmn., Pa. Republican Platform Com., 1958, 62. Mem. Pa., McKean County bar assns., Alpha Tau Omega. Home: 409 Franklin St Smethport PA 16749 Office: Longworth Office Bldg Washington DC 20515

JOHNSON, ALBERT WILLARD, coll. dean; b. Belvidere, Ill., July 29, 1926; s. Foster D. and Frida (Heinemann) J.; B.S., Colo. A. and M. Coll., 1949; M.S., U. Colo., 1951, Ph.D., 1956; m. Beverly M. Baynes, Aug. 3, 1945; children-Mark A., Curtis N., Christopher S. Research asst. U. Colo. Inst. Arctic and Alpine Research, 1951-56, instr. biology, 1955; instr., asst. prof., asso. prof. botany U. Alaska, 1956-62; research biologist U. Cal. at Los Angeles, 1962-64; asso. prof., prof. biology San Diego State Coll., 1964- 70, dean Coll. Scis., 1969—. Pres. Citizens Coordinate for Century III, San Diego; bd. dirs. Thorne Found., San Diego Natural History Mus. Served with USAAF, 1945. Mem. A.A.A.S. (past exec. sec. Alaska div.), Ecol. Soc. Am., Soc. for Study Evolution, Sigma Xi. Home: 4363 Middlesex Dr San Diego CA 92116

JOHNSON, ALDEN PORTER, editor, pub.; b. Worcester, Mass., Mar. 24, 1914; s. Charles Warren and Ruby (Allen) J.; student Princeton, 1937; m. Mary Chandler Bullock, Sept. 17, 1938; children—Judith A., Lisa, Peter C. Pres., Johnson-deVou, Inc., Worcester, 1942-46, Barre Gazette, Barre Publ. Co. (Mass.), 1946—. Trustee Worcester Found. Exptl. Biology; chmn. George I. Alden Trust, 1950—; trustee Worcester Natural History Soc., Worcester Art Mus., Clark U.; pres. Stetson Home for Boys, Barre, Mass.; bd. dirs. Salisbury Mansion Assos. Mem. Am. Antiquarian Soc. (v.p.), Imprint Soc. (pres.), Mass., Worcester hist. socs., Colonial Soc. Mass. Clubs: Odd Volumes (Boston); Grolier (N.Y.C.). Home: 4 Paul Revere Rd Worcester MA 01609 Office: Barre Publishing Co Barre MA 01005

JOHNSON, ALDEN W., pres., chief exec. officer So. Cal. 1st Nat. Bank of San Diego. Address: 1007 5th Av San Diego CA 92112*

JOHNSON, ALEX, baseball player; b. Helena, Ark., Dec. 7, 1942; s. Arthur and Wille Mae (Mayo) J.; grad. high sch.; m. Julia Augusta, Feb. 2, 1963; 1 dau., Jeniffer. Mem. baseball team Miami-Fla. State, 1962-63, Magic Valley-Pioneer, 1963-64, Ark.-Pacific Coast, 1964, Phila. Phillies, 1964-65, St. Louis Cardinals, 1966-67, Tulsa Oilers, 1966, Cin. Reds, 1968-69; outfielder Cal. Angels, Anaheim, 1970—. Recipient Come Back Player of the Year award Nat. League Baseball, 1968; Bat Champ award Am. League Baseball, 1970. Home: 19474 Birwood St Detroit MI 48221 Office: Cal Angels Baseball Club Anaheim CA 92802

JOHNSON, ALFRED EUGENE, civil engr., engring. assn. exec.; b. Harrison, Ark., July 10, 1907; s. Charles Edwin and Anna Maude (Doolin) J.; B.S. in Civil Engring., U. Ark., 1929; m. Irene Walker, Mar. 7, 1936; children—Alfred Eugene, Frank Edwin. With Ark. Hwy. Dept., 1927-55, successively rodman, instrumentman, designer, research observer, resident engr., asst. chief engr., chief engr., 1947-55; exec. dir. Am. Assn. State Hwy. Ofcls., 1955—. Exec. com. hwy. research bd. NRC; mem. nat adv. council urban transp. U.S. Dept. Transp., 1969; mem. nat adv. council water data for pub. use Dept. Interior; conf. reporter of middle East, Internal. Road Fedn., 1967; vice chmn. steering com. Paan Am. Hwy. Congress, 1962. Recipient Thomas H. MacDonald award for outstanding contbn. to hwys., 1959; Bartlett award for outstanding contbn. to hwy. progress, 1962; Hwy. Research Bd.- Crum award for outstanding contbn. to hwy. research, 1970. Registered profl. engr., Ark. Fellow Am. Soc. C.E. (dir. Mid-South sect. 1942-55); mem. Inst. Traffic Engrs., Am. (chmn. planning and design policy com. 1951-55, pres. 1954), Southeastern (pres. 1949) assns. state hwy. ofcls., Nat. Assn. Counties (hon.), Inst. Hwy. Engrs. Gt. Britain (hon.), Theta Tau (hon.). Clubs: Little Rock Engrs. (pres. 1949), Ark. Engrs. (pres. 1950). Home: 3154 Patrick Henry Dr Falls Church VA 22044 Office: Nat Press Bldg Washington DC 20004

JOHNSON, ALLAN RAYMOND retail exec.; b. Phila., Aug. 2, 1916; s. Francis Raymond and Susan Wallace (Taylor) J.; student U. Pa., 1935-37; m. Frances Elizabeth Mora, Nov. 21, 1947; children—Jane (Mrs. Robert T. Fell), Barbara Hobin, Kathy Allan, Elaine Susan; m. 2d, Joan Banks Lovejoy, Feb. 14, 1969. Asst. personnel dir. N.Y. Shipbldg. Corp., Camden, N.J., 1940-42; personnel dir. Saks Fifth Avenue, N.Y.C., 1945- 48, gen. mgr., Detroit, 1948-54, gen. mgr. all stores, 1954-61, exec. v.p., gen. mgr. all Saks Fifth Avenue stores, 1961-69; chmn. Saks & Co., N.Y.C.,1969—, chief exec. officer, 1970—; pres., dir. Lockharts Co., St. Lowis, Fashions for Men, N.Y.C., dir. Gimbel Bros., Inc. Mem. Westchester C. of C., 1952; pres. Detroit Conv. and Tourist Bur., 1951-52. Dir. N.Y. State Council Retail Mchts.; v.p., dir. Fifth Av. Assn.; bd. dirs. The Lighthouse (N.Y. Assn. for Blind), Fashion Inst. Tech., N.Y. Sales Execs. Club, Ireland-U.S.Council for Commerce and Industry; mem. exec. bd. New York council Boy Scouts Am.; chmn. exec. com. Mchts. Council, N.Y.U. Inst. Retail Mgmt.; mem. exec. bd. City Coll. Sch. Retailing; pres. N.Y. Met. Retail Mchts. Assn., 1968—. Served as 2d lt. USAAF, 1942-45. Mem. Eta Mu Pi, Delta Upsilon. Home: 150 E 72d St New York City NY 10021 Office: 611 Fifth Av New York City NY 10022

JOHNSON, ALTON CORNELIUS, educator; b. Argyle, Wis., Apr. 27, 1924; s. Herman A. and Cora E. (Hendrickson) J.; B.A., St. Olaf Coll., 1949; M.B.A., U. Wis., 1953, Ph.D., 1957; m. Virginia R. Kroener, Aug. 15, 1959; children—Vance, Brian. Partner, Johnson Motor Service, Argyle, Wis., 1949-52; instr. U. Okla., Norman, 1953-55; asst. prof. U. Wis., Madison, 1957-62, asso. prof., 1962-65, prof., 1965—, chmn. dept. mgmt., 1966—; cons. to industry and govt. First v.p. Madison Area Assn. for Retarded Children, 1970—. Earhart Found. fellow, 1956-57; research grantee Ford Found., 1960-63, U.S. Office Edn., 1965-66. Mem. Acad. Mgmt., Indsl. Relations Research Assn., Am. Soc. Personnel Adminstrs., Am. Mgmt. Assn., Gerontological Soc., Phi Kappa Phi. Lutheran (pres. ch. 1969, sec. So. Wis. dist. Brotherhood 1964-68). Author articles, monographs. Home: 641 Chatham Terrace Madison WI 53711

JOHNSON, ALVIN CARL, banker; b. Chgo., Apr. 9, 1919; s. Alvin A. and Gertrude M. (Schau) J.; student Am. Inst. Banking, 1935-37, Sch. Commerce, Northwestern U., 1937- 41, 46-47, Stonier Grad. Sch. Banking, 1958; m. Eileen Myrtle Weise, May 25, 1946; children—Kristine Ann, Lisa Ellen, Alvin Carl, Paul Andrew. With First Nat. Bank Chgo., 1935-, v.p. charge div. I, 1963-. Treas., chmn. finance com. Swedish Covenant Hosp., 1960-65; v.p. Cathedral Shelter of Chgo. Mem. Am. Petroleum Inst., Mid-Continent Oil and Gas Assn. Episcopalian. Clubs: Bankers, Chicago Athletic Assn., Swedish, Oil Mens (Chgo.); Hinsdale Golf. Home: 635 W North St Hinsdale IL 60521 Office: Division I First Nat Bank Chicago One First Nat Plaza Chicago IL 60670

JOHNSON, ALYN WILLIAM, univ. dean; b. Calgary, Alta, Can., Dec. 16, 1933; s. Alyn C. and Irene (Johnston) J.; B.Sc., U. Alta., 1954; Ph.D., Cornell U., 1957; m. M. Joan Auger, July 26, 1956; children—Patricia, Nancy, Robert, Katherine. Came to U.S., 1954. Research fellow Mellon Inst., Pitts., 1957-60; asst., then asso. prof. chemistry U. N.D., 1960-65; asso. prof., chmn. dept. chemistry U. Sask., 1965-67; dean Grad. Sch., dir. research and devel., prof. chemistry U. N.D., 1967—. Fellow Chem. Inst. Can.; mem. Am. Chem. Soc., N.D. Acad. Sci., Sigma Xi. Episcopalian. Clubs: Curling (pres.), Grand Forks Country (bd. dirs.) (Grand Forks). Author: Ylid Chemistry, 1966; also articles. Address: Univ N D Grand Forks ND 58201

JOHNSON, AMOS NEILL, physician; b. Garland, N.C., June 5, 1908; s. Jefferson Deems and Mary Lily (Wright) J.; A.B., Duke, 1929; med. student U. N.C., 1929-31; M.D., U. Pa., 1933: m. Mary Porter Allan, Mar. 16, 1934; children—Mary Allan (Mrs. William R. Watts III), Amos Neill. Intern, Jackson Meml. Hosp., Miami, Fla.; pvt. gen. med. practice, Garland, 1934—; mem. staff Sampson County Meml., Bladen County Meml. hosps.; instr. gen. practice Duke Med. Sch. 1944—. Mem. Bd. Med. Examiners N.C., 1950-56, pres., 1955; chief staff Sampson County Meml. Hosp., 1952; adviser Sears Roebuck Med. Found., 1962—; mem. N.C. Bd. Hosp. Controls, 1948-52; med. adviser U.S. Dept. Health, Edn. and Welfare, 1963—, mem. med. assistance adv. com.; mem. Gov's Commn. to Study Pub. Sch. System N.C., Gov.'s Commn. on Econ. Devel.; med. adviser N.C. State Bd. Mental Health, 1964—. Dir. Lundy Packing Co., Universal Edn. Corp., Inc., Media Medica, Cape Fear Bank & Trust Co. Mem. Sampson County Bd Edn. 1950-62; mem. Gov. N.C. bd. dirs. Am. Bd. Family Physicians. Com. Court Reform, 1956. Trustee Greater Univs. of N.C., Family Health Found. Am.; Mem. Am. Acad. Gen. Practice (pres. N.C. 1952-53, chmn. edn. con. N.C. 1953-60; nat. chmn. com. edn. 1961-62, com. sci. assembly 1960-61, nat. bd. dirs. 1961-64, chmn. bd. dirs. 1962-64, pres. 1965- 66, chmn. family health care services), A.M.A. (mem. commn. accreditation hosps. 1960-70), Med. Soc. N.C. (pres. 1960-61), Sampson County (pres. 1947), 3d Dist. (pres. 1948) med. socs., Sigma Chi, Omicron Delta Kappa. Democrat. Presbyn. Address: Garland NC 28441

JOHNSON, ANDREW, lawyer; b. Huntingdon, Tenn., Oct. 11, 1918; s. Franklin Everett and Martha (Young) J.; student Bethel Coll., McKenzie, Tenn. 1936-37, U. Tenn. Jr. Coll., Martin, 1937-38; LL.D., U. Tenn., 1948; m. Mary Nell Greer, Oct. 32, 1959; children—Frank L., (stepsons) James P., William G., Russell G., John G. Brownlow. Admitted to Tenn. bar, 1948, since practiced in Knoxville; partner Kramer, Dye, Greenwood, Johnson & Rayson, 1949—. Pres. bd. edn., Knoxville, 1956- 58. Served with AUS, 1943- 46. Mem. Am., Tenn., Knoxville bar assns., Order of Coif, Phi Delta Phi, Phi Kappa Phi. Presbyn. (deacon). Club: Cherokee Country (Knoxville). Home: 6915 Stone Mill Rd Knoxville TN 37919

JOHNSON, ANDREW N., lawyer; b. Sparta, Wis., Nov. 10, 1887; s. Marcus M. and Susanne (Jensen) J.; A.R., Northwestern, 1913, LL.B., 1915; m. Louise C. Weaver, Sept. 13, 1916 (dec. May 7, 1949); children—Douglas W., Alice J. (Mrs. Richard C. Keller), Gordon A. Admitted to Minn. bar, 1916; partner Mercer & Jonson, Mpls., 1920-25, Sweet & Johnson, 1925-30, Sweet, Johnson & Sands, 1930-37, Johnson, Sands & Brumfield, 1937- 47, Johnson, Sands, Brumfield & Maloney, 1947, now Johnson and Sands; dean, trustee Mpls.-M.nn. Coll. of Law, 1940-56; pres., trustee William Mitchell Coll. Law, 1956—; gen. counsel N. Am. Life & Casualty Co., 1946-62, dir. 1950-54; dir. Pure Milk Products Co., 1951-70, B.F. Griebenow, 1947-70. Vice consul of Denmark, Minn., 1927-47, consul, 1947-58, consul gen. Minn., B.D., S.D., Mont. 1958—. Pres., Mpls. council Camp Fire Girls, 1948-49, nat. bd. dirs., 1962—, chmn. nat finance com. exec. com . Camp Fire Girls, Inc., 1962-65. Decorated knight Order Danish Flag, King Christian X Medal Liberation, knight 1st class Order of Danish Flag (Denmark); knight 1st class Order of Vasa (Sweden). Mem. Minn. State, Hennepin County, Am. Bar Assns., Mpls. Bus. Mens Assn. (past pres.), Order of Coif, Alpha Delta Phi, Delta Theta Phi. Clubs: Six O'Clock, Minneapolis, Minneapolis Athletic, Skylight. Author: Marcus and Susanne The Johnson (sen) Family, 1965. Home: 19 S 1st St Minneapolis MN 55401 Office: First Nat Bank Bldg Minneapolis MN 55402

JOHNSON, ARCHIBALD DEBAUN, holding co. exec.; b. Chilpencingo, Mexico, Nov, 3, 1898; s. George and Florence (DeBaun) J.; A.B., Princeton, 1919; m. Margaret Louise Jones, Mar. 29, 1934; children—Gwenyth Howell (Mrs. John W. Roberts), Tracy Todd (Mrs. John W. Wurts, Jr.). Mgr., Drexel & Co., Phila., 1923-45; v.p. Phila. Nat. Bank, 1945-63; sec.-treas. Penn Central Co., 1970—; dir. market devel. Gen. Bldg. Contractors Assn., Inc., Phila., 1963—; pres. Phila. Transp. Co., 1968—; dir. Am. Locker Co., Inc., N. Shore Corp., Clearfloat, Inc., Security Columbian Bank Note Co. Pres. Children's Country Week Assn., Phila.; chmn. adv. com. Presbyn. Home Aged, Phila.; treas. Presbyn. Children's Village, Rosemont, Pa., Shipley Sch., Bryn Mawr, Pa. Mem. St. Andrews Soc. Phila. (pres.). Republican. Presbyn. (trustee). Home: 621 Old Gulph Rd Bryn Mawr PA 19010 Office: 2 Penn Center Philadelphia PA 19102

JOHNSON, ARNO HALLOCK, economist; b. Jacksonville, Fla., Jan, 12, 1901; s. John M. and Mabel (Hallock) J.; B.S., in Engring., Mich. State Coll., 1922; M.B.A., Harvard, 1924; m. Marian Lettenberger, July 8, 1925; children—Elliott Hallock, Dean Marshall. Research supervisor, bureau of bus. research, Harvard, 1924-26; market analyst, J. Walter Thompson Co., N.Y.C., 1926- 29, dir. research, 1932-42, dir. media and research, 1942-57, v.p., 1946- 57, v.p., sr. economist, 1957—; dir. research J. Walter Thompson Co., Ltd., Montreal, Que., Can., 1930-31, London, 1931-32. Chmn. bd. Advt. Research Found. Mem. Advt. Fedn. Am. (dir.), Sales Execs. Club N.Y. (dir.), Internat. Platform Assn., Market Research Council of N.Y. (past sec.-treas., past v.p., pres. 1940-41). Recipient Hall of Fame in Distbn.; Mich. State U. Centennial award, 1955. Mem. Am. Statis. Assn., Am. Marketing Assn. (v.p. 1954-55), Tau Beta Pi, Alpha Delta Sigma, Pi Alpha Mu, Scabbard and Blade, Acacia. Mason. Republican. Club: Harvard (N.Y.C.). Mem. editorial bd. Harvard Bus. Rev. Author: several books on econ. including, Market Potentials, 1948; (pamphlet) Consumer Purchasing Power, 1949; Marketing Opportunities, 1950; Hidden Pressures for Expansion, 1953; Setting Our Sights For the '60s, 1960; Selling to Tomorrows Consumers, 1961; Advertising—A Dynamic Force in Economic Growth, 1961; Are We Shackling Economic Growth by Overlooking the Consumer, 1962; The Decade of Opportunity Worldwide, 1966-75, 1965; The American Market of the Future, 1967. Contbr. to journals. Delivered speech"57 Million Jobs-A Postwar Goal and Opportunity" before Governor's Conf. Mackinac Island, July 1945, and to clubs. Initial winner of annual Am. Marketing Assn. award for "Leadership in Marketing" 1946; (film and booklet) Challenge to America, 1955. Home: 701 E Camino Real Boca Raton FL 33432 Office: care J Walter Thompson Co 420 Lexington Av New York City NY 10017 ☆

JOHNSON, ARNOLD WALDEMAR, educator; b. Buffalo, June 24, 1900; s. Sam R. and Hulda F. (Nelson) J.; B.B.A., U. Wash., 1927; M.B.A., Harvard, 1929. Purchasing agt. Ford Motor Co., 1922-26; job analyst Gillette Safety Razor Co., 1929; asst. prof. accounting W.Va. U., 1929-33; asso. prof. W.Va. Inst. Tech., 1933-35; asst. dir. budget State of W. Va., 1935; successively asst. prof., asso prof., prof. U. Okla., 1935-42; prof. Tulane U., 1942-46; prof., chmn. dept, Syracuse U., 1946-51; prof. N.Y.U. Grad. Sch. Bus. Adminstrn., 1952-54, prof., chmn. dept. Sch. Commerce N.Y.U., 1954-65; vis. prof. accounting U. Fla. 1966-68, Fla. Atlantic U., 1968-70. Recipient Wisdom award of Honor, 1970, Centennial medal Syracuse U., 1970. C.P.A., Okla., La. Mem. Am. Inst. C.P.A.'s, Am. Accounting Assn. (v.p. 1956-57). Author: Principles of Accounting, 1937; Elementary Accounting, 1962; Advanced Accounting, 1968; Case Problems in Auditing, 1958; Auditing: Principles and Case Problems, 1959; (with E. S. Germain) C.P.A. Problems and Solutions, 1959; (with Oscar Kriegman) Intermediate Accounting, 1964. Home: 633 S W 4th St Boca Raton FL 33432

JOHNSON, ARTHUR E., oil exec.; b. Colorado Springs, Colo., Sept. 4, 1892; s. Nels and Laura Johnson; ed. Colorado Springs High Sch.; hon. D.Sc.; m. Helen Kenney, Apr. 12, 1918; 1 dau., Helen Barbara (Mrs. Gerald R. Hillyard). Oil bus., 1913—; dir. United Banks of Colo. Trustee Lovelace Found. Med. Edn. and Research; bd. dirs. USAF Acad. Found. Served to 1st lt. U.S. Army, 1917-19. Clubs: Denver, Cherry Hills, Denver Country, Wigwam, Garden of the Gods Hiwan Country Home: 2423 E Exposition Av Denver CO 80209 Office: 1700 Broadway Denver CO 80202

JOHNSON, ARTHUR GERALD, retail chain store exec.; b. Mpls., Mar. 6, 1908; s. Andrew and Hulda (Pearson) J.; student Dunwoody Inst., Mpls., 1922-23; m. Louise Elizabeth Donaldson, June 24, 1939; children—David Paul, Susan Kathryn. Mgr. replacement parts div. Dodge Bros., Mpls., 1923-28, Standard United Parts, Mpls., 1928-37; with Gamble-Skogmo, Inc., Mpls., 1937—, v.p. merchandising, 1964-68, exec. v.p. buying and merchandising, 1968—, also dir. dir. Gambles Continental State Bank, Red Owl Stores, Inc.; dir., mem. exec. com. Gambles Import Corp.; mgmt. com. Marshall Wells Canada, Ltd., Chmn. mgmt. com. Northside YMCA, Mpls., 1960-61, also chmn. several sustaining membership drives. Dir. Mpls. Soc. for Blind. Mem. Quarter Century Group. Lutheran (chmn. trustees 1961-62). Mason. Clubs: Minneapolis Athletic, Minneapolis Golf. Home: 2560 Brookridge Av Minneapolis MN 55422 Office: 5100 Gamble Dr Minneapolis MN 55416

JOHNSON, ARTHUR MENZIES, educator, historian; b. Waltham, Mass., July 24, 1921; s. Frederick P. and Florence (Bishop) J.; grad. Philips Exeter Acad., 1940; B.A., Harvard, 1944, M.A., 1948; Ph.D., Vanderbilt U., 1954; m. Emily Ann Wilford, Dec. 28, 1946; children—Robert Menzies, Nancy Revell. Instr., Thayer Acad., Braintree, Mass., 1946-47, Cambridge Sch., Weston, Mass., 1948-50; asst. prof. U.S. Naval Acad., 1954-58; faculty Harvard Grad. Sch. Bus. Adminstrn., 1958-70, prof. bus. history, 1966-70; 1970—, U. Me., 1969-70, A & A Bird prof. Am. history, 1970-69, Sec., New Eng. Econ. Edn. Council, 1967-69, pres. Bus. History and Econ. Life Program, 1968- 70 chmn., 1970—. Vice chmn. Me. Council on Econ. Edn., 1969—; mem. adv. com. Eleutherian Mills Hist. Library, 1967-70 Me. State Archives, 1969—. Served to capt. USAAF, 1943-46, USAF, 1951. 53. Mem. Am. Hist. Assn. (Beveridge prize 1954), Orgn. Am. Historians, Econ. History Assn., Me. Hist. Soc. Author: Development of American Petroleum Pipelines, 1956; Government Business Relations, 1965; Petroleum Pipelines and Public Policy, 1967; (with Barry E. Supple) Boston Capitalists and Western Railroads, 1967; Winthrop W. Aldrich. Lawyer, Banker, Diplomat, 1968. Home: Seaward Castine ME 04421

JOHNSON, AUBREY KENNETH, farm credit ofcl.; b. Benton Harbor, Mich., Mar. 8, 1922; s. Kenneth O. and Maude (Krieger) J.; B.S. Mich. State U., 1948; m. Joan Elna Fredeen, Sept. 25, 1947; children-Brian Lee, Terry Alan. Field asst. Fed. Land Bank Assn., St. Joseph, Mih., 1948-51, mgr., sec.-treas., St. Johns, Mich., 1951-52, regional mgr., St. Paul, 1952-57; asst. to pres. Fed. Inter-mediate Credit Bank, St. Paul, 1957-60, treas., 1960-64, sec. 1960- 69, v.p. 1964-68,1st v.p., 1968-69; dep. gov., dir. prodn. credit service Farm Credit Adminstrn., 1969—; chmn., gov. Nat. Coop. Mgmt. Devel. Served with AUS, 1942-45. Named State Farmer, 1940. Mem. Phi Kappa Phi, Alpha Zeta. Mason. Mem. United Ch. Christ (moderator 1960, 67). Home: 1900 E Eads Arlington VA 22202

JOHNSON, AVERY FISCHER, artist; b. Wheaton, Ill., Apr. 3, 1906; s. Nicholas L. and Faith (Fischer) J.; B.A., Wheaton Coll., 1928; grad. Sch. Art Inst. Chgo., 1933; m. Nina Gertrude Ryder, Mar. 7, 1935; children— Sandra (Mrs. John E. Van Hoven, Jr.), Susan, Stephanie (Mrs. Robert Pasco). Murals in U.S. post offices in Marseilles, Ill., Liberty, Ind., Lake Village, Ark., Catonsville, Md., Bordentown, N.J., North Bergen, N.J.; rep. permanent collections Newark Mus., Montclair, (N.J.) Mus., Philbrook Mus., Tulsa, Holyoke (Mass.) Mus., Library of Congress; exhbns. include Met. Mus., 1967, Mexico City, 1968, numerous others; instr. Newark Sch. Fine and Indsl. Art, 1947-60, Montclair Art Mus., 1940-70. Civilian with OWI, 1944- 45. Recipient awards Am. Watercolor Soc., Montclair Mus., N.J. Water Color Soc. A.N.A. Mem. Am., N.J. watercolor socs., Audubon Artists. Address: RFD 1 Cooper Rd Dover NJ 07801

JOHNSON, BENJAMIN EDGAR, clergyman; b. Sterling, Colo., Oct. 30, 1921; s. A. Judson and Elsie (Marks) J.; A.B., Pasadena Coll., 1943; D.D., 1964; m. Kathryn Pierret, Feb. 8, 1944; children—Lois, Janet. Ordained to ministry Ch. of Nazarene, 1943; pastor in Los Angeles, Whittier, Santa Ana and Upland, Cal., 1943-64; dist. sec. So. Cal. Dist. Ch. Nazarene, 1950-64; gen. sec. Ch. of Nazarene 1964—. Trustee Pasadena Coll., 1943-46, 57-64. Editor So. Californian, 1950-56. Home: 701 E 90th St Kansas City MO 64131 Office: 6401 The Paseo Kansas City MO 64131

JOHNSON, BENJAMIN FRANKLIN, Jr., univ. dean; b. Carrollton, Ga., Sept 30, 1914; s. Benjamin Franklin and Grace (Veal) J.; A.B., U. Ga., 1937; J.D., Emory U., 1939; LL.M., Duke, 1949; m. Stella Darnell, June 8, 1938; children—Benjamin Franklin III, Sherman Darnell. Admitted to Ga. bar, 1939; practiced in Atlanta, 1940- 43; asso. Sutherland, Tuttle & Brennan; prof. law Emory U., 1946—, dean Sch. Law 1961—. Mem. Ga. Senate from 42d Dist., 1963-68. Served to lt. USNR., 1943-46. Mem. Am. Ga., Atlanta bar assns., Atlanta Lawyers Club, Omicron Delta Kappa, Phi Delta Phi, Sigma Pi. Home: 1035 Clifton Rd N E Atlanta GA 30307

JOHNSON, BERKELEY DANIELS, banker; b. Hopedale, Mass., June 29, 1906; s. Arthur C. and Grace (Daniels) J.; grad. Wesleyan U., 1929; m. Helen C. Mitchell, June 14, 1930; children—Berkeley D., Craig M., Lee (Mrs. W.J. Corbett), Gay (Mrs. R. K. Rogers). With U.S. Trust Co. of N.Y., 1929—, asst. sec., 1941, asst. v.p., 1944, v.p., 1950, vice chmn. bd., trustee, 1962—; dir. Prudential Ins. Co., Gt. Britain, Hudson Ins. Co., Celanese Corp., Josten's, Inc., Gen. Portland Cenebt Co., Jeffrey Co., U.S. Leasing Realty Investors, Gen. Cable Corp., mem. exec. com. Skandia Ins. Co. Trustee, exec. com. N.Y. State YMCA; adv. bd. Salvation Army, N.Y.C.; trustee Wesleyan U. Clubs: Down Town Association, River (N.Y.C.); Lost Tree (N. Palm Beach, Fla.); Everglades (Fla.). Home: 12167 Turtle Beach Rd North Palm Beach FL 33403 Office: 45 Wall St New York City NY 10005

JOHNSON, BERT WILLARD, county mgr.; b. Marinette, Wis., Apr. 1, 1915; s. Lawrence and Hanna (Johnson) J.; Ph.B. in Municipal Administrn. and Finance, U. Wis., 1939; grad. study U. Chgo., 1941-42; m. Dorothy June Stauffacher, June 22, 1940; children—L. Kirk, June C., Ralph W., Ernest W., Cynthia M. Participant research and field projects, 1939-40; finance dir., Winnetka, Ill., 1940-48; city mgr., Lebanon, Mo., 1948-50, Boulder, Colo., 1950-53, Evanston, Ill., 1953-62; lectr. Northwestern U., 1954- 62; county mgr., Arlington, Va., 1962—. Finance cons. Govt. V.I., 1969; mem. Census Adv. Com. on State and Local Statistics, 1968-71. Trustee Evanston YMCA, 1960-62. Asso., Northwestern U. U.S. rep. Caribbean Seminar, 1964. One of four city mgrs. selected for study tour Republic West Germany, 1953; named one of top ten city mgrs., 1963. Served with USNR, 1943-46. Mem. Internat. City Mgmt. Assn. (pres. 1963-64, exec. bd. 1960-61, 63-69) Am. Soc. Pub. Adminstrn. (nat. council), Nat. League Cities (mem. bd. cons. for com. on parking), Nat. Municipal League, Nat. Acad. Pub. Adminstrn., U. Wis. Alumni Assn. Presbyn. Club: Army-Navy Country (Arlington). Home: 3621 38th St N Arlington VA 22207 Office: Court House Arlington VA 22207

JOHNSON, BJARNE, lawyer; b. Dutton, Mont., Dec. 24, 1917; B.A., Mont. State U., 1940, LL.B., 1942. Admitted to Mont. bar, 1942; dep. county atty., 1942-46; now partner Church, Harris, Johnson & Williams, Great Falls, Mont. Mem. Great Falls Sch. Bd., 1963-69. Fellow Am. Coll. Probate Counsel (regent 1966—, v.p. 1970); mem. Am., Mont., Cascade County (pres. 1967) bar assns., Phi Delta Phi. Office: Great Falls Nat Bank Bldg Great Falls 59401*

JOHNSON, BRIARD POLAND army officer; b. Lynn, Mass., Feb. 5, 1905; s. Justin Brown and Bertha (Poland) J.; B.S. in Civil Engring., Norwich U., 1927, LL.D., 1963; grad. Army Command and Gen. Staff Coll., 1947, Air War Coll., 1950; m. Helen Sigrid Nelson, June 15, 1929; children—Eleanor June (Mrs. John Merritt Archibald), Barbara Phyllis (Mrs.Charles F. Muckenbirn), Helen Sigrid (Mrs. Bernard Roy Johnson). Civil engr., 1927-33; commd. 2d lt. (Res.) cav., U.S. Army, 1927, advanced through grades to maj. gen., 1958; served in Morocco, Sicily, Normandy, No. France, Ardennes, Rhineland, Central Europe, World War II; comdr. 67th Armored Regt., 2d Armored Div., 1945-46; assigned Office Sec. Def. for Research and Development 1949; comdr. Combat Command B. 2d Armored Div., 1951-53; assigned U.S. Army Gen. Staff, research and devel. 1954; chief Mich. Mil. Dist., also comdr. Ft. Wayne, Mich., 1955; chief Army Maneuver Test and Evaluation Group, 1955-56; comdr. 8th U.S. Army Support Command, Korea, 1956-57, XIV U.S. Group to Thailand, 1959-62; asst. chief of staff U.S. Continental Army Command, Ft. Monroe, Va., 1962-63, chief of staff, 1963. Trustee Norwich U., 1964-69. Decorated Silver Star, Legion of Merit, Bronze Star with 1 oak leaf clusters, D.S.M., numerous service medals; Legion of Honor, Croix de Guerre with palm (France); Order of Fatherland 1st class (USSR). Mem. Assn. U.S. Army, U.S. Armor Assn. Home: 125 Horseshoe Dr Queen's Lake Williamsburg VA 23185

JOHNSON, BRUCE, civil engr.; b. Grand Forks, N.D., June 17, 1912; s. Thomas Garfield and Mildred Henderson (Smith) J.; B.S. in C.E., U. N.D., 1934, Profl. Engr. (hon.), 1949; m. Lola C. Hoover, Feb. 22, 1964; children—Nancy Kay (Mrs. Curtis Thorpe), Margaret Helen (Mrs. Rudy J. Beres); stepdaus.-Mary Sue (Mrs. William Miles), Penelope Ann (Mrs. Robert Gordon). Constrn., then design engr. N.D. Hwy. Dept., 1934-40; engr. Bur. Reclamation, 1940-49, dist. mgr., Bismarck, 1949-60, reg. dir. Billings, Mont., 1960-64, planning officer Missouri River Basin, Omaha, 1964-66; dir. East Asia Office Engring., AID, Dept. State, 1966, chief industry and engring. Seoul, Korea, 1968-69, chief capital assistance and engring., Saigon, Vietnam, 1970—. Mem. Am. Soc. C.E., Sigma Xi, Phi Delta Theta, Sigma Tau. Home: USAID care Am Embassy APO San Francisco CA 96301 Office: Dept of State AID Washington DC 20523

JOHNSON, BRUCE BIRMINGHAM exec.; b. Lima, O., Apr. 1, 1932; B.S., U. San Francisco, 1954; M.S., Stanford University, 1956; m. Rosemarie Lois Brown, May 15, 1955; 1 son, Anthony Robinson. Sales rep. Ames-Brockton Fabricated Products, Akron, O., 1956-58, sales mgr. Coshocton, Ohio, 1959-61, gen. manager plant, 1961-68, v.p. sales, 1968--. Instr. bus. Coshocton Jr. College, 1968-69. Mem. Coshocton C. of C. (vice president 1967-68, pres. 1969-70), English Speaking Union, Coshocton Sertoma Club, Nat. Assn. Mfrs., Sales Executives Institute, Phi Beta Kappa, Sigma Chi, Phi Mu. Democrat. Mem. Christian Ch. (lay reader). Mason (32, Shriner). Clubs: Coshocton Country, Coshocton City, Running Deer Country. Home: 2d Av Coshocton OH Office: 3d Av Coshocton OH

JOHNSON, BRUCE CONNOR, educator, biochemist; b. Regina, Sask., Can., Apr. 28, 1911; s. Wilfred Connor and Edna (Young) J.; B.A., McMaster U., 1933, M.A., 1934; Ph.D., U. Wis., 1940; m. Elizabeth Marie Peterson, Sept. 7, 1940; children—Bruce Connor II, Peter Y., Stephen P., Lisa C., Christina M.; m. 2d, Halina V. Bogdanska, 1966; 1 dau., Margaret E. Chemist, Canadian Canners, Ltd., Hamilton, Ont., 1934-37; grad. asst. U. Wis., 1937-40; postdoctoral fellow U. Ill., 1940-42; research biochemist Golden State Co., San Francisco, 1942-43; mem. faculty U. Ill., 1943-65, prof. biochemistry, 1951-65; pro. biochemistry, chmn. dept. biochemistry and molecular biology U. Okla. Coll. Medicine, 1965—; head biochem. sect. Okla. Med. Research Found., 1965—. Mem. Atoms for Peace Mission to S. Am., 1956; State Dept. cons. Orgn. European Econ. Coop., 1958. Guggenheim fellow, 1955; recipient Nutrition Council award, 1960; NSF fellow, 1961-62. Mem. Am. Soc. Biol. Chemistry, Am. Inst. Nutrition, Biochem. Soc. (Great Britain), Am. Chem. Soc., A.A.A.S., N.Y. Acad. Sci., Soc. Exptl. Biology and Medicine. Author: Methods of Vitamin Determination, 1948; also numerous articles. Research field vitamin requirements of new born calves, lambs, pigs; first discovery of B-vitamin deficiencies in these species; metabolism of vitamins with discovery of a new metabolite of niacin; studies of function of vitamin B12, A, K and E; role of vitamin B12 in mammalian enzyme reactions; role of vitamin K in prothrombin biosynthesis; nutrition and enzyme induction. Home: 4409 Thompson Av Oklahoma City OK

JOHNSON, BRUCE HAVENS, lawyer; b. Greencastle, Ind., Apr. 7, 1913; s. J. Paul and Helen (Havens) J.; A.B., Butler U., 1933; J.D., Ind. U., 1936; m. Frances E. Richman, June 17, 1939; children—Judith Ellen, Gregory Bruce. Admitted to Ind. bar, 1936, Okla. bar, 1951; mem. firm Olive, McCurdy & Johnson, Indspl., 1937-43, Ross McCord Ice & Miller, Indspl., 1943-47; with interpretative div. Office Chief Counsel, Internal Revenue Service, 1947- 51, asst. head div., 1950-51; mem. Crowe, Dunlevy, Thweatt, Swinford, Johnson & Burdick, and predecessor firms, 1951—; asso. faculty mem. Oklahoma City Univ. Sch. of Law, 1960, 66, also lectr. at various law insts. throughout U.S. Trustee Okla. Bar Found. Mem. Am. (chmn. natural resources com., taxation sect. 1958, mem. council sect. 1964-66), ind. (sec. taxation sect. 1943-47), Okla. (chmn. taxation sect. 1955), Fed. (pres. Oklahoma City chpt. 1965-66) bar assns., Oklahoma City Tax Lawyers Assn. (pres. 1956-57). Am. Law Inst., Am. Judicature Soc. Home: 1419 Sherwood Lane Oklahoma City OK 73116 Office: Liberty Tower Oklahoma City OK 73102

JOHNSON, C. DALE, educator; b. Alexandria, Minn., June 30, 1924; s. Clarence Ellsworth and Alphia (Danielson) J.; A.B., U. Minn., 1950, M.A., 1952, Ph.D., 1961; m. Beda Irene Caroline Felt, Aug. 22, 1948; children—Kathryn Elizabeth, Timothy Dale, Michael Richard. Asst. prof. sociology St. Olaf Coll., Northfield, Minn., 1953-59; instr., then asst. prof. U. Kan., 1959-63; mem. faculty San Diego State Coll., 1963—, now prof. sociology, chmn. dept.; cons. in field. Served with USAAF, 1943-46. Recipient Distinguished Teaching award Cal. State Colls., 1969. Fellow Am. Sociol. Assn.; mem. Midwest Sociol. Soc., Pacific Sociol. Assn., Soc. Sci. Study Religion, Am. Assn. U. Profs. Author: (with others) Social Profile of a Poverty Area, 1966. Home: 8590 Renown Dr San Diego CA 92119

JOHNSON, CARL LEE, oral surgeon, anesthesiologist; b. Greensboro, N.C., Dec. 23, 1928; s. Andrew and Camilla L. (Coffin) J.; B.S., Hampton Inst., 1948; D.D.S., Meharry Med. Coll., 1953; postgrad. U. Pa. Grad. Sch. Medicine, 1956; married June 10, 1952; children—Carl Reginald, Rodney Derrick, Cheryl Densie, Dwain Richard. Intern Harlem Hosp., N.Y.C., 1953-54, resident anesthesia, 1954-55; resident oral surgery Grasslands Hosp., Valhalla, N.Y., 1956-57; practice dentistry, specializing in oral surgery and anesthesiology, Phila.,, 1957—; chief anesthesiologist Mercy Douglass Hosp., Phila., 1958-62, asst. chief anesthesiology, 1962-68, sr. attending oral surgeon, 1958—; sr. oral surgeon John F. Kennedy Hosp., 1960—; instr. Grad. Sch. Medicine, U. Pa., 1960—. Served to maj. USAF, 1965-68. Mem. Am., Del. socs. oral surgeons, Am. Soc. Dental Anesthesia (regional pres. 1965), Phila. County Med. and Dental Soc., James R. Cameron Honor Soc., Black Doctors Assn., N.A.A.C.P., Alpha Phi Alpha, Alpha Kappa Mu, Beta Kappa Chi. Home: 6904 Lincoln Dr Philadelphia PA 19119 Office: 1736 Pine St Philadelphia PA 19103

JOHNSON, CARL MILTON, physician; b. York, Pa., Aug. 13, 1905; s. Milton Smith and Minnie Elisabeth (Weiser) J.; B.S., Mt. Union Coll., 1929; Sc. D., Johns Hopkins, 1931; M.D., Leland Stanford Jr. U., 1949; m. Mildred Francis Davis, Feb. 9, 1928; children—Barbara Lee, Carl Milton, Richard Alan. Teaching fellow parasitology Johns Hopkins U. 1930-31; fellow med. scis. NRC, 1931-33; asst. dir. Gorgas Meml. Lab., Republic of Panama, 1935-45, dir., 1954-64, dir. emeritus, chief exptl. pathology, 1964—; cons. parasitologist Panama Hosp., Herrick Clinic, 1935-45; responsible investigator OSRD, 1942-44; intern medicine Stanford Hosp., 1948-49; resident pathology Gorgas Hosp., 1949-51, pathologist, 1953-54, expert med. officer parasitology and tropical diseases, 1956—; chief health officer Canal Zone govt., Panama, 1951-53; cons. pathology United Fruit Med. Dept., 1954—; former prof. extraordinario ad honorem U. Panama Sch. Medicine; spl. cons. lab. tropical virology Nat. Inst. Allergy and Infectious Diseases, Middle Am. research Unit, Bethesda, Md., 1960—; adv. com. tropical medicine Nat. Sci.-NRC, 1960—; clin. prof. tropical medicine La. State U. Sch. Medicine, 1962. Decorated Order Vasco Nuez de Balboa (Panama). Recipient Robins award, 1962. Diplomate Am. Bd. Preventive Medicine, Am. Bd. Pathology. Mem., Acad. of Medicine and Surgery, Panama, Am. Soc. Parasitologists, N.Y. Acad. Sci., Am. Pub. Health Assn., Am. Coll. Preventive Medicine, Alpha Tau Omega, Phi Sigma, Alpha Kappa Kappa, Delta Omega. Clubs: Union (Panama); Cosmos (Washington). Address: Apartado 6991 Panama Republic of Panama

JOHNSON, CARLETON WARE, editor; b. Springfield, Mo., Feb. 23, 1909; s. Frank Tatham and Katherine (Taylor) J.; A.B., U. Ill., 1930, M.A., 1932; m. Martha Byrd Baker, June 1, 1934; children—Martha Ann, Barbara Ruth. Mem. news staff Tampa Tribune, 1937-42, asst. editor, 1942-58; editor Tampa Times, 1958—. Mem. Fla. Soc. of Editors, Nat. Conf. Editorial Writers, Sigma Delta Chi (past pres. Fla. West Coast chpt.), Alpha Chi Rho. Presbyn. Mason (33, Shriner, Jester). Club: Palma Ceia Golf (Tampa). Home: 3126 Oaklyn Dr Tampa FL 33609 Office: Tampa Times Tampa FL 33602

JOHNSON, CECIL AUGUST, lawyer; b. Stratford, Ia., June 9, 1905; s. Franklin A. and Louise (Erickson) J.; student Ia. State Coll., 1922-23; LL.B., Southeastern U., 1936, M.P.L., 1938, B.S.C., 1939; LL.M., Columbus U., Washinton, 1937; LL.D., (hon.), Midland Lutheran Coll., 1964; m. Esther M. Nelson, June 30, 1926 (dec. Aug. 1959); children—Newell D., M. Nadyne, Franklin C., Richard A.; m. 2d, Harriet L. Paige, Sept. 1, 1960. Pvt. bus., Ames, Ia., 1926-33; exec. asst. A.A.A., U.S. Dept. Agr., 1933-35, dir. commodity loans, 1935-38; sec. and asst. mgr. Federal Crop Ins. Corp., Washington, 1938-42; directed reorgn. Office Civilian Def., Washington, 1942, asst. to gov. of U.S. Farm Credit Adminstrn., Kansas City, Mo., 1942-44; admitted to Ia. bar, 1936, D.C. bar, 1937, Ill. bar, 1945, Neb. bar, 1950; partner law firm Ekern, Meyers & Matthias, Chgo., 1944-51; mem. of firm Barton & Johnson, Washington 1951-66, Johnson & Hunter, Omaha, 1951-64, Johnson & Ilich, 1964—; gen. counsel C. A. Swanson & Sons, Omaha, 1951-55, Butter Nut Foods Co. 1955-64, Swanson Enterprises, Omaha, 1955—. Dir. adv. indsl. alcohol productions, govt. alcohol plant, 1944-49; lay mem. Nat. Adv. Council for Neurol. Diseases and Blindness, USPHS, 1950-51. Trustee, exec. com. Immanuel Med. Center; chmn. bd. trustee Lutheran Ch. of Am. Found., U. Neb. Found., Midland Lutheran Coll. Mem. Am., Ia., Ill., Neb., Chgo. bar assns., Am. Judicature Soc., Theta Chi. Democrat. Lutheran. Mason. Co-author Fed. Crop Ins. act and Nat. All Risk Crop Ins. program. Home: 8717 Capitol Av Omaha NB 68114 Office: 8401 Dodge St Omaha NB 68102

JOHNSON, CECIL C., ins. exec.; b. Mexico, Mo., Oct. 13, 1903; B.S. in Elec. Engring., U. Mo., 1928; M.B.A., U. Denver, 1941; student advanced mgmt. program Harvard, 1956; m. Ola B. Bentley, June 15, 1927; 1 son, C. Bryce. Vice chmn., dir. Tenneco Inc., until 1968; chmn. investment com., dir. Phila. Life Ins. Co., Tenn. Life Ins. Co.; dir. Houston Nat. Bank. Mem. Tau Beta Pi, Eta Kappa Nu. Presbyn. Clubs: Wall Street (N.Y.C.); River Oaks Country, Ramada (Houston). Home: 3726 Inwood Dr Houston TX 77019 Office: P O Box 2511 Houston TX 77001

JOHNSON, CECIL EARL, educator; b. Sweetwater, Tex., Feb. 11, 1924; s. Asberry and Jewel Dicey (Headrick) J.; B.A. cum laude, Baylor U., 1949, M.A., 1950; Ph.D. (Univ. fellow), U. Tex., Austin, 1954; m. Ruth Wade, Aug. 26, 1950. Asst. prof. Tex. Technol. Coll., 1955-60; prof., chmn. dept. polit. sci. So. Meth. U., Dallas, 1960—; research asso. Columbia, 1966-68. Bd. dirs. Arnold Found., Houston. Served with USAAF, 1943-46. Named Outstanding Prof., So. Meth. U., 1964, 66. Sr. fellow Research Inst. on Communist Affairs, Columbia, 1968. Mem. Am. Polit. Sci. Assn., Assn. for Asian Studies, Pi Sigma Alpha, Phi Alpha Theta, Alpha Chi. Democrat. Author: The Domestic Policies of the Castro Regime, 1961; Communist China and Latin America, 1959-1967, 1970. Home: 914 Wedgewood Way Richardson TX 75080 Office: So Meth U Dallas TX 75222

JOHNSON, CECIL SLATON, educator; b. Jackson, Ga., Mar. 2, 1900; s. John Lipscomb and Sue Bell (Moody) J.; A.B., Miss. Coll., 1922; A.M., U. Va., 1924; Ph.D., Yale, 1932; LL.D., William Carey Coll., 1960; m. Lucia Lockwood Porcher, May 30, 1929; children—Lucia Porcher (Mrs. John C. Rather), Rosalind Toy (Mrs. Zell A. McGee). Teaching asst., Miss. Coll., 1920; various teaching positions, 1920-29; prof. history, personal rep. of pres. Miss. Woman's Coll., Hattiesburg, 1929-30; instr. history U. N.C., 1931-35, asst. prof., 1935-41, asso. prof. 1941-46, prof. 1946-65, prof. emeritus, 1965—; adviser in gen. coll., 1936-61, acting dean, 1942-45, asso. dean, 1946-55, dean gen. coll. 1955-61, acting sec. of faculty, 1962-63; vis. prof. U. N.M. summer 1948, 51. Served with S.A.T.C., Miss. Coll., 1918. Mem. State Lit. and Hist. Assn. of N.C. (2d v.p. 1944-45). Hist. Soc. N.C. (sec.-treas. 1945-50); Am., So. hist. assns. Baptist. Author: British West Florida, 1763-1783, 1943. Editor: Autobiographical Notes of John Lipscomb Johnson, 1958. Address: 800 S Columbia St Chapel Hill NC 27514 ☆

JOHNSON, CHARLES BARTLETT, mut. fund exec.; b. Montclair, N.J., Jan. 6, 1933; s. Rupert Harris and Florence (Endler) J.; B.A., Yale, 1954; m. Ann Demarest Lutes, Mar. 26, 1955; children—Charles E., Holly, Sarah, Gregory, William, Jennifer, Mary. With R.H. Johnson & Co., N.Y.C., 1954-55; pres. Franklin Distbrs., Inc., N.Y.C., 1957—; dir. Franklin Custodian Funds Inc., Gen. Host Corp. Mem. alumni bd. dirs. Yale. Served to 1st lt. AUS, 1955-57. Mem. N.Y.C. C. of C. Clubs: Morris County (N.J.) Golf; Downtown Athletic (N.Y.C.). Home: Village Rd New Vernon NJ 07976 Office: 99 Wall St New York City NY 10005

JOHNSON, CHARLES BERT, Jr., former petroleum engr.; b. Warren, Pa., Sept. 23, 1907; s. Charles Bert and Maude (Metzgar) J.; student U. Tulsa, 1927-28; B.S., U. Okla., 1932; m. Juliette Charitat, May 27, 1934; 1 dau., Barbara Marie. Petroleum engr. Bransdall Oil Co., 1932-37; research engr. Bransdall Research Corp., 1937-42; on loan to Seismograph Service Corp., Venezuela, 1942-44; dist. engr. Champlin Petroleum Co. (formerly Chgo. Corp.), Ft. Worth, 1944-45, chief engr., 1945-51, mgr. natural gas operations, 1951-54, vice president of natural gas operations, 1954-55, vice pres. natural gas operation, engring., products pipeline, 1955-60, sr. v.p. natural gas operations, pipelines, refinining, 1960-65, executive vice v.p., dir., 1965-69, also petroleum cons.; chmn. bd. Champlin Pipe Line Co., 1967-69, Pontiac Refining Corp., Corpus Christi, Tex., 1967—; cons. refining natural gas operations, pipelines, 1969—. Mem. Am. Petroleum Inst., Soc. of Petroleum Engrs. Home: 3805 Overton Park E Fort Worth TX 76109 Retired

JOHNSON, CHARLES CHRISTOPHER, Jr., assn. exec.; b. Des Moines, Sept. 6, 1921; s. Charles C. and Haley Dale (Evans) J.; student Dowling Jr. Coll., Des Moines, 1941-42; B.S. in Civil Engring., Purdue U., 1947, M.S., 1957; m. Betty Jean Tanner, Dec. 25, 1947; children—Charles Christopher III, Teresa Ilene. Commd. jr. grade officer USPHS, 1947, advanced through ranks to asst. surgeon gen., 1968; chief sanitation facilities constrn. br. Div. Indian Health, 1960-66, chief office environmental health, 1966-67, adminstr. consumer protection and environmental health service Dept. Health, Edn. and Welfare, Washington, 1968-69, adminstr. environmental health service, 1970; asso. exec. dir. Am. Pub. Health Assn., N.Y.C., 1970—; asst. commr. health for environmental health N.Y.C. Health Dept., 1967-68. Adj. asso. prof. N.Y. U. Sch. Environmental Medicine, 1967-68; cons. Booz, Allen & Hamilton, N.Y.C., 1967, Bd. dirs. Urban Am., Nat. Cath. Found. Episcopal Ch. Am., Washington; mem. adv. council Sch. Engring. Stanford U., 1970—. Served with USMCR, 1942-46. Registered profl. engr., D.C. Recipient Meritorious Pub. Service Award Gov. D.C., 1967; Distinguished Engring. Alumnus award Purdue U. Sch. Engring., 1969. Diplomate Am. Acad. Environmental Engrs. Mem. Commd. Officers Assn., Am. Pub. Health Assn. Contbr. articles to profl. jours. Home: 615 Eye St SW Washington DC 20204 Office: 1740 Broadway New York City NY 10019

JOHNSON, CHARLES EDWARD, III, army officer; b. Edgefield, S.C., Nov. 20, 1911; s. Charles Edward and Beulah (Barron) J.; student U. S.C., 1929-30; B.S., U.S. Mil. Acad., 1934; grad. Inf. Sch., 1938, Strategic Intelligence Sch., 1949, Army War Coll., 1953, Airborne Sch., 1956; m. Betty Betz, Mar. 9, 1939; children—Patricia A., Charles Edward IV. Commd. 2d lt., inf. U.S. Army, 1934, advanced through grades to maj. gen., 1963; various assignments U.S., 1934-42; assigned command and staff 3d Inf. Div., N. Africa, Sicily, Italy, France, Germany, Austria, 1942-45; sec. Inf. Sch., Ft. Benning, 1945-49; asst. army attache, Rome, Italy, 1949-52; dep. chief pub. information Dept. Army, 1953-54; comdg. officer 7th Inf. Regt., 3d Inf. Div., Korea, 1954; asst. chief staff G-2, 8th Army, Korea, 1954-55; instr. Army War Coll., 1955-56; chief staff 101st Airborne Div., Ft. Campbell, Ky., 1956-57; dep. asst. chief staff G-2, Hdqrs. USAREUR, Heidelberg, Germany, 1957-58, chief staff Office U.S. Comdr. Berlin, Germany, 1958-60; comdg. gen. Berlin Command, 1960-61; dir. fgn. intelligence Dept. Army, 1961-62; dep. spl. asst. for counterinsurgency and spl. activities Joint Chiefs Staff, 1962-63; chief plans and policy div., region II, J-5, Joint Chiefs Staff, 1963-64; dep. chief staff intelligence Hdqrs. USAREUR, Heidelberg, 1964; chief U.S. Mil. Supply Mission to India, 1965-66; chief staff, dep. comdr. 1st U.S. Army, Ft. Meade, Md., 1966-67, ret., 1967; dir. regional activities Assn. U.S. Army, 1967—. Decorated D.S.M. with oak leaf cluster, Legion of Merit, Bronze Star with oak leaf cluster; Croix de Guerre with palm, Fourragere (France); UN medal; Ulchi Distinguished Mil. Service medal with silver star (Korea). Mem. Kappa Alpha (So.). Presbyn. Club: Army-Navy Country (Arlington, Va.). Home: 3806 26th N Arlington VA 22207 Office: 1529 18th St N W Washington DC 20036

JOHNSON, CHARLES KOBLER, fgn. service officer; b. Chgo., Feb. 10, 1923; s. Charles Ackerman and Dorothy (Kobler) J.; student U. Cal. at Los Angeles, 1940-42; B.A., M.A., Stanford; m. Ruth Elizabeth Reed, Jan. 23, 1954; children—Karen Louise, Bruce Reed, Lauren Elizabeth, Mark Kobler, Keith James. With State Dept., 1950—; intelligence specialist, internat. relations officer Office Intelligence Research and German Affairs, Washington, then U.S. mission in Berlin; assigned Exec. Secretariat State Dept., officer-charge Soviet Zone and All-German Affairs, Office German Affairs, 1963-65; became dep. prin. officer Am. Consulate Gen., Milan, Italy, 1965. Mem. Phi Beta Kappa, Beta Theta Pi. Presbyn. Address: care State Dept Fgn Service Washington DC

JOHNSON, CHARLES RANDALL, lawyer; b. Tacoma, Mar. 18, 1927; s. John Lloyd and Martha (Lodge) J.; LL.B., U. Wash., 1957, J.D., 1968; m. Theodora Marie Schroeder, Sept. 18, 1949; children-Charles Theodore, Christopher Sanford. Admitted to Wash. bar, 1957, since practiced in Tacoma; dep. prosecuting atty., Pierce County, Wash., 1957-58; asst. atty. gen. State of Wash., 1959; partner Gordon, Honeywell, Malanca, Peterson & Johnson, 1959—. Chmn. bd. Thurston County Bank, Olympia, Wash., Mid Valley Bank, Omak, Wash.; vice chmn., bd. dirs. Bank of Tacoma. Pres., bd. dirs. Jesse Dyslin Boys Ranch. Served with USMCR, 1943-46; PTO. Mem. Chi Psi, Phi Delta Phi. Clubs: Tacoma Country and Golf, Tacoma. Home: 1349B Regents Blvd Tacoma WA 98466 Office: 1 Washington Plaza Tacoma WA 98402

JOHNSON, CHARLES SIDNEY, Jr., educator; b. Albany, Ga., Mar. 7, 1936; s. Charles Sidney and Mary Virginia (Reid) J.; B.S. in Chemistry, Ga. Inst. Tech., 1958; Ph.D. in Phys. Chemistry, Mass. Inst. Tech., 1961; m. Ellen Cook McFarland, Sept. 3, 1958; children—David Mason, Daniel Cook. Nat. Acad. Sci-NRC postdoctoral fellow, instr. U. Ill., 1961-62; asst. prof. Yale, 1962-66, asso. prof., 1967; prof. chemistry U.N.C., 1967—. NSF fellow, 1958-61; Yale Faculty fellow, 1966-67; Alfred P. Sloan fellow, 1966. Mem. Am. Phys. Soc., A.A.A.S., Am. Assn. U. Profs., Phi Kappa Phi, Sigma Xi, Tau Beta Pi. Editorial bd. Jour. Magnetic Resonance, 1971—. Contbr. articles profl. jours. Home: 1833 N Lake Shore Dr Chapel Hill NC 27514

JOHNSON, CHARLOTTE BUEL, art historian, educator; b. Syracuse, N.Y., July 21, 1918; d. Edward Sullivan and Mary Frances (Power) Johnson; B.A. in Art History, Barnard Coll., 1941; M.A. in Art History, N.Y. U., 1951. Tchr., Vincent Smith Sch., Port Washington, N.Y., 1941-42; tchr. art and art history St. Mary's Sch. for Girls, Peekskill, N.Y., 1942-45, Calhoun Sch., N.Y.C., 1946-47; instr. art history Hollins Coll., 1947-48; instr., then asst. prof. charge art Maryville (Tenn.) Coll., 1948-52; mus. instr. Worcester (Mass.) Art Mus., 1952-57; vis. lectr. art history Clark U., Worcester, summer 1957; lectr. Albright-Knox Art Gallery, Buffalo, 1957- -, curator edn., 1958—, part-time lectr. Am. studies U. Buffalo, 1957- 68. Travel to European galleries summers 1949, 50, 62, 68, 69, Mexico, summer 1961; Kinnicutt travel award to Greece, summer 1954; participant UNESCO Museums Seminar, Athens, 1954. Mem. Coll. Art Assn. Am., Barnard Coll. Club Western N.Y. (past pres.). Author articles profl. jours. Contbg. editor Sch. Arts Mag., 1963-70. Home: 121 Park St Buffalo NY 14201 Office: 1285 Elmwood Av Buffalo NY 14222

JOHNSON, CHESTER LEE, army officer; b. Halsey, Ore., June 3, 1915; s. Tracy Keeler and Rose (Lunau) J.; B.S., U.S. Mil. Acad., 1937; M.A. in Polit. Sci., Harvard, 1947; postgrad. Columbia, 1948; grad. Arty. Sch., 1951, Command and Gen. Staff Coll., 1952, Army War Coll., 1956; m. Katherine Evelyn Downs, June 10, 1940 (dec. Oct. 1962); children—Peter Lee Chittenden, Tracy Keeler Truman; m. 2d, Mary Elizabeth Dowling vonWellsheim, July 10, 1964; stepchildren—Anita vonWellsheim, Eugene Joseph vonWellsheim. Commd. 2d lt. F.A., U.S. Army, 1937, advanced through grades to maj. gen., 1964; various arty. assignments, U.S., Philippines, 1937-41; exec. officer 1st Bn., 24th F.A., Bataan campaign, 1941-42; Japanese prisoner of war, 1942-45; asst. prof. social scis. U.S. Mil. Acad. 1947-50; comdg. officer 74th Armored F.A. Bn., exec. officer VII Corps Arty., Germany 1952-55; faculty Army War Coll., 1956-59; with Office Dep. Chief Staff Mil. Operations, Dept. Army, 1959-60; with office asst. sec. Def. (internat. relations), 1960-61; attache, Mexico, 1961-63; asst. div. comdr. 5th Inf. Div., 1963-64; comdg. gen. II Army Corps, 1964-65, 7th Inf. Div., Korea, 1965-66; dep. asst. chief staff intelligence Dept. Army, 1966-67; comdr. U.S. Army Forces So. Command, Ft. Amador, C.Z., 1967-70; dep. comdg. gen. 5th U.S. Army, Ft. Sam Houston, Tex., 1970—. Decorated Silver Star, Legion of Merit with oak leaf cluster, D.S.M., Bronze Star with oak leaf cluster; Order Mil. Merit (Mexico); Order Service Merit (Republic Korea), Order Merito Militar (Brazil). Mem. P.E. Ch. Address: Dep Comdg Gen 5th US Army Fort Sam Houston TX 78234

JOHNSON, CLARENCE G., ins. co. exec.; b. Omaha, Nov. 2, 1915; LL.B., U. Neb. at Omaha. Admitted to Ia. bar; claim atty. Fidelity & Casualty of N.Y., Omaha, 1941; regional claim mgr., Employers Mut. Wausau, N.Y.C., 1942-53; claim mgr. Indsl. Indemnity Co., San Francisco, 1954-62, now sr. v.p., sec. Mem. Am. (chmn. com. on workmen's compensation and Employer's liability law), Cal. San Francisco, Neb., Utah bar assns., Pacific Claims Execs. Assn. (past pres.), Cal. Workmen Compensation Inst. (chmn. mgmt. com.). Home: 14132 Seven Acres Lane Los Altos CA Office: 255 California St San Francisco CA 94120*

JOHNSON, CLARENCE JOSEPH former machine co. exec.; b. N.Y.C., Aug. 12, 1907; s. William Charles and Maria T. (Weiss) J; ed. Pace Inst., 1931; m. Mary Eymard Morrissey, Nov. 30, 1933; children—Mary Louise (Mrs. Sam Sottosanti), William C. Clk. cashier's office Bklyn. plant Am. Machine & Foundry Co., 1928-29, asst. to sec. exec. offices, N.Y.C., 1929-33, confidential sec. to pres. and chmn. bd., 1933-43, sec. bd. dirs., exec. com. Bklyn. plant, 1943-44, asst. sec., 1944-46, asst. to pres., 1944-46, became corp. sec., 1946, v.p., 1961; sec. dir. numerous other subsidiaries Am. Machine & Foundry Co. Mem. Am. Soc. Corp. secretaries (sec.). Home: Wooleys Dr Southampton NY 11968 also 333 E 34th St New York City NY 10016

JOHNSON, CLARENCE LEONARD, aircraft engr.; b. Ishpeming, Mich., Feb. 27, 1910; s. Peter and Christine (Anderson) J.; B.S. (Sheehan fellow 1932), U. Mich., 1932, M.S., 1933, D. Eng. (hon.), 1964; D.Sc., U. So. Cal., 1964; LL.D., U. of Cal. at Los Angeles, 1965; m. Mayellen Elberta Meade. With Lockheed Aircraft Corp., Burbank, Cal., 1933—, chief research engr., 1938-52, chief engr., 1952-56, v.p. charge research and devel., 1956-58, v.p. advanced devel. projects. 1958—, also mem. bd. dirs. Recipient of the Lawrence Sperry award Inst. Aero. Scis. 1937, Sylvanus A. Reed award, 1956, 66; Wright Bros. medal Soc. Automotive Engrs., 1941; named aviation man of year Airlines Activities Com.; Coller award for design of air frame, 1959; Distinguished Alumnus award in engring. U. Mich., 1953; Gen. Hap Arnold gold medal award Vets. Fgn. Wars, 1960; Collier trophy Nat. Aero. Assn., Look Mag., 1964, Theodore Von Karman award Air Force Assn., 1963; Presdl. Medal of Freedom, 1964, Nat. Medal of Sci., 1966, Thomas D. White Nat. Def. award USAF Acad., 1966; Billy Mitchell award Post 743, Am. Legion, 1969; hon. mem. Aerospace Med. Assn., 1963. Fellow Inst. Aero. Scis. (chmn. W. Coast sect. 1946-47, nat. v.p. 1948-53), Nat. Acad. Engring., Nat. Acad. Scis., Soc. Automotive Engrs., Los Angeles C. of C., Phi Kappa Phi, Sigma Xi, Tau Beta Pi (hon.). Club: Lakeside Golf (Hollywood, Cal.). Home: 16801 Oak View Dr Encino CA 91316 Office: 2555 Hollywood Way Burbank CA 91502

JOHNSON, CLIFFORD FRANCIS, govt. ofcl.; b. Waverly, Neb., May 18, 1922; s. Francis A. and Esther V. (Pearson) J.; student Dickinson Bus. Sch., Omaha, Am. U., U. Md.; m. Ruth H. Miller, Dec. 4, 1943; children—Steven, Gregory, Clifford Junior, Patricia (dec.), Jill, Jeffry, Pamela, Jeanna, Thomas, Robert. Clk., Council Bluffs Seed Co., Omaha, 1938-40; personnel clk. Office Surgeon Gen., War Dept., 1941-42; mgmt. analyst Office Army Surgeon Gen., 1946-47; newswriter, copy editor Bull. U.S. Army Med. Dept., 1947- 48, mng. editor, 1948-49; information specialist, tech. information office Office Army Surgeon Gen., 1949-50, asst. chief tech. information office, 1950-57; information officer NIH, 1957-59, chief pub. information sect., 1959-60, chief Office Research Information, 1960-67, dir. information, 1967-70, grantee relations officer, 1970—. Served with AUS, 1942-46. Mem. Am. Pub. Health Assn., Am. Coll. Pub. Relations Assn. Home: 4017 Byrd Rd Kensington MD 20795 Office: Pub Health Service NIH Bethesda MD 20014

JOHNSON, CRAWFORD, business exec.; b. Chattanooga, Tenn., Oct. 22, 1898; s. Crawford Toy and Anne Caroline (Acree) J.; student The Lawrenceville (N.J.) Sch., 1913-17; B.S., Yale, 1920; Yale, 1920; m. Mary-Stuart Snyder, Apr. 30, 1921 (dec. May 1963); children—Crawford Toy, Frederic Stuart; m. 2d Mary Neuman Bartow, Nov. 4, 1965. Clk. Birmingham Coca-Cola Bottling Co. (Ala.), 1920-24, sales mgr., 1924- 26; v.p. Crawford Johnson & Co., Inc., 1926-42, pres., 1942-56, chmn. bd., 1956-65, also dir.; pres., chmn. or dir. numerous Coca-Cola Coca-Cola Bottling Cos.; dir. 1st Nat. Bank of Birmingham, Ala. Metal Industries Corp. Served as chief Q.M., Naval Aviation, World War I; lt. col. Fiscal Div., U.S. Army, 1942-45. mem. Book and Snake Soc. Republican. Episcopalian. Clubs: Augusta (Ga.) Nat. Golf; Racquet and Tennis, Links, Leash, River (N.Y.C.); Birmingham Country (pres. 1938), Mountain Brook Country (pres. 1947) (Birmingham); Minneapolis, Woodhill (Mpls.); Louisiana (New Orleans); Rolling Rock (Ligonier, Pa.); Royal and Ancient Golf of St. Andrews (Scotland); Somerset Hills Country, Essex Hunt. Home: Mount Harmony Rd Far Hills NJ 07931 (summer) Clay Cliffe Excelsior MN 55331 Office: 230 Park Av New York City NY 10017 ☆

JOHNSON, CURTIS LEE, editor, writer; b. Mpls., May 26, 1928; s. Hjalmar N. and Gladys (Goring) J.; B.A., U. Ia., 1951, M.A., 1952; m. Jo Ann Lekwa, June 30, 1950; children—Mark Alan, Paula Catherine. Mag. and ency. editing and writing, Chgo., 1953-60; textbook and edn!. editing and writing Chgo., 1960-66; editor, pub. December mag. 1962—; free-lance editing and writing 1966—. Served with USNR, 1946-48. Mem. Phi Beta Kappa, Phi Eta Sigma. Author: How to Restore Antique and Classic Cars (with George Uskali), 1954; (novel) Hobbledehoy's Hero, 1959; Short Stories from the Literary Magazines (with Jarvis Thurston), 1970; Best Little Magazine Fiction:1970, 71; also fiction articles. Cons. editor Panache mag., 1967-. Home: 4146 Grand Av Western Springs IL 60558 Office: Box 274 Western Springs IL 60558

JOHNSON, DAVID ALFRED, hosp. adminstr.; b. Gary, Ind., Sept. 9, 1929; s. George Kasper and Edla (Gustafson) J.; A.B. in Bus. Administrn., Augustana Coll., Ill., 1951; M.B.A., U. Chgo., 1957; adminstrv. resident U. Md., 1954-55; m. Joyce Ann Graham, May 4, 1957; children—Keith, Lisa, Kevin, Lori. Asst. dir. Miami Valley Hosp., Dayton, O., 1955-62; asst. adminstr. Deaconess Hosp., Inc., Evansville, Ind., 1962-64, exec. dir., 1965- -. Mem. adv. hosp. and health facilities planning council Ind. Bd. Health, 1968-70; mem. Ind. Regional Med. Program, 1966—, mem. subcom. regional characteristics and med. manpower and facility requirements, 1966—; chmn., mem. health occupations adv. bd., sch. practical nursing and surg. tech. aide program Evansville-Vanderburgh Sch. Corp., 1966-69; mem. council health and welfare services United Ch. Christ, 1964-71, pres., 1968-70. Bd. dirs. Tri-State Area. Health Planning Council, Evansville Assn. for Retarded children. council health and welfare services United Ch. Christ, 1964—, pres., Served with AUS, 1951-53, Mem. Am. (chmn. com. library services for hosps. 1965-66), Ind. (pres. Evansville 1962, dir. Am. Protestant (del. at large 1966-67, chmn. council assn. devel. 1967-71, trustee 1968-71) hosp. assns.; Am. Coll. Hosp. Adminstrs., Nat. League Nursing. Kiwanian. Home: 2411 E Chandler Av Evansville IN 47714 Office: 600 Mary St Evansville IN 47710

JOHNSON, DAVID BUTLER, educator; b. Madison, Wis., July 24, 1918; s. Paul Browning annd Helen Armine (Fay) J.; B.A., Antioch Coll., 1942; M.S., U. Wis., 1948, Ph.D., 1955; m. Marjorie Ann Kaun, Dec. 27, 1941; children—Timothy E., Deborah D., David D. Field examiner NLRB, Cin., 1946-47; chief contractor personnel br. div. orgn. and personnel U.S. AEC, Washington, 1950-57; asst. prof. U. Wis., Madison, 1957-59, asso. prof., 1959-63, prof., 1963—, chmn. dept. econs., 1965-68. Served with AUS, 1942-45. Mem. Am. Econ. Assn., Am. Assn. U. Profs., Am. Arbitration Assn., Indsl. Relations Research Assn. (nat. sec.-treas. 1962—). Democrat. Unitarian. Home: 5806 Anchorage Av Madison WI 53705

JOHNSON, DAVID FOOTE SELLERS, ins. co. exec.; b. Chattanooga, Feb. 8, 1916; s. Joseph Wilson and Nell (Evans) J.; grad. Hun Sch., 1935; ed. Vanderbilt U., 1939; m. Elise Elrod, Apr. 9, 1938; children—Anita (Mrs. William Branch Hamilton), Sarah (Mrs. DeWitt Malone Shy). With Interstate Life & Accident Ins. Co., Chattanooga, 1936—, v.p., mgr. agys., mem. exec.. com., 1953-64, exec. v.p., mem. finance com., 1964—, also dir.; v.p., dir. Interstate Fire Ins. Co., 1953—; mem. exec. com., dir. The Interstate Corp., 1969—; dir. Invesco, Inc.; mem. exec. com. br. offices Hamilton Nat. Bank, Chattanooga, 1955—. Chmn. Nat. Alliance Businessmen, Chattanooga, 1969-70. Del. Republican Nat. Conv., 1960; chmn. Finance Com. Rep. Party Tenn., 1963-65. Bd. dirs. Evans Found.; trustee Finch Coll., N.Y.C. Mem. Life Ins. Agy. Mgmt. Assn. (chmn. combination co. com.), C. of C. (pres. Chattanooga Chamber Found.), Phi Delta Theta. Mem. Christian Ch. Rotarian. Clubs: Chattanooga Yacht; Yachting of America (Ft. Lauderdale, Fla.); Capitol Hill (Washington). Home: 211 Sylvan Dr Lookout Mountain TN 37350 Office: 540 McCallie Av Chattanooga TN 37402

JOHNSON, DAVID GALE, economist; b. Vinton, Ia., July 10, 1916; s. Albert D. and Myra Jane (Reed) J.; B.S., Ia. State Coll., 1938; M.S., U. Wis., 1939; student U. Chgo., 1930-41; Ph.D., Ia. State Coll., 1945; m. Helen Wallace, Aug. 10, 1938; children—David Wallace, Kay Ann. Research asso. Ia. State Coll., 1941-42, asst. prof. econs., 1942-44; with dept. econs. U. Chgo., 1944- -, beginning as research asso., successively asst. prof., asso. prof., 1944-54, prof., 1954—, asso. dean div. social scis., 1957-60, dean 1960-70; economist OPA, 1942, Dept. State, 1946, Dept. Army, 1948; cons. TVA and Rand Corp., A.I.D. 1962-68. Pres., Nat. Opinion Research Center, 1962-67; agrl. adviser Office of President's Spl. Rep. for Trade Negotiations; mem. Pres.'s Nat. Adv. Commn. on Food and Fiber, 1965-67; adv. bd. Policy Planning Council State Dept., 1967-69, Nat. Commn. on Population Growth and the Am. Future, 1970—. Mem. Social Sci. Research Council (dir. 1954-57), Am. Econ. Assn., Am. Statis. Assn., Am. Farm Econ. Assn. (pres. 1964- 65), Phi Kappa Phi, Alpha Zeta. Author: Forward Prices for Agriculture, 1947; Trade and Agriculture, 1950; (with Robert Gustafson) Grain Yields and the American Food Supply, 1963; The Struggle Against World Hunger, 1967. Address: 5617 S Kenwood Av Chicago IL 60637

JOHNSON, DAVID LIVINGSTONE, educator; b. Gustavus, O., Feb. 17, 1915; s. David Charles and Margaret (Delaney) J.; A.B., Berea Coll., 1936; M.A., State U. Ia., 1938, B.S. in Elec. Engring., 1942; M.S., Okla. State U., 1950, Ph.D., 1957; m. Eugenia Gibson McQuarie, Jan. 23, 1954. Instr., U.S. Naval Tng. Sch., Okla. State U., 1942-44; field engr. Airborne Coordinating Group, 1944-45; instr. Spartan Sch. Aeros., Tulsa, 1945-48; asst. prof. Okla. State U., 1948-55; prof., head dept. elec. engring. La. Tech. U., Ruston, 1955—. Registered profl. engr., La., Okla. Mem. A.A.A.S., I.E.E.E., Am. Soc. Engring. Edn., Assn. Computing Machinery, Nat.. Soc. Profl. Engrs., Soc. Indsl. and Applied Math., Am. Assn. U. Profs., Am. Documentation Inst., Instrument Sco. Am., Sigma Xi, Eta Kappa Nu, Phi Kappa Phi, Pi Mu Epsilon, Sigma Tau, Tau Beta Pi. Home: 1610 Valley St Ruston LA 71270

JOHNSON, DAVID SIMONDS, govt. ofcl., meteorologist; b. Porterville, Cal., June 29, 1924; s. Frank David and Wanda (Simonds) J.; student U. Cal. at Berkeley, 1942- 43, Reed Coll.; 1943-44, Harvard 1945; A.B., U. Cal. at Los Angeles, 1948, M.A., 1949; m. Betty Jeanne Reed, June 19, 1943. Meteorol. aid U.S. Weather Bur., Boise, Ida., 1946-47; research asst. to asst. meteorologist U. Cal. at Los Angeles, 1947-52; asso. meteorologist Pineapple Research Inst., Honolulu, 1952-56; with U.S. Weather Bur. 1956- 65, dir. Nat. Weather Satellite Center, 1964-65; dir. Nat. Environmental Satellite Center, Environmental Sci. Services Adminstrn., Washington, 1965-70; dir. Nat. Environmental Satellite Service, Nat. Oceanic and Atmospheric Adminstrn., Washington, 1970—. Mem. working group II com. space research Internat. Council Sci. Unions, 1965-69, working wort VI, 1965—, chmn. panel neutral atmosphere, 1966-69; mem. panel edn. and manpower com. atmospheric scis. Nat. Acad. Sci., 1967-69; mem. Gov. Md. Sci. Resources Adv. Bd., 1963-67. Served with USAAF, 1943-46. Recipient Gold medal Dept. Commerce, 1965; Exceptional Service medal NASA, 1966. Fellow American Meterol. Soc. (councilor 1963- 65, 68-70, exec. com. 1969-70, chmn. com. atmospheric measurements 1965- 68); asso. fellow Am. Inst. Aeros. and Astronautics; mem. Am. Geophys. Union, A.A.A.S., Sigma Xi. Mem. United Ch. Christ. Club: Cosmos (Washington). Co-author: Studies of the Structure of the Atmosphere over the Eastern Pacific Ocean in Summer, 1961. Mem. editorial bd. Jour. Remote Sensing of Environment, 1967—. Home: 237 Panorama Dr Washington DC 20021 Office: Nat Environmental Satellite Service Washington DC 20233

JOHNSON, DONAL DABELL, univ. dean; b. Rigby, Ida., July 20, 1922; s. Alfred Tom and Jennie (Dabell) J.; B.S., Brigham Young U., 1948; M.S., Cornell U., 1950, Ph.D., 1952; m. Ruth Beardall, Aug. 22, 1945; children-Kemp B., Alfred Tom, Donal B. Pre-doctoral fellow AEC, 1952; mem. faculty Coll. Agr., Colo. State U., Ft. Collins, 1952—, prof., 1962—, asso. dean, 1967, dean, 1968—; coordinator agrl. devel. Colo. State U.-AID, Eastern Nigeria, 1964-68. Served with USAAF, 1943-47. Mem. A.A.A.S., Am. Soc. Agronomy, Soil Sci. Soc. Am., Sigma Xi, Gamma Sigma Delta. Home: 1812 Orchard Pl Fort Collins CO 80521

JOHNSON, DONALD CAMPBELL, advt. exec.; b. Faribault, Minn., June 20, 1910; s. Loren Jesse and Grace (Hatfield) J.; B.S., Carleton Coll., Northfield, Minn., 1933; student U. Minn. Sch. Bus., 1934; m. Mary Eleanor Poseley, Oct. 27, 1945; children—James Campbell (dec.), Margaret Grace. With McCann- Erickson, Mpls., 1935-41, McCarthy Co., Los Angeles, 1946-48, Batten, Bartin, Durstine & Osborn, Los Angeles, 1946-53; with Davis, Johnson, Mogul & Colombatts, Inc., Los Angeles 1953—, now sr. v.p., sec. Mem. Catholic Press Council, 1959—. Bd. dirs. Cath. Big Bros., Los Angeles, 1968-. Served with AUS, 1942-45. Mem. Los Angeles Advt. Club. Clubs: Los Angeles, Westlake Golf. Home: 4343 Coronet Dr Encino CA 91316 Office: 3810 Wilshire Blvd Los Angeles CA 90005

JOHNSON, DONALD EDWARD, farm supply exec., govt. ofcl.; b. Cedar Falls, Ia., June 5, 1924; s. Chris E. and E. Jacolyn (Johnson) Hansen; student Ia. State U., 1941-42, 46, Eastern Ore. Coll. Edn., LaGrande, 1943; LL.D., Ia. Wesleyan Coll., 1971; m. Mary Jean Suchomel, Oct. 13, 1947; children—Alan, David, Brian, Kevin, Julie, Kurt, Joan, Robert, Beth. Sec.-treas. Johnson Hatcheries Inc., West Branch, Ia., 1947-61; pres. D.J. Services, Inc., 1961—, West Branch Farm Supply, Inc., 1961- -; sec.-treas. S. J. Poultry Co., Inc., West Branch and Waterloo, 1956—; v.p. ME-JON Fertilizers Inc., Oxford, Ia., 1956-65; chmn. bd. Protein Blenders Inc., Iowa City, 1961-66; Mem. adminstr. vets. affairs VA Central Office, Washington, 1969—. Mem. Am. Legion, 1945—, comdr. Ia., 1952-53, mem. nat. exec. com. from Ia., 1957-61, nat. comdr., 1964-65, dir., 1969—. Chmn. Ia. chpt. Crusade for Freedom, 1954, 57, U.S. Civil Rights Commn., 1958; Ia. adv. mem. U.S. Commn. Civil Rights, 1959-60; pres. West Branch Community P.T.A., 1960, West Branch Heritage Found. 1956-66. Councilman, West Branch, 1948-49, 66-67. Served with inf. AUS, 1942-46;ETO. Decorated Bronze Star medal; Croix d'Officer de la Reconnaissaince (Belgium), 1964; named Iowan of Year, Ia. Radio and Television Broadcasters, 1965. Mem. Ia. Feed and Grain Assn., Am. Feed Mfrs. Assn., West Branch C. of C. (pres. 1947-48). Republican. Roman Catholic (chmn. bldg. com. 1959). Home: Alexandria VA 22308 Office: 810 Vermont Av NW Washington DC 20420

JOHNSON, DONALD ELLIS, educator; b. Plaistow, N.H., Apr. 7, 1918; s. Ellis Clark and Donna (Hills) J.; B.S. in Edn., Mass. State Coll., 1940; A.M. Clark U., 1941, Ph.D. in History and Internat. Relations, 1953; m. Ruby Frances Evans, Nov. 8, 1942: children—Donald Clark, Roberta Joan, Jacqueline Evans. Mem. faculty Worcester Poly. Inst., 1946—, prof. history 1966—, head dept. history and modern langs., 1968—; vis. lectr. U.S. diplomatic history Coll. Holy Cross. 1968. Bd. govs. Worcester Jr. Coll., 1956-62. Served with USAAF, 1942- 46. Mem. New Eng. Forensic Conf. (sec. 1951-52, pres. 1955-56), Am. Hist. Assn., Am. Soc. Engring. Edn., Am. Assn. U. Profs., Worcester Assn. Historians and Polit. Scientists, Phi Gamma Delta. Author: (with J.E. Mooney) Pioneer Class, 1966. Home: 16 Lowell Av Holden MA 01520 Office: Worcester Poly Inst Worcester MA 01609

JOHNSON, DONALD MILTON, ins. co. exec.; b. Los Angeles, Cal., Feb. 15, 1920; s. Oscar E. and Maude F. (Philips) J.; B.S., U. Cal. at Los Angeles, 1941; m. Marguerite Glaze, Feb. 14, 1942; children—Stephen, Thomas, Andrew, Kenneth. Field rep. Aetna Casualty & Surety Co., Los Angeles, 1946-50, supt. agy. dept., 1950-55, mgr., 1956-60, gen. mgr., 1960-61, asst. v.p. exec. dept., Hartford, 1960-65, v.p. corporate services Aetna Life & Casualty, 1965-66, v.p. exec. dept., 1966-67, sr. v.p., 1968, exec. v.p. ins. operations, adv. Pres. ins. operations, dir., mem. exec. com., 1970—; pres., dir. Aetna Fund; dir. Excelsior Life Ins.; adv. bd. Farmington Av. br. Hartford Nat. Bank; trustee Northeast Utilities; dir. Participating Annuity Life Ins. Co., Gen. Adjustment Bur., Nat. Bd. Fire Underwriters Bldg. Corp. Bd. dirs. Greater Hartford YMCA; asst. v.p., bd. dirs. Greater Hartford Community Chest; trustee Hartford Sem. Found. Served to maj. O.M.C., AUS, 1942-46. Mem.

Health Ins. Assn. Am. (dir.) Nat. Assn. Casualty and Surety Execs. (mem. exec. com.), Ins. Inst. Am. (bd. govs.), Am. Inst. for Property and Liability Underwriters (trustee). Conglist. Clubs: Hartford, Hartford Golf. Home: 44 Uplands Dr West Hartford CT 06107 Office: 151 Farmington Av Hartford CT 06115

JOHNSON, DONOVAN ALBERT, educator; b. Litchfield, Minn., Aug. 2, 1910; s. John Alfred and Elizabeth (Erickson) J.; B.S., U. Minn., 1931, M.A., 1933, Ph.D., 1948; m. Alice Isabel Carlson, June 5, 1935. High sch. tchr., Stillwater, Minn., 1933-36, Sheboygan, Wis., 1936-39; office mgr. Social Security Bd., Bloomington, Ill., 1939-42; instr. Naval Tng. Sch., St. Paul, 1942- 44; head math. dept. Univ. High Sch., prof. edn. U. Minn., 1944—; vis. prof. U. Colo., summer 1951, San Diego State Coll., summer 1953, Stanford, summer 1960, U.B.C., summer 1963, Mem. mgmt. com. Univ. YMCA. Mem. Nat. Council Tchrs. Math. (bd. dirs. 1950-53. v.p. 1957-58. pres. 1966-68), Conf. Bd. of Math. Scis., Central Assn. Sci. and Math. Tchrs. (bd. dirs. 1960-62), Math. Assn. Am., N.E.A., A.A.A.S., Am. Edn. Research Assn., Phi Delta Kappa. Author: (with G. Lester Anderson, Dale Carpenter) The World of Mathematics, 1951; (with William H. Glenn) Exploring Mathematics on Your Own, 1961, Invitation to Mathematics, 1962; Reasoning and Logic in Mathematics, Probability and Chance. The Curves of Space, 1963; (with Gerald R. Rising) Guidelines for Teaching Mathematics, 1967; (with John J. Kinsella) Algebra, Its Structure and Application, 1967; (with Herman Rosenberg) Geometry, A Dimensional Approach, 1967; (with Viggo P. Hansen, others) Activities in Mathematics, 1971. Editor: Evaluation in mathematics, yearbook Nat. Council Tchrs. Mathematics, 1961. Contbr. articles profl. jours. Home: 2225 W Hoyt Av St Paul MN 55117 Office: U of Minn Minneapolis MN 55455

JOHNSON, DORIS, dietitian; b. Woodstock, Ill., Sept. 18, 1910; d. Alfred E. and Flora (Longanecker) Johnson; B.S., U. Wis., 1932, M.S., 1938, Ph.D., 1951 Dietetic intern Johns Hopkins Hosp., 1933; dietitian St. Joseph's Hosp. Milw., 1934-36. Wis. State Sanatorium, 1938-40, Hines Hosp., 1940, Columbia-Presbyn. Med. Center, N.Y.C., 1941-48; asst. prof. U. Wis., 1951-1952; dir. dietetics, lectr. pub. health Yale-New Haven Med. Center, 1952—. Recipient Marjorie Hulsizer Copher award, 1967. Fellow Am. Pub. Health Assn.; mem. Am. Dietetic Assn. (treas. 1956-58, pres. 1959-61, treas. Found. 1966- 69). Am. Bd. Nutrition, Am. Home Econs. Assn., Am. Heart Assn., Am. Soc. for Clin. Nutrition, Am. Inst. Nutrition, Sigma Xi, Sigma Delta Epsilon. Omicron Nu. Phi Upsilon Omicron. Phi Kappa Phi. Club: Quota (New Haven). Author: Modern Dietetics, 1951; Laboratory Manual in Cookery. Home: 5 Cole Rd Hamden CT 06518 Office: 789 Howard Av New Haven CT 06504

JOHNSON, DOUG, advt. exec.; b. Watertown, N.Y., Aug. 16, 1919; s. H. Douglas and Clare (Lane) J.; student pub. schs.; m. Geraldine Evans, Aug. 11, 1943; children—Andrew P., Molly E., Faith D. Pres., Doug Johnson Assos., pub. relations, Syracuse, N.Y., 1949-61, Barlow/Johnson, Inc., advt. and pub. relations, Syracuse, 1961—; dir. First Trust & Deposit Co., Syracuse. Home sec. to congressman, 1949-65. Mem. pres.'s assos. LeMoyne Coll. Bd. dirs. Everson Mus., Urban League Onondaga County, Better Bus. Bur. Greater Syracuse, N.Y. State Bus. and Tech. Adv. Corps. Served with AUS, 1941-45. Decorated Purple Heart with 3 oak leaf clusters. Mem. Pub. Relations Soc. Am., Am. Assn. Advt. Agys., Syracuse C. of C. (pres. 1968-69). Clubs: Century, Press (Syracuse); Cazenovia (N.Y.) Ski. Home: 10 Thornwood Lane Fayetteville NY 13066 Office: 117 Highbridge St Fayetteville NY 13066

JOHNSON, DOUGLAS MURDOCH, nuclear co. exec.; b. Albany, Ore., Jan. 18, 1920; s. O.V. and Grace (Murdoch) J.; B.S., U. Cal., Berkeley, 1940; m. Phyllis Smith, July 18, 1940; children—Kay (Mrs. David F. Wilson), Lynn (Mrs. Gerald Andrews). Various accounting positions Gen. Electric Co., Schenectady, 1940-53, mgr. finance Hanford Atomic Products div., Richland, Wash., 1953-61, Western region mgr. finance and service Gen. Electric Co., San Francisco, 1961-65, mgr. finance nuclear energy div., San Jose, Cal., 1965-67; v.p. finance United Nuclear Corp., Elmsford, N.Y., 1967—, dir., 1968—. Served to lt. (j.g.) USNR, 1944-46. Mem. Financial Execs. Inst. Home: 49 Marcourt Dr Chappaqua NY 10514 Office: Grasslands Rd Elmsford NY 10523

JOHNSON, DUANE EARL, former hosp. adminstr.; b. Salt Lake City, Jan. 24, 1926; s. Norman M. and Peal (Tripp) J.; student Kan. State Tchrs. Coll., 1944; B.S., U. Okla., 1948; M.H. A., Washington U., St. Louis, 1950; m. Nancy Elizabeth McCaul, Oct. 15, 1949; children—Christina Elizabeth, Duane Earl, Mark Bryan. Adminstrv. resident Clarkson Hosp., Omaha, 1949-50; adminstrv. asst. Latter Day Saints Hosp., Salt Lake City, 1950-51; adminstr. Audubon (Ia.) County Hosp., 1951-52, U. Neb. Hosp., Omaha, 1953-62, Milw. County Gen. Hosp., Milw., 1962-69. Cons. C. Louis Meyer Therapy Center for Children, Omaha, 1955. Mem. budget com. Omaha Community Chest, 1960; mem. blood bank com. Omaha chpt. A.R.C., 1958-61. Served to lt. USNR, 1943-47. Named Boss of Year, Omaha chpt. Nat. Secs. Assn., 1957. Mem. Am. Coll. Hosp. Adminstrs., Am. Hosp, Assn. (chmn. planning council and research and edn. trust 1961-62), Assn. Am. Med. Colls. (sec. teaching hosp. sect. 1958-60). Presbyn. (elder). Kiwanian. Home: 8843 Watertown Plank Rd Wauwatosa WI 53226

JOHNSON, DWIGHT BENJAMIN, former army officer; b. Nekoosa, Wis., Sept. 5, 1907; s. Edward and Nellie C. (Nelson) J.; student Northwestern U., 1927-28; B.S., U.S. Mil. Acad., 1932; grad. Army-Navy Staff Coll., 1944, Indsl. Coll. Armed Forces, 1952; m. Elizabeth W. Rule, June 14, 1933; children—Dwight Benjamin, Hugh Rodman, Christine Elizabeth (Mrs. Michael J. Fowles). Commd. 2d lt. arty. U.S. Army, 1932, advanced through grades to maj. gen., 1961; various assignments U.S. and Philippines, 1932-43; tng. insp. Hdqrs. Antiaircraft Command, Richmond, Va., 1943-44; asst. G-3, Hdqrs. Army Ground Forces, 1945; with Gen. MacArthur's hdqrs., Manila, 1945; operations staff officer GHQ, Southwest Pacific Area and Allied Forces Pacific, 1945-47; mem. orgn. and tng. div. War Dept. Gen. Staff, 1947-49; dep. spl. asst. civilian component affairs Office Chief Staff, U.S. Army, 1949-51; chief tng. br. orgn. and tng. div. NATO Hdqrs., Naples, Italy, 1952-54, dep. chief staff div., 1954-55; Comdr. 19th A.A.A. Group, 1955-56; chief staff U.S. Army Air Def. Command, Colorado Springs, Colo., 1956- 60; dep. comdr. field command Def. Atomic Support Agy., also comdg. gen. U.S. Army Element of Field Command, 1960-61; dep. comdr. 32d region N.Am. Air Def. Command, also dep. comdr. 32d region N.Am. Air Def. Command, 1961-62; dep. comdr., chief staff U.S. Army Air Def. Command, Colorado Springs, 1962-65; chief mil. assistance adv. group Republic of China, 1965-67, ret., 1967. Campaign chmn. Pikes Peak chpt. United Fund, 1970. Bd. govs. Wagon Wheel council Girl Scouts Am. Decorated D.S.M., Legion of Merit, Bronze medal. Mem. Ret. Officers Assn. (pres. Pikes Peak chpt. 1971), Assn. U.S. Army (v.p. Pikes Peak chpt. 1971), Colorado Springs C. of C. (mem. mil. affairs com.), West Point Soc. of Pikes Peak, Colorado Springs Fine Arts Center. Clubs: Broadmoor Golf; Officers (Ft. Carson); Winter Night. Home: 40 Marland Rd Broadmoor Colorado Springs CO 80906

JOHNSON, EARL GILIUS, educator; b. Duluth, Minn., May 18, 1916; s. Johan Albert and Ellen M. (Giliuson) J.; grad. Duluth Jr. Coll., 1936; M.B.A., U. Chgo., 1963; m. Lillian Lois Ericson, Nov. 2, 1940; children—Linda Beth (Mrs. William McK. Riggs), Michael Gilius. Sec.-treas., dir. Lowenberg Bakery, Inc., Ottumwa, Ia., 1946-54; gen. plant mgr. Wagner Baking Corp., Chgo., 1954- 58; gen. mgr. Midwest div. Pepperidge Farm, Inc., 1958-63; exec. dir. Am. Marketing Assn., 1964-69; asso. prof. mgmt. Grad. Sch. Bus., Loyola U., Chgo. 1969—; cons. in field. Mem. Am. Econ. Assn., Acad. of Mgmt., Am. Marketing Assn., Econ. Club of Chgo., Bakery Engrs., Swedish Pioneer Hist. Soc. Presbyn. Mason (Shriner). Club: Lake Shore (Chgo.). Home: 880 Lake Shore Dr Chicago IL 60611 Office: 820 N Michgan Av Chicago IL 60611

JOHNSON, EARL MORTIMER, hotel exec.; b. Chgo., May 2, 1908; s. Francis Royal and Hilda Louise (Rapp) J.; B.S., Northwestern U., 1932; m. Dolores Wetzel, Jan, 18, 1936; children—Dianne Marie, Dennis Dolan, Dolores Michelle, Valerie Ann, Bruce Anthony, Francis Jerome. Pres., Johnson Land & Timber Co., 1936—, Earl M. Johnson, realtors, 1945—; owner Johnson's Rustic Resort, (all Houghton Lake, Mich.), 1936—. Mem. exec. com. Mich. Indsl. Ambassadors. Pres., Michigan Tourist Council, 1953-54. Bd. dirs. Mich. Accident Fund. Served to lt. USNR, 1943-45. Recipient Citizen award Mich. Ho. of Reps. Mem. Hotel Assn. Redbook Directory Corp. (dir.), Am. (resort com., past pres., hon. mem.), Mich. (past pres., hon. life dir.) hotel assns., Am. Hotel and Motel Assn. (hon. life dir.), East Mich. Tourist Assn. (past pres.), Paul Bunyan Bd. Realtors (past pres.), Theta Xi. Clubs: Tavern (N.Y.C.); Chicago Culver, Executive (Chgo.). Address: Johnson's Rustic Resort Houghton Lake MI 48651

JOHNSON, EARLE BERTRAND, ins. co. exec.; b. Otter Lake, Mich., May 3, 1914; s. Bertrand M. and Blanche (Sherman) J.; B.S., U. Fla., 1937, J.D., 1940; m. Frances Pierce, Oct. 12, 1940; children—Earle Bertrand, Victoria, Julia, Sheryl. With State Farm Ins. Cos., Bloomington, Ill., 1940—, regional agy. dir., 1958-60, regional v.p., 1960-65, v.p., sec. State Farm Mut. Automobile Ins. Co., 1965—, dir., 1967—, also mem. exec. com. chmn. bd. State Farm Life Ins. Co., 1970—, also mem. exec. com.; v.p., dir. State Farm Fire & Casualty Co., also mem. exec. com., sr. v.p., treas. State Farm County Mut. Ins. Co. Tex., dir. State Farm Gen. Ins. Co. 1st v.p., dir. S.W. Ins. Information Service, 1963-65; mem. U. Tex. Ins. Adv. Bd., 1964—. Mem. Gen. Agy. Mgmt. Assn., Agy. Officers Round Table (exec. coms.), Am., Fla. bar assns., Phi Alpha Delta, Phi Kappa Tau. Home: 215 Imperial Dr Bloomington IL 61701 Office: 112 E Washington St Bloomington IL 61701

JOHNSON, EDGAR, educator; b. N.Y.C., Dec. 1, 1901; s. Walter Conover and Emily Mathilde (Haas) J.; A.B. with honors, Columbia, 1922, postgrad. Sch. Architecture, 1922-23, Grad. Sch., 1923- 24, 26-27, m. Eleanor Kraus, June 21, 1933; children—Judith Emlyn, Laurence Michael. Instr. English, Columbia, 1922-24, Washington U., 1924-26, Hunter Coll., 1926-27; instr. English City Coll. of City U. N.Y. 1927—, asso. prof. and chmn. English dept., 1949-64, prof., 1953—, distinguished prof. English lit., 1970; Carnegie vis. prof. English, U. Hawaii, 1955; lectr. New Sch. for Social Research, 1933-46; vis. asso. prof. Vassar Coll., 1943; lectr. N.Y. U., 1946-50; Frederick Ives Carpenter vis. prof. U. Chgo., summer 1956; Fulbright sr. scholar U. Edinburgh, 1956-57; Guggenheim fellow, 1957-58, 66-67; Ford Found. lectr. Harvard, 1960, Sir Walter Scott lectr. U. Edinburgh, 1967; adv. bd. 19th Century Fiction, The Pilgrim edition of Letters of Charles Dickens; adv. editorial bd. Funk & Wagnall's New Standard Dictionary; vis. prof. Princeton, 1968; Kenan Distinguished vis. prof. Vanderbilt U., 1969-70. Ednl. adv. bd. John Simon Guggenheim Meml. Found., 1970. Decorated officer l'Ordre des Palmes Académiques (France). Fellow Royal Soc. Arts (Eng.); mem. Alumni Fedn. Columbia, Modern Lang. Assn., Dickens Fellowship (v.p.), Phi Beta Kappa. Clubs: Century, Lotus (N.Y.C.); P.E.N. (pres. 1961-63, v.p. 1963- 65). Author: several books including: One Mighty Torrent, 1937; Charles Dickens: His Tragedy and Triumph, 1952; Sir Walter Scott: The Great Unknown, 1970 (winner Am. Heritage prize for biography 1969). Editor and author: A Treasury of Satire, 1945. Editor: A Treasury of Biography, 1940; The Last Days of Pompeii (Bulwer Lytton): A Christmas Carol, 1956; Oliver Twist, 1957; Tale of Two Cities (Dickens), 1958; Rob Roy (Scott), 1956; David Copperfield (Dickens), 1962; The Dickens Theatrical Reader, 1964; Pickwick Paners (Dickens), 1964; Waverley (Scott), 1964; Martin Chuzzlewitt, Bleak House (Dickens). Contbr. numerous revs., critical articles, poems, essays to mags., newspapers. Mem. Council Basic Edn., 1956—. Mem. adv. com. Satire News Letter. Home: 320 Central Park W New York City NY 10025

JOHNSON, EDWARD CROSBY, 2d, investment exec.; b. Boston, Jan. 19, 1898; s. Samuel and Josephine (Forbush) J.; student Milton Acad., 1916; A.B., Harvard, 1920, LL.B., 1924; m. Elsie Livingston Johnson, Oct. 18, 1924; m. Elsie Livingston Johnson Oct. 18, 1924: children—Elsie Pierrepont (Mrs. John Mitchell), Edward Crosby 3d. Admitted Mass. bar, 1924; asso. law firm of Ropes & Gray, Boston, 1925-39; v.p., treas. Incorporated Investors, Boston, 1939- 45; pres., dir. Fidelity Fund, Inc., 1943—, Puritan Fund, Inc., 1946—, Fidelity Capital Fund, Inc., 1958—, Fidelity Trend Fund, Inc., 1958—; v.p., trustee Milton Savs. Bank; v.p., dir. Crosby Corp., Boston; pres., dir. Fidelity Mgmt. & Research Co. Congress Street Fund, Inc., 1960—, Essex Fund, Inc., 1961—, Dow Theory Investment Fund, Inc. 1963—, FMR Investment Management Service Inc., 1964—, 2d Congress St. Fund, Inc., 1964—; dir. Crosby Corp. Chmn. bd. appeals, mem. bd. pub. welfare, Milton, Mass. Mem. investment com., trustee Children's Hosp.: mem. corp. Milton Hosp.; trustee Mary A. Cunningham Fund. Clubs: Milton-Hoosic; Harvard, Union, Down Town (Boston); La Gorce Country (Miami, Fla.); Brae Burn Country (Newton, Mass.). Home: 1196 Canton Av Milton MA 02186 Office: 35 Congress St Boston MA 02109

JOHNSON, EDWARD DUDLEY HUME, educator; b. Alton, O., Nov. 29, 1911; s. Charles Cooke and Margaret Fuller (Jones) J.; grad. St. Paul's Sch., Concord, N.H., 1930; A.B., Princeton, 1934; B.A. (Rhodes scholar), Oriel Coll., Oxford (Eng.) U., 1936; Ph.D., Yale, 1939; m. Mary Laura Vance, Aug. 11, 1947; children—Alexander Buchanan Vance, Geoffrey McClure, Victoria Taylor. Faculty, Princeton, 1939—, Phillip Freneau preceptorship, 1950-52, prof. English, 1961—, chmn. dept. 1968—. Served to lt. comdr. USNR, 1941-46. Mem. Modern Lang. Assn., Phi Beta Kappa. Mem. P.E. ch. Clubs: Elizabethan (New Haven); Century Assn. (N.Y.C.). Author: The Alien Vision of Victorian Poetry, 1952; The World of the Victorians 1964; The Poetry of Earth, 1965; Charles Dickens: An Introduction To His Novels, 1969. Contbr. articles to profl. jours. Home: 19 Linden Lane Princeton NJ 08540

JOHNSON, EDWARD ELEMUEL, psychologist, educator; b. Jamaica, B.W.I., July 25, 1926; s. Edward and Mary Elizabeth (Blake) J.; B.S., Howard U., 1947, M.S., 1948; Ph.D., U. Colo., 1952; m. Beverley Jean Morris, Jan. 26, 1955; children—Edward Elemuel, Lawrence Palmer, Robin Jeannine, Nathan Jerome, Cyril Ulric. Came to U.S., 1941, naturalized, 1948. Asso. prof. psychology Grambling Coll., La., 1954-55; prof. So. U., Baton Rouge, 1955-60, prof., head dept. psychology, 1960—69, asso. dean univ., 1969—, also dir. Regional Head Start Evaluation and Research Center; clin. prof. La. State U. Sch. Medicine, New Orleans; dir. Exptl. Curriculum Devel. Program. Cons. collaborative child devel. project State Indsl. Sch. Scotlandville, La.; vocational cons. U.S. Dept. Health, Edn. and Welfare. Served to 1st lt. AUS, 1951-53. Fellow A.A.A.S.; mem. Am. Psychol. Assn. (mem. com. on adv. services for edn. and tng. 1968—), N.Y. Acad. Scis. (life), Sigma Xi. Mason (33). Home: P O Box 9884 Baton Rouge LA 70813 Office: Southern Univ and A and M Coll Baton Rouge LA 70813

JOHNSON, EDWARD LEWIS, wholesale food distbn. exec; b. Heath Springs, S.C., June 1, 1912; s. Edward Banks and Mary (Cole) J.; student Furman U., 1929-31; m. Margaret Elizabeth Thomasson, Apr. 23, 1933; children—Gerald L., Donna Ann, James Robert. With Jewel Tea Co., Inc., 1933-67, So. region sales mgr., 1953- 59, gen. sales mgr., 1959-67, v.p., 1961-67; pres. JFG Coffee Co., 1967- -. Home: 9600 Tunbridge Lane Route 5 Concord TN 37720 Office: 200 W Jackson Av Knoxville TN 37902

JOHNSON, EDWARD QUIVRON, r.r. exec.; b. Globe, Ariz., Apr. 22, 1917; s. John C. and Rosalie (Quivron) J.; B.S. in Transp. Engring., U. Mich., 1938; m. Elizabeth Barber, Mar. 21, 1941; children—Edward Q., Jeffrey B., Richard K., Jill Ann. With C., R.I. & P. Ry., 1938, C.B. & Q. R.R., 1939; with Wabash R.R., 1939-41, 47-55, 57-64, chief engr., 1963-64; asst. engr. Ann Arbor R.R., 1941-44, supr., 1944-46; asst. engr. Fla. East Coast R.R., 1946-47; gen. mgr. Des Moines Union R.R., 1955-57, v.p., dir., 1964—; chief engr. N. & W. Ry., Roanoke, Va., 1964-71; asst. gen. mgr. maintenance staff C&O/B&O Rys., 1971—. Mem. Am. Ry. Engring. Assn. (pres. 1970-71), Roadmasters and Maintenance of Way Assn., Va. C. of C., Sigma Phi Epsilon. Republican. Presbyn. Home: 225 Stanwick Rd Phoenix MD 21131 Office: 2 N Charles St Baltimore MD 21201

JOHNSON, EDWIN HENNESSY, educator; b. Boulder, Colo., Sept. 21, 1914; s. John Hartwell and Martha Winnifred (Hennessy) J.; B.A., U. Colo., 1936; M.A., U. Mo., 1938; m. Charlotte Marie Kennedy, Dec. 31, 1938. Asst. advt. mgr. A. P. Green Fire Brick Co., Mexico, Mo., 1939; reporter Ft. Morgan (Colo.) Herald, 1940; high sch. tchr., Walsenburg, Colo., 1941; editor Trenton (Mo.) Missourian, 1941-42; asst. prof. journalism S.D. State Coll., 1946-48; head, journalism dept. U. Tulsa, 1948—. Served with USAAF, 1943-46. Mem. Assn. for Edn. Journalism, Pub. Relations Soc. Am. (sec.-treas.), Internat. Council Indsl. Editors, Am. Fedn. Advt., Tulsa Advt. Fedn., Indsl. Editors of Tulsa (dir.), Am. Soc. Journalism Sch. Adminstrs., Am. Acad. Advt., Sigma Delta Chi, Pi Alpha Mu. Methodist. Home: 114 N College St Tulsa OK 74110

JOHNSON, EDWIN WALLACE, lawyer; b. Spartanburg, S.C., July 24, 1904; s. Edwin Wallace and Jesse (Dean) J.; student Wofford Coll., 1923-24, Citadel, 1921-23; LL.B., U. S.C., 1930; m. Eppes Jones, Mar. 3, 1934; children—Wallace Eppes (Mrs. Mabrey W. Vannerson, Jr.), Frances (Mrs. George Brown Sibert, Jr.). Admitted to S.C. bar, 1930, since practiced law Spartanburg; mem. firm Johnson & Smith, 1957—; spl. judge Ct. Common Pleas, 1948, 62. Chmn. spl. com. on redrafting probate ct. law Jud. Council S.C., 1962-65, chmn. spl. com. on redrafting criminal statutes and procedure, 1966—. Vice chmn. S.C. Wildlife Resources Commn., 1952- 62, chmn., 1962-65. Mem. S.C. Ho. of Reps., 1944. Named S.C. Conservationist of Year, 1965. Mem. Am., S.C. (pres. 1965-66), Spartanburg County (pres. 1957) bar assns., Am. (S.C. v.p. 1958-60, gov. 1963-65), S.C. (pres. 1958-59) trial lawyers assns., Am. Judicature Soc., Internat. Soc. Barristers. Elk (hon. life). Home: 460 Mockingbird Lane Spartanburg SC 29302 Office: 220 N Church St Spartanburg SC 29301

JOHNSON, ELDON LEE, univ. ofcl.; b. Putnam County, Ind., Nov. 5, 1908; s. Alfred L. and Nora Belle (Sims) J.; A.B., Ind. State U., 1929; Ph.M., U. Wis., 1933; Ph.D., 1939; postgrad. London Sch. Econ and Polit. Sci., 1951; LL.D. U. R.I., 1959, U. Me., 1961, Dartmouth, 1963, U. N.H., 1964; L.H.D., Western New Eng. Coll., 1960; Catedratico honorario, U. San Marcos, Lima, Peru, 1958; m. Lois Howelll, Apr. 8, 1934; children—Judith (Mrs. Thomas P. French, Jr.), Sue (Mrs. Robert G. Peterson). High sch. tchr.; Ind., Wis., 1929-32, 34- 36; teaching asst., fellow U. Wis. 1936-38; orgn., mgmt. analyst U.S. Dept. Agr., 1938-40, adminstr. Grad. Sch., 1940-41, dir., 1941-45; prof. polit. sci., head dept. U. Ore., 1945-47; acting dir. summer sessions, 1946; dean Coll. Liberal Arts and Grad Sch., 1947-55, pres. U. N.H., 1955-62; pres. Gt. Lakes Coll. Assn., 1962-66; lectr.-cons. Center Study Higher Edn., U. Mich., 1963-66; v.p. U. Ill., Urbana, 1966—. Nat. acad. dir. Army Air Forces Premeteorol. Tng. Programs (25 colls. and univs.), 1943-44; ednl. cons. ICA, B.W.I., 1961. Chmn., New Eng. Bd. Higher Edn., 1958-61; mem. exec. overseas liaison com. Am. Council on Edn.; 1964—; mem. Overseas liaison com. Am. Council on edn.; 1964—; mem. provisional council U. Nigeria, 1959-61, U. Malawi, 1965—, council U. Coll. Nairobi, Kenya, 1966—; ednl. cons. Ford Found., S. Africa, 1965, Edn. and World Affairs, Nigeria, 1965, Am. Council on Edn., So. Africa, 1970, chmn. Nyasaland Ednl. Survey for Am. Council on Edn., 1963. Recipient Alexander Meiklejohn award for acad. freedom, 1958 Mem. Pacific N.W. (pres. 1954-55), Am. polit. sci. assns., Am. Soc. Pub. Adminstrn. Author: From Riot to Reason, 1971; co-author Study of Comparative Government, 1949; Higher Education-Some Newer Developments, 1965. Editor; Personnel Adminstrn ., 1942-43. Contbr. articles to profl. jours. Home: 306 W Florida Urbana IL 61801

JOHNSON, ELLIOTT AMOS, lawyer; b. Soldier, Ia., Feb. 21, 1907, s. John C. and Sarah (Knutson) J.; Ph.B., U. Chgo., 1928, J.D., 1931; student Northwestern U., 1923-24, 34- 36; LL.B., South Tex. Coll., 1937; m. Katherine Ryckman, Oct. 17, 1936; children—Nancy, Glenn, Karen. Prin., coach Melvin (Ia.) High Sch., 1928- 29; admitted to Ill. bar, 1931, Tex. bar, 1937; atty. Chgo., 1931-36; with Schlumberger Well Surveying Corp., Houston, 1936-68, formerly v.p. finance, treas., gen. counsel; former v.p. Schlumberger Tech. Corp.; partner in firm Johnson, Cox & Miller, Houston, 1968—. Dir., East End State Bank. Councilman-at-large city of Houston, 1945-47. Bd. Dirs Travelers Aid Soc., Houston, 1946-60, pres. 1958-60; bd. dirs. Profit Sharing Research Found., 1958-60, 69—; chmn. bd. S. Tex. Jr. Coll., 1967—. Mem. Council Profit Sharing Industries (dir. 1951-62, chmn. 1958-60), Am. Petroleum Inst. (dir. 1960-62), Petroleum Equipment Suppliers Assn. (dir. 1951—, pres. 1960-61), Houston Soc. Financial Analysts (pres. 1957-58), Tax Research Assn. (pres. Houston 1952-53), Tex. Mfrs. Assn. (dir. 1956-59), Am., Tex., Houston bar assns., Phi Delta Theta, Alpha Kappa Psi. Presbyn. Mason. Clubs: Houston, Houston Country, Kiwanis (pres. 1964). Home: 502 W Friar Tuck Lane Houston TX 77024 Office: Post Oak Bank Bldg Houston TX 77027

JOHNSON, ELLSWORTH JOHN, state govt. ofcl.; b. Huxley, Ia., Dec. 24, 1927; s. Miller C. and Edna (Havens) J.; B.S. in Bus. Adminstrn., Drake U., 1961; m. Juanita A. Jenkin, Nov. 23, 1949; children—Marc L., Scott A., Brett A. Supr. prodn. control and contract adminstrn. Solar Aircraft Co., Des Moines, 1955-59; indsl. devel. rep. Ia., 1959-62; dir. devel. Ia., 1962—. Served with AUS, 1946-47. Mem. Am. Indsl. Devel. Council, Assn. State Planning and Devel. Agys. Democrat. Lutheran. Mason (Shriner). Home: 2831 Forest Dr Des Moines IA 50312 Office: Jewett Bldg Des Moines IA 50309

JOHNSON, ELLWOOD WAGNER, banker; b. St. Louis, Nov. 23, 1904; s. Reno DeOrville and Estelle Elizabeth (Wagner) J.; ed. pub. schs. m. Madeleine Grace Reed; 1 son, Ellwood Dennis. Formerly with Chino Copper Co., Hurley, N.M.; grove owner, Fla., until 1927; began with First Nat. Bank Tampa (Fla.), 1927, former vice-chmn., dir.; dir. Broadway Nat. Bank, Tampa, Gradiaz-Annis Cigar Co., Brinson-Allen Constrn. Co. Mem. Tampa C. of C. Kiwanian. Home: 5017 Leona St Tampa FL 33609

JOHNSON, ELMER DOUGLAS, librarian; b. Durham, N.C., Aug. 2, 1915; s. Ulysses and Nancy (Smith) J.; A.B., U. N.C., 1936, A.M., 1942, Ph.D., 1951; m. Rosa Shepherd, Nov. 7, 1936; children—Eric S., Lynn D., Elaine C., Giles K. Camp librarian TVA, Guntersville Dam, Ala., 1936-40; circulation supr. U. N.C. Library, 1940-42; librarian, prof. Am. history Limestone Coll., Gaffney, S.C., 1944-53; asso. librarian, prof. library sci. East Carolina Coll., Greenville, N.C., 1953-54; dir. libraries U. Southwestern La., Lafayette, 1954-63; librarian, prof. history Radford (Va.) Coll., 1963—; mng. editor Radford Rev., 1965—. Research analyst War Dept., Washington, 1942-44. Mem. A.L.A., Bibliography Soc. Am., Phi Beta Kappa, Phi Alpha Theta. Author: Communication, 1955, Japanese trans., 1969; Of Time and Thomas Wolfe, a bibliography, 1959; A History of Libraries in the Western World, 1965; Thomas Wolfe: A Checklist, 1970; South Carolina: A Documentary Profile, 1971. Contbr. articles to library jours. Home: 1200 Milton Lane Radford VA 24141

JOHNSON, ELTON LOYD, food co. exec.; b. Florence, Colo., June 6, 1918; s. Alzanon S. and Hanie Frances (Lomax) J.; B.S.A., Okla. State U., 1940; M.S., Purdue U., 1942, Ph.D., 1948; m. Marjorie Blanche Tobias, Sept. 26, 1942; children—Carol Frances, David Lawrence. Research asst. Purdue U., 1940-42, 46-48; research, tchr. avian sci. Ia. State U., 1948-53; faculty U. Minn., 1953-66, prof., head dept. poultry sci., 1953-66; dir. internat. rural devel. office Assn. State Univs. and Land-Grant Colls., 1964-66; prof. animal sci. U. Minn., St. Paul, 1967; dir. research Ralston Purina Eastern, 1967-71, pres., 1971—. Cons., writer in field. Pres. Alphaturk, 1960-64. Served to capt. AUS, 1942-46; lt. col. Res. Mem. Soc. Internat. Devel., Poultry Sci. Assn., Am. Soc. Animal Sci., Assn. Inst. Biol. Scis., World Poultry Sci. Assn., Am. Inst. Nutrition, Ia. Acad. Sci., Sigma Xi, Alpha Zeta, Gamma Sigma Delta. Club: International (Washington). Home: 3 Old Peak Rd Hong Kong British Crown Colony Office: 44 New Henry House 10 Ice House St Hong Kong British Crown Colony

JOHNSON, EMERY ALLEN, health services adminstr.; b. Sioux Falls, S.D., Apr. 16, 1929; s. Emery Albert and Florence (Johnson) J.; B.S., Hamline U., 1951; M.D., U. Minn., 1954; M.P.H., U. Cal. at Berkeley, 1964; m. Nancy Mourning, June 19, 1954; children—Steven C., Scott E., Jennifer L., Jill M. With USPHS, 1955—, asst. surgeon gen. USPHS, dir. Indian Health Service, Health Services and Mental Health Adminstrn., Dept. Health, Edn. and Welfare, Rockville, Md., 1969—. Mem. A.M.A., Am. Pub. Health Assn., Assn. Office: 5600 Fishers Lane Rockville MD 20852

JOHNSON, ERIC FOLKE, assn. exec.; b. Oyster Bay, N.Y., Mar. 6, 1916; s. Johannes Stefanus and Anna Alida Jansson; A.B., Antioch Coll., 1939; m. Catherine Myers, Sept. 6, 1947. With Wilcox & Follett Co., Chgo., 1939-40; with Am. Water Works Assn., N.Y.C., 1940—, editor, dir. publs. 1946-47, asst. sec., 1947-67, dir. pub. relations, 1961-67, exec. dir., 1967—; exec. bd. Internat. Water Supply Assn. Served with USMCR, 1943-46. Mem. Am. Water Works Assn., Westchester Water Works Conf., N.Y. Soc. Assn. Execs., Inst. Water Engrs. (profl. asso.), Am. Soc. Assn. Execs., Am. Pub. Health Assn., Brit. Waterworks Assn. (hon.), Water Conditioning Assn. Internat. (hon.), Am. Pub. Works Assn. Home: 22 Sprain Valley Rd Scarsdale NY 10583 Office: 2 Park Av New York City NY 10016

JOHNSON, ERIC G., business exec.; Middletown, Conn., Oct. 11, 1898; s. Joseph Johnson and Hannah Amanda (Ericson) J.; student U. Pitts., 1919-23. Agt., Penn. Mut. Life Ins. Co. of Phila., 1928-30, asst. mgr. 1930-39; mgr. 1939-41, v.p., 1941-50; v.p. Colonial Life Ins. Co. Am., 1951-59; v.p., dir. Northeastern Life Ins. Co. of N.Y., N.Y.C., 1961-65; v.p. Fidelity Bankers Life Ins. Co., 1965-68; v.p. Fidelity Corp., 1968-69, cons., 1969—. Chmn., Southeastern Pa. U.S.O. Fund Raising campaign, 1946. Served to lt. col. Adj. Gen. Dept., AUS, 1942-45. Mem. Life Ins. Agy. Mgmt. Assn. (chmn. compensation com. 1947-49), Pitts. Life Underwriters Assn. (pres.), Pa. Assn. Life Underwriters (v.p.), Sigma Alpha Epsilon. Republican. Mason. Clubs: University (Pitts.); Racquet (Phila); Greenwich Country; Union League (N.Y.C.). Home: Lake Av Greenwich CT 06830 Office: Fidelity Bldg Richmond VA 23219

JOHNSON, ERLING OLAF, supt. schs.; b. Wells, Minn., July 8, 1909; s. John L. and Josephine (Olson) J.; B.A., Luther Coll., Decorah Ia., 1931, D.H.L., 1962; M.A., U. Minn., 1938; LL.D., Hamline U., 1963; m. Geneva Nyberg, Aug. 3, 1937; children—James Erling, Katherine Eleanor, William Edward. Tchr. history and music Janesville (Minn.) High Sch., 1931-33; supt. schs., Verdi, Minn., 1933-37, Janesville, 1937-42, Mountain Lake, Minn., 1942-45, Northfield, Minn., 1945-53, Mankato, Minn., 1953-61; commr. edn. Minn., 1962-64; supt. schs. Anoka (Minn.) Hennepin Sch. Dist. 11, 1964—. Recipient Outstanding Achievement award U. Minn., 1958. Mem. N.E.A., Am. Assn. Sch. Adminstrs., Phi Delta Kappa. Home: 832 Eastwood Lane Anoka MN 55303 Office: Office Supt Schs Anoka MN 55303

JOHNSON, ERNEST ALFRED, Jr., educator; b. Methuen, Mass., Sept. 3, 1917; s. Ernest Alfred and Mary (Lamont) J.; grad. Phillips Acad., 1935; A.B., Amherst Coll., 1939; M.A., U. Chgo., 1940; M.A., Harvard, 1941, Ph.D., 1950; m. Elizabeth Faber Fischer, Dec. 28, 1940; children—Peter Faber, Frederick Lamont, Emily Hix, Christopher Hall. Mem. faculty Amherst Coll., 1941-42, 48—, prof. Romance langs., 1962—, chmn. Spanish dept., 1948-68; mem. grad. faculty U. Mass., 1960—. Guest lectr. U. Merida (Venezuela), 1968. Mem. Amherst Sch. Com., 1959-62; active Amherst Community Opera, local Boy Scouts Am. Served to lt. USNR, 1942-45. Rockefeller traveling fellow, S. Am., 1947-48. Mem. Am. Assn. Tchrs. Spanish and Portuguese, Am. Assn. U. Profs., Chi Psi. Rotarian (sec. Amherst 1963-66, v.p. 1968-69, pres. 1969-70). Contbr. profl. jours. Home: 195 West St Amherst MA 01002

JOHNSON, ERNEST FREDERICK, Jr., chem. engr., educator; b. Jamestown, N.Y., Apr. 4, 1918; s. Ernest Frederick and Esther Marie (Engstrom) J.; B.S., Lehigh U., 1940; Ph.D., U. Pa., 1949; m. Marjorie Ruth McMullin, July 15, 1944; children—David S., Carolyn L., Arthur B., Melissa A. Research engr., tech. supr. synthetic organic chems. mfr. Barrett div. Allied Chem. Corp., Phila., 1940-46; asst. prof. dept. chem. engring. Princeton, 1948-54, asso. prof., 1954-59, prof., 1959—, acting chmn. dept. chem. engring., 1959- 60, asso. dean faculty, 1962-66, asso. Plasma Physics Lab., 1955—; cons. petroleum, chem., engring. firms, 1949—. Dir. Autodynamics, Inc. Mem. adv. bd. Indsl. and Engring. Chemistry, 1964-67. Trustee Asso. Univs., Inc., 1962-68 chmn. exec. com., chmn. bd., 1965-67. Fellow A.A.A.S., Am. Inst. Chemists; mem. Am. Chem. Soc. (exec. com. div. indsl. and engring. chemistry 1965-67), Am. Soc. Engring. Edn., Am. Inst. Chem. Engrs., Am. Swedish Hist. Found., Sigma Xi, Tau Beta Pi, Phi Eta Sigma. Presbyn. (elder). Club: Adirondack Mountain. Author: Automatic Process Control, 1967. Contbr. Advances in Chemical Engineering, 1958, Ency. Chemistry, also articles to sci. jours. Home: 90 Galbreath Dr Princeton NJ 08540

JOHNSON, ERNEST PARKER, psychologist, educator; b. Springfield, Mass., Aug. 30, 1917; s. Ernest Parker and Priscilla (Billings) J.; B.S., Springfield (Mass.) Coll., 1938; M.S., Brown U., 1940, Ph.D., 1947; m. Judith Kennedy, June 8, 1942; children—Stephen, Rebecca Tyyne. Instr., asst. prof., asso. prof. Bowdoin Coll., 1947-55; prof., head dept. edn. and psychology Colby Coll, 1955-61, dean faculty, 1960-7O, Dana prof. psychology, 1970—, vis. research prof. psychology Brown U., 1967-68. Chmn. Me. Democratic Party Platform Com., 1970. Served flight lt. med. br. RCAF, 1941- 45. Fellow Am. Psychol. Assn.; mem. Me. Psychol. Assn., Psychonomic Soc., Optical Soc. Am., A.A.A.S., Am. Conf. Acad. Deans (chmn. 1970-71), Internat Soc. Clin. Electroretinography. Home: Rural Route 1 Oakland ME 04901 Office: Colby Coll Waterville ME 04901

JOHNSON, ERNEST WILEY, lawyer; b. Corsicana, Tex., Mar. 17, 1908; s. Ernest Newton and Bessie (Pullen) J.; LL.B., So. Meth. U., 1932; m. Elizabeth Lyle, June 26, 1935; children—Ernest Wiley, Elizabeth Lyle. Admitted to Tex. bar, 1932, since practiced in Dallas; mem. firm Johnson, Bromberg, Leeds & Riggs. Dir., Los Angeles Biltmore Hotel Co., Dallas Hotel Co., Corrigan Properties, Inc., L. & L. Realty Corp., Bank Bldg. Corp. Mem. Am. Bar Assn. Home: 6136 Mimosa Lane Dallas TX 75230 Office: 1500-211 N Ervay St Dallas TX 75201

JOHNSON, EUGENE INGWALL, educator; b. Houston, Oct. 22, 1912; s. Ingwall Martin and Ella Sophia (Baas) J.; B.A., Am. U., 1938; exchange student Lingnan U., Canton, China, 1936-37; M.A., Stanford, 1949, Ed.D., 1952; m. Barbara Jewell Davis, June 17, 1943; 1 son, Evans Carlson. With Asso. Bds. Christian Colls. in China, 1946, Brotherhood R.R. Trainmen, Cleve., 1946- 47, Nat. Inst. Social Relations, Washington, also Los Angeles, 1947-48; dir. adult edn. and community services Fall River (Cal.) Unified Sch. Dist., 1950-52; dir. community edn. project Ford Found. Fund for Adult Edn., San Bernardino, Cal., 1952-56; dir. Civic Edn. Center, Washington U., St. Louis, 1956-63, asso. prof. edn., asst. dean Univ. Coll., 1956- 63; exec. com. Adult Edn. Assn. U.S., Washington, 1959-62, v.p., 1962- 63. exec. dir., 1963-68; prof. adult edn. U. Ga., Athens, 1968—. Cons., U.S. Office Edn., 1959, 64, asst. sec. health, edn. and welfare, 1967, Nat. Commn. Hunger, 1967, Nat. Council Chs., 1962-65, Urban Emphasis, 1963-67; cons. United Ch. of Christ, 1963—, mem. adv.com. dept. urban ch.; mem. inst. edn. Council Chs. Greater Washington, 1965-68; surgeon gen. adv. com. health commn. and edn. USPHS, 1965-66, nat. adv. com. div. hosps. med. service, 1965-67; chmn. tech. adv. com. adult edn. commrs. D.C., 1967-68; mem. nat. bd. Citizens Crusade Against Poverty, 1964-68; nat. tng. com. Campfire Girls, 1968—; dir. Latin Am. Adult Edn. Study Project AID, 1965-66; dir. pilot program edn. aging Adminstrn. Aging, Health, Edn. and Welfare, 1967-68; ednl. cons., dir. Seminars Urban Specialists, Dept. Housing and Urban Devel., 1967—; cons. manpower devel. TVA, 1970—; adv. com. community leadership lab. Nat. Tng. Labs., 1960—; founding mem., 1st chmn. Nat. Com. on Urban Life, 1960-62; chmn. Nat. Conf. on Urban Life, 1962. Served to maj. AUS, 1942- 46; CBI. Decorated Bronze Star medal; recipient Best Program award Missouri Valley Adult Edn. Assn., 1959, spl. citation Citizens Council on Housing and Community Planning, St. Louis, 1963, Delbert Clark award for nat. services in adult edn., 1969. Mem. N.E.A., Adult Edn. Assn., Assn. Higher Edn., Nat. Assn. Pub. Sch. Adult Edn., Phi Delta Kappa. Mem. United Ch. of Christ. Clubs: International (Washington); University (Athens, Ga.). Author: The Community Education Project: A Four year Report, 1956; Metroplex Assembly, 1965. Contbr. chpts. to books, articles to profl. jours. Home: 370 S Pope St Athens GA 30601 Office: Dept Adult Edn U Ga Athens GA 30601

JOHNSON, EVERETT RAMON, coll. dean; b. Bklyn., Dec. 18, 1915; s. George and Margaret (Nelsen) J.; B.A., U. Ia., 1937; M.A., Harvard, 1940; Ph.D., U. Rochester, 1949; M.S. in Engring. (hon.), Stevens Inst. Tech., 1960; m. Lucy Anna Rossini, June 27, 1942; children—Thomas G., Lisa M., Aimee A. Scientist, Brookhaven Nat. Lab., 1949-53; research engr. RCA Labs., 1953-54; prof. chemistry Stevens Inst. Tech., 1954-62; phys. sci. adminstr., div. research AEC, 1964-66; program mgr. Nat. Standrad Reference Data System, Nat. Bur. Standards, 1966; asso. dean U. Md. Coll. Engring., College Park, 1966—. Served to 1st lt. AUS, 1943-46. Mem. Radiation Research Soc., Am. Chem. Soc., Sigma Xi. Author: Chemistry and Physics of High Energy Reaction, 1969; Radiation Induced Decomposition of Inorganic Molecular Ions, 1970. Asso. editor Jour. Chem. and Engring. Data, 1966—. Home: 6810 Connecticut Av Chevy Chase MD 20015 Office: Coll Engring U Md College Park MD 20742

JOHNSON, F.A., former mfg. exec.; b. Endicott, N.Y., Dec. 5, 1908; s. George W. and Lulu Estelle (Seagers) J.; student Hill Sch., Pottstown, Pa., 1927-30; m. Jane Twining, June 25, 1932; children—Ann T., Judith E., Barbara A. Began with Endicott Johnson Corp., 1931, became chmn. bd., 1962; dir. First City Nat. Bank of Binghamton, Security Mut. Life Ins. Co. N.Y., Liberty Mut. Ins. Co., Commerce and Industry Ins. Co. N.Y.C., Columbia Gas N.Y. Inc.; adv. bd. Liberty Mut. Ins. Co. N.Y. State. Dir. Blind Work Assn. Binghamton, Dir. Asso. Industries, N.Y. State, Inc., Wilson Meml. Hosp.; adv. bd. Salvation Army Binghamton, Vols. of Am. Binghamton; mem. Valley Devel. Found., Inc.; trustee So. Tier Ednl. TV Assn., Nat. Jewish Hosp., Denver. Mem. Broome County C. of C. (dir.). Home: Southwood Dr Vestal NY 13850

JOHNSON, FALK SIMMONS, educator; b. Wake Forest, N.C., Oct. 17, 1913; s. Walter Nathan and Eva (Coppedge) J.; B.A., Wake Forest Coll., 1935, M.A., 1936; postgrad. Northwestern U., 1937-40; Ph.D., U. Chgo., 1956; m. Laura Frances Stark, June 11, 1940; children—Mark Hartman, Bruce Walter, Martha Frances, Craig Falk. Tchr. English, Campbell Coll., N.C., 1936-37; mem. pub. relations staff Northwestern U., 1937-38; tchr. English, Mars Hill Coll., 1938-40; instr. English, Northwestern U., 1945-49; mem. faculty U. Ill., Chgo., 1949—, prof. English, 1966—. Served to 1st lt., Signal Corps AUS, 1942- 45. Mem. Linguistic Soc. Am., Nat. Council Tchrs. English, Conf. Coll. Composition and Communication (sec. 1959-60), Coll. English Assn., Am. Assn. U. Profs., Modern Lang. Assn. Author: A Spelling Guide and Workbook, 1959, How To Organize What You Write, 1964, Improving What You Write, 1965, A Self-Improvement Guide to Spelling, 1965. Editor Bobbs-Merrill Series in Composition and Rhetoric, ednl. TV, 1958-60. Home: 7624 Maple St Morton Grove IL 60053

JOHNSON, FRANCIS SEVERIN, physicist; b. Omak, Wash., July 20, 1918; s. Ralston Severin and Elizabeth (Gruenes) J.; B.Sc. with honors in Physics, U. Alta. (Can.), 1940; M.A. in Physics and Meteorology, U. Cal. at Los Angeles, 1942, Ph.D. in Meteorology, 1958; m. Maurine Marie Green, Sept. 12, 1943; 1 dau., Sharan Kaye. Head, high atmosphere research sect. U.S. Naval Research Lab., Washington, 1946-55; mgr. space physics research Lockheed Missiles & Space Co., 1955-62; head, atmospheric and space scis. div. S.W. Center Advanced Studies, Dallas, 1962-64, dir. earth and planetary scis. lab., 1964-69; acting pres. U. Tex. at Dallas, 1969-71, dir. Center for Advanced Studies, 1971—; dir. Space Scis. Center, So. Meth. U., 1968—. Cons. ionospheric physics subcom., space scis. steering com. NASA, 1960-62, mem. planetary atmospheres subcom., space scis. steering com., 1962-67, chmn. lunar atmospheric measurements team. Apollo sci. planning teams, 1964-67, mem. adv. bd. Mars space missions, 1964-67, mem. lunar and planetary missions bd., 1967-71; mem. adv. panel atmospheric scis. NSF, 1962-67; tech. adv. com. Inst. Tech. and Applied Scis., So. Meth. U., 1965—; mem. working group IV, Com. Space Research, 1965—; chmn. U.S. commn. IV, Internat. Union Radio Sci., 1964-67, sec. U.S. Nat. Com., 1967-70, v.p., 1970—; mem. Nat. Acad. Scis. panel adv. to central radio propagation lab. Nat. Bur. Standards, 1962-65; mem. panel weather and climate modification Nat. Acad. Scis., 1964—; adv. com. research to coordinating bd. Tex. Coll. and Univ. System, 1966-67; mem. space sci. bd. Nat. Acad. Sci., 1967—; mem. Nat. Acad. Scis. com. adv. to Environmental Sci. Services Adminstrn., 1966-71; mem. sci. adv. bd. USAF, 1968—; mem. nat. adv. com. Oceans and Atmosphere, 1971—. Served with USAAF, 1942- 46. Decorated Bronze Star medal. Fellow Am. Geophys. Union (vice chmn. sect. geomagnetism and aeronomy 1964-68, pres. sect. solar planetary relationships 1970-72), A.A.A.S. (council mem. 1968-72), Am. Meteorol. Soc.; asso. fellow Am. Inst. Aeros. and Astronautics (chmn. tech. com. space and atmospheric physics 1961-64; Space Sci. award 1966); sr. mem. I.E.E.E.; mem. Am. Phys. Soc., Am. Astron. Soc., Internat. Assn. Geomagnetism and Aeronomy (exec. com. 1967—), Internat. Union Radio Sci., Sigma Xi. Author: Satellite Environment Handbook, 1965; also numerous articles. Home: 13619 Sprucewood Dr Dallas TX 75240 Office: PO Box 30365 Dallas TX 75230

JOHNSON, FRANK HARRIS, cell physiologist, microbiologist; b. Raleigh, N.C., July 31, 1908; s. A.R.D. and Mary Victoria (Harris) J.; ed. Gilman Country Sch., Balt.; A.B., Princeton, 1931, Ph.D., 1936; M.A., Duke, 1932; postgrad. N.C. State Coll., 1933, Vanderbilt U., 1934; m. Mary Frances McGhee, June 11, 1933; children—Virginia Lane, Mary Frances, Charlotte Elizabeth. Teaching fellow Vanderbilt U.; grad. research fellow Woods Hole Oceanographic Inst.; Eli Lilly & Co. research fellow biology Princeton, 1936-37, instr. biology, 1937-41, asst. prof., 1941-46, asso. prof., 1946-56, prof., 1956—, Edwin Grant Conklin prof. biology, 1969—. Vis. prof. U. Utah, 1950-51. Program dir. developmental, environmental and systematic biology NSF, 1952-53, cons., 1953-56; com. photobiology NRC, 1952-64. Rockefeller Found. fellow for biophysics and microbiol. research, Netherlands, 1939; Guggenheim fellow, 1944-46, 50-51. Recipient award (with D.E. Brown, D.A. Marsland) for research basic mechanism in biol. effects of temperature, pressure and narcotics A.A.A.S., 1942. Fellow Am. Acad. Microbiology; mem. Am. Soc. Zoology, Am. Physiol. Soc., Am. Soc. for Microbiology, Soc. Exptl. Biology and Medicine, Soc. Gen. Physiology, A.A.A.S., Art Students League N.Y. (life), Sigma Xi, Phi Beta Kappa. Clubs: Princeton, Quadrangle (Princeton, N.J.). Author: (with H. Eyring, M.J. Polissar) The Kinetic Basis of Molecular Biology, 1954. Editor: The Luminescense of Biological Systems, 1955; The Influence of Temperature on Biological Systems, 1957; (with Y. Haneda) Bioluminescence in Progress, 1966. Editorial bd. Am. Jour. Physiology, Jour. Applied Physiology, 1958-64; fgn. editor Canadian Jour. Microbiology, 1953-57; hon. editor Photochemistry and Photobiology, 1961-66. Contbr. articles to profl. jours. Home: 590 Lake Dr Princeton NJ 08540

JOHNSON, FRANK LESHER, Naval officer; b. Delaware City, Del., July 21, 1907; s. Frank Brazilla and Elsie (Nickle) J.; B.S., U.S. Naval Acad., 1930; grad. Chem. Warfare Sch., 1936, Naval Postgrad. Sch. 1937, Naval War Coll., 1951; m. Nina Elizabeth McAlister, Aug. 25, 1934; children—Sandra Gay (Mrs. B.J. Taylor), Wendy Leigh (Mrs. Francis M. Bunch III). Commd. ensign, U.S.N., 1930, advanced through grades to rear adm., 1958; various assignments battleships, cruisers, destroyers; officer charge Fire Control Sch., Naval Gun Factory, Washington, 1937; comdg. officer destroyers U.S.S. Fletcher, U.S.S. Purdy, participated Pacific Ocean campaigns including Marshall Islands, Shangrila, Coral Sea, Midway, Guadalcanal, Okinawa, 1942-45; chief staff officer to Comdr. Task Flotilla 5, Korean and Chinese waters, then awards officer Comdr. Destroyer Force Pacific Fleet, Pearl Harbor, 1945-46; head, dept. ordnance and gunnery Naval Sch. of Gen. Line, Newport, R.I., 1946-49; comdr. Destroyer Div. 52, Pacific, 1949-50; student, mem. faculty Naval War Coll., Newport, R.I., 1950-53; comdg. officer attack cargo ship U.S.S. Seminole, Amphibious Transport Squadron 1, Pacific Fleet, 1953- 54; head, strategic studies br., then joint and internat. plans br. Office Chief Naval Operations, Washington, 1954-56; comdr. Destroyer Squadron 30, Atlantic Fleet, Suez Canal operation and Jordan Crisis, 1956-57; comdr. Mil. Sea Transp. Service, Eastern Atlantic and Mediterranean area, 1957-59; comdr. Destroyer Flotilla 6, Atlantic Fleet, 1959-60; dir. shore activities devel. and control div. Office Chief Naval Operations, 1960-63; comdr. Mil. Sea Transp. Service, Atlantic Area, 1963-65; comdr. U.S. Naval Forces, Japan, 1965-68; commandant 13th Naval Dist., Seattle, 1968-69, ret., 1969. Decorated Navy Cross with gold star, Silver Star, Legion of Merit with V and gold star, Bronze Star with V, Navy Unit commendation, Navy Commendation ribbon with combat V. Mem. Nat. Def. Transp. Assn., Naval Acad. Athletic Assn., Naval Acad. Alumni Assn., U.S. Naval Hist. Soc. Clubs: Army-Navy Country; Belle Haven Country; New York Yacht.

JOHNSON, FRANK MINIS, Jr., lawyer, U.S. dist. judge; b. Haleyville, Ala., Oct. 30, 1918; s. Frank M. and Alabama (Long) J.; grad. Gulf Coast Mil. Acad., Gulfport, Miss., 1935, Massey Bus. Coll., Birmingham, 1937; LL.B., U. Ala., 1943; m. Ruth Jenkins, Jan. 14, 1938; 1 son, James Curtis. Admitted to Ala. bar, 1943, pvt. practice in Haleyville and Jasper, since 1946, mem. firm Curtis, Maddox & Johnson, 1946-53; U.S. atty. No. Dist. Ala. 1953-55; U.S. dist. judge Middle Dist. Als., 1955—. Served from pvt. to capt. inf., AUS. 1943-46. Decorated Purple Heart with oak leaf cluster, Bronze Star medal. Republican (past mem. state exec. com.). Home 118 N Haardt Dr Montgomery AL 36105 Office: Fed Bldg Montgomery AL

JOHNSON, FRANKLYN ARTHUR, educator; b. Rochester, N.Y., Nov. 6, 1921; s. Robert B. and Olyve C. (Eckler) J.; B.A. magna cum laude, Rutgers U., 1947; M.A., Harvard, 1949, Ph.D. (faculty scholar 1951), 1952; Fulbright scholar, London (Eng.) Sch. Econs., 1951-52; L.H.D., Jacksonville (Fla.) U. 1961; Litt.D., Mt. Senario Coll., 1971; m. Emily B. Lingle, Aug. 15, 1945; children—Franklyn Arthur, Terri A., Sandra C. Br. chief, intelligence officer CIA, 1949-51, cons., 1951-52; asst. prof. govt. Rollins Coll., 1952-55, asso. prof., 1955-56, chmn. div. social scis. and bus., 1954-56; pres., prof. govt. Jacksonville (Fla.) U., 1956-63, Cal. State Coll. at Los Angeles, 1963-65; dir. Job Corps, Office Econ. Opportunity, 1965-66; pres., trustee William H. Donner Found., N.Y.C., 1966-71; cons. Arthur Vining Davis Founds., 1970—; lectr. in govt. Hunter Coll., 1967-68; prof. govt. City U., N.Y., 1968-70, prof. pub. adminstrn. Fla. Atlantic U., Boca Raton, 1970—; lectr., speaker; Social Sci. Research Council fellow, London, 1962; vis. lectr. Inst. Commonwealth Studies, U. London, 1962, Univ. ROTC units. Dir. 1st Bank & Trust Co., Jacksonville, Fla., 1960-63; pres. Chaseville Corp., 1957-70. Co- founder, 1st state dir. Fla. Citizenship Clearing House, 1954-56, exec. com., 1954-57; chmn. Gov. Fla. UN 10th Anniversary Com., 1955. Mem. 3d Army Adv. Com., 1955-63; council Nat. Strategy Information Center, 1969—. Trustee Edn. Television, Inc., Jacksonville Art Mus., 1958-63, Founds. Luncheon

Group N.Y., 1968-71, Fuller Child Devel. Center, 1970—, Helen Dwight Reid Found. of Washington, Inst. Am. Univs., Aix-en-Provence, France, Southeastern Council Founds. Served from 2d lt. to 1st lt. 1st Inf. Div. AUS, 1942-45; ETO. Decorated Silver Star, Bronze Star Medal with 3 oak leaf clusters, Purple Heart with 2 oak leaf clusters, Distinguished Unit citation, Conspicious Service Cross (U.S.): Croix de Guerre (France); Ky. col.; So. Fellowships Fund fellow, 1957; co-recipient George Washington honor medal Freedoms Found., 1956; recipient Outstanding Prof. award Rollins Coll., 1956; Mershon fellow 1967, 69. Mem. commn. coll. and soc. Assn. Am. Colls., 1965-66; pres. Fla. Assn. Colls. and Univs., 1959-60; mem. Am. So. polit. sci. assns., Am. Mil. Inst., Am. Assn. U. Profs., Am. Assn. Un (chmn. Fla. 1954-56), Inst. Strategic Studies, S.A.R., Jacksonville Symphony Assn. (dir.), Jacksonville Area, Arlington (gov.) chambers commerce, Fla. Ednl. Television Task Force, Phi Beta Kappa (corr. sec.), Zeta Psi, Tau Kappa Alpha, Scabbard and Blade. Presbyn. Clubs: Torch (dir. 1958); Harvard (N.Y.); Oxford, Cambridge University (London, Eng.). Author: One More Hill, 1949; Defence by Com.: The Committee of Imperial Defence, 1960; Defence by Ministry, 1964; co- author: Political-Military Relations and U.S. Foreign Policy, 1966. Contbr. articles profl. jours. and Ency. Americana. Home: 612 SW 44th Av Fort Lauderdale FL 33314 Office: 1st Nat Bank Bldg Miami FL 33131 also Fla Atlantic U Boca Raton FL 33432

JOHNSON, FRED GILBERT, former banker; b. Buxton, Ore., July 5, 1908; s. J.F. and Sarah (Olson) J.; B.S., Ore. State U., 1930; m. Mabel Strandberg, May 16, 1936; 1 son, Fred Gilbert. Asst. cashier U.S. Nat. Bank-Ore., Portland, 1944-46, asst. v.p., 1946-51, v.p., 1951-56, sr. v.p., 1966-70, ret.; dir. Ore. Mutl. Ins. Co., McMinnville. Mem. C. of C., Acadia. Mason. Home: 906 SW Chestnut St Portland OR 97219 Retired

JOHNSON, FREDERICK AUGUSTUS, food co. exec.; b. Dallas, Jan. 7, 1926; s. Frederick Augustus and Marie (Fourcade) J.; B.S., U.S. Mil. Acad., 1949; M.B.A., N.Y.U., 1952; m. Dolly M. Wishnack, June 7, 1949; children-Frederick Augustus III, Dolly M. Branch mgr. Armour & Co., 1949-60; gen. mgr. Kroger Co., 1960-65; devel. mgr. Gen. Foods., 1965-67; v.p. marketing United Fruit Co., 1967- 69; v.p. marketing Agway, Inc., Syracuse, N.Y., 1969—; dir. Curtice Burns, Inc., Rochester, N.Y. Decorated knight legion of Honor (France). Mem. West Point Soc. N.Y., West Point Assn. Grads. Author articles. Home: Stonehedge Lane Manlius NY 13104 Office: Agway Inc Box 1333 Syracuse NY 13201

JOHNSON, FREDERICK JACKSON, transport exec.; b. Norfolk, Neb., Feb. 11, 1905; s. Oscar Jackson and Winifred (Leffert) J.; B.S., U. Colo., 1927, E.E., 1933; m. Alice Connett, Feb. 28, 1929 (dec. 1960); 1 son, Frederick Kennedy; m. 2d, Laurice Settle Girdler, Dec. 1, 1961. Jr. engr. Henry L. Doherty & Co., 1927-28; transp. engr. St. Joseph Ry., Light, Heat & Power Co. (Cities Service Co.), 1928-36; spl. engr. Honolulu Rapid Transit Co., Ltd., 1937- 38, asst. mgr., 1938-42, v.p., 1942-49, asst. mgr., 1942-49, dir., 1945- 49, operating v.p., 1949, pres. 1950; pres., chmn. exec. com., dir. Louisville Transit Co., 1950-55, dir., 1955-58; pres., dir. Milw. and Surburban Transport Corp., 1955—, Louisville Transit Co., 1958- -; chmn. bd., dir. Indpls. Transit System, Inc., 1956—, Transport-Ads of Milw. Inc., 1955-67; pres. Louisville Investment Co., 1967—; dir. Louisville Investment Co., Mid Empire Corp., Citizens Fidelity Bank & Trust Co. Commr. Met., Sewer Dist., Louisville, 1953-55; v.p., dir. Lousville Safety Council 1952-55; mem. Greater Milw. Com., 1955—, Met. Study Com.-Transp. Com., 1958—, Registered Profl. engr., Hawaii, Ky. Mem. Hawaii Employers Council (v.p., dir. 1943-50), I.E.E.E., Inst. Traffic Engrs., Am. Transit Assn. (pres. 1961- 62), Beta Theta Pi. Clubs: Pacific (Honolulu); Pendennis, Harmony Landing Country, Filson (Louisville); University, Milwaukee (Milw.); Columbia (Indpls.). Home: 1801 Sulgrave Rd Louisville KY 40205 Office: 4212 Highland Blvd Milwaukee WI 53208

JOHNSON, FREDERICK WILLIAM, pub. relations exec.; b. Los Angeles, Nov. 6, 1913; s. Ralph Elmer and Jennie Mary (Seaman) J.; student U. So. Cal., 1931-34, Am. Inst. Banking, 1935-41; m. Sibyl Marie Acord, Feb. 20, 1940; children—Michael Morey, Timothy Lee. Exec. sec. Los Angeles County br. Am. Cancer Soc., 1947-52; v.p., gen. mgr. Asso. In-Group Donors, Los Angeles, 1952-56; exec. dir. Republican Central Com. Cal., 1956-58; dir. pub. relations, pub. services Rexall Drug & Chem. Co., 1958-60; chmn. bd. dirs. Galaxy Advt., Inc., 1960-61; owner, pres. Fred W. Johnson & Co., Los Angeles, 1961-69; v.p., dir. Coastal Dynamics Corp., Venice, Cal., 1966-69; pres., chief exec. officer, dir. Long Beach Store Fixture Co. (Cal.), 1970—; dir. pub. relations Rev. Pub. Corp. Instr. pub. speaking profl. orgns., 1942-46; prof. U. So. Cal., 1944-45. Mem. pub. relations com. United Hosp. Fund, 1960-62; chmn. pub. relations com. Ch. Fedn. Los Angeles, 1961-62; chmn. Speakers Bur. Community Chest, 1946; v.p. Hemophilia Found. vice chmn. Go-AID program campaign, 1960; vice chmn. pub. relations council U. So. Cal. Trustee, treas., chmn. finance and budget com. Chapman Coll., Orange, Cal.; trustee Bapt. Boys Home. Mem. Pub. Relations Soc. Am. (dir.), Ind. Businessmen's Assn. Long Beach (dir.), Order Golden Key (past pres.), Delta Phi Epsilon. Baptist (deacon, trustee). Club: Los Angeles Athletic. Home: 4111 Fairway Blvd Los Angeles CA 90043 Office: 330 Locust Av Long Beach CA 90812

JOHNSON, GARDINER, lawyer; b. San Jose, Cal., Aug. 10, 1905; s. George W. and Izora (Carter) J.; A.B., U. Cal., 1926, J.D., 1928; m. Doris Louise Miller, Sept. 28, 1935; children—Jacqueline Ann, Stephen Miller. Admitted to Cal. bar, 1928, since practiced in San Francisco; partner Johnson & Stanton, 1952—. Mem. nat. drafting com. Council State Govts., 1944-47; chmn. Gov.'s Conf. on Edn., 1955; chmn. Cal. delegation White House Conf. on Edn., 1955. Mem. Cal. Legislature, 18th Assembly Dist., 1935- 47, speaker pro tempore, 1940; mem. Republican State Central Com., 1934- 46, 1950—; mem. Alameda County Rep. Central Com., 1934-47, 59—; alternate del. Rep. Nat. Conv., 1940, del., 1956, 60, 64, 68; pres. Cal. Rep. Assembly, 1959; mem. Rep. Nat. Com., 1964-68; mem. Citizens Legislative Adv. Commn., 1957-61. Bd. dirs. U. Cal. Hosps. Aux., 1960-70, pres., 1962, 64-65; bd. dirs. Florence Crittenton Home, San Francisco, 1960-69, pres., 1967-69; bd. dirs. Florence Crittenton Assn. Am., 1969—; bd. dirs. Spring Opera of San Francisco, 1963—; bd. govs. San Francisco Heart Assn., 1963-69, chmn., 1966- 69. Fellow Am. Coll. Trial Lawyers; mem. Internat. (alternate del. 8th Conf., Salzburg, 1960), Inter-Am., Am. (com. state legislation 1957-59, vice chmn. com. pub. contracts 1959) bar assns., State Bar of Cal. (exec. com. Conf. State Bar Dels. 1953-56, chmn. 1956-57, chmn. legislative com. 1956), Bar Assn. San Francisco (dir. 1951-57, pres. 1958-59), Cal. Hist. Soc. (trustee 1961—, pres. 1968-70), San Francisco C. of C. (dir. 1964-67, v. p. 1967), Phi Beta Kappa, Phi Delta Phi, Kappa Delta Rho. Republican. Episcopalian. Clubs: Pacific-Union, Claremont Country, Lawyers (San Francisco); Commonwealth of Cal. (chmn. sect. adminstrn. justice 1950-53, bd. govs. 1954-64, pres. 1958-59. Home: 329 Hampton Rd Piedmont CA 94611 Office: 221 Sansome San Francisco CA 94104

JOHNSON, GEORGE D., hotel co. exec.; b. Manassas, Va., July 15, 1906; s. R. E. Lee and Emma C. (Dawson) J.; student pub. schs.; m. Lula M. Hixson, Oct. 8, 1932; 1 dau., Nancy Kathryn (Mrs. Frank J. Stanley III). Vice pres., gen. mgr. Washington Properties, Inc., 1931-53; sr. v.p., dir. Sheraton Corp. Am., Boston, 1953—, dir. all Sheraton subsidiaries. Home: 790 Boylston St Boston MA 02199 Office: 470 Atlantic Rd Boston MA 02210

JOHNSON, GEORGE DAVID educator, biologist; b. Ames, Ia. Instr., Ia. State U., 1946-47; asst. prof. biology Johns Hopkins, 1947-50, asso. prof., 1950-62, prof., 1962--, chmn. dept., 1963-69; vis. lectr. Stanford, 1970-71. Active Boy Scouts Am., 4-H Club. Served with AUS, 1940-46. Mem. Am. Soc. Biologists, Md. Biologists, A.A.A.S., Am. Acad. Arts and Scis., Phi Beta Kappa.

JOHNSON, GEORGE EDWARD, former ins. cons.; b. St. Joseph, Mo., Nov. 9, 1905; s. George E. and Minnie (Adams) J.; A.B., U. Neb., 1928, LL.B. magna cum laude, 1929; m. Elizabeth Durisek, Jan. 3, 1930; children—George Edward III, Robert Alan, Susan Elizabeth. Owner, operator radio sta. WLAF, Lincoln, Neb., 1920-29; sec.-treas. Econ. Bridge Assn., Lincoln, 1924-29, Lincoln Sch. Aviation, 1926-29; admitted to N.Y. bar, 1930; asso. Root, Clark, Buckner, Howland & Ballantine, N.Y.C., 1929-35; atty. Tchrs. Ins. & Annuity Assn., N.Y.C., 1935-39, sec., 1939-51, v.p., gen. counsel, 1951-55; v.p., gen. counsel Coll. Retirement Equities Fund, N.Y.C., 1952- 55; pres., chmn. Variable Annuity Life Ins. Co. Am., Washington, 1955-56; pres. Equity Annuity Life Ins. Co., Washington, 1956-58, chmn., 1958-59; pres., chmn. bd. Non-Profit Equities Fund, Inc.; trustee, mem. exec. com., chmn. ins. com., mem. trustees longrange planning com. and v.p. Nat. Health and Welfare Retirement Assn., Inc., acting pres., 1956-66; trustee of Health and Welfare Life Ins. Assn., Inc., acting pres., 1956-66; trustee Health and Welfare Life Ins. Assn., Inc., acting pres., 1966—; mem. investment adv. com. TVA Retirement System, 1957; variable annuities cons. Met. Life Ins. Co., 1967-69, N.Y. Life Ins. Co., 1969-70. C.L.U. Fellow Life Office Mgmt. Assn. Inst., Gerontol. Soc.; mem. Order Coif, Phi Delta Phi, Delta Sigma Rho, Phi Gamma Delta. Club: Century Association. Home: 18811 Walkers Choice Rd Gaithersburg MD 20760

JOHNSON, GEORGE HOWARD, Jr., realtor; b. Collingdale, Pa., Aug. 19, 1916; s. George Howard and Mildred S. (Moore) J.; student Mercersburg (Pa.) Acad., 1934-35, Princeton, 1935-39; m. Elizabeth Garland Fisher, Sept. 28, 1940: children—George Howard III, David Hays, Peter Milan. With Albert M. Greenfield & Co., Inc., Phila., 1939—, pres., 1968—; dir. Bankers Bond and Mortgage Co., Lizbar, Inc.; founding dir. Nat. Land and Investment Co. Served to lt. (s.g.) USNR, 1942-46. Mem. Phila. Bd. Realtors, Nat. Assn. Real Estate Brokers. Clubs: Princeton, Union League, Phila. Country, Kiwanis (Phila.). Home: 1300 Wendover Av Rosemont, PA 19010 Office: Bankers Securities Bldg 1315 Walnut St Philadelphia PA 19107

JOHNSON, GEORGE MARION, educator; b. Albuquerque, May 22, 1900; s. William Sloan and Ella (Alexander) J.; A.B., U. Cal. at Berkeley, 1923, LL.B., 1929, J.S.D. (Sheffield-Sanborn scholar 1929-30), 1936; LL.D., U. Nigeria, 1964; m. Evelyn Williams, July 3, 1954. Pres. Student Inst. Pacific Relations, 1927; admitted to Cal. bar, 1929; tax counsel Cal. Bd. Equalization, 1933-40; dep. chmn., acting gen. counsel Pres.'s Com. Fair Employment Practice, 1942- 45; with Assn. Am. Law Schs., 1945-58, chmn. com. legal edn. and nat. def., 1953; prof. law Howard U., 1940-41, 45-58, dean, 1946-58, panelist 14th ann. conf. div. social scis., 1951; mem. U.S. Commn. Civil Rights, 1958- -; adv. com. D.C. Juvenile Ct., 1958—; guest lectr. Cath. U., Rio de Janeiro, 1959; seminar panelist U. Notre Dame, 1959; guest lectr. Douglass Coll., 1960; vice chancellor U. Nigeria, 1960-64; prof. edn. Mich. State U., East Lansing, 1960-68, asst. to pres., 1968- 69. Bd. dirs. D.C. Legal Aid Bus., 1955—; mem. D.C. Auditorium Commn., 1956-57. Recipient D.C. Inspiration House Achievement award, 1954. Mem. Am., Nat. bar assns., Am. Judicature Soc., Am. Assn. U. Profs. N.A.A.C.P., Nat. Orgn. on Legal Problems Edn. (bd. dirs. 1967-69, mem. exec. com. 1967-69), Alpha Phi Alpha. Rotarian. Author: Education Law, 1969. Co-author: New Universities in the Modern World, 1966. Home: 1350 Ala Moana Blvd Apt 401 Honolulu HI 96814

JOHNSON, GEORGE MARVIN, Jr., air force officer; b. Fort Valley, Ga., Apr. 11, 1918; s. George Marvin and Louise (Halliburton) J.; B.S. in Mil. Sci., U. Md., 1960; M.A. in Internat. Affairs, George Washington U., 1963; grad. Air Force Flying Sch., 1942, Air Command and Staff Sch., 1950, Air War Coll., 1959; m. Betty Herrington, Oct. 3, 1945; children—George Marvin III, Jean. Commd. 2d lt. USAAF, 1942, advanced thru grades to maj. gen. USAF, 1967; comdr. 96th Troop Carrier Squadron, ETO, World War II, 8th Troop Carrier Squadron, 1947-51; assigned Joint Air Transp. Bd., Ft. Bragg, N.C., 1951- 55; dep. and chief, air force sect. Mil. Assistance Adv. Group, Japan, 1955-58; assigned Hdqrs. USAF, 1959-65, dir. mil. assistance, 1964- 65; dep. chief staff materiel Hdqrs. USAFE, Europe, 1965-68; comdr. Air Materiel Area, Oklahoma City, 1968—. Decorated Legion of Merit, D.F.C., D.S.M., also Air Medal with oak leaf cluster, Air Force Commendation medal; Croix de Guerre (France). Home: 143 Buford Pl Macon GA 31204 Office: Hdqrs OCAMA (OCG) Tinker Air Force Base OK 73145

JOHNSON, GEORGE ROBERT, educator; b. Caledonia, N.Y., Aug. 2, 1917; s. Arthur E. and Mary J. (Sinclair) J.; B.S., Cornell U., 1939; M.S., Mich. State U., 1947, Ph.D., 1954; m. Beatrice E. Caton, Nov. 7, 1942; children—Diane K., Jane A., Rosemary E., Martha L. Tchr., Corfu-E. Pembroke Central Sch., Corfu, N.Y., 1939-42; asst. agrl. country agt. St. Lawrence (N.Y.) County, 1942-43; instr. animal husbandry Cornell U., 1943-47, asst. prof., 1947-48, asso. prof., 1948-55; asso. prof. Ohio State U., 1955- 58, prof., chmn. dept. animal sci., 1958—. Mem. Am. Soc. Animal Sci., Sigma Xi, Alpha Zeta, Gamma Sigma Delta. Home: 251 Fairlawn Dr Columbus, OH 43214.

JOHNSON, GEORGE STEPHEN, educator; b. Wilsonville, Neb., Sept. 10, 1899; s. Dr. Frank B. and Cora (Austin) J.; A.B., U. Neb., 1921, B.Sc., 1922, M.D., 1924; m. Marian Eleanor Nye, Dec. 22, 1923. Instr., U. Colo., 1926-28, asst. prof., 1928-31, acting head dept., 1931-32, asso. prof., 1932-33; asst. dir. Colo. Psychopathic Hosp., 1927-31; lectr. psychiatry U. Denver, 1930-33; prof. neuropsychiatry, exec. div. Stanford, 1933- 53, prof. psychiatry, exec. dept., 1954-58, prof. psychiatry, 1958-64, prof. psychiatry emeritus, 1964—. Pres., Cal. Bd. Med. Examiners, 1961; med. adviser Cal. Div. Mental Hygiene; cons. Surgeon Gen. U.S. Army, U.S. VA, U.S. Dept. Justice. Diplomate Am. Bd. Psychiatry and Neurology. Fellow A.M.A., A.C.P., Am. Psychiat. Assn., Am. Orthopsychiat. Assn., A.A.A.S.; mem. Assn. for Research in Nervous and Mental Diseases, Am. Psychosomatic Soc., Am. Acad. Neurology, Sigma Xi, Alpha Omega Alpha, Phi Gamma Delta, Phi Rho Sigma. Clubs: Bohemian: San Francisco Golf. Home: 1960 Vallejo St San Francisco CA 94123 Office: 909 Hyde St San Francisco CA 94109

JOHNSON, GEORGE WILLIAM, coll. dean; b. Jamestown, N.D., July 5, 1928; s. George Carl and Mathilde (Trautman) J.; B.A., Jamestown Coll., 1950; M.A., Columbia, 1953, Ph.D., 1960; m. Joanne Ferris, June 11, 1955; children—Robert, Garth. Instr. U. Mo., 1954-56; mem. faculty Temple U., 1957—, chmn. dept. English, 1967-68, prof. English, 1968—, dean Coll. Liberal Arts, 1968—. Served with AUS, 1951-52. Mem. Modern Lang. Assn., Nat. Council Tchrs. English, Am. Assn. Higher Edn., Am. Council Acad. Deans, Am. Council Edn. Home: 351 Waverly Rd Glenside PA 19038 Office: Coll Liberal Arts Temple U Philadelphia PA 19122

JOHNSON, GERALD EDWIN, lawyer; b. Warren, Pa., Sept. 2, 1907; s. Albert Edwin and Selma C. (Nelson) J.; A.B., Wittenberg U., 1929; J.D., Case Western Res. U., 1932; m. Gertrude Blomquist, Aug. 14, 1937; children—Christina (Mrs. Robert J. Woltersdorf), Paul L. Admitted to Ohio bar, 1932, since practiced in Cleve.; partner Jamison, Ulrich, Johnson, Burkhalter & Hesser, 1954-69; partner firm Johnson and Umstead, 1969—; chief rent atty. Cleve. area OPA, 1942-43. Pres. trustees Albert Rees Davis Endowment Fund, 1960-70. Fellow Am. Coll. Probate Counsel; mem. Am., Ohio (council dels.), Cleve. (exec. com.) bar assns., Court Nisi Prius (judge 1968-69), Order of Coif, Alpha Tau Omega (pres. 1958-62, treas. 1968-70), Phi Delta Phi, Tau Kappa Alpha. Clubs: Union, Singers (pres. 1952) (Cleve.) Home: 12700 Lake Av Lakewood OH 44107 Office: National City Bank Bldg Cleveland OH 44114

JOHNSON, GERALD WALTER, air force officer; b. Owenton, Ky., July 10, 1919; s. James Benjamin and Attie A. (Reeves) J.; student Eastern State Coll., Richmond, Ky., 1939-41; B.S., Boston U., 1950; postgrad. George Washington U., 1962-63; m. Lou Ann Schaefers, July 7, 1946 (dec.); children—Gerald Walter, Deborah A. Commd. 2d lt. USAAF, 1941, advanced through grades to lt. gen. USAF, 1971; comdr. 508th Strategic Fighter Wing and 4080th Strategic Reconnaissance Wing, Turner AFB, Ga., 1955-57; dir. plans 7th Air Div., U.K., 1957-59; dir. plans and asst. dep. chief of staff personnel Hdqrs. SAC, Offutt AFB, Neb., 1959-62; comdr. 95th Bomb Wing, 305th Bomb Wing and 825th Air Div., 1963-68; vice comdr. 2d Air Force, Barksdale AFB, La., comdr. 1st Strategic Aerospace Div., Vandenburg AFB, Cal., 1968-69; dep. chief of staff operations Hdqrs. SAC, Offutt AFB, 1969-71; comdr. 8th Air Force, 1971—. Decorated D.S.C., Air Force D.S.M., Legion of Merit with two oak leaf clusters, D.F.C. with 4 oak leaf clusters, Bronze Star, Air medal with 3 oak leaf clusters, Army Commendation medal, Air Force Commendation medal; French Croix de Guerre with silver gilt star. Mem. Am. Fighter Aces Assn., Air Force Assn., Am. Legion, Beta Gamma Sigma. Address: APO San Francisco CA 96334

JOHNSON, GERALD WHITE, newspaper man; b. Riverton, N.C., Aug. 6, 1890; s. Archibald and Flora Caroline (McNeill) J.; A.B., Wake Forest Coll., 1911; Litt.D., 1928; studies U. of Toulouse, France; LL.D., Coll. of Charleston, S.C., 1935; LL.D., U. N.C., 1937; D.C.L., U. South, 1942; LL.D., U. N.C. at Greensboro, 1966; Litt.D., Goucher Coll., 1969; m. Kathryn Hayward, Apr. 22, 1922; 2 daughters. Established Thomasville (N.C.) Davidsonian, 1910; with Lexington (N.C.) Dispatch, 1911-13; with Greensboro (N.C.) Daily News, 1913-24; prof. journalism, U. N. C., 1924-26; editorial writer Balt. Evening Sun, 1926-39, The Sun, 1939-43, free-lance, 1943—; news commentator on station WAAM-TV, 1952-54; contbg. editor The New Republic, 1954—. Served with 321st Infantry, 81st Div., U.S. Army, 1917-19; with A.E.F. France 1 yr. Recipient DuPont Commentators' award, 1953; Sidney Hillman Found. award, 1954; George Foster Peabody award, 1954; Gold medal State of N.C., 1964; Andrew White medal Loyola Coll., Balt., 1969. Mem. Phi Beta Kappa. Democrat. Author: The Story of Man's Work (with W. R. Hayward), 1925; The Undefeated, 1926; What Is News? 1926; Andrew Jackson-An Epic in Homespun, 1927; Randolph of Roanoke—A Political Fantastic, 1929; By Reason of Strength, 1930; Number Thirty Six, 1933; The Secession of the Southern States, 1933; The Sunpapers of Baltimore (with Frank R. Kent, H.L. Mencken and Hamilton Owens), 1937; A Little Night Music, 1937; The Wasted Land, 1937; America's Silver Age, 1939; Roosevelt: Dictator or Democrat?, 1941; American Heroes and Hero-Worship, 1943; Woodrow Wilson, 1944; An Honorable Titan, 1946; The First Captain, 1947; Liberal's Progress, 1948; Our English Heritage, 1949; Incredible Tale, 1950; This American People, 1951; Pattern for Liberty, 1952; Lunatic Fringe, 1957; Peril and Promise, 1958; The Lines Are Drawn, 1958; America: A History for Peter (3 vols.), 1959-60; The Man Who Feels Left Behind, 1960; Hod-Carrier, 1964; Communism; An American's View; Franklin D. Roosevelt, 1967; The Imperial Republic, 1972. Clubs: West Hamilton Street; Century (N.Y.C.). Home: 217 Bolton Pl Baltimore MD 21217

JOHNSON, GERALD WOODROW, physicist; b. Spangle, Wash., Sept. 16, 1917; s. James Clinton and Garnet Elva (Ogden) J.; student Eastern Wash. State Coll., 1933-35; B.S., Wash. State U., 1937. M.S. 1939; Ph.D., U. Cal. at Berkeley, 1947; m. Mary Kay Skidmore, Aug. 19, 1940; children—Susan Elizabeth, Russell Dana, Richard Kent. Asst. prof. physics Wash. State U., 1947-49; asso. physicist Brookhaven Nat. Lab., Upton, N.Y., 1949-51; chief analysis br. Armed Forces Spl. Weapons Project, Washington, 1951-53; spl. asst. to dir. research AEC, Washington, 1953; asso. dir. for weapons testing and peaceful applications Lawrence Radiation Lab. U. Cal. at Livermore, 1953- 61, asso. dir., 1963-66; dir. Navy Labs., 1966-68, mgr. explosives engring. services Gulf Energy and Environmental Systems, 1968—; chmn. mil. liaison com., asst. to sec. defense for atomic energy, 1961-63. Served from ensign to lt. comdr., USNR, 1941-46, comdr., 1951-53; capt. Res. Mem. Am. Phys. Soc., Am. Geophys. Soc., U.S. Naval Inst., Sigma Xi. Office: Lawrence Radiation Lab University of Cal Livermore CA 94550

JOHNSON, GIFFORD K., bus. exec.; b. Santa Barbara, Cal., June 30, 1918; s. Elvin Morgan and Rosalie Dorothy (Schlagel) J.; student Santa Monica (Cal.) City Coll., 1938-39, U. Cal. at Los Angeles, 1940, Harvard Bus. Sch., 1944; m. Betty Jane Crockett, June 10, 1944; children—Craig, Dane, Janet. With N. Am. Aviation, Inc., 1935-41; chief indsl. engr. Consol. Vultee Aircraft Corp., 1941-48; prodn. mgr. to pres. Chance Vought Aircraft Corp., 1950- 61; pres., chief operating officer Ling-Temco-Vought, Inc., 1961-64; pres. S.W. Center Advanced Studies, 1965-69; pres. Am. Biomed. Corp., 1969—; v.p., dir. Ranch Foods, Inc., dir. Oak Cliff Savs., Dallas, Richardson (Tex.) Heights Bank & Trust; v.p., trustee Excellence in Edn. Found.; councilor Tex. A. and M. Research Found. Clubs: Northwood Country, White Mountain Country (Ariz.); Salesmanship (Dallas). Home: 7517 Baxtershire Dr Dallas TX 75225 Office: 7007 Preston Rd Dallas TX 75225

JOHNSON, GLEN R., investment banking exec.; b. Lake Lillian, Minn., May 2, 1929; s. Oscar A. and Ruth (Anderson) J.; student Gustavus Adolphus Coll., 1946-47, Minn. Sch. Bus., 1947-48; m. LaVonne Corley, Jan. 7, 1949; children—Vicki, David, Lori. Founder, Lake Lillian Crier, 1949 editor, pub., 1949-61; pub. Fishing and Boating News, 1959-61; dep. dir., area mgr. for Minn. U.S. Savs. Bonds, 1961-62, dir. Minn., 1962-67, nat. dir., 1967-69; v.p. Motivational Systems, Inc., N.Y.C., 1969-70; pres. Mutual Fund for Investment in U.S. Govt. Securities, 1970—. Pres. Weekly Press Assn. Kandiyohi County, Minn., 1957-59; pres. Lake Lillian C. of C., 1955-60. Chmn. Kandiyohi County chpt. Minn. Mental Health Assn., 1960. Campaign mgr. 7th dist. Senator Hubert H. Humphrey, 1960. Named Twin City Civil Service Employee of Year, 1965; recipient Certificate of Merit, Treasury Dept., 1965, Distinguished Service award Lutheran Brotherhood, 1968. Hon. mem. Minn. Newspaper Assn. Lutheran (sec. Congregation 1954-56). Clubs: Minn. Press (charter); New York Athletic. Home: 1702 Greenbrier Circle Reston VA 22070 Office: 421 7th Av Pittsburgh PA 15230

JOHNSON, GLENDON ELWOOD, lawyer; b. Cleveland, Utah, Feb. 19, 1924; s. John Ivan and Hildur Elizabeth (Johnson) J.; B.S., U. Utah, 1948; LL.B., Harvard, 1952; m. Bobette Peterson, Aug. 15,

1949; children—Glendon Elwood, Eric, Tawny. Admitted to Utah bar, 1953; law clk. Utah Supreme Ct., 1953-54; practice law, Salt Lake City, 1953-54; adminstrv. asst. to U.S. Senator Bennette, 1954-58; with firm Ray, Rawlins, Jones & Henderson, Salt Lake City, 1959; asso. gen. consel Am. Life Conv., 1959-61, gen. counsel, 1962-68, v.p., 1966-68; sr. exec. vp. Gt. So. Life Ins. Co., Houston, 1968—; chmn. bd. Terracor, Salt Lake City; vice chmn., sec., dir. State Savs. & Loan Assn., Salt Lake City; dir. Securities Mgmt. Corp., Dallas; co-owner of Notomvideo Ranches, Notom, U. Missionary, Ch. Jesus Christ Latter-Day Saints, 1948-49, mem. bishopric Chevy Chase ward, 1960-66. Instl. rep. Nat. Capital area council Boy Scouts Am., 1960—. Served to maj., inf., AUS, 1942-46; ETO. Mem. Am., Fed., Utah bar assns., Assn Life Ins. Counsel, Am. Judicature Soc., Phi Beta Kappa, Phi Kappa Phi, Beta Gamma Sigma, Phi Eta Sigma, Alpha Kappa Psi (medallion for scholastic excellence 1947), Sigma Chi, Owl and Key, Skull and Bones. Clubs: Kenwood Golf and Country (Chevy Chase); University (Washington). Contbr. articles in field to profl. jours. Home: 2929 Buffalo Speedway Houston TX 77006 Office: 3121 Buffalo Speedway Houston TX 77001

JOHNSON, GLENNA BEACH (Mrs. Axel H. Johnson), social worker; b. Bristol Center, N.Y., Feb. 23, 1905; d. Stephen H. and Estella (Warfield) Beach; B.A. magna cum laude, Syracuse U., 1926; M.S. in Social Adminstrn., Case-Western U., 1928; certificate psychiat. social work U. Buffalo, 1938; m. Axel H. Johnson, Apr. 24, 1931; children—David Axel, Karen Ann (Mrs. Wilfrid Kitchen), Eric Warfield. Caseworker, student supr. Family Service Assn., Cleve., 1928-30, dist. sec. 1931-33; dist. sec. Cuyahoga County Relief Adminstrn., Cleve., 1933- 34; casework supr. Family Service Soc., Buffalo, 1934-41; caseworker Family Service Soc., Cleve., 1941-42; case cons. Children's Bur. Cleve., 1941-42; dir. social work for emergency child care Welfare Fedn., Cleve., 1942-45; dir. social work Summit County Child Welfare Bd., Akron, O., 1945-46; child care supr. Family Service Soc., Akron, 1946- 53; pvt. practice psychiat. social work, psychiat, social worker Akron, 1953-56, 57-58; dir. social services Summit County Mental Hygiene Clinic, Akron, 1956-57; exec. sec. Travelers Aid Soc., Akron, 1958-61; dir. casework Family Service-Travelers Aid, Des Moines, 1961-66; pvt. practice counselling, Des Moines, 1961-68; chmn. Des Moines br. Women's Internat. League for Peace and Freedom, 1962-65, exec. dir., Phila., 1968—. Named Woman of Distinction, Buffalo Courier Express, 1940. Mem. Nat. Assn. Social Workers (co-chmn. legislative com. Central Ia. chpt.), Acad. Certified Social Workers, Am. Civil Liberties Union, CORE, Conf. Advancement Pvt. Practice in Social Work (nat. bd.), N.A.A.C.P., Phi Beta Kappa. Unitarian. Contbr. articles profl. jours. Home: 7520 Crittenden St Philadelphia PA 19119 Office: 2006 Walnut St Philadelphia PA 19103

JOHNSON, GLOVER, lawyer; b. Perth Amboy, N.J., Dec. 1, 1900; s. Arthur Glover and Lillian M. (Miller) J.; student Trinity Sch., N.Y.C., 1919; A.B. (Lemuel Curtis scholar), Trinity Coll., 1922, LL.D., 1960; LL.B. (Kent scholar), N.Y. Law Sch., 1925; m. Dorothy Murray Algeo, Nov. 27, 1926; children—Margaret Murray (Mrs. Charles J. Werber), Patricia Hinckley. With Morgan Guaranty Trust Co., N.Y.C., 1922-26; admitted to N.Y. bar, 1926, since practiced in N.Y.C.; with White & Case, 1926—, partner, 1936—; vice chmn., dir. Internat. Minerals & Chem. Corp., Chgo., Genung's Inc., White Plains, N.Y., 1955-68; chmn. exec. com., dir. F. & M. Schaefer Corp.; sole trustee R. J. Schaefer Trust; dir. Agfa-Gevaert, Inc. F. & M. Schaefer Brewing Co., Fed. Paper Bd. Co., Inc., N.Y.C., Topper Corp. Chmn. lawyers div. A.R.C., N.Y.C., 1958. Bd. govs. New Rochelle Hosp. Assn., 1955—, pres., 1963-68, chmn. 1968—; pres. N.Y. Sch. for Deaf, 1949-63, chmn., 1963—; life trustee Trinity Schs., N.Y.C., Pawling, N.Y., 1944—, pres., 1967—; life trustee Trinity Coll., Hartford, Conn., 1962—, chmn. com. on admissions, sr. fellow, 1956-62. Mem. S.R. (bd. mgrs. 1959), Am. (chmn. com. fed. regulation of securities 1953- 54), N.Y. State, Westchester County, N.Y.C. bar assns., Nat. Legal Aid Assn., Alumni Assn. Trinity Coll. (pres. 1947-49, 60-62), Delta Kappa Epsilon, Phi Delta Theta. Episcopalian (sr. warden 1944-47). Clubs: Down Town Assn., Wall Street, The Brook, Board Room, Yale (N.Y.C.); Larchmont (N.Y.) Yacht (trustee 1939—, sec. 1939-54), Siwanoy (Bronxville, N.Y.); Blind Brook (Rye, N.Y.). Home: Brookside Wilmot Rd New Rochelle NY 10804 Office: 14 Wall St New York City NY 10005

JOHNSON, GORDON, lawyer; b. San Jose, Cal., Aug. 10, 1905; A.B., J.D., U. Cal. Admitted to Cal. bar, 1928, since practiced in San Francisco; mem. firm Thelen, Marrin, Johnson & Bridges. Trustee Scripps Coll., Claremont, Cal. Mem. Am. Bar Assn., Bar Assn. San Francisco, State Bar Cal., Am. Coll. Trial Lawyers, Phi Beta Kappa, Phi Delta Phi. Office: 111 Sutter St San Francisco CA 94104

JOHNSON, GORDON FRANKLIN, food processing co. exec.; b. Racine, Wis., Dec. 18, 1920; s. Archibald Lester and Ruth (Stransky) J.; B.B.A., U. Wis., 1950; m. Jane Margaret Grassick, Oct. 2, 1943; children—Elizabeth Jane (Mrs. William Harry Stroven), Christopher Gordon, Susan Mary, Sarah Ruth. With Haskins & Sells, C.P.A.'s, Milw., 1950-54; controller Gerber Products Co., Fremont, Mich., 1954—, also v.p. Served with USAAF, 1942-46; CBI. C.P.A., Wis. Mem. Mich. Assn. C.P.A.'s, Am. Legion. Republican. Episcopalian. Mason, Moose, Rotarian. Home: 2474 Wisner Dr Fremont MI 49412 Office: 445 State St Fremont MI 49412

JOHNSON, GORDON HARMON, advt. exec.; b. Ft. Nelson, B.C., Can., July 1, 1912; s. Nelson H. and Lillian (Barmore) J.; came to U.S., 1917, naturalized, 1936; B.S., Cornell Coll., Mt. Vernon, Ia., 1933; m. Agnes E. Munks, Aug. 4, 1934; 1 son, William E. With Montgomery Ward & Co., 1934-44, nat. mdsg. mgr., 1942-44; with Dancer-Fitzgerald-Sample, Inc., 1944—, sr. v.p., 1958-62, exec. v.p., 1962-66, dir. advt. com. U.S. Olympic Com., 1963—; active scholarship fund Cornell Coll., 1961—, mem. bd. trustees, 1968—. Adv. bd. Trinity Sch., N.Y.C., 1958—. Mem. Alpha Theta Alpha. Republican. Clubs: Minneapolis, Minneapolis Golf Marco Polo, Sky (N.Y.C.). Home: 50 E 72d St New York City NY 10021 Office: 347 Madison Av New York City NY 10017

JOHNSON, GORDON SWANTE, hosp. adminstr.; b. Salt Lake City, Mar. 20, 1919; s. Swante and Regina (Seequist) J.; B.A., U. Utah, 1941; M.D., U. Louisville, 1944; m. Grace Kendall, Sept. 14, 1946; children—Evelyn Regina, Patrician Ann, Kristine, Gordon Stephen, Michael Cory, Mary Julene (adopted). Gen. practice, Eureka, Utah, 1947-50; dist. health officer Utah Dept. Health, 1950-52; staff psychiatrist U.S. VA Hosp., Salt Lake City, 1952-53; sr. psychiatrist Utah State Hosp., 1957-61; dir. Bur. Mental Health, Nev. Dept. Health, dir. Mental Health Clinic, Las Vegas, dir. Care Program Rose de Lima Hosp., Henderson, Nev., 1961-63; supt. Utah State Hosp., 1963—; clin. instr. dept. psychiatry U. Utah, 1959-61, 64—, faculty Brigham Young U., 1963—; psychiat. cons. to AEC, 1961-63. Active United Fund. Trustee, Central Utah Alcoholism Council; mem. Utah State Adv. Com. for Handicapped. Served with USNR, 1942-44, 45-46, 53-55. Fellow Am. Psychiat. Assn.; mem. Provo C. of C., A.M.A., Utah State, County med. socs., Utah, Intermountain psychiat. socs., Nat. Assn. Med. Supts. Mental Hosps., Nat. Assn. State Mental Health Program Dirs., Pi Chi. Mem. Ch. of Jesus Christ of Latter-day Saints. Elk. Home: 1079 E Center St Provo UT 84601 Office: Box 270 Provo UT 84601

JOHNSON, GOVE GRIFFITH, Jr., economist; b. N.Y.C., Aug. 15, 1912; s. Gove Griffith and May Francelia (Russell) J.; A.B., Harvard, 1934, A.M., 1936, Ph.D., 1938; m. Janet Clementson Young, 1936; children—Carol Lynne, Gove Griffith III. With U.S. Treasury Dept., 1936-37, 1938-39, Nat. Def. Adv. Commn., 1940-41, OPA, 1941-46; cons. economist Nathan Assos., 1946-47; dir. Econ. Stabilization Div., Nat. Security Resources Bd., 1948-49; asst. chief fiscal div., chief economist U.S. Bur. Budget, 1949-50; asst. adminstr. econ. policy Econ. Stabilization Agy., 1950-52; economist Motion Picture Assn. Am., 1952, v.p., 1952-62, exec. v.p., 1971—; asst. sec. econ. affairs Dept. of State, 1962-65; exec. v.p. Motion Picture Export Assn. Am., 1965—. Former mem. council Harvard Found. Advanced Study and Research, vis. com. Harvard Sch. Pub. Adminstrn. Mem. Am. Econ. Assn., Delta Upsilon. Clubs: Columbia Country (Chevy Chase); University (Washington); Harvard (N.Y.C.). Author: The Treasury and Monetary Policy, 1939; Economic Effects of Federal Public Works Expenditures (with J.K. Galbraith), 1940. Home: 5100 Dorset Av Chevy Chase MD 20015

JOHNSON, GUSTAVE FREDERICK, former utility co. exec.; b. Eveleth, Minn., Jan. 14, 1906; s. Ernest and Rina (Sanden) J.; B.S. in Elec. Engring., U. Minn., 1927; m. Vera C. Edblom, Jan. 1, 1936; children—Lois Ann, Constance E., Dorothy M. With No. States Power Co., Mpls., 1927-71, v.p. finance, treas., 1967-71, ret., 1971; dir. Midland Nat. Bank, Mpls. Registered profl. engr., Minn. Republican. Lutheran. Clubs: Minneapolis Athletic, Engineers (Mpls.); Interlachen (Edina, Minn.). Home: 4721 Annaway Dr Minneapolis MN 55436

JOHNSON, GUY DIBBLE, corp. exec.; b. New Orleans, Oct. 8, 1885; s. Homer Alonso and Mary (Dibble) J.; ed. pub. schs. New Orleans; m. Helen Perez. Railroad work in Central Am., 1902-05; with Nat. Paper & Type Co., N.Y.C., 1907, v.p., gen. mgr. Buenos Aires br., 1930-45, pres., 1945-53; pres. Guy D. Johnson, Inc., 1953—. Clubs: Metropolitan (N.Y.C.). Home: 969 Park Av New York City NY 10028 Office: 667 Madison Av New York City NY 10021

JOHNSON, HAL HAROLD GUSTAV, educator; b. Saginaw, Mich., Apr. 30, 1915; s. Harold Hjalmar and Ruth W. (Broman) J.; B.S., Beloit Coll., 1936, M.S., 1938; Ph.D., U. Wis., 1941; m. Elizabeth Schreiner, June 15, 1940; children—Judith Lynn, David Schreiner, John Bradley, Instr., Beloit Coll., 1935-38; asst. U. Wis., 1938-41; organic chemist Comml. Solvents Corp., Terre Haute, Ind., 1941-45; asst. gen. mgr. Dykem Co., St. Louis, 1945-46; mgr. Organic div. Monsanto Co., St. Louis, 1946-49, asst. dir. gen. devel. dept., 1949-52, dir. research and devel. Western div., San Francisco, 1952-54, dir. gen. devel. dept. research and engring. div., 1954-57; dir. chem. and rubber div. Bus. and Def. Services Adminstrn., Dept. Commerce, Washington, 1957; v.p. Vick Chem. Co. (now known as Richardson-Merrell Co.), N.Y.C., 1957-59, cons. chems. mgmt., 1959-62; v.p. marketing, dir. S.W. Potash Corp. div. Am. Metal Climax, 1962-66; mgmt. cons. Consol. Cons., Hal Johnson & Assos., 1966-69; dir. comml. devel. Borg-Warner Corp., 1969-71; prof. marketing No. Ill. U., DeKalb, 1971—. Bd. trustees Beloit Coll. Mem. Am. Chem. Soc. (chmn. St. Louis sect.; chmn. chem. marketing and econs. div.), Am. Inst. Chem. Engrs., Am. Inst. Chemists, A.A.A.S., Comml. Devel. Assn. (past pres.), Phi Beta Kappa, Sigma Xi, Sigma Alpha Epsilon, Gamma Alpha. Clubs: Cosmos, Congressional Country (Washington); Parkersburg (W.Va.) Country. Patentee. Contbr. sci. articles. Home: Apt 118A Saint Albans Green Sycamore IL 60178 Office: Dept Marketing No Ill U DeKalb IL 60115

JOHNSON, HAROLD ELLIS, ins. co. exec.; m. Elma Lowry, Oct. 29, 1938; children—JoAnn (Mrs. Jon R. Rampton), Patricia (Mrs. John Hunter), Harold Ellis. Exec. v.p. Continental Corp., Continental Ins. Co.; trustee Queens County Savs. Bank; dir. Colonial Penn Group, Inc. Dir. Diners Club, Afco, Inc. Trustee Village of Munsey Park, 1961-63, mayor, 1963-68. Clubs: Down Town Assn. (N.Y.C.); Manhasset Bay Yacht. Home: Forest Dr Sands Point Port Washington NY 11050 Office: 80 Maiden Lane New York City NY 10038

JOHNSON, HAROLD G., mfg. co. exec. Sec., Fuller Brush Co., East Hartford, Conn. Office: 88 Long Hill St East Hartford CT 06108*

JOHNSON, HAROLD KEITH, ret. army ofcr.; b. Bowesmont, N.D., Feb. 22, 1912; s. Harold C. and Edna M. (Thomson) J.; B.S., U.S. Mil. Acad., 1933; grad. Command and Gen. Staff Coll., 1947, Armed Forces Staff Coll., 1950, Nat. War Coll., 1953; D.Edn. (hon.), Park Coll., 1962; LL.D., Yankton Coll., 1963, Ill. Coll., 1965, U. Akron, 1968, Pa. Mil. Colls., 1968; H.H.D., N.D. State Univ., 1966; D.Sc., Norwich U., 1968; m. Dorothy Rennix, Apr. 13, 1935; children—Harold Keith, Ellen Kay, Robert James. Commd. 2d lt. U.S. Army, 1933, advanced through grades to gen., 1964; assigned successively to 3d Infantry, 28th Inf., Philippine Scouts, prior to World War II; survivor Bataan death march, prisoner of Japanese, 1942-45; bn. regt. comdr. 1st Cav. Div., also G-3 1st U.S. Corps, 1951; assigned G-3 Dept. of Army, asst. div. comdr. 8th Inf. Div., 1956-57; chief staff 7th Army, 1957-59, G-3 U.S. Army Europe, 1959; chief staff Central Army Group, Europe, 1959-60; comdt. U.S. Army, Command and Gen. Staff Coll.,Ft. Leavenworth, Kan., 1960-63; dep. chief of staff for mil. operations, 1963-64; chief of staff U.S. Army, 1964-68, ret., 1968; Pres. Herbert Hoover Predsl. Library Assn., 1969—; dir. Genesco, Inc., Research Analysis Corp. Decorated D.S.C., Legion of Merit with 3 clusters. Distinguished Unit citation with two clusters, Bronze Star medal, D.S.M. with cluster; Presdl. Unit citation (Republic of Korea) (P.I.); Legion of Honor (France) (P.I.); Order Mil. Merit (Brazil); Cross Venezuelan Ground Forces; Knight Grand Cross of Most Exalted Order White Elephant (Thailand); Order Mil. Merit Taeguk (Korea); White Cross Mil. Merit and Greatest Grade (Spain); Nat. Order, 2d Class (Republic of Vietnam); recipient Silver Beaver and Silver Buffalo awards Boy Scouts Am. Mason (33) Office: 1776 K St NW Washington DC 20006

JOHNSON, HAROLD LESTER, astronomer, educator; b. Denver, Apr. 17, 1921; s. Averill C. and Marie (Sallach) J.; B.S., U. Denver, 1942; Ph.D., U. Cal. at Berkeley, 1948; m. Mary Elizabeth Jones, July 1, 1954; children—August Harold, Selma Marie. Asst. prof. astronomy U. Chgo., 1950-52; astronomer Lowell Obs., Flagstaff, Ariz., 1952-59; prof. astronomy U. Tex., 1959-61, chmn. dept., 1961; research prof. lunar and planetary lab. U. Ariz., 1962-69, asso. dir. lab., 1967-69, astronomer Steward Obs., research prof. Optical Scis. Center, 1969—; investigator Titular, Instituto de Astronomia, Universidad Nacional Autonomo de Mexico, Mexico, D.F., 1968—. Mem. Am. Astron. Soc. (Helen B. Warner prize 1956), Astron. Soc. Pacific, N.Y. Acad. Scis., Internat. Astron. Union, Nat. Acad. Scis. Home: 8431 E Appomattox St Tuscon AZ 85710

JOHNSON, HAROLD T., congressman; b. Yolo County, Cal., student U. Nev.; m. Albra I. Manuel; 2 children. State senator, Cal., 1948-58; mem. 36th-91st Congresses, 2d Cal. Dist. Former mayor Roseville. Mem. Brotherhood of Ry. Clks., Lambda Chi Alpha. Democrat. Eagle, Moose, Elk. Home: Roseville CA 95678 Office: House Office Bldg Washington DC 20525

JOHNSON, HARRIETT, music critic, editor; b. Mpls., Aug. 31; d. Albert and Mary Dora (Steele) Johnson; B.A. cum laude, U. Minn.; fellow grad. student Juilliard Sch. Music; studied with Olga Samaroff Stokowski, Rubin Goldmark, Bernard Wagenaar, Antonio Lora, Donald Ferguson; m. Hubert Norville (div. 1952) 1 son, Craig Hubert. Artistic dir., lectr. Layman's Music Courses, Town Hall, N.Y.C., 1939-42; non-resident head music dept. Foxcroft Sch., Middleburg, Va., 1936-40; traveling lectr.; dir. symphony course Berkshire Symphonic Festival, Lenox, Mass., 1938-42; music critic, editor N.Y. Post, 1943—; editor billboard Music Yearbook, 1945; record reviewer Met. Opera program, 1945-56. Mem. Nat. League Am. Pen Women, Newspaper Guild, A.S.C.A.P., Phi Beta Kappa, Sigma Alpha Iota. Author: Your Career in Music. Composer (orch.): Chuggy and the Blue Caboose, Pet of the Met, Five Preludes for String Quartet and Wind Instruments; also hymns, piano music, songs. Contbr. articles mus. publs. Home: 162 W 54th St New York City NY 10019 Office: care New York Post 210 South St New York City NY 10002

JOHNSON, HARRY GORDON, economist; b. Toronto, Ont., Can., May 26, 1923; s. Henry Herbert and Frances (Muat) J.; B.A., U. Toronto, 1943, M.A., 1947; B.A., U. Cambridge (Eng.), 1946, M.A., 1951; A.M., Harvard, 1949, Ph.D., 1958; M.A. Manchester (Eng.) U., 1960; LL.D., St. Francis Xavier U., N.S., Can., 1965, U. Windsor, Ont., Canada, 1966, Queen's U., Can., 1967, U. Sheffield, 1969, Carleton U. (Canada), 1970; m. Elizabeth Scott Serson, May 28, 1948; children—Steven Ragnar, Karen Eve. Came to U.S., 1959. Lectr., Cambridge U., also fellow King's Coll., 1949-56; prof. econ. theory U. Manchester, 1956-59; prof. econs. U. Chgo., 1959—; prof. London (Eng.) Sch. Econs. and Polit. Sci., 1966—; Wicksell lect., 1968. Mem. U.S. Rev. Com. Balance of Payments Statistics, 1963-65. Served with inf. Royal Canadian Army, 1944-46. Fellow Brit. Acad.; mem. Canadian Polit. Sci. Assn. (pres. 1965-66), Am. Assn. (exec. com. 1964- 66), also mem. Am. Acad. of Arts and Scis., Royal Econ. Soc., Econometric Soc. Author: Internat. Trade and Economic Growth, 1958; Money, Trade and Economic Growth, 1962; The Canadian Quandary, 1963; The World Economy at the Crossroads, 1965; Economic Policies Toward Less Developed Countries, 1967; Essays in Monetary Economics, 1967; Comparative Cost and Commercial Policy Theory for a Developing World Economy, 1968, Aspects of Tariff Theory, 1971; The Two-Sector Model of General Equilibrium, 1971. Home: Bedford Ct Mansions Bedford Av London WC1 England Office: 1126 E 59th St Chicago IL 60637

JOHNSON, HARRY JULIUS, physician; b. N.Y.C., June 4, 1902; s. Peter M. and Caren (Johnson) J.; A.B., Columbia, 1924; M.D., Harvard, 1930; m. Teresa Hirle, Sept. 20, 1935; children—Michael D., Harry Keith, Intern, N.Y. Postgrad. Hosp., 1930-32, resident, 1932-33; sr. attending physician French Hosp., N.Y.C., 1936—, mem. exec. con., 1950—; became med. dir. Life Extension Inst., 1937, now chmn. med. bd.; asst. prof. clin. medicine N.Y. Post Grad. Med. Sch., Columbia, 1940-50. Mem. Bd. Med. Examiners State N.Y. Mem. exec. bd. nat. council Boy Scouts Am., 1961—, chmn. nat. council, 1961—, chmn. health and safety com., 1967- -; pres. Life Extension Found., 1953—; bd. dirs. Nat. Soc. for Prevention Blindness, Inc. Lutheran. Mason. Club: Harvard (N.Y.C.). Author: (with Lea and Febiger), Dietetics for the Clinician, 1950; Invitation to Health, 1945; Guide to Better Health 1959; Keeping Fit in Your Executive Job, 1963; Eat, Drink, Be Merry and Live Longer, 1968. Home: 911 Park Av New York City NY 10021 Office: 11 E 44th St New York City NY 10017

JOHNSON, HARRY LEE, educator; b. Saltville, Va., Apr. 18, 1929; s. Jerry D. and Zella (Henderson) J.; B.A., Emory and Henry Coll., 1952; M.A., U. Va., 1957, Ph.D., 1959; m. Jean Doyle Youell, Jan. 29, 1955. Asso. prof. La. Poly. Inst., 1959-60; prof. U. Ala., 1961-64; asso. prof. U. Tex., Austin, 1964-66; prof., head dept. finance U. Tenn., Knoxville, 1966—. Dir. The Nucleus, Vol. State Bank. Chmn. E.Tenn. Econ. Devel. Finance Com., 1969- 70. Bd. dirs. Tenn. Banking Sch., Florence Crittenton Agy. Served with U.S. Army, 1952-54. Mem. Am., Royal, So. econ. assns., Am., So. finance assns., Bank Mgmt. Inst. (dir.). Club: Fort Loudoun Yacht (dir.) (Concord, Tenn.). Author: (with others) The Labor Force in Virginia, 1959. Editor: Monetary Issues of the 1960s, 1968; State and Local Tax Problems, 1969. Contbr. articles profl. jours. Home: 640 Kenesaw Av Knoxville TN 37919

JOHNSON, HARRY MORTON, educator, sociologist; b. Cambridge, Mass., Oct. 25, 1917; s. Harry Morton and Helen (Roche) J.; A.B., Harvard, 1939, M.A., 1942, Ph.D., 1949; postgrad. Tulane U., 1940-41; m. Danielle Cousin, Jan. 25, 1970. Instr. to prof. Simmons Coll., Boston, 1942-64; asso.. prof., prof. Mass. Coll. Art Boston, 1945-55; asso. prof., prof. U. Ill. at Urbana, 1964—. Mem. Am. Sociol. Assn. Author: Sociology: A Systematic Introduction, 1960. Asso. editor Am. Sociol. Rev., 1964-66. Home: 804 W Indiana Av Urbana IL 61801

JOHNSON, HARVEY LEROY, educator; b. Cleburne, Tex., Sept. 12, 1904; s. John Andrew and Ida May (Johnson) J.; A.B., Howard Payne Coll., Brownwood, Tex., 1925; A.M., U. Tex., 1928; Ph.D., U. Pa., 1940; student U. Mexico, summer 1930; U. Madrid, summer 1931, Sorbonne (Paris), summer 1935; m. Margaret Burkhardt, Aug. 31, 1950; children—Harvey, Harold. Tchr. high schs. in New Mexico and Texas, 1925-27, 1928-30; instr., Rice Inst., Houston, 1930-36; prof. Cedar Crest Coll., Allentown, Pa., 1937-40; instr. in Romance langs., Northwestern U., 1940- 42, asst. prof., 1942-44, asso. prof., 1944-50, prof. and counselor to fgn. students, 1950-51; prof. Spanish and Portuguese Ind. U., 1951-65, chmn. Houston, 1965—. Cons. Hispanic Found. of Library Congress, Dept. Health, Edn. and Welfare. Hon. doctorate U. Mayor de San Andres, La Paz, Bolivia, 1948. Life fellow Internat. Inst. Arts and Letters, Asociacion Internacional de Hispanistas; mem. Ind. Modern Fgn. Lang. Tchrs. Assn. (pres.), Assn. Coll. Honor Socs. (pres.), Southwest Council Latin Am. Studies (pres.), Modern Lang. Assn., Am. Assn. Tchrs. Spanish and Portuguese Alpha Chi Scholarship Soc., Sigma Delta Pi, Phi Sigma Iota (nat. pres.). Democrat. Author: An Edition of Triunfo de los Santos with a Consideration of Jesuit School Plays in Mexico Before 1650, 1941; La America Espanola, 1949; An Edition of El Diablo Nocturno, 1956; translation with introduction and notes Altamirano's La Navidad en las Montanas; Aprende a hablar espaol, 1963; Student's Laboratory Manual to accompany, 1965. Contbr. to Revista Ibero-Americana, Nueva Revista de Filologia Hispanica, Hispania, Hispanic Rev. Ency. Brit. Year Book, World Book Ency., Handbook of Latin American Studies, and others. Home: 5307 Dumfries St Houston TX 77035

JOHNSON, HAYDEN BRIGGS, city planner; b. Cleve., Apr. 24, 1917; s. Roger Arthur and Elizabeth (Briggs) J.; B.A., Amherst Coll., 1937; B.Arch., Columbia, 1941, M.S. in Planning and Housing, 1942; m. Jean Ruth Noland, Oct. 15, 1945; children—Courtney Hayden and Hardy Elizabeth (twins). Community planner TVA, 1942-44; exec. dir. Tenn. Planning Commn., 1944-48, Poughkeepsie (N.Y.) Area Devel. Assn., 1948-51; city mgr., Poughkeepsie, 1952-55; chief planning div. Port N.Y. Authority, 1955-61, dep. dir. port devel., 1961-66, dep. dir. planning and devel., 1966—; lectr. urban planning N.Y.U., 1956—. Bd. dirs. Am. Soc. Planning Ofcls., 1953-57, pres. 1962-63; bd. dirs. Citizens Housing and Planning Council N.Y.; U.S. mem. bur. Internat. Fedn. Housing and Planning, 1967—. Mem. Am.

Inst. Planners (pres. N.Y. Met. chpt. 1963-65), Internat. City Mgrs. Assn., Am. Soc. Pub. Adminstrn. Episcopalian. Club: Poughkeepsie Tennis. Home: 37 Richards Rd Port Washington NY 11050 Office: 111 8th Av New York City NY 10011

JOHNSON, HAYNES BONNER, journalist; b. N.Y.C., July 9, 1931; s. Malcolm Malone and Ludie (Adams) J.; B.J., U. Mo., 1952; M.S., U. Wis., 1956; m. Julia Ann Erwin, Sept. 21, 1954; children—Katherine Adams, David Malone, Stephen Holmes, Sarah Brooks, Elizabeth Haynes. Reporter, Wilmington (Del.) News-Jour., 1956- 57; with Washington Star, 1957-69; nat. corr. Washington Post, 1969—. Lectr. colls., univs. Served to 1st lt. AUS, 1952-55. Recipient Pub. Service prize and Grand award for reporting Washington Newspaper Guild, 1962, 68, Interpretive Reporting award, 1965, Nat. Reporting award, 1968; Pulitzer Prize for nat. reporting, 1966, Headliners award for nat. reporting, 1968; Sigma Delta Chi gen. reporting award, 1969. Mem. Phi Gamma Delta. Democrat. Episcopalian. Club: National Press (Washington). Author: Dusk at the Mountain, 1963; The Bay of Pigs, 1964; (with Bernard M. Gwertzman) Fulbright: the Dissenter, 1968. Home: 2316 Valley Dr Alexandria VA 22302 Office: 1515 L St NW Washington DC 20005

JOHNSON, HELMER O., exec. v.p. United Cal. Bank until 1969; chmn. bd. Fidelity Financial Corp., San Francisco, Fidelity Savs. and Loan Assn., San Francisco. Trustee Lomas and Nettleton Mortgage Investors, Dallas; dir. Pacific States Steel Co., Union City, Cal. Address: 260 California St San Francisco CA 94111

JOHNSON, HELMER ROBERT, lawyer; b. Grant County, S.D., Jan. 9, 1913; s. Emil and Tecla (Carlson) J.; B.S., Lewis Inst., Chgo., 1934; J.D., Northwestern U., 1937; m. Ramona Grattan, Dec. 30, 1939; children—Robert Grattan, William Hall, Craig Frederick. Admitted to Ill. bar, 1937, N.Y. bar, 1947; atty. SEC, 1938-40; with adv. commn. Council Nat. Def., 1940-41, Dept. Justice, 1941-42, Office Alien Property, 1942-46; with firm Willkie, Farr & Gallagher, N.Y.C., 1946—, partner, 1953—. Dir., gen. counsel Continental Can Co., Inc., 1962—. Fellow Am. Bar Found.; mem. Am., Fed., N.Y. State bar assns., Bar Assn. City N.Y., Northwestern U. Sch. Law Alumni Assn. (regional v.p.), Manhasset Bay Power Squadron. Club: Wall Street (N.Y.C.). Home: 149 Columbia Heights Brooklyn NY 11201 Office: 1 Chase Manhattan Plaza New York City NY 10005

JOHNSON, HENRY CLAY, ins. co. exec., lawyer; b. Canton, O., Mar. 16, 1910; s. Henry Moore and Bertha (Burns) J.; A.B. magna cum laude, U. Notre Dame, 1932, LL.B., 1934; LL.M., Cath. U. Am., 1935; m. Rosemary Fitzpatrick, 1945; children—Michael Clay, Peter H., Catherine S., Anne M. Admitted to Ind. bar, 1934; individual practice, South Bend, 1934-35; counsel RFC, 1935- 41; mem. law faculty Cath. U. Am., 1935-41; spl. asst. to pres. N.Y. Stock Exchange, 1941-42; v.p., gen. counsel Rubber Res. Co., 1942-45; dir., gen. counsel Rubber Devel. Co., 1943-45; v.p. War Damage Corp., 1942-45; exec. v.p., gen. counsel, dir. Royal-Globe Ins. Cos., 1945-65, now pres. and chmn. bd.; mem. adv. bd. for lower Manhattan Chem. Bank, N.Y.; dir. Lincoln 1st Banks, Inc., Rochester, N.Y., Nat. Bank Westchester, N.Y., Underwriters Salvage Co.; chmn. Underwriters' Labs.; chmn. Gen. Adjustment Bur. Pres., Ins. Information Inst., 1964-65. Mayor city of Rye, 1962-65. Mem. adv. council U. Notre Dame; mem. adv. bd. Salvation Army. Pres., trustee United Hosp., Port Chester, N.Y.; bd. dirs., v.p. Beekman Downtown Hosp.; dir. Downtown-Lower Manhattan Assn., Am. Arbitration Assn. Knight of Malta. Mem. Pilgrims U.S., Am. Bar Assn. Roman Catholic. Clubs: Lawyers, University, Economic (N.Y.C.); Manursing Island (Rye, N.Y.). Home: 164 Grandview Av Rye NY 10580 Office: 150 William St New York City NY 10038

JOHNSON, HENRY JOSEPH, naval officer; b. N.Y.C., Apr. 10, 1916; s. Fred and Louise (Jensen) J.; B.C.E., Bklyn. Poly. Inst., 1938; postgrad. Pa. State Coll., 1941; m. Mary Jane Grace, Mar. 29, 1941; 1 dau., Mary Louise (Mrs. Robrt Henry Armsby). Commd. ensign USNR, 1940, advanced through grades to rear adm., 1969; comdr. U.S.S. Grainger, 1945-46; civil engr., 1947—; officer charge constrn., Vietnam, 1969-70; naval facilities engring. command, San Bruno, Cal., 1970—. Decorated D.S.M., Legion of Merit. Registered profl. engr., N.Y. Fellow Am. Soc. C.E.; mem. Soc. Am. Mil. Engrs., Naval Inst., Am. Pub. Works Assn., Tau Beta Pi. Home: 2 Whiting Way Yerba Buena Island San Francisco CA 94130 Office: Naval Facilities Engring Command PO Box 727 San Bruno 94066

JOHNSON, HENRY STANLEY, Jr., geologist; b. Augusta, Ga., Apr. 16, 1926; s. Henry Stanley and Susie Garland (Dawson) J.; B.S., U. S.C., 1947; m. Stephanie Louise Kruse, Dec. 19, 1954; children—Helen Mary, Robert Andrew, David Patrick, Katherine Anne. With U.S. Geol. Survey, 1948-49, 52-57, Zonolite Co., 1950-52; with div. geology S.C. Devel. Bd., Columbia, 1957-69, state geologist, 1958-69, cons. geologist, 1969—; pres. Sandhill Resources, Inc.; v.p. Orion Exploration, Ltd. Served with USMCR, 1943-45. Mem. Geol. Soc. Am., Soc. Econ. Geologists. Home: 1721 Maplewood Dr Columbia SC 29205 Office: Box 11726 Columbia SC 29211

JOHNSON, HERBERT, former steel exec.; b. Janesville, Wis., Jan. 10, 1911; s. Wilford A. and Edla C. (Moldstad) J.; A.B., Luther Coll., 1932; LL.B., Harvard, 1940. With Jones & Laughlin Steel Corp., Pitts., 1940-71, v.p., 1953-71, ret. Dir. iron and steel div. NPA, 1952. Bd. Dirs. Met. Pitts. Ednl. Television; trustee Econ. and Bus. Found. Mem. Am. Iron and Steel Inst. Club: Duquesne. Home: 130 Richland Lane Pittsburgh PA 15208 Retired

JOHNSON, HERBERT CONRAD, utilities exec.; b. S.I., N.Y., Mar. 25, 1909; s. Conrad and Clara Marie (Olson) J.; B.S., N.Y. U., 1937; m. May Helene Welzin, July 3, 1940; children—Keith Eldridge, Douglas Welzin. Various positions natural gas interests Standard Oil Co. (N.J.), 1927-43; asst. treas. Consol. Natural Gas Co., 1943-51, treas., 1951-58, dir., 1955—, v.p., 1956-63, exec. v.p., 1963-66, pres., 1966-70, chmn., 1970—. Mem. Bus. Adv. Council Religion in Am. Life. Trustee Inst. Gas Tech., Am. Fund Dental Edn. Mem. N.Y. C. of C., Newcomen Soc., Am. Gas Assn., Nat. Petroleum Council, Beta Gamma Sigma. Republican. Episcopalian. Clubs: Richmond County Country (pres.) (S.I.); University, New York University (N.Y.); Duquesne (Pitts.); Eastwand Ho Country (Chatham, Mass.). 76 Romer Rd Staten Island NY 10304 Office : 30 Rockefeller Plaza New York City NY 10020

JOHNSON, HERBERT HOWARD, architect; b. El Campo, Tex., June 24, 1913; s. Algot and Ann Elizabeth (Schutte) J.; B.A., Rice U. 1935, B. Arch., 1936; certificate naval arch., U.S. Naval Postgrad. Sch., 1944; m. Elizabeth Ann Westerdahl, Sept. 25, 1943; children—Herbert Warren, Lawrence Algot. Pvt. practice architecture, Houston, 1940-42, Miami, Fla., 1946—; partner Weed-Johnson Assos., 1957-62, Herbert H. Johnson Assos., 1962—; prin. works include Sears, Roebuck & Co. store, Tampa, Fla., 1957, First Nat. Bank, Miami, 1959, Nat. Airlines hanger, Miami, 1957, Jordan Marsh store, Miami, 1955, Lehigh Cement Co. office, Miami, 1958, Copperstone Co. bldg., Miami, 1960, D.C. Nat. Bank, Washington, 1962, Am. embassy, Leopoldville, Congo, 1957. Mem. Miami Downtown Devel. Com., vice chmn. Dade County Planning Adv. Bd. Dade County Indsl. Devel. Com. Recipient Silver medal Pan Am. Congress Architects, 1950, award internat. exhbn. architecture, Sao Paolo, 1961. Fellow A.I.A. (awards 1959, 60); mem. Fla. Assn. Architects (2 awards, 1956, 2 awards 1957), Fla., Dade County chambers commerce, Bldg. Research Inst. Elk. Home: 2587 Bayshore Rd Miami FL 33133 Office: 950 S Miami St Miami FL 33130

JOHNSON, HERBERT MARTIN, lawyer; b. Woodhull, Ill., May 11, 1904; s. Otto A. and Emma A. (Samuelson) J.; A.B., Agustana Coll., 1926; postgrad., U. Chgo., 1927-28; J.D., Northwestern U., 1932; m. Shirley Elizabeth Oliver, Feb. 6, 1932 (dec. Aug. 1956); children—Judith E. (Mrs. Steve R. Brown), James; m. 2d, Gladys P. Murray, May 17, 1958; 1 dau., Marilyn R. (Mrs. Richard Fredrichsen). Instr. English, Harvard Sch. for Boys 1927-28; admitted to Ill. bar, 1933; asso. Schuyler, Wienfeld & Hennessy, Chgo., 1929-37; atty. Chgo. Rapid Transit Co., 1937-47; gen. atty. Chgo. N. Shore & Milw. Ry. Co., Chgo., 1947-49; former sr. mem. firm Johnson, Zahler, Campbell, Boughner & Stitt, Chgo.; sr. v.p., gen. counsel, sec. Ill. Mid-Continent Life Ins. Co., 1957-64, pres., 1964; pres. Combination Investments, Inc., 1963-65; now sr. mem. law firm Johnson, Snow, Holmgren and Burden. State senator 19th Dist. Ill., 1956-58. Chmn. bd. dirs. Beverly YMCA, 1951-52; pres. bd. trustees Garrett Theol. Sem.; pres. Ridge Civic Council, 1948-50. Recipient Outstanding Meth. Churchman award, 1952; Outstanding Citizen citation Augustana; voted Outstanding Senator Ill. News All-Alumni, 1956. Mem. Am. Ill., Chgo. bar assns., I.V.I., 1957; Am. Judicature Soc., Chgo. Art Inst. (life), Chgo. Natural History Mus., Nordic Law Club, Newcomen Soc. Republican. Methodist (lay leader, 1946-52). Clubs: University, Executives (Chgo.). Home: 1855 Norman Blvd Park Ridge IL 60068 Office: 29 LaSalle St Chicago IL 60603

JOHNSON, HERMAN E., pub. co. exec.; b. 1913; ed. Northwestern U., Marquette U.; married. With Western Pub. Co., Racine, Wis., 1929—, became asst. mgr., 1955, pres., 1958, now chmn., chief exec. officer, dir. Office: 1220 Mound Av Racine WI 53404

JOHNSON, HOMER FIELDS, educator, chem. engr.; b. Lynchburg, Va., Sept. 8, 1920; s. Homer Fields and May (Royall) J.; B.Chem. Engring., U. Va., 1942; M.Engring., Yale, 1944, D.Engring., 1946; m. Virginia Lee Cain, May 17, 1947; children-Philip Royall, Richard Wesley, Lee Duncan, Jeffrey Alan. Grad. asst., instr. Yale, New Haven, Conn., 1942-45; chem. engr. Standard Oil Devel. Co., Linden, N.J., 1945-49; asst. prof. U. Tenn. at Knoxville, 1949-51, asso. prof. 1951-58, prof., 1958—, head dept. chem. and metall. engring., 1960—; cons. engring. Oak Ridge Nat. Lab., 1951—. Registered profl. engr., Tenn. Mem. Am. Inst. Chem.Engrs. (chmn. Knoxville-Oak Ridge sect. 1955), Am. Soc. Engring. Edn., Am. Assn. Univ. Profs., Raven Soc., Sigma Xi, Phi Kappa Phi, Alpha Chi Sigma, Tau Beta Pi. Contbr. articles on mass transfer and drop phenomena, chem. engring. edn. profl. jours. Home: 3612 Timberlake Rd Knoxville TN 37920

JOHNSON, HORACE RICHARD, electronics co. exec.; b. Jersey City, Apr. 26, 1926; s. Horace Adam and Grace (Lower) J.; B.Elec. Engring. with distinction, Cornell U., Ithaca, N.Y., 1946, postgrad., 1947; Ph.D. in Physics, Mass. Inst. Tech., 1952; m. Mary Louise Kleckner, July 29, 1950; children—Lucinda Louise, Karen Ann, Richard Adam, Russell Kleckner, David Thorp. Mem. tech. staff Hughes Aircraft Co., 1952-57; co-founder Watkins-Johnson Co., Palo Alto, Cal., 1958, pres., 1967—. Lectr. engring. U. Cal. at Los Angeles, 1956- 57, Stanford, 1958-68; chmn. Los Angeles Profl. Group on Electron Devices, 1955-56; dir. WEMA, 1971—, Vols. Internat. Tech. Assistance, 1971—. Pres., Stanford Area council Boy Scouts Am., 1968-70, bd. mem., 1970—; campaign chmn. Palo Alto-Stanford chpt. United Fund, 1967. Research Lab. for Electronics fellow, 1947-51. Served with USNR, 1943-46. Fellow I.E.E.E.; mem. Am. Phys. Soc., Research Soc. Am., Newcomen Soc. N. Am., Sigma Xi, Eta Kappa Nu, Tau Beta Pi, Phi Kappa Phi, Gamma Alpha. Club: Commonwealth of California. Contbr. articles to profl. jours. Patentee in field. Home: 1336 Cowper St Palo Alto CA 94301 Office: 3333 Hillview Av Palo Alto CA 94304

JOHNSON, HOWARD ALBERT, clergyman, b. Atlantic, Ia., Oct. 8, 1915; s. Mark Peter and Jessie (Howard) J.; B.A., U. Cal. at Los Angeles, 1936; B.D., P.E. Theol. Sem. in Va., 1939, D.D., 1965; postgrad. Princeton, 1942, (fellow Am.-Scandinavian Found.), U. Copenhagen, 1946-48; S.T.M., Union Theol. Sem., N.Y.C., 1949; D.D., Upsala Coll., 1956, Episcopal Theol. Sem. in Ky., 1964. Ordained priest P.E. Ch., 1940; Served parishes in Cal., Washington, 1940-45; asso. prof. sch. theology U. of South, 1949-53; lectr. Kierkegaard, Japanese colls. and univs., 1952; fellow St. Augustine's, Central Coll. of Anglican Communion, Canterbury, 1953-54; adj. prof. religion Columbia, 1954-58; ednl. cons. Diocese of Hong Kong and Macao, 1970; editorial asst. Soren Kierkegaard Inst., Copenhagen, 1971—. Canon theologian Cathedral of St. John the Divine, 1954-64. Mem. Soc. Theol. Discussion; corr. mem. Soren Kierkegaard Soc. Copenhagen. Author: Kierkegaard Rikaino Kagi, 1953; (with James A. Pike) Man in the Middle, 1956; Global Odyssey, 1963. Contbr. to Sons of the Prophets, 1963, Modern Canterbury Pilgrims, also Dr. Lowrie of Princeton & Rome; Editor: Preaching the Christian Year; This Church of Ours; Either/OR (Soren Kierkegaard), rev. translation 1959; co-editor: A Kierkegaard Critique, 1962. Contbr. articles to profl. jours. Home: Cathedral Heights New York City NY 10025

JOHNSON, HOWARD B., restaurant and motel co. exec.; b. Boston, Aug. 23, 1932; s. Howard D. and Bernice (Manley) J.; grad. Andover Acad., 1950; B.A., Yale, 1954; student Harvard Bus. Sch.; m. Patricia A. Bates, Jan. 17, 1958; children—Howard Bates, Marissa Turull. Pres., dir., chmn. bd. Howard Johnson Co.†

JOHNSON, HOWARD BERGSTROM, former steel co. exec.; b. Tallapoosa, Ga., Oct. 28, 1912; s. Carl F. and Alma (Bergstrom) J.; B.C.S., Ga. Inst. Tech., 1934; m. Lillouise Buffington, Aug. 21, 1937; 1 dau., Judith E. With Atlantic Steel Co., Atlanta, 1933-69, beginning as credit clk., successively cost accountant, asst. sec., v.p. finance, v.p. sales and finance, dir., exec. v.p., 1933-56, pres., 1956-65, chmn., chief exec. officer, 1965-69; Bd. trustees Georgia Tech. Found. Home: 3030 Nancy's Creek Rd NW Atlanta GA 30327

JOHNSON, HOWARD CARROL, air force officer; b. Knoxville, Tenn., Feb. 2, 1920; s. Roscoe Howard and Clara (Coker) J.; student U. Louisville, 1938-42, 47; m. Doris Holder, Feb. 20, 1943; children—Ted, Carol, William. Commd. aviation- cadet USAAF, 1943, advanced through grades to col., 1964; assigned tng. command, Laredo, Tex., World War II; with 41st Fighter Squadron, Japan, 12th and 44th fighter Squadrons, P.I., 1948-51; with 18th Fighter Group, Korea, 1950-51, 59th Fighter Squadron, Otis AFB, Miss., 1951-53; leader flight of first fighters to Thule, Greenland; with fighter squadrons of 285th Air Div., Hamilton AFB, Cal., 1953-57, tactical evaluation team Hdqrs. Air Def. Command, Ent AFB, Colorado Springs, Colo., 1957-60; sr. tactical air adviser to German Air Force, Mil. Air Adv. Group, Bonn, 1960-63; operations officer 476th Squadron, 1963-64; comdr. 436th Tactical Fighter Squadron, 1964-65; dep. for operations 479th Tactical Fighter Wing, 1965-66; dir. for operations 388th Tactical Fighter Wing, 1966-67; dep. comdr. for operations 507th Fighter Wing, Kincheloe Air Force Base, 1967-68, dep. comdr. operations 4780th Air Def. Wing, Perrin Air Force Base, 1968—. Decorated D. F. C., Air medals; recipient Collier trophy for altitude record, 1959. Mem. Red River Valley Fighter Pilots Assn. (founder, 1st pres.). Holder world's altitude record, 1958. Home: 125 Vandenberg Dr Sherman TX 75090 Office: Comdr Detachment 1 Air Def Weapons Center Perrin Air Force Base TX 75090

JOHNSON, HOWARD COOPER, Jr., banker: b. Germantown, Pa., Feb. 7, 1909; s. Howard Cooper and Edith (Lamb) J.; grad. William Penn Charter Sch., 1926; A.B., Swarthmore Coll., 1930; M.B.A., Harvard, 1932; grad. Centre de Préparation aux Affaires, Chambre de Commerce de Paris, 1933; m. Betty Doan Young, Aug. 24, 1945; children—Pamela, Richard, Christina. Investment banker, 1933- 41, Stroud & Co., 1933-34, Lazard Fréres & Co., 1934-36, Morgan Stanley & Co., 1936-41; USN Material Inspection Administrn., Washington, 1941- 43, asst. to sec. Joint Chiefs of Staff, USN, Washington, 1943-45; in Office Sec. Navy, UN Conf. on Internat. Orgn., San Francisco, 1945; with Office UN Affairs, Dept. State, 1945-52, asst. chief, div. Internat. Security Affairs, 1947, chief, 1947-49, adviser on planning in charge UN Planning Staff, 1949-51; attended Nat. War Coll., 1951-52; with Ford Found., 1952-55; asst. to chmn. bd. firs. U.S. Steel Corp., 1955-60, dir. stockholder relations, 1961- 63; dir. N.Y. Office Internat. Bank for Reconstrn. and Devel., Internat. Finance Corp., 1963-67; pres. World Banking Corp., Nassau, Bahamas, 1968—. Trustee Woods Hole Oceanographic Instn. Mem. Council Fgn. Relations. Mem. Soc. of Friends. Home: P O Box 6343 Nassau Bahama Office: P O Box 100 Nassau Bahama

JOHNSON, HOWARD E., paper co. exec.; b. Virginia, Minn., July 24, 1924; s. Ernest and Anna Elizabeth (Nordstrom) J.; B.B.A., Northwestern U., 1949; m. Mary Jean Hughes, Aug. 29, 1947; children—Amy, Grant, Martha, Philip, Seth, Sarah. With trust dept. Northwestern Nat. Bank, Mpls., 1949-50; with Peat, Marwick, Mitchell & Co., Mpls., 1950-54; v.p., dir. The Creamette Co., Mpls., 1954-63; sec., dir. Creamette Co. Can. Ltd., 1960-63; with Hoerner Waldorf Corp., St. Paul, 1963—, corporate controller, 1968—, also dir. subsidiaries. Served with AUS, 1943-46. C.P.A., Minn. Mem. Am. Inst. C.P.A.'s, Minn. Soc. C.P.A.'s, Tax Execs. Inst. Home: 5311 Oaklawn Av Minneapolis MN 55424 Office: 22250 Wabash Av St Paul MN 55114

JOHNSON, HOWARD WESLEY, univ. pres.; b. Chgo., July 2, 1922; s. Albert H. and Laura (Hansen) J.; B.A., Central Coll., Chgo., 1943; M.A., U. Chgo., 1947, certificate Glasgow (Scotland) U., 1946; recipient numerous hon. degrees; m. Elizabeth J. Weed, Feb. 18, 1950; children—Stephen Andrew, Laura Ann, Bruce Howard. From asst. to asso. prof., dir. mgmt. research U. Chgo., 1948-51, 53-55; asst. to v.p. personnel adminstrn. Gen. Mills, Inc., 1952-53; asso. prof., dir. exec. programs, asso. dean Sloan Sch. Mgmt., Mass. Inst. Tech., 1955-59, prof., dean, 1959-66, pres. Mass. Inst. Tech., 1966—; exec. v.p. Federated Dept. Stores, 1966, now dir.; chmn. Fed. Res. Bank Boston, 1968-69; dir. Hitchiner Mfg. Co., John Hancock Mut. Life Ins. Co., U.S. Plywood Champion Papers, Inc.; trustee Putnam Funds. Mem. Pres.'s Adv. Com. on Labor-Mgmt. Policy, 1966-68. Trustee Com. Econ. Devel., Wellesley Coll.; bd. dirs. WGBH Ednl. Found., Mus. Sci., Cambridge, Mass.; overseer Boston Symphony Orch., 1968—; mem.-at-large Boy Scouts Am. Served with AUS, 1943-46. Fellow Am. Acad. Arts and Scis., A.A.A.S.; mem. Council Fgn. Relations, Phi Gamma Delta. Clubs: University, Harvard (N.Y.C.); Algonquin, Commercial, Tavern, St. Botolph (Boston). Home: 111 Memorial Dr Cambridge MA 02142

JOHNSON, HUBERT DEE, lawyer; b. Lytle, Tex., Mar. 16, 1915; s. Hubert Dee and Onab (Dollahite) J.; LL.B., U. Tex., 1937; m. Emme Lou Brown, Feb. 12, 1941; children—Hubert Dee, Linda Lou. Admitted to Tex. bar, 1937; asso. atty. firm Locke, Stroud & Randolph, Dallas, 1937-41; gen. counsel Fed. Res. Bank Dallas, 1945-48: partner firm Carrington, Gowan, Johnson & Walker, Dallas, 1948-58, Carrington, Johnson & Stephens, Dallas (now Johnson, McElroy & Cravens), 1958—; instr. Acad. Am. and Internat. Law, Dallas, 1964—. Dir. Mercantile Nat. Bank, Dallas. Served with USNR, 1942-45. Mem. State Bar of Texas, Am., 1942-45. Mem. State Bar of Tex., Am., Dallas (bd. dirs. 1961—, pres. 1964) bar assns., Am. Judicature Soc., Am. Law Inst., Phi Delta Phi, Order of Coif. Methodist. Home: 3720 Marquette St Dallas TX 75225 Office: Mercantile Bank Bldg Dallas TX 75201

JOHNSON, HUNTER, former educator, composer; b. Benson, N.C., Apr. 14, 1906; s. Amos Cephus and Martha (Barbour) J.; student U. N.C., 1924-26, Mus. D. (hon.), 1960; Mus. B., Eastman Sch. Music, 1929. Mem. faculty U. Mich., 1929- 33, U. Man., 1944-47, Cornell U., 1948-53, U. Ill., 1959-65, U. Tex., 1966-71. Recipient Rome prize, 1933, award Nat. Inst. Arts and Letters, 1958; fine arts award N.C., 1965. Guggenheim fellow, 1941-54. Composer: Symphony I, 1932; Piano Sonata, 1934-36; Concerto for Piano and Chamber Orchestra, 1936; For An Unknown Soldier, 1938; Music for String Orchestra, 1939; (ballet) In Time of Armament, 1939; (ballet, commd. by Martha Graham) Letter to the World, 1940; (ballet commnd. by Martha Graham) Deaths and Entrances, 1942; Concerto for Orchestra, 1944; Trio for Flute, Oboe and Piano, 1954; concert suite from Letter to the World, 1959; North State (for orch. commn. by Carolina Charter (Corp.), 1963; Past the Evening Sun (for orch.), 1964. Home: Benson NC 27504

JOHNSON, IRVING HARDING, (Mrs. Curtis B. Johnson), ret. bus. exec.; b. Davidson, N.C., Nov. 10, 1889; d. Richmond and Mildred (Berry) Harding; A.B., Queens Coll., 1909, LL.D., 1959; m. Rev. Dr. Archibald McGeachy, July 14, 1910 (dec. 1928); m. 2d, Curtis Boyd Johnson, May 1942 (dec. 1950). Editor syndicated problem column under name of Caroline Chatfield, 1932-42; chmn. bd. Observer Co., Charlotte, N.C., 1951-53; pres. Charlotte Observer, Charlotte Observer Transp. Co. Mem. bd. United Community Services. Trustee Queens Coll.; bd. visitors Davidson Coll. Democrat. Presbyn. Club: City, Charlotte Country. Home: 2225 Pembroke Av Charlotte NC 28207

JOHNSON, IRVING MCCLURE, author; b. Hadley, Mass., July 4, 1905; s. Clifton and Anna (McQueston) J.; grad. Hopkins Acad., 1923; m. Electa Search, Sept. 15, 1932; children—Arthur Cook, Robert Parkin. Sailed around Cape Horn in 4 mast bark "Peking," 1929; mate of "Shamrock V," America's cup challenger, on crossing back to Eng., 1930 owner pilot schooner, "Yankee," sailed three times around world with amateur crews, 1933-41; discovered and charted 5 islands north of New Guinea, 1934; owner brigantine "Yankee," sailed around world, 1947-49, 50-52, 53-55, 56-58, lectr., writer, 1929—. Served from lt. comdr. to comdr. USNR, 1941-46; Recipient Spl. Service award for diving work in the South Pacific, 1942, 1943. Mem. Mystic Seaport Marine Mus. Conn. (life mem.; trustee). Clubs: Royal Ocean Racing (Eng.); Adventurers (Chgo.); Cruising of America, Explorers (N.Y.C.); Cruising of Hawaii. Author several books, 1931-38; Yankee's Wander World, 1949; Yankee's People and Places, 1955; Yankee Sails Across Europe, 1962; Yankee Sails the Nile, 1966. Contbr. articles to mags. Now sailing European waters in ketch Yankee. Address: Hockanum Rd Hadley MA 01035

JOHNSON, IVAN EARL, art educator; b. Denton, Tex., Sept. 23, 1911; s. Ivan E. and Dorothy (Williams) J.; B.S., N. Tex. State U., 1932, B.A., 1933; M.A., Columbia, 1936; Ed.D. (Founders Day award

1960), N.Y. U., 1960; m. Inez Stocker, Oct. 24, 1942; children—Ivan Earl III, Lynn, Joseph, Susan, Jean. Art instr. S.W. Tex. State Coll., San Marcos, 1936-39; design cons. Dept. Agr., head dept. art edn. and constructive design Fla. State U., 1952—; mem. staff Seminar for Art Suprs., U.S. Office Edn., 1970. Pres., Tallahassee Jr. Mus. 1964-65; chmn. bd. Tallahassee chpt. A.R.C., 1965-67. Served to lt. comdr. USNR, 1942-46. Univ. Research Council grantee, Denmark 1971. Mem. Nat. Art Edn. Assn. (v.p. 1953-55, pres. 1955-57, mem. tng. inst. 1969), Western Arts Assn. (pres. 1950-52), Am. Inst. Designers, Kappa Delta Pi, Phi Delta Kappa, Pi Kappa Alpha. Author: (with C. Stafford) Art for Living, 1952, Art for You, 1956; (with G. Hubbard) Instructor Modern Art Portfolio, 1965; (with J. Hausman, others) Report of Commission on Art in Education, 1965. Book editor Arts and Activities mag., 1952—. Mem. editorial bd. Jour. Art Edn., 1962-70. Home: 2304 Charles Ct Tallahassee FL 32303

JOHNSON, JACK THOMAS, educator; b. Burlington, Ia., July 16, 1915; s. James H. and Emily L. (Holihan) J.; B.A., State U. Ia., 1935, M.A., 1936, Ph.D., 1938; m. Margaret L. Gill, Sept. 1, 1938. Asst. in instrn. State U. Ia., 1936-40, instr. polit. sci., 1940-42, asst. prof., 1942-47, asso. prof., 1947-51; asst. adminstr. tng. and edn. Office FCDA, 1951-53; provost Hofstra Coll., 1953-57, v.p. 1957-62; vis. prof. polit. sci. N.M. Western Coll., 1962-63; dir. Bur. Govt. Research, Ind. State U., 1964-65; asso. dir. Inst. Higher Edn., Tchrs. Coll., Columbia, 1965-68; asso. dean arts and scis. Ind. State U., 1968-70, dir. spl. gen. edn. projects, 1970—. Rockefeller Found. fellow 1946. Served to ensign USNR, 1944-46. Mem. Phi Beta Kappa, Pi Gamma Mu, Omicron Delta Kappa, Alpha Tau Omega, Pi Delta Epsilon, Sigma Kappa Alpha. Author: A Railroad to the Sea, 1939; Peter A. Dey, 1939; A Handbook for Iowa Mayors, 1943; Iowa Government, 1951; The Changing Mission of Home Economics, 1968. Contbr. profl. jours. Home: 1901 N 7th St Terre Haute IN 47804

JOHNSON, JALMAR EDWIN, newspaper editor; b. Clarkfield, Minn., Sept. 25, 1905; s. Julius Sven and Emma (Walgren) J.; student U. Ore., 1923-26; m. Dorothy Dolores Hegeman, May 14, 1932; children—Harry H., Judith Irene (Mrs. Albert A. Cohen, Jr.). Reporter, Eugene (Ore.) Register, 1925-29; mem. staff The Oregonian, Portland, 1929—, asso. editor editorial page, 1951—. Mem. Citizens Adv. Zoning Com., Portland, 1959-61; Rural Areas Devel. Com., 1965—, Police Sunshine Div., 1951—. Recipient Merit award Printing House Craftsmen, 1951, award Appreciation Forest Industries, 1960, Citizens award A.I.A., 1964, Smokey Bear award, 1970. Mem. Am. Forest Assn., Portland C. of C., Ore. Hist. Soc., Sigma Delta Chi. Republican. Presbyn. Author: Builders of the Northwest, 1963. Home: 2714 NE Dunckley St Portland OR 97212 Office: 1320 SW Broadway Portland OR 97201

JOHNSON, JAMES, librarian; b. Roswell, N.M., June 28, 1917; s. Leonard J. and Blanche (Davenport) J.; B.A., Eastern N.M. Coll., 1941; B.S. in L.S., U. Denver, 1947; m. Leah Johnson, June 2, 1939; children—Timothy, Robert, Judith. Tchr., N.M. pub. schs., 1936-47; asst. librarian N.W. Mo. State Coll., Maryville, 1948-49, librarian, 1949—. Danforth asso., 1956—. Mem. Mo. Library Assn. Kiwanian (pres. 1967). Home: 218 S Munn St Maryville MO 64468

JOHNSON, JAMES DOUGLAS, Jim, lawyer; b. Crossett, Ark., Aug. 20, 1924; s. Thomas William and Maudie Myrtle (Long) J.; LL.B., Cumberland U., 1947; m. Virginia Morris, Dec. 21, 1947; children—Mark Douglas, John David and Joseph Daniel (twins). Admitted to Ark. bar, 1948; practice in Crosset, 1945-58; asso. justice Supreme Ct. Ark., 1958-66; practice law, Little Rock, 1966- -. Mem. Ark. Senate 22d Senatorial Dist., 1950-54. Served with USMCR, World War II. Mem. Ark. Jud. Council, Lamda Chi Alpha. Democrat. Methodist. Mason (32, Shriner). Home: Conway AR 72032 Office: Union Life Bldg Little Rock AR 72201

JOHNSON, JAMES EDWARD, govt. ofcl.; b. Madison, Ill., Mar. 3, 1926; s. Richard and Veola (Thompson) J.; student George Washingon U., 1958-59, U. Md., 1960-61, Chapman Coll., 1962-65, Santa Ana, 1965-67; B.S., George Washington, U., 1970; m. Juanita Virginia Butler, Sept. 25, 1948; children—Kenneth Edward, Janice Vernea, Kurtis James, Juan Eric. Served as officer USMC, 1944-65; resigned, 1965; exec. spl. agt. Prudential Ins. Co. Am., Anaheim, Cal., 1965-67; dir. Cal. Dept. Vets. Affairs, 1967-69; vice chmn. U.S. Civil Service Commn., 1969—. Finance chmn. Planned Parenthood Assn.; pres. Orange County chpt. Childrens Asthma Research Inst. and Hosp.; bd. dirs. United Givers Fund; mem. D.C. Health and Welfare Council. Mem. Orange County Republican Assn.; finance chmn. Life Ins. Underwriters Orange County for Gov. Ronald Reagan, 1966; chmn. Orange County interested minority com. Orange County Rep. Central Com.; asst. Cal. chmn. Commitment '68 for Nixon presdl. campaign; asso. mem. Cal. Central Rep. Com. Bd. govs. Anaheim YMCA; bd. dirs. Golden Empire council Boy Scouts Am., also mem. Nat. Exec. bd. and mem. adv. bd. Nat. Capital area council; bd. dirs. United Christian Centers, Sacramento Safety Council. Mem. AMVETS, Am. Legion, V.F.W. Club: Toastmasters Internat. (area gov.). Home: 2816 Blue Spruce Lane Wheaton MD 20906 Office: 1900 E St NW Washington DC 20415

JOHNSON, JAMES GLOVER, coll. prof., clergyman; b. Jacksonville, Ala., Nov. 30, 1901; s. Allison James and Minnie Ross (Glover) J.; student prep. dept., Ala. Presbyn. Coll. 1916-18; A.B., Mercer U., 1922, A.M., 1922; Th.M., So. Bapt. Theol. Sem., 1924, Th.D. (fellow missions and comparative religion 1924- 26), 1927; Ph.D., Yale, 1936; m. Mary Jessie Pearce, Aug. 2, 1939. Ordained to ministry Bapt. Ch., 1924; master Mount Hermon (Mass.) Sch. for Boys, 1936-46, head Bible dept. and chaplain, 1940-46; prof. religion Marietta Coll., 1946-53, prof. religion and philosophy, 1953—, chmn. dept., 1953-67; minister Putnam Congl. Ch., Marietta, O., 1949-61; vis. lectr. Ohio U., 1953-69. Mem. exec. com. Marietta United Appeal Bd., 1953-60; chmn. com. on homes Marietta chpt. Am. Field Service, 1959-61; mem. corp. Marietta (O.) Meml. Hosp., 1960—; Marietta Coll. Danforth asso. The Danforth Found., 1949—. Recipient Wisdom award Wisdom Soc., 1970. Mem. Am. Ohio acads. religion, Nat. Council Chs. (profs. and research sect. div. Christian edn.; chmn. profs. sect. 1948-50), Metaphys. Soc. Am. Soc. for Sci. Study Religion, Am., Ohio philos. assns., Religious Edn. Assn., Classical Assn. of Middle W. and S. Royal Inst. of Philosophy (London), Acad. Religion and Mental Health. Mem. United Ch. Christ. Mason. Clubs: Rotary, Exec. (pres. 1957-59), Reading (Marietta). Author: Highroads of the Universe, An Introduction to Christian Philosophy, 1944, rev. 1971. Contbr. articles and book reviews to profl. jours. Home: 428 Victoria Av Williamstown VA 26187 Office: Marietta Coll Marietta OH 45750

JOHNSON, JAMES KIMBALL, II, found. exec.; b. Maywood, Ill., Nov. 16, 1901; s. James Kimball and Harriet (Nelson) J.; B.S., Case Inst. Tech., 1924, M.S., 1930; m. Minerva S. Buttorff, Feb. 24, 1928 (dec. Jan. 1959); 1 son, James Kimball, III; m. 2d, Virginia Knapp Wright, May 7, 1960. Civil and sanitary engineer, 1924-32, resident engr., Havana, Cuba, 1929- 30; in charge Civil Works Adminstrn., Cleve., 1933-34; bus. mgr. Cuyahoga County Relief Adminstrn., 1935-36; mgr. Akron (O.) field office U.S. Social Security Bd., also regional rep. Bur. Unemployment Compensation, 1937-41; dep. dir. War Manpower Commn., 1944-45; regional dir. U.S. Employment Service, 1946-48, Dept. Health, Edn. and Welfare, Cleve., Chgo., 1948-54; dir. Cleve. Found., 1954-68, cons., 1968—. Bd. mem. Conf. Social Welfare, Council on Founds., Shaker Heights Pub. Library, Ohio Citizens Council for Health and Welfare; mem. numerous coms. and agys. affiliated with Cleve. Welfare Fedn. Recipient Distinguished Service award United Appeal, 1959 Ky. col. Mem. Am. Soc. Pub. Adminstrn., C. of C., Phi Kappa Psi, Tau Beta Pi. Episcopalian. Contbr. tech., pub. welfare articles various mags. Home: 2547 N Moreland Blvd Cleveland OH 44120 Office: National City Bank Bldg Cleveland OH 44114

JOHNSON, JAMES LOUIS, (J.J. Johnson), musician; b. Indpls., Jan. 22, 1924; s. James Hartly and Nina (Gieger) J.; grad. high sch.; m. Vivian Freeman, Sept. 23, 1946; children—William Freeman, Kevin Louis. Trombone soloist, composer, arranger Benny Carter Orch., 1942-44, Count Basie Orch., 1945-47; free lance work in radio, TV, concert tours abroad, 1948-56; mem. J. J. Johnson Quintet and Sextet, 1957-61; soloist with Miles Davis Orch., 1961—; recording recording artist Columbia Records. Mason. Composer: Poem for Brass, 1956; Perceptions, 1961. Home: 1365 S St Nicholas St New York City NY 10033

JOHNSON, JAMES MYRON, educator, psychologist; b. Sauk Centre, Minn., Aug. 4, 1927; s. Walfred and Sophie (Koelzer) J.; B.A., U. Minn., 1948; M.A., Clark U., 1950; Ph.D., Columbia, 1958; m. Constance Mary Blodgett, Apr. 15, 1950; children—Kathryn, Peter, Donna, Daniel, Amy, Linda, Eric, Christian. Adj. prof. Grad. Sch. Indsl. Engring., N.Y.U., 1963-66; dep. dir. lab. psychol. studies Stevens Inst. Tech., 1964-67, dir., 1967—, research prof. mgmt. sci., 1966—; cons. to industry. Pres. Darien (Conn.) Mental Health Assn., 1961-64, 68-70. Mem. Darien Democratic Town Com. Bd. dirs. Stamford (Conn.) Psychiat. Clinic Children. Served with USNR, 1945-46. Mem. Am., N.J. psychol. assns., N.Y. Acad. Sci., Met. N.Y. Assn. Applied Psychology (pres. 1966-67), A.A.A.S., Inst. Mgmt. Sci., Am. Assn. U. Profs., Sigma Xi. Home: 62 Brookside Rd Darien CT 06820 Office: Stevens Inst Tech Lab Psychol Studies Castle Point Sta Hoboken NJ 07030

JOHNSON, JAMES NOEL, mfg. co. exec.; b. Stevens Point, Wis., Oct. 7, 1919; s. Benjamin Alfred and Margaret (Masters) J.; Ph.B., Marquette U., 1941; LL.B., Cornell U., 1943; m. Jane Ellen Cantwell, Feb. 6, 1943; children—Jane (Mrs. John B. Winston), Craig, Randall, Karen (Mrs. David Pressley), Scott, Gary, Todd, Philip, Erik. Admitted to Wis. bar, 1943; asso. firm Olwell & Brady, Milw., 1943-46; asso. of James D. Porter, Milw., 1946-50; partner firm Porter, Johnson, Quale & Porter, Milw., 1950-61; sec., gen. counsel A. O. Smith Corp., Milw., 1961-67, v.p., sec., gen. counsel, 1967—; proctor Marquette U. Law Sch., 1957-61. Pres., Health Service Data Wis., Milw., 1966-68; chmn. Milw. Med. Resources Study Com., 1965-68. Chmn. bd. govs. Dominican Coll., Racine, 1968—. Mem. Am. Soc. Corp. Secs., Am., Internat., Inter-Am., Wis., Milw. Bar assns. Club: Blue Mound Golf and Country (Wauwatosa, Wis.). Contbr. legal jours. Home: 13550 Wrayburn Rd Elm Grove WI 53122 Office: 3533 N 27th St Milwaukee WI 53201

JOHNSON, JAMES WINSTON, educator; b. Quinton, Okla., May 25, 1930; s. Fred M. and Lois Amelia (Sands) J.; B.S. in Chemistry-Math., Southeastern Okla. U., 1953; B.S. in Chem. Engring., Mo. Sch. Mines and Metallurgy, 1957, M.S. in Chem. Engring. (AEC fellow), 1958; Ph.D. (NSF fellow), U. Mo., 1961; m. Vera Mae Hamman, Oct. 17, 1953; children—Christopher James, Victor Andrew. Instr., Mo. Sch. Mines and Metallurgy, 1958-60, asst. prof., 1961-62; research asso. U. Pa., 1962-63; asso. prof. U. Mo. at Rolla, 1963-66, prof. chem. engring., 1966—, research asso. Grad. Center Materials Research, 1965—. Served with AUS, 1953-55. Mem. Am. Inst. Chem. Engrs., Nat. Assn. Corrosion Engrs., Electrochem. Soc., Faraday Soc., Blue Key, Sigma Xi, Tau Beta Pi, Alpha Chi Sigma, Sigma Pi Sigma, Phi Kappa Phi, Kappa Delta Pi, Sigma Tau Gamma. Republican. Contbr. articles tech. jours. Home: PO Box 486 Rolla MO 65401

JOHNSON JESS WALTER, coll. pres.; b. Kansas City, Mo., May 19, 1917; s. Walter O. and Vada (Vanderberg) J.; B.Th., N.W. Christian Coll., Eugene, Ore., 1942; student U. Ore., 1940-41, summer 1945, Union Theol. Sem., N.Y.C., summer 1944; B.D., Christian Theol. Sem., Indpls., 1951; postgrad. Butler U., 1947-51; LaSalle Extension U., 1966; D.D., Milligan Coll., 1959; m. Mary M. Sargent, June 15, 1941; children—Rose Mary (Mrs. Arthur A. Cantrell). Cecil W., Susan Diane, Kevin Lee. Ordained to ministry Christian Ch., 1940; minister in Tillamook, Ore., 1942-47, Frankfurt, Ind., 1947-49, Indpls., 1949-51, Portland, Ore., 1951-59, Johnson City, Tenn., 1959-65; v.p. devel. Milligan Coll., 1965-66, exec. v.p. 1966-68, pres., 1968—. Mem. bd. European Evangelistic Soc., 1952—, Christian Missionary Fellowship, 1950—, Ore. Christian Missionary Soc., 1945, 47, 53, 54; mem. continuation com. N.Am. Christian Conv., 1951-64, 69—, chmn. local arrangements com., 1958, v.p., 1959; pres. Christian Missionary Fellowship, 1962-64, N. Area Coordinating Council, 1955; chmn. Johnson City Preaching Mission, 1962, exec. sec., 1965; chmn. Appalachian Preaching Mission; 1971. Vice pres. North. Portland YMCA, 1958; chmn. Johnson City-Washington county chpt. A.R.C., 1967-69; commr. Johnson Housing Authority, 1968—. Mem. Am. Assn. Ind. Coll. Presidents, Am. Sci. Affiliation, Elizabethan C. of C. (bd. mem.), Soc. Sci. Study Religion, Internat. Platform Assn. Kiwanian. Home: 104 Ridgemont Rd Johnson City TN 37601 Office: Box E Milligan College TN 37682

JOHNSON, JESSE CHARLES, mining engr.; b. Clallam, Wash., Feb. 22, 1894; s. Robert R. and Mary (Rosebrook) J.; B.S., U. Wash., 1919; m. Alice Frein, Nov. 14, 1925; 1 dau., Mary Virginia. Cons. mining engr., Seattle, 1919-26; securities bus., 1926-42; engr. R.F.C., Washington, 1943, chief engr., 1943-45, dep. dir. in charge domestic and fgn. metal procurement, 1946-47; dep. dir. div. raw materials A.E.C. Washington, 1948-49, dir., 1950-63, Distinguished Service award, 1956; cons., adviser U.S. del. Internat. Confs. Peaceful Uses Atomic Energy, Geneva, Switzerland, 1955, 58. Recipient Ambrose Monnell medal and prize, 1961. Mem. Am. Mining and Metall. Soc., Am. Inst. Mining and Metall. Engrs., Sigma Xi, Tau Beta Pi, Alpha Delta Phi. Club: Cosmos (Washington). Home: 5900 Bradley Blvd Bethesda MD 20014

JOHNSON, JESSE GEARING, former naval officer; b. Bridgeton, N.J., Jan. 9, 1895; s. George Alexander and Mary Harper (Buckman) J.; student Swarthmore Coll., 1916- 17, U. Hawaii, 1935-36; m. Elisabeth Harrold, June 11, 1921; children—Joan (Mrs. Allan Hugh McKinley), Suzanne (Mrs. Adolf Gunnar Mellberg), Adrianne (Mrs. Vernon Keith Little). Commd. ensign USN, 1918, advanced through grades to rear adm., 1947; served on destroyers, transports, U.S.S. Langley, U.S.S. Ranger, aircraft carriers 1918-38; served as a naval aviator, Pensacola, Fla., 1924; served in various fleet squadrons and U.S. Naval Acad., 1926- 28; mapped Wake Island, 1935, built air base, Russell Islands, 1943; exec. officer, asst. task force comdr. U.S.S. Guadalcanal, Atlantic, 1943-44; captured German submarine U-505 June 4, 1944 (now on exhbn. Mus. Sci. and Industry, Chgo.); comdr. U.S.S. Webster, Pacific, 1945; ret. Jan. 1947; now engaged in pub. relations; philatelic writer. Mem. exec. com. Fedn. Internat. Philatelic Congress, Istanbul, Paris, Vienna, Munich. Health campaign drive March of Dimes. Decorated Bronze Star medal, Legion of Merit, Mem. Am. Philatelic Soc. (sec.) Am. Air Mail Soc. (past pres.), Kappa Sigma. Presbyn. Mason (Shriner). Clubs: Virginia, Norfolk German, Cosmopolitan International. Author: Sourdough Flights (history of Alaskan flights), 1940; Old Bay Line Mail: (biography) Blue Skies Ahead. Asso. editor American Air Mail Catalogue 1967-71. Home: Cardinal Point Norfolk VA 23508

JOHNSON, JOHN AUGUST, former coll. dean; b. Twin Valley, Minn., May 15, 1904; s. John August and Mary Frances (Day) J.; B.Edn., Mankato (Minn.) State Tchrs. Coll., 1931; M.A., U. Minn., 1939; D. Edn., U. Colo., 1956; m. Virginia I. Ellis, Dec. 26, 1931 (dec. Sept., 1954); children—John August, Charles E.; m. 2d, Elizabeth V. Davidian, Aug. 20, 1955. Tchr., Lake Crystal (Minn.) High Sch., 1929-30; prin. Mountain Lake (Minn.) High Sch., 1931-36, supts. schs., 1936-42; supt. schs. Wayzata (Minn.) pub. schs., 1942-48; dir. placement Mankato State Tchrs. Coll., 1948-56, chmn. div. profl. edn. and psychology, 1956-64, dean Sch. Edn., 1964-70, now ret., rep. to Am. Assn. Colls. Tchr. Edn., 1960-70. Sec-treas. No. Intercollegiate Conf., 1963-64; mem. Minn. Adv. Com. Tchr. Edn., 1956-69. Chmn. fund raising Mankato Community Chest, 1953. Mem. Nat., Minn. edn. assns., Asso. Alumni Mankato State Tchrs. Coll. (sec. 1948-58), Phi Delta Kappa. Mason. Kiwanian. Home: 219 Bahia Vista Dr Englewood FL 33533

JOHNSON, JOHN BOCKOVER, Jr., univ. provost; b. Chicago, Sept. 21, 1912; s. John Bockover and Mary Clyde (Wiltshire) J.; A.B., Williams Coll., 1934; Ph.D., U. Chgo., 1942; LL.D., Ripon (Wis.) Coll., 1953; m. Cloyd Stifler, Apr. 18, 1942; children—David Stifler, Randall Wharton, Lucy Burnley. With Dun & Bradstreet, Inc., Louisville, 1935-38, credit analyst, 1936- 38, Chgo., 1942; mem. faculty Park Coll., Parkville, Mo., 1946-51, chmn. social sci. div., 1947-51, chmn. polit. sci. dept., 1946-51; pres. Milw. Downer Coll., 1951-64; provost Old Dominion U., Norfolk, Va., 1964—. Mem. instructional programs adv. com. State Council Higher Edn. for Va. Mem. Council United Community Services of Greater Milw., Inc., 1951-64; adv. bd. Girl Scouts U.S., 1951-64; cons. bd. World Affairs Council, 1951-64. Exec. com. Wis. Found. Ind. Colls., Inc., 1951-64, also past pres.; joint liaison com. Old Dominion Coll., Norfolk Gen. Hosp., Norfolk Area Med. Center Authority. Served with AUS, 1942-46. Recipient Army Commendation award, 1946 for 2 vol. history. Mem. Continuing Conf. on Gen. Edn. and The Social Sci. (Carnegie Corp.), 1950- 51. Mem. Norfolk Mus. Arts and Scis., Assn. Wis. Pres. and Deans (past pres.), Greater Milw. Assn. Phi Beta Kappa (past pres.), Delta Upsilon. Author: (with Irving Lewis) Registration for Voting in the United States, 1941; (with Graves T. Wilson) history of World War II Research and Development of Medical Field Equipment, 2 vols., 1946. Home: 505 Brackenridge Av Norfolk VA 23505

JOHNSON, JOHN BRYAN, Jr., lawyer; b. Little Rock, Dec. 12, 1933; s. John Bryan and Frances (Regenold) J.; B.B.A., U. Okla., 1955, LL.B., 1957; LL.M., Harvard, 1961; m. Laura Anne Francis, June 21, 1956; children-John Bryan III, Laura Francis. Admitted to Okla. bar, 1957; practice in Tulsa, 1961—; mem. firm Gable, Gotwals, Hays, Rubin & Fox, 1967—. Dir. Marion Corp. Served with USAF, 1957-60. Decorated Commendation medal; recipient Jr. award Tulsa County Bar Assn., 1967. Mem. Tulsa Estate Planning Forum (past pres.), Harvard Law Sch. Alumni Assn. Okla. (past pres.). Methodist (adminstrv. bd.). Elk, Mason. Home: 2909 E 56th Ct Tulsa OK 74105 Office: Fourth Nat Bank Bldg Tulsa OK 74119

JOHNSON, JOHN CHARLES, physicist, educator; b. Pike County, Ill., June 19, 1920; s. John Creston and Florence Ellen (Bradbury) J.; B.A., Culver Stockton Coll., 1942; postgrad. Ohio State U., 1942-43; M.A., U. Mich. 1947, Ph.D., 1950; m. Lorraine Irene Ura, Oct. 14, 1950; children—John Anthony, James Andrew, William Dean. Tech. supr. Tenn. Eastman Corp., Oak Ridge, 1944- 46; research asst., research physicist U. Mich., 1946-59; prof. engring research Pa. State U., 1959—, dir. Ordnance Research Lab., 1959—, chmn. grad. program engring. acoustics. Mem. USN Research and Devel. Planning Council; mem. com. on fed. labs. Fed. Council for Sci. and Tech., 1969—. Bd. dirs. United Campus Ministry and United Fund Coll. Area. Registered profl. engr., Pa. Fellow Acoustical Soc. Am. (pres. 1971-72), A.A.A.S.; mem. Am. Soc. Engring. Edn., Am. Ordnance Assn., Am. Phys. Soc., Sigma Xi. Presbyn. Mason. Clubs: Centre Hills Country, Centre Squares Dance. Asso. editor: U.S. Navy Jour. Underwater Acoustics, 1961-66. Home: Boalsburg PA 16827 Office: PO Box 30 State College PA 16801

JOHNSON, JOHN CLARK, educator; b. Waterbury, Conn., Aug. 17, 1919; S. John Mauritz Eugene and Aletha (Clark) J.; A.B., Middlebury Coll., 1941; S.M., Mass. Inst. Tech., 1946; Sc.D., 1948; m. Frances Elizabeth Barrett, July 1, 1941 (div. June 1961); children—Eric Arthur, Signe Lee. Asst. prof. Mass. Inst. Tech., 1950-53; lectr., research asso. Tufts U., 1953-54; faculty Worcester (Mass.) Poly. Inst., 1954—, prof. physics, 1965—. Served to 1st lt. USAAF, 1941-45; ETO. Decorated Air medal. Mem. Am. Phys. Soc., Am. Meteorol. Soc., Optical Soc. Am., Am. Assn. Physics Tchrs., Sigma Xi, Alpha Sigma Phi. Author: Physical Meteorology, 1954. Home: 147 Milk St Westboro MA 01581 Office: 222 Olin Hall Worcester Poly Inst Worcester MA 01609

JOHNSON, JOHN H., editor, pub.; b. Arkansas City, Ark., Jan. 19, 1918; student U. Chgo., Northwestern U.; LL.D., Central State Coll., Shaw U., N.C. Coll.; m. Eunice Johnson; children—John Harold, Linda. Editor, pub. Negro Digest, Chgo., 1942-51; pres. Johnson Pub. Co., Inc., Chgo. and N.Y.; pub., editor Ebony, Black Stars, Jet and Black World mags.; pres., chief exec. officer Supreme Life Ins. Co. Am.; dir. Marina City Bank, Chgo., Service Fed. Savs. & Loan Assn. Mem. Pres.'s Nat. Adv. Commn. on Selective Service; mem. exec. com. Internat. Exec. Service Corps. Trustee Inst. Internat. Edn. Recipient Horatio Alger award, 1966; John Russwurm award Nat. Newspaper Pubs. Assn., 1966, Spingarn medal N.A.A.C.P., 1966. Mem. Mag. Pubs. Assn. (dir.), Chgo. Assn. Commerce and Industry (dir.), Nat. Conf. Christians and Jews (dir.). Club: Chicago Press. Office: 1820 S Michigan Av Chicago IL 60616 also 1270 Avenue of Americas New York City NY

JOHNSON, JOHN HENRY, pub. relations exec.; b. Waterproof, La., Nov. 24, 1929; s. Foster and Ella (Johnson) J.; student St. Mary's Coll., 1949-53; B.A. in Edn., Ariz. State U., 1955; postgrad. Duquesne U., 1965; m. Leona Butts, June 3, 1967; children—Kathrine, Michael, Toni and Terri (twins), Carol, John Henry. Football player San Francisco 49ers, 1953-56, Detroit Lions, 1957-60, Pitts. Steelers, 1960-67; stock broker, mem. N.Y. Stock Exchange with Universal Diversified Services, Pitts., 1965-67; salesman Carling Black Label-Goebel Brewing Co., 1961-64; cons. Westinghouse Electric Co., Boise Cascade Co., Gen. Electric Co. Pres. John Henry Johnson Youth Found.; bd. dirs. Athletic Sick Cell Anemia. Recipient citation for work with youth in CORE City-Camping and Counseling Program, 1965; named Football All Pro, 1962, 64, 65, Personality of Year, Talk Mag., 1970; selected to Pro Bowl Team 8 times. Mem. Pub. Relations Soc., N.A.A.C.P., Nat. Football League Players Assn., Kappa Alpha Psi. Lion. Club: Lunch (Pitts.). Home: 5730 Holden St Pittsburgh PA 15230

JOHNSON, JOHN HOWARD, profl. basketball player; b. Carthage, Miss., Oct. 19, 1947; s. James and Lonnie (Leflore) J.; A.A., Northwest Community Coll., 1966-68; B.A., U. Ia., 1968-70; m. Marca Hogan, Aug. 15, 1970. Basketball player Cleve. Cavaliers, 1971—. Democrat. Roman Catholic. Home: 4400 Clarkwood Pkwy Warrensville Heights OH 44128

JOHNSON, JOHN J., educator, historian; b. White Swan, Wash., Mar. 26, 1912; s. George E. and Mary (Whitford) J.; B.A., Central Wash. Coll., 1940; M.A., U. Cal. at Berkeley, 1943, Ph.D., 1947; postgrad., U. Chgo., 1943-44, U. Chile, 1946; m. Maurine Amstutz, June 8, 1942; 1 son, Michael G. Tchr. pub. schs., Wash., 1935-41; mem. faculty Stanford, 1946—, prof. history, 1958—, chmn. com. Latin Am. studies, 1966—; acting chief S. Am. br., div. research Am. Republic, State Dept., 1952-53; lectr. U. Ariz. Summer Sch., Guadalajara, Mexico, 1955, 58, 61; cons. to industry and govt., 1959—. Recipient Bolton prize Conf. Latin Am. History, 1959. Mem. Am. Hist. Assn. (chmn. conf. Latin Am. history 1961), Latin Am. Studies Assn. (pres. 1970). Club: Cosmos. Author: Pioneer Telegraphy in Chile, 1948; Political Change in Latin America; The Emergence of the Middle Sectors, 1958; The Military and Society in Latin America, 1964; Simon Bolivar and Spanish American Independence: 1783-1830, 1967. Editor, contbr.: Role of the Military in Underdeveloped Countries, 1962; Continuity and Change in Latin America, 1964; The Mexican American: A Selected and Annotated Bibliography, 1969. Home: 774 Esplanada Way Stanford CA 94305

JOHNSON, JOHN RAUCHE, mfg. co. exec.; b. Webster City. Ia., July 23, 1920; s. Ernest Sidney and Elizabeth (Rauche) J.; student Westminister Coll., Fulton, Mo., 1943; B.S., Northwestern U., 1946; m. Joan Lloyd Treece, Nov. 16, 1945; children—Sydney, John Rauche. With Standard Kollsman Industries, Melrose Park, Ill., 1946-59, sr. v.p., 1957-59; with Royal Industries, Pasadena, Cal., 1959—, pres., 1959—, also dir.; dir. Acme Gen. Corp. Asso. U. So. Cal., 1965—; trustee Westminister Coll., 1967—. Served to 2d lt. USMCR, 1942-46. Mem. Aircraft Owners and Pilots Assn. Clubs: Annandale Golf (Pasadena); California (Los Angeles). Home: 1006 Fallen Leaf Rd Arcadia CA 91006 Office: 980 S Arroyo Pkwy Pasadena CA 91105

JOHNSON, JOHN ROCHELLE LEE, Jr., lawyer, chem. co. exec.; b. Franklin, Va., July 19, 1906; s. John Rochelle Lee and Susie (Rawls) J.; student Radford (Va.) State Tchrs. Coll., 1924-26; A.B., Coll. William and Mary, 1928, M.A., 1929; LL.B., Harvard, 1935; m. Josephine Lucas, Sept. 5, 1936; children—Susan C. (Mrs. C. William Tulloch), John Rochelle Lee, 3d, De Forest. Asst. librarian Coll. William and Mary, 1930-32; admitted to Va. bar. 1932, Del. bar, 1937; atty. SEC, Washington, 1935-36; counsel Radford Ordnance Works, 1940-41, Vol. Ordnance Works, Chattanooga, 1941-42; asst. gen. counsel legal dept. Hercules, Inc., Wilmington Del., 1936-40, 42-49, gen. counsel, 1949-55, v.p., mem. exec. com., 1955—, dir., 1954—. Mem. Am., Del. bar assns., Phi Beta Kappa, Phi Kappa Phi, Sigma Phi Sigma, Sigma Nu. Baptist. Clubs: Wilmington, Wilmington Country. Home: Hillendale Rd RD 1 Chadds Ford PA 19317 Office: 910 Market St Wilmington DE 19801

JOHNSON, JOHN S., business exec.; b. 1930; B.A., Yale, 1952, LL.B., 1955; married. With law firm Chadbourne, Parke, Whiteside & Wolff, 1959-64; with Anaconda Co., N.Y.C., 1964-70, asst. sec., 1967-68, sec.-treas., 1968-70; v.p., sec., gen. counsel, treas. Warnaco Inc., 1970—. Served with USNR, 1955-59. Office: 350 Lafayette St Bridgeport CT 06602

JOHNSON, JOHN SEWARD, bus. exec.; b. New Brunswick, N.J., 1895; s. Robert Wood and Evangeline (Armstrong) J.; student Yale; m. Esther Mead Underwood; children—Mary Lea (Mrs. William Ryan), Elaine (Mrs. Keith C. Wold), John Seward, Diana (Mrs. Richard G. Stokes), Jennifer (Mrs. Peter H. Gregg), James Loring. Vice pres. Johnson & Johnson, New Brunswick, N.J., 1931-, dir., 1921—, chmn. finance com. Trustee, Hunterdon County Med. Center. Served to lt. (j.g.) USN, 1917. Clubs: Cruising of America, New York Yacht, Royal Thames Yacht, Kringl Svenske Saleskant. Office: Johnson & Johnson 501 George St New Brunswick NJ 08903

JOHNSON, JOHN WILLIAM, Jr., lawyer; b. Landgale, Ala., July 19, 1920; s. John Will and Cordelia (Harrell) J.; B.S, U. Ala., 1942, LL.B., 1947; m. Elsie Brinson, June 24, 1950; children-John Will III, Robert Lee, Curti Morrell. Admitted to Ala. bar, 1947, since practiced in Lanett. Pres., dir. First Fed. Savs. and Loan Assn., W. Point, Ga.; dir. Citizens Nat. Bank, Shawmut, Ala. Mem. Ala. Senate, 1951-55. Served to 1st lt. AUS, 1943-46. Home: 6105 26th Av Langdale AL 36864 Office: Johnson Bldg Lanett AL 36863

JOHNSON, JOSEPH ESREY, former found. exec.; b. Longdale, Va., Apr. 30, 1906; s. Joseph Esrey and Margaret Hill (Hilles) J.; S.B., Harvard, 1927, A.M., 1932, Ph.D., 1943; LL.D., Williams Coll., 1951, Bowdoin Coll., 1967, L.I.U., 1969; m. Catherine D. W. Abbot, Dec. 31, 1930; children—Anne (Mrs. Herbert S. Stone III), William R. A. Instr. history Bowdoin Coll., 1934-35; instr. Williams Coll., 1936-38, asst. prof. history, 1938-47, on leave, 1942-47, prof., 1947-50; pres., trustee Carnegie Endowment for Internat. Peace, 1950-71, pres. emeritus, 1971—. Officer, Dept. State, 1942-47, acting chief. div. Internat. Security Affairs, 1944-45, chief 1945-47; adviser U.S. del. Dumbarton Oaks Conf., 1944, Inter- Am. Conf. on Problems War and Peace, Mexico City, 1945; expert, U.S. del. UN Conf. Internat. Orgn., San Francisco, 1945; adviser U.S. del. 1st session Gen. Assembly of UN, London, N.Y., 1946; adviser, U.S. rep. UN Security Council, London, N.Y., 1946; policy planning staff, Dept. of State, 1947; dep. U.S. rep. Interim Com. UN Gen. Assembly, 1948; adviser U.S. govt., dels. Internat. Labor Conf., 1957, 58; spl. rep. UN Conciliation Commn. for Palestine, 1961-62; alt. U.S. rep. 24th UN Gen. Assembly, 1969. Trustee, World Peace Found.; bd. dirs. Council Fgn. Relations, UN Assn. U.S. Fellow Am. Acad. Arts and Scis.; mem. Am. Hist. Assn., Inst. Strategic Studies (London) (v.p.). Clubs: Harvard, American Alpine, Century (N.Y.C.); Cosmos (Washington); Alpine (London). Home: 22 Winant Rd Princeton NJ 08540

JOHNSON, JOSEPH STUART, coll. dean b. Gower, Mo., May 8, 1912; s. Roy Ivan and Maud (Stuart) J.; B.S., U. Mo., 1932, M.S., 1934; Ph.D., Ia. State Coll. 1937; Sc.D., Lawrence Inst. Technology, 1963; m. Lucille Woodson, Dec. 23, 1934; children—Russell Ivan, Martha Maud (Mrs. Thomas Grant III), Sylvia. Grad. asst. Ia. State Coll., 1934-36, instr., 1936-37; instr., asst. prof. Mo. Sch. Mines, 1937-44; asso. research engr. U. Fla., 1946-47, asst. dean. prof. elec. engring., 1947-54; head Sch. Elec. Engring., Purdue U., 1954-57; dean Coll. of Engring., Wayne State U., 1957-67; dean Sch. Engring. U. Mo., Rolla, 1967—. Served as lt., USNR, 1944-46. Fellow Inst. Elec. and Electronic Engrs.; mem. Am. Soc. Engring. Edn. (v.p. 1963-65), Nat. Soc. Profl. Engrs., Phi Kappa Phi, Phi Eta Sigma, Gamma Alpha, Scabbard and Blade, Pi Mu Epsilon, Sigma Pi Sigma, Sigma Tau, Triangle, Sigma Xi, Tau Beta Pi, Eta Kappa Nu. Presbyn. Home: 1000 Vista Dr Rolla MO 65401

JOHNSON, JOSEPH YANDELL, architect; b. St. Louis, Oct. 1, 1911; s. Joseph Yandell and Bertha (Seitz) J.; B.Arch., Washington U., 1933, M.Arch., 1934; m. Mary Louise Pipkin, July 1, 1931. Pvt. archtl. practice, Little Rock, 1946-67; adminstr. Erhart, Eichnabaum, Rauch & Blass, Little Rock, 1970—; works include Nat. Old Line Ins. Co. bldg. and addition, 1st Christian Ch. of Jonesboro (Ark.). Mem. Ark. Bd. Architects, 1953-61, sec., 1954-61; pres., chmn. Ark. Festival of Arts, 1965. Dir. Family Service Agy., 1965-68. Served with USNR, 1942-45; PTO. James Harrison Steadman fellow, 1936. Fellow A.I.A. (pres. Ark. 1952-53). Home: 5117 Crestwood Dr Little Rock AR 72207 Office: Continental Bldg Little Rock AR 72201

JOHNSON, JOSEPHINE WINSLOW, (Mrs. Grant G. Cannon), author; b. Kirkwood, Mo., June 20, 1910; d. Benjamin H. and Ethel (Franklin) Johnson; student Washington U., 1933, L.H.D. (hon.), 1970; m. Grant G. Cannon, Apr. 5, 1942; children—Terence, Jane Ann, Carol Lynn. Author: Now in November, 1934 (Pulitzer prize 1935); Jordanstown, 1937; Wildwood, 1947; (short stories) Winter Orchard, 1936; (poetry) Years End, 1939; (novel) The Dark Traveler, 1963; The Sorcerer's Son (short stories), 1965; The Inland Island, 1969; also writer numerous stories in Best Short Stories, other anthologies 1944-46, (O'Henry Meml. award 1934, 35, 42-45). Recipient Alumnae citation Washington U., 1955; Cin. Inst. Fine Arts award, 1964; Ohioana Library citation, 1964; Sarah Chapman Francis medal Ganden Club Am., 1970. Mem. Authors Guild. Home: 4907 Klatte Rd Cincinnati OH 45244

JOHNSON, JULIAN, surgeon; b. Cox's Creek, Ky., July 3, 1906; s. John Robert and Julia Ann (Spight) J.; A.B., Maryville Coll., 1927; M.D., U. Pa., 1931, D.Sc., 1939; m. Mary Christine Benn, June 30, 1933; 1 dau., Joan Ellen. Intern, Hosp. U. Pa., 1931-33, surg. fellow, 1933-39; asso. surgery U. Pa., 1939-45, asst. prof. surgery, 1945-47, asso. prof., 1947-49, prof., 1950- -. Served as lt. col. AUS, 1942-46. Mem. Am. Surg. Soc., Am. Assn. Thoracic Surgery, Soc. Clin. Surgery, Soc. Vascular Surgeons, Am. Coll. Chest Physicians, Phila. Acad. Surgery. Author: (with C.K. Kirby) Surgery of the Chest 1952, 4th edit. (with H. McVaugh Jr., J. Waldhausen), 1970. Home: 31 Righter's Mill Rd Gladwyne PA 19035 Office: 3400 Spruce St Philadelphia PA 19104

JOHNSON, KARL RICHARD, coll. pres.; b. Galesburg, Ill., Feb. 28, 1907; s. Charles Theodore Emanuel and Sigrid (Swanson) J.; B.S., Knox Coll., 1929; M.S., U. Colo., 1932, Ph.D., 1939; m. Evelyn Jo Hilander, August 7, 1943; children—Thomas Arthur, Anne Christine. Instr. in sci. and music Toluca (Ill.) High Sch., 1929-31, Abingdon (Ill.) High Sch., 1932-35; instr. sci. Thornton Twp. High Sch., Harvey, Ill., 1935- 37; asst. in biology U. Colo., 1931-32, 1937-39; instr. biology Knox Coll., 1939-40; head, sci. dept. Nat. Coll. Edn., Evanston, Ill., 1940- 48, vice chmn. adminstrv. council and asst. to pres., 1945-48; pres., 1949—; asso. prof. biology Augustana Coll., 1948-49. Vice pres. Fedn. Ill. Colls.; pres. Asso. Colls. Ill.; trustee Luth. Student Found. Active in civilian def. work tng. instrnl. staff and operation of control center, Evanston, World War II. Recipient Alumni Achievement award Knox Coll.; award in air-age edn. Air Force Edn. Fellow A.A.A.S., Ill. Acad. Sci., Am. Assn. U. Profs.; mem. Nat. Intercollegiate Flying Assn. (dir.), Nat. Aviation Edn. Council (pres.), Nat. Aeros. Assn. (dir.), Asso. Colls. Ill. (pres.), C. of C. (dir.), Ecol. Soc. Am., Sigma Xi, Beta Beta Beta. Lutheran. Rotarian. Clubs: University, Economic, Executives. Contbr. articles to U. of Colo. Studies and Ecology. Office: National College of Education Evanston IL 60201

JOHNSON, KEACH, educator; b. East Moline, Ill., June 21, 1910; s. Arthur B. and Mable (Doyel) J.; B.A., Ill. Coll., 1932; M.A., U. Ill., 1935; Ph.D., U. Ia., 1949; postgrad. Cornell U., 1937, U. Chgo., 1941; m. Elizabeth Ruth Bishop, Apr. 2, 1944; children—Martha, Jeanne, Carole. Tchr. high sch., Jacksonville, Ill., 1936-41; instr. Ill. Coll., Jacksonville, 1941-44; historian USAAF Hist. Office, Wright Field, 1944-45; instr. U. Ia., 1946-48, U. Me., 1949-52; instr. Drake U., 1952-53, asst. prof., 1953-62, asso. prof., 1962-68, prof. history, 1968—, chmn. dept., 1967—. Mem. Am. Hist. Assn., Orgn. Am. Historians, Am. Assn. U. Profs., Phi Beta Kappa. Mem. Unitarian Ch. Contbr. articles profl. jours. Home: 1106 44th St Des Moines IA 50311

JOHNSON, KEITH, Jamaican diplomat; b. Spanish Town, St. Catherine, Jamaica, July 29, 1921; s. Septimus A. and Emily Johnson; grad. Kingston Coll., Jamaica, 1937; grad. studies demography, Columbia, 1950-51; children—Hope and Marie (twins). With Jamaica Civil Service, 1939-48, statistician, 1946- 48; research asst. Bur. Applied Social Research, Columbia, 1948-49; profl. trainee various positions, then social affairs officer UN population br., dept. social and econ. affairs UN, 1949-62; formerly consul gen. for Jamaica in U.S.; Jamaica's permanent rep. to UN; Non-resident ambassador to Republic of Argentina, 1969—. Recipient Jamaica Ind. medal, 1963; Internat. Relations award West Indian Students Assn. Inc., U.S. and City Coll. chpt., 1963; Human Relations award West Indian Cultural Soc., Boston, 1965; Humanitarian award West Indian Celebration Com., 1966; Franklin Mint Peace medal, 1967; grand marshall Martin Luther King Jr. Meml. Day Parade, 1968; Comdr. Order of Distinction, Jamaica, 1970. Mem. 369th Vets.' Assn. (hon.), Inst. Sci. Study Population, Soc. Fgn. Consuls, West Indian Students Assn. (pres. 1954-57, chmn. adv. com. 1958- -). Address: Permanent Mission of Jamaica to UN 235 E 42d St New York City NY 10017

JOHNSON, KELLUM, ins. co. exec.; b. Wortham, Tex., Oct. 29, 1904; s. William J. and Emma (Alston) J.; student So. Meth. U.; m. Louise Gaston, Dec. 2, 1950 (dec.); m. 2d, Jean Sheppard, June 29, 1962; children—Marilyn, Nina, Kellum. Treas., St. Mary's Coll., Dallas, 1925-27; with Gulf Ins. Co., Dallas, 1927—, v.p., treas,, 1944-56, sr. v.p., treas., 1956-71, cons., 1971—, also dir.; sr. v.p., treas., dir. subsidiaries Atlantic Ins. Co.; Select Ins. co.; dir. UCC Financial Corp., Reliance Chem. Co., Sci. Assos. Inc., Triton Oil and Gas Corp., First Nat. Bank, Lafayette, La. Foreman, Dallas County Grand Jury, 1948. Head delegation Cultural Exchange Program sponsored by U.S. Dept State to USSR, 1958. Pres. Dallas Council Camp Fire Girls, 1947-48, S.W. area council YMCAs, 1956-57; chmn. Downtown YMCA, Dallas, 1956-57. Trustee N. Dallas-Park Cities Kiwanis Trust Fund. Recipient Outstanding Service award S.W. YMCA Phys. Edn. Congress, 1950, Distinguished Service award, 1959; named Sportsman- of-the-Month, Dallas C. of C., 1958; Silver Beaver award Boy Scouts Am. Mem. Amateur Athletic Union U.S. (pres. 1958-59), U.S. Olympic Com. (dir. 1956-64), Ins. Accounting and Statistical Assn. (dir. 1960-64), Dallas Personnel Assn. (past pres.), Ins. Club Dallas, Order Blue Goose. Episcopalian. Clubs: Admiral's, Kiwanis (pres. N. Dallas- Park Cities 1952), Chaparral, Cipango. Home: 9324 Waterview Rd Dallas TX 75218 Office: PO Box 1771 Dallas TX 75221

JOHNSON, KENNETH LAWSON, army officer; b. Portland, Ore., Sept. 10, 1919; s. Bernhard and Irene (Lawson) J.; B.S., U. Md., grad. Inf. Officer Candidate Sch., 1942, Inf. Advanced Course, 1950, Command and Gen. Staff Coll., 1953, Army War Coll., 1959; m. Charlotte Katherine Kuzawski, Dec. 4, 1945; 1 son, Michael Kenneth. Enlisted Minn. N.G., 1940, called to active duty, 1941, commd. 2d lt. U.S. Army, 1942, advanced through grades to maj. gen., 1969; Assigned N. Ireland, Normandy, Holland invasions, Battle of Bulge, 1943-45; G-3 40th Inf. Div., Korea, 1953-54; officer assignment div. Hdqrs. Dept. Army, 1954-58; joint plans officer CINCPAC, exec. asst. dept. chief staff fgn. affairs and logistics, 1959-61; battle group comdr. 25th Inf. Div., 1961-63; assigned Office Personnel Operations Hdqrs. Dept. Army, 1963-64; chief spl. rev. div. ODCSPER, 1964-66; asst. div. comdr. 2d Inf. Div., Korea, 1966-67; dir. enlisted personnel Dept. Army, 1967-68; dir. procurement and distbn. ODCSPER, 1968-70; comdg. gen. 7th Inf. Div., Korea, 1970; dep. chief Office Personnel Operations, Dept. Army, 1970—. Decorated D.S.M., Silver Star, Legion of Merit with 2 oak leaf clusters, Bronze Star with V device and oak leaf cluster, Commendation medal with 3 oak leaf clusters, Purple Heart; Belgium Fourragere; Mil. Order Wilhelm of Orange; French Fourragere; Netherlands Orange Lanyard. Mem. U.S. Army Assn. Club: Army Navy Country. Home: 2111 Jefferson Davis Hwy Arlington VA 22202 Office: Office Personnel Operations Dept Army Washington DC 20310

JOHNSON, KENNETH LEROY, physiologist, educator; b. Wausa, Neb., May 24, 1914; s. Victor August and Mathilda (Anderson) J.; B.S., Bethany (Kan.) Coll., 1934; M.S., U. So. Cal., 1940, Ph.D., 1950; m. Katherine Louise Watts, June 5, 1938. Instr. sci. and speech Canton (Kan.) High Sch., 1934-37; asst. prof. biol. sci., dean men Bethany Coll., 1937-43; instr. Navy V-5 Program, U. Kan., 1943-44; instr. physiology Ia. State Coll., 1944-45; instr. biol. sci., dean men Reedley (Cal.) Jr. Coll., 1945-46; asst. prof. physiology San Jose (Cal.) State Coll., 1947-51; mem. faculty Long Beach (Cal.) State Coll., 1951—, prof. physiology, 1952-, chmn. div. natural sci., 1952-67; mem. Cal. State Colls. State Acad. Senate, 1968-71; spl. research hypothermia-metabolism relationships. Mem. A.A.A.S. Cal., So. Cal. acads. scis., Sigma Xi, Pi Delta Kappa, Phi Kappa Phi. Home: 636 Flint Av Long Beach CA 90814

JOHNSON, KENNETH OWEN, audiologist, assn. exec.; b. St. Paul, Jan. 26, 1920; s. Ernest Wilbert and Anna Mae (Little) J.; B.A., Macalester Coll., St. Paul, 1946; M.A., U. Minn., 1948; Ph.D., Stanford, 1952; m. Dorothy Schlesselman, Sept. 5, 1949. Chief, audiology and speech correction program VA, Washington, 1954- 56, past. cons. acoustical audiology; dir. San Francisco Hearing and Speech Center, 1956-57; asst. clin. prof. dept. surgery Stanford Med. Sch., 1957; exec. sec. Am. Speech and Hearing Assn., 1957—, dir. Deafness, Speech and Hearing Publs., 1959—, past pres.; chmn. Coalition Ind. Health Professions, 1970—; cons. for speech, hearing and lang. to Head Start program; mem. research fellowship bd. U.S. Vocational Rehab. Adminstrn., 1964-71. Bd. dirs. Com. Handicapped People to People Program; trustee Am. Speech and Hearing Found. Certified in speech pathology and audiology Am. Speech and Hearing Assn. Fellow Am. Speech and Hearing Assn. (editor jour.); mem. A.A.A.S., Am. Phychol. Assn., Speech Assn. Am., Internat. Assn. Logopedics and Phoniatrics. Home: 7303 Broxburn Ct Bethesda MD 20034 Office: 9030 Old Georgetown Rd Washington DC 20014

JOHNSON, KIMBELL, govt. ofcl.; b. Brundidge, Ala., Dec. 16, 1913; s. Arthur Lee and Estelle (Kimbell) J.; student Birmingham So. Coll., 1930-31, Ala. State Tchrs. Coll., Troy, 1931-33; B.S., U. Ala., 1936; m. Mary Hill McGilvray, Sept. 23, 1934; children—Frances Kaye (Mrs. Kenneth Duncan), Sara Ann. Tchr. pub. schs. Ala., 1934-39; with U.S. Civil Service Commn., Washington, 1939—, dir. Bur. Personnel Investigations, 1954—. Recipient U.S. Commr's Distinguished Service Medal, 1966. Mem. Fed. Law Enforcement Assn., Mason-Dixon Outdoor Writers Assn. Methodist. Home: 6700 Bellcrest Rd Hyattsville MD 20782 Office: U S Civil Service Commn 1900 E St Washington DC 20415

JOHNSON, LADY BIRD, (b. Claudia Alta Taylor) (Mrs. Lyndon Baines Johnson); b. Karnack, Tex., Dec. 22, 1912; d. Thomas Jefferson Taylor; B.A., U. Tex., 1933, B. Journalism, 1934; LL.D., Tex. Woman's U., 1964; Litt.D., U. Tex., 1964, Middlebury (Vt.) Coll., 1967; L.H.D., Williams Coll., 1967; H.H.D., Southwestern U., 1967; m. Lyndon Baines Johnson (36th Pres. U.S.), Nov. 17, 1934; children—Lynda Bird (Mrs. Charles S. Robb), Luci Baines (Mrs. Patrick J. Nugent). Mgr. husband's congl. office, Washington, 1941-42; owner, operator radio-TV sta. KTBC, Austin, Tex., 1942—, cattle ranches, Tex., 1943—, also cotton and timberlands, Ala. Hon. chmn. numerous civic and charitable orgns., drives; founder Com. for more Beautiful Capital, 1965; mem. Adv. Bd. Nat. Parks, Historic Sites, Bldgs. and Monuments; co- chmn. Nat. Cultural Center; mem. nat. com. Helen Keller World Crusade for Blind; active environmental, nat. beautification projects. Hon. trustee Washington Gallery Modern Art; regent U. Tex. Recipient Togetherness award McCall's Mag., 1958, Crystal citation Fashion Group Phila., 1961, Distinguished Achievement award Washington Heart Assn., 1962, citation Nat. Assn. Colored Women's Clubs, 1962, Humanitarian award Ararat chpt. B'nai B'rith, Industry citation Am. Women in Radio and TV, 1963, Humanitarian citation Vols. Am., 1963; numerous others. Mem. Federated Bus. and Profl. Women's Club, (Business woman's award 1961), Am. Assn. U. Women (life Tex. div.), Internat. Club II, Theta Sigma Phi (citation 1961), others. Episcopalian. Author Memoirs. Narrator TV prodn. A Visit to Washington with Mrs. Lyndon B. Johnson, 1965. Address: L B J Ranch Stonewall TX 78671

JOHNSON, LAMONT, stage and film dir.; b. Stockton, Cal. Sept. 30, 1922; s. Ernest Lamont and Ruth Alice (Fairchild) J.; student U. Cal. at Los Angeles, 1942-43; m. Toni Merrill, July 27, 1945; children—Jeremy Carolyn, Christopher Anthony. Produced, appeared in leading role in world premiere Gertrude Stein's Yes Is For A Very Young Man, 1946; dir. world premiere 2 Thornton Wilder one act plays, Berlin, 1957; dir. 8 profl. Theatre Group's prodns. U. Cal., Los Angeles, including premiere prodn. Under Milkwood, 1959; founder, mem. exec. com. Theatre Group, 1959—; dir. Iphigenie en Tauride with Marilyn Horne and Los Angeles Philharmonic Orch., 1964, Warner Bros. film, A Covenant with Death, 1966-67, Universal film My Sweet Charlie, 1969 United Artist film The McKenzie Break, 1970, Paramount film A Gunfight, 1970. Recipient Screen Dirs. Guild Most Distinguished Directorial Achievement in Television award for premiere Profiles in Courage, 1964, 70 for My Sweet Charlie. Address: 601 Paseo Miramar Pacific Palisades CA 90272

JOHNSON, LEE HARNIE, coll. dean; b. Houston, Jan. 4, 1909; s. Lee Harnie and Isabelle (Smart) J.; B.A., Rice Inst., 1930, M.A. 1931; M.S., Harvard, 1932, Sc.D., 1935; m. Eulalie Woolverton McKay, Oct. 19,1940; children—Lee McKay, William Irving. Fellow in math. Rice Inst., 1930-31; asst. in civil engring. Harvard, 1932-35; asst. engring. aide, United States Waterways Expt. Station, Vicksburg, Miss., 1935-36; asst. to engr. in charge design, U.S. Engr. Office, Mobile, Ala., 1936-37; dean engring. and prof. civil engring. U. Miss., 1937-50, dir. def., war tng. program, 1941-45; dean engring., prof. civil engring. Tulane U. 1950—. Graham Baker and Hohenthal scholar Rice Inst.; Hilton Scholar Harvard Mem. Am. Soc.E., Am. Soc. Engring Edn., La. Engring Soc., Phi Beta Kappa, Kappa Delta Phi, Tau Beta Pi, Chi Epsilon, Gamma Alpha, Omicron Delta Kappa. Democrat. Presbyn. Clubs: New Orleans Country, Boston (New Orleans); Stratford, Lake Shore. Author: The Slide Rule, 1947; Nomography and Empirical Equations, 1952; Engineering: Principles and Problems, 1960. Contbr. to engring. jours. Home: 1338 Audubon St New Orleans LA 70118

JOHNSON, LELAND H., banker; b. Duluth, Minn., Oct. 9, 1915; s. John O. and Christie (Evans) J.; student Pacific U., Pacific Coast Banking Sch.; certificate Am. Inst. Banking; m. E. Gray Cravat, Oct. 12, 1940; children—Leland Robbin, Lynn Cravat. With Bank of Cal.,

N.A., 1952—, sr. v.p., mgr. Portland (Ore.) br., 1962-64, exec. v.p., San Francisco, 1964—. Dir. Fred Meyer Inc. Bd. dirs. Pacific U., Herbert A. Templeton Found. Served with AUS, 1943-46; PTO. Clubs: San Francisco Golf, Family, Stock Exchange (San Francisco). Home: 81 Melanie Lane Atherton CA 94025 Office: 400 California St San Francisco CA 94104

JOHNSON, LELAND PARRISH, educator, biologist; b. Ponemah, Ill., Nov. 14, 1910; s. Carl W. and Dora M. (Parrish) J.; B.S., Mommouth Coll., 1932; M.S., State U. Ia., 1937; Ph.D., 1942; Ford faculty fellow, Harvard, 1955-56; m. Marion E. Schiess, Aug. 25, 1940; children—Christine Ann, Don Alan. Sci. tchr., Reynolds (Ill.) High Sch., 1930-36; mem. faculty Drake U., 1937—, prof. biology, 1947—, chmn. dept., 1956—, coordinator sci. div., 1958, dean Coll. Liberal Arts, 1971—, dir. cancer research, 1958—. Dir. insts. tchr. research participation programs NSF, 1959—; cons. gen. edn. Ia. League Nursing, 1958—; ednl. adv. bd. Ia. Meth. Hosp., 1952—; chmn. Ia. Bd. Basic Sci. Examiners, 1957—. Recipient Distinguished Alumni award Monmouth Coll., 1957. Mem. N.E.A., A.A.A.S., Am. Micros. Soc., N. Y., Ia. (pres. 1965-66) acads. sci., Soc. Protozoologists, Am. Inst. Biol. Scis., Nat. Assn. Research Sci. Teaching Nat. Assn. Biology Tchrs., Assn. Midwest Biology Tchrs. (pres. 1958). Soc. History Sci., Phi Beta Kappa, Sigma Xi. Contbr. lab. manuals, monographs, articles. Home: 3223 Cottage Grove Des Moines IA 50311

JOHNSON, LEROY DENNIS, univ. dean; b. Langhorne, Pa., Oct. 4, 1908; s. Thomas Pierson and Gertrude (Danson) J.; A.B., Lincoln U. (Pa.), 1931; M.S., U. Pa., 1934, Ph.D., 1954; m. Goldye Hortense Kent, Dec. 21, 1940; children—Jacquelyn Ann (Mrs. Val Jordan), Leroy Kent. Prof. chemistry, dean Storer Coll., 1934-54; asso. prof. chemistry, prof. chemistry, dean, registrar Lincoln U., 1955—. Chmn. blood program Brandywine br. A.R.C., 1968—; pres. Oxford Area Civic Assn., 1970-71. Bd. dirs. Opportunities Industrialization Centers. Recipient NSF fellowships and grants, 1960-68. Fellow Am. Inst. Chemists; mem. Am. Chem. Soc., Sigma Xi. Presbyn. Mason. Author: Gen. Sci. Lab. Manual, 1946. Contbr. articles profl. jours. Home: Box 98 Lincoln University PA 19352

JOHNSON, LESTER ELWIN, hosp. adminstr.; b. Winthrop, Minn., Apr. 2, 1923; s. Louis Magnus and Blenda (Nelson) J.; A.B. in Econs., Ill. Coll., 1948; M.Hosp. Adminstrn., Washington U., St. Louis, 1954; m. Margaret Lenore Foley, Oct. 7, 1945; children—Stephen Willard, Blenda Alice, Katherine Sue, Peter Eric. Br. office cashier Swift and Co., Jacksonville, Ill., 1948- 49; prodn. cost accountant Eli Bridge Co., Jacksonville, 1949-51; asst. adminstrn. Bapt. Hosp., Alexandria La., 1954-56; asst. supt. Willmar (Minn.) State Hosp., 1956-61, adminstr., 1961—. Treas., Kandiyohi County Hist. Soc., 1966-68, bd. dirs., 1971—. Served with AUS, World War II. Decorated Purple Heart, Bronze Star medal. Fellow Am. Coll. Hosp. Adminstrs., Royal Soc. Health; mem. Am. Hosp. Assn., Internat. Hosp. Fedn. Presbyn. (deacon, elder). Kiwanian (dir. 1962-63, pres. Willmar 1968). Home: 901 W 3d St Willmar MN 56201 Office: Box 1128 Willmar MN 56201

JOHNSON, LEWIS KERR, educator; b. Staunton, Va., Aug. 4, 1904; s. Walter Bell and Lee (Giles) J.; B.S. in Commerce. U. Va., 1927, M.S. in Econs., 1928; Ph.D., Ohio State U., 1943; m. Margaret Lupton, Dec. 21, 1927; 1 dau., Martha Kerr. Asst. prof. econs. Mercer U., 1928-33; faculty Washington and Lee U., 1933—, prof. commerce, 1948—, head dept., Sch. Commerce and Adminstrn., 1950-68; vis. prof. U. N.C., summer 1961; prin lectr. 2d annual tng. program Roanoke (Va.) Personnell Assn., 1956; mem. Ford Ednl. Symposium, Ford Motor Co., 1955; lectr. CIO Steelworkers Workshop, U. Va., 1961. Mem. com. markets and marketing Adv. Council Va. Economy, 1948—. Served to lt. comdr. USNR, 1943-46. Mem. Phi Eta Sigma, Beta Gamma Sigma, Lambda Chi Alpha, Delta Sigma Pi. Baptist. Author. Marketing in Virginia, 1950; Sales and Marketing Management, 1957; also articles.Home: 32 University Pl Lexington VA 24450

JOHNSON, LINCOLN F., Jr., educator, art and film historian; b. Lynn, Mass., May 21, 1920; s. Lincoln F. and Theresa (McGowan) J.; A.B., Bowdoin Coll., 1942; M.A., Harvard, 1947; Ph.D., 1956. Vis. lectr. Wellesley Coll., 1949-50; mem. faculty Goucher Coll., 1950—, chmn. dept. fine arts, 1959-69, prof. art, 1963—, art critic Balt. Sun, 1971—. Mem. accessions com. Balt. Mus. Art, 1963-69; mem. Balt. Municipal Arts. Commn., 1960—. Trustee Md. Inst. Coll. Art, 1957—. Served with USAAF, 1942-46. Longfellow fellow, 1942; Beacon fellow, 19498-49; Fulbright fellow, 1962. Mem. Coll. Art Assn., Am. Assn. U. Profs., Phi Beta Kappa. Home: 111 Crosskeys Rd Baltimore MD 21211 Office: Goucher Coll Towson MD 21204

JOHNSON, LINDSAY FRANKLIN, mining cons.; b. Greensboro, N.C., Oct. 28, 1907; s. Lindsay F. and Flora McA. (Long) J.; student Eldon Coll. (N.C.), Columbia; m. Elsie M. Taverna, Apr. 9, 1934; 1 dau., E. Kerala. Resident-mcht., Malabar Coast, S. India, 1928-41; with N.J. Zinc Co., N.Y.C., 1942-70, successively adminstrv. asst., asst. to v.p., asst. gen. mgr. Palmerton (Pa.) plants, asst. to pres., 1942-55, v.p., 1955-66, pres., 1966-70, also treas., dir.; mining cons., 1970—. Mem. Am. Inst. Mining Metall. and Petroleum Engrs. Presbyn. (elder). Clubs: Saucon Valley Country (Bethlehem, Pa.); Down Town Assn., Union, Mining (N.Y.C.); Country of North Carolina (Pinehurst). Home: Polk Valley Rd R D 1 Hellertown PA 18055 Office: 140 SW Broad St Southern Pines NC 28387

JOHNSON, LOFTIN, utility exec.; b. Fair Bluff, N.C., Dec. 15, 1910; s. James Edwin and Mary Elizabeth (Loftin) J.; B.S. in Elec. Engring., U. Fla., 1934; m. Melvene Young, July 2, 1939; children—James Loftin, David Heywood. With Fla. Power & Light Co., 1935—, supt. transmission and distbn., 1952-56, operating v.p., 1956—. Served to lt. USNR, World War II. Methodist. Home: 6150 Chapman Field Dr Miami FL 33156 Office: 4200 W Flagler St Miami FL 33134

JOHNSON, LORAND VICTOR, ophthalmologist; b. Blockton, Ia., May 28, 1905; s. Silas Weygandt and Julia Ann (Peters) J.; A.B., Huron Coll., 1927; M.A., Boston U., 1931; M.D., 1933; postgrad., Harvard, 1937; m. Dorothy Storm, 1941; children—Carolyn Jane (Mrs. Robert F. Parker), Madelyn Mayhew (Mrs. Robert Zolto), Lorand Victor. Grad. asst. Mass. Eye & Ear Infirmary, 1933, resident, 1935-37; intern Salem (Mass.) Hosp., 1934-35; practice medicine, specializing in ophthalmology, Cleve., 1937—; instr. ophthalmology Western Res. U., U. Hosps. Cleve., 1937-40, sr. instr., 1940-45, asst. clin. prof., 1945-48, asso. clin. prof., 1948-51, clin. prof., 1951-70, emeritus, 1970—, ophthalmologist in charge, 1950-60, also dir. lab. research in ophthalmology; cons. Nat. Soc. Prevention Blindness. Vice chmn. Wise Owl Club Ohio Safety Council, 1945-48. Recipient certificates of award Pan-Am. Assn. Ophthalmology, 1948, Am. Acad. Ophthalmology and Otolaryngology, 1954. Diplomate Nat. Bd. Med. Examiners, Am. Bd. Ophthalmology. Mem. Assn. for Research Ophthalmology (trustee E. Central sect., past sec.-treas.), S.A.R., Cleve. Mus. Art, Western Res. Hist. Soc., Cleve. Ophthal. Club, Pan-Am. Ophthal. Assn., Am. Ophthalmology Soc., A.C.S., A.A.A.S., Assn. Coll. Profs., Cleve. Diabetes Club, Cuyahoga County Med. Library Assn., Med. Arts Club, Cleve. Clin. Club, Sigma Xi. Baptist. Clubs: Cleveland Skating, University (both Cleve.). Author: The Descendants of William and John Johnson, Colonial Friends of Virginia, 1942. Contbr. Blakiston's New Gould Med. Dictionary, 1957 articles ophthal. jours. Home: 17600 Parkland Dr Shaker Heights OH 44120 Office: 10515 Carnegie Av Cleveland OH 44106

JOHNSON, LOWELL FERRIS, drug and food mfr.; b. Butler, N.J., Sept. 21, 1912; s. George F. and Eliza (James) J.; B.S., N.J. State U., 1934; Ed.M., Rutgers U., 1938; postgrad. N.Y. U; m. Josephine Herche, July 7, 1939 (dec. Jan. 5, 1964); children—Don W., Joy C. Johnson; m. 2d, Beverly Herman, Sept. 25, 1965. Mem. faculty Rutgers U., 1941-45; with Am. Home Products Corp., N.Y.C., 1945, mem. operations com., 1957—, v.p. indsl. relations, 1959-61, v.p., 1961—; v.p., dir. Citizen's Realty Co.; dir. Bankers Nat. Ins. Co.,United Nat. Bank Central Jersey, North Plainfield Savs. & Loan Assn., LOR, Inc.; former spl. lectr. Rutgers U., Columbia, N.Y. U., George Washington U., U. Md. Mgmt. team U.S. State Dept. Mission to Guatemala, 1961. Bd govs. Mulhlenberg Hosp.; chmn. bd., chmn. exec. com., mem. internat. com. Am. Heart Assn.; trustee N.J. State Coll. Recipient Boss-of-the-Year award N.Y. chpt. Nat. Sec. Assn., 1959. Mem. N.J. C. of C. (chmn. mgmt.-employee relations com.), Commerce and Industry Assn. (chmn. state and local affairs com, mem. mems. council), U.S. C. of C., Council State Chambers Commerce U.S., Soc. Advancement Mgmt., Am. Arbitration Assn. (nat. labor panel), Am. Mgmt. Assn. (personnel planning council), Nat Indsl. Conf. Bd., N.Y. Indsl. Relations Assn. (past pres.) Home: 40 Mali Dr North Plainfield NJ 07060 Office: 685 3d Av New York City NY 10017

JOHNSON, LUDWELL HARRISON, III, educator; b. Charleston W.Va., Mar. 30, 1927; s. Ludwell Harrison, Jr. and Sarah (Graham) J.; B.A., Johns Hopkins, 1952, Ph.D., 1955, m. Pamela Doreen Cartin, Apr. 7, 1957; 1 dau., Abigail Cabell. Acting asst. prof. history Coll. William and Mary, 1955-56; asst. prof. history Fla. State U., 1956-58; mem. faculty Coll. William and Mary, 1958—, prof. history, 1965—, chmn. dept., 1966—. Served with USNR, 1945-46. Mem. Am. Hist. Assn., Phi Beta Kappa. Author: Red River Campaign: Politics and Cotton in the Civil War, 1958. Home: 109 Willow Dr Williamsburg VA 23185

JOHNSON, LYNDON BAINES, former Pres. U.S.; b. nr. Stonewall, Tex., Aug. 27, 1908; s. Samuel Ealy and Rebekah (Baines) J.; B.S., Southwest Tex. State Coll., San Marcos, Tex., 1930; Postgrad. Georgetown Law Sch., 1935; LL.D. (hon.) Southwestern U., 1943, Howard Payne U., 1957, Brown U., 1959, Bethany Coll., 1959, U. Hawaii, 1961, U. Philippines, 1961, Gallaudet Coll., 1961, East Ky. State Coll., 1961, William Jewell Coll., 1961, Elon Coll., 1962, Southwest Tex. State Tchrs. Coll., 1962, Wayne State U., 1963, Jacksonville U., 1963, McMurray Coll., 1963, U. Md., 1963, Tufts U., 1963; U. Cal., 1964, U. Tex., 1964, Swarthmore Coll., 1964, Syracuse U., 1964, Georgetown U., 1964; U. Ky., 1965, Baylor U., 1965, Howard U., 1965, Catholic U., 1965; D.C.L., Holy Cross Coll., 1964, U. Mich., 1964; L.H.D., Oklahoma City U., 1960, Yeshiva U., 1961; m. Claudia Taylor, Nov. 17, 1934; children—Lynda Bird (Mrs. Charles Robb), Luci Baines (Mrs. Patrick J. Nugent). Tchr. Houston (Tex.) public schs., 1930-31; sec. Congressman Richard M. Kleberg, Tex., 1931-35; state dir. Nat. Youth Adminstrn. of Tex., 1935-37; elected to 75th Congress (1937-38) to fill unexpired term of Congressman James P. Buchanan, 10th Tex. Dist.; re-elected to 76th to 80th Congresses (1938-48); U.S. senator, 1949-61, minority leader, 83d Congress, majority leader, 84th-86th Congresses; v.p. U.S., 1961-63; 36th pres. U.S. (succeeded to the Presidency of U.S. Nov. 22, 1963 on death of Pres. John F. Kennedy), elected Pres., Nov. 3, 1964, took office Jan. 20, 1965. Chmn. Pres.'s Com. on Equal Employment Opportunity; chmn. Nat. Aeronautics and Space Council; chmn. Peace Corps Adv. Council; mem. NSC Council. Comdr. USNR, active duty, 1941-42. Democrat. Mem. Christian Ch. Address: LBJ Ranch Stonewall TX 78671

JOHNSON, MALCOLM BLAINE, newspaper editor; b. Wardner, Ida., Feb. 13, 1913; s. James Blaine and Winifred (Ashley) J.; B.S., U. Fla., 1936; m. Dorothy Lucile Burt, Oct. 23, 1937; 1 dau., Donna Burt (Mrs. Sam H. Moorer, Jr.). Reporter, Jacksonville (Fla.) Jour., 1936-37; city editor Tallahassee (Fla.) Democrat, 1937-40, editor, 1954—; corr. A.P., 1940-54; cons. World Book Ency., Kiplinger Fla. Letter. Pres. Tallahassee Hist. Soc., Founders, Inc.; bd. dirs. Fla. Heritage Found., Audubon Soc. Recipient Centennial award for meritorious service U. Fla., 1953, Fla. Bar award for outstanding journalistic contbn. to adminstrn. of justice, 1956, 60, 67, Freecom Found. citation, 1959, George Washington medal, 1961, Fla. Assn. Architects award as outstanding journalist, 1965, Tallahassee Jr. C. of C. award for outstanding contbn. to better govt., 1965, Fla. Legislators Press award as outstanding columnist, 1967, Fla. Hist. Soc. award to merit, 1968, Colonial Dames award, 1968. Mem. Fla. (dir.), Am.. socs. newspaper editors, Fla. Capital Press Club (past pres.), Nat. Conf. Editorial Writers. Rotarian (past pres.). Club: Torch (past pres.) (Tallahassee). Home: 2933 Meridian Rd Tallahassee FL 32303 Office: 277 N Magnolia Dr Tallahassee FL 32302

JOHNSON, MARSHALL LAMOINE, food co. exec.; b. Eau Claire, Wis., June 17, 1931; s. Guy G. and Mary (McMahon) J.; student U. Wis., 1929-30; m. Mildred I. Poff, May 6, 1935. Asst. purchasing agt., sales mgr. Kroger Co., Madison, Wis., 1930-35; with Kellog Sales Co., 1935-70, v.p., Western regional mgr., Kansas City, Mo., 1954-59, v.p. central regional mgr., Chgo., 1959-63, v.p. Eastern regional mgr., N.Y.C., 1963-64, v.p. central regional mgr., 1964-70; pres., chief exec. officer, vice chmn. bd., dir. Salada Foods Ltd., Don Mills, Ont., Can., 1970—; pres., Milamar Co.; pres., dir. Bell-Noll Woman's Bakery Ltd., Brit. Honduras Fruit Co. Ltd., Canadian Food Products Ltd., Canadian Food Products Sales Ltd., Chip- Boy Ltd., Coffee Co. Jamaica Ltd., Erindale Foods Ltd., Etobicoke Pancake Kitchens Ltd., La Bonne Boulangere Ltee, Les Produits Salda Ltee., Made-Rite Potato Chips Ltd., Pancake Kitchens Can. Ltd., Prior's Foods, Ltd., Regus Corp. Ltd., Salda Foods Jamaica Ltd., Salada Realty Ltd., Salada Sales Co. Ltd., Scarborough Pancake Kitchens Ltd., Shirriff's (Jamaica) Ltd., Sun Pep Co., Vigneux Foods Ltd., Watson Food Products Ltd. K.C. Clubs: Lambton Golf (Toronto); Sara Bay Country (Sarasota, Fla.). Office: 855 York Mills Rd Don Mills Ontario Canada

JOHNSON, MARTIN WIGGO, scientist; b. Chandler, S.D., Sept. 30, 1893; s. Christian Hans and Julia M. (Hansen) J.; grad. Pacific Luth. Acad., 1918; B.S., cum laude, U. Wash., 1924, M.S., 1930, Ph.D., 1931; m. Lelia T. Clutter, Apr. 16, 1924; children—Byron M., Phyllis T. Tchr. high schs., Seattle, 1924; Curator, Puget Sound Biol. Sta., 1924-29; biologist Internat. Passamaquoddy Fisheries Commn., 1932- 33; research asso. U. Wash., 1933-34, asso. prof. summers 1941, 47, prof., summers, 1960, 62; faculty Scripps Instn. Oceanography, U. Cal. at La Jolla, 1934—, successively instr., asst. prof., asso. prof. marine biology, 1934-49, prof. marine biology, 1949-62, prof. emeritus and research marine biologist, 1962—; marine biologist U. Cal. Div. War Research, 1942-46. Mem. staff Operation Crossroads, USN, 1946; NRC co-chmn. com. on marine biology 6th Pacific Sci. Congress, 1939; del. NRC, also U. Cal., 7th and 8th Pacific Sci. Congresses, New Zealand, 1949, P.I., 1953; adv. com. Pacific Sci. Bd. NRC, 1946-59; UNESCO adv. com. for Biol. Center, India, 1962-64; rev. cons. NSF, AEC. Served as musician with CAC, U.S. Army, World War I. Recipient certificate commendation for Outstanding Research, World War II, USN; Agassiz medal for contbn. to field of oceanography Nat. Acad. Scis., 1959; Distinguished Alumnus Pacific Lutheran U., 1966. Fellow Cal. Acad. Scis., San Diego Soc. Naturalists (pres. 1949), A.A.A.S.; mem. Am. Soc. Limnology and Oceanography (pres Western sect. 1952), Western Soc. Naturalists (pres. 1953), Ecol. Soc. Am. (editorial bd. 1950-52), Am. Micros. Soc. (v.p. 1952), Soc. Systematic Zoology, Sigma Xi. Author: (with H. U. Sverdrup, R.H. Fleming) The Oceans 1942; also profl. papers. Home: 2524 Ellentown Rd La Jolla CA 92037 Office: Scripps Instn Oceanography La Jolla CA 92037

JOHNSON, MARVIN JOYCE, educator; b. McIntosh, Minn., Nov. 25, 1906; s. Joseph and Clara Tina (Hanson) J.; B.A., U. Wis., 1927, Ph.D., 1932; m. Gisela Hildegard Mueller, July 27, 1934; children—Edith (Mrs. Richard Radder), David. NRC fellow Deutsche Technische Hochschule, Prague, 1932-33; research asso. U. Wis., 1933-40, asst. prof., 1940-41, asso. prof., 1941-46, prof. biochemistry, 1946—. Mem. Am. Chem. Soc. (chmn. div. microbial chemistry 1962-63, Distinguished Service award microbial chemistry div. 1968), Am. Soc. Biol. Chemists, Biochem. Soc., Am. Soc. for Microbiology, Soc. for Gen. Microbiology (pres. sect. econ. and applied microbiology 1964-66), Internat. Assn. Microbiol. Socs. Contbr. numerous research articles on microbial biochemistry to tech. jours. Home: 733 Miami Pass Madison WI 53711

JOHNSON, MARVIN RICHARD ALOIS, architect, state ofcl.; b. Humphrey, Neb., Aug. 13, 1916; s. Otto Henry and Reenste (Berends) J.; A.B., U. Neb., 1943; B.A. in Architecture, U. Neb., 1943; M.Architecture, Harvard, 1948. Designer, draftsman firm Clark & Enersen, Lincoln, Neb., 1946-47, 48-50; consulting architect div. sch. planning N.C. Dept. Pub. Instrn., Raleigh, 1950—; cons. HEW, Washington, 1960. Served with USNR, 1943-46. Fellow A.I.A. (recipient Distinguished Service citation N.C. chpt. 1960); mem. Council Ednl. Facility Planners, Am. Assn. School Adminstrs., Bldg. Research Inst., N.C. Arts Soc., Phi Beta Kappa. Democrat. Lutheran. Contbr. profl. jours. Home: L5 Raleigh Apts 1020 W Peace St Raleigh NC 27605 Office: NC Dept Pub Instrn Edn Bldg Raleigh NC 27602

JOHNSON, MAURICE DEVERE SANFORD, banker; b. Anoka, Minn., Dec. 4, 1911; s. Allen DeVere Warner and Nora Marie (Bergslien) J.; student Coe Coll., 1930-31; B.A. in Journalism, U. Minn., 1935; grad. U. Wis. Sch. Banking, 1960-63; LL.D., Kan. State U., 1969; m. Kathryn Genevieve Casey, Jan. 16, 1937; children—Sandra (Mrs. David F. Patzman), Martha DeVere, Nancy Kay. With Miller Pub. Co., 1935-45, mgr. Southwestern div., Kansas City, Mo., 1942-45; with Staley Milling Co., Kansas City, Mo., 1945-60, exec. v.p., 1958-60; with 1st Nat. Bank Kansas City (Mo.), 1960-67, exec. v.p., 1964-67; pres. Citizens Fidelity Bank & Trust Co., 1967-70, chmn., 1970—; dir. Orion Broadcasting Co., Louisville Gas & Electric Co., Percy Kent Bag Co. Bd. dirs. Norton- Children's Hosp. Mem. Sigma Delta Chi. Episcopalian. Home: 19 River Hill Rd Louisville KY 40207

JOHNSON, MAURICE O., educator; b. Rosemont, Neb., July 18, 1913; s. Oscar Theodore and Alice Welthia (Cook) J.; A.B., U. Neb., 1935, A.M., 1936; Ph.D., Columbia, 1949; m. Nancy Coe Dilworth, Oct. 21, 1945; children—Laurie, Kate, Scott Dilworth, Amy. Instr. English lit. and lang. U. Neb., 1936-38, Carnegie Inst. Tech., 1939-42; asst. prof. Syracuse U., 1948-50; mem. faculty U. Pa., 1950—, prof. English, 1962—, chmn. grad. English dept., 1962-65; vis. lectr. Columbia, summer 1956. Served with AUS, 1942-46. Mem. Modern Lang. Assn., Delta Upsilon, Sigma Upsilon. Author: Walt Whitman as a Critic of Literature, 1938; The Sin of Wit: Jonathan Swift as a Poet, 1950; Fielding's Art of Fiction, 1961; also articles. Asso. editor Prairie Schooner, 1933-38; adv. editor Satire Newsletter, 1964—. Home: 119 S Princeton Av Swarthmore PA 19081 Office: Dept English U Pennsylvania Philadelphia PA 19104

JOHNSON, MAURITZ, univ. dean; b. N.Y.C., Jan 7, 1922; s. Mauritz and Alma (Hanson) J.; A.B., State U. N.Y. at Albany, 1942, M.A., 1947; Ph.D., Cornell U., 1952; m. Shirley Jane Busacker, June 29, 1945; children—William, David, Carl, Linnea, Elizabeth. Tchr. sci. and math. Bombay (N.Y.) High Sch., 1942-44; tchr. sci. Goshen (N.Y.) High Sch., 1946-48; prin. Moravia (N.Y.) High Sch., 1948-50; research asso. N.Y. State Dept. Edn., 1952- 53; prof. edn. State U. N.Y. at Albany, 1953-60, 68—; prof. edn. Cornell U., 1960-68, dean Sch. Edn., 1966-68. Served with USNR, 1944-46. Mem. Am. Ednl. Research Assn., Ednl. Research Assn. N.Y. State (pres. 1958-60), Phi Kappa Phi, Phi Delta Kappa, Kappa Phi Kappa. Author: (with Leese and Frasure) Teacher in Curriculum Making, 1961; (with Busacker and Bowman) Junior High School Guidance, 1961; American Secondary Schools, 1965. Home: 111 Berwick Rd Delmar NY 12054 Office State U NY Albany NY 12203

JOHNSON, MILLARD WALLACE, Jr., educator; b. Racine, Wis., Feb. 1, 1928; s. Millard Wallace and Marian Manilla (Rittman) J.; B.S. in Applied Math. and Mechanics, U. Wis., 1952, M.S., 1953; Ph.D. in Math., Mass. Inst. Tech., 1957; m. Ruth Pugh Gifford, Dec. 26, 1953; children—Millard Wallace III, Jeannette Marian, Charles Gifford, Peter Allen. Research asst. Mass. Inst. Tech., 1953-57, lectr., 1957-58; mem. staff Math. Research Center, prof. mechanics U. Wis., 1958-63, prof. mechanics and math., 1964—, mem. staff Rheology Research Center, 1970—. Served with USN, 1946-48. Mem. Soc. Rheology, Soc. Indsl. and Applied Math., Am. Soc. M.E., Am. Inst. Aero. and Astronautics, Soc. Engring. Sci., Phi Beta Kappa. Contbr. articles profl. jours. Home: 802 Blue Ridge Pkwy Madison WI 53705

JOHNSON, MILTON AXEL, lawyer; b. Marinette, Wis., July 10, 1906, s. Charles Alfred and Hilma (Lindlof) J.; LL.B., Ind. U., 1930; m. Clara Bauer, Sept. 6, 1934; 1 dau., Linda C. (Mrs. James F. Hayden). Admitted to Ind. bar, 1930, since practiced in South Bend; mem. firms Hammerschmidt & Johnson, South Bend, 1935-56, Jones, Obenchain, Johnson, Ford & Pankow, 1957—, Dir. H.G. Christman Constrn. Co., Inc. City chmn. Republican party, 1942. Mem. Am., Ind. (bd. govs. 1949-51), St. Joseph County (pres. 1944) bar assns., Ind. Soc. Chgo., Lambda Chi Alpha, Phi Delta Phi. Club: Kiwanis, Elks, Indiana (South Bend). Home: 605 W North Shore Dr South Bend IN 46617 Office: Bank Bldg South Bend IN 44601

JOHNSON, NEIL ALBERT, prof. basketball player; b. Jackson, Mich., Apr. 17, 1943; s. Edward and Harriette (Michaels) J.; student Creighton U., 1966—; m. Susan Mae Tancer, Mar. 21, 1967; 1 dau., Alison Beth. Profl. basketball player N.Y. Knickerbockers, 1966-68, Phoenix Suns, 1968-70, Virginia Squires, 1970—. Athletic camp cons. Pub. relations adviser Eugene McCarthy for Pres. Mem. Am. Basketball Assn. All-Star Team, 1971. Mem. Virginia Beach Volleyball Assn., Am. Motorcycle Assn. Home: 108 Smythe Ct Virginia Beach VA 23452

JOHNSON, NELS CLARENCE, naval officer; b. Auburn, N.H., July 9, 1912; s. Claus and Adolfina (Wennerstrand) J; B.S., U.S. Naval Acad., 1934; grad. Nat. War Coll., 1956; m. Dorothea Lindall, June 16, 1936; 1 dau., Veronica Marie (Mrs. William D. Hohmann). Commd. ensign U.S. N., 1934, advanced through grades to vice adm., 1967; assigned various ships, 1934-46 comdr. officer U.S.S. Witek, 1946-47; fleet anti-submarine warfare officer, staff comdr. in chief Atlantic Fleet, 1947-50, planning officer N. Atlantic Ocean regional planning group NATO, 1950-51, staff supreme allied comdr. Atlantic, 1951; comdr. Destroyer Div. 262, 1951-53; head, command policy sect., strategic plans div. Office Chief Naval Operations, 1953-55; comdg. officer U.S.S. Arneb, 1956-57; head, joint and internat. plans br., strategic plans div. Office Chief Naval Operations, 1957-59; comdg. officer U.S.S. Helena, 1959-60; chief staff, aide to comdr. 7th Fleet, 1960-61; comdr. Amphibious Group 3, 1961-63; dep. dir. gen. planning and programming Office Chief Naval Operations, 1963; chief stategic plans and policy div. Office Joint Chiefs Staff, 1963-66; dep. chief staff, fgn. mil. aid, logistics and adminstrn. to comdr. in chief Pacific, 1966-67; dir. plans and policy, J-5, Joint Chiefs Staff, 1967-68; dir. joint staff Joint Chiefs Staff, 1968-70; comdr. amphibious force U.S. Pacific Fleet, 1970—. Decorated D.S.M., Legion of Merit with gold star and combat V. Joint Service Commendation medal with oak leaf cluster. Mem. Naval Inst. Home: Quarters E US Naval Air Sta North Island San Diego CA 92135 Office: COMPHIBPAC San Diego CA 92155

JOHNSON, NICHOLAS, govt. ofcl.; b. Iowa City, s. Wendell A.L. and Edna (Bockwoldt) J.; B.A., U. Tex., 1956, LL.B., 1958; m. Karen Mary Chapman, 1952; children—Julie, Sherman, Gregory. Admitted to Tex. bar, 1958, D.C. bar, also U.S. Supreme Ct., 1963; law clk. U.S. 5th Circuit Ct. Appeals Judge John R. Brown, 1958-59, to U.S. Supreme Ct. Justice Hugo L. Black, 1959-60; acting asso. prof. law U. Cal. at Berkeley, 1960-63; asso. firm Covington & Burling, Washington, 1963-64; adminstr. Maritime Adminstrn., U.S. Dept. Commerce, 1964-66; commr. FCC, 1966—; adj. prof. law Georgetown U., 1971—. Named 1 of 10 Outstanding Young Men in U.S., Jr. C. of C., 1967; recipient New Republic Pub. Defender award, 1970. Mem. Am., Fed. bar assns., State Bar Tex., Internat. Soc. Gen. Semantics (dir.), Phi Beta Kappa, Order of Coif, Phi Delta Phi, Phi Eta Sigma, Pi Sigma Alpha. Democrat. Unitarian. Author: How to Talk Back to Your Television Set, 1970. Contbr. legal and gen. publs. Office: FCC Washington DC 20554*

JOHNSON, NORMAN L., journalist. Editorial writer Louisville Times. Office: 525 W Broadway Louisville KY 40202*

JOHNSON, NORMAN STANLEY, county ofcl., assn. exec.; b. Los Angeles, June 27, 1912; s. Neil C. and Nora (Johnson) J.; B.S. in Pub. Adminstrn., U. So. Cal., 1934; student Woodbury Coll., Los Angeles, 1930; S. Western U., Los Angeles, 1936-37; m. Dorothy Harragan, May 18, 1940; 1 son, Steven K. Field auditor County Los Angeles 1934-41, budget analyst, 1946-48, bus. mgr. county fire dept., 1950-52; exec. asst. County Parks and Recreation Dept., 1950-55, dir. dept., 1955—. Pres. Am. Inst. Park Execs., 1963-64; chmn. Cal. Suprs. Adv. Parks Commn., 1960—; mem. adv. com. Cal. Dept. Parks and Recreation, 1964—. Trustee, mem. exec. com. Nat. Recreation and Park Assn. Mem. Cal. Assn. Park and Recreation Execs., Govt. Accounting Soc., Western Govt. Research Assn. Home: 437 W Duarte Rd Arcadia CA 91006 Office: 155 W Washington St Los Angeles CA 90015

JOHNSON, NORRIS OLIVER, economist; b. Jamestown, N.Y., Dec. 29, 1905; s. Nicholas Oscar and Emma Augusta (Otander) J.; B.S., Syracuse U., 1927; A.M., Harvard, 1932, Ph.D., 1934; m. Patricia Bartel, Sept. 28, 1935, children—Diana Lansbury, Eric Niles. Statistician, Am. Tel & Tel. Co., 1927-28; statistician, editor Investors Research Bur., 1928-30; instr. Giffin Coll., 1933-34; statistician Fed. Res. Bank of N.Y., 1934-38, chief domestic research div., 1938-42, mgr. research dept., 1942-44; treas.- gen. of Iran, 1945; asst. v.p. Nat. City Bank of N.Y., 1946-54, v.p., 1954-55; v.p. First Nat. City Bank of N.Y., 1955-62, sr. v.p., economist, 1962-66; prof. econs. New Coll., 1966-67; Me. Bankers Assn. prof. econs. U. Me., 1967-71. Chmn. bd. Excelsior Ins. Co. Trustees Syracuse U. Recipient Arentz medal Syracuse U., 1962. Fellow Royal Econ. Soc.; mem. Am. Econ. Assn., Am. Finance Assn. (pres. 1955), Met. Econ. Assn. (pres. 1959), Conf. Bus. Economists (chmn. 1967), Nat. Econ. Club, Internat. C. C. (exec. com. U.S. council), Alpha Tau Omega, Pi Delta Epsilon. Mason (32). Clubs: Teheran (Iran); University (N.Y.C.). Contbr. profl. jours. Home: Westwinds Halifax VT 05301 Office: Gedney P O Box 57 White Plains NY 10605

JOHNSON, NUNNALLY, writer; b. Columbus, Ga., Dec. 5, 1897; s. James Nunnally and Pearl (Patrick) J.; educated grade and high schs., Columbus, Ga.; m. Dorris Bowdon, Feb. 4, 1940; children—Christie, Roxanna, Scott Bowdon; children by previous marriages—Marjorie, Nora. Newspaperman, 1916; reporter on Columbus Enquirer Sun, Savannah (Ga.) Press, N.Y. Tribune Brooklyn Daily Eagle, N.Y. Herald Tribune; columnist Bklyn. Daily Eagle, N.Y. Evening Post and PM; writer stories and articles for Saturday Evening Post and other mags.; writer and producer of films, 1932—; wrote screenplays, The House of Rothschild; The Country Doctor; Jesse James; Grapes of Wrath; Holy Matrimony; The Gunfighter; The Mudlark; The Desert Fox; How to Marry a Millionaire. Wrote, produced and directed Night People; Black Widow; Oh, Men, Oh. Women; The Three Faces of Eve. Wrote and directed: The Man in the Gray Flannel Suit; writer screenplay The World of Henry Orient, (with Lukas Heller) The Dirty Dozen, 1967. Served in the U.S. Army, 1916-18. Author: There Ought to Be a Law (short stories), 1930. Home: 33 Grosvenor Sq London W1 England

JOHNSON, OLIVER ADOLPH, educator; b. Everett, Wash., Feb. 16, 1923; s. Gustaf Adolph and Olga (Toll) J.; B.A., Linfield Coll., McMinnville, Ore., 1944; postgrad., U. Ore., 1946-47; Oxford (Eng.) U., 1950-51; M.A., Yale, 1950, Ph.D., 1951; m. Carol Jeanne Pence, Mar. 21, 1946; children—Julie Mae, Stuart Earle, Elizabeth Ann, Melinda Jean. Instr. philosophy Yale, 1951- 52; fellow Inst. Philos. Research, San Francisco, 1952-53; mem. faculty U. Cal. at Riverside, 1953—, prof. philosophy, 1965—. Served to lt. (j.g.) USNR, 1943-46. Mem. Am. Philos. Assn. (div. sec.-treas.), Royal Inst. Philosophy. Author: Ethics, 1958; Heritage of Western Civilization 1958; Rightness and Goodness, 1959; Man and His World, 1964; Moral Knowledge, 1966; The Moral Life, 1969. Home: 4381 Picacho Dr Riverside CA 92507

JOHNSON, ORIS BAKER, air force officer; b. Ashland, La., June 20, 1920; s. Henry Baker and Mary (Pullen) J.; B.S., Northwestern State Coll., La., 1939; m. Katherine Shaw, Dec. 8, 1945; children—Charles Henry, Judith Sue. Joined USAAF, 1940, commd. 2d lt., 1941, advanced through grades to maj. gen. USAF, 1966; comdr. 422 Night Fighter Squadron, ETO, World War II; assigned Hdqrs. Tactical Air Command, 1946-47, Hdqrs. USAF, 1947-50, 57-59, Hdqrs. Far East Air Forces, 1951-53; comdr. 56th Fighter Group, 1953-56; assigned Hdqrs. Air Def. Command, 1956-57, Hdqrs. USAF, Europe, 1960-63; comdr. Washington Air Def. Sector, 1963-66; assigned Hdqrs. N.Am. Air Def. Command, 1966; student Imperial Def. Coll., London, Eng., 1960; comdr. 9th Aerospace Def. Div., Ent AFB, Colo., 1966-68; comdr. 14th Aerospace Force Ent AFB, Colo., 1968-69, 313th Air Div. Kadena AFB, Okinawa, 1969-71, DCS/Materiel, Ent Air Force Base, Colo., 1971—. Decorated D.S.M., Legion of Merit with 3 oak leaf clusters, D.F.C., Air medal. Mem. Sigma Tau Gamma, Lambda Delta Lambda. Address: Hq ADC PO Box 23 Ent AFB CO 80912

JOHNSON, PAMELA HANSFORD, (The Lady Snow) writer; b. London, Eng., May 29, 1912; d. Reginald Kenneth and Amy Clotilda (Howson) Johnson; educated Clapham County Sch., London; D. Litt. (hon.), Temple U., York U., m. Gordon Neil Stewart, Dec 15, 1936; children—Andrew Morven, Lindsay Jean; m. 2d, Charles Percy Snow, July 15, 1950; 1 son Philip Charles Hansford. Novelist, critic and broadcaster, 1945; mem. panel Brains Trust on BBC, 1956—, Critics on BBC, 1953—. Fellow Centre Advanced Studies, Wesleyan U., Middletown, Conn., 1961; Timothy Dwight fellow arts and letters Yale, 1961. Fellow Royal Soc. Lit.; mem. Societe Europeene de Culture. Author: (novels) This Bed Thy Centre, 1935; Too Dear for My Possessing, 1940; An Avenue of Stone, 1947; A Summer to Decide, 1948; Catherine Carter, 1952; An Impossible Marriage, 1954; The Last Resort (in U.S., The Sea and The Wedding), 1956; The Unspeakable Skipton, 1959; The Humbler Creation, 1959; An Error of Judgement, 1962; Night and Silence Who is Here?, 1963; Cork Street, Next to the Hatter's, 1965; (criticism) Thomas Wolfe, a Critical Study, 1947, (in U.S. as The Art of Thomas Wolfe, 1963), I. Compton-Burnett, 1953; Social Criticism: On Iniquity, 1967; (play) Corinth House, 1948; (radio series) Six Proust Reconstructions, 1948. Translator: (with Kitty Black) Anouilh's The Rehearsal, 1962; (novel) The Survival of the Fittest, 1968; The Honours Board, 1970. Address: care MacMillan Ltd Little Essex St Strand London WC 2 England

JOHNSON, PAUL CARLTON, mfg. exec.; b. Muskegon, Mich. Apr. 1, 1907; s. Charles E. and Gunnelia (Selim) J.; student u. Mich.; grad. Babson Inst., 1929; m. Ann Lovelace, Sept. 26, 1933; children—Charles Edward II, Paul Carlton, Jeffrey Elston. With Sealed Power Corp., Muskegon, Mich., 1929—, beginning in mfg. div., successively staff original equipment, sales div., mgr. original equipment sales, v.p. charge sales, exec. v.p., 1929-52, pres., 1952-68, now chmn. Dir. Mich. Steamship Agys.; mem. Harbors Exec. Com., 1954. Dir. Greater Muskegon Community Fund, 1952-58, Hackley Hosp., 1956. Mem. Greater Muskegon C. of C. (dir. 1953-56). Clubs: Muskegon County; Century; Detroit Athletic. Home: Circle Dr North Muskegon MI 49445 Office: 2001 Sanford St Muskegon Heights MI 49444

JOHNSON, PAUL CORNELIUS, former editor; b. Lakeville, Minn., Aug. 17, 1904; s. Peter Christian and Ingeborg (Alfson) J.; A.B., St. Olaf Coll., 1928, L.H.D. (hon.), 1952; m. Eveline Lenore Ellingson, Aug. 5, 1931; children—David, Linda. Editor Worthington (Minn.) Daily Globe, 1935-40; asso. prof. agr. extension U. Minn., 1940-47; editor, also editorial dir. Prairie Farmer, Wallace Farmer, Wis. Agriculturist, 1947-70; dir. Prairie Farmer Pub. C. Trustee Farm Found., Found. Human Ecology, Butler Meml. Trust; bd. regents Augustana Coll., Sioux Falls, S.D. Awarded Am. Farmer degree (hon.), 1951; Reuben Brigham award in Agrl. Journalism, 1954. Mem. Am. Agrl. Editors Assn. (pres. 1951-52). Home: 1115 S Maple St Northfield MN 55057

JOHNSON, PAUL EMANUEL, former educator; b. Niantic, Conn., Feb. 19, 1898; s. John Edward and Martha (Cadwallader) J.; A.B., Cornell Coll., 1920, D.D., 1939; A.M., U. Chgo., 1921; S.T.B., Boston U., 1923, Ph. D., 1928; m. Evelyn Grant, June 2, 1922; children—Lois Kathay (Mrs. George A. Cummings), Mona Margaret (Mrs. William Valentine). Asst. in philosophy Brown U., 1924-25; instr. ethics West China Union U., 1926-27; asso. prof. philosophy Hamline U., 1928-36; dean, prof. philosophy and religion Morningside Coll., 1936-41; prof. psychology of religion Boston U. Sch. Theology, 1941-57, Danielsen prof. psychology and pastoral counseling, 1957-63, prof. emeritus, 1963- -, dir. pastoral counseling service, 1952-63 Vis. prof. Kwansei Gakuin, Aoyama Gakuin, Toyko Union Theol. Sem., Doshisha U. (all Japan), 1963-64, Christian Theol. Sem., Indpls., 1966-71; dir. Indpls. Pastoral Counseling Center, 1965-68; lectr. Duke, Garrett Theol. Sem., U. So. Cal. Sch. Religion, Pacific Sch. Religion, Sch. Theology at Claremont (Cal.), Union Coll. of B.C., Vancouver Diplomate Am. Assn. Pastoral Counselors; Fellow Am. Psychol. Assn.; mem. Am. Philos. Assn., Am. Acad. Religion, Acad. Religion and Mental Health, Assn. Clin. Pastoral Edn., Soc. Group Psychotherapy and Psychodrama, Am. Protestant Hosp. Assn., Phi Beta Kappa. Author: Who Are You, 1937; Psychology of Religion, 1945, rev. 1959; Psychology of Pastoral Care, 1953; Personality and Religion, 1957; Person and Counselor, 1967; The Middle Years, 1971; (with Lowell Calston) Personality and Christian Faith, 1972. Contbg. editor Community Mental Health. Contbr. articles to religious publs., philos. and psychol. jours. Home: 213 Lakeside Dr Centerville MA 02632

JOHNSON, PAUL HOUSTON, lawyer; b. Tulsa, Aug. 19, 1926; s. James B. annd Pearl (Houston) J.; B.S., Okla. State U., 1950; J.D., U. Tulsa, 1957; m. Ruth Jones, June 19, 1951; children-Jeffrey James, Lisa Ann. Purchasing agt. Sinclair Oil & Gas Co., Tulsa, 1952-60; admitted to Okla. bar, 1957: practiced in Tulsa, 1960—; mem. firm Head & Johnson. Vice chmn. Housing Authrotiy Tulsa; bd. dirs. Family and Childrens Service; sec. exec. com. Thomas Gilcrease Inst. Am. History and Art. Served with USNR, 1944-46. Registered profl. engr., Okla. Mem. Okla., Patent Office, Tulsa County bar assns., Sigma Tau, Eta Kappa Nu. Lion. Club: Green T (past pres.) (Tulsa). Home: 4259 E 62d St Tulsa OK 74135 Office: Beacon Bldg Tulsa OK 74103

JOHNSON, PAUL POLLARD, mfr. textile machinery; b. Cleve., May 7, 1907; s. Paul Moxon and Emily (Pollard) J.; Ph.B., Brown U., 1929; student Cleve. Law Sch., 1930, Cleve. Coll., 1931, Case Inst. Tech., 1933; grad. Advanced Mgmt. Program, Harvard, 1943; m. Luella Moore, Sept. 8, 1934; children—Judith A. (Mrs. David M.M. Catmur), Paula E.(Mrs. John Waterman), Paul Pollard. With firm Thompson Products, Inc., Cleve., 1931-48, mgr. aircraft accessories div., 1943-48; pres. Waltham Watch Co., 1948-49; ind. indsl. cons., 1949-51; with Leesona Corp., Providence, 1951—, v.p., 1951-53, exec. v.p., dir. 1953-67, pres. and chief exec. officer, 1967-70, now vice chmn.; dir. Leesona Holt, Ltd., 1959-61, Tech. Operations, Inc., 1951-59; mem. cor. Providence Instn. Savs. Councilman, Town of N. Kingstown, R.I., 1958-62. Dir. Madison Industries, Inc., R.I. Med. Soc. Physicians Service. Trustee N. Kingstown Free Library, Mem. corp. Rogers Williams Coll. Mem. Am. Mgmt. Assn., Am. Ordnance Assn., Research Inst. Am., Providence C. of C. Brown U. Alumni Assn. Clubs: Hope (Providence). Home: RFD 71 Saunderstown RI 02874 Office: 333 Strawberry Field Rd Warwick RI 02886

JOHNSON, PHILIP CARL, educator, physician; b. White Plains, N.Y., Nov. 12, 1924; s. Philip Carl and Josephine (Losee) J.; B.S., U. Mich., 1948, M.D., 1949; m. Virginia Snyder, July 1, 1950; children—Philip Carl III, Christopher Carl. Faculty, U. Mich., 1952-54, asst. chief radioisotope lab. U. Mich. Hosp., 1954; chief radioisotope service, asst. chief profl. service for research VA Hosp., Oklahoma City, 1955-60; asso. prof. medicine U. Okla., 1958-60; dir. radioisotope lab. Meth. Hosp., Houston, 1960—; asso. prof. medicine Baylor U., Houston, 1960-67, prof. medicine, 1967—. Mem. A.M.A., A.A.A.S., Central Soc. for Clin. Research, Nuclear Medicine Soc., A.C.P., Sigma Xi. Research, publs. on use radioisotopes in clin. medicine, thyroid, cardiac function, drugs. Home: 12122 Rip Van Winkle St Houston TX 77024

JOHNSON, PHILIP CORTELYOU, architect; b. Cleve., July 8, 1906; s. Homer M. and Louise (Pope) J.; A.B. Harvard, 1930, B.Arch., 1943. Architect Mus. Modern Art Annex and Sculpture Ct.; N.Y. State Theater, Lincoln Center, N.Y.C.; Glass House, New Canaan, Conn.; co-architect Seagram Bldg., N.Y.C. Dir. dept. architecture and design Mus. Modern Art, 1930-36, 46-54, trustee, 1958—. Mem. Nat. Inst. Arts and Letters (council). Author: The International Style, Architecture Since 1922 (with Henry-Russel Hitchcock), 1932; Mies van der Rohe, 1947, rev., 1953. Home: Ponus St New Canaan CT 06840 Office: 375 Park Av New York City NY 10022

JOHNSON, RALPH M., educator; b. Ririe, Ida., Apr. 9, 1918; s. Ralph Melvin and Millie (Marler) J.; B.S., Utah State U., 1940; M.S., U. Wis., 1947, Ph.D., 1948; m. Genevieve Porter, Aug. 8, 1940; children—Karen (Mrs. Warren Eugene Babcock), Robert Christian, Wilford Preece. Fellow, Wis. Alumni Research Found., U. Wis., 1940-41, 46-47; fellow NIH, 1947-48; research asso., asst. to sci. dir. Detroit Inst. Cancer Research, 1948-59; research prof., dir. research labs. Inst. Nutrition and Food Tech., Ohio State U., Columbus, 1959-63, dir. Inst. Nutrition, 1963-66, dean Coll. Biol. Sics., 1966-68; dean Coll. Sci., Utah State U., 1968—; asst. prof. physiol. chemistry Coll. Medicine, Wayne State U., 1951-59. Served to maj. AUS, 1941-46. Mem. Am. Soc. Biol. Chemists, Am. Inst. Nutrition, Sigma Xi, Phi Kappa Phi, Gamma Sigma Delta. Republican. Mem. Ch. of Jesus Christ of Latter-day Saints (pres. stake). Contbr. articles profl. jours. Home: 2044 N 13th E Logan UT 84321

JOHNSON, RAY, painter; b. Detroit, 1927; student Art Students' League, N.Y.C., Black Mountain Coll. Asso. with Am. Abstract Artists, 1949-52; founded N.Y. Corr. Sch. Art, 1962; exhibited one-man shows Willard Gallery, N.Y.C., 1965, 66, 67, Feigen Gallery, Chgo., 1966, 67; exhibited group shows including Boylston St. Print Gallery, Cambridge, Mass., 1955, contemporary Arts Assn. Houston, 1959, Batman Gallery, San Francisco, 1961, Pitts. Internat., Carnegie Inst., 1961, AG Gallery, N.Y.C., 1961, Oakland Art Mus., 1963, Mus. Modern Art, N.Y.C., 1966, Finch Coll. Mus. Art, N.Y.C., 1967; Chgo. Mus. Contemporary Art, 1967. Recipient award Nat. Inst. Arts and Letters, 1966. Pub. The Paper Snake, 1965. Address: care Feigen Gallery 24 E 81st St New York City NY 10028

JOHNSON, RAY CLIFFORD, cons. engr., educator; b. Canton, O., Aug. 26, 1927; s. Olaf Andreas and Hilma D. (Blomberg) J.; B.S. with distinction, U. Rochester, 1950, M.S., 1954; m. Helen Frances Lindgren, July 2, 1949; children—Glen Eric, Barbara Ann, Carol Marie. Mech. designer Gleason Works, Rochester, N.Y., 1950-51; instr. U. Rochester, 1951-54; sr. design engr. Eastman Kodak Co., 1954- 58; asst. prof. mech. engring. Yale, 1958-61; staff engr. IBM Corp., 1961-62; John Woodman Higgins prof. mech. engring. Worcester Poly. Inst., 1962—; lectr. and cons. to major univs. and industries, 1957—. Served with USNR, 1945-46. Recipient Emil Kuichling prize U. Rochester, 1948; Wisdom Award of Honor, 1970. Registered profl. engr., N.Y., Conn., Mass., Mich. Mem. Am. Soc. M.E., Soc. Exptl. Stress Analysis, Am. Soc. Engring. Edn., Am. Assn. U. Profs., Phi Beta Kappa, Sigma Xi, Tau Beta Pi, Pi Tau Sigma. Author: Optimum Design of Mechanical Elements, 1961; Mechanical Design Synthesis with Optimization Applications, 1971; also tech. papers. Patentee in field. Home: 58 Birchwood Dr Holden MA 01520 Office: Worcester Poly Inst Worcester MA 01609

JOHNSON, RAY G., govt. ofcl.; b. Fresno, Cal., Apr. 12, 1902; s. Ray George and Daisy Muriel (Browne) J.; B.S., Ore. State Coll., 1924, grad. student plant ecology, 1935; m. Helen Illidge, Apr. 24, 1925; children—Dorothy Patricia (Mrs. Frederick P. Erickson), Kathryn (Mrs. Garvin Lovejoy). Cattle, wheat rancher, Wasco County, Ore., 1924-28; county agrl. agt., Grant County, Ore., 1928-35; prof. dept. animal husbandry Ore. State U., 1935-42, prof., head, animal husbandry dept., 1944-47, also mem. nat. range sheep breeding com., nat. range beef cattle breeding com.; agrl. edn. adviser Chinese Nat. Govt., Dept. State, 1942-43; staff Internat. Basic Econ. Corp., Venezuela, 1947-49; range mgmt. specialist Mont. Extension Service, 1950-51; dir. agr. program ICA and predecessor agys., P.I., 1952-55, dir. agrl. adv. program in Iran, 1955-59, dep. dir. over-all programs in Iran, 1959-61; chief Office of Food and Agr., TCM. India, 1961-65; food and agrl. officer AID, Egypt, 1965-67 cons. contractor, 1970. Decorated by Shah of Iran, 1959. Mem. Am., Western Socs. animal prodn., Nat., Western socs. range mgmt., Sigma Alpha Epsilon, Alpha Zeta, Phi Kappa Phi, Gamma Sigma Delta, Epsilon Sigma Phi. Democrat. Mason Contbr. articles agrl. jours. Nat. Geog. Mag. Home: 1724 Minnewawa Clovics CA 93612

JOHNSON, RAYMON DUDLEY, univ. dean; b. Sparta, Tenn., May 15, 1915; s. S.B. and Mollie (Bohanon) J.; B.S., Tenn. Tech. U., 1939; M.A., U. Ky., 1941, Ed.D., 1952; m. Margaret Tully Norwood, Mar. 6, 1943; children—Sandra, Pamela. High sch. tchr. and coach, 1939-41; instr. Commerce Morehead State U., 1941-42; chief advisement VA, 1946-49; mem. faculty U. Ky. 1952—, dean univ. extension, asso. prof. edn., 1964. Served with USNR, 1942-45; PTO. Mem. Am., Ky. personnel and guidance assns. Phi Delta Kappa. Kiwanian (past pres. past lt. gov.). Home: 222 Jesselin Dr Lexington NY 40503

JOHNSON, RAYMOND COLES, ins. exec.; b. Bisbee, Ariz., June 19, 1907; s. Ira J. and Carolyn (Coles) J.; B.S., U. Ariz., 1928; m. Alice Elizabeth Abbott, June 21, 1930 (dec. July 21, 1949); children—Carolyn C. (Mrs. Thomas H. Smith), Eleanor (Mrs. R.N. Palmer, Jr.); m. 2d, Alice Hall Willard, July 16, 1954. With N.Y. Life Ins. Co., 1927—, agt., Phoenix, 1927-29, asst. mgr., Ariz. br., 1929-33, mgr., 1933-38, mgr. Los Angeles br., 1938-42, supt. agys. home office, N.Y.C., 1942- 43, asst. v.p. 1942-49, agy. v.p. and exec. officer, 1949-51, v.p. charge agy. admistrn., 1951-56, v.p. charge agy. affairs, 1956-59, v.p. charge marketing, 1959-62, exec. v.p., 1962-69, dir., 1968—, vice chmn., 1969—. Bd. govs. Internat. Ins. Seminars, 1968—; agy. chmn. Am. Life Conv., 1962. Mem. Cardinal's Com. of Laity. Mem. Republican Nat. Finance Com. Mem., trustee Midtown Hosp. Corp., 1965; chmn. N.Y. chpt. A.R.C., 1966—, treas., chmn. 1968—; trustee Ednl. Broadcasting Corp., 1966, Notre Dame Coll. S.I., Ind. Coll. Funds Am. Recipient U. Ariz. Alumni Achievement award, 1956. C.L.U. Chmn. joint com. on pub. relations Am. Coll. Life Underwriters (life trustee) and Am. Soc. C.L.U. Mem. Life Ins. Agy. Mgmt. Assn. (dir. past pres.), Better Bus. Bur. Met. N.Y. (dir. 1968, council 1969), Piligrams U.S., Newcomen Soc., Phi Delta Theta, Pi Delta Epsilon, Alpha Kappa Psi. Knight of Malta. Clubs: University (N.Y.C.); Atlantic Beach (gov. 1964); California, Metropolitan (Los Angeles); Sales Executives (dir.); Economic; Capitol Hill; Metropolitan; Confrerie des Chevaliers Tastevin. Contbr. articles mags. and trade jours. Home: 1020 Park Av New York City NY 10028 Office: 51 Madison Av New York City NY 10010

JOHNSON, RAYMOND EDWARD, editor; b. McEwen, Tenn., Feb. 27, 1904; s. Edward and Lina (Adams) J.; grad. high sch.; m. Mae Louthan, July 30, 1908; children—Robert Edward, Raymond Eugene. Office boy Nashville Tennessean, 1918-20, sports writer, 1920-25, asst. sports editor, 1926-37, sports editor, 1937-70; sports editor Evening Tennessean, 1925-26; pres. Nat. Turf Writers Assn., 1970—. Mem. Football Writers Assn. Am. (past pres.), Amateur Softball Assn. Am. (past pres.), Golden Gloves Nat. (past pres.), So. Assn. Baseball Writers (past pres.), Nat. Turf Writers Assn. Am., Golf Writers Am.

(life), Nat. Assn. Softball Writers, Southeastern Amateur Athletic Union (past pres.), Sigma Delta Chi. Democrat. Lutheran. Mason (Shriner), Rotarian, Elk. Home: 1604 17th Av Nashville TN 37212 Office: 1100 Broadway Nashville TN 37202

JOHNSON, REX D., banker; b. Ardmore, Okla., Sept. 19, 1926; s. Robert Bruce and Opal (Williams) J.; B.B.A., U. Okla., 1949; M.B.A., Stanford, 1951; m. Helen Anne Duboc, Dec. 28, 1957; children—Dianne Elizabeth, Bradley Duboc. With Republic Nat. Bank Dallas, 1951—, staff credit analyst, 1951-53, asst. cashier comml. loans, 1953-57, asst. v.p. comml. loans, 1957-60, v.p. comml. loans, 1960-66, sr. v.p. comml. loans, 1966-67, exec. v.p. finance, administrn., 1967—; dir. Stewart Engring. Co. Dir. Tejas council Girl Scouts U.S.; mem. Children's Med. Center Devel. Council, Dallas. Served with USMCR, 1944-46. Mem. Phi Kappa Sigma, Delta Sigma Pi. Presbyn. Mason (Shriner). Home: 5941 Averill Way Dallas TX 75225 Office: Republic Nat Bank Dallas PO Box 5961 Dallas TX 75222

JOHNSON, RICHARD ABRAHAM, historian, educator; b. Moline, Ill., Apr. 17, 1910; s. Andrew and Harriet May (Abrahamson) J.; A.B., Augustana Coll., 1932; M.A., U. Tex., 1933, Ph.D., 1938; m. Irene E. Beam, July 15, 1946; children—Christina Anne, Richard Alexander, Daniel Anders Lowell. Instr. Montezuma Coll., 1933-34, U. Tex., 1935-38; prof. Augustana Coll., Rock Island, Ill., 1938-40; apptd. fgn. service officer, 1940; vice consul, Naples, Italy, 1940-41; vice consul, 3d sec., London, 1941- 46; U.S. observer Conf. Allied Ministers Edn., 1943-45; tech. sec. U.S. delegation U.N. Conf. Orgn. of UNESCO, 1945, acting rep. preparatory com., 1945-46, adviser U.S. del. 1st Gen. Conf. UNESCO, 1946; staff Dept. State, 1946-48; consul, 1st sec., La Paz, Bolivia, 1948-50; consul, prin. officer, Guadalajara, Mex., 1950-51; consul, 1st sec., dep. chief mission, Ciudad Trujillo, 1952-54, Nat. War Coll., 1954-55; counselor of Embassy, Madrid, Spain, 1955-57; dep. dir. Office of Intelligence and Research, Dept. of State, Washington, 1957-59; dir. Office Functional and Biographic Intelligence, 1959-61; exec. dir. Bd. Examiners for Fgn. Service, 1961-62; consul gen. Monterrey, Mexico, 1962-65; prof., coordinator Inter-Am. studies Trinity U., San Antonio, 1965-70, dir. Interdisciplinary Area Tng. Program, 1966-70. Lectr. George Washington U., 1959-60. Chmn. edn1. exhibits com. Hemis Fair, 1966- 68. Mem. Am. Hist. Soc.,Am. Fgn. Service Assn., Mexican Acad. Internat. Law (academician), Am. Polit. Sci. Assn. Author: The Mexican Revolution of Ayutla, 1939; the Administration of U.S. Fgn. Affairs, 1971. Contbr. articles profl. publs. Home: RR4 Box 760 New Braunfels TX 78130

JOHNSON, RICHARD CLAYTON, physicist; b. Eveleth, Minn., May 9, 1930; s. Elvin and Sadie (Abramson) J.; B.S. in Physics, Ga. Inst. Tech., 1953, M.S., 1958, Ph.D., 1961; m. Sallie Staples Hairston, Aug. 2, 1958 (div. 1971); children—Karen Louise, Diana Elizabeth. Co-op student Ga. Power Co., 1949-51; with Ga. Inst. Tech., 1952—, prin. research physicist, 1967—, chief, electronics div., 1968- -; cons. to govt. and industry, 1966—. Served to lt. (j.g.) USNR, 1953- 55. Registered profl. engr., Ga. Mem. Am. Phys. Soc., I.E.E.E., Sigma Xi, Phi Kappa Phi, Tau Beta Pi, Phi Eta Sigma, Sigma Pi Sigma, Phi Kappa Sigma. Contbr. research papers, chpt. in book. Patentee in field. Home: 2572 G6 Lenox Rd NE Atlanta GA 30324

JOHNSON, RICHARD CRAIG, lawyer; b. Mpls., Dec. 9, 1929; s. Hilmer Henry and Alma (Swanson) J.; B.A., U. Minn., 1951, LL.B., 1956 (now J.D.); m. Nancy E. Van Tassel, Sept. 29, 1951; children—Craig R., Leslie E., Kent P.D.; m. 2d, Aline Monique Hartl, Sept. 3, 1970. Admitted to Minn. bar, 1956; atty., leasing agt. Am. Shopping Centers, Inc., Mpls., 1956-57; atty., asst. counsel, asso. counsel, counsel, gen. counsel, asst. sec. and gen. counsel, sec. and gen. counsel, v.p., sec. and gen. counsel Red Owl Stores, Inc., Mpls., 1957—. Mem. Gov. Minn. Commn. on Law Enforcement, 1967-68; pres. Hopkins (Minn.) Babe Ruth League, 1967; mem. Edina (Minn.) Commn. on Human Rihts, 1968-69; vol. Amicus, Inc., 1969—. Councilman, Edina, 1966—. Served with USMC, 1954-56. Mem. Am., Fed. (pres. Twin Cities chpt.), Minn. (bd. govs.) bar assns., Corporate Counsel Assn. Minn. (pres.), Anchor and Chain, Phi Delta Phi. Republican. Conglist. (Chmn. bd. trustee). Home: 5400 W 70th St Edina MN 55435 Office: 215 E Excelsior Av Hopkins MN 55343

JOHNSON, RICHARD DAVID, librarian; b. Cleve., Juen 10, 1927; s. Robert Emanuel and Emma LLindhorst) J.; B.A., Yalele, 1948; M.A. in Internat. Relations, U. Chgo., 1950, M.L.S., 1957; m. Harriet Herzog, Sept. 8, 1956; children-Ruth Ellen, Royce Emanuel, Librarian, Nat. Opinion Research Center, U. Chgo., 1956-57; reference librarian Stanforrd, U., 1957-59, cataloguer, 1959-60, 61-62, adminstrv. asst. to dir., 1960-61, head acquisitions, 1962-64, chief librarian tech. services, 1967-68; librarian HOnnold Library, Claremont (Cal.) Colls., 1968—. Served with inf. AUS, 1952-54. REcipient Bronze Star. Mem. A.L.A., Cal., Spl. library assns., Am. Soc. Information Sci., Beta Phi Mu. Oresbyn. Editor: California Libbrarian, 1966-68. Home: 571 Northwestern Dr Claremont CA 91711 Office: Honnold Library Claremont CA 91711

JOHNSON, RICHARD GARON, fgn. service officer; b. New Haven, Oct. 6, 1921; s. Harold Augustus and Ruth Hubbard (Spang) J.; B.A., Yale, 1946; M.A., Sch. Advanced Internat. Studies, Washington, 1947; m. Adaline Rockwell, Oct. 4, 1947; children—Susan Rockwell, Richard Garon. Joined U.S. fgn. service, 1947; vice consul, Florence, Italy, 1947-49; 3d sec. Am. embassy, Prague, Czechoslovakia, 1949-51; consul, Frankfurt, Germany, 1952; assigned Office Eastern European Affairs, State Dept., 1953-56, Polish lang. officer, 1956; 1st sec. Am. embassy, Warsaw, Poland, 1956-58; consul, Algiers, 1959-62; prin. officer, Asmara., Ethiopia, 1962; dep. chief of mission Am. embassy, Sofia, 1967-70; now dir. for Yugoslavia, Romania, Bulgaria, Albania. Home: 6 Warren Pl Montclair NJ 07042 Office: Dept State Washington DC 20250

JOHNSON, RICHARD HAROLD, army officer; b. Beaumont, Tex., Mar. 5, 1923; s. William Bernard and Lena (Nershon) J.; B.S., U.S. Mil. Acad., 1945; postgrad. Columbia, 1949-50; M.S. in Bus. Adminstrn., George Washington U., 1966; m. Jean Alice Robinson, Sept. 18, 1948; children—William Webb, Frederick Mershom, Harold Whelan, Robert Waite. Commd. 2d lt. U.S. Army, 1945, advanced through grades to brig. gen., 1969; mem. faculty U.S. Mil. Acad., 1950-54; mem. staff U.S. Army, Europe, 1955-58; assigned Staff Coll., Leavenworth, Kan., 1958-59; exec. officer, asst. chief staff G-3, Hdqrs. 8th Army, Korea, 1959-60; comdg. officer Leghorn Gen. Depot, dep. G-H, Hdqrs. So. Task Force, Italy, 1960-63; assigned 4th Div., 1963-65, Mil. Assistance Command, Vietnam, 1966-68; exec. officer Office Chief Staff Army, 1968-69; chief of staff First Field Force, Vietnam, 1969-70; asst. dep. chief staff for logistics Hdqrs. Continental Army Command, Ft. Monroe, Va., 1970—. Decorated D.S.C., Legion Merit with 3 oak leaf clusters, Air medal with 9 oak leaf clusters, Army Commendation medal with V and 2 oak leaf clusters. Home: 75 Ingalls Rd Fort Monroe VA 23351 Office: ADCSLOG Hdqrs CONARC Fort Monroe VA 23351

JOHNSON, RICHARD LOUIS, paper mfg. co. exec.; b. Madison, Wis., May 16, 1916; s. Harry J. and Louise (Nisalk) J.; B.A., U. Wis., 1939, LL.B., J.D., 1942; m. Virginia Eckman, Jan. 1, 1943; children—Gregg E., Timothy D. Admitted to Wis. bar, 1942; atty. Internal Revenue Chief Council Office, Washington, 1943-44; gen. atty, tax mgr., asst. controller Marathon Corp., Menasha, Wis., 1944-55; controller Menasha (Wis.) Corp., 1955-60, pres., dir., 1960—; dir. N.E. Wooden Ware Co., Wis. Mich. Power Co., Menasha Wood Ware Co., 1st Nat. Bank Menasha, John Strang Paper Co., Neenah- Menasha Water Power Co. Mem. Phi Delta Phi. Republican. Presbyn. Club: North Shore Golf. Home: 856 Bayview Rd Neenah WI 54956 Office: Menasha Corp Hwy 41 Neenah WI 54956

JOHNSON, RICHARD MERRILL, educator; b. Ft. Wayne, Ind., Oct. 31, 1934; s. Merrill C. and Blanche A. (Haberkorn) J.; B.A., Miami U., Oxford, O., 1956; M.A., Am. U., 1961; Ph.D., U. Ill., 1965; m. Nancy K. Burris, Apr. 20, 1957; children-Kathleen A., Deborah L. Instr. U.S. Naval Acad., Annapolis, Md., 1959-61; staff asst. Gov. Ill., 1963; instr. U. Ill. at Urbana, 1963-64; asst. prof. polit. sci. State U. N.Y. at Buffalo, 1964-68, asso. prof., 1968-69, vice-chmn. dept., 1966-68; prof., head dept. polit. sci. U. Ill. at Chgo. Circle, 1969—. Served to lt. USNR, 1956- 61. Mem. Am., Midwest polit sci. assns. Democrat. Unitarian. Author: The Dynamics of Compliance; Supreme Court Decision-Making From a New Prespective, 1967. Home: 2753 Girard Evanston IL 60201

JOHNSON, RICHARD NEWHALL, bus. exec.; b. Colorado Springs, Colo. Feb. 13, 1900; s. Otis Stafford and Annie (Fisher) J; A.B., Harvard, 1922, M.B.A., 1923; m. Margaret L. Paisley, July 4, 1924; children—Gordon Otis Fraser, Kathleen Fisher, Margaret Paisley; m. 2d, Phyllis Rising Walker, Feb. 25, 1950. With Pacific Mills, Boston, 1925-29; pres. and treas. Hillsboro Woolen Mills Co., 1929-36; v.p. Bldg. Products Inc., 1936-39; pub. Boston Evening Transcript, 1939-42; with WPB 1942-45; asst. treas. Export-Import Bank Washington 1945-50; fgn-trade policy adviser to the White House staff, 1950-51; asst. dir. mut. security Exec. Office of Pres., 1951-53; ass. dir. Fgn. Operations Administrn., 1953-54; pres. Logetronics, Inc., Springfield, Va., 1955-67, chmn. bd., 1968—. Served with USN AS, 1918. Home: Bywater Rd Annapolis MD 21401 Office: 7001 Loisdale Rd Springfield VA 22150

JOHNSON, RICHARD TENNEY, govt. ofcl.; b. Evanston, Ill., Mar. 24, 1930; s. Ernest Levin and Margaret Abbott (Higgins) J.; A.B. with high honors, U. Rochester, 1951; Postgrad., Trinity Coll., Dublin, Ireland, 1954-55; LL.B., Harvard, 1958; m. Marilyn Bliss Meuth. May 1, 1954; children—Ross Tenney, Lenore, Jocelyn. Trainee, Office Sec. Def., 1957-59; admitted to D.C. bar, 1959; atty. Office Gen. Counsel. Dept. Def., 1959-63; dep. gen. counsel Dept. Army, 1963-67, Dept. Transp., 1967-70; gen. counsel CAB, 1970—. Served to lt. USNR, 1951-54. Mem. Am., Fed. bar assns., Phi Beta Kappa, Theta Delta Chi. Home: 8424 Magruder Mill Ct Bethesda MD 20034 Office: 1825 Connecticut Av NW Washington DC 20428

JOHNSON, RICHARD TIDBALL, educator, neurologist; b. Grosse Pointe Farms, Mich., July 16, 1931; s. Horton Antonius and Katharine (Tidball) J.; A.B. cum laude, U. Colo., 1953, M.D., 1956; m. Frances Wilcox, Sept. 18, 1954; children—Carlton, Erica, Matthew, Nathan. Intern Stanford Hosps., 1956-57; resident Mass. Gen. Hosp., Boston, 1959-62; teaching fellow neurology Harvard Med. Sch., 1959-62; temporary 1st asst. neurology U. Newcastle-Upon-Tyne (Eng.), 1962; hon. fellow microbiology Australian Nat. U., 1962-64; asst. prof. Case-Western Res. U. Sch. Medicine, 1964-68, asso. prof., 1968-69; Eisenhower prof. neurology, asso. prof. microbiology Johns Hopkins U. Sch. Medicine, 1969—; neurologist Johns Hopkins Hosp., 1969—. Chmn. neurol. sci. tng. com., adv. bd. to Dept. Health, Edn. and Welfare, 1970-72. Served to capt., M.C., AUS, 1957-59. Recipient Weil award Am. Assn. Neuropathologists, 1967. Mem. Am. Neurol. Assn., Am. Soc. Clin. Investigation, Johns Hopkins Med. Soc. (pres. 1970-71), Phi Beta Kappa, Alpha Omega Alpha. Contbr. articles sci. jours.. Research on effect viruses on nervous system. Home: 107 Ridgewood Rd Baltimore MD 21210

JOHNSON, RICHARD WALTER, accountant; b. Mpls., Oct. 2, 1928; s. Walter Benjamin and Evelyn (Peterson) J.; B.B.A., with distinction, U. Minn., 1949; m. Patricia Gail Farrey, Nov. 16, 1963. With Arthur Andersen & Co., C.P.A.'s, 1949- , mng. partner, Omaha, 1960—. Bd. dirs., exec. com. Jr. Achievement Omaha, 1962—, v.p. finance, 1964—, chmn. fund raising com., 1963, pres., 1966-67; chmn. pilot div. United Community Services fund raising campaign, 1965, chmn. pacemaker sect. fund raising campaign, 1964, chmn. corporate standards com., 1966, asso. gen. chmn. 1968, treas., mem. exec. com., 1969; treas., dir. Neb. World Trade Devel. Council; bd. dirs. Mid-Am. council Boy Scouts of Am., Omaha Symphony Assn., Omaha Big Bros. Assn., Omaha Playhouse Assn. Mem. Aspen Inst. Humanistic Studies; trustee Fontenelle Forest Assn. Recipient One of Outstanding Young Men in Am. award, 1965. C.P.A., Neb., Ill. Mem. Am. Inst. C.P.A.'s, Neb. Soc. C.P.A.'s, Omaha-Lincoln Soc. Financial Analysts, Omaha C. of C. (chmn. membership relations com. 1962—, bd. dirs., 1965—, mem. exec. com., v.p. 1968), Beta Gamma Sigma, Beta Alpha Psi. Mason (K.T.). Clubs; Executives, Mid-Am. (Chgo.); Garden of the Gods (Colorado Springs); Omaha, Omaha Country; Univ. Minn. Alumni (Mpls.); Lincoln Univ.; La. Gorce Country (Miami Beach, Fla.); Palm Bay, Surf (Miami). Home: 1435 S 85th Av Omaha NB 68124 Office: 1700 Farnam St Omaha NB 68102

JOHNSON, ROBERT AVERY, lawyer; b. Chgo., Sept. 19, 1910; s. Philip Sidney and Belle (Root) J.; A.B., Calvin Coll., 1935; J.D., U. Mich., 1937; m. Barbara Harrigan Schmitt, Oct. 4, 1950; children—Camilla, Joni (Mrs. James E. Hadden), Sally (Mrs. Alan Tassler), Nancy (Mrs. John T. Connolly), Herbert F.N. Schmitt, Avery, Robert Avery, Lucia. Admitted to Mich. bar, 1937; since practiced in Grand Rapids; partner Miller, Johnson, Snell & Cummiskey. Mem. Am., Mich. bar assns., Am. Judicature Soc. Clubs: Kent Country, University (Grand Rapids). Home: 801 Cambridge Dr SE Grand Rapids MI 49506 Office: Old Kent Bldg Grand Rapids MI 49502

JOHNSON, ROBERT BRITTEN, educator; b. Cortland, N.Y., Sept. 24, 1924; s. William and Christine (Hofer) J.; student Wheaton (Ill.) Coll., 1942-43, 46-47; A.B. summa cum laude, Syracuse U., 1949, M.S., 1950; Ph.D., U. Ill., 1954; m. Garnet Marion Brown, Aug. 30, 1947; children—Robert Britten, Richard Karl, Elizabeth Anne. Asst. geologist Ill. Geol. Survey, 1951-54; asst. prof. geology Syracuse U., 1954-55; sr. geologist and geophysicist C. A. Bays & Asso., Urbana, Ill., 1955-56; from asst. prof. to prof. engring. geology Purdue U., 1956-66, head, engring. geology dept., 1964-66; prof. geology DePauw U., 1966-67, head, dept. geology, 1966-67; prof. geology Colo. State U., 1967—, acting chmn. dept. geology, 1968, chmn. dept., 1969—; cons. in field, 1957—. Active local Boy Scouts Am., 4-H Club, Sci. Fair. Served with USAAF, 1943-46. Fellow Geol. Soc. Am.; mem. Soc. Econ. Paleontologists and Mineralogists, Paleontol. Soc., Nat. Assn. Geology Tchrs., Assn. Engring. Geologists, Geosci. Information Soc., Rocky Mountain Assn. Geologists, Phi Beta Kappa. Republican. Baptist. Home: 2309 Moffett Dr Fort Collins CO 80521

JOHNSON, ROBERT BRUCE, pub. relations exec.; b. Mpls., Sept. 10, 1912; s. Edward and Kristine (Anderson) J.; A.B., Colo. Coll., 1934; m. Grace Burns, Dec. 8, 1943; children—Randi Elizabeth, Kristin Anne. Advt. supr. Proctor & Gamble, 1939-42; dir. pub. relations Marshall Field & Co., Chgo., 1945-49; sales promotion mgr. Mdse. Mart, Chgo., 1949-56; v.p., dir. merchandising Harshe-Rotman, Inc., Chgo., 1956-57; mng. dir. State St. Council, Chgo., 1957-64; pres. Robert Bruce Johnson & Assos., Inc., 1964- -. Trustee, Chgo. YWCA, Mus. Contemporary Art; bd. dirs. Inst. Internat. Edn. Adult Edn. Council Chgo., Chgo. Maternity Center. Served to lt. comdr. USNR, 1942-45. Mem. Pub. Relations Soc. Am., Chgo. Federated Advt. Clubs, Soc. Typographic Arts, Soc. Contemporary Am. Art, Am. Marketing Assn., Internat. Downtown Execs. Assn., Phi Delta Theta. Clubs: Chicago Press, Arts, Publicity (past pres.), University, Economic (Chgo.). Home: 489 Willow Rd Winnetka IL 60093 Office: 520 N Michigan Av Chicago IL 60611

JOHNSON, ROBERT CLYDE, educator; b. Knoxville, Tenn., Aug. 17, 1919; s. Robert Clyde and Lucille (Davis) J.; B.S., Davidson Coll., 1941, D.D., 1963; postgrad. Princeton Theol. Sem., 1941-43; B.D., Union Theol. Sem., N.Y.C., 1944, S.T.M., 1953; M.A., Columbia, 1947, Yale (hon.), 1963; D.D., Tusculum Coll., 1953; Ph.D., Vanderbilt U., 1957; m. Elizabeth Childs, June 26, 1942; children—Robert Clyde III, Richard Albert, Catherine Barton, Anne Elizabeth. Ordained to ministry Presbyn. Ch., 1943; minister in Shrewsbury. N.J., 1943-47, Greeneville, Tenn., 1947-55; asst. prof. theology Pitts. Theol. Sem., 1955-57, prof., 1957- 63; prof. thelogy Yale Div. Sch. 1963—, dean, 1963-69, fellow ezra Stiles Coll., Yale, 1963—. Served as chaplain USNR, 1944-46. Mem. Am. Theol. Soc. Author: The Meaning of Christ, 1958; Authority in Protestant Theology, 1959; The Church and its Changing Ministry, 1962. Editorial council Theology Today. Home: Candlewood Trails RD 2 New Milford CT 06776 Office: Yale Div Sch 409 Prospect St New Haven CT 06510

JOHNSON, ROBERT CURTIS, chem. engr., educator; b. Danville, Ill., Oct. 8, 1922; s. George Ernest and Jessie Rae (Tuttle) J.; B.S., U. Ill., 1944, M.S., 1946; Ph.D., Pa. State U., 1951; m. Claranne Von Fossen, Aug. 26, 1944; 1 dau., Julie Anne. Instr., Pa. State U., 1946-51; asst. prof., asso. prof. Washington U., 1951-57; dir. sci. computation Compumatix, St. Louis, 1957-58; assoo. mgr. process analysis dept. domputer div. TRW, Los Angeles, 1958- 64; prof., chmn. chem. engring. dept. U. Colo., Boulder, 1964—; cons. Mitsubishi-TRW, Tokyo, 1962-63. Mem. Am. Inst. Chem. Engrs., Am. Chem. Soc., A.A.A.S., Sigma Xi, Beta Theta Pi, Tau Beta Pi, Sigma Tau. Author: (with Edwin T. Williams) Stoichiometry for Chemical Engineers, 1958. Home: 1400 Mariposa St Boulder CO 80302

JOHNSON, ROBERT EDWARD, gas co. exec.; b. Ottumwa, Ia., July 5, 1921; s. Carl William and Beulah Margaret (Boyles) J.; B.A., George Washington U., 1950; m. Alice Charline Chandler, July 14, 1946; children—Robert Carl, Deborah Lea. Financial analyst SEC, Washington, 1941-57; asst. treas. Mich.-Wis. Pipe Line Co., Washington, 1958-62; v.p., controller Wis. Gas Co., Milw., 1963—. Served with USCGR, 1942-46. Episcopalian. Clubs: University, Milw. Yacht (Milw.). Home: 2631 E Shorewood Blvd Milwaukee WI 53211 Office: Wisconsin Gas Co 626 E Wisconsin Av Milwaukee WI 53201

JOHNSON, ROBERT ELLIOTT, airline exec.; b. Granger, Wash., July 10, 1907; s. Ashby William and Katherine (Pence) J.; A.B., U. Wash., 1929; m. Rosalie Gimple, May 14, 1937. Mgr. advt. and publicity Boeing Aircraft Co., Seattle, 1929-32; Pacific N.W. publicity rep. United Air Lines, asst. v.p. traffic, Chgo., 1932-38, dir. advt., 1938-50, asst. to pres., dir. pub. relations and advt., 1950-51, v.p., asst. to pres. charge sales, pub. relations and advt., 1951-58, sr. v.p. charge sales and advt., 1958-63, sr. v.p. marketing and services, 1963-71, exec. v.p., 1971—, dir., 1954—. Served to lt. USNR, World War II. Mem. Sales and Marketing Execs. Internat. (pres. 1962-63), Nat. Travelers Aid Soc. (dir.). Pi Sigma Epsilon, Chi Phi, Sigma Delta Chi. Clubs: Saddle and Cycle, Tavern; Thunderbird Country (Palm Springs, Cal.). Author: Flight Seven 1940; Pilot Jack Knight, 1950. Home: 1550 N State Pkwy Chicago IL 60610 Office: PO Box 66100 Chicago IL 60666

JOHNSON, ROBERT EMERSON LAMB, mcht.; b. Phila., Aug. 24, 1905; s. Howard Cooper and Edith (Lamb) J.; grad. Chestnut Hill Acad., 1923; A.B., Swarthmore Coll., 1927: postgrad., Harvard Bus. Sch., 1929; m. Mary Livingston Marshall, Sept. 14, 1929; children—Anne Livingston (Mrs. John W. M. Clark), Robert Emerson Lamb. Service mgr., asst. buyer, br. store mgr. Strawbridge & Clothier, Phila., 1929-42; exec. v.p. Good House Stores, Inc., Phila., 1946-48; successively asst. v.p., v.p., exec. v.p. and dir. Woodward & Lothrop, Inc., Washington, 1948—, later chmn. bd., chief exec. officer, now dir., mem. exec. com.; dir., chmn. exec. com. Frederick Atkins, Inc., N.Y.C. 1955-56, pres., 1957, chmn. bd., 1958-59; dir., mem. exec. com. Fed. Res. Bank Richmond, 1960-67. Bd. dirs. Me. Coast Meml. Hosp., Landon Sch., Bethesda, Md.; pres. Gibson Island Corp., 1969, also dir. Served to lt. comdr. USNR, 1942-46. Mem. Met. Washington Bd. Trade (dir. 1962-65), Dixie Dist. Lightning Class Assn. (commodore 1953), Central Soup Soc. (past v.p., dir.), Pa. Soc., Newcomen Soc., Gibson Island Yacht Squadron, Eta Mu Pi, Delta Upsion. Mem. Soc. Friends. Clubs: Northeast Harbor (Me.) Yacht; Causeway, (pres. 1970-71, dir.) (Southwest Harbor, Me.); Metropolitan; Alfalfa; Gibson Island (dir., sec. 1967-69); Southwest Harbor (Me.) Fleet (commodore 1963-65). Home: Gibson Island MD 21056 Office: Broadwater Way Gibson Island MD 21056

JOHNSON, ROBERT EUGENE, physiologist; b. Conrad, Mont., Apr. 8, 1911; s. Arthur and Florence May (Disbrow) J.; B.S. in Chemistry, Univ. Wash., 1931; A.B. in Physiology (Rhodes scholar), U. Oxford (Eng.), 1934, D.Phil. in Biochemistry, 1935; M.D., Harvard, 1941; m. Margaret Hunter, Jan. 12, 1935; children—Thomas Arthur, Charles William, Katherine Helen (dec.). Research asst. advancing to asst. prof. indsl. physiology Harvard Fatigue Lab., 1935-46; expert cons. QMC 3 AUS, 1941-46; dir. U.S. Army Med. Nutrition Lab., Chgo., 1946-49; prof. physiology U. Ill. at Urbana, 1949—, head dept., 1949-60, univ. dir. honors program, 1959-67, acting dean Grad. Coll., U. Ill., 1952-53. Nat. Sci. Found. Sr. Postdoctoral Research fellow, 1957-58; Guggenheim Meml. Found. fellow, 1964-65. Mem. Am. Soc. Clin. Investigation, Am. Soc. Biol. Chemists, Am. Physiol. Soc., Am. Inst. Nutrition. Author: Metabolic Methods, 1951; co-author Physiological Measurements of Metabolic Functions in Man, 1963; also articles in profl. jours. Home: 804 W Green St Urbana IL 61801

JOHNSON, ROBERT H., constrn. co. exec.; b. Phoenix, Feb. 26, 1916; s. Alfred and Bessie (Hornbeck) J.; grad. high sch.; m. Ella Mae Douglas, Apr. 15, 1939; children—Susan (Mrs. John Lane), Lawrence Alfred. With Del E. Webb Corp., 1935—, mgr. Los Angeles dist. office, 1944-47, v.p. corp., Phoenix, 1947-61, sr. v.p., 1961-67, pres., 1967—; dir. Cypress Ins. Co., Congress Ins. Co., Congress Ins. Co. Mem. Asso. Gen. Contractors Am. (past pres. So. Cal. chpt.). Clubs: Jonathan; Verdugo; Annandale Country; Indian Wells Country; La Quinta Country; Phoenix Country. Home: 77055 Desi Dr Indian Wells CA also 400 Georgian Rd Pasadena CA 91103 Office: PO Box 7588 Phoenix AZ 85011

JOHNSON, ROBERT HENRY, educator; b. Hannaford, N.D., Jan. 23, 1921; s. Albert Idan and Alma (Peterson) J.; B.A., Concordia Coll., Moorhead, Minn., 1942; M.S. Syracuse U., 1943; Ph.D., Harvard, 1949; m. Jean Vivian Ostby, June 21, 1943; children—Mark Olin, Eric

Lowell, Hilary Jean. Teaching fellow Harvard, 1948-49, instr. govt., 1949-51; asst. to exec. sec. NSC 1951-54, mem., sec. spl. staff, 1954-59, dir. planning bd. secretariat, 1959-61; mem. policy planning council State Dept., 1962- 67; sr. fellow Brookings Instn., 1966-68; Harvey Picker vis. prof. internat. relations Colgate U., 1968—. Served USNR, 1943-46. Fellow Social Sci. Research Council, 1948-49; recipient Rockefeller Pub. Service award, 1958. Mem. Am. Polit. Sci. Assn., Assn. for Asian Studies. Conglist. Home: 3710 N 38th St Arlington VA 22207 Office: Political Science Dept Colgate U Hamilton NY 13346

JOHNSON, ROBERT HUGH, bus. exec.; b. Franklin, Ind., Sept. 12, 1899; s. Newton Carr and Mary (Vornauf) J.; A.B., Oakland City Coll., 1921; B.S., U. Chgo., 1922, A.M., 1923, honor scholarship in math., Grad. Sch.; spl. work Mass. Inst. Tech., 1923-24; m. Kathleen McElroy, Nov. 30, 1933; children—Robert Hugh, John William, Mary (Mrs. W.J. Carney, Jr.) and Kathleen (Mrs. Moses Feldman) (twins). Rep. in Phila. dist., Ingersoll-Rand Co., 1924-30, mgr. Houston br., 1930- 31, central mgr. railroad dept., 1931-34, mgr. Cleve. br., 1934, Chgo. br., 1935-39, asst. v.p., 1939-45, v.p., N.Y.C., 1945- 55, 1st v.p., 1955, pres., 1955-59, chmn. bd., 1959-67, chmn. exec. com., 1967-70; dir., mem. exec. com. Western Electric Co.; dir. Ingersoll-Rand Co. Mem. Soc. Automotive Engrs., Am. Inst. Mining, Metall. and Petroleum Engrs. Republican. Baptist. Clubs: Siwanoy Country (Bronxville, N.Y.); India House (N.Y.C.); Blind Brook (Port Chester, N.Y.). Home: 1 Crown Circle Bronxville NY 10708 Office: Ingersoll-Rand Co 55 Broad St New York City NY 10004

JOHNSON, ROBERT IVAR, bus. exec.; b. Chgo., Aug. 18, 1933; s. Ivar Carl and Anna Elina (Wirkula) J.; diploma Wright Jr. Coll., 1953; A.B., Northwestern U., 1957; postgrad. U. Mich., 1958-59; m. Patricia A. Horgan, June 30, 1962; children—Christine Anne, Selenie Anne. Research asst. Dearborn Obs., Northwestern U., 1953-54, 57; planetarium tech. Adler Planetarium and Astron. Mus., 1953-55, asst. dir., acting dir., 1959, dir., 1960-68, staff Mus. Expdn. Observation Total Solar Eclipse, 1954, 63; dir. Kan. City Mus. History and Sci., 1966-70; exec. v.p., asst. sec., asst. treas., dir. Envirec, Inc., Northbrook, Ill., 1970—; spectrographic astronomy U. Mich., 1958-59; adult edn. faculty Central YMCA, Chgo., 1959-61; cons. Hubbard Sci. Com., 1961—, Coll. Am. Pathologists, 1970—. Lectr. astronomy Chgo. Acad. Scis., 1959-66, Chgo. Tchrs. Coll., 1960-66; spl. lectr. astronomy Ind. U., 1960-65; cons. Field Enterprises Ednl. Corp., 1960- 66, Replogle Globe Co., 1962-63, 68, Compton's Ency., 1961—, No. Ill. U., 1961-65, Ency. Brit. Films, Inc., 1962-64, McGraw-Hill, Inc., 1963, Museum Sci. and Tech., Tel Aviv, Israel, 1965-70, Rand McNally & Co., 1966, NSF Earth Sci. Curriculum Project, 1966; dir. NSF Summer Inst. in Astronomy, 1963, 64, 66; partner TBM Investments Co., 1964-65; tech. cons. Follett Pub. Co., 1966-68. Mem. citizens adv. com. for natural scis. Lake Forest Coll., 1961-66; bd. advisers World Book Ency. Sci. Service, 1964-66; program adv. bd. Inter-Univ. Center, 1966- -; mem. Am. Nat. ICOM Com. Edn. and Cultural Action; cons. astronomy and allied scis., planetarium design and ednl. films prodn. various orgns. Sci. fair judge high sch. div. Chgo. Bd. Edn., Parochial Schs., 1959-66; mem. U.S. com. for ednl. and cultural affairs Internat. Council Museums, 1966-70; mem. fine arts com. Ill. Sesquicentennial Commn., 1967-68; mem. Model Cities Com., Liberty Meml. Exhbn. Com., 1967-70 (both Kansas City); mem. Regional Health and Welfare Council, 1967-70, Kansas City Assembly on U.S. and Eastern Europe, 1968; mem. NSF panel Summer Inst. for Secondary Schs., 1968—; mem. Midwest Mus. Conf., 1964-70, finance com., 1967-70; mem. spl. events com. Kansas City Jewish Community Center, 1968-70. Bd. govs. Bacchus Cultural and Ednl. Found., 1968-70, Served with AUS, 1955-56; intelligence analyst Chgo.-Gray Nike Def. Hdqrs. Recipient certificate for service Gary (Ind.) Pub. Schs.; named One of 10 Outstanding Young Men, Chgo. Jr. C. of C. and Industry, 1961. Fellow A.A.A.S.; mem. Am. (co-chmn. com. spl. events 1964), Chgo. astron. socs., Internat. Platform Assn., Chgo. Planetarium Soc., Chgo. Physics Club (dir., pres. 1960-66), Assn. Sci. Mus. Dirs., Chgo. Geog. Soc., Adult Edn. Council Greater Chgo. (speakers bur., dirs.), Am. Assn. Museums (chmn. planetarium sect. 1962-66, program chmn. 1966), Northwestern U. Alumni Assn., Royal Astron. Soc. Can., Nat. Adult Edn. Assn. (tours com. 1966), Mu Beta Phi (hon.). Clubs: Physics (pres. 1963-64), Executives (Chgo.); Carriage. Author: Teachers Guide for the Celestial Globe, 1961; Astronomy-Our Solar System and Beyond, 1963; Galaxy Model Study Guide, 1963; The Story of the Moon, 1963, rev. edit., 1968, 2d revision, 1971; Celestial Planetarium Guide Book, 1964; Meteorite Kit Study Guide, 1968; Sundials, 1968. Editorial bd. Space Frontiers, 1962- 66. Contbr. articles to profl. jours., other publs. Home: 3 Overlook Dr Golf IL 60029 Office: 801 Skokie Blvd Northbrook IL 60062

JOHNSON, ROBERT JOSEPH, physician, educator; b. Toppenish, Wash., Feb. 8, 1915; s. Joseph Oliver and Minnie M. (Godfrey) J.; student Ia. State Coll., 1932-37; M.D., U. Ia., 1943; m. Dorothy Etsinger, Dec. 23, 1941; children—Lynn S., Patricia E., Nora J. Intern U. Ia. Hosps., 1943; from instr. to prof. anatomy U. Wash. Sch. Medicine, 1946-57; from asso. prof. to prof. surgery U. Wash., 1951-57; prof., chmn. dept. gross and neurol. anatomy U. W.Va., 1957-63; prof., chmn. dept. anatomy Grad. Sch. Medicine, U. Pa., 1963—; basic sci. examiner anatomy Wash. State, 1948-57; coroner Monongalia County, W.Va., 1961-63. Pres. W.Va. div. Am. Cancer Soc., 1961-63. Served with M.C., AUS, 1944-46, col. Res. Mem. Am. (exec. com. 1960-64), Canadian assns. anatomists, Am. Acad. Forensic Scis., Anat. Soc. Gt. Britain and Ireland, Halsted Soc. Home: 1234 Wyngate Rd Wynnewood PA 19096 Office: U Pa Philadelphia PA 19104

JOHNSON, ROBERT KELLOGG, librarian; b. Grand Rapids, Mich., July 27, 1913; s. Maurice Flower and Hazel Jeannette (Kellogg) J.; A.B., U. Mont., 1937; B.A. in Librarianship, U. Wash., 1938; M.S., U. Ill., 1946, Ph.D., 1957; m. Mary Loretta Franks, Aug. 22, 1950; children—Phillip, Emily (dec.), Peter, Sarah, Robert Kellogg. Reference asst. Library Assn. Portland (Ore.), summer 1938; circulation and reference librarian, instr. French, Pacific U., 1938-39, acting librarian, instr. library sci. 1939-40, head librarian, asso. prof. library sci., acting head audio-visual dept., 1946-48; head librarian, instr. library sci. Central Coll., Fayette, Mo., 1940-42; payroll auditor, spl. asst. to plant exec. central devel, and expt. unit Gen. Motors Corp., 1942-43; bibliographer U.Ill. Library, 1948-50, cataloguer, 1950-52; mem. staff Air U. Library, Maxwell AFB, Ala., 1952-59, asst. dir. libraries Drexel Inst. Tech., 1959-62, prof. library sci. Grad. Sch. Library Sci., 1959-64, dir. libraries, 1962-64; univ. librarian, prof. library sci. U. Ariz., 1964—. Chmn., Library Council Met. Phila., 1963- 64; mem. Pa. Com. Research Library Network, 1963-64; mem. Ariz. Library Survey Adv. Com., 1966-68; mem. Com. Jr. Colls. in Phila. Area, 1962-63; mem. Media (Pa.) Free Library Bd., 1959-60; mem. exec. and editorial bds. Seminar Acquisition Latin Am. Library Materials, 1969—. cons. in field. Mem. del. County Com. Career in Social Work, 1962-64. Trustee, Bibliog. Center for Research, Rocky Mountain Region, Inc., 1970-71. Served with USNR, 1943-46. Mem A.L.A., (council 1969—), Ariz. Library Assn. (exec. bd. 1965-66, v.p., exhibits chmn. 1967-68, pres. 1968-69) Assn. Coll. and Research Libraries (bd. dirs. 1969—). Contbr. numerous articles in field. Home: 3020 E 3d St Tucson AZ 85716

JOHNSON, ROBERT LAWRENCE, mech. engr.; b. Glasgow, Mont., June 18, 1919; s. Elmer and Hilma Otilia (Lindstrom) J.; B.S. in Mech. Engring., Mont. State U., 1942; m. Josephine Marie Saetre, Feb. 3, 1945; children—Robert Lawrence, Elizabeth Marie, Richard Paul. Research mech. engr. NACA, Langley Field, Va., 1942-43, project engr., then head lubrication sect., Cleve., 1943-58; chief lubrication br. NASA, Cleve., 1958—. Cons. in field; lectr. lubrication Gordon Research Confs., 1960—. Fellow Am. Soc. Lubrication Engrs. (Alfred E. Hunt award 1961, 65, IR100 award, 1966, nat. award, 1971, nat. pres. 1968-69); mem. Am. Assn. Testing Materials, A.A.A.S., Soc. Automotive Engrs., Lambda Chi Alpha. Lutheran. Mason (Shriner). Contbr. articles to profl. jours. Patentee in field. Home: 4503 W 224th St Fairview OH 44126 Office: NASA 21000 Brookpark Rd Cleveland OH 44135

JOHNSON, ROBERT LEE, lawyer; b. Yuman, Ariz., June 28, 1938; s. Charles A. and Ruth (Frame) J.; LL.B. cum laude, U. Ariz., 1962; m. Nancy Lou Thomason, Aug. 15, 1959; children-Sandra Jean, Susan Marie, Joan Leslie. Admitted to Ariz. bar, 1962, since practiced in Phoenix; mem. firm Jennings, Strouss & Salmon, 1962—; adj. prof. internat. comml. law Thunderbird Grad. Sch. for Internat. Mgmt., Phoenix, 1968-69. Mem. Am., Ariz. bar assns., Am. Bd. Trial Advs. Home: 1458 E Tuckey Lane Phoenix AZ 85014 Office: 111 W Monroe St Phoenix AZ 85003

JOHNSON, ROBERT LOUIS, govt. ofcl.; b. Winslow, Ariz., May 16, 1920; s. Ernest Conrad and Carrie (Saunders) J.; m. Betty Louise Tuft, Oct. 24, 1942; children-Jeanne, Robert, Louis, Bruce, Kirk. Missile design engr. Douglas Aircraft Co., Santa Monica, Cal., 1946-55, asst. chief engr. missile design engr. missile and space systems, 1955-58, chief engr. missile and space systems 1958-61, v.p. research and engring. missile and space systems, 1961-64; v.p. Manned Orbital Lab. program McDonnell Douglas Astronautics Co., 1964-69; asst. sec. army (research and devel.), 1969—; cons. research and devel. bd. Dept. Defense, 1952-61. Served with USNR, 1942-46. Recipient James H. Wyld Meml. award Am. Rocket Soc., 1960. Asso. fellow, Am. Inst. Aero.; mem. U. Cal. Engring. Adv. Council (vice chmn. 1963-69), Cal. State Tech. Services Adv. Council (vice chmn. 1966-69); Sigma Xi, Tau Beta Pi. Episcopalian. Home: 6823 Melrose Dr McLean VA 22101 Office: Dept Army Pentagon Washington DC 20310

JOHNSON, ROBERT MAX LOUIS, city mgr.; b. Des Moines, Jan. 6, 1921; s. Max Louis and Nell (Landfear) J.; student Coe Coll., Cedar Rapids, Ia., 1942; m. Edna Mae Haldy, July 20, 1941; children—R. Kimberlee, Kristine K. Newspaper reporter, columnist, Eldora, Ia., 1946, Waterloo, Ia., 1946-52; news editor WMT stas., Cedar Rapids, 1952-57; commr. pub. safety, Cedar Rapids, 1957-59; sales account exec.; 1960-61; mayor of Cedar Rapids, 1962-68; partner Growth & Development, Inc., subsidiary Condon Real Estate, Inc., Cedar Rapids, 1968—. City mgr., Marion, Ia., 1970—. Republican candidate for Congress, 2d dist. Ia., 1966. Served with inf. AUS, World War II; PTO. Recipient Distinguished Service award Sales Execs. Club, 1963, Recognition award Optimists Club, 1963, Upper Case award Cedar Rapids Press Club, 1963; named Boss of Year Criabwa chpt. Am. Bus. Women's Assn., 1965; DeMolay Legion of Honor, 1966. Mem. League Ia. Municipalities (chmn. pub. information com. 1963, chmn. larger cities group 1965), Am. Pub. Works Assn., Am. Legion. Presbyn. (past trustee). Mason (Shriner). Clubs: Optimist, High 12, Executives (Cedar Rapids). Contbr. articles. Home: 1515 Brookman Av Marion IA 52302 Office: City Hall Marion IA 52302

JOHNSON, ROBERT MERRILL, coll. adminstr.; b. Detroit, Sept. 17, 1926; s. Austin George and Jeanne Maude (Parkin) J.; B.S., U. Detroit, 1951, M.S., 1953; Ph.D., Mich. State U., 1957; m. Eleonore Maria Wegele, June 14, 1947; children-Barbara Jeanne (Mrs. Patrick Burns), Eric Merrill, Kristopher James, Kim Marie. Grad. teaching fellow U. Detroit, 1951-52; mfr. agt. Baker & Collinson, Detroit, 1953-54; grad. asst. Mich. State U., 1954- 57; instr. Colo. STate U., 1957-58, asst. prof., 1958-61, asso. prof., 1961-64, prof., 1964—, asst. dir.research found., 1958-62, dir. facilities devel., 1964-66; program dir. NSF, Washington, 1962-64, staff Asso., 1966-68; grad. dean, dir. research Fla. State U., 1968—. Served with USAAF, 1944-46. MEm. Am. Physiol. Soc., A.A.A.S., Electron Microscope Soc. Am., Sigma Xi. Contbr. articles to profl. jours. HOme: 306 Saratoga Dr Tallahassee FL 32303

JOHNSON, ROBERT RAYMOND, govt. ofcl.; b. Anthony, Kan., Feb. 22, 1917; s. Wallace Blaine and Marie Frances (Mulholland) J.; B.S., Northwestern U., 1939; postgrad. U. Ore., 1951-55, U. Pitts., 1964; m. Elizabeth Forsythe Griffin, Feb. 5, 1941; children—Elizabeth Ann, Alan, Brian, Eleanor. Personnel examiner City of Kansas City, Mo., 1940-41; cons. Pub. Adminstrn. Service Chgo., 1941-46; dir. Ore. Civil Service Commn., 1946-51; exec. dir. Ore. Legislative Commn. State Govt. Reorgn., 1949- 50; civil govt. adviser to Greece, ECA, 1951-55; exec. dir. Ore. Legislative Commn. Local Govt. Orgn., 1955-56; dir. Ore. Dept. Finance and Adminstrn., 1956-57; cons. League Ore. Cities, 1957-58; orgn. and mgmt. adviser to India, ICA, 1958-61; chief public adminstrn. adviser to Iran, AID, 1961-64, asst. dir. for East Pakistan, Dacca, 1965-67, asst. dir. pub. adminstrn. AID mission to Vietnam, 1967-68; asso. dir. for local devel., Vietnam, 1968-69; dir. tech. assistance AID, East Asia Bur., Washington, 1969—. Mem. Ore. Interstate Coop. Commn., 1957-58; U.S. observer pub. sect. mgmt. UN-ECAFE, 1959. Mem. Am. Soc. Pub. Adminstrn. (pres. Ore. 1957-58), Asia Soc., Middle East Inst., Eastern Region Orgn. Pub. Adminstrn., Indian Inst. Pub. Adminstrn., Sigma Alpha Epsilon. Rotarian, Mason. Home: 8500 Cherry Valley Lane Alexandria VA 22309

JOHNSON, ROBERT REED, paper co. exec.; b. Plainfield, Wis., June 1, 1919; s. Buchanan and Grace (Walker) J.; Ph.B., U. Wis., 1941, LL.B., 1948; m. Anna M. Buschor, June 1, 1946; 1 son, Reed Buchanan. Admitted to Wis. bar, 1948; practice in Plainfield, 1948-49; with Nekoosa-Edwards Paper Co., 1949—, sec., 1962—, also dir.; pres., dir. Nekoosa-Port Edwards Savs. and Loan Assn., 1959—; sec., gen. counsel Butler Paper Co., 1963- -. Justice of peace, Port Edwards, Wis., 1952-53; mem. bd. suprs., Wood County, Wis., 1963—. Bd. visitors U. Wis. Law Sch., 1966-69, chmn., 1968-69; bd. dirs., sec. Nekoosa-Edwards Found., 1956—; bd. dirs. S. Wood County YMCA, 1957—. Served with AUS, 1941-45. Mem. State Bar Wis. (bd. dirs. corp. counsel sect. 1955-58), Wis. Law Alumni Assn., Wood County Bar Assn., Tri-City Bar Assn., U. Wis. Law Sch. Benchers Soc., Chi Psi. Methodist (trustee). Rotarian.

JOHNSON, ROBERT W., bus. exec.; b. 1926; B.S., Carnegie-Mellon U., 1949, M.S., 1950; m. Mgr., Touche, Ross & Co., 1950-62; corporate controller Teledyne, Inc., 1962-65; v.p. M & M/Mars, 1965-69; v.p. Titan Group, Inc., 1969-70; v.p. finance, treas. Ronson Corp., 1970—. Served with USNR, 1945-46. Address: 1 Ronson Rd Woodbridge NJ 07095*

JOHNSON, ROBERT WILLARD, educator; b. Denver, Dec. 23, 1921; s. Ernest A. and Edith (Glassford) J.; student Lake Forest Acad., 1935-39, Oberlin Coll., 1939-42; M.B.A., Harvard, 1946; Ph.D., Northwestern U., 1952; m. Mary McCormack, Jan. 7, 1945; children—Judith L., Cynthia L. Asst. prof. Southwestern at Memphis, 1948-50; lectr. Mfrs. and Traders Trust Co., prof. finance, dir. exec. devel. program, dir. mgmt. tng. program chmn. dept. U. Buffalo, until 1959; economist Fed. Res. Bd., 1956-57; prof. financial adminstrn. Mich. State U., 1959-64; prof. indsl. adminstrn. Purdue U., Lafayette, Ind., 1964—. Reporter-economist National Conf. Commrs. on Uniform State Laws, 1964-71. Fellow Inst. Basic Math. for Application to Bus., Harvard, 1959-60; mem. Nat. Commn. Consumer Finance, 1969-72. Served with Supply Corps, USNR, 1943-46. Mem. Am. Finance Assn., Am. Econs. Assn., Inst. Mgmt. Scis., Financial Mgmt. Assn. (pres. 1971). Author: Financial Management, 1959; 4th edit., 1971; co-author: Self-Correcting Problems in Finance, 2d edit., 1970; Capital Budgeting, 1970. Home: 1001 Digby Dr Lafayette IN 47905

JOHNSON, ROSSALL JAMES, educator; b. Evanston, Ill., Dec. 31, 1918; s. James G. and Birdie (Barber) J.; A.A., Kendall Coll., 1939; B.S., Northwestern U., 1942, M.B.A., 1946; Ph.D., Purdue U., 1954; m. Helen Lauriente, Oct. 1, 1944; children—Clifford R., Kurtis F., Keith M. Asst. prof. mgmt. Miss. State Coll., 1949-51; prof. adminstrn., organizational behavior Northwestern U., 1954—; dir. Exec. Devel. Program U. Indonesia, 1959-61; sr. research prof. Ford Found. in India, 1964-66; cons. to industry. Mem. Am. Psychol. Assn., Acad. Mgmt. Author: Personnel and Industrial Relations, 1960; Executive Decisions, 1963, 2d edit., 1970; Business Environment in an Emerging Nation, 1966. Home: 638 Garrett Pl Evanston IL 60201

JOHNSON, ROY LEWIS, mfg. co. exec.; b. Lebanon, O., Mar. 19, 1913; s. George B. and Maude (Griswold) J.; A.B., Ohio Wesleyan U., 1934; m. Beatrice Valetta Robitzer, Oct. 27, 1934; children—Douglas (dec.), Gary F., Suzanne. With Gen. Electric Co., 1934-64, 66—, mgr. financial personnel service, 1960-64, v.p. mgmt. manpower services, 1966-70, v.p. exec. manpower, 1970—; v.p. Dun & Bradstreet, Inc., 1964-65, exec. v.p., 1965-66, also dir.; dir. Reuben H. Donnelley Corp., 1965-66, also dir. Gen. Learning Corp., 1967—. Mem. Financial Execs. Inst., Phi Beta Kappa, Omicron Delta Kappa, Alpha Tau Omega. Conglist. (trustee). Home: Mirror Lake Tuftonboro NH 03853 also 400 E 56th St New York City NY 10022 Office: 570 Lexington Av New York City NY 10022

JOHNSON, RUSSELL HARRISON, ret. banker; b. Montreal, Can., Jan. 2, 1911; s. Harrison T. and Rosemond (Overton) J.; student St. Paul's Sch., 1924-27; m. Mary Jane Miller, Feb. 28, 1936; children—Judith, Russell Harrison, Marus, Mary Jane. With U.S. Trust Co., N.Y.C., 1928-70, exec. v.p., 1961-70; ret., 1970. Club: Plantation (Hilton Head Island, S.C.). Address: 1 Woodbine Pl Sea Pines Plantation Hilton Head Island SC 29928

JOHNSON, RUSSELL MELVIN, savs. and loan assn. exec.; b. Scandia, Minn., Mar. 19, 1909; s. Henry A. and Minnie (Allenson) J.; B.A., Gustavus Adolphus Coll., St. Peter, Minn., 1931; m. Ruth M. Johnson, July 28, 1934; children—Stephen, Susan (Mrs. Jay Diebold), Lynn (Mrs. Mark Anderson). Engaged as realtor, 1931- 37; with Twin City Fed. Savs. and Loan Assn., 1937—, v.p., 1951- 66, pres., dir., 1966—; dir. N. Central Co., N. Central Life Ins. Co., Continental Mortgage Ins. Co., Madison, Wis. Bd. dirs. Better Bus. Bur. Mpls.; mem. Minn. Savs. and Loan Adv. Council. Vice pres. Arthritis and Rheumatism Found. Minn.; bd. dirs. Goodwill Industries St. Paul, Minn. Blue Cross, Mpls. Downtown Council, Mpls. YMCA. Recipient Distinguished Alumni award Gustavus Adolphus Coll., 1969. Mem. U.S. Savs. and Loan League (past bd. dirs.), Savs. and Loan Council Twin Cities (past pres.), Savs. and Loan League Minn. (past pres.). Kiwanian (treas.), Mason (Shriner). Clubs: Minnesota, Town and Country, St. Paul Athletic (past bd. dirs.), Midway Civic (St. Paul), Minneapolis. Home: 666 S Mississippi River Blvd St Paul MN 55116 Office: 801 Marquette Av Minneapolis MN 55402

JOHNSON, RUTH CARTER, (Mrs. J. Lee Johnson III), civic worker; b. Ft. Worth, Oct. 19, 1923; d. Amon Giles and Nenetta (Wiess) Carter; B.A., Sarah Lawrence Coll., 1945; m. J. Lee Johnson III, June 8, 1946; children—Sheila Broderick (Mrs. John V. Lindley, Jr.), J. Lee IV, Karen Carter, Catherine Lehane, Mark Lehane Pres., Ft. Worth Jr. League, 1954-55, chmn. bd. Amon Carter Mus. Western Art, Ft. Worth, 1961- -; pres. Arts Council Greater Ft. Worth, 1963-64; bd. regents U. Tex. at Austin, 1963-69; v.p. internat. council Mus. Modern Art, 1965—; bd. mem. Nat. Trust Historic Preservation, Nat. Coll. Fine Arts, Smithsonian Instn., Washington, 1966-70. Roman Catholic. Home: 1200 Broad Av Fort Worth TX 76107

JOHNSON, R.W., business exec. Controller Clevite Corp., Cleve. Office: 17000 St Clair Av Cleveland OH 44110*

JOHNSON, SAM HOWARD, univ. dean; b. Henning, Tenn., June 27, 1907; s. Sam Howard and Harriet (Poston) J.; B.S., Memphis State U., 1931; M.A., Columbia Tchrs. Coll., 1939; Ed.D., N.Y. U., 1954; m. Ruth Amelia Fritsche, June 2, 1938. Tchr., supervising prin. pub. schs., Tenn., 1933-43; propr. Johnson Brokerage Co., Jacksonville, Fla., 1945-49; mem. faculty Memphis State U., 1949- 58, 63—, prof. edn., 1954-58, dean Sch. Edn., 1961-70; prof. ednl. adminstrn. and supervision N.Y. U., 1958-61; cons., speaker regional, state, nat. edn. and hosp. teaching groups; participant Research Study N.Y. State, N.Y. U., 1960; cons. Western Tenn. Elementary Prins. Assn.; univ. rep. Am. Assn. Colls. Tchrs. Edn.; summer tchr. N.Y. U. courses for Puerto Rican tchrs., San Juan, 1956-60. Mem. Nat. Com. of Edn. in Family Finance; cons., speaker family finance edn., Okla., Ark.; cons. Sch. to Sch. project Am. Sch. Guatemala. Past v.p., now bd. dirs. Memphis Speech and Hearing Center. Chmn. Memphis Consumer Affairs Com.; mem. Tenn. Adv. Commn. on Certification and Edn. Mem. Am. Assn. Sch. Adminstrs., N.E.A., Assn. Supervision and Curriculum Devel. (past pres.), Phi Delta Kappa. Mason, Lion (past v.p. East Memphis). Contbr. articles ednl. jours. Home: 5376 Rolling Oaks Dr Memphis TN 38117

JOHNSON, SAMUEL CURTIS, wax co. exec.; b. Racine, Wis., Mar. 2, 1928; s. Herbert Fisk and Gertrude (Brauner) J.; B.A., Cornell U., 1950; M.B.A., Harvard, 1952; m. Imogene Powers, May 8, 1954; children—Samuel Curtis III, Helen Powers, Herbert Fisk III, Winifred Conrad. With S.C. Johnson & Son Inc., Racine, 1954—, internat. v.p., 1962-63, exec. v.p., 1963-66, pres., 1966—, chmn. bd., 1967—; chmn. bd., pres. Johnson Diversified, Inc., Racine, Heritage Bank Racine; chmn. bd. Triple E Corp., Racine; dir. Johnson Wax cos. in U.S., Eng., France, Italy, Germany, Netherlands, Philippines, Japan, Venezuela, Switzerland and Can., Cutler-Hammer, Inc., Milw.; dir., mem. exec. com. Inland Financial Corp., Milw. Mem. Bus. Council, Conf. Bd., Bus. Com. for Arts; mem. exec. com. Nat. Urban Coalition. Bd. dirs. Am. Host Found.; trustee Eisenhower Exchange Fellowships, Am. Crafts Council, Com. for Econ. Devel.; trustee, exec. com. of bd. Cornell U.; pub. trustee Mayo Found.; chmn. bd. Johnson Found., Inc., Prairie Sch., Mem. Internat. C. of C. (trustee, mem. exec. com. U.S. council), Young Pres.' Orgn., Chi Psi. Clubs: Cornell (N.Y.C., Milw.); University (Milw.); Racine Country; American. Home: 16 N Vincennes Circle Racine WI 53402 Office: 1525 Howe St Racine WI 53403

JOHNSON, SEARCY LEE, lawyer; b. Dallas, Aug. 30, 1908; s. Jesse Lee and Annie Clyde (Searcy) J.; A.B., Williams Coll., 1929, LL.B., U. Tex., 1933; m. Lillian Cox; 1 dau., Susan Lee. Admitted to Tex. bar., 1933; since practiced in Dallas; partner Lawther, Cramer, Perry

& Johnson, 1941, then Johnson, Guthrie, White & Stanfield, now Johnson & Guthrie. Pres., Allen Co., publishers, Dallas. Legal adv. Gen. Hershey on vets. reemployment, 1944-45; spl. asst. to U. S. Atty. Gen., organizer, chief Veterans Affairs Sect., Dept. Justice, 1945-47. Served as lt. comdr. USNR, 1941-45. Decorated Army Commendation award. Mem. Am., Washington, Tex., Dallas (spl. prosecutor 1938) bar assns., Am. Legion, Amvets (charter mem.), Dallas Hist. Assn., A.S.C.A.P., Am. Authors and Composers, S.A.R., Am. Judicature Soc., Fellows Tex. Bar, English-Speaking Union, Psi Upsilon. Mason (33, Shriner, K. T.), Blue Goose, Royal Order of Scotland. Clubs: Chaparal Dallas, City, Insurance, Williams, Dallas Athletic, Dallas Country; National Press (Washington). Author; Marbel Model; In Loco Parentis; Feast of Tabernacles. Contbr.; Hildebrand's Texas Corporations, 1942; also articles to legal jours. Composer: Sama Veda, Sweet Bird of Youth, Votive Offering, The Ballad of the Thresher, others. Home: 3901 Gillon Av Dallas TX 75205 Office: Republic Nat Bank Bldg Dallas TX 75201

JOHNSON, SHERMAN ELBRIDGE, clergyman; b. Hutchinson, Kan., Mar. 7, 1908; s. Walter Ambrose and Josie Augusta (Enderton) J.; student George Washington U., 1923-29; A.B., Northwestern U., 1933; B.D., Western Theol. Sem., 1933; S.T.M., Seabury-Western Theol. Sem., 1934; Ph.D., U. Chgo., 1936; S.T.D. (hon.), Nashotah (Wis.) House, 1940, Seabury-Western, 1952, Ch. Divinity Sch., 1971; D.D. (hon.), Occidental Coll., 1959, Episcopal Theol. Sch., Cambridge, Mass., 1967, Pacific Sch. Religion, 1971; m. Jean Henkel Rogers, June 10, 1935; 1 son, David Enderton; stepchildren —Carol Julia (Mrs. Dana B. Malone), Marcia Jean. Ordained to ministry Episcopal Ch., 1933; pastor Trinity Ch., Belvidere, Ill., and tutor Seabury-Western Theol. Sem., 1933-36; prof. New Testament, Nashotah House, 1936-40; asst. prof. New Testament Episcopal Theol. Sch., Cambridge, Mass., 1940-46, prof., 1946-51; ann. prof. Am. Sch. Oriental Research, Jerusalem, Palestine, 1947-48; dean Ch. Divinity Sch. of Pacific, Berkeley, Cal., 1951—; lectr. Union Theol. Sem., 1945, Yale Divinity Sch., 1950; Fulbright prof. U. Utrecht, Netherlands, 1962; Weigle prof. Yale Divinity Sch., 1967- 68; scholar in residence Ecumenical Inst., Jerusalem, 1971-72. Mem. Joint commn. approaches to unity Protestant Episcopal Ch., 1944-49, 56-61, exec. council, 1964-70; archaeologist expdn. to el-Jib, Jordan, 1956, Sardis, Turkey, 1958. Mem. Archaeol. Inst. Am., Soc. Bibl. Lit. and Exegesis. Author: The Septuagint Translators of Amos, 1936; Commentary on Matthew in The Interpreter's Bible, 1951; Jesus in His Homeland, 1957; The Gospel According to St. Mark, 1960; The Theology of the Gospels, 1966; translator (with others) Johannes Weiss, History of Primitive Christianity, 1937. Editor: (with M.H. Shepherd, Jr.) Munera Studiosa, 1946; The Joy of Study, 1951; Anglican Theol. Rev., 1956-59. Contbr. numerous articles and book revs. in theol. jours. Home: 569 Forest Hill Rd Mansfield OH 44907 (summer) Jacksonville Stage Rd Charlemont MA 01339

JOHNSON, SHERMAN ELLSWORTH, econ. cons.; b. Scandia, Minn., July 31, 1896; s. Emil and Eva (Johnson) J.; B.S., U. Minn., 1924, M.S., 1926; Ph.D., Harvard, 1938; m. Evelyn Hedin, June 27, 1925; children—Lenore (Mrs. W. W. Cowan), Paul, Katherine (Mrs. R.R. Nelson). Instr. agrl. econs. U. Minn., 1924- 25; asst. economist La. State U., 1925; asst., asso. prof. Montana State Coll., 1926-29; head, dept. agrl. econs., S.D. State Coll., 1930-33; wheat specialist Brookings Instn., 1933-34; regional dir. land utilization program U.S. Dept. Agr., 1934-36; prin. agrl. economist, Bur. Agrl. Econs., 1936-37, head. div. farm mgmt. and costs, 1937-46, asst. chief Bur. Agrl. Econs. 1946-53, dir. farm and land mgmt. research Agrl. Research Service, 1954-56, chief economist, 1957- 60; dep. adminstr. Econ. Research Service, 1961-65, collaborator, 1965—; econ. cons., 1965—. Dir., Food Prodn. Br., War Food Adminstrn., World War II. Recipient Outstanding Achievement award U. Minn., 1956; Distinguished Service award, Dept. Agr., 1958; Pres.'s award Distinguished Civilian Service, 1963. Fellow Am. Farm Econ. Assn. (pres. 1943); mem. Internat. Assn. Agrl. Economists (pres. 1958-61), Am. Econ. Assn., Agrl. History Soc., Alpha Zeta, Gamma Sigma Delta. Presbyn. Sr. author: Managing a Farm; Getting Started in Farming; also agrl. and tech. bulls.; contbr. to profl. jours. Home: Virginia Circle Strasburg VA 22657

JOHNSON, SHIRLEY BEATRICE, (Mrs. Asher B. Lans), educator; b. Wichita, Kan., Mar. 27, 1934; d. Howard A. and Kathryn (Wiebe) Johnson; B.A. magna cum laude, Radcliffe Coll., 1956; M.A. (Marshall scholar), U. Edinburgh, 1958; Ph.D., Columbia, 1966; m. Asher B. Lans, June 28, 1967; 1 dau., Andrea Elisabeth. Hon. Woodrow Wilson scholar, 1956-58; instr. econs. Mt. Holyoke Coll., 1958-59; lectr. City Coll. N.Y., 1959-62; instr. Barnard Coll., Ford research scholar, Columbia U. Labor Workshop fellow, 1962-65; asst. prof. N.Y.U., 1965-67; asso. prof. econs. Vassar Coll., Poughkeepsie, N.Y., 1967—; vis. prof. Sarah Lawrence Coll., 1970-71. Sec. Columbia Seminar on Maladaptation in Modern Soc., 1967-70. Recipient Gold medal in polit. economy U. Edinburgh, 1958. Mem. Am. Econ. Assn., Phi Beta Kappa. Club: N.Y.C. Radcliffe (dir.). Contbr. articles profl. jours. Home: 24 Gramercy Park South New York City NY 10003 Office: Vassar Coll Dept Econs Poughkeepsie NY 12603

JOHNSON, SIDNEY MALCOLM, educator; b. New Haven, Conn., Aug. 17, 1924; s. Everett Caswell and Eleanor (Eckman) J.; B.A., Yale, 1944, M.A., 1948, Ph.D., 1953; m. Lora Louise Dunbar, Sept. 29, 1945; children—Thomas Malcolm, Frederick William, Karl Everett. Asst. instr. Yale, 1946-51; instr. U. Kan., 1951- 53, asst. prof., 1953-58, asso. prof., 1958-62, prof., 1962-65; prof. German, chmn. dept. Emory U, 1965—. Served to lt. (j.g.) USNR, 1943- 46. Research grantee Am. Philos. Soc., 1963. Mem. Modern Lang. Assn., S. Atlantic Modern Lang. Assn., Am. Assn. Tchrs. German, Am. Assn. U. Profs., Wolfram von Eschenbach Gesellschaft, Internat. Assn. for Germanic Studies. Contbr. articles on medieval German lit. profl. jours. Home: 878 Barton Woods Rd NE Atlanta GA 30307

JOHNSON, STANFIELD BRYANT, r.r. ofcl., lawyer; b. Omaha, Nov. 8, 1907; s. Alvin F. and Marie (Bryant) J.; A.B., Dartmouth, 1929; LL.B., Creighton U., 1932; m. Jean Redick, Jan. 6, 1934; children—Alvin F., William Stanfield. Admitted to Neb. bar, 1932, D.C. bar, 1946, Cal. bar, 1955; practice law, Omaha, 1932- 34, Washington, 1934-42; atty. U.P. R.R., 1945-55; legal rep. So. Pacific Co., Washington, 1945-55, gen. solicitor, San Francisco, 1955- 58; chmn. Assn. Southeastern R.R.'s, 1958—. Served as maj., Gen. Staff, AUS, 1942-45. Mem. Nat. Def. Transp. Assn. (v.p., gen. counsel 1966), Alpha Delta Phi, Phi Sigma Rho, Delta Theta Phi, Alpha Sigma Nu. Clubs: Metropolitan, Burning Tree, Chevy Chase (Washington); Burlingame (Cal.) Country. Home: 2814 R St NW Washington DC 20007 Office: 1710 H St N W Washington DC 20006

JOHNSON, STURE ARCHIE MANSFIELD, educator, physician; b. Morgan, Ore., Apr. 24, 1907; s. Per and Olga (Miller) J.; Ph.C., N. Pacific Coll., 1928; B.A., U. Ore., 1934, M.D., 1938; m. Geneva Frances Beane, June 7, 1936. Intern, Multnomah County Hosp., Portland, Ore., 1938-39; resident U. Ore. Med. Sch., Clinics and Hosps., 1939-41; N.Y. Skin and Cancer Hosp., 1941-42; research asso. U. Mich. Med. Sch., 1942-44, asst. prof. dermatology, 1944-46; prof. dermatology, head dept. U. Wis. Med. Sch., Madison, 1946—; chief cons. dermatology VA Hosp., Madison, 1961—. Fellow A.C.P.; mem. Am., Pacific (hon. corr.) dermatol. assns., Soc. Investigative Dermatology (v.p. 1956), Acad. Dermatology, Wis. (past pres.), Chgo. (v.p. 1959), dermatol. socs. Pan Am. Med. Assn. (diplomate). Mem. sptly. editorial bd. Postgrad. Medicine, 1960—. Home: 313 New Castle Way Madison WI 53704

JOHNSON, TERRY WALTER, Jr., educator; b. Waukegan, Ill., Jan. 13, 1923; s. Terry Walter and Cora (Anderson) J.; B.S., U. Ill., 1948; M.S., U. Mich., 1949, Ph.D., 1951; m. Anita May Johnson, Sept. 4, 1948; children—Sharon Lee, Laura Ann, Betty Louise. Instr., U. Mich., 1950-51; mycologist Chem. Corps, Ft. Detrick, Md., 1951-53; asst. prof. biology U. Miss., 1953-54; asst. to prof. dept. botany Duke, 1954—, chmn. botany dept., 1963-71; vis. prof. U. Wash., summer 1962, U. Minn., summer 1967. Mem. adv. panel NSF, 1963- 66. Served with AUS, 1943-47. Guggenheim fellow, 1960-61. Mem. Mycol. Soc. Am., Bot. Soc. Am., N.C. Acad. Sci., Brit. Mycol. Soc. Lutheran. Research on aquatic fungi. Contbr. numerous articles profl. jours. Home: 2408 Prince St Durham NC 27707

JOHNSON, THEODORE REYNOLD, finance co. exec.; b. Knoxville, Ia., Jan. 24, 1911; s. Hans Theodore and Edith (Reynolds) J.; student U. Utah, 1935, Am. Inst. Banking, 1936, Indsl. Coll. Armed Forces, 1951; m. Virginia Coleman, Mar. 20, 1937; children—Judith (Mrs. Alan Hay Pierrot), Susan (Mrs. Gordon N. Elliott). With Salt Lake City br. Fed. Res. Bank of San Francisco, 1929-36; with Bank of Vernal, Vt., 1937-41; with ins. mgmt. T.R. Johnson & Co., Denver, 1946-52; exec. v.p. Kassler & Co., mortgage bankers, Denver, 1952-64; dir., sec.-treas. Tri State Finance Corp., Denver, 1964—; dir. Blvd. Nat. Bank, 1964—; v.p., treas., dir. Blvd. Corp., 1969—. Mem. Colo. and Denver Met. Safety Council, 1953-55. Pres. Denver President's Round Table, 1959; bd. dirs. Denver Better Bus. Bur.; nat. trustee Voice of Youth; chmn. adv. bd. Salvation Army, 1966. Served from 1st lt. to col., C.E., AUS, 1941-45. Decoraed Bronze Star medal. Mem. Denver Insurors (dir. 1953-55). Episcopalian. Mason, Kiwanian (internat. pres., past trustee). Home: 1515 E 9th Av Denver CO 80218 Office: 900 E Louisiana Av Denver CO 80210

JOHNSON, THOMAS HERBERT, educator; b. Bradford, Vt., Apr. 27, 1902; s. Herbert T. and Myra (Burbeck) J.; A.B., Williams Coll., 1926, L.H.D. (hon.), 1949; A.M., Harvard, 1929, Ph.D., 1934; Litt.D., Marlboro Coll., 1955, Rutgers U., 1956, Middlebury Coll., 1967; m. Catherine Rice, Sept. 11, 1934; children—Laura Bradley, Thomas. Instr. English, Rutgers U., 1928-29, Williams Coll., 1929-31; lectr. in English, summers, Rutgers, 1930-32, U. Ia., 1936, Chautauqua, 1937; lectr. New Sch. Social Sci., 1943-44; tchr. English, Lawrenceville (N.J.) Sch., 1937—, dept. chmn., 1944-67; vis. prof. Am. lit. U. Copenhagen, 1951-52, U. Pa., 1958- 59, N.Y. U., 1959-60; bibliographer Am. lit., Modern Lang. Assn., 1943-47; lectr English, summers, Columbia, 1948, Harvard, 1950; Berg prof. N.Y. U., 1959-60; judge nonfiction Nat. Book award, 1959. Recipient Chap Book award, 1956; Guggenheim fellow, 1951-52. Fellow Soc. Am. Historians, Soc. for Am. Studies; mem. Colonial Soc. Mass., Bibliog. Soc. Am., Modern Lang. Assn. Am., Delta Upsilon. Conglist. Clubs: Century, Grolier. Author: (with Perry Miller) The Puritans, 1938; A Bibliography of the Printed Works of Jonathan Edwards, 1940; Emily Dickinson: An Interpretive Biography, 1955; Oxford Companion to American History, 1966. Editor: (with Clarence Faust) Jonathan Edwards, Representative Works, 1935; The Poetical Works of Edward Taylor, 1939; Men of Tomorrow, 1942; Return to Freedom, 1944; A Man's Reach, 1947; In Defense of Democracy, 1949; The Poems of Emily Dickinson, (3 vols.), 1955; The Letters of Emily Dickinson, 3 vols. 1958. Co-Editor; (with Spiller, Thorp and Canby) Literary History of the U.S., 1948; Final Harvest: Emily Dickinson's Poems, 1968; Emily Dickinson: Selected Letters, 1971. Contbr. Ency. Brit. Address: Lawrenceville NJ 06848

JOHNSON, THOMAS J., former banker; b. Pitts., Dec. 29, 1905; s. Howard M. and Eleanor (Conaway) J.; student Wharton Sch. U. Pa., 1928; m. Dorothy Slocum, Oct. 18, 1929; children—Thomas J. III, Walter J., Stephen C., Theodore C. With Mellbank Corp., Pitts., 1930-35; asst. v.p. Mellon Securities Corp., Pitts., 1935- 46; v.p. First Boston Corp., N.Y.C., 1946-70, ret., 1970; dir. McLouth Steel Corp., Detroit, N.H. Robertson Co., Pitts. Home: 15 Payne Whitney Lane Manhasset NY 11030

JOHNSON, THOMAS JOSEPH, Jr., mgmt. cons.; b. Burlington, N.J., Nov. 16, 1916; s. Thomas Joseph and Sara (Riley) J.; B.S., La. State U., 1939; m. Martha G. Gossett, Dec. 25, 1944; children—Thomas Joseph III, Timothy A. Mng. dir. mgmt. scis. Ebasco Services, Inc., N.Y.C., 1967—; pres. Tomac Devel. Corp. Served to maj. AUS, 1941-45. Mem. Edison Elec. Inst., Am. Gas Assn., Phi Delta Theta. Home: 3 Bingham Hill Circle Rumson NJ 07760 Office: 100 Church St New York City NY 10007

JOHNSON, THOMAS MARION, investment banker; b. Columbus, Ga., July 26, 1901; s. John Thomas and Elizabeth (Mountcastle) J.; student Pape and Lind and Myers pvt. schs., 1907-16, Gordon Mil. Inst., 1916-17; A.B., U. Ga., 1921; m. Kathryn May Twiggs, July 24, 1924; children—Thomas Marion, John David Twiggs, Robert Bradley, Kathryn (Mrs. Harcourt E. Waller, Jr.), Elizabeth Mountcastle. With Citizens & So. Co., Savannah, Ga., 1921-33, v.p., sec., 1925-33; chmn. bd., dir. Johnson, Lane, Space, Smith & Co., Inc., Savannah, 1933—; dir. Hanna Mfg. Co. (Athens, Ga.), Central of Ga. R.R., Airpax Electronic, Inc. (Ft. Lauderdale, Fla.). Trustee Episcopal Church Pension Fund, N.Y. Mem. N.Y. Stock Exchange, Investment Bankers Assn. Am. (past v.p.), Am. Stock Exchange. Clubs: Oglethorpe, Savannah Yacht and Country, Chatham (Savannah). Home: 31 Island Dr Savannah GA 31406 Office: 101 E Bay St Savannah GA 31401

JOHNSON, THOMAS PHILLIPS, lawyer; b. New Castle, Pa., June 8, 1914; s. Charles H. and C. Grace (Phillips) J.; A.B., Rollins Coll., 1934; LL.B., Harvard, 1937; LL.D., Culver-Stockton Coll., 1959; m. Jane Moore, June 28, 1934; children—Thomas P., James M. Admitted to Pa. bar, 1937, and practiced as asso. firm Reed, Smith, Shaw & McClay, Pitts., 1937-42; partner firm Kirkpatrick, Lockhart, Johnson & Hutchison, Pitts. Dir., v.p. N.Am. Rockwell Corp., Rockwell Standard Co., Pitts., Hall Johnson Constrn. Co.; pres., dir. Castle Motels, Inc.; chmn. Lawrence Savs. & Trust Co.; v.p., sec., dir. Pitts. Athletic Co.; sec. 525 Wm. Penn Pl. Corp., Park View Corp.; dir. Robroy Industries, Inc., Pa. Investment & Real Estate Co., Trion, Inc., T.W. Phillips G & O, Rockwell Mfg. Co., Cyclops Corp., Blair Strip Steel Co. Trustee, Rollins Coll., Presbyn. Hosp., St. Francis Hosp., Bethany Coll. Served to lt. comdr. USNR, 1944-46. Awarded Sec. of Navy Commendation. Mem. Am., Pa., Allegheny County bar assns., Am. Law Inst., Newcomen Soc. Eng., Kappa Alpha, Omicron Delta Kappa, Pi Gamma Mu. Clubs: Duquesne, Harvard-Yale-Princeton, University, Pittsburgh Athletic Association, Variety, International, Allegheny (Pitts.); Pinnacle, Press (N.Y.C.); Fox Chapel Golf; LyFord Cay (Nassau); Cat Cay (Bimini). Home: W Woodland Rd Pittsburgh PA 15232 Office: Oliver Bldg Pittsburgh PA 15222

JOHNSON, THOR, musician, educator; b. Wisconsin Rapids, Wis., June 10, 1913; s. Rev. Herbert B. and Anna Josephine (Reusswig) J.; A.B., U. N.C., 1934, Mus.D., 1951; Mus.M., U. Mich., 1935; Hon. Mus., Davidson Coll., 1947; Hon. Dr. Mus., Cin. Conservatory Music, 1948, U. N.C., 1952, Moravian Coll., 1953, Northwestern U., 1953, Baldwin Wallace Coll., 1956, U. Wis., 1960; LL.D., Beloit Coll.; Litt.D., Miami U., 1950; studied under Felix Weingarter, Bruno Walter, Nicolai Malko at Salzburg Mozarteum (Beebe Found. scholarship awarded 1935 for European study), 1936-37; studied conducting under Hermann Abendroth, conservatory of Leipzig; pvt. study in Prague; studied conducting under Dr. Serge Koussevitsky, Berkshire Music Center (scholarships), summers 1940, 41; unmarried. Organized and conducted an orchestra of 17 players, Winston-Salem. N.C., age of 13; asst. conducter N.C. State Symphony, 1932-34; condr. U. of Mich. Little Symphony, 1934- 36, 1938-42, Grand Rapids (Mich.) Symphony Orch., 1940-42, Univ. Musical Soc. (choral union and May festival), Ann Arbor, 1939-42 and since 1947; asst. prof. music, U. of Mich., 1937-42; founder and condr. Asheville (N.C.) Mozart Festival, 1937-41; orchestral condr. Juillard Sch. of Music, N.Y.C., 1946-47; permanent condr. Cin. Symphony Orch., 1947-58; mem. music dept. Northwestern U., 1958-64, prof., 1958-64; dir. Interlochen (Mich.) Arts Acad., 1964-67; music dir. Nashville Symphony Orch., 1967—; condr. Chgo.'s Little Symphony Orch., 1967—; condr. Chicago's Little Symphony, 1960—; guest condr. N.Y. Philharmonic Symphony Orch., Phila. Orch., Chicago Symphony, Boston Symphony Orch.; founder-conductor Pennisula Music Festival (Wis.), 1953; co-conductor Symphony of the Air, Asia, 1955. Enlisted AUS, 1942; as warrant officer band leader founded 1st soldier symphony orch. in army; conducted Am. Univ. Symphony Orch., Shrivenham Eng., on tour of Eng., 1945-46; served in France; disch. June 1946. Awarded Alice B. Ditson prize, 1949; Sachs award, 1950. Mem. Nat. Assn. Am. Composers and Conductors, Am. Fedn. Musicians, Phi Beta Kappa, Phi Kappa Phi, Phi Mu Alpha Sinfonia (received 1951 Nat. Man of Music award), Order of the Golden Fleece. Member Moravian Ch. (Protestant). Address: 823 Cammack Ct Nashville TN 37205

JOHNSON, TOM, hockey team coach. NHL defenseman with Canadiens for 13 years; asst. to gen. mgr., now coach Boston Bruins Hockey Club. Recipient Norris Trophy, six Stanley Cups. Address: 150 Causeway St Boston MA 02114*

JOHNSON, TRUMAN, savs. and loan assn. exec.; b. Des Moines, July 17, 1897; s. Rufus Alvin and Martha (Gelhorn) J.; A.B., Occidental Coll.; m. Eva Atkinson, July 3, 1924; children—Barbara Ann (Mrs. Russell Cole), Truman, Kent. Asst. cashier Pacific S.W. Trust & Savs. Bank, Pasadena, Cal., 1923-26; mgr. Am. Oriental Banking Corp., Shanghai, China, 1926-31; pres. Asia Elec. Co., Shanghai, 1932-35, Pacific Banking Corp., Shanghai, 1934- 35; v.p. Pasadena 1st Nat. Bank, 1936-37; v.p. Young & Koenig Co., Inc., Los Angeles, 1937-40; exec. dir. U.S.O. Los Angeles area, 1942-45; pres. Truman Johnson Investment Co., Pasadena, Cal., 1945-57; pres. Sterling Savs. & Loan Assn., Riverside, Cal., 1957-65, chmn. bd., 1966-68, chmn. bd. emeritus, bd. dirs., 1968-69; pres. Fidelity Land Escrow Service, Inc., El Monte, Cal., 1967—; chmn. Golden Bear Constrn. Corp., Riverside, 1968—; dir. Suburban Water Co. Trustee, Covina Union High Sch. Dist., 1946-52, Mt. San Antonio Jr. Coll., Walnut, Cal., 1955-62, Occidental Coll., 1962—, San Francisco Theol. Sem., 1962—; pres. San Gabriel Valley YMCA, 1955-56; bd. dirs. Riverside, YMCA, Riverside Art Assn., Riverside Opera Assn., Riverside Symphony Soc., World Affairs Council, Riverside. Mem. Kappa Sigma. Mason (32), Rotarian. Home: 2599 Field Lane Riverside CA 92501

JOHNSON, U. ALEXIS, govt. ofcl.; b. Falun, Kan., October 17, 1908; s. Carl Theodore and Ellen (Forsse) J.; A.B., Occidental Coll., 1927-31, LL.D., 1957; postgrad. Georgetown U., 1931-32; m. Patricia Ann Tillman, Mar. 21, 1932; children—Judith (Mrs. Mason S. Zerbe, Jr.), Stephen Tillman, William Theodore, Jennifer (Mrs. Maitri Mojdara). Lang. attache Am. embassy, Tokyo, 1935-37; vice consul, Seoul, Korea, 1937-39, Tientsin, China, 1939, Mukden, Manchuria, 1940-42; 2d sec., Am. embassy, Rio de Janeiro, 1942-44; U.S. Army Civil Affairs Tng. Sch., U. Chgo., 1944; Am. consul, Manila, P.I., 1945; detailed to GHQ SCAP, Tokyo, Japan, Aug. 1945; Am. consul, Yokohama, Japan, Apr. 1946, Am. consul gen., 1947-49; dep. dir. Office NE Asian Affairs, Dept. State, 1949-51, dir., 1951; dep. asst. sec. state for Far Eastern affairs, 1951-53; U.S. ambassador to Czechoslovakia, 1953-58, to Thailand, 1958-61; dep. under sec. state for polit. affairs, 1961-64; dep. ambassador to Vietnam, Saigon, 1964-65; dep. undersec. of state polit. affairs, 1965-66; U.S. ambassador to Japan, 1966-69; under sec. of state polit. affairs, 1969—; coordinator U.S. delegation Geneva Conf., 1954; U.S. rep. for ambassadorial level talks with Chinese Communists, 1955-58, SEATO council, 1958-61. Recipient Medal of Freedom award, 1945, Career Service award Nat. Civil Service League, 1964, Rockefeller Pub. Service award, 1965; Pres.' award for distinguished fed. civilian service, 1971. Mem. Am. Fgn. Service Assn. (pres. 1963-66), Phi Beta Kappa. Clubs: International (Washington); Chevy Chase. Address: 2101 Connecticut Av NW Washington DC 20008

JOHNSON, UNA E., mus. curator, writer; b. Dayton, Ia.; d. W. O. and Linda E. (Putzke) Johnson; A.B., U. Chgo., 1928; M.A., Western Res. Univ., 1937; Carnegie fellow for European travel, 1939. Asst., Cleve. Mus. Art, 1931-37; staff Bklyn. Mus., 1937—, curator prints and drawings, 1941-69; curator collection Storm King Art Center, Mountainville, N.Y., 1969-71; Rockefeller Found. grantee for research 20th Century prints, 1957. Adv. bd. Pratt-Contemporaries Graphic Workshop; dir. Print Council Am. Author: Drawings of the Twentieth Century, vols. I, II, 1964. Contbr. articles profl. publs. Home: 341 W 24th St New York City NY 10011

JOHNSON, UWE, author; b. Cammin, Pomerania, July 20, 1934; s. Erich and Erna (Straede) J.; student Rostock, 1952-54; diploma philology U. Leipzig (Germany), 1956; m. Elisabeth Schmidt. Feb. 28, 1962; 1 dau., Katharina. Recipient Fontane prize West Berlin, 1960; Internat. Pubs. prize, 1962. Author: Speculations About Jakob, 1963; The Third Book About Achim, 1967; Two Views, 1966. Home: Stierstrasse 3 West Berlin 41 Germany

JOHNSON, VALDEMAR NELS LUTHER, fgn. service officer; b. Wells, Minn., Oct. 4, 1912; s. John Lewis and Josephine (Olson) J.; B.A., Luther Coll., 1933; postgrad. Northwestern U., summers 1934-35; M.S., U. So. Cal., 1941; student Russian U. Colo., 1944-45; m. Alice Griswold, May 9, 1936 (div. Dec. 1965); children—D. Paul, Annalee (Mrs. James D. Platt, Jr.), Allan G.; m. 2d, Geraldine Stibbe, Nov. 26, 1966. Tchr. history, 1933-44; with Dept. State, 1946—; joined U.S. Fgn. Service, 1952; asst. naval attache, Oslo, Norway, 1952-54; 2d sec., Warsaw, Poland, 1954-55, 1st sec., 1955-57; internat. relations officer, Washington, 1957-60, mem. sr. seminar fgn. policy, 1960-61; 1st sec., Reykjavik, Iceland, 1961-62, counselor, 1962-66; sr. state dept. fellow U. Minn., 1966-67; consul gen., Calgary, Alta., Can., 1967—. Served to comdr. USNR, 1944-46, 52-54. Home: 1138 Prospect Av SW Calgary 3 Alberta Canada Office: 805 8th Av SW Calgary 2 Alberta Canada

JOHNSON, VAN, movie actor; b. Newport, R.I.; s. Charles and Loretta Johnson; grad. high sch.; m. Eve Abbott Wynn, Jan. 25, 1947; 1 dau., Schuyler Van. Began as worker in father's plumbing office, 1936; 1st stage appearance in chorus of musical, New Faces, 1937; later toured as singer with vaudeville act; joined Eight Men of Manhattan, appearing with Mary Martin at Rainbow Room; appeared in roles in Too Many Girls, 1940, Pal Joey, 1941; in motion pictures 1941—, role in Murder in the Big House; joined Metro-Goldwyn-Mayer, 1942; now free lancing; has appeared in numerous pictures, latest being: Grounds for Marriage, Minister in Washington, Three Guys Named Mike, Go for Broke!, Too Young to Kiss, When in Rome, Invitation, 1951; Washington Story, Plymouth Adventure, A Steak for Connie, Remains To Be Seen, 1952; Easy to Love, 1953; Brigadoon, 1954; The End of the Affair, 1955; Kelly and Me, 1956; Action of the Tiger, 1956; Subway In the Sky, 1957; The Last Blitzkrieg, 1958; Beyond This Place, 1958; Wives and Lovers, 1963. Toured in musicals Music Man, Bye Bye Birdie, Damn Yankees, summer 1963; appeared in Mating Game (comedy), 1965. Home: 801 N Foothill Beverley Hills CA 90210 ☆

JOHNSON, VAN CHARLES, educator; b. nr. Vermillion, S.D., Nov. 17, 1913; s. Charles E. and Mattie J. (Christopherson) J.; B.A., St. Olaf Coll., 1935; M.A., U. S.D., 1951; Ph.D., Mich. State U., 1963; m. Ruth J. Ljostveit, Aug. 23, 1939; children—Thomas C., Timothy P., Julie Anne. Tchr., prin., supt. schs. S.D. Pub. Schs., 1935-46; prof., dean student affairs U. S.D., Vermillion, 1947-68; guest lectr. Mich. State U., East Lansing, 1961-63, prof. higher edn., 1968—; cons. Am. Sch. Internat. Schs., The Hague, Netherlands, 1967, Netherland-Am. Ednl. Found., 1970, Netherland Ministry Edn., 1970, Ministry Edn. in Saigon, S. Vietnam, 1971. Served to lt. USNR, 1943-47. Recipient Kemp award for outstanding person in guidance and counseling in S.D., 1967. Mem. S.D. Guidance and Personnel Assn. (past pres.), Blue Key, Phi Delta Kappa. Home: 2031 Osage Dr Okemos MI 48864 Office: Mich State U East Lansing MI 48823

JOHNSON, VAN LORAN, educator; b. Medford, Wis., Jan. 18, 1908; s. William and Rossie (Olson) J.; A.B., U. Wis., 1930, A.M., 1931, Ph.D., 1935; A.B., Oxford U., 1934, A.M., 1938; m. Marjorie Jean Carr, June 30, 1934; children—Karen Christine, Eric Van. Rhodes scholar at Corpus Christi Coll., Oxford, 1931-34; Markham traveling fellow U. Wis., 1935-36; instr. in classics, 1936-37; instr. Latin, Tufts Coll., 1937-41, asst. prof., 1941-47, asso. prof., 1947-52, prof., 1952—, chmn. dept. classics, 1952-69; gen. sec. Archaeol. Inst. Am., 1948-51, also editor Bull., 1949-51; cons. Fulbright program, 1949; organized New Eng. Latin Workshop, 1955; regional asso. Am. Council Learned Socs., 1956-59; organized classical year in Naples, Italy, 1961; mem. mng. com. Am. Sch. Classical Studies, Athens; mem. council Am. Sch. Classical Studies, Rome. Fellow Internat. Acad. Arts and Letters; mem. Am. Assn. U. Profs. (pres. Tufts chpt. 1948-49), Am. Classical League (pres. 1953-60, hon. pres. 1960—), Am. Philol. Assn., Archaeol. Inst. Am., Am. Assn. Rhodes Scholars, Classical Assn. of N.E. (sec.-treas. 1947-49), Council for Basic Edn. (senate 1957-59), Phi Beta Kappa. Author: Roman Origins of Our Calendar, 1958, 2d edit., 1969; Tenuis Musa, book of Latin verse, 1960; contbr. articles, revs. and notes in various periodicals. Translated: Euripides' Andromache in Six Greek plays (editor D. Fitts), 1955. Home: 40 Tesla Av Medford MA 02155

JOHNSON, VERDENAL HOAG, educator, art editor, writer; b. Newark, Nov. 22, 1924; d. Philip Osborne and Frances (Verdenal) Hoag; B.A., Swarthmore Coll., 1945; postgrad. Temple U., 1945-46, Rutgers U., 1956-57, Newark State Coll., 1961-63; m. Edward F. Johnson, June 29, 1945; children—Candida Ann, David Bladen, Frances Verdenal. Psychometrician VA, Phila., Bklyn., 1944-46; founder, dir. Argus Gallery, Madison, N.J., 1961-67; psychol. cons. Hooper Holmes Bur., Basking Ridge, N.J., 1965—; art editor Newark Star Ledger, 1969—; tchr. English, Morristown (N.J.) High Sch., 1963—, chmn. dept., 1970—; lectr., art judge. Active Girl Scouts Am., A.R.C., various community activities; mem. Gov.'s Commn. Study Arts N.J., 1965-66. Mem. Nat. Council Tchrs. English, N.E.A., N.J. Edn. Assn. Originator Coll.-Univ. Arts Faculty Show, Painters of N.J. Scene, Me. Through Eyes of Its Artist, Brit. Printmakers Council exhbn. Home: 88 Garfield Av Madison NJ 07940 Office: Star-Ledger Plaza Newark NJ 07101

JOHNSON, VERNON A., business exec. Sr. v.p., asst. sec. Fram Corp., East Providence, R.I. Office: 105 Pawtucket Av East Providence RI 02916*

JOHNSON, VERNON ARTHUR, aircraft mfr.; b. Heavener, Okla., Dec. 15, 1914; s. Arthur and Lillian Bell (Bradley) J.; A.B., U. Cal., 1936; postgrad. Harvard Advanced Mgmt. Program, 1963; m. Dorothy Lee Thompson, June 18, 1939; children—Brian A., Curtis B., Shirley L. (Mrs. Joseph E. Henderson). Asst. mgr. San Bernardino (Cal.) C. of C., 1937-38, mgr., Redlands, Cal., 1939-40, Bakersfield, 1941-42; staff assembly div. Lockheed Aircraft Corp., 1943, asst. pub. relations mgr., 1944-47, staff Washington office, asst. to pres., 1948-54, Washington mgr., 1954-58, v.p. Eastern Region, 1958—. Conglist. Clubs: Aero (pres. 1953), Congressional Country (v.p. 1957-58), Burning Tree (pres. 1970-71), Metropolitan (Washington); Lost Tree (North Palm Beach, Fla.). Home: 8709 Fenway Dr Bethesda MD 20034 also 11796 Lost Tree Way North Palm Beach FL Office: 900 17th St N W Washington DC 20006

JOHNSON, VICTOR, physiologist; b. Chgo., Jan. 19, 1901; s. Eric and Carrie (Pearson) J.; Ph.B., U. Chgo., 1926, Ph.D., 1930, M.D., 1939; D.Sc., Rockford Coll., 1954; m. Maria Bacca, Jan. 12, 1962; 1 son, Victor Raymond. Instr. physiology U. Chgo., 1929-36, asst. prof., 1936-40, asso. prof. physiology, dean students in biology and medicine, 1940-44; professorial lectr. physiology, 1944-47; sec. council on med. edn. and hosps. A.M.A., 1943-47, mem., 1946-58; dir. Mayo Found. and Mayo Grad. Sch. Medicine, Rochester, Minn.; prof. physiology U. Minn., 1947-66; cons. Edn. and Tng. Div., Office Surgeon Gen., AUS, 1958-66; sci. writer Majorca Daily Bull., Palma, Spain, 1969—. Dir. Am. Med. Edn. Found., 1950-61; adv. council Nat. Fund for Med. Edn., 1950-62; mem. sci. adv. council Inst. Advancement Med. Communication, 1960-66; research inst. com. Upper Midwest Research and Devel. Council, 1961-66; nat. civilian cons. to surgeon gen. USAF, 1961-66. Mem. Adv. Com. Fed. Hosp. Council, FSA, 1946-48; mem. Citizens Fed. Adv. Com., U.S. Office Edn. 1946-50; mem. adv. com. Civilian Prodn. Bd. 1944-50; mem. adv. bd. on health services A.R.C., 1945-48; mem. bd. hon. civilian cons. to Surgeon Gen. Navy, 1951-54, v.p. World Conf. Med. Edn., 1953, dep. pres., program com. chmn., 1957-59; dir. U.S. Com. World Med. Assn., 1954-65. Mem. Am. Assn. U. Profs., A.A.A.S., A.M.A., A.C.P., Am. Physiol. Soc., Royal Acad. Medicine Mallorca (corr.), Phi Beta Kappa, Sigma Xi, Alpha Omega Alpha (dir. 1959-66, pres. 1963-66). Co-author: Elements of Electrocardiographic Interpretation, 1944; Machinery of the Body, 1941, 5th edit., 1961. Contbr. sci. articles to Am. Jour. Physiology. Home: Frente Hotel Forte Cala Vinas Urbanizacion Bahia Palma Cala Vinas Mallorca Spain Office: Mayo Grad Sch Rochester MN 55901

JOHNSON, VICTOR HENRY, library adminstr.; b. Salamanca, N.Y., Aug. 10, 1909; s. Victor S. and Jennie (Prusinowski) J.; B.A., U. Buffalo, 1933, B.S.L.S., 1939; M.A., U. Mich., 1954; m. Margery Zeilman, Aug. 2, 1941. With Buffalo and Erie County Library, 1933-43, head young adults dept., 1939-43; head circulation dept. Amherst (Mass.) Coll. Library, 1946-49; dir. Norwich U. Library, Northfield, Vt., 1949—. Chmn. Zoning Bd. Northfield, 1968—; mem. Planning Bd., Northfield. Trustee Vt. State Library, Northfield Pub. Library. Served with USAAF, 1943-45. Mem. Am. Assn. U. Profs., Am. Library Assn., Am., Eastern N.Y. (past v.p.), Vt. (past pres.) library assns., Assn. Coll. and Research Librarians. Clubs: Green Mountain (Rutland, Vt.); Appalachian Mountain, Four Thousand Footer (Boston). Home: 11 Slate Av Northfield VT 05663 Office: Norwich U Library Northfield VT 05663

JOHNSON, VICTOR LONG, sugar exec.; b. Norfolk, Va., Aug. 24, 1914; s. Lindsay Franklin and Flora (Long) J.; B.S., Columbia, 1936, Chem.E., 1937; m. Erica E. Ehrentraut, Feb. 21, 1942; children—Linda Ann, Erica Ellen, David Lindsay. Chem. engr. Amstar Corp., 1937—, v.p., 1949—, dir., 1966—; dir. Duff-Norton Co., Inc., Charlotte, N.C. Bd. dirs. Internat. Sugar Research Found., Bethesda, Sugar Assn., N.Y.C. Mem. Am. Inst. Chem. Engrs., Am. Chem. Soc., Inst. Food. Technologists. Home: Box 423 Sparta NJ 07871 Office: 1251 Av of Americas New York City NY 10020

JOHNSON, VICTOR SAMUEL, Jr., coll. trustee, mfg. exec.; b. Chgo., June 12, 1916; s. Victor Samuel and Minnie F. (Neumann) J.; A.B., Amherst Coll., 1938; LL.B., Yale, 1941; m. Nancy McKisson, Nov. 9, 1946; children—Victor Samuel III, Christine Louise. Admitted to Ill. bar, 1941, also U.S. Circuit Ct., U.S. Supreme Ct.; law clk. Judge Otto Kerner, Chgo., 1941-42; atty. WPB, Washington, 1942; pres. Aladdin Industries, Inc., Nashville, 1943—, chmn., 1951—; dir. Alladin Industries, Ltd., London, Eng., Alladin Products of Can., Ltd., Toronto; dir. Tenn. Natural Gas Lines. Mem. Com. Fgn. Relations, Nashville; chmn. Tenn. Adv. Com. on Atomic Energy; chmn. exec. com. So. Interstate Nuclear Bd., 1968-70; mem. Charter Comm., Nashville and Davidson County, 1957-58, 1961- 62. Chmn. trustees Meharry (Md.) Coll.; chmn. admissions and allocations United Givers Fund, Nashville, 1954, trustee, 1955-58, 66—. Mem. Nashville C. of C., Chgo. Bar Assn., Round Table of Nashville. Presbyn. Home: 970 Overton Lea Rd Nashville TN 37220 Office: 703 Murfreesboro Rd Nashville TN 37210

JOHNSON, VINTON CHARLES, investment fund trustee; b. Galesburg, Ill., Sept. 10, 1904; s. Charles E. and Blenda (Johnson) J.; A.B., Knox Coll., 1926; M.B.A., Harvard, 1929; m. Frances Lamont, Sept. 10, 1930 (dec. May 1939); children—Harriet A., Colin L.; m. 2d, Marion Spearin, Apr. 1944 (dec. July 1947); m. 3d, Lanora Fritch, Apr. 6, 1950. With 1st Boston Corp., 1929-51, v.p., 1949-51; trustee Century Shares Trust, Boston, 1951—, vice chmn. trustees, 1954-59, chmn. trustees, 1959-69; dir. Depositors Fund, Inc., Boston Common Stock Fund, Boston Fund, Inc., Diversification Fund, Inc., Exchange Fund Boston, Capital Exchange Fund, Inc., Fiduciary Exchange Fund, Inc., Leverage Fund Boston, 2d Fiduciary Exchange Fund, Inc.; trustee Boston Five Cent Savs. Bank. Mem. Beta Theta Pi. Home: 770 Boylston St Boston MA 02199 Office: 111 Devonshire St Boston MA 02109

JOHNSON, VIRGINIA ESHELMAN, (Mrs. William H. Masters), psychologist; b. Springfield, Mo., Feb. 11, 1925; d. Harry Hershel and Edna (Evans) Eshelman; student music Drury Coll., Springfield, 1940-42, U. Mo., 1944-47; Washington U., St. Louis, 1964; m. George Johnson, June 13, 1950 (div. 1956); children—Scott Forstall, Lisa Evans; m. 2d, William H. Masters, Jan. 7, 1971. With St. Louis Daily Record, 1947-50, radio sta. KMOX, St. Louis, 1950-51; with div. reproductive biology, dept. obstetrics and gynecology Washington U. Sch. Medicine, 1957-63, research instr., 1962-64; research asst. Reproductive Biology Research Found., St. Louis, 1964—. Fellow Soc. Sci. Study Sex; mem. Soc. for Study Reprodn., Internat. Sec. for Research in Biology Reprodn. Episcopalian. Author: (with Dr. William H. Masters) Human Sexual Response, 1966; Human Sexual Inadequacy, 1970. Home: 50 Salem Estates St Louis MO 63124 Office: 4910 Forest Park St Louis MO 63108

JOHNSON, WALLACE EDWARDS, motel chain exec. and builder; b. Edinburg, Miss., Oct. 5, 1901; s. Felix A. and Josephine (Edwards) J.; student Moorhead (Miss.) Jr. Coll.; LL.D., Gordon Coll., 1968, Harding Coll., 1970; m. Alma McCool, Aug. 10, 1924. Co-founder, vice chmn. Holiday Inns, Inc. (formerly Holiday Inns of Am., Inc.), Memphis, 1953—; founder, chmn. Wallace E. Johnson Enterprises (formerly Wallace E. Johnson, Inc.), builders, Memphis, 1941—; pres. Service Mortgage & Investment Co., Memphis, 1945—; co-founder, chmn. bd. Medicenters of Am., Inc., Memphis, 1966—, Alodex Corp., Memphis, 1967—. Adv. bd. Bapt. Hosp., Memphis; chmn. exec. com. Religious Heritage Am., Inc., Washington; trustee Gordon Coll., Wenham, Mass., LeTourneau Coll., Longview, Tex. Named Layman of Yr., Religious Heritage Am., Inc., 1965; Horatio Alger award, 1968. Kiwanian (life). Home: 3395 Waynoka St Memphis TN 38111 Office: P O Box 18127 Memphis TN 38118

JOHNSON, WALTER, educator; b. Nahant, Mass., June 27, 1915; s. Alfred and Annie (Hogan) J.; A.B., Dartmouth, 1937; M.A., U. Chgo., 1938, Ph.D., 1941; m. Bette Gifford, Sept. 13, 1955; 1 son, Gifford; children by previous marriage—Deborah, Richard. Instr. history U. Chgo., 1940-43, asst. prof., 1943-49, asso. prof., 1949-50, prof., 1950-66, chmn. dept., 1950- 61, Preston and Sterling Morton prof. history, 1963-66; prof. history U. Hawaii, 1966—; Harmsworth prof. Am. history Oxford U., 1957-58. Mem. U.S. Adv. Commn. Internat. Ednl. and Cultural Affairs. Bd. fgn. scholarships Fulbright Program, 1947-54, chmn. bd., 1950-53. Co- chmn. Nat. Com. Stevenson for Pres., 1952. Recipient $1000 prize for excellence in teaching U. Chgo., 1943; accompanied Gov. Stevenson around the world, 1953; Newberry Library fellow, 1945. Mem. Am., Miss. Valley hist. assns., Am. Polit. Sci. Assn. Author: The Battle Against Isolation, 1944; William Allen White's America, 1947; (with Avery Craven) The United States; Experiment in Democracy, 1947; How We Drafted Adlai Stevenson (book), 1955; American Studies Abroad, 1963; co-author: The Fullbright Program: A History, 1965. Editor: Selected Letters of William Allen White, 1947; Roosevelt and The Russians; The Yalta Conference (Edward R. Stettinius, Jr.), 1949; Turbulent Era: A Diplomatic Record of Forty Years (Ambassador Joseph C. Grew), 1952; 1600 Pennsylvania Avenue: Presidents and the People, 1929-59, 1960; The Papers of Adlai E. Stevenson. Home: 53-109 Kam Hwy Punaluu Oahu HI 96717 Office: Dept History U Hawaii Honolulu HI 96822

JOHNSON, WALTER CONRAD, banker; b. Mpls., Oct. 4, 1925; s. John Conrad and Edna (Gustafson) J.; B.B.A., U. Minn., 1948; m. Janet Patricia Baker, Aug. 27, 1949; children—Karen, Steven, James. Accountant, George Rossetter & Co., Chgo., 1949-53, Peat, Marwick, Mitchell & Co., Mpls., 1953-57; controller NW Bancorp., Mpls., 1959-71, treas., 1962—, v.p., 1967—; treas., dir. N.W. Optimation Services, Inc.; dir. Ia. Securities Co.; treas., dir. Union Investment Co., Northwestern Mortgage Co., N.W. Computer Services, Inc., Northwestern Financial Center, Inc., Lease N.W., Inc.; treas. N.W. Internat. Bank. Mem. Mpls. Citizens League. Served to ensign, AC USNR, 1943-46. C.P.A., Minn., Ill. Mem. Financial Execs. Inst. (nat. dir. 1971—), Am. Inst. C.P.A.'s, Minn. Soc. C.P.A.'s, Bank Adminstrn. Inst., Am. Inst. Banking, U. Minn. Sch. Bus. Adminstrn. Alumni Assn. (dir. 1967-70), Beta Alpha Psi. Lutheran. Kiwanian. Clubs: Minneapolis; Wayzata (Minn.) Country. Home: 4743 E Coventry Rd Minnetonka MN 55343 Office: Northwestern Bank Bldg Minneapolis MN 55480

JOHNSON, WALTER CURTIS, educator; b. Weikert, Pa., Jan. 6, 1913; s. David C. and Mary (Ely) J.; B.S., Pa. State Coll., 1934, E.E., 1942; m. Carolyn Shirk, Sept. 1, 1934; children—Walter Curtis, William Stanford, David Edward. Engr., Gen. Elec. Co., Schenectady, 1934-37; instr., dept. elec. engring. Princeton, 1937, prof. elec. engring., 1948—, Arthur LeGrand Doty prof. engineering, 1963—, chmn. dept., 1950-65; engring. cons. various cos.; resident visitor Bell Telephone Labs., 1968. Recipient Western Elec. award for excellence in engring. edn. Am. Soc. Engring. Edn., 1967. Fellow I.E.E.E. (profl. groups on edn., electron devices); mem. Am. Soc. Engring. Edn. (chmn. elec. engring. div. 1955-56), Sigma Xi. Presbyn. Author: Mathematical and Physical Principles of Engineering Analysis, 1944; Transmission Lines and Networks, 1950; (with P.R. Clement) Electrical Engineering Science, 1960; articles tech. and sci. publs. Home: 20 McCosh Circle Princeton NJ 08540

JOHNSON, WALTER H., Jr., airline exec.; b. N.Y.C., Jan. 3, 1917; s. Walter H. and May E. (McCarthy) J.; student Fordham Prep. Sch., 1930-34, Fordham U., 1934-35; A.B., U. Notre Dame, 1939; m. Marcella Rheume, July 1, 1944; children—Regina May, Walter H., Kevin McCarthy, Bruce Rheaume. Reservations agt. Am. Airlines, Inc., N.Y.C., sales rep., Chgo., 1940- 41, gen. supt. express traffic, 1942-43, dir. sales, 1946-47, regional v.p., 1947-48, sec., asst. to pres., 1948-51, v.p.-properties and facilities, 1951-54, v.p., sales mgr., 1954-58; sr. v.p.-marketing, dir. Capital Airlines, Inc., 1958-60, dir., 1960; v.p. McCann-Erickson, U.S.A., Inc., 1960; exec. v.p. a div., Market Research Corp., 1960; now v.p. Interpub. Group Cos., Inc.; chmn. bd. Central Air Terminal, Inc., East Side Airline Terminal, West Side Airline Terminal (all N.Y.C.), Myers-Fisher-Infoplan, Internat. dir. Air Cargo, Inc. Nat. dir. Jr. Achievement, Inc., Travlers Aid. Served with U.S. Marine Corps., 1944-46. Mem. Nat. Sales Exec. (vice chmn. bd.), Am. Soc. Traffic and Transp. (founding mem.). Clubs: Sales Execs., Pinnacle, Wings (N.Y.C.); Nat. Aviation, F Street (Washington); Campfire of Am. Home: McLean VA 22101 Office: 1271 Av of Americas New York City NY 10019

JOHNSON, WALTER J., publisher; b. July 29, 1912; ed. U. Heidelberg, U. de Paris á la Sorbonne, Paris, U. Coll., London; married. Founder, pres. Walter J. Johnson, Inc., N.Y.C. and London, 1942--; founder, pres. Academic Press, N.Y.C. and London, 1942--; founder, pres. Johnson Reprint Co., N.Y.C. and London, 1946--(became subsidiary of Academic Press 1967); sr. v.p., dir. Harcourt Brace Jovanovich, Inc. (merger of Academic Press and Harcourt Brace Jovanovich), N.Y.C., 1969--; also chief exec. officer Academic Press and Johnson Reprint Corp. and pres. overseas div. Harcourt Brace Jovanovich; founder, pres. Seminar Press (subsidiary Academic Press), N.Y.C., and London, 1970--. Trustee Albany (N.Y.) Med. Coll. Fellow Pierpont Morgan Library. Served with Nat. Guard, 1941-44. Mem. A.L.A., Am. Med. Library Assn., Friends of Columbia U. Club: Grolier (N.Y.C.). Office: 111 Fifth Av New York City NY 10003

JOHNSON, WALTER SAMUEL, lumber co. exec.; b. East Saginaw, Mich., Nov. 10, 1884; s. Alfred A. and Mary (Calkins) J.; LL.B., U. Cal., 1914; m. Mabel Brady, Nov. 18, 1914; m. 2d, Pauline Cook, May 11, 1938 (div. 1964); m. 3d, Margherita Dan, Apr. 3, 1965. Circulation mgr. San Francisco Bull.; pres., mgr. Johnson's Inc., book stores, 1906-11; admitted to Cal. bar, 1914, practiced in San Francisco, 1914-17; organized Am. Box Corp., now Am. Forest Products Corp., pres., 1928-56, chmn. bd., 1956-70; pres. Friden, Inc., 1945-63, chmn. bd., 1963-65. Served to capt. Signal Corps U.S. Army, 1917-19. Mason (32, Shriner). Clubs: Bohemian, Castlewood Country, Commonwealth. Home: Route 1 Box 426 Pleasanton CA 94566 Office: 2740 Hyde St San Francisco CA 94119

JOHNSON, WARREN C., educator, univ. exec.; b. Otter Lake, Mich., Sept. 22, 1901: s. Grant W. and Elizabeth (Osborne) J.; B.S., Kalamazoo Coll., 1922, D.Sc., 1946; M.A., Clark U., 1924; Ph.D., Brown U., 1925, D.Sc., 1960; m. Florence Louise Campbell, June 27, 1928; children—Barbara Ann, Margaret Louise, Mary Elizabeth. Research instr. chemistry Brown U., 1925-27; instr. chemistry U. Chgo., 1927-28, asst. prof., 1928-32, asso., 1932-43, prof., 1943—, dean div. phys. scis., 1955-58, v.p., prof., 1958—. Dir. chemistry div. Clinton Labs., Oak Ridge, 1943-45; cons. Union Carbide Corp., 1962—; dir. Oak Ridge Inst. Nuclear Studies, 1953—. Mem. gen. adv. com. AEC, 1954-60, chmn., 1956-60; cons. NSF. Trustee Mellow Inst., Kalamazoo Coll., Inst. Def. Analysis. Recipient citation amd medal U.S. AEC, 1961. Fellow A.A.A.S.; mem. Am. Chem. Soc., Am. Nuclear Soc., Chgo. Planetarium Soc. (trustee), Ill. Acad. Sci., Sigma Xi. Clubs: Cosmos (Washington); Quadrangle (Chgo.) Author textbooks. Home: 5825 Dorchester Av Chicago IL 60637

JOHNSON, WARREN CHARLES, lawyer; b. Wahoo, Neb., Mar. 22, 1920; s. Wilmer G. and Florence (Slama) J.; B.S. in Bus. Adminstrn. with high distinction, U. Neb., 1942, J.D. magna cum laude, 1948; m. Janet Muriel Ralston, Feb. 14, 1943; children—Warren W., Lucinda A., Lauri D., Genevieve H. Admitted to Neb. bar, 1948, since practiced in Lincoln; partner firm Cline, Williams, Wright, Johnson & Oldfather, 1951—. Dir. Messenger Corp., First Nat. Bank & Trust Co. Lincoln, First Nat. Bank, Fairbury, Neb., Utah Gas Service Co. Pres. Neb. Conf. United Ch. Christ, 1962-68, S.W. Community Center, 1963-67. Served with USAAF, 1942-46. Mem. Am., Neb., Lincoln (pres. 1966-67) bar assns., Beta Gamma Sigma, Delta Upsilon, Phi Delta Phi. Mason. Home: 6800 Old Cheney Rd Lincoln NB 68516 Office: First Nat Bank Bldg Lincoln NB 68508

JOHNSON, WAYNE EATON, journalist; b. Phoenix, May 9, 1930; s. Roscoe and Marion (Eaton) J.; B.A., U. Colo., 1952; postgrad. Duke, 1952-53; (KLM polit. reporting fellow 1957) U. Vienna (Austria), 1955-56; M.A., U. Cal., Los Angeles, 1957; m. N. Becky Trabing, Mar. 4, 1962; children—Jamie, Katherine, Jeffrey. Reporter, Internat. News Service, Des Moines, 1958, Wheat Ridge (Colo.) Advocate, 1957, Pueblo (Colo.) Chieftain, 1959; reporter Denver Post, 1960, editorial writer, music critic, 1961-65; arts and entertainment editor Seattle Times, 1965-; instr. journalism Colo. Woman's Coll., 1962. Served with CIC, AUS, 1953-55. Home: 11303 Durland PL NE Seattle WA 98125 Office: Seattle Times Fairview Av N and John St Seattle WA 98111

JOHNSON, WENTWORTH PAUL, banker; b. Nashville, May 29, 1897; s. Wentworth Paul and Nannie (Williams) J.; grad. Hotchkiss Sch.; Ph.B. cum laude, Yale, 1917; J.D., N.Y. U., 1936; m. Dorothy Elizabeth Leahey; children—Shelby Mackay, Hope, Elizabeth W., Wentworth Paul III, Melinda. Staff accountant Lybrand, Ross Bros. & Montgomery, 1919-23; v.p. Irving Trust Co., 1923-48; sr. v.p., dir. Fidelity-Phila. Trust Co., 1949—; dir. Glen Alden Corp. (Wilkes-Barre, Pa.), Phila Suburban Water Co., Edo Corp. (N.Y.C.), Curtis Pub. Co., Phila., Electrocopy Corp., Fidelity Internat. Corp. Co. for Investing Abroad. Bd. dirs. Agnes-Irwin Sch. Mem. Phila. Com. on Fgn. Relations. Trustee, Temple U. Served to 1st lt. U.S. Army, 1917-19; AEF. Decorated Croix de Guerre. Mem. Am., Pa. bankers assns., Soc. Cin., Phila. C. of C. (dir.), Mil. Order Fgn. Wars, Soc. Colonial Wars, Phi Delta Phi. Clubs: Merion Cricket, Racquet, Mid-day (Phila.); University (N.Y.C.). Home: 714 Woodleave Rd Bryn Mawr PA 19010 Office: 135 S Broad St Philadelphia PA 19109

JOHNSON, WESLEY MARTIN, govt. ofcl.; b. Spencer, Tenn., Aug. 11, 1918; s. Ira Otis and Sallie (Mohon) J.; B.S. in Elec. Engring., U. Tenn., 1946; m. Pauline Peden, Aug. 24, 1940; 1 son, Wesley Martin. With AEC, 1946—, dep. mgr. N.Y. Operations Office, 1960-64, mgr., 1964—. Served with USNR, 1942-46. Mem. Fed. Exec. Bd. N.Y. (vice chmn. 1966-67), Fed. Bus. Assn. N.Y. (v.p. 1965-67). Mem. Ch. of Christ (pres. 1961-65). Home: 44 E 80th St New York City NY 10021 Office: 376 Hudson St New York City NY 10017

JOHNSON, WESLEY ROBERT, corp. exec.; b. Cleve., Dec. 27, 1919; s. Fritz G. and Marguerite (Smith) J.; B.S., Ohio State U., 1948; M.B.A., Northwestern U., 1949; postgrad. Northwestern U., Columbia, 1950-53; m. Doris F. Meadows, Feb. 14, 1945; children—Elizabeth N., Wesley Robert, Philip Meadows, Gillian Smith. Mgmt. cons. George Fry & Assos., Chgo., 1949-51; v.p. internat. Ill. Tool Works Inc., Chgo., 1951-62; pres. Woodall Industries Inc., Detroit. Mem. assembly United Community Services Met. Detroit. Bd. govs. Greater Mich. Found.; adv. bd. Coll. Engring. U. Detroit; trustee Traffic Safety for Mich. Served to capt. USAAF, World War II. Mem. Brit. Inst. Dirs., Am. Marketing Assn., Greater Detroit C. of C. Mason. Clubs: Columbia U. (N.Y.C.); Detroit Athletic, Country, Economic (dir.) (Detroit); Am. (London, Eng.). Home: 207 Ridge Rd Grosse Pointe Farms MI 48236 Office: 7565 E McNichols Rd Detroit MI 48234

JOHNSON, WILFRID ESTILL, govt. ofcl.; b. Whitley Bay, Eng., May 24, 1905; s. Arthur Nicholas and Edith (Peace) J.; came to U.S., 1920, naturalized, 1928; B.S., Ore. State U., 1930, M.E., 1939, D.Sc. (hon.), 1959; m. Esther Taylor, Dec. 31, 1930; children—Anita Louise (Mrs. Clark B. McKee), Arthur Robert, Richard Beeson. Engr. refrigeration Gen. Elec. Co., Schenectady, 1930- 36, Ft. Wayne, Ind., 1936-40, mgr. engring. aircraft engines, Lynn, Mass. and Syracuse, N.Y., 1940-46, mgr. engring. air conditioning, Bloomfield, N.J., 1946-48; gen. mgr. Hanford Atomic Works, Richland, Wash., 1948-66; commr. AEC, Washington, 1966—. Mem. Richland Community Council, 1966; mem. Wash. Citizens Council, 1953-58; mem. vis. com. Sch. Bus. Adminstrn. U. Wash., 1961-66. mem. Recipient Pi Tau Sigma award, 1938, AEC citation, 1965. Fellow Am. Soc. M.E., Am. Nuclear Soc.; mem. Acad. Polit. and Social Scis., Am. Soc. for Engineering Edn. (asso. mem.), Nat. Acad. Engring., Sigma Xi, Phi Kappa Phi, Tau Beta Pi, Sigma Tau. Elk. Clubs: University (Washington); Washington Athletic (Seattle). Contbr. profl. jours. Patentee in field. Home: 12711 River Rd Potomac MD 20854 Office: US AEC Washington DC 20545

JOHNSON, WILLARD LYON, orgn. exec.; b. Sterling, Ill., Dec. 1, 1905; s. James William and Anna Laura (Lyon) J.; A.B., Drake U., 1930, M.A., 1932; B.D., Colgate- Rochester Div. Sch., 1933; m. Marjorie Elta Hackenberg, Feb. 9, 1936; children—Willard Lyon, Miriam Ellen. Ordained to ministry Disciples of Christ Ch., 1930; asso. minister Plymouth Congl. Ch., Des Moines, 1939- 41; dean men, dir. personnel Drake U., 1934-38; regional dir. Nat. Conf. Christians and Jews, 1938-42, 58, dir. Chgo., 1955-58; asst. to pres., 1942-45, v.p., 1945-47, nat. program dir., 1947-51, European dir. World Brotherhood, 1951, sec.-gen., 1951-55; pres. Com. Internat. Econ. Growth, 1958-60; v.p. Am. Edn. Found., Geneva, Switzerland, sec. human rights com., 1947-49; chief mission CARE, Berlin, Germany, 1960-62; exec. dir. Unitarian Universalist Service Com., 1962-65; exec. dir. Am. Freedom from Hunger Found., Inc., FAO, 1965-66; exec. dir. Center for Research and Edn., 1966-67; dir. internat. devel. Cal. Western U., 1967- 68; exec. dir. Planned Parenthood, San Diego, 1968-70; 1st v.p. Zero Population Growth, Inc., 1971—. Cons. State Dept., Germany, 1950; gen. sec. U.S. com. UN Genocide Conv., 1948; exec. com. Nat. Assn. Intergroup Relations Ofcls., 1950—; cons. nat. radio network programs Light of the World and Superman; religious news reporter sta. WHO, Des Moines, 1938-41, sta. KWK, St. Louis, 1941-42; asst. commentator Religion in the News, NBC, 1947-49; del. World Council Chs. Consultations, Salonika, Greece, 1959. Trustee Bur. Intercultural Edn., Inst. Am. Democracy, World Alliance Internat. Friendship Through Religion; chmn. scholarship fund, Pleasantville, N.Y. Recipient Distinguished Service award Drake U., 1956. Mem. Religious Radio Assn. (pres. 1947-49), Soc. Psychol. Study Social Issues, Soc. Internat. Devel. (mem. council; pres. Boston chpt.), UN Assn. (pres. San Diego 1970-72), Phi Beta Kappa, Omicron Delta Kappa, Psi Chi. Unitarian. Author: Population and Quality of Life, 1971. Contbr. chpts., articles, various publs. to profl. jours. Home: 4149 6th Av San Diego CA 92103 Office: 4149 6th Av San Diego CA 92103

JOHNSON, WILLIAM BENJAMIN, transp. co. exec.; b. Salisbury, Md., Dec. 28, 1918; s. Benjamin A. and Ethel (Holloway) J.; A.B. maxima cum laude, Washington Coll., 1940; LL.B. cum laude, U. Pa., 1943; m. Mary Barb, Dec. 19, 1942; children—Benjamin H., Kirk B., John P., Kathleen M. Editor-in-chief U. Pa. Law Rev.; admitted to Md. bar, 1946, Pa. bar, 1947; atty. U.S. Tax Ct., 1945-47; asst. solicitor Pa. R.R., 1947-48, asst. gen. solicitor, 1948-51, asst. to gen. counsel, 1951-52, asst. gen. counsel, 1952-59; pres., dir. Ry. Express Agy., Inc., N.Y.C., 1959-66, chmn. bd., 1966; pres., chief exec. officer, dir. Ill. Central Industries and I.C. R.R., 1966-68; chmn., pres., chief exec. officer Ill. Central Industries, 1968—; chmn., chief exec. Officer I.C. R.R., 1969—; dir. Conill Corp., Chgo., Abex Corp., N.Y.C., Aetna Life Ins. Co., and affiliated co's., Hartford, TransUnion Corp., Chgo., Swiff & Co., Chgo., Pepsi-Cola Gen. Bottlers, Inc., Chgo. Bd. dirs. Chgo. Central Area Com.; trustee Michael Reese Hosp., Mus. Sci. and Industry, Com. for Econ. Devel.; mem. citizens bd. U. Chgo.; governing mem. Shedd Aquarium; bus. adv. council Grad. Sch. Bus. Northwestern U. Served as spl. agt., Security Intelligence Corps, AUS, 1943-45. Mem. Am., Phila. bar assns., ICC Practitioners Assn., Juristic Soc., Assn. Am. R.R.s (dir.), Assn. Western Rys. (dir.), Assn. Southeastern R.R.s (dir.), Newcomen Soc. N.Am., Transp. Assn. Am. (dir.), Nat. Def. Transp. Assn. (life; chmn. bd.), U.S. C. of C. (mem. coms.), Md. Soc. Pa., S.A.R., Order of Coif, Kappa Alpha, Omicron Delta Kappa. Baptist. Clubs: Sky, Economic (N.Y.C.); Carlton (Washington); Commercial, Economic, Chicago, Executives, Mid-America (Chgo.); Shoreacres (Lake Bluff); Onwentsia (Lake Forest); Old Elm (Highland Park); Ponte Vedra (Fla.). Home: 971 N Hawthorne Pl Lake Forest IL 60045 Office: 135 E 11th Pl Chicago IL 60605

JOHNSON, WILLIAM HAROLD, mfg. co. exec.; b. Iron Mountain, Mich., Sept. 28, 1920; s. Elmer S. and Emma Catherine (Weidemeyer) J.; B.A., Lake Forest (Ill.) Coll., 1943; student Ill. Tech. Coll., 1945-46, Northwestern U., 1949-51; m. Olga E. Castori, Aug. 16, 1941; children—Paula Karen, Nancy Rae. Office mgr. Hansell Elcock Co., Chgo., 1945-48; controller Chgo. Foundry Co., 1948- 51; with White Motor Co., 1951-56, asst. v.p. finance, 1954-56; exec. v.p., White Consol. Industries, Inc., Cleve., 1945-59, pres., 1969—; dir., v.p. Domestic Sewing Machine Co., Apex Fibre-Glass Products, Inc.; dir. White Sewing Machine, Limited. Elk. Clubs: Cleve. Athletic, Treasurer (Cleve.); Shaker Heights Country. Home: 3127 Bremerton Rd Cleveland OH 44124 Office: 117700 Berea Rd Cleveland OH 44111

JOHNSON, WILLIAM HOWARD, educator, agrl. engr.; b. Sidney, O., Sept. 3, 1922; s. Russell Earl and Dollie (Gamble) J.; B.S., Ohio State U., 1948, M.S., 1953; Ph.D., Mich. State U., 1960; m. Wyoma Jean Swift, Oct. 2, 1943; children—Lawrence Alan, Cheri Ellen, Dana Sue. Mem. faculty Ohio Agrl. Expt. Sta., Wooster, 1948-64; mem. faculty Ohio Agrl. Research and Devel. Center, Wooster, 1964-70, prof., asso. chmn. dept. agrl. engring., 1959-70; part-time prof. Ohio State U., 1964-70; prof., head dept. agrl. engring. Kan. State U., Manhattan, 1970—; cons. farm equipment cos. Mem. Am. Soc. Agrl. Engrs., Sigma Xi, Tau Beta Pi. Author: (with B. J. Lamp) Principles, Equipment and Systems for Corn Harvesting, 1966; also articles. Research on soil-plant-machine relationships, harvesting, design for soiltillers, planters, harvesters. Home: 2025 Blue Hills Rd Manhattan KS 66502

JOHNSON, WILLIAM HYATT, steel mfr., b. ville, Tex., Dec. 29, 1911; s. Rufus Edward and Robin (Matlock) J.; A.A., Schreiner Inst., 1930-32; B.B.A., U. Tex., 1934; m. Ruth Hobbs, Jan. 4, 1946; children—Gayl Hyatt, William Hyatt Sr. accountant Haskins & Sells, 1935-47; asst. treas. Lone Star Steel Co., 1947-48, v.p., asst. treas., 1948-50, v.p., controller, asst. treas., 1950, exec. v.p., 1950-64, v.p., 1964—. Mem. Financial Execs. Inst., N.A.M., Am. Iron and Steel Inst. Episcopalian. Rotarian. Home: 4715 S Lindhurst Dr Dallas TX 75229 Office: 4501 W Mockingbird Lane Dallas TX 75209

JOHNSON, WILLIAM LEE, lawyer, corp. exec.; b. N.Y.C., Jan. 11, 1929; s. Reginald Lee and Dorothy (Maloney) J.; grad. Horace Mann Sch., N.Y.C., 1946; A.B., Princeton, 1950; LL.B., Columbia, 1955; m. Marjory Bruce Hughes, Apr. 26, 1952; children—Susan D., Helen W., Marjory S. Admitted to N.Y. bar, 1955; asso. firm Hughes, Hubbard, Blair & Reed, 1955-61; sec., gen. counsel Otis Elevator Co., N.Y.C., 1968—. Trustee Village of Irvington, N.Y., 1963-67. Mem. Am. Bar Assn., Assn. Bar City N.Y. Clubs: Princeton, Riverdale Yacht (N.Y.C.); St. Andrew's Golf (Westchester County); Ardsley Curling (Ardsley-on-Hudson). Home: 240 Harriman Rd Irvington-on-Hudson NY 10533 Office: 260 11th Av New York City NY 10001

JOHNSON, WILLIAM LOUIS, educator; b. Silver Point, Tenn., July 3, 1908; s. William Louis and Mary Lou (Johnson) J.; B.S., Bowling Green Bus. U., 1932; J.D., Cumberland U. (now Samford U.), 1934; M.A., Northwestern U., 1940; m. Virginia Wilcox, June 4, 1931; children—William Louis, John Wilcox. Tchr., Andrew Jackson Bus. U., Nashville, 1932-33, Castle Heights Mil. Acad., Lebanon, Tenn., 1933-34; Massey Bus. Coll., Houston, 1934-35; chmn. accounting dept. Tenn. Technol. U., Cookeville, 1936-40, asst. prof., then asso. prof. bus. adminstrn., 1942-43, chmn. dept. bus. adminstrn., 1944-45, dir. Coll. Bus. Adminstrn., 1945-64, dean coll., 1964—; chmn. dept. bus. E. Tenn. State Coll., 1941-42; tax cons. U.S. Steel Corp., 1942-43; admitted to Tenn. bar, 1934; pvt. part-time practice law and taxation, 1945-. Pres. Tenn. Municipal League, 1948-49. Commr. finance and taxation City of Cookeville, 1947-53; mem. Tenn. Adminstrv. Adv. Council , 1962-66. Mem. bd. dirs. Middle Tenn. council Boy Scouts Am., 1956-58, United Givers Fund Cookeville, 1963-68. Mem. Am. Accounting Assn., Am. Bus. Law Assn., Tenn. Edn. Assn., N.E.A., Cookeville C. of C. (bd. dirs.), S.A.R. Pi Omega Pi, Phi Delta Kappa, Phi Kappa Delta, Sigma Iota Epsilon, Phi Kappa Phi. Methodist (chmn. ofcl. bd. 1966-67). Mason, Rotarian (pres. Cookville 1947-48), Lion (dir. Cookeville 1961-68, pres., 1966-67). Home: 729 Woodlawn Dr Cookeville TN 38501

JOHNSON, WILLIAM MCKINLEY, Jr., fgn. service officer; b. Columbus, O., June 15, 1920; s. William McKinley and Maria Valentine (Pierce) J.; A.B., Princeton, 1941; M.A., Fletcher Sch. Law and Diplomacy, 1947; m. Margaret Hodge Urban, Oct. 23, 1948; children—Mary V., Christopher H., Margaret P. With various intelligence depts. U.S. Govt., 1947-50; joined U.S. fgn. service, 1950; 3d sec., vice consul, Munich and Regensburg, Germany, 1950-52; 2d sec., consul Am. embassy, Pretoria, Union S. Africa, 1952-55; internat. affairs officer African Bur., Dept. of State, 1955-59; 1st sec., consul Am. embassy, Rabat, Morocco, 1959-63, Canadian Def. Coll., Kingston, Ont., 1963-64; polit. counselor Am. embassy, Ottawa, Ont., Can., 1964-69; country dir. for Can. Dept. State; 1969—. Served to lt. USNR, 1942-46. Episcopalian. Club: Rideau. Home: 3514 Leland St Chevy Chase MD 20015

JOHNSON, WILLIAM SUMMER, educator; b. New Rochelle, N.Y., Feb. 24, 1913; s. Roy Wilder and Josephine (Summer) J.; grad. Gov. Dummer Acad., 1932; B.A., Amherst Coll., 1936; M.A., Harvard, 1938, Ph.D., 1940, Sc.D., Amherst Coll., 1956, L.I. U., 1968; m. Barbara Allen, Dec. 27, 1940. Instr., Amherst Coll., 1936-37; research chemist Eastman Kodak Co., summers, 1936-39; instr. Univ. Wis., 1940-42, asst. prof., 1942-44, asso. prof., 1944-46, prof., 1946-60, Homer Adkins prof. chemistry, 1954- 60; prof. dept. chemistry Stanford, 1960—, chmn. dept., 1960-69; vis. prof. Harvard, 1954-55. Mem. exec. bd. Jour. Organic Chemistry, 1954- 56; mem. chem. adv. panel NSF, 1952-56; sec. organic sect. Internat. Congress Pure and Applied Chemistry, 1951. Recipient award for creative work in synthetic organic chemistry, 1958; medal Synthetic Organic Chem. Mfrs. Assn., 1963; Nichols medal award Am. Chem. Soc. 1968; Roussel prize, 1970. Fellow London Chem. Soc.; mem. Am. Acad. Arts and Scis., Swiss Chem. Soc., Am. Chem. Soc. (chmn. organic div. 1951-52), Nat. Acad. Scis., Phi Beta Kappa, Sigma Xi. Contbr. chpts. to chemistry books; articles assn. jours. Bd. editors Organic Syntheses, vol. 34, 1954; Jour. Am. Chem. Soc., 1956-65; Jour. Organic Chemistry, 1954-56, Tetrahedron, 1957—. Home: 191 Meadowood Dr Portola Valley CA 94025 Office: Dept Chemistry Stanford U Stanford CA 94305

JOHNSON, WILLIAM WEBER, writer; b. Mattoon, Ill., Dec. 18, 1909; s. Finis Ewing and Jessie (Weber) J.; B.A., De Pauw U., 1932; M.A., U. Ill., 1933; m. Elizabeth Ann McMurray, Oct. 7, 1951; stepson, Richard; children (by previous marriage)—Peter William, Jane. Reporter on Decatur (Ill.) Herald, 1933; asso. with various Ill. newspapers, 1933-37; with A. P., Detroit 1937-39; pub. relations adviser N. W. Ayer, Chgo. and N. Y., 1939-40; contbg. editor Time, Inc., 1940-43; war corr. Time and Life, ETO 1944-45, fgn. corr., chief of Time and Life Mexico Bur., 1945-47, chief Time & Life bur. Buenos Aires, 1947- 48, chief Time & Life Southwestern bur., Dallas, 1949, later chief Boston Bur. corr. Time, Inc., Beverly Hills, Cal., 1958- 61; prof. U. Cal. at Los Angeles, 1961-71, chmn. dept. journalism, 1968-71, prof. emeritus, 1971—. Recipient Gold medal for non-fiction Commonwealth Club, 1969; Guggenheim fellow, 1958. Mem. Delta Kappa Epsilon. Author: Sam Houston, The Tallest Texan, 1953; Kelly Blue, 1960; Birth of Texas, 1960; Captain Cortes Conquers Mexico, 1960; Mexico, 1961; The Andean Republics, 1965; Heroic Mexico, 1968. Home: Warner Springs CA Office: Journalism Dept U Cal Los Angeles CA 90024

JOHNSON, WILLIAM WOODWARD, banker; b. Augusta, Ga., Feb. 16, 1931; s. Dewey H. and Mabel (Woodward) J.; student U. S.C., 1949-53; m. Sarah Pierrine Baker, July 26, 1951; children—Jennifer, Marie, Salley, Jane. With State Bank & Trust Co., Columbia, S.C., 1953—, asst. cashier, 1954-56, asst. v.p., 1956-59, v.p., 1959-60, sr. v.p., 1960-63, exec. v.p., 1963-65, pres., 1965—; pres., dir. Augwood Life & Accident Ins. Co.; v.p., dir. Emerald Fire & Casualty Ins. Co.; asst. exec. trustee, asst. sec. State Real Estate Investment Trust. Campaign chmn. United Fund, 1964, mem. exec. bd., 1965—; mem. adv. bd. Salvation Army, 1965—; mem. S.C. Gen. Assembly, 1956-57; mem. S.C. State Ports Authority, 1965-; mem. Richland Tech. Edn. Commn., 1964-65. Treas., Richland County Democratic Party, 1965-66. Bd. dirs. U. S.C. Ednl. Found. Mem. Columbia C. of C. (v.p.), S.C. Young Bankers Assn. (past pres.), S.C. Bankers Assn. Methodist (chmn. ofcl. bd.). Clubs: Pine Tree Hunt, Spring Valley Country, Palmetto. Home: 5011 Quail Lane Columbia SC 29206 Office: 1244 Main St P O Box 448 Columbia SC 29202

JOHNSON, WILSON SUNDAY, assn. exec.; b. Mappsville, Va., July 26, 1914; s. William Thomas and Cecie Frances (Robinson) J.; Columbia Union Coll., 1935-39; B.A., U. Md., 1940; m. Vera Mae Koseruba, 1941 (div.); children—Donald Wilson, Carol Evelyn (Mrs. Bill Toll), Helen Marguerite (Mrs. Roger Cain); m. 2d, Dorothy Elizabeth Kesserling, Apr. 8, 1961 (dec. Dec. 1969); m. 3d, Charlotte Ann VanHorn, Sept. 5, 1970. Ordained to ministry Seventh-Day Adventist Ch., 1942; minister, 1939-49; mem. staff Nation's Bus. dept. U.S. C. of C., Phila. dist., 1949-51, mgr. Nation's bus. dept., Balt. dist., 1951-58; mgr. Atlanta div. Nat. Fedn. Ind. Bus., 1958-61, Eastern field dir., N.Y.C., 1951-69, dir., 1964—, pres., San Mateo, Cal., 1969—. Recipient awards Cal. Dept. Human Resources Devel., 1970, U.S. Small Bus. Adminstrn., 1971. Home: 151 W 3d Av San Mateo CA 94402 Office: 150 W 20th Av San Mateo CA 94403

JOHNSON, ZACHARY TAYLOR, coll. pres.; b. Athens, Ga., June 18, 1897; s. John Gilbert and Julia Frances (Snipes) J.; A.B., Asbury Coll., Wilmore, Ky., 1925; A.M., U. Ky., 1926; Ph.D., George Peabody Coll. for Tchrs., Nashville, 1929; LL.D., Taylor U., 1942; D.D., Houghton (N.Y.) Coll., 1948; m. Sadie Eloise Mershon, Sept. 11, 1916; children—Walter Henry, Zachary Taylor, Olive Mershon. Minister, 1916-26; tchr. Asbury Coll., 1924-26, Peabody Coll., 1927-29; head history dept. State Teachers Coll., Hattiesburg, Miss., 1929-34; minister Wilmore (Ky.) Meth. Ch., 1934-35; exec. v. p. Asbury Coll., Wilmore, 1935-40, pres., 1940—. Mem. Phi Delta Kappa, Kappa Delta Pi. Democrat. Methodist. Author: Career of Howell Cobb, 1929; Topical Survey of Civilization, 1931; What Is Holiness?, 1935; Sins and Faults, 1939; Methodism and Holiness, 1942; Limiting God, 1947; We Believe, 1957; History of Asbury College, 1970. Contbr. to ednl. and religious jours. Home: Wilmore KY 40390

JOHNSON, ZANE QUENTIN, oil co. exec.; b. Bristow, Okla., Mar. 5, 1924; s. Sylvester B. and Meta (Biggs) J.; B.S., U. Okla., 1947; m. Nila Jean Caylor, June 4, 1949; children—Zane Quentin, Mark C., Janis L. With Gulf Oil Co., 1947—, exec. v.p., Gulf Oil Co.-U.S., Houston, 1968-69, pres., chief operating officer Gulf Gen. Atomic, Inc., San Diego, 1969-70, exec. v.p. Gulf Oil Corp., Pitts., 1970—. Mayor, Port Arthur, Tex., 1957-58. Bd. dirs. United Community Services San Diego County, Scripps Meml. Hosp., San Diego, San Diego Symphony Orch. Assn. Served to 1st lt. USAAF, 1943-46; PTO. Decorated Air medal with three oak leaf clusters. Mem. Am. Inst. Chem. Engrs., Am. Petroleum Inst. Presbyn. Clubs: Duquesne, Pittsburgh, Longue Vue (Pitts.). Home: 580 Squaw Run Rd Pittsburgh PA 15238 Office: Gulf Bldg Pittsburgh PA 15230

JOHNSTON, ALEXANDER HYATT mfg. exec.; b. Lima, O., Apr. 1, 1932; B.S., U. San Francisco, 1954; M.S., Stanford University, 1956; m. Rosemarie Lois Brown, May 15, 1955; 1 son, Anthony Robinson. Sales rep. Ames-Brockton Fabricated Products, Akron, O., 1956-58, sales mgr. Coshocton, Ohio, 1959-61, gen. manager plant, 1961-68, v.p. sales, 1968--. Instr. bus. Coshocton Jr. College, 1968-69. Named Man of Year, Coshocton Junior Chamber of Commerce, 1968. Mem. Coshocton C. of C. (vice president 1967-68, pres. 1969-70), English Speaking Union, Coshocton Sertoma Club, Nat. Assn. Mfrs., Sales Executives Institute, Phi Beta Kappa, Sigma Chi, Phi Mu. Democrat. Mem. Christian Ch. (lay leader). Mason (32, Shriner). Clubs: Coshocton Country, Coshocton City, Running Deer Country. Home: 2d Av Coshocton OH Office: 3d Av Coshocton OH

JOHNSTON, ANDERSON chemist, educator; b. Chicago, 1928; B.S. in Physics, Yale, 1950; Ph.D. in Chemistry, Harvard, 1956; m. Sally Ann Jones, July 5, 1957; children--Kenneth J., Nancy A. Chemist, Acme Chem. Co., Blue Island, Ill., 1950-51; director of Research Lab., Indsl. Chemicals Corp., Cambridge, Mass., 1956-60; project coordinator environmental sect. Steinmetz Assos., Chgo., 1960-61; v.p. for research Bauer Bros. Chem. Co., Inc., Memphis, 1961-64; asst. prof. chemistry Washington U., St. Louis, 1964-66, asso. prof., 1966-70, prof., 1970--, head of chemistry dept., 1970-71. Vis. prof. So. Ill. U., summer 1967, U. of Ore., 1969. Scoutmaster, Boy Scouts America, University City, Mo., 1968-70. Bd. dirs. Rest Haven Home for Elderly, 1960-61; trustee of the Lutheran Hosp., 1965-71. Served from lt. to capt., AUS, 1951-53. Mem. Am. Chem. Soc., Sci. Research Soc. Am. (chpt. treas. 1967), Sigma Xi. Author: (with others) Basic Inorganic Chemistry, 1971. Home: Fairfax Apts 7291 Windermere Dr University City MO 63105

JOHNSTON, BENJAMIN BURWELL, Jr., composer, educator; b. Macon, Ga., Mar. 15, 1926; s. Benjamin Burwell and Janet (Ross) J.; student Cath. U. Am., 1944-45; B.A., Coll. William and Mary, 1949; M. Mus., Cin. Conservatory Music, 1950; M.A., Mills Coll., 1952; postgrad. U. Cal. at Berkeley, 1950, U. Ill. at Urbana, 1952- 54; student Composition with Darius Milhaud, Burrill Phillips, Robert Palmer, Harry Partch, John Cage; m. Dorothy Haines, June 1947 (div.); m. 2d, Betty Ruth Hall, Apr. 14, 1950; children—Sibyl Bulluck, Ross Burwell, Christopher Alan. Prof. music Sch. Music, U. Ill. at Urbana, 1951—, chmn. music planning com. for univ. Festival Contemporary Arts, 1962-65, asso. mem. Center Advanced Studies, 1966. Served with USNR, 1944-46. Guggenheim fellow, 1959- 60; Summer Research fellow U. Ill., 1958; Research Bd. grantee, 1965; Nat. Found. Arts and Humanities grantee, 1966. Mem. A.S.C.A.P., Am. Soc. U. Composers, Societe des Auteurs et Compositeurs Dramatiques, Phi Beta Kappa, Omicron Delta Kappa, Pi Kappa Lambda. Composer: (orch.) Passacaglia and Epilogue, 1955, 60, Quintet for Groups, 1965; (ballets) Gambit, 1959, St. Joan, 1955; (operas) Gertrude, or Would She Be Pleased to Receive It?, 1956, Carmilla, 1970; (cantata) Night, 1955; (chamber music) Nine Variations for String Quartet, 1959, String Quartet No. 2, 1964, String Quartet No. 3, 1966; Sonata for Two (violin and cello), 1960, Knocking Piece (2 percussionists and grand piano), 1962, Duo (flute and string bass), 1963; One Man (solo for trombone and percussion), 1967; (piano music) Satires, 1953, Celebration, 1953, Sonata for Microtonal Piano, 1965; (for jazz band) Ivesberg Revisited, 1960, Newcastle Troppo, 1960; (songs) Three Chinese Lyrics, 1955, Five Fragments, 1960, A Sea Dirge, 1962, Seven, 1970 Knocking Piece II, Recipe for a Casta Conference, 1968; (with Jaap Spek) score for orientation film Mus. History and Tech., Smithsonian Instn., 1968, Automobile, 1969, Kindergarden lieder, 1969; Knocking Piece Collage, 1969. Contbr. articles. Home: 1003 W Church St Champaign IL 61820 Office: Sch Music Univ Illinois Urbana IL 61801

JOHNSTON, BRUCE GILBERT, civil engr.; b. Detroit, Oct. 13, 1905; s. Sterling and Ida (Peake) J.; B.S. in Civil Engring., U. Ill., 1930; M.S., Lehigh U., 1934; Ph.D. in Sci., Columbia, 1938; m. Ruth Elizabeth Barker, Aug. 5, 1939; children—Sterling, Carol Anne (Mrs. John Snow), David. Engaged in engring. constrn. with Coolidge Dam, Ariz., 1927-29; in design office Roberts & Schaefer Co., Chgo., 1930; instr. civil engring. Columbia, 1934-38; charge structural research Fritz Engring. Lab., Lehigh U., 1938-50, dir., 1947, tchr. grad. work structures and materials 1938-50, asst. prof. civil engring., 1938, prof. 1945- 50; prof. structural engring. U. Mich., 1950-68, prof. emeritus,

1968- -; prof. civil engring. Ariz., Tucson, 1968-70; lectr., 1970—; with John Hopkins Lab. Applied Physics, Silver Spring, Md., 1942-45. Chmn. Column Research Council, 1956-62. Registered profl. engr., N.Y., Mich. Hon. mem. Am. Soc. C.E. (J.J.R. Cross medalist 1937-54, chmn. engring. mech. div. 1961-62, chmn. structural div. 1965-66); mem. Am. Soc. Testing Soc. Engring. Edn., Am. Inst. Steel Constrn., Assn. Iron and Steel Engrs., Sigma Xi, Phi Kappa Phi, Tau Beta Pi, Chi Epsilon. Methodist. Contbr. tech. papers in field. Editor column Research Council Design Guide, 1960—. Home: 5025 E Calle Barril Tucson AZ 85718

JOHNSTON, CHARLES OLIVER, communications co. exec.; b. Cumberland, Md., Nov. 16, 1927; s. Thomas Paul and Margaret (Hunt) J.; B.S. in Econs., Wharton Sch., U. Pa., 1952; m. Arla Lethian Claar, June 21, 1952; 1 son, Randal Charles. With Gen. Elec. Co., 1952-58; dir. finance Litton Industries, 1958-64; v.p., comptroller Western Union Co., 1964—; v.p. finance Western Union Corp.; chmn. bd. Western Union Realty Corp.; v.p. finance, treas., dir. Computer Utilities Jacksonville; treas. Western Union Hawaii, Western Union Data Services; dir., chief financial officer Teleprocessing Industries, Inc.; dir. Western Union Telegraph Co., Gray Mfg. Co., Distronics Corp. Served with USNR, 1946-47. Mem. Financial Execs. Inst., Am. Mgmt. Assn., Sigma Tau Gamma, Beta Alpha Psi. Mason. Home: 611 Dakota Trial Franklin Lakes NJ 07417 Office: 60 Hudson St New York City NY 10013

JOHNSTON, CLEMENT DIXON, bus. exec., b. Crestwood, Ky., Nov. 7, 1895; s. Clement B. and Lula G. (Johnston) J.; B.S., Centre Coll., Danville, Ky., 1916, LL.D., 1951; student Harvard Med. Sch., 1916; L.H.D., William Jewell Coll., 1954; m. Lutie Walcott Douthat, July 21, 1950. Sales mgr. Johnston Bros. Co., Inc., Louisville, 1919-26; founder Roanoke Pub. Warehouse (Va.), 1926, since pres.; Bristol Grocery Co. (Va.) 1937—, Williamson Grocery Co. (W.Va.), 1935—; v.p . Abingdon Grocery Co. (Va.), Huff, Andrews & Thomas, Bluefield, W.Va.; mgr. Morris Plan Bank Va.; dir. Mullens Grocery Co., (W.Va.), F.B. Thomas & Co., Roanoke, So. Investment Co., Roanoke, Sublette Feed & Supply Co., Bluefield, W.Va., Walker Machine & Foundry Corp., Roanoke, Moore of Bedfore Inc. (Va.). Mem. Tabor Com. (investigative staff Ho. Reps. appropriations com.), 1953; nat. chmn. Project Adequate Roads, 1953—; cons. warehousing Office Def. Transp., RFC; chmn. warehouse industry adv. com. OPA; dept. dir. Office Civil Def. Planning Washington, 1948; chmn. study group U.S. Commn. Intergovtl. Relations, 1954-55; nat. council, exec. com. region III Boy Scouts Am., 1934—; vice chmn. United Community Campaigns Am.; spl. rep. U.S. Senate fgn. relations com. for aid program in S.E. Asia, 1956-57; pub. mem. 12th selection bd. Dept. State. Bd. regents James Monroe Meml.; trustee Community Hosp. Roanoke Valley. Served to capt., 33d Inf., U.S. Army, World War I; lt. col. ordnance dept., control div. services of supply, Washington, also ordnance supply officer East China, World War II. Decorated Legion of Merit. Mem. Internat. (mem. Am. com., U.S.) (past pres., chmn. 1955—), Va. (pres.) chambers commerce, Conf. Nat. Orgns. (nat. chmn.), Am. Warehousemen's Assn. (pres.), Am. Chain Warehouses (pres.), Omicron Delta Kappa, Beta Theta Pi, Alpha Kappa Psi. Methodist. Rotarian (dist. gov.). Clubs: Pendennis (Louisville); Shenandoah, Roanoke Country (Roanoke); Metropolitan (Washington). Address: Blue Hills Farm Turner Creek Lane Roanoke VA 24019

JOHNSTON, DANIEL WEBSTER, banker; b. White Bluff, Tenn., Sept. 30, 1903; s. James Crawford and Dixie (White) J.; student pub. schs.; m. Elizabeth Sudekum, Dec. 28, 1943; children—Frances J. (Mrs. W. Earthman), Daniel W., Tony S. With Cumberland Valley Nat. Bank, 1919, Am. Nat. Bank, 1921-27; exec. v.p., dir. Third Nat. Bank, Nashville, 1952-64, sr. chmn., 1964-70, dir., 1964—; dir. Farmer Bank, White Bluff, Tenn., 1945—; chmn., dir. Crescent Co., Nashville; dir. Ashland City Bank & Trust Co. (Tenn.). Chmn. bd. trust Martin Coll., Pulaski, Tenn.; trustee Scarritt Coll. for Christian Workers; chmn. finance com. Martin Coll., Pulaski, Tenn. Mason (32, Shriner). Clubs: Belle Meade, The Cumberland (Nashville). Home: 400 Jackson Blvd Nashville TN 37205 Office: 201 4th Av N Nashville TN 37219

JOHNSTON, DAVID IAN, mfr.; b. Ottawa, Ont., Can., Mar. 11, 1932; s. Wilbur Austin and Florence (Tucker) J.; B.A., McGill U., 1953, B.C.L., 1957, LL.M., 1961; B.Sc., Sir George Williams U., 1956; m. Patricia D. Lowe, June 7, 1952; children—David Ian, Cynthia Lowe, Peter Doyle. European tech. rep. Canadair, Ltd., 1954-55; solicitor Canadair, Ltd., 1957-64; v.p. legal CAE Industries, Ltd., Montreal, 1964-67, exec. v.p., 1967—; dir. N.W. Industries, Ltd., CAE Aircraft, Ltd., Canadian Bronze Co., Ltd., Union Screen Plate Co., Ltd., CAE Machinery, Ltd., Oneida Electronics, Inc. Served with R.C.A.F., 1948-52. Mem. Inst. Internat. Air Law Assn. (past pres.), Canadian (bar counsel 1964-66), Que. (bar counsel 1964-66) bar assns., Law Soc. Alta., Assn. Canadian Gen. Counsel, Lambda Chi Alpha. Clubs: Hillside Tennis (past pres.), Montreal Badminton and Squash, St. James (Montreal). Contbr. articles profl. jours. Home: 3220 Ridgewood Av Montreal 247 Quebec Canada Office: CAE Industries Ltd Place Ville Marie Montreal 113 Quebec Canada

JOHNSTON, ERNEST R., educator; b. Galesburg, Ill., Feb. 9, 1907; s. Emmee and Nellie (Gale) J.; B.Ed., Ill. State Normal U., 1937; M.S., U. Ill., 1938; Ph.D., U. Minn., 1954; m. Lucille Z. West, Dec. 25, 1939. Teacher, prin. Ill. pub. schs., 1926- 37; instr. U. Ill., 1939-40; instr. Austin Jr. Coll., 1940-42; engr. Naval Ordnance Lab., 1942-47; asst. prof. math. U. Minn., 1947-53; prof. math. Wis. State Coll., 1953-55; mem. faculty Ind. U., also Purdue U. at Indpls., 1955—, prof., head dept. math. sci., 1960—. Home: 4338 E 39th St Indianapolis IN 46226

JOHNSTON, ERVIN GLENN, lawyer; b. Sedan, Kan., June 27, 1926; s. George E. and Gertrude (Glenn) J.; B.A., Kan. U., 1949, LL.B., 1951; m. Jean Trantum, Oct. 6, 1951; children—Jo Lynn, Robert. Admitted to Kan. bar, 1951; law clk. U.S. dist. judge Arthur Melloett, Kansas City, Kan., 1951-52; atty. Kan. Tax Commn., Topeka, 1952-55; asso. mem. firm Stanley, Stanley, Schroeder, Weeks, Thomas, Kansas City, Kan., 1955-57; partner Weeks, Thomas, Lysaught, Bingham, Johnston, Kansas City, Kan., 1957—. Dir. Home State Bank, Process Solvent Co., Inc., Larsen Brothers, Inc., Kan. Assn. Profl. Corps., Topeka, Fashion, Inc. Leader Jayhawk Council Boy Scouts Am., 1953-55; mem. fund com. Camp Fire Girls, 1958-63, Kaw Valley Heart Assn., 1965-68. Kan. rep. for liaison com. Regional Commn. Internal Revenue Service, IRS, 1960-63. Trustee Stumpff Student Loan Fund. Mem. Kan. Bar Assn. (chmn. taxation com. 1955-61), Wyandotte Co., Kan. bar assns., Pi Kappa Alpha, Phi Alpha Delta. Republican. Methodist. Author: (with J.K. Logan) Kansas Estate Administration, 1967. Home: 5620 W 84th Terrace Shawnee Mission KS 66207 Office: Home State Bank Bldg Kansas City KS 66101

JOHNSTON, EVERETT DALE, lawyer; b. nr. Findlay, O., Sept. 12, 1904; s. Frederick Harvey and Metta Viola (Householder) J.; student Tiffin (O.) Bus. U., 1922-23; A.B., George Washington U., 1927, LL.B., 1931; m. Dorothy Jane Nuckles, Mar. 2, 1935; children—Joan Page (Mrs. William Ewart Gladstone), David Frederick. Employee U.S. Govt., 1923-34; admitted to D.C. bar, 1931; specializing in communications law, 1934—; asso. firm Dow & Lohnes, 1934-43, Kirkland, Fleming, Green, Martin & Ellis, 1943-50; spl. partner Roberts & McInnis, Washington, 1951-60, partner, 1960-65; partner firm McInnis, Wilson, Munson & Woods, 1965-70. Mem. No. Va. Regional Planning and Econ. Devel. Commn., 1959-62, vice chmn., 1962. Mem. City Council Falls Church, Va., 1959-62. Mem. Fed. Communications Bar Assn. (sec. 1953), Am. Bar Assn., Bar Assn. D.C., Am. Judicature Soc., Delta Theta Phi. Republican. Methodist. Home: 2902 Dadmun Ct Fairfax VA 22030 Office: 1150 Connecticut Av NW Washington DC 20036

JOHNSTON, FRONTIS WITHERS, coll. dean; b. Summerville, S.C., Oct. 31, 1908; s. Thomas Dabney and Mary Elizabeth (Withers) J.; A.B., Davidson Coll., 1930; Ph.D., Yale, 1938; m. Lucy Martin Currie, Dec. 22, 1936; children—Letitia Dabney (Mrs. Lawrence M. Kimbrough), Archibald Currie, Martha Elizabeth. Mem. faculty Davidson Coll., 1935—, prof. history, 1941—, dean faculty, 1958—; vis. prof. history summers Emory U., 1950, Duke, 1953, 55, 58; lectr. FBI Nat. Acad., 1949—. Trustee Edgar Tufts Meml. Assn., 1959—, N.C. Agrl. and Tech. Coll., 1960—. Ford Found. faculty fellow, 1954-55. Mem. Am., So. hist. assns., N.C. Lit. and Hist. Assn. (pres. 1951-53), Hist. Soc. N.C. (sec.-treas. 1950-55, pres. 1963), Soc. Am. Historians, Phi Beta Kappa, Beta Theta Pi, Omicron Delta Kappa. Presbyn. (elder). Editor: The Papers of Zebulon B. Vance, Vol. 1, 1963. Home: 209 Grey Rd Davidson NC 28036

JOHNSTON, GEORGE, univ. dean; b. Clydebank, Scotland, June 9, 1913; s. William George and Jenny (McKeown) J.; M.A., Glasgow U., 1935, B.D., 1938, D.D. (hon.), 1960; Ph.D., Cambridge U., 1941; m. Alexandra Gardner, Aug. 6, 1941; children—Christine (Mrs. Hamilton McClymont III), Ronald, Janet. Ordained to ministry Ch. Scotland, 1940; minister in St. Andrews, Fife, Scotland, 1940-47; asso. prof. Hartford (Conn.) Theol. Sem., 1947-52; prof. N.T., Emmanuel Coll., Toronto, 1952-59; prof. N.T., McGill U., 1959—, dean faculty religious studies, 1970—; prin. United Theol. Coll., Montreal, 1959-70. Commr. gen. council United Ch. Can., 1958, 66, 68; del. World Council Chs., New Delhi, 1961, Montreal, 1963. Active St. Andrews Boys Club, 1942-47; mem. Port Credit (Ont.) Library Com., 1958-59. Served with Brit. Army, World War II. Faculty fellow Am. Assn. Theol. Schs., 1967. Author: The Church in the New Testament, 1943; The Secrets of the Kingdom, 1954; Ephesians, 1967; The Spirit-Paraclete in the Gospel of John, 1970. Home: 8-44 Academy Montreal Quebec Canada 215

JOHNSTON, GEORGE BURKE, educator; b. Tuscaloosa, Ala., Sept. 8, 1907; s. George D. and Eleanor (McCorvey) J.; A.B., U. Ala., 1929; A.M., Columbia, 1930, Ph.D., 1943; m. Mary Tabb Lancaster, Dec. 28, 1936; children—Elizabeth Carrington (Mrs. C.L. Lipscomb, III), Thomas McCorvey, George Burke, Mary Tabb. Instr. English, Va. Polytech. Inst., Blacksburg, Va., 1930-33, dean Sch. Applied Scis. and Bus. Adminstrn., 1950-61, dean Sch. Sci. and Gen. Studies, 1961-63, dean Coll. of Arts and Scis., 1963-65, Miles prof. English, 1965—; instr. English, U. Ala., 1935-41, asst. prof., 1941-46, asso. prof., 1946-50, prof., 1950, asst. dean coll. arts and scis., 1946-50; Served as 2d lt., CA-Res., 1929, 1st lt., 1932; from 1st lt. to lt. col., AUS, 1941-45. Mem. Modern Lang. Assn., Phi Beta Kappa, Omicron Delta Kappa, Delta Kappa Epsilon, Alpha Kappa Psi, Phi Kappa Phi. Episcopalian. Author: Ben Jonson: Poet, 1945; Reflections, 1965; contbr. poems and articles periodicals. Editor: Poems of Ben Johnson, 1954; Alabama Historical Sketches (T.C. McCorvey), 1960. Home: 804 Gracelyn Ct Blacksburg VA 24060

JOHNSTON, GEORGE PALMER, Jr., newspaper writer; b. Cheyenne, Wyo., July 5, 1918; s. George Palmer and Fanny (Phelps) J.; B.A., U. Wyo., 1941; m. Margaret F. Hanson, Dec. 19, 1941; children—Lawrence George, Christopher Alan. Reporter, Wyo. State Tribune, 1941, reporter, asst. city editor, 1946-48; city editor Wyo. Eagle, 1948-52, mng. editor, 1952-55, editor, 1955-62; staff writer Denver Post, 1962-63, night city editor, 1963-65, dir. bus. news dept., 1965-66, exec. news editor, 1966-71, financial editor, 1971—. Served to 1st lt. Q.M.C., AUS, 1943- 46. Mem. Kappa Sigma. Rotarian. Club: Denver Press. Home: 2841 S Locust St Denver CO 80222 Office: Denver Post Denver CO 80202

JOHNSTON, GEORGE WASHINGTON, educator, botanist; b. Quitman, Miss., Feb. 1, 1910; s. Jerry Myer and Annie Elizabeth (Fairchild) J.; B.S., Miss. State U., 1933, M.S., 1938; Ph.D., Duke, 1940; m. Ruby Lee, June 15, 1935; children—Carol Myers, George Brooks. High. sch. prin. and supt., Miss., 1933-36; grad. asst. botany Miss. State U., 1936-38, Duke, 1938-40; mem. faculty Miss. State U., 1940—. prof. botany, 1956—, head dept., 1962—; asso. agronomist Miss. Expt. Sta., 1942-45, botanist, 1960-; botanist Miss. Extension Service, 1960—. Bd. dirs. Community Bible Study; Baptist lay lectr. Mem. Bot. Soc. Am., Internat. Soc. Plant Morphologists, Sigma Xi, Sigma Chi, Omicron Delta Kappa, Blue Key. Lion. Author: (with F.S. Batson) Wild Flowers of Mississippi, 1945; Wild Flowers of Mississippi. Home: Box 621 State College MS 39762

JOHNSTON, HAROLD, advt. agy. exec. Pres. Leo Burnett Co. of Can. Ltd. Office: 165 University Av Toronto 1 Ontario Canada*

JOHNSTON, HAROLD JOHN, banker; b. Elizabeth, N.J., June 18, 1919; s. Walter Jones and Pearl (Markle) J.; student Am. Inst. Banking; m. Doris Catherine Eckert, May 23, 1942; children—Todd Douglas, Mark Gordan. With Central Hanover Bank, N.Y.C., 1936-54; trust officer 1st Mechanics Nat. Bank, Trenton, N.J., 1954-61; exec. v.p., trust officer Trenton Trust Co., 1961—; dir. Taylor Provisions Co., Trenton. Treas. N.J. Hist. Drama Assn. Trustee Colligan's Stockton Inn Pension Plan. Served with USAAF, 1942-45. Mem. Trenton C. of C. (chmn. finance com.), N.J. Bankers Assn. (chmn. exec. com. trust div. 1969), Am. Bankers Assn. (nat. legislative council). Presbyn. (pres., trustee 1968). Home: 2210 Stackhouse Dr Yardley PA 19067 Office: 28 W State St Trenton NJ 08605

JOHNSTON, HAROLD P., banker; b. Danville, Que., Can., Sept. 20, 1904; s. George H. and Ethel M. (Waller) J.; ed. pub. schs. Western Can.; m. Alice Poole, Mar. 15, 1924 (dec. Apr. 1962); 1 dau., Shirley Ann (Mrs. Paul A. Mumford). Came to U.S., 1924, naturalized. Sr. v.p. Central Nat. Bank Chgo., 1965-67; pres., dir. First State Bank & Trust Co. of Park Ridge (Ill.), 1967-70; mem. adv. com. Peterson State Bank, Chgo., 1971—. Mem. Robert Morris Assos. (life; past pres. Chgo.). Mason (Shriner). Clubs: Union League (Chgo.); LaGrange (Ill.) Country. Home: 4015 Franklin Av Western Springs IL 60558

JOHNSTON, HAROLD SLEDGE, univ. dean; b. Woodstock, Ga., Oct. 11, 1920; s. Smith L. and Florine (Dial) J.; A.B., Emory U., 1941, D.Sc., 1965; Ph.D., Cal. Inst. Tech., 1948; m. Mary Ella Stay, Dec. 29, 1948; children—Shirley Louise, Linda Marie, David Finley, Barbara Dial. From instr. to asso. prof. chemistry Stanford, 1947-56; asso. prof. Cal Inst. Tech., 1956-57; prof. chemistry U. Cal. at Berkeley, 1957—, dean Coll. Chemistry, 1966-70. Mem. Am. Chem. Soc. (Gold medal Cal. sect. 1956), Am. Phys. Soc., Nat. Acad. Sci. Author: Gas Phase Reaction Rate Theory, 1966. Home: 132 Highland Blvd Berkeley CA 94708

JOHNSTON, HARRY DRISCOLL, JR., banker; b. Los Angeles, July 14, 1922; s. Harry Driscoll and Vera (Garrison) J.; student Pasadena (Cal.) Jr. Coll., 1940-41, U. Tulsa, 1946, Boise Jr. Coll., 1947; m. B. Maxine Gross, Sept. 29, 1946; children-Gary, Linda. Loan collection mgr. Pacific Finance Co., 1950-53; with First Nat. Bank Ariz., Phoenix, 1953—, adminstrv. v.p., 1965—. Mem. adminstrv. com. and adb. bd. Western Bancorp. retirement plan and supplemental retirement plan. Served with USAAF, 1942-45. Decorated D.F.C., Air medal with silver cluster. Mem. Ariz. Tax Research Assn. (treas.), Ariz. Bankers Assn. (chmn. legislative com.). Home: 6812 E Bonita Dr Scottsdale AZ 85251 Office: 411 N Central Av Phoenix AZ 85004

JOHNSTON, HENRY POELINITZ, broadcasting exec.; b. Uniontown, Ala., Jan. 26, 1908; s. Charles P. and Eloise (White) J.; student Culver Mil. Acad., 1923-25; grad. Washington and Lee U., 1929; m. Louise Feagin, Dec. 26, 1946; children—Henry Poellnitz, Margaret Ann. With Kelly Smith, newspaper advt., N.Y.C., 1929- 30; nat. advt. dept. Birmingham News-Age Herald, 1930-31, local advt. mgr., 1934-37; pub. Huntsville (Ala.) Times, 1931-34, pres., 1934-56; liaison between Birmingham News-Age Herald and radio sta. WSGN, 1936, v.p. Birmingham News Co., 1936-56; mng. dir. WSGN, 1936-53; pres., mng. dir. Ala. Broadcasting System, 1953-57; chmn. bd. Planters & Merchants Bank of Uniontown (Ala.); dir. Southern Airways; mem. adv. bd. So. div. 1st Nat. Bank, Birmingham. Mem. Jefferson County Personnel Bd.; former mem. adv. com. Voice of Am.; chmn. Interracial Council, 1954-56. Nat. dir. Ala. div. Am. Cancer Soc.; bd. dirs. Alabama Found. for Hearing and Speech; chmn. Jefferson County A.R.C., former chmn. regional blood program Jefferson County. Recipient plaque Ala. Broadcasters Assn., 1956. Mem. Nat. Assn. Broadcasters (dir. 1947-49), Ala. Broadcasters Assn. (1st pres.), Soc. Colonial Wars (charter mem. Ala.), S.A.R. (Ala. pres.), Sons of War of 1812, N. C. Soc. of Cin., Huguenot Soc. of S.C., Sales Execs. Club, Omicron Delta Kappa, Alpha Tau Omega, Sigma Delta Chi, Pi Delta Epsilon, Alpha Epsilon Rho. Democrat. Presbyn. Rotarian. Clubs: Down Town, Birmingham Country, Mountain Brook Country, The Club, Quarterback (Birmingham); Nat. Press (Washington). Author: Little Acorns from the Mighty Oak; Pioneers in Their Own Right; The Gentle Johnstons; Around the World in 42 Days; Me and My Gals. Home: 3123 Overhill Rd Birmingham AL 35223 Office: P O Box 7661 Birmingham AL 35223

JOHNSTON, HENRY RUST, retired banker; b. Chgo., Feb. 13, 1888; s. James Wright and Bessie (Rust) J.; A.B., Williams Coll., 1909; LL.B., cum laude, New York Law Sch., 1912; m. Helen Earle, May 20, 1914; children—Douglas Earle, David Prince, Alexander Rust. Admitted to N.Y. bar, 1912, and began practice at N.Y.C., mem. Greene & Hurd until 1917; asst. to pres. Mercantile Trust Co., 1919-21; with Chatham Phenix Nat. Bank & Trust Co. (now Mfrs. Trust Co.), 1921-33, was v.p. and dir.; v.p. and dir. Case, Pomeroy & Co., 1933-38, pres. 1938-41; ret., 1942; dir. Lord, Abbett group Investment Trusts, since 1946; treas., exec. dir. Com. for Econ. Devel., 1943-49. Chmn. Nat. Inter-fraternity Conf., 1925-26, instituting system of annual surveys of scholarship of male students in 120 colleges and univ. of U.S. Mem. Borough Council of Essex Fells, N.J., 2 terms 1929-35, pres. 1935; mem. N.J. State Prison Bd., Trenton, 1934-48; pres. Ponte Vedra Community Assn., 1951. Trustee, v.p. Citizens Budget Comm., N.Y.C., 1946-50; trustee Williams Coll., 1926-31, pres. Soc. Alumni, 1933-36. Served in U.S. Navy Flying Corps, World War I. Mem. Delta Kappa Epsilon (Council of Fgn. Relations). Republican. Episcopalian. Clubs: University, Williams, Down Town Assn. (New York); Pine Valley Golf. Donor of Amherst-Williams Trophy of Trophies, 1919. Home: Ponte Vedra Beach FL 32082

JOHNSTON, JAMES JORDAN advt. exec.; b. Sedalia, Mo., Jan. 17, 1931; s. E.O. and Hildah (Pease) J.; student U. Cal., 1951-52, U. Mo., 1955-56, U. Wichita, 1956-57; m. Patricia Rose Curnutt, 1951; children—Shelley Rose, Douglas Tiffany. Operations mgr. KTVH-TV, Wichita, Kan., 1956-57; dir. advt. and promotion WMBD-TV, Peoria, Ill., 1957-59; v.p., creative dir. Kane Advt., Bloomington, Ill., 1959-62; partner Howard Advt., Raleigh, N.C., 1962-64; v.p., creative dir. Griswold-Eshleman Co., Cleve., 1964—, pres., 1969—, chief exec. officer, 1970—. Promotion chmn. Cleve. Plan, 1968—. Served with USAF, 1951-55. Named Man of Year, Cleve. Soc. Communicating Arts, 1968. Mem. Am. Assn. Advt. Agys. (chmn. Cleve. council, gov. Central Region), Cleve. Soc. Communicating Arts (past dir.), A.I.M. (president's council). Home: 16401 Fernway Rd Shaker Heights OH 44120 also 250 E 63d St New York City NY 10021 Office: 55 Public Sq Cleveland OH 44113

JOHNSTON, JOHN CLIFFORD, Jr., lawyer; b. Wooster, O., July 30, 1916; s. John Clifford and Estella Marie (Smith) J.; B.A., Coll. Wooster, 1938; J.D., U. Mich., 1941; m. Marie Wolf, Sept. 6, 1947; children—John Clifford,. Gordon Wolf. Admitted to Ohio bar, 1941; since practiced in Wooster, 1945—. Mem. alumni bd. Coll. Wooster, 1948-50. Served to capt. AUS, 1941-45. Recipient Distinguished Alumni award Coll. Wooster, 1963. Fellow Am. Bar Found.; mem. Am., Ohio (pres. 1961-62) bar assns., Am. Judicature Soc. (dir. 1970-71), Alumni Assn. Coll. Wooster (past pres.), Phi Beta Kappa, Delta Sigma Rho. Home: 1118 Quinby Av Wooster OH 44697 Office: 225 N Market St Wooster OH 44691

JOHNSTON, JOSEPH FORNEY, lawyer; b. Birmingham, Ala., July 31, 1906; s. Forney and Clara (Cocke) J.; A.B., Princeton, 1927; LL.B., Harvard, 1930; m. Elizabeth Whipple White, June 13, 1931; 1 son, Joseph Forney. Admitted to Ala. bar, 1929, Va. bar, 1939; asst. gen. counsel, also gen. solicitor Seaboard Air Line Ry., 1938-43; partner firm Cabaniss, Johnston, Gardner & Clark, Birmingham, 1946—. Dir. Hayes Internat. Corp., McWane Cast Iron Pipe Co. Mem. Ala, Constl. Com. Bd. mem. Birmingham Mus. Art; chmn. trustees Birmingham YWCA. Served to lt. col. AUS, 1943-46; ETO, PTO. Decorated Legion of Merit. Mem. Am., Ala. (chmn. com. constl. revision), Va., Birmingham bar assns., Am. Law Inst. (council 1950-). Clubs: Commonwealth (Richmond); Mountain Brook Country, Relay House (Birmingham); Metropolitan (Washington); Princeton (N.Y.C.). Home: 2825 Overton Rd Birmingham AL 35223 also Bremo Bremo Bluff VA 23022 Office: First Nat So Natural Bldg Birmingham AL 35203

JOHNSTON, JOSEPH REX, govt. ofcl.; b. Iredell, Tex., Apr. 24, 1915; s. Marion Benjamin and Minnie Lorena (Hensley) J.; B.S. in Agronomy, Tex. Tech. Coll., 1933-36; Ph.D. in Soil Sci., Ia. State Coll., 1941; m. Selma Louise Lider, June 1, 1941; children—Joseph Edward, Janice Marie, George Lider. With Soil Conservation Service Dept. Agr., Wis., Ia., Tex., 1938-48; supt. Blackland Expt. Sta., Temple, Tex., 1948-51; asst. dir. Tex. Agrl. Expt. Sta., College Station, Tex., 1951-54; agrl. adminstr. Soil and Water Conservation Research Div., Agrl. Research Service, 1954—, chief So. Plains br. Mem. research com. Gt. Plains Agrl. Council, Nat. Water Resources Assn., West Tex. Water Inst. Dist. chmn. Heart O' Tex. council Boy Scouts Am., 1948-50. Fellow Soil Conservation Soc. Am. (pres. elect 1971); mem. Soil Sci. Soc. Am., Am. Soc. Range Mgmt., Internat. Soc. Soil Sci., Sigma Xi, Gamma Sigma Delta, Alpha Chi. Kiwanian. Contbr. articles to profl. jours. Home: 1231 Bonham St Amarillo TX 79102 Office: SWC-ARS-USDA Bushland TX 79012

JOHNSTON, LOGAN T., steel co. exec.; b. Pitts., Sept. 1, 1900; s. William G. and Emily (Truax) J.; B.Sc., Carnegie Inst. Tech., 1923; D.C.S. (hon.), U. Cin., 1962; LL.D., Miami U., 1963; m. Janet Rutherford, Jan. 5, 1923; 1 son, Logan T. With Columbia Steel Co., 1925-27, co. acquired by Armco Steel Corp., 1927, exec. v.p., 1958-60, pres., 1960-65, chmn. bd., 1965- -, also dir.; dir. Union Central Life Ins. Co., Cin., Standard Oil Co. (Ind.), Cin. Gas & Elec. Co. Trustee Automotive Safety Found., Hwy. Users Fedn. Safety and Mobility; chmn., dir. Internat. Iron and Steel Inst.; trustee Carnegie Mellon U., Miami U., Oxford, O., Regenstrief Found. Clubs: Laurel Valley (Ligonier, Pa.); Sky (N.Y.C.); Lyford Cay (Nassau, Bahamas); Moraine Country (Dayton, O.); Duquesne (Pitts.); Commercial (Cin.). Home: 2705 McGee Av Middletown OH 45042 Office: 703 Curtis St Middletown OH 45042

JOHNSTON, MARK W., banker. Vice chmn. bd. Union Bank and Trust Co., Montgomery, Ala. Office: PO Box 2191 100 Commerce St Montgomery AL 36103*

JOHNSTON, MARY ELIZABETH, journalist; b. Austin, Tex.; d. Harry M. and Winifred (Graham) Johnston; B.A., Rice U., 1941. Reporter Houston Post, 1942-49; Houston corr. Christian Sci. Monitor, 1947-49; researcher Time mag., 1949-51; researcher Fortune mag., 1951-52, asst. chief of research, 1952- 55, chief of research, 1955, mem. bd. editors, 1956—. Home: 249 E 48th St New York City NY 10022 Office: Time Inc Rockefeller Center New York City NY 10020

JOHNSTON, MEANS, Jr., naval officer; b. Schlater, Miss., Dec. 5, 1916; s. Means and Annie Cecil (Wilsford) J.; B.S., U.S. Naval Acad., 1939; J.D., Georgetown U., 1950; grad. Nat. War Coll., 1959; m. Hope Manning Larkin, June 29, 1946; children—Hope Larkin, Means III. Commd. ensign U.S. Navy, 1939, advanced through grades to rear adm., 1966, assigned U.S.S. Oklahoma, 1939-40, U.S.S. Borie, 1940-42, Bomb Disposal Sch., 1942-43; exec. officer, later comdg. officer U.S.S. Flaherty, 1943-44, comdr. U.S.S. Hanna, 1945-46, U.S.S. Halford, 1946, U.S.S. Frank E. Evans, 1946; U.S. Senate Navy liaison officer, 1946-48; aide to chief naval personnel, 1948-49; comdr. U.S. Beatty, 1950-52; aide, flag sec. to comdr. U.S. Pacific Fleet, 1952- 53; asst. for Congl. and legal matters to chmn. Joint Chiefs Staff, 1953- 56; mil. advisor to Pres. Citizens Advisers or Mut. Security Programs, 1956-57; comdr. Destroyer Div. 222, 1957-58; mem. staff comdr. in chief Allied Forces, So. Europe, 1959-60; mil. asst. to Sec. Def., 1960- 61; comdr. U.S.S. Capricornus, 1961-62, Destroyer Squadron 26, 1962-63; asst. to dir. Navy Program Planning Office, Office Chief Naval Operations, 1963-65, mem. Sec. Navy Task Force on Personnel Retention, Office Sec. Navy, 1965; comdr. Naval Base, Newport, R.I., 1966-68; comdt. 1st Naval Dist. Boston, 9 months; comdr. Cruiser-Destroyer Flotilla 10, 1968-69; chief legislative affairs Navy Dept., 1969—. Decorated Bronze Star with gold star and combat V, also numerous unit and area ribbons. Home: 1134 Litton Lane McLean VA 22101 Office: The Pentagon Washington DC 20350

JOHNSTON, NEIL, ins. co. exec.; b. Chgo., July 12, 1920; B.S., U. Chgo. With Employers Muts. Cos., 1953—, sr. v.p., treas. Employers Mut. Liability Ins. Co. Wis., Employers Mut. Fire Ins. Co.; v.p., treas. Employers Life Ins. Co.; dir. Wausau Paper Mills, Central Nat. Bank, Wis. Valley Trust- Co. Bd. dirs. Wausau Hosps. Mem. YMCA Found. Mem. Wausau C. of C. (dir.), Alpha Delta Phi. Clubs: Wausau Country, Wausau Curling. Home: 3714 Riverview Dr Wausau WI 54401 Office: 2000 Westwood Dr Wausau WI 54401

JOHNSTON, PAUL, lawyer; b. Birmingham, Ala., Feb. 6, 1908; s. Forney and Clara (Cocke) J.; A.B., Harvard, 1930; LL.B., Yale, 1933; m. Isabelle Berry, Apr. 23, 1938; children-Thomas B., Paul C., Caryl, John H.C. Admitted to Ala. bar, 1933; practice in Birmingham 1935—; atty. RFC. Washington, 1933- 35; mem. firm Cabaniss, Johnston, Gardner & Clark, 1935-65, Johnston & Shores, 1966—. Chmn. Citizens Com. for Fluoridation, Jefferson County, Ala., 1954, Citizens Com. for Indigent Med. Care for Jefferson County, 1957-58; mem. overseers com. to visit Center for Behavioral Scis., Harvard, 1965-67. Pres., bd. dirs. Jefferson County Assn. for Mental Health; bd. dirs. Nat. Assn. for Mental Health. Served to lt. USNR, 1943- 45. Recipient Birmingham Man of Year award, 1958, William Cranford Gorgas award Med. Assn. Ala. for distinguished vol. service in field pub. health, 1960. Mem. Am., Ala., Birmingham bar assns., Am. Law Inst., Birmingham C. of C. (dir.), Harvard Alumni Assn. (regional v.p.), Yale Law Sch. Assn. (past mem. exec. com.). Home: 32 Ridge Dr Birmingham AL 35213 Office: Brown-Marx Bldg Birmingham AL 35203

JOHNSTON, PAUL ALEXANDER, bus. exec.; b. Smithfield, N.C., May 17, 1916; s. Albert S. and Gayle (Makepeace) J.; A.B., U. N.C., 1950, LL.B., 1952; m. Margaret McGirt, Aug. 31, 1949; 1 son, Paul A. Admitted to N.C. bar, 1952; asso. Satterlee, Warfield and Stephens, N.Y.C., 1952; asst. dir. Inst. Govt., U. N.C., 1953; adminstrv. asst. to Gov. Luther H. Hodges, 1954- 57; dir. adminstrn. N.C., 1957-60; asst. to controller Burlington Industries, Greensboro, N.C., 1960; exec. asst. to sec. Dept. Commerce, 1961; v.p. contracts Martin Co. div. Martin Marietta Corp., 1961-63, pres. cement and lime div., N.Y.C., 1963-65; v.p. Martin Marietta Corp., 1963-65; pres. Glen Alden Corp., 1965—; chmn. bd. Panacon Corp., Cin., 1966—. Served with AUS, 1944-46. Mem. N.C. State Bar, N.C. Bar Assn., Bar Eastern Dist. N.C., Order of Coif, Phi Delta Phi. Democrat. Methodist. Editor-in- chief N.C. Law Rev., 1952. Office: 888 7th Av New York City NY 10019

JOHNSTON, RICHARD JAMES HUMPHREYS, newspaperman; b. N.Y.C., May 20, 1910; s. Edward Brooks and Helen Marie (Humphreys) J.; grad. Dean Acad., 1930; A.B., U. Ala., 1934; m. Elizabeth Meyers, June 30, 1936; 1 son, Richard Henry Meyers. Mem. staff N.Y. Times, 1934—, successively reporter, war corr. Europe and Korea, fgn. corr. Europe and Far. East, 1934-52, Chgo.-Midwest corr., 1952-59, Far East corr., 1960, mgr. spl. projects, 1962-63, UN corr., 1967-69; journalism instr. Armed Forces Inst., 1945-49; lectr. Trustee, Dean Jr. Coll., Franklin, Mass., 1965—. Decorated Purple Heart; Independence medal (Korea); citation for war correspondence U.S. War Dept., 1945. Mem. UN Corrs. Assn., N.Y. Reporters Assn., Soc. of Silurians, Sigma Delta Chi, Alpha Phi Delta. Clubs: Chicago Press (gov.); Overseas Press (pres. 1962-63); Lambs; New York Times 30 Year (pres. 1967-68). Author: (with mems. Overseas Press Club) Off the Record, 1952; (with others) Around the U.S.A. in 1,000 Pictures, 1955; The Two Koreas, 1965; (with others) the Pope's Journey to the United States, 1965; (with others) How I Got That Story, 1967. Address: 229 W 43d St New York City NY 10036

JOHNSTON, RICHARD WYCKOFF, journalist; b. Eugene, Ore., Mar. 21, 1915; s. Claude D. and Sarah (Wyckoff) J.; student U. Ore., 1936-38; m. Laura M. Smith, July 5, 1939; children—Dana, Elisa. Sports editor Eugene Register-Guard, 1933-35; city editor Eugene Daily News, 1937-38; domestic corr. U.P., 1939-42, war corr., Pacific and Far East, 1943-45; free-lance lectr., 1946; with Time mag., 1946-47, fgn. corr. and fgn. news writer, 1947; with Life mag., 1947-53, asst. copy editor, 1951-53; with Sports Illustrated mag., 1953- -, asst. mng. editor, 1954-63, exec. editor, 1963-70, spl. contbr., 1971—. Recipient Nat. Headliners award, 1943. Mem. 2d Marine Div. Assn. (hon. life), Sigma Delta Chi. Author: Follow Me!, 1948; (with Mrs. Johnston) (juvenile) Elizabeth Enters, 1952. Copy editor: Picture History of World War II, 1950. Home: 5575 Pia St Honolulu HI 96821

JOHNSTON, ROBERT ATKINSON, educator, psychologist; b. Allentown, Pa., July 8, 1931; s. Robert and Marion (McBride) J.; A.B., Haverford Coll., 1952; M.A. State U. Ia., 1954, Ph.D., 1955; m. Constance L. Moffet, Aug. 29, 1953; children—Robert Paul, Kenneth Moffett, Scott Andrew. Intern, VA Hosp., Knoxville, Ia., 1955-56; staff psychologist VA Hosp., Coatesville, Pa., 1956; asso. prof. psychology, dir. Univ. Center for Psychol. Services, U. Richmond, 1957-63; prof. psychology, asso. dean faculty Coll. William and Mary, 1963—. Pres., Williambsburg P.T.A. Council, 1967-69. Chmn. bd. dirs. Williambsburg Pre-sch. for Spl. Children, 1968-69. Mem. Am., Eastern psychol. assns., Va. Acad. Sci., Am. Assn. U. Profs. Home: 118 Ware Rd Williambsburg VA 23185

JOHNSTON, RODERICK WALKER STRACHAN, lawyer; b. Toronto, Ont., Can., Nov. 23, 1904; s. Strachan and May Murray (Walker) J.; B.A., U. Toronto, 1927; postgrad. Osgoode Hall; m. Gladys L.K. Pennock, June 1930; children—Gladys, David, Catharine. Admitted to Ont. bar, 1930; now partner firm Lash, Johnston, Sheard & Pringle, Toronto. Mem. Zeta Psi. Anglican religion. Clubs: Toronto Golf, Toronto. Home: 42 Castle Frank Rd Toronto 5 Ontario Canada Office: 21 King St E Toronto 1 Ontario Canada*

JOHNSTON, RUSS, marketing and advt. exec.; b. Gutherie, Okla., Sept. 13, 1908; s. Thomas Francis and Cleo Ethel (Stephens) J.; ed. Central High Sch., Oklahoma City, 1922-26; m. Margery Luce, Nov. 10, 1952; children-Robert Stephen, David Luce. Radio announcer sta. WKY, Oklahoma City, 1924; mgr. sta. WDAH, El Paso, Tex., 1927-30; producer Freeman Lang Studios, Hollywood, Cal., 1931-34; program dir. CBS, Hollywood, 1937-42; mgr. Hollywood Office McCann-Erickson, 1942, sr. v.p., dir., N.Y.C., 1960—; dir. TV film div. NBC, N.Y.C., 1947-52; gen. corporate exec. Interpub. Group, 1958—; mng. dir. Russ Johnston Assos Marketing Cons.; dir. Ryder-Stilwell Co., Inc., Hollywood. Chmn. adv. com. Hollywood YMCA, 1968; mem. finance com. Radio and Motion Picture Fund of Unitedd Fund, Hollywood, 1968; pub. relations adviser Children's Village, Dobbs Ferry, N.Y. Broadcast specialist Office Coordinator Information, Washington, 1942. Mem. Sales and Marketing Execs. Internat. (chmn. internat. com. 1966-68). Contbr. articles profl. jours. Home: 57 Judson Av Dobbs Ferry NY 10522 Office: 485 Lexington Av New York NY 10017

JOHNSTON, SAMUEL PAUL, aviation consultant; b. Pitts., Aug. 3, 1899; s. James Irvin and Bertha Wilson (Gill) J.; student Carnegie Inst. Tech., 1917-19; B.S. in Mech. Engring., Mass. Inst. Tech., 1921; D.Sc. (hon.), Adelphi Coll., 1957; m. 4th, Virginia Thomas, 1956; children—Mary (Mrs. Thomas Ballard), James Irvin II. With Aluminum Company Am., 1921-29; writer, editor, 1930-40; coordinator of research NACA, 1940-42; with Curtiss-Wright Corp., 1942-43; dir. Inst. Aero. Scis., N.Y.C., 1946-64; dir. Nat. Air and Space Mus., Smithsonian Instn., Washington, 1964-69; dir. Chesapeake Bay Maritime Mus., St. Michaels, Md., 1969-71; sr. asso. R. Dixon Speas Assos., Manhasset, N.Y., 1971—. Exec. dir. Pres.'s Air Policy Commn., 1948; cons. Mass. Inst. Tech. Lexington Project, 1948; exec. dir. Pres.'s Airport Commn., 1952; mem. aero. com. on research and devel. Dept. Def., 1949-53; cons. DoT/NASA CARD project, 1971. Bd. dirs. Flight Safety Found. N.Y.; chmn. aero. engring. adv. com. Princeton U.; trustee Acad. aeros., N.Y.C.; bd. govs. CBMM, St. Michaels, Md. Served with U.S. Army, 1918; from lt. comdr. to capt. USNR, 1944-46; ETO, PTO. Decorated Legion of Merit. Fellow Am. Inst. Aeros. and Astronautics, Royal Aero. Soc. Clubs: Cosmos, Army and Navy; Talbot County Country. Author 4 vols. aviation history, aviation sect. Brit., Jr., Brit. Yr. Book; also numerous articles various publs. Editorial adviser aero., aero. biography. Home: LK Atterrissage Mulberry Point Boxman MD 21612 Office: ChesapeaKe Bay Maritime Mus St Michaels MD 21663

JOHNSTON, STEWART ARCHIBALD, educator, chemist; b. Fort William, Ont., Can., Aug. 22, 1911; s. Thomas Stewart and Ada Emily Eva Gill (Murchison) J.; B.Sc. with honors (Isbister scholar 1929-31, gold medal 1932), U. Man., 1932, M.Sc., 1937; Ph.D. (Lever Bros. Co. fellow), Stanford, 1940; m. Amelia Alice Alston, Feb. 4, 1932; children—Shirley (Mrs. Milan Merhaut), Betty-Jean (Mrs. Richard Blades), Suzanne (Mrs. Geoffrey Reddall). Came to U.S., 1938, naturalized, 1946. Lectr., United Coll., Winnipeg, Man., 1934-38; research chemist Va. Chem. Corp., 1940-41; engr. Western Elec. Co., 1941-42; instr. Western Wash. Coll., Bellingham, 1942-43, head dept. math., 1946-52; asst. prof. U. So. Cal., 1943-44; research chemist, chief chemistry sect. jet propulsion lab. Cal. Inst. Tech., 1944-46, staff engr. jet propulsion lab., 1952-53; prof. chemistry Cal. State Coll. at Los Angeles, 1953—, chmn. div. sci. and math., 1953-64, dir. research and govtl. relations, 1964-67. Cons. rocket fuels Ramo-Wooldridge Corp., 1954-58, Space Tech. Labs., 1958-60, Aerospace Corp., 1960-69. Mem. Am. Chem. Soc., A.A.A.S., N.E.A., Sigma Xi. Home: 1340 S Oak Knoll Av Pasadena CA 91106 Office: 5151 State College Dr Los Angeles CA 90032

JOHNSTON, THOMAS ALEXANDER III, lawyer; b. Mobile, Ala., Sept. 7, 1916; s. Thomas Alexander, Jr. and Pauline (Sheldon) J.; J.D., U. Ala., 1938; m. Helen Torrey DuBois, July 16, 1941; children-Helen DuBois (Mrs. P. Thomas Sargent), Leslie Sheldon, Thomas Alexander IV. Admitted to Ala. bar, 1938, since practiced in Mobile; partner Howell, Johnston, Langford & Finkbohner and predecessor firms, 1938—. Mem. Ala. Ho. of Reps., 1941-49; mem. Ala. Senate, 1949-53; mem. Ala. Constl. Revision Com., 1970—. Pres. Mobile Wildlife Conservation Assn. Holder Brit. title 13th Baronet of Caskieben. Mem. Am., Ala., Mobile County (past pres.) bar assns., Pi Kappa Phi. Clubs: Mobile Country, Athelstan (Mobile). Home: 350 W Delwood Dr Mobile AL 36606 Office: 903 E A Roberts Bldg Mobile AL 36601

JOHNSTON, THOMAS MCELREE, lawyer; b. Ben Avon, Pa., Dec. 19, 1897; s. Samuel Lawrence and Eunice Isabel (McElree) J.; B.S., Westminster Coll., New Wilmington, Pa., 1920; LL.B., U. Pa., 1924; m. Lorine Davis, July 11, 1933; children—Thomas McElree, Anne Lorine (Mrs. Fred W. Beesley, Jr.), Mary Margaret (Mrs. Charles P. Munroe), Shepherd. Admitted to Pa. bar, 1924, Fla. bar, 1925; practice in Miami, 1925—; asso. Evans & Mershon, 1925-38; partner Evans, Pershon, Sawyer, Johnston & Simmons, 1938-64, Mershon, Sawyer, Johnston, Dunwody and Cole, 1965—; spl. asst. to atty. gen. U.S. to handle Okeechobee Flood Control Project, 1933-45. Mem. Welfare Planning Council, Miami, 1952-53; mem. Govt. Research Council. Bd. dirs. Vis. Nurses Assn.; bd. dirs., mem. exec. com. Ednl. Television Found.; chmn. bd. Coral Gables YMCA; bd. dirs., v.p. bd. Met. YMCA, Miami. Recipient Spl. award for meritorious service to YMCA, 1951. Fellow Am. Bar Found.; mem. Am., Fla., Dade County bar assns., Am. Law Inst. Presbyn. Clubs: Biscayne Bay Yacht (commodore 1967-68), Miami Fla.; Riviera Country; Coral Gables (Fla.) Country. Home: 2800 Alhambra Circle Coral Gables FL 33134 Office: First Nat Bank Bldg Miami FL 33131

JOHNSTON, WILLIAM C., forensic psychiatrist; b. Kippen, Ont., Can., July 17, 1902; s. William H. and Sarah (Blake) J.; M.B., U. Toronto; m. Marian Elizabeth Collings, Oct. 2, 1926; 1 son, Peter B. Asst. physician Foord Sanitarium, Kerhonkson, N.Y., 1926-33; physician Wallkill (N.Y.) Prison, 1933-40; psychiatrist Matteawan State Hosp., Beacon, N.Y., 1940-49, asst. dir., 1948-58, supt., 1962—; supt. Beacon State Instn.; dir. Dannemora (N.Y.) State Hosp., 1958-62. Served to comdr. M.C., USNR, 1943-46. Diplomate in psychiatry Am. Bd. Psychiatry and Neurology. Fellow Am. Psychiat. Assn. (past pres. Mid- Hudson br.); mem. A.M.A., Med. Corr. Assn. Elk, Kiwanian. Contbr. articles profl. publs. Address: Matteawan State Hosp Beacon NY 12508

JOHNSTON, WILLIAM DRUMM, Jr., geologist; b. Garrett, Ind., Nov. 3, 1899; s. William Drumm and Jessie Mae (Kane) J.; B.S., U. Chgo., 1921; Ph.D., George Washington U., 1932; m. Madeline A. Thomas, 1931; children—William Drumm III, John Thomson, Richard Thomas, Elizabeth Louise. Faculty dept. geology U. Cin., U. Ky., N.M. Sch. Mines, 1922-28; geologist U.S. Geol. Survey, 1928-41, chief sect. fgn. geology, 1945-48, chief Alaskan and fgn. geology br., 1949-51, chief fgn. geology branch, 1951-64, staff geologist, 1965-70; with Bd. Econ. Warfare, Brazil, 1942-45. Del., 3d Pan-Am. Consultation on Cartography, Caracas, 1946; 2d Pan- Am. Congress Mining Engring. and Geology, Rio de Janeiro, 1946; U.S. govt. delegation Internat. Geol. Congress, Eng., 1948, Algiers, 1952, Mexico, 1956, Denmark, 1960, New Delhi, India, 1964, Prague, Czechoslovakia, 1968; del. to 4th Empire Mining and Metall. Congress, Eng., 1949; adv. Joint Brazil-U.S. Tech. Commn., Rio de Janeiro, 1948; chief U.S. Geol. Mission to Thailand, 1949-50; del. Indian Sci. Congress, Bangalore, 1951, centenary of Geol. Survey of India, Calcutta, 1951; adviser coms. on iron and steel and indsl. devel. Econ. Commn. for Asia and Far East, Lahore, 1951, chmn. U.S. delegation 1st Symposium on Devel. Petroleum in Asai, Delhi, 1958, adviser 2d Symposium, Tehran, 1962, 3d Symposium, Tokyo, Japan, 1965, Canberra, Australia, 1969; chmn. U.S. delegation Seminar on Devel. and Use Natural Gas in Asia, Tehran, 1964; del. working party geol. map Asia, ECAFE, Calcutta, 1957, Tokyo, 1960, Manila, 1963, Bangkok, 1966, Terhan, 1968; del. Nat. Acad. Sci., Pacific Sci. Congress, Bangkok, 1958, Tokyo, 1966; observer 4th Inter-Territorial Geol. Conf., Entebbe, 1951; Inter- Guianean Geol. Conf., Georgetown, 1959; adviser conf. on application sci. and tech. for benefit underdeveloped nations UN, Geneva, 1963; del. UNESCO Conf. on Application Sci. and Tech. to Devel. Latin Am., Santiago, Chile, 1965; v.p. for N.A., Internat. Geol. Congress Commn. for Geol. Map of World, 1956-66; mem. U.S. Commn. Geology, 1961—. pres. sub-com. for Metallogenic Map of World, 1957—; mem. NAS-NRC com. Inter-Am. Sci. Coop., 196O-62, Latin Am. Sci. Bd., 1963-69. Decorated Cruizeiro de Sul (Brazil), 1952; recipient Distinguished Service medal Dept. Interior, 1959; Jose Bonifacio de Andrade medal Geol. Soc. Brazil, 1959, Leipold von Buch medal German Geol. Soc., 1963; named prof. honoris causa Fed. U. Rio de Janeiro (Brazil), 1970. Fellow Am. Acad. Arts and Scis., Geol. Soc. Am., Mineral. Soc. Am.; mem. Soc. Econ. Geologist (sec. 1938-41, v.p. 1957), Geol. Soc. Washington (pres. 1957), Pan-Am. Inst. Mining, Engring. and Geology (chmn. U.S. sect. 1948-49), Am. Rhododendron Soc., Sigma Xi; corr. mem. geol. socs. Argentina, Brazil, W. Germany, Peru, Brazil Acad. Sci. Clubs: Cosmos (Washington); Engenharia (Rio de Janeiro). Contbr. articles on geology and ore deposits to tech. jours. Home: 1620 Rigg Pl NW Washington DC 20009

JOHNSTON, WILLIAM NOEL, coll. pres.; b. Balt., Mar. 21, 1919; s. Howard Thomas and Irene Louise (Noellert) J.; A.B., Johns Hopkins, 1949, M.Ed., 1951; LL.D., Heidelberg Coll., 1965; m. Virginia Miles Vogts, Sept. 26, 1943; children—Virginia Gail, William Noel, Jeffrey. Asst. dir. pub. relations Johns Hopkins, 1947-49; supr. personnel Locke dept. Gen. Elec. Co., 1949-51; dir. pub. relations Goucher Coll., 1951-53; asst. to pres. Evansville (Ind.) Coll., 1953-54, Pratt Inst., Bklyn., 1954-56; exec. dir. Am. Coll. Pub. Relations Assn., 1956-59; v.p. Ohio Wesleyan U., 1959-64; pres. Defiance (O.) Coll., 1964—. Dir. summer insts. coll. devel. officers, 1959, 60, 61, 63, 64; adv. com. pub. relations Assn. Ch. Related Colls., 1961—; trustee Am. Coll. Pub. Relations Assn., 1960-63; mem. exec. com. Ohio Coll. Assn. Chmn. United Ch. Christ Council Higher Edn., 1966, 67; mem. joint com. on ch.-coll. relationships United Ch. Christ 1968- 69; trustee United Colls. Fgn. Study and Exchange. Served with F.A. AUS, 1941-45; ETO. Mem. Ohio Coll. Assn. (pres. 1971—). Methodist. Rotarian (pres. Delaware, O. 1962-63). Home: 705 E High St Defiance OH 43512

JOHNSTON, WILLIAM REDMOND, chemist; b. Chgo., June 26, 1907; s. Henry and Ida (Redmond) J.; B.S., U. Wash., 1930; Ph.D., Johns Hopkins, 1933; m. Felicie Johnston, Oct. 28, 1942; 1 dau., Wendy Lynne. Research chemist Fleischmann Lab., N.Y.C., 1933-38, head phys. lab., 1938-44, head phys. div., 1944-48; dir. research Standard Brands, Inc., N.Y.C., 1948- 50, v.p. charge research, 1950-61; v.p. research and devel. Internat. Multifoods Inc., 1961-71; ret. Mem. Am. Chem. Soc., Am. Inst. Chemists, Inst. Food Technologists, Am. Soc. Bakery Engineers, N.Y. Acad. Sci., Am. Assn. Cereal Chemists, Soc. Rheology, Am. Inst. City N.Y., Phi Beta Kappa, Sigma Xi, Phi Lambda Upsilon. Club: Wayzata (Minn.) Country. Home: 1506 Holdridge Lane Wayzata MN 55391

JOHNSTONE, BURTON KENNETH, architect; b. Chgo., Jan. 20, 1907; s. Burton Clermont and Margaret (Wulff) J.; B.S. in Architecture, U. Ill., 1928; B.F.A., Yale, 1929; fellow Am. Acad. in Rome (Italy), 1929-32; student Lake Forest (Ill.) Found. for Architecture and Landscape Architecture, summer 1928; m. Helene Estelle Hetzel, Aug. 27, 1938; children—Dorn Kenneth, Robert Philip. Began as draftsman Granger and Bollenbacher, Chgo., 1924; teaching asst. U. Ill., 1928, Yale, 1929; mem. faculty Pa. State Coll. 1933—, successively asst. prof. architecture, asso. prof., prof. and head dept. architecture, 1938- 45; dean Coll. Fine Arts, Carnegie Inst. Tech., 1945-52. Recipient Rome prize in Architecture, 1929, Scarab gold medal, 1941. Fellow A.I.A.; mem. Pa. Soc. Architects, Assn. Collegiate Schs. Architecture (past pres.), Tau Beta Pi, Sigma Tau, Phi Eta Sigma, Pi Kappa Alpha, Scarab (past nat. pres.). Author: (with others) Building or Buying a House, 1945. Contbr. to professional jours. Home: 4625 5th Av Pittsburgh PA 15213 Office: Law and Finance Bldg Pittsburgh PA 15219

JOHNSTONE, DONALD BOYES, microbiologist, educator; b. Newport, R.I., July 25, 1919; s. Fred W. and Reba (Boyes) J.; B.S., U. R.I., 1942; M.S., Rutgers U., 1943, Ph.D., 1948; m. Helen Beardslee, Aug. 20, 1949; children—Elizabeth, Margaret, Fred. Bacteriologist, Woods Hole Oceanographic Inst., 1942-43, 46; microbiologist Bikini Atomic Bomb Tests in Pacific, 1946; mem. faculty U. Vt., Burlington, 1948—, prof. microbiology, chmn. agr. biochemistry 1958-69, dean Grad. Sch., prof. agrl. biochemistry and med. microbiology, 1969—. Fellow Am. Acad. Microbiology, Am. Inst. Biol. Scis., Soc. Am. Microbiology, A.A.A.S. Contbr. articles profl. jours. Home: Box 2192 South Burlington VT 05401

JOHNSTONE, EDMUND FRANK, advt. exec.; b. Rochester, N.Y., Apr. 28, 1909; s. Charles T. and Ida M. (Hilgenreiner) J.; student Ohio State U., 1928; m. Margaret Horan, Apr. 1, 1940; children—Heather, Dawn; m. 2d, Janet Olcott, June 2, 1951; children—Charles, Jill, Edmund, Chauncey, Rita. With E. F. Johnstone Advt. Co., 1939-51;

exec. v.p. Dowd, Redfield & Johnstone, Inc., (both N.Y.C.), 1951—; vice chmn. bd. Calkins Holden. Inc., advt. agency, 1959; sr. v.p. Fletcher Richards, Calkins & Holden, N.Y.C., 1959-60; exec. v.p. Kastor Hilton Advt. Agy., 1960-; vice chmn. exec. com., dir. Kastor, Hilton, Chesley, Clifford and Atherton, Inc., 1960—. Served as lt. col. USAAF, WW II. Mem. Mil. Order Fgn. Wars. Episcopalian. Clubs: New York Athletic, St. Bartholomew's (N.Y.C.); New Canaan Field. Contbr. articles to trade jours. Home: 635 Park Av New York City NY 10021 also Trinity Pass Rd Pound Ridge NY 10576 Office: 575 Lexington Av New York City NY 10022

JOHNSTONE, FRANCIS ELLIOTT, Jr., educator; b. Georgetown County, S.C., Apr. 22, 1911; s. Francis Elliott and Eleanor (Nicholson) J.; B.S., Clemson Coll., 1932; M.S., La. State U., 1937; Ph.D., Cornell U., 1940; m. Monah Colvin, Mar. 12, 1936; children—Sylvia Colvin, Isabel Jane. Engaged in farming, 1932-33; pub. sch. tchr., 1933-34; asst. plant pathology S.C. Agrl. Expt. Sta., 1934-35; camp adminstrv. officer Civilian Conservation Corps, 1935-36; grad. asst. La. State U., 1936-37; research asst. Cornell U., 1937-40; from asst. prof. to prof. horticulture Auburn U., 1940-41, 46-47; agronomist Nat. Cottonseed Products assn., 1947-48; prof. horticulture Ohio State U., 1948-50; prof. horticulture U. Ga., Athens, 1951—, head dept., chmn. div., 1951-67, dir. Bot. Gardens, 1968—. Adviser horticulture Nat. Coll. Agr., Cambodia, 1960- 62; pres. Belle Isle Gardens, Georgetown, S.C., 1952-55; cons. Ga. Acad. Blind, 1955-60, Ida Cason Callaway Gardens, Pine Mountain, Ga., 1959-60. Mem. adv. council on naval affairs Sixth Naval Dist., 1966-68; adv. com. Callaway Gardens, 1971—; chmn. U. Ga. Bot. Garden steering com., 1969—. Served to comdr. USNR, 1941-46; capt. Res. Fellow A.A.A.S.; mem. Am. Soc. Hort. Sci., Ga. Acad. Sci., So. Agrl. Workers Assn., Ga. Plant Food Ednl. Soc. (charter), Res. Officers Assn. (pres. Ga. 1960), Ga. Hort. Soc. (charter, pres. 1967-69), Nat. Agrl. Plastics Conf. (sec.-treas. 1964, pres. 1965), Sigma Xi, Alpha Zeta, Gamma Sigma Delta, Phi Kappa Phi. Episcopalian. Rotarian. Contbr. numerous articles to profl. jours. Home: 395 Parkway Dr Athens GA 30601

JOHNSTONE, HARRY INGE, architect; b. Mobile, Ala., Nov. 27, 1903; s. Charles Albert Lesesne and Virginia (Inge) J.; student Univ. Mil. Sch., Mobile, 1912-21; B.Arch., Cornell, 1927; m. Kathleen Cawthorn Yerger, June 24, 1930; children—Montgomery Inge, Yerger, Douglas. Archeol. research restoration, Mexico, 1926; draftsman, designer Shreve & Lamb, N.Y.C., 1927-28; archtl. study, England, Italy, 1928-29; designer T. O. Foster, London, 1928-29; instr. archtl. design, theory architecture Cornell, 1929-30; chief designer Marston-Maybury, Pasadena, Cal., 1930-31; asso. Douglas Honnold, Los Angeles, 1931; instr. architecture John Herron Art Sch. Indpls., 1933-36; pvt. practice architecture, Indpls., 1933-36, Mobile, 1937—; propr. Harry Inge Johnstone, 1937—; partner J.B. Converse & Co., Inc. & Harry Inge Johnstone, 1950—. Served as maj. AUS 1943-45. Fellow A.I.A. (v.p. Ala. chpt. 1940); mem. Ala (pres. 1941, 47), Mobile (pres. 1959), assns. architects, Am. Malacological Union, Phi Delta Theta. Episcopalian. Office: 115 Charles St Mobile AL 36604

JOHNSTONE, HENRY WEBB, JR., educator; b. Montclair, N.J.,Feb. 22, 1920; s. Henry Webb and Beatrice (Grieb) J.; grad. Hill Sch., 1938; B.S., Haverford Coll., 1942; M.A., Harvard, 1947, Ph.D., 1950; m. Margery Vaughan Coffin, July 17, 1948; children-Barbara C., Anne C., Henry Webb III. Instr. philosophy Williams Coll., 1948-52; mem. facutulty Pa. State U., 1952—, prof. philosphy, 1961—, asst. to v.p. for research, 1966-70, dir. Inst. Arts and Humanistic Studies, 1968-70. Served to capt. AUS 1942-46. Author: Elementary Deductive Logic, 1954; Philosphy and Argument, 1959; (with J.M. Anderson) Natural Deduction, 1962; What is Philosphy?, 1965; (with M. Natanson) Philosphy, Rhetoric and Argumentation, 1965; The Problem of Self, 1970. Contbr. articles profl. jours. Home: 262 Woodland Dr State College PA 16801

JOHNSTONE, JAMES RODERICK, former fgn. service officer; b. New Rochelle, N.Y., Jan. 6, 1911; s. Alexander and Elizabeth (Lawler) J.; grad. high sch.; m. Mozina Louise Dubberly, Dec. 6, 1935; children—Elizabet (Mrs. Donald Schoeb), Joye (Mrs. Patrick Costinett), Judy, Jill, James A. Engaged in pvt. bus., 1929-35; with U.S. Dept. Agr., 1935-42, Office Emergency Mgmt., 1942-45; fgn. service officer Dept. State, 1945—; counselor for adminstrn., Tokyo, Japan, 1954-58; exec. dir. Bur. Far Eastern Affairs, Dept. State Washington, 1958-61, dep. asst. sec. for fgn. bldgs., 1961-65; former consul gen. Frankfurt, Germany. Dir. Dept. State Fed. Credit Union. Club: Kronberg Golf and Country. Home: 8616 Ewing Dr Bethesda MD 20014

JOHNSTONE, QUINTIN, legal educator; b. Chgo., Mar. 29, 1915; s. Quintin and Wegia (Metsker) J.; A.B., U. Chgo., 1936, J.D., 1938; LL.M., Cornell U., 1941; J.S.D., Yale, 1951; m. Nancy McMullen, Oct. 15, 1948; children—Robert Dale, Katherine Mary. Admitted to Ill. bar, 1939, Ore. bar, 1948; individual practice law, Chgo., 1939-41; atty. OPA, 1941-47; mem. law faculty U. Willamette, 1947-50, U. Kan., 1950-55; mem. law faculty Yale, 1955—, Justus S. Hotchkiss prof., 1969—; dean law, prof. Haile Sellassie I U., Ethiopia, 1967-69. Mem. Am., Conn., Ore. bar assns. Author: (with D. Hopson) Lawyers and Their Work, 1967; (with A. Axelrod and C. Berger) Land Transfer and Finance, 1971. Contbr. articles profl. jours. Home: 22 Morris St Hamden CT 06517 Office: Yale Law Sch New Haven CT 06520

JOHNSTONE, RUSSELL R., corp. exec.; b. Ashley, N.D., 1913; ed. U. N.D., 1936. Sec. Roadway Express, Inc. Home: 1321 Lisa Ann Dr Akron OH 44313 Office: 1077 Gorge Blvd Akron OH 77410*

JOHNSTONE, WILLIAM CRANE, univ. prof.; b. Denver, Colo., Sept. 2, 1901; s. William Clelland and Kathern (Parmer) J.; A.B., U. Denver, 1924, A.M., 1927; Ph.D., Stanford, 1932; m. Anne Davis Hartwell, Nov. 29, 1929; children—Delight Davis (Mrs. Stephen A. Wallace), Kathern Parmer (Mrs. Thomas E. Hinrichs). Faculty George Washington U., Washington, as instr. in polit. science, 1930-31, asst. prof., 1931-34, asso. prof., 1934-38, prof., 1938—, acting dean jr. coll., 1934-35, dean, 1935-44, dean sch. govt., 1944-46; chief Pub. Affairs Officer, Am. Embassy, New Delhi, India, 1946-48; adviser to U.S. Spl. Diplomatic Mission to Nepal, 1947; dir. Office Ednl. Exchange, Dept. State, 1948-52, dep. adminstr. field programs U.S. Internat. Information Adminstrn., Dept. State, 1952-53; prof. Asian studies, Sch. Advanced Internat. Studies, Johns Hopkins U., 1953-70, prof. emeritus, 1970—; co-dir. Rangoon-Hopkins Center for South East Asian Studies, Rangoon U., Rangoon, Burma, 1957-59; sr. specialist East-West Center, Honolulu, 1966-67. Recipient Distinguished Citizen award, City Denver, 1958. Mem. Am. Polit. Sci. Assn., Assn. Asian Studies, Phi Beta Kappa, Beta Theta Pi. Club: Cosmos (Washington). Author: The Future of Japan, 1945; Burma's Foreign Policy, 1963; several others. Contbr. profl. jours. Home: 4831 N Via Entrada Tucson AZ 85718

JOHNSTONE, WYCLIFFE mfg. exec.; b. Lima, O., Apr. 1, 1932; B.S., U. San Francisco, 1954; M.S., Stanford University, 1956; m. Rosemarie Lois Brown, May 15, 1955; 1 son, Anthony Robinson. Sales rep. Ames-Brockton Fabricated Products, Akron, O., 1956-58, sales mgr. Coshocton, Ohio, 1959-61, gen. manager plant, 1961-68, v.p. sales, 1968--. Instr. bus. Coshocton Jr. College, 1968-69. Secretary Coshocton YMCA, 1960-61; active Boy Scouts of America. Named Man of Year, Coshocton Junior Chamber of Commerce, 1968. Mem. Coshocton C. of C. (vice president 1967-68, pres. 1969-70), English Speaking Union, Coshocton Sertoma Club, Nat. Assn. Mfrs., Sales Executives Institute, Phi Beta Kappa, Sigma Chi, Phi Mu. Democrat. Mem. Christian Ch. (lay leader). Mason (32, Shriner). Clubs: Coshocton Country, Coshocton City, Running Deer Country. Home: 2d Av Coshocton OH Office: 3d Av Coshocton OH

JOICE, JAMES PORTEUS, packing co. exec.; b. Scarborough, Eng., June 8, 1909; s. James Porteus and Alice M. (Robinson) J.; brought to U.S., 1910, naturalized, 1914; B.A., Wesleyan U., Middletown, Conn., 1931; M.B.A., N.Y.U., 1940; m. Virginia D. Hoskins, Jan. 20, 1950; 1 stepson, Robert H. Warren. Self employed ins. broker, 1931-36; security analyst Reynolds & Co., N.Y.C., 1936-39; staff accountant Arthur Andersen & Co., C.P.A.'s, N.Y.C., 1939- 40; spl. agt. FBI, 1940-46; with Internat. Packers Ltd., Chgo., 1946-69, sec., 1951-62, controller 1952-69, v.p., 1962-69, also dir.; v.p. Deltec Internat. Ltd., Nassau, 1969—, also controller. Mem. Chgo. Crime Commn., 1954-69. C.P.A., N.Y. Mem. Am. Inst. C.P.A.'s, Ill., N.Y. State socs. C.P.A.'s, Financial Execs. Inst., Soc. Former Agts. FBI, Am. Soc. Corporate Secretaries. Clubs: Union League (Chgo.); Glen Oak Country; Coral Harbour Country. Home: Conchrest Apts P O Box 6343 Nassau Bahamas Office: 401 N Michigan Av Chicago IL 60611 also Deltec House PMB 29 Nassau Bahamas

JOINER, CHARLES WYCLIFFE, univ. dean; b. Maquoketa, Ia., Feb. 14, 1916; s. Melvin William and Mary (von Schrader) J.; B.A., U. Ia., 1937, J.D., 1939; m. Ann Martin, Sept. 29, 1939; children—Charles Wycliffe, Nancy Caroline, Richard Martin. Admitted to Ia. bar, 1939, Mich. bar, 1947; with firm Miller, Huebner & Miller, Des Moines, 1939-47; part-time lectr. Des Moines Coll. Law, 1940- 41; faculty U. Mich. Law, 1947-68, asso. dean, 1960-65, acting dean, 1965-66; dean Wayne State U. Law Sch., Detroit, 1968—; asso. dir. Preparatory Commn. Mich. Constl. Conv., 1961, co-dir. research and drafting com., 1961-62; civil rules adv. com. U.S. Jud. Conf. Com. Rules Practice and Procedure, 1959-70, evidence rules adv. com., 1965-70; rep. Mich., Atty. Gens. Com. Ct. Congestion, 1959-60. Mem. charter rev. com. Ann Arbor Citizens Council, 1959-61; mem. Mich. Commn. on Uniform State Laws, 1963—. Mem. Ann Arbor City Council, 1955-59. Served to 1st lt. USAAF, 1942-45. Mem. Am. Bar Assn. (chmn. com. specialization 1952- 56, spl. com. uniform evidence rules fed. cts. 1959-64; adv. bd. jour. 1961-67, spl. com. on specialization 1966—, ethics com. 1961-70, council mem. sect. individual rights and responsibilities 1967—), State Bar Mich. (pres. 1970-71; chmn. joint com. Mich. procedural revision 1956-62, commr. 1964—), Am. Judicature Soc. (chmn. publs. com. 1959- 62), Am. Law Student Assn. (bd. govs.), Am. Law Inst., Am. Bar Found., Scribes (pres. 1963-64). Author: Civil Justice and the Jury, 1962; Trials and Appeals, 1957; Trial and Appellate Practice, 1968. Co-author: Introduction to Civil Procedures, 1949; Jurisdiction and Judgments, 1953; (with Delmar Karten) Trials and Appeals, 1971. Home: 1345 Glendaloch Circle Ann Arbor MI 48104 Office: Law Sch Wayne State U Detroit MI 48202

JOINER, OTIS WILLIAM, grain co. exec.; b. Maquoketa, Ia., Jan. 10, 1919; s. Melvin William and Mary (von Schrader) J.; student Maquoketa Jr. Coll., 1936-38; B.A. in Econ., U. Ia., 1940; m. Josephine Jennette McElhinnet, June 8, 1941; children—Cherie (Mrs. David Hartley Root), Mary (Mrs. John Jauchen), Thekla, Amy. Business trainee Gen. Electric Co., Schenectady, N.Y., 1940-44; with Kent Feeds Inc., Muscatine, Ia., 1946—, v.p., gen. mgr., 1966—, also dir.; exec. v.p. Grain Processing Co., Muscatine, 1966—, also dir.; dir. Muscatine Corp. Mem. adv. bd. Muscatine Community Coll. Feed Technology, 1966—. Bd. dirs. Salvation Army, Muscatine. Served with USNR, 1944-46. Presbyn. (elder). Rotarian. Home: RR 4 Muscatine IA 52761 Office: 40 Kent Feeds Oregon St Muscatine IA 52761

JOINER, TRUMAN, constrn. co. exec.; b. Twin Fall, Ida., June 1, 1910; s. Arthur A. and Exa I. (Harris) J.; student Linfield Coll., McMinnville, Ore., 1929-32; m. Anna C. George, Aug. 30, 1936; 1 dau., Ina Cynthia (Mrs. Richard L. Shropshire). With First Security Bank, Nampa, Ida., 1928-29; engaged in pub. accounting, Boise, Ida., 1933-42; dir. Ida. Bur. Pub. Accounts, 1938-40; dep. tax commnr. Ida., 1940; controller Morrison-Knudsen Co., Inc., Boise, 1942-69, v.p. econ. research, 1969—; pres. S. Fork Lodge, Inc., Lowman, Ida., 1956—, Gem State Bindery, Inc., Boise, 1956—. Bd. dirs. Asso. Taxpayers Ida., 1946—, pres., 1953-58; pres. Boise-Stanley Hwy. Assn., 1958—; chmn. Boise Redevel. Agy., 1967—. Trustee Boise Community Christian Center, Linfield Coll. C.P.A., Ida. Mem. Am. Inst. C.P.A.'s, Ida. Soc. C.P.A.'s, Am. Mgmt. Assn., Financial Execs. Inst., Hist. Soc. (chmn. bd. trustees, 1968—). Baptist. Home: 1014 Houston Rd Boise ID 83704 Office: 319 Broadway Boise ID 83707

JOLDERSMA, ALFRED T., elec. equipment co. exec.; b. Mount Vernon, N.Y., Oct. 17, 1918; s. Alfred C. and Antoinette (Rosendahl) J.; A.B., Hope Coll., 1940; M.B.A., U. Mich., 1942; m. Mildred Potter, June 24, 1942; children—Diane (Mrs. R.S. Portenga), Thomas, Jane. Accountant, Arthur Andersen & Co., C.P.A.'s, Detroit, 1942-43; treas. Detroit Harvester Co., 1943-56; v.p. finance Kawneer Co., Niles, Mich., 1956-62; v.p. finance, sec. treas. Harvey Hubbell, Inc., Bridgeport, Conn., 1962—, also dir.; trustee Merchants and Farmers Savs. Bank, Bridgeport. Mem. Financial Execs. Inst. (bd. dirs., pres.), Tax Execs. Inst. Home: 13 Berndale Dr Westport CT 06880 Office: Harvey Hubbell Inc State St and Bostwick Av Bridgeport CT 06602

JOLITZ, CHARLES EDWARD, ret. chain food store exec.; b. Deadwood, S.D., Aug. 18, 1914; s. August Albert and Augusta (Duennermann) J.; student U. Denver, 1931; B.S., U. Neb., 1937; grad. Advanced Mgmt. Program, Harvard, 1957; m. Christine Hilda Sparrow, May 3, 1940; 1 son, William Robert. With Gen. Foods Corp., 1935-58, gen. mgr., 1956-58; pres. Cal. Vegetable Concentrates, Inc., 1958-61; v.p. Kroger Co., 1961-66, exec. v.p., dir., 1966-68; vice chmn. Alled Supermarkets, 1968-71; dir. Stockton Terminal & Eastern R.R. Exec. bd. Boy Scouts Am. Served with AUS, 1940-46. Decorated Medal of Merit; recipient N.Y. State Distinguished Service Cross; Silver Beaver, Boy Scouts Am., also Silver Antelope award; named Ky. Col., 1962. Mem. Nat. Assn. Food Chains (dir.), Inst. Food Tech. Home: 1100 Orchard Ridge Rd Bloomfield Hills MI 48013

JOLIVET, ANDRE, composer; b. Paris, France, Aug. 8, 1905; s. Victor Ernest and Madeleine (Perault) J.; ed. Lycée Colbert, Ecole Normale de Paris, Paris; m. Hilda Guigue, Sept. 26, 1933; children—Pierre-Alain, Christine, Merri. dir. music Comédie-Francaise, Paris, 1945-59; prof. composition Conservatoire Nat. Supérieur de Musique, Paris, 1966—; tech. counselor Arts, Letters Gen. Direction, 1959-62; mus. expert UNESCO, 1958—. Served with French Army, 1939-40. Decorated officer Legion of Honor, Croix de Guerre; recipient Arts and Letters award. Mem. Concerts Lamoureux (pres.), Syndicate Artists and Musicians France (hon. pres.). Composer: (piano) Mana, 2 sonatas; (chamber music) Quatuor, Suite Delphique, Rhapsodie à 7, Pastorales de Noël, Suite Rhapsodique pour Violon seul, Suite en Concert pour Violoncelle seul, Cinq Incantations pour Flte; (vocales) Trois complaintes du Soldat, Deux Messes, Poèmes intimes, Epithalame, Madrigal; (symphonies) Cinq Danses rituelles, Trois musiques de scène. Address: 59 Rue de Varenne Paris VIIe France

JOLLES, PAUL RODOLPHE, Swiss diplomat; b. Berne, Switzerland, Dec. 25, 1919; s. Leo and Ida (Hegnauer) J.; student Berne, Lausanne univs., Switzerland; M.A., Harvard, 1943, Ph.D., 1945; m. Erna Ryffel, 1956. Attache Swiss Legation, Washington, 1943-49; staff Swiss Fgn. Office, Berne, 1949-56, head secretariat in charge multilateral trade programs, Swiss Div. Commerce, 1955; mem. Swiss delegation Orgn. European Econ. Coop., Paris, 1955-56; sec. Swiss-Inter-Deplt. Com. Atomic Energy Questions, 1955; mem. Swiss delegation negotiating bilteral agreement with U.S. on cooperation atomic energy, 1956; exec. sec. preparatory commn. Internat. Atomic Energy Agy., 1956, sec.-gen. 1st Gen. Conf., 1957, dep. dir.-gen. for adminstrn., liaison and secretariat, 1957-61; del. Fed. Council of Switzerland for Trade Agreements, rank minister plenipotentiary, 1961; chief interdepartmental office for questions of European Integration, 1962-66; dir. Fed. Div. Commerce, 1966—. Head Swiss delegation UN Trade and Devel. Bd., 1965, pres., 1967—; head Swiss delegation for negoiations with European Communities, 1970—. Address: 23 Herrengasse Bern Switzerland

JOLLEY, ELMER OTIS, Jr., distillery co. exec.; b. Richwood, O., Aug. 28, 1913; s. Elmer Otis and Harriet (Wilson) J.; B.S., Northwestern U., 1935, M.B.A., 1941; m. Jean C. Olson, Dec. 20, 1943; 1 dau., Susan (Mrs. Rodney M. Ficker). Faculty, Northwestern U. Sch. Bus., 1935-41; officer Mr. Boston Distiller Corp., Boston, 1946—, now exec. v.p., treas., dir.; dir. J.C. Hall Co., Inc. Served from ensign to lt. comdr., USNR, 1941-45. Mem. Am. Econ. Assn., Am. Finance Assn. Home: 180 Meadowbrook Rd Weston MA 02193 Office: 1010 Massachusetts Av Boston MA 02118

JOLLEY, HOMER RICHARD, govt. ofcl.; b. Morgan City, La., May 28, 1916; s. Homer Levi and Frances (Shannon) J.; A.B., Gonzaga U., 1938, M.A., 1939; M.S., Fordham U., 1941; S.T.L., St. Louis U., 1946; Ph.D. (Allied Chem. & Dye fellow), Princeton, 1951; Fulbright fellow, U. Nottingham (Eng.), 1950-51. Entered Soc. of Jesus, 1932; ordained priest Roman Catholic Ch., 1945; asst. prof. chemistry Loyola U., New Orleans, 1951-54, asso. prof., 1954- 58, prof., 1958-70, chmn. chemistry dept., 1956-64, v.p. devel., 1964-66, pres., 1966-70; dir. innovation Medicaid program Dept. Health, Edn. and Welfare, Washington, 1970—; summer research participant Oak Ridge Nat. Lab., 1957-64, cons., 1964—. Bd. dirs. Gulf South Research Inst., Total Community Action, Internat. House, Internat. Trade Mart., Met Area com. La. Council for Music and Performing Arts, Fgn. Relations Assn., New Orleans, Nat. Found. (New Orleans chpt.); trustee Greater New Orleans Ednl. TV Found.; mem. adv. bd. La. Council Human Relations; mem. Adv. Council Naval Affairs New Orleans; mem. adv. bd. Delta Regional Primate Research Center. Fellow Am. Inst. Chemists (past chmn. La. chpt.); mem. Chem. Soc. London, Faraday Soc., N.Y. Acad. Sci., Am. Chem. Soc. (past chmn. La. sect.), New Orleans Jr. Acad. Sci. (past pres.), Sigma Xi. Clubs: Princeton (N.Y.C.); Plimsoll. Home: Georgetown Univ Washington DC 20007

JOLLIE, WILLIAM PUCETTE, educator; b. Passaic, N.J., June 27, 1928; s. William Pucette and Katharina (Grau) J.; B.A., Lehigh U., 1950, M.S., 1952; Ph.D., Harvard, 1959; m. Ludmila Georgieva, Dec. 28, 1950; children—William Pucette, Michael K. Instr. natural scis. Bradford Jr. Coll., Haverhill, Mass., 1959; lectr. histology-embryology Queen's U., Kingston, Ont., 1959-61; asst. prof. anatomy Tulane U., 1961-65, asso. prof., 1965-68, prof., 1968-69; prof., chmn. dept. anatomy Va. Commonwealth U., Richmond, 1969—. Served with Chem. Corps, AUS, 1953-55. Mem. Am. Assn. Anatomists, Assn. Anatomy, Soc. Cell Biology, Soc. Study Reprodn., Electron Microscope Soc. Am., So. Soc. Anatomists, Perinatal Research Soc. Research and publs. on ind. investigations on ovoimplanatation, placental formation, maternofetal exchange, parturition. Home: 8304 River Rd Richmond VA 23229

JOLLIFFE, ELWIN TEBBITT, univ. adminstr.; b. Ottosen, Ia., Aug. 6, 1909; s. Frank Elwin and Charlotte, Maude (Tebbitt) J.; B.S.C., State U. Ia., 1932; m. Helen Lucille Hughes, Dec. 17, 1933; children—Karma Kay (Mrs. James S. Rife), James Elwin. Mem. staff State U. Ia., 1932—, sec., bus. mgr., 1954-58, v.p. bus. and finance, 1958—. Mem. exec. com. Central Assn. Coll. and Univ. Bus. Officers, 1960-61, 70-71; joint bus. officers com. State Univs. Assn. and Nat. Assn. Land Grant Colls. and State Univs., 1959-61; mem. com. taxation and fiscal reporting on fed. govt. Am. Council Edn., 1957- 58; bd. dirs. Midwestern Univs. Research Assn., 1955-57, 60-62, 64- 72; bd. dirs., Measurement Research Center, 1954-68, treas., 1954-68. Dir. Aeromotor Corp., 1957-58; treas. Ia. Meml. Union Corp., 1954-69; bd. dirs. Ia. City Bldg. and Loan Assn., 1956-70, v.p., 1957-65, pres., 1965-70; dir. 1st Fed. Savs. and Loan Assn. Iowa City. Bd. dirs. Iowa City Community Sch. Dist., 1955-61, pres., 1957-58; mem. project com., mental health program NIH, 1962-67. Bd. dirs. Ia. Measurement Research Found., 1968—, treas., 1968—; nat. adv. council U.S. Aid Fund, 1969-71; trustee Argonne Univs. Assn. Mem. Iowa City C. of C., Nat., Cent. assns. coll. and univ. bus. officers, Beta Gamma Sigma, Phi Tau Theta. Mason, Kiwanian. Home: 1502 Muscatine Av Iowa City IA 52240

JOLLS, THOMAS HALDANE, educator; b. Dunkirk, N.Y., Sept. 17, 1909; s. Frank S. and Anna (McDonald) J.; A.B., U. Mich., 1930, J.D., 1933; m. Frances R. Talcott, Jan. 1, 1932; children—Thomas H., Katherine M. (Mrs. Macit Guçol), Robert T. Admitted to Ill. bar, 1933; asso. Packard, Barnes, McCaughey & Scumacher, Chgo., 1933-37; with No. Trust Co., Chgo., 1937-68, v.p., 1955-68; prof. law Coll. William and Mary, 1968—. Dir. Mut. Trust Life Ins. Co. (Chgo.). Mem. Highland Park (Ill.) Bd. Edn., 1957-61. Mem. Am., Chgo. bar assns., Am. Soc. Corporate Secs. (dir. 1963-65), Law Club Chgo., Am. Assn. Univ. Profs., Order of Coif, Phi Delta Phi. Contbr. articles profl. jours. Home: 12 Huntington Dr Williamsburg VA 23185

JOLLY, JOHN PERSHING, nat. guard officer; b. Taiban, N.M., Aug. 28, 1919; s. G. W. and Ruth (McCollough) J.; B.A., N.M. State U., 1950; m. Lydia Lea Goodin, May 24, 1942; childrenBarbara Ann, Sharon Kay, Jennifer Lee. Tchr., coach high sch., Almgordo, N.M., 1945-46; tng. officer VA, N.M. State U., 1946-47, postmaster, 1947-56; adminstrv. asst. city mgr., Las Cruces, N.M., 1956- 58, city clk., 1958—; mem. N.M. Nat. Guard, 1947—, maj. gen., 1959- -; gen. of N.M.; State dir. Selective Service, Civil Def. Mem. Adj. Gens. Assn. (exec. com.), N.G. Assn. U.S., Nat. Assn. Postmasters. Lion. Office: PO Box 4277 Santa Fe NM 87501

JOLLY, LEWIS FOSTER, rubber co. exec.; b. Waterloo, Ia., Sept. 15, 1917; s. Kendrick P. and Louise (Foster) J.; B.S.C., U. Ia., 1939; m. Polly Forinash, Dec. 28, 1939; children—Polly (Mrs. Michael J. McNeill), Catherine (Mrs. John G. McGinnis), Lewis, James. Sr. accountant R.G. Rankin & Co., C.P.A.'s, Chgo., 1939-43; treas. Armstrong Rubber Mfg. Co., Des Moines, 1946-47; controller Armstrong Rubber Co., New Haven, 1968—. Served with inf. AUS, 1943-46. Mem. Financial Execs. Inst., Beta Gamma Sigma. Home: 955 Mix Av Hamden CT 06514 Office: 500 Sargent Dr New Haven CT 06507

JOLLY, WILLIAM LEE, educator; b. Chgo., Dec. 27, 1927; s. John McGowen and Marjorie (Farmer) J.; B.S., U. Ill., 1948, M.S., 1949; Ph.D., U. Cal. at Berkeley, 1952; m. Frances Anne Adams Bartholomew, Nov. 18, 1950; children-Jeffrey Lee, Steven William, Jennifer Frances. Instr. chemistry dept. U. Cal. at Berkeley, 1952-53, group leader Radiation Lab., Livermore, 1953-55, asst. prof., asso. prof., prof. chemistry, Berkeley, 1955—, prin. investigator inorganic materials research div. Lawrence Radiation Lab., Berkeley, 1955—. Guggenheim fellow, 1960. Mem. Am. Chem. Soc., A.A.A.S., Chem. Soc. London, Sigma Xi, Alpha Chi Sigma. Authoor: The Synthesis and Characterization of Inorganic Compounds, 1970. Editor: Preparative Inorganic Reactions, Vols. 1-7, 1964—. Mem. editorial bd. Inorganic Syntheses, 1959—. Home: 2621 La Honda St El Cerrito CA 94530 Office: Chemistry Dept U Cal Berkeley CA 94720

JOLSON, MARVIN ARNOLD, educator; b. Chgo., June 7, 1922; s. George and Bess (Sweetow) J.; B.E.E., George Washington U., 1949; M.B.A., U. Chgo., 1965; Ph.D., U. Md., 1968; m. Betty Harris, July 8, 1944; children—Robert, Nancy. With Ency. Brit., Inc., Chgo., 1946-68; mgr. Eastern nat. sales, 1960-62, sr. v.p., 1962-68; prof. bus. adminstrn. U. Md., College Park, 1968—. Served with Signal Corps, AUS, 1944-46. Mem. Sales Exec. Club, Am. Marketing Assn., Am. Mgmt. Assn., Beta Gamma Sigma. Mason. Author: Consumer Attitudes Toward Direct-To-Home Marketing Systems, 1970; Quantitative Techniques For Marketing Decisions. Contbr. articles to profl. jours. Office: U Md College Park MD 20740

JONAH, DAVID ALONZO, librarian; b. Sackville, N.B., Can., Mar. 19, 1909; s. Alonzo Dow and Jennie (Cochran) J.; B.S., Mt. Allison U., 1929; M.S., Brown U., 1931; postgrad. Columbia, summer 1940; LL.D., Mount Allison U., 1960; m. Elizabeth Rhodes Wright, Nov. 18, 1937. Came to U.S., 1929, naturalized, 1938. Instr. math. Brown U., Providence, 1932-34, 1942- 44, gen. asst. library, 1935-38, in charge phys. scis. library, 1938-43, 1944-46, acting librarian, 1946-48, asso. librarian, 1948-49, librarian, 1949-60, librarian univ. library and dir. libraries, 1960—, asst. prof., 1945-51, asso. prof. bibliography, 1951-53, John Hay prof. bibliography, 1953—. Mem. A.L.A., R.I. Library Assn. (pres. 1956- 58), Medieval Acad. Am., East Greenwich Free Library Assn. (pres. 1958- 71), Bibliog. Soc. Am., Sigma Xi. Episcopalian. Clubs: Caxton, Grolier, University, Odd Volumes. Home: 4474 Post Rd East Greenwich RI 02818 Office: Brown U Library Providence RI 02912

JONAS, CHARLES RAPER, congressman; b. Lincolnton, N.C., Dec. 9, 1904; s. Charles A. and Rosa (Petrie) J.; A.B., U. N.C., 1925, J.D., 1928; m. Annie Elliott Lee, Aug. 14, 1928; children—Charles Raper, Richard Elliott. Admitted to N.C. bar, 1929, asst. U.S. atty. Western dist. N.C., 1931-33; mem. 83d-87th Congresses, 10th Dist., N.C., mem. 88th-91st Congresses, 8th N.C. Dist.; mem. 91st-92d Congresses, 9th N.C. Dist. Mem. N.C. Bd. Law Examiners, 1947-48. Served with U.S. Army, 1939-46; ret. col. N.C. N.G. Mem. D.C., N.C. (pres. 1946-47), Lincoln County bar assns., Order of Coif, Phi Delta Phi, Chi Phi. Republican. Methodist. Rotarian. Home: Lincolnton NC 28092 Office: House Office Bldg Washington DC 20515

JONAS, FRANZ, fed. pres. of Austria; b. Vienna, Oct. 4, 1899; s. Josef and Katharine (Rokos) J.; ed. Workers' High Sch., univ. extension; m. Margarethe Towarek, Dec. 23, 1922. Type-setter, proof-reader, 1919-32; sec. Social Democratic Dist. Orgn. Vienna XXI, 1932-35; arrested for polit. reasons, accused of high treason, 1935; clk. in factory, 1938-45; chmn. local council Vienna XXI, 1946-48; city councillor for food supplies and agr., 1948, for housing, 1950; gov., mayor Vienna, 1951-65; mem. Austrian Fed. Council, 1951-53, Austrian Nat. Council, 1953-65; fed. pres. Republic Austria, 1965—. Chmn., Fedn. Austrian Citires, 1951- 65; mem. exec. com., also chmn. European com. Internat. Fedn. Communities, 1955-65; mem. presdl. council Council European Communities, 1963-65; Austrian del. local govt. conf. Council of Europe, 1956-65. Decorated Grand Golden Order Merit with star, Grand Silver Order of Merit with ribbon, grand star Order of Merit (Austria); grand cross Order Ethiopian Star; grand cross of merit with star and ribbon Order Merit Fed. Republic Germany; grand cross with ribbon Persian Homayoun Order 1st class; comdr. cross with star Greek Order King George I; Bavarian Order Merit; grand cross Finland Order Lion; grand cross Dutch-Oranien-Nassau Order; grand cross Danish Danebrog Order; grand cross Thailand Crown Order; named hon. citizen Vienna, hon. senator Vienna U. and Vienna U. Tech.; dr. hon. causa Thammasat U., Bangkok, Thailand; Thai Rajamitraphorn Order; Most Honourable Order Bath, spl. degree; grand cross Norwegian Order St. Olav with Collane Grand Cross; Iranian Pahlavi Order Collane; Grand Star of Yugoslavia; Grand Star Liechtenstein Order of Merit; others. Address: Hofburg Vienna Austria

JONAS, HANS, educator; b. Monchengladbach, Germany, May 10, 1903; s. Gustav and Rosa (Horowitz) J.; Ph.D. summa cum laude, U. Marburg (Germany), 1928; D.H.L. (hon.), Hebrew Union Coll.-Jewish Inst. Religion, 1962; m. Eleonore Weiner, Oct. 6, 1943; children—Ayalah, Jonathan, Gabrielle. Came to U.S., 1955, naturalized, 1960. Lectr. philosophy Hebrew U., Jerusalem, 1938-39, 46-48, Brit. Council Sch. Higher Studies, Jerusalem, 1946- 48; teaching fellow McGill U., 1949-50; asso. prof. Carleton U., Ottawa, Can., 1950-54; prof. grad. faculty New Sch. Social Research, 1955—, chmn. philosophy dept., 1957-63, Alvin Johnson prof. philosophy, 1966—; vis. lectr. Princeton, 1958,.61-62; Ingersoll lectr. Harvard, 1960-61; vis. prof. Columbia, 1961, 66-67, Hunter Coll., 1963-64, Union Theol. Sem., N.Y.C., 1966-67, Com. Social Thought, U. Chgo., 1968, 69, 70. Served with Royal Brit. Arty., 1940-45, with Israeli Army, 1948-49. Lady Davis fellow, Can., 1949-50; Rockefeller fellow, Europe, 1959-60; fellow Center Advanced Studies, Wesleyan U., Middletown, Conn., 1964-65. Mem. Am. Philos. Assn., Am. Soc. Study Religion, Inst. Soc. Ethics and Life Scis. Author: Augustin und das paulinische Freiheitsproblem, 1965; Gnosis und spatantiker Geist, I, 1964, II, 1966; The Gnostic Religion, 2d edit., 1963, 3d rev. edit., 1970; Zwischen Nichts und Ewigkeit, 1963; The Phenomenon of Life, 1966; Wandel and Bestand, 1970; also papers. Home: 9 Meadow Lane New Rochelle NY 10805 Office: 66 W 12th St New York City NY 10011

JONAS, JOHN, Jr., lawyer, accountant; b. Chgo., June 21, 1922; s. John and Louisa (Wilde) J.; student Western Mich. Coll., 1941-43; B.B.A., U. Mich., 1947, M.B.A., 1948; LL.B., Wayne State U., 1951; m. Katharine Schreier, Oct. 2, 1965; 1 dau., Katharine Ann. Tax accountant Ernst & Ernst, Detroit, 1951-53; tax analyst Gen. Motors Corp., Detroit, 1953-55; tax adminstr. Isenberg Newman & Co., Detroit, 1955-58; tax counsel Burroughs Corp., Detroit, 1958-67; tax atty., treas. CTS Corp., Elkhart, Ind., 1967—. Bd. dirs. Elkhart County Cystic Fibrosis Found. Admitted to Mich. and Ind. bars. Served with USAAF, 1943-45; ETO. C.P.A., Ind. Mem. Tax Execs. Inst. (v.p. Western Mich. chpt.), Mich., Ind. socs. C.P.A.'s, Elkhart C. of C. (bd. dirs.). Presbyn. Club: Rotary (Elkhart). Home: 1520 Ash Dr E Elkhart IN 46514 Office: 905 Northwest Blvd Elkhart IN 46514

JONAS, MANFRED, historian, educator; b. Mannheim, Germany, Apr. 9, 1927; s. Walter and Antonie (Dannheisser) J.; came to U.S., 1937, naturalized, 1944; B.S., City Coll. N.Y., 1949; A.M., Harvard, 1950, Ph.D. (Teaching fellow), 1959; m. Nancy Jane Greene, July 19, 1952; children—Andrew Miles, Kathryn Leslie, Emily Susan, Matthew Greene. Mil. intelligence analyst U.S. Dept. Def., 1951-54; teaching fellow Harvard, 1954-59; vis. prof. Am. history Free U., Berlin, 1959-62; asso. prof. PMC Colls., 1962-63; faculty Union Coll., Schenectady, 1963—, dir. Grad. Program Am. Studies, 1964—, prof. history, 1967—, chmn. dept. history, 1970—, chmn. div. Social Sci., 1971—; lectr. City Coll. N.Y., 1950, U. Md. Extension, 1954, Northeastern U., 1958; dir. Nat. Def. Edn. Act Insts. for Advanced Study in History, 1966-68; cons. U.S. Office Edn., 1966. Mem. N.Y. State Coll. Proficiency Exam. Com. in Am. History, 1970—. Moderator, Forum 17 WMHT-TV, 1965. Bd. dirs. Freedom Forum, Ins., 1965—, chmn., 1969-70. Served with USNR, 1945-46. Mem. Am. Hist. Assn., Orgn. Am. Historians, Soc. for Historians Am. Fgn. Relations, Am. Assn. U. Profs. (chpt. pres. 1969-71), German Assn. Am. Studies, Phi Beta Kappa, Phi Alpha Theta. Author: Die Unabhängigkeitserklärung der Vereinigten Staaten, 1964; Isolationism in America, 1935-41, 1966; American Foreign Relations in the Twentieth Century, 1967. Contbr. articles profl. jours. Home: 2471 Hilltop Rd Schenectady NY 12309

JONASSEN, HANS BOEGH, educator, chemist; b. Seelze, Hannover, Germany, Aug. 18, 1912; s. Hans Adolph Leire Boegh and Ida (von Droege) J.; Abitur, Leibniz Real- gymnasium (Germany), 1931; came to U.S., 1940, naturalized, 1943; B.S., Tulane U., 1942, M.S., 1944; Ph.D., U. Ill., 1946; m. Fannie Taylor Baumgartner, Aug. 30, 1939; children—Hans Boegh, Ida Frances, Ellen Taylor. Instr., Tulane U., 1942-44, asst. prof., 1946-48, asso. prof., 1948- 52, prof., 1952-, chmn. dept. chemistry, 1962—. Sci. liaison officer London br. Office Naval Research, 1958-59; mem. Nat. Adv. Council Coll. Chemistry, 1962-66; mem. divisional coms. for postdoctoral fellowship Nat. Acad. Scis.-NRC, 1960-63; Reilly lectr. U. Notre Dame, 1964; 5th F.P. Dwyer Meml. lectr., Sydney, Australia, 1967. Bd. dirs. New Orleans YMCA, 1950, trustee, 1963—; mem. internat. com. YMCA, So. area chmn. for La. Recipient So. Chem. award, 1954, Coll. Chem. Tchrs. award Mfg. Chemist's Assn., 1959; Fulbright-Hayes sr. scholar fellow U.Sydney (Australia), 1971. Fellow A.A.A.S.; mem. Am. Chem. Soc., Am. Assn. U Profs., Chem. Soc. London. Presbyn. (elder). Asso. editor Chem. Rev., 1959-62; bd. editors Jour. Am. Chem. Soc., 1960—, Jour. Inorganic and Nuclear Chemistry, 1961—, Inorganic and Nuclear Letters, 1966—; bd. advisers Chem. and Engring. News, 1962-65; co-editor Techniques of Inorganic Chemistry, 1962-64; bd. cons. editors Inorganic and Nuclear Chemistry Letters, 1965—. Home: 7729 Belfast St New Orleans LA 70125

JONATHAN, JOSEPH LEABUA, prime minster of Lesotho; b. Oct. 30, 1914; ed. Mission Sch., Leribe. Mine worker, S. Africa, 1933-37; returned to Basutoland, 1937; ct. pres., 1938; mem. Dist. Council, Leribe, 1956, Nat. Council, Maseru, 1956; mem. panel of 18, 1956-59; founder Basutoland Nat. Party, 1959, leader, 1959—; mem. Legislative Council, 1960-64; del. at Constl. Conf., 1964; prime minster Lesotho (formerly Basutoland), 1965—. Office: Prime Minister's Office PO Box 527 Maseru Lesotho*

JONCICH, MICHEAL JOSEPH, chemist, educator; b. San Pedro, Cal., Dec. 9, 1921; s. Marion and Florence (Felando) J.; student Compton Coll., 1941-42; B.Chem. with distinction, U. Minn., 1946-48; M.S., Ore. State U., 1950; Ph.D., U. Tex., 1952; m. Jane Kathryn Leach, July 22, 1944 (div. 1970); children—David Michael, Mary Jane. Research scientist U. Tex., 1950-52; research asso. Northwestern U., 19b52-53; asst. prof. U. Tenn., 1953-59; asso. program dir. for chemistry NSF, 1959-61; prof., head dept. chemistry No. Ill. U., 1961-68; asst. chmn. spl. tng. div. Oak Ridge Asso. Univs., 1968—. Dir. Central States Univs. Served with USNR, 1941-45. Mem. Am. Chem. Soc., Electrochem. Soc., Biophys. Soc., Am. Assn. U. Profs., Faraday Soc., Sigma Xi, Phi Lambda Upsilon. Home: 122 Latimer Rd Oak Ridge TN 37830

JONDAHL, DONALD EDWARD, ins. co. exec.; b. Chester, Ia., Aug. 12, 1916; s. Edward P. and Bertha (Bell) J.; B.B.A., U. Minn., 1939; M.B.A, Harvard, 1941; m. Leona M. Lawson, Apr. 24, 1947; children—Bruce, Linda, David, Kenneth, Elizabeth Susan. Investment analyst Continental Casualty Co., Chgo., 1941-42, 46- 47; v.p. finance Northwestern Nat. Life Ins. Com., Mpls., 1947-69, sr. v.p., 1969—; dir. N. Atlantic Life Ins. Co., Mineola, N.Y. Mem. adv. com. Minn. Investment Bd.; mem. investment com. Minn. Ordnance Assn. Trustee, mem. investment Com. Minn. Med. Found. Served with CIC, AUS, 1942-46. Mem. Twin Cities Soc. Security Analysts (past pres.). Home: 302 Parkers Lake Rd Wayzata MN 55391 Office: 20 Washington Av S Minneapolis MN 55440

JONES, A. QUINCY, architect; b. Kansas City, Mo., Apr. 29; s. Archibald Quincy and Floye (Osborn) J.; B.Arch., U. Wash., 1936; m. Ruth E. Schneider (div.); m. 2d, Anne B. Austin (div.); children—Michael Bruce, Hillary Anne, Timothy Quincy; m. 3d, Elaine Kollins Sewell, June 26, 1962. Pvt. practice architecture, 1945-50; partner archtl. firm, Los Angeles 1950—; prin. works include Am. Consulate-Gen. bldg., Singapore, early merchant-built house, (First Honor award A.I.A. 1950), Grad. Research Library, U. Cal. at Los Angeles, 1963; designer merchant-built houses for Eichler Homes, 1951—; vis. prof. Sch. Architecture, U. So. Cal., 1951—; vis. critic Cornell U., Rice U., others. Mem. design com. Los Angeles Music Center, 1962-63. Served with USNR, World War II. Recipient Spl. Service award St. Louis U.; Golen Scissors award Cal. Fashion Creators. Fellow A.I.A. (pres. So. Cal. chpt. 1960, mem. housing com. 1963-64, 69—, mem. internat. relations com. 1966—). Co-author: Builders Homes for Better Living, 1957. Contbr. articles archtl. jours. Home: 11320 Joffre St Los Angeles CA 90049 Office: 12248 Santa Monica Blvd Los Angeles CA 90025

JONES, ALAN PORTER, food co. exec.; b. Ft. Atkinson, Wis., July 6, 1897; s. Edward Cole and Charlotte (Brown) J.; B.S., Dartmouth, 1919; m. Eleanor Pratt Bright, June 10, 1924; children—Alan Porter, William Bright, Milo Cole. With Jones Dairy Farm, Ft. Atkinson, 1920—, treas., 1920-61, pres., 1961-66, chmn. bd., 1966—; pres., co-founder Uncle Josh Bait Co., Ft. Atkinson, 1924; dir. First Nat. Bank Ft. Atkinson. Mem. Episcopal diocesan standing com. Diocese Milw., 1956-66. Served with Air Force, USNRF, 1918. Mem. Wis. C. of C. (bd. dirs. 1964-66), Sigma Chi. Clubs: Union League (Chgo.), University (Milw.). Home: 432 Jones Av Fort Atkinson WI 53538 Office: Jones Dairy Farm Fort Atkinson WI 53538

JONES, ALEXANDER ELVIN, univ. pres.; b. Independence, Mo., Oct. 11, 1920; s. Joseph Elvin and Tessie (Watson) J; B.A. with high distinction, DePauw U., 1942, LL.D., (hon.), 1964; M.A., U. Minn., 1949, Ph.D., 1950: LL.D., U. Ark., 1967; D.H.L., Indiana Central Coll., 1970; m. Sara Elisabeth Mullins, Jan. 16, 1946; children—Jo Ellen, Sara Elisabeth. Mem. faculty U. Minn., 1949-50, U. Ark., 1950-56, MacMurray Coll., 1956-59; dean Coll. Liberal Arts and Scis., prof. English, Butler U., 1959-63, pres., 1963—. Dir. Am. United Life Ins. Co. Bd. dirs. Ind. Ednl. Services Found.; mem. exec. com. Ind. Conf. Higher Edn. Served with USNR, 1942-45. Mem. Am. Lit. Group, Coll. English Assn., Am. Assn. Presidents Am. Colls. and Univs. (2d v.p.), Modern Lang. Assn. Am., Nat. Council Tchrs. English, Ind., Indpls. (dir.) chambers commerce, Newcomen Soc. in N.Am., English Speaking Union (local dir.), Phi Beta Kappa, Phi Eta Sigma, Phi Kappa Phi, Kappa Delta Pl. Kiwanian (pres. 1971) Clubs: Torch, Athenaeum Turners, Indianapolis Athletic, Columbia, Woodstock, Indianapolis Literary, Riviera (Indpls.). Author: Creative Exposition 1957; co-author: Writing Good Prose, 1961, 2d edit., 1968, 3d Edit., 1971; also articles on Mark Twain, other Am. writers. Home: 530 W Hampton Dr Indianapolis IN 46208

JONES, ALFRED LAMONT, banker; b. Cleve., Dec. 1, 1907;; s. John Earl and Olive (Fosnaugh) J.; student Cleve. Coll., 1927-30, Grad. Sch. Banking, Wis., 1948-50; m. Marie Catherine Scharf, Aug. 20, 1930. Sr. examiner 4th Dist., Fed. Res. System, Cleve., 1932-53; 1st v.p. Harter Bank & Trust Co., Canton, O., 1953-56; asst. v.p. Union Commerce Bank, Cleve., 1956, v.p., 1957-64, , sr. v.p., 1964-68, pres., 1968-70, chmn. bd., 1970—; dir. Forest City Devel. Co., Union Commerce Capital Co. Treas., Growth Bd. Cleve., 1969-; asst. treas. United Appeal Greater Cleve., 1969—. Trustee Cleve. Found., Dyke Coll.; bd. govs. Am. Indsl. Conf. Mem. Bluecoats, Inc., Citizens League, Cleve. Council World Affairs. Clubs: Union, Cleveland Athletic, (Cleve.); Lakewood Country (Westlake, O.). Home: 22429 Blossom Dr Rocky River OH 44116 Office: 3 9th add Euclid Av Cleveland OH 44101

JONES, ALFRED WELWOOD, educator; b. N.Y.C., July 6, 1915, s. Adam Leroy and Lily (Murray) J.; B.A., Columbia, 1937, M.A., 1939, Ph.D., 1944; m. Pierrette Jeanine Petas, Feb. 22, 1962; children—K. Darcy (Mrs. Howard K. Fuguet), Laurie H. (Mrs. Gordon W. Adams), Alison M. (Mrs. Robert Spencer, Jr.), Leroy W., Bruce M. Instr. math. U. Me., 1939-42, Yale, 1942-44; asst. prof. Mich. State U., 1944-47; asso. prof. Rensselaer Poly. Inst., 1947-57; systems engr. Bell Telephone Labs., 1957-64; sr. research staff Inst. Def. Analysis, 1964-69; prof. operations research, chmn. dept. indsl. engring. and operations research Coll. Engring., Wayne State U., 1959—; vis. mem. Inst. Advanced Study, Princeton, 1950—; cons. in field; flutist in civic symphonies, 1939-68. Mem. Operations Research Soc., Inst. Mgmt. Scis., Soc. Indsl. and Applied Math., Am. Inst. Indsl. Engrs., Phi Beta Kappa, Sigma Xi. Presbyn. (ruling elder 1961—). Co-author: Continuum Mechanics, 1971. Home: 5369 Hickory Bend Bloomfield Hills MI 48013 Office: Coll Engring Wayne State Univ Detroit MI 48202

JONES, ALFRED WILLIAM, bus. exec.; b. Dayton, O., 1902; s. Samuel Rufus and Mary Adele (Yost) J.; student Moraine Sch., Dayton, 1917-20, U. Pa., 1920-23; m. Katharine Houk Talbott, Sept. 6, 1928; children—Alfred, Marianna (Mrs. David L. Kuntz), Katharine (Mrs. Paul O'Connor), Howard. Mgr., Sapeloe Plantation, Ga., 1925-28; pres. Sea Island Co., developers of resorts, 1928-44, chmn. bd., 1944—; dir. Brunswick Paper & Pulp Co.; v.p., dir. Seaboard Constrn. Co.; dir. Mead. Corp., Westinghouse Elec. Corp., Ga. Kraft Co., First Nat. Bank Atlanta. Grad. mem. Bus. Council. Mem. Phi Kappa Psi. Methodist. Home: Sea Island GA 31561

JONES, ALTON, pianist; b. Fairfield, Neb., Aug. 3, 1899; s. Merton Lester and Clara (Palmer) J; Mus. B., Drake U., 1919; grad. Inst. Musical Art, N.Y.C., 1921, diploma in artists course, with honors, 1923; unmarried. Début, Aeolian Hall, N.Y.C., 1925; soloist Am. Orchestral Soc., 1924; N.Y. Philharmonic Symphony; mem. of faculty Juilliard Sch. of Music 1921-71; chmn. piano faculty, 1957-59; faculty mem. Columbia Summer School, 1929-41; Juilliard Summer Sch., 1933-52; U. N.C. Summer Sch., 1949. Mem. Music Tchrs. Nat. Assn., Am. Liszt Soc., Am. Fedn. Musicians, Music Edn. League (chmn. piano judges), League of Composers, Am. Musicol. Soc., Juilliard Sch. Alumni Assn. (pres. 1959-65), Pi Kappa Lambda. Republican. Mason. Club: Bohemians. Recital appearances in many parts of U.S. Died 1971.

JONES, ANNE PRIOLEAU, educator; b. Urbana, Ill., Aug. 22, 1911; d. Harry Stuart Vedder and Margaret (Walker) Jones; B.A., U. Ill., 1932, M.A., 1934; postgrad. Sorbonne, Paris, 1932-33, U. Munich (Germany), also Columbia. Tchr. French, Knox Sch., Cooperstown, N.Y., 1935-37; from instr. to prof. French, Lawrence U., 1937—, Bergstrom prof. French, 1960—, chmn. modern fgn. lang. dept., 1954-62, chmn. freshman studies, 1948-53, 63- 65, chmn. French dept., 1965-68. Fellow Fund for Advancement Edn., 1953-54. Decorated Chevalier des Palmes Academiques. Mem. Modern Lang. Assn. Am., Assn. Tchrs. French, Phi Beta Kappa. Author: (with Germaine Brée) Hier et Aujourd'hui, 1958; also profl. articles. Editor: André Malraux: Lectures Choisies, 1965. Address: Lawrence U Appleton WI 54911

JONES, ARCHER, educator, historian; b. Richmond, Va., Oct. 14, 1926; s. Montgomery Osborne and Helen Rutherfoord (Johnston) J.; student St. John's Coll., 1943-46; B.A., Hampden-Sydney Coll., 1949; M.A., U. Va., 1953, Ph.D., 1958; m. Louise Fairfax Coleman, June 16, 1956; 1 son, Caruthers Coleman. Part-time instr. Randolph-Macon Woman's Coll., 1953-54, U. Va., 1954-55; instr. Hampden-Sydney Coll., 1957-58; dean, asso. prof. history Clinch Valley Coll., U. Va., 1958-61; prof. history, chmn. dept. history and polit. sci. Va. Polytech. Inst., 1961-66; asso. dean arts and scis., prof. history U. S.C., 1966-68; prof. history, dean Coll. Arts and Scis., N.D. State U. Served to 1st. lt. AUS, 1946-47, 55-57. Mem. Am., So. hist. assns., Va. Hist. Soc., Raven Soc., Phi Beta Kappa, Omicron Delta Kappa, Chi Phi. Author: Confederate Strategy from Shiloh to Vicksburg, 1961. Contbr. Civil War books. Home: 1358 N 3d St Fargo ND 58102

JONES, ARCHIE HARRISON, coll. dean; b. Kenosha, Wis., Feb. 17, 1920; s. Archie Harrison and Frances A. (Glaves) J.; B.A., Carroll Coll., Waukesha, Wis., 1947; M.A., U. Chgo., 1949, Ph.D., 1954; m. Phyllis Kathryn Rutherford, Dec. 26, 1941; childrenMichael Rutherford, Carolyn Frances. Asst. prof. history Hastings (Neb.) Coll., 1949-51, 54-55, chmn. dept., 1950-51, dir. summer session, 1955; asst. prof. history and philosophy, chmn. div. social sci. Humboldt State Coll., Arcata, Cal., 1955-59; cons. history Cal. Com. Revision Social Studies Curriculum, 1957-59; asso. dir. Chgo. Hist. Soc., 1959-63; prof. Am. Studies Bowling Green (O.) State U., 1963-70, dean Coll. Liberal Arts, 1963-68; dean Sch. Arts and Scis., Ft. Lewis Coll., Durango, Cal., 1970—. Served to capt. USAAF, 1941-46. Mem. Am. Hist. Assn., Orgn. Am. Historians, Am. STudies Assn. Clubs: Literary, Caxton (Chgo.). Editor: History of American Literature, 1607-1783 (Moses coit Tyler), 1967. Home: 1005 Balsam Dr Durango CA 81301

JONES, ARCHIE NEFF, univ. dean; b. Atlantic, Ia., Sept. 20, 1900; s. Archie Israel and Edith Lorraine (Neff) J.; diploma U. Neb., 1925; B.S., U. Minn., 1929, M.A., 1931; Mus. D. (hon.), MacPhall Coll., 1940; m. Gladys Miller Allen, Aug. 30, 1969; children by previous marriage—Catherine (Mrs. John Longenecker), Elizabeth, (Mrs. Allen R. Moers), Archie Alan. Supr. music, Marshall, Minn., 1924-27; dir. music State tchrs. Coll., La Crosse, Wis., 1927-28; chmn. music edn. dept. U. Minn., 1928-35; dir. music U. Ida., 1935-40; prof. music edn. U. Tex., 1940-59; dean Conservatory Music, U. Mo. at Kansas City, 1959-70; guest prof. U. So. Cal., U. Mont., U. Wyo., U. S.D., Okla. U., U. Denver., Brigham Young U., Mich. State U., Colo. Coll. Mem. Nat. council U.S.O., 1961-71, chmn. nat. music council-Dept. Def. overseas tours com., 1961-71. Pres. Sinfonia Found., 1960-64. Distinguished Service award Mu Phi Epsilon, 1964; Distinguished Service award USO Bd. Govs., 1971; Distinguished Service citation Nat. Fedn. Music Clubs, 1971. Mem. Am. Choral Dirs. Assn. (pres. 1958-60), Internat. Assn. Concert Mgrs. (pres. 1958-61), Music Tchrs. Nat. Assn., Music Educators Nat. Conf. (life;

past pres. Southwest div.), Phi Mu Alpha (pres. 1950-60, recipient Man of Music award 1964), Omicron Delta Kappa, Sigma Nu, Phi Delta Kappa, Pi Kappa Lambda, Kappa Delta Pi. Mason (Shriner), Rotarian. Author: Introduction to Musical Knowledge, 1935; Pronouncing Guide to French, German, Italian and Spanish, 1948; Techniques in Choral Conducting, 1949; First Steps to Choral Music, 1957; Music Education In Action, 1960. Contbr. articles to profl. jours. Compositions for mixed chorus. Home: 2516 Enfield Rd Austin TX 78703

JONES, ARNOLD ROOSEVELT, educator; b. Haddam, Kan., May 30, 1904; s. John H. and Miriam G. (Jones) J.; B.S. in Bus., U. Kan., 1927; grad student, Kan. State Coll., 1930-31, U. Denver, summer 1931, U. Kan., summer 1932, U. Colo., 1953-54; m. Ruth D. Cress, Nov. 6, 1927, children—A. Richard, Virginia L. Accountant, Peat, Marwick, Mitchell & Co., Kansas City, Mo., also Ozark Oil Co., Joplin, Mo., 1928; C.P.A. practice as Stewart & Jones, A. R. Jones & Co. and Breisford, Gifford & Jones, Manhattan and Topeka, Kan., 1929-42; instr., asst. prof. accounting Kan. State Coll., 1928-33; asst. budget dir. and state accountant, Kan., 1933-37; lectr. accounting Washburn U., 1935-39, treas., bus. mgr., 1937-39; mem. Kan. Corp. Commn., 1939-42; dir. div. adminstrn. Office Gov. Kan., 1951-53; dean financial adminstrn., chief financial officer Kan. State Coll., 1945-58, prof. accounting, 1945-58; dep. dir. U.S. Bur. Budget, 1956-57; Distinguished lectr. in accounting U. South Fla., Tampa, 1966-67. Mem. Def. Mobilization Bd.; adv. bd. Econ. Growth and Stability; alt. budget dir. N.S.C. and Pres.'s Cabinet; chmn. Interdepartmental Com. on User Charges; vice chmn. bd. dirs. TVA, 1957-66; Mem. Kan. bd. Edn., 1969; vol. Internat. Exec. Service Corps, 1970—. Mem. bd. C.P.A. Examiners, 1941-44. Trustee, sec.-treas. Kan. State U. Endowment Assn., 1947-56. Served from 1st lt. to capt., AUS, 1942-45. C.P.A., Kan. Mem. Am. Inst. C.P.A.'s, Am. Accounting Assn., Kan. C. of C., Kan. Soc. C.P.A.'s (exec. dir. 1968-69), Phi Kappa Phi, Phi Sigma Kappa (nat. financial v.p.), Alpha Kappa Psi; hon. mem. Tenn. Soc. C.P.A.'s. Home: 4200 Ironwood Circle Bradenton FL 33505

JONES, ARTHUR CARHART, physician; b. Oberlin, O., Sept. 4, 1896; s. Burton Howard and Angeline (Tallmon) J.; B.A., Pacific U., 1921, L.H.D., 1963; M.A., U. Or., 1925, M.D., 1926; postgrad. Northwestern U., 1928; m. Doris Winifred Wolcott, Sept. 18, 1924 (dec. 1964); children—Ardis Carolyn (Mrs. David G. Hitchcock), Irving Wolcott; m. 2d, Freeda Hartzfeld, Oct. 1965. Intern St. Luke's Hosp., Chgo., 1926-27; faculty mem. U. Ore. Med. Sch., 1927-69, prof. phys. medicine, 1957-69; dir. depts. phys. medicine Good Samaritan, U. Ore. hosps., 1929-67; cons. San Francisco area office VA, Madigan Army Hosp.; med. dir., co-founder Rehabilitation Inst. of Ore., 1947-61. Dir., co-founder Ore. chpt. Arthritis and Rheumatism Found.; dir. Scientists of Tomorrow. Served with machine gun bn., U.S. Army, 1910-19; chief phys. medicine Letterman Gen. Hosp., Mitchell Convalescent Hosp., 1942-46. Diplomate Am. Bd. Phys. Medicine and Rehabilitation. Fellow Am. Acad. Phys. Medicine; mem. A.M.A., Ore. Med. Soc., Portland Acad. Medicine, Am. Rheumatism Assn., World Med. Assn., Internat. Soc. Welfare Cripples, Nat. Rehabilitation Assn., U. Ore. Med. Sch. Alumni Assn. (past pres.), Geol. Soc. Ore. (charter mem., past pres.), Soc. Mayflower Descs. (vice gov., gov., counselor), Am. Congress Phys. Medicine and Rehabilitation (pres. 1958- 59), Alcohol Rehabilitation Assn. (co-founder). Republican. Unitarian. Contbr. articles profl. jours. Home: 3300 S W Heather Lane Portland OR 97201 Office: 712 S W 12th Av Portland OR 97205

JONES, ARTHUR EDWIN, Jr., educator, librarian; b. Orange, N.J., Mar. 20, 1918; s. Arthur Edwin and Lucy (Alpaugh) J.; A.B., U. Rochester, 1939; M.A., Syracuse U., 1941, Ph.D., 1950; M.L.S., Rutgers U., 1964; m. Rachel Evelyn Mumbulo, Apr. 24, 1943; 1 dau., Carol Rae Jacobus. Instr. English dept. Syracuse U., 1946-49; faculty Drew U., 1949—, successively instr., asst. prof., 1949-54, asso. prof., 1954-62, prof., 1962—, librarian, 1955-63, dir. libraries Drew U., 1963- -. Served from sgt. to 1st lt., inf., AUS, 1941-46. Mem. Modern Lang. Assn., Coll. English Assn., Nat. Council Tchrs. English, Am. Assn. U. Profs., A.L.A., Am. Theol. Library Assn. (pres. 1967-68), Phi Beta Kappa. Home: 24 Rose Av Madison NJ 07940

JONES, ARTHUR GRIFFITH, found. exec.; b. Utica, N.Y., Sept. 25, 1912; s. John Griffith and Edith (Edwards) J.; grad. Utica Free Acad.; 1931, A.B., Hamilton Coll., 1935; postgrad. Syracuse U., 1935-37; grad. Nat. War Coll., 1958; postgrad. Am. Univ., 1964-66; m. Maragret A. Childs, May 2, 1941; (dec. Sept. 1966); children—Jonathan D., Constance G. Personnel staff TVA, 1937-47; adminstrn. activities Dept. of State, 1947-56; fgn. service officer, 1956-63, counselor Embassy for adminstrn., New Delhi, India, 1958-62; asso. dir. Com. on Fgn. Affairs Personnel, 1961-62; chief personnel policy council Dept. of State, 1963-64, asst. dir. for personnel operations, 1964, chief fgn. affairs personnel planning, 1965-66, fgn. service insp., 1967-68; dir. GAO Reports and Liason Program, 1968, project specialist Ford Found., 1968—. Chmn. Am. Embassy Commissary Assn.; treas., mem. bd. U.S. Ednl. Found. India; mem. bd. govs. Am. Sch., New Delhi. Recipient meritorious service award Dept. State. Mem. Phi Beta Kappa. Presbyn. (elder). Author: The Evolution of Personnel Systems for U.S. Foreign Affairs, 1965. Home: 722 C St NE Washington DC 20002 Office: care Ford Found 11 Gifford Rd PO Box M270 Accra Ghana

JONES, B. FRANK, educator; b. Amarillo, Tex., Apr. 15, 1936; s. B. Frank and Elizabeth (Glenn) J.; B.A., Rice U., 1958, Ph.D., 1961; m. Beverly June Carter, June 8, 1957; children—Marianna, Elaine, David. Vis. mem. Courant Inst. Math. Scis., N.Y. U., N.Y.C., 1961-62; mem. faculty dept. math. Rice U., Houston, 1962—; mem. Inst. for Advanced Study, Princeton, N.J., 1965-66; vis. prof. U. Minn., Mpls., 1969-70. Mem. Am. Math. Soc., Math. Assn. Am. Home: 417 Lindenwood St Houston TX 77024

JONES, BARRY, actor; b. Guernsey, Channel Islands, England Mar. 6, 1893; s. William John and Amerial Hammond (Robilliard) J.; student Elizabeth Coll., St. Peter Port, Guernsey. State debut with Shakespearean co. Grand Theatre, Leeds, Eng., 1921; appeared with Shakespearean co., London, Stratford-on-Avon, Oslo, Norway, as mem. stock co., appeared in Toronto, later Boston; N.Y. debut in Man and the Masses, Garrick Theatre, 1924, on Broadway in the Bully, 1924; on tour with The Road to Rome, 1928; formed managerial partnership Colbourne-Jones Co., 1928, toured U.S., Can. with repertory George Bernard Shaw plays, 1928-31; toured Italy, Austria, Germany in The Apple Cart, 1946; appeared numerous plays, including Charles the King, 1936, The Curtain Rises, 1940, Private Lives, Doctor's Dilemma, 1941, The Browning Version, 1949, Mrs. Inspector Jones, 1950, Barefoot in Athens, 1951, Misalliance, 1953, The Cave Dwellers, 1957-58; motion pictures includes Arms and the Man, 1931, Seven Days to Noon, 1950, The Clouded Yellow, 1951, White Corridors, 1952, Plymouth Adventure, 1952, Return to Paradise, 1953, Demetrius and the Gladiators, 1954, Brigadoon, 1954, Glass Slipper, 1955, Alexander the Great, War and Peace, 1956; Dancing with Crime, Freida, Uneasy Terms, Prince Valiant; the Heroes of Telemark, 1965; had made numerous television appearances in U.S.; exhibited oil paintings. Served with Royal Guernsey Light Inf., Royal Irish Fusiliers, Brit. Army, 1914-20; spl. constable Royal Naval Vol. Res., 1945; head Entertainments Nat. Service Assn., 1945- 56. Club: Variety (Pitts.) Home: 48 Campden Hill Sq London, England Also St Peter Port Guernsey Channel Islands England

JONES, BENJAMIN FRANKLIN, III, former steel mfr.; b. Pitts., Mar. 15, 1895; s. Benjamin Franklin, Jr., and Sue Duff (Dalzell) J.; prep. edn. St. Paul"s Sch., Concord, N. H.; student Princeton, 1915-17; LL.D., Geneva Coll., 1954; m. Katharine W. Holdship, June 27, 1917; children—Benjamin Franklin IV, Frederick Holdship, Peter Dalzell. Asst. treas., asst. sec. Jones & Laughlin Steel Co., 1919-23; sec. Jones & Laughlin Steel Corp., 1923- 27, v.p., sec., 1927-60; dir. Mellon Nat. Bank & Trust Co. Bd. dirs. Allegheny Gen. Hosp. 2d lt. F.A. Res. Corps, 1917-18. Republican. Presbyterian. Clubs: Edgeworth (Pa.); Pittsburgh, Harvard, Yale Duquesne, Princeton, Pittsburgh Golf (Pitts.); Racquet and Tennis, Princeton (N.Y.C.); Allegheny Country, Sewickley Heights Golf (Sewickley). Home: 203 Creek Drive Sewickley PA 15143 Office: Union Trust Bldg Pittsburgh PA 15219

JONES, BENJAMIN ROWLAND, judge; b. Wilkes-Barre, Pa., May 29, 1906; s. Benjamin Rowland and Margaret Hannah (Williams) J.; Wyoming Sem., Kington, Pa., 1923; A.B., Princeton, 1927; LL.B, U. Pa., 1930; m. Jane Randall Griffith, 1956; children—Benjamin Rowland III, Morgan R.; 1 stepson, Edward Griffith II Admitted to Pa. bar, 1930; partner Bedford, Waller, Jones & Darling, Wilkes-Barre, 1930-51; pres. judge Orphans' Ct. of Luzerne County, 1952- 57; justice Supreme Ct, Pa., 1957—. Trustees Wyoming Sem. Served with USNR, 1944-45. Mem. AM., Pa. bar assns., Wilkes-Barre Law and Library Assn (past pres) Home: R D 2 Benton PA 17814 Office: Court House Wilkes Barre PA 19001 also City Hall Philadelphia PA 19001

JONES, BILLY MAC, univ. pres.; b. Abilene, Tex., Apr. 5, 1925; s. William Anderson and Faye (Barton) J.; B.A., Vanderbilt U., 1950; M.A., George Peabody Coll., 1952; Ph.D., Tex. Tech. U., 1963; postgrad. U. Colo., 1967-68; m. Doris Jane Hudson, Mar. 10, 1948; children—Jeffrey Hudson, Woodrow Edward, Russell Anderson, Scott Ellis. Tchr.-coach Hillsboro High Sch., Nashville, 1950-54, Middle Tenn. State U., 1954-58, Tex. A. and M. U., 1958-59; chmn. social scis. San Angelo Jr. Coll., 1959-61; instr. Tex. Tech. U., 1961-63; chmn. history dept., dean of students Angelo State U., San Angelo, Tex., 1963-67, chmn. history dept., dir. curriculum devel., 1968-69; Am. Council on Edn. fellow U. Colo., 1967-68; pres. S.W. Tex. State U., San Marcos, 1969—. Vice pres. Tom Green County Hist. Soc.; bd. dirs., mem. exec. council, chmn. youth com. YMCA; bd. dirs. S. Tex. Heart Assn., Ft. Concho Mus. Served with USNR, 1943-46. Piper prof., 1967; acad. adminstrn. intern Am. Council on Edn., 1967-68. Fellow Am. Council on Edn., Tex. Hist. Assn. (life mem.; v.p.); mem. N.E.A. (life), W. Tex. Hist. Assn. (exec. com.), Phi Theta Kappa, Phi Alpha Theta, Phi Kappa Phi, Phi Delta Kappa. Rotarian. Author: Search for Maturity, 1965; Health Seekers in Southwest, 1967. Contbr. chpts. to Protest, Student Activism in America, 1969; Rangers of Texas, 1969; Capitols of Texas, 1970. Contbr. articles profl. jours. Home: 301 Roanoke St San Marcos TX 78666

JONES, BOB, Jr., educator, lectr., minister; b. Montgomery, Ala., Oct. 19, 1911; s. Bob and Mary Gaston (Stollenwerck) J.; grad. Bob Jones Coll., 1930; M.A., U. Pitts., 1932; student U. Chgo., U. Ala., Northwestern U.; hon. Litt. D., Asbury Coll., Wilmore, Ky., 1935; L.H.D., John Brown U., Siloam Springs, Ark., 1941; LL.D. Houghton Coll., 1943; D.D., Northwestern Schs., Mpls., 1950; m. Fannie May Holmes, 1938; children—Bob III, Jon Edward, Joy Estelle. Acting pres. Bob Jones Coll., 1932-47; pres. Bob Jones U., 1947-71, chmn. bd. trustees, 1964—, chancellor, 1971—. Shakespearean authority and interpreter. Col., Gov's. Staff, S.C., Tenn., Ala. Fellow Royal Geog. Soc.; mem. Gospel Fellowship Assn. (pres. bd.). Minister, lectr., radio speaker. Author: All Fulness Dwells; How to Improve Your Preaching; As the Small Rain; Inspirational and Devotional Verse; Showers Upon the Grass; Wine of Morning (historical novel); Ancient Truths for Modern Days; Prologue: A Drama of Jon Hus. Contrbr. writings to various religious and profl. periodicals. Author weekly syndicated article. A Look at the Book. Home: Greenville SC 29614

JONES, BOLLING, Jr., stove and range mfr.; b. Bristol, Va., Mar. 16, 1897; s. Samuel Dews and Elizabeth (Harrison) J.; B.S., U. Ga., 1916; m. Dorothy Hodgson, Jan. 3, 1920; children—Bolling III, Saunders II. With Atlanta Stove Works, Inc., 1917—, pres. 1926—, chmn. bd., 1969—, also dir.; pres. Birmingham Stove & Range Co. (Ala.), 1930-69, chmn. bd., 1969—. Served to ensign USN, 1917-18. Mem. Am. (past pres.), So. (past pres.) stove assns., Sigma Alpha Epsilon. Clubs: Piedmont Driving, Capital City (Atlanta). Home: 1145 W Paces Ferry Rd NW Atlanta GA Office: 112 Krog St Atlanta GA

JONES, BOOKER TALIAFERRO, musician, bandleader; b. Memphis, Nov. 12, 1944 s. Booker T. and Lurline (Newell) J.; student Memphis State U., 19xx; B. Mus. Edn., Ind. U., 1966; m. Willette Gigi Armstrong, Nov. 8, 1963; children—Booker Taliferro III. Staff studio musician, artist, producer Stax Records, Memphis, 1961—; tours colls., univs. and auditoriums, U.S., 1962—, also in France, Eng., Norway, Denmark, Sweden, Scotland and Wales; TV appearances, U.S. and Europe, 1965—; free band concerts for Heart Fund, Memphis Park Commn.; donated free services and royalties to Stay in School project, 1967. Recipient Gold Record, Record Industry Am., 1966; named Leader Number One Nat. Instrumental Combo, Billboard mag., 1968. Mem. Am. Fedn. Musicians, Composers and Lyricists Guild Am., Broadcast Music, Inc., Nat. Acad. Recording Arts and Scis., Kappa Alpha Psi. Composer: Green Onions, 1962; Soul Limbo, 1968; Uptight, 1968. Home: 670 Edith Av Memphis TN 38126 Office: 926 E McLemore Av Memphis TN 38106

JONES, BURTON WADSWORTH, educator; b. Redwood Falls, Minn., Oct. 1, 1902; s. Arthur Julius and Ethel (Rounds) J.; A.B., Grinnell Coll., 1923; M.A., Harvard, 1924; Ph.D., U. Chgo., 1928; m. Marian Grace Snelling, Sept. 10, 1932; children—Marian Louise, Christopher, Phyllis Wadsworth. Instr. math. Western Res. U., 1924-26; asst. prof. then asso. prof., prof. math. Cornell U., 1930-48; prof. math. U. Colo., 1948—, chmn. dept., 1949-63. Fellow NRC, 1929-30. Mem. Am. Math. Soc., Math. Assn. Am. (bd. govs.), Nat. Council Tchrs. Math. (bd. dirs.), Sigma Xi, Phi Beta Kappa. Kiwanian (pres. Boulder). Author: A Table of Eisenstein-Reduced Positive Ternary Quadratic Forms, 1935; Elementary Concepts of Mathematics, 1940, 3d edit., 1970; The Arithmetic Theory of Quadratic Forms, 1948; The Theory of Numbers, 1955; Modular Arithmetic, 1964; Introduction to Number Systems, 1966. Address: U Colo Boulder CO 80302

JONES, BUTLER ALFONSO, educator, sociologist; b. Birmingham, Ala., July 22, 1916; s. Jackson C. and Nettie (Butler) J.; A.B., Morehouse Coll., 1937; A.M., Atlanta U., 1938; Ph.D., N.Y.U., 1955; m. Lillian E. Webster, Dec. 27, 1939. Tchr., Atlanta U. Lab. Schs., 1938-42; prof. social scis. Talladega Coll., 1943-52; asso. prof., prof. sociology Ohio Wesleyan U., Delaware, 1952-69; prof., chmn. dept. sociology Cleve. State U., 1969—; vis. prof. Oberlin Coll., 1962-63, Hamline U., 1966-67. Mem. Am. Sociol. Assn., Soc. for Study Social Problems, Ohio Valley Sociol. Soc., Assn. for Study Negro Life and History, Soc. for Applied Anthropology. Research on effectiveness of law as an instrument for creating and directing social change along a predetermined path, comparison of conditions obtaining before intervention, cases taken primarily from sch. segregation litigation in U.S. Home: 13855 Superior Rd Cleveland OH 44118

JONES, CARL ALLEN, newspaper pub.; b. Bristol, Tenn-Va., Oct. 13, 1912; s. Carl Allen and Edith (Carr) J.; B.Sc., Ohio State U., 1934; m. Kathryn Alice Paxton, Nov. 16, 1934; children—Alice Carr, Timothy Paxton, Carleton Allen III, John Arnold. Bus. mgr. Johnson City (Tenn.) Press (afternoon and Sunday paper), 1934-35; consol. Press with Evening Staff- News and assumed charge of Morning Chronicle, Johnson City, 1935, gen. mgr. both publs., 1935, pub. since 1939; pub. treas. Press Inc., Johnson City, 1939-50, pres., pub., 1950—; pres., pub. Lebanon Democrat and Covington Leader; pres. Erwin Record; pres. East Tenn. Broadcasting Co., Appalachian League, 1944-46, dir. Dixie Coca-Cola Bottling Co., H.P. King Co. (Bristol, Tenn.). Pres. Johnson City Baseball Club, sec. Johnson City Planning Commn., 1951-52; pres. Community Chest, 1952-53; mem. Johnson City Power Bd., 1960-61; nat. assoc. Boys' Clubs Am., 1954-56, 61-65; chmn. Tenn. Alcoholic Beverage Commn. Mem. Gov.'s Staff. Trustee, Tenn. Tb Hosps. Mem. Tenn. Press Assn. (pres. 1956-57) Johnson City C. of C. (dir.), Sigma Delta Chi, Kappa Sigma. Democrat. Methodist Church. Clubs: Rotary (dist. gov. 1967-68). Country, Hurstleigh (Johnson City, Tenn.); Overseas Press (asso. N.Y.C.); National Press (Washington). Home: 806 Hillrise Blvd Johnson City TN 37601 Office: care Press-Chronicle Johnson City TN 37601

JONES, CARL TRAINER, educator, chemist; b. Allentown, Pa., Dec. 31, 1910; s. John Richard and Beulah (Trainer) J.; B.A., Columbia Union Coll., 1933; M.S., Cath. U. Am., 1939; Ph.D., Ore. State U., 1959; m. Lucile Hall, Aug. 30, 1938; children—John Richard, Carl Leighton. Instr. chemistry Atlantic Union Coll., 1937-38; sci. tchr. Takoma Acad., also instr. chemistry Columbia Union Coll., 1938-45; head sci. dept. Philippine Union Coll., 1945-51; prof. chemistry, chmn. dept. Walla Walla Coll., 1952—. Mem. Am. Chem. Soc. Home: 207 N E A College Place WA 99324

JONES, CARLYLE HERMAN, mfg. co. exec.; b. Vincent, O., Jan. 15, 1914; s. Herman L. and Ella Blanche (Shaw) J.; R.S. in Bus. Adminstrn., Miami U., Oxford, O., 1936; m. Virginia A. Sloat, July 1, 1939; children—Carleton Shaw, Beverly Ann (Mrs. Willis). With mfg. div. Marshall Field & Co., 1936-41, asst. dept. sales mgr., 1938-41; with Sperry Gyroscope Co., 1941-68, dir. pub. relations, 1953-63, v.p. pub. relations, 1963- 68, dir. pub. relations Sperry Rand Corp., 1968-. Vice pres. L.I. Assn, 1964, pres., 1965-66, chmn. bd., 1966-68, chmn. govt. affairs com., 1961-63; chmn. Protestant faith com. Boy Scouts Am., 1959; mem. N.Y. State Pub. Affairs Group, 1961—. Citizens for Steven B. Derovnian, 1962—, Trustee L.I. Fund, 1957-61, Nassau County Health Services Found., 1967—; adv. bd. Abilities Inc., 1957-64. Human Resources Found., 1967—. Served to lt. j.g. USNR. 1944-46; PTO. Named Advt. Man of Year on L.I., L.I. Advt. Assn., 1963. Mem. Aerospace Industries Assn. (chmn pub. relations com. 1964—), Aviation Writers Assn., Navy League, Assn. U.S. Army, Air Force Assn. Republican. Conglist. (Chmn. trustees 1952). Clubs: Wings (N.Y.C.); Nat. Press (Washington); Cherry Valley (L.I.). Home: 4939 Crescent St Chevy Chase MD 20016 Office: Sperry Rand Corp 1290 Av of Americas New York City NY 10019

JONES, CATESBY BROOKE, banker; b. Lexington, Va., Mar. 7, 1925; s. Catesby and Elizabeth (Cox) J.; grad. St. Paul's Sch., 1943; B.A. in Econs., Yale, 1949; student Stonier Grad. Sch. Banking, Rutgers U., 1956, U. Va. Grad. Sch. Bus., 1961; m. Margaret Gordon Gaffney, June 13, 1953; children—Catesby II, Margaret Brooke, Elizabeth Gordon. With United Va. Bank State Planters, Richmond, 1949—, sr. v.p., head nat. div., 1965—. Chmn. finance com., dir. Richmond Area Community Council, 1959-63; div. chmn. United Givers Fund, 1965. Served to 1st lt. AUS, 1944-46. Mem. Am. Inst. Banking, Robert Morris Assos., Va. (treas., dir. 1964-67), Richmond (chmn. membership relations com. 1957-59) chmabers commerce, Soc. Colonial Wars in Va. (treas., dir.), Soc. Cincinnati in Va. (treas., dir.), Jamestown Soc., Newcomen Soc., Beta Theta Pi. Episcopalian. Clubs: Yale of Va. (past pres.); Yale (N.Y.C.); Country of Va. (Richmond). Home: 1 Greenway Lane Richmond VA 23226 Office: 900 E Main St Richmond VA 23219

JONES, CECIL DERWENT former publisher; b. Thompson Station, Tenn., July 9, 1905; s. James Allen and Cammye Sowell (Evans) J.; student Battle Fround Acad., Franklin, Tenn., Emory U., 1924-26; m. Allie Tucker Yarbrough, July 17, 1929; children—Cecil Derwent, David Sterling. With Meth. Pub. House Nashville, 1926—; clk, 1926-27, asst. credit mgr., 1927-30, v.p., 1956- -; with Abingdon Press 1930-64, salesman, 1930-40, asst. mgr., 1940-56, mgr. 1956-63; v.p. charge pub. div. Meth. Pub. House, Nashville, 1963- 64, became exec. v.p., 1964. Mem. Nat. Council Chs., C. of C., Protestant Church-Owned Pub. Assn. Sigma Chi. Rotarian. Home: 2020 Stonehurst Dr Nashville TN 37203

JONES, CHARLES E., lawyer; b. Kingfisher, Okla., Mar. 25, 1908; s. Charles Edward and Geneva (Reese) J.; A.R. Wichita State U., 1930; LL.B., U. Mich., 1933; m. Nina Kirky, June 4, 1936; children—Darlynn (Mrs. Ronald Walker), Reese Jones, Mary Kay (Mrs. Lawrence Hickerson), Charles E. III. Admitted to Kan. bar 1933, since practiced in Wichita. Co-owner, mgr. Crystal Labs., Inc., Wichita; mgr. radio sta. KAKE; v.p., dir gen. counsel Am. Savs. Assn. Wichita; sec., dir. KAKE Broadcasting Co., KAKE- TV and Radio, Inc., Wichita. Mem. Am., Kan., Wichita (pres 1952) bar assns., Beta Theta Pi. Conglist. Mason (Shriner). Clubs; Wichita, Wichita Country; Farm and Ranch. Home: RR 4 Box 176A Wichita KS Office: 201 n Main St Wichita KS 67201

JONES, CHARLES EDWARD, advt. exec.; b. Mound City, Ill., Oct. 1, 1918; s. William M. and Daisy D. (Rivers) J.; student McKendree Coll., Lebanon, Ill., 1936-38; B.J., U. Mo., 1940; m. Doris E. Hogendobler, June 26, 1938; children Eleanor Ann, Philip Alan; m. 2d, Greta Jane Houston., Dec. 3O, 1955; 1 dau., Emily Susan. Account supr. Schwimmer & Scott, Ins., Chgo., 1950- 52; adminstrv. v.p., dir. Potts-Woodbury, Inc., 1952-60, pres., chmn. bd., chief exec. officer, 1962-67; sr. v.p. Biddle Advt., 1967—; pres. Blue Anchor Marina, Inc., 1969—; gen. sales mgr. WHB Radio, Kansas City, Mo., 1960-62. Dir. Greater Kansas City Sports Comn.; bd. govs. Am. Royal; active local United Fundi bd. dirs. Kansas City Assn. Mental Health. Served as 1st lt. USMC, 1943-46. Mem. Kansas City C. of C. (dir.), Kansas City Advt. and Sales Execs. Club. Mason. Club: Kansas City. Home: 5240 Foxridge Dr Mission KS 66202 Office: 1125 Grand Av Kansas City MO 64106

JONES, CHARLES FRANCIS, banker; b. Chgo., 1905. Vice pres., dir. Burlington Marine Bank (Wis.); dir. Marine Nat. Exchange Bank, Milw.; dir. Aluminum Splty. Co., Frabill Mfg. Co. Home: 3227 Menomonee River Pkwy Milwaukee WI 53222 Office: 1 Marine Plaza Milwaukee WI 53201

JONES, CHARLES FRANKLIN, petroleum co. exec.; b. Bartlett, Tex., Nov. 23, 1911; s. Charles Edward and Pearl Lee (Keeton) J.; B.S. in Chem. Engring., U. Tex., 1933, M.S. in Chem. Engring., 1934, Ph.D. in Phys. Chemistry, 1937; LL.D., Autin Coll., 1965; m. Edith Temple Houston, Apr. 1, 1938; children—Dianne (Mrs. Orson C. Clay), Kenneth Franklin. With Humble Oil and Refining Co., 1937-47, 49-63, mgr. econs. and planning dept., Houston, 1960-62, gen. mgr. central region, Tulsa, 1962-63; asst. to mgr. coordination and econs. dept. Standard Oil Co. (N.J.), 1947-49; pres., dir. Esso Research and Engring. Co., Linden, N.J., 1963-64; exec. v.p. Humble Oil & Refining Co., Houston, 1964, pres., 1964-68, vice chmn., 1970—, also dir.; chmn. bd. Fed. Res. Bank of Dallas. Mem. Nat. sci. bd. NSF; mem. Nat. Indsl. Conf. Bd.; chmn. Tex. Research League; pres. Houston Symphony Soc. Registered profl. engr., Tex. Recipient Distinguished Engring. Grad. award, U. Tex., 1964. Mem. Am. Petroleum Inst., A.A.A.S., Am. Chem. Soc., Soc. Automotive Engrs., Soc. Chem. Industry, Am. Inst. Chem. Engrs., Sigma Xi, Tau Beta Pi, Phi Lambda Upsilon. Presbyn. (elder). Home: 3706 Del Monte Houston TX 77019 Office: PO Box 2180 Houston TX 77001

JONES, CHARLES H., former bus. exec.; b. Brookline, Mass., Mar. 20, 1902; s. Charles Henry and Bessie (Roberts) J.; B.S., Dartmouth, 1923; postgrad., Harvard Bus. Sch., 1924; m. Margaret French, Sept. 10, 1927; children—Charles H., Leslie. With Commonwealth Shoe & Leather Co. (now Kayser-Roth Shoes, Inc.), Whitman, Mass., 1923-68, v.p., 1933-49, pres., 1949-64, chmn. bd., 1964- 68. Mem. Nat. Shoe Mfrs. Assn. (hon. chmn.). Home: Little Island Rd West Falmouth MA 02574

JONES, CHARLES OSCAR, educator; b. Worthing, S.D., Oct. 28, 1931; s. Llewellyn F. and Marjorie (Tye) J.; B.A. magna cum laude U. S.D., 1953; M.S., U. Wis., 1956, Ph.D., 1960; student London Sch. Economics and Polit. Sci., 1956-57; m. Vera B. Mire, June 6, 1959; children—Joseph B., Daniel C. Instr. Wellesley Coll., 1959-61, asst. prof., 1961-62; vis. lectr. U. Wis., summer 1961; asso. prof. U. Ariz., 1963-65, prof., 1965-69; Maurice Falk prof. politics U. Pitts., 1969—; asso. dir. Nat. Center for Edn. in Politics, N.Y., 1962-63; cons. for elections analysis NBC News, N.Y.C., 1964, 1966. Mem. Commn. on Polit. Activity of Govt. Personnel U.S. Congress, 1966-67. Served with AUS, 1953-55. Mem. Am. Polit. Sci. Assn. (mem. council 1967-69), Phi Beta Kappa, Pi Sigma Alpha. Author: The Republican Party in American Politics, 1965; Every Second Year: Congressional Behavior and the Two-Year Term, 1967; The Minority Party in Congress, 1970. Home: 609 Ravencrest Rd Pittsburgh PA 15215

JONES, CHARLES RICHARD, devel. co. exec.; b. Mannington, W. Va., May 30, 1935; s. Donley and Mildred Janice (Ryan) J.; A.B., Rutgers U., 1957; M.B.A. with distinction, U. Mich., 1961. Audit mgr. Lybrand, Ross Bros. & Montgomery, N.Y.C., 1961-70; asst. v.p., gen. controller Gen. Devel. Corp., Miami, Fla., 1970—. Served with AUS, 1958-60. C.P.A., N.J., N.Y. Mem. Am. Inst. C.P.A.'s, N.Y. State Soc. C.P.A.'s, Am. Accounting Assn., Tax Execs. Inst., Am. Inst. Corporate Controllers, Accounting Research Assn. Home: 14760 S W 79th Ct Miami FL 33158 Office: 1111 S Bayshore Dr Miami FL 33131

JONES, CHARLES SHERMAN, aviator; b. Castleton, Vt., Jan. 11, 1894; s. John and Helen (Sherman) J.; student Middlebury (Vt.) Coll., Harvard Sch. Phy. Edn.; m. Marguerite Williams, Oct. 31, 1917 (dec. July 1967); children—Charles Sherman, Deborah Harrison; m. 2d, Hulda Cole, Nov. 26, 1967. With Curtiss Wright Corp., airplane mfrs., 1919-33; founder, pres. Casey Jones Sch. Aeros., Newark, 1932-56, Acad. Aeros., La Guardia Field, N.Y., 1940-63, chmn bd., 1964—; pres J. V. W. Corp., 1933-41, partner, 1942-64. Mem U.I. Port Authority, 1968—. Served with AC U.S. Army, 1917-18. Recipient John J. McGraw award, 1956. Fellow Am. Inst. Aeros. and Astronautics; mem. Am. Soc. Engring. Edn., Phi Beta Kappa, Chi Psi, Club: Wings (past pres.) (N.Y.C.). Winner 2d pl. N.Y.-Toronto race, 1919, Am. Derby, Kansas City, Mo., 1921, winner 2 1st pl. and 2d pl. Nat. Air Races Omaha, 1921, 2d pl. On to Detroit race, 1922, On to St. Louis race, 1923, On to Dayton race, 1924, Central Union Speed race, 1924; won 2 events Nat. Air Races, Mitchel Field, 1925, 1st and 2d pl., Phila., 1928; winner of race for cabin ships, Chgo 1930 Home: PO Box 412 St Thomas Virgin Islands Office: Acad Aeros La Guardia Field NY

JONES, CHARLES WILLIAMS, educator; b. Lincoln, Neb., Sept. 23, 1905; s. Charles Williams and Grace Elizabeth (Cook) J.; A.B., Oberlin Coll., 1926; Litt.D. (hon.), 1951; A.M., Cornell U., 1930, Ph.D., 1932; m. Sarah Frances Bosworth, June 30, 1928; children—Frances Elizabeth, Charles Bosworth (dec.), Lawrence Wager, Gregory Hunt. Rep. Allyn and Bacon, ednl. pubs., 1926-29; instr. English, Oberlin Coll., 1932-35; instr. English, Cornell U., 1936-38, asst. prof., 1938-41, asso. prof., 1941-48, prof. 1948-54, dir. summer sessions, 1946-48, dean Grad. Sch., 1948-53; prof. English U. Cal., Berkeley, 1954; dir. U.S. Mil. Acad. Preparatory, 1943-45. Research fellow Am. Council Learned Socs., 1935-36; Guggenheim Meml. Found., 1939-40, 1945-46. Author: Bedae Pseudepigrapha, 1939; Writing and Speaking (with others), 1943, Bedae Opera de Temporibus, 1943; Saints, Lives and Chronicles of Early England, 1947; Medieval Literature in Translation, 1950; The St. Nicholas Liturgy, 1963; Bedae Opera Exegetica: in Genesim, 1967. Editor or contbr. Ency. Brit., Dictionary Sci. Biography, others. Home: 766 Spruce St Berkeley CA 94707

JONES, CHESTER MORSE, physician; b. Portland, Me., Mar. 29, 1891; s. Harry Lee and Marie Albertina (Morse) J.; B.A., Williams Coll., 1913, D.Sc., 1942, M.D., Harvard, 1919; m. Kathleen Holmes, June 7, 1920; children—Robert H., Elizabeth M. (Mrs. Sam L. Clark, Jr.), Anne K. (Mrs. Ward Stoops). Intern Mass. Gen. Hosp., 1918-19, various staff positions, 1919- 57, bd. conss., 1957-64, hon. physician, 1964—; mem. of faculty Harvard Med. Sch., 1921—, clin. prof. medicine, 1940-57, prof. emeritus, 1957—, also spl. cons. to dean William O. Moseley Jr. traveling fellow (Harvard) to Strasbourg, France, 1924-25; Henry Pickering Walcott fellow clin. medicine, 1925-28; acting asso. prof. medicine Vanderbilt U., 1940-41; cons. medicine Surg. Gen. U.S. Army, 1944-46; mem. Unitarian Service Com., Med. Missions to Austria, Greece, Italy, 1947-48; Shattuck lectr. Mass. Med. Soc., 1958. Recipient Rogerson Cup and medal Williams Coll., 1956. Diplomate Am. Bd. Internal Medicine (chmn. 1955 ' 57). Fellow Royal Coll. Physicians and Surgeons of Can. (hon.); mem. Am. Soc. for Clin. Investigation, Assn. Am. Physicians, Harvard Med. Alumni Assn. (pres.-elect), Am. Gastroent. Soc. (pres 1936), Am. Clin. and Climatol. Soc. (pres. 1951), A.C.P. (mem. bd. regents; mastership 1958; pres., 1961-62). Author: Digestive Tract Pain, 1938, Editorial bd. New Eng. Jour. Medicine, Gastroenterology, Annals of Internal Medicine. Contbr. med. articles on digestive tract physiology and disease. Home: 11 Emerson Pl Boston MA 02114 Office: Mass Gen Hosp Boston MA 02114

JONES, CLAIBORNE STRIBLING, educator; b. Petersburg, Va., Dec. 20, 1914; s. Claiborne Turner and Elizabeth (Stribling) J.; A.B., Hampden-Sydney Coll., 1935; M.A., U. Va., 1940, Ph.D., 1944; m. Annie Goodwyn Boisseau, June 12, 1940; children—Anne Goodwyn, Maria de Saussure, Elizabeth Claiborne. Faculty U. N.C., 1944—, prof. zoology, 1955—, asso. dean Gen. Coll., 1958-65, asst. vice chancellor, 1965-66, asst. to chancellor, 1966—. Trustee St. Augustine's Coll., Raleigh, N.C. Mem. Am. Soc. Zoologists, A.A.A.S., N.C. Acad. Sci., Phi Beta Kappa, Sigma Xi, Omicron Delta Kappa, Pi Kappa Alpha. Democrat. Episcopalian. Home: 419 Westwood Dr Chapel Hill NC 27514

JONES, CLEON, baseball player; b. Mobile, Ala. Outfielder, N.Y. Mets baseball team. Address: care Dir Pub Relations NY Mets Baseball Team William A Shea Stadium Roosevelt Av and 126th St Flushing NY 11368*

JONES, CLIFFORD AARON, lawyer; b. Long Lane, Mo., Feb. 19, 1912; s. Burley Monroe and Arlie Mary (Benton) J.; LL.B., U. Mo., 1938; m. Oklabelle Malone, Jan. 31, 1942; children—Clifford Aaron II, Joni Lee. Admitted to Nev. Bar, 1938, practiced in Las Vegas, 1938- -, sr. partner law firm Jones, Jones, Close, Bilbrary, Kaufman & Olsen, Ltd.; majority leader, Nev. Legislature, 1941; dist. judge for 8th Jud. Dist., Nev., 1945-46; lt. gov. State of Nev., 1947-54; Dem. chmn. Clark Co. Nev., 1948; chmn. bd., dir. Thunderbird Hotel, Inc., Las Vegas, 1948-64; pres., dir. Income Investment, Inc., 1963-65; pres. Caribbean-Am. Investment Co., Inc., 1960—; sr. v.p., dir. First Western Financial Corp., 1963-66; sec., dir. 1st Western Savs. & Loan Assn., 1954-66; dir. Barrington Industries, Inc., 1966-70. Served as lt. col, F.A., 1942-45. Mem. Am. Legion, V.F.W., Phi Delta Phi, Kappa Sigma. Democrat. Protestant. Elk, Lion (past pres. Las Vegas). Home: 892 Vegas Valley Dr Las Vegas NV 89109 Office: 1st Nat Bank Bldg Las Vegas NV 89101

JONES, CLIFFORD BARTLETT, banker; b. Rico, Colo., Apr. 9, 1885; s. Charles Adam and Virginia (Bartlett) J.; grad. high sch.; LL.D., McMurray Coll., Abilene, Tex., 1939; LL.D., Southwestern U., Georgetown, Tex., 1941; LL.D., Tex. Technol. U., Lubbock, 1941; m. Alice Louise Palmer, June 24, 1908 (dec. May 1919); m. 2d, Audrey Lynn Barber, Sept. 27, 1922 (dec. May 1969). Purchasing agt. Kansas City Bag Mfg. Co. (Mo.), 1904-07; v.p., treas. Jacques Steel Co., Kansas City, 1907-10; asst. ranch mgr. S.M. Swenson & Sons of N.Y.C., Spur, Tex., 1911-13, ranch mgr., 1913-38; pres. Tex. Technol. U., 1938-44; pres. Spur Nat. Bank, 1936-55, chmn. bd., 1955-62; pres. Spur Cattle Loan Co., 1914-19; pres. Dickens County Agrl. Credit Corp.; dir., chmn. bd. Lubbock Nat. Bank, 1944—; dir. Ft. Worth & Denver R.R. Co., Merc. Nat. Bank, Dallas, Southwestern Pub. Service Co., Merc. Security Life Ins. Co., Dallas, Fed. Regional Agrl. Credit Corp., Ft. Worth. Organizer, pres. Ft. Worth-Roswell Hwy. Assn., 1914; v.p. Tex. Hwy. Assn., Austin; pres. Tex. Transcontinental Trail, Ft. Worth. Mem. Tex. Centennial Commn., 1936—; chmn. Dickens County Draft Bd., World War I; mem. Dist. Appellate Draft Bd., No. Judicial Dist. Tex., World War I; regional adviser PWA for Tex., La. and N.M., 1934. Mayor, Spur, 19-. Pres., bd. dirs. Tex. Tech. Found.; bd. dirs. Tex. Safety Council, Tax Conservation Council Tex., Scottish Rite Found. Tex., Lubbock Symphony, W.Tex. Mus.; trustee Tex. Technol. U. Sch. Law. Recipient Good Citizenship award Tex. Soc. S.A.R., 1959, MacArthur award S.A.R., 1965. Named spl. Tex. Ranger. Fellow Tex. Acad. Sci.; mem. Tex. Cowboy Reunion Assn. (life), Lubbock C. of C., Philos. Soc. Tex., Am. Inst. Banking, A.A.A.S., Acad. Polit. Sci., Tex., W.Tex. hist. assns., N.E.A., Tex. Soc. S.A.R. (pres., life mem.), Sons Republic Tex., Knights of San Jacinto, Phi Delta Theta. Episcopalian. Mason (33, K.T., Shriner), Rotarian. Clubs: Ft. Worth, Lubbock, Block and Bridle Tex. Technol. U. (Lubbock). Home: 1108 Altura Towers 1617 27th St Lubbock TX 79405 Office: Lubbock Nat Bank PO Box 421 Lubbock TX 79408 also 916 Main St Lubbock TX 79401

JONES, CLIFTON CLYDE, educator; b. Huntington, W.Va., Dec. 21, 1922; s. Clifton Clark and Goldie (Williams) J.; A.B., Marshall Coll., 1944; student Bethany Coll., 1943; M.A., Northwestern U., 1950, Ph.D., 1954; m. Margaret Esther Scheldrup, 1948; children—Karen Eileen, Kristin Ann, Clifton Carl. Instr. dept. bus. history Northwestern U., 1951-53; asst. prof. econs. Atlanta div. U. Ga., 1953-55; asst. prof. econs. U. Ill., 1955-58, asso. prof., 1958-60; prof., head dept. bus. adminstrn. Kan. State U., 1960- 62, dean Coll. Commerce, 1962-67, v.p. univ. devel., 1966-70 prof. bus. adminstrn., 1970—. Dir. Manhattan Fed. Savs. and Loan Assn., Mid-Am. Lines, Inc., Kansas City, Mo., Kan. State Bank. Mem. Kansas Council for Econ. Analysis, 1963-67; pres. Kan. Council Econ. Edn., 1965-66. Served from ensign to lt. (j.g.), USNR, 1944-46. Mem. Econ. History Assn., Agrl. History Soc. (pres. 1967-68), Manhattan C. of C. (pres. 1965), Delta Sigma Pi. Presbyn. Rotarian. Author: (with D.L. Kemmerer) American Economic History, 1959. Editor: Agricultural History, 1958-60. Home: 2008 Arthur Dr Manhattan KS 66502

JONES, CRANSTON EDWARD, mag. editor, writer; b. Albany, N.Y., Mar. 12, 1918; s. Edward Thomas and Katharine Phoebe (Lamson) J.; grad Phillips Acad., Andover, Mass., 1936; B.S., Harvard, 1940; m. Jean Campbell, Dec. 24, 1949; children—Abigail Ainsworth, Baird Campbell. Corr. for Time-Life mag., San Francisco, London and Paris, 1946-52, bur. chief, Rio de Janeiro, 1952-55; mem. staff Time mag., 1955-69, sr. editor, 1961-69; editor-in- chief Travel & Camera, 1969-70, Travel & Leisure, 1970-71; exec. v.p. U.S. Camera Pub. Corp., 1969-71; exec. dir. Atlas Mag., 1971—. Bd. dirs. Bear Run Found. Served to lt. USNR, 1941- 45. Recipient award for excellence in archtl. journalism A.I.A., 1956, 58, 59, 60. Mem. Municipal Art Soc., Soc. Mayflower Descs., St. Andrews Soc., Soc. Archtl. Historians. Clubs: Century; Edgartown Yacht. Author: Architecture Today and Tomorrow, 1961; Homes of American Presidents, 1962; Marcel Breuer: Works and Projects, 1921-1961, 1963: also articles. Home: 8 E 96th St New York City NY 10028 Office: 1170 Av of Americas New York City NY 10036

JONES, CURTIS EDISON, banker; b. Bellevue, Pa., Oct. 21, 1918; s. Chester D. and Jane (Green) J.; B.S; U. Pitts., 1950; m. Margaret R. McFarland, Apr. 21, 1943; children—Craig W., R. Scott. With Union Trust Co., Pitts., 1936-46; Mellon Bank (merger Union Trust Co. and Mellon Bank), Pitts., 1946—, asst. cashier, 1950-53, asst. v.p., 1953-56, v.p., 1956-70, sr. v.p., 1970—; dir. Koppers Co., Inc., Martin Marietta Corp., Oliver Tyrone Corp., Tyrone Hydraulics, Inc. Trustee Allegheny County Med. Soc. Found., Koppers Found.; bd. dirs. Pitts. chpt. A.R.C.; v.p., dir. Suburban Gen. Hosp. Served to lt. col. AUS. 1941-46. Mem. Assn. Res. City Bankers. Mason. Clubs: Board Room (N.Y.C.); Laurel Valley Golf (Ligonier, Pa.); Duquesne, Fox Chapel Golf (Pitts.). Home: 110 Forest Dr Pittsburgh PA 15238 Office: Mellon Nat Bank & Trust Co Mellon Sq Pittsburgh PA 15230

JONES, CURTIS FULLER, fgn. service officer; b. Maine, Oct. 25, 1921; B.A., Bowdoin Coll., 1942 married. Assigned Diplomatic Service, Dept. State. 1946; 3d sec., vice consul, Lebanon, 1946-47; 3d sec., vice consul, Addis Ababa, Ethiopia, 1947-49, 2d sec., vice consul, 1949; assigned Dept. State, Washington, 1949; Arabic lang. tng. Fgn. Service Inst., 1949; Arabic lang.-area study, U. Pa., 1949; vice consul, Tripoli, Libya, 1950-52, 2d sec., vice consul, 1952; prin. officer Port Said, 1952, consul, 1952-55; intelligence research specialist Dept. State, 1955-58; consul, Damascus, 1958-61, 1st sec., consul, 1961-63; officer-in-charge UAR-Syrian Arab Republic affairs, Dept. State, 1963-65; consul gen. Aden, also Muscat and Oman, 1965—. Served with AUS, 1942-45. Address: 2706 31st St SE Washington DC 20018*

JONES, DACE WILLETT, utility exec.; b. Burlington, N.C., 1906; ed. Elon Coll. Vice pres., dir. Duke Power Co.; dir. Allsheer Hosiery Co., J.P. Stevens & Co. Home: 2636 Chilton Pl Charlotte NC 28207 Office: 422 S Church St Charlotte NC 28202

JONES, DALLAS L., Jr., economist; b. Shreveport, Aug. 29, 1914; s. Dallas L. and Mabel Adelaide (Scanland) J.; B.A., Centenary Coll., 1935; B.S., Georgetown U., 1946; M.A., Yale, 1958; m. Alice Gretchen Edgar, Nov. 7, 1938; children—Dallas L. III, Alice Gretchen. Internat. trade specialist Dept. Commerce, 1946- 49; joined U.S. fgn. service, 1949; dep. chief econ. sect. Am. embassy, Oslo, Norway, 1949-52; chief spl. trade staff Am. embassy, Paris, France, 1952-55; spl. asst. internat. finance div. Dept. State, 1956-60; mem. NATO Def. Coll., Paris, 1960-61; chief financial and econ. div. Am. Embassy, Madrid, Spain; former conselor econ. affairs U.S. Mission to OECD, Paris, France; now mem. planning and coordination staff U.S. Dept. State. Chmn. U.S. delegation GATT Balance of Payments Consultations, Tokyo, Japan, 1959. Served to lt. (j.g.) USNR, 1943-45. Author articles. Office: 7206 Denton Rd Bethesda MD 20014

JONES, DAN HENLEY, psychologist: b. Amherstburg. Ont., Can., June 17, 1924 (parents U.S. citizens); s. George Hayward and Helen (Henley) J.; A.B., U. Ky., 1948, M.A., 1949; Ph.D., Mich. State U., 1956; m. Winifred BeGole, Sept. 7, 1946; children—George H., Charles G., Dan H., Christopher B., Sara E. Rehab. psychologist Herman Kiefer Hosp., Detroit, 1949-51; indsl. psychologist Gen. Motors Corp., Flint Mich., 1951-56; asso. prof., prof., chmn. psychology dept., U. Detroit, 1956-66; selected as expert in indsl. psychology by UN for tng., research Indian Industry, New Delhi, 1962-63; engaged in testing programs AID, Seoul, Korea, 1966-68; exec. Scientist Asia/Pacific office Am. Insts. for Research, 1966-71; dir. Korean Inst. for Research in Behavioral Scis., 1968-69; sr. research team mem. U.S. Dept. Def. study in Assessment Methodology, Bangkok, Thailand, 1970-71; dir. advanced planning Am. Insts. for Research, Pitts., 1971—. Mem. Am. Psychol. Assn., Am. Mgmt. Assn., Am. Assn. U. Profs. Address: 710 Chatham Center Pittsburgh PA 15219

JONES, DANIEL JOHN, educator; b. Kansas City, Mo., Aug. 30, 1914; s. Edward Daniel and Ruby Knondez (Heller) J.; B.S., U. Okla., 1933, M.S., 1934; Ph.D., U. Chgo, 1938; m. Alice Evelyn Hamilton, June 15, 1938; children—Edward Hamilton, Donald Daniel. Research geologist, then chief, geol. research Phillips Petroleum Co., 1937-50; mem. faculty U. Utah, 1950-70, prof. geology, 1959-70; chmn. dept. earth scis. Cal. State Coll., Bakersfield, 1970—; project cons. AEC, 1953-54; vis. prof. U. So. Cal., 1957-58; hon. research asso. Univ. Coll., London, Eng., summer 1962; asso. dir. earth sci. curriculum project American Geol Inst., 1963-65. Member Am. Assn. Petroleum Geologists, Soc. Econ. Paleontologists and Mineralogists (sec.-treas. 1962-63), Geol. Soc. Am., Phi Beta Kappa, Sigma Xi, Sigma Gamma Epsilon. Author: Introduction to Microfossils, 1956. Address: Earth Scis Cal State Coll Bakersfield CA 93309

JONES, DARRELL G., educator; B.S., M.A., No. Ia. U.; Ph.D., Mich. State U. Prof., head dept. bus. edn. and adminstrv. services Western Mich. U., Kalamazoo. Office: Dept Bus Edn and Adminstrv Services Western Mich U Kalamazoo MI*

JONES, DAVID, singer; b. Manchester, Eng. Actor musical Oliver, Pickwick (both N.Y.C.); now singer with group Monkees, performer NBC TV, also recordings. Address: David Pearl 7033 Sunset Blvd Hollywood CA 90028

JONES, DAVID ALLEN, health facility exec.; b. Louisville, Aug. 7, 1931; s. Evan L. and Elsie F. (Thurman) J.; B.S., U. Louisville, 1954; LL.B., Yale, 1960; m. Betty L. Ashbury, July 24, 1954; children—David, Susan, Daniel, Matthew, Carol. Founder, chief exec. officer Extendicare, Inc., operators hosps. and related med. facilities, Louisville, 1961—; admitted to Ky. bar, 1960; partner firm Greenebaum, Grissom, Doll, Matthews & Boone, and predecessor, Louisville, 1965-69, of counsel, 1969—; dir. First Nat. Bank Louisville, Ky. Cols. Profl. Basketball Team. Bd. dirs. Louisville Community Chest. Served to lt. (j.g.) USNR, 1954-57. Mem. Louisville Area C. of C. (bd. dirs.). Home: 35 Poplar Hill Rd Louisville KY 40207 Office: PO Box 1438 Louisville KY 40201

JONES, DAVID CARLTON, oil co. exec.; b. Calgary, Alta., Can., Dec. 14, 1914; s. D. Charles and Norah (Browne) J.; student U. Alta., 1933-35; B.Eng., McGill U., 1937; postgrad. Harvard, 1963; m. Marian Lilian Glover, Nov. 30, 1940; children—Donna Marian (Mrs. Jeffrey King Motherwell), Linda Noreen. Engr., Dominion Bridge Co., Calgary, 1944; engr. Canadian Western Natural Gas Co., 1945-51; cons. engr. Denton Spencer Co., Calgary, 1951-54; engr. Hudson's Bay Oil & Gas Co., Ltd., Calgary, 1955-59, v.p. prodn., 1960-66, exec. v.p., 1966-69, pres., 1970—; pres. Petroleum Recovery Research Inst.; v.p., dir. Alta. Gas Trunk Line. Vice pres., bd. dirs. Calgary Philharmonic Soc., Calgary YMCA; mem. bd. mgmt. Foothills Gen. Hosp. Mem. Assn. Profl. Engrs. Alta. (pres. 1960). Home: 1411 Beverley Pl Calgary 9 Alberta Canada Office: 320 7th Av SW Calgary 2 Alberta Canada

JONES, DAVID JOHN, oil co. exec.; b. Chgo., July 12, 1920; s.Robert Thomas and Florence (Phillips) J.; student London Sch. Econs., 1937-40, Columbia Grad. Sch., 1946; M.B.A., Harvard, 1947. Asst. treas. Esso Export Corp., London, Eng., 1950-52; financial mgr. Esso Standard Societe Anonyme Francaise, Paris, 1953-57; with Standard Oil Co. (N.J.), 1947—, mgr. coordination and planning dept., 1963-65, treas., 1965-70, v.p. finance, 1970—. Served to 1st lt. AUS, 1942- 45. Decorated Legion of Merit; Croix de Guerre, (France); Valore Militare (Italy). Mem. Am. Petroleum Inst., Am. Econ. Assn., Council Fgn. Relations, Am. Acad. Polit. Sci. Home: 14 Sutton Pl S New York City NY 10022 Office: 30 Rockefeller Plaza New York City NY 10020

JONES, DEAN CARROLL, actor; b. Morgan City, Ala., Jan. 25, 1935; s. Andrew Guy and Nolia Elizabeth (Wilhite) J.; student Asbury Coll., U. Cal. at Los Angeles, 1957; m. Mae Inez Entwisle, Jan. 1, 1954 (div.); children—Carol Elizabeth, Deanna Mae. Blues singer, New Orleans; actor films including Handle With Care, That Darn Cat; actor TV series Ensign O'Toole, What's It All About, World?; appeared Broadway plays Under the Yum-Yum Tree, Company; recording artist. Mem. Acad. Motion Picture Arts and Scis., Acad. TV Arts and Scis., Acad. Recording Arts and Scis. Address: care Walt Disney Prodns 500 S Buena Vista Burbank CA 91503

JONES, DEXTER, (Charles Dexter Weatherbee Jones III), Sculptor; b. Haverford, Pa., Dec. 17 1926; s. Charles Dexter Weatherbee and Edna (Shadle) J.; student Pa. Acad. Fine Arts, 1947-49, (scholar) Charles Rudy and Walker Hancock, 1951-52; student, asst. Jo Davidson, 1948-50, Paul Manship, 1950-52; student museums Europe, 1955- 57, Accademia de de Belle Arti, Florence, Italy, 1955-56; 1 child, Pagan J. Exhbns. include N.A.D. anns., 1950-51, 58-60, 67-68, Nat. Sculpture Soc. anns., 1959-62, Phila. Mus. Art, 1959, 62, 64, Smithsonian Instn., 1968, Carnegie Hall, 1961, Nat. Arts Club, 1961, 63- 65, Phila. Art Alliance, 1951, 58, 62, 64-65, Corning Glass Works, 1964, Allied Artists Am. anns., 1959-63,

65-66, A.I.A., Phila., 1962-64, 66, Pa. Soc. Architects, 1962-63, 65, 67, N.J. Soc. Architects, 1966-67, Archtl. League N.Y., 1959-62, 64-67, N.Y. State Assn. Architects, 1967; represented inpermanent collections N.A.D., Pa. Acad. Fine Arts, Woodmere Gallery, Germantown, Pa., Omaha Airport, Moravian Coll., Bethlehem, Pa., Bradford Nat. Bank (Pa.), St. Paul's Luth. Ch., Warren, O., Wittenberg U., Springfield, O., Nat. Presbyn Ch., Washington, Child and Youth Center Phila. Psychiat. Hosp., Phila. Zoo, Municipal Services Bldg., Pa. Hosp., John H. Webster Pub. Sch., Fire Sta., Independence Mall (all Phila.); executed numerous portrait medals, busts. Recipient John Harbeson prize Pa. Acad. Fine Arts, 1950; Mrs. Louis Bennett prize 43d Nat. Sculpture Soc. Ann. Bas-Relief Exhbn., 1959; Daniel Chester French prize Allied Artists Am., 1959; Lindsay Morris award, 1962; Helen Foster Barnett prize N.A.D., 1960; Silver medal 19th Ann. DaVinci Alliance Exhbn., 1960; John Gregory award Nat. Sculpture Soc., 1961; award for excellence Art. Dirs. Club Phila., 1966. Fellow Nat. Sculpture Soc., Pa. Acad. Fine Arts (bd. mgrs. 1953-55); mem. Allied Artists Am, Nat. Arts Club, craft asso. A.I.A. Home: 2124 Lombard St Philadelphia PA 19146 Office: 1611 Sansom St Philadelphia PA 19103

JONES, DON ARDEN, govt. ofcl.; b. Waldron, Mich., Sept. 16, 1912; s. Willard M. and Jessie L. (Weaver) J.; B.S., Mich. State U., 1933; grad. Armed Forces Staff Coll., Norfolk, Va., 1956; m. Frances Dean Lutz, Nov. 7, 1964; children—Alicia E., Radford W., Donna L. Franz. Civil Service employee U.S. Coast and Geodetic Survey, Washington, Balt., 1933-39; apptd. commd. officer, 1940, advanced through grades to rear adm., 1967; shipboard assignments include comdg. officer Ship SOSBEE, 1946-47; officer-in-charge North party, Arctic field party, 1947-51; chief of party conducting triangulation surveys Eastern U.S. and Bahama Islands, also comdg. officer wire-drag vessels East Coast U.S., 1951-57; chief Geodetic Control Project, Blue Nile River Basin, Ethiopia, 1957-61; asst. chief Geodesy div. Washington Office, 1961-63; exec. and comdg. officer Ocean Survey Ship Surveyor conducting extensive oceanographic surveys Pacific Ocean, 1963-65; asso. dir. Office Hydrography and Oceanography, Rockville, Md., 1966; asso. adminstr. Environmental Sci. Services Adminstrn., 1967-68; dir. Coast and Geodetic Survey, 1968-70; acting dir. Nat. Ocean Survey, 1970, dir., 1971—. Served with OSS, AUS, 1942-45. Recipient Exceptional Service award U.S. Dept. Commerce, 1962. Mem. Soc. Am. Mil. Engrs., Am. Congress on Surveying and Mapping, Marine Tech. Soc., Am. Shore and Beach Preservation Assn., U.S. Power Squadrons. Mason (32, Shriner), Elk. Home: 6716 Sulky Lane Rockville MD 20852 Office: 6001 Executive Blvd Rockville MD 20852

JONES, DONALD EDWARD, advt. exec.; b. Jamestown, N.Y., June 2, 1922; s. Albin Ernest and Anna (Anderson) J.; student Mass. Inst. Tech., 1943-44; B.S., U. Mich., 1948; m. Marilyn Ahlstrom, June 26, 1948; children—Jeffrey, Barbara, Cynthia, Kathleen. Bus. mgr. Rogers Pub. Co., Detroit, 1948-54; with MacManus, John & Adams, Inc., Bloomfield Hills, Mich., 1954—, v.p., mgr., Los Angeles, 1958-64, exec. v.p., mgr. N.Y. office, 1964-69, exec. v.p. central operations, 1969—, dir., 1964—; exec. v.p., dir. D'Arcy-MacManus-Intermarco, Inc. Served with Signal Corps, AUS, 1943-46. Home: 124 Dunning Rd New Canaan CT 06840 Office: 10 W Long Lake Rd Bloomfield Hills MI 48013

JONES, DONALD PRENTISS, oil co. exec.; b. Providence, July 25, 1908; s. Arthur Julius and Ethel Louise (Rounds) J.; A. R., Grinnell Coll., 1930; M.B.A., Harvard, 1932; m. Ethel Grace Turner, Jan 13, 1934; children—Arthur W., D. Elizabeth, Lawrence T. With Sun Oil Co., 1932—, successively auditor, mgr. gen. accounting dept., asst. comptroller, 1932-47, comptroller, dir., 1947-68, v.p., dir., 1968-70, sr. v.p., dir., 1970—. Pres. sch. bd., Swarthmore, 1953-61; trustee, pres. Financial Execs. Research Found.; past pres. Delaware County unit Am. Cancer Soc., treas., chmn. finance com. Pa. div. Chmn. bd. trustees Community Coll. Delaware County; pres. bd. mgrs. Taylor Hosp. Mem. Am. Petroleum Inst., (gen. vice chmn. 1952, gen. chmn. financial and accounting com. 1953, v.p. div. finance and accounting 1963- 64), Financial Execs. Inst. (pres. Phila. control 1954-55. nat. v.p. 1957-58, 59-60, nat. bd. dirs., 1955-58, 69—). Newcomen Soc. Phila. C. of C., Phi Beta Kappa. Presby. (elder) Club: Union League (Phila.). Home: 120 Mansion Dr Rose Tree Media PA 19063 Office: 1608 Walnut St Philadelphia PA 19103

JONES, DONALD WAYNE, publisher; b. LaCrosse, Wis., Sept. 25, 1922; s. Lester Martin and Nelle (Roach) J.; A.B., DePauw U., 1943; m. Barbara Causey, Sept. 2, 1950; children—Donald Wayne, Nona Lane, Clayton. Sci. editor Prentice-Hall, Inc., 1946-56; editor-in-chief Allyn & Bacon, Inc., 1956-58; pres. Addison-Wesley Pub. Co., Reading, Mass., 1958—; dir. Ealing Corp. Vice pres. Am. Ednl. Pubs. Inst., 1967-69. Served with USAF, 1943-46. Mem. Woods Hole Oceanographic Inst. (asso.), Assn. Am. Pubs., Sierra Club, Sigma Chi. Club: Woods Hole (Mass.) Golf. Home: 90 Sears Rd Wayland MA 01778 Office: Addison Wesley Pub Co Reading MA 01867

JONES, DOROTHY MAY, lawyer, assn. ofcl.; b. North Little Rock, Ark., June 26, 1917; d. Elet Sidney and Jeannette Viola (Armstrong) May; LL.B., Ark Law Sch., 1938; m. Edmund N. Orsini, July 31, 1935 (div. 1966); children—Edmund N., David, Merrily Ann; m. 2d. Joseph P. Jones, Jr., Sept. 24, 1966. Admitted to Ark. bar, 1938; practice of law with H.B. Stubblefield, Little Rock, 1945-54; exec. dir. Ark. Bar Assn., 1954-66; bus. mgr. Women Lawyers Jour., 1958-59. Mem. Nat. Assn. Women Lawyers (corr. sec. 1959-60, treas. 1960-61, v.p. 1961-62, pres. 1962-63, past state del., regional dir., mem. bd., editor Women Lawyers Jour., 1968-69), Little Rock Assn. Women Lawyers (past pres.), Jefferson County Women Lawyers Assn. Phi Delta Delta. Home: 800 S 4th St Louisville KY 40203

JONES, DOUGLAS EPPS, educator, geologist; b. Tuscaloosa, Ala., May 28, 1930; s. Walter Bryan and Hazel (Phelps) J.; B.S., U. Ala., 1952; Ph.D., La. State U., 1959; m. Bonnie Ann Cook, June 4, 1955; children—Susan Lucile, Elizabeth Tannahill, Walter Bryan II. Research geologist La. Geol. Survey, 1955- 58; mem. faculty U. Ala., 1958—, prof. geology, head dept. geology and geography, 1966-68, asst. dean Coll. Arts and Scis., 1967-68, interim dean, 1968-69, dean, 1969—. Served with AUS, 1952-54. Mem. Am. Assn. Petroleum Geologists, Geol. Soc. Am., Am. Inst. Profl. Geologists, Sigma Xi. Contbr. articles on gulf coastal plain paleontology and stratigraphy. Home: 23 High Forest St Tuscaloosa AL 35401 Office: PO Box 2926 University AL 35486

JONES, ED, congressman; b. Yorkville, Tenn., Apr. 20, 1912; s. William Frank and Hortense (Pipkin) J.; B.S., U. Tenn., 1934; student U. Wis., 1944, U. Mo., 1945; m. Mary Llewellyn Wyatt, June 9, 1938; children-Mary Llew (Mrs. Robert S. McGuire), Jennifer Wilson. With Tenn. Dept. Agr., 1934- 41, Tenn. Dairy Products Assn., 1941-43; agrl. agt. Ill. Central R.R., 1943-49, 52-59; Tenn. commnr. agr., 1949-52; mem. 91st Congress 8th dist. Tenn. Dir. Nat. Telephone Coop. Assn., 1965—; chmn. Tenn. Agrl. Stblzn. Conservation Commn., 1952-69. Trustee Bethel Coll., McKenzie, Tenn. Named Man of Year, Progressive Farmer mag., 1951, Memphis Agrl. Club, 1957; recipient Distinguished Dairy Service award U. Tenn. Dairy Club 1966. Mem. Alpha Gamma Rho. Democrat. Presbyn. Mason (Shriner), Elk. Home: G Yorkville TN 38389 Office: House Office Bldg Washington DC 20515

JONES, EDGAR ALLAN, Jr., educator, arbitrator, lawyer, television performer; b. Bklyn., Jan. 8, 1921; s. Edgar Allan and Isabel (Morris) J.: B.A., Wesleyan U., 1942; LL.B., U. Va., 1950; m. Helen Callaghan, Sept. 15, 1945; children—Linda Marie, Anne Marie, Carol Marie, Edgar Allan III, Denis James, Robert Morris, David Llewellyn, Therese Marie, Catherine Marie, Nancy Marie, Daniel Anthony. Admitted to Va. bar, 1948; faculty U. Cal. at Los Angeles Law Sch., 1951—, prof. law, 1958—, asst. dean, 1957-58, dir. Law-Sci. Research Center, 1963-66; labor dispute arbitrator, mediator, fact finder for pvt. and pub. employers and unions, 1953—, appeared as judge network TV programs Accused, 1958-59, Traffic Court 1958-61, Day in Court, 1958-64; moderator ednl. TV program Forum West, 1966. Pres. Creddalt Research, Inc., 1959—: dir. Capital for Tech. Industries, Inc., 1962-66. Pub. mem. Cal. Commn. Manpower Automation and Tech., 1963-67, cal. Manpower Adv. Com., 1964-67; nat. enforcement commr. WSB, 1951. Sec. Californians for Kennedy, 1960. Served to 1st lt. USMCR, 1942-45. Mem. Nat. Acad. Arbitrators (bd. govs. 1966-68, chmn. law and legislative com., 1965-7O, v.p. 197O-71), Am. Bar Assn., Am. Law Inst., Va. State Bar, A.F.T.R.A. Author: (with Charles O. Gregory) Labor and the Law, 3d edit., 1971; also numerous articles. Editor: Law and Electronics: The Challenge of a New Era, 1960. Office: 405 Hilgard Av Los Angeles CA 90024

JONES, EDGAR WAGSTAFF, lawyer; b. Bellevue, Ky., Mar. 6, 1908; s. Harry Ross and Madeline (Pocock) J.; grad. Phillips Exeter Acad., 1925; A.B., Yale, 1929; LL.B., Harvard, 1932; m. Christine Oby, Aug. 24, 1929; children—Anne- Christine (Mrs. Thomas S. Jenkins), Edgar Wagstaff. Admitted to Ohio bar, 1933; practice in Canton, 1933—; partner firm Amerman, Burt, Shadrach, McHenry & Jones, and predecessors, 1940—. Dir. Canton Nat. Bank, Union Metal Mfg. Co., Canton Hardware Co., Olympic Plating Industries, Inc., Adamson- Alliance Co., Ltd., Maritime Products Inc. Pres. Aultman Hosp. Assn., 1943-45, 47-50, trustee, 1938—; pres., trustee Hosp. Service (Blue Cross), 1938—; gen. chmn. Canton United Fund campaign, 1943, 47. mem. A.R.C. campaign, 1943, Hosp. Bldg. Fund campaign, 1950; pres. Canton Welfare Fedn., 1946-53. Served with USNR, 1943-46; ETO. Mem. Am., Ohio, Stark County bar assns., Internat. Assn. Ins. Counsel, Alpha Chi Rho. Episcopalian. Clubs: Canton, Brookside Country (Canton; Toledo Yacht; Great Lakes Cruising; Catawba Island. Home: 3443 Parkridge Circle NW Canton OH 44718 Office: Peoples Merchants Trust Bldg Canton OH 44702

JONES, EDITH AUGUSTA, dietitian; b. Muscle Shoals, Ala.; d. Leonidas and Ora (Phillips) Jones; B.S., U. Ala., 1941; M.S., U. Tenn., 1949. Dietetic intern Johns Hopkins Hosp., 1941-42, staff dietitian, 1942-43, dir. student curriculum Sch. Dietetics, 1946-49; nutritionist Bur. State Services, USPHS, 1950-51, dietitian cons. hosp. facilities div. Bur. Med. Service, 1951-52; chief, Nutrition dept. Clin. Center, NIH, Bethesda, Md., 1952—. Chnm., Internat. Com. Dietetic Assns., 1965-69; gen. chmn. 5th Internat. Congress Dietetics, 1969. Recipient Distinguished Service award U. Ala, 1956; McLester award Assn. Mil. Surgeons U.S., 1957; Meritorious Achievement award USPHS, 1971. Fellow Am. Pub. Heath Assn.; mem. Am. (pres 1962-63), D.C. (rep. ho. dels. Am. assn.) dietetic assns., Am. Home Econs. Assn., Mortar Bd., Alpha Chi Omega (award achievement 1962), Phi Kappa Phi, Phi Upsilon Omicron, Alpha Lambda Delta, Omicron Nu. Contbr. articles in field. Address: 4977 Battery Lane Bethesda MD 20014

JONES, EDMUND LYDDANE, lawyer; b. Rockville, Md., Feb. 6, 1894; s. Charles Benedict and Lavinia (Lyddane) J.; LL.B., Georgetown U., 1916; m. Bettina Evans Prescott, Nov. 17, 1917 (dec. Oct. 1967); children—Bettina (Mrs. John Curtis), Edith Kellogg (Mrs. Edward Picken), Edmund Lyddane; m. 2d, Bessie Lewis, Sept. 14, 1968. Admitted to D.C. bar, 1916; practice law, Washington, 1916—; mem. firm Hogan & Hartson, 1938—. Chmn. com. admissions and grievances U.S. District Ct. for D.C. Served from 2d lt. to 1st lt., U.S. Army, 1917-18, AEF. Fellow Am. Coll. Trial Lawyers; mem. Am. Bar Assn., Bar Assn. D.C., Delta Theta Phi. Clubs: Lawyers, Metropolitan, Barristers, Burning Tree, Chevy Chase (Washington). Home: 3006 45th St Washington DC 20016 Office: 815 Connecticut Av Washington DC 20006

JONES, EDMUND RUFFIN, Jr., zoologist, educator; b. Charlottesville, Va., Oct. 1, 1905; s. Rev. Edmund Ruffin and Jane Bell (Dabney) J.; B.A., U. Va., 1927, B.S., 1927, M.A., 1928, Ph.D., 1930; m. Helen Purdum Bell, June 11, 1936; children—Helen Bell (Mrs. William Edward Kerby), Frances Dabney (Mrs. Donald Moore Giles). Lectr. biology Dalhousie U., Halifax, N.S., 1930- 31; asso. prof. Norfolk Div. of Coll. of William and Mary, 1931-37, prof., 1937-46, chmn. div. natural sci., 1940-46, chmn. faculty, 1941- 42, dir. summer session, 1941-44, dir. evening coll. and adult edu., 1942-44; instr. Mt. Lake Biol. Station, 1935, 45, 46, 50, 56, also acting dir., 1945; asso. prof. U. Fla., Gainesville, 1946-47, prof., 1947—, dir. pre-prof. counseling, 1958-69, asst. dean Grad. Sch., 1961-64, asst. dean arts and scis., 1964-70; instr. zoology Marine Biol. Lab., Woods Hole, Mass., 1940, 41; cons. USPHS, 1940-42. Dir. Civilian Def. Tng. Schs. for Norfolk, Va., 1942-44; treas. for Eastern Va. of Young Am. Wants to Help (div. Brit. War Relief Soc.), 1940-42; treas. United Community Fund, Gainesville, 1959-62. Fellow A.A.A.S. (pres. acad. conf. 1962); mem. Am. Soc. Zoologists, Assn. Southeastern Biologists (pres. 1963- 64), Soc. Systematic Zoology, Nat. Inst. Dental Research (tng. com. 1962-66, chmn. 1966-67, Am. Microscopic Soc., Corp of Marine Biol. Lab., Assn. U. Profs., Va., Fla. (pres. 1959) acads. sci., Townsmen's Soc. of Norfolk (past pres.), Phi Beta Kappa, Sigma Xi, Phi Sigma, Phi Delta Theta. Democrat. Episcopalian. Rotarian. Contbr. articles to sci. and tech. publs. Home: Gale Hill Route 3 Box 200 B-1 Gainesville FL 32601

JONES, EDWARD COLE, meat packing co. exec.; b. Fort Atkinson, Wis., May 10, 1902 s. Edward C. and Charlotte W. (Brown) J.; student Dartmouth, 1920-22, U. Wis., 1922-24; m. Helen E. Schlosser, Jan 23, 1926: childrenFrances Cole (Mrs. F.J. Paddock), Deborah Wells (Mrs. Malcolm Donaldson), Edward Cole. With Jones Dairy Farm, Ft. Atkinson, 1922—, pres., 1966—. Bd. dirs. Am. Meat Inst., 1948—, treas., 1964-68, chmn. bd., 1968—, recipient Community Relations award, 1958; pres. Wis. Live Stock and Meat Council, 1963—. Mem. Gov. Wis. Council Econ. Devel., 1965—. Pres. bd. trustees Ft. Atkinson Meml. Hosp., 1943-. Recipient award outstanding service and leadership Wis. Live Stock Breeders Assn., 1964; hon. recognition U. Wis., 1967; award distinguished community service Ft. Atkinson Lions Club, 1968; recognition and appreciation award, Wis. Live Stock and Meat Council, 1969. Mem. N.A.M. (past bd. dirs.), Wis. Mfrs. Assn. (past bd. dirs.; recognition outstanding service to Am. bus. 1969), Def. Orientation Conf. Assn. (bd. dirs.), Sigma Chi. Republican. Episcopalian. Clubs: University (Milw.); Chicago, Union League (Chgo.); Rolling Rock (Ligonier, Pa.); Capitol Hill (Washington); Lake Zurich (Ill.) Golf. Home: 424 W Milwaukee Av Fort Atkinson WI 53538 Office: PO Box 25 Fort Atkinson WI 53538

JONES, EDWARD D., bus. exec. Pres., dir. Griesedieck Co., mem. Edw. D. Jones & Co.; dir. Carthage (Mo.) Marble Corp., Hydraulic Press Brick Co., Securities Investment Co., St. Louis, Brewers Yeast Corp., Key Co., East St. Louis, Ill., Mid West Wax Paper Co.; sec., dir. Champion Shoe Machinery Co., St. Louis. Mem. Chicago Bd. of Trade, Stock Exchange. Home: 6349 Ellenwood Av Clayton MO 63105 Office: Edward D Jones & Co 4th & Olive St St Louis IL 63102*

JONES, EDWARD FAUCETT, assn. exec.; b. Lawrenceburg, Tenn., Mar. 10, 1924; s. Osceola Gordon and Zana Dee (Benson) J.; student Washington and Lee U., 1942-43; m. Wanda Smith Tindall, Jan. 8, 1960. Staff dir. Congl. Traffic Safety Com., 1959-63; press sec. to Tenn. gov. Frank G. Clement, 1963-67; exec. v.p. Nashville Area C. of C., 1967—. Bd. dirs. Chet Atkins Guitar Found. Served to 1st lt. USAAF, World War II; ETO. Decorated Air medal with 4 oak leaf clusters. Mem. Pub. Relations Soc. Am., Am. Assn. C. of C. Execs., Am. Legion. Democrat. Kiwanian. Club: Nashville City. Home: 118 Keyway Dr Nashville TN 37205 Office: 161 4th Av N Nashville TN 37219

JONES, EDWARD LOGAN, food co. exec.; b. Montreal, Que., Can., May 27, 1914; s. Edward David and Pearl (Logan) J.; B. Commerce, McGill U., 1936; chartered accountant, 1944; M.B.A., N.Y. U., 1945; m. Ruth Dorothy Burns, Oct. 24, 1942; children—Susan Ruth (Mrs. John Yu), Raun Elizabeth, Edward David, Reed Catherine, Kim Larraine. Auditor, P.S. Ross & Sons, chartered accountants, 1936-40; finance officer Brit. Ministry of Supply Mission, 1941-46; v.p., sec-treas. George Weston Ltd., 1947-67; sr. v.p., sec- treas. Loblaw Co., Ltd., 1968—, also dir.; dir. Loblaw Groceries Co. Ltd., G. Tamblyn Ltd., Nat. Tea Co., Loblaw Inc. Mem. Financial Execs. Inst., Am. Mgmt. Assn., Phi Kappa Pi. Clubs: National, Toronto, St. Georges Golf and Country, Boulevard, Empire (Toronto). Home: 17 Whitney Av Toronto Ontario Canada Office: 545 Lakeshore Blvd W Toronto Ontario Canada

JONES, EDWARD MAGRUDER, TV producer-writer, corr.; b. Orlando, Fal., Feb. 25, 1928; s. Peter Brown and Edna Marguerite (Moor) J.; student U. Minn., 1945-46, N.Y. U., 1947-49, 52-53; m. Margaret Ann Sutherland, June 29, 1957; children—Victoria Leigh, Tracy St. Clair, Robert Sutherland. Copy-boy, N.Y. Times, 1947- 48; freelance writer, 1949-50; from mail boy to producer CBS, 1952-62, prodns. including See It Now, Small World, CBS Reports; producer news and pub. affairs WABC-TV, 1963-66, prodns. including The Big News, Page One, New York, New York, also specials; producer-writer-dir., ABC News, 1966-67, "Africa,", "Nurses: Crisis in Medicine", Westinghouse Broadcasting Co., co-producer, dir. "One Nation, Indivisible", 1968; producer, writer, director "Night Call" for Television Radio Film Commn., United Meth. Ch., 1968; producer, writer, editor news and pub. affairs spls. Nat. Ednl. TV, 1969, now producer, writer, corr. news and pub. affairs spls. and series WHYY-TV. Served with the AUS, 1945-47, USAF, 1951. Recipient Brotherhood award Nat. Conf. Christians and Jews, 196l, 1969; award Overseas Press Club, 1962; Freedoms Found. award, 1968, 69; Emmy award, 1964, 66, 1968; Peabody award, 1968, 1969; Albert J. Lasker Med. Journalism award, 1966; TV Pub. Service award, Sigma Delta Chi, 1966. Home: Riverside Marina Riverside NJ Office: 4548 Market St Philadelphia PA 19139

JONES, EDWARD MARSHALL, automotive parts distbg. co. exec.; b. Decatur, Ga., Feb. 3, 1926; S. Henry L. and Stella (Moessner) J.; student Ga. Inst. Tech., 1946-48, Ga. State Coll., 1948-49; m. Shirlie McCleary, June 13, 1947; children—Glenn Steven, Gary Lynn, Michael Alan. With Genuine Parts Co., Atlanta and Jacksonville, Fla., 1947—, asst. to pres., 1961-65, treas., 1965—, v. p. operations, 1967—. Active local Community Chest, United Appeal. Served with USAAF, 1944-45. Lutheran (council). Club: Atlanta Optimist. Home: 6175 Old Hickory Point NW Atlanta GA 30328 Office: 299 Piedmont Av Atlanta GA 30312

JONES, EDWARD NEWLON, educator; b. Downs, Kan., Apr. 15, 1899; s. Charles Dudley and Florence (Newlon) J.; B.S., Ottawa U., Kan., 1921; Ph.D., U. Ia., 1925; LL.D., Ottawa U., 1940; LL.D., Baylor U., 1961; m. Ruth Scharl Bowerman, June 12, 1923 (dec. Aug. 31, 1927); l son, Robert Bowerman; m. 2d, Florence George Maulsby, May 31, 1930 (dec. Dec. 20, 195O); children—Florence Elaine, Allen Maulsby; m. 3d, Fannie Woodson Wheat, June 8, 1952. Fellow in botany, U. of Ia., 1924-25; prof. botany and chmn. dept., Baylor U., 1925-32, prof. biology and chmn. dept., 1932-42, dean Coll. Arts and Scis., 1935-39, dean univ., 1939-42; pres. Tex. Coll. of Arts and Industries, 1942-48; v.p. Tex. Tech. Coll., 1948-52, pres., 1952-59; dean instrn. Midwestern U., 1959-60; sec. Christian edn. commn. Bapt. Gen. Conv. Tex., Dallas, 1960-67; adminstrv. asso. Dallas Bapt. Coll., 1968—; mem. edn. commn. So. Bapt. Conv., 1961-67; interim pres. U. Corpus Christi, 1965-66. Trustee Bishop Coll., Ottawa U.; regent Midwestern U., 1962—, chmn. bd. regents, 1968—. Pres., State Bapt. Young Peoples Union of Kan., 1919; head ranger nat. Ednl. Div., Yellowstone Nat. Park, summers 1928-30; mem. Gov.'s Bi-Racial Commn., 1946; edn. com. Bapt. Gen. Conv. of Tex., 1953-60; Fellow A.A.A.S., Tex. Acad. Sci. (past pres.); mem. Assn. Tex. Colls. (pres. 1936-37; mem. com. on standards, 1938-43); S. Assn. of Colls. and Secondary Schs. (mem. commn. on colls. and univs. 1957-60), Tex. Council of Church-Related Coll. (organizer and 1st chmn., 1937-38); Sigma Xi, Gamma Alpha, Tri Beta, Pi Kappa Delta, Phi Kappa Phi. Democrat. Baptist. Rotarian (past pres.). Contbr. to mags.; lecturer. Home: 9009 Villa Park Circle Dallas TX 75225

JONES, EDWIN CHANNING, retired engring. educator; b. Smithburg, W.Va., July 20, 1903; s. Edwin Camden and Georgia (Smith) J.; B.S., W. Va. U., 1925; M.S., U. Ill., 1929; m. Helen Sterrett, July 27, 1929 (dec. 1959); children—Edwin Channing, Harriet C.; m. 2d, Ruth Knoch, July 2, 1961. Grad. asst. elec. engring. dept., W.Va. U., 1925-26, instr. elec. engring. dept., 1926-35, asst. prof. 1935-41, asso. prof., 1941-47, prof., 1947-70, head elec. engring. dept., 1948-60, chmn., 1960-69, elec. engr., Engring. Expt. Sta., 1948-70, ret., 1970; with Gen. Elec. Co., summers 1930, 40, 41. Registered profl. engr., W.Va. Fellow I.E.E.E.; mem. Am. Soc. Engring. Edn., Nat. Soc. Profl. Engrs., Tau Beta Pi, Eta Kappa Nu, Pi Kappa Phi. Methodist. Mason (Shriner), Rotarian (pres. 1950-51) Home: 1380 Western Av Morgantown WV 26505

JONES, EDWIN DONATUS, Jr., lawyer; b. Washington, Sept. 19, 1919; s. Edwin Donatus and Kathryn (Sullivan) J.; A.B., Stanford, 1941, LL.B., 1950; m. Ann Ellen Harris, Feb. 17, 1945; children—Susan, Laura, Andrew, Sarah. Admitted to Cal. bar, 1950; with firm Betts, Ely & Loomis, Los Angeles, 1950-53; partner firm Hoge, Fenton, Jones & Appel, San Jose, 1953—. Legal adviser Jr. League San Jose; past v.p., bd. dirs. Family Service Assn., San Jose. Trustee San Jose Unified Sch. Dist.; bd. dirs. Goodwill Industries Santa Clara County. Served to lt. comdr. USNR, World War II. Fellow Am. Coll. Trial Lawyers; mem. Am., Cal., Santa Clara County (trustee), Monterey County bar assns., Am., Santa Clara County (past pres.) trial lawyers assns., Assn. Def. Counsel, Internat. Assn. Ins. Counsel, Am. Judicature Soc., Def. Research Assn., R.R. Trial Counsel, Am. Arbitration Assn. (nat. panel). Episcopalian (past sr. warden). Rotarian. Clubs: San Jose Country, Sainte Claire (San Jose). Home: 1942 University Av San Jose CA 95126 Office: 28 N 1st St San Jose CA 95113

JONES, EDWIN LEE, Jr., constrn. co. exec.; b. Charlotte, N.C., May 6, 1921; s. Edwin Lee and Annabel (Lambeth) J.; student U.S. Mil. Acad., 1940-41; B.S. in Civil Engrng., Duke, 1948; m. Lucille Finch, Oct. 16, 1943; children—Edwin Lee III, Annabel Lambeth (Mrs. Henry W. Link), Sam Finch, John Wesley, David Gilchrist. With J.A. Jones Constrn. Co., Charlotte, N.C., 1948—; pres., 1960-71, pres., chief exec. officer, 1971—; dir. Charlotte br. First Union Nat. Bank, William L. Crow Constrn. Co., Charles H. Tompkins Co. Charlotte met. chmn. Nat. Alliance Businessmen, 1969—. Mem. Gen. Bd. Evangelism; bd. dirs. United Community Services, Constrn. Edn. Found. N.C.; mem. capital funds bd. Charlotte YMCA; trustee Scarritt Coll., Am. U., Duke, Lake Junaluske, Super Annotated Endowment Fund, Found. Evangelism; J.A. Jones Constrn. Co. Found. Mem. Assn. Gen. Contractors (bd. dirs. 1969- 72, mem. exec. com. 1965-67, chmn. heavy duty div. 1966-67), Cons. Constructors Council Am., Beavers, Moles, Chi Epsilon, Omicron Delta Kappa, Pi Mu Epsilon, Pi Kappa Phi. Kiwanian. Home: 3715 Pomfret Lane Charlotte NC 28211 Office: 521 E Morehead St Charlotte NC 28201

JONES, EDWIN S., banker; b. St. Louis, Dec. 16, 1915; s. C. Norman and Josephine (Calhoun) J.; student Yale, 1934-36, U. Wis., 1948; m. Hope DePew, Nov. 3O, 1946; children—Stephen C., Douglas D., Hope F. With Ely & Walker, Inc., St. Louis, 1936-41; with 1st Nat. Bank St. Louis, 1946—, exec. v.p., 1960-68, pres. 1968-70, chmn. bd., 1970—, also dir.; dir. Gen Steel Industries, Pet, Inc., Interco, Gen. Am. Life Ins. Co., Alton Box Co., Interco, Inc., McDonnell-Douglas Corp., Vico Corp.; pres., chief operating officer First Union, Inc. Trustee Washington U., St. Louis, St. Louis Council Boy Scouts Am., St. Louis YMCA, St. Louis Jr. Achievement; bd. dirs. Barnard Skin and Cancer Hosp., St. Louis. Served to capt. USAAF, 1941-46. Decorated D.F.C., Air medal. Mem. Res. City Bankers Assn., St. Louis C. of C. (dir.). Clubs: St. Louis, Noonday, St. Louis Country, Log Cabin, Racquet (St. Louis). Home: 765 Cella Rd St Louis MO 63124 Office: 510 Locust St St Louis MO 63101

JONES, EIDDON LLOYD, banker; b. Utica, N.Y., Oct. 25, 1904; s. David and Jane (Lloyd) J.; student pub. schs., Utica; m. Ruth A Davies, Apr. 23, 1932 (dec. Apr. 1964); 1 son, Robert E; m. 2d, Alice Liddy, Aug. 30, 1965. With Marine Midland Trust Co. of Mohawk Valley (formerly 1st Bank and Trust Co.), Utica, 1923—, v.p., 1950-62, exec. v.p., 1962-64, pres., chmn. bd., 1964-68, chmn. bd., chief exec. officer, 1968-69, also dir. until 1971, now mem. adv. com.; exec. council Marine Midland Bank, 1964-69; asst. sec., adminstr. shopping centers Cole Devel. Corp., 1971—. Asst. treas. Greater Utica Community Chest, 1955, treas., 1956, campaign mgr., 1957—, pres., 1959- -; chmn. Utica Cerebral Palsy and Handicappped Children's Assn., 1950—; campaign chmn. United Fund Campaign, 1957. Mem. planning bd. City of Utica, 1950—. Trustee St. Luke's Meml. Hosp. Mem. N.Y. State Bankers Assn. (chmn group IV, 1955-56), Greater Utica C. of C. (pres. 1967-69). Home: 143 Eastwood Av Utica NY 13501 Office: 520 Seneca St Utica NY 13502

JONES, ELI STANLEY, missionary; b. Balt., Jan. 1, 1884; s. Albin Davis and Sarah Alice (Peddicord) J.; A.B., Asbury Coll., 1906, A.M., 1912; D.D., Duke U., 1928; S.T.D., Syracuse U., 1928; m. Mabel Lossing, Feb. 11, 1911; 1 dau., Eunice Treffry (Mrs. J.K. Mathews). Evangelist to high castes of India, 1907—; elected bishop M.E. Ch., 1928, resigned to continue missionary work; founder two Christian Ashrams at Sat Tal and Lucknow, India, a Psychiatric Center at Lucknow, also active Christian Ashram Movement U.S. and Europe. Chmn. Assn. for United Ch. Am. Author: The Way, 1948; Mahatma Gandhi; An Interpretation, 1948; The Way to Power and Poise, 1950; How to be a Transformed Person, 1951; The Word Became Flesh, 1966; Victory Through Surrender, 1967; A Song of Ascents, 1968; also numerous others. Contbr. articles Christian Herald Christian Advocate. Address: care Methodist Div World Missions 475 Riverside Dr New York City NY 10027

JONES, ELIZABETH ORTON, artist, author; b. Highland Park, Ill., June 25, 1910; d. George Roberts and Jessie (Orton) Jones; student Highland Hall, Hollidaysburg, Pa.; grad. House in the Pines, Norton, Mass., 1929; Ph.B., U. Chgo. 1932; diploma Ecole des Beaux Arts, France, 1932; student Art Inst. Chgo., 1932; M.A. (hon.) Wheaton Coll., 1955. Artist, author, illustrator, exhibited O'Brien Galleries (Chgo.), Smithsonian Inst., and other galleries; murals, Crotched Mountain Center, Greenfield, N.H., U. N.H. Library. Recipient Charles Muller prize Chicago Soc. Etchers, 1939, Caldecott Medal for illustrations for Prayer for a Child, 1944. Mem. Delta Kappa Gamma (hon.). Illustrator. a variety of pubs., including A Prayer for Little Things, by Eleanor Farjeon, 1945; Secrets, 1945; A Little Child, 1946, by Jessie Orton Jones. Author and illustrator; Song of the Sun, by St. Francis of Assisi. Author: books, latest ones being; Little Red Riding Hood (A Little Golden Book), 1947; Big Susan, 1947; This is the Way, 1951; How Far Is it to Bethlehem, Ragman of Paris, Minnie the Mermaid, Maminka's Children, Twig. Author, editor: Mason, N.H. 1768-1968. Editor: Song of the Sun. Address: Mason NH 03244 ☆

JONES, ELMER ALONZO, orgn. exec.; Mpls., Aug. 11, 1902; s. Irvin P. and Christine (Gordon) J.; E.M., U. Minn., 1924; m. Celeste Stanley Phillips, Jan. 15, 1926; children—Stanley Gordon, James Irvin, John Thomas, Celeste Phillips. Engr. Minn. Hwy. Dept., 1924-25; mining engr. Ducktown Sulfur Copper & Iron Ltd., Copperhill, Tenn., 1925-26; with St. Joseph Lead Co., 1926-67, mgr. S.E. Mo. mining and milling div., 1953-67, dir.; v.p., mgr., dir. Mo. Clay Products Co., 1967; chmn. Lead-Zinc Producers Com., Washington, 1968—; v.p., dir. Meramec Mining Co.; dir. Mine La Motte Corp., Bonne Terra Farming & Cattle Co., Lead Belt Water Co. Vice pres. St. Louis council Boy Scouts Am.; mem. Bonne Terre Sch. Bd. Bd. dirs. Bonne Terre Hosp. Assn. Recipient Outstanding Achievement award U. Minn., 1960. Mem. Am. Inst. Mining Engrs. (past dir.), Soc. Mining Engrs. (past pres.; Saunders Gold Medal award 1969), Mining and Metall. Soc., Sigma Alpha Epsilon, Theta Tau. Conglist. (bd.). Mason. Home: 27 Stanmore Ct Potomac MD 20854 Office: 1145 19th St NW Washington DC 20036

JONES, ELVIN RAY, drummer; b. Pontiac, Mich., Sept. 9, 1927. Played with bands. Detroit, 1952-56; with Pepper Adams-Donald Byrd quintet, other combos. N.Y.C.; joined John Coltrane Quartet, 1960, Duke Ellington, 1966, then Tony Scott; now free-lance with own group; recording artist for Atlantic, River. Impulse records. Address: 151 W 16th St New York City NY 10011*

JONES, ELWOOD M., Jr., bus. exec.; b. Manila P.I., Mar. 19, 1914; s. Elwood M. and Nami (Jones) J.; ed. U. So. Calif; m. Jarjorie Cameron, June 14, 1936; children—Richard C., Elwood M. III. With Am. Airlines, Jan. 1936-July 1937; became v.p. and gen. sales mgr. Rubberset Co., Newark, N.J., 1937, also of William Peterman, Inc., 1937; now dir. and pres. Rubberset Co. Home: 1 Stanley Oval Westfield NJ 07090 Office: Haves and Lincoln Hwy Newark NJ 07090

JONES, EMILY STRANGE, ednl. cons.; b. Rochester, N.Y., June 24, 1919; d. Leonard Warburton and Helen (Stone) Jones; A.B., Vassar Coll., 1940. Asst. in children's room N.Y. Pub. Library, 1941-43; editorial asst. Trained Nurse mag., 1943-44; film prodn. asst. Emerson Yorke Studio, 1944-46; adminstrv. dir. Ednl. Film Library Assn., Inc., N.Y.C., 1946-69; ednl. film cons., 1969—. Exec. dir. Am. Film Festival 1959-69; treas., bd. dirs. Ednl. Media Council, 1965-68; chmn. bd. dirs. Dance Films, Inc., 1966-69; sec. bd. dirs. Internat. Film Found., 1970—; mem. internat. jury Teheran Festival Films for Children, 1970, mem. adv. com. N.Y. Council on Arts, 1969—. Girl Scout leader, N.Y.C., 1944-49. Mem. Council Scout leader, N.Y.C., 1944-49. Mem. Council Internat. Non-Theatrical Events (dir.). Author: (with Jessie Kitching) Index to Selected Film Lists, 1950; Films and People, 1951; Manual on Film Evaluation, 1968; also articles in mags. Editor; Sightlines Mag., 1966-69; supervising editor Film Evaluation Guide. Address: 72-61 113th St Forest Hills New York City NY 11375

JONES, EMLYN DAVID, educator; b. Seattle, Nov. 27, 1912; s. David and Anna (Gabriel) J.; student Western Wash. Coll., 1930-33; B.A., U. Wash., 1936; M.A., Stanford, 1942, Ph.D., 1954; m. Gertrude Augusta Ey, Aug. 4, 1941; children—Gregory, Monica Ann. Elementary sch. tchr., Selleck and Woodinville, Wash., 1936-39; jr. high sch. tchr., Auburn, Wash., 1939- 41; high sch. tchr., head dept. history, Seattle, 1946-49; dir. social studies Seattle pub. schs., 1949-60; prof. history and edn. U. Wis., 1960-65, chmn. dept. curriculum and instrn.; prof. history, chmn. div. history and social scis. Green River Coll., Auburn, Wash., 1965—; vis. summer instr. Stanford, 1953, U. Me., 1955, 57, Seattle U., 1960, U. Hawaii, 1966, Western Wash., 1965, 68. Editor Civic Edn. Service Publs., 1956-64; cons. editor United World Films, Inc., 1960-64; cons. editor McGraw Hill Text Films, 1964-66, Universal Edn. Films, 1966-70; adviser Hoover Commn., 1949-52, Ednl. Policies Commn., 1956-59. Guest of Japanese Govt. at Diplomatic Centennial, 1960. Served to lt. comdr., USNR, 1942-46. Mem. Nat. (pres.). Wis., Puget Sound (hon. life) councils social studies, N.E.A., Am. Hist. Assn. Co-author: We Live in Washington, 1954; Beyond Our Borders, 1964; Within Our Borders, 1964; Within the Americas, 1967; Our Washington, 1965; Exploring the Northwest, 1969; Beyond the Oceans, 1961; America de Todos, 1968. Home: 31815 W Valley Hwy Auburn WA 98002 Office: Green River Coll Auburn WA 98002

JONES, ERNEST ALBIN, advt. exec.; b. Jamestown. N.Y., June 18, 1915; s. Albin E. and Anna (Anderson) J.; B.A., U. Mich., 1938; m. Marian Wellman, June 28, 1939; children—Ernest Albin III, Christine Wellman, Stephen Wellman, Janet Marian, Mark Gregory. With MacMannus, John & Adams, Inc., Bloomfield Hills, Mich., 1958—, account exec., 1946-51, v.p., 1951-53, exec. v.p., 1953-55; pres., 1955-67, chmn. bd., chief exec. officer, 1967-71; chmn. bd., co-chief exec. officer D'Arcy-MacManus-Intermarco, Inc., 1971—. Chmn. bd. dirs. Birmingham-Bloomfield United Found., 1956; bd. dirs. Detroit Symphony, Mich. C. of C.; trustee Cranbrook Acad. Art, Interlochen Art Acad. Assn. Advt. Agencies (dir., 1955-56, central regional chmn., 1955-56, com. advt. relations 1956-57); Nat. Outdoor Advt. Bur. (dir. 1955-56). Clubs. University, Fifth Av. (N.Y.C.); Univ. Mich., Recess, Detroit, Detroit Athletic (Detroit); Bloomfield Hills Country; Bloomfield Open Hunt; Old Club (Harsens Island, Mich.); Otsego Ski (Mich.). Home: 990 Cranbrook Rd Bloomfield Hills MI 48013 Office: D'Arcy-MacManus-Intermarco Inc Bloomfield Hills MI 48013

JONES, ERNEST CARL, educator; b. Atlanta, La., Feb. 17, 1921 s. Rufus T. and Nena (Franks) J.; B.S., Southwestern La. Inst., 1941; M.S., La. State U., 1947, Ph.D., 1962; m. Helen L. Worsham, Dec. 25, 1944; children—Kenneth Carl, Carol Annette. Grad. research asst. agr. econs. La. State U., 1945-57; faculty La. Poly Inst., Ruston, 1947—. prof. econs., 1962—, head dept. econs. and finance, 1964—. Cons. Gulf South Research Inst., 1966, La. Revenue Dept., 1970-71. Served with AUS, 1942-45. Mem. So. Econs. Assn., Southwestern Social Scis. Assn., La. Tchrs. Assn. (unit pres. 1963- 64), Beta Gamma Sigma, Delta Sigma Pi, Omicron Delta Epsilon, Omicron Delta Kappa. Lion (chmn. edn. com. 1967-68, 1st v.p. 1968, pres. 1969). Club: National Block and Bridle (hon. Ruston). Author: An Analysis of the Farm Real Estate Market, Lincoln Parish, Louisiana, 1939-57, 1957; An Economic Appraisal of Public Revenues and Expenditures in Lincoln Parish, Louisiana, 1962; A Severance Damage Study on Interstate System, Louisiana, 1967. Home: 921 Robinette Dr Ruston LA 71270

JONES, EUINE FAY, educator, architect; b. Pine Bluff, Ark., Jan. 31, 1921; s. Euine Fay and Candie Louise (Alston) J.; B.Arch., U. Ark., 1950; M.Arch., Rice U., 1951; m. Mary Elizabeth Knox, Jan. 6, 1943; children—Janis Fay (Mrs. Robert M. Carney), Jean Cameron (Mrs. Fred W. Stone). Asst. prof. architecture U. Okla., 1951-53; Frank Lloyd Wright Taliesin fellow, 1953; prof. architecture U. Ark., 1953—, chmn. dept., 1966—; pvt. practice architecture, 1953—. Served as lt. USNR, 1942-45. Recipient nat. awards for archtl. design. Mem. A.I.A., Assn. Collegiate Schs. Architecture, Soc. Archtl. Historians. Home: 1330 N Hillcrest St Fayetteville AR 72701

JONES, EVERETT HOLLAND, clergyman; b. San Antonio, June 9, 1902; s. Richard Clarence and Enid (Holland) J.; A.R., U. Tex., 1922; student Columbia U., 1923-24, Union Theol. Sem., 1924-25; B.D., Va. Theol Sem., 1927, D.D., 1943; D.D., U. of South, Sewanee, Tenn., 1943; LL.D., Trinity U., San Antonio Tex., 1944; m. Helen Miller Cameron, Nov 25, 1940; 1 stepdau., Flora Cameron (Mrs. Holt Athenton). Reporter, San Antonio Express, 1918-22; instr. Tex. Mil. Inst. (then West Tex. Mil. Acad.), 1922-23; ordained to ministry Protestant Episcopal Ch., 1927; rector, Grace Ch., Cuero, Tex., 1927-30, St. Paul's Ch., Waco, Tex, 1930-37; canon chancellor Nat. Cathedral, Washington, 1938; rector St. Mark's Ch., San Antonio, 1938-43; bishop Diocese of West Tex. Protestant Episcopal Ch. in U.S.A., 1943-68. Pres. bd. trustees St. Mary's Hall, Tex. Mil. Inst. Mem. nat. council P.E. Ch., 1938-43, 52-58. Chmn. bd. trustees Episcopal Theol. Sem. S.W., 1965-66. Rotarian. Author: Finding God, 1943- 68; A Bishop Looks at Life, 1967. Home: 330 Westover Rd San Antonio TX 78209 Office: 7809 Broadway San Antonio TX 78209

JONES, F. P., Jr., oil co. exec.; b. Leesville, La., 1906; ed. La. State U., 1930. Exec. v.p., dir. Superior Oil Co. Home: 3859 Chevy Chase Houston TX 77019 Office: PO Box 11521 Houston TX 77001*

JONES, FELIX CLARKE, former labor union exec.; b. Houston County, Ga., Dec. 20, 1909; s. William Reese and Eula Maudie (Clarke) J.; grad. high sch.; m. Mary Chesley Whitworth, June 8, 1934. Local union officer United Cement, Lime and Gypsum Workers, 1934-39, dist. pres., 1939, dist. rep., 1940-48, asst. to gen. pres., 1948-54, gen. pres., 1955-70, gen. bd. mem. AFL-CIO, 1956-70. Home: Route 9 Alkid St Rome GA 30161

JONES, FERDINAND TAYLOR, Jr., educator, psychologist; b. N.Y.C., May 15, 1932; s. Ferdinand Taylor and Esther (Haggie) J.; A.B., Drew U., 1953; Ph.D., U. Vienna, Austria, 1959; m. Antonina Laub, Sept. 26, 1953, (div. Mar. 1967); children—Joanne Esther, Terrie Lynn; m. 2d, Myra Jean Rogers, Nov. 26, 1967. Staff psychologist Riverside Hosp., Bronx, N.Y., 1959-62; chief psychologist Westchester County Community Mental Hosp. Bd., White Plains, N.Y., 1962-67; tng. cons. Lincoln Hosp. Mental Health Services, Bronx, 1967-69; tchr. psychology, black social change, Sarah Lawrence Coll., Bronxville, N.Y., 1968—; Cons. St. Peter's Head Start, Yonkers, N.Y., 1967-71, Bronx State Hosp., 1969—. Served with AUS, 1953-56. Mem. Am. Group Psychotherapy Assn., Am., Eastern, Westchester County (past pres.) psychol. assns., Assn. Black Psychologists, Soc. Psychol. Study Social Issues. Developed (with Myron W. Harris) small group method for reduction of distance and dissonance in interracial communication. Home: 167 Concord Av Hartsdale NY 10530

JONES, FRANCES DOWNEY, (Mrs. Vern B. Jones), orgn. exec. sec.; b. Lincoln. Neb., Feb. 25, 1911; d. How and Dora (Unitt) Downey; student Van Sant Coll., 1928-29; m. Vern B. Jones, Jan. 19, 1934; 1 son, Richard David. Exec. sec. Nat. Conf. Commrs. Uniform State Laws, 1948—. Home: 5801 N Sheridan Rd Chicago IL 60626 Office: 1155 E 60th St Chicago IL 60637

JONES, FRANK ANDERSON, pub. relations; b. Los Angeles, Jan. 29, 1921; s.Fred C. H. and Ellen (Anderson) J.: A.B., Occidental Coll., 1943; postgrad. U. So. Cal., 1955-57; m. Roberta Jane Ludgate, June 30, 1950; children—Janis Elaine, Jeffrey Frank, Gordon Robert, Karen Elizabeth. Field dir. Eberle Econ. Service, Pasadena, Cal., 1946-47; exec. mgr. Pasadena Automobile Parking Assn. (Cal.), 1947-48; mng. dir. Nat. Safety Council, Pasadena dist. chpt., 1948-50; pub. relations mgr. Consol. Electrodynamics Corp., Pasadena, 1952-60; dir. pub. relations Bell & Howell Co., Chgo., 1960- 66, sec., 1963-66, asst. to chmn. bd., 1963, v.p. pub. relations, 1966-67; v.p. pub. relations Hunt Foods and Industries, Inc., 1967-68, Norton Simon, Inc., Fullerton, Cal, 1968-70; lectr. Western Inst. Traffic Tng., U. Cal. at Los Angeles, 1950. Mem. Pres.'s Conf. Indsl. Safety, Washington, 1949; chief pub. information Civil Def., Pasadena, 1955-60; mem. bd. Niles Twp. Safety Council, 1961-62. Bd. dirs. Bell & Howell Profit Sharing, pres. Bell and Howell Found. Served with USNR, 1943-46, 50-52. Mem. Pub. Relations Soc. Am., Navy Res. Assn., Occidental Coll. Alumni Assn., Pasadena Tournament Roses Assn., Navy League U.S., Phi Gamma Delta. Republican. Presbyn. Address: 236 Via Eboli Newport Beach CA 92660

JONES, FRANK CATER, lawyer; b. Macon, Ga., June 19, 1925; s. Charles Baxter and Carolyn (Cater) J.; B.B.A., Emory U., 1947; LL.B., Mercer U., 1950; m. Annie Gantt Anderson, Mar. 31, 1951; children—Eugenia Anderson, Annie Gantt, Carolyn Cater, Frank Cater. Admitted to Ga. bar, 1950, since practiced in Macon; mem. firm Jones, Cork, Miller & Benton, and predecessor, 1952- . Dir. First Nat. Bank & Trust Co., Macon, Macon Fed. Savs. & Loan Assn., So. Trust Ins. Co., Cornell Young Co. Pres. United Givers Fund Macon-Bibb County, 1965; chmn. Macon chpt. A.R.C., 1958-60. Trustee Wesleyan Coll., Macon; v.p., chmn. local bd. Meth. Home of So. Ga. Conf. Served to lt. USNR, 1943-46. Mem. Macon (pres. 1954), Ga. (pres. young lawyers assn. 1956-57) bar assns., State Bar Ga. (pres 1968-69), Greater Macon C. of C. (pres. 1965) Home: 3395 Osborne PL Macon GA 31204 Office: First Nat Bank Macon GA 31201

JONES, FRANK EDWARD, educator; b. Montreal, Que., Can., Oct. 28, 1917; s. Richard Thomas and Victoria Lemire (Hughes) J.; B.A. in Sociology Harvard, 1954; m. Jean E. McEachran, Sept. 14, 1946; children—David, Dilys. Chief research div. Canadian Citizenship Bd., Dept. Citizenship and Immigration, Ont., 1953-55; asst. prof. sociology McMaster U., 1955-59, chmn. dept., 1959-64, asso. prof., 1959-64, prof., 1964—; vis. prof. U.B.C., summers 1957-67, Australian Nat. U., 1961, 71, McGill U., 1966-67. Mem. Social Planning Research Council, Hamilton, Ont., Can. Served with Royal Canadian Navy, 1940-45. Author: An Introduction to Sociology, 1961; (with others) Canadian Society Sociological Persectives, 1961, 64, 68, 70. Editor Canadian Review of Sociology and Anthropology, 1968—; also articles. Home: 19 Brentwood Dr Dundas Ontario Canada

JONES, FRANK GARFIELD, box mfg. exec.; b. Cin., Mar. 5, 1914; s. Frank G. and Agnesse (Evans) J.: B.S., U. Cin., 1936, Chem. Engr., 1937; m. Mildred A. Simon, May 27, 1938. With Container Corp. Am., 1937—, beginning as indsl. engr., successively personnel mgr., plant mgr., div. gen. mgr., 1937-57, v.p. charge corrugated box plants, 1957-59, mfg. asst. to v.p. 1959- 63, v.p., dir. mfg., 1963—. Mem. Tau Beta Pi. Home: Banbury Rd Inverness Palatine IL 60067 Office: 500 E North Av Carol Stream IL 60187

JONES, FRANK LOWE, oil co. exec.; b. Taft, Tex., July 18, 1918; s. Fred L. and Ethel (Harrell) J.; B.S. in Natural Gas Engring., Tex. Coll. Arts and Industries, 1941; m. Ann Toland, Aug. 22, 1942. With Louisville Gas and Electric Co., 1941-42; with Chicago Corp., Ft. Worth, 1945-55, chief engr., 1951-55; asst. v.p. Champlin Oil & Refining Co., Ft. Worth, 1955- 65; v.p. charge natural gas operations Champlin Petroleum Co., Ft. Worth, 1965-68, sr. v.p. in charge natural gas operations, engring. and producing operations, 1968—, sr. v.p. natural secondary recovery and environmental control, 1970—; pres. Midland Gasoline Corp. Served with USAAF, 1942-45. Mem. Natural Gas Processors Assn. (dir.), Ind. Petroleum Assn. Am. (dir.), Am. Inst. Mining, Metall. and Petroleum Engrs., Petroleum Engrs. Club, Natural Gas Men. Houston. Clubs: Ridglea Country (Ft. Worth); Petroleum. Home: 6412 Drury Lane Fort Worth TX 76116 Office: 5301 Camp Bowie Blvd Fort Worth TX 76107

JONES, FRANK PIERCE, educator; b. Appleton, Wis., Apr. 10, 1905; s. George W. and Maud F. (Sackett) J.; student Lawrence Coll., 1922-23, U. Wis., 1923-24; B.A., Stanford, 1926, M.A., 1928; postgrad., U. Chgo. 1929-30; Ph.D., U. Wis., 1937; m. Helen Bartlett Rumsey, Aug. 10, 1931; children—Thomas R., Emlen V. (Mrs. Michael A. O'Keeffe), John Evan. Asst. in gen. lit. Reed Coll., 1927-29; instr. Greek, Latin classics Brown U., 1937-41, asst. prof., 1941-44; asst. prof. Pa. Mil. Coll., 1944-45; pvt. teaching, research in kinesthetic perception, Boston, N.Y.C., 1945-54; research asso. Inst. for Psychol. Research, Tufts U., 1954-68, lectr. classics, 1955-64, prof. classics, 1964-70, lectr. psychology, 1968-70, prof. emeritus classics, 1970—. Carnegie grantee, 1954-56; USPHS grantee, 1956-64, 66-67. Mem. Am. Philol. Assn., Am., New Eng. psychol. assns., A.A.A.S., Phi Beta Kappa, Sigma Xi. Contbr. articles on classical subjects, kinestetic perception of postural reflex patterns to profl. jours. Home: 33 Lexington Av Cambridge MA 02138 Office: 490 Boston Av Medford MA 02155

JONES, FRED EUGENE, lawyer; b. Detroit, Aug. 22, 1926; s. Fred McKinley and Thelma (Riddell) J.; student Miami U., Oxford, O., 1944-45, Ohio State U., 1946-48; LL.B., Salmon P. Chase Coll. Law, 1951; m. Colleen F. Cranmer, July 19, 1948; children-Jennifer Lynn, Daniel Frederick, Matthew Charles, Barbara Ellen. Admitted to Ohio bar, 1951, since practiced in Lebanon; pros. atty. Warren County, 1957-61; mem. firm Young & Jones, 1954—. Chmn. Warren County Republicans, 1962-68; mem. Warren County Bd. Elections, 1962-70; state committeeman Ohio 24th Dist., 1966-70; del. Rep. Nat. Conv., 1964-68; Rep. candidate for Congress, 1970. Served with AUS, 1944-45. Home: R R 1 Drake Rd Lebanon OH 45036 Office: P O Box 280 Lebanon Citizens Bank Bldg Lebanon OH 45036

JONES, FRED NOWELL, Jr., educator; b. Santa Monica, Cal., Aug. 16, 1912; s. Fred Nowell and Jane (Seddon) J.; A.B., U. Cal. at Los Angeles, 1934, M. A., 1937; Ph.D., Cornell U., 1939; m. Margaret Russell Hubbard, June 19, 1939; 1 dau., Lynne Hubbard. Instr., asst. prof. psychology U. Ala., 1939-42, 43-45; time- study man Bridgeport

Brass Co. (Conn.), 1942; with personnel dept. Lockheed Aircraft Co., Burbank, Cal., 1943; asst. prof. psychology U. Wis., 1945-56; asso. prof., chmn. dept. psychology Wash. State Coll., 1946-49; asst prof. to prof. U. Cal. at Los Angeles, 1949—, chmn. dept. psychology, 1962-71. Mem. food acceptance adv. com. Q.M.C., 1958-61; sub-com. psychology mental health tng. com. USPHS, 1964-68. Fellow Am. Psychol. Assn. (policy and planning bd. 1963- 66), A.A.A.S.; mem. Inst. Food Technologists, Western Psychol. Assn., Phi Beta Kappa, Sigma Xi, Theta Chi, Phi Kappa Phi. Club: South Coast Corinthian Yacht. Contbr. articles psychol. jours. Home: 467 Denslow Av Los Angeles CA 90049

JONES, FREDERICK LAFAYETTE, educator; b. Spartanburg, S.C., Dec. 5, 1901; s. Frederick Sinclair and Leila Jane (Marchbanks) J.; A.B., Furman U., Greenville, S.C., 1921; A.M., Cornell U., 1922, Ph.D., 1925; Litt.D. (hon.), Furman U., 1951; m. Lucile Smith, Aug. 30, 1927; children—Frederick Lafayette, William Cecil. Instr. English, Cornell U., 1923-24; asst. prof. English, Baylor U., 1925-28; prof. English and chmn. dept., Mercer U., Macon, Ga., 1928-47, chmn. Grad. Div., 1941-47; prof. English, U. of Pa., 1947—, grad. chmn. English Dept., 1952-54, 58-60; mem. faculty Duke U., summer, 1939, U. N.C., summer 1947. Postwar Rockefeller fellow in Humanities, 1946; research fellow abroad, Gen. Edn. Bd., 1936-37. Served as lt. and lt. comdr., U.S.N.R., 1943-46. Mem. Mod. Lang. Assn. Am., South Atlantic Modern Lang. Assn. v.p. 1941, 46, pres. 1942-43), Keats-Shelley Assn. Am., Modern Humanities Research Assn., Am. Assn. U. Profs., Phi Delta Kappa. Democrat. Baptist. Author: (with N. I. White and K.N. Cameron), An Examination of The Shelley Legend, 1952. Editor: The Letters of Mary W. Shelley, 2 vols., 1944, Mary Shelley's Journal, 1947; Maria Gisborne and E. E. Williams: Their Journals and Letters, 1952; Percy Bysshe Shelley. Selected Poems (Crofts Classics), 1956; The Diary of Harriet Grove, in Shelley and his Circle, vol. 2, 1961; The Letters of Percy Bysshe Shelley, 2 vols., 1964. Contbr. articles to profl. jours. Address: 4537 Pine St Philadelphia PA 19143

JONES, FREDERICK MASON, Jr., musician, educator; b. Hamilton, N.Y., June 16, 1919; s. Frederick Mason and Elizabeth (Piotrow) J.; student Curtis Inst. Music, 1936-38; Mus. D. (hon.), Colgate U., 1970; m. Eve Furlong, July 20, 1941; children—Frederick Mason III, Saralinda Mason. Mem. Phila. Orch., 1938—, first hornist, 1940—, personnel mgr., 1963- -; tchr. horn Curtis Inst. Music, 1946—; condr. Episcopal Acad. Orch., 1958-60; founder-mem. Phila. Woodwind Quintet, 1950—; co-founder Phila. Brass Ensemble, 1957—; asst. condr. Phila. Chamber Orch., 1961-64. Served with USMC, 1942-46. Recipient C. Hartman Kuhn award for service to Phila. Orch., 1953, 56, 68. Episcopalian. Clubs: Union League (Phila.); Merion (Pa.) Golf. Editor: Solos for the Horn Player, 1962. 20th Century Orch. Studies, 1971. Home: 1124 Rose Glen Rd Gladwyne PA 19035 Office: 230 S 15th St Philadelphia PA 19102

JONES, FREDERICK WILLIAM PRYCE, educator; b. London Ont., Can., Aug. 17, 1910; s. Joseph W.P. and Gertrude R. (Whittaker) J.; B.A. with honours in Bus. Adminstrn., U. Western Ont., 1933; m. Elsie Dearborn, Aug. 22, 1936 (dec.); children—Deborah Anne Pryce, Gwyneth, Elaine Pryce; m. 2d. Aileen Tyrell Douglas, Aug. 25, 1967. Area mgr. Kellogg Co., Can. Ltd., 1933- 36; successively v.p., mng. dir., pres. Hobbs Glass Ltd., 1936-52; v.p. Canadian Pitts. Industries Ltd., 1952-53, dir., 1952—; dean Sch. Bus. Adminstrn. U. Western Ont., 1953-63, prof. bus. adminstrn., 1963—. Vice pres. Canadian Scudder Investments; dir. Avco, Inc., Can. Ltd., Econ. Investment Trust, Ellis-Don Ltd., Grouped Income Shares Ltd., No. Life Assurance Co., Scudder Internat., Gen. Products Ltd., Supertest Petroleum Corp., Kemp Products, Emco., Ltd., Gen. Products Mfg. Corp., Ltd., Commonwealth Holiday Inns Ltd., M.G.F. Mgmt., Ltd., Union Gas Co. of Canada. Dir. mgmt. tng. sect. Wartime Prices and Trade Bd., Ottawa, 1942-43; chmn. Province Ont. Agrl. Marketing Commn., 1959-62; project supr. Ont. Econ. Council, 1964. Bd. dirs. Addictions Research Found. Mem. London C. of C. (dir. 1956-58). Clubs: London, London Hunt and Country; University (Toronto); Caledon Mountain (Inglewood Ont.). Home: 35 Doncaster Av London 72 Ontario Canada

JONES, GALEN, edn. council exec.; b. Grundy Center, Ia., July 12, 1896; s. Jesse Edwin and Etta Maria (Strickler) J.; A.B., McPherson (Kan.) Coll., 1918; A.M., Tchrs. Coll., Columbia U., 1921, Ph.D., 1935; LL.D., Upsala Coll., 1946; m. Grace Everts, Aug. 14, 1922; children—Royce Emerson (dec.), Galen Everts, Thomas Hugh. Tchr., prin., supt. pub. schs., 1919-33; prin. Plainfield (N.J.) High Sch., 1934-42, E. Orange High Sch., 1942- 45; tchr. grad. div., U. Mo., Columbia, summers 1927-28; Ohio State U., Columbus, 1930-32; Pa. State Coll., State College, Pa., 1936- 37; Alfred (N.Y.) U., 1938; U. Pa., Phila., 1939, 40, 41; Harvard, 1942, Tchrs. Coll., Columbia, Saturdays, 1942-43, 1943-44; Lehigh U., Bethlehem, Pa., Saturdays, 1944-45; U. N.H., Durham, summers 1944-45; dir. div. secondary edn., U. S. Office Edn., 1945- 51, dir. orgn., instrn. and services br., 1951-54; dir. Council for Advancement of Secondary Edn.; cons. ednl. relations Field Enterprises Ednl. Corp., 1965-67. Served with F.A. Central Officers Tng. Sch., Camp Taylor, Louisville, Ky., 1918. Chmn. U.S. del. 10th, 11th, 14th, Internat Conf. Pub. Edn., Geneva, 1947, 48, 51; del. I.L.O. adv. com. on salaried employees and profl. workers, Geneva, 1954; mem. U.S. nat. com. UNESCO, 1954-59. Mem. Middle States Assn. Colls. and Secondary Schs. (pres. 1947-48; v.p. 1946-47). N.E.A., Nat. Assn. Secondary Sch. Prins. (pres. 1947-48), Headmasters Assn. (hon.), Phi Delta Kappa, Kappa Delta Pi. Mason. Author books on edn. Home: Becky Branch Rd at Crest Southern Pines NC 28387 Office: 1201 16th St NW Washington DC 20036 ☆

JONES, GALEN EVERTS, microbiologist, educator; b. Milw., Sept. 9, 1928; s. Galen and Grace (Everts) J.; A.B., Dartmouth, 1950; M.A., Williams Coll., 1952; Ph.D., Rutgers U., 1956; m. Edith Agnes Boehme, July 17, 1954; children—Randolph, Gwenith Grace, Christopher Thomas. With Scripps Inst. Oceanography, U. Cal. La Jolla, 1955-63, asst. research microbiologist, 1957-63; asso. prof. biology Boston U., 1963-66; prof. microbiology, dir. Jackson Estuarine Lab., U. N.H., Durham, 1966—. Fellow A.A.A.S.; mem. Am. Inst. Biol. Sci., Soc. Gen. Microbiology, New Eng. Estuarine Research Soc., Nat. Oceanography Assn., Western Soc. Naturalists, Geochem. Soc., Am. Soc. Mircrobiology, Am. Soc. Limnology and Oceanography, Am. Soc. Oceanography, Internat. Oceanographic Found., Marine Tech. Soc., Sigma Xi, Phi Sigma. Contbr. articles profl. jours. Home: 22 Faculty Rd Durham NH 03824

JONES, GEOFFREY JOHN CHARLES, paper co. exec.; b. Bromley, Kent, Eng., Feb. 21, 1927; s. Frederick John Charles and Grace Margaret (Prior) J.; student Eltham Coll., 1938-43; B.A., U. Manchester, 1951; m. Alice Walmsley, Aug. 18, 1951; children—Christopher John Geoffrey, Briony Helen Kezia, Katherine Rosemary Alexandra, Heather Ceinwen Grace. Financial accountant Bowater Paper Corp., Ltd., London, 1955-64, chief accountant, 1965-68, controller, 1969—; dir. Bowater Packaging, Ltd. Served to lt. Brit. Army, 1945-48. Fellow Inst. Chartered Accountants in Eng. and Wales. Clubs: Savile (London); Blue Circle Sailing (Cliff, Kent, Eng.). Home: 11 Beadon Rd Bromley Kent BR 2 9AS England Office: Bowater House Knightbridge London SW1X 71R England

JONES, GEORGE HENRY GABRIEL, librarian; b. Mt. Vernon, O., Oct. 25, 1909; s. George Henry and Mary (Randall) J.; B.A., Oberlin Coll., 1931; M.A., Harvard, 1949, Ph.D. 1966; M.L.S., Kent State U., 1957; m. Elizabeth Clisby, Aug. 1, 1937; 1 son, Randall Clisby. Art dealer, Oberlin, 1932-40; instr. U. Rochester, 1942-43; asst. prof., then asso. prof. art Lawrence Coll., 1946-53; librarian, Northfield, O., 1955-57, Youngstown (O.) U., 1957—. Bd. dirs. Youngstown Mental Health Assn.; trustee Arms Hist. Mus. Served with USNR, 1943-45. Mem. A.L.A., Am. Assn. U. Profs. Unitarian. Home: 417 S Main St Poland OH 44514 Office: Youngstown U Library Youngstown OH 44503

JONES, GEORGE LEWIS, Jr., gov. ofcl.; b. Balt., Jan. 18, 1907; s. Geogre Lewis and Emma (Little) J.; grad. Boys' Sch., Balt., 1925; B.S., Harvard, 1929; student Christ's Coll., Cambridge, Eng., 1929-30, London Sch. Econ, 1930-31; grad. Nat. War Coll., 1950; m. Polly Cooke, Nov. 30, 1935; children—Virginia Lewis, Christopher George Lewis, Andrew Calder Lewis. Clk. to the U.S. comml. attaché assignments U. S. and abroad, 1930-42; Near Eastern Div., Dept. of State, charge Turkish Affairs, 1942-45, asst. chief Div. Nr. Eastern Affairs, 1945-46; assigned 2d sec., London, 1946, 1st sec., 1947; detailed to Nat. War Coll., 1949-50; mem. policy planning staff Dept. of State, 1950, dir. Office Nr. Eastern Affairs; 1950-52; consul gen. Tunis, 1952-53; counselor of embassy, Cairo, Egypt, 1953-55, dep. chief of mission, Tehran, with personal rank of minister, 1955-56; first U.S. ambassador to Tunisia, 1956-59; asst. sec. state, for Near East and South Asian affairs, 1959-61; minister Am. Embassy, London, Eng., 1961- 64; coordinator Sr. Seminar in Fgn. Policy, Dept. State, 1964—; spl. negotiator with personal rank of ambassador, 1964. Clubs: Chevy Chase, Metropolitan (Wash.); Travelers, Garrick, American (London, Eng.). Home: 1644 Avon Pl NW Washington DC 20007; also Jones Reach Yarmouth Port Mass 02657 Office: Dept of State Washington DC 20525

JONES, GILBERT EDWARD, bus. machine co. exec.; b. Convent, N.J., Jan. 8, 1917; s. Gilbert Edward and Leila Ingersoll (Haven) J.; grad. St. Mark's Sch., 1934; A.B., Harvard, 1938; m. Jean Coats Morse, June 3, 1942; children—Leila Haven (Mrs. Jonathan Scranton Linen), Jean (Mrs. Anson Beard, Jr.), Pamela (Mrs. Lewis Atterbury Clarke, Jr.), Gilbert Edward. With IBM Corp and subsidiaries, 1938—, exec. v.p., dir. IBM World Trade Corp., 1962-63, pres., dir., 1963-67, chmn., 1971—, sr. v.p. IBM Corp., 1967-70, dir., 1970—; dir. Continental Oil Co., Webster Apts trustee U.S. Trust Co. Mem. devel. com., trustee Internat. House; dir. Fund for Overseas Grants and Edn., Inc., Com. Nat. Trade Policy; vice chmn. U.S. adv. com. European Inst. Bus. Adminstrn.; mem. adv. council Internat. Center N.Y., Inc.; trustee Com. Econ. Devel., Vassar Coll. Mem. Inst. Internat. Edn. (trustee), Nat. Inst. Social Scis., Pilgrims, Newcomen Soc. Clubs. Economic, Union (N.Y.C.). Home: Close Rd Greenwich CT 06830 Office: 821 UN Plaza New York City NY 10017

JONES, GIRAULT MCARTHUR, clergyman; b. Centerville, Miss., June 30, 1904; s. Ackland Hartley and Elizabeth Girault (Shaifer) J.; student Staunton (Va.) Mil. Acad., 1921; A.B., U. Miss., 1925; B.D., U. of South, Sewanee, 1928, D.D., 1949; m. Virginia Wallace, Apr. 22, 1930 (dec. Nov. 1930); m. 2d, Kathleen Platt, July 9, 1935; children—Virginia Kathleen, Elizabeth Girault. Ordained to ministry, Protestant Episcopal Ch., 1928; served as rural missionary, Miss., 1928-31; rector, Trinity Ch., Pass Christian, Miss., 1931-361 St. Andrew's Ch., New Orleans, 1936-49; bishop of Diocese of La., 1949-69. Chancellor U. of South, 1967—. Chmn. Episcopal Radio-TV Found., 1961-65. Mem. Phi Beta Kappa. Address: PO Box 57 Sewanee TN 37375

JONES, GORDON, banker; b. Atlanta, Jan. 14, 1918; s. Harrison and Kathryn (Gordon) J.; B.S., U. Ga., 1940; m. Ann Creekmore, Oct. 8, 1940; children—Harrison II, Caroline C., Ann Gordon, Kathryn Helene. With Fulton Nat. Bank of Atlanta, 1941—, successively asst. cashier, asst v.p., v.p., exec. v.p., 1941-58, pres., 1958—; dir. Atlanta Stove Works, Inc., Haventy Furniture Cos., Inc., Atlanta Gas Light Co., Coastal States Life Ins., Co., So. Cross Industries, Inc. Bd. dirs. Atlanta Symphony Guild; mem. finance com. Jr. League Sch. Speech Correction; trustee U. Ga. Found., Met. Found. Atlanta. Mem. Ga. State (dir.), Atlanta (dir.) chambers commerce, Assn. Res. City Bankers (exec. council) Am Bankers Assn (exec council) Home: 660 W Paces Ferry Rd NW Atlanta GA 30327 Office: 55 Marietta St NW Atlanta GA 30303

JONES, GORDON BURR, ins. co. exec.; b. Peabody, Mass., Sept. 10, 1918; s. Burr Frank and Helen (Robinson) J.; A.B., Colby Coll., 1940; M.B.A., Harvard, 1942; m. Geraldine A. Stefko, Sept. 12, 1942; children—Carol L., Gordon Burr, David R., Valerie G., Allison G., Randall B. Investment analyst Provident Mut. Life. Ins. Co. Phila., 1945-48; investment analyst John Hancock Mut. Life Ins. Co., Boston, 1948-52, asst. treas., 1952- 57, 2d v.p., 1957-66, v.p., 1966, sr. v.p., 1966-68, exec. v.p., 1968—, also chmn. finence com., dir.; corporator, trustee Eliot Savs. Bank, Boston; dir. Servend-Seiler Corp., John Hancock Advisers, Inc., John Hancock Growth Fund., John Hancock Signature Fund, Inc., John Hancock Realty Devel. Corp., John Hancock Investors, Inc., Raytheon Co.; cons. investment com. Arkwright-Boston Mfrs. Mut. Ins. Co. Gen. Campaign chmn. Ford Found. Challenge Campaign, Colby Coll., 1962- 65. Chmn. bd. trustees, dir. Needham YMCA; dir., mem. investment com. Mass. Soc. Prevention Cruelty to Animals; trustee, mem. exec. com., chmn. investment com. Colby Coll. Recipient Man of Year award Colby Coll. Club, 1955. Mem. Am. Petrolium Inst., Newcomen Soc. N.Am., Boston Security Analysts Soc., Phi Beta Kappa. Republican. Conglist. Clubs: Brae Burn Country; Boston Madison Square Garden Union (Boston) Home: 495 South St Needham MA 02192 Office: 200 Berkeley St Boston MA 02117

JONES, GORDON MERRILL, publisher; b. Oak Park, Ill., Dec. 12, 1896; s. Nathaniel M. and Mary (Merrill) J.; A.B., Northwestern U., 1918, LL.B., 1922; m. Kathleen Row, May 24, 1922; children—Laura Row, Gordon Row. Sec.-tres. Row Peterson & Co., Evanston, Ill., 1924-42, pres., 1942-60, chmn. bd., 1960-62; chmn. bd. Harper & Row, pubs., 1962-67, chmn. exec. com., 1967—; dir. State Nat. Bank, Evanston, Ill. Power Co. Mem. Evanston Zoning Bd. Appeals, 1953-65; pres. Evanston United Fund, 1959-60; dir. North Shore Jr. Achievement Bd.; trustee Nat. Coll. Edn. Served as capt. USNR. Mem. Am. Textbook Pubs. Inst. (pres. 1948-49), Ill. C. of C. (pres. 1952-53; dir.), Evanston Hist. Soc. (dir. 1950-65), U.S. C. of C. (edn. com.), Beta Theta Pi, Phi Delta Phi. Methodist. Home: 603 Trinity Ct Evanston IL 60201 Office: 2500 Crawford Av Evanston IL 60201

JONES, GORMAN ROBINSON, Jr., lawyer; b. Sheffield, Ala., Oct. 19, 1919; s. Gorman Robinson and Aline (Drake) J.; student Marion Mil. Inst., 1937-38; A.B., U. Ala., 1940, LL.B., 1943; m. Llewellyn Childress, Oct. 25, 1941; children—Aline Llewellyn (Mrs. Don R. Parks), Elizabeth Cecelia, Martha Shaler, Gorman Robinson III. Admitted to Ala. bar, 1943; law clk. U.S. dist. judge, 1943-45; asst. U.S. atty., 1945-47; practice law, Sheffield, 1947—; partner McDonnell & Jones, 1947—. Sec., dir. So. Tire Co., Inc., Asso. Developers, Inc. Mem. Commn. on Minister and His Work N.Ala. Presbytery, Presbyn. Ch. in U.S., 1969-72, commr. Gen. Assembly, 1969. Pres., Colbert County United Fund, Sheffield City Bd. Edn. Mem. Colbert C. of C. (past pres.). Author: (with others) Alabama Appellate Practice, 1963. Home: 120 Rivermont Ct Sheffield AL 35660 Office: Sheffield Fed Savs & Loan Bldg Sheffield AL 35660

JONES, GREYDON G., retail store exec.; b. Warsaw, N.Y., Feb. 16, 1926; s. Onias S. and Dorothy M. (Goetz) J.; student Syracuse U., 1943-44, Ohio State U., 1944-45, Tex. A. and M. U., 1945; B.C.S., Auerswald Bus. U., 1949; m. Janis R. Anderson, June 21, 1946; children—Carrell (Mrs. James L. Tysver), Melodee K. (Mrs. Rolf G. Krueger). Partner, V.L. Maxfield & Co., Seattle, 1949-57; prin. Haskins & Sells, Seattle, 1958-68; v.p., treas. Weisfield's, Inc., Seattle, 1968—. Served with AUS, 1943-46. C.P.A., Wash. Mem. Wash. Soc. C.P.A.'s, Am. Inst. C.P.A.'s, Financial Execs. Inst. Office: Home: 12302 Marine View Dr Edmonds WA 98020

JONES, GWYNETH, dramatic soprano; b. Pontnewynydd, Monomouthshire, S. Wales, Nov. 7, 1937; d. Edward George and Violet (Webster) Jones; student Royal Coll. Music, London, Eng., 1956-60, Acad. Chigiana, Siena, Italy, 1960, Internat. Opera Centre, Zurich, Switzerland, 1961-62. Mem. Zurich Opera House, 1962-63, Royal Opera House, Convent Garden, London, 1963—, Vienna (Austria) Staatoper, 1966—; appearances include Berlin (Germany) Deutscheoper, Munich (Germany) Staatsoper, Hamburg (Germany) Staatsoper, Paris, France, Bayreuth (Germany) Festival, La Scala, Milan, Italy, Rome, Italy, Teatro Colon, Buenos Aires, Argentina. Dallas, N.Y.C., San Francisco; Chgo., Los Angeles, Tokyo, Japan. TV appearances and recs. for EMI, DGG, Decca, CBS. Address: Box 8040 Zurich Switzerland

JONES, HALBERT MCNAIR, cotton mfr.; b. Laurinburg, N.C., Aug. 13, 1909; s. James A. and Mary (McNair) J.; B.S., U. N.C.; M.B.A., Harvard, 1931; H.H.D. (hon.) N.C. State Coll., 1958; m. Elizabeth Munroe, Apr. 6, 1943; children—Elizabeth M., Mary Ellen, Halbert McNair, James. Pres., treas. Waverly Mills. Inc., 1934—; v.p., treas. Scotland Mills, Inc., 1939-63. treas. Morgan Jones, Inc., N.Y.C., 1946-63. Chmn. Laurinburg Sch. B. 1953-68. Acting pres., chmn. bd. trustees Flora McDonald Coll., Red Springs, 1948-49; vice chmn. bd. trustees St. Andrews Presbyn. Coll., 1958—. Served to maj. AUS, 1942-46. Mem. Card Yarn Assn. (pres. 1951-52), Am. Cotton Mfrs. Inst. (pres. 1958-59), N.C. Textile Mfrs. Assn. Presbyn. (elder) Rotarian (pres 1946-47) Home: 308 Prince St Laurinburg NC 28352 Office: Waverly Mills Inc Laurinburg NC 28352

JONES, HARMON WOODROW, govt. ofcl.; b. Gilmer, Tex., Mar. 4, 1918; s. Fred J. and Mary O. (Ridgeway) J.; student Tex. A. and M. U., 1938; m. Troy Tracy Lansdale, Oct. 15, 1938; children—Patricia Annette (Mrs. Harlyn D. Pope), Judy Carolyn (Mrs. George Kirkland Grimes, Jr.). With Dept. Agr., 1940—, exec. dir. Agrl. Stablzn. and Conservation Service, 1943—. Legislative coordinator Nat. Assn. Agrl. Stblzn. and Conservation County Office Employees, 1968—, pres. Tex. assn., 1959-62, nat. pres., 1962-68, mem. exec. com., 1960—. Served with USNR, 1945-46. Recipient Superior Service award Dept. Agr., 1968. Baptist (deacon, former Sunday sch. supt.). Lion. Home: 404 S Ellis St New Boston TX 75570 Office: 2000 S Merrill St New Boston TX 75570

JONES, HAROLD, banker. Pres., City Nat. Bank Wichita Falls (Tex.). Office: Corner 8th and Scott Sts Wichita Falls TX 76307*

JONES, HARRY LEE II, army officer; b. Kansas City, Mo., Oct. 27, 1918; s. Harry Lee and Hazel (Hixon) J.; student Washington U., St. Louis, 1937-40; A.B., George Washington U., 1950, M.A., 1963; M.B.A., Harvard, 1953; grad. Army War Coll., 1963; m. Gloria Carolyn Raeder, Mar. 26, 1947; children—Patricia (Mrs. Frederick H. French), Harry Lee. Joined U.S. Army, 1940, commd. 2d lt., 1943, advanced through grades to maj. gen., 1970; finance officer 24th Inf. Div., 1942-46; mem. Gen. Staff, 1958-62; adv. to dir. finance and audit Ministry Def., Vietnam, 1963-65; chief finance and accounting Office Comptroller Army, 1967-70; asst. comptroller for information systems, Washington, 1969-70; chief Army Audit Agy., Washington, 1970—; instr. U. Md., Heidelberg, Germany, 1953-56. Bd. dirs. Army Mut. Aid Assn., Fort Myer, Arlington, Va., 1967—. Decorated Legion Merit with 2 oak leaf clusters, Bronze Star, Army Commendation medal with oak leaf cluster; Medal Honor 1st class (Republic Vietnam). Mem. Assn. U.S. Army, Army Finance Assn. (nat. pres., 1967-70), Am. Soc. Mil. Comptrollers (nat. v.p.). Home: 8906 Captains Row Alexandria VA 22308 Office: 5611 Columbia Pike Falls Church VA 22041

JONES, HARRY LEROY, lawyer; b. Summitville, Ind., June 28, 1895; s. Arthur H. and Daisy (Bake) J.; A.B., Ind. U., 1916; J.D., Northwestern U., 1922; m. Gladys Moon, Jan. 1, 1922; children—Susan Cornelia (Mrs. John O. Gouge), Tenley Moon. Admitted to Ill. bar, 1922, D.C. bar, 1929; pvt. practice, Chgo., 1922-26; lectr. Northwestern U. Law Sch., sec. Am. br. Assn. Internat. de Droit Penal, 1922-26; spl. atty. Bur. Internal Revenue, 1926-29; pvt. practice, Washington, 1930-33; chief atty. alien property bur. Dept. Justice, in charge gold litigation from monetary legislation 73d Congress, 1934-42, 1st asst., chief alien property litigation sect., war div., 1942-47, chief hearing examiner Office Alien Property, 1948-59; dir. Commn. Internat. Rules Jud. Procedure, 1959-66; exec. dir. World Assn. Judges, 1966-68. Adviser jud. assistance Harvard Research Internat. Law, 1937-39; chief cons. project internat. procedure Columbia Law Sch., 1960-62; vis. lectr. seminar Am. jurisprudence Sch. Law U. Parana (Brazil), 1961. Painting represented in permanent collection Corcoran Gallery Art. Served as 1st. lt. U.S. Army, 1917-20; AEF. Mem. Am. (chmn. com. transnat. jud. procedure, sect. internat. and comparative law 1962-63; editors Internat. Lawyer), Internat. (chmn. com. internat. jud. coop. 1950-59), Inter-Am. (chmn. com. internat. jud. procedure), Fed. bar assns., Inst. Jud. Adminstrn., Am. Soc. Internat. Law (exec. council 1955-58). Washington Fgn. Law Soc. (v.p. 1955-57), Consular Law Soc. (hon. fellow, bd. govs.), Am. Law Inst., Am. Fgn. Law Assn., World Peace Through Law Center, Order of Coif, Phi Delta Theta, Phi Delta Phi, Delta Sigma Rho, Tau Kappa Alpha. Contbr. numerous articles to profl. jours. Chief student editor Ill. Law Rev., 1921-22. Home: 1310 34th St NW Washington DC 20007

JONES, HARRY R., lawyer; b. Hubbard, Tex., Nov. 16, 1902; s. James R. and Ida (Walton) J.; A.B., Baylor U., 1923, LL.B., 1926; m. Hazel Tanner, Aug. 7, 1929; children—Mary Owen (Mrs. Charles M. Sloan), Janet (Mrs. Thomas Garth), Harry R., Steven E. Admitted to Tex. bar, 1926, since practiced in Waco and Houston; partner firm Andrews, Kurth, Campbell & Jones, 1936—; gen. counsel dir., mem. exec. com. Southwest Forest Industries, Inc. Mem. Am., Tex. Houston (pres. 1952) bar assns., Am. Law Inst., Am. Bar Found., Am. Coll. Trial Lawyers. Kiwanian (pres. Houston 1949). Home: 6046 Riverview Way Houston TX 77027 Office: Humble Bldg Houston TX 77002

JONES, HARRY WILLMER, prof. law; b. N.Y.C., Mar. 4, 1911; s. Harry and Leona May (Coffin) J.; student Westminster Coll., Fulton, Mo., 1929-31; LL.B., Washington U., St., Louis, 1934, A.B., 1937; postgrad. Oxford U. (Eng.) (Rhodes scholar), 1934-35; LL.M., Columbia, 1939; LL.D., Jewish Theol. Sem. Am., 1967; m. Shirley O'Neal Coggeshall, Nov. 21, 1935 (dec. 1955); m. 2d, Alice Neuburger Katz, July 11, 1956. Admitted to Mo. bar, 1934, Cal. bar,

1946; part-time law practice, lecture series on public and internat. affairs, 1935-38; instr., asst. prof. law Washington U., 1935-39; vis. lectr. in law, Columbia, 1939- 40, Stanford, summer 1940; asso. prof. law U. Cal., 1940-41, prof. 1946; prof. law, Columbia, 1947-57, Cardozo prof. jurisprudence, 1957—; prof. law U. Chgo., 1963-64; dir. research Am. Bar Found., 1963-64; with O.P.A., Washington, 1941-43, successively as head, research and opinion unit, chief appellate litigation branch, asst. gen. counsel, dir. food enforcement div.; vis. prof., Columbia, summer 1947; vis. prof. law U. Delhi (India), 1968. Chmn. O.D.M. shipbldg. industry panel, summer 1952; research dir. Am. Assembly, 1953; faculty Salzburg Seminar in Am. Studies, summers 1955-59. Trustee W.E. Meyer Research Inst. Law, 1957—. Served as asst. counsel Bur. Aercs. and counsel for Bur. Aeronautics gen. rep., Western Dist., with rank of lt. (j.g.) and lt. comdr. USNR, 1943-46; cons. on legislative research and drafting problems for conl. and state legislative coms. Recipient Alumni citation Washington U., 1958, Westminster Coll., 1960. Mem. Am. Law Inst., Am. Philos. Soc., Am. Acad. Arts and Scis. Am. Bar Assn., Order of Coif, Phi Delta Theta, Phi Delta Phi. Democrat. Presbyn. Author: Materials for Legal Method (with N.T. Dowling, E.W. Patterson and R.R. Powell), 1952; Economic Security for Americans, 1954; Legal Realism and Natural Law (Riverside lectures), 1956; Cases on Contract (with E.W. Patterson and G.W. Goble), 1957: The Courts, The Public and The Law Explosion, 1965; (with E.A. Farnsworth, William F. Young) Cases and Materials on Contracts, 1965; Law and the Social Role of Science, 1966; The Efficacy of Law, 1969. Editor in charge of dept. legislation Am. Bar Assn. Jour., 1948-51. Directing editor Univ. Textbook Series. Home: RFD 1 Box 142 Kent CT 06757 Office: Columbia Law School New York City NY 10027

JONES, HENRY, actor; b. Phila., Aug. 1, 1912; s. John F.X. and Helen (Burk) J.; A.B., St. Joseph's Coll., Phila., 1935; m. Yvonne Bergere, Jan. 1942 (dec. Oct. 1942); m. 2d, Judy Briggs, June 1946 (div. 1961); children—David, Jocelyn. Actor starring in Broadway shows, motion pictures and television; theatrical credits include Hamlet, Henry IV, Part 2, The Time of Your Life, Village Green, My Sister Eileen, This Is the Army, January Thaw, Alice in Wonderland, How I Wonder, Kathleen, Town House, They Knew What They Wanted, Metropole, A Story for a Sunday Evening, The Solid Gold Cadillac, The Bad Seed, Sunrise at Campobello, Advise and Consent; films include This Is the Army, The Lady Says No, The Bad Seed, The Girl He Left Behind, The Girl Can't Help It, Will Success Spoil Rock Hunter?, 310 to Yuma, Vertigo, Cash McCall, Bramblebush, Angel Baby, Never Too Late, The Champagne Murders, Project X, Stay Away Joe, Support Your Local Sheriff, Rascal, Angel in My Pocket, Butch Cassidy and the Sun Dance Kid, Rabbit Run, Cock-eyed Cowboys of Calico, Dirty Dingus Magee, Support Your Local Gunman, Skin Game; numerous TV appearances. Served with AUS, 1942-45. Recipient Tony award for Sunrise at Campobello, 1958; winner Variety N.Y. Drama Critics Poll for Sunrise at Campobello, 1958. Club: Players (N.Y.C.). Home: Malibu CA 90265

JONES, HENRY CAMPBELL, ins. co. exec.; b. Westfield, Mass., Feb. 25, 1902; s. Henry C. and Casandra (Martin) J.; M.E., Northeastern U., Boston, 1925, LL.D., 1962; m. Mildred Shirley, Sept. 15, 1928; children—Ronald L., David H. Fire prevention engr. Asso. Factory Mut. Fire Ins. Cos., Boston, 1926-34, fire prevention engr. Arkwright Mut. Fire Ins., Co., Boston, 1934-40, asst. v.p., 1940-42, v.p., 1942-49, pres., dir., 1949-68; chmn. bd., dir. Arkwright-Boston Mfrs. Mut. Ins. Co., 1968-71, hon. chmn., dir., 1971—, Mut. Boiler and Machinery Ins. Co., Waltham, Mass.; adv. dir. New Eng. Mchts. Nat. Bank. Exec. com. Nuclear Ins. Rating Bur. Mem. corp., trustee Northeastern U. Mem. Nat. Fire Protection Assn., U.S. C. of C., Tau Beta Pi. Conglist. Mason. Clubs: Downtown, Union (Boston); Brae Burn Country (Newton) Home: 34 Ruthven Rd Newton MA 02158 Office: 225 Wyman St Waltham MA 02154

JONES, HENRY WILLIAMS, former petroleum co. exec.; b. Ambler, Pa., Dec. 22, 1904; s. Charles Wyne and Winifred Wilton (Williams) J.; B.S., Mass. Inst. of Tech., 1926; m. 3d, Pauline Ash Juska, June 10, 1966; children by previous marriage—Stephen, Diane Elizabeth. With Atlantic Richfield Co., Phila., 1926-69, successively chem. engr., adminstrv. supr., research and devel. dept., mgr. indsl. relations, gen. mgr. indsl. relations, 1926-53, v.p., 1953-69, gen. mgr. employee and pub. relations, 1960-68, v.p. minority affairs, 1968-69, now ret. Mem. MIT corp. vis. com. Mass. Inst. Tech.; chmn. bd. trustees Community Coll. Phila.; mem. bd. Family Service Phila.; vice chmn. bd. Asso. Hosp. Service Phila. Republican. Club: Philadelphia Cricket. Contbr. articles on engring., indsl. relations to profl. jours. Home: 233 W Allens Lane Philadelphia PA 19119

JONES, HERBERT ARTHUR, banker; b. Maryland, N.Y., June 30, 1903; s. Edward Walker and Amelia A. (Fenn) J.; student Northwestern U., 1958; m. Annette Nusbaum, Apr. 6, 1940; children—Patricia Ann (Mrs. G. David Repp, Jr.), Pamela Ruth (Mrs Ernest H. Lawrence, Jr.), Herbert Arthur. With Nat. Comml. Bank & Trust Co., Albany, N.Y., 1924- -, now sr. v. p. cons.; trustee Home Savs. Bank, (Albany). Dist. chmn. U.S. Savs. Bond Com., 1962—; past pres. N.E. N. Y. Estate Planning Council. Pres. Albany Inst. History and Art. Bd. dirs. Albany County chpt. A.R.C. Mem. N.Y. State Bankers Assn. (past chmn. trust div.). Home: 5 N Helderberg Pkwy Slingerlands NY 12159 Office: 60 State St Albany NY 12201

JONES, HERBERT L., educator; b. Copperton, N.M., Dec. 2, 1904; s. Herbert M. and Myra E. (Lukens) J.; B.A., U. Ore., 1926; M.A., Ore. State Agrl. Coll., 1934, Ph.D., 1936; m. Margaret Zimmerman, Mar. 23, 1928; children—Margaret Elizabeth, Herbert Edmund. Telephone engr. Pacific Tel. & Tel., 1926-29; radio telephone engr. Bell Telephone Labs., 1929-32; instr. physics Ore. State Coll., 1935-36; instr. elec. engring. U. N.M., 1936-46; prof. elec. engring. Okla. State U., 1946-70 research prof., dir. severe storm lab. emeridus, 1970—, dir. tornado lab., 1947- -. NSF grantee, 1959. Registered profl. engr., N.M. Okla. Mem. Am. Assn. U. Prof., I.E.E.E., Internat. Platform Asso., Nat., Okla. soc. profl. engrs., Am. Meteorol. Soc., Am. Geophys. Union, Phi Beta Kappa, Sigma Xi, Sigma Phi Epsilon, Phi Kappa Phi, Sigma Tau, Pi Mu Epsilon, Kappa Mu Epsilon, Eta Kappa Nu. Lutheran. Mason, Elk, K.P. Author: The Identification of Lightning Discharges by Speric Characteristics, 1958: The Tornado Pulse Generator: A Reality, 1960; The Tornado Pulse Generator as a Criteria for the Definition of the Severe Storm, 1963; The Tornado Pulse Generator: Weatherwise, 1967; The Hurricane Pulse Generator, 1969. Discoverer tornado pulse generator and hurricane pulse generator. Home: 18450 Scott Av Tuma AZ 85364

JONES, HOMER, banker; b. Ainsworth, Ia., June 25, 1906; s. John Crawford and Nellie (Pearson) J.; A.B., State U. Ia., 1927, M.A., 1928; Ph.D., U. Chgo., 1949; m. Alice Cable Hanson, Apr. 21, 1930; children—Robert Hanson, Richard John, Douglas Coulthurst. Mem. faculty U. Pitts., 1929-30, Rutgers U., 1930-32; with Brookings Instn., 1934-35, FDIC, 1935-46, Com. Econ. Devel., 1946-49, Fed. Res. Bd., 1949-58; with Fed. Res. Bank St. Louis, 1958—, sr. v.p., 1969—, dir. econ. research, editor monthly rev., 1958—; sometime vis. prof. Washington U., St. Louis; regent's lectr. U. Cal. at Los Angeles; econ. adviser Republic of Korea. Fellow Royal Econ. Soc.; mem. Am. Statis. Assn. (past pres. Washington and St. Louis chpts.), Am. Finance Assn., Phi Beta Kappa. Author articles in field. Home: 404 Yorkshire Pl Webster Groves MO 63119 Office: 411 Locust St St Louis MO 63102

JONES, HORACE CHARLES, sales co. exec.; b. Benton, Ky., Nov. 12, 1910; s. Horace Cleveland and Evalena (Darnall) J.; diploma commerce, Northwestern U., 1929-35; m. Loretta Louise Schille, June 12, 1937; children—Charles D., Margaret L. Investment analyst City Nat. Bank & Trust Co., Chgo., 1930-38; treas. Fed. Home Loan Bank of Chgo., 1938-43; with Hickman, Williams & Co., Cin., 1947—, v.p., 1959-64, pres., 1964—. Treas. YMCA of No. Ky., 1965—; exec. allocation bd. Community Chest of Cin., 1969; mem. adv. council William Booth Meml. Hosp., Covington, Ky., 1967—. Served to lt. USNR, 1943-46. C.P.A., Ohio. Mem. Am. Iron and Steel Inst., Am. Inst. C.P.A.'s. Baptist. Clubs: Fort Mitchell (Ky.) Country; Cincinnati. Home: 625 Sunset Ct Covington KY 41011 Office: First Nat Bank Bldg Cincinnati OH 45201

JONES, HOWARD MUMFORD, author; b. Saginaw, Mich., Apr. 16 1892; s. Frank Alexander and Josephine Whitman (Miles) J.; student State Normal Sch., La Crosse, Wis., 1910-12; B.A., U. Wis., 1914; M.A., U. Chgo., 1915; Litt.D., Harvard, 1936; L.H.D., Tulane U., 1938, Ohio State U., Hebrew Union Coll., 1962, Northwestern U., 1966, Clarkson Coll. Tech., 1968; Litt.D., U. Colo., 1938, Western Res. U., U. Wis., 1948, Clark U., 1952; LL.D., Colby Coll., 1962, U. Utah, 1966, U. Windsor, 1969., Litt.D., N.Y.U., 1969; m. Clara Edgar McLure, July 13, 1918; 1 dau., Eleanor McLure; m. 2d, Bessie Judith Zaban, June 11, 1927. Asso. prof. comparative lit. U. Tex., 1919-25; asso. prof. English, Univ. of N.C., 1925-27, prof. English lit., 1927-30, prof. English, U. Mich., 1930-36; prof. English, Harvard, 1936-60, Lawrence Lowell prof. humanities, 1960-62, prof. emeritus, 1962—, editor, Harvard Library Bull., 1966-68, dean Grad. Sch. Arts and Scis., 1943-44, ednl. cons. Provost Marshal Gen's Office, 1945, Chmn. Am. Council Learned Socs., 1955-59; chmn. Weil Inst., 1959-60; Paley vis. prof. Hebrew U., Jerusalem, 1964. Guggenheim fellow, 1964-65. Mem. Mass. Hist. Soc., Modern Lang. Assn. Am., Colonial Soc. Mass., Tex. Philos. Soc. Am. Acad. Arts and Scis. (pres. 1944-51), Am. Philos. Soc., Phi Beta Kappa, Sigma Delta Chi, Delta Sigma Rho. Author: A Little Book of Local Verse, 1915; Gargoyles (poems), 1918; (play) The Shadow (in Wisconsin Plays) 1917; (brochure) The King in Hamlet, 1921; (with R.H. Griffith) A Bibliography of Works and Mss. of Byron, 1924; America and French Culture (1750-1848), 1927; The Romanesque Lyric (with P.S. Allen), 1928; The Life of Moses Coit Tyler, 1933; They Say the Forties, 1937; The Harp That Once, 1937; Ideas in America, 1944; Education and World Tragedy, 1946; The Theory of American Literature, 1948; The Frontier in American Fiction, 1956. Translated Heine's poem The North Sea, 1918, The Bright Medusa, 1952; The Pursuit of Happiness, 1953; American Humanism, 1957; Reflections on Learning, 1958; One Great Society, 1959; Emerson on Education; 1966, History and the Contemporary, 1964; O Strange New World, 1964 (Pulitzer prize for gen. nonfiction 1964; Emerson prize Phi Beta Kappa); Jeffersonianism and the American Novel, 1966; Belief and Disbelief in American Literature, 1967; The Literature of Virginia in the Seventeenth Century, 1968; The Age of Energy, 1971. Editor: The Poems of Edgar Allan Poe, 1929; Plays of Restoration and Eighteenth Century (with D. MacMillan), 1930; Major American Writers (with E.E. Leisy), 1935; The College Reader (with R.M. Lovett), 1936; Oliver Wendell Holmes (with S.I. Hayakawa), 1939; Primer of Intellectual Liberty, 1949; Modern Minds (with Richard Ludwig and Marvin Perry), 1949; Letters of Sherwood Anderson (with Walter B. Rideout), 1953; Guide to American Literature and Its Backgrounds Since 1890, 1959, rev. (with Richard M. Ludwig), 1964; A Treasury of Scientific Prose (with I. Bernard Cohen) 1963. Contbr. to periodicals. Address: Harvard U Cambridge MA 02138

JONES, HOWARD PALFREY, journalist, educator, diplomat; b. Chgo., Jan. 2, 1899; s. William Cadwallader and Ida May (Noble) J.; student U. Wis., 1917-20; Litt.B., Columbia, 1921; postgrad. U. Mich., 1925-27, Columbia, 1929- 30; LL.D., Farileigh-Dickinson U., 1962, U. Wis., 1971; L.H.D., Juniata Coll., 1970, m. Mary Rendall, Oct. 22, 1921; 1 dau., Patricia Ann (dec.). Newspaper work, 1921-39, including instr. journalism U. Mich., 1925-27; pub. relations sec. Nat. Municipal League, 1929-33, sec. league, editor Nat. Municipal Rev., 1933-39; civil service commr. N.Y. State, 1939-43, dep. comptroller, 1943; fgn. service officer Dept. State, 1948-65; chief U.S. Element Finance Br., Bipartite Control Office, Germany, 1947-48; dep. dir. Berlin office U.S. High Commr. for Germany, Berlin rep. ECA spl. mission to Germany, 1949-51, dir. Berlin element, 1951; counselor embassy Am. embassy China, 1952, charge d'affaires, 1952; chief of mission U.S. Fgn. Operations mission to Indonesia, 1954-55; dep. asst. sec. state for Far Eastern Affairs, 1955-58; ambassador to Indonesia, 1958-65; dean diplomatic corps, Djakarta, 1962- 65; chancellor East-West Center, U. Hawaii, 1965-68; research fellow Hoover Inst. on War, Revolution and Peace, Stanford, 1968-69; trustee Christian Sci. Pub. Soc.; Boston, 1969—, chmn., 1970-71. Cons. Va. Commn. on County Govt., 1931; dir. N.Y. State Commn. on Revision of Tax Laws, 1936-38; cons. Gov.'s Commn. on N.Y. State Constl. Conv., 1938; mem. gov. bd. U.S. Pub. Adminstrn. Service 1933-40; del. representing U.S. State Dept., Internat. Union of Cities, Lyons, France, 1934; U.S. delegation Colombo Plan Conf., Singapore, 1955; chmn. U.S. delegation UN Econ. Commn. for Asia and Far East, Bangolore, India, 1956; Sladen lectr. Colby Jr. Coll., 1970. Served from maj. to col. AUS, 1943-47. Fellow Oberlaender Trust of Carl Schurz Meml. Found. to study pub. adminstrn. in Germany, 1934. Recipient 50th Anniversary award Columbia U. Grad. Sch. Journalism, 1963; Distinguished Honor award Dept. State, 1964. Mem. Indonesian Soc. U.S., Sigma Nu, Sigma Delta Chi. Mason. Clubs: Columbia University, Cosmos (Washington); Algonguin (Boston). Author: Indonesia-The Possible Dream, 1971. Home: 790 Boylston St Boston MA 02199 Office: 1 Norway St Boston MA 02115

JONES, HOWARD ROBERT, coll. dean; b. St. Paul, Mar. 17, 1911; s. Fred and Jessie Floy (Salsbery) J.; B.S., U. Minn., 1933, M.A., 1936; Ph.D., Yale, 1940; L.H.D., U. N.H., 1971; m. Helen Louise Cook, Dec. 27, 1934; children—Richard Howard, Harriet Louise (Mrs. Garry Rechnitz), Virginia Cook (Mrs. Kent Tunks). Tchr., guidance counselor Sheridan Elementary and Jr. High Sch., Mpls., 1934-38; instr. edn., U. Conn., 1938; teaching asst. edn. Yale, 1938-40; asst. prof. edn. U. N.H., 1940-41, counselor charge student personnel program, 1941-42, asso. prof., asst. to dean Coll. Liberal Arts, 1942-43; supt. schs., New Canaan, Conn., 1943-46; part- time lectr. sch. adminstrn. Yale, 1943-45; pres. Plymouth (N.H.) State Coll., 1946-51; vis. prof. edn. U. Cal. at Los Angeles, summer 1957, U. Colo., summer 1961; prof. ednl. adminstrn. U. Mich., 1951-62; dean Coll. Edn., prof. edn. State U. Ia., 1962—, dir. summer session, 1962-68. U.S. rep. UNESCO seminar, 1946; mem. com. religion and pub. edn. Nat. Council Chs., 1948-55; instl. rep. Am. Assn. Colls. Tchr. Edn., 1946-51, 62—; cons. adminstrv. orgn. Centro dr Adiestriemiento de Operadores, Mexico City, 1956; mem. Mich. Ednl. Finance Adv. Com., 1952-61, chmn., 1954, 56; study tchr. edn., India, 1963, Africa, 1968. Trustee Univ. Council Ednl. Adminstrn., 1961-64; v.p. Sceva Speare Meml. Hosp. Assn., Plymouth, 1947-51, hon. life dir., 1951—. Recipient Outstanding Achievement award U. Minn., 1970. Mem. Am. Assn. U. Profs., Am. Edn. Research Assn., Am. Assn. Sch. Adminstrs. (life), N.E.A. (life), Phi Kappa Phi, Phi Delta Kappa, Kappa Delta Pi. Episcopalian. Rotarian. Author: Financing Public Elementary and Secondary Education, 1966. Contbr. profl. jours. Home: RFD 2 Solon IA 52333

JONES, HOWARD WILBUR, Jr., gynecologist; b. Balt., Dec. 30, 1910; s. Howard Wilbur and Ethel Ruth (Marling) J.; A.B., Amherst Coll., 1931; M.D., Johns Hopkins, 1935, Dr. Honoris Causa, Cordoba, 1968; m. Georgeanna Emory Seegar, June 22, 1940; children—Howard Wilbur III, Georgeanna S., Lawrence M. Intern, asst. resident, resident gynecology Johns Hopkins Hosp., 1935-37, 46-48; asst. resident, resident surgery Ch. Home and Hosp., Balt., 1937-40; practice medicine, specializing in obstetrics and gynecology, Balt., 1948—; instr., asst. prof., asso. prof., prof. gynecology and obstetrics Sch. Medicine Johns Hopkins, 1948—; nat. cons. USAF, 1968. Dir. William & Wilkins Co. Served to maj., M.C., AUS, 1943-46. Decorated Bronze Star medal. Mem. A.M.A., Am. Assn. Cancer Research, Am. Cancer Soc. (dir. Md. div.), Am. Coll. Obstetrics and Gynecology, Soc. Pelvic Surgeons, Sociedad de Obstetricia Y Gynecologia die Buenos Aires, Sociedad Peruana de Obstetricia Y Ginecologia. Author: (with W.W. Scott) Hermaphroditism, Genital Anomalies and Related Endocrine Disorders, 1958, rev. edit., 1971; (with E.R. Novak and G.S. Jones) Textbook of Gynecology, 1965, 8th edit., 1971; (with R. Heller) Pediatric and Adolescent Gynecology, 1968. Editor in chief (with G.E.S. Jones) Obstetrical and Gynecological Survey, 1957—. Contbr. articles to profl. jours. Home: 325 Hawthorne Rd Baltimore MD 21210 Office: 601 N Broadway Baltimore MD 21205

JONES, HUGH HENRY, Jr., banker; b. Pitts., Apr. 22, 1930; s. Hugh H. and Merriem (Robinson) J.; A.B., Lafayette Coll., 1952; M.B.A., N.Y. U.; grad. Stonier Grad. Sch. Banking, New Brunswick, N.J.; m. Mary Joyce Mackie, Feb. 5, 1955; children—Cynthia Arlene, Merriem Ruth, Laura Elizabeth. With Chem. Bank N.Y. Trust Co., 1954-69; sr. v.p. Barnett First Nat. Bank, Jacksonville, Fla., 1970—; 1st v.p., dir. Barnett Banks Fla., Inc. Presbyn. Home: 4933 Long Bow Rd Jacksonville FL 32210

JONES, HUGH MCKITTRICK, architect; b. St. Louis, Oct. 6, 1919, s. Hugh McKittrick and Carroll (West) J.; B.S., Harvard, 1940, B.Arch., 1942, M.Arch., 1947; m. Elizabeth Siddons Mowbray, Sept. 9, 1940; children—Cynthia Siddons (Mrs. Paul Charles Hachten), Terry West (Mrs. James Henry Eddy, Jr.), Hugh McKittrick III, Timothy Millard. Trainee, Office Walter Bogner, Cambridge, Mass., 1945-47, Office Douglas Orr, New Haven, 1947-49; architect Jones & Mowbray, New Haven and Guilford, Conn., 1949-54; architect Office Hugh Jones, Guilford, 1954—; corporator, trustee Guilford Savs. Bank, 1954—. Mem. Guilford Republican Party Town Com., 1952—; mem. Guilford Town Planning Commn., 1953-58, chmn., 1956; mem. Regional Planning Agy., 1961-69; rep. Conn. Ho. Reps., 1963-67; mem. Conn. Commn. to Study Metro Govt., 1965-67; mem. Guilford Land Conservation Trust, 1965—. Served to lt. USNR, 1942-46; PTO. Registered profl. architect, N.Y., Conn. Fellow A.I.A. (pres. Conn. chpt., 1962, 63; dir., pres. New Eng. regional council 1970—), Guilford C. of C., Sierra Club. Rotarian. Clubs: New Haven Lawn; Sachems Head Yacht (Guilford). Principal works include Country Sch., Madison, Conn., Fire House, Fishers Island, N.Y., Stevens residence, Guilford, Russell residence, W. Hartford. Home: 265 Dromara Rd Guilford CT 06437 Office: 71 Whitfield St Guilford CT 06437

JONES, IRENE ANN, former ch. exec.; b. Carbondale, Pa.; d. Daniel and Harriet Ann (Mason) Jones; A.B., Cornell U., 1926; M.A., Columbia, 1936; Ph.D., U. Pa., 1947; M.R.E., Eastern Bapt. Theol. Sem., 1943. Tchr., Jermyn, Pa. until 1933; dean women Eastern Bapt. Theol. Sem., 1934-43; home sec. Woman's Am. Bapt. Fgn. Mission Soc. (merged into Am. Bapt. Fgn. Mission Soc. 1955), 1943-55; asso. dir. pub. relations Am. Bapt. Fgn. Mission Socs., 1955-56, asso. gen. sec., 1956-66; asso. exec. sec. div. fgn. missions Nat. Council Chs., 1956-64, exec. dir. dept. specialized ministries, 1965-66, del. nat. assembly, 1966—, vice chmn. div. overseas ministries, 1969-71, Vice chmn Internat. Missionary Council, 1958-61; del. 3d assembly World Council Chs., New Delhi, India, 1961, mem. div. com., div. world mission and evangelism, 1961-63, del. meeting commn. world mission and evangelism, Mexico City, 1963—, del. 4th Assembly, Uppsala, Sweden, 1968; chmn. Com. on Christian Lit. for Women and children in Mission Fields, 1969—. Author: Adult Guide on India, Pakistan, Ceylon, 1954; Into All the World Together, 1960; also articles. Home: 100 LaSalle St New York City NY 10027

JONES, J. ELIAS, librarian; b. Cleve., Oct. 18, 1916; s. John Elias and Mary Margaret (Johnstone) J.; student Oberlin Coll., 1936-37; A.B., Case- Western U., 1941, B.L.S., 1942, A.M., 1951, Ph.D., 1961; m. Loretta Ann Bucher, July 2, 1942; children—Richard Lloyd, Laura Louise, Hilary Margaret, Mark Edwin. Asst. bus. information bur. Cleve. Pub. Library, 1942, asst. sci. and tech. div., 1945-47,, asst. head sci. and tech. div., 1949-52, chief cataloging dept., 1952-57; research librarian Ferro Corp., Cleve., 1947- 49; mng. editor Enamelist mag., 1948-50; dir. libraries Drake U., now asso. librarian, chief bibliographer, asso. prof.; vis. instr. Rutgers U. School Library Service, summer 1956, U. Denver Sch. Librarianship, summer 1957; instr. Russian, Community Coll., Drake U., 1960-. Served with AUS, 1943-45. Mem. A.L.A., Ia. Library Assn., Adult Edn. Assn. U.S., Bibliog. Soc. Am., History of Sci. Soc., Phi Sigma Iota. Episcopalian. Mason. Club: Torch (Des Moines). Home: 1332 40th St Des Moines IA 50311 Office: Cowles Library 28th and University Av Des Moines IA 50311

JONES, J. RAYMOND, politician; b. Virgin Islands, 1900. Mem. N.Y. City Council. Chmn. N.Y. County Dem. Orgn. (Tammany Hall) Address: 270 Convent Av New York City NY 10031*

JONES, JACK vocalist. Address: care Kappa Records Inc 136 E 57th St New York City NY 10022*

JONES, JAMES author; b. Robinson, Ill., Nov. 6, 1921; s. Ramon and Ada (Blessing) J.; student U. Hawaii, 1942, N.Y. U., 1945; m. Gloria Mosolino, 1957; children—Kaylie, Jamie. Served with U.S. Army, 1939-44. Decorated Purple Heart, B.S.M. Author: From Here to Eternity (Nat. Book award), 1951; Some Came Running, 1957; The Pistol, 1959; The Thin Red Line, 1962; Go to the Widow-Maker, 1967; The Ice-Cream Headache, 1968; The Merry Month of May, 1971. Home: 10 Quai d'Orleans Ile Saint Louis Paris 4e France Office: care Dell Pub Co Inc 750 3d Av New York City NY 10017

JONES, JAMES, basketball player; b. Tallulah, La., Jan. 1, 1945; s. Arthur Williams and Lubertha Jones Herring; B.S., Grambling Coll., 1967; m. Jean Randle, Apr. 3, 1965; 1 son, Michael. Formerly guard for New Orleans Buccaneers, now for Memphis Pros. Mem. All-Rookie team, 1967-68, All-league team, 1968-69, All-Star team, 1968-71. Home: 4074 Tarry Wood St Memphis TN 38118 Office: Mid-South Collesium Memphis TN 38118

JONES, JAMES BEVERLY, educator, engr.; b. Kansas City, Mo., Aug. 21, 1923; s. Alonzo Lewis and Bertha (Crockett) J.; B.S., Va. Poly. Inst., 1944; M.S. in Mech. Engring., Purdue U., 1947, Ph.D., 1951; m. Jane Hardcastle, Oct. 20, 1945; children—Ellen Elizabeth, Warren Howard. Asst. mech. engr. Engr. Bd., U.S. War Dept., Ft.

Belvoir, Va., 1944-45; devel. engr. Gen. Electric Co., Schenectady, 1951-52; asst. instr. Purdue U., Lafayette, Ind., 1945-47, instr., 1947-51, asst. prof., 1951-54, asso. prof., 1954-57, prof., 1957-64; prof., head dept. mech. engring. Va. Poly. Inst. and State U. at Blacksburg, 1964—; faculty fellow Swiss Fed. Inst. Tech. at Zurich, 1961-62; cons. mech. engring. Mem. Am. Inst. Aeros. and Astronautics, Am. Soc. M.E., Am. Soc. Engring. Edn., Nat. Soc. Profl. Engrs. Presbyn. Rotarian. Club: Torch (Blacksburg). Author: (with G.A. Hawkins) Engineering Thermodynamics, 1960. Home: 1503 Palmer Dr SE Blacksburg VA 24060

JONES, JAMES EARL, actor; b. Tate County, Miss., Jan. 17, 1931; s. Robert Earl and Ruth (Williams) J.; B.A., U. Mich., 1953; diploma Am. Theatre Wing, 1957. Appeared in plays Romeo and Juliet, 1955, Wedding in Japan, 1957, Sunrise at Campobello, 1958, The Pretender, 1959, The Cool World, 1960, King Henry V., 1960, Measure for Measure, 1960, The Blacks, 1961, A Midsummer Night's Dream, 1961, The Apple, 1961, Moon on a Rainbow Shawl, 1962, Infidel Caesar, 1962, The Merchant of Venice, 1962, The Tempest, 1962, Toys in the Attic, 1962, P.S. 193, 1962, Macbeth, 1962, The Love Nest, 1963, The Last Minstrel, 1963, Othello, 1963, 68, The Winter's Tale, 1963, Mr. Johnson, 1963, Next Time I'll Sing to You, 1963, Bloodknot, 1964; appeared in movie Dr. Strangelove, 1963; TV appearances include The Defenders, 1962, East Side/West Side, 1963, Camcer 3, 1963, Look Up and Live, 1963. Mem. Nat. Council of Arts. Recipient The Village Voice Off- Broadway awards, 1962, Theatre World award, 1962; Tony award for best actor in Great White Hope, 1969. Address: 19 Allen St New York City NY 10002 *

JONES, JAMES HAROLD, banker; b. Harrison, Ark., Aug. 26, 1930; s. Charlie Mac and Pearl Mary (Wood) J.; B.S. in Bus. Adminstrn., U. Ark., 1953; grad. Southwestern Grad. Sch. Banking, So. Meth. U., 1960, Advanced Mgmt. Program Harvard; m. Peggy Lou Bort, Apr. 2, 1960; children— James Bort, Cliff O., Lee-C. With Lakewood State Bank, Dallas, 1953-54; with Republic Nat. Bank of Dallas, 1954—, v.p., 1960—, sr. v.p., 1963-67, exec. v.p., 1967-69, also chmn. real estate loan com., mem. exec. and sr. loan coms.; pres., dir. Nat. Bank Commerce New Orleans (name changed to First Nat. Bank Commerce 1971, 1969—; v.p. Howard Corp., Dallas, Rheims Corp.; chmn., dir., chief exec. officer First Commerce Real Estate Corp.; chmn., dir., pres. First Commerce Corp., 1971—; trustee Lomas & Nettleton Mortgage Investors. Chmn., lectr. real estate div. Southwestern Grad. Sch. Banking, 1964-65; faculty mem. Banking Sch. of South, La. State U.; mem. bus. sch. council Tulane U. Grad. Sch. Bus. Mem. New Orleans Bd. City Trusts. Bd. dirs., mem. exec. com., finance com., annuity bd. So. Bapt. Conv. Mem. Am. Bankers Assn. (urban affairs com.), Assn. Res. City Bankers, U. Ark. Alumni Assn., C. of C. Greater New Orleans (treas. 1971, dir.), Young Pres. Assn., La. Bankers Assn., Phi Lambda Chi. Clubs: Dallas Athletic Country, Club de Banqueros de Mexico; New Orleans Country, International House (v.p. 1971). Home: 440 Walnut St New Orleans LA 70118 Office: PO Box 60279 New Orleans LA 70160

JONES, JAMES REES, oil co. exec.; b. Britton, S.D., Nov. 26, 1916; s. Buell Fay and Florence (Bockler) J.; B.S. in Accountancy, U. Ill., 1938; m. Betty Jane Preston, May 23, 1943; children—Quentin Buell, Newton James, Preston Lee. From accountant to sr. accountant Ernst & Ernst, C.P.A.'s, ., Detroit and Kalamazoo, 1938-41; auditor, then div. auditor, chem. plant office mgr. Pan Am. Petroleum Corp., 1948-56; comptroller Amoco Chems. Corp., Chgo., 1956-62; mgr. auditing Standard Oil Co. Ind., 1962-63; controller Murphy Oil Corp., El Dorado, Ark., 1963—, dir., 1968—; controller Ocean Drilling & Exploration Co., El Dorado, 1963-66, dir., 1966—; v.p., controller, director Deltic Farm & Timber Co., Inc., El Dorado, 1963—. Mem. El Dorado Water Utilities Commn. Past pres., bd. dirs. United Campaign EL Dorado. Served to capt. AUS, 1941-46. Mem. Financial Execs. Inst., Am. Petroleum Inst., Mid-Continent Oil and Gas Assn., Phi Kappa Psi. Clubs: Internat. (Washington); El Dorado Golf and Country. Home: 2001 W Oak St EL Dorado AR 71730 Office: 200 Jefferson Av EL Dorado AR 71730

JONES, JAMES VICTOR, mfg. co. exec.; b. Toronto, Ont., Can., Dec. 4, 1913; s. Robert Victor and Elizabeth Ann (Abraham) J.; came to U.S., 1924, naturalized, 1931; Ph.B., U. Chgo., 1936; m. Beatrice Carolyn Beal, Apr. 5, 1941; children—Carol Ann, Roberta Beth, Ellen Gav, Jennifer Vee. With Armstrong Cork Co., 1936—, v.p., gen. mgr. bldg., industry and def. products, 1963-68, exec. v.p., 1968—. Home: 300 Eshelman Rd Lancaster PA 17601 Office: Armstrong Cork Co Lancaster PA 17604

JONES, JAMES VICTOR, librarian; b. Willard. O., May 14, 1924 s. Harry D. and Hazel (Kuhn) J.; student Fenn Coll., 1942-43, U. Ala., 1943-44; B.S. magna cum laude, John Carroll U., 1949; M.S., Western Res. U., 1950; m. Elizabeth Jean Stillions, Aug. 17, 1946; children—Kathryn Lee, Kenneth James, Richard Joseph, Christopher John. Student library asst. Fenn. Coll., 1942-43, John Carroll U., 1947-48; student library asst. Western Res. U., 1948- 49, reference asst., 1950; librarian Sch. Commerce and Finance St. Louis U., 1950-52, asst. dir. libraries, 1952-55, dir. libraries, 1955-66; dir. libraries Cleve. State U., 1966-68; dir. univ. libraries Case Western Res. U., Cleve., 1968—. Asso. Leadership Tng. Project, N. Central Assn. Colls. and Secondary Schs., 1962-63, examiner, cons., 1963—. Mem. bd. govs. Case Western Res U., 1965-67, chmn. vis. com. Sch. Library Sci., 1966-68; bd. overseers Case Western Res. U., 1967-68; council Center Research Libraries, 1965-66. Mem. Ohio, Cath. (pres. Greater St. Louis unit 1959-61, chmn. scholarship com. 1959-63), Am. (mem. council 1959-61) library assns., Spl. Libraries Assn. (conv. chmn. 1964), Assn. Coll. and Research Libraries (past chmn. com. liaison with accrediting agys.), Am. Soc. for Information Sci., St. Louis Library Club (past pres.), Beta Phi Mu. Roman Catholic. Adv. editor Manuscripta, 1957-66. Contbr. articles to profl. jours. Home: 2841 Berkshire Rd Cleveland Heights OH 44118 Office: Freiberger Library Case Western Reserve U 11161 East Blvd Cleveland OH 44106

JONES, JAMESON MILLER, clergyman, coll. dean; b. Corinth, Miss., Jan. 8, 1916; s. Paul Tudor and Sara (Shelton) J.; A.B., Southwestern, 1936; B.D., Louisville Presbyn. Theol. Sem., 1939; Ph.D., Duke U., 1942; m. Clarece McElroy Nichols, Aug. 16, 1945 (dec. Apr. 1950); children—Calvin Nichols, Samuel Nichols; m. 2d, Dorothy Darnell, June 17, 1952; children—John, Sara. Ordained to ministry Presbyn. Ch. U.S., Transylvania Presbytery, 1942; prof. religion and philosophy Poly. Inst. of P.R., 1948-49, Centre Coll. of Ky., Danville, 1942-48, dean, 1949-55; dean, Southwestern at Memphis, 1955-71; asso. dir. Memphis Acad. Arts, 1971—. Mem. Phi Beta Kappa, Omicron Delta Kappa. Home: 1747 Forrest Av Memphis TN 38112

JONES, JAREN LLOYD, real estate developer; b. Bountiful, Utah, Nov. 26, 1909; s. Joseph P. and Martha L. (Tolman) J.; LL.B., U. Utah, 1934; married Betty Callister, October 2, 1933; children—Betty M. (Mrs. Jerold L. Davis), Sharon (Mrs. Gordon R. Clawson). Janet (Mrs. Robert Flegal), Susan (Mrs. Steven G. Westerberg). Admitted to Utah bar, 1934, since practiced Salt Lake City: pres., dir. Rainbow Randevu, Inc., 1936—; pres. Cottonwood Hills, 1962—; pres., dir. Oak Hills, Inc., 1952—; dir., mem. exec. com. Hotel Utah, 1958—. Mem. Rep. Nat. Com. for Utah, 1956-61, mem. exec. com., 1958-61. Chmn. Utah Legislative Council, 1957-58; mem. Utah Com. Indsl. and Employment Planning. Utah Coordinating Bd. Higher Edn., Utah Civil Defense Bd. Utah Constl. Study Group. Mem. Utah Ho. of Reps., 1951-58, speaker, 1957-58. Mem. Nat. Assn. Home Builders, Nat. Assn. Real Estate Bds., Nat. Inst. Real Estate Brokers. Clubs: Salt Lake Country (sec.-treas., dir.), Alta (Salt Lake City). Home: 998 Oak Hills Way Salt Lake City UT 84108 Office: Continental Bank Bldg Salt Lake City UT 84101

JONES, JENKIN LLOYD, editor, publisher; b. Madison, Wis., Nov. 1, 1911; s. Richard Lloyd and Georgia (Hayden) J.; student Culver (Ind.) Mil. Acad., 1925, The Tome Sch., Port Deposit, Md., 1926-29; Ph. B., U. Wis., 1933; m. Juanita Carlson, Nov. 12, 1935; children—Jenkin, David, Georgia. Reporter and columnist Tulsa (Okla.) Tribune, 1933-36, mng. editor, 1936-38, asso. editor, 1938-41, editor, 1941—, also pub.; v.p. Tulsa Tribune Co., 1938—; writer weekly newspaper column syndicated by Gen. Features Corp.; dir. Newspaper Printing Corp. Served as communications officer USNR. 1944-46; took part in Iwo Jima and Okinawa campaigns aboard U.S.S. Makassar Strait, CVE 91, 1945; lt. comdr. USNR, ret. Recipient William Allen White award, 1957. Mem. Am. Soc. Newspaper Editors (pres. 1956), V.F.W., U.S. C. of C. (pres. 1969), Phi Gamma Delta, Sigma Delta Chi. Republican. Unitarian. Clubs: National Press, Southern Hills Country. Author: The Changing World. Home: 2272 E 38th St Tulsa OK 74105 Office: Tulsa Tribune Tulsa OK 74103

JONES, JENNIFER, actress; b. Tulsa, Okla., d. Philip R. and Flora Mae (Suber) Isley; ed. pub. schs., Tulsa, Oklahoma City, Okla., Dallas, Tex.; Monte Cassino Jr. Coll.; Northwestern U.; Am. Acad. Dramatic Arts; m. Robert Walker, Jan. 2, 1939 (div. June 1945); children—Robert Hudson, Michael Ross; m. 2d, David O. Selznick, July 13, 1949 (dec. 1965); 1 dau., Mary Jennifer, m. 3d, Norton Simon, May 30, 1971. Appeared stock cos.; actress in motion pictures, 1943—, The Song of Bernadette; Since You Went Away; Cluny Brown; Love Letters; Duel in the Sun; We Were Strangers; Madame Bovary; Portrait of Jennie; Carrie; Wild Heart; Ruby Gentry; Indiscretion of an American Wife; Beat the Devil; Love is a Many-Splendored Thing; Good Morning, Miss Dove; The Man in the Gray Flannel Suit; The Barretts of Wimpole Street, A Farewell to Arms; Tender Is The Night, The Idol. Recipient Acad. Motion Pictures Arts and Scis. award for best performance by an actress (for work in Song of Bernadette), 1943; Winged Victory award (France), 1948; Triunfo award (Spain). 1953; Film Critics Award (Japan), 1953; First Annual Audience award, 1955; winner Nat. Critics Poll, 1955; award Stars and Stripes; citation for war work A.R.C.; medal and citation for work at front during Korean War. ‡

JONES, JENNINGS HINCH, educator; b. Petrolia, Pa., Aug. 19, 1913; s. George Findred and Florence Jennings (Hinch) J.; B.S., Pa. State U., 1934, M.S., 1937, Ph.D., 1941; m. Katherine E. Campbell, Nov. 16, 1940; children—Ellen F. (Mrs. James F. Balsley), Trudy K. (Mrs. Micheal Schobinger). Chemist, Pa. Coal Products Co., Petrolia, 1934-36; faculty Pa. State U., University Park, 1941—, prof. chem. engring., 1941—. Cons. in field. Fellow Am. Inst. Chemists; mem. Am. Chem. Soc., Am. Inst. Chem. Engrs., Sigma Xi, Phi Lambda Upsilon. Patentee in field. Home: 229 S Gill St State College PA 16801 Office: Chem Engring Bldg University Park PA 16802

JONES, JERRY DILMAN, resort exec.; b. San Francisco, Apr. 1, 1942; s. Prentice Ray and Bernadine (Fields) J.; student Boise Coll., 1960-61, San Francisco State Coll., 1961-62, Merritt Davis Sch. Commerce, 1961; m. Julie Hurst, Oct. 19, 1966. Front office mgr. Hotel Boise (Ida.), 1960-61, Sir Francis Drake Hotel, San Francisco, 1961-63; room clk. Princess Kaiulani Hotel, Honolulu, 1963; asst. mgr. Hotel Boise, 1964-65; asst. mgr. Sun Valley Lodge (Ida.), 1965-66; reservation and conv. mgr. Sun Valley Co., Inc., 1966-68, dir. hotel operations, dir. marketing, 1968—; v.p. Sun Valley Co. Inc., 1971—. Arrangements chmn. Nat. Rep. Gov.'s Conf., 1970, Brown Bros. Harriman World Bank meeting, 1968; prodn. coordinator Peggy Fleming at Sun Valley TV spl., 1971. Dir. Employees United Fund, 1964. Served as sgt., Air N.G., 1968. Named promoter of the week for Ida., 1969. Mem. Ida. Hotel Assn. (dir.), Am. Soc. Travel Agts., Western Am. Conv. and Travel Inst. Home: PO Box 423 Sun Valley ID 83353 Office: Sun Valley Co Inc Sun Valley ID 83353

JONES, JOE CHESTER, govt. ofcl.; b. Birmingham, Ala., Sept. 18, 1922; s. James Marion and Cynthia (Byram) J.; B.S. in Aero. Engring., Auburn U., 1943; S.M. in Indsl. Mgmt. (Sloan fellow), Mass. Inst. Tech., 1957; m. Mary Emma Bowdon, Aug. 17, 1940; children—Cynthia Louise (Mrs. Dennis William Wertz), Cheri Lynn (Mrs. William Carroll Dyer), James Marion, Joe Chester. Organizer, head Air Force Engring. Field Orgn., Air Research and Devel. Command, 1947-50, founder, tech. dir. nuclear powered aircraft div., 1951-55; spl. asst. to comdr. Wright Air Devel. Center, 1955; tech. dir. Nuclear Bomber Weapons System, 1956; tech. dir. Joint Air Force/AEC Aircraft Nuclear Propulsion Office, AEC, Germantown, Md., 1958-60; dep. dir. tech. operations div. Advanced Research Projects Agy., 1960-61, dir. plans div., 1961; staffmem., dep. for devel. asst. sec. Air Force for research and devel., Dept. Air Force, Washington, 1961-66, dep. asst. sec. for research and devel., 1966—. Mem. research and tech. adv. com. on aeronautics NASA, 1968, 69, 70. Served from 2nd lt. to captain USAAF, 1943-46. Recipient Exceptional Civilian Service award USAF, 1965 and 1969. Mem. Soc. Sloan Fellows, Sigma Nu. Home: 909 Hyde Rd Silver Spring MD 20902 Office: Deputy Asst Sec Air Force Research and Devel Dept of Air Force Pentagon Washington DC 20330

JONES, JOHN CLIFTON, surgeon; b. Steubenville, O., Nov. 18, 1903; s. James Cornelius and Sarah Ann (Evans) J.; B.A., Ohio Wesleyan U., 1925; M.D., U. Mich., 1929; D.Sc. (hon.), Ohio Wesleyan U., 1969. Intern, St. Vincent's Charity Hosp., Cleve., 1929-30; fellow surgery Cleve. Clinic, 1930-32; asst. surgery (thoracic) U. Mich. Hosp., 1932-34; pvt. practice medicine, Los Angeles, 1934—; clin. prof. surgery U. So. Cal. Med. Sch., 1952—; chief thoracic surgery Children's Hosp., Los Angeles County Gen. Hosp., Barlow Sanatorium, Good Hope Med. Found.; attending surgeon Hosp. of Good Samaritan, St. Vincent's Hosp.; cons. thoracic surgeon Santa Fe Hosp. Assn. Trustee Children's Hosp., Los Angeles, Barlow Sanatorium. Diplomate Am. Bd. Thoracic Surgery (founder), Am. Bd. of Surgery. Fellow A.C.S. (past 1st v.p.); mem. Soc. Thoracic Surgeons (a founder), Am., Western, Pacific Coast (past pres.) surg. assns., Am. Assn. Thoracic Surgery (past pres.), Internat. Cardiovascular Soc., Soc. Vascular Surgery, Nat. Tb Assn., Am. Trudeau Soc., A.M.A., Internat. Soc. Surgery. Home: 545 S Figueroa St Los Angeles CA 90017 Office: 1136 W 6th St Los Angeles CA 90017

JONES, JOHN GRANDEL, mfg. co. exec.; b. Mpls., 1920; ed. U. Minn., 1941; postgrad. Harvard Bus. Sch., N.Y. U. Former treas., dir. Chesebrough-Pond's, Inc., N.Y.C.; controller, gen. mgr. container Machinery Bostitch div. Textron, East Greenwich, R.I., 1948-62; mgmt. positions Gen. Electric Co., Bridgeport, Conn., 1941-42, 45-46; v.p. finance, dir. Econs. Lab. Inc., St. Paul, 1970—; dir. Real Petroleum Co., Wichita, Kan. Mem. Financial Execs. Inst., Am. Mgmt. Assn. Clubs: Marco Polo (N.Y.C.); Town and Country (St. Paul). Home: 320 S Mississippi River Blvd St Paul MN 55105 Office: Osborn Bldg St Paul MN 55102

JONES, JOHN HARRIS, lawyer, banker; b. New Blaine, Ark., Apr. 9, 1922; s. Ira Burton and Byrd (Harris) J.; A.B., State Coll. Ark., 1941; postgrad. George Washington U. Law Sch., 1941-42; LL.B., Yale, 1947; m. Mardis Bennett, May 25, 1951. Communications clk. FBI, 1941-42; admitted to Ark. bar, 1946, also U.S. Supreme Ct.; practice in Pine Bluff, 1947—; spl. judge Circuit Ct., 1950. Chmn. bd. Pine Bluff Nat. Bank, 1964—, pres., 1966- -. Mem. Ark. Bd. Law Examiners, 1953-59. Vice pres., dir. John Rust Found., 1953-60. Served to 1st lt. USAAF, 1943-45. Decorated Purple Heart, Air medal. Mem. Am., Ark., Jefferson County (pres. 1959-60) bar assns., Am. Judicature Soc., Res. Officers Assn. Mem. Christian Ch. (elder 1963-65, trustee 1965—). Club: Pine Bluff Country. Home: 3711 Mulberry St Pine Bluff AR 71601 Office: National Bldg Pine Bluff AR 71601

JONES, JOHN HAYDN, educator; b. Utica, N.Y., Feb. 16, 1910; s. John G. and Edith H. (Edwards) J.; student Utica Free Acad., 1924-27; A.B., Hamilton Coll., 1931, A.M., 1934, L.H.D., 1961; m. Charlotte Jane Weaver, June 29, 1940; children—Jeremy, Peter Jeffrey, John Christopher, Charlotte, Jennifer. Instr. pub. speaking Hamilton Coll., 1931-33; tchr. English Deerfield Acad., 1935-49; headmaster Riverdale Country Sch. for Boys, N.Y.C. 1945—. Bd. dirs. Camp Dudley, Westport, N.Y., Forest Neighborhood House, N.Y.C. Mem. Country Day Sch. Headmasters' Assn., Headmasters Assn. Republican. Episcopalian. Home: Riverdale Country Sch 253rd St and Fieldston Rd New York City NY 10471

JONES, JOHN HUGH MOWBRAY, bus. exec.; b. Sault Ste. Marie, Ont., Can., Aug. 24, 1905; s. Charles Hugh L. and Elisabeth (Kennedy) J.; student Upper Can. Coll.; B.S. with honors, U. Toronto, 1927; D.Eng., N.S. Tech. Coll., 1959; m. Phyllis L. Hodges, Apr. 7, 1934; children—Jenepher, Sandra Stephanie, Daryl, Dereck. With engring. dept. Spanish River Pulp & Paper Co., Ltd., 1927-28; engr. Abitibi Power & Paper Co., Sault Ste. Marie, 1928; with Bowaters Mersey Paper Co., Ltd. (formerly Mersey Paper Co.), Liverpool, N.S., 1928—, successively resident engr., chief engr., mill mgr., 1928- 47. v.p., dir., 1947-58, pres., gen. mgr., dir., 1958-62, chmn., 1962- 67, now dir.: pres., dir. Glencannon Corp., Ste. Foy, Chateau Bonne Entente, Ste. Foy, White Point Beach Lodge, Ltd. (N.S.); dir., chmn., mem. exec. com. Hermes Electronics Can., Ltd., Dartmouth, N.S.; dir. Kenting, Ltd., Calgary, Bank of Montreal, Dresden Arms, Ltd., Crown Life Ins. Co., Toronto, Minas Basin Pulp & Power Co., Ltd., Hantsport, N.S., N.S. Light & Power Co., Ltd., Maritime Paper Products, Ltd., Halifax, Halifax Devel. Ltd., Bowater Paper Corp., London, Eng., Bowater U.S. Corp., Ben's Holdings, Ltd., Argyle Securities, Ltd., Grand Hotel Co. Ltd., Yarmouth, N.S., Maritime Cans Ltd., Brit. Nfld. Corp., Halifax Internat. Containers Ltd. Serving brother order St. John Jerusalem. Chmn. bd. Queens Gen. Hosp. Assn., Liverpool, N.S.; gov. Royal Edward Hosp. Served to maj. Res. Army, 1943-45. Mem. Assn. Profl. Engrs. N.S. (pres. 1944), Engring. Inst. Can. (life), Delta Kappa Epsilon. Conservative. Anglican. Kiwanan (lt. gov. Maritime div. 1937) (Liverpool). Clubs: Mount Royal, Montreal Badminton and Squash (Montreal): Garrison (Quebec): Halifax, Royal Nova Scotia Yacht Squadron, Ashburn Golf (Halifax); Liverpool Golf and Country (Liverpool). Home: 250 Clarke Av Westmount Montreal 215 Quebec Canada

JONES, JOHN PAUL, transit exec.; b. Cin., June 12, 1916; s. Edward William and Lily (Morrissey) J.; B.B.A., U. Cin., 1939; m. Dorothy Pearl Hoffhouse, Apr. 27, 1944; children—Gerald Paul, Julia Ann. With Cin. Transit Co., 1937- -, successively traffic researcher, claim investigator, staff asst., asst. to pres., dir. pub. relations, 1937-55, pres., dir., 1956—. Served to 2d lt., AUS, 1941-45. Mem. Pub. Relations Soc. Am., Ohio Transit Assn. (pres. 1959-63, 70-71), Young Presidents Orgn., Cincinnatus Assn., Cin. C. of C. (dir. 1967—), Am. Transit Assn. (pres. 1969-70), Cin. Conv. Bur. (pres. 1962-64), Cin. Hist. Soc., Newcomen Soc., Ohio C. of C., Cin. Council World Affairs. Clubs: University, Queen City, Cincinnati Country (Cin.); Literary. Home: 3561 Bayard Dr Cincinnati OH 45208 Office: 6 E 4th St Cincinnati OH 45202

JONES, JOHN ROBERT, educator, physician, surgeon; b. Pandora, O., Feb. 18, 1924; s. Lawrence E. and Edna (Gardner) J.; B.S., U. Mich., 1946, M.D., 1951; m. Mildred Ann LaRue, Apr. 27, 1946; children—Larry, Susan, Sharon, Nancy. Intern, U. Hosp., Ann Arbor, Mich., 1951-52; resident Ohio State U., 1952-54, chief resident dept. anesthesia, 1953-54, instr. dept. anesthesia, 1956-58, asst. prof., 1958-59; asso. prof. dept. anesthesia Marquette U., 1960-62; prof. surgery sect. anesthesia U. Neb. Coll. Medicine, Omaha, 1962—, prof. oral surgery dept. oral surgery Coll. Dentistry, 1969—. Mem. Westside Community Council, Sch. Dist. 66, 1966-67; treas. Arbor Heights Jr. High Sch. Booster Club, 1967-68. Served with USNR, 1954-56. Recipient Golden Apple award Student Am. Med. Assn., 1967-68; named Best Clin. Instr., U. Neb. Coll. Medicine, 1963-64. Hon. Adm. Neb. Navy, 1966; Shackelford prof. surgery (anesthesia), 1969. Diplomate Am. Bd. Anesthesia. Fellow Am. Coll. Anesthesiologist (bd. govs., com. chmn.); mem. A.M.A., Am. (com. chmn.), Neb. socs. anesthesiologists, Internat. Anesthesia Research Soc., Neb., Douglas County med. socs., Omaha Midwest Clin. Soc., Assn. U. Anesthetists, Soc. Acad. Anesthesiologists (chmn.), Neb. Heart Assn., Sigma Xi, Alpha Omega Alpha. Contbr. articles profl. jours. Home: 712 S 94th Av Omaha NB 68114

JONES, JOHN TILFORD, Jr., broadcasting exec.; b. Dallas, Dec. 2, 1917; s. John Tilford and Margaret (Wilson) J.; student N.M. Mil. Inst., 1935-38, U. Texas, 1938- 40; m. Winifred Ann Small, Oct. 20, 1945; children—Melissa Ann, Jesse Holman II, John Clinton. Pres. Houston Chronicle Pub. Co., 1949-66, Houston Consol. TV Co., 1954-67, Rusk Corp., 1965—; broadcast exec. KTRH-AM, KLOL-FM; pres. Battlegroung Corp.; dir. Fischback & Moore, Inc., Am. Gen. Ins. Co. Vice pres., dir. Tex. Med. Center, Inc. Served from lt. to capt., AUS, ETO, 1940-45. Presbyn. Office: Gulf Bldg Houston TX 77002

JONES, JOHN WESLEY, past ambassador; b. Sioux City, Ia., June 4, 1907; s. Edward Hannibal and Ida May (Murrison) J.; student Morningside Coll., Sioux City, 1926- 28, LL.D., 1964; A.B., George Washington U., 1930; m. Katharine N. del Valle, May 21, 1938; children—Peter Edward, Valentine Sevier, Frances Thornton. Joined U.S. Fgn. Service, 1930; vice consul, Saltillo, Mexico, 1931-32, Calcutta, India, 1932-35; vice consul, Rome, Italy, 1935-37, consul, 1937-41; assigned State Dept., 1941-45, asst. chief S. European affairs, 1944-45; 1st sec. embassy, Rome, 1945-48; counselor embassy, Nanking, China, 1948-49, Madrid, Spain, 1949-53; dir. Office Western European Affairs, State Dept., 1953-57; dep. asst. sec. state, 1957-58; U.S. ambassador to Libya, 1958-62, to Peru, 1963-69; dep. comdt. Nat. War Coll., Washington, 1969-71, now ret. Home: Flat Rock NC

JONES, JOSEPH FRECH, food co. exec.; b. DeSoto, Mo., Nov. 5, 1914; s. Roscoe B. and Eva (Frech) J.; B.S. in Mech. Engring., U. Mo., 1936; m. Frances K. McLaughlin, June 27, 1945; children—Michael F., Christopher J., Mark J., Nancy K., Sarah M. With prodn. dept. Ralston Purina Co., St. Louis, 1936- 42, mgr. prodn. div., 1945-60; v.p. Central Soya Co., Inc., Ft. Wayne, Ind., 1960-65, exec. v.p., dir., 1965-70, pres., 1970—. Served to lt. comdr. USNR, 1942-45.

Registered profl. engr., Ind., Mo. Home: 1340 Westover Rd Fort Wayne IN 46807 Office: Ft Wayne Nat Bank Bldg Fort Wayne IN 46802

JONES, JOSEPH HAROLD, textile co. exec.; b. Knoxville, Mo., July 4, 1914; s. Albert E. and Ina B. (Stratton) J.; student Lewis Inst. Tech., 1937; m. Geraldine Kuper, July 20, 1943; children—Frederick K., Jeral Lynn, Jamie Anne, Janis Sue, Jacqueline Marie. With Phoenix Dye Works, Cleve., 1933—, exec. v.p., 1961-65, pres., 1965-. Mem. Am. Assn. Textile Chemists and Colorists (pres. 1969-70). Home: 6836 Wallings Rd Brecksville OH 44141 Office: 4855 W 150th St Cleveland OH 44135

JONES, JOSEPH L., newspaperman; b. Moody, Mo., June 18, 1897; s. Charles Warren and Cora (Powell) J.; A.B., Drury Coll., Springfield, Mo. 1921, LL.D. (hon.), 1957; B.Litt., Columbia, 1922; m. Helen Sullivan, Sept. 24, 1924; children—Peter Taylor, Elizabeth Townsend, Constance Hamilton. Began as office boy West Plains (Mo.) Jour., 1914; with U.P.I., 1921—, fgn. editor, 1924, assigned to London, 1925-26, to Lima, Santiago, Buenos Aires and Caracas, 1928-29, gen. fgn. mgr., 1937—, v.p. 1942-64, cons. to internat. dept., 1965- -; asso. in journalism Columbia, 1932-55. Presbyn. Club: University. Home: 302 Monterey Av Pelham NY 10803 Office: 220 E 42 St New York City NY 10017

JONES, JOSEPH LOUIS, Jr., bldg. materials co. exec.; b. Sheppards, Va., Feb. 27, 1923; s. Joseph Louis and Edna (Elcan) J.; B.A., Va. Poly Inst., 1947; m. Dorothy Jeanne Jennings, June 21, 1949; children-Joseph, Catherine, Carolyn. With Armstrong Cork Co., Lancaster, Pa., 1947—, prodn. mgr., 1961-68, v.p. carpet operations, 1968—. Served to capt., inf., AUS, 1943-46. Decorated Bronze Star medal. Mem. Lancaster C. of C. Republican. Presbyn. (trustee). Club: Lancaster Country. Home: 1131 Country Club Dr Lancaster PA 17601 Office: Liberty and Charlotte Sts Lancaster PA 17604

JONES, JOSEPH MARION, Jr., fgn. policy writer, educator; b. Lockhart, Tex., Oct. 29, 1908; s. Joseph Marion and Helen (Davis) J.; A.B., Baylor U., 1928, D. Lit., 1945; A.M., U. Pa., 1929, Ph.D., 1935; Postgrad. London Sch. Econs., 1932-33; m. Sarah Plant Harrison, Aug. 17, 1935; children—Clergue, Clarissa Harrison; m. 2d, Lilian Grosvenor Coville, Nov. 1956. Economist U.S. Tariff Commn., Washington, 1933-37; divisional asst. Dept. of State, 1937-43; asso. editor Fortune mag., 1943-46; spl. asst. to asst. sec. of state for pub. affairs, 1946-48; spl. asst. to administr. ECA, 1949-52, to U.S. rep. in Europe, Paris, 1952-53; fellow Yale, 1954; spl. asst. to gov. of N.Y., 1955-59; cons. to research and edn. com. Lasker Found., 1959-62; research asso. Fletcher Sch. of Law and diplomacy, 1965-67; adj. prof. Center for Advanced Internat. Studies U. Miami, 1968—. Club: Cosmos (Washington). Author: Tariff Retaliation,1934; A Modern Foreign Policy For the United States, 1944; The Fifteen Weeks, 1955; Does Overpopulation Mean Poverty, 1962; The United Nations at Work, 1965. Contbr. to Harper's, The Reporter, Fortune, other mags. Home: 3333 S Moorings Way Coconut Grove Miami FL 33133

JONES, JOSEPH SEVERN, lawyer; b. Montpelier, Ida., Mar. 23, 1905; s. John Joseph and Elizabeth (Severn) J.; B.A., U. Utah, 1927; J.D., U. Chgo., 1930; m. Marjorie Allen, June 24, 1931; children—Allen Severn, John Samuel Roger, Joseph Stephen Lowry. Admitted to Utah bar, 1929; practice in Salt Lake City, 1930—; sr. partner firm Jones, Waldo, Holbrook & McDonough, 1958—. Dir. Walker Bank & Trust Co., Mountain Fuel Supply Co., Interstate Brick Co., A. Keyser Co. Pres. Utah Bar Found., 1968. Served to comdr. USNR, 1942-45. Mem. Am., Utah bar assns. Democrat. Mem. Ch. of Jesus Christ of Latter Day Saints. Home: 268 10th Av Salt Lake City UT 84103 Office: Walker Bank Bldg Salt Lake City UT 84111

JONES, JOSEPH WEST, beverage co. exec.; b. Georgetown, Del., Oct. 9, 1912; s. John Arters and Sallie Emma (West) J.; B.C.S., Beacom Coll., Wilmington, Del., 1932; m. Hattie Johns Bryan, Mar. 3, 1935 (div. 1946); 1 son, Joseph Wayne, m. 2d, Virginia Lee Rhoads, June 14, 1947; children—John Vernon, Terry Lee. With Coca-Cola Co., 1935—, asst. sec., 1956-59, asst. sec.-asst. treas., 1959-61, sec., asst. treas., 1961—; chmn., bd. dirs., pres. Whitehead Holding Co. Treas., trustee Trebor Found., Atlanta; trustee Great So. Real Estate Trust; chmn. bd. trustees Joseph B. Whitehead Found, Lettie Pate Evans Found.; mem. governing bd., chmn. finance com. Woodward Acad., College Park, Ga. Mem. Phoenix Soc. Clubs: Atlanta Athletic; Peachtree Racket. Home: 3840 Randall Ridge Rd NW Atlanta GA 30327 Office: 310 North Av NW Atlanta GA 30313

JONES, KENNETH LESTER, educator, botanist; b. Keweenaw Bay, Mich., Dec. 3, 1905; s. Charles Schuyler and Sarah Minnie (Geertz) J.; A.B., Syracuse U., 1928; Ph.D., U. Mich., 1933; m. Wilma Gertrude Oppenborn, June 15, 1929; children—Hannah Pierson (Mrs. Hannah Chamberlin), Roland Leo. Instr. botany U. Mich., 1931-37, asst. prof., 1937-45, asso. prof., 1945-51, prof. 1951—, chmn. dept. botany, 1950-63, great ooks staff, 1964—; research in antibiotics Comml. Solvents Corp., 1948-50. Fellow A.A.A.S., Am. Acad. Microbiology; mem. Bot. Soc. Am. (chmn. teaching sect. 1951), Soc. Am. Bacteriologists, Mich. Acad. Sci. Arts and Letters, N.Y. Acad. Sci., Sigma Xi (pres. U. Mich. chpt. 1962-63), Phi Sigma. Author: Botanical Essays and Plants in Our Lives; also articles articles on biology of Ambrosia and Streptomycetes. Home: 607 W Davis St Ann Arbor MI 48103

JONES, KENSINGER, advt. exec.; b. St. Louis, Oct. 18, 1919; s. Walter C. and Anna (Kensinger) J.; student Washington U., 1938-39; m. Alice May Guseman, Oct. 7, 1944; children—Jeffrey, Janice A. (Mrs. Jeffrey Geary). Exec. v.p., creative dir. Campbell-Ewald Co., Detroit, 1960-68; sr. v.p., creative dir. D.P. Brother & Co., Detorit, 1968-70; sr. v.p., exec. creative dir. Leo Burnett Co., Inc., Chgo., 1970—. Mem. exec. com. Detroit area council Boy Scouts Am., mem. pub. relations com. Nat. council; mem. exec. com. World Medical Relief, Inc.; dir. Mich. Soc. Mental Health. Mem. Nat. Def. Exec. Res. (dir. Mich. chpt.). Clubs: The Players; Recess; Circumnavigators; Chicago Advertising; Adcraft of Detroit. Home: 425 Pritchardville Rd Hastings MI 49058 also 900 N Michigan Av Chicago IL 60611 Office: Leo Burnett Co Inc Prudential Plaza Chicago IL 60601

JONES, L. BRUCE, music educator; b. Aurora, Ill., Oct. 11, 1905; s. Warren and Anne Wallace (Gehring) J.; B.S., Northeast Mo. State Teachers Coll., 1926; Mus. B., U. Ill., 1928; M.A., George Peabody Coll., 1942; m. Mary Floy Crossgrove, Aug. 29, 1928; children—Robert Bruce, Shirley Louise, Mary Carolyn, Evelyn Denise. Dir. of bands and orch., Little Rock (Ark.) Sr. High Sch., 1928-45; supr. instrumental music Little Rock pub. schs., 1932-45; chmn. music edn. program, prof. music La. State U., 1945—, dir. bands, 1945-59, band cons., 1959—; dir. music Immanuel Baptist ch., Little Rock, 1942-45; concert master Ark. State Symphony, 1940-42, condr., 1942-43; dir. music dept. 1st Bapt. Ch., Baton Rouge, 1945-67; condr. U.S.A. Band & Chorus tour Eastern U.S. and Can., 1966; guest condr. state and nat. clinics, univ. summer sch. music groups. Owner, operator Sandy Creek Farm, cattle and horses, 1952—. Mem. Am. Guild Organists (choir dirs. sect.), Ark. Sch. Band and Orch. Assn. (organizer and 1st pres.), Dixie Band and Orch. Assn. (organizer and 1st pres.), Music Educators Nat. Conf., Nat. Competition Festivals (chmn. region 7), Nat. Sch. Band Assn. (pres. 1940-45), Coll. Band Dirs. Nat. Assn. (pres. 1951-53), Am. Bandmasters Assn., Phi Mu Alpha Sinfonia, Kappa Delta Phi, Phi Delta Kappa. Mason (32). Author: Building the Instrumental Music Department. Home: 625 Delgado Dr Baton Rouge LA 70808 ☆

JONES, L. DAVIS, former advt. exec.; b. Mt. Pleasant, Pa., Oct. 9, 1914; s. Howard Fothergill and Katharine E. (Davis) J.; B.S. in Econs., Franklin and Marshall Coll., 1936; m. Meade A. Barner, Jan. 19, 1946; children—Davis M., J. Brinton, Carter. With N.W. Ayer & Son, Inc., 1936-71, v.p. exec. service, 1957-67, exec. v.p., 1967-71, also dir. Trustee Phila. Coll. Art. Served to lt. USNR, 1942-46. Mem. Phi Kappa Tau, Alpha Delta Sigma. Republican. Mem. Soc. of Friends. Home: Yellow Springs Rd Paoli PA 19301

JONES, L. MEYER, educator; b. Hartford City, Ind., Mar. 2, 1913; s. Robert Wilkins and Kate Alice (Sands) J.; A.B., DePauw U., 1935; D.V.M., M.S., Ia. State U., 1939; Ph.D., U. Minn., 1945; m. Mary Elizabeth Homer, Sept. 10, 1935; children—Larry Wilkins, Ronald Lee, Charlotte Kathryn. From asst. to prof. Ia. State U., 1935-60; dir. sci. activities Am. Vet. Med. Assn., Chgo., 1960-66; dean U. Ga. Sch. Vet. Medicine, 1966-68; dean U. Ill. Coll. Vet. Medicine, Urbana, 1968—; cons. Am. Vet. Med. Assn., Research Fellow Am. Vet. Med. Assn., 1942-44, Fulbright prof. to Austria, 1953-54. Mem. Am. Vet. Med. Assn., Am. Soc. Pharmacology and Exptl. Therapeutics, Soc. Toxicology, Sigma Xi, Phi Kappa Phi, Phi Zeta. Rotarian. Author: Veterinary Pharmacology and Therapeutics, 1954. Home: 2110 Grange Dr Urbana IL 61801

JONES, LAFLIN CLIFFORD, ins. co. exec.; b. Milw., Feb. 14, 1908; s. Evan D. and Mary (Laflin) J.; A.B., Dartmouth, 1929; m. Marjorie Ogden, Apr. 22, 1939; 1 son, Timothy O. With Northwestern Mut. Life Ins. Co., Milw., 1929—, v.p., dir. markets research, 1963-65, v.p. insurance, 1965-69, now sr. v.p. corporate planning and devel. Chmn. World Affairs Council, Milw., 1955-57; treas. Lad Lake, Inc., 1962—. Mem. Pension Research Council U. Pa. Served to lt. USNR, 1943-46. Mem. Am. Soc. Chartered Life Underwriters. Clubs: University, Tripoli Country. Home: 4530 N Murray Av Milwaukee WI 53211 Office: 720 E Wisconsin Av Milwaukee WI 53202

JONES, LANDON Y., food co. exec.; b. St. Louis, 1915; grad. Washington and Lee U., 1938; married. With Price Waterhouse & Co., C.P.A.'s, 1938-51; dir. group hosp. service Blue Cross, 1951-56; controller Pet Inc., St. Louis, 1959, v.p. finance, 1962-66, sr. v.p. finance and adminstrn., 1966-68, exec. v.p. finance, 1968—, also dir. Address: 400 S 4th St St Louis MO 63166

JONES, LAUMAR SESSEND diversified mfg. co. exec.; b. Cin., May 21, 1910; grad. Phillips Acad., Andover, Mass., 1927; B.S., Princeton, 1931; postgrad. Mass. Inst. Tech., 1931-33; m. Jean R. Holland, June 16, 1935; children--Lois A., Andrew M., James. Salesman, Brown Mfg. Co., Boston, 1932-33; jr. engr. Ball Metals Co., Carson City, Nev., 1933-36, engr., 1936-37, sr. engr., 1937-40; project engr. Kingston Engrng. Co., Los Angeles, 1940-43; with dept. engrng. City of Denver, 1946-50, dep. head, 1950-52; 2d v.p. Johnson Mfg. Co., Kansas City, Kansas, 1952-54, v.p. for engrng., 1954-57; v.p. research Consol. Industries, Inc., South Bend, Ind., 1957-60, exec. v.p., 1960-65, pres., 1965-70, chmn. bd., chief exec. officer, 1970--, also dir.; dir. ABC Chem. Co., 2d Nat. Bank, Country Food Storage Co., Providence Indsl. Corp. (Ind.), Wilson Investment Co., Inc., Hammond Life Ins. Co., Inc. Pres., Dewey High Sch., Kansas City, Mo., 1953-54; fund chmn. local div. Salvation Army, 19560. Mem. South Bend Republican Com., 1964-68. Bd. dirs. Ind. council Boy Scouts Am., 1969-71; trustee Lovell Found. Served to lt., Corps Engrs., AUS, 1943-45. Decorated Bronze Star medal. Member N.A.M., South Bend C. of C. (v.p. 1963-65, dir. 1965-70), Am. Mgmt. Assn., Ind. Engrs. Soc. (program com. 1961-62), Princeton Alumni Assn. Episcopalian. Home: 6823 Broad Terrace Av South Bend IN 46505

JONES, LAWRENCE BRENTON, steel co. exec.; b. Colorado Springs, Colo., Jan. 3, 1902; s. Thomas Jefferson and Grace (Mosher) J.; B.S., U. Tex., Austin, Tex., 1924; m. Letha Cowart Rhodes, Oct. 9, 1954. With Mosher Steel Co., 1924—, pres., chief exec. officer, Dallas, 1954-60, chmn. exec. com., 1960-63, 70—, chmn. bd., 1963-70; dir. Mercantile Nat. Bank Dallas, Traders & Gen. Ins. Co., Astoria-Fibra Steel Co., Astoria, Ill. Mem. Dallas Citizens Council, 1960—; indsl. chmn. Tex. Soc. Engrng. Found. U. For Preventions Blindness, 1960—. Mem. Dallas C. of C. (past dir.), Tex. Mfrs. Assn. (past pres.), Newcomen Soc. of N. Am., Chi Epsilon, Tau Beta Phi. Clubs: Rotary, Salesmanship, City, Dallas Country, Petroleum, Imperial, Chaparral, Executives Dinner. Home: 6328 Bandera St Dallas TX 75225 Office: P O Box 5651 Dallas TX 75222

JONES, LAWRENCE NEALE, seminary pres.; b. Moundsville, W.Va., Apr. 24, 1921; s. Eugene Wayman and Rosa (Bruce) J.; B.Ed., W. Va. State Coll., 1942, LL.D., 1965; M.A., U. Chgo., 1948; B.D., Oberlin Grad. Sch., 1956; Ph.D., Yale, 1961; LL.D., Jewish Theol. Sem., 1971; m. Mary Ellen Cooley, Mar. 29, 1945; children—Mary Lynn (Mrs. Gary C. Walker), Rodney Bruce. Ordained to ministry, United Ch. Christ, 1956; student Christian Movement Middle Atlantic Region, 1957-60; dean chapel Fisk U., 1960-65; dean students Union Theol. Sem., N.Y.C., 1965-71, prof. Afro- Am. Ch. History, 1970, dean, 1971, acting pres., 1970—. Pres. Civil Rights Coordinating Council Nashville, Tenn., 1963-64. Bd. dirs. Sheltering Arms and Children's Service; bd. dirs. Inst. Social and Religious Studies Jewish Sem.; bd. dirs. United Ch. Bd. for World Ministries. Served with AUS, 1943-46, 47-51. Rockefeller Doctoral grantee, Lucy Monroe scholar, Rosenwald scholar, Am. Assn. Theol. Schs. Study grantee. Mem. Am. Ch. History Soc., Am. Acad. Religion, Nat. Com. Black Churchmen. Home: 99 Claremont Av New York City NY 10027

JONES, LEMUEL THEOPHILUS, candy mfr. and retailer, civic and religious leader; b. Ebensburg, Pa., Jan. 23, 1896; s. Thomas Daniel and Mary Ann (Hughes) J.; A.B., U. Ia., 1921; LL.D., Parsons Coll., 1950; L.H.D., Tarkio Coll., 1950; m. Jessie E. Stover, Dec. 22, 1921; children—Lemuel Theophilus, Russel Stover, Thomas (dec.), Sally Jacquelyn, Mary Ann, John Paul. High sch., coll. instr., 1921-28; partner Russell Stover Candies, Kansas City, Mo., 1928- 60; pres. Russell Stover Candies, Inc., 1960-61; pres. Russell Corp.; v.p., dir. Empire State Bank, Kansas City, Mo., dir. Millcon Corp., Lincoln Redevel. Corp., sr. v.p. Logistics Research, Inc., Aviation Research, Inc. Industry World Alliance Cocoa Producers, Chocolate Mfrs. and Confectioners, London, 1957; industry adviser Am. delegation FAO Cocoa Study Group, Nigeria, 1957, Ghana, 1961. Mem. Kansas City Crime Commn., 1951—; Commn. Charitable Solicitations, 1953-63; adv. com. Regional Health and Welfare Council; bd. Nat. Council Community Chests Am.; dir. Helping Hand Inst., United Funds Kansas City, Kansas City Community Chest (past pres); Urban League of Kansas City exec. bd., chmn. career fair; nat. dir. Nat. Conf. Christians and Jews. 1953-56; a founder, dir. Kansas City Conf. Christians and Jews; mem. nat. council United Negro Coll. Fund, 1949-54; bd. govs. Am. Royal; nat. dir. YMCA, 1952-55, pres. West Central area, 1946-50, dir. Kansas City, 1942—, former v.p., nat. council; co- chmn. Billy Graham Heart of Am. Crusade, 1967. Chmn., Mo. Republican Finance Com., 1960-62, Mo. State Rep. Com., mem. Rep. Nat. Finance Com. Pres. bd. trustees State Ia. Found., Mo. Valley Coll.; trustee Mo. Bible Coll., Meml. Hosp., 1947-67, Kansas City Conservatory of Music, 1951—; member bd. dirs. Am. Humanics Found., YMCA Rockies Starlight Theater. del. Served as ensign, USN, 1917-19. Recipient Silver Beaver award Boy Scouts. Mem. Mo. C. of C. (dir.) C. of C. U.S., Kansas City C. of C., N.A.M., Nat. Assn. Confectioners, Nat. Council Chs. Christ in Am. (pres. United Ch. Men 1950-54, gen. bd. mem., Nat. Council Presby. Men pres. 1950-52, exec. com., nominating com.), Religion in Am. Life (laymen's com.), Am. Bible Soc. (chmn. Kansas City 1943-50), Mo. (past v.p.), Kansas City (exec. com. mem. at large) councils of chs., Sunday Sch. Union (hon. v.p.). Presbyn. (elder). Mason, K.P. Home: 803 W 54th Terrace Kansas City MO 64112 Office: Waltower Bldg Kansas City MO 64106

JONES, LEO BOND, army officer; b. Stuart, Ia., Mst. 28, 1918; s. Levi B. and Eva Belle (Bond) J.; B.S., Ia. State U., 1941; postgrad. Army Command and Gen. Staff Coll., 1954, Army War Coll., Carlisle Barracks, Pa., 1957-58, Nat. War Coll., 1966; m. Embry Pryor Wilson, June 26, 1948; children—Janelle Wilson, Fadra Rebecca. Commd. 2d lt. U.S. Army, 1941, advanced through grades to maj. gen., 1969; comdg. officer 11th F.A. Bn., Army Forces Far East, 1954-55, asst. chief of staff G-4 24th Inf. Div., 1955; comdg. officer 23d F.A. Bn., Ft. Benning, Ga., 1956-57; staff officer Office Asst. Chief of Staff for Mil. Operations, Dept. Army, Washington, 1958-60, Far East br. J-3 Office Joint Chiefs of Staff, Washington, 1960-62; comdg. officer 72d Arty. Group, 1962-63; asst. comdr. VII Corps Arty., 1963-64; asst. chief of staff G-4, VII Corps, 1964-65; faculty Nat. War Coll., Washington, 1965-66; dir. plans ODCSLOG, Washington, 1966-67; dep. comdg. gen. 1st Logistical Command, Vietnam, 1967-68; chief of staff U.S. Army, Vietnam and comdg. gen. Support Troops, Vietnam, 1968-69, Hdqrs. U.S. Army Materiel Command, Washington, 1969-70; asst. dep. chief of staff for logistics Dept. Army, Washington, 1970—. Decorated D.S.M., Legion of Merit with oak leaf cluster, Bronze Star medal. Mem. Scabbard and Blade, Cardinal Key, Sigma Phi Epsilon. Home: Quarters 21A North Post Fort Myers VA 22211 Office: Asst Dep Chief of Staff for Logistics Dept Army Washington DC 20310

JONES, LEROI (Imamu Baraka), author; b. Newark, Oct. 7, 1934; s. Coyette LeRoi and Anna Lois (Russ) J.; B.A., Howard U., 1954; m. Hettie Roberta Cohen, Oct. 13, 1958 (div. Aug. 1965); children—Kellie Elisabeth, Lisa Victoria Chapman; m. 2d., Sylvia Robinson, Aug. 1966; children— Obalaji Malik Ali, Ras Jua Al aziz. Faculty, New Sch. for Soc. Research, Columbia. Author: Preface to a Twenty Volume Suicide Note, 1961; Blues People, 1963; The Moderns, 1963; Dutchman and The Slave, 1964; The Dead Lecturer, 1964; The System of Dante's Hell, 1965; Home, 1966; Black Music, 1966; Tales, 1967; Black Art, 1967; Black Magic, 1969; 4 Black Revolutionary Plays, 1969; In Our Terribleness, 1971; Raise——, 1971. Major theatrical prodns. include: Dutchman (Off- Broadway award best Am. play 1964), The Slave (2d prize Internat. Art Festival, Dakar 1966), The Toilet, The Baptism, Jello, A Black Mass; theatrical works produced in major U.S. cities, also Dakar, Paris, Berlin. Dir. Spirit House, Newark; coordinator creativity workshops Black Power Conf., 1968. Served with USAF, 1954-57. Whitney fellow, 1960- 61; Guggenheim fellow, 1965-66. Mem. Black Acad. Arts and Letters. Address: care Hobbs Agy 211 E 43d New York City NY 10017

JONES, LEROY, state ofcl.; b. Santa Ana, Cal., Aug. 30, 1921; s. LeRoy and Wilhemina (Barth) J.; grad. Fullerton Jr. Coll., 1940; B.A., Whittier Coll., 1942; LL.B., U. Conn., 1960; m. Marilyn Bredenberg, Oct. 21, 1944; children—Daniel, Kathryn. Dir. convs. and publicity Springfield (Mass.) C. of C., 1946-48; exec. v.p. Norwich (Conn.) C. of C., 1948-51, 53; with Conn. Devel. Commn., Hartford, 1954-67, mng. dir., 1962-67; commr. Conn. Dept. Community Affairs, 1967-71; devel. adminstr. City of New Haven, 1971—; admitted to Conn. bar, 1960. Mem. Conn. Indsl. Devel. Council. Bd. dirs. Church Homes. Served with USNR, 1942-46, 51-53. Mem. Am., Conn., Hartford County bar assns., Assn. State and Planning and Devel. Agys., Am. Inst. Planners, Northeastern Trade Assn. Comml. Execs., Hartford Auto Club (dir.), Nat. Assn. Redevel. Officials (dir.). Rotarian. Home: Crown Towers 123 Yovk St New Haven CT 06511 Office: City Hall 161 Church St New Haven CT 06510

JONES, LOUIS CLARK, assn. exec.; b. Albany, N.Y., June 28, 1908; s. Charles Edward and Mable (Clark) J.; A.B., Hamilton Coll., 1930, L.H.D., 1962; A.M., Columbia, 1931, Ph.D., 1941; m. Hazel Williams, June 25, 1932 (div.); children—Peter, Carol (Mrs. Raymond Loomis), David; m. 2d, Agnes Halsey, Oct. 25, 1953. Instr. English, L.I.U., Bklyn., 1931-32; Syracuse U., 1933-34; asso. prof. N.Y. State U., Albany 1934-46; exec. dir. N.Y. State Hist. Assn. and Farmers Mus., 1946—. Chmn. N.Y. State Hist. Trust; mem. N.Y. Nature and Hist. Preserve Trust; exec. com. State Council Parks, N.Y. State Council on Arts; state Liaison officer Nat. Register Hist. Pls. Adv. bd. Mystic Seaport; mem. Cooperstown Sch. Bd., 1951-58. Guggeheim fellow, 1946; Rochester Mus. fellow. Fellow Am. Folklore Soc.; mem. Am. Assn. Museums (council 1952-70), Am. Assn. State and Local History (award distinction 1969, exec. council 1950- 58), N.Y. State Hist. Assn. (Trustee, exec. dir.), Am., So. Hoosier, N.Y. (a founder, editor Quar. 1945-50), Western folklore socs. N.Y. Hist Soc. (hon. asso.) Clubs: Emerson Literary (Clinton, N.Y.); Century Assn. (N.Y.C.). Author: Clubs of the Georgian Rakes, 1942; Spooks of the Valley, 1948; Cooperstown 1949; (with Marshall Davidson) American Folk Art, 1952; Things That Go Bump in The Night, 1959; (with Agnes H. Jones) New Found Folk Art of the Young Republic, 1960; Growing up in the Cooper Country, 1964. Editor: New York History, 1947-52: mem. editorial bd. American Heritage. Contbr. articles, verse to various mags., scholarly jours., Dictionary of Folklore, 1951. Home: Pomeroy Pl Cooperstown NY Office: NY State Hist Assn Cooperstown NY 13326

JONES, LYLE VINCENT, educator; b. Grandview, Wash., Mar. 11, 1924; s. Vincent F. and Matilda M. (Abraham) J.; student Reed Coll., 1942-43; B.S., U. Wash., 1947, M.S., 1948; Ph.D., Stanford, 1950; m. Patricia Edison Powers, Dec. 17, 1949; children—Christopher V., Susan E., Tad W. Nat. Research fellow, 1950-51; asst. prof. psychology U. Chgo., 1951-57; vis. asso. prof. U. Tex., 1955-57; asso. prof. U.N.C., 1957-60, prof., 1960—, Alumni distinguished prof., 1969—, dir. L.L. Thurstone Psychometric Lab., 1957—, vice-chancellor, dean The Grad. Sch., 1969—; cons. in field. Served with USAF, 1943-46. Fellow Center Advanced Study in Behavioral Scis., 1964-65; grantee NIH, 1957-63, NSF, 1960-63, 71—, Nat. Inst. Mental Health, 1963—. Fellow A.A.A.S., Am. Psychol. Assn. (pres. div. 1963-64); mem. Psychometric Soc. (pres. 1962-63, trustee 1968—), Am. Statis. Assn., Psychonomic Soc. Author: (with others) Studies in Aphasia: An Approach to Testing, 1961; The Measurement and Prediction of Judgment and Choice, 1968. Mng. editor Psychometrika, 1956-61. Editorial com. for psychology Mc-Graw-Hill, 1965—. Contbr. articles profl. jours. Home: Route 1 Pittsboro NC 27312 Office: South Bldg U NC Chapel Hill NC 27514

JONES, MACLEAN EVERETT, lawyer; b. Calgary, Alta., Can., Nov. 28, 1917; s. Edgar Ward and Adelaide Belle (Graham) J.; B.A., LL.B., U. Alta.; m. Yolande Adele Partridge, Dec. 27, 1941; 2 sons, 1 dau. Admitted to Alta. bar, 1940, Sask. bar, 1959; now partner firm

Saucier, Jones, Peacock, Black, Gain, Stratton & Laycraft, Calgary. Dir. Canadian Imperial Bank of Commerce, 1966—. Pub. sch. trustee, 1956-60, chmn., 1959-60; mem. Calgary Police Commn., 1961-66. Mem. Canadian, Calgary bar assns., Law Soc. Alta. (bencher 1966-68), Phi Kappa Phi. Anglican religion. Rotarian. Clubs: Ranchmen's; Glencoe; Calgary Golf and Country. Office: 444 7th Av SW Calgary 2 Alberta Canada*

JONES, MALCOLM GWYNNE, business exec.; b. Nanticoke, Pa., Sept. 17, 1902; s. Evan L. and Emma Jane (Edmunds) J.; B.S. in Chemistry, Bucknell U., 1926; m. Mary Woodford White, July 13, 1931; children—Malcolm Gwynne, Nancy Kent. Gen. engring. constrn., 1926-29; foreman acetate rayon plant, E. I. duPont de Nemours, Waynesboro, Va., 1929-31, supr., 1931-37, chief supr., 1937-46, plant mgr., 1946-48, dir. prodn. acetate rayon, orlon acrylic fibers, Wilmington, Del., 1948-50, dir. nylon sales, 1950, dir. sales synthetic fibers, 1951-53; pres., dir. Robbins Mills, Inc., 1953-54. chmn. bd., pres., 1954; dir. Sidney Blumenthal & Co., Inc., 1954-56, also mem. exec. com.; pres., dir. Shelton Looms Distbg. Corp., 1954-56; pres. Wayne Devel. Co., Inc., 1957—; mgmt. cons. Hercules Powder Co., 1960-70, dir. am. Thread Co., Jefferson Cables Corp.; adv. bd. dirs. 1st & Mchts. Nat. Bank Va. Chmn. bd. trustees Blue Ridge Community Coll. Mem. Phi Gamma Delta, Pi Delta Epsilon. Presbyn. Mason. Club: Waynesboro Country (Va.). Address: 1080 Fairway Dr Waynesboro VA 22980

JONES, MARK MANDERVILLE, pvt. mgmt. cons., b. Cedar Falls, Ia.; s. Fred Soule and Ada (Thompson) J.; student East Waterloo (Ia.) High Sch., 1903-05; LL.D., Bethany Coll., 1940; m. May Irene Rinehart, 1916; 1 dau., Helen May (Mrs. Franks G. Evatt, Jr.). Successivley chief clk. to gen. mgr. and traffic mgr. Waterloo, Cedar Falls and No. Ry.; traffic mgr. William Galloway Co., Waterloo, Ia.; successively indsl. sec. Chamber of Commerce, Oakland, Cal.; dir. personnel Thomas A. Edison Industries, Orange, N.J.; dir. econ. staff Curtis, Fosdick and Belknap, N.Y.C., on affairs of John D. Rockefeller, Jr., 1921-26; mgmt. cons. and cons. economist, N.Y.C. and Princeton, N.J., 1926—. Cons. to pres. U.S. Steel Corp., 1953-59; pres. Akron Belting Co., 1934- 54, Leadership Publs., Inc., 1948-54; editor Execs. Policy Letter, 1948-53; pres. Nat. Econ. Council, 1963-69. Mem. N.J. thoroughbred Breeders Assn. (treas. 1945—). Republican. Presbyn. Clubs: Union League (N.Y.C.); Nassau, Princeton. Editor: Economic Council Letter, 1963-69. Address: P O Box 268 159 Library Pl Princeton NJ 08540

JONES, MARSHALL P., fgn. service officer; b. Columbus, Ind., Apr. 7, 1915; s. Frank S. and Mae (Wood) J.; A.B., DePauw U., 1937; student U. Colo., 1937, Harvard Bus. Sch., 1942; m. Virginia J. Spitler, Apr. 24, 1941; children—Marshall P. II, Tarpley Brooks, Zachary Chaffin. Salesman, U.S. Rubber Co., 1939-40, sales supr., 1940-42; coordination and planning officer VA, 1946-51; orgn. and methods examiner Dept. State, Washington, 1951-54; 1st sec. Am. embassies, Tel Aviv and Belgrade, 1954-59; budget dir. Dept. of State, Washington, 1959-61, exec. asst. Bur. Adminstrn., 1961-62; counselor Am. embassy, Seoul, Korea, 1962-64; exec. dir. Bur. Far Eastern Affairs, Dept. State, 1964-65; A.E. and P. to Republic of Malawi, 1965-70. Served to maj. USAAF, 1942-45. Home: 1313 Main St Murray KY 42071 Office: Dept State Washington DC 20521

JONES, MARSHALL ROBERTSON, educator, psychologist; b. Charter Oak, Ia., June 5, 1910; s. Henry Asa and Nelle Verne (Robertson) J.; student Ia. state Coll., 1928-29; A.B., Drake U., 1932, M.A., 1935; student U. Ill., 1935-37; Ph.D., Yale, 1940; m. Carolyn L. Ewers, Dec. 31, 1937; children—Marshall Robertson, Scott Lincoln. From asst. to asst. prof. Cornell U. Med. Coll., 1939-46; asst. prof. psychology State U. Ia., 1946-49; prof. psychology U. Neb., 1949- 63; prof. psychology, chmn. dept. U. Miami (Fla.), 1963—; cons. clin. psychology VA, 1948-63, 67—; research cons. Neb. Dept. Vocational Rehab., 1961-66; organizer, editor U. Miami Symposium on Prediction of Behavior, 1967, 68. Bd. dirs. United Health Found., Miami. Mem. Fla. State Bd. Examiners Psychology, 1965-71. Served with USNR, 1943-46. Diplomate Am. Bd. Profl. Psychology. Fellow Am. Psychol. Assn.; mem. Southeastern, Fla. psychol. assns., Am. Assn. U. Profs., Sigma Xi. Organizer, editor Neb. Symposium on Motivation, 1953-63. Home: 6801 SW 135th St Miami FL 33156 Office: Dept Psychology Univ Miami Coral Gables FL 33124

JONES, MARVIN, judge; b. nr. Valley View, Tex.; s. H.K. and Dosia J.; A.B., Southwestern U., 1905; LL.B., U. Tex., 1907; LL.D., Tex A. and M. Coll. Admitted to Tex. bar, 1907; praticed at Amarillo; appted. chmn. bd. legal examiners 7th Supreme Jud. Dist. Tex., 1913; mem. 65th to 76th Congresses (1917-41), 18th Tex. Dist., chmn. House Com. on Agr.; 1931-40; judge U.S. Ct. Claims, 1940-45, on leave 1943-45; chief justice. U.S. Ct. Claims, Washington, 1947-64, sr. judge, 1964—. Asst. to Hon. James F. Byrnes 1943; pres. UN Conf. on Food and Agr., 1943; mem. War Moblzn. Com., U.S. food adminstr., 1943-45. Mem. Am. Legion, Order of Coif (hon.). Democrat. Methodist. Mason, Woodman, Elk. Author: How War Food Saved American Lives; Should Uncle Sam PayWhen and Why? Home: 2807 Hughes St Amarillo TX 79109

JONES, MARY GARDINER, lawyer, govt. ofcl.; b. N.Y.C., Dec. 10, 1920; d. Charles Herbert and Anna Livingston (Short) Jones; B.A., Wellesley Coll., 1943; LL.B., Yale, 1948. Intern tchr. George Sch., Newtown, Pa., 1943-44; research analyst, research and analysis br. Internat. Law sect. OSS, Washington, 1944-46; admitted to N.Y. bar, 1949; asso. firms Donovan, Leisure, Newton and Irvine, 1948-53, Webster, Sheffield, Fleischmann, Hitchcock & Chrystie, 1961-64 (both N.Y.C.); trial atty. antitrust div. Dept. Justice, N.Y.C., 1953-61; commr. FTC, Washington, 1964—. Mem. Am., Fed. bar assns., Internat. Law Assn., Assn. Bar City N.Y., Am. Arbitration Assn., Contbr. articles law jours. Home: 3037 W Lane Keys NW Washington DC 20007 Office FTC 6th and Pennsylvania Av NW Washington DC 20580

JONES, MERLE GRANT, mfg. co. exec., church ofcl.; b. Trenton, Neb., Aug. 6, 1909; s. John J. and Emma Gertrude (Leighton) J.; student Doane Coll., Crete, Neb., 1926- 29, L.H.D. (hon.), 1954; m. Jennie Elizabeth Noyce, Sept. 20, 1931; children—Mary Jane (Mrs. Everett Knoche), Barbara Louise (Mrs. William C. Marten), John Joseph. With Store Kraft Mfg. Co., Beatrice, Neb., 1929- -, pres., 1945—, treas., 1950-67. Mem. United Presbyn. Ch. U.S.A., 1931- -, now elder, tchr, Sunday sch. local ch.; mem. Radio and TV Dept., 1956-62, Commn. Ecumenical Mission and Relations, 1958-66, Commn. Evangelism, 1952-58, commr. Gen. Assembly, 1939, 63, vice moderator, 1963-64, mem. Capital Funds Commn., 1963-66; ofcl. del. 18th gen. council World Presbyn. Alliance, Sao Paulo, Brazil, 1959; pres. Nat. Council Presbyn. Men, 1955-56; moderator Synod of Neb., 1952-53; del. gen. assembly Nat. Council Ch., 1957, bd. mgrs. dept. united churchmen, 1955-56; sec. Neb. Council Chs. and Christian Edn., 1951-54. Mem. Gov. Neb. Com. Human Relations, 1954; pres. Asso. Industries Neb., 1951-53, Neb. Tax Research Council, 1964-66, Beatrice Community Chest, 1944; mem. Cornhusker council Boy Scouts Am., 1954-61, Beatrice Bd. Edn., 1956-64; mem. Neb. Bd. Vocational Edn., 1950-54; mem. adv. com. vocational edn. to Neb. Bd. Edn., 1965—. Trustee Doane Coll., 1958—, chmn., 1961—; mem. Neb. Ind. Coll. Found., 1954—; trustee Hastings (Neb.) Coll., 1949- 58; adv. bd. Beatrice Salvation Army, 1937; bd. dirs. Mennonite Hosp. Found., 1954—, chmn., 1970—; bd. dirs. Gage County Polio Com., 1938—. Named Outstanding Young Man, Beatrice Jr. C. of C., 1944, Outstanding Boss, 1956; named Bus. and Industry Man of Year, Asso. Industry Neb., 1958. Mem. N.A.M. (bd. 1960-63), Internat. Platform Assn., U. S., Beatrice (past bd. dirs.) chambers commerce, Pi Kappa Delta, Alpha Kappa Psi (hon.). Mason (K.T.), Kiwanian (pres. Beatrice 1938; Distinguished Service medal Lincoln club 1955). Address: 421 N 16th St Beatrice NB 68310

JONES, MERLE SILAS, TV exec.; b. Omaha, Neb., Aug. 14, 1905; s. Alan W. and Ida (O'Donnell) J.; LL.B., U. Neb., 1929; m. Frances Evelyn Green, Mar. 21, 1932. Admitted to Neb. bar, 1929, practiced law, 1929-32; mem. sales dept. Radio Sta. WAAW, Omaha, 1932-34; nat. sales mgr., Radio Sta. KMBC, Kansas City, Mo. 1934-36; asst mgr. Radio Sta. KMOX, St. Louis, 1936-37, gen. mgr., 1937-44; v.p., gen. mgr. Cowles Broadcasting Co., Washington, 1944-47; gen. mgr. Radio Sta. WCCO, Mpls., 1947-49; gen. mgr. Radio Sta. KNX and Columbia Pacific Network and TV Sta. KTSL, Los Angeles, 1949-July 1951; v.p. chare co. owned stas. and gen. services. CBS TV, N.Y.C., 1951-56, exec. v.p., 1956, pres., 1956-58; pres. CBS Films, Inc., also pres. Terrytoons div., 1958- 69, CBS Japan, Inc., 1964-69; chmn. bd. CBS Ltd., London, 1958-69, CBS (Europe) S.A., Zug, Switzerland, 1959-69. Dir. Bus. Council for Internat. Understanding. Mem. TV Bur. Advt. (dir.), Nat. Assn. Radio and TV Broadcasters (dir.), Radio Pioneers (dir.), Broadcast Pioneers (pres. 1960), TV Program Export Assn. (dir.), Alpha Tau Omega, Phi Delta Phi. Home: 10800 Chalon Rd Bel-Air Los Angeles CA 90024

JONES, MORGAN, Jr., banker; b. Abilene, Tex., Sept. 5, 1910; s. Morgan and Jessie Kenan (Wilder) J.; B.S. in Mech. Engring., Rice U., 1932; M.A., Wharton Sch. of U. Pa., 1934; m. Mary Elizabeth Whatley, June 3, 1937; children—Harriet Jane, Elizabeth Kenan. Engaged in engring. and sales Hydril Co., Houston, 1934-40; mgmt. duties with div. Morgan Jones Estate, Abilene, Tex., 1940-45; engaged in mgmt. trusts and investments, 1945—; partner Jones & Fulgham, real estate and oil, 1948—; v.p., dir. S.W. Savs. and Loan Assn., Abilene, 1953-68; chmn. bd. Bank of Commerce, Abilene, 1968—; dir. Lone Star Gas Co., Santa Anna Tile Co. Mem. Gov.'s Com. on Pub. Edn., 1966-69; Mem. Abilene Sch. Bd., 1951—, pres., 1956-69; mem. exec. com. Tex. Sch. Bd. Assn., 1957-62; del. White House Conf. Edn., 1955; chmn. Abilene United Fund, 1957-58, bd. dirs., 1955—; pres. W. Tex. council Girl Scouts U.S. 1952-56. Trustee, endowment com. McMurry Coll. Named Outstanding Citizen Abilene, 1958, Outstanding Citizen Contbg. Most to Edn., 1956; recipient Thanks Badge award Girl Scouts U.S., 1955. Registered profl. engr., Tex. Mem. Abilene C. of C. (pres. 1956), Rice U. Alumni Assn., Tex. Soc. Profl. Engrs., Tau Beta Pi. Methodist (ofcl. bd.). Home: 3435 S 9th St Abilene TX 79605 Office: PO Box 1320 Abilene TX 79604

JONES, NARD, author; b. Seattle, Apr. 12, 1904; s. Nelson Hawk and Edythe (Benedict) J.; A.B., Whitman Coll., Walla Walla, Wash., 1926; m. Elisabeth Dunphy, June 21, 1928 (dec.); 1 son, Blair Anthony; m. 2d, Anne Marie Mynar, Nov. 21, 1942; children—Lawrie Anne, Deborah Anne. Reporter, Walla Walla Dally Bull., 1922-26; editor Pacific Motor Boat, 1926-40. Served to lt. comdr. USNR, 1940-44. Mem. Authors League Am., Zeta Phi Epsilon. Clubs: Internat. Flattie Yacht Racing Assn. (N.Y.C.); College (Seattle). Author: Oregon Detour, 1930; The Petlands, 1931; Wheat Women, 1933; All Six Were Lovers, 1934; West, Young Man, 1937; The Case of the Hanging Lady, 1938; Swift Flows the River, 1940; Scarlet Petticoat, 1942; Still to the West, 1946; Evergreen Land, 1947; The Island, 1948; I'll Take What's Mine, 1954; Ride the Dark Storm, 1955; The Great Command, 1959; Pacific Northwest, 1962. Contbr. fiction to mags., indsl. writing on wood cellulose. Home: 9124 Lake Washington Blvd Bellevue WA 98004

JONES, NELL CHOATE, artist; b. Hawkinsville, Ga.; d. James Dearborn and Sarah Cornelia (Rocquemore) Choate; student Adelphi Acad., Fontainebleu Sch. Art, 1929; art criticisms from John Carlson, Frederick K. Boston; m. Eugene A. Jones Artist, 1933—; painted in N.E. and So. states, S.W., Eng., France, Italy, Switzerland; seven one-woman shows, N.Y.C., Boston, Adelphi Coll., Garden City, N.Y.; represented in permanent mus. collections, also pvt. collections; exhibited N.Y. Acad. Design, Allied Artists, Audubon Artists, N.Y. Water Color Soc., Brooklyn Mus., One World art show Argent Gallery, N.Y.C., 1947, N.Y. World's Fair, 1939 and others; exhibited in museums throughout U.S., 1946—; exhibited, Paris, 1957, Athens and Salonika, Greece, 1958, Brussels Worlds Fair, Belgium, 1958; exhibited with water color groups, Amsterdam, Brussels, Antwerp, Ostenda, Bern, Switzerland, 1956, 57. 1st prize Pen and Brush, N.Y., 1946, Founders prize, 1951; 1st prize C.L.W. Club, 1950; medal of honor Nat. Assn. Women Artists, 1955, Lena Newcastle water color prize, 1958; several hon. mentions. Fellow Swiss Internat. Inst. Arts and Letters; mem. Internat. Council Women, N.Y. Council Women, Nat. Assn. Women Artists (hon. life mem., pres. 1951-55), Nat. Council Am. Women, Internat. Council Am. Women, Bklyn. Soc. Artists (pres. 1949-52), Studio Traveling Guild, So. States Art Assn. Clubs: Boston Art, Pen and Brush (N.Y.C.); Fontainebleu Art Assn. (France). Home: 296 Clermont Av Brooklyn NY 11205 Office: Argent Gallery 236 E 60th St New York City NY 10022

JONES, NELSON, lawyer; b. Quitman, Tex., Oct. 26, 1909; s. Walter Neilson and Alberta Margaret (Mayer) J.; A.B., So. Meth. U., 1929; LL.B., U. Tex., 1933; advanced mgmt. program Harvard, 1952; m. Lena Louise Ward, Feb. 24, 1934; children—Elizabeth Louise, Celia Ann. Admitted to Tex. bar, 1933; asst. dist. atty. 9th Jud. Dist. Tex., 1933-37; law dept. Humble Oil & Refining Co., Houston, 1937—, gen. atty, 1948-56, dir. and gen. counsel, 1956, now v.p., dir.; dir. Humble Pipe Line Co., 1943-48, v.p., 1947-48; vis. prof. law U. Tex., 1951. Trustee St. Joseph Hosp. Fellow Am. Coll. Trial Lawyers; mem. Am., Tex., Houston bar assns., Am. Petroleum Inst., Phi Delta Phi, Phi Delta Theta. Episcopalian. Clubs: Houston Country, Ramada. Home: 2030 Persa St Houston TX 77019 Office: Humble Bldg Houston TX 77001

JONES, NORMAN EDWARD, iron and steel mfg. co. exec.; b. Sydney, Australia, Aug. 2, 1904; s. Edward J. and Eliza Esther (Swain) J.; honours diploma in chemistry, Newcastle (New S. Wales) Tech. Coll., 1925; D.Sc. (hon.), U. New S. Wales, 1955, U. Newcastle, 1966; m. Mabel Elizabeth Swainson, Nov. 17, 1928; 1 son, Ian Edward. With Broken Hill Proprietary Co. Ltd., Melbourne, Australia, 1921—, chief gen. mgr., 1950-52, mng. dir., 1952-67, dir., 1967—; dir. Nat. Bank of Australia, Ltd., Australian Paper Mfrs. Ltd., Colonial Mut. Life Assurance Soc., Ltd. Dep. chmn. Australian Adminstrv. Staff Coll.; v.p. Victorian Chamber Mfrs. Mem. council U. Melbourne; bd. dirs. Alfred Hosp., Melbourne. Hon. mem. Am. Iron and Steel Inst.; mem. Am. Inst. Mining, Metall. and Petroleum Engrs., Iron and Steel Inst. London (pres. 1967-68), Australian Inst. Mining and Metallurgy, Australian Inst. Metals, Australian Inst. Mgmt. Home: 136 Kooyong Rd Toorak Victoria Australia Office: 460 Bourke St Melbourne Victoria Australia

JONES, OAKAH L., utility exec.; b. Boston, Mar. 9, 1901; s. Louis L. and Eloise (Stevens) J.; ed. Brown U., U. Tulsa; m. Dorothy Eleanor Wilson, May 8, 1927; one son, one dau. Clk., Stone & Webster, Boston, 1917, Cape Breton Electric Co. Ltd., Sydney, N.S., Can., 1919; accountant Conn. Power Co., 1922, Blackstone Valley Electric Co., Pawtucket, R.I., 1923; asst. sec., treas. Okla. Natural Gas Co., Tulsa, 1935-51, v.p., 1951-54; with Consumers Gas Co., Toronto, Can., 1954—, now pres., gen. mgr.; v.p. Niagara Gas Transmission Ltd.; dir. Can. Permanent Trust Co. Boiler Insp. and Ins. Co. Can. Rubbermaid (Can.) Ltd. Nat. pres. Nat. Office Management Assn., 1946-47; pres. Tulsa C. of C., 1953-54; cons. prof. mgmt. Okla. A. and M. Coll., 1949-54. Mem. adv. council U. Tulsa, 1949- 54; bd. dirs. Toronto Symphony Orch. Assn., Boy Scouts Assn.; bd. govs. Ont. Research Found., Trinity Coll.; mem. nat. exec. council Canadian Mfrs. Assn.; adv. bd. Toronto Redevel. Authority; mem. Ont. Econ. Council; bd. regents Mt. Alison U.; v.p. Met. Toronto Indsl. Commn. Relations Inst.; exec. com. Ont. Centre Sci. and Tech. Mem. Toronto Bd. Trade. Mem. Anglican Ch. Rotarian. Clubs: York; National; Granite; Toronto; Toronto Hunt; Royal Canadian Yacht. Home: 3 Highland Av Toronto Ontario Canada Office: 19 Toronto St Toronto Ontario Canada*

JONES, OLIVER HASTINGS, assn. exec.; b. Altoona, Pa., Dec. 9, 1922; s. Oliver Hastings and Mary (Herman) J.; B.A., St. Francis Coll., Loretto, Pa., 1948; M.A., Pa. State U., 1949, Ph.D., 1961; m. Margaret Ann Vogel, July 4, 1942; children—Thomas, William, David, Robert, Richard. Analyst, div. bank operations, bd. govs. Fed. Res. System, 1951-55; sr. economist, research dept. Fed. Res. Bank Cleve., 1955-59; asso. research economist, real estate research program Grad. Sch. Bus. Adminstrn., U. Cal. at Los Angeles, 1959-61; economist Stanford Research Inst., 1961-62; dir. research Mortgage Bankers Assn. Am., 1962-67; cons. economist Oliver Jones & Assos., Washington, 1967-68; exec. v.p. Mortgage Bankers Assn. Am., 1968—; professorial lectr. Am. U., 1967—. Served with AUS, 1942-45. Mem. Am. Statis. Assn., Am. Econ. Assn., Am. Finance Assn., Nat. Assn. Bus. Economists, Lambda Alpha. Club: Cosmos (Washington). Author: (with Leo Grebler) The Secondary Mortgage Market, 1961. Home: 10417 Burnt Ember Dr Silver Spring MD 20903 Office: 1125 15th St NW Washington DC 20015

JONES, OLIVER OWENSBORO mfg. exec.; b. Lima, O., Apr. 1, 1932; B.S., U. San Francisco, 1954; M.S., Stanford University, 1956; m. Rosemarie Lois Brown, May 15, 1955; 1 son, Anthony Robinson. Sales rep. Ames-Brockton Fabricated Products, Akron, O., 1956-58, sales mgr. Coshocton, Ohio, 1959-61, gen. manager plant, 1961-68, v.p. sales, 1968--. Instr. bus. Coshocton Jr. College, 1968-69. Mem. Coshocton C. of C. (vice president 1967-68, pres. 1969-70), English Speaking Union, Coshocton Sertoma Club, Nat. Assn. Mfrs., Sales Executives Institute, Phi Beta Kappa, Sigma Chi, Phi Mu. Democrat. Mem. Christian Ch. (lay reader). Mason (32, Shriner). Clubs: Coshocton Country, Coshocton City, Running Deer Country. Home: 2d Av Coshocton OH Office: 3d Av Coshocton OH

JONES, OLIVER PERRY, anatomist hematologist; b. West Chester, Pa., May 13, 1906; s. Oliver Perry and Helen Evelyn (Mackey) J.; A.B., Temple U., 1929; Ph.D., U. Minn., 1935; M.D., U. Buffalo, 1956; m. Cathryn Margaret Knights, Apr. 17, 1935; children—Helen C. (Mrs. Helen J. Brown), Oliver Perry, Carolyn M. (Mrs. Ramsdell Gurney, Jr.), Ann L. (Mrs. Henry Davidson). Instr. anatomy U. Minn., 1935-37; asst. prof. U. Buffalo, 1937-43, asso. prof., 1943, prof., 1943-71, Distinguished prof., 1971—, head dept. 1943-71, asst. dean Sch. Medicine, 1946- 54; vis. prof. Grad. Research Inst., Baylor U., 1951-52, Nat. U., Mexico, 1956; Buswell research fellow, 1957-62, 67—. Mem. Am. Assn. Anatomists (program sec. 1954-66), Histochem. Society, Internat. Soc. Hematology (counselor 1952-58, v.p. 1958-62, historian 1962—), Electron Microscope Soc. Am., Am. Soc. Hematology (adv. council), Nat. Soc. Med. Research (dir. 1956-61), Am. Assn. U. Profs., A.A.A.S., Soc. Exptl. Biology and Medicine (pres. Western N.Y. sect. 1951-52), Am. Soc. Cell Biology, Internat. Soc. Cell Biology, Swiss, Italian, European socs. hematology (corr. mem.), Mexican Soc. Anatomy (hon.). Unitarian. Contbr. Folia Haematologica, 1937-49. Asso. editor Anatomical Record, 1955-68; editorial bd. Blood, 1946-55. Home: 23 Berkley Pl Buffalo NY 14209

JONES, OTIS HUNTER, obstetrician and gynecologist; b. Wake Forest, N.C., Sept. 11, 1908; s. Ira Otis and Elizabeth (Freeman) J.; B.S., Wake Forest Coll., 1929, B.S. in Medicine, 1931; M.D., Columbia, 1933; m. Nancy McGee Hovis, May 3, 1941; children—Nancy Louise (Mrs. Sherman E. Crites, Jr.), Frances Hovis (Mrs. Martin L. Brackett, Jr.), Elizabeth Hunter. Intern, Meth.-Episcopal Hosp., Bklyn., 1933- 35; resident Sloane Hosp. Women, N.Y.C., 1935-36, Meth.-Episcopal Hosp., 1937—; individual practice, Charlotte N.C., 1937—; mem. staff Charlotte Meml. Hosp., 1940—, chief dept. obstetrics and gynecology, 1964—. Trustee, Florence Crittenton Home, Charlotte, 1967—. Served to capt. M.C., AUS, 1942-45. Mem. A.M.A., N.C., Mecklenburg County med. socs., Charlotte Gynecol. and Obstet. Soc. (pres. 1963-64), N.C. Obstet. and Gynecol. Soc. (pres. 1965-66), S. Atlantic Assn. Obstetricians and Gynecologists (v.p. 1965-66), Alumni Assn. Meth.-Episcopal Hosp., Ex- Interns Soc. Sloane Hosp. Women, Theta Kappa Nu, Phi Chi. Baptist (deacon). Rotarian. Home: 1710 Queens Rd W Charlotte NC 28207 Office: Doctors Bldg 1012 Kings Dr Charlotte NC 28207

JONES, OWEN TENBROECK, banker; b. Springfield, Ill., Jan. 9, 1904; s. John Tenbroeck and Alice (Conner) J.; student Bradley U., 1926-27; m. Anne Holliday, May 5, 1928; children—Janet Anne (Mrs. Donald Templeman), Susan Holliday (Mrs. Robert J. Goudy), Barbara Hale. With Ill. Mchts. Trust Co., Chgo., 1921-26; partner N.H. Stronck and Co., Chgo., 1927-32; U.S. comptroller currency, 1933; examiner Fed. Deposit Ins. Corp., 1933-35; with Wells Fargo Bank, and predecessor, San Francisco, 1935-69, v.p., controller, 1949-62, sr. v.p., 1962-69; with Internat. Exec. Service Corps, Thailand, 1969, Malaysia, 1970, Taiwan, 1970. Mem. Gov. Cal. Survey Efficiency and Cost Control, 1967—. Mem. Nat. Assn. Bank Auditors and Controllers (dir. at large 1965-67), Financial Execs. Inst. (dir. 1949-52). Republican. Conglist. Rotarian. Home: 809 Wilmington Rd San Mateo CA 94402 Office: 464 California St San Francisco CA 94120

JONES, MRS. PAUL MCCLELLAN, (Mildred Elizabeth FitzHenry), assn. exec.; b. Bloomington, Ill.; d. Louis and Lottie (Rankin) FitzHenry; A.B., Ill. Wesleyan U., 1933; A.M., U. Chgo., 1935; m. Paul McClellan Jones, 1941; children—Paul McClellan, Charlotte FitzHenry (Mrs. Bob S. Moore). With YWCA, 1943—, bd. dirs. Memphis YWCA, 1945-49, White Plains, N.Y., 1954-60, mem. nat. bd., 1953—, chmn. nat. pub. affairs com., 1954-58; v.p. YWCA of U.S.A., 1958-64, v.p. at large, 1967-70; mem. World YWCA Council, 1958—, exec. com., 1963—; mem. nat. bd. trustees YWCA, 1962—. Trustee Nat. Assembly for Social Policy and Devel., 1968—. Home: 27 Hotel Dr White Plains NY 10605

JONES, PETER D'ALROY, educator, author; b. Hull, Eng., June 9, 1931; s. Alfred and Margery (Rutter) J.; B.A., Manchester (Eng.), U. 1952, M.A., 1953; Ph.D., London U., 1963; postgrad. Brussels (Belgium) U., 1954; m. Beau Fly, June 10, 1961; children—Kathryn Beauchamp, Barbara Collier. Came to U.S., 1959, naturalized, 1968. Freelance editor, London, Eng., 1953-56; lectr. U.S. history and instr. Dept. Am. Studies, Manchester U., 1957-58; vis. asst. prof. econs. Tulane U., 1959-60; from asst. to full prof. Smith Coll., 1960-68; prof. history U. Ill. at Chgo., 1968—; vis. prof. Columbia, U. Mass. Mem. com. examiners Grad. Record Exams Ednl. Testing Service,

Princeton, N.J., 1966-70; adviser pubs. Served with RAF, 1956-57. Mem. Am. Hist. Assn., Orgn. Am. Historians, Econ. History Assn., Am. Sociol. Assn. Author: Economic History of U.S.A. since 1783, 2d edit., 1965; The Story of the Saw, 1961; America's Wealth, 1963; The Consumer Society, 2d edit., 1967; The Christian Socialist Revival, 1968; The Robber Barons Revisited, 1968; Robert Hunter's Poverty; Social Conscience in the Progressive Era, 1965; La Sociedad Consumidora, 1968. Editor Pegasus, 1966-68. Home: 429 10th St Wilmette IL 60091 Office: Dept History U Ill Chgo Circle Campus Chicago IL 60680

JONES, PHILIP DAVIS, editor; b. Kingston, Pa., Mar. 24, 1932; s. Scott and Catherine (Davis) J.; B.S., Wilkes Coll., 1954; m. Kay Wharen, July 7, 1957; (div. Nov. 1965); children—Philip B., Bradford D.; m. 2d, Jean Elizabeth LeGwin, Aug. 26, 1967. Rep. Ronald Press Co., 1956-59; editor Macmillan Co., 1959-62, Random House-Alfred A. Knopf, 1964-67; editor-in-chief U. Chgo. Press, 1967—. Served with USAF, 1954-56. Mem. Am. Hist. Assn. Club: Quadrangle (Chgo.). Home: 5807 S Dorchester Av Chicago IL 60637 Office: U Chgo Press 5801 Ellis Av Chicago IL 60637

JONES, PHILIP LEROY, banker; b. Youngstown, O., Nov. 1, 1907; s. Harrison H. and Mary (Steber) J.; student Youngstown U., 1934-37; m. Marian L. Jones, July 14, 1937; children-Philip D., Marianne (Mrs. Mark Aber). with Mahoning Nat. Bank, Youngstown, 1925—, pres., 1967—, also dir. Bd. dirs., v.p. exec. com. Youngstown Area C. of C.; bd. dirs., treas., mem. exec. com.. Youngstown Area Devel. Found. Mem. Am. Inst. Banking (past instr.), Bank Adminstrn. Inst. (past pres. Youngstown). Presbyn. (past trustee). Mason (32). Clubs: Youngstown, Youngstown Country. Home: 1000 Westport Dr Youngstown OH 44511 Office: 23 Central Sq Youngstown OH 44501

JONES, PUTNAM FENNELL, educator; b. Amsterdam, N.Y., Aug. 22, 1902; s. Leslie Wallace and Frances (Fennell) J.; A.B., Cornell, 1924, A.M., 1926, Ph.D. (Goldwin Smith fellow in English, 1926-27), 1927; m. Margaret E. Dillig, Apr. 20, 1935; m. 2d; Margaret L. Peterson, Aug. 11, 1951; 1 dau., Phyllis Margaret. Instr. English, Cornell U.; 1924-26; asst. prof. English, U. Pitts., 1927-32, asso. prof., 1932-46, prof. English; 1946-60, chmn. English dept., 1947-55, acting dean grad. sch., 1955-56, asso. dean coll., 1954-56, acting dean coll., 1956, dean grad. faculty, 1956-68, dean emeritus grad. faculty, prof.-at-large, 1968—; acting dean Sch. Liberal Arts, 1964-65. Councillor Mediaeval Acad. Am. 1960-63; mem. Commn. on Higher Edn., Middle States Assn., 1965-71. Mem. Modern Lang. Assn. Am. (chmn. Old English research group 1933), Mediaeval Acad. Am., Nat. Council Tchrs. English, Coll. English Assn., Phi Beta Kappa, Alpha Tau Omega. Presbyn. Author: A Concordance to the Historia Ecclesiatica of Bede, 1929. Editor: The Constitution of the United States, 1787-1962, 1962. Contbr. articles and reviews in profl. jours. Home: 346 Churchill Rd Pittsburgh PA 15235 Office: U Pitts Pittsburgh PA 15213

JONES, QUINCY, composer, arranger, condr., trumpeter; b. Chgo., Mar. 14, 1933; ed. Seattle U., Berklee Sch. Music, Boston Conservatory Trumpeter arranger Lionel Hampton Orch., 1950-53; arranger for orchs., singerds including Ray Anthony, Count Basie, Sarah Vaughan, Peggy Lee; organizer, trumpeter Dizzy Gillespie Orch. for Dept. of State tour of Near East. Middle East, S.Am., 1956; music dir. Barchlay Disques, Paris, France; leader own orch., European tour, concerts, TV, radio, 1960; music dir. Mercury Records, 1961, v.p., 1964; composer fill background scores The Boy in the Tree; conductor film music The Pawnbroker, Mirage, The Slender Thread; composer, actor film Blues for Trumpet and Koto. Recipient Grammy award, award German Jazz Fedn., Edison Internat. award of Sweden. Address; care dir pub relations A & M Records 1416 N La Brea Hollywood CA 90028*

JONES, R. BRUCE, advt. exec.; b. Phila., Aug. 29, 1912; s. Clifford B. and Elizabeth (Ferguson) J.; B.S., Haverford Coll., 1934; M.A., U. Pa., 1938; m. Jeanne E. Tousaw, June 20, 1936; children—Margaret L., Eric N. With N.W. Ayer & Son, Inc., Phila., 1934—, treas., 1956-60, sec.-treas., 1960—. Chmn. bd. Christian Hall Library, Phila., 1960-65; sec.-treas. W. M. Armistead Found., 1960—; bd. dirs. Friends Edn. Fund, 1957-64; trustee Friends Central Sch., 1969—. Author: Greene Street Friends School, 1955. Home: 127 W Chestnut Hill Av Philadelphia PA 19118 Office: N W Ayer & Son Inc W Washington Sq Philadelphia PA 19106

JONES, RALPH, Jr., educator, physician; b. Parkersburg, W.Va., Mar. 16, 1918; s. Ralph and I. (Holden) J.; A.B., W.Va. U., 1939; M.D., U. Pa., 1943; m. Marian Gresh, Sept. 16, 1944; children—Ralph, Amy. Intern Hosp. U. Pa., 1943- 44, resident, 1947-49; research asso. urology U. Chgo., 1946, research biochemistry, 1947; mem. faculty U. Pa. Sch. Medicine, 1948- 55, asso. prof. medicine, dir. C. Willard Robison Found., U. Miami (Fla.) Med. Sch., 1955-63, prof. medicine, chmn. dept., 1964-70, chief cancer research Internist Roswell Park Meml. Inst., Buffalo, 1964-70, Providence Med. Assos., 1971—. Chmn. coordinating com. Nat. Chemotherapy Program; fellowship com. NSF; chmn. new drug com., clin. panel Cancer Chemotherapy Center, 1955- 60; mem. cancer chemotherapy study sect. USPHS, 1955-60; exec. com., chmn. medicine test com. Nat. Bd. Med. Examiners cons. to surgeon gen. USPHS, surgeon gen. U.S. Army; NRC fellow medicine, 1948- 49; Markie scholar med. scis., 1949-54. Diplomate Am. Bd. Internal Medicine. Fellow A.C.P.; affiliate fellow Royal Coll. Medicine Gt. Britain; mem. Soc. Pharmacology and Exptl. Therapeutics, N.Y. Acad. Scis., A.A.A.S., A.M.A., Am. Assn. Cancer Research, Physiol. Soc. Phila., Phila. Coll. Physicians, Am. Soc. Tropical Medicine and Hygiene, Assn. Am. Med. Colls., Am. Chem. Soc., Am. Assn. U. Profs., Am. Fedn. Clin. Research, So. Soc. Clin. Research, Am. Med. Edn. Found., Am. Soc. Toxicology, Sigma Xi, Alpha Omega Alpha. Home: 132 Cleveland Av Buffalo NY 14222 Office: 549 4th St Niagara Falls NY

JONES, RALPH WALDO EMERSON, coll. pres.; b. Lake Charles, La., Aug. 6, 1905; s. John Sebastian and Maria (Morrison) J.; A.B., So. U., Baton Rouge, 1925; A.M., Columbia, 1932; LL.D., La. Tech. U., 1970; m. Mildred Shay, Apr. 11, 1937; children—Ralph, John Arthur. Tchr., Lampton Coll., Alexandria, La., 1925-26; instr. Grambling (La.) Coll., 1926-27, dean, 1927-36, pres., 1936—. Baptist. Mason (33). Home: Grambling College Grambling LA 71245

JONES, RALPH WOOD, educator; b. Streator, Ill., July 9, 1918; s. Ralph A. and Jane (Wood) J.; B.Mus., Ill. Wesleyan U., 1940; M. Mus. Edn., Okla. U., 1941; postgrad., U. Mich., 1946; Ph.D., U. Tex., 1959; m. Ruthelle Lorraine Schroeder, June 20, 1942; children—Kyra Lee (Mrs. Kyra Lee Osmus), Amelia Kay (Mrs. Milton Ward). Asso. prof., head wind instrument dept. Southwestern U., Georgetown, Tex., 1946-57, asso. prof., then prof. history, 1957-61; prof., chmn. dept. history and philosophy edn. U. Ala., 1961-68; prof., dir. grad. studies Coll. Edn. U.S. Ala., 1968-71. Served to lt. (j.g.) USNR, 1942-46. Fellow Philosophy Edn. Soc.; mem. Am. Edn. Research Assn., Phi Delta Kappa, Phi Mu Alpha. Author: A History of Southwestern University, 1960; (with others) Problem Solving Processes in Social Studies, 1968. Home: 1242 Anchor Dr Mobile AL 36609

JONES, RAY LOCKWOOD, lawyer; b. Cordell, Okla., May 30, 1908; s. LeRoy and Laura E. (Resseguie) J.; student Western Okla. Christian Coll., 1925-26; LL.B., U. Okla., 1930; m. Ellen Jones, Sept. 8, 1935; childrenJanet, Ray Lockwood. Admitted to Okla. bar, 1930, practiced in Cordell, 1933-; county atty., Washita County, 1931-32. Mem. Subversive Activities Control Bd., Washington, 1956-60. Okla. State Republican committeeman, 1936—; del. Rep. Nat. Conv., 1944; mem. Okla. State Exec. Com. Mem. Okla. State Soc. of Washington (pres.), Am. Okla. bar assns., Phi Alpha Delta, Acacia. Republican. Presbyn. Mason, Kiwanian. Home: 922 922 N Temple Cordell OK 73630 Office: Johnston Bldg Cordell OK 73632

JONES, RAYMOND ALLEN, Jr., constrn. co. exec.; b. Charlotte, N.C., Jan. 19, 1925; s. Raymond Allen and Lucille (Hubbard) J.; B.C.E., Ga. Inst. Tech., 1949; m. Donna Louise Bridges, Dec. 28, 1946; children—Sharon Lucille, Donna Lee, Raymond Allen III. Exec. v.p. J.A. Jones Constrn. Co., Charlotte; pres. J.A. Jones Internat., Inc.; v.p. William L. Crow Constrn. Co., N.Y.C.; dir. Environs Co., Atlanta; pres. Peachtree Hills Apts. Corp., Atlanta; chmn. bd. Cloudland Ridge Corp., Atlanta. Nat. adv. bd. Ga. Tech. Trustee Pfeiffer Coll., Mosenheimer, Charlotte Country Day Sch.; bd. dirs. Goodwill Industries, Charlotte Arts Council. Served with AUS, World War II. Mem. Am. Soc. C.E., Newcomen Soc. N.Am. Methodist. Rotarian. Home: 335 Eastover Rd Charlotte NC 28207 Office: 521 E Morehead St Charlotte NC 28203

JONES, RAYMOND EDWARD, Jr., brewing exec.; b. New Bern, N.C., Jan. 27, 1927; s. Raymond Edward and Ellen LaVerne (Mallard) J.; B.S., U. Md., 1953; LL.B., U. Balt., 1962; m. Sarra Gordon O'Bryan, Aug. 29, 1958; children—Leslie Anne, Raymond Edward III. Office mgr. Hopkins Furniture Co., Annapolis, Md., 1953-55; v.p. legal, sec. Nat. Brewing Co., Balt., 1956—; house counsel and/or officer Divex, Inc., Laco Products, Inc., Laco Corp., C.W. Abbott, Inc., Pompeian, Inc., Interhost Corp., Solarine Co., Balt. Baseball Club, Inc.; admitted to Md. bar, 1962. Bd. dirs. Soc. Preservation Md. Antiquities, 1969—. Served with USNR, 1942-45. Mem. U.S. Brewers Assn., Am., Md., Balt. City bar assns., Sigma Chi, Sigma Delta Chi. Democrat. Presbyn. Home: 2500 Pickwick Rd Baltimore MD 21207 Office: 225 N Calvert St Baltimore MD 21207

JONES, RAYMOND WATERS, wholesale co. exec.; b. Honey Grove, Tex., May 12, 1900; s. John Royal and Kathryn Lee (Temple) J.; grad. high sch.; m. Harriet Jack Cocke, Feb. 12, 1926; children—Jack Raymond, Robert Temple, Janet Dona. Gen. mgr. J.H. Newbauer & Co., Modesto, Cal., 1924-26; pres. Jones & Co., 1926-33; sales mgr. Safeway Store, So. Cal. div., 1934; owner Thrifty Mart, Modesto, 1935-40; pres., gen. mgr. Central Valley Grocers, 1940-55; sr. v.p. Market Wholesale Grocery Co., Modesto, 1970—. Served with USN, 1917-19. Mason. Clubs: Rotary (pres. 1944-45), Del Rio Golf and Country (pres. 1955) (Modesto). Home: 1118 Amherst St Modesto CA 95350 Office: 1324 Coldwell Av Modesto CA 95352

JONES, REESE D., banker; b. Kingston, Pa., Mar. 22, 1929; s. Scott D. and Catherine Davis (Jones) J.; B.A., Wilkes Coll., 1956; M.A., U. Pa., 1958; m. Anne Swortwood, June 22, 1957; children—Abigail Lee, Scott Davis. With Fed. Res. Bank, Phila., 1955-57; sr. v.p. Studley, Shupert & Co., Phila., 1957-67; pres. First Valley Bank (formerly Nat. Bank & Trust Co.), Bethlehem, Pa., 1967—; dir. William Gillespie & Son, Inc., Phila., United Life Ins. Co., Educators Mut. Life Ins. Co., Lancaster, Pa., Lehigh Valley Indsl. Park; adj. prof. econs. Lehigh U. Chmn. adv. bd. Bethlehem Central Bus. Dist. Asso. gen. chmn. United Fund Appeal, 1969; chmn. spl. gifts div. Historic Bethlehem Preservation Fund. Served with USAF, 1948-53. Mem. Bethlehem C. of C. (dir., 2d v.p.), Am. Finance Assn., Omicron Delta Upsilon. Mem. Moravian Ch. Home: 704 Pine Top Dr Bethlehem PA 18017 Office: 535 Main St Bethlehem PA 18018

JONES, REGINALD HAROLD, elec. mfg. co. exec.; b. Stoke-on-Trent, Staffordshire, Eng., July 11, 1917; s. Alfred John and Gertrude (Cartlidge) J.; came to U.S., 1925, naturalized, 1930; B.S. in Econs., U. Pa., 1939; m. Grace Butterfield Cole, Mar. 2, 1940; children—Keith Edwin, Grace Seymour. With Gen. Electric Co., Bridgeport, Conn., 1939—, bus. trainee and traveling auditor, 1939-50, asst. to comptroller, apparatus dept. assignments, 1950-56, gen. mgr. Air Conditioning div., 1956-58, gen. mgr. Gen. Electric Supply Co. div., 1958-61, v.p. parent co., 1961-70, gen. mgr. constrn. industries div., 1964-67, group exec., 1967-68, v.p. finance, 1968-70, sr. v.p., 1970—. Home: 742 Lake Av Greenwich CT 06830 Office: 570 Lexington Av New York City NY 10022

JONES, RICHARD EARLE, lawyer; b. Jones Mill, Monroe Co., Ala., Apr. 5, 1894; s. James Wiley and Mary Frances (Hughes) J.; A.B., U. Ala., 1914, M.A., 1915, LL.B., 1919; m. Lucile Foster, June 10, 1922; children—Richard Earle, Sara Frances. Admitted to Ala. bar, 1919; partner firm Knox, Jones, Woolf & Merrill, Anniston; dir. First Nat. Bank of Anniston, Classe Ribbon Co. Inc. Mem. Ala. State Democratic Exec. Com., 1924-40, elected pres. and v.p., 3 terms. Mem. City Bd. Edn., Anniston, 1935-46; chmn. merit system council Co. Depts. Pub. Welfare, 1947-51. Capt. F. A., AUS, World War I. Mem. Anniston C. of C., Am., Calhoun County bar assns., Ala. State Bar, Phi Beta Kappa, Baptist. Kiwanian. Home: 1420 Woodstock Av Anniston AL 36201 Office: Comml Nat Bank Bldg Anniston AL 36201

JONES, RICHARD GREGG, hosp. adminstr.; b. Kent, Wash., Apr. 20, 1914; s. Robert Chapin and Hattie (Richardson) J.; B.A., U. Wash., 1938; m. Olga Petric, Apr. 4, 1946; children—Marilyn Diana, Susan Carol. With VA, 1946-68, hosp. dir. VA Hosp., Walla Walla, Wash., 1962-65, VA Hosp., Livermore, Cal. Pres. Walla Walla Community Services Council, 1963; campaign chmn. Walla Walla County United Fund, 1965. Bd. dirs. Walla Walla unit A.R.C., 1963-65, Oakland-S. Alameda County chpt., 1967—. Served with USAAF, 1942-45; ETO. Fellow Am. Coll. Hosp. Adminstrs.; mem. Am. Hosp. Assn., Assn. Western Hosps., Am. Legion, V.F.W., Livermore C. of C. (dir. 1968—; foreman Livermore Corral Club, 1968). Rotarian, Elk, Mason. Address: 1375B Camino Peral Moraga CA 94556

JONES, RICHARD HUTTON, educator; b. Rye, Colo., Aug. 11, 1914; s. John Wiley and Jessie (Hutton) J.; B.A., U. No. Colo., 1934, M.A., 1937; Ph.D., Stanford, 1947; m. Alyce Decker, Aug. 15, 1935; 1 son, Robert Charles. High sch. tchr., Ft. Lupton, Colo., 1934-38; instr. Stanford, 1940-41; mem. faculty Reed Coll., 1941—, Richard F. Scholz prof. history, 1949- -; profector Ore. Shakespearean Festival, 1964. Chmn. com. European history Coll. Entrance Exam. Bd., 1960-67, mem. com. exams., 1965-68; spl. cons. Ednl. Assos., Inc., 1968-70. Pub. mem. Ore. Legislative Interim Com. Labor, 1958-60; mem. Ore. Commn. Constl. Revision, 1961, 62; exec. sec. Citizens Com. Constl. Revision, 1963-65, Ore. chmn. Rep. Com. Arts and Scis., 1965-66; chmn. Ore. Reps. for McCarthy, Social Sci. Research Council faculty fellow, 1951- 53; Ford Found. fellow, 1953-54; sr. fellow law and behavioral sci. U. Chgo., 1956. Author: The Royal Policy of Richard II, 1968. Home: 3908 S E Reedway Portland OR 97202

JONES, RICHARD LLOYD, Jr., newspaper exec.; b. Nyack, N.Y., Feb. 22, 1909; s. Richard Lloyd and Georgia (Hayden) J.; student Culver Mil. Acad., 1925. Tome Sch., Port Deposit, Md., 1926; Ph.B., U. Wis., 1932; m. Martha Meredith Corder, Mar. 4, 1933; children—Richard, Dana. Apprentice, mech. depts. Tulsa Tribune, 1933-34; telegraph desk, 1935, desplay advt. dept., 1935-38, v.p., now pres., gen. mgr.; v.p. bus. mgr. Newspaper Printing Corp., 1941-51, pres. 1951—; v.p., treas. Hennepin Paper Co., Little Falls, Minn., 1953- 56; dir. Brookside State Bank, Tulsa, N.Y. World's Fair, 1964-65, Douglas Aircraft Co. Dir. 1964—. Chmn. Tulsa Airport Authority; dir. state fair, livestock expn., Tulsa. Served to lt. U.S.N.R., World War II. Mem. Tulsa C. of C. (dir. 1954—, pres. 1960-61). So. Newspaper Pubs. Assn. (chmn. labor com. 1948-52, pres. 1953-54, chmn. of board 1954-55), Am. Newspaper Pubs. Assn. (chmn. bd. bur. advt. 1956-58). Aviation Writers' Assn., Phi Gamma Delta. Unitarian. Club: Southern Hills Country (Tulsa). Home: 1754 E 30th St Tulsa OK 74114

JONES, RICHARD MONTGOMERY, assn. exec.; b. Portland, Ore., Sept. 23, 1907; s. Horace Tillard and Marie (Neuhausen) J.; student U. Ore.; 1925-28; m. Nancy Guild, June 19, 1935 (div. 1966); children—Gary Guild, Nancy Lynn, Susan Elizabeth; m. 2d, Elizabeth Mansfield, 1967. Reporter, sportswriter, city editor. Asso. Press corr. on newspapers in Portland, Eugene, Pendleton, Ore., 1928-29, 1937-38; pub. relations Western Airlines and Trans World Airline, Portland, Seattle, San Francisco, 1929- 31; spl. agt. div. investigations Fed. Works Agency, Portland, 1933-37, 1938-40; civilian chief A.A.F., Intelligence div., Wright Field, Dayton, O., 1940-43; chief plant protection Douglas Aircraft, Chgo. plant, 1943-45; pub. relations dir. Blue Cross Commn., 1945-47; dir. Blue Cross Commn., Am. Hosp. Assn., Chgo., 1947-60; asso. sec. Council Blue Cross Prepayment and Financing, 1960-63; exec. dir. Hosp. Planning Council Met. Portland Area, Portland, 1963-64; exec. sec. Ore. Dental Assn., 1965-69; asst. to pub. Asso. Publs. Inc., 1969—, pub. relations cons., 1970—; dir. Health Service, Inc. Vice pres., adv. bd. Mt. St. Joseph Residence and Nursing Home. Fellow Am. Coll. Hosp. Adminstrs. (hon.); mem. Am. Hosp. Assn., Mystic Order Rose, Sigma Chi. Club: City (Portland). Address: 2670 SW Grenwolde Pl Portland OR 97201

JONES, RICHARD STANLEY, lawyer, milk co. exec.; b. Shelbyville, Ind., Apr. 8, 1908; s William Stanley and Bess Adeline (Trout) J.; B.S., Ind. U., 1930; LL.B., Harvard, 1933; m. Laura Gray, Sept. 28, 1935; children—Mary Stephens, Elizabeth Stanley. Admitted to Mo. bar, 1933; since practiced in St. Louis; mem. firm Williams, Nelson & English, partner, 1940-43; gen. counsel Pet, Inc., St. Louis, 1943-44, gen. counsel, asst. sec., 1944-52, v.p., dir., 1951-66, sr. v.p. corporate devel., dir., 1966—; dir. A.B. Chance Co. Chmn. Dairy Industry Com., 1953-54. Pres. Health and Welfare Council Met. St. Louis, 1967-70. Bd. mgrs. Central Inst. for Deaf, 1942—, pres. bd. mgrs., 1960-62; curator Stephens Coll., 1963—; dir. Playgoers of St. Louis, 1952—, pres., 1961-62. Mem. State Guard, Mo., 1942-43. Mem. Mo., St. Louis bar assns., Kappa Sigma, Alpha Kappa Psi, Beta Gamma Sigma. Clubs: Noonday, St. Louis Country. Home: 23 Picardy Lane Saint Louis MO 63124 Office: Pet Plaza 400 S 4th St Saint Louis MO 63166

JONES, RICHARD THEODORE, educator; b. Portland, Ore., Nov. 9, 1929; s. Lester Tallman and Olene (Johnson) J.; student Cal. Inst. Tech., 1948-51, Ph.D., 1961; B.S., U. Ore., 1953, M.S., M.D., 1956; m. Marilyn Virginia Beam, June 20, 1953; children—Gary Richard, Alan Donald, Neil William. Student asst. dept. physiology U. Ore. Med. Sch., Portland, 1953-56, asst. prof., 1961-64, asso. prof. exptl. medicine and biochemistry, 1964-67, prof., chmn. dept. biochemistry, 1967—; intern Hosp. U. Pa., 1956-57; research asst. dept. chemistry Cal. Inst. Tech., 1959-60. Mem. biochemistry tng. com. Nat. Inst. Gen. Med. Scis., NIH, 1968-71; biochemistry test com. Nat. Bd. Med. Examiners, 1968—. Mem. Am. Soc. Biol. Chemists, Am. Chem. Soc., A.A.A.S., Sigma Xi, Alpha Omega Alpha, Tau Beta Pi. Republican. Contbr. articles profl. jours. Home: 9615 SW Eagle Ct Beaverton OR 97005 Office: 3181 SW Sam Jackson Park Rd Portland OR 97201

JONES, RICHARD W., chmn., chief exec. officer investment banking firm Mitchum, Jones & Templeton, Inc.; dir. Gen. Telephone & Electronics Corp., Wayne Mfg. Co., Strolee of Cal., Wyle Labs., West Bay Financial Corp., Gen. Telephone Directory Co., Charter Life Ins. Co. Vice chmn. bd. govs. Pacific Coast Stock Exchange. Address: 510 S Spring St Los Angeles CA 90013*

JONES, ROBERT ALFRED, educator; b. Bayonne, N.J., Feb. 14, 1928; A.B., Catholic U., 1951, M.A., 1953, Ph.D., 1957; married; 1 child. From staff psychologist to research coordinator clin. psychology VA Regional Office, N.J., 1957-60; asst. prof. psychology Rutgers U., New Brunswick, N.J., 1960-62; asso. prof. Seton Hall U., South Orange, N.J., 1962-66, prof., 1966—, chmn. dept. psychology, 1962—. Cons. Asso. Cath. Charities, 1960—; mem. bd. psychology examiners N.J. sect. Am. Bd. Examiners Profl. Psychologists. Served with AUS, 1946-47. Mem. A.A.A.S., Am. Psychol. Assn. Office: Seton Hall U South Orange NJ*

JONES, ROBERT COPELAND, investment banker; b. Washington, Aug. 23, 1898; s. Wentworth C. and Elizabeth (Tolson) J.; student schs., Washington, also Md.; m. Virginia C. Lewis, Mar. 26, 1921 (dec. 1959); children—Robert Copeland, Kenneth Page, Virginia Aline; m. 2d, Jille Romney, 1959. With John L. Edwards & Co., investment securities, Washington; co-mgr. at Washington for N.Y. Stock Exchange Ho. of G.M.P. Murphy & Co., 1927-30; established investment banking house of Robert C. Jones & Co., 1939, became sr. partner; sr. partner Jones, Kreeger & Hewitt, mem. N.Y. Stock Exchange, 1952—; partner Jones, Kreeger & Co., Washington, 1959—. Served from 2d lt. to capt., U.S. Army, World War I; AEF; from lt. col. to col., USAAF, World War II. Decorated Legion of Merit. Mem. Washington Bd. Trade, N.Y. and Washington Stock Exchange, Soc. Colonial Cavaliers, Soc. Colonial Wars, Soc. War of 1912, Soc. of Cincinnati, S.A.R. Clubs: Army and Navy, Army-Navy Country, University (Washington). Home: Knollwood Rockville MD 20850 Office: 1625 Eye St NW Washington DC 20006

JONES, ROBERT E., Jr., congressman, lawyer; b. Scottsboro, Ala., June 12, 1912; s. Robert E. and Augusta (Smith) J.; LL.B., U. Ala., 1937; m. Christine Francis, Apr. 9, 1938; 1 son, Robert E. Admitted to Ala. bar, 1937; established law practice with firm, Brewton and Jones, Scottsboro, Ala.; elected judge, Jackson County Ct., 1940, reelected in absentia, 1945; elected to 80th Congress in spl. election to fill vacancy created by John J. Sparkman's election to U.S. Senate; mem. 81st-87th, 89th-92d Congresses, 8th Ala. Dist., mem. 88th Congress at large. Served as gunnery officer, USNR, 1942-46, Atlantic and Pacific theaters of operations. Mem. V.F.W., Am. Legion, Kappa Alpha. Home: Scottsboro AL 35768 Office: House Office Bldg Washington DC 20515

JONES, ROBERT EDWARDS, religious exec.; b. Holyoke, Mass., Apr. 8, 1927; s. Carleton Parker and Ruth (Adams) J.; B.A. cum laude, Amherst Coll., 1949; m. Mary Phillips Leszkiewicz, Aug. 8, 1954; children—Miriam Ellis, Edmund Adams. Staff reporter Holyoke Transcript-Telegram, 1949-55, Springfield (Mass.) Daily News,

1955-56; cons. survival planning project Mass. Civil Def. Agy., 1956-58; dir. news and information Greater Boston C. of C., 1958-60; campaign press sec. to Gov. Volpe of Mass., 1960; dir. pub. information Mass. Dept. Pub. Works, 1961-62; exec. dir. Unitarian Universalist Fellowship for Social Justice, 1962-64; dir. Washington office, div. social responsibility Unitarian Unversalist Assn., 1964-69, exec. dir. Joint Washington Office for Social Concern, rep. Am. Ethical Union- Am. Humanist Assn., Unitarian Universalist Assn., 1969—. Mem. New Eng. regional com. Am. Unitarian Youth, 1946-47; pres. Samuel Atkins Eliot chpt. Unitarian Laymen's League, 1959. Mem. Fellowship for Equal Rights S. Prince George's, 1962—; sec. Nat. Civil Liberties Clearing House, 1966-67. Mem. bd. Nat. Rural Housing Coalition, 1970—, Internat. Devel. Conf., 1969—. Chmn. Amherst Democratic Town Com., 1952-54; Dem. nominee for Mass. Ho. of Reps., 1954; del. Mass. Dem. Conv., 1952, 54. Recipient Eagle Scout award Boy Scouts Am., 1945; Franklin medal excellence Am. history S.A.R., 1944. Mem. Am. Acad. Polit. and Social Sci., Am. Dem. Action, Am. Civil Liberties Union. Contbr. articles, reports. Home: 5062 Temple Hills Rd Temple Hills MD 20031 Office: 100 Maryland Av NE Washington DC 20002

JONES, ROBERT ELLIOTT JONAH, trumpet player; b. Louisville, Dec. 31, 1909. Played with Wallace Bryant on Miss. riverboats, 1929; also with Wesley Helvey, 1930, Jimmie Lunceford, 1931, Stuff Smith, 1932-34, 36-40, 53, McKinney's Cotton Pickers, 1935, Fletcher Henderson, 1940, Benny Carter, 1940-41, Cab Calloway, 1941-52; with Joe Bushkin at Embers, 1952; on tour with Earl Hines, 1952-53, Porgy and Bess pit band, 1953; on tour Europe, 1954; numerous recordings with Teddy Wilson, Billie Holiday, Lil Armstrong, others; appeared Fred Astaire TV Show, 1958, 59. Address: care Sam Berk 160 W 46th St New York City NY 10036*

JONES, ROBERT EUGENE, architect; b. Lawton, Okla., Nov. 13, 1930; s. James Cecil and Ernestine Alberta (Huber) J.; B.Arch., U. So. Cal., 1955; m. Sara Carol Price, Dec. 31, 1955; children—Brent, Brigette. Partner, Hester-Jones & Assos., La Jolla, Cal., 1962-64; prin. Robert E. Jones, Architect, La Jolla, 1964-66; partner Robert E. Jones & Edwin K. Hom, architects, La Jolla, 1966-69, pres., 1969—. Planning commr. City of Del Mar, Cal., 1970—; mem. Design Rev. Bd., City of Del Mar, 1970—, Urban Design Center, S.E. San Diego Model Cities Area, 1970. Served to 1st lt. USAF, 1955-57. Recipient 13 nat. and local A.I.A. design awards; named One of 12 Top Performers of 1969 by House & Home Mag. for contbn. of patio-home concept to housing industry. Mem. A.I.A., San Diego C. of C., Urban Land Inst., Nat. Council Archtl. Registration Bds., Blue Key, Skull and Dagger, Tau Sigma Delta, Scarab. Important works include Bruck Residence, La Jolla, 1st patio home community, Casas Capistrano, 2d patio home community, Westlake Village, Jones Residence, Del Mar, Busch Residence, Del Mar. Home: 2041 Balboa St Del Mar CA 92014 Office: 7911 Herschel Av La Jolla CA 92037

JONES, ROBERT GEAN, educator; b. Magnolia, Ark., Feb. 17, 1925; s. Emless Bunyan and Eunice (Gean) J.; B.A. cum laude, Baylor U., 1947; B.D. cum laude, Yale, 1950, M.A., 1957, Ph.D., 1959; m. Marian Laverne Alexander, July 23, 1946; 1 dau., Carolyn Ann. Ordained to ministry Bapt. Ch., 1946; minister Deep River (Conn.) Bapt. Ch. and First Bapt. Ch. of Saybrook, 1950-59; asst. prof. religion George Washington U., Washington, 1959-61, asso. prof., 1961-64, prof., 1964—, chmn. dept. religion, 1963—, univ. marshal, 1969—. Mem. Soc. Bibl. Lit. and Exegesis, Am. Acad. Religion, Alpha Chi, Omicron Delta Kappa. Author: The Rules for the War of the Sons of Light With the Sons of Darkness, 1957; The Manual of Discipline (1QS), The Old Testament and Persian Religion, 1964. Home: 11835 Goya Dr Potomac MD 20854 Office: George Washington U Washington DC 20006

JONES, ROBERT HAYDON, advt. exec.; b. N.Y.C., July 15, 1910; s. Haydon and Emma (Voos) J.; B.A. cum laude, Harvard, 1930; m. Florence Joan Shaw, May 15, 1937; children-Robert Haydon, Christopher Shaw, Jeffrey Owen, Jeremy Mary, Jude Anne, Pamela Cathlyn. Advt. and pub. relations exec. R.H. Macy & Co., N.Y.C., 1932-34; dir. advt. and pub. relations Doubleday, Dora & Co., 1934-37; asst. to pres. Condé Nast Publns., 1937-40; dir. advt. and pub. relations John Wanamaker, N.Y.C. and Phila., 1940-41; account exec. Batten, Barton Durstine & Osborn, 1941-45; dir. Alley & Richards Co., Boston, 1945-47; sales mgr. Glenwood Range Co., Taunton, Mass., 1947-49; pres. Robert Haydon Jones Assos., Westport, Conn., 1949-51; partner, v.p. Marschalk & Pratt Co., N.Y.C., 1951-54; v.p. McCann-Erickson, Inc., N.Y.C., 1954-60; sr. v.p. McCann-Erickson Internatt., N.Y.C., 1960—; dir. Westport Co., London Co., Ltd. Mem. Staples tuition grants com., Wesport, 1955-70. Mem. Westport Repulbican Town Com., 1948-56. Served with N.Y. State N.G., 1942-46. Mem. Assn. Ex-Mems. Squadron A. K.C. Club: Harvard (N.Y.C.). Home: 17 Appletree Trail Westport CT 06880 Office: 485 Lexington Av New York NY 10017

JONES, ROBERT HUHN, educator; b. Chgo., July 30, 1927; s. Merton Oakes and Ethel (Huhn) J.; A.B., U. Ill. at Champaign, 1950, M.A., 1951, Ph.D., 1957; m. Estelle Marie Long, June 12, 1948; children—Judith Caroline, Robert Paul. Mem. faculty Kent (O.) State U., 1957-65, Case Western Res. U., Cleve., 1965-71, prof. history, chmn. dept. U. Akron, 1971—; vis. research prof. U. Ill. at Champaign, 1962-63, Lilly Endowment postdoctoral fellow, 1964. Mem. Stow (O.) City Sch. Dist. Bd. Edn., 1968—; pres. Stow Bd. Edn., 1971—. Served with Signal Corps, AUS, 1945-47. Mem. Ohio Acad. History (chmn. standards com. 1970-71), Am. Hist. Assn., Western History Assn., Orgn. Am. Historians. Author: The Civil War in the Northwest, 1960; (with Fred A. Shannon) The Centennial Years, 1967; The Roads to Russia: United States Lend-Lease to the Soviet Union, 1969. Home: 3967 Darrow Rd Stow OH 44224

JONES, ROBERT LEE, educator; b. Sapulpa, Okla., June 17, 1920; s. Clyde William and Arminia (Harris) J.; B.A, Oklahoma City U., 1948; B.D., So. Methodist U., 1951. M.A., 1952; Ph.D., St. Mary's Coll., U. St. Andrews, Scotland, 1956; m. Mary Claire Collingsworth, June 12, 1948; 1 dau. Mary Lee. Ordained to ministry Meth. Ch., 1952; asso. pastor Wesley Meth. Ch., Oklahoma City, 1947-48, Wesley Meth. Ch., Dallas, 1948-52; pastor Grove (Okla.) Meth. Ch., 1952-54; pastor Ch. of Scotland, 1954-56; pastor, dir. Wesley Found. Meth. Ch., Goodwell, Okla., 1956-57; asst. prof. religion Oklahoma City U., 1957-61, asso. prof., 1961-65, prof., 1965—, dean of men, 1960-62, asso. dean Coll. A. and S., 1962-63, dean, 1963-70, v.p. acad. affairs, 1970—; del. 3d Oxford Inst. Meth. Theol. Studies, 1965. Internat. Conf. on Higher Edn., Oxford, Eng. 1965. Chmn. com. on edn. Community Relations Commn., Oklahoma City, 1966—, vice chmn. Commn., 1970. Serve with F.A., AUS, 1941-45. Decorated Bronze Star medal. Mem. Am. Acad. Religion, Am. Assn. Higher Edn. Home: 3240 N W 18th St Oklahoma City OK 73107 Office: N W 23d at Blackwelder Oklahoma City OK 73106

JONES, ROBERT LEON, educator; b. Halstead, Kan., Sept. 6, 1921; s. Henry Arthur and Leona (O'Keefe) J.; B.A., U. Wichita, 1942; M.A., U. Minn., 1947, Ph.D., 1951; m. Betty Ann McClure, Aug. 5, 1944; children—Kevin Arthur, Kathryn Alison, Barrett Jerome. Instr. dept. psychology U. Minn., 1948-50, asst. dir. research div. Sch. Journalism, U. Minn., 1950-51, asso. prof., 1952- 57, prof., 1957, dir. Sch. Journalism, 1958—, acting chief intelligence research br. Human Resources Research Inst., 1951-52. Minn. Bd. Examiners in Psychology. Served to 1st lt. USAAF, 1942-46. Mem. Am. Psychol. Assn., Am. Assn. Pub. Opinion Research, Am. Marketing Assn., Assn. for Edn. Journalism (past pres.), Am. Council on Edn. for Journalism, Sigma Xi, Sigma Delta Chi. Adv. editorial bd. Journalism Quar. Home: 1596 Vincent St St Paul MN 55108 Office: U Minn Minneapolis MN 55455

JONES, ROBERT LESLIE, educator; b. Cobden, Ont. Can., Apr. 4, 1907; s. Robert and Martha (Caswell) J.; A.B., Queen's U., 1927, A.M., 1928; A.M., Harvard, 1932, Ph.D., 1938; postgrad. Ont. Coll. Edn., 1928-29, U. Chgo., summer 1931; m. Maude Lacey, Dec. 25, 1939; children—Constance Helen, Natalie Ruth. Came to U.S., 1938, naturalized, 1945. High sch. tchr., Lindsay, Ont., 1929-30, Napanee, 1930-31, Pembroke, 1933-34; instr. history Marietta (O.) Coll., 1938-43, asst. prof. of history, 1943-45, prof., head dept., 1945—, Andrew U. Thomas prof. history, 1966—. Mem. Agrl. History Soc., Am., Can., Minn., Miss. Valley, Wis. hist. socs.; Canadian Polit. Sci. Assn. Conglist. Lion. Author: History of Agriculture in Ontario, 1613-1880, 1946. Contbr. articles to profl. jours. Home: 206 Brentwood St Marietta OH 45750

JONES, ROBERT MARION, book and mag. editor; b. Fulda, Minn., May 31, 1919; s. John Webster and Emma Louella (Price) J.; B.A., U. Minn., 1940; m. Mary Catherine Burd, Nov. 16, 1940; children—Sheila (Mrs. Richard S. Reagan), Robert Michael, Jeffrey Paul, Molly, Christopher Francis. Newspaper reporter Hennepin County (Minn.) Rev., 1938-40, Madison (S.D.) Daily Leader, 1940-42, Sioux Falls (S.D.) Daily Argus-Leader, 1942-45; editorial asst., asso. editor, mng. editor Better Homes & Gardens, Meredith Pub. Co., Des Moines, 1945-54; editor Family Circle, N.Y.C., v.p. Family Circle, Inc., 1955-67; home services editor Time-Life Books Time, Inc., 1967—. Mem. Mag. Publishers Assn., Univ. Minn. Alumni Assn., Am. Soc. Mag. Editors, Sigma Delta Chi. Editor: Better Homes and Gardens Handyman's Book, 1951; Can Elephants Swim? Unlikely Answers to Improbable Questions, 1969; The Time-Life Book of Family Finance, 1969; The Time-Life Ency. of Gardening, 1971. Home: 611 Long Hill Rd Briarcliff Manor NY 10510 Office: Time-Life Books Time Inc New York City NY 10020

JONES, ROBERT MEAD, lawyer, indsl. relations exec.; b. Chgo., July 26, 1918; s. Walter D. and Mary (Mead) J.; grad. Peddie Sch., 1937; B.S. in Econs., U. Pa., 1941, J.D., 1948; m. Constance Rommel, Dec. 29, 1941; children—Suzanne D. Clark, Robert Mead. Admitted to Pa. bar, 1948; with Philco Corp., Phila., 1948-64, successively asst. counsel, dir. indsl. relations for mfg. plants outside Phila., dir. pub. relations, 1957-60, dir. personnel, 1960-61, v.p. personnel, 1961-62, v.p. indsl. relations, 1961-64; v.p. personnel U.S. Plywood Corp., N.Y.C., 1965-70; v.p. Motorola, Inc., Franklin Park, Ill., 1970-71; dir. Huston Assos., Inc., Phila., Twenty Herman St. Corp., Phila. Served to captain USAAF, 1941-45. Mem. Am., Pa., Phila. bar assns., Am. Indsl. Relations Council of U. Pa., Indsl. Relations Assn. Phila., Indsl. Relations Research Assn. Lutheran. Clubs: Union League (Phila.); Seaview Country (Absecon, N.J.). Home: 1616 Sheridan Rd Wilmette IL 60091 Office: 9401 W Grand Av Franklin Park IL 60131

JONES, ROBERT STEWART, educator; b. Omaha, June 10, 1918; s. R. Martin and Anisia (Stewart) J.; B.A., U. Omaha, 1946; M.A., Ohio State U., 1949, Ph.D., 1950; m. M. Louise Harvey, Feb. 14, 1942; children-James S., Linda L. From asst. prof. to prof. chmn. dept. ednl. psychology U. Ill., Urbana, 1950—. Served to capt., AUS, 1941-45. Fellow Am. Psychol. Assn. Author: Educational Psychology, 1968; Psychology of Adolescence for Teachers, 1964. Home: 508 E Harding Av Urbana IL 61801

JONES, ROBERT TRENT, golf course architect; b. nr. Ince, Eng., June 20, 1906; s. William Rees and Jane (Sothern) J.; came to U.S., 1911, derivative citizenship; spl. student Cornell, 1927-30; m. Ione Tefft Davis, May 11, 1934; children—Robert Trent, Jr., Rees Lee. Partner Stanley Thompson, Canadian golf course architect, N.Y.C., 1930-40; pvt. practice as golf course architect, 1940—. Mem. Delta Kappa Epsilon (exec. dir. Delta Chi). Episcopalian. Clubs: Montclair (N.J.) Golf; Pine Valley Golf (Clementon, N. J.); Ponte Vedra (Fla); Yale (N.Y.C.); Coral Ridge Country (pres.; Fort Lauderdale, Fla.); Royal and Ancient Golf (St. Andrews, Scotland); Cotton Bay (dir.); Eleuthera (Bahamas); Burning Tree, Chevy Chase (Washington); Oakmont Country (Pitts.); Sleepy Hollow Country (Scarborough, N.Y.); Metropolitan (N.Y.C.); Spyglass Hill (Pebble Beach, Cal.). Co-author: The Complete Golfer, 1954; Golf-Its History, People and Events, 1966. Contbr. articles golf publs. Designed more than 350 world's most outstanding courses. Home: 173 Gates Av Montclair NJ 07042 also Breakwater Towers Fort Lauderdale FL 32016 Office: P O Box 304 Montclair NJ 07042 also P O Box 4121 Fort Lauderdale FL 33304 Also 705 Forest Av Palo Alto CA 94301

JONES, ROBERT V., electric co. exec.; b. Lincoln, Neb., June 6, 1916; s. James R. and LuLu (Crump) J.; Ph.B. in Accounting, U. Wis., 1939; m. Dorothy I. Casey, Jan. 25, 1941; children—Mary Kathleen (Mrs. James Langlois), Richard James. With Am. Steel and Wire Co., 1941-46; with Marathon Electric Co., Wausau, Wis., 1946—, pres., 1960—; dir. First Am. Nat. Bank, Mosinee Paper Corp. (both Wausau). Mem. Am. Mgmt. Assn., President's Profl. Assn., Wausau C. of C. (bd. dirs. 1965), Alpha Kappa Psi. Republican. Catholic. Clubs: Wausau Country, Wausau, Rotary (pres. 1962-63) (Wausau). Home: 801 13th St Wausau WI 54401 Office: Box 1407 Wausau WI 54401

JONES, ROBERT VAUGHAN, comptroller; b. Phila., Dec. 16, 1908; s. Thomas Gaun and Mary Frances Mary Frances (Vaughan) J.; B.S., Lehigh U., 1930; m. Evelyn Elizabeth Horton, July 15, 1933; 1 dau., Elizabeth E. Sheehan. Comml. engr., accountant N.Y. Telephone Co., 1927-29, accountant, chief toll supr., chief supervising supervising accountant, 1930-45; with Am. Tel. & Tel. co., 1945-54, successivly accountant, supervising accountant, gen. accountant, staff asst. revenue requirements, asst. comptroller, 1952-54; comptroller New Eng. Telephone & Telegraph Co., Boston, 1955-57 v.p., comptroller, 1957-63; v.p.- finance, treas., 1963-65, v.p., comptroller, 1965-67, v.p. finance, comptroller, 1967-69. Home: 35 W 18th St Ocean City NJ 08226

JONES, ROBERT VERNON, lawyer; b. Peterson, Ia., Sept. 16, 1901; s. Alonzo W. and Ada Marian (Dunn) J; A.B., Northwestern U., 1923, J.D., 1926; LL.D., Buena Vista Coll., Storm Lake, Ia., 1961; m. Elsie Pierce Brown, 1926 (div. 1963); children—Richard Vernon, Nancy Gwendolyn Green, David Owen, Robert Alonzo; m. 2d, Adelaide Peterson, 1963. Lectr. in econ., Northwestern U., 1924-26; admitted to Ill. bar, 1926; law clk. firm Foreman, Bluford, Steele & Schultz, Chgo., 1926-28; partner, Stearns & Jones, Chgo., 1928-42; practiced law, 1942-45; with U.S. group Control Council for Germany, 1945; pres. Noble Mfg. Co.; v.p. Sac City State Bank; pres. R.V. Jones & Co., Inc.; prof. bus. and govt. Northwestern U. Sch. Commerce, 1946-48. Governing mem. Orchestral Assn., Chgo. Mem. Am., Ill., Chgo. bar assns., Am. Econ. Assn., Northwestern U. Asso., Phi Beta Kappa, Alpha Delta Phi, Phi Alpha Delta, Order of Coif. Clubs: Law, University (Chgo.); Glen View. Author: The Challenge of Liberty, 1956. Contbr. articles to mags. Home PO Box 485 Mundelein IL 60060

JONES, RODERIC MILLER, lawyer; b. Newark, O., June 21, 1911; s. Roderic and Iris (Miller) J.; A.B., Denison U., 1933; J.D., U. Cin., 1936; m. Frances Upson Flory, Dec. 27, 1939 (dec., May 1956); children-Georgia Flory (Mrs. John E. Schultheiss), Sarah Sheffield; m. 2d, Dora Jones Tanner, July 8, 1960. Admitted to Ohio bar, 1936, since practiced in Newark; partner Jones, Kibler, Norpell & Hervey, 1968—. Pres. Bd. Edn. Newark, 1965. Served to 1st lt., Judge Adv. Gen. Corps, AUS, 1943-46. Mem. Licking County Bar Assn. (past pres.), Newark Area C. of C. (past dir.), Order of Coif, Phi Gamma Delta, Phi Delta Phi. Democrat. Episcopalian. Home: 881 N Village Dr Newark OH 43055 Office: Trust Bldg Newark OH 43055

JONES, ROGER WARREN, govt. ofcl.; b. New Hartford, Conn., Feb. 3, 1908; s. Henry Roger and Eleanor (Drake) J.; A.B., Cornell U., 1928; M.A., Columbia, 1931; LL.D., Otterbein Coll., 1962, Princeton, 1962; D.P.S., George Washington U., 1969; m. Dorothy Heyl, Feb. 1, 1930; children—Cynthia (Mrs. John Hodges), Roger H., Edward C. Instr., Coral Gables Mil. Acad., 1928-29; clk., asst. mgr. Doubleday Doran Book Shops, N.Y.C., 1929-31; tutor, 1932-33; clk., asst. exec. officer Central Statis. Bd., Washington, 1933-39; adminstrv. officer U.S. Bur. of Budget, 1939-42, successively budget examiner, asst. to dir., dep. asst. dir., asst. dir. legislative reference, asst. dir., 1945-58, dep. dir., 1958-59; chmn. U.S. Civil Service Commn., 1959-61; dep. under sec. state adminstrn., 1961-62; sr. cons., spl. asst. to dir. Bur. Budget, 1962-68, asst. dir. Office Mgmt. and Budget, 1969-71, cons., 1971—. Mem. Commn. Polit. Activity Govt. Employees, 1967; exec. in residence Woodrow Wilson Sch. Pub. and Internat. Affairs, Princeton, 1968-69, sr. fellow, 1969-72. Chmn., Conference Pub. Service, 1964-70; treas., dir. Worldwide Assurance Employees Pub. Agys., Inc. Mem. Washington Bd. Higher Edn., 1968—. Vice pres United Givers Fund, Washington, 1959-62, bd. dirs., 1959-65; bd. govs. Washington Inst. Mental Hygiene, 1938-61, v.p., 1953-60. Recipient Stockberger award outstanding contbn. to personnel administrn. Served from capt. to col., AUS, 1942-45. Decorated Legion of Merit; Order. Brit. Empire; recipient Career Service award Nat. Civil Service League; Pres.'s award for distinguished fed. civilian service. Mem. Nat. Acad. Pub. Adminstrn., Sigma Phi Epsilon, Delta Theta Phi, Pi Sigma Alpha. Episcopalian. Club: Cornell (Washington). Home: 3912 Leland St Chevy Chase MD 20015 Office: Office Mgmt and Budget Washington DC 20503

JONES, RONALD WADE, economist; b. Agency, Mo., Sept. 2, 1916; s. Floyd Lester and Mary Elizabeth (Barnes) J.; B.S., U. Mo., 1937. M.A., 1941; student U. Chgo., 1947-48: m. Effie Lelah Henderson, July 11, 1942; children—Janice Lee (Mrs. Douglas L. Vogel), Judith Ann (Mrs. Robert A. Hutwich). Agrl. economist Dept. Agr., 1941-50; economist Office Food and Agr., ICA, and predecessor agys., 1950-52, 55-57; Ford Found. cons. to Govt. India 1952-55; chief career devel. div. ICA, 1957-59; asst. dir. U.S. Operations Mission to Turkey, 1959-61; dir. Office Afghanistan and Pakistan Affairs, AID, 1962-65; dep. dir. AID Mission to Afghanistan, 1963-64; research asso. and asso. dir. CIC-AID Rural Devel. Research Project, U. Wis., 1965-68; staff coordinator Bur. Near East and S. Asia, AID, 1968-69, dir. Office Population Programs, 1969—. Mem. Am. Econ. Assn., Am. Farm Econ. Assn., Soc. Internat. Devel. Author papers in field. Home: 4902 Southland Av Alexandria VA 22312 Office: 1061 New State US Dept State Washington DC 20525

JONES, RONALD WINTHROP, educator; b. Louisville, July 5, 1931; s. August Fabel and Bess (White) J.; A.B., Swarthmore Coll., 1952; Ph.D., Mass. Inst. Tech., 1956; m. Catherine Maitland, June 14, 1969; children—Deane Elizabeth, Laura Denise. Instr. econ. Mass. Inst. Tech., Cambridge, 1955-56; instr. Swarthmore Coll., 1956-57; mem. faculty U. Rochester, N.Y., 1958—, prof., 1964-68, John Munro Prof. of Econ., 1968—; mem. editorial bd. Am. Econ. Rev., Jour. Internat. Econ. Cons. NSF. Served with AUS, 1957. Mem. Econometric Soc., Am. Econ. Assn. Contbr. profl. jours. Home: 1301 Highland Av Rochester NY 14620 Office: U Rochester Rochester NY 14627

JONES, ROY WINFIELD, educator; b. Shawnee, Okla., Sept. 16, 1905; s. William Winfield and Grace (McCreery) J; A.B. magna cum laude, Oklahoma City U., 1927; M.S., Kan State U., 1928; Ph.D., U. Okla., 1937; m. Maurine King, Sept 1, 1928; children—Neil Winfield, Marian King. Lab. asst. biology Oklahoma City U., 1925-27; research asst. parasitology Kan. State U., 1927-28; high sch. tchr., Alexandria. La., 1928; mem. faculty Central State Coll., Edmond, Okla., 1929-47, dean coll., acting dean men, 1939-47, prof. biology, head dept., 1936-47; prof. zoology, chmn. biol. sci. course Okla. A. and M. Coll., 1947-51; prof. zoology, head dept. Okla. State U., 1951-71, emeritus, 1971—. Chmn., Okla. Com. Improvement Sci. Instrn., 1958-68. Served to lt. comdr. USNR, 1942-45. Collecting Net scholar Marine Biol. Sta., Woods Hole, Mass., 1934. Fellow A.A.A.S., Okla. Acad. Sci. (pres. 1941); mem. Am. Biology Tchrs. Assn., N.E.A., Okla. Edn. Assn., Am. Soc. Zoologists, Am. Micros. Soc., Soc. Exptl. Biology and Medicine, Nat. Sci. Tchrs. Assn., Am. Inst. Biol. Scis., Am. Legion, Sigma Xi, Phi Kappa Phi, Kappa Delta Pi, Beta Beta Beta, Phi Sigma, Sigma Phi Epsilon, Pi Kappa Delta. Methodist. Lion. Author: (with I.E. Wallen) Biological Science Notebook, 1957; also articles. Home: 2030 W Admiral Rd Stillwater OK 74074

JONES, RUDOLPH, coll. pres.; b. Winton, N.C., June 27, 1910; s. E. R. and Annie (Walden) J.; A.B., Shaw U., 1930; M.A., Cath. U. Am., 1947, Ph.D., 1952; m. Mildred O. Parker, Feb. 16, 1935; 1 son, Rudolph Bernard Jones. Prin. Currituck County Tng. Sch., Snowden, N.C., 1931-37; sr. interviewer N.C. Employment Service, Rocky Mount, N.C., 1938-40; student work supr. Nat. Youth Adminstrn., Raleigh, N.C., 1940-42, finance officer master project, Washington, 1942-43; tchr. math. Dunbar High Sch., Washington, 1949-50; tchr., acting dean, then dean Fayetteville Tchrs. Coll., 1952-56, pres., 1956—. Bd. dirs. Fuller Sch. Exceptional Children Fayetteville. Price economist OPS, Washington, 1951-52. Served as seaman 1/c USNR. 1944-45 Mem. Fayetteville Area C. of C. (bd. dirs.), N.E.A., N.C. Coll. Conf., Am. Legion, Alpha Phi Alpha, Pi Gamma Mu. Presbyn. Mason. Address: Fayetteville State Coll Fayetteville NC 28301

JONES, RUSSELL reporter; b. Mpls., Jan. 5, 1918; s. Lewis Russell and Elizabeth (McLeod) J.; student pub. schs., Mpl. and Stillwater, Minn.; m. Martha 'Sennyey von Kissenye, July 29, 1955; step children—Jozsef Karolyi van Nagykaroly, Erzsebet Karoli von Nagykaroly. Reporter, radio columnist St. Paul Dispatch 1938-41; co-founder, combat reporter The Stars and Stripes, 1942-45, civilian reporter, 1947-48; co-owner, editor for or Germany, Weekend mag., Paris, 1948-49; with U. P., 1949—, London, Prague, Vienna, Frankfurt, chief Eastern European corr., 1956-58; Middle Eastern corr. CBS News. 1958—. Recipient Pulitzer, Sigma Delta Chi prizes for fgn. corr., George Polk Meml. award for reporting under hazardous conditions (coverage Hungarian Re- volution Oct. 1956). Author:(with others) This is Germany, 1950. Home: Hotel St George Beirut Lebanon

JONES, SAMUEL, conductor; b. Iverness, Miss., June 2, 1935; s. Samuel Leander and Ella Mae (Spencer) J.; B.A., Millsaps Coll., 1957; M.A. (Woodrow Wilson fellow), Eastman Sch. Music, U. Rochester, 1958, Ph.D., 1960; m. Nancy Ruth Peacock, Jan. 29, 1957; children—Rachel Ann, Alison Frances. Dir. instrumental music Alma (Mich.) Coll., 1960-62, instr., 1960-61, asst. prof., 1961-62; founder

Alma Symphony, 1961; condr. Saginaw (Mich.) Symphony, 1962-65, also dir. Saginaw Choral Soc.; composer-in-residence Delta Coll., University Center, Mich., 1964-65; founder, conductor Festival Orch., University Center, 1964-65; with Rochester Philharmonic Orch., 1965—, resident condr., 1971—. Guest condr. Pitts. Symphony, Buffalo Philharmonic, Shenandoah Valley Music Festival, Naumberg Symphony, others; asso. dir. Condr. Study Inst., Am. Symphony Orch. League. Recipient Founders medal Millsaps Coll., 1957. Mem. Am. Symphony Orch. League, Rochester Musicians Assn., Nat. Assn. Am. Composers and Condrs., Nat. Assn. Humanities Edn., Omicron Delta Kappa, Lambda Chi Alpha. Methodist. Rotarian. Composer: Symphony 1, 1960; In Retrospect (small orch.), 1959; Overture for a City, 1964; Festival Fanfare (commd. Am. Symphony Orch. League), 1964; Elegy in Memory of John Fitzgerald Kennedy, 1917-63, 1963. Writer/narrator Man in his Music, The World of Music (ednl. TV series for N.Y. State Dept. Edn.). Home: 153 Tobey Rd Pittsford NY 14534 Office: 60 Gibbs St Rochester NY 14604

JONES, SAMUEL SHEPARD, educator, political scientist; b. Arcadia, Fla., Nov. 11, 1909; s. William Bristow and Flora Belle (Shepard) J.; A.B., Georgetown (Ky.) Coll., 1930, LL.D., 1967; A.M., U. Ky., 1931; postgrad. Harvard, 1932-33, Geneva Sch. Internat. Relations, summer 1934; D.Phil., Oxford U., Eng. (Rhodes scholar), 1936. Mem. instructional staff various ednl. instns., 1930-42; with Office of Facts and Figures, 1942, Dept. State, Washington, 1942-56; spl. asst. U.S. delegation to UN conf., San Francisco, 1945; exec. officer, planning staff Allied Mission to Observe Greek Elections, 1946; chief Div. Pub. Studies, Dept. State, 1947-50; officer-in-charge pub. affairs Bur. Near Eastern, South Asian and African Affairs 1950-53, chief pub. affairs officer Am. embassy, Karachi, Pakistan, 1953-54, Amman, 1954-55; v.p. U. N.C., Chapel Hill, 1955-56, Burton Craige prof. polit. sci., 1956—, acting chmn. dept., 1959-60. Guest lectr. Air War Coll., USAF, 1957, 58; guest lectr. Naval War Coll., 1962, 64, 66, cons. on internat. relations 1963; lectr. Sch. Advanced Internat. Studies, John Hopkins, 1961. Chmn. chancellors com. on internat. studies, 1959-62. Recipient Alumni Achievement award Georgetown Coll., 1969. Mem. Am. Polit. Sci. Assn., Am. Assn. Rhodes Scholars, Middle East Inst., Middle East Studies Assn. N.Am., Kappa Alpha Order, Pi Kappa Delta (Alumni award 1963), Pi Sigma Alpha. Baptist. Author: The Scandinavian States and the League of Nations, 1939, 69. Editor: Documents on American Foreign Relations (with D.P. Myers) vols. I, II, III; America Looks Ahead (pamphlet series); America's Role in the Middle East, 1958, 61, 63, 65. Address: Dept Polit Sci University NC Chapel Hill NC 27514

JONES, SARAH DOWLIN, librarian; b. Media, Pa., Sept. 20, 1916; d. William Dowlin and Elsie May (Lutton) Jones; A.B., U. Pa., 1937, M.A., 1939, Ph.D., 1954; B.L.S., Pratt Inst. Library Sch., 1944. Reference asst. Pratt Inst. Library, 1944-45; reference librarian Am. Library, London, 1945-47; head, math. physics library U. Pa., 1947-49; head reference dept. U. Pa. Library, 1949-52; librarian Goucher Coll., 1952—. Mem. Modern Lang. Assn., A.L.A. (council 1967-71), Md. Library Assn., Assn. Coll. and Reference Libraries, Women's Internat. League, Am. Assn. U. Women, Am. Assn. U. Profs., Phi Beta Kappa, Mortar Bd. Home: 24 Aylesbury Rd Timonium MD 21093 Office: Goucher Coll Towson Baltimore MD 21204

JONES, SCOTT, pub. relations counsel; b. Chgo., Mar. 12, 1914; s. Thomas S. and Mary (McDaniel) J.; A.B., Princeton, 1936; m. Helen B. Hench, Aug 15, 1942; children—Thomas Scott, Robert C., Katharine H., Marilyn McD. Traffic mgr. Batten, Barton, Durstine & Osborn, Inc., advt., Chgo., 1936-37; copy writer, account exec. Weiss & Geller, Inc., advt., Chgo., 1938-40; pub. relations counsel Mitchell McKeown Orgn., Chgo., 1940-42, 46-47; co- founder, partner Gardner, Jones & Cowell, Inc., Chgo., pub. relations, and prin., 1960—. Trustee Found. Pub. Relation Research and Edn. (pres. 1969-70). Trustee Village of Hinsdale, Ill., 1953-57, 59-61. Bd. assos. Chgo. Theol.; bd. dirs. Health Edn. Inst., Inc. Served as editor and war corrs., information and ednl. div., AUS, 1943-45; ETO. Recipient Presdl. citation for meritorious service Pub. Relations Soc. Am., 1957, 60, 68. Mem. Pub. Relations Soc. Am. (charter; dir. 1955- 56, chmn. eligibility com. 1957, pres. Chgo. chpt. 1955, sec., chmn. counselors sect.), Community Renewal Soc. (dir.). Moderator Union Ch., Hinsdale. Clubs: Economic, Chicago, University, Princeton (Chgo.); Hinsdale Golf. Home: 138 E 4th St Hinsdale IL 60521 Office: 79 W Monroe St Chicago IL 60603

JONES, SHIRLEY, actress, singer; b. Smithton, Pa., Mar. 31; d. Paul and Marjorie (Williams) Jones; grad. high sch., 1952; student Pitts. Playhouse; m. Jack Cassidy, Aug. 5, 1956; children—Shaun, Patrick, Ryan. Appeared with chorus South Pacific, 1953, also Broadway prodn. Me and Juliet (leading role in road tour); role of Laurey, motion picture Oklahoma, 1954 (later stage tour of Paris and Rome, sponsorship U.S. Dept. State); Am. stage in summer stock 1960; appeared in role of Julie, motion picture Carousel, 1956; other films include April Love, 1957, Never Steal Anything Small, 1959, Elmer Gantry, 1960, Pepe, 1960, The Music Man, 1962, A Ticklish Affair, 1963, Bedtime Story, 1964, The Secret of My Success, 1965, Fluffy 1965; appeared in a night club tour with husband, 1958, later TV and summer stock; appeared in CBS-TV prodn. Victor Herbert operetta The Red Mill, 1958; appeared in Broadway play Maggie Flynn, 1968; star TV series The Partridge Family, 1970—; TV role Playhouse 90 drama, The Big Slide. Recipient Acad. award for best supporting actress in Elmer Gantry, 1961. Address: care of Aarons Mgmt 9601 Oak Pass Rd Beverly Hills CA 90210

JONES, STANLEY LLEWELYN, educator; b. Shell Lake, Wis., Sept. 7, 1918; s. Owen and Esther (Isack) J.; B.S., U. Wis., 1940, M.A., 1941; Ph.D., U. Ill., 1947; m. Adele Joan Tuman, Dec. 18, 1942; children—Glenna, Maia, Lois. Faculty U. Ill. at Chgo. Circle, 1947-70, prof. history, 1963-70, chmn. dept., 1964-68, acting dean Coll. Liberals Arts and Scis., 1965-66; prof. history U. N.C. at Greensboro, 1971—, vice chancellor acad. affairs, 1971—. Served with AUS, 1942-45. Mem. Phi Beta Kappa. Author: The Presidential Election of 1896, 1964. Home: 610 Rockford Rd Greensboro NC 27408 Office: Adminstrn U NC Greensboro NC 27412

JONES, STEPHEN BARR, educator; b. Seattle, Feb. 23, 1903; s. Richard Saxe and Margaret (Barr) J.; B.S., U. Wash., 1924; M.A., Harvard, 1929, Ph.D., 1934; m. Marjorie Jean Sadler, Sept. 2, 1933; 1 son, Douglas Barr. Instr. geography Ore. Coll. Edn., 1932-35, U. Hawaii, 1935-42; geographer Dept. State, 1942- 43; asso. prof. geography Yale, 1943-48, prof. geography, 1948-71, prof. emeritus, 1971—, chmn. dept., 1948-52, sr. faculty fellow, 1963-64. Research staff Office Naval Research, 1953-54; mem. U.S. Delegation Internat. Geog. Congress, 1964. Fellow Am. Geog. Soc. (hon.); mem. Assn. Am. Geographers (hon. pres.), Internat. Geog. Union (spl. U.S. rep. regional conf. in Japan 1957), Am. Meteorol. Soc. Author: Boundary Making, 1945; Geography and World Affairs, 1953, rev., 1962, 1970. Contbr. geog. publs. Home: 10935 Tropicana Circle Sun City AZ 85351

JONES, T. EMBURY civic worker; b. Ilion, N.Y., Mar. 9, 1907; s. William O. and Anna (Crowner) J.; A.B., Columbia, 1927, M.E., 1930; m. Leah A. Pettit, June 10, 1930; children—T. Embury, Pearl Anne (Mrs. L. F. Warner, Jr.) With Fed. Machine & Welder Co., Warren, O., 1930-45, v.p., mgr. welder div., 1942-45; pres., treas., dir. Precision Welder and Machine Co., Cin., 1945-64, Precision Welder & Flexopress Corp., Cin., 1952-69, Precision Welder & Flexopress (Can.) Ltd., 1959-69; cons. Precision- Cin., 1969. Vol. worker, dir. Action Housing of Greater Cin. Mem. council Columbia Coll., 1961-65. Mem. Am. Welding Soc. (pres. 1964-65), Cin. C. of C. (past v.p. and dir.). Republican. Methodist (nat. bound. evangelism). Mason (Shriner). Clubs: Cincinnati, Hyde Park Golf and Country, Queen City, Rotary (Cin.); Royal Poinciana Golf (Naples, Fla.). Home: 1001 Rockwood Dr Cincinnati OH 45208 Office: Action Housing of Greater Cin Fed Res Bank Bldg Cincinnati OH 45202

JONES, TAYLOR, lawyer; b. Thomasville, Ga, Apr. 2, 1911; s. Henry Taylor and Mamie (Libby) J.; LL.B., Washington and Lee U., 1934; m. Nona Broadfield Johnson, Aug. 8, 1940. Admitted to Fla. bar, 1934, since practiced in Jacksonville; partner firm Rogers, Towers, Bailey, Jones & Gay, 1951-. Served with USNR, 1943-46; lt. comdr. Res. Mem. Phi Beta Kappa, Order of Coif. Home: 904 Granada Blvd S Jacksonville FL 32207 Office: 110 W Forsyth St Jacksonville FL 32202

JONES, THEODORE W., banker; b. Warren, O., Mar. 28, 1924; s. Sydney W. and Mareen (Herlinger) J.; A.B., Western Res. U., 1947, LL.B., 1951; m. Jeanne Williams, Apr. 18, 1953; children—Jenny Beth, Pamela. Admitted to Ohio bar, 1951, since practiced in Cleve.; with firm Burgess, Fullmer, Parker & Steck, 1951-61; asst. gen. counsel Glidden Co., 1961-66; v.p., gen. counsel Nat. City Bank Cleve., 1966-70, sr. v.p., 1970—. Trustee Cuyahoga County (O.) Hosps. Served with AUS, 1943-46. Mem. Am., Ohio, Cuyahoga County, Cleve. (trustee, treas., exec. com.), bar assns., Am. Inst. Banking. Home: 5308 Golfway Lane Lyndhurst OH 44124 Office: 623 Euclid Av Cleveland OH 44101

JONES, THOMAS E., banker; b. Greenville, Tex., 1933; grad. U. Tex., 1956. Pres., Nat. Bank Commerce; dir. Bonanza Internat. Inc. Mem. adv. council Coll. Arts & Scis. U. Tex. Home: 3545 Caruth St Dallas TX 75225 Office: 1525 Elm St Dallas TX 75201*

JONES, THOMAS FRANKLIN, Jr., univ. pres., elec. engr.; b. Henderson, Tenn., July 9, 1916; s. Thomas Franklin and Addye Mac (Moore) J.; B.S., Miss. State Coll., 1939; M.S., Mass. Inst. Tech., 1940, Sc.D., 1952; LL.D., The Citadel, 1966; m. Mary Katherine Butterworth, March 9, 1942; children—Thomas James, Jonathan, Katherine, Andrew. Physicist underwater sound, harbor def. Naval Research Lab., 1941-47; instr. Mass. Inst. Tech., 1947, research asso. guided missiles, analog computation and analysis, 1948-49, asst. prof., 1949-54, instr. exptl. methods, 1952- 54, asso. prof. charge circuits, electronics and measurements labs., 1954-58; head Purdue U. Sch. Elec. Engring., 1958-62; pres. U. S.C., 1962—. Dir. Citizens & So. Nat. Bank, Indsl. Electronetics Corp.; chmn. tech. adv. bd. Western Union Telegraph Co., 1967-70. Spl. adviser NSF, Assn. State Univs. and Land-Grant Colls., 1970; participant Council on Higher Edn. in Am. Republics, Lima, Peru, 1968, Bogota, Columbia, 1969, Buenos Aires, Argentina, 1970, Lima; Peru, 1971. Bd. dirs. Nat. Electronics Conf. 1959-62; mem. Nat. Sci. Bd., 1966—, exec. com., vice chairman long range planning com. Recipient Meritorious Civilian Service award USN; named South Carolinian of Yr., 1966. Fellow I.E.E.E. (v.p. profl. group on edn.; dir. 1963-66; exec. com. editorial bd., publs. bd. 1963-66, chmn. external awards com., fellow com. 1971); mem. Engrs. Council Profl. Devel. (dir.), Am. Soc. Engring. Edn., Newcomen Soc., Nat. Acad. Scis. (ad hoc com. on postdoctoral edn. 1966-67, exec. com. hwy. research bd. 1967—), Nat. Acad. Engring. (nominating com.), Sigma Xi, Phi Eta Sigma, Kappa Mu Epsilon, Tau Beta Pi, Eta Kappa Nu, Theta Xi, Phi Mu Alpha. Clubs: Kosmos (Columbia, S.C.); University (N.Y.). Home: President's Home University SC Columbia SC 29208

JONES, THOMAS PIERCE, elec. mfg. co. exec.; b. Renovo, Pa., Nov. 19, 1908; s. Edward Pierce and Mary (Van Gorden) J.; B.S. in Elec. Engring., Pa. State U., 1930; postgrad. Harvard Grad. Sch. Bus. Adminstrn., 1951; m. Eleanor R. Green, June 27, 1936; 1 dau., Patricia (Mrs. David H. Beary). With Westinghouse Electric Corp., 1930—, regional mgr., Phila., 1956-58, v.p., 1958-65, v.p. marketing, Pitts., 1965—. Mem. Nat. Elec. Mfrs. Assn. (bd. govs.), Sigma Nu. Clubs: Seaview Country (Absecon, N.J.); Duquesne, Longue Vue, Fox Chapel Golf (Pitts.); Pine Valley (N.J.) Golf. Home: 8 James Ross Pl Fox Chapel Pittsburgh PA 15215 Office: Westinghouse Bldg Gateway Center Pittsburgh PA 15222

JONES, THOMAS VICTOR, aero. exec.; b. Pomona, Cal., July 21, 1920; s. Victor March and Elizabeth (Brettelle) J.; student Pomona Jr. Coll., 1938-40; B.A. with great distinction, Stanford, 1942; LL.D., George Washington Univ., 1967; m. Ruth Nagel, Aug. 10, 1946; children—Ruth Marilyn, Peter Thomas. Engr., El Segundo div. Douglas Aircraft Co., 1941-47; tech. adviser Brazilian Air Ministry, 1947-51; prof., head dept. Brazilian Inst. Tech., 1947-51; staff cons. Air Staff of USAF, Rand Corp., 1951- 53; asst. to chief engr. Northrop Corp., 1953, dep. chief engr., 1954-56, dir. devel. planning, 1956-57, corporate v.p., 1957, sr. v.p., 1958-59, pres., 1959, chief exec. officer, 1960, chmn. bd., 1963; dir. Times Mirror Co., U.S. Steel Corp., Wells Fargo Bank. Mem. men's adv. com. County-U. So. Cal. Med. Center Aux.; v.p., treas., dir. Los Angeles World Affairs Council; vis. com. U. Cal. at Los Angeles Grad. Sch. Bus. Adminstrn.; trustee Cal. Inst. Tech., Stanford U., Inst. for Strategic Studies, London, Eng.; bd. govs. Internat. Sci. Found. Fellow. Am. Inst. Aeros. and Astronautics; mem. Los Angeles C. of C., Stanford Research Inst. Council, Navy League U.S. (life), Aerospace Industries Assn. (gov.), So. Cal. Symphony Assn., U. So. Cal. Assos., Town Hall. Clubs: California, Los Angeles Country; The Beach (Santa Monica); Georgetown; California Yacht. Author: Capabilities and Operating Costs of Possible Future Transport Airplanes, 1953. Home: 1050 Moraga Dr Los Angeles CA 90049 Office: 1800 Century Park E Century City Los Angeles CA 90067

JONES, TIMOTHY SELDEN lawyer, corp. exec.; b. Kent, O., 1922; B.A., Yale, 1943, LL.B., 1944; m. Mae Reed, May 2, 1949; 1 son. Admitted to Massachusetts bar, 1944; practiced in Boston, 1947--. Home: 23 Beacon St Boston MA 02107

JONES, TOM, playwright, lyricist; b. Littlefield, Tex., Feb. 17, 1928; s. W.T. and Jessie (Bellomy) J.; B.F.A. in Drama, 1947, M.F.A., 1951; m. Elinor Wright, June 1, 1963. Author books and lyrics for the Fantasticks, 1961, 110 In The Shade, 1963, I Do, I Do, 1966, Celebration 1969, Colette, 1970. Served with AUS, 1951-53. Recipient Vernon Rice award for contbn. Off-Broadway Theatre, 1961. Home: West Cornwell CT Office: 7 W 96th St New York City NY 10025

JONES, TOM, singer, entertainer; b. Pontypridd, Wales, June 7, 1940; s. Thomas and Freda (Jones) Woodward; m. Malinda Trenchard, 1956; 1 son, Mark. Appeared at local pubs and workingmen's clubs, Pontypridd, until 1963; 1st hit recording, 1964; appeared Brit. TV shows Beat Room, Top Gear, Thank Your Lucky Star, Sunday Night at the London Paladium, from 1965; toured U.S., 1965, 70; appeared Ed Sullivan Show; starred TV series This Is Tom Jones. Named Britain's Most Popular Male Singer, 1967, 68. Home: Weybridge Surrey England Office: care A/A Ltd 24/25 New Bond St London W1 England*

JONES, TOM BARD, educator; b. Dunkirk, N.Y., June 21, 1909; s. Charles Champlin and Bettie Vedder (Bard) J.; A.B., U. Mich., 1931, M.A., 1937, Ph.D., 1934. Faculty history U. Minn., 1935—, prof., 1949—, Regents' prof., 1970—. Served with USNR, 1942- 46. Fellow Am. Numis. Soc.; mem. Am. Oriental Soc. (pres. Midwest br. 1959), Am. Hist. Assn., Archeol. Inst. Am. Author: South America Rediscovered, 1949; Ancient Civilization, 1960; Sumerian Economic Texts, 1961; The Silver-Plated Age, 1962; Paths to the Ancient Past, 1967; The Figure of the Earth, 1967; The Sumerian Problem, 1969. Editorial bd. Am. Hist. Rev., 1967—. Home: 3911 E 50th St Minneapolis MN 55417

JONES, TONY EVERETT, educator; b. Leonard, Tex., Sept. 5, 1920; s. Pink and Nancy Lee (Duvall) J.; B.S., U. Tex., 1948, M.S., 1950; Ph.D., U. Colo., 1957; m. Imogene Brown, May 28, 1947; children—Everett Eugene, Susan Renee. With Inst. Pharm. Chemistry, U. Tex., Austin, 1949-53; registered pharmacist M.D.'s Pharmacy, Austin, 1949-51, Seton Hosp., Austin, 1951-54; asst. prof. pharm. chemistry U. Tex., 1953-54; asst. prof. U. Colo., Boulder, 1956-59, asso. prof., 1959-63, prof. pharm. chemistry, 1964—; dir. pharm. research, also cons. Carbisulphoil Co., Dallas, 1954—. Mem. adv. bd. Nat. Investors Life Ins. Co., 1962—. Served with USNR, World War II. Mem. Am. Pharm. Assn., Am. Chem. Soc., Sigma Xi, Phi Delta Chi, Rho Chi, Phi Lambda Upsilon. Baptist (exec. bd. Colo. Baptist Conv. 1968—). Research and publ. in local anesthetics, toxicology, drug assay. Home: 7631 Watonga Way Boulder CO 80303

JONES, TRACEY KIRK, Jr., clergyman; b. Boston, Mar. 16, 1917; s. Tracey Kirk and Marion (Flowers) J.; B.A., B.D., D.D., Ohio Wesleyan U.; B.D., Yale Div. Sch., 1942; m. Martha Clayton, Sept. 12, 1942; children—Judith Grace (Mrs. Larry Watson), Tracey Kirk Jones, III, Deborah Anita Jones. Ordained to ministry Meth. Church, 1945; liaison officer Chinese Govt., 1945; missionary Meth. Ch., China, 1946-50, Malaya, 1952-55; exec. bd. mission Meth. Ch., 1955; exec. sec. S.E. Asia, 1955-62, asso. gen. sec. div. world missions, 1962-64, asso. gen. sec. world div., 1964-68, gen. sec. bd. missions, 1968—. Mem. theol. edn. fund World Councils Chs., of 1965—, chmn. div. world mission and evangelism. Author: Our Mission Today, 1963. Home: 38 Aubrey Rd Montclair NJ 07043 Office: 475 Riverside Dr New York City NY 10027

JONES, VINCENT STARBUCK, editor; b. Utica, N.Y., Dec. 4, 1906; s. William Vincent and Susan B. (Starbuck) J.; A.B., Hamilton Coll., 1928; postgrad. Harvard, 1929-30; LL.D., Hamilton Coll., 1971; m. Nancy van Dyke Parsons, May 25, 1940; children—Suzanne van Dyke, Margot Cauldwell. Reporter, Utica Daily Press, 1928-29, night city editor, 1930-37, city editor, 1937-38, mng. editor, 1938; mng. editor, Utica Observer- Dispatch, 1938-42; exec. editor, Utica Observer-Dispatch and Utica Daily Press, 1942-50; dir. news and editoral office Gannett Newspapers, 1950- 55, exec. editor, 1955-70, v.p., 1965-70; exec. v.p. Gannett Found., 1970—, also sec. bd. dirs. Lectr. Am. Press Inst. 1948-68. Member Utica City Planning Bd., 1946-50; v.p. St. Lukes Meml. Hosp., Utica, N.Y., 1950; bd. govs. Genesee Hosp., Rochester, 1957—; treas. Gannett Newspaperboy Scholarships, Inc., 1967—; bd. dirs. Rochester Civic Music Assn., 1954-62; trustee Monroe Community Coll., Rochester (chmn. 1969—), George Eastman House, Rochester (vice chmn. 1970—); past trustee Hamilton Coll.; lectr., writer newspaper readership, readability, photography; dir. Kent State U. photo short course, 1952. Recipient distinguished service medal Syracuse Journalism Sch., 1969. Mem. N.Y. State Asso. Press Assn. (pres. 1947), Am. Soc. Newspaper Editors (dir. 1962-70, pres. 1968-69), Asso. Press Mng. Editors Assn. (dir. 1949-56, pres. 1955), N.Y. State Soc. Editors (pres. 1962-63), Internat. Press. Inst. (chmn. Am. com. 1965-68), Nat. Press Photographers Assn. (Sprague award 1954), Sigma Delta Chi, Psi Upsilon. Episcopalian. Clubs: Genesee Valley, Country, Torch (Rochester.) Directed, edited: The Road to Integration (Pulitzer prize citation 1964). Home: 5 Highland Heights Rochester NY 14618 Office: 55 Exchange St Rochester NY 14615

JONES, VIRGINIA LACY (Mrs. E.A. Jones), librarian; b. Cin., June 25, 1912; d. Edward and Ellen Louise (Parker) Lacy; B.S., Sch. Edn., Hampton Inst., 1936, B.S. in L.S., 1933; M.S. in L.S., U. Ill. (Gen. Edn. Bd. fellow 1937-38). 1938; Ph.D., Chgo. (Gen. Edn. Bd. fellow 1943-45), 1945; m. Edward Allen Jones, Nov. 27, 1941. Asst. Librarian Louisville Municipal Coll., 1934-35, librarian, 1936-37; asst. circulation dept., Hampton Inst. Library, 1935-36; dir. dept. library sci. Prairie View (Tex.) State Coll., summers 1936-39; catalog librarian Atlanta U., 1939-41, instr. Sch. Library Service, 1941-43, dean, 1945—. Mem. A.L.A. (exec. bd. 1971—), Assn. Am. Library Schs. (pres. 1967-68), N.A.A.C.P., Delta Sigma Theta, Beta Phi Mu. Democrat. Conglist. Home: 1341 Thurgood St SW Atlanta GA 30314

JONES, WALK CLARIDGE, Jr., architect; b. Memphis, July 18, 1904; s. Walk Claridge and Sophy (Winkelman) J.; student Washington and Lee U., 1922-23, U. Ill., 1923-26; B.F.A., Yale, 1928; m. Lelia Gray, Oct. 30, 1929; 1 son, Walk Claridge III. Jr. partner Jones, Furbringer & Jones, Architects, Memphis, 1931- 35; partner firm Walk C. Jones-Walk C. Jones, Jr., Architects, Memphis, 1935-53; prin. Walk C. Jones, Jr., Architects, Memphis, 1963- 66; partner Walk Jones/Mah & Jones/Architects/Inc., 1966—; prin. works include Bapt. Meml. Hosp. (Modern Hosp. mag. award 1957), 1956, Meth. Hosp. (food service facilities award Instns. mag. 1959), 1958, U. Tenn. Med. Sch., 1956, Burrow Library at Southwestern Coll., 1953, Dormitory- Student Union at Wofford Coll., 1958, French Camp Acad., 1959, Christ Meth. Ch. (Gulf State regional dist. A.I.A. award 1958, Ch. Archtl. Guild Am. award 1959, food services facilities award Instns. mag. 1959), 1958, Memphis Country Club (food service facilities award Instns. mag. 1958), 1957, Ely & Walker Distbn. Center, 1956, Orgill Bros. & Co. Distbn. Center, 1954, parts dept. Internat. Harvester Co., 1948, parts dept. Allis-Chalmers Mfg. Co., 1947, Grace Chem. Co., 1954. Mem. adv. bd. Memphis Bur. Bldgs., 1957—. Pres. Shelby United Neighbors, 1960—; adv. com. bd. trustees Bapt. Meml. Hosp., 1958—; trustee Miss Hutchinson's Sch., 1958—; sec. Memphis Acad. Arts, 1949-50. Recipient Certificate of Achievement, Brookings Instn., 1963. Fellow A.I.A. (pres. Memphis 1947; Gulf States regional dist. award DeSoto County Jail 1956, Gulf States regional dist. Outstanding Community Service award 1958, 1st Honor award 12th Ann. Conf. Gulf States Region 1963); mem. Am. Planning and Civic Assn., Church Archtl. Guild Am. (award Ch. Holy Communion 1954), Tenn. Soc. Architects, Bldg. Research Inst., Yale Arts Assn. (pres. 1960-62), Am. Hosp. Assn., Guild Religious Architecture, Bldg. Research Inst., Memphis Chamber of Commerce (past dir.), Omicron Delta Kappa, Kappa Sigma. Presbyn. (elder). Clubs: Engineers, Rotary (pres. 1947), Memphis Country, University (Memphis). Home 727 S Perkins Rd Memphis TN 38117 Office: 1215 Poplar Av Memphis TN 38104

JONES, WALLACE SYLVESTER, lawyer; b. N.Y.C., May 23, 1917; s. Adam Leroy and Lily Sylvester (Murray) J.; A.B., Columbia, 1938, J.D. (Kent Scholar 1941, editor Law Rev. 1939-41), 1941; m.

Barbara Hardenbergh Ostgren, June 7, 1941 (dec. Dec. 1964); children—Karen Ostgren (Mrs. John Gordon Fraser, Jr.), Ellen Wallace, Mark Lawrence, Sara Sylvester, Caroline; m. 2d, Helen Marion Nelson Anderson, Jan. 7, 1967. Admitted to N.Y. bar, 1941, U.S. Supreme Ct., 1948; asso. firm Davis Polk & Wardwell, and predecessors, N.Y.C., 1941—, mem., 1957—. Mem. Essex Fells (N.J.) Bd. Edn., 1955-58; commr. Essex County Ednl. Audio-Visual Aid Commn., 1955-58; pres. W. Essex Regional Sch. Dist., Essex County, 1957- 60; Moderator No. N.J. Assn., United Ch. Christ, 1966-67, moderator Central Atlantic Conf., 1969-70. Trustee Barnard Coll., 1958—, chmn. bd., 1967- -, Seeing Eye, Inc., 1971—; bd. dirs. Kimberly Sch., Montclair, N.J., 1968-70, United Ch. Homes N.J., 1967—. Served to lt. comdr. USNR, 1942-46; PTO. Mem. Am., N.Y. State bar assns., Assn. Bar City N.Y., N.Y. County Lawyers Assn., Psi Upsilon, Phi Delta Phi. Conglist. (trustee). Clubs: Ausable (St. Huberts, N.Y.); Fells Brook (Essex Fells); Adirondack Mountain (chmn. Hurricane Mountain chpt. 1952-53); Union League, Down Town, Wall Street (N.Y.C.); Farmington Country (Charlotteville, Va.). Home: 21 Inwood Rd Essex Fells NJ 07021 Office: 1 Chase Manhattan Plaza New York City NY 10005

JONES, WALTER BEAMON, congressman; b. Fayetteville, N.C., Aug. 19, 1913; s. Walter George and Fannie (Anderson) J.; B.S., N.C. State U., 1934; m. Doris Long, Apr. 26, 1934; children—Mrs. Dotdee Move, Walter Beamon II. Mem. N.C. Gen. Assembly, 1955- 59; mem. N.C. Senate, 1965; mem. 90th-92d Congresses 1st Dist. N.C. Dir. Security Savs. & Loan Assn., Farmville, N.C. Mayor, Farmville, 1949-53. Recipient Watchdog of Treasury award Nat. Assn. Businessmen, 1966; named Farmville Man of Year, 1955. Democrat. Baptist (deacon). Mason (32, Shriner), Elk, Rotarian, Moose. Home: May Blvd Farmville NC 27828 Office: Cannon Bldg Washington DC 20515

JONES, WALTER CLYDE, Jr., lawyer; b. Chgo., Dec. 7, 1902; s. Walter Clyde and Emma (Boyd) J.; B.A., Yale, 1925; J.D., Northwestern U., 1928; m. Emily Watt, June 12, 1929; children—Mary Helen (Mrs. Stuart A. McKeldin), Emily Hubbard (Mrs. John G. Meeker), Walter Clyde III, William Watt. Admitted to Ill. bar, 1928; asso. firm Jones, Addington, Ames & Seibold, Chgo., 1928-31, Cutting, Moore & Sidney, now Sidley and Austin, Chgo., 1931- 36; asst. gen. atty. Ill. Bell Telephone Co., Chgo., 1936-40, gen. atty. 1940-51, gen. solicitor, 1951-67; dir. State Nat. Bank Evanston, Pickard, Inc. Mem. Am., Ill., Chgo. bar assns., Beta Theta Pi, Phi Delta Phi, Order of Coif. Clubs: Chicago; Skokie Country (Glencoe). Home: 624 Drexel Av Glencoe, IL 60022. Office: 225 W Randolph St Chicago IL 60606

JONES, WALTER LOUIS, editor; b. Bloomington, Ill., Nov. 30, 1928; s. Squire and Ethel (Berry) J.; student Ill. State U., 1948, Tenn. State U., 1949-51, U. Ill., 1955-57; m. Cleo Estella Brooks, June 18, 1955; children—Walter Louis, Stephen Brooks, Joy Valerie. Mng. editor Gary (Ind.) Crusader Newspaper, 1961-62; mng. editor Info Newspaper, Gary, Ind., 1962-64, Milw. Courier, 1971—; editor, pub. Greater Milw. Star, 1964-71, editor, 1971—. Pres. Northside Bus. Assn., 1966. Served with USAAF, 1946-47, USAF, 1951-53. Recipient Best Editorial, Best Column, Best News Story awards Nat. Newspaper Pubs. Assn., 1965-68. Mem. Milw. Advt. Club, Sigma Delta Chi, Alpha Phi Alpha. Methodist. Home: 4149 N 23d St Milwaukee WI 53209 Office: 2431 W Hopkins St Milwaukee WI 53206

JONES, WALTER PARKER, newspaper editor; b. Sacramento, July 4, 1894; s. William Edmund and Phoebe (Parker) J.; ed. grade and high schs., Sacramento; m. Kathleen Adelle Jones, Aug. 12, 1916; children—Mary Elizabeth, Walter Parker. Reporter, Sacramento Star, 1912-16, Marysville (Cal.) Democrat and Appeal, 1916-17; state capital corr. Scripps papers Cal., 1917- 18, San Francisco and Los Angeles Examiners, 1918-19; polit. reporter Sacramento Bee, 1919-33, McClatchy Newspapers Cal., 1922-33; news editor, mng. editor Sacramento Bee, 1933-34; editorial dir. McClatchy Newspapers Cal., 1934-36, editor, 1936—. Mem. C. of C., Am. Soc. Newspaper Editors. Presbyn. Rotarian. Clubs: Sutter, Del Paso Country (Sacramento). Home: 3361 Sierra Oaks Dr Sacramento CA 95825 Office: Sacramento Bee Sacramento CA 95825

JONES, WARREN LEROY, judge; b. Gordon, Neb., July 2, 1895; s Lauren and Katherine (Ballengee) J.; LL.B. cum laude, U. Denver, 1924; LL.D., Stetson U., 1955; m. Edith Ann Le Prouse, Dec. 23, 1921; 1 dau., Dorothy Lauren (Mrs. Robert P. Shakely). Admitted to Colo. bar, 1924; dep. dist. atty. City and County Denver, 1924; mem. firm Jones, Gandy & Wilson, Denver, 1925; admitted to Fla. bar, 1926; asso. firm Fleming, Hamilton, Diver & Lichliter, Jacksonville, 1926-37; mem. firms Fleming, Hamilton, Diver & Jones, 1938-41, Fleming, Jones, Scott & Botts, 1942- 55, sr. mem., 1948-55; U.S. circuit judge 5th Circuit, 1955-65; sr. circuit judge, 1965—. Sec., dir. Jacksonville Blood Bank, 1942-55. Recipient Lincoln diploma of honor Lincoln Meml. U., 1971. Mem. Fla., Jacksonville (pres. 1955) chambers commerce, S.A.R., Am. Judicature Soc., Am. Law Inst., Am., Fla. (pres. 1944), Jacksonville (pres. 1939) bar assns., Nat. Lawyers Club (Washington), Newcomen Soc., Phi Alpha Delta. Episcopalian. Mason (33, Shriner). Clubs: Timuquana Country; Florida Yacht; Seminole; River; Civitan (past pres.); University (Jacksonville). Collector Lincolniana. Home: 1081 Arbor Lane Jacksonville FL 32207 Office: US PO and Ct House Bldg Jacksonville FL 32202

JONES, WAYNE VAN LEER, cons. geologist; b. Chgo., June 18, 1902; s. Frank Edgar and Josephine Louella (Van Leer) J.; A.B., Northwestern U., 1923; m. Elizabeth Rieke, Jan. 14, 1926; 1 son, Wayne Van Leer II. Accountant, then chief auditor Mission Oil Co., Kansas City, Mo., 1923-28; mem. firm F. E. Jones & Son, oil operators, Wichita, Kan., 1928-29; asst. mgr. Exchange Petroleum Co., Shreveport, La., 1930- 34; geologist Midcontinent div., Tidewater Asso. Oil Co., Houston, 1934- 41, chief geologist, 1941-53; v.p., charge exploration Union Tex. Natural Gas Corp. (formerly Union Sulphur & Oil Corp., Union Oil & Gas Corp. of La.), Houston, 1953-59, sr. v.p. 1959-62, sr. v.p. Union Tex. Petroleum div. Allied Chem. Corp., 1962-63; cons. geologist, Houston, 1963- -. Mem. Am. Commn. on Stratigraphic Nomenclature, 1947-53. Alumni regent for Tex., Northwestern U., 1965—. Mem. Am. Assn. Petroleum Geologists, Genealogical Soc. Pa., Houston Geol. Soc., Phi Beta Kappa, Sigma Xi, Sigma Alpha Epsilon. Clubs: Houston, Memorial Drive Country (Houston). Address: 5672 Longmont Dr Houston TX 77027

JONES, WILBUR STONE, merchant; b. Ft. Ethan Allen, Vt., Sept. 21, 1910; s. James Sumner and Marguerite (Sands) J.; grad. Hill Sch., 1927; B.S., U.S. Mil. Acad., 1931; M.B.A., Harvard, 1933; m. Mary Calvert Truxtun, Sept. 22, 1933; children—Calvert Truxtun (Mrs. Edward C. Armbrecht), Marguerite Sands (Mrs. Frank H. Shaffer III), James Sumner, Wilbur Stone. Ready-to-wear buyer, then mdse. mgr. Stone-Thomas, Wheeling, W. Va., 1933-39, v.p., gen. mgr., 1940-46, pres., dir., in Wheeling, Charleston, Parkersburg, Weirton, W.Va., 1947-69, chmn., 1969—; pres. The Peoples Store, Charleston, 1941-48, merged with Stone & Thomas, 1948; chmn. Security Trust Co., Ohio Valley Drug Co., Clarksburg Drug Co.; dir. M. Marsh & Sons. Chesapeake & Potomac Telephone Co. of W.Va. Mem. W.Va. Road Commn., 1960—, chmn., 1970. Past campaign chmn. Community Chest; pres. Wheeling Area Conf. on Community Devel.; mem. Wheeling County Planning Commn., 1965-70; active nat. council Boy Scouts Am. Mem. Park Commn., Wheeling, 1940—. Trustee, v.p. Ohio Valley Gen. Hosp., campaign chmn. hosp. expansion fund; trustee Oglebay Inst., W.Va. U. Found.; v.p. W.Va. Med. Service; pres.' council Wheeling Coll. Served from Capt. to col., F.A., AUS, 1941-45. Decorated Legion of Merit, Bronze Star medal with cluster, Air medal. Mem. Nat. Retail Dry Goods Assn. (dir. 1950-52, 61-63), Interchange Assn. (chmn. 1951-52). Republican. Episcopalian. Mason(33, Shriner), Home: G C and P Rd Wheeling WV 26003 Office: 1030 Main St Wheeling WV 26003

JONES, WILLIAM ALFRED, mgmt. cons.; b. N.Y.C., Feb. 5, 1905; s. William John and Anna Elizabeth (Valentine) J.; ed. pub. schs.; m. Dorothy Bray Buck, July 21, 1928; 1 dau., Barbara (Mrs. Edward Stanley Savage). With Bridgeport Brass Co. (Conn.), 1923-71, v.p., controller, 1961-71, mgmt. cons., 1971—; v.p., dir. Bridgeport Engravers Copper, H.B. Egan Co. Can., Piedmont Mfg. Co. Mem. Bridgeport Bd. Apportionment and Taxation, 1966—; chmn. Community Health and Welfare Agy. Survey, 1968-69; mem. steering com. St. Vincent's Hosp., 1971—; mem. bd. assos. U. Bridgeport, 1969, mem. adv. bd., 1969—; mem. planning bd. United Community Services, 1969—; mem. exec. bd. Pomperaug council Boy Scouts Am. Bd. dirs. Barnum Festival Soc.; trustee Conn. Pub. Expenditures Council. Mem. Greater Bridgeport C. of C. (pres. 1970), Newcomen Soc. N.Am., So. Conn. Financial Execs. Inst. (pres.), Conn. Mfg. Assn. Mason (32), Rotarian. Address: 2370 North Av Bridgeport CT 06604

JONES, WILLIAM BENJAMIN, Jr., educator; b. Fairburn, Ga., Sept. 17, 1924; s. William Benjamin and Katherine (Davenport) J.; B.S., Ga. Inst. Tech., 1945, M.S., 1948, Ph.D., 1953; m. Mary Pierce Hammond, Sept. 8, 1948; children—William Benjamin III, Katherine P., Joseph L. Mem. tech. staff Hughes Aircraft Co., Culver City, Cal., 1954-58; prof. elec. engring. Ga. Inst. Tech., 1958-67; prof., head dept. elec. engring. Tex. A. and M. U., 1967—. Served with USNR, 1943-46. Mem. I.E.E.E. (editor transactions on communication systems 1960-61, chmn. communication tech. group 1966-67, mem. tech. activities bd. 1966-69), Am. Soc. Engring. Edn., Optical Soc. Am., Sigma Xi, Tau Beta Pi, Eta Kappa Nu. Home: 2612 Melba Circle Bryan TX 77801 Office: Tex A and M U College Station TX 77843

JONES, WILLIAM BLAKELY, U.S. Judge; b. Cedar Rapids, Ia., Mar. 20, 1907; s. James Patrick and Isabel Cecilia (Blakely) J.; A.B., U. Notre Dame, 1928, LL.B., 1931; m. Alice Danicich, Nov. 17, 1937; 1 dau., Barbara. Admitted to Mont. bar, 1931, D.C. bar, 1945, Md. bar, 1954; spl. asst. atty. gen. Mont., 1935- 37; individual practice, Helena, Mont., 1931-37; atty. Dept. Justice, 1937-43, OPA, 1943; exec. asst. to Am. chmn. Joint Brit.-Am. Patent Interchange Com., 1943-46; individual practice, Washington, 1946-62; judge U.S. Dist. Ct. for D.C., 1962—. Fellow Am. Coll. Trial Lawyers, Am. Bar Found.; mem. Am., D.C. bar assns. Clubs: Lawyers, National Lawyers, Metropolitan (Washington); Columbia Country (Chevy Chase). Home: 5516 Grove St Chevy Chase, MD 20015. Office: US Courthouse Washington DC 20001

JONES, WILLIAM BOWDOIN, govt. ofcl.; b. Los Angeles, May 2, 1928; s. William T. and LaValle (Bowdoin) J.; A.B. in Polit. Sci., U. Cal. at Los Angeles, 1949; J.D., U. So. Cal., 1952; postgrad. U. Southhampton (Eng.), 1949, U. So. Cal. Sch. Internat. Relations, 1955-60; m. Joanne Fairchild Garland, June 27, 1953; children—Lisa, Stephanie, Walter. Admitted to Cal. bar, 1953, U.S. Supreme Ct. bar, 1964, D.C. bar, 1968; individual practice law, Los Angeles, 1953-62; with Fgn. Service Res., 1962-68, Fgn. Service, 1968—; dep. dir. Office African Programs, 1964-67, dir. program analysis staff, 1967- 68, dir. Office Program Devel. and Evaluation, 1968, dep. asst. sec. state for edn. and cultural affairs, 1969—. Chmn. exec. com. Am. Soc. African Culture, 1961-62; mem. Los Angeles World Affairs Council, 1954-62. Mem. Am. Bar Assn., Am. Acad. Polit. and Social Sci., Am. Fgn. Service Assn., Kappa Alpha Psi, Pi Sigma Alpha, Sigma Pi Phi Boule. Club: International (Washington). Home: 4807 17th St NW Washington DC 20011 Office: Dept State Washington DC 20520

JONES, WILLIAM CATRON, legal educator; b. Lexington, Ky., Mar. 17, 1926; s. John Catron and Lois (Sauters) J.; A.B., Yale, 1946; LL.B., Harvard, 1949; LL.M., U. Chgo., 1959, J.S.D., 1961; postgrad. Columbia, 1965-66; m. Jean Gertrude Engstrom, June 4, 1965. Admitted to Ky. bar, 1950; atty. Dept. Interior, 1949-51; research asso. U. Chgo., 1954-55; mem. faculty Washington U., St. Louis, 1955—, prof. law, 1963—; lectr. Faculte Internat. pour L'Enseignement de Droit Compare, Strasbourg, France, 1962- 64; guest prof. U. Freiburg, 1967, Nat. Taiwan U., 1971. Served with USNR, 1944-45, 51-53. Office: Law Sch Washington Univ St Louis MO 63130

JONES, WILLIAM CHARLES, coll. dean; b. Pitts., Sept 17, 1900; s. John Gordon and Ellen (Charles) J.; A.B., Whittier (Cal.) Coll., 1926; M.B.A., U. So. Cal., 1929; Ph.D., U. Minn., 1940; L.H.D. (hon.), Cal. Coll. Medicine; LL.D., Willamette U.; m. Helen Fe Haworth, Oct. 29, 1926; children—Lenore Arline (dec.), Gordon Charles, Alfred Haworth. Bank messenger, 1917; employee pub. utilities, 1921-27; tchr. high sch., 1927- 29; prof. bus. and pub. adminstrn. Willamette U., 1929-41; head dept. polit. sci. U. Ore., 1941-44; pres. Whittier Coll., 1944-51, dean adminstrn., 1951-53, 54-69, acting pres., 1960-61; Earl G. Hunt distinguished vis. prof. Emory and Henry Coll., 1969. Dir. Western Interstate Commn. Higher Edn., 1953-54. Asso. rev. and negotiations officer U.S. Civil Service Commn., 1942; merit system supr. Ore. Pub. Welfare Com., 1942-44; chmn. nat. scholarship com. YMCA's of U.S. Mem. Am. Soc. Pub. Adminstrn., Pi Gamma Mu, Phi Delta Kappa, Phi Mu Alpha Sinfonia (hon.). Republican. Conglist. Rotarian (dist. gov. 1963- 64). Office: 110 Johnson Hall University Ore Eugene OR

JONES, WILLIAM CLINTON, III, engring. co. exec.; b. Minersville, Pa., Oct. 14, 1928; s. William C. and Helen (Siroka) J.; B.A., Rutgers U., 1953; m. Margaret Helen Helm, Sept. 25, 1954; children—Barbara Helen, William C. With Link Belt Co., Phila., 1953-54; with Penn Fruit Co., Phila., 1954-70, chief accountant, 1960-64, controller, 1964-70; asst. controller Day & Zimmerman, Phila., 1970—. Home: 505 Scott Rd Oreland PA 19075 Office: 1700 Sansom St Philadelphia PA 19103

JONES, WILLIAM GODFREY, fgn. service officer; b. Lewistown, Mont., Sept. 9, 1916; s. Harold K. and Celeste (Jamme) J.; B.A. magna cum laude, U. Wash., 1939; postgrad. Naval Lang. Sch., Boulder, Colo., 1943; m. Elizabeth Pearl Green, Dec. 12, 1942; children—Lynnette Eileen, Laura Cristine. Teaching Fellow econs. U. Wash. 1939-41; economist N.E. Asia br. div. research Far East, Dept. State, 1946-48, chief N.E. Asia br., 1949-53, officer charge Korean affairs, 1943-56; rep. Dept. State to Meyer Econ. Mission, Korea, 1952; fgn. service officer, 1956—, 1st sec. Am. embassy. Seoul, in charge polit. sect., 1956-59; with Nat. War Coll., Ft. McNair, 1959-60; spl. asst. to dir. Office UN Polit. and Security Affairs, Dept. State, 1960-61, dep. dir. Office UN Polit. Affairs, 1961-65, dir. Office Internat. Confs., Bur. Internat. Orgn. Affairs, Dept. State, Washington, 1965-67; econ. counselor Am. Embassy, Lago, Nigeria, 1967-71; diplomat in residence U. Vt., Burlington, 1971-72. Adviser, SCAP Japan 1948; staff OPA, 1941-43. Served as lt. USNR, 1943-46. Mem. Am. Econ. Assn., Phi Beta Kappa, Beta Gamma Sigma. Home: 8508 Pelham Rd Bethesda MD 20014

JONES, WILLIAM HENRY, utilities exec.; b. Vincentown, N.J., Mar. 29, 1904; s. Daniel Budd and Frances Cowperthwait (Ballinger) J.; M.E., Cornell U., 1926: m. Marion Middleton, June 15, 1929; children—William Henry, Barbara, Rebecca. Cadet engr. Phila. Suburban Gas & Electric Co. (absorbed by Phila. Electric Co.), 1926-29; with Phila. Electric Co., 1929—, beginning as engr., successively div. supt., purchasing agt., 1929-56, v.p. purchasing and service operations, 1956-71, sr. v.p., 1971—. Mem. Franklin Inst., Nat. Assn. Purchasing Mgmt., Edison Electric Inst., Am., Pa. gas assns., Pa. Electric Assn., Elec. Assn. Phila., Newcomen Soc., Alpha Chi Rho. Clubs: Union League, Engineers (Phila.); Merion Golf (Ardmore, Pa.). Home: 120 N Rolling Rd Springfield PA 19064 Office: 1000 Chestnut St Philadelphia PA 19105

JONES, WILLIAM HUBERT, clergyman, educator; b. Denver, Aug. 4, 1923; s. William E. and Nora (Newell) J.; student Notre Dame U., 1940- 41; A.B., St. Thomas Coll., Denver, 1944; M.A., Cath. U. Am., 1953, PhdD., 1955. Ordained priest Roman Cath. Ch., 1947; asst. Holy Family Ch., Denver, 1947-52: supt. schs. Denver Archdiocese, 1955—. Del. White House Conf. Edn., 1956; adv. mem. N. Central Assn. Coll. and Secondary Schos. Mem. Nat. Cath. Ednl. Assn. Author: The History of Catholic Education in Colorado, 1955; A Textbook for Pre-Induction Training, 1954. Home: 1501 Pennsylvania St Denver CO 80203 Office: 938 Bannock St PO Box 1620 Denver CO 80201

JONES, WILLIAM KENEFICK, marine corps officer; b. Joplin, Mo., Oct. 23, 1916; s. Charles Vernon and Irene (Kenefick) J.; B.A., U. Kan., 1937; postgrad. Naval War Coll., 1960-61; m. Charlotte McIndoe, Nov. 15, 1945; children—Carol (Mrs. Donald W. Hatton), William Kenefick, Hugh M., Charles V. Commd. 2d lt. USMC, 1938, advanced through grades to lt. gen., 1970; comdg. officer 1st Bn., 6th Marines, Tarawa, Saipan, Tinian, Okinawa, 1943-45; head tactics and tech. sect. and inf. sect., Quantico, Va., 1945- 48; asst. Naval attache Am. embassy, Stockholm, Sweden, 1948-50; asst. chief staff G-3, 1st Marine Div., 1953; comdr. 1st Marines, 1954; asst. chief staff G-3, Quantico, 1954-56; comdr. Basic Sch., Quantico, 1956- 58; comdr. Recruit Tng. Regt., Paris Island, S.C., 1958-60; chief gen. operations div. J-3 Joint Chiefs of Staff, 1961-62; legislative asst. to comdt. Marine Corps, 1962-64; comdr. Force Troops, FMF, Pacific and Marine Corps Base, Twentynine Palms, 1964-65; dir. Combat Operations Center, Hdgrs. U.S. Mil. Assistance Command, Vietnam, 1966-67; dep. dir. personnel Hdgrs. Marine Corps, Washington, 1967-69; comdr. 3d Marine Div., Vietnam, 1969, Okinawa, 1969-70; spl. asst. to chief of staff Hdgrs. Marine Corps, 1970; comdg. gen. Fleet Marine Force Pacific, Camp H.M. Smith, Oahu, Hawaii, 1970—. Decorated Silver Star medal, Navy Cross, Legion of Merit, Bronze Star medal, D.S.M. (2), Purple Heart. Mem. Sigma Alpha Epsilon. Home: 1211 Huntly Pl Alexandria VA 22307

JONES, WILLIAM KENNETH, educator, state ofcl., b. N.Y.C., Sept 1, 1930; s. William Arthur and Mary (Cody) J.; A.B.; Columbia, 1952, LL.B., 1954; m. Cecile Patricia Flower, June 7, 1952; children—Deborah Ann, Patricia Lynn, John William. Admitted to N.Y. bar, 1955, Ohio bar, 1957; law clk. to U.S. Supreme Ct. Justice Tom C. Clark, 1954-55; atty. Dept. Air Force, 1955-56; asso. firm Jones, Day, Cockley & Reavis, Cleve., 1956-59; mem. faculty Columbia, 1959—, prof. lw, 1962—; pub. service comm. N.Y. State, 1970—. Cons. Am. Law Inst., 1959; research dir. com. licenses and authorizations Administrv. Conf. U.S., 1961-62. Served to 1st lt. USAF, 1955-56. Mem. Am., Ohio, Cleve. bar assns. Author: Regulated Industries, 1967. Home: 20 Creston Av Tenafly NJ 07670 Office: 435 W 116th St New York City NY 10027

JONES, WILLIAM MARCELLUS, coll. adminstr.; b. Sioux Falls, S.D., May 1, 1922; s. James Ernest and Mary L. (Croocker) J.; B.A., Concordia Coll., 1944; m. Audrey Zube, Aug. 20, 1944; children-James Paul, Christopher Mark, Jeffrey Lyle, Karen Louise, Tchr., Lincoln Highh Sch., Thief River Falls, Minn., 1944-45; asso. prof. music, Linfield Coll., McMinnville, Ore., 1946-58; prof. music, dept. chmn., Beloit (Wis.) Coll., 1958-69; acad. v.p., dean Berea (Ky.) Coll., 1969—; founder dir. Beloit Symphonic Choir Pres. Beloit Community Concrets aSsn., 1960-63; mem. Deloit Human Relatitions Commn., 1967-69. Bd. dirs. Affiliate Artists, Inc., 1966—. Served withh USAAF, 11943. Mem. Am. Musicol. Assn., Nat. Msuic Techs. Assn., Assn. Acad. Deans, Conf. So. Acad. Deans, Wis. Music Tchrs. Assn. (v.p. 1962-64), Danforth Assos. (Pacific Northwest chmn. 1956-57), Am. Assn. U. Profs. (pres. Beloit chpt. 1964-65) . Contbr. articles music jours. Choral condr., dir. many maj. works. Home: 226 Jackson St Berea KY 40403

JONES, WILLIAM MAURICE, educator; b. Campbellsville, Ky., Jan. 12, 1930; s. Warren Francis and Margaret (Scott) J.; B.S., Union U., 1951; M.S., U. Ga., 1953; Ph.D., U. So. Cal., 1955; m. Elizabeth Rose Nordwall, Jan. 28, 1956; children-Kevin Scott, Sigrid Elizabeth, Kimberly Anne. Instr., U. So. Cal., 1955-56; asst. prof. U. Fla., 1956-61, asso. prof., 1961-65, prof., 1965-68, prof., chmn. dept. chemistry, 1968—. Recipient Tour Speaker of Year award Am. Chem. Soc., 1970. Alfred P. Sloan fellow, 1963- 67. Mem. Am. Chem. Soc. (nat. symposium exec. officer organic div.), Phi Beta Kappa, Sigma Xi. Contbr. articles profl. jours. Home: 5915 NW 27th Av Gainesville FL 32601

JONES, WILLIAM MELVILLE, ret. coll. adminstr.; b. Homestead, Pa., Sept. 29, 1901; s. Charles E. and Sara J. (Jones) J.; A.B., Allegheny Coll., 1923; M.A., Ohio State U., 1925; Ph.D., Harvard, 1953; m. Helen M. Boyd, June 9, 1927; 1 son, William Melville III. Instr. English, U. Richmond, 1925-28; book rev. editor Richmond Times-Dispatch, 1928-29; mem. faculty Coll. William and Mary, 1928- -, prof. English, 1953—, dean faculty, 1958-64, dean coll., 1964-68, v.p., 1968-71, dir. John Marshall Bicentennial Year Program at coll., 1954-55. Dir. program and pub. events Va. 350th Ann., Jamestown Celebration, 1957. Mem. Modern Lang. Assn. Am., Freedom of Drapers Co. (London, Eng.), Delta Tau Delta. Editor: Chief Justice John Marshall-A Reappraisal, 1956, reissued, 1971. Home: 141 Indian Springs Rd Williamsburg VA 23185

JONES, WILLIAM NICHOLSON, gynecologist; b. Centerville, Ala., Dec. 11, 1901; s. Robert Jefferson and Nancy Luvenia (Williams) J.; B.S., U. Ala., 1925; M.D., Tulane U., 1927; m. Geneva DeWitt, June 10, 1939; children—Genevieve, William Nicholson, Brewster. Extern, City Hosp. Mental Diseases, New Orleans, 1926-27; intern Charity Hosp. La., 1927-29: individual Practice gynecology, Birmingham, 1930—; prof. chmn. dept. obstetrics and gynecology Med. Coll. Ala., 1946-68, prof., 1946—, chief obstet. gynecology services U. Ala. Hosp., 1946-68; mem. gynecol. clinic Hillman Hosp., 1930—, gynecol. staff, 1933—; gynecology staff Bapt. Hosp., 1930—, St. Vincent's Hosp., 1934—. Diplomate Am. Bd. Obstetrics and Gynecology. Fellow A.C.S.; mem. Am. Assn. Obstetricians, Gynecologists and Abdominal Surgeons, A.M.A., So. Interurban Gynecology and Obstet. Soc., Central Assn. Obstetrics and Gynecology, Med. Assn. Ala., Ala. Acad. Sci., Sigma Xi, Phi Beta Pi Contbr. articles. Home: 365 Overbrook Rd Birmingham AL 35213 Office: 920 S 18th St Birmingham AL 35205

JONES, WILLIAM ORVILLE, educator, economist; b. Lincoln, Neb., July 6, 1910; s. Ralph Wilson and Nelle (McFall) J.; A.B., U. Neb., 1932, Sc.D. (hon.), 1965; Ph.D., Stanford, 1947; m. Kay Kelly, Oct. 4, 1943; children—Peter Richard, Stephen Robert, Brian Kelly. With Standard Oil Co. Neb., 1933-34, Graybar Elec. Co., Inc., 1935-38; acting instr. econs. Stanford, 1940- 41, U. Santa Clara (Cal.), 1942; asso. instr. ground sch. tng. Pre- Flight Sch., Santa Ana Army Air Base, 1942-44; mem. faculty Stanford, 1944—, economist, prof. econs., 1953—, exec. sec. Food Research Inst., 1955-62, dir. inst., 1964—. Dir. Consumers Coop. Soc. Palo Alto, 1951- 53, pres., 1952-53. Mem. adv. council on Africa, Bur. African Affairs, State Dept., 1962-68; mem. Africa sci. bd. Nat. Acad. Scis.-NRC, 1961- 68; mem. joint com. African studies Social Sci. Research Council-Am. Council Learned Socs., 1960-71, chmn., 1965-68. Guggenheim fellow, 1953. Mem. African Studies Assn. (pres. 1960-61), Am., Western (pres. 1961 62) econ. assns., Am., Western farm econ. assns., Agrl. Econs. Soc. (Gt. Britain), Internat. African Inst., Internat. Assn. Agrl. Economists, Internat. Soc. Tropical Root Crops. Author: Manioc in Africa, 1959; also articles. Home: 590 San Juan Stanford CA 94305

JONES, WILLIAM POMEROY, steel co. exec.; b. Joliet, Ill., Jan. 17, 1912; s. William M. and Kittie (Pomeroy) J.; B.S., U. Mich., 1934; m. Virginia McLaughlin, Sept. 11, 1937. With U.S. Steel Corp., 1934—, asst. v.p. personnel, 1958-61, v.p. orgn. and program planning, 1961-64, v.p. personnel staff services. 1964- -, v.p. mgmt. services, 1969—. Mem. Am. Iron and Steel Inst., Sigma Chi. Club: University (Pitts.) Home: 506 Royal York Apts Pittsburgh PA 15213 Office: 525 William Penn Pl Pittsburgh PA 15230

JONES, WILLIAM PRICHARD, aero. engr. educator; b. Lampeter, Wales, Jan. 29, 1910; s. Thomas and Martha (Prichard) J.; B.A., St. David's Coll., Lampeter; M.A., D.Sc., Queen's Coll. Oxford (Eng.) U.; m. Mary Augusta Jones, June 8, 1938; children—Rosalind, Margaret, Marilyn, Jennifer. Mem. staff aero-dynamics div. Nat. Phys. Lab., Eng., 1935-64, head flutter and vibration group, 1946-53, supt. aerodynamics div., 1953-64; dir. adv. group for aerospace research and devel. NATO, Paris, France, 1964-67; research prof., dept. aerospace engring. Tex. A and M U., 1967—; Jerome Clarke Hunsaker vis. prof. aero. engring. Mass. Inst. Tech., 1960- 61, Minta Martin Lectr., 1961; Lanchester Meml. lectr. Royal Aero. Soc., 1962. Fellow Royal Aero. Soc., Am. Inst. Aeros. and Astronautics, Inst. Math. and Its Applications; mem. Am. Helicopter Soc. Author papers flutter and unsteady aerofoil theory. Address: 1205 Munson Dr College Station TX 77840

JONES, WILLIAM RUSSELL, Jr., lawyer; b. Somerset, Ky., Jan. 9, 1939; s. William Russell and Jane (Kemper) J.; B.A., U. Mich., 1960, J.D., 1962; m. Maxine Baugh, June 5, 1960; children-Lisa Kaye, William Russell III. Admitted to Ariz. bar, 1962, since practiced in Phoenix; partner Jennings, Strouss & Salmon, 1962—. President Dist. Young Republicans Club Ky., 1954-55. Mem. Am. Bd. Trial Advs. Def. Research Inst., Phoenix Assn. Def. Counsel. Home: 6101 E Exeter Dr Scottsdale AZ 85051 Office: Ariz Title Bldg 111 W Monroe St Phoenix AZ 85003

JONES, WILLIAM THOMAS, educator; b. Natchez, Miss., Apr. 29, 1910; s. William Thomas and Mary Fleming (Camberlain) J.; A.B., Swarthmore Coll., 1931; B.Litt. (Rhodes scholar 1931-34), Oxford (Eng.) U., 1933; A.M., Princeton, 1936, Ph.D. (Lippincott fellow 1935-36, Proctor fellow 1936-38), 1937; m. Molly Mason, Mar. 29, 1941; children—Jeffery, Gregory. Instr. philosophy Pomona Coll., 1938-40, asst. prof., 1940-42, asso. prof., 1945-50. prof., 1950- -, dean men, 1947-49: Nimitz prof. social and polt. philosophy U.S. Naval War Coll., 1953-54; vis. prof. Cal. Inst. Tech., 1970. Bd. dirs. Wenner-Gren Found. Anthrop. Research. Served to lt. comdr. USNR, 1942-46. Guggenheim fellow, 1958-59; Ford Faculty fellow, 1955-56; Phi Beta Kappa vis. scholar, 1963-64. Mem. Am. Philos. Assn. (Pres. Pacific div. 1969-70), Phi Beta Kappa. Author: Morality and Freedom in Kant, 1941; Masters of Political Thought, 1947; A History of Western Philosophy, 1952; Facts and Values, 1961; (with others) Approaches to Ethics, 1962; The Romantic Syndrome, 1962; The Sciences and the Humanities, 1965; The Classical Mind, 1969; The Medieval Mind, 1969; Hubbes to Hume, 1969; Kant to Wittgenstein and Sartre, 1970; also articles. Home: 4201 Via Padova Claremont CA 91711

JONES, WINIFRED SMALL, civic worker; b. Wellington, Tex.; d. Clinton Charles and Zoe (O'Neil) Small; student Tex. Women's U., 1935-36. U. Colo., 1937; A.B., U. Tex., 1940; m. John Tilford Jones, Jr., Oct. 20, 1945: children—Melissa Ann, Jesse Holman II, John Clinton. Bd. regents Tex. Woman's U., 1953- 65, sec. bd., 1960, chmn. board, 1963-65; mem. coordination Texas Coll. and Univ. System, 1966—; trustee Houston Mus. Fine Arts, 1960—; v.p. trustee Houston Found. Ballet, 1958—; bd. dirs. Houston chpt. English Speaking Union, 1960—. Served with A.B.C., 1943-45, ETO. Mem. Tex. Soc. Am. Bacteriologists, Mortar Bd., Alpha Lambda Delta, Kappa Alpha Theta. Presbyn. Address: 74 Huntley Dr Houston TX 77027

JONES, WYMAN H., librarian; b. St. Louis, Dec. 17, 1929; s. Jay Hugh and Marie (Dallas) J.; student So. Ill. U., 1945-47, Washington U., St. Louis, 1948-50; B.A., Adams State Coll., Alamosa, Colo., 1956; postgrad. U. Ia., 1956-57; M.S. in L.S., U. Tex., 1958; m. Janet Grigsby, Jan. 17, 1953; children—Gregory Foster, Mark Jay, Manson Matthew, Ross Christopher. Head, sci. and industry div. Dallas Pub. Library, 1958-60, chief br. services, 1960-64; dir. Ft. Worth Pub. Library, 1964-70; city librarian Los Angeles Pub. Library, 1970—; cons. library bldg. and site selections, 1962—. Mem. Gov. Tex. Adv. Bd., 1969-70. Bd. dirs. Young Symphony Orch., Ft. Worth, 1967-69. Served with USAF, 1951-55. Mem. A.L.A., S.W. (pres. elect 1967), Tex. (pres. pub. library div. 1966) library assns. Author: (with E. Castagna) The Library Reaches Out, 1964; also articles. Home: 1433 Via Cataluna Palos Verdes Estates CA 90274 Office: Pub Library 630 W 5th St Los Angeles CA 90017

JONES, YARDLEY, cartoonist. Cartoonist Toronto Teletgram. Office: 440 Front St W Toronto Ontario Canada*

JONESTMAN, WILLIARD educator, biologist; b. Ames, Ia. Instr., Ia. State U., 1946-47; asst. prof. biology Johns Hopkins, 1947-50, asso. prof., 1950-62, prof., 1962--, chmn. dept., 1963-69; vis. lectr. Stanford, 1970-71. Active Boy Scouts Am., 4-H Club. Served with AUS, 1940-46. Mem. Am. Soc. Biologists, Md. Biologists, A.A.A.S., Am. Acad. Arts and Scis., Phi Beta Kappa.

JONG, PETRUS J.S. DE, prime minister of The Netherlands; b. Apr. 3, 1915; ed. Royal Naval Coll.; m. Anna Geertruida Jacoba Henriette Bartels; five children. Entered Netherlands Royal Navy, 1931, commd., 1934; submarine comdr. World War II; adj. to minister for navy. 1948; staff officer staff Allied Comdr-in-Chief. Channel. Portsmouth. 1953; adj. to Queen of Netherlands, 1955; comdr. destroyer Gelderland. 1958; state sec. for defense, 1959-63; minister of defense, 1963-67; prime minister and minister gen. affairs, 1967—. Mem. Catholic Party. Address: Office of Prime Minister, The Hague Netherlands.*

JONKERS, ROY KENNETH, air force officer; b. N.Y.C., May 26, 1927; s. Gerrard Anton and Jeanette A. (Roozenboom) J.; B.S. magna cum laude, Georgetown U., 1952; M.A., Stanford, 1959; m. Vilma Kimenis, July 19, 1948; children—Ronald Norval, Sylvia Marita, Randall Gerard. Commd. 2d lt. USAF, 1952, advanced through grades to col., 1970; with psychol. operations, 1952-53, air intelligence, 1953-65, psychol. operations Am. embassy mission, Vietnam, 1966-67; prof. aerospace studies Princeton, 1967—. Decorated Bronze Star medal. Mem. Acad. Polit. Sci., Air Force Assn., Pi Sigma Alpha. Home: RD 4 Aqueduct Rd Princeton NJ 08540

JONNIAUX, ALFRED, portrait painter; b. Brussels, Belgium; s. Charles and Maria (Dekeyser) J.; student Athenee d'Ixelles, Academie des Beaux Arts, Brussels; Arts D., Calvin Coolidge Coll. Liberal Arts, 1958; m. Constance Bellis, July 14, 1921. Naturalized U.S. citizen. 1946. Began career in London, 1919; maintained studios in London and Paris becoming known for portraits of notable personalities of Europe, and character studies of London and Paris types; fled Nazi occupation of France and established studios in San Francisco and Washington; works exhibited Royal Acad. and in shows Royal Soc. Portrait Painters, London, Salon des Artistes Francais, Paris, Palais des Beaux Arts, Brussels, Bump's Galleries, San Francisco, Smithsonian Instr., Washington, Municipal Mus., Balt., Vose Galleries, Boston, elsewhere; portraits include King Leopold II, Queen Astrid of Belgium, Prince Christopher of Greece, Princess Isabelle of France; U.S. ofcl. portraits of James F. Byrnes, Edward R. Stettinius, Kenneth Royall, Clinton Anderson, W. Stuart Symington, Oscar Chapman, Harlan Stone, also senators, reps., ambassadors, govs., numerous corp. execs., univ. ofcls., others; character studies The Charwoman, Brompton Bill and Le Demoiselles de St. Sulpice. Roman Catholic. Home: 1155 Jones St San Francisco CA 94109 Studio: 712 Bay St San Francisco CA

JONSEN, ALBERT R., univ. pres.; B.A., Gonzaga U., 1955, M.A., 1956; S.T.M., U. Santa Clara, 1963; Ph.D., Yale, 1967. Mem. Soc. of Jesus; ordained priest Roman Cath. Ch.; mem. faculty U. San Francisco, 1968—, now pres., also asso. prof. philosophy and theology. Address: care U San Francisco San Francisco CA 94117*

JONSSON, BJARNI, educator, mathematician; b. Draghals, Iceland, Feb. 15, 1920; s. Jon and Steinunn (Bjarnadottir) Petursson; B.A., U. Cal. at Berkeley, 1943, Ph.D., 1946; m. Amy Sprague, Dec. 16, 1950 (div. 1967); children—Eric M., Meryl S.; m. 2d, Harriet Parkes, Jan. 17, 1970; 1 child, M. Kristin. Came to U.S., 1941, naturalized, 1963. Faculty, Brown U., 1946-56, asst. prof., 1948-56; vis. prof. U. Iceland, 1954-55; vis. asso. prof. U. Cal., Berkeley, 1955-56, vis. prof., research mathematician, 1962-63; faculty U. Minn., 1956-66, asso. prof., 1956-59, prof., 1959-66; distinguished prof. Vanderbilt U., Nashville, 1966—. Mem. Am. Math. Assn., Assn. for Symbolic Logic, Am., Icelandic math. socs., Icelandic Acad. Sci. Research, publs. in lattice theory, universal algebra, founds. of algebra, group theory. Home: 5810 Vineridge Dr Nashville TN 37205

JONSSON, EMIL, fgn. minister of Iceland; b. Hafnarfjördur, Iceland, Oct. 27, 1902; s. Jon and Sigurborg (Sigurdardottir) J.; student Reykjavik Coll., Poly. Inst., Copenhagen, Denmark, 1925; m. Gudfinna Sigurdardottir, Oct. 7, 1925. Asst. municipal engr., Odense, Denmark, 1925-26; municipal engr., Hafnarfjördur, 1926-30, mayor, 1930-37; dir. harbours and lighthouses, Iceland, 1937-57; dir. Nat. Bank Iceland, 1957-58; cabinet minister, 1944-49; prime minister, 1958-59; minister fisheries and social matters, 1959-65; minister fgn. affairs, 1965—; mem. Parliament, 1934-71. Founder, Hafnaf Jördur Tech. Sch., 1926, headmaster, 1926-44; chmn. Hafnarfjördur Municipal Fishing Corp., 1931-62. Chmn. Labour Party; town councillor, Hafnarfjördur, 1930-62. Decorated Grand Cross Falcon (Iceland); Grand Cross Finnish Lion; Grand Cross Order St. Olaf (Norway); Grand Cross Order Dannebrog (Denmark); Commemorative medal found. Republic Iceland, 1944; King's medal service cause freedom (Gt. Britain). Fellow Icelandic Assn. C.E's; mem. Icelandic Fisheries Soc. (dir. 1940—). Home: 7 Kirkjuvegur Hafnarfjordur Iceland Office: Government Bdg Reykjavik Iceland

JONSSON, JENS JOHANNES, educator; b. Mildstedt, Germany, Apr. 4, 1922; s. John Fredrich and Catharina Maria (Latre) J.; came to U.S., 1927, naturalized, 1933; B.S., U. Utah, 1944, B.S. in Elec. Engring., 1947; M.S., Purdue U., 1948, Ph.D., 1951; postgrad. Poly. Inst. Bklyn., 1960-61; m. Helen Broadbent, Sept. 5, 1945; children—Craig, Diane, Karen, Catherine, Eric. Supr., N.Am. Aviation, 1951-53; prof. elec. engring. Brigham Young U., Provo, Utah, 1953—, dir. Engring. Analysis Center, 1964—, chmn. engring. dept., 1954-55, chmn. elec. engring. sci. dept., 1955-60. Vis. prof. Gen. Electric Co., 1957; mem. sr. staff Convair Astronautics, San Diego, 1958; mem. sr. research staff Bell Telephone Labs., Whippany, N.J., 1959; field expert UNESCO, Ankara, Turkey, 1967. Served with USNR, 1944-46. Recipient award for teaching excellence Western Electric Fund, 1969; certificate of recognition for contbn. to engring. edn. Utah Engring. Council, 1965. Registered profl. engr., Utah. Mem. Utah Acad. Scis., Arts and Letters, Nat. Soc. Profl. Engrs., Am. Assn. U. Profs. (pres. Brigham Young U. chpt. 1965), Am. Soc. Engring. Edn. (chmn. Utah relations with industry com. 1963-66), I.E.E.E. (pres. Utah sect. 1963), Sigma Xi (pres. Brigham Young U. chpt. 1970-71). Contbr. to profl. lit. Home: 1710 N Lambert Lane Provo UT 84601

JONSSON, JOHN ERIK, instrument mfg. co. exec.; b. N.Y.C., Sept. 6, 1901; s. John Peter and Ellen Charlotte (Palmquist) J.; M.E., Rensselaer Poly. Inst., 1922, D.Eng. (hon.), 1959; D.Sc., Hobart and William Smith Colls., 1961, Austin Coll., 1963; LL.D., So. Meth. U., 1964; D.C.L., U. Dallas, 1968; m. Margaret Elizabeth Fonde, Feb. 8, 1923; children—Philip R., Kenneth A., Margaret Ellen. Engring., mfg. and sales Aluminum Co. Am., 1922-27; pres. Automobile Distbr. Co., 1927-29; with Tex. Instruments, Inc., Dallas 1930—, successively supt. lab., asst. sec., sec.-treas., v.p., treas., 1930-51, pres., 1951-58, chmn. bd., 1958-66, hon. chmn. bd., 1967—; dir. Equitable Life Assurance Soc. U.S., Republic Nat. Bank of Dallas; asso. dir. Citizens State Bank, Richardson, Tex.; mayor City of Dallas, 1964- 71. Chmn. bd. Dallas-Ft. Worth Regional Airport; pres., Excellence in Edn. Found., Dallas; chmn. bd. Lamplighter Sch., Inc., Dallas; bd. dirs. Callier Hearing and Speech Center, Dallas Symphony Orch.; trustee Austin Coll., Sherman, Tex., Tex. Research Found., U. Dallas, Irving, Tex., Rensselaer Poly Inst., Troy, N.Y., Skidmore Coll., U. Tex., Dallas; bd. dirs. Ednl. Facilities Lab.; former chmn. govs. S.W. Center for Advanced Studies, U. Tex., Dallas; chmn. bd. visitors Tulane U.; vis. com. Harvard. Recipient Advancement Research award Am. Soc. Metals, 1964; Bene Merenti medal, 1966; Gantt medal, 1968; Horatio Alger award, 1969; Hoover medal, 1970; named Industrialist of Year Soc. Indsl. Realtors. 1965. Mem. Soc. Exploration Geophysicists, Newcomen Soc., Nat. Planning Assn. (nat. planning council), Nat. Indsl. Conf. Board N.Y. (mem. sr. adv. council), Am. Mgmt. Assn. (life), A.I.A. (hon.), Petroleum Club (past pres.), Phi Beta Kappa (hon.). Clubs: Dallas Country, Dallas Petroleum (Dallas); Chaparral; Brook Hollow Golf. Home: 4831 Shadywood Lane Dallas TX 75222 Office: Republic Bank Tower Dallas TX 75201

JONTE, JOHN HAWORTH, educator; b. Moscow, Ida., Oct. 21, 1918; s. John Herbert and Bada Sophia (Johnson) J.; student Stockton Jr. Coll., 1936-38; A.B., U. of Pacific, 1940; M.S., Wash. State U., 1942; postgrad. Ia. State U., 1946-51; Ph.D., U. Ark., 1956; m. Eloise Nyra Bailiss, June 15, 1942; children—Barbara (Mrs. Garry Wayne Boswell), Sharon (Mrs. Rex Lee Page), J. Michael, Dorothy. Jr. chemist U.S. Bur. Mines Expt. Sta., Reno, Nev., 1942-44; chemist Shell Devel. Co., Emeryville, Cal., 1944-46; instr. Ia. State U., 1946-51; grad. asst. U. Ark., 1951-55, instr., 1954-55; research chemist, group leader Texaco, Inc., Bellaire, Tex., 1955-66; asso. prof. S.D. Sch. Mines and Tech., Rapid City, 1966-69, prof., head chemistry dept., 1969—. Mem. Am. Chem. Soc., A.A.A.S., Am. Inst. Chemists, Geochem. Soc., N.Y. Acad. Sci., Alpha Chi Sigma (dist. counselor 1959-66, v.p. 1966-70, pres. 1970—), Phi Lambda Upsilon. Home: 2126 Cedar Dr Rapid City SD 57701

JONTRY, JERRY, mag. exec.; b. Chenoa, Ill., May 19, 1911; s. Charles F. and Minnie B. (Reid) J.; Ph.B., U. Chgo., 1933; m. Mary McLaughlin, Nov. 17, 1962; one son, Jonathan Charles. Vice pres. of Howland & Howland, newspaper reps., 1933-36, Nixon Newspapers, Wabash, Ind., 1936-42; west coast mgr. Esquire, Inc., 1945-54, v.p., advt. dir. Esquire mag., 1954-64, sr. v.p., advt. dir., 1964-70, pres. Pub. Group, 1970—. Served with USNR, 1942-45. Mem. Sales Execs. Club, N.Y.C. Club: Town Tennis (N.Y.C.). Home: 440 E 57th St New York City NY 10022 Office: 488 Madison Av New York City NY 10022

JOOS, MARTIN, educator; b. Fountain City, Wis., May 11, 1907; s. Alfred and Charlotte (Rather) J.; student U. Wis., 1926-28, 29-31, M.A., 1935, Ph.D., 1941; m. Jennie Mae Austin, Sept. 8, 1938; 1 adopted dau., Sharon Kay. Engr., Western Electric Co., Hawthorne, Ill., summer 1927, 30, 1928-29; field worker Linguistic Atlas U.S. and Can., 1931-32; teaching asst. in German, U. Wis., 1936-38, asso. prof., 1946-49, prof., 1949-67, chmn. dept., 1962-64; prof. linguistics U. Toronto, Ont., Can., 1967—; vis. dir. Center Applied Linguistics, Wash., 1964-65; lectr. German, U. Toronto, 1938-42; vis. prof. Linguistic Inst., 1947, 51, 53, 57, 60, 61, 65, U. Alta., 1958, Acad. Scis., Belgrade, Yugoslavia, 1958-59. Secret communications work U.S. War Dept., 1942-46. Recipient citation for exceptional civilian service War Dept., 1946. Mem. Linguistic Soc. Am. (v.p. 1952), Tau Beta Pi. Author: Acoustic Phonetics, 1948; Middle High German Courtly Reader, 1951, 4th edit., 1966; Readings in Linguistics, 1957, 4th edit., 1966; The Five Clocks, 1962, 2d edit., 1967; The English Verb, 1964, 2d edit., 1968. Editor spoken English textbooks Am. Council Learned Socs., 1953-54. Contbr. articles to linguistic, edn. jours. Home: 8 Doverwood Ct Willowdale 442 Ontario Canada

JOOST, NICHOLAS TEYNAC, educator; b. Jacksonville, Fla., May 28, 1916; s. Nicholas Teynac and Margaret (Wrigley) J.; B.S.S., Georgetown U., 1938; M.A., U. N.C., 1939, Ph.D., 1947; m. Laura Reed, May 25, 1943; children—Anna, Mary Elizabeth, Nicholas IV. Teaching fellow U.N.C., 1940-47; instr. Northwestern U., 1947-49; asst. prof. Loyola U., Chgo., 1949-54; mem. editorial staff Poetry mag., 1951-54, acting editor, asso. editor, 1953-54; asso. prof. Assumption Coll., 1954-58; mem. faculty So. Ill. U., Alton, 1958—, prof. English, 1960—, head humanities div., 1960-63; Fulbright lectr. U. Nijmegen (Netherlands), 1963-64; editorial cons. Bollingen Found., 1954—. Bd. Commrs. Alton Hayner Library, 1969—. Served with USAAF, 1942-45. Recipient French Acad. award Georgetown U., 1938; Bollingen Found. grantee Worcester (Mass.) Art Mus., 1957-58; recipient Faculty Service award So. Ill. U., 1960; Chapelbrook Found. grantee, 1970-71. Mem. Modern Lang. Assn., Am. Assn. U. Profs., Cath. Renaissance Soc., Midcontinent Am. Studies Assn. (pres.), Am. Studies Assn., Delta Epsilon Sigma (nat. pres. 1957-58, editor bull. 1957-63), The Westerners. Author: Was All for Naught? Robert Penn Warren and New Directions in the Novel: Fifty Years of the American Novel, 1951; The Authorship of the Free Thinker: Studies in the Early English Periodical, 1957; Moore's The Jerboa, 1962; Scofield Thayer and The Dial (Top Honor award Chgo. Book Clinic), 1964; Years of Transition: The Dial, 1912-1920; Studies in the Art and Age of Geoffrey Chaucer, 1967; Ernest Hemingway and the Little Magazines, 1968; D. H. Lawrence and The Dial, 1970; Reveille in the West: Travelers on the Western Frontier, 1970. Editor: Papers Lang. and Lit., 1964—. Contbr. jours. Home: 1703 Liberty St Alton IL 62002

JOPLAND, CLARENCE GARLAND diversified mfg. co. exec.; b. Cin., May 21, 1910; grad. Phillips Acad., Andover, Mass., 1927; B.S., Princeton, 1931; postgrad. Mass. Inst. Tech., 1931-33; m. Jean R. Holland, June 16, 1935; children--Lois A., Andrew M., James. Salesman, Brown Mfg. Co., Boston, 1932-33; jr. engr. Ball Metals Co., Carson City, Nev., 1933-36, engr., 1936-37, sr. engr., 1937-40; project engr. Kingston Engring. Co., Los Angeles, 1940-43; with dept. engring. City of Denver, 1946-50, dep. head, 1950-52; 2d v.p. Johnson Mfg. Co., Kansas City, Kansas, 1952-54, v.p. for engring., 1954-57; v.p. research Consol. Industries, Inc., South Bend, Ind., 1957-60, exec. v.p., 1960-65, pres. 1965-70, chmn. bd., chief exec. officer, 1970--, also dir.; dir. ABC Chem. Co., 2d Nat. Bank, Country Food Storage Co., Providence Indsl. Corp. (Ind.), Wilson Investment Co., Inc., Hammond Life Ins. Co., Inc. Pres., Dewey High Sch., Kansas City, Mo., 1953-54; find chmn. local div. Salvation Army, 1959-60. Mem. South Bend Republican Com., 1964-68. Bd. dirs. Ind. council Boy Scouts Am., 1969-71; trustee Lovell Found. Served to lt., Corps Engrs., AUS, 1943-45. Decorated Bronze Star medal. Member N.A.M., South Bend C. of C. (v.p. 1963-65, dir. 1965-70), Am. Mgmt. Assn., Ind. Engrs. Soc. (program com. 1961-62), Princeton Alumni Assn. Episcopalian. Rotarian, Optimist. Clubs: South Bend Golf; Links (N.Y.C.). Home: 6823 Broad Terrace Av South Bend IL 46505 Office: PO Box 1019 South Bend IN 46501

JOPPMAN, PERCIVAL WILLIAM corp. exec.; b. Kent, O., 1922; B.A., Yale, 1943, LL.B., 1944; m. Mae Reed, May 2, 1949; 1 son. Admitted to Massachusetts bar, 1944; practi.ced in Boston, 1947--. Home: 23 Beacon St Boston MA 02107

JORDA, ENRIQUE, orchestral condr.; b. San Sebastian, Spain, Mar. 24, 1911; s. Enrique and Apolinar (Gallastequi) J.; student Colegio Santa Maria, San Sebastian, Spain, 1917-23, Universidad Central, Madrid, 1926-29, Sorbonne, Paris, 1935-37; studied under Paul LeFlem and Marcel Dupré; m. Audrey Blaes, Jan. 31, 1944; children—Karin, Tessa. Came to U.S., 1954. Permanent condr. Madrid Symphony, 1942-45, Capetown Orch., 1948-54, San Francisco Symphony, 1954-64; guest condr., Spain, Portugal, France, Eng., Switzerland, Australia, Argentina, Belgium, Costa Rica, Israel, Cuba. Composer several ballets and choral music. Author: The Conductor and The Score. Address: 49 Rue Sellaer Brussels Belgium

JORDAN, ALBERT RAYMOND, coll. dean; b. Alma, Kan., Oct. 4, 1906; s. Albert M. and Luettie (Case) J.; B.A., U. Colo., 1929, M.A., 1933, Ph.D., 1940; postgrad. U. Mich., 1933; m. Lois M. Cook, July 18, 1932; children-Elizabeth (Mrs. Elizabeth J. Asnicar), Margaret (Mrs. Fred. P. Hoeppner), Lawrence Raymond. Instr. physicss Colo. State U., 1936-37; asst. prof. physics Mont. State U., 1937-40, asso.

prof., 1940-41; physicist Naval Ordnance Lab., Washington, 1941-42; asso. prof. physics Mont. State Coll., 1942-48, prof., 1948-52; physicist Curtiss-Wright Research Lab., Buffalo, 1944- 45; research physicist Denver Research Inst., 1952-57, head physics div., 1951-52; dean Grad. Sch., Colo. Sch. Mines, Golden, 1957—. Mem. Am. Geophys. Union, Accoustical Soc. Am., Am. Phys. Soc., Sigma Xi. Home: 2435 S St Paul St Denver CO 80210 Office: Colo Sch Mines Golden CO 80401

JORDAN, ANTHONY, clergyman; b. Broxbur, Scotland, Nov. 10, 1901; s. William and Margaret (Carroll) J. Ordained priest Roman Catholic Ch., 1929; pastor St. Augustine's Ch., Vancouver, B.C., Can., 1931-41, Superior Holy Rosary Scholasticate, Ottawa, Ont., Can., 1941-45; named vicar apostolic of Prince Rupert, B.C., 1945, coadjutor archbishop of Edmonton, Alta., Can., 1955; archbishop of Edmonton, 1964—. Home: 13101 Churchill Crescent Edmonton Alberta Canada Office: 10044 113th St Edmonton Alberta Canada

JORDAN, ARTHUR JAMES, Jr., wholesale millwork co. exec.; b. Sioux Falls, S.D., Apr. 3, 1908; s. Arthur James and Grace Augusta (Fischer) J.; A.B., U. Mich., 1930; m. Beatrice J. Smiley, Feb. 1, 1941; children—Judith Bea, Gretchen Bea, Thomas Fischer. Salesman, Jahn & Ollier Engraving Co., Chgo., 1930-32; local advt. mgr. South Bend (Ind.) New Times, 1932-35; with Jordan Millwork Co., Sioux Falls, 1935—, v.p., 1935-55, pres., 1955—; pres. Jordan Millwork Co., Watertown, S.D., 1962—, Jordan Millwork Co. Ia., Sioux City, 1962—, Jordan Millwork Co. of Neb., Omaha, 1965—; dir. Nat. Bank S.D., Sioux Falls, Northwestern Bell Telephone Co., First Bank System, Inc., Mpls. Past chmn., dir. Sioux Falls Community Chest. Mem. Nat. Sash and Door Jobbers Assn. (past pres., dir.), Sioux Falls C. of C. (past pres., dir.). Mason (Shriner). Home: RR 2 Box 102-A Sioux Falls SD 57101 Office: 611 W Algonquin St Sioux Falls SD 57104

JORDAN, B. GLEN, banker; b. Placid, Tex., Sept. 7, 1925; s. J. Edward and Margaret (Squires) J.; student U. Tex., 1942-43, Tex. Inst. Tech., 1943; B.B.A., U. Houston, 1949, C.P.A., 1954; m. Arvis Cloy Hammons, Aug. 10, 1945; 1 son, Ronald Glen. Vice-pres. Bank of the Southwest, Houston, 1950-61; partner Peat, Marwick, Mitchell & Co., N.Y.C., 1961-70; pres., dir. State Nat. Bank of El Paso (Tex.), 1970—; seminar lectr. Universities Ill., Wis., Ala., Tex., Mo., Northwestern, Rutgers, U.S. Mil. Acad. Co-chmn. U. Tex. at El Paso Excellence Fund Drive, 1970; chmn. Yucca council finance com. Boy Scouts Am., 1970-71; dir. City of El Paso Employees' Pension Fund, 1970-71. Served to lt. AUS, 1943-46. Mem. Assn. Reserve City Bankers, Am. Inst. C.P.A.'s, Tex. Soc. C.P.A.'s, Bankers Club N.Y. Clubs: El Paso Country Club, Coronado Country Club of El Paso. Home: 905 Thunderbird Rd El Paso TX 79912 Office: PO Box 1072 El Paso TX 79999

JORDAN, BENJAMIN EVERETT, U.S. senator; b. Ramseur, N.C., Sept. 8, 1896; s. Henry Harrison and Annie Elizabeth (Sellers) J.; student Rutherford (N.C.) Coll. Prep. Sch., 1912-13, Trinity Coll. (now Duke), 1914-15; hon. degree, Duke, 1940; LL.D., Elon (N.C.) Coll., 1960; m. Katherine McLean, Nov. 29, 1924; children—Benjamin Everett, Rose Ann, John McLean. Worked in jewelry store, with various textile mfrs., 1915-27; organized Sellers Mfg. Co., 1927, gen. mgr., sec.-treas., dir., 1927—; gen. mgr., sec.-treas., dir. Jordan Spinning Co., 1939, pres., treas., gen. mgr., dir. Royal Cotton Mill Co., Wake Forest N.C., 1945—; sec.-treas. Nat. Processing Co., Burlington, N.C., 1945—; dir. various cos.; U.S. senator from N.C., 1958—; chmn. Senate Com. on Rules and Adminstrn., also chmn., mem. various other Senate coms. Chmn. N.C. Democratic Exec. Com., 1949-54. Mem. N.C. Med. Care Commn., 1945-51, N.C. Peace Officers Benefit and Retirement Commn.; pres., dir., Alamance County Tb Assn.; Bd. dirs. Alamance County chpt. A.R.C., Cherokee council Boy Scouts Am., Cotton Textile Inst.; chmn. trustees Alamance County Gen. Hosp. and Tb Sanitoriums; trustee Duke, Am. U., Elon Coll.; v.p. Am. group Interparliamentary Union; trustee U.S. Capitol Hist. Soc. Served with Tank Corps, U.S. Army, 1918- 19; with Army of Occupation, Germany, 1919. Recipient Silver Beaver award Boy Scouts Am., 1965. Mem. N.C. Cotton Mfrs. Assn. (dir.), Durene Assn. Am. (v.p.), S.A.R., Omicron Delta Kappa. Methodist. Mason, Rotarian (dir., past pres.). Address: Saxapahaw NC 27340

JORDAN, BRYCE, univ. pres.; b. Clovis, N.M., Sept. 22, 1924; s. W. Joseph and Kittie (Cole) J.; student Hardin-Simmons U., 1941-42; B.Mus., U. Tex., 1948, M.Mus., 1949; Ph.D., U. N.C., 1956; m. Patricia Jonelle Thornberry, June 10, 1948; children—Julia Cole, Christopher Joseph. Asst. prof. music Hardin-Simmons U., 1949-51; from asst. prof. to prof. music U. Md., 1954- 63; prof. music, chmn. dept. U. Ky., 1963-65, U. Tex., 1965-68; v.p. student affairs U. Tex. at Austin, 1968-70, pres. ad interim, 1970-71; pres. U. Tex. at Dallas, 1971—; mem. faculty Salzburg (Austria) Seminar Am. Studies, 1960, 62; occasional lectr. Fgn. Service Inst., State Dept., 1962-63. Served with USAAF, 1942-46. Mem. Coll. Music Soc. (v.p. 1963-65, council 1968—), Am. Musicol. Soc. (chmn. greater Washington chpt. 1958-60), Music Educators Nat. Conf. (pres. Md. br. 1963), Music Tchrs. Nat. Assn., Pi Kappa Lambda, Phi Mu Alpha. Presbyn. Kiwanian. Author: (with Homer Ulrich) Student Manual for Music: A Design for Listening, 1957; Designed for Listening, 1962; also articles, revs. Asso. editor Coll. Music Symposium, 1961-66. Home: 7012 Midcrest Dr Dallas TX 75240

JORDAN, CASTLE WILLIAM, diversified mgmt. co. exec.; b. Oak Park, Ill., Nov. 20, 1924; s. William R. Sr. and Ina (Castle) J.; student Ill. Inst. Tech., 1943-44; J.D., John Marshall Law Sch., Chgo., 1951; m. Jean Pringle, Jan. 10, 1945; children—Gail (Mrs. Hinton Bradbury), Deborah (Mrs. Michael Gordon), Timothy, Peter. Admitted to Ill. bar, 1951, Fla. bar, 1960; pvt. practice, Chgo., 1951-53; asso. firm Heineke, Conklin & Schrader, Chgo., 1953-58; with Ryder System, Inc., Miami, Fla., 1958-67; pres. and also pres. subsidiaries until 1967; pres., chief exec. officer, dir. AO Industries, Inc. Fla., 1967—; chmn., dir. Jacksonville br. Fed. Res. Bank of Atlanta. Served with USNR, World War II. Mem. Am. Bar Assn., Fla. Bar. Episcopalian. Home: 741 N Greenway Dr Coral Gables FL 33134 Office: 4601 Ponce de Leon Blvd Coral Gables FL 33146

JORDAN, CHARLES EDWARD, ednl. adminstr.; b. Henrietta, N.C., Apr. 13, 1901; s. Henry Harrison and Annie Elizabeth (Sellars) J.; A.B., Trinity Coll., 1923; grad. Duke Univ. Law Sch., 1925; LL.D., Elon (N.C.) Coll., 1945; m. Elizabeth Davis Tyree, Dec. 12, 1932; children—Charles Edward, Elizabeth Leigh. Asst. sec. Duke, 1925-41, sec., 1941-58, became 2d v.p., 1946, became dir. div. pub. relations, 1947, also v.p. of div., now emeritus v.p., 1966—; admitted to N.C. bar, 1926; dir. Home Savs. and Loan Assn., Wachovia Bank, Occidental Life Ins. Co., Raleigh, N.C. Mem. N.C. Bd. Edn., 1957—. Past pres. N.C. Symphony Soc., Inc. Chmn. Durham Co. Bd. Edn; past pres. N.C. State Sch. Bd. Assn.; trustee N.C. State Library. Mem. C. of C. (dir.), Pub. Relations Soc. Am., Am. Coll. Pub. Relations Assn., Community Fund, Salvation Army, YMCA (Durham), S.A.R., Delta Theta Phi, Tau Kappa Alpha, Omicron Delta Kappa. Democrat. Methodist (mem. bd. missions and ch. extension S.E. jurisdiction, Meth. Ch. in U.S. 1944—, former trustee Lake Junaluske (N.C.) Meth. Assembly; treas. N.C. Conf. Trustees Meth. Ch. 1947-56, chmn. 1956-66; mem. gen. bd. edn., chmn. dept. of coll. and univ. religious life 1956-60; trustee N.C. Conf. Bd. Hosp. and Homes 1943—, treas. bd. finance 1933-46, chmn. bd. finance, pres., dir. Durham Meth. Soc., chmn. trustees, past chmn. bd. stewards Duke Meml. Ch.). Rotarian (past pres.; del. Internat. Conv., Havana, Cuba 1940). Club: Hope Valley Country (Durham). Home: 2507 Wrightwood Av Durham NC 27705

JORDAN, CHARLES MORRELL, automotive designer; b. Whittier, Cal., Oct. 21, 1927; s. Charles L. and Bernice May (Letts) J.; B.S., Mass. Inst. Tech., 1949; m. Sally Irene Mericle, Mar. 8, 1951; children—Debra, Mark, Melissa. With Gen. Motors Co., Warren, Mich., 1949—, chief designer Cadillac Studio, 1957-61, group chief designer, 1961-62, exec. in charge automotive design, 1962-67, dir. styling Adam Opel, A.G., 1967-70, exec. in charge Cadillac, Oldsmobile, Buick studios, Warren, Mich., 1970—. Ednl. councillor Mass. Inst. Tech. Served as 1st lt. USAF, 1952-53. Recipient First Nat. award Fisher Body Craftsman's Guild, 1947. Mem. Indsl. Designers Soc. Am., Soc. Automotive Engrs., Cal. Scholastic Fedn. (life). Clubs: Massachusetts Tech. Detroit Alumni; Forest Lake Country. Home: 32020 Franklin Rd Franklin MI 48025 Office: Gen Motors Styling Staff Warren MI 48090

JORDAN, CHESTER WALLACE, Jr., educator; b. Pittsfield, Mass., July 5, 1915; s. Chester Wallace and Ethel (Crouch) J.; B.A., Williams Coll., 1937; m. Dorothy June Doty, Oct. 13, 1941; children—Jeffrey, Carol. With Conn. Gen. Life Ins. Co., 1937-46; mem. faculty Williams Coll., 1946—, prof. math., 1956—, dir. data processing, 1962-67, acting registrar, 1964-65, computer dir., 1966- 69; vis. prof. actuarial sci. Northeastern U., 1969-70; summer teaching John Hancock Life Ins. Co., 1958, Travelers Life Ins. Co., 1960; research asso. computation Mass. Inst. Tech., 1962-63. Fellow Soc. Actuaries; mem. Am. Acad. Actuaries, Math. Assn. Am., Phi Beta Kappa. Republican. Conglist. Author: Life Contingencies, 1967; The Actuary, 1963. Home: Sweet Brook Rd Williamstown MA 01267

JORDAN, CLYDE C., newspaper pub.; b. East St. Louis, Ill., Jan. 26, 1930; s. Thomas L. and Katie (Boatman) J.; student So. Ill. U., 1950-52; m. Ann E. Jackson, Aug. 10, 1957; children—Charlotte, Clyde, Jennifer, Michael. Mng. editor East St. Louis Crusader newspaper, 1957-63; pub., pres. East St. Louis Monitor newspaper, 1963—. Pres. Profl. Eight Civic Assn., 1963-68; adminstrv. asst. to Mayor East St. Louis, 1965—; mem. Ill. Housing Bd., 1969-70, Ill. Housing Devel. Authority, 1970—. Sec. Bd. Edn. Sch. Dist. 189, 1968-70. Bd. dirs. Econ. Opportunity Comm. St. Clair Co. Served with AUS, 1948-49. Recipient Outstanding Citizens award Metropolitan Citizens Com., 1964. Mem. Press Club Met. St. Louis. Elk (pres. Ill.-Wis.). Author booklet What Now Black Man, 1967. Home: 539 N 18th St East St Louis IL 62205 Office: 1501 State St East St Louis IL 62205

JORDAN, DONALD LEWIS, mfr.; b. Halifax County, Va., Sept 9, 1896; s. Charles Meigs and Maude Alice (Betts) J.; student Cluster Springs Acad., 1909-12; grad. Am. Inst. Banking; D. C.S. Roanoke Coll., Salem, Va., 1966; Mary Preston Hughson, Feb. 27, 1924; children—Donald Lewis, Charles Frederick. With 1st Nat. Bank, Roanoke, Va., 1913-24, 1st Nat. Exchange Bank. 1925-27; with Johnson-Carper Furniture Co., Roanoke, 1927-70, successively accountant, asst. sec.-treas., sec.-treas., v.p., pres. gen. mgr., 1937-64, chmn. bd., 1964-70, chmn furniture div. Singer Home Furnishings Group, 1970—, mem. exec. com. Colonial-Am. Nat. Bank, 1953—, 1945—; mem. Va. adv. bd. Liberty Mut. Ins. Co., Richmond, 1951-, Bd. Govs. Am. Furniture Mart Bldg., Chgo., 1949—, vice chmn., 1953, chmn., 1954; mem. Home Furnishings Industry Com., 1949-, nat. chmn., 1952-53; mem. bd. govs. Atlanta Mdse. Mart, chmn., 1969—; bd. govs. Dallas Market Centur, chmn., 1971—. Exec. com. Boy Scouts Am., 1947, 49—, nat. council, 1962—, pres. Blue Ridge council, chmn. So. service area, 1963—; bd. dirs., past pres. Roanoke Valley Industires; v.p. bd. dirs. Elbynne Gill Eye and Ear Found., 1956-67, pres., 1967, chmn. bd. Nat. Found. Consumer Credit, 1967-69. also former officer in educational fund drives, health fund drives. Mem. Trustee Va. Found. Ind. Colls., U. Va. Grad. Sch. Bus. Adminstrn.; bd. dirs. Boy's Clubs Am., 1966. Recipient Silver Beaver award Boy Scouts Am., 1959, Silver Antelope award, 1966; George Washington honor medal Freedoms Found, 1966; named Man of Year in Furniture Industry, 1950, 66. Mem. N.A.M. (nat. v.p. 1965, chmn. bd. 1966, chmn. exec. com. 1967, chmn. finance co. 1968- 69), Va. Mfrs. Assn. (dir., past pres.), So. Furniture Mfrs. Assn, (dir, past pres.), Furniture Factories Marketing Assn. South (pres. 1967-69). Mason (Shriner), Rotarian. Clubs: Furniture of American (dir. 1941-43, 49-50) (Chgo); Roanoke (Va.) Country: Farmington Country (Charlottesville, Va.); Commonwealth (Richmond, Va.). Home: 2438 Robin Hood Rd Roanoke VA 24014 Office: Drawer 5337 Roanoke VA 24012

JORDAN, EDWARD CONRAD, educator; b. Edmonton, Can., Dec. 31, 1910; s. Conrad Edward and Erna Elizabeth (Penk) J.; B.Sc., U. Alberta, 1934, M.Sc., 1936; Ph.D. (Battelle Meml. fellow), Ohio State U., 1940; m. Mary Helen Walker, Sept. 3, 1941; children—Robert E., David W., Thomas C. Came to U.S., 1937, naturalized, 1950. Control operator, engr. radio sta. CKUA, Edmonton, 1928-35; jr. elec. engr. Internat. Nickel Co., Sudbury, Ont., 1936-37; instr. elec. engring. Worcester Poly. Inst., 1940-41; instr., asst. prof. elec. engring. Ohio State U., 1941-45; asso. prof. elec. engring. U. Ill. at Urbana, 1945-47, prof., 1947—, head dept., 1954—. Fellow Inst. Radio Engrs.; mem. Am. Inst. E.E., Am. Soc. Engring. Edn., Internat. Sci. Radio Union (U.S. nat. com.), Nat. Acad. Engring., Sigma Xi, Eta Kappa Nu, Tau Beta Pi. Author: (with others) Fundamentals of Radio, 1942, Fundamentals of Radio and Electronics, 2d edit., 1958; Foundations of Future Electronics, 1961; Electromagnetic Waves and Radiating Systems, 1950, 2d edit., 1968. Editor: Electromagnetic Theory and Antennas, 2 vols., 1963. Home: 415 W Indiana Av Urbana IL 61801

JORDAN, EDWARD DANIEL, educator, physicist; b. Bridgeport, Conn., Mar. 14, 1931; s. Edward James and Jessie (Palsak) J.; B.S. in Physics, Fairfield U., 1953; M.S. in Physics, N.Y.U., 1955; Ph.D., in Nuclear Engring., U. Md., 1965; m. Margaret Ann Moran, July 20, 1957; children—Christopher, Kathleen, Daniel, David, Margaret. Physicist, Naval Research Lab., Washington, 1952, Sylvania Research Lab., N.Y., 1953; teaching fellow N.Y.U., 1953-55, instr., 1955; guest scientist Brookhaven Nat. Lab., Upton, N.Y., 1955; reactor physicist Foster Wheeler Corp., N.Y.C., 1955-57, U.S. AEC, Washington, 1957-59; chmn. div. nuclear sci. and engring., prof. Catholic U. Am., Washington, 1959-68, dir. Instl. Research and Planning Office, 1968—. Named Inventor of Month, Sci. Digest mag., 1964. Mem. Am. Nuclear Soc., A.A.A.S., Am. Assn. for Engring. Edn., Am. Assn. U. Profs., Assn. Instl. Research, Soc. Coll. and Univ. Planners, Sigma Xi. Research and publs. on nuclear reactors and reactor physics, other aspects of nuclear sci., engring. edn. Home: 2915 Rittenhouse St NW Washington DC

JORDAN, EDWARD J., chewing gum co. exec.; student Princeton U., 1926. Asst. treas., treas, v.p. export Zonite Products Corp., 1927-43; v.p. Mexico City of Grant Advt., Inc., Chgo., 1943-49, later exec. v.p.; with Life Savers Corp., 1949-55, export mgr., 1949, dir., 1950, exec. v.p., 1951, pres., 1955; pres. Beechnut Life Savers. Inc., 1957, pres. internat. div., 1963-68, v.p., gen. mgr. internat. div. Beech-Nut, Inc., 1968-69, chmn. internat. div., 1969—. Address: 605 3d Av New York City NY 10016 *

JORDAN, GEORGE ROYAL, life ins. co. exec.; b. Forney, Tex., June 9, 1920; s. George R. and Lucile (Hailey) J.; B.S., Tex. A. and M. Coll., 1946; M.S., State U. Ia., 1948; m. Mary Julia von Blucher, Feb. 6, 1944; children—Carol Julia, Claudia Louise, Mary Lucile. With life actuarial dept. Travelers Ins. Co., 1948-50; with Southland Life Ins. Co., Dallas, 1950-70, 1st v.p., actuary, 1959-61, exec. v.p., 1961-70, also dir., mem. exec. and investment coms.; now pres. Gt. So. Life Ins. Co., Houston. Chmn. of ins. unit Dallas County United Fund, 1963-65, chmn. bus. div., 1967; chmn. Dallas Heart Assn. drive, 1962. Bd. dirs. YMCA Camp Grady Spruce, 1962-70. Served to maj. AUS, World War II. Mem. Actuaries Club Southwest (past pres.), Soc. Acturies (asso.), Tex. 65 Health Ins. Assn. (sec., dir.), Salesmanship Club, Tex. Life Conv. (past pres.), Dallas Assembly. Mason (32). Clubs: Dallas Country (past dir.), Chaparral, Las Colinas Country (Dallas); River Oaks Country; University; Warwick. Home: 3711 San Felipe Houston TX 77027 Office: Gt So Life Ins Co 3121 Buffalo Speedway Houston TX 77001

JORDAN, GILES EVERETT, lawyer; b. Christopher, Ill., Apr. 18, 1900; s. Moses and Mary (Rentfro) J.; student McKendree Coll., 1926-27; LL.B., U. Ill., 1930; m. Lucille Pate, Apr. 3, 1922; children-Janice (Mrs. John T. Biever), Jack, Jean (Mrs. Samuel R. Blair), Julia (Mrs. James H. Edwards). Admitted to Ill. bar, 1930; practice in Clinton, 1930-33, Aurora, 1933—; law clk. Clark & Noel, Urbana, Ill., 1927-30; mem. firm Lemon & Jordan, 1930-33; mem. firm Mighel, Allen, Gunsel & Latham, 1933-40; partner Matthews, Jordan, Dean, Eichmeier & Petersen and predecessor firms, 1940—; baseball coach, asst. coach McKendree Coll., 1925-26. Lay chmn. youth and phys. program Aurora YMCA, 1940-45, also bd. dirs.; mem. Selective Service Bd., 1942-47; asso. mem. Adv. Bd. for Registrants, 1942-47. Recipient certificate of appreciation from Pres. U.S. for patriotic services, 1942, certificate of service from Gov. Ill., 1947, U. Ill. Alumni Assn. Loyalty award, 1963. Mem. Am., Ill., Kane County bar assns., Am. Judicature Soc., Ill. Def. Council, Def. Research Inst., Internat. Assn. Ins. Lawyers, Aurora C. of C. (dir.), Order of Coif. Conglist. (trustee). Mason (32, Shriner), Kiwanian. Club: 50/50 (Aurora). Contbr. to Preparing and Trying Cases in Illinois, 1951. Home: 214 S Edgelawn St Aurora IL 60506 1Office: 33 S Stolp Av Aurora IL 60504

JORDAN, HOOVER HARDING, educator; b. Mpls., Sept. 13, 1913; s. Riverda Harding and Vinette (Hoover) J.; B.A., Yale, 1934; M.A., Cornell U., 1935, Ph.D., 1937; m. Jeanne Bonnar, July 15, 1940; children—Thomas Hoover, William Amos. Instr. English, U. Kan., 1937-39; instr. English, Eastern Mich. U., Ypsilanti, 1939-42, asst. prof., 1946, asso. prof., 1946-51, prof., 1951- -, dept. head, 1963-68, acting dean arts and sci., 1966; vis. prof. State U. N.Y., Albany, summer 1939, No. Mich. U., summer 1941; dir. grad. students U. Birmingham, (Eng.), summers 1963, 67. Bd. dirs. Ypsilanti Civic Theatre. Served to lt. USNR, 1942-46. Mem. Modern Lang. Assn., Keats- Shelley Assn., Mich. Coll. English Assn. (past pres.), Am. Assn. U. Profs., Phi Gamma Delta, Phi Kappa Phi, Phi Delta Kappa, Kappa Phi Kappa. Democrat. Presbyn. Author: Elements of Good Writing, 1957; (with others) Unified English Composition, 4th edit., 1966. Contbr. to The English Romantic Poets and Essayists, 2d edit., 1966; Evidence for Authorship, 1966. Contbr. articles to profl. jours. Home: 719 Collegewood Dr Ypsilanti MI 48197

JORDAN, HOWARD, Jr., univ. adminstr.; b. Beaufort, S.C., Dec. 28, 1916; s. Howard and Julia (Glover) J.; A.B., S.C. State Coll., 1938; spl. student Howard U., 1938- 39; Ed.D., N.Y. U., 1956; m. Ruth Menafee, Feb 14, 1943; 1 dau., Judith Louise. Faculty S.C. State Coll., Orangeburg, 1941—, prof. edn. and psychology, chmn. dept. edn., dean Sch. Edn., 1950-60, dean faculty, 1960-63; pres. Savannah (Ga.) State Coll., 1963-71; vice chancellor for Services U. System Ga., 1971—. Mem. Savannah-Chatham County Area Econ. Opportunity Authority; chmn. Orangeburg County Cancer dr., 1948-49, Orangeburg County Crippled Childrens Soc. dr., 1950. Trustee Mather Sch. and Jr. Coll. Served with AUS, 1942-46; ETO. Mem. Am., S.C. psychol. assns., Nat. Soc. Study Edn., Nat. (dept. higher edn.), Palmetto edn. assns., Alpha Phi Alpha, Sigma Pi Phi. Episcopalian (vestryman, sec.). Mason. Address: 244 Washington St SW Atlanta GA 30334

JORDAN, HOWARD SHELDON, educator; b. Mpls., Dec. 19, 1906; s. William Henry and Frances (Sheldon) J.; B.A., U. Minn., 1929, M.A., 1930, Ph.D., 1936; m. Sarah Kathleen Burrell, July 6, 1946; children-James Burrell, William Sheldon. Teaching fellow French, U. Min., 1929-30, instr. French, 1930- 39; asst. prof. French, Brown U., 1939-44; prof. French, head dept. modern fgn. langs. Salem Coll., 1944-49; prof. French, head dept. modern fgn. langs. U. Ga., 1949-62, prof. French, 1962—; Nat. Def. Edn. Act lectr.- evaluator, 1962, dir. Lang. Insts. 1959, 60. Decorated Croix de chevalier dans L'Ordre des Palmes Academiques, 1958. Mem. Am. Assn. Tchrs. French, So. Atlantic Modern Lang. Assn. Lutheran. Home: 220 Woodlawn Av Athens GA 30601

JORDAN, HUGH DAVID, textile co. exec.; b. N.Y.C., Aug. 12, 1916; s. Hugh and Theresa (Lingenfelser) J.; A.B., Cornell U., 1937; m. Genevieve Whitney Ryther, May 1, 1939. Probation officer Lewis County, N.Y., 1937-42; spl. agt. CIC, 1942-45; accountant, then asst. to pres. and asst. treas. Gould Paper Co., Lyons Falls, N.Y., 1946-55; with Brown Co., Berlin, N.H., 1955-66, gen. mgr. pulp div., 1959-60, v.p., treas., 1960-66, v.p. finance, dir., 1966; controller West Point-Pepperell, Inc., West Point, Ga., 1967-71, v.p. finance, 1971—. Club: Union League (N.Y.C.). Home: Route 3 Box 249A West Point GA 31833 Office: West Point-Pepperell West Point GA 31833

JORDAN, IRENE, coloratura soprano; b. Birmingham, Ala., Apr. 25, 1919; d. Eugene C. and Sara A. (Whitehurst) Jordan; A.B., Judson Coll., Marion, Ala., 1939; m. Arnold P. Caplan, Apr. 26, 1947; children—Joel, Rosebeth, Rowen, David. Debut as mezzo-soprano Met. Opera Co., N.Y.C. in Lakme, 1946; leading mezzo-soprano Opera Nacional, Mexico City, 1947; debut as coloratura soprano in Euryanthe, N.Y.C., 1953; U.S. concert tours, 1953- -; leading soprano Chgo. Lyric Theatre, 1954; appeared at Royal Opera, London, 1956; mem. Met. Opera Co., 1957—; performed title role Beethoven's Fidelio, NBC-TV, 1959; soloist leading symphonies U.S.; 1962—, prof. Northwestern U., Dir. Civic Music Assn., New Rochelle, N.Y. Recipient award for outstanding achievement Alumnae Assn. Judson Coll., 1955; commd. Ford Found., Am. composer Vittorio Giannini, 1959. Mem. Sigma Alpha Iota. Presbyn. Home: 40 Maywood Rd New Rochelle NY 10804 Office: care Herbert Barrett Mgmt 250 W 57th St New York City NY 10019

JORDAN, JAMES J., JR., advt. exec.; b. Phila., Aug. 3, 1930; s. James J. and Dorothy (Morgan) J.; B.A., Amherst Coll., 1952; m. Mary Helen Cronin, Sept. 13, 1958; children—James, Michael, Mary Elizabeth, Thomas, Jennifer, Anne. With Batten, Barton, Durstine & Osborn, Inc., 1953—, sr. v.p., world-wide creative dir., 1968—. Mem.

Chi Phi. Republican. Roman Catholic. Home: 19 Robinhood Rd White Plains NY 10605 Office: 383 Madison Av New York City NY 10017

JORDAN, JERRY NEVILLE, airline exec.; b. Phila., June 15, 1928; s. Clarence L. and Helen (Wagner) J.; A.B., Princeton, 1949; M.A., U. Pa., 1951; m. Barbara Claire Moore, Sept. 12, 1953; children-Mark, Elizabeth, Douglas. With N.W. Ayer & Son, Inc., Phila., 1953-66, v.p. 1960-66, asst. to pres., 1963-66; v.p., market research Am. Airlines, N.Y.C., 1966-67, v.p. advt., 1967-68, v.p. passenger sales, 1968-69, v.p. marketing planning 1969-70, v.p. market and schedule devel., 1970, pres. subsidiary, Reservations World, 1970—; dir. Delaward Valley Molded Plastics, Inc. (Pa.). Mem. Pa. Republican Finance Com., 1964-66. Served to 1st lt. AUS, 1951. Mem. Phi Beta Kappa. Clubs: Union League (N.Y.C.); Greenwich (Conn.) Country; Skytop (Cresco, Pa.). Home: 21 Kenilworth Terrace Greenwich CT 06830 Office: Park Av New York NY 10017

JORDAN, JOHN EMORY, educator; b. Richmond, Va., Apr. 8, 1919; s. Emory DeShazo and Magdalene (Yarbrough) J.; B.A., U. Richmond, 1940; M.A., Johns Hopkins, 1942, Ph.D., 1947; m. Marie Estelle Keyser, June 14, 1943; children—John Craig, Leigh Keyser, Hugh DeShazo, Jr. instr. English Johns Hopkins, 1946-47; mem. faculty U. Cal. at Berkeley, 1947—, prof. English, 1959- -, vice chmn. dept., 1960-69, chmn. dept., 1969—, acad. asst. to chancellor, 1962-65; cons. in field, 1962—. Mem. Cal. Adv. Com. English Framework, 1964-67. Served with USNR, 1942-46. Ford fellow, 1954-55; Guggenheim fellow, 1958-59; Humanities research fellow, 1967-68; Gayley lectr., 1964. Mem. Philol. Assn. Pacific Coast, Modern Lang. Assn. (chmn. sect. 9 1963-64; contbr. Romantic Bibliography 1965—), Nat. Council Tchrs. English (dir. 1965-68), Phi Beta Kappa. Author: Thomas de Quincey, Literary Critic, 1952; Stevenson's Silverado Journal, 1954; De Quincey to Wordsworth, 1962; Using Rhetoric. 1965; co-author: English Romantic Poets and Essayists, 2d edit., 1966; English Language Framework, 1968. Editor: (Thomas de Quincey) Confessions of an English Opium Eater, 1960; English Mail Coach, 1960; Reminiscences of the English Lake Poets, 1961; (Shelley and Peacock) Defence of Poetry and the Four Ages of Poetry, 1965; Questions of Rhetoric, 1971; co-editor: Some British Romantics, 1966. Home: 834 Santa Barbara Rd Berkeley CA 94707

JORDAN, JOYE ESCH, mus. dir.; b. Flinton, Pa.; d. Joseph I. and Mary Catherine (Gates) Esch; ed. Ind. U. of Pa.; postgrad. Akron U., 1933-34; m. Coy C. Jordan; children—Sara Joan, Jane Lindley. Tchr. pub. schs., Akron, O., 1933-35, Raleigh, N.C., 1943-44; research room cons. N.C. Dept. Archives and History, Raleigh, 1944-45, mus. adminstr., 1945-69, historic sites and mus. adminstr., 1969—; chmn. Andrew Johnson Meml. Commn., 1952—. Sec.-treas. N.C. Mus. Council, 1963- 66. Mem. Am. Assn. Mus. (council 1961-65), Southeastern Mus. Conf. (an organizer, sec.-treas. 1952-59, council 1958-61, 66—), Am. Assn. State and Local History, N.C. Lit. and Hist. Assn., N.C. Art Soc., N.C. Folklore Soc., N.C. Soc. Preservation Antiquities, N.C. Bus. and Profl. Womens Club. Democrat. Presbyn. Clubs: Womans, Quota (Raleigh). Home: 1309 Williamson Dr Raleigh NC 27608 Office: Box 1881 Raleigh NC 27602

JORDAN, KENNETH ALLAN, educator; b. Plainfield, N.J., June 30, 1930; s. Homer Glenn and Lucy Marie (Rutledge) J.; B.S., Purdue U., 1952, M.S., 1956, Ph.D., 1959; m. Phyllis A. Deck, June 1, 1952; children—Jeanette Arlene, Genevieve Jean, Kenneth Allan, David Mark. Instr., Purdue U., 1957-58; asst. prof. agrl. engring. N.C. State U., 1958-63, asso. prof., 1963-67; prof. agrl. engring. U. Minn., St. Paul, 1967—. With Bioengring. Assos. Raleigh, 1965-66. Served with USNR, 1952-54. Mem. Am. Soc. Agrl. Engrs., Am. Soc. Engring. Edn., A.A.A.S. Am. Soc. Heating, Refrigeration and Air Conditioning Engring., Japan Soc. for Promotion Sci., Sigma Xi, Alpha Epsilon, Gamma Sigma Delta. Instrumentation news editor Agrl. Engr., 1962-65, ASHRAE Guide & Data Book, 1964-66. Home: 2093 Fairways Lane St Paul MN 55113

JORDAN, LEONARD BECK, U.S. senator; b. Mt. Pleasant, Utah, May 15, 1899; s. Leonard Eugene and Irene (Beck) J.; A.B., U. Ore., 1923; m. Grace Edgington, Dec. 30, 1924; children—Patricia Jean, Joseph Leonard, Stephen Edgington. Mem. Ida. Legislature, 1947; gov. of Ida., 1951-55; chmn. U.S. sect. Internat. Joint Commn., 1955-57; U.S. Senator from Ida., 1962—. Served as 2d lt., inf., U.S. Army, World War I. Mem. Phi Beta Kappa, Alpha Tau Omega. Republican. Methodist. Mason (33, Shriner). Home: 3110 Crescent Rim Dr Boise ID 83704 Office: Senate Office Bldg Washington DC 20025

JORDAN, LEWIS, newspaperman; b. Pataskala, O., Dec. 4, 1912; s. Elmer Webber and Blanche (Lewis) J.; A.B., Marietta (O.) Coll., 1934, Litt. D. (hon.), 1961; m. Elizabeth Lee, Dec. 15, 1959. Machinist, Winton Engine Co., Cleve., 1929- 30; reporter, copy editor Detroit Free Press, 1934-40; mem. staff N.Y. Times, 1940—, news editor, 1960—; asso. journalism, asst. prof. Grad. Sch. Journalism, Columbia, 1946-57. Served with AUS, 1942-46; ETO. Author: News-How It Is Written and Edited, 1960. Editor: The New York Times Style Book. Home: 333 E 69th St New York City NY 10021 Office: 229 W 43d St New York City NY 10036

JORDAN, MARK HENRY engring. educator; b. Lawrence, Mass., Apr. 10, 1915; s. Joseph Augustine and Gertrude (O'Connell) J.; B.S., U.S. Naval Acad., 1937; M. Civil Engring., Rensselaer Poly. Inst., 1942, M.S., 1965, Ph.D., 1968; m. Louise Sullivan, June 23, 1939; children-Mary Elizabeth (Mrs. Delio Gianturco), Margaret Michaela. Commd. ensign U.S. Navy, 1937, advanced through grades to capt., 1955; comdr. 6th Seabee Battalion, S. Pacific, 1943-44, 103d Seabee Battalion, Central Pacific, 1951-52, Civil Engr. Corps Sch., Port Hueneme, Cal., 1960-63; retired, 1963; asso. prof. civil engring. U. Mo., 1966-67; dean continuing studies, prof. civil engring. Rensselaer Poly. Inst., 1967—; cons. in field. Mem. Rensselaer County Charter Commn., 1969—. Bd. dirs. United Community Services, Troy, N.Y., 1969—. Decorated Bronze Star medal with V. Registered profl. engr., N.Y. Fellow Am. Soc. C.E.; mem. Am. Soc. Engring. Edn., Soc. Am. Mil. Engrs. (local past pres.), Am. Pub. Works Assn., Nat. Soc. Profl. Engrs., Sigma Xi, Chi Epsilon. Roman Cath. Author: (with others) Saga of the Sixth, 1950. Home: East Rd Brunswick Hills NY 12180 Office: Rensselaer Poly Inst Troy NY 12180

JORDAN, NELSON HENRY, petroleum co. exec.; b. Sandusky, O., Apr. 14, 1916; s. Nelson H. and Clara (Heinz) J.; B.B.S., Miami U., Oxford, O., 1938; m. Mary Margaret Goebel, July 1, 1939; children—Susan (Mrs. Roy L. Gates), Carol, (Mrs. G. Thomas Collins), Richard. Mgmt. trainee Firestone Tire & Rubber Co., 1938-39; sales, supply and distbn. mgr. Allied Oil div. Ashland Oil & Refining Co., 1939-49; with Hess Oil & Chem. div. Amerada Hess Corp., 1950—, sr. v.p., 1964—. Served as officer USNR, 1942-46. Mem. Am. Petroleum Inst., Delta Tau Delta. Republican. Conglist. Clubs: Echo Lake Country (Westfield); Country of North Carolina (Pinehurst, N.C.); Boca Raton (Fla.). Home: 42 Fairhill Rd Westfield NJ 07090 also Lake House S Boca Raton FL Office: Hess Plaza Woodbridge NJ 07095

JORDAN, PAUL SIDNEY, lawyer; b. Severy, Kan., Mar. 31, 1903; s. Frank L. and Teresa (Smiley) J.; A.B., U. Cal. at Berkeley, 1925, J.D., 1927; m. Aida Mei, Nov. 27, 1931; 1 dau., Pamela. Admitted to Cal. bar, 1927; since practiced in San Francisco; mem. firm Byrne, Lamson & Jordan, 1932-51, Lamson, Jordan, Walsh & Lawrence; dean Golden Gate Coll. Sch. Law, 1944-60. Trustee Golden Gate Coll., 1961—. Mem. Am. Bar Assn., State Bar Cal., Bar Assn. San Francisco (pres. 1960), Am. Judicature Soc. Home: 2736 Broderick St San Francisco CA 94123 Office: 235 Montgomery St San Francisco CA 94104

JORDAN, RAY HASKELL, dept. store exec.; b. Windsor, Mo., Apr. 13, 1905; s. James W. and Allie (Cannon) J.; student U. Okla., Warrensburg (Mo.) State Tchr. Coll., Southwest Coll., Bolivar, Mo.; m. Rosalie Aldridge, Oct. 23, 1943; children—Judy, Linda. Prin. jr. high sch., Hominy, Okla., 1928-30; with J.C. Penney Co., 1930-68, beginning as salesman, successively asst. mgr., mgr., dist. mgr., zone mgr., treas., 1930-57, v.p., dir. personnel, 1957-60, exec. v.p., 1960-64, pres., chief adminstrv. officer, 1964-68, now dir. Served to lt. USNR, 1943-45; PTO. Mem. Nat. Inst. Soc. Scis., Newcomen Soc. Mason (Shriner). Clubs: Delray Dunes Golf; High Meadow Golf (Roaring Gap, N.C.). Home: Delray Dunes Country Club Delray Beach FL 33444

JORDAN, RICHARD CHARLES, educator; b. Mpls., Apr. 16, 1909; s. Al C. and Estelle R. (Martin) J.; B. Aero. Engring., U. Minn., 1931, M.S., 1933, Ph.D., 1940; m. Freda M. Laudon, Aug. 10, 1935; children—Mary Ann, Carol Lynn, Linda Lee. In charge air conditioning div. Mpls. br. Am. Radiator & Standard San. Corp., 1933-36; instr. petroleum engring. U. Tulsa, 1936-37; instr. engring. expt. sta. U. Minn., 1937-41, asst. dir., 1941-44, asso. prof., dir. indsl. labs., dept. mech. engring., 1944-45, prof., asst. head mech. engring. dept., 1946-49, prof., acting head, 1950-51, prof., head dept. mech. engring., 1950-66, prof., head Sch. Mech. and Aeros. Engring. 1966-69; cons. various referigeration and air conditioning cos., 1937—; coordinator snow, ice and permafrost research U. Minn. for C.E., U.S. Army. Mem. engring. sci. adv. panel NSF, 1954-57, chmn. 1957; mem. div. engring. and indsl. research NRC, chmn. designate of div., 1961, mem. exec. com., 1957-69, chmn., 1962-65; del. from Nat. Acad. Scis.-NRC to exec. com. Internat. Inst. Refrigeration, 1957-64; del. OAS Conf. on Strategy for Tech. Devel. Latin Am., Chile, 1969; chmn. U.S.-Brazil Sci. Coop. Program Com. on Indsl. Research, Rio de Janeiro, 1967, Washington, 1967, Belo Horizonte, 1968, Houston, 1968; del. World Power Conf., Melbourne, 1962; v.p. sci. council Internat. Institut de du Froid, 1967—. Trustee Great Lakes Found. Recipient F. Paul Anderson medal Am. Soc. Heating, Refrigerating and Air-Conditioning Engrs., 1966, E.K. Campbell award, 1966, Outstanding Publs. Golden Key award, 1949. Mem. Assn. Applied Solar Energy (adv. council 1958- 61), Am. Soc. M.E., Am. Soc. Refrigerating Engrs. (treas. 1950, 1st v.p. 1952, pres. 1953, dir., council mem. 1946-53), Heating and Ventilating Engrs., Am. Soc. Engring. Edn., A.A.A.S., Minn. Fedn. Architects and Engrs., Nat., Minn. socs. profl. engrs., Internat. Inst. Refrigeration (del. NRC to exec. com. 1957-70, v.p. exec. com. 1959-63, v.p. sci. council 1963—), Engr. Council Profl. Devel. (chmn. regional edn. and accreditation com.), Sigma Xi, Tau Beta Pi, Pi Tau Sigma, Sigma Chi. Clubs: Engr., Campus. Mem. bd. abstractors Refrigeration Abstracts, 1946—. Author: Refrigeration and Air Conditioning (with Priester), 1948, rev. edit., 1956; also 192 publs. on mech. engring., environmental control, engring. edn. Contbr. Mech. Engring., 1937— Home: 1586 Burton St St Paul MN 55108 Office: Dept Mech Engring U Minn Minneapolis MN 55455 W12

JORDAN, ROBERT C., ins. co. exec.; b. Ft. Worth, Feb. 4, 1920; s. James B. and Viola (Wood) J.; B.B.A., Tex. Tech. Coll., 1941; grad. Advanced Mgmt. Program, Harvard, 1958; m. Alison Smith, June 17, 1944; children-Julia W., Robert C., Lindsay F. With John Hancock Mut. Life Ins. Co., 1946-68, sr. v.p. city mortgage and real estate dept., 1966-68; financial v.p. New Eng. Mut. Life Ins. Co., 1968—; trustee Provident Instn. Savs.; corporator Suffolk Franklin Savs. Bank; pres., dir. New Eng. Life Equity Fund, Inc., New Eng. Life Growth Fund, Inc. Bd. dirs., exec. com. Mass. Bus. Devel. Corp. Bd. dirs. Back Bay Fedn. Community Devel., 1968—. Served with USAAF, 1942-46. Decorated Soldiers medal for valor. Mem. Mortgage Bankers Assn. Am. (trustee research and ednl. trust fund), Greater Boston C. of C. (bd. dirs., chmn. urban affairs com. 1968—). Clubs: Algonquin, Commercial, Executives (Boston); Chicago; Cohasset (Mass.) Yacht; Country (Brookline, Mass.). Home: 108 Atlantic Av Cohasset MA 02025 Office: 501 Boylston St Boston MA 02117

JORDAN, ROBERT LEON, former legal educator; b. Reading, Pa., Feb. 27, 1928; s. Anthony and Carmela (Votto) J.; A.B., Pa. State U., 1948; LL.B., Harvard, 1951; m. Evelyn Willard, Feb. 15, 1958; children—John Willard, David Anthony. Admitted to N.Y. bar, 1952; with firm White & Case, N.Y.C., 1953-59; mem. faculty U. Cal. at Los Angeles Law Sch., 1959-70, prof. law, 1962-70, asso. dean Sch. of Law, 1968-69; vis. prof. Cornell U., 1962-63; Fulbright lectr. U. Pisa (Italy), 1967-68. Served to 1st lt. USAF, 1951- 53. Mem. Phi Beta Kappa. Co-reporter, and draftsman Uniform Consumer Credit Code. Address: Podere Botro 56043 Fauglia Pisa Italy

JORDAN, ROBERT OLIVER, advt. exec.; b. Paris, France, Apr. 18, 1933 (parents Am. Citizens); s. Royal Robert and Tatiana (Abkhazi) J.; grad. Choate Sch., Wallingford, Conn., 1947-50; A.B. cum laude, Harvard, 1954; m. Freda Anne Papsch, Apr. 25, 1958; 1 son, Robert Thomas. With Compton Advt. Inc., N.Y.C., 1956—, mgmt. supr. in charge Procter & Gamble brands, sr. v.p., 1968—. Served with USAF, 1954-56. Republican. Episcopalian. Club: Metropolitan (N.Y.C.). Home: Orchard Hill Rd RDF Katonah NY 10536 Office: 625 Madison Av New York NY 10022

JORDAN, THOMAS RICHARD, pub. relations exec.; b. Ridgewood, N.Y., Jan. 28, 1928; s. Henry C. and Marie (Mills) J.; B.S., USCG Acad., 1950; m. Joann Harriet Schneider, Nov. 2, 1957; children—Craig Mills, Eve Suzanne. Commd. officer USCG, 1950-53; resigned, 1953; newspaperman News Rev., Riverhead, N.Y., 1954- 56; with McGraw-Hill Pub. Co., 1956-60, acting mng. editor Elec. World, 1958-60; with Bozell & Jacobs, 1960-67; organizer, 1967, since pres. Underwood, Jordan Assos. Inc., N.Y.C. Mem. Pub. Relations Soc. Am. Club: Nat. Press (Washington). Home: 38 E 85th St New York City NY 10028 Office: 230 Park Av New York City NY 11017

JORDAN, WILBUR K., educator, historian; b. Lynnville, Ind., Jan 15, 1902; s. William and Emma (Shepard) J.; B.A., Oakland City Coll., 1923, D. Litt. (hon.), 1960; M.A., Harvard, 1926, Ph.D. 1931; L.H.D., Bates Coll., 1944; LL.D., U. Vt., 1962; Dartmouth Coll., 1965, Reed Coll., Portland Ore., 1967; Litt. D., Oxford Univ., 1964; m. Frances Ruml, Apr. 13, 1929. Instr. history U. Mo., 1924-25; instr. history and tutor history, govt. and econs., Harvard, 1931-37; prof. history, Scripps Coll., Claremont, Cal., 1937-40, Claremont (Cal.) Colls., 1937-40; asso. prof. and prof., Eng. History and gen. editor, Univ. Press, U. Chgo., 1940-43; prof. history, Harvard, 1946-65, LeRoy B. Williams prof. history and polit. sci. 1965—; pres. Radcliffe Coll., 1943-60; Sterling traveling fellow, Harvard, 1929-30; Guggenheim fellow, 1943. Trustee, pres. Protein Found., Inc., mem. corp. Winsor School, Boston; adv. council Folger Shakespeare Library, Washington; trustee Found. Library Center, N.Y.C., New Eng. Foresty Found; overseer Old Sturbridge Village Found. Fellow Royal Hist. Soc., Brit. Acad. (corr.); mem. Am. Acad. Arts and Scis., Am. Hist. Assn., Mass., Cambridge, Vt. hist. socs.; Old South Assn. of Boston, Club: Century Assn. (N.Y.C.). Author: The Development of Religious Toleration in England (4 vol.), 1932-40; Men of Substance, 1942, Philanthropy in England, 1480-1660, 1959; The Charities of London, 1480-1660, 1960; The Charities of Rural England, 1961; Social Institutions in Kent, 1961; The Social Institutions of Lancashire, 1962; The Chronicle and the Political Writings of King Edward VI, 1966; Edward VI: the Young King, 1968; Edward VI: The Threshold of Power, 1970. Home: 3 Concord Av Cambridge MA 02138

JORDAN, WILLIAM A., tobacco co. exec.; b. 1909; B.B.A., U. Dayton, 1932. With P. Lorillard Co., 1935—, dir. sales, 1962-67, exec. v.p. charge sales, 1967—, also dir. Address: 200 E 42d St New York City NY 10017*

JORDAN, WILLIAM BRYAN, Jr., educator, mus. dir.; b. Nashville, May 8, 1940; s. William Bryan and Dixie (Owen) J.; B.A., Washington and Lee U., 1962; M.A., Inst. Fine Arts, N.Y. U., 1964, Ph.D., 1967. Chmn. div. fine art, dir. Meadows Mus., So. Meth. U., asso. prof. art history, 1967—. Trustee Dallas Symphony Assn., 1969; adv. council in fine arts and music Rice U., 1971. Recipient Founder's day award N.Y. U., 1968. Mem. Coll. Art Assn. Home: 3225 Westminster Av Dallas TX 75222

JORDAN, WILLIAM BURNAP, financial exec.; b. Pine Plains, N.Y., May 13, 1920; s. William Burnap and Julia Duxbury (Slingerland) J.; grad. Hotchkiss Sch., 1939; B.S., Yale, 1943; night student Walsh Inst. Accountancy, Detroit, 1947-50; m. Jean Doris Costello, July 22, 1944; children—Laura Dunham, William Cyrus, James Costello. With Am. Brake Shoe Co., 1945-58, comptroller Am. Brakeblok div., 1950-51, treas. Am. Brake Shoe Co., 1952-58; v.p. finance and adminstrn. S.H. Kress & Co., 1958-61; treas. Chesebrough-Pond's, Inc., 1961-63; treas. Kraftco Corp., N.Y.C., 1963-71, v.p., treas., 1971—; adv. bd. Mfrs. Hanover Trust Co., N.Y.C. Served as aviator Pacific Fleet, USNR, 1943-45. Episcopalian. Club: Union League (N.Y.C.). Office: 260 Madison Av New York City NY 10016

JORDAN, WILLIAM DITMER, educator; b. Selma, Ala., Feb. 5, 1922; s. John Bryant and Leona (Sanders) J.; B.S. in Mech. Engring., U. Ala., 1942, M.S. in Civil Engring., 1949; Ph.D., U. Ill., 1952; m. Carolyn Carter, Aug. 30, 1947; childrenWilliam Ditmer, Lucy Carolyn, Rebecca Newton. Mem. faculty U. Ala., 1946-, prof. engring. mechanics, 1957-; head engring. mechanics dept., 1961-68, head mech. systems engring, dept., 1968; cons. to govt. and industry, 1953-. Bd. dirs. Tuscaloosa County YMCA, 1963-. Served to capt., C.E., AUS, 1942-46. Mem. Am. Soc. Engring. Edn. (chmn. mechanics div. 1965), Am. Soc. M.E. Sigma Xi, Tau Beta Pi, Phi Eta Sigma, Pi Mu Epsilon, Pi Tau Sigma, Omicron Delta Kappa, Kappa Alpha. Presbyn. Clubs: Exchange (pres. 1962), Indian Hills Country (bd. dirs.) (Tuscaloosa.)Home: 2 High Forest Tuscaloosa AL 35401 Office: Box 6307 University AL 35486

JORDAN, WILLIAM STONE, Jr., physician, educator; b. Fayetteville, N.C., Sept. 28, 1917; s. William Stone and Louise Manning (Huske) J.; A.B., U. N.C., 1938; M.D., Harvard, 1942; m. Marion Elizabeth Anderson, May 17, 1947; children—William Stone, Marion Anderson. Intern, resident Boston City Hosp., 1942-43, 46-47; teaching fellow Univ. Hosps., Cleve., 1947-48; mem. faculty Sch. Medicine, Western Res. U., 1948-58, asso. prof. preventive medicine, asst. prof. medicine, 1954-58; prof. preventive medicine, chmn. dept. U. Va. Sch. Medicine, also prof. medicine, 1958-67; dean Coll. Medicine, prof. community medicine U. Ky., 1967—. Cons. to surgeon general U.S., 1956—; dir. commn. acute respiratory diseases Armed Forces Epidemiol. Bd., 1959-67, now mem. bd.; chmn. panel on respiratory and related viruses NIH, 1960-64, mem. bd. for virus reference reagents, 1962-64, mem. vaccine devel. com., 1967-70; chmn. pub. health and preventive medicine test com. Nat. Bd. Med. Examiners, 1962-65; mem. com. epidemiology and vet. followup studies Nat. Acad. Scis-NRC, 1965—, health adv. com. Region III, Dept. Health, Edn. and Welfare, 1967-71; mem. infectious diseases adv. com. Nat. Inst. Allergy and Infectious Diseases, 1970—, chmn., 1970-71; sci. adv. com. Nat. Found., 1959—. Served to lt. USNR, 1943-46. Markle scholar med. sci., 1953-58. Diplomate Am. Bd. Preventive Medicine, Am. Bd. Microbiology. Mem. Assn. Am. Physicians, A.M.A., Am. Acad. Microbiology, Am. Epidemiol. Soc., A.A.A.S., Am. Thoracic Soc., Infectious Diseases Soc. Am., Am. Assn. Im- munologists, Am. Soc. Clin. Investigation, Am. Fedn. Clin. Research, Am. Pub. Health Assn., Soc. Med. Cons. Armed Forces, Central Soc. Clin. Research (sec.-treas. 1957), So. Soc. Clin. Research, Soc. Exptl. Biology and Medicine, Assn. Tchrs. Preventive Medicine (sec. 1965-67), Phi Beta Kappa, Sigma Xi, Alpha Omega Alpha, Alpha Tau Omega. Episcopalian. Contbr. sci. papers. Editorial bd. Am. Rev. Respiratory Diseases, 1962-65. Home: 1775 Mooreland Dr Lexington KY 40502

JORDAN, WINTHROP DONALDSON, educator, historian; b. Worchester, Mass., Nov. 11, 1931; s. Henry Donaldson and Lucretia Mott (Churchill) J.; grad. Phillips Acad., Andover, Mass., 1949; student Marlborough (Eng.) Coll., 1949-50; A.B., Harvard, 1953; M.A., Clark U., 1957; Ph.D., Brown U., 1960; m. Phyllis Henry, Aug. 30, 1952; children—Joshua H., J. Mott, W. Eliot. With Prudential Life Ins. Co., 1953-54; instr. Phillips Exeter Acad., 1955- 56; lectr. Brown U., 1959-61; fellow Inst. Early Am. History and Culture, Williamsburg, Va., 1961-63; mem. faculty U. Cal. at Berkeley, 1963—, prof. history, 1969—, asso. dean minority group affairs, grad. div., 1968-70. Recipient Ralph Waldo Emerson award, 1968; Parkman prize, 1969; Nat. Book award in history and biography, 1969; Bancroft prize, 1969; Guggenheim fellow, 1966; Social Sci. Research Council fellow, 1966; fellow Charles Warren Center Study Am. History, 1966. Author: White Over Black: American Attitudes toward the Negro 1550-1812, 1968. Home: 1107 Milvia St Berkeley CA 94707

JORDAN, ZACHARY mfg. exec.; b. Lima, O., Apr. 1, 1932; B.S., U. San Francisco, 1954; M.S., Stanford University, 1956; m. Rosemarie Lois Brown, May 15, 1955; 1 son, Anthony Robinson. Sales rep. Ames-Brockton Fabricated Products, Akron, O., 1956-58, sales mgr. Coshocton, Ohio, 1959-61, gen. manager plant, 1961-68, v.p. sales, 1968--. Instr. bus. Coshocton Jr. College, 1968-69. Secretary Coshocton YMCA, 1960-61; active Boy Scouts of America. Named Man of Year, Coshocton Junior Chamber of Commerce, 1968. Mem. Coshocton C. of C. (vice president 1967-68, pres. 1969-70), English Speaking Union, Coshocton Sertoma Club, Nat. Assn. Mfrs., Sales Executives Institute, Phi Beta Kappa, Sigma Chi, Phi Mu. Democrat. Mem. Christian Ch. (lay leader). Mason (32, Shriner). Clubs: Coshocton Country, Coshocton City, Running Deer Country. Home: 2d Av Coshocton OH Office: 3d Av Coshocton OH

JORDEN, WILLIAM JOHN, govt. ofcl.; b. Bridger, Mont., May 3, 1923; s. Hugh G. and Jane Ann (Temple) J.; B.A. with honors, Yale, 1947; M.S., Columbia, 1948; m. Eleanor Harz, Mar. 3, 1944; children—William Temple, Eleanor Harz, Marion Telva. Instr. Japanese, Yale, 1945-46: reporter Vineyard Gazette, Edgartown,

Mass., 1947; radio news writer N.Y. Herald Tribune, 1948; fgn. corr. A.P., Japan and Korea, 1948-52, N.Y. Times, Japan and Korea, 1952-55, USSR, 1956-58, Washington bur., 1958-61; mem. Policy Planning Council, State Dept., 1961-62, spl. asst. to under sec. polit. affairs, 1962-65, dep. asst. sec. state pub. affairs, 1965-66; sr. mem. staff NSC, 1966-68; mem., spokesman Am. delegation Vietnam Peace Talks, Paris, France, 1968-69; asst. to former Pres. Lyndon B. Johnson, 1969—. Pulitzer traveling fellow, 1948-49; Council Fgn. Relations fellow, 1955-56. Mem. Council Fgn. Relations, Austin Com. on Fgn. Relations. Clubs: Yale (Austin); Foreign Correspondents of Japan (pres. 1952-53). Co- author: Japan Between East and West. Home: Westgate Apts Austin TX 78701 Office: Fed Office Bldg Austin TX 78701

JORDY, WILLIAM HENRY, educator; b. Poughkeepsie, N.Y., Aug. 31, 1917; s. Elwood Banjamin and Caroline May (Hill) J.; B.A., Bard Coll., 1939, L.H.D., 1968; postgrad. Inst. Fine Arts, N.Y. U., 1939-42; Ph.D., Yale, 1948; m. Sarah Stoughton Spock, July 25, 1942. Instr., then asst. prof. art and Am. civilization Yale, 1948-55; faculty Brown U., Providence, 1955—, prof. art, 1960—, chmn. dept., 1963-66. Mem. Coll. Art Assn., Soc. Archtl. Historians, Am. Studies Assn., Victorian Soc. Author: Henry Adams, Scientific Historian, 1952. Editor: (with Ralph Coe) Montgomery Schuyler, American Architecture and Other Writings, 1961. Cons.: Arts of the United States, 1960. Contbr. articles to profl. jours. Home: 55 Bond Rd Riverside RI 02915 Office: Brown U Providence RI 02912

JORGENSEN, ARNOLD TANG, utility exec.; b. Huntington, N.Y., Feb. 14, 1914; s. John T. and Ketty (Rasmussen) J.; B.S., N.Y.U., 1937; m. Francise Chouteau, Nov. 26, 1936; children—Erik, Karen (Mrs. Lionel Tremblay), Mark. Cadet engr. L.I. Lighting Co., N.Y., 1941-42, various positions in operations, 1942-65, v.p. charge prodn., gas prodn. operations, 1965-69, sr. v.p., Mineola, N.Y., 1969—. Mem. Am. Soc. M.E., Engrs. Club N.Y.C., Am. Gas Assn., Edison Electric Inst., L.I. Assn. Club: Huntington (N.Y.) Country. Home: Split Rock Rd East Norwich NY 11732 Office: 250 Old Country Rd Mineola NY 11501

JORGENSEN, CHARLES JOSEPH, educator; b. Springfield, Ill., Feb. 17, 1910; s. C. Chris and May (Bishop) J.; B.S., U. Ill., 1931; Ph.D., U. Wash., 1962; m. Mary A. Huston, Dec. 1, 1935; children—Jane (Mrs. J.C. Russell), Margaret (Mrs. T.R. Dick). Commd. 1st lt., arty., U.S. Army, 1941, advanced through grades to lt. col., 1951; comdg. officer F.A. batteries, 1941-42, 50-51, 52-53; assigned F.A. Sch., 1942-44, staff 1st Army, 1953-56; retired, 1958; asst. prof. econs. U. Wash., 1962-63; prof. econs., head dept. econs. and bus. adminstrn. Norwich U., Northfield, Vt., 1962-70; prof. econs. Rollins Coll., Winter Park, Fla., 1970—. Decorated Bronze Star. Mem. Am. Econ. Assn., Am. Econ. History Assn. Home: 1640 Forest Av Winter Park FL 32789

JORGENSEN, EARLE MOGENSEN, steel distbr.; b. San Francisco, June 22, 1898; s. Neils Frederick Daniel and Maren (Mogensen) J.; ed. pub. schs.; m. Beatrice Griffin, Sept. 27, 1924 (dec.); children—John W., Earle M., B. Wayne (Mrs. Ted Beem), Maren (Mrs. Jorgensen Cummings); m. 2d, Marion Newbert. Founder, Earle M. Jorgensen Co., Los Angeles, 1923, now chmn. bd., chief exec. officer; dir. Northrop Corp., Rheem Mfg. Co., Kerr McGee Corp. Trustee Cal. Inst. Tech. Clubs: Pacific Union (San Francisco); Los Angeles Country, California (Los Angeles); Hollywood Turf (dir.). Office: 10650 S Alameda St Los Angeles CA 90054

JORGENSEN, JENS, mill operator, rancher; b. Yacolt, Wash., Feb. 27, 1906; s. Jens and Elise (Gabriel) J.; ed. pub. schs.; m. Ellen May Schnick, May 9, 1938; children—Phyllis Anne (Mrs. Darrel Mulkey), Richard Jens. Engaged in sawmilling, logging, 1932; with Port Orford Cedar Co., 1932-42, Coos Bay Lumber Co., 1942-56; with Ga.-Pacific Corp., 1956-71, gen. mgr. Western plywood and lumber prodn., 1963-64, v.p. plywood prodn., 1964-71; now Sawmill and cedar shake mill operator, rancher. Co.-chmn. bldg. com. Coquille Community Bldg., 1951—. Recipient President's Achievement award Ga. Pacific Corp., 1964. Elk, Mason. Home: Route 1 Box 400 Coquille OR 97423

JORGENSEN, JOHN WARREN, steel co. exec.; b. Los Angeles, July 25, 1925; s. Earle M. and Beatrice (Griffin) J.; student Tex. A. and M. Coll., 1944; B.A., Pomona Coll., 1948; m. Jacquelyn Luckow, Jan. 22, 1949; children—Maren R., Sidney Jill, John Warren. With Earle M. Jorgensen Co., Los Angeles, 1949—, v.p., 1962-67, pres., chief adminstrv. officer, 1967—, also dir., mem. exec. com. Bd. dirs. Los Angeles YMCA; chmn. bd. trustees Flintridge Prep. Sch., Pasadena. Served with USNR, World War II. Mem. Steel Service Center Inst. (chmn. exec. com.), Nat. Assn. Aluminum Distbrs. (v.p., dir.). Clubs: California, Los Angeles Yacht (Los Angeles); Pacific Union, Family (San Francisco); Annandale Golf (Pasadena); Indian Wells Country (Palm Desert, Cal.). Home: 1590 Shenandoah Rd San Marino CA 91108 Office: 10650 S Alameda St Los Angeles CA 90054

JORGENSEN, OVE WOODROW, electrical products mfg. co. exec.; b. Erwin, S.D., Aug. 19, 1915; s. Jorgen and Thora (Christensen) J.; student Minot (N.D.) Tchrs. Coll., 1933-35, Minot Bus. Inst., 1935—, La Salle Extension U., 1940-42, Alexander Hamilton Bus. Inst., 1949-51; m. Winifred Mae Bakeman, Dec. 24, 1939; children—Susan Gay, Jay Ove. Accountant, Internat. Harvester Co., Minot, 1936-42; with Packard Motor Car Co., 1944-56, adminstrv. asst. to v.p. finance, asst. sec., 1954-62; v.p. finance Essex Wire Corp., Ft. Wayne, Ind., 1956-65, exec. v.p. finance, 1966—, also dir., mem. exec. com.; dir. 1st Fed. Savs. & Loan, Ft. Wayne. Bd. dirs. Parkview Hosp., Fort Wayne, Jr. Achievement, Ft. Wayne. Served with USAAF, 1942-44. Mem. Financial Exec. Inst. (adv. counsel), Am. Legion (past post comdr.). Presbyn. Clubs: Pere Marquette Rod and Gun (Baldwin, Mich.); Ft. Wayne Country, 100, Executives, Summit (dir.) (Ft. Wayne); Thunderbird Country (Palm Springs, Cal.). Home: 2934 Covington Lake Dr Fort Wayne IN 46804 Office: 1601 Wall St Fort Wayne IN 46804

JORGENSEN, PAUL ALFRED, educator; b. Lansing, Mich., Feb. 17, 1916; s. Karl and Rose Josephine (Simmons) J.; A.B., Santa Barbara State Coll., 1938; M.A., U. Cal. at Berkeley, 1940, Ph.D., 1945; m. Virginia Frances Elfrink, Jan. 3, 1942; children—Mary Catherine, Elizabeth Ross. Instr. English, Bakersfield (Cal.) Jr. Coll., 1945-46, U. Cal. at Berkeley, summer 1946, U. Cal. at Davis, 1946-47; mem. faculty U. Cal. at Los Angeles, 1947—, prof. English, 1960—; vis. prof. U. Wash., summer 1966; mem. editorial com. U. Cal. Press, 1957-60; humanities inst. U. Cal., 1967-69. Guggenheim fellow, 1956-57. Mem. Modern Lang. Assn., Shakespeare Assn. Am. (bibliographer 1954-59), Renaissance Soc. Am., Philol. Assn. Pacific Coast (exec. com. 1962-63). Episcopalian. Author: Shakespeare's Military World, 1956; (with Frederick B. Shroyer) A College Treasury, rev. edit., 1967; (with Shroyer) The Informal Essay, 1961; Redeeming Shakespeare's Words, 1962. Editor: The Comedy of Errors, 1964; Othello: An Outline- Guide to the Play, 1964; (with Shroyer) The Art of Prose, 1965; Lear's Self-Discovery, 1967; Our Naked Frailties; Sensational Art and Meaning in Macbeth, 1971. Mem. bd. editors Film Quar., 1958-65, Huntington Library Quar., 1965—, Coll. English, 1966-70. Home: 234 Tavistock Av Los Angeles CA 90049

JORGENSEN, ROBERT RICHARD, retail store exec.; b. Chgo., Aug. 7, 1911; s. Robert and Mary Blanche (Moore) J.; Ph.B., U. Chgo., 1933; J.D., DePaul U., 1943; m. Meta Elizabeth Bixby, Nov. 23, 1940; children—Marta Kay, Laura Christine. Karen (Mrs. Dowling). Admitted to Ill. bar, 1943; with Sears, Roebuck & Co., Chgo., 1933—, dir. taxes, 1953-65, divisional v.p. taxes, 1965-68, v.p. taxes, 1968—; instr. taxation U. Chgo., 1946-51. Served to lt. USNR, 1944-46. Mem. Am., Fed., Chgo. bar assns., Tax Execs. Inst. Presbyn. Clubs: Mid-Day (Chgo.); Capital Hill, Nat. Lawyers (Washington); Glen Oak Country (Glen Ellyn). Home: 654 Park Blvd Glen Ellyn IL 60137 Office: 925 S Homan Av Chicago IL 60607

JORGENSEN, WILLIAM ERNEST, librarian; b. Heber, Utah, Oct. 13, 1913; s. George Michael and Mary Annette (Jackman) J.; B.A. summa cum laude, U. Ida., 1938; certificate librarianship U. Cal. at Berkeley, 1940; M.A., Ore. State U., 1942; m. Margaret Louise Boyle, May 25, 1940; children—Robert Ernest, Barry Steven, Mollie Ann. Engring. librarian Ore. State U., 1940-42; supr. tech. data sect., frequency change dept. So. Cal. Edison Co., 1945-46; chief librarian research library Naval Electronics Lab. Center, San Diego, 1946—; John Cotton Dana lectr. U. Cal. at Los Angeles, 1964. Mem. investment bd. Coronado Mgmt. Corp., 1970—. Mem. inter-library task group San Diego Ednl. Resources Project, 1960—; library com. Fine Arts Soc. San Diego, 1965-67; chmn. 10th Mil. Librarian Workshop, 1966; mem. Navy Research Library Council W. Coast, 1955—; expert examiner U.S. Civil Service Examiners for So. Cal. Navy Labs., 1951-68; mem. Com. for Assos. Sci. Libraries San Diego, 1963—; adv. council edn. for Librarianship U. Cal., Berkeley, Los Angeles, 1965-68. Bd. dirs. San Diego chpt. Am. Civil Liberties Union, 1971—. Served to lt. comdr. USNR, 1942-45. Mem. Cal. Library Assn. (pres. Palomar dist. 1963, councilor 1967-70), Spl. Libraries Assn. (chmn. engring. sect. 1950), U. Cal. Schs. Librarianship Alumni Assn. (pres. 1963), Am. Badminton Assn., Phi Beta Kappa, Phi Kappa Phi. Author: The Use of a Technical Library, 1942; Naval Electronics Laboratory Reliability Bibliography, 1956-58; Navy Electronics Laboratory and the Point Loma Military Reservation, A Collection of Historical Photographs, 1966. Editor: procs. Tenth Military Librarians Workshop, 1966. Contbr. articles to profl. jours. Home: 4139 Atascadero Dr San Diego CA 92107 Office: 271 Catalina Blvd San Diego CA 92152

JORGENSON, DALE WELDEAU, economist, educator; b. Bozeman, Mont., May 7, 1933 s. Emmett B. and Jewell (Torkelson) J.; B.A., Reed Coll., 1955; A.M., Harvard, 1957, Ph.D., 1959; m. Margaret Irma Jefraim, Aug. 17, 1957 (dec. Mar. 1970). Mem. faculty U. Cal. at Berkeley, 1959-69, prof. econs., 1963-69; prof. econs. Harvard, 1969—; Ford research prof. econs. U. Chgo., 1962-63. Fellow Econometric Soc., Am. Statis. Assn. (asso. editor Jour. 1962-64); mem. Am. Econ. Assn., Royal Econ. Soc. Author: (with J.J. McCall, R. Radner) Optimal Replacement Policy, 1967. Am. editor Rev. Econ. Studies, 1964-67; editor Am. Econ. Rev., 1967—. Contbr. articles profl. jours. Home: 1010 Memorial Dr Cambridge MA 02138

JORN, ASGER, artist; b. Mar. 3, 1914. Studied with Leger; collaborator with Le Corbusier on Temps Nouveaux Pavailion, Paris Universal Exhbn., 1937; co- founder Cobra internat, group; exhibited paintings, engravings, sculpture, ceramics at First Exhbn. Exptl. Art, Amsterdam, Netherlands, 1949, Brussels (Belgium) Internat. Exhbn., 1958, Dunn Internat. Exhbn., London, Eng., 1963. numerous others. Address; 28 rue du Tage Paris 13e, France.*

JORSTAD, LOUIS HELMAR surgeon; b. Morris, Ill., Sept. 16, 1896; s. Omund L. and Rebecca (Larson) J.; student U. Ill., 1917-19; M.D., Washington U., St. Louis, 1924; m. Cleone Branian, Dec. 26, 1924; 1 dau., Meredith. Asst. prof. bacteriology and pathology Washington U. Sch. Dentistry, 1926-39, asso. prof. oncology, 1949—; dir. pathology Barnard Free Skin and Cancer Hosp., 1926-38, surgeon-in-chief head and neck service, 1938-47; cons. surgeon U.S. Marine Hosp., Kirkwood, Mo., 1940-53; surgeon, gen. staff St. Lukes, Jewish, Mo. Bapt. hosps., 1931-61; cons., surg. staff Ellis Fischel State Cancer, St. Lukes, Frisco hosps. Mem. profl. bd. Am. Cancer Soc., 1943-45, Mo. chmn., 1938-48 Recipient Distinguished Service award Miss. Valley Med. Soc., 1948. Mem. A.M.A., Internat. Coll. Surgeons, Am. Radium Soc., Am. Assn. Cancer Research, A.C.S., Am. Assn. Advancement Oral Diagnosis, Soc. Exptl. Biology and Medicine, So. Med. Assn., Miss. Valley Med. Soc. Republican. Mason. Club: University (St. Louis). Author: Surgery of the Breast, 1964. Contbr. articles to profl. publs Home: 7314 Westmoreland Drive St Louis MO 63130 Office: 3720 Washington Blvd St Louis MO 63108

JORY, WILLIAM HENRY, shipbuilder; b. Glenburnie, Md., Sept. 19, 1910; s. William Henry and Helena (Helmer) J.; student naval architecture Md. Inst., 1935; m. Mary Ellen Seidenstricker, Mar. 1, 1932; children—John Helmer, William Henry, Holly. Salesman, then estimator, asst. to v.p. Md. Shipbuilding & Dry Dock Co., 1928-46, asst. to pres., 1946-51, v.p., 1951-56, sr. v.p., dir., 1956-62; pres. Am. Shipbldg. Co., Lorain, 1962-67, also dir., former chief exec. officer; pres., dir. Modern Terminals, Inc., Wayne, Mich.; chmn. Am. Submarine Div., Lorain, O.; chmn. Cin. Sheet Metal & Roofing Co.; chmn. Automobile Transport. Inc., Wayne, Mich.; dir. Lorain Nat. Bank. Mem. Soc. Naval Architects and Marine Engrs., Am. Bur. Shipping, Soc. Naval Engrs., Shipbuilders Council Am. (v.p., dir.), Greater Lorain C. of C. (dir.). Clubs: Union, Cleve. Athletic; Propeller U.S.; University, Whitehall. Home: 260 Overbrook Rd Gulf Farms Elyria OH 44035

JOSE, JAMES ROBERT, coll. dean; b. Pitts., Jan. 7, 1939; s. John Frederick and Helen Louise (Hunter) J.; B.A., Mt. Union Coll., 1960; M. Internat. Relations, Am. U., 1962, Ph.D., 1968; m. Joyce Ann Mosser, June 10, 1961; children—Anna Mansfield, Andrew Douglass. Registrar, adminstrv. asst. to acad. dean, instr. polit. sci. Mt. Union Coll., 1963-65; asst. dean, asst. prof. internat. relations Am. U., 1965-70; dean of coll., prof. polit. sci. Lycoming Coll., 1970—; lectr. U.S. Mil. Acad., Fgn. Service Inst., U.S. Dept. State. Bd. dirs. UN Assn. of U.S.A. Named Outstanding Young Man of Am., U.S. Jr. C. of C., 1967. Mem. Am. Polit. Sci. Assn., Phi Kappa Phi, Pi Gamma Mu, Pi Sigma Alpha. Author: An Inter-American Peacekeeping Force Within the Framework of the Organization of American States, 1970; The Political Dynamics of International Organization, in preparation. Contbr. to America's World Role in the 70's (A.A. Said, Ed.), 1970. Home: 816 Faxon Pkwy Williamsport PA 17701

JOSEPH, ALEXANDER HENRY, mag. editor; b. Pitts., July 30, 1911; s. Charles Homer and Caroline (Schoenfeld) J.; grad. Shady Side Acad., Pitts., 1930; A.B., Princeton, 1934; m. Betty York, Mar. 31, 1941 (dec. 1970); children—Alexander Henry, Ann; m. 2d, Ruth Y. Magid, May 31, 1971. Reporter, picture editor Pitts. Sun-Telegraph, 1934-41; picture editor, asst. news editor Phila. Inquirer, 1941-53; asso. editor TV Guide Radnor, Pa., 1953-59, mng. editor, 1959—. Spl. lectr. journalism U. Pa., 1945-54. Home: 1610 Cloverly Lane Rydal PA 19046 Office: TV Guide Radnor PA 19087

JOSEPH, BURTON M., grain mcht.; b. Mpls., Apr. 2, 1921; s. I.S. and Anna J.; B.A., U. Minn., 1942; m. Geraldine, Apr. 2, 1953; children—Shelley, Scott, Jonathan. Vice pres. I.S. Joseph Co., Inc., Mpls., 1945-53, pres., 1953- -. Commr., Duluth Port Authority, Mpls. Human Relations Commn.; treas. Nat. Commn. Anti-Defamation League. Trustee Am. Freedom from Hunger Found.; trustee, bd. govs. Hebrew Union Coll.- Jewish Inst. Religion. Home: 5 Red Cedar Lane Minneapolis MN 55410 Office: Flour Exchange Bldg Minneapolis MN 55415

JOSEPH, DANIEL DONALD, educator, aero. engr.; b. Chgo., Mar. 26, 1929; s. Samuel and Mary (Simon) J.; M.A., U. Chgo., 1950; B.S. in Mech. Engring., Ill. Inst. Tech., 1959, M.S., 1960, Ph.D., 1963; m. Ellen Broida, Dec. 18, 1949; children—Karen, Michael, Charles. Asst. prof. mech. engring. Ill. Inst. Tech., 1962-63; mem. faculty U. Minn., 1963—, asso. prof. fluid mechanics dept. aeros. and engring. mechanics, 1965-69, prof. aerospace engring. and mechanics, 1969—. Guggenheim fellow, 1969-70. Mem. Am. Phys. Soc., Am. Soc. M.E. (sponsor in hydrodynamics 1966—), Soc. Nat. Philol. Contbr. articles to sci. jours. Asso. editor Archtl. Rating Mech. Jour., Jour. Applied Mechanics. Contbns. to math. theory of hydrodynamic stability; methods for determining quantitative conditions for change of one fluid motion into another, e.g. laminar to turbulent flow. Home: 3156 Shorewood Dr St Paul MN 55112 Office: U Minn Minneapolis MN 55455

JOSEPH, EDWARD DAVID, psychiatrist; b. Pitts., Aug. 26, 1919; s. A. Pinto and Hortense (Ury) J.; B.Sc., McGill U., 1941, M.D., C.M., 1943; postgrad. N.Y. Psychoanalytic Inst., 1949-55; m. Harriet Bloomfield, Aug. 16, 1942; children—Leila, Alan, Brian. Intern, Montreal (Que., Can.) Gen. Hosp., 1943-44; resident, fellow in psychiatry Mt. Sinai Hosp., N.Y.C., 1947-49, coordinator in-patient psychiat. service, 1965-71, clin. dir. psychiatry, 1971—, attending psychiatrist, 1949—; practice medicine, specializing in psychiatry and psychoanalysis, N.Y.C., 1949—; tng. analyst N.Y. Psychoanalytic Inst., 1964—, lectr., 1962—; prof. psychiatry Mt Sinai Med. Sch., N.Y.C., 1968—. Served to capt., M.C., AUS, 1944-46. Mem. Am. Psychoanalytic Assn. (exec. councilor 1962-67, treas. 1967-72, pres. 1972-73), N.Y. Psychoanalytic Soc. (sec. 1965-67), Am. Psychiat. Assn., A.A.A.S., Westchester Mental Health Assn. Club: Town (Scarsdale). Editor: Kris Monograph Series, 1965—; asso. editor Psychoanalytic Quar., 1965—. Contbr. articles profl. jours. Home: 9 Putnam Rd Scarsdale NY 10583 Office: 1 E 100th St New York City NY 10029

JOSEPH, GABE, newspaper exec.; b. Fargo, N.D., July 6, 1907; s. Abraham and Mabel (Scoth) J.; B.A., U. Mich., 1930; m. Janet Bachenheimer, June 25, 1938; 1 dau., Betty (Mrs. Jerome Abeles). With Chicago Tribune, 1930-41; joined Chgo. Sun-Times, formerly Chgo. Sun, 1941, asst. advt. dir. and retail mgr., 1950-52, advt. mgr., 1952-63; v.p., advt. mgr. Chgo. Sun- Times and Chgo. Daily News, 1963—, also mem. newspaper div. exec. com. and mgmt. bd. Vice chmn. Chgo. Better Bus. Bur., 1960—. Mem. advt. com. Chgo., 1957—; chmn. Glencoe (Ill.) Park Bd., 1957; pres. Glencoe Adv. Com., 1964; mem. Glencoe Youth Activities Com., 1959. Mem. Newspaper Advt. Execs. Assn. Clubs: Standard (Chgo.); Northmoor Country (Richland Park, Ill). Home: 611 Longwood Dr Glencoe IL 60022 Office: 401 N Wabash Av Chicago IL 60611

JOSEPH, GEORGE G., life ins. co. exec; b. Sault Ste. Marie. Mich., Nov. 9, 1918; B.A., Wooster Coll., 1940. With New Eng. Mut. Life Ins. Co., Boston 1947—. dir. agys., 1959-60, 2d v.p., 1960-64, now sr. v.p. Pres. Newark Assn. Life Underwriters, 1956, N.J. Life Underwriters Assn., 1958, N.J. Gen. Agts. and mgrs. Assn., 1955. C.L.U. Mem. Boston Life Underwriters Assn. Home: 21 Greylock Rd Wellesley MA Office: 501 Boylston St Boston MA*

JOSEPH, JAMES, educator, physicist; b. Berlin, Germany, Feb. 3, 1926; s. Nathan and Janet (Glatzer) J.; came to U.S., 1934, naturalized, 1942; B.S., Bklyn. Coll., 1949; Ph.D., State U. Ia., 1956; m. Phyllis Patricia Schuman, Aug. 16, 1952; children—Jonathan Brian, Stephen Philip. Asst. prof. physics Ia. State U., 1955-57; asso. prof. physics St. John's U., N.Y.C., 1957-63, prof., chmn. dept. physics, 1964—; vis. prof. physics Inst. Theoretical Physics, U. Geneva, 1963-64; prin. investigator NASA grant, 1962-64; cons. investigator grants by NSF and Air Force Office Sci. Research. Served with AUS, 1944-45. Mem. Am. Phys. Soc., Sigma Xi. Home: 9 Hartley Rd Great Neck NY 11023 Office: St Johns U Dept Physics Jamaica NY 11432

JOSEPH, JOHN J., lawyer; b. Marathon, O., July 27, 1899; s. Frank A. and Ella Maria (Hensel) J.; A.B., Ohio Wesleyan U., 1920; LL.B., Western Res. U., 1928; LL.D., Bowling Green (O.) State U., 1943; m. Dorothy S. Griswold, Dec. 21, 1952. Serveral positions 1917-1928, including instr. polit. sci. Western Res. U., instr. Law Sch., 1942—; admitted to Ohio bar. 1928, practiced in Cleve., 1928-29; with Ohio Bell Telephone Co., 1929—, plant supr., 1929-33, directory advt. sales mgr., 1933-35, asst. to v.p., 1935-37. asst. v.p., 1937-48, v.p. charge pub. relations, 1948-63; asso. firm Claypool & Joseph. Columbus, O., 1963—; owner Clermont Farms, Danville, O., 1949—; exec. v.p., Citizens Holding Co., Columbus, 1965—; v.p. Am. Securities Co., Columbus; chmn. bd. dirs. Clinton Energy Producers Inc.; dir. First State Bank & Trust Co. of Columbus, Colonial Heritage Life Ins. Co., Danville Bank (O.), Ohio Farmers Ins. Co., The Ohio Farmers Indemnity Co. Mem. Selective Service Bd., Cleveland. 1941-46. Bd. dirs. Ohio Council on Econ. Edn.; life trustee Ohio Wesleyan U. Mem. Am., Ohio bar assns., Am. Judicature Soc., Ohio C. of C., U.S. C. of C., Omicron Delta Kappa, Phi Delta Phi, Alpha Tau Omega (chmn. high council 1954-58, Province chief, Ohio, 1937-46), Republican. Methodist. Mason. Clubs: Advertising, Athletic (Cleve.); University (Columbus). Home: Clermont Farms Danville KS 43014 Office: 88 E Broad St Columbus OH 43215

JOSEPH, JULES KAUFMAN, pub. relations exec.; b. Cin., Jan. 18, 1925; s. Leslie Bloch and Ellen (Kaufman) J.; B.A., U. Wis., 1946; m. Elizabeth Levy, Sept. 9, 1948; children—Ellen Beth, Barbara Ann, John Charles. Reporter, Cin. Enquirer, 1946; asst. editor Hosp. Mgmt., Chgo., 1947-48; mem. press relations staff Gimbels, Milw., 1948-52; bur. chief Fairchild Publs., Milw., 1952-60; co-founder, co-owner, exec. v.p. Zigman-Joseph Associates in Pub. Relations, Milw., 1960—. Pres. Friends of Art, of Milw. Art Center, 1961-62; v.p. Milwaukee County Mental Health, 1967. Bd. dirs. Milw. Repertory Theatre, Episcopalian Camp Webb; v.p. bd. dirs. Mid-Am. Ballet Co. Served with USNR, World War II. Mem. Pub. Relation Soc. Am. (treas. Wis.), Sigma Delta Chi, Phi Kappa Phi. Esiscopalian. Home: 5028 N Lake Dr Milwaukee WI 53217 Office: 208 E Wisconsin St Milwaukee WI 53202

JOSEPH, KEITH SINJOHN, Brit. govt. ofcl.; b. London, Eng., Jan. 17, 1918; s. Samuel and Edna Cicely (Philips) J.; ed. Harrow, 1931-36; M.A., Magdalen Coll., Oxford U., 1939, fellow All Souls Coll., 1946-60; m. Hellen Louise Guggenheimer, July 6, 1951; children—James, Emma, Julia, Anna. In bldg. constrn., 1945-59; mem. Parliament for Leeds North East, 1956—; parliamentary sec. to Ministry Housing and Local Govt., 1959-61; minister of state Bd. of Trade, 1961-62; minister housing and local govt., also minister for Welsh affairs, 1962-64. Dir. Gilbert-Ash Ltd., 1949-59; Bovis Holdings Ltd., 1951-59, deputy chmn., 1964- -; chmn. Bovis Ltd., 1958-59; founder, first chmn. Mulberry Housing Trust, 1964-70.

Co-founder, 1st chmn. Found. for Mgmt. Edn. Served with Brit. Army, 1939-45. Succeeded to baronetcy, 1943. Jewish religion. Address: 23 Mulberry Walk London SW 3 England

JOSEPH, RICHARD, writer, travel commentator; b. N.Y.C., Apr. 24, 1910; s. Isaac and Harriet Maurine (Isaacson) J.; B.S., Ohio State U., 1932; postgrad. Alliance Francaise, Paris, France, 1937-38; m. Morgan Howard, Sept. 5, 1954; children—Jamieson Anne, Richard Matthew. Reporter, Columbus (O.) Citizen, 1932, N.Y. Evening Jour., 1933-37, N.Y. Post, 1939-40; dir. Walt Disney-Mickey Mouse, S.A., Paris, 1937-39; engaged in pub. relations, 1940-42; asso. editor Esquire mag., 1946-47, travel editor, 1947—; travel columnist N.Y. Post, Chgo. Tribune-N.Y. News Syndicate, 1959- -; travel commentator NBC TV, 1956-59, CBS Radio Network, 1961-65. Served AUS, 1942-46; ETO. Decorated Croix de Guerre (France) Recipient Star of Solidarity (Italy); Travel Journalism award Am. Soc. Travel Agts., 1950, 51, 56; Pacific Area Travel Assn., 1961, 62, 65, 67, Ethiopian Airlines, 1964, Trans World Airlines, 1952-62, 64-69; Strebig Dobben award, 1963; George Hedman Meml. award, 1966; officer Ordre de Merite Touristique (France), 1962. Mem. Soc. Am. Travel Writers (bd. govs. 1960-63), N.Y. Travel Writers Assn. (pres. 1949-51). Club: Overseas Press, Silurians (N.Y.C.). Author: Your Trip Abroad, 1950; Your Trip to Britain, 1951; Richard Joseph's World Wide Travel Guide, 1952; A Letter to the Man Who Killed My Dog, 1956; Richard Joseph's Comprehensive Guide to Europe, 1956; Esquire's Europe in Style Contbr. numerous articles to various publs. Home: Goshen CT also 303 E 33d St New York City NY 10016 Office: 488 Madison Av New York City NY 10022

JOSEPHS, DEVEREUX COLT, bus. exec.; b. Newport, R.I., Oct. 16, 1893; s. Lyman Colt and Alice Vernon (Wilson) J.; grad. Groton (Mass.) School, 1911; A.B., Harvard, 1915, LL.D., 1957; m. Margaret Thayer Graham, June 26, 1922; children—Margaret G. (Mrs. Peter B. Nalle). Devereux Colt. In investment banking, 1915-39; with Tchrs. Ins. and Annuity Assn., 1939-45; pres. Carnegie Corp. of N.Y., 1946-48; retired as chmn. bd. N.Y. Life Ins. Co., 1959; bd. Ednl. Broadcasting Corp. (channel 13). Dir. Met. Mus. Art, N.Y. Pub. Library. Republican. Episcopalian. Clubs: Century Assn., Harvard (N.Y.C.). Home: 200 E 66th St New York City NY 10021 Office: 51 Madison Av New York City NY 10010

JOSEPHS, JESS J., educator, physicist; b. N.Y.C., Jan. 4, 1917; s. Jacob I. and Mollie (Barouch) J.; A.B., N.Y. U., 1938, M.Sc., 1940, Ph.D., 1943; m. Margaret Milroy, June 22, 1962; children—John Lewis III (stepson), Kenneth, Nancy Lewis (stepdau.), David. Instr. phys. chemistry Northwestern U., 1946- 47; asst. prof. phys. scis. U. Chgo., 1947-50; asst. prof. physics Boston U., 1950-56, prof. physics Atmosphere Physics Lab., Boston U., 1951-54; faculty Smith Coll., 1956—. Served with USNR, 1943-46. Mem. Am. Phys. Soc., Am. Assn. Physics Tchrs., Am. Chem. Soc., Sigma Xi, Phi Lambda Upsilon. Author: The Physics of Musical Sound, 1967. Home: 56 Ward Av Northampton MA 01060

JOSEPHS, RAY, pub. relations cons., writer; b. Phila., Jan. 1, 1912; s. Isaac and Eva (Borsky) J.; student U. Pa., 1927-29; m. Juanita Wegner, Feb. 22, 1941. Staff writer Phila. Evening Bull., 1929-40; columnist Buenos Aires Herald, 1940-44; Latin-Am. corr., 1940—, representing at various times Wash. Post, Christian Sci. Monitor, Pitts. Post-Gazette, Newark Star Ledger, Chgo. Sun, P.M., Variety, Nat. Monthly, others; pres. Internat. Pub. Relations Co., Ltd., N.Y.C.; pres., chmn. bd. Ray Josephs Pub. Relations, Ltd., Ray Josephs Assos., Inc., pub. relations cons. maj. industries, comml. concerns. Lectr., Columbia Inst. Arts and Scis., Ind. U., Cornell Coll., Sweet Briar, Union Coll., Town Hall of West, San Francisco, Detroit, Indpls., Atlanta, Louisville, Spokane, Los Angeles Town Halls, numerous forums, town meetings from coast to coast; broadcaster NBC, CBS, MBS, cons. on Latin Am. affairs to coordinater Inter-Am. Affairs Brit. Ministry Information, RKO Radio Pictures, Asso. Export Adv. Agys. Mem. Brandels U. Devel. Council. Mem. Writers Guild Am., Soc. Mag. Writers. Author: Argentine Diary, 1944; Spies and Saboteurs in Argentina, 1943; Latin America: Continent in Crisis, 1948; (with former Ambassador James Bruce) Those Perplexing Argentines, 1952; How to Make Money from Your Ideas. 1954; How to Gain an Extra Hour Every Day, 1955; (with David Kemp) Memoirs of a Live Wire, 1956; Streamlining Your Executive Workload, 1958; (with Oscar Steiner) Our Housing Jungle and Your Pocketbook, 1960; (with Stanley Arnold) The Magic Power of Putting Yourself Over with People, 1962 (books pub. in Brit., French, Japanese, Spanish, Italian, German edits.). Clubs: American (Buenos Aires); Overseas Press (N.Y.C.) Home: 415 E 52d St New York City NY 10022 Office: 230 Park Av New York City NY 10017

JOSEPHSON, DONALD VICTOR, educator; b. Stillwater, Minn., Mar. 16, 1911; s. Joseph N. and Edna H. (Anderson) J.; B.S., U. Minn., 1935; Ph.D., Pa. State U., 1943; m. Ada Clarice Burris, Sept. 29, 1933; children—Donald B., Ronald V. Research chemist Borden Co., 1937-38; instr., then asst. prof. Pa. State U., 1938-45, prof., head dept. dairy sci., 1948—, chmn. div. food sci., 1965—; asso. prof. Ohio State U., 1945-48; cons. in field. Bd. dirs. Dairy Remembrance Fund, 1950—, v.p., 1960—, chmn. scholarship com., 1950—. Fellow A.A.A.S.; mem. Am. Dairy Sci. Assn. (pres. 1958), Am. Chem. Soc. (Borden award in chemistry milk 1954), Inst. Food Technologists, Sigma Xi, Gamma Sigma Delta, Alpha Zeta, Alpha Gamma Rho. Author papers in field. Home: 317 E Park Av State College PA 16801 Office: Borland Lab Penn State Univ University Park PA 16802

JOSEPHSON, JOSEPH PAUL, govt. ofcl.; b. Trenton, N.J., June 3, 1933; s. David S. and Jenny (Randelman) J.; B.A., U. Chgo., 1953; J.D., Cath. U. Am., 1960; m. Karla Zander, May 29, 1960; children-Peter, Andrew, Sara. Admitted to Alaska bar, 1961, since practiced in Anchorage; mem. firms Pollock & Josephson, 1966-68. Legislative asst. to territorial del. and U.S. Senator from Alaska, Washington, 1957-60; mem. Alaska Ho. of Reps., Juneau, 1963-67; acting mayor Anchorage, 1968; mem. Alaska Senate, 1969—; candidate U.S. Senate, 1970. Chmn. S. Central Alaska A.R.C., 1964-65. Served with AUS, 1955-57. Mem. Am., Alaska, Anchorage bar assns. Democrat. Editorial bd. Cath. U. Am. Law Review, 1959-60. Home: 1526 F St Anchorage AK 99501 Office: 326 H St Anchorage AK 99501

JOSEPHSON, MATTHEW, author; b. Bklyn., Feb. 15, 1899; s. Julius and Sarah (Kasindorf) J.; A.B., Columbia, 1920; m. Hannah Geffen, May 6, 1920; children—Eric Jonathan, Carl Philip Emmanuel. Editor, Broom, 1922- 24; Am. editor Transition. 1928-29; asst. editor New Republic, 1931-32. Elected mem. Nat. Inst. Arts and Letters 1948. Author: Galimathias, 1923; Zola and His Time, 1928; Portrait of the Artist as American, 1930; Jean-Jacques Rousseau, 1932; The Robber Barons, 1934; The Politicos, 1938; The President Makers, 1940; Victor Hugo, 1942; Empire of the Air, 1944; Stendhal: or the Pursuit of Happiness, 1946: Sidney Hillman: Statesman of American Labor, 1952; Union House, Union Bar, 1956; Edison: A Biography (Francis Parkman prize Soc. Am. Historians 1960), 1959; Life Among the Surrealists: a Memoir, 1962: The Infidel in the Temple: a Memoir of the 1930's, 1967; (with Hannah Josephson) Al Smith: Hero of the Cities (Van Wyck Brooks prize for biography and history), 1969. Contbr. to mags. Guggenheim traveling fellow for creative lit., 1933-34. Address: Sherman CT 06784

JOSEPHSON, R.M., car leasing co. exec.; b. 1923; B.A., Luther Coll.; married. With Arthur Anderson & Co., C.P.A.'s, 1952-62; with Hertz Corp., 1962—, v.p. administrn. and budget Control, 1968—. Served with USAAF, World War II. Address: 660 Madison Av New York City NY 10021

JOSEPHSON, WILLIAM HOWARD, lawyer; b. Newark, Mar. 22, 1934; s. Maurice and Gertrude (Brooks) J.; A.B., U. Chgo., 1952; J.D., Columbia, 1955; commoner St. Antony's Coll., Oxford (Eng.) U., 1958-59. Admitted to N.Y. bar, 1956. D.C. bar, 1966, U.S. Supreme Ct. bar, 1959; asso. Paul, Weiss, Rifkind, Wharton & Garrison, N.Y.C., 1955-58; Far East regional counsel ICA, 1959-61; spl. asst. to dir. Peace Corps, 1961-62, dep. gen. counsel, 1961-63, gen. counsel, 1963-66; asso. Joseph L. Rauh, Jr., Washington, 1959; asso. Fried, Frank, Harris, Shriver & Jacobson, N.Y.C., 1966-67, partner, 1968—. Instr., George Washington U. Law Sch., 1960. Treas., Adams-Morgan Planning Com., Washington, 1963-65; spl. counsel N.Y.C. Human Resources Adminstrn., 1966-67, N.Y.C. Bd. Edn., 1968-71. Recipient William A. Jump award exemplary achievement pub. adminstrn., 1965. Mem. Assn. Bar City N.Y. (spl. com. on Congl. ethics, 1968-70). Democrat. Jewish religion. Bd. editors Columbia Law Rev., 1953-55. Home: 58 S Oxford St Brooklyn NY 11217 Office: 120 Broadway New York City NY 10005

JOSEPHY, ALVIN M., Jr., author, editor; b. Woodmere, N.Y., May 18, 1915; s. Alvin M. and Sophia (Knopf) J.; student Harvard, 1932-34; m. Elizabeth Carlisle Peet, Mar. 13, 1948; children—Diane (Mrs. Charles D. Burgin), Alvin M. III, Allison Elizabeth, Katherine Anne. Screen writer M.G.M., 1934-35; ednl. editor, reporter, corr. N.Y. Herald Tribune, Mexico, 1937; news and spl. features dir. radio sta. WOR, 1938-42; screen writer M.G.M., Warner Bros., United Artists, 1944-51; mng. editor Santa Monica (Cal.) Ind., 1949-51; asso. editor Time mag., 1951-60; v.p., editorial dir. gen. books Am. Heritage Pub. Co., 1960—, mem. editorial adv. bd. mag., 1961—. Chief spl. events, domestic radio bur. Office Facts and Figures, OWI, 1942-43; cons. sec. Dept. interior, 1963, commnr. Indian Arts and Crafts Bd., 1966-70, vice chmn., 1967-70; contbg. editor Indian Historian, 1966-69; mem. Conn. adv. bd Small Bus. Adminstrn., 1961-63; adv. bd. Atlantic chpt. Sierra Club, 1966—; cons. Nat. Congress Am. Indians, 1958-65; exec. com. Assn. Am. Indian Affairs, 1967- -; nat adv. bd. Indian work Episcopal Ch., 1962-69; mem. council Indian Affairs, 1961-69; writer spl. report on Am. Indian for Pres. Nixon, 1969; cons. Pub. Land Rev. Commn., 1970. Vice chmn. Am. Vets. Com. Cal., 1947-48; pres. Young Democratic Club, Greenwich, Conn., 1952-55; v.p. Conn. Young Dem. Clubs, 1953-55; mem. Conn. Dem. Central Com., 1956-60; Dem. candidate for Conn. Legislature, 1958, 60. Served with USMCR, 1943-45; PTO. Decorated Bronze Star. Recipient Western Heritage award Cowboy Hall of Fame, 1962, 65; Eagle Feather award Nat. Congress Am. Indians, 1964; award of merit Am. Assn. State and Local History, 1965; Golden Saddleman, Golden Spur and Buffalo awards for history, 1965. Guggenheim fellow 1966-67. Mem. Soc. Am. Historians, Western History Assn., Am. Indian Ethnohistoric Conf., 3d Marine Div. Assn., N.Y. Westerners. Clubs: Harvard, Players, Overseas Press (N.Y.C.). Author: (with others) The U.S. Marines on Iwo Jima, 1945; The Long and The Short and The Tall, 1946; (with others) Uncommon Valor, 1946; (with others) American Heritage Book of the Pioneer Spirit, 1959; The Patriot Chiefs, 1961; The Nez Perce Indians and the Opening of the Northwest, 1965; (with others) American Heritage Pictorial Atlas of U.S. History, 1966; The Indian Heritage of America, 1968; The Artist Was A Young Man, 1970; Red Power, 1971. Editor: American Heritage Book of Indians, 1961; Horizon History of Africa, 1971. Contbr. articles to various jours. Home: 4 Kinsman Lane Bruce Park Greenwich CT 06830 also Joseph OR Office: 551 Fifth Av New York City NY 10017

JOSETTA, SISTER MARY, educator; b. Chgo. Dec. 27, 1904; d. Thomas F. and Mary (Fitzpatrick) Butler; B.S., St. Xavier Coll., Chgo., 1935; M.S., U. Ill., 1936, Ph.D., 1939. Joined Religious Sisters of Mercy; prof. chemistry St. Xavier Coll., Chgo., 1940- 63, dean coll. 1941-56, exec. v.p., 1956-60, pres. 1960-63; nat. exec. sec. Conf. Maj. Superiors of Women's Insts. in U.S. 1963-64; mem. Am. promoting group. Better World Movement, Washington, 1963-72, exec. com., 1969-72; vicar gen. The Religious Sisters of Mercy, 1972—. Dir. McAuley House, Washington, 1966-69, nat. chmn. Overseas Edn. Program, 1958-70. Mem. Am. Chem. Soc., Nat. Cath. Ednl. Assn., Sigma Xi, Iota Sigma Pi. Address: Sisters of Mercy Generalate 10000 Kentsdale Dr West Bethesda MD 20034

JOSIF, HAROLD GEORGE, fgn. service officer; b. Burma, June 16, 1920 (parents U.S. citizens); s. George Demetrius and Esther (Wright) J.; student Redlands U., 1937- 39; B.A., U. Chgo., 1941; M.A., Sch. Advanced Internat. Studies, Johns Hopkins, 1947; student S. Asia lang. and area. U. Pa., 1951; m. Sylvia Estfan, Sept. 14, 1943; 1 dau., Elaine Ann. Joined U.S. Fgn. Service, 1947; 3d sec., vice consul embassy, Karachi. Pakistan, 1948-49; vice consul consulate. Oporto, Portugal, 1950, consulate gen., Madras, India. 1951-53; India desk officer State Dept., 1954-57; consul, Tabriz, Iran, 1957-59; 1st sec., consul embassy. Colombo. Ceylon, 1959-62; assigned Air War Coll., 1962-63; officer in charge Pakistan Afghanistan affairs Dept. State, 1963-64, faculty, Nat. War Coll., Washington, 1964-66, dir. dept. polit. affairs, 1965-66; counselor of Am. embassy, Mogadiscio, Somali Republic, 1966-71; dep. chief of mission, Tripoli, Libya, 1971—. Office: Am Embassy Tripoli Libya

JOSLIN, ALFRED HAHN, state justice; b. Providence, Jan. 29, 1914; s. Philip C. and Dorothy (Aisenberg) J.; grad. Mercersburg Acad., 1931; A.B. magna cum laude, Brown U., 1935; LL.B. cum laude, Harvard, 1938; m. Roberta Grant, Mar. 9, 1941; children—Andrew J., Susan A. Admitted to R.I. bar, 1938, practiced in Providence, 1938-63; asso. justice Supreme Ct. R.I., 1963- -. vice pres. R.I. Health Facilities Planning Council; v.p., budget chmn. United Fund R.I., 1955-57; mem. com. to revise corp. laws R.I., 1949-50, com. to revise election laws R.I., 1959- 60; pres. Butler Hosp., 1957-65, emeritus, 1965—. Trustee Brown U., 1963-69, vice chancellor, 1968-69, fellow, 1969—; bd. dirs. R.I. Legal Aid Soc., Jewish Children's Home R.I., R.I. region Nat. Conf. Christians and Jews; trustee Miriam Hosp. Served from lt. (j.g.) to lt. comdr. USNR, 1942-45. Recipient Big Bro. of Year award in R.I., 1957; Outstanding Accomplishment citation Brown U., 1959. Mem. Am. (chmn. jr. bar conf. R.I. 1940-41), R.I. (chmn. exec. com. 1962-63) bar assns., Alumni Assn. Brown U. (dir.), Phi Beta Kappa, Phi Alpha Delta, Pi Lambda Phi. Clubs: University, Ledgemont Country; Bristol Yacht. Home: Mulberry Rd Bristol RI 02809 Office: Supreme Ct of RI RI

JOSLIN, ENNIS SCOTT, utility exec.; b. San Gabriel, Tex., Aug. 14, 1902; s. Andrew J. and Lula (Dunn) J.; m. Virginia Campbell, Dec. 17, 1931. Began career with mercantile co., Alice, Tex. 1923-27; with Central Power and Light Co., Corpus Christi, Tex., 1927—, v.p., 1953-64, pres., chief exec. officer, 1964-69, now dir. Vice chmn. Corpus Christi Area Devel. Com.; bd. dirs. Tex. Research League. Mem. Corpus Christi (v.p., dir.), S. Tex. (exec. com.) chambers commerce. Lion (past Pres.). Home: 242 Ohio St Corpus Christi TX 78404 Office: 120 N Chaparral St Corpus Christi TX 78403

JOSLIN, G. STANLEY, educator; b. Sextonville, Wis., July 20, 1911; s. G. Stanley and Mable (Starks) J.; B.A., Cornell Coll., 1934; LL.B., U. Wis., 1939, J.D., 1968; LL.M., U. Mich., 1952; postgrad. law; Eng., 1963-64; m. Eleanor Strickland, Nov. 25, 1948; children—George Stanley, Edith Strickland. Admitted to Wis. bar, 1939, Ga. bar, 1955; practiced law, Portage, Wis., 1939-42; instr. law U. Ky., 1947; prof. law Emory U., Atlanta, 1947—, Charles Howard Candler prof., 1960—, acting dean Law Sch., 1960- 61; interim judge Ga. Ct. Appeals, 1967. Research asst. Ga. Ct. Appeals, 1960; legal counsel Atlanta-Fulton Sch. Study Commn.; mem. U.S. Supreme Ct. Adv. Com. on Bankruptcy Rules, 1962—. Mem. DeKalb County Republican Exec. Com., 1958. Served with USAAF, 1942-45. Grantee Ford Found., 1963-64. Mem. Nat. Assn. Law Schs., Assn. Am. Law Schs. (chmn. council on securities regulation, chmn. creditors rights com. 1960, fgn. exchange law faculties com. 1970—), Am. Bar Assn., Euthanasia Soc. Am., Tau Kappa Alpha, Phi Delta Phi. Methodist. Club: Lawyers (Atlanta). Author: Minister Law Handbook, 1962; Law for the High School, 1968; Everyman's Law, 1968, contbr. articles to profl. jours. Home: 822 Houston Mill Rd NE Atlanta GA 30329

JOSLIN, MURRAY, consultant; b. Independence, Ia., Nov. 21, 1901; s. William H. and Genevieve (Murray) J.; B.S., Ia. State Coll., 1923; m. Mary Kallal, Apr. 21, 1926 (dec. oct. 1945); children-Mrs. Barbara Wilkie, William M., Jr., Thomas J., Charles W., Mrs. Mary C. Phelan, John J. Various engring., operating positions Commonwealth Edison Co., 1923-66, v.p., 1953-66; nuclear power cons. Gen. Electric Co., 1966—. Mem. Ill. AEC. Recipient U.S. AEC citation, 1968; U.S. Engrs. citation, 1970. Trustee, exec. com. Argonne Univs. Assn. Fellow I.E.E.E.; mem. Western Soc. Engrs., Am. Nat. Standards Inst. (nuclear tech. adv. bd.), Am. Soc. M.E., Phi Kappa Theta, Phi Delta Phi, Eta Kappa Nu, Tau Beta Pi. Home: 110 N Kenilworth Av Oak Park IL 60302 Office: 840 S Canal St Chicago IL 60680

JOSLYN, MAYNARD ALEXANDER, educator; b. Alexandrovsk, Russia, July 7, 1904; s. Alexander Leo and Anna (Kalutsky) J.; came to U.S., 1913, naturalized, 1922; B.S. in Chemistry, U. Cal. at Berkeley, 1926, M.S. in Agrl. Tech., 1928, Ph.D. in Chemistry, 1935; m. Golda Fischer, Apr. 19, 1947. Supr. prodn. Nat. Juice Corp., Tampa, Fla., 1930-31; faculty U. Cal. at Berkeley, 1927—, prof. dept. food tech., 1949-61, prof. food tech dept. nutritional scis., 1963—. Cons. Cal. Dept. Health, 1958—; food processing adviser, Australia, 1942-45, New Zealand, 1944, China, 1945, Israel, 1951, 58-59, 60, 64, 68; vis. prof. food tech. Mass. Inst. Tech., 1960; mem. adv. com. on food chems. code NRC. Mem. vis. com. Mass. Inst. Tech. Served from capt. to col. AUS, 1942-46. Decorated Legion of Merit (Australia), Bronze Star medal (China), spl. breast Order Yun Hai (Nat. Govt. China); recipient prize for book on table wines Office Internat. du Vin, Paris, France, 1951, prize for book on dessert wines, 1965; Man of Year award Cal.- Israel C. of C., 1955; Fulbright research award, Ireland, 1970-71. Fellow A.A.A.S., Am. Inst. Chemists; mem. N.Y. Acad. Sci., Asso. Armed Forces Food and Container Research Inst., Am. Soc. Enologists, Soc. Cryobiology, Am. Chem. Soc., Am. Soc. Plant Physiologists, Inst. Food Tech. (Internat. award 1961, Babcock-Hart award 1963, Nicholas Appert award, 1966; pres. 1965-66, mem. council 1966—), Plant Phenolics Group N.Am., Am. Soc. Biol. Chemistry, Am. Inst. Nutrition, Am. Pub. Health Assn., Am. Soc. Microbiology, Soc. Ind. Microbiology, Plant Phenolics Group Gt. Britian, Sigma Xi, Phi Beta, Gamma Alpha, Phi Lambda Upsilon, Asso. editor Advances in Food Research; editorial bd. Food Tech., Jour. Biochem. and Microbiol. Tech., IFT jours. Home: 1317 Spruce St Berkeley CA 94709

JOSLYN, PAUL WILLIAM, former business exec.; b. Chgo., Nov. 3, 1902; s. Wallace William and Maude Elizabeth (Reyer) J.; student pub. schs.; m. Helen Janette Elkin, Apr. 16, 1921; children—Paul William, Dorothy Ann (Mrs. Machamer). Mem. Chgo. Bd. Trade, 1940-70, dir. 1948-54. Home: 1514 Byron St Chicago IL 60613

JOSSELSON, HARRY HIRSCH, educator, linguist; b. Tartu, Estonia, Apr. 23, 1906; s. Adolf and Etta (Stark) J.; came to U.S., 1926, naturalized, 1938; A.B., Detroit City Coll., 1930; postgrad. U. Paris (France), 1930-31; M.A., Wayne State U., 1938; Ph.D., U. Mich., 1952; m. Evelyn S. Shorr. Dec. 27, 1936; children—Arnold Robert, Robert Howard. Faculty Wayne State U., 1938- -, prof. Slavic, gen. linguistics, 1959—, chmn. dept. Slavic and Eastern langs., 1946—. Fulbright lectr., Rome, Italy, 1955-56. Mem. subcom. linguistics statistics Permanent Internat. Com. Linguistics, 1957-62. Mem. Central States Modern Tchrs. Assn. (pres. 1950-52), Assn. Machine Transl. and Computational Linguistics (sec.-treas. 1962-70), Am. Assn. Tchrs. Slavic and East European Langs. (pres. 1953). Author: Russian Word Count, 1953; (with Fan Parker) From Pushkin to Pasternak, 1963; Russian-English Plastics Dictionary, 1970; Automatic Translation of Languages since 1960—A Linguist's View, 1970. Home: 18470 South Dr Southfield MI 48076 Office: Wayne State U Detroit MI 48202

JOSSELSON, JACK BERNARD, lawyer; b. Ashland, Ky., June 25, 1905; s. Frank R. and Bella (Goodman) J.; A.B., U. Cin., 1926; LL.B., Harvard, 1929; m. Beatrice Elaine Lichtenstein, Dec. 26, 1933; children—Jill (Mrs. Stanley Kamin), John and Frank (twins). Admitted to Ohio bar. 1930; asst. pros. atty. Hamilton County, O., 1931-32; spl. asst. solicitor City of Cin., 1933; practice in Cin., 1933—; mem. firm Schmidt, Effron, Josselson & Weber, 1944—. Instr. transp. law U. Cin., 1948-50. Pres. Children's Heart Assn., 1967-69; trustee Cin. Legal Aid Soc., Ohio State Bar Assn. Found. Fellow Am. Bar Found.; mem. Am., Ohio (exec. com.; adminstrv. law com.), Cin. (pres. 1965-66) bar assns., Motor Carrier Lawyers Assn. (pres. 1960-61), Harvard Law Sch. Assn. Clubs: Civic (pres. 1946), Harvard, Losantville Country (Cin.). Home: Regency Apts 2444 Madison Rd Cincinnati OH 45208 Office: Atlas Bank Bldg Cincinnati OH 45202

JOSSELYN, CALVIN EVERIST, mfg. co. exec.; b. Cambridge, Mass., Jan. 14, 1919; s. P. Edward and Ruth (Hendrickson) J.; B.S., Northeastern U., 1941; m. Barbara Jane Scott, June 2, 1951; children—Jill Valerie, Janet Eve. Various positions in accounting and finance Dennison Mfg. Co., Framingham, Mass., 1946—, treas., 1964—, also dir. Served to capt. USAF, 1941-45; ETO. Mem. Financial Execs. Inst., Treasurers Club Boston, Newcomen Soc. N.Am. Home: Tower Dr Dover MA 02030 Office: 300 Howard St Framingham MA 01701

JOSSEM, EDMUND LEONARD, educator, physicist b. Camden, N.J., May 19, 1919; s. Morris Henry and Fannie (Siris) J.; B.S., Coll. City N.Y., 1938; M.S., Cornell U., 1939 Ph.D., 1950. Instr., Cornell U., 1942-45, research asso., 1950-55, asst. prof., 1955-56; with Los Alamos Sci. Lab., 1945-46; faculty Ohio State U., Columbus, 1956—, prof. physics, 1964—, chmn. dept., 1967- -. Chmn., Commn. Coll. Physics, 1966—; cons. in field, 1950—. Mem. nat. adv. council Edn. Professions Devel., 1967-70; mem. edn. and manpower council Am. Inst. Physics; mem. physics survey panel on physics edn. Nat. Acad, Scis.- NRC, 1970-71. Fellow A.A.A.S. (council 1966-70); mem. Am. Phys. Soc., Am. Assn. Physics Tchrs. (v.p. 1971-72, Distinguished Service citation 1970), Am. Assn. U. Profs., Sigma Xi. Research x-ray spectroscopy and solid state physics. Home: 25 Westview Av Columbus OH 43214 Office: 174 W 18th Av Columbus OH

JOURDAN, LOUIS, actor; b. Marseille, France, June 19, 1921; s. Henry Gendre and Yvonne Jourdan; ed. pvt. schs., m. Berthe Frederique, Mar. 11, 1946; 1 son, Louis II. Came to U.S., 1946. Profl. actor, 1940—; appeared in French motion pictures, 1940-46; Am. motion picture appearances include The Paradine Case, 1946, No Minor Vices, 1947, Letter from An Unknown Woman. 1948, Madame Bovary, 1949, Bird of Paradise, 1950, Anne of the Indies, 1950, Three Coins in the Fountain, 1953, The Swan, 1955, Julie, 1956, Gigli, 1957, Best of Everything, 1959; Can-Can, 1960, The V.I.P.'s, 1963; Made in Paris, 1966; various Broadway appearances include The Immoralist, Tonight at Sammarkand; numerous appearances in U.S., Eng. Home: 712 N Crescent Dr Beverly Hills CA 90210 Office: CMA Inc 8899 Beverly Blvd Los Angeles CA 90048

JOURDONAIS, LEONARD FRANCIS, educator, physician; b. Havre, Mont., July 27, 1904; s. Lucien A. and Camille (Wyrn) J.; B.A., U. Mont., 1926; M.A., Northwestern U., 1932, M.D., 1933; m. Ruth Anderson, Sept. 1, 1927. Intern, Evanston Hosp., 1933- 34; fellow N.Y. Postgrad. Med. Sch. and Hosp., 1936-37; prof. medicine Northwestern U. Med. Sch., 1964—; chmn. dept. medicine Evanston Hosp., 1956—, Louise W. Coon chair dept. medicine, 1970—. Diplomate Am. Bd. Preventive Medicine. Fellow A.C.P.; mem. Am. Diabetes Assn., A.M.A., Endocrine Soc., Chgo. Soc. Internal Medicine, Assn. Tchrs. Preventive Medicine, Alpha Omega Alpha. Home: 525 Grove St Evanston IL 60201 Office: 2650 Ridge Av Evanston IL 60201

JOVA, JOSEPH JOHN, ambassador; b. Danskammer, Newburgh, N.Y., Nov. 7, 1916; s. Joseph Luis and Maria Josefa (Gonzalez-Cavada) J.; A.B., Dartmouth, 1938; grad. sr. seminar on fgn. policy Fgn. Service Inst., 1959; m. Pamela Johnson, Feb. 9, 1949; children—Henry Christopher, John Thomas, Margaret Ynes. With Guatemala div. United Fruit Co., 1938-41; fgn. service officer Dept. State, 1947—, vice consul, Basara, 1947-49, 2d sec., vice consul, Tangier, 1949-51, 2d sec., consul, 1951; consul, Oporto, 1952-54; 1st sec., Lisbon, 1954-57, officer-in-charge French-Iberian affairs, 1957-58, asst. chief personnel operations div., 1959-60, chief personnel operations div., 1960-61, counselor, dep. chmn. mission, Santiago, Chile, 1961-65, ambassador U.S. embassy, Tegucigalpa, Honduras, 1965-69; ambassador to rep. OAS, Washington, 1969—. Trustee Mt. St. Mary's Coll. Served to lt. (s.g.) USNR, 1942-47. Named knight Malta-Am. Assn., recipient Grand Cross, Order Morazan (Honduras). Mem. Am. Fgn. Service Assn., Am. Soc. Pub. Adminstrn., Sigma Phi Epsilon. Rotarian. Roman Catholic. Office: Dept of State Washington DC 20525

JOVANOVICH, WILLIAM ILLYA, publisher; b. Louisville, Colo., Feb. 6, 1920; s. Iliya M. and Hedviga (Garbatz) J.; A.B., U. Colo., 1941; grad. study Harvard, 1941-42, Columbia, 1946-47; Litt.D., Colo. Coll., 1966, U. Colo., 1971; m. Martha Evelyn Davis, Aug. 21, 1943. With Harcourt Brace Jovanovich, Inc., N.Y.C., 1947—, asso. editor, 1947-53, v.p., dir., 1953-54, pres., and dir., 1955-70, chmn., chief exec. officer, dir., 1970—; chmn., dir. Longmans Can., Ltd., 1961—. Recipient Norlin award distinguished achievement U. Colo., 1963. Mem. Phi Beta Kappa. Club: Union League. Author: Now Barabbas, 1964. Office: 757 3d Av New York City NY 10017

JOY, NED VERNON, coll. dean; b. San Rafael, Cal., Sept. 30, 1920; s. Allen Patrick and Pansy (Peterson) J.; A.B. in Polit. Sci., U. Cal. at Berkeley, 1946, Ph.D., 1952; m. Dorothy Mae Berry, Mar. 10, 1946; children—Thomas Patrick, Kathryn Ann. Jr. adminstrv. asst. civilian personnel div. War Dept., 1941-42; instr. polit. sci. Princeton, 1949-52; faculty San Diego State Coll., 1953-69, prof., 1961-69, chmn. dept. polit. sci., 1966-69, dean undergrad. studies, 1969—. Chmn. San Diego chpt. Am. Civil Liberties Union, 1960-61. Served with USAAF, 1942-45. Decorated Air medal with 3 oak leaf clusters, D.F.C. Mem. Am. Assn. U. Profs. (pres. San Diego State Coll. chpt. 1966-67), Am. Western polit. sci. assns., Pi Sigma Alpha, Phi Kappa Phi. Home: 10041 Resmar Pl La Mesa CA 92041 Office: San Diego State Coll San Diego CA 92115

JOYCE, AUBREY LAVELLE, actuary; b. Mt. Pleasant, Ont., Can., Dec. 30, 1905; s. Walter and Mary Elizabeth (Tye) J.; A.B., U. Toronto, 1927; m. Isobel L. Brewster, June 21, 1933; children—John, Roger. Came to U.S., 1927, naturalized, 1941. Joined Conn. Gen. Life Ins. Co., Hartford, 1927, actuary, 1950—, v.p., 1954, v.p., controller, 1956—. Fellow Soc. Acturaries. Home: Montevideo Rd Avon CT 06001

JOYCE, EDMUND PATRICK, Jr., clergyman; univ. exec.; b. Tela, Honduras (parents U.S. citizens), Jan. 26, 1917; s. Edmund Patrick and Genevieve (Block) J.; B.S.C., U. Notre Dame, 1937; postgrad. Holy Cross Coll., 1945-49, Oxford U., 1950-51; LL.D., St. Thomas Coll., St. Paul, 1958; L.H.D., Belmont Abbey Coll., 1967. C.P.A., Spartanburg, S.C., 1939; entered Congregation of Holy Cross, 1943; ordained priest Roman Cath. Ch., 1949; tchr. religion U. Notre Dame, 1949-51, v.p. bus. affairs, 1951 -52, exec. v.p., 1952—. U.S. del. Atlantic Congress, London, 1959. Trustee Jr. Achievement; bd. visitors U.S. Naval Acad. Mem. S.C. Assn. C.P.A.'s, Oxford Soc. K.C. Home: Corby Hall Notre Dame IN 46556

JOYCE, JAMES AVERY, internat. lawyer, economist, author; b. London, Eng., May 24, 1902; s. George Thomas Simeon and Mary Elizabeth (Leng) J.; student Geneva (Switzerland) Sch. Internat. Studies; Ph.D.; B.Sc. in Econs., London U.; grad. Inns of Ct. Law. Sch. Lectr., London U.; called to bar to practice common and criminal law on S.E. Circuit, also before High Ct. in London; popular law broadcasts BBC; faculty U. Denver Inst. Internat. Adminstrn., also Inst. Internat. Affairs at Grinnell Coll., San Diego State Coll., N.Y.U. vis. lectr. other U.S. univs., colls., also New Delhi U.; speaker auspices Am. Friends Service Com., Midwest and N.E. communities, 1948—; distinguished prof. Lambuth Coll., 1969-70. Founder World Unity Movement, 1939, later became World Citizenship Movement; founder, 1929, nat. chmn. League of Nations Youth Movement; staff League of Nations Union; sec. Internat. Conf. Minorities of Lang., Race and Religion; Brit. sec. Internat. Assn. Labour Legislation; staff Internat. Labour Office, Geneva; cons. UNESCO and ECOSOC of UN. Candidate for Parliament from Oldham, 1951, Lambeth, 1955. Fellow Royal Geog. Soc., Royal Statis. Soc., Royal Econ. Soc.; mem. Royal Inst. Pub. Adminstrn., Internat. Law Assn., Howard League, World Calendar Assn. (UN rep.), Parliamentary Labour Assn., Brit. Inst. Internat. and Comparative Law, Internat. Lawyers Club, Internat. Center Criminological Studies (v.p.), Soc. Labour Lawyers, Internat. P.E.N., Translators Assn., Am. Assn. U. Profs., Am. Polit. Sci. Assn., UN Assn. Mem. Labour Party. Methodist. Author: World Organization, 1944; Justice at Work, 1950; World in the Making, 1953; Revolution on East River, 1956; Red Cross International, 1959; Capital Punishment, A World View, 1960; Target for Tomorrow, 1962. Going One Way, 1963; Worker's Education Handbook, 1963; Education and Training, 1963; The Story of International Cooperation, 1964; World of Promise, 1965; Decade of Development , 1966; End of An Illusion, 1969; Story of The League of Nations, 1970; Which Way Europe, 1971. Contbr. articles to profl. jours., nat. mags. Address: 161 Lexington Av New York City NY 10016 also 3 King's Bench Walk Temple London EC4 England also care Am Friends Service Com 44 A Brattle St Cambridge MA 02138

JOYCE, JAMES NEAL, educator, psychologist; b. Buhl, Ida., July 8, 1925; s. Patrick William and Margaret (McFerran) J.; student Ida. State Coll., 1946-48; B.A., Ind. U., 1950; M.A., Ohio State U., 1952, Ph.D., 1955; m. Maxine Petterborg, Aug. 29, 1948; children—Jeffrey Neal, Timothy Kevin, Patricia Alice, Michael David. Psychologist, Columbus (O.) Sch. Retarded, 1955; from asst. prof. to asso. prof. Coe Coll., Cedar Rapids, Ia., 1955-60; faculty Western Ill. U., Macomb, 1960—, prof. psychology, 1966—, chmn. dept., 1962-70, acting dean Sch. Arts and Scis., 1969-70. Mem. Gov. Ill. Com. Mental Retardation, Zeller Zone; cons. Ill. planning com. White House Conf. Served with USNR, 1943-46. Mem. Am. (editor newsletter div. 2, mem. council), Midwestern, Ill. psychol. assns., Am. Assn. U. Profs., A.A.A.S. Home: 514 N McArthur St Macomb IL 61455

JOYCE, JAMES VINCENT, pub. relations exec.; writer; b. Port Chester, N.Y., Jan. 14, 1925; s. James R. and Frances M. (Joyce) J.; B.A. cum laude, U. Pitts., 1949; m. Sevim Lokman, June 16, 1954; children—Cecelia M., Rosemary, James. Pub. relations dept. Batton, Barton. Durstine & Osborne, 1949-51; joined U.S. Fgn. Service, 1951; assigned Turkey, 1951-52, Iran, 1953-54, India, 1954- 55; pub. affairs officer, Jordan, 1960-63; counsellor of embassy for pub. affairs, Athens, Greece, 1963-64; counselor for pub. affairs U.S. delegation to NATO, 1964-67; pub. affairs dir. Europe, First Nat. City Bank. Served with parachute Troops, AUS, 1943-46; ETO. Author stage and TV plays, novels, articles, studies. Home: 54 Av de New York Paris 16 France

JOYCE, JOHN MICHAEL, Jr., bus. exec.; b. Grand Rapids, Mich., Sept. 18, 1908; s. John Michael and Mary Agnes (McCann) J.; B.C.S., St. Louis U., 1930; LL.D., Ia. Coll., 1962; m. Catherine Bernice Peet, Oct. 16, 1934; children—John Michael III, Thomas Patrick, Patricia Anne, Mary Catherine, Anne Elizabeth, Timothy Joseph, Cathleen. Agt., Travelers Ins. Co., 1930-37; with Joyce 7-Up, Chgo., 1937-39; pres. N.Y. Seven-Up Bottling Co., New Rochelle, 1939-65, chmn. bd., 1965—, also dir. affiliates, Chgo., Madison, Wis., Joliet, Ill.; pres., dir. Washington Seven-Up Co.; dir. Peoria Seven-Up Co., D.D. Bean & Sons; trustee Emigrant Savs. Bank, N.Y.C.; chmn. exec. com. Nat Bank of Westchester, White Plains, N.Y., 1960—, dir., mem. exec. com. Lincoln First Banks, Inc., Rochester, N.Y., dir. Bookmatches, Inc., Jaffrey, N.H. Bd. dirs., bd. govs. New Rochelle Hosp., now chmn. bd. govs; trustee Iona Coll., New Rochelle; mem. pres.'s com. Notre Dame U. Recipient Merit award St. Louis U., Bro. William B. Cornelia Founders award Iona Coll., 1965. Knight of Malta, Knight of Holy Sepulchre. Mem. New Rochelle C. of C. (past pres.). Roman Catholic. Clubs: Westchester Country; Minocqua (Wis.) Country; Metropolitan (bd. govs. N.Y.C., Washington); St. Louis; Lyford Cay (Nassau). Home: 7 Forest Circle New Rochelle NY 10804 Office: Joyce Rd New Rochelle NY 10802

JOYCE, PETER J., diversified industry exec.; b. 1922; B.B.A., John Carroll U., 1948; married. Mem. accounting staff Diamond Shamrock Corp., Cleve., 1948-52, mgr. accounting, 1952-60, asst. controller, 1960-69, controller, 1969—. Served with AUS, 1942-46. Office: Union Commerce Bldg Cleveland OH 44115*

JOYCE, PHILIP HALTON, journalist; b. Albany, N.Y., Dec. 15, 1928; s. Raymond F. and Edna (Crist) J.; B.A. in Sociology, Siena Coll., 1952; m. Mary Frances Tessier, Feb. 11, 1961; children—Marie Elizabeth, Thomas Patrick. Sports writer Glens Falls (N.Y.) Post-Star, 1954-55; reporter The Saratogian, Saratoga, N.Y., 1955-56, Times-Union, Albany, N.Y., 1956-62; reporter Buffalo Courier-Express, 1962-64, legislative corr., 1965, copy editor, 1966-68; editorial writer Phila. Inquirer, 1968—. Served with AUS, 1952-54. Roman Catholic. Home: 22 Erindale Dr Marlton NJ 08053 Office: Phila Inquirer 400 N Broad St Philadelphia PA 19101

JOYCE, REGINALD, research exec., mech. engr.; b. Crewe, Cheshire, Eng., July 17, 1906; s. John and Alice (Rixon) J.; Nat. Diploma Engring. with distinction Crewe Tech. Inst., 1925; Advanced Nat. Diploma Engring. Inst. of M.E., London, Manchester Coll. of Tech, 1928; m. Beatrice D. Beisel, Aug. 4, 1934; children—Alice, Reginald John. Came to U.S., 1929, naturalized, 1936. Apprentice to engring. trades, Crewe, Eng., 1920-27; cost and estimate engr., London Midland & Scottish Ry. Co., Crewe, England. 1927-28, draftsman and designer locomotive works, Crewe, Eng., 1928-29; draftsman and designer Central R.R. of N.J., Elizabeth, 1929-30; draftsman and designer Combustion Engring. Corp., N.Y.C., 1930; time study engr. United Dry Docks, Inc., Staten Island, N.Y., 1931; mech. engr. Consumers' Research, Inc., 1932-35; sec., editor, asst. to tech. dir., v.p. Consumer's Research, Inc., Washington, N.J., 1935-70. Mem. Am. Soc. M.E., Soc. Automotive Engrs., Photographic Soc. of Am. Past pres. Washington Township Bd. Edn. Republican. Episcopalian. Home: Route 4 Box 210 Washington Warren County NJ 07882 Office: Consumers' Research Inc Washington NJ 07882

JOYCE, ROBERT FRANCIS, bishop; b. Proctor, Vt., Oct. 7, 1896; s. Patrick J. and Helen (Connor) J.; Ph.B. cum laude, U. Vt., 1917, D.D., 1955; S.T.L. summa cum laude, U. Montreal, 1923; LL.D., St. Michael's Coll., Winnoski, Vt., 1956; L.H.D., Norwich U., 1957; LL.D., Stonehill Coll., 1962. Priest, Roman Cath. Church, in 1923; prin. Cath. High Sch., Burlington, Vt., 1927-32; pastor, Northfield, Vt., 1932-43, Rutland, Vt., 1946-57; aux. bishop Diocese of Burlington, 1854-57, bishop, 1957—. Dir. Holy Name Soc. Diocese Burlington, 1947-57; pro-Synodal judge Diocese Burlington, 1938-57. Mem. Fulbright Scholarship Com. for Vt., 1952-58, Trustee Vt. Cancer Soc., Vt. Arthritis and Rheumatism Found., Vt. Multiple Sclerosis Soc., Champlain Coll. Served as maj. (chaplain) AUS, 1943-46. Mem. Am. Legion, V.F.W., Phi Beta Kappa. K.C. (4). Address: 52 Williams St Burlington VT 05401

JOYCE, W. SEAVEY, coll. pres., clergyman; b. Boston, Sept. 3, 1913; s. William Patrick and Katherine Mary (Abele) J.; B.A. Boston Coll., 1937; M.A., Georgetown U., 1940; S.T.L., Weston Coll., 1944; Ph.D., Harvard, 1949. Instr. Holy Cross Coll., 1939-40; asst. prof. Boston Coll., 1949-52, asso. prof., 1952—. chmn. dept. econs., 1949-57, dean Coll. Bus. Adminstrn., trustee, 1953—, pres., 1968—; ordained priest Roman Cath. Ch., 1943. Mem. planning com. Boston Citizens' Seminars; chmn. Boston Citizens Adv. Com. Bd. dirs. Boston Municipal Research Bur. Recipient citizenship award Nat. Municipal League, 1959; Adult Edn. award Mass., 1959. Mem. Greater Boston, C. of C. (dir., v.p.), Boston Conf. Distbn., Nat. Municipal League, Am., Cath. econ. assns., Am. Finance Assn., Beta Gamma Sigma. Address: Boston Coll Chestnut Hill MA 02167

JOYCE, WALTER FARRELL, Jr., editor; b. Cleve., Jan. 1, 1923; s. Walter Farrell and Catherine (Gatz) J.; B.J., Ohio U., 1948; m. Elaine Plomske, Apr. 20, 1946; 1 dau., Karen. Editor, Printers' Ink. Served as 1st lt. USAAF, 1942-45. Decorated D.F.C., Air medal, Dept. of Commerce, 1950; Godlove award 1960, 61, 63. Author: The Propaganda Gap. 1963. Home: 7 Wake Robin Rd Norwalk CT 06851 Office: 501 Madison Av New York City NY 10022

JOYCE, WILLIAM JOSEPH, Jr., automotive exec.; b. Columbus, O., Aug. 10, 1905; s. William Joseph and Helen (Black) J.; M.E., Cornell U., 1927; m. Dorthy Margaret Spegal, Sept. 30, 1950; children—William Baxter, Winifred (Mrs. Hunter Bennett, Jr.), LeRoy Thomas Hinman (stepson). Comml. mgr. Ohio Bell Telephone Co., 1927-36; exptl. engr. Gen. Motors Corp., 1937-40; devel. engr. Am. Optical Co., 1941-43; chief engr. Raybestos-Manhattan, Inc., 1944-48; research dir. Wayne Pump Co., 1949-51; sales mgr. Dana Corp., 1952- 53; v.p. charge internat. operations, automotive divs. N.Am. Rockwell Corp., Detroit, 1954-70; cons. internat. operations, 1970—. dir. Rubery Owen Can., Ltd. Decorated Order Indsl. Merit (Brazil). Registered profl. engr., Pa., Ohio, Ind. Mem. Soc. Automotive Engrs., A.S.C.A.P., Phi Kappa Psi. Episcopalian. Elk. Clubs: Duquesne (Pitts.); Cornell (N.Y.C.); Detroit Athletic. Holder 15 patents. Home: 8104 E Jefferson Av Detroit MI 48214 Office: Broderick Tower Detroit MI 48226

JOYES, PRESTON POPE, ins. co. exec.; b. Louisville, Ky., Dec. 25, 1918; s. Preston Pope and Nina (Bingham) J.; A.B., Dartmouth Coll., 1940; m. Adele Albright Palmer, Oct. 30, 1948; children—Adele Palmer, Caroline Preston. With Commonwealth Life Ins. Co., Louisville, Ky., 1946—, v.p. underwriting and ins. services, 1956—, also sec., 1968—, v.p. ins. operations Commonwealth Fire & Casualty Ins. Co., Louisville, 1964-68, pres., 1968—. Chmn. gen. campaign Community Chest Louisville and Jefferson Co., 1955. Bd. dirs. Falls Region Health Council; bd. mgrs. Cave Hill Cemetery. Served to capt. Q.M.C., AUS, 1942-46. Mem. Kappa Sigma. Clubs: Wynn Stay, Louisville Country (Louisville). Home: 3706 Pennington Lane Louisville KY 40207 Office: PO Box 2141 Louisville KY 40201

JOYNER, JAMES CRAIG, proctologist; b. Durham, N.C., Sept. 23, 1898; s. Patrick Henry and Mary (Craig) J.; student Elon Coll. and U. of North Carolina; M.D., U. of Maryland. 1918; spl. study in Vienna and Paris; m. Lucie B Alcott, Nov. 10, 1948. Connected with various hospitals in N.Y.C.; recognized authority on rectal disease. Served as lt. (s.g.), USN World War I. Mem. N.Y. State and County Med. Socs., N.Y. Acad. Medicine. A.M.A. Clubs: Union, Long Island Country. Author various med. publs. Home: 720 Park Av New York City NY 10021 Office: 718 Park Av New York City NY 10021

JOYNER, LEON FELIX, univ. adminstr.; b. Savannah, Ga., Nov. 20, 1924; s. Leon Felix and Sarah (Thompson) J.; student Harvard, 1944-45; A.B., Berea Coll., 1947; postgrad. Univs. Ala., Tenn., Ky., 1947-48; m. Margaret Ruth Barrett, June 28, 1944; children-Leon Stephens, Barrett Ray. Mem. budget staff Ky. State Govt., 1948-55; mem. field staff Pub. Adminstrn. Service, Chgo., 1956-60; commr. personnel Ky. State Govt., 1960-62, health welfare adminstr., 1962-63, commr. finance, 1963-67; v.p. finance U. N.C., 1968—; cons. Govts. of Burma, Thailand, 1956-59, Auditor-Gen. Pakistan, 1968. Chmn. Commn. on Reorganization of Exec. Br. State Govt. Ky., 1962. Bd. dirs. Research Triangle Found. N.C. Served to lt. (j.g.), Supply Corps, USNR, 1943-46. Named Pub. Adminstr. of Year, Ky. chpt. Am. Soc. Pub. Adminstrn., 1961. Mem. Am. Soc. Pub. Adminstrn. (past pres. Ky. chpt.), Nat. Assn. State Budget Officers (past mem. exec. com.), Internat. Bridge, Tunnel and Turnpike Assn. (past dir.), Chapel Hill C. of C., Phi Kappa Phi. Democrat. Presbyn. Home: 616 Churchill St Chapel Hill NC 27514

JOYNER, WEYLAND THOMAS, educator, physicist; b. Suffolk, Va., Aug. 9, 1929; s. Weyland T. and Thelma (Neal) J.; B.S., Hampden-Sydney Coll., 1951; M.A., Duke, 1952, Ph.D., 1955; m. Marianne Steele, Dec. 3, 1955; children—Anne, Weyland, Leigh. Teaching fellow Duke, 1954, research asso., 1958; physicist Dept. Def., Washington, 1954-57; research physicist U. Md., 1955-57; asst. prof. physics Hampden-Sydney Coll., 1957-59, asso. prof., 1959-63, prof., 1963—, physics chmn., 1968—; research asso. Ames Lab. AEC, 1964-65; vis. prof. Pomona Coll., 1965; staff Commn. on Coll. Physics, Ann Arbor, Mich., 1966-67; mem. Panel on Preparation Physics Tchrs., 1967-68; nuclear phys. cons. Oak Ridge Inst. Nuclear Studies, 1960-67, Pres. Piedmont Farms, Inc., 1958—; Ednl. cons. numerous colls. and univs., 1965—; Pres. Windsor Supply Corp., 1966—; mgmt. cons., 1966—; pres. Windsor Seed & Livestock Co., 1969—. Fellow A.A.A.S.; mem. Am. Phys. Soc., Am. Assn. Physics Tchrs., I.E.E.E., Va. Acad. Sci. (past mem. council, sect. pres.), Am. Angus Assn., Am. Internat. Charolais Assn., Am. Inst. Physics (regional counselor, past dir. Coll. Program), Phi Beta Kappa, Sigma Xi, Lambda Chi Alpha. Presbyn. (deacon). Contbr. articles profl. jours. Home: 2 Wilson Dr Hampden-Sydney VA 23943

JOYNER, WILLIAM T., lawyer; b. Goldsboro, N.C., Apr. 11, 1891; s. James Yadkin and Effie E. (Rouse) J.; A.B., U. N.C., 1911; LL.B., Harvard, 1916; m. Sue Arrington Kitchin, Apr. 17, 1920 (dec. Aug. 6, 1954); children—Sue Kitchin, William T., Walton Kitchin. Instr. Woodberry Forest (Va.) Sch., 1911-13; admitted to N.C. bar, 1915, D.C. bar, 1932; in gen. practice of law, Raleigh, N.C., 1916-17, 1919—; asst. gen. solicitor So. Ry. Co., Washington, 1932-37, div. counsel, 1937—; counsel for all railroads of Southeastern U.S. in minimum wage case, 1940, in nat. wage cases, 1941, 42, 43. Vice chmn. N.C. Adv. Com. on Edn., 1954-56; chmn. N.C. Hwy. Commn., 1957; chmn. steering com. for planning study for N.C. constn., 1967-68. Sec. Elections, 1943-47. State Democratic Exec. Co., 1921-23; chmn. N.C. State Bd. Elections, Served as capt. 113th F.A., U.S. N.A., Aug. 1917-Aug. 1918, maj. 45th F.A., Aug.-Dec. 1918; instr. F.A. Sch. of Fire, Fort Sill, Okla., 1918; lt. col. 113th F.A., N.C. Nat. Guard, 1923, col., 1924-32; mem. War Dept. adv. com. on mil, justice, 1946-47; cons. War Dept. on govt. operation of railroads, May-Aug. 1948. Mem. Gen. Alumni Assn. U. N.C. (pres. 1945-46), Am. Legion (nat. exec. committeeman, 1930-33), Am., N.C., Wake Country bar assns., Am. Coll. Trial Lawyers, Zeta Psi, Phi Beta Kappa. Democrat. Baptist. Kiwanian. Home: 621 N Blount Raleigh NC 27604 Office: Wachovia Bank Bldg Raleigh NC 27601

JOYNES, WALTER COOPER, Jr., former cement co. exec.; b. Norfolk, Va., Oct. 13, 1909; s. Walter Cooper and Rosalind (Cox) J.; student pub. schs., Norfolk; m. Mildred Bittle, Sept. 15, 1936; children—Walter Cooper III, William A. Began with Lone Star Cement Co., N.Y.C., 1928, former treas. Home: 50 Frame Rd Briarcliff Manor NY 10510

JOYNT, ROBERT JAMES, physician; b. Le Mars, Ia., Dec. 22, 1925; s. Robert J. and Mayme (Teefey) J.; B.A., Westmar Coll., 1949, D.Sc., 1964; M.D., U. Ia., 1952, M.S., 1963, Ph.D., 1963; m. Margaret McGivern, Aug. 23, 1953; children—Robert, Patricia, Mary, Anne, Thomas, Kathleen. Intern Royal Victoria Hosp., Montreal, Can., 1952-53; resident neurology U. Ia., 1954- 57, asso., 1957-58, asst. prof., 1958-61, asso. prof. neurology, 1961- 66; prof., chmn. dept. neurology U. Rochester, 1966—. Served with AUS, 1944-46. Fulbright scholar Cambridge (Eng.), U. 1953-54; named Penfield lectr. Am. U., Beirut, 1969; recipient Distinguished Alumni award U. Ia., 1970. Mem. Am. Neurol. Assn., Am. Acad. Neurology, Am. EEG Soc., Am. Assn. Neurol. Surgeons, A.M.A. Home: 32 Sandpiper Lane Pittsford NY 14534 Office: 260 Crittenden Blvd Rochester NY 14620

JUARISA, JOHN B., mfg. co. exec.; b. 1911; married. Founder Admiral Corp., 1935-59; chmn. bd. United Equity Corp., 1959-64, also partner Jay Bee Enterprises, Chgo.; with Standard Kollsman Industries Inc., 1964—, chmn. bd., chief exec. officer, 1969—, also dir. Address: 2085 N Hawthorne Av Melrose Park, IL 60160.*

JUCKEM, WILFRED PHILIP, mfg. co. exec.; b. Sheboygan, Wis., Apr. 27, 1915; s. Arvin M. and Martha (Henning) J.; grad. Sheboygan Bus. Coll., 1934; m. Dorothy Iris Dean, Dec. 8, 1941; children—Jean

Audrey, Philip Dean. With Jenkins Machine Co., Sheboygan Falls, Wis., 1933-34, Kohler of Kohler (Wis.), 1934-42, Rock Island (Ill.) Arsenal, 1942-45; with Eagle Signal Corp., Moline, Ill., 1947-63, v.p. mfg., 1958-63; asst. to pres. E.W. Bliss Co., Canton, O., 1963-64, adminstrv. v.p., 1964-66, v.p. press div., 1966-67, v.p. corporate devel., 1967-68, v.p., div. mgr. Eagle Signal div., 1968—. Mem. Am. Ordnance Assn., Davenport C. of C., Quad City Devel. Assn., Asso. Industries Quad Cities. Lutheran. Clubs: Town, Outing, Davenport, Iowa, Rock Island Arsenal Golf. Home: 2626 Ridgewood Av Davenport IA 52803 Office: 320 LeClaire St Davenport IA

JUCKETT, JACOB WALTER, religious assn. ofcl.; b. West Springfield. Mass., May 26, 1908; s. Frank A. and Laura P. (Fassett) J.; B.S. in Elec. Engring., Norwich U. 1930, D. Sc. (hon.), 1962; m. M. Elizabeth Brown, Aug. 24, 1940; children—David Warren, Nancy Elizabeth. With Hurlbut Paper Co., 1930-36, asst. treas., 1935-36; office mgr. Sandy Hill Corp. (formerly The Sandy Hill Iron & Brass Works), Hudson Falls, N.Y., 1936-42, asst. treas., 1937-42, sec., asst. treas., 1942- 49, sec.-treas., and gen. mgr., 1952-57, pres., 1957—, also dir.; pres. Richmor Aviation, Inc.; dir. Glens Falls Ins. Co., Kamyr. Inc., also Glens Falls Nat. Bank & Trust Co. Mem. area adv. com. N.Y. Bus. Devel. Corp. Mem. Nat. Harbor and Rivers Congress 1961—. Pres. bd. edn. Hudson Falls Central Sch. Dist., 1957—; mem. exec. com. Nat. Bd. Missions Commn. on Evangelism. United Presbyn. Ch. U.S., 1954-59; mem. gen. council Presbytery of Albany, United Presbyn. Ch. U.S., 1958-61, mem. gen. council Presbyn. Ch. U.S., 1959-60, exec. com. cons. conf. missions under gen. council; mem. at large Nat. council Boy Scouts Am. Trustee Sandy Hill Found., 1951—, Norwich U., 1958—, Citizens Pub. Expenditure Survey Inc. in N.Y. State; trustee Adirondack Community Coll. Served to capt. AUS, 1942-45. Recipient Silver Beaver award Boy Scouts Am. Mem. Nat. Council United Presbyn. Men (pres. 1959-60), Nat. Council Chs. (mem. dept. evangelism 1958-60). T.A.P.P.I. (asso.), Newcomen Soc. in N.Am., Tau Beta Pi. Presbyn. (elder). Home: 31 Pearl St Hudson Falls NY 12839 Office: 27 Allen S Hudson Falls NY 12839

JUDD, BRIAN RAYMOND, educator, physicist; b. Chelmsford, Eng., Feb. 13, 1931; s. Harry and Edith (Saltmarsh) J.; B.A., Brasenose Coll., Oxford U., 1952, M.A., 1955, D.Phil., 1955. Fellow, Magdalen Coll., Oxford U., 1955-62; instr. U. Chgo., 1957-58; asso. prof. U. Paris, 1962-64; staff mem. Lawrence Radiation Lab., Berkeley, Cal., 1964-66; prof. physics Johns Hopkins, Balt., 1966—. Vis. Erskine fellow U. Canterbury Christchurch, New Zealand, 1968. Author: Operator Techniques in Atomic Spectroscopy, 1963; Second Quantization and Atomic Spectroscopy, 1967, (with J.P. Elliott) Topics in Atomic and Nuclear Theory, 1970. Office: Physics Dept Johns Hopkins Baltimore MD 21218

JUDD, DEANE BREWSTER, color scientist; b. South Hadley Falls, Mass., Nov. 15, 1900; s. Horace and Etta Lois (Gerry) J.; A.B., Ohio State U., 1922, M.A., 1923; Ph.D., Cornell U., 1926; m. Elizabeth Melamed, Aug. 7, 1926; children—Dean Burritt, Audrey Lois. Physicist optics Nat. Bur. Standards, Washington, 1927-70; pres. Munsell Color Found., 1943—. Am. rep. Internat. Commn. Illumination, 1931, 35, 48, secretariat dir., 1951; Am. rep. Internat. Commn. Optics, 1948; studies color measurement, color differences, color perception, color blindness; invited prof. Instituto de Optica, Madrid, 1956-57. Recipient Jour. award Soc. Motion Picture Engrs., 1936; Exceptional Service award Gold medal Dept. Commerce, 1950; Samuel Wesley Stratton award Nat. Bur. Standards, 1966. Mem. Illuminating Engring. Soc. (Gold medal 1961), Optical Soc. Am. (Herbert E. Ives medal 1958, pres. 1953-55, asso. editor jour. 1936-60, editor 1961-63), Inter-Soc. Color Council (Godlove award 1957, chmn. 1940-44). Author: Color in Business, Science and Industry, 1952, (with G. Wyszeck) 2d edit., 1963; Home: 3115 Leland St Chevy Chase MD 20015

JUDD, DONALD CLARENCE, artist; b. Excelsior Springs, Mo., June 3, 1928; s. Roy Clarence and Effie (Cowsert) J.; student Art Students League, N.Y.C., 1949-53; B.S., Columbia, 1953; m. Margaret Hughan Finch, Mar. 14, 1964. Exhbns. include Green Gallery, N.Y.C., 1963, VIII Sao Paulo Bienal, 1965, Castelli Gallery, N.Y.C., 1966-67, 69-70, Blum Gallery, Los Angeles, 1967-70, Whitney Mus. Am. Art. 1968, Met. Mus. Art, N.Y. Painting and Sculpture, 1940-70, Sonnabend Gallery, Paris, 1969, Zwirner Gallery, Cologne, 1969, Helman Gallery, St. Louis, 1970, Eindhoven, Netherlands, 1970, Essen, Germany, 1970, Hanover, Germany, 1970, Guggenheim Mus. Internat., 1971, others. Served with AUS, 1946-47. Mem. Cactus and Succulent Soc. Am. Address: 101 Spring St New York City NY 10012

JUDD, EDWARD STARR, surgeon; b. Rochester, Minn., Oct. 16, 1911; s. Edward Starr and Helen (Berkman) J.; grad. Deerfield Acad., 1928; A.B., Dartmouth, 1932; M.D., Rush Med. Coll., 1936; M.S. in Surgery, U. Minn., 1940; m. Virginia Helm, June 24, 1936; children—Thomas, Jill. Intern, Geisinger Meml. Hosp., 1936-37; fellow surgery Mayo Found., 1937-42, prof. surgery 1957- -; staff surgeon Mayo Clinic, 1942—. Served to maj. M.C., AUS, 1942- 46. Fellow A.C.S. (2d v.p.); mem. Am. (2d v.p.), Western, Central (pres.) surg. assns., Am. Thyroid Assn., A.M.A., Mayo Assn. (bd.), Sigma Xi, Psi Upsilon, Nu Sigma Nu. Contbr. numerous articles to profl. jours. Home: 1319 7th St Rochester MN 55901 Office: Mayo Clinic Rochester MN 55901

JUDD, FRANK, tobacco co. exec.; b. Berlin, Germany, Dec. 20, 1907; s. Simon and Johanna (Fuchs) Juda; D.Oeconomiae, Grad. Sch. Bus., Berlin, 1931; m. Claire Loeb, May 27, 1945; children—Naomi Ann, Deborah Sue. Came to U.S., 1934, naturalized, 1940. Jr. accountant S.D. Leidesdorf & Co., N.Y.C., 1934-36; financial analyst Lehman Corp., 1936-41; br. chief OPA, Washington, 1941-43, div. dir. in accounting, 1945-46; sect. head cost analysis CAB, 1946-47; cost analyst Brown & Williamson Tobacco Corp., Louisville, 1947-49, asst. treas., 1949-51, asst. controller, 1951-59, controller, 1959—, dir. long range planning, spl. studies. Faculty, Univ. Coll., U. Louisville, 1948-66. Mem. Jewish communal affairs com. Am. Jewish Com., 1963-67; mem. exec. com. Louisville Conf. Jewish Orgns.; past pres. Louisville Bur. Jewish Edn. Served with USAAF, 1942-45. C.P.A., N.Y. Mem. Am. Econ. Assn., Am. Inst. C.P.A.'s, Nat. Assn. Accountants (past pres. Louisville chpt., nat. dir.), Nat. Soc. for Bus. Budgeting (past pres. Louisville chpt., regional dir.). Home: 2411 Woodbourne Av Louisville KY 40205 Office: 1600 W Hill St Louisville KY 40201

JUDD, GEORGE EZRA, physician; b. Coalville, Utah, Mar. 11, 1901; s. George Thomas and Margaret Jeanette (Lewis) J.; A.B., U. Utah, 1923, student Med. Sch., 1923-25; M.D., U. Pa., 1927; m. Emmeline Lund, Sept. 1, 1925 (dec. June 1960); children—Lewis Lund, Howard Lund; m. 2nd, Olive Romney Marshall, Aug. 6, 1962. Intern Bklyn Hosp., 1927-29; resident physican Hollywood (Cal.) Hosp., 1929-30; pvt. practice specializing in obstetrics and gynecology, Los Angeles, 1930—; jr. attending obstetrician Los Angeles County Gen. Hosp., 1934-40, sr. attending gynecologist, 1940-50; mem. attending staff Good Samaritan Hosp., 1930—, chief obstetrics and gynecology, 1947-51; attending staff Good Hope Clinic, 1934-42; med. dir. Planned Parenthood, Los Angeles, 1966-68; instr. Coll. Med. Evangelists, 1934-40; asst. clin. prof. obstetrics and gynecology U. So. Cal. Med. Sch., 1940-50, U. Cal. at Los Angeles, 1971—. A founder, 1st gen. chmn. Obstet. and Gynecol. Assembly So. Cal., 1946-47. Fellow Royal Coll. Obstetricians and Gynecologists; mem. Am. Coll. Obstetrics & Gynecology (vice chmn. dist. VIII, 1955-57, chmn. 1957-60. 1st v.p. 1960-61, pres. 1963-64), Internat. Fedn. Obstetrics and Gynecology (exec. bd.), A.C.S. (bd. govs. 1957-63), Pacific Coast (pres. 1959-60), Los Angeles County (pres. 1944- 45) obstet. and gynecol. socs., Symposium Soc. Los Angeles (pres. 1946- 47), Cal. Med. Assn. (chmn. sect. obstetrics and gynecology 1956-57), Sigma Nu, Phi Beta Pi (pres. 1924). Mem. Ch. of Jesus Christ of Latter- day Saints (high council Los Angeles stake 1954-62). Rotarian. Clubs: Los Angeles Country, Jonathan (Los Angeles). Author med. papers. Asst. editor Western Jour. Surgery Gynecology and Obstetrics, 1947-55. mem. editorial bd., 1955—. Home: 1755 Hillcrest Av Glendale CA 91202

JUDD, JOHN HEWITT, ophthalmologist; b. Dawson, Neb., May 12, 1899; s. Delbert B. and Linda (Helm) J.; B.S., U. Neb., 1922, M.D., 1924; m. Ellanore Baxter, Sept. 14, 1935; 1 dau. Katherine Hewitt. Intern, Luth. Hosp., Beatrice, Neb., 1924-25; postgrad. tng. U. Vienna, 1925- 26; pvt. practice ophthalmology, Omaha, 1930—; faculty, U. Neb. Coll. Med., since 1930—, prof. ophthalmology, chmn. dept., 1942-64, prof. emeritus ophthalmology, 1964—. Fellow A.C.S., Am. Acad. Ophthalmology and Otolaryngology: mem. A.M.A., Am. Assn. Research in Ophthalmology, Royal, Am. numis. socs., Am. Numis- Assn. (past pres.), A.A.A.S., Archeol. Inst. Am., Neb. Med. Soc., Alpha Omega Alpha, Phi Rho Sigma. Republican. Episcopalian. Mason. Author: United States Pattern, Experimental and Trial Pieces. Home: 680 N 56 St Omaha NB 68131 Office: Doctors Bldg Omaha NB 68131

JUDD, MATTHEW BLATCHFORD diversified mfg. co. exec.; b. Cin., May 21, 1910; grad. Phillips Acad., Andover, Mass., 1927; B.S., Princeton, 1931; postgrad. Mass. Inst. Tech., 1931-33; m. Jean R. Holland, June 16, 1935; children--Lois A., Andrew M., James. Salesman, Brown Mfg. Co., Boston, 1932-33; jr. engr. Ball Metals Co., Carson City, Nev., 1933-36, engr., 1936-37, sr. engr., 1937-40; project engr. Kingston Engring. Co., Los Angeles, 1940-43; with dept. engring. City of Denver, 1946-50, dep. head, 1950-52; 2d v.p. Johnson Mfg. Co., Kansas City, Kansas, 1952-54, v.p. for engring., 1954-57; v.p. research Consol. Industries, Inc., South Bend, Ind., 1957-60, exec. v.p., 1960-65, pres., 1965-70, chmn. bd., chief exec. officer, 1970--, also dir.; dir. ABC Chem. Co., 2d Nat. Bank, Country Food Storage Co., Providence Indsl. Corp. (Ind.), Wilson Investment Co., Inc., Hammond Life Ins. Co., Inc. (Ind.), Prudential Ins. Co., Haverford Mfg. Co., Leader Pub. Co. Pres., Dewey High Sch., Kansas City, Mo., 1953-54; fund chmn. local div. Salvation Army, 1959-60. Mem. South Bend Republican Com., 1964-68. Bd. dirs. Ind. council Boy Scouts Am., 1969-71; trustee Lovell Found. Served to lt., Corps Engrs., AUS, 1943-45. Decorated Bronze Star medal. Member N.A.M., South Bend C. of C. (v.p. 1963-65, dir. 1965-70), Am. Mgmt. Assn., Ind. Engrs. Soc. (program com. 1961-62), Princeton Alumni Assn. Episcopalian. Rotarian, Optimist. Clubs: South Bend Golf; Links (N.Y.C.). Home: 6823 Broad Terrace Av South Bend IN 46505 Office: PO Box 1019 South Bend IN 46501

JUDD, ROBERT CARPENTER, educator; b. Maui, Hawaii, July 6, 1921; s. Robert Augustine and Marguerite (Schoonmaker) J.; A.B., U. Chgo., 1942; Ph.D., U. Wis., 1963; m. Dorothy May Heiple, Sept. 19, 1964; children—Dianna Kay (Mrs. Joseph R. Carlisi), Nancy Carol (Mrs. David E. Wilber), Linda Sue, Patricia Ann (Mrs. Robert L. King); (step-daus.) Catherine Rafferty, Deborah Rafferty, Nancy Rafferty. Statis. analyst Montgomery Ward & Co., 1943; statis. mgr. Manning, Maxwell & Moore, Inc., 1943-46; market research engr. R.G. LeTourneau, Inc., 1946-47; instr. statistics Bradley U., 1947-50; spl. risks supr. Continental Casualty Co., 1950-52; asst. to v.p. Mut. of Omaha, 1952-55; Eastern regional mgr. Fed. Life & Casualty Co., 1955-57; asst. prof. econs. and bus., dir. continuing edn. Beloit Coll., 1957-62; asst. prof. bus. orgn. and mgmt. U. Neb., 1962-63; asso. prof. marketing DePaul U., 1963-66; asso. prof. marketing No. Ill. U., 1966-68; prof. operations analysis U. Toledo, 1968—, chmn. dept. operations analysis, 1968-71; adj. prof. math. medicine Med. Coll. Ohio, 1969—. Mem. Am. Marketing Assn., Operations Research Soc. Am., Am. Statis. Assn., Assn. Instl. Research, Internat. Soc. Ednl. Planners, Delta Sigma Pi. Contbr. articles profl. jours. Home: 3422 Pelham Rd Toledo OH 43606

JUDD, THOMAS MARSHALL, fgn. service officer; b. Washington, May 18, 1920; s. Maurice and Ruth M. (Chapman) J.; A.B., Princeton, 1941; M.S. Internat. Affairs, George Washington U., 1968; m. Mary M., Greenlaw, Jan. 10, 1945; children—Mary Margaret, Thomas Marshall, Leslie-Victoria. Joined U.S. fgn. service, 1945; vice consul, Bucharest, 1946-48; polit. adviser, Trieste, 1948-50; assigned Athens, Greece, 1950-54; assigned Benghazi, Libya, 1954-57; prin. officer, 1956-57; assigned Dept. State, 1957—, chief fgn. service placement br., 1958-60; counselor embassy, Mogadiscio, Somali Republic, 1960-62; charge d'Affaires Embassy Mogadiscio, 1962-63; assigned officer in charge U.K. affairs Dept. State 1963-67; Nat. War Coll., 1967-68; polit. counselor Am. embassy, Seoul, Korea, 1968-70; faculty Nat. War Coll., 1970—. Served from pvt. to capt., USAAF. 1941-45; Africa, Italy. Decorated Distinguished Flying Cross, Air medal with 5 oak leaf clusters, Purple Heart. Home: 1610 Greenbrier Ct Reston VA Office: Dept of State Washington DC 20525

JUDD, WALTER H., physician, missionary; b. Rising City, Neb., Sept. 25, 1898; s. Horace Hunter and Mary Elizabeth (Greenslit) J.; B.A., U. Neb., 1920; M.D., 1923; fellow surgery Mayo Found. U. Minn., 1932-34; hon. doctorate degrees, numerous univs., colls.; m. Miriam Louise Barber, Mar. 13, 1932; children—Mary Louise (Mrs. Norman Carpenter), Carolyn Ruth, Eleanor Grace (Mrs. Paul J. Quinn). Instr. zoology U. Omaha, 1920-24; intern U. Hosp., Omaha, 1922-24; traveling sec. Student Vol. Movement colls., univs., 1924-25; med. missionary Congl. Fgn. Mission Bd., Nanking, China, 1925-26, Shaowu, Fukien, China, 1926-31, Fenchow, Shansi, China, 1934-38; lectr. throughout U.S. on Am. fgn. policy, interests in Pacific, 1938-40; physician, surgeon, Mpls., 1941-42. Mem. 78th to 87th Congresses, 5th Minn. Dist.; U.S. del. 12th Gen. Assembly UN; radio commentator. Founder, Aid Refugee Chinese Intellectuals; co-founder World Neighbors; vice chmn. Am. Emergency Com. Tibetan Refugees; v.p. Am. Bur. Med. Aid to China. Dir. Good-Will Industries, Inc.; co-founder Com. of One Million Against Admission Communist China to UN Bd. dirs. Met. YMCA, Washington. Founder, Republican Workshops. Served from pvt. to 2d lt. F.A., U.S. Army 1918-19. Recipient CARE-MEDICO Humanitarian award, 1962; George Washington Honor medal Freedoms Found., 1959, 61, 62, 64, 67; Great Living Am. award U.S. C. of C., 1963; Outstanding Achievement award U. Minn., 1964; Lay Churchman of Year, Religious Heritage Am., 1966. Mem. A.M.A. (Distinguished Service award 1961), (jud. council 1963—), Minn. Med. Assn., Am. Acad. Gen. Practice, Am. Legion, China Soc., Phi Beta Kappa, Alpha Omega Alpha, Phi Rho Sigma, Omicron Delta Kappa. Republican. Conglist. Mason (33, Shriner). Contbg. editor Readers Digest, 1963—. Home: 3083 Ordway St NW Washington DC 20008

JUDD, WILLIAM EDWARD, mfg. co. exec.; b. Chgo., Sept. 1, 1919; s. Frank and Frances (Meitz) J.; ed. Loyola U. and Law Sch., Chgo., 1937-42; m. Dorothy R. Neunuebel, Aug. 1, 1942; children—Robert A., Patricia R., Donald E. With firm Willians, Bradbury, McCaleb & Hinkle, patent law, 1936-42; with Stewart-Warner Corp., 1942—, gen. mgr. heating and air conditioning div., 1956- -, v.p. corp., 1960—. Bd. dirs. Nat. Oil Fuel Inst. chmn. bd., 1970-71. Mem. Soc. Automotive Engrs., Nat. Warm Air Heating and Air Conditioning Assn. (pres. 1968, trustee), Am. Gas Assn., Nat. Petroleum Council, Am. Ordnance Assn., Newcomen Soc. Clubs: Glen Country (Lebanon, Ind.). Meridian Hills Country. Home: 8020 N Meridian St Indianapolis IN 46260 Office: Stewart-Warner Corp Lebanon IN 46052

JUDE, ROBERT BOARDMAN, broker; b. Bradford, Pa., Nov. 8, 1906; s. George Washington and Pearl (Boardman) J.; B.S. in Bus. Adminstrn., Syracuse U., 1928; m. Ardelle Zoret, June 8, 1929; children—Robert Bradley, Mary Milda. With Spencer Kellogg & Sons, Inc., Buffalo, 1929-62, asst. v.p., 1948-52, v.p., 1952- 62; v.p. Clayton Brokerage, Chgo., 1962—. Mem. Bd. Econ. Warfare, Washington, Brazil, 1942-43. Served as lt. USNR, 1943-46; PTO. Mem. Chgo. Bd. Trade, Mpls. Grain Exchange, Sigma Phi Epsilon. Home: 1149 Woodview Rd Hinsdale IL 60521 Office: Bd of Trade Bldg Chicago IL 60604

JUDELL, ROBERT LEWIS, food co. exec.; b. Mpls., Nov. 28, 1920; s. Philip and Lena (Krause) J.; B.S., Harvard, 1942; M.B.A., Columbia, 1948; C.P.A., N.Y., 1951; m. Mary Hatheway, Feb. 28, 1948; children—David H., Douglas L. With Hurdman & Cranstoun, C.P.A.'s, N.Y.C., 1947-52; with Welch Foods Inc., Westfield, N.Y., 1952-56, 62—, v.p., treas., 1964—, also dir.; asst. treas. Chemway Corp., 1956-62. Instr., Jamestown Community Coll., 1964-67, State U. N.Y. at Fredonia, 1968-71. Bd. dirs. Asso. N.Y. State Food Processors, 1971—. Mem. Pequannock (N.J.) Twp. Bd. Edn., 1961-62. Served to 1st lt. USAAF, 1942-46. Mem. Am. Inst. C.P.A.'s, N.Y. State Soc. C.P.A.'s, Nat. Soc. Accountants for Coops. Home: 305 Chestnut St Fredonia NY 14063 Office: Main and Portage Sts Westfield NY 14787

JUDELSON, DAVID N., bus. exec.; b. 1928; B.S. in Mech. Engring., N.Y.U., 1949; m. Chmn. bd. Oscar I. Judelson, Inc., mfrs. indsl. equipment, Jersey City, 1949-58; with Gulf & Western Industries, Inc., 1958—, v.p., dir., 1959-61, mem. exec. com., 1961-65, chmn. exec. com., 1965-66, exec. v.p., 1966-67, pres., 1967—, also dir.; dir. Ward Foods, Inc., Paramount Pictures Corp. Address: 437 Madison Av New York City NY 10022*

JUDGE, JOHN EMMET, mfg. co. exec.; b. Grafton, N.D., May 5, 1912; s. Charles and Lillian (Johnson) J.; B.S. in Elec. Engring., U. N.D., 1935; m. Clarita Garcia, Apr. 18, 1940; children—Carolyn (Mrs. Daniel Belanger), John Emmet, (Maureen, Eileen, Susan. Asst. to adminstr. Fed. Works Agy., Washington, 1939-42; staff Wallace Clark & Co., mgmnt. cons., N.Y.C., 1942-46; v.p. Margan Furniture Co., Asheville, N.C., 1946-48; mgr. financial analysis Lincoln-Mercury div. Ford Motor Co., 1949-53, asst. gen. purchasing agt., 1953-55, mgr. dsg. and product planning, 1955-58, marketing mgr., 1958-60, product planning mgr., Dearborn, Mich., 1960-62; v.p. marketing services Westinghouse Elec. Corp., Pitts., 1963-67; v.p. marketing Indian Head, Inc., 1967-68; marketing cons., 1969—; dir. Capital Corp. of Am., investments, Intertek Industries, Krotos, Inc. Mem. adv. com. to U.S. sec. of commerce. Chmn. Birmingham Library Com., 1957; mem. bd. Boysville of Mich., 1957—. Dir. tng. Oakland County (Mich.) Republican Com., 1962. Mem. Am. Ordnance Assn., Soc. Advancement Mgmt., N.A.M. (chmn. marketing com.), Am. Soc. M.E., Engring. Soc. Detroit, Nat. Assn. Accountants, Soc. Automotive Engrs., Sigma Tau, Alpha Tau Omega, Roman Catholic. Clubs: Detroit Athletic, Economic (Detroit); Orchard Lake (Mich.) Country. Home: 2147 Yarmouth Rd Birmingham MI 48009 Office: Birmingham MI 48009

JUDGE, THOMAS LEE, advt. exec., lt. gov. Mont.; b. Helena, Mont., Oct. 12, 1934; s. Thomas Patrick and Blance (Guillot) J.; B.A., U. Notre Dame, 1957; student U. Louisville, 1958-60; m. Carol Anderson, Jan. 29, 1966. Sales exec. Nat. Starch Products & Chem. Co., Louisville, 1957-58; merchandising dir. Louisville Courier-Jour., 1958-60; owner, pres. Judge Advt.-Pub. Relations, Helena, 1960—; exec. sec. Mont. Broadcasters Assn., 1961—, Mont. Savs. and Loan League, 1965—; advt. dir. Glacier Park, Inc.; lt. gov. of Mont., 1969—. Mem. Mont. Ho. of Reps., 1960-65, asst. minority leader, 1962; mem. Mont. Senate, 1967-69, chmn. natural resources com. Bd. dirs. YMCA, 1962-64. Served with AUS, 1958-59. Named Outstanding Young Man of Mont., Jr. C. of C., 1966, Notre Dame Man of Year for Mont., 1966. Mem. Pub. Relations Soc. Am., Nat. Conf. Lt. Govs. (exec. com. 1970—), Am. Soc. Assn. Execs. Democrat. K.C., Elk, Eagle. Home: 1619 Highland Av Helena MT 59601 Office: State Capitol Bldg Helena MT 59601

JUDIS, JOSEPH, coll. dean; b. Toledo, Sept. 23, 1929; s. Max and Thelma (Rabinovitz) J.; B.S. in Pharmacy, U. Toledo, 1949; M.S., Purdue U., 1951, Ph.D., 1954; m. Hana Kiryati, Mar. 20, 1955; children-Linda Susan, Allen Sydney. Postdoctoral research fellow microbiology Western Res. U. Med. Sch., 1954-55; research microbiologist Toledo Hosp. Inst. Med. Research 1955-56; mem. faculty U. Toledo, 1956—, prof. pharmacy, 1962—, chmn. dept. biology, 1964-66, dean Coll. Pharmacy, 1966—. Mem. Am. Pharm. Assn., Am. Chem. Soc., Am. Soc. Microbiology, Soc. Gen. Microbiology (London), A.A.A.S., Sigma Xi, Phi Lambda Upsilon, Rho Chi, Phi Kappa Phi. Author articles in field. Home: 2806 Meadowwood Dr Toledo OH 43606

JUDKINS, DONALD WARD, banker; b. Seattle, Apr. 2, 1912; s. Earl Henry and Laura (Lundberg) J.; student U. Minn. 1929-32; grad. Am. Inst. Banking, 1937; m. Elizabeth Waltz, Jan. 23, 1954. With First Nat. Bank, Mpls., 1933-41, 46-49; cashier First Hennepin State Bank, Mpls., 1949-56; pres. First Southdale Nat. Bank, Mpls., 1956—. Bd. dirs. Walker Art Center, Mpls., 1953—, pres. bd. dirs., 1955-58, bd. dirs. Center Opera Co., 1968—, v.p., 1969-71, pres., 1971—; bd. dirs. Ft. Snelling State Park Assn; bd. dirs. treas. Southdale Center Mchts. Assn., 1956-68. Mem. Greater Southdale Area C. of C. (pres. 1967-68). Rotarian. Clubs: Minneapolis; Mill Reef (Antigua, B.W.I.); Home: 2310 Huntington Point Rd W Wayzata MN 55391 Office: 226 Southdale Minneapolis MN 55435

JUDKINS, WESLEY PARKHURST, horticulturist; b. Oakland, Me., Sept. 27, 1911; s. Wallace Howard and Ida Estelle (Mosher) J.; B.S. in Horticulture. U. Me., 1934; M.S., Ohio State U., 1937, Ph.D., 1941; m. Helen Elizabeth Starr, Dec. 31, 1939; children—Susan J., Mary B., James S., Nancy R., Anne L. Instr. vocational agr. North Yarmouth Acad., 1934-35; instr. horticulture U. Me., 1935-36, N.M. A. and M. Coll., 1937-38; asst. prof. horticulture U. Conn., 1940-43; asso. prof. Ohio State U., 1943-49; prof., head dept. horticulture Va. Poly Inst., Blackburg, 1949-67, prof. horticulture, extension specialist, 1967—. Pres., P.T.A. Mem. Am. Inst. Biol. Sci., Am. Soc. for Hort. Sci., Am. Pomological Soc., Nat. Council State Garden Clubs (nat. chmn. horticulture), Sigma Xi, Phi Kappa Phi, Alpha Zeta, Gamma Sigma Delta, Phi Epsilon Phi, Pi Alpha Xi. Presbyn. Editor: Fruit Varieties and Horticulture Digest, 1946-49. Contbr. articles to profl., popular publs. Home: 317 Country Club Dr Blacksburg VA 24060

JUDKINS, WINTHROP OTIS, educator; A.B., M.A., Ph.D., Harvard. Prof. art McGill U., Montreal, Que., Can., also chmn. dept. Home: 40 Hillcrest Av Pointe Clair Quebec Canada

JUDSON, EVERETT GIFFORD, ins. co. exec.; b. Bronx, N.Y., Aug. 4, 1917; s. Charles Everett and Sadie (Gifford) J.; grad. Columbia, 1938; grad. advanced mgmt. program, Harvard, 1952; m. Sarah Elizabeth Henckel, Mar. 1, 1941; children-Nancy, Barbara (Mrs. Lawrence Colvin), Cynthia. With N.Y. Life Ins. Co., 1938- 61, v.p., 1958-61; v.p., dir. First Boston Corp., 1961-62; v.p., First Nat. City Bank, N.Y.C., 1962-64; sr. v.p., dir. Keystone Custodian Funds, 1964-68; v.p. Nat. Life Ins. Co., Montpelier, Vt., 1968-69, sr. v.p. investments, 1969—; pres., dir. Nat. Life Investment Mgmt. Co., Montpelier,, 1969—; dir. Adminstrv. Services, Inc., Equity Services, Inc., Sentinel Growth and Income Funds. Mem. investment coom. Vt. Coll., Montpelier. Bd. dirs. Vt. Childrens Aid Soc. Mem. Life Ins. Assn. Am. Mem. United Ch. of Christ. Club: Union League (N.Y.C.). Home: Westwood Dr Montpelier VT 05602 Office: Nat Life Ins Co Nat Life Dr Montpelier VT 05602

JUDSON, FRANKLYN SYLVANUS, lawyer, mfg. co. exec.; b. Cleve., May 13, 1915; s. Calvin Albert and Beatrice (Harding) J.; A.B., Case Western Res. U., 1938, J.D., 1940; m. Nancy E. Nevin, July 29, 1939; children—Franklyn N., William W., Ann Louise, Kenneth G., Carolyn. Admitted to Ohio bar, 1940, Pa. bar, 1954; law librarian Western Res. U., Cleve., 1940-41; jr. atty., prin. trial atty., asst. regional adminstr. SEC, Cleve., 1942-53; atty., asst. sec. I-T-E Circuit Breaker Co., Phila., 1953-55, sec., 1955- 67; sec., gen. counsel I-T-E Imperial Corp., 1967—, v.p., sec., gen. counsel, 1969—; dir. Elkhart Products Corp., Chase-Shawmut Co. Chmn. div. C maj. firms dept. United Fund, Phila., 1957-59; trustee I-T-E Found. Bd. dirs. Health and Welfare Council, 1963, United Cerebral Palsy Assn. Phila.; Pres. bd. trustees Friends' Central Sch. Mem. Am., Cleve., Phila. bar assns., Am. Soc. Corp. Secs. (past pres. Middle Atlantc regional group, bd. dirs. 1968). Mem. Soc. Friends (trustee Old Haverford monthly meeting). Clubs: Union League (Phila.). Home: 820 Colony Rd Bryn Mawr PA 19010 Office: 1900 Hamilton St Philadelphia PA 19130

JUDSON, JAY RICHARD, educator; b. N.Y.C., July 5, 1925; s. Bernard and Sylvia (Siegl) J.; grad. Horace Mann Sch., 1943; B.A., Oberlin Coll., 1948; M.A., N.Y. U., 1952; Ph.D., Kunsthistorisch Inst., U. Utrecht (Netherlands), 1956; m. Carolyn French, June 20, 1953; children—Pieter Moulton, Matthew Bowditch, Sarah Mercer, Nicolaas French. Faculty, Smith Coll., 1956- -, prof. art, 1967—; chmn. dept., 1967-69; vis. asso. prof. Columbua, 1966- 67. Bd. dirs. Am. Assn. Commn. Relief in Belgium Alumni. Mem. selection com. Netherlands-Woodrow Wilson Fellowships, 1965. Served with USNR, 1943-44. Commn. Relief in Belgium fellow, summer 1953; Fulbright grantee, 1954-55, 55-56; Guggenheim fellow, 1960-61; Fulbright research grantee, guest prof. U. Utrecht, 1963-64. Mem. Coll. Art Assn., Soc. Bentvogels. Club: Nantucket (Mass.) Yacht. Author: Gerrit van Honthorst, A Discussion of his Position in Dutch Art, 1959; Catalogue of Paintings, Rembrandt After three Hundred Years (Art Inst. Chgo.), 1969. Dirck Barendsz, 1534-1592, 1971; Jacob de Gheyn, 1971; Home: 187 Elm St Northampton, MA 01060.

JUDSON, ROBERT DRAKE, banker; b. Lake Forest, Ill., Mar. 5, 1925; s. Frank M. and Gladys (Stahl) J.; A.B., Princeton, 1947; m. Mary Douglass Scribner, Nov. 26, 1948; children—Robert D., Gilbert H., Frank V.D., Hunter R., Douglass S., Duncan S. With First Nat. Bank of Chgo., 1948—, v.p., 1962—; dir. Teco, Inc., Unarco Industries, Inc. Served with USNR, 1943-46. Clubs: Indian Hill, Princeton (N.Y.C.) University, Commonwealth (Chgo.); Old Elm; Minneapolis; Pine Valley Golf. Home: 9 Indian Hill Rd Winnetka IL 60093 Office: 1 First Nat Plaza Chicago IL 60670

JUDSON, SHELDON, educator; b. Utica, N.Y., Oct. 18, 1918; s. Salmon Sheldon and Dorothy (Eurich) J.; A.B., Princeton, 1940; M.A., Harvard, 1946, Ph.D., 1948; m. Anne Perrin Galpin, Feb. 13, 1943; children—Stephanie Dean, Anne Perrin Lucy Sheldon. Faculty U. Wis., 1948-55, asso. prof. geology, 1955- 64; Knox Taylor prof. geology Princeton, 1964—, chmn. dept., 1970— Dir. Princeton Coop. Sch. Program, 1964-66; pres. Princeton Jr. Mus., 1964-67. Trustee Daily Princetonian; Served to lt. USNR, 1942-46. Faculty fellow Fund Advancement Edn., 1954-55; Guggenheim fellow, 1960-61, 66-67; Fulbright fellow, 1960-61. Fellow A.A.A.S., Geol. Soc. Am.; mem. Arctic Inst., Sigma Xi. Author articles in field. Asso. editor, Am. Scientist, 1956-69. Home: 18 Aiken Av Princeton NJ 08540

JUDSON, SYLVIA SHAW, (Mrs. Sidney Haskins), sculptor; b. Chgo., June 30, 1897; d. Howard and Frances (Wells) Shaw; student Sch. Art Inst. Chgo., 1916-20; studies in Paris, 1920-21; Dr. Sculpture (hon.), Lake Forest Coll., 1952; m. Clay Judson, Sept. 3, 1921 (dec. Nov. 1960); children—Alice Clay (Mrs. Edward L. Ryerson, Jr.), Clay; m. 2d, Sidney Gatter Haskins, Dec. 1, 1963. Exhibiting sculptor, 1922—; one man shows Art Inst. Chgo., 1938 (tour of 5 other middle western museums 1938), Arden Gallery, N.Y.C., 1940, Ill. State Mus., Springfield, 1948, Chgo. Pub. Library, 1955, Sculpture Center N.Y., 1957; exhibited Phila. Mus. Art, Whitney Mus. Art, Mus. Modern Art, Met. Mus., Century of Progress Exhbns. at Chgo. Art Inst., N.Y., San Francisco world's fairs; mus. collections Chgo. Art Inst., White House, Phila., Dayton, O., Springfield, Ill., Davenport, Ia. Recipient Logan prize, 1929, hon. mention, 1925, 35, 45, Clyde Carr prize, 1947; Art Inst. Chgo.; hon. award in fine arts Chgo. chpt. A.I.A., Chgo. Assn. Commerce and Industry, 1956; Municipal Art League prize Chgo. No. Jury Show, 1957; Speyer prize Am. Acad. Design, 1957; medal Garden Club of Am., 1957. Fellow Nat. Sculpture Soc.; mem. N.A.D. Mem. Soc. of Friends. Author: The Quiet Eye, 1954; For Gardens and Other Places, 1968. Address: 1230 Green Bay Rd Lake Forest, IL 60045.

JUDY, HUBERT STONEWALL, def. industry cons.; b. Woodward, Okla., June 20, 1915; s. Hubert Stonewall and May (Sheets) J.; B.S. in Bus. Adminstrn., Okla. U., 1940; grad. Advanced Flying Sch., Kelly Field, Tex., 1941, Air War Coll., 1952, Nat. War Coll., 1959, Advanced Mgmt. Program Harvard, 1956; m. Mae Summers, Oct. 10, 1942. Commd. 2d lt. USAAF, 1941, advanced through grades to brig. gen. USAF, 1962; various assignments in U.S., 1941-43; dep. comdr., then comdr. 448th Heavy Bomb Group, Eng., 1943-45; plans and operations staff officer SHAPE, air dep. to air comdr. Office Allied Mil. Govt., Berlin, Germany, 1945-46; staff plans and operations officer, directorate plans and operations Hdqrs. USAF, 1946- 48; USAF liasion officer to State Dept., 1948-49; asst. exec., exec. directorate plans and operations Hdqrs. USAF, 1949-51; asst. chief staff, plans and operations NATO, 1952-55; dep. comdr. Air Force Missile Devel. Center, Holloman AFB, N.M., 1955-58; asst. chief staff, plans and operations, J-3, Hdqrs. Alaskan Command, 1959-62; comdr. Montgomery Air Def. Sector, Gunter AFB, Ala., 1962-64, 32 NORAD/CONAD Region, 1963-64; dep. dir. plans for advanced planning, directorate plans, DCS/P&O, Hdqrs. USAF, 1964-65; dep. dir. plans NATO Mil. Com. and Standing Group, Washington, 1965-67, ret., 1967; now cons. to def. industry, rancher. Decorated Legion Merit with 2 oak leaf clusters, D.F.C. with 2 oak leaf clusters, Bronze Star with oak leaf cluster, Air medal with 3 oak leaf cluster; Croix de Guerre with palm (France). Home: Box G Star Route Hot Springs VA 24445

JUDY, JOHN WAYNE, Jr., veterinary educator; b. Indpls., Oct. 11, 1931; s. John Wayne and Doris Lucile (Lane) J.; student Wabash Coll., 1949-52; B.S., Purdue U., 1954, Ph.D.; D.V.M., Kan. State U., 1958; m. Shirley Nell Brooks, Aug. 15, 1953; children—Charles W., Martha L., Douglas B. Individual practice vet. medicine, Greencastle, Ind., 1958-61; research fellow Coll. Vet. Medicine Ia. State U., 1961-62; instr. Purdue U., 1962-68, asst. to dean, 1964-66, asst. prof., 1968-69; prof., head dept. med. and surgery Coll. Vet. Medicine U. Ga., 1969-71; prof. comparative medicine and clin. medicine Coll. Vet. Medicine, U. Ill., 1971—; vet. cons. Named Tchr. of Year, 1969. Mem. Am., Ill., Ga., Ind. vet. med. assns., Am. Farm Econ. Assn., Sigma Xi, Sigma Chi, Phi Zeta. Republican. Methodist. Mason. Contbr. articles profl. jours. Home: 802 W Delaware Av Urbana IL 61801

JUDY, PAUL RAY, investment banker; b. Portland, Ind., Feb. 18, 1931; s. Paul R. and Mary E. (Hanlin) J.; A.B., Harvard, 1953, M.B.A., 1957; m. Mary Ann Dorsey, Nov. 27, 1954; children—Carol Ann, Mary Hannah, John Hanlin, Beth Ellen. With A.G. Becker & Co. Inc., Chgo., 1958—, v.p. corp. finance, 1961- 65, chmn. exec. com., 1965—, pres., chief exec. officer, 1968—; dir. Mohawk Data Sci. Corp. Bd. govs. N.Y. Stock Exchange, 1968-71. Trustee Chgo. Orch. Assn., Hadley Sch. for Blind. Served to 1st lt. USMCR, 1953-55. Clubs: Harvard, Economic (dir.), Chicago (Chgo.); Indian Hill; Sunset Ridge; Recess (N.Y.C.). Home: 14 Country Lane Northfield IL 60093 Office: 2 First Nat Plaza Chicago IL 60670

JUERGENS, WILLIAM GEORGE, dist. judge; b. Steeleville, Ill., Sept. 7, 1904; s. H.F. William and Mathilda (Nolte) J.; A.B., Carthage Coll., 1925, LL.D., 1970; J.D., U. Mich., 1928; m. Helen A. Young, Dec. 14, 1929 (dec. Feb. 1966); children—Jane (Mrs. Donald L. Hays), William G.; m. 2d, Charlotte Louise Mann, Mar. 18, 1967. Admitted to Ill. bar, 1928; county judge Randolph County, 1938-50; judge 3d Jud. Circuit Ct. of Ill., 1951-56, U.S. Dist. Ct., Eastern Dist. of Ill., 1956—, now chief judge. Adv. bd. Inst. Juvenile Research, Ill., 1945-56. Recipient 1st Ann. Honor Alumnus award Carthage Coll., 1961. Mem. Fed. Ill., Randolph County bar assns., Bar Assn. 7th Fed. Circuit. Republican. Presbyn. Mason (32, Shriner), Lion. Home: 1836 Swanwick St Chester IL 62233 Office: First Nat Bank Bldg Chester IL 62233

JUGO, LAURENCE, actor; b. Berkeley, Cal; ed. U. Cal. Broadway appearances include Skin of Our Teeth, Decision, Born Yesterday, Stalag 17; TV appearances include Studio One, Omnibus, Danger, The Web; featured on The Web, CBS- TV network. Address: 157 Taft Crescent Centerport NY 11721*

JUHL, JOHN HAROLD, educator, physician; b. Thompson, Ia., Nov. 21, 1913; s. Hans Peter and Helen (Halverson) J.; A.B., U. Mich., 1936, M.D., 1940; m. Helen B. Harris, Sept. 12, 1938; children—John Harold, Susan. Intern, U. Hosp., Madison, Wis., 1941, resident radiology, 1946-49; faculty U. Wis. Med. Sch., 1949-52, 54—, prof. radiology, 1960—, chmn. dept., 1963—; radiologist St. Barnabas Hosp., Mpls., also engaged in private practice, 1952-54. Served with USNR, 1943-46. Diplomate Am. Bd. Radiology. Fellow Am. Coll. Radiology; mem. Assn. U. Radiologists, Radiol. Soc. N.AM., Wis. Radiol. Soc., A.M.A., Wis., Dane County med. socs. Author: (with L. W. Paul) Essentials of Roentgen Interpretation, 2d edit., 1965. Home: 40 N Roby Rd Madison, WI 53705.

JUKES, RICHARD STARR, mining and mfg. co. exec.; b. S. Mountain, Ont., Can., Dec. 6., 1906; s. Arthur Starr and Annie Florance (Norris) J.; grad. St. Edmund's Sch., Canterbury, Eng., 1923; m. Ruth Mary Wilmot, Sept. 21, 1935; children—Richard Wilmot Starr, Ann Starr (Mrs. David Bucks), Romola Starr. Sec., accountant Gyproc Products Ltd., 1934-39, dir., 1930—; dir. BPB Industries, Ltd., London, Eng., 1943—, deputy chmn., 1962—, chmn. mgmt. com., 1964-69, chmn. bd., 1965—; chmn. Gypsum Industries Ltd., S. Africa, 1952—; dir. S.A. Gyproc-Benelux, Belgium, dir. Svenska Aktiebolaget Gyproc, Placoplatre S.A., Platrieres-Modernes de Grozon S.A., Umtali Board and Paper Mills (pvt.) Ltd. Mem. bd. referees U.K. Taxation Court. Fellow Inst. of Chartered Accountants. Clubs: Bath (London); Island Sailing (Cowes, Eng.); Sandy Lodge Golf (Middlesex, Eng.); Moor Park Golf (Hertfordshire Eng.); Sundsvalls Golf (Sweden). Home: White House Watford Rd Northwood Middlesex England Office: Ferguson House 15-17 Marylebone Rd London NW 1 England

JUKES, THOMAS HUGHES, biol. chemist; b. Hastings, Eng., Aug. 25, 1906; s. Edward Hughes and Ann Mary (Barton) J.; B.S.A., U. Toronto, 1930, Ph.D., 1933; NRC fellow med. scis. U. Cal. at Berkeley, 1933-34; m. Marguerite Esposito, July 2, 1942; children—Kenneth Hughes, Caroline Elizabeth (Mrs. Nicholas Knueppel), Dorothy Mavis. Came to U.S., 1925, naturalized,, 1939. Instr., asst. prof. U. Cal. at Davis, 1934-42; with pharm. div. Lederle Labs., 1942-45, dir. nutrition and physiology research sect. research div. Am. Cyanamid Co., Pearl River, N.Y., 1945-58, dir. research agrl. div., 1958-59, dir. biochemistry, 1960-62; vis. sr. research fellow in biochemistry Princeton, 1962-63; prof. in residence div. med. physics, research biochemist Space Scis. Lab., U. Cal. at Berkeley, 1963—, asso. dir., 1968-70, lectr. nutritional scis. cons. C.W.S., AUS, 1944-45, NASA, 1969-70; guest lectr. various univs. Recipient Borden award Poultry Sci. Assn., 1947. Fellow Am. Soc. Animal Sci.; mem. Am. Soc. Biol. Chemists, Biophys. Soc., Am. Inst. Nutrition (council 1941-45), Soc. for Exptl. Biology and Medicine, Am. Chem. Soc., Trustees for Conservation (San Francisco), Sigma Xi, Delta Tau Delta. Republican. Clubs: Am. Alpine, Explorers (N.Y.C.); Sierra (San Francisco). Author: B Vitamins for Blood Formation, 1952; Antibiotics in Nutrition, 1955; Molecules and Evolution, 1965. Editorial bds. Biochem. Genetics, Jour. Molecular Evolution, other sci. jours. Contbr. articles to profl. jours. Home: 170 Arlington Av Berkeley CA 94707

JULES, MERVIN, artist; b. Balt., Mar. 21, 1912; s. Sidney and Anna (Goldenberg) J.; student Balt. City Coll., 1930, Md. Inst. Fine Arts, 1930-33, Art Students League, 1933-34; m. Rita Albers, Apr. 20, 1940; children—Gabriel, Fredrick. Instr. art Fieldston Sch., N.Y.C., 1942-44, Mus. Modern Art, 1943-44, 1946-48, War Vets. Art Center, 1944; vis. artist Smith Coll., 1945-45, asso. prof. art, 1946-63, prof., 1963—, chmn. art dept., 1963-67; prof., chmn. art dept. Coll. City N.Y., 1969—; mem. staff, univ. extension div., dept. edn. Commonwealth Mass., 1950-52. Lectr., U. Wis., summer 1951; staff George Vincent Smith Mus., Springfield, 1952-53. Held many one man shows including A.A.A. Gallery, N.Y.C., 1961; represented in collections including Met. Mus. Art, Mus. Modern Art, Art Inst. Chgo., Mus. Fine Arts Boston, Portland (Ore.) Mus., Library Congress, Balt. Mus. Art, Duncan Phillips Gallery, Walker Art Center, Tel Aviv Mus., N.Y. Library, La. Art Commn., Fogg Mus., Carnegie Inst., colls., univs. Lectr., Hillyer Coll., Hartford, Conn., 1953, fellow McDowell Colony, 1938, 61, Yaddo, 1941. Trustee Cummington Sch. Arts; mem. governing bd. Inst. for Study Art in Edn. Recipient Wilson Levering Smith medal, 1939, 41; Purchase prize Balt. Mus. Art, 1941, Mus. Modern Art, 1941, Library Congress, 1945, Bklyn. Mus., 1946; Springfield Art League prize, 1952, 1st prize, 1955; 1st prize Cape Cod Art Assn., 1957; Hollis M. Carlyle purchase prize Eastern States Art Exhbn., 1957; grant to study in Japan, Asian African Study Program, 1967. Mem. Provincetown Art Assn. (trustee), Audubon Artists, Artists League Am., Com. Art Edn., Soc. Am. Graphic Artists, Artist Equity Assn., Springfield Art League, Boston Printmakers (hon. mention 19th Ann. Exhbn. 1967), Am. Assn. U. Profs. Adv. editor School Arts. Home: 720 Burns St Forest Hills Gardens NY 11375

JULIA, GILDA, realtor, mem. Republican Nat. Com.; b. San Juan, P.R., Nov. 18, 1927, d. Enrique and Emilia (MartineZ) Julia; B.S. in Math., U. Va.; div.; children—Maria Emilia, Luis Esteban, Mario Enrique, Maria Luisa, Andres Eduardo, Miguel Antonio, Maria Alexandra. Originated 1st condominium apt. bldg. in U.S., 1st condominium office bldg. in U.S., 1st condominium parking garage in U.S., indsl. real estate developer in P.R. Del., Republican Nat. Conv., 1968; mem. Rep. Nat. Com. for P.R., 1968—. Club: Sleepy Hollow Country. Home: Mallorca 37 Hato Rey PR 00917 Office: Box 11605 Santurce PR 00910

JULIAN, ANTHONY, judge; b. Italy, Mar. 25, 1902; s. Francesco and Maddalena (Ventresca) Giuliani; A.B., Boston Coll., 1925, LL.D., 1961; J.D., Harvard, 1929. Came to U.S., 1913, naturalized, 1923. Admitted to Mass. bar, 1929; practiced law, Boston, 1929-53; town counsel Watertown, 1930-32, 41-43; faculty Boston Coll., 1934-37; U.S. atty. Dist. Mass., 1953-59; U.S. dist. judge Dist. 1934-37; U.S. atty. District Mass., 1953-59; U.S. dist. judge Dist. of Mass., 1959—. Mem. Mass. State Legislature, 1937-38. Mem. adv. bd. Don Orione Home for Aged. Served as maj. Judge Adv. Gen. Corps., AUS, World War II. Decorated knight Order Holy Sepulchre of Jerusalem; Star of Solidarity (Italy). Home 790 Boylston St Boston MA 02199

JULIAN, LEO SEASE, lawyer; b. Prosperity, S.C., May 29, 1892; s. A.J.P. and Lilly Agnes (Sease) J.; B.S., Va. Mil. Inst., 1912; LL.B., U. Va., 1920; grad. Saumur F. A. Sch., France, 1918; grad. study U. Clearmont, France, 1919; m. Dorothy Wellborn Johnson, Nov. 11, 1920; children—Eleanor (Mrs. Richard E. Cotton), William Alexander. Admitted to Fla. bar, 1915; practicing lawyer, Miami, 1920—; trial counsel Shutts, Bowen, Simmons, Prevatt & Julian 1930-57. Apptd. judge Circuit Ct. 11th Jud. Circuit, Dade Co., Fla., 1940 (did not accept); lt. col. Fla. Gov's. staff, 1949-52. Served as lt., F.A., U.S. Army, 1917-19, A.E.F., France, 1918-19. Mem. Internat. Bar Assn., Am., Fla., Dade Co. (pres. 1944-45) bar assns., Phi Sigma Kappa. Democrat. Episcopalian. Mason. Compiler: Florida Law Digest, Martindale Law Directory, 1924-30. Home: 1009 Hardee Rd Coral Gables FL 33134

JULIAN, ORMAND CLINKINBEARD, surgeon; b. Omaha, May 6, 1913; s. William Harold and Ella (Clinkinbeard) J.; B.S., U. Chgo., 1934, M.D., 1937, Ph.D., 1941; m. Rosemary Stirling Becker, Sept. 14, 1935; children—William H., Gail Elizabeth. Intern St. Luke's Hosp., Chgo., 1937-38; resident U. Chgo. Clinics, 1938-42; practice medicine, specializing in cardiovascular surgery, Chgo., 1945—; prof. surgery U. Ill. Coll. Medicine, 1947-71; chmn. div. surgery Presbyn.-St. Luke's Hosp., Chgo.,, 1965-70, chmn. dept. cardiovascular-thoracic surgery, 1970—; prof. Rush Med. Coll. Rush-Presbyn.-St. Luke's Med. Center, Chgo., 1971—. Served to maj. M.C., AUS, 1942-45. Fellow A.C.S.; mem. Am. Surg. Assn., Soc. Clin. Surgery, Internat. Cardiovascular Soc., Soc. Vascular Surgery. Home: 1110 N Lake Shore Dr Chicago IL 60611 Office: 1725 W Harrison St Chicago IL 60612

JULIAN, PERCY LAVON, chemist; b. Montgomery, Ala., Apr. 11, 1899; s. James S. and Elizabeth Lena (Adams) J.; A.B., DePauw U., 1920, D.Sc., 1947; A.M., Harvard, 1923; Ph.D., U. Vienna, 1931; D.Sc., Fisk U., 1947, W.Va. State Coll., 1948, Northeastern U., 1948, Morgan Coll., 1950, Northwestern U., 1951, Howard U., 1951, Lincoln U., 1954, Roosevelt U., 1961, Va. State Coll., 1962, Morehouse Coll., 1963, Oberlin Coll., 1964, Ind. U., 1969; LL.D., Lafayette Coll., 1969; L.H.D., MacMurray Coll., Jacksonville. Ill., 1969, Ind. U., 1969; m. Anna Johnson, Dec. 24, 1935; children—Percy Lavon, Faith Roselle. Instr. chemistry Fisk U., 1920-22; Austin fellow chemistry Harvard, 1922- 23, research fellow biophysics, 1923-24, George and Martha Derby scholar chemistry, 1924-25, univ. scholar, 1925-26; prof. chemistry W.Va. State Coll., 1926-27; asso. prof. chemistry, acting head dept. Howard U., 1927-29, prof., head dept. chemistry, 1931-32; Gen. Edn. Bd. fellow U. Vienna, 1929-31; research fellow, tchr. organic chemistry DePauw U., 1932-36; dir. research Soya Products div. Glidden Co., 1936-45, dir. research, mgr. fine chems., 1945-53; pres. Julian Labs., Inc., Laboratorios Julian de Mexico, S.A., 1953-64, Julian Research Inst. Julian Assos., Inc., 1964—. Spl. cons. Nat. Inst. Arthritis and Metabolic Diseases, NIH. Exec. bd. Chgo. chpt. Nat. Conf. Christians and Jews, v.p. bus. adv. council Chgo. Urban League; chmn. Commonwealth Edison Environmental Adv. Council; bd. regents State Ill. Trustee DePauw U., Greencastle Ind., Fisk U., Nashville, Howard U., Washington, So. Union Coll., Wadley, Ala., Roosevelt U. bd. dirs. Chgo. Theol. Sem., Chgo., Fund for Republic- Center for Study Democratic Instns. Recipient Spingarn medal, 1947; Distinguished Service award 1949-50 Phi Beta Kappa Assn., Chgo. 1949; Chicagoan of Year award Chgo. Sun-Times, 1950; Chem. Pioneer award, 1968; Merit award Chgo. Tech. Socs. Council (1967; others. Fellow Chem. Soc. London, N.Y. Acad. Sci., Am. Inst. Chemists (Honor Scroll award 1964); mem. Phi Beta Kappa Assos., Sigma Xi, Phi Beta Kappa. Conbr. articles to profl. jours. Holder patents. Address: Julian Research Inst 9352-58 W Grand Av Franklin Park IL 60131

JULIANA, JAMES NICHOLAS, corp. exec.; b. Camden, N.J., Apr. 1, 1922; s. Nicholas and Rosa (de Noti) J.; B.S., Washington Coll., Md., 1944; m. Elizabeth D. Sutton, Nov. 8, 1947; children—James S., Patrick C., Mary E., Thomas E., David J., Richard S., Robert Francis and Ronald Joseph (twins). Spl. agt. FBI, Washington, 1947-53; asst. exec. dir., exec. dir. U.S. Senate Com. on Govt. Operations, 1953-55, chief counsel to minority Senate Permanent Sub-com. on Investigations, 1955-58; exec. dir. CAB 1958-61; pres., dir. Internat. Fact Finding Inst., 1961- 62; pres. James N. Juliana Assos., Washington, 1962—. Mem. Pres. Com. on Mental Retardation, 1971—. Served with USNR, 1944-46. Mem. Soc. Former Spl. Agts. FBI, Assn. former Senate Aides, Kappa Alpha, Omicron Delta Kappa. Clubs: International, Georgetown. Home: 11013 Rosemont Dr Rockville MD 20852 Office: 1812 K St NW Washington DC 20006

JULIANA, LOUISE EMMA MARIE WILHELMINA, Queen of the Netherlands; b. 1909; d. Henry Wladimir Albert Ernst, Duke of Mecklenburg-Schwerin. and Wilhelmina, Queen of the Netherlands; ed. pvtly. and at U. of Leyden; m. Bernhard (Leopold Frederic Everhard Jules Curt Charles Godfrey Pierre), Prince of Lippe-Biesterfeld, Jan. 7, 1937; children—Beatrix Wilhelmina Armgard, Irene Emma Elisabeth, Margriet Francisca, Maria Christina. Became princess regent, 1948, queen Sept. 1948—. Address: Palace of Soestdijk Soestdijk The Netherlands

JULIBER, EDWARD BROWNE, investment consultant; b. N.Y.C., Oct. 11, 1912; s. Philip Herché and Leah (Browne) J.; B.S., U. N.C., 1937, M.S., 1938; m. Linda Porter Cromwell, May 30, 1940. Mng. dir. So. States Oil Co., Charleston, S.C., 1940-42; dep. dir. petroleum div. Office Q.M., Gen., Washington, 1945- 47; dep. dir. Trans. Planning, SCAP, Tokyo, Japan, 1947-50; chief Ryukyus Import-Export Mission, 1950; pres., dir. Am. Inst. for Fgn. Trade, Phoenix, 1952—, chmn. exec. com., bd. dirs.; exec. v.p. Phoenix Title and Trust Co.; v. chmn. Rustproofing, Inc.; pres., dir. Transam. Devel. Co., 1963-68, chief exec. officer, 1966-68, chmn., 1967-68; dir. Ariz. Ban-corp., Transam. Title Ins. Co., Title Guaranty Co. Denver, Valley Fair Corp., Allied Constrn. Co., Guarantee Title & Trust Co., Pioneer Title & Trust Co., Southwest Title & Trust Co., Title & Trust Realty Tax & Service Co. Bd. dirs. Heard Mus., Phoenix Symphony, Roosevelt council Boy Scouts Am. Served with USNR, 1942-45; now lt. comdr., inactive res.; dep. comptroller Trans. Corps, AUS, 1951-52. Mem. Q.M. Assn., Nat. Trans. Assn., Ariz. Coll. Assn. Clubs: Industrial (Japan); Rotary, Paradise Valley Country (dir.), Arizona, Press (Phoenix). Author articles. Home: P O Box 913 Scottsdale AZ 85252 Office: 3800 N Central Av PhoeniX AZ 85012

JULIBER, IRVING GERARD, corp. exec.; B. Bklyn., May 22, 1913; s. Irving and Lillian (Faltman) J.; B.S., N.Y. U., 1934, postgrad., 1940; M.A., Columbia, 1936; m. Roslyn E. Wolff, June 30, 1940; children—Ilene H., Lois D. Dep. mgr. N.Y. State Employment Service, 1938-41; dir. personnel OWI, 1941-43, Philharmonic Radio Corp., N.Y.C., 1943-46; dir. personnel, labor relations Waldes Kohinoor, Inc., N.Y.C., 1946-50; with Revlon, Inc., N.Y.C., 1950-71, v.p. indsl. relations, 1950-56, v.p., operations, 1956-60, sr. v.p. adminstrn., 1960-70; owner I. Gerard Juliber Assos., N.Y.C., 1971—; dir. Medispas, Inc. Employer-trustee Dist. 65 Welfare and Pension Fund, Distributive Workers Am. Comml., labor arbitrator Am. Arbitration Assn. Mem. Am. Soc. Personnel Adminstrn. Clubs: N.Y. University, Varsity Letter; Pine Hollow Country (East Norwich, L.I.). Home: 635 Bryant Av Roslyn Harbor NY 11576 Office: 40 W 55th St New York City NY 10019

JULIEN, RICHARD EDWARD HALE, lawyer; b. Detroit, Mar. 20, 1900; s. Edward H. and Katherine (Heard) J.; A.B., U. Cal. at Berkeley, 1923; LL.B., Harvard, 1926; m. Sophie Hill, Aug. 30, 1926; children—Joan Mary, Richard Edward Hale. Corporate fiduciary banking, N.Y.C., San Francisco, 1927-35; admitted to Cal. bar, 1935, since practiced in San Francisco. Dir. Travelers Aid Soc. San Francisco, 1963-69. Life mem. Am. Bar Assn. (mem. ho. dels. 1952—, chmn. com. on hearing 1960-62, rep. Conf. Lawyers and C.P.A.'s 1963-65, mem. bd. govs. 1964-67); mem. Bar Assn. San Francisco (bd. dirs., chmn. com. judiciary 1958-59), State Bar Cal. (chmn. com. on taxation, com. on Jour. 1958-60), Am. Law Inst., Practicing Law Inst., Am. Bar Found. (charter life fellow), Am. Judicature Soc., Am. Acad. Polit. Sci., Soc. Cal. Pioneers San Francisco County (v.p.), Am. Legion (past post comdr.), Phi Delta Theta, Phi Alpha Delta (hon.). Republican. Clubs: Commonwealth of Cal. (chmn. sect. on adminstrn. of justice), Harvard, Olympic. Contbr. articles to banking, legal jours. Home: 2640 Steiner St San Francisco CA 94104. Office: Mills Tower 220 Bush St San Francisco CA 94104

JUMP, CHESTER JACKSON, Jr., clergyman, ch. ofcl.; b. Covington, Ky., Mar. 31, 1918; s. Chester Jackson and Inez (Moore) J.; A.B., Albright Coll., 1938; M.A., Columbia, 1940; B.D., Union Theol. Sem. N.Y.C., 1943; postgrad. Ecole Coloniale, Brussels, Belgium, 1950-51; D.D., Eastern Bapt. Theol. Sem., 1965; m. Margaret Elizabeth Savidge, Sept. 5, 1942; children—Karen Jane, Richard Alan, Catherine Louise, Robert Jon. Ordained to ministry Bapt. Ch., 1943; pastor N.E. Larger Parish, Lyndon Center, Vt., 1943-44; missionary Belgian Congo, Republic of Congo, 1945-62; regional rep. Am. Bapt. Fgn. Mission Socs., Valley Forge, Pa., 1961-64, gen. sec., 1965—. Asso. gen. sec. Am. Bapt. Conv., 1965—; mem. gen. bd. Nat. Council Chs., 1965—, mem. program bd., exec. com. div. overseas ministries, 1965—; mem. exec. com. Bapt. World Alliance, 1965—; mem. Bapt. Joint Com. on Pub. Affairs, 1965-67. Trustee Eastern Bapt. Theol. Sem.; bd. dirs. Japan Internat. Christian U. Found. Mem. Pi Gamma Mu. Author: (with wife) Congo Diary, 1950; Coming, Ready or Not, 1959. Home: 31 Reeceville Rd Coatesville PA 19320 Office: Am Bapt Fgn Mission Socs Valley Forge PA 19481

JUMP, ELLIS BURNETT, educator; b. New Britain, Conn., Dec. 16, 1909; s. Herbert and May (Brock) J.; grad. Taft Sch., 1928; A.B., Dartmouth, 1932; D.M.D., Harvard, 1936; Ph.D., U. Chgo., 1944; m. Margaret Endicott, Aug. 25, 1945; children—Constance, Leyton, Janet. Fellow stomatology Boston Children's Hosp., Harvard, 1936-38; asst. prof. anatomy Coll. Dentistry, U. Cal. at San Francisco, 1943-46; asso. prof. U. Ore. Dental Sch., 1947, prof. anatomy, head dept. 1947—. Dir. refugee services Am. Friends Service Com., Germany, Austria, 1953-55. Mem. Am. Assn. Dental schs., Am. Assn. Anatomy, Internat. Assn. Dental Research. Home: 3027 NE Ainsworth St Portland OR 97211

JUNG, ALLEN F., educator, ednl. adminstr.; b. Chgo., July 8, 1924; A.B., Loyola U., 1942, B.S., 1944; M.B.A., U. Chgo., 1947, Ph.D. in Marketing, 1957; married, 1946; 8 children. Instr. math., Stanford, 1945-46; asst. prof. marketing U. Mo., 1947-48, U. Ill., 1948-58; dir. M.B.A. program downtown campus, U. Chgo., 1958-65; prof. marketing, dir. Grad. Sch. Bus. Loyola U., Chgo., 1965—. Cons. to U.S. State Dept., Santiago, Chile, 1961. Mem. Am. Marketing Assn., Am. Econ. Assn. Contbr. articles to profl. publs. Office: Grad Sch Bus Loyola U 820 N Michigan Av Chicago IL 60611*

JUNG, CHARLES CHESTER, bus. exec.; b. Delavan, Wis., Sept. 11, 1903; s. Charles Eugene and Hattie (Seston) J.; A.B., U. Mich., 1926; m. Gwen Drew, Dec. 16, 1927; children—Nancy Ellen, Constance Drew, Charles Chester; m. 2d, Margaret Elizabeth Norse, 1951. Asso. Halsey, Stuart & Co., Chgo., 1926-28, A. G. Becker & Co., 1928-34; exec. v.p., gen. mgr., dir. Sheridan, Farwell & Morrison, Chgo., 1940-49; pres., dir. Scudder, Stevens & Clark, Inc., Chgo., 1949-53, dir., 1953-60; v.p. Calument & Hecla, Inc., Chgo., 1953-62, chmn. bd., 1962-68, chief exec. officer, 1965- 68, also dir.; chmn. bd. Cal. Cold Storage & Distbg. Co., Long Beach; chmn. bd. Hayward Marum, Inc.; dir. State Nat. Bank, Evanston, Gen. Finance Corp., Evanston, Universal Oil Products Co., Des Plaines, Ill. Past pres., dir. Glencoe Community Chest; past pres. Glencoe Park Bd.; dir. YMCA Hotel, Chgo. Mem. Beta Phi Theta, Acacia. Mason (K.T.). Clubs: Skokie Country (Glencoe); University (Chgo., Evanston and Milw.); Swedish, Executives (Chgo.). Home: 3150 Lake Shore Dr Chicago IL 60657 Office: 3150 Lake Shore Dr Chicago IL 60657

JUNG, LEO, rabbi; b. Ung. Brod, Moravia, June 20, 1892; s. Maurice Tzevi and Ernestine (Silbermann) J.; B.A., London U., 1918, Ph.D., 1921; B.A., Cambridge U., 1920, M.A., 1926; D.D., Yeshiva U., 1950; H.L.D., N.Y. U., 1955; Rabbinic diploma Hildesheimer Sem., Berlin, 1920; m. Irma Rothschild, Feb. 28, 1922; children—Erna (Mrs. Miguel Villa), Rosalie (Mrs. Leonard Rosenfeld), Julie (Mrs. Michael Etra), Marcella (Mrs. E.D. Rosen). Rabbi, Congregation Knesset Israel, Cleve., 1920-22, Jewish Center, N.Y.C., 1922—; prof. ethics Yeshiva U., 1931-67, prof. emeritus, 1968—. Pres., Rabbinical Council, 1926-34, Jewish Acad. Arts and Scis., 1950—; chmn. N.Y. State Govt. Adv. Bd. for Kosher Law Enforcement, 1935-65, Cultural Religious Commn., Joint Distbn. Com., 1941—. Pres., Milah Bd. of N.Y.; chmn. bd. Womens Social Service of Israel. Recipient Congl. medal for work in World War II. Mem. Am. Assn. U. Profs., Rabbonim Aid Soc. (hon. pres.). Author numerous books on Jewish law and lore, comparative folklore. Editor: The Jewish Library (8 vols.), 1928—. Home: 241 Central Park W New York City NY 10024 Office: 131 W 86th St New York City NY 10024

JUNG, NAWAB ALI YAVAR, former Indian diplomat; b. Hyderabad, India, Feb. 16, 1905; s. Nawab Khedive and Tyeba (Begum) J.; student Nizam Coll., Hyderabad, 1916-21; B.A., Queen's Coll., Oxford 1927, LL.D. (hon.) 1958; m. Zehra Begum, Aug. 29, 1939; children—Bilqis (Mrs. Lateef), Adil Yar Khan, Nasreen (Mrs. Kulsum Dubash), Asad Karim Khan, Azeez Mehdi Khan. Prof. history Osmania U., Hyderabad, 1927-35, pres., 1945-46, pres., 1948-52; dir. information Hyderabad State, 1935-37; sec. Hyderabad Govt. for constl. Affairs, Information and Broadcasting, 1937-42; sec. to Govt. for Constl. Affairs and Home. 1942-45; minister Constl. Affairs, Edn., Pub. Health and Local Govt., 1946-47; ambassador to Argentina and Chile, 1952- 54, to Egypt, Lebanon and Libya, 1954-58, to Yugoslavia, Bulgaria and Greece, 1958-61, to France, 1961-65; pres. Aligarh Muslim U., 1965-68; former ambassador to U.S.A.; del of India to UN. 1946-55, dep. leader, 1956, 57, 60; leader Indian Delegation to Econ. and Social Council, 1953. Recipient Padma Bhushan award for distinguished and meritorious service Pres. of India, 1959. Home: Banjara Hills Hyderabad India

JUNGE, JAMES F., corp. exec.; b. Chgo., June 18, 1921; s. William F. and Eleanore (Rauch) J.; B.A. in Chem. Engring., U. Ill., 1943; m. Bethel Pitcairn, Sept. 4, 1943; children—Danna, Jan, Dirk, Wenda, Kim, Nita, Kaye. Engr., Gulf Oil Corp., 1943-49; partner Custom Refining Co., 1949-54; cons. engr. Welling & Woodward, Inc., 1954-58; exec. v.p. Pitcairn Co., Jenkintown, Pa., 1958-63, pres., 1963-70, pres. Pitcairn Inc., 1971—, also dir.; dir. PPG Industries, Inc., Commonwealth Oil Refining Co., Inc., Westmount Life Ins. Co., Bluemount Resources Ltd., Fidelity Bank. Mem. Am. Chem. Soc., Am. Inst. Chem. Engrs. Home: 3192 Buck Rd Bryn Athyn PA 19009 Office: Jenkintown Plaza Jenkintown PA 19046

JUNGEBLUT, CLAUS WASHINGTON, bacteriologist; b. St. Paul, June 12, 1897; s. Nicholas and Gertrude (Kypke) J.; student Kaiser Friedrich Gymnasium, Berlin, 1903- 15; M.D., U. Bern, (Switzerland), 1921; m. Dora Blom, Mar. 5, 1923 (div.); 1 son, Roland; m. 2d, June Magor Beckwith, Dec. 14, 1951. Vol. asst. Robert Koch Inst., Berlin, 1921-22, Inst. Exptl. Therapy, Berlin- Dahlem, 1922-23; bacteriologist N.Y. State Dept. of Health, 1O23-27; fellow in med NRC, 1927; asso. prof. bacteriology and exptl. pathology Stanford, 1927-29; asso. prof. bacteriology Columbia, 1929-36, prof. bacteriology, 1936-62; research cons. microbiology Lenox Hill Hosp., N.Y.C., 1962—. Engaged in study infectious diseases, infantile paralysis, exptl. tumors; Fulbright vis. lectr. Cairo U., UAR, 1960-61; vis. prof. microbiology Postgrad. Med. Center, Karachi, Pakistan, 1962-63. Fulbright award for research in Netherlands, 1951. Mem. N.Y. State Bd. Med. Examiners, 1946-55. Mem. A.M.A., N.Y. Acad. Scis., Am. Soc. for Exptl. Pathology, Soc. Exptl. Biology and Medicine. Lutheran. Contbr. articles to med. jours. Home: 63 Cross Hwy Westport CT 06880 Office: Lenox Hill Hosp Park Av and 77th St New York City NY 10021

JUNIPER, KERRISON, Jr., physician, educator; b. St. Petersburg, Fla., Aug. 3, 1924; s. Kerrison and Dorothy (Drew) J.; student Duke, 1941-43, U. Miss., 1943-45; M.D., Emory U., 1949; m. Catherine Durant, July 10, 1943; children—Kevin Alan, Karen Ann. Intern Roper Hosp., Charleston, S.C., 1949-50; resident VA Hosp., Atlanta, 1950-51, 52-54; asst. in medicine Boston U., 1954-56; asst. prof. medicine U. Ark. Med. Center, Little Rock, 1956-62, asso. prof., 1962-67, prof., 1967—, chief gastroenterology sect., 1956-70, dir. Postgrad. Tng. Program in Gastroenterology, 1960-70, dir. Office Biomedical Communications, 1969-70, coordinator tech. research med. edn., 1970—; vis. prof. Nat. Def. Med. Center, Taipei, Taiwan, 1971-72; attending physician in medicine VA Hosp., Little Rock, 1956-62, cons. in medicine, 1962—. Mem. health occupations adv. bd. Met. High Sch., Little Rock; cons. in continuing edn. Ark. Regional Med. Programs, 1970—. Served with AUS, 1943-46, to capt., 1951-52. Decorated Bronze Star medal. USPHS postdoctoral research fellow in gastroenterology Boston U., 1954-56. Diplomate Am. Bd. Internal Medicine, Am. Bd. Gastroenterology, Am. Bd. Microbiology. Mem. A.A.A.S., Am. Fedn. Clin. Research, A.C.P., So. Soc. Clin. Investigation, Central Soc. Clin. Research, Am. Gastroenterol. Assn., Am. Soc. Tropical Medicine and Hygiene, So. Gut Club, So. Med. Assn., Health Sci. Communication Assn., Nat. Audio Visual Assn., Ark. Med. Soc., Sigma Xi. Mem. editorial bd. Am. Jour. Digestive Diseases, 1966-68. Home: 224 Kingsrow Dr Little Rock AR 72207

JUNIPER, WALTER HOWARD, coll. ofcl.; b. Nelsonville, O., Oct. 25, 1911; s. Charles Walter and Lucena E. (Howard) J.; A.B., B.S., Ohio State U., 1933, A.M., 1934, Ph.D., 1937; postgrad. (Martin Kellogg Fellow in classics), Yale, 1934-35; m. Helen Marjorie Howery, May 25, 1935; 1 dau., Margaret Helen. Instr. classical langs. Ohio State U., 1934-37, instr. English, 1946; instr. French and Latin, dean men Cumberland Coll., Williamsburg, Ky., 1937-38; asst. prof. Latin Baylor U., 1938-41, asst. dean, prof. Latin, 1946-49; dean W. Tex. State U., Canyon, 1949-66, acad. v.p., 1966—. Moderator, Waco Jr. Town Meeting, 1947-49. Served with AUS, 1941-46. Mem. Tex. Assn. for Ednl. Television, N.E.A., So. Conf. Acad. Deans, Am. Assn. U. Profs., Am. Philol. Assn., Tex. Classical Assn. Presbyn. Mason, Rotarian. Author, producer: Jukebox of Yesteryear, 1948-52. Contbr. to profl. jours. Home: 2516 6th Av Canyon TX 79015

JUNKIN, MARION MONTAGUE, artist, educator; b. Chunju, Korea, Aug. 23, 1905 (parents Am. citizens); s. William McCleery & Mary (Leyburn) J.; A.B., Washington and Lee U., 1927, Arts D., 1949; student Art Students League N.Y., 1937-30; studied with Luks, Locke & McCartan, 1930-32; m. Marguerite Eddy, Sept. 16, 1933; children—Michael Eddy, Margo Patricia. Prof. fine arts, asso. dir. Richmond Sch. Arts, Coll. William and Mary, 1933-42; prof., head dept. fine arts Vanderbilt U., 1941-49; prof., head dept. fine arts Washington and Lee U., Lexington, Va., 1949—; exhbt. in one man shows at Joseph Luyber Gallery, N.Y.C., 1946, 47, Va. Mus. Fine Arts, 1948; exhbt. in group shows at Whitney Mus., 1936, Corcoran Gallery, 1933, Art Inst. Chgo., 1933, N.Y. Worlds Fair, 1939, Pa. Acad. Fine Arts, 1933, Butler Art Inst., 1943, Carnegie Inst., 1949; fresco paintings in Memphis, Richmond, Roanoke, Va. Mem. Va. Fine Arts Commn., 1939-42. Recipient awards from Va. Mus. Fine Arts, Richmond Acad. Fine Arts, Butler Art Inst., IBM Corp., Brooks Meml. Gallery. Mem. Omicron Delta Kappa. Episcopalian. Home: 801 Stonewall St Lexington VA 24450

JUNOR, JOHN, newspaper exec.; b. Glasgow, Scotland, Jan. 15, 1919; s. Alexander and Margaret (Dickie) J.; M.A., Glasgow U., 1939; m. Pamela Welsh, Apr. 21, 1942; children—Roderick, Penelope Jane (Mrs. James Leith). Editor Sunday Express, London, Eng., 1954—, chmn., 1969—. Served to lt. Royal Navy. Presbyn. Club: Royal and Ancient. Home: Wellpools Farm Charlwood Surrey England Office: Sunday Express Fleet St London England

JURA, GEORGE, educator, chemist; b. N.Y.C., Nov. 18, 1911; s. Joseph and Mary (Kunda) J.; B.S., Ill. Inst. Tech., 1939; Ph.D., U. Chgo., 1942; m. Rose G. Bell, Aug. 23, 1937; children—George Henry, Michael Alan, Russell David. Asst. prof. U. Chgo., 1942-46; mem. faculty U. Cal. at Berkeley, 1946—, prof. chemistry, 1955—, now dir. Inst. Nuclear Tech. for Coll. Tchrs. Mem. chemistry adv. panel USAF Office Sci. Research. Guggenheim fellow, 1953. Mem. Am. Phys. Soc. spl. research surfaces of solids, effect high pressure on elec. and magnetic properties of solids. Home: 36 Arlington Av Kensington CA 94707

JURAN, JOSEPH MOSES, engr.; b. Braila, Rumania, Dec. 24, 1904; s. Jakob and Gitel (Goldenberg) J.; brought to U.S., 1912, naturalized, 1917; B.S. in Elec. Engring., U. Minn., 1924; J.D., Loyola U., 1935; m. Sadie Shapiro, June 5, 1926; children—Robert, Sylvia, Charles, Donald. Admitted to Ill. bar; with Western Electric Co., Inc., 1924-41; asst. adminstr. Office Lend-Lease Adminstrn., 1941-43; asst. adminstr. Fgn. Econ. Adminstrn., 1943-45; prof., chmn. dept. adminstrv. engring., N.Y.U., 1945-51; cons. numerous indsl. cos. and govt. agys., 1951—; dir. Dennison Mfg. Co., Ideal Corp., vis. lectr. numerous Am. and Fgn. univs. Recipient alumni medal U. Minn., 1954, Scroll of Appreciation, Japanese Union Scientists and Engrs., 1961, 250th Anniversary medal Czech Higher Inst. Tech., 1965, Wallace Clark medal, 1967, ann. medal technikhaza Eszterdom, Hungary, 1968, medal Fedn. Tech. and Sci. Industries (Hungary), 1968; medal of honor camera Official de la Industria, Madrid, 1970. Registered profl. engr., N.Y. State, N.J. Fellow Internat. Acad. Mgmt., A.A.A.S., Am. Soc. for Quality Control (hon., Brumbaugh award 1958, Edwards medal 1962, Eugene L. Grant medal 1967), Am. Inst. Indsl. Engrs., Am. Mgmt. Assn., Am. Soc. M.E. (Warner medal 1945); mem. sometime officer many profl. assns., Sigma Xi, Tau Beta Pi, Alpha Pi Mu. Club: Engineers (N.Y.C.). Editor: Quality Control Handbook, 2d edit., 1962 (translated into Japanese, Spanish, Russian, Hungarian). Author numerous books in the field quality control; Case Studies in Industrial Management, 1955; Managerial Breakthrough, 1964; (with J.K. Louden) the Corporate Director, 1966; (with F.M. Gryna, Jr.) Quality Planning and Analysis, 1970. Lectr., author, numerous papers on mgmt. Address: 860 UN Plaza New York City NY 10017

JURETSCHKE, HELLMUT J(OSEPH), physicist, educator; b. Berlin, Germany, Aug. 9, 1924; s. Alfred Hans Anton and Gertrude J. (Joseph) J.; came to U.S., 1940, naturalized, 1945; B.S., Harvard 1944, M.S., 1947, Ph.D., 1950; m. Ruth Marion Tarno, Feb. 11, 1950; children-Susan, Annette. Instr., asst. prof., asso. prof. Polytech. Inst. Bklyn., 1950-59, prof. physics, 1959—, acting head physics dept., 1965-66, head physics dept., 1966—. Served with AUS, 1944-46. Fellow Am. Phys. Soc.; mem. Am. Assn. Physics Tchrs., Phi Beta Kappa, Sigma Xi. Home: 41 Eastern Pkwy Brooklyn NY 11238 Office: 333 Jay St Brooklyn NY 11201

JURGENSEN, CHARLES ANDREW, mfr.; b. Goshen, N.Y., July 23, 1909; s. Christian Andrew and Mary (Stahigren) A.; B.S., Rutgers U., 1931; m. Ann Clara Jaeger, June 5, 1936; children—Alice, Charles II, J. Craig. With firm of DeLaval, Turbine, Inc. Trenton, N.J., 1931-66, successively shop worker to foreman, supt., work mgr., 1931-52, v.p. mfg., 1952-66; became v.p. operations DeLaval Separator Co., Poughkeepsie, N.Y., 1966, now exec. v.p., also dir.; dir. DeLaval Devel. Corp., G & H Products Co., Am. Heat Reclaiming Corp. Member exec. com. Del. United Fund. Trustee Rutgers U. Mem. Am. Soc. M.E. (exec. com., mem. bd. on edn.), Soc. Naval Architects and Marine Engrs., Soc. Advancement Mgmt. Engring. Council for Profl. Devel. (council mem.), also a member of the organization Council for Internat. Progress in Mgmt. (council mem.). Home: Maple Av Millbrook NY 12545 Office: DeLaval Separator Co Poughkeepsie NY 12602

JURGENSEN, WARREN PETER, educator, psychiatrist; b. Sioux City, Ia., June 30, 1921; s. Matthias Peter and Dagmar (Jensen) J.; B.S., Northwestern U., 1945; M.D., Creighton U., 1950; m. Gwenda Doris Downey, Mar. 30, 1946; children—Gail Ruth, Karen Sue, Timothy Allan. Intern Edward W. Sparrow Hosp., Lansing, Mich., 1950-51; regional health dir., then asst. chief U.S. Health Mission to Iran, 1951-54; psychiat. resident USPHS Hosp., Lexington, Ky., 1955-57, Cin. Gen. Hosp., 1957-58; with USPHS, 1951-70, chief Clin. Research Center, Nat. Inst. Mental Health, Ft. Worth, 1969-70; dir. student health services U. Tex. at Arlington, 1970—; clin. asst. prof. psychiatry U. Tex. Southwestern Med. Sch., 1966—; vis. research scientist Inst. Behavorial Research, Tex. Christian U., 1967—; vis. lectr. Regional Tng. Center, N. Central Tex. Council Govts., 1967—. Served with USNR, 1942-45. Diplomate Am. Bd. Psychiatry and Neurology. Fellow Am. Psychiat. Assn., Am. Pub. Health Assn. Epsicopalian. Home: 5000 Marble Falls Rd Fort Worth TX 76103 Office: Univ Texas 3d and West Sts Arlington TX 76010

JURINAC, SREBRENKA SENA, opera singer; b. Travnik, Yugoslavia, Oct. 24, 1921; d. Ludwig Jurinac and Christine Cerv; ed. Musical Acad.; m. Josef Lederle, 1961. Made first appearance on stage as Mimi in La Bohème, with Zagreb Opera, 1942; mem. Vienna State Opera, 1944—; numerous appearances Glyndebourne Festivals, 1949-56, Salzburg Festivals, 1957-67; regular guest artist LaScala, Covent Garden; prin. parts include Donna Elvira in Don Giovanni, Elisabeth in Tannhauser, Madame Butterfly, Mimi in La Boheme, Marschallin in Der Rosenkavalier, Elisabeth in Don Carlos, Desdemona in Othello, Tosca, others. Recipient Kammersängerin award, 1951; Ehrenkreuz für Wissenschaft and Kunst, 1961; Grosses Ehrenzeichen für Verdienste umdie Republik Osterreich, 1967. Address: care Vienna State Opera Austria

JURIST, JAMES ALFRED, business exec.; b. Chgo., Dec. 9, 1924, s. Alfred Edward and Rachel (Graff) J.; B.A., Columbia, 1947, M.B.A., 1949; m. Janet C. Calodny, June 28, 1953; children—Louis Michael, Carolyn Ruth. Staff accountant Arthur Young & Co., N.Y.C., 1949-51, 52-56; various financial mgmt. positions NBC, N.Y.C., 1956-65; controller Columbia Pictures Corp., N.Y.C., 1965-67; v.p., sec. John Blair & Co., N.Y.C., 1967- -. Served to 1st lt. USAAF, 1943-46, USAF, 1951-52. C.P.A., N.Y. Mem. Am. Inst. C.P.A.'s, N.Y. State Soc. C.P.A.'s, Phi Beta Kappa, Beta Gamma Sigma. Home: 210 DeMott Av Rockville Centre NY 11570 Office: 717 Fifth Av New York City NY 10022

JURJI, EDWARD J., educator; b. Latakia, Syria, Mar. 27, 1907; s. Jabra and Mary (Jureidini) J.; B.A., Am. U., Beirut, Lebanon, 1928, M.A., 1934; Ph.D., Princeton, 1936, B.D., 1942; m. Nahia K. Khuri, Aug. 20, 1932 (dec. April 1957); children—Layla (Mrs. Willard G. Oxtoby), Edward David; m. 2d, Ruth Guinter, Nov. 27, 1958. Came to the U.S., 1933, naturalized, 1947. Tchr. dept. edn., Iraq, 1928-30, Am. Sch. for Boys, Baghdad, 1930-33; mem. Inst. Advanced Study Princeton, 1936-38, faculty Theol. Sem. since 1939, lectr. in Arabic, 1942-52, book review editor Princeton Sem. Bull., 1945—; asso. prof. Islamics, comparative religion, 1946-54, prof., 1954-63, prof. history religions, 1963—. Vis. prof. numerous colls., univs., sems.; lectr. Middle East internat. and intercultural affairs; Haskell lectr. Oberlin, 1959; Fulbright research prof. U. Madras, India, 1960. Mem. Presbytery of N.Y.C.; chmn. Sesquicentennial Comparative Religion Conf., 1963; dir. World Religious Conf., 1964, 66. Edward F. Gallahue grantee, Member Soc. for Scientific Study of Religion, Internat. Assn. for History of Religions, Am. Assn. U. Profs. Author: Illumination in Islamic Mysticism, 1938; Christian Interpretation of Religion, 1952; The Middle East, Its Religion and Culture, 1957; The Phenomenology of Religion, 1963. Editor: Great Religions of the Modern World, 1947; The Ecumenical Era in Church and Society, 1959; Religious Pluralism and World Community, 1969. Co-editor Proc. of First Gallahue Conf. on World Religions, 1966. Collaborator:

Tarikh el Arab (3 vols.); Saudi Arabia. Contbr. articles on fgn. affairs, intercultural dialogue, world religions to profl. publs. Cons. staff: Random House Dictionary of the English Language, 1966, coll. edit., 1968. Home: 89 Castle Howard Ct Princeton NJ 08540

JUROW, IRVING H., lawyer; b. N.Y.C., Sept. 10, 1905; s. Benjamin and Helen (Nachman) J.; B.S., N.Y. U., 1926; J.D. cum laude, Harvard, 1929; m. Mae Wechsler, July 4, 1929. Admitted to N.Y. bar, 1930, U.S. Supreme Ct. bar, 1944; pvt. practice, N.Y.C., 1929-31; atty. N.Y. State Banking Dept., 1931-33; asst. to gen. counsel N.Y. State Ins. Dept., 1934-42; atty., sr. examiner Office Alien Property, 1942-43; legislative counsel Fed. Deposit Ins. Corp., 1943-48; gen. counsel Schering Corp., 1948-53, sec., gen. counsel, 1953-59, v.p., gen. counsel, 1959-70. Mem. Am. (sec. div. food drug and cosmetic law of corp., banking and bus. law sect.), N.Y. State (sec. food drug and cosmetic law sect. 1958-61) Bar Assn., Assn. Bar City New York. Club: Harvard (N.Y.C.). Office: 60 Orange St Bloomfield NJ 07003

JUST, CAROLYN ROYALL, lawyer; b. Shanghai, China, Sept. 15, 1907; d. Francis Martin and Mary Dunklin (Sullivan) Royall; Ph.B., U. of Chicago, 1934; J.D., DePaul U., 1938; LL.M., George Washington U., 1940; grad. Inter-Am. Acad. Comparative Internat. Law. Havana, Cuba, 4th Session, 1949, 5th Session, 1950; 7th Session, 1955, 9th Session, 1957; Certificate, Hague Acad. Internat. Law, 31st Session, 1960; m. Robert Just, Dec. 17, 1925 (dec. Nov. 1943). Violin tchr., 1925-30; chief of staff Concessions Dept., Century of Progress Chicago Exposition, 1933; editorial asst., sec. to Dr. Forest Ray Moulton, permanent sec. A.A.A.S., 1930-38; admitted to D.C. bar, 1938, practiced law at Washington, D.C., 1938; admitted to Ill. bar, 1940; admitted to bar of Supreme Court of U.S., 1941; with U.S. Dept. of Justice, atty. Lands Div., 1938-43; atty. Antitrust Div., 1943-50; atty. Tax Div., 1950—. Mem. D.C. Citizenship (formerly I Am An American) Day Com. (chmn. com. citizen- ship recognition, 1946, gen. sec., 1947-50); mem. Atty. Gen's. Adv. Com. on Citizenship and del. representing Dept. of Justice to nat. confs. on citizenship at Phila., 1946. Washington, 1947, 48, and 1950-55, N.Y.C., 1949. Mem. Am. Bar Assn. (sects. of taxation, antitrust internat. law, chmn. com. on relations with internat. bar orgns; adv. com. on pub. relations 1962-65; mem. com. facilities Law Library Congress 1952-59), Fed. Bar Assn. (formerly asst. editor Fed. Bar Jour.); Nat. Assn. Woman Lawyers, Bar Assn. of D.C., Women's Bar Assn. D.C., Internat. Bar Assn. (charter parton, del. to confs. N.Y.C., 1947, London, England, 1951, Madrid, 1952, Salzburg, 1960, Mexico City, Mexico, 1964; chmn. credentials com. Madrid 1952), Inter-Am. Bar Assn. (delegate to first conference Havana, Cuba, 1941, 3d and 4th confs., Mexico City, 1944, santiago, Chile, 1945, 5th Conf., Lima. Peru, 1947 6th conf. Detroit, 1949, 8th conf. Sao Paulo, Brazil, 54, 9th conf. Dallas, 1956, 10th conf. Buenos Aires, 1957, 11th conf. Miami 1959, 12th conf. Bogota, Colombia, 1961, 15th conference San Jose Costa Rica 1967; reporter general; council 1945—), Am. Law Inst., Am. Soc. Internat. Law, George Washington U. Alumni Assn., U. Chgo. Alumni Assn., Am. Judicature Soc., Am. Assn. U. Women, Club de las Americas (pres. 1964-65), D.A.R., Internat. Law Assn. (Am. br.), Internat. Fiscal Assn., Pi Gamma Mu, Kappa Beta Pi, Phi Delta Gamma. Mem. George Washington U. Symphony Orch., Gault Chamber Music Players, Amateur Chamber Music Players, Friday Morning Music Club. Home: Harbour Sq 520 N St S W Washington DC 20024 Office: U S Dept of Justice Washington DC 20530

JUST, WARD SWIFT, journalist; b. Michigan City, Ind., Sept. 5, 1935; s. F. Ward and Elizabeth (Swift) J.; student Lake Forest (Ill.) Acad., 1949-51. Cranbrook (Mich.) Sch., 1951-53, Trinity Coll., Hartford, Conn., 1953- 57; m. Jean Ramsay, Jan. 23, 1957 (div. Mar.1967); children—Jennifer Ramsay, Julia Barnett. Reporter, Waukegan (Ill.) News-Sun. 1957-59, Newsweek, 1959-61, Reporter mag., 1962-63; corr. Newsweek, 1962-65, Washington Post, 1965—. Clubs: Fed. City (Washington); Cercle Sportif (Saigon). Home: 22 Nguven Hue Saigon Republic of Vietnam Office: care of Washington Post 1515 L St N W Washington DC 20005

JUSTICE, JACK, realtor; b. Birmingham, Ala., Nov. 9, 1903; s. William James and Elizabeth Justice; m. Katherine Helga Wivestad, May 20, 1942; children—Romer B., Elizabeth Christine. Sales mgr. Kelvinator Corp., S. Am., 1934-36; distributor Frigidaire products, 1936-40; propr. firm Jack Justice, realtor, Miami Beach, Fla., 1940—; dir. First National Bank of Nay Harbor Islands. Chmn. the Florida Real Estate Commission, 1971. Councilman, Town Bay Harbor Islands, 1948-51; village mgr., Indian Creek Village, 1959-64. Served with AUS, World War II. Mem. Nat. Assn. Real Estate bds. (pres. 1966). Nat. Inst. Farm and Land Brokers (pres. 1963), Fla. assn. Realtors (pres. 1956), Miami Beach Bd. Realtors (pres. 1949), AMVETS (comdr. Fla. 1952), Am. Legion, Internat. Real Estate Fedn. (v.p. 1971), Nat. Real Estate Flyers Assn. (pres. 1958), Dade County Police Chiefs Assn., Fraternal Order Police, Interama C. of C. Mason (Shriner), Kiwanian (pres. N. Shore club 1962). Home: 9564 Byron Av Surfside FL 33154 Office: 1143 Kane Concourse Miami Beach FL 33154

JUSTICE, WILLIAM WAYNE, judge; b. Athens, Tex., Feb. 25, 1920; s. William Davis and Jackie May (Hanson) J.; LL.B., U. Tex., 1942; m. Sue Tom Ellen Rowan, Mar. 16, 1947; 1 dau., Ellen Rowan. Admitted to Tex. bar; partner firm Justice & Justice, Athens, 1946-61; city atty. Athens, 1948-50, 52-58; U.S. atty. Eastern Dist. Tex., 1961-68; U.S. dist. judge Eastern Dist. Tex., Tyler, 1968—. Vice pres. Young Democrats Tex., 1948; adv. council Dem. Nat. Com., 1954; alternate del. Dem. Nat. Conv., 1956; presdl. elector. 1960. Served to 1st lt. F.A., AUS, 1942-46; CBI. Mem. Am. Judicature Soc., V.F.W. (past post comdr.). Baptist. Rotarian (pres. Athens 1961), Mason (K.T.). Home: 324 W 8th St Tyler TX 75701 Office: Fed Bldg Tyler TX 75701

JUSTIN, BROTHER CORNELLUS, (Joseph M. Brennan), educator; b. Bklyn., Jan. 21, 1901; s. John and Mary (Culleton) B.; A.B., Manhattan Coll., 1925; M.A., Columbia, 1932. Mem. teaching order Bros. of Christian Schs.; founder, 1947, dir. Westchester Labor Sch., Yonkers, N.Y.; head dept. labor-mgmt. Manhattan Coll., 1947—. Lectr., U.S. Dept. State, Venezuela, 1965, Colombia, 1966. Mem. N.Y.C. Mayor's Action Panel To Study Problems of Job Discrimination, 1963—, N.Y. State Pub. Employment Relations Bd. Recipient Quadragesimo Anno medal Assn. Cath. Trade Unionists, 1950; John Acropolis Found. award, 1957. Mem. Am. Arbitration Assn., Indsl. Relations Research Assn., Cath. Bus. Edn. Assn., Acad. Polit. Sci., Am. Mgmt. Assn., Am. Acad. Polit. and Social Sci. Home: Manhattan Coll New York City NY 10471

JUSTIS, GUY R., pub. welfare adminstr.; b. Topeka, Kan., Dec. 27, 1911; s. Guy Tracy and Amy (Reynolds) J.; M.A., U. Denver, 1953; student U. Chgo., 1936; m. Ardis Caroline Larson, July 20, 1936: children—Joan Roslyn (Mrs. Brent Shaw), Richard Alan, Robert Tracy. Research cons. Colo. Emergency Relief Adminstrn., 1934-35; dist. supr. Colo. Dept. Pub. Welfare, 1935-42, supr. field services, 1942-43, dir. dept., 1954-64; adminstv. cons. Am. Pub. Welfare Assn., 1947-52, pres., 1963-64, dir., 1964—; mgr. welfare Denver Dept. Welfare, 1952-54; cons. on aging to sec. health, edn. and welfare, 1963-66, mem adv. council on pub. welfare, 1964-66. Served with USNR, 1943-45; PTO. Office: 1313 E 60th St Chicago IL 60637

JUSTUS, ROY BRAXTON, cartoonist; b. Avon, S.D., May 16, 1901; s. Augustus Braxton and Eliza Jane (Ruch) J.; student Morningside Coll., 1920-23, LL.D., (hon.), 1956; m. Ruth Eleanor Langley, Aug. 25, 1928. Polit. cartoonist Sioux City (Ia.) Tribune, 1924-26, 27- 41; editorial cartoonist Sioux City Jour., 1941-44, Mpls. Star & Tribune, 1944—; engaged in polit. cartoon syndication from Washington, 1927; mem. A.P. art staff, N.Y.C., 1927. Recipient Nat. Headliners' Club cartoon award; 1944 Freedoms Found. awards, 1949-56; Christopher award, 1955; Grenville Clark editorial page award, 1962, 65; Sigma Delta Chi award, 1965. Mem. Assn. Am. Editorial Cartoonists (pres. 1958-59). Club: Minnesota Press (Mpls). Home: 19 S 1st St Minneapolis MN 55401 Office: 425 Portland Av Minneapolis MN 55415

JUTEN, JOHN RUSSELL, mfg. co. exec.; b. Sparta, Minn., June 20, 1907; s. John Amandus and Edith (Nelson) J.; B.S. in Chem. Engring., Cath. U. Am., 1929; J.D., Georgetown U., 1933; m. Beunah Greenstreet, June 16, 1930; 1 dau., Joan Alice (Mrs. Richard Dube Casper). Admitted to D.C. bar, 1932, also Supreme Ct.; atty. U.S. Patent Office, 1929-31; practice patent law, Washington and N.Y.C., 1931-40; legal counsel, dir. indsl. relations Keuffel & Esser Co., Morristown, N.J., 1940—, v.p., sec., gen. counsel, 1960—. Mgmt. mem. labor-mgmt. com. def. manpower region II, Dept. Labor, 1951—. Mem. bd. edn., West Orange, N.J., 1967—, pres., 1971. Mem. Am., Fed. bar assns., N.Y., N.J. patent law assns., Am. Soc. Corporate Secs. Home: 7 Undercliff Terrace West Orange NJ 07052 Office: 20 Whippany Rd Morristown NJ 07960

KABALEVSKY, DMITRI BORISOVITSH, composer; b. Leningrad, Russia, Dec. 30, 1904; s. Boris and Nadejda (Kabalevskaja) K.; student composition Moscow State Conservatorium, 1925- 29, student piano, 1925-30, arts degree, 1935; m. Larissa Tchegodaeva, Nov. 29, 1937; children—Maria, Juri. Pianist, 1930—; conductor, 1948—; prof. Moscow State Conservatorium, 1938—; editor Soviet Music mag., 1940-47; head music dept. USSR Radio Com., 1943-45, music sect. Inst. History and Arts, USSR Acad. Scis., 1949-51; sec. Union of Composers, 1951—; v.p. Internat. Soc. Music Edn.; Academician, Acad. Pedagogic Scis. USSR. Works performed by numerous orchs. and conductors, Europe and U.S. Composer: (operas) Colas Breugnon, 1937, In Flames, 1942, The Taras Family, 1947, Nikita Vershinin, 1954, The Sisters, 1967; (operatta) Spring Song, 1957; (cantatas) Our Great Native Country, 1942, The Song of Morning, Spring and Peace, 1957-58. The Leninists, 1959, Requiem, 1962, About the Native Land, 1966; 4 symphonies, 1932, 33, 34, 56; The Comedians, 1940, Romeo and Juliet; musical sketches for symphony orch., 1956; concertos for piano and orch., for violin and orch., for cello and orch., also numerous children's pieces, sonnets by Shakespeare for voice and piano, chorus, music for films. Home: Nejdanova St 8/10 Moscow K-9 USSR Office: Union of Soviet Composers Nejdanova St 8/10 Moscow USSR

KABANDA, CELESTIN, former diplomat of Rwanda; b. Rusagara, May, 1936; s. Jean Ruhingo and Marie (Nyiratuza) K.; Philosophie of et Lettres, U. Lovanium (Congo); m. Felicite Nyirabagenzi, Aug. 24, 1963; children—Marie-Cecile, Jean-Marie, Jean-Pierre. Sec. to pres. Republic Rwanda, then sec. to cabinet and sec.- rapporteur for council of govt.; formerly ambassador to U.S., also to UN and Can. Mem. MDR-Parmehutu Party. Mem. Am. Acad. Polit. and Social Sci. Club: International (Washington). Home: 1752 Sycamore St NW Washington DC 20012 Office: 1714 New Hamptonshire Av NW Washington DC 20009

KABBANI, MAJATL, ambassador of Lebanon to U.S. Address: 2560 28th St NW Washington DC 20008*

KABELKA, KENNETH J., banker; b. Columbus, O., Sept. 28, 1928; s. Karl Franz and Marie (Glauder) K.; B.S. in Bus. Adminstrn., Ohio State U., 1951; grad. Am. Inst. Banking; m. Melbe Golder, May 26, 1956; children—Karen Maria, Karl Franz. With Huntington Nat. Bank, Columbus, 1946—, now sr. v.p.; occasional tchr. Am. Inst. Banking. Pres. trustees Columbus Tech. Inst. Served to lt. (j.g.) USCGR, 1951-53. Mem. Financial Execs. Inst. (sec.- treas. Columbus). Home: 358 Arden Rd Columbus OH 43214 Office: 17 S Hight St Columbus OH 43214

KABLE, EDWARD EVERETT, textile co. exec.; b. Bklyn., Feb. 17, 1939; s. Charles W. and Ruth E. (Combs) K.; B.A., Williams Coll., 1961; LL.B., Harvard, 1964; LL.M., N.Y. U., 1967; m. Lynn Waterson Middleton, June 1, 1958; 1 dau., Lisa Middleton. Admitted to N.Y. bar, 1965; asso. firm Curtis, Mallet-Prevost, Colt & Mosle, N.Y.C., 1965-67; asso. counsel Greenwood Mills, Inc., N.Y.C., 1967—, sec., asst. treas., 1969—. Mem. N.Y. State Bar Assn., Bar Assn. City N.Y., Am. Textile Mfrs. Inst. Home: 161 W 75th St New York City NY 10023 Office: 111 W 40th St New York City NY 10018

KABOTIE, FRED, artist, educator; b. Shongopavi, Ariz., Feb. 20, 1900; s. Lolomayoma and Seka (Vanka) K.; ed. pub. schs.; m. Alice Talay, June 30, 1931; children—Hattie (Mrs. Hattie K. Lomayesva), Michael. Tchr. art, 1937—; organizer, dir. Hopi Arts and Crafts and Silverscraft Coop. Guild, Oraibi, 1949—; organizer, pres. Hopi Cultural Center, Second Mesa, Ariz., 1965- -; chmn. archtl. com. Hopi Tribe; arts and crafts specialist Indian Arts and Crafts Bd., 1960—; exhbns. include Ariz. State Fair Fine Art, Phoenix, Inter-Tribal Indian Ceremonial, Gallup, N.M., Rockwell Art Gallery, Kansas City, Mo., Chgo. Art Inst., Dallas Art Mus., San Francisco World's Fair, Soc. of Four, Miami, Fla.; works rep. permanent collections Sante Fe Art Mus., Mus. No. Ariz., Flagstaff, Denver Art Mus., Mus. Modern Art, Mus. Am. Indian, N.Y.C., De Young Mus., Cal. Palace Legion of Honor, Newark Art Mus.; asso. Mus. No. Ariz., 1949—; demonstrated Am. Indian painting, silversmithing, carving at World Trade Fair, New Delhi, 1959-60. Trustee Louis Comfort Tiffany Found. Recipient certificate Indian Arts and Crafts Bd., 1959; medallion Republique Francaise Ministere de L'Education Nationale, 1956; Guggenheim fellow, 1945; medallion achievement Indian Council Fire, 1949, U. Ariz., 1961. Mem. Nat. Fedn. Fed. Employees, No. Ariz. Soc. Sci. and Art (asso.), Inter-Tribal Indian Ceremonial Assn., Author: Designs from Membrenos with Interpretations, 1949. Illustrator many books of S.W. Indians. Address: PO Box 37 Second Mesa AZ 86043

KAC, MARK, educator, mathematician; b. Krzemieniec, Poland, Aug. 3, 1914; s. Bencion and Chana (Rojchel) K.; Magister of Philosophy, U. Lwow (Poland), 1935, Ph.D., 1937; D.Sc. (hon.), Case Inst. Tech., 1966; m. Katherine Elizabeth Mayberry, Apr. 4, 1942; children—Michael Benedict, Deborah Katherine. Came to U.S., 1938, naturalized, 1943. Teaching asst. U. Lwow, 1935-37; jr. actuary Phoenix Co., Lwow, 1937-38; fellow Parnas Found., Johns Hopkins, 1938-39; instr. Cornell U., 1939-43, asst. prof., 1943-46, prof. math., 1947-61, Andrew D. White prof.-at- large, 1965-71; mem. Inst. Advanced Study, Princeton, 1951-52; prof. Rockefeller U., N.Y.C., 1961—. H.A. Lorentz vis prof. U. Lelden (Netherlands), 1963; vis. fellow Brasenose Coll., sr. vis. fellow Oxford (Eng.) U., spring, 1969. Guggenheim fellow, 1946-47; recipient Chauvenet prize for paper Random Walk and the Theory of Brownian Motion, Math. Assn. Am., 1950, for paper Can One Hear the Shape of A Drum, 1968. Mem. Am. Acad. Arts and Scis., Am. Philos. Soc., Am. Math. Soc., Math. Assn. Am., Nat. Acad. Scis., Inst. Math. Statistics. Sigma Xi. Contbr. articles profl. jours. Home: 6 Rectory Lane Scarsdale NY 10583 Office: Rockefeller U New York City NY 10021

KACHADOORIAN, ZUBEL, painter; b. Detroit, 1924; student Meinzinger Art Sch., Detroit, Saugatuck (Mich.) Art Sch., Skowhegan (Me.) Art Sch., Colorado Springs (Colo.) Fine Arts Center. Exhbns. include U. Ill., 1959-61, Milw. Art Center, 1945, Am. Annual, Chgo., 1961, Pepsi-Cola Fellowship Exchange, 1947, Va. Mus. Fine Arts, 1947, 49, Pa. Acad. Fine Arts, 1948, 49, Cal. Palace Legion of Honor, 1946, 47, Pasadena (Cal.) Mus. Art, 1945, also France, Eng., Italy, 1957-59; 15 one man exhbns., 1943-62; rep. permanent collections Art Inst. Chgo., Detroit Inst. Art, Muskegon (Mich.) Art Mus., Tate Gallery, London, Eng., Worcester (Mass.) Mus. Art, Norton Gallery, Palm Beach, Fla., Nelson Gallery Art, Kansas City, Mo. Recipient Prix-de-Rome fellowship Am. Acad. in Rome, 1956-59; purchase award Mich. Acad. Arts and Letters, 1956; Kirk-in-the-Hills award, 1954, 55; Gold medal Scarab Club, 1947; award Mich. Watercolor Soc., 1946; Pepsi-Cola Midwest fellow, 1946-47; Rosenthal award Nat. Inst. Arts and Letters. Mem. Mich. Acad. Arts and Letters. Address: Nicola Fabrizi 8 Rome Italy*

KACHLEIN, GEORGE FREDERICK, Jr., lawyer, assn. exec.; b. Tacoma, May 9, 1907; s. George Frederick and Edna June (Burt) K.; A.B., Stanford, 1929; LL.B., Harvard, 1932; m. Retha Hicks, Aug. 30, 1930; 1 son, George Frederick. Admitted to Wash. bar, 1933; asso. firm Bogle, Bogle & Gates, Seattle, 1933-37, partner, 1937-42, 46-65; asst. gen. mgr., asst. sec. Seattle-Tacoma Shipbldg. Corp., 1942-46; sec. Greater Seattle, Inc., 1952-57, pres., 1958-59; pres. Am. Automobile Assn., 1962-64, exec. v.p., 1965-70. cons. internat. affairs, 1971—, also trustee; v.p. Orgn. Mondiale de Tourisme et del'Automobile. Mem. Pres.'s Nat. Hwy. Safety Adv. Com.; sec. King Neptune VI, 1955-56. Named Seattle's Man of Year, 1963. Mem. Inter-Am. Fedn. Touring and Automobile Clubs (1st v.p.). Am., Wash., Seattle bar assns., C. of C. Clubs: Rainier; Seattle Golf; Thunderbird Country; Wash. Athletic (sec. 1950-51); Broadmoor Golf (pres. 1950-51). Home: Sandy Point Langley WA 98260 Office: 1712 G St NW Washington DC 20006

KACY, HOWARD WILLIAM, former ins. exec.; b. Huntington, Ind., Sept. 19, 1899; s. William J. and Augusta (McNabb) K.; LL.B., Ind. U., 1921; m. Anne Millsaps, Mar. 1, 1924; children—Anne (Mrs. Herbert S. Ainsworth), Howard William. Admitted to Ind. bar, 1921, D.C. bar, 1923; with Acacia Mutual Life Ins. Co., Washington, 1923-70, successively asst. counsel, counsel, gen. counsel, v.p. and gen. counsel, 1st v.p., exec. v.p., 1923-55, pres., 1955-67, chmn. of the board, 1967-70, dir., 1935-70; dir. Am. Security & Trust Co. Bd. dirs. Boys Club Met. Police D.C., Group Hospitalization, Inc., D.C. div. Am. Cancer Soc., D.C. chpt. A.R.C., YMCA, Nat. Capital area council Boy Scouts Am. Mem. Washington Bd. Trad (dir.), Soc. Friendly Sons St. Patrick (dir., past pres. Washington), Sigma Alpha Epsilon, Phi Delta Phi. Mason (hon. mem. DeMolay Legion of Honor). Clubs: Alfalfa, Metropolitan (Washington); Columbia Country (Chevy Chase, Md.); Rotary. Home: 1011 N Noyes Dr Silver Spring MD 20910 Office: 51 Louisiana Av Washington DC 20001

KADANE, DAVID KURZMAN, educator, lawyer; b. N.Y.C., Apr. 9, 1914; s. Joseph Carlisle and Fannie (Kurzman) K.; B.S.S., Coll. City N.Y., 1933; LL.B., Harvard, 1936; m. Helene Born, Oct. 5, 1936; children—Joseph B., Kathryn Ann (Mrs. Garry Crane). Asst. counsel U.S. Senate com. on interstate commerce investigation r.r. finance, N.Y.C., 1936-38; atty. SEC, Washington and Phila., 1938-41, spl. counsel and asst. dir., 1942-46; asst. to fed. housing expediter and nat. housing adminstr., Washington, 1946; gen. counsel L.I. Lighting Co., 1949-70; on leave as vol. Peace Corps, 1964-66; prof. law Hofstra Law Sch., 1970—. Chmn. Nassau County Youth Bd. Jewish religion. Home: 190 Voorhis Av Rockville Centre NY Office: 250 Old Country Rd Mineola NY

KADAR, JAN, motion picture director; b. Budapest, Hungary, Apr. 1, 1918; s. Rudolf and Luisa (Tyroler) K.; student Charles U., Prague, Czechoslovakia; m. Judith Sacher, Mar. 12, 1958. Engaged in documentary film business since World War II; script writer, asst. dir. Barrandov Feature Film Studio, 1947—; co-dir. with Elmer Klos: Kidnapped, 1952, Death is Called Engelchen (1st gold medal Moscow Film Festival), 1963, The Accused, 1964, The Defendent (grand prize Karlovy Vary Internat. Film Festival), 1964, Shop on Main Street (Acad. award for best fgn. lang. picture), 1965. Decorated State prize Czechoslovakia, 1964, 66; named Artist of Merit, 1965. Address: 3 Vlkova Prague Czechoslovakia

KADAR, JANOS ex-premier of Hungary; b. Hungary, 1912; student village sch. Apprentice toolmaker, then locksmith, streetcar condr.; leader Communist Youth Group, 1931; mem. Communist Party, 1932; a leader of Resistance in World War II; dep. police chief, 1945; mem. Parliament, 1945—; dep. sec.-gen. Communist Party, 1947, minister of interior, Hungary, 1949, also became head secret police AVO; arrested, imprisoned, 1951-53; mem. nat. com. Communist-dominated fatherland front, 1954, party 1st sec., 1955—, elected mem. Politburo, 1956; dep. premier, 1955, minister of state, 1957-61, premier of Hungary, 1956-58, 1961-65. Author: Firm People's PowerIndependent Hungary, 1958. Address: Budapest Hungary* *

KADEL, WILLIAM H., pres. Fla. Presbyn. Coll. Address: 5401 34th St S St Petersburg FL 33731*

KADES, CHARLES LOUIS, lawyer; b. Newburgh, N.Y., Mar. 12, 1906; s. Louis and Carrie (Kahn) K.; A.B., Cornell U., 1927; LL.B., Harvard, 1930; grad. Inf. Sch., 1942, Command and Gen. Staff Sch., 1943; m. Dorothy Lawrence (dec.); m. 2d, Patricia Minchin (div.); 1 dau., Caroline Jeanne; m. 3d, Phyllis Taber. Admitted to N.Y. bar, 1931, also D.C. bar; atty. Hawkins. Delafield & Longfellow, N.Y.C.; asst. gen. counsel Treasury Dept., 1938-42; commd. 2d lt. inf. U.S. Army Res., 1928, advanced through grades to col.; assigned to duty with gen. staff War Dept. 1943-45; served with Hdqrs. 7th Army and 1st Airborne Task Force in So. France operation, 1944-45; dep. chief govt. sect. G.H.Q., SCAP, 1945-49; partner Hawkins, Delafield & Wood, attys. and counselors, N.Y.C., 1949—. Decorated Legion of Merit with oak leaf cluster. Mem. Am., N.Y. State (past chmn. sect. on taxation) bar assns., Assn. Bar City N.Y., Tax Inst., N.Y. County Lawyers Assn., Japan Soc., Sphinx Head (Cornell U.), Phi Beta Kappa, Phi Kappa Phi. Democrat. Clubs: Harvard; City Mid-Day; Nat. Lawyers. Home: Green Bough Heath MA 01346 Office: 67 Wall St New York City NY 10005

KADING, DANIEL, educator; b. Juneau, Wis., May 5, 1921; s. August and Ida (Becker) K.; B.A., U. Wis., 1943, M.A., 1947; Ph.D., Cornell U., 1949; m. Elizabeth Anne Bland, May 29, 1947; children-Anne, Hume, Jefferson, Thomas, Sarah. Asst. prof., asso. prof. philosophy U. Tex., Austin, 1949-67; prof., chmn. philosophy dept. Kenyon Coll., Gambier, O., 1967—. Mem. Austin bd. Am. Civil Liberties Union. Served with USAAF, 1943-46. Mem. Am. Assn. U. Profs., Am. Philos. Assn. Home: 306 Gaskin St Gambier OH 43022

KADISH, MORTIMER RAYMOND, educator, philosopher; b. N.Y.C., Dec. 2, 1916; s. Samuel and Frances (Klein) K.; B.S.S., Coll. City N.Y., 1938; M.A., Columbia, 1939, Ph.D., 1950; m. Ruth Morman, Feb. 10, 1948; 1 dau., Joanne. Lectr., City Coll. N.Y., 1947-48; faculty Case-Western Res. U., Cleve., 1948—, prof. philosophy, 1962—, chmn. dept., 1957-67, dir. program philos. studies, 1964-66, co-dir., 1966-67; vis. lectr. U. Mich., 1960. Served with AUS, 1941-45; ETO. Guggenheim fellow, 1954-55; Spl. Rockefeller fellow, 1952; fellow Am. Council Learned Socs. 1967-68. Mem. Am. Philos. Assn., Am. Soc. Legal and Polit. Philosophy, Am. Assn. U. Profs. Author: (novel) Point of Honor, 1952; Reason and Controversy In The Arts, 1968; also articles. Home: 13855 Superior Rd Cleveland OH 44118

KADISH, SANFORD HAROLD, legal educator; b. N.Y.C., Sept. 7, 1921; s. Samuel J. and Frances R. (Klein) K.; B.S.S., Coll. City N.Y., 1942; LL.B., Columbia, 1948; m. June Kurtin, Sept. 29, 1942; children—Joshua, Peter. Admitted to N.Y. bar, 1948, Utah bar, 1954; practice law, N.Y.C., 1948-51; prof. law U. Utah, 1951-60, U. Mich., 1961-64, U. Cal. at Berkeley, 1964—; vis. prof. Harvard, 1960- 61, Freiburg U., 1967; lectr. Salzburg Seminar Am. Studies 1965; vis. fellow Inst. Criminology, Cambridge (Eng.) U., winter 1968. Reporter, Cal. Legislative Penal Code Project, 1964-68; public mem. Wage Stblzn. Bd., region XII, 1951-53; cons. Pres.'s Commn. on Law Enforcement, 1966; mem. Cal. Council Criminal Justice, 1968-69. Served to lt. USNR, 1943-46. Fulbright lectr. Melbourne (Australia) U., 1956; fellow Center Advanced Study Behavioral Scis., 1967-68. Mem. Am. Assn. U. Profs. (nat. pres.), Nat. Acad. Arbitrators, Am. Soc. Legal and Polit. Philosophy, Am. Assn. Law Sch. (exec. com. 1960), Phi Beta Kappa, Order of Coif (exec. com. 1966-67). Author: Criminal Law and Its Processes, 2d edit., 1969; also articles. Home: 774 Hilldale St Berkeley CA 94708

KADISON, ALEXANDER, author, editor; b. N.Y.C., Feb. 23, 1895; s. Bernard James and Ethel (Baszenska-Silberdicht) K.; B.A., Coll. City N.Y., 1915 (class orator); M.A., Columbia, 1916; m. Isabel Dean, Nov. 23, 1921 (dec. 1967). Free lance writer, N.Y.C., 1915; ofcl. translator U.S. Govt., Washington, 1917-18; head editorial dept. J. J. Little & Ives Co., N.Y.C., 1921-23; with Alfred A. Knopf, Inc., pubs., 1923-26; cons. editor and lit. adviser to pubs., 1926-29; with P. F. Collier & Son Co., pubs., 1929-30; local rep. Brit. Rationalist Press, 1930—; editor, pub. Kadison's News Letter. Cited by Archbishop O'Boyle of Washington for discovery omission in New Cath. Ency. Fellow Royal Geog. Soc.; mem. Sci. League Am., Rationalist Press Assn. (London, Eng.). Republican. Club: Sunrise (N.Y.C.). Author: Through Agnostic Spectacles, 1919; Immortality, 1922. Represented in New Learned History for Ready Reference, Biographical Dictionary of Modern Rationalists (London), others. Contbr. essays and poems to Am. and Brit. periodicals; cons. on newspaper problems; originator, 1931, of editorial policy for more effective opposition by newspapers to spread of communism in U.S. Literary executor of the late Annie S. Peck; lectr. social and polit. topics. Owner large collection of letters and diaries dealing with Am. life before, during and after Civil War. Actively identified since June 1942, with movement for postwar dismemberment of Germany. Author of several widely circulated pamphlets. Issued documented exposé of communism in U.S. Bureau of Census, Dept. Commerce, 1950. Contbr. The American Language, Supplement Two, H. L. Mencken; Excerpts from Tributes by H.L. Mencken, 1918-1948, 1968. Creator bus. slogans for nat. advertisers; cons. on trade names, trademark phraseology, spl. comml. neologisms. Authority on place names and Am. colonial surnames. Address: 35 Fifth Av New York City NY 10003

KADNER, CARL GEORGE, educator; b. Oakland, Cal., May 23, 1911; s. Adolph L. and Otillia (Pecht) K.; B.S., U. San Francisco, 1933; M.S., U. Cal. at Berkeley, 1936, Ph.D., 1941; m. Mary E. Moran, June 24, 1939; children—Robert Joseph, Elizabeth Grace, Carl Louis. Asst. prof. biology Loyola U., Los Angeles, 1936-41, prof., chmn. dept. biol., 1941-43, 1946—, now also trustee. Served to maj. AUS, 1943-46. Mem. A.A.A.S., Entomol. Soc. Am., Western Soc. Naturalists, Am. Soc. Microbiology, Sigma Xi. Home: 8100 Loyola Blvd Los Angeles CA 90045

KAEBNICK, HERMANN WALTER, bishop; b. Brookston, Pa., Feb. 13, 1898; s. Julius Frederick and Caroline (Bloedow) K.; student Warren Conservatory Music, 1919-22; B.A., Central U., 1926; postgrad. N.Y. Theol. Sem., 1925-26; B.D., United Theol. Sem., 1927; postgrad. U. Pitts., 1927-28; S.T.M., Luth. Theol. Sem., 1933; postgrad. Yale, 1948; LL.D., Albright Coll., 1960; D.D., Lycoming Coll., 1964; L.H.D., Lebanon Valley Coll., 1965; m. Gertrude Lillian Strehler, Aug. 4, 1927; childrenWarren W., Winifred L. Recitalist, oratorio singer, 1922-28; ordained to ministry Evang. U.B. Ch., 1928; pastor, Forest Hills, L.I., N.Y., 1925-26, Freedom, Pa., 1927- 28, Altoona, Pa., 1928-30, Somerset, Pa., 1930-39; supt. Pitts. Conf. Evang. Ch., 1939-50; gen. ch. treas. Evang. U.B. Ch., 1951-54; exec. sec. Gen. Council Adminstrn. Evang. U.B. Ch., Dayton, O. 1954-58; bishop Eastern Area, Harrisburg, Pa., 1959-67; bishop United Meth. Ch., Harrisburg, 1967-; tchr. Schuylkill Coll., 1925-26. Trustee Albright Coll., Lebanon Valley Coll., United Theol. Sem., Evang. Theol. Sem. Served to lt. (j.g.) USNRF, World War I. Mason, Kiwanian. Author: Education for Alcohol Problems, 1948. Contbr. articles to profl. jours. Home: 3018 Green St Harrisburg PA 17110 Office: 3 Riverside Office Center 2101 N Front St Harrisburg PA 17110

KAEL, PAULINE, author; b. Petaluma, Cal., June 19, 1919; d. Isaac Paul and Judith (Friedman) Kael; student U. Cal. at Berkeley, 1936-40; 1 dau., Gina James. Movie critic New Republic mag., 1966-67, New Yorker mag., 1968—. Author: I Lost it at the Movies, 1965; Kiss Kiss Bang Bang, 1968; Going Steady, 1970. Guggenheim fellow, 1964. Address: 25 W 43d St New York City NY 10036

KAELIN, EUGENE FRANCIS, educator; b. St. Louis, Oct. 14, 1926; s. Albert Aloysius and Bertah (Erni) K.; B.A. with distinction, U. Mo., 1949, M.A., 1950; D.E.S., U. Bordeaux (France), 1951; Ph.D., U. Ill., 1954; m. Pierrette Nicole Demartini, Dec. 30, 1952; children-Valerie Chantal, Carolyne Pascale, Martine Laurence. Instr. philosophy U. Mo., 1952-53; fellow philosophy U. Ill., 1953-54, post-doctoral fellow, 1954-55; instr. philosophy U. Wis., 1955-57, asst. prof., 1957-61, asso. prof., 1961-65; asso. prof. Fla. State U., 1965-67, prof., 1967—, chmn. dept., 1969—; mem. nat. adv. bd. Aesthetic Edn. Program (Central Midwestern regional ednl. lab.), 1968—. Served with USMC, 1945-46. Recipient William Henry Kiekhofer Meml. Teaching award, U. Wis., 1959. Mem. Am. Philos. Assn., Am. Soc. Aesthetics, Am. Soc. Phenomenology and Existential Philosophy, Fla. Philos. Assn. Author: An Existentialist Aesthetic, 1962; Art and Existence, 1970. Home: 604 Hillcrest St Tallahassee FL 32303

KAEP, LOUIS JOSEPH, artist; b. Dubuque, Ia., Mar. 19, 1903; s. Henry John and Mayme (Eulberg) K.; grad. Loras Coll., 1921, Chgo. Art Inst., 1924; fgn. travel and study Julien Acad., Paris, 1928-31; m. Marion Luey, Feb. 10, 1934. Art dir. J. Walter Thompson, Chgo., 1923-29, Montgomery Ward & Co., N.Y.C., 1942-54; exec. v.p., gen. mgr. Vogue Wright Studios, N.Y.C., 1954-68; pres. Electrographic Corp., N.Y.C., 1968—; exhibited Met. Mus. Art, Chgo. Art Inst., Wadsworth Atheneum, Hartford, Conn., Nat. Acad., U.S. Nat. Mus., Washington, John Herron Art Inst., Indpls., Chgo. galleries, others; commd. by USN to execute series of paintings in Mediterranean Area, 1960, in Pacific and Far East, 1961. Recipient gold medal Hudson Valley Assn. Artists, 1955, 70; 1st honor award Profl. Art League N.Y., 1956, award, 1965; Grand Nat. award Am. Artists Profl. League, 1956, Winsor Newton award, 1964; A.I.A. award, 1958; 1st award Art League L.I., 1958; Katharine M. Howe Meml. Fund award Knickerbocker Artists, 1961; Jane Peterson award 33d Ann. Hudson Valley Art Assn., 1961; USN Meritorious Pub. Service citation, 1963; Sidney Taylor Meml. award 1965; Muriel Alvord award, 1966; Katharine Howe Meml. award, 1968. Mem. Artists and Writers Assn., N.A.D., Am. Watercolor Soc. (1st v.p. 1962-66, citation for outstanding service 1965), Knickerbocker Artists, London Soc. Royal Arts, Balt. Watercolor Club, Allied Artists Am. (Asso. Mems. award), Greenwich Soc. Artists (treas. 1953-57), Springfield (Mass.) Art League, Chgo. Painters and Sculptors, Chgo. Galleries Assn., Ia., Westport artists assns., Soc. Illustrators. Club: Salmagundi (Clark Boyson award 1958, award for best in show 1969) (N.Y.C.). Contbr. Am. Artist. Home: 14 Anderson Rd Greenwich CT 06830

KAESER, CLIFFORD RICHARD, mfg. co. exec.; b. Boise, Ida., Feb. 17, 1936; s. Clifford Morgan and Bertha (Minton) K.; B.A., Coll. Ida., 1959; LL.B., Yale, 1962; m. Nan E. Wilson, May 29, 1965; children—Richard L., Cindy Marie. Admitted to Cal. bar, 1962; asso. atty. firm Lawler, Fexlix & Hall, Los Angeles, 1962-63; asst. counsel Lockheed Aircraft Co., 1963-64; successively div. counsel, group counsel, asst. sec. and acquisition counsel Litton Industries, Inc., 1964-69; v.p., gen. counsel HITCO, Los Angeles, 1969-70, adminstrv.

v.p., 1970—; v.p., dir. Wickes Industries, Inc., Bathey Mfg. Co., Conn. Hard Rubber Co., Rubber Fabricators, Inc.; mem. gen. mgmt. com. ARMCO Steel Corp. Mem. Am., Cal. bar assns., Am. Mgmt. Assn. Republican. Club: Sertoma (Bd. dirs.) (Marina del Rey). Home: 13210 F Admiral Av Marina del Rey CA 90201 Office: 533 S Fremont Av Los Angeles CA 90017

KAESS, FREDERICK WILLIAM U.S. judge; b. Detroit, Dec. 1, 1910; s. Fred C. and Dorothy (Koch) K.; student U. Mich., 1927-28; LL.B., Detroit Coll., 1932; m. Phyllis Danckmeyer, Dec. 31, 1931; 1 son, Frederick Charles. Admitted to Mich. bar, 1932; pvt. practice law, 1932-33; municipal justice St. Clair Shores, Mich., 1932-33; claims mgr. Mich. Mut. Liability Co., Detroit, 1933-39, 41-45; dep. commr. Mich. Dept. Labor and Industry, 1939-40; mem. firm Davidson, Kaess, Gotshall & Kelly, 1945-53; U.S. atty. Eastern Dist. Mich., 1953-60, U.S. dist. judge, 1960—. Chmn. Wayne County Republican Com., 1948-62; gen. counsel Nat. Fedn. Young Reps. Chosen Outstanding Fed. Adminstr. of 1959. Mem. Am., Mich., Fed. (pres. Detroit chpt. 1955-59) bar assns., Internat. Assn. Ins. Counsel, Sigma Delta Kappa. Mason (33, Shriner). Clubs: Univ. Mich., Yacht (Detroit); City (Lansing, Mich.). Home: 971 North Oxford Rd Grosse Pointe Woods MI 48236 Office: Fed Bldg Detroit MI 48226

KAFKA, ALEXANDRE, economist; b. Prague, Czechoslovakia, Jan. 25, 1917; s. Bruno and Jana Bondy (de Bondrop) K.; student Grad. Sch. Internat. Studies, Geneva, Switzerland, 1937-38; B.A., Balliol Coll., Oxford (Eng.) U., 1940, M.A., 1946; m. Rita Petschek, Sept. 6, 1947; childrenDoris, Barbara. Prof. econs. U. Paulo, Sch. Sociology and Politics, 1941-49; asst. div. chief Internat. Monetary Fund, 1949-51, exec. dir., rep. Brazil, Colombia, Dominican Republic, Haiti, Panama and Peru, 1966- -; dir. Brazilian Inst. Econs., 1951-63; prof. econs. U. Va., 1959-61, 63—, acting chmn. dept. econs. 1965-66; adv. Superintendency of Money and Credit, Brazil, 1951-56, UN, 1956-59. Adviser, Brazilian Ministry Finance, 1964-65; mem. tech. council Nat. Confedn. Commerce, Rio de Janeiro. Registered mem. Conselho Regional dos Economistas Professionais, Rio de Janeiro. Mem. editorial bd. So. Econ. Jour., 1966-68. Office: Internat Monetary Fund 19th and H Sts NW Washington DC 20006 also Rouss Hall U. Va Charlottesville VA 22904

KAFKA, MAXIMILIAN MARTYN surgeon; b. Warsaw, Poland, Apr. 1, 1900; s. Hirsch H. and Mildred M. (Dreyer) K.; brought to U.S., 1902, naturalized, 1907; student Columbia, 1918-20; S.B. in Medicine, U. Ark., 1922; M.D., U. Md., 1924; student N.Y. Postgrad. Med. Sch., Columbia, 1932-33, 35-36; m. Irma May Leonard, June 28, 1932; children—Malcolm Edmund, Stephen David. Intern Bellevue and allied hosps., 1924-26; first surg. asst. A. Roth Ear, Nose and Throat Hosp., N.Y.C., 1926-31; staff and faculty appointments N.Y.C., Bklyn., 1933-39; aviation med. research; attending flight surgeon Republican Aviation Corp., 1942—; cons. plastic surgeon and chief ear, nose, and throat dept. Meml. Hosp., Queens, L.I.; cons. plastic surgeon Doctors Hosp., Queens; courtesy surgeon N.Y. Eye and Ear Infirmary, N.Y.C.; ophthalmic med. examiner CAA, also mem. safety council same orgn.; cons. flight surgeon United Air Lines; mem. ophthalmology staff N.Y. Post Grad. Hosp. and Med. Sch. Commd. med. officer U.S. Army Res., 1927; certified flight surgeon USAAF, 1936-39; active mil. service as U.S. Army flight surgeon, 1940; retired as flight surgeon, capt., 1941. Decorated Congl. medal SSS, 1945. Diplomate Am. Bd. Preventive Medicine, Am. Bd. Otolaryngology, Am. Bd. Aviation Medicine. Fellow Am. Coll. Preventive Medicine, Am. Aviation Med. Assn., Am. Med. Writers Assn., N.Y. State Acad. Preventive Medicine, Am. Assn. Aviation Med. Examiners, Internat. Coll. Surgeons, Am. Acad. Ophthalmology and Otolaryngology; mem. nat. state and local gen. and spl. med. assns., Am. Assn. Motor Vehicle Safety (founder; pres.). Newcomen Soc. N.A. (mem. com. N.Y.), Foman Rhino-Plastic Surg. Group. Asso. editor Jour. of Safety. Clubs: Lions, City. Author several books in field of specialty and aviation medicine. Contbr. numerous articles various jours. Address: 147 Alhambra Circle Coral Gables FL ☆

KAFOED, E. J., banker; b. New Orleans, July 31, 1914; s. Harold James and Marie (Bouchon) K.; student Spencer Bus. Coll.; m. Ruth Gertrude Hingle, Aug. 3, 1940; 1 son, LeRoy John (dec. 1960). With Hibernia Nat. Bank, New Orleans, 1935—, sr. v.p., 1968—; cons. M&L Mortgage Co., New Orleans; adviser LaMor Land Co. Active local Boy Scouts Am. Served with USNR, 1942-46. Mem. New Orleans C. of C. Clubs: Internat. House, Vista Shores Country (New Orleans). Home: 6208 Bertha Dr New Orleans LA 70122 Office: PO Box 61540 New Orleans LA 70160

KAGAN, DONALD, historian, educator; b. Kurshan, Lithuania, May 1, 1932; s. Max and Leah (Benjamin) K.; brought to U.S., 1934, naturalized, 1940; A.B., Bklyn. Coll., 1954; M.A., Brown U., 1955; Ph.D., Ohio State U., 1958; m. Myrna Dabrusky, Jan. 13, 1955; children—Robert William, Frederick Walter. Instr. history Pa. State U., Univ. Park, 1959-60; asst. prof. ancient history Cornell, 1960-64, asso. prof., 1964-67, prof., 1967; prof. history and classics Yale, 1969—. Mem. Am. Hist. Assn., Am. Philol. Assn. Author: The Great Dialogue, 1965; The Outbreak of the Peloponnesian War, 1969. Home: 10 Fairy Glen Dr North Haven CT 06473 Office: Phelps Hall Yale Univ New Haven CT

KAGAN, JEROME, educator, psychologist; b. Newark, Feb. 25, 1929; s. Joseph and Myrtle (Liebermann) K.; B.S., Rutgers U., 1950; Ph.D., Yale, 1954; m. Cele Katzman, June 20, 1951; 1 dau., Janet Ina. Instr. psychology Ohio State U., 1954-55; research asso. Fels Research Inst., Yellow Springs, O., 1957-59, chmn. dept. psychology, 1959-64; asso. prof. psychology Antioch Coll., 1959-64; prof. social relations Harvard, 1964—. Adv. com. Nat. Inst. Child Health and Devel. Served with AUS, 1955-57. Fellow Am. Psychol. Assn., Am. Acad. Arts and Scis., Soc. Research Child Devel.; mem. Midwest Psychol. Assn. Author: (with G.S. Lesser) Contemporary Issues in Thematic Apperceptive Methods, 1961; (with Moss) Birth to Maturity, 1962; (with Mussen and Conger) Child Development and Personality, 3d edit., 1969; (with Havemann) Psychology, 1968; (with Janis, Mahl and Holt) Personality, 1969; Understanding Children, 1971. Home: 210 Clifton St Belmont MA 02178 Office: William James Hall Harvard U Cambridge MA 02138

KAGAN, SIOMA, educator; b. Riga, Russia, Sept. 29, 1907; s. Jacques and Berta (Kaplan) K.; Diplom Ingenieur, Technische Hochschule, Berlin, Germany, 1931; M.A., Am. U., 1949; Ph.D. in Econs., Columbia, 1954; m. Jean Batt, Apr. 5, 1947 (div. 1969). Came to U.S., 1941, naturalized, 1950. Sci. asst. Heinrich Hertz Inst., Berlin, 1931-33; partner Laboratoire Electro-Acoustique, Neuilly-sur-Seine, France, 1933-48; chief French Mission Telecommunications, French Supply Council in N.Am., Washington, 1943-45; mem. telecommunications bd. UN, 1946-47, econ. affairs officer, 1947-48; econs. cons. to govt. and industry; asso. prof. econs. Washington U., St. Louis, 1956-59; staff economist Joint Council Econ. Edn., N.Y.C., 1959-60; prof. internat. bus. U. Ore., Eugene, 1960- 67, U. Mo. at St. Louis, 1967—; faculty leader exec. devel. programs Columbia, Northwestern U., others. Served with Free French Army, 1941- 43. Decorated Legion of Honor (France). Fellow Latin Am. Studies Assn.; mem. Am. Econ. Assn., Acad. Polit. Sci., Assn. Asian Studies. Clubs: University (St. Louis); Conanicut Yacht (Jamestown, R.I.). Contbr. numerous articles profl. publs. Home: 18 S Kingshighway St Louis MO 63108

KAGANOFF, NATHAN M., librarian; b. Gaisin, Russia, Apr. 8, 1926; s. David Kaganoff and Miriam (Drazhner) K.; came to U.S., 1932, naturalized, 1937; B.A., Northwestern U., 1947; rabbi, Hebrew Theol. Coll., Chgo., 1948; M.A., Am. U., 1956, Ph.D., 1961; m. Baila Wolk, June 14, 1950 (dec. 1968); children—Joshua, Jeremy, Abbe-Gail, David, Moshe Mordecai; m. 2d, Rosalyn Winchester, Apr., 1970. Librarian, specialist religion and Judaica, Library of Congress, 1950-62; librarian Am. Jewish Hist. Soc., N.Y.C., 1962-69, librarian-editor, 1969—; lectr. history Coll. Jewish Studies, Washington, 1955-56; prin. Midrasha Community Hebrew High Sch., Washington, 1960-62; vis. prof. Brandeis U., 1969—. Mem. council, chmn. PTA YRSRH Edl. Instns., N.Y.C., 1964-68; mem. bd. edn., bd. dirs. Hebrew Acad., Washington 1952-62. Served as chaplain AUS, 1951-53. Named Father of Year, Hebrew Acad., Washington, 1962. Mem. Religious Zionists. Am. (pres. Washington 1960-62, nat. exec. council 1962—), Assn. Jewish Libraries (chmn. tech. processes com. 1966—, pres. research and spl. library div. 1968-70, pres. assn. 1970—), Am. Hist. Assn., Assn. Coll. and Research Libraries, Rabbinical Council Am., A.L.A., Inst. Early N.Y. History, Phi Beta Kappa, Phi Eta Sigma, Pi Mu Epsilon. Contbr. articles profl. jours. Home: 86 Greenough St Brookline MA 02146 Office: 2 Thornton Rd Waltham MA 02154

KAGEI, UMEO, Japanese diplomat; b. Tottori Prefecture, Japan, Mar. 9, 1920; s. Nobuharu and Tomeko (Akimoto) K.; grad. in law, Tokyo U., 1941; m. Sakiko Saito, Dec. 15, 1949; children—Ichiro, Yoko, Emiko, Joji, Sumiko, Saburo, Fumiko, Tomiko. Sec., Ministry Fgn. Affairs, 1945-53; assigned embassy, Washington, 1953-54; 2d sec. UN, 1954-55; 1st sec. embassy, Philippines, 1955-56; assigned Japanese Cabinet, 1956-58; chief S.E. Asia bur. Ministry Fgn. Affairs, 1958-60; 1st sec. embassy, Canberra, Australia, 1960-62, counselor, 1962-64; minister embassy, Thailand, 1964-66; consul gen. in Chgo., 1967—. Decorated 2d Order White Elephant (Thailand), 1967. Home: 1201 Sheridan Rd Evanston IL 60202 Office: 625 N Michigan Av Chicago IL 60611

KAGEL, MAURICIO, composer; b. Buenos Aires, Argentina, 1931. Pianist, conductor in Argentina, 1947-57, formerly dir. Argentinian Chamber Opera, Teatro Colon; prof. Berlin Acad. Film and TV; tchr. composition Darmstadt, Germany, Buffalo, Stockholm, Sweden; mem. staff Studio for Electronic Music, West German Radio, Cologne, 1957—; conductor numerous concerts modern music throughout Europe; recording artist for Times Records. Composer: Transicion I, Anagrama, Phonophonie, Diaphonie, Musik für Renaissance Instruments, Sur Scerie, Pas-de-cing, Match for 3, Transicion II for piano, percussion and two magnetic tapes, 1959. Address: Cologne-Lithal 83 Gleuelerstrasse West Germany*

KAGEL, SAM, lawyer; b. San Francisco, Jan. 24, 1909; s. Hyman and Jennie (Osiawich) K.; B.A., U. Cal. at Berkeley, 1929, LL.B., 1948; m. Sophia Rae Hornstein, Jan. 10, 1932; children—John, Peter, Katharine Margaret. Admitted to Cal. bar, 1949; labor economist, 1931-43; war manpower dir. No. Cal., 1943-45; labor arbitrator, 1945—; permanent arbitrator in San Francisco for Ladies' Garment Industry, 1945—, Pacific Coast Longshore Industry, 1948—; prof. labor law Sch. Law, U., Cal. at Berkeley, 1952-70. Mem. Gov. Cal. Adv. Com. Dept. Employment, 1959-67; mem. arbitrators panel Fed. Mediation and Concilation Service, 1946—; mem. panel Cal. Concilation Service, 1946—. Bd. dirs. A.R.C., 1962—. Mem. Cal. (chmn. com. labor relations 1962—), San Francisco bar assns., Am. Arbitration Assn. (panel 1946—). Author articles, booklets, monographs, reports. Home: 470 Vassar Av Berkeley CA 94708

KAHAN, ARCADIUS, educator, economist; b. Lodz, Poland, Jan. 16, 1920; s. Boruch M. and Sophie (Stupel) K.; student law and econs., Stefan Batory U., Vilno, Poland, 1936-38, econs. Free U. Warsaw (Poland), 1938-39; M.A., Rugters U., 1955, Ph.D., 1959; m. Pearl Ellenbogen, Nov. 12, 1946; children—Vivian Sarah, Miriam Israela. Came to U.S., 1950, naturalized, 1955. Research asso. U. Chgo., 1955-57, mem. faculty, 1957—, prof. econs., 1965—, master social scis. collegiate div., asso. dean of coll. of univ.; vis. prof. London (Eng.) School Econs., 1963; Fulbright prof. Hebrew U., 1967-68; cons. RAND Corp., 1959, Nat. Bur. Econ. Research, 1963-66. Fellow Russian Research Center, Harvard, 1961; NSF grantee, 1963-66; Guggenheim fellow, 1964. Mem. Am. Econ. Assn., Econ. History Assn., Econ. History Soc., Am. Assn. Advancement Slavic Studies. Home: 5539 S Blackstone Av Chicago IL 60637

KAHAN, IRVING, editor; b. Passaic, N.J., Feb. 12, 1912; s. Harry R. and Sonia (Abbot) K.; B.A., State U. Ia., 1935, certificate in journalism, 1935; m. Minna Richman, Sept. 11, 1941; children—Harriet R., Justine S. Editor, Passaic Citizen, 1936-38, Paterson (N.J.) Sunday Chronicle, 1939-40, Textile Dyer, Paterson, 1940-48; mng. editor Textile Labor mag., N.Y.C., 1949- 56, editor, 1957-69; pub. relations dir. Textile Workers Union Am., AFL- CIO, 1957—, publns. dir., 1969—. Publicity dir. United Italian Appeal, Paterson, 1946. Served with inf. AUS, 1943-45. Recipient Scholarship award Sigma Delta Chi, 1935. Author: Behind Taft-Hartley's Mumbo-Jumbo, 1949; The TWUA Story: They Said it Couldn't Be Done, 1964. Home: 466 Essex Av Bloomfield NJ 07003 Office: 99 University PL New York City NY 10003

KAHANE, HENRY, educator, linguist, medievalist; b. Berlin, Germany, Nov. 2, 1902; s. Arthur and Paula (Ornstein) K.; student univs. Berlin, Rome and Greifswald, 1922-30; Ph.D., U. Berlin, 1930; alumnus Am. Sch. Classical Studies, Athens; m. Renée Toole, Dec. 5, 1931; children—Roberta (Mrs. Marshall Ash), Charles. Came to U.S., 1939, naturalized, 1945. Asst. prof. Romance linguistics U. Berlin, 1932; lectr. U. Florence (Italy), 1934-38; research asst. U. So. Cal., 1939-41; mem. faculty U. Ill. at Urbana, 1941—, now prof. Spanish and linguistics, also prof. Center Advanced Study at univ. Bd. dirs. Mediterranean Linguistic Atlas, Venice, Italy, Linguistic Research, Inc. Guggenheim fellow, 1956, 62. Mem. Linguistic Soc. Am., Modern Lang. Assn., Arthurian Soc., Linguistic Soc. Paris, Soc. Romance Linguistics. Author: (mostly in coop. with wife) Italian Placenames in Greece, 1940; Spoken Greek, 1945-46; Descriptive Studies in Spanish Grammar, 1954; Development of Verbal Categories in Child Language, 1958; Lingua Franca in the Levant, 1958; Structural Studies on Spanish Themes, 1959; The Krater and the Grail, 1965; Glossary of Old Italian Portolani, 1967; also articles. Asso. editor Romance Philology, 1947—. Home: 808 W Oregon St Urbana IL 68101

KAHANE, MELANIE, interior and indsl. designer; b. N.Y.C., Nov. 26, 1910; d. Morris and Rose (Roth) Kahane; grad. Parsons Sch. Design, N.Y.C., 1931, Paris, France, 1932; m. Theodore Earl Ebenstein; Dec. 22, 1934 (div. 1945); 1 dau., Joan Lynn; m. 2d, Ben Grauer, Sept. 25, 1954. Illusr., Tobias Green Advt. Co., 1931-32; designer Lord & Taylor, 1933-34; founder, pres. Melanie Kahane, Inc., 1935-52; founder, 1952, since pres. Melanie Kahane Assos., indsl. design; designer for SBF Dept. and suburban stores St. Louis 1958—, Charles of Ritz beauty salons throughout U.S., 1957—, Playbill Restaurant, N.Y.C., 1958, Children's Mus., Ft. Worth, 1955, Ziegfield Theatre, N.Y.C., 1963, Gov. Shivers mansion, Austin, Tex., 1957, Pres. Goheen of Princeton ofcl. residence, 1958, Reid Hall, Paris, France, 1948, First Nat. Bank, Ft. Worth, 1962, others; dir. styling and design Sprague & Carleton Furniture Co., Inc., 1962—; lectr. Parsons Sch. Design, 1950—; design, color and fabric cons., 1952—. Mem. commn. to S.E. Asia for N.Y. World's Fair 1964-65; mem. Nat. Panel Arbitrators, 1963—; mem. NBC Monitor program mission to Russia, 1959. Chmn. Greater N.Y. Fund, 1961. Named hon. citizen, Knoxville, Tenn., Wichita, Kan. and Houston; recipient Decorator of Year award Carpet Assn. Am., 1953; Designer citation U.S. Commnr. Gen. Cullman, 1958; award Brussels World Fair, 1958; Career Key award Girl's Club Am., 1961; chosen as one of 100 American Women of Accomplishment, Harper's Bazaar mag., 1967. Fellow Am. Inst. Interior Designers (past nat. sec., bd. dirs., past pres. N.Y. chpt., nat. treas. 1971—), Municipal Art Soc., Decorator's Club N.Y.C., Archtl. League N.Y., Illuminating Engring. Soc., Inter-Soc. Color Council, Nat. Home Fashions League, Inst. Practising Designers (Eng.), Am. Theatre Wing. Contbr. books, encys. Author: There's a Decorator in Your Doll House, 1968. Prod. documentary film, Decorating, A Way of Life, 1949. Home: 29 E 63d St New York City NY 10022 Office: 25 E 61st St New York City NY 10021

KAHL, JOSEPH ALAN, educator; b. Chgo., July 26, 1923; s. Samuel and Lillian (Simon) K.; A.B., U. Chgo., 1947, A.M., 148; Ph.D., Harvard, 1952. Instr. Harvard, Cambridge, Mass., 1951-54; asst. prof. U. N.C., 1955; asst. prof. Washington U., St. Louis, 1956-59, asso. prof., 1959-63, prof., 1963-69; prof. sociology Cornell U., 1969—; vis. prof., Mexico, 1955—, Brazil, 1960, U. Leister (Eng.), 1966. Served with AUS, 1943-46. Author: American Class Sturcture, 1957, Measurement of Modernism, 1968. Editor: La Industrialización en América Latina, 1965, Comparative Perspectives on Stratification, 1968. Home: 101 Maple Av Ithaca NY 14850

KAHL, WILLIAM CARL, state edn. ofcl.; b. Mt. Horeb, Wis., Sept. 19, 1908; s. John C. and Augusta (Heuser) K.;B.A. in Social Sci. and Econs., U. Wis., 1931, M.A. in Ednl. Adminstrn., 1937; m. Bernice Lauder, Nov. 14, 1939; 1 dau., Karen (Mrs. Roberts). Tchr., Albany (Wis.) pub. schs., 1931-33; supervising prin., Albany, 1933-44; supt. schs., Lancaster. Wis., 1944- 49; supr. elementary instrn. Wis., Madison, 1949-54, dir. state aids, 1954-56, asst. supt. sch. finance, 1956-62, dept. state supt. pub. instrn., 1966—. Mem. Wis. Coordinating Com. for Higher Edn. 1966—, State Bd. Vocation Tech. and Adult Edn., 1966—, Ednl. Broadcasting Bdl., 1966—, Bd. regents U. Wis., state univs.; chmn. bd. dirs. Project Pub. Information, Mem. Am. Council on Edn. (mem. com. on accreditation of service experiences 1966—). Edn. Commn. States Council Chief State Sch. Officers. Home: 113 Richland Lane Madison WI 53705 Office: 126 Langdon St Madison WI 53702

KAHLE, LOUIS GEORGE, educator; b. St. Louis, Nov. 20, 1912; s. George L. and Martha (Kaminski) K.; B.A., U. Tex., 1935, M.A., 1937, Ph.D., 1951; m. Barbeth Staffel, Aug. 20, 1938; 1 son, Stephen L. Instr. modern langs. Wentworth Mil. Acad., Lexington, Mo., 1936-40; mem. faculty U. Mo., 1946—, prof. polit. sci., 1957—, chmn. dept., 1964-67, chmn. univ. tenure com., 1967-71. Chmn. regional selection com. Woodrow Wilson Fellowship, 1954-58. Served with AUS, 1943-45. Mem. Am., Southwestern polit. sci. assns., Am. Acad. Polit. and Social Sci., Internat. Studies Assn., Latin Am. Studies Assn., Pi Sigma Alpha, Phi Theta Kappa, Sigma Delta Pi. Home: 923 La Grange Rd Columbia MO 65201

KAHLER, ELIZABETH SARTOR, (Mrs. Ervin Newton Chapman), physician; b. Washington, Oct. 20, 1911; d. Armin Adolphus and Lenore Elome (Sartor) Kahler; B.S., George Washington U., 1933, M.A., 1935, M.D. with distinction, 1940; m. Dr. Ervin Newton Chapman, Feb. 24, 1942. Intern Gallinger Municipal Hosp. (now D.C. Gen. Hosp.), Washington, 1940-41 resident Children's Hosp., Washington, 1941-42; practice medicine, Washington, 1942—; asso. univ. physician George Washington U., 1942-50; examining physician YWCA, 1942-45; courtesy staff Washington Hosp. Center, Doctor's Hosp., George Washington U. Hosp.; alternate physician to wards Bd. Pub. Welfare, Dept. Pub Welfare D.C., 1953—; sch. physician Burdick Vocational High Sch., 1959—. Mem. cons. com. D.C. Pub. Schools for practical nursing program, 1962—. Trustee Wilson Coll. Mem. Women's Med. Soc. D.C. (pres. 1950-51), Am. Med. Women's Assn. (pres. 1957-58), A.M.A., Med. Soc. D.C. (chmn. com. on medicine and religion 1967—), D.C. Assn. Mental Health, Am. Heart Assn., Camp Fire Girls Inc. (nat. program com.), Columbian Women of George Washington U. (life). Home: 2600 36th St NW Washington DC 20007 Office: 3601 Davis St NW Washington DC 20007

KAHLER, HERBERT FREDERICK, mfg. co. exec.; b. St. Augustine, Fla., Sept. 20, 1936; s. Herbert E. and Marie (Strieter) K.; A.B., Johns Hopkins, 1958; LL.B., Harvard, 1961; m. Erika Rozsypal, May 16, 1964; children—Erik, Stephen, Christopher. Admitted to N.Y. bar, 1962; with firm Simpson, Thacher & Bartlett, N.Y.C., 1961-65; sec., gen. counsel Insilco Corp., Meriden, Conn., 1965-70; pres., chief exec. officer W.H. Hutchinson & Son, Inc., Chgo., 1970—. Bd. corporators Meriden Hosp. Served to lt., arty. AUS, 1962-64. Mem. Am. Bar Assn., Bar Assn. City N.Y., Phi Beta Kappa, Alpha Tau Omega. Republican. Lutheran. Club: Copper Valley (Meriden). Office: 1031 N Cicero Av Chicago IL 60651

KAHLER, WOODLAND, orgn. ofcl., author; b. Dallas, Feb. 6, 1895; s. Harry Adams and Beulah (Pace) K.; grad. Phillips Acad., 1914; B.A., Yale, 1918; student Faculte des Lettres, Paris, 1923; hon. degree Internat. Pythagorean Philos. Soc., London; m. Baroness Olga Clewesahl-Steinheil, May 3, 1932. Officer, Am. Trust Co., N.Y.C., 1919-22; pub. relations exec. Alfred A. Knopf, 1928-29. Rep. UNESCO, Paris; pres. Internat. Vegetarian Union; pres. World League for Protection of Animals; v.p. Beauty without Cruelty, Inc.; pres. World Orgn. Culture; adv. editor Voice of Ahinsa, Aliganj, India; hon. com. Terre Et Cosmos (1st interplanetary exhbn. in world). Served with U.S. Army, World War I. Created marquis d'Orlier de St. Innocent; decorated Hon. Diploma Vie et Action, chevalier Order of Merit, Livre d'Or (France); chevalier San Juan Bautista, Heraldica, Madrid, Order St. John of Cross (Spain). Fellow Am. Natural Hygiene Soc. (exec. com.), Indian Vegetarian Congress (life), Nilgiri Humanitarian League (exec. com.), All-Indian Animal Welfare Assn. (exec. com.), World Jain Mission (exec. com.), Men of the Trees (London), Friends of Buddhism (Paris), Millenium Guild (N.Y.C.); mem. S.R. (life N.Y. State), Vegetarian Soc. Eng. (v.p.), Authors League Am., S.A.R. (life), Psi Upsilon, Cercle de L'Union, Union Interalliée (Paris, France), Federacion Vegetariana Espanola (hon. pres.). Clubs: Polo de Barcelona; Polo (Paris, France); Ootacamund (India). Author: Early to Bed, 1928; Smart Setback, 1930; False Front, 1937; Giant Dwarf, 1942; Portrait in Laughter, 1946; Almighty Possibility, 1958; Cravings of Desire, 1960. Contbr. newspaper, mags.; books and art translated into Swedish, French, German, Hebrew, Hindi, Spanish. Home: Chateau la Budallera Barcelona (Vallvidrera) Spain

KAHN, ALBERT M., bus. exec.; b. Lithuania, Nov. 5, 1897; s. Maurice and Sarah (Cole) K.; brought to U.S., 1907, naturalized, 1920; student Rensselaer Poly. Inst., 1915-17, C.E. (hon.), 1954; m. Mildred Gilman, June 20, 1920; children—Shirley (Mrs. William

Ross), Marilyn (Mrs. G. de Turenne); m. 2d, Lillian Feldman, Apr. 25, 1955. Various positions Consol. Products Co., Inc., 1919-25, pres., 1925-51; rehab. Spreckles Sugar Refinery, Yonkers, N.Y., 1935-39, Franklin Foundry & Machine Co., Providence, Farr-Alpaca, Holyoke, Mass., 1939-42; treas. Winter & Co., 1942-45, dir., 1945-58; rehab. High Rock Knitting Co., Philmore, N.Y., 1943-45; pres. Acme Hamilton Mfg. Co, 1945—, also chmn. bd.; pres. Spear & Co., 1951; chmn. bd. Ludwig Baumann-Spear's, 1952-53. Pioneer in orgn. United Jewish Appeal. Trustee Jewish Hosp., Bklyn. Mem. Alumni adv. council, gen. devel. council Rensselaer Poly. Inst.; founder Albert Einstein Coll. Medicine; bd. dirs. Weizmann Inst. Sci., Am. Friends of Hebrew U., Albert Einstein Coll. Medicine Hosp. Mem. Am. Legion, Phi Epsilon Pi. Mason. Home: 45 Sutton Pl S New York City NY 10022 Office: 666 Fifth Av New York City NY 10019

KAHN, ALFRED EDWARD, coll. dean, economist; b. Paterson, N.J., Oct. 17, 1917; s. Jacob and Bertha (Orlean) K.; A.B., N.Y.U., 1936, M.A., 1937; postgrad. U. Mo., 1937-38; Ph.D., Yale, 1942; m. Mary Simmons, Oct. 10, 1943; children—Joel, Rachel, Hannah. Mem. staff Brookings Inst., 1940, 51- 52; with anti-trust div. Dept. Justice, 1941-42, Dept. Commerce, 1942, WPB, 1943; economist on Palestine surveys, 1943-44, Twentieth Century Fund, 1944-45; asst. prof., chmn. dept. econs. Ripon Coll., 1945-47; asst. prof. Cornell U., 1947-50, asso. prof., 1950-55, prof., 1955—, chmn. dept. econs., 1958-63, Robert Julius Thorne prof. econs., 1967—, dean Coll. Arts and Scis., 1969—. Dir. Tompkins Co., Econ. Opportunity Corp., 1968-69. Mem. atty. gen.'s nat. com. to study anti-trust laws, 1953-55; sr. staff U.S. Council Econ. Advisers, 1955-57; spl. cons. Boni, Watkins, Jason & Co., N.Y.C., 1957-61, Nat. Econ. Research Assos., 1961—, U.S. Fgn. Agrl. Service, Israel, 1960-61, Dept. Justice, 1963-64, FTC, 1965, Ford Found., 1967; econ. adv. council Am. Tel. & Tel. Corp., 1968—; mem. econ. adv. com. U.S. C. of C., 1964-66. Fulbright research fellow, Italy, 1954-55. Mem. Am. Econ. Assn., Phi Beta Kappa. Author: Great Britain in the World Economy, 1946; (with J.B. Dirlam) Fair Competition, The Law and Economics of Anti-trust Policy, 1954; (with M.G. de Chazeau) Integration and Competition in the Petroleum Industry, 1959; The Economics of Regulation, 2 vols., 1970, 71. Bd. editors Am. Econ. Rev., 1961-64. Home: RD 3 Trumansburg NY 14886

KAHN, ALFRED JOSEPH, educator, social worker and planner; b. N.Y.C., Feb. 8, 1919; s. Meyer and Sophie (Levine) K.; B.S.S., Coll. City N.Y., 1939; B. Hebrew Lit., Sem. Coll. Jewish Studies, N.Y.C., 1940; M.S., Columbia, 1946, D.Social Welfare, 1952; m. Miriam Kadin, Sept. 3, 1949; 1 dau., Nancy Valerie. Psychiat. social worker Jewish Bd. Guardians, N.Y.C., 1946-47; mem. faculty Columbia Sch. Social Work, 1947—, prof., 1954—; staff cons. Citizens Com. for Children, N.Y.C., 1948—; mem. summer faculty Smith Coll. Sch. Social Work, 1949-54; cons. in field to govts., founds., vol. agys., 1949- -. Corporate mem. Nat. Assembly Social Policy and Devel., 1969—. Bd. dirs. Day Care and Child Devel. Council, 1967—; adv. com. Inst. Research Poverty, U. Wis. Served with USAAF, 1942-46. Fellow Am. Social. Assn.; mem. Nat. Assn. Social Workers (chmn. div. practice and knowledge 1963-66, bd. dirs. 1967-70), Council Social Work Edn., Am. Assn. U. Profs. Author: A Court for Children, 1953; Planning Community Services for Children in Trouble, 1963; Neighborhood Information Centers, 1966; (with Anna Mayer) Day Care as a Social Instrument, 1966; Theory and Practice of Social Planning, 1969; Studies in Social Policy and Planning, 1969; contbr. monographs, articles to profl. jours., chpts. to books. Editor: Issues in American Social Work, 1959. Home: 76 Hampton Rd Scarsdale NY 10583 Office: Columbia Univ New York City NY 10025

KAHN, BENJAMIN MAURICE, rabbi, educator; b. Lowell, Mass., Nov. 10, 1913; s. Gabriel and Celia (Leibowitz) K.; A.B magna cum laude, Harvard, 1934; rabbi, M.H.L., Jewish Theol. Sem., N.Y.C., 1938; L.H.D. (hon.), Alfred (N.Y.) U., 1962; D.H.L. (hon.), Jewish Theol. Sem., N.Y., 1969; m. Rosalind Aronson, June 26, 1938; children—Simon Hirsh, Jenette Sarah. Asst. rabbi Anshe Emet Synagogue, Chgo., 1938-40; dir. B'nai B'rith Hillel Found., Pa. State U., 1940-44, 45-59, McGill U., 1944-45; lectr. Hebrew Pa. State U., 1947-59; internat. dir. of B'nai B'rith Hillel Founds., Washington, 1959—. Mem. acad. council Am. Friends Hebrew U.; bd. overseers Lown Inst. Contemporary Jewish Studies, Brandeis U.; mem. exec. com. Rabbinical Assembly. Mem. Nat. Peace Corps Adv. Council, 1963-69. Mem. Nat. Assn. Hillel Dirs. (pres. 1952-54), Am. Assn. U. Profs., Rabbinical Assembly, Nat. Assn. Profs. Hebrew, Author: (with Harshbarger and Mourant) Exploring Religious Ideas: The Great Western Faiths, 1959; Sabbath Eve Services in Hillel Foundations, 1957. Editorial bd. Jewish Heritage 1960—. Home: 7907 Rocton Av Chevy Chase MD 20015 Office: 1640 Rhode Island Av NW Washington DC 20036

KAHN, CHARLES HENRY, educator; b. New Iberia, La., May 29, 1928; s. Harold A. and Selma (Meyer) K.; B.A., U. Chgo., 1946, M.A., 1949; Ph.D., Columbia, 1958; student U. Paris (France), 1949-50, Free U. Berlin, 1955; m. Denise Bouvy, Feb. 10, 1951; children—Philip A., Maria I. From instr. to asso. prof. Greek and Latin, Columbia, 1957-65; asso. prof. philosophy U. Pa., 1965-68, prof., 1968—. Served with Signal Corps, AUS, 1953-55. Am. Council Learned Socs. research fellow, 1963-64. Mem. Am. Philos. Assn., Am. Philol. Assn. Author: Anaximander and the Origins of Greek Cosmology, 1960. Co-editor Archiv fur Geschichte der Philosophie, 1965—. Home: 4621 Larchwood Av Philadelphia PA 19143

KAHN, EDGAR ADOLPH, neurosurgeon; b. Detroit, Aug. 17, 1900; s. Albert and Ernestine (Krolik) K.; student Phillips Andover Acad., 1918; B.S., U. Mich., 1924, M.D., 1924; m. Rose Parker, Apr. 24, 1949; children—Barbara Jean, Elizabeth Ellen, Carol Rose. Intern U. Mich. Hosp., 1925-26; practicing as specialist in neurosurgery, 1926—; mem. faculty U. Mich. Med. Sch., 1926-71, instr., 1926-29, asst. prof., 1929-34, asso. prof., 1934-50, prof. surgery, neurosurgery sect., 1950-71, emeritus, 1971—. Served with M.C., AUS, 1942-45; chief surgery 298th Gen. Hosp. Mem. Am. Neurol. Soc., Harvey Cushing Soc., Soc. Neurol. Surgeons, Central Surg. Soc., A.M.A., Sigma Xi, Nu Sigma Nu. Author: The Journal of a Neurosurgeon, 1971. Sr. editor: Correlative Neurosurgery, 1969. Home: 500 Burson Pl Ann Arbor MI 48104

KAHN, EDWIN LEONARD, lawyer; b. N.Y.C., Aug. 1, 1918; s. Max L. and Julia (Rich) K.; A.B., U. N.C., 1937; LL.B. cum laude, Harvard, 1940; m. Myra J. Green, Oct. 20, 1946; children—Martha Lynn, Deborah Jane. Admitted to N.C. bar, 1940, D.C. bar, 1949; atty., asst. head legislation and regulations div. Office Chief Counsel, Internal Revenue Service, 1940-52, dir. tech. planning div., 1952-55; partner firm Arent, Fox, Kintner, Plotkin & Kahn, Washington, 1955—. Dir. Rentex Services Corp. Lectr. tax insts. N.Y.U., Coll. William and Mary, U. Chgo., U. Tex. Mem. adv. bd. N.Y.U. Tax Inst., 1959-70; chmn. N. Va. Extension Jewish Community Center, 1970—. Served with AUS, 1943-46; ETO. Decorated Bronze Star. Mem. Am. (mem. council, 1963-66, vice chmn., 1965-66, sect. of taxation), Fed. (chmn. taxation com. 1967-68), D.C. bar assns., Tax Inst. Am. (adv. council 1967-69, dir. 1969-71), Am. Law Inst., Phi Beta Kappa. Jewish religion. Editor: Harvard Law Rev., 1939-40. Home: 4104 N 40th St Arlington VA 22207 Office: 1815 H St Washington DC 20006

KAHN, ELY JACQUES, architect; b. N.Y.C., June 1, 1884; s. Jacques and Eugenie (Maximilian) K.; A.B., Columbia, 1903, B.Arch., 1907; grad. Ecole Des Beaux Arts, Paris, 1911; m. Liselotte Hirshman, Jan. 1964; children— Ely Jacques, Joan, Olivia. Architect, 1911—; prof. architecture Cornell U., 1915; architect for various govt. and state projects and many tall buildings in N.Y.C.; chmn. adv. commn. Sch. Indsl. Art. Mem. N.Y. State Adv. Bd. City Planning; former adviser U.S. Housing Authority. Benjamin Franklin fellow Royal Soc. Arts. Fellow A.I.A.; mem. Archtl. League N.Y. (past pres.), Municipal Art Soc. (past pres.), Beaux Arts Inst. Design. (past chmn. bd.). Author: Design in Art and Industry, 1937. Contbr. articles Ency. Brit., other jours. Home: 1185 Park Av New York City NY 10028

KAHN, ELY JACQUES, Jr., writer; b. N.Y.C., Dec. 4, 1916; s. Ely Jacques Kahn and Elsie Plaut Mayer; grad. Horace Mann School, 1933; A.B., Harvard, 1937; m. Virginia Rice, 1945 (div. 1969); children—Ely Jacques III, Joseph Plaut, Hamilton Rice; m. 2d, Eleanor M. Frankfurter, 1969. Writer and reporter, N.Y.C., 1937. Bd. dirs. Asso. Harvard Alumni. Served with AUS, 1941-45. Mem. Authors Guild Am., Phi Beta Kappa, Kappa Alpha Tau. Author: The Army Life, 1942; G. I. Jungle, 1943; McNair: Educator of an Army, 1945; The Voice, 1947; Who, Me?, 1949; The Peculiar War, 1952; The Merry Partners, 1955; The Big Drink, 1960; A Reporter Here and There, 1961; The Stragglers, 1962; The World of Swope, 1965; A Reporter in Micronesia, 1966; The Separated People, 1968; Harvard: Through Change and Storm, 1969. Contbr. New Yorker, other nat. mags. Home: 1095 Park Av New York City NY Address: The New Yorker 25 W 43d St New York City NY 10036

KAHN, GORDON BARRY, lawyer; b. Mobile, Ala., Dec. 3, 1931; s. Al and Molly (Prince) K.; B.S., U. Ala., 1953, LL.B., 1958; LL.M., N.Y.U., 1959; postgrad. U. London, 1957—; m. Christine Fortier, JJune 5, 1968; 1 son, Andrew Fortier. Admitted to Ala. bar, 1958; practice in Mobile, 1959—; mem. firm Lyons, Pipes & Cook, 1959—. Chmn. Mobile United Jewish Appeal, 1963-64. Pres. Friends of Mobile Pub. Library; bd. dirs. Mobile Symphony. Served to 1st lt. U.S. Army, 1953-55. Mem. Am., Ala., Mobile County bar assns., English Speaking Union. Democrat. Jewish religion. Mason (Shriner). Clubs: Internat. Trade,, Highland Country (Mobile). Home: 62 Clarise Circle Mobile S1AL 36608 1Office: First Nat Bank Bldg Mobile AL 36601

KAHN, HERMAN, archivist; b. Rochester, N.Y., Aug. 13, 1907; s. Isadore and Dora (Schoenberg) K.; A.B. summa cum laude, U. Minn., 1928, A.M., 1931; Univ. fellow in history Harvard, 1933-34; m. Anne Elizabeth Suess, Sept. 13, 1936; children—Michael Frederick, Melinda Deborah (Mrs. Kenneth Devens). Teaching asst. history U. Minn., 1928-31; asst. prof. history (Peru) Neb. State Tchrs. Coll., 1931-33; historian Nat. Park Service, 1934-36; archivist Nat. Archives, 1936-41; chief div. interior dept. archives, Nat. Archives, 1942-46, dir. nat. resources records office, 1947-48; dir. Franklin D. Roosevelt Library Hyde Park, 1948-61; asst. archivist for civil archives Nat. Archives, 1961-63, asst. archivist for presdl. libraries, 1964-68; asso. librarian for manuscripts and archives, also lectr. in history Yale U., 1968- -; fellow Timothy Dwight Coll., 1969—; vis. lectr. history Bard Coll., 1957; lectr. history Columbia, 1960- 61. Pres. Dutchess County Council Social Agys., 1957. Mem. Nat. Archives Adv. Council, 1971—. Recipient Gen. Services Adminstrn. Distinguished Service award, 1960. Fellow Soc. Am. Archivists (v.p. 1968-69, pres. 1969-70, mem. council); mem. Am., Miss. Valley hist. assns., Conn. Acad. Arts and Scis. Contbr. articles to hist., archival jours. Home: 98 Everit St New Haven CT 06511

KAHN, HERMAN, def. analyst; b. Bayonne, N.J., Feb. 15, 1922; s. Abraham and Yetta Kahn; student U. So. Cal., 1940-41; B.A., U. Cal. at Los Angeles, 1945; M.S., Cal. Inst. Tech., 1948; m. Rosalie Jane Heilner, Mar. 31, 1953; children—Deborah Yetta, David Joshua. Mathematician, Douglas Aircraft Co., 1945, lab. analyst on project for RAND Corp., 1947-48; teaching asst. U. Cal. at Los Angeles, 1946; mathematician Northrop Aviation, 1947; sr. physicist, mil. analyst RAND Corp., 1948-61; with assos., established Hudson Inst., Croton-on-Hudson, N.Y., 1961, now dir. Staff tech. adv. group AEC, 1950; cons. Oak Ridge Nat. Lab., 1950-52, Gaither Com. on Strategic Warfare, 1957, Stanford Research Inst. Non-Mil. Def., 1958; tech. adviser Boeing Aircraft, RCA; cons. design of mech. drum computers, reactor calculations; mem. computing council Nat. Bur. Econ. Research. Served with AUS, 1942-45. Mem. Am. Phys. Soc., Council on Fgn. Relations, Center for Inter-Am. Relations, Am. Polit. Sci. Assn. Author: On Thermonuclear War, 1960; Thinking About the Unthinkable, 1962; On Escalation Metaphors and Scenarios, 1965; (with Anthony Wiener) The Year 2000, 1967; (with others) Can We Win in Viet Nam, 1968; Why ABM, 1969; The Emerging Japanese Superstate - Challenge and Response, 1970. Contbr. numerous articles to sci. jours., popular mags. Home: 19 Birch Lane Chappaqua NY 10514 Office: Hudson Inst Croton-on-Hudson NY 10520

KAHN, HERMAN BERNARD, constrn. co. exec.; b. Cleve., Feb. 12, 1923; s. Myron Bernard and Bessie (Shur) K.; B.S. in Gen. Engring., N.C. State U., 1949; m. Revera C. Toloshko, Aug. 1, 1948 (div. Feb. 1970); children—Meryl Denise, David Geoffrey, Paula Louise. Partner M.B. Kahn Constrn. Co., Columbia, S.C., 1949—; pres. M.B. Kahn Constrn. Co., Inc., 1965—; dir. Habak, Inc., Nix Volkswagens, IK Corp., Stadium Realty Co., S.R. Charles, Inc., S.R. Tenn., Inc. (all Columbia). Mem. adv. bd. S.C. Fire Marshall, 1969—, UN Day com., 1969—. Bd. dirs. M.B. Kahn Found. Served with AUS, 1943-46. Mem. Civitan Internat., Asso. Gen. Contractors Am., Columbia Contractors Assn. Jewish religion. Home: Senate Plaza Columbia SC 29201 Office: 1113 Blossom St Columbia SC 29201

KAHN, HERMAN HEYWOOD, banker; b. N.Y.C., Aug. 3, 1909; s. Joseph Paul and Fannie (Gisnet) K.; grad. N.Y.U., 1931; m. Ruth Schulman, Mar. 25, 1934; children—Samuel Sidney, Geraldine, Frederick Seth. With Lehman Bros., N.Y.C., 1928—, securities analyst, 1928, with indsl. dept., 1935, mgr. financial engring. div. until 1950, partner, 1950—; dir. Avco Corp., Dayco Corp., Allied Stores Corp., Microwave Assos., Inc., United Merchants and Mfrs., Inc. Republican. Jewish religion. Clubs: Preakness Hills Country; Harmony (N.Y.C.). Home: 334 Robin Rd Englewood NY 07631 also 956 Fifth Av New York City NY Office: 1 William St New York City NY 10004

KAHN, HERTA HESS, (Mrs. Howard Kahn), stockbroker; b. Wuerzburg, Germany, Apr. 1, 1919; d. Ferdinand and Lilly (Suesser) Hess; student Northwestern U. Sch. Commerce, 1947-49, 51-56; m. Herbert Levy, Jan. 4, 1947 (dec. 1966); 1 dau., Linda, m. 2d. Howard Kahn, 1970. Came to U.S. 1939, naturalized, 1944. With Paine, Webber, Jackson & Curtis, 1941-44, registered rep., 1955—. Mem. nat. budget com., Chgo. exec. com., Anti-Defamation League B'nai B'rith. Mem. bd. Found. Hearing and Speech Rehab., Michael Reese Hosp.; trustee Highland Park Hosp. Mem. N.Y. Soc. Security Analysts, C. of C., Investment Analysts Soc. Chgo., Stockbrokers Assoc. Chgo. Clubs: Northmoor Country, (Chgo.); Tamarisk Country (Palm Springs, Cal.). Author: What Every Woman Should Know About Investing Her Money, 1968. Home: 1000 Lake Shore Plaza Chicago IL 60611 Office: 208 S LaSalle St Chicago IL 60604

KAHN, IRVING, stock brokerage co. exec.; b. N.Y.C., Dec. 19, 1905; s. Saul Henry and Esther (Friedman) K.; student Coll. City N.Y., Columbia Sch. Bus.; m. Ruth Perl, June 21, 1931; children—Donald, Alan, Thomas. Partner Abraham & Co., mems. N.Y. Stock Exchange, 1917—; dir. Grand Union Co., Willcox & Gibbs Corp. Trustee Ednl. Found. Office: 120 Broadway New York City NY 10005

KAHN, IRVING B., communications exec.; b. N.Y.C., Sept. 30, 1917; s. Abraham and Ruth (Baline) Kahn; B.S., U. Ala., 1939; m. Elizabeth Heslin, Sept. 17, 1949; children—Ruth, Jean. Advt., publicity mgr. Wilby-Kincey theatres, Tuscaloosa, Ala., 1935-38; publicity mgr. orchs., 1938- 39; radio contact, advt. and publicity dept. 20th Century Fox, 1939-42, radio mgr., 1945-46, TV program mgr., spl. asst. to Spyros P. Skouras, 1946-51; pres., chmn. TelePrompTer Corp., 1951—; pioneered closed-circuit TV for teaching missile men Redstone Arsenal, Huntsville, Ala.; co-designer automated electronic audio-visual systems; staging cons. Dem. and Rep. nat. convs., 1952, 56, 60; pioneered large-screen closed-circuit telecasts; dir. Nat. Cable TV Assn., 1965-68. Served as 1st lt. with USAAF, 1942-45. NCTA Larry Boggs Man of Yr. award, 1970. Mem. Soc. Motion Picture and TV Engrs., Internat. Radio and TV Soc. N.Y., Am. Rocket Soc., Young Pres. Orgn., Phi Sigma Delta. Clubs: National Press (Washington); Variety of America. Home: 1260 Flagler Dr Edgewater Point Mamaroneck NY 10543 Office: 50 W 44th St New York City NY 10036

KAHN, IRWIN, constrn. co. pres.; b. Cleve., Mar. 17, 1912; s. Myron B. and Ethel (Kaufman) K.; B.S., U. S.C., 1935; m. Katie Bogen, Oct. 18, 1936; children—Alan Bruce, Deborah, (Mrs. Michael Rubin). With Myron B. Kahn Constrn. Co., Inc., Columbia, S.C., 1935—, pres., 1960-65, chmn. bd., 1965—; officer So. Plastics Co., Columbia, 1943—; pres., Kahn-Jackson Inc., Columbia, 1945—, Palmetto Radio Corp., Columbia, 1956—; dir. New S. Life Ins. Co., Columbia; mem. adv. bd. dirs. 1st Nat. Bank, Columbia, 1963—. Pres. United Fund, 1964; mem. Columbia Bi-Racial Com., 1966—, Columbia Bldg. Code Com., 1952. Bd. dirs. Columbia Art Mus., Philharmonic Orch., M.B. Kahn Found.; pres. Columbia Jewish Center. Mem. S.C. Soc. Engrs. Democrat. Jewish religion. Mason. Club: Columbia Country. Home: 3811 Kilbourne Rd Columbia SC 29205 Office: Box 1608 Columbia SC 29202

KAHN, JOSEPH GABRIEL, newspaperman; b. N.Y.C., May 11, 1913; s. Max and Helen (Tigner) K.; student Nat. Acad. Design; m. Lenore Ferber, June 12, 1947; children—Richard, Robert, William. With N.Y. Post, 1942—, reporter, 1943—; free-lance writer nat. mags.; water colorist. Recipient Nat. Journalism award Assn. Improvement Mental Hosps., 1953, Albert Lasker award, 1959, Page One award Newspaper Guild, 1959, 60, Service award N.Y. City Protestant Council, 1959, award Planned Parenthood Fedn. Am., 1959, Heywood Broun meml. award, 1960, George Polk meml. award, 1960. Reporters Assn. N.Y.C. award, 1960. Home: 160 W 96th St New York City NY 10025 Office: 210 South St New York City NY 10006

KAHN, LAWRENCE R., investment co. exec.; b. N.Y.C., May 15, 1912; s. Sigmund and Emma (Isenberg) K.; B.S.S., Coll. City N.Y., 1937; M.A., Columbia, 1939; m. Helen Beling, Sept. 30, 1937; children—Kathe (Mrs. James H. Mayer), Vicki (Mrs. Craig Hodgetts). Economist, asst. gen. mdse. mgr. Bloomingdale Bros. Inc., N.Y.C., 1942-47; mdse. mgr. Oppenheim Collins & Co., N.Y.C., 1947-49; propr. L. R. Kahn Co., N.Y.C., 1949-51; dir. research E. F. Hutton & Co., N.Y.C., 1951-55; v.p. research A. G. Becker & Co. Inc., N.Y.C., 1955-62; sr. v.p. investments Nat. Securities & Research Corp., N.Y.C., 1962—; pres. NSR Adv. Corp., 1969—; asso. prof. marketing Pace Coll., 1952- 62. Bd. dirs., mem. exec. com. George Jr. Republic, 1964—; bd. dirs. Westchester Ethical Soc., 1960-65. Mem. N.Y. Soc. Security Analysts (pres. 1959-60, bd. dirs. 1954- 66), Phi Beta Kappa (bd. dirs. 1965—). Club: Lawyers (N.Y.C.). Home: 287 Weyman Av New Rochelle NY 10805 Office: 120 Broadway New York City NY 10005

KAHN, LOUIS I., architect; b. Island of Saarama, Estonia, Feb. 20, 1901; s. Leopold and Bertha (Mendelsohn) K.; grad. Pub. Industrial Art Sch., 1917; student Graphic Sketch Club, 1916-20; B. of Arch., U. Pa., 1924; D.Arch., Poly. Inst. Milan (Italy), 1964; H.H.D., U. N.C., 1964; A.F.D., Yale 1965, Md. Inst. Coll. Art, 1968, Bard Coll., 1970, U. Pa., 1971; LL.D., LaSalle Coll., Philadelphia, 1967; m. Esther Virginia Israeli, Aug. 9, 1930; 1 dau., Sue Ann. Brought to U.S., 1905, naturalized, 1915. Chief of design Sesqui-Centennial Exposition, 1925-26; study and travel in Europe, 1928-29; organized Archtl. Research Group, 1931-33; pvt. practice architecture, 1935—; cons. architect for Phila. Housing Authority, 1937, for U.S. Housing Authority, 1939; asso. with George Howe, 1941-42, asso. with George Howe, Oscar Stonorov, 1942-43, asso. with Oscar Stonorov, 1943-47; prof. architecture Yale, 1947-48; res. architect Am. Acad. in Rome, 1950-51; Albert Farwell Bemis prof. Mass. Inst. Tech., 1956; prof. architecture, U. Pa., 1956—, Paul Philippe Cret prof., 1966-71, emeritus, 1971—. Recipient Arnold Brunner prize, Nat. Inst. Arts and Letters, 1960; Phila. Art Alliance medal, 1962; Frank P. Brown medal Franklin Inst., Phila., 1964; medal of honour Danish Archt. Assn., 1965; Internat. Silver medal U. Conn., 1969; Phila. Book award, 1971; Golden Plate award Am. Acad. 1971. Fellow World Acad. Arts and 1971. Sci., A.I.A. (regional urban planning com.; gold medal Phila. chpt. 1969, gold medal N.Y. chpt. 1970, nat. gold medal 1971); Royal Soc. Arts; mem. Royal Swedish Acad. Fine Arts, Nat. Inst. Arts and Letters, Nat. Coll. Architects Peru, Phila. Art Commn. Jewish religion, Club: Print. Prin. works include: numerous govt. housing projects, 1941-47, Yale Art Gallery, U. Pa. Biology Labs, Salk Inst. Biol. Studies, La Jolla, Cal., First Unitarian Ch., Rochester, N.Y., Second Capitol of Pakistan, Dacca, Indian Inst. Mgmt. Ahmedabad, India, Theatre Performing Arts, Fort Wayne, Ind., Kimball Mus. Art, Fort Worth, Library and dining hall bldgs. Phillips Exeter Acad., factory Olivetti Corp. Am., Harrisburg, Pa., Temple Beth El, Chappaqua, N.Y. Author: (books) Why City Planning Is Your Responsibility. (with Oscar Stonorov). 1943; You and Your Neighborhood (with Oscar Stonorov). 1944; contbr. articles on architecture to jours. and mags. Home: 921 Clinton St Philadelphia PA 19107 Office: 1501 Walnut St Philadelphia PA 19102

KAHN, LUDWIG WERNER, educator; b. Berlin, Germany, Oct. 18, 1910; s. Bernhard and Dora (Frishberg) K.; student U. Berlin, 1938-33, U. Paris, 1931; M.A., U. London, 1936; Ph.D., U. Berne, 1934; m. Tatyana Uffner, July 12, 1941; children—Andrée S., Miriam. Came to U.S., 1936, naturalized, 1943. Staff mem. Warburg Inst., London, 1934-36; asst. lectr. Univ. Coll., U. London, 1935-36; instr. U. Rochester, 1936-40, Bryn Mawr Coll., 1940-42; editor Strategic Index of Latin Am., 1942-43; instr. Vassar Coll., 1942- 45, asst. prof., 1945-47; asst. prof. Coll. City N.Y., 1947-53, asso. prof., 1953-62, prof., 1963-67, chmn. dept. Germanic and Slavic langs., 1961-67; prof. Columbia, 1967—; vis. prof. Yale Grad. Sch., 1968, Tech. U., Stuttgart, Germany, 1959-60. Mem. regional selection com. Woodrow Wilson Found., 1962-66. Sr. Fulbright lectr.; Faculty fellow Fund Advancement Edn., 1951-52; Guggenheim fellow, 1969-70; Fulbright research fellow, 1969-70. Mem. Modern Lang. Assn. (sect. chmn. 1955), Am. Assn. U. Profs., Am. Assn. Tchrs. German. Author: Shakespeares Sonette in Deutschland, 1935; Social Indeals in German

Literature, 1939; Literatur and Glaubenskrise, 1964; contbr. numerous articles profl. jours. Home: 9 Atherstone Rd Scarsdale NY 10583 Office: Hamilton Hall Columbia U New York City NY 10027

KAHN, MARK LEO, economist, educator; b. N.Y.C., Dec., 16, 1921; s. Augustus and Manya (Fertig) K.; B.A., Columbia, 1942; M.A., Harvard, 1948, Ph.D., 1950; m. Ruth Elizabeth Wecker, Dec. 21, 1947; children—Ann Mariam, Peter David, James Allan, Jean Sarah. Asst. economist U.S. OSS, Washington, 1942-43; teaching fellow Harvard, 1947-49; dir. case analysis U.S. WSB, Region 6- B Mich., 1952-53; econs. faculty Wayne State U., Detroit, 1949—, prof., 1960—, dept. chmn., 1961-68; mem. faculty council Inst. Labor and Indsl. Relations U. Mich.-Wayne State U.; arbitrator union-mgmt. disputes. Trustee Jewish Vocational Service and Community Workshop, Detroit, 1965—, exec. com., 1968-70. Served to capt. AUS, 1943-46. Decorated Bronze Star medal. Mem. Indsl. Relations Research Assn. (past chpt. pres.), Am. Econ. Assn., Am. Assn. U. Profs. (past chpt. pres.), Nat. Acad. Arbitrators. Contbr. articles to profl. jours. Home: 19541 Cranbrook Dr Detroit MI 48821

KAHN MAX lithographer; B.S., Bradley U.; student Art Inst. of Chgo., Beaux Arts, N.Y.C. studied with Bourdelle, Despiau, Friesz, Paris. Instr. Lithography, Graphics, painting U. Chgo. Exhibited U.S Eng., S.A. France, Switzerland; Represented in collections Art Inst. Chgo. Mus modern Art, other U.S. galleries. Recipient awards Art Inst. Chgo., San Francisco Water Color Show, Phila. Color Print Soc., Phila. Print Club, Am. Jewish Artists, Old Northwest Territory Exhbn., Asso. Am. Artists. Recipient awards from Corcoran Gallery, Washington, Pa. Acad., Ford Found. purchase prize, Sun Times Chgo. Address: 1759 N Cleveland Av Chgo IL 60614

KAHN, RAYMOND LEE, lawyer; b. Chgo., Apr. 2, 1917; s. William and Gertrude (Weinberg) K.; A.B., U. So. Cal., 1938, LL.B., 1940; m. Gloria Kornberg, Feb. 20, 1949; children—Patricia Ellen, Carol Eileen. Admitted to Cal. bar, 1940; law clk. to justice U.S. Ct. of Appeals, Washington, 1940-41; practice in Beverly Hills, 1945—; pvt. practice, 1945-70; v.p. bus. affairs Aaron Spelling Prodns., Inc., Hollywood, Cal., 1970—. Served to capt. USAAF, 1941-45. Mem. Am., Cal., Los Angeles County, Beverly Hills bar assns., Los Angeles Copyright Soc. Home: 5241 Purdue Av Culver City CA 90230 Office: 132 S Rodeo Dr Beverly Hills CA 90212

KAHN, REUBEN LEON, educator, bacteriologist; b. Kovno, Lithuania, July 26, 1887; s. Lazarus and Lottie (Wolpert) K.; brought to U.S., 1899; A.B., Valparaiso (Ind.) U., 1909, LL.D., 1943; M.S., Yale, 1913; D.Sc., N.Y. U., 1916; D.Sc., Institutum Diui Thomae, Cin., 1954; M.D. (hon.), Med. Sch., Nat. U., Athens, 1963; Ph.D. (hon.), Far Eastern U., Manila, P.I., 1964; m. Dina Hope Weinstein, May 31, 1917 (dec. May 1967); children—Lyra Justine (Mrs. Frank S. Morgan), David Curry. Research chemist Harriman Research Lab., N.Y.C., 1916-17; immunologist Mich. Dept. Health, Lansing, 1920-28; dir. labs. Univ. Hosp. and asst. prof. bacteriology U. Mich., 1928-48, asso. prof., 1948-51, prof. serology, 1952-57, emeritus, 1957—; past chief serology lab. Univ. Hosp.; prof. microbiology Howard U. Coll. Medicine, 1968—; vis. prof. immunology Inst. Divi Thomae, Cin. Served as 1st lt., San. Corps, U.S. Army, 1917-18, capt., 1918-19. Published the standard Kahn Test in 1923. Recipient 11th ann. award A.A.A.S., 1933, for paper Tissue Reactions in Immunity; gold medal Phi Lambda Kappa for contbns. to med. scis., 1937; bronze medal for 25th anniversary of Kahn Reaction, 1948. Fellow A.A.A.S.; mem. Am. Soc. Microbiology, Soc. Exptl. Biology and Medicine, Am. Assn. Immunologists, Am. Assn. Pathologists and Bacteriologists, Am. Pub. Health Assn., Mich. Acad. Sciences, Sigma Xi, Phi Delta Epsilon; hon. mem. numerous med. orgns. Jewish religion. Clubs: Research; Cosmos (Washington). Author books including; Tissue Immunity, 1936; Serology with Lipid Antigen, 1950; An Introduction to Universal Reaction in Health and Disease, 1951. Contbr. to sci. and med. jours. Home: 2100 Massachusetts Av NW Washington DC 20008 ☆

KAHN, ROBERT LUDWIG, educator; b. Nuremberg, Germany, Apr. 22, 1923; s. Gustav and Beatrice (Freudenthal) K.; B.A., Dalhousie U., 1944, M.A., 1945; Ph.D., U. Toronto, 1950; m. Liselott M. Kupfer, Aug. 27, 1951; children—Peter Gustavus, Beatrice Margaret. Came to U.S., 1948, naturalized, 1956. Teaching fellow U. Toronto, 1946-48; acting instr. U. Wash., 1948- 50, instr., 1950-55, asst. to dean arts and scis., 1951-54, asst. prof., 1955-60, asso. prof., 1960-62; prof. German lit. Rice U., 1962—, chmn. dept. fgn. langs., 1963-64, chmn. dept. Germanics, 1964—; guest lectr. U. B.C., 1958; guest prof. German Summer Sch. of Pacific, 1965, 66, 68. Alexander von Humboldt Found. fellow, 1961-62; grantee Deutsche Acad. Austaushdienst, 1967. Mem. Am. Assn. U. Profs. (pres. Rice U. chpt. 1964-65), Modern Lang. Assn., Am. Assn. Tchrs. German, Schiller Gesellschaft, S.Central Modern Lang. Assn., Delta Phi Alpha. Editor: Georg Forster's Werke, Vol. I. Contbr. articles to profl. jours. Home: 4106 Merrick Dr Houston TX 77025

KAHN, SANDERS ARTHUR, realty cons.; b. N.Y.C., Jan. 20, 1919; s. Robert and Hattie (Grossman) Miriam Lefkowitz, Mar. 19, 1948; children—Leslie Arlene, Susan Betty, Richard Steven. With Adams & Co., Real Estate, Inc., 1939-42; v.p. Walter Oertly Assos., Inc., 1946-48; with Dwight-Helmsley, 1948-49; asst. prof. real estate U. Fla., 1949-50; mgr. real estate planning div. Port N.Y. Authority, 1951-53; pres., dir. Sanders A. Kahn Assos., Inc. N.Y.C., 1953—; pres. Transp. Realty Devel. Corp., Teaneck, N.J., 1965- -; adj. prof., supr. real estate edn. Coll. City N.Y., 1953—. Bd. dirs. Citizens Housing and Planning Council N.Y. Pres. adv. bd. Mercy Coll., Dobbs Ferry, N.Y. Served with USAAF, 1942-45. Fellow Valuers and Auctioneers Instn. (Gt. Britain); mem. Am. Soc. Planning Ofcls., Soc. Bus. Adv. Professions, Am. Soc. Appraisers (past chmn. internat. edn. com., past internat. gov.), So. Econ. Assn., Am. Right of Way Assn. (past state pres., nat. bd. dirs., chmn. Valuation com.), Urban Land Inst., Am. Arbitration Assn., Lambda Alpha, Alpha Epsilon Pi. Elk. Clubs: Nat. Arts, N.Y.U. Alumni (N.Y.C.). Author: (with others) Real Estate Appraisal and Investment. Contbr. articles to profl. jours. Home: 428 Green Hill Rd Smoke Rise Kinnelon NJ 07405 Office: 535 Fifth Av New York City NY 10017 also Peoples Trust Co Bldg 352 Cedarlane Teaneck NJ 07666 and 23 Lawrence Lane London EC 2 England

KAHN, THEODORE CHARLES, educator, behavioral scientist; b. Germany, Oct. 13, 1912; s. Samuel and Julia (Mayer) K.; came to U.S., 1922, naturalized, 1927; B.A., Yale, 1935; M.A., Columbia, 1940; Ph.D., U. So. Cal., 1950; M.A., Mills Coll., 1952; Doktor Rerum Naturalium, Johannes Gutenberg U., Mainz, Germany, 1960; m. Shirley Rich, June 7, 1948; children—Donald Alan, Susan, Steven James. Sr. counselor Vocational Guidance Center, U. Cal. at Los Angeles, 1947-49; psychologist Los Angeles city schs., 1949-51; prof. behavioral sci., chmn. dept. So. Colo. State Coll., 1965—. Mem. tech. rev. bd., aeromed. div. USAF, 1963-65, task scientist biomed. service corps., 1963- 65; cons. psychiatry Wilford Hall USAF Hosp., 1966-69; liaison fellow Am. Anthrop. Assn. 1958-60. Served to maj. AUS, 1940-46; to col. USAF, 1951-65. Decorated Purple Heart, N.Y. State Distinguished Service Cross. Fellow Am. Psychol. Assn., A.A.A.S.; mem. Internat. Soc. Study Symbols (founder, pres. 1958-61), Deutsche Gesellschaft fuer Anthropologie, USAF Soc. Psychologists (hon. past pres.), Japanese Soc. (hon. pres.). Author: Kahn Test of Symbol Arrangement, 1947; Audio-visual-tactile Rhythm Therapy Experiments, 1950-53: Kahn Intelligence Test, 1958; (with M.B. Giffen) Psychological Techniques in Diagnosis and Evaluation, 1960; Introduction Hominology, 1965; Introduction to Hominology—The Study of the Whole Man, 1969. Founder Hominology, 1965. Home: 2103 Comanche Rd Pueblo CO 81001

KAHN, TOM, assn. exec.; b. N.Y.C., Sept. 15, 1938; s. David and Adele (Klaus) K.; student Bklyn. Coll., 1955-57; B.A., Howard U., 1963. Asst. organizer Youth Marches for Integrated Schs., 1958-59; mem. staff Am. Com. Africa, 1959-60; mem. Com. to Defend Martin Luther King, 1960-61; asst. dep. dir. March on Washington for Jobs and Freedom, 1963; exec. dir. League Indsl. Democracy, N.Y.C., 1964—; mem. faculty Urban Affairs Center, New Sch. Social Research, 1969—. Co-chmn. ad hoc com. to defend right to teach, 1968; chmn. ad hoc com for justice in schs., 1968; mem. guiding com. Nat. Com. for A Polit. Settlement in Vietnam, 1968—. Mem. nat. action com. Socialist party U.S., 1965—. Bd. dirs. A. Philip Randolph Inst., Nat. Com. Against Discrimination in Housing, Workers Def. League. Leadership Conf. on Civil Rights, N.Y. Friends; co-dir. Norman Thomas Fund. Mem. Center War/Peace Studies. Editorial bd. Dissent mag. Contbr. articles to various jours. Office: 112 E 19th St New York City NY 10003

KAHN-FREUND, OTTO, legal educator, author; b. Nov. 17, 1900; s. Richard and Carrie Kahn- Freund; D.Laws, U. Frankfurt (Germany), 1925; M.Laws, U. London (England), 1935; Dr. Jur. (h.c.), univs. Bonn, Stockholm, Brussels; m. Elisabeth Klaiss, 1933; 1 dau. Judge in German cts., 1928-33; barrister-at-law, Middle Temple, 1936—; asst. lectr., then lectr. and reader in law U. London, London Sch. Econs. and Polit. Sci., 1935-51, prof. law, 1951-64; prof. comparative law U. Oxford, 1964-71; co-editor Modern Law Rev. Hon. pres. Internat. Soc. Labour Law and Social Legislation; mem. Royal Commn. Trade Unions and Employers Assn., 1965-68. Author: Law of Carriage by Inland Transport, 4th edit., 1965; The Growth of Internationalism in English Private International Law, 1960; Labour Law and Social Security, 1960; co-author: The System of Industrial Relations in Great Britain, 1954; Matrimonial Property Law, 1955; Law and Opinion in England in the Twentieth Century, 1959. Co-editor: (Dicey) Conflict of Laws, 8th Edit., 1967; (Renner) Institutions of Private Law and Their Social Functions, 1949. Address: Roundabouts Shottermill Haslemere Surrey England

KAHT, JOSEPH EDWARD, banker, lawyer; b. Bklyn., Feb. 4, 1928; s. Joseph Martin and Isabelle (Stewart) K.; student St. Francis Coll., 1946-48; LL.B., N.Y. Law Sch., 1952; m. Rose Perazzo, Apr. 24, 1954; 1 dau., Jo Ann. Admitted to N.Y. bar, 1953; asso. atty. Dewey, Ballantine, Bushby, Palmer & Wood, N.Y.C., 1952-61; house counsel Irwin, Wolfson, N.Y.C., 1961-63; asst. v.p., atty. Dry Dock Savs. Bank, 1963-67, v.p., atty., 1967-69, sr. v.p., 1970—; lectr. real estate Practicing Law Inst., 1965—; mem. adv. bd. Security Title & Guaranty Co., N.Y.C., 1961—. Mem. Am., N.Y. State bar assns., Catholic Lawyers Guild. Club: Hempstead (N.Y.) Golf. Home: 3309 Milburn Av Baldwin Harbor NY 11510 Office: 742 Lexington Av New York City NY 10022

KAIER, EDWARD A., lawyer; b. Mahanoy City, Pa., July 26, 1908; s. Edward John and Catharine (Gorman) K.; A.B., Pa. State U., 1930; LL.B., U. Pa., 1933; m. Mary Patricia Crimmins, Apr. 15, 1940; children—Anne, Edward John. Admitted to Pa. bar, 1933; with Pa. R. R., 1933-70, law clk., Phila., asst. solicitor, asst. gen. solicitor, Chgo., 1935-44, asst. gen. counsel, Pitts., 1944-48, dir. pub. relations, Phila., 1948-49, gen. atty., Phila., 1949-58, gen. solicitor, Phila., 1958-69; gen. counsel Penn Central Co., Phila., 1969-70, v.p., 1970; pvt. practice, Phila., 1970—; chief counsel all U.S. railroads in nationwide freight rate cases ICC; bd. mgrs. Beneficial Mut. Savs. Bank, Phila.; dir. Continental Bank, Phila. Mem. alumni council Pa. State U. Mem. Am., Pa., Phila. (chmn. com. corporate counsel 1962-63) bar assns., Assn. ICC Practitioners. Roman Catholic. Clubs: Racquet, Philadelphia Country. Home: 803 N Pennstone Rd Bryn Mawr PA 19010 Office: 3 Penn Center Plaza Philadelphia PA 19102

KAIN, JOHN FORREST, educator; b. Ft. Wayne, Ind., Nov. 9, 1935; s. Forrest and Bessie (Wilder) K.; B.A. with honors in Econs. and Polit. Sci., Bowling Green State U., 1957; M.A., U. Cal. at Berkeley, 1961, Ph.D., 1961; m. Mary Fan Kiracofe, Aug. 17, 1957; children-Mary Jo, Joanna. Grad. research asst. U. Cal. at Berkeley, 1957-59, lectr. bus. adminstrn. and econs., extension div., 1959-61; research economist RAND Corps., 1961-62; mem. faculty Harvard, 1966—, prof. econs., 1969—; sr. staff mem. Nat. Bur. Econ. Research, 1967—; cons. to govt. Mem. task force housing Urban Coalition. Served to 1st lt. USAF, 1962-65. Mem. Am. Econ. Assn., Am. Statis. Assn., Econometric Soc., Regional Sci. Assn. Author: (with John R. Meyer and Martin Wohl) The Urban Sci. Assn. Author: (with John R. Meyer and Martin Wohl) The Urban Transportation Problem, 1965; also articles. Editor: Race and Poverty: The Economics of Discrimination, 1969. Home: 66 Watson Rd Belmont MA 02178 Office: Littauer Center Harvard Univ Cambridge MA 02138 Cambridge MA 02138

KAIN, RICHARD MORGAN, educator, author; b. York, Pa., Dec. 19, 1908; s. George Hay and Cara (Watt) K.; A.B with highest honors, Swarthmore Coll., 1930; M.A., U. Chgo., 1931, Ph.D., 1934; grad. student Harvard, 1931-32; research Yale, Brit. Museum, also Nat. Library Ireland; m. Louise Kinsey Yerkes, June 16, 1931; children—Richard Yerkes, David Hay, Constance Louise (Mrs. H. Hudson Milner). Asso. prof. English, Augustana Coll., Sioux Falls, S.D., 1933-34; asst. prof. Ohio Wesleyan U., 1934-40; mem. faculty U. Louisville, 1940—, prof. English, 1947—, acting chmn. dept., spring 1953, chmn. div. humanities, 1963-69; vis. prof. Northwestern U., summer 1948, Harvard, summer 1950, U. Colo., summer 1959, Yeats Internat. Summer Sch., Sligo, Ireland, 1961, 67; Fulbright lectr. Univ. Inst., Venice, Italy, 1961-62, Am. Seminar, Rome, Italy, 1962; lectr. James Joyce Tower, Dublin, Ireland, 1962; Centennial lectr. U. Mass., spring 1963; vis. prof. N.Y.U., summer 1963; Peters Rushton lectr. U. Va., 1964; vis. prof. U. Wash., summer 1966, Univ. Coll., Dublin, spring 1972. Mem. James Joyce Tower Com., Dublin, 1960-62; mem. screening com. internat. exchange of persons, conf. bd. Asso. Research Councils, 1962-65; pres. Friends Ky. Libraries, 1957-58; chmn. Save Our Parks Com., 1958- 59. Bd. dirs. Louisville Orch., 1951-65; trustee James Joyce Found., 1967—; bd. overseers U. Louisville, 1970—. Mem. Modern Lang. Assn. (chmn. comparative lit. discussion group I, 1963), S. Atlantic Modern Lang. Assn., Modern Humanities Research Assn., James Joyce Soc., Am. Com. Irish Studies, Am. Assn. U. Profs., Phi Beta Kappa, Phi Delta Theta, Delta Sigma Rho, Pi Delta Epsilon, Phi Kappa Phi. Author: Fabulous Voyager: James Joyce's Ulysses, 2d edit., 1959; (with Marvin Magalaner) Joyce: The Man, The Work, The Reputation, 2d edit., 1962; Dublin in the Age of William Butler Yeats and James Joyce, 1962; (with Robert Scholes) The Workshop of Daedalus, 1965. Editorial bd. James Joyce Quar., 1963—, U. Ky. Press, 1969-71. Contbr. articles profl. jours., chpts. to books. Home: 564 Sunset Rd Louisville KY 40206

KAIN, RONALD STUART, editor, writer; b. nr. Helena, Mont., Mar. 5, 1899; s. Henry and Fanny (Clift) K.; M.A., Columbia, 1936; m. Olive McKay, June 29, 1929. Asso. editor Mont. Banker, Great Falls, 1922; reporter Yakima (Wash.) Herald, 1923, Butte (Mont.) Miner, 1923-25; editorial staff N. Y. Herald Tribune, 1926-29; editor for Am. Biography, supplement New Internat. Ency., 1929, asso. editor, 1932-44; fgn. editor New Internat. Year Book, 1929-31; fgn. news editor, N.Y. office, news and features div. Outpost Service Bur., OWI, 1944, Psychol. Warfare Dept., SHAEF, London, 1944-45; chief press sect. Netherlands Unit of OWI in London, 1945, Brussels, 1945, The Hague, 1945 (attached as press officer to psychol. warfare consolidation team 11, Allied mil. mission to Netherlands); chief press and photo sects. USIS, Am. embassy, The Hague, 1945- 1946; with State Dept., 1946; free-lance writer and editorial cons., 1946-49; sr. rev. officer Dept. State, 1949-51, chief rev. officer, 1951-54, dep. coordinator, chief rev. officer, 1954-61; dir. internat. surveys staff Office Sec. Dept. Health, Edn. and Welfare, 1961-66; free-lance writer, 1967—; visited Netherlands and Indonesia to study Indonesian revolution during 1947. Mem. English Speaking Union. Unitarian. Club: Cosmos (Washington). Author: Europe: Versailles to Warsaw, 1939. Contbr. articles mags. Home: 3611 N St NW Washington DC 20007

KAINEN, JACOB, museum curator, artist; b. Waterbury, Conn., Dec. 7, 1909; s. Joseph and Fannie (Levin) K.; grad. Pratt Inst., 1930; grad. study N.Y.U., 1936-38, George Washington U., 1944-46; m. Bertha Friedman, Aug. 28, 1938; children—Paul Chester, Daniel Bernard; m. 2d, Ruth Priscilla Cole, Feb. 19, 1969. Aide div. graphic arts U.S. National Mus., Smithsonian Instn., Washington, 1942-44, asst. curator, 1944-46, curator, 1946-66, curator Nat. Collection Fine Arts, 1966-70, spl. cons., 1970—; lectr. painting and history graphic arts U. Md., 1970-71; work rep. permanent collections Met. Mus. Art, Bklyn. Mus., Corcoran Gallery of Art, Phillips Collection, Carnegie Inst., Balt. Mus. Art, Bklyn. Pub. Library, East Tex. State Tchrs. Coll., H. Biggs Meml. Hosp., Ithaca, Queens Coll., Howard U., Bezalel Nat. Mus., Jerusalem. Recipient research grant Am. Philos. Soc., 1956. Mem. Print Council Am. (bd. dirs.). Author: George Clymer and the Columbian Press, 1950; The Haltone Screen, 1951; Why Bewick Succeeded, 1959; John Baptist Jackson: 18th Century Master of the Color Woodcut, 1962; The Etchings of Canaletto, 1967; also articles. Home: 27 W Irving St Chevy Chase MD 20015 Office: Nat Collection Fine Arts Washington DC 20001

KAISER, EDGAR FOSBURGH, corp. exec.; b. Spokane, July 29, 1908; s. Henry J. and Bessie (Fosburgh) K.; student U. Cal., 1927-30; LL.D., U. Portland, Pepperdine Coll., Mills Coll.; L.H.D., U. Cal.; m. Sue Mead, Aug. 24, 1932; children—Carlyn, Becky, Gretchen, Edgar Fosburgh, Henry Mead, Kim John. Constrn. supt. natural gas line Kan. to Tex., 1930-32; shift supt. Boulder Dam, Nev., 1932-33; adminstrv. mgr. Columbia Constrn. Co., Bonneville (Ore.) Dam, 1934-38, Consol. Builders, Inc., Grand Coulee Dam, Wash., 1938-41; v.p., gen. mgr. Ore. Shipbldg. Corp. and Kaiser Co., Inc., Portland and Vancouver, 1941-45; pres., dir. Kaiser Motors Corp., 1945-56; chmn., dir. affiliated Kaiser cos. and subsidiaries, principally: Kaiser Industries Corp., Kaiser Steel Corp., Kaiser Aluminum & Chem. Corp., Kaiser Cement & Gypsum Corp., Kaiser Aerospace & Electronics Corp., Kaiser Broadcasting Corp., Kaiser Found. Health Plan, Inc., Kaiser Found. Hosps., Kaiser Engrs., Kaiser Sand & Gravel; chmn. bd., pres. Nat. Steel & Shipbldg. Co.; dir. Bank Am. Corp. Past mem. Pres.'s Com. on Equal Employment Opportunity, Pres.'s Missile Sites Labor Commn., Pres.'s Adv. Com. Labor- Mgmt. Policy; past chmn. Pres.'s Com. on Urban Housing; past mem. adv. council Stanford U. Grad. Sch. Bus.; past nat. chmn. UN Day; mem. Business Council, Internat. Indsl. Conf.; corp. support com. Nat. Urban League; chmn. incorporators Nat. Corp. for Housing Partnerships. Vice chmn. bd. dirs. Stanford Research Inst., Nat. Opportunities Industrialization Center, Bus. Com. for Arts; trustee Center for Inter-Am. Relations, San Francisco Bay Area Council; hon. trustee Toledo Mus. Art; mem. bd. Council for The Americas; vice chmn. United Community Campaigns Am.; hon. chmn. Oakland Mus. Founders' Fund; past mem. bd. incorporators Communications Satellite Corp.; v.p., dir. Oakland-Alameda County Coliseum; bd. dirs. Oakland Museum Assn.; chmn. bd. Oakland Symphony Orch. Assn.; mem. San Francisco Opera Co. Recipient numerous honors and awards, most recent being: Ann. Moles award for outstanding achievement in constrn. industry, 1962; Achievement award Bldg. and Industry Conf. Bd., 1968; Mgmt. Achievement award Loyola U., 1968; Hoover medal, 1969; Presdl. Medal of Freedom, 1969; 1st annual Internat. Key award Opportunities Industrialization Center, 1970. Named Industrialist of Year, Cal. Mus. Sci. and Industry, 1966, Constrn.'s Man of Year, Engring., News-Record, 1968, Alunmus of Year, U. Cal., 1969. Fellow Am. Acad. Arts and Scis. Clubs: Moles, Pacific Union (San Francisco); Commonwealth of Cal. Home: Lafayette CA 94549 Office: 300 Lakeside Dr Oakland CA 94604

KAISER, FRED, regulator co. exec.; b. Bklyn., Nov. 22, 1906; s. Fred and Elizabeth (Kleber) K.; student indsl. electricity Pratt Inst., 1922; grad. Marconi Inst., 1924; m. Jeannette Nelson, June 17, 1930; children—Carol (Mrs. Gene L. Oliver), Janice (Mrs. Donald P. Smith). Comml. radio operator on shipboard Tropical Radio Co., 1925-26; with Mpls.-Honeywell Regulator Co., 1926—, regional Midwest mgr., Chgo., 1942-50, field sales mgr., 1950-53, regional mgr. Eastern states, N.Y.C., 1953-60, v.p., 1960-64, v.p. So. area, 1964—. Mem. Am. Soc. Heating and Air Conditioning Engrs., N.Y.C. Sales Execs. Club. Clubs: Atlanta Athletic; Lanier Yacht. Home: 525 Londonberry Rd NW Atlanta GA 30327 Office: 6 W Druid Hills Dr NE Atlanta GA 30329

KAISER, GRAND EDWIN, educator; b. Kitchener, Ont., Can., Aug. 6, 1926; s. Lorne and Frieda (Reuber) K.; B.A., Waterloo Coll., 1949; M.A., U. Western Ont., 1950; French Govt. fellow U. Bordeaux (France), 1950-51; Ph.D. (Univ. and Fels scholars), Brown U., 1957; m.; children—Warren Dean, Bradley Ross. Teaching fellow U. Western Ont., 1949-50; instr. French, U. R.I., summer 1954; lectr. Carlton U., 1955-56; faculty Emory U., 1956—, prof. Romance langs., 1965—, chmn. dept., 1962—. Mem. Modern Lang. Assn., Am. Assn. U. Profs., Am. Council Teaching Fgn. Langs., Asso. des Amuis D'Andre Gide, Am. Assn. Tchrs. French, S. Atlantic Modern Lang. Assn., Malraux Soc. Contbr. articles to profl. jours. Home: 1120 McConnell Dr Decatur GA 30033

KAISER, IRWIN HERBERT, educator, physician; b. N.Y.C., Jan. 27, 1918; s. Leon S. and Helen (Kessler) K.; B.A., Columbia, 1938; M.D., Johns Hopkins, 1942; Ph.D., U. Minn., 1953; m. Barbara J. Lieberman, June 12, 1938; children—Susan (Mrs. R. L. Currier), Peter, Richard, Margaret, Steven, James. Intern Johns Hopkins Hosp., 1942-43; research fellow embryology Carnegie Instn., Washington, 1946-47; resident physician Sinai Hosp., Balt., 1947-50; from instr. to asso. prof. U. Minn., 1950-59; prof. obstetrics and gynecology, chmn. dept. U. Utah Med. Sch., 1959-68; prof. gynecology and obstetrics Albert Einstein Coll. Medicine, 1968—. Served to capt., M.C., AUS, 1943- 46. Home: 20 Dimitri Pl Larchmont NY 10538

KAISER, JOSEPH A., banker; b. Bklyn., June 14, 1906; s. Joseph A. and Elizabeth A. (Turner) K.; student Fordham U., 1926, St. John's Law Sch., 1929; m. Marian M. Mullen, Oct. 22, 1932; children—Robert J., Patricia Ann. With Williamsburgh Savs. Bank since 1926, exec. v.p., 1945-53, trustee since 1950, pres., 1953—, also treas.; dir. Savs. Bank Trust Co., Instnl. Securities Corp., Insco Systems Corp. Mem. Banking Bd. N.Y. State, 1959—; mem. adv.

com. N.Y. Fed. Res. Bank, 1960—. Bd. dirs. Bklyn. chpt. A.R.C; Mem. Comptroller's Com. for Investment Pension Funds, N.Y.C., trustee Indsl. Home for Blind (Bklyn.). Mem. Bklyn. C. of C., Downtown Bklyn. Assos. Clubs: Union League (N.Y.C.); Garden City (N.Y.) Golf; Montauk (Bklyn.); Garden City Country. Home: 82 Whitehall Blvd Garden City NY 11530 Office: 1 Hanson Pl Brooklyn NY 11217

KAISER, LLOYD EUGENE, broadcasting exec.; b. Alpena, Mich., Aug. 1, 1927; s. Albert W. and Adele V. (Diemond) K.; B.A., U. Mich., 1950, M.A., 1951; m. Barbara Jane Wieand, June 17, 1957; children—Kristina, Timothy. Communications instr. Fla. secondary schs., 1951-52; instr. radio and tv Lehigh U., Bethlehem, Pa., 1952-54; asst. prof. communications State U. N.Y., Fredonia, 1954-58; ednl. TV programming exec. Rochester (N.Y.) Ednl. Television Assn., 1958-63; founder, gen. mgr. sta. WITF-TV, Hershey, Pa., 1963-70; pres., gen. mgr. WQED/WQEX-TV, pub. broadcasting, Pitts., 1970—. Vice chmn. bd. Pub. Broadcasting Service, 1969—; v.p. Eastern Ednl. Network, 1970—. Bd. dirs. Pitts. March of Dimes Adv. bd. Point Park Coll., Pitts. Mem. Nat. Ednl. TV Affiliates Council (sec. 1967-68), Nat. Assn. Ednl. Broadcasters (bd. dirs., sec. Ednl. TV Stas. 1968—), Pitts. C. of C. (edn. com. 1970—). Rotarian. Home: 1204 Hulton Rd Oakmont PA 15139 Office: 4802 5th Av Pittsburgh PA 15213

KAISER, PAUL ROBERT, baking co. exec.; b. Washburn, Wis., Oct. 24, 1916; s. Paul Christian and Nell (Johnson) K.; student Pa. State Coll., 1935-36, Va. Poly. Inst., 1936-38, Rutgers U., 1938-39; LL.D. (hon.), Hobart Coll., 1963; m. Louise Philippine Baur, July 1, 1941; children—Geoffrey David, John Philip. Agt., Conn. Gen. Life Ins. Co., Phila., 1943-52; pres., chmn. bd. Tasty Baking Co., Phila., 1952—, also dir.; dir. Central Penn. Nat. Bank, Phila., Fidelity Mut. Life Ins. Co., Pa. Lumbermens Mut. Ins. Co., Phila., Phila. Electric Co. Bd. dirs. Blue Cross Greater Phila.; trustee Found. Ind. Colls. Pa., Tasty Baking Found. Served with AUS, 1942-43. Mem. Million Dollar Round Table, 1949, 51-52. Republican. Episcopalian. Clubs: Union League, Cricket (Phila.); Pine Valley Golf (Clementon, N.J.); Atlantic City Country (Northfield, N.J.); Ocean Reef (Key Largo, Fla.). Home: Box 377 Gwynedd Valley PA 19437 Office: 2801 Hunting Park Av Philadelphia PA 19129

KAISER, PHILIP M., former diplomat; b. Bklyn., July 12, 1913; s. Morris and Temma (Sloven) K.; A.B., U. Wis., 1935; B.A., M.A. (Rhodes scholar), Balliol Coll., Oxford (Eng.) U., 1939; m. Hannah Greeley, June 16, 1939; children—Robert Greeley, David Elmore, Charles Roger Kaiser. Economist, mem. bd. govs. Fed. Res. System, 1939-42; chief, project operations staff, also chief, planning staff, enemy br. Bd. Econ. Warfare and Fgn. Econ. Adminstrn., 1942-46; expert on internat. orgn. affairs State Dept., 1946; exec. asst. to asst. sec. labor, charge internat. labor affairs, 1946-47; dir. Office Internat. Labor Affairs, Dept. Labor, 1947-49; asst. sec. labor for internat. labor affairs, 1949-53; mem. U.S. govt. bd. fgn. service State Dept., 1948-53; U.S. govt. mem. governing body ILO, 1948-53, chief U.S. delegation to confs., 1949-53; labor adviser to Com. for Free Europe, 1954; spl. asst. to gov. N.Y., 1955-58; prof. internat. labor relations, dir. program for overseas labor and indsl. relations, Sch. International Service, Am. U., 1958-61; U.S. ambassador. Republic Senegal, Islamic Rep. Mauritania, 1961-64; minister Am. embassy, London, Eng., 1964-70. Mem. interdepartmental com. which assisted in developing programs under Marshall Plan, 1947-48; mem. interdepartmental com. which developed Greek-Turkish aid and Point 4 Tech. Assistance programs, 1947-49. Mem. Gov.'s Spl. Com. Unemployment, 1954. Mem. Am. Assn. Rhodes Scholars, Council Fgn. Relations, Am. Polit. Sci. Assn., Phi Beta Kappa. Home: 9133 McDonald Dr Bethesda MD 20034

KAISER, RAYMOND FRANCIS, pub. health officer; b. Ellis, Kan., Dec. 25, 1911; s. John B. and Barbara (Weigle) K.; M.D., U. Colo., 1937; M.P.H., Harvard, 1942; m. Alice Elizabeth Tuleen, Oct. 22, 1938; 1 dau., Candace Barbara. Various assignments clin. and preventive medicine, USPHS, 1937-47, asst. chief cancer control br. Nat. Cancer Inst., 1947-51, chief, 1951-54, chief field investigations and demonstrations br., 1954-61; chronic diseases cons. region IX USPHS, chief chronic diseases services, 1961-63, asso. health dir. region IX, 1963-67, asso. regional health dir. for health manpower, 1967—, dep. regional health director, San Francisco, 1967—; clin. asst. prof. oncology Georgetown U. Sch. Med., Washington; cons. Children's Med. Center, Boston. Served with USPHS, World War II. Diplomate Am. Bd. Preventive Med. Mem. A.M.A., Inter- Soc. Cytology Council, Pub. Health Cancer Assn. (nat. com. careers in med. tech.), A.C.S., Am. Cancer Soc. (clin. fellowships commn.). Author articles on cancer control, edn., diagnosis. Home: 433 Dellbrook Av San Francisco CA 94131 Office: Fed Office Bldg 50 Fulton St San Francisco CA 94101

KAISER, ROBERT LOUIS, steel co. exec.; b. Elyria, O., Apr. 2, 1914; s. L.P. and Elsie (Hahn) K.; A.B. cum laude, Miami U., Oxford, O., 1935; J.D., summa cum laude, Cleve. Law Sch., 1940; m. Ruth Gill, Aug. 19, 1939; children—Tom, Sally, Mary Elizabeth. From auditor to asst. sec. Nat. Refining Co., 1935-43; admitted to Ohio bar, 1940; with Otis & Co., Cleve., 1946-, v.p., 1950- -, sec., 1947—, also dir., now v.p. of finance; with Portsmouth Steel Corp., Cleve., 1950-60, v.p., 1959-50, sec., 1950- 60, also dir.; co. acquired by Detroit Steel Co., 1960, now v.p. finance, also dir.; v.p. Cleve. Indians Inc., 1962-66; dir. Iron Ores Ltd., Steep Rock Iron Mines, Limited, 1968-. Served to lt. (j.g.) USNR, 1943-46. Mem. Am. Iron and Steel Inst., Am. Ordnance Assn., Ohio Bar Assn., Econ. Club Detroit, Phi Beta Kappa. Home: 77 Merriweather Rd Grosse Pointe Farms MI 48236 Office: 1025 S Oakwood St Detroit MI 48209

KAISER, WALTER JACOB, educator; b. Bellevue, O., May 31, 1931; s. Walter O. and Joyce (Drexel) K.; grad. Phillips Acad., Andover, 1946-49, Shrewsbury Sch., Eng., 1949-50; A.B., Harvard, 1954, Ph.D., 1960; postgrad. U. Paris, 1954-55, Ecole Normale Superieure (Paris), 1955-56; m. Neva Goodwin Rockefeller, Dec. 17, 1966; children—David Walter, Miranda Margaret. Instr. Harvard, 1960-62, asst. prof., 1962-65, asso. prof. English and comparative lit., 1965-69, prof., 1969—, chmn. dept. comparative lit., 1969—. Mem. vis. com. Boston Mus. Fine Arts, 1971—. Fulbright fellow, 1954-55; Tower fellow, 1955-56; Am. Council Learned Socs. fellow to Rome, 1964-65; recipient faculty prize, Harvard U. Press, 1963. Mem. Renaissance Soc. Am., Am. Comparative Literature Assn., Modern Greek Studies Assn., Signet Soc. Phi Beta Kappa. Author: Praisers of Folly: Erasmus, Rabelais, Shakespeare, 1963. Editor: Selected Essays of Montaigne, 1941. Translator: Three Secret Poems (George Seferis), 1969. Home: 88 Appleton St Cambridge MA 02138

KAISER, WILLIAM MARTIN, Jr., investment exec.; b. Portland, Ore., Apr. 7, 1921; s. William Martin and Lillian (Martin) K.; grad. Deerfield Acad., 1939; A.B., Brown U., 1943; M.B.A., U. Chgo., 1947; m. Barbara Bellows, Sept. 25, 1948; children—William Martin III, Anne Gilbert. With Studebaker Corp., 1947-50, A.O. Smith Corp., 1950-55; controller Consol. Foundries & Mfg. Corp., Chgo., 1956-59; asst. to treas. Miehle-Dexter-Goss, Inc., Chgo., 1959-64, controller, 1964-70; treas. Miehle-Goss-Dexter Americas Co., 1964-70. Regional chmn. Brown U. Devel. Fund, 1966-67. Served with USAAF, 1943-46. C.P.A., Wis. Mem. Financial Execs. Inst., Am. Inst. C.P.A.'s Ill. Soc. C.P.A.'s, Nat. Assn. Accountants, Brown U. Alumni Assn. (bd. dirs. 1965-67), Phi Delta Theta. Episcopalian. Home: 1248 Northport Dr Sarasota FL 33581 Office: 5111 Ocean Blvd Sarasota FL 33578

KAJECKAS, JOSEPH, diplomat; b. Shenandoah, Pa., June 17, 1897; s. Peter and Ona (Malakauskas) K.; diploma U. Montpellier (France), 1929, also Ecole Libre des Scis. Politiques, Paris; m. Ona Viburis, Feb. 16, 1931; 1 son, Gabriel. With Lithuanian Ministry Fgn. Affairs, 1929—; 1st sec. Lithuanian legation, London, 1930-35; with Lithuanian Fgn. Ministry, 1935-39; counselor Lithuanian Legation, Berlin, 1939-40, Washington, 1940—; charge d'affaires of Lithuania, 1957—. Sec. gen. Lithuanian Red Cross Soc., 1935-39. Address: 2622 16th St NW Washington DC 20009

KAKUTANI, SHIZUO, educator, mathematician; b. Osaka, Japan, Aug. 28, 1911; s. Kakujiro Kakutani and Chiyo; M.A., Tohoku U., 1934; Ph.D., Osaka U., 1941; M.A. (hon.), Yale, 1953; m. Kay Uchida, Jan. 12, 1952; 1 dau., Michiko. Research mem. Inst. Advanced Study, 1940-42, 48-49; asst. prof. Osaka U., 1942-48; asst. prof. Yale, 1949-50, asso. prof., 1950-53, prof. math., 1953-62, Eugene Higgins prof. math., 1962—. Mem. Am. Math. Soc., Math. Soc. Japan, Am. Acad. Arts and Scis. Home: 32 Round Hill Rd North Haven CT 06473 Office: Yale University New Haven CT 06520

KALA, TOIVE ILMARI, Finnish diplomat; b. Helsinki, Finland, Mar. 19, 1909; s. Johan Herik and Maya (Forsgren) K.; B. Bus. Adminstrn., Helsinki Sch. Econs., 1931; M.B.A., 1933, B.A., 1953; M.A., U. Helsinki, 1950; m. Quita Carpelan, July 7, 1942; children-Ann. Matt Ilmari, Johan Ilmari. Engaged in banking, 1930-31, in edn., 1931-32; joined Finnish Diplomatic Service, 1933; assigned Tokyo, Japan, 1933-39, Shanghai, 1939-41, Ankara, Turkey, 1941-47, Budapest, Hungary, 1951, Tel-Aviv, Israel, 1952-58, Sydney, Australia and Wellington, New Zealand 1959-63; consul gen. in N.Y.C., 1967—. Decorated comdr. Order White Rose; comdr. Order Lion of Finland; medal Finno-Soviet War, 1939-40. Home: 857 Fifth Av New York NY 10021 Office: Consulate Gen of Finland 200 E 42d St New York NY 10017

KALAHER, WILLARD MICHAEL, banker; b. Milw., June 4, 1909; s. Michael William and Ella (Dassler) K.; B.S., Marquette U., 1929; postgrad. U. Wis., 1955; m. Mildred May Koch, July 2, 1938; children—Richard Alan, Bonnie (Mrs. Richard Bell). Teller, Am. Nat. Bank, 1926-38; auditor First Wis. Nat. Bank, Milw., 1938-54, asst. cashier, 1954-63, cost controller, 1963-65, cashier, 1965- -. Mem. Badger Bankers, Nat. Assn. Bank Auditors and Controllers, Adminstrv. Mgmt. Soc., Milw. Assn. Commerce, Milw. Clearing House Assn. Lutheran. Mason, Elk. Clubs: Milwaukee Athletic, Milwaukee Press. Home: 4364 N Alpine Av Milwaukee WI 53211 Office: 743 N Water St Milwaukee WI 53202

KALB, BERNARD, TV journalist. TV journalist CBS, N.Y.C. Recipient Asian Mag. award for TV program The Viet Cong. Office: 51 W 52d St New York City NY 10019*

KALB, HAROLD WATKINS, banker; b. Tremont, Pa., Apr. 17, 1913; s. George V. and Emily (Watkins) K.; B.A., Pa. State U., 1935; postgrad. Stonier Grad. Sch. Banking, Rutgers U., 1958; m. Elizabeth A. Bathurst, Aug. 28, 1937; children—Linda Elizabeth, George Bathurst. With Tremont Nat. Bank (Pa.), 1935-44; asst. to auditor Girard Trust Bank, Phila., 1946-51, asst. auditor, 1951-53, asst. treas., 1953-56, asst. v.p., 1956-60, v.p., 1960—, auditor, 1969—. Chmn. bank United Fund campaign, 1966. Served with AUS, 1944-46; ETO. Recipient Certificate of Appreciation, City Phila., 1958, award Data Processing Mgmt. Assn., 1958. Mem. Am. Inst. Banking (pres. Phila. 1960), Bus. Electronics Round Table (chmn. 1963), Bank Automation Soc. Del. Valley (pres. 1957), Phila. Clearing House Assn. (chmn. automation sub-com. 1961), Bank Adminstrn. Inst., Pi Kappa Alpha. Presbyn. Mason. Clubs: Lehigh (Allentown, Pa.); Alpha (Phila.). Contbr. articles banking jours. Home: 150 Terminal Av Philadelphia PA 19118 Office: 1 Girard Plaza Philadelphia PA 19101

KALB, MARVIN LEONARD, radio and TV corr.; b. U.S., June 9, 1930; s. Max and Bella (Portnoy) K.; B.S.S., Coll. City N.Y., 1951; M.A., Harvard, 1953, Ph.D. candidate, 1955; m. Madeleine J. Green, June 1, 1958; children—Deborah, Judith. Press attache Am. embassy, Moscow, 1956-57; corr. CBS News, Moscow, 1960-63, diplomatic corr., Washington, 1963—. Served with AUS, 1953-55. Recipient award for best radio analysis Overseas Press Club, 1962, award for best TV analysis, 1965; award for best interpretation fgn. news on TV, Internat. Cinema Soc., 1967. Mem. Overseas Writers (pres.), State Dept. Corrs. Assn. Clubs: Nat. Press (Washington); Harvard (N.Y.C.), Author: Eastern Exposure, 1958; Dragon in the Kremlin, 1961; The Volga, A Political Journey Through Russia, 1967; introduction to One Day in Life of Ivan Denisovich, 1964; (with Elie Abel) Roots of Involvement: The U.S. in Asia 1784-1971, 1971. Office: 2020 M St Washington DC 20036

KALBERER, ALFRED FREDRICH, ret. air force officer; b. Lafayette, Ind., Jan. 1, 1907; s. Ernest I. and Charlotte (Rover) K.; grad. Army Air Corps Primary and Adv. Flying Sch., 1928; m. Charlotte Wolber, June 12, 1953. Commd. 2d lt. USAAF, 1927, advanced through to maj. gen. USAF, 1953; assigned 1st Pursuit Group, Selfridge Field, Mich., 1928-29; attached task force, Egypt, in raids against Italian Fleet, also Ploesti oil fields, 1942, 43; comdr. 462d Bomb Group, Indian and China, 1944; later led move to Tinian and air action against Japan; intelligence officer task force, Bikini Bomb tests, Kwajalein, 1946; chief intelligence 8th Air Force, 1946-48; dir. pub. information Hdqrs. SAC, later spl. asst. to Gen. Curtis E. LeMay, 1948- 52; comdr. 55th Reconnaissance Wing, Ramey AFB, P.R., 1952- 55, 14th Air Div., Travis AFB, Cal., 1955-57; dep. comdr. 15th Air Force, March AFB, Cal., 1957-59; vice comdr. Continental Air Command, N.Y., 1959-61; chief staff Air South, NATO, 1961-62; ret.; now pres. Safety Products, Inc. Decorated Silver Star, Legion of Merit with cluster, Air Medal with clusters, D.F.C. with cluster, Presidential Unit citation with clusters, D.S.M. (U.S.); Order Brit. Empire. Mem. Order Daedalians. Contbr. short stories, articles to tech. publs. and nat. mags. Home: 223 Fairfax Rd Bellevue NB 68005 Office: PO Box 427 Bellevue NB 68005

KALBFLEISCH, GIRARD EDWARD, U.S. judge; b. Piqua, O., Aug. 3, 1899; s. Oscar Conrad and Lena (Gerstmeyer) K.; LL.B., Ohio No. U., 1923, LL.D., 1960; m. Chattie Lenore Spohn, May 1, 1929. Admitted to Ohio bar, 1924; practice in Manfield; pros. atty., Richland County, 1928-32; judge Municipal Ct., 1936-43, Common Pleas Ct., 1943-59; judge U.S. Dist. Ct., No. Dist. Ohio, 1959—. Dir. Civilian Def., 1941-45. Served as pvt. U.S. Army, 1918. Mem. Common Pleas Judges Assn. Ohio (pres. 1952). Mason. Home: 545 Stewart Lane Mansfield OH 44907 Office: US Dist Ct Federal Bldg Cleveland OH

KALCKAR, HERMAN M., educator, scientist; b. Copenhagen, Denmark, Mar. 26, 1908; s. Ludvig and Bertha (Melchior) K.; M.D., U. Copenhagen, 1933, Ph.D., 1938; M.A. (hon.), Harvard U.; D.Sc. (hon.), Washington U., St. Louis; children—Sonja, Nina, Niels. Came to U.S., 1953, naturalized, 1956. Sci. asst. Inst. Med. Physiology, U. Copenhagen, 1934-37, instr. physiology, 1934-37, asst. prof., 1937; Rockefeller research fellow Cal. Inst. Tech., Hopkin Marine Sta. of Stanford and Washington U. Sch. Medicine, 1939-42; research asso. Pub. Health Research Inst., N.Y.C., 1943-46; asso. prof. physiology U. Copenhagen 1946-49, research prof., dir. Inst. for Cytophysiology, 1949- 54; vis. scientist NIH, Bethesda, Md., 1953-56, chief sect. metabolic ezymes, 1956-58; prof. biology and biochemistry, dept. biology Johns Hopkins, 1958-61; prof. biol. chemistry Harvard Med. Sch., 1961—; chief biochemistry, biochem. research lab. Mass. Gen. Hosp., Boston, 1961—. Recipient Presdl. award Internat. Poliomyelities Congress, 1956, Medaille Internat., Societe de Chimie Biolgique, Paris, 1957. Fellow Am. Acad. Arts and Scis.; mem. Soc. Biol. Chemists. Harvey Soc. (hon.), Kongelige Danske Videnskabernes Selskab (fgn.), Nat. Acad. Scis. Author numerous articles, monographs on phosphorylation and galactose metabolism. Office: Mass Gen Hosp Boston MA 02114

KALERGIS, JAMES GEORGE, army officer; b. Lowell, Mass., Jan. 13, 1917; s. George and Nellie (Vassilakos) K.; B.S., Boston U., 1938; M.A. in Internat. Affairs, George Washington U., 1961; grad. Advanced Mgmt. Program, Harvard, 1966; m. Norma Frances Butler, Feb. 11, 1940; children—George J., James B., David G., Sandra P. Enlisted as pvt. U.S. Army, 1941, advanced through grades to maj. gen., 1971; comdg. officer 597th Armored F.A. Battalion, Germany, 1952-54; comdg. gen. I Field Force, Arty. Vietnam, 1967-68; comptroller hdqrs. Material Command, Washington, 1969-70; dep. comdg. gen. for logistics support, Hdqrs. U.S. Army, 1970—. Decorated D.S.M., Legion of Merit, Bronze Star, Air medal. Mem. Assn. U.S. Army, Armed Forces Mgmt. Assn. Home: 7854 Midday Lane Alexandria VA 22306 Office: Bldg T-7 Gravelly Pt VA Washington DC 20315

KALES, MORRIS LEON, educator; b. N.Y.C., Aug. 26, 1910; s. Louis and Sophia (Bergman) K.; B.S. in Math., Mass. Inst. Tech., 1933, M.S., 1934; Ph.D., Brown U., 1936; m. Rose Moskovitz, Oct. 11, 1931; children—Arthur Norman, Eugene Laurence. Instr. Brown U., 1936-37, U. Mich., 1937-39, Tulane U., 1939-42, U. Me., 1942-44; mem. sci. staff radiation lab. Mass. Inst. Tech., 1944-45; with U.S. Naval Research Lab., 1945-65; prof. U.S. Naval Acad., Annapolis, 1965—. Recipient Award Merit, Navy Dept., 1959, also Superior Accomplishment award, 1961; Applied Sci. award Research Soc. Am., 1959. Mem. Math. Assn. Am., A.A.A.S., Research Soc. Am., Sigma Xi. Patentee in micro-wave antenna and ferrite device field. Contbr. profl. jours. Home: 6408 Marjory Lane Bethesda MD 20034 Office: US Naval Acad Annapolis MD 21402

KALES, ROBERT GRAY, mgmt., finance, mfg., real estate exec.; b. Detroit, Mar. 14, 1904; s. William R. and Alice (Gray) K.; grad. Phillips Exeter Acad., 1923; B.S., Mass. Inst. Tech., 1928; M.B.A., Harvard, 1933; m. Jane Webster, Nov. 27, 1932; children—Jane (Mrs. William H. Ryan), Robert Gray, William R., Anne W. (Mrs. Jeffrey Howson); m. 2d, Miriam Wallin, Jan. 6, 1945; 1 son, David Wallin; m. 3d, Herma Lou Boyd, Mar. 6, 1951; m. 4th, Shirley L. McBride, Feb. 14, 1961; children—John Gray, Nancy Davis. With Whitehead & Kales Co., Detroit, 1928-31, 43—, v.p., 1943—, now chmn. bd., River Rouge, Mich., also dir.; with Union Guardian Trust Co., Detroit, 1933-34; analyst, sec.-treas. Investment Counsel, Inc., Detroit, 1934-35; organizer Kales Kramer Investment Co., Detroit, 1935, pres., dir., 1935—; pres., dir. Indsl. Resources, Inc., 1955—, Automotive Bin Service Co., Inc., 1955—, Jefferson Terminal Warehouse, 1934—, Kales Bldg. Co., 1944—, Kales Realty Co., 1935—, Midwest Underwriters, Inc., 1938—, Modern Constrn., Inc., 1938— (all Detroit); v.p., dir. Basin Oil Co., Metamora, Mich., 1947—; dir. Independent Liberty Life Ins. Co., Grand Rapids, Mich. Chmn. vets. com. Detroit Armed Forces Week. Adv. bd. Patriotic Edn., Deland, Fla.; chmn. trustees, pres. Kales Found. Served to lt. comdr. USNR, 1942-45; capt. Res. Mem. Am. Legion, Navy League U.S. (pres. Southeastern Mich. council), Mil. Order World Wars (past nat. comdr.-in-chief), Nat. Sojourners, Naval Order U.S., S.A.R., U.S. Naval Inst., Sigma Chi. Episcopalian. Mason (K.T., Shriner). Clubs: Army and Navy, University (Washington); Bayview Yacht, Detroit Country, Detroit Athletic, Detroit, Curling, Detroit Power Squadron, The Players, St. Clair Yacht, Scarab, University (Detroit); Black River Ranch (Onaway, Mich.); Longwood Cricket, Union Boat (Boston); Stone Horse Yacht (Harwich, Mass.); Triton Fish and Game (Quebec, Can.); Grosse Pointe (Mich.) Hunt, Grosse Pointe Yacht. Home: 87 Cloverly Rd Grosse Pointe Farms MI 48236 Office: 58 Haltiner St River Rouge MI 48218 also Kales Bldg 76 Adams Av Detroit MI 48226

KALEY, H.E., steel co. exec. Comptroller Pitts.-Des Moines Steel Co. Office: Neville Island Pittsburgh PA 15225*

KALIJARVI, THORSTEN VALENTINE, retired diplomat, educator; b. Gardner, Mass.; s. Gustaf and Ida Christina (Kuniholm) K.; A.B., Clark U., 1920, A.M., 1923; Carnegie Endowment fellow, Harvard, 1920-22; LL.B., LaSalle; Ph.D., U. Berlin, 1935, also A.L.M.; student Hague Acad. Internat. Law, Geneva Sch. Internat. Studies, 1929; m. Dorothy Corbett Knight, Sept. 4, 1926; 1 dau., June. Head dept. polit. sci. U. N.H., 1927, prof. govt., 1939-45; exec. dir. N.H. Planning and Devel. Commn., mem. nat., state, regional commns., 1942-47; prin. analyst European affairs Legislative Reference Service, Library Congress, 1947; research counsel internat. relations, 1947-50, sr. specialist fgn. affairs, 1950-52; staff asso., cons. Senate Fgn. Relations Com., 1947-53, dep. asst. sec. state for econ. affairs, 1953-57, asst. sec. state for econ. affairs, 1957; acting under-sec. state for econ. affairs, 1956-57; U.S. ambassador to El Salvador, 1957-61; cons. Dept. of State, 1961; Distinguished prof. internat. and pub. affairs Pa. State U., 1962-64; dean faculty Cape Cod Com. Coll., 1964-68, prof. emeritus, 1968—; lectr. history and govt. Am. U., 1947-53, dir. Insts. on Communism and Am. Constitutionalism, 1963, adj. prof., 1964- 66; lectr. Johns Hopkins 1952-53; lectr., cons. internat. affairs. Pub. panel mem. War Labor Bd., Region I; arbitrator labor disputes; cons. Planning Research Corp., 1968-70; dir. Manchester Pub. Forum, 1937. Served in S.A.T.C., 1918. Fellow Am. Acad. Scis.; mem. U.S. C. of C. (internat. com.), Am. Legion, Phi Kappa Phi, Pi Gamma Mu. Clubs: Dacor, Cosmos (Washington). Author: Recent American Foreign Policy, 1952; Modern World Politics, 1953; Soviet Power and Policy, 1954; Central America, Land of Lords and Lizards, 1962. Editor: Congress and Foreign Relations, 1953, Fascism in Action, 1948. Contbr. articles jours. Address: 1552 33d St NW Washington DC 20007 also Seascape Popponesset Beach MA 02560 and Blue Blinds Barnstable MA 02630

KALIL, MARGARET, singer; b. Monroe, La.; d. Fred and Anna (Shamis) Kalil; B.S., Columbia, 1949, M.A., 1950; postgrad. Julliard Sch. Music, 1956-60. Soloist, N.Y. Philharmonic, Boston Symphony orchs., Dallas, Detroit Symphonies, 1959- 64; resident artist N. Tex. State U., 1960-64; mem. faculty Columbia Tchrs. Coll., 1964—; operatic performer, debut in donna Anna, Chataqua Opera Co., 1959. Town Hall, N.Y.C., 1963, Met. Opera in Celestial Voice, 1965; mem. Met. Opera Assn. Recipient aid to Music award Martha Baird Rockefeller, 1957, Concert Artists Guild award, 1963, James Loeb Meml. hon. award Julliard Sch. Music, 1959-60. Mem. Nat. Assn. Tchrs. Singing, Sigma Alpha Iota, Pi Kappa Lambda. Home: 600 W 111th St New York City NY 10025 Office: Metropolitan Opera Assn Lincoln Center New York City NY 10023

KALIMOS, LEON GUS, ballet mgr.; b. Astoria, Ore., June 7, 1917; s. Constantine and Athena (Gavalos) K.; student San Francisco Coll., 1934-42, U. Cal., 1936-38; m. Wana Josephine Williams, Feb. 29, 1955; 1 dau., Tina. Mng. dir. San Francisco Ballet, 1956—; exec. dir. Marin Meml. Theatre Performing Arts, 1969—. Vice pres. Ballet Mgrs. Assn.; bd. dirs. San Francisco Ballet Guild, Bay Area Arts Council; dir. 3d v.p. Dance Companies; pres. Assn. Am. Dance Companies. Served with AUS, World War II. Club: Press, Commonwealth (San Francisco). Home: 1 Ardenwood Way San Francisco CA 94132 Office: 378 18th Av San Francisco CA 94121

KALINOWSKY, LOTHAR BRUNO, neuropsychiatrist; b. Berlin, Germany, Dec. 28, 1899; s. Alfred and Anna (Schott) K.; student univs. Berlin, Heidelberg, Munich, 1917-22; M.D., U. Berlin, 1922, U. Rome, 1934; m. Hilda Pohl, Mar. 7, 1925; children—Marion, Ellen. Asst. neuro-psychiatry univ. hosps. Berlin, Hamburg, Breslau, Vienna, 1922-32; asst. Univ. Hosp. for Nervous and Mental Diseases, Rome, 1933-39; guest physician various European hosps., 1939-40, Pilgrim State Hosp., 1940-43; attending psychiatrist N.Y. Psychiat. Inst. and Hosp., N.Y.C., 1940-58; asso. neurologist Neurol. Inst., N.Y.C., 1940-57; attending psychiatrist St. Vincent's Hosp., N.Y.C., 1957—; specializing chiefly in somatic treatment in psychiatry, 1938—; teaching, research asso. psychiatry Coll. Phys. and Surg., Columbia, 1942-58; asso. prof. neuropsychiatry N.Y. Sch. Psychiatry, 1958—; clin. prof. psychiatry N.Y. Med. Coll., 1961—. Diplomate Am. Bd. Neurology and Psychiatry. Mem. Brit. Med. Assn., A.M.A., Am. Psychiat. Assn., Am. Neurol. Assn., N.Y. Acad. Medicine, Internat. League Against Epilepsy, Royal Medico-Psychol. Assn. (corr.), German Neuropsychiat. Soc. (hon.). Author: (with Paul H. Hoch) Somatic Treatments in Psychiatry, 1961; (with H. Hippius) Pharmacological, Convulsive and Other Somatic Treatments in Psychiatry, 1969. Contbr. numerous articles sci. jours. Home: 242 Lakeview Av E Brightwaters NY 11718 Office: 115 E 82d St New York City NY 10028

KALISH, DONALD, educator; b. Chgo., Dec. 4, 1919; s. Lionel and Mildred (Paneira) K.; A.B., U. Cal. at Berkeley, 1943, M.A. in Psychology, 1945, Ph.D. in Philosophy, 1949. Instr. Swarthmore Coll., 1946-47, U. Cal. at Berkeley, 1947-48; mem. faculty U. Cal. at Los Angeles, 1949—, prof. philosophy, 1964—, chmn. dept., 1964-70. Co-chmn. Nat. Mblzn. Com. to End War in Vietnam, 1967-68; mem. steering com. Resist, 1967—. Mem. Am. Assn. U. Profs., A.A.A.S., Am. Philos. Assn., Assn. Symbolic Logic, Am. Fedn. Tchrs., New Univ. Conf., Sigma Xi. Author: (with Richard Montague) LogicTechniques of Formal Reasoning, 1964; also articles.

KALISH, HARRY ALEXANDER, lawyer; b. Phila., Nov. 30, 1907; s. Louis and Elizabeth (Silverstein) K.; LL.B., Dickinson Sch. Law, 1928; m. Ada Sablosky, Mar. 18, 1933. Admitted to Pa. bar, 1930; a founder, 1933, since partner firm Dilworth, Paxson, Kalish, Kohn and Levy, Phila.; farmer, 1940—; a founder drive-in theatre industry, 1948; a developer North Cape May (N.J.) community, 1950; atty. for Levitt and Sons, Inc., in devel. Levittown, Pa., 1952—. Dir. Crime Commn. Phila.; vice chmn. Phila. City Planning Commn., 1956-58; chmn. Mayor's Com. Light and Sound, Independence Hall. Trustee Phila. Community Found., Inc.; bd. dirs. Eagleville Sanatorium, Found. Cardiovascular Research, Pa. Soc. Advancement Med. Research. Served from 1st lt. to maj., USAAF, 1942-45. Mem. Am., Phila., Phila. County, Pa. bar assns., Brandeis Lawyers Soc. (bd. govs.), Judge Advocates Assn., Tau Epsilon Rho, Woolsack. Clubs: Lawyers, Midday, Mid-City (Phila.); Philmont (Pa.) Country; Lotos (N.Y.C.). Home: 250 S 17th St Philadelphia PA 19103 Office: Fidelity-Phila Trust Bldg Philadelphia PA 19109

KALISH, HARRY ISIDORE, univ. dean; b. N.Y.C., Apr. 4, 1921; s. Max and Pearl (Pollack) K.; B.A., U. Ia., 1949, M.A., 1951, Ph.D., 1952; m. Mildred Armstrong, Apr. 27, 1944; children—Douglas, Gregory. Postdoctoral trainee VA Hosp., Iowa City, 1952-53; vis. prof. Duke, 1953-55; asst. prof. U. Mo., 1955-56; asso. prof. Adelphi U., Garden City, N.Y., 1956-61; prof., chmn. dept. psychology State U. N.Y. at Stony Brook, 1961-71, dean profl. and para-profl. programs, 1971—; cons. VA. Mem. Psychology adv. bd. N.Y. State Edn. Dept. Diplomate Am. Bd. Examiners Profl. Psychology. Fellow Am. Psychol. Assn., A.A.A.S.; mem. Psychonomic Soc., Sigma Xi. Contbr. articles profl. jours. Home: 14 Childs Lane Setauket NY 11733

KALISH, MYRON, lawyer, rubber co. exec.; b. N.Y.C., Dec. 3, 1919; s. Louis and Bertha (Nacht) K.; B.S. in Social Sci., Coll. City N.Y., 1940; LL.B. cum laude, Harvard, 1943; m. Evelyn J. Zobler, Apr. 1, 1944; children—Nita Jane, Pamela Sue. Admitted to N.Y. bar, 1944, since practiced in N.Y.C.; sr. partner firm Arthur, Dryt & Kalish, and predecessors, 1961—; gen. counsel UNIROYAL, Inc., 1961—; dir. Paul B. Mulligan & Co., Inc. Adv. bd. Southwestern Legal Found. Served to lt. (s.g.) USNR, 1943-46. Mem. Am., N.Y. State bar assns., Assn. Bar City N.Y., N.A.M. Mason. Clubs: Old Westbury Golf and Country; Harvard. Editor: Harvard Law Rev., 1942-43. Home: 430 Bryant Av Roslyn Harbor NY 11576 Office: 1230 6th Av New York City NY 10020

KALISS, NATHAN, research biologist; b. N.Y.C., Aug. 1, 1907; s. Philip and Anna (Breslovsky) Kalish; B.S., Coll. City N.Y., 1929; M.A. in Zoology, Columbia, 1931, Ph.D. in Zoology, 1938; m. Rebecca B. Weiss, Nov. 5, 1928; children—Anthony M., Jeffrey D., W. Edwin. Research asso. Cornell U. Med. Coll., 1940-43; med. statistician VA, 1946-47; sr. fellow cancer reserach Am. Cancer Soc., Jackson Lab., Bar Harbor, Me., 1947-50, research asso., 1950-57, staff scientist, 1957-59, sr. staff scientist, 1959—, asst. dir. research, 1958-62; research asso. surgery Harvard Med. Sch., 1966—. Spl. research immunology tissue grafting, cancer immunology and biology. Guggenheim fellow, 1956-57. Served to capt. USAAF, 1943-46. Fellow A.A.A.S., N.Y. Acad. Scis.; mem. Transplantation Soc. (exec. bd.), Am. Assn. Immunologists, Am. Assn. Cancer Research, Soc. Exptl. Biology and Medicine. Editor monographs. Mng. editor Transplantation Bull., 1953-62; editor Transplantation, 1963—; editorial adv. bd. proc. Transplantation Soc., 1968—, Cancer Research, 1969—. Office: Jackson Lab Bar Harbor ME 04609

KALKBRENNER, JUERGEN, German diplomat; b. Luebeck, Germany, Aug. 6, 1924; s. Georg and Ida (Meyer) K.; Dr. jur., Kiel U., 1951; postgrad. U. Wash., Seattle, 1951-52; m. Renate Fuerstenwerth, June 18, 1955; children—Joerg, Jens, Julia. With German Fgn. Service, 1955—; asst. to Pres. Commn. European Econ. Community, Brussels, 1963-67; counselor for cultural and ednl. affairs Germany embassy, Washington, 1970—. Served with German Army, 1942-45. Home: 6013 Claiborne Dr McLean VA 22101 Office: 4645 Reservoir Rd NW Washington DC 20007

KALLAI, GYULA, Hungarian govt. ofcl. Formerly journalist, fgn. affairs adviser; dep. premier Hungary, 1960-65, premier, 1965-67; speaker Hungarian Parliament, 1967—. Address: Parliament Bldg Budapest Hungary*

KALLAND, EARL STANLEY, clergyman, educator; b. Superior, Wis., June 26, 1910; s. Matt and Hilda (Hagan) K.; Th.B., Bible Inst. Los Angeles, 1936; Th.B., Gordon Coll. Theology and Missions, Boston, 1937, B.D., Gordon Div. Sch., 1940, Th.D., 1942; D.D., Conservative Bapt. Sem., Denver, 1954; m. Kathryn Jean Morris, Aug. 30, 1936; children—Charles Morris, Eric Lance, Cheryl Earlene, Betty Darlene. Ordained to ministry Bapt. Ch., 1940; pastor Rock Hill Ch., Boston, 1936-42, First Ch., Sayre, Pa., 1942-44, Calvary Bapt. Ch., Burbank, Cal., 1944-45; prof. Bibl. lit. and exegesis Los Angeles Bapt. Theol. Sem., 1944-45; prof. O.T. and Hebrew, Cal. Bapt. Theol. Sem., Los Angeles, 1945-46; dean Western Bapt. Theol. Sem., Portland, Ore., 1946-47, prof. O.T. and Hebrew, 1946-56, pres., 1947-56; dean, asso. prof. O.T., Conservative Bapt. Theol. Sem., Denver, 1956-58, dean prof. O.T., 1958- -. Mem. Com. Bible Translation, 1965—. Mem. bd. Concern, Inc., 1962-65. Mem. Am. Schs. Oriental Research, Evang. Theol. Soc. (treas. 1960-63), Soc. Bibl. Lit. and Exegesis, Nat. (chmn. sem. div. edn. com. 1959-62, v.p. edn. com. 1960-62, chmn. edn. com. 1962-65, exec. com. Commn. higher edn. 1966—), Colo. (bd. dirs. 1960-62), Denver (pres. 1958-59, 1st v.p. 1960-62), assns. evangelicals, Assn. Higher Edn., N.E.A., Colo. Temperance Fedn. (bd. 1958-62), Internat. Oceanographic Found., Nat. Wild Life Fedn., Smithsonian Instn., Americans United, Phi Alpha Chi. Republican. Home: 3090 S High St Denver CO 80210 also (summer) Indian Hills CO 80454 Office: PO Box 10000 University Park Sta Denver CO 80210

KALLEN, ARNOLD MILTON, physician; b. Newark, 1912; M.D., U. Glasgow (Scotland), 1937. Intern, Med. Center of Jersey City, 1937-39; resident in psychiatry Winter VA Hosp., Topeka, Kan., 1948-50; fellow Menninger Found. Sch. Psychiatry, Topeka, 1948-50; staff psychiatrist Council Child Devel. Center, N.Y.C.; dir. Essex County Guidance Center, Cedar Grove, N.J.; supt., med. dir. Essex Co. Hosp., Cedar Grove; clin. asso. prof. child psychiatry N.J. Coll. Medicine. Served to col. M.C., USAF. Diplomate in psychiatry Am. Bd. Psychiatry and Neurology. Fellow Am. Psychiat. Assn., A.C.P.; mem. Soc. Adolescent Psychiatry, Eastern Psychoanalytic Assn., Am. Assn. Community Clinic and Center Psychiatrists, Am. Orthopsychiat. Assn., A.M.A., Am. Group Psychotherapeutic Assn. Office: 125 Fairview Av Cedar Grove NJ 07009*

KALLEN, HORACE MEYER, retired educator; b. Berenstadt, Silesia, Germany, Aug. 11, 1882; s. Jacob David and Esther Rebecca (Glazier) K.; came to U.S., 1887; A.B. magna cum laude, Harvard, 1903, Ph.D., 1908, L.H.D., 1948; post-grad. Princeton, Oxford U. and Paris; Litt.D., Hebrew Union Coll., Jewish Inst. Religion, 1953, L.H.D., 1965; m. Rachel Oatman Van Arsdale, 1926; children—Harriet S., David J. Asst., lectr. philosophy Harvard, 1908-11; instr. logic Clark Coll., Worcester, Mass., 1910; instr. philosophy and psychology U. Wis., 1911-18; prof. New School for Social Research, N.Y.C., 1952, research prof. social philosophy, 1952-69, emeritus, 1969—, dean grad. faculty polit. and social sci. 1944-46; Distinguished Seminar prof. L.I.U., 1964-68. Mem. labor com. Adv. Commn. Council Nat. Def.; mem. Commn. Inquiry on Terms of Peace, N.Y.C. Mayor's Com. on City Planning; chmn. commn. on edn. Am. Labor Conf. on Internat. Relations, Presdl. Commn. on Higher Edn.; cons. N.Y.C. Commn. on Intergroup Relations, 1961. Named by Wm. James editor of unfinished book, 1910; lit. executor Benjamin Paul Blood, 1920. Trustee Rochdale Inst., N.Y.C., Found. Study Modern Sci., Found. Oceanic Edn. Recipient Bernard Semel award, Mark Eisner Edn. medal, Frank Weill award, Acad. Div. United Jewish Appeal award. Fellow Jewish Acad. Arts and Scis., Internat. Inst. Arts and Letters; mem. Am. Jewish Congress (hon. v.p.), World Jewish Congress (exec. com.), Internat. League for Rights Man, Am. Philos. Soc., Soc. Sci. Study Religion (pres.), Am. Assn. Jewish Edn. (v.p.). Translator: Criminal Psychology (Hans Gross), 1910. Author: Decline and Rise of the Consumer, 1936; Art and Freedom, 2 vols., 1942; Modernity and Liberty, 1947; The Liberal Spirit, 1948; Ideals and Experience 1948; The Education of Free Men, 1949, (translated in Italian), 1964; Patterns of Progress, 1950; Democracy's True Religion, 1951; Secularism is the Will of God, 1954; Cultural Pluralism and the American Idea, 1956; Utopians at Bay, 1958; The Book of Job as Greek Tragedy, 1959; A Study of Liberty, 1959; Philosophical Issues in Adult Education, 1962; Freedom, Tragedy and Comedy, 1963; Liberty, Laughter and Tears, 1968; What I Believe and Why-Maybe, 1971. Editor: The Bertrand Russell Case (with John Dewey), 1941. Contbr. to periodicals. Address: 66 W 12th St New York City NY 10027

KALLENBERG, WILLIAM GRAHAM, investment co. exec.; b. Cedar Rapids, Ia., Jan. 30, 1925; s. Edwin Frank and Thelma (Graham) K.; student U. Tenn., 1948-49; B.S. in Indsl. Econs., Ia. State U., 1950; m. June George, Nov. 26, 1948; children—William Graham, Betsy E., Edwin Parke. Vice pres. Joel H. Clark & Assos., Union City, Tenn., 1953-62; regional v.p. Crosby Corp., Atlanta, 1962-68, v.p. sales, Boston, 1968-69, exec. v.p., 1969, pres., 1969—, also dir.; dir. Crosby Plans Corp. Served to 1st lt. USAAF, 1943-46. Mem. Union City C. of C. (pres. 1961-62). Rotarian (pres. 1961). Home: 45 Berkeley Rd Avondale Estates GA 30002 Office: 225 Franklin St Boston MA 02110

KALLET, ARTHUR, med. editor, engr.; b. Syracuse, N.Y., Dec. 15, 1902; s. Barnett and Etta (Kaplan) K.; B.S., Mass. Inst. Tech., 1924; m. Opal Boston, Apr. 27, 1927 (dec. 1952); 1 son, Anthony; m. 2d, Mary R. Fitzpatrick, January 28, 1954; children—Cynthia, Lisa. Engaged in editorial work N.Y. Edison Co., 1924-26, then asst. mgr. editorial bur., 1927; mem. staff Am. Standards Assn. and editor, Indsl. Standardization, 1927-34; with publicity dept. Regional Plan N.Y., 1929-32; prin. founder, dir. Consumers Union U.S., 1936-57; exec. dir. The Med. Letter Drugs and Therapeutics, 1958—; pres. Med. Letter, Inc., 1958—, Buyers Lab., Inc., 1961—. Author: 100,000,000 Guinea Pigs (with F. J. Schlink), 1933; Counterfeit, 1935. Home: 224 Broadview Av New Rochelle NY 10804 Office: 56 Harrison St New Rochelle NY 10801

KALLIO, REINO EMIL, educator, microbiologist; b. Worcester, Mass., July 6, 1919; s. Emil N. and Hulda (Ilen) K.; B.S., U. Ala., 1941; M.S., U. Ia., 1948, Ph.D., 1950; m. Rebecca Deems, Feb. 28, 1942; children—Leonard Emil, Sandra Ellen, Siska Elaine. Sr. supr. Trojan Powder Co., Sandusky, O., 1941-44; from instr. to prof. U. Ia., 1959-62; Career Research grantee USPHS, 1962-65; prof. microbiology, dir. Sch. Life Scis., U. Ill., Urbana, 1965—. Served with USNR, 1944-46. Mem. Am. Acad. Microbiology (sec.- treas. 1965—), Am. Soc. Microbiology (councilor at large 1964-66, nat. program chmn. 1962-64), Am. Chem. Soc., Soc. Gen. Microbiology. Editorial bd. Jour. Bacteriology, 1964—. Contbr. numerous articles profl. jours. Home: 37 Sherwin Circle Urbana IL 61801

KALLIOKOSKI, JORMA OSMO, educator, geologist; b. Finland, Nov. 23, 1923; s. August and Naima (Bastman) K.; came to U.S., 1953, naturalized, 1963; B.Sc., U. Western Ont., 1947; Ph.D., Princeton, 1951; m. Saara Rauha, Oct. 1, 1949; children—Donald, Susan, Karen. With Geol. Survey Can., 1949-53, Newmont Exploration Ltd., 1953-56; mem. faculty Princeton, 1956-68, asso. prof., 1951-68; prof., head dept. geology and geol. engring. Mich. Tech. U., Houghton, 1968—; bus. editor Econ. Geology Pub. Co., 1971—; geol. field work in U.S., Can., Alaska, Turkey, Venezuela. Fellow Geol. Soc. Am.; mem. Canadian Inst. Mining and Metallurgy, Soc. Econ. Geologists (sec. 1965-67, asso. editor jour. 1969-72). Am. Inst. Mining and Metall. Engrs. Editor: Role of Governments in the Exploration for Mineral Resources, 1964. Home: 1010 E 7th Av Houghton MI 49931

KALLIR, JOHN, advt. exec.; b. Vienna, Austria, Apr. 23, 1923; s. Otto and Francisca (Countess zu Lowenstein) K.; B.S. in Chemistry, Manhattan Coll., 1943; A.M. in History, Columbia, 1950; m. Joyce Rubin, Apr. 16, 1949; children—Jane Katherine, Barbara Sue. Research librarian S.B. Penick & Co., Jersey City, 1946; asst. editor E.R. Squibb & Sons, Bklyn., 1947- 49; copy writer Paul Klemtner & Co., Newark, 1950-51; with William D. McAdams, Inc., N.Y.C., 1952-61, account exec., 1954-56, v.p., 1956-61; founder, 1962, since pres. Kallir, Philips, Ross, Inc. Trustee Columbia Coll. Pharmacy. Served with M.C., AUS, 1943- 46. Mem. A.A.A.S., Am. Med. Writers Assn., Pharm. Advt. Club, Am. Hist. Assn., N.Y. Acad. Scis. Home: High Point Lane Scarsdale NY 10583 Office: 919 3d Av New York City NY 10722

KALLMANN, GERHARD MICHAEL, prof. architecture Harvard. Address: 127 Tremont St Boston MA 02108 also 3 Concord Av Cambridge MA 02138

KALLSEN, THEODORE JOHN, educator; b. Jasper, Minn., Mar. 27, 1915; s. Bernhart H. and Irene (Wehrman) K.; B.S., Mankato State Coll., 1936; M.A., U. Ia., 1940, Ph.D., 1949; m. Marvel J. Stordahl, Aug. 27, 1939; children—Carolyn Irene (Mrs. Harold Pate), Tonya Jo. Various teaching positions, Minn., Mo., Ia., 1936-49; asst. prof. integrated studies W.Va. U., Morgantown, 1949-55; prof. English, head dept. Stephen F. Austin State U., Nacogdoches, Tex., 1955-65, prof., dean Sch. Liberal Arts, 1965—. Cons. English curriculum pub. schs.; communications cons. to industries; co-dir. schs., colls., Beaumont region, Tex. Safety Assn., 1965. Served to lt. (j.g.) USNR, 1944-46. Mem. Nat. Council Tchrs. English, Conf. Coll. Composition and Communication (past mem. exec. com.), Am. Assn. U. Profs., Tex. Conf. Coll. Tchrs. English, Tex. Coll. English Assn., Modern Lang. Assn., So. Humanities Conf. Club: Piney Woods Country (past dir. Nacogdoches). Author: Modern Rhetoric and Usage, 1955; (with D.E. McCoy) Reading and Rhetoric: Order and Idea, 1963; Teachers' Use of Dictating Machines, 1965. Home: 600 Bostwick Lane Nacogdoches TX 75961

KALMAN, ANDREW, corp. exec.; b. Hungary, Aug. 14, 1919; s. Louis and Julia (Bognar) K.; m. Violet Margaret Kish, June 11, 1949; children—Andrew Joseph, Richard Louis, Laurie Ann. Came to U.S., 1922, naturalized, 1935. With Detroit Engring. & Machine Co., 1947-66, exec. v.p., gen. mgr., 1952-66; exec. v.p. Indian Head, Inc., 1966—, also dir.; dir. Acme Precision Products. Trustee Alma (Mich.) Coll. Home: 11 Shady Hollow Dr Dearborn MI 48124 Office: 21800 Greenfield Rd Detroit MI 48237

KALMAN, CHARLES ARNOLD, mgmt. cons.; b. St. Paul, Aug. 20, 1919; s. Charles Oscar and Alexandra (Robertson) K.; S.B., Mass. Inst. Tech., 1941; m. Marie Dickey, Oct. 3, 1942; children—Eric, Kristina. With N.C. Shipbldg. Co., Wilmington, 1941-43; with Springfield Machine & Foundry Co. (Mass.), 1943-44, Cramp Shipbldg. Co., Phila., 1944-46, Am. Machine & Foundry Co., Bklyn., 1946-50; with Booz, Allen & Harmilton, N.Y.C., 1950—, partner, 1956-62, v.p., 1962-70, sr. v.p., 1970—; dir. Bliss & Laughlin, Inc., Oakbrook, Ill., 1948—, chmn. exec. com., 1960—; dir. Servotronics, Inc., Buffalo; dir. Electronic Memories Magnetics Corp., Domain Industries. Mem. Soc. Automotive Engrs. Home: 9 Conant Pl Salem Straits Darien CT 06820 Office: 245 Park Av New York City NY 10017

KALMAN, RUDOLF EMIL, research mathematician, engr.; b. Budapest, Hungary, May 19, 1930; s. Otto and Ursula (Grundmann) K.; B.S., Mass. Inst. Tech., 1953, M.S., 1954; D.Sc., Columbia, 1957; m. Constantina Stavrou, Sept. 12, 1959; children—Andrew E.F.C., Elisabeth K.U. Staff engr. IBM Research Corp., Poughkeepsie, N.Y., 1957-58; research mathematician Research Inst. Advanced Studies, Balt., 1958-64; prof. engring. mech. and elec. engring. Stanford 1964-67, prof. math. system theory, 1967—; dir. Centre d'Automatique, Elde Nationale Superieure de Mines de Paris, 1968—; mem. sci. adv. bd. Laboratorio di Cibernetica, Napoli, 1970—. Named outstanding young scientist Md. Acad. Sci., 1962. Home: 169 Eleanor Dr Woodside CA 94602 Office: 114 Encina Commons Dept Operations Research Stanford CA 94305

KALMBACH, ALBERT CARPENTER publisher; b. Sturgeon Bay, Wis., June 25, 1910; s. Maurice Frederick and Mae Louise (Carpenter) K.; B.S., Marquette U., 1932; student eve. classes U. Wis., 1937-41; m. Bernice Irene Graham, Oct. 22, 1933 (dec. 1960); children—Kathryn (Mrs. George Mahnke), Elizabeth (Mrs. James Cole), Charles Albert, William Henry; m. 2d, Pauline L. Gaenslen, Jan. 21, 1961 (dec. 1965). Part-time worker circulation department Milw. Jour., 1928-30; gen. mgr. Milw. Press, 1932-33; founder Kalmbach Publishing Company, pres. 1933, now chmn. bd., publisher various mags.; founder and editor of several of which now only publisher, usually in model making and transportation; pres. K-P-K Corp., Milw. Mem. Mag. industry adv. com. N.P.A., 1951-52; mem. policy com. Smaller Magazines Postal Com., 1950—; chairman budget com. of United Community Welfare. Vice pres. Nat. Railroad Museum, Inc.; trustee Town Hall, Milwaukee, Wis. Director Model Industry Assn.; mem. Lexington Group; chmn. Met. Transp. Com., Milw., 1948-60; chmn. Mayor's adv. com. Met. Transit Authority. Recipient Distinguished Service award Hobby Industry Assn., 1965; Spl. Founder's award Nat. Model R.R. Assn., 1965. Mem. Assn. R.R. Advt. Mgrs. (hon. life), Employing Printers Assn. Milw. (pres. 1960-63), Nat. Ry. Hist. Soc. (hon. life mem.), Nat. Model R.R. Assn. (hon.), Ry. and Locomotive Hist. Soc., Railroadians America, Model Industry Association (president 1952-54), Newcomen Society North America, Sigma Delta Chi, Pi Mu Epsilon. Clubs: Press, Athletic (Milw.). Author: Model Railroader Cyclopedia, 1936-43; Model Railroad Track and Layout, 1940; Railroad Panorama, 1944. Home: 4625 N Cramer St Whitefish Bay WI 53211 Office: 1027 Seventh St N Milwaukee WI 53233 ☆

KALMBACH, HERBERT WARREN, lawyer; b. Port Huron, Mich., Oct. 19, 1921; s. Carl Malen and Doris Estelle (Wallace) K.; B.S., U. So. Cal., 1949, J.D., 1951; m. Barbara Helen Forbush, June 12, 1948; children—Kurt Warren, Lauren Ann, Kenneth Malen. Admitted to Cal. bar, 1952; v.p., dir. Security Title Ins. Co., Los Angeles, 1952-57; pvt. practice law, Newport Beach, Los Angeles, 1957-61, 62-64; pres., dir. Ariz. Title Ins. & Trust Co., Phoenix, 1961; v.p., gen. counsel, dir. Macco Realty Co., Newport Beach, 1964-67; sr. partner Kalmbach, DeMarco, Knapp & Chillingworth, Newport Beach, Los Angeles, 1967—. Asso. finance chmn. Nixon for Pres. campaign, 1968; exec. vice chmn. Republican Nat. Finance Com., 1968-69. Bd. dirs. Hoag Hosp. 552 Support Group, Newport Beach; sec., trustee Richard Nixon Found. Served to lt. (j.g.) USNR, 1942-47. Mem. Am., Cal., Los Angeles, Orange County bar assns., Los Angeles, Orange County world affairs councils, Legion Lex, Town Hall, Delta Tau Delta, Phi Delta Phi. Clubs: Los Angeles Country; California (Los Angeles); Irvine Coast Country, Balboa Bay, Big Canyon Country (Newport Beach); Lincoln (dir. Orange County). Home: 1056 Santiago Dr Newport Beach CA 92660 Office: 550 Newport Center Dr Newport Beach CA 92660 also 515 S Flower St Los Angeles CA 90071

KALMBACH, LELAND JOHN, ins. co. exec.; b. Chelsea, Mich., Apr. 30, 1901; s. John and Cora (Lutz) K.; A.B., U. Mich., 1923; LL.D. (hon.), Am. Internat. Coll.; L.H.D., Springfield Coll.; Litt.D., Western New Eng. Coll.; m. Letha Grace Alber, Sept. 1, 1931; 1 son, Dohn Leland. With actuarial dept. Cleve. Life Ins. Co., 1923; with Lincoln Nat. Life Ins. Co., Ft. Wayne, Ind., 1924-47, v.p., 1939-47, 1st v.p., 1947, dir., 1937-47; v.p. Mass. Mut. Life Ins. Co., Springfield, Mass., 1948-50, pres., 1950-62, chmn. bd., 1962-66, hon. chmn. 1966—, dir., 1948—; dir. N.E. Tel. and Tel. Co. Fellow Soc. Actuaries; mem. Life Ins. Assn. Am. (past chmn.), Phi Beta Kappa, Delta Sigma Pi. Republican. Methodist. Clubs: Colony (Springfield); Longmeadow (Mass.) Country; Augusta (Ga.) Nat. Golf; Presidents (U. Mich.); Blind Brook (Port Chester, N.Y.). Home: Somers CT 06071 Office: 1295 State St Springfield MA 01101

KALMENSON, BENJAMIN, retired pictures exec.; b. Pitts., Jan. 3, 1899; s. Charles and Gail K.; m. Norma Goldman, Dec. 28, 1926; children—Mrs. Burton Levine, Howard. Began career with Crucible Steel Co. of Am.; in motion picture industry 1927-69; with First Nat. Exchange, 1934; joined Warner Bros., 1934; pres. Warner Bros. Distbg. Corp., 1941; exec. v.p. Warner Bros. Pictures, Inc., 1956-66, pres., chief exec. officer, 1966-67; pres., dir. Warner Bros-Seven Arts, Ltd., 1967-69.

KALMUS, HENRY PAUL, physicist; b. Vienna, Austria, Jan. 9, 1906; s. Ignatz and Grete (Kruger) K.; Dipl. Eng., Vienna Tech. U., 1930, Dr. Tech., 1960; m. Diana Denny, Feb. 27, 1954; children—Angela, Josephine. Came to U.S., 1938, naturalized, 1944. Physicist, Emerson Radio Corp., N.Y.C., 1938-41; research physicist Zenith Radio Corp., Chgo., 1941-48; cons. W. M. Welch Mfg. Co., Chgo., 1948—; physicist Nat. Bur. Standards, Dept. Commerce 1948-53; chief scientist, asso. dir. research and devel. Harry Diamond Labs., Dept. Army, Washington, 1953—. Recipient Exceptional Service award Dept. Commerce, 1954; Exceptional Service award Dept. Army, 1961; named Master Designer, Product Engring., 1967; recipient Gravity Found. award, 1966; Distinguished Service award Def. Dept., 1970; Sperry award Instrument Soc. Am., 1970. Fellow I.E.E.E. Patentee field physics. Contbr. articles sci. jours. Home: 3000 University Terrace NW Washington DC 20016 Office: Harry Diamond Labs Dept Army Washington DC 20438

KALODNER, HARRY ELLIS U.S. judge; b. Phila., Mar. 28, 1896; s. David and Ida (Miller) K.; LL.B., U. Pa., 1917; L.H.D., Yeshiva U., 1950; m. Tillie Poliner, Dec. 20, 1925; children—Philip Poliner, Howard Isaiah. Admitted to Pa. bar, 1917; practice in Phila.; mem. staff Phila. N. Am., 1919-25; financial and polit. editor Phila. Record, 1928-34; sec. revenue Commonwealth Pa., 1935; judge Ct. Common Pleas, No. 2, Philadelphia County, 1936 -37, U.S. Dist. Ct., Eastern Dist. Pa., 1938-46, U.S. Ct. Appeals, 3d Circuit, 1946—. Bd. dirs. Independence Hall Assn., Phila. Psychiat. Hosp., Fedn. Jewish Agys. Greater Phila.; trustee Yeshiva U.; mem. nat. council Am. Jewish Joint Distbn. Com. Served with Judge Adv. Gen.'s Dept., U.S. Army, France and Germany, during World War. Recipient hon. mention for Pulitzer prize for journalism, 1931, 32. Mem. Phila., Pa., Am. bar assns., Lawyers Club Phila., Am. Legion, Brandeis Lawyers' Soc. Democrat. Club: Socialegal. Home: The Wellington 19th and Walnut Sts Philadelphia PA 19103 Office: US Court House Philadelphia PA 19107

KALOUPEK, WALTER EVERETT, educator, polit. scientist; b. Elberon, Ia., Nov. 23, 1907; s. Emil and Augusta (Rohlck) K.; A.B., U. Ia., 1929, A.M., 1936, Ph.D., 1938; m. Virginia Cox, Oct. 9, 1933; 1 son, John L. Prin., Ferguson (Ia.) High Sch., 1929- 31; prof., chmn. dept. history and govt. Huron (S.D.) Coll., 1938- 41; asst. prof. polit. sci. U. N.D., 1941-43, asso. prof., 1943-45, prof., chmn. dept. polit. sci., 1945-63, prof. polit. sci., 1963—, dir. Bur. Govtl. Research, 1963-70. Mem. Am. Polit. Sci. Assn., Am. Assn. U. Profs., Am. Acad. Polit. and Soc. Sci. Mason (33, Shriner). Author: History and Administration of Iowa Highway Patrol, 1938; Alive Nelson Page, 1946; North Dakota Government, 1957; Administration Election Laws in North Dakota, 1960; North Dakota Government, 1963; Opinion Survey of Civil Defense in North Dakota, 1965; Influential Leaders Civil Defense in North Dakota, 1966; Municipal County Finance Officers Training Program in North Dakota, 1967; North Dakota Government, 1970; also various articles and revs. Contbr. County Government Across the Nation, 1950. Home: 1711 21st Av S Grand Forks ND 58201

KALP, EARL SHERMAN, assn. exec.; b. Navarre, O., Apr. 7, 1901; s. Charles Robert and Ella Nora (Sherman) K.; A.B., Sioux Falls Coll. and Des-Moines U., 1923; A.M., Drake U., 1935; grad. study U. Ia., U. Denver; m. Mabel Michael Branson, Sept. 1, 1922; 1 son, Richard Charles. Tchr. social scis. Des Moines high schs., 1932-36, coordinator exptl. curriculum, 1936-42; dir. Office Pub. Information, Drake U., 1943-48; ednl. dir. Midwest div. Nat. Conf. Christians and Jews, 1948-53, asso. nat. dir. edn., 1953-54, exec. dir. Cleveland and No. Ohio region, 1954-58, Chgo. and No. Ill. region, 1958—, dir. program devel. for ednl. orgns., 1963-65, national director of education, Des Moines, 1965—; mem. Presbytery of Des Moines. Mem. Nat. Assn. Intergroup Relations Ofcls., Delta Sigma Rho, Pi Kappa Delta. Author: Democracy and Its Competitors, 1940; In the Service with Uncle Sam, 1942; Defense of the Western Hemisphere, 1941. Contbr. articles to profl. jours. Home: 2223 63d St Des Moines IA 50322 Office: Empire Bldg Des Moines IA 50309

KALPADAKIS, EMMANUEL EVANGHELOS, diplomat; b. Athens, Greece, Feb. 8, 1936; s. Evanghelos Emmanuel and Mary (Androulaki) K.; law degree, Athens U., 1958. With Greek Ministry Fgn. Affairs, 1963-65; vice consul, Edirne, Turkey, 1965-67; consul of Greece, N.Y., 1967-70, also mem. delegation UN Gen. Assembly, 1969; 1st sec. Greek embassy, Washington, 1970—. Served with Greek Army, 1959-60. Home: 4201 Cathedral Av NW Washington DC 20016 Office: 2221 Massachusetts Av NW Washington DC 20008

KALTENBORN, HOWARD SCHOLL, educator; b. Pitts., Jan. 21, 1907; s. Philip and Sarah (Scholl) K.; B.S., Carnegie Inst. Tech., 1928; M.S., U. Mich., 1931, Ph.D., 1934; m. Helen Bertisch Houghtaling, Sept. 3, 1937; children—Alice M. (dec.), Sara H. Instr. math. Carnegie Inst. Tech., 1928-32, U. Mich., 1934-37, U. Tex., 1938-39; asso. prof. La. Poly. Inst., 1939-43, U. Ida., 1945-46; prof. math., chmn. dept. Memphis State U., 1946—; dir. insts. for tchrs. sponsored by NSF, 1959-65, mem. staff insts., 1961, 63, 66. Served to 1st lt. USAAF, 1945. Mem. Math. Assn. Am. (vis. lectr. secondary schs. 1959-62), Tenn. Math. Tchrs. Assn. (co-founder, 1st pres.), Phi Beta Kappa, Sigma Xi (charter mem., past pres. Memphis State U. chpt.). Author: Meaningful Mathematics, 1951; (with others) Basic Mathematics, 1958. Home: 169 S Mendenhall St Memphis TN 38117

KALTENBORN, HOWARD STANLEY, elec. corp. exec., economist; b. Waco, Neb., Sept. 20, 1917; s. Ernest J. and Frances (Anstine) K.; A.B., U. Neb., 1937, M.A., 1938; Ph.D., U. Wis., 1942; m. Myrna M. McGaffin, Aug. 21, 1938 (dec.); children—Douglas R., H. Stanley, Kent E. Instr. econs. U. Neb., 1941-42; asst. wage stblzn. dir., asso. disputes dir., chmn. appeals div. regional war labor bds., Detroit and Chgo., 1942-44; wage and salary adminstr. Curtiss-Wright Corp., 1944-45, dir. indsl. relations, 1945-50; prof. bus. adminstrn. Coll. Bus. Adminstrn., research asso. Inst. Indsl. Relations, U. Cal. at Berkeley, 1950-52; v.p. Indsl. Relations Counselors, Inc., also Indsl. Relations Counselors Service, Inc., N.Y.C., 1952-59; v.p., dir. Westinghouse Electric Corp., Pitts., 1959—. Chmn., pub. mem. National Airframe Panel, 1952. Social Sci. Research Council fellow. Mem. Phi Beta Kappa, Beta Gamma Sigma. Home: W Waldheim Rd Pittsburgh PA 15215 Office: Westinghouse Electric Corp 3 Gateway Center Pittsburgh PA 15222

KALTER, SEYMOUR SANFORD, educator, virologist; b. N.Y.C., Mar. 19, 1918; s. Aaron H. and Jessie (Schulman) K.; B.S., St. Joseph's Coll., Phila., 1940; M.A., U. Kan., 1943; postgrad. U. Pa., 1943-45; Ph.D., Syracuse, 1947; m. Gloria V. Verstein, Mar. 3, 1946; children—Susan P., Steven P., Debra I. Asst. instr. bacteriology U. Kan., 1940-43; research asst. dept. med. bacteriology U. Pa., 1943-45; from asst. to asso. prof. med. microbiology Upstate Med. Center, N.Y. State U., Syracuse, 1945-56; cons. virology Pan Am. San. Bur., Cologne (Germany) U.; adj. prof. Trinity U., San Antonio, 1966—, U. Tex. Med. Sch. at San Antonio, 1971—; bacteriologist Syracuse Dept. Health, 1945-56; chief virus diagnostic methodology unit Contagious Disease Center, USPHS, Atlanta, 1956-60; chief virology sect. Sch. Aviation Medicine, Brooks AFB, Tex., 1960-63; chmn. dept. microbiology Southwest Found. Research and Edn., 1963-66, dir. div. microbiology and infectious diseases, 1966—, chmn. dept. infectious diseases, 1967—; cons. study zoonoses of primates WHO. Mem. biohazards control and containment sect. Nat. Cancer Inst.; chmn. com. simian viruses WHO/FAO. Diplomate Am. Bd. Microbiology. Fellow A.A.A.S., Am. Pub. Health Assn.; mem. Am. Acad. Microbiology, Am. Assn. Immunologists, Soc. Exptl. Biology and Medicine, N.Y., Tex. acads. scis., Am., Tex. socs. microbiologists, Am. Soc. Tropical Medicine and Hygiene, Royal Soc. Health (Eng.), Tex. Soc. Electron Microscopy, Am. Soc. Cryobiology, Wildlife Diseases Assn., Research Soc. Am., Sigma Xi. Home: 1418 Haskin St San Antonio TX 78209 Office: PO Box 28147 San Antonio TX 78228

KALTINICK, PAUL R., retail trade co. exec.; b. N.Y.C., Dec. 1, 1932; s. Morris and Vera (Halpern) K.; B.B.A., Pace Coll., 1954; m. Alice Levy, Dec. 26, 1954; children—Vera, Marjorie, Pamela. Accountant, also mgmt. cons. Peat, Marwick, Mitchell & Co., N.Y.C., 1956-63; exec. v.p. Mr. Christmas, Inc., N.Y.C., 1963-64; with J.C. Penney Co., Inc., N.Y.C., 1964—, asst. treas., 1966-69, treas., 1969—; dir., pres. J.C. Penney Financial Corp., Wilmington, Del., 1969—. Served with USMCR, 1954-56. C.P.A., N.Y. Mem. Am. Inst. C.P.A.'s, N.Y. State Soc. C.P.A.'s. Club: The Treasurers Group (N.Y.C.). Home: 352 IU Willets Rd Roslyn Heights NY 11577 Office: JC Penney Co Inc 1301 Av Americas New York City NY 10019

KALUDIS, GEORGE, univ. adminstr.; b. Balt., Oct. 7, 1938; s. Steven George and Theresa (Topal) K.; student Lehigh U., 1955-56; B.A., U. Md., 1960, M.Ed., 1965; Ph.D., Fla. State U., 1968; m. Eugenia Leone Mihalakis, July 21, 1962; children—Stephen George, Michele Maria, William Michael, Kirk Jamie. Asst. dean student life U. Md., 1960-65; resident instr. U. South Fla., 1965-66; dir. div. planning and evaluation Fla. Bd. Regents, 1966-70; vice chancellor operations and fiscal planning, asso. prof. mgmt. Vanderbilt U., 1970—. Mem. tech. council Nat. Center Higher Edn. Mgmt. Systems; pres., dir. Fraternity Advisors Group, Inc., Tallahassee, Fla., 1968-70. Served with AUS, 1962-64. Mem. Am. Assn. Higher Edn., Assn. Instnl. Research, Nat. Assn. Coll. and Univ. Bus. Officers, Omicron Delta Kappa, Pi Sigma Alpha, Sigma Phi Epsilon. Greek Orthodox (v.p. bd. trustees). Mem. Order of Ahepa. Home: 2127 Chickering Lane Nashville TN 37215

KALVEN, HARRY, Jr., educator, lawyer; b. Chgo., Sept. 11, 1914; A.B., U. Chgo., 1935, J.D., 1938; m. Betty Rymer, June 16, 1924; children—James, Michael, Peter, Catherine. Admitted to Ill. bar, 1939; with Frantz & Johnson, 1939-42; instr. Law. Sch., U. Chgo., 1945, asst prof., 1946-49, asso. prof., 1949- 53, prof., 1953—, also leader U. Chgo. Jury Project, interdisciplinary study basic issues of modern jurisprudence. Mem. com. for standard jury instrns. Ill. Supreme Ct., 1957—. Served with Armed Forces, 1942-45. Mem. Am., Chgo. bar assns. Author: (with Walter J. Blum) The Uneasy Case for Progressive Taxation, 1953; (with Hans Zeisel, Bernard Buchholz) Delay in the Court, 1959; (with Charles O. Gregory) Cases and Materials in Torts, 1959; (with Walter J. Blum) Public Law Perspective on a Private Law Problem: Auto Compensation Plans, 1964; The Negro and the First Amendment, 1965; (with Hans Zeisel) The American Jury, 1966. Home: 4925 S Woodlawn Av Chicago IL 60615 Office: 935 E 60th St Chicago IL 60637*

KAMAN, CHARLES HURON, corp. exec.; b. Washington, June 15, 1919; s. Charles W. and Mabel (Davis) K.; B.S. in Aero. Engring. magna cum laude, Cath. U. Am., 1940; m. Helen Sylvander, Oct. 20, 1945 (div.); children—Charles William II, Cathleen, Steven Wardner; m. 2d, Roberta C. Hallock, Sept. 1, 1971. With Hamilton Standard Propellers div. United Aircraft Corp., E. Hartford, Conn., 1940-45; chmn. bd., pres. Kaman Corp., Bloomfield, Conn., 1945—; dir. Kaman Scis., Inc., Airkaman, Inc. Chmn. Vertical Life Aircraft Council, 1954, 64. Mem. Jr. Achievement; bd. govs. Cath. U. Am. Recipient Distinguished Service award Conn. Jr. C. of C., 1953, Engr. of Year award, 1961. Fellow Am. Helicopter Soc. (pres. 1958, bd. dirs. 1959-61); mem. Conn. Bus. and Industry Assn. (dir., exec. com.), Nat. Acad. Engring., Conn. Soc. Profl. Engrs., Pi Tau Sigma (hon.). Home: PO Box 145 Bloomfield CT 06002 Office: Old Windsor Rd Bloomfield CT 06002

KAMARCK, ANDREW MARTIN, economist; b. Newton Falls, N.Y., Nov. 10, 1914; s. Martin and Frances (Earl) K.; B.S. summa cum laude, Harvard, 1936, M.A., 1939, Ph.D. in Polit. Sci. and Govt., 1951; m. Margaret Ellen Goldenweiser, Oct. 25, 1941; children—Ellen Mary, Elizabeth Anne, Martin Alexander. Economist, Fed. Res. Bd., 1939-40; confidential adv. to sec. treasury, 1940-42; dep. dir. finance div. U.S. group Allied Control Council, Germany, 1945; chief nat. adv. council internat. monetary and financial problems Treasury Dept., 1946-48; U.S. Treasury rep., chief financial rep. Marshall Plan Mission, Rome, Italy, 1948-50; econ. adviser World Bank, 1950-64, dir. econs. dept., 1965-71, dir. Econ. Devel. Inst., 1971—; lectr. Sch. Advanced Internat. Studies, Johns Hopkins, 1958—; Regents prof. U. Cal. at Los Angeles, 1964. Mem. internat. council Soc. Internat. Devel. Served to maj. F.A., AUS, 1942-44; Italy. Recipient Certificate of Merit, War Dept., 1945. Fellow African Studies Assn.; mem. Am. Econ. Assn. (policy bd. Econs. Inst.), Council Fgn. Relations, Dacor House Washington, Phi Beta Kappa. Democrat. Unitarian. Author: (with others) The Economic Development of Uganda, 1962; (with others) The United States and Africa, 1963; (with others) The African World, 1965; The Economics of African Development, 1967. Home: 126 3d St SE Washington DC 20003 Office: 1818 H St NW Washington DC 20433

KAMATS, GEORGE MICHAEL, airline exec.; b. Emporium, Pa., May 7, 1935; s. George and Clara (Zoschg) K.; B.B.A., U. Miami, 1964; m. Kathleen D. Sinnes, Feb. 14, 1959; children—Cynthia Louse, Richard Joseph, George Michael, Susan Kathleen. Jr. accountant John J. Barry C.P.A., Coral Gables, Fla., 1959-61; chief accountant Saturn Airways, Inc., Oakland, Cal., 1961-65, comptroller, 1965-67, asst. sec., asst. treas., 1967-69, treas., 1969—, also dir. Served with USAF, 1955-59. C.P.A., Cal. Home: 26842 Jennings Way Hayward CA 94544 Office: P O Box 2426 Internat Airport Oakland CA 94614

KAMB, WALTER BARCLAY, educator, geologist; b. San Jose, Cal., Dec. 17, 1931; s. Karl Walter and Eleanor (Williams) K.; B.S. in Physics, Cal. Inst. Tech., 1952, Ph.D. in Geology, 1956; m. Linda Helen Pauling, Sept. 8, 1957; children—Barclay James, Carl Alexander, Anthony Pauling, Linus Peter. Mem. faculty Cal. Inst. Tech., 1956—, prof. geology and geophysics, 1961—. Guggenheim fellow, 1960; Sloan fellow, 1964. Fellow Geol. Soc. Am., Mineral. Soc. Am. (award 1968); mem. Am. Geophys. Union, Am. Crystallographic Assn. Home: 3500 Fairpoint St Pasadena CA 91107

KAMBERG, KENNETH EDWARD, savs. and loan assn. exec.; b. Kansas City, Mo., July 25, 1915; s. William J. and Harriet (Block) K.; ed. U. Kansas City, 1935; m. Frances Reichard, May 17, 1936; 1 son, John Bruce. Vice pres. Home Savs. Assn., Kansas City, Mo., 1949-51, exec. v.p., mng. officer, 1951-61; exec. v.p., dir. Coral Gables Fed. Savs. and Loan Assn. (Fla.), 1961-66, pres., 1966—; dir. Continental Mortgage Ins., Inc., Madison, Wis. Pres. Bus., Inc., Miami, Fla., 1968; bd. dirs. Indsl. Devel. Corp. Fla.; chmn. Coral Gables Com. 21, 1970. Past mem. citizens bd. U. Miami. Served with USNR, World War II. Mem. U.S. (bd. dirs. 1969-71), Fla. (pres. 1968) savs. and loan leagues, Coral Gables C. of C. (pres. 1967). Clubs: Rotary (pres. 1969), Riviera (pres. 1969-70, Century (bd. govs.) (Coral Gables). Home: 1326 Mendavia St Coral Gables FL 33146 Office: 2501 Ponce de Leon Blvd Coral Gables FL 33134

KAMEN, MARTIN DAVID, educator, biochemist; b. Toronto, Ont., Can., Aug. 27, 1913; s. Harry and Goldie (Achber) K.; came to U.S., 1913, naturalized, 1938; B.S. cum laude, U. Chgo., 1933, Ph.D. in Phys. Chemistry, 1936, Sc.D. (hon.), 1969; Dr. Hon. causa, Sorbonne, U. Paris, 1969; m. Beka Doherty, Mar. 16, 1949 (dec. Nov. 1963); 1 son, David Martin; m. 2d, Virginia L. Swanson, Apr. 29, 1967. Prof. biochemistry U. Cal. at San Diego, 1961—, chmn. grad. council, 1961-63, chmn. commn. ednl. policy, 1964, acting dean grad. studies, 1965-66, chmn. dept. chemistry, 1970-72; project dir. Lab. de Photo-Synthese, C.N.R.S., France, 1967-69; group leader Manhattan Project, 1941-44. Recipient C. F. Kettering Research award Am. Soc. Plant Physiologists, 1968. Mem. Nat. Acad. Scis., Am. Chem. Soc. (counsellor 1963; award applications nuclear chemistry 1963), Radiation Research Soc., Am. Acad. Arts and Scis., Phi Beta Kappa, Sigma Xi. Editoral board Jour. Biol. Chemistry, 1959-64, Ann. Revs. Biochemistry, 1963-68. Contbr. numerous articles profl. jours. Co-discoverer long-lived radioactive carbon isotope C-14; spl. research heme compounds. Home: 800 Prospect Dr La Jolla CA 92037

KAMENY, NAT, advt. exec.; b. N.Y.C., Nov. 6, 1923; s. Michel and Bessie (Sunchine) K.; student Coll. City N.Y., 1941-42, 46-47; m. Ruth Zatal, Mar. 27, 1943; children—Ellen, Leslie, Debra. Propr., Camenard Studios, profl. photographers, 1945; founder, pres. Kameny Assos., advt., N.Y.C., 1946—; pres. Israel Communications, Inc., pub. relations, 1969—; exec. v.p. George T. Abrams & Asso., N.Y.C., 1971—; dir. Agnekolor Systems Corp. Vice pres. Jewish Welfare Council Bergen County; vice chmn. pub. relations com. Council Jewish Fedns.; chmn. Arab boycott com., co-chmn. Mid-East affairs com., mem. nat. exec. com. Anti-Defamation League; v.p. U. Haifa Found.; sec. Photography for Youth Found.; asst. to mayor Bergenfield, N.J., 1960-62, indsl. commnr. Bergenfield, 1960-64; vice chmn. Bergenfield Planning Bd., 1960-67. Chmn., Bergen County Democratic Campaign Com., 1960-61. Mem. Am. Assn. Advt. Agys., Photographic Adminstrs., League Advt. Agys. (pres. 1962-63). Mem. B'nai B'rith. Home: 85 Thames Blvd Bergenfield NJ 07621 Office: 110 E 59th St New York City NY 10022

KAMERICK, JOHN JOSEPH, univ. pres.; b. Ottumwa, Ia., Dec. 30, 1919; s. Harry Herman and Catherine Cecilia (Doyle) K.; B.A., St. Ambrose Coll., 1943; M.A., State U. Ia., 1947, Ph.D., 1950; m. Elaine Elizabeth Lenny, Aug. 7, 1948; children—Maureen Margaret, Michael John, Sheila Catherine, Kathleen, Eileen, Megan. Reporter, 1940-43; instr. U. Ia., 1948-50; asst. prof. Marycrest Coll., 1950-51; dean studies Lewis Coll. Sci. and Tech., 1951- 56; asst. dean Coll. Arts and Scis., Kent State U., 1956-59, dean Coll. Fine and Profl. Arts, 1959-63, v.p., dean faculties, 1963-66, v.p., provost, 1966-68; pres. N. Tex. State U., Denton, 1968-70, U. No. Ia., Cedar Falls, 1970—. Served to lt. (s.g.) USNR, 1943-46. Mem. Assn. Higher Edn., Am. Hist. Assn., Am. Cath. Hist. Assn. Democrat. Roman Catholic. Home: 2501 College St Cedar Falls IA 50613

KAMERLING, SAMUEL EDWARD, retired educator; b. Paterson, N.J., Nov. 14, 1903; s. Henry and Clara (Van Haste) K.; B.S., N.Y.U., 1926, M.S., 1927; Ph.D., Princeton, 1933; m. Helen Frances Hawes, July 9, 1932; childrenMary C., Clara H. Research asst. chemistry Harvard, 1930-32; research asst. gen. physiology Rockefeller Inst., 1932-34; mem. faculty Bowdoin Coll., 1934—, prof. chemistry, 1946-69, Charles Weston Pickard prof., 1952-69, prof. emeritus, 1969—. Pres. Girl Scouts of Pine Tree State 1959- -. Fellow A.A.A.S.; mem. Am. Chem. Soc. (sect. officer), Phi Beta Kappa, Sigma Xi, Phi Kappa Tau. Home: 18 McLellan St Brunswick ME 04011

KAMIHIRA, BEN, artist; b. Yakima, Wash., Mar. 16, 1925; s. Jujiro and Hatsuno (Kumamoto) K.; student Pa. Acad. Fine Arts, 1948-52; m. Elizabeth Hetherington Spencer, May 24, 1952; children—Miyo, Anita, Tomi, Padl, Eben, Owen, Ronda Maria. Instr. Pa. Acad. Fine Arts, Phila.; exhibited N.A.D., 1952, 54, 56, 57, 58, Pa. Acad. Fine Arts Ann., 1954, 58, Butler Art Inst., 1953, 57, 58, Mus. Modern Art, 1962; one-man shows Dublin Gallery, 1952, Phila. Art Alliance, 1954, Pa. Acad. Fine Arts, 1956, Janet Nessler Gallery, N.Y.C., 1962; rep. permanent collections Friends Central, Phila., J. Ringling North, Pa. Acad. Fine Arts, Whitney Mus. Am. Art. Recipient Cresson traveling scholarship, 1951; Scheidt traveling scholarship, 1952; Louis C. Tiffany scholarship, 1952, 58; 1st Hallgarten prize N.A.D., 1952; Altman art prize, 1958; Lippincott prize Pa. Acad. Fine Arts, 1958; Guggenheim fellow, 1955-56, 56-57; 2d prize with silver medal Concoran Biennal, 1961; 1st Altman prize N.A.D., 1962; Johnson prize New Eng. Ann., 1961; 1st prize Chatauqua Nat. Exhbn., 1962. Served as pvt. inf., AUS, 1944- 46. Fellow Pa. Acad. Fine Arts, N.A.D. Home: Cheyney Rd Cheyney PA 19319

KAMIN, LEON J., educator; b. Taunton, Mass., Dec. 29, 1927; s. Jonas and Jean (Rybak) K.; B.A., Harvard, 1949, Ph.D., 1954; m. Marie-Claire Fay, Apr. 21, 1970; children—John, Katherine. Prof. psychology McGill U., 1954-55, Queen's U., 1955-57, McMaster U., 1957-68; Dorman T. Warren prof. psychology, chmn. dept. Princeton, 1968—. Served with AUS, 1946-47. Mem. Soc. Exptl. Psychology, Am. Psychol. Assn., Psychonomic Soc. Cons. editor Jour. Comparative and Physiol. Psychology. Home: 84 Maclean Circle Princeton NJ 08540

KAMINO, SIDNEY EDWARD, chain dept. store exec.; b. Utica, N.Y., Dec. 7, 1920; s. Harry and Jennie (Cohen) K.; grad. pub. schs.; m. Lillian Mettol, Mar. 17, 1946; children—Diane, Eric. Store mgr. Enterprise Stores, Boston, 1946-55; v.p. Easy Bargain Center, Syracuse, N.Y., 1955-60, pres., 1960—; pres. Family Bargain Centers, Inc., State St. Mill Bargain Center, Syracuse, 1960—, Kenton Corp.

Vice pres., bd. dirs. Jewish Home of Aged, Syracuse; mem. adv. bd. Small Bus. Assn. Served with AUS, 1942-46. Mem. Lafayette C. of C. (bd. govs.), A.I.M. (pres.'s council). Club: Lafayette Country (pres.). Home: 16 Lyndon Rd Fayetteville NY Office: 742 James St Syracuse NY 13203

KAMINS, ROBERT MARTIN, educator; b. Chgo., Mar. 10, 1918; s. Philip Eugene and Lena (Silverman) K.; student U. Cal., Los Angeles, 1936-37; A.B., U. Chgo., 1940, M.A. (Walgreen fellow), 1948, Ph.D., 1950; m. Shirley Ritter, Oct. 14, 1940; children—Diane Eve (Mrs. Richard Quinn), Melissa. Research asst. dept. econs. U. Chgo., 1939-41, Fedn. Tax Adminstrs., Pub. Adminstrn. Clearing House, Chgo., 1941-42; asso. economist Fed. Bd. Investigation and Research, Washington, 1942; faculty U. Ill., 1946-47; faculty U. Hawaii, Honolulu, 1947—, prof. econs., 1963—, dean acad. devel., 1963—; vis. prof. Inst. for Social Studies, The Hague, 1953. Dir. research Hawaii Constl. Conv., 1950; adminstrv. asst. U.S. Senator Oren Long, 1959-61. Served with USNR, 1943-45. Ford Found. grantee, 1963; East-West Center sr. scholar, 1968. Mem. Am., Western, Hawaii econ. assns., Am. Assn. U. Profs. (nat. council 1956-58), Nat. Tax Assn., Am. Soc. Pub. Adminstrn., UN-U.S.A. Assn. (pres. Hawaii chpt. 1952). Author: The Tax System of Hawaii, 1952. Contbr. articles profl. jours. Home: 2400 Parker Pl Honolulu HI 96822

KAMINSKA, IDA, actress, director; b. Odessa, Russia, Nov. 4, 1899; d. Abram Izzehak and Ester Rachel (Halpern) Kaminski; grad. Gymnasium, Warsaw, Poland, 1916; m. Zygmunt Turkow, Aug. 1918; 1 dau., Ruth; m. 2d, Mirian Melman, July 1936. Mem. Kaminski Theatre, Warsaw, Poland, 1916-23, Warsaw Theatre WIKT, 1923-31; dir. Ida Kaminska Ensemble, Warsaw, 1930-39, Jewish State Theatre of W. Ukrainia, Lwow, 1940-41, theatre in Frunze, Middle Asia, 1941-44, Jewish Theatre, Warsaw, 1947—; appearances in 200 parts, dir. 100 prodns.; dir. film Shop on Mainstreet, 1965; tchr. Theatre Studio, Warsaw, 1965—. Recipient State Nat. award Poland, 1955, Czechoslovakia, 1966; decorated 1st and 2d class Polish Nat. Flag Labor. Mem. Assn. Theate Writers, Polish Theatre and Film Actors Assn. Home: 101 m11 Al Jerozolimskie Warsaw Poland Office: 13 Ul Krolewska Warsaw Poland

KAMINSTEIN, ABRAHAM LOUIS, govt. ofcl., lawyer; b. N.Y.C., May 13, 1912; s. Max and Sarah (Shulman) K.; B.S. in Social Sci., Coll. City N.Y., 1932; LL.B., Harvard, 1935; LL.M., 1936; m. Barbara Glesin, Apr. 28, 1941; 1 son, Dana Seth. Research fellow Harvard Law Sch., 1936-37; admitted to N.Y. bar, 1935; chief examining div. U.S. Copyright Office, 1947-60, dep. register, 1959-60, acting register, 1960, register copyrights, 1960—. Adviser U.S. delegation at meeting preliminary draft Universal Copyright Conv. prepared 1951; chmn. panel cons. gen. revision U.S. Copyright Law, 1960—; chmn. U.S. Delegation Neighboring Rights Diplomatic Conf., 1961. Mem. Am., Fed. bar assns., Copyright Soc. U.S. Author: Divisibility of Copyrights, 1957. Office: Library of Congress Washington DC 20540

KAMISAR, YALE, educator; b. N.Y.C., Aug. 29, 1929; s. Samuel and Mollie (Levine) K.; A.B., N.Y.U., 1950; LL.B., Columbia, 1954; m. Esther Englander, Sept. 7, 1953; children—David Graham, Gordon, Jonathan. Research asso. Am. Law Inst., N.Y.C., 1953; admitted to D.C. bar, 1955; asso. firm Covington & Burling, Washington, 1955-57; asso. prof. law, then prof. U. Minn. Law Sch., 1957-64; prof. law U. Mich. Law Sch., 1965—; vis. prof. law Harvard, 1964-65. Cons. to Nat. Adv. Commn. Civil Disorders, 1967-68, Nat. Commn. Causes and Prevention Violence, 1968-69. Served to 1st lt. AUS, 1951-52. Mem. adv. com. model code pre-arraignment procedure Am. Law Inst., 1965—. Author: (with W.B. Lockhart and J.H. Choper) Constitutional Law: Cases, Comments and Questions, 3d edition, 1970; (with others) Modern Criminal Procedure: Cases and Commentaries, 3d edit., 1969; (with F. Inbau and T. Arnold) Criminal Justice in Our Time, 1963. Contbr. articles to profl. jours. Home: 2 Lndonberry Circle Ann Arbor MI 48104

KAMM, HERBERT, newspaper editor; b. Long Branch, N.J., Apr. 1, 1917; s. Louis and Rose (Cohen) K.; student Monmouth Jr. Coll., 1935; m. Phyllis I. Silberblatt, Dec. 6, 1936; childrenLaurence R., Lewis R., Robert H. Reporter, sports editor, Asbury Park (N.J.) Press, 1935-42; with A.P., 1942-43; with N.Y. World-Telegram and Sun, 1943-66, successively rewrite man, picture editor, asst. city editor, feature editor, mag. editor, asst. mng. editor, 1943-63, mng. editor, 1963-66; exec. editor, N.Y. World Jour. Tribune, 1966-67; editorial cons. Scripps-Howard Newspapers, 1967-69; asso. editor Cleve. Press, 1969—; radio and TV news commentator and panelist, 1950—. Mem. A.F.T.R.A., Sigma Delta Chi. Jewish religion (bd. dirs. temple 1957-60). Club: National Press. Contbr. articles mags. Asso. editor Jr. Illus. Ency. Sports, 1960, rev. edit., 1963, 66, 70. Home: 12700 Lake Av Lakewood OH 44107 Office: 901 Lakeside Av Cleveland OH 44114

KAMM, JACOB OSWALD, corp. exec.; b. Cleve., Nov. 29, 1918; s. Jacob and Minnie K. (Christensen) K.; A.B. magna cum laude, Baldwin-Wallace Coll., 1940, LL.D., 1963; A.M., Brown U., 1942; Ph.D., Ohio State U., 1948; LL.D., Erskine Coll., 1971; m. Judith Steinbrenner, Apr. 24, 1965; children—Jacob Oswald II, Christian. Asst. econs. Brown U., 1942; instr. Ohio State U., 1945; instr. Baldwin-Wallace Coll., 1945-46, asst. prof., 1947-48, asso. prof., 1948, prof., dir. Sch. Commerce, 1948- 53; econ. cons. to U.S. P.O., 1951; exec. v.p. Cleve. Quarries Co., 1953- 55, pres., 1955-67, chmn. bd., chief exec. officer, 1967—; pres., treas., dir. Am. Shipbldg. Co., 1967-69; dir., exec. com. United Screw & Bolt Corp., Nordson Corp.; dir. Lorain Av. Greenhouse Co., Second Fed. Savs. & Loan Assn., First Ohio Service Corp.; weekly columnist econ. affairs Cleve. Plain Dealer, 1964-68. Exec. bd. Lorain County Met. Park Bd., 1961—; hon. mem. Mental Health Com., 1964-69; mem. St. Luke's Hosp. Assn., 1967—; mem. adv. council Natural Sci. Mus., 1967-69; bd. regents State of Ohio; pub. mem. Underground Gas Storage Com. Ohio, 1964—. Chmn. Lorain County Republican Finance Com., 1968-70, mem. exec. com., 1969-70; mem. Ohio Rep. Finance Com., 1970—. Mem. bd. counselors Erskine Coll., 1962—; trustee (life fellow) Cleve. Zool. Soc., Lake Erie Jr. Nature and Sci. Center; trustee Baldwin-Wallace Coll., 1953—, mem. exec. and investment coms., 1956—. Recipient Alumni Merit award Baldwin-Wallace Coll., 1956; Wisdom award of honor, 1970. Mem. Am. Econs. Assn., Am. Finance Assn., Am. Assn. U. Profs., Indsl. Assn. N. Central Ohio (pres. 1960), Ohio Mfrs. Assn. (v.p., exec. com. 1970—, trustee); Newcomen Soc. N.Am., Assn. Ohio Commodores, Royal Econ. Soc., Nat. Alumni Assn. Baldwin-Wallace Coll. (pres. 1961-63), Phi Alpha Kappa, Delta Phi Alpha, Delta Mu Delta, Beta Gamma Sigma. Methodist. Mason (Shriner, 32). Clubs: Brown University (N.Y.C.); Union (Cleve.); Duquesne (Pitts.); Clifton (Lakewood, O.); Lake Placid. Author: Decentralization of Securities Exchanges, 1942; Economics of Investment, 1951; Making Profits in the Stock Market, 3d rev. edit., 1961; Investor's Handbook, 1954. Contbg. author: An Introduction to Modern Economics, 1952; Essays On Business Finance, 1953. Contbr. articles profl. jours. Home: RD 1 Huron OH 44839 Office Amherst OH 44001

KAMM, ROBERT B., univ. pres.; b. W. Union, Ia., Jan. 22, 1919; s. Balthasar and Amelia (Etter) K.; B.A., U. No. Ia., 1940; M.A., U. Minn., 1946, Ph.D., 1948; m. Maxine Moen, July 10, 1943; children—Susan, Steven. Tchr., Belle Plaine (Ia.) High Sch., 1940-42; research asst., counselor Gen. Coll., U. Minn., 1946-48; dean students Drake U., 1948-55; dean student personnel services Tex. A. and M. U., 1955-56, dean basic div. and student personnel services, 1956-58; dean Coll. Arts and Scis., Okla. State U., 1958-65, v.p. acad. affairs, 1965-66, pres., 1966—. Mem. commn. coll. student Am. Council Edn., 1957-60; chmn. div. arts and scis. Assn. State Univs. and Land-Grant Colls., 1963-64, co-chmn. home econs. commn., 1968-70; chmn. Mid-Am. State Univs. Assn., 1968-69; mem. adv. panel USAF R.O.T.C., 1967-69; mem. nat. vocational rehab. and edn. adv. com. VA, 1970-72; mem. President Nixon's Commn. Observance 25th Anniversary UN, 1970-71. Pres. Bi-State Mental Health Assn., 1967-69; v.p. Will Rogers council Boy Scouts Am., 1965-66. Bd. visitors Air U., 1968-70; v.p. Frontiers Sci. Found. Okla., Inc., 1966-69; chmn. bd. dirs. Wesley Found., 1962-64. Civilian radio instr. USAAF, 1942-44, coordinator on staff, 1944; naval aviation radar technician, USNR, 1944-46. Recipient Alumni Achievement award U. No. Ia., 1970; Outstanding Achievement award U. Minn., 1971. Fellow Am. Psychol. Assn.; mem. Am. Coll. Personnel Assn. (exec. council 1954-56, pres. 1957), Am. Personnel and Guidance Assn., Assn. Higher Edn., Nat. Vocational Guidance Assn., N.E.A. (div. higher edn.), Okla. Edn. Assn. (pres. Okla. State U. chpt. 1962-63), Assn. Gen. and Liberal Studies, C. of C. (dir., v.p. 1965, 66), Kappa Kappa Psi, Omicron Delta Kappa, Phi Delta Kappa, Psi Chi, Kappa Delta Pi, Theta Alpha Phi, Kappa Mu Epsilon, Alpha Phi Omega, Phi Mu Alpha Sinfonia, Phi Kappa Phi, Blue Key. Methodist. Rotarian (pres. 1962-63). Contbr. articles on student personnel work and higher edn. profl. jours. Home: 1600 N Monroe Stillwater OK 74074

KAMM, ROBERT WILLIAM, univ. ofcl.; b. Mpls., July 10, 1917; s. Gerald Edward and Matilda (Kraus) K.; B.Aero, Engring., N.Y.U., 1939; m. Mary Anne Roper, Apr. 27, 1946; children—Mary Lou, Salliie Anne, Stacey Carolyn; 1 stepson, John Paul Campbell, Jr. Aero. engr. NACA, Langley AFB, Va., 1940-46; sr. aerodynamist Glenn L. Martin Co., Balt., 1946-48; exec. dir. panel facilities com. aero. Research and Devel. Bd., Dept. Def., 1948-50; with USAF Arnold Engring. Devel. Center, 1950-59, chief plans and policy office, 1957-59; dir. Western Support Office, NASA, 1959-68, cons. NASA Hdqrs., 1969—; asst. to dir. U. Tenn. Space Inst., Tullahoma, 1968-69, exec. asst. to dir., 1970—. Chmn. Joint Coll. Fed. Council So. Cal., 1966-67; chmn. Los Angeles Fed. Exec. Bd., 1966-68; mem. Mayor Los Angeles Space Adv. Com., 1964-68, chmn. subcom. utilization space tech., 1964- 66. Asso. fellow Am. Inst. Aero. and Astronautics; mem. Psi Upsilon, Perstare et Praestare. Home: 407 E Fort St Manchester, TN 37355. Office: Univ Tenn Space Inst Tullahoma TN 37388

KAMMEN, MICHAEL GEDALIAH, educator, historian; b. Rochester, N.Y., Oct. 25, 1936; s. Jacob M. and Blanche (Lazerow) K.; A.B., George Washington U., 1958; M.A., Harvard, 1959, Ph.D. (Bowdoin prize), 1964; m. Carol Koyen, Feb. 26, 1961; children—Daniel Merson, Douglas Anton. Mem. faculty Harvard, 1964-65; mem. faculty Cornell U., 1965—, prof. Am. history, 1969—, acting chmn. dept. Semitic langs. and lits., 1970-71; asso. faculty seminar early Am. history and culture Columbia, 1967—, faculty council reps., 1971—, bd. editors U. Press, 1971—; cons. Ednl. Services, Inc., Cambridge, Mass., 1965, Ednl. Testing Services, Princeton, N.J., 1970—. Mem. Internat. Commn. History of Parliamentary and Rep. Instns., 1966, N.Y.C. Com. Sociol. History, 1970—, Coll. Conf. N.Y. History, 1970—. Fellow Nat. Endowment for Humanities, 1967, Humanities Center, Johns Hopkins, 1968-69. Mem. Am. Hist. Assn., Orgn. Am. Historians, Am. Soc. Legal History (bd. dirs. 1971—), Colonial Soc. Mass., Hakluyt Soc., Econ. History Assn., Phi Beta Kappa. Author: A Rope of Sand: The Colonial Agents, British Politics and The American Revolution, 1968; Politics and Society in Colonial America: Democracy or Deference, 1967; Deputyes and Libertyes: The Origins of Representative Government in Colonial America, 1969; Empire and Interest: The American Colonies and the Politics of Mercantilism, 1970; The Contrapuntal Civilization: Essays Toward a New Understanding of the American Experience, 1971. Co-editor: The Glorious Revolution in America, Documents on Colonial Crisis of 1689, 1964. Home: 1326 E State St Ithaca NY 14850

KAMMER, EDWARD JOSEPH, clergyman, educator; b. New Orleans, Apr. 23, 1908; s. Edward William and Mary Catherine (Kane) K.; B.A., St. Mary's Sem., 1933; M.A., Cath. U. Am., 1939, Ph.D., 1941. Joined Congregation of the Mission (Vincentian Fathers), 1927; ordained priest Roman Cath. Ch., 1933; prof. history and sociology St. Mary's Sem., Perryville, Mo., 1933-37; prof. history Kenrick Sem., Webster Groves, Mo., 1937-38; prof. sociology De Paul U., Chgo., 1941-60, dean Downtown Coll. Liberal Arts and Scis., 1943-46, Coll. Commerce, 1946-50, faculties, 1950-60, v.p., 1944-55, exec. v.p., 1955-60, trustee, 1944-60; prof. social scis. St. Mary's Sem., Houston, 1960-63; rector Assumption Sem., San Antonio, 1963-67; asso. v.p. univ. planning DePaul U., 1967—. Mem. Higher Edn. Commn. Ill. Mem. Assn. Instl. Research, Soc. Coll. and U. Planning, Marquis Biographical Soc., Blue Key (hon.), Delta Epsilon Sigma, Pi Gamma Mu, Phi Kappa Alpha. Author: A Socio-economic Survey of the Marsh Dwellers of Four South Eastern Louisiana Parishes, 1941. Home: 2233 N Kenmore Av Chicago IL 60614

KAMMERER, CHARLES FRANCIS, Jr., banker; b. White Plains, N.Y., Nov. 19, 1921; s. Charles Francis and Angela (Cantwell) K.; student Columbia, 1940-42; m. Pam Tatanni, Oct. 8, 1949; children-Lynn Marie, Wendy Ann. With County Trust Co., White Plains, 1940—, asst. treas., 1952-59, v.p., 1959-67, sr. v.pp., 1967—; tchhr. Am. Inst. Baniing. Served with AUS, 1942-45. Mem. Nat. Assn. Cost Accountants, Financial Execs. Inst., Mun icipal Finance Officers Am. (dir.), White Plams (N.Y.) C. of C. (past treas.) Home: 136 Rolling Hills Rd Thornwood NY 10594 Office: 235 Main St White Plains NY 10502

KAMMERER, HERBERT LEWIS, sculptor; b. N.Y.C., July 11, 1915; s. Louis Joseph and Christine A. (Von Wlodeck) K.; B.F.A., Yale, 1941; fellow Am. Acad. in Rome, 1949-51; married to Mary Margaret Naphen, 1947; children—Seth Lewis, Cornelia Ann, Mary Susan. Works exhibited nat. shows, 1941—; executed Skinner Meml., Oswego, N.Y., Va. Mil. Inst. Meml., Frederick May Eliot Tablet, St. Paul, St. Christopher Shrine, Chgo., Leader Meml., Yale; executed medals Soc. Prevention of Blindness, Elston Nat. Bank Centenary, research medal Am. Soc. Tool Engrs., Centenary medal Beloit Iron Works, commemorative medal St. Lawrence Hydro-Electric Power Project; rep. pub., pvt. collections U.S. and abroad; portrait busts, pvt. collections, B. Barnes Coll., others; now professor of sculpture State U., New Paltz, N.Y. Recipient George D. Widener gold medal Pa. Acad. ann., 1948; Fulbright fellow, 1949; Procter portrait prize Nat. Acad. Design, 1952; grant in sculpture Nat. Inst. Arts and Letters. Fellow Nat. Sculpture Soc. (pres. 1965-67). Club: Century Assn. Home: 64 Plains Rd New Paltz NY 12561

KAMMERER, WEBB LOUIS, mfg. exec.; b. St. Louis, June 3, 1893; s. William Alexander and Harriet (Webb) K.; B.S. in Civil Engring., Washington U., 1916; m. Else Marie Eyssell, Jan. 18, 1919; children—Marjorie Anne (Mrs. Gary B. Wood), Virginia Else (Mrs. L. W. Bergesch). In melting dept. foundry Warren Steel Casting Co., St. Louis, 1916-18, asst. supt., 1918-20, supt., 1920-23; salesman Midvale Mining & Mfg. Co., 1923-30, v.p., 1930- 40, pres., 1940-65, chmn. of the board, 1965—; pres. Midvale Material Handling Equipment Co., St. Louis, 1952-60; dir. McQuay- Norris Mfg. Co., St. Louis, General chmn. Mo. Valley regional tech. conf., Rolla, Mo., 1955; life dir. Washington U.; adv. Com. Foundry Edn. Found. (trustee), U. Mo. Sch. Mines and Met.; trustee of Training and Research Inst., Chicago. Profl. engr., Missouri. Served as observer USAC, 1918, 1st lt. res., 1919-24. Mem. Acad. Scis (St. Louis), Am. Foundrymen's Soc., (nat. dir., 1958-61), C. of C., Mo. Hist. Soc., Ducks Unlimited, Conservation Fedn. Mo., Kappa Alpha. Republican. Methodist. Mason. Clubs: University, Mo. Duck Hunters, Rotary, Mo. Athletic (St. Louis). Home: 9066 Monmouth Dr St Louis MO 63117 Office: 6310 Knox Industrial Dr St Louis MO 63139

KAMMERER, WILLIAM HENRY, physician; b. Logansport, Ind., Mar. 4, 1912; s. Henry and Margaret (Halpin) K.; student U. Notre Dame, 1928-31; M.D., Ind. U., 1935; m. Edith B. Langley, Feb. 12, 1938; children—Dr. William S., Kelly C., Athleen B. (Mrs. William Ellington), Hilary J. Intern U.S. Marine Hosp., Staten Island, N.Y., U. Chgo. Clinics, fellow gastro-enterology Lahoy Clinic, Boston; asst. resident N.Y. Hosp., 1935-39; pvt. practice specializing internal medicine and rheumatology, N.Y.C., 1939—; clin. prof. medicine Cornell Med. Coll.; attending physician N.Y. Hosp., Hosp. Special Surgery. Served from lt. to lt. col., M.C., AUS, 1942-46; PTO. Diplomate Am. Bd. Internal Medicine. Fellow A.C.P.; mem. Harvey Soc., Am. Rheumatism Assn., Century Assn. Home: 215 149th St Whitestone NY 11357 Office: 449 E 68th St New York City NY 10021

KAMMERMEYER, KARL, educator, chem. engr.; b. Nuremberg, Germany, June 15, 1904; s. Eberhard and Margaret (Reuther) K.; came to U.S., 1925, naturalized, 1931; B.S. in Chem. Engring., B.S. in Math., U. Mich., 1930, M.S. in Engring. (Tau Beta Pi fellow), 1931, D.Sc., 1932; m. Cordelia G. Myers, May 24, 1930; 1 son, John Karl. Research asso. U. Mich., 1930-32; devel. engr. Standard Oil Co. Ind., Whiting, 1933-36; refinery chief chemistry, chem. engr. Pure Oil Co., Toledo refinery, 1936-39; asst. prof. chem. engring. Drexel Inst. Tech., 1939-42; dir. research Publicker Industries, Inc., 1942-47; mgr. research and devel. chem. div. Glenn L. Martin Co., Balt., 1947-49; prof. chem. engring., head dept. U. Ia., 1949- -; cons. instruments and life support div. Bendix Corp., Fed. Water Pollution Control Adminstrn., Monsanto Research Corp., VA Hosp., Iowa City. Chmn. Gordon Research Conf. Separation and Purification, 1957. Recipient Distinguished Service award Ia. Engring. Soc., 1965. Mem. A.A.A.S., Am. Assn. U. Profs., Am. Inst. Chem. Engrs., Am. Soc. Engring. Edn., Am. Chem. Soc., Nat. Soc. Profl. Engrs., Sigma Xi, Tau Beta Pi. Home: 116 Ferson Av Iowa City IA 52240

KAMMHOLZ, THEOPHIL CARL, lawyer; b. Jefferson County, Wis., Mar. 23, 1909; s. Frederic Carl and Emma (Donner) K.; LL.B., U. Wis., 1932; m. Lura Walker, Apr. 22, 1935; children—Carolyn (Mrs. John Arthur Smith), Robert. Admitted to Wis. bar, 1932, Ill. bar, 1945, D.C., 1964; asso. Stephens, Sletteland & Sutherland, Madison, Wis., 1932-34, Bogue & Sanderson, Portage, Wis., 1934-35; partner Bogue & Sanderson & Kammholz, Portage, 1935-42; regional counsel War Labor Bd., Chgo., 1943; partner Pope and Ballard, Chgo., 1944-52, Vedder, Price, Kaufman & Kammholz, Chgo., 1952-55, 57—. Exec. dir. Chgo. Foundrymen's Assn., 1952; gen. counsel NLRB, Washington, 1955-57; dir. Edward H. Anderson & Co. Chgo., Fosdick Enterprises, Inc. Adviser U.S. Govt. delegation, ILO Conf., Geneva, Switzerland, 1954. Mem. Am., Ill., Wis., Chgo., Fed. bar assns., Internat. Soc. Labor Law (U.S. exec. com.), Wis. Law Alumni Assn. (pres. Chgo. 1953-55), Chgo. Assn. Commerce and Industry (chmn. labor-mgmt. relations com. 1966-68, v.p. govtl. affairs 1968-70, dir., mem. policy com. 1968—), Order of Coif, Delta Sigma Rho, Lambda Chi Alpha. Clubs: North Shore Country (bd. govs.), Law, Executives, University (Chgo.); Kenwood Country (Washington). Co-author: Practice and Procedure Before the NLRB. Contbr. articles profl. jours. Home: 1323 Sunview Lane Winnetka IL 60093 Office: 39 S LaSalle Chicago IL 60603 also 1750 Pennsylvania Av Washington DC 20006

KAMOWITZ, HERBERT MEYER, educator; b. Bklyn., Dec. 31, 1931; s. William and Sylvia (Abelson) K.; B.S., Coll. City N.Y., 1952; Sc.M., Brown U., 1954, Ph.D., 1960; m. Elaine Frances Heyman, Dec. 24, 1955; children—David Louis, Sylvia Jean, Anne Lisa. Mathematician Avco Corp., Wilmington, Mass., 1957-66; asso. prof. math. U. Mass. at Boston, 1966-70, prof., 1970—. Mem. Am. Math. Soc., Sigma Xi, Phi Beta Kappa. Contbr. math. jours. Home: 11 Jacobs Terrace Newton Centre MA 02159 Office: Math Dept U Mass Boston MA 100 Arlington St Boston MA 02116

KAMP, CARL OTTO, Jr., govt. ofcl.; b. St. Louis, Dec. 20, 1924; s. Carl Otto and Nancy Leach (Smith) K.; student U. Okla., 1945; B.S., Washington U., St. Louis, 1952; m. Willena G. Busby, May 17, 1946; children—Carl Otto III, William Linn, Wakefield Taylor. With Conservative Fed. Savs. & Loan Assn., St. Louis, 1948-69, pres., dir., 1962-69; mem. Fed. Home Loan Bank Bd., Washington, 1969—; dir. Fed. Home Loan Mortgage Corp., 1970—; dir. Fed. Home Loan Bank of Des Moines, 1961-65. Mem. St. Louis Bicentennial Sub-com. on Downtown St. Louis Beautification Com., 1963-64. Bd. dirs. Better Bus. Bur. Served with USNR, 1943-46. Winner Am. Savs. and Loan Inst. Nat. Speech Contest, Washington, 1950. Mem. Am. Savs. and Loan Inst. (pres. St. Louis chpt. 1953), Mo. (dir. 1961-62), Greater St. Louis (pres. 1956) savs. and loan leagues. Republican. Lion (v.p., dir. 1961). Office: 101 Indiana Av NW Washington DC 20552

KAMPELMAN, MAX M., lawyer; b. N.Y.C., Nov. 7, 1920; s. Joseph and Eva (Gottlieb) Kampelmacher; A.B., N.Y.U., 1940, LL.B., 1945; M.A., U. Minn., 1946, Ph.D., 1951; m. Marjorie Buetow, Aug. 21, 1948; children—Anne, Jeffrey, Julie, David, Sarah. Admitted to N.Y. bar, 1947, D.C. bar, 1950, Md. bar, 1956; research staff Internat. Ladies Garment Workers Union, N.Y.C., 1940-41; law clk. Phillips, Nizer, Benjamin & Krim, N.Y.C., 1941- 43; instr. polit. sci. U. Minn., 1946-48; mem. faculty dept. polit. economy Bennington Coll., 1948-50; legislative counsel to Senator Hubert H. Humphrey, Washington, 1949-55; partner firm Fried, Frank, Harris, Shriver & Kampelman, Washington, 1956—; sr. adviser U.S. mission to UN, 1966-67; mem. faculty Sch. for Workers, U. Wis., summers 1947-48; vis. professorial lectr. Howard U., 1954-56; vis. distinguished prof. polit. sci. Claremont Colls., summer 1963. Chmn. exec. com., dir. D.C. Nat. Bank, 1962-66. Vice chmn. Mayor Mpls. Com. Charter Reform, 1947-48; pres. Friends of Nat. Zoo, 1958-60. Bd. dirs. Nat. Tng. Labs., Atlantic Council of U.S.; trustee Fed. City Council, Inst. Am. Univs. (Aix-en-Provence, France), Helen Dwight Reid Ednl. Found.; hon. chmn. bd. trustees Greater Washington Ednl. TV Assn., Inc.; bd. overseers Coll. V.I. Mem. Am., Fed. bar assn., Bar Assn. D.C., Am. (counsel, past treas.), D.C. (past pres.) polit. sci. assns., Am. Judicature Soc. Clubs: Cosmos, Federal City, Nat. Press (Washington). Author: The Community Party vs. The C.I.O.: A Study in Power Politics, 1957; (with Kirkpatrick) The Strategy of Deception, 1963. Contbr. articles profl. publs. Home: 3154 Highland Pl NW Washington DC 20008 Office: 600 New Hampshire Av NW Washington DC 20037

KAMPHOEFNER HENRY LEVEKE, ednl. adminstr.; b. Des Moines, May 5, 1907; s. Charles Herman and Mary Amelia (Leveke) K.; student Morningside College, Sioux City, Ia., 1924-26, D.F.A., 1967; B.Arch., U. Ill., 1930; M.Arch., Columbia, 1931, Schermerhorn fellowship (alternate), 1939; Edward Langley scholar., A.I.A., 1940; m. Mabel C. Franchere, Jan. 5, 1937. Architect, Sioux City, 1932-36; asso. architect Rural Resettlement Adminstrn., 1936-37; prof. architecture U. Okla., 1937- 48; dean Sch. Design, N.C. State U., 1948—, lectr. various univs. and colls. Photographs of works exhibited Royal Inst. Brit. Architects, London, Nat. Gallery, Washington, U. Miami. Served as asso. architect U.S. Navy, summers 1938, 39, 41. Fellow A.I.A. (nat. com. edn. 1949-50); mem. Assn. Collegiate Schs. Architecture (pres. 1963-65), Raleigh Chamber Music Guild (pres. 1954-56), Raleigh Council Architects, Am. Assn. U. Profs. Author: Cities Are Abnormal (with others), 1946; Churches and Temples (with Richard Bennett and Paul Thiry), 1953; The South Builds (with Edward and Elizabeth Waugh), 1960. Contbr. archtl. articles to profl. jours. Home: 3060 Granville Dr Raleigh NC 27609

KAMPMAN, ROBERT RAY, banker; b. Pueblo, Colo., June 8, 1932; s. Raymond Ray and Nellie (Rakestraw) K.; student N.W. Mo. State Coll., 1955; B.S., U. Mo., 1960; postgrad. Colo. Sch. Banking, 1963-65, IBM Exec. Sch., 1966, U. Wis., 1967-69; m. Alberta Lea Fulton, Feb. 14, 1958; children-Roger, Steve, Bruce. Auditor, Colo. Nat. Bank, Denver, 1960—. Cubmaster, Denver Area council Boy Scouts Am., 1970. Served with USAF, 1950-54. Mem. Nat. Assn. Bank Auditors and Controllers (past dir. Denver chpt.). Home: 4731 Marshall St Wheat Ridge CO 80033 Office: 17th and Champa Sts Denver CO 80217

KAMPMANN, FLORA CAMERON, political worker; b. Waco, Texas; d. William Waldo and Helen Emelyn (Miller) Cameron; A.B., Sweet Briar Coll., 1946; m. Ike Simpson Kampmann, Jr., Nov. 1, 1947; children—Ike Simpson III, Megan Cameron. Active Rep. Party of Tex., 1952—. mem. hdqrs. com., 1957-58, vice chmn. state exec. com., 1958-60; mem. Rep. Nat. Com. for Program and Progress, 1959; mem. Rep. Nat. Com. for Tex., 1960-65; asst. to exec. dir. platform com., del. Rep. Nat. Conv., 1960, del., 1960, 64; mem. Rep. Nat. Finance Com., 1965-. Pres. Kamko Found.; trustee Southwest Foundation Research and Education, Trinity U., San Antonio; bd. dirs. Bexar County Tb Assn., Bexar County Legal Aid Soc., San Antonio Fair Assn.; member nat. council Met. Opera. Mem. Jr. League San Antonio, Colonial Dames Am. Home: 315 Westover Rd 78209 Office: 4600 Broadway San Antonio TX 78209

KAMPMEIER, RUDOLPH HERMAN, physician; b. Butler County, Ia., Jan. 15, 1898; s. August and Mary (Ehrlicher) K.; A.B., State U. Ia., 1920, M.D., 1923; m. Blanche Davis, June 18, 1922; 1 dau., Joan. Research fellow U. Chgo. Med. Coll., 1925; asst. prof. medicine Vanderbilt U. Sch. Medicine, 1936-38, asso. prof., 1938-53, prof. 1953-63, acting dir. dept. medicine, 1944-46, dir. postgrad. med. 1946-63, prof. emeritus, 1963—, dir. continuing edn., 1963-66; vis. physician Vanderbilt U. Hosp.; dir. med. edn. Saint Thomas Hosp., 1960-64; sr. cons. Central State Psychiat. Hosp., 1938-68, med. dir., 1968—. Mem. adv. com. cancer control program USPHS, 1963-67, cons. cancer control, 1967—, cons. venereal disease br., 1964—; mem. nat. commn. venereal disease Dept. Health, Edn. and Welfare, 1971—; chmn. adv. com. for White House Conf. Aging to Tenn. Commn. Aging, 1970—; mem. exec. com. Nashville Met. Regional Health Planning Council, 1964—; exec. com. Nashville Health and Hosp. Planning Council; adv. com. Tenn. Midsouth Regional Med. Program; cons. surg.-gen. U.S. Army, 1944-45; made nutrition surveys in civilian population Am. zone in Germany, including Berlin, summer 1945. Diplomate Am. Bd. Internal Medicine, 1937. Fellow A.C.P. (regent 1961-66, 68-71, pres. 1967-68), Royal Coll. Physicians (London), Royal Coll. Physicians Ireland (hon.); mem. A.M.A. (sec. sect. internal medicine 1956-59, chmn. 1960), Nashville Acad. Medicine (pres. 1951), Tenn. (editor jour. 1950-71, pres. 1964). So. (editor jour. 1954—, pres. 1965) med. assns., Am. Clin. and Climatol. Assn., Assn. Am. Physicians, So. Soc. Clin. Research (hon.), Sigma Xi, Alpha Kappa Kappa, Alpha Omega Alpha, Unitarian. Author: Essentials of Syphilology, 1943; Physical Examination in Health and Disease, 4th edit., 1969. Home: 4424 Alcott Dr Nashville TN 37215 Office: Vanderbilt U Hosp Nashville TN 37203

KAMRATH, KARL, architect; b. Enid, Okla., Apr. 25, 1911; s. G. A. and Martha (Kreplin) K.; B. Arch., U. Tex., 1934; m. Enginie Sampson, June 27, 1934; children—Karl, Eugenie Martha, John, Robert, Thomas Ramser. Designer Pereira & Pereria, Chgo., 1934-36; chief architect interior studios Marshall Field & Co., Chgo., 1936; partner MacKie & Kamrath, Houston, 1937—; vis. archtl. critic U. Ill., U. Ore., U. Tex., U. Ark., Tex. A. and M. Coll., Tex. Tech., La. State U. Mem. four man U.S. archtl. team inspecting W. Germany planning and reconstrn., 1954; chmn. Tex. Planning Com., 1949-56; dir., founder Contemporary Arts Assn. Mus., Houston, 1948-52. Served to capt. C.E., AUS, 1942-45. Registered architect, Tex., Ill., Okla., La. Fellow A.I.A. (dir. pres. Houston chpt., chmn. Frank Lloyd Wright Meml. Com. 1959, 60); mem. Tex. Soc. Architects, Am. Planning and Civic Assn. (dir.), Nat. Council Archtl. Registration Bds., Houston Fine Arts Mus., Alpha Rho Chi. Clubs: Racquet, River Oaks Country (Houston). U.S. nat. tennis champion boys doubles, 1927, intercollegiate doubles, 1931, father and son, 1952. Home: 8 Tiel Way Houston TX 77019 Office: 2713 Ferndale Pl Houston TX 77006

KAN, Y.K., banker. Chmn., Bank of East Asia, Ltd., Victoria, Hong Kong. Office: 10 Des Voeux Rd Victoria Hong Kong*

KANAKARATNE, NEVILLE, diplomat from Ceylon; b. Colombo, Ceylon, July 19, 1923; s. Abilion De Silva and Mildred (DeSilva) K.; student Royal Coll. Colombo; B.A., U. Ceylon; M.A., U. Cambridge, 1950, LL.B., 1948; Barrister-at-law, Middle Temple, London, 1951; advocate Supreme Ct. Ceylon; crown counsel Dept. Atty. Gen. Ceylon, 1951-57; 1st sec., legal adviser, permanent mission UN, N.Y.C., 1957-61, legal adviser to Sec.-Gen.'s spl. rep. in Congo, 1961-62, polit. and legal adviser, to comdr. UN Emergency Force in Middle East, 1962-64, legal adviser to comdr. UN Peace-Keeping Force, Cyprus, 1964-65; sr. fellow Centre for Internat. Studies, N.Y. U., 1965-66; mem. Ceylon del., 21st session Gen. Assembly UN, 1966—; minister econs. affairs, London, 1967-70; ambassador to U.S. and Mexico, Washington, 1970—. Participant Harvard Internat. Seminar on Current Affairs, 1956. Mem. Royal Commonwealth Soc. London (central council 1969—). Home: 2503 30th St NW Washington DC Office: 2148 Wyoming Av NW Washington DC

KANALY, EARL DEANE, banker; b. Oklahoma City, July 23, 1930; s. Cecil P. and Louise (Schwan) K.; B.B.A., U. Okla., 1952, M.B.A., 1953; m. Virginia Dee Johnson, Aug. 24, 1952; children—Steven Patrick, Jeffery Craig, Andrew Deane. Vice pres., trust officer Bank of the S.W. Nat. Assn., Houston, 1955, then v.p., exec. trust officer, mgr. trust div.; now with River Oaks Bank & Trust Co., Houston; dir. Fish Internat. Constructors, Inc., F & C Engrng. Co., F & C Equipment Co., Chambco, Inc.; instr. U. Houston, 1955-61, Am. Inst. Banking, 1963—; lectr. Women's Inst. Houston. Served from 2d lt. to 1st lt., USAF, 1953-55. Mem. Houston Bus. and Estate Planning Council, Houston Estate and Financial Forum, Phi Kappa Psi, Phi Eta Sigma, Delta Sigma Rho, Beta Gamma Sigma. Presbyn. Clubs: Houston Country, Petroleum (Houston). Contbr. articles bus. publs. Home: 514 Clear Spring Dr Houston TX 77024 Office: 2119 Westheimer St Houston TX 77001

KANANE, MARY CATHARINE, orgn. exec., judge; b. Kenilworth, N.J., Sept. 1; d. John Thomas and Jane Sara (Gillooly) Kanane; student Fordham U., Seton Hall U. Surrogate, 1963—; lectr. Nat. regent Catholic Daus. Am. Past pres. Union County Women's Republican Club. Dir. Eastern Union County Community Services. Recipient Pro Ecclesia et Pontifice citation, 1954. Mem. Bus. and Profl. Womens Club. Author: Come Along With Me, 1959. Home: 912 Lakeside Pl Union NJ 07083 Office: Court House Elizabeth NJ 07207

KANATZAR, CHARLES LEPLIE, coll. dean; b. St. Elmo, Ill., Apr. 12, 1914; s. Charles Leplie and Cora (Gray) K.; B.Ed., Eastern Ill. U., 1935; M.S., U. Ill., 1936, Ph.D., 1940; m. Marjorie M(ae) Walls, Feb. 18, 1940; children—Constance Jean, Phyllis Rae. Engaged in real estate investment, 1940-43; mem. faculty MacMurray Coll., Jacsonville, Ill., 1946—, prof. biology, head dept., 1948-61, dean faculty, 1961-67, prof. sci., 1961, dean coll., 1967—. Mem. bd. Ill. State Mus., 1962—, chmn., 1970—. Served with AUS, 1943-46. Mem. Ill. Acad. Sci. (pres. 1959-60), A.A.A.S. Democrat. Methodist. Mason (Shriner). Home: 1841 Mound Rd Jacksonville IL 62650

KANBARA, BERTRAM TERUO, state ofcl.; b. Honolulu, Jan. 7, 1926; s. Matsuichi and Hama (Hamamura) K.; B.A., U. Hawaii, 1950; J.D., Harvard, 1953. Admitted to Hawaii bar, 1953, also U.S. Dist. Ct. Hawaii, U.S. Supreme Ct., 9th Circuit Ct. of Appeals; dep. corp. counsel City and County of Honolulu, 1954-62; dep. atty. gen. State of Hawaii, 1963-68, asst. atty. gen., 1968-69, atty. gen., 1969—. Served with AUS, 1946-47; PTO. Mem. Nat. Assn. Attys. Gen. (v.p.), Nat. Conf. Commrs. on Uniform State Laws, Am., Hawaii (dir. 1965, pres. Jr. Bar sect. 1960) bar assns., Hawaii Jr. C. of C. (legal counsel 1959), Harvard Law Sch. Assn., U. Hawaii Alumni Assn., Honolulu Acad. Arts. Home: 1429 Auld Lane Honolulu HI 96817 Office: State Capitol Honolulu HI 96813

KANDER, JOHN, composer; b. Kansas City, Mo., Mar. 18, 1927; s. Harold S. and Bernice (Aaron) K.; B.A., Oberlin Coll., 1951; M.A., Columbia. Composer: A Family Affair, 1963; Flora, the Red Menace, 1965; Cabaret (Tony award 1967, N.Y. Drama Critic's Circle award) 1966; The Happy Time, 1967; Zorba, 1968; 70 Girls 70, 1971.

KANE, ANTHONY, r.r. exec., lawyer; b. Delano, Minn., Jan. 9, 1912; s. Joseph Patrick and Isabelle V. (Browne) K.; LL.B., U. Wash., 1935; m. Margaret Mary Moore, Feb. 26, 1942; children—Thomas Patrick, Mary Kathleen, Nicholas, Gerald, Timothy, Keelin Moore, Susan, Dennis D. Admitted to Wash. State bar, 1935, practiced in Seattle, 1935-37; mem. legal dept. G.N. Ry., 1937- 70, asst. gen. counsel, 1946-50, gen. solicitor, 1950-57, v.p., 1957-70; mem. law dept. Burlington No. Inc., 1970—, v.p. law, 1970—. Served as lt. col. AUS, 1942-46. Mem. Sigma Chi. Roman Catholic. Clubs: Metropolitan (Washington); Minnesota (St. Paul); Union League (Chicago). Home: 1365 Summit Av St Paul MN 55105 Office: Burlington Northern Bldg St Paul MN 55101

KANE, CHARLES ARTHUR, physician; b. Boston, Oct. 2, 1917; s. Meyer C. and Alice (Richardson) K.; A.B., Havard, 1939, M.D. cum laude, 1943; m. Mildred Elizabeth Jonson, Sept. 8, 1944 (div. Nov. 1966); children—Charles Arthur, Priscilla E., Richard J.; m. 2d, Rita M. Earnshaw. Intern Boston City Hosp., 1942; asst. resident Goldwater Meml. Hosp., N.Y.C., 1944, Lakeside Hosp., Cleve., 1947; resident VA Hosp., Bronx, N.Y., 1948- 49; practice medicine specializing in neurology, Boston, 1951-66; instr. Cornell U., 1949-51, Harvard, 1951-66; group practice Med. Assos. Mass. Meml. Hosps., 1951-60; vis. neurologist Boston VA Hosp., City Hosp., Carney Hosp., Univ. Hosps., 1951-66; prof. neurology Sch. Medicine Boston U., 1956-66; chief sect. neurology Permanente Group, Hayward, Cal., 1966—. Served from capt. to maj., M.C., AUS, 1944-46. Mem. A.M.A., Am. Acad. Neurology (pres. 1965-66), Nat. Com. Research Neurol. Disorders (chmn. legislative com.), Sigma Xi, Alpha Omega Alpha. Contbr. articles med. jours. Home: 7498 Hillsboro Av San Ramon CA 94583 Office: 27400 Hesperian Blvd Hayward CA 94545

KANE, DANIEL HIPWELL, lawyer; b. Far Rockaway, N.Y., Aug. 18, 1908; s. David and Bertha (Schilling) K.; B.S., N.Y.U., 1929, J.D., 1931; m. Helen Shirkey, July 30, 1931; children—Ailene (Mrs. Edward Lee Rogers), Daniel Hipwell, Patricia (Mrs. Patrice Hennin), Kevin Kane. Admitted to N.Y. bar, 1932, since practiced in N.Y.C., specializing in patents; sr. partner Kane, Dalsimer, Kane, Sullivan & Kurucz, 1946—; mem. faculty N.Y.U. Sch. Law, 1947—, adj. prof., 1964—; lectr. Practising Law Inst., 1951—. Vice pres., dir. Dzus Fastener Co., Inc., West Islip, N.Y., 1941—; dir. Pickering & Co., Inc., Plainview, N.Y., 1965—. Pres. bd. edn. Union Free Sch. Dist. 6, Huntington, N.Y., 1954-55. Trustee William Dzus Fund; bd. dirs. Ukrainian Inst. Am. Mem. Assn. Bar City N.Y., Am. Bar Assn., Am., N.Y. patent law assns., Am. Judicature Soc., Phi Delta Phi. Clubs: N.Y.U. (N.Y.C.); Centerport Yacht. Author article. Home: 22 Spring Hollow Rd Centerport NY 11721 Office: 420 Lexington Av New York City NY 10017

KANE, DAVID SCHILLING, lawyer; b. Far Rockaway, N.Y., Jan. 20, 1907; s. David and Bertha Dorothy (Schilling) K.; student N.Y. U., 1924-26, LL.B., 1930; m. Mildred Irene Thompson, Sept. 23, 1931; children—David H. T. Sheila, Kathleen. Admitted to N.Y. State bar, 1931; asso. Duell, Dunn & Anderson, N.Y.C., 1931-34; partner Duell & Kane, 1934, sr. partner, 1942-52; sr. partner Kane, Dalsimer & Kane, 1952-65, Kane, Dalsimer, Kane & Smith, 1965-67, Kane, Dalsimer, Kane, Sullivan and Smith, 1967-69, Kane, Dalsimer, Kane, Sullivan & Kurcz, 1969—; pres. Camloc Fastener Corp., 1942-44; dir. Becton, Dickinson & Co., C. F. Mueller Co.; lectr. grad. div. N.Y. U. Sch. Law, 1946-59, adj. asso. prof. law, 1960-64, adj. prof., 1964—. Mem. sch. bd., Port Washington, N.Y., 1948-50; mem. bd. appeals Inc. Village Sands Point, N.Y., 1948- 63, trustee, 1963-65, major, 1965-69. Trustee N.Y. U. Law Center Found., C.F. Mueller Scholarship Found.; dir. N.Y. U. Vanderbilt Assos. Awarded 1950 Certificate Meritorious Service, N.Y. U. Law Center Found. Mem. Am. Judicature Soc., Nat. Council Patent Law Assn. (chmn. 1963-64), Am. (pres. 1962-63), N.Y. (pres. 1958-59) patent law assns., Am., N.Y.C. bar assns., N.Y. County Lawyers Assn., N.Y. State Bar Assn., N.Y. U. Law Alumni Assn. (dir.), Fed Bar Council, Nat. Lawyers Club, Am. Trial Lawyers Assn., Phi Delta Phi Assn. N.Y. Mason. Clubs: Union League, Pinnacle, New York University (founder member) (N.Y.C.); Sands Point Bath and Tennis Club; Manhasset Bay Yacht; Naples Yacht; Royal Poinciane Golf; Naples Yacht. Contbg. author: Survey American Law, 1942-45. Home: Cornwell's Beach Rd Sands Point Long Island NY 12123 also 140 2d Av N Naples FL 33940 Office: 420 Lexington Av New York City NY 10017

KANE, EDWIN C., banker. Vice chmn. bd., pres. First Nat. Bank, Little Rock. Office: PO Box 1471 3d and Louisiana Sts Little Rock AR 72203*

KANE, FRANK EDWARD, lawyer; b. N.Y.C., June 14, 1923; s. Frank E. and Margaret (Shannon) K.; B.S., Ohio State U., 1950, J.D. cum laude, 1951; m. Eleanora Van Winkle, Aug. 7, 1948; children-John Francis, Joan Elizabeth. Instr. legal writing Ohio State U. Coll. Law, 1952; admitted to Ohio bar, 1952, since practiced in Toledo; asso. Eastman, Stichter, Smith & Bergman, 1952-60, partner, 1960—; instr. trial practice Coll. Law, U. Toledo, 1959-60. Pres. Community Improvement Corp., Perrysburg, 1967-68. Arbitrator, Am. Arbitration Assn. Served with AUS, 1941-45. Mem. Am., Ohio, Toledo, Lucas County bar assns., Toledo Zool. Soc., Order of Coif, Beta Gamma Sigma, Phi Eta Sigma, Delta Theta Phi. Republican. Roman Catholic. Editor-in-chief Ohio State Law Jour., 1951. Contbr. articles profl. jours. Home: 4547 River Rd Toledo OH 43614 Office: 240 Huron St Toledo OH 43604

KANE, BROTHER GABRIEL, educator, physicist; b. Bklyn., July 17, 1909; s. Charles A. and Jeannette (Morrissy) K.; A.B., Manhattan Coll., 1932; Ph.D., Cath. U. Am., 1939; M.A., Notre Dame U., 1952. Joined Bros. of Christian Schs.; tchr. grammar sch., 1929-33, high sch., 1933- 36; instr. De La Salle Coll., Washington, 1936-39; instr. Manhattan Coll., N.Y.C., 1939-41, asst. prof. 1941-43, head dept. physics, 1941- 60, prof., 1943—. Mem. N.Y. Gov.'s Gen. Adv. Com. on Atomic Energy. Mem. Am., Italian phys. socs., Sigma Xi, Sigma Pi Sigma. Co-author: The Physical Universe, 1941; Foundations of Catholic Belief, 1942. Contbr. articles profl. jours. Dir. constrn. first critical reactor, N.Y.C. Research in cosmic rays, nuclear physics, elementary particles, structure liquids. Home: Manhattan Coll New York City NY 10471

KANE, HARNETT THOMAS, author, critic; b. New Orleans, La., Nov. 8, 1910; s. William J. and Anna (Hirt) K.; B.A., Tulane U., New Orleans, 1931, grad. work in sociology, 1932-33; unmarried. Reporter with New Orleans Item-Tribune, 1928-43, assignments covered welfare, business, labor, politics; teacher of journalism, Loyola U. (New Orleans), 1943-44. Del. of New Orleans Item-Tribune to Cities Investment Trust Foundation Safety Seminar, N.Y. City, 1937. Mem. bd. New Orleans Cultural Attractions Fund. Pres. La. Council for Vieux Carre. Mem. Lyceum Assn. (mem. bd. dirs.), Authors Guild of Am., Soc. of Midland Authors, New Orleans Art Assn.; v.p. English Speaking Union of New Orleans, Chevaliers de Tastevin, France d'Amerique, Athenee Louisianaise, board of Louisiana Landmarks Soc., Am. Newspaper Guild, Sigma Delta Chi, Theta Nu, Kappa Delta Phi. Received Dorothy Dix journalism award, 1930, Ala. Writers' Assn. award for distinguished writing on the South, 1958, Chevalier de Palmes Academiquest award, France, 1958, Guggenheim fellowship for study of southern problems, 1943-44, 44-45. Democrat. Roman Catholic. Club: Arts and Crafts (New Orleans). Author: Louisiana Hayride: The American Rehearsal for Dictatorship, 1941; Bayous of Louisiana, 1943; Deep Delta Country; Plantation Parade-the Grand Manner in Louisiana, 1945; New Orleans Woman, 1946; Natchez on the Mississippi, 1947; Bride of Fortune, 1948; Queen New Orleans, 1949; Pathway to the Stars, 1950; Scandalous Mrs. Blackford, 1951; Gentlemen, Swords and Pistols, 1951; Dear Dorothy Dix (biography with Ella B. Arthur), 1952; The Lady of Arlington, 1953; Spies for the Blue and Gray, 1954; The Smiling Rebel, 1955; (with Inez Henry) Miracle in the Mountains, 1956; The Gallant Mrs. Stonewall, 1957; The Southern Christmas Book, 1958; The Golden Coast, 1959; The Ursulines, Nuns of Adventure, 1959; Have Pen, Will Autograph, 1959; Gone Art the Days, 1960; The Romantic South, 1961; The Amazing Mrs. Bonaparte, 1963; Young Mark Twain and the Mississippi; published in 1966; also author of several articles pub. in Colliers, Gourmet; Reader's Digest, Am. Mercury, National Geographic and articles and book reviews to newspapers and nat. mags.; also series of articles on leprosy in La. and history of New Orleans and Louisiana. Home: 5919 Freret St New Orleans LA 70115

KANE, HARRY JOSEPH, lumber products exec.; b. Spokane, Jan. 5, 1923; s. Harry J. and Ann (Hartmeier) K.; B.A., U. Wash., 1948; m. Antoinette M. Van Parys, Oct. 28, 1944; 1 son, Thomas Robert. With Arthur Anderson & Co., C.P.A.'s, Seattle, 1948-55; v.p. Ga.-Pacific Corp., Portland, Ore., 1955- 66, exec. v.p., 1966—, also dir. C.P.A., Ore., Wash. Mem. Financial Execs. Inst., Ore., Wash. socs. C.P.A.'s. Home: 9950 S W Hawthorne Lane Portland OR 97225 Office: Equitable Bldg Portland OR 97207

KANE, IRVING, lawyer; b. Kiev, Russia, Jan. 24, 1908; s. Aaron and Clara (Blazer) K.; brought to U.S., 1913, naturalized, 1924; student U. Mich., 1924-25; B.A., Western Res. U., 1928, LL.B., 1930; L.H.D. (hon.), Hebrew Union Coll.-Jewish Inst. Religion, 1964; m. Adeline Faller, June 26, 1932; children—Kathie (Mrs. Melvin D. Kraft), Bonnie (Mrs. Erwin Raffel). Admitted to Ohio bar, 1930, since practiced in Cleve. Pres. Hosp. Specialty Co., Cleve., 1941-62; bus. and financial cons. Irving Kane Assos., 1962—. Asso. chmn. Am. Jewish Tercentenary, 1954; life trustee, v.p. Jewish Community Fedn. Cleve.; mem. Cleve. Community Relations Bd., 1950-61; vice chmn. Joint Distbn. Com.; campaign cabinet United Jewish Appeal; chmn. Am. Israel Public Affairs Com. Trustee emeritus Brandeis U.; bd. dirs. Am. Jewish Hist. Soc., Am. Friends Hebrew U., Am. Ort Fedn.; bd. govs. Am. Jewish Com. Recipient gold certificate merit exceptional service Jewish War Vets., 1952, Distinguished Citizenship award Fedn. Jewish Women's Orgns. Cleve., 1954, Haym Solomon award of Del., 1962, Eleanor Roosevelt Humanities award, 1964, Distinguished Service award United Appeal Greater Cleve., 1968. Mem. Nat. Community Relations Adv. Council (past chmn.), Council Jewish Fedns. and Welfare Funds (past pres.; life trustee), Jewish Community Council Cleve. (past pres.), Am. Arbitration Assn. (nat. panel), Phi Sigma Delta, Delta Sigma Rho. Clubs: Harmonie (N.Y.C.); Oakwood (Cleve.). Home: 13800 Shaker Blvd Cleveland OH 44120

KANE, JOHN FRANCIS, physician and surgeon; b. Hampton, Va., Oct. 29, 1919; s. John and Veronica (Koch) K.; student St. Louis U., 1936-39; M.D., Marquette U., 1943; m. Jeannette M. Bergan, Nov. 28, 1947. Intern St. Anne's Hosp., Chgo., 1943-44; resident gen. surgery Hines (Ill.) VA Hosp., 1946-49; with VA, 1949—, chief staff VA Hosp., Portland, Ore., 1960-69, Livermore (Cal.) VA Hosp., 1969—; asst. clin. prof. surgery U. Ore. Med. Sch., 1960-69. Served to maj. M.C., AUS, 1944-46; ETO. Diplomate Am. Bd. Surgery. Mem. A.M.A., Am. Geriatrics Soc., Portland Surg. Soc. Address: VA Hosp Livermore CA 94558

KANE, JOHN JOSEPH, educator, sociologist; b. Phila., Apr. 20, 1909; s. John Joseph and Marie Cornelia (O'Hara) K.; A.B., St. Joseph's Coll., Phila., 1939; M.A., Temple U., 1946; Ph.D., U. Pa., 1950; m. Anne Marie Hilly, Oct. 18, 1941 (dec. Dec. 1966); children—Gerald (dec.), Marianne, Joan, Patricia. Instr. sociology St. Joseph's Coll., 1946-48; prof. sociology U. Notre Dame, 1948-67, head dept., 1964-67; acting chmn., vis. prof. sociology Loyola Coll., Montreal, Que., 1967-68; now prof. sociology U. Notre Dame. Dir. Ind. conf. Nat. Conf. Christians and Jews, 1950- 52; social sci. com. N.A.A.C.P. on desegregation, 1955-56. Mem. Am. Cath. Sociology Soc. (pres. 1952), Ind. Conf. Family Relations (v.p.), Am. Sociology Soc., Nat. Council Family Relations, Alpha Sigma Nu. Roman Catholic. Author: Marriage and the Family: a Catholic Approach, 1952; Protestant-Catholic Conflicts in America, 1955; Together in

Marriage, 1957; Social Problems, 1962. Contbr. articles profl. jours. and periodicals, chpt. to Catholicism in America, 1954. Home: 230 Ardennes Av Mishawaka IN

KANE, MARGARET BRASSLER, sculptor; b. East Orange, N.J., May 25, 1909; d. Hans and Mathilde (Trumpler) Brassler; student Packer Collegiate Inst., 1920-26, Syracuse U., 1927, Art Students League, 1927-29, N.Y. Coll. Music, 1928- 29, John Hovannes Studio, 1932-34; m. Arthur Ferris Kane, June 11, 1930; children—Jay Brassler, Gregory Ferris. Work has appeared at Jacques Seligmann Gallery, N.Y., Whitney Ann. Exhbns., all Sculptors Guild Mus. and Outdoor Shows, Nat. Sculpture Soc. Ann. Bas-Relief Exhbn., 1938, Whitney Mus. Sculpture Festival, 1940, Bklyn. Mus. Sculptors Guild, 1938, Bklyn. Soc. Artists, 1942, Lawrence (Mass.) Art Mus., 1938, N.Y. World's Fair, 1939, Sculptors Guild World's Fair Exhbn., 1940, Robinson Gallery, N.Y., 1939, Traveling Museums and Instns., 1938, Lyman Allyn Mus., 1939, Met. Mus., Internat. Exhbns., 1940, 1949, Roosevelt Field Art Center, N.Y.C., 1957, Phila. Mus., N.Y. Archtl. League, Nat. Acad., Penn. Acad., Chgo. Art Inst., Am. Fedn. Arts, Riverside Mus., Montclair Mus., Grand Central Art Galleries, Lever House (N.Y.C.), 1959-70, Rye (N.Y.) Library, 1962, and exhbns. of nat. scope, 1938—; solo sculpture exhbn. Friends Greenwich (Conn.) Library, 1962; executed plague for Burro Monument, Fairplay, Colo.; exhibited N.Y. Bank for Savs., 1968, Mattatuck Mus., Con., 1967, Lamont Gallery, N.H., 1967. Head craftsman for sculpture, arts and skills unit, A.R.C., Halloran Gen. Hosp., N.Y., 1942-43; 2d v.p. Nat. Assn. Woman Artists, Inc., 1943-45; sec. to exec. bd. Sculptors Guild, Inc., 1942-45; chmn. exhbn. com. Sculptors Guild, Inc., 1942, 44. Fellow Internat. Inst. Arts and Letters (life); mem. Sculptors Guild, Nat. Assn. Women Artists, Artists Council, U.S.A., Bklyn. Soc. Artists, Greenwich Soc. Artists (council mem.), Pen and Brush, Silvermine Guild Artists. Recipient Anna Hyatt Huntington award, 1942; Am. Artists Profl. League and Montclair Art Assn. Awards, 1943; 1st Henry O. Avery Prize, 1944; Sculpture Prize, Bklyn. Soc. Artists, Bklyn. Mus., 1946, John Rogers Award, 1951; Lawrence Hyder Prize, 1952, 54; David H. Zell Meml. Award, 1954, 63, hon. mention U.S. Maritime Commn., 1941 and A.C.A. Gallery Competition, 1944, Nat. Assn. Med. of honor for sculpture, 1951, Nat. Assn. Women Artists, Nat. Acad. Galleries, N.Y.; prize for carved sculpture, 1955, animal sculpture, 1956, 1st award for sculpture, Greenwich Art Soc., 1958, 60. Annual New Eng. Exhbns., Silvermine, Conn. Jury mem. Bklyn. Mus., 1948, Am. Machine & Foundry Co., 1957; com. mem. An American Group, Inc. Contbr. articles to magazine. Reprodns. in Contemporary Stone Sculpture, 1970. Home and studio: 30 Strickland Rd Cos Cob CT 06807

KANE, MICHAEL MYRON, architect; b. Cleve., Mar. 10, 1922; s. Abraham Jacob and Anne (Solomon) K.; B.A., U. Mich., 1943; postgrad. Western Res. U., 1946, Case Inst. Tech., 1946; B.Arch., U. Mich., 1949; postgrad. Ecole du Louvre, La Sorbonne, Scola Cantorum, Paris, France, 1960-61; m. Leila Nedda Goold, July 21, 1967; children—Anina Jo, Carolyn Laurie. Prin., Michael M. Kane & Assos., architects, Cleve. and Lorain, O., Buena Park, Cal., 1950-62; architect adviser, cons. AID, Dept. State, 1962-63; cons. architect World Bank, Mission to Nigeria, 1963-64; regional architect for Central Am. and Panama, Am. Inst. for Free Labor Devel., Washington, 1964-68; adviser for campus and facilities devel. to the pres. Queensborough Community Coll., City U. N.Y., 1968-71, vis. lectr. on urban environment, 1968; v.p. Synoptic Design Corp. an affiliate of Consol. Housing Corp., St. Croix, V.I., 1971—; invited speaker XXXVII Congresso Internacional de Americanistas, Buenos Aires, Argentina, 1966. Mem. Mayor's Com. on Housing, Cleve., 1950-52; profl. adviser Cerebral Palsy Found., Cleve., 1953-57; charter mem. Alley Restoration Com., Bayside, N.Y., 1969-71. Bd. dirs. Celo Health and Edn. Corp., Arthur Morgan Sch., Celo, N.C., 1963-68. Served to lt. USNR, 1943-46; PTO, ETO, MTO. Recipient Boursier Govt. France, 1960-61, Fulbright Travel grant, 1960-61, Turtle award Queensborough Community Coll. Student Assn., 1970, numerous other awards for archtl. work. Mem. A.I.A., Ohio Soc. Architects, Am. Assn. Jr. Colls., Council of Ednl. Facilities Planners, Soc. for Coll. and Univ. Planners, V.I. Assn. Architects, Engrs. and Land Surveyors, Am. Inst. Planners (affiliate mem.), UN Assn. U.S.A., Pi Lambda Phi. Jewish religion. Club: Oakwood Country (Cleve.). Contbr. articles profl. jours. Important works include Walban Apts., Painesville, O., Kane Co. Showrooms, Cleve., Pvt. Enterprise Redevelopment Corp., Cleve., Byron Jr. High Sch., Shaker Heights, O., Ednl. Auditorium Addition to The Temple, Cleve., Instituto Superior de Agricultura, Santiago de los Caballeros, Dominican Republic, Colonia FESITRANH, Honduras. Home: 3 North St Christiansted St Croix VI 00820 Office: The Lodge Box 2561 43-A Queen St Christiansted St Croix VI 00820

KANE, RICHMOND KEITH, lawyer; b. San Francisco, July 3, 1900; s. Daniel H. and Beryl (Keith) K.; grad. St. George's Sch., 1918; A.B., Harvard, 1922, LL.B., 1926; student Balliol Coll., Oxford (Eng.) U., 1922-23; m. Amanda Bryan, May 21, 1930; children—Shelah Keith, Anne Tennant, Hope Stewart, Constance Henley. Admitted to N.Y. bar, 1926; with firm Cadwalader, Wickersham & Taft, 1926-32, mem., 1932-40, 46—; spl. asst. to atty. gen. U.S., 1940-42; spl. asst. to sec. navy, 1943-45, Trustee U.S. Trust Co. N.Y.; dir. Amerada Hess Corp., Crowell-Collier & Macmillan, Inc. Served with USNRF, 1918, U.S. Marine Corps, 1918; lt. comdr. USNR, 1937-40. Fellow Am. Bar Found.; mem. Assn. Bar City N.Y., N.Y. State, Am., D.C. bar assns., Am. Law Inst. Democrat. Episcopalian. Clubs: Somerset, Tavern, Harvard (Boston); Union, Harvard, Century, Downtown Assn., Knickerbocker, River (N.Y.C.); Metropolitan (Washington); Commonwealth, Country of Va. (Richmond, Va.). Home: 121 E 78th St New York City NY 10021 Office: 1 Wall St New York City NY 10005

KANE, ROBERT JOSEPH, univ. athletic director; b. Ithaca, N.Y., Apr. 24, 1911; s. Frank J. and Mary (Purcell) K.; B.S., Cornell U., 1934; m. Ruth Mary Brosmer, Aug. 17, 1937; children—Christopher, Karen. Asst. athletic dir. Cornell U., 1939-41, acting athletic dir., 1941-44, athletic dir., 1944—. Mem. exec. com. Eastern Coll. Athletic Conf., 1947-50, 53-55, 57-59, 64—; bd. dirs. U.S. Olympic Com., 1952—; adminstrv. dir. U.S. Olympic Team, Tokyo (Japan) Games, 1964. Trustee Gunnery Sch. Home: 109 Cayuga Heights Rd Ithaca NY 14850

KANE, RUSSELL WILLIAM, editor, author; b. Duluth, Minn., Apr. 2, 1925; s. Ralph W. and Mary (Cotton) K.; B.A., Ohio State U., 1948; m. Lois Arlene Morgan, Mar. 20, 1948 (div.); children-Barbara L., Robert W., Alan R. News editor Chagrin Valley Herald, Chagrin Falls, O., 1949-52; with Cleve. Plain Dealer, 1952—, Sunday mag. editor, 1969—. Served with AUS, 1943-45. Decorated Purple Heart with cluster. Mem. Am. Newspaper Guild (bd. dirs. local). Democrat. Clubs: City, Press (Cleve.). Author: Zoo Who's, 1971. Home: 8228 Maple Dr Chesterland OH 44026 Office: 1801 Superior Av Cleveland OH 44114

KANE, STANLEY BRUCE, food co. exec.; b. N.Y.C., June 5, 1920; s. Jacob and Anna (Epstein) K.; student N.Y.U., 1938-39; m. Janet Marilyn Haas, May 23, 1948; children—Katherine, Betsy, Priscilla. With Kane-Miller Corp., N.Y.C., 1938—, chmn. bd., 1959—. Served with USAAF, 1942-45. Home: 290 Bedford Center Rd Bedford Hills NY 10507 Office: 355 Lexington Av New York City NY 10017

KANE, WILBUR PRICE, govt. ofcl.; b. Altoona, Pa., Feb. 5, 1916; s. Charles Ray and Grace Irene (Price) K.; student Johns Hopkins, 1943-45, Am. U., 1947-48; LL.B., Nat. U., 1942; m. Lois Irene Humphries, June 3, 1944; children—Sean, Christina, Cort, Kerry. With PWA, 1938-40; with Dept. Interior, 1940—, asst. commnr. Bur. Reclamation, 1963—. Admitted to D.C. bar, 1942. Chmn. bd. Oakview Recreation Corp. Served with USCGR, 1942-45. Named citizen of the year Oakview, Md., 1964. Methodist. Mason. Home: 13232 Clifton Rd Silver Spring MD 20904 Office: Dept of Interior Washington DC

KANE, WILLARD WEIR, retired govt. ofcl.; b. Bennett, Colo., Jan. 14, 1908; s. Van Ness and Edith (Weir) K.; B.B.A., U. Colo., 1931, B.A., 1932; M.A., Am. U., 1942; m. Mary Herndon Morse, Mar. 3, 1939; children—Virginia Morse (Mrs. James George Monsour), Margaret Edith. Tchr., coach Iliff (Colo.) High Sch., 1932-34; statis. clk., economist, textile specialist U.S. Tariff Commn., Washington, 1934-43, 46-57, asst. to dir. investigation, 1957-62, dir. investigation, 1962-69, chmn. staff coordinating com., 1966-69; negotiator, cons. internat. trade agreements, Geneva, 1947, 56, Annecy, France, 1949, Torquay, Eng., 1950-51. Served with USAAF, 1943-46. Mem. Phi Kappa Tau. Democrat. Episcopalian. Contbr. govt. publns. Home: 933 E Taylor Run Pkwy Alexandria VA 22302

KANE, W.J., formerly pres. Great Atlantic & Pacific Tea Co., now chmn. bd., chief exec. officer. Address: 420 Lexington Av New York City NY 10017

KANIA, EUGENE BENEDICT, transp. co. exec.; b. Chgo., Mar. 21, 1928; s. Frank J. and Lillian (Miller) K.; B.S., Ind. U., 1950, M.B.A., 1951; m. Mary Rafacz, Sept. 5, 1950; children—Ann, Joan. Supr. materials control Cummins Engine Co., Columbus, Ind., 1952-57; dir. accounting Pacific Intermountain Express Co., Oakland, Cal., 1958-61, controller, 1964-67; v.p. finance Nat. Carloading Corp., 1968—; controller Schwabacner Frey, San Francisco, 1926-64; cons. Pacific Industries, San Francisco, 1964. Served with AUS, 1946-48. Mem. Tax Execs. Inst., Financial Execs. Inst., Operations Research Soc. Am. Home: 1293 Quandt Ct La Fayette CA 94549 Office: 1801 Edgewater Dr Oakland CA 94612

KANIG, JOSEPH LOUIS, educator; b. N.Y.C., July 11, 1921; s. Jack and Molly (Singer) K.; B.S., L.I.U., 1942; M.S., Columbia, 1949; Ph.D., N.Y.U., 1960; m. Thelma Yospin, Aug. 23, 1947; children—Steven Paul, Gary Roy, David Ross. Mem. faculty Columbia Coll. Pharm. Scis., 1949—, prof. pharmaceutics, 1962- -, dean, 1965—, dir. indsl. pharmaceutics labs., 1958—, dir. aerosol research lab., 1958-65; cons. in field, since 1952. Mem. adv. panel Nat. Formulary, 13th edit. Served with USCGR, 1942-46. Recipient Chem. Industries Buyers and Suppliers Assn. award, 1962; N.J. Pharm. Research Discussion Group award, 1966; Man of Year award Drug and Allied Products Guild, N.Y.C., 1967. Fellow Am. Coll. Apothecaries, A.A.A.S., Am. Inst. Chemists; mem. Am. Pharm. Assn., N.Y. Acad. Scis., Soc. Pharmacists in Industry, Am. Soc. Hosp. Pharmacists, Soc. Cosmetic Chemists, Am. Assn. U. Profs., Am. Pub. Health Assn., Assn. Higher Edn., Acad. Pharm. Scis., Am. Bur. Med. Aid to China, Am. Soc. Pharmacognosy, Am. Inst. History Pharmacy, Royal Soc. Health, Am. Bd. Diplomates in Pharmacy (charter), Internat. Narcotic Enforcement Officers Assn., Pharm. Soc. State N.Y., A.M.A. (asso.), N.Y. City Soc. Hosp. Pharmacists, N.Y. State Council Hosp. Pharmacists, Sigma Xi, Rho Chi. Contbg. author: Remington's Pharmaceutical Scis., 11th, 12th, 13th edits., 1956-65; Pharmacotherapeutics of Oral Disease, 1964. Co-editor: The Theory and Practice of Industrial Pharmacy, 1970. Contbr. numerous articles in field to profl. jours. Home: 889 Baldwin Dr Westbury NY 11590 Office: 115 W 68th St New York City NY 10023

KANIN, GARSON, playwright, dir.; b. Rochester, N.Y., Nov. 24, 1912; s. David and Sadie (Levine) K.; grad. Am. Acad. Dramatic Arts, N.Y.C., 1933; m. Ruth Gordon, Dec. 4, 1942. Actor appearing on Broadway stage in Little Ol' Boy, Spring Song, Ladies Money, Three Men on a Horse, The Body Beautiful, Boy Meets Girl, Star Spangled, 1933-36; asst. dir. to George Abbott for Three Men on a Horse, Boy Meets Girl, Room Service, Brother Rat, 1935-37; dir. Hitch Your Wagon, 1936, Too Many Heroes, 1937; mem. prodn. staff Samuel Goldwyn, Hollywood, Cal., 1937; dir. films for R.K.O.; A Man to Remember, 1938, Next Time I Marry, 1938, The Great Man Votes, 1939, Bachelor Mother, 1939, My Favorite Wife, 1940, They Knew What They Wanted, 1940, Tom, Dick and Harry, 1941; dir. play The Rugged Path, with Spencer Tracy; writer, dir. play Born Yesterday, 1946; dir. plays Years Ago by Ruth Gordon (Mrs. Kanin) With Frederic March and Florence Eldridge, 1946; How I Wonder, 1947; The Leading Lady, 1948; The Diary of Anne Frank, 1955; Small War on Murray Hill, 1957; A Hole in the Head, 1957; writer, dir. Smile of the World, 1949; The Rat Race, 1949; The Live Wire, 1950; Do Re Me, 1961; The Good Soup, 1960; Sunday in New York, 1961; Funny Girl, 1964; I Was Dancing, 1964; A Very Rich Woman, 1965; We Have Always Lived in the Castle, 1966; adapted and directed A Gift of Time, 1962; co-author (with Ruth Gordon) (films) A Double Life (nominated Acad. Award, 1948); Adam's Rib, 1949; Pat and Mike, 1952; The Marrying Kind, 1952; (screenplays) From This Day Forward (adaptation); The Right Approach; It Should Happen to You, 1953; The Rat Race, 1959; original story High Time, 1960; wrote New English libretto and directed Fledermaus, Met. Opera Co., 1950, 66; author fiction Do Re Mi, 1955; Little Brown, 1955; Blow Up a Storm, 1959; The Rat Race, 1960; (collections): The Bedside Playboy, Second Science Fiction Anthology; contbr. Atlantic Monthly, Cosmopolitan, Esquire, Good Housekeeping, Playboy, McCall's, Vogue, others. Served to capt. AUS, 1941-45; co-dir. with Carol Reed, Gen. Eisenhower's film report The True Glory, named best film of 1945 by Nat. Bd. Review. Recipient Acad. Award; citation N.Y. Film Critic's Circle; following awards for play, Born Yesterday; Sidney Howard Memorial award; Donaldson award for best 1st play of season, 1945-46, Donaldson award for best dir. of season, 1945-46. Mem. Jewish Theatrical Guild, Soc. Stage Directors and Choreographers, ANTA, Writer's Guild, Dramatist Guild, Acad. Motion Picture Arts and Sci., Authors League, Authors Guild, A.S.C.A.P., Actors Fund, A.F.T.R.A. Clubs: The Players, The Friars, The Lamb's, Coffee House (N.Y.C.). Office: 1650 Broadway New York City NY 10019

KANITZ, ERNEST, composer; b. Vienna, Austria, Apr. 9, 1894; s. Sigmund and Eugenie (Stricker) K.; Dr. Jur., U. Vienna, 1918; student composition with R. Heuberger and Franz Schreker, 1912-20; m. Gertrude Reif, June 28, 1920; children—Elizabeth (Mrs. John O. Canfield), Thomas R., Kane Mary Brigit (Mrs. William D. Lavender). Came to U.S., 1938, naturalized, 1944. Prof. music theory New Vienna Conservatory, 1922-38; asst. prof. music Winthrop Coll., Rock Hill, S.C., 1938-41; prof. music, chmn. dept. Erskine Coll., Due West, S.C., 1941-44; prof. composition U. So. Cal., 1945-59, 60-61; lectr. music Marymount Coll., Palos Verdes, Cal., 1960- 63; founder, conductor Vienna Women's Chamber Chorus, 1930-38. Mem. Assn. Am. Composers and Conductors (bd. dirs. 1958—), League Composers, Cal. Music Tchrs. Assn. (hon.), A.S.C.A.P., Phi Mu Alpha (hon.), Pi Kappa Lambda. Composer, 1907—, most important compositions being: Ballet Music, 1936i concert piece for Trumpet and Orch., 1951; concerto for Chamber Orch., 1957; concerto for Bassoon and Orch., 1962; Visions at Twilight, 1962; Sinfonia Seria, 1963; 2d Symphony, 1965; Sinfonia Concertante for Violin and Cello (3d Symphony), 1967; Cantata 1961 for mixed chorus and 2 pianos, 1961; Perpetual (opera), 1960; Concertino for Five Players, 1957; 2d sonata for Violin and Piano, 1965; sonata for Bassoon and Piano, 1966. Address: 6206 Murietta Av Van Nuys CA 91401

KANN, ROBERT ADOLF, educator, historian; b. Vienna, Austria, Feb. 11, 1906; s. Leo and Louise (Eisenschitz) K.; Dr.Jur., U. Vienna, 1930; Ph.D., Columbia, 1946; m. Marie Breuer, Jan. 26, 1937; children—Peter R., Marilyn B. Came to U.S., 1939, naturalized, 1944. Legal work Austrian cts., 1931-36; pvt. practice law, Vienna, 1936-38; mem. Inst. Advanced Study, Princeton, 1942-45; mem. faculty Rutgers U., 1947—, prof. history, 1956- -; vis. prof. Columbia, 1957, 62-64, 66-67; research asso. Princeton, 1952-53, vis. prof., 1966. Rapporteur, Internat. Congress Hist. Scis., 1965. Guggenheim fellow, 1949-50; Social Sci. Research Council fellow, 1960; recipient award for research Lindback Found., 1969. Mem. Am. Hist. Assn. (exec. sect. com. research Hapsburg monarchy, 1968-70, chmn. conf. group Central European history 1964); life corr. mem. Austrian Acad. Author: The Multinational Empire, 2 vols., 1950; The Hapsburg Empire, 1957; A Study in Austrian Intellectual History, 1960; Die Sixtusaffaire, 1966; The Problem of Restoration, 1968; co-author: Political Community and North Atlantic Area, 1957; Spectrum Austriae, 1957; Historica, 1965; Quantitative History, 1969. Editorial bd. Austrian History Yearbook, 1965-70, Central European History, 1968—. Home: 143 Loomis Ct Princeton NJ 08540 Office: Grad Dept History Rutgers Univ New Brunswick NJ 08903

KANNER, LEO, medical educator; b. Klekotow, Austria, June 13, 1894; s. Abraham and Klara (Reisfeld) K.; grad. Sophiengymnasium, Berlin, 1913; M.D., U. Berlin, 1921; m. June Lewin, Feb. 11, 1921; children—Anita (Mrs. Theodore Gilbert), Albert Victor. Came to U.S., 1924, naturalized, 1930. Vol. asst. Charité Hosp., Berlin, Germany, 1920-23; pvt. practice medicine, Berlin, 1921-23; sr. asst. physician Yankton (S.D.) State Hosp., 1924-28; Commonwealth Fund fellow psychiatry Johns Hopkins, 1928- 30, Josiah Macy Jr. Found. research fellow child psychiatry, 1930-32, asso. psychiatry, 1932-33, asso. prof. psychiatry, 1948—, prof. child psychiatry, 1957-59, prof. emeritus child psychiatry, 1959—; dispensary psychiatrist Johns Hopkins Hosp., 1928-30, psychiatrist charge children's psychiat. service, 1930-59, hon. cons., 1959—, asst. psychiatrist, 1933-42, asso. psychiatrist, 1942-47, psychiatrist, 1947- -, pediatrician, 1948—; cons. psychiatrist Juvenile Ct. Balt., 1930- 41; vis. lectr. Dalhousie U., 1937, U. Mich., 1945, U. Minn., 1946, Goucher Coll., 1948-51, U. Tex., 1951, Mt. Sinai Hosp., N.Y.C., 1956; Kemper Knapp distinguished vis. prof. U. Wis., 1956. Dir. Child Study Center Md., 1937-44, League Emotionally Disturbed Children; exec. com. Children's Guild Balt.; adv. bd. Woods Schs., Langhorne, Pa., Devereux Schs., Devon, Pa., Cove Sch., Racine, Wis. Recipient award outstanding contbn. field medicine Assn. Help Retarded Children, 1954; 1st ann. award. Nat. Orgn. Mentally Ill Children, 1960; Gutheil Meml. medal Am. Assn. Advancement Psychotherapy, 1962; Stanley R. Dean award 1965. Fellow Am. Psychiat. Assn. (chmn. sect. child psychiatry 1942-43), Am. Assn. Mental Deficiency, Am. Acad. Child Psychiatry, Am. Orthopsychiat. Assn.; mem. Nat. Assn. Retarded Children (research adv. com.), Md. Psychiat. Soc. (pres. 1957-58), Assn. History Medicine, A.A.A.S., Internat. League Against Epilepsy, Md. Soc. Med. Research, Balt. City Med. Soc., Am. Assn. U. Profs., Johns Hopkins Med. Soc. Author: Folklore of the Teeth, 1928; In Defense of Mothers, 1941; Miniature Textbook of Feeblemindedness, 1949; Child Psychiatry, rev. edit., 1957; A Word to Parents About Mental Hygiene, 1957; History of the Care and Study of Mentally Retarded, 1964. Contbr. articles profl. jours. Editor Jour. Autism and Childhood Schizophrenia. Home: 4000 W Charles St Baltimore MD 21218

KANSARA, T. D., banker. Chmn., Bank of India, Ltd., Bombay. Office: 70-80 Mahatma Gandhi Rd 1 Bombay India*

KANTE, MAMADOU BOUBACAR, former ambassador of Mali to UN. Address: 111 E 69th St New York City NY 10021 *

KANTER, JOSEPH HYMAN, banker, community developer; b. Tarrant, Ala., Nov. 15, 1923; s. Harry O. and Sylvia (Klein) K.; student U. Ala., 1942, Georgetown U., 1943; m. Nancy Reed, July 26, 1953; children—Harry, Hilary, Mary Ellen, John. Pres., dir. Airo-Jet Indsl. City, Miami, Fla., Kanko Devel. Corp., Miami; pres., treas., dir. B.M.R. Industries, Inc., Cin., Forest Park Realty Inc., Cin., Hilary Farms, Inc., Cin., Internat. Bancorp. Cin., Kanter Corp., Cin., Kanter Farms, Inc., Cin., Park Farms, Inc., Cin., Southwestern Leasing Corp. Cin., Kanter Corp. Mo., Keystone Financial Corp., Cin., Northland Constrn. Inc., Riddle Properties Inc., Cin.; limited partner Towne House, St. Louis; pres., treas., dir. Essex Devel., Inc., Indpls.; pres., dir. Housing Corp. Am., Cin.; chmn. bd. ITI Corp. (Am. stock exchange), N.Y.C.; v.p., dir. Forest Park, Inc. Cin.; pres., trustee Joseph H. Kanter Found., Cin.; stockholder Keystone Savs. Assn., Cin.; chmn. bd. First Builders Bancorp., San Francisco; spl. partner Oppenheimer & Co., N.Y.C. Finance chmn. for Fla., U.S. Com. for UN, 1958, for Ohio, 1959-60; mem. bus. leadership adv. council Office Econ. Opportunity, 1967. Past gen. chmn. Xmas Seal campaign Anti-Tb League, Cin.; nat. chmn. young leadership cabinet United Jewish Appeal, 1963-65; chmn. State Israel Bonds drive, Cin., 1966; chmn. Cin. com. Ohio Council Econ. Edn., 1966; nat. chmn. Israel Ednl. Fund of United Jewish Appeal, 1967-7O, leading gifts chmn. Jewish Welfare Fund Cin., 1967; nat. chmn., founder internat. young leadership cabinet United Jewish Appeal, 1967; hon. pres. Am. Friends of Tel Aviv U., 1968—. Bd. assos. Brandeis Univ.; bd. govs. Jewish Community Relations Com.; bd. dirs. Am. Jewish Com., Jewish Welfare Bd. Cin., Am. Com. for Weizmann Inst. Sci., Ohio Council Econ. Edn., Am. Friends of Hebrew U.; mem. exec. com. United Jewish Appeal, 1964-7O; mem. exec. com. State Israel Bonds, 1964- -; trustee United Israel Appeal, Inc.; chmn. Greater Miami Fedn. and United Jewish Appeal Campaign, 1970-71. Chmn. Nat. Coordinating Com. Hubert Humphrey, 1968. Served with AUS, World War II. Named one of fifty four outstanding bright young men in sci., politics, arts and bus. Esquire mag., 1958; recipient Leadership award United Jewish appeal, 1962, 63, Herbert Lehman award, 1965. Mem. Guardsmen (past bd. mem.), Am. Legion (past post comdr.), Young Pres. Orgn., Jewish War Vets., Ala. Soc., V.F.W. Mason (Shriner); mem. B'nai B'rith. Home: 6010 N Bay Rd Miami Beach FL 33140 also Dixie Dale Farm 1651 Waycross Rd Cincinnati OH 45240 Office: 690 Northland Rd Cincinnati OH 45240

KANTER, RICHARD S., musician; b. Chgo., July 7, 1935; s. Martin J. and Audrey M. (Kobb) K.; diploma Curtis Inst. Music; m. Janet Shagom, Dec. 15, 1969. With Lyric Opera of Chgo., Grant Park Symphony Orch. of Chgo.; mem. Chgo. Symphony Orch., 1961—. Served with USNR, 4 years. Home: 2743 N Pine Grove Chicago IL 60614 Office: 220 S Michigan Av Chicago IL 60604

KANTNER, ARTHUR HENRY, banker; b. N.Y.C., Sept. 4, 1918; s. Rudolph Julius and Anna (Westen) K.; diploma, N.Y. State A. and M. Inst., Farmingdale, 1938; B.S., Cornell U., 1949, M.S., 1950, Ph.D., 1952; m. Shelton Valeria Richardson, Dec. 15, 1944; children—Leslie Anne, Neil Arthur, Alyce Marie. Serviceman, Coop. Grange League Fedn., Bridgehampton, L.I., N.Y., 1938-42; research asst. Coll. Agr., Cornell U., 1949-52; jr. economist, economist, sr. economist Fed. Res.

Bank of Atlanta, 1952-62, asst. cashier, 1963-66, asst. v.p. New Orleans br., 1966-68, v.p. in charge, 1968—. Served to 1st lt. USAAF, World War II; PTO. Mem. Greater New Orleans C. of C.. Presbyn. (elder). Home: 81 Dove St New Orleans LA 70124 Office: 525 St Charles Av New Orleans LA 70160

KANTNER, JOHN F., educator; b. Somerset, Pa., July 17, 1920; s. Joseph M. and Ethel (McDonald) K.; A.B., Franklin & Marshall Coll., 1942; M.A., U. Mich., 1947, Ph.D., 1953; m. Jane Boose Kantner, June 6, 1943; children—Andrew, JoAnn, Christopher, Julia. Asst. prof. Coll. William and Mary, 1950-53; statistician U.S. Bur. Census, 1953-60; asso. Population Council N.Y., 1960-65; chmn. dept. sociology U. Western Ont., 1965-68; prof. dept. population dynamics Johns Hopkins U., 1968—. Served with AUS, 1943-45. Fellow Am. Sociol. Assn.; mem. Population Assn. Am., Internat. Union for Scientific Study of Population, Am. Statist. Assn. Home: 1306 Wine Spring Lane Towson MD 21204 Office: Sch Hygiene and Pub Health Johns Hopkins U Baltimore MD 21205

KANTOR, HARRY SIMKHA, retired govt. ofcl.; b. Russia, Nov. 3, 1903; s. David and Freda Susan (Grabois) K.; brought to U.S., 1904; B.A., Columbia, 1924, M.A., 1925, grad. study, 1927, 29, 31; m. Anne Golden, Oct. 17, 1936; children—Paul, Fred, Freda Susan. Mem. staff Dept. Agr., other govt. agencies, 1926-38; with Dept. Labor, 1938—, successively price analyst, economist, statistician, 1938- 55, asst. adminstr. wage and hour and pub. contracts div., 1955-58, analyst Office Research and Devel., Office Sec. Labor, 1958-64, analyst with Office of Policy Planning, 1964-69, cons. Office Sec., 1969—. Mem. U.S. delegation to negotiate current trade agreement Republic of Philippines, 1954; mem. Nat. Inventor's Council, Dept. of Labor. Recipient Distinguished Service award Dept. Labor for work in enactment first minimum wage law in P.I., 1951. Mem. Am. Econ. Assn., Am. Statis. Assn., Phi Beta Kappa. Home: 2806 Woodstock Av Silver Spring MD 20910

KANTOR, JACOB ROBERT, psychologist; b. Harrisburg, Pa., Aug. 8, 1888; s. Julius and Mary (Slocum) K.; Ph.B., U. Chgo., 1914, Ph.D., 1917; D.Sc. (hon.), Denison U., 1961; LL.D. (hon.), U. Akron, 1970; m. Helen Rich, Sept. 2, 1916 (dec.); 1 dau., Helene Juliette. Instr. philosophy and psychology U. Minn., 1915-17; instr. psychology U. Chgo., 1917-20; asst. prof. psychology Ind. U., 1920-21, asso. prof., 1921-23, prof., 1923-59, prof. emeritus, 1959—; research asso. U. Chgo., 1964- -; vis. prof. psychology N.Y.U., 1962-63, U. Md., 1963-64, U. Chgo., 1925, Ohio State U., 1928, 38; editor Principia Press, 1931—. Fellow A.A.A.S.; mem. Am. Philos. Assn., Am. Psychol. Assn., History Sci. Soc., Sigma Xi. Author books including: Psychology and Logic, Vol. I, 1945, vol. II, 1950; Problems of Physiological Psychology, 1947; The Logic of Modern Science, 1953; Interbehavioral Psychology, 1959; The Scientific Evolution of Psychology, Vol. I, 1963, Vol. II, 1968. Contbr. chpts. and articles to sci. publs. Address: 5743 S Kimbark Av Chicago IL 60637

KANTOR, LESTER JOEL, hosp. adminstr.; b. Chicopee, Mass., Feb. 13, 1909; s. Moses Daniel and Rose (Sisitsky) K.; M.D., D.P.H., U. Brussels, 1936; married Apr. 2, 1937; children—Diane Danielle (Mrs. Joseph Shrager), Judith J. (Mrs. Joseph Clark). Intern USPHS hosps., 1936-39, various assignments, 1939-51; chief staff, dir. profl. services VA hosps., Albuquerque, Kerrville, Tex., 1951-57, hosp. dir., Lebanon, Pa., 1957—. Diplomate Am. Bd. Preventive Medicine. Fellow Am. Coll. Preventive Medicine; mem. A.M.A., Am. Coll. Hosp. Adminstrs., Am. Hosp. Assn. Address: 135 Forest Av Hershey PA 17033

KANTOR, MACKINLAY, novelist; b. Webster City, Ia., Feb. 4, 1904; s. John Martin and Effie Rachel (McKinlay) K.; grad. Webster City High Sch., 1923; student high schs., Des Moines, Ia. and Chgo.; D. Litt., Grinnell Coll., 1957, Drake U. 1958, Lincoln (Ill.) Coll., 1959, Ripon Coll., 1961; LL.D., Ia. Wesleyan Coll., 1961; m. Florence Irene Layne, July 2, 1926; children—Carol Layne, Thomas MacKinlay. Reporter, Webster City Daily News, 1921-24; worked as advt., claim corr., Chgo., 1925-26; reporter Cedar Rapids (Ia.) Republican, also free lance writer, 1927; columnist Des Moines Tribune, 1930-31; scenario writer Paramount Prodns., Metro-Goldwyn-Mayer, 20th Century Fox, Samuel Goldwyn; mem. uniformed div. N.Y.C. Police Dept., 1948-50. Mem. Nat. Council Boy Scouts Am. Trustee Lincoln Coll., 1960-68, hon. trustee, 1968—; hon. cons. Am. letters Library of Congress, 1967—. War corr. ETO with Brit. and U.S. Air Forces, 1943, 45; war corr. Korean war, 1950; tech. cons. USAF, 1951-53; studied personnel, equipment, tng., operations at Mediterranean bases Italian and Royal Hellenic (Greece) air forces, 1963. Recipient Medal of Freedom. Fellow Soc. Am. Historians, Am. Soc. Psychical Research; mem. Nat. Assn. Civil War Musicians, Sons Union Vets., Military Order Loyal Legion (hereditary companion). Author: Diversey, 1928; El Goes South, 1930; The Jaybird, 1932; Long Remember, 1934; Turkey in the Straw (verse), 1935; The Voice of Bugle Ann, 1935; Arouse and Beware, 1936; The Romance of Rosy Ridge, 1937; The Noise of Their Wings, 1938; Here Lies Holly Springs, 1938; Valedictory, 1939; Cuba Libre, 1940; Gentle Annie, 1942; Angleworms on Toast (juvenile), 1942; Happy Land, 1943; Author's Choice, 1944; Glory for Me, 1945; But Look, The Morn, 1947; Midnight Lace, 1948; Wicked Water, 1949; The Good Family, 1949; Signal Thirty-two, 1950; Lee and Grant at Appomattox (juvenile), 1950; Don't Touch Me, 1951; Warwhoop, 1952; Gettysburg (juvenile), 1952; The Daughter of Bugle Ann, 1953; God and My Country, 1954; Andersonville (Pulitzer prize 1956) 1955; Lobo, 1957; The Work of St. Francis, 1958; If the South had won The Civil War, 1961; Spirit Lake, 1961; (with Gen. Curtis LeMay) Mission With LeMay: My Story, 1965; Story Teller, 1967; Beauty Beast, 1968; The Day I Met A Lion, 1968; Missouri Bittersweet, 1969; (with Tim Kantor) Hamilton County, 1970. Contbr. Sat. Eve. Post, Atlantic Monthly, other mags. Address: Sarasota FL 33581

KANTOR, MORRIS, artist, painter; b. Russia, Apr. 15, 1896; s. Benjamin and Rebecca (Margolin) K.; student Ind. Sch. of Art, N.Y.C.; m. Martha Ryther, Mar. 7, 1928. Exhibited, 1928—; at Brummer Gallery, Rehn Gallery (N.Y.C.), also in nat. shows in U.S., 1929—; one-man shows, 1930, 32, 35, 38, 40, 43, 45, 47, 49, 53; rep. permanent collections Met. Mus. Art, Modern Mus. Art, Whitney Mus. Am. Art, Art Inst. Chgo., Pa. Acad. Fine Arts, Phillips Meml. Gallery (Washington), other museums throughout U.S. Recipient 1st prize and Logan medal Art Inst. Chgo., 1931; 3d Clark prize Corcoran Gallery, 1939; Temple medal Phila. Acad., 1940; Purchase prize U. Ill., 1951. Address: 45 S Mountain Rd New York City NY 10956

KANTROWITZ, ADRIAN, surgeon, educator; b. N.Y.C., Oct. 4, 1918; s. Bernard Abraham and Rose (Esserman) K.; A.B., N.Y.U., 1940; M.D., L.I. Coll. Medicine, 1943; postgrad. physiology Western Res. U., 1950; m. Jean Rosensaft, Nov. 25, 1948; children—Niki, Lisa, Allen. Gen. rotating intern Jewish Hosp. Bklyn., 1944; asst. resident, then resident surgery Mt. Sinai Hosp., N.Y.C., 1947; asst. resident Montefiore Hosp., N.Y.C., 1948, asst. resident pathology, 1949, fellow cardiovascular research group, 1949, chief resident surgery, 1950, adj. surg. service, 1951-55; USPHS fellow cardiovascular research, dept. physiology Western Res. U., 1951-52, teaching fellow physiology, 1951-52; instr. surgery N.Y. Med. Coll., 1952-55; cons. surgeon Good Samaritan Hosp., Suffern, N.Y., 1954-55; asst. prof. surgery State U. N.Y. Coll. Medicine, 1955-56, asso. prof. surgery, 1957-64, prof., 1964-70; dir. cardiovascular surgery Maimonides Med. Center, Bklyn., 1955-64, dir. surgery, 1964-70; chmn. dept. surgery Sinai Hosp. Detroit, 1970—; prof. surgery Wayne State U. Sch. Medicine, 1970—; Served from 1st lt. to capt., M.C., AUS, 1944-46. Recipient H.L. Moses prize to Montefiore Alumnus for outstanding research accomplishment, 1949; 1st prize sci. exhibit Conv. N.Y. State Med. Soc., 1952; Gold Plate award Am. Acad. Achievement, 1966; Max Berg award for outstanding achievement in prolonging human life, 1966; Theodore and Susan B. Cummings humanitarian award Am. Coll. Cardiology, 1967. Diplomate Am. Bd. Surgery, Am. Bd. Thoracic Surgery. Fellow N.Y. Acad. Sci., A.C.S.; mem. Internat. Soc. Angiology, Am. Soc. Artificial Internal Organs (pres. 1968-69), N.Y. County Med. Soc., Harvey Soc., N.Y. Soc. Thoracic Surgery, N.Y. Soc. Cardiovascular Surgery, Am. Heart Assn., Am. Physiol. Soc., Am. Coll. Cardiology, Am. Coll. Chest Physicians, Bklyn. Thoracic Surgery Soc. (pres. 1967-68), Pan Am. Med. Assn., Soaring Soc. Am., Am. Ski Assn. Contbr. articles profl. jours. Pub. pioneer motion pictures taken inside living heart, 1950; contbr. to devel. pump- oxygenators for human heart surgey; pioneer devel. mech., artificial hearts; performed 1st permanent partial mech. heart surgery in humans, 1966; 1st use phase-shift intra-aortic balloon pump in patient in cardiogenic shock; 1st human heart transplant in U.S., Dec. 1967. Home: 70 Gollogly Rd Pontiac MI 48053 Office: 6767 W Outer Dr Detroit MI 48253

KANTROWITZ, ARTHUR, physicist; b. N.Y.C., Oct. 20, 1913; s. Bernard A. and Rose (Esserman) K.; B.S., Columbia, 1934, M.A., 1936, Ph.D., 1947; m. Rosalind Joseph, Sept. 12, 1943; children—Barbara Ann, Lore Ellen, Andrea Ruth. Physicist NACA, 1935-46; asso. prof., then prof. aero. engring. and engring. physics Cornell U., 1946-56; dir. Avco-Everett Research Lab., Everett, Mass., 1955—; v.p., dir. Avco Corp., 1956—; vis. lectr. Harvard, 1952; fellow Sch. Advanced Study, Mass. Inst. Tech., 1957, vis. inst. prof., 1957-58, 61-64; Fulbright and Guggenheim fellow Cambridge and Manchester univs., 1954. Trustee, mem. mech. engring. adv. com. U. Rochester; mem. adv. council dept. aero. engring. Princeton. Recipient Theodore Roosevelt Distinguished Service medal. Mem. Internat. Acad. Astronautics, Am. Acad. Arts and Scis., Am. Phys. Soc., Nat. Acad. Scis., Am. Assn. U. Profs., A.A.A.S. Contbr. articles profl. jours. Home: 25 Spring Valley Arlington MA 02174 Office: Avco-Everett Research Lab Everett MA 02149

KANTZER, KENNETH SEALER, clergyman, coll. dean; b. Detroit, Mar. 29, 1917; s. Edwin Frederick and Clara (Sealer) K.; A.B., Ashland Coll., 1938; M.A., Ohio State U., 1939; B.D., Faith Theol. Sem., 1942; S.T.M., 1943; postgrad. (Hopkins scholar) Harvard, 1944-46, Ph.D., 1950; postgrad. Goettingen U., Germany, 1954- 55, Basel U., Switzerland, 1955; m. Ruth Forbes, Sept. 21, 1939; children—Mary Ruth, Richard Forbes. Ordained to ministry Evang. Free Ch., 1948; instr. King's Coll., 1941-43, Gordon Div. Sch., 1944-46; pastor Pigeon Cove Community Ch., 1945-46; faculty Wheaton Coll., 1946- 63, Charles Deal Found. prof., 1954-63, chmn. dept. Bible and philosophy, 1950-59, chmn. div. Bibl. edn., 1957-63; dean Trinity Evang. Div. Sch., Bannockburn, Ill., 1963—, v.p. grad. studies, 1968—; prof. theol. Young Life Summer Inst., summers 1956-63; Griffith Thomas lectr., Dallas, 1957. Mem. bd. Evang. Alliance Mission, Wheaton, Ill. Mem. Evang. (book editor of Jour.), Am. theol. socs. Cons. editor His mag. Home: 1752 Spruce Highland Park, IL 60035. Office: Trinity Evang Div Sch Bannockburn Deerfield IL 60015

KAPEL, KLAUS OTTO, Danish diplomat; b. Gentofte, Denmark, Nov. 19, 1931; s. Otto and Esther (Bartholdy) K.; B.A., Lincoln Coll. Oxford, 1954, M.A., 1958; M.Sc., U. Copenhagen, 1961; m. Inge Baek, Mar. 3, 1962; 1 son, Christian. With Danish Fgn. Service, 1961—; sec. Royal Danish embassy, Peking, 1964-65, Ministry Fgn. Affairs, Copenhagen, 1966-68; assigned Office Prime Minister, Copenhagen, 1968-69; 1st sec. Royal Danish embassy, Washington, 1969—. Home: 34 Nordre Strandvej Elsinore 3000 Denmark Office: 3200 Whitehaven St NW Washington DC 20008

KAPELL, BERNARD LEONARD, mfg. co. exec.; b. N.Y.C., July 22, 1926; s. Harry and Edith (Wolfson) K.; A.B., Princeton, 1948; J.D., U. Mich., 1953; m. Lydia Ann Goodman, Aug. 26, 1950; children—Andrea, Jennifer, Lydia, William, Rachel. Tax mgr. Arthur Andersen & Co., N.Y.C., 1953-61; v.p. finance Transcontinental Investing Corp., N.Y.C., 1961-63; corp. controller taxes U.S. Industries, Inc., N.Y.C., 1964—; lectr. N.Y.U. Tax Siminars. Served with USNR, 1944-46. Mem. Internat. Tax Assn., Tax Execs. Inst., Sigma Xi. Club: Princeton (N.Y.C.). Home: 50 E 91st St New York City NY 10028 Office: 250 Park Av New York City NY 10017

KAPELNER, ALAN, novelist. Author: Lonely Boy Blues; All the Naked Heroes. Address: care George Braziller Inc 215 Park Av S New York City NY 10003*

KAPITZA, PETER LEONIDOVICH, Russian physicist; b. Kronshtadt, Russia, July 29, 1894; s. Leonid and Olga (Stebnitsckiy) K.; grad. Petrograd Polytechnic Inst., 1919; D.Ph., Cambridge U., 1923, fellow, 1923-24, fellow Trinity Coll., 1925-34; D.Sc. (hon.), Algiers U., 1944, Sorbonne (U. Paris), France, 1945; D.Ph. (hon.), Oslo U., 1946; Dr. Sc. hon. causa, Yagellonian U., Cracow, Poland, 1964, Technische U., Dresden, Germany, 1964, Karlova U., Czechoslovakia, 1965, Delhi U., 1966, Columbia, 1969; m. Nadezhda Tschernovsvitova (dec.); m. 2d, Anna Krylova; 2 sons. Lectr. Petrograd Polytechnic Inst., 1919-21; asst. dir. magnetism research Cavendish Lab., Cambridge, Eng., 1924-32; dir. Royal Soc. Mond Lab., 1930-34, Inst. Physical Problems, Acad. Scis., Moscow, 1934—; developer processes for liquifying helium, Decorated Order of Yugoslav Banner with ribbon; recipient State prize, 1941, 43, Order of Lenin, 1943, 44, 45, 64, 71, Hero Socialist Labour, 1945, Order Red Banner of Labour, 1954 (USSR); Faraday medal Inst. Elec. Engrs. (Eng.), 1942; medal Franklin Inst. (U.S.), 1944; diploma Royal Danish Acad., 1946; Sir Devaprasad Sarbadhikari gold medal (U. Calcutta), 1955; Kothenius Gold medal Acad. Leopoldina, 1959; Lomonosov Gold medal Acad. Sci. USSR, 1960; Great medal Exhbn. Econ. Achievements, USSR, 1962; medal for merits in sci. and to mankind Czechoslavak Acad. Sci., 1964; Nils Bohr gold medal Danish Engrs. Soc., 1964; Rutherford medal Inst. Physics and Phys. Soc., Eng., 1966; Golden Kamerlingh Onnes medal Netherlands Soc. Refrigeration, 1968; hon. fellow Trinity Coll., Eng., 1966. Fellow Brit. Royal Soc., Inst. Physics (Eng.), Nat. Acad. Sci. India (hon.); fgn. hon. mem. Am. Acad. Arts and Scis.; hon. mem. Inst. Metals (Eng.), Franklin Inst., N.Y. Acad. Sci. (U.S.A.), Royal Irish Acad.; mem. Nat. Acad. Sci. U.S., Acad. Scis. USSR, Deutsche Akademie der Naturforscher (hon.), Internat. Acad. Astronautics; fgn. mem. Royal Netherlands Acad. Scis., Royal Acad. Sci., Sweden, Polish Acad. Sci. Holder U.S. patent on turbine device for prodn. liquid air. Address: Inst Physical Problems Academy Scis Vorobyvskoe shosse 2 Moscow USSR

KAPLAN, ABBOTT, coll. pres.; b. N.Y.C., Jan. 12, 1912; s. Nahum and Leah (Beilowitz) K.; B.S., Columbia, 1933, M.A., 1934, Ph.D., 1942; B.J.P., Jewish Theol. Sem. Am., 1933; m. Beatrice Dresher, Nov. 1, 1936. Tchr., 1933-37; asst. prin. Chestnut St. Jr. High Sch., Springfield, Mass., 1937-38; prin. High Sch. Commerce, Springfield, 1938-39; dir. adult edn., guidance and placement pub. schs., Springfield, 1939-43; dir. for France, Am. Joint Distbn. Com., 1945-46; head extension services Inst. Indsl. Relations, U. Cal. at Los Angeles, 1946-49, asst. dir. Inst., 1950- 52, asso. dir. Inst., asst. dir. univ. extension, 1952-57, asso. prof., 1955-64, prof. edn., 1964-66, dir. univ. extension South area, 1960-66, asso. dean (statewide), 1960, prof. theater arts, asso. dean Coll. Fine Arts, 1966; pres. State U. N.Y. Coll. at Purchase, N.Y., 1967—. Founder, chmn. bd. Theatre Group Los Angeles, 1959-67; chmn. Cal. Arts Commn., 1964-66; vice chmn. Cal. Commn. Compensatory Edn., 1965-66. U.S. rep. UNESCO internat. meeting of experts, France, 1953; panel mem. Rockefeller Bros. Fund Study of Performing Arts Am., 1963; mem. State Cal. Commn. on Cultural Arts. Served as lt. comdr. USNR, 1943-45. Fulbright fellow, 1949-50. Mem. Adult Edn. Assn. U.S. (pres. 1960-61), Am. Acad. Arbitrators, Indsl. Relations Research Assn. Clubs: Century, Columbia Univ. (N.Y.C.). Author: Adventures in Growing Up, 1941; Socio-Economic Circumstances and Adult Participation in Educational Activities, 1943; Study Discussion in the Liberal Arts, 1960. Editor: The Cultural Arts in California, 1964. Home: Purchase St Purchase NY 10577

KAPLAN, ABRAHAM, conductor; b. Tel-Aviv, Israel, May 5, 1931; s. Shlomo and Sara (Elazar) K.; diploma Israel Acad. Music, Jerusalem, 1953, Juilliard Sch. Music, 1957; m. Davida Florence; children—David Elazzar, Dafna Judith. Condr., Kol Israel Chorus, 1953-54, 58-59, Haifa Oratorio Soc., 1958- 59; founder, 1960, since condr. Camerata Singers, N.Y.C.; dir. choral music Juilliard Sch. Music, 1961—; music dir. Collegiate Chorale, 1961—; condr. Henry Street Settlement Orch., 1963-68, Henry Street Settlement Chamber Orch., 1964—; music dir., condr. Symphonic Choral Soc. N.Y., Inc.; toured with Camerata Singers, 1968-69; guest condr. Kol Israel Orch., Israel Philharmonic, Goldman Band, Orch. da Camera, St. Louis Little Symphony, Orch. of Am.; regular appearances on CBS-TV; spl. guest on conducting faculty Berkshire Music Center, Tanglewood, summer 1963; vis. prof. music, dir. Choral Condrs. Forum, Boston U., summer 1965; faculty Sch. Sacred Music, Union Theol. Sem. Editor choral works pub. by Mercury Music Corp., Alexander Broude, Inc., Lawson & Gould Pubs., Mills Music. Home: 150 West End Av New York City NY 10023 Office: Symphonic Choral Society of NY 250 W 57th St New York City NY 10019

KAPLAN, ABRAHAM, educator; b. Odessa, Russia, June 11, 1918; s. Joseph and Chava (Lerner) K.; brought to U.S., 1923, naturalized, 1930; B.A., Coll. St. Thomas, 1937; student U. Chgo., 1937-40; Ph.D., U. Cal. at Los Angeles, 1942; D.H.L., U. Judaism, 1962; m. Iona Judith Wax, Nov. 17, 1939; children—Karen Eva (Mrs. Shlomo Diskin), Jessica Ariya. Instr., N.Y.U., 1944-45; asst. prof. U. Cal. at Los Angeles, 1946-49, asso. prof., 1949- 55, prof., 1955-63, chmn. philosophy dept., 1952-56; vis. prof. Harvard, 1953, 63, Columbia, 1955; prof. philosophy U. Mich., 1963—; cons. Rand Corp., 1952-64; mem. faculty Brandeis Inst., 1954-62, Hebrew Union Coll., Los Angeles, 1959-62; bd. editors Philosophy East and West, Honolulu, Inquiry, Oslo, Norway; dir. E.-W. Philosophers' Conf., vis. prof. U. of Hawaii, 1967—. Mem. nat. bd. Joint Distbn. Com. Mem. Nat. Hillel Commn. Fellow Center Advanced Study in Behavioral Scis., 1960-61, Center Advanced Studies, Wesleyan U., 1962- 63, Hudson Inst.; Guggenheim fellow, 1945-46, Rockefeller fellow, 1957- 58; vis. fellow Western Behavioral Scis. Inst., 1966. Mem. Am. Philos. Assn. (pres. Pacific div. 1957-58), Am. Soc. Aesthetics, Assn. Legal and Polit. Philosophy, Assn. Jewish Philosophy, Acad. Psychoanalysis, Nat. Tng. Labs. Author: (with H. D. Lasswell) Power and Society, 1950; The New World of Philosophy, 1962; American Ethics and Public Policy, 1963; The Conduct of Inquiry, 1964. Bd. editors Jour. Applied Behavioral Sci. Home: 1745 Westridge Rd Ann Arbor MI 48105

KAPLAN, ALICE MANHEIM, (Mrs. Jacob Merrill Kaplan), civic worker; b. Budapest, Hungary, Nov. 27, 1903; d. Armin and Theresa (Quittner) Manheim; came to U.S., 1905, naturalized, 1912; student Tchrs. Coll. Columbia, 1920-24, M.A. in History Art, 1966; D.F.A. (hon.), Cedar Crest Coll., Allentown, Pa., 1968; m. Jacob Merrill Kaplan, June 30, 1925; children—Joan (Mrs. C. Girard Davidson), Elizabeth Ann (Mrs. Gonzalo Fonseca), Richard David, Mary Ellen. Co-chmn. 50th anniversary exhbn. Army Show, 1963; mem. adv. council dept. art and archaeology Columbia, 1965—. Inst. Fine Arts, N.Y.U., 1965—; mem. creative arts awards commn. Brandeis U., 1964—; mem. adv. bd. Mus. Am. Folk Art, 1963; Mem. Fine Arts Commn. N.Y.C., 1969—. Trustee Am. Fedn. Arts, 1958—, pres., 1967—; trustee Mus. City N.Y.; trustee J.M. Kaplan Fund, 1944—, v.p., 1958—; bd. dirs. Henry St. Settlement, Friends of Whitney Mus.; council fellows Morgan Library; chmn. adv. com. Cooper-Hewitt Mus., Smithsonian Instn., 1968—. Ford Found. grantee, 1966. Mem. Municipal Arts Soc., Nat. Trust. Club: Women's City (N.Y.C.). Originator, chmn. film program Curriculum in Visual Edn., Am. Fedn. Arts, 1964. Home: 760 Park Av New York City NY 10021 Office: 41 E 65th St New York City NY 10021

KAPLAN, ARTHUR MARK, univ. adminstr., psychologist; b. Bronx, N.Y., Nov. 15, 1927; s. Max and Clara (Yegerman) K.; B.A., U. Me., 1949; M.A., Boston U., 1950; Ph.D., Cornell U., 1956; m. Doris Ray Flax, Mar. 21, 1953; children—Caren Jane, Mitchell David. Chief psychologist Augusta (Me.) State Hosp., 1950-53; instr. psychiatry and neurology Washington U. Sch. Medicine, St. Louis, 1955-58; dir. Eastern Me. Guidance Center, Bangor, also lectr. psychology U. Me. and mental health cons. to Bangor pub. schs., 1958-63; prof. psychol., head dept. U. Me., 1963-69, dir. South Campus, Bangor, Me., 1968-69, dean students, 1969—, v.p. student affairs, 1970—; cons. Peace Corps tng. programs at univ., summers 1962, 63. Mem. sch. com. Cerebral Palsy Sch., Bangor; chmn. Me. Bd. Examiners Psychols. Mem. Am., Me. (past pres.) psychol. assns., Soc. Research Child Devel., Sigma Xi. The Practice of Psychotherapy with Children. Home: 117 Forest Av Orono ME 04473

KAPLAN, BENJAMIN, legal educator; b. N.Y.C., Apr. 9, 1911; s. Morris and Mary (Berman) K.; A.B., Coll. City N.Y., 1929; LL.B., Columbia, 1933; A.M. (hon.), Harvard, 1948; m. Felicia Lamport, Apr. 16, 1942; children—James L., Nancy L. Admitted to N.Y. bar, 1934, Mass. bar 1950; asso., then mem. firm Greenbaum, Wolff & Ernst, N.Y.C., 1933-42, 46; vis. prof. law Harvard, 1947, prof. law, 1948—, Royall prof. law, 1961—. Reporter to adv. com. on civil rules Jud. Conf. U.S., 1960-66, mem., 1966—; co-reporter restatement (2d) of law judgements to Am. Law Inst., 1970—; mem. com. on law Yale U. Council, Panel Consultants on Gen. Revision Copyright Law. Served to lt. col. AUS, 1942-46; mem. Justice Jackson's staff Nuremberg Trial, 1945. Mem. Am. Law Inst., Assn. Bar City of N.Y., N.A.A.C.P. (bd. advisors Legal Def. and Ednl. Fund, Assn. Am. Indian Affairs (bd. dirs.), Phi Beta Kappa. Author: An Unhurried View of Copyright, 1967; co-author: Materials for a Basic Course in Civil Procedure, 2d edit., 1968; Cases on Copyright, 1960. Home: 2 Bond St Cambridge MA 02138

KAPLAN, BENJAMIN, educator; b. Rechicha, Minsk, Russia, May 10, 1906: s. Joseph and Pesha (Greenman) K.; B.A., Tulane U., 1928, M.A., 1929; student N.Y. Sch. Social Work, also N.Y. U., 1930, Colo. U., 1948; Ph.D., La. State U., 1952; m. Yetive Tatar, May 14, 1933; 1 dau., Barbara Kathleen. Supr., parish dir. La. Dept. Pub. Welfare, 1931-40; faculty U. Southwestern La., 1940—, prof. sociology, 1954-66, Frank A. Godchaux prof. sociology, 1966—. Dep. dir. personnel charge tng. Southeastern area A.R.C., 1942-45, chmn. Lafayette Parish chpt., 1946-47; participant White House Conf.

Children and Youth, 1960, White House Conf. Aging, 1961; mem. La. Adv. Com. Aging, 1962-64. Mem. exec. com. Evangeline Area council Boy Scouts Am., 1942-55, Bayou council Girl Scouts Am., 1946-56. Fellow Am. Sociol. Assn.; mem. Am. Assn. U. Profs., Theta Xi, Phi Epsilon Pi, Kappa Delta Pi, Phi Kappa Phi. Jewish religion (pres. congregation 1951-52). Rotarian; mem. B'nai B'rith. Author: The Eternal Stranger, A Study of The Small Jewish Community, 1957; Jews and Social Equality, 1963; The Jew and His Family, 1967. Home: 216 Stephens St Lafayette LA 70501

KAPLAN, EUGENE, physician; b. N.Y.C., Sept. 5, 1912; s. Phoebus and Jennie (Hartman) K.; B.A., Dartmouth, 1933; M.D., N.Y.U., 1937; m. Jane Markowitz, Sept. 1, 1938 (dec. Aug. 1962) children—Joseph, Nora, Nancy, Sally; m. 2d, Mildred Fine, Nov. 25, 1963; 1 son, Jonathan. Rotating intern Jewish Hosp., Bklyn., 1937-39; pediatric resident Children's Med. Center, Boston, 1939-42; tchr. pediatrics, also investigator N.Y.U., 1945-46, Wayne State U., 1946-54, La. State U., 1954-55; pediatrician-in-chief Sinai Hosp., Balt., 1962—; asso. prof. pediatrics Johns Hopkins Med. Sch., 1959—. Served with AUS, 1942-45. Mem. A.M.A., Pediatric Research Soc., Am. Pediatric Soc., Am. Acad. Pediatrics. Spl. research hematology in newborn. Home: Longacre Lane Stevenson MD 21153 Office: Sinai Hosp Belvedere Av Baltimore MD 21215

KAPLAN, FRED, educator; b. Bklyn., Sept. 2, 1934; s. Harry and Isabelle (Chernofsky) K.; B.A., N.Y. U., 1955; postgrad. Brandeis U., 1955-58; Ph.D., Yale, 1960; m. Phyllis Deen Rowe, Aug. 19, 1957; children—Harold Deen, Madeleine Marie. USPHS postdoctoral fellow Fed. Inst. Tech., Zurich, Switzerland, 1959-60; postdoctoral fellow Cal. Inst. Tech., Pasadena, 1960-61; instr., asst. prof., asso. prof., prof. chemistry U. Cin., 1961—. USPHS spl. fellow, 1968-69. Mem. Am. Chem. Soc., Chem. Soc. (London), Am. Assn. U. Profs., A.A.A.S., Am. Civil Liberties Union, Sigma Xi, Phi Lambda Upsilon. Democrat. Contbr. articles to profl. jours. Home: 140 Wentworth Av Cincinnati OH 45220

KAPLAN, HAROLD, fgn. service officer; b. Newark, July 29, 1918; s. Samuel and Celia (Greestein) K.; student U. Ill., 1936-38; B.A., U. Chgo., 1940, M.A. (fellow), 1941; m. Celia Scop, Nov. 19, 1938; children—Leslie, Roger Francis, Lionel Philip. Instr. U. Chgo., 1940-41; writer, editor OWI, 1942, with Psychol. Warfare br., North Africa, 1943-44, Paris, 1945; embassy press officer, 1945-47, chief information officer, 1952-57; acting chief information bur., UNESCO, 1947-50; information officer Marshall Plan, ECA-Mut. Security Adminstrn., France, 1950-52; policy officer European affairs U.S. Information Agy., 1957-59, dep. pub. affairs officer, Germany, 1959-62, director Berlin Task Force, 1962-63, pub. affairs counselor, Geneva, Switzerland, 1963-65, chief press relations, Saigon, S. Viet Nam, 1965-66; dep. asst. sec. state pub. affairs, 1966-68; U.S. spokesman, chief briefing officer U.S. delegation Vietnam Peace Talks in Paris, 1968—; Paris corr. Partisan Rev., 1947-50. Member Phi Beta Kappa. Author: The Plenipotentiaries, 1949; The Spirit and the Bride, 1952. Contbr. articles to periodicals, U.S. and France. Home: 250 Prospect St East Orange NJ 07017 Office: Bur Pub Affairs State Dept Washington DC 20525

KAPLAN, HAROLD MORRIS, physiologist, educator; b. Boston, Sept. 4, 1908; s. Max and Mollie (Smith) K.; A.B., Dartmouth, 1930; A,M. (Jeffries Wyman scholar), Harvard, 1931, Ph.D., 1933; m. Bernice Stone, June 1935; children—Elaine Beth, Joyce M., Lee Allan. Asst. instr. Harvard, 1933-34; prof. Middlesex Med. Sch., 1934-35, Middlesex Vet. Sch., 1945-47; writer Washington Inst. Medicine, 1946-49; asso. prof. U. Mass., 1947-48; prof. So. Ill. U., 1948—, now also chmn. dept. psysiology; Asso. editor, bd. dirs. Animal Care Panel, 1959, pres., 1966-67; chmn. editorial bd. Lab. Animal Scis., 1959—. Fellow A.A.A.S.; mem. Am. Soc. Zoology, Ill. Acad. Sci. (pres. 1968-69), Ill. Soc. Med. Research (dir. 1966—), Inst. Lab. Animal Resources (past adv. council), Am. Physiol. Soc., Electron Microscope Soc. Am., Midwest Soc. Electron Microscopists, Am. Soc. Ichtyologists and Herpetologists, Am. Assn. Lab. Animal Sci. (pres., exec. bd. 1969-70), Sigma Xi, Phi Kappa Phi, Phi Eta Sigma. Home: 106 N Almond St Carbondale IL 62901

KAPLAN, HENRY SEYMOUR, educator, radiologist; b. Chgo., Apr. 24, 1918; s. Nathan M. and Sarah (Brilliant) K.; B.S., U. Chgo., 1938; M.D., Rush Med. Coll., 1940; M.S. in Radiology, U. Minn., 1944; m. Leah Hope Lebeson, June 21, 1942; children—Ann Sharon, Paul Allen. Intern Michael Reese Hosp., Chgo., 1940- 41, resident radiation therapy and tumor clinic, 1941-42; tng. fellow Nat. Cancer Inst., 1943-44; instr. radiology Yale Med. Sch., 1944-45, asst. prof., 1945-47; radiologist Nat. Cancer Inst., 1947-48; prof. radiology, exec. chmn. dept. Sch. Medicine, Stanford, 1948—, dir. biophysics lab., 1957-64; mem. sci. adv. com. St. Jude's Children's Hosp., Memphis, 1970—. Mem. com. radiology NRC, 1950-56; gastrointestinal cancer com. Nat. Cancer Inst.; mem. panel path. effects radiation Nat. Acad. Sci.-NRC; adv. com. biology Oak Ridge Nat. Lab.; subcom. radiation carcinogenesis (chmn. 1957-58), commn. on research Internat. Union Against Cancer; nat. adv. cancer council Nat. Cancer Inst., USPHS, 1959-63; adviser cancer council Cal., 1959-62; nat. panel cons. on cancer U.S. Senate, 1970-71. Decorated Légion d'Honneur (France); Order of Merit (Italy); Shabbanou award (Iran); recipient Lila Motley Cancer Found. award; Atoms for Peace award, 1969; Modern Medicine award for distinguihed achievement, 1968; Lucy W. James award James Ewing Soc., 1971; R.R. de Villiers award Leukemia Soc., 1971; Commonwealth Fund fellow, vis. scientist NIH, 1954-55. Mem. Am. Soc. Exptl. Pathology, Assn. Univ. Radiologists (pres. 1954-55), Radiol. Soc. N.A., Am. Coll. Radiology (chmn. commn. on cancer, bd. chancellors 1970—), A.A.A.S., Soc. Exptl. Biology and Medicine, Radiation Research Soc. (pres. 1956-57), Western Soc. Clin. Research, Am. Assn. Cancer Research (bd. dirs. 1954-56, 64-67, pres. 1966-67), Am. Soc. Therapeutic Radiologists (pres. 1966- 67, chmn. bd. dirs. 1967-68), Internat. Club Therapeutic Radiologists, Am. Soc. Biol. Chemists, Am. Acad. Arts and Sci., Harvey Soc. N.Y. Author: Congenital Heart Disease: An Illustrated Diagnostic Approach (with S.J. Robinson), 1954, 2d edit. (with H. L. Abrams and S. J. Robinson), 1965; Angiocardiographic Interpretation in Congenital Heart Diseases (with H.L. Abrams), 1955; Hodgkins Disease, 1971. Editorial adv. bd. Cancer; editorial com. Ann. Rev. Nuclear Sci., 1966-70. Home: 631 Cabrillo Av Stanford CA 94305

KAPLAN, IRVING, physicist; b. N.Y.C., Dec. 1, 1912; s. Charles and Pauline (Nadell) K.; A.B., Columbia, 1933, Ph.D., 1937; m. Ruth Evelyn Stern, May 20, 1945; children—Paul, Paul, Daniel, Judith. Research chemist Michael Reese Hosp., Chgo., 1937-41; physicist div. war research S.A.M. Labs., Columbia, 1941-44, S.A.M. Labs., Carbide & Carbon Chem. Corp., 1941-46; sr. physicist Brookhaven Nat. Lab., 1946-57; Gordon McKay vis. lectr. nuclear engring. Harvard, 1956; vis. prof. nuclear engring. Mass. Inst. Tech., 1947, prof. nuclear engring., 1958—. Mem. adv. com. reactor physics AEC. Fellow Am. Nuclear Soc., Am. Acad. Arts and Scis.; mem. Am. Phys. Soc., Fedn. Am. Scientists. Author: Nuclear Physics, 1955. Home: 9 Essex Rd Belmont MA 02178 Office: Nuclear Engring Dept Mass Inst Tech Cambridge MA 02139

KAPLAN, IRVING M.J., steel co. exec.; b. Pitts., Sept. 5, 1919; s. Frank R.S. and Madeline (Roth) K.; grad. Shady Side Acad., 1937; B.A., Princeton, 1941; m. Joan Marie Meyerhoff, Nov. 10, 1955; children—William A., Thomas R., Fred M. Vice pres., sec., dir. Copperweld Steel Co., Pitts., 1954—. Republican ward committeeman 14th Ward, Pitts., 1964—; mem. exec. bd. Rep. Finance Com. Allegheny County, 1966—; Rep. state committeeman 43d Dist., 1966- -. Pres. Vocational Rehab. Center 1961-63, bd. dirs., 1955—; bd. dirs. Community Chest, Planned Parenthood Center Pitts., Tb League Pitts.; trustee Alumni Council Shady Side Acad., 1960-63; mem. men's adv. com. Home for Crippled Children, Health and Welfare Assn. Allegheny County, Citizens Assembly. Mem. Am. Iron and Steel Inst., Newcomen Soc., Am. Ordnance Assn., Am. Soc. Corporate Secs., Am. Soc. Metals, Pa. Soc. Commerce, Pitts. C. of C., Amen Corner. Jewish religion (trustee congregation). Mason. Clubs: Concordia, Standard, Harvard-Yale-Princeton. Home: 5469 Northumberland St Pittsburgh PA 15217 Office: Frick Bldg Pittsburgh PA 15219

KAPLAN, JARRIL FALIS, lawyer; b. Houston, Sept. 18, 1929; s. Ervin and Libby (Gandelson) K.; B.B.A., U. Tex., 1949; J.D., U. Ariz., 1953; m. Jeanette R. Gold, Mar. 29, 1953; children—Susan M., Robert L., David B. Admitted to Ariz. bar, 1953, since practiced in Phoenix; partner firm Moore, Romley, Kaplan, Robbins & Green, 1959—. Chmn., Phoenix Human Relations Commn., 1966-69; pres. Phoenix Jewish Fedn., 1969-70, Phoenix Jewish Family and Children's Service, 1962-64, Phoenix chpt. Am. Jewish Com., 1961-63; mem. Phoenix Solicitations Bd., 1964-66. Chmn. bd. regents Brophy Coll. Preparatory, 1966—. Mem. Am., Maricopa County bar assns., State Bar Ariz. (chmn. com. econs. practice 1968—), Am. Judicature Soc., Fedn. Ins. Counsel, Law Soc. Ariz. State U. (trustee), Ariz. Acad. Club: Lawyers, Kiva, Arizona (Phoenix). Home: 4514 Calle del Notre Phoenix AZ 85018 Office: Ariz Title Bldg Phoenix AZ 85003

KAPLAN, JEREMIAH, publisher, editor; b. N.Y.C., July 15, 1926; s. Samuel H. and Fannie (Brafman) K.; m. Charlotte R. Larsen, June 16, 1945; children—Ann Frances, Susanna Ruth, Margaret Jane, David Baruch. Vice pres. Free Press Glencoe, Inc. (Ill.), 1947-60, pres., 1960-64; editorial dir. gen. pub. div. Crowell-Collier Pub. Co., 1960-62, v.p., 1962-67, sr. v.p., 1967—; chmn. bd. Sci. Materials, Inc., 1962-63; v. p. Macmillan Co., 1960- 63, exec. v.p., 1963-65, pres., 1965—; exec. v.p. Crowell Collier and Macmillan, Inc., 1968—, dir., 1969—; professorial lectr. behavioral scis. Grad. Sch. Bus., U. Chgo., 1960-63. Trustee Telladega Coll., Stoneleigh-Burnham Sch., U. Rochester; nat. adv. council Hampshire Coll. Mem. Am. Sociol. Assn. Clubs: Quadrangle (Chgo.); Dutch Treat, Lotos (N.Y.C.). Home: Willow Walk Westport CT 06880 Office: 866 3d Av New York City NY 10022

KAPLAN, JOHN, legal educator; b. N.Y.C., July 9, 1929; s. Edward I. and Dorothy (Saron) K.; A.B. in Physics, Harvard, 1951, LL.B., 1954; m. Elizabeth Brown, Nov. 5, 1960. Admitted to N.Y., Cal. and D.C. bars; law clk. to U.S. Supreme Ct. Justice Tom C. Clark, 1954-55; spl. atty. Dept. Justice, 1957-58; asst. U.S. atty. No. Dist. Cal., 1958-61; asso. prof. law Northwestern U. Law Sch., 1962-64; vis. asso. prof. law U. Cal. at Berkeley Law Sch., 1964-65; prof. law Stanford Law Sch., 1965—. Author: (with Jon R. Waltz) The Trial of Jack Ruby, 1965; (with David Louisell and Jon R. Waltz) Cases and Materials on Evidence, 1968; (with David Louisell and Jon R. Waltz) Principles of Evidence and Proof, 1968; Marijuna—The New Prohibition, 1970. Office: Stanford Law Sch Stanford CA 94305

KAPLAN, JOSEPH, retired educator; b. Tapolcza, Hungary, Sept. 8, 1902; s. Henry and Rosa (Lowy) K.; brought to U.S., 1910; B.S., Johns Hopkins, 1924, A.M., 1926, Ph.D., 1927; D.Sc., U. Notre Dame, 1957, Carleton Coll., 1957; L.H.D., Hebrew Union Coll., Yeshiva U., 1958; L.H.D., U. Judaism; m. Katherine E. Feraud, June 24, 1933. Research fellow Princeton, 1927; asst. prof. physics U. Cal., 1928-35, asso. prof., 1935-40, prof., 1940-70, prof. emeritus, 1970—, chmn. dept. of physics and meteorology, 1938-44, dir. Inst. Geophysics, 1946-47; nat. Sigma Xi lectr., 1948-49, Vice pres. Internat. Geodesy and Geophysics, 1960- 63, pres., 1963-67; rep. com. space research Internat. Council Sci. Unions, 1958-67, also mem. exec. bd.; chmn. West Los Angeles Co-ordinating Council; mem. Commn. 22, Internat. Astron. Union; mem. Internat. Conf. Sci. Advancement New States, Weizmann Inst., Israel, 1960, also gov. Weizmann Inst.; chmn. U.S. Nat. Com. Internat. Geophys. Yr., 1953-63; chmn. panel geophys. research Sci. Adv. Bd., USAF, also chmn. sci. adv. group Office Aero-space Research, 1963-69. Past chmn. acad. council Am. Friends Hebrew U. Hon. mem. bd. govs. Hebrew U., Jerusalem; past bd. govs. Hebrew Union Coll.-Jewish Inst. Religion; past bd. dirs. Reiss-Davis Clinic Child Guidance; past mem. Cal. adminstrv. bd. Hebrew Union Coll.-Jewish Inst. Religion. With USAAF 1943-45. Decorated for exceptional civilian service War Dept., 1947, USAF, 1960, 69; recipient Achievement award Tau Delta Phi; Distinguished Service award Phi Delta Epsilon, 1956; Astronautics award Am. Rocket Soc., 1956; Fellowship award Inst. Aero. Scis.; recipient Hodgkins medal and award Smithsonian Instn., 1965. Fellow Am. Physical Soc., Am. Inst. Aeros. and Astronautics, Am. Geophys. Union (John A. Fleming award 1969); mem. Nat. Acad. Scis., Am. Astron. Soc., Am. Meteorol. Soc. (hon.), Tau Beta Pi, Tau Delta Phi, Scabbard and Blade. Republican. Jewish religion. Club: West Los Angeles Rotary (pres. 1938; hon.). Co-author: Physics and Medicine of the Upper Atmosphere, 1951; Across the Space Frontier, 1951; Great Men of Physics, 1969. Contbr. articles to Phys. Rev., other sci. publs. Discover lab. prodns. auroral spectrum, light of night sky. Home: 1565 Kelton Av Los Angeles CA 90024

KAPLAN, JOSEPH, artist; b. Minsk, Russia, Oct. 3, 1900; s. Samuel and Mary (Cohen) K.; student Nat. Acad. Design, N.Y.C.; m. Virginia Haber, Nov. 1928. Exhibited one-man shows major cities, U.S.; exhibited group shows major cities U.S.; represented collections Newark Museum, U. Ky., Butler Inst. Am. Art, Decatur Art Center; represented numerous pvt. collections. Recipient Adolph and Clara Obrig prize, 1967; Proctor prize, 1970. Mem. Audubon Artists, Artists Equity (dir. N.Y. chpt. 1960-63), Provincetown Art Assn. (trustee 1959-61, 69-71). Jewish religion. Address: 463 West St New York City NY 10014 also 638 Commercial St Provincetown MA 02657

KAPLAN, JUSTIN, author; b. N.Y.C., Sept. 5, 1925; s. Tobias D. and Anna (Rudman) K.; B.S., Harvard, 1944, postgrad., 1944-46; m. Anne F. Bernays, July 29, 1954; children—Susanna Bernays, Hester Margaret, Polly Anne. Free-lance editing, writing, N.Y.C., 1946-54; sr. editor Simon & Schuster, Inc., N.Y.C., 1954-59; lectr. English, Harvard, 1969. Recipient Pulitzer prize for biography, 1967, Nat. Book award in arts and letters 1967. Club: Tavern (Boston). Author: Mr. Clemens and Mark Twain, 1966. Editor: Dialogues of Plato, 1948; With Malice Toward Women, 1949; The Pocket Aristotle, 1956; The Gilded Age, 1964; Great Short Works of Mark Twain, 1967; Mark Twain, A Profile, 1967. Contbr. Atlantic Monthly, Harper's, N.Y. Times, Boston Globe. Home: 16 Francis Av Cambridge MA 02138

KAPLAN, LEON, lawyer; b. N.Y.C., Mar. 27, 1908; student U. Cal. at Los Angeles; A.B., U. So. Cal., 1930, LL.B., 1932. Admitted to Cal. bar, 1932; now partner firm Kaplan, Livingston, Goodwin, Berkowitz & Selvin, Beverly Hills, Cal. Mem. Am., Beverly Hills, Hollywood bar assns., State Bar Cal., Los Angeles Copyright Soc., Order of Coif. Address: 450 Roxbury Dr Beverly Hills CA 90210

KAPLAN, LOUIS, librarian; b. N.Y.C., Jan. 27, 1909; s. Barney and Fanny (Radin) K.; B.S., U. Chattanooga, 1930; B.L.S., U. Ill., 1937; Ph.D., Ohio State U., 1939; m. Esther L. Alk, Sept. 3, 1939. Instr. history U. Chattanooga, 1930-31; head reference dept. U. Wis. Library, 1937-45, asso. dir., 1946, dir., 1957-71, prof. Library Sch., 1971—. Mem. Assn. Research Libraries (chmn. Farmington plan com., dir.), A.L.A. (chmn. research planning com. Assn. Coll. and Reference Libraries 1951-53). Author: Research Materials in the Social Sciences, 1939; History of Reference Work in the United States, 1952; A Bibliography of American Autobiographies, 1961. Editor: A Reader in the Computer and Library Services, 1971. Home: 5725 Elder Pl Madison WI 53705

KAPLAN, MARVIN WILBUR, actor, writer; b. N.Y.C., Jan. 24, 1927; s. Isidore Edward and Ruth (Rothman) K.; student N.Y.U., 1943; A.B., Bklyn. Coll., 1947; postgrad. U. So. Cal., 1947-48, 58. Actor appearing in motion pictures and television; motion pictures include Adams Rib, Francis, It's a Mad, Mad World, The Great Race; television includes Alfred Prinzmetal in Meet Millie series, 1952-56, Choo Choo in Top Cat cartoon series, 1961, Marvin in Chgo. Teddy Bears series, 1971; writer segment for Bill Cosby Show, 1969, Mod Squad, 1970; writer sketches and parodies for AFTRA Fed. Credit Union annual shows; substitute tchr. Los Angeles high schs., 1958-66. Dir. Los Angeles AFTRA-SAG Fed. Credit Union, 1966—. Mem. AFTRA (dir. Los Angeles), Television Acad. Arts and Scis., Motion Picture Acad. Arts and Scis., Writers Guild Film Soc., Actors Equity (West Coast adv. bd.), Stage Soc., Theatre Rapport. Author: The Convention, 1968; Hairless, 1970. Office: Mishkin Agency 9255 Sunset Blvd Los Angeles CA 90069

KAPLAN, MELVIN HYMAN, medical educator; b. Malden, Mass., Dec. 23, 1920; s. Harry and Rena (Chernoff) K.; A.B., Harvard, 1942, M.D., 1952. Intern Boston City Hosp., 1952; research fellow medicine House of Good Samaritan, Boston, also asst. bacteriology and immunology Harvard Med. Sch., 1953, research asso. medicine, instr., also established investigator Am. Heart Assn., 1954-57, asso. bacteriology and immunology, 1957-58; practice medicine, specializing in rheumatology and clin. immunology, Cleve., 1958—; asst. prof. medicine Sch. Medicine Western Res. U., 1958-60, asso. prof., 1960-65, prof., 1965—; asso. physician Cleve. Met. Gen. Hosp., 1958-62, physician, 1962—. Cons. allergy and immunology study sect. USPHS, 1964- 69; asso. mem. com. streptococcal diseases Armed Forces Epidemiological Bd., 1956—; temp. adviser WHO Study Cardiomyopathies in Africa, 1965. Served with AUS, 1942-46. Recipient Research Career award USPHS, 1964. Mem. Am. Soc. Clin. Investigation, Am. Rheumatism Assn., Am. Assn. Immunologists, Central Soc. Clin. Research, Am. Soc. Microbiology, Soc. Exptl. Biology and Medicine, Am. Heart Assn. Asso. editor, Jour. Lab. and Clin. Medicine, 1963-68, Jour. Clin. and Exptl. Immunology, 1965-71. Contbr. articles profl. jours. Home: 13855 Superior Rd East Cleveland OH 44118 Office: 3395 Scranton Rd Cleveland 44109

KAPLAN, MILTON LEWIS, journalist; b. Mpls., May 8, 1920; s. Hyman David and Esther (Codden) K.; B.A., U. Minn., 1943; children by previous marriage—Judith (Mrs. Orlin Silverman), James; m. 2d, Doris Willens, May 26, 1949; children —Jeffrey, Andrew, Dan. Gen. assignment reporter, feature writer, asst. city editor Mpls. Tribune, 1943-48; feature writer I.N.S., 1948-49, fgn. corr., 1950-55, feature editor, 1955-58; editor Hearst Headline Service, 1958-68; chief Washington bur. Hearst Newspapers, 1963-66, nat. editor, 1966-68; exec. v.p. King Features Syndicate, 1968-69, pres., gen. mgr., 1969—. Clubs: Nat. Press (Washington); Overseas Press (N.Y.C.). Contbr. articles to mags. Home: 64 Edgecliff Terrace Yonkers NY 10705 Office: 235 E 45th St New York City NY 10017

KAPLAN, MORRIS, educator, ophthamologist; b. Minsk, Russia, Apr. 21, 1912; s. Joseph and Pesha (Greenman) K.; came to U.S., 1915, naturalized, 1917; B.S., Tulane U., 1931, M.D., 1935; certificate ophthalmology, U. Ill.; m. Saucil Kirschstein, Aug. 8, 1936; children—Phyllis (Mrs. David DeLoach), Vicki. Rotating intern St. Joseph's and Children's Hosp., Denver, 1935-36; pvt. practice, Denver, 1938—; mem. faculty U. Colo. Med. Sch., 1938—, asso. clin. prof. ophtalmology, 1957—; surg. dir. Colo. Eye Bank, 1955—; cons. to govt., 1950—; spl. assignment Care Medico, Algeria, 1963; research frozen tissue of eyes, San Salvador, 1965; research trachoma for Govt. Samoa, 1962. Pres. Gibraltar Savs. & Loan Assn., Denver, 1963- 65. Bd. dirs. Colo. Partners of the Alliance. Served to lt. col. M.C., USAAF, 1941-46; CBI; col. Res. Diplomate Am. Bd. Ophthalmology. Fellow A.M.A., A.C.S.; mem. Am., Colo. (pres. 1962-63), Pan-Am. ophthal. socs., Eye Bank Assn. Am. (pres. 1967-69, bd. dirs.), Am. Acad. Ophthalmology and Otolaryngology, Nat. Soc. Low Vision People (pres. 1967—), Phi Delta Epsilon. Democrat. Jewish religion. Editor Newsight mag., 1961-65. Home: 522 Monaco Blvd Denver CO 80220 Office: 3705 E Colfax Av Denver CO 80206

KAPLAN, MORRIS AARON, physician, educator; b. Bklyn., Apr. 5, 1907; s. David and Eva (Erenberg) K.; student Crane Jr. Coll. and Lewis Inst., 1924-27; B.S., U. Ill., 1929, M.S. (Sigma Xi prize for undergrad. research), 1931, M.D., 1932, grad. study, 1931-41, Nat. Naval Med. Sch., 1943-44; m. Celia S. Furlett, Dec. 27, 1931. Intern, Cook County Hosp., 1931—33; pvt. practice, specialist in allergy, Chicago, 1933—; instr. physiol. chemistry coll. medicine U. Ill., 1929-31, asst. medicine, 1933-37, instr., 1937-41, asso., 1941-46, clin. asso., 1946-50, lectr. allergy, dept. physiol. chemistry, 1933-50, cons. allergy, dept. pediatrics, 1946- 50, instr. post-grad. clin. allergy, 1946-50, attending physician allergy clinics Research and Ednl. Hosp., 1933-50, chief allergy clinics, 1946-50; asst. attending physician Michael Reese Hosp., 1946-52, attending physician allergy Mandel Clinic, 1946- 52, lectr. allergy Nurses Tng. Sch., 1946-52; instr. allergy post-grad. instrn. course Am. Coll. Allergists, 1948, 51, 53-58; dir. allergy research unit Chgo. Med. Sch. and Mt. Sinai Research Found., 1954—, also asso. prof. clin. medicine; research asso. prof. div. enzymology and exptl. hypersenitivity Chgo. Med. Sch., clin. prof. biochemistry, 1969—; clin. prof. biochemistry Grad. Sch., Chgo. Med. Sch., U. Health Scis., 1969—; attending physician Mount Sinai Hosp., 1953—, Weiss Meml. Hosp., 1955—; allergy cons. Chgo. Bd. Edn.; regional cons. allergy Nat. Jewish Home for Asthmatic Children. Denver, 1951—; staff mem. Franklin Blvd. Hosp., 1946—, Roosevelt Meml. Hosp., 1966—. cons. Asthmatic Children's Found. Pres., Ill. Found. for Asthma. Bd. dirs. Ill. Found. Asthma; bd. dirs. Chgo. chpt. Am. Found. for Allergic Diseases; mem. med. adv. bd. Asthmatic Children's Aid; bd. dirs. Allergy Found. Am. Served from lt. to lt. comdr. M.C., USNR, World War II; lt. comdr. M.C., Vol. Med. Unit 9-20, 1946—. Fellow Am. Coll. Allergists (past pres.; chmn. bd. dirs.), Am. Acad. Allergy, Internat. Assn. Allergy, Am. Med. Writers Assn., Am. Coll. Chest Physicians; Chgo. Inst. Medicine, mem. Am. Assn. Immunology, Assn. Am. Med. Coll., A.M.A., Soc. Exptl. Biology and Medicine, Am. Fedn. Clin. Research, Assn. Allergists Mycological Investigation, Chgo. Soc. Allergy (sec.-treas. 1947, pres. 1949, exec. com. 1949—), Ill. State (chmn. sect. allergy), Chgo. med. socs., A.A.A.S., N.Y. Acad. Sci., Internat. Corr. Soc. Allergy, Ill. Acad. Sci., Asthma and Allergy Fedn. Greater Chgo. (dir.). American, Chgo. assns. immunologists, Sigma Xi, Phi Delta Epsilon. Jewish religion. B'nai B'rith, Mason. Editorial bd. Annals of AllergV, 1948. Contbr. med. publs. Home: 3150 Lake Shore Dr Chicago IL 60657 Office: 111 N Wabash Av Chicago IL 60602

KAPLAN, MORTON A., educator; b. Phila., May 9, 1921; s. Lewis J. and Anthea (Ginsberg) K.; B.S., Temple U., 1943; Ph.D., Columbia, 1951; m. Azie Mortimer, 1967. Instr. Ohio State U., 1951-52; asst. prof. polit. sci. Haverford Coll., 1953-54; mem. staff Brookings Instn., Washington, 1954-55; asst. prof. polit. sci. U. Chgo., 1956-61, asso. prof., 1961-65, chmn. com. internat. relations, 1958—, prof. polit. sci., 1965—; research asso. Center of Internat. Studies, Princeton, 1958-61; vis. asso. prof. polit. sci. Yale, 1961-62; staff mem. Hudson Inst., 1961—; lectr. Command and Gen. staff Coll., 1965- 67, Fgn. Service Inst., 1967, Air War Coll., 1967-69, Nat. Def. Coll. Can., 1970—; Gabrielson Distinguished lectr. Boudoin Coll., 1968; Nulton Distinguished lectr. Goucher Coll., 1969; Pres. Cetra Music Corp., 1962—, Moraz Prodns., Inc., 1963—. Cons. Com. Econ. Devel., 1965, Braddock, Dunn and McDonald, 1969, 71. Served with AUS, 1943-46. Fellow Center Internat. Studies, Princeton, 1952-53, Center Advanced Study in Behavioral Scis., 1955-56; Carnegie fellow, 1959-60; fellow Fgn. Policy Research Inst., 1968—. Mem. A.A.A.S., Am. Soc. Internat. Law, Am., Internat. (v.p. standing com. on sociology internat. relations 1970—) polit. sci. assns., Inst. Strategic Studies London. Author: System and Process in International Politics, 1957; Some Problems in the Strategic Analysis of International Politics, 1959; The Communist Coup in Czechoslovakia, 1960; (with Nicholas de B. Kaztenbach) The Political Foundations of International Law, 1961; (with Reitzel and Coblenz) United States Foreign Policy, 1944-55, 1956; Macropolitics Essays on the Philosophy and Science of Politics, 1969; On Historical and Political Knowing: An Inquiry into Some Problems of Universal Law Freedom, 1971; Dissent and the State in Peace and War: An Essay on the Grounds of Public Morality, 1970. Editor: The Revolution in World Politics, 1962—; The New Approaches to International Politics, 1968; editor, contbg. author: Great Issues of International Politics; asso. editor Jour. Conflict Resolution, 1962—; mem. editorial bd. World Politics, 1961-71, ORBIS, 1968—. Home: 5446 S Ridgewood Ct Chicago IL 60615

KAPLAN, NATHAN ORAM, educator, biochemist; b. N.Y.C., June 25, 1917; s. Philip and Rebecca (Uttef) K.; A.B., U. Cal. at Los Angeles, 1939, Ph.D., 1943; m. Goldie Levine, Feb. 9, 1947; 1 son, Jerold Laurence. Research asso. Mass. Gen. Hosp., Boston, 1945-49; asst. prof. biochemistry U. Ill., 1949-50; asst. prof. biology Johns Hopkins, 1950-52, asso. prof., 1952-56, prof., 1956-57; prof. biochemistry, chmn. grad. dept. biochemistry Brandeis U., 1957-68; prof. chemistry U. Cal. at San Diego, 1968—; cons. Inst. Child Health and Devel. Recipient Sugar Research award, 1946, Eli Lilly award in biochemistry, 1952, travel award NSF, 1952; Guggenheim fellow, 1965. Mem. Am. Chem. Soc., Am. Soc. Biochemist, Nat. Acad. Scis., Am. Soc. Bacteriologists, A.A.A.S., Nat. Cancer Inst. (spl. cons.), Am. Assn. U. Profs., Am. Acad. Arts and Scis., Sigma Xi. Home: 8587 La Jolla Scenic Dr La Jolla CA 92037

KAPLAN, NATHANIEL R., lawyer; b. N.Y.C., Oct. 5, 1909; B.S., N.Y. U., 1930, J.D., 1932. Admitted to N.Y. State bar, 1933; mem. firm Tenzer, Greenblatt, Fallon and Kaplan, N.Y.C. Mem. N.Y. County Lawyers Assn., N.Y. State Bar Assn., Am. Judicature Soc. Office: Pfizer Bldg 235 E 42d St New York City NY*

KAPLAN, OSCAR JOEL, educator; b. N.Y.C., Oct. 21, 1915; s. Philip and Rebecca (Uttef) K.; A.B., U. Cal. at Los Angeles, 1937, M.A., 1938; Ph.D., U. Cal. at Berkeley, 1940; m. Rose Zankan. Dec. 28, 1942; children—Stephen Paul, Robert Malcolm, David T.A. Instr., then asso. prof. psychology So. br. U. Ida., 1941-46; asst. prof. psychology San Diego State Coll., 1946-49, prof., 1952—, chmn. dept. psychology, 1950-52, 63-66, dir. center for survey research; cons. geronotology USPHS, 1946-50; vis. prof. pub. health U. Cal. at Los Angeles, 1965-66; cons. clin. psychology VA, 1962—. Mem. planning com. 1st Nat. Conf. Aging, 1951; mem. Nat. Council on Aging, 1954—; mem. Gov.'s Adv. Com. on Aging, 1963-67. Fellow Social Sci. Research Council, 1951; travel fellow NSF, 1954. Mem. Am. Assn. Pub. Opinion Research (council Pacific chpt. 1963—), Am. Psychol. Assn. (pres. div. on maturity and old age 1954-55), Western Gerontological Soc. (pres. 1956-57), Gerontological Soc. (editor Newsletter 1954-60), A.A.A.S. (council Pacific div. 1958-59). Author: Mental Disorders in Later Life, 2d edit., 1956. Editorial bd. Jour. Gerontology, 1946-60, VOX MEDICA, 1960—, Geriatrics, 1970—; editor-in-chief The Gerontolgist, 1961-66; internat. bd. editors Gerontology and Geriatrics, Amsterdam, 1958—; editorial bd. Geriatrics, 1970—. Home: 5409 Hewlett St San Diego CA 92115

KAPLAN, SAMUEL, educator, mathematician; b. Detroit, Sept. 13, 1916; s. Isaac and Fanny (Steinberg) K.; student Wayne State U., 1933-35; B.S., U. Mich., 1937, M.S., 1938, Ph.D., 1942; m. Marjorie Lois Penniman, June 25, 1953; children—Katherine Margaret, David Tai. Postdoctoral student Princeton, 1946-47; mem. Inst. Advanced Study, Princeton, 1947-48, 56-57; asst. prof. math. Wayne State U., 1948-56, asso. prof., 1956-60, prof., 1960-61; prof. math. Purdue U., 1961—. Served with AUS, 1942-46. Mem. Am. Math. Soc., Am. Assn. Univ. Profs. Contbr. articles profl. jours. Home: 1014 Sunset Ct West Lafayette IN 47906 Office: Purdue Univ Lafayette IN 47907

KAPLAN, SHELDON, corp. exec.; b. 1927; B.S. in Mech. Engring., Mass. Inst. Tech., 1948; M.A. in Bus. Adminstrn., Harvard and Mass. Inst. Tech., 1949; married. Asst to pres. Hyman Michaels Co., 1949-59; exec. v.p. U.S. Ry. Equipment Co., 1959-65; company acquired by Evans Products Co., 1965; exec. v.p. U.S. Ry. Equipment Co. div. Evans Products Co., 1965—, v.p., gen. mgr. transp. equipment group, 1966, exec. v.p. indsl. products group, 1966—, also dir. Address: 1121 SW Salmon St Portland, OR 97205.*

KAPLAN, SHELDON, lawyer; b. Mpls., Feb. 16, 1915; s. Max Julius and Harriet (Wolfson) K.; B.A. Summa cum laude, U. Minn., 1935; LL.B., Columbia, 1939; m. Helene Bamberger, Dec. 7, 1941; children—Jay Michael, Mary Jo, Jean Burton, Jeffrey Lee. Admitted to N.Y. bar, 1940, Me. bar, 1946; practice in N.Y.C., 1940-42, Mpls., 1946—; mem. firm Lauterstein, Spiller, Bergerman & Dannett, N.Y.C., 1939-42; partner firm Maslon, Kaplan, Edelman, Borman, Brand & McNulty, Mpls., 1946—. Dir. Nat. Presto Industries, Inc., N.Am. Life & Casualty Co., Investment Corp. Am., Nat. Packaging Corp., Nat. Bldg. Centers, Inc., Century Metalcraft Corp. Served to capt., AUS, 1942-46. Mem. Minn. Bar Assn., Phi Beta Kappa. Home: Box 276C Rt 2 Excelsior MN 55331 Office: Maslon Kaplan Edelman Borman Brand & McNulty Builders Exchange Minneapolis MN 55402

KAPLAN, SHELDON Z., internat. lawyer; b. Boston, Nov. 15, 1911; s. Jacob and Lizzie (Strogoff) K.; grad. Boston Latin Sch., 1928; A.B., Yale, 1933; student Harvard Law Sch., 1933-34; B.A. in Jurisprudence, Oxford (Eng.) U., 1937, M.A. 1945; internat. law student U. Paris and L'Ecole Libre des Sciences Politques, 1945; Dr. honoris causa, Inca Garcilasoda la Vega U., Lima, Peru, 1970; m. Megan Vondersmith, May 8, 1947; children—Eldon, Deborah. Daniel, Philip, Rebecca, Abigail. Research asso. Elder, Whitman and Weyburn, Boston, 1937-40; admitted to Mass. bar, 1940, D.C. bar, 1957, also Supreme Court; law practice, Boston, 1940-42; asst. to legal adviser Dept. State, Washington, 1947- 49; staff cons. House Fgn. Affairs, Com., 1949-57; legal counsel to Govt. Guatemala in U.S., 1960-62; gen. counsel Latin Am. and C.Am. Sugar Council, 1963-65; counsel Central Bank Honduras, 1962-64; partner Dodd & Kaplan, Washington, 1957-58; counsel firm Martin & Burt, 1959-62, Wilkinson, Cragun & Barker, Washington, 1962-67. Mem. U.S. Spl. Mission to Costa Rica, 1949, El Salvador, 1950, Europe, 1951, 53, Pakistan, India, Thailand, Indochina, 1953, Latin Am., 1954, Uruguay, 1955, C.A., 1955, Guatemala, 1957, Europe, 1957; congl. adviser, mem. U.S. delegation to 10th Gen. Assembly of UN, 1955; del. Govt. Nicaragua 18th, 19th Sessions Internat. Sugar Council, London, 1964, 65. Mem. bd. Glaydin School, Leesburg, Va., 1965—. Served to capt. AUS, 1942-46; E.T.O. Decorated La Medaille de la Reconnaissance Francaise (France); Bronze Star, (U.S.); Orden Del Quetzal (Guatemala); Orden al Merito (Peru). Mem. Am., Inter-Am., D.C. (com. internat. law) bar assns., Brasenose Soc. (Oxford, Eng.), A.S.C.A.P., Am. Soc. Internat. Law, Washington Fgn. Law Soc. Jewish religion. Clubs: Sugar Lawyers, Nat. Steeplechase and Hunt Assn., Brit. Schs. and Universities, Yale (N.Y.C.); Cosmos, Yale, Army and Navy, Federal City (Washington). Author govt. pub. documents, reports on fgn. affairs. Contbr. legal and fgn. affairs jours. Composer popular songs. Home: 7810 Moorland Lane Bethesda MD 20014 Office: 1001 Connecticut Av NW Washington DC 20036

KAPLAN, SIDNEY JOSEPH, educator, sociologist; b. Malden, Mass., Feb. 1, 1924; s. Harry and Rena (Chernoff) K.; B.A. magna cum laude, Boston U., 1949, M.A., 1950; Ph.D., Wash. State U., 1953; m. Patricia Carter, Mar. 2, 1957 (div. 1968); children—Carter, Cydney Rena. From instr. to asso. prof. sociology U. Ky., 1953-62; prof. sociology, chmn. dept. sociology and anthropology U. Toledo, 1962-66, 69—, prof. sociology, 1962—, asso. dean Coll. Arts and Scis., 1962-68. Served with USAAF, 1946-47. Mem. Am. Sociol. Assn., Am. Assn. U. Profs., Ohio Valley Sociol. Soc. (V.P. 1964-65), Phi Beta Kappa. Home: 6632 Maplewood Av Sylvania OH 43560 Office: Univ Toledo Toledo OH 43606

KAPLAN, STEVEN MAX, steel co. exec.; b. Chgo., Apr. 20, 1942; s. Stanley M. and Corinne (McCoy) K.; B.A., U. Cal. at Los Angeles, 1965; A.M., Harvard, 1968; m. Ethel Rosenberg, July 1, 1965; 1 son, Stanley M. With M.S. Kaplan Co., Chgo., 1967—, treas., 1970—; instr. econs. Roosevelt U., Chgo., 1969—. Woodrow Wilson fellow, 1965-66. Mem. Phi Beta Kappa. Home: 5135 S Cornell Av Chicago IL 60615 Office: 69 W Washington St Chicago IL 60602

KAPLAN, WALTER FRANCIS, dept. store exec.; b. El Paso, Tex., July 29, 1900; s. Albert and Hannah (Kirske) K.; J.D., Golden Gate Coll., 1924; m. Margaret Jacob, Apr. 18, 1929; children—Margery (Mrs. Leon Myron Blum), Charles. Controller, Emporium Capwell Co., San Francisco, 1930-42, sec.-treas., 1942—; pres. San Francisco Downtown Parking Corp. Chmn. San Francisco Redevel. Agy., 1966—. Pres. Goodwill Industries San Francisco. Served to col. USAF, 1951-52. Mem. Retail Merchants Assn. (past pres.). Mason. Contbr. articles profl. jours. Home: 1875 Broadway San Francisco CA 94109

KAPLANSKY, IRVING, educator, mathematician; b. Toronto, Ont., Can., Mar. 22, 1917; s. Samuel and Anna (Zuckerman) K.; B.A., U. Toronto, 1938, M.A., 1939; Ph.D., Harvard, 1941; LL.D. (hon.), Queen's U. 1969; m. Rachelle Brenner, Mar. 16, 1951; children—Steven, Daniel, Lucille. Came to U.S., 1940, naturalized, 1955. Instr. math. Harvard, 1941-44; mem. faculty U. Chgo., 1945—, prof. math., 1956—, chmn. dept., 1962—, George Herbert Mead Distinguished Service prof. math., 1969—. Mem. exec. com. div. math. NRC, 1959-62. Mem. Nat. Acad. Scis. Author books, tech. papers. Home: 5825 S Dorchester Av Chicago IL 60637

KAPLON, MORTON F., coll. provost; b. Phila., Feb. 11, 1921; s. Myer and Ida (Abramson) K.; B.Sc., Lehigh U., 1941, M.S., 1947; Ph.D., U. Rochester, 1951; m. Anita Joanne Harle, June 16, 1946; children—Keith Victor, Bryna Myra, Andrea Joanne. Research asso. physics U. Rochester, 1951-52, mem. faculty, 1953- 71, prof. physics, 1960—, asso. dean Coll. Arts and Scis., 1963-64, chmn. dept. physics and astronomy, 1964-69; asso. provost City Coll. N.Y., 1971—; spl. research cosmic ray physics, fundamental particles, origin cosmic radiation, very high energy interactions, gamma ray astronomy. Served to 1st lt. USAAF, 1942- 46. NSF Sr. Postdoctoral fellow, 1959-60. Fellow Am. Phys. Soc.; mem. Italian Phys. Soc., Am. Geophys. Union, Am. Astrophys. Soc., A.A.A.S., Am. Assn. U. Profs., Sigma Xi. Contbr. profl. jours. Editor: Homage to Galileo, 1965. Home: 11 White Birch Dr Pomona NY 10970

KAPLOWITZ, PAUL, lawyer; b. Atlantic City, Apr. 22, 1906; s. Morris and Dora (Pollock) K.; LL.B., Am. U., 1928; m. Dora Berkman, Jan. 24, 1938; 1 son, Morris. Admitted to D.C. bar, 1935; asst. gen. counsel U.S. Tariff Commn., 1943-50, gen. counsel, 1950-64: adviser U.S. delegation 2d meeting UN Prep. Com. Internat. Conf. Trade and Employment, Geneva, Switzerland, 1947, meeting Contractive Parties to Gen. Agreement Tariffs and Trade, Torquay, Eng., 1951; tariff cons. ways and means com. U.S. Ho. of Reps., 1965; chmn. U.S. Tariff Commn., 1966-67. Jewish religion. Home: 5135 Linnean Av Washington DC 20008

KAPNER, ROBERT SIDNEY, chem. engr., educator; b. N.Y.C., Dec. 23, 1927; s. Irving and Dora (Rosenberg) K.; B. in Chem. Engring., Poly. Inst. Bklyn., 1950; M.Sc., U. Cin., 1952; D.Eng., Johns Hopkins, 1959; m. Leonore Elizabeth Ginsberg, Sept. 4, 1955; children—Richard Joseph, Kevin Lynn. Devel. engr. Gen. Foods Corp., 1952-53; research and devel. engr. Gen. Aniline & Film Corp., 1953-55; instr. McCoy Coll., Johns Hopkins, Balt., 1956-57; asso. prof. chem. engring. Rensselaer Poly. Inst., Troy, N.Y., 1959-68; prof., head dept. chem. engring. Cooper Union, 1968—; cons. chem. and metal div. Gen. Electric Corp., 1960-67, chem. devel. operation, 1965-67; cons. Gen. Motors Corp., 1967-69. Served with AUS, 1945-47; ETO. Mem. A.A.A.S., Am. Inst. Chem. Engrs., Am. Soc. Engring. Edn. Home: 8 Midvale Av West Caldwell NJ 07006 Office: Cooper Union 51 Astor Pl New York City NY 10003

KAPNICK, HARVEY E., Jr., accounting co. exec.; b. Palmyra, Mich., June 16 1925; s. Harvey E. and Beatrice (Bancroft) K.; student James Miliken U., 1942-44; B.S., Cleary Coll., 1947, D.Sc. in Bus. Adminstrn. (hon.), 1971; postgrad. U. Mich., 1947-48; m. Jean Bradshaw, Apr. 5, 1947 (dec. 1962); m. 2d. Mary Redus Johnson, Aug. 5, 1963; children—David Johnson, Richard Bradshaw, Scott Bancroft. Mem. staff, mgr. Arthur Andersen & Co., C.P.A.'s Chgo., 1948-56, partner, 1956-62, partner in charge, Cleve., 1962-70, chmn., chief exec., 1970—. Vice chmn. met. div. Boy Scouts Am., 1965-66; pres. Cuyahoga unit Am. Cancer Soc., 1968-69, chmn. Ill. crusade, 1972; asst. treas. Lake Erie Opera Theatre; vice pres. of Soc. for Crippled Children; mem. Ambassador's Com. Greater Cleve. Growth Bd., Lake Erie Opera Assn. Treas. Christ Ch. Found., 1965-70; trustee Cleve. Plan Citizens League Greater Cleve., Ravinia Festival Assn. Served to 2d lt. USAAF, 1943-46. C.P.A., Ill. Mem. Ill. Soc. C.P.A.'s, Assn. Ohio Commodores, U.S. (pvt. pension plans com.), Ill. (dir. 1970—) chambers commerce, Northwestern U. Assos., Am. Inst. Pub. Accountants, Nat. Assn. Accountants, Am. Accounting Assn., Bluecoats. Clubs: Shaker Heights Country (past pres.); (Cleveland); Mid-America (gov. 1971—), Chicago, University, Executives, Exmoor Country, Economic (Chgo.). Home: 100 Woodley Rd Winnetka IL 60093 Office: 69 Washington St Chicago IL 60602

KAPP, MARY EUGENIA, chemist, educator; b. Mt. Airy, N.C., Apr. 15, 1909; d. Eugene C. and Lillie (Sides) Kapp; B.A., U. N.C., 1930, Ph.D., 1938; M.A., Duke, 1931. Head sci. dept. Blackstone (Va.) Coll., 1931-34; head sci. dept. Averett Coll., Danville, Va., 1938-39; instr. chemistry Sophie Newcomb Coll., New Orleans, 1939-40; head chemistry dept. Richmond (Va.) Profl. Inst., 1940-42, prof., chmn. Sch. Sci., 1946-66; asst. chief chemist E.I. duPont de Nemours & Co., Richmond, 1942-46; chmn. chemistry dept. Va. Commonwealth U., Richmond, 1966—. Recipient Distinguished Service award Va. sect. Am. Chem. Soc., 1969. NSF Faculty fellow, 1959. Mem. Am. Chem. Soc. (chmn. Va. sect.), Va. Acad. Sci., Am. Assn. U. Women, Fan Dist. Assn., Sigma Xi. Author: Laboratory Manual for General Chemistry, 1947-60; Laboratory Manual for Survey of Chemistry, 1958-70. Home: 208 N Vine St Richmond VA 23220

KAPP, MAX ADOLPH, religious adminstr.; b. Herkimer, N.Y., Feb. 1, 1904; s. Adolph and Matilda (Wagner) K.; A.B., St. Lawrence U., 1926, B.D., 1928, D.D., 1943; M.S.T., Harvard, 1931; m. Dorothy Louise Filene, Sept. 26, 1932; children—Martin S., Christopher F. Ordained to ministry Universalist Ch.; minister Newtonville (Mass.) Universalist Ch., 1928-31, Fitchburg Universalist Ch., 1931-38, Rochester Universalist Ch., 1938-42; mem. faculty Theol. Sch. St. Lawrence U., 1942-65, dean, 1960-65; dir. overseas and interfaith relations Unitarian Univ. Assn., Boston, 1965-69: pres. N.Y. State Conv. Universalists, Gen. Sunday Sch. Assn.; v.p. Internat. Assn. for Religious Freedom; mem. adv. com. Inst. on Religion in Age of Sci. Mem. Phi Beta Kappa. Home: W Chap Rd Vineyard Haven MA 02568

KAPP, MILTON L., pub. utility exec.; b. 1900; ed. Tulsa U.; married. With Chandler Electric Co., 1918-21, Okla. Natural Gas Co., 1921-36; operations supt., v.p., dir. Mich. Pub. Service Co., 1936-39; with Interstate Powder Co., Dubuque, Ia., 1939—, exec. v.p., asst. sec., 1949-53, pres., 1953-66, chmn. bd., 1966—, also dir.; dir. Am. Trust & Savs. Bank, A.Y. McDonald Mfg. Co. Home: 1297 Dunleith Ct Dubuque IA 52001 Office: 1000 Main St Dubuque IA 52001

KAPP, RONALD ORMOND, educator; b. nr. Ann Arbor, Mich., Mar. 10, 1935; s. Ormond Emanuel and Anna Louise (Heller) K.; B.A., U. Mich., 1956, M.S., 1957, Ph.D., 1963; m. Phyllis Isabel Moreen, Jan. 30, 1960; children—Lisa, Marda, Sara. Instr., Alma (Mich.) Coll., 1957-60, asst. prof., 1960-64, asso. prof., 1964-69, prof., provost, 1969—. Mem. Gov.'s Com. on Natural Areas, 1971—. Fellow A.A.A.S.; mem. Ecol. Soc. Am., Mich. Acad. Sci. (dir.), Mich. Natural Areas Council, Phi Beta Kappa, Sigma Xi. Author: How to Know Pollen and Spores, 1969. Contbr. articles to profl. jours. Home: 6193 Winans Rd Alma MI 48801

KAPP, WILLIAM EDWARD, architect; b. Toledo, Aug. 20, 1891; s. John and Charlotte (Remmert) K.; spl. student architecture, U. Pa., 1912-14; m. Helen Ida Jochen, Sept. 23, 1916; children—Mary Louise (dec.), John William. Archtl. practice, Toledo, 1909-16, Detroit, 1919—; mem. firm Smith, Hinchman & Grylls, 1919- 41; pvt. practice, 1941—; designer important religious, ednl., commml. and indsl. bldgs. Detroit area. Bd. trustees Cranbrook Inst. Sci., 1945—. Served as lt., constrn. division U.S. A.C., 1917- 18; AEF. Registered architect, Mich., 1938, nat. registration, 1943. Fellow A.I.A. (pres. Detroit chpt. 1942-44); mem. Mich. Soc. Architects, Engring. Soc. Detroit, Detroit Hist. Soc., Detroit Astron. Soc., Cranbrook Inst. Sci., Am. Legion. Republican. Lutheran. Mason. Club: Players (pres. 1940). Home: 3250 Sherbourne Rd Detroit MI 48221 Office: Buhl Bldg Detroit MI 48226

KAPPAUF, ROBERT EDWIN, former railroad exec.; b. N.Y.C., Oct. 17, 1915; s. William Emil and Juliet T. (Bonnlander) K.; B.S., Columbia, 1936, M.S., 1937; m. Laura E. Garrigus, Nov. 23, 1940; children—Robert Laurance, David Garrigus, Donald Wayne. With Price Waterhouse & Co., C.P.A.'s, N.Y.C., 1937-54, Newark, 1954-56; asst. comptroller N.Y.C. R.R. Co., 1956-57, comptroller, 1957-68; asst. v.p. Penn Central, 1968-70; v.p., asst. to pres. Lehigh Valley R.R., 1969-70. C.P.A., N.Y., N.J. Mem. Am. Inst. C.P.A.'s, Nat. Assn. Accountants, Assn. Am. Railroads. Home: Laurel Lane Oakhurst Route 1 Center Valley PA 18034

KAPPAUF, WILLIAM EMIL, Jr., educator, psychologist; b. N.Y.C., Oct. 2, 1913; s. William Emil and Juliet Theodora (Bonnlander) K.; A.B., Columbia, 1934; M.A., Brown U., 1935; Ph.D., U. Rochester, 1937; m. Catharine Anne Hamilton, June 16, 1945; children—Barbara, Charles, Katharine, William. Instr. psychology U. Rochester, 1937-41; research projects under NDRC and OSRD, 1941-46; asso. prof. Princeton, 1946-51; prof. U. Ill., Champaign, 1951—; cons. Bell Telephone Labs.; cons., panel mem. Mil. Agys., NSF, NIH. Recipient Presidential certificate of merit, 1948. Mem. Am., Midwestern psychol. assns., Soc. Exptl. Psychologists (sec.-treas. 1967-70), Am. Assn. U. Profs., A.A.A.S., Phi Beta Kappa, Sigma Xi. Contbr. articles profl. jours. Home: 1401 Waverly Dr Champaign IL 61820

KAPPEL, FREDERICK RUSSELL, former bus. exec.; b. Albert Lea, Minn., Jan. 14, 1902; s. Fred Albert and Gertrude May (Towle) K.; B.S.E. U. Minn., 1924; LL.D., Lehigh U., 1958, Knox Coll., 1959, Ohio Wesleyan U., 1960, Columbia, 1962, Williams Coll., 1962, U. N.H., 1963, Mich. State U., 1963, Pace Coll., 1965, Butler U., 1966, Colgate U., 1967, Yale, 1967; D.C.L., Union Coll., 1959; D.Engring., Rensselaer Poly. Inst. 1961, U. Minn., 1966; m. Ruth Carolyn Ihm, June 18, 1927; children—Carolyn Elaine (Mrs. William N. Boak), Kathleen Marjorie (Mrs. Jerry Lee Rose). Ground man Northwestern Bell Tel. Co., Minn., 1924, various engring. positions with co. until 1933, area plant engr., Neb., S.D., 1934-36, plant operations supr., Omaha, 1937- 38, asst. v.p. operations, 1939-42, v.p. operations, dir. 1942- 48; asst. v.p. Am. Tel. & Tel. Co., 1949, v.p., 1949-53, pres., chief exec. officer, 1956-61, chmn. bd. chief exec. officer, 1961-67, chmn. exec. com., 1967-69; pres. Western Electric Co., 1954-56; chmn. bd. Internat. Paper Co., 1969-70; trustee Aerospace Corp.; dir. Standard Oil Co. (N.J.), 1967-70, Whirlpool Corp., Chase Manhattan Bank, Met. Life Ins. Co., Gen. Foods Corp., Internat. Paper Co. Bd. govs. U.S. Postal Service. Bd. dirs. Boys' Clubs Am.; trustee U. Minn. Found., Tax Found., Presbyn. Hosp. Gov.; bd. govs. A.R.C., 1961-67, chmn. nat. finance com., 1964-67; adv. bd. Salvation Army; bd. visitors U.S. Mil. Acad., 1967-69. Recipient Outstanding Achievement award U. Minn., 1954; Sat. Rev.'s Businessman of Year citation, 1962; Silver Quill award, 1963; Wm. Penn award, 1963; Presdl. Medal of Freedom, 1964; John Fritz medal, 1965; decorated Cross Comdr. of Postal award (France). Fellow I.E.E.E., mem. Com. Econ. Devel. (trustee), Bus. Council (chmn. 1963-64), U.S. C. of C., Am. Soc. Metals, Triangle, Tau Beta Pi, Eta Kappa Nu, Beta Gamma Sigma, Phi Sigma Phi. Presbyn. Mason (33). Clubs: University, Economic, Links (N.Y.C.); Blind Brook (Portchester, N.Y.); Siwanoy Country (Bronxville). Author: Vitality in a Business Enterprise, 1960; Business, Purpose and Performance, 1964. Home: 17 Hewitt Av Bronxville NY 10708 Office: 195 Broadway New York City NY 10007

KAPPEL, PHILIP, artist, author; b. Hartford, Conn., Feb. 10, 1901; s. Morris and Anna (Superior) K.; grad. Pratt Inst., 1924; A.F.D. (hon.), Trinity Coll., Hartford, 1966; m. Theresa M. Pentz, Apr. 3,

1935 (dec. Mar. 1962). Numerous sketches, etchings of scenes along N.E. coast, Mediterranean ports, North Africa, Near East, Far East, Haiti, W.I., coast of Venezuela, interior of Colombia; print in permanent collection Bibliothéque Nationale, Paris: etchings and prints appear in museums throughout U.S., including Met. Mus., U.S. Nat. Mus., Coll. W.I., Jamaica; rep. permanent collections Bklyn. Mus. Art, Carnegie Art Inst., others; artist for several indsl. orgns. Mem. Conn. Commn. Arts, 1966—. Recipient Bijur prize Bklyn. Soc. Etchers, 1926; prize Marblehead (Mass.) Art Assn., 1926; Purchase prize Asso. Am. Artists 1st Ann. Nat. Art Competition, 1946; Dr. Marvin F. Jones prize for best etching, 1947; Herman Wunderlich Meml. prize best work reflecting industry Soc. Am. Graphic Artists, 1952; others. Mem. Soc. Am. Etchers, Conn. Acad. Fine Arts, Washington Art Assn. (pres. Washington Depot), Salmagundi Club; asso. mem. N.A.D. Author, illustrator: Louisiana Gallery, 1950; Jamaica Gallery, 1961; New England Gallery, 1966; illustrator: Timothy Dexter Revisited (by John Marquand), 1960. Contbr. maritime art Yachting mag. Address: Church St Roxbury CT 06783

KAPPES, CHARLES WILLIAM, ins. co. exec., lawyer; b. Union Hill, N.J., July 5, 1912; s. Charles William and Erna (Braunston) K.; A.B., Princeton, 1933; postgrad. Am. Acad., Rome, 1934; LL.B., Yale, 1937; m. Nancy Jean Macfarlan, Nov. 29, 1941; children—Prudence (Mrs. Clark Taylor Montgomery), Leslie, Judith, Robert Addison. Admitted to N.J. bar, 1937, since practiced in Newark; asso., then partner Riker, Emerv & Danzig, 1939-50; asst. counsel Mut. Benefit Life Ins. Co., 1950, asso. counsel, 1951-60, counsel, 1960-64, v.p., counsel, 1964—. Pres. Youth Consultation Service, Newark, 1949-56, Newark Council Social Agys., 1954-55; chmn. Planning Bd., Ridgewood, 1955-63; pres. Hosp. and Health Council Newark and Vicinity, 1962; mem. Bd. Edn., Ridgewood, 1963-70, pres., 1967-70. Pres., bd. mgrs. State Home For Boys, Jamesburg, 1958; trustee N.J. Health Facilites Planning Council. Served to col. F.A., AUS, 1940-45; CBI. Decorated Bronze Star. Mem. Assn. Life Ins. Counsel (past pres.), Nat. Conf. Lawyers and Life Ins. Cos. Episcopalian. Home: 128 West End Av Ridgewood NJ 07450 Office: 520 Broad St Newark NJ 07101

KAPRELIAN, EDWARD K., mech. engr., physicist; b. Union Hill, N.J., June 20, 1913; s. Karnig and Haiganoosh (Tatarian) K.; M.E., Stevens Inst. Tech., 1934; student law, George Washington U., 1937-38, physics, 1943-44; m. Lucy Ainilian, Feb. 29, 1936; children—Charles E., Harold R., Helen L. (Mrs. Stuart Ward, Jr.). Patent examiner for U.S. Patent Office, 1936-42; physicist Bd. Econ. Warfare, 1942-45: patent adviser U.S. Army Signal Corps, 1945-46; chief photo br. Signal Corps Engring. Labs., Ft. Monmouth, 1946-52; dir. research and engring. Kalart Co., Plainville, Conn., 1952-55; pres. Kaprelian Research & Devel. Co., Simsbury, Conn., 1955-57; dep. dir. research U.S. Army Signal Research & Devel. Lab., Ft. Monmouth, 1957-62; tech. dir. U.S. Army Limited War Lab., Aberdeen Proving Ground, Md., 1962-67; v.p., tech. dir. Keuffel & Esser Co., 1967- -. Mem. NRC-Nat. Acad. Scis., 1957-66. Recipient Exceptional Civilian award U.S. Army, 1963. Registered profl. engr., N.J., Md. Fellow Soc. Photog. Scientists and Engrs. (past pres.): sr. mem. I.E.E.E.; mem. Am. Soc. M.E., Optical Soc. Am., Phys. Soc. (London, Eng.), Soc. Motion Picture and TV Engrs., Royal Photog. Soc. (Eng.), Patent Office Soc., N.Y. Patent Law Assn., Am. Ordnance Assn., Armed Forces Communications and Electronics Assn., A.A.A.S., Am. Mgmt. Assn., Armed Forces Mgmt. Assn., N.Y. Acad. Sci., Sigma Xi. Club: Chemists (N.Y.C.). Author, patentee in field. Home: Lowery Lane Mendham NJ 07945 Office: 20 Whippany Rd Morristown NJ 07960

KAPRIELIAN, ZOHRAB ARAKEL, educator; b. Aleppo, Syria, Sept. 23, 1923; s. Arakel and Vartouhi (Lusigian) K.; B.A., Am. U. in Beirut, Lebanon, 1942, M.A., 1943; Ph.D., U. Cal., Berkeley, 1954; Came to U.S., 1949, naturalized, 1961. Research fellow, instr. Cal. Inst. Tech., 1954-57; asst. prof. elec. engring. U. So. Cal., Los Angeles, 1957-58, asso. prof., 1958-62, chmn. elec. engring. dept., 1962-70, dir. Grad. Center for Engring. Scis., 1968—, dir. Seaver Solid State Scis. Center, 1968—, acting dean Sch. Engring., 1969-70, dean, 1970—, v.p. acad. planning and research, 1970—; mem. vis. com. Jet Propulsion Lab. Recipient Distinguished Faculty award U. So. Cal. Sch. Engring., 1965. Fellow I.E.E.E.; mem. Am. Phys. Soc., Sigma Xi, Tau Beta Pi, Eta Kappa Nu. Home: 2396 Roscomare Rd Los Angeles CA 90024

KAPROW, ALLAN, educator, artist; b. Atlantic City, Aug. 23, 1927; s. Barnet and Evelyn (Lecomowitz) K.; student painting Hans Hofmann Sch. Fine Arts, N.Y.C., 1947-48; B.A., N.Y.U., 1949, postgrad., 1949-50; M.A., Columbia, 1952; student music composition under John Cage, N.Y.C., 1957-59; m. Vaughan Peters, Mar. 24, 1955; children—Anton, Amy, Marisa. Instr. dept. fine arts Rutgers U., New Brunswick, N.J., 1953-56, asst. prof., 1956-61; lectr. aesthetics, dept. fine arts Pratt U., Bklyn., 1960-61; asso. prof. fine arts State U. N.Y. at Stony Brook, 1961-66, prof., 1966; now asso. dean Sch. Art, Cal. Inst. Arts, Valencia; dir. criticism, exptl. research Inst. Contemporary Art Boston, 1965-66; cons. Berkeley Pub. Sch. System, 1968-69; co-founder Hansa Gallery, N.Y.C., 1952, Reuben Gallery, N.Y.C., 1959; dir. Judson Gallery, N.Y.C., 1960, co-dir., 1961; composer music for Living Theatre, N.Y.C., 1960; one-man shows N.Y.C. area, Provincetown, Mass., 1953-57, Pasadena (Cal.) Art Mus., 1967; exhibited in group shows U.S. and Europe; creator Environments, Happenings, 1958—. Grantee Katherine White Found., 1951, Rutgers U. Research Fund, 1957, State U. N.Y. at Stony Brook, 1963, Office Fgn. Area Studies, State U. N.Y., 1965; recipient Copley Found. award, 1962; Guggenheim Found. fellow, 1967. Author numerous books, articles. Address: 270 Wigmore Dr Pasadena CA 91105

KAPSTEIN, ISRAEL J., educator; b. Fall River, Mass., Jan. 16, 1904; s. Bernard and Fanny (Silver) K.; A.B., Brown U., 1926, A.M., 1928, Ph.D., 1933; m. Stella Cohen, Dec. 23, 1928; children—Judith Deborah (Mrs. David J. Brodsky), Jonathan. Faculty Brown U., 1928—, beginning as instr. English dept., successively asst. prof., asso. prof., 1928-50, prof. English, 1950—. Trustee Miriam Hosp., Providence, Jewish Bd. of Edn., Providence, Providence Pub. Library; bd. dirs. Jewish Family and Children's Service R.I. Awarded Guggenheim, Sharpe fellowships. Smith-Mundt vis. prof. lit., U. Saigon, 1960-61. Mem. Modern Lang. Assn., Phi Beta Kappa. Home: 63 Dexterdale Rd Providence RI 02906

KARABAICH, NICK JOHN, hosp. adminstr.; b. Wilson, Pa., Dec. 6, 1919; s. Anthony and Mary (Vitkay) K.; R.N., Central Islip Sch. Nursing, 1943; B.S., N.Y. U., 1948; M.S. in Hosp. Adminstrn., 1953; m. Esther Ann Fee, June 17, 1944; children—Bryan, Anne. Asst. adminstr. Croton Manor, Croton-on-Hudson, 1948-49; adminstr. Prospect Heights Hosp., Bklyn., 1953-57; asso. hosp. cons. J.G. Steinle, Garden City, N.Y., 1957-59; adminstr. Boulevard Hosp., Long Island City, N.Y., 1959; asst. hosp. adminstr. Dept. Hosps., N.Y.C., 1960—, asst. adminstr. Met. Hosp., 1965—. Mem. Am. Coll. Hosp. Adminstrs., Am. Hosp. Assn., Hosp. Mgmt. Systems Soc. Author: Research Into Costs of Disposable Syringes, 1958; Survey of D.C. General Hospital, 1958. Home: 300 Knickerbocker Rd Tenafly, NJ 07670 Office: 1901 1st Av New York City NY 10029

KARABATSOS, GERASIMOS JOHN, educator, chemist; b. Chomatada, Greece, Apr. 17, 1932; s. John P. and Athena (Papadopoulou) K.; came to U.S., 1950, naturalized, 1963; B.A. magna cum laude, Adelphi Coll., 1954; M.A., Harvard, 1956, Ph.D., 1959; m. Marianna Marris, Dec. 16, 1956; children—Lelena, Yanna, Jason. Asst. prof. Mich. State U., East Lansing, 1959-63, asso. prof., 1963-65, prof. chemistry, 1966—; NSF sr. postdoctoral fellow U. Cal., Berkeley, 1965-66; Ford Found. vis. prof. San Marcos U., Peru, 1967. Sloan Found. fellow, 1962-66. Recipient Sigma Xi Jr. Research award, 1970, Am. Chem. Soc. award in petroleum chemistry, 1971. Mem. Greek Acad. of Athens (corr.), Am. Chem. Soc., Chem. Soc. London, Sigma Xi. Editor: Advances in Alicyclic Chemistry, 1966. Contbr. articles profl. jours. Home: 1623 Old Mill Rd East Lansing MI 48823

KARABERIS, CONSTANTINE ARTHUR, former naval officer, banker; b. Lewiston, Me., Aug. 4, 1912; s. Arthur Manthas and Malpo (Zartha) K.; B.S., U.S. Naval Acad., 1935; grad. U.S. Naval War Coll., 1951; m. Avis Estelle Moore, Mar. 6, 1946. Commd. ensign USN, 1935, advanced through grades to rear adm., 1963; naval aviator aboard U.S.S. Honolulu, Pearl Harbor, 1941; served in carriers U.S.S. Shamrock Bay, U.S.S. Wake Island, World War II; exec. officer Naval Air Sta., Alameda, Cal., 1951-53, chief staff officer to comdr. Fleet Air Wing Two, 1953-54; comdg. officer Air Transp. Squadron 23, Japan, Far East, 1954-56; with Bur. Aeros., Navy Dept., Wash., 1956-58; chief staff to comdr. Antisubmarine Def. Force, U.S. Atlantic Fleet, Norfolk, Va., 1958-60; comdr. U.S.S. Wasp, 1960-61; dep. asst. chief naval personnnel, 1961-63: comdr. Carrier Div. 15, 1963-64; mgr. Anti-Submarine Warfare Project Office, Navy Dept., Washington, 1964-67; comdr. Fleet Air, San Diego, 1967-69; ret., 1969; community relations officer So. Cal. First Nat. Bank, San Diego, 1969—. Decorated Bronze Star, Legion of Merit. Methodist. Home: 820 Armada Terrace San Diego CA 92106 Office: So Cal 1st Nat Bank San Diego CA 92101

KARAGHEUSIAN, CHARLES ARSHAG, rug mfg. exec.; b. Istanbul. Turkey, Aug. 1, 1903; s. Arshag and S. (Shabaz) K.; A.B., Williams Coll., 1925; student Law Harvard, 1925-26, Came to U.S., 1920, naturalized, 1925. With A. & M. Karagheusian, Inc., N.Y.C., 1926—, successively in purchasing dept., treas., dir., v.p., chmn. 1948—. Served as capt., Army Intelligence, 1942-45. Mem. Carpet Inst. (chmn., trustee), Delta Phi. Episcopalian. Clubs: Larchmont Shore, Williams, Nantucket Yacht. Home: 145 Central Park West New York City NY 10023 Office: 295 Fifth Av New York City NY 10017

KARAGHEUZOFF, THEODORE, city ofcl.; b. Bklyn., Mar. 2, 1935; s. Sarkis and Anne (Papasian) K.; B.C.E., Coll. City N.Y., 1955; traffic inst. certificate Northwestern U., 1956; LL.B., Bklyn. Sch. Law, 1961; m. Odette Mary Chambart, May 23, 1964; children—Patricia, Nicole, Steven, Christopher. Admitted to N.Y. State bar, 1961; traffic engr., asst. to dir. traffic signals N.Y.C. Traffic Dept., 1955-59, asst. dir. traffic signals, 1959-61, asst. to commr., 1961- 63, dep. commr., chief engr., 1963-68, traffic commr., 1968—. Asst. prof. N.Y. U. Center for Safety Edn.; cons. engr. traffic problems. Mem. nat. com. for Uniform Traffic Laws. Registered profl. engr., N.Y. Mem. Inst. Traffic Engr., Am. Soc. Municipal Engrs., Am. Soc. C.E., Queens County Bar Assn, Chi Epsilon. Home: 75-02 193d St Fresh Meadows NY 11366 Office: 28-11 Bridge Plaza North Long Island City NY 11101

KARAKASH, JOHN J., coll. dean; b. Istanbul, Turkey, June 14, 1914; s. Joachim Theodore and Irene (Georges) K.; student Robert Coll., Istanbul, 1932-35; B.S., Duke, 1937; M.S. (Moore fellow), U. Pa., 1938; D.Engring. (hon.), Lehigh U., 1971; m. Marjorie Rutherford, June 21, 1945; 1 son, John Thomas. Came to U.S., 1936, naturalized, 1948. Instr. U. Pa., 1938-40, project engr. Moore Sch. Elec. Engring., 1944- 46; research engr. Am. TV Labs., Chgo., 1940-42; edn. dir. 6th Service Command Signal Corps Radar Sch., Chgo., 1942-44; asst. prof. elec. engring. Lehigh U., 1946-50, asso. prof., 1950-55, prof., head dept., 1955—, Distinguished prof., 1962—, dean Coll. Engring., 1965—, project engr. UHF filters, 1950-54, project dir. active networks Signal Corps. 1954-60; cons. Bell Telephone Labs., Murray Hill, N.J., 1950-56. Recipient Alfred Nobel Robinson award for service to univ., 1948, Hillman award for distinguished service Lehigh, 1962, Outstanding Tchr. award, 1968; Pa. Profl. Engring. award for distinction, 1965. Registered profl. engr., Pa. Fellow I.E.E.E.; mem. Am. Soc. Engring. Edn., Engring. Council for Profl. Devel. (nat. accreditation com. for engring. 1970—), Franklin Inst., Pergamon Inst. (hon. adv. bd.), Phi Beta Kappa, Sigma Xi, Tau Beta Pi, Omicron Delta Kappa, Eta Kappa Nu, Iota Gamma Pi. Author: Transmission Line and Filter Networks, 1950; also articles. Home: 1732 Chelsea Av Bethlehem PA 18013

KARALES, JAMES HARRY, photo-journalist; b. Canton, O., July 15, 1930; s. Harry and Mary (Fisher) K.; B.F.A., Ohio U., 1955; m. Eleanor Ann Cecilia Francis, Sept. 28, 1957; children—Joseph Harry, Jams Demetrios. Asst. to W. Eugene Smith, 1955-58; free-lance, 1958-60; staff photographer Look mag., 1960- 71; one man exhbns. include Limelight Gallery, N.Y.C., 1958, Leitz Gallery, N.Y.C., 1965, Portland, Ore., 1959; rep. permanent collection Mus. Modern Art; important pictures include Rendville, O., 1956, Logging, 1958, Gheel, Belgium, 1961, Vietnam, 1964, 65, 66, Turning Point for the Church, Selma, Ala., 1965. Recipient award Pictures of year, 1965; Page One citation Newspaper Guild N.Y., 1966; 2d award 35th nat. competition Inst. Outdoor Advt.; certificate of merit Art Dirs. Club N.Y., 1966, 68, medal, 1969; 2d place award Overseas Press Club, 1970. Home: 217 Cleveland Dr Croton-on-Hudson NY 10520 Office: 488 Madison Av New York City NY 10022

KARANIKAS, ALEXANDER, educator; b. Manchester, N.H., Sept. 23, 1916; s. Stephen and Vaia (Olgas) K.; student U. N.H., 1934-36; A.B. cum laude, Harvard, 1939; M.A., Northwestern U., 1950, Ph.D. in English, 1953; m. Helen J. Karagianes, Jan. 2, 1949; children-Marianthe Vaia, Diana Christine, Cynthia Maria. With N.H. Writers Project, 1940-41; radio news commentator sta. WMUR, Manchester, 1946; grad. asst. Northwestern U., 1950-52; instr. Kendall Coll., Evanston, Ill., 1952-53, Northwestern U., 1953-54, 57-59; mem. faculty U. Ill. at Chgo. Circle Campus, 1954—, prof. English, 1966—; cons. in field. Publicity dir. N.H. Independent Voters, 1946; sec. Manchester Vets. Council, 1946. Democratic candidate for Congress, 1948. Served with USAAF, 1942-45. Mem. Modern Lang. Assn., Am. Assn. U. Profs., P.T.A., Soc. Study So. Lit., Friends of Lit., Phi Eta Sigma, Order Ahepa (dist. sec. 1946).. Mem. Greek Orthodox Ch. Club: Harvard (Chgo.). Author: When A Youth Gets Poetic, 1934; In Praise of Heroes, 1945; Tillers of a Myth: The Southern Agraians as Social and Literary Critics (Friends of Lit. award 1967), 1966; Elias Venezis (with Helen Karanikas), 1969. Home: 618 N Harvey Av Oak Park IL 60302 Office: Univ of Ill at Chicago Circle Chicago IL 60680

KARARA, HOUSSAM MAHMOUD, educator; b. Cairo, Egypt, Sept. 5, 1928; s. Mahmoud Mohammed and Amna Fahmy (El-Kashef) K.; B.S., Cairo U., 1949; Dr.Sc.techn., Swiss Fed. Inst. Tech., Zurich, 1956; m. Albertina Gulietta Panchetti, May 14, 1955; children—Anna Maria, Mervet. Came to U.S., 1957, naturalized, 1962. Engr., Ministry Pub. Works, Egypt, field engr. Idfina Dam constrn., 1949-51; field engr. on La Grande Dixence Dam constrn. La Grande Dixence Co., Sion, Switzerland, 1952; sci. collaborator Inst. Photogrammetry, Swiss Fed. Inst. Tech., 1955-56; asst. prof. U. Ill., Urbana, 1957-61, asso. prof., 1961-66, prof. civil engring., 1966—. Cons. photogrammetric engring. to industry and govtl. mapping agys., U.S., abroad. Mem. Am. Soc. Photogrammetry (dir., Talbert Abrams award 1959, 61, Presdl. Meritorious award 1966, 71), Am. Congress on Surveying and Mapping, Am. Soc. C.E. (Research prize 1963), Canadian Inst. Surveying, Brit., French, German, Italian, Japanese, Swiss socs. photogrammetry. Contbr. articles to profl. jours. Home: 1913 Moraine Rd Champaign IL 61820 Office: Dept Civil Engring U Ill Urbana IL 61801

KARAS, MILAN RICHARD, educator; b. Youngstown, O., Oct. 25, 1911; s. Nicholas and Catherine (Anderson) K.; B.A., Ohio Wesleyan U., 1937; M.A., Kent State U., 1942; Ph.D., Ohio State U., 1951; m. Mary Louise Howard, Sept. 16, 1943; 1 dau., Patricia Louise. Store mgr. B.F. Goodrich Co., Butler, Pa., 1937- 40, dist. sales promotion mgr., 1940-41; instr. marketing Ohio State U., 1946-48; asst. prof. U. Cin., 1948-52, asso. prof., 1952-55, prof., 1955- -, chmn. indsl. mgmt. dept., 1955-58, asso. dean Coll. Bus. Adminstrn., 1958-64, chmn. marketing dept., 1964—. Served with AUS, 1942-46. Mem. Am. Marketing Assn., Nat. Sales Exec. Council, Phi Beta Kappa, Beta Gamma Sigma (nat. sec.-treas. 1951-58, editor Exchange 1951-58, mem. nat. exec. com. 1958—). Home: 3603 Mound Way Cincinnati OH 45227

KARASAPAN, ERDINC, Turkish diplomat; b. Ankara, Turkey, June 8, 1930; s. Celal Tevfik and Fatma (Nevzat) K.; M.A., N.Y.U., 1959; m. Simru Uluman, Dec. 19, 1953; children—Mehmet Omer, Ceylan, and Atilla (twins). With Turkish Fgn. Ser., 1960—; 2d sec. Turkish embassy, Nicosia, Cyprus, 1961, Warsaw, Poland, 1962; 1st sec. Turkish embassy, Algeria, 1963-66; dir. tech. assistance sect. Ministry Fgn. Affairs, Ankara, 1966-68; 1st sec. Turkish embassy, Washington, 1968-70, counselor, 1970—. Served with Signal Corps. Turkish Army, 1955-57. Home: 5956 Wilson Blvd Arlington VA 22205 Office: 1606 23d St NW Washington DC 20008

KARASICK, JOSEPH, clergyman; b. Minsk, Russia, June 7, 1922; s. Jacob and Mary (Katzman) K.; came to U.S., 1923, naturalized, 1929; B.A., Yeshiva U., 1943; postgrad. McGill U., 1945-46; rabbi Isaac Elchanan Theol. Sem., 1945; m. Pepa Wakmann, Mar. 3, 1946; children—Bernice (Mrs. Benjamin Mandel), Mark Wakmann, George David. Rabbi, Spanish Portuguese Synagogue, Montreal, Que., Can., 1945-47; treas. Union Orthodox Jewish Congregations Am., 1962-64, pres., 1966—; chmn. Am. sect. World Jewish Congress, 1971—. Pres. Wakmann Co. Inc., N.Y.C.; 1956—. Bd. govs. World Jewish Congress; bd. dirs. Jewish Meml. Found., Yeshiva U., Nat. council Boy Scouts Am. Recipient Bernard Revel Meml. award, 1969; Orthodox Union Nat. award, 1965. Mem. Religious Zionists Am. (bd. dirs.), Nat. Torah Schs., Yeshiva Coll. Alumni Assn. (pres. 1964-66), Day Sch. Home: 451 West End Av New York City NY 10024 Office: 597 Fifth Av New York City NY 10017

KARASICK, RICHARD, investment adviser; b. N.Y.C., Mar. 20, 1929; s. Abraham S. and Dora (Rubin) K.; student Cornell U., 1948; B.S., N.Y.U., 1950; m. Helene C. Cohen, Aug. 11, 1957; children—Emily Jeanne, Elizabeth Amy. Partner A.S. Karasick & Co., N.Y.C. (now subsidiary McDonnell & Co., Inc.), 1953-59, exec. v.p., dir., 1959-69; v.p., dir. Peoples Planning Corp. Am., N.Y.C. (subsidiary McDonnell & Co., Inc.), 1958-69; officer, dir. Peoples Securities Corp., N.Y.C., 1955-65, pres., dir., 1965-69; v.p., dir. Goodkind & Co., Inc., mem. N.Y. Stock Exchange, N.Y.C., 1969-70; v.p. Model, Roland & Co., mems. N.Y. Stock Exchange, N.Y.C., 1970—. Served with AUS, 1951-53. Home: 25 New York Av White Plains NY 10606 Office: 711 Fifth Av New York City NY 10022

KARASIK, MONROE, lawyer; b. Bklyn., May 24, 1911; s. Louis and Tillie (Teplitz) K.; B.A., Dartmouth, 1931; LL.B., Bklyn. Law Sch., 1935; m. Joan Pascal, Sept. 7, 1944; children—David, Michael, Judy, Paul. Admitted to N.Y. bar, 1936, D.C. bar, 1947; pvt. practice, N.Y.C., 1936-38; with Dept. Justice, 1938-42, Office Alien Property Custodian, 1942, State Dept., 1945-50; partner firm Surrey, Karasik & Greene, and predecessors, 1950—. Counsel, bd. dirs. Day Care and Child Devel. Council Am., 1968- -; trustee Green Acres Sch., 1960-66, 68-70, pres., 1962-63. Served to 1st lt. AUS, 1943-45. Mem. Am., Fed. bar assns., N.Y. County Lawyers Assn., Bar Assn. D.C., Plowman and Fisherman. Democrat. Home: 9 W Lenox St Chevy Chase MD 20015 Office: 1156 15th St NW Washington DC 20005

KARBER, JAMES WINFIELD, pub. utility cons.; b. Elizabethtown, Ill., July 8, 1914; s. James F. and Myrtle (Tyer) K.; A.B., U. Ill., 1934, LL.B., 1936, J.D., 1968; m. Irma I. Cox, Aug. 15, 1935; 1 dau., Karen Sue (Mrs. Thomas Purvis). Admitted to Ill. bar, 1936; Ill. State's Atty. Gallatin County, Ill., 1936-40; practiced in Ridgeway and Shawneetown, Ill., 1936-61; pres. Gallatin County State Bank, 1947-53; chmn. Ill. Commerce Commn., Chgo., 1961-69; now pub. utility cons.; pres. Ill. Title Assn., 1946-47; owner, operator Gallatin County Abstract & Title Co., 1937-47. Mem. Ill. Ho. of Reps., 1947-50; Dem. State Central Committeeman, 1943-46. Mem. White-Gallatin- Edwards County Bar Assn., Nat. Assn. Regulatory Utility Commrs. (mem. exec. com. 1962-, pres. 1968), Midwest Assn. R.R. and Utilities Commrs. (pres. 1964-). Mason (32, Shriner). Home: PO Box 298 Ridgway IL 62979 Office: PO Box 298 Ridgway IL 62979

KARCH, GEORGE FREDERICK, banker; b. Barberton, O., May 1, 1907; s. Charles Matthew and Nina (Close) K.; student St. Lawrence U., 1924-26; LL.B., Cleve. Law Sch., 1930; grad. Rutgers U. Grad. Sch. Banking, 1940; LL.D., Cleveland Marshall Law Sch., Baldwin Wallace Coll.; m. Mary Sargent, Aug. 2, 1932; children—George Frederick, Sargent, Mary K. Wilson, Jane. With Cleve. Trust Co., 1926—, mem. officers exec. com., 1954—, exec. v.p., 1960-62, pres., 1962-66, chmn., pres., 1966-69, chmn. bd., 1969—, also dir.; mem. exec. com. Standard Brands, Inc.; pres. dir. Gund Realty Co. Oglebay Norton Co.; exec. com., dir. Reliance Electric Co.; dir. Cleve.-Tusc. Corp., Harbel Corp.; dir., mem. exec. com. Medusa Portland Cement Co., Warner & Swasey Co., Brush Berylium Co.; dir. Am. Greetings Corp., Fed. Res. Bank Cleve., White Motor Corp., N.Am. Rockwell Corp., Park- Ohio Industries, Inc., Firestone Tire & Rubber Co. Trustee Am. Greetings Found.; bd. dirs., treas. George Gund Found.; treas., trustee Health Hill Home for Convalescent Children; trustee Cleve. Clinic Found., Ednl. Research Council Am., Coll. of Wooster, Cleve. Clinic Ednl. Found., Medusa Found., Sherwick Found., Southwaite Found., Warner and Gwasey Found., Cleve. Soc. for Blind, Oglebay Norton Found.; treas. Council for High Blood Pressure, Salvation Army, Cleve. Devel. Found.; chmn. bd. trustees com. Cleve. Found.; mem. exec. com. University Circle; mem. adv. com. Cleve. Plan; bd. dirs. Greater Cleve. Growth Assn. Mem. Assn. Res. City Bankers, Citizens League, Council World Affairs, Am. Heart Soc., Cleve. C. of C., Beta Theta Pi. Presbyn. Clubs: Canterbury Golf; Union, 50 (Cleve.); Princeton (N.Y.); Pepper Pike; Clevelander. Home: 2720 Wicklow Rd Shaker Heights OH 44120 Office: 916 Euclid Av Cleveland OH 44115

KARCHER, JOHN CLARENCE, geophysicist; b. Dale, Ind., Apr. 15, 1894; s. Leo and Mary (Madlon) K.; B.S., U. Okla., 1916; Ph.D., U. Pa., 1920; m. Lydia Kilborn, Oct. 16, 1920 (div. June 1952);

children—Colleen M. (Mrs. David J. Stone), John Paul. Attached U.S. embassy, Paris, France, 1918; research analysis M-series x-ray spectra, physicist Bur. Standards, 1920-21, 22-23; devel. gauge for measurement pressure curves, powder chamber arty. pieces, 1920; developed reflection seismograph for oilfield exploration, 1920-30; div. engr. Western Electric Co., 1923-25; v.p. Geophys. Research Corp., 1925-30; pres. Geophys. Service, Inc., 1930-39, Coronado Exploration Corp., 1936-50, Coronado Corp., 1939-41, Comanche Corp., 1945-48; pres., dir. Concho Petroleum Corp., 1950—; dir. Rep. Nat. Bank. Past pres., dir. Mid-Continent Oil and Gas Assn. Trustee Tex. Research Found. Served with U.S. Army, 1917-18. Fellow A.A.A.S., Am. Phys. Soc.; mem. Dallas Council World Affairs (dir.), Ind. Petroleum Assn. (dir.), Soc. Exploration Geophysicists (past pres.), Am. Assn. Petroleum Geologists, Am. Inst. Mining and Metall. Engrs., Phi Beta Kappa, Sigma Xi, Sigma Tau Tau Beta Pi (hon.). Home: Melrose Hotel Dallas TX 75219 Office: Adolphus Tower Dallas TX 75201

KARCZMAR, ALEXANDER GEORGE, educator, pharmacologist; b. Warsaw, Poland, May 9, 1918; s. Stanislaus and Helena (Billauer) K.; came to U.S., 1940, naturalized, 1946; student J. Pilsudski U., Warsaw, 1934-39; M.A., Columbia, 1941, Ph.D., 1947; m. Marion Hope Allen, Jan. 18, 1946; children—Gregory Stanislaus, Christopher Anthony. Research asst. N.Y.U., 1942-44; research asso. Amherst Coll., 1944-45; teaching fellow Columbia, 1945-46; lectr. Charleston (S.C.) Coll., 1946; mem. faculty Georgetown U. Med. Center, 1948-54; asso. Sterling-Winthrop Research Inst., 1954-56; professorial lectr. Albany (N.Y.) Med. Coll., 1954-56; prof., chmn. dept. pharmacology and therapeutics Stritch Sch. Medicine, Loyola U., Chgo., 1956—; cons. Emerson Drug Co., 1952-54, Ill. Psychiat. Inst., 1960—; research cons. Hines VA Hosp., 1959—; prin. investigator grants USPHS, 1950—, also Ill. Psychiat. Tng. and Research Fund, 1956—; dir. tng. grant USPHS, 1960—; sr. co-dir. Inst. Mind, Drugs and Behavior, 1965—. Mem. Ill. Krebiozen Com., 1963—; mem. Internat. Brain Research Orgn. Symposium on Neuropharmacology, Warsaw, Poland, 1963, Symposium on Aggressive Behavior and Fedn. Am. Societies Exptl. Biology, 1968; chmn. Symposium on Central Cholinergic Transmission; mem. pharmacology study sect. A, NIH, 1968—. Guggenheim fellow Istituto Superiore di Sanita, 1968-69. Fellow A.A.A.S.; mem. Internat. Brain Research Orgn., Am. Soc. Pharmacology and Exptl. Therapeutics, Am. Soc. Zoologists, Am. Assn. Anatomists, N.Y. Acad. Scis., Soc. Exptl. Biology and Medicine, Am. Coll. Neuropsycho- pharmacology (charter, council), Sigma Xi. Co-author: Experimental Pharmacodynamics, 3d edit., 1964. Contbr. chpts. books. Editorial bd. Internat. Jour. Neuropharmacology, 1963—; editorial bd., sect. editor Internat. Ency. Pharmacology and Therapeutics; editorial bd. Exptl. Brain Research, 1968—. Home: 327 N Euclid Av Oak Park IL 60302 Office: PO Box 1336 Hines IL 60141

KARDELJ, EDWARD, mem. council Fed. Assembly Yugoslavia; ed. as tchr., also spl. studies in econs. and polit. sci.; married; 2 children. Active in polit. affairs from early years; imprisoned, 1930-32; lived abroad, 1934-37; an organizer Liberation Front in Slovenia and Ygoslavia, becoming mem. Nat. Army of Liberation, 1941; served as v.p., minister Constituent Assembly; vice premier, fgn. minister 1948-53; v.p. Federal Exec. Council, 1953- 63; pres. Fed. Assembly, 1963-67, now mem. council; pres. Commn. for Constl. Affairs, 1960-63. Head of Yugoslav delegation to Peace Conf., Paris, 1946, to U.N. Gen. Assembly, 1946, 1947-50. Sec. central com. Communist League Yugoslavia, 1948-66, mem. presidium of central com., 1966—; mem. exec. bur. of presidium League Communists of Yugoslavia, 1969—. Author publs. on polit. and social subjects. Address: Council of the Fedn Novi Beograd Yugoslavia

KARDINER, ABRAM, educator, psychiatrist; b. N.Y.C., Aug. 17, 1891; s. Isaac and Mildred (Wolff) K.; B.A., Coll. City N.Y., 1912; M.D., Cornell U., 1917; m. Ethel D. Rabinowitz, Dec. 3, 1948; 1 dau., Elin A. Apprenticeship with Freud, 1921-22; mem. faculty N.Y. Psychoanalytic Inst., 1922-44; instr. psychiatry Cornell U., 1923-29; asso. psychiatry Columbia, 1929-32, asso. dept. anthropology and sociology, 1939-52, asst. clin. prof. psychiatry, 1944- 49, clin. prof., 1949-55, dir. psychoanalytic clinic, 1955-61; research prof. psychiatry. Emory U., 1961—. Mem. Am. Psychiatric Assn., Am. Psychol. Assn., N.Y. Acad. Medicine. Author: The Individual and His Society, 1939; The Psychological Frontiers of Society (with others), 1945; The Mark of Appression (with L. Ovesey), 1951; Sex and Morality, 1954; They Studied Man (with Edward Preble), 1961: also numerous articles. Address: Emory Univ Atlanta GA 30322

KARDON, ROBERT, corp. exec.; b. Phila., Mar. 8, 1922; s. Morris and Sophie (Winkleman) K.; student U. Miami (Fla.), 1940-42, Shriveham Am. U., Swindon, Eng., 1945-46; m. Janet Stolker, Nov. 19, 1949; children—Roy, Nina, Ross. Chmn. bd. B.T. Babbitt Co., Inc., 1964-66; pres., dir. Pitts. Mortgage Corp., 1964—, Murphree Mortgage Co., Nashville, 1966—; pres., dir. Kardon Investment Co., 1945—; pres., dir. Peoples Bond & Mortgage Co., Phila., 1950—; pres., dir., v.p. United Container Co., Phila., 1938—. Mem. Merion Civic Park Assn. Served with AUS, 1942-46. Mem. Young Pres. Orgn. Clubs: Green Valley Country, Locust (Phila.). Home: 523 How Rd Merion Station PA 19066 Office: 1201 Chestnut St Philadelphia PA 19107

KARELSEN, FRANK EPHRAIM, lawyer; b. N.Y.C., Jan. 3, 1892; s. Frank E. and Emma (Williams) K.; student N.Y.U., 1912-15; m. Sophie Van Raalte, June 1917; children—June (Mrs. Wm. W. Goodman), Ellen (Mrs. Robert L. Solender), Frank Ephraim III. Admitted to N.Y. bar, 1915, partner Karelsen & Karelsen N.Y.C., 1919; now sr. partner Karelsen Karelson Lawrence & Nathan, N.Y.C. Past chmn. bd. State Bank of Long Beach; counsel Met. Ednl. TV Assn. Mem. N.Y. State com. White House Conf. on Edn., 1955; chmn. adv. com. human relations Bd. Edn., N.Y.C., 1943-45; commr. Community Mental Health Bd., N.Y.C. Dir., sec. Irvington House Cardiac Children; mem. bd. Henry Ittelson Center Child Research, Ramapo Anchorage Camp; past treas. nat. Sch. Volunteer Program, Inc.; hon. v.p. Jewish Bd. Guardians; mem. N.Y. State Com. White House Conf. Youth, 1960; hon. gov., past chmn. admissions com. Ethical Culture Schs.; past mem. Nat. Adv. Council Edn. Disadvantaged Children Under Title I. Del. Democrat Nat. Conv., 1964. Asso. trustee N.Y.U. Med. Center Bd. Served as lt. (j.g.) anti-submarine service, USN, World War 1. Decorated Navy cross. Mem. Bar Assn. City N.Y., Am., N.Y. State bar assns., N.Y. County Lawyers Assn., Ams. for Dem. Action (nat. bd.), Am. Jewish Com. (nat. exec. com., exec. com. N.Y. chpt., hon. chmn.), All Day Neighborhood Schools (hon. pres.), Child Study Assn. Am. (v.p.), Pub. Edn. Assn. (hon. v.p., past chmn. exec. com.). Clubs: City, Harmonie, National Democratic (N.Y.C.). Author: Human Relations, A Challenge to Our Public Schools, 1947; A Layman Looks at Academic Freedom, 1949; also articles. Home: 1130 Park Av New York City NY 10028 Office: 230 Park Av New York City NY 10017

KARFF, SAMUEL EGAL, rabbi; b. Phila., Sept. 19, 1931; s. Louis and Reba (Margalith) K.; Hebrew tchr. certificate, Gratz Coll. Jewish Studies, 1949; A.B., Harvard, 1952; M.H.L., Hebrew Union Coll.-Jewish Inst. Religion, 1956, D.H.L., 1961; m. Joan Gabrielle Mag, June 29, 1959; children—Rachael, Amy, Elizabeth. Ordained rabbi, 1956; asst. rabbi Congregation Beth Israel, Hartford, Conn., 1958-60; rabbi Temple Beth El, Flint, Mich., 1960-62, Chgo. Sinai Congregation, 1962—; Lectr. Jewish thought and Am. culture U. Chgo., 1969—. Exec. bd. Chgo. Conf. Religion and Race. Served as chaplain USAF, 1956-58. Mem. Central Conf. Am. Rabbis (editorial bd. jour.), Assn. Jewish Chaplains, Acad. Religion and Mental Health, Alumni Assn. Hebrew Union Coll.-Jewish Inst. Religion (pres. 1970-71). Home: 5490 South Shore Dr Chicago IL 60615 Office: 5350 South Shore Dr Chicago IL 60615

KARGER, DELMAR WILLIAM educator; b. Cape Girardeau, Mo., May 9, 1913; s. Ernest J. and Clara M. (Hellewege) K.; student S.E. Mo. State Coll., 1931-32; B.S. in Elec. Engring., Valparaiso U., 1935; M.S. in Gen. Engring., U. Pitts., 1947; m. Paula E. Miller, July 5, 1935 (dec. Nov. 1958); children—Bonnie E., Karen R., Joyce P.; m. 2d, Edith Kennedy Loring, Jan. 11, 1962 (dec. Aug. 1969); m. 3d, Ruth Lounsberry Rivard, Oct. 31, 1970. Insp., surveyor C.E., U.S. Army, 1935; asst. chief electrician Internat. Harvester Co., 1935-41, asst. plant engr., 1941-42; head mfg. engr. Westinghouse Electric Corp., 1942-45, mgr. coop. edn., 1945-47; plant mgr. Pa. Electric Coil Corp., Pitts., 1947-48; mgr. orgn. systems and procedures RCA, 1948-50; chief indsl. engr. RCA Service Corp., 1950- 51; mgmt. cons. Booz, Allen & Hamilton, N.Y.C., 1951; chief plant and indsl. engr. Magnavox Co., 1951-56, mgr. new products devel., 1956- 59; prof. mgmt. Rensselaer Poly. Inst., Troy, N.Y., 1959—, chmn. dept. mgmt. engring., 1959-68, dean Sch. Mgmt., 1963-70, Ford Found. prof. mgmt., 1970—. Dir. Fiber Glass Industries, Inc., Amsterdam, N.Y., Wellington Tech. Industries, Englewood, N.J., Golub, Corp., Schenectady, Wellington Computer Graphics, Inc., Englewood; ind. mgmt. cons. Mem. finance com., bd. dirs. N.Y. div. Am. Cancer Soc. Registered profl. engr. Fellow Am. Inst. Indsl. Engrs. (past nat. v.p., dir. inter-soc. affairs), Soc. Advancement Mgmt., A.A.A.S.; mem. Am. Statis. Assn., Eastern Acad. Mgmt., Methods Time Measurement Assn. Standards and Research (pres. 1958-60), Am. Inst. Plant Engrs., Am. Soc. Engring. Edn., Council Internat. Progress Mgmt. (past bd. dirs.), Am. Assn. U. Profs., Inst. Mgmt. Scis., Internat. U. Contact Mgmt. Edn. Presbyn. Mason. Clubs: Lake Placid (N.Y.); DeFuniak Springs Country (Fla.); Santa Rosa (Fla.) Golf and Beach. Author: (with F. Bayha) Engineered Work Measurement, rev. edit., 1966; The New Product, 1960: La Mesure Rationelle du Travail, 1962; (with R.G. Murdick) Managing Engineering and Research, rev. edit., 1969; (with A.B. Jack) Problems of Small Business in Developing and Exploiting New Products, 1963; (with R.G. Murdick) New Product Venture Management, 1972. Contbr. numerous articles profl. jours. Home: 5 Whitman Ct Troy NY 12180

KARHOHS, FRED ERNEST, army officer; b. Silesia, Germany, Dec. 22, 1923; s. Ernest Henry and Magdelene (Immig) K.; brought to U.S., 1926, naturalized, 1932; B.S., Omaha U., 1959; M.A., George Washington U., 1964; grad. Advanced Mgmt. Program, Harvard, 1968; m. JoAnn VanWagoner, Sept. 9, 1950; children—Jeffrey Wayne, James Vernon. Enlisted in U.S. Army, 1944, commd. 2d lt., 1945, advanced through grades to maj. gen., 1971; assigned Europe, 1944-45, Korea, 1953; battalion and brigade comdg. officer, Vietnam, 1966-67; adj. 24th Mechanized Dic., 1968-69; dep. dir. plans ODCSOPS, Dept. Army, 1969-70; dir. Vietnam Task Force, Office Asst. Sec. Def., 1970—, Decorated Silver Star with oak leaf cluster, Legion of Merit, D.F.C. with 2 oak leaf clusters, Bronze Star with 2 oak leaf clusters, Air medal with 22 oak leaf clusters, Army Commendation medal with 4 oak leaf clusters. Home: 4141 N 27th St Arlington VA 22207 Office: Director Vietnam Task Force Office Asst Sec Defense Washington DC 20301

KARIEL, HENRY S., educator, author; b. Plauen, Germany, July 7, 1924; B.A., U. Wash., 1948; M.A., Stanford, 1950; Ph.D., U. Cal. at Berkeley, 1954: m. Sheila Madden, June 16, 1950; children—David, Rachel. Mem. faculty Harvard, 1955-58, Bennington Coll., 1958-64, U. Hawaii, 1964—. Served with AUS, 1943-46. Grantee Rockefeller Found., 1954-55, Huber Found., 1962-63, Volker Found., 1958-59. Mem. Am. Polit. Sci. Assn., Am. Soc. Legal and Polit. Philosophy, Caucus for a New Polit. Sci., Phi Beta Kappa. Author: The Decline of American Pluralism, 1961; In Search of Authority, 1964; Sources in Twentieth Century Political Thought, 1964; The Promise of Politics, 1966; Open Systems, 1969; The Politcal Order, 1970; Frontiers of Democratic Theory, 1970; also articles. Home: 3811 Tantalus Dr Honolulu HI 96822

KARIM, MUHAMMAD ENAYET, Pakistan diplomat; b. Dacca, Pakistan, Aug. 31, 1927; s. Muhammad and Syedun Nesa (Ali) Yasin; B.A., U. Dacca, 1949, M.A., 1949; m. Hosneara, Sept. 20, 1950; children—Luna Karim, Shahla Karim. Lectr. econs. U. Dacca, 1950-52; joined Pakistan Fgn. Service, 1952; 3d sec. U.K. and India, 1955-59; 2d sec., Iran, 1960-63; 1st sec., Burma and India, 1964-66; counsellor, India, 1966-67; dir. Fgn. Office, Islamabad, 1967-69; counselor, minister Embassy of Pakistan, Washington, 1970—. Decorated Tamgha-e-Pakistan. Home: 2822 Arizona Terrace NW Washington DC 20016 Office: Embassy of Pakistan 2315 Massachusetts Av NW Washington DC 20008

KARINEN, ARTHUR ELI, educator; b. Comptche, Cal., Feb. 25, 1919; s. Eli and Anna (Koskelo) K.; A.B., U. Cal. at Berkeley, 1944, M.A. in Geography, 1948; Ph.D. in Geography, U. Md., 1958; m. Florence Irene Wickstrom, Apr. 12, 1946; children—Sandra Jean (Mrs. Charles Robert McCormick), Nancy Ruth, Patricia Anna (Mrs. Alan Stanley Hightman), Judith Riike. Cartographer, OSS, 1942-43; instr. Ohio State U., 1946-47; asst. prof. geography U. Md., 1948-59; prof., chmn. dept. geography Chico (Cal.) State Coll., 1959—; Fulbright lectr. U. Oulu (Finland), 1970. Mem. Assn. Am. Geographers, Am. Congress Surveying and Mapping, Am. Geog. Soc., Cal. Council Geog. Edn. (pres. 1965-66). Presbyn. Author: (with others) California: Land of Contrast, 2d edit., 1970. Home: 834 Arbutus Av Chico CA 95926

KARINSKA, BARBARA, costume designer; b. Kharkov, Russia, Oct. 1886; d. Andrei Zhmoudsky; m. 2d, Karinsky. Editor socialist paper, H Kharkov; owner embroidery and dress show, Moscow; exhibited paintings in group shows, Moscow; costume maker, Paris, 1932, U.S., 1938; costume designer Bourée Fantasque, N.Y. City Ballet Co., 1949, The Nutcracker, 1954, Liebeslider Walzer, 1960, Valses et Variations, 1961, Midsummer Night's Dream, 1962, Western Symphony, 1968; also made costumes for prodns. Met. Opera Co.; costumer for films Lady in the Dark, 1944, Gaslight, 1944, Frenchman's Creek, 1944, Kismet, 1944, Kitty, 1945. Recipient (with Dorothy Jeakins) Oscar for costumes Joan of Arc, Acad. Motion Picture Arts and Scis., 1948. Address: 20 W 57th St New York City NY 10021*

KARJALAINEN, AHTI KALLE SAMULI, prime minister Finland; b. Hirvensalmi, Finland, Feb. 10, 1923; s. Anshelm and Anna (Viherlehto) K.; Ph.D. in Econs. Helsinki U., 1959; m. Pälvi Helinä Koskinen, May 17, 1947; children—Kerkko, Kimmo, Kukka- Maaria, Tero. Sec. to prime minister, 1950-56; minister of finance, 1957-58, of trade and industry, 1959-61, of fgn. affairs, 1961-62; prime minister, 1962-63, 70—; bd. govs. Bank of Finland, 1958—; minister of fgn. affairs, 1964-70; mem. Parliament, 1966—; chmn. Econ. Council, 1962-66. Chmn. bd. adminstrn. Rauter-uukki Steelworks, 1960—. Decorated grand cross Order White Rose, comdr. Order Lion, Medal of Liberty 2d class (Finland); great golden decoration and ribbon Order Merit (Austria); grand cross Order St. Olav (Norway), grand cross Order Republic (Tunis); grand cross Order Aztec Eagle (Mexico); grand officer Order Poland Restored; grand cross Order Pius; 1st class Order Republic (UAR); 1st class Order People's Republic (Bulgaria); grand cross Order North star (Sweden); grand cross Order Independence (Tunisia); grand cross Order Crown (Belgium); grand cross Order Icelandic Falcon; grand cross Most Distinguished Order St. Michael and St. George; Order Banner Hungarian People's Republic 1st class; Order White Lion 1st class (Czechoslovakia); Tudor Vladimirescu 1st class (Rumania). Author: A National Economy Based on Wood 53, The Relation of Central Banking to Fiscal Policy in Finland in 1811-1953, 1959. Home: 13 Perustie Helsinki Finland Office: Valtioneuvosto Helsinki 17 Finland

KARK, ALLAN EUGENE, educator, surgeon; b. Bethal, Transvaal, S. Africa, Aug. 16, 1921; s. Robert Julius and Sara (Hirschowitz) K.; B.Sc., U. Witwatersand (S. Africa), 1940, M.B., B Ch., 1944; m. Sharon Freda Phillips, Oct. 28, 1954; children—Vanessa Ann, Eden Paul Andre. Came to U.S., 1961, naturalized 1967. Intern Royal Berkshire Hosp., 1945-46; resident Royal No. Hosp., 1947, St. Paul's Hosp. Genito Urinary Disease, 1948, Hillingdon County Hosp., 1948, Ealing Gen. Hosp., 1949-50; grad. research work Chgo., 1951-52 U. London (Eng.) Postgrad Sch. Medicine, 1953-54; chmn. dept. surgery U. Natal, Durban, S. Africa, 1954-60, Mt. Sinai Sch. Medicine, N.Y.C., 1961—. Fellow Royal, Am. colls. surgeons. Home: 152 E 82d St New York City NY 10028

KARK, ROBERT M., educator, physician; b. Cape Town, Union S. Africa, Aug. 29, 1911; s. Ezekiel and Rebeccah (Kark) K.; B.A., U. Cape Town, 1931; M.R.C.S., L.R.C.P., Guy's Hosp. Med. Sch., London, Eng., 1935; m. Julia Rieck, Aug. 21, 1935; children—Pieter, John, Elizabeth. Came to U.S., 1938, naturalized, 1948. House physician Guy's Hosp., 1935-36; registrar, demonstrator pathology Guy's Hosp. Med. Sch., 1937-38; Adrian Stokes fellow Thorndike lab. Boston City Hosp., 1938, Rockefeller fellow, 1939; research fellow Harvard Med. Sch. 1938-41; asst. dir. Med. Nutriton Lab., Chgo., 1947-50; prof. medicine U. Ill., 1950—, Rush Med. Coll., Chgo., 1971—; Harvelan lectr., London, 1958; Pfizer lectr. Royal Australasian Coll. Physicians, 1959; physician Presbytn. Hosp., Chgo., 1951—; attending physician Cook County and U. Ill. Hosps., Chgo.; spl. cons. to USPHS. Mem. adv. com. medicine Office Surgeon Gen., U.S. Army; mem. food and nutrition bd. NRC. Mem. bd. Lawrence Hall, Chgo. Served to lt. col. M.C., Royal Canadian Army, 1941-46. Decorated Burma Star. Guggenheim fellow, 1961-62. Fellow Royal Coll. Physicians (London), A.C.P. (gov. No. Ill.), Royal Soc. Medicine; mem. A.M.A., Am. Soc. Clin. Investigation, Assn. Physicians Gt. Britain and Ireland. Home: 220 E Walton Pl Chicago IL 60611 Office: 122 S Michigan Blvd Chicago IL 60603

KARKOW, RICHARD ELLIS, tool co. exec.; b. Chgo., July 3, 1928; s. Conrad and Florence (Ellis) K.; A.B., Kenyon Coll., 1948; M.B.A., Harvard, 1950; J.D., Loyola U., Chgo., 1958; m. Ruth Ehrlin, Jan. 29, 1955; children—Catherine Elizabeth, Douglas Paul. With Northern Trust Co., Chgo., 1954-59; sec. H.M. Byllesby & Co., Chgo., 1959-60; treas. Pet Milk Co., St. Louis, 1961-62; treas. Kroger Co., Cin., 1963-66, v.p., treas., 1966-70; v.p. Ill. Tool Works, Inc., 1971—. Home: 40 N Hart Rd Barrington IL 60010 Office: 8501 W Higgins Rd Chicago IL 60010

KARL, JOHN JOSEPH, former hotel exec.; b. Altoona, Pa., Mar. 21, 1927; s. Andrew and Anne (McGraw) K.; B.A. in Hotel Mgmt., Pa. State U., 1950; m. Romayne Rutter, Feb. 27, 1954; children—Connie, Andrew, Daniel, Therese, Mary. With Sheraton Hotel Corp., 1950-70, gen. mgr. Sheraton Delta Hotel, New Orleans, 1967- 70. Served with USNR, 1944-46. Mem. Hotel Sales Mgrs. Assn., Skal Council N. Am., New Orleans C. of C., Sales Execs. Club New Orleans. 1732 Canal St New Orleans LA 70112

KARLEN, DELMAR, educator, author; b. Chgo., Jan. 6, 1912; s. Carl and Esther (Norman) K.; B.A., U. Wis., 1934; LL.B., Columbia, 1937; m. Alice Mary McGushon, July 12, 1940; children—Delmar, Karen Elise. Admitted to N.Y. bar, 1938, Wis. bar, 1946; with firm Simpson, Thacher & Bartlett, N.Y.C., 1937-46; mem. faculty U. Wis. Law Sch., 1946-52; prof. law N.Y.U., 1952—; asso. dir. Inst. Jud. Administrn., N.Y.C., 1952-62, dir., 1962-71, v.p., 1969—. Am. co-dir. Legal Research Inst., Ankara, Turkey, 1956-57; pres. Found. for Overseas Libraries Am. Law, 1969—. Mem. sch. bd., Garrison, N.Y., 1955-56. Democratic candidate county judge, Putnam County, N.Y., 1958. Bd. visitors Judge Adv. Gen. Sch., 1960-65. Served with AUS, 1942- 46. Mem. Am. Bar Assn., Assn. Bar City N.Y., Phi Beta Kappa, Order of Coif. Author: Primer of Procedure, 1950; Civil Litigation in Turkey, 1957; Cases and Materials on Pleading and Procedure Before Trial, 1961; Cases and Materials on Trials and Appeals, 1961; Appellate Courts in the United States and England, 1963; Law in Action, 1964; The Citizen in Court, 1963; Anglo-American Criminal Justice, 1967; Judicial Administration, 1970; also monographs, articles. Home: Garrison NY Office: 40 Washington Sq S New York City NY 10012

KARLEN, GOTTFRIED EMANUEL, lumber mfr., distbr.; b. Helena, Mont., Oct. 12, 1893; s. Gottfried and Emily Maude (Betchen) K.; ed. pub. schs., Long Prairie, Minn.; m. Anastatia Baldwin, July 6, 1921 (dec. Apr. 1963). Car loader Red River Lumber Co., Akeley, Minn. 1911-13; checker Internat. Lumber Co., International Falls, Minn., 1913, Shevlin-Clarke Co., Ft. Frances, Ont., Can., 1914; foreman, asst. supt. St. Paul & Tacoma Lumber Co., 1915-17; buyer J. E. Morris Lumber Co., Seattle, 1919-22; v.p. Schwager-Karlen Lumber Co., 1922-28; pres. Karlen-Davis Co., Tacoma, 1928—; sr. partner Eatonville Lumber Co. (Wash.), 1943-53; partner Tacoma Lumber Fabricating Co., 1945-51; pres. Timber Devel. Co., Inc., Tacoma, 1937-54, Orwaca Land Co., 1951—, Thunderbird Park, Inc., 1954—; chmn. Fed. Home Loan Bank of San Francisco, 1958-61; dir. Am. Mail Line, Financial Fedn., Inc., Los Angeles; adv. bd. Puget Sound Nat. Bank. Past campaign chmn. Tacoma Community Chest and Council. Bd. dirs. Tacoma Gen. Hosp.; hon. trustee U. Puget Sound. Served with U.S. Army, 1917-19. Mem. Nat. Lumber Mfrs. Assn. (past dir., v.p.), N.A.M., Indsl. Conf. Bd. Tacoma, W. Coast Lumbermen's Assn. (past pres.), Wash. Hist. Soc., Tacoma C. of C. Republican. Mason (Shriner), Rotarian. Clubs: Rainier, Wash. Athletic (Seattle; Tacoma Country and Golf (past pres.), Tacoma, Tacoma Lumbermens (past pres.). Arlington (Portland, Ore.); Pacific-Union, Bohemian (San Francisco); Thunderbird County (past pres.), O'Donnell Golf, Committee of Twenty-Five (Palm Springs, Cal.); Bohemian (San Francisco). Home: 7606 North St SW Tacoma WA 98498 Office: Washington Bldg Tacoma WA 98401

KARLIN, SAMUEL, educator; b. Yonava, Poland, June 8, 1923; B.S., Ill. Inst. Tech., 1944; Ph.D. in Math., Princeton, 1947; married; 3 children. Naturalized U.S. citizen. Asst. prof. math. Cal. Inst. Tech., 1949-50, 51-54, asso. prof., 1954-56; vis. asst. prof. Princeton, 1950-51; prof. math. and statistics Stanford, 1956—. Cons. Rand Corp., 1948—. Mem. Am. Math. Soc., Inst. Math. Statistics, Am. Statis. Assn. Contbr. articles to profl. jours. Office: Math Dept Stanford U Stanford CA 94305*

KARLING, JOHN S., educator; b. Austin, Tex., Aug. 2, 1899; s. Theodore L. D. and Mary Ruth (Jacobson) K.; student Tex. Wesleyan Coll., Tex., 1914-15; A.B., U. Tex., A.M., 1920; postgrad. U. Mexico City, 1920, Oxford U. (Eng.), 1923; Ph.D., Columbia, 1925; m. Page Burwell Johnston, Aug. 10, 1940; 1 dau., Sayre Christian. Dean, Tex. Wesleyan Coll., 1919- 20; instr. U. Tex., 1920; fellow Columbia, 1924; asst. prof. botany, 1926-35; asso. prof., 1935-48; prof., chmn. dept. biol. scis. Purdue U., dir. Ross Biol. Res. 1948-59, John Wright distinguished prof. biol. scis., 1959-65; Fulbright- Hays fellow, New Zealand, 1965-66. Dir. chicle research Tropical Plant Research Found., British Honduras, 1927- 32, research fellow Bermuda Biol. Sta., 1942; field dir. exploration dept. U.S. Govt. Rubber Devel. Corp. in Brazil, 1942- 43. Vis. prof. botany La. State U., 1947; vis. prof. mycology Mt. Lake Biol. Sta., U. Va., 1948; vis. prof. research U. Coll. W.I., Jamica, 1958: research fellow Chesapeake Biol. Lab., Solomans, Md., spring 1948; mem. NRC Com. on Orgn. Am. Inst. Biol. Scis., 1946-48; Sir C.V. Roman vis. prof. U. Madras (India); marine mycologist Internat. Indian Ocean Expdn., 1963. Served with AC, U.S. Army, World War 1. Fellow A.A.A.S. (council v.p., sect. chmn. 1950), Royal Soc. Arts London; mem. Bot. Soc. Am. (sec. mem. edit. bd. 1945-50, v.p. 1951), Am. Soc. Indsl. Microbiol., Am. Biol. Soc. (sec.), Torrey Bot. Soc. (pres. 1941, historian), Am. Assn. U. Profs., Ind. Acad. Sci., Mycol. Soc. Am., Am. Phytopath. Soc., Union Biol. Socs. (sec.), Brit. Mycol. Soc., Sigma Xi. Democrat. Rotarian. Clubs: Explorers, Columbia (N.Y.); Wabash Valley Torch, Town and Gown, University. Author: The Plasmodiophorales, 1942: The Simple Holocarpie Riflagellate Phycomvcetes, 1942; Synchtrium, 1963; Contbr. many articles to profl. jours. Cons. editor: Bot. Revs. Home: 1219 Tuckahoe Lane Lafayette IN 47906

KARLINSKY, SIMON educator; b. Harbin, Manchuria, Sept. 22, 1924; s. Aron and Sophie (Levitin) K.; B.A., U. Cal. at Berkeley, 1960, Ph.D., 1964; M.A., Harvard, 1961. Came to U.S., 1938, naturalized, 1944. Conf. interpreter, music student, Europe, 1947-57; teaching fellow Harvard, 1960-61; asst. prof. Slavic langs. and lits. U. Cal. at Berkeley, 1963-65, prof., 1967—, chmn. dept. 1967-69; vis. asso. prof. Harvard, 1966. Served with AUS, 1944-46. Woodrow Wilson fellow, 1960-61; Guggenheim fellow, 1969- 70. Mem. Phi Beta Kappa. Author: Marina Cvetaeva: Her Life and Her Art, 1966. Contbr. articles profl. jours. Composer: (ballet) Souvenirs, 1956. Home: 250 Kenyon Av Kensington CA 94708 Office: U Cal Berkeley CA 94720

KARLOS, ANTHONY CHRIST, food co. exec.; b. Chgo., Sept. 24, 1912; s. Christ A. and Angeline (Simoulis) K.; student pub. schs., Chgo.; m. Demetrea Ganos, June 11, 1944; children—Chris, Dean, Stephanie. Mgr. family-owned business, 1930- 37; with Gen. Foods Corp., 1937-43; with Grocerland Co-op, Inc., Chgo., 1943—, gen. mgr., 1949—, vice chmn. bd., 1961-63, chmn. bd., chief exec. officer, 1963—; sec., dir., founder O'Hare-Chgo. Corp. (O'Hare Inn), 1960- -; sec., dir., founder Century Broadcasting Corp.; dir. Archer Nat. Bank Chgo.; partner Seven Eagles Restaurant, Des Plaines, Ill.; speaker to food industry assns. Bd. dirs., hon. parish council mem. United Greek Orthodox Chs. Chgo.; nat. bd. trustees City of Hope. Recipient Golden Torch of Hope, City of Hope, 1965; named Man of Year, Ill. and Chgo. wholesale grocers assns., 1961. Mem. Chgo. Wholesale Grocers Assn. (dir., past pres.), Nat. Restaurant Assn., Ill. Food Retailers Assn., Chgo. Natural History Mus. (life asso.), Chgo. Council Fgn. Affairs, Order of Ahepa Mason (32). Club: Executives (Chgo.). Home: 6747 Minnehaha Av Lincolnwood IL 60646 Office: 3636 W 51st St Chicago IL 60632

KARLS, HAROLD M., banker, lawyer; b. Saginaw, Mich., Dec. 5, 1906; s. Herman B. and Anna (Meister) K.; B.A., U. Mich., 1929, J.D., 1931; m. Mary E. Spencer, Dec. 24, 1938; children—Lois (Mrs. Kurtz S. Downer), John, James, Mark. Admitted to Mich. bar, 1931; practice in Saginaw, 1931-34; with Second Nat. Bank Saginaw, 1934—, exec. v.p., 1965-68, pres., 1968-71, chmn. bd., 1971—, also dir. Mem. Saginaw Bd. Edn., 1959—, pres. 1962-63; del. World Meth. Conf., 1966, 71; del. several Meth. Gen. Confs. Bd. dirs. Saginaw United Fund, Saginaw Jr. Achievement; adv. council Asbury Theol. Sem. Recipient Arnold Boutell Meml. award for community service, 1969. Mem. Am., Mich. (past dir. probate and trust law sect.), Saginaw County bar assns., Am. Judicature Soc., Mich. Bankers Assn. (past mem. trust com.), Saginaw C. of C. (bd. dirs.). Rotarian. Club: Saginaw. Home: 20 Hammond Rd Saginaw MI 48602 Office: Second Nat Bank Saginaw MI 48607

KARLSON, ALFRED GUSTAV, educator, microbiologist; b. Virginia, Minn., Apr. 26, 1910; s. Knute John and Pauline Henrietta (Johnson) K.; B.S., Ia. State U., 1934, D.V.M., 1935, M.S., 1938; Ph.D., U. Minn., 1942; m. Janice Ruth Stillians, June 24, 1938; children—Alfred Lennart, Karl John, Kathy Jean, Trudy Ann, Julie Kay. Instr. bacteriology Ia. State U., 1935-38; fellow exptl. medicine Mayo Grad. Sch., U. Minn., 1938-39, faculty, 1946—, prof. comparative pathology, 1962—; cons. exptl. medicine Mayo Clinic, 1946-53, cons. microbiology, 1953—. Sec., Conf. Research Workers Animal Diseases, 1948-64; mem. Nat. Bd. Vet. Examiners, 1948-64. Served to lt. col. Vet. Corps, AUS, 1941-45. Alumni Achievement award I. State U., 1965. Diplomate pub. health and med. microbiology Am. Bd. Microbiology; diplomate Am. Coll. Vet. Pathologists (pres. 1949). Fellow Am. Acad. Microbiology, Am. Vet. Med. Assn.; mem. Am. Thoracic Soc., Soc. Am. Bacteriologists, Soc. Exptl. Biology and Medicine, Sigma Xi. Unitarian-Universalist. Sect. editor Biol. Abstracts, 1940—; editorial bd. Jour. Bacteriology, 195056, Am. Jour. Vet. Research, 1952—, Applied Microbiology, 1967—. Contbr. articles to sci. jours. Home: 428 16th Av SW Rochester MN 55901 Office: Mayo Clinic Rochester MN 55901

KARLSON, PHIL, film dir.; b. Chgo., July 2, 1908; student Loyola Schs., Chgo. and Los Angeles. With May Co. Dept. Store, 1928-32; entered motion picture industry with Universal Studios in prop dept.; promoted to asst., then dir. Leatherneck series; mgr. Iryon Foy for one year; tech., asso. dir. with Stuart Walker; asst. dir. Universal, then producer, 1940; dir. numerous films, 1945—, including Scandal Sheet, Mask of Avenger, The Brigand, Kansas City Confidential, 99 River Street, They Rode West, Tight Spot, Hell's Island, Five Against the House, Phoenix City Story, The Silencers. Address: care Columbia Pictures Corp 711 Fifth Av New York City NY 10022*

KARLSSON, ERIK LENNART, economist; b. Stenbrohult, Sweden, Nov. 25, 1918; s. Karl Hjalmar and Jenny (Pettersson) K.; student Stockholm Sch. Social Work and Pub. Adminstrn., 1949-53, U. Stockholm, 1950-54; m. Maj-Lis Wannefors, Oct. 20, 1953; children—Hans Jorgen, Mats Lennart, Bo Erik, Per Ola, Sven Erland. With Swedish State Rys., 1939-52, Govt. Commn. of Full Employment and Monetary Stability, 1953-55, Nat. Debt Office, Ministry Finance and Nat. Inst. Econ. Research, 1956-60, Central Bank of Sweden, 1960-67, IMF, 1967-68; exec. dir. representing Denmark, Finland, Iceland, Norway and Sweden, World Bank, Washington, 1968—. Home: 6909 N 28th St Arlington VA 22213 Office: World Bank 1818 H St Washington DC 20433

KARMIN, MONROE WILLIAM, journalist; b. Mineola, N.Y., Sept. 2, 1929; s. Stanley Albert and Phyllis Rae (Appelbaum) K.; B.A., U. Ill., 1950; M.S., Columbia, 1953; m. Mayanne Sherman, Oct. 30, 1955; children—Paul Nance, Betsy Anne. Staff writer Wall St. Jour., N.Y.C. and Washington, 1953—. Served with USAF, 1951-52. Recipient Pulitzer prize for nat. reporting, 1967. Mem. Nat. Press Club, Sigma Delta Chi (Distinguished Service award for gen. reporting 1967), Sigma Alpha Mu. Home: 7011 Beechwood Dr Chevy Chase MD 20015 Office: Nat Press Bldg Washington DC 20004

KARNER, HERBERT RUDOLF, editor, ret. army officer; b. Coyle, Okla., June 5, 1915; s. Rudolf and Elma (Myer) K.; student U. Tulsa, 1937-57; m. Ruth Della Bredehoeft, Jan. 1, 1938; children—Donald (dec.), Gary, Valarie (Mrs. Terry Kolkmann), Kenneth. Enlisted as pvt. U.S. Army, 1942, advanced through grades to maj., 1952; served in Pacific, 1942-46, Korea, 1949-52; retired, 1960; editor Ranch and Farm World, Tulsa, Okla., 1957—. Decorated Bronze Star. Recipient J.S. Russell meml. award for outstanding contbn. to agrl. journalism, 1969. Mem. Newspaper Farm Editors Am. (pres. 1965), Sigma Delta Chi (v.p. Eastern Okla. chpt. 1970). Lutheran (dir. pub. relations Okla. dist. 1970-74). Home: RFD 2 Box 69 Broken Arrow OK 74012 Office: 315 S Boulder St Tulsa OK 74102

KARNES, HOUSTON THURMAN, educator; b. Mt. Juliet, Tenn., Aug. 9, 1905; s. Walter Lipscomb and Annie Rebecca (Hatfield) K.; A.B., Vanderbilt U., 1928, A.M., 1929; Ph.D., Peabody Coll., 1940; summer student U. Wis., 1930, U. Mich., 1936; m. Julia May McDaniel, Mar. 30, 1956. Prof. math. and biology Northwestern Jr. Coll., Orange City, Ia., 1929-35; prof. math., head dept., also dean of men Harding Coll., 1935-36; tchr. math., dept. head Nashville City Sch. System, 1936-38; mem. faculty La. State U., 1938—, prof. math., 1953—, dean men, 1945-46, dir. Math. Inst., 1959—; vis. prof. math. U. Allahabad (India), summer 1965; mem. writing team Sch. Math. Study Group, 1958-61. Cons. NSF; cons., mem. adv. com. Southwest Ednl. Devel. Lab. Pres. Baton Rouge Community Concert Assn., 1959-63, mem. bd., 1945—; trustee Harding Coll. (pres. 1964-68); pres. bd. Lambda Chi Alpha Ednl. Found., 1955—; trustee National Interfraternity Found., 1960—. Fellow A.A.A.S.; mem. Am. Math. Soc., Math. Assn. Am., Nat. Council Tchrs. Math. (sec. 1954-65, mem. bd. 1965-69), Nat. Interfraternity Conf. (pres. 1958), Phi Kappa Phi, Omicron Delta Kappa, Pi Mu Epsilon (nat. v.p.), Phi Delta Kappa, Kappa Delta Pi, Lambda Chi Alpha (pres. 1950-54). Clubs: Baton Rouge Country, Kiwanis (mem. bd., pres. 1968), Knife and Fork (past mem. bd.) (Baton Rouge). Home: 5576 Sandalwood Dr Baton Rouge LA 70806

KARNES, WILLIAM GEORGE, foods co. exec.; b. Chgo., Mar. 24, 1911; s William and Ida (Carson) K.; B.S., U. Ill., 1933; J.D., Northwestern U., 1936; m. Virginia Kelly, May 1, 1937. Admitted to Ill. bar, 1936; atty. law dept. Beatrice Foods Co., 1936-39, head employee relations dept., 1939-43, v.p., asst. to pres., 1943-47, dir., 1947—, exec. v.p., 1948-52, pres., chief exec. officer, 1952—; dir. Borg-Warner Corp., LaSalle Nat. Bank, Chgo., Vaughan's Seed Co., Am. Biomed. Corp. Mem. N.Y. Merc. Exchange. Mem. vis. com. Div. Sch. U. Chgo.; mem. pres.'s club U. Ill.; mem. finance com. Ill. Council on Econ. Edn.; mem. sponsors council Nat. 4-H Found.; chmn. adv. com. Coll. Commerce and Bus. Adminstrn. U. Ill.; mem. vis. com. div. biology Cal. Inst. Tech. Mem. Chgo. Crime Commn.; governing bd. Passavant Hosp. Trustee Knox Coll., U. Ill. Found., Nat. Jewish Hosp., Denver; bd. dirs. Internat. Dairy Show; governing mem. Glenwood Sch. Boys. Recipient Horatio Alger award, 1961; Alumni Achievement award U. Ill., 1965; Nat. Conf. Christians and Jews Food Industry award, 1969; Am. Jewish Com. Human Relations awards, 1970. Mem. U.S. (membership com.), Ill. chambers commerce, Ireland-U.S. Council for Commerce and Industry (bd. dirs. Mid-Am. chpt.), Chgo. Assn. Commerce and Industry (bd dirs.), Am. Mgmt. Assn., Am. Judicature Soc., Newcomen Soc. N.Am., Phi Gamma Delta, Beta Gamma Sigma, Phi Delta Phi. Clubs: Mid-Day, University, Commercial (Chgo.); Seventy-One; Whitehall. Home: Butterfield Lane Flossmoor IL 60422 Office: 120 S LaSalle St Chicago IL 60603

KARNOSH, LOUIS JOSEPH, retired physician, educator; b. Bellaire, O., Mar. 30, 1892; s. John Joseph and Katherine (Stock) K.; B.S., Berea Coll., 1913, Sc.D., 1926; M.D., Western Res. U., 1920; m. Eva Pauline Milton, Dec. 28, 1923; children- -Patricia (Mrs. Albert Charles Lammert), Joan Louise, Katherine (Mrs. Yngyar Lovat Fraser Hvistendahl, Jr.). Intern Cleve. City Hosp., 1920- 21, dir. neuropsychiatry, 1928-46; dir. neuropsychiatry Cleve. Clinic, 1946-58; clin. prof. neurology Western Res. U. Med. Sch., 1946-63, emeritus clin. prof. neurology, 1963—. Cons. SSS, 1942-45; mem. council Ohio Dept. Mental Hygiene, 1957—. Trustee Berea (Ky.) Coll. Diplomate Am. Bd. Psychiatry and Neurology (dir. 1947-51). Fellow Am. Psychiat. Assn.; mem. Am. Neurol. Assn., Soc. Biol. Psychiatry (v.p.), Central Neuropsychiat. Assn. (pres. 1941), Am. Acad. Neurology, Alpha Omega Alpha. Author: Handbook of Psychiatry, 1944; Psychiatry for Nurses, rev. edit., 1958. Home: 22299 Parnell Rd Shaker Heights OH 44122 Office: Ingleside Hosp Cleveland OH 44106

KARNOVSKY, MANFRED LESLIE, educator; b. Johannesburg, S. Africa, Dec. 14, 1918; s. Herman L. and Florence (Rosenberg) K.; B.Sc., U. Witwatersrand, Johannesburg, 1940, M.Sc., 1942; Ph.D., U. Capetown (S. Africa), 1946; m. Ann Rosenblum, July 31, 1952. Came to U.S., 1947, naturalized, 1956. Mem. faculty Harvard Med. Sch., 1952—, acting head dept. biol. chemistry, 1959-60, chmn. dept., 1969—, prof. biol. chemistry, 1962—, now Harold T. White prof. biol. chemistry. Recipient 2d award Glycerine Producers Assn., 1953; Lederle Med. Faculty award, 1955-58. Mem. Am. Soc. Biol. Chemists, Histochem. Soc., Am. Chem. Soc., Biophys. Soc., Am. Soc. Cell Biology, Sigma Xi. Asso. editor Jour. Histochemistry and Cytochemistry, 1954-59, Jour. Biol. Chemistry, 1961- 69; editorial bd. Jour. Cell Biology, 1964-68. Home: 10 Wyman Rd Cambridge MA 02138

KARNOW, STANLEY, journalist; b. N.Y.C., Feb. 4, 1925; s. Harry and Henriette (Koeppel) K.; B.A., Harvard, 1947; student U. Paris (France), 1948-49, Inst. d'Etudes politiques, Paris, 1949-50; m. Claude Sarraute, July 15, 1948 (div. 1955); m. 2d, Annette Kline, Apr. 21, 1959; children—Cutis Edward, Catherine Anne, Michael Franklin. Corr., Time mag., Paris, 1950-57; bur. chief N. Africa, Time-Life, 1958-59, Hong Kong, 1959-62; spl. corr. Time, Inc., 1962-63; Far East corr. Sat. Eve. Post, 1963-65, Washington Post, 1965-71; mem. Washington bar. Washington Post, 1971—. Served with USAAF, 1943-46. Neiman fellow Harvard, 1957- 58; recipient citation Overseas Press Club, 1966, Ann. award for best newspaper interpretation of foreign affairs Overseas Press Club, 1968; fellow Inst. Politics, John F. Kennedy Sch. Govt., also fellow E. Asian-Research Center, Harvard, 1970-71. Mem. Signet Soc. Clubs: Harvard, Foreign Correspondents, Shek-O (Hong Kong). Author: Southeast Asia, 1963; also articles. Home: Office: Washington Post 1515 L St NW Washington DC 20005

KARNS, HARRY EDWARD, journalist; b. Columbus, Kan., Oct. 29, 1921; s. Harry Vaughn and Gertrude (Howe) K.; B.A., U. Okla., 1950; m. Carol Mary Hanson, Feb. 3, 1945; children—Katherine (Mrs. John Weddle), Martin Edward, Samuel Patrick, Martha Susan. Reporter, Enid (Okla.) Morning News, 1937-39; news editor Fairview (Okla.) Republican, 1939-40; news editor radio sta. KCRC, Enid, 1946-48; editorial page editor Press-Telegram, Long Beach, Cal., 1950-65; editor, writer corp. staff Lockheed Aircraft Corp., 1965- 66; asso. editor Orange County News, Garden Grove, Cal., 1966-67; editorial writer Detroit News, 1967—. Tchr. writing techniques adult div. Long Beach City Coll., 1957-60; syndicated columnist Newsday, Inc., 1964-68. Served with USNR, 1942-45. Recipient 1st pl. best series editorials Cal. Newspaper Pubs. Assn., 1964. Mem. Nat. Conf. Editorial Writers, Sigma Delta Chi. Republican. Presbyn. Club: Detroit Press. Home: 31831 Shiawassee Rd Farmington MI 48024 Office: 615 W Lafayette St Detroit MI 48231

KARNS, RUSSELL DALE, petroleum corp. exec.; b. Oswego, Kan., Oct. 6, 1909; s. James Henry and Rutha E. (Tower) K.; grad. Harvard, Advanced Mgmt. Program, 1951; m. J. Anita Spivey, Feb. 1, 1930; 1 dau., Ina Kay (Mrs. Donald E. Loeffler). With Phillips Petroleum Co., 1928-34; with Pan Am. Petroleum Corp., 1934- -, asst. treas., 1959-63, treas., 1963—. Hon. mem. staff gov. Okla., 1955. Bd. dirs. Asso. Industries Okla. Mem. Tulsa C. of C., Am. Petroleum Inst. Presbyn. Clubs: Oaks Country, Petroleum (Tulsa). Home: 1502 S Boulder St Tulsa OK 74119 Office: PO Box 591 Tulsa OK 74102

KARP, DAVID, writer; b. N.Y.C., May 5, 1922; s. Abraham and Rebecca (Levin) K.; B.S.S., Coll. City N.Y., 1948; m. Lillian Klass, Dec. 25, 1944; children—Ethan Ross, Andrew Gabriel. Continuity dir. radio sta. WNYC, N.Y.C., 1948-49; free-lance writer for radio, mags., motion pictures, novels, 1949—; guest lectr. Coll. City N.Y., 1964; pres. Leda Prodns., Inc., 1968—. Served with AUS, 1943- 46; PTO. Guggenheim fellow, 1956; recipient Emmy award for writing, 1964- 65; Ohio State U. award, 1956; Look mag. award, 1958; Mystery Writers Am. award, 1960. Mem. Writers Guild Am. West (council 1967—, pres. TV radio br. 1969-71), P.E.N., Nat. Acad. TV Arts and Scis. (editorial bd. TV Quar. 1965-71), Nat. Acad. Motion Picture Arts and Scis. Author: One, 1953; (under pseudonym) Platoon, 1953; The Day of the Monkey, 1955; All Honorable Men, 1956; Leave Me Alone, 1957; Enter, Sleeping, 1960; (with Murray D. Lincoln) Vice President In Charge of Revolution, 1960; The Last Believers, 1964. Home: 1116 Corsica Dr Pacific Palisades CA 90272 Office: care Frank Cooper Assos 9000 Sunset Blvd Los Angeles CA 90069

KARP, RUSSELL, film co. exec.; b. N.Y.C., 1929; B.A., Washington U., St. Louis, 1951; LL.B., Yale, 1954; m. Asso. Jaffe & Stein, attys., 1954-57; with Screen Gems, Inc. div. Columbia Pictures Industries, Inc., 1957-68, sec., 1961, v.p., 1962, v.p., treas., 1965, v.p. Columbia Pictures Industries, Inc., 1968—, treas., 1969—. Home: 4925 Arlington Av Riverdale NY 10471 Office: 711 Fifth Av New York City NY 10022

KARPEN, RICHARD LOUIS, data processing co. exec.; b. Hasting, Minn., Feb. 21, 1926; s. John P. and Agnes (Heinen) K.; student St. Thomas Coll., 1943, 46-47; B.E.E., U. Minn., 1950; m. Patricia Ann Jacques, June 9, 1951; children—Richard, Katherine, Thomas, Mary, Carol, James, Karen, William. Supr. computer maintenance Lawrence Radiation Lab., Livermore, Cal., 1950-55; group mgr. comml. computers Sperry Rand-Univac div., St. Paul, 1955-64; dir. engring. govt. systems div. Control Data Corp., Mpls., 1965-67; exec v.p., dir. operations. bd. dirs. Mohawk Data Scis. Corp., Herkimer, N.Y., 1967—; dir. Atron Corp. Served with USAAF, 1944-46. Mem. I.E.E.E., Zeta Psi. Roman Catholic. K.C. Home: 401 N Prospect St Herkimer NY 13350 Office: Palisades St Herkimer NY 13350

KARPLUS, MARTIN, educator; b. Vienna, Austria, Mar. 15, 1930; s. Hans and Isabella (Goldstern) K.; came to U.S., 1938, naturalized, 1945; B.S., Harvard, 1951; Ph.D., Cal. Inst. Tech., 1953. NSF postdoctoral fellow Oxford (Eng.) U., 1953-55; from instr. to asso. prof. chemistry U. Ill., 1955-60; asso. prof., then prof. Columbia, 1966; prof. chemistry Harvard, 1966—. Recipient Fresenius award Phi Lambda Upsilon, 1965; Harrison Howe award Rochester sect. Am. Chem. Soc., 1967. Mem. Am. Phys. Soc., Nat. Acad. Sci., Am. Acad. Arts and Scis. Research in theoretical chemistry. Office: Dept Chemistry 12 Oxford St Harvard U Cambridge MA 02138

KARPLUS, ROBERT, educator, physicist; b. Vienna, Austria, Feb. 23, 1927; s. Hans and Isabella (Goldsten) K.; came to U.S., 1938, naturalized, 1944; B.S., Harvard, 1945, M.A., 1946, Ph.D., 1948; m. Elizabeth Frazier, Dec. 27, 1948; children—Beverly, Margaret, Richard, Barbara, Andrew, David, Peter. Asst. prof. physics Harvard, 1950-54; mem. faculty U. Cal. at Berkeley, 1954—, prof., 1958—, dir. Sci. Curriculum Improvement Study, 1961—; asso. dir. Lawrence Hall of Sci., 1969—. Research in analytical chemistry, quantum field theory of elementary particles, geomagnetism, magnetohydrodynamics, microwave spectroscopy, molecular structure, field theories, sci. edn. Home: 57 Overhill Rd Orinda CA 94563 Office: Dept Physics U Cal LeConte Hall Berkeley CA 94720

KARPOWICZ, RAY ANTHONY, broadcasting exec.; b. Madison, Ill., Feb. 6, 1925; s. Anthony and Mary (Pero) K.; B.S., U. Mo., 1949; m. Virginia Lee Mitchell, Aug. 9, 1952; children—Paul, James, Christy, Laurie, Lisa. Account exec. WTMV Radio, East St. Louis, Ill., 1949-51; account exec., sales mgr. WEW Radio, St. Louis, 1951-54; account exec. KTVI-TV, St. Louis, 1954-55, KSD-TV, St. Louis, 1955-61, sales mgr., 1961-69, gen. mgr., 1969—. Served with USAAF, 1943-46; PTO. Decorated D.F.C., Air medal with 6 oak leaf clusters. Mem. St. Louis Advt. Club, Mo. Bradcasters Assn., Nat. Assn. Broadcasters, Nat. Acad. TV Arts and Sci., Media Club, Stadium Club St. Louis. Author: Effects of Wired Music, 1953. Home: 525 Oak Valley Dr St Louis MO 63131 Office: 1111 Olive St St Louis MO 63101

KARR, GARY, double bassist; b. Los Angeles, 1943; student U. So. Cal.; pupil of Herman Reinshagen; student Northwesten; pupil of Stuart Sankey; student (Naumberg scholar), Juillard Sch. Music. Formerly mem. and featured soloist orchs. of Peter Meremblum; tour with Chgo. Little Symphony; later played in Leonard Bernstein's Young Peoples Concerts; guest artist Brevard (N.C.) Music Festival. Address: care Chgo Symphony Orchestra Chicago IL 60604*

KARR, J. HAROLD, elec. mfg. co. exec.; b. Enterprise, Kan., Mar. 17, 1909; s. Ernst F. and Harriet (Lash) K.; B.S. in Elec. Engring., Kan. State Coll., 1930; M.S. in Engring., Purdue U., 1936; m. Ruth Macomber, Aug. 29, 1931. Mem. faculty Purdue U., Sch. Engring., 1930-41; electric motor designer Robbins & Myers Inc., Springfield, O., 1941-44, asst. chief engr., 1941- 56, product mgr., 1956-61, v.p., 1961-63, exec. v.p., 1963-65, pres., 1965—. Home: 3435 Derr Rd Springfield OH 45503 Office: Robbins & Myers Inc Springfield OH 45501

KARR, LLOYD, lawyer; b. Monticello, Ia., May 19, 1912; s. Charles L. and Margaret E. (Houston) K.; m. Margaret E. Phelan, May 14, 1938; children—Janet A., Richard L. Admitted to Ia. bar, 1937, since practiced in Webster City; county atty. Hamilton County, 1940-48. Pub. Webster City Daily Freeman Jour., 1952-55, Winter Park (Fla.) Sun-Herald, 1959-63. Mem. adv. council naval affairs 6th Naval Dist., 1959-62. Served with AUS, 1943- 45. Recipient Award of Merit, Ia. Bar Assn., 1968. Fellow Am. Coll. Probate Counsel; mem. Am., Ia. (bd. govs. 1959-61, pres. 1962- 63), 11th Jud. Dist., Hamilton County (pres. 1951) bar assns., DeMolay Legion of Honor, Sigma Delta Chi. Mason, Elk. Home: 1420 Wilson Av Webster City IA 50595 also 711 Des Moines St Webster City IA 50595

KARR, PAYNE, lawyer; b. Seattle, Feb. 15, 1909; s. Day and Jessie (Glick) P.; A.B., U. Wash., 1929; LL.B., George Washington U., 1932; m. Susan Hovey Fitch, Feb. 2, 1933; children—Susan Day (Mrs. Robert Kuebler), Robert Payne, William Thomas, Cynthia Hovey (Mrs. Richard T. Feerick). Admitted to Wash. bar, 1932, since practiced in Seattle; sr. partner firm Karr, Tuttle, Koch, Campbell, Mawer & Morrow, 1949—. Commnr., Seattle Transp. System, 1943-49, Seattle Planning Commn., 1942-43; bd. mem. Seattle SSS, 1943-47, govt. appeal agt., 1947-67. Mem. Internat. Assn. Ins. Counsel (pres. 1961-62), Am., Wash. (pres. 1968-69), Seattle bar assns., Am. Judicature Soc., Am. Coll. Trial Lawyers, Order of Coif, Sigma Nu, Phi Delta Phi, Pi Sigma Alpha. Home: Bainbridge Island WA 98110 Office: Seattle First Nat Bank Bldg Seattle WA 98101

KARRAS, ALEX, football player; Gary, Ind., July 15, 1935; m. Player, Detroit Lions; host NFL Preview ABC-TV. Named All-Pro, 1960, 61, 63, 65; recipient Outland award, 1947. Office: 1401 Michigan Av Detroit MI 48216*

KARRER, LAWRENCE EDISON, utilities cons.; b. Roslyn, Wash., Dec. 22, 1904; s. Frank and Theresa (Braun) K.; B.S., U. Wash., 1927; m. Roberta Mudgett, June 14, 1930; children—Joan, Robert L. Meter tester Puget Sound Power & Light Co., Seattle, 1927, engr., 1927-30, asst. to v.p., 1930-38, mgr. North Coast Lines (subsidiary), 1938-42, v.p. company, 1942-47, exec. v.p., 1947-65, sr. v.p., 1965-70; cons. Gulf Gen. Atomic, Inc., Bonneville Power Adminstrn., 1970—. Trustee Seattle Com. Fgn. Relations. Mem. Acad. Polit. Sci., Newcomen Soc. Engrs., Am. Nuclear Soc., Edison Elec. Inst., Northwest Power and Light Assn., Seattle Hist. Soc., Am. Inst. E.E., Seattle C. of C. (trustee, v.p.), Pacific N.W. Trade Assn., Sigma Xi, Tau Beta Pi, Theta Chi. Mason (Shriner), Rotarian. Clubs: Yacht, Washington Athletic (Seattle). Home: 130 W Lake Sammamish Blvd SE Bellevue WA 98008 Office: PO Box 801 Bellevue WA 98009

KARRER, MAX RAYMOND, rubber co. exec.; b. nr. York, Neb., June 21, 1907; s. Frederick William and Zena M. (Pyle) K.; B.S., U. Neb., 1928; m. Nedra E. King, June 19, 1929; 1 son, Max C. Research and devel. B.F. Goodrich Co., Akron, O., 1929-39; chmn. bd., pres., chief exec. officer Electric Hose & Rubber Co., Wilmington, Del., 1939—; dir. Bank of Del., Continental Investment Co., Retirement Living; mem. Del. adv. bd. Liberty Mut. Ins. Co. Vice pres., bd. dirs. Del. Safety Council; trustee Brandywine Coll. Recipient Distinguished Service award U. Neb. Alumni Assn., 1970. Mem. Del. C. of C. (dir., past pres.), Rubber Mfr. Assn. (dir.), Soc. Plastics Industry, Am. Soc. Testing Materials, Am. Chem. Soc. Home: PO Box 56 RD # 2 Heyburn Rd Chadds Ford PA 19317 Office: PO Box 910 Wilmington DE 19899

KARRER, SEBASTIAN, physicist; b. Rich Hill, Mo., Apr. 10, 1889; s. Frank Xavier and Theresa (Braun) K.; A.B., A.M., U. Wash., 1913; Ph.D., U. Ill., 1918; m. Annie May Hurd, Aug. 3, 1923. Instr. physics U. Ill., 1918-19; chief physics div. Fixed Nitrogen Research Lab., Dept. of Agr., 1919-26; dir. research Consol. Gas, Electric Light & Power Co., Balt., 1926-46; cons. Nat. Def. Research Com.; chief cons., research and devel. div. N.M. Sch. Mines, 1946-48; dir. research Baso, Inc., 1948-58, v.p., 1955-58; asso. dir. central research Minn. Mining and Mfg. Co., 1960-61; research asso. Georgetown Univ. Obs., 1964-68. Recipient Modern Pioneer award Am. Mfrs. Assn.; Merit award Navy Ordnance Dept. Mem. A.A.A.S., Am. Phys. Soc., Am. Chem. Soc., Am. Optical Soc., Md. Acad. Scis. (past pres.), Philos. Soc. Washington, Washington Acad. Scis., Newcomen Soc., Phi Beta Kappa, Sigma Xi, Gamma Alpha. Patentee thermoelectric materials and devices. Address: Port Republic MD 20676

KARSCH, DANIEL SELWYN, advt. exec.; b. N.Y.C. Jan. 28, 1921; s. Samuel and Louise (Gold) K.; B.A., U. Va., 1942; grad. student Princeton, 1942-43; m. Shirley Sperans, Nov. 24, 1949; children—Andrew, Thomas. With advt. dept. Warner Bros. Pictures, 1945-46; account exec. Ray Austrian & Assos., 1946-52; pres. Daniel & Charles, Inc., N.Y.C., 1952-70, chmn. exec. com., 1970—. Served with AUS, 1942- 45. Club: Lotos (N.Y.C.). Home: 1010 Fifth Av New York City NY 10028 Office: 261 Madison Av New York City NY 10016

KARSH, BERNARD, educator; b. Chgo., Aug. 25, 1921; s. David and Harriett (Pugach) K.; student Roosevelt U., 1946; M.A., U. Chgo., 1948, Ph.D., 1953; m. Annette Eleanor Shier, June 9, 1946; children—Paul I., Aaron N. Research asst., then asst. prof. U. Chgo., 1948-53; mem. faculty U. Ill. at Champaign, 1954—, prof. sociology, 1961—; vis. lectr. U. Kan., 1951, U. Ind., 1952; vis. prof. Keio U., Tokyo, Japan, 1966; cons. in field. Served with USAAF, 1939-43.. Fulbright scholar, 1960. Fellow Am. Sociol. Assn.; mem. Assn. Asian Studies, Indsl. Relations Research Assn., Am. Assn. U. Profs., Midwest Conf. Asian Studies (v.p. 1970-71). Author: Diary of a Strike, 1957; Worker Views His Union, 1958; The Japanese Industrial Relations System, 1971; also articles. Home: 1412 W William St Champaign IL 61820

KARSH, YOUSUF, photographer, portraitist; b. Mardin, Armenia (Turkey), Dec. 23, 1908; s. Amsih and Bahia (Nakash) K.; student photography, art and design, Boston; LL.D. (hon.), Carleton U., 1960, Queen's U., 1960; D.H.L., Dartmouth, 1962, Ohio U., 1965, Mt. Allison U., N.B., 1968, Emerson Coll., 1969; D.C.L., Bishop's U., Que., 1969; m. Solange Gauthier, Apr. 27, 1939 (dec. 1961); m. 2d, Estrellita Nachbar, Aug. 28, 1962. Came to Can., 1924, citizen, 1947. Photographer, photog. studio, Ottawa, Ont. 1933—; portrait photographer numerous statesmen, celebrities, including Winston Churchill, King George VI of Eng., Thomas Mann, Lord Beaverbrook, Elizabeth II, Albert Schweitzer, Albert Einstein, Jean Sibelius, Picasso, Pablo Casals, Ernest Hemingway; Karsh photographs on stamps Churchill, Queen Elizabeth, Prince and Princess Monaco, others; photograph Atlas Steel, Ltd., Welland, Ont., 1950-51, Ford of Can., Ltd., 1951. Rep. collections Eastman House, Inc., Rochester, N.Y., Royal Photog. Soc., London, Eng., Mus. Modern Art, N.Y.C., Chgo. Art Inst., Nat. Gallery Can., Phila. Art Mus., Tokyo Mus. Modern Art; one-man shows Expo 67, Montreal, Montral Mus. Fine arts, 1968, Boston Mus. Fine Arts, 1968, Corning Mus., 1968, Greensboro (N.C.) Mus., Corcoran Gallery, Washington, 1969, Detroit Art Inst., 1969, Seattle Art Mus., 1969-70, Japan, 1970, Kalamazoo Inst. Arts, 1971, Phila. Civic Center, 1971, Grand Rapids (Mich.) Art Mus., 1971, Hackley Art Gallery, Muskegon, Mich., 1971; vis. prof. photography and fine arts Ohio U., Athens, 1967-69; photog. adviser Expo 70, Osaka, Japan, 1969. Chmn. subcom. immigrant problems Canadian Citizenship Council. Trustee Photog. Arts and Scis. Found.; nat. v.p. Muscular Dystrophy Assn. (citation 1971), 1969-71. Decorated Order of Can.; recipient Can. Council medal, 1965, centennial medal, 1968; named hon. fellow, Hon. Master Photog. Arts, Inst. Incorporated Photographers Gt. Britain, 1970. Hon. fellow Royal Photog. Soc. (Eng.); fellow Photog. Soc. Am.; mem. Canadian Photog. Soc. (hon. life), Canadian Armenian Congress (hon. pres.). Photographer: Faces of Destiny (photog. portraiture collection), 1947; This Is the Mass, 1958, rev., 1965; This is Rome, 1960; This is the Holy Land, 1961; In Search of Greatness (autobiography), 1962; These Are the Sacraments, 1963. Author: Portraits of Greatness, 1960; (with John P. Frank) The Warren Court, 1964; Karsh Portfolio, 1967; Faces of Our Time, 1970. Home: Little Wings Prescott Hwy Ottawa Ontario Canada Office: 130 Sparks St Ottawa Ontario Canada

KARSLAKE, JAMES SPIER, educator; b. Iowa City, May 8, 1905; s. William Jay and Grace Frederick (Gookin) K.; B.A., U. Mich., 1926; M.A. in Physics, Harvard, 1937; M.A. in Edn., U. Ia., 1937; Ph.D. in Psychology, Purdue U., 1940; m. Ruth Elizabeth Henion, Dec. 31, 1938; children—Allison Grace, Charles Kent. Instr. psychology Hiram Coll., 1939-40, Ohio State U., 1940-42; adminstrv. asst. War Dept., Wright-Patterson Field, Dayton, O., 1942-44; staff psychologist Stevenson, Jordan & Harrison, Chgo., 1944- 45; cons. psychologist, 1945-46; dir. research Rohrer, Hibler & Replogle, Chgo., 1946-48; mem. faculty Mich. State U., 1948—, prof. psychology, 1959—, chmn. dept., 1962-64. Mem. profl. adv. council Lansing Rehab. Med. Center, Rehab. Industries. Past pres., bd. dirs. United Cerebral Palsy Assn. Lansing; bd. dirs. United Cerebral Palsy Assn. Mich., Easter Seal Soc. Ingham County. Diplomate Indsl. Psychology. Mem. Pan Am. Union, Nat. Wildlife Fedn., Wilderness Soc., Nat. Parks Assn., Assn. Am. Indian Affairs, S.W. Indian Found., Appalachian Trail Conf., Am., Midwest psychol. assns., A.A.A.S., Am. Assn. U. Profs., Sigma Xi, Psi Chi. Contbr. articles profl. jours. Patentee in field. Home: 933 Lantern Hill Dr East Lansing MI 48823

KARSON, EMILE, grain co. exec.; b. Berlin, Germany, Sept. 10, 1921; s. Bogdon and Zorka (Natowa) Karastoyanoff; LL.B., U. Sofia, 1944; LL.B., U. Paris, 1946, LL.D., 1948; LL.M., Yale, 1951, J.S.D., 1953; m. Lilia Usunowa, Dec. 31, 1944; 1 dau., Danielle. Came to U.S., 1948, naturalized, 1956. Lawyer World Bank, Washington, 1951-55; subsidiary coordinator Lockheed Aircraft Internat., Los Angeles, 1955-63; dir. European treas.'s office Litton Industries, Inc., 1963-69; treas. Continental Grain Co., N.Y.C., 1969—; vis. prof. law U. P.R., 1957. Mem. Rep. Assos., 1954-56. Treas. Continental Found., Fribourg Found. Fellow French Govt., 1945-48. Mem. World Peace Through Law, Am. Soc. Internat. Law. Clubs: Yale So. Cal., Lions (Los Angeles). Home: 1 Deer Hill Rd Alpine NJ 07520 Office: 2 Broadway New York City NY 10004

KARSON, SAMUEL, educator, psychologist; b. Balt., Jan. 3, 1924; s. Norman Jacobson and Annie (Raskin) K.; B.S., L.I.U., 1948; Ph.D., Washington U., St. Louis, 1952; m. Dorothy Faye Libert, Sept. 5, 1946; children—Linda, Michael. Asst. prof. U. N.H., 1957-58; research asst. prof. dept. nursing U. Miami (Fla.), 1959-62; chief psychologist, dir. research Dade County Child Guidance Clinic, Miami, 1958-62; spl. asst. for clin. psychology FAA, 1962-66, guest lectr. aviation med. examiner seminars, 1966—; prof., chmn. dept. psychology Eastern Mich. U., 1966—; cons. in field 1966—. Served with USAAF, 1942-45, USAF, 1955-57. Fellow Am. Orthopsychiat. Assn.; mem. Soc. Multivariate Exptl. Psychology, Aerospace Med. Assn., Am. Psychol. Assn., Sigma Xi, Psi Chi. Research in automazed 16PF personality interpretations, 2d order personality factors in sky marshalls and air traffic control specialists, also psychology skyjackers. Home: 1730 Roosevelt Blvd Ypsilanti MI 48197

KARSTEN, CHRISTIAN FRIEDRICH, banker; b. Assen, Netherlands, July 1, 1917; s. R. and M. (Graf) K.; master's degree, Netherlands Econ. U., 1940, doctor's degree, 1952; m. Carolina Johanna Wilhelmina van Waard, May 27, 1942; children—Peter, Cardina, Frederik, Roelof. Economist, Rotterdamsche Bank N.V., 1945-48, sec. to mng. dirs., 1948-52, asst. mng. dir., 1952-55, mng. dir., 1955-65, mng. dir. successor firm Amsterdam-Rotterdam Bank N.V., 1965—. Decorated knight Order Dutch Lion. Home: 15 Rijksweg Oost Laren Netherlands Office: 595 Herengracht Amsterdam Netherlands

KARSTEN, THOMAS LOREN, realtor lawyer; b. Mpls., Sept. 4, 1915; s. H.A. and Ida D. (Karsten) K.; A.B., U. Chgo., 1937, LL.D., 1939; m. Marilyn R. Herst, Nov. 26, 1950; children—Lesley, Thomas, Liza, Timothy. Admitted to Ill. bar, 1938, N.Y. bar, 1948; exec. asst. to under sec. interior, 1942; naval aide to gov. P.R., also lectr. adminstrv. law U. P.R. and alternate mem. Anglo-Am. Caribbean Commn., 1943-45; asso. prosecutor Internat. Mil. Tribunal, Nuremberg, Germany, 1945-46; mem. firm Schwartzreich & Mathias, N.Y.C., 1946-50; spl. counsel to Spl. Senate Com. to Investigate Organized Crime in Interstate Commerce, 1950; dir. consumer goods div. OPS, Washington, 1951-52; asst. to pres. Am. Trading & Prodn. Corp., Balt.; v.p. No. Properties, Inc.; v.p., dir. Blaustein Industries, Inc., Am. Trading Corp., Wilshire Properties, Inc., Atapco-Valley, Inc., Atapco-Valley Land Corp., Atanco- San Diego, Inc.; v.p. Charles St. Devel. Corp., 1953-68; exec. v.p. Ogden Devel. Corp., also vice chmn. Greenwood Village, Inc., 1968-70; now pres. Thomas L. Karsten Assos. Mem. Mayor's Com. on P.R. Affairs, 1949-50; v.p. A Fair Deal for N.Y. County, 1949-50; commr. Balt. County Redevel. and Rehab. Commn.; v.p. Green Spring Valley Area Planning Council; exec. v.p., dir. Planned Parenthood Assn.; dir. Nat. Travelers Aid Assn.; commr. Md. Gambling Study Commn. Served to lt. comdr. USNR, 1942-46. Mem. UN Assn. (v.p., bd. dirs.). Club: Standard (Chgo.). Collaborating author: Handbook of Federal Indian Law, 1941. Home: 1521 Amalfi Dr Pacific Palisades CA 90272 Office: 10889 Wilshire Blvd Los Angeles CA 90024

KARTALIA, MITCHELL P., mfr. elec. equipment; b. Yukon, Pa., Mar. 31, 1913; s. Peter and Julia (Juras) K.; E.E., U. Cin., 1940; m. Rebecca Dunham, Oct. 7, 1939; children—David E., Janet E., Diane S., Peter J., Mitchell J. With Am. Rolling Mill Co., Butler, Pa., 1939-40; with Square D Co., Park Ridge, Ill., 1940—, v.p., 1958-65, exec. v.p., 1965-68, pres., chief exec. officer, 1968—, dir., 1963—; dir. Warner Electric Brake & Clutch Co., Rex Chainbelt Inc., Hobart Mfg. Co. Mem. Nat. Elec. Mfrs. Assn. (vice chmn. bd. govs.), Ill. Mfrs. Assn. (bd. dirs.), Eta Kappa Nu. Mason (Shriner). Home: 212 Biltmore Dr Barrington IL 60010 Office: Square D Co Executive Plaza Park Ridge IL 60068

KARTH, JOSEPH EDWARD, congressman; b. New Brighton, Minn., Aug. 26, 1922; s. William Albert and Wilhelmina (Kurst) K.; student U. Neb. Sch. Engring.; m. Charlotte J. Nordgren, Mar. 17, 1950; children—Kevin, Bradley, Brian. Various jobs labor-mgmt. relations, 1947-58; mem. Minn. Legislature, 1950-58; mem. 86th-92d Congresses, 4th Dist. Minn. Mem. Minn. Fedn. Legislative Com. Active Indianhead council Boy Scouts. Served with AUS, World War II. Mem. V.F.W., Am. Legion. Home: 2233 E Lydia North Saint Paul MN 55109 Office: Rayburn Office Bldg Washington DC 20525

KARTMAN, BEN, editor; b. Chgo., Mar. 8, 1901; s. Abraham and Etta (Landau) K.; A.B., U. Ill., 1923; m. Leah Affron, Jan. 11, 1927 (dec.); children—Keith Harris, Edwin Affron. Instr. English and journalism U. Ill., 1923-25; copyreader Chgo. Daily jour. 1925-26; copyreader Chgo. Daily News, 1926-28, make-up editor, 1928-44; asso. editor Coronet mag., 1945-52; editorial dir. Family Weekly, 1954-59, exec. editor, 1959-65; editorial writer Hollister Newspapers, 1966-66; prodn., editor Popular Mechanics, Do-It-Yourself Ency., 1967-68; instr. Medill Sch. Journalism, Northwestern U., 1952-65; instr. mag. non-fiction Midwestern Writers Conf., 1945-54; lectr. humanities U. Chgo., 1952-53. Bd. govs. Midwestern Writers Conf. Pres. Assn. Family Living, 1958-60. Bd. dirs. Youth Orch. Greater Chgo., 1952-65, Lawson YMCA; pub. relations com. Met. Chgo. YMCA; v.p. bd. dirs. Wilmette Vol. Pool. Mem. Soc. Midland Authors (v.p. 1955-57, pres. 1957-61), Phi Epsilon Pi (nat. v.p, 1925-27, nat. editor 1924-28), Sigma Delta Chi, Pi Delta Epsilon. Jewish religion. Editor: Disaster!, 1948. Editorial bd. Viewpoint mag. Contbr. Ency. Brit. Book Year, 1945, Am. People's Ency. Yearbook, 1954, 55. Home: 208 Golf Terrace Wilmette IL 60091

KARZON, DAVID THEODORE, educator, pediatrician; b. N.Y.C., July 8, 1920; B.S., Ohio State U., 1940, M.S., 1941; M.D., Johns Hopkins, 1944; m. Allaire Urban, May 18, 1946; children—David Theodore, Elizabeth U. Intern, them resident Johns Hopkins Hosp., 1944-45; resident N.Y.-Cornell Med. Center, 1945-46; mem. faculty State U. N.Y. at Buffalo Sch. Medicine, 1952-68, prof. pediatrics, 1963-68; asso. attending physician Children's Hosp., Buffalo, 1952-64, attending physician, 1964-68; prof. pediatrics, chmn. dept. Vanderbilt U. Sch. Medicine, 1968—; cons. USPHS, NIH. Mem. spl. adv. com. immunization practice to surgeon gen., 1964-70. Served to capt. M.C., AUS, 1946-48. Lowell M. Palmer sr. fellow, 1953-56; Markle scholar, 1956-61; recipient Research Career award NIH, 1962-68. Diplomate Am. Bd. Pediatrics, Am. Bd. Microbiology. Mem. Am. Acad. Pediatrics, Soc. Pediatric Research, Assn. Med. Schs. Pediatric Dept. Chairmen, So. Soc. Pediatric Research, Am. Pediatric Soc., Am. Acad. Microbiologists, Am. Soc. Microbiology, Am. Epidemiological Soc., N.Y. Acad. Sci., Am. Assn. Immunologists, Soc. Exptl. Biology and Medicine, Phi Beta Kappa. Asso. editor Am. Jour. Epidemiology, 1966—. Home: 1049 Overton Lea Rd Nashville TN 37220

KASCH, EDWARD G., cheese mfr.; b. Chgo., Sept. 8, 1906; s. John Louis and Elizabeth (Hedtke) K.; night student, Northwestern U., DePaul U., Central Coll.; m. Ethel Beckman, Oct. 4, 1930. With Kraft Foods Co., Chgo., 1928—, successively adjustment clk., credit mgr., asst. dir. personnel, mgr. labor relations, gen. personnel mgr., v.p. personnel, 1954—. Bd. dirs. English Dist. Luth. Ch. Mo. Synod; pres. Luth. Charities Fedn. Mem. U.S., Ill. chambers commerce, Indsl. Relations Assn. Chgo. (v.p.). Home: 191 Exmoor Av Glen Ellyn IL 60137 Office: 500 Peshtigo Ct Chicago IL 60690

KASCH, JOHN EDWARD, oil co. exec.; b. Bloomington, Ind., Sept. 3, 1916; s. Charles H. and Nellie D. (St. Clair) K.; B.S. in Chem. Engring., U. Tex., 1938, M.S., 1939, Ph.D., 1943; grad. Advanced Mgmt. Program, Harvard, 1957; m. Lady Katherine Lenoir, Sept. 28, 1940; children—John Adkins, Barbara Kay. Research fellow, instr. U. Tex., 1939-41; chem. engr. Pan Am. Refining Corp., 1942-44, econ. analyst Petroleum Adminstrn. War, 1944-45; sect. head, asso. dir. research and devel., 1946-52; with Am. Oil Co., 1952- 65, gen. mgr. supply and transp., also dir., 1957-65; v.p. prodn., mfg., transp., engring., purchasing, research and devel. Standard Oil Co. (Ind.), 1965-66; exec. v.p., dir. Am. Internat. Oil Co., 1966—; chmn. Colonial Pipeline Co., Atlanta, 1965-68. Mem. adv. council Coll. Engring. Found., U. Tex. Trustee Chgo. Med. Sch., 1965—. Recipient Distinguished Grad. award U. Tex., 1960. Registered profl. engr., Tex. Mem. Am. Inst. Chem. Engrs., Am. Chem. Soc., Soc. Automotive Engrs., Am. Petroleum Inst., Transp. Club Petroleum Industry, Newcomen Soc. N.Am., Sigma Xi, Phi Lambda Upsilon. Presbyn. (trustee). Clubs: Chicago Athletic Assn., Executives (Chgo.); Economic (N.Y.C.). Home: 909 Holly Ct Northbrook IL 60062 Office: 500 N Michigan Av Chicago IL 60680

KASDORF, DONALD LEE, pharm. co. exec.; b. Chgo., July 13, 1929; s. Harry E. and Frances (Granquist) K.; B.S. in Bus. Adminstrn., Northwestern U., 1959; m. Carol Jean Gaebel, July 21, 1951; children-Leslie Lynne, Donna Lee. Controller Wells Mfg. Co., Skokie, Ill., 1955-63; divisional controller Lamb Industires, Milw., 1963; corporate controller Abbott Labs., N. Chgo., Ill., 1963—. Mem. Lake Bluff Sch. Bd. Caucus, 1966-69; mem. health and resources com. Lake County Hosp. Assn., 1970—. Served with AUS, 1951- 53. Mem. Nat. Assn. Accountants. Club: Northwestern Chgo. Home: 1918 W Hackberry Lake Forest IL 60045 Office: Abbott Park North Chicago IL

KASE, NATHAN GINDEN, physician, educator; b. N.Y.C., Apr. 6, 1930; s. Joseph and Flora (Ginden) Kosovsky; A.B., Columbia, 1951, M.D., 1955; M.A. (hon.), Yale, 1969; m. Judith Caryl Glass, July 8, 1956; children—Deborah, James, Nancy. Intern Mt. Sinai Hosp., N.Y.C., 1955-57, resident, 1960-62; USPHS trainee steroid biochemistry Clark U. and Worcester (Mass.) Found. Exptl. Biology, 1959-60; mem. faculty Yale Med. Sch., 1962—, prof. obstetrics and gynecology, chmn. dept., 1969—; attending clin. labs. Yale-New Haven Hosp., also chief service obstetrics and gynecology; mem. cons. staff Griffin Hosp., Derby, Conn., New Britain (Conn.) Gen. Hosp., St. Raphael Hosp., New Haven, Stamford (Conn.) Hosp., Norwalk (Conn.) Hosp., William W. Backus Hosp., Norwich, Conn. Served to capt., M.C., USAF, 1957-59. Recipient Francis Gilman Blake award Yale Sch. Medicine, 1967. Diplomate Am. Bd. Obstetrics and Gynecology, Fellow Am. Coll. Obstetricians and Gynecologists; mem. Am. Fertility Soc., Endocrine Soc., N.Y. Acad. Scis., Soc. Gynceol. Investigation, Sigma Xi, Alpha Omega Alpha. Author: (with Robert H. Glass) Woman's Choice, 1970; also articles. Home: Robin Rd Woodbridge CT 06525 Office: 333 Cedar St New Haven CT 06510

KASELOW, JOSEPH, advt. exec.; b. N.Y.C., Oct. 21, 1912; s. Frederick and Louise (Lehanka) K.; B.A., Cornell Coll., Mt. Vernon, Ia., 1934; m. Alice Davidson, Jan. 12, 1940; children—Evelyn, Joseph Andrew, Frederick Lee. With Cowan & Dengler, Inc., advt., 1934-36; mem. staff N.Y. Herald Tribune (briefly known as World Jour. Tribune), 1937-67, bus. news writer, 1939-52, columnist Along Madison Avenue with Kaselow, 1952- 67; employed Sullivan, Stauffer, Colwell & Bayles, Inc., advt. agy., N.Y.C., 1967-68; v.p.-corporate relations Cunningham & Walsh, Inc., 1968—; broadcaster radio sta. WOR, 1956, MBS, 1962, WINS, 1963-64; editor Ad World, sta. WOR-TV, 1958. Dir. N.Y. area Decade of Growth campaign Cornell Coll., 1963-64. Bd. mgrs. Glen Rock (N.J.) Community Chest, 1959- 62. Served with USNR, 1943-45. Recipient Alumni Achievement award Cornell Coll., 1962; annual award League Advt. Agys., 1962. Mem. N.Y. Financial Writers Assn., Cornell Coll. Alumni Assn. (pres. N.Y. area 1957-59). Silurians, Kappa Tau Alpha, Alpha Delta Sigma, Sigma Delta Chi. Contbr. articles nat. mags. Home: 4 Diamond Ct Glen Rock NJ 07452 Office: 260 Madison Av New York City NY 10016

KASER, DAVID, librarian; b. Mishawaka, Ind., Mar. 12, 1924; s. Arthur Leroy and Loah (Steele) K.; A.B., Houghton Coll., 1949; M.A., U. Notre Dame, 1950; A.M. in L.S., U. Mich., 1952, Ph.D., 1956; m. Jane Jewell, Sept. 1, 1950; children—John Andrew, Kathleen Jewell. Serials librarian, instr. library sci. Ball State Tchrs. Coll., 1952-54; asst. in exchanges U. Mich. Library, 1954-56; chief acquisitions Washington U. Libraries, St. Louis, 1956-59, asst. dir., 1959-60; prof. English, Vanderbilt U., also prof. library sci. Peabody Coll. and dir. joint univ. libraries, 1960-68; dir. libraries Cornell U., 1968—. Guggenheim fellow, 1967. Mem. A.L.A., Bibliog. Soc. Am., Assn. Coll. and Research Libraries (pres. 1968-69), Assn. Southeastern Research Libraries (chmn. 1966-68), Tenn. Library Assn. (pres. 1968-69), Am. Antiquarian Soc., Grolier Club, Phi Beta Kappa, Beta Phi Mu. Rotarian. Author: Messrs. Carey & Lea of Philadelphia, 1957; Washington University Manuscripts, 1958; Cost Book of Carey & Lea, 1825-1838, 1963; Joseph Charless, Printer in the Western Country, 1963; Books in America's Past, 1966; Book Pirating in Taiwan, 1969; Library Development in Eight Asian Countries, 1969. Editor Mo. Library Assn. Quar., 1958-60, College and Research Libraries, 1963-69. Home: 116 Crest Lane Ithaca NY 14850

KASER, RUDOLPH THEODORE, ins. broker; b. Antelope, Ore., Dec. 5, 1908; s. Jacob and Lena (Yaisli) K.; B.S., Ore. State U., 1931; m. Virginia Ruth Adams, May 29, 1932; children—Carolyn Ruth (Mrs. Robert Fairman), Kathryn Ann (Mrs. Nicholas Dodge). Engr., Ore. Ins. Rating Bur., Portland, Ore., 1931-43; with Marsh & McLennan, Portland, 1943—, engr., 1943-50, mgr. engring. dept., 1950-55, v.p., asst. mgr. Ore. operations, 1955-65, sr. v.p., mgr. Ore. operations Marsh & McLennan-D.K. MacDonald & Co., Inc., 1965-70, dir., 1970-71, v.p., dir. mgr. Marsh & McLennan, Inc. of Ore., 1970-71, v.p., sr. cons. dir., 1971—, v.p. Marsh and McLellan, Inc. (Bel.), 1970-71, v.p., dir., 1971—. Mem. Soc. Fire Protection Engrs. (charter), Am. Risk and Ins. Assn., Am. Forestry Assn., Asso. Gen. Contractors Am. (asso.), Nat. Fire Protection Assn., Nat. Rifle Assn., Pacific N.W. Trade Assn. (past regional v.p.), Lang Syne Soc., Royal Rosarians (life), Portland C. of C. (past chmn. trade and commerce com.), Order Blue Goose (past pres. Ore.; past dep. Ore. and Wash.), Order of Antelope (life). Presbyn. Clubs: Arlington, University, City, International (Portland). Home: 722 SW Westwood Dr Portland OR 97201 Office: Georgia-Pacific Bldg Portland OR 97204

KASHA, LAWRENCE NATHAN, producer, dir. theatrical prodns.; b. Bklyn., Dec. 3, 1934; s. Irving and Rose (Katz) K.; B.A., N.Y.U., 1954, M.A., 1955. Theat. dir. and producer; works include nat. co. L'il Abner, 1958, nat. tour Camelot, 1963-64, Anything Goes off-Broadway co., 1962, Broadway co. Bajour, 1964, nat. co. Funny Girl, 1965, London co., 1966, Show Boat revival, 1966, nat. co. Cactus Flower, 1968, nat. co. Star Spangled Girl, 1968, London co. Mame, 1969, Lovely Ladies, Kind Gentlemen, 1970; producer off-Broadway prodn. Parade, 1960, Broadway prodn. She Loves Me, 1963, Hadrian VII, 1969, Broadway prodn. Applause, 1970. Recipient Tony award, 1970. Mem. Directors Guild Am., Actors Equity Assn. Playwright: (with Lionel Wilson) Where Have You Been, Billy Boy?, 1969; (with Hayden Griffin) The Pirate, 1968. Home: 60 W 57th St New York City NY 10019 Office: 1650 Broadway New York City NY 10019

KASHA, MICHAEL, educator, phys. chemist; b. Elizabeth, N.J., Dec. 6, 1920; s. Stephen and Mary (Ficula) K.; B.S., U. Mich., 1943; Ph.D., U. Cal. at Berkeley, 1945; m. Lilli Cohn, Dec. 14, 1947; 1 son, Nicolas. Research chemist plutonium project U. Cal. at Berkeley, 1944-46, univ. fellow, instr., 1946, research asso., 1946-49; fellow AEC, U. Chgo., 1949-50; Guggenheim fellow, spl. lectr. U. Manchester (Eng.), 1950-51; prof. chemistry Fla. State U., 1951—, chmn. dept., 1959-61, dir. Inst. Molecular Biophysics, 1960—; vis. prof. Harvard, 1959-60. Named Distinguished Prof. of Year, Fla. State U., 1962; recipient Charles F. Kettering Research award, 1962. Mem. Am. Acad. Arts and Scis., Am. Chem. Soc., Biophys. Soc., Radiation Research Soc., Sigma Xi. Author: (with L. Kasha) Molecular Electronic Bibliography, Vol. 1, 1958. Editor: (with B. Pullman) Horizons in Biochemistry, 1962. Translator (with M. Oppenheimer, Jr.) Theory of Molecular Excitons (Davydov), 1962. Home: Route 4 Box 622 Tallahassee FL 32301

KASHI, ALIZA, actress; b. Tel-Aviv, Israel, Apr. 5, 1940; d. Ben and Sarah (Kaly) Kashi; ed. Ayanot Agr. Sch., Coll. of Jerusalem; m. Daniel H. Wolfe, Oct. 30, 1968. Came to U.S., 1964. Actress appearing in clubs, theatre, TV. Named Miss Ziegfield, 1968, Woman of Year, Variety Club, 1970; recipient award of merit, United Cerebral Palsy, 1971, award of merit, Anti-Defamation League, 1970. Served with Israeli Army, 1966-67. Office: 5 E 51st St New York City NY 10022

KASHIWA, SHIRO, lawyer, govt. ofcl.; b. Kohala, Hawaii, Oct. 24, 1912; s. Ryuten and Yuki (Matsubara) K.; B.S., U. Mich., 1934, LL.B., 1936; m. Mildred Yamagata, Mar. 15, 1941; children—Gregg R., Wendy Yuki. Admitted to Hawaii bar, 1937, since practiced in Honolulu, mem. firm Kashiwa & Kashiwa, 1950-69; atty gen., Hawaii, 1957, 59-69; asst. atty. gen. land and natural resources div. Dept. Justice, 1969—. Vice chmn. Republican Party of Hawaii, 1956-57. Dir. Kuakini Hosp., 1956-57; v.p. Honpa Hangwanji Missions of Hawaii, 1958; dir., mem. exec. com. Honolulu Community Chest, 1958-59. Mem. Internat. Acad. Trial Lawyers (dir.), Hawaii Legal Aid Soc. (pres. 1954, past dir.). Home: 5375 Kalanianaole Hwy Office: Dept of Justice Washington DC 20530

KASISCHKE, RICHARD REINHOLD, newspaperman; b. St. Joseph, Mich., Sept. 22, 1911; s. Ludwig and Anna (Rexine) K.; grad. high sch.; 1 dau., Kathleen C. Fgn. corr. A.P., 1943-67, chief bur., Prague, 1949-50, chief corr., Berlin, 1950- 51, Bonn, 1951-53, chief bur., Moscow, 1953-55. Vienna, 1956-60, So. Africa at Johannesburg, 1960-63, corr. London, 1963-67; with AP World Services N.Y., 1967—. Home: 1919 Forres Av Saint Joseph MI 49085

KASK, JOHN LAURENCE, biologist; b. Red Deer, Alta., Can., Mar. 21, 1906; s. John Michael and Minnie Melanie (Walters) K.; A.B., U. B.C., 1928; Ph.D., U. Wash., 1936; m. Doris Mary Hunter, June 29, 1935; children—Janet Doris, Melanie Margaret. Biol. asst. Biol. Bd. Can., Nanaimo, B.C., 1928; asst. scientist and asso. scientist Internat. Fisheries Commn., Prince Rupert, B.C. and Seattle, 1929-38; asso. scientist, dep. dir. Internat. Pacific Salmon Fisheries Commn., New Westminster, B.C., 1938-43; spl. lectr. fisheries U. Wash., 1935-43; curator aquatic biology Cal. Acad. Scis., San Francisco, 1943-47; spl. cons. in fisheries Govt. Costa Rica, 1947, Dept. State, Washington, 1947; chief biologist fisheries div. FAO of UN, 1948-51, cons. fisheries and oceanography, 1970—; chief sect. research and devel., asst. dir. Pacific Oceanic Fishery Investigations, Fish and Wildlife Service, Dept. Interior, Honolulu, T.H., 1951, chief fgn. activities, 1952, asst. dir. (fisheries), Washington, 1952-53; permanent chmn. Fisheries Research Bd. Can., Ottawa, 1953-63; lectr. marine zoology U. Hawaii, 1951; commr. Internat. Commn. for. N.W. Atlantic Fisheries, 1952, chmn., 1953; dep. commr. Inter-Am. Tropical Tuna Commn., 1952, Internat. Whaling Commn., 1952; commr. Internat. Commn. for Sci. Investigation of Tuna, 1952; dir. investigations Inter Am. Tropical Tuna Commn., research asso. Scripps Instn. Oceanography, La Jolla, Cal., 1963-70. Fellow Cal. Acad. Scis.; mem. Hawaiian, Wash. acads. scis., Am. Fisheries Soc., Am. Soc. Limnology and Oceanography, Am. Soc. Icthyologists and Herpetologists, A.A.A.S., Sigma Xi, Phi Sigma. Contbr. articles profl. jours. Home: 5191 Mt Alifan Dr San Diego CA 92111 Office: Dir Investigations Inter-Am Tropical Tuna Commn care Scripps Instn Oceanography La Jolla CA 92037

KASKE, ROBERT EARL, educator; b. Cin., June 1, 1921; s. Herman Charles and Ann (Laake) K.; B.A., Xavier U., 1942; M.A., U. N.C., 1947, Ph.D., 1950; 1 son by previous marriage, David Louis; m. 2d, Carol Margaret Vonckx, June 4, 1958; 1 son, Richard James. Instr., then asst. prof. Washington U., St. Louis, 1950-57; asst. prof. Pa. State U., 1957-58; asso. prof. U. N.C. at Chapel Hill, 1958-61; prof. U. Ill. at Urbana, 1961-64; prof. English, Cornell U., 1964—. Served to 1st lt. AUS, 1942-46. Mem. Modern Lang. Assn., Mediaeval Acad. Am., Dante Soc. Am., Internat. Assn. U. Profs. of English. Contbr. profl. jours. Home: 121 N Quarry St Ithaca NY 14850

KASKELL, PETER HOWARD, mfg. co. exec., lawyer; b. Berlin, Germany, Mar. 29, 1924; s. Joseph and Lilo (Schaeffer) K.; grad. Horace Mann Sch. N.Y.C., 1940; B.A., Columbia, 1943, LL.B., 1948; m. Joan Folsom Macy, Nov. 30, 1968; stepchildren—Brenda, Alison. Admitted to N.Y. bar, 1948; asso mem. firm White & Case, N.Y.C., 1948-51; atty., Nat. Prodn. Authority, Washington, 1951-53, W.R. Grace & Co., N.Y.C., 1952-54; div. counsel Curtiss-Wright Corp., Buffalo, 1954-56; with Olin Corp., Stamford, Conn., 1956—, sec., asso. gen. counsel, 1969—; dir. Ormet Corp., Hannibal, O., Yeonas Co., Vienna, Va., Morrison Homes Corp., Oakland, Cal., Md. Housing Corp., Balt., Tourism Promotion Services, Ltd., Nairobi, Kenya. Trustee Boys' Athletic League, N.Y.C. Served with Intelligence Ser. AUS, 1943-45; ETO. Decorated Bronze Star medal. Mem. Am. Bar Assn., Assn. Bar N.Y.C. Home: 31 DeForest Rd Wilton CT 06897 Office: 120 Long Ridge Rd Stamford CT 06904

KASMAS, JASQUES, artist. Address: care Coda Gallery 89 E 10th St New York City NY 10003*

KASMIRE, ROBERT DIAZ, broadcasting co. exec.; b. New Bedford, Mass., May 7, 1926; s. Robert Diaz and Bertha B. (Parkins) K.; A.B. cum laude, Brown U., 1951; m. Angela Anne Viggiani, May 28, 1957. Reporter, Meriden (Conn.) Record, 1951-52, Providence Jour., sta. WJAR-TV-AM-FM, 1952-53; reporter, editor A.P., 1953-55; dir. bus. publicity State N.Y., 1956; asst. to sec. to N.Y. Gov., 1956-58; with NBC, 1959—, dir. corp. information, 1962-63, v.p., 1963—. Mem. joint com. Research TV and Children. Bd. dirs. Internat. Radio and TV Found., N.Y. County chpt. Multiple Sclerosis Soc. Served with AUS, 1944-46. Recipient Distinguished Service award R.I. Broadcaster's Assn., 1969. Mem. Acad. TV Arts and Scis., Internat. Radio and TV Soc., New Eng. Soc. N.Y., Phi Beta Kappa. Club: Brown University (N.Y.C.); University (Providence). Home: 40 E 9th St New York City NY 10003 Office: NBC 30 Rockefeller Plaza New York City NY 10020

KASPER, RUSSELL RICHARD, air conditioning co. exec.; b. Milw., Nov. 23, 1932; s. Bruno and Frances (Lisiecki) K.; B.B.A., U. Wis., 1955; m. Sandra J. Weston, July 9, 1960; children—Kathleen D., Robert R., Janet M. Auditor, Arthur Young & Co., C.P.A.'s, Milw., 1955-61; controller James Mfg. Co., Ft. Atkinson, Wis., 1961-64, Marmon Group, Chgo., 1964-68, Trane Co., LaCrosse, Wis., 1968—. Served with AUS, 1955-57. C.P.A., Wis. Mem. Am. Inst. C.P.A.'s, Nat. Assn. Accountants. Home: 870 W Janice Ct La Crosse WI 54601 Office: 3600 Pammel Creek Rd La Crosse WI 54601

KASRIEL, ROBERT HERMAN, educator, mathematician; b. Tampa, Fla., Oct. 18, 1918; s. David and Sophie (Kornblum) K.; B.S. in Edn. and Math., U. Tampa, 1940; M.A. in Math., U. Va., 1949, Ph.D. in Math., 1953; m. Ernestine Moskowits, Jan. 31, 1946; children—Sarita Gay, David A. Coordinator war tng. courses U. Tampa (Fla.), 1940-42; instr. math. U.S. Maritime Acad., Pass Christian, Miss., 1945-47; staff aero. research NACA, 1952-54; asst. prof. math. Ga. Inst. Tech., Atlanta, 1954-57, asso. prof., 1957-62, prof., 1962—; vis. faculty mem. U. Va., summer 1956, U. Wis., summer 1963—. Served with AUS, 1942-45; to lt. (j.g.) U.S. Maritime Service, 1945-47. Mem. Am. Math. Soc., Math. Assn. Am., Sigma Xi (pres. Ga. Tech. chpt. 1966-67, M.A. Ferst research award 1962). Nat. Alumni Council U. Tampa. Author: Undergraduate Topology, 1971. Home: 1162 Franklin Circle NE Atlanta GA 30324

KASSABAUM, GEORGE EDWARD, architect; b. Atchison, Kan., Dec. 5, 1920; s. George A. and Dorothy (Gaston) K.; B. Arch., Washington U., St. Louis, 1947; m. Marjory Verser, Jan. 22, 1949; children—Douglas George, Ann Denise, Karen Jane. Faculty, Washington U., 1947-50; asso. Hellmuth, Yamasaki & Leinweber, 1950-55; prin. Hellmuth, Obats & Kassabaum, St. Louis, 1955—. Chmn. bd. mgrs. Downtown br. YMCA. Served with USAAF, 1945-46. Fellow A.I.A. (pres. 1968- 69). Important works include Planetarium St. Louis, U. W. Indies, Bur. Reclamation Office Bldg. (Denver), dormitories, classroom bldgs. U. Mo., U. Washington. Home: 761 Kent Rd St Louis MO 63124 Office: 315 N 9th St St Louis MO 63101

KASSANDER, ARNO RICHARD, Jr., research adminstr.; b. Carbondale, Pa., Sept. 10, 1920; s. Arno Richard and Elsa (Hausstein) K.; B.A., Amherst Coll., 1941; M.S., Okla. U., 1943; Ph.D., Ia. State U., 1950; m. Sara Witmer Nollen, May 15, 1943; 1 dau., Helen Ann. Asst. geologist Tex. Co., 1941; research asst. Magnolia Petroleum Co., 1942; asst. prof. Ia. State U., 1950-54; asso. dir. Inst. Atmospheric Physics, U. Ariz., Tucson, 1954-56, dir., 1956-65, dir. Water Resources Research Center, Tucson, 1965—. Trustee Univ. Corp. Atmospheric Research. Mem. Presidents Sci. Adv. Com. Panel on Environment, 1969—. Bd. dirs. Ariz.-Sonora Desert Mus. Served with AUS, 1943-46. Mem. A.A.A.S., Ariz. Acad. Sci., Am. Phys. Soc., Am. Geophys. Union, Am. Meteorol. Soc., Sigma Xi, Theta Delta Chi. Presbyn. (trustee). Rotarian. Home: 3341 E 4th St Tucson AZ 85716

KASSEBAUM, VERNON BENJAMIN, lawyer; b. Pittsburg, Kan., May 25, 1907; s. John Benjamin and Louise (Dryer) K.; J.D., U. Mo., 1929; m. Helen Louise Woodsmall, Oct. 15, 1932; children—Martha (Mrs. Charles Russell Luger, Jr.), James Warren. Admitted to Mo. bar, 1928, since practiced in Kansas City; partner firm Watson, Ess, Marshall & Enggas, and predecessors, 1943—. Dir. Cook Chem. Co., United Farm Agy., Inc., Luce Press Clippings, Inc. Hon. trustee local Boy Scouts Am. Mem. Am., Mo. bar assns., Lawyers Assn. Kansas City (Mo.), Kansas City (Mo.) C. of C., English-Speaking Union (bd. dirs. Kansas City, Mo. chpt.), Sigma Nu, Phi Delta Phi. Clubs: University, Mission Hills Country (Kansas City, Mo.). Home: 1215 W 59th St Kansas City MO 64113 Office: Home Savings Bldg Kansas City MO 64106

KASSIM, BEN HUSSEIN, Malaysian diplomat; b. Ipoh, Malaysia, Feb. 14, 1928; s. Mohamad Hussein and Puteh Sapiah (OSman) K.; student Malay Coll., U. Malaya; m. Miss Koeswardani, Dec. 30, 1962; children—Rini, Aziah, Srikandi, Kamarul. With Fgn. Service Malaysia, 1958—, minister fgn. affairs, Kuala Lampur, counsellor, Manila, Philippines, also Cairo, UAR; charge d'affaires, Addis Ababa, Ethiopia; now minister to Washington. Clubs: Selangor, Subang Golf, Sentul Golf, Indian Spring Golf. Home: 4704 Linnean Av NW Washington DC 20008 Office: 2401 Massachusetts Av Washington DC 20008

KASSMAN, HERBERT SEYMOUR, camera mfg. co. exec.; b. Binghamton, N.Y., June 13, 1924; s. Maurice Pincus and Clara (Wolkenstein) K.; A.B., Harvard, 1947, LL.B., 1953; m. Deborah Gordon Newman, Aug. 22, 1948; 1 dau., Judith Clare. Engr., writer, editor Jackson & Moreland, cons. engrs., Boston, 1948-50; admitted to Mass. bar, 1953; with Polaroid Corp., Cambridge, Mass., 1953- -, asst. sec., 1961-65, sec., 1965—. Chmn. tax com. Asso. Industries Mass., 1970—. Bd. dirs., clk. Chorus Pro Musica, Boston, 1955—; dir. Met. Cultural Alliance, 1969—. Served to lt. (j.g.) USNR, 1943-46. Mem. Am., Mass., Boston bar assns., Boston Patent Law Assn. Home: 5 Stonewall Rd Lexington MA 02173 Office: 549 Technology Sq Cambridge MA 02139

KAST, CHARLES HOWARD, accountant; b. Rock Rapids, Ia., Dec. 11, 1921; s. Charles A. and Ethel (Howard) K.; B.C.S., Drake U., 1947; m. Rose Bosovich, Mar. 25, 1945; children—Peter C., David H., Carol Ann. With Haskins & Sells, C.P.A.'s, Chgo., 1946-47, Denver, 1947, mem. firm, 1958—. Mem. Colo. Bd. Accountancy, 1965— (past pres.). Past pres., campaign chmn. Mile High United Fund. Served with AUS, 1942-46. Mem. Am. Inst. C.P.A.'s, Colo. Soc. C.P.A.'s (past pres.; past pres., dir. ednl. found.), Mountain States Council C.P.A.'s (past chmn.), Nat. Assn. State Bds. Accountancy (bd. dirs. 1968-70), Denver C. of C. (past treas., bd dirs.), Nat. Assn. Accountants. Clubs: Denver (past dir., treas.), Denver Country; El Paso (Colorado Springs). Home: 3520 S Dahlia St Denver CO 80237 Office: 621 17th St Denver CO 80202

KASTEL, HOWARD LESLIE, lawyer; b. Chgo., Jun 11, 1932; s. William A. and Beatrice (Seltzer) K.; A.B., Harvard, 1954; J.D. cum laude, Loyola U., Chgo., 1960; m. Joan Barbara Herron, Dec. 20, 1953; children-Mark Alan, Jeffrey Lawrence. News reporter, corr. Boston Post, 1951-53; personnel dir. Chgo. Roto Print Co., 1953-56; asst. to chmn. spl. standing com. on labor relations Am. Newspaper Pubs. Assn., Chgo., 1956-60; admitted to Ill. bar, 1960 since practiced in Chgo.; asso. Aaron, Aaron, Achimberg & Hess, 1961-62; gen. mgr., atty. Gary (Ind.) Post-Tribune, 1961-63; asso. Altheimer, Gray, Naiburg, Strasburger & Lawton, 1962-66, partner, 1966—; lectr. in field. Served with USMCR, 1954-56. Mem. Am., Ill., Chgo. (sub-com. chmn. 1967-69) bar assns., Phi Alpha Delta. Club: Winnetka (Ill.) Yacht. Author articles. Home: 156 LaPier St Glencoe IL 60022 Office: N Lasalle St Chicago IL 60602

KASTELIC, ROBERT FRANK, banker; b. Granite City, Ill., July 17, 1934; s. Joseph and Anna M. (Kries) K.; B.S., U. Ill., 1956; postgrad. U. Heidelberg (Germany), 1957- 58; m. Patricia Ann Dalton, Apr. 8, 1961; children—Michael J., Robert J., Constance A. Accountant, Price Waterhouse & Co., C.P.A.'s, St. Louis, 1956-63; mgr. accounting and auditing Nat. Rejectors, Inc., St. Louis, 1963-64; comptroller Merc. Trust Co. N.A., St. Louis, 1964—; v.p. comptroller Merc. Bancorp. Inc., St. Louis, 1964—. Chmn. audit com. United Fund, 1967-69. Served with AUS, 1956-58. C.P.A., Mo. Mem. Am. Inst. C.P.A.'s, Mo. Soc. C.P.A.'s, Financial Execs. Inst. (bd. dirs.), Bank Adminstrn. Inst., Nat. Assn. Accountants, Delta Chi. Home: 5 Sunnybrae Ct Baldwin MO 63011 Office: PO Box 524 St Louis MO 63166

KASTEN, GEORGE FREDERICK, banker; b. Milw., Feb. 2, 1912; s. Walter and Anita (Heinemann) K.; A.B., Williams Coll., 1933; m. Janet Mackie, Apr. 26, 1935; children— Walter II, George Frederick, Alexander Mitchell, Janet Elizabeth. Asso. First Wis. Nat. Bank, Mill., 1934—, now chmn., dir.; sec., dir. Toepfer & Sons, Inc.; pres., dir. First Wis. Bankshares Corp.; dir. Wis. Power & Light Co., Krause Milling Co., Hometown, Inc., First Wis. Trust Co., Harnischfeger Corp., Northwestern Nat. Ins. Co. Clubs: Milwaukee, Town, Milw. Athletic, Milw. Country (Milw.). Home: 4645 N Wilshire Rd Milwaukee WI 53211 Office: 743 N Water St Milwaukee WI 53202

KASTENDIECK, MILES MERWIN, educator, music critic; b. Bklyn., Apr. 16, 1905; s. Julian T.W. and Lizbeth Burr (Gaylor) K.; A.B., Yale, 1927, Mus.B., 1928, Ph.D., 1932; m. Clementine Hall, June 12, 1943; children—Carol Lizbeth, Richard Merwin and Jon Gaylor (twins). Music critic New Haven Jour.- Courier, 1929-38, Bklyn. Eagle, 1937-46, N.Y. Jour. Am., 1946-66, World Jour. Tribune, N.Y.C., 1966-67; tchr. Poly. Prep. Country Day Sch. 1932—, chmn. English dept., 1955- -; lectr. music Bklyn. Inst. of Arts and Scis., 1942-57, 60- 67; music corr. Christian Sci. Monitor, 1945—; dir. Am. Mus. Digest, 1967-70. Mem. exec. com. Friends of Bklyn. Pub. Library, 1939-62, sec. 1945-62; dir. Bklyn. Kindergarten Soc., 1939-69, pres. 1940-42, 46-56, hon. pres., 1956—; bd. dirs. Bklyn. Philharmonic Soc. Recipient Gold Key award Columbia Scholastic Press Assn., 1966; certificate merit Yale Sch. Music Alumni, 1969. Mem. Music Critics Assn. (a founder; pres. 1957-60), Music Critics Circle N.Y.C. (a founder; pres. 1945-51, 53-56, 61-62) Poly Prep Alumni Assn. (sec. 1935—), Phi Beta Kappa. Author: England's Musical Poet-Thomas Campion, 2d edit., 1963; The Story of Poly, 1940. Editorial adv. bd. Mus. Am., 1958-64. Home: 30 Orange St Brooklyn NY 11201 Office: Poly Prep Country Day Sch 92d St and 7th Av Brooklyn NY 11228

KASTENDIECK, RAYMOND STONE, architect; b. Billings, Mont., Aug. 31, 1894; s. John Herman and Mary M. (Stone) K.; B. Archtl. Engring., Washington U., St. Louis, 1923; m. Marion E. Williams, Aug. 3, 1941. With archtl. firm William B. Ittner, St. Louis, 1923-33; propr. Raymond Stone Kastendieck, architect, Gary, Ind., 1933—; projects include housing projects, schs., chs., including Andrean High Sch. and Residences, 1959, (asso. architect) Ind. State Office Bldg., 1959-60. Past rep. Nat. council Sauk Trails council Boy Scouts Am., also mem. exec. bd. Calumet council; bd. dirs. Gary YMCA; pres. bd. trustees A.I.A. Found., 1968—. Served to 1st lt., F.A., U.S. Army, World War I; AEF in France. Recipient Silver Beaver award Boy Scouts America. Fellow A.I.A. (bd. dirs. Great Lakes dist. 1953-56, nat. treas. 1956-63, bursar Coll. of Fellows, 1964-68; advanced fellowship, 1959; mem. nat. jud. bd. 1963-68); mem. Ind. Soc. Architects (pres. 1948-50), Gary C. of C. (past bd. dirs.), No. Ind. Artists Assn., Am. Legion, Tau Beta Pi. Mason (Shriner, Jester), Rotarian (past gov. Dist. 224). Clubs: Gary Country, Gary University; Lake Shore (Chgo.) Home: 128 Glen Park Av Gary IN 46408 Office: 673 Broadway Gary IN 46402

KASTENMEIER, ROBERT WILLIAM, congressman; b. Beaver Dam, Wis., Jan. 24, 1924; s. Leo Henry and Lucille (Powers) K.; LL.B., U. Wis., 1952; m. Dorothy Chambers, June 27, 1952; children—William, Andrew, Edward. Dir. br. office claims service War Dept., P.I., 1946-48; admitted to Wis. bar, 1952; practice in Watertown until 1959; justice of the peace, 1955-58; mem. 86th-92d Congresses 2d Dist. Wis.; mem. com. on judici subcom., chmn. subcom. house jud. com., mem. com. on interior and insular affairs. Mem. Nat. Commn. to Reform Fed. Criminal Laws. Chmn. Jefferson County Democratic Central Com., 1953-56; del. Dem. Nat. Conv., 1956, 64, 68; mem. Wis. Dem. Central Com., 1955-56. Served from pvt. to 1st lt., inf., AUS, 1943-46. Home: 300 N Water St Watertown WI 53094 Office: House Office Bldg Washington DC 20515

KASTLER, ALFRED, educator, scientist; b. Guebwiller, Upper Rhine, May 3, 1902; s. Frederick and Anna (Frey) K.; teaching degree, also D. Phys. Sci.; hon. degrees univs. Louvain, Pisa, Oxford, Laval Quebec, Edinburgh, Jerusalem, Hebraic U. Jerusalem, Belgrad, Bucarest; m. Elise Cosset, Dec. 27, 1924; children—Daniel, Mireille, Claude-Yves. Prof. Lycees de Mulhouse, Colmar, Bordeaux, France, 1926- 31; asst. to sci. faculty U. Bordeaux, 1931-36; lectr. sci. faculty Clermont-Ferrand, 1936-38; prof. faculty scis. U. Bordeaux, 1938-41; asso. prof., then prof. faculty scis. U. Paris (France), 1941-68; Francqui prof. U. Louvain (France), 1953-54. Recipient grand prize de la Recherche sci. decerne par l'Academie des scis., 1956; grand prize sci. de la Ville de Paris, 1963; Nobel Prize in physics, 1966; C.E.K. Mees medal Optical Soc. Am., 1962; decorated officer Legion of Honor (France). Mem. Inst. Acad. Sci., French Phys. Soc. (hon.), Optical Soc. Am. (hon.), Polish Phys. Soc. (hon.), Acad. Scis. Poland (hon.) Deutsche Akakemie du Wissenschaften zu Berlin (hon.), Indian Acad. Sci. (hon.), Deutsche Akademie der Naturforsher Leopoldina (hon.), Flemish Royal Acad. Spl. research on magnetic resonance and optical pumping. Home: 1 rue du Val-de-Grace Paris 5 France

KASTLER, BERNARD ZANE, Jr., natural gas co. exec.; b. Billings, Mont., Oct. 30, 1920; s. Bernard Zane and Elsie (Grossman) K.; student U. Colo., 1940-41; LL.B. with high honors, U. Utah, 1949; m. Donna Irene Endicott, July 24, 1948; children—Lynn (Mrs. John Edwards), Kerry Sue. Admitted to Mont. bar, 1948, Utah bar, 1949; pvt. practice law, 1949-52; counsel Civil Service Commn. Salt Lake City, 1949-50; with Mountain Fuel Supply Co., 1952—, financial v.p., treas., 1968—; legal officer Utah wing Civil Air Patrol, 1956-68. Mem. Salt Lake City Traffic Adv. Com., 1950; exec. sec. Utah Bd. Pardons, 1951; legal counsel Salt Lake Area Transp. Study Com., 1955-57; instr. law U. Utah Sch. Law, 1950-51. Dir. Wasatch Chem. Co., Zions Savs. & Loan Assn., Walker Bank & Trust Co. Active Utah Heart Assn., 1958-64, Great Salt Lake council Boy Scouts Am., 1960-63; div. chmn. Westminster Coll. Devel. Fund, 1958; campaign chmn. Greater Salt Lake Area United Fund, 1959, chmn. spl. events, 1960, v.p., 1961, bd. dirs., 1959-65, pres., 1964; mem. legislative com. Pro Utah, Inc., 1965; adv. com., div. continuing edn. U. Utah, 1964—; mem. Utah Bd. Bonding Commrs., 1965—; chmn. Traffic Citizenship Com., 1964—; adv. com. to Utah rep. to Pub. Land Law Rev. Commn., 1967-69; mem. ad hoc com. to rev. functions and financial adminstrn. div. continuing edn. U. Utah, 1968—; mem. Utah Legislative Conf., 1957—, v.p., 1965—, mem. constl. revision com., 1969—; mem. selection com., scholarship award Utah Pub. Employees Assn., 1967. Republican chmn. legislative dist. 17, 1960-64; mem. Utah Ho. of Reps. 17th Dist., 1963-64. Bd. dirs. Utah Mental Health Assn., 1960-61, Blue Shield, 1964-65; bd. dirs. U. Utah Alumni Assn., 1967-69, nat. chmn. alumni fund drive, 1969; trustee Utah Heritage Found., 1967- -. Served with USNR, World War II. Mem. Am., Utah, Salt Lake County, Mont., Fed. bar assns., Ind. Natural Gas Assn., Ind. Petroleum Assn. Am. Pacific Gas Assn. (chmn. legal com. 1967-68), Rocky Mountain Oil and Gas Assn., Rocky Mountain Mineral Found. (trustee 1959-63, 65—, chmn. scholarship com. 1963-64). Nat. Assn. Congl. Christian Chs. (moderator 1955-56, mem. exec. com. 1969-70), Salt Lake City C. of C. (chmn, aviation com. 1963—, bd. govs. 1967-70, v.p. govt. and pub. affairs council 1968-70), Order of Coif, Phi Kappa Phi, Phi Delta Phi. Conglist. (deacon 1951-57, chmn. ch. bd. 1957- 58). Mason, Kiwanian (pres. Salt Lake City 1967). Contbr profl. jours. Home: 3777 E Millstream Dr Salt Lake City UT 84109 Office: PO Box 11368 Salt Lake City UT 84111

KASTOR, FRANK SULLIVAN, educator; b. Evanston, Ill., Aug. 19, 1933; s. Herman Walker and Rebecca (Sullivan) K.; B.A., U. Ill., 1955, M.A., 1956; Ph.D., U. Cal. at Berkeley, 1963; m. Sue Schurman (div. 1962); in 2d, Sue Dirksen, Dec. 27, 1964; children—Jeffrey, Mark, Harlan. Teaching asst. U. Ill., 1955-56; teaching asst. U. Cal. at Berkeley, 1960-63; asst. prof. English U. So. Cal., 1964-6, 67-68; asso. prof. English No. Ill. U., 1968-69; prof., chmn. dept. Wichita State U., 1969—. Served with USAF, 1956-59. Research grantee U. Cal. at Berkeley, 1962, U. So. Cal., 1964, No. Ill. U., 1969, Wichita State U., 1970; Fulbright lectureship, Spain, 1966-67; recipient Nat. Endowment Humanities award, 1971. Mem. Modern Lang. Assn., Midwest Modern Lang. Assn., Philol. Assn. Pacific Coast (sec. chmn. 1969), Milton Soc. Am., Am. Assn. U. Profs., Comparative Lit. Assn. Western States. Contbr. The Milton Ency., 1972. Author articles. Home: 28 Willowbrook Rd Wichita KS 67207

KASWELL, ERNEST RALPH, chemist; b. Boston, Mar. 21, 1917; s. Louis and Goldie (Jacobs) K.; B.S., Mass. Inst. Tech., 1939, M.S., 1941; m. Yolande Romsey, Aug. 15, 1943; children—Jeanne (Mrs. Jeanne Kaswell Sager), Gordon David, Stuart Joel. Research asso. Mass. Inst. Tech., 1939-41, 60-61; chemist Am. Cyanamid Co., 1941-42; pres. Fabric Research Labs., Inc., Dedham, Mass., 1942—; spl. research mech. properties textiles, plastics and polymers, parachutes. Fellow Brit. Textile Inst.; mem. Fiber Soc. (pres. 1960), Am. Assn. Textile Chemists and Colorists (pres. 1963-64; Olney medal 1971), Am. Chem. Soc., Am. Assn. Textile Technologists, Textile Research Inst., A.A.A.S., British Soc. Dyers and Colourists, Sigma Xi. Mason. Author: Textile Fibers, Yarns and Fabrics, 1953; Handbook of Industrial Textiles, 1963; also articles. Home: 67 Paulson Rd Waban MA 02168 Office: 1000 Providence Hwy Dedham MA 02026

KASZNAR, KURT SEWISCHER, actor; b. Vienna, Austria, Aug. 12, 1913; s. Nathan and Leopoldine (Schweiger) Serwischer; grad. Schuttel Gymnasium, Vienna, 1930, Max Rheinhard Sem., 1932; m. Cornelia Woolley, 1938 (dec. 1947); m. 2d, Leora Sheppherd Dana, June 29, 1952 (div.). Actor starring motion pictures, Broadway shows, TV; theatrical credits include Don Juan in Hell, Joy to the World, Montserrat, The Happy Time, Seventh Heaven, Six Characters in Search of an Author, Waiting for Godot, Look After Lulu, The Sound of Music, Barefoot in the Park, My Three Angels, Once More with Feeling, The Little Hut, Arms and the Man; films include The Happy Time, Valley of the King, Lonely to Look At, Glory Alley, Talk About a Stranger, Anything Can Happen, All the Brothers Were Valiant, Kiss Me, Kate, Give a Girl a Break, Sombrero, Ride Vaquero, Lili, The Last Time I Saw Paris, Jump Into Hell, Flame of the Islands, My Sister Eileen, Anything Goes, The Light Touch, Legend of the Lost, A Farewell to Arms, For the First Time, The Journey, 55 Days at Peking; TV role in Land of the Giants. Served with Signal Corps, AUS, World War II.‡

KATCHER, DAVID A., consultant; b. Bklyn. Apr. 28, 1915; s. Morris M. and Leah (Meltzer) K.; B.A., U. Wis., 1936; m. Shirley Mingins Nibley, Mar. 29, 1947; children—Philip Royall Nibley, Katherine Liza. Founding editor Physics Today, monthly mag., N.Y.C., 1948; with Operations Research Office, Johns Hopkins, 1951-56; with Inst. Def. Analyses, 1956-66, Arthur D. Little Co., Inc., Cambridge, Mass., 1966—. Served to 1st lt., AUS 1943- 46. Mem. Operations Research Soc. Am. (treas. 1959-62). Home: Arena Terrace Concord MA 01792 Office: 35 Acorn Park Cambridge MA 02140

KATELL, SIDNEY, cost engr.; b. N.Y.C., Feb. 2, 1915; s. Aaron and Gusta (Ornstein) K.; B.Chem. Engring., N.Y. U., 1941; m. Elvie League, July 4, 1948; children—Alan David, Barry Steven. Chem. engr. design U.S. Bur. Mines, Louisiana, Mo., 1948-53, chem. engr., Morgantown, W.Va., 1954-55, chief gas treating and testing sect., 1955-57, chief process evaluation group, Morgantown, 1957—; chem. engr. Westinghouse Electric Co., Pitts., 1953-54. Vis. asso. prof. W.Va. U., 1969—. Mem. Am. Assn. Cost Engrs. (pres. 1970-71), Am. Chem. Soc., Am. Inst. Chem. Engrs.; Am. Gas Assn. (Operating Sect. award merit 1955), Morgantown C. of C. (chmn. pollution control com.). Jewish religion (pres. congregation). Mem. B'nai B'rith. Contbr. articles to profl., govtl. jours. Home: 1464 Dogwood Av Morgantown WV 26505 Office: PO Box 880 Morgantown WV 26505

KATES, CHARLES, mfg. co. exec.; b. Hamilton, Ont., Can., Mar. 13, 1918; s. William and Rose (Levin) K.; student U. Toronto, 1936-38; m. Phyllis M. Jacobson, Feb. 24, 1946; children—Kenneth William, Patti Jane. Came to U.S., 1939, naturalized, 1943. Sales promotion Monogram Pictures, also Warner Bros. Pictures, 1939-42; with Union Malleable Mfg. Co. 1947—, dir., 1948—, sec., purchasing agt. (corp. and subsidiaries), 1949-52, v.p., sales mgr., 1952-53, pres., gen. mgr., 1953—; sec., works mgr. Union Brass & Copper Co., 1948; mem. adv. bd. First Nat. Bank, Mansfield, O. Mem. pres.'s council Ashland (O.) Coll. Served with USAAF, 1942-46. Mem. Ohio, Ashland chambers commerce, N.A.M. Home: 17800 Shaker Blvd Shaker Heights OH Office: Clark St Ashland OH

KATIMS, MILTON, conductor; b. Bklyn., s. Harry and Caroline K.; A.B., Columbia; Mus.D. (hon.), Whitworth Coll., 1959; m. Virginia Katims; children- -Peter Michael, Pamela Artura. With Budapest String Quartet, 1940-54; first desk violist under Arturo Toscanini, NBC Symphony, 1943; staff condr. NBC, 1944-54; mem. faculty Juilliard Sch. Music, 1946-54; guest conductor NBC Symphony, 1947-54, also Boston, Cleve., Phila., N.Y., Chgo., Paris, Brussels, Barcelona, Israel, Hollywood Bowl, London, Eng., Vancouver Festival; mus. dir., condr. Seattle Symphony, 1954—; guest condr. Philharmonia Orch., London, 1961; condr. Seattle World's Fair Festival, 1962; mus. dir. Menton Festival, 1963, La Jolla (Cal.) Festival, summers 1964-68; guest conductor Mozart Festival at Lincoln Center, 1966, Japan Philharmonic, Tokyo, 1967. Mem. music adv. panel State Dept. Cultural Presentations, 1968. Recipient Columbia U. medal, 1953, Alice M. Ditson Condr. award, 1963. Editor various works. Contbr. articles to N.Y. Times, Sat. Rev., Music Pubs. Jour., Columbia Records and RCA, Victor Records. Office: Seattle Symphony 4th and Pike Bldg Seattle WA 98104

KATKE, MARVIN LEO, automobile mfg. co. exec.; b. Big Rapids, Mich., Feb. 8, 1908; s. John F. and Laura (Holt) K.; student Mich. State Coll., 1937-39; m. Maisie Cope, Nov. 1, 1925; children—John, David. With Oldsmobile div. Gen. Motors Corp., 1928-49; plant mgr. automatic transmission div. Ford Motor Co., Dearborn, Mich., 1949-51, asst. group exec., 1952-53, gen. mgr. automatic transmission div., 1953-57, then group exec., now v.p.; dir. Southwestern Water Co., Cin. Mem. Navy League U.S., Soc. Automotive Engrs., Am. Ordnance Assn., Soc. Tool Engrs., Livonia (Mich.), Cin. chambers commerce. Clubs: Detroit Athletic, Oakland Hills Country (Detroit); Bloomfield Hills Country. Home: 1401 Kirkway Dr Bloomfield Hills MI 48013 Office: Ford Motor Co American Rd Dearborn MI 48121

KATONA, GEORGE, social scientist; b. Budapest, Hungary, Nov. 6, 1901; s. Siegmund and Olga (Wittmann) K.; Ph.D., U. Goettingen (Germany), 1921; m. Marian Beck, Nov. 2, 1929. Came to U.S., 1933, naturalized, 1939. Asso. editor Der Deutsche Volkswirth, Berlin, Germany, 1926-33; investment counsel, N.Y.C., 1933-36; lectr. New Sch. Social Research, N.Y.C., 1936-42; research dir. com. on price control Cowles Commn., U. Chgo., 1943-45; sr. study dir. div. program surveys Dept. Agr., Washington, 1945-46; program dir. survey research center, prof. econ. and psychol. U. Mich., 1946—; vis. prof. Mass. Inst. Tech., 1961, N.Y.U., 1964. Recipient grant Carnegie Found., 1938-40; fellow Guggenheim Meml. Found., 1940-42; winner 1st Dr. Hegemann prize, Dusseldorf, Germany, 1963. Mem. Am. Psychol. Assn., Am. Econ. Assn., Am. Statis. Assn. Author: Organizing and Memorizing, 1940; War Without Inflation, 1942; Price Control and Business, 1945; Psychological Analysis of Economic Behavior, 1951; Consumer Attitudes and Demand, 1953; Consumer Expectations, 1956; Business Looks at Banks, 1957; The Powerful Consumer, 1960; The Mass Consumption Society, 1964; Private Pensions and Individuals Saving, 1965; Consumer Response to Income Increases, 1968; Aspirations and Affluence, 1971. Home: 1615 Brooklyn Av Ann Arbor MI 48104

KATORI, YASÛE, former diplomat of Japan; b. Sendai, Japan, July 16, 1921; s. Ryuzo and Kaoruko (Shoda) K.; m. Nobuko Ichikawa, June 6, 1947; children—Yoshinori, Mayuni. Joined Japanese Fgn. Service, 1943; 2d sec. embassy, Bonn, Germany, 1953-55, 1st sec., 1959-63; head Western European div. Fgn. Office, 1964-67; consul gen. in Seattle, 1967-70. Hon. v.p. Japan-Am. Soc., Seattle, 1968-70. Club: Rainier (Seattle). Home: 2217 W Viewmont Way Seattle WA 98199 Office: Norton Bldg Seattle WA 98104

KATSH, ABRAHAM ISAAC, univ. pres.; b. Poland, Aug. 10, 1908; s. Reuben and Rachel (Maskilleison) K.; came to U.S., 1925, naturalized, 1932; B.S., N.Y.U., 1931, A.M., 1932, J.D., 1936; postgrad. Princeton 1941; Ph.D., Dropsie U., 1944; D.H.L. (hon.), Hebrew Union Coll.-Jewish Inst. of Religion, 1964, Coll. of Jewish Studies, Chgo., 1968; D.D. (hon.), Christian Theol. Sem., 1970, U. Dubuque; LL.D. (hon.), Lebanon Valley (Pa.) Coll.; m. Estelle Wachtell, Feb. 20, 1943; children—Ethan, Salem, Rochelle. Instr. Hebrew, N.Y.U., 1934-37, exec. dir. Jewish Culture Found., 1937-44, exec. chmn., 1944-67, instr. edn., 1937-44, asst. prof., 1944-45, asso. prof., 1945-47, prof. edn., 1947-66, prof. Hebrew and Near Eastern studies Grad. Sch. Arts and Scis., 1966-67, dir. Inst. Hebrew Studies, 1962-67, Arabic instr., 1942-43, dir. Library Judaica and Hebraica, 1942, curator, 1952-67, chmn. dept. fgn. langs., 1953-54, chmn. dept. Hebrew culture edn., 1953—, dir. Hebrew lang. and lit. sect. Wash. Sq. Coll., 1957-66, distinguished prof. research, 1967-68; lectr. New Sch. Social Research; pres. Dropsie U., Phila., 1967—, research prof. Hebraica, 1967—; dir. Am. Workshop on Israel Life and Culture, held in Israel sponsored by N.Y.U., 1949-67; asst. editor charge Hebrew, Modern Lang. Jour., 1949—; mng. editor Jour. Ednl. Sociology, 1948-51; editor Bar Mitzvah, 1955; lectr. at internat. congress and world congress. Mem. exec. bd. License for Tchrs. and Prins. of Jewish Sch., N.Y.C.; chmn. Nat. Bd. of License for Tchrs. and Colls. field Hebrew Studies, 1957—; spl. examiner N.Y.C. Bd. Edn. Trustee Dropsie U., A.S.O.R.; bd. govs. World Hebrew Acad. Recipient Bnai Zion Meritorius key, 1944; Founders citation N.Y.U. Chair Hebrew Culture Edn., 1953; Brith Abraham Gold Medal, 1952; Tercentary citation Jewish Book Council Am., 1954; 1st prize Hebrew Acad. Am., 1956; Matz Found. prize, 1956, 1st prize Hebrew Acad. Histadruth Ivrith, 1957; Dropsie Coll. Jubilee citation, 1957; named Ky. Col., 1957; prof. chair named in honor, N.Y.U., 1957; recipient Am. Assn. Jewish Edn. award, 1959; Ernest O. Melby award, 1962. Mem. N.Y. State Fedn. Fgn. Lang. Tchrs. (dir.), World Congress Hebrew Lang. and Culture (exec. com.), Jewish Book Council Am. (nat. com.), Zionist Orgn. Am. (nat. chmn. 1949-51), Nat. Council Jewish Edn. (exec. com.), Jewish Acad. Arts and Sci. (chmn. exec. bd.), Nat. Assn. Profs. Hebrew in Am. Instns. Higher Learning (founder, pres. 1951- 53, hon. pres., 1953—), Am. Assn. Jewish Edn. (nat. chmn. bd. licenses), Hadoar Assn. (exec. bd.), Inst. Internat. Edn., Modern Lang. Assn. (chmn. evaluation modern Hebrew materials), Am. Jewish Congress, World Hebrew Congress, Phi Delta Kappa. Author: Einstein's Theory of Relativity (Hebrew), 1937; Hebrew in American Higher Education, 1941; Hebraic Contributions to American Life. 1941; Krochmal and the German Idealists, 1948; Hebrew Language, Literature and Culture in American Institutions of Higher Learning, 1950; Education and Racial Prejudices; Democracy and Interfaith; Hebraic Backgrounds of American Democracy, 1951; Judaism in Islam, 1954; Judaic Backgrounds of Islam (Hebrew), 1957; The Bible and the Koran, 1962; The Antonin Genizah Collection in the USSR, 1963; Yiggal Hazon, 1964; The Scroll of Agony (Hebrew), 1964, (English), 1966; Megilat Yessurin (Hebrew), 1966, Chronique D'une Agonie (French), 1966, Dodens Dokument (Swedish) 1967, Buch der Agonie (German); Midrash David Hanagid (Hebrew), vol. I, 1967, vol. II, 1968; Ginze Mishna, 1971. Editor-in-chief Hebrew Abstracts, 1950—; asso. editor Universal Jewish Ency., 1958-59; editorial com. Nat. Study Jewish Edn., 1957; co-editor Jewish Quar. Rev., 1968—; chmn. editorial bd. Jewish Apocryphal Literature, 1968—. Contbr. jours. and encys. articles. Home: 1520 Spruce St Philadelphia PA 19102

KATSOYANNIS, PANAYOTIS GEORGE, educator; b. Athens, Greece, Jan. 7, 1924; s. George P. and Moira (Armiriotis) K.; M.S. in Organic Chemistry, U. Athens (Greece), 1948, Ph.D. in Organic Chemistry, 1952; m. Frieda Kontos, June 4, 1955; children—Miranda, George. Came to U.S., 1952, Naturalized, 1962. Head div. biochemistry Med. Research Center Brookhaven Nat. Lab., Upton, N.Y., 1964-68; Dorothy H. and Lewis Rosenstiel prof. biochemistry, chmn. dept. Mt. Sinai Sch. Medicine, City U. N.Y., 1968—; Edwin J. Cohn Meml. lectr., 1963. Served with Greek Army, 1950-52. Found. Greece fellowship, 1952-54; recipient career devel. award USPHS, 1963. Corr. mem. Nat. Acad. Greece. Contbr. articles profl. jours. Synthesis Human and Animal Insuline. Home: 69 Drake Lane Manhasset NY 11030 Office: Mt Sinai Sch Medicine 10 E 102d St New York City NY 10029

KATTEL, GUSTAVE EDWARD, financial cons.; b. N.Y.C., June 27, 1908; B.C.S., N.Y.U., 1930; m. Dorothea Fleming, June 12, 1930; children—Edward, Richard. With Grace Nat. Bank, N.Y.C., 1951-65, exec. v.p., 1955-65, past dir.; exec. v.p. Marine Midland Grace Trust Co., N.Y.C., 1965-69; chmn. Kattel, Inc., Coral Gables, Fla., 1969—; dir. Rotron, Inc., Woodstock, N.Y. Mem. Delta Sigma Pi. Mason. Clubs: Athletic, India House (N.Y.C.); Miami (Fla.); Key Biscayne Yacht. Home: 615 Ocean Dr Key Biscayne FL 33149 Office: 316 Minorca Av Coral Gables FL 33134

KATTEL, RICHARD L., banker; b. N.Y.C., 1936; grad. Emory U., 1958; postgrad. Harvard Bus. Sch. Program Mgmt. Devel.; married. With Citizens and So. Nat. Bank, Savannah, Ga., 1958—, asst. to pres., 1966-68, exec. v.p. in charge Savannah bank, 1968—, also dir.; pres., dir. C & S Community Devel. Corp. Bd. dirs. Candler Gen. Hosp., YMCA, United Community Services. Served with AUS. Home: 2912 Atlantic Av Savannah GA 31404 Office: 300 Bull St Savannah GA 31402*

KATTUS, ALBERT ADOLPH, Jr., medical educator; b. Cin., Oct. 8, 1917; s. Albert A. and Matilda (Gerling) K.; A.B., Ohio Wesleyan U., 1939; M.D., U. Rochester, 1943; m. Mary Clare Fallon, June 23, 1945; children—Frank, Mary Jo, Gretchen, Sarah, Jane, Patricia, Thomas, Successively intern, asst. resident, clin. fellow, research fellow Johns Hopkins Hosp., 1944-51; asst. prof. medicine U. Cal. at Los Angeles Med. Sch., 1951-56, asso. prof., 1956-62, prof., 1962—; vis. prof. medicine Vanderbilt U., 1968-69. Served to lt. (j.g.) M.C., USNR, 1945-46, as maj. M.C., AUS, 1956-57. Fellow A.C.P.; mem. Am. (v.p. research com.), Cal. heart assns., Mission Drs. Assn., Assn. U. Cardiologists, Western Assn. Physicians, Western Soc. Clin. Investigation, A.M.A. Research in effect of exercise tng. in coronary insufficiency and angina pectoris. Home: 10647 Eastborne Av Los Angeles CA 90024

KATZ, ABRAHAM, fgn. service officer; b. Bklyn., Dec. 4, 1926; s. Alexander and Zina (Rabinowitz) K.; B.A. cum laude, Bklyn. Coll., 1948; student Hebrew U., Jerusalem, 1946-47, Harvard, 1956-57; M.I.A., Columbia, 1950; Ph.D., Harvard, 1968; m. Carmella Furman, June 18, 1947; children—Tamar, Jonathan, Naomi. Joined U.S. Fgn. Service, 1951; vice consul, prin. officer, Merida Yucatan, Mexico, 1951-53; 2d sec., vice consul, Mexico City, 1953-55; with bur. intelligence Office Undersec., State Dept., 1957-59; 1st sec. U.S. missions to NATO and OECD, Paris, France, 1959-64; sec. U.S. delegation to OECD, 1959-64; counselor of embassy, Moscow, USSR, 1964-66; fellow Center Internat. Affairs, Harvard, 1966-67; dir. OECD, Office European Community and Atlantic Polit. Econ. Affairs, Dept. of State, 1967—. Recipient Commendable Service award State Dept., 1952, Meritorious Service award, 1963. Mem. Am. Assn. Advancement Slavic Studies, Am. Soc. Study Soviet Type Econs., Am. Fgn. Service Assn., Am. Polit. Sci. Assn. Author: The Politics of Economic Reform in the Soviet Union. Home: 3309 Shirley Lane Chevy Chase MD 20015 Office: Dept State EURRPE Washington DC 20523

KATZ, ALEX, artist; b. Bklyn., July 24, 1927; s. Isaac and Ella (Marion) K.; certificate, Cooper Union, 1949; m. Ada Del Moro, Feb. 1, 1958; 1 son, Vincent. One man exhbns. include Roko Gallery, N.Y.C., 1954, 57, Fischbach Gallery, N.Y.C., 1964-71, Stable Gallery, N.Y.C., 1960-61, Tanager Gallery, N.Y.C., 1959, 62, Martha Jackson Gallery, N.Y.C., 1962, Grinnell Gallery, Detroit, 1964, Sun Gallery, Provincetown, Mass., 1958- 59, Pa. State Coll., 1957, Mili-Jay Gallery, Woodstock, N.Y., 1961, David Stuart Gallery, Los Angeles, 1966, Bertha Eccles Art Center, Ogden, Utah, 1968, Towson State Coll., Balt., 1968, Phyllis Kind Gallery, Chgo., 1969-71, W.Va. U., 1969; group shows include Pa. Acad., 1960, Va. Mus., Richmond, 1960, Whitney Mus., 1960, 67-68, Art Inst. Chgo., 1961, 62, 64, Yale Mus., 1962, Colby Coll., 1961, 63, 64, Am. Fedn. Art., 1964-65, Mus. Modern Art, 1964-66, Milw. Arts Center, 1966, 69, R.I. Sch. Design, 1966, Cin. Art Mus., 1968, Am. Acad. Design, 1968, U. Cal. at LaJolla, 1969, numerous others; vis. critic Yale, 1960-63; rep. permanent collections Whitney Mus., Mus. Modern Art, Brandeis U., N.Y.U., Bowdoin Coll., Detroit Mus., Allentown (Pa.) Mus., Weatherspoon Gallery Art, Greensboro, N.C., Tokyo (Japan) Gallery, Allen Meml. Art Mus., Oberlin, O. Address: 435 W Broadway New York City NY 10012

KATZ, ARTHUR JASON, educator; b. N.Y.C., June 27, 1924; s. Samuel and Eva (Rosenthal) K.; B.S., City U. N.Y., 1947; M.S., Columbia, 1952; Ph.D., N.Y. U., 1968; m. Eleanor Landa, July 3, 1947; children—Susan (Mrs. Steven Morris), Johathan, Samuel, Daniel. Exec. dir. East Tremont Center, N.Y.C., 1953-56; dean, prof. Grad. Sch. Social Work, Adelphi U., Garden City, N.Y., 1956-62; exec. v.p. Jewish Theol. Sem. Am., N.Y.C., 1962-65; asso. prof. Grad. Sch. Social Work, N.Y.U., 1965-68; dean, prof. Sch. Social Welfare, U. Kan., Lawrence, 1968—; cons. OEO, Office Child Devel., Office Edn., Dept. Health, Edn. and Welfare; dir. Camp Ray Hill, Mt. Kislo, N.Y., 1953—, Vacation Camp for Blind, Spring Valley, N.Y., 1948-50, Camp Hawthorne, St. Louis, 1955—. Mem. Am. Civil Liberties Union, N.A.A.C.P., N.Y. State Citizens Council. Bd. dirs. Health and Welfare Council Nassau County; v.p. Vocational Found. N.Y. Served with USAAF, 1942-46. Recipient City U. Alumni award, 1947, Sen. Robert F. Wagner award Columbia 1956, N.Y.U. Founders award, 1968. Mem. Lawrence C. of C. Nat. Assn. Social Workers, Council Social Work Edn., Am. Assn. U. Profs., Nat. Conf. Social Welfare, Internat. Council Social Welfare. Home: 2549 Jasu Dr Lawrence KS 66044

KATZ, DANIEL, psychologist; b. Trenton, N.J., July 19, 1903; s. Rudolph and Regina (Fleischer) K.; A.B., U. Buffalo, 1925 A.M., Syracuse U., 1926, Ph.D., 1928; m. Christine Ross Braley, Sept 1, 1930; children—Joanna Braley, Jean Braley. Instr. psychology Princeton, 1928-31, asst. prof., 1931-40, asso. prof., 1940-43; prof. psychology, chmn. dept. Bklyn. Coll., 1943-47; prof. psychology U. Mich., 1947—, program dir. Survey Research Center, 1947-50, research asso., 1950—. Research dir. surveys div. OWI, 1943-44. Fellow Center Advanced Study Behavioral Scis., 1960-61. Mem. Am.

Psychol. Assn. (dir. 1960-63), Indsl. Relations Research Assn., Soc. Psychol. Study Social Issues (sec.- treas., 1945-48, pres., 1949-50), Phi Beta Kappa, Sigma Xi. Author: Students Attitudes, 1931; (with R.L. Schanck) Social Psychology, 1938; (with Henry Valen) Political Parties in Norway, 1964 (with R. L. Kahn) The Social Psychology of Organizations, 1966. Editor: Research Methods in the Behavioral Sciences (with Leon Festinger), 1953; Public Opinion and Propaganda, 1954. Editorial bd. Pub. Opinion Quar., 1939-50, Jour. Conflict Resolution 1957—; editor Jour. Abnormal and Social Psychology, 1962-64, Jour. Personality and Social Psychology, 1965-67. Contbr. articles profl. jours. Home: 1789 Country Club Rd Ann Arbor MI 48105

KATZ, DONALD LAVERNE, chem. engr.; b. nr. Jackson, Mich., Aug. 1, 1907; s. Gottlieb and Lucy (Schnackenberg) K.; B.S., U. Mich., 1931, M.S., 1932, Ph.D., 1933; m. Lila Maxine Crull, Sept. 17, 1932 (dec. 1965); children—Marvin LaVerne, Linda Maxine; m. 2d, Elizabeth Harwood Correll, Nov. 26, 1965; stepchildren—Ricard, Steven, Jonathan H. Research engr. Phillips Petroleum Co., Bartlesville, Okla., 1933- 36; asst. in depts. chemistry and chem. engring. U. Mich., 1930-33, asst. prof. chem. engring., 1936-42, asso. prof., 1942-43, prof. chem. engring., 1943-66, Alfred H. White univ. prof. chem. engring., 1966—, chmn. dept. chem. and metall. engring., 1951-62; cons. engr., 1936—. Trustee Ann Arbor pub. schs. (pres. 1953-56), Engring. Index, 1966—. Recipient Hanlon award Natural Gasoline Assn. Am., 1950; named Mich. Engr. Yr., Mich. Soc. Profl. Engrs., 1959; recipient John Franklin Carll award Soc. Petroleum Engrs., 1964; Founders award Am. Inst. Chem. Engrs., 1964; Warren K. Lewis award, 1967; W.H. Walker award, 1968; Mineral Industry Edn. award Am. Inst. Mining and Metall. Engrs., 1970. Fellow A.A.A.S., American Nuclear Soc., Am. Inst. Chem. Engrs. (bd. dirs. 1955-57, v.p. 1958, pres. 1959, sec. commn. engring. edn. 1962-64); mem. Am. Chem. Soc., Am. Inst. Mining and Metall. Engrs., Am. Soc. M.E., Am. Soc. Engring. Edn., Am. Gas Assn., Ann Arbor Council Chs. (pres. 1944-46), Nat. Soc. Profl. Engrs., Nat. Acad. Sci. (chmn. USCG com. on hazardous materials 1964—, mem. sci. and tech. communications com. 1967-69), Engrs. Council Profl. Devel. (bd. dirs., mem. exec. com. 1959-65, trustee EDUCOM 1967—, chmn. bd. trustees 1969—), Nat. Acad. Engring., Sigma Xi, Tau Beta Pi, Phi Lambda Upsilon (hon.), Phi Kappa Phi, Alpha Chi Sigma. Methodist. Contbr. articles profl. publs. Home: 2011 Washtenaw Av Ann Arbor MI 48104

KATZ, EARL SIDNEY, merchant; b. Kansas City, Mo., Aug. 28, 1907; s. Isaac and Minnie V. (Baranov) K.; B.S. in Econs., Wharton Sch. of U. Pa., 1929; m. Dorothy Hoffman, Aug. 15, 1934; children—Stephen, Earl Sidney, Leslie Jo, Ward Allen. Buyer, v.p. Katz Drug Co., Kansas City, Mo., 1929-46, pres., 1946- 60, vice chmn., 1960-62, chmn., 1962-69; vice chmn. Bdg. Skaggs Companies, Inc., Kansas City, Mo., 1970—. Bd. dirs. Am. Royal Assn., Starlite Theater Assn., Kansas City Philharmonic Orch.; trustee Isaac and Minnie Katz Found. Served to capt. USAAF, 1942-45. Office: 1130 Walnut St Kansas City MO 64106

KATZ, EDWARD MORRIS, banker; b. Passaic, N.J., Apr. 18, 1921; s. David and Badane (Gubersky) K.; B.A., Bklyn. Coll., 1947; M.A., N.Y. U., 1948; m. Phyllis Kushner, June 20, 1948; children—David, Alan, Michael. Auditor, Amalgamated Bank N.Y., N.Y.C., 1951-55, cashier, 1955—, v.p., 1957-61, sr. v.p., 1961-71, exec. v.p., 1971—, dir., 1966—. Served with USAAF, 1941-45. Mem. Nat. Assn. Bank Auditors, Am., N.Y. State bankers assns. Home: 48 Windsor Rd Great Neck NY 11020 Office: 11-15 Union Square New York City NY 10003

KATZ, EUGENE R., corp. exec.; b. Woodbine, N.J., Dec. 1, 1909; s. Isaac and Fanny (Askoff) K.; student Dickinson Coll., 1927-28; LL.B., Cumberland U., 1932; m. Muriel Sylvia Klubock, Mar. 28, 1943; children—Barbara Ann, Janet F. Admitted to Ga. bar, 1932; gen. practice law, 1932-35; with UN, 1945-48, Warren Industries, 1948-64; v.p. Jim Walter Corp., 1966—, also dir.; pres. Celotex Corp., 1966—, also dir.; dir. Celotex Ltd. (London), Crawford Door European COAB (Torslanda, Sweden). Home: 1524 Cecilia St Coral Gables FL 33146 Office: 1500 N Dale Mabry St Tampa FL 33607

KATZ, HERBERT MELVIN, editor; b. N.Y.C., Nov. 13, 1930; s. Dr. Charles and May (Tonkin) K.; B.A., N.Y.U., 1951; M.A., Columbia, 1952; m. Marjorie Phillis Pearle, Jan. 5, 1957; children—Daniel Seth, Nina Judith. Publicity writer Viking Press, 1952-53; editor-in-chief Pyramid Books, 1953-55; editorial dir. Funk & Wagnalls Co., also Wilfred Funk, Inc., 1955-61; editor G.P. Putnam's Sons, 1961-63; v.p., editor-in-chief M. Evans & Co., 1964—. Author: (with Mrs. Katz) Museums, U.S.A.: A History and Guide, 1965; Museum Adventures: An Introduction to Discovery, 1969. Office: 216 E 49th St New York City NY 10017

KATZ, HILDA, artist; b. June 2, 1909; d. Max and Lina (Schwartz) Katz; student Nat. Acad. Design (3 awards; New Sch. Social Research scholarship), 1940-41. One-woman exhbns. include Bowdoin Coll. Art Mus., 1951, Cal. State Library, 1953, U. Me., 1955, 58, Jewish Mus., 1956, Pa. State Tchrs. Coll., 1956, Massillon Mus., 1957, Ball State Tchrs. Coll., 1957, Springfield (Mass.) Art Mus., 1957, Miami Beach (Fla.) Art Center, Richmond (Ind.) Art Assn., 1959, Old State Capitol Mus. La.; other exhbns. include Corcoran Bienniale Library of Congress, Am. in the War Exhbn. (26 museums), Am. Drawing anns. at Albany Inst., Nat. Acad. Design, Conn. Acad. Fine Arts, Bklyn. Mus., Delgado Mus., Art-U.S.A., 1959, Congress for Jewish Culture, Met. Mus. Art., Springfield (Mo.) Art Mus., Children's Mus. Hartford, Conn., Miniature Printers, Peoria (Ill.) Art Center, Pa. Acad. Fine Arts, Originale Contemporate Graphic Internat., France, Bezalel Nat. Mus., Israel, Venice (Italy) Bienniale, Royal Etchers and Painters Exchange Exhibit, Eng., Bat Yam Mus., Israel, Paris, France, 1958, 59, Am.-Italian Print Exchange, numerous libraries, artists socs.; invitational exhbns. include Rome, Turin, Venice, Florence, Naples (all Italy), Nat. Academe Muse, France, Israel, USIA exhbts. in Europe, S. Am., Asia, Africa; rep. permanent collections U.S. Nat. Mus., U. Me., Library of Congress, Met. Mus. Art, Nat. Gallery Art, Nat. Collection Fine Arts, Nat. Air and Space Mus., Balt. Mus. Art, Franklin D. Roosevelt, Fogg Mus. (Harvard), Santa Barbara (Cal.) Art Mus., Syracuse U., Colorado Springs Fine Arts Center, Pennell Collection, Am. Artists Group Prize at Samuel Golden Coll., U. Minn., Cal. State Library, Pa. State Library, Bezalel Nat. Mus., Newark Pub. Library, Addison Gallery Am. Art, Bat Yam Municipal Mus., Safed Mus., Israel, Pa. State Tchrs. Coll., Richmond Art Assn., Peoria Art Center, Boston Pub. Library, St. Margaret Mary Sch. Art. Recipient award Miss. Art Assn. Internat. Water Color Club, 1947, 51, New Haven Paint and Clay Club; purchase award Peoria Art Center, 1950, Print Club Albany, 1962, also Library of Congress, U. Minn., Cal. State Library, Met. Mus. Art, Pa. State Tchrs. Coll., Art Assn. Richmond, Ind., N.Y. Pub. Library, Newark Pub. Library, St. Margaret Mary Sch. Art Coll.; landscape award Soc. Miniature Painters, Gravers and Sculpture; life fellow Met. Mus. Art; named to Exec. and Profl. Hall of Fame (plaque of honor 1966). Mem. Soc. Am. Graphic Artists (group prize 1950), Print Club Albany (N.Y.), Boston Printmakers (recipient award 1955), Washington Printmakers (exhbns.), Conn. Acad. Fine Arts, Am. Color Print Soc., Audubon Artists (group exhbns., award 1944), Phila. Water Color Club (group exhbns.), Nat. Assn. Women Artists (award 1945, 47), Print Council Am., Hunterdon Art Center, Internat. Platform Assn. Address: 915 West End Av New York City NY 10025

KATZ, HILLIARD JOEL, physician; b. Stockton, Cal., May 26, 1918; s. Nelson and Pauline (Landman) K.; A.B., U. Cal. at Berkeley, 1939; M.D., U. Cal. at San Francisco, 1942; m. Jeanette Lillian Gordon, Aug. 18, 1946; children—Stephanie, Steven Nelson, Hilary. Intern U. Cal. Hosps., San Francisco, 1942-43, asst. resident internal medicine, 1943-44, attending physician, electrocardiographer, 1948—, chief staff, 1964-66, physician charge coronary care unit, 1966—; resident, sr. resident internal medicine San Francisco VA Hosp., 1946-48; clin. instr. medicine U. Cal. Sch. Medicine, San Francisco, 1948-53, asst. clin. prof., 1953-61, asso. clin. prof., 1961-70, clin. prof., 1970—; practice medicine specializing in internal medicine and cardiology, San Francisco, 1948—. Trustee Grad. Physiology Fund. Served to capt. M.C., AUS, 1944-46. Diplomate Am. Bd. Internal Medicine. Fellow Am. Coll. Cardiology (gov. No. Cal.), A.C.P., Am. Heart Assn. (fellow council clin. cardiology 1963, Distinguished Service award 1963, Service Recognition award 1964); mem. Cal. (bd. dirs. 1956—), San Francisco (pres. 1955-57, Distinguished Service certificate 1959) heart assns., Cal. Acad. Medicine (pres. 1965), U. Cal. Sch. Medicine Alumni-Faculty Assn. (pres. 1961-62), Soc. Med. Friends Wine (pres. 1968, bd. govs.), Phi Beta Kappa, Alpha Omega Alpha. Home: 223 Cherry St San Francisco CA 94118 Office: 450 Sutter St San Francisco CA 94108

KATZ, ISADOR I., lawyer; b. Rock Island, Ill., Oct. 29, 1905; student Augustana Coll.; B.S.L., Northwestern U., 1927, J.D., 1930. Admitted to Ill. bar, 1930; atty. for Rock Island, 1933-34; now partner firm Katz, McAndrews, Durkee & Telleen, Rock Island. Fellow Am. Coll. Trial Lawyers; mem. Am., Ill., Rock Island County bar assns., Order of Coif. Office: 1st Nat Bank Bldg Rock Island IL 61201*

KATZ, J. LAWRENCE, educator, physicist; b. Bklyn., Dec. 18, 1927; s. Frank and Rose (Eidenberg) K.; B.S. in Physics, Poly. Inst. Bklyn., 1950, M.S., 1951, Ph.D., 1957; m. Gertrude Seidman, June 17, 1950; children—Robyn Laurie, Andrea Lee, Talbot Michael. Teaching fellow physics, research fellow, instr. math. Poly. Inst. Bklyn., 1950-56; faculty Rensselaer Poly. Inst., Troy, N.Y., 1956—, prof. physics, 1967—. Summer research asso. Wright Aero. Co., 1956, Knolls Atomic Power Lab., Schenectady, 1957; hon. research asst. Crystallography Univ. Coll., London, 1959-60; vis. prof. biomed. engring., oral biology U. Miami (Fla.), 1969-70; vis. scientist physics Am. Assn. Physics Tchrs.-Am. Inst. Physics, 1970-72; cons. in field, 1950—; dir. Bioanalytical Labs., Inc., Troy; mem. engring. biology and medicine tng. com. NIH; mem. U.S. Standards Inst. Com. N44, chmn. subcom. diagnostic radiology. Mem. organizing com. Black Arts Council, 1969-70. Mem. exec. com. Schenectady County Liberal Party, 1963—; chmn. 4th jud. dist. nominating conv. Liberal party, 1967-68; Liberal party candidate for U.S. Congress, 1968; committeeman Liberal party, 1968—; asst. chmn. Schenectady County Liberal party, 1969—. Sponsor tri-city div. United Negro Coll. Fund, 1967-68. Served with USNR, 1946-48. NSF sci. faculty fellow, 1959-60. Mem. Am. Crystallographic Assn. (chmn. crystal data com.), Am. Inst. M.E. (chmn. dental med. tech. com.), Am. Phys. Soc., Am. Assn. U. Profs., Biophys. Soc., Orthopaedics Research Soc., Internat. Assn. Dental Research, Fedn. Am. Scientists, Sigma Xi, Sigma Pi Sigma. Jewish religion (trustee temple 1962-63, mem. social action com. 1968-69). Contbr. papers to profl. lit., chpts. to books. Home: 838 Maxwell Dr Schenectady NY 12309 Office: Rensselaer Poly Inst Troy NY 12181

KATZ, JOSEPH JACOB, educator, chemist; b. Apr. 19, 1912; s. Abraham and Stella (Asnin) K.; B.Sc., Wayne U., 1932; Ph.D., U. Chgo., 1942; m. Celia S. Weiner, Oct. 1, 1944; children—Anna, Elizabeth, Mary, Abram. Research asso. chemistry U. Chgo., 1942-43; asso. chemist metall. lab. U. Chgo., 1943-45; sr. chemist Argonne (Ill.) Nat. Lab., 1945—; chmn. dept. chemistry Argonne Sch. Nuclear Sci. and Tech., 1955—; lectr. chemistry U. Wis., summer 1954; vis. prof. chemistry U. Chgo., 1955; professorial lectr., 1964—; spl. grad. lectr. chemistry Ill. Inst. Tech., 1955, Robert A. Welch Found. lectr., 1959. Tech. adviser U.S. delegation UN Conf. on Peaceful Uses Atomic Energy, Geneva, Switzerland, 1955; chmn. A.A.A.S. Gordon Research Conf. on Inorganic Chemistry, 1953-54. Recipient Distinguished Alumnus award Wayne U., 1955; Guggenheim fellow, 1956-57. Mem. Am. Chem. Soc. (award for nuclear applications in chemistry 1961, sec.-treas. div. phys. chemistry 1966—), Am. Nuclear Soc., Phi Beta Kappa, Sigma Xi. Author: (with A.V. Crewe) Research USA, 1964. Am. editor Jour. Inorganic and Nuclear Chemistry, 1955—; editorial bd. Inorganic Syntheses, 1955—. Home: 5658 Blackstone Av Chicago IL 60637 Office: 9700 S Cass Av Argonne IL 60439

KATZ, JOSEPH MORRIS mfg. co. exec.; b. Iampole, Russia, July 7, 1913; brought to U.S., 1914; s. Samuel and Sarah (Averbach) K.; student U. Pitts., 1931-34; m. Agnes Roman, 1937; children—Marshall, Andrea. Published own mag. Boy's Ideal, 1928-30; propr. Printers' Paper Supply Co., Pitts., 1936, became Joseph M. Katz & Co., 1942; founder, chmn. bd., pres. Papercraft Corp., Pitts., 1945—; pres. Marshand, Inc., LePage's, Inc., Gloucester, Mass., Am. Universal Plastics, Inc., N.J.; chmn. bd. CPS Industries, Inc., Knomark, Inc., Kim Color Corp., Tolin Mfg. Co., Merit Mfg. Co., Puerto Rico, Knomark of Can., Ltd., Columbia Pen & Pencil Corp., Modern Orthopedic Appliance Co., Esquire Aktiebolag, Stockholm, Sweden. Chmn. United Jewish Fedn. campaign, 1961-62; mem. Gov.'s Fiscal Task Force, 1970; Pitts. Symphony, Pitts. council Boy Scouts Am., Am. Wind Symphony, Nat. Cabinet United Jewish Appeal. trustee, Point Park Coll., Pitts.; bd. visitors U. Pitts.; mem. pres.'s adv. bd. Carlow Coll.; bd. govs. Am. Jewish Com. Katz Found., Montefiore Hosp. Clubs: Westmoreland Country, Concordia (Pitts.); Harmonie (N.Y.C.). Home: Gateway Towers Pittsburgh PA 15222 also 795 Fifth Av New York City NY 10021 Office: Papercraft Corp Papercraft Park Pittsburgh PA 15238

KATZ, JULIUS LOUIS, govt. ofcl.; b. N.Y.C., Mar. 9, 1925; s. Morris and Bertha (Altneu) K.; student Bklyn. Coll., 1942-43; A.A., George Washington U., 1948, A.B., 1949; m. Charlotte Friedman, Sept. 19, 1948; children—Barbara Joan, Linda Rae, Lawrence Robert. With State Dept., 1950—, economist Eastern European affairs, 1950-59, econ. adviser Eastern European affairs, 1959- 63, dep. dir. Office Internat. Trade, 1963-65, dir., 1965-67; dir. Office Internat. Commodities, 1967-68; dep. asst. sec. of state for internat. resources and food policy, 1968—. Served with AUS, 1943-45; ETO. Mem. Am. Econ. Assn., Artus. Home: 5617 Newington Rd Bethesda MD 20016 Office: Dept of State Washington DC 20520

KATZ, LEO, math. statistician; b. Detroit, Nov. 29, 1914; s. Max and Mollie (Gastman) K.; B.S. in Elec. Engring., Lawrence Inst., 1936; M.A., Wayne U., 1938; Ph.D., U. Mich., 1945; postdoctoral study U. Cal., 1948, 52- 53, U. N.C., 1950, Stanford, 1952-53; m. Jean Prepsky, Sept. 5, 1936; children—Michael, Daniel. Statistician, Mich. Dept. Labor, 1941-42; mathematician Gen. Motors Corp., 1942-46; asst. prof. math., asso. prof. statistics Mich. State U., 1946-56, prof. chmn. dept. statistics, 1956-63, dir. statis. lab., 1959-; vis. prof. biostatistics Coll. Medicine, U. Cin., 1963-66; vis. prof. indsl. engring. U. Pitts., 1966- 68, 69-70; Alcoa Found. vis. prof., 1968-69; prin. investigator Office Naval Research, 1951-58, NSF Research, 1958—; vis. lectr. statistics NSF, 1963-65, 71—; cons. editor Wadsworth Pub. Co., 1963-66; statis. cons. European sci. liaison officer for math. and statistics Office Naval Research, U.S. Navy, 1959-60; Ford Found. vis. distinguished prof. U. N.C., 1961-62. Exec. sec. Inst. Math. Statistics, 1968—; chmn. Mich. Consumer Council, 1967-70; cons.-examiner N. Central Assn. Commn. Colls. and Univs., 1968—. Fellow Inst. Math. Statistics, Am. Statis. Assn., Royal Statis. Soc., A.A.A.S.; mem. Am., London math. socs., Psychometric Soc., Biometric Soc., Am. Assn. U. Profs., Inst. Math. Statistics (council), Am. Civil Liberties Union, Internat. Statis. Inst., Sigma Xi, Phi Kappa Phi. Contbr. articles profl. jours. Home: 425 Durand St East Lansing MI 48823

KATZ, LEWIS, educator; b. Fond du Lac, Wis., Mar. 19, 1923; s. Alex and Rivka (Tabajovich) K.; student N.D. State U., 1940-42; B.Chem., U. Minn., 1946, Ph.D., 1951; m. Shirley Rita Robbins, Sept. 12, 1948; children—Susan Theresa, Deborah Ann. Instr. chemistry U. Conn., 1952-55, asst. prof., 1955-59, asso. prof., 1959-64, prof., 1964—; cons. Pratt & Whitney Aircraft. Served with AUS, 1943-46. Postdoctoral fellow Cal. Inst. Tech., 1951-52; Nat. Sci. Found. sci. faculty fellow Cambridge U., 1961-62. Mem. Am. Chem. Soc., Am. Crystallog. Assn., Am. Assn. Univ. Profs., Phi Beta Kappa, Sigma Xi, Phi Lambda Upsilon. Contbr. articles profl. jours. Home: 8 Eastwood Rd Storrs CT 06268

KATZ, LOUIS NELSON, medical research; b. Pinsk, Poland, Aug. 25, 1897; s. Harry J. and Sarah (Rosenberg) Kates; came to U.S., 1900, naturalized, 1904; A.B., Western Reserve U., 1918, M.D., 1921, M.A., 1923, D.Sc. honoris causa, 1965; m. Aline Grossner, June 15, 1928; one son, Arnold Martin. Intern and asst. res. medicine Cleve. City Hosp., 1921-23; dir. Cardiovascular Inst., Michael Reese Hosp. and Med. Center, Chgo., 1930-67, emeritus, 1967—; dir. dept. cardiovascular disease div. medicine, 1962-67, emeritus, 1967—; asst. prof. physiology U. Chgo., 1930-41, professorial lectr. physiology 1941-67, emeritus, 1967, vis. prof. physiology, 1967—. Attending physician Michael Reese Hosp. since 1947. Served as private, S.A.T.C., 1918. Pres. III Inter- Am. Cardiol. Congress 1948. Recipient Lasker award Am. Heart Assn., 1956; permanent hon. pres. Inter-Am. Cardiol. Soc. Fellow A.C.P., A.A.A.S.; mem. Am. (pres. 1951-52, chmn. sci. council, 1952-53), Chgo. (pres. 1954-57, chmn. sci. council, 1952-53) heart assns., Am. Soc. Clin. Investigation, Central Soc. Clin. Research, Am. Soc. Study Arteriosclerosis (pres. 1954-55), Internat. Cardiol. Soc., A.M.A., Am. Physiol. Soc. (pres. 1956-57), Phi Beta Kappa, Sigma Xi, Alpha Omega Alpha. Jewish religion. Author books; co-author publs. including: Experimental Atherosclerosis, 1953; Clinical Electrocardiography, 1956; Nutrition and Atherosclerosis, published 1958. Mem. editorial board Acta Cardiologica; editor sect. cardiovascular system Biol. Abstracts, Phila.; bd. editors Circulation, 1958—. Contbr. to nat. internat. med. jours. Home: 601 E 32d St Chicago IL 60616 Office: Michael Reese Hosp and Med Center 29th and Ellis Av Chicago IL 60616 ☆

KATZ, MAURICE HARRY, lawyer, educator; b. N.Y.C., Jan. 18, 1937; s. Milton and Florence (Davies) K.; A.B. cum laude, Columbia, 1958; LL.B., Harvard, 1961; m. Margery E. Rosenberg, May 6, 1962; children-Brian, Bradley, Andrew. Admitted to Cal. bar, 1963, N.Y. bar, 1962, also U.S. Supreme Ct; mem. firms Loeb and Loeb, Los Angeles, 1962-64, Freshman, Marantz and Comsky, Beverly Hills, Cal., 1964-66, Reinstein, Lanoe and Katz, Los Angeles, 1966—; prof. U. San Fernando Sch. Law, Los Angeles, 1965—; judge pro tem Beverly Hills Mun. Ct., 1968-70. Served with USMCR, 1961-62. Mem. State Bar Cal., Am., Los Angeles County, Beverly Hills bar assns., Phi Beta Kappa. Jewish religion. Home: 315 N McCadden Pl Los Angeles CA 90004 Office: 1880 Century Park E Los Angeles CA 90067

KATZ, MILTON, legal educator; b. N.Y.C., Nov. 29, 1907; s. Morris and Clara (Schiffman) Katz; A.B. Harvard U., 1927, J.D., 1931; m. Vivian Greenberg. July 2, 1933; children—John, Robert, Peter. Mem. anthrop. expedn. across Central Africa for Peabody Mus., Harvard, 1927-28; admitted to N.Y. bar, 1932, Mass. bar, 1959; various ofcl. posts with U.S. Govt., 1932-39; prof. law Harvard, 1940— (leaves of absence 41-46, 48-50), Henry L. Stimson prof. law, also dir. internat. legal studies, 1954—, dir. internat. program in taxation, 1961-63; solicitor WPB, 1941-43; U.S. exec. officer Combined Prodn. and Resources Bd., 1942- 43; with OSS, 1943-44; U.S. spl. rep. in Europe, with rank ambassador extraordinary and plenipotentiary, 1950-51; chief U.S. delegation Econ. Commn. for Europe, 1950-51; chmn. Def. Financial and Econ. Com. N. Atlantic Treaty, 1950-51; asso. dir. Ford Found., 1951-54, cons., 1954-66; cons., asst. sec. edn. Dept. Health, Edn. and Welfare, 1967. Pres. Cambridge Community Services, 1959-61; dir. Internat. Friendship League; chmn. com. manpower White House Conf. Internat. Cooperation, 1965; chmn. com. on life scis. and social policy Nat. Acad. Sci.-NRC.; mem. panel tech. assessment Nat. Acad. Sci., 1968-69. Trustee Case Western Res. U., Brandeis U., Inter.-Am. U. Found.; mem. corp. Boston Mus. Sci.; chmn. bd. trustees Carnegie Endowment Internat. Peace; trustee, mem. exec. com. Internat. Legal Center, World Peace Found., Citizen's Research Found. Served with USNR, 1944-46; MTO, ETO; lt. comdr. Res. Decorated Legion of Merit. Fellow Am. Acad. Arts and Scis. (councillor); mem. Harvard Alumni Assn. (bd. dirs. 1952-55). Author: Cases and Materials in Administrative Law, 1947; Government Under Law and the Individual (with others), 1957; Law of International Transactions and Relations (with Kingman Brewster, Jr.), 1960; The Things That Are Caesar's, 1966; The Relevance of International Adjudication, 1968; (with other) Man's Impact on the Global Environment; 1970; also articles. Home: 6 Berkeley St Cambridge MA 02138

KATZ, NATHAN, retail chain store exec.; b. Bklyn., Mar. 20, 1920; s. Oscar and Celia (Litwer) K.; student Rutgers U., 1936-37, N.Y.U., 1937-43; m. Rosalyn Anker, June 1, 1943; 1 son, Jeffrey Owen. With I. J. Skolnick & Co., C.P.A.'s, N.Y.C., 1940-56; treas., dir., mem. exec. com. Franklin Stores Corp., N.Y.C., 1956—. Served with USAAF, 1943-46. C.P.A., N.Y. Mem. Women's Apparel Chains Assn. (v.p., dir.), N.Y. State Soc. C.P.A.'s. Home: 2924 Wynsum Av Merrick NY 11566 Office: 815 Hutchinson River Pkwy Bronx NY 10465

KATZ, OSCAR, TV exec.; b. N.Y.C., Apr. 12, 1913; s. Louis and Celia (Sellinger) K.; B.S., Coll. City N.Y., 1942; m. Rose Wolfe, Sept. 11, 1938; children—Marjorie, Joan. With Nat. Market Analysis, also Houser Assos., ind. research firms, until 1938; mem. research dept. CBS, 1938-56, dir. research CBS-TV, until 1956, v.p. charge daytime programs CBS-TV Network New York City, 1956-59, v.p. network programs, 1959-64; exec.-v.p. charge prodn. Desilu Prodn., Inc., 1964-66; sr. v.p. TV div. Gen. Artist Corp., 1966—; faculty eve. session Sch. Bus., Coll. City N.Y., 1946-47; chief audience response sect. domestic bur. intelligence, O.W.I., then cons. radio bur. div. research and analysis. Mem. Am. Statis. Assn., Market Research Council. Clubs: Friars, Players (N.Y.C.). Author articles on radio and TV research. Home: 325 N Carolwood Dr Los Angeles, CA 90024. Office: 9025 Wilshire Blvd Beverly Hills CA 90212

KATZ, PAUL, educator, conductor; b. N.Y.C., Nov. 2, 1907; s. Nathan and Molly (Rothenberg) K.; B.M. in Theory, Cleve. Inst. of Music, 1931; postgrad. Am. Cons. of Music, Fountainbleau, France;

student of Sevcik, Ysaye, Auer, Boulanger; hon. degrees U. Dayton, Central State U.; m. Phyllis Margolis, July 29, 1934; 1 son, Nevin. Conductor Dayton Philharmonic Orch., 1933—; tchr., conductor, chmn. orch. dept. Cin. Coll. Cons. Music; lectr., tchr. U. Dayton, Wright State U. Mem. Audubon Soc. Jewish religion. Composer. Home: 1710 Academy Pl Dayton OH 45406

KATZ, ROBERT ARVIN, corp. exec., lawyer; b. Boston, Jan. 14, 1927; s. Morris Wolf and Freda (Cohen) K.; A.B., Harvard, 1946, postgrad., 1947-48; LL.B., Boston U., 1954; m. Tracy Oppenheimer, Dec. 28, 1952; children—Terry Alison, Robin Elizabeth, Wendy Arete, Michael Edward. Admitted to Ill. bar, 1954, Conn. bar, 1960, N.Y. bar, 1966; practice in Chgo., 1954-59; asso. firm Peebles, Greenberg & Keele, and predecessors, 1954-59; asst. sec. Revlon, Inc., N.Y.C., 1961-65; sec. Joseph E. Seagram & Sons, Inc., N.Y.C., 1965-69; chmn. exec. com., dir. Bevis Industries, Inc., Providence, 1969—; dir. E.P. Dutton Co N.Y.C., Oppenheimer Casing Co., Chgo., Thomas Doran Co., Inc., White Plains, N.Y. Bd. dirs., pres. Robert J. Strickman Found., N.Y.C. Served to ensign USNR, 1944-46. Home: Woods Rd Palisades NY 10964 Office: 375 Park Av New York City NY 10022

KATZ, ROBERT LEE, natural resource co. exec.; b. San Francisco, Jan. 8, 1926; s. Adrian Joseph and Anne (Schallman) K.; A.B., U. Cal. at Berkeley, 1945; M.B.A., Stanford, 1948; D.C.S., Harvard, 1956; m. Susan Elinor Goldsmith, June 14, 1953; children—Andrew Lee, Peter Michael, Jeffrey David. Asst. prof. Amos Tuck Sch. Bus. Adminstrn. Dartmouth, 1953-56; asst. prof. Harvard, 1956-60; exec. v.p. Opto-Electronic Devices, Inc., Mountain View, Cal., 1960-64; lectr. bus. mgmt. Stanford, 1960-68; prof. bus. mgmt. l'Inst. pour L'Etude des Methodes de Direction de l'Enterprise, Lausanne, Switzerland, 1966-7; pres. Robert L. Katz and Assos., 1953-69, U.S. Natural Resources, Inc., Menlo Park, Cal., 1969—; mng. partner Ranchita Cattle Co., Pinnacles Investment Co.; dir. Lincoln Consol., Inc.; dir. Yosemite Park & Curry Co. Chmn. planning commn., Portola Valley, Cal., 1964-66. Served to lt. (j.g.) USNR, 1945-46. Mem. Acad. Mgmt. Republican. Clubs: Harvard (N.Y.C.); Stanford Golf (Palo Alto, Cal.). Author: Cases and Concepts in Corporate Strategy, 1970; Management of the Total Enterprise, 1970; Organizational Behavior and Administration, 1961. Contbr. articles profl. jours. Home: 155 Mapache Dr Portola Valley CA 94025 Office: 3000 Sand Hill Rd Menlo Park CA 94025

KATZ, SAMUEL, educator; b. Berlin, Germany, Feb. 13, 1923; s. Herman and Bertha (Low) K.; came to U.S., 1934, naturalized, 1940; B.S., U. Mich., 1943; A.M., Columbia, 1947, Ph.D. 1955; m. Jean Barbara Parker, July 10, 1953; children—David R., Daniel M., Miriam E. With radiation lab. Mass. Inst. Tech., 1943-46; mem. sci. staff Lamont Geol. Obs., Columbia, 1948-53; sr. physicist Stanford Research Inst., 1953-57; mem. faculty Rensselaer Poly Inst., 1957—, prof. geophysics, 1962—, chmn. dept. geology, 1964- 69. Mem. Am. Geophys. Union, Soc. Explorations Geophysicists, Am. Phys. Soc., Seismol. Soc. Am., Sigma Xi. Contbr. articles in field to profl. jours. Home: 908 Karenwald La Schenectady NY 12309 Office: Rensselaer Poly Inst Troy NY 12181

KATZ, SIDNEY LEON, architect; b. N.Y.C., Oct. 7 1914; B.Arch., N.Y.U., 1935, M. Arch., 1936. Archtl. designer Peter Copeland, N.Y.C., 1934-38; archtl. designer and city planner Norman Bel Geddes, N.Y.C., 1938-39; archtl. designer Erling Oure, N.Y.C. Tunnel Authority, 1939-40; with A. Gordon Lorimer, N.Y.C. Dept. Pub. Works, 1940-41; architect and site planner Antonin Raymond, N.Y.C., 1941-42; archtl. designer William Lescaze, N.Y.C., 1942-44; now with Katz, Waisman, Weber, Strauss & Joseph Blumenkranz, N.Y.C.; acting dean Pratt Inst. Architecture, 1970—; prin. works include Dretzin residence, Chappaqua, N.Y., 1948, Sarkes Tarzian factory, Bloomington, Ind., 1954, Bay View Houses, Castle Hill Houses, Bronx, Pub. Sch. 46, Bklyn., 1960. Recipient numerous citations, awards. Fellow A.I.A. Address: 305 E 45th St New York City NY 10017

KATZ, SOL, advt. exec.; b. N.Y.C., Jan. 6, 1925; s. Samuel and Lillie (Freiwald) K.; B.S., Coll. City N.Y., 1948; M.B.A., N.Y.U., 1952; m. Alice Wetreich, Feb. 19, 1949; children—William, Douglas. Cons. research mgr. Biow Co., N.Y.C., 1949-53; asst. research dir. Geyer Advt., N.Y.C., 1953-55; research dir. Donahue & Coe, N.Y.C., 1955-60; sr. v.p. Warwick & Legler, Inc., N.Y.C., 1960—. Served with USAAF, 1943-46. Mem. Am. Assn. Pub. Opinion Research, Nat. Assn. Bus. Econs., Am. Marketing Assn., Conererie de la Chaine der Rotisseurs, Chevalier du Tastevin. Home: 8100 Bay Pkwy Brooklyn NY 11214 Office: 375 Park Av New York City NY 10022

KATZ, SOLOMON, univ. ofcl.; b. Buffalo, June 10, 1909; s. Saul and Sophia (Gelber) K.; A.B., Cornell U., 1930, Ph.D., 1933; student Sorbonne U., 1932-33; m. Marcia Geller, Sept. 6, 1931; children—Kenneth, Cynthia. Asst. prof. Greek, U. Ore., 1935-36; mem. faculty U. Wash., 1936—, successively instr., asst. and asso. prof., prof. history, 1936—, chmn. dept., 1954-60, v.p. acad. affairs, 1967—, dean Coll. Arts and Scis., 1960-66, provost, 1965—. Served from 1st lt. to maj., USAAF, 1942-46. Decorated Bronze Star; George C. Boldt traveling fellow, Europe, 1932-33; fellow Am. Council Learned Socs., Europe, 1934-35; Fulbright research scholar, France, 1952-53, Guggenheim fellow, Italy, 1953-54; Danforth grantee, Europe, 1970. Mem. Am. Hist. Assn. (pres. Pacific Coast br.), Am. Philol. Assn., Archaeol Inst., Medieval Acad., Am. Assn. U. Profs., Phi Beta Kappa. Author: Jews in Visigothic and Frankish Kingdoms of Spain and Gaul, 1937; The Decline of Rome and the Rise of Medieval Europe, 1955; also articles. Home: 7708 56th Pl N E Seattle WA 98115

KATZ, THOMAS JOSEPH, educator, chemist; b. Prague, Czechoslovakia, Mar. 21, 1936; s. Francis and Ida (Jungmann) K.; came to U.S., 1940, naturalized, 1945; B.A., U. Wis., 1956; M.A., Harvard, 1957, Ph.D., 1959; m. Meta Oehmsen, Dec. 27, 1963; 1 son, Joshua Timothy. Mem. faculty Columbia, 1959—, prof. chemistry, 1968—. Mem. Am. Chem. Soc., Chem. Soc. (U.K.). Author research papers organic chemistry. Home: 375 Riverside Dr New York City NY 10025

KATZ, WILBER GRIFFITH, retired educator; b. Milw., June 7, 1902; s. George H. and Jessie (Griffith) K.; A.B., U. Wis., 1923; LL.B., Harvard, 1926, S.J.D., 1930; m. Ruth Weaver, Dec. 30, 1926; 1 dau., Elisabeth. Admitted to N.Y. bar, 1927, Ill. bar, 1935; practice with Root, Clark, Buckner & Ballantine, N.Y.C., 1927-29; asst. prof. law U. Chgo. Law Sch., 1930-33, asso. prof., 1933-36, prof., 1936-62, dean Law Sch., 1939-50; prof. law U. Wis.-Madison, 1962-70. Episcopalian. Home: 435 Starin Rd Whitewater WI 53190

KATZ, WILLIAM LOREN, author; b. Bklyn., June 2, 1927; s. Bernard and Phyllis (Brownstone) K.; B.A., Syracuse U., 1950; M.A., N.Y.U., 1952; m. Glorida Gray, Apr. 6, 1952 (div. Apr. 1969); children—Naomi, Michael; m. 2d, Jacqueline Hunt, Mar. 6, 1970. Tchr. Am. history, N.Y.C., 1954-60, Hartsdale, N.Y., 1960-68; author, 1968—; cons. N.Y. State Edn. Dept., 1967-68; research fellow Columbia Tchrs. Coll., 1971—. Served with USNR, 1945-46. Author: Eyewitness: The Negro in American History, 1967 (Gold Medal award for non-fiction Nat. Conf. Christians and Jews 1968); Teachers' Guide to American Negro History, 1968; (with Warren J. Halliburton) American Majorities and Minorities: A Syllabus of United States History for Secondary Schools, 1970; The Black West: A Documentary and Pictorial History, 1971. Gen. editor: The American Negro: His History and Literature, 147 vols., 1968-71. Mem. editorial bd. jour. Black Studies, 1970—. Contbr. articles Sat. Rev., Jour. Negro History, Jour. Negro Edn., Crisis, Freedomways, Jour. Black Studies. Home: 130 W 16th St New York City NY 10011

KATZ, BENJAMIN JOSEPH, educator; b. Bklyn., July 13, 1923; s. Louis H. and Sarah (Golinsky) K.; A.B., Bklyn. Coll., 1946; A.M., Harvard, 1949, Ph.D. (Ford fellow), 1954; m. Kaila Goldman, Aug. 11, 1957; children-Frederic M., Daniel L., Shira. Asst. prof. econs. U. N.H., 1949-54, asso. prof., 1954-57; asso. prof. N.Y.U., 1957-65, prof., 1965—, chmn. dept. econs., 1968—. Cons. N.H. Mfgr.'s Assn., 1954-55, Joint Council on Econ. Edn., 1958. Served with AUS, 1943-46. Home: 287 Beechwood Rd Oradell NJ 07649 Office: New York Univ Coll Bronx NY 10453

KATZELL, RAYMOND A., educator, psychologist; b. Bklyn., Mar. 16, 1919; s. Abraham and Fannie (Skoblow) K.; B.S., N.Y.U., 1939, A.M., 1941, Ph.D., 1943; postgrad. Columbia, 1939; m. Florence Joyce Goldstein, Sept. 7, 1941; m. 2d, Mildred Engberg, May 11, 1953. Research asst. psychology NRC grant for research on selection and tng. pilots N.Y.U., 1939-42, instr. psychology, 1942-43, adj. asso. prof. psychology, 1951-53; instr. eve. Sch. Bus. Adminstrn., Coll. City N.Y., 1942-43; asst. prof. psychology U. Tenn., 1945-46, asso. prof., 1946-48; asso. prof. personnel psychology, dir. psychol. service center Syracuse U. 1948-51; lectr. psychology Columbia, 1955-57; cons. personnel psychology in indsl. orgns., 1945-57; v.p. Richardson. Bellows, Henry & Co., Inc., 1951-57, dir. 1947-68; prof. mgmt. engring. and psychology and dir. research center indsl. behavior N.Y.U., 1957-63, prof., head dept. psychology, 1963—; cons. N.Y.C. Dept. Personnel, 1967—, U.S. Dept. Labor, 1968—, U.S. Dept. Health, Edn. and Welfare, 1968-70, U.S. Dept. Justice, 1969—. Chmn. Adv. Council Psychologists, N.Y. State, 1963-68; Expert cons. USAF, 1950-51; personnel psychologist personnel research sect. Adj. Gen.'s office, U.S. War Dept., 1943-45. Diplomate Am. Bd. Examiners in Psychology. Fellow Am. Psychol. Assn. (pres. div. indsl. psychology 1960-61), A.A.A.S.; mem. Soc. Advancement Mgmt. (pres. Central N.Y. chpt. 1949-51), N.Y. State Psychol. Assn. (pres. 1958-59). Co-author: Testing and Fair Employment, 1968. Author articles profl. jours. Home: 112 Waverly Pl New York City NY 10011

KATZENBACH, EDWARD LAWRENCE, Jr., univ. ofcl.; b. Trenton, N.J., Feb. 24, 1919; s. Edward Lawrence and Marie (Hilson) K.; grad. Lawrenceville (N.J.) Sch., 1936; A.B., Princeton 1940, Ph.D., 1953; LL.D., L.I.U., 1963; m. Maude Thomas, Apr. 26, 1942 (div. 1963); children—Edward L., Matilda, Eldridge Thomas; m. 2d, Dolores Fiala, Apr. 11, 1963; children—Hadley Hadley Stephenson, Karen Ann, William Hunt. Instr. Princeton, 1946-48, 50; dep. dir. hist. sect. Dept. Def., 1951; research asso. Inst. War and Peace Studies, Columbia, 1952-55; dir. def. studies program Harvard, 1955-59; dir. acad. devel. Brandeis U., 1958-60; dep. asst. sec. def. edn. and manpower resources, 1961-64; dir. commn. on adminstrv. affairs Am. Council Edn., 1964-66; v.p. edn. Raytheon Corp., Lexington, Mass., 1966-68; v.p. for research and pub. service U. Okla., 1968-71; v.p. charge program devel. N.Y. Inst. Tech., 1971—. Served with USMCR, 1942-45, 50-52; col. Res. Mem. Am. Hist. Assn., Acad. Polit. Sci., Council Fgn. Relations, Conf. on Pub. Service. Episcopalian. Club: Federal City. Contbr. articles profl. jours. Office: NY Inst Tech New York City NY

KATZENBACH, G. RICHARD, corp. exec.; b, 1921; ed. Franklin and Marshall Coll., 1943. Chmn. bd. Thriftway Foods, Inc.; v.p. finance, dir. Fleming Co. Address: Thriftway Foods Inc Church and Henderson Sts King of Prussia, PA 19406.*

KATZENBACH, L. EMERY, investment banker; b. St. Paul, Dec. 18, 1915; s. L. Emery and Mary (Whittredge) K.; grad. Berkshire Sch., 1933; m. Marjorie Pell, Sept. 4, 1937; children—Varick (Mrs. Nicholas Niles Jr.,), Susan (Mrs. William A. Barker), L. Emery, Christian; m. 2d, Kathleen Dixon Hartford, Feb. 20, 1965. Partner firm White, Weld & Co., N.Y.C., 1950—; dir. Am. Cyanamid Co., Molybdenum Corp. Am., Southwest Forest Industries. Home: 814 West Rd New Canaan, CT 06840. Office: 20 Broad St New York City NY 10005

KATZENBACH, NICHOLAS DEBELLEVILLE, corp. exec.; b. Phila., Jan. 17, 1922; s. Edward Lawrence and Marie Louise (Hilson) K.; grad. Philips Exeter Acad., 1939; B.A., Princeton, 1945; LL.B., Yale, 1947; Rhodes scholar Balliol Coll., Oxford (Eng.) U., 1947-49; m. Lydia King Phelps Stokes, June 8, 1946; children—Christopher Wolcott, John Strong Minor, Maria Louise Hilson, Anne deBelleville. Admitted to N.J. bar, 1950, Conn. bar, 1955; with firm Katzenbach, Gildea & Rudner, Trenton, N.J., 1950; atty.-adviser Office Gen. Counsel Air Force, 1950-52, part-time cons., 1952-56; asso. prof. law Yale Law Sch., 1952-56; prof. law U. Chgo. Law Sch., 1956-60; asst. atty. gen. Dept. Justice, 1961-62, dep. atty. gen., 1962-64, acting atty. gen., 1964, atty. gen., 1965-66; under sec. state, 1966-69; v.p., gen. counsel IBM Corp., 1969—. Served to 1st lt. USAAF, 1941-45. Decorated Air medal with three clusters; Ford Found. fellow, 1960-61. Mem. Am. Law Inst., Am. Bar Assn., Am. Judicature Soc. Democrat. Episcopalian. Author: (with Morton A. Kaplan) The Political Foundations of International Law, 1961. Editor-in-chief Yale Law Jour., 1947. Contbr. articles profl. jours. Home: 5225 Sycamore Av Riverdale NY 10471 Office: IBM Corp Armonk NY 10504

KATZMAN, DANIEL, mfg. co. exec.; b. Omaha, Aug. 24, 1924; s. Meyer and Nettie (Gerelick) K.; B.S. in Bus. Adminstrn., U. Neb., 1948; m. Ruth Goldberg, Aug. 24, 1947; children—Steven Edward, Saragail. Hotel exec., 1948-52; co- founder Commodore Corp., mobile home mfrs., 1952, pres., 1967—; dir. U.S. Nat. Bank, Omaha. Del. Reconstructed Assembly of Jewish Agy. Jerusalem, 1971. Trustee Omaha Jewish Fedn., Archbishop Bergen Meml. Hosp., Omaha; bd. dirs. nat. cabinet United Jewish Appeal, Am. Friends Hebrew U. Served with AUS, 1943-46. Mem. Mobile Homes Mfrs. Assn. (treas., bd. dirs.). Home: 6617 Cuming St Omaha NB 68132 Office: 8712 W Dodge Rd Omaha NB 68114

KATZMAN, ROBERT educator, physician; b. Denver, Nov. 29, 1925; s. Maurice and Leah (Schnitt) K.; B.S., U. Chgo., 1949, M.S. 1951; M.D. cum laude, Harvard, 1953; m. Nancy Bernstein, Sept. 2, 1947; children—David Jonathan, Daniel Mark. Intern Boston City Hosp., 1953-54; chief resident neurologist Neurol. Inst., Columbia Presbyn. Hosp., N.Y.C., 1956-57; mem. faculty Albert Einstein Coll. Medicine, 1957—, prof. neurology, chmn. dept., 1964—. Mem. research rev. panel Nat. Multiple Sclerosis Soc., 1964-70, mem. adv. com. fellowships, 1970—; cons. Jewish Bd. Guardians, 1962-68. Recipient Borden undergrad. research award Harvard Med. Sch., 1953; sr. fellow neurophysiology USPHS, 1961-62, Career Research Devel. grantee, 1962-66; recipient ann. prize Neuropathology Soc., 1962; NATO sr. fellow, 1969. Diplomate Nat. Bd. Examiners, Am. Bd. Neurology and Psychiatry. Fellow Am. Acad. Neurology (Weir Mitchell award 1960, chmn. neurochemistry sect. 1965-67); mem. Am. Neurol. Assn., Am. Electroencephalographic Soc., Am. Physiol. Soc. (cons. bd. 1968-71), N.Y. Neurol. Soc. (councillor 1968-69, pres. 1970-71), Am., Internat. socs. neurochemistry, Harvey Soc., Soc. Exptl. Biology and Medicine, Phi Beta Kappa, Sigma Xi, Alpha Omega Alpha. Editorial bd. Neurology, 1963—; editorial adv. bd. Jour. Neuropathology and Exptl. Neurology, 1964—. 1300 Morris Park Av New York City NY 10469

KAUFERT, FRANK HENRY, univ. dean; b. Princeton, Minn., Dec. 2, 1905; s. Frank and Mary Amelia (Kraft) K.; B.S., U. Minn., 1928, M.S., 1930, Ph.D., 1935; student U. Halle, Halle A. Saale, Germany, 1931; m. Ione Elizabeth Mossman, Oct. 28, 1938; 1 son, Joseph Mossman. Asst. prof. U. Minn., 1936; research chemist E.I. du Pont de Nemours, Wilmington, Del., 1936- 40; asso. prof. forestry U. Minn., 1940-42, prof., dir. Sch. Forestry, 1946-70, dean Coll. Forestry, 1970—; asst. adminstr. Coop. State Research Service, U.S. Dept. Agr., 1963-64; sr. wood technologist U.S. Forest Service Forest Products Lab., Madison, Wis., 1942-45; dir. forestry research project Soc. Am. Foresters, 1954. Pres. Keep Minn. Green, 1951-64. Mem. Forest History Found. (pres. 1956-57), Soc. Am. Foresters (council 1950, 53), Am. Wood Preservers Assn., Assn. State Coll. and Univ. Forestry Research Orgns. (pres. 1966-68), A.A.A.S., Forest Products Research Soc. (pres. 1957- 58), Sigma Xi, Xi Sigma Pi, Gamma Sigma Delta, Alpha Zeta. Conglist. Author (with others): Wood Aircraft Fabrication and Inspection, 1944; Forestry and Related Research in North America, 1955. Home: 2337 Carter Av Saint Paul MN 55108

KAUFFMAN, CRAIG ROBERT, artist; b. Los Angeles, Mar. 31, 1932; s. Kurtz and Margret (Buchanan) K.; student Sch. Architecture, U. So. Cal., 1950-52; M.A. in Painting, U. Cal. at Los Angeles, 1956. Instr. art U. Cal. at Irvine; one man shows include Felix Landau Gallery, Los Angeles, 1953, Dilexi Gallery, San Francisco, 1958, 60, Ferus Gallery, Los Angeles, 1958-62, 63, 65, Ferus Pace Gallery, Los Angeles, 1967, Pace Gallery, N.Y.C., 1967, 69, Irving Blum Gallery, Los Angeles, 1969; group exhbns. include San Francisco Mus. ann., 1952, 54, 59, 60, 61, Mus. Modern Art, 1953, Merry- Go-Round show, Los Angeles, 1955, Artists Under 35, Dickson Art Center, U. Cal. at Los Angeles, 1959, 50 Paintings by 37 Painters, U. Cal. at Los Angeles, 1960, U. Ill. ann., 1961, 67, 5 at Pace, Pace Gallery, 1964, Los Angeles Now, Robert Fraser Gallery, London, 1966, Image, Color, Form, Detroit Inst. Arts, 1967, Ten from Los Angeles, Seattle Art Mus., 1966, The 1960's, Mus. Modern Art, 1967, Plastics West Coast, Hansen Gallery, Los Angeles, 1967, Recent Acquisitions, Whitney Mus., 1967, A New Aesthetic, Washington Gallery Modern Art, 1967, V Paris Biennale, 1967, Contemporary Am. Painting and Sculpture, Krannert Art Mus., U. Ill., 1967, Plastics Plantings and Sculpture, Cal. State Coll., Los Angeles, 1968, California at Janie C. Lee Gallery, Dallas-Fort Worth, 1968, L.A.-N.Y., U. Cal. at San Diego, 1968, Painting: Out From the Wall, Des Moines, 1968, Los Angeles 6, Vancouver Art Gallery, 1968. Faculty 1968, U. Cal. at Irvine, 1968, Whitney Sculpture ann., 1968, Late Fifties at the Ferus, Los Angeles County Mus. Art, 1968, New Media exhbn., traveling, 1969, Three from L.A., Dunkelman Gallery, Montreal, Can., 1969, Recent Am. Sculpture, Walker Art Center, 1969, Plastic New Art, Inst. Contemporary Art, U. Pa., 1969; rep. permanent collections Mus. Modern Art, Whitney Mus. Am. Art, Albright Knox Art Gallery, Larry Aldrich Mus., Ridgefield, Conn., Pasadena (Cal.) Mus. Art, U. Ariz., Los Angeles County Mus. Home: 160 La Brea Laguna Beach CA 92651

KAUFFMAN, GEORGE WHITTEN, wholesale drug exec.; b. Columbus, O., May 28, 1915; s. George H. and Marguerite (Fair) K.; A.B. cum laude, Harvard, 1937; m. Jean Leckie, June 20, 1941; children—Sally Point, Nancy Whitten, Jean Stuart. With Kauffman-Lattimer Co., Columbus, 1937—, pres., 1949—; dir. Druggists Service Council, N.Y.C. 1957-63, Ohio Nat. Bank of Columbus. Bd. dirs. United Appeals Franklin County, 1955-65, pres., 1961; trustee Children's Hosp., 1951—, pres., 1962-64. Served to capt. U.S. Army, 1942- 46. Mem. Nat. Wholesale Druggists Assn. (bd. dirs. 1951-54. pres. 1953), Nat. Assn. Wholesalers (pres., 1956-57), Columbus C. of C. (bd. dirs. 1963-66), Columbus Better Bus. Bur. (bd. dirs. 1949-51). Clubs: Columbus, Country (Columbus); Rocky Fork Golf. Home: 393 Brookside Dr Columbus OH 43209 Office: 1200 E Fifth Av Columbus OH 43216

KAUFFMAN, JOSEPH FRANK, coll. pres., b. Providence, Dec. 2, 1921; s. Frank J. and Lena (Andelman) K.; B.A., U. Denver, 1948; M.A., Northwestern U., 1950; Ed.D., Boston U., 1958; m. Gladys Davidson, June 20, 1943; children—Marcia Lee, Glenn Frank. Asst. to pres., dean student Brandeis U., 1952-60; exec. vp. Jewish Theol. Sem. Am., 1960-61; dir. tng. Peace Corps, 1961-63; staff asso. Am. Council Edn., 1963-65; dean student affairs, prof. counseling U. Wis., 1965-68; pres. R.I. Coll., 1968—. Cons. in field, 1964—; chmn. nat. com. student higher edn. Hazen Found., 1966—; mem. Peace Corps Nat. Adv. Council, 1968-69. Bd. dirs. R.I. Council Community Services, Urban Coalition R.I. Served with inf. AUS, 1942-45. Fellow Am. Sociol. Assn.; mem. Am. Personnel and Guidance Assn., Nat. Assn. Student Personnel Adminstrs., Am. Council Edn. (dir.), Phi Beta Kappa. Jewish religion. Author: Education, 1966. Editor: (with L.E. Dennis) The College and the Student, 1966. Contbr. articles to profl. jours. Home: 255 Fruithill Av North Providence, RI 02911. Office: 600 Mount Pleasant Av Providence RI 02908

KAUFFMAN, MARK, photographer; b. Los Angeles, Sept. 3, 1922; s. Mitchell and Anna (Bearman) K.; grad. vocational photography, John C. Fremont Sch., 1940; m. Anita Jansson, May 18, 1948; children—Linda, Yvonne, Lenita, Sylvia Ann. Photographer Life mag. 1941-57, Los Angeles, Chgo., 1941-46, Far East, China, 1946-47, London, Eng., 1948- 49, Paris, France, 1950, Washington, 1950-57, London Bur. Time-Life, 1957- 61; photography editor Playboy mag., 1971—. Winner first place U. Mo. Sch. Journalism News Pictures Contest, 1951; recipient Grand award Whitehouse Photographers Assn., 1953; 1st place award color photography Ency. Brit. and Nat. Press Photographers Assn., 1959; named Photographer of Year by U. of Mo. and Ency. Brit. Home: Brookwillows Woodlands Rd Harrison NY 10528 Office: Playboy Mag 919 N Michigan Av Chicago IL 60611

KAUFFMAN, SANFORD BOGERT, airline exec.; b. Baldwin, L.I., N.Y., Aug. 8, 1907; s. William A. and Minnie (Moore) K.; Ph.B., Yale, 1928; student Harvard Grad. Sch. Bus. Adminstrn., 1933-34; m. Betty Gay Symington, Aug. 11, 1939; children—Pamela, Lelia, Robert, Margaret, Virginia. Exchange worker Deutsche Lufthansa, Berlin, 1928-29; with Pan Am. World Airways, Inc., N.Y.C., 1929—, v.p. engring., 1963-68, v.p. tech. staff, 1968-70, v.p., exec. asst., 1970—. Office: Pan American Bldg New York City NY 10017

KAUFFMANN, FRED MARIX, investment banker; b. Chgo., Jan. 14, 1904; s. Fred Marix and Stella (Winkler) K.; ed., U. Mich.; m. Patricia Born, Aug. 28, 1947. With investment bankings firms Dean, Onativia & Co., Chgo., 1923-25, S.W. Straus & Co., Chgo., 1925-27, Louchheim, Minton & Co., N.Y.C., 1929-31, Sour & Kauffmann, N.Y.C., 1931-35, Bull & Eldredge, N.Y.C., 1935-38; with Hallgarten & Co., N.Y.C., 1927-29, 38-42, 45—, now gen. partner; dir. Burton Dixie Corp., Crown Central Petroleum Corp., Ludowici-Celadon Co., Chgo. Served with AUS, 1942-45. Clubs: Mid-Am. (Chgo.); Lake Shore Country (Glencoe, Ill.); Stock Exchange Luncheon (N.Y.C.); Curzon House, Clermont (London). Home: 465 Park Av New York City NY 10022 Office: 144 Wall St New York City NY 10005

KAUFFMANN, JOHN HOY, newspaper exec.; b. Washington, Jan. 21, 1925; s. Samuel H. and Miriam (Hoy) K.; grad. Choate Sch., 1943; A.B., Princeton, 1947; m. Laura Allen, July 15, 1946 (div. 1958); children—Bruce Gordon, Louise Miriam, Margaret Ellen, Samuel Hay IV; m. 2d, Patricia Bellinger, Feb. 8, 1958; 1 son, John Hoy II. With Eve. Star, Washington, 1949—, v.p., bus. mgr., 1957-68, pres., dir., 1968—; v.p., dir. Columbia Plenograph Co.; dir. Spruce Falls Power & Paper Co., Toronto, Can., Sta. WCIV, Charleston, S.C., Sta. WMAL, Washington, Sta. WLVA, Lynchburg, Va., Am. Security Corp., Tal-Star Computer Systems, Inc., Magnavox Co., Peoples Life Ins. Co. Mem. fed. laws come Nat Newspaper Pubs. Assn.; mem. exec. com. Greater Nat. Capitol com. Washington bd. Trade; bd. dirs. Audit Bur. Circulations. Vice pres., dir. Health and Welfare Council Met. Washington; bd. dirs. A.R.C., Washington Better Bus. Bur., Nat. Symphony Orch., Jr. Achievement Met. Washington; trustee Am. Cancer Soc., Am. U., Washington Center Met. Studies. Served with USAAF, 1943-45. Decorated Air medal; recipient Community Service award. Clubs: Metropolitan, Variety, Alfalfa, Advertising (Washington); Chevy Chase (Md.). Home: 620 Boyle Lane McLean VA 22101 Office: 225 Virginia Av SE Washington DC 20003

KAUFFMANN, STANLEY JULES, author; b. N.Y.C., Apr. 24, 1916; s. Joseph H. and Jeannette (Steiner) K.; B.F.A., N.Y.U., 1935; m. Laura Cohen, Feb. 5, 1943. Mem. Washington Sq. Players, 1931-41; asso. editor Bantam Books, 1949-52; editor-in-chief Ballantine Books, 1952- 56; editor Alfred A. Knopf, 1959-60; film critic New Republic, N.Y.C., 1958-65, 67—, asso. lit. editor, 1966-67, theater critic, 1969—; drama critic N.Y. Times, 1966; conductor program The Art of Film, Channel 13, N.Y.C., 1963-67; vis. prof. drama Yale, 1967-68, 69—. Ford Found. fellow for study abroad, 1964, 71; hon. fellow Morse Coll., Yale, 1964. Author: The Hidden Hero, 1949; The Tightrope, 1952; A Change of Climate, 1954; Man of the World, 1956; A World on Film, 1966; Figures of Light, 1971. Address: 10 W 15th St New York City NY 10011

KAUFMAN, ALEX, corp. exec.; b. Lemburg, Poland, Sept. 9, 1924; s. Isadore and Bronislava (Halpern) K.; degree in chemistry, Stuttgart Poly. Inst. (Germany); m. Amalia Fuss, Sept. 6, 1951; children—Bernice, Irene, Mark. Came to U.S. 1950, naturalized, 1955. With Hatco Chem. div. W.R. Grace & Co., Fords, N.J., v.p., 1961-62, pres. parent co., 1962—, corporate v.p., 1967, exec. v.p., 1968—, also dir., group exec. Hatco Group; pres. Grace Petrochems., Inc., P.R., 1969—; dir. Bekaert-Belgium/Bekaert, Australia, Mid-Jersey Nat. Bank, Woodbridge, N.J. Mem. Soc. Plastics Industry Mfg. Chemists Assn., A.I.M. (pres.'s council), Woodbridge C. of C. Home: 57 Century Lane Watchung NJ 07060 Office: King George Post Rd Fords NJ 08863

KAUFMAN, ALLAN NATHAN, physicist, educator; b. Chgo., July 21, 1927; s. Justin and Millie (Low) K.; Ph.B., U. Chgo., 1947, B.S., 1949, M.S., 1951, Ph.D., 1953; m. Louise E. Lazarus, Apr. 14, 1957; children—Joel, Janet. Staff, Lawrence Radiation Lab., Livermore, Cal., 1953-64; sr. lectr. U. Cal. at Los Angeles, 1964-65; asso. prof. physics U. Cal. at Berkeley, 1965-67, prof., 1967—. Fellow Am. Phys. Soc. Contbr. articles profl. jours. Home: 7041 Devon Way Berkeley CA 94705

KAUFMAN, ARNOLD, electronic co. exec.; b. Ft. Wayne, Ind., Oct. 12, 1921; s. Albert Fred and Ellenora (Meyer) K.; B.S. in Elec. Engring., Tri-State Coll., Angola, Ind., 1946; m. Pauline Werling, May 26, 1946; children—Michael, Scott. Salesman, Gen. Electric Co., Chgo., 1947-50; gen. mgr. Utah Radio Products Co., Huntington, Ind., 1950-56; pres. Utrad Corp., Huntington, 1956—, Triad Transformer Corp., Los Angeles, 1961—; v.p. Litton Industries, Inc., Litton Precision Products Inc. Served with USAAF, 1942-44. Mem. I.E.E.E. Home: RR 8 Flaxmill Rd Huntington IN 46750

KAUFMAN, ARNOLD SAUL, educator, philosopher; b. Hartford, Conn., Sept. 14, 1927; s. Louis A. and Norma (Grant) K.; B.S.S., City Coll. N.Y., 1949; Ph.D., Columbia, 1955; m. Elizabeth Williams, Feb. 3, 1954; children—Margaret Ann, William Louis. Mem. faculty U. Mich., 1955-69; prof. philosophy U. Cal. at Los Angeles, 1969—. Mem. nat. bd. SANE, 1967—; nat. steering com. New Democratic Coalition, 1969—; a founder Vietnam Teach-In Movement, 1965. Served with USNR, 1945-46. Fulbright scholar, 1953-55; fellow Center Advanced Study Behavioral Scis., 1962-63. Mem. Am. Philos. Assn. Author: The Radical Liberal, 1968. Home: 10514 Wyton Dr Los Angeles CA 90024

KAUFMAN, BEL, author, educator; b. Berlin, Germany; d. Michael J. and Lala (Rabinowitz) Kaufman; B.A. magna cum laude, Hunter Coll.; M.A. with highest honors, Columbia; LL.D., Nasson Coll., Me.; div.; children—Jonathan Goldstine, Thea Goldstine. Adj. prof. English, Borough Manhattan Community Coll.; lectr. throughout country, also appearances on TV and radio. Recipient plaque Anti-Defamation League; award and plaque United Jewish Appeal; Paperback of Year award; Bell Movie award. Mem. Author's Guild, Dramatists Guild, P.E.N. (exec. bd.), English Grad. Union, Phi Beta Kappa. Author: Up the Down Staircase, 1965; also short stories, translations of Russian, lyrics for musicals. Address: 1020 Park Av New York City NY 10028

KAUFMAN, CHARLES RUDOLPH, lawyer; b. Chgo., Dec. 25, 1908; s. Aaron C. and Miriam (Eisenstaedt) K.; A.B., U. Mich., 1930; LL.B. magna cum laude (Fay diploma), Harvard, 1933; m. Violet-Page Koteen, Feb. 20, 1936; children—Thomas H., Constance Page (Mrs. Peter K. Dickinson), Christopher Lee. Admitted to D.C. bar, 1935, Ill. bar, 1938; legal sec. Judge Learned Hand, U.S. Ct. of Appeals, 1933-34; supervising atty. SEC, Washington, 1934-37; pvt. practice Pope & Ballard, 1937-52, Vedder, Price, Kaufman & Kammholz, Chgo., 1952—, Former mem. New Trier Twp. High Sch. Bd. Edn.; active in various charitable law sch. programs Trustee Hadley Sch. for Blind. Mem. Am., Ill., Chgo. (legal aid, judiciary coms.) bar assns., Chgo. Law Club. Legislative editor Harvard Law Rev., 1932-33. Home: 844 Prospect Av Winnetka IL 60093 Office: 39 S LaSalle St Chicago IL 60603

KAUFMAN, CHARLES WESLEY, research adminstr.; b. Thomas, W.Va., Nov. 26, 1911; s. Marion Ellsworth and Ethel B. (Burch) K.; B.S., Washington and Lee U., 1933; M.S., Ph.D., U. Ariz.; student W.Va. U., U. Cal.; m. Colleen V. Over, Feb. 24, 1935; 1 dau., Janet Burch. Research chemist Nat. Fruit Products Co., 1933-36, Nat. Canners Assn., 1936-39; research chemist Gen. Foods Corp., 1939-44, asst. dir. research, 1944-47, dir. research 1947-50, exec. council, 1950; food cons. O.Q.M.G., 1941-50, v.p. subsistence lab. Research and Devel. Assn.; v.p., exec. dir. research, exec. com. Kraft Foods Co., 1950—, dir., 1953—; pres. research and devel. div. Nat. Dairy Products Corp., 1958—; v.p. Foremost Dairies, Inc., San Francisco, 1962—, private cons.; v.p. Mars, Inc. Washington; asso. prof. U. Ariz., 1964—; v.p. adminstrn. Pima Coll. Adv. com. S.W. Ednl. Research Lab., 1965—; trustee Shimer Coll., 1958-61. Registered prof. engr., Ariz. Mem. Am. Chemical Soc., Packaging Inst. (pres. 1959-60), Inst. Food Technologists (exec. com. 1956-57), Refrigeration Research Found. (bd. advisers), Research and Devel. Asso. (v.p.), Indsl. Research Inst. Clubs: Olympic (San Francisco); Forty Niner's Country (pres. 1963-64), El Con (Tucson). Contbr. articles on food processing to profl. jours. Patentee. Home: Colyancha Ranch R F D 2 Box 800 K Tucson AZ 85715 Office: 2500 N Soldier Trail Tucson AZ 85715

KAUFMAN, CLEMENS MARCUS, educator; b. Moundridge, Kan., Aug. 27, 1909; s. Andrew H. and Magdalena (Krehbiel) K.; A.B., Bethel Coll., N. Newton, Kan., 1936; M.S., U. Minn., 1938, Ph.D., 1943; m. Alice Lucile Woolery, May 10, 1941; children—Joan Carol, Randolph Lee, Sandra Merry. Extension asst. forester U. Minn., 1940-42, research asst., 1942-43; from asst. prof. to prof. forest mgmt. N.C. State Coll., 1943-51; dir. Sch. Forestry, U. Fla., Gainesville, 1951-62, prof. forestry, 1962—. Mem. Soc. Am. Foresters, Ecol. Soc. Am., Sigma Xi, Xi Sigma Pi. Methodist. Rotarian. Home: 2150 NW 8th Av Gainesville FL 32601

KAUFMAN, DENVER, lawyer; b. Freeman, S.D., Nov. 11, 1929; s. Albert T. and Lydia (Schrag) K.; student Freeman Jr. Coll., 1947-49; B.S., U. S.D., 1952, LL.B., 1958; postgrad. U. Colo., summer 1950; m. Sharol Ann Amundson, Jan. 7, 1961; children—Mary Kathryn, Thomas Denver. admitted to S.D. bar, 1958, Minn. bar, 1959; with Hanley, Costello & Porter, Rapid City, S.D., 1958, Gordon Berg, Mpls., 1959-61; mem. firm Popham, Haik, Schnobrich, Kaufman & Doty, Ltd., Mpls., 1961—; instr. William Mitchell Coll. Law, St. Paul, 1963-65. Served with CIC, AUS, 1953-55. Mem. Hennepin County, Minn., Am. bar assns., Delta Tau Delta, Delta Sigma Phi, Phi Delta Phi. Lutheran. Editor-in-chief S.D. Law Rev., 1957-58. Constbr. Minn. Estate Adminstrn., 1968. Home: 2960 Tonkaha Dr Wayzata MN 55391 Office: Farmers and Mechanics Bldg Minneapolis MN 55402

KAUFMAN, DONALD LEROY, aluminium co. exec.; b. Erie, Pa., May 9, 1931; s. Isadore H. and Lena (Sandler) K.; B.Sci. in Bus. Adminstrn., Ohio State U., 1953; LL.B., 1955; m. Estelle Friedman, Aug. 15, 1954; children—Craig Ivan, Susan Beth, Carrie Ellen. Admitted to Ohio bar, 1955; exec. v.p., dir. operations, dir. Alside, Inc., Akron, O. Mem. adv. com. U. Akron. Dir. Archtl. Aluminum Mfrs. Assn. Trustee Jewish Welfare Fund, Akron, 1958-65, young leaders div., 1961-65; bd. dirs. Kaufman Found., sec., 1956—. Served to 1st lt. USAF, 1955- 57. Mem. Akron Bar Assn., Sigma Alpha Mu, Tau Epsilon Rho. Club: Rosemont Country (Akron). Home: 545 Hampshire Rd Akron OH 44313 Office: P O Box 1261 Akron OH 44309

KAUFMAN, ELKIN, tobacco co. exec.; b. Louisville, May 23, 1905; s. Edwin and Adele (Straus) K.; student Harvard, 1927; m. Gertrude Winkler, Nov. 24, 1934; 1 son, Eli Winkler. Sales promotion mgr. Esquire mag., 1934-40; co-founder, exec. v.p., dir. William H. Weintraub & Co., Inc., 1941-55, name changed to Norman, Craig and Kummell Inc., pres., 1955-57; sr. v.p. Lennen & Newell, Inc., 1957-66; mgr. spl. projects Philip Morris, Inc., N.Y.C., 1966—. Bd. dirs. Grand St. Settlement, Altro Health and Rehab. Services (Tb rehab.), George Jr. Republic. Club: Harvard (N.Y.C.). Home: 480 Park Av New York City NY 10022 Office: 100 Park Av New York City NY 10017

KAUFMAN, FRANK ALBERT, U.S. dist. judge; b. Balt., Mar. 4, 1916; s. Nathan Hess and Hilda (Hecht) K.; A.B. summa cum laude, Dartmouth, 1937; LL.B. magna cum laude, Harvard, 1940; m. Clementine Alice Lararon, Apr. 22, 1945; children—Frank Albert, Peggy Ann (Mrs. Fred Wolf III). Admitted to Md. bar, 1940; atty. Office Gen. Counsel Treasury, 1940-41, Office Gen. Counsel, Lend Lease Adminstrn., 1941-42; lend lease rep. Turkey, 1942- 43; asst. to chief Psychol. Warfare Bd., Allied Forces Hdqrs., N. Africa, 1943-44; chief leaflet div., psychol. warfare div. SHAEF, 1944-45; asst. to gen. counsel FEA, 1945; asso. firm Frank, Bernstein, Conaway, Kaufman & Goldman, Balt., 1945-47, partner, 1948-66; U.S. dist. judge Md., 1966—; lectr. adminstrv. law U. Balt., 1948-62; lectr. contracts U. Md. Law Sch., 1953-54. Mem. Gov. Md. Commn. Study and Report Certain Aspects Mgmt. and Labor Relations, 1960; mem. Gov. Md. Commn. to Study and Report Uniform Comml. Code 1961; chmn. Gov. Md. Commn. Study Sentencing Criminal Cases, 1962-66; mem. Gov. Md. Ad Hoc Com. Health Problems, 1968. Mem. nat. exec. bd. Am. Jewish Com., 1960-70, exec. bd. Balt. chpt., 1948-70, pres., 1955-56; bd. overseers Goucher Coll., 1957—; bd. dirs. Md. Inst. Coll. Art, 1956—, vice chmn. bd., 1962-70; bd. dirs. Park Sch., Balt., 1956—, pres., 1963-66; bd. dirs. Sinai Hosp. Balt., 1957—, mem. exec. com., 1964—, v.p., 1967-70; past bd. dirs. Balt. chpt. Nat. Conf. Christians and Jews; bd. dirs. Balt. Jewish Council, 1954-66, pres., 1964-66; bd. dirs. Jewish Family and Children's Service, Balt., 1946-54, pres., 1953-54; bd. dirs. Asso. Jewish Charities and Welfare Fund, Balt., 1953-54, Jewish Welfare Bd., Balt., 1965-67, Md. Partners of Alliance, 1965—, Good Samaritan Hosp., Balt., 1967—. Mem. Fed., Am., Md. (chmn. com. grievences 1957-58, chmn. com. jud. rev. sentences criminal cases 1961-65, chmn. criminal law and procedure sect. council 1965-66), Balt. chmn. pub. relations com. 1965- 66, mem. exec. com. 1965-66) bar assns., Am. Law Inst., Harvard Law Sch. Assn. Md. (past pres.; past chmn. Md. com. for fund), Phi Beta Kappa. Jewish religion (bd. dirs. congregation 1947-48, 60-62). Clubs: Suburban (bd. dirs. 1941-42, 53-60, pres. 1956-60), Rule Day (past chmn.), Wranglers Law (past chmn.), Roundtable, Hamilton Street, Center (Balt.). Home: 7 Clovelly Rd Pikesville MD 21208 Office: Post Office Bldg Baltimore MD 21202

KAUFMAN, FREDERICK ALLEN, steel co. exec.; b. Ellwood City, Pa., Dec. 14, 1919; s. William Jackson and Clara (DeArment) K.; B.S., Grove City Coll., 1941, D.Sc., 1967; m. Martha C. Harlan, Nov. 20, 1948; children—Lynn Louise, Martha Elizabeth. Mem. staff Mellon Inst. Indsl. Research, Pitts., 1944-46; v.p. McKay Co., 1946-58; v.p. Universal-Cyclops Corp., Bridgeville, Pa., 1958-65, gen. mgr. Universal- Cyclops Splty. Steel div., 1965-68, pres., 1959-68, also dir.; v.p., group exec. Teledyne, Inc., Pitts., 1968—. Trustee St. Clair Hosp., Pitts. Mem. Am. Inst. Iron and Steel, Am. Soc. Mech. and Metall. Engrs. Presbyn. (trustee). Mason (32 Shriner). Home: 851 Valleyview Rd Pittsburg PA 15216 Office: Manor Oak 2 Bldg 1910 Cochran Rd Pittsburg PA

KAUFMAN, GERALD SAMUEL, hotel exec.; b. N.Y.C., Mar. 8, 1935; s. Benjamin and Rita (Skydell) K.; A.B., Columbia, 1956; LL.B., N.Y.U., 1960; m. Carol F. Fuchs, Dec. 21, 1957; children—Miriam, Michael, Daniel, Jeremy. Admitted to N.Y. bar, 1960; practice in N.Y.C., 1960-63; formerly exec. v.p., mng. dir. Sherman House, Chgo., now pres., mng. dir.; gen. partner Esquire Realty Co., JKFK Realty Co., Bronx River Realty Co.; pres. Tiffany Prodns., Inc., Chgo., Mill Run Coast Prodns., San Carlos, Cal. Bd. dirs. Portas Cancer Prevention Center, Chgo. Served with Med. Service Corps, AUS, 1957. Clubs: Executives, Standard, City, Variety (Chgo.). Mem. B'nai B'rith. Home: 3240 N Lake Shore Dr Chicago IL 60657 Office: Sherman House Clark and Randolph Sts Chicago IL 60601

KAUFMAN, GORDON DESTER, educator, theologian; b. Newton, Kan., June 22, 1925; s. Edmund George and Hazel (Dester) K.; A.B. summa cum laude, Bethel (Kan.) Coll., 1947; M.A. in Sociology, Northwestern U., 1948; B.D. magna cum laude, Yale, 1951, Ph.D. in Philos. Theology, 1955; m. Dorothy Wedel, June 11, 1947; children—David W., Gretchen E., Anne Louisa, Edmund G. Ordained to ministry Mennonite Ch., 1953; asst. prof. religion Pomona Coll., 1953- 58; asso. prof. theology Vanderbilt U., 1958-63; prof. theology Harvard Div. Sch., 1963—, Edward MallincKrodt Jr. prof. div., 1969—. Bd. dirs. Bethel Coll. Mem. Soc. Religion Higher Edn., Am. Philos. Assn., Am. Assn. U. Profs., Metaphys. Soc. Am., Am. Theol. Soc. Democrat. Author: Relativism, Knowledge and Faith, 1960; The Context of Decision, 1961; Systematic Theology; a Historicist Perspective, 1968; God the Problem, 1972. Home: 4 Thoreau Rd Lexington MA 02173 Office: 45 Francis Av Cambridge MA 02138

KAUFMAN, HAROLD FREDERICK, educator; b. nr. Greenville, O., May 6, 1911; s. Charles E. and Trecy (Valentine) K.; A.B., U. Mo., 1938, A.M., 1939; Ph.D., Cornell U., m. Lois Cook, June 8, 1939; 1 son, Harrell Lynn. With U.S. Forest Service, summers 1938, 45; asst. rural sociology Cornell U., 1939-42; instr. U. Mo., 1942-45; asst. prof. U. Ky., 1945-48; chmn. dept. sociology and rural life Miss. State U., State College, 1948-61, prof. sociology, 1948- -, dir. Social Sci. Research Center, 1960-69, research prof. sociology, 1969—; seminar participant, Caribbean, 1961, Mexico, 1964, N. Europe, 1968; vis. lectr. Columbia, 1952-53, U. Wis., 1954. Recipient Faculty award for research, 1970; Fulbright research scholar to India, 1961, field research, 64. Fellow Soc. Applied Anthropology, Am. Sociol. Assn.; mem. So. (pres. 1959), Rural (pres. 1962), Indian sociol. socs., European Rural Sociology Soc., Assn. U. Profs. Contbr. numerous monographs, articles to profl. lit. Home: 204 N Nash St Starkville MS 39759 Office: Box 5161 State College MS 39762

KAUFMAN, HERBERT, educator, polit. scientist; b. N.Y.C., Sept. 21, 1922; s. Benjamin Harry and Gertrude (Meltzer) K.; B.S.S., Coll. City, N.Y., 1942; M.A., Columbia, 1946, Ph.D., 1950; m. Ruth L. Davis, Mar. 19, 1967. Research analyst Pres.'s Com. Civil Rights, 1947; research asso. Inst. Pub. Adminstrn., N.Y.C., 1948-49; lectr. govt. Coll. City N.Y., 1951-53; mem. faculty Yale, 1953-69, prof. polit. sci., 1963-69, chmn. dept., 1964-67; sr. fellow Brookings Instn., Washington, 1969—; cons. U.S. Bur. Budget, Econ. Stblzn. Agy., Mayor N.Y.C. Com. Mgmt. Survey, State Com. to Study Orgnl. Structure Govt. N.Y.C., N.Y. State Health Dept., Mayor N.Y.C. Task Force City Personnel. Mem. New Haven Plan Commn. 1963—, chmn., 1964-66; chmn. New Haven Housing Authority, 1966-67. Served with AUS, 1942-46. Fellow Center Advanced Study Behavioral Scis., 1959-60; co- recipient Fruin-Colnon award Nat. Municipal League, 1961. Mem. Am. Polit. Sci. Assn. (council 1966-67), Democrat. Jewish religion. Author: The Forest Ranger: A Study in Administrative Behavior, 1960; (with Wallace S. Sayre) Governing New York City, 2d edit., 1965; Politics and Policies in State and Local Government, 1963. Office: Brookings Institution Washington DC 20036

KAUFMAN, HERBERT EDWARD, ophthalmologist, educator; b. N.Y.C., Sept. 28, 1931; s. Benjamin and Claire (Krinsky) K.; A.B. magna cum laude, Princeton, 1952; M.D. magna cum laude, Harvard, 1956; m. Eleanor Rosenblum, June 30, 1957; children— Stephen, Joshua, Claire. Intern Mass. Gen. Hosp., Boston, 1956-57; resident Mass. Eye and Ear Infirmary Boston, 1959-62; practice medicine, specializing in ophthalmology, Gainesville, Fla., 1962—; prof., chmn. dept. ophthalmology Coll. Medicine, U. Fla., 1964—; cons. NIH, Surgeon Gen. USAF. Chmn. tng. com. Nat. Eye Inst., 1970-71. Served with USPHS, 1957-59. Recipient Lions Humanitarian award, 1968; named one of Ten Outstanding Young Men in Am., 1964. Fellow A.A.A.S., A.C.S.; mem Am. Assn. Immunologists, Am. Assn. Ophthalmology, Am. Fedn. Clin. Research, A.M.A., Am. Soc. Microbiology, Am. Soc. Clin Investigation, Assn. Research Ophthalmology (sec-treas.), Am. Assn. U. Profs., Assn. U. Profs. Ophthalmology, Am. Acad. Ophthalmology and Otolaryngology, Eye Bank Assn. Am. (bd. dirs.), Pan Am., So., Fla., Alachua County med. assns., Nat., Fla. rehab. assns., Fla. Soc. Ophthalmology, Fla. Soc. Prevention Blindness, N.Y. Acad. Scis., Mass. Eye and Ear Infirmary Alumni Assn., Pan-Am. Assn. Ophthalmology, Pan Pacific Surg. Assn., Soc. Cryobiology, Soc. Exptl. Biology and Medicine, Royal Soc. Medicine, Sigma Xi. Contbr. articles profl. jours. Office: Coll of Medicine U Fla Gainesville FL 32601

KAUFMAN, HYMAN, educator, mathematician; b. Lachine, Que., Can., Feb. 2, 1920; s. Solomon and Anna (Sabesinsky) K.; B.Sc., McGill U., 1941, M.Sc., 1945, Ph.D., 1948; postgrad. Brown U., 1945-46, Yale, 1948-49; m. Sylvia Van Straten, June 21, 1959. Research geophysicist Continental Oil Co., Ponca City, Okla., 1949-50; mem. theory group Lab. for Electronics, Boston, 1950-52; faculty McGill U., Montreal, Que., 1952—, prof. math., 1963—; cons. to pvt. cos. Mem. Am. Math. Soc., Math. Assn. Am., I.E.E.E., Canadian Math. Congress, Soc. for Indsl. and Applied Math., Soc. for Exploration Geophysics, Canadian Operations Research Soc., Operations Research Soc. Am. Author: (with G.E. Roberts) Table of LaPlace Transforms, 1966; also articles. Research on properties correlation function in statis. communication theory, spl. properties differential equations. Home: 533 Querbes St Montreal 153 Quebec Canada

KAUFMAN, IRA JEFFREY, investment banker; b. Chgo., Mar. 4, 1928; s. Hy and Gertrude (Schwartz) K.; student Chgo. Mil. Acad., 1938-41, Northwestern Mil. and Naval Acad., 1941-45, U. Ill., 1945-46; m. Audrey Becker, Jan. 12, 1969; 1 dau., children—Stephen, Stacy, Elizabeth, Jonathan. Pres., chmn. bd. Rodman & Renshaw, Inc., 1958—; chmn. exec. com. Skyline Corp.; dir. Dan River Mills, Inc. Mem. Chgo. Merc. Exchange, Chgo. Bd. Trade. Clubs: Standard, Attic (Chgo.); Palm Bay. Home: 2479 Woodbridge Lane Highland Park IL 60035 Office: 209 S LaSalle St Chicago IL 60604

KAUFMAN, IRVING ROBERT, U.S. judge; b. N.Y.C., June 24, 1910; s. Herman and Rose (Spielberg) K.; LL.B., Fordham U., 1931; LL.D., Jewish Theol. Sem. Am., Oklahoma City U.; m. Helen Ruth Rosenberg, June 23, 1936, children— Robert Howard, James Michael, Richard Kenneth. Admitted to N.Y. bar, 1932; spl. asst. to U.S. atty. So. Dist. N.Y.; asst. U.S. atty., spl. asst. to atty. gen. U.S. charge of lobbying investigation; set up permanent lobbying unit for Dept. Justice, served as head; pvt. practice law, N.Y.C.; partner firm Simpson, Brady, Noonan & Kaufman, Noonan, Kaufman & Eagan; U.S. dist. judge So. Dist. N.Y., 1949-61; circuit judge U.S. Ct. Appeals, 2d circuit, 1961- -. U.S. del. 2d UN Congress Prevention Crime and Treatment Offenders. Trustee emeritus Riverdale Country Sch. Recipient certificate of honor Va. State Assn. B'nai B'rith; citation N.Y. State Fedn. Women's Clubs; Chief Justice Harlan Fiske Stone award Assn. Trial Lawyers City N.Y.; 1st ann. Thomas Jefferson award Unitarian Universalist Ch.; Encaenia award Fordham Coll. Fellow Inst. Jud. Adminstrn. (pres. 1969-71; chmn. exec. com., chmn. juvenile justice standards project); mem. Am. Law Inst., Assn. Bar City N.Y., Fed., N.Y., Am. (mem. sect., Jud. adminstrn.; chmn. com. operations jury system 1966—) bar assns., Am. Judicature Soc., Jud. Standards Com., Fordham Law Alumni Assn. (dir.; Achievement award), Tau Epsilon Phi (Man of Year citation), Phi Alpha Delta (hon.). Eleventh ann. James Madison lectr.: The Message, The Medium and the First Amendment; Contbr. articles to profl. jours. Home: 1185 Park Av New York City NY 10028 Office: U S Courthouse Foley Sq New York City NY 10007

KAUFMAN, JEROME J., aluminum co. exec.; b. Cleve., Nov. 27, 1917; s. Isadore and Lena (Sandler) K.; grad. Erie Acad. High Sch., 1935; m. Janet Levine, Jan. 16, 1939; children—Jeffrey, James, Joel. Pres. Alside, Inc., Akron, O., 1947—, dir.; pres. Lifewall Corp.,

Akron, 1949—, Aluma-King Corp., Akron, 1949—, Ohio Aluminum Supply Co., Akron, 1955-, Alside Acceptance Corp., Akron, 1961- -; dir. First Nat. Bank Akron, 1961—. Trustee Akron City Hosp., Rehab. Center Summit County; adv. com. U. Akron; pres. United Found. Summit County. Served with inf. AUS, World War II. Recipient Kovod award United Jewish Appeal, 1956. Clubs: Rosemont Country (bd. dirs.) (Akron); Westview Country (Miami, Fla.); Tamarisk Country, Racquet (Palm Springs, Cal.); Hillcrest Country (Los Angeles). Home: 275 N Portage Path Akron OH 44303 Office: PO Box 1261 Akron OH 44309

KAUFMAN, JOHN S., ins. co. exec.; b. Phila., Dec. 31, 1908; A.B., U. Pa., 1930. With Gen. Accident, Fire & Life Assurance Corp., 1930—, agy. supt., 1945-49, agy. mgr. charge agys. and br. offices, 1949-50, asst. U.S. mgr., also v.p. Potomac Ins. Co., 1950-53, gen. mgr., 1953-55, sr. v.p. Pa. Gen. Ins. Co., 1955-63, exec. v.p. Potomac Ins. Co., Pa. Gen. Ins. Co., 1963-66, exec. v.p. Camden Fire Ins. Assn., 1966-67, dep. gen. atty. Gen. Accident Co., 1967-69, vice chmn. Potomac Ins. Co., Camden Fire Ins. Assn., Pa. Gen. Ins. Co., 1969—. Mem. Phi Beta Kappa. Clubs: Union League, Racquet. Home: R F D East Greenville PA 18041 Office: 414 Walnut St Philadelphia PA 19106*

KAUFMAN, JOSEPH LAWRENCE, stock broker; b. N.Y.C., Sept. 30, 1922; s. Marcus and Anna (Low) K.; B.S. in Mech. Engring., Mass. Inst. Tech., 1947; m. Muriel D. Berkson, May 23, 1957; children—Lucas Ian, Abigail Charlotte. Design and project engr. Cinecolor Corp., Los Angeles, 1947-48, Houston Corp., 1948-49, Rhodes Lewis Corp., 1949-50, Gray & Huleguard, Inc., 1950-52; sales engr. E. F. Hauserman, N.Y.C., 1953-56; mem. Am. Stock Exchange, 1956—, gov., 1965—, now sr. floor ofcl.; dir. Am. Stock Exchange Clearing Corp. Served to ensign USNR, 1942-45. Registered profl. engr., Cal. Home: 390 West End Av New York City NY 10024 Office: 74 Trinity Pl New York City NY 10006

KAUFMAN, JOSEPH WILLIAM, lawyer; b. N.Y.C., Mar. 27, 1899; s. Samuel and Adelaide (Brenner) K.; A.B., Columbia, 1920, LL.B., 1923, J.D., 1969. Former law sec. Judge John C. Knox; active practitioner law, N.Y.C., Washington; mem. Col. William J. Donovan's legal staff in bankruptcy investigation, 1932; spl. trial examiner N.Y. N.Y. Labor Relations Bd., 1939-41; gen. counsel Smaller War Plants Corp., Dept. Commerce, World War II; dep. chief counsel Nuremberg War Crime Trials, chief prosecutor Krupp case, 1947; chief counsel Ho. Reps. Small Bus. Com., 1949-50; referee appeals council Social Security Adminstrn., 1956-61; trial examiner FTC, 1961-69; spl. master U.S. Ct. Appeals, 1965—. Recipient Distinguished Service award and citation, 1969. Mem. nat. and labor panel arbitrators Am. Arbitration Assn.; mem. panel Nat. Mediation Bd.; lectr. law schs. Served with U.S. Army, World War I. Mem. Am., Fed. bar assns., Assn. Bar City N.Y. Contbr. articles to profl. jours.

KAUFMAN, KARL LINCOLN, coll. dean; b. Attica, O., 1911; s. S.F. and I. (Huffman) K.; B.Sc., Ohio State U., 1933; Ph.D., Purdue U., 1936; m. Mary Jo Rettig, 1936; children—Karl, James, Robert. Instr., then asst. prof. Wash. State Coll., 1936-40; asso. prof. Med. Coll. Va., 1940-45, prof., head dept., 1945- 49· cons. pharm. mfrs.; exec. officer Coll. Pharmacy, Butler U., Indpls., 1949- 52, dean, 1952—; project dir. several drug abuse edn. projects. Past pres. Ind. Health Careers, Inc.; pres. Comprehensive Health Planning Council; pres. elect Marion County Heart Assn.; bd. Am. Cancer Soc.; past chmn. Sci. Fair Council; founder, sec.- treas. Ind. Sci. Edn. Fund; coordinator Ind. Regional Sci. Fairs; past pres. Ind. Interprofl. Health Council. Mem. Am., Ind. pharm. assns., Am. Chem. Soc., Sigma Xi, Phi Sigma, Rho Chi. Republican. Episcopalian. Mason (32). Clubs: Internat. Torch (internat. past pres.). Co-author: American Pharmacy, vol. I, 1945-48. Contbr. World Book Ency., Am. Mercury; articles to profl. jours. Home: 4905 N Illinois St Indianapolis IN 46208

KAUFMAN, LEONARD, lawyer; b. N.Y.C., Apr. 30, 1913; s. Louis and Lillian (Brown) K.; student Coll. City N.Y., 1929-31; LL.B., Fordham U., 1936; m. Rita Dembitz, Aug. 9, 1940; children—Lawrence J., Robert I. Admitted to N.Y. bar, 1937; staff law offices Nathan Burkan, N.Y.C., 1933-36, Schwartz & Frohlich, N.Y.C., 1936-49; legal staff Paramount Pictures Corp., N.Y.C., 1949-59, gen. house counsel, 1959-64, gen. counsel, 1964-67; pvt. practice of law, 1968—; mem. firm Kaufman & Kaufman, 1969—. Served with AUS, 1943-45; CBI. Mem. Am., N.Y. State bar assns., Assn. Bar N.Y.C., Copyright Soc. U.S.A. Mem. B'nai B'rith. Home: 400 Orienta Av Mamaroneck NY 10543 Office: 342 Madison Av New York City NY 10017

KAUFMAN, MARJORIE RUTH, educator; B.S., Wis. State Coll.; A.M., U. Wash.; Ph.D., U. Minn. Prof. English, Mt. Holyoke Coll., South Hadley, Mass. Office: Dept English Mt Holyoke Coll South Hadley MA 01075*

KAUFMAN, MOSES RALPH, psychiatrist; b. nr. Beltz, Bessarabia, Russia, Oct. 5, 1900; s. Jakov and Sarah (Straker) K.; came to U.S., 1925, naturalized, 1937; M.D., McGill U., 1925; m. Ida Elizabeth Esack, Sept. 2, 1925; children—Paul, Bettina Deborah. Intern Manhattan State Hosp., Ward's Island, N.Y., also asst. Vanderbilt Clinic, N.Y.C., 1925-26; resident neurol. staff Montefiore Hosp., 1926-27; asst. sr. physician Boston Psychopathic Hosp., 1927-28; Commonwealth Research fellow Harvard, Vienna, 1928-31; clin. dir. McLean Hosp., Waverly, Mass., 1931- 33; chief psychiatrist Mt. Sinai Hosp., N.Y.C., 1945—, emeritus dir. dept. psychiatry Inst. Psychiatry; prof. psychiatry Mount Sinai Med. Sch., 1964—; clin. prof. psychiatry Columbia Coll. Phys. and Surg., 1948-68; Esther and Joseph Klingenstein prof. psychiatry emeritus Mount Sinai Sch. Medicine; dean emeritus Page and William Black Post- Grad. Sch. Medicine. Past chmn. med. adv. bd. Hebrew U., Hadassah Med. Sch., Jerusalem, Israel. Served from maj. to col., M.C., AUS, 1942-45. Diplomate Bd. Psychiatry and Neurology, 1935. Fellow A.M.A., N.Y. Acad. Medicine (v.p.), Am. Psychiat. Assn. (v.p. 1963-64); mem. Am. Psychoanalytic Assn. (past pres.) Assn. Research Nervous Mental Disease, Am. Psychosomatic Soc., Harvey Soc., N.Y. Psychoanalytic Soc., N.Y. Soc. Clin. Psychiatry, A.A.A.S. Clubs: Harvard (Boston and N.Y.C.). Home: 1170 Fifth Av New York City NY Office: Mt Sinai Hosp New York City NY 10029

KAUFMAN, ORVAL JOSEPH, lawyer; b. Moundridge, Kan., Apr. 25, 1927; s. Jacob N. and Amelia (Goering) K.; B.S., U. Kan., 1948, J.D., 1952; m. Barbara Jean Olson, Jan. 27, 1951; children—Allen Robert, Craig Howard, Brian Nelson, David Joseph. Admitted to Kan. bar, 1952; partner Weigand, Curfman, Brainerd, Harris & Kaufman, Wichita, 1952—. Mem. Wichita C. of C., Wichita, Kan., Am. bar assns., Order Coif, Sigma Alpha Epsilon, Alpha Kappa Psi, Phi Delta Phi. Methodist. Mason (32, Shriner). Home: 661 N Mission St Wichita KS 67206 Office: First Nat Bank Bldg Wichita KS 67202

KAUFMAN, PHILLIP, film producer; b. Chgo., Oct 23, 1936; s. Nathan and Elizabeth (Brandau) K.; B.A. with honors, U. Chgo., 1958, postgrad., 1960; postgrad Harvard Law Sch., 1959; m. Rose Fisher, June 14, 1959; 1 son, Peter. Co-author, dir., producer motion picture Goldstein, 1963; author, dir., producer Frank's Greatest Adventure, 1965; pres. Jericho Prodns., Inc., film producers, Chgo., 1965—; dir.-writer-producer Universal City Studios (Cal.). Recipient Prix de la Nouvelle Critizue for Goldstein, Cannes Film Festival, 1964. Home: care N Kaufman 730 Elder Ct Glencoe IL 60022 Office: Universal City Studios Universal City CA 91608

KAUFMAN, RAYMOND HENRY, physician; b. Bklyn., Nov. 24, 1925; s. Morris and Anne (Markewich) K.; student Coll. William and Mary, 1942-43, U. N.C., 1943-44; M.D., U. Md., 1948; m. Patricia Ann Judson, June 23, 1946; children—Susan Jo (Mrs. Edward B. Kahn), Wendy Beth, Marri Ellen, Elisabeth Ann. Intern, Beth Israel Hosp., N.Y.C., 1948-49, resident obstetrics and gynecology, 1949-53; fellow pathology Meth. Hosp., Houston, 1955-58; asst. prof. obstetrics, gynecology, pathology Baylor Coll. Medicine, Houston, 1959-65, asso. prof., 1965—, acting chmn. dept., 1968—. Served with USNR, 1943-45; to capt. USAF, 1953-55. Diplomate Am. Bd. Obstetrics and Gynecology; mem. Am. Coll. Obstetrics and Gynecology, A.C.S., Central Assn. Obstetrics and Gynecology (chmn. com. for cons. gynecol. pathology 1968—), Tex. Assn. Obstetrics and Gynecology (v.p. 1971—), Houston Obstet. and Gynecol. Soc. (pres. 1971—), Am. Cytology Soc., Am. Fertility Soc., Am. Soc. Colposcopy, Phi Delta Epsilon (nat. sec. 1970—). Author: (with H.L. Gardner) Benign Diseases of Vulva and Vagina, 1969; also articles. Home: 11002 Hunters Park Dr Houston TX 77024

KAUFMAN, STEPHEN ALLAN, city planner; b. N.Y.C., Sept. 6, 1911; s. Milton and Bertha (Rosenthal) K.; B.A., Princeton, 1932, M.F.A., 1935; M.City Planning, Mass. Inst. Tech., 1940; m. Jean F. Friedman, Feb. 27, 1941; children—Jonathan A., Barbara S., Martha R. Research asst. Regional Plan Assn. N.Y., N.Y.C., 1940-41, City Planning Commn. N.Y.C., 1941-42; project planner regional office PHA, N.Y.C., 1942-43; city planner City Planning Commn., Cleve., 1943-48; with Regional Planning Commn. Cleve., 1948—, acting dir., dep. 1961—; spl. lectr. Case Inst. Tech., 1956-66, 68-69; dir. Ohio Planning Conf., 1956, pres., 1967-69. Chmn. periodic rev. com. Welfare Fedn. Cleve.; chmn. census tract adv. com. for Cuyahoga County, U.S. Bur. Census; dir. N.E. Ohio Aviation Council, 1968—, pres., 1971. Mem. Am. Inst. Planners (past pres. N. Ohio chpt., nat. sec.-treas. 1964- 66, v.p. 1966-68), Phi Beta Kappa. Home: 16100 Chadbourne Rd Cleveland OH 44120 Office: 415 The Arcade Cleveland OH 44114

KAUFMANN, BERWIND PETERSEN, biologist; b. Phila., Apr. 23, 1897; s. Rudolph and Ida (Petersen) K.; B.S., U. Pa., 1918; A.M., 1920, Ph.D., 1925; m. Jessie Thomson McCulloch, Apr. 12, 1924; children—Berwind Norman, Carl Bowman, Anders Joseph. Asst. dept. biology U. Pa., 1916-24; tchr. biology Northeast High Sch., Phila., 1919-25; prof. biology Southwestern U., Memphis, 1926-28; prof., head dept. botany U. Ala., 1928-36; NRC fellow in biol. sci. Cal. Inst. Tech., 1932-33; guest investigator dept. genetics Carnegie Instn., 1936, 37, resident investigator, 1937-62, acting dir., 1960-61, dir., 1961-62; prof. zoology and botany, sr. research scientist U. Mich. at Ann Arbor, 1962-67, prof. emeritus, 1967—; co-prin. investigator sci. research program USPHS; guest investigator Brookhaven Nat. Lab., 1955-63; dir. grad. program devel. Adelphi Coll., 1962-64. Mem. Biology Council; mem. exec. com. NRC; mem. Marine Biol. Corp., Woods Hole, Mass.; mem. Biol. Stain Commn. Fellow A.A.A.S.; mem. L.I. Biol. Assn. (asst. sec., dir.), Am. Soc. Cell Biology, Am. Soc. Naturalists (v.p. 1951), Bot. Soc. Am., Am. Soc. Zoologists, Genetics Soc. Am. (sec.-treas. 1941-43, v.p. 1944, pres. 1961), Soc. Cell Biology, Nat. Acad. Scis., Soc. for Study Evolution, Radiation Research Soc., Soc. for Study Devel. and Growth, Phi Beta Kappa, Sigma Xi, Omicron Delta Kappa, Alpha Epsilon Delta, Lambda Chi Alpha. Author: (with M. Demerec) Drosophila Guide. Editor: gen. animal, human cytology and cytochemistry sect. Biol. Abstracts; asso. editor Jour. Morphology, The Nucleus, Internat. Jour. Radiation Biology. Author articles on plant and animal cytology and cytology and cytogenetics. Home: 2650 Heather Way Ann Arbor MI

KAUFMANN, CECIL DAVID, jeweler; b. Detroit, Sept. 18, 1904; s. Saul and Cora (Samter) K.; student U. Pa., 1922-23; m. Isabelle Gotta Dec. 14, 1923; children—Jean Carol, Edmund I., Cora Lee (Mrs. Max S. Gross). With Hadley Furniture Co., Springfield, Mass., 1924-25, Hecht Co., Washington, 1925-26; buyer furniture Kaufmann Furniture Co., Washington, 1926-29; pres. Franc Jewelry Co., Washington 1929-34; supr. Midwestern stores Kay Jewelry Stores, Inc., Washington, 1934-35, chmn. bd., 1935-46, pres., 1946—; pres. Ad-Masters Advt. Agy., Washington, 1936-46, Fairfax Distbg. Co., Inc., Washington, 1953—. Bd. dirs. Laurel Harness Racing Assn., Ky. Harness Racing Assn., Federal City Council. Co-founder, past pres. Jewelry Industry Council, Nat. Found. Consumer Credit. Pres. Cora and Saul Kaufmann Meml. Found., Jewish Fund for Med. Research, Kay Asso. Stores Charitable Found.; founder, hon. pres., Kaufmann Camp for Washington Boys and Girls; hon. life mem. bd. dirs. Jewish Community Center, Washington; bd. dirs. Washington chpt. A.R.C., Washington Heart Assn., Washington council Boy Scouts Am.; mem. Washington Businessmens' Assn. (past pres.). Balt.-Washington Mfg. Assn. (past pres.), Advt. Club Washington, Washington Bd. Trade, Zeta Beta Tau. Mason. Clubs: Variety (Washington); African Safari (Washington and Fla.); Woodmont Country. Home: 2812 Chesterfield P1 NW Washington DC 20008 Office: 1328 New York Av NW Washington DC 20005

KAUFMANN, HANNS LUCAS, hosp. adminstr.; b. Berlin, Germany, Oct. 26, 1911; s. Georg and Margarethe (Pflessor) K.; B.A., U. Zurich (Switzerland), 1929; postgrad. U. Cal. at Los Angeles, 1931-32; m. Evelyn Minette Neill, June 7, 1935; children—Julia Minette, Mark Georg. Came to U.S., 1931, naturalized 1941. Sec., asst. producer United Players Prodns., Inc., 1933-39; timekeeper Capital Co., also war plant constrn. office mgr. Cahill Bros., San Francisco, 1940-43; officer mgr., asst. gen. mgr. Clementina Co., San Francisco, 1946-51; controller-asst. dir. Childrens Hosp., San Francisco, 1951-57; dir. publs., asst. dir. Menorah Med. Center, Kansas City, Mo., 1960; adminstr. Fresno County (Cal.) Gen. Hosp., 1961-69, French Hosp., San Francisco, 1969—. Pres. Fresno Hosp. Council, 1964; bd. dirs. South San Joaquin Valley Hosp. Conf., 1965, San Francisco Hosp. Conf., 1970-71, Fresno Community Council, 1962. Served with AUS, 1943-46; ETO. Mem. Am. Coll. Hosp. Adminstrs., Cal. Hosp. Assn. (chmn. county hosp. com. 1964). Episcopalian. Home: 2149 Lyon St San Francisco CA 94115 Office: 4131 Geary Blvd San Francisco CA 94118

KAUFMANN, HENRY HANS, grain research mgr., author; b. Hanau, Germany, June 5, 1919; s. Arthur and Lilly (Weil) K.; came to U.S., 1939, naturalized, 1943; B.S. in Food Tech., U. Minn., 1953; m. R. Marianne Rosenstock, Dec. 20, 1949; children—Anita L., Wendy E., Kenneth M., Ronald S., Daniel G. Mgr. grain research lab. Cargill, Inc., Mpls., 1953—, gen. grain supt., 1971—. Served with AUS, 1942-46. Decorated Bronze Star medal. Mem. Am. Assn. Cereal Chemists, Am. Soc. Agrl. Engrs., Grain Elevator and Processing Soc. (dir.), Nat. Grain and Feed Assn., Minn. Engring. Soc. Author: (with C.M. Christensen) Grain Storage, 1969 (recipient McKnight award U. Minn. Press, 1970). Contbr. articles to mags. Patentee in fields grain handling, storage. Home: 1605 Fairway Lane Minneapolis MN 55426 Office: Cargill Bldg Minneapolis MN 55402

KAUFMANN, HENRY WILLIAM, educator; b. Cambridge, Mass., Oct. 23, 1913; s. Otto and Mary (Korman) K.; Mus.B., Yale, 1945, Mus.M., 1946; Ph.D., Harvard, 1960; m. Helen Stwart Sanderson, Jan. 29, 1950. Faculty, U. Wis., 1948-50, Boston U., 1950-56, Ohio State U., 1958-62; faculty Rutgers U., New Brunswick, 1962—, prof. music history, 1948—. Trustee Proctor Found. Mem. Am. Musicological Soc. (council), Coll. Music Soc. (exec. sec.). Episcopalian. Author: Nicola Vicentino Opera Omnia, 1963; The Life and Works of Nicola Vicentino, 1966. Home: 3 Radio Ct Somerset NJ 08873 Office: Music Dept Rutgers U New Brunswick NJ 08903

KAUFMANN, HERBERT, author; b. Cologne, Germany, Aug. 24, 1920; s. Paul and Trude (Neitzel) K.; D. Philosophy (social Anthropology), U. Cologne, 1958; m. Gertrud Lesker, June 30, 1945; children—Judith, Michael. Engaged in chem. industry, 1934-50; ethnol. studies and social changes studies, Africa 1951-61; correspondent German Broadcasting Service for East and Central Africa Affairs, Nairobi, Kenya; also corr. Frankfurter Allgemeine Zeitung. Mem. Gesellschaft für Erd Kunde zu Berlin, also The Internat. African Inst. in London, England. Author: (travel) Rote Strassen, 1955; Der verlorene Karawanenweg (juvenile, trans. The Lost Sahara Trail), 1955; Der Teufel tanzt im JuJu-Busch (juvenile), 1956; Die Stadt unter dem Wüstensand (juvenile), 1957; Roter Mond und Heisse Zeit (prize Best youthbook in Germany 1958, hon. list Internat. Christian Andersen Prize 1960; trans. Red Moon and High Summer, trans. Adventure in the Sahara, (Children's Spring Book Festival award 1961), 1957; Des Königs Krokodil (novel) (Friedrich Gerstäcker prize 1960), 1958; Pfeile und Flöten (novel), 1960; Sulei-Ein Kleiner Negerjunge, (juvenile), 1959; (travel) Nigeria, rev. edit., 1961, Congo, 1959; Afrikas Weg in die Genewart, 1963; books translated into French, Spanish, Dutch, Danish, Swedish, Japanese, Afrikaans. Address: Box 2738 Nairobi Kenya

KAUFMANN, RALPH JAMES, educator; b. Grand Forks, N.D., Aug. 2, 1924; s. Ralph Jennings and Mary (Allyn) K.; B.A., Grinnell (Ia.) Coll., 1947; M.A., Princeton, 1949, Ph.D., 1953; postgrad. Univ. Coll., London, Eng., 1950-51; m. Ruth Joan Hackett, June 30, 1944 (div.); children—James, Margaret, Mary and Sarah (twins); m. 2d, Leslie Delaney Connor, May 31, 1969; children—Christopher, Courtney. Instr. English, Princeton, 1949-53; asst. prof. English, Wesleyan U., Middletown, Conn., 1953-55; mem. faculty U. Rochester, 1955-69, prof. history, English, 1964-69, asso. dean Coll. Arts and Scis., 1961-63, chmn. history dept., 1966-68; prof. English, U. Tex., Austin, 1969—, asso. dean Coll. Humanities, 1971—; presdl. cons. Wesleyan U. Served with USNR, 1943-46. Woodrow Wilson fellow, 1947-48; Fulbright fellow, 1950-51; Folger fellow, 1961; Guggenheim fellow, 1964-65; recipient Curtis prize for excellence in teaching U. Rochester, 1964; Harbison award for distinguished teaching Danforth Found., 1968. Mem. English Inst., Am. Hist. Assn., Modern Langs. Assn. Am. Asso. dir. Center Contemporary Cultural Studies, Birmingham, Eng. Author books and essays on Renaissance and modern culture. Home: 1516 Forest Trail Austin TX 78703

KAUFMANN, ROBERT JOSEPH, tobacco co. exec.; b. Bruchsal, Germany, Nov. 10, 1910; s. Simon and Helene (Tuwiner) K.; student Höhere Handelschule, Bruchsal, 1927-30; m. Suzanne Belle Sloss, Dec. 26, 1941; 1 son, Robert Joseph. Came to U.S., 1938, naturalized, 1943. Vice pres. H. Duys & Co., N.Y.C., 1946-52; sr. v.p., dir. Consol. Cigar Corp., N.Y.C., 1952—. Served with USAAF, 1942- 45. Mem. Cigar Mfrs. Assn. (chmn. agrl. com. 1966—, also treas.) Home: 62 Laurel Ledge Rd Stamford CT 06903 Office: 1 Gulf and Western Plaza New York City NY 10023

KAUFMANN, THEODORE, cigar mfg. exec.; b. Bruchsal, Germany, Oct. 11, 1909; s. Simon and Helene (Tuwiner) K.; student Sch. Economics, Karlsruhe, Germany; m. Johanna Brod, July 21, 1936; children—Anthony Steven, Christine Babette. Naturalized U.S. citizen, 1940. With Pappenheim's Tabakshandel, Amsterdam, Netherlands, to 1932; exec. v.p. General Cigar Co., Inc., N.Y.C., 1932—, now also vice chmn., also dir.; pres. General Cigar Internat., Inc., Gen. Cigar de Utuado S.A. Bd. dirs. Epilepsy Found. Home: 2110 Cedar Swamp Rd Brookville Glen Head NY Office: 605 3d Av New York City NY 10016 also 305 E 40th St New York City NY 10016

KAUFMANN, WALTER ARNOLD, educator, author; b. Freiburg, Germany, July 1, 1921; s. Bruno and Edith (Seligsohn) K.; came to U.S., 1939, naturalized, 1944; B.A., Williams Coll., 1941; M.A., Harvard, 1942, Ph.D., 1947; m. Hazel Dennis, July 12, 1942; children—Dinah, David. Mem. Princeton, 1947—, prof. philosophy, 1962—; vis. prof. Cornell U., 1952, Columbia, 1955, U. Wash., 1958, U. Mich., 1959, Purdue U., 1966; Fulbright research prof. Heidelberg U., 1955-56; Fulbright prof. Hebrew U. Jerusalem, 1962-63; Phi Beta Kappa vis. scholar, 1971-72. Mem. adv. screening com. philosophy and religion Com. Internat. Exchange of Persons, 1957-61, chmn., 1959-61; co-founder, chmn. bd. InterFuture (student exchange program), 1970-71. Served with M.I., AUS, 1944-46. Recipient Internat. Leo Baeck prize, 1961. Mem. Phi Beta Kappa. Author: Nietzsche, 1950, rev., enlarged 3d edit., 1968; Critique of Religion and Philosophy, 1958; From Shakespeare to Existentialism, 1959, rev., enlarged edit., 1960; Twenty German Poets, 1961; Cain and Other Poems, 1962, enlarged edit., 71; Hegel, 1965; Tragedy and Philosophy, 1968; Beyond Guilt and Justice, 1972. Translator: Leo Baeck's Judaism and Christianity, 1958; Goethe's Faust, 1961. Editor: Existentialism from Dostoevsky to Sartre, 1956; Hegel's Political Philosophy, 1970; ten of Nietzche's works in The Portable Nietzsche, 1954; The Will to Power, 1967; Basic Writings of Nietzsche, 1968; Martin Buber's I and Thou, 1970. Contbr. encys., anthologies. Home: 429 Prospect Av Princeton NJ 08540

KAUL, ANDREW, III, carbon mfg. exec.; b. St. Marys, Pa., July 4, 1907; s. Frank A. and Jane (Mallison) K.; B.S., Yale, 1929; grad. Harvard Sch. Bus. Adminstrn., 1930; m. Libby Morrow, June 18, 1930 (dec. July 1953); children—Andrew IV, Jane (Mrs. Hugh Morrow III); m. 2d, Marie Dillman, Feb. 20, 1960. With Speer Carbon Co., St. Marys, Pa., 1931—, sales mgr. Internat. Graphite & Electrode div., 1937-44, sec. Speer Carbon Co., 1944, pres., dir., 1944-60, chmn. bd., chief exec. officer, 1960-61, chmn., chief exec. officer Speer Carbon Co. div. Air Reduction Co., Inc., 1961-63; pres., chief exec. officer, Airco Speer (formerly Speer Carbon Co.), 1964-70, adviser to Airco Speer Divs., 1970—; dir. Speer Carbon Co. Can., Ltd.; dir. Air Reduction Co., Inc., 1961-70; pres., dir. Kaul Land Co.; v.p., dir. Kaul & Hall Oil & Gas Co.; chmn., dir. Airco Singapore Pvt. Ltd., Elk County Bank & Trust Co. Asso. judge Elk County Ct. Common Pleas, 1956—. Bd. dirs. St. Marys chpt. A.R.C.; pres., bd. dirs. Boys Club Holding Corp.; bd. dirs. Boys Club St. Marys; chmn. bd. trustees Andrew Kaul Meml. Hosp.; pres., bd. dirs. DuBois Ednl. Found. Recipient Freedoms Found. award Valley Forge, Pa., 1951. Mem. Pa. C. of C. (dir.), Aurelian Honor Soc. Elk. Clubs: Yale (N.Y.C.); St. Elmo's (New Haven); Skytop (Pa.); St. Mary's Country; Pennhills, Bradford (Pa.). Home: Kaulwald Trout Run Rd RFD St Marys PA 15857 Office: Airco Speer Divs 800 Theresia St St Marys PA 15857

KAULA, WILLIAM MASON, educator, geophysicist; b. Sydney, Australia, May 19, 1926 (parents U.S. citizens); s. Edgar Louis and Edna (Mason) K.; B.S., U.S. Mil. Acad., 1948; M.S. in Geodesy, Ohio

State U., 1953; m. Denise Bouche, June 11, 1949; children—Anne, Jacqueline, Charles, Marie. Commd. 2d lt. C.E., U.S. Army, 1948; advanced through grades to capt., 1953; resigned, 1957; geodesist U.S. Army Map Service, 1957-60; researcher orbital dynamics and planetary structure NASA, 1960-63; prof. geophysics U. Cal. at Los Angeles, 1963—. Mem. Nat. Acad. Sci. adv. coms. to NASA and Environmental Sci. Service Adminstrn. Fellow Am. Geophys. Union. Author: Theory of Satellite Geodesy, 1966; Introduction to Planetary Physics, 1968. Editor Revs. of Geophysics and Space Physics. Contbr. papers profl. lit. Home: 1035 Centinela Av Santa Monica CA 90403 Office: Dept Planetary and Space Sci U Cal Los Angeles CA 90024

KAULBACK, FRANK SANFORD, Jr., ednl. adminstr.; b. Pitts. May 5, 1912; s. Frank Sanford and Elizabeth Flavia (McGuire) K.; B.S., U. Va., 1934, M.A., 1942, Ph.D., 1945; m. Mildred Virginia Van Lear, July 3, 1941; 1 son, Frank Sanford III. With sales dept. Bridgeport Brass Co., 1935-37, Am. Radiator Standard San. Corp., 1937-40; mem. faculty U. Va., Charlottesville, 1946—, dean McIntire Sch. Commerce, 1955—; mem. faculty U. Cal., 1947; dir. Nat. Bank & Trust Co. Charlottesville. Cons. U.S. Gen. Accounting Office, OPS, 1951-52. Served to lt. USNR, World War II. Mem. Am. Accounting Assn. (past pres.), Raven Soc., Beta Gamma Sigma, Alpha Kappa Psi. Clubs: Farmington Country, Colonnade (Charlottesville). Home: 215 Montebello Circle Charlottesville VA 22903

KAUNDA, KENNETH DAVID, pres. Republic of Zambia; b. Lubwa Mission, Chinsali, No. Rhodesia, Apr. 28, 1924; s. David and Helen Kaunda; ed. Lubwa Tng. Sch., Munali Secondary Sch.; m. Betty Banda, Aug. 24, 1946; children—Panji, Wazamanzana, Nqeaweze, Tilyenji, Masuzyo, Kaweche, Musata, Kambarage Cheswa. Tchr., Lubwa Tng. Sch., 1943, headmaster, 1944-47; sec. Chinsali Young Men's Farming Assn., 1947; welfare officer Chingola Copper Mine, 1948-49; tchr. sch., 1948-49; founder, sec. Lubwa br. African Nat. Congress, 1950, dist. organizer, 1951, provincial organizer, 1952, sec.-gen. for No. Rhodesia, 1953; broke away to form Zambia African Nat. Congress, 1958; pres. United Nat. Independence Party, 1960—; minister local govt. and social welfare No. Rhodesia, 1962-64, prime minister, 1964; pres. Pan-African Freedom Movement for East, Central and South Africa, 1963; 1st pres. Zambia, 1964—. Decorated Order of Collar of Nile; knight of collar Order Pius XII; Order Queen of Sheba. Author: Zambia Shall be Free; A Humanist in Africa; Humanism in Zambia. Address: Office of President State House Lusaka Republic of Zambia

KAUPER, PAUL GERHARDT, educator; b. Richmond, Ind., Nov. 9, 1907; s. Frederick J. and Mary (Tubesing) K.; A.B., Earlham Coll., 1929, LL.D., 1958; J.D., U. Mich., 1932; LL.D., Capital U., 1956, Valparaiso (Ind.) U., 1959, Tex. Luth. Coll., 1965; J.D. honoris causa, Heidelberg U., 1970; m. Anna Marie Nicklas, Sept. 22, 1934; children—Thomas Eugene, Carolyn Ann. Admitted to N.Y. bar, 1936; practice with firm White & Case, N.Y.C., 1934-36; legal research asst. U. Mich. Law Sch., Ann Arbor, 1932-34, asst. prof. law, 1936-39, asso. prof., 1939-46, prof., 1946-65, Henry M. Butzel prof. law, 1965—, Henry Russell lectr., 1971; guest prof. Max Planck Inst., Heidelberg, 1959, 66; Rosenstiel Distinguished vis. prof. law U. Ariz., 1971; mem. legal dept. Pan Am. Petroleum & Transport Co., N.Y.C., 1942-45. Chmn. Gov.'s Transp. Study Commn., 1950; mem. Ann Arbor Charter Revision Commn., 1953, Ann Arbor Planning Commn., 1956-59. Recipient Distinguished Faculty Achievement award U. Mich., 1959. Mem. Am., Mich. bar assns., Order of Coif (pres. 1965-67, exec. com. 1968-70), Tau Kappa Alpha. Lutheran (mem. bd. coll. edn. Am. Luth. Ch. 1960-66, trustee Luth. Student Found. Ann Arbor, mem. commn. on ch.-state relations Luth. Ch. Am.). Author: Cases on Constitutional Law, 1954; Frontiers of Constitutional Liberty, 1957; (with E. Blythe Stason) Cases on Municipal Corporations, 1959; Civil Liberties and the Constitution, 1961; Religion and the Constitution, 1964; also articles. Home: 1702 Shadford Rd Ann Arbor MI 48104

KAUSLER, DONALD HARVEY, educator; b. St. Louis, July 16, 1927; s Charles Richard and Pauline Ann (Svejkovsky) K.; A.B., Washington U., St. Louis, 1947, Ph.D., 1951; m. Martha Blanche Roeper, Oct. 25, 1952; children—Rene, Donald Harvey, Jill, Barry. Research psychologist USAF, Mather AFB, Cal., 1951-55; asst. prof., then asso. prof. U. Ark., 1955-60; asso. prof., then prof. St. Louis U., 1960-70, chmn. dept. psychology, 1963-70; prof. psychology U. Mo.-Columbia, 1970—. Mem. Am. Psychol. Assn., Am. Assn. U. Profs., Phi Beta Kappa, Sigma Xi. Editor: Readings in Verbal Learning; Contemporary Theory and Research 1966—. Contbr. articles profl. jours. Home: 3905 Faurot Dr Columbia MO 65201

KAUTZ, LYNFORD ENGLISH, ednl. adminstr.; b. W. Chester, Pa., Apr. 5, 1915; s. Jacob R. and Martha S. (Sharples) K.; teaching certificate W. Chester State Coll., 1936-37, Jourdan Sch. Publicity and Promotion, Phila., 1945-46, Am. TV Inst., Chgo., 1947-48; m. Jacqueline Jean Paul, Jan. 24, 1950; children—Jill Louise, Jacqueline Jean. Instr. Booth Sch., Rosemont, Pa., 1939-41; promotional dir. Black Hills Passion Play Am., Spearfish, S.D., 1947-49; dir. funds Chgo. office Nat. Conf. Christians and Jews, 1949-52; regional dir. Nat. Fund Med. Edn., Chgo., 1952-54; dir. devel. and pub. relations Northwestern U., 1954-62; v.p. devel. Boston U., 1962-67; dir. resources Fletcher Sch. Law and Diplomacy, 1967-69; dir. office devel. Smithsonian Instn., 1969—; ednl. cons., 1958—. Trustee Arden Shore Assn., Lake Bluff, Ill. Served with inf. AUS, 1941-45; ETO. Decorated Purple Heart. Mem. Am. Pub. Relations Assn., Am. Alumni Council, Pub. Relations Soc. Am., Pith Helmut Soc. Presbyn. Clubs: Chicago, Economic (Chgo.); Longwood Cricket (Chestnut Hill, Mass.); Algonquin (Boston). Home: 1002 Abbey Way McLean VA 22101

KAUTZ, RICHARD CARL, chem. and feeds co. exec.; b. Mucatine, Ia., Aug. 1, 1916; s. Carl and Leah (Amlong) K.; student U. Ariz., 1936-37; B.S. with high distinction, State U. Ia., 1939; m. Mary Elda Stein, Dec. 24, 1939; children—Linda (Mrs. Thomas P. Smith), Judith (Mrs. James L. Howell), John Terry, Thomas R., Susan E., Sarah J., Mary Catherine, Jennifer W. Supr. finance dept. Gen. Electric Co., 1939-43; with Grain Processing Corp. and Kent Feeds, Inc., Muscatine, Ia., 1943—, chmn. bd., dir., mem. exec. com., 1966—. Mem. U. Ia. Alumni Council; mem. State Ia. Old Capitol Restoration Com.; mem. research com. Ia. Coll.-Community Research Center; mem. Upper Miss. Valley Flood Action Exec. Com.; industry chmn. Nat. Bible Week, 1968-69, mem. tech. assistance com. White House Conf. Children and Youth; chmn. bd. Nat. Council YMCA, 1970—. Republican finance chmn. 1st Dist. Ia.; chmn. Rep. Nat. Finance Com. for Ia.; mem. Rep. Nat. Finance Com. Mem. N.A.M. (bd. dirs., chmn. membership com.), Am. Mgmt. Assn., Muscatine C. of C., DeMolay Legion of Honor, Beta Gamma Sigma, Sigma Chi. Presbyn. Mason (Shriner), Elk, Rotarian. Clubs: Union League (Chgo.); Capitol Hill (Washington); Canadian (N.Y.C.); University Athletic (Iowa City); Des Moines, Embassy, Lincoln (Des Moines). Home: RR4 Muscatine IA 52761 Office: 1600 Oregon St Muscatine IA 52761

KAUZMANN, WALTER JOSEPH, educator; b. Mt. Vernon, N.Y., Aug. 18, 1916; s. Albert and Julia Maria (Kahle) K.; B.A., Cornell U., 1937; Ph.D., Princeton, 1940; m. Elizabeth Alice Flagler, Apr. 1, 1951; children—Charles Peter, Eric Flagler, Katherine Elizabeth Julia. Westinghouse research fellow Westinghouse Mfg. Co., E. Pittsburgh, Pa., 1940-42; mem. staff Explosives Research Lab., Bruceton, Pa., 1942-44, Los Alamos Lab., 1944-46; asst. prof. Princeton, 1946-51, asso. prof., 1951-60, prof. chemistry, 1960—, chmn. dept., 1964-68, David B. Jones prof. chemistry, 1963—. Jr. fellow Soc. Fellows, Harvard, 1942; Guggenheim fellow, 1957. Recipient Linderstrom- Lang medal, 1966. Fellow Am. Acad. Arts and Scis.; mem. Nat. Acad. Scis., Am. Soc. Biol. Chemists, Am. Chem. Soc., Am. Phys. Soc., A.A.A.S., Fedn. Am. Scientists, Sigma Xi. Author: Quantum Chemistry, 1957; Kinetic Theory of Gases, 1966; Thermal Properties of Matter, 1967; (with D. Eisenberg) Structure and Properties of Water, 1969. Home: 4 Newlin Rd Princeton NJ

KAVANAGH, EDWARD JOHN, found. exec.; b. Phila., Oct. 25, 1906; s. Thomas and Catherine (Maher) K.; ed. parochial schs.; m. Alice M. Kelly, Oct. 12, 1935; children—Joan (Mrs. James E. Feeney), Kevin E., Thomas E., Eileen R. (Mrs. James L. Murcko), Katherine B. With Wheatland Tube Co. (Pa.), 1932-69, pres., 1965-69; v.p., dir. John Maneely Co., 1953-69; pres. Wheatland Steel Products Co., 1965-69; dir. First Fed. Savs. & Loan Assn., Sharon, Pa. Bd. dirs., v.p. Maneely Fund Pa., 1953-69. Pres., Sharon Gen. Hosp., 1964—, Edward J. Kavanagh Found., 1969—. Mem. Am. Iron and Steel Inst. Republican. K.C., Elk. Home: 655 Woodlawn Dr Sharon PA 16146 Office: 811 E State St Sharon PA 16146

KAVANAGH, JOHN FRANCIS, utility exec.; b. Indpls., Jan. 20, 1915; s. Bartholomew P. and Delia (Cunningham) K.; B.S. cum laude, Butler U., 1936; m. Lucille M. Kuhn, Oct. 2, 1940; children—John M., Bernard P., Sharon M. (Mrs. Timothy Hurley), Rita K. (Mrs. Robert Campbell), Richard T., Marianne L., Dennis J., Kevin F., Thomas V., Grace E., Maureen E. Gen. accountant Pub. Service Co. Ind., Indpls., 1937-45; with Ind. Gas Co., Inc., Indpls., 1945—, treas., 1955-69, v.p., 1962-69, dir., 1964—, exec. v.p., 1969—. Mem. Am. Gas Assn., Financial Execs. Inst. Roman Catholic. Home: 4106 Washington Blvd Indianapolis IN 46205 Office: 1630 N Meridian St Indianapolis IN 46202

KAVANAGH, L.J., paper mfg. exec.; b. N.Y.C., June 22, 1903; s. Edward William and Katherine (Reany) K.; student pub. schs.; m. Sadie E. Creighton, Aug. 19, 1928. With W. Va. Pulp and Paper Co., 1919—, now treas.; dir. U.S. Envelope Co. Mem. N.A.M. (chmn. auditing com.). Home: 2 Tudor City Pl New York City NY 10017 Office: 299 Park Av New York City NY 10017

KAVANAGH, PRESTON BRECKENRIDGE, utility exec.; b. Washington, Aug. 15, 1932; s. Preston Breckenridge and Mary Lucille (Day) K.; B.A., Princeton, 1954; S.T.B., Harvard, 1960; m. Lois Lapham, Feb. 10, 1956; children—Katherine, Preston III, Evan. Ordained to ministry United Ch. of Christ, 1961; parish minister inner city, Cleve., 1960-61; minister Chgo. City Missionary Soc., 1961-63; with Commonwealth Edison Co., Chgo., 1963—, sec., 1970—. Bd. dirs. Ada S. McKinley Community Services, Community Renewal Soc. Served with USNR, 1954-57. Club: Princeton (Chgo.). Contbr. articles to profl. jours. Home: 620 Exmoor Av Kenilworth IL 60043 Office: PO Box 767 Chicago IL 60690

KAVANAGH, THOMAS CHRISTIAN, educator, cons. engr.; b. N.Y.C., Aug. 17, 1912; s. Patrick F. and Anna C. (Unger) K.; student Tech. U., Berlin, Germany, 1930-31; B.S., Coll. City N.Y., 1932. M.S. in Civil Engring., 1933; M.B.A., N.Y.U., 1942, Sc.D. in Engring., 1948; m. Kerstin E. Berglund, Sept. 18, 1937; children—Patricia Frances, Kenneth Thomas, Susan Karin. Tech. asst. to research dir. Johns-Manville Corp., 1935-37; structural engr., designer, squad and sect. leader Devenco, Inc., Frederick R. Harris, Inc., M.W. Kellogg Inc., Fairchild Aircraft, Office Chief Engr. City N.Y., 1933-45; asst. prof. civil engring. N.Y.U., 1945-48, chmn. dept. civil engring., prof. structural engring., 1952-54, adj. prof., 1954-55; adj. prof. civil engring. Columbia, 1956—; prof. civil engring. Pa. State U., 1948-52; partner Praeger- Kavanagh-Waterbury, cons. engrs.-architects, 1953-69, v.p., 1969—; v.p. Madigan-Hyland, Inc., 1969—; cons. atomic blast protection U.S. govt. Recipient awards profl. bridge design Lincoln Arc Welding Found., 1949- 50-52; Gold Medal award engring. Archtl. League N.Y., 1954; N.Y.U. Centennial citation; Lincoln Progress award, 1956; Steinman award N.Y. Acad. Scis., 1957; Ernest E. Howard award Am. Soc. C.E., 1969; David B. Steinman medal Coll. City N.Y., 1969. Fellow N.Y. Acad. Scis., Am. Soc. C.E. (bd. dirs.); mem. Am. Inst. Cons. Engrs., Nat. Soc. Profl. Engrs., Am. Concrete Inst., A.A.A.S., Am. Soc. Engring. Edn., Internat. Assn. Bridge and Structural Engring., Am. Welding Soc., Column Research Council Engring. Found., Nat. Acad. Engring. (founding mem., treas.), Am. Soc. Testing Materials, Marine Tech. Soc., Internat. Assn. Shell Structures, N.Y. Assn. Cons. Engrs., Municipal Engrs. N.Y., Engrs. Joint Council (bd.), Offshore Tech. Conf., Bldg. Research Adv. Bd., N.Y. Bldg. Congress, Phi Beta Kappa, Sigma Xi, Tau Beta Pi, Chi Epsilon. Co-author: (text) Design of Foundations for Buildings; author sects. in various engring. handbooks, Contbr. papers profl. lit. Home: 71 Dorchester Av Hastings-on-Hudson NY 10706 Office: 200 Park Av New York City NY 10017

KAVANAGH, THOMAS MATTHEW, state justice; b. Carson City, Mich., Aug. 4, 1909; s. Thomas and Margaret (Barrett) K.; J.D., U. Detroit, 1932; m. Agnes C. Miller, Oct. 27, 1930; children—Doris Jeanne (Mrs. Donald Closser), Donna Joan (Mrs. Thomas Baker), Patricia (Mrs. Owen Kean), Kathleen (Mrs. Harry Zipperer). Admitted Mich. bar, 1932; practice in Detroit, 1932-35, Carson City, 1935-55; city atty., Carson City and Perrington, Mich., 1943-54; village clk. Carson City, 1943-54; atty. gen. Mich., 1954-57; justice Mich. Supreme Ct., 1957—, chief justice, 1964- 67, 71—. Chmn. Gt. Lakes Commn. Candidate for Mich. Legislature, 1938. Mem. Am., Ionia-Montcalm (pres.), Ingham County bar assns., State Bar Mich. Roman Catholic, K.C. (state dep. 1952-54; now mem. supreme bd. dirs.). Lion (pres. 1941- 42). Home: 3934 Barton Rd Lansing MI 48917 Office: Seven Story Bldg Lansing MI 48933

KAVANAU, LAWRENCE LEWIS, systems engring. exec.; b. Detroit, Oct. 16, 1926; s. George and Bessie (Leitson) K.; B.S. in Math., B.S. in Aero. Engring., U. Mich., 1948, M.S. in Aero. Engring., 1949; Ph.D. in Engring., U. Cal. at Berkeley, 1954; m. Shirley Buckler, Dec. 28, 1947 (dec.); children—Jerard Irving, Laura Sue, Sandra Lee. Test engr. guided missile div., cold weather test USAAF, 1945-46; aerodynamic research U. Mich., 1947-49; head wind tunnel operations Jet Propulsion Lab., Cal. Inst. Tech., 1949-51; rarified gas dynamics research U. Cal. at Berkeley, 1951-54; head aerodynamics and thermodynamics, research and devel. lab., missile systems div. Lockheed Aircraft Corp., 1954-56; mgr. research, planning, spl. projects, vehicle devel., mgr. aerospace scis., aeronutronics div. Ford Motor Co., 1956-61; spl. asst. for space, dir. def. research engring. Dept. Def., 1961-63; exec. v.p. tech., space and information systems div. N.Am. Aviation, Inc., 1963-65, asst. to pres., chmn. bd., 1965-66; pres. Systems Assos., Inc., Long Beach, Cal., 1966—; dir. Tasker Industries. Trustee Long Beach Community Hosp.; bd. councillors U. So. Cal. Mem. Am. Inst. Aeros. and Astronautics, Am. Soc. M.E., Am. Soc. Engring. Edn., I.E.E.E., A.A.A.S., Long Beach C. of C. (bd. dirs.), Sigma Xi. Home: 5361 El Parque Long Beach CA 90815 Office: 444 W Ocean Blvd Long Beach CA 90802

KAVANAUGH, JAMES, author, lectr.; b. Kalamazoo, Sept. 17, 1928; s. Frank P. and Hazel (Wendell) K.; Ph.D., Cath. U. Am., 1966; m. Patricia Jean Walden, Dec. 16, 1967 (div.). Priest Roman Cath. Ch., 1954-67; asso. prof. psychology U.S. Internat. U., San Diego. Author: There's Two of You, 1964; A Journal of Renewal, 1965; Man in Search of God, 1966; A Modern Priest Looks at His Outdated Church, 1967; The Struggle of the Unbeliever, 1968; Birth of God, 1969; (poetry) There Are Men Too Gentle To Live Among Wolves, 1970, Will You Be My Friend?, 1971; (juvenile) The Crooked Angel, 1970; (with Dr. E. Shostrom) Between Man and Woman. Mailing Address:

KAVASS, IGOR IVAR, educator; b. Riga, Latvia, July 31, 1932; s. Nicolas and Iraida (Kushnarev) K.; LL.B., U. Melbourne, Australia, 1956; LL.B., U. Adelaide, Australia, 1959; m. Irene Dmitrijevs, Feb. 17, 1956 (dec. Sept. 1970); children—Sybilla, Ariane, Lara. Sr. lectr. law U. Adelaide, 1959-63; sr. lectr. law U. Melbourne, 1964-66; asso. prof. law Monash U., 1967-68; prof. law, dir. law library U. Ala., 1968-70; prof. law, law librarian Northwestern U., Chgo., 1970—; barrister, solicitor, Australia; law library cons.; comml. arbitrator, Australia, 1960-66. Mem. Assn. Am. Law Schs., Internat., Am. assns. law libraries, Brit. Inst. Internat. and Comparative Law, Australian Inst. Mgmt., Order of Coif. Author: (with Paterson, Ednie and others) Australian Company Law, 1963; Australian Supplement to Modern Company Law, 2d edit., 1970. Contbr. articles profl. jours. Home: 2808 Garrison Av Evanston IL 60201 Office: 357 E Chicago St Chicago IL 60611

KAVESH, ROBERT ALLYN, economist, educator; b. N.Y.C., Sept. 12, 1927; s. Samuel and Pearl (Berlin) K.; B.S., N.Y.U., 1949; A.M., Harvard, 1950, Ph.D., 1954; m. Ruth Freidson, June 24, 1951; children)Richard, Laura, Andrew, Joseph. Asst. prof. econs. Dartmouth, 1953-56; bus. economist Chase Manhattan Bank, N.Y.C., 1956-58; prof. econs. and finance Grad. Sch. Bus. Adminstrn., N.Y.U., 1958—, chmn. dept. econs., 1968—. Dir. Londontown Mfg. Corp., VLN Corp. Recipient Danforth Found. prize distinguished teaching, 1968. Mem. Am. Finance Assn. (exec. sec.-treas.), Regional Sci. Assn. (past sec.), Am. Econ. Assn. Author: Businessmen in Fiction, 1955; (with W.F. Butler) How Business Economists Forecast, 1966, also articles. Asso. editor Bus. Economics, 1965—. Home: 390 Highland Av Upper Montclair NJ 07043 Office: 100 Trinity Pl New York NY 10006

KAVINOKY, EDWARD H.; Lawyer; b. Buffalo, May 29, 1903; s. Samuel and Caroline (Cohn) K.; B.A., Harvard, 1923, LL.B., 1926; m. Irene Rose, July 1, 1926; children-Katherine (Mrs. Henry Goldman), Andrew. Admitted to N.Y. bar, 1926, since practiced Buffalo; pres. Kleinhans Hall Mgmt., Inc.; sr. partner Kavinoky, Cook, Hepp, Sandler & Gardner. Dir. Marine Midland Bank Western, Gomco Surg. Mfg. Corp., Buffalo Ry. Equipment Co., Inc., Arnold Equipment Corp., Internat. Life Ins. Corp., Welcome Radio, Inc. Pres. Council Social Agys., Buffalo, 1944, nat. bd. Community Chests and Councils, 1946; pres. Jewish Fedn. Buffalo, 1948, Jewish Welfare Soc., 1935-41; chmn. Buffalo chpt. A.R.C., 1950-53, adv. com. Atlantic Area, 1951-53; mem. Buffalo regional state Commn. Against Discrimination in Employment, 1941-68; hon. chmn. Brotherhood Week, 1951; mem. exec. com. Buffalo Philharmonic Orch. Soc., Inc., 1946—, pres., 1954; mem. White House Conf. on Aging, 1961; chmn. Commn. Human Relations City Buffalo, 1966. Bd. dirs. Community Chest, Buffalo Studio Theatre, D'Youville Coll., Buffalo; trustee, chmn. Buffalo and Erie County Library. Fellow Brandeis U. Mem. Am., N.Y. State, Erie County (past trustee, pres.) bar assns., Buffalo Lawyers Club, Buffalo Roundtable Christians and Jews (co- chmn. 1953-55, nat. award 1960), Council World Affairs (chmn. Buffalo chpt.), Am. Law Inst. Clubs: Harvard (N.Y.C.); Marshall, Harvard (pres. 1950). (Buffalo). Home: 332 Middlesex Rd Buffalo NY 14216 Office: 120 Delaware Av Buffalo NY 14202

KAWABATA, YASUNARI, Japanese writer; b. 1899; B.A., Tokyo U. Mem. editorial staff jour. Bungei Shunjū 1025. Bd. dirs. PEN Club. Recipient Bungei Konwa Kai prize, 1937. Goethe medal, 1959, Nobel prize for lit., 1968. Author: Dancers of Izu Province, 1925; Red Group of Asakusa, 1925; Snow Country; Thousand Cranes. Address: 264 Hase Kamakura-shi Kanagawa Prefecture Japan*

KAWALEK, THADDEUS P., coll. pres.; b. Chgo., Aug. 22, 1921; s. Peter John and Anastasia (Wojtas) K.; B.E., No. Ill. U., 1942; M.A., U. Chgo., 1951, Ph.D., 1959; m. Lorriane A. Wielgos, June 18, 1949; children—Paul Edward, Nadine Ann, Nina Marie. Tchr., dir. instrumental music Tobin Grade Sch., Oak Lawn, Ill., 1942; teller, cashier Am. Express Co., 1945; tchr. music Marshall and Harrison high schs., 1954-56; part-time life ins. agt., 1946; tchr., dir. instrument music O.W. Holmes Sch. Oak Park, Ill., 1946- 47; counselor malajusted children, Oak Park, 1947-51; prin. Horace Mann Sch., Oak Park, 1952; supt. schs., sch. dist. 152/ Hazel Crest, Ill., 1952-58; instr. DePaul U. Grad. Sch., winter 1961; supt. sch. dist. 95, Brookfield, Ill., 1958-62; prof. Roosevelt U. Grad Sch., Chgo., 1960-62; asst. supt. schs. Gary, Ind., 1926-64; dean faculties, prof. edn. adminstrn. Roosevelt U., 1963-66; v.p., dean Columbia Coll., Chgo., 1966-67; pres. Chgo. Coll. Osteopathy, 1967—. Mem. coordinating com. med. schs. and teaching hosps. Ill. Regional Med. Program; Ill. statewide adv. council Div. Health Planning and Resource Devel.; adv. com. Ill. Bd. Higher Edn.; Osteo. Progress Fund Com. Am. Osteo. Assn.; dir. various programs in field, also dir. sch. property tax assessment surveys. Pres., Interfaith Council LaGrange Park. Bd. dirs. S.E. Chgo. Commn., Hyde Park YMCA. Served with AUS, 1942-45. Mem. Adult Edn. Council Greater Chgo., Am. Assn. Sch. Adminstrs., Am. Assn. Osteo. Colls., Am. Assn. Ind. Coll. and Univ. Presidents, Ill. Pub. Health Assn., N.E.A., Nat. Soc. Edn., Phi Delta Kappa. Home: 700 N LaGrange Rd LaGrange Park IL 60625 Office: 5200 S Ellis Av Chicago IL 60615

KAWECKI, HENRY CASIMIR, retired chem. co. exec.; b. Chgo., July 5, 1912; s. Casimir and Stephanie (Dobkowski) K.; B.S. in Electro-chem. Engring., Mass. Inst. Tech., 1934; D.Sc., Alliance Coll., 1964; m. Clara Gregonis, June 27, 1938; children—Elizabeth Louise, Henry John, Margaret Anne. Dir. research Beryllium Corp., Reading, Pa., 1934-49; pres. Kawecki Chem. Co., Boyertown, Pa., 1949-59, chmn. bd., 1959—; hon. chmn. bd. Kawecki- Berylco Industries, 1968-71. Mem. Electrochem. Soc., Am. Chem., Soc., Am. Soc. Metals. Republican. Roman Catholic. Contbr. articles profl. publs. Home: Lenhartsville PA 19534

KAY, ALBERT, retired govt. ofcl.; b. Bklyn., Apr. 3, 1914; s. Herman and Tillie (Handmaker) K.; A.B., Columbia, 1935, grad. work econs., 1935-36, 38-40; m. Lucie Breyer, June 20, 1942; children—Jeffrey Albert, Carol Ann. Econ. analyst Office Adminstr., Nat. Housing Agency, 1946-47; econ. analyst, material div. Exec. Office Sec., Navy Dept., 1947-48; chief manpower div. Munitions Bd., Office Sec. Def., 1948-51; dep. dir. Office Manpower Supply, Office Asst. Sec. Def., 1951-53, dir. Office Manpower Supply, 1953-70. Served to capt. AUS, 1941-46. Mem. Phi Beta Kappa. Club: Westwood Country. Home: 204 E Columbia St Falls Church VA 22046

KAY, BRIAN ROSS, former educator; b. Gisborne, New Zealand, May 8, 1924; s. Leslie V. and Lilian (Jessup) K.; B.A., U. B.C., 1948, M.A., 1949; Ph.D., U. London, 1951; m. Eleanor I. Smith, Sept. 16,

1947; 1 son, Bruce C. Came to U.S., 1954, naturalized, 1960. Def. research scientist Dept. Def. Can., 1952-54; research coordinator Human Relations Area Files, Yale, 1954-56; asst. prof., asso. prof., prof. U. N.H., 1956-66; prof. psychology New Coll., Sarasota, Fla., 1967-68; prof. psychology, head dept. behavioral scis. Rollins Coll., Winter Park, Fla., 1968-70, ret., 1970. Dir. comprehensive mental health planning state N.H. Served with Royal New Zealand Navy, 1941- 1941- 43, Canadian Army, 1944-45. Mem. Am., N.H. (past pres.) psychol. assns., Brit. Psychol. Soc., Sigma Xi, Phi Kappa Phi. Author: (with S. Palmer) The Challenge of Supervision, 1961; (with R. Clough) Cases in Supervision, 1962; Supervision In Industry, 1966. Home: 829 Nicoma Trail Maitland FL 32751

KAY, EARLE B., cardiovascular surgeon; b. Battle Creek, Mich., July 29, 1911; s. James Roy and Bess (Gaffield) K.; B.A., U. Mich., 1933, M.D., 1936, M.S. in Surgery, 1940; D.Sc. (hon.), John Carroll U., 1961; m. Dorothy Imrie, June 18, 1940 (dec. 1952); children—Carole Ann (Mrs. Richard E. Combs, Jr.), David Alan, Nancy Elizabeth, Richard Bradley; m. 2d, Florence Fawick, Dec. 26, 1953; children—Thomas Fawick, Debra. Intern, U. Mich. Hosps., 1936-37, resident, 1937-42, instr. surgery, 1941-42; practice thoracic and cardiovascular surgery, Cleve., 1946-; chief thoracic and cardiovascular surgery, dir. cardiovascular research St. Vincent Charity Hosp., Cleve., 1944—; asso. surgeon thoracic surgery St. Lukes Hosp., Cleve., 1952—. Pres., trustee Heart Assn. N.E. Ohio, 1960-61; trustee Ohio Heart Assn. (1959-61); pres. staff St. Vincent Charity Hosp., 1961- 64. Bd. dirs. Earle B. Kay Research Found. Served to lt. col. AUS, World War II. Recipient Page One award, 1957; citation, guest lectr. Japanese Assn. Thoracic Surgery, 1962; recipient Theodore and Susan B. Cummings Humanitarian award, 1964; hon. fellow for 1st open heart surgery in S. Am., Brazilian Coll. Surgeons, 1956; recipient citation Pres. Johnson for overseas diplomatic lecture mission, 1964, Vice Pres. Humphrey for overseas diplomatic lecture mission, 1966. Honors Achievement award Angiology Research Found., 1968; hon. prof. U. Santo Domingo (Dominican Republic), 1968; decorated Heraldic Order Cristobal Colon (Dominican Republic), 1968. Fellow A.C.S., Am. Coll. Cardiology (v.p., trustee), Am. Coll. Chest Physicians, Colegio Brasileira for Cirurgioes; mem. Am. Assn. Thoracic Surgery, Soc. Thoracic Surgeons, Am. Heart Assn., Cardiovascular Surgeons Club, Internat. Cardiovascular Soc., Am. Soc. Artificial Internal Organs, Am. Thoracic Soc., Chest Club, Internat. Coll. Surgeons, Am. Broncho-Esophageal Assn., Internat. Broncho-Esophageal Assn., N.Y. Acad. Scis., Soc. Vascular Surgery, Central Surg. Soc., A.M.A., Ohio Med. Soc., Heart Assn. N.E. Ohio, Acad. Medicine. Pioneer open heart surgery; co-developer heart and lung disc oxygenator, 1956, discoid valve to replace diseased human heart valve, 1964, also new surg. technics. Home: 3125 SOM Center Rd Hunting Valley Chagrin Falls OH 44022 Office: 2475 E 22d St Cleveland OH 44115

KAY, GEORGE MARSHALL, univ. prof., geologist; b. Paisley, Ont., Can., Nov. 10, 1904; s. George Frederick and Bethea (Hopper) K.; B.A., U. Ia., 1924, M.S., 1925; U. Chgo., 1924; Ph.D., Columbia, 1929; m. Inez Margaret Clark, June 8, 1935; children—Elizabeth (Mrs. R.A. Berner), Katherine (Mrs. D.B. Vielmetti), Robert, Richard. Lectr. Barnard Coll., 1929-30, instr., 1930-31; instr. Columbia, 1931-37; asst. prof., 1937-42, asso. prof., 1942-44, prof. geology, 1944-67, exec. officer dept., 1953-56, Newberry prof. geology, 1967—; adminstrn. com. war research, 1944-46. Mem. bd. mgrs. N.Y. Botanical Garden. Awarded George F. Kunz prize, N.Y. Acad. Sci., 1941. Del Internat. Geol. Congress, Moscow, 1937. London, 1948; Copenhagen, 1960. Fellow Geol. Soc. Am., A.A.A.S., Paleontol. Soc. (v.p. 1945), N.Y. Acad. Sci. (v.p. 1944-45), Ia. Acad. Sci., Am. Assn. Petroleum Geologists, Paleontol. Assn. Soc. Econ. Paleontologists and Mineralogists, Am. Geophys. Union, Geol. Soc. London (hon. fgn.), Geol. Soc. Stockholm (hon. corr.), Phi Beta Kappa, Sigma Xi (nat. bd. 1968—). Presbyn. Author: North American Geosynclines, 1951; (with E.H. Colbert) Stratigraphy and Life History, 1965. Editor North Atlantic-Geology and Continental Drift, 1969. Contbr. articles to profl. jours. Home: 175 Glenwood Av Leonia NJ 07605 Office: Schermerhorn Hall Columbia U New York City NY 10027 ☆

KAY, HERSHY, composer-arranger; b. Phila., Nov. 17, 1919: s. Louis H. and Ida (Aisen) K.; student cello Curtis Inst., 1936-40. Composer-arranger scores for Broadway shows including On the Town, 1944, A Flag is Born, 1947, Peter Pan, 1950, Golden Apple, 1954, Sand Hog, 1955, Candide 1956, Once Upon a Mattress, 1958, Juno, 1958, Livin' The Life, 1959, Happiest Girl in the World, 1961, Milk and Honey, 1961, 110 in the Shade, 1963, Kelly, 1965, Coco, 1969; prepared ballet scores for Martha Graham Co., 1947, Thief Who Loved a Ghost, Ballet Theatre, 1950, Cakewalk, 1951, Western Symphony, 1954, Stars & Stripes, 1958, Who Cares?, 1970 (all for N.Y.C. Ballet), The Concert for Ballets USA, 1956, L'Inconnue for Am. Ballet Theatre, 1965, The Clowns for Joffrey Ballet Co., 1968, Grand Tour for Royal Ballet, London, 1971, Meadowlark and Cortege Burlesque for Eliot Feld Co., 1969; orchestrated film scores including Man With a Gun, 1955, King and Four Queens, 1956, Cinerama (South Seas), 1958, Girl of the Night, 1960; orchestral plays Kelly, 1965, (with Clare Grundman) Drat! The Cat!, 1965; TV scores include Valiant Years, 1962, FDR series, 1964, Twentieth Century, 1963, This Nation at War, Startime, 1959, spl. projects, 1963 (all NBC). Composer original background music Cyril Ritchard's Mother Goose recording, 1958; completed opera Good Soldier Schweik for composer Robert Kurka (dec.), 1959; reconstructed, orchestrated Louis M. Gottschalk's Grande Tarantelle for piano and orch., 1957. Address: 205 W 57th St New York City NY 10019

KAY, JACK GARVIN, educator, chemist; b. Scott City, Kan., July 11, 1930; s. Albert Edward and Ellamay (Garvin) K.; A.B. (NROTC felloe), U. Kan., 1952, Ph.D., 1960; m. Gloria Patricia Johnson, June 4, 1952; children—Morris Martin, Maren Patricia. Research asst. U. Kan., 1956-59, Monsanto research fellow, 1958-59; instr. chemistry U. Ill., Urbana, 1959-62, asst. prof., 1962-66; prof. chemistry U. Toledo, 1966-69, chmn. dept. chemistry, 1966-68, dir. chemistry Ph.D. program devel., 1966-68; prof., head chemistry dept. Drexel U., Phila., 1969—; vis. research chemist Bell Telephone Labs., Inc., Murray Hill, N.J., summer 1961, Sandia Corp., Albuquerque, summer 1964; cons.. Chemotronics, Inc., AVCO, Inc. Prin. investigator U.S. AEC, 1960-69. Served from ensign to lt. (j.g.), USNR, 1952-55. Fellow Am. Inst. Chemists; mem. Am. Chem. Soc., Am. Phys. Soc., Faraday Soc., A.A.A.S., Sigma Xi, Alpha Chi Sigma, Lambda Chi Alpha, Sigma Pi Sigma, Phi Lambda Upsilon. Presbyn. (elder). Mason. Contbr. articles profl. jours. Home: 500 Valley View Rd Merion Station PA 19066 Office: Dept Chemistry Drexel U Philadelphia PA 19104

KAY, ROBERT LEO, educator; b. Hamilton, Ont., Can., Dec. 13, 1924; s. Norman Robert and Elizabeth (Blatz) K.; B.A., U. Toronto, 1949, M.A., 1950, Ph.D., 1952; m. Ann Donata Morrow, Sept. 12, 1952; children—David Robert (Dec.), Theresa Ann, Joanne Frances, Robert Leo. With Rockefeller Inst. for Med. Research, N.Y.C., 1952-56; asst. prof. chemistry Brown U., Providence, 1956-63; sr. fellow Mellon Inst., Pitts., 1963-67; prof. chemistry Carnegie-Mellon U., Pitts., 1967—. Served with Canadian Army, 1943-46. Merck of Can. Postdoctoral fellow, 1952; research grantee Research Corp., 1957-59, NSF, 1959-60, AEC, 1959-63, Office Saline Water, U.S. Dept. Interior, 1963-70. Mem. Biophys. Soc., A.A.A.S., Am. Chem. Soc., Pitts. Chemists Club. Contbr. articles sci. jours. Editor Jour. Solution Chemistry, 1971—. Home: 221 Parkway Dr Pittsburgh PA 15228

KAY, THOMAS, city mgr.; b. Detroit, Nov. 25, 1924; s. Frederick Thomas and Elizabeth Josephine (Knowles) K.; B.A., Mich. State U., 1948; m. Rose Helen Smith, Sept. 24, 1949; children—Mary Jane, Frederick, Sharon, Patricia, Colleen. Newspaper reporter, 1949-53; adminstrv. asst. to city mgr., Flint, Mich., 1953-57, dep. city mgr., 1957-62, city mgr., 1963—. Chmn. Flint Transp. Authority. Mem. central budget com. Flint Red Feather Fund. Served with USMCR, 1942-45, 50-51. Named Outstanding Young Man of Year, Flint Jr. C. of C., 1958. Mem. Internat. City Mgrs. Assn. Home: 3221 Yale St Flint MI Office: 1101 S Saginaw St Flint MI 48502

KAY, ULYSSES, educator, composer; b. Tucson, Jan. 7, 1917; s. Ulysses Simpson and Elizabeth (Davis) K.; B.Mus., U. Ariz., 1938; M.Mus., Eastman Sch. Music, 1940; postgrad. Yale, 1941-42, Columbia, 1946-49; Mus. D., Lincoln Coll., 1963, Bucknell U., 1966, U. Ariz., 1969; D.H.L., Ill. Wesleyan U., 1969; m. Barbara Harrison, Aug. 20, 1949; children—Virginia, Melinda, Hillary. Editorial adviser Broadcast Music, Inc., N.Y.C., until 1968; prof. music Herbert H. Lehman Coll., City U. N.Y., 1968—; guest condr. N.Y. Little Symphony, Tucson Symphony; commd. by Louisville Symphony Orch., Koussevitzky Music Found., DePaul Inf. Chorus, Quincy (Ill.) Fine Arts Soc.; vis. prof. Boston U., 1965, U. Cal. at Los Angeles, 1966-67. Mem. 1st ofcl. delegation U.S. composers to USSR, State Dept. Cultural Exchange Program, 1958. Served with USNR, 1942-46. Alice M. Ditson fellow, 1945; Julius Rosenwald fellow, 1948, Fulbright fellow, Italy, 1950-51; Guggenheim fellow, 1964-65; recipient ABC prize, 1946; 3d Ann. Gershwin Contest, 1947; Rome prize in Composition, 1949-50, 51-52. Mem. Corp. of Yaddo, Am. Fedn. Musicians, League of Composers, Phi Mu Alpha-Sinfonia. Club: Federal City (Washington). Composer: (operas) The Boor; The Juggler of Our Lady; The Capitoline Venus; ballet Danse Calinda; overture New Horizons; Suite for Strings; Concerto for Orchestra; (film) The Quiet One; Two Symphonies; Three Pieces after Blake (soprano and orch.); Serenade for Orchestra; male chorus Triumvirate; cantata Song of Jeremiah; cantata Phoebus, Arise, Inscription from Whitman; other orch.; choral, chamber music works. Address: care Music Dept Herbert H Lehman Coll Bedford Park Blvd W Bronx NY 10468

KAY, WEBSTER BICE, educator; b. Hammond, Ind., Dec. 8, 1900; s. Howard Lincoln and Bessie (Bice) K.; B.Chem. Engring., Ohio State U., 1922; Ph.D., U. Chgo., 1926; m. Ruth Eloise St. John, June 4, 1939; children—Bonnie Jean, Bruce Webster. Research phys. chemist Standard Oil Co., Whiting, Ind., 1926-47; prof. chem. engring. Ohio State U. at Columbus, 1947—; cons. Battelle Meml. Inst., Wright-Patterson AFB, Dayton, O. Grantee Petroleum Research Fund, NSF, Am. Petroleum Inst. Mem. Am. Chem. Soc., Am. Inst. Chem. Engrs., Am. Soc. Engring. Edn., A.A.A.S., Sigma Xi. Methodist. Club: Ohio State U. Faculty. Contbr. research papers on thermodynamic properties of liquid mixtures. Patentee. Home: 214 E Weber Rd Columbus OH 43202

KAYE, DANNY, actor, comedian; b. N.Y.C., Jan. 18, 1913; s. Jacob and Clara (Nemerovsky) K.; m. Sylvia Fine, Jan. 3, 1940; 1 dau., Dena. Appeared on stage in Straw Hat Revue, Ambassador Theatre, N.Y.C., 1939, Lady in the Dark, 1940, Let's Face It, 1941; on screen with Samuel Goldwyn, Inc., 1943-48, motion pictures include: Up In Arms, 1943; Wonder Man, 1944; Kid from Brooklyn, 1945; Secret Life of Walter Mitty, 1946, A Song is Born, 1947; Inspector General, 1948; On The Riviera, 1950; Hans Christian Anderson, 1952; Knock on Wood, 1954; White Christmas, 1954; The Court Jester, 1955; Merry Andrew, 1957; Me and the Colonel, 1958; The Five Pennies, 1959; On the Double, 1961; The Man from the Diner's Club, 1962; star TV show The Danny Kaye Show; broadway play; Two by Two, 1970-71. Ambassador-at-large UN Childrens Fund. Recipient Emmy award for Danny Kaye Show, 1963, George Foster Peabody award for Danny Kaye Show, 1963. Jewish religion. Home: Beverly Hills CA 90213 Office: 9171 Wilshire Blvd Beverly Hills CA 90212

KAYE, NORA, ballerina; b. N.Y.C., d. Gregory and Lisa Koreff; married third to Herbert Ross, August 21, 1959. Prima ballerina, Ballet Theatre, 1940-50; joined N.Y.C. Ballet Co., 1951; asst. dir. Am. Ballet Theatre, 1964—. Home: 619 N Hillcrest Rd Beverly Hills CA 90210 Office: care Am Ballet Theatre 1790 Broadway New York City NY 10019

KAYE, NORMAN ERNEST, dairy exec.; b. Swift Current, Sask., Can., Oct. 26, 1918; s. Charles Robert and Letitia Mary (Carr) K.; student extension courses; m. Ethel Christine Eckel, May 25, 1944; 1 dau., Diane Cheryl. With Silverwood Dairies, Ltd., London, Ont., Can., 1941—, chmn. bd., pres., chief exec. officer, 1969—, also dir. Rotarian. Clubs: London, London Hunt and Country. Home: 1567 Ryersie Rd London 72 Ont Can Office: 75 Bathurst St London Ont Can

KAYE, SAMMY, orchestra leader; b. Lakewood, O., Mar. 13, 1913; s. Samuel and Mary (Zarnocay) K.; B.S. in Civil Engring., Ohio U., 1933; m. Ruth Knox Elden, Mar. 2, 1940, (div. 1956). Band leader, 1933—; recording artist with Columbia Records; motion picture, radio and TV appearances. Mem. Winter Golf League of Advt. Interests, Theta Chi. Address: 607 5th Av New York City NY 10017

KAYE, SYDNEY MILTON, lawyer; b. N.Y.C., Feb. 3, 1900: s. Ludwig and Elvira (Metz) K.; student Townsend Harris Hall, 1914-17; A.B., Columbia, 1921, LL.B., 1923; m. Muriel Gray, Aug. 21, 1941. Admitted to N.Y. bar, 1924; mem. firm Rosenman, Colin, Kaye, Petschek, Freund and Emil, N.Y.C., 1961—. Chmn. bd. Broadcast Music, Inc. Mem. U.S. delegation Conf. Copyright Experts Am. Republics, Washington, 1952, Inter-Govtl. Copyright Conf., Geneva, Switzerland, 1952, Diplomatic Conf. Protection Performer's Rights, Rome, 1962, Intellectual Property Conf., Stockholm, 1967, Inter-Govtl. Conf. Revision Copyright Treaties, Paris, 1971; mem. panel cons. Gen. Revision Copyright Law and Neighboring Rights Panel, U.S. Copyright Office; mem. internat. copyright panel Dept. State. Trustee N.Y. Cancer Research Inst., Inc. Recipient Broadcast Pioneers award, 1960, Richard Strauss medal, 1971. Mem. Am. (com. program revision copyright law), N.Y. State, Fed. Communications bar assns., Copyright Soc. U.S.A. (trustee), Assn. Bar City N.Y. (copyright com.), N.Y. County Lawyers Assn. (dir.), Broadcast Pioneers (bd. dirs.). Clubs: Overseas Press, Lotos (N.Y.C.). Mem. publs. com. Commentary mag. Home: 12 E 88th St New York City NY 10028 Office: 575 Madison Av New York City NY 10022 also Cornwall Bridge CT 06754

KAYE, SYLVIA FINE, composer; b. N.Y.C., Aug. 29, 1917; d. Samuel and Bessie Fine; m. Danny Kaye, Jan. 3, 1940; 1 dau., Dena. Author spl. material for husband; composer songs including Bali Boogie, Pavlova, Melody in 4F, Anatole of Paris, Straw Hat Review, Let's Face It, Ludwig Von Stickfitz; many popular songs including main title for Man With The Golden Arm; (scores) for Up In Arms, Wonder Man, Secret Life of Walter Mitty; asso. producer Inspector General, Knock on Wood, Court Jester; producer several TV spls. Mem. A.S.C.A.P. Home: 1103 San Ysidro Dr Beverly Hills CA 90210 Office: 9171 Wilshire Blvd Beverly Hills CA 90210

KAYIBANDA, GREGOIRE, pres. Rwanda; b. 1924; ed. Kabgayi and Nyakibanda, Rwanda. Tchr., Kigali, 1949-53; information officer, Kabgayi, 1953-55; editor L'Ami, 1953-55, Kinyamateka, 1955-58; founder Rwanda Coop. Movement, 1952, Hutu Social Movement, 1957. Democratic Republican Movement, 1959; pres. TRAFIPRO Coop., Kabgayi; pres. Democratic Republic Movement; pres. Rwanda, 1960—. Address: Office of the President Kigali Rwanda*

KAYNOR, SANFORD BULL, lawyer; b. Waterbury, Conn., Nov. 24, 1926; s. Warren Fox and Margaret (Smith) K.; B.S., Yale, 1949; LL.B., Columbia, 1952: m. Laura Sanford, June 6, 1953; children—Laura Smith, Sanford Bull, Frederick Kirk. Admitted to N.Y. bar, 1953; asso. firm Havens, Wandless, Stitt & Tighe, N.Y.C., 1952-58; atty. U.S. Industries, Inc., N.Y.C., 1958—, sec., 1961- -, v.p., gen. counsel, 1967—. Served with AUS, 1945-46. Mem. St. Elmo Soc., Phi Delta Phi. Republican. Episcopalian. Club: Yale of N.Y.C. Home: 21 Old Stone Rd Darien, CT 06820. Office: 250 Park Av New York City NY 10017

KAYRUKTIS, A.E., bank exec.; b. Newark, 1909; grad. N.Y. U., 1931. Vice pres., cashier Sterling Nat. Bank and Trust Co., N.Y.C.; v.p., treas., dir. Sterling Safe Deposit Co. Home: 1346 Port Washington NY 11050 Office: 1410 Broadway New York City NY 10018*

KAYS, WILLIAM MORROW, educator; b. Norfolk, Va., July 29, 1920; s. Herbert Emery and Margaret (Fechteler) K.; A.B., Stanford, 1942, M.S. in Engring., 1947, Ph.D. in Engring., 1951; m. Alma Campbell, Sept. 14, 1947; children—Nancy, Leslie, Margaret, Elizabeth. Mem. faculty Stanford, 1951—. prof. mech. engring., 1957—, exec. head dept., 1961—. Fulbright fellow Imperial Coll. Sci. and Tech., London, Eng., 1959-60. Mem. Am. Soc. M.E., Am. Soc. Engring. Edn., Sigma Xi. Home: 852 Pine Hill Rd Stanford CA 94305

KAYSEN, CARL, economist; b. Phila., Mar. 5, 1920; s. Samuel and Elizabeth (Resnick) K.; A.B., U. Pa., 1940; postgrad. Columbia, 1940-42; A.M., Harvard, 1947, Ph.D., 1954; m. Annette Neutra, Sept. 13, 1940; children—Susanna (Mrs. Wylie), Laura. Researcher, Nat. Bur. Econ. Research, 1940-42; economist OSS, 1942; jr. fellow Soc. Fellows, Harvard, 1947-50, asst. prof. econs., 1950-55, asso. prof., 1955-57, prof., 1957-66, asso. dean Grad. Sch. Pub. Adminstrn., 1960-66, Lucius N. Littauer prof. polit. economy, 1964-66; dir. Inst. Advanced Study, Princeton, N.J., 1966—. Dep. spl. asst. to Pres. Kennedy for nat. security affairs, 1961-63; mem. Carnegie Commn. on Higher Edn., 1968—. Trustee U. Pa. Sr. Fulbright research scholar London Sch. Econs., 1955-56; Guggenheim fellow 1955-56. Served to capt. air intelligence, AUS, 1942-45. Mem. Am. Philos. Soc., Am. Acad. Arts and Scis., Phi Beta Kappa. Home: 97 Olden Lane Princeton NJ 08540

KAYSER, ELMER LOUIS, educator, historian; b. Washington, Aug. 27, 1896; s. Samuel Louis and Susie Brown (Huddleston) K.; B.A., also Bachelor's Diploma in Edn., George Washington U., 1917, M.A., 1918, LL.D., 1948; Ph.D., Columbia, 1932; m. Margery Ludlow, Feb. 11, 1922; 1 dau., Katherine Ludlow (Mrs. Arthur Hallett Page III). Asst. in history George Washington U., 1914-17, instr., 1917-20, asst. prof., 1920-24, asso. prof., 1924-32, prof. 1932-67, emeritus, 1967—, asst. librarian, 1917-18, recorder, 1918, sec. 1918-29, dir. summer sch., 1925-29, dir univ. students, 1930-34, dean, 1934-62, dean emeritus, 1967—, univ. historian, 1962—, asso. chmn. sch. of govt., 1957-58; radio commentator on world affairs, 1940-45. Sec.-treas. Gen. Alumni Assn., George Washington U., 1918-24, pres. 1950-53; vice-chmn. bd. trustees Mt. Vernon Sem., 1946-66; past chmn. com. improvement Adminstrn. Justice D.C.; past bd. govs. Nat. Cathedral Sch.; chmn. sec. navy's adv. com. naval history. Dir. Am. Peace Soc. Served with O.T.S. Camp Zachary Taylor, Ky., World War I. Recipient Alumni Achievement award George Washington U., 1941; comdr. Nat. Order of Merit (Ecuador). Mem. Inst. Jud. Adminstrn., Am. Hist. Assn. (treas.), Columbia Hist. Soc. (v.p.), Am. Assn. Univ. Profs. (council 1952-54), Sigma Phi Epsilon, Pi Gamma Mu, Omicron Delta Kappa, Delta Phi Epsilon, Gate and Key. Club: Nat. Press. Author: The Grand Social Enterprise, 1932; A Manual of Ancient History, 1937; The George Washington U., 1821-1966, 1966; Washington's Bequest to a National University, 1965; Luther Rice, Founder of Columbian Coll., 1966; Bricks Without Straw, 1970; co-author: Contemporary Europe, 1941. Past mem. bd. editors World Affairs. Historian, Nat. Capital Sesquicentennial Commn., 1950. Home: 2921 34th St NW Washington DC 20008 Office: George Washington U Washington DC 20006

KAYSER, PAUL, business exec.; b. Tyler, Tex., Feb. 10, 1887; s. Albert and Mary Louise (Lawrence) K.; A.B., Baylor U., 1909, LL.D. (hon.), 1953; legal edn. by correspondence, U. Tex.; LL.D. (hon.), U. Ariz., 1957; m. Elizabeth Harris Clegg, Sept. 1, 1910; children—Betty and Jean (twins). Prin. high sch., Gatesville, Tex., 1909-11; admitted to Tex. bar, 1913; practice in Houston, 1913-29; mem. firm Huggins, Kayser & Liddell; pres. El Paso Natural Gas Co., Houston, Texas, 1929-60, chmn. and chief exec. officer, 1960-65, hon. chmn., 1965-66, dir., 1966—; pres. Western Natural Gas Co., 1935-63; mem. adv. bd. First Nat. Bank of San Antonio (Tex.), Tex. Nat. Bank Commerce, Houston. Served as capt., 7th Cav., N.G., World War I. Mem. Ind. Natural Gas Assn. (pres. 1951-52). Episcopalian. Clubs: Houston, River Oaks Country (Houston); University (Chgo.); Recess (N.Y.C.). Contbr. articles profl. jours. Home: 3260 Del Monte Dr Houston TX 77019 Office: 1006 Main St Houston TX 77002

KAYSER, PAUL WILLIAM, mgmt. cons.; b. N.Y.C., Feb. 28, 1918; s. Paul G. and Julia M. (Buttlar) K.; student Hill Sch., Pottstown, Pa., 1936; B.A., Wesleyan U., Middletown, Conn., 1940; m. Mary Viola Snell, Feb. 21, 1942 (div.); 1 son, Craig; m. 2d, Jane M. Satter, Oct. 1, 1965. Mem. faculty Blair Acad., Blairstown, N.J., 1940-41, 42- 43; with L. Bamberger & Co., Newark, 1941-42, Walter Kidde & Co., Belleville, N.J., 1943-47; dir. personnel, dir. Permacel Tape Corp., New Brunswick, N.J., 1947-52; dir. indsl. relations P. Lorillard Co., N.Y.C., 1952-55; v.p. personnel Am. Airlines, Inc., N.Y.C., 1955- 62, Anderson, Clayton & Co., Houston, 1962-65; v.p., dir. indsl. relations Pepsi Co. Inc., N.Y.C., 1965-70; adminstrv. v.p. King Resources Co., Denver, 1970-71; partner Golightly & Co. Internat., Inc., cons. to mgmt., N.Y.C., 1971—. Pres. Nat. Alliance Businessmen, 1969—. Mem. Newcomen Soc., N.Y. Indsl. Relations Assn., Am. Mgmt. Assn., Alpha Delta Phi. Club: Union League (N.Y.C.), Home: 605 Park Av New York City NY 10021 Office: 1 Rockefeller Plaza New York City NY 10020

KAZ, NATHANIEL, sculptor; b. N.Y.C., Mar. 9, 1917; s. I. Rudolph and Ida (Elkan) K.; student Art Students League; children—Naomi Della, Eric Justin. One-man shows Downtown Gallery, 1939, Asso. Am. Artists, 1946, Grand Central Moderns, 1954, Joan Avnet Gallery, 1965; exhbns. Whitney Mus., Met. Mus. Art, Bklyn. Mus., Art Inst. Chgo., U. Neb., Phila. Mus. Fine Arts, Mus. Modern Art, N.Y. and San Francisco world's fairs; rep. permanent collections Bklyn. Mus., Whitney Mus., Met. Mus., pvt. collections; designed and executed 10 ft. carving in limestone for Fine St. Temple, Nashville,

6 ft. bronze for Pub. Sch. 59, Bklyn.; exhibited 4 ritual works Grand Central Moderns, 1957, Temple of Beth Emeth, Albany, N.Y., 1965; designed and executed two 7 ft. colored aluminum reliefs of Thespians-Tragedy and Comedy for Jr. High Sch. 164, Queens, New York, 1958; tchr. Art Students League, N.Y.C. Recipient Mich. Sculpture award, 1929, Sect. Fine Arts award, 1940, Artists for Victory award, 1942, Audubon Artists 6th ann. award, 1947, Bklyn. Soc. Artists 32d ann. award, 1948, Sculpture prize Bklyn. Mus., 1952; Alfred G. B. Steel Meml. prize, 148th ann. exhibit Pa. Acad. Fine Arts, 1953; winner nationwide competition UN monument design Nat. Council for U.S. Art. Mem. Sculptors Guild. Home: 160 W 73rd St New York City NY 10023 Studio: 253 W 26th St New York City NY 10001

KAZAKOFF, JOHN, utility exec.; b. Kamsack, Sask., Can., Mar. 14, 1913; s. Peter E. and Parana (Ogloff) K.; student U. Sask., Saskatoon, Can., 1931-33; B.Eng. in Elec. Engring., McGill U., Montreal, Que., Can., 1935; m. Ellen Elizabeth Parsons, July 25, 1942; children—Valerie Judith (Mrs. Richard D. Byrne), Michael Angus. With Canadian Ingersoll Rand Co., 1935-38; with Bolivian Power Co., 1938-42, 47-48, supt. operations, 1941-42, acting mgr. Oruro div., 1947-48; with Montreal Engring. Co. Ltd., 1942-46, 48-60; asst. v.p. Internat. Power Co. Ltd., 1960-63, v.p. 1963-66; with Canadian Internat. Power Co., Montreal, 1966—, exec. v.p., 1968-69, pres., 1969—; pres., dir. Internat. Power Co. Ltd., C I Power Services Ltd., Compania Boliviana de Energia Electrica, S.A., Bolivian Power Co. Ltd.; dir. Barbados Light & Power Co. Ltd., Monterey Ry., Light & Power Co., Compania de Alumbrado Electrico de San Salvador. Gov. The Canadian Assn. for Latin Am. Mem. Corp. Engrs. Que., Engring. Inst. Can., Inst. Elec., Electronics Engrs., Canadian Elec. Assn., Engrs. Club Montreal. Mem. United Ch. Clubs: Engineers, St. James's (Montreal); Summerlea Golf and Country (Dorion, Que.); Lachine (Que.) Curling. Home: 749 44th Av Lachine 610 Quebec Canada Office: 276 St James St W Montreal 126 Quebec Canada

KAZAN, ELIA, theatrical and motion picture exec.; b. Constantinople, Turkey, Sept. 7, 1909; s. George and Athena (Sismanoglou) K.; A.B., Williams Coll., 1930; postgrad. Yale, 1930-32; M.F.A., Wesleyan U., Middletown, Conn., 1955; m. Molly Day Thacher, Dec. 2, 1932 (dec.); children—Judy, Chris, Nick, Katharine; m. 2d, Barbara Loden, June 5, 1967. Actor with Group Theatre, 1932- 39; dir. stage plays, 1940-55, including Skin of Our Teeth, Harriet, Jacobowsky and the Colonel, All My Sons, Deep Are the Roots, A Streetcar Named Desire, Death of a Salesman, Camino Real, Tea and Sympathy, Cat on a Hot Tin Roof, The Dark at the Top of the Stairs, J.B. (Antoinette Perry award direction 1958), Sweet Bird of Youth, After the Fall, But for Whom Charlie, The Changeling; dir. numerous motion pictures, 1944—, including A Tree Grows in Brooklyn, Boomerang, Gentlemen's Agreement (Acad. award best direction, 1947), Pinky, Panic in the Streets, Streetcar Named Desire, Zapata, Man on a Tight Rope, On the Waterfront (1954 Acad. Award for best direction), East of Eden, Baby Doll, A Face in the Crowd, Wild River, Splendor in the Grass, America, America. Co-founder Actors Studio. Author: The Arrangement, 1967 (producer, dir. film 1968). Office: 1545 Broadway New York City NY 10036

KAZDIN, MELVIN MAXWELL, lawyer; b. Bklyn., Mar. 22, 1933; s. Frank and Anna (Rifkin) K.; B.B.A., Coll. City N.Y., 1954; LL.D., N.Y.U., 1957; m. Phyllis Morgenstern, July 14, 1957; children—Loren, Miriam, Marjorie. Admitted to N.Y. bar, 1957, since practiced in N.Y.C.; mem. firm Booth, Lipton & Lipton, 1957-61; pvt. practice, 1961-68; partner firm Kazdin & Weinstein, 1968—. Sec. J.W. Mays, Inc., N.Y.C., 1964—. Bd. dirs., pres. Roslyn Country Club Civic Assn.; bd. dirs. J. Weinstein Found., N.Y.C., Laurelton Lodge Masonic Found., N.Y.C. Mason (past master). Home: 33 Shadetree Lane Roslyn Heights NY 11577 Office: 2 Pennsylvania Plaza New York City NY 10001

KAZEMZADEH, FIRUZ, educator, historian; b. Moscow, USSR, Oct. 27, 1924; s. Kazem and Talieh (Yevseyev) K.; came to U.S., 1944, naturalized, 1955; B.A., Stanford, 1946, M.A., 1947; Ph.D., Harvard, 1951; m. Caterina Bosio, Jan. 5, 1959; children—Tatiana, Allegra, Monireh. Research fellow Hoover Inst., Stanford, Cal., 1949-50; cons. publs. State Dept., 1951-52; head Soviet affairs unit, information dept. Radio Free Europe, 1952-54; research fellow Russian Research Center, Center Middle Eastern Studies, Harvard, 1954-56, instr. history and lit., 1955-56; mem. faculty Yale, 1956—, prof. history, 1967—, chmn. council Russian and East European studies, 1968-69. Morse fellow, 1958-59; Ford fellow internat. affairs, 1966. Mem. Bahá'í Faith and Nat. Spiritual Assembly Bahá'ís of U.S.; editor World Order, Bahá'í mag., 1966—. Author: The Struggle for Transcaucasia, 1917-1921, 1952; Russia and Britain in Persia, 1864-1914; A Study in Imperialism, 1968. Home: 231 Colony Rd New Haven CT 06511

KAZEN, ABRAHAM, Jr., congressman; b. Laredo, Tex., Jan. 17, 1919; student U. Tex., 1937-40, Cumberland Law Sch., Lebanon, Tenn., 1941; m. Consuelo Raymond; children—Abraham III, Mrs. E.C. Dillman, Jr., Christina (Mrs. Ronald K. Attal), Catherine, Jo-Betsy. Admitted to Tex. bar, 1942; mem. firm Raymond, Alvarado & Kazen, Laredo, 1946-55; pvt. practice, Laredo, 1955-67; mem. Tex. Ho. of Reps., 1947-52; mem. Tex. Senate, 1952-66, pres. pro tempore, 1959; acting gov. Tex. 1959; mem. 90th-92d congresses 23d Dist. Tex. Past mem. Tex. Legislative Council. Sponsor pre-sch. program for non-English speaking children. Served to capt. USAAF, World War II; ETO, CBI. Named Man of Year, Father of Year, Laredo. Mem. Tex., Laredo bar assns., Laredo Internat. Fair and Expn., Washington's Birthday Celebration Assn., Am. Legion, U. Tex. Ex-Students Assn. Democrat. K.C. Home: Laredo TX 78040 Office: House Office Bldg Washington DC 20515

KAZIN, ALFRED, writer; b. Bklyn., June 5, 1915; s. Charles and Gita (Fagelman) K.; B.S.S., Coll. City of N.Y., 1935; A.M., Columbia, 1938; Litt. D., Adelphi U., 1965; m. Caroline Bookman, May 23, 1947 (div.); 1 son, Michael; m. 2d, Ann Birstein, June 26, 1952; 1 dau., Cathrael. Lit. editor New Republic, 1942-43, contbg. editor, 1943-45; contbg. editor Fortune Mag., 1943-44; lectr. Black Mountain Coll. Fall, 1944; vis. prof. U. Minn., summer 1946, 50, lectr. Harvard, 1953; William Allan Neilson research prof. Smith Coll., 1954-55; Berg professor of lit. N.Y. U., 1957; prof. Am. studies Amherst Coll., 1955-58; vis. prof. Coll. City N.Y., 1962; Beckman prof. U. Cal., 1963; Distinguished prof. English, State U. N.Y. at Stony Brook, 1963—. Guggenheim fellow, 1940, 1947, Rockefeller fellow study of trade-union and Army popular edn. movements in Gt. Britain, 1945. Recipient George Polk Meml. award for criticism, 1966. Mem. Nat. Inst. Arts and Letters, Am. Acad. Arts and Scis. Author books including: On Native Grounds, 1942; A Walker in the City, 1951; The Inmost Leaf, 1955; Contemporaries, 1962; Starting Out in the Thirties, 1965; co-author Introduction to the Works of Anne Frank, 1959; General Introduction to Dell Edition of the Novels of Theodore Dreiser, 1960; others. Editor publs. including: The Viking Portable William Blake, 1946; F. Scott Fitzgerald, The Man and His Work, 1951; Moby-Dick, 1956; Introduction to Selected Stories of Sholem Aleichem, 1956; The Open Form: Essays For Our Time, 1961; The Selected Short Stories of Nathaniel Hawthorne, 1966. Co- editor: The Stature of Theodore Dreiser, 1955; Emerson: A Modern Anthology, 1958; The Ambassadors (James), 1969. Contbr. articles to newspapers, mags. Home: 440 West End Av New York City NY 10024

KAZMAYER, ROBERT HENDERSON, bus. analyst, publisher; b. Rush, N.Y., Nov. 1908; s. Jacob and Viola (Darron) K.; student U. Rochester, 1929-31, Colgate-Divinity Sch., 1931-34; LL.D., Salem Coll., Salem. W.Va., 1956; m. Clara V. Rapp. July 29, 1936 (div.); 1 son, Robert L.; m. 2d, Ida L. Wright, Nov. 18, 1955. Ordained deacon M.E. Ch., 1932; ordained elder, 1934; held pastorates at Indian Falls, 1930-31; Lewiston M.E. Ch., Rochester, N.Y., 1931-34; Monroe Av M.E. Ch., 1934-38; left ministry to devote full time to writing, lecturing, 1939; travelled annually in Central and S. Am., Australia, Far East, Eng., much of continental Europe, Russia, 1929-41; in 22 months following Pearl Harbor, travelled numerous states addressing over 400 audiences, lecturing on Germany, Russia, Japan, internat. politics; originator and for two years moderator of Rochester Town Hall of the Air, WHEC; three years as radio ch. editor, WSAY; originator of Kazmayer Seminar Tours; publishes news letter for U.S., British bus. men; Things to Watch, Watch For, bimonthly travel letters. Lectured throughout U.S., Can., Europe, the East; mem. bd. lectrs. Freedoms Found. Valley Forge. Recipient L'Accueil De Paris, Conseil Municipal Paris, 1956; Geo. Washington Honor medal, Freedoms Found., 1961. Life mem. Acad. Polit. Sci., 1952; charter mem. Anglo-Am. Goodwill Assn. (British), Authors League; mem. Am. Acad. Polit. and Social Sci. Methodist. Mason (32, Shriner). Clubs: Rotary, Union League (Chgo.); Adventurers (Chgo., N.Y., London); Overseas Press (N.Y.C.). Author: Out of the Clouds, 1944; New Strength for America (speeches). Contbr. We Believe in Prayer. Conducted Pastor's Exchange in Christian Advocate, 1935-36. Home: Kendall NY 14476 Office: 84 Rand St Rochester NY 14615

KEACH, STACY, Jr., actor, director; b. Savannah, Ga., June 2, 1941; s. Stacy and Mary Cain (Peckham) K.; A.B. in English and Drama, U. Cal. at Berkeley, 1963; student Yale Drama Sch., 1963-64, London Acad. Dramatic Art, 1964-65. Asso. prof. drama Yale, 1967-68; Broadway debut in Indians; off-Broadway appearances in Macbird, The Niggerlovers, Peer Gynt, Henry IV, 1 and 2, Hamlet; mem. Lincoln Center Repertory Co., also Long Warf Theatre; film appearances include The Heart is a Lonely Hunter, End of the Road. Peer Gynt; dir. Pullman Car Hiawatha, 1964-65, The Stronger 1964-65, The Maids, 1964-65. Recipient Oliver Thorndike acting award Yale Drama Sch., 1963-64; Best Actor award U. Cal., 1963; Best Actor award Ore. Shakespeare award, 1963; Obie award, 1967; Vernin Rice Drama Desk award, 1967; Sat Rev. award, 1967; Fulbright award, 1964-65.

KEADY, GERALD JOSEPH, steel mfr.; b. Rochester, N.Y., Sept. 25, 1900; s. Mitchell B. and Anna J. (Duffy) K.; B.S., U. Pa., 1925; m. Eleanor Shelburne Russell, June 10, 1927; children—Eleanor K. Whitcomb, Robert R., Linda K. Boyd. Office boy Dillon, Read & Co., N.Y.C., 1926, mgr. br. office, 1926-30, sales mgr., 1930-32; sales mgr. Container Corp. Am., Chgo., 1932-37; with Sharples Corp., Phila., 1937-56, exec. v.p., 1938-48, pres., 1948-56; pres. Phila. Steel & Iron Corp., 1956-67, chmn., 1967—; v.p., exec. com., dir. Old Phila. Devel. Co.; dir. 1st Pa. Banking & Trust Co., Potomac Ins. Co., Phila., Athena Controls, Inc.; chmn. adv. com. U.S. br. Gen. Accident Fire & Life Assurance Corp., Ltd., Perth Scotland; dir. Pa. Gen. Ins. Co., Phila., Camden Fire Ins. Assn. Bd. dirs. Univ. City Sci. Center; trustee Moore Sch. Elec. Engring., Phila. Mem. Delta Kappa Epsilon. Clubs: Racquet, IV Street (Phila.); Santee (S.C.); Merion Cricket (Haverford, Pa.); Merion Golf (Ardmore, Pa.); Chemists (N.Y.C.); St. James' London, (Eng.); Faculty (U. Pa.). Home: 410 Hillbrook Rd Bryn Mawr PA 19010 Office: Walnut St and Washington Av Conshohocken PA 19428

KEAGLE, LEROY CURTIS, coll. dean; b. Bloomington, Pa., Feb. 18, 1919; s. Lawrence E. and Bertha (Clarkson) K.; B.S. in Pharmacy, Rutgers U., 1940; Ph.D., U. Md., 1944; postgrad. fellow Purdue U., 1944-45; m. Jane A. Beckman, Aug. 1, 1942; children—Douglas Lee, Pamela Jane, Cynthia Ann. Asst. prof. Rutgers U. Coll. Pharmacy, 1945-49; prof. pharmacy, chmn. dept. U. Buffalo, 1949-53, asst. dean, 1950-53; sr. scientist Warner-Lambert Pharm. Co., Morris Plains, N.J., 1953-57; pres., dean New Eng. Coll. Pharmacy, Boston, 1957-62; dean Coll. Pharmacy, Northeastern U., Boston, 1962—. Pres. Manor Park Assn., also rep. to Joint Civic Com. Westfield, N.J., 1956-57; mem. ednl. facilities com. Westfield P.T.A. council, 1956-57. Served with AUS, 1944-45. Mem. Am., Mass., N.H. (hon.) pharm. assns., Am. Chem. Soc., A.A.A.S., New Eng. Coll. Pharmacy Alumni Assn. (honorary), Conference Tchrs., Am. Assn. Colls. Pharmacy, Mass. Soc. Hosp. Pharmacists, Sigma Xi. Rho Chi, Kappa Psi, Alpha Zeta Omega (hon.), Phi Kappa Phi, Mason. Home: 20 Richfield Rd West Newton MA 02165 Office: 360 Huntington Av Boston MA 02115

KEALLY, FRANCIS architect; b. Pitts., s. Charles L. and Bertha (Loeffler) K.; A.B., Carnegie-Mellon U.; B.S. in Architecture, U. Pa.; 1916; m. Mildred Fessenden Taber, Apr. 4, 1923; 1 son, Francis Taber. Mem. design staff, Rice Inst., Houston, 1915-16, U. Minn., 1916-17, Sch. Architecture Columbia U., 1927-30, Sch. Architecture N.Y. U., 1930-31, N.Y. Sch. Applied Design for Women, 1930-34. Began practice N.Y.C., 1927. Designed nat. pioneer monument erected at Harrodsburg, Ky. in collaboration with Ulric Ellerhusen (sculptor); in assn. with Trowbridge & Livingston, designed Ore. State Capitol, Salem; with Alfred Morton Githens designer Bklyn. Pub. Library, Concord (N.H.) Pub. Library, consultants on Va. State Library, Richmond, Joint Univs. Library, Nashville; designed Communications Bldg., N.Y. World's Fair, 1939; devel. campus plan for Carnegie-Mellon U. In association with Cass Gilbert, Jr. architect for new addition to Detroit Pub. Library, architect for U.S. Mil. Cemetery, Hamm, Luxembourg. apptd. cons. architect of Am. Hotel Assn.; cons. architect Am. Meml., Free U. Libraries, Berlin, Germany, addition to Ore. State Capitol, Salem, Emancipation Proclamation Shrine State N.Y., Albany. Architect for Oswego Tchrs., Coll., George Westinghouse Vocational High Sch., Bklyn., in assn. with Charles K. Hirzel, architect for Greek Orthodox Ch. Complex, Tenafly, N.J., downtown branch Bklyn. pub. library. Retained by Icelandic Govt. to develop sketches for a modern hotel for Reykjavik, Iceland, 1946. Apptd. mem. A.I.A. Com. to analyze plans for putting 200,000 unemployed to work in N.Y., 1933. Apptd. camouflage specialist for 2d Civilian Defense Region, U.S. Office of Civilian Defense, N.Y.C., Aug. 24, 1942. Architect Iranian Embassy, Washington. Award of Merit, Carnegie Inst. of Technol. Alumni Fedn., 1954; citation, senate of Berlin, 1954; Golden Plate award Am. Acad. Achievement, 1966. Mem. War Meml. Adv. Council; mem. Library Bldgs. com., A.L.A. Dir. Greater N.Y. Civic Center Assn., Allen-Stevenson Sch. Fellow Am. Inst. Architects (pres. N.Y. chpt., 1951-52); mem. Nat. Acad. Design (treas. N.Y.), Fine Arts Fedn. N.Y. (pres., 1957-59), Archtl. League, N.Y., Beaux-Arts Inst. Design, Soc. Medalist, Municipal Arts Soc. N.Y. (pres. 1952-54), Psi Upsilon; hon. mem. Nat. Soc. Mural Painters, Nat. Sculpture Soc. Clubs: University (chmn. art com. N.Y.); Grolier; Cosmos (Washington). Contributed various articles to Pencil Points, Archtl. Forum, Archtl. Record. Home: 131 E 66th St New York City NY 10021 Office: 227 E 44th St New York City NY 10017

KEAN, BENJAMIN HARRISON, physician; b. Chgo., Dec. 2, 1912; s. Harrison and Tillie (Rhodes) K.; A.B., U. Cal., 1933; M.D., Columbia, 1937. Intern Gorgas Hosp., C.Z., Panama, 1937-39; pvt. practice medicine, N.Y.C., 1946—; clin. prof. tropical medicine Cornell U. Med. Coll.; attending physician N.Y., Doctors hosps.; dir. parasitology lab. N.Y. Hosp.; med. cons. Ford Found., Travelers Health Inst., Devel. and Resources Corp. Served to lt. col. M.C., AUS, 1942-46. Recipient Presdl. Award of Golden Heart, Philippines Govt., 1968. Fellow A.C.P.; mem. A.M.A., Royal Soc. Tropical Medicine and Hygiene, Am. Soc. Clin. Pathology, Am., N.Y. socs. tropical medicine, Am. Assn. Pathology and Bacteriology. Author: (with Breslau) Parasites of the Human Heart, 1964; (with Tucker) Traveler's Health Guide, 1965, Traveler's Medical Guide for Physicians, 1966. With Dr. Edward I. Goldsmith developed surg. procedure for extracorporeal hemofiltration. Home: 435 E 70th St New York City NY 10021 Office: 728 Park Av New York City NY 10021

KEAN, BETTY WYNN, comedienne; b. Hartford, Conn., Dec. 15, 1918; d. Robert Samuel and Annette Helen (Hansen) K.; m. Lew Parker, Mar. 9, 1955; 1 dau., Deirdre (Mrs. John Mahon). Appearances vaudeville, Broadway, movies, TV appearances. Home: 1850 N Cherokee St Hollywood CA 90028 Office: care Lou Irwin Agy 9165 Sunset Blvd Hollywood CA 10069

KEAN, HELEN ELIZABETH, educator; b. Detroit, Feb. 11, 1914; d. Peter Francis and Lillian (McDonnell) Kean; A.B. summa cum laude, Marygrove Coll., Detroit, 1934; A.M., U. Detroit, 1944. Asst. dir. Pre-Coll. Counseling Bur., U. Detroit, 1935-63, dean women, 1942-68, asso. dean students, 1968-70, dean students, 1970-71, asst. prof. counselor edn., 1971—. Mem. Am. Assn. U. Women, Nat., Mich. assns. women deans and counselors, Guidance Assn. Met. Detroit, Mich. Coll. Personnel Assn., Am. Personnel and Guidance Assn., Mich. Assn. Counselor Edn., Kappa Gamma Pi. Roman Catholic. Co-pub. ann. guidance bulls. U. Detroit, 1935-64. Home: 16500 N Park Dr Southfield MI 48075

KEAN, ROBERT W., Sr., gas co. exec. Chmn. Elizabethtown Gas Co. Office: 1 Elizabethtown Plaza Elizabethtown NJ 07207*

KEAN, WILLIAM FRANCIS, ednl. adminstr.; b. Buffalo, Sept. 24, 1913; s. Thomas Chester and Lillian Alice (Cunningham) K.; B.S., Buffalo State Tchrs. Coll., 1936; M.Ed., U. Buffalo, 1939, Ed.D., 1957; m. Doris Elizabeth Koch, Apr. 6, 1940; children—Janet Elizabeth, William Francis, Arthur Thomas, John Francis, Robert Thomas, Tchr., Kenmore (N.Y.) pub. schs., 1936-43; supr. service reps. tng. sch. Bell Aircraft Corp., 1943-44, job analyst, 1944- 45; chief registration and research VA, Buffalo, 1945-47; asst. prof. edn. Canisius Coll., Buffalo, 1947-57, asso. prof., 1957-61, prof. edn. 1961—, acting chmn. dept. edn., acting dir. grad. div., 1958, chmn. dept. edn., dir. grad. div., 1959-65, dean grad. div., 1965—; lectr. D'Youville Coll., 1951-54, St. John Vianney Sem., E. Aurora, N.Y., 1961-66. Coordinator, Buffalo Community Resources Workshop, 1956-68. Mem. Am. Assn. U. Profs. (past chpt. pres.), Jesuit Ednl. Assn. (chmn. conf. on grad. schs. 1967-70), Assn. Grad. Schs. In Cath. Univs. (sec.-treas. 1967-69, chmn. 1969-71), Phi Delta Kappa (past pres. chpt.). Home: 417 Argonne Dr Kenmore NY 14217 Office: 2001 Main St Buffalo NY 14208

KEANE, DANIEL B., business exec. Sec.-treas. H.C. Christians Co., Chgo. Office: 1325 W 15th St Chicago IL 60608*

KEANE, GUSTAVE ROBERT, architect; b. Vienna, Austria, Jan. 7, 1914; s. Robert Kien and Frances (Partl) K.; archtl. engr., State U. Czechoslovakia, 1937; m. Constance van Lennep, Jan. 30, 1940; children—Robert van Lennep, John Francis. Came to U.S., 1938, naturalized, 1945. Designer, Harvey Wiley Corbett, N.Y.C., 1940-43; with Eggers Partnership, N.Y.C., 1945—, partner, 1963—; guest lectr. Bd. dirs. Bldg. Research Inst., Washington, Nat. Bd. Accreditation in Concrete Constrn. Past chmn. architects com. United Hosp. Fund. Fellow A.I.A., Am. Soc. Testing Materials; mem. Am. Assn. Hosp. Planning. Prin. works include Def. Intelligence Agy., North River Devel. N.Y., Am. Embassy, Ankara, Turkey, U.S. Naval Hosp., P.R. Contbr. books, jours. Home: 7 Harmony Rd Huntington NY 11743 Office: 100 Park Av New York City NY 10017

KEANE, MARK EDWARD, assn. exec.; b. Chgo., Sept. 10, 1919; s. Fred J. and Mary E. (Sullivan) K.; B.S. in Pub. Service Engring., Purdue U., 1941; m. Carolyn Mims, Sept. 12, 1942; children—Mark Edward, Daniel, Dennis, Brian, Mary, Peter, Barry. Intern pub. adminstrn. Nat. Inst. Pub. Affairs, Washington, 1941-42; staff cons. Pub. Adminstrn. Service, Chgo., 1945- 48; asst. to city mgr., Wichita, Kan., 1948-49; city mgr., Shorewood, Wis., 1950-53, Oak Park, Ill., 1953-62, Tucson, 1962-66; dir. land and facilities devel. adminstrn. Dept. Housing and Urban Devel., Washington, 1966-67; exec. dir. Internat. City Mgmt. Assn., Washington, 1967—. Served to maj. AUS, 1942-45. Mem. Nat. Acad. Pub. Adminstrn. Home: 3522 Rittenhouse St Washington DC 20015 Office: 1140 Connecticut Av NW Washington DC 20036

KEANE, PETER LEO, lawyer; b. N.Y.C., Apr. 19, 1917; s. Patrick and Katherine (Collins) K.; student N.Y.U., 1935-38; LL.B., St. Lawrence U., 1941; m. Susan Hughes, Nov. 20, 1948; children—Peter Kevin, Susan. Admitted to N.Y. bar, 1942, since practiced in N.Y.C.; asso. Lord, Day & Lord, 1941-54, partner, 1954—. Chmn. bd., dir. Am. Export Industries, Inc.; dir. Grow Chem. Corp. Trustee Kips Bay Boys Club. Served with USAAF, 1942- 45. Mem. Am., N.Y. State bar assns., Assn. Bar City N.Y., Maritime Law Assn. Home: 35 Stone Fence Rd Allendale NJ 07401 Office: 25 Broadway New York City NY 10004

KEANE, WALTER STANLEY, artist; b. Lincoln, Neb., Oct. 7, 1920; s. William Robert and Alma (Johnson) K.; B.A., Armstrong Coll., Berkeley, Cal., 1941; student Grande Chaumiere, also Beaux-Arts, Paris, France, 1945-46; pupil of Danlos, Bruges, Belgium, 1947; m. Margaret Doris Hawkins, Dec. 28, 1955 (div. Aug. 1965); 1 dau., Susan Hale. Exhbns. include Royal Hawaiian Hotel, Honolulu, 1955, Court of Two Sisters, New Orleans, 1956, Little Gallery, Boston, 1956-59, Hotel Sherman Art Gallery, Chgo., 1957, Harry Marks Gallery, N.Y.C., 1957-59, Little Gallery, Honolulu, 1957, 58, 60, 61, Brussels World Fair, 1958, Galleries Phila., 1957-59, Little Gallery, Phila., 1956-58, Galleries Philadlphie, Paris, 1958-59, Am. Cultural Center, Tokyo, 1960, Shamrock Hotel, Houston, 1961, W.&J. Sloane Co. in Beverly Hills, Cal., 1961-63, in Palm Springs, Cal., 1965, Boise (Ida.) Mus. Art, 1963, Contemporary Mus. Art, Madrid, 1965, Keane Art Galleries, San Francisco and N.Y.C., 1958—; rep. permanent collections Nat. Mus. Western Art, Tokyo, Contemporary Mus. Art, Madrid, Spain, Internat. Art Center, Honolulu, Mus. Modern Art, Mexico, UN Bldg., Groeninge Mus. Art, Bruges, also numerous pvt. collections. Donor Keane Found., scholarships for art students, 1962. Fellow Soc. Western Artists (trustee 1964-65); mem. De Young Mus., San Francisco Mus. Art, Mus. Modern Art, N.Y.C., San Francisco C. of C. Address: 494 Broadway San Francisco CA 94133

KEAR, FRANK GREGG, cons. radio engr.; b. Minersville, Pa., Oct. 18, 1903; s. Frank G. and Kathryn (Snyder) K.; E.E., Lehigh U., 1926; S.M. Mass. Inst. Tech., 1928, Sc.D., 1933; m. Virginia Graham Leach,

Jan. 30, 1940; children—Nancy Graham (Mrs. J.H. Glass), Walter, Frank, Rhys. Asso. Dr. V. Bush and Dr. H. L. Hazen in devel. of product integraph and differential analyzer, 1926-28; physicist staff Nat. Bur. Standards, 1928-33; one of group which developed radio range beacon and 1st instrument landing equipment for aircraft; participated in work terminating in 1st blind airplane landing, developed 1st combined radio beacon and radio telephone transmitter, 1931; developed practical means for stabilizing directional pattern of complex antenna array; participated in devel. radio beacon system free from night effect; chief engr. Washington Inst. Tech., 1933-41; continued devel. of radio landing systems for aircraft, rep. various radio stas. before F.C.C., pioneered in Application of directional Antennas to broadcasting participated in devel. of Earth Inductor Compass as applied to problems in air and water nav.; lectr. elec. commns. U. Md., 1936-41; holder numerous patents in field of communication U.S. and Eng.; electronics devel. cons. Am. Broadcasting Co.; engr. in charge Empire State Bldg. TV project. Served as head radio sect. Bur. Aeros., U.S.N.; east coast stas. Navy Dept., Eng. and France, World War II; tech. adv. 3d C.E.R.C.A., London, Eng., 1945; capt. USNR. Govt. St. Albans Sch., 1955-63 (chmn. 1959-61); mem. bd. trustees Lehigh U. Fellow I.E.E.E.; mem. A.A.A.S., Lehigh U. Alumni Assn. (pres. 1966-67), Phi Beta Kappa, Sigma Xi, Eta Kappa Nu, Tau Beta Pi, Scabbard and Blade. Republican. Methodist Episcopalian. Mason (K.T.) Clubs: University, Cosmos. Author articles tech. publs. Home: 3913 Leland St Chevy Chase, MD 20015. Office: 1302 18th St NW Washington DC 20036

KEARINS, MICHAEL JOSEPH, Jr., cutting tools mfgr.; b. Chgo., Aug. 8, 1892; s. Michael J. and Elizabeth (Gannon) K.; ed. Crane Tech. High Sch. and De La Salle Inst., Chgo.; m. Mildren Mary O'Neill, Sept. 29, 1923; children—Jean Anne (dec.), Patricia J., Barbara M. Past pres. Whitman & Barnes Mfg. Co., Detroit, mfrs. drills, reamers, cutters; chmn. J.H. Williams Co.; formerly chmn. United Drill & Tool Co., Chgo. (merged with United Greenfield Corp. 1958); now chmn. United Greenfield Corp. Served with 16th Engineers, U.S. Army, 1917-19; overseas, also with AS, 22 months. Clubs: Chicago Athletic Assn.; Detroit Athletic; Oakland Hills Country. Home: 51 Fairford Rd Grosse Pointe MI 48236 Office: 411 W Ontario St Chicago IL 60611

KEARL, BRYANT EASTHAM, educator; b. Paris, Ida., Sept. 21, 1921; s. Chase and Hazel (Loveless) K.; student U. Ida., 1936-37; B.S., Utah State U., 1941; M.S., U. Wis., 1942; Ph.D., U. Minn., 1951; m. Ruth Warr, Sept. 5, 1941; children—Susan (Mrs. Dick DeJongh), Richard, Kathryn, Robert. Corr., Salt Lake Tribune, 1935-38, Denver Post, 1940-41; mem. faculty U. Wis. Madison, 1942—, prof. agrl. journalism, 1954—, chmn. dept., 1952-64, asso. dean Grad. Sch., 1963- 67, vice chancellor univ., 1967-70; lectr. U. Minn., 1947-48; cons. W. German Ministry Agr., 1952; vis. prof. U. Bonn (Germany), 1961-62; planning officer U. East Africa, 1964-65; exec. dir. Asia office Agr. Devel. council, 1970—. Served to lt. (j.g.) USNR, 1944-46; PTO. Mem. Am. Assn. U. Profs., Assn. Edn. Journalism, Am. Agrl. Coll. Editors Assn. (pres. 1963-64), Epsilon Sigma Phi, Sigma Alpha Epsilon. Mem. Ch. of Jesus Christ of Latter-day Saints. Home: 2807 Ridge Rd Madison WI 53705

KEARL, CHASE DELMAR, educator, assn. exec.; b. Provo, Utah, July 26, 1917; s. Chase and Hazel (Loveless) K.; student U. Ida., 1935-37; B.S., Utah State U., 1941; M.S., Cornell U., 1947, Ph.D., 1949; m. Marjorie Lee Lail, Feb. 1, 1943; children—Sandra, Steven, Gail, Kenneth, Rodney, Debra Ann, Shari Lynn. Missionary, Latter-day Saints Ch., Eng., 1937-39; with Adel Precision Products, 1941-42; from asst. to prof. Cornell U., 1949—; vis. asso. prof. U. Philippines, 1954-56; farm planning adv. Dept. Agr., Uganda, 1960. Served to 1st lt. AUS, 1942- 46. Mem. Am. Farm Econ. Assn. (sec.-treas.), Internat. Conf. Agrl. Economists, Alpha Zeta, Phi Kappa Phi, Pi Gamma Mu, Sigma Alpha Epsilon. Mem. Ch. Latter-day Saints. Author articles agrl. econs. Home: 255 Perciville Rd RD 1 Freville NY 13068

KEARNEY, FRANCIS WILLIAM, educator; b. Stoneboro, Pa., Feb. 16, 1912; s. William F. and Julia (Tobin) K.; B.A., St. Bonaventure (N.Y.) U., 1934; M.A., Columbia, 1942; Ph.L., Laval (Qua.) U., 1944, Ph.D., 1945. Joined Order of Friars Minor, ordained priest Roman Cath. Ch., 1938; prof. philosphy St. Bonaventure U., 1939-41, dean dept., 1949-53, pres. univ., 1961-67; prof. philosophy St. Stephen's Coll., Croghan, N.Y., 1949-53; rector St. Francis Coll., Rye Beach, N.H., 1953-61; prof. philosophy Siena Coll., Loudonville, N.Y., 1967-70. Address: Siena Coll Loudonville NY 12211

KEARNEY, JAMES EDWARD, retired bishop; b. Red Oak, Ia., Oct. 28, 1884; s. William Patrick and Rosina (O'Doherty) K.; student N.Y. Tchrs. Coll., N.Y.C., 1901-03, St. Josephs Sem., Dunwoodie, Yonkers, N.Y., 1903-08; S.T.B., Catholic U. Am., 1909, J.C.L., 1909. Ordained priest Roman Cath. Ch., 1908; asst. rector St. Cecilia's Ch., N.Y.C., 1909-28; founder, 1928, pastor, 1928-32, Ch. of St. Francis Xavier, N.Y.C.; prof. apologetics Good Counsel Coll., N.Y.C., 1928-32; bishop of Salt Lake, 1932-37, of Rochester, N.Y., 1937-66; retired, 1966. Home: 947 East Av Rochester NY 14607

KEARNEY, JOHN WALTER, sculptor, painter; b. Omaha, Aug. 31, 1924; s. John F. and Ruth (Masters) K.; student Cranbrook Acad. Art, 1946-48; m. Lynn Haigh, June 2, 1951; children—Daniel Raymond, Jill Ann. Sculptor, painter, 1946—; tchr., 1948—; co-founder, 1950, since co-dir. Contemporary Art Workshop Chgo.; one man shows in N.Y.C., 1964, 69, Rome, Italy, 1964, 68 Chgo., 1966, Ft. Wayne (Ind.) Mus., 1966, A.C.A. Gallery, 1964, 69, Galleria Schneider, Rome, Italy, 1969, Cedar Rapids, Ia., 1969; rep. permanent collections Chrysler Art Mus., Provincetown, Mass., Norfolk (Va.) Art Mus., Ft. Wayne Art Mus., St. Paul Mus., also pvt. collections; spl. sculpture in bronze and silver, also kinetic sculpture, steel bumpers sculpture. Served with USNR, World War II; PTO. Recipient prizes for sculpture and painting, 1952, 53, 60, 61, 64; named Man of Year in Arts in Chgo., 1963; Fulbright grantee, 1963-64; Italian Govt. grantee, 1963-64; grantee Nat. Found. Arts and Humanities, 1968. Mem. Provincetown Art Assn. Home: 747 W Montrose St Chicago IL 60613 Studio: 542 W Grant Pl Chicago IL 60614

KEARNEY, RICHARD DAVID, govt. ofcl.; b. Dayton, Ky., Jan. 3, 1914; s. David Richard and Mary (Manouge) K.; A.B., Xavier U., 1935; LL.B., U. Cin., 1938; m. Margaret Helen Murray, Nov. 22, 1944. Admitted to Ohio bar, 1938; asst. gen. counsel U.S. High Comr., Germany, 1949-50; dep. U.S. mem. Validation Bd. for German Dollar Bonds, 1953-56; asst. legal adviser European affairs State Dept., 1956-62, prin. dep. legal adviser, 1962- 1967, mem. with personal rank of ambassador UN Internat. Law Commn., 1967—, 1st v.p. commn., 1970. chmn., Sec. State's Adv. Com. Pvt. Internat. Law, 1964—, head U.S. delegation Conf. Uniform Internat. Sales Law, 1964, The Hague Conf. Pvt. Internat. Law, 1964-68, conf. on Enforcement Fgn. Judgements, 1966, UN Conf. on Law of Treaties, 1968- 69, Inter-Am. Conf. on Human Rights, 1969. Mem. governing council Internat. Inst. for Unification of Pvt. Law,, 1968—. Served to maj. AUS, 1942-46; ETO. Mem. Am. Soc. Internat. Law, Am. Acad. Polit. Sci., Am. Bar Assn., Fgn. Service Assn., Order of Coif. Democrat. Roman Catholic. Clubs: Landsdowne (London, Eng.); Lakewood Country (Rockwood, Md.). Home: 1409 4th St. S W Washington, DC 20024. Office: Dept of State Washington DC 20520

KEARNS, AMOS RAGAN, hosiery mfr.; b. High Point, N.C., July 22, 1905; s. Gurney Harriss and Katherine (Ragan) K.; A.B., Duke, 1927; m. Louise Copeland, Nov. 25, 1933; children—Amos Ragan, Jane (Mrs. James Marlowe). Sec.-treas., dir. Crown Hosiery Mills, Inc., High Point, 1927-62, pres., treas., 1962—; pres. Asso. Industries, Inc., 1946-48; v.p., treas. G.A.C. Corp., real estate, 1935-62, v.p., sec., 1962—; dir. High Point Bank & Trust Co., Tom Haggai & Assos. Chmn. finance com. High Point City Council, 1939-48, mayor, 1951-53; dir. Bd. Conservation and Devel. N.C., 1953-61, past chmn. state parks div.; mem. of Electoral Coll., 1949, del. Democratic Nat. Conv., 1956. Trustee Duke Endowment; bd. dirs., mem. exec. com. N.C. Citizens Assn.; past regional dir. Com. Econ. Devel.; past dir. Research Triangle Found., N.C.; trustee, mem. exec. com. Duke, chmn. bd. visitors Med. Center, 1963-67; mem. adv. council Maryfield Nursing Home; hon. trustee emeritus for life High Point Meml. Hosp.; mem. adv. bd. Westchester Acad.; trustee Angie B. Duke Meml. Mem. High Point C. of C. (past pres.), Duke Alumni Assn. (past pres.), Newcomen Soc., Alpha Tau Omega. Methodist (bd. stewards). Rotarian. Clubs: Emerywood Country (past pres.); Union League (N.Y.C.); String and Splinter (past pres.). Home: 600 Emerywood Dr High Point NC 27262 Office: 449 S Wrenn St High Point NC 27260

KEARNS, CARROLL D., ex-congressman, metalcraft co. exec., b. Youngstown, O., May 7, 1900; s. Patrick Henry and Ida May (Carroll) K.; Mus. B., Chgo. Mus. Coll., 1921, D.Mus., 1948; B.S., Westminster Coll., Pa., 1933; M.Ed., U. Pitts., 1938; m. Nora Lynch, Aug. 30, 1933. Asst. dir. spl. schs., Chgo., 1922-25; supr. music, Greenville, Pa., 1931-38; head dept. music Slippery Rock (Pa.) State Tchrs. Coll., 1938-41; supt. Farrell (Pa.) Schs., 1941-46; mem. 80th to 82d congresses 28th Pa. Dist., 83d-87th congresses 24th Pa. Dist.; dir., Shenengo Metalcraft Co. Recipient Farrell C. of C. award, 1946; Am. Legion Distinguished Service award, 1946; Benjamin Rush medal, 1950; 1st Alumni Achievement award Westminster Coll., 1955. Mem. Northwestern Pa. Sportsmen's Assn. (hon.), Phi Mu Alpha (life). Republican. Lutheran. Elk, Odd Fellow, K.P., Mason (Shriner). Clubs: Congressional Country (Washington); Iroquois, Conneaut Lake (Pa.). Home: (winter) Ocean Summit Fort Lauderdale FL 33308 (summer) Conneaut Lake PA 16316

KEARNS, CHARLES MAXWELL, Jr., mfr. aircraft accessories,; b. Beavertown, Pa., Mar. 20, 1915; s. Charles Maxwell and Margaret (McCormick) K.; B.S. in Elec. Engring., Pa. State Coll., 1936; m. Margaret Baker, Apr. 26, 1943; children—Elizabeth, Margaret, Deborah, Charles Maxwell III, Christopher. With Hamilton Standard div. United Aircraft Corp., 1936-61, asst. gen. mgr., 1957-58, gen. mgr. div. 1958-61, v.p. corp., 1960—, v.p. research, 1967—; div. pres. United Aircraft Corporate Systems Center, 1961-68. Trustee Julius Hartt Mus. Found., U. Hartford (Conn.). Recipient Lawrence Sperry award Inst. Aero. Scis., 1939; Longstreth medal Franklin Inst., 1942. Home: 648 Ridge Rd Wethersfield CT 06109 Office United Aircraft Research Labs Hartford CT 06103

KEARNS, DAVID RICHARD, educator; b. Urbana, Ill., Mar. 20, 1935; s. Clyde W. and Camille V. (French) K.; B.S. Chemistry, Cemistry, U. Ill., 1956; Ph.D., U. Cal. at Berkeley, 1960; m. Alice Chen, July 5, 1958; children—Jennifer, Michael. USAF U. postdoctoral fellow U. Chgo., 1960-61, Mass. Inst. Tech., 1961-62; asst. prof. chemistry U. Cal. at Riverside, 1962-63, asso. prof., 1964-67, prof., 1968—. Sloan Found. fellow, 1965-67; Guggenheim fellow, 1969-70. Mem. Am. Chem. Soc., Am. Phys. Soc. Asso. editor Molecular Photochemistry, 1969—, Photochemistry and Photobiology, 1971—. Home: 4187 Swain Ct Riverside CA 92507

KEARNS, FRANCIS EMNER, bishop; b. Bentleyville, Pa., Dec. 9, 1905; s. George Verlinda and Jennie Mae (McCleary) K.; A.B., Ohio Wesleyan U., 1927, D.D., 1954; S.T.B., Boston U. Sch. Theology, 1930; postgrad. U. Berlin (Germany), U. Edinburgh (Scotland), 1930-31; Ph.D., U. Pitts.; LL.D., Mt. Union Coll., 1965; L.H.D., Ohio No. U., 1965; Pd.D., Baldwin-Wallace Coll., 1966; m. Alice Margaret Thompson, Sept. 1, 1933; children—Rollin Thompson, Margaret (Mrs. Richard E. Baldwin), Francis Emner II. Ordained to ministry Meth. Ch., 1931; pastor, Dravosburg, Pa., 1931-32; asso. pastor Christ Meth. ch., Pitts., 1932-35, Ben Avon Meth. Ch., 1935-40, Asbury Meth. Ch., Uniontown, Pa., 1940-45, Wauwatosa (Wis.) Meth. Ch., 1945-64; bishop Meth. Ch., 1964—; dean Wis. Area Pastors' Sch., Appleton, 1948-60. Mem. gen. bd. edn., curriculum com. Meth. Ch., 1956-64, mem. gen. bd. evangelism, 1965-68, vice chmn. gen. bd. edn., 1968—, chmn. div. curriculum resources, 1968—, mem. program council, 1968—, mem. Meth. Corp., 1968—; mem. gen. assembly Nat. Council Chs.; pres. Ohio Council Chs., 1969—; chmn. faith and order dept. Wis. Council Chs., 1960-63; chmn. Meth. Interbd. Com. on Christian Vocations, 1964- 68; chmn. Faith and Order Commn., Ohio Council Chs., 1965-69; mem. Meth. Interbd. Commn. on Town and Country, 1964-68. Trustee Baldwin-Wallace Coll., Mt. Union Coll., Ohio No. U., Ohio Wesleyan U., Meth. Theol. Sch. in Ohio, Otterbein Coll., United Theol. Sem. Mem. Phi Beta Kappa. Mason (32), Rotarian. Author: The Church is Mine, 1962. Contbr. articles profl. jours. Home: 340 Lakecrest Dr NW Canton OH 44709 Office: 1226 N Market St Canton OH 44714

KEARNS, FREDERICK RONALD, aircraft mfg. co. exec.; b. Quyon, Que., Can., Mar. 11, 1924; s. Thomas and Inez (Whelan) K.; student St. Patrick's Coll., Ottawa U., 1945-46, McGill U., 1949; m. Elizabeth M. Black, July 3, 1948; children—Sandra, Michael, John, Stephen, Jane. Clk., Dept. Nat. Def., Ottawa, 1940-42; with Canadair Ltd., Montreal, 1949—, exec. v.p., 1960- 65, pres., chief exec. officer, 1965-70, pres., 1970—; dir. Asbestos Corp., Ltd., AIAC. Life gov. Douglas Hosp., Verdun, Quebec, Can., 1966—, Notre Dame Hosp., Montreal, 1960—; bd. govs. Loyola Coll., Montreal, 1964—. Served as fighter pilot Royal Canadian Air Force, 1942-45. Home: 5 Edgehill Rd Westmount Quebec Canada Office: PO Box 6087 Montreal Quebec Canada

KEARNS, HENRY, corp. exec., former govt. ofcl.; b. Salt Lake City, Apr. 30, 1911; s. Henry A. and Mary (Orilla) K.; student U. Utah Sch. Engring., 1929- 31; grad. Internat. Corr. Schs., 1935; D.Bus. Adminstrn. (hon.), Woodbury Coll., 1960; D.Econs. (hon.), Chung Aug U., Seoul, Korea, 1971; m. Marjorie Harriett Prescott, Aug. 30, 1938; children—Patricia (Mrs. Patricia Kearns Calubaugh), Henry Timothy, Michael and Mary (Mrs. David George Rohe) (twins). Salesman, Loesch & Osborne Motor Co., Pasadena, Cal., 1933- 34; service sta. salesman Shell Oil Co., 1934-35; new car salesman Uptown Chevrolet Co., Pasadena, 1935-37, new car sales mgr., 1937-38, gen. sales mgr., 1938-39; partner David H. Lane Chevrolet Co., Pasadena, 1939-41; organizer, v.p., gen. mgr. Victory Mfg. Co., Los Angeles, 1942-43, pres., gen. mgr., 1943—, established plastic devel. sect., 1943; asst. sec. internat. affairs Dept. Commerce, 1957-60, 60-69, now cons. internat. trade and finance; owner Kearns Car Rental, Orange Oaks Ranch; pres. San Gabriel Valley Motors, Rio Hondo Devel. Co., Policyholders Ins., Co., Sharder Water Co., Kearns Internat., Am. Capital Corp.; v.p., dir. Pike Corp. Am., 1966-67; pres., chmn. Export Import Bank U.S., 1969—; pres. Nat. Sci. Engring. Co., 1966-67; adviser to bd. dirs. Philippine Investment Mgmt. Inc., Manila, 1964-66. Mem. Nat. Adv. Com. on Internat. Monetary and Fiscal Policy. Vice pres., dir. C. of C. U.S.; pres. U.S. Jr. C. of C. 1945-46, Cal. Jr. C. of C., 1944, Pasadena Jr. C. of C., 1943-44; dir. Alhambra C. of C.; mem. nat. council cons. Small Bus. Adminstrn.; mem. spl. Pasadena War Meml. Com.; chmn. Pasadena Freedom Train Com.; exec. bd., com. for Young Men in Govt.; vice mem. Task Force Intelligence Activities, Hoover Commn., 1965-66. Republican central committeeman Los Angeles County; pres. Pasadena Rep. Club, Pasadena Rep. Assembly; chmn. Eisenhower-Nixon campaign So. Cal., 1956; mem. exec. com. Cal. Rep. Central Com.; chmn. Rep. Nat. Finance Com. Trustee Pasadena Boys Club, Hazel Hurst Found. Blind; bd. dirs. Pasadena Civic Music Assn. Recipient Distinguished Service award City of Pasadena, 1943; designated Outstanding Young Man of Cal., 1944; decorated knight grand cross Most Exalted Order of White Elephant (Thailand); grand officer de l'Ordre Nat. (Republic Ivory Coast). Fellow A.I.M.; mem. So. Cal. Sales Mgrs. Council (past pres.), Tournament Roses Assn. (pres. 1966-67), Nat. Indsl. Information Com. Mason (32). Clubs: Chevy Chase; Burning Tree; San Gabriel Country; Lotus (N.Y.C.). Home: 4903 Rockwood Pkwy NW Washington DC 20016 Office: 811 Vermont Av NW Washington DC 20571

KEARNS, JEROME BARTON, banker; b. Ft. Wayne, Ind., Apr. 28, 1939; s. Bernard T. and Dolores Ann (Krouse) K.; B.S. in Finance, U. Notre Dame, 1961; m. Judith L. Christie, Aug. 25, 1962; children—Margaret Christie, Sean Barton. Credit analyst to sr. credit analyst Nat. Bank Detroit, 1961-64; asst. v.p. comml. loans St. Joseph Bank & Trust Co., S. Bend, Ind., 1964-65, v.p., 1965-68, sr. v.p., 1968-70, exec. v.p., 1970—. Adv. council Ind. Small Bus. Adminstrn., 1969—. Div. chmn. United Way, 1971—. Mem. finance com. S. Bend Democratic Party, 1966—. Bd. dirs. Cath. Social Service, 1968—, pres., 1969—; bd. dirs. Citizens for Decent Lit., Model Neighborhood Planning Agy. Mem. No. Ind. Group Robert Morris Assos. (dir.), South Bend-Mishawaka Area C. of C., Ind. Assn. Credit Mgmt., Am., Ind. bankers' assns. Clubs: Notre Dame of St. Joe Valley (past pres., dir.), S. Bend Country, Indiana (S.Bend). Home: 1344 E Wayne St South Bend IN 46615 Office: 202 S Michigan St South Bend IN 46601

KEARNS, ROBERT JOHN, librarian, clergyman; b. Detroit, Aug. 9, 1919; s. Hugh Bernard and Evelyne Margaret (Mathers) K.; A.B., Loyola U., Chgo., 1944, M.A., 1946; Ph.L., West Baden (Ind.) Coll., 1947, S.T.L., 1953; Ph.D. in English, U. Mich., 1958. Joined Soc. of Jesus, 1939, ordained priest Roman Cath. Ch., 1952; asst. prof. English, U. Detroit, 1958-60, dir. libraries, 1960—, Jesuit superior, 1964-67. Mem. Am., Cath., Mich. Cath. library assns., Jesuit Library Conf., Modern Lang. Assn., Nat. Council Tchrs. English. Address: U Detroit Detroit MI 48221

KEARNS, WILLIAM HARLAND, advt. exec., b. Beatrice, Neb., Sept. 29, 1908; s. William Harris and Jennie May (Keever) K.; A.B., U. Neb., 1929, LL.D., 1968; m. Caroline Dodge, Oct. 25, 1930 (dec. Oct. 1957); m. 2d, Margaret A. Draper, Sept. 5, 1958. Partner, Buchanan-Thomas Advt. Co., Omaha, 1929-36; account exec. Blackett-Sample-Hummert, Inc., Chgo., 1936-39; v.p. H.W. Kastor & Sons, 1939-42; v.p. Ted Bates, Inc., N.Y.C., 1942-48, partner, 1948-55; pres. Ted Bates & Co., Inc., 1955-59, vice chmn. bd., chmn. exec. com., 1959-71, cons., 1971—; dir. Companion Life Ins. Co. Served to lt. USNR, 1943-45. Mem. Phi Delta Theta, Alpha Delta Sigma. Clubs: Stanwich Country; Princeton, University (N.Y.C.). Home: Cedar Cliff Rd Riverside CT 06878 Office: 666 Fifth Av New York City NY 10019

KEARNS, WILLIAM MICHAEL, ins. exec.; b. Gardiner, Me., May 1, 1899; s. Peter and Mary (Barron) K.; B.A., U. Me., 1923; LL.B., N.J. Law Sch., 1934; m. Doris Mae Hodgkinson, Aug. 19, 1933; children—William Michael, Joan. Br. mgr. Liberty Mut. Ins. Co., Newark, 1923-33, Am. Lumbermans Mut. Ins. Co., N.Y.C., 1934-35; asst. sec. Sun Indemnity Co. of N.Y., 1936, sec., 1938, v.p., dir., 1948, pres. 1950-55 (merged with Patriotic Ins. Co. Am., Sun Underwriters Ins. Co. N.Y.), pres. Sun Ins. Co. of N.Y., 1955-57, chmn. bd., 1957-64; U.S. gen. atty. Sun. Ins. Office Ltd., 1957-64; past financial sec., dir. Albany Ins. Co., Provident Ins. Co.; past financial sec. Atlas Assurance Co., Ltd., Royal Assurance Co., Ltd. Past mem. U.S. adv. com. Brit. Marine Trust Fund; past mem. exec. com. Nat. Bd. Fire Underwriters. Mem. Beta Theta Pi, Kappa Phi Kappa. Club: University. Home: 567 Prospect St Maplewood NJ 07040

KEARNS, WILLIAM MICHAEL, Jr., investment banker; b. Orange, N.J., June 26, 1935; s. William Michael and Doris Mae (Hodgkinson) K.; A.B., U. Me., 1957; student Boston Coll. Law Sch., 1957-58; A.M., N.Y. U., 1960, student Grad. Sch. Bus. Adminstrn., 1960-64; m. Patricia Anne Wright, Aug. 17, 1957; children—William Michael III, Susan Elizabeth, Kathleen Anne, Michael Patrick. With Chase Manhattan Bank, 1958-59; security analyst Hayden, Stone & Co., Inc., N.Y.C., 1960-62; asso. instl. sales and syndicate dept. Kuhn, Loeb & Co., N.Y.C., 1962-64, asst. v.p., 1964-66, v.p., 1966-68, sales mgr., 1968-70, gen. partner, 1970—; mem. faculty Fairleigh Dickinson U. Coll. Bus. Adminstrn., 1959-68; instr. security analysis N.Y. Inst. Finance, 1961-67; adj. prof. Grad. Sch. Bus. Adminstrn., N.Y.U., 1971—. Trustee Morris Mus. Arts and Sci. Served with USMCR, 1955-61. Mem. Investment Assn. N.Y. (v.p. 1970), Investment Bankers Assn. Am. (mem, exec. com. N.Y. group), New Eng. Soc., Beta Theta Pi, Kappa Phi Kappa. Clubs: Down Town Assn., University, Bond (N.Y.C.); Morris County Golf (Convent Station, N.J.). Home: Dellwood Dr Madison NJ 07940 Office: 40 Wall St New York City NY 10005

KEARTON, FRANK, industrialist; b. Feb. 17, 1911; s. Christoper John and Lillian (Hancock) K.; student St. John's Coll., Oxford U.; m. Agnes Kathleen Brander, 1936; 2 sons, 2 daus. With Imperial Chem. Industries, Billingham div., 1933; with Atomic Energy project U.K., also U.S., 1940- 45; part-time mem. U.K. Atomic Energy Authority, 1955—; charge chem. engring. Courtaulds, Ltd., 1946—, chmn., 1964—; chmn. Industrial Reorganization Corp., 1966—; formerly chmn. Brit.-Celanese, Ltd. Mem. Electricity Supply Research Council, 1954—, chmn., 1960—; mem. Dept. Sci. and Indsl. Research, 1955—; mem. Windscale Accident Com., 1957, Tropical Products Inst. Com., 1958—; mem. spl. adv. group Brit. Transp. Commn., 1960; mem. Adv. Com. Tech., 1964—, Nat. Econ. Devel. Council, 1965—. Decorated Order Brit. Empire; created life peer, 1970. Fellow Royal Soc. Address: The Old House Whitchurch nr Alesbury Buckshire England

KEAST, WILLIAM REA, educator; b. Malta, Ill., Nov. 1, 1914; s. Perce Marwood and Helen Gertrude (Dusher) K.; A.B., U. Chgo., 1936, Ph.D. (Rockefeller Postwar fellow in humanities), 1947; LL.D., U. Mich., 1967; m. Mary Alice Hart, Aug. 21, 1938; children—Sara Hart, Stephen Calhoun, Emily Wrightsman. Instr. English, U. Chgo., 1938-47, asst. prof., 1947-51; asso. prof. English, Cornell U., 1951-57, prof. English, chmn. dept., 1957-62, dean Coll. Arts and Scis., 1962-63, v.p. acad. affairs, 1963-65; pres. Wayne State U., Detroit, 1965- 71, chmn. commn. acad. tenure, 1971-72; vis. com. Mass. Inst. Tech., U. Chgo. Served from pvt. to maj., AUS, 1941-46. U. Chgo. fellow, 1936-38; faculty fellow Fund Advancement Edn., 1955-56; Guggenheim fellow, 1958-59. Mem. Modern Lang. Assn. Am.,

Johnsonians, Bibliog. Soc., Shakespeare Assn. Am., Am. Council Edn. (commn. on acad. affairs), Mich. Acad. Sci., Arts and Letters (pres. 1969-70), Phi Beta Kappa, Phi Kappa Phi. Clubs: Cosmos (Washington); Grolier (N.Y.C.). Author: (with R.R. Palmer and B.I. Wiley) Procurement and Training of Ground Combat Troops, 1948; (with others) Critics and Criticism, 1952; (with R.E. Streeter) The Province of Prose, 2d edit., 1959; Seventeenth-Century English Poetry, 2d edit., 1971. Contbr. articles profl. jours., revs. Home: 6140 Midnight Pass Rd Sarasota FL 33581

KEAT, JAMES SUSSMAN, journalist; b. N.Y.C., Dec. 25, 1929; s. Harold Edward and Ida (Sussman) K.; B.A., Brown U., 1951; M.S., Columbia, 1952; postgrad. Harvard, 1953- 54, U. Pa., 1954; m. Betty Yurina, Dec. 24, 1955. Reporter financial news N.Y. Herald Tribune, 1952-53; Ford Found. fellow India Studies, 1953-56; reporter, fgn. corr., editorial writer Balt. Sun, 1956-67, editor Perspective sect., 1968-69, foreign editor, 1969—. Pulitzer fellow Columbia University, N.Y.C., 1952, Ford Foundation fellow, 1953. Mem. Nat. Press Club Washington. Home: 326 Taplow Rd Baltimore MD 21212

KEATHLEY, GEORGE EDWARD, theatre dir.; b. Key West, Fla., June 27, 1925; s. James H. and Angelita (Martinez) K.; B.A., New Sch. Social Research, 1949. Theatrical dir. Studio M, Miami, Fla.; artistic dir. Playhouse in the Park, Phila., 1959-64; now dir. Ivahoe Theater, Chgo. Served to 1st lt., AUS, 1943-46. Recipient Joseph Jefferson award as best dir., 1969, award of merit for distinguished service to performing arts, Cliff Dwellers, 1970; recipient Presdl. invitation to direct The Glass Menagerie at 1st annual White House Festival of Arts. Director: Sweet Bird of Youth (Tennessee Williams); The Square Root of Wonderful (Carson McCullars); The Glass Menagerie; The Immoralist; Rooms; The Golden Screw; A View from the Bridge (Arthur Miller). Home: 2800 Lake Shore Dr Chicago IL 60657 Office: 3000 N Clark St Chicago IL 60657

KEATING, JAMES W., educator; b. Wilkes Barre, Pa., Feb. 23, 1924; s. Paul T. and Ella M. (Tigue) K.; B.S., Dickinson Coll.; M.A., Cath. U., 1951, Ph.D., 1953; m. Ann K. Rodden, July 24, 1954; children—Carol Ellen, Paula Marie, Michelle Therese, Patrick James, Marianne. Asst. prof. Lewis Coll., 1953- 56, dean coll., 1956-60; asso. prof. De Paul U., 1961-64, prof., 1964-70; spl. research philosophy of athletics, sport, amateurism. Mem. Mayor Chgo. Cultural and Econ Com. Served with USAAF, 1943-46. Mem. Am. Philos. Assn., Am. Sociol. Assn., Am. Psychol. Assn., Am. Assn. Health, Phys. Edn. and Recreation. Author numerous articles in field. Home: 106 Reyton St Chicago Heights IL 60411 Office: 2322 Kenmore Av Chicago IL 60614

KEATING, KENNETH B., ambassador; b. Lima, N.Y., May 18, 1900; s. Thomas Mosgrove and Louise (Barnard) K.; student Genesee Wesleyan Sem., 1911-15, A.B., U. Rochester, 1919, LL.D., 1954; LL.B., Harvard, 1923; m. Louise Depuy, Apr. 11, 1928 (dec.); 1 dau., Judith. Law practice, Rochester, N.Y., 1923-48; mem. firm Harris, Beach, Keating, Wilcox, Dale & Linowitz; mem. 80th-82d congresses 40th N.Y. Dist.; 83d-85th congresses 38th N.Y. Dist.; U.S. senator from N.Y., 1958-65; asso. justice N.Y. Ct. Appeals, 1966-69; ambassador to India, 1969—. Mem. Congl. delegation Council of Europe, Interparliamentary Union, Washington, 1953, Vienna, 1954, Helsinki, 1955, Bangkok, 1956, London, 1957; del. intergovtl. com. European Migration Confs., 1956, 57. Served with U.S. Army World War I; from maj. to brig. gen., AUS, World War II. Decorated Legion of Merit with oak leaf cluster, Order of Brit. Empire. Mem. Am. Legion, V.F.W., Res. Officers Assn., Am., N.Y. State, Rochester bar assns., U. Rochester Alumni, S.A.R., Empire State Soc., Phi Beta Kappa, Delta Upsilon. Republican. Presbyn. Mason (33, Shriner), Moose, Eagle, Elk. Clubs: Brook, Sky (N.Y.C.); University (Rochester); F Street (Washington). Office: 2 State St Rochester NY 14614

KEATING, LOUIS CLARK, educator; b. Phila., Aug. 20, 1907; s. Louis Alcloma and Blanche Augusta (DeYoung) K.; A.B., Colgate U., 1928; A.M., Harvard, 1930, Ph.D., 1934; postgrad. Sorbonne, 1932-33, Middlebury Spanish Sch., summers 1928, 29, Heidelberg U., summer 1931, Centro de Esudios Historicos, summer 1933; m. Lucille Elizabeth Tate, July 23, 1936; children—Richard Clark, Geoffrey Tate, Anne Elizabeth. Saltonstall travelling scholar Harvard, 1932-33; instr. Romance langs. Colgate U., 1928-29; asst. prof. Spanish, Macalester Coll., 1934-36; asst. prof. Romance langs. Monticello Coll., 1936-37; asso. Romance langs. U. Ill., 1937-39; asst. prof. Romance langs. George Washington U., 1939-40, asso. prof., 1940-46, prof., exec. officer dept. Romance langs., 1946-57; vis. prof. U. Tenn., summer 1947; resident dean U. Md. Grad. Fgn. Study Center, Paris, 1949-50; head dept. Romance langs. U. Cin., 1957-60; edn. adviser USOM, Peru, 1960-62; prof. Romance langs. U. Ky., Lexington, 1962—, chmn. dept. modern fgn. langs., 1963-66; vis. prof. U. Calgary, Alta., Can., 1969-70. Mem. Arlington County (Va.) Sch. Bd., 1953-57, chmn. bd., 1956-57. Served from 1st lt. to capt., Signal Corps, AUS, 1943-46. Decorated officier d'Academie (France). Mem. Am. Assn. U. Profs. (past pres. George Washington U. chpt.), Modern Lang. Assn., Am. Assn. Tchrs. Spanish and Portuguese, Am. Assn. Tchrs. French (past pres. Minn. chpt., D.C. chpt., Ky. chpt.), Fed. Schoolmens Club, Phi Beta Kappa. Presbyn. Author: Studies on the Literary Salon in France, 1550- 1615, 1941; Critic of Civilization, Georges Duhamel, 1965; Andre Maurois, 1969; Du Bellay, 1971; articles, revs. in lang. jours. Translator, editor. Home: 608 Raintree Rd Lexington KY

KEATING, STEPHEN FLAHERTY, corp. exec.; b. Graceville, Minn., May 6, 1918; s. Luke J. and Blanche (Flaherty) K.; B.S., U. Minn., 1940, LL.B., 1942; m. Mary E. Davis, Dec. 14, 1945; children—Stephen, Elizabeth, Thomas, Mary. Admitted to Minn. bar, 1942; spl. agt. FBI, Norfolk, Va., Detroit, 1942-43; asso. Otis, Faricy & Burger, St. Paul, 1946-48; mgr. mil. contracts, aero div. Mpls. Honeywell Regulator Co., 1948-54, divisional v.p., 1954-56, v.p., 1956-61, exec. v.p., 1961-65; pres., dir. Honeywell Inc., 1965—; dir. 1st Bank System, Inc., Gen. Mills, Inc., Toro Mfg. Corp., Dayton Hudson Corp. Trustee Mayo Found. Served as air combat intelligence officer USNR, 1943- 46. Mem. Order of Coif. Clubs: Minneapolis, Woodhill. Home: 688 Hillside Dr Wayzata MN 55391 Office: 2701 4th Av S Minneapolis MN 55408

KEATING, WILLIAM CLEVELAND, Jr., state ofcl.; b. Sacramento, May 17, 1920; s. William Cleveland and Vern (Francis) K.; student U. Cal. at Berkeley, 1938-39; B.S., St. Mary's Coll., Moraga, 1942; M.D., Tulane U., 1947; certificate Menninger Found. Sch. Psychiat. Hosp. Adminstrn., 1957; m. Verna E. Carlson, May 17, 1942; children—Karen, William Cleveland III, Robert L. Intern, resident surgeon Sacramento County Hosp., 1947-49; practice medicine specializing in psychiatry, Sonoma, Cal., 1949-60, Vacaville, Cal., 1960—; ward physician, dir. outpatient and preadmission dept. Sonoma State Hosp., 1949-56, acting asst. supt., asst. supt., 1957-60; supt. Cal. Med. Facility, 1960-66; asst. dep. dir. Cal. Dept. Mental Hygiene, 1966—. Served with AUS, 1942-44, to capt. M.C., 1952-54. Mem. Am. Assn. Mental Deficiency, Am. Acad. Med. Adminstrs., Am. Psychiat. Assn. Home: 1426 Carrousel Lane Sacramento CA 95822 Office: 744 P St Sacramento CA 95814

KEATING, WILLIAM HOWARD, govt. ofcl.; b. Trenton, Mo., Sept. 15, 1916; s. George M. and Pearl (Ormsby) K.; B.S. in Elec. Engring., U. Mo., 1949; m. Margaret H. Hickman, May 11, 1943; 1 dau., Elaine Ann. Elec. engr. U.S. Bur. Reclamation, Casper, Wyo., 1949-57, Denver, 1957-61, Sacramento, 1961-64, supr. of power, Washington, 1964-70, asst. commr., Washington, 1970—. Served to 1st lt., arty., AUS, 1940-46. Mason, Elk. Mem. Christian Ch. Home: 6115 Thomas Dr Springfield VA 22150 Office: Interior Bldg 19th and C Sts Washington DC 20240

KEATING, WILLIAM JOHN, congressman; b. Cin., Mar. 30, 1927; s. Charles H. and Adele (Kipp) K.; B.B.A., U. Cin., 1950, J.D., 1950; m. Nancy Nenninger, Sept. 22, 1951; children—Nancy C., Willaim J., Michael K., Daniel N., Susan M., Thomas J., John S. Admitted to Ohio bar, 1950; asst. aty. gen. Ohio, 1957-58; judge Cin. Municipal Ct., 1958-65, presiding judge, 1962-63; judge Ct. Common Pleas, Hamilton County, O., 1965-67; mem. Cin. City Council, 1967-70, majority leader. chmn. finance com.; mem. 92d Congress Dist. Ohio. Bd. dirs. Friars Club, Nat. Multiple Sclerosis Assn., Nat. Found., Cin. Pepsi Marlins, Cin. Big Bros., K.C. Served wtih USNR, World War II. Mem. Am. Legion. Republican Club: Mt. Lookout Civic (Cin.). Home: 2959 Alpine Terrace Cincinnati OH 45208 Office: Longworth House Office Bldg Washington DC 20515

KEATLEY, ROBERT LELAND, journalist; b. Astoria, Ore., Feb. 14, 1935; s. R. L. and Eva S. (Porsky) K.; B.A., U. Wash., 1956; M.A., Stanford, 1959; married Anne Greene. Mem. staff Wall St. Jour., 1959—, Asian bur. chief, Hong Kong, 1964-68, diplomatic corr., Washington, 1968—. Served as officer USNR, 1956-58. Clubs: Nat. Press (Washington); Foreign Correspondents, Royal Jockey (Hong Kong). Address: 139 North Carolina Av SE Washington DC

KEATS, DONALD HOWARD, composer, educator; b. N.Y.C., May 27, 1929; s. Bernard and Lillian (Katz) K.; Mus.B., Yale, 1949; M.A., Columbia, 1951; Ph.D., U. Minn., 1962; Fulbright scholar Staatliche Hochshcule fur Musik, Hamburg, Germany, 1954-56; m. Eleanor Steinholz, Dec. 13, 1953; children-Jeremy, Jennifer, Jeffrey, Jocelyn. Teaching fellow Yale U. Sch. Music, 1948-49; instr. music theory U.S. Naval Sch. Music, Washington, 1953-54; post music dir. Ft. Dix, N.J., 1956-57; faculty Antioch Coll., Yellow Springs, O., 1957—, prof., 1967—, chmn. music dept. 1967—; Guggenheim fellow, Europe, 1964-65; vis. prof. music U. Wash. Sch. Music, 1969-70. Served with U.S. Army, 1952-54. Recipient A.S.C.A.P. awards, 1964—; awards from Ford, Danforth and Lilly founds., Nat. Endowment for Arts; winner Rockefeller Found. Symphonic Competitions, 1965, 66. Mem. A.S.C.A.P., Coll. Music Center Composer: Divertimento For Winds and Strings, 1949., The Naming of Cats, 1951; The Hollow Men, 1952; String Quartet 1952; Concert Piece for Orchestra, 1952; Variations for Piano, 1955; Symphony 1957; Piano Sonata, 1961; An Elegiac Symphony, 1962; Anyone Lived in a Pretty How Town, 1965; (Ballet) New Work, 1966; Polarities for Violin and Piano, 1968-70; String Quartet 1969; A Love Triptych, 1970. Home: Meredith Rd Yellow Springs OH 45387

KEATS, EZRA JACK, illustrator, author; b. Bklyn., Mar. 11, 1916; s. Benjamin and Augusta (Podgainy) K.; ed. pub. schs. Tchr. Famous Artists Sch., Westport, Conn., 1955-58, Workshop Sch., N.Y.C., 1955-57, Sch. Visual Arts, N.Y.C., 1947-48; exhibited Asso. Am. Artists Gallery, N.Y.C., 1950- 54; mag., advt. illustrator, 1947—. Pres. Ezra Jack Keats Found. Mem. P.E.N., Author's Guild, Soc. Illustrators. Author, illustrator: The Snowy Day (Newbery-Caldecott medal 1963), 1962; Whistle For Willie; Peters Chair; John Henry; A Letter to Amy; Jennie's Hat; Goggles, 1970; Hi, Cat! (Boston Globe-Horn book award 1970); Apt. 3. Editor, illustrator: God Is In The Mountain; illustrator Christcard series UNICEF, 1966, The King's Fountain. Editor: Night. Address: 444 E 82d St New York City NY 10028

KEATS, HAROLD ALAN, corp. exec.; b. Bridgeport, Conn., Oct. 25, 1913; s. Abraham and Jeannette (Boges) C.; student University Sch., Bridgeport, Conn., 1928- 31, Washington U., 1932-33; m. Charleen Turner, Dec. 19, 1953; children—Candace, Harold Alan. Owner, Harold A. Keats Constrn. Co., Fort Lauderdale, 1936, Keats S.S. & Tourist Agy.; pres. Indian Citrus Groves, Inc., Fla. Sunshine Groves, Inc., Harold A. Keats Investment Co., Inc., Englewood Mailing Lists, Inc.; partner Keats, Allen & Keats; pres. Rocking K Ranch Inc. Nat. vice comdr. Amvets, 1947, nat. comdr., 1948-49. Liaison officer to White House, 1949—; counselor Amvets Nat. Service Found., 1949—, U.S. commr. Am. Battle Monuments Commn., 1950-53. Past nat. chmn. Vets. Democratic com.; dir. vets. div. Nat. Dem. Com. Served with USNR, 1942-45, 51; commd. lt., intelligence Pub. Information, 1949; Mem. Mil. Order World Wars, Past Nat. Comdrs. Orgn. (nat. chmn.), Am. Yachtsmen's Assn. (nat. pres.), Knights Round Table Assn. (pres.). Mason (32, Shriner). Club: African Safari of Fla. (sec.-treas.). Home: 3608 NE 25th Terrace Ft Lauderdale FL 33308 Office: 3034 E Commercial Blvd Fort Lauderdale FL 33308

KEATS, THEODORE ELIOT, educator, physician; b. New Brunswick, N.J., June 26, 1924; B.S., Rutgers U., 1945; M.D., U. Pa., 1947; m. Margaret E. McNamara, Aug. 27, 1959; children—Matthew Mason, Ian Stuart B. Intern U. Pa. Hosp., Phila., 1947-48; resident U. Mich. Hosp., Ann Arbor, 1948-51; instr. U. Cal. Sch. Medicine, San Francisco, 1953-54, asst. prof., 1954-56; asso. prof. U. Mo. Sch. Medicine, Columbia, 1956-59, prof. radiology, 1959-63; prof., chmn. dept. radiology U. Va. Sch. Medicine, Charlottesville, 1963- -; vis. prof. Karolinska Hosp., Stockholm, Sweden, 1963-64. Mem. Com. on Radiology Nat. Acad. Scis.-NRC; mem. adv. council Greenbrier Clinic. Served with AUS, 1943-47; to capt., M.C., AUS, 1951- 53. Fellow Am. Coll. Radiology; mem. A.M.A., Am. Roentgen Ray Soc., Radiol. Soc. N. Am. (counselor for Va.), Soc. Chmn. Acad. Radiology Depts., Assn. U. Radiologists, Soc. Pediatric Radiology, So. Med. Assn., Phi Beta Kappa, Sigma Xi, Alpha Omega Alpha. Author: (with Lee B. Lusted) Atlas of Roentgenographic Measurement, 2d edit., 1967. Home: 1102 Rugby Rd Charlottesville VA 22903

KEAVY, HUBBARD, newspaper editor; b. Mpls., Dec. 24, 1902; s. Timothy and Katherine (Dolan) K.; student Columbus Coll., Sioux Falls, S.D., 1921-23; m. Harriett McGraw, Nov. 21, 1928; children—John Timothy, Michael Hubbard. Various positions with newspapers, S.D., Des Moines, Milw. and Toledo; mng. editor Bloomington (Ill.) Pantagraph, 1927; with A.P., Chgo., 1928, Hollywood, 1929-68, writer movie column to 1939, news staff, 1939-42, chief bur., 1942-67, exec. rep., Cal.-Nevada, 1967-68; exec. editor South Coast News-Post, Laguna Beach, Cal., 1968-71; founder, writer syndicated column Good News From Everywhere, 1970—; condr. better writing campaign for A.P. 1958, 59. Mem. Cath. Press Council So. Cal. (founder, pres. 1951). Author: (with Howard Heyn) Writing for the AP, 1960. Home: 23406 Via Jacinto Laguna Hills CA 92653

KEAY, JAMES WILLIAM, banker; b. Manley, Ia., Nov. 16, 1921; s. William J. and Valborg (Biorn) K.; B.A. in Econs., U. Colo., 1947; M.B.A., Northwestern U., 1948; grad. Rutgers U. Grad. Sch. Banking, 1956, Harvard Advanced Mgmt. Program, 1964; m. Frances Lee Oglesby, Mar. 20, 1954; children—Martha Evelyn, James William, Stuart Enslie. With Republic Nat. Bank, Dallas, 1949—, asst. cashier, 1953, asst. v.p., 1953-56, v.p., 1956-61, sr. v.p., 1961- 63, mem. exec. com., 1962—, exec. v.p. loans, 1963-65, exec. v.p. adminstrn., 1965, pres., dir., 1965—, also dir.; dir. United Fidelity Life Ins. Co., Howard Corp., Dallas Power & Light Co., Gen. Automotive Parts Corp. Bd. dirs. State Fair of Dallas, Dallas Assembly, Dallas County United Fund. Served with AUS, World War II; ETO, MTO. Mem. Pi Gamma Mu. Lutheran (elder). Clubs: Idlewild, Brook Hollow Golf, City, Dallas, Terpsichorean, Preston Trail Golf, Petroleum (Dallas). Home: 3920 Gillon St Dallas TX 75205 Office: Pacific at Ervay St Dallas TX 75222

KEAY, RONALD WILLIAM JOHN, scientist; b. Richmond, Eng., May 20, 1920; s. Harold John and Marion (Flick) K.; M.A., B.Sc., St. John's Coll., Oxford (Eng.) U., 1946, B.Sc., 1949, D.Phil., 1963; m. Joan Mary Walden, Aug. 18, 1944; children—Alison (Mrs. Alan Eldridge), Hilary, Martin. With Nigerian Forest Service, 1942-62, assigned Kew Gardens, 1951-57, dir. forest research, 1960-62; dep. exec. sec. Royal Soc., 1962—. Mem. spl. com. Internat. Biol. Programme, 1964—, Spl. Com. on Problems Environment, 1971—. Decorated officer Order Brit. Empire. Fellow Inst. Biology, Linnean Soc. (v.p. 1965-68); mem. Brit. Ecol. Soc. (council), Sci. Assn. Nigeria (pres. 1961-62, 71—). Author numerous papers in field. Home: Little Hill Claremont Lane Esher Surrey England Office: 6 Carlton House Terrace London SW1 England

KEBKER, VANT WILMOT, educator; b. Grayslake, Ill., July 12, 1909; s. Henry and Maude (Wilmot) K.; B.A. cum laude, U. Minn., 1931, M.A., 1933, Ph.D., 1940; m. Dorothy Ford, Dec. 24, 1938; children—Ruth Estelle, Ann Erlynne, David Ford. Instr. econs. N.D. Agrl. Coll., 1934-36, U. Minn., 1936-38; instr. econs. and marketing U. Kan., 1938-42; asso. economist WPB, 1942-43; market analyst War Food Adminstrn., 1943; asso. prof. econs. and bus. adminstrn. Ohio Wesleyan U., Delaware, 1946-53, White Found. prof. econs. and bus. adminstrn., 1953—. Cons. marketing and statistics; fellow Coll.- Bus. Exchange Program, 1952. Served from lt. (j.g.) to lt. USNR, 1944-46; comdr. Res. Mem. Am., Midwest econ. assns., Am. Marketing Assn., Tri-State Tchrs. Marketing, Ohio Assn. Economists and Polit. Scientists (v.p. 1954-55, pres. 1955-56). Methodist. Kiwanian. Author: (with Kercher, Leland) Consumers' Cooperatives in the North Central States, 1940. Contbr. articles to Jour. Marketing. Home: 267 N Washington St Delaware OH 43015

KECK, GEORGE E., former airlines co. exec.; b. Chgo., Feb. 26, 1912; s. Edwin L. and Anna (Sass) K.; B.S., U. Ill., 1932; m. Harriet E. Clausen, June 20, 1936; children—Leslie Ann (Mrs. John Herzog), Georgia (Mrs. E.S. Witherspoon). Employed with the Owens-Illinois Can Co., 1938-42, acting plant mgr., Chgo., 1941-42; with United Air Lines, 1946-53, 54-71, v.p. base maintenance, 1959-61, exec. v.p. operations, 1961-63, pres., 1963-71, also dir.; dir. Continental Ill. Nat. Bank & Trust Co., Sears, Roebuck & Co., Internat. Harvester Co.; cons. engr. A.T. Kearney Co., Chgo., 1953. Mem. Bus. Council. Mem. exec. bd. Chgo. Area council Boy Scouts-Am. Dir. Mid-Am. chpt. Am. Nat. Red Cross. Served to capt. C.E., AUS, 1942-46. Mem. Am. Inst. Aero. and Astronautics, Chgo. Assn. Commerce and Industry (dir.). Clubs: Mid-America, Glen View, Commercial, Chicago, Economic (Chgo.); International (Washington); Wings, Sky (N.Y.C.). Home: 177 N Dewey Rd Palatine IL 60067

KECK, HAROLDSON ALEXANDERmfg. exec.; b. Lima, O., Apr. 1, 1932; B.S., U. San Francisco, 1954; M.S., Stanford University, 1956; m. Rosemarie Lois Brown, May 15, 1955; 1 son, Anthony Robinson. Sales rep. Ames-Brockton Fabricated Products, Akron, O., 1956-58, sales mgr. Coshocton, Ohio, 1959-61, gen. manager plant, 1961-68, v.p. sales, 1968--. Instr. bus. Coshocton Jr. College, 1968-69. Named Man of Year, Coshocton Junior Chamber of Commerce, 1968. Mem. Coshocton C. of C. (vice president 1967-68, pres. 1969-70), English Speaking Union, Coshocton Sertoma Club, Nat. Assn. Mfrs., Sales Executives Institute, Phi Beta Kappa, Sigma Chi, Phi Mu. Democrat. Mem. Christian Ch. (lay leader). Mason (32, Shriner). Clubs: Coshocton Country, Coshocton City, Running Deer Country. Home: 2d Av Coshocton OH Office: 3d Av Coshocton OH

KECK, JAMES COLLYER, physicist, educator; b. N.Y.C., June 11, 1924; s. Charles and Anne (Collyer) K.; B.A., Cornell U., 1947, Ph.D., 1951; m. Margaret Ramsey, Sept. 6, 1947; children—Robert Lyon, Patricia Anne. Research asst. Cornell U., 1951-52; sr. research fellow Cal. Inst. Tech., 1952-55; prin. scientist Avco-Everett Research Lab., Everett, Mass., 1955-65, dep. dir., 1960-64; Ford prof. engring. Mass. Inst. Tech., Cambridge, 1965—. Served with AUS, 1944-46. Mem. Am. Phys. Soc., Phi Beta Kappa, Sigma Xi, Phi Kappa Phi. Research high energy photonuclear reactions, theory of chem. reaction rates, high temperature gas dynamics. Office: Mass Inst Tech Cambridge MA 02139

KECK, JAMES MOULTON, air force officer; b. Scranton, Pa., Sept. 4, 1921; s. Richter L. and Helen (Walker) K.; student Brown U., 1940; B.S., U.S. Mil. Acad., 1943; postgrad. Naval War Coll., 1951-52, Nat. War Coll., 1959-60; m. Barbara Brown Fleck, June 2, 1943; children—Bonnilyn (Mrs. Richard E. Gardner), Thomas J., Allison (Mrs. Richard E. Pickens). Commd. 2d lt. USAAF, 1943, advanced through grades to maj. gen. USAF, 1970; staff officer Office Sec. Def., 1958-60; wing and div. comdr. SAC, 1960-69; dir. plans Hdqrs. USAF, Washington, 1970—. Decorated Legion Merit with oak leaf cluster, D.F.C. with oak leaf cluster, Air medal with 3 oak leaf clusters. Mem. Order Dadaelians. Home: 7372 Montcalm Dr McLean VA 22101 Office: Hdqrs USAF XOX The Pentagon Washington DC 20330

KECK, RICHARD MCCUTCHEN lawyer; b. Boston, Dec. 10, 1906; s. Herbert Allen and Harriett (McCutchen) K.; A.B., U. Ill., 1928, LL.B., 1930; m. Leonora Barr Welborn, Feb. 6, 1932. Admitted to Ill. bar, 1930, since practiced in Chgo.; partner firm Chadwell, Keck, Kayser, Ruggles & McLaren, 1940—. Served to maj., ordnance dept., AUS, 1942-45. Mem. Am., Ill., Chgo. bar assns., Order of Coif, Phi Gamma Delta, Phi Delta Phi. Clubs: Law, University, Mid-Day, Economic (Chgo.); Westmoreland Country (Wilmette, Ill.). Home: 211 Abingdon Av Kenilworth IL 60043 Office: 135 S LaSalle St Chicago IL 60603

KECK, ROBERT CLIFTON, lawyer; b. Sioux City, Ia., May 20, 1914; s. Herbert Allen and Harriet (McCutchen) K.; A.B., Ind. U., 1936; J.D., U. Mich., 1939; m. Ruth P. Edwards, Nov. 2, 1940; children—Robert, Laura E. Simpson, Gloria E. Admitted to Ill. bar. 1939, since practiced in Chgo., mem. firm Price, Cushman, Keck & Mahin, 1939—, partner, 1946—. Dir. Am. Hosp. Supply Corp.; sec., dir. Methode Electronics, Inc.; dir. Signode Corporation, Rustoleüm Corp., Union Spl. Machine Corp., First Nat. Bank & Trust Co., Evanston. Pres. bd. trustees Nat. Coll. Edn., 1955—. Served with USNR, 1943- 45. Fellow Am. Coll. Trial Lawyers; mem. Am., Fed., Ill., Chgo. assns., Bar Assn. Seventh Fed. Circuit (bd. govs.), Phi Gamma Delta. Republican. Methodist. Mason. Clubs: Westmoreland Country (Wilmette); Executives (dir.), Chicago, Mid-Day, Union League (Chgo.); Biltmore Forest Golf (Asheville, N.C.); Glen View (Golf, Ill.). Contbr. legal jours. Home: 1043 Seneca Rd Wilmette IL 60091 Office: 134 S LaSalle St Chicago IL 60603

KECK, SHELDON WAUGH, art conservator; b. Utica, N.Y., May 30, 1910; s. Fred Rutherford and Myra Edna (Waugh) K.; A.B., Harvard, 1932; m. Caroline Martin Kohn, Oct. 31, 1933; children—Albert C., Lawrence W. Apprentice art restoration Fogg Mus., Cambridge, Mass., 1932-33; conservator Bklyn. Mus., 1934-61; dir. conservation center Inst. Fine Arts, N.Y.U., 1961-65; prof. fine arts N.Y.U., 1964-66, adj. prof., 1966-69; prof. conservation historic and artistic works Cooperstown Grad. Programs, State U. Coll. at Oneonta and N.Y. State Hist. Assn., 1969—; cons. conservator pvt. practice Mus. Modern Art, Guggenheim Mus., N.Y. State Hist. Assn., Newark Mus., Colonial Williamsburg, others, 1934-61. Mem. governing com. Bklyn. Mus.; visual arts adv. panel N.Y. State Council Arts. Served to 2d lt. AUS, 1943-46. Fulbright fellow, fall 1959; Guggenheim fellow, 1959-60. Fellow Internat. Inst. Conservation Historic and Artistic Works; mem. Internat. Council Museums (com. conservation), Cooperstown (N.Y.) Art Assn. (dir.). Clubs: Century Assn. (N.Y.C.); Rembrandt, (Bklyn.). Contbr. articles profl. jours. Home: Byberry Cottage River St Cooperstown NY 13326

KECK, WILLIAM, architect; b. Watertown, Wis., Dec. 1, 1908; s. Fred George and Amalie (Henze) K.; student Northwestern U., 1926-27; B.S., U. Ill., 1931; m. Stella M. McLeish, Oct. 23, 1937; 1 dau., Margaret M. Draftsman, specifications writer, Chgo., 1931-42; site planner, specifications writer U.S. C.E., Chgo., 1942-43; partner George Fred Keck & William Keck, architects, Chgo., 1946—. Cons. regional office Housing and Urban Devel.; dir. Hyde Park-Kenwood Community Conf., Chgo., 1953-55, mem. planning com., 1952—; Mem. planning com. Housing Code Modernization Met. Housing and Planning Council. Served to lt. USNR, 1943-46. Fellow A.I.A.; mem. Alpha Rho Chi. Prin. works include; Kunstadter House, Highland Park, Ill., 1953, Prairie Cts. Housing Project, Chgo., Blair House, Lake Bluff, Ill., 1958, Hirsch House, Highland Park, Ill., 1963, Child Care Center, Chgo., Kenwood Park Housing project, Chgo., 1970. Home: 5551 University Av Chicago IL 60637 Office: 612 N Michigan Av Chicago IL 60611

KECK, WINFIELD, educator; b. Clifton Heights, Pa. Sept. 15, 1917; s. Charles Winfield and Orpha (McNeil) K.; B.A., Amherst Coll., 1937; M.A., U. Pa., 1938; Ph.D., Brown U., 1949; m. Margaret Ann Yuza, Sept. 23, 1944; children—Peter, Lindsey, Jonathan, Timothy. Instr., Franklin and Marshall Coll., 1939-40, Muhlenberg Coll., 1941-46, Brown U., 1946-48; faculty Lafayette Coll., 1949—, prof. physics, 1961—, chmn. dept., 1960—. Mem. Am. Assn. Physics Tchrs., Math. Assn. Am., Am. Assn. U. Profs., A.A.A.S., Sigma Xi. Home: PO Box 155 Martins Creek PA 18063 Office: Lafayette Coll Easton PA 18042

KEDAH, SULTAN OF (Abdul Halim Mu'azzam Shah ibni Almarham Sultan Badlishah), ruler Malaysian state of Kedah; b. Nov. 28, 1927. Succeeded as Kedah state ruler, Malaysia, 1958; King of Malaysia, 1970—. Address: Alor Star Kedah Malaysia*

KEDROVA, LILA, recipient Acad. Award for best supporting actress in Zorba the Greek, 1964. Address: care Twentieth Century Fox Film Corp New York City NY 10019 *

KEE, HOWARD CLARK, educator; b. Beverly, N.J., July 28, 1920; s. Walter Leslie and Regina (Corcoran) K.; A.B., Bryan (Tenn.) Coll., 1940; Th.M., Dallas Theol. Sem., 1944; postgrad. Am. Sch. Oriental Research, Jerusalem, 1949-50; Ph.D., Yale, 1951; m. Janet Burrell, Dec. 15, 1951; children—Howard Clark III, Christopher Andrew, Sarah Leslie. Instr. religion and classics U. Pa., 1951-53; from asst. prof. to prof. N.T., Drew U., 1953- 68; Rufus Jones prof. history, chmn. dept. religion Bryn Mawr (Pa.) Coll., 1968—; vis. prof. religion Princeton, 1954-55; mem. archaeol. teams at Roman Jericho, 1950, Shechem, 1957, Mt. Gerizim, 1966, Pella, Jordan, 1967, Ashdod, Israel, 1968. Bd. mgrs. Am. Bible Soc., 1956, chmn. translations com., 1970—. Mem. Montgomery County (Pa.) Democratic Com., 1970—; Two Brothers fellow Yale, 1949; fellow Am. Assn. Theol. Schs., Germany, 1960; Guggenheim fellow, Israel, 1966-67. Mem. Soc. Religion Higher Edn., Am. Acad. Religion, Soc. Bibl. Lit., Studiorum Novi Testamenti Societas. Presbyn. Author: Understanding the New Testament, 2d edit., 1965; Making Ethical Decisions, 1958; The Renewal of Hope, 1959; Jesus and God's New People, 1959; Jesus in History, 1970. Home: 129 Fishers Rd Bryn Mawr PA 19010

KEE, JAMES, congressman; b. Bluefield, W.Va., Apr. 15, 1917; s. John and Elizabeth (Simpkins) K.; ed. Southeastern U., Georgetown U.; m. Helen Lee Chapman, Sept. 7, 1939; children—Kirsten (Mrs. John C. Cook), Kathleen (Mrs. Ronald Reagle), Karen. Mem. 89th-92d congresses 5th Dist. W.Va. Democrat. Home: 105 Oakhurst Av Bluefield WV 24701 Office: House Office Bldg Washington DC 20525

KEE, SARAH JANICE, govt. ofcl., librarian; b. Spring Creek, Tex., Feb. 23, 1908; d. Richard Alexander and Rosalinde May (Dow) Kee; B.S., Tex. Wesleyan Coll., 1935; M.S., Tex. State Coll. for Women, 1951. Tchr. pub. schs., Anson, DeLeon, Tex., 1927-35; high sch. librarian, Gladewater and Beaumont, 1935-41; county librarian, Beaumont, 1941-43; Army librarian, Independence, Kan., 1943-45;AAF Command librarian, Randolph Field, Tex., 1945-47; extension librarian, acting state librarian Mo. State Library, Jefferson City, 1947-50; dir. state film circuit, pub. libraries, Mo., 1948-50; instr. library sci. U. Mo., summer 1949, U. Wis., 1950-52; exec. sec. pub. libraries div. A.L.A., Chgo., 1952-56; exec. sec. Wis. Free Library Commn., 1956-65; lectr., cons. dept. librarianship Kan. State Coll., Emporia, 1965-67; library program officer Region VI, U.S. Office Edn., Dallas, 1967—. Chmn., Wis. Interdepartmental Com. on Aging Population, 1959; gov's designee White House Conf. Aging, 1961. Mem. Am., Tex., Southwestern library assns., adult edn. Assn. U.S., Am. Assn. U. Women, Wis. Arts Found. and Council, Wis. Acad. Scis. Arts and Letters. Contbr. articles to profl. jours. Home: 4218 Prescott Av Dallas TX 75219 Office: Office Edn US Dept Health Edn and Welfare 1114 Commerce St Dallas TX 75202

KEECH, RICHMOND B., U.S. judge; b. Washington, Nov. 28, 1896; s. Leigh R. and Anne L. (Contee) K. LL.B., Georgetown U., 1922, LL.M., 1923; m. Alice Cashell Berry, Sept. 24, 1957. Pvt. practice law, Washington, 1922-25; asst. corp. counsel D.C., 1925- 30, people's counsel, 1930-34; law mem. and vice chmn. Pub. Utilities Commn., 1934-40, corp. counsel, gen. counsel, 1940-45; adminstrv. asst. to Pres. U.S., 1945-46; judge U.S. Dist. Ct. for D.C., 1946-66, chief judge, 1966, sr. dist. judge, 1967—. Served in trans. service USN, World War I. Mem. Bar Assn. D.C., Am. Legion, Barristers, Masters of Foxhounds Assn. Am., Phi Alpha Delta. Episcopalian. Rotarian. Clubs: Nat. Press, Potomac Hunt, Lawyers, Metropolitan (Washington); Chevy Chase (Md.); American Foxhound; Virginia Foxhound. Home: 12930 Travilah Rd Potomac MD 20854 Office: US Dist Ct for DC Washington DC 20001

KEEDICK, ROBERT LEE, lecture bur. exec.; b. N.Y.C., Dec. 2, 1919; s. Lee and Mabel (Ferris) K.; B.A., Brown U., 1941; m. Harriet Byrnes, May 29, 1958; children—Theodore Lee, Lauri Lynne. With Keedick Lecture Bur., N.Y.C., 1941—, pres., 1957—; v.p. Keedick Press, 1964—; dir. Nutmeg Products Co. Served to lt. USNR, 1942-46. Clubs: Dutch Treat (bd. dirs.), Brown U. (N.Y.C.); Aspetuck Valley Country. Home: 138 Greens Farms Rd Westport CT 06880 Office: 475 Fifth Av New York City NY 10001

KEEFE, DONALD FORAN, lawyer; b. New London, Conn., Mar. 12, 1917; s. Arthur T. and Mabel (Foran) K.; grad. Taft Sch., 1934; B.A., Yale, 1938, LL.B. cum laude, 1946; postgrad. King's Coll., Cambridge (Eng.), U., 1938-39; m. Kate Stevens Hemingway, Apr. 8, 1942; children—Sarah, Nicholas, Thomas. Admitted to Conn. bar, since practiced in New Haven; partner firm Tyler, Cooper, Grant, Bowerman & Keefe, and predecessor, 1949—. Dir. Second Nat. Bank New Haven; v.p., dir. New Haven Water Co. Pres. United Fund Greater New Haven, 1964-66, bd. dirs., 1961-67; mem. sch. bd. Cath. Archdiocese Hartford, 1966-69. Adv. bd. Albertus Magnus Coll., New Haven; trustee Conn. Med. Service. Served to comdr. USNR, 1941-45. Decorated knight St. Gregory. Mem. Am., Conn., New Haven County bar assns., Am. Judicature Soc., New Haven C. of C. (v.p., dir.). Republican. Roman Catholic. Clubs: Graduate's, Quinnipiac, Lawn (New Haven). Home: 30 Old Orchard Rd North Haven CT 06473 Office: 205 Church St New Haven CT 06509

KEEFE, GEORGE EVANS, publishing co. exec.; b. Lawrenceville, N.J., Nov. 28, 1909; s. David and Sabina (Mulligan) K.; B.A., U. Pa., 1930; m. Ruth A. Brockmann, Dec. 16, 1933; children—Ruth K. Clary, David B. With Dun & Bradstreet, Inc. as dist. mgr. Pitts. and Richmond, Va., gen. reporting and service mgr., N.Y.C., 1931-57, v.p., N.Y.C., 1960-68, sr. v.p., 1968—; gen. mgr., dir. Moody's Investors Service Inc., N.Y.C., 1970—; v.p., gen. mgr. Dun & Bradstreet Publs. Corp.; pres. dir. Nat. Credit Office, Inc., N.Y.C., 1957-60; v.p., dir. Fantus Co., N.Y.C., 1966—, Thomas Y. Crowell Co., N.Y.C. Home: 46 Wordsworth Rd Short Hills NJ 07078 Office: 99 Church St New York City NY 10007

KEEFE, ROGER MANTON, banker; b. New London Conn., Feb. 26, 1919; s. Arthur T. and Mabel (Foran) K.; grad. Taft Sch., 1936; student Coll. St. Gregory, Downside Abbey, Eng., 1936-37; B.A. in History and Internat. Relations, Yale, 1941; m. Ann Hunter, June 4, 1949; children—Christopher Hunter, Matthew Foran and Michael Devereux (twins), Susan Ann, Robin Mary, Victoria Morrill. With Chase Manhattan Bank, N.Y.C., 1945—, sr. v.p. charge div. financing devel. and tech. services, 1966—; mem. finance com. Fund Am. Companies. Treas., mem. exec. council Yale Class of 1941; mem. bd. edn., Norwalk, Conn. Mem. Nat. Republican Finance Com., also treas. adv. finance com.; mem. N.Y. State Rep. Finance Com. Treas., trustee St. Thomas More Corp. Served to maj. AUS, World War II; ETO. Decorated Silver Star, Bronze Star with cluster, Purple Heart. Mem. Am. Forestry Assn., Am. Arbitration Assn., N.Y.C. C. of C. Home: Nathan Hale Rd Wilson Point South Norwalk CT 06854 Office: 1 Chase Manhattan Plaza New York City NY 10015

KEEFE, WILLIAM CARROLL, natural gas co. exec.; b. Clinton, Ia., Jan. 18, 1914; s. William J. and Anna B. (Carroll) K.; A.B., U. Notre Dame, 1935; J.D., Harvard, 1938; m. Barbara J. Lilly, Feb. 14, 1942; children—Robert J., Carol A. Admitted to N.Y. bar, 1940; practice in N.Y.C., 1940-50; with Panhandle Eastern Pipe Line Co., N.Y.C., 1950—, sec., 1956—, v.p., 1961-68, pres., 1968—; v.p. finance, dir. subsidiary Trunkline Gas Co., 1965-68, pres., 1968—, vice chmn., 1970—; dir. Nat. Distillers & Chem. Corp., 20th Century Fox Film Corp., Kansas City Life Ins. Co., Anadarko Prodn. Co., Nat. Helium Co. Mem. Am. Gas Assn. (bd. dirs.). Clubs: Wall Street, N.Y. Athletic (N.Y.C.); Siwancy Country (Bronxville); Houston, Houston Country, Ramada, Petroleum (Houston). Home: 5413 Sturbridge Houston TX 77027 Office: 3000 Bissonnet St Houston TX 77005

KEEFE, WILLIAM JOSEPH, educator; b. Piper City, Ill., Nov. 28, 1925; s. Joseph and Elfreda (Huxtable) K.; B.S., Ill. State U., 1948; M.A., Wayne State U., 1949; Ph.D., Northwestern U., 1951; m. Martha Maria Schroeder, Dec. 22, 1948; children— Kathryn, Robert, Nancy, Mary Jo, John. Asst. prof. polit. sci. U. Ala., 1951-52; mem. faculty Chatham Coll., Pitts., 1952-68, asso. prof., 1955-61, prof., 1961-68; prof., chmn. dept. polit. sci. U. Pitts., 1968—. Mem. adv. com. Eagleton Inst. Politics, Rutgers U., 1965—. Served with USNR, 1944-46. Mem. Am. Polit. Sci. Assn. (chmn. Congl. fellowship program). Author: (with Morris Ogul) The American Legislative Process: Congress and the States, 3d edit., 1972; Parties, Politics and Public Policy in America, 1972. Contbr. profl. jours. Home: 838 7th St Oakmont PA 15139 Office: Dept Polit Sci U Pitts Pittsburgh PA 15213

KEEFER, CHESTER SCOTT, physician; b. Altoona, Pa., May 3, 1897; s. John Henry and Gertrude (Scott) K.; B.S., Bucknell U., 1918, M.S., 1922, D.Sc., 1944; M.D., Johns Hopkins, 1922; D.Sc., Boston U., 1944, Bates Coll., 1962; m. Jean Balfour, Aug. 11, 1928; 1 dau., Ishbel McGill. Resident house officer Johns Hopkins Hosp., 1922-23, asst. resident physician, 1923-26; asst. in medicine Johns Hopkins Med. Sch., 1923-25, instr. in medicine, 1925-26; resident physician Billings Hops., Univ. Clinics, U. Chgo., 1926-28; asso. prof. medicine Peiping (China) Union Med. Coll., 1928-30; asst. prof. medicine Harvard Med. Sch., 1930-36, asso. prof., 1936-40; asso. physician Thorndike Meml. Lab., Boston City Hosp., 1930-40, cons. physician, 1940—; jr. vis. physician Boston City Hosp., 1937—; dir. 2d and 4th Med. Services (Harvard), Boston City Hosp., also chief 4th Med. Service, 1939-40; Wade prof. medicine Boston U. Sch. Medicine, 1940-64, Wade prof. emeritus, 1964—; dir. Robert Dawson Evans Meml., 1940-59; physician in chief Mass. Meml. Hosp., 1940-59; dir. Boston U. Sch. Medicine, 1955-59, Boston U.-Mass. Meml. Hosps. Med. Center, 1959-60. Adminstrv. officer com. med. research OSRD, 1944, 46; spl. asst. to sec. health, edn. and welfare, 1953, 55. Decorated Medal of Merit (U.S.); His Majesty's medal. Diplomate Am. Bd. Internal Medicine. Fellow A.C.P. (pres. 1960, regent), Am. Acad. Arts and Scis.; mem. Am. Soc. Clinic Investigation, Assn. Am. Physicians, Am. Clin. and Climatol. Assn., A.M.A., Am. Phila. Soc., Interurban Clin. Club, Phi Beta Kappa, Phi Gamma Delta, Phi Chi, Alpha Omega Alpha. Republican. Presbyn. Clubs: Harvard, St. Botolph (Boston); Cosmos, Capitol Hill (Washington); Country (Brookline); Harvard (N.Y.C.); Hunt (London, Ont.). Home: 71 Upland Rd Brookline MA 02146 Office: 80 E Concord St Boston MA 02118

KEEFER, RAYMOND MARSH, educator, chemist; b. Twin Falls, Ida., Apr. 29, 1913; s. William Raymond and Mary Catherine (Marsh) K.; student Fresno (Cal.) State Coll., 1930-32; B.S. in Chemistry, U. Cal. at Berkeley, 1934, Ph.D., at Davis, 1940; m. Hilda Ottilie Zimmerman, Jan. 6, 1943; children—Raymond Marsh, Katherine Jean, James Otto. Mem. faculty U. Cal. at Davis, 1936- -, prof. chemistry, 1956—, prof. chmn. dept., 1962—; spl. research interaction ions and dipolar ions, complex ions amino acids, molecular complexes, kinetics reactions in solution. Served to lt. comdr. USNR, 1942-45; capt. Res Mem. Am. Chem. Soc., Sigma Xi. Author: (with Andrews) Molecular Complexes in Organic Chemistry, 1964. Home: 3 Willowbank St Davis CA 95616

KEEFER, RICHARD EDWARD, r.r. assn. ofcl.; b. Washington, Feb. 23, 1910; s. Edward Albert and Gertrude (Dooley) K.; B.C.S., Benjamin Franklin U.; m. Winifred Ann Jones, May 14, 1938; children—Richard Edward, Sheila M., Patricia A., J. Stephen, Michael C., Thomas D. Stenographer, Ry. Accounting Officers Assn., 1928-32; sec. to v.p. R.R. Credit Corp., 1932-36, asst. comptroller, asst. sec., 1937-43, comptroller, asst. sec., 1943-47; sec. joint com. traffic execs. and accounting officers Assn. Am. R.R.'s, 1934-36, asst. to sec. finance, accounting, taxation and valuation dept., 1936-37, asst. to sec., then office mgr., 1947-52, sec. dept., also accounting and treasury divs., 1952-57, asst. sec.-treas. assn., Washington, 1957-58, sec.-treas., 1958-64, sec.-treas., adminstrv. asst. to pres., 1964-66, exec. asst. to pres., sec.- treas., 1966—. Served with AUS, 1944-46. Mem. Am. Soc. Assn. Execs. Roman Catholic. Clubs: Traffic (Washington); Kenwood Golf and Country. Home: 5612 Cromwell Dr (Springfield Maryland) Washington DC 20016 Office: Am Railroads Bldg Washington DC 20036

KEEFER, ROY J., lawyer; b. Webster Mills, Pa., Jan. 22, 1902; A.B., Lafayette Coll., 1926; LL.B., Harvard, 1929. Admitted to Pa. bar, 1930, U.S. Supreme Ct. bar, 1945; partner firm Metzger, Hafer, Keefer, Thomas and Wood, Harrisburg, Pa. Mem. Am., Pa., Dauphin County bar assns., Phi Beta Kappa. Office: 208-210 Walnut St Harrisburg PA 17108*

KEEFLER, RALPH HOLLEY, retired electric co. exec.; b. Toronto, Can., Sept. 12, 1902; s. J. K. and Margaret (Holley) K.; B.A.Sc. in Mech. Engring., U. Toronto, 1924; m. Beatrice Taschereau, Sept. 14, 1927; children—Robert, Lois (Mrs. Edward Kehoe). With Bell Telephone Co. of Canada, 1924-61, v.p., 1954- 61; pres., chmn. Northern Electric, 1961-67, chmn., 1961-70. Served from maj. to maj. gen., arty. and inf., Canadian Army, 1940-46; ETO. Decorated comdr. Order British Empire, Distinguished Service Order; Legion of Honor, Croix de Guerre with palm (France). Home: Bayswater Pitts Bay Rd Bermuda Bahamas

KEEGAN, DAVID CHARLES, lawyer, business exec.; b. Elgin, Ill., Sept. 18, 1929; s. Walter C. and Arline (Gallagher) K.; A.B., Johns Hopkins, 1951; J.D., Northwestern U., 1954; m. Lorraine Suchy, Aug. 23, 1950; children-Anne, David Charles, Susan. Admitted to Ill. bar, 1955, snce praciced in Chgo.; mem. firm Winston, Strawn, Smith & Patterson, 1954—, partner, 1962—. Sec. Chamberlain Mfg. Co., Elmhurst, Ill.; dir. Multnomah Co. Mem. bd. edn. Sch. Dist. 41, Glen Ellyn, Ill.; mem. Glen Ellyn Community Relations Commn. Bd. dirs. Glen Ellyn (Ill.) Youth Center. Mem. Ill. Bar Assn., Order of Coif, Phi Alpha Delta, Alpha Tau Omega. Roman Catholic. Club: Glen Oak Country. Home: 617 Riford Rd Glen Ellyn Il 61037 Office: 1 First Nat Plaza Chicago IL 60670

KEEGAN, JAMES BENNETT, banker; b. Santa Rosa, Cal., Nov. 28, 1915; s. James W. and Effie (Bennett) K.; m. Edith J. Newman, Oct. 14, 1939; children—Micheal Joel, James Bennett. With Wells Fargo Bank, 1937—, asst. v.p., mgr. Santa Rosa Office, 1955-60, v.p., mgr., 1960-65, Redwood Empire Dist. v.p. for Cal. North Coast counties, 1965—. Pres. Santa Rosa Bd. Edn., 1965-69; mem. Cal. Water Quality Control Bd., 1971—. Sec. bd. dirs. Santa Rosa Found.; bd. dirs. Santa Rosa Meml. Hosp.; treas., bd. dirs. Redwood Region Conservation Council; bd. govs. San Francisco Bay Area Council; mem. exec. bd. Mendocino and Sonoma council Boy Scouts Am. Served to capt., inf., AUS, 1942-46. Decorated Bronze Star medal, Purple Heart; recipient Cal. medal of merit, 1961, Silver Beaver award Boy Scouts Am., 1960. Mem. Cal. Bankers Assn. (past group pres.), Am. Inst. Banking (past pres. Redwood Empire chpt.), Cal. C. of C. Club: Santa Rose Golf and Country. Home: 1559 E Foothill Dr Santa Rosa CA 95404 Office: 49 Old Courthouse Sq Santa Rosa CA 95402

KEEHN, GRANT, corporate dir.; b. Kenilworth, Ill., Oct. 11, 1900; s. George Washington and Jeannette Sophronia (Shipman) K.; A.B., Hamilton Coll., Clinton, N.Y., 1921; M.B.A., Harvard, 1923; m. Marjorie Elliott Burchard, July 30, 1923 (dec. Jan. 1961); children—Nora, Gretchen, Silas; m. 2d, Veronika Marietta Rona, Mar. 31, 1962; children—Dorka, Fruzsina. With Goldman Sachs and Co., 1923-31; partner, 1931; independent financial cons.; v.p. Kelsey Hayes Wheel Corp., Detroit, 1932-33; officer, dir. Equity Corp. and asso. cos., 1934-38; partner Grant Keehn & Co., 1939-42; v.p. 1st Nat. Bank City N.Y., 1945-50, exec. v.p. 1950-55, dir. 1951-55; exec. v.p. 1st Nat. City Bank N.Y., 1955-58; sr. v.p., dir. Equitable Life Assurance Soc. U.S., 1958-64, pres., dir., 1964-67, vice chmn. bd., dir. 1967-69, chmn. finance com., dir., 1969-71; dir. Burlington No., Inc., St. Paul, Kelsey Hayes Co., Detroit, G. D. Searle & Co., Chgo., Chem. Bank & Chem. N.Y. Corp., Amerada Hess Corp.; trustee Equitable Life Mortgage & Realty Investors, Boston. Chmn. N.Y. State comptroller's investment adv. com. N.Y. State Common Retirement Fund. Trustee Hamilton Coll., 1948—, chmn., 1963-69; trustee, treas. N.Y. Pub. Library; trustee Kirkland Coll. Served from maj. to col., AUS, 1942- 45; liaison officer Army Service Forces, Chgo. Mem. Phi Beta Kappa, Alpha Delta Phi. Clubs: Harvard, Bond, River, Links (N.Y.C.); Blind Brook (Port Chester, N.Y.); Chicago; Nat. Golf (Augusta, Ga.). Home: 45 Sutton Place S New York City NY 10022 Office: 1285 Av of Americas New York City NY 10019

KEEHSAN, SISTER MARGARET MARY, former coll. pres.; b. Albany, N.Y., May 10, 1915; d. Clarence S. and Elizabeth (Flanagan) Keeshan; B.S., Coll. St. Rose, Albany, 1950, M.A., 1952; Ph.D., St. John's U., N.Y.C., 1958. Tchr., Albany Diocese, Troy. N.Y., 1936-42, 47-51, Syracuse (N.Y.) Diocese, 1942-47; mem. faculty Coll. St. Rose 1951-70, chmn. biology dept., 1961-66, pres., 1966-70. Mem. A.A.A.S., Soc. Protozoology, Am. Soc. Zoology, Am. Inst. Biol. Sci., N.Y. Acad. Sci., Delta Epsilon Sigma. Contbr. articles profl. jours. Address: Coll of St Rose Albany NY 12203

KEEL, HOWARD actor, singer; b. Gillespie, Ill., Apr. 13, 1919; m. Helen Anderson (div. Nov. 1970); children—Kaija Liane, Gunnar, Kristine; m. 2d, Judith Ann Magamoll, Dec. 21, 1970. Concert singer, also appeared in music festivals Mississippi Valley area, Chgo.; stage debut in Carousel, 1945; screen debut The Small Voice, 1948; numerous motion pictures, latest being Annie Get Your Gun, 1950, Show Boat, 1951, Kiss Me Kate, 1953, Seven Brides for Seven Brothers, 1954, Floods of Fear, The Big Fisherman, 1959, Waco, Red Tomahawk, Bushwackers, 1966, War Wagon, 1967; leading role in mus. Saratoga, 1959. Home: 14000 Palawan Way Marina Del Ray CA 90291 Office: Ashley Famous Agy 9255 Sunset Blvd Los Angeles CA

KEELAN, KEVIN ROBERT, coll. pres., clergyman; b. Elizabeth, N.J., Mar. 4, 1921; s. Patrick Joseph and Ellen Cecelia (McNesby) K.; student Seton Hall U., 1940-42; B.A., St. Francis Coll., 1945; S.T.L., Cath. U. Am., 1949; Ph.L., Pontificum Athenaeum Angelicum, Rome, Ph.D., 1951. Joined Third Order Regular of St. Francis, 1942, ordained priest Roman Cath. Ch., 1949; instr. philosophy, dean students St. Francis Coll., Loretto, Pa., 1951-53, pres., 1956-59; asst. prof. philosophy, dean Coll. of Steubenville, O., 1953-56, pres., 1959-62, vice chmn. bd. trustees, exec. v.p., 1966-69, pres., 1969—; minister provincial Province Most Sacred Heart Jesus, 1962-66. Recipient Porter W. Averill award Thomas Jefferson High Sch., 1955. Mem. N.E.A., Nat. Cath. Edn. Assn., Am. Cath. Philos. Assn. K.C.; mem. Ancient Order Hibernians. Home: Holy Spirit Monastery Franciscan Way Steubenville OH 43952

KEELAN, MARY FLORENCE, librarian; b. Prelate, Sask., Can., Oct. 31, 1920; d. John Joseph and Florence (Axford) Keelan; ed. Sacred Heart Acad. (Regina, Sask.). Sec. McColl-Frontenac Oil Co., Ltd., Regina and Calgary, Alta., 1937-45, UNRRA, Washington and

China, 1945-47; sec. to exec. v.p. Great-West Life Assurance Co., Winnipeg, Can., 1947-66, librarian, 1967—. Mem. Man. Library Assn. Liberal. Roman Catholic. Clubs: Charleswood Golf, Charleswood Curling (Winnipeg). Home: 580 Centennial St Winnipeg 9 Manitoba Canada Office: 60 Osborne St N Winnipeg 1 Manitoba Canada

KEELE, HAROLD M., lawyer; b. 1901; A.B., U. Ill., 1923, LL.B., 1927. Admitted to Ill. bar, 1928; asst. states atty., 1928-32; now partner firm Pebbles, Greenberg, Keele, Lunn & Ford, Chgo. Mem. Am., Ill. bar assns., Phi Beta Kappa, Phi Delta Phi. Office: 1 N LaSalle St Chicago IL 60602*

KEELER CHARLES ADDISON, lawyer; b. Binghamton, N.Y., Apr. 11, 1897; s. Charles and Aldruda (Addyman) K.; A.B. Hamilton Coll., 1920; m. Esther Montgomery, Aug. 8, 1929; children—Charles Addison, Emily Ann (Mrs. James M. Ludwig, Jr.), John Montgomery. Admitted to N.Y. bar, 1924; mem. firm Lewis & Keeler, Binghamton, 1925-26, Hinman, Howard & Kattell, Binghamton, 1926- -. Dir. Haywood Lumber & Mining Co. Chmn., Broome County (N.Y.) Council Commn. Against Discrimination, 1945- 55; pres. N.Y. State Assn. YMCA's, 1958-65, past pres., Binghamton, mem. nat. council, bd. and exec. com., 1956—; pres. bd. visitors Binghamton State Hosp., pres. Binghamton Community Chest, 1931, Broome County United Fund, 1956. Chmn. trustees Link Found. Served with U.S. Army, 1918-19; with AEF in France. Fellow Am. Coll. Trial Lawyers; mem. Am., N.Y. State (past pres., past chmn. exec. com., pres. Found. 1960), Broome County (past pres.) bar assns., Assn. Bar City N.Y., Binghamton (past pres.), Empire State (past dir.) chambers commerce, Am. Legion (past post and county comdr.). Presbyn. (trustee, chmn. bd. trustees Presbytery Susquehanna Valley). Club: Binghamton (past pres.). Home: 14 Campbell Rd Ct Binghamton NY 13905 Office: Security Mut Life Bldg Binghamton NY 13901

KEELER, RUBY, actress; b. Halifax, N.S., Canada, Aug. 25, 1910; d. Ralph and Elnora (Laby) Keeler; m. Al Jolson, 1928 (dec. 1939); 1 son; m. 2d, John Lowe, Oct. 29, 1941; 1 son, 3 daus. Debut in N.Y.C. in chorus The Rise of Rosy O'Reilly, 1923, later appeared in Bye-Bye, Bonnie, 1927, Lucky, 1927, The Sidewalks of New York, 1927, Show Girl, 1929 (all N.Y.C.), Hold Onto Your Hats, Chgo., 1940; appeared in films including 42nd Street, 1933, Gold Diggers of 1933, Footlight Parade, 1933, Dames, 1934, Flirtation Walk, 1934, Go Into Your Dance, 1935, Shipmates Forever, 1935, Colleen, 1936, Ready, Willing and Able, 1937, Mother Carey's Chickens, 1938, Sweetheart of the Campus, 1941; appeared on TV in Jackie Gleason Show, This Is Your Life, Jerry Lewis Show, The Greatest Show on Earth. Mem. Actors Equity Assn., Screen Actors Guild.*

KEELER, W. W., petroleum exec.; b. Dalhart, Tex. Apr. 5, 1908; s. William and Sarah (Carr) K.; student Kansas U., 1926-29; LL.D., Coll. of Ozarks; E.D., Colo. Sch. Mines; m. Sept. 15, 1933; children—William Robert, Bradford Roger, Kenneth Richard. Asst. chemist Phillips Petroleum Co., Bartlesville, Okla., 1929-34, chemist, 1934, control chemist, 1934-37, engr., 1937-38, chief chemist, 1938-39, night supt., 1939-40, asst. mfg. supt., 1940-41, chief engring. div., 1941, process engr., 1941, chief engr., 1941-43, tech. asst. to v.p., 1943-45, mgr., 1945-47, v.p., 1947-56, exec. v.p., 1956-62, chmn. exec. com., 1962- 67, pres., chief exec. officer, 1967-68, chief exec. officer, chmn. bd., 1968—; officer subsidiary cos.; dir. First Nat. Bank, Bartlesville. Spl. cons. sec. interior, 1961; head delegation U.S. Oil Men to Russia, 1960. Dir. Dwight Presbyn. Mission; mem. Commn. on Rights, Liberties and Responsibilities of Am. Indian; prin. chief Cherokee Nation, 1949. Recipient Silver Beaver award Boy Scouts Am.; named to Okla. Hall of Fame. Mem. Am. Petroleum Inst., Mid-Continent Oil and Gas Assn., Ind. Natural Gas Assn., Nat. Petroleum Assn. (trustee), Ind. Petroleum Assn. Am., Nat. Petroleum Council, Def. Orientation Conf. Assn., C. of C., N.A.M. (chmn. 1969-70, exec. com. 1971—), Sigma Chi, Sigma Tau. Mason. (33, Shriner); mem. Legion Honor Order DeMolay. Club: Hillcrest Country. Home: 1118 S Dewey Av Bartlesville OK 74003 Office: Phillips Bldg Bartlesville OK

KEELEY, BENJAMIN JOSEPH, educator, sociologist; b. Wilmington, Del., Sept. 14, 1917; s. Daniel J. and Gertrude M. (McManus) K.; B.A., Neb. State Tchrs. Coll., 1947; M.A., U. Neb., 1950, Ph.D., 1954; m. Helen Irene Moon, Aug. 19, 1944; 1 son, Michael Clark. Mem. faculty Ill. State U., Normal, 1952—, prof. sociology, 1961— head dept. social scis., 1961-66, acting dean Coll. Liberal Arts and Scis., 1966-67; research asso. U. Cal. at Berkeley, 1963-64; postdoctoral fellow Center Study World Religions, Harvard, 1971-72. Fellow Am. Sociol. Assn.; mem. Soc. Sci. Study Religion, Am. Soc. Value Inquiry, Midwest Social. Soc., Am. Assn. U. Profs., Religious Research Council, Pi Gamma Mu, Alpha Kappa Delta. Unitarian. Author: The Bloomington Survey; Opinions of Voters on Their City, Its Government, and Some of Its Problems, 1958. Home: 214 Imperial Dr Bloomington IL 61701 Office: Ill State U Normal IL 61761

KEELEY, EDMUND LEROY, educator; b. Damascus, Syria, Feb. 5, 1928; s. James Hugh and Mathilde (Vossler) K.; came to U.S., 1939; B.A., Princeton, 1949; D. Phil., Oxford (Eng.) U., 1952; m. Mary Stathatos-Kyris, Mar. 18, 1951. Fulbright tchr. English, Am. Farm Sch., Salonika, Greece, 1949-50; Woodrow Wilson fellow, 1950-51; instr. English, Brown U., 1952-53; Fulbright lectr. Salonika U., 1953-54; instr. English, Princeton, 1954-57, asst. prof., 1957-63, asso. prof., 1963-70, prof. English and creative arts, 1970—, co-chmn. program in comparative lit., 1964-65, dir. creative arts program, 1966-71, dir. program creative writing and the performing arts, 1971—; lectr. dept. Byzantine and Modern Greek, Oxford (Eng.) U., 1960; writer in residence Knox Coll., spring 1963; vis. lectr. Writers Workshop, U. Ia., 1962-63. Mem. scholarship fund com. Am. Farm Sch., Salonika, Greece; chmn. McCarter Theatre Com., 1969. Served with USNR, 1945-46. Jr. fellow Council Humanities, 1956-57; Rome prize fellow Am. Acad. Arts and Letters, 1959-60; Guggenheim fellow, 1959-60; McCosh Faculty fellow, 1969-70. Mem. Authors Guild, Comparative Lit. Assn., Internat. Soc. Neo-Hellenic Studies, Modern Lang. Assn. Modern Greek Studies Assn. (pres. 1969—), Phi Beta Kappa. Author: The Libation, 1958; (with Philip Sherrard) Six Poets of Modern Greece, 1960, George Seferis: Collected Poems, 1924-1955, 1967; The Gold-Hatted Lover, 1961; The Impostor, 1970; (with George Savidis) C.P. Cavafy: Passions and Ancient Days, 1971; C.P. Cavafy: Selected Poems, 1972. Translator (with Mary Keeley) The Plant, the Well, the Angel (V. Vassilikos), 1964. Editor: (with Peter Bien) Modern Greek Writers, 1972. Home: 140 Littlebrook Rd Princeton NJ 08540

KEELEY, JAMES ARTHUR, banker; b. Waseca, Minn., Aug. 4, 1922; s. Arthur Henry and Emma (Gregor) K.; student St. Johns U., Collegeville, Minn., 1939-42; B.A., St. Marys Coll., Richardton, N.D., 1944; postgrad. U. Wash., 1951; m. Irene M. Cocke, June 6, 1948; children—Donald Edward, Marcia Diane. Tchr., Assumption Abbey, Richardton, 1945-47; v.p., sr. trust officer Crocker Citizens Nat. Bank, San Francisco, 1947—. Affiliate, Stanford Research Inst. Mem. Am. Soc. Corp. Secretaries, San Francisco C. of C. Club: Olympic (San Francisco). Home: 1432 Beacon Av San Leandro CA 94579 Office: 1 Montgomery St San Francisco CA 94120

KEELEY, JOHN LEMUEL, surgeon; b. Streator, Ill., Apr. 12, 1904; s. John William and Mary Catherine (Fife) K.; B.S., Loyola U., Chgo., 1927, M.D., 1929; m. Mary Edith Schneider, Oct. 14, 1937; children—John Lemuel, George William, James Michael. Asst. physician dept. student health U. Wis., 1931-33, resident surgery Wis. Gen. Hosp., Madison, 1933-36; Arthur Tracy Cabot fellow in surgery Harvard, 1936-37, Harvey Cushing fellow surgery, research fellow surgery, acting resident urology Peter Bent Brigham Hosp., Boston, 1937-38; instr. surgery La. State U., 1938-40, asst. prof., 1940- 41; vis. surgeon Charity Hosp., New Orleans, 1938-41; asst. clin. prof. surgery Loyola U. Sch. Medicine, Chgo., 1941-43, asso. clin. prof., 1943- 54, prof. surgery, 1954—, asst. chmn. dept. Stritch Sch. Medicine, 1954-58, chmn., 1958-69; asso. attending surgeon Cook County Hosp., Chgo., 1941-52, attending surgeon, 1952—; sr. attending surgeon Mercy Hosp. Chgo., 1941- -, chmn. dept., 1958-67; chmn. dept. surgery Loyola U. Hosp., 1968-69; attending gen. and thoracic surgeon West Side VA Hosp., 1953-63; surgical cons. Hines VA Hosp., 1963—; surg. cons. Woodlawn, South Shore, Little Co. Mary hosps. Diplomate Am. Bd. Surgery, Am. Bd. Thoracic Surgery. Fellow A.C.S.; mem. Chgo. Med. Soc., Chgo. Surg. Soc., Am. Central, Western surg. assns., Am. Assn. for Thoracic Surgery. Am. Coll. Chest Physicians, Soc. for Vascular Surgery, Am. Acad. Pediatrics (surg. affiliate), Phi Chi, Alpha Omega Alpha. Roman Catholic. Clubs: University, South Shore Country (Chgo.). Author articles surg. subjects. Home: 7116 S Coles Av Chicago IL 60649 Office: 2160 S 1st Av Maywood IL 60141

KEELEY, JOSEPH CHARLES, author; b. Wilkes-Barre, Pa., Aug. 10, 1907; s. William Thomas and Martha (McCole) K.; Litt.B., Columbia, 1930; m. Helen Elizabeth Klein, June 22, 1931; children—Jean Helen, Thomas Charles. Mem. pub. relations staff N. W. Ayer & Son, N.Y.C., 1930-38; dir. pub. relations dept. J. M. Mathes Inc., 1938-44; editor Am. Legion mag., 1949-63. Served as staff sgt. USMCR, 1944-45, also mng. editor Marine Corps Gazette. Author: They Sold Themselves (with Howard Stephenson), 1937; Making Inventions Pay, 1950; Taking It Easy with Your Camera, 1957; Photography For Your Family, 1964; China Lobby Man, 1969; The Left-Leaning Antenna, 1971. Contbr. nat. mags. Address: Clifton Rd Star Route Gouldsboro PA 18424

KEELING, EDWARD WOOD, food chain exec.; b. Santa Anna, Tex., Nov. 16, 1920; s. John J. and Safrohie Ann (Lee) K.; gard. high sch.; m. Verma Rhea Lovelace, Dec. 21, 1941; 1 dau., Karen Ann. Meat cons. Safeway Food Stores, 1952-55; with Shop Rite Food, Inc., 1955—, exec. v.p., gen. mgr., 1970—. Served with USMCR, 1942-46. Home: 4237 Glenview Ct Fort Worth TX 76118 Office: 1106 Highway 30 Grand Prairie TX 75050

KEELING, GERALD FAY, former air force officer, aircraft co. exec.; b. Lockney, Tex., Oct. 23, 1915; s. Lewis Wilson and Beulah (Berry) K.; student Colo. State U., 1935-39, U. Pitts., 1949; grad. Army Command and Gen. Staff Coll., 1945, Air Command and Staff Sch., 1948, Air War Coll., 1954; m. Maxine Margarita Guillot, Nov. 24, 1951; 1 son, Richard Gerald. Commd. 2d lt. USAAF, 1940, advanced through grades to maj. gen. USAF, 1961; chief aircraft and missiles div. Directorate Procurement and Prodn., Air Material Command, 1949-53; exec. to dep. chief staff material Hdqrs. USAF, 1955-58; USAF plant rep. N. Am. Aviation. 1958-60; comdr. Western Contract Mgmt. Region, Mira Loma, Cal., 1960-62; dep. chief staff procurement and prodn. Hdqrs. USAF Systems Command, 1962-67; asst. dep. chief staff systems and logistics Hdqrs. USAF. 1967-69, ret. 1969; with Hughes Aircraft Co., Culver City, Cal., 1969—. Decorated Legion of Merit, D.S.M. Mem. Nat. Contract Mgmt. Assn., Sigma Tau, Sigma Phi Epsilon. Methodist. Home: 1346 Brinkley Av Los Angeles CA 90049

KEELING, THOMAS CALLENDER, Jr., business exec.; b. Baton Rouge, Nov. 19, 1912; s. Thomas Callender and Bessie Lee (Sperry) K.; B.S. in Chem. Engring. and Bus. Adminstrn., Mass. Inst. Tech., 1935; grad. Harvard Advanced Mgmt. Program; m. Jessie Parkes Stites, Sept. 23, 1938; children—Thomas Callender, Louise Armistead. Sales engr. Niagara Alkali Co., N.Y.C., 1935-41; asst. v.p., sales mgr. chem. div. Koppers Co., Inc., Pitts., 1945-53, asst. v.p., 1952-53, 54-58, mgr. Aniline Products unit, 1956-58, v.p., gen. mgr. chems. and dyestuffs div., 1958- 63, v.p., gen. mgr. internat. div., dir. co., 1964—; pres. Koppers Internat., C.A., 1963—, Mathieson Hydrocarbon Chems. div. Mathieson Chem. Corp., Balt., 1953-54. Dir. chem. division NPA., 1952-53. Served to lt. col. USAAF 1941-46. Decorated commendatore al Merito della Repubblica Italiana. Mem. Armed Forces Chem. Assn., Sigma Chi. Clubs: Chemists (N.Y.C.); Duquesne (Pitts.); Rolling Rock (Ligonier,Pa.); St. Clair Country; Plantation (Hilton Head Island, S.C.). Home: 1719 Hastings Mill Rd Pittsburgh PA 15241 Office: Koppers Bldg Pittsburgh PA 15219

KEELOR, THOMAS HOWARD, r.r. co. exec.; b. Chgo., Dec. 14, 1912; s. Ralph Parker and Florence (Clancy) K.; student Northwestern U., 1953; m. Bernice Barbara Stockhausen, Feb. 4, 1937; children—Barbara (Mrs. David Larson), Patricia (Mrs. Everett Fertig), Virginia L. (Mrs. Morris Watson), Richard H., David H., Thomas H. With C. & O. Ry., Cleveland, Ohio, 1931—, asst. sec., asst. treas., 1948-51, sec., 1951—; sec. B. & O. R.R. Capt. transp. div. United Appeal Greater Cleve., 1949-65. Mem. Am. Soc. Corporated Secs. (dir., past nat. pres.), Stockholder Relations Soc. N.Y. Club: Westwood Country (Rocky River). Home: 19555 Story Rd Rocky River OH 44116 Office: Terminal Tower Cleveland OH 44101

KEENAN, BOYD RAYMOND, educator; b. Parkersburg, W.Va., June 29 1928; s. Claude Joseph and Lillie (Sayre) K.; A.B., U. Ky., 1949, M.A., 1957; Ph.D., U. Ill., 1960; m. Donna May Booth, June 9, 1951; childrn—Kevin Lee, Karen Ruth. Reporter, Parkersburg News, 1949-50; state editor Lexington (Ky.) Herald, 1950-52; news editor U. Ky., 1952-55, dir. news bur., 1955-57; teaching asst. U. Ill., 1957-58, Charles E. Merriam fellow polit. sci., 1958-59; asst. to dir. Com. Instl. Coop., 1959-60; asst. prof. polit. sci. Marshall U., Huntington, W.Va., 1960-62; vis. prof. polit. sci. Purdue U., asso. dir. Com. Instl. Coop., 1962-64, prof. polit. sci., head dept., 1964-67; prof. polit. sci. U. Ill., Chgo. Circle, 1967- -. Dep. dir. Ill. Bd. Higher Edn., chmn. Ill. Sci. Adv. Council; sci. adviser Ill. Gov., 1969-70. Mem. Am. Polit. Sci. Assn., Midwest Conf. Polit. Scientists, Am. Soc. Pub. Adminstrn. Editor, contbr.: Science and the University, 1966. Contbr. articles profl. jours. Home: 271 Boyd Av Elmhurst IL 60126 Office: Box 4348 U Ill Chicago IL 60680

KEENAN, EDWARD LOUIS, Jr., govt. ofcl.; b. Somerville, N.J., Jan. 21, 1911; s. Edward Louis and Eva (Voorhees) K.; B.S.C., Temple U., 1933; m. Edith Emily Campbell, May 29, 1936; children—Edward Louis 3d, Barry Campbell. Research work and interviewer Phila. Employment Center, 1932-33; asst. personnel dir. Lit Brothers Dept. Store, Phila., 1933-34; supr. Nat. Re- employment Service and Pa. Employment Service, 1934-36; student social ins. systems, Eng., Germany and Scandinavian countries, 1936; tech. adviser unemployment compensation Social Security Bd., Washington, 1936-37, regional rep., bur. employment security, Ohio, Mich. and Ky., 1937-42, dep. regional manpower dir. for Ohio, Mich. and Ky., 1942-43; Ohio manpower dir., 1943-45; regional manpower dir. for Ohio, Mich. and Ky., 1945; dep. dir. U.S. Employment Service, Dept. of Labor, 1945-48; dep. dir. Bur. Employment Security, Social Security Adminstrn., 1948-49; dep. dir. Bureau Employment Security, Dept. of Labor, 1949-58; dir. field operations Def. Manpower Adminstrn. 1951; dep. asst. dir. manpower OCDM, 1958-62; dir. Manpower and Services Office, Office Emergency Planning, 1962-63, dir. Resource Readiness Office, 1964-68, dir. field services, 1968-70; cons. ICA, govts. Turkey and Libya, 1960. Adviser on labor and manpower Joint Brazil-U.S. Tech. Commn., Rio de Janeiro, Brazil, 1948; U.S. del. Latin Am. Tech. Manpower Conf., Peru, 1952; adviser to U.S. dels. 41st session Internat. Labor Conf. (maritime), ILO, Geneva, 1958; cons. ICA, Govt. Turkey, 1960; cons. AID, Govt. Jordan, 1965. Mem. Am. Soc. Pub. Adminstrn., Sigma Delta Chi. Home: 11304 South Shore Rd Reston VA 22070

KEENAN, EDWARD LOUIS, Jr., educator; b. Buffalo, May 13, 1935; s. Edward Louis and Emma (Boudiette) K.; A.B., Harvard, 1957, M.A., 1961, Ph.D., 1966; postgrad. Leningrad State U., 1959-61; m. Joan Glasser, Nov. 25, 1961; children-Edward, Christopher, Nicholas, Matthew. Teaching fellow Harvard, Cambridge, Mass., 1962-63, instr., 1965-68, lectr., 1968-70, prof. history, 1970—; lectr. Slavic Workshop, Inc. U., 1962-64. Guggenheim fellow, 1970—. Mem. Cambridge Civic Assn. Contbr. articles profl. jours. Office: 1737 Cambridge St Cambridge MA 02138

KEENAN, FRANK J., mfg. co. exec.; b. 1915; married. With Lybrand, Ross Bros. & Montgomery, 1939-57; asst. controller Gen. Refractories Co., Phila., 1957-63, controller, 1963—. C.P.A., Pa. Office: 1520 Locust St Philadelphia PA 19102*

KEENAN, GERALD, retired univ. dean; b. Hornell, N.Y., June 21, 1906; s. John Francis and Laura (Lenahan) K.; Mus.B. (scholar), Eastman Sch. Music, 1933, Mus.M., 1940, Ph.D., 1953; spl. student Alfred U., 1934-35, W. Chester State Coll., 1943; m. Elizabeth Jane Landis, July 21, 1945; children—Mary Ann, Gerald Patrick. Violinist, Rochester Philharmonic, 1931-34; tchr. Elmira (N.Y.) pub. schs., 1934-39, Westchester State Tchrs. Coll., 1939-54; exec. dir. Duquesne U. Sch. Music, Pitts., 1954-56, dean, 1956-71, dean emeritus, 1971—. Mem. adv. bd. Bach Choir Pitts.; performed own violin concerto with Rochester Civic Orch., 1933; guest condr., adjudicator mus. events. Mem. Nat. Cath. Music Edn. Assn. (head music edn. 1956-57, head coll. dept. 1958-61), Pa., Pitts. music edn. assns., Pa. Music Tchrs. Assn. (pres. 1965), Music Educators Nat. Conf., Music Tchrs. Nat. Assn., Pitts. Chamber Music Soc. (dir.), Phi Mu Alpha. Composer: Violin Sonata, 1932; Concerto for Violin, String Orch. and Piano, 1933; The Sunken Bell, 1940; Pages From a Child's Story Book, 1942; Sonatina for Violin and Piano, 1945; Missa Brevis for unaccompanied male voices, 1950; Concerto for Viola and Orchestra, 1953. Editorial adv. bd. Musart, 1963-66. Home: RFD 1 Graysville PA 15337

KEENAN, J. MICHAEL, educator; B.A., M.S., U. Colo.; Ph.D., Ohio State U. Prof., chmn. dept. mgmt. Western Mich. U., Kalamazoo. Office: Dept Mgmt Western Mich U Kalamazoo MI*

KEENAN, JOHN ARTHUR, pen co. exec., b. Beloit, Wis., Apr. 29, 1908; s. John and Mae (Ehrler) K.; B.S., U. Wis., 1930, M.S., 1932, Ph.D., 1934; m. Marian Stevens Hill, June 21, 1935; children—Stephen, Douglas, Judith Ann, Robert Mark, Priscilla Ann. Asso. research dir. Wis. Alumni Research Found., 1934-36; dir., v.p. charge prodn. Nat. Dairy Products Corp., 1936-41; dir. research Carnation Co., 1941-43; exec. v.p. Standard Packaging Corp., N.Y.C., 1943-45, pres., 1945-65; pres. W.A. Sheaffer Pen Co., Ft. Madison, Ia., 1965-71, Speidel Co., Providence, 1971—. Mem. Am. Chem. Soc., Sigma Xi, Alpha Chi Sigma, Phi Sigma, Phi Lambda Upsilon. Office: 70 Ship St Providence RI 02902

KEENAN, JOSEPH HENRY, educator, engr.; b. Wilkes-Barre, Pa., Aug. 24, 1900; s. Joseph Henry and Wilhelmina (Maurer) K.; B.S., Mass. Inst. Tech., 1922; LL.D., U. Glasgow, 1966; m. Isabel Morrison, Jan. 30th, 1924; children—Esther Marie (Mrs. Johm W. Carr III), Matthew Arnold. Steam turbine engr. Gen. Electric Co., Schenectady, 1922-28; asst. prof. mech. engring. Stevens Inst. Tech., 1928-34; asso. prof. Mass. Inst. Tech., 1934-39, prof. 1939-66, prof. emeritus, sr. lectr., 1966-71, head dept. mech engring., 1958-61; Fulbright lectr. Cambridge U., Imperial Coll. Sci. and Tech., 1951. Dir. Thermo Electron Corp., No. Research & Engring. Corp. Del. Internat. Confs. on Properties of Steam, 1929—. Served to lt. comdr. USNRF, 1940-53. Fellow Am. Acad. Arts and Scis., Am. Soc. M.E. (hon.; Worcester Reed Warner medal 1954); mem. Inst. Aero. Scis., Am. Soc. Engring. Edn., Am. Assn. U. Profs., Tau Beta Pi, Sigma Xi. Clubs: Siasconset (Mass. Casino); Belmont Hill; Harvard Musical Assn.; Nantucket (Mass.) Yacht. Author: Steam Tables and Mollier Diagram, 1930, Thermodynamic Properties of Steam (with F.G. Keyes), 1936, Thermodynamics, 1941; Gas Tables (with J. Kaye), 1948; (with G.N. Hatsopoulos) General Thermodynamics, 1965; (with F.G. Keyes, P.G. Hill and J.G. Moore) Steam Tables, 1969. Contbr. numerous papers to profl. lit. Patentee equipment for processing coffee, cocoa; devices for separating dust from gas streams. Home: 11 Howells Rd Belmont MA 02178

KEENAN, RICHARD HENRY, banker; b. Renovo, Pa., June 24, 1909; s. John Joseph and Elnora (Ranck) K.; student Pa. State U., 1927-28; B.S. in Commerce, Temple U., 1931; m. Anne C. Hall, Sept. 17, 1932. With Central Pa. Natl. Bank, Phila., 1929—, v.p., 1954-63, sr. v.p., 1963—. Treas. Heart Assn. Southeastern Pa., 1958—. Asst. treas. Republican Finance Com. Pa., 1962—. Served with USNR, 1943-45. Home: 1152 Lindsay Lane Rydal PA 19046 Office: Central Pa Nat Bank Broad and Walnut Sts Philadelphia PA 19101

KEENE, CHRISTOPHER, condr.; b. Berkeley, Cal., Dec. 21, 1946; s. James Phillip and Yvonne San Jule Yvette (Cyr) K.; ed. U. Cal. at Berkeley, 1963-67; m. Sara Frances Rhodes, Dec. 21, 1967; 1 son, Anthony Alexander. Appearances with Spoleto Festival, 1968, 69, 71; mus. dir. Am. Ballet Co., 1969-70; with Santa Fe Opera, 1971; now with N.Y. City Opera, Met. Opera. Home: 650 West End Av New York City NY 10024 Office: N Y City Opera Lincoln Center New York City NY 10023*

KEENE, CLIFFORD HENRY, med. adminstr.; b. Buffalo, Jan. 28, 1910; s. George Samuel and Henrietta Hedwig (Yeager) K.; A.B., U. Mich., 1931, M.D., 1934, M.S. in Surgery, 1938; m. Mildred Jean Kramer, Mar. 3, 1934; children—Patricia Ann (Mrs. William S. Kneedler), Martha Jane (Mrs. William R. Sproule), Diane Eve. Resident surgeon, instr. surgery U. Mich., 1934-39; cons. surgery of cancer Mich. Med. Soc. and Mich. Dept. Health, 1939-40; pvt. practice surgery, Wyandotte, Mich., 1940-41; med. dir. Kaiser-Frazer Corp., 1946-53; instr. surgery U. Mich., 1946-54; med. adminstrv. positions with Kaiser Industries and Kaiser Found., 1954—, v.p., 1960—; v.p., gen. mgr. Kaiser Found. Hosps. and Kaiser Found. Health Plan, 1960—; med. dir. Kaiser Found. Sch. Nursing, 1954—; dir. Kaiser Found. Research Inst., 1958—; pres. Kaiser Found. Hosps. Health Plan, Sch. Nursing; chmn. editorial bd. Kaiser Found. Med. Bull., 1954—; lectr. med. econs. U. Cal. at Berkeley, 1956—; mem. vis. com. Med. Sch. Stanford, 1966—, Harvard, 1967—. Mem. Presdl. Panel Fgn. Med. Grads. (Nat. Manpower Commn.), 1966—. Served to lt. col. M.C., AUS, 1942-46. Diplomate Am. Bd. Surgery, Am. Bd. Preventive Medicine (occupational medicine). Fellow A.C.S.,; mem. Am. Assn. Indsl. Physicians and Surgeons, Frederick A. Coller Surg.

Soc., Cal., Am. med. assns., Alpha Omega Alpha. Mem. Community Ch. Contbr. papers to profl. lit. Home: 1000 Mason St San Francisco CA 94108 Office: Kaiser Center 300 Lakeside Dr Oakland CA 94604

KEENE, JAMES CALVIN, educator; b. Enders, Pa., July 29, 1908; s. James E. and Nora (Kershner) K.; A.B., Lebanon Valley Coll., 1930; Ph.D., Yale, 1937; m. Elsa Feichtinger, Apr. 20, 1934; children—Lenore (Mrs. Stephen Congdon), James, Joan W. Instr., Internat. Coll., Izmir, Turkey, 1931-34, Colgate U., 1937-43; from asst. prof. to prof. Howard U. Sch. Religion, 1943-58; prof. religion, chmn. dept. St. Lawrence U., Canton, N.Y., 1958—. Vis. prof. Am. U. Beirut, 1949-50. Recipient Alumni Assn. citation Lebanon Valley Coll., 1971. Lilly Found. grantee, 1966-67. Mem. Am. Theol. Soc. (v.p. 1962-63, sec. 1964-71), Am. Acad. Religion (v.p. 1947-48), Am. Assn. U. Profs. Mem. Soc. of Friends. Rotarian. Author: Meditations on the Gospels, 1959. Editor, reviser: Western Heritage of Faith and Reason, 1963; editor Jour. Religious Thought, 1953-58. Contbr. articles to profl. jours. Home: 13 College St Canton NY 13617

KEENE, KENNETH E., advt. exec.; b. Connersville, Ind., June 21, 1918; s. Thomas and Nettie A. (Arnett) K.; grad. high sch.; m. Virginia Lee Fowler, July 1, 1945; 1 son, Kenneth Edward. With Quinlan Keene Peck & McShay, Inc., Indpls., 1934—, pres., 1967—, chmn. bd., 1968—. Mem. bd. Indpls. Airport Authority, 1970—; mem. Ind. Armory Bd., 1965. Bd. dirs., v.p. 500 Festival Assn., 1960-67. Served to maj. USAAF, USAAF, 1941-45. Decorated D.F.C., Air medal (6), Bronz Star. Mem. Assn. Indsl. Advertisers (pres. 1949), Sales and Marketing Execs. (v.p. 1971). Mason (Shriner). Clubs: Indianapolis Athletic; Hillcrest Country (Indianapolis). Home: 811 Ellenberger Pky Indianapolis IN 46219 Office: PO Box 1962 Indianapolis IN 46206

KEENEN, JOSEPH DANIEL, labor union ofcl.; b. Chgo., Nov. 5, 1896; s. Edward and Mary (Curtin) K.; ed. St. Jarloth's Sch., Chgo.; elec. apprentice course Crane Tech. High Sch., Chgo.; children—John E. Joseph D. Cable splicer Chgo. Telephone Co., 1915-23; supt. elec. constrn., Fed. Electric Co., Chgo., 1921-30; elec. engr. charge North side treatment plant, Chgo., 1930-37; sec. Chgo. Fedn. Labor, 1937—; dir. WCFL, Chgo., 1937-40; labor advisor to asso. dir. gen., OPM, 1940-41; asso dir. Labor Prodn. Bd., 1942; v. chmn. labor prodn., WPB Washington, 1943-45; labor adviser to Gen. Clay, Berlin, Germany, 1945-47; dir. Labor's League for Polit. Edn.; asst. to dir. ODM, 1953—; sec. Elec. Workers Union No. 134; sec.-treas. Bldg. and Constrn. Trades Dept., A.F.L., 1950-54; internat. sec. Internat. Brotherhood Elec. Workers, 1954—. Democrat. Roman Catholic. Eagle. Club: Irish Fellowship. Home: 2727 29th St NW Washington DC 20008

KEENER, HARRY ALLAN, coll. dean; b. Greensboro, Pa., Dec. 22, 1913; s. Franklin Hodson and Mary Ann (Kelley) K.; B.S., Pa. State U., 1936, Ph.D., 1941; M.S., W.Va. U., 1938; m. Elizabeth Margaret Hartley, July 26, 1941; children—Allan Wayne, William Franklin. Grad. asst. W.Va. U., 1936-38, Pa State U., 1938-41; mem. faculty U. N.H., Durham, 1941—, prof. dairy sci., 1950—, dir. agr. expt. sta., 1958—, dean Coll. Life Sci. and Agri., 1961—. Mem. bd. collaborators U.S. Plant, Soil and Nutrition Lab., 1956-59, U.S. Pasture Research Lab., 1952-62; mem. N.H. Conservation Com., 1958—, N.H. Milk Sanitation Bd., 1963—, Dept. Agr. Com. Nine, 1963-66, Expt. Sta. Com. on Orgn. and Policy, 1966-69. Mem. N.Y. Acad. Sci., Am. Soc. Animal Sci., Am. Dairy Sci. Assn., Sigma Xi, Phi Kappa Phi, Alpha Zeta, Gamma Sigma Delta, Alpha Gamme Rho. Author: (with H.F. Judkins) Milk Production and Processing, 1960, Spanish edit., 1962. Home: Canney Rd Durham NH 03824

KEENER, JEFFERSON WARD, business exec.; b. Portersville, Ala., Aug. 6, 1908; s. Joseph Ward and Mary Elizabeth (Boston) K.; A.B., Birmingham-So. Coll., 1928, LL.D., 1955; M.A., U. Chgo., 1930; postgrad. Ohio State U., 1931; LL.D., Ohio Wesleyan U., 1959; D.C.S. (hon.), Milliken U., 1959; m. Marian Feudner, Sept. 19, 1931; children—Jefferson Ward, Harry Alan, Robert Lee. Instr., then asst. prof. econs. Ohio Wesleyan U., 1929-37, 38-39; dir. bus. research B.F. Goodrich Co., 1939-42, asst. to financial v.p., asst. to pres., 1942-46, v.p., 1946-56, exec. v.p. 1956-57, pres., dir., mem. exec. com., 1957-58, pres., chief exec. officer, dir., mem. exec. com., 1958-67, chmn., chief exec. officer, 1967—; dir. Campbell Soup Co., Ohio Bell Telephone Co., B.F. Goodrich Australia Pty., Ltd., B. F. Goodrich Liberia, Inc., B. F. Goodrich Can., Ltd., Internat. B. F. Goodrich Corp., Fed. Res. Bank Cleve. Mem. Wage Stblzn. Bd., 1950-51, Mut. Security Program Evaluation Study of Germany, 1953; mem. adv. com. on civilian personnel mgmt. U.S. Army, 1954-56; mem. The Bus. Council; mem. balance payments adv. com. to sec. commerce, 1965-68; mem. Pres.' Adv. Com. Labor-Mgmt., 1966-68; sr. mem. Nat. Indsl. Conf. Bd.; mem. Indsl. Relations Counselors. Emeritus trustee City Hosp. Akron; trustee Western Res. Acad., Cleve. Clinic Found. Recipient AUS medal for exceptional civilian achievement, 1956. Mem. Rubber Mfrs. Assn. (dir.), Bus. Council, Phi Gamma Delta, Kappa Phi Kappa. Delta Sigma Pi. Republican. Lutheran. Clubs: City, Portage Country (Akron); Economic, Links, Fifth Avenue (N.Y.C.); Naples Yacht, Hole-in-the-Wall (Naples, Fla.). Home: 265 Hampshire Rd Akron OH 44313 Office: BF Goodrich Co 500 Main St Akron 1 OH 44311

KEENER, LEE LANAM, rubber co. exec.; b. Alliance, O., Aug. 16, 1910; s. Hayes Harold and Rose (Lenam) K.; student Mt. Union Coll., 1928-29; B.S. in Bus. Adminstrn., U. Ariz., 1933; m. Lucy Jessica Hicks, Feb. 18, 1938; 1 son, Lee Lanam. Pub. accountant Ernst & Ernst, C.P.A.'s Canton, O., 1939-40; travelling auditor B.F. Goodrich Co., Akron, O. 1940-43; chief accountant B.F. Goodrich Chem. Co., Cleve., 1946-53; sec. treas. B.F. Goodrich Can. Ltd., Kitchener, Ont., 1954—. Mem. Civic Centre Com. Kitchener, 1966—. Served with USAF, 1943-46. Mem. K-W Art Gallery Assn. (pres. 1962-65) K-W Art Gallery Assn. (pres. 1963-70), Canada Mfrs. Assn., Rubber Assn. Canada, Kitchener C. of C., Waterloo C. of C. Anglican. Club: Westmount Golf and Country (Kitchener). Home: 170 John Blvd Waterloo Ontario Canada Office: 409 Weber St W Kitchener Ontario Canada

KEENEY, BARNABY CONRAD, ednl. adminstr.; b. Halfway, Ore., Oct. 17, 1914; s. Robert Mayro and Maud Barnaby (Conrad) K.; A.B., U. N.C., 1936; A.M., Harvard, 1937; Ph.D., 1939; Guggenheim Post Service fellow, 1945-46; LL.D., Tufts Coll., 1955, U. N.C., 1956, Princeton, 1956, Franklin and Marshall Coll., 1957, U. R.I., 1958, Boston Coll., 1958, Northwestern U., 1958, Columbia, 1959, Lafayette Coll., 1958, Brown U., 1967, Providence Coll., 1959, Yeshiva U., 1961; Ed.D., R.I. Coll. Edn., 1959; J.D., Portia Law Sch., 1959; L.H.D., Ohio U., 1962, L.H.D., Brandeis U., 1966; D.Sc., Bryant Coll., 1962; Litt. D., Clark U., 1964; m. Mary E. Critchfield, June 27, 1941; children—Barbara Alice (Mrs. Michael Clark), Thomas, Elizabeth. Tutor, instr. history Harvard, 1939-42; asst. prof. history Brown U., 1946-49, asso. prof., 1949-51, prof., 1951, asso. dean Grad. Sch., 1948, dean, 1949-53, dean of coll., 1953-55, pres. univ., 1955-66; chmn. Nat. Endowment for Humanities, Washington, 1966-70; chief exec. officer Consortium of Universities, Washington, 1970-71; pres. Claremont Grad. Sch., 1971—. Served to capt. AUS, 1942-45; hdqrs., 35th Inf. Div. Decorated Purple Heart, Bronze Star, Silver Star; recipient Jaffe medal for service to humanities, 1970. Fellow Am. Acad. Arts and Scis.; mem. R.I., Mass. hist. socs., Mediaeval Acad. Am., Am. Hist. Assn., Am. Philos. Soc. Phi Beta Kappa. Clubs: Cosmos (Washington); Century, Hope (Providence). Author: Judgment by Peers, 1949; also articles and revs. profl. jours. Asst. editor Speculum, 1947-50, adv. bd., 1950-61. Home: 7908 Glendale Rd Chevy Chase MD 20015 Office: Claremont Grad Sch Claremont CA

KEENEY, EDMUND LUDLOW, physician; b. Shelbyville, Ind., Aug. 11, 1908; s. Bayard G. and Ethel (Adams) K.; A.B., Ind. U., 1930; M.D., Johns Hopkins, 1934; m. Esther Cox Loney Wight, Mar. 14, 1950; children—Edmund Ludlow, Eleanor Seymour (Mrs. Cameron Leroy Smith). Intern Johns Hopkins Hosp. Balt.,, 1934-37, vis. physician, instr. internal medicine Sch. Medicine and Hosp., 1940- 48; practice medicine, specializing internal medicine, San Diego, 1948- 55; dir. Scripps Clinic and Research Found., La Jolla, 1955-67, pres., 1967-. Dir. research on fungus infections OSRD, 1942-46; cons. U.S. Navy, 1948—, VA, 1954—. Bd. dirs. Allergy Found. Am. Diplomate Am. Bd. Internal Medicine. Fellow A.C.P.; mem. A.M.A., Am. Soc. Clin. Investigation, Am. Acad. Allergy (pres. 1964), Western Assn. Physicians, Cal. Med. Assn., Western Soc. Clin. Research, Phi Beta Kappa, Alpha Omega Alpha, Beta Theta Pi. Republican. Presbyn. Rotarian. Club: Cuyamaca. Author: Practical Medical Mycology, 1955. Contbr. articles on allergy, immunology and mycology to med. jours. Home: 338 Via del Norte La Jolla CA 92037 Office: 476 Prospect St La Jolla CA 92038

KEENLEYSIDE, HUGH LLEWELLYN, Canadian business cons.; b. Toronto, Ont., July 7, 1898; s. Ellis William and Margaret Louise (Irvine) K.; B.A., U. B.C., 1920, LL.D., 1945; M.A., Clark U., 1921, Ph.D., 1923, LL.D., 1951; LL.D., Carleton Coll., Northfield, Minn., 1947, McMaster U., Ont., 1949, Saint Ambrose Coll., Davenport, 1954, Carleton Coll., Ottawa. 1956; D.Sc., New Sch. Social Research, 1958; m. Katherine Hall Pillsbury, Aug. 11, 1924; children—Mary (Mrs. Sydney Segal), Miles, Anne (Mrs. J.A. McCullum), Lynn (Mrs. Gordon C. Jackson), Lectr. history U. B.C., 1925-27; staff Dept. External Affairs, Ottawa, 1928; counsellor, 1940-41; 1st sec. Canadian legation, Tokyo, Japan, 1929-36, asst. under-sec. state for external affairs, 1941-44; Canadian ambassador to Mexico, 1944-47; del. gen. assembly UN, 1946; dep. minister Mines and Resources, 1947-50; head Can. delegation UN Sci. Conf. on Conservation and Utilization of Resources, 1949; chief UN Tech. Assistance Mission to Bolivia, 1950; dir. gen. tech. assistance adminstrn. UN, 1950-58; under-sec. for pub. adminstrn. UN, 1959; chmn. Power Commn., B.C. Can., 1959-62, Hydro and Power Authority, 1962-69. Mem. Can.-U.S. Joint Bd. Def., 1940-45, War Tech. and Sci. Devel. Com., 1941-45; mem. N.W. Tys. Council, 1941-45, chmn. council, 1947- 50. Bd. govs. Carleton Coll.; trustee Clark U.; mem. senate U. B.C., 1963-69; chancellor Notre Dame U., Nelson, B.C., 1969—. Served with 2d tank bn. Canadian Army, World War I. Recipient Haldane medal Royal Inst. Pub. Adminstrn., 1954; named Companion of Can., 1969. Fellow Royal Geog. Soc. Gt. Britain, Royal Hist. Soc. Gt. Britain, Asiatic Soc. Japan; mem. Arctic Inst. N.Am., Canadian Inst. Pub. Adminstrn. (Vanier medal 1962), Canadian Geog. Soc., Assn. Canadian Clubs (pres. 1948). Unitarian. Author: (with A.F. Thomas), History of Japanese Education, 1937; Canada and the United States, last edit., 1952; International Aid: A Summary, 1966. Address: 3470 Mayfair Dr Victoria British Columbia Canada

KEENY, SPURGEON MILTON, Jr., govt. ofcl.; b. N.Y.C., Oct. 24, 1924; s. Spurgeon Milton and Amelia (Smith) K.; B.A., Columbia, 1944, M.A. in Physics, 1946, postgrad. Sch. Internat. Affairs and Russian Inst., 1946-47; m. Sheila Spear, May 3, 1952; children-Christopher Spear, Christy Virginia, Spurgeon Milton III. Chief spl. weapons sect. Directorate of Intelligence, Hdqrs. USAF, 1950- 55; staff mem. Panel on Peaceful Uses Atomic Energy, Joint Congl. Com. Atomic Energy, Washington, 1955-56; chief atomic energy div. Office of Asst. Sec. Defense for Research and Engring., Washington, 1956-57; mem. Gaither security resources panel Exec. Office of Pres., 1957; tech. asst. to President's Sci. Adviser, Washington, 1958-69; Sr. staff mem. Nat. Security Council, 1963-69; asst. dir. sci. and tech. Arms Control and Disarmament Agy., Washington, 1969—. Mem. U.S. delegation to Geneva Conf. Experts on Nuclear Test Detection, 1958, Geneva Conf. on Discontinuance of Nuclear Weapons Tests, 1958-60. Served to 1st lt., USAF, 1948-50. Recipient Rockefeller pub. Service award, 1970. Mem. Am. Phys. Soc., Phi Beta Kappa. Home: 3600 Albemarle St N W Washington DC 20008 Office: U S Arms Control and Disarmament Agency Washington DC 20451

KEEPPER, WENDELL EDGAR, economist, univ. dean; b. Hillsboro, Ill., Sept. 7, 1910; s. Edgar Roy and Elizabeth (Haywood) K.; student Blackburn Coll., 1928-30; B.S., U. Ill., 1934; M.S., Cornell U., 1936, Ph.D., 1938; m. Alta Hyde Lewis, Dec. 22, 1934; children—Carolyn Grace, Roger Allan, Christopher Colin, Holly Elizabeth. Rural sch. tchr., Montgomery County, Ill., 1930-32; asst. agrl. econs. Cornell U., 1934-37, instr. Agrl. Econs. Extension 1938; asst. prof. Pa. State Coll., 1938-41, asso. prof., 1941-43, prof., 1943-50; prof., chmn. agr. dept. So. Ill. U., Carbondale, 1950-57, acting dir. div. rural studies, 1953-55, dean Sch. Agr., 1955—. On leave as adviser to Spl. Funds Project, FAO Agrl. Office, Rome, Italy, 1960-62; cons. economist Inter-Am. Inst. Agrl. Scis., Turrialba, Costa Rica, 1948-49; mem. adv. bd. Ill. Farmer Home Adminstrn., 1953-54; mem. Ill. bd. agrl. advisers Dept. Agr., 1953—; mem. Ill. Agrl. Export Adv. Com., 1964-66; agrl. officer FAO, Station-Caracas, Venezuela, 1956; cons. FAO, Teheran, Iran, 1965—, UN Spl. Fund, Cochabamba, Bolivia, 1964, Internat. Bank Reconstrn. and Devel., Venezuela, 1966. Mem. Am. Farm Econs. Assn., Alpha Zeta, Gamma Sigma Delta, Phi Kappa Phi, Alpha Tau Alpha. Methodist. Contbr. articles to profl. jours. Office: Sch Agr So Ill U Carbondale IL 62901

KEESHAN, BOB, TV producer-actor; b. N.Y.C., June 27, 1927; s. Joseph and Margaret (Conroy) K.; student Fordham U., 1946-49; Pd.D., R.I. Coll., 1969; D.H.L., Alfred U., 1969; m. Anne Jeanne Laurie, Dec. 30, 1950; children—Michael Derek, Laurie Margaret, Maeve Jeanne. Appeared as Clarabell on Howdy Doody Show, NBC-TV, 1947-52, as Corny the Clown on Time for Fun, ABC-TV, 1953-55; producer, also appeared as Tinker the Toymaker on Tinker's Workshop, ABC-TV, 1954-55; producer, appearing as Captain Kangaroo on Captain Kangaroo, CBS-T'V, 1955—; producer, appeared as Mr. Mayor and The Town Clown on Mr. Mayor, CBS-TV, 1964-65; pres. Robert Keeshan Assos., 1955—. Mem. bd. edn., W. Islip, N.Y., 1953- 58; pres. Suffolk County Hearing and Speech Center; mem. Suffolk County council Boy Scouts Am. Bd. dirs. Nat. Assn. Hearing and Speech Agys., Good Samaritan Hosp., West Islip, N.Y., United Fund L.I. Served with USMCR, 1945- 46. Recipient Sylvania award, 1956, Peabody award, 1958, Jr. Membership award Cal. Fedn. Women's Clubs, 1961, 62, Freedom Found. award, 1962, Page One award, 1965, Ursula Laurus award Coll. New Rochelle, 1958. Clubs: L. I. Yacht (commodore 1964-65) (Babylon); Southward Ho Country (Bashore, N.Y.). Author: (juvenile) She Loves Me... She Loves Me Not..., 1963. Home: 20 Melbury Rd Babylon NY 11702 Office: 1271 6th Av New York City NY 10009

KEESHAN, SISTER MARGARET MARY, coll. pres.; b. Albany, N.Y., May 10, 1915; d. Clarence S. and Elizabeth (Flanagan) Keeshan; B.S., Coll. St. Rose, Albany, 1950, M.A., 1952; Ph.D., St. John's U., N.Y.C., 1958. Tchr., Albany Diocese, Troy N.Y., 1936-42, 47-51, Syracuse (N.Y.) Diocese, 1942-47; faculty Coll. St. Rose, 1951—, chmn. biology dept., 1961-66, pres., 1966—. Mem. A.A.A.S., Soc. Protozoology, Am. Soc. Zoology, Am. Inst. Biol. Sci., N.Y. Acad. Sci., Delta Epsilon Sigma. Contbr. articles profl. jours. Address: Coll of St Rose Albany NY 12203

KEESING, FRANS ARNOLD GEORGE, economist; b. Hilversum, The Netherlands, Aug. 7, 1913; s. Arnold and Francisca (Gunzel) K.; Ph.D. in Econs., U. Amsterdam, 1939; m. Geertruida Kok, Apr. 4, 1939; children—Frans J., Wouter, Hugo A., Joost. With Unilever Bros., London, Eng., 1937-39, Ministry Commerce, The Hague, 1939-45, Ministry Finance, 1945-51; with Internat. Monetary Fund, Washington, 1951—, dir. fund's inst., 1964—; prof. money and credit U. Amsterdam, 1946-51. Decorated Lion of Netherlands; Crown of Belgium; Legion of Honor (France). Author books and articles in field. Home: 7809 Greentwig Rd Bethesda MD 20034 Office: Internat Monetary Fund Washington DC 20431

KEESLING, FRANCIS VALENTINE, Jr., ins. co. exec.; b. San Francisco, Mar. 3, 1908; s. Francis Valentine and Haidee (Grau) K.; grad. Phillips Acad., Andover, Mass.; A.B., Yale, 1930; LL.B., Stanford, 1933; m. Mary Heath, Mar. 20, 1935; 1 son, Francis Valentine III. Admitted to Cal. bar, 1934; practice in San Francisco, 1934-55; asst. counsel West Coast Life Ins. Co., San Francisco, 1936-38, counsel, 1938-45, v.p., gen. counsel, 1945-47, 1st v.p., gen. counsel, 1949-63, dir., 1954—, pres., 1963-68, chmn. bd., 1968—. Chief liaison and legislative officer nat. headquarters SSS, Washington, 1940-45, spl. adv. to dir., 1945—; Washington rep. City and County of San Francisco, 1948-55. Mem. welfare com. City and County of San Francisco, 1946-47; mem. San Francisco Bay Area Council; chmn. task force alcohol and drugs Gov.'s Com. on Traffic Safety; mem. adv. com. on alcoholism Cal. Dept. Pub. Health; sr. council, past pres. San Francisco YMCA. Bd. dirs. Cal. Traffic Safety Found., Nat. Council on Alcoholism San Francisco Area. Served from lt. to col. U.S. Army. Decorated D.S.M. Mem. Assn. Life. Ins. Counsel (exec. com., pres. 1956-57), Am. Life Conv. (legal sect., past state v.p., del. ho. dels. Am. Bar Assn. 1962-63), Nat. Conf. Lawyers and Life Ins. Cos., Health Ins. Assn. Am., Cal., San Francisco bar assns., San Francisco Art Assn. (past pres.), Cal. Ins. Fedn. (v.p., past pres.), Chi Psi, Phi Delta Phi. Mason. Clubs: Stock Exchange, Bankers, Pacific Union (San Francisco); Capitol Hill (Washington). Home: 930 Chestnut St San Francisco CA 94109 Office: 605 Market St San Francisco CA 94105

KEESLING, FRANK MORTON, lawyer; b. Dos Palos, Cal., Sept. 5, 1907; s. Isaac James and Mary (Graham) K.; student Fresno State Coll., 1924-26; A.B., U. Cal. at Berkeley, 1928; LL.B., Boalt Hall of Law, Berkeley, 1931; m. Wilhelmina Smythe, May 11, 1931; children—William S., Alan F., Admitted to Cal. bar 1931; research asst. Cal. Bd. Equalization, Sacramento, 1931-32; asst. legal adviser Tax Research Bur., Sacramento, 1932-33; asst. sec. Cal. Bd. Equalization, Sacramento, 1933-35; counsel Cal. Franchise Tax Commn., Sacramento, 1935-38; asso. Loeb & Loeb, 1939-43, now partner; Cal. lectr. U. Cal. Law Sch. at Berkeley, 1950—, U. Cal. Law Sch. at Los Angeles, 1950—. Mem. Am. Law Inst., Assn. State Tax Adminstrs., Nat. Tax Assn., Town Hall. Co-author: Allocation of Income on State Taxation, 1946-50; contbr. numerous articles pub. in profl. jours. Home: 2356 Hollyridge Dr Los Angeles CA 90028 Office: One Wilshire Bldg Wilshire Blvd at Grand Av Los Angeles CA 90017

KEETON, MORRIS TEUTON, coll. adminstr.; b. Clarksville, Tex., Feb. 1, 1917; s. William Robert and Ernestine (Tuten) K.; B.A., So. Meth. U., 1935, M.A., 1936; M.A., Harvard, 1937, Ph.D., 1938; m. Ruth Urice, Jan. 9, 1944; children—Gary KaDel, Scot, Gerlinde Joan. Instr. philosophy and social sci. So. Meth. U., 1938-41; ednl. sec. Brethren Civilian Pub. Service, 1942-45; ordained to ministry Meth. Ch., 1946; mem. faculty Antioch Coll., 1947—, prof. philosophy and religion, 1956—, coll. pastor, 1947-60, dir. Carnegie study Antioch ednl. program, 1956-60, dean faculty, 1963-66, acad. v.p., 1966—; Coll. examiner N. Central Assn. Colls. and Secondary Schs., 1960—; mem. bd. edn. Yellow Springs Exempted Village Sch. Dist., 1961-65; mem. personnel guidelines com. Ohio Sch. Bds. Assn., 1963-64; head mission in Germany, Am. Friends Service Com., 1953-55, chmn. internat. confs. and seminars program com., 1959-63, chmn. diplomats conf., Clarens, Switzerland, 1961, chmn. mission to Germany, 1963. Guggenheim fellow, 1946. Fellow Soc. Religion Higher Edn.; mem. Am. Philos. Assn. (sec.-treas. Western div. 1959-61, chmn. Carus Lectures com. 1965-69), Am. Assn. U. Profs., Assn. Higher Edn. (exec. com. 1965-66, dir. campus governance program 1966-69, pres. 1972-73). Democrat. Author: The Philosophy of Edmund Montgomery, 1950; Values Men Live By, 1960; Shared Authority on Campus, 1971; Models and Mavericks—A Profile of Liberal Arts Colleges, 1971; co-author: Journey Through a Wall, 1964; Ethics for Today, 4th edit., 1966; Struggle and Promise: A Future for Colleges, 1969. Editor: (with Harold Titus) The Range of Ethics, 1966. Home: 10989 Swansfield Rd Columbia MD 21043

KEETON, ROBERT ERNEST, educator, lawyer; b. Clarkeville, Tex., Dec. 16, 1919; s. William Robert and Ernestine (Tuten) K.; B.B.A., U. Tex., 1940, LL.B., 1941; S.J.D., Harvard, 1956; m. Betty E. Baker, May 28, 1941; children—Katherine, William Robert. Admitted to Tex. bar, 1941, Mass. bar, 1955; asso. firm Baker, Botts, Andrews & Wharton, and successors, Houston, 1941-42, 45-51; asso. prof. law So. Meth. U., 1951-54; Thayer teaching fellow Harvard, 1953-54, asst. prof., 1954-56, prof. law, 1956—. Commnr. on Uniform State Laws from Mass., 1971—. Served to lt. comdr. USNR, 1942-45. Decorated Bronze Star. Mem. Am. Bar Assn., State Bar Tex., Am. Law Inst., Am. Risk and Ins. Assn., Am. Assn. U. Profs., Chancellors, Friars, Order of Coif, Beta Gamma Sigma, Beta Alpha Psi, Phi Delta Phi, Phi Eta Sigma. Author: Trial Tactics and Methods, 1954; (with Page Keeton) Cases and Materials on the Law of Torts, 1971; Basic Text on Insurance Law, 1971; Legal Cause in the Law of Torts, 1963; (with Jeffrey O'Connell) Basic Protection for the Traffic Victim; A Blueprint for Reforming Automobile Insurance, 1965; After Cars Crash—The Need for Legal and Insurance Reform, 1967; Venturing To Do Justice, 1969; also articles. Home: 25 Avon St Cambridge MA 02138

KEETON, WERDNER PAGE, univ. dean; b. Clarksville, Tex., Aug. 22, 1909; s. William Robert and Mildred Ernestine (Tuten) K.; B.A., LL.B., U. of Tex., 1931; S.J.D., Harvard, 1936; m. Madge Anna Stewart, Mar. 4, 1934; children—Richard Page, Carole Stewart. Asst. prof. law U. Tex., 1932-35, asso. prof. law, 1936-39, prof. law, 1939-42; dean Sch. Law, U. of Okla., 1946-49, dean U. Tex. Law Sch., 1949—. Served successively as chief counsel fuel div. and price exec. petroleum br. OPA, Washington, 1942-45; asst. chief counsel Petroleum Adminstrn. for War, Washington, 1945. Pres. Assn. Am. Law Schs., 1962, mem. panel of law sch. advisers to exec. com., 1948; mem. Jud. Council of Okla., 1946-49; mem. Law Enforcement Study Commn. Tex., 1958. Fellow Am. Bar Found. (bd. dirs.); mem. Tex., Okla., Am. bar assns., Phi Beta Kappa, Order of Coif, Phi Delta Phi, Alpha Tau Omega, Pi Sigma Alpha. Democrat. Methodist. Home: 5316 Western Hills Dr Austin TX 78731

KEETTEL, WILLIAM CHARLES Jr., physician, educator; b. Lyons, Neb., Apr. 30, 1911; s. William Charles and Eunice Una (Rohde) K.; A.B., B.Sc., U. Neb., 1932, M.D., 1936; m. Mary Helen Shinn, June 30, 1940; 1 son, William David. Rotating intern U. Ind., 1936-37; resident obstetrics and gynecology State U. Ia., Iowa City, 1937- 40, asst. prof., 1946-49, asso. prof., 1949-53, prof., 1953—, head dept. obstetrics and gynecology, 1959—; postgrad. instr. State Dept. Health, U. Wis. Med. Sch., 1940-42. Mem. reviewing bd. maternal deaths in Ia. Dir. Am. Bd. Obstetrics and Gynecology. Fellow A.C.S. (tripartite residency review com. obstetrics and gynecology, residency rev. com.); mem. Am. Coll. Obstetricians and Gynecologists, Am., Central assns. obstetricians and gynecologists, Central Travel Club Obstetricians and Gynecologists, Ia. Obstet. and Gynecol. Soc., Am. Gynecol. Soc. Contbr. articles to profl. jours. Home: 343 Hutchinson Av Iowa City IA 52240

KEFFER, FREDERIC, physicist, educator; b. Anaconda, Mont., May 23, 1919; s. Robert and Placie (Munter) K.; B.S., Wash. State U., 1945; Ph.D., U. Cal. at Berkeley, 1952; m. Lore Maria Sanders, Apr. 24, 1949; children-Thomas, Leslie. Faculty physics U. Pitts., 1952—, prof., 1959—, ept. chmn., 1963—; vis. prof. physics U. Cal. at Berkeley, 1959-60. Cons. Westinghouse Research Labs., 1952-55, Bell Telephone Labs., summer 1961. Mem. A.A.A.S., Am. Phys. Soc. Contbr. articles profl. jours. Home: 235 Woodside Rd Pittsburgh PA 15221

KEFFER, WILLIAM WARD, ins. co. exec.; b. Hartford, Conn., Mar. 19, 1922; B.A. in Math., Brown U., 1943; m. Kathleen E. Lard, June 11, 1949. With Conn. Gen. Life Ins. Co., Hartford, 1946—, v.p., 1965-69, sr. v.p., 1969—. Home: Barnes Hill Rd Burlington CT 06022 Office: Conn Gen Life Ins Co Hartford CT 06115

KEFFORD, NOEL PRICE, educator, botanist; b. Melbourne, Australia, Feb. 5, 1927; s. Richard Alfred and Mary (Price) K.; came to U.S., 1965; B.Sc., U. Melbourne, 1948, M.Sc., 1950; Ph.D., U. London (Eng.), 1954; m. Helen Marion Hanna, Aug. 19, 1950; children—Michele Jean, Louise Judith, Hugh Donald. Prin. research officer, div. plant industry Commonwealth Sci. and Indsl. Research Orgn., Canberra, Australia, 1950-65; prof. botany, chmn. depts. botany and plant physiology U. Hawaii, Honolulu, 1965—; research fellow Harvard, 1953-54; research asso. Yale, 1962-63. Mem. Am., Australian soc. plant physiologists, Hawaiian Bot. Soc., Sigma Xi. Contbr. articles to profl. jours. Home: 1903 Puu Nanea Pl Honolulu HI 96822

KEGEL, CHARLES HERBERT, coll. dean; b. Chgo., Aug. 16, 1924; s. Charles and Helene (Schwaldt) K.; A.B., Alma (Mich.) Coll., 1947; M.A., Northwestern U., 1948; Ph.D., Mich. State U., 1955; m. Carol Drown, June 24, 1950; children—Erik Anders, Garth Calvin. Instr., Mich. State U., 1951-56; faculty Ida. State U., Pocatello, 1956—, prof. English 1962—, head div. humanities, 1960-63, dean Coll. Liberal Arts, 1963-67, dean faculties, 1966-68, acad. v.p., 1968—. Vice chmn. Ida. Commn. for Arts, 1966; mem. Bonneville Power Authority Adv. Com., 1963—; pres. Pocatello Civil Rights Com., 1964-66. Served with USNR, 1943-46. Mem. Modern Lang. Assn., Philol. Assn. Pacific Coast, Rocky Mountain Modern Lang. Assn. Author: Communications Principles and Practice, 1958; Glossary for College English, 1966; Lyric Poems on Twelve Themes, 1969. Editor: Earl Miller's Recollections of the Ruskin Cooperative Association, 1958. Contbr. articles to profl. jours. Home: 161 16th Pl Pocatello ID 83201

KEGELES, GERSON, educator, chemist; b. New Haven, Apr. 23, 1917; s. Alex and Jennie (Wilder) K.; B.S. in Chemistry, Yale, 1937, Ph.D., 1940, postgrad., 1940-41; postdoctoral research U. Wis., 1945-47; m. Bertha Webber, Apr. 16, 1944; children—Winifred, Lawrence, Stanley, Gloria, Joyce. Research phys. chemist Nat. Cancer Inst., 1947-51; mem. faculty Clark U., Worcester, Mass., 1951-68, prof. chemistry, 1956-68, chmn. dept., 1960-63; prof. biophys. chemistry U. Conn., Storrs, 1968—; cons. to industry, 1954—. Served with AUS, 1941-45. Mem. Am. Acad. Arts and Scis., Am. Chem. Soc., Am. Soc. Biol. Chemists, Biophys. Soc., Washington Acad. Scis. Contbr. articles profl. jours., sects. books. Home: Oakwood Dr RFD2 Stafford Springs CT 06076 Office: U Conn Storrs CT 06268

KEGLEY, CHARLES WILLIAM, educator; b. Chgo., Feb. 17, 1912; s. Charles R.W. and Orpha M. (Koch) K.; B.A., Northwestern U., 1933, M.A., 1937, Ph.D., 1943; B.D., Chgo. Luth. Sem., 1936; children—Charles, John Franklyn, Jacquelyn Ann; m. 2d, Jacquelyn Ann Kovacevic, June 12, 1965. Ordained to ministry Luth. Ch., 1937; pastor Luth. Ch., Evanston, Ill., 1940-45; chmn. univ. bd. religion and dir. John Evans Religious Center, Northwestern U., 1944-46; lectr. philosophy Northwestern U., 1946-50; prof. philosophy religion and ethics, dean Grad. Sch., Chgo. Luth. Theol. Sem., Maywood, Ill., 1945-50; prof. philosophy Wagner Coll., N.Y.C., 1949-69; prof. philosophy, chmn. dept. philosophy and religious studies Cal. State Coll., Bakersfield, 1969—; Rockefeller vis. prof. philosophy U. Philippines, 1965. Condr. study tours, Europe, Far East, 1939—; del. XIII Internat. Congress Aesthetics, 1964, XIV Congress, 1968; chmn. Am. Luth. delegation World Conf. Christian Youth, Amsterdam, 1939; lectr. Internat. Congress, Philosophy, Brussels, 1953, Venice, 1958, Athens, 1960, Mexico, 1963. Mem. Am. Philos. Assn., Am. Soc. Reformation Research, European Soc. Culture, Am. Soc. Ch. History, Am. Theol. Soc., Omicron Delta Kappa. Clubs: Rich County Country (N.Y.C.); University (Chgo.). Author: Protestantism in Transition, 1965; Politics, Religion and Modern Man, 1968; co-author: Religion in Modern Life, 1956; Existence Today, 1957. Founder, editor Library of Living Theology; co-editor: The Theology of Paul Tillich, 1952; Reinhold Niebuhr—His Religious, Social and Political Thought, 1956; editor: The Theology of Emil Brunner, 1966; The Theology of Rudolph Bultman, 1970; The Philosophy and Theology of Anders Nygren, 1970. Home: 7115 Mesa Verde Way Bakersfield CA 93309

KEHART, MARTIN WILLIAM, civil engr., retired naval officer; b. Rathmel, Pa., June 17, 1902; s. William and Pearl (Koval) K.; B.S., U. Ill., 1926; m. Louise Martin, Feb. 14, 1931; 1 dau., Charlotte (Mrs. Dennis LeRoy Lang). Jr. engr. U.S. Army Engrs., Peoria, Ill., 1926-27; bridge designer, resident engr. bridge constrn. Bridge Dept. Ark., 1927, 33-38; constrn. engr. Lakeside Bridge & Steel Co., Milw., 1928-33; resident engr. insp. Pub. Works Adminstrn., Little Rock, also Texarkana, 1938-39; commd. lt., C.E., USN, 1939, advanced through grades to rear adm., 1956; successively resident officer charge constrn., Palmyra Island, project mgr. constrn., Pearl Harbor, officer charge constrn. Naval Tng. Sta., Farragut, Ida., pub. works officer Naval Operating Base, Norfolk, Va., asst. and acting chief insp. Bur. Yards and Docks, Washington, officer charge constrn. Alaska Contracts, Adak, dist. pub. works officer 3d Naval Dist., N.Y.C., asst. chief for operations Bur. Yards and Docks, dist. pub. works officer 14th Naval Dist., Pearl Harbor, dir. Atlantic div. Bur. Yards and Docks, N.Y.C., 1939-58, insp. gen. Bur. Yards and Docks, Washington, 1958-59, dir. Atlantic div. and area pub. works officer N.Y., 1959-61, cons. engr., mem. Internat. Tech. Commn. Locate Site for Capital Proposed Independence of W.I., 1961-62; partner Singstad & Kehart, N.Y.C., 1962—. Registered profl. civil engineer, Ark. N.Y., Conn., Va., Mich., N.H. Mem. Internat. Assn. Bridge and Structural Engrs., Moles, Soc. Am. Military Engrs. (past pres. Washington post, also N.Y.C. post), Am. Soc. C. E., Am. Concrete Inst., Am. Inst. Cons. Engrs. Mason. Clubs: Downtown Athletic, N.Y. Yacht, Engineers (N.Y.C.), Army-Navy Country (Washington). Home: 88 Poplar St Garden City NY 11530 Office: 17 Battery Pl New York City NY 10004

KEHL, WILLIAM LOUIS, physicist; b. Canton, O., Apr. 14, 1915; s. Herman E. and Lela (Shepherd) K.; A.B., Washington and Jefferson Coll., 1938; M.S., State U. Ia., 1941; postgrad. U. Pitts., 1944-47; m. Marie E. Clark, Nov. 28, 1942; children—Dennis W., Lorraine E. Sr. research physicist Gulf Research & Devel. Co., Pitts., 1941—. Sec.-treas. U.S. Nat. Com. for Crystallography, 1971—. Pres. Fox Chapel Water Authority, 1968-70. Mem. Am. Crystallographic Assn. (sec. 1964-69), Am. Phys. Soc., Sigma Xi, Phi Kappa Psi. Contbr. articles profl. jours. Patentee in field. Home: 1942 Fox Chapel Rd Pittsburgh PA 15238 Office: PO Drawer 2038 Pittsburgh PA 15230

KEHOE, EDWARD MARTIN, banker; b. Lynn, Mass., Mar. 7, 1911; s. John C. and Dorothy (Hennion) K.; student Boston U., 1930; student Grad. Sch. Banking at Rutgers U., 1952; student Mgmt. Devel. Program, U. Mass., 1969; m. Margaret E. Deacon, July 7, 19937; children-Edward R., Barbara L. (Mrs. Gerald Weber), Peter A. With Suffolk Franklin Savs. Bank, Boston, 1928—, sr. v.p., 1966-67, exec. v.p., 1968-69, pres., 1969—; dir. treas. Met. Mortgage Bur., Boston, 1966—. Mem. Greater Boston Real Estate Bd., Boston, 1960—. Mason. Home: 116 Boardman Av Melrose MA 02176 Office: 45 Franklin St Boston MA 02110

KEHOE, THOMAS JOSEPH, instrument co. exec.; b. Bisbee, Ariz., June 16, 1919; s. Dennis A. and Alice Mary (Nikodem) K.; B.S., Loyola U., Los Angeles, 1941; m. Regina Mary Wallace, Apr. 22, 1950; children—Patricia Ann, Kathleen Marie, Judith Ann, John Thomas, Mary Jean, Joseph Thomas. Supr. research and devel. dept. Am. Potash & Chem. Corp., Trona, Cal., 1941-49; cons. indsl. waste treatment, 1949-54; mgr. application engring. dept., process instrument div. Beckman Instruments, Inc., Fullerton, Cal., 1954—. Mem. Grand Jury Orange County, 1964. Fellow Instrument Soc. Am. (dir., v.p., pres. 1969-70), Am. Inst. Chemists; mem. Am. Chem. Soc., Am. Inst. Chem. Engrs. Contbr. chpt. to Treatise in Anal. Chemistry, 1964. Home: 920 N Grandview St Fullerton CA 92632 Office: 2500 Harbor Blvd Fullerton CA 92634

KEHR, AUGUST ERNEST, geneticist; b. Frankfort, Ky., Mar. 2, 1914; s. Carl Adolf and Anna Esther (Heller) K.; B.S., Cornell U., 1936, M.S., 1947, Ph.D., 1950; m. Mary Louise Coon, Dec. 26, 1942; 1 dau., Janet Marie. Tchr. sci. and agr., Unadilla, N.Y., 1936-42, Hudson, N.Y., 1942-47; research asst. plant breeding Cornell U., 1947-50; asso. prof. horticulture La. State U., 1950-54; with Dept. Agr., also prof. horticulture Ia. State U., 1954- 58; asst. br. chief, vegetables and ornamentals research br. Dept. Agr., Beltsville, Md., 1958-65, br. chief, 1965—. Mem. fellowship evaluation com. NSF, 1957-59; rep. Assn. Coll. Honor Socs. for Phi Kappa Phi, 1957-60. Mem. Am. Genetics Assn. (pres. 1964-66), Soc. Study Growth and Devel., Am. Potato Assn., Am. Soc. Hort. Sci., Sigma Xi, Phi Kappa Phi, Gamma Sigma Delta. Club: Cosmos. Contbr. articles to profl. jours., chpts. to books. Home: 10202 Green Forest Dr Silver Spring MD 20903 Office: Plant Industry Sta Beltsville MD 20705

KEHR, PHILIP B., ins. co. exec.; b. Prescott, Ariz. Mar. 11, 1908; A.B., Stanford, 1930; LL.B., Harvard, 1933. Admitted to Cal. bar; underwriter Swett & Crawford, Los Angeles, 1940-43; mgr. surety claims dept. Pacific Indemnity Co., Los Angeles, now sec., treas. Mem. Am., Los Angeles bar assns., Cal. State Bar, Surety Underwriters Club Los Angeles, Am. Soc. Corporate Secs., Inc. Home: 837 S Windsor Blvd Los Angeles CA 90005 Office: 3200 Wilshire Blvd Los Angeles CA 90054

KEIFER, LOUIS FREDERICK, newspaper pub.; b. Indpls. July 14, 1894; s. Andrew Charles and Ella (Conroy) K.; Ph.B., Notre Dame U., 1916; m. Marguerite Katherine McCauley, Nov. 5, 1924; 1 son, Louis Frederick. Automobile editor and advt. Terre Haute (Ind.) Tribune, 1916-17, nat. advt. mgr., 1919-31; nat. advt. mgr. Tribune & Star, 1931-35; asst. gen. mgr., v.p. Tribune- Star Pub. Co., Inc., Terre Haute 1935-40, gen. mgr., v.p., 1940-66, pres., gen. mgr., 1966—; v.p. Wabash Fed. Savs. & Loan Assn. Pres., Vigo County Tb Soc.; treas. Family Service Assn. Bd. dirs. YMCA, Goodwill Industries Nat. Found., Fresh Air Camp. Served to 1st lt. U.S. Army, 1917-19. Mem. Am. Legion, 40 and 8, 82d Div. Assn., Terre Haute C. of C. (past pres.). Roman Catholic. K.C., Rotarian (past pres.). Clubs: Country of Terre Haute (past pres.), Aero (past chmn. bd.), Serra (Terre Haute). Home: Allendale Terre Haute IN 47808 Office: 721 Wabash Av Terre Haute IN 47808

KEIGHLEY, WILLIAM J., motion picture dir.; b. Phila., Aug. 4, 1889; s. William Jackson and Mary (Hausel) K.; m. Genevieve Tobin, Sept. 19, 1938. Stage dir., N.Y.C., 1925-30; motion picture dir. Warner Bros., Burbank, Cal., 1930- 42; films directed include: Green Pastures, Robin Hood, The Man Who Came to Dinner, Varsity Show, 1936, Each Dawn I Die, Easy to Love, 1938, Yes My Darling Daughter, 1939, The Fighting 69th, 1940, No Time for Comedy, 1941, George Washington Slept Here, 1942; dir. Street with No Name, 20th Century-Fox, also films Rocky Mountain, Close to My Heart, Master of Ballantrae; producer Lux Radio Theatre; prod., dir. documentary Target for Today, selected by U.S. Treasury, 6th war loan drive; pioneer film selected for hist. library films U.S. Archives; compiled photog. documentation in color France's hist. monuments, serving base for lectures given ann., Musee des Arts Decoratifs, Paris. Served from lt. col. to col., USAAF, 1942-45; chief motion picture div., organized combat camera units. Decorated Legion of Merit; Silver medal City of Paris; fellow in perpetuity Met. Mus. Art, N.Y.C., 1959; chevalier des Arts et Lettres; chevalier de la Legion d' Honneur; Comdr. Legion de Merit (Spain). Address: 75 Av Foch Paris 16eme France

KEIGHTON, WALTER BARKER, Jr., educator, chemist; b. Swarthmore, Pa., June 17, 1901; s. Walter Barker and Jennie Hunter (Johnston) K.; B.A., Swarthmore Coll., 1923; Ph.D. (John Lockwood fellow), Princeton, 1933; m. Eleanor Mary Paxson, Aug. 21, 1926; children—Charles Earl, Robert Laurie, June (Mrs. Jerome K. Furlow), James Douglas, Walter Leslie. Chemist, E.I. duPont de Nemours & Co., Inc., 1923-25, Sharples Splty. Co., 1925-29; mem. faculty Swarthmore Coll., 1931—, prof., 1952—, Edmund Allen prof. chemistry, 1961—, chmn. dept., 1958—; chemist Sinclair Oil Co., summers 1938-40; tchr. Pa. State Coll., summer 1941; cons. Pa. Salt Co., 1948, Frankford Arsenal, 1951, Bartol Research Found., 1946-59; chemist U.S. Geol. Survey, 1951—. Mem. Am. Chem. Soc., Am. Geophys. Union, Am. Assn. U. Profs., N.E. Assn. Chemistry Tchrs., Delaware Valley Ornithol. Club, Am. Water Resources Assn., Phi Beta Kappa, Sigma Xi, Sigma Tau. Mem. Soc. of Friends. Author: The Investigation of Chemical Quality of Water in Tidal Rivers, 1954; (with C.N. Durfor) Chemical Characteristics of Delaware River Water, 1954; (with Garald Parker, Allen Hely, Franklin Olmsted) Quality of Water Resources of the Delaware River Basin, 1960; Quality of Delware River Water at Trenton, N.J., 1964; other publs. dealing with quality natural waters, chem. hydrology. Contbr. articles tech. jours. Home: 311 Cedar Lane Swarthmore PA 19081

KEIL, ALFRED ADOLF HEINRICH, ednl. adminstr.; b. Konradswaldau, Germany, May 1, 1913; s. Kurt Alfred and Marie (Berger) K.; Dr. nat. sc., U. Breslau (Germany), 1939, m. Ursula Leppelt, Oct. 15, 1943; children—Michael G., Juergen G. Came to U.S., 1947, naturalized, 1954. Research asst. U. Breslau, 1939-40; research asso. Chem.-Phys. Research Establishment, Kiel, Germany, 1940- 45; chief scientist underwater esplosive research div. Norfolk Naval Shipyard, Portsmouth, Va., 1947-59; tchr. dir. structural mech. lab. David Taylor Model Basin, 1959-63, tech. dir. basin, 1963-66; prof., head dept. naval architecture and marine engring. Mass. Inst. Tech., 1966-71, dean Sch. Engring., 1971—. Served with German Army, 1939-40. Recipient Civilian Distinguished Service award Navy Dept., 1963; Gibbs Bros. gold medal for naval architecture Nat. Acad. Scis., 1967. Mem. Nat. Acad. Engring., Am. Soc. Naval Engrs. (Gold Medal award 1964), Soc. Naval Architects and Marine Engrs., Am. Phys. Soc. Contbr. articles profl. jours. Home: 39 Hillside Terrace Belmont MA 02178 Office: Mass Inst Tech Cambridge MA 02139

KEIM, ADDISON JOHN, banker; b. Albany, N.Y., July 23, 1917; s. Addison and Emma (Pfeil) K.; B.S., Syracuse U., 1939; postgrad. Grad. Sch. Banking, Rutgers U., 1951; m. Marjorie Meuser, July 24, 1945; children—Joan Lynn, Addison John. With sales dept. Tobin Packing Co., 1939-41; with Nat. Comml. Bank & Trust Co., Albany, 1946-48; mortgage clk., sec., v.p., exec. v.p. Albany Exchange Savs. Bank (name now Mechanics Exchange Savs. Bank), Albany, 1948—, pres., 1963—, trustee, 1957—; dir. Albany Parking, Inc., Albany Park & Shop. Mem. Albany County Mental Health Assn., 1962-69; mem. budget panel Albany Community Chest, 1958-63; chmn. Russell Sage Coll. fund drive, Albany, 1958. Treas., bd. dirs. Northeastern N.Y. Speech Center, St. Agnes Fathers Assn.; bd. dirs. Albany Acad. Fathers Assn., Practical Nurser Tng. Sch.; trustee Savs. Bank Life Ins. Fund; mem. adv. com. N.Y. State Tchrs. Retirement System-Mortgage. Served from 2d lt. to lt. col., USAAF, 1941-46. Mem. Mortgage Bankers Assn., N.Y. State Savs. Banks Assn. (past chmn.), Investment Officers Assn. of Savs. Banks (past pres.), Greater Albany C. of C. (past v.p. dir.,). Rotarian. Clubs: University Albany; Schuyler Meadows Loudonville; New York Athletic; Fort Orange (trustee). Home: 4 S Loudon Lane Loudonville NY 12211 Office: 111 Washington Av Albany NY 12201

KEIM, CHARLES JOSEPH, educator; b. Judith Gap, Mont., Nov. 2, 1922; s. Francis Folmer and Jennie May (Thayer) K.; B.A. in Journalism, U. Wash., 1948, M.A. in History, 1950; m. Betty Joyce Boyd, Apr. 16, 1944; children—Janet Marie, Ann Theresa, Bruce Charles. Reporter, U.P.I., 1940; part-time asso. journalism U. Wash. Sch. Journalism, 1949; news editor Port Angeles (Wash.) Eve. News, 1950-54; tchr. adult evening edn. program Port Angeles Sch. Dist., 1953; faculty U. Alaska, College, 1954—, prof. journalism and English, 1961—, dean Coll. Arts and Letters, 1963-70. Mem. Fairbanks adv. bd. Alaska Dept. Fish and Game, 1963-70. Served with inf. AUS, 1940- 45; PTO. Decorated Bronze Star, Combat Inf. badge; recipient awards for writing Wash. Press Club, 1954, Alaska Press Club, 1955, 57, 64, 70; Centennial Lit. Achievement award, 1967; named Outstanding Prof., U. Alaska Alumni Assn., 1962, Alaska 49'er, Alaska Press Club, 1964. Mem. Nat. Riflemens Assn. (life), Sigma Delta Chi. Roman Catholic. Club: Explorers (N.Y.C.). Author: Aghvook, White Eskimo, 1969; The Gallant Try, 1970. Contbr. articles mags., author short stories. Home: Box 80-242 College AK 99701

KEIM, CHRISTOPHER PETER, educator; b. Tecumseh, Neb., Apr. 6, 1906; s. Jacob Henry and Mary (Pohlenz) K.; A.B., Neb. Wesleyan U., 1927, D.Sc., 1959; M.Sc., Neb. U., 1932, Ph.D., 1940; m. Lucille Parli, June 25, 1929; children—Virginia Ann Hayes, Robert Churistopher. With Lincoln Telephone & Telegraph Co. (Neb.), 1928-31; prof. phys. scis. York (Neb.) Coll., 1933-37; research fellow Neb. U., 1937-40; mem. chemistry faculty Tulsa U., 1940-41; research engr. Sylvania Electric Products Corp., Salem, Mass., 1941-42; research fellow Mellon inst., Pitts. 1942-44; sr. physicist Tenn. Eastman Corp., Oak Ridge, 1944-47, Union Carbide Corp., 1947; dir. Stable Isotope Research and Prodn. div. Oak Ridge Nat. Lab., 1947-57, dir. tech. information div., 1957-71; dir. field services Roane State Jr. Coll., 1971—. Dir. Mgmt. Services, Inc. Mem. tech. information panel AEC, 1957-71. Dir. Oak Ridge Utilities Bd. Recipient Alumni Achievement award Neb. Wesleyan U. Fellow Am. Phys. Soc., Tenn. Acad. Sci. (pres. 1960), A.A.A.S.; mem. Am. Mgmt. Assn., Am. Chem. Soc., Am. Nuclear Soc., Sigma Xi, Phi Lambda Upsilon, Sigma Pi Sigma. Methodist. Mason (32, Shriner), Rotarian. Contbr. articles sci. and edn. jours. Home: 102 Orchard Lane Oak Ridge TN 37830

KEIM, LEWIS PARKER, pub. relations exec.; b. Chgo., Oct. 15, 1930; s. Charles Perry and Ruby Marie (Parker) K.; B.A., U. Mont., 1953; m. Carol Cushman, Dec. 29, 1953; children—Kelly, Kathlyn, Jennifer, Mary, Karin. Reporter, Spokane (Wash.) Chronicle, 1953; capitol corr. U.P., Helena, Mont., 1953-55; dir. pub. relations Mont. C. of C., Helena, 1955-57; corporate pub. relations staff Allis-Chalmers, Milw., 1957-62; account exec. Burson-Marsteller, Chgo., 1962-64, v.p., 1964—. Mem. Pub. Relations Soc. Am., Chgo. Athletic Assn. Elk. Home: 603 E Euclid St Arlington Heights IL 60004 Office: 1 E Wacker Dr Chicago IL 60601

KEIM, ROBERT PHILLIP, advt. exec.; b. Ridgewood, N.Y., Jan. 28, 1920; s. William John and Josephine (Becht) K.; B.A. magna cum laude, Queen's Coll., student Grad. Sch. Internat. Relations, U. Md., 1950-51; m. Gloria Kathleen Smith, Jan. 24, 1943; children—William Gary, Barbara Kathleen. trainee Compton Advt., N.Y.C., 1942; campaigns mgr. Advt. Council, Inc., N.Y.C., 1954-61, pres., 1966—, also dir.; 2d. v.p. marketing service Chase Manhattan Bank, N.Y.C., 1962-66; dir. Valley Broadcasting Co., Ansonia, Conn., 1956-70: cons. supt. USAF Acad., 1958. Mem. Air Force Res. Policy Com., 1961 63; del. White House Conf. Edn., 1956: mem. Pres.'s Com. Traffic Safety, 1957-62; mem. pub. relations adv. com. Inst. Internat. Edn., 1963-65; mem. Nat. Adv. Council on Minority Bus. Enterprise. Mem. exec. com. Air Force Acad. Found. for Falcon Stadium Fund, 1960-61. Served as officer USAAF, 1942-54. Decorated Commendation ribbon; scholar Queens Coll., 1941; recipient Dept. English 1st in class award, 1942. Mem. Air Force Assn., Iron Gate Squadron, Assn. Nat. Advertiser, Nat. Reading Council. Clubs: Wings, Union League (N.Y.C.). Methodist (elder, past steward). Author: Air Force Academy Cadet Procurement Study, 1958; Reserve Forces Utilization Study, 1962; writer, prod. Air Force Hour, 1946-49, Armed Forces Hour, 1949-50.‡

KEIM, S. T., Jr., educator; B.A., Tex. A. and M. U., 1938, M.S., 1940; I.A., Harvard, 1953; Ph.D., U. Cal., 1954. Prof., chmn. dept. econs. U. Tex. at Arlington. Office: Dept Econs U Tex Arlington TX 76010*

KEIPER, BERNARD STEPHEN, grocery co. exec.; b. N.Y.C., Apr. 11, 1921; s. Stephen John and Tillie (Schnatz) K.; B.A., Fordham U., 1940; m. Grace L. Briza, May 30, 1952; children—Bernadette, Elizabeth, Stephen, Kathrine. Dir. data processing Snow Crop Co., 1952-56; dir. mgmt. information system Compton Advt., 1956-57; treas. Asso. Grocers Fla., Inc., Miami, 1957—; lectr. U. Miami, 1958—; cons. data processing. Served with USMCR, 1941-45; PTO. Decorated Purple Heart. Mem. Nat. Machine Accountants Assn.

(past v.p.). K.C., Kiawanian. Contbr. trade jours. Home: 13911 Lake Claire Ct Miami Lakes FL 33014 Office: 6695 NW 36th Av Miami FL 33152

KEISER, DAVID M., retired sugar co. exec.; b. Milw., Feb. 13, 1906; s. George Edward and Mary (Camp) K.; A.B., Harvard, 1927; m. Sylvia Kodjbanoff, Aug. 11, 1938; children—Basil Edward, David Spencer, Florence (Mrs. Romanov), Peter Camp. With N.Am. Sugar Industries, 1927-71, retired as pres., dir. Trustee Am. Farm Sch., Salonica, Greece, Juilliard Mus. Found., Sarah Lawrence Coll., Wooster Sch.; hon. chmn., bd. dirs. N.Y. Philharmonic Symphony Soc.; chmn. bd. dirs. Juilliard Sch. Music; bd. dirs. Lincoln Center for Performing Arts. Mem. Squadron A N.Y. N.G. (cav.), 1932-36. Mem. Soc. Mayflower Descs., Soc. Colonial Wars, Clubs: University, Harvard, Century Assn., Knickerbocker (N.Y.C.); Riding Club (Wilton). Home: 105 Seeley Rd Wilton CT 66897 Office: 500 Fifth Av New York City NY

KEISER, PAUL HAROLD, hosp. adminstr.; b. Dalton, O., June 1, 1927; s. Austin R. and Elrena (Tschantz) K.; B.S., Mt. Union Coll., Alliance, O., 1948; M.S. in Hosp. Adminstrn., Northwestern U., 1952; m. Nancy Fairchild Homan, May 27, 1950; children—James William, Martha Ann, Elizabeth Louise, Patricia Elrena. Bookkeeper, adminstrv. asst., adminstrv. resident Wesley Meml. Hosp., Chgo., 1949-52; adminstr. Community Hosp., Evanston, Ill., 1952-54, Burlington (Ia.) Hosp., 1954-67; adminstr. York (Pa.) Hosp., 1967-68, pres., 1968—; lectr., seminar leader Northwestern U. Program Hosp. Adminstrn., 1952-54, State U. Ia. Program Hosp. Adminstrn., 1955-59; lectr. health care George Washington U., 1969—. Pres. Ia. Interprofl. Assn., 1963-64; mem. Gov. Ia. Adv. Com. Pub. Health, 1963-66. Named Outstanding Young Man, Burlington C. of C., 1960. Fellow Am. Coll. Hosp. Adminstrs. (regent Ia. 1965-67), Royal Soc. Health; mem. Am. (del. 1963-66), Ia. (pres. 1961-62) hosp. assns., Northwestern U. Hosp. Adminstrn. Alumni (pres. 1958-59), Sigma Alpha Epsilon. Rotarian (pres. Burlington 1958-59). Contbr. articles profl. jours. Home: 721 Greendale Rd York PA 17403 Office: 1001 S George St York PA 17405

KEISLER, HOWARD JEROME, educator; b. Seattle, Dec. 3, 1936; s. Harry Benton and Marion (Siegel) K.; B.S., Cal. Inst. Tech., 1959; Ph.D., U. Cal., 1961; m. Lois Joyce Hoffman, May 1, 1959; children—Randall Benjamin, Jeffrey Michael, Thomas David. Mathematician Inst. Def. Analysis, Princeton, 1961-62; asst. prof. math. U. Wis., 1962-64, asso. prof., 1964-67, prof., 1967—; vis. prof. U. Cal. at Los Angeles, 1967-68. Alfred P. Sloan fellow, 1966-69. Mem. Am. Math. Soc., Assn. Symbolic Logic (exec. com. 1968-71). Jewish religion. Author: (with C.C. Chang) Continuous Model Theory, 1966, Model Theory, 1972; Model Theory for Infinitesimals Logic, 1971; Elementary Calculus: an Approach Using Infinitesimals, 1971. Home: 6318 Masthead Dr Madison WI 53705

KEITEL, GLENN HOWARD, educator; b. Chgo., Feb. 16, 1930; s. Fred and Harriet (Johnson) K.; B.S. magna cum laude, U. Wash., 1952, M.S., 1954; Ph.D., Stanford, 1955; student Cambridge (Eng.) U., 1955-56; m. Laurel Josephine Lund, June 12, 1953; children—Kristin Marie, Karin Anne. Mem. tech. staff Gen. Electric Co., Palo Alto, Cal., 1956-59; mgr. communications scis. dept. Philco Corp., Palo Alto, 1959-62; prof. elec. engring., chmn. dept. San Jose (Cal.) State Coll., 1962-69; electronics liaison scientist U.S. Office Naval Research, London, Eng., 1963-64; prof. elec. engring., chmn. dept. Drexel U., 1969—; cons. to industry. Mem. I.E.E.E., A.A.A.S., Am. Soc. Engring. Edn., Phi Beta Kappa, Sigma Xi, Tau Beta Pi, Eta Kappa Nu, Pi Mu Epsilon. Club: Stanford (bd. dirs.) (Phila.). Home: 756 Camp Woods Rd Villanova PA 19085 Office: Drexel Univ Philadelphia PA 19104

KEITH, CHARLES WILKES, petroleum co. ofcl.; b. Dallas, Nov. 4, 1913; s. Charles Marvin and Alice (Wilkes) K.; student U. Tulsa; m. Mary Ellen Lewis, Feb. 19, 1938; children—Caroline, Jan, Bonnie, Richard. With Service Pipe Line Co., Tulsa, 1930-69, office boy, accounting clk., sr. clk., supr. taxes, 1930-48, treas., 1948-50, comptroller, 1950-58, financial v.p., 1958-69; sr. tax mgr. Standard Oil, Chgo., 1969—. Home: 1346 Western Av Flossmoor IL 60422 Office: 910 S Michigan Av Chicago IL 60605

KEITH, CHARLES WILLIAM, univ. dean; b. nr. New Concord, O., Jun 9, 1917; s. Clark Raymond and Elizabeth (Dennis) K.; B.S., Ohio State U., 1949; M.A., Mich. State U., 1954; Ph.D., 1964; m. Ruth Helene Smith, June 21, 1947; children—Gregory, Deborah, Marsha. Tool designer Crutiss Wright Corp., 1939-42, Oldsmobile div. Gen. Motors Corp., 1950-51; machine designer B.F. Goodrich Corp., 1956; mgr. engring. services, tool designer Lamb elec. div. Ametek Corp., 1955; drafting and tool design Lansing (Mich.) pub. schs., 1949-54; prof. indsl. tech. and profl. courses Kent State U., 1954-69, also coordinator indsl. tech. div., 1956-67, chmn., dir. Sch. Tech., 1967—, asst. dean Coll. Fine and Profl. Arts, 1967—. Mem. Ohio Bd. Regents Adv. Com. to Tech Edn., 1967—; co-chmn. Ohio Regional Conf. of Danforth Assos., 1968. Served with USAAF, 1943-45. Mem. Nat. Assn. Indsl. Tech. (trustee), Ohio Assn. Engring. Graphics (pres. 1966), Am. Soc. Engring. Edn., Am. Indsl. Arts Assn., Soc. Mfg. Engrs., Epsilon Pi Tau. Mason. Author: (with Farnham and McCabe) Mechanical Drafting Essentials, 1967. Home: 322 Valley View Dr Kent OH 44240

KEITH, DAMON JEROME, U.S. judge; b. Detroit July 4, 1922; s. Perry A. and Annie L. (Williams) K.; S.B., W.Va. State Coll., 1943; LL.B., Howard U., 1949; LL.M., Wayne State U., 1956; m. Rachel Boone, Oct. 18, 1953; children—Cecile Keith, Debbie, Gilda. Admitted to Mich. bar, 1949; atty. Office Friend of Ct., Detroit, 1951-55; sr. partner firm Keith, Conyers Anderson, Brown & Wahls, Detroit, 1964-67; mem. Wayne County Bd. Suprs., 1958-63; U.S. judge Eastern Dist. Mich., 1967—. Co-chmn. Mich. Civil Rights Commn., 1964-67; pres. Detroit Housing Commn., 1958-67; commnr. State Bar Mich., 1960-67; mem. legal staff Detroit Bd. Edn. Vice pres. United Negro Coll. Fund Detroit; 1st v.p. Detroit chpt. N.A.A.C.P. Served with AUS, World War II. Recipient Alumni citation Wayne State U., 1968. Mem. Am., Nat., Mich., Detroit bar assns., Nat. Lawyers Guild, Am. Judicature Soc. Baptist (deacon). Club: Detroit Cotillion. Contbr. legal jours. Home: 3130 W Outer Dr Detroit MI 48221 Office: 231 W Lafayette St Detroit MI 48226

KEITH, DAVID, (pseudonym); see Steegmuller, Francis.

KEITH, EDWARD GORDON, educator; b. Brockton, Mass., July 8, 1905; s. Edward A. and Grace (Coggins) K.; A.B., Amherst Coll., 1927; Ph.D., Harvard, 1937; m. Margaret Soutter Woods, Aug. 27, 1938; children—Robert, Philip, Stephen, Janet, Douglas. Instr. econs. Amherst Coll., 1934-35; instr. econs., tutor div. history, govt. and econs. Harvard, 1935-38; research asso. Nat. Bur. Econ. Research, 1938-39; research staff Social Sci. Research Council, 1939-41; instr., asst. prof. finance U. Pa., 1939-41, successively asso. prof., prof., 1946—, asso. dean Wharton Sch. Finance and Commerce, 1960-70; economist div. tax research U.S. Treasury, 1941-46; sr. economist Council Econ. Advisers, 1954-55. Dir. Drexel Equity Fund, Inc. Mem. Am. Econ. Assn., Nat. Tax Assn., Am. Finance Assn., Lower Merion Library Assn. (dir., chmn. 1968—). Presbyn. Home: 434 Levering Mill Rd Merion PA 19066 Office: U Pa Philadelphia PA 19104

KEITH, EVERETT EARNEST, edn. assn. exec.; b. Buffalo, Mo., Sept. 1, 1906; s. William Anderson and Nora (Woods) K.; B.S., S.W. Mo. State Coll., 1929; M.A., U. Mo. 1932, Gregory scholar, 1933-35; LL.D., Lindenwood Coll., 1957; m. Anna Catherine Blanchard, June 1, 1933; 1 dau., Katherine Anne. Elementary tchr., elementary prin., high sch. tchr., supt. schs., Buffalo, 1926-33; instr. U. Mo., 1935; sch. supr., dir. supervision Mo. Dept. Edn., 1935- 38; dir. pub. relations Mo. Tchrs. Assn., Columbia, 1938-41, exec. sec., 1941—; pres. Mo. Bd. Edn., 1946-47, mem. bd., 1946-54. Dir. Horace Mann Ins. Cos. Del. White House Conf. Edn., 1955, 65; del. World Confederation Orgns. Teaching Professions, Ottawa, Ont., 1950, Stockholm, Sweden, 1962; mem. Mo. Delegation Edn. Commn. of States, 1965-. Hon. col. Gov's. Staff, 1961-65. Recipient citation of merit Coll. Edn. and Alumni Assn. U. Mo., 1957. Mem. N.E.A. (past chmn. legislative com.), Am. Assn. Sch. Adminstrs., Nat. Assn. Secs. State Tchrs. Assns. (mem. exec. bd., past pres.), Phi Delta Kappa, Alpha Pi Zeta, Pi Gamma Mu, Phi Sigma Sigma. Methodist. Mason (33, Shriner), Kiwanian; mem. Order Eastern Star. Home: 23 Bingham Rd Columbia MO 65201 Office: 405 S 6th St Columbia MO 65201

KEITH, GRAEME M., banker; b. Greenwood, S.C., 1932; grad. Davidson Coll., 1954. Exec. v.p. First Union Nat. Bank N.C., Charlotte. Home: 3724 Pomfret Lane Charlotte NC 28211 Office: 301 S Tryon St Charlotte NC 28291*

KEITH, HADDOW MACDONNELL, pediatrician; b. Toronto, Ont., Can., May 20, 1899; s. George A. and Bessie (Haddow) K.; M.B., U. Toronto, 1924; m. Marion Fraser, Aug. 20, 1927; children—Fraser, Alison; m. 2d, Katherine Roberts, Aug. 31, 1957. Came to U.S., 1924, naturalized, 1944. Intern, asst. in medicine Henry Ford Hosp., 1924-26; resident Strong Meml. Hosp., Rochester, N.Y., 1926- 28; asst., cons. Mayo Clinic, Rochester, Minn., 1928-32, asso. prof., prof. pediatrics Mayo Clinic, Mayo Found., 1939-64, emeritus prof. pediatrics, 1964—; asst., asso. prof. McGill U., 1932-39, traveling fellow, 1934-35. Cons. pediatrician Minn. State Dept. Health, 1965—; cons. City Rochester Dept. Health, 1965-67. Dist., council offices Boy Scouts Am., 1942—. Served with RAF, 1917-19. Mem. Am., Canadian, Northwest pediatric socs., Midwest Soc. Pediatric Research, A.M.A., Am. Acad. Pediatrics (affiliate) Royal Soc. Medicine (asso.), Am. Acad. Neurology. Author Convulsive Disorders in Children, 1961. Home: 924 9th Av SW Rochester MN 55901 Office: 200 1st St SW Rochester MN 55901

KEITH, HASTINGS, congressman; b. Brockton, Mass., Nov. 22, 1915; s. Roger and Carolyn (Hastings) K.; grad. Deerfield Acad.; B.S., U. Vt., 1938; grad. study Harvard; grad. Command and Gen. Staff Sch.; m. Louise Harriman, Aug. 31, 1943; children—Helen (Mrs. Arthur M. Brink, Jr.), Carolyn. Mgmt. tng. Equitable Life of U.S., 1938, agt., 1938-40, asst. mgr. Boston agy., 1946-52; incorporator People's Savs. Bank; partner Roger Keith & Sons, gen. ins., Brockton, Mass.; senator, Mass., 1952-56, chmn. com. mercantile affairs, election laws, chmn. spl. coms. to study flouridation pub. water supplies, planning zoning and subdiv. control Commonwealth Mass., chmn. recess commn. to study uniform small boat regulations; ranking minority mem. spl. house subcom. maritime edn.; mem. 86th-87th congresses 9th Dist. Mass., 88-92d congresses 12th Dist.; mem. interstate and fgn. commerce com., also merchant marine and fisheries com. Congl. adviser 1971 session Conf. Com. Disarmament, Geneva, Switzerland. Mem. House Republican Policy Com., 1962-64. Mem. Mass. N.G., 1940-42; served from maj. to lt. col., AUS, 1942-45, col. Res. Mem. Aircraft Owners and Pilots Assn., Am. Legion, V.F.W., Sigma Phi. Conglist. Elk, Mason. Clubs: Capitol Hill, Congressional Country (Washington); University. Home: 91 River St West Bridgewater MA 02324 Office: House Office Bldg Washington DC 20515

KEITH, JOHN MCDONELL, tobacco co. exec.; b. Omemec, Ont., Can., June 9, 1906; s. John Paterson and Cora (McDonell) K.; B.A.Sc. in Chem. Engring., U. Toronto, 1929; m. Mary Kathleen Dobie, Aug. 30, 1932; children—John James, Mary Helen (Mrs. Brian P. Gibbs). With Tuckette Tobacco Co., 1929-33; with Imperial Tobacco Co., Montreal, 1933-70, chmn. bd., 1969-70, also dir.; dir. Innotron Internat. Ltd., Innotron Inc., Redwood Food Packing and Progresso Inc. Mem. Montreal Bd. Trade. Mem. adv. com. bus. adminstrn. Bishop's U.; finance and extension bd. Montreal Presbytery, United Ch. Can.; hon. pres. Constance Lethbridge Centre; bd. dirs. Red Feather Services; dir. adv. com. Soc. des Relations d'Affaires H.E.C. Inc. Mem. Chem. Inst. Can., Corp. Profl. Chemists Que., McGill U. Assos., U. Montreal Assos., Mil. and Hospitaller Order St. Lazarus Jerusalem, Phi Gamma Delta. Clubs: University, Mount Royal, Kanawaki Golf (Montreal). Home: 250 Clarke Av Westmount Montreal Quebec Canada Office: 3810 St Antoine St Montreal Quebec Canada

KEITH, LANCE MALCOLM Jr. chemist, educator; b. Chicago, 1928; B.S. in Physics, Yale, 1950; Ph.D. in Chemistry, Harvard, 1956; m. Sally Ann Jones, July 5, 1957; children--Kenneth J., Nancy A. Chemist, Acme Chem. Co., Blue Island, Ill., 1950-51; director of Research Lab., Indsl. Chemicals Corp., Cambrige, Mass., 1956-60; project coordinator environmental sect. Steinmetz Assos., Chgo., 1960-61; v.p. for research Bauer Bros. Chem. Co., Inc., Memphis, 1961-64; asst. prof. chemistry Washington U., St. Louis, 1964-66, asso. prof., 1966-70, prof., 1970--, head of chemistry dept., 1970-71. Vis. prof. So. Ill. U., summer 1967, U. of Ore., 1969. Bd. dirs. Rest Haven Home for Elderly, 1960-61; trustee of the Lutheran Hosp., 1965-71. Served from lt. to capt., AUS, 1951-53. Mem. Am. Chem. Soc., Sci. Research Soc. Am. (chpt. treas. 1967), Sigma Xi. Author: (with others) Basic Inorganic Chemistry, 1971. Home: Fairfax Apts 7291 Windermere Dr University City MO 63105 Office: Dept Chemistry Washington University St Louis MO 63130

KEITH, NATHANIEL S., urban planner; b. Cin., Dec. 30, 1906; s. Nathaniel S. and Alice (Munhall) K.; A.B. magna cum laude, Brown U., 1929; m. Marjorie MacDonald, May 21, 1932; children—Anthony, Penelope. Staff writer covering automobile, aviation, r.r. and rubber industries Wall St. Jour., N.Y.C., 1929-38, specializing in govt. finance, Washington, 1938-40; bus. editor PM, N.Y.C., 1940; editor Insured Mortgage Portfolio (pub. Fed. Housing Adminstrn.), 1941, asst. dir. pub. relations FHA, 1942; asst. dir. information Nat. Housing Agy., 1943-44, spl. asst. to adminstr. responsible for liaison with Congress, 1944-47; asst. to Housing and Home Finance Adminstr., responsible for liaison with Congress and with nat. orgns. active in housing, 1947-49, dir. slum clearance and urban devel. 1949-53; housing and redevel. cons., 1953- -, (Washington, Buffalo, San Juan, P.R., V.I., other cities). Mem. adv. com. on housing and urban devel. AID. Mem. Nat. Capitol Democratic Club, Washington. Trustee Found. Coop. Housing. Mem. Nat. Assn. Housing and Redevel. Ofcls., Nat. Housing Conf. (pres.), Phi Beta Kappa, Phi Kappa Psi. Clubs: Cosmos, National Communications. Author: (with Charles C. Colt) 28 Days, A History of Banking Crisis, 1933; (with James W. Rouse) No Slums in 10 Years, 1955; (with Carl Feiss) A Report on the Renewal Possibilities of the Historic Triangle of the City of San Jaun; (with C. Feiss) The Future of Buffalo, 1958, The Community Renewal Program for Rochester, N.Y., 1963, Community Renewal Program for the Virgin Islands, 1966; The Future of Downtown Rochester, 1965; Housing America's Low and Moderate Income Families, 1968. Home: 3212 Macomb St Washington DC 20008 Office: 1250 Connecticut Av Washington DC 20036

KEITH, NOEL LEONARD, educator; b. Cassville, Mo., Feb. 1, 1903; s. Otis Parker and Vesta Pearl (Kelly) K.; B.A., Tex. Christian U., 1938, B.D., 1940, M.A., 1949; Th.D., Iliff Sch. Theology, 1953; m. Beulah Irene Dorsey, Aug. 27, 1927; 1 son, Marvin Russell. Ordained to ministry Christian Ch., 1929; minister in Okla., Kan., Tex., 1927-46; mem. faculty Tex. Christian U., Fort Worth, 1946—, spl. asst. to pres., chmn. dept. ch. history Brite Coll., 1946-52, chmn. dept. religion univ., 1953-68, John F. Weatherly prof. N.T., 1959—; speaker weekly program sta. WBAP-TV, 1961—; chmn. Tex. Christian U. Press, 1948—. Recipient citation for TV weekly program Planning for Tomorrow, Ft. Worth Area Council Chs., 1962. Mem. Nat. Assn. Bibl. Instrs., Disciples of Christ Hist. Soc. Mason, Kiwanian. Author: Worship Highways, 1943; (fable for children) The Green Horse, 1950; The Story of D.S. Burnet, 1954; The Human Rift, 1963; Religion: An Introduction and Guide to Study, 1965; Paul's Message for Today, 1970. Home: 3882 S Hills Circle Fort Worth TX 76109

KEITH, NORMAN CLINTON, petroleum co. exec.; b. Bridgewater, Mass., Nov. 19, 1912; s. Clarence L. and Christie May (Smith) K.; B.S., Springfield Coll., 1936, H.H.D., 1966; m. Kathleen Hanley, Aug. 2, 1967; children—Clinton, Ralph, Quentin, Jocelyn, Jonathan. With Standard Oil Co. N.Y. (now Mobil Oil Corp.), Phila., 1936-41; pres., founder Petroleum Export Co., Washington, also London, Paris, Rome, Bombay, 1945-71; pres. Petroleum Marketing Corp. (merged Commonwealth Oil Refining Corp. 1970), Washington, 1947-70; pres., dir., chmn. exec. com., chief exec. officer Commonwealth Oil Refining Co., San Juan, P.R., 1971—. Trustee Springfield Coll., chmn. bd. trustees, 1962-69, acting pres. coll., 1965. Served as lt. USNR, 1942. Am. Petroleum Inst., Nat. Petroleum Council. Clubs: Chevy Chase, Burning Tree, Metropolitan (Washington); Pine Valley (Clementon, N.J.); Maidstone (East Hampton, N.Y.); Lyford Cay (Nassau, Bahamas); Racquet (Phila.); Merion Golf (Ardmore, Pa.). Bankers (San Juan); Sky, Union (N.Y.C.). Home: Laguna Terrace Condominium 9 Joffre St Santurce PR 00907 Office: Banco Popular Center Hato Rey San Juan PR 00918

KEITH, ROBERT J., flour co. exec.; b. Eau Claire, Wis., Mar. 23, 1914; s. Alexander J. and Katharine (Kennedy) K.; student pub. schs.; m. Freda Christensen, Mar. 29, 1937; children—Katharine K. (Mrs. Jackson), Robert J. With No. States Power Co., 1931-33, Nat. Pressure Cooker Co., 1934-35; joined Pillsbury Co. (formerly Pillsbury Mills, Inc.), 1935, v.p., 1950-56, exec. v.p., 1956-65, pres., 1965-67, chmn., chief exec. officer, 1967—, also dir.; dir. First Bank System, Inc., McQuay, Inc., Dayton Hudson Corp. Clubs: Woodhill, Minneapolis. Home: Wayzata MN 55391 Office: Pillsbury Co Pillsbury Bldg Minneapolis MN 55402

KEITH, WARREN GRAY, engring. educator; b. Anamosa, Ia., Sept. 16, 1908; s. Roy Theo and Jessie (Gray) K.; B.S. in Civil Engring., Ia. State U., 1934; M.S. in Civil Engring., U. Mo. 1948; m. Fannie Luella Bare, Aug. 22, 1937; children—James Warren, Carolyn Luella. Engr., Chicago County, Minn., 1937-41; stress analyst Goodyear Aircraft Corp., Akron, O., 1943-45; mem. faculty U. Ala., 1941-43, 45—, prof. civil engring., head dept., 1964-68; partner Woodman-Keith Engring. Co., cons. engring., 1949-. Registered profl. engr., Ala., Miss., Ia. Mem. Am. Soc. Civil Engrs. (pres. Ala. 1954), Am. Soc. Engring. Edn., Nat., Ala. socs. profl. engrs., Chi Epsilon (nat. council 1958-69, nat. pres. 1964-66). Home: 1611 27th Av East Tuscaloosa AL 35401 Office: PO Box Z University AL 35486

KEITH, WILLARD WOODWARD, business exec.; b. Fresno, Cal., Aug. 25, 1899; s. Charles B. and Pleasance A. (Peck) K.; ed. grammar sch.; LL.D., Loyola U., Los Angeles, U. So. Cal.; m. Adeline N. Donnelly, Nov. 5, 1919; children—Willard W. (dec.), Donald R. With Niagara Fire Ins. Co., 1914-17; with Cosgrove & Co., Inc., 1918—, pres. Los Angeles and N.Y. offices, v.p., San Francisco office (merged with Marsh & McLennan's Pacific orgn.), became pres. Marsh & McLennan-Cosgrove & Co., Los Angeles, 1956, also dir.; dir. Lockheed Aircraft Corp., Investment Co. Am., Am.-Hawaiian S.S. Co., Norris Industries Inc., Marineland of Pacific, Inc. Dir. So. Cal. sector Office Civilian Def. 1942-44, Cal. War Council. Trustee Crippled Children's Soc. Los Angeles, U. So. Cal.; bd. dirs. Cal. Inst. Assos.; bd. govs. Los Angeles area Boy Scouts Am.; mem. scholarship com. Helms Found. Mem. Navy League (adv. bd.), Cal. Hist. Soc. Club: Los Angeles Country (Los Angeles). Office: 9896A Wilshire Blvd Beverly Hills CA 90210

KEITHAHN, EDWARD LINNAEUS, former museum curator, author; b. Tenino, Wash., May 15, 1900; s. Henry John and Lola Mae (Swift) K.; A.B., U. Wash., 1938; m. Marie Antoinette La Chance, June 15, 1923; children—Yvonne (Mrs. Gale Mueller), Loretta (Mrs. Richard Penrod), Richard Edward. Tchr., Wash., 1920-23, Alaska, 1923-41; curator Alaska Hist. Library and Mus., 1941-65. Mem. Alaska adv. com. Bd. Geog. Names, 1948—; chmn. Alaska Geog. Bd., 1963- -. Served with U.S. Army, 1918. Recipient plaque for distinguished service to Alaska, 1948; Outstanding Citizen award Alaska Press Club, 1964; certificate of merit State of Alaska, 1965. Fellow A.A.A.S., mem. Am. Assn. Museums, Soc. Am. Archaeology, Alaska Pioneers, Am. Legion. Democrat. Elk, Rotarian. Author: Igloo Tales, 1944; (with Juliet Morgan) Alaska and Hawaii, 1956; Native Alaskan Art, 1959; Eskimo Adventure, 1963; Monuments in Cedar, 1963; Alaska for the Curious, 1966. Contbr. articles to profl. jours. Address: 45 Oak Ct Eugene OR 97405

KEITHLEY, JEROME, city manager Oakland, Cal. Address: City Hall Oakland CA 94612

KEITH-LUCAS, ALAN, educator, social worker; b. Cambridge, Eng., Feb. 5, 1910; s. Keith Lucas and Alys Hubbard; came to U.S., 1937, naturalized, 1942; B.A. with 1st class honors, Cambridge U., 1931, M.A., 1935; M.S. in Social Adminstrn., Western Res. U., 1939; Ph.D., Duke, 1955; m. Georgia Work, July 8, 1939; children—Susan Carson, Timothy. Prin. pvt. sch. in Eng., 1933-37; caseworker, supr. Cleve. Humane Soc., 1939-44; child welfare cons., supr. children's services La. Dept. Pub. Welfare, 1944-50; mem. faculty U. N.C. Sch. Social Work, Chapel Hill, 1950—, Alumni Distinguished prof. social work, 1961—, asso. dean, 1964-65, acting dean, 1951-52, 65-66, 71—; vis. prof. London Sch. Econs., 1966; dir. Group Child Care Project, 1956-69, Chapel Hill Workshops for Instl. Personnel, 1951—; cons. Children's Bur., Child Welfare League Am., others; spl. cons. staff devel. Me. Dept. Health and Welfare, 1959-70; K.L.M. Pray vis. prof. U. Pa., 1969. Mem. Acad. Certified Social Workers, Nat. Conf. Social Welfare (divisional planning com.), Council Social Work Edn. (past mem. bd.), Am. Pub. Welfare Assn., Nat. Assn. Social Workers (com. ethics), Phi Beta Kappa. Presbyn. (elder, bd. ch. extension). Author: Decisions About People in Need, 1957; Some Casework Concepts for the Public Welfare Worker, 1957; The Church Children's Home in a Changing World, 1962; The Church and Social Welfare, 1963; Christian Education for Disturbed Children, 1967. Editor: Chapel Hill

Workshop Reports, 1953—; Readings for Houseparents in Children's Institutions, 1957; Problems and Programs in Child Welfare, 1964. Contbr. articles profl. jours. Home: 705 Greenwood Rd Chapel Hill NC 27514

KEKICH, EMIL AUGUSTINE, former fgn. service officer; b. St. Louis, Aug. 6, 1893; s. Thomas M. and Ellen (Keserich) K.; A.B., St. Viator Coll., Bourdonnais, Ill., 1913; postgrad. U. Montpellier (France), 1919; B.F.S., Georgetown U., 1921; m. Xenia Obolsky, Jan. 7, 1923. Reporter, Alton (Ill.) Daily Telegraph, 1919-20; asst. to U.S. trade commr., Vladivostok, Siberia, Harbin, Manchuria, Shanghai, China, Riga, Latvia, 1921-24; U.S. comml. attache, Helsinki, Finland, Stockholm, Sweden, Belgrade, Yuguslavia, 1924-33, Bucharest, Rumania, 1946, Prague, Czechoslovakia, 1947-49, Ottawa, Can., 1953-55, London, Eng., 1955-61; exec. dir. Am. C. of C., London. Exec. sec. Am. Match Mfrs. Assn., N.Y.C., 1934-44. Adviser, WPB, 1942. Served with U.S. Army, 1917-19; AEF in France. Decorated comdr. Brit. Empire, 1967. Mem. Delta Phi Epsilon. Clubs: University (Washington); American (London). Contbr. numerous govt. publs. Home: 4000 Massachusetts Av NW Washington DC 20016

KEKKONEN, URHO KALEVA, pres. of Finland; b. Pielavesi, Finland, Sept. 3, 1900; s. Juho and Emilia (Pylvanainen) K.; LL.D., U. Helsinki, 1936; Dr. h.c., univs. Moscow, Aix-en-Provence. Waterloo, Warsaw, Delhi, Budapest, Prague; m. Sylvi Uino, Apr. 4, 1926; children—Tanell and Matti (twins). Minister of justice, Finland, 1936-37, 44-46, minister of interior, 1937-39, 50-51, prime minister, 1950-53, 54-56, fgn. minster, 1952-53, 54; mem. bd. mgmt. Bank Finland, 1946-56; mem. of Diet, 1936-56, 2d speaker, 1946-47, speaker, 1948-50; pres. Finnish Republic, 1956—. Pres. com. for Olympic Games in Finland, 1938-46. Decorated Grand Cross. White Rose with Collar, Grand Cross of Liberty, Grand Cross of Lion, Grand Cross Holy Lamb, Gold Cross of Merit of Finnish Sports, Olympic Cross of Merit (Finland); numerous fgn. decorations. Mem. Sport Assn. Finland (pres. 1932-47). Lutheran. Address: Presidential Palace Helsinki Finland

KELAKOS, MICHAEL GEORGE, fgn. service officer; b. Lowell, Mass., Sept. 15, 1913; s. George Michael and Eleni (Zarouli) K.; S.B., Mass. Inst. Tech., 1935; m. Theresa Plakias, Sept. 27, 1953; children—George Michael, Eleni Maria. Chem. engr. Mathieson Alkali Works, Niagara Falls, N.Y., 1936-42; dep. chief Inter-Allied Reparation Agy. Mission Berlin, Germany, 1946-48; chief programming div., spl. asst. to sec. gen., Inter-Allied Reparation Agy., Brussels, Belgium, 1948-50; econ. devel. officer Office S. Asian Affairs Dept. State, Washington, 1951-54; country chief Refugee Relief Program, Am. embasssy, Athens, Greece, 1954-56, Stuttgart, Germany, 1956-57; officer-in-charge econ. affairs Bur. Internat. Orgns. Affairs, Dept. State, Washington, 1957-61; dep. permanent rep. UNESCO, Paris, France, 1961-63; sci. attache Am. embassy, Rome, Italy, 1963-66, Tel Aviv, Israel, 1966—. Served to lt. col. AUS, 1942-46; ETO. Decorated Bronze Star; Crois de Guerre (France). Mem. Am. Fgn. Service Assn., Res. Officers Assn. U.S. Address: Am Embassy Tel Aviv Israel

KELB, NORMAN ERNEST, indsl. exec.; b. Toledo, Apr. 2, 1893; s. Frank F. and Theresa (Himmelmann) K.; student pub. schs.; m. Carrie Bernice Schill, Aug. 15, 1917 (dec. 1948); 1 son, Edwin D.; m. 2d, Zelma Bird, 1952. With France Stone Co., 1913-29; sec.-treas., mgr. Erie Stone Co., 1929- 39; pres., dir. High Point Oil Co., 1925—, Refiners Transport, Inc., Cumberland Quarriers, Inc., 1940—; pres. Ayrshire Collieries Corp., 1957-70. Served with U.S. Army, World War I. Mem. Nat. Coal Assn., Nat. Crushed Stone Assn. (pres. 1956, 57), Ind., Indpls. chambers commerce. Mason (Shriner). Clubs: Columbia (Indpls.); Ulen Country. Home: 3919 Meadows Dr PO Box 55211 Indianapolis IN 46205 Office: 3919 Meadows Dr Indianapolis IN 46205

KELCE, MERL C., ret. coal co. exec.; b. Pittsburg, Kan., 1905. Formerly exec. v.p., later pres., dir. Peabody Coal Co., chmn. exec. com.; past v.p., dir. Broken Aro Coal Co., Key Coal Co., Rogers County Coal Corp., Victoria Coal Corp., Sentry Royalty Co.; past pres., dir. Tecumseh Coal Corp., No. Ill. Coal Co., Sinclair Mines (Can.), Ltd. Home: 400 Mansion House Center St Louis MO 63102

KELCEY, GUY, cons. engr.; b. Dunchurch, Ont., Can., June 1, 1889; s. George Henry and Jane (Tuily) K.; brought to U.S., 1899; B.S., Carnegie Inst. Tech., 1914; D. Engring., Newark Coll. Engring., 1958; m. Grace Elizabeth Saxe, Oct. 2, 1918 (dec. May 1965); children—Theodosia (Mrs. Raymond Moyer Dean), Virginia (Mrs. George Havens Leland); m. 2d, Jane Townsend Dowell, June 1966. With City Engr.'s Office, Lackawanna, N.Y., 1907-08, Peoples Savs. & Trust Co., also E.W. Clark & Co., Pitts., 1914-17, Rush Machinery Co., Pitts., 1919-20; mgr. traffic engring. div. Am. Gas Accumulator Co., Elizabeth, N.J., 1920-41; pres. Vehicular Parking, Ltd., Newark, 1941-42; regional dir. So. states, div. local transport Office Def. Transp., Atlanta, 1942-44; hwy. transp. analyst Port of N.Y. Authority, 1944-45; partner Edwards & Kelcey, engrs., 1945- 58; chmn. Edwards & Kelcey, Inc., Newark, 1957—; participated as cons. engr. N.J. Turnpike, N.Y. Thruway, N.J. Garden State Pkwy., urban expressways in Conn., Mass., also Spain and other countries; traffic and transp. studies N.Y., other met. areas. Charge mission Am. Engrs., hwy. program in Iraq; adv. com. dept. civil engring, Newark Coll. Engring.; mem. nat. coms. on engring. and econ. problems of transp., traffic, hwys.; vis. lectr. transp. and hwy. traffic Yale, Harvard, other univs. Res. mil. adviser AC, U.S. Army, 1917-19. Life fellow Am. Soc. C.E.; mem. Inst. Traffic Engrs. (hon. life; Motson award 1966), Am. Inst. Cons. Engrs., Hwy. Research Bd., Am. Road Builders Assn. (dir. and pres. engring div.), Internat. Rd. Fedn., Legion Aviators Post, Delta Upsilon, Chi Epsilon. Episcopalian. Clubs: Quiet Birdmen, Adventurers, Engineers (N.Y.C.); Essex (Newark). Author tech. publs. Home: 739 Highland Av Westfield NJ 07090 Office: 8 Park Pl Newark NJ 07102

KELCH, DAVID ERDMAN, utility exec.; b. New Orleans, July 19, 1928; s. Raymond Ellsworth and Norma (Erdman) K.; student Coll. Wooster, 1946; student Trinidad (Colo.) State Coll., 1948-49; m. Maxine Jones, Oct. 16, 1949; children—Mary Louise, David Carter. Asst. chief accountant Zia Co., Los Alamos, 1951-55; with Tex. Electric Service Co., Ft. Worth, 1955—, sec., asst. treas., 1966—; sec., asst. treas. subsidiary Old Ocean Fuel Co., 1966—. Mem. methods and procedures com. Edison Electric Inst., 1962-65. Served with AUS, 1946-48. Home: 2101 Yosemite Ct Fort Worth TX 76112 Office: 408 W 7th St Fort Worth TX 76101

KELCH, RAY ALDEN, educator; b. Logan, O., Sept. 13, 1923; s. Albert Robison and Clara (Lindsey) K.; A.B., Ohio State U., 1947, M.A., 1949, Ph/D., 1955. Mem. faculty Stephens Coll., Columbia, Mo., 1953-57; mem. faculty San Francisco State Coll., 1957—, prof. history, 1964—, chmn. dept., 1964-70; vis. prof. Ariz. State U., Tempe, 1970-71. Served with AUS, 1943-46. Mem. Am. Hist. Assn., Conf. Brit. Studies, Am. Assn. U. Profs. Democrat, Protestant Episcopalian. Home: 310 Arballo Dr San Francisco CA 94132

KELDYSH, MSTISLAV VSEVOLODOVICH, scientist; b. Riga, Latvia, Feb. 10, 1911; s. Vsevolod Michailovich Keldysh; ed. mech. and math. dept., Moscow State U., 1927-30; m. Stanislava Valerianovna, children—Pyotr, Svetlana. Asst., Moscow Machinetool and Instruments Inst., 1931; engr., group chief Central Aerohydrodynamics Inst., Moscow, 1931-41; docent Moscow State U., 1932- 36, prof., 1937-47; doctorant Math. Inst. of USSR Acad. Scis., 1934-37, chief researcher, 1937-41, sec. dept. phys. and math. scis., 1953-55; chief mechanics dept. Math. Inst., Moscow, 1944-53, asst. dir., 1946-51; mem. presidium USSR Acad. Scis., 1953, v.p., 1960, pres., 1961. Dep., Supreme Soviet USSR. Named Hero Socialist Labour; recipient State prize, Lenin prize (2), Order Lenin (6), Order Red Banner Labour (3). Mem. Polish, Mongolian, Rumanian (hon.), Bulgarian (hon.), Saxony (corr.), Leipzig (corr.), German (corr. Berlin) acads. sciences, Acad. Scis. Czechoslovakia, Am. Acad. Arts and Sciences (foreign member), also German Leopold Acad. of Naturalists. Author: About Air Stream Vibration of the Wing, 1938. The Solvation and Stability of Dirichl's Problem, 1940: The Function Presentation of the Complex of Polynom Variable in a Locked Region, 1945; The Proper Value and Proper Function of Some Classes of Non Conjugated Directions, 1951. Address: 14 Leninsky Prospect Moscow USSR

KELEHAN, JAMES LAWRENCE, steam generating equipment co. exec.; b. Mpls., Oct. 30, 1914; s. James H. L. and Sadie (Moran) K.; B.S., U. Minn., 1936, J.D., 1938; m. Mary Donahue, Jan. 3, children—Catherine childrenCatherine M. (Mrs. Fred Reinis), Paul J. Asso. dir. Defense Plant, RFC, Washington, 1946-48; asst. gen. mgr. AEC, 1954-56; asst. to v.p. Boiler div. Babcock & Wilcox, 1957-60; pres., dir. Air Preheater Co., Inc., Wellsville, N.Y., 1961-64; v.p. mfg. Cumbustion Engring., Inc., Windsor, Conn., 1964-67, v.p. indsl. group, 1967-; asso. dir. Hartford branch Conn. Bank & Trust Co. Vice pres., dir. Junior Achievement of Hartford. Recipient of the Outstanding Service award AEC, 1956. Member Greater Hartford C. of C. (dir.), Mfrs. Assn. Hartford County (dir.). Clubs: Wampanoag Country (West Hartford); Congressional Country (Washington). Home: 7 Hollister Dr West Hartford CT 06117 Office: Windsor CT 06095

KELEHER, EDWIN WILLIAM, banker; b. Cambridge, Mass., Apr. 24, 1919; s. Charles H. and Margaret (Leary); B.S. cum laude, U. Notre Dame, 1941; m. Elaine M. Newton, Nov. 8, 1947; 1 dau., Kathleen M. With E.I. duPont de Nemours & Co., Inc., 1941-42, Charles S. Rockey, C.P.A.'s, Phila., 1947-50; controller Gordon Davis Co., Phila., 1951-52; treas. Slater System, Inc., Phila., 1952-61; controller Automatic Retailers Am., 1962-67; v.p., comptroller Provident Nat. Bank, Phila. Served to maj. AUS, 1942-46. C.P.A., Pa. Mem. Financial Execs. Inst., Am. Inst. C.P.A.'s. Home: 26 Kynlyn Rd Wayne PA 19087 Office: Stock Exchange Bldg Philadelphia PA 19103

KELEHER, GREGORY CHARLES, former coll. adminstr.; b. Somerville, Mass., Sept. 9, 1919; s. Edwin James and Gertrude (Lynch) K.; A.B., St. Anselm's Coll., Manchester, N.H., 1943; postgrad. St. Basil's Sem., 1943-44, U. Toronto, 1944-45, St. Anselm's Sem., 1945-47; M.A., U. Notre Dame, 1951, Harvard, 1951, 52. Benedictine monk; ordained priest Roman Cath. Ch., 1946; mem. faculty St. Anselm's Coll., 1947-67, acad. dean, 1964-67; acad. dean St. Bernard Coll., Cullman, Ala. 1967-68, exec. v.p., 1968-70. Chmn. com. orgn. N.H. Council Colls. and Univs., 1966-67; v.p. N.H. Ednl. Broadcasting Council, WEHN-TV, 1957, pres., 1958, bd. dirs., 1959-62. Mem. History Edn. Assn., Comparative Edn. Assn., Soc. Advancement Edn., Nat. Soc. Study Edn., Assn. Higher Edn. Address: St Anselm Abbey Manchester NH 03102

KELEHER, WILLIAM ALOYSIUS lawyer; b. Lawrence, Kan., Nov. 7, 1886; s. David and Mary Ann (Gorry) K.; LL.B., Washington and Lee U., 1915; hon. M.A. U. N.M., 1946, LL.D., 1968; LL.D., U. Albuquerque, 1960; m. Mae J. Kelly, 1918 (dec. 1923); 1 dau., Mary Ann; m. 2d, Loretta Barrett, 1932; children—William Barrett, Michael Lawrence, John Gorry, Thomas Franklin. With Western Union Telegraph Co., Albuquerque, N.M., 1900-06; clk. bd. edn., Albuquerque, 1907-08; reporter, city editor Albuquerque Jour. and Albuquerque Herald, 1908-13; practiced law 1915—. Chmn. Democratic State Central Com., 1928. Mem. N.M. State Finance Bd., 1932-49; pres. bd. regents N.M. Coll. Agr. and Mech. Arts, 1941-42. Certificate Recognition, Nat. Conf. Christians and Jews, 1966; elected N.M. Hall Fame, 1964. Mem. Am., N.M. bar assns., Phi Beta Kappa, Sigma Chi, Phi Delta Phi. Democrat Roman Catholic. Club: Albuquerque Country. Author: Maxwell Land Grand, a New Mexico Item, 1943; The Fabulous Frontier, 12 New Mexico Items, 1945; Turmoil in New Mexico 1846-1868, 1952; Violence in Lincoln County, a New Mexico Item, 1957; Memoirs 1892-1969, a New Mexico Item, 1969. Home: 123 15th St SW Albuquerque NM 8710 Office: Public Service Bldg Albuquerque NM 87101

KELEMEN, MILKO, composer; b. Podravska Slatina, Yugoslavia, Mar. 30, 1924; s. Dragutin and Maria (Tobisch) K.; ed. Acad. Music, Zagreb, Yugoslavia, Conservatoire de Paris (France), Musikakademie Freiburg im Bresgau (W. Germany); m. Mira Jurisic, June 9, 1964. Docent composition Acad. Music, Zabreb, 1954—, pres. music biennale Festival Internat. Modern Music, Zagreb 1960—. Recipient Beethoven prize, Bonn, Germany, 1963, prize of Zagreb, 1955, prize Rome, Italy, 1963. Mem. Heinrich Schütz Gesellschaft. Composer: Transfigurations for Piano and Orchestra, 1960; Equilibres for Two Orchestra, 1961; Le Nouveau Locataire (opera), 1963- 64; also ballets, others. Home: Vocarsko Naselje 102 Zagreb Yugoslavia Office: Gunduliceva 6 Zagreb Yugoslavia

KELEMEN, PAL, archeologist, art historian; b. Budapest, Hungary, Apr. 24, 1894; s. Joseph and Jenny (Gratt) K.; ed. univs. Budapest, Munich and Paris; mus. research, Budapest, Vienna, Florence, London, Madrid, Seville; m. Elisabeth Hutchings Zulauf, May 2, 1932. Came to U.S., 1932, naturalized, 1939. Made 10 survey trips, Latin Am., since 1933, 2 for cultural div. Dept. State, to Mexico, Guatemala, Honduras, El Salvador, Nicaragua, Panama, Colombia, Ecuador, Peru, Bolivia; survey and lecture trip for Dept. State to Portugal, Spain, Switzerland, Hungary, Czechoslovakia, Belgium, 1948; lecture tour univs., mus. in Southwest, Pacific coast, Can., 1952; vis. prof. U. Tex., 1953; survey, Mex., 1953, 63, 64, 67; research Portugal, Italy, Sicily, 1954, Eng., Switzerland, Italy and Spain, 1959; lectr. Nat. Gallery Art (Washington), Met. Mus. Art (N.Y.C.), and other univs. and mus.; U.S. specialist lecture tour for Dept. State to Portugal, Spain, Italy, also Istanbul, Athens, Thessaloniki; London, 1956. Trustee Textile Mus. (Washington). Hon. presbiter First Magyar Ref. Ch., N.Y. Officer, 4 yrs., World War I; mem. Commn. for Protection and Salvage of Artistic and Historic Monuments in War Areas, World War II. Comdr. Order of Merit Ecuador. Fellow Royal Anthropol. Inst.; mem. various sci. societies in U.S., Latin Am., Europe. Author: Battlefield of the Gods, Essays on Mexican Art, History and Exploration, 1937 (travel book of the month; trans. Hungarian and German); Medieval Am. Art, 2 vols., 1943, 44, 46, 67; Baroque and Rococo in Latin Am., 1951, 68; earlier publs. in Hungarian and German; Medieval American Art, Masterpieces of the New World before Columbus, 1 vol., 1956; El Greco Revisited; Candia, Venice, Toledo, 1961, Spanish edit., 1965; El Greco Revisited: His Byzantine Heritage, 1962; paperbacks ancient, colonial art of Ams., Dutch, 1962, German, 1964, French, 1965, Spanish, 1967, Portuguese, 1969; Art of the Americas: Ancient and Hispanic, 1969, paperback, 1970. Contr. to Ency. Brittanica, also contbr. Stauffacher's World Art History, leading periodicals in Europe, U.S., Latin Am. From consideration of early Christian art, turned since coming in U.S. to pre-Colombian and colonial art in Latin Am. Address: Loon Meadow Dr Norfolk CT 06058

KELL, REGINALD, educator, musician; b. York, Eng., June 8, 1906; s. Fred and Edith (Porter) K.; student Royal Acad. Music, London, 1929-31; m. Diana Holbrooke, Aug. 23, 1936; 1 son, Jeffrey. Came to U.S., 1948. Violinist, clarinetist, 1926—; prof. clarinet Royal Acad. Music, 1936—; prin. clarinetist Royal Philharmonic, London Philharmonic, London Symphony, Royal Opera Covent Garden, Toscanini Festival orchs.; solo, chamber music recs. RCA Victor, Columbia, Decca, Mercury, H.M.V., London record cos. Fellow Royal Acad. Music. Author clarinet study books. Home: Box 4779 Carmel CA 93921

KELL, WALTER GERRY, educator; b. Chgo., Dec. 23, 1921; s. Walter Frederick and Iva Beatrice (Gerry) K.; B.B.A., U. Mich., 1946, M.B.A., 1947; Ph.D., U. Ill., 1952; m. Dorothy Marie Polk, June 28, 1946; children—Linda Lee, Gary Walter, Gayanne Marie, William Arthur. Instr. U. Ill., 1947-51; asst. prof. Mich. State U., 1951-53; asso. prof., chmn. accounting dept. Syracuse U., 1953-58, prof., chmn. dept., 1959-62; prof. accounting U. Mich., Ann Arbor, 1962—. Mem. N.Y. State Council on Accountancy, 1960-62. C.P.A., Ill. Mem. Mich. Assn. C.P.A.'s, Am. Accounting Assn. (chmn. com. scope four-year accounting maj. 1968, v.p. 1959, pres. 1963), Am. Inst. C.P.A.'s (chmn. com. personnel testing 1960, mem. com. auditing procedure 1970), Beta Alpha Psi, Beta Gamma Sigma. Editor, contbg. author: Accountants Handbook, 4th edit., 1956; cons. editor: Accounting Principles, 8th edit., Accountants Handbook, 5th edit., 1970; contbg. author: Financial Handbook, 4th edit., 1964. Home: 2432 Londonderry Rd Ann Arbor MI 48104

KELLAM, RICHARD B., judge. Judge U.S. Dist Ct., Norfolk, Va. Office: US Courthouse Norfolk VA*

KELLAM, WILLIAM PORTER, librarian; b. McLeansville, N.C., Oct. 9, 1905; s. Henry Davis and Matilda Dee (Wyrick) K.; student Trinity Park Sch., Durham, 1921-22; A.B., Duke U., 1926. A.M., 1929; A.B. in Library Science, Emory U., 1931; m. Mary Carrington Umstead, Dec. 27, 1926; children— William Porter, Mary Umstead (Mrs. Fred H. Mewhinney). Tchr., Mangum Township High Sch., Durham County, N. C., 1926-27, prin. Glenn Elementary Sch., 1927-28; asst., Duke U. Library, 1928-29, head circulation dept., 1929-30; edn. librarian U. N.C., 1931, head, circulation dept., 1932-34; librarian, N.C. State Coll., Raleigh, 1934- 39, W.Va. U., Morgantown, 1939-46, U. S.C., 1946-47; asst. librarian U. N.C., 1947-50; dir. libraries U. Ga., 1950—. Bd. dirs. Assn. College and Research Libraries, 1948-49. Chmn. Oberly Meml. Award Com., Am. Library Assn., 1944-48. Pres. W. Va. Library Assn., 1943-45. Chmn. W.Va. Library Commn., 1941- 46. Received Rosenwald scholarship in library work. Mem. A.L.A. (chmn. membership com. 1955-59), Am. Assn. Univ. Profs., Ga. (pres. 1955- 57), Southeastern (sec.-treas. 1948-50, v.p. 1968-70, pres. 1970-72) library assns. Rotarian. Editor: Southeastern Librarian, 1952-61. Contbr. to library mags. Home: 399 Parkway Dr Athens GA 30601

KELLAR, CURTIS BRADBURY, oil co. exec.; b. Albert Lea, Minn., July 16, 1916; s. Horatio Ellsworth and Laura (Koontz) K.; B.A., U. Minn., 1938, LL.B., 1940; m. Mary Ames, July 10, 1943 (div. 1967); children—Lucia Ames, Curtis Bradbury, William Ellsworth, Mary Elizabeth, Martha Hartwell; m. 2d, Amy Vanderbilt, Mar. 1, 1968. Admitted to Minn. bar, 1940, N.Y. bar, 1946; with firm Winthrop, Stimson, Putnam & Roberts, N.Y.C., 1945-54; atty., asst. sec. W.R. Grace & Co., 1954-58; counsel Mobil Oil Corp., 1958-61, Mobil Petroleum Co. Inc., 1961-65; gen. counsel Mobil East Region, 1965-68, Mobil Petroleum Co. Inc., 1965-69; asst. gen. counsel internat. div. Mobil Oil Corp., 1968—; dir. Daisyfields Corp. Served to lt. comdr. USNR, 1941-45; PTO, ETO. Decorated Bronze Star. Mem. Am. Bar Assn., Assn. Bar City N.Y., Phi Gamma Delta, Phi Delta Phi, Grey Friars. Republican. Episcopalian. Mem. student editorial bd. Minn. Law Rev., 1939-40. Home: 438 E 87th St New York City NY 10028 Office: 150 E 42d St New York City NY 10017

KELLAR, MELVIN E., textile co. exec.; b. Atlanta, Oct. 26, 1920; s. Spencer F. and Lois (Mason) K.; student King's Coll., New Castle, Del., 1941-42; m. Jane E. McNutt, Dec. 21; children—Jane Evelyn, Daniel Allen. With control div. E.I. duPont de Nemours & Co., 1944-46; resident mgr. W.W. Stribling & Co., C.P.A.'s, 1946-54; v.p., treas., dir. E.T. Barwick Mills, Inc., 1954-66, sr. v.p., treas., dir. 1966-70; sr. v.p., treas., dir. E.T. Barwick Mills, Inc., Nev., 1966-70; chief financial officer Barwick Industries, Inc., vice chmn., 1968-70; v.p., treas. Monarch Rug Mills, Inc. Treas., trustee E.T. Barwick Found., Columbia Bible Coll.; trustee Ben Lippen Sch., Carver Fgn. Missions, Rocky Acres Bible Camp. Served with AUS, 1942-44. Mem. Tufted Textile Mfrs. Assn. (1st v.p. dir.), Gideons Internat. (state sec.). Baptist. Clubs: Athletic, Capital City (Atlanta). Home: 354 Lake Forrest Lane NE Atlanta GA 30305 Office: 5025 New Peachtree Rd Chamblee GA 30005

KELLEHER, HARRY BARTLETT, lawyer; b. New Orleans, Apr. 21, 1909; s. William J. and Harriet I. (Perrin) K.; A.B., LL.B., Tulane U., 1931; m. Nellie May Bartlett, Feb. 4, 1936; children—Nellie May (Mrs. James A. Churchill), Harry Bartlett. Admitted to La. bar, 1931, also U.S. Supreme Ct; practice in New Orleans, 1931—; sr. partner firm Lemle, Kelleher, Kohlmeyer, Matthews & Schumacher. Mem. exec. com. Pub. Affairs Research Council. Mem. com. Nat. Soc. Crippled Children and Adults; hon. life chmn. trustees Crippled Childrens Hosp., New Orleans; chmn. trustees Metairie Park Country Day Sch.; past pres. New Orleans chpt. Travelers Aid Soc.; mem. devel. council Tulane U.; chmn. bd. adminstrs. Tulane Ednl. Fund; trustee Episcopal Diocese La.; council trustees Gulf South Research Inst.; bd. dirs., past pres. Council Better La., Met. Area Com. Fellow Am. Coll. Trial Lawyers; mem. Am., La. (past sec.-treas., vice chmn. com. profl. grievances and ethics), New Orleans bar assns., Am., La. law insts., Assn. Bar City N.Y., Order of Coif (hon.), Delta Kappa Epsilon, Omicron Delta Kappa. Episcopalian (past sr. warden, vestryman). Clubs: Boston, Louisiana, New Orleans Country, Internat. House, Round Table, Plimsell (New Orleans); Delta Kappa Epsilon (N.Y.C.). Home: 2001 Palmer Av New Orleans LA 70118 Office: Nat Bank of Commerce Bldg New Orleans LA 70112

KELLEHER, PATRICK JOSEPH, educator, museum dir.; b. Colorado Springs, Colo., July 26, 1917; s. Patrick and Mary (Devaney) K.; A.B., Colo. Coll., 1939; M.F.A., Princeton, 1942, Ph.D. (Procter fellow), 1947; postgrad fellow Am. Acad. in Rome, 1947-49; m. Marion Mackie, Mar. 14, 1948; children—George, Maria. Chief curator art Los Angeles County Mus., 1949; lectr. U. Buffalo, 1950-51; curator collections Albright-Knox Art Gallery, Buffalo, 1950-54; curator European art Nelson Gallery-Atkins Mus., Kansas City, Mo., 1954-59; dir. Art Mus., Princeton, 1960—, prof. art and archeology, 1962—. Served to maj. AUS, 1942-46. Mem. Assn. Mus. Dirs., Phi Beta Kappa. Home: 176 Parkside Dr Princeton NJ 08540

KELLEHER, RITA PATRICIA, coll. dean; b. Hingham, Mass., Mar. 21, 1908; d. John J. and Mary E. (Fee) Kelleher; R.N., Faulkner Hosp. Sch. Nursing, 1929; B.S., Columbia Tchrs. Coll., 1936; M.Ed., Boston

U., 1945; LL.D., Villa Maria Coll., 1962; D.Sc., Boston Coll., 1968. Pvt. duty nurse, Cuba, 1930; instr. scis. Clinton, Quincy, Mass., Mass. Gen. hosps., 1931-44; ednl. dir., dir. sch. Quincy City Hosp., 1944-47; asso. prof. nursing edn. Boston Coll. Sch. Nursing, 1947-50, prof. nursing edn., 1950-68, acting dean, 1947-50, dean, 1950-68. Mem. council Conf. Cath. Schs. Nursing; mem. nursing conf. Jesuit Schs. Nursing; chmn. nursing council, mem. com. health hosp. and med. care div. United Community Services; chmn. bd. registration in nursing Mass., 1950-56; chmn. Mass. Approving Authority for Schs. Nursing, 1950-56; dir. Mass. Com. on Children and Youth, 1965; mem. Mass. Com. on Status Women, 1965. Mem. Mass. Nurses Assn. (chmn. legislative com.), Greater Boston Nursing Council (chmn.), Mass. (pres. 1947-48), Nat. leagues nursing, Am. Nurses Assn., Adminstrv. Women in Edn., N.E. Pub. Health Assn. Home: 205 Otis St Hingham MA 02043 Office: Boston Coll Sch Nursing Chestnut Hill MA 02167

KELLEHER, ROBERT JOSEPH, lawyer; b. N.Y.C., Mar. 5, 1913; s. Frank and Mary (Donovan) K.; A.B., Williams Coll., 1935; LL.B., Harvard, 1938; m. Gracyn W. Wheeler, Aug. 14, 1940; children-R. Jeffrey, Karen Kathleen. Admitted to N.Y. bar, 1939, Cal. bar, 1942, also U.S. Supreme Ct.; atty. War Dept., 1941-43; Asst. U.S. atty. So. Dist. Cal., 1948-50; pvt. practice, Beverly Hills, 1951—. Mem. So. Cal. Com. Olympic Games, 1964; capt. U.S. Davis Cup Team, 1962-63; treas. Youth Tennis Found. So. Cal., 1961-64. Served to lt. USNR, 1942-45. Mem. So. Cal. Tennis Assn. (v.p. 1958-64), U.S. Lawn Tennis Assn. (pres. 1967-68), Delta Kappa Epsilon. Harvard of So. Cal.; Williams (N.Y.C.); La Jolla (Cal.) Beach and Tennis. Home: 1672 Waynecrest Dr Beverly Hills CA 90210 Office: 424 S Beverly Dr Beverly Hills CA 90212

KELLEN, STEPHEN MAX, investment banker; b. Berlin, Germany, Apr. 21, 1914; s. Max and Leonie (Marcuse) Katzenellenbogen; grad. Royal French Coll., Berlin, 1932; m. Anna-Maria Arnhold, Mar. 7, 1940; children—Marina (Mrs. Heinz Gundlach), Michael. Came to U.S., 1936, naturalized, 1944. With Berliner Handels- Gesellschaft, Berlin, 1932-35, Lazard Bros. Ltd., London, Eng., 1936, Loeb, Rhoades & Co., N.Y.C., 1937-40; with Arnhold and S. Bleichroeder, Inc., N.Y.C., 1940—, pres., 1955—; dir. Pittway Corp., Deutsches Theater, Inc., Siemens Overseas Investments Ltd. Can. Bd. dirs. Friends of Animals; trustee N.Y. Cancer Research Inst. Mem. Investment Bankers Assn. Am. (bd. govs.). Clubs: Bond, Wall Street (N.Y.C.); Club du Chateau (Castellaras, France). Home: 784 Park Av New York City NY 10021 Office: 30 Broad St New York City NY 10004

KELLENBERG, WALTER P., bishop; b. N.Y.C., 1901; student St. Joseph's Sem., Yonkers, N.Y.; spl. student Columbia; LL.D., Fordham U., 1954, St. Michael's Coll., 1959. Ordained priest Roman Cath. Ch., 1928; apptd. mem. N.Y. Archdiocese Curia, 1934, asst. chancellor, 1939, vice chancellor, 1942, chancellor, 1947, sec. Cardinal Spellman, 1947-50, moderator coordinating com. Cath. Lay Orgns. of Archdiocese, 1948; papal chamberlain, 1943, domestic prelate, 1948; aux. bishop of N.Y., 1953; bishop of Ogdensburg, 1954, of Rockville Center, 1957—. Address: St Agnes Cathedral Rectory 29 Quealy Pl Rockville Centre NY 11570

KELLENBERGER, GORDON EDWARD, banker; b. Balt., Nov. 5, 1911; s. Frank Albert and Helen Gertrude (Knauff) K.; student Johns Hopkins, 1928-30, 34-35; J.D., U. Balt., 1939; m. Dorothy Catherine Hoxter, Jan. 14, 1933; children—Joan C. (Mrs. George Frederick Gardner, Jr.), Dorothy L. (Mrs. James Arthur Donovan). Admitted to Md. bar, 1939; asst. trust officer Mercantile Trust Co. Balt., 1942-47; trust officer Mercantile Safe Deposit & Trust Co., Balt., 1947-53, v.p., 1953, sr. v.p., 1953—; pres., dir. Orange Central Corp., Balt., 1966—; v.p., dir. Balt. Chair Co., 1950—; dir. F.H. Shallus Co., Chartwell Holding Co. Life mem. Glen Burnie Improvement Assn., 1941—, pres., 1950-51; mem. Severna Park Improvement Assn., 1953—, bd. dirs., 1954-57; mem. Anne Arundel County adv. bd. Am. Automobile Assn., 1969—. Pres., bd. dirs. R.C. Heller Found., since 1964—; bd. dirs. Anne Arundel Community Coll. Fund. Mem. Am. Judicature Soc., Am., Md. bar assns., Bar Assn. Baltimore City, Heuisler Honor Soc. Republican. Episcopalian. Kiwanian (past pres., now dir.), Mason (32, Shriner). Clubs: Merchants (Balt.); Chartwell Golf & Country Severna Park. Home: 115 Avondale Circle Severna Park MD 21146 Office: 2 Hopkins Plaza Box 2257 Baltimore MD 21203

KELLENBERGER, HUNTER, retired educator; b. Newark O., Feb. 14, 1904; s. Charles William and Helen (Hunter) K.; A.B., Kenyon Coll., 1925; A.M., Princeton, 1928, Ph.D., 1931; m. Esther Rodman Stone, May 3, 1941; children—Gordon Hunter, Judith Rodman. Latin master DeVeaux Sch., 1925-27; French master Northwood Sch., Lake Placid Club, N.Y., 1931-33; travelling fellow Am. Council Learned Socs., 1933-34; instr. French, Princeton, 1934-35, 37-38; asst. prof. Brown U., 1938-46, asso. prof., 1946-47, prof. French, 1947-71, emeritus, 1971—, chmn. div. modern langs., 1946-60, chmn. dept. French, 1960-64. Chmn. New Eng. Conf. Teaching Fgn. Langs., 1954. Mem. Modern Lang. Assn. Am., Am. Assn. Tchrs. French, New Eng. Fgn. (pres. 1961-62), R.I. (pres. 1968-69) fgn lang. assns. Episcopalian. Author: The Influence of Accentuation on French Word Order, 1932; contbg. author The Case for Basic Education 1959. Editor com. reports. Home: 3 Angell Ct Providence RI 02906

KELLER, CHARLES, Jr., constrn. co. exec; b. Detroit, Oct. 20, 1908; s. Charles and Frances (Rosenfield) K.; B.S., U.S. Mil. Acad., 1930; B.S. in Mech. Engring., Mass. Inst. Tech., 1933; m. Rosa Freeman, Dec. 28, 1932; children—Charles III, Mary (Mrs. Luis M. Zervigon), Caroline (Mrs. Philip H. Loughlin III). Commd. 2d lt. C.E., U.S. Army, 1930. advanced through grades to col., 1944; resigned, 1945; with Nat. Am. Bank, New Orleans, 1939-41; pres. Keller Constrn. Corp., New Orleans, 1946—. Pres., Pub. Affairs Research Council La., 1960-61, United Fund Greater New Orleans Area, 1955; chmn. Central Area Com., New Orleans, 1959-61. Trustee Com. Econ. Devel. Decorated Bronze Star with 2 oak leaf clusters, Legion of Merit with oak leaf cluster; Legion of Honor (U.S.); Croix de Guerre with palm (France). Registered profl. engr., La. Mem. Asso. Gen. Contractors Am. (pres. 1963), Am. Soc. C.E., Soc. Am. Mil. Engrs., Nat. Soc. Profl. Engrs. Home: 1701 Arabella St New Orleans LA 70115 Office: PO Box 50039 New Orleans LA 70150

KELLER, CHRISTOPH, Jr., bishop; b. Bay City, Mich., Dec. 22, 1915; s. Christoph and Margaret Ely (Walter) K.; grad. Lake Forest (Ill.) Acad., 1934; B.A., Washington and Lee U., 1939; student Grad. Sch. Theology, U. South, 1954; certificate spl. work, Gen. Theol. Sem., N.Y.C., 1957; S.T.D. (hon.), Gen. Theol. Sem.; D.D. U. South; m. Caroline P. Murphy, June 22, 1940; children—Caroline, Cornelia, Cynthia, Kathryn, Christoph, Elisabeth. Planter, Alexandria, La., 1940—; pres. Deltic Farm & Timber Co., El Dorado, Ark., 1948-51; exec. v.p. Murphy Corp., El Dorado, 1951-54, dir., 1948—; ordained priest P.E. Ch., 1957; rector, Harrison, Ark., also charge missions in Eureka Springs and Mountain Home, Ark., 1957-61; rector St. Andrews Episcopal Ch., Jackson, Miss., 1962-67; dean St. Andrews Cathedral, Jackson, until 1967; bishop coadjutor Diocese of Ark., 1967-70, diocesan bishop, 1970—. Dir. Tallalah State Bank (La.), 1950-51. Bd. trustees P.E. Diocese Ark., 1957-62, mem. exec. council, 1958-60, chmn. dept. promotion, 1958-60; exec. committee P.E. Diocese Miss., 1963-65; dep. Gen. Conv. P. E. Ch., 1958 61, 64, 67. Pres. La. Aberdeen Angus Breeders Assn., 1947, La. Delta Council, 1950; chmn. United Fund El Dorado, 1952. Mem. Madison Parish (La.) Sch. Bd., 1952-53. Trustee All Saints Jr. Coll., Vicksburg, Miss., 1949-51, Kent Sch., Conn., U. South; bd. overseers Sweet Briar Coll. Served as officer USMCR, World War II. Mem. Pi Kappa Alpha (pres. 1939). Kiwanian. Home: 1809 Beechwood Rd Little Rock AR 72205 Office: 300 W 17th St Little Rock AR 72206

KELLER, CLARENCE CHRISTIAN, corp. exec., elec. engr.; b. Orrville, O., Dec. 6, 1907; s. Charles and Emma (Zimmerman) K.; B.Elec. Engring., Ohio State U., 1929, E.E., 1935; m. Nellie Grubb, Sept. 8, 1928; children—Jacquelyn (Mrs. S. Gilbert), Barbara (Mrs. J. Wilkens), Patricia (Mrs. W. Button), Clarence Christian, Sarah (Mrs. J. Filippini), S. Lee, Marjorie. With Holophane Co., Newark, O., 1929—, successively test engr., mgr. application engring., N.Y.C., asst. sales mgr., gen. sales mgr., v.p. charge sales, dir. parent co. and subsidiaries, v.p., 1929-59, exec. v.p., pres, 1961—, chief exec. officer, 1966—; pres., dir. Holophane S.A. de C.V. Mexico City, Mex.; chmn. bd. Holophane Co., Ltd., Can., Holophane Ltd. Bletchley, Bucks, Eng., Mobilite, Inc., Woodbro Corp., Van Nuys, Cal.; dir. Spheres, Inc., Strong Electric Corp. Mem. School Board, Yorkstown, N.Y., 1965-67, Zoning bd. Appeals, Yorktown. Pres. Charles Franck (Holophane) Found., Inc. Mem. Illuminating Engring. Soc. (regional v.p. 1942-44, dir. 1944-47, gen. sec. 1951-53 v.p. 1964-66), pres. 1966-67), Nat. Elec. Mfrs. Assn. (chmn. indsl. and comml. lighting equipment sect., v.p., bd. govs., pres. 1969), Engrs. Club N.Y.C. Clubs: Sedgwood Country (Carmel, N.Y.); Kiwanis (past pres.). Home: 3020 Old Yorktown Rd Yorktown Heights NY 10598 Office: 1120 Av of Americas New York City NY 10036

KELLER, DEANE, artist; b. New Haven, Dec. 14, 1901; s. Albert Galloway and Caroline Louise (Gussmann) K.; A.B., Yale, 1923, B.F.A., 1926, M.A., 1948; fellow Am. Acad. in Rome, 1926-29; student Art Students' League, N.Y.C., 1922- 23; m. Katherine P. Hall, July 16, 1938; children—Deane Galloway, William. Portrait, mural and landscape painter, 1929; passt. prof. Yale Sch. Fine Arts, 1930-36, asso. prof., 1936-48, prof., 1948—; prin. works include: mural (with Rancel La Farge) New Haven Pub. Library "Valley Forge, " Nat. Mus., Washington 1933, ofcl. portrait Conn. Gov. John Lodge, 1954, portrait Sen. Robert A. Taft, Taft Sch. and Senate Reception Chamber of Capitol Bldg., portrait Herbert Hoover for Boys' Club Am.; murals Shriver Hall, Johns Hopkins, 1958; rep. permanent collections Yale; Bishop Mus., Honolulu; Hosp. San Salvador, Santiago, Chile; Wayne County Med. Soc., Detroit; Boston State House; Emerson Elec. Mfg. Co., gun turret div., St. Louis; Capt. Colin P. Kelly; N.A.D., N.Y.C.; U. N.C. Served from capt. to maj., AUS, 1943-46. Decorated Legion of Merit (U.S.A.); Order Brit. Empire; Crown of Italy, Partisan medal (Italy); Order of St. John Lateran (Vatican); recipient Prix de Rome, 1926; figure painting prize New Haven Paint and Clay Club 1926, 41, 47; portrait prize Conn. Acad., 1940. Mem. Grand Central Galleries N.Y., Alumni Assn. Am. Acad. Rome, Conn. Acad. Fine Arts, Fifth Army Assn., Portraits, Inc. Clubs: Paint and Clay (past pres.), Graduate, Century (New Haven). Home: 18 Brookhaven Rd Hamden CT 06517 Office: Yale Art Gallery New Haven CT 06520

KELLER, DOLORES ELAINE, educator, biologist; b. N.Y.C., Oct. 29, 1926; d. Louis and Ada Betsy (Ross) Greene; certificate Northwestern U., 1942; B.S. magna cum laude, L.I.U., 1945; M.A., N.Y.U., 1947, Ph.D., 1956; postgrad. oceanography Columbia, 1961, marine biology, U. Hawaii, 1964, animal behavior, U. N.C., 1969, primate behavior, U. Cal. at Davis, 1971; certificate electron microscopy, U. Cal. at Berkeley, 1966; m. Martin Edward Keller, July 27, 1946; children—Steven Edward, Kevin Edward, Wendy Anne. Instr. biology, chmn. dept. N.Y.C. High Sch., 1952-54; instr., asst. dean L.I.U., 1954-56; asso. prof., chmn. dept. sci. Fairleigh Dickinson U., 1956-66; prof. biology, chmn. dept. Pace Coll., 1966—; asso. dir. adult edn. Union Free Dist. 5, 1952-56; lectr. sex edn., 1952—; Haskins Labs. research asso., 1965—. Mem. exec. com. Project Hope; mem. Juvenile Delinquency Commn. Bergen County; curriculum chmn. Bergen Coll.; exec. dir. N.J. Acad. Scis.; dir. NSF grants, Allied Health grants. Fellow A.A.A.S.; mem. Electron Microscopic Soc. Am., Soc. Protozologists, N.Y. Acad. Sci., Am. Zool. Soc., Am. Inst. Biol. Scis., Animal Behavior Soc. Author: Sex and the Single Cell, 1971; also articles. Home: 96 Cypress St Woodcliff Lake NJ 07680 Office: Pace Coll Plaza New York City NY 10038

KELLER, EDWARD LUTHER, retired educator; b. Harrisburg, Pa., Mar. 8, 1904; s. Harry Levi and Ida (Windsor) K.; B.S., Pa. State Coll., 1925; D.Sc., Elizabethtown (Pa.) Coll., 1965; m. Dessa Belle Buoymaster, Nov. 6, 1926; 1 son, Edward Windsor. Salesman, John J. Nesbitt Co., 1925; instr. engring. extension Pa. State U., 1926-30, asst. prof., 1930-34, asso. prof., 1934, acting head dept., 1934, dir. dept., 1935, prof. engring. extension, 1937-69, exec. asst. central extension, 1942-51, asst. dir. gen. extension, 1951-53, dir., 1953-59, dir. continuing edn., 1959-64, v.p. pub. affairs, 1964-69. Dir. Nat. Univ. Extension Assn., 1946-49; mem. nat. panel arbitrators, Am. Arbitration Assn.; chmn. council on gen. extension Assn. Land-Grant Colls. and Univs., 1950-51; mem. Nat. Adv. Council Extension and Continuing Edn. Chmn. Central Pa. Heart Assn. Campaign chmn. Coll. area United Fund, 1967—; mem. Nat. Tech. Inst. Deaf. Pres. State Coll. borough council, 1946-51. Mem. Nat. Acad. Arbitrators, Pa., Am. vocational assns., Pa. State Assn. Adult Edn., Nat. U. Extension Assn. (pres. 1949-50). Am. Mgmt. Assn., Am. Soc. Engring. Edn., Pa. Heart Assn. (chmn. 1959-61), Council Nat. Orgns. (treas.), Engrs. Joint Council (vice chmn. govtl. liaison com.), Alpha Tau Omega (nat. vocational adv. bd.), Gamma Omega, Alumni Assn. of Alpha Tau Omega (pres.). Republican. Presbyn. Club: Centre Hills Country (State College). Home: 610 N Burrowes St State College PA 16801

KELLER, FRANK J., publishing co. exec.; b. N.Y.C., May 22, 1911; s. August and Bertha (Fisher) K.; B.S.S., N.Y.U., 1931; m. Ruby C. Carrigan, Oct. 20, 1935; children—Bruce, Valerie (Mrs. Anthony Stuart), Randall, Regina. Accountant, Seidman & Seidman, C.P.A.'s, 1932-34; treas. J.L. Hopkins & Co., 1934-38; with Funk & Wagnalls, Inc., 1939—, chmn. bd., 1971—. Pres., Property Owners Assn. Harbor Acres, N.Y., 1958-59, Assn. Roslyn Estates, N.Y., 1967-68; Frank J. Keller Found. Trustee Village of Roslyn Estates, USPS Meml. and Gifts Found. for Edn. C.P.A., N.Y. Mem. Nat. Assn. Accountants, U.S. Power Squadrons. Roman Catholic. K.C. Home: 66 The Oaks Roslyn Estates NY 11576 Office: 53 E 77th St New York City NY 10021

KELLER, GEOFFREY, coll. dean; b. N.Y.C., June 12, 1918; s. Franklin Jefferson and Evelyn (Miles) K.; B.S., Swarthmore Coll., 1938; Ph.D., Columbia, 1948; m. June McNicol, June 9, 1950; children—Gregory, Wendy. Asso. physicist Bur. Naval Ordnance, 1941-45; from instr. to asso. prof. physics and astronomy Ohio State U., Columbus, 1948-57, dean Coll. Math. and Phys. Scis., 1968—; dir. Perkins Obs., Delaware, O., 1952- 59; program dir. for astronomy NSF, 1957-61, div. dir. math. and phys. scis., 1961-66, dep. planning dir., 1966-68. Mem. Am. Astron. Soc., Am. Phys. Soc. Club: Cosmos (Washington). Home: 410 Highgate Av Worthington OH 43085 Office: 164 W 17th Av Columbus OH 43210

KELLER, GEORGE M., Jr., grocery mfg. co. exec.; b. N.Y.C., Apr. 18, 1921; s. George M. and Marion (Hicks) K.; grad. Middlesex Sch., Concord, Mass., 1938; student Stanford, 1938-39; B.A. in Econs. cum laude, Princeton, 1942; m. Joan Van Buren, Apr. 3, 1959; children—Susan, Michael M., Lynn M., Steven Van Buren, George M. III, Andrew M., Jane Stewart. With Seeman Bros., 1946-52; v.p. Internat. Milk Processors, 1952-53; cons. Booz-Allen & Hamilton, 1953-55; asst. to pres. John Shaw Advt., 1955-56; with Armour & Co., 1956-67, group v.p., 1966-67; pres. Keebler Co., Elmhurst, Ill., 1967—, also dir. Served as fighter pilot USNR, 1942-45. Mem. Phi Beta Kappa. Clubs: Economic, Executives, Racquet (Chgo.); Princeton (N.Y.C. and Chgo.); Onwentsia (Lake Forest). Home: 435 E Illinois Rd Lake Forest IL 60045 Office: 677 Larch Av Elmhurst IL 60125

KELLER, HARRY ADOLPH, editor, author; b. Phila., Nov. 1, 1894; s. Ernst Adolph and Ella (Whetstone) K.; ed. Bklyn. Boys High Sch., also pvt. tutors; m. Florence Broadhurst, June 25, 1915 (div. 1920); 1 dau., Dorothy Knox (Mrs. John Leahey); m. 2d, Margaret Achatz, Feb. 13, 1935 (dec. 1954); m. 3d, Lilly Holland Blish, Aug. 12, 1954. Asso. editor, then editor Street & Smith Publs., 1915-22; editor True Detective mag. 1923-26, Phys. Culture mag., 1926-28; fiction editor Dell Publs., 1928-29, Mackinon-Fly Publs., 1930-33; editor ofcl. Detective Stories mag., Phila., 1933-64, Tragedy-of-the-Month, 1949-50; editor, compiler Ofcl. Detective Omnibus, 1949; lectr. radio How to Write and Sell Short Stories, 1929-30, My Most Exciting Case, radio sta. WFIL, Phila., 1948-50; master of ceremonies Pub. Prosecutor, WFIL-TV, 1951; cons. editor, 1957-60; editorial cons. MacFadden-Bartel Corp., N.Y.C. Hon. staff mem. Wills Eye Hosp., Phila.; recipient Humanitarism award for outstanding vol. services, 1970. Republican. Episcopalian. Author: If You Must Write, 1930; Picture Bride, 1930; Sacred Sin, 1931; Death Sits In, 1932; Debtors Holiday, 1933; Yesterday's Sin, 1933. Home: 405 A The Kenilworth Alden Park Philadelphia PA 19144 Office: 205 E 42d St New York City NY 10017

KELLER, HENRY, Jr., textile co. exec.; b. Harrisburg, Pa., May 9, 1922; s. Henry and Susanna (Safnauer) K.; student U. Ga., 1947-51; LL.B., Woodrow Wilson Coll. Law, 1953; m. Jane Palmer, Apr. 9, 1944; children—Julia Louise, Jan Elaine. With U.S. Treasury Dept., Atlanta, 1948-53; spl. assignments West Point Mfg. Co. (Ga.), 1953-57, asst. treas., 1957-62, sec., 1962-65; sec. West Point-Pepperell, Inc., 1965-70, asst. treas., 1970—. Sec. Community Service Assn., Shawmut, Ala., 1962-70, W. Point Pepperell Found., 1962-70. Served with AUS, 1942-45; ETO. Mem. Ga. Bar Assn., Ga. Soc. C.P.A.'s. Baptist (deacon). Home PO Box 547 West Point GA 31833 Office: West Point-Pepperell Inc West Point GA 31833

KELLER, HENRY HERMAN, newspaper pub.; b. Durhamville, N.Y., Oct. 23, 1902; s. Herman Frederick and Charlotte Elizabeth (Skinner) K.; B.S., Wharton Sch., U. Pa., 1924; m. Rebecca Elliott Donohue, Apr. 18, 1925. With Nation's Business, U.S. C. of C., Washington, 1924-26; dir., pres. Post-Standard Co., Syracuse, N.Y., 1926-70, v.p., 1926-61, pres. 1961-70, also publisher. Dir. Met. Devel. Assn. Mem. Nat. Advt. Execs. Assn., N.Y. State Pubs. Assn. (dir.), Am. Newspaper Publs. Assn., Pi Kappa Alpha, Alpha Delta Sigma. Episcopalian. Clubs: University, Kiwanis, U. Pa. Central N.Y. (past pres.) (Syracuse). Home: 1221 Euclid Av Syracuse NY 13210 Office: 300 E Fayette St Syracuse NY 13202

KELLER, IRA C., business exec.; b. Portland, Me., Feb. 2, 1899; s. Charles and Frances Keller; M.E., Rensselaer Poly. Inst., 1920; m. Lauretta Brownson Taylor, Apr. 5, 1924; 1 son, Richard Brownson. Apprentice, Westinghouse Electric Co., 1920; later employed Union Carbide & Carbon Co., Nat. Acme Co., Cleve.; with Container Corp. Am., Chgo., 1926-53, exec. v.p., 1946-53; chmn., dir. Western Kraft Corp., Western Sales Co. (Portland), Western Corrugated, Inc. (Cal.); vice chmn., dir. Willamette Industries, Inc., Portland, Ore. Chmn. Portland Devel. Commn. Vice chmn. Ore. Grad. Center. Served with U.S. Army, World War I. Mem. Alpha Tau Omega. Unitarian. Clubs: Racquet (Chgo.); Arlington, Waverly Country, University, (Portland). Home: 4700 S W Northwood Av Portland OR 97201 Office: Standard Plaza Portland OR 97204

KELLER, JACK (John A.C. Keller), newspaperman; b. Columbus, O., Oct. 23, 1911; s. Edwin Louis and Mildred Elizabeth (Riedel) K.; B.Sc., Ohio State U., 1933; m. Claire Elizabeth Schrader, June 10, 1931; children—John Jay, Patricia Mae. With Columbus Citizen-Jour., 1933—, as reporter, sports editor, city editor, news editor, 1933-54, mng. editor, 1954—. Mem. Olympian. Mem. 1932 Olympic Track Team, high hurdles, world record holder 220 yd. low hurdles. Home: 1452 Cottonwood Dr Columbus OH 43229 Office: 34 S 3d St Columbus OH 43215

KELLER, JAMES G., retired clerygman; b. Oakland, Cal., June 27, 1900; s. James and Margaret (Selby) K.; student St. Patrick's Coll., 1920-24; M.A., Cath. U., 1925; LL.D., Mt. Mary Coll., 1949, Canisius Coll., 1949. Ordained priest Roman Cath. Ch., 1925; founder, dir. The Christophers, Inc., N.Y.C., 1945; now retired. Author: The Priest and A World Vision, 1946; You Can Change The World, 1948; Three Minutes a Day, 1949; Careers That Change Your World, 1950; One Moment Please, 1950; Government is Your Business, 1951; Just for Today, 1952; All God's Children, 1953; Stop, Look and Live, 1954; Give Us This Day, 1956; It's Your Day, 1957; A Day At a Time, 1958. Home: 121 E 39th St New York City NY 10016

KELLER, JOHN ESTEN, educator; b. Lexington, Ky., Sept. 27, 1917; s. Owen Bullitt and Mary Louise (Welsh) K.; A.B., U. Ky., 1940, M.A., 1942; Ph.D., U. N.C., 1946; m. Dinsmore Davis, Sept. 2, 1942; children—John E., Laura Dinsmore. Instr. U. N.C., 1943-46; asso. prof. U. Tenn., 1947-50; mem. faculty U. N.C., 1950-67, prof., 1957-67; prof., chmn. dept. Spanish and Italian, asso. dean arts and scis. U. Ky., Lexington, 1967—. Mem. Mediaeval Acad. Am., Modern Lang. Assn., S. Atlantic Modern Lang. Assn. (pres. 1967-68); corr. mem. Consejo Superior de Investigaciones Cientificas Madrid, Spain. Author: Alfonso X, El Sabio, 1967. Editor: (Calila e Digna) Medieval Spanish, 1957; Libro de los Gatos, 1958; Libro de los Engannos 1959; Libro de los Exenplos, 1961. Home: 802 Chinoe Rd Lexington KY 40502

KELLER, JOSEPH ADREON, Jr., business exec.; b. Balt., Oct. 3, 1918; s. Joseph Adreon and Teresa (Latchford) K.; grad. Balt. Poly. Inst., 1936; B.S. in Mech. Engring., Ga. Inst. Tech., 1939, M.S., Lehigh U., 1941; m. Patricia Powers, June 10, 1944; children—Blanid T., Joseph Adreon III, James W., Sarah L., Suzanne L., Paul P., Katharine A., Christian. Foreman, Bethlehem Steel Corp., Sparrows Point, Md., 1939-41; spl. engr. Carnegie-Ill. Steel Corp., Chgo., 1941-45; v.p. George Fry & Assos., Chgo., 1947-54; v.p. operations Mergenthaler Linotype Co., Bklyn., 1955-57, exec. v.p., 1957, pres., 1958—, also dir.; pres., dir. Eltra Corp. Served as ensign, Civil Engring. Corps, USNR, 1945-46. Mem. Am. Mgmt. Assn., Am. Ordnance Assn., Beta Theta Phi. Clubs: Univ. Chicago; Plandome Country. Home: 76 Papermill Rd Plandome NY 11030 Office: 2 Pennsylvania Plaza New York City NY 10001

KELLER, JOSEPH BISHOP, mathematician, educator; b. Paterson, N.J., July 31, 1923; s. Isaac and Sally (Bishop) K.; B.A., N.Y.U., 1943, M.S., 1946, Ph.D., 1948; m. Evelyn Fox, Aug. 29, 1963; children-Jeffrey M., Sarah N. Prof. math Courant Inst. Math. Scis., N.Y.U., 1948—, chmn. dept. math. Univ. Coll. Arts and Scis. and Grad. Sch. Engring. and Sci., 1967—. Mem. Am. Math. Soc., Am. Phys. Soc. Contbr. articles profl. jours. Home: 4 Washington Square Village New York NY 10012 Office: Dept Math Sch Engring N Y U University Heights Bronx NY 10453

KELLER, LEROY, press assn. exec.; b. Longmont, Colo., Aug. 31, 1905; s. Samuel Ashby and Vinnie Alice (Howard) K.; A.B., U. Colo., 1929; m. Winifred Cora Allen, Mar. 31, 1935; children—John, Winifred (Mrs. E.J. Andrews). Joined United Press Assns., 1929, staff writer, 1929-33, syndicate rep., 1933- 35, bus. rep., 1936-45, asst. bus. mgr., 1945-48, gen. sales mgr., 1948- 64, v.p., 1952—, dir. client relations, 1959-64, v.p., gen. mgr. internat. divs., 1964—; v.p. United Features Syndicate; dir. UPI Newsfilm, Inc., UPI Ltd. of Canada, U.P.I., 1958-61, United News Services, Internat. News Service, Wire Service Supply Co. Adv. com. World Press Inst., ANPA-World Press Achievement Awards. Mem. Inter-Am. Press Assn., Internat. Press Inst., Sigma Delta Chi, Sigma Alpha Epsilon. Clubs: University (N.Y.C.); Scarsdale Golf, Fox Meadow Tennis (Scarsdale). Home: 23 Old Army Rd Scarsdale NY 10583 Office: 220 E 42d St New York City NY 10017

KELLER, LOUIS, physician, educator; b. N.Y.C., 1906; M.D., St. Louis U., 1937. Intern, St. Louis U. Group Hosps., 1937-38, fellow, clin. asst., jr. resident, 1949, resident, 1949-51, asst. dermatologist, 1951-56, asso. dermatologists, 1956—; mem. vis. staff St. Louis City Hosp.; clin. prof., chmn. dept. dermatology St. Louis U. Served to capt. M.C., AUS, 1942-46. Diplomate Am. Bd. Dermatology. Fellow Am. Acad. Dermatology; mem. A.M.A. Office: 221 N Grand Blvd St Louis MO 63103*

KELLER, MORTON, educator, historian; b. Bklyn., Mar. 1, 1929; s. Jacob and Anita (Sherman) K.; B.A., U. Rochester, 1950; M.A., Harvard, 1952, Ph.D., 1956; m. Phyllis Daytz, Sept. 7, 1951; children—Robin, Jonathan. Instr. history U. N.C., 1956-58; asst. prof., asso. prof. U. Pa., 1958-63; vis. lectr. Harvard, 1963-64; prof. history Brandeis U., Waltham, Mass., 1964—, chmn. dept., 1965-70. Dir. Telluride Assn. Summer Program, Stanford, 1962. Served as officer USNR, 1953-56. Mem. Am. Hist. Assn., Orgn. Am. Historians, Phi Beta Kappa. Author: In Defense of Yesterday—James M. Beck and the Politics of Conservatism, 1958; The Life Insurance Enterprise (Kulp award 1964), 1963. Editor: The New Deal, 1963; (E.L. Godkin) Problems of Modern Democracy, 1966; The Art and Politics of Thomas Nast, 1968. Home: 29 Raymond St Cambridge MA 02140 Office: Dept History Brandeis U Waltham MA 02154

KELLER, RAYMOND NEVOY, educator, chemist; b. Wolcott, Ind., Apr. 21, 1909; s. Benjamin and Priscilla (Blume) K.; A.B., Ind. U., M.A., 1937; Ph.D., U. Ill., 1940; m. Mollie Goodrich, Dec. 19, 1936; children—Roger Raymond, Mark Douglas, Janet Mollie. Teaching asst. dept. chemistry Ind. U., 1936; teaching asst. dept. chemistry U. Ill., Urbana, 1937-39, fellow, 1939-40; instr. chemistry U. Wis., 1940-42; instr. U. Mich., 1942-45, asst. prof., 1945-51; research chemist Argonne Nat. Lab., Chgo., 1950-51; asst. prof. chemistry U. Colo., 1951-52, asso. prof., 1952-60, prof., 1960—. Mem. Am. Chem. Soc., Chem. Soc. London, Colo.-Wyo. Acad. Sci., Sigma Xi, Phi Beta Kappa, Phi Kappa Phi, Phi Lambda Upsilon. Republican. Presbyn. Contbr. articles profl. jours. Research in inorganic chemistry, especially pseudohalide complexes and boroxines. Home: 3781 N 26th St Boulder CO 80302

KELLER, REXFORD CURTIS, educator, condr., organist; b. Buchanan, Mich., Apr. 6, 1904; s. William Howard and Harriet Louise (Dwire) K.; sr. diploma Chgo. Mus. Coll., 1923; B.M., U. Mich., 1931, M.M., 1932; organ study under Wilhelm Middleschulte, Palmer Christian, Marcel Dupre; m. Margaret Stuart, Nov. 14, 1926; children—Mary Stuart, Alice Anne. Organist, Meth. Peace Temple and 1st Bapt. Ch., Benton Harbor, Mich., 1921-23; minister music 1st Bapt. Ch., South Bend, Ind., 1925-27, 1st Meth. Ch., Ypsilanti, Mich., 1928-33; instr. theory, piano, organ Nashville Conservatory, 1933-34; organist, dir. choral groups Vanderbilt U., 1933-34; dir. choral groups, instr. organ and theory Ohio Wesleyan U., 1934—, head music dept., 1936— (on leave, 1945); minister music N. Broadway Meth. Ch., Columbus, O., 1944-47, 49-59; tchr. European Army U., Biarritz Am. U., France, 1945. Recipient Albert A. Stanley medal U. Mich., 1932. Mem. Music Tchrs. Nat. Assn., Music Educators Nat. Conf., Ohio Music Educators Assn. (past chmn. coll. div.), Am. Guild Organists, Nat. Assn. Schs. of Music chmn. region 5 1962), Phi Mu Alpha Sinfonia, Pi Kappa Lambda, Omicron Delta Kappa, Phi Kappa Phi. Methodist. Research in Am. folk music, psychology of memorizing music. Home: 67 Griswold St Delaware OH 43015

KELLER, ROBERT FRANKLIN, govt. ofcl.; b. Washington, Aug. 22, 1913; s. Paul D. and Edna S. (Wells) K.; student George Washington U., 1931-32; LL.B., Washington Coll. Law, 1937; B.C.S., Benjamin Franklin U., 1952; m. Mary Benton Robinson, Nov. 11, 1939; children—Elizabeth Wright (Mrs. Edward L. Koepenick) Katherine Wells. Admitted to D.C. bar, 1936; with Gen. Accounting Office, 1935-42, 46—, gen. counsel, 1958-69, dep. controller gen. U.S., 1969—; legislative atty. Office Comptroller Gen. U.S., 1946-50, asst. to comptroller gen., 1950-53, prin. asst., 1953-58. Trustee Govt. Services, Inc. Served from ensign to lt., USNR, 1942-45; asst. to officer charge Navy Purchasing Office, San Francisco, also gen. counsel. Recipient commendation sec. navy; Rockefeller Pub. Service award, 1965. Mem. Fed., Am. bar assns., Nat. Contract Mgmt. Assn. (bd. advisers), Sigma Nu Phi. Lion. Club: Kenwood Golf and Country (Bethesda, Md.). Home: 5604 Namakagan Rd Washington DC 20016 Office: 441 G St NW Washington DC 20548

KELLER, ROBERT JOHN, educator; b. White Bear Lake, Minn., May 25, 1913; s. John Joseph and Lillie (Olson) K.; B.E., Winona (Minn.) State Tchrs. Coll., 1937; M.A., U. Minn., 1940, Ph.D., 1947; m. Alice Maurine Fawcett, Dec. 29, 1943; children—Janet Maurine, Marilyn Jean. Rural sch. tchr., 1931-32; tchr., prin. Ramsey County, Minn., 1932-38; high sch. tchr., N. St. Paul, Minn., 1938-40; teaching research asst. U. Minn., 1940-42, 45-46; civilian research psychologist, 1946-47; asst. prof. U. Minn., Mpls., 1947, asso. prof., 1948, prof. edn., 1951—, dir. Univ. High Sch., 1956-64, dean Coll. Edn., U. Minn., 1964-70; Carnegie vis. prof. U. Hawaii, 1957-58; vis. prof. U. Hawaii, 1970-71; AID cons. Ministry Edn., Republic Korea, 1971—. Asso. dir. Bur. Instnl. Research, 1947-50, dir., 1950- 54; chmn. Senate Com. on Instnl. Relationships, 1948-64; dir. Gov.'s Com. on Higher Edn., 1956-57, Legislative Interim Commn. on Higher Edn., 1958-59, Kan. Study Higher Edn., 1959-60; mem. Coll. Entrance Exam. Bd., 1964-67; mem. exec. com. Minn. Council Econ. Edn.; bd. mem. Upper Midwest Research and Devel. Council; mem. exec. bd., commn. instns. higher edn. N. Central Assn., 1967-71, bd. dirs. assn., 1969—; v.p. Am. Assn. Higher Edn., 1968-69, pres., 1969-70. Served with USAAF, 1942- 45. Fellow A.A.A.S.; mem. Am. Psychol. Assn., Am. Assn. Sch. Adminstrs., Am. Statis. Assn., Am. Ednl. Research Assn., Psychometric Soc., N.E.A., Nat. Assn. Secondary Sch. Prins., Am. Assn. Jr. Colls., Phi Delta Kappa, Kappa Delta Pi. Author: (with Ruth Eckert) A University Looks at its Program, 1954; Minnesota's Stake in the Future, Higher Education 1956-70, 1957; Higher Education for Our State and Times, 1959; (with Otto Domian) Comprehensive Educational Survey of Kansas, Vol. IV, 1960; (with D.R. Bruning) St. Paul Junior High School Study, 1962; Educational Survey for Wisconsin Evangelical Lutheran Synod, Vols. I-II, 1962; (with R.C. Gibson, A.O. Pfinster) Expansion and Coordination of Higher Education in Missouri, 1962; (with others) Education and Economic Growth, 1964. Home: 1989 W Shryer Av St Paul MN 55113 Office: Burton Hall U Minn Minneapolis MN 55455

KELLER, ROBERT KARL, lawyer; b. Seattle, Sept. 19, 1916; s. John Storey and Mary (Daniels) K.; B.A. in Econs. and Bus., U. Wash., 1938, LL.B., 1940; m. Esther Francis Elliott, Mar. 8, 1944; children—John Elliott, Robert Karl, Deborah Lee, Jennifer Francis. Admitted to Wash. bar, 1940; practiced in Seattle, 1946—; partner firm Horswill, Keller, Rohrbach, Waldo & Moren, and predecessor firm, 1952—. Dir. Pioneer Mut. Savs. Bank, Seattle. Served to lt. comdr. USNR, World War II. Mem. Wash., Seattle, King County bar assns., Am. Arbitration Soc. Club: Wash. Athletic (Seattle). Home: 11085 Arroyo Beach Pl SW Seattle WA 98146 Office: IBM Bldg Seattle WA 98101

KELLER, STANLEY ELLIS, educator, dentist; b. Medford, Mass., Sept. 9, 1921; s. Adrian C. and Jeannie (Ellis) K.; D.M.D. cum laude, Tufts U., 1944; M.S., U. Ala., 1962; m. Constance Berry, Apr. 7, 1945; children—David R., Bonnie, Robert A., Bruce P. Pvt. practice dentistry, Boston and Springfield, Mass., 1947-57; instr. clin. dentistry Tufts Dental Sch., Boston, 1947-58; prof. dentistry U. Ala., Birmingham, 1957—, dir. clinics, chmn. dept. oral diagnosis, 1959—. Cons. oral diagnosis VA Hosp., Birmingham. Served to capt., Dental Corps. AUS, 1944-47. Mem. Am. Coll. Dentists, Am. Dental Assn., Internat. Assn. Dental Research, Am. Assn. Dental Schs., Ala. Acad. Sci., Orgn. Tchrs. Oral Diagnosis, Sigma Xi, Omicron Kappa Upsilon. Home: 3144 Dolly Ridge Dr Birmingham AL 35243

KELLER, WALTER DAVID, geologist; b. N. Kansas City, Mo., Mar. 13, 1900; s. Theodore and Marie A. (Schulz) K.; A.B., U. Mo., 1925, Ph.D., 1933; B.S., Mo. Sch. Mines, 1930; A.M., Harvard, 1932; m. Lillian Madge Jones, Dec. 1936; children—David Eugene, Dwight Milton. Instr. geology U. Mo., Columbia, 1926-29, asst. prof., 1932-36, asso. prof., 1936-42, prof. geology, 1942-70, prof. emeritus, 1970—, chmn. dept. geology, 1941-45; ceramic technologist A.P. Green Fire Brick Co., Mexico, Mo., 1929-31; lectr. geology U.S. Army U., Florence, Italy, 1945; cons. in geology, microscopy, ceramics; Distinguished lectr. Am. Assn. Petroleum Geologists, 1954-55; lectr. Am. Geol. Inst., 1959-60; vis. prof. geology U.S. Fla., Tampa, 1970-71. Chmn. clay minerals com. Nat. Acad. Scis., NRC, 1957-60. Served as pvt. U.S. Army, 1918. Recipient Neil Miner award Nat. Assn. Geology Tchrs.; Faculty Alumni award, 1968; Distinguished Faculty Mem. award, 1969; Outstanding Educator award, 1970, 71. Fellow Geol. Soc. Am., Mineral Soc. Am., A.A.A.S.; mem. Am. Ceramic Soc., Brit. Mineral. Soc., Am. Inst. Mining and Metall. Engrs., Am. Assn. Petroleum Geologists, Soc. Econ. Paleontologists and Mineralogists, Am. Geophys. Union, Clay Minerals Soc. (hon.), Phi Beta Kappa, Sigma Xi, Alpha Chi Sigma, Sigma Gamma Epsilon, Gamma Alpha. Mem. United Ch. Christ. Mason. Club: University. Author: Common Rocks and Minerals of Missouri, rev. edit., 1962; (with Branson, Tarr) Introduction to Geology, 1952; Principles of Chemical Weathering, rev. edit., 1957; Chemistry in Introductory Geology, Mineralogy, Ceramics; contr. articles to sci. jours., Ency. Brit., Ency. Chem. Tech., Ency. Sci. and Tech. Home: 403 W Stewart Rd Columbia MO 65201

KELLER, WILLIAM KARL, educator; b. Louisville, Aug. 4, 1906; s. William August and Necia (Hamby) K.; A.B., U. Louisville, 1930, M.D 1931; m. Elizabeth Trawick, June 13, 1931; childrenn-Elizabeth T., Martha Kendrick (Mrs. Donald E. Jansen). Intern Louisville Gen. Hosp., 1931-32, resident medicine, 1932- 34; resident psychiatry Johns Hopkins Hosp., 1934-35, N.Y. Hosp., 1935- 37; Rockfeller fellow neurology, London, Eng., 1937-38; mem. faculty U. Louisville Sch.. Medicine, 1938—, prof. psychiatry, 1949—, chmn. dept., 1964—. Served with M.C., USNR, 1942-45. Recipient Distinguished Alumnus award U. Louisville, 1968. Fellow A.C.P., Am. Coll. Psychiatrists, Am. Psychiat. Assn.; mem. Ky., Jefferson County med. socs., A.M.A., Am. Assn. Automotive Medicine (pres. 1963-64), Central Neuropsychiat. Assn. (pres. 1968-69), Kappa Alpha, Alpha Kappa Kappa, Alpha Omega Alpha. Contbr. med. jours. Home: 4013 St Ives Ct Louisville KY 40207

KELLER, WILLIAM LEONARD, lawyer; b. Dallas, Aug. 7, 1922; s. Lawrence L. and Irene (Meadows) K.; LL.B., So. Methodist U., 1950; LL.M., George Washington U., 1953, postgrad., 1953-54; m. Carol Y. Klotz, Dec. 26, 1964; children—William Leonard, John L. Admitted Tex. bar, 1949, U.S. Supreme Ct.; practice in Dallas, 1950-51, 56-67, mem. firm Clark, Coon, Holt & Fisher, 1950-56; legislative atty. Econ. Stblzn. Agy., 1951-52; legal adviser NLRB, 1952- 56; partner Clark, West, Keller, Clark & Ginsberg, 1956-67; lectr. Labor Law Insts., Seminars. Served to 1st lt. USAAF, 1942-46. Mem. Am., Fed., Dallas (sect. chmn.) bar assns., State Bar Tex. (past sect. chmn., bd. govs. labor law sect.), Southwestern Legal Found. Am. Judicature Soc., Internat. Soc. for Labor Law and Social Legislation, Inter-Am. Bar Assn., Am. Mgmt. Assn., U.S. C. of C. (chmn. labor law sect., chmn. Labor Law Inst.), Dallas Council World Affairs, Barristers, Delta Theta Phi. Lion. Home: 5371 Montrose St Dallas TX 72509 Office: First Nat Bank Bldg Dallas TX 75202

KELLER, WILLIAM MARTIN, corp. exec.; b. Wilkes-Barre, Pa., Oct. 26, 1916; s. Roy S. and Alice (Obrien) K.; A.B., Syracuse U., 1939; grad. Advanced Mgmt. Program, Harvard; LL.D. in Internat. Relations, U. Liberia (W. Africa); m. Mary Anne Davis, Oct. 25, 1939; chiildren—Anne Elizabeth Hufford, William Martin III. Indsl. engr. Montgomery Ward & Co., 1939-40, Armstrong Cork Co., Inc., 1941-42; with Owens-Corning Fiberglas Corp., N.Y.C., 1942-62, mgr. indsl. engring., plant mgr., gen. factories mgr., 1942-54, v.p., gen. sales mgr. textile products div., 1954-57, v.p., gen. mgr. reinforced plastics div., 1958-62, v.p. internat., 1964-67; dir. AID, Monrovia, Liberia, 1962- 64; pres., dir. Marianne Rd., Inc.; pres. W.M. Keller Assos., 1968—; bus., govt. cons. to fgn. countries. Chmn. bd. trustees Cherry Lawn Sch., Darien, Conn. Decorated Star of Africa (Republic of Liberia). Mem. Pa. Soc. Mason (Shriner), Elk, Kiwanian. Clubs: N.Y. Sales Executive, Pinnacle, N.Y. Athletic (life), Harvard Business (N.Y.C.); Woodway Country; Metropolitan (Washington). Home: 20 Marianne Rd Darien CT 06820 Office: 180 Central Park S New York City NY 10019

KELLER, J. H., partner charge North Central dist. Ernst and Ernst, C.P.A.'s Address: Union Commerce Bldg Cleveland OH 44115

KELLERMAN, MRS. GEORGE, (Elizabeth Rountree Kellerman), mem. Republican Nat. Com.; b. High Point, N.C., Sept. 1, 1906; d. James B. and Elizabeth (Anderson) Rountree; A.B., Sweet Briar Coll., 1926; LL.B., Columbia, 1933; m. George H. Kellerman, Oct. 8, 1940; children—George R., R., James P. Admitted to N.Y. bar, 1934; atty. RFC, Washington, 1933, Fed. Emergency Adminstrn. Pub. Works, Washington, 1933-37; TV commentator on nat. and internat. affairs, 1965-70. Del. Hawaii Constl. Conv., 1950; mem. Republican Nat. Com. for Hawaii 1963—, mem. exec. com., 1964-68. Sec. Hawaii Council on Crime and Delinquency. Trustee Hawaii-Pacific Coll. Mem. Am. Assn. U. Women (v.p. Hawaii br. 1957-58, pres. 1958-60), World Brotherhood (co-chmn. Hawaii chpt. 1953-57), Hawaii Congress Parents and Tchrs. (legislative chmn. 1950-52), N.Y. State Bar Assn., We the Women of Hawaii, Nat. League Am. Pen Women, Phi Beta Kappa. Episcopalian. Club: Oahu League Republican Women. Home: 104 Wailupe Circle Honolulu HI 96821

KELLERMAN, KARL FREDERIC, engr.; b. Washington, May 11, 1908; s. Karl Frederic and Gertrude (Hast) K.; student Friends Sch., Washington, 1917-21; E.E., Cornell, 1929; grad. study in bus. law, management; C.L.U., Am. Coll. Life Underwriters, 1938, Northwestern U. Inst. Mgmt., 1961; m. Margaret Phillips, June 2, 1934; 1 son, Karl Frederic III. Communications engr. N.Y. Tel. Co., 1929-36; asst. br. mgr. and cons. on bus. econs. and taxation N.Y. Life Ins. Co., N.Y.C., 1936-42; charge tech. product sales devel. Aircraft Radio Corp., Boonton, N.J., 1946-47; exec. dir. com. on guided missiles Research and Devel. Bd., Washington, 1947-49; mgr. Washington office for Brush Devel. (electronics) 1949-53; pres. Kellerman & Co., cons. engrs., 1953-55; asso. dir. systems planning Bendix Aviation Corp., 1955-57, asst. v.p. engring., 1957-60, asst. to exec. v.p. 1960-62; pres. Microwave Devices, Inc., Rockville, Md., 1962- 64; sci. adviser USAF Systems Command, 1964—. Mem. council Cornell U., 1954-60. Served to comdr. USNR, World War II; head electronics coordination br. engring div., Bur. Aeros. Recipient ofcl. Navy commendation for initiation and supervision electronic test equipment standardization program, 1945. Registered profl. engr. Sr. mem. I.R.E.; mem. Cornell Soc. Engrs., A.A.A.S., Aircraft Owners and Pilots Assn., Am. Ordnance Assn., Air Force Assn., Tau Beta Pi, Eta Kappa Nu, Delta Upsilon. Clubs: Cosmos, Columbia Country (Washington); Cornell (N.Y.C.); Plantation (South Carolina). Initiated establishment new radio frequency standards lab. at Nat. Bur. Standards, 1944. Writer, speaker of airborne electronics, measurements and guided missiles. Pvt. pilot; golfer (former sect. champion, pres. D.C. Golf Assn. 1959, v.p. Middle Atlantic Golf Assn. 1967—). Home: 10500 Rockville Pike Rockville MD 20852

KELLERMANN, HENRY JOSEPH, govt. ofcl.; b. Berlin, Germany, Jan. 12, 1910; student U. Freiburg, 1928, U. Heidelberg, 1929-30; J.D., U. Berlin, 1937; fellow by courtesy, polit. sci., Johns Hopkins, 1937-38; diploma, N.Y. Sch. Social Work, Columbia, 1941; m. Mignon Lunt Pauli; children—David B., Thomas A., Susan. Columnist, also free lance and editorial writer European newspapers, 1933-37; dir. youth orgn., Berlin, 1934-36; dir. div. for social and cultural adjustment Nat. Refugee Service, N.Y.C., 1938-39; research asst. N.Y. Sch. Social Work, 1940-41; study dir. Welfare Council of N.Y.C., 1941-42; propaganda analyst Fgn. Broadcast Intelligence Service, Washington, 1942-44; research analyst OSS, 1944-45; chief research and cons. Office U.S. Chief for Prosecution of Axis Criminality, Nuremberg, 1945; research analyst office research and intelligence Dept. State, 1945, regional specialist div. occupied areas, 1946, chief German and Austrian area, pub. affairs overseas program staff, 1948, chief div. German and Austrian information and reorientation affairs, 1949, dir. German and Austrian pub. affairs; fgn. service officer, 1956; acting pub. affairs adviser Bur. European Affairs, Dept. State, 1956; spl. asst. to asst. sec. of state for pub. affairs, 1956; U.S. permanent rep. UNESCO, counselor of embassy, Paris, France, 1956-61; UN adviser to asst. sec. state for European affairs, 1961-62; counselor, dep. chief mission Am. embassy, Bern, Switzerland, 1962-65, chargé d'affaires, 1965-66; cons. policy planning council Dept. State, Washington, 1966-68; spl. asst. to dir. internat. scientific and technological affairs, 1968-70; exec. div. com. internat. environmental programs Nat. Acad. Scis., 1970—; cons. Rand Corp., 1953-55. Mem. U.S. Survey Missions to Germany, 1948, 49; U.S. del. 6th Session Council Fgn. Ministers, Paris, 1949; chmn. internat. environmental com. Fed. Council Sci. and Tech.; chmn. U.S. delegation Conservation Conf., Council Europe. Recipient Superior Honor award State Dept. Mem. Am. Polit. Sci. Assn., Assn. N.Y. Sch. Social Work. Author articles in field. Office: 2101 Constitution Av Washington DC 20418

KELLEY, ALBERT JOSEPH, Coll. dean; b. Boston, July 27, 1924; s. Albert Joseph and Josephine (Sullivan) K.; B.S., U.S. Naval Acad., 1945; B.S. in Elec. Engring., Mass. Inst. Tech., 1948, Sc.D. in Aero. Engring., 1956; postgrad. U.S. Naval Postgrad. Sch., 1953-54; m. Virginia Marie Riley, June 7, 1945; children—Mark Shaun, David. Commd. ensign USN, 1945, advanced through grades to comdr.; fire control officer U.S.S. Flint, 1945-46, U.S.S. Rochester, 1946-47; carrier squadron pilot, electronics officer USN Carrier Air Group 2, 1950-51; exptl. test pilot, project dir. U.S. Naval Air Test Center, Patuxent River, Md., 1951-53; asst. head air-to-air missile br. Bur. Aeros., 1956-57, asst. head guided missile guidance br., 1957-58, project dir. Eagle missile system, 1958- 60; program mgr. Agena launch vehicle NASA, 1960-61, dir. electronics and control, 1961-64, mgr. electronics research task group, 1963-64, dep. dir. Electronics Research Center, Cambridge, Mass., 1964-67, cons. 1967-70; dean Boston Coll., Sch. Mgmt., 1967—; mgmt. and investment cons.; cons. U.S. Dept. Transp., 1971—. Dir. Ventron Corp., Baird-Atomic Corp. Chmn. bd. econ. advisers Commonwealth Mass., 1970—. Decorated Air medal; recipient NASA Exceptional Service medal, 1967. Fellow Am. Inst. Aeros. and Astronautics (asso.), I.E.E.E.; mem. Armed Forces Communications and Electronics Assn. (nat. v.p., dir.), Internat. Acad. Astronautics, Sigma Xi, Tau Beta Pi, Eta Kappa Nu, Sigma Gamma Tau, Beta Gamma Sigma. Home: 79 Hinckley Rd Milton MA 02187 Office: Boston Coll Chestnut Hill MA 02167

KELLEY, ALBERT SUMTER, educator, artist; b. Slocomb, Ala., Jan. 12, 1909; s. Albert Clyde and Gertrude (Ausley) K.; Ph.B., Emory U., 1930; M.A., Columbia, 1946; Met. scholar Art Students League N.Y., 1932-35; studied with Nicolaides Miller, Ringling Art Sch., Sarasota, Fla. Dir. Civic Art Inst., Jacksonville, Fla., 1940-41; instr. painting Franklin Sch. Art, N.Y.C., 1946-48; prof., chmn. art dept. Adelphi U., Garden City, N.Y., 1950—; mem. adv. art commn. Nassau County, N.Y., 1963—; nine murals in children's ward Lincoln Hosp., Bronx, N.Y.; rep. collections Emory U., Adelphi U., also pvt. collections; exhbt. London, Paris, Entretat (France), Academie de la Grand Chaumier, Paris, N.Y.C., Fla., group and one man shows. Served with camouflage unit AUS, 1941-45; ETO. Louis Tiffany Found. fellow, 1935. Life mem. Art Students League N.Y.; mem. Coll. Art Assn., Am. Fedn. Art, N.Y. Art Tchrs., Met. Opera Guild, Kappa Alpha, Omicron Delta Kappa. Methodist. Home: 6 Sealy Av Hempstead NY 11550 Office: Art Dept Adelphi U Garden City NY 11530

KELLEY, ALVIN MARSHALL, govt. ofcl.; b. Brilliant, O., June 14, 1915; s. Frank A. and Maude (Reed) K.; student Cleve. Coll., 1945-48, Cin. U., 1948-49; m. Mary Ellen Glenn, Oct. 18, 1937; children—Larry Alvin, Lynda Kaye, Patricia Ellen, Pamela Sue, Deborah Eileen. With Civil Service Commn., Cin., 1939- 52, asst. chief exam. div., 1950-52; with Internal Revenue Service, 1953- -, dir., St. Louis, 1960-62, dir., Boston, 1962-65, regional commnr. Midwest region, Chgo., 1966- 71, asst. commnr. planning and research, 1971—; lectr. on mgmt., 1958—. Dir. projects for Hoover commn., 1948; dir. orgn. field offices OPA, War Assets Adminstrn., World War II. Bd. dirs. govt. div. United Fund campaign, St. Louis, 1962. Recipient Commnrs. award outstanding service Internal Revenue Service, 1964.

Mem. Internat. Platform Assn. Episcopalian (past vestryman, dir. brotherhood; bishop's com. 1967—). Mason (K.T., 32, Shriner). Home: 113 Parkchester Rd Elk Grove Village IL 60007 Office: 35 E Wacker Dr Chicago IL 60601

KELLEY, ANDREW JOSEPH, business exec.; b. Boston, 1919; grad. Boston U., 1941, LL.B., 1950. Treas., controller, dir. United-Carr, Int., Boston. Home: 145 Hinckley Rd Milton MA 02187 Office: Prudential Center Boston MA 02199*

KELLEY, BETHEL BOWLES, lawyer; b. Bardstown, Ky., Dec. 6, 1912; s. John S. and Myrtle (Troutman) K.; A.B., U. Mich., 1934, J.D., 1937; m. Jane Hamilton, Dec. 21, 1940; children—Patricia, Nancy, Mary Beth. Admitted to Ky. bar, 1936, Mich bar, 1937; asso. firm Harold R. Smith, Detroit, 1937-40, Grafton & Grafton, Louisville, 1940-41; mem. firm Cross, Wrock, Miller, Vieson & Kelley, Detroit, 1941-67, Dykema, Wheat, Spencer, Goodnow & Trigg, Detroit, 1967—. Dir. Mich.-Ohio Pipeline Corp., Mt. Pleasant, Mich. Trustee Alma Coll. Served to lt. USNR, 1943-46. Mem. Am., Detroit bar assns., State Bar Mich., Delta Kappa Epsilon. Republican. Clubs: Detroit Athletic, Pere Marquette Rod and Gun, Secord, Detroit Players; Orchard Lake Country. Home: 640 Henley Dr Birmingham MI 48008 Office: Penobscot Bldg Detroit MI 48226

KELLEY, CHARLES MANFORD, architect, educator; b. Eutaw, Ala., May 8, 1919; s. Charles Manford and Laura Aldora (Lett) K.; B.Arch., Auburn U., 1942; M.Arch., Harvard, 1952; m. Sally Dortch Kershaw, Dec. 27, 1957; children—Charles Manford III, John Robert Kenan. With archtl. office Wurster, Bernardi & Emmons, San Francisco, 1946, Sherlock, Smith & Adams, Montgomery, Ala., 1947-50; pvt. practice, Montgomery, 1950-52; asso. Sherlock, Smith & Adams, 1952-55, partner, 1955-56; prof. Auburn U. Sch. Architecture and Arts, 1956-57, head dept., 1957-63; now prof. U. Wash. Coll. Architecture, Seattle. Recipient medal Alpha Rho Chi, 1941, honor awards Progressive Architecture mag., 1954, 55. Mem. A.I.A. (student award 1941, nat. honor award 1951), Omicron Delta Kappa, Lambda Chi Alpha, Scarab (pres. 1961-63). Episcopalian. Home: 3612 E Union St Seattle WA 98122

KELLEY, CLARENCE ALFRED, transp. exec.; b. Corning, N.Y., Apr. 25, 1903; s. Ernest and Barbara (Metz) K.; LL.B., Akron U., 1931; m. Mary Musser, June 9, 1934; children—David, Susan I. Admitted to Ohio bar, 1931; gen. practice law specializing in transp., 1931-38; gen. counsel Dixie Ohio Express, Inc., Akron, O., 1935-55, pres., 1956-70; v.p. Coastal Industries, 1971—. Chmn. Share in Am. campaign Summit County Savs. Bond campaign; pres. YMCA, 1966-67, United Found., 1966-67. Mayor, Silver Lake Village, 1950-54. Bd. dirs. Valparaiso U.; adv. com. Akron U. Mem. Am. Trucking Assns., Inc. (exec. com. 1957—, pres. 1961-62, chmn. bd. 1962-63), Ohio Trucking Assn. (pres. 1955-57). Lutheran. Rotarian (past pres. Cuyahoga Falls). Home: 2982 Silver View Dr Silver Lake Estates Cuyahoga Falls OH 44224 Office: 215 E Waterloo Rd Akron OH 44319

KELLEY, CLARENCE MARION, city ofcl.; b. Kansas City, Mo., Oct. 24, 1911; s. Clarence Bond and Minnie (Brown) K.; A.B., U. Kan., 1936; LL.B., U. Mo., 1940; m. Ruby Dyeantha Pickett, Aug. 28, 1937; children—Mary Ruth (Mrs. Edward Ragland Dobbins, Jr.), Kent Clarence. With FBI, 1940-61, spl. agt. in charge, Memphis, until 1961; chief of police, Kansas City, Mo., 1961—. Bd. dirs. Boys' Club, United Fund, Starlight Theatre Assn. (all Kansas City, Mo.). Served with USNR, 1943-46. Mem. Ex-FBI Agts., Internat. Assn. Chiefs of Police, Mo. Police Chiefs, Tenn.-Miss. Peace Officers, Mo. Peace Pfficers (past pres.), Phi Delta Phi, Sigma Nu. Mem. Christian Ch. (deacon). Home: 1260 W 72d St Kansas City MO 64114 Office: 1125 Locust St Kansas City MO 64106

KELLEY, CLINTON MONROE, retired educator; b. Portland, Ore., July 19, 1913; s. Curtis and Alice (Chick) K.; B.S., Ore. State Coll., 1934; Ph.D., U. Wash., 1941; m. Virginia A. Robinson, May 1, 1948; 1 dau., Joan R. Instr. chemistry Western Wash. Coll. Edn., 1941; instr. Tex. A. and M. Coll., 1941-43, asso. prof., 1949-50; mem. staff Radiation Lab., Mass. Inst. Tech., 1943-46; asso. dir. Naval Research Lab. Field Sta., Boston, 1946; asst. prof. U. Denver, 1946-49; research Chemist Stanford Research inst., 1950-55, chmn. chem. physics dept., 1955-61, dir. chem. physics div., 1961- 62; chmn. chemistry dept. U. Denver, Colo., 1962-71. Mem. A.A.A.S., Am. Phys. Soc., Am. Chem. Soc., Sci. Research Soc. Am., Phi Kappa Phi, Phi Lambda Upsilon. Home: 10590 W 8th Av Lakewood CO 80215

KELLEY, DANIEL FRANCIS, Jr., lawyer; b. San Juan, P.R., Oct. 5, 1919; s. Daniel Francis and Consuelo (Porrata-Doria) K.; grad. Loomis Sch., 1937; A.B., Cornell U., 1941; Indsl. Adminstr., Harvard, 1943; LL.B., Yale, 1947; m. Katherine Joan MacKenzie, May 2, 1953; children—Brenda, Jean, Robin. Admitted to N.Y. bar, 1949, P.R. bar, 1951; asso. firm Sullivan & Cromwell, N.Y.C., 1947- 49, Charles R. Hartzell, San Juan, P.R., 1949-54; sr. partner McConnell, Valdes, Kelley & Sifre, Hato Rey, P.R., 1954—. Served to capt. AUS, 1943-46. Mem. Sigma Chi. Home: 509 Tintillo Rd Bayamon PR 00619 Office: Pan Am Bldg Hato Rey PR 00917

KELLEY, DARIUS MUNRO, banker; b. St. Johnsbury, Vt., Aug. 30, 1912; s. William D. and Jessie H. (Munro) K.; B.S. in Bus. Adminstrn., Boston U., 1937; m. Frances E. West, Dec. 18, 1941. Asst. cashier Nat. Bank Newport (Vt.), 1937-47; asst. examiner FDIC, 1947-48; exec. v.p., cashier, dir. Shelburne Falls Nat. Bank (Mass.), 1948-57; exec. v.p., dir. Orange Nat. Bank (Mass.), 1957-59, pres., trust officer, 1959-69; pres., dir. Franktin County Trust Co., Greenfield, Mass., 1969—. Trustee Franklin County Soc. Prevention Cruelty to Children, Franklin County Pub. Hosp., United Fund Franklin County; trustee, mem endowment and trust com. Athol (Mass.). Home: 1200 Bernardston Rd Greenfield MA 01301 Office: 324 1 Main St Greenfield MA 01301

KELLEY, DAVID OTIS, univ. librarian; b. Newport, Tex., Sept. 27, 1908; s. William Oliver and Beulah (Milburn) K.; A.B., U. So. Cal., 1932, A.M., 1934; postgrad. U. Chgo., summers 1939-43; m. Onetia May Nettles, June 29, 1930; children—Onetia Jean, Robert Otis. Tchr., librarian Burbank (Cal.) Secondary Schs., 1934-37; asso. prof. social sci. George Pepperdine Coll., Los Angeles, 1937-38, librarian, 1938-45; divisional librarian in social studies U. Neb., 1945-48, asst. dir. libraries, 1947-48; head dept. library sci. U. Ky., 1948-49; librarian U. N.M., head div. library sci., Albuquerque, 1949—. Mem. Am., S.W. (pres. 1967-68), N.M. (pres. 1963), library assns., Pi Sigma Alpha, Phi Delta Kappa, Phi Kappa Phi. Mem. Ch. of Christ. Home: 3417 Groman Ct NE Albuquerque NM 78110

KELLEY, DEAN MAURICE, ch. exec.; b. Cheyenne, Wyo., June 1, 1926; s. Mark M. and Irene (Lancester) K.; A.B., Denver U., 1946; Th.M., Iliff Sch. Theology, Denver, 1949; postgrad. Columbia, 1949-50; m. Maryon M. Hoyle, June 9, 1946; 1 dau., Lenore Hoyle. Ordained to ministry Meth. Ch., 1946; pastor in Oak Creek, Colo., 1946-49, East Meadow, N.Y., 1950-52, Westhampton Beach, N.Y., 1952-55, Queens, N.Y., 1955-56, Bronx, N.Y., 1957-60; exec. dir. religious liberty Nat. Council Chs., 1960—. Home: Monsey NY 10952 Office: 475 Riverside Dr New York City NY 10027

KELLEY, DONALD E., judge; b. McCook, Neb., Jan. 29, 1908; s. Charles W. and Elsie (Asten) K.; LL.B., U. Neb., 1930; m. Georgia E. Pyne, June 21, 1930; children—John Michael, Donald Pyne. Gen. practice law, McCook, 1930- 38; asst. atty. gen. Neb., Lincoln, 1939-41; county atty. Red Willow County, Neb., 1942-44; gen. practice law, Denver, 1945-53; U.S. atty. Dist. Colo., 1953-59; city atty. City and County of Denver, 1959-61; state senator Colo., 1963-67; justice Colo. Supreme Ct., Denver, 1967—. Chmn. bd. trustees Colo. div. Am. Cancer Soc. Mem. Am., Fed. (pres. Denver), Colo. (gov.), Neb., Denver bar assns., Nat. Inst. Municipal Law Officers (regional v.p. 1959-61), Am. Law Inst., Am. Judicature Soc. (dir.), Phi Delta Phi, Delta Upsilon. Mason (Shriner), Rotarian. Home: 3144 S Columbine Denver CO 80210 Office: State Capitol Bldg Denver CO 80203

KELLEY, ESTEL WOOD, food products mfr.; b. Sharpsville, Ind., Mar. 24, 1917; s. Floyd and Maude (Wood) K.; B.A., Ind. U., 1939, LL.D., 1971; m. Wilma Lipert, June 17, 1939; children—E. Wood, Wayne L., Karen. Controller, treas., dir., mem. exec. com. R.H. Macy & Co., Kansas City, Mo., 1951-56; asst. to exec. v.p. Gen. Foods Corp., 1956-57, gen. mgr. distbn., sales services div., 1957-59, treas., 1960-61, gen. mgr. Birds Eye div., v.p. corp., 1961-64; exec. v.p., dir. Heublein, Inc., Hartford, Conn., 1964-68; pres. Consumer Products group Gulf and Western Industries, Inc., pres. subsidiary Consol. Cigar Corp., 1968-70; pres. Consol. Brands, Inc., 1970—; chmn. Polly Bagan Co., 1971—; pres. Kelley, Inc., RCE, Inc., Prairie Builders (all Kokomo, Ind.). Bd. dirs. Ind. U. Found. C.P.A., Ind. Mem. Nat. Assn. Accountants (chmn. com. accounting devel. 1959-61, past nat. dir.), Controllers Inst. Am., Mgmt. Assn. Clubs: Avon (Conn.) Country; Metropolitan, Marco Polo (N.Y.C.); Kokomo County; Lake Region Yacht and Country (Fla.). Home: 101 Central Park W New York City NY 10023 Office: 1 Gulf and Western Plaza New York City NY

KELLEY, FRANCIS PATRICK, hosp. adminstr., educator; b. Lynn, Mass., Apr. 7, 1925; s. Arthur L. and Beatrice (Noone) K.; B.S., Bridgeport (Conn.) U., 1949; M.A., Columbia, 1954, also doctoral work; m. Mildred Bourne, Apr. 7, 1945; children—Linda, Claudia, Sarah, Vincent, Mark, Garth. Tchr., supr. recreation Southbury (Conn.) Tng. Sch., 1949-54; asst. supt. Ladd Sch., N. Kingston, R.I., 1955-63; supt. Mansfield (Conn.) State Tng. Sch., 1963—. Mem. President's Council on Mental Retardation; mem. adminstrv. council mental retardation Conn. Dept. of Health; cons. on mental retardation, also residential care and recreation; cons. Nat. Assn. Retarded Children, Joseph P. Kennedy Jr. Found., Nat. Inst. Mental Health. Served with USMCR, 1943-46; PTO, China. Recipient Rosemary F. Dybwad Internat. award. Mem. Am. Assn. Mental Deficiency (councilor), Nat. Assn. Retarded Children (chmn. recreation com. 1962-63), Nat. Recreation Soc. Rotarian. Clubs: Eastern Conn. Sportsmen, U. Conn. Faculty (Storrs, Conn.). Author articles in field. Address: Box 51 Mansfield Depot CT 06251

KELLEY, FRANK JOSEPH, state govt. ofcl.; b. Detroit, Dec. 31, 1924; s. Frank Edward and Grace Margaret (Spears) K.; pre-law certificate U. Detroit, 1948, LL.B., 1951; m. Josephine Palmisano, June 30, 1945; children—Karen Karen Ann, Frank Edward, Jane Francis. Admitted to Mich. bar, 1952; gen. practice law, Detroit, 1952-54, Alpena, 1954-61; atty. gen. Mich., Lansing, 1962—. Instr. econs. Alpena Community Coll., 1955-56; instr. pub. adminstrn. Alpena County, 1956; atty. city real estate law U. Mich. Extension, 1957-61. Mem. Alpena County Bd. Suprs., 1958-61; pres. Alpena Community Services Council, 1956. Founding dir., 1st sec. Alpena United Fund, 1955; founding dir., 1st pres. Northeastern Mich. Child Guidance Clinic, 1958; pres., bd. dirs. Northeastern Mich. Cath. Family Service, 1959. Mem. Am., 26th Jud. Circuit (pres. 1956) bar assns., State Bar Mich., Internat. Movement Atlantic Union, Alpha Kappa Psi. K.C. (4, past legal adv.). Home: 4267 Mar-Moor Dr Lansing MI 48917 Office: Capitol Bldg Lansing MI 48933

KELLEY, GEORGE WALTER, educator; b. Winfield, Kan., Dec. 5, 1921; s. George Walter and Lela (Bonewell) K.; B.S., U. Neb. 1947; M.S., U. Ky., 1950; Ph.D., U. Neb., 1953; m. Ava Bargar, Dec. 25, 1942; children—James Alan, Kathy Ann, Jeanne Margaret. Asst. parasitologist U. Ky., 1948-50; parasitologist Neb. Health Dept., 1950-53; asso. prof. U. Neb., Lincoln, 1953-64; marketing specialist Eli Lilly Internat. Corp., Indpls., 1964-67; chmn. dept. biology, prof. Youngstown (O.) State U., 1967—; spl. coop. agt. Dept. Agr., 1954-57; tech. cons. pharm. firms. Mem. com. environmental health planning Mahoning Valley Health Planning Assn., Youngstown, 1970—; chmn. com. higher edn. for crossroads Resource Conservation and Devel., Youngstown, 1970—. Trustee William Holmes McGuffy Hist. Soc. Served with AUS, 1942-45: ETO. Decorated Bronze Star, Purple Heart. Mem. Am. Soc. Parasitologists, Am. Inst. Biol. Scis., A.A.A.S., Sigma Xi. Contbr. profl. jours. Home: 4141 Windsor Rd Youngstown OH 44512

KELLEY, H. ROY, architect; b. Mattewan (now Beacon), N.Y., May 2, 1893; s. Seth and Anna (Carey) K.; student Cornell (Sands Meml. medal 1915), 1912-15, Paris Ateliers, 1919; m. Thyra Hoyer, Dec. 17, 1941. With architects in N.Y., Chgo. and Indpsl., 1915-26; ind. practice, Los Angeles, 1926-58; cons. camouflage, other passive def. design features Douglas Aircraft Co., 1942-43; cons. architect for West, Good Housekeeping mag., 1929-39; architect Rand Corp., Santa Monica, 1950-56. Profl. adviser Ft. Moore Meml., Los Angeles, 1952-53; mem. adv. commn. Claremont Colls., 1957-67; mem. Los Angeles Welfare Planning Council, 1963-70. Bd. dirs. John Tracy Clinic, Los Angeles. Served as 1st lt., inf., U.S. Army, World War I, AEF in France. Recipient medals Beaux Arts Soc., 1914-15, 1st prize Own Your Own Home, Nat. Contest, 1927, 1st prize House Beautiful Nat. Contest, 1928, 34, 35, hon. mention, 1929, 30, 31, 1st prize Nat. Better Homes award by Home Owners Inst., 1929, 1st prize Better Homes Contest Los Angeles Times, 1929, medal Better Homes in Am., 1930, 9 honor awards A.I.A., 1927-50; Distinguished Architecture award Archtl. League N.Y., 1938. Fellow A.I.A. (past bd. dirs.); mem. Los Angeles C. of C. (constrn. industries com. 1937-55), Los Angeles Archtl. Club (past pres.), Gargoyle Soc., Cal. Assn. Architects (regional bd. dirs. 1929-30), Am. Legion, Town Hall, Mason. Clubs: University, Chapparal, Curfew, Men's Garden, Cornell of So. Cal. (Los Angeles); San Gabriel (Cal.) Country. Architect: Hdqrs. Bldgs Rand Corp., Santa Monica, Cal., 1950-56, Inst. Aero. Scis., Los Angeles, 1946, Nurses Home and Auditorium Hollywood Hosp., 1954, 25th Ch. Christ Scientist, Los Angeles, 1935. Contbr. popular, tech. mags. Home: 1320 Oak Grove Av San Marino CA 91108

KELLEY, SISTER HELEN, coll. pres.; b. Cedar Rapids, Ia., May 21, 1925;. d. William John and Frances Jane (Heenan) Kelley; B.A., Immaculate Heart Coll., Los Angeles, 1949; M.A., St. Louis U., 1954, Ph.D., 1958. Tchr. grammar sch., Visalia, Cal., 1947-48; tchr. history Immaculate Heart High Sch., Los Angeles, 1948-55; tchr. sociology Immaculate Heart Coll., 1958-63, pres., 1963—, also mem. bd. regents. Fellow Radcliffe Inst., 1963. Mem. Am. Sociol. Assn., Soc. Sci Study Religion, Assn. Higher Edn., Nat. Cath. Ednl. Assn. Democrat. Roman Catholic. Contbr. articles to profl. jours. Home: 5515 Franklin Av Los Angeles CA 90028

KELLEY, JAMES E., lawyer; b. Pinnconning, Mich., Dec. 3, 1895; s. Joseph Samuel and Electa Alvina (Segur) K.; LL.B., St. Paul Coll. Law, 1917; m. Margaret Louise Hamm, Sept. 19, 1923; 1 dau., Cynthia Hampton (Mrs. James C. O'Neill). Admitted to Minn. bar, 1917, ince practiced in St. Paul; mem. firm Kelley & O'Neill. Pres. Kelley Land Cattle Co. Vice pres. St. Paul Bur. Municipal Research. Bd. dirs. Hamm Found., Inc.; bd. dirs., treas. Margaret H. and James E. Kelley Found.; trustee, v.p. William Mitchell Coll. Law; trustee Northland Coll., Ashland, Wis., St. Luke's Hosp., St. Paul. Served in Chem. Warfare Service, U.S. Army, 1918-19. Mem. Am., Minn., St. Paul, Ramsey County bar assns., Mason (Shriner). Club: Minnesota (St. Paul). Home: 2901 E Old Shakopee Rd Bloomington MN 55420 Office: Hamm Bldg St Paul MN 55102

KELLEY, JOHN D., oil co. exec.; b. 1910; LL.B., Houston Law Sch. Admitted to Tex. bar, 1937; with Continental Oil Co., 1951—, sec., 1968—. Address: 30 Rockefeller Plaza New York City NY 10020*

KELLEY, JOHN DENNIS librarian; b. Nov. 3, 1900; s. John H. and Nora J. (Mullen) K.; A.B., Boston Coll., 1922; M.B.A., N.Y.U., 1927; m. Mary Agnes Barry, June 29, 1940; children—John H., Thomas B., Dennis J., David B. Shoe buyer Nat. Cloak & Suit Co., N.Y.C., 1922-27; mdse. mgr. Gilchrist Co., Boston, 1928-31; office mgr. Carew & McGreenery, investments, 1932-37; librarian, dir. Somerville (Mass.) Pub. Library. Pres., dir. Central Coop. Bank; corporator Somerset Savs. Bank. Commr. Div. Pub. Libraries Mass., 1950—. Trustee Somerville Hosp. Mem. Am., Mass. (past pres.) library assns. Rotarian. Club: Boston Review. Home: 178 Central St Somerville MA 02145 Office: Highlands Av and Walnut St Somerville MA 02143

KELLEY, JOHN F., mfg. exec.; b. Rockford, Ill., Feb. 21, 1917; s. John F. and Mary V. (Carey) K.; B.S., B.A., Northwestern U., 1943; m. Mary Jean Fairbairn, Nov. 27, 1948; children—Maureen L., John, Paul, Nancy, James, Brian. With Continental Ill. Nat. Bank & Trust Co., Chgo., 1937-46; asst. credit mgr. Am. Smelting & Refining Co., Whiting, Ind., 1946-52; with Pullman-Standard Car Mfg. Co., Pullman-Standard Car Export Corp., Chgo., 1952-59, treas., 1953-59; with Pullman, Inc., 1952—, treas., 1955—; treas. Pullman Transp. Leasing Co., Transp. Leasing Co., 1959—. Home: 425 Pinecrest Lane Wilmette IL 60091 Office: 200 S Michigan Av Chicago IL 60604

KELLEY, JOHN LEROY, educator; b. Kan., Dec. 6, 1916; s. Charles G. and Estella France (Hogan) K.; B.A., U. Cal. at Los Angeles, 1936, M.A., 1937; Ph.D., U. Va., 1940; m. Nancy Elizabeth Bruce, June 9, 1938 (div. 1960); children—John Leroy, Bruce, Paul; m. 2d, Betty Ying Lee, June 15, 1963; children—Max, Sara. Mathematician, Aberdeen Proving Grounds, 1942-45; mem. faculty U. Notre Dame, 1940-42, U. Chgo., 1945-47, Tulane U., 1950-52, U. Kan., 1952-53; mem. faculty U. Cal. at Berkeley, 1947—, prof. math., 1953—, chmn. dept., 1957-60; tchr. Indian Inst. Tech., Kanpur, India, 1964; lectr. Continental Classroom, NBC, 1960. Fellow Inst. Advanced Study, Princeton, 1945-46; NSF postdoctoral fellow, 1953-54; Fulbright research prof. Cambridge (Eng.) U., 1957-58. Mem. Am. Math. Soc., Math. Assn. Am. Author: (with MacShane, Reno) Exterior Ballistics, 1950, General Topology, 1955; Introduction to Modern Algebra, 1960; (with Isaac Namioka, others) Linear Topological Spaces, 1963; (with Dan Richert) Elementary Mathematics for Teachers; also articles. Address: U Cal Berkeley CA 94720

KELLEY, JOHN WILLIAM, gas co. exec.; b. Sugar Grove, O., Dec. 4, 1910; s. William Spence and Zella Gay (Cumpston) K.; student Marshall Coll., 1928-29, Carnegie Inst. Tech., 1927; m. Louise Virginia Wade, May 22, 1916; children-Mary Louise (Mrs. George Robert Moore), Ellen Wade (Mrs. Kemble Widmer, II). Supr., Va. Gas Transmission Co., Lexington, 1930-43; supt. transmission United Fuel Gas Co., Huntington, W. Va., 1943-47; v.p. Atlantic Seaboard Corp., Falls Church, Va., 1952-59; pres. Columbia Gulf Transmission Co., Columbia Gas Devel. Corp., Houston, 1959—; dir. Columbia Gas System Service Corp., Wilmington, Del., 1959—. Mem. Falls Church Sch. Bd., 1957-59; area chmn. Washington Campfire Girls, 1957-59. Mem. So., Am. gas assns., Independent Natural Gas Assn., Houston C. of C. Presbyn. Clubs: Lakeside Country Houston, Petroleum, University Internat. (Houston). Home: 17 Creekside Circle Houston TX 77024 Office: 3805 W Alabama St 1Houston TX 77027

KELLEY, NOBLE HENRY, former psychologist, educator; b. Thamesville, Ont., Can., Aug. 10, 1901; s. Isaac Wesley and Louisa (Ross) K.; A.A., Graceland Coll., 1931; A.B., State U. Ia., 1933, A.M., 1935, Ph.D., 1936; m. Ethel B. Patterson, July 9, 1927; 1 son, Alan Douglas. Eastman research fellow dept. psychology U. Ia., 1936-37; 1st asst. prof. dept. psychology U. Louisville, 1937-43, asso. prof., 1943-46, prof., head dept. psychology, 1946-51, clin. psychologist, dir. psychol. services center, 1946-51; prof., chmn. dept. psychology, dir. psychol. services So. Ill. U., Carbondale, 1951-60, research prof. psychology, 1960-69. Adv. bd. Inst. for Juvenile Research, 1957-59; mem. Ill. Psychiat. Tng. and Research Authority, 1957-65. Certified clin. psychologist, Ky., Ill. Bd. Examiners; diplomate in clin. psychology, sec.-treas. Am. Bd. Profl. Psychology, 1951-61, exec. officer, 1961- 70; chmn. adv. com. supt. pub. instrn. Ill., 1954-61. Fellow clinic and cons. divs. Am. Psychology Assn. (mem. council reps.); pres. Conf. State Psychol. Assn., 1949-51. Mem. bd. Council Analysis Orgnl. Structure. Mem. Assn. Midwestern Coll. Psychiatrists and Clin. Psychologists (pres. 1948-49), Am. (edn. and tng. bd. 1956-59, council of reps., pres. div. cons., psychology 1966-67), Midwestern, Ill. (pres. 1957, bd. examiners 1959-63), psychol. assns., Am. Assn. U. Profs., Sigma Xi, Alpha Epsilon Delta, Lambda Chi Alpha. Democrat. Unitarian. Lion. Author: Work book for General Psychology, 1940; A Manual for General Psychology, 1942. Home: Point Brittany 5108 Brittany Dr S St Petersburg FL 33715

KELLEY, NORMAN DURASK, tenor, actor; b. Eddington, Me., Aug. 27, 1917; s. John W. and Janet E. (Shiels) K.; student Leland Powers Sch. of Theatre, Pasadena Jr. Coll., Eastman Sch. Music; m. Maria L. Paradiso, June 26, 1943; children—John M., Paul R. Debut, Phila. La Scala, 1947; also appeared with Opera Nacional de Bellas Artes, Mexico City, 1948, Central City Opera Co., Colo., 1949, San Carlo Opera Co., N.Y.C., 1948—; appeared in The Consul, N.Y.C., 1950, London, Paris, 1951, N.Y.C. premiere Troilus and Cressida, 1955, world premiere The Good Soldier Schweik, N.Y.C. Opera Co., 1958; U.S. premiere Voyage to the Moon, 1958, Maria Golovin, 1958, Der Corregidor, 1958, Der Apotheker, 1959; appeared as Koko in Mikado, Duke of Plaza Toro in The Gondoliers, mem. Met. Opera Co., 1956-, also N.Y.C. Center Gilbert & Sullivan Opera Co., N.Y.C. Opera Co. Served as capt. AUS, 1940-46. Mem Actors Equity, Am. Fedn. Radio Actors, Am. Guild Musical Artists. Home: 5611 Highgate Dr Baltimore MD 21215

KELLEY, RALPH HOUSTON, lawyer; b. Chattanooga, Sept. 23, 1928; s. Glenn Blair and Louise (Hobson) K.; student U. Md., 1948-49; B.A., U. Chattanooga, 1951; LL.B., Vanderbilt U., 1954; m. Barbara Ann Fahl, June 24, 1960; children—Laura Lee, Ellen Kay, Karen Lynn. Page boy U.S. Ho. of Reps., 1941-46; admitted to Tenn. bar, 1954; partner firm Kelley, Dirisio & Shattuck, Chattanooga, 1954-69; mayor City of Chattanooga, 1963-69; referee in bankruptcy U.S. Dist. Ct. for Eastern Dist. Tenn., 1969—; mem. faculty English and speech dept. U. Chattanooga Eve. Coll., 1954-58. Pres. Hamilton County Young Democratic Club, 1956-60; mem. Tenn. Ho. of Reps. 1959-61. Served with USAAF, 1946-49. Mem. Am., Tenn., Chattanooga bar assns., Am. Judicature Soc., Jr. C. of C., Chattanooga C. of C., Delta Theta Phi, Lambda Chi Alpha. Democrat. Methodist. Clubs: Boating (dir., past commodore), Exchange, Mountain City (Chattanooga). Home: 18 Sweetbriar Av Chattanooga TN 37411 Office: Federal Bldg Chattanooga TN 37402

KELLEY, RAYMOND F., corp. exec.; b. 1899. With Am. Brake Shoe Co., 1925-52, asst. to pres., 1945-52; v.p. Dynamics Corp. Am., 1952-58, pres., chief exec. officer, chmn. bd., 1958-70, chmn. bd., 1970—. Dir. Internat. Elec. Research Corp. Office: 501 Fifth Av New York City NY 10017

KELLEY, RICHARD AUGUSTUS, coll. dean; b. Boston, July 9, 1916; s. Everett Augustus and Jessie Priscilla (Dixon) K.; B.S., Tufts Coll., 1937, Ed.M., 1938; m. Mary Elizabeth Donning, Aug. 26, 1940; children—Warren Donning, Donna Dixon, Tchr., coach asst. prin. Northboro (Mass.) High Sch., 1938-41; asst. to v.p. Tufts Coll., Medford, Mass., 1941-51, instr. edn., 1941-47, asst. prof. edn., 1947-53, asso. prof., 1953—, dir. student activities, 1941-52, asst. dean div. spl. studies, 1951-52, dean Coll. Spl. Studies, 1952—, acting research coordinator, 1956-58, asso. coordinator, 1958-67, cons. univ. com. tchr. edn., 1962-63, chmn. joint council coordination and devel. tchr. edn., 1963-64, dir. Tufts U. Overseas Programs, Italy, 1963-68, Paris, 1965—, Germany, 1965—, Eng., 1967—, Mexico, 1970—; coordinator edn., regional research and tng. center in rehab. Tufts New Eng. Med. Center, 1964-67. Dir. Winter Hill Fed. Savs. & Loan Assn. Cons. Lincoln Filene Center Citizenship and Pub. Affairs 1959-63; chmn. colls. sect. Greater Boston United Red Feather campaign, 1952; mem. Mass. Citizens Com. for Ednl. Television, 1953; New Eng. rep. nat. adv. com. on spl. edn. United Cerebral Palsy Assn., 1963-67; mem. U.S. adv. bd. Venice Island Studies, U. Venice (Italy), 1969—; mem. rehab. council United Community Services of Greater Boston. mem., affiliate bd. dirs. Nat. Council Alcoholism, N.Y.; trustee Somerville (Mass.) Hosp.; mem. corp., trustee Curry Coll., Milton, Mass., vice chmn. bd. trustees, 1968—, chmn. com. acad. affairs, 1968—. Served as communications officer USNR, 1945-46, PTO. Mem. Mass. Schoolmasters Club, Somerville C. of C. (dir.), Tufts U. Tchrs. Assn., Nat. Council U. Research Adminstrs., Delta Tau Delta. Unitarian. Home: 15 Talbot Av Medford MA 02155

KELLEY, RICHARD EASTLAND, banker; b. Cleve., Jan. 26, 1922; s. Henry Eastland and Ethel (Gibbs) K.; B.A. cum laude, Amherst Coll., 1944; M.B.A., Harvard, 1948; m. Dorothy Louise Desmond, Dec. 9, 1944. Treas., dir. Plastic & Rubber Products Co., and subsidiaries, Los Angeles, 1951-58; pvt. practice as mgmt. cons., Los Angeles, 1958-61; pres., dir. Keyfax Publs., Inc., Los Angeles, 1961-64; v.p., dir. Directors Financial Corp., Los Angeles, 1962-64; nat. adminstr. small bus. investment companies, dep. adminstr. Small Bus. Adminstrn., 1964-66; v.p. First Nat. Bank Chgo., 1966-70; speaker, cons. in field. Pres. MacNeel Pierce Found., Los Angeles, 1953- 58. Served to lt. USNR, 1944-46. Recipient Superior Service award Small Bus. Adminstrn., 1965. Mem. Cal. State Soc., Psi Upsilon. Republican. Clubs: Harvard (N.Y.C. and Washington); Harvard Business School (Washington). Author: The SBIC's in Action, 3d edit., 1963. Home: 1310 Ritchie Ct Chicago IL 60610 Office: 38 S Dearborn St Chicago IL 60690

KELLEY, ROBB BEARDSLEY, ins. co. exec.; b. Des Moines, Jan. 21, 1917; s. Lawrence Elam and Susan (Gunn) K.; B.A., Dartmouth, 1938; m. Winifred Gray Murray, June 21, 1951; children—Bruce Gunn, Carolyn Robb, Sarah Gordon. With Employers Mut. Casualty Co., 1939—, pres., treas., 1963—; pres., treas. ENCASCO Ins. Co., Employers Modern Life Co.; chmn. bd., treas. Union Mut. Ins. Co., Providence, 1968—; dir. Bankers Trust Co., Des Moines. Gen. chmn. Des Moines YWCA New Bldg. Program, 1967—, Greater Des Moines United Campaign, 1962. Trustee, asst. sec., treas. Drake U., trustee, sec. Ia. Methodist Hosp., trustee Hawley Found. Recipient Distinguished Community Service award Des Moines Tribune, 1970. Served with AUS, 1942-44. Recipient Brotherhood award Nat. Conf. Christians and Jews, 1967. Mem. Nat. Soc. Chartered Property and Casualty Underwriters (pres. 1970), Am.'Inst. Property and Liability Underwriters (trustee), Ins. Inst. Am. (trustee). Home: 4321 Greenwood Dr Des Moines IA 50312 Office: 210 7th St Des Moines IA 50309

KELLEY, ROBERT E., electric co. exec.; b. 1916; B.A., Harvard, 1938; LL.B., Boston Coll., 1942; m. With Sprague Electric Co., 1945—, sec., clk., 1962-64, sr. v.p., sec., 1964—, also dir. Address: 87 Marshall St North Adams MA 02147

KELLEY, ROGER TIMOTHY, govt. ofcl.; b. Milw., Jan. 14, 1919; s. John P. and Eleanor C. (Purcell) K.; B.S. in Econs., Holy Cross Coll., 1941; student Grad. Sch. Bus. Adminstrn., Harvard, 1941-42; m. Mary Gertrude Keogh, Oct. 18, 1947; children—Timothy David, Roger John, Peter Aherne, Stephen Michael, Paul Edward, Mary Ellen. With Caterpillar Tractor Co., and subsidiaries, 1946-69, dir. edn. and tng., 1962-64, v.p., 1964-69; asst. sec. def. manpower and res. affairs, Washington, 1969—. Served to lt. USNR, 1942-46. Club: Country of Peoria (Ill.). Home: 7008 Heatherhill Rd Bethesda MD 20034 Office: Pentagon Washington DC 20301

KELLEY, ROY SKILES, army officer; b. Plano, Ky., Oct. 23, 1915; s. H. Lee and Sallie (Potter) K.; B.S. in physics, Western Ky. U., 1935; B.S., U.S. Mil. Acad., 1941; M.S. in Civil Engring., Cal. Inst. Tech., 1948; grad. Army War Coll., 1958; m. Catherine Lahey, Dec. 10, 1945; children—Linda, Regina, Roy Skiles, Frederick. Commd. 2d lt. U.S. Army, 1941, advanced through grades to brig. gen., 1967; various mil. command and staff assignments, U.S. and Europe, 1941-48; asso. prof. engring. U.S. Mil. Acad., 1948-52; engr. staff officer U.S. Army Forces Far East, Tokyo, 1953-55; dep. dist. engr. U.S. Army Engr. Dist., Pitts., 1955-57; dir. personnel Corps. Engrs., 1958-62; engr. 7th Army, Stuttgart, Germany, 1965-67, U.S. Army Europe, Heidelberg, Germany, 1967-69; div. engr. U.S. Army Engr. Div., N. Pacific, 1969—. Mem. Permanent Internat. Assn. Navigation Congresses; mem. U.S. Entity for Columbia River Treaty with Canada; mem. Pacific N.W. River Basin Commn.; mem. policy com., chmn. community service and pub. affairs com. Portland Fed. Exec. Bd.; past chmn. coordinating com. Nat. Capital Planning Commn. Decorated D.S.M., Bronze Star (2), Legion of Merit, Army Commendation medal. Fellow Am. Soc. C.E.: mem. Soc. Am. Mil. Engrs., Am. Pub. Works Assn. Registered profl. civil engr., D.C. Home: 18665 NW Tolovana St Portland OR 97229 Office: Custom House Portland OR 97209

KELLEY, ROYDEN KRUEGER, food co. exec.; b. Elkhart, Ind., June 8, 1911; s. Chester R. and Carrie B. (Krueger) K.; student Wabash Coll., 1933; grad. Advanced Mgmt. Program, Harvard, 1953; m. Grace K. Baumhart, June 12, 1937; 1 son, Charles Keith. Chmn. Nabisco Foods, Ltd., Eng., 1954-56, exec. v.p. Dromedary Co. div. Nat. Biscuit Co., 1956-57, pres., 1957-58, v.p. parent co., 1958—; chmn. Nabisco-Astra Nutrition Products, Inc., 1970—. Mem. nat. para-profl. personnel com. Boy Scouts Am.; nat. adv. com. White House Conf. on Children, 1970. Bd. dirs., exec. com., finance com. Jr. Achievement. Served with AUS, 1943-46, PTO. Mem. Beta Theta Pi. Home: North Broadway White Plains NY 10603 Office: 425 Park Av New York City NY 10022

KELLEY, STANLEY, Jr., educator; b. Detroit, Kan., Dec. 7, 1926; s. Stanley and Stella Elma (Marts) K.; A.B., U. Kan., 1949, M.A., 1951; postgrad. U. Rome (Italy), 1953-54; Ph.D., Johns Hopkins, 1955. Research asst. Brookings Instn., 1956- 57; faculty Princeton, 1957—, prof. politics, chmn. dept., 1964- 66. Served with AUS, 1945-47. Mem. Am. Polit. Sci. Assn., Phi Beta Kappa. Author: Professional Public Relations and Political Power, 1956; Political Campaigning, 1960. Contbr. to books, articles to profl. jours. Home: 120 Prospect Av Princeton NJ 08540

KELLEY, THOMAS BASIL, ins. co. exec.; b. Syracuse, N.Y., Aug. 4, 1917; s. John Otis and Martha Grace (Blake) K.; B.S., Hamilton Coll., 1938; m. Mary McPheeters Kincheloe, Aug. 14, 1943; children—Thomas Basil 3d, Martha Maywood. With Comml. Union Ins. Group, N.Y.C., 1938-68, dep. U.S. mgr., 1958-60, U.S. mgr., 1960-68; pres., dir. Comml. Union Ins. Co. of N.Y., 1962-68, Pa. Ins. Co., 1962-68; sr v.p. Crum & Forster, 1969—; sr. v.p., dir. U.S. Fire Ins. Co., N. River Ins. Co., Westchester Fires Ins. Co., Internat. Ins. Co.; v.p., dir. Am. Eagle Life Ins. Co.; dir. Constn. Reins Co., Internat. Excess & Surplus Lines Ins. Co. Trustee Hamilton Coll. Served to maj. USAAF, World War II. Mem. Ins. Soc. N.Y., Alpha Delta Phi. Clubs: Union League (N.Y.C.); Ekwanok Country (Manchester, Vt.); Baltusrol Golf (Springfield, N.J.). Home: 110 W Hanover Av Morristown NJ 07960 Office: Madison Av at Canfield Rd PO Box 2387 Morristown NJ 07960

KELLEY, VERNE FRANCIS, Jr., public relations exec.; b. Oak Park, Ill., July 29, 1928; s. Verne F. and Irene (Plamondon) K.; B.A., U. Notre Dame, 1950; m. Lois Phillips, Nov. 25, 1954. Sales, mdsg. exec. Proctor & Gamble, 1951-52; pub. relations exec. United Air Lines, 1952-53; TV writer and producer, account exec. Ruthrauff & Ryan, Inc., 1953-57; v.p. advt. and pub. relations Greyhound Corp., Chgo., 1957-66; v.p. creative services, dir. AM-AD, Inc., Chgo., 1966-68; pres. Daniel J. Edelman, Inc., Chgo., 1969-70, sr. v.p., 1970—; owner Kelley Co., 1966—. Mem. Pub. Relations Soc. Am., Western Advt. Golfers Assn., Assn. Nat. Advertisers. Clubs: Publicity, Notre Dame, Advertising, Ill. Athletic (Chgo.); Broadcast Advertising; Midwest Travel Writers; Barclay, Ltd.; Whitehall. Home: 78 W Schiller St Chicago IL 60610 Office: 221 N LaSalle St Chicago IL 60601

KELLEY, VINCENT COOPER, former educator; b. Seattle, July 6, 1904; s. Seth Foster and Sara Eleanor (Cooper) K.; B.A., U. Cal. at Los Angeles, 1931; M.S., Cal. Inst. Tech., 1932, Ph.D., 1937; m. Carol Harwood, May 27, 1929 (div. 1944); 1 son, David F.; m. 2d, Anne Robertson, Aug. 15, 1946; children—John R., Robert B., Paul C. Mem. faculty U. N.M., Albuquerque, 1937-70, prof. geology, 1938-70, chmn. dept., 1960-70, prof. emeritus, 1970—; with U.S. Geol. Survey, 1938—; cons. AEC, 1953-57; cons., panelist NSF, 1964-65. Fellow Geol. Soc. Am. (councilor 1960-62, chmn. Rocky Mountain sect. 1962-63); mem. N.M. Geol. Soc. (hon.), Albuquerque Gem and Mineral. Soc. (hon.), N.M. Mining Assn. (dir., past v.p.), Soc. Econ. Geologists (councilor 1960-62), Am. Inst. Mining and Metall. Engrs., A.A.A.S., S.A.R., Sigma Xi. Rotarian. Home: 606 Vassar Dr NE Albuquerque NM 87106

KELLEY, WENDELL J., utilities exec.; b. Champaign, Ill., May 2, 1926; s. Victor W. and Erma (Dalrymple) K.; B.S., U. Ill., 1949; m. Evelyn Kimpel, June 12, 1947; children—Jeffrey, David, Alan, Stephen, John. With Ill. Power Co., Decatur, 1949—, mgr. personnel, 1959-61, v.p., 1961-66, pres., 1966—, also dir.; dir. Millikin Nat. Bank, Decatur, Electric Energy, Inc. Mem. exec. com., former chmn. Mid-Am. Interpool Network. Mem. Ill. Council on Econ., Edn.; mem. citizens com. U. Ill.; mem. U. Ill. Found. Mem. adv. bd. St. Mary's Hosp., Decatur. Served with USAAF, 1944-45. Registered profl. engr., Ill. Mem. I.E.E.E. (chmn. centre Ill. sect.), Elec. Engring. Alumni Assn. U. Ill. (past pres.), Ill. C. of C. (dir.), U. Ill. Alumni Assn. (dir.), Am. Soc. Profl. Engrs., Nat. Assn. Electric Cos. (dir.), Eta Kappa Nu. Mem. Ch. of Christ (elder). Home: 65 Dellwood Dr Decatur IL 62521 Office: 500 S 27th St Decatur IL 62525

KELLEY, WILBUR EDRALD, cons. nuclear engr.; b. Birmingham, Ala., Dec. 2, 1908; s. Wilbur Edrald and Madeleine (Whitfield) K.; B.S., U. Louisville, 1931, C.E., 1940, D.Engring. (hon.), 1950; m. Elizabeth Lindley Wells, June 18, 1932; children—Wilbur E. and William L. (twins), Elizabeth Anne. Engaged in navigation and flood control structure design and constrn. U.S. Engrs., Rock Island, Ill. and Galveston, Tex., 1931-40, bombproof structure design and constrn., Panama Canal, 1940-42, design and constrn. Atomic Bomb project, 1942-46; U.S. rep. tech. staff. UN AEC, 1946-47; mgr. N.Y. operations office AEC, 1946- 53; v.p. charge of engring. Catalytic Constrn. Co., Phila., 1953- 56; pres. Asso. Nucleonics (formerly Walter Kidde Nuclear Labs., Inc.), Garden City, N.Y., 1956—, Asso. Engrs. & Consultants, Inc., Garden City; v.p., mgr. Stone & Webster Engring. Corp., Garden City, 1966-70. Served to lt. col. C.E., AUS, 1943-46. Decorated Legion of Merit. Mem. Theta Tau. Home: 35 Rhodes St New Hyde Park NY 11040

KELLEY, WILLIAM, author; b. S.I., N.Y., May 27, 1929; B.A., Brown U., 1955; M.A., Harvard, 1957; m. Cornelia Ann; 1 dau., Maura. Author: Gemini, 1959; The God Hunters. Home: PO Box 565 Coronado CA 92118*

KELLEY, WILLIAM ANDREW GRESHAM, lawyer; b. Buffalo, Feb. 4. 1911; s. Harry Joseph and Helen (O'Malley) K.; B.A. cum laude, St. Francis Xavier U., 1930; LL.B., Dalhousie U. (Can.), 1935; postgrad. Harvard, 1935-36; m. Isavel MacKay Ross, Aug. 24, 1937; 1 dau., Mary Jane. Admitted to N.S. bar, 1936, Ont. bar, 1937; now partner firm Borden, Elliot, Kelley & Palmer, Toronto. Mem. Canadian Bar Assn., Phi Delta Phi. Roman Catholic. Clubs: Rosedale Golf; York; Nat.; Briars Golf and Contry; Toronto Hunt; Granite; Echo Beach Fishing. Home: 80 Chestnut Park Rd Toronto 5 Ontario Canada Office: 250 University Av Toronto 110 Ontario Canada*

KELLEY, WILLIAM FREDERICK, ednl. adminstr.; b. Madison, Wis., Feb. ll, 1914; s. William and Elizabeth Anne (Harrington) K.; A.B., St. Louis U., 1936, Ph.L., 1938, M.A., 1939, S.T.L., 1945; Ph.D., U. Minn., 1950. Joined Soc. of Jesus, 1931; ordained priest Roman Catholic Ch., 1944; instr. English, speech St. Louis U. High Sch., 1938-41; asst. to pres. Creighton U., Omaha, 1950- 51, dean coll. arts and scis., 1951-58, acad. v.p., 1958-62, asst. to pres., 1967—; pres. Marquette U., 1962-65; dir. Study Am. Jesuit Higher Edn., Washington, 1965-67. Mem. Father Marquette Tercentenary Commn.; mem. commn. on colls. and univs. N. Central Assn., commn. on tchr. edn. Assn. Am. Colls.; vice chmn. State Commn. for Acad. Facilities, 1964; mem. Wis. Indsl. Research Council; sponsor Atlantic Council U.S.; vice chmn. Assn. Urban Univs., 1964. Bd. dirs. Coll. Entrance Exam. Bd. Mem. N.E.A., Jesuit Ednl. Assn., Nat. Cath. Edn. Assn. (chmn. Midwest sect. 1961, nat. exec. com. higher edn. sect.), Nat. Jesuit Deans' Inst., Am. Council on Edn., Am. Conf. Acad. Deans (exec. com. 1956), Phi Delta Kappa. Address: Creighton U Omaha NB 68131

KELLEY, WILLIAM MELVIN, writer; b. 1937. Recipient Rosenthal Found. award Nat. Inst. Arts and Letters, 1963. Author: A Different Drummer, 1962; A Drop of Patience, 1965; dem, 1967; Dunfords Travels Everywheres, 1970; (short stories) Dancers on the Shore (Transatlantic Rev. award), 1964. Contbr. short stories to Mademoiselle, Saturday Evening Post, Black World, Cavalier. Address: care Doubleday & Co Inc 277 Park Av New York City NY 10017

KELLEY, XAVIER JAMES, Jr. mfg. exec.; b. Lima, O., Apr. 1, 1932; B.S., U. San Francisco, 1954; M.S., Stanford University, 1956; m. Rosemarie Lois Brown, May 15, 1955; 1 son, Anthony Robinson. Sales rep. Ames-Brockton Fabricated Products, Akron, O., 1956-58, sales mgr. Coshocton, Ohio, 1959-61, gen. manager plant, 1961-68, v.p. sales, 1968--. Instr. bus. Cosyshocton Jr. College, 1968-69. Secretary Coshocton YMCA, 1960-61; active Boy Scouts of America. Trustee Coshocton Animal Welfare League, Curry Home for the Aged. Named Man of Year, Coshocton Junior Chamber of Commerce, 1968. Mem. Coshocton C. of C. (vice president 1967-68, pres. 1969-70), English Speaking Union, Coshocton Sertoma Club, Nat. Assn. Mfrs., Sales Executives Institute, Phi Beta Kappa, Sigma Chi, Phi Mu. Democrat. Mem. Christian Ch. (lay leader). Mason (32, Shriner). Clubs: Coshocton Country, Coshocton City, Running Deer Country. Home: 2d Av Coshocton OH Office: 3d Av Coshocton OH

KELLIHER, PETER MAURICE, arbitrator; b. Chgo., Dec. 23, 1912; s. Edward J. and Catherine (Rooney) K.; A.B., U. Chgo., 1935, J.D., 1937; m. Virginia Dowdle, Jan. 21, 1942; children—Diane, Peter. Admitted to Ill. bar, 1938; spl. asst. corp. counsel City Chgo., 1940-41; U.S. commnr. conciliation, 1941-42; arbitrator-umpire labor diputes, 1945—. Pres. Kelliher Co., Inc.; developer Hemingway House and Huntington Hills. Past commnr. Chgo. Urban Renewal Commn.; bd. dirs. Greater N. Michigan Av. Assn. Served to capt. AUS, 1942-45. Mem. Nat. Acad. Arbitrators (pres.), Wine and Food Soc. Clubs: Irish Fellowship (v.p.), Tavern Lake Shore Athletic (Chgo.). Home: 109 E Bellevue Pl Chicago IL 60611 Office: 77 W Washington St Chicago IL 60602

KELLIHER, THOMAS GEORGE, oil co. exec.; b. Salem, Mass., Feb. 20, 1905; s. Thomas Francis and Margaret Theresa (O'Connell) K.; A.B., Boston Coll., 1926; LL.B., Georgetown U., 1931; m. Dorothy Josephine Gaffey, Nov. 19, 1932; 1 son, Thomas George. With FBI, 1931-34; with dept. investigation Dept. Interior, 1934-36; with Getty Oil Co. (Tidewater Oil Co. merged into Getty 1967) Houston, 1936—, v.p., gen. mgr. So. div., now group v.p., gen. mgr., dir. Mid-Continent div. Vice chmn. Internat. Oil and Gas Ednl. Center, Dallas, 1963—. Bd. dirs. Jr. Achievement Houston; mem. adv. bd. St. Joseph's Hosp. Mem. Am. Petroleum Club, Am. Assn. Petroleum Landmen (past pres.), Phi Alpha Delta. Clubs: Houston; Serra. Home: 5211 Memorial Dr Houston TX 77007 Office: PO Box 1404 Houston TX 77001

KELLIN, MIKE, actor; b. Hartford, Conn., Apr. 26, 1922; s. Samuel and Sophie (Botuck) K.; student Bates Coll., 1939-40, Boston U., 1940-41; A.B., Trinity Coll., 1943; postgrad. Yale, 1947-48; m. Sally Moffet, Aug. 3, 1966; 1 dau., Shauna. Actor appearing in TV, stage, films; co-star TV series The Wackiest Ship in the Army; appeared on Broadway in Mother Courage, The Odd Couple, Stalag 17, Pipe Dream, the Emperor's Clothes, 25 others; films include the Great Imposter, Fools' Parade, The Boston Strangler, Riot!, Banning, Invitation to a Gunfighter, 30 others; regional theatre credits include 3 Sisters, Rocket to the Moon, Tchin Tchin, King Lear, Oliver!, Fiddler on the Roof, Taming of the Shrew; conducted Nyack (N.Y.) Actors Workshop. Dir. Fortune Soc., 1968—; sponsor Synanon, 1965-66; pres. Rockland County (N.Y.) friends of Fortune. Served with USNR, World War II. Composer, performer record album: And the Testimony's Still Comin' In, 1967; Composer series of songs for Sierra Club Survival Songbook. Home: 23 Clinton Av Nyack NY 10960 Office: care International Famous Agency Inc 9255 Sunset Blvd Los Angeles CA 90069

KELLMAN, MAX, apparel products co. exec.; b. Poland, Dec. 30, 1906; s. Benjamin David and Esther (Mondz) K.; came to U.S., 1920, naturalized, 1920; B.S., Washington Sq. Coll., N.Y.U., 1930, J.D., Law Sch., 1932, LL.M., 1934; m. Belle Weiss, Dec. 19, 1931; children—Eilene R. (Mrs. Robert Kahn), Lester R. With Best Form Founds., Inc. and Lily of France, Inc., N.Y.C., 1934—, now exec. v.p. Bd. govs. United Home for Aged Hebrews, New Rochelle, N.Y. Jewish religion (bd. govs. temple). Mason. Club: Fenway Golf (White Plains, N.Y.). Office: 90 Park Av New York City NY 10016

KELLN, ELMER ELLSWORTH, dental educator; b. Cymeric, Sask., Can., Nov. 6, 1926; s. Adam and Kathrine Marie (Herb) K.; student Walla Walla Coll., 1943-45; B.S., U. Neb., 1949, D.D.S., 1949; M.S.D., U. Minn., 1960; m. Jeanette Kyle Ackerman, July 15, 1948; children—Elmira Jean, Wayne James, Lois Jeannine. Individual practice gen. dentistry, B.C., 1949-57; asso. prof. pathology U. W. Va., 1960-66; prof. oral medicine Loma Linda U., 1966—, asso. dean Sch. Dentistry, 1971—; mem. staff W. Va. U. Med. Center, 1960-65, Loma Linda U. Med. Center, 1967—. Bd. dirs. Am. Cancer Soc., 1965-66. NIH fellow U. Minn., 1958-60. Fellow Am. Coll. Dentists, Am. Acad. Oral Pathology. Lion. Contbr. articles profl. jours. Home: 24917 Lawton St Loma Linda CA 92354

KELLNER, AARON, med. educator; b. N.Y.C., Sept. 24, 1914; s. Louis and Rose (Horn) K.; B.A., Yeshiva Coll., 1934; M.S. in Pub. Health, Columbia, 1936; M.D., U. Chgo., 1939; m. Zira DeFries, May 4, 1942; children—David, William, Charles. Intern Michael Reese Hosp., Chgo., 1939-41; resident Montefiore Hosp., N.Y.C., 1941; with N.Y. Hosp.-Cornell Med. Center, 1946—, attending pathologist, 1960—, dir. central labs., 1948-64; clin. prof. pathology Cornell U. Med. Sch., 1968—; dir. Community Blood Council Greater N.Y. and N.Y. Blood Center, 1964—; cons. clin. pathology and blood banking Community Hosp. Glen Cove, N.Y., 1955—, Univ. Seminar asso. Columbia, 1964-70. Served with USAAF, World War II. Research fellow Life Ins. Med. Research Fund, 1947-48. Diplomate Am. Bd. Pathology. Mem. Am. Assn. Blood Banks (pres. 1954), Am. (chmn. council arteriosclerosis 1960), N.Y. (sci. council) heart assns.). Home: 40 E 83d St New York City NY 10028

KELLNER, EDWIN GORDON, state govt. ofcl.; b. Dell. Mont., Oct. 29, 1914; s. Leslie B. and Merle (Kenison) K.; B.A., Tex. Christian U., 1942; M.A., Mont. State U., 1948; postgrad. U. Wash.; m. Ruth Ratliff, Aug. 15, 1941; children—Stephen Stuart. Faculty, U. Mont., 1950-54; safety dir. No. Tank Line, 1954-57; mgr. N.D. Motor Transport Assn., 1957-60; mgr. Mont. C. of C., Helena, 1960-67; dir. Mont. Dept. Instns., 1967—; cons. personnel psychology. Chmn., Mont. Safety Council. Served to maj. AUS, 1942-46; ETO. Mem. Sigma Phi Epsilon, Psi Chi. Baptist. Mason, Elk. Home: 620 N Warren St Helena MT 59601 Office: 1326 6th St Helena MT 59601

KELLOGG, CHARLES EDWIN, soil scientist; b. Ionia County, Mich., Aug. 2, 1902; s. Herbert Francis and Eunice Irene (Stocken) K.; B.S., Mich. State Coll., 1925, Ph.D., 1929; D.Sc., U. Gembloux (Belgium), 1960 U. Ghent (Belgium), 1963, N.D. State U., 1962; m. Lucille Jeanette Reasoner, Dec. 25, 1925; children—Robert Leland, Mary Alice. Fellow in soils Mich. State Coll., 1926-28; soil scientist

Wis. Geol. Natural History Survey, 1928-30; asst. prof., then prof. soils N.D. Agrl. Coll., Fargo, 1930-34; chief soil survey U.S. Dept. Agr., 1934—, asst. adminstr., soil conservation service, 1953-63, dep. adminstr., 1963—. Del. 3d Internat. Congress Soil Sci., Oxford, Eng., 1935, gen. assembly Internat. Inst. Agr., Rome, 1938, 2d Inter-Am. Conf. Agr., Mexico City, 1942, 7th Pacific Sci. Congress, New Zealand, 1949; head U.S. delegation 4th Internat. Congress Soil Sci., Amsterdam, 1950, 5th Internat. Congress Soil Sci., Leopoldville, 1954, 6th Internat. Congress Soil Sci., Paris, 1956; chmn. U.S. Mission on Soil Sci. to USSR, 1958; guest scientist India, 1958, 59, S. Viet Nam, 1959; Messenger lectr. Cornell U., 1945; Sigma Xi lectr., 1947; guest Acad. Scis. USSR for Jubilee Anniversary Sessions, Moscow and Leningrad, 1945; guest scientist, France, 1947, Belgian Congo, 1947, Britain, 1948, Ireland, Portugal and Iceland, 1950, Israel, 1952, Gold Coast, 1954. Recipient Distinguished Service award, gold medal U.S. Dept. Agr., 1950; Distinguished service citation Mich. State U., 1955. Fellow A.A.A.S., Am. Soc. Agronomy; mem. Assn. Am. Geographers, Internat. Soc. Soil Sci., Soil Sci. Soc. Am. (pres. 1941), Royal Soc. New Zealand (hon.), Indian Soc. Soil Sci. (hon.), Sigma Xi, Phi Kappa Tau, Alpha Zeta. Mason. Club: Cosmos (Washington). Author: Soil Survey Manual; Our Garden Soils, 1952; (with D.C. Knapp) The College of Agriculture-Science in the Public Service, 1966. Contbr. numerous bulls. and papers to profl. lit. Home: 4100 Nicholson St Hyattsville MD 20782 Office: US Dept Agr Washington DC 20251

KELLOGG, EDMUND HALSEY, educator; b. Morristown, N.J., Mar. 8, 1912; s. Frederic Rogers and Cornelia Van Wyck (Halsey) K.; student Groton Sch.; A.B., Princeton, 1934; diplome U. Dijon, France, 1932; LL.D., Harvard, 1937; m. Celina Robbins, June 9, 1938; children—Eliza Darcy, Celina Robbins, Roger Bradford, Edmund Drake. Admitted to N.Y. bar, 1938; asso. firm Davis, Polk, Wardwell, Gardiner & Reed, N.Y.C., 1937-41; asst. to asst. sec. state Adolph Berle, 1941-42; staff bur. UN affairs State Dept., 1946-54; fgn. service officer, 1954-68; fgn. service insp., counselor Am. embassy, Phnom Penh, Cambodia, 1954-60; spl. asst. dir. Disarmament Adminstrn., Dept. State, 1960-61; consul gen., Duesseldorf, Germany, 1961- 67; spl. asst. to sec. state for population matters, 1967-68; dep. exec. dir. Pathfinder Fund, Boston, 1968-71; dep. dir. law and population program Fletcher Sch. Law and Diplomacy, 1971—. Served from 2d lt. to maj., AUS, 1942-46. Decorated Bronze Star. Mem. Fgn. Service Assn., Soc. Preservation New Eng. Antiquities (trustee). Clubs: Metropolitan (Washington); Colonial (Princeton); Somerset (Boston). Mem. staff Harvard Law Rev., 1935-37. Home: Bedford Rd Lincoln MA 01773 Office: Fletcher Sch Law Medford MA 02155

KELLOGG, FRANCIS LEONARD, corporate dir.; b. N.Y.C., Jan. 5, 1917; s. Frank Leonard and Emily Humphries (Baker) K.; grad. Choate Sch., 1936, Phillips Exeter Acad., 1937; B.A., Princeton, 1940; m. Fernanda Munn, Oct. 12, 1942; children—Christopher, Fernanda. With John Wanamaker, N.Y.C., 1946-55, exec. asst. to pres., 1950, v.p. charge br. stores, 1950-55, now dir.; chmn. bd., chief exec. officer, pres. Nat. Dept. Stores Corp., N.Y.C., 1955-58; pres. Internat. Mining Corp., 1958-70, now dir.; pres., dir. John Wanamaker Liberty St., Inc.; dir. John Wanamaker Phila., John Wanamaker Wilmington, A.T. Stewart Realty Co., Molybdenum Corp. Am., Perry Industries, Inc., Hunter Industries, S.A., Fresnillo Co., Canton Co. of Balt., L.E.R. Distbg. Corp., 920 Fifth Av. Corp. Trustee Estate of Rodman Wanamaker. Dir., chmn. exec. com. Internat. Rescue Com. Mem. Am. Immigration and Citizenship Conf. (treas.), Eta Mu Pi. Clubs: Union, Racquet and Tennis (N.Y.C.); Travellers (Paris, France). Home: 920 Fifth Av New York City NY 10021 Office: 280 Park Av New York City NY 10017

KELLOGG, FREDERIC HARTWELL, engr.; b. Pitts., July 31, 1904; s. Frederic Sherlock and Gertrude (Chew) K.; Geol. Engr., Colo. Sch. Mines, 1927; A.M., Johns Hopkins, 1929, Ph.D., 1934; m. Helen Bishop, Apr. 8, 1937; children—Frederic H., Walter Whitney. Engring. geologist Panama Canal, 1929-34; engr. soils and founds., constrn. dept. TVA, 1934-45; engr. U.S. Engrs., Mo. Valley Devel., 1945-46; prof. civil engring. U. Miss. 1946-65, chmn. dept. civil engring., 1947-65, dean engring., 1950-65; now dean emeritus engring. Memphis State U.; cons. Engr. found. and earthworks phases of constrn., 1946—; cons. TVA, Govt. of Bombay (India), Punjab, others. Mem. Miss. Bd. Engring. Examiners, 1958-64; mem. Miss. River Commn. Fellow Am. Soc. C.E. (J. James R. Croes medal 1950); mem. Memphis Engrs. Club, Omicron Delta Kappa, Kappa Sigma, Chi Epsilon. Author: Construction Methods and Machinery, 1954. Home: 4722 Gwynne Rd Memphis TN 38117

KELLOGG, GEORGE EDGAR, railroad ofcl.; b. Galva, Ia., Oct. 1, 1922; s. Lloyd Leslie and Bessie Bernice (Whitsitt) K.; student Coll. Advanced Traffic, Chgo., 1946; m. LaVonne Gertrude Stanley, Mar. 5, 1946; children—Georgia Kay, Peggy Louise, Robert Wesley, Rodney Leslie. With C.G.W. R.R., 1946-65, sec., comptroller, 1961-62, v.p., sec., comptroller, 1962-65; v.p., sec. Kansas City So. Industries, Inc., K.C.S. Ry. and subsidiaries, 1967—, La. & Ark. Ry. Co., 1967—. Served with AUS, 1942-45. Mem. Tax Execs. Inst., Assn. Am. Railroads, Ry. Systems and Mgmt. Assn., Am. Soc. Corporate Secs., Nat. Investor Relations Inst. Methodist. Club: Union League (Chgo.). Home: 4 W Bridlespur Dr Kansas City MO 64114 Office: 114 W 11th St Kansas City MO 64105

KELLOGG, GRACE (Mrs. Clarendon Waite Smith), author; b. Bangor, Me.; d. Charles Carroll and Eva M. (Crosby) K.; A.B., Smith Coll., 1908; M.A., U. Vt., 1953; m. M.D. Griffith (div. 1934); children—Grace Callaway (Mrs. Douglas W. Edmondson), Thomas Dison (dec. 1964), Barbara Kellogg (Mrs. Herbert P. Beam), Charles Kellogg; m. 2d, Clarendon Waite Smith, 1942 (dec. 1951). Faculty Am. Coll. for Women, Istanbul, 1915-17; campaigned for enfranchisement of women, Phila., 1918; vol. editorial work office Margaret Sanger, birth control, N.Y.C., 1931-32; weekly column for peace Provincetown Advocate, 1962-63; summer faculty, dept. English, St. Michael's Coll., Burlington, Vt., 1962. Mem. Authors League Am., Am. Soc. Friends, Am. Civil Liberties Union, Fellowship Reconciliation, Com. for Nonviolent Action, Author: A Keeper of the Door; The Mould; The House; The Silent Drum; Windy; inn; The Beloved Tenant (London); Escape Me Never; The Two Lives of Edith Wharton (biography), 1965. Contbr. short stories, articles to popular mags., anthologies. Home: Aldridge Hotel Shawnee OK 74801

KELLOGG, HAMILTON HYDE, retired bishop; b. Skaneateles, N.Y., Sept. 6, 1899; s. Walter Hamilton and Jennie Louise (Kellogg) K.; student Syracuse U., 1917-18, LL.D., 1956; A.B., Williams Coll., 1921, D.D., 1944; grad. Gen. Theol. Sem., N.Y.C., 1924, S.T.D., 1946; M.A., Columbia, 1924; D.D., U. of South, 1946, Hamilton Coll., 1954, Seabury-Western Theol. Sem., 1957; m. Mildred Sarah Haley, June 10, 1929. Ordained deacon and priest P.E. Ch., 1924; priest-in-charge St. Alban's Ch., Syracuse, N.Y., also St. Mark's Ch., Jamesville, N.Y., 1924-25; curate Christ Ch., Greenwich, Conn., 1925-29; rector St. James' Ch., Danbury, Conn., 1929-41, Christ Ch., Houston, 1946-49; 1st dean Christ Ch. Cathedral, Houston, 1949-52; consecrated bishop coadjutor Diocese of Minn., 1952; bishop of Minn., 1956-70. Dir. Ministers Life & Casualty Union, 1957. Past mem. bd. dirs. of United Fund, Mpls.; past pres. bd. trustees Breck Sch., Mpls., St. James Sch., St. Mary's Hall, Shattuck Sch.; dir. Bishop-Seabury Mission, Faribault, Minn.; hon. trustee Seabury-Western Theol. Sem., Evanston, Ill., 1952-58, chmn., 1958, 67-69; trustee Carleton Coll., 1956-70, St. Barnabas Hosp., Mpls., St. Luke's Hosp., St. Paul, 1956-70; past trustee Gen. Theol. Sem., N.Y.C., St. Stephen's Sch. and Sem. of S.W., Austin, Tex. Served as sgt. USMC, World War I; 1st lt. Chaplain's Corps, U.S. Army, 1928-29; capt. Conn. N.G., 1929-41; col. AUS, World War II. Decorated Bronze Star (U.S.); Croix de Guerre with palm (Belgium). Mem. Mil. Order World Wars, Delta Kappa Epsilon. Mason. Clubs: Minneapolis, Minikahda (Mpls.); Town and Country, University (St. Paul); Waizata (Minn.) Country. Home: 1805 S Logan Av Minneapolis MN 55403 Office: 1917 Logan Av S Minneapolis MN 55403

KELLOGG, HERBERT HUMPHREY, educator, metallurgist; b. N.Y.C., Feb. 24, 1920; s. Herbert H. and Gladys (Falding) K.; B.S., Columbia, 1941, M.S., 1943; m. Jeanette Halstead, July 20, 1940; children—Thomas Bartlett, Jane Falding, David Humphrey, Elizabeth Ann. Asst. prof. mineral preparation Pa. State U., State Coll., 1942-46; faculty Columbia, N.Y.C., 1946—, Stanley-Thompson prof. chem. metallurgy, 1968—. Chmn. titanium adv. com. Office Def. Mblzn., 1954-58. Recipient Best Paper award extractive metals div. Am. Inst. Metall. Engrs. Mem. Am. Inst. Mining, Metall. and Petroleum Engrs. (chmn. extractive metallurgy div. 1958), Am. Chem. Soc., Electrochem. Soc., Am. Soc. for Metals, Sigma Xi, Tau Beta Pi. Research; contbr. numerous articles to publs. Home: Closter Rd Palisades NY 10964 Office: Columbia New York City NY 10027

KELLOGG, JAMES CRANE, III, broker; b. N.Y.C., May 14, 1915; s. James C. and Etti (Cissel) K.; student Williams Coll., 1937; m. Elizabeth Irwin, June 18, 1937; children—James Crane, Peter Rittenhouse, Richard Irwin, Morris Woodruff. Partner, Spear & Leeds, brokers, N.Y.C., 1945; now sr. partner Spear, Leeds & Kellogg; chmn. bd. Newex Corp., N.Y. Stock Exchange Bldg. Co., N.Y. Stock Exchange Aviation Corp., N.Y. Stock Exchange Clearing Corp.; pres., dir. J.C. Kellogg & Sons, Inc.; v.p. Maymount Co., Bayhead, N.J.; pres., dir. Bayhead Improvement Corp.; v.p., dir. Bay Head Corp., Tampa, Fla.; chmn. bd. govs. N.Y. Stock Exchange, 1956-58; dir. City Fed. Savs. Bank, Central Home Trust Co., De Laval Steam Turbine Co., De Laval Turbine Co., Manhattan Shirt Co., Mutual Benefit Life Ins. Co. Pres. Assn. Stock Exchange Firms. Commnr., vice chmn. finance com. N.Y. Port Authority. Trustee Elizabeth Community Chest; chmn. bd. J. C. Kellogg Found Mem. Westminster Ch. Clubs: Town and Country (dir.) (Elizabeth); Bay Head (pres.) (N.J.); Bay Head Yacht (trustee). Home: 42 Aberdeen Rd Elizabeth NJ 07208 Office: 11 Wall St New York City NY 10005

KELLOGG, MARION KNIGHT, lawyer, educator; b. Bowling Green, Ky., July 24, 1904; s. Robert Marion and Nelle (Willis) K.; B.A., Va. Mil. Inst., 1925; LL.B Yale, 1928; m. Virginia Dryden, Oct. 3, 1931. Admitted to N.Y. bar, 1929, Mich. bar. 1932, Va. bar, 1961; practiced in N.Y.C., 1928-32, Detroit, 1932-56, Charlottesville, 1956-; asso. firm Chadbourne, Hunt, Jaeckel & Brown, Cravath, de Gersdorf, Swaine & Wood, 1928-32; pvt. practice, 1932-56; mem. firm Kellogg, Fulton & Donovan, 1942-46; lectr. law Sch. Law U. Va., 1956-64, prof. law, exec. dir. Law Sch. Found., 1964—. Pres. Charlottesville- Albermarle United Givers Fund, 1964; mem. Charlottesville Community Relations Com., 1964-65; mem. steering com. United Negro Coll. Fund, Shenandoah Area, 1966—. Served to lt. col., Q.M.C., AUS, 1942-45. Mem. Am., N.Y., Mich., Va., Charlottesville-Albermarle, Detroit, Fed., Inter-Am. bar assns., Internat. Law Assn., Am. Law Inst., Charlottesville Com. Fgn. Relations (past pres.), Order of Coif (hon.), Phi Delta Phi. Presbyn. Clubs: Farmington Country, Farmington Hunt, Commonwealth (Richmond, Va.); Nat. Lawyers (Washington); Torch (past pres.), Colonnade (Charlottesville). Yale (N.Y.C.); Graduate (New Haven). Home: Farmington PO Box 3755 University Station Charlottesville, VA 22903.

KELLOGG, PAUL JESSE, educator, physicist, b. Tacoma, Nov. 6, 1927; s. Jesse I. and Irma (Kennedy) K.; B.S., Mass. Inst. Tech., 1950; Ph.D., Cornell U., 1955; m. Dorothy Del Bourgo, June 10, 1951 (div. Nov. 1964); children—Kenneth, David; m. 2d, Janet Schuffenhauer, Apr. 26, 1969; children—Deidre, Todd. Research fellow U.S. Naval Research Lab., 1955-56; research asso., U. Minn., Mpls., 1956-57, faculty, 1957—, prof. physics, 1964—. Fellow Am. Phys. Soc.; mem. Am. Geophys. Union, Am. Assn. U. Profs. Research, publs. on theory of radiation belt, shock wave around earth, waves in plasma, observation solar corona. Home: Route 2 Box 395 N Shore Clear Lake Forest Lake MN 55025

KELLOW, WILLIAM F., univ. dean; b. Geneva, N.Y., Mar. 14, 1922; s. Robert Leo and Mary Loretta (Kelley) K.; B.S., U. Notre Dame, 1943; M.D., Georgetown U., 1946; D.Sc. (hon.), St. Joseph's Coll., 1967; m. Stella Margaret Toczylowski, Apr. 21, 1951; children—Suzanne, Joanne, Jennifer, Mary Jeanne, Kathleen. Intern D.C. Gen Hosp., 1946-47; resident internal medicine and pulmonary diseases D.C. Gen. Hosp., Georgetown U. Hosp., Walter Reed Med. Center, 1947-51; mem. faculty U. Ill. Coll. Medicine, 1953-61, asso. prof. medicine, assc. dean, 1959-61; prof. medicine, dean Hahnemann Med. Coll., Phila., 1961-67; prof. medicine, dean, v.p. Jefferson Med. Coll., Phila., 1967—. Trustee Eastern Pa. Psychiat. Inst., Ednl. Council Fgn. Med. Grads. Served to capt. M.C., USAF, 1951-53. Diplomate Am. Bd. Internal Medicine, Am. Bd. Pulmonary Diseases. Mem. A.C.P. (trustee), Am. Fedn. Clin. Research, Am. Thoracic Soc., Sigma Xi. Club: Union League (Phila.). Home: 457 Moreno Rd Wynnewood PA 19096 Office: 1025 Walnut Philadelphia PA 19107

KELLY, ALFRED HINSEY, educator, historian; b. Pekin, Ill., June 23, 1907; s. Raymond Ransom and Bessie Mae (Case) K.; Ph.B., U. Chgo., 1931, A.M., 1934, Ph.D., 1938; m. Emily May Peterson, Sept. 22, 1935; children—Elizabeth Marie (Mrs. Donald Breneau), Virginia Jayne, Alfred Herbert. Mem. faculty Wayne State U., Detroit, 1935—, prof. history, chmn. dept., 1952—. Tech. adviser preparation Supreme Ct. brief Brown vs. Board, N.A.A.C.P., 1953; apptd. to Oliver Wendell Holmes Devise, 1970. Mich. co-chmn. Vols. for Stevenson, 1952, Detroit chmn., 1956. Served to lt. USNR, 1944-46. Mem. Am., So. hist. assns., Orgn. Am. Historians. Club: Orphens (Detroit). Author: (with W. A. Harbison) The American Constitution: Its Origins and Development, 4th edit., 1970. Editor, author: American Foreign Policy and American Democracy, 1954; Foundations of Freedom, 1958. Contbr. articles profl. jours. Home: 1013 Balfour St Grosse Pointe Park MI 48232 Office: Dept History Wayne State U Detroit MI 48202

KELLY, ARTHUR, judge; b. Toronto, Ont., Can., Dec. 28, 1900; s. Hugh T. and Mary (Hynes) K.; B.A., U. Toronto, 1920; legal edn. Osgoode Hall Law Sch., Toronto; m. Aileen McDonagh, Oct. 24, 1928; children—Carol, Miriam, Hugh, Kevin, Called to Canadian bar, 1923, apptd. Queen's Counsel, 1944; practiced Toronto; with Day, Wilson, Kelly, Martin & Campbell (and predecessors), 1928-60, partner, 1931-60; justice Ct. of Appeals of Ont., 1960—. Gov., U. Toronto, 1944-70, chmn. insulin com., 1949-60; chmn. Connaught Med. Research Labs., 1956- 66. Chmn., Ont. Mental Health Found. 1962-69. Decorated knight comdr. Order St. Gregory. Mem. Canadian Bar Assn. (pres. 1957-58), County of York (pres. 1948) bar assns., Theta Delta Chi. Home: 3 Mckenzie Av Toronto 5 Ontario Canada Office: Osgoode Hall Toronto 1 Ontario Canada

KELLY, BALMER HANCOCK, clergyman, educator; b. Wytheville, Va., June 12, 1914; s. James Montgomery and Caroline Balmer (Hancock) K.; A.B., King Coll., Tenn., 1934, D.D., 1960; B.D., Union Theol. Sem. in Va., 1939, Th.M., 1940; Th.D., Princeton, 1947; postgrad. U. Zurich (Switzerland), 1951; m. Ann Franklin Wood, Sept. 2, 1944; children—Ruth Wood, Caroline Ann, Franklin Wood. Ordained to ministry Presbyn. Ch., 1941; prof. Bible, King Coll., 1940-41; asso. prof. Bible, Union Theol. Sem. in Va., 1943-47, prof. Bibl. theology, 1947—, dean faculty, 1965—. Mem. Soc. Bibl. Lit. Editor: Layman's Bible Commentary, 1959-64; Tools for Bible Study, 1958. Co-editor: Interpretation, 1947-65; Ezra, Nehemiah, Esther, Job, vol. 8, Layman's Bible Commentary, 1962. Contbr. articles to various publs. Home: 1012 Melrose Av Richmond VA 23227

KELLY, BERNARD M., Cath. aux. bishop Diocese Providence, titular bishop of Tegea. Address: 92 Hope St Providence RI 02906*

KELLY, BURNHAM, educator; b. Evanston, Ill., Jan. 23, 1912; s. George Thomas and Margaret (Burnham) K.; diploma U. Paris (France), 1932; A.B., Williams Coll., 1933, L.H.D., 1963; LL.B., Harvard, 1936; M.C.P., Mass. Inst. Tech., 1941; m. Jean McKee Kingery, Sept. 14, 1939; children—Leila McKee, Sherman, Katharine, Wells, Hugh. Admitted to R.I. bar, 1937; asso. Greenough, Lyman & Cross, Providence, 1936-38; asst. exec. officer com. on fortification design NRC, Washington, 1941-44; mem. adv. com. Office Civil Def., 1942-43; spl. asst. to chief div. 2, NDRC, 1942-44; field service cons. OSRD, 1944-45; mem. Alsos mission in Europe, U.S. Army Intelligence, 1945; research asso. city and regional planning dept. Mass Inst. Tech., 1945-46, asst. prof., 1946-50, asso. prof., 1950-60; asst. dir. Bemis Found., 1945-58, dir. 1948-54; dean Cornell U. Coll. Architecture, 1960-71, now prof. Vice chmn. Nat. Fine Arts Commn., 1963-67, N.Y. State Council Architecture, 1968—. Mem. Am. Inst. Planners, A.I.A., Am. Soc. Planning Ofcls., Phi Beta Kappa, Delta Kappa Epsilon. Author: The Prefabrication of Houses, 1950; (with others) Design and the Production of Houses, 1959. Home: 200 Forest Home Dr Ithaca NY 14850

KELLY, CHARLES JAMES, lawyer; b. St. Johns, Nfld., Can. Aug. 22, 1892; s. Michael J. and Mary (Meehan) K.; student St. Bonaventures Coll., St. Johns; LL.B., U. Colo., 1925; m. Marjorie Fleming, Dec. 21, 1922; children—John Fleming, Mary Ellen (Mrs. Thomas Page Owen). Admitted to Colo. bar, 1925, since practiced in Denver; mem. firm Lee, Shaw & McCreery, 1944-48, Lee, Bryans, Kelly & Stansfield, 1948—. Dir. Pub. Service Co. Colo. Served with U.S. Army, 1917-18. Mem. Am., Colo (pres. 1954-55), Denver bar assns., Phi Delta Phi, Phi Delta Theta. Republican. Roman Catholic. Clubs: City, University, Denver Country (Denver). Home: 155 Gaylord St Denver CO 80206 Office: Pub Service Co Bldg Denver CO 80202

KELLY, CHARLES SCOTT, lawyer; b. Hudson, Wis., Sept. 16, 1899; s. Arthur David and Addie Elizabeth (Scott) K.; student River Falls (Wis.) State Normal Sch., 1917- 19; LL.B., U. Minn., 1925; m. Bess Loftis, June 1927; children—Charles Arthur, Ann. Admitted to Minn. bar, 1925, Ill. bar, 1930; practice law, St. Paul and Mpls., 1925-29, Chgo., 1930—; now mem. firm Hubachek, Kelly, Rauch and Kirby. Chmn. presidents Quetico-Superior com. for study internat. conservation, recreation program Rainy Lake Watershed, Minn. and Ontario. Mem. Am., Ill., Chgo. bar assns., Phi Delta Phi. Republican. Clubs: U. Chgo., Mid-Am. (Chgo.). Home: 210 Davis St Evanston IL 60201 Office: Prudential Bldg Chicago IL 60601

KELLY, CROSBY MOYER, mgmt. cons.; b. Hinsdale, Ill., Mar. 23, 1918; s. Thomas Cowen and Mary Emma (Moyer) K.; B.A., U. Ariz., 1939; postgrad. U. Mexico, 1939-40; m. Willah Mary Smith, Mar. 12, 1951. With Ford Motor Co., 1941-48; dir. advt. and pub. relations Rapid Standard Co., Inc., Grand Rapids, Mich. 1949; exec. dir. Chgo Fair of 1950; sales rep. Central Services, Inc., Kansas City, Mo., 1951; owner-mgr. importing-distbg. co., Havana and Camaguey, Cuba, 1952-55; v.p., dir. advt. and pub. relations, asst. to chief exec. officer Litton Industries, Inc., Beverly Hills, Cal. 1959- 65; now chmn. bd. Crosby M. Kelly, Robert L. Bliss, Inc.; chmn. Pres. Advt. Measurements, Inc., 1965-70; owner AMPR Assos., Inc., Paris, Dusseldorf, Hamburg, Brussels, 1966—; dir. Western World Ins. Co., 1970—; chmn. bd. Performance Measurements Co., Detroit, 1968—; cons., insp. gen. Fgn. Assistance, State Dept., 1962—; guest lectr. European Inst. Bus. Adminstrn. Fontainebleau, France, 1966. Head Am. delegation Internat. Congress Air Force Assns., Turin, Italy, 1964; del. UN Indsl. Devel. Orgn. 1st World Symposium. Trustee Albertus Magnus Coll. Decorated commendatore Order of Merit Republic Italy, 1969. Mem. Def. Orientation Conf. Assn., Pub. Relations Soc. Am., Fgn. Policy Assn., Aviation Writers Assn. Clubs: Los Angeles Country; Litchfield Country; University, Netherlands, Bankers (N.Y.C.). Home: Butternut Brook Farm Litchfield CT 06759 Office: 1 Rockefeller Plaza New York City NY 10020

KELLY, CULLEN J., banker; b. Rosebud, Tex., Jan. 25, 1922; s. R. T. and Gladys (Braden) K.; student N. Tex. State Tchrs Coll., Denton; m. Mary Frances Rhodes, June 14, 1946. Formerly file clk. Denton County Nat. Bank, also asst. bank examiner, 1944-48; with First Nat. Bank, Midland, Tex., 1948—, pres., 1962—. Trustee Mary Hardin-Baylor Coll., Belton, Tex. Mem. Tex. Ex- Examiners Assn., Young Pres.'s Orgn. Clubs: Petroleum, Midland Country, Exchange (Midland). Home: 2001 Humble St Midland TX 79701 Office: 303 W Wall St Midland TX 79701

KELLY, DANIEL EDMUND, advt. exec.; b. Loudon, Tenn., Dec. 6, 1925; s. Daniel James and Martha (McQueen) K.; B.J., U. Mo., 1949; m. Carol Joan Maurek, Oct. 30, 1954; children—Daniel A., Megan M., Erin L., Brian W. Copywriter, Buchen Co., Chgo., 1949-53; copy supr. Needham, Louis & Brorby, Chgo., 1962; copywriter Foote, Cone & Belding, Chgo., 1953-62, sr. v.p., creative dir., 1962—. Area chmn. New Trier Twp. Democratic Orgn., Winnetka, Ill., 1966—. Served with USAAF, 1943-45. Mem. Alpha Delta Sigma, Sigma Alpha Epsilon. Home: 715 Laurel Av Wilmette IL 60091 Office: 401 N Michigan Av Chicago IL 60611

KELLY, DAVID, retired lawyer; b. Hudson, Mass., May 20, 1899; s. William Powers and Lillian (Lee) K.; Litt.B., Rutgers U., 1920; LL.B., Harvard, 1926; m. Katharine Houghton, Jan 26, 1927 (dec. July 1945); children—David, Dana Kimball; m. 2d, Marion T. Hakanson, Aug. 1, 1947 (dec. Mar. 1964); adopted children—Peter G. Hakanson, Ellen M. (Mrs. Edward G. Hixson); m. 3d, Gaynor B. Hewett, Sept. 28, 1964. Mem. firm Turk, Marsh, Kelly & Hoare, and predecessors, N.Y.C., 1939-69; now ret. Mem. Madison Bd. Edn., 1937-46, pres., 1942-46. Trustee Colonial Little Symphony Soc., Madison, 1954-62, pres., 1957-62; trustee Madison Pub. Library, 1951-57, pres., 1953-57. Mem. Am., N.Y. State bar assns., Bar Assn. City N.Y. Club: Mountain View Country (Greensboro, Vt.). Home: 107 Whispering Sands Dr Sarasota FL 33581

KELLY, DAVID J., business exec. Controller Econs. Lab., Inc., St. Paul. Office: Osborn Bldg St Paul MN 55102*

KELLY, DOROTHY ANN, coll. dean; b. Bronx, July 26, 1929; d. Walter David and Sarah (McCauley) Kelly; B.A., Coll. New Rochelle, 1951; M.A., Catholic U., Washington, 1958; Ph.D., U. Norte Dame,

1970. Mem. faculty Coll. New Rochelle (N.Y.), 1957—, chmn. dept. history, 1965-67, acad. dean, 1967—, acting pres., 1970-71. Mem. com. New Rochell Hosp. Sch. Nursing, 1970—. Mem. Am. Assn. U. Profs., Am. Hist. Assn., Eastern Assn. Coll. Deans. Address: Coll New Rochelle New Rochelle NY 10801

KELLY, EDWARD JAMES educator; b. Middletown, N.Y., July 10, 1920; s. Edward Joseph and Florence (Atwell) K.; A.B., Defiance Coll., 1942; M.A., State U. Ia., 1948, Ph.D., 1953; m. Betty Ruth Elder, Oct. 15, 1944; children—Paul E., Brian E. Tchr., Keckuk, Ia., 1946-47; prin., Washington, Ia., 1948-51; research asst. State U. Ia., 1951-53; vis. lectr. U. S.D., 1953; prof. Colo. State Coll., 1953-57, chmn. edn. div., 1957—, dean Sch. Edn., 1965-70; dean Coll. Edn., U. No. Colo., 1970-72, prof. edn., 1972—; cons. tchr. edn. AID, Thailand, 1971. Served to lt. (s.g.) USNR, 1942-46. Mem. N.E.A., Colo. Edn. Assn., Am. Research Assn., Assn. Higher Edn., Nat. Soc. Study Edn., Phi Delta Kappa. Contbr. articles profl. jours. Home: 2109 Buena Vista Dr Greeley CO 80631

KELLY, EDWARD JOSEPH, stock broker; b. N.Y.C., July 25, 1911; s. William E. and Rose (DeLorenzo) K.; Ph.B., Notre Dame U., 1932; m. Bernadette Maher, May 30, 1937; children—Sheila, (Mrs. Joel Ihlefeld), William E., Edward J., Peter, Bernadette, Barbara, John R. Mgr. trading dept. Loeb, Rhoades & Co., N.Y.C., 1940—, partner, 1961—; pres. Nat. Security Traders Assn., Inc., 1960-61, Security Traders Assn. N.Y., 1957-58. Mem. Notre Dame Alumni Assn. Clubs: Bankers America (N.Y.C.); Larchmont (N.Y.) Yacht; Boca Raton. Home: 252 Silver Palm Rd Boca Raton FL 33432 Office: 42 Wall St New York City NY 10005

KELLY, ELIZABETH BAKER, (Mrs. John J. Kelly), retired coll. dean; b. Glendive, Mont., July 4, 1908; d. Arthur A. and Carol (Walt) Baker; B.A., Mt. Holyoke Coll., 1943; L.H.D., Middlebury Coll., 1970; m. John J. Kelly, Apr. 4, 1949. Mem. staff Los Angeles Pub. Library Tng. Sch., 1926-27, Plentywood (Mont.) County Library, 1929-31, Havre (Mont.) High Sch. Library, 1936-38, Mt. Holyoke Library, 1938-43; mem. A.R.C. staff overseas hosps., Australia, New Guinea, P.I., 1943-46; social dir. Middlebury Coll., 1946-49, dean women, 1949-70. Mem. Am. Assn. U. Women. Home: 106 Norton St Bennington VT 05201

KELLY, ELLSWORTH, artist; b. Newburgh, N.Y., May 31, 1923; student Boston Mus. Fine Arts Sch., also Ecole des Beaux-Arts, Paris, 1946-48. Works exhibited Salon de Realities Nouvelles, Paris, 1950, 51, Mus. Modern Art, N.Y.C., 1956, 60, 64, 68, 69, Whitney Mus., 1957, 60-68, Carnegie Inst., 1958, 61, 64, 67, Am. Pavilion, Brussels World's Fair, 1958, Seattle World's Fair, 1962, Sao Paulo Biennial, 1961, Tokyo Internat., 1963, Documenta III, Germany, 1964, Documenta IV, 1968, Venice Biennale, 1966, Expo 67, Montreal, Guggenheim Internat., 1967; one man shows Galerie Arnaud, Paris, 1951, Galerie Maeght, Paris, 1958, 64, Sidney Janis Gallery, N.Y.C., 1965, 67, 68, Betty Parsons Gallery, N.Y.C., 1956, 57, 59, 61, 63, Toth Gallery, London, 1962, Washington Gallery Modern Art, 1964, Inst. Contemporary Art, Boston, 1964; rep. permanent collections Mus. Modern Art, Met. Mus., Whitney Mus., Carnegie Inst., Albright Art Gallery, Chgo. Art Inst., Worcester Mus., Toronto (Can.) Mus., Tate Gallery, London, Eng., Walker Art Center, Guggenheim Mus., N.Y.C., Los Angeles County Mus., Stedlijk Mus., Amsterdam, others; sculpture in lobby Transp. Bldg., Phila. Recipient Brandeis painting award, 1963; Edn. Minister award Tokly Internat, 1963; Carnegie Inst. 4th prize, 1962, painting prize, 1964; Flora Mayor Witkowsky prize Chgo. Art Inst., 1964.‡

KELLY, EPWORTH CONSTATINE mfg. exec.; b. Lima, O., Apr. 1, 1932; B.S., U. San Francisco, 1954; M.S., Stanford University, 1956; m. Rosemarie Lois Brown, May 15, 1955; 1 son, Anthony Robinson. Sales rep. Ames-Brockton Fabricated Products, Akron, O., 1956-58, sales mgr. Coshocton, Ohio, 1959-61, gen. manager plant, 1961-68, v.p. sales, 1968--. Instr. bus. Cosyhocton Jr. College, 1968-69. Secretary Coshocton YMCA, 1960-61; active Boy Scouts of America. Trustee Coshocton Animal Welfare League, Curry Home for the Aged. Named Man of Year, Coshocton Junior Chamber of Commerce, 1968. Mem. Coshocton C. of C. (vice president 1967-68, pres. 1969-70), English Speaking Union, Coshocton Sertoma Club, Nat. Assn. Mfrs., Sales Executives Institute, Phi Beta Kappa, Sigma Chi, Phi Mu. Democrat. Mem. Christian Ch. (lay leader). Mason (32, Shriner). Clubs: Coshocton Country, Coshocton City, Running Deer Country. Home: 2d Av Coshocton OH Office: 3d Av Coshocton OH

KELLY, ERNEST BYRON, Jr., investment banker; b. Chgo., Oct. 27, 1915; s. Ernest Byron and Clara (Johnson) K.; A.B. U. Ill., 1937; m. Kathryn Sumner Canfield, Mar. 7, 1942; children—Ernest Byron III, Michael W. Sales trainee Halsey, Stuart & Co. Inc., Chgo., 1937-39, salesman, Detroit, 1940-41, mgr. Detroit 1946-65, pres., chief exec. officer Chgo., 1968-70, chmn., chief exec. officer, 1970—; v.p. Blyth & Co., Inc., 1965-67; dir. Chgo. Title & Trust Co. Pres., Grosse Pointe Little League, 1963-64; chpt. chmn. United Found. Torch Dr., 1961-63; mem. Wayne County Bd. Suprs., 1965-68, City Council Grosse Pointe, Mich., 1963-68. Bd. govs. Chgo. Assn. Stock Exchange Firms, 1970—. Served with USNR, 1941-45. Mem. Financial Analysts Soc. Detroit, Am. Ordnance Assn., Mil. Order World Wars, U. Ill. Alumni, Midwest, Phila.-Balt.-Washington stock exchanges, Delta Kappa Epsilon. Republican. Presbyn. Clubs: Country, Bond (pres. 1952-53) (Detroit). Home: 501 Cambridge Lane Lake Bluff IL 60044 Office: 123 S LaSalle St Chicago IL 60690

KELLY, EUGENE F., business exec.; b. 1926; ed. Seton Hall U., married. With Gen. Banking Co., 1943-48, Boyce, Hughes & Farrell, C.P.A.'s, 1948-51, Price Waterhouse & Co., C.P.A.'s, 1951-64; controller Rheingold Corp., N.Y.C., 1964-66, controller, asst. sec., 1966—, also treas., 1968—. Office: Rheingold Corp 41 E 42d St New York City NY 10017

KELLY, EVERETT LOWELL, educator, psychologist; b. Kokomo, Ind., Nov. 15, 1905; s. Alva Elmont and Maude (Vickery) K.; B.S., Purdue U., 1926, D.Sc., 1955; A.M., Colo. Coll. Edn., 1928; Ph.D., Stanford, 1930; m. Lillian Isaacs, Dec. 25, 1938; children—Patricia Ann (Mrs. Paul Klinger), Paul Alan, Pamela Jane. High sch. prin., tchr. Taiban (N.M.) pub. schs., 1926-27; asso. prof. psychology, dir. admissions U. Hawaii, 1930-32; Social Science Research Council fellow, study in Germany, Austria, 1932-33; chmn. dept. psychology U. Conn., 1933-39; asso. prof. psychology, dir. psychol. clinic Purdue U., 1939-42; br. chief clin. psychologist VA, 1946-47; prof. psychology U. Mich., Ann Arbor, 1946—, chmn. dept. psychology, 1958-62; dir. Bur. Psychol. Services, 1950-71, Inst. Human Adjustment 1971—; cons. USPHS, USN, VA. Adviser to dir. SSS; dir. selection Peace Corps, Washington, 1961-62. Served with USNR, 1942-46; comdr. Res. Recipient letter of commendation (with ribbon) sec. navy, 1945. Mem. Am. (pres. 1954-55), Mich. (pres. 1948-49) psychol. assns. Home: 2559 Blueberry Lane Ann Arbor MI 48103

KELLY, FRANCIS D., newspaper exec. Business mgr. Milw. Jour. Office: 333 W State St Milwaukee WI 53201*

KELLY, FRANCIS T., film co. exec.; b. 1907; B.S., N.Y. U., 1927; m. With Twentieth Century- Fox Film Corp. and predecessor, 1935—, treas., 1962—, v.p., 1967—. Address: 444 W 56th St New York City NY 10019

KELLY, GENE CURRAN, dancer, actor, dir., b. Pitts., Pa., Aug. 23, 1912; s. James Patrick Joseph and Harriet (Curran) K.; A.B., U. Pitts., 1933; m. Betsy Blair, September 22, 1941 (div. in 1957); 1 daughter, Kerry; m. 2d, Jeanne Coyne, Aug. 6, 1960; children—Timothy, Bridget. Has appeared in N.Y. prodns.: Leave It To Me, 1938; Time of Your Life, 1940; One for the Money, 1939; Pal Joey, 1941; staged: Billy Rose's Diamond Horseshoe, 1940; Best Foot Forward, 1941; dir. dances for motion pictures Anchors Aweigh, 1944, The Pirate, 1948, Living in a Big Way, 1947; appeared in Me and My Girl, 1942, The Pirate, 1948, The Three Musketeers, An American in Paris, 1950, The Devil Makes Three, 1952, Brigadoon, 1954, Inherit the Wind, 1960, Gigo, 1961, others; co.-dir. On the Town, 1949, Singin, in the Rain, 1951, It's Always Fair Weather, 1955; dir. Invitation to the Dance, 1953; producer and dir. The Happy Road, France, 1956; Flower Drum Song, musical, 1958. Served as a lt. (j.g.) USNR, 1944-46. Mem. Chgo. Dance Masters Assn., Screen Actors Guild (v.p.), Phi Kappa. Author: Take Me Out to the Ball Game, 1948. Home: 725 N Rodeo Dr Beverly Hills CA 90210 Office: Universal Studios Universal City CA 91608

KELLY, GEORGE, dramatist; b. Phila., Pa., Jan. 16, 1887; s. John Henry and Mary (Costello) K.; ed. privately; A.F.D. (hon.), LaSalle Coll. of Pa., 1962; unmarried. Début in juvenile roles, N.Y.C., 1912, later with touring companies; author of a succession of one-act plays, of which Finders Keepers was the first; among full length plays are The Torchbearers (a satire on the little theatre movement in America); The Show-Off; Craig's Wife (Pulitzer prize 1925); Daisy Mayme, 1926; Behold the Bridegroom, 1927; Maggie the Magnificant, 1929; Philip Goes Forth, 1931; Reflected Glory, 1936; The Deep Mrs. Sykes, 1945; The Fatal Weakness, 1946. Recipient medal of Achievement and Creative Arts award Brandeis U., 1959; Phila. Creative Arts Theatre award, 1962; Gold medal Women's Theatre Club, N.Y.C.; Drama Award of Distinction, Cal. Alpha chpt. Theta Alpha Phi, 1968. Home: 1823 Old Gulph Rd Villanova PA 19085

KELLY, GEORGE LOFTUS, retail sales exec.; b. Hornell, N.Y., Sept. 24, 1907; s. John G. and Ruby (Loftus) K.; student pub. and parochial schs.; m. Marion Shoffner, June 15, children—Barry, Beth. With Newberry Co., N.Y.C., 1930—, store mgr. to 1935, dist. supt., 1935-46, div. mdse. mgr., 1946, asst. div. mgr., 1947-54, div. mr., 1954-58, v.p., 1958—, Eastern regional mgr., 1966-69; v.p. Britt's Dept. Store Corp., 1962-69, Britt's div. mgr., 1969—; pres. J.J. Travel, 1970—. Served from 1st lt. to lt. col., AUS, 1942-45. Club: Larchmount Shore. Home: 10 Iselin Terrace Larchmont NY 10538 Office: 245 Fifth Av New York City NY 10016

KELLY, GRACE; see Grimaldi, Princess Grace of Monaco.

KELLY, HARRY CHARLES, univ. adminstr.; b. Wilkes Barre, Pa., Sept. 3, 1908; s. Thomas A. and Josephine Magdalene (Reilly) K.; B.S., Lehigh U., 1931, M.S., 1933; Ph.D., Mass. Inst. Tech., 1936; LL.D., U. Hokkaido (Japan); m. Irene E. Andes, Dec. 14, 1940; children—Henry C., William T. Teaching fellow Lehigh U., 1931-33; teaching fellow Mass. Inst. Tech., 1933-36, research asso. radiation lab., 1942-46; research engr. Am. Thermos Co., Conn., 1936-37; asst. prof., then asso. prof. physics Mont. State Coll., 1937-41; dir. labs. St. John's Coll., Md., 1941-42; chief sci. and tech. div., spl. projects unit U.S. Army Occupation, Japan, 1945-50; head sci. sect. Office Naval Research, Chgo., 1950-51; asst. dir. NSF, 1951-62, head div. sci. personnel and edn., 1951-59, asso. dir, ednl. and internat. activities, 1959-62; dean facullty N.C. State U., Raleigh, 1962-67, provost, 1967—, vice chancellor, 1971—. Co-chmn. U.S.-Japan Com. Sci Coop., 1961-69. Recipient commendation for meritorius civilian service U.S. Occupation Forces, 1949; Order Sacred Treasure, Japan, 1969; certificate of merit State Dept., 1969. Fellow Am. Acad. Arts and Scis., A.A.A.S.; mem. Phys. Soc. Japan (hon.), Phi Beta Kappa. Club: Cosmos (Washington). Author: A Textbook in Electricity and Magnetism, 1941; also articles. Home: 613 Macon Pl Raleigh NC 27609

KELLY, HUGH JOSEPH, corporation dir.; b. N.Y.C., Apr. 5, 1905; s. Hugh and Elizabeth (Dunne) K.; grad. Columbia, 1926; m. Catherine Rice, Nov. 11, 1933; children—Hugh J., Agnes Rice (Sister Agnes), Edmund, Neill, Daniel, Christopher (dec.). Asst. to dir. Columbia U. Press, 1926-27, trustee, 1959—, treas., 1961—; with McGraw Hill, Inc., N.Y.C., 1927-70, asst. to pres., 1932-37, dir. Whittlesey House, 1937-42, became sr. v.p., dir., 1944, apptd. v.p. mfg. and service McGraw-Hill, Inc., 1953, exec. v.p. 1956-67, pres. real estate and gen. services div., 1967-70, now dir.; dir. Fed. Paper Board Co., Inc. Newton Falls Paper Co. Mem. council friends Columbia U. Library. Served to maj. AUS, 1942-45. Decorated Army Commendation medal. Mem. Phi Beta Kappa. Roman Catholic. Knight of Malta. Clubs: Columbia, Dutch Treat, University, Players (N.Y.C.); Army and Navy (Washington); Pelham (N.Y.) Country. Home: Stone Ridge NY 12484

KELLY, J. HOWARD, lawyer; b. Wingham, Ont., Can.; s. Thomas J. and Mary E. (Clifford) K.; B.A., LL.B., U. Alta.; m. Leona A. Lemieux, Sept. 14, 1933; children—Anne K. (Mrs. Hawitt), John Howard. Called to Alta. bar, 1928, created King's counsel, 1952; former mem. firm Jones, Prescod & Adams; dir. Burns Foods Ltd., Zurich Life Ins. Co. Can., P. Burns Ranches Ltd., Burns Coal Mines Ltd., Hydro Carbons Pipelines Ltd., Revelstake Bldg., Materials Ltd., Canadian Hydro Carbons Ltd. Adv. bd. Can. Permanent Trust Corp. Bd. dirs. Burns Found. Ltd., Canadian Council Retarded Children; trustee Med. and Edn. Research Found. Mem. Canadian (past dir.), Calgary (past pres.) chambers commerce. Alta. Law Soc. Clubs: Ranchmens, Calgary Golf and Country, Glencoe (Calgary). Home: 4219 Britannia Dr Calgary Alberta Canada Office: 307-330 9th Av SW Calgary Alberta Canada

KELLY, JACK, (John A. Kelly, Jr.), actor; b. Astoria, L.I., N.Y., Sept. 16, 1927; s. John A. and Ann M. (Walsh) K.; student U. Cal. at Los Angeles, 1947; m. Donna Lee Hickey, Nov. 10, 1956. Child actor, Broadway and radio, until 1938, then mem. company Circle Theatre, Los Angeles; featured role in Anna Lucasta, Los Angeles; motion pictures include Fighting Man of the Plains, 1950, Where Danger Lives, Submarine Command, Rough Company, To Hell and Back, Black Tuesday, Terror in the Night, Kings Row, Love and Kisses; radio and television appearances include Lux Radio Theatre, Suspense, Tell it Again, and also Romance of the Ranchos, Studio One, Kraft Theatre, Philco Playhouse; star television series Maverick; appeared in play Night Life, 1962. Served with USAAF, World War II. Democrat. Roman Cath. Address: care Louis Berke 120 El Camino Dr Beverly Hills CA 90212

KELLY, JAMES BARTON, engring. co. exec.; b. St. Louis, Feb. 12, 1927; s. James Christopher and Hazel Jean (Barton) K.; B.S., U.S. Merchant Marine Acad., 1949; LL.B., St. Johns U., 1954; LL.M., N.Y.U., 1957; m. Eileen Mary Redling, Oct. 16, 1949; children—James Patrick, Stephen Robert, Michael Matthew, Daniel Joseph. Engr., Combustion Engring., Inc., N.Y.C., 1949-56, asst. sec., 1956-63, sec., 1963-67, v.p., sec., 1967—; admitted to N.Y. bar, 1954, also U.S. Supreme Ct.; dir. Combustion Engring.-Superheater, Ltd., Montreal, Combustion Engring. Overseas, Inc. Windsor, Conn., Combustion Chems., N.Y.C. Recipient U.S. Merchant Marine Acad. Alumni award for outstanding profl. achievement, 1964. Mem. Am., N.Y. State bar assns., Assn. Bar City N.Y., Newcomen Soc., Engrs. Club: Canadian. Home: Kinnicutt Rd Pound Ridge NY 10576 Office: 277 Park Av New York City NY 10017

KELLY, JAMES FRANCIS, dept. store exec.; b. Mt. Vernon, N.Y., Nov. 7, 1906; s. Hugh and Elizabeth (Dunne) K.; LL.B., St. John's U., 1930; m. Ruth Wellington Dee, Oct. 19, 1935; children—Barbara (Mrs. John G. Ryden), Hampton Merrill (stepson). Admitted to N.Y. bar, 1940; with Asso. Dry Goods Corp., 1934—, sec., 1956—, also v.p. Clubs: Lambs (N.Y.C.); Pelham (N.Y.) Country. Home: The Balfour 112-20 72d Dr Forest Hills NY 11375 Office: 417 Fifth Av New York City NY 10016

KELLY, JAMES FRANCIS, univ ofcl.; b. Washington, Aug. 5, 1915; s. James Francis and Mary (Carr) K.; student bus. adminstrn. Columbus U., Washington; J.D., Cath. U. Am., 1939; D. Polit. Sci., U. Pacific, 1969; D.Sc., N.Y. Med. Coll., 1970; m. Gloria Mary Soule, Mar. 21, 1941; children—Mary Carol, Joan Frances, James Francis, Laurel Ann, David Carr, Elizabeth Soule, John Quentin. Admitted to D.C. bar; with Pub. Housing Adminstrn. and predecessor agys., 1934-54; with Dept. Health, Edn. and Welfare, 1954-70, deptl. budget officer, 1954-61, deptl. comptroller, 1961-66, asst. sec. comptroller, 1966-70; v.p. for adminstrv. affairs Georgetown U., Washington, 1970—, lectr. pub. adminstrn., 1955—. Chmn. adv. com. St. Elizabeth Parish, Rockville, Md. Served to lt. USNR, 1943-46. Recipient Superior Service award Pub. Housing Adminstrn., 1954; Superior Service award Dept. Health, Edn. and Welfare, 1958, Distinguished Service award, 1960; Career Service award Nat. Civil Service League, 1968. Mem. Fed. Govt. Accountants Assn. (Leadership award 1966), Am. Soc. Pub. Adminstrn., Am. Acad. Polit. and Soc. Sci., Am. Pub. Health Assn., Nat. Assn. Coll. and Univ. Bus. Officers, Assn. Jesuit Colls. K.C. (3). Home: 7115 Plantation Lane South Rockville MD 20852 Office: 37th and O St NW Washington DC 20007

KELLY, JAMES JOSEPH, oil co. exec.; b. El Reno, Okla., Dec. 8, 1912; s. John P. and Helen (Weber) K.; student Cameron State Jr. Coll.; B.S. in Civil Engring., Okla. State U., 1936; m. Lue Elsie Daley, Oct. 29, 1938; children—Karen Batchelor, Thomas J. State engr. Nat. Youth Adminstrn., 1936-37; v.p. Allied Materials Corp., 1937-46; pres. Kerr-McGee Chem. Corp., Oklahoma City; exec. v.p. Kerr-McGee Corp., Oklahoma City; chmn. bd. Borax & Chems., Ltd., London, Eng., G.H. Poole & Son (Bootle) Ltd., London; dir. Silobar S.A., Paris, France. Chmn. bd. dirs. St. Gregory's Coll.; bd. dirs. Okla. State U. Devel. Found. Mem. Asphalt Inst., Asphalt Refiners Assn. (dir.), Am. Petroleum Inst., Am. Soc. Mil. Engrs., Twenty-Five Year Club Petroleum Industry, Newcomen Soc. Clubs: Beacon, Petroleum, Oklahoma City Golf and Country (Oklahoma City); Chicago Oil Men's. Home: 1609 Queenstown Rd Oklahoma City OK 73116 Office: Kerr-McGee Bldg Oklahoma City OK 73102

KELLY, JAMES WOODROW, naval chaplain; b. Carthage, Ark., Dec. 24, 1913; s. Miles D. and Mary Susan (Hodges) K.; B.A., Ouachita U., Arkadelphia, Ark., 1936, D.D., 1958; Th.M., So. Bapt. Theol. Sem., 1940; student U. Chgo., 1952; m. Frances Evelyn Morton, Aug. 29, 1939; children—Judith Love (Mrs. John T. Davis, Jr.), Ruth F. (Mrs. Michael G. Brown), James Morton, Miles Dawson, Ann Marie. Commd. lt. (j.g.), Chaplain Corps, U.S. Navy, 1942, advanced through grades to rear adm., 1963; served aboard U.S.S. Mobile, 1943-44, U.S.S. Alaska, 1946; assigned Naval Air Test Center, Patuxent River, Md., 1946-48; Great Lakes Naval Tng. Center, 1950-51, U.S. Naval Acad., 1960-63; dir. chaplains div. Navy Dept., 1963-65, chief chaplains, 1965-. Pres. NATO Chaplains Conf., Copenhagen, Denmark, 1967; chmn. Armed Forces Chaplains Bd., 1968-69. Decorated Bronze Star with combat V, Purple Heart. Home: 2513 N 23d Rd Arlington VA 22207 Office: Chaplains Div Bur Naval Personnel Navy Dept Washington DC 20370

KELLY, JOHN EDWARD, retired army officer; b. Washington, July 10, 1911; s. Michael Andrew and Eleanor (Johnston) K.; B.S., U.S. Mil. Acad., 1936; M.A. in Langs., Laval (Que.) U., 1941; grad. Army War Coll., 1953; m. Jane E. Oseth, Dec. 29, 1937; children—Jane M. (Mrs. Stanley H. Quigg), Patrick O., John Edward, Richard A., Maureen E., Timothy J., Erin M. Commd. 2d lt. U.S. Army, 1936, advanced through grades to lt. gen., 1968; instr. U.S. Mil. Acad., 1941-43; comdr. inf. battalion, World War II; comdr. regt. in 40th Div., Korea, 1954, 27th Wolfhounds of 25th Inf. Div., 1958-59; established 1st mil. supply mission to India, 1962; comdg. gen. 2d Armored Div., 1965- 67; mem. staff Dept. Army, 1967-68; comdt. Nat. War Coll., 1968-70; retired; now pres. Ga. Security Systems, Inc., Atlanta. Decorated D.S.C., D.S.M., Legion of Merit with oak leaf cluster, Bronze Star with 2 oak leaf clusters, Silver Star. Mem. Assn. Army, U.S. Armor Assn., Res. Officers Assn. Kiwanian; mem. Woodmen of World. Author articles in field. Home: 15 Lake Forest Lane NE Atlanta GA 30342 Office: 1145 Peachtree St NE Atlanta GA

KELLY, JOHN MARTIN, petroleum cons.; b. Chelsea, Mass., Oct. 1, 1914; s. James B.A. and Elizabeth B.A. (Ford) K.; B.S., N.M. Sch. Mines, 1936, Petroleum Engr., 1939; D.Sc., N.M. Inst. Mining and Tech., 1963; m. Esther E. Ladenburg, Dec. 29, 1938; children—Joseph J., Patricia E., Mary Ann, J. Michael. Mining engr. Rosedale Gold Mines, 1936; mine chemist Am. Metal Co., 1936-37; petroleum engr. Lea County Operators Com., 1937-41; state geologist N.M., 1941-45; exec. sec. mem., dir. N.M. Oil Conservation Commn., dir. N.M. Bur. Mines and Mineral Resources, coordinator mines in N.M. for WPB, 1941-45; cons. mining, petroleum engr., geologist, mineral adviser N.M. State Land Commr., 1945-61; pres. Elk Oil Co., 1945-61; dir. Yucca Water Co.; asst. sec. for mineral resources Dept. Interior, Washington, 1961-65; petroleum cons., Washington, 1965—. Mem. N.M. Bd. Ednl. Finances; adv. bd. Small Bus. Adminstrn. Decorated knight St. Gregory, knight Holy Sepulchre; Distinguished Service Honor award Dept. Interior, 1966. Registered profl. engr., N.M. Mem. Am. Inst. Mining Engrs., Am. Assn. Petroleum Geologists, Am. Assn. Petroleum Landmen, Am. Inst. Profl. Engrs., Am. Petroleum Inst., Ind. Petroleum Assn. Am., Mining Club N.Y.C., N.M. Oil and Gas Assn. (dir.), N.M. Mining Assn., N.M. Landmens Assn., N.M., Roswell geol. socs., Rocky Mountain Coal Mining Inst., A.A.A.S., Geol. Soc. Am., Mining and Metall. Soc. Am. Home: Box 310 Roswell NM 88201 Office: 1001 Connecticut Av Washington DC 20036

KELLY, JOHN PATRICK, educator; b. Sigourney, Ia., Sept. 30, 1924; s. John Walter and Vena (Wraight) K.; B.A., U. Ia., 1948, M.A., 1953, Ph.D., 1959; B.Mortuary Sci., Coll. Mortuary Sci., St. Louis, 1950; m. Jean Ann Donohue, June 14, 1947 (dec. 1971); children—Michael, Camilla, Carol. Mem. faculty U. Nev., Reno, 1955- -, prof. elementary edn., 1968—. Served with USNR, 1943-46. William H. Carpenter fellow, 1950; Kellogg Found. fellow, 1965. Mem. Nat. Council Tchrs. English, Internat., Sierra Chpt., Western Region Coll. reading assns., Phi Delta Kappa, Phi Delta Theta. Elk, K.C. Co-editor: Basic Reading. Contbr. articles profl. jours. Home: 790 Brookfield Dr Reno NV 89503

KELLY, JOHN PATRICK, newspaper editor; b. Winston-Salem, N.C., July 16, 1927; s. John Patrick and Emma Gray (Hunter) K.; A.B., U. N.C., 1947; postgrad. (Nieman fellow) Harvard, 1958-59; m. Jane Watson, Aug. 29, 1953; children—Jane Megan, John Patrick, Ann Perrin, Kathleen Hayes. Reporter, Winston-Salem Jour., 1947-49, copy desk editor, 1949-51, telegraph editor, 1951-54; Sunday editor Winston-Salem Jour. and Sentinel, 1954- 55, exec. editor, 1964—; mng. editor Raleigh (N.C.) Times, 1955-57; telegraph editor Atlanta Jour., 1957-59, mng. editor, 1960-64; Sunday editor Atlanta Jour. and Constn., 1959-60. Chmn. adv. com., courses for practicing newsmen U. N.C. Pres. Piedmont Sigma Delta Chi. Found. Mem. Sigma Delta Chi. Office: Piedmont Pub Co Winston-Salem NC 27102

KELLY, JOHN SAMUEL, physicist; b. Louisville, Jan. 24, 1922; s. James and Mary Elizabeth (Turner) K.; B.Sc., Western Ky. State Coll., 1946; postgrad. Ohio State U., 1947-48; m. Juanita Lewis, Dec. 24, 1945; children—John Lawrence, Mary Kathryn, Nancy Linda, Barbara, Carolyn. Research asst. instrumentation Allegany ballistics lab. Hercules Powder Co., 1946-47; project engr. infrared detection systems Navy Dept., 1948-54, supervisory engr. radiation monitoring systems for nuclear powered submarines, 1954-56; physicist AEC, 1956-, dir. div. peaceful nuclear explosives, 1961—. Served with AUS, 1942-43. Methodist. Home: 15 Orchard Way N Rockville MD 20854 Office: AEC Washington DC 20525

KELLY, JOSEPH LUTHER, Jr., lawyer; b. Bristol, Va., Aug. 27, 1912; s. Joseph Luther and Mary (Hull) K.; student King Coll., Bristol, 1928-30; B.A., U. Va., 1932, LL.B., 1935; m. Belle Faucette, May 8, 1954; children—Joseph Luther III, Mary Nash, Kathleen Hull. Admitted to Va. bar, 1935; spl. asst. to atty. gen. Va., 1935-38; asst. atty gen. Va., 1938-42; partner firm Williams, Worrell, Kelly & Worthington, and predecessors, Norfolk, 1948—. To lt. (j.g.) USCGR, 1942-46. Mem. Am., Va., Norfolk and Portsmouth (pres. 1962- 63) bar assns., Am. Law Inst. Home: 936 Graydon Av Norfolk VA 23507 Office: 234 Monticelli Av Norfolk VA 23510

KELLY, KEVIN, author; b. Boston, Aug. 5, 1934; s. St. Clair and Joan (Sinnott) K.; A.A. (New England Scholastic Press Assn. scholar), Boston U., 1950, B.A., 1952, M.A., 1953. Mem. staff Boston Globe, 1958—, drama critic, 1962—, critic-at-large, 1966—, film critic, 1969—; local theatre critic for Show Bus. Illus., 1960-62; speaker in field. Bd. overseers Brandeis U. Recipient Boston Globe award, 1946, 47. Contbr. to mags. Home: 39 Mount Hope Norwell MA 02061 Office: 135 Morrissey Blvd Boston MA 02107

KELLY, LAWRENCE VINCENT, opera producer; b. Chgo., May 30, 1928; s. Patrick James and Thelma (Seabott) K.; student Chgo. Music Coll., 1942-45, Georgetown U., 1950, DePaul U. Law Sch., 1950-51. Office mgr. Kelly Bros. Realty Inc., Chgo., 1950, sec.-treas., 1951—, also dir.; v.p. Dearborn Supply Co., 1951-52, also dir.; ins. broker, 1953—. Co-founder Lyric Theatre of Chgo., 1953, sec.-treas., 1953-56, mng. dir., 1954-56; founder Dallas Civic Opera, 1957, gen. mgr., 1957—; co-founder, producer Performing Arts Found. of Kansas City, 1965—. Republican. Roman Catholic. Home: 3327 Douglas Dallas TX Office: Reliance Life Bldg Dallas TX 75201

KELLY, LEON, artist; b. Perpignan Pyrenees-Orientale, France, Oct. 1, 1901; ed. Phila. Mus. Sch., Pa. Acad. Fine Arts. Exhibited in one-man shows at Gallery of Contemporary Art, Phila., 1925, 32, Galerie du Printemps, Paris, France, 1926, Contemporary Arts Gallery, N.Y.C., 1933, Julien Levy Galleries, N.Y.C., 1942, 44, 45, Hugo Gallery, N.Y.C., 1950, Hewitt Gallery, N.Y.C., 1956, Alexander Iolas Gallery, 1959, 61, Phila. Art Alliance, 1943, Zabriskie Gallery, 1963, Galleria Amici di Francia, Milan. Italy, 1954; exhibited in group shows European Internat., 1927, A Century of Progress, Chgo., 1933-34, U. Neb., others; represented in permanent collections in U.S., William and Noma Copley Found. grantee, 1959, France, Tel Aviv Mus. Israel, other countries. Cresson fellow, Pa. Acad. Fine Arts, 1924. Address: care Richard Feigen Gallery 226 E Ontario St Chicago IL 60611

KELLY, LEROY, profl. football player; b. Phila., May 20, 1942; s. Orvin and Argie (Watson) K.; student Morgan State Coll., 1960-64. Offensive halfback Cleve. Browns, 1964—. Served with AUS. Named All-Pro halfback, 1966-69. Home: 13855 Superior Av Cleveland OH 44118 Office: Cleveland Stadium Cleveland OH

KELLY, LUTHER WRENTMORE, Jr., physician; b. Charlotte, N.C., June 9, 1925; s. Luther Wrentmore and Charlotte (Abbott) K.; student U. N.C., 1942-44, certificate of medicine, Sch. Medicine, 1946; M.D., Harvard, 1948; research fellow Western Res. U. Sch. Medicine, 1954; m. Susan F. Bowman, Dec. 1, 1956; children—Abbott Bowman, Mary Luther. Intern, then resident medicine Univ. Hosps, Cleve., 1948-53; staff physician Nalle Clinic, Charlotte, N.C., 1955—; chmn. dept. medicine Charlotte Meml. Hosp., 1964-68; clin. asst. prof. medicine U. N.C. School Medicine, 1966-69, clin. asso. prof., 1969—. Mem. adv. com. aging Family Service Assn. Am., 1961—. Bd. dirs. Family and Childrens Service Mecklenburg County, 1955—, pres., 1958-61; bd. dirs. N.C. Council Human Relations, 1955—. Pres. Community Health Assn. Charlotte; project dir. diabetes cons. and edn. service N.C. Regional Med. Program. Served with USNR, 1950-52. Fellow A.C.P.; mem. Endocrine Soc., Am., N.C. (pres. 1968-69) diabetes assns., Am., Charlotte (past pres.) socs. internal medicine. Author articles thyroid and adrenal gland function. Home: 2510 Forest Dr Charlotte NC 28211 Office: 1350 S Kings Dr Charlotte NC 28201

KELLY, NANCY, actress; b. Lowell, Mass., Mar 25, 1921; student Immaculate Conception Acad., L.I., N.Y., St. Lawrence Acad., N.Y., Bentley Sch., N.Y.; m. Warren Caro, 1955; 1 dau., Kelly Lurie. Child actress; appeared stage prodn. Susan and God, N.Y.C., 1937, The Big Knife, N.Y.C., 1949, Season in the Sun, 1950-51, Bad Seed (also appeared in movie version), 1954-55 , Giants Sons of Giants, 1962, Who's Afraid of Virginia Woolfe?, 1963, Sons of Giants, 1962, Box-Quotations from Mao Tse-Tung-Box, 1968; appearances in motion pictures include Jesse James, Stanley and Livingston, Show Business, Murder in the Music Hall, Crowded Paradise, The Genius and The Goddess, The Rivalry, Torando, Women in Bondage, Gamblers Choice, Double Exposure, Song of the Sarong, Woman Who Came Back. Recipient Antoinette Perry award, 1955; Sarah Siddons award, 1956, 63-64; Laurel award, 1956-57. Home: 40 Central Park S New York City NY 10019

KELLY, PATRICK, educator; b. Denver, June 8, 1936; s. Jack M. and Nellie Jo (Hitt) K.; B.A., Emory U., 1958, M.A., 1962, Ph.D., 1966; postgrad. Stanford, 1966-67; m. A. Jean Wade, June 9, 1956; children—D. Kathleen, Todd P., Leigh Ann. Mem. faculty Ga. Inst. Tech., Atlanta, 1959—, head dept. social scis., 1969—. Mem. Ga. Philos. Soc., So. Soc. for Philosophy and Religion, Am. Soc. Engring. Edn., Omega Delta Kappa. Home: 1293 Vista Leaf Dr Decatur GA 30333 Office: 225 North Av Atlanta GA 30332

KELLY, PATRICK DALE, univ. dean; b. Buckingham, Ia., Jan. 1, 1924; s. Raymond W. and Mabel (McKenna) K.; B.A., U. No. Ia., 1947; student Purdue U., 1943-44, J.D., Drake U., 1953; m. Mary Catherine Heath, Apr. 26, 1945; children—Daniel D., Kevin P., Kathleen M. (dec.). Secondary sch. tchr., Doon, Ia., 1947- 48; gen. ins. agt., Ida Grove, Ia., 1948-51; admitted to Ia. bar, 1953, Mo. bar, 1962; asso., then partner Steward, Crouch & Kelly, Des Moines, 1953-61; prof. law U. Mo., Kansas City, 1961-66, dean Sch. Law, 1966—; lectr. appellate practice Drake U. Law Sch., 1959-61. Pres., Am. Law Student Assn., 1952-53, jr. bar sect. Ia. Bar Assn., 1959-60. Served with USNR, 1942-46. Mem. Am. Judicature Soc., Am., Mo., Kansas City (Ann. Achievement award 1967) bar assns., Lawyers Assn. Kansas City, Delta Theta Phi. Author: Case Investigation and Preparation, vol. 1, Automobile Law and Practice, 3d edit., 1965; Evidence, Blashfield, vol. 11 and 12, 1968; co-author, editor Medical-Legal Preparation, vol. 9, 1967. Home: 631 W 66th Terrace Kansas City MO 64113

KELLY, PATRICK MICHAEL, sculptor: b. Steubenville, O., May 4, 1939; s. Joseph George and Zelma (Cline) K.; B.F.A., Ohio U., 1964, M.F.A., 1966; m. JoHanna Holligan, June 9, 1962; children—Karen Jeanne, Mary Margaret. Grad. asst. Ohio U., 1964-66; asst. prof. art Northland Coll., Ashland, Wis., 1966-68, chmn. dept. art, 1967-68; asso. prof., chmn. sculpture dept. N.S. Coll. Art, Halifax, 1968—. One-man exhbns. include Flair House Gallery, Cin., 1965, Ohio No. U., 1965; exhbt. 160th annual exhbn. Am. painting and sculpture Pa. Acad. Fine Arts, 1964. Recipient purchase award Ford Found., 1964; Can. Council grantee, 1970. Home: 599 Stanhope St Halifax Nova Scotia Canada

KELLY, PAUL L., corp. exec.; b. Salem, Mass., May 7, 1939; s. Lawrence J. and Edith (Rioux) K.; student Phillips Acad., 1956-58; B.A., Yale U., 1962, LL.B., 1965; m. Grace Anita Doyle, Dec. 24, 1966; 1 son, Paul Lance. Admitted to Tex. bar, 1965; atty. firm Fulbright, Crooker, Freeman, Bates & Jaworski, Houston, 1965-67; asst. sec. Anderson, Clayton & Co., Houston, 1967-69; sec. Zapata Norness Inc., Houston, 1969, v.p. adminstrn., sec., 1970—. Mem. Am., Inter-Am. bar assns., Am. Soc. Internat. Law, State Bar of Tex., Am. Soc. Corp. Secs. Home: 6122 San Felipe Rd Houston TX 77027 Office: Southwest Tower 910 Milam Houston TX 77002

KELLY, RICHARD SMITH, mfg. co. exec.; b. Chgo., Jan. 18, 1925; s. Frank Brazzil and Adelaide (Smith) K.; B.A., U. Mich., 1948; J.D., Northwestern U., 1951; m. Nancy G. Kelly, Aug. 26, 1950; children—Richard Smith, Mark F., David G., Peter M., Anne M., John T., Paul T. Admitted to Ill. bar, 1951; partner firm Springer, Bergstrom & Crowe, Chgo., 1951-55; with firm McDermott, Will & Emery, Chgo., 1955-60; atty. Container Corp. Am., Chgo., 1960-67, asst. gen. counsel, 1967-69, gen. counsel, 1969-71, v.p., gen. counsel, 1971—; sec., asst. gen. counsel Marcor Inc., Chgo., 1968-71, sec., gen. counsel, 1971—. Served with AUS, 1943-46. Mem. Am., Ill., Chgo. bar Assns. Clubs: Law, University, Michigan Shores (Chgo.). Home: 423 Laurel Av Wilmette IL 60091 Office: 1 First Nat Plaza Chicago IL 60670 also 619 W Chicago Av Chicago IL 60607

KELLY, ROBERT GORRELL, lawyer; b. Sutton, W.Va., Apr. 30, 1898; s. Lon Hamman and Bertha (Gorrell) K.; student Washington and Lee U., 1917-18; LL.B., W.Va. U., 1923; m. Irma King, Oct. 30, 1926; children—Robert K., Carol (Mrs. S.W. Pickering III, dec.), Sally (Mrs. W.T. Slicer, Jr.). Agt., FBI, 1919-20; admitted to W.Va. bar, 1923, since practiced in Charleston; partner firm Mohler, Peters & Kelly, 1926-30, Jackson, Kelly, Holt & O'Farrell, 1931- -; atty. Kanawha County, 1931-32. Former chmn. bd. W.Va. Water Co.; dir. Carbon Fuel Co., Ky-Carbon Corp., Vann Industries, Inc., Kanawha Valley Bank. Mem. W.Va. Conservation Com., 1935-40; chmn. W.Va. Aeros. Com., 1947-52; Co-founder Nat. History Mus. Chmn., W. Va. Democratic Exec. Com., 1932-36. Served with U.S. Army, 1918-19, USAAF, 1942-43. Mem. Am., Inter-Am., Internat., W.Va., Kanawha County bar assns., U.S. (past dir.), W.Va. (past pres.) chambers commerce, Sigma Chi, Phi Delta Phi, Presbyn. Rotarian. Clubs: N.Y. Athletic, Explorers (N.Y.C.); Army and Navy (Washington). Author: Trails, Trouts and Tigers, 1961. Contbr. articles profl. jours. Home: 1879 Louden Heights Rd Charleston WV 25314 Office: PO Box 553 Charleston WV 25322

KELLY, ROGER MICHAEL, pub. accountant; b. Balt., Nov. 4, 1910; s. Patrick J. and Margaret E. (Hughes) K.; grad. Calvert Hall, 1928; student U. N.C., 1933; m. Dorothy Morrell, Oct. 13, 1943; children—Patricia Ann, Michael Clark. With Stewart, Watts & Bollong, C.P.A.'s N.Y.C., 1945-55, partner, 1947-55; exec. v.p. Phila & Reading Corp., 1956-70, also dir.; chmn. finance com., dir. Northwest Industries, Inc. Clubs: Chesapeake Bay Yacht, Talbot Country; N.Y. Athletic, Union League (N.Y.C.). Home: Brightwaters Farm Oxford NY 13830 Office: 400 Park Av New York City NY 10022

KELLY, SIDNEY, automobile co. exec.; b. N.Y.C., Jan. 26, 1922; s. Sidney and Helen (Young) K.; B.A.,Columbia, 1943, LL.B., 1948; postgrad. N.Y.U., 1943-44; m. Marion Cecil Steele, July 1, 1950; children-Sidney Johnston, Ann Cecil. Admitted to N.Y. bar, 1949, W.Va. bar, 1959, Mich. bar, 1969; with Office of Counsel to Gov. N.Y. State, 1951-55; asst. atty. gen. N.Y. State Dept. Law, 1955-57; adminstrv. asst. to Senator J.K. Javits, U.S. Senate, 1957-58; asst. sec., asst. gen. counsel Wheeling Steel Corp., 1958-67; corporate cousel, sec. Ford Motor Co., Dearborn, Mich., 1967—. Served with USAAF, 1943-46. Mem. Am. Bar Assn., Am. Soc. Corporate Secs. Home: 1199 Buckingham Rd Birmingham MI 48008 Office: The American Rd Dearborn MI 48121

KELLY, STEPHEN JOHN, educator, ophthalmologist; b. Milbank, S.D., Apr. 4, 1925; s. Stephen John and Gretchen (Roggenbuck) K.; A.B., Stanford, 1946, M.D., 1950; m. Patricia L. White, Mar. 27, 1946; children—Pamela, Christopher. Intern St. Francis Hosp., Wichita, 1949-50; resident Washington U. Hosp., St. Louis, then U. Ala. Med. Centers 1950-54; mem. faculty Med. Coll. Ala., 1953—, asso. prof., co-chmn. dept. ophthalmology, 1956—. Served with USNR, 1943-46, with USAF, 1950-53. Diplomate Am. Bd. Ophthalmology. Home: 3636 Rock Hill Rd Birmingham AL 35223

KELLY, THOMAS LAUGHLIN, dept. store constrn. exec.; b. N.Y.C., July 21, 1918; s. Joseph and Mary Ann (McQueeney) K.; B.C.E., N.Y. U., 1941, M.C.E., 1951; m. Agnes Bryan McGreevy, Oct. 15, 1948; children—Kieran Michael, Thomas Laughlin, Jaime Kathleen, Sean Owen. Structural engr. for cons. firms, N.Y.C., 1940-43; with Gen. Electric Co., 1948-60, constrn. mgr., 1956-60; chief engr. Montgomery Ward & Co., 1961-62; v.p. engring. and constrn. R.H. Macy & Co., Inc., N.Y.C., 1962-67, sr. v.p., 1967—. Served with USNR, 1943-46. Registered profl. engr., N.Y. Mem. Navy League, Am. Arbitration Assn., Tau Beta Pi. Home: 9 Robinhood Rd Summit NJ 07901 Office: 151 W 34th St New York City NY 10001

KELLY, THOMAS PAINE, Jr., lawyer; b. Tampa, Fla., Aug. 29, 1912; s. Thomas Paine and Beatrice (Gent) K.; A.B., U. Fla., 1935, J.D., 1936; m. Jean Baughman, July 25, 1940; children—Carla (Mrs. Henry Dee), Thomas Paine III, Margaret Jo. Admitted to Fla. bar, 1936, since practiced in Tampa; jr. partner McKay, Macfarlane, Jackson & Ferguson, 1939-48; partner Macfarlane, Ferguson, Allison & Kelly, 1948—. Chmn. Tampa Com. 100, 1960-61; pres. Tampa Citizens' Safety Council, 1961-62. Bd. dirs. Tampa chpt. A.R.C., 1955-62, pres., 1958- 59; bd. dirs. Boys Clubs Tampa, 1956-67, pres., 1966-67. Served to col. F.A., AUS, 1940-45. Decorated Silver Star. Fellow Am. Coll. Trial Lawyers, Internat. Acad. Trial Lawyers; mem. Am. Bar Assn., Bar Assn. Tampa and Hillsborough County, Fla. Bar (chmn. com. profl. ethics 1953-58, chmn. com. ins. and negligence law 1962- 63, chmn. fed. rules com. 1969-70). Democrat. Episcopalian. Home: 5426 Lykes Lane Tampa FL 33611 Office: 512 Florida Av Tampa FL 33601

KELLY, WALT, cartoonist; b. Phila., Aug. 25, 1913; s. Walter Crawford and Genevieve (MacAnnulla) K.; student pub. schs., Bridgeport, Conn. Newspaper work, Bridgeport, 1928-35; animator Walt Disney Studio, 1935-41; comml. artist N.Y.C., 1941-48; polit. cartoonist N.Y. Star, 1948-49; author Pogo comic strip, also Pogo books; East of Berlin and Short of the Moon, 1961.

KELLY, WILLIAM C., lawyer; b. Mpls., 1918; B.S., U. Minn., 1940, LL.B., 1942. Admitted to Minn. bar, 1942, D.C. bar 1966. Mem. firm O'Connor, Green, Thomas, Walters & Kelly, Mpls. Mem. Hennepin County, Minn., Am. bar assns., Gamma Eta Gamma. Office: 845 Northwestern Bank Bldg Minneapolis MN*

KELLY, WILLIAM CLARK, sci. adminstr.; b. Braddock, Pa., Mar. 18, 1922; s. Clark William and Alma (Wilhelm) K.; B.S., U. Pitts., 1943, M.S., 1946, Ph.D., 1951; m. Gertrude Clark Blackwood, Sept. 8, 1947; children—Emily Clark, William Blackwood. From asst. physics to asso. prof. U. Pitts., 1943-58; Ford faculty fellow, 1954-55; dir. dept. edn. and manpower Am. Inst. Physics, 1958-65; dir. fellowships NRC, Washington, 1965-67, dir. Office Sci. Personnel, 1967- -. Sec. Internat. Commn. Physics Edn., Internat. Union Pure and Applied Physics, 1966—. Fellow A.A.A.S.; mem. Am. Assn. Physics Tchrs. (Distinguished Service citation 1959), Am. Phys. Soc., Sigma Xi. Club: Cosmos (Washington). Author: (with others) General Physics, 3d edit., 1963; (with others) High School Physics, rev. edit., 1958; (with T.D. Miner) Physics for High School, 1967. Home: 9320 Renshaw Dr Bethesda MD 20034 Office: 2101 Constitution Av Washington DC 20418

KELLY, WILLIAM HAROLD, educator; b. Rich Hill, Mo., July 2, 1926; s. George Samuel and Ola (Ayers) K.; A.A., Graceland Coll., 1948; B.S., U. Mich., 1950, M.S., 1951, Ph.D., 1955; m. Altabelle Dougherty, Sept. 1, 1950; children—Douglas Scott, Linda Sue, Brian Patrick. Eastman Kodak predoctoral fellow in physics U. Mich., 1954-55; asst. prof. physics and astronomy Mich. State U., 1955-61; physicist U.S. Naval Research Lab., Washington, 1956; physicist Lawrence Radiation Lab., Berkeley, Cal., 1961-62; asso. prof. physics Mich. State U., 1961-67, prof., 1967—, asso. chmn. undergrad. programs, 1968—; summer research participant Oak Ridge (Tenn.) Nat. Lab., 1964; physicist Lawrence Radiation Lab., Berkeley, Cal., 1967-68. Served with USNR, 1944-46. Fellow Am. Phys. Soc.; mem. Am. Assn. Physics Teaches, Tau Beta Pi, Sigma Xi, Phi Kappa Phi. Mem. Reorgn. Ch. Jesus Christ of Latter-day Saints (high priest 1971—, elder 1956—). Research, articles nuclear structure physics. Home: 2184 Belding Ct Okemos MI 48864 Office: Physics Dept Mich State U East Lansing MI 48823

KELLY, WILLIAM HENDERSON, educator; b. Bisbee, Ariz., Nov. 23, 1902; s. William Beatty and Ruth (Guernsey) K.; B.A., U. Ariz., 1936; M.A., Harvard, 1941, Ph.D., 1944; m. Frances A. Buntin, May 25, 1963; 1 stepson, Donald. Editor, pub. Tombstone (Ariz.) Epitaph, 1925-30; advt. mgr. Ariz. Daily Star, Tucson, 1930-34; teaching fellow, instr., Harvard, 1940-46; asst. prof. anthropology U. Minn., asso. prof. anthropology McGill U., 1947-52; prof. anthropology, dir. bur. ethnic research U. Ariz., 1952—. U.S. rep. to bd. govs. Inter-Am. Indian Inst., 1961-68. Fellow Am. Anthrop Assn., Soc. Applied Anthropology (exec. com.), Am. Sociol. Assn.; mem. Sigma Xi. Author: Indians of the Southwest, 1952; also numerous reports, articles in sci. jours. Home: 5837 E Hawthorne St Tucson AZ 85711

KELLY, WILLIAM ROBERT, lawyer; b. Mound City, Mo., Feb. 22, 1883; s. David and Christian (Kennish) K., B.A., U. Colo., 1905, LL. B., 1907; m. Caroline Ettella Smith, June 29, 1911; 1 son, David Potter. Admitted to Colo. bar, 1908; practiced at Ft. Collins, 1908, Greeley 1908—; referee in water adjudication, Dists. 1 and 2, under Denver and Weld county courts, 1911- 25; city atty., Greeley, 1916-21, county atty., Weld County, 1921-28; spl. counsel U.S. Supreme Ct. Wyo. vs. Colo., Neb. vs. Colo., 1930-38; atty. No. Colo. Water Conservancy Dist., 1935-56; partner Kelly & Snyder, 1941-48, Kelly and Clayton, 1949-56. Mem. Greeley Pub. Library Bd., 1912-38; chmn. bar com. Supreme Ct., Bd., of Law Examiners, 1920-37. Mem. 2d O.T.C., Aug. 1918; chmn. bd. Instrn. Registered Men, 1918; mem. Local Draft Bd. No. 14, 1940-41. Pres. Greeley C. of C., 1916; mem. Weld County Hosp. Bd., 1944- 54; dir. Colo. Bar. Assn. Found., 1941-70. Recipient award 4 States Irrigation Council, 1967. Fellow Am. Bar Found., Newcomen Soc.; mem. Am., Colo. (pres. 1940), Weld County bar assns., Order of Coif, Phi Delta Phi, Alpha Tau Omega. Episcopalian (vestryman 29 yrs.). Republican. Clubs: Greeley Rotary (pres. 1932), Westerners. Author: Navigation and Irrigation in the Mountain States, 1945; also articles in revs. and jours. Home: Route 2 Box 369 Greeley CO 80631 Office: 1st Nat Bank Bldg Greeley CO 80631

KELLY, WILLIAM TOLSON, Jr., former mfg. exec.; b. Mobile, June 5, 1907; s. William Tolson and Helen Rhodes (Prince) K.; grad. Phillips Acad., 1924; B.S., Yale, 1928; m. Mary Kelly Vizard, Sept. 17, 1929; children—William Tolson III, J. Douglas, Eugene V. With Am. Brake Shoe Co. (name changed to Abex Corp.), 1928-70, asst. to gen. purchasing agt., 1933-40, gen. purchasing agt., 1940-44, exec. v.p. Kellog div., 1944-45, pres. div., 1945-58, pres. engineered castings div., 1946-48, exec. v.p. Am. Brakeblok div., 1947-50, pres., 1950-53, pres. Sintermet div., 1954-55, v.p. corp., N.Y.C., 1946-64, 1st v.p., 1964-66, dir., 1955-70, pres., chief operating officer, 1966-69, chmn., chief exec. officer, 1969-70; vice chmn. Ill. Central Industries, 1969-70. Chmn. industry adv. com. Iron and steel Scrap Industry, OPA; mem. adv. coms. Ferrous Foundry and Iron and Steel Scrap, WPB, World War II. Mem. Am. Iron and Steel Inst., Berzelius Soc., Torch Honor Soc. Episcopalian. Club: Wee Burn Country (Darien, Conn.); Royal Poinciana (Naples). Home: 2601 Gulf Shore Blvd N Naples FL

KELLY, WILLIAM WATKINS, coll. pres.; b. Asheville, N.C., Sept. 21, 1928; s. John Jackson and Trula (Watkins) K.; B.A., Va. Mil. Inst., 1950; A.M., Duke U., 1955, Ph.D., 1957; m. Lura Jane Kelly, Feb. 14, 1953; children—William Watkins, Robert Jackson, Blair Massey, Gregory Clark. Commandant cadets, tchr. English John Marshall High Sch., Richmond, Va., 1950-52; instr. English Va. Mil. Inst., 1952-53; instr. English Air Force Acad., 1957-58, asst. prof., 1958-60; asst. prof. English Va. Mil. Inst., 1960-62; asst. prof. Am. thought and language Mich. State U., 1962-65, asso. prof., 1965-69, asso. dir. The Honors Coll., 1965-68, dir. 1968-69; pres. Mary Baldwin Coll., 1969—. Mem. adv. bd. First & Merchants Nat. Bank. Served with USAF, 1957-60. Danforth fellow, 1953-57, Duke scholar, 1954-55, Ellis L. Phillips Found. intern Rutgers U., 1964-65. Mem. Modern Language Assn., Am. Assn. U. Profs., Am. Studies Assn., Soc. Religion in Higher Edn., Am. Assn. Higher Edn., Nat. Collegiate

Honors Council, Staunton C. of C. (dir. 1970), Phi Beta Kappa, Omicron Delta Kappa. Rotarian. Author: Ellen Glasow: A Bibliography, 1964. Home: 46 Ridgeview Rd Staunton VA 24401

KELLY, WYNTON CHARLES, pianist; b. Bklyn., Dec. 2, 1931; s. Milton and Ethel (Miller) K.; student High Sch. Music and Art, 1946-47. Played with Hot Lips Paige, 1948, Eddie Lockjaw Davis, 1949-50, Dinah Washington (also Dizzy Gillespie), 1950-58, Miles Davis, 1958-63, Wynton Kelly Trio, 1963-; organist St. Simons Ch., Bklyn, 1946-49. Served with AUS, 1952-54. Recipient plaque Playboy mag. 1960. Episcopalian. Composer: Little Tracy, 1967. Home: 586 Lincoln Pl Brooklyn NY 11238 Office: care Shaw Artists 565 Fifth Av New York City NY 10017

KELLY, J. M., banker. Sr. v.p., sr. trust officer First Nat. Bank Tampa. Office: 414-16 Franklin St Tampa FL 33601*

KELM, ERWIN EDWARD, mfr. agrl. products; b. Grand Rapids, Minn, Nov. 4, 1911; s. Edward Louis and Adele (Hachez) K.; B.B.A., U. Minn., 1933; m. Joyce M. Bangson, June 15, 1935; children—David E., Susan J. With Cargill, Inc., Mpls., 1933—, v.p., 1946-57, exec. v.p., 1957-60, pres., 1960-68, chmn. bd. 1968—, also dir.; dir. Kansas City So. Industries, First Nat. Bank Mpls. Conglist. Clubs: Minneapolis, Minikadha (Mpls.); Hazetine Nat. Golf. Home: 4601 Townes Rd Minneapolis MN 55424 Office: Cargill Bldg Minneapolis MN 55402

KELMAN, ARTHUR, educator, plant pathologist; b. Providence, Dec. 11, 1918; s. Philip and Minnie (Kollin) K.; B.S., U. R.I., 1941; M.S., N.C. State U., 1946; Ph.D., 1949; postgrad. U. Wis., 1947-48; m. Helen Moore Parker, June 22, 1949; 1 son, Philip Joseph. Faculty, N.C. State U., Raleigh, 1948-65, prof., 1957-65, W.N. Reynolds distinguished prof. plant pathology, 1961-65; chmn. dept. plant pathology U. Wis., Madison, 1965—. Vis. investigator Rockefeller Inst., 1953-54; cons. United Fruit Co., 1958-64; vis. lectr. Am. Inst. Biol. Sci., 1961-62. Served with AUS, 1942-45. NSF sr. postdoctoral fellow, 1971-72. Fellow Am. Phytopath. Soc. (chmn. sourcebook com., councilor-at-large, v.p. 1965-66, pres. 1966-67); mem. Internat. Soc. Plant Pathology (v.p. 1968—), Am. Soc. Foresters, Soc. Gen. Microbiology, Am. Soc. Microbiology, Am. Inst. Biol. Sci., Sigma Xi, Alpha Zeta, Gamma Sigma Delta, Phi Kappa Phi, Phi Sigma, Xi Sigma Pi. Author: The Bacterial Wilt Caused by Pseudomonas solanacearum, 1953; (with A. Husain) Tissue is Disintegrated in Plant Pathology, 1959; (with I. Buddenhagen) Biological and Physiological Aspects of Bacterial Wilt, 1964. Asso. editor Phytopathology, 1953-56; editor: Am. Phytopath. Soc. Sourcebook Lab. Exercises in Plant Pathology, 1967. Home: 234 Carillon Dr Madison WI 53705

KELMAN, HERBERT CHANOCH, educator; b. Vienna, Austria, Mar. 18, 1927; s. Leo and Lea (Pomeranz) K.; came to U.S., 1940, naturalized, 1950; B.A., Bklyn. Coll., 1947; B.H.L., Sem. Coll. Jewish Studies, N.Y.C., 1947; M.S., Yale, 1949, Ph.D., 1951, A.M. (hon.), Harvard, 1969; m. Rose Brousman, Aug. 23, 1953. Research asst. Yale, 1947- 51; research fellow Johns Hopkins, 1951-54; fellow Center Advanced Study Behavioral Scis., 1954-55, 67; research psychologist Nat. Inst. Mental Health, 1955-57; lectr. social psychology Harvard, 1957-62; fellow Inst. Social Research, Oslo, Norway, 1960-61; prof. psychology U. Mich., 1962- 69, chmn. doctoral program social psychology, 1966-67, research psychologist Center for Research on Conflict Resolution, 1962-69; Richard Clarke Cabot prof. social ethics Harvard, 1968—. Chmn. internat. conf. social-psychol. research in developing countries U. Ibadan (Nigeria), 1966. Mem. adv. com. govt. programs behavioral sci. NRC-Nat. Acad. Sci., 1966-69; nat. field rep. Congress Racial Equality, 1954-60; nat. adv. council War Resisters League, 1952—; bd. sponsors Nat. Com. for Sane Nuclear Policy, 1966—; mem. psychology tng. rev. com. Nat. Inst. Mental Health, 1969—. Recipient Socio-Psychol. prize A.A.A.S., 1956. Western Behavioral Scis. Inst. fellow, 1964. Fellow Soc. Psychol. Study Social Issues (pres. 1964- 65), Am. Psychol. Assn. (com. on sci. and profl. ethics and conduct 1968—, council 1968—, pres. div. on personality and social psychology 1970-71), Am. Sociol. Assn.; mem. Soc. Exptl. Social Psychology, Internat. Studies Assn., Internat. Peace Research Assn., Interam. Soc. Psychology, Inst. Soc. Ethics and Life Scis. (dir.), Internat. Soc. Applied Psychology, Peace Research Soc. Author: A Time to Speak—on Human Values and Social Research, 1968; co-author Cross-National Encounters, 1970. Editor, co-author: International Behavior—A Social-Psychological Analysis, 1965. Contbr. articles to profl. jours. Home: 984 Memorial Dr Cambridge MA 02138

KELMAN, WOLFE, rabbi; b. Vienna, Austria, Nov. 27, 1923; s. Hersh Leib and Mirl (Fish) K.; B.A., U. Toronto, 1946; M.H.L., Jewish Theol. Sem. Am., 1950; m. Jacqueline Levy, Mar. 2, 1952; children—Levi Yehuda, Naama Kathrine, Abigail, Tobie. Came to U.S., 1946, naturalized, 1962. Rabbi various congregations; vis. rabbi West London Congregation Brit. Jews, London, Eng., 1957-58; exec. v.p. Rabbinical Assembly, 1951—, rep. to U.S. com for UN, 1951—; dir. joint placement commn. Rabbinical Assembly, United Synagogue Am. and Jewish Theol. Sem. Am., 1951-66; vis. prof. homiletics Jewish Theol. Sem. Am., 1966—. Mem. governing bd. World Jewish Congress, 1968—. Served with RCAF, 1943-45. Home: 845 West End Av New York City NY 10025 Office: 3080 Broadway New York City NY 10027

KELMENSON, LEO ARTHUR, advt. exec.; b. N.Y.C., Jan. 3, 1925; s. Joseph A. and Ruth (Rothberg) K.; B.S., Columbia, 1951, postgrad. Grad. Sch. Bus., 1952; div.; children—Todd-Arthur, Joel Adam. From TV prodn. to sr. v.p., asst. to pres. Lennen & Newell, 1951-65; exec. v.p., mem. exec. com. Norman Craig & Kummel, 1965-66; sr. v.p., dir., mem. exec. com. Kenyon & Eckhardt, 1967-68; pres. Kenyon & Eckhardt Advt. Inc., 1968—; pres., chief exec. officer, chmn. exec. com. Kenyon & Eckhardt Inc., C.P.V., 1970—; pres. Kelmerson Funds Ltd.; dir. Locations Unlimited; lectr. New Sch. Social Research. Adviser communications office U.S. Atty. Gen., 1960-63; spl. project officer State Dept., 1952-64; v.p., dir. African Research Found., 1957—; mem. pub. relations com. Nat. Cancer Found., 1958—; adv. com. Nat. Cultural Center, 1962; pres. Shoes for Little Souls, 1960, Remsenburg Assn., 1968. Served with USMCR, 1942-46. Recipient Theodore Roosevelt Man of Year award, 1955; Silver Quill Poetry award 1955; Res. Officers Assn. award, 1965; Guggenheim World Peace award, 1951. Mem. U.S. Olympic Com., N.Y. Advt Club, Soc. Am. Businessmen Club, Sigma Phi Epsilon. Clubs: Sands Point (N.Y.) Yacht; L.I. Polo. Author: (poetry) Epilogue, 1964; also short stories. Home: 145 Central Park West New York City NY 10023 Office: 200 Park Av New York City NY 10017

KELNER, ALBERT, educator, biologist; b. Phila., Sept. 7, 1912; s. Jacob and Eva (Maimon) K.; A.B., U. Pa., 1940, Ph.D., 1943; M.S., N.C. State Coll., 1942; m. Adelyn Uswald, Dec 14, 1946; children—Robert, Margaret, Carole. Fellow Wm. Pepper Lab. Clin. Medicine, Med. Sch. U. Pa., 1943-46; bacteriologist L.I. Biol. Lab., Cold Spring Harbor, N.Y., 1946-49; research fellow biology Harvard, 1949-51; asst. prof. biology Brandeis U., Waltham, Mass., 1951-61, prof., 1961—, now Burg prof. microbiology; cons. microbiology to industry. Recipient Finsen Gold medal for research in photorestoration 4th Internat. Congress Photobiology, Oxford, 1964. Mem. Soc. Am. Microbiologists (past pres. N.E. chpt.), A.A.A.S., Genetics Soc. Am., Radiation Research Soc., Sigma Xi. Home: 303 Florence Rd Waltham MA 02154

KELSEY, FLOYD LAMAR, Jr., architect; b. Colorado Springs, Colo., Jan. 2, 1925; s. Floyd Lamar and Myrtice (Graves) K.; student Colo. Coll., 1942-44; B.S. in Arch. with honors, U. Ill., 1947; m. Ruth Ann Witty, June 22, 1946; children—Patricia Ann, Carol Susan. Partner, Bunts & Kelsey, architects, Colorado Springs, Colo., 1952-66; prin. Lamar Kelsey & Assos., architects planners, Colorado Springs, 1966—; cons. design rev. bd. U. Colo., 1969-70, adv. panel, region 8, GSA, 1969-70; vis. lectr. U. Colo., 1960, U. Denver, 1958. Bd. dirs. YMCA. Recipient design awards A.I.A., 1961-63, Am. Inst. Steel Constrn., 1967, Am. Assn. Sch. Adminstrs., 1966-68, Nation's Schs. mag., 1963-67. Fellow A.I.A.; mem. Colorado Springs C. of C. (bd. dirs.), Gargoyle Archtl. Hon. Soc., Phi Delta Theta. Methodist. Clubs: El Paso, Colorado Springs Country, Broadmoor Golf (Colorado Springs). Author: Schools for America, 1967; Open Space Schools, 1971. Contbr. profl. jours. Architect Auditorium-Gymnasium Colo. State U., 1966, Mitchell Sr. High Sch., 1965 and Grant Elementary Sch., 1966 (both Colorado Springs), Evergreen Jr. High Sch., Jefferson County, Colo., 1969. Home: 4423 Valli Vista Rd Colorado Springs CO 80915 Office: 430 N Tejon St Colorado Springs CO 80902

KELSEY, FRANCES OLDHAM, (Mrs. Fremont Ellis Kelsey), govt. ofcl.; b. Vancouver Island, B.C., Can., July 24, 1914; d. Frank Trevor and Katherine (Stuart) Oldham; B.Sc., McGill U., 1934, M.Sc., 1935; Ph.D., U. Chgo., 1938, M.D., 1950; m. Fremont Ellis Kelsey, Dec. 6, 1943; children—Susan Elizabeth, Christine Ann. Came to U.S., 1936, naturalized, 1956. Instr., asst. prof. pharmacology U. Chgo., 1938- 50; editorial asso. A.M.A., Chgo., 1950-52; asso. prof. pharmacology U. S.D., 1954-57; med. officer FDA, Washington, 1960—, dir. div. sci. investigations, 1967—. Recipient Pres.'s award for Distinguished Fed. Civilian Service (refusal to approve coml. distbn. Thalidomide in U.S.), 1962. Mem. Am. Soc. Pharmacology and Exptl. Therapeutics, Soc. Exptl. Biology and Medicine, Am. Med. Writers Assn., N.Y. Acad. Scis., Teratology Soc., Sigma Xi. Author: (with F.E. Kelsey, E.M.K. Geiling) Essentials of Pharmacology, 1960. Home: 5811 Brookside Dr Chevy Chase MD 20015 Office: Food and Drug Adminstn Washington DC 20204

KELSEY, GEORGE DENNIS SALE, educator; b. Columbus, Ga., July 24, 1910; s. Andrew Zadok and Marie (Haywood) K.; A.B., Morehouse Coll., 1934; B.D., Andover Newton Theol. Sem., 1937; Ph.D., Yale, 1946; m. Leola Brunette Hanks, Dec. 29, 1930; children—Goerge Dennis Sale II, Everett Newton. Ordained to ministry Baptist Ch., 1938; prof. religion and philosophy Morehouse Coll., 1938- 45, dir. Sch. Religion, 1945-58; asso. dir. field dept. Nat. Council Chs., 1948-52; asso. prof. Christian ethics Drew U., 1952-57, prof., 1957—. Bd. dirs. Morris County Urban League; trustee-at-large Morris County Community Chest, Mem. Assn. Profs. Christian Ethics, Nat. Council Religion Higher Edn., Fellowship So. Churchmen. Author: Racism and the Christian Understanding of Man; also numerous articles in field. Home: 5 Cedar St Madison NJ 07940

KELSEY, HAROLD, newspaper exec.; Business mgr. Seattle-Post-Intelligence. Office: 6th and Wall Sts Seattle WA 98121*

KELSEY, HARVEY MARION, Jr., corp. exec.; b. Plattsburg, N.Y., Aug. 23, 1923; s. Harvey M. and Marguerite (Finn) K.; grad. Phillips Acad., 1941; B.A., Princeton, 1945; B.A., Harvard U., 1949; m. Anne Talcott, Sept. 6, 1947; children—Harvey Marion III, James T., Peter B., Karen M., Marguerite S. With James Talcott Inc., N.Y.C., 1949—, v.p., 1956-62, sr. v.p., 1962-69, exec. v.p. finance, 1969—, dir., 1957—; exec. v.p.- finance, dir. Talcott Nat. Corp.; dir. Seabrook Foods Inc.; dir. Market Research Corp. of Am. Served with AUS, 1942-46. Mem. Soc. Colonial Wars, Phillips Acad. Alumni Assn. N.Y. (pres. 1971), Alumni Council Princeton U. Republican. Roman Catholic. Clubs: American Yacht (trustee 1969—); Princeton N.Y.; Manursing Island; Storm Trysail; Appalachian Mountain. Home: 121 Apawamis Av Rye NY 10580 Office: 1290 Av of the Americas New York City NY 10019

KELSEY, JOHN EUGENE, electronics engr., former army officer; b. Newport News, Va., Jan. 8, 1915; s. Harry Ray and Bart (Downing) K.; student Va. Poly. Inst., 1932-33; B.S., U.S. Mil. Acad., 1938; M.S., Mass. Inst. Tech., 1948; m. Myrtle McCormick, Feb. 11, 1939; children—John Stuart, Anne Catherine. Commd. 2d lt. U.S. Army, 1938, advanced through grades to brig. gen., 1965; signal officer 99th Inf. Div., 1942-44, XXIV Corps and U.S. Army Forces, Korea, 1944-47, Signal Corps. Engring. Lab., 1948-51; student Naval War Coll., 1954-55; dep. chief research and devel. Office Chief Signal Officer, 1955-60; asst. chief staff communications Allied Land Forces Central Europe, 1960-64; dep. comdg. gen. U.S. Army Strategic Communications Command, 1965-66; comdg. gen. U.S. Army STRACOM-EUROPE, also dep. chief staff C.E., U.S. Army, Europe, 1966; now systems mgr. DataCom systems Burroughs Corp. Decorated D.S.M., Legion of Merit with oak leaf cluster; Order Mil. Merit (Brazil). Mem. I.R.E., Sigma Xi. Home: 4123 N 27th St Arlington VA 22207 Office: 7726 Old Springhouse Rd McLean VA 22101

KELSEY, JOHN FIELD, architect; b. Los Angeles, Dec. 7, 1925; s. Van Rensslaer and Tomasa (Stiles) K.; B.Arch., U. So. Cal., 1954; m. Donna Fischer, Oct. 15, 1967; children by previous marriage—Elizabeth, Jennifer, Brent. Asso., Thornton, Ladd & Assos., architects, Pasadena, Cal., 1954-58; partner Ladd & Kelsey, architects, Pasadena, 1958—. Served with USAAF, 1944-45. Mem. A.I.A., Nat. Council Archtl. Registration Bds., Tau Sigma Delta, Kappa Sigma. Important works include Pasadena Art Mus., 1969, Busch Gardens, Van Nuys, Cal., 1967, Cal. Inst. Arts, 1971. Hollywood Presbyn. Hosp., 1971. Home: 110 Los Altos Dr Pasadena CA 19903

KELSEY, PAUL JAMES, food co. exec.; b. Allendale, Ill., May 14, 1919; s. James G. and Ella (Buchanan) K.; B.S., U. Ill.; postgrad. Lockyears Bus. Coll., Evansville, Ind.; m. Dorothy Gober, May 15, 1949; children—Gregory Allan, Karl Timothy, Kurt Lewis. With Pillsbury Co., Mpls., 1949—. dir. corp. planning, 1965-66, v.p. corp. planning, 1966-67, v.p., controller, 1967—. Past moderator Presbytery Mpls.; past pres. local P.T.A. Served with AUS, 1942-46. Mem. Nat. Assn. Accountants (past pres. Mpls.). Home: 1650 Utah Dr St Louis Park MN 55426 Office: 608 2d Av S Minneapolis MN 55402

KELSO, ALEC JOHN, educator; b. Chgo., Dec. 5, 1930; s. Alexander Joseph and Collette Mary (Scanlon) K.; B.S., No. Ill. U., 1952; M.A., Ph.D., U. Mich., 1958; m. Mary Gemeny, Dec. 29, 1951; children—Colette, Williams. Teaching fellow U. Mich., 1955-57; instr. Wayne State U., Detroit, 1957; faculty U. Colo., Boulder, 1958—, prof. anthropology, 1967—, chmn. dept., 1963-68, 71—, dir. Summer Inst. Anthropology, 1961-62, 64, 68-70. Asst. dir. USAF Anthropometric Research Project, Antioch Coll., 1958; Distinguished vis. prof. Ore. State U., 1971. Mem. Am. Anthrop. Assn., Am. Assn. Phys. Anthropoligists (exec. com. 1961-64), Internat. Assn. Human Biologists, Sigma Xi. Author: Introduction to Physicial Anthropology Laboratory Manual, 1962; Physical Anthropology, 1970. Editor Yearbook of Physical Anthropology, 1962, 63.

KELSO, JAMES LEON, archaeologist, author; b. Duluth, Minn., Oct. 21, 1892; s. Evan E. and Bertha (Walle) K.; A.B., Monmouth (Ill.) Coll., 1916, D.D., 1926, LL.D., 1951; Th.M., Xenia Theol. Sem., St. Louis, 1918, Th.D., 1927; A.M., Ind. U., 1921; m. Adolphina Pearson, Jan. 28, 1920. Ordained to ministry U.P. Ch., 1918; pastor Bloomington, Ind., 1918-23; prof. O.T., Xenia Theol. Sem., 1923-30, Pitts.-Xenia Theol. Sem., 1930-59; prof. O.T. history and bibl. archaeology Pitts. Theol. Sem., 1960-63, prof. emeritus, 1963—; staff archaeol. excavations Tell Beit Mirsim, Palestine, 1926, 30, 32; pres. staff Bethel Archaeol. expdn., 1934; dir. excavations Tulul Abu el Alayiq and Nitla, Jordan, 1950; dir. Bthel Archaeol. Expdn., 1954, 57, 60; pres. asst. dir. staff Tell el Ful excavations, 1964. Moderator, U.P. Ch., 1952. Dir. Am. Sch. Oriental Research, Jersualem, 1949-50; pres. bd. trustees Palestine Archaeol. Mus., Jerusalem, 1949-51. Mem. Am. Oriental Soc., Archaeol. Inst. Am., Soc. Bibl. Lit. Republican. Author: The Ceramic Vocabulary of the Old Testament; The Excavation of New Testament Jericho, 1955; Archaeology and Our Old Testament Contemporaries, 1966; The Excavations of Bethel, 1934-60; Archaeology and the Ancient Testament, 1968; An Archaeologist Looks at the Gospels, 1969; An Archaeologist Fellow, the Apostle Paul, 1970. Contbr. numerous archael. articles to various tech. jours. Archeol editor S.S. Times, 1934-43. Home: 129 Altadena Dr Mt Lebanon PA 15228

KELSO, JOHN HODGSON, govt. ofcl.; b. Iowa City, June 16, 1925; s. Edward Lewis and Eliza (Hodgson) K.; B.A., State U. Ia., 1949, M.A., 1950; m. Marian Louise Towers, Aug. 22, 1948; 1 son, John T. Occupational research analyst Bur. Naval Personnel, Dept. Navy, Washington, 1951-55; orgn. and methods examiner Agr. Research Services, Dept. Agr., Washington, 1955-57; mgmt. analyst mgmt. adv. br. Bur. State Services, USPHS, Dept. Health, Edn. and Welfare, Washington, 1957-58, chief survey group, 1958-60, chief mgmt. adv. br., 1960-62, asst. exec. officer, 1962-66, exec. officer, Bethesda, Md., 1966-68; asst. adminstr. mgmt. Health Services and Mental Health Adminstrn., 1968—. Served with AUS, 1943-46. Mem. Am. Pub. Health Assn., Am. Soc. Pub. Adminstrn., Assn. Mgmt. in Pub. Health, Sigma Alpha Epsilon. Methodist. Home: 2332 N Early St Alexandria VA 22302 Office: 5600 Fischer's Lane Rockville MD 20852

KELSO, LOUIS ORTH, lawyer; b. Denver, Dec. 4, 1913; s. Oren S. and Nettie (Wolfe) K.; B.S. cum laude, U. Colo., 1937, LL.B, 1938; D.Sc., Araneta U., Manila, 1962; m. Betty Hawley, Aug. 6, 1938; children—Martha Jennifer, Katherine Elizabeth. Admitted to Colo. bar, 1938, Cal. bar, 1946; practice law, Denver, 1938-42, San Francisco, 1946—; asso. Pershing Bosworth, Dick & Dawson, 1938-42; partner Broebeck, Phleger & Harrison, 1946-59; sr. partner Kelso, Cotton, Seligman & Ray, 1959-70; asso. prof. law U. Colo., 1946. Mng. dir. Louis O. Kelso, Inc., San Francisco, 1970—. Dir. Precision Instrument Co., Bangert & Co., Inc., Statesman Group, Inc., Kilburg Geochron Corp., Aetna Participating Annuity Life Ins. Co., Polak, Winters & Co. Pres. Inst. Study Econ. Systems, San Francisco; sec. Journey for Perspective Found. Bd. dirs. Inst. Philos. Research, Chgo.; founding trustee Crystal Springs Sch. Girls, Hillsborough, Cal. Served to lt. USNR, 1942-46. Mem. Am., Cal., San Francisco bar assns. Clubs: Pacific-Union, Bohemian, Bankers, Villa Taverna (San Francisco). Author: (with Mortimer J. Adler) The Capitalist Manifesto, 1958, The New Capitalists, 1961; (with Patricia Hetter) Two-Factor Theory The Economics of Reality, 1968. Editor-in-chief Rocky Mountain Law Rev., 1938. Contbr. articles profl. jours. Home: 520 Costa Rice Av San Mateo CA 94402 Office: 111 Pine St San Francisco CA 94111

KELSO, ROBERT CHARLES, lawyer; b. New Salem, Ind., Nov. 13, 1916; s. Rayburn and Amy (Hargitt) K.; student U. Ill., 1934-37; J.D. cum laude, John Marshall Law Sch., 1942; postgrad. law, Goethe U., Frankfurt, Germany; m. Evelinne M. Bursch, Nov. 8, 1941; children-Robinne Sue (Mrs. Rex Hornbaker), Margaret Anne. Admitted to Ill. bar, 1942, Ariz. bar, 1948, D.C. bar, 1960; asst. states atty., Rockford, Ill., 1945-47; city atty., Springerville and Eagar, Ariz., 1948-51; practice in Springerville, 1948- 51; spl. counsel European and internat. law Def. Dept., 1951-56; sr. partner firm Lewis, Roca, Beachamp & Linton, Phoenix, 1959—; asso. prof. internat. comml. law Am. Inst. Fgn. Trade, 1958-68. Mem. Regional Export Expansion Council; chmn. Ariz.-Mexican Trade Commn., 1965-67; del. Internat. Congress Jurists, Hamburg, Germany, 1953; hon. consul Fed. Republic Germany, 1961—. Bd. govs. Ill. Young Republicans, 1946-47; del. Ill. Rep. Conv., 1946; chmn. Apache County Republican Com., 1950; del. Aro. Rep. Com.,1 1950. Named to Order John Marshall, 1942. Mem. Am., Ill., Ariz., Am., Internat. bar assns., Fedn. Ins. Counsel, Theta Chi. Presbyn. Mason (32, Shriner), Rotarian. Clubs: Ariz. Yacht, Arizona, Hiram (Phoenix). Author: Legal Problems Arising Out of Industrial Use of Atomic Energy, 1956; International Law of Commerce, 1961; co-author: International Trade Handbook, 1963; also articles. Home: 5315 E Royal Palm lRd Phoenix AZ 85253 Office: Title and Trust Bldg Phoenix AZ 85003

KELSON, ROBERT NATHANIEL, educator; b. Boston, May 8, 1927; s. Philip and Lena (Silbert) K.; A.B., Boston U., 1948, A.M., 1949; Fulbright student Victoria U. Coll., U. New Zealand, 1953; Ph.D. (Commonwealth Studies Center fellow 1956-58), Duke, 1959; m. Cara Hall, May 7, 1955; 1 son, Stanley Crispin. Instr. polit. economy Boston U., 1950-52, teaching fellow polit. sci., 1952; jr. lectr., then lectr. Victoria U. Coll., 1954-55; traveling fellow Commonwealth Studies Center in S. And S.E. Asia and U.K., 1955-56; acting asst. prof. polit. sci. U. Colo., 1958-59; asst. prof. polit. sci U. Western Ont., 1959-62, asso. prof., 1962-64; Fred Morgan Kirby prof. civil rights, head dept. govt. and law, Lafayette Coll., 1964—; lectr. Canadian Nat. Def. Coll., 1960-66. Mem. N.Y. Regents Fellowship Bd., 1966. Vice chmn. Easton-Phillipsburg Human Relations Commn., 1965-61. Candidate for Democratic Nat. Nominating Conv., 1952; mem. Mass. Kefauver for Pres. Com., 1952. Served with USNR, 1945-46. Recipient award Canadian Social Sci. Research Council, 1961; grantee Can. Council Research, 1962. Mem. Am., Pa., New Eng. polit. sci. assns., Am. Assn. U. Profs. Unitarian. Author: The Private Member of Parliament, 1964; Canadian Overseas Aid, 1964; also articles, chpts. in books. Editorial cons. U. Toronto Press, 1963-64. Home: 410 Hamilton St Easton PA 18042

KELTNER, JOHN WILLIAM, educator; b. Literberry, Ill., June 20, 1918; s. Claude and Geno Blanche (Lewis) K.; B.E., Ill State Normal U., 1940, M.A., Northwestern U., 1943, Ph.D., 1947; m. Alberta Cochran, Jan. 1, 1941; children—Mary Jean, Lewis Dean. Instr. speech, English, social studies, drama and correction Oak Park (Ill.) jr. high schs., 1940-43; instr. pub. speaking Pekin (Ill.) Community High Sch., 1943-44; teaching asst., lectr. speech Northwestern U., 1944-46; asst. prof. speech Ia. State Tchrs. Coll., 1946-48; asso. prof. speech U. Okla., 1948-54; prof. speech, head dept. Kan. State Coll., 1954-58; lab. coordinator Human Relations Tng. Lab., 1955-58; commr. Fed. Mediation and Conciliation Service, 1958-61; nat. office rep. and tng. officer, 1961-64; prof. speech, chmn. dept. speech communication Ore. State U., Corvallis, 1963-71, prof. speech communications, 1971—; pub. and pvt. mediator and arbitrator; cons. human relations and communications. Prin., Cons. Assos., 1960—, also dir. Mem. Am. Arbitration Assn.(pub. employees panel), Indsl. Relations Research Assn., Adult Edn. Assn. Am., Am. Soc. Tng. Dirs., Western (v.p. 1970-71), Central States (pres. 1951-52) speech assns., Speech Communication Assn., Am. Assn. U. Profs., Delta Sigma Rho (nat. v.p. 1950-53, exec. sec. 1953-58, editor Gavel 1953-58) Pi Kappa Delta, Theta Alpha Phi. Author: Group Discussion Processes, 1957; (with L. Harter) Labor in America, 1966; Interpersonal Speech Communication, 1970. Home: 2770 SW De Armond Way Corvallis OR 97330

KELTON, JOHN T., lawyer; b. Bay City, Mich., Mar. 12, 1909; s. Frank P. S. and Jessie Eleanor (Tremain) K.; student Culver (Ind.) Mil. Acad., 1925-28; B.S. in Chem. Engring., Mass. Inst. Tech., 1932; LL.B., Harvard, 1935; m. Carol E. Copeland, July 9, 1935; children-Carol E.M., Joy T. Admitted to N.Y. bar, 1935; practiced patent law as asso. and mem. Watson, Bristol, Johnson & Leavenworth, N.Y.C., 1935-40, 46-49; mem. Watson, Johnson, Leavenworth & Blair, 1950-53, Watson, Leavenworth, Kelton & Taggart, 1954—. Served from 2d lt. to lt. col., AUS, 1940-46. Mem. Assn. Bar City N.Y., Am. (bd. mgrs. 1964-67), N.Y. (pres. 1967) patent law assns. Conglist. Clubs: Harvard, Chemists, Union League (N.Y.C.). Home: Nutmeg Lane Westport CT 06880 Office: 100 Park Av New York NY 10017

KEMBALL-COOK, DENIS BASIL, oil co. exec.; b. London, Eng., 1910; s. Sir Basil Alfred and Nancy (Pavit) Kemball-C.; student Balliol Coll., Oxford U.; m. Virginia Ricks, 1935; children—Richard McNaughton, Denis Stephen, Virginia. Came to U.S., 1932, naturalized, 1940. With Shell Oil Co., Boston, 1932, St. Louis, 1933, 37, Houston, 1934, 38, N.Y.C., 1958—, exec. v.p., 1958-69, chief operating officer, 1968-69, pres., chief exec. officer, 1970—, also dir.; with Shell, Caracas, Venezuela, 1945, dir., 1953; v.p., dir. Shell Caribbean, N.Y.C., 1957-58. Vice chmn. bd. trustees Skidmore Coll., Saratoga Springs, N.Y. Fellow Royal Soc. Arts; mem. Am. Petroleum Inst. (dir., exec. com.). Clubs: New York Yacht; Noroton Yacht. Home: Andrews Dr Darien CT 06820 Office: 50 W 50th St New York City NY 10020

KEMBLE, EDWIN CRAWFORD, retired educator, physicist; b. Delaware, O., Jan. 28, 1889; s. Duston and Margaret Agnes (Day) K.; student Ohio Wesleyan U., 1906-07; B.S., Case Sch. Applied Sci., 1911, D.Sc., (hon.) 1931; A.M., Harvard, 1914, Ph.D., 1917; Ed.D., R.I. Coll. Edn., 1957; m. Harriet Mary Tindle, Sept. 8, 1920; children—Robert Day, Jean Allen. Asst. instr. physics Carnegie Inst. Tech., 1911-13; engring. physicist Curtiss Motor Corp., 1917-18; instr. physics Williams Coll., 1919; instr. physics Harvard, 1919-23, asst. prof., 1923-27, asso. prof. 1927- 30, prof., 1930-57, prof. physics emeritus, 1957—, chmn. dept., 1940-45. Guggenheim fellow, 1927; recipient Oersted medal Am. Assn. Physics Tchrs., 1969. Fellow Am. Phys. Soc., Am. Acad. Arts and Scis., Nat. Acad. Scis.; mem. A.A.A.S., Sigma Xi, Tau Beta Pi, Phi Kappa Psi. Conglist. Author: Fundamental Principles of Quantum Mechanics, 1937; Physical Science: Its Structure and Development, vol. I, 1966; co-author: Report on Molecular Spectra in Gases, 1926. Contbr. to Phys. Rev. Home: 8 Ash Street Pl Cambridge MA 02138

KEMBLE, JOHN HASKELL, educator; b. Marshalltown, Ia., June 17, 1912; s. Ira Oscar and Caroline (Haskell) K.; B.A., Stanford, 1933; M.A., U. Cal. at Berkeley, 1934, Ph.D., 1937. Faculty, Pomona Coll., 1936—, prof. history, 1951—. Vis. lectr. history U. Cal. at Los Angeles, 1948-49; vis. prof.mil. history U.S. Naval War Coll., Newport, R.I., 1952-53; vis. prof. history U. Tex., 1967; sec. Navy Adv. Com. Naval History, 1961—. Served to lt. comdr. USNR, 1941-46; PTO. Fellow Rockefeller Found., 1947-48, Guggenheim Found., 1956-57. Fellow Cal. Hist. Soc.; mem. Am. Hist. Assn. (sec.-treas. Pacific Coast br. 1941-42, 45-49), Am. Antiquarian Soc., Soc. Nautical Research, S.S. Histo. Soc., Hist. Soc. So. Cal. (pres. 1967-70), Zamorano, Odd Volumes, Westerners, E. Clampus Vitus. Republican. Episcopalian. Author: The Panama Route, 1848-1869, 1943; San Francisco Bay: a Pictorial Maritime History, 1957. Editor: Journal of a Cruise to California and the Sandwich Islands...1841-1844 (William H. Myers), 1955; Two Years Before the Mast (Richard Henry Dana, Jr.), 1964; To California and the South Seas: The Diary of Albert G. Osbun, 1849-1851, 1966; Sketches of California and Hawaii...1842-1843 (William H. Meyers), 1970. Home: 452 W 6th St Claremont CA 91711

KEMBLE, WILLIAM TYSON, investment banker; b. Washington, Aug. 26, 1911; s. John and Jeanne (Tyson) K.; student Harvard, 1934; m. Madeleine Powers, Apr. 29, 1938. With Estabrook & Co., Boston, 1929-30, 33—, successively salesman, sales mgr., 1929-30, 33-51, partner 1951—; dir. Davis & Furber Machine Co., SLM Corp. of Am., Boston Pro Football Team. Mem. Am., Boston, N.Y. stock exchanges. Served to comdr. USNR, World War II. Decorated Bronze Star. Mem. Investment Bankers Assn. Am. (v.p. 1961-63), Assn. Stock Exchange Firms (gov. 1961-63, pres.). Clubs: Somerset (Boston); Myopia Hunt (Hamilton, Mass.); Midocean (Bermuda). Home: South Hamilton MA 01982 Office: 15 State St Boston MA 02109

KEMELMAN, HARRY, author; b. Boston, Nov. 24, 1908; s. Isaac and Dora (Prizer) K.; A.B., Boston U., 1930; M.A., Harvard, 1931; m. Anne Kessin, Mar. 29, 1936; children—Ruth (Mrs. George Rooks), Arthur Frederick, Diane (Mrs. Stanley Neustadter). Tchr., Boston pub. schs., 1935-41, eve. div. Northeastern U., 1938-41; chief job analyst and wage adminstr. Boston Port Embarkation, 1942-49; free-lance writer, 1949-63; tchr. Franklin Inst., Boston, 1963-64, State Coll., Boston, 1964—. Recipient Edgar award for best first novel, 1965; Faith and Freedom Communications award, 1967. Mem. Author's League, Mystery Writers Assn. Author: Friday the Rabbi Slept Late, 1964; Saturday the Rabbi Went Hungry, 1966; The Nine Mile Walk, 1967; Sunday the Rabbi Stayed Home, 1969; Commonsense in Education, 1970; Monday the Rabbi Took Off, 1972. Address: 47 Humphrey St Marblehead MA 01947

KEMENY, JOHN GEORGE, coll. pres.; b. Budapest, Hungary, May 31, 1926; s. Tibor and Lucy (Fried) K.; came to U.S., 1940, naturalized, 1945; B.A., Princeton, 1947, Ph.D., 1949, LL.D., 1971; D.Sc., Middlebury Coll., 1965; LL.D., Columbia, 1971; m. Jean Alexander, Nov. 5, 1950; children—Jennifer M., Robert A. Asst. theoretical div. Los Alamos Project, 1945-46; asst. teaching and research Princeton, 1946-48, Fine instr., Office Naval Research fellow math., 1949-51, asst. prof. philosophy, 1951-53; research asst. to Dr. Albert Einstein, Inst. Advanced Study, 1948-49; prof. math. Dartmouth, 1953-70, chmn. math. dept., 1955- 67, Albert Bradley 3d Century prof., 1969—, pres., 1970—; coordinator ednl. plans and devel., 1967-69; lectr. in Austria, Israel, India, Japan, 1964-65. Cons. Rand Corp., Santa Monica, Cal., 1953-69; mem. nat. commn. libraries and information sci. Dept. Health, Edn. and Welfare, Regional Director's Adv. Com.; chmn. U.S. Commn. on Math. Instrn., 1958-60; mem. NRC, 1963-66; Mem. Hanover (N.H.) Sch. Bd., 1961-64. Trustee Found. Center, Carnegie Found. Advancement Teaching. Served with AUS, 1945- 46. Mem. Assn. Symbolic Logic, Math. Assn. Am. (chmn. New Eng. sect. 1959-60, bd. govs. 1960-63, chmn. panel biol. and social scis. 1963-64), Am. Math. Soc., Am. Philos. Assn., Am. Acad. Arts and Scis., Phi Beta Kappa, Sigma Xi (nat. lectr. 1967). Author: A Philosopher Looks at Science—Random Essays; co-author: Introduction to Finite Mathematics; Finite Mathematical Structures; Finite Markov Chains; Mathematical Models in the Social Sciences; Finite Mathematics with Business Applications: Denumerable Markov Chains; Basic Programming, 1967. Contbr. to Ency. Brit., articles to profl. jours. Cons. editor Jour. Symbolic Logic, 1950-59; asso. editor Jour. Math. Analysis and Applications. Home: Hemlock Rd Hanover NH 03755

KEMLETTER, JAMES PHILIP chemist, educator; b. Chicago, 1928; B.S. in Physics, Yale, 1950; Ph.D. in Chemistry, Harvard, 1956; m. Sally Ann Jones, July 5, 1957; children--Kenneth J., Nancy A. Chemist, Acme Chem. Co., Blue Island, Ill., 1950-51; director of Research Lab., Indsl. Chemicals Corp., Cambridge, Mass., 1956-60; project coordinator environmental sect. Steinmetz Assos., Chgo., 1960-61; v.p. for research Bauer Bros. Chem. Co., Inc., Memphis, 1961-64; asst. prof. chemistry Washington U., St. Louis, 1964-66, asso. prof., 1966-70, prof., 1970--, head of chemistry dept., 1970-71. Vis. prof. So. Ill. U., summer 1967, U. of Ore., 1969. Scoutmaster, Boy Scouts America, University City, Mo., 1968-70. Bd. dirs. Rest Haven Home for Elderly, 1960-61; trustee of the Lutheran Hosp., 1965-71. Served from lt. to capt., AUS, 1951-53. Mem. Am. Chem. Soc., Sci. Research Soc. Am. (chpt. treas. 1967), Sigma Xi. Author: (with others) Basic Inorganic Chemistry, 1971. Home: Fairfax Apts 7291 Windermere Dr University City MO 63105 Office: Dept Chemistry Washington University St Louis MO 63130

KEMMERER, DONALD LORENZO, univ. prof.; b. Manila, P.I., Dec. 24, 1905; s. Edwin Walter and Rachel (Dickel) K.; A.B., Princeton, 1927; A.M., 1931, Ph.D., 1934; m. Mirjane Strong, Nov. 27, 1934; children—Jane S., Edwin Walter II. Asst. sec. to financial adv. commns. to Chile, 1925, Poland, 1926, China, 1929; instr. econs., Lehigh U., 1934-37; asso. econ. U. Ill., 1937-39, asst. prof., 1939-45, asso. prof., 1945-49, prof. econs., 1949—; vis. prof. N.Y. U., summer 1952, U. Melbourne, Australia, 1958; cons. Kabul Univ., Afghanistan, 1959; Fulbright prof. U. Montpelier, France, 1960, U. Munich, 1964; econ. adv. Republican Party's platform planning com. 1944, Pa. R.R., 1945, Investors Mgmt. Co., 1950-57; dir. Fundamental Investors, Inc. Cons. European Productivity Agy., 1955; v.p. Economists Nat. Com., 1957-67, pres., 1967—; mem. U.S. Assay Com., 1967. Pres. Lincoln Ednl. Found., 1958—. Mem. Midwest Econ. Assn. (2d v.p. 1950), Am. Econ. and Finance Assn., Am. Hist. Assn., Orgn. Am. Historians, Bus. and Econ. Hist. Assns., Econ. Nat. Com. Monetary Policy, Phi Beta Kappa. Clubs: Mont Pelerin, Rotary Internat. Author: Path to Freedom, 1940; Economic History of American People (with E. I. Bogart) 1942, rev. 1947; ABC of Federal Reserve System (with E.W. Kemmerer), 12th edit., 1950; (with R H. Blodgett) Comparative Economic Development, 1956; (with C. C. Jones) American Economic History, 1957, rev. edit. 1959; also articles profl. jours. Home: 1006 W Armory Av Champaign IL 61820 Office: David Kinley Hall Urbana IL 61801

KEMMERER, JOHN L., Jr., mining co. exec. Chmn. bd. Kemmerer Coal Co., Wyo.; pres. Kemmerer Corp.; dir. Bralorne Can-Fer Resources Ltd., Bralorne Oil & Gas Ltd., Bituminous Coal Research, Latrobe Steel Co., Penn Va. Corp., Steel Heddle Mfg. Co., Whitehall Cement Mfg. Co., First Nat. Bank Kemmerer, Wyndham Securities Corp. Former officer Nat. Coal Assn., Washington. Address: 120 Broadway New York City NY 10005

KEMMERER, RUSSELL EDWIN, holding co. exec.; b. Easton, Pa., Sept. 21, 1919; s. Russell B. and Laura (Clause) K.; grad. Bethlehem (Pa.) Bus. Coll., 1940; student N.Y.U., 1947-49; m. Audry C. Kirtland, Nov. 21, 1947. With GAC Miami, Fla., 1940—, treas., 1959—, v.p., 1965—. Mem. Nat. Assn. Accountants, Financial Execs. Inst. Club: Miami Jockey. Home: 2451 Bricknell Av Miami FL 33129 Office: 825 S Bayshore Dr Miami FL 33131

KEMNITZER, WILLIAM JOHNSON, econ. geologist; b. Sacramento, Sept. 2, 1898; s. Louis Henry and Emma Charlotte (Johnson) K.; A.B., Stanford, 1923, research petroleum geology and econs. Cal. Inst. Tech., 1928-31; m. Jacqueline Thomas Baldwin, Nov. 20, 1954. Geologist, engr. various mining and petroleum cos., U.S., Mexico, 1923-27, 31-37; expert Fed., Cal. State govts. on investigations and litigation petroleum lands, 1937-41; mem. U.S.-Mexico Oil Commn., 1942; mem. U.S. Indsl. Mission to Brazil, 1942-43; chief fuel specialist Fgn. Econ. Adminstrn., 1943-45; ind. contractor negotiating devel. petroleum lands between Govt. Bolivia and U.S. pvt. interest, 1945-51; engaged personal interests, 1952—; research Sch. Mineral Sci. Stanford, 1959—; lectr. Hispanic Am. Studies, Stanford, 1960—, Am. Inst. Fgn. Trade, Phoenix, 1962-63. Served with USNR, 1918-22, lt. comdr., 1937-56. Recipient Order Condor de los Andes, Bolivia, 1944. Mem. Inst. Petroleum Tech. (London), Delta Upsilon. Club: Commonwealth (San Francisco). Author: (with R. Arnold) Petroleum in the United States and Possessions, 1931; Rebirth of Monopoly, 1938. Contbr. tech. articles to petroleum jours. U.S., Europe, also newspapers, other publs. Home: 988 Monte Rosa Dr Menlo Park, CA

KEMP, ARTHUR, educator; b. Buffalo, Jan. 29, 1916; s. Arthur and Caroline (Durk) K.; B.A., U. Buffalo, 1939; M.B.A., Northwestern U., 1940; Ph.D., N.Y. U., 1949; m. Helene L. Morlock, Aug. 23, 1940. Instr. Yale, 1941-43; asst. prof. N.Y. U., 1946-53; prof. Claremont (Cal.) Mens Coll., 1953—; dir. dept. econ. research A.M.A., 1959-60. Research asst. to chmn. Hoover Commn., 1947-49. Served to 1st lt. USAAF, 1943-46. Recipient citation of merit U. Buffalo, 1962. Mem. Am., Western econ. assns., Am. Finance Assn., Econ History Assn., Mont Pelerin Soc., N.A.M. (past v.p.), Phila. Soc. (pres., dir.). Author: The Legal Qualities of Money, 1956; The Role of Government in Developing Peaceful Uses of Atomic Energy, 1960; The Role of Gold, 1963. Home: 1541 Lafayette Rd Claremont CA 91711

KEMP, BARRETT GEORGE, lawyer; b. Dayton, O., Feb. 22, 1932; s. Barret M. and Gladys (Linkhart) K.; B.S., Ohio U., 1954; J.D., Ohio No. U., 1959; m. Patricia A. Picard, June 23, 1956; children-Becky Ann, Barrett George II. Admitted to Ohio bar, 1959; spl. agt. FBI, 1959-61; pvt. practice, St. Marys, O., 1961- -; city solicitor, St. Marys, 1964—. Sec. Community Improvement Corp., 1966—. Cubmaster, Boy Scouts Am., 1966—. Trustee United Fund, 1966—. Served with AUS, 1954-56. Mem. Am. Judicature Soc., Am., Ohio Auglaize County (pres. 1969) bar assns., St. Marys C. of C. (trustee 1962-65, v.p. 1965). Mason, Rotarian (bd. dirs. 1962-64. v.p. 1968-69). Mem. United Ch. Christ (treas. 1963-66). Home: 107 N Wayne St St Marys OH 45885 Office: Home Bank Bldg St Marys OH 45885

KEMP, HARRIS ATTERIDGE, architect; b. Kewanee, Ill., July 3, 1912; s. John Edward and Pauline (King) K.; B.S., U. Ill., 1934, M.S., 1935; M.Arch., Mass. Inst. Tech., 1937; m. Carol Western, Sept. 18, 1937; children—David Anders, Peter Alan, Constance Susan. Francis J. Plym fellow in architecture to Europe, 1937-38; designer Wis. State Architects Office, 1938-40; supr. plant layout dept. N.Am. Aviation Corp., 1940-44; asso., chief designer George L. Dahl- Architects and Engrs., Dallas, 1944-55; partner Harper & Kemp-Architects, Dallas, 1955—. Dir. Dallas Central Bus. Dist. Assn., 1968—; mem. pub. adv. panel Gen. Services Adminstrn., Region 7, 1969—. Fellow A.I.A. (pres. Dallas chpt. 1957); mem. Tex. Soc. Architects (dir. 1964-67), Phi Celta Theta. Presbyn. (elder). Kiwanian. Club: Dallas Country. Important works include Denton State Sch., Dallas Livestock Coliseum, Gt. Am. of Dallas Bldg., Dallas Municipal Adminstrn. Center. Home: 5328 Waneta Dr Dallas TX 75209 Office: 2020 Live Oak St Dallas TX 75201

KEMP, J. ROBERT, meat packing co. exec.; b. Seattle, Nov. 4, 1920; s. S.H. and Bertha (Bankhead) K.; B.S. in Agr., U. Ida., 1943; m. Mary M. Filer, Sept. 23, 1942; children—Kandace, Kathy, Karen, Kay. With Armour & Co., 1946-62, plant mgr. various plants, 1955-62; v.p., gen. plant mgr. Ia. Beef Processors, Inc., Fort Dodge, 1962-63, v.p. sales, mem. exec. com., 1963, exec. vp., 1968—, dir., co-chmn., 1970—. Served with USAAF, 1943-46; PTO; 1st lt. Res. Mem. Phi Delta Theta. Elk, Kiwanian. Home: 2619 E Solway St Sioux City IA 51104 Office: Ia Beef Processors Inc Gen Office Dakota City NB

KEMP, JACK F., congressman; b. Los Angeles, July 13, 1935; B.A., Occidental Coll., 1957; postgrad. Long Beach State U., Cal. Western U. m. Joanne Main; children—Jeffrey, Jennifer, Judith. Spl. asst. to gov. of Cal., 1969; elected to 92d Congress, 1970—; profl. football player for 13 years; TV and radio commentator for nat. networks and local stas.; pub. relations officer Marine Midland Bank of Buffalo. Named Outstanding Young Man of Year, Buffalo Jr. C. of C.; recipient Distinguished Service award N.Y. State Jaycees; Outstanding Citizens award Buffalo Evening News. Republican. Mem. Nat. Assn. Broadcasters, Engrs. and Technicians, Buffalo Area C. of C., Sierra Club, Pres.'s Council on Phys. Fitness and Sports, Am. Football League Players Assn. (cofounder and pres. 1965-70), Nat. Football League Players Assn. (exec. com. and player pension bd.). Address: 28 Calvin Ct S Buffalo NY*

KEMP, JAMES DUDLEY, air force officer; b. Spring Ranch, Neb., Mar. 28, 1918; s. Oakley Charles and Ruby (Shipmab) K.; B.A. in Geography, U. Wash., 1947; grad. Army Command and Staff Coll., 1946, Air Force Command and Staff Sch., 1956, Air War Coll., 1958; m. Edna Ellestad, Dec. 10, 1949; 1 son, Phillip Michael. Commd. 2d lt., pilot, USAAF, 1940, advanced through grades to brig. gen. US Air Force, 1965; comdr. B-17, B-24 squadrons Guatemala, and C.Z., 1943-45, 452d and 17th Light Bombardment groups, Korea, 1951-52; dep. insp. gen. Far East Air Forces, Tokyo, 1952; chief personnel requirements div. Hdqrs. USAF, Washington, 1953-56; comdr. 10th Tactical Reconnaissance Wing, Germany, 1959-60, Eng., 1960-62; dir. operations TAC Hdqrs., Langley AFB, Va., 1962-64; comdr. 831st Air Div., TAC, George AFB, Cal., 1964-66; chief joint war games agy. Joint Chiefs Staff, Washington, 1966-68; vice comdr. San Antonio Air Materiel Area, 1967; asst. chief staff for operations, dir. U.S./Korea Operational Planning Staff, UN Command, Korea, 1968-70; comdr. Def. Gen. Supply Center, Richmond, Va., 1970—. Decorated D.S.M., Legion Merit with 2 oak leaf clusters, D.F.C., Bronze Star medal, Air Medal with 2 oak leaf clusters, Air Force, Army (with 2 oak leaf clusters) commendation medals; Order of Nat. Security Merit 3d class (Republic Korea), 1970. Address: Def Gen Supply Center Richmond VA 23219

KEMP, LEBBEUS COURTRIGHT, Jr., petroleum exec.; b. Houston, Oct. 8, 1907; s. Lebbeus C. and Della (Courtright) K.; B.S. in Chem. Engring., Rice Inst., 1929; m. Alice Richter, Aug. 1, 1936; children—Henry Richter, May Courtright. With Tex. Co., 1929—, petroleum research, dir. research, asst. to v.p., asst. to sr. v.p., gen. mgr. petrochems. dept., 1929-57, v.p., 1957-59, v.p. research, 1959-68, v.p. spl. assignments, 1968—; dir. Jefferson Chem. Co., Tex. U.S. Chem. Co., Texaco Devel. Corp., Noches Butane Products Co. Registered profl. engr., N.Y., Tex., Va. Fellow A.A.A.S.; mem. Am. Inst. Chem. Engrs., Am. Chem. Soc., Am. Petroleum Inst., Soc. Chem. Industry, N.Y. Acad. Sci., Tau Beta Pi. Clubs: Houston; Chemists (N.Y.C.). Home: 12318 Huntingwick Houston TX 77024 Office: 1111 Rusk Av Houston TX 77002

KEMP, ROBERT D., corp. exec.; b. South Bend, Ind., 1918. Exec. v.p., dir. Allen Industries, Inc.; dir. Dayco Corp., Dayton, O. Home: 76 Webber Pl Grosse Pointe Shores MI 48236 Office: 1927 Leland Av Detroit MI 48207

KEMP, VERBON ERIC, former assn. exec.; b. Oneonta, Ala., Oct. 27, 1899; s. Wilson T. and Zula (Bynum) K.; student Washington and Lee U., 1918-21; m. Ann Litchford, Apr. 22, 1924; children—Verbon Eric, Ann L. (Mrs. W.E. Des Portes), Wilson E. Field sec. Washington and Lee U., 1920-24, alumni sec., 1924- 29; exec. sec. Charlottesville C. of C., 1929-35; gen. sec. Va. C. of C., Richmond, 1935-38, exec. dir., 1938-64; sec. Christian Children's Fund, Inc., 1945-64, exec. dir. 1964-70. Mem. Va. 350th Anniversary Commn., 1950-64, Jamestown Corp., 1948—, Woodrow Wilson Centennial Commn., 1950-60, James Monroe Centennial Commn., 1954-62, Va. Econ. Adv. Council, 1948-58. Bd. dirs., vice chmn. Internat. Prayer Fellowship U.S.A. Mem. Newcomen Soc., Beta Theta Pi, Omicron Delta Kappa. Presbyn. (elder). Kiwanian. Founder, editor Alumni mag. Washington and Lee U., 1927-29; pub. Commonwealth, Mag. of Va., 1938-64. Home: 5909 D Willow Oaks Dr Richmond VA 23225

KEMP, J. E., savs. and loan assn. exec. Exec. v.p., mgr. Equitable Savs. and Loan Assn., Palo Alto, Cal. Office: 180 University Av Palo Alto CA 94302*

KEMPE, CHARLES HENRY, educator, physician; b. Breslau, Germany, Apr. 6, 1922; A.B., U. Cal. at Berkeley, 1942, M.D., at San Francisco, 1945; m. Ruth Svibergsen, Sept. 29, 1948. Intern pediatrics U. Cal. Med. Sch., San Francisco, 1945-46, instr. pediatrics, 1949-51, asst. prof., 1951-56, lectr. social welfare, 1940, lectr. Sch. Nursing, 1949; fellow Fleischner Fund. Children's Hosp., San Francisco, 1946; asst. virologist med. dept. Research and Grad. Sch., Washington, 1946-47; chief virologist 6th Army Area, Presidio of San Francisco, 1947-48; virologist med. dept. Research and Grad. Sch., Washington, 1948; asst. pediatrics Yale Sch. Medicine, 1948-49; cons. surgeon gen. Dept. Def., 1950—; cons. influenza commn., mem. epidemiol. bd. U.S. Army; ad hoc cons. smallpox WHO, Geneva Switzerland; Fulbright research scholar, Rome, 1955-56; prof. pediatrics, chmn. dept. U. Colo., 1956—. Mem. Soc. Pediatric Research (council), Am. Assn. Immunologists, Western Soc. Pediatric Research (pres. 1960), No. Cal. Pediatric Soc., Am. Acad. Pediatrics (E. Mead Johnson award), Am. Pub. Health Assn., Am. Fedn. Clin. Research, Western Soc. Clin. Research. Author: Handbook of Pediatrics, 1971; Healthier Babies, 1960. Co-editor: The Battered Child, 1968. Home: 154 S Jersey St Denver CO 80222

KEMPE, RUDOLF, orch. conductor; b. Dresden, Germany, June 14, 1910; student State Orchestra Sch., Dresden. Prin. oboist and repetitor, Gewandhaus, Leipzig, 1929-36; conductor, Leipzig, 1936; dir. music State Orchestra, Dresden, 1949, State Opera of Munich (Germany), 1952; conductor Salzburg, Edinburgh, Bayreuth festivals; sometime condr. Met. Opera N.Y.C., Opera Covent Garden; conductor numerous orchestras and appeared various opera houses, also conductor for broadcasts and recs; artistic dir. Royal Philharmonic Orch., London, 1963—, Tonhalle Orch., Zürich, 1965—; gen. music dir. Münchemer Philharmoniker, München, 1967—. Address: 8 Munchen 2 Loristrasse 24 West Germany

KEMPER, ARTHUR BERNARD, retired educator, chemist; b. Crafton, Pa., Jan. 5, 1912; s. Francis Joseph and Rose Marie (Kreaps) K.; student Grove City (Pa.) Coll., 1928-29; B.S., Carnegie Inst. Tech.,

1933; Ph.D., Catholic U. Am. (K.C. fellow, 1933- 36), 1936; m. Mary Elizabeth O'Donnell, Apr. 15, 1942; children—Margaret Rose, Mary Frances. Mem. faculty Manhattan Coll., N.Y.C., 1936-69, prof. chemistry, 1945-69, prof. emeritus, 1969—, head dept. chemistry, 1945-66; chem. cons. (particularly photography), 1942—. Fellow Am. Inst. Chemists; mem. Am. Chem. Soc., Am. Assn. U. Profs. Home: 22 Metropolitan Oval New York City NY 10462

KEMPER, HATHAWAY GASPER, former mut. ins. exec.; b. Van Wert, O., Feb. 10, 1893; s. Hathaway and Mary (Scott) K.; student U. Wis.; m. Grace Clark Stover, Feb. 4, 1928; 1 son, Hathaway Clark. Mem. First Officers Tng. Camp, Fort Sheridan, Ill., 1915, served in F.A. until end World War I. Started with Kemper orgn., 1912; chmn. sr. council, dir. Lumbermens Mut. Mut. Casualty Co., Am. Motorist Ins. Co.; chmn. sr. council Am. Mfrs. Mut. Ins. Co., N.Y.C., Fed. Mut. Ins. Co., Boston. Mem. Chgo. Crime Commn. Republican. Presbyn. Clubs: Committee of Twenty-Five, Thunderbird Country, Racquet (Palm Springs, Cal.); Tavern, Chicago (Chgo.). Home: 71 Westlake Circle Palm Springs CA 92262 Office: Kemper Ins Bldg Chicago IL 60606

KEMPER, JAMES MADISON, Jr., banker; b. Kansas City, Mo., Oct. 10, 1921; s. James M. and Gladys (Grissom) K.; B.A., Yale, 1943; m. Mildred Lane, Mar. 30, 1948; children—Laura Lane, David, Jonathan McBride, Julie Ann. Pres. McBride Realty Co., Kansas City, Mo.; with Commerce Trust Co., Kansas City, 1946- -, asst. cashier, 1946-48, v.p., 1948-53, exec. v.p., 1953-55, pres., 1955—, also chmn.; dir. Missouri Pacific R.R. Co., St. Louis, Owens- Corning Fiberglas Corp., Gas Service Co., Kansas City, Mo., Panhandle Eastern Pipe Line Co., N.Y., Paul Mueller Co., Springfield, Mo.; pres., chmn., dir. Commerce Bancshares, Inc., Kansas City, Mo. Trustee Com. Econ. Devel. Office: Commerce Trust Co Kansas City MO 64106

KEMPER, JAMES SCOTT, ins. co. exec.; b. Van Wert, O., Nov. 18, 1886; s. Hathaway and Mary Jane (Scott) K.; ed. pub. and high schs., Van Wert; LL.D., Miami U., Oxford, O., Ripon (Wis.) Coll., Wittenberg Coll., Middle bury Coll., Northwestern U., 1963, Ill. Inst. of Tech., 1964; m. Mildred Estelle Hooper, Apr. 5, 1913 (dec. Nov. 27, 1927); children—James Scott, Rosemary, Mildred Jean; m. 2d, Mrs. Gertrude Ziesing Stout, Jan. 17, 1931. Spl. agt. in Ind. and Western Ohio, Central Mfrs., 1907-11; mgr. western dept., Chicago, same orgn., also mgr. Asso. Lumber Mutuals and Lumbermens & Mfrs. Ins. Agy., 1911; v.p., gen. mgr. Lumbermens Mutual Casualty Co., Chgo., 1912-19, pres., 1919-45, chmn. 1946-57, chmn. bd., 1958—; chmn. bd., pres. Fidelity Life Assn.; chmn. bd. Am. Motorists Ins. Co., Fed. Kemper Life Assurance Co.; chmn. bd. Am. Mfrs. Mut. Ins. Co. (N.Y.), James S. Kemper & Co. (Chgo.), Econ. Fire and Casualty Co., Freeport, Ill., Sequoia Ins. Co., Menlo Park, Cal., Fed. Mut. Ins. Co., Chgo., Lumbermens & Mfrs. Mut. of Ill.; officer or dir. several ins. orgns.; dir. S.C. Johnson & Son, Inc. U.S. ambassador to Brazil, 1953-55. U.S. sec. Inter-Am. Council Commerce and Prodn., past pres. Trustee Ill. Inst. Tech., Chgo. Wesley Meml. Hosp.; Chmn. James S. Kemper Found.; bd. dirs. Inst. Am. Strategy; mem. adv. bd. Greater Chgo. Safety Council; dir. Boys Clubs of Am. Chmn. Republican Nat. Finance Com., 1944- 46; treas. Rep. Nat. Com., 1946-48; del. nat. convs., 1936, 40, 44, 48, 52, 64; Rep. Nat. Committeeman, Ill., 1960—. Decorated grand cross Order So. Cross (Brazil); comdr. Order of Merit (Ecuador); recipient Thomas F. Cunningham award for outstanding service in Inter-Am. Relations, 1948; Internat. Chicagoan of Year award, 1962, Chgo. medal of merit, 1962; named Businessman of Americas, U.S. sect. Inter- Am. C. of C. and Prodn., 1963. Mem. Nat. Indsl. Conf. Bd. (res. fund com.), YMCA (life mem. Rio de Janeiro), Internat. Assn. Chiefs Police (distinguished life), U.S.C. of C. (bd. dirs. 1920-28, v.p., 1937-40, pres., 1940-41; mem. sr. council), Internat. C. of C. (trustee), Ins. Forum San Francisco (hon.), Am. C. of C. for Brazil (hon. pres.), Am. Inst. Property and Liability Underwriters (trustee), Alpha Kappa Psi, Iota Nu Sigma. Clubs: Casino, Chicago, Glen View, Racquet, Saddle and Cycle, Tower, Executives, Post and Paddock (Chgo.); California (Los Angeles); Racquet, Thunderbird, Com. of Twenty-five, El Dorado (Palm Springs); Bohemian (San Francisco); Bath and Tennis, Everglades (Palm Beach); Metropolitan, Downtown Assn. (N.Y.C.); Chevy Chase, Metropolitan, Capitol Hill (Washington). Home: Green Meadow Farms Barrington IL 60010 Office: Kemper Insurance Bldg Chicago IL 60606 also 345 Via Las Palmas Palm Springs CA 92262

KEMPER, JAMES SCOTT, Jr., ins. co. exec.; b. Chgo., Apr. 8, 1914; s. James Scott and Mildred Estelle (Hooper) K.; B.A., Yale, 1935; LL.B., Harvard, 1938; m. Joan Hoff, Dec. 27, 1960; children by previous marriages—James Scott III, Linda S., Stephen H., Judith, Robert C. Admitted to N.Y., Ill., Cal. bars; with anti-trust div. Dept. Justice, 1938-40; practice in N.Y.C., 1940-42, Chgo., 1946-52, Los Angeles, 1952-60; vice chmn. Lumbermens Mut. Casualty Co., Chgo., 1960-63, pres., 1963—, also dir.; pres., dir. Am. Motorists Ins. Co., Chgo., Am. Mfrs. Mut. Ins. Co.; sr. v.p. Fed. Mut. Ins. Co.; chmn. bd., dir. Economy Fire & Casualty Co. Pres., trustee James S. Kemper Found.; bd. dirs. Nat. Council Alcoholism. Served to lt. comdr. USNR, World War II. Mem. Alpha Sigma Phi. Home: 530 Ash St Winnetka IL 60093 Office: 4750 N Sheridan Rd Chicago IL 60640

KEMPER, JOHN DUSTIN, univ. dean; b. Portland, Ore., May 29, 1924; s. Clay Wallace and Leona (Bell) K.; B.S., U. Cal. at Los Angeles, 1949, M.S., 1959; Ph.D., U. Colo., 1969; m. Barbara Jeanne Lane, June 28, 1947; 1 dau., Kathleen Lynne. Engr. Telecomputing Corp., North Hollywood, Cal., 1949-52, chief mech. engr., 1952-55; chief mech. engr. H.A. Wagner Co., Van Nuys, Cal., 1955-56; chief engr. Marchant div. SCM Corp., Oakland, Cal., 1956-60, v.p engring., 1960-62; prof. Coll. Engring., U. Cal. at Davis, 1962-69, dean, 1969—. Served with USAAF, 1944-46. Sci. faculty fellow NSF, 1965-68. Mem. Am. Soc. M.E., Am. Soc. Engring. Edn., Sierra Club, Tau Beta Pi. Author: The Engineer and His Profession, 1967; also articles. ‡

KEMPER, JOHN MASON, headmaster; b. Fort D.A. Russell, Wyo., Sept. 1, 1912; s. James Brown and Mercer (Mason) K.; B.S., U.S. Mil. Acad., 1935; M.A., Columbia, 1942; L.H.D., Williams Coll., 1948, Colby Coll. 1958; Litt.D., Tufts Coll., 1952; LL.D., Harvard, 1962; m. Sylvia Mayo Pratt, June 9, 1936 (dec. Sept. 1961); children—Cecily Thomson (Mrs. David Wood Gillespie), Lucy Ord (Mrs. Jerome Alec Pieh), Rosamond Pratt; m. 2d, Abby Castle, Dec. 27, 1963. Commd. 2d lt. U.S. Army, 1935, advanced through grades to col., 1944; chief hist. br. War Dept., World War II; headmaster Phillips Acad., Andover, Mass., 1948—. Decorated Legion of Merit (2). Mem. Headmasters Assn. (pres. 1970-71), Nat. Assn. Ind. Schs. (chmn. 1955-57). Clubs: Century Assn., University (N.Y.C.); Tavern (Boston). Home: 189 Main St Andover MA 01810 Office: Phillips Acad Andover MA

KEMPER, MARK, ins. co. exec.; b. Van Wert, O., Oct. 7, 1901; s. Hathaway and Mary Jane (Scott) K.; B.S., Northwestern U., 1924; M.B.A., Harvard, 1927; m. Annabel Wagner, Jan. 4, 1934; children—John Scribner, Mary Ann (Mrs. Robert P. Sowersby), Barbara (Mrs. Donald Chalice). With Lumbermens Mut. Casualty Co., Chgo., 1919—, mgr. investment dept., 1930-67, dir., 1936- -, treas., 1941-55, sec., 1947-67, financial v.p., 1955-67, chmn. finance com., 1968—; dir. Am. Mfrs. Mut. Ins. Co., Chgo., Fed. Mut. Ins. Co., Am. Motorists Ins. Co., Chgo.; mem., chmn. finance com. all cos. Kemper Group; chmn., dir. Bank Chgo.; dir., chmn. finance com., mem. exec. com. Fidelity Life Assn., Fulton, Ill.; dir. Economy Fire & Casualty Co., Kemper Security Ins. Co., Empire State Mut. Life Ins. Co., Jamestown, N.Y., Sequoia Ins. Co., Menlo Park. Mem. adv. bd. Jr. Achievement, Boy Scouts Am.; mem. citizens bd. U. Chgo.; bd. dirs., v.p. James S. Kemper Found.; bd. dirs. Theol. Sem. Mem. Am. Statis. Soc., Am. Finance Assn., Investment Analysts. Presbyn. (trustee). Clubs: Chicago, University, Mid- Day, Economic, Tower (Chgo.). Home: 903 Private Rd Winnetka IL 60093 Office: 20 N Wacker Dr Chicago IL 60606

KEMPER, ROBERT LOUIS, banker; b. Sacremento, Dec. 1, 1928; s. Paul L. and Vivienne E. (Mehl) K.; B.S.C., U. Santa Clara (Cal.), 1950; C.P.A., Cal., 1955; grad. Stonier Grad. Sch. Banking, Rutgers U., 1963; m. Dorothy I. Shanks, May 2, 1954; children—Catherine A., Susan D. Staff auditor Arthur Andersen & Co., San Francisco, 1950-56; with Am. Trust Co., San Francisco, 1956—, controller, 1962—, v.p., 1964-68, sr. v.p., 1968—, cashier, 1967—. Mem. Bank Adminstrn. Inst. (past pres. Golden Gate chpt.), Financial Execs. Inst. (past pres. San Francisco Chpt.), Am. Inst. C.P.A.'s, Cal. Soc. C.P.A.'s. Home: 80 Logan Lane Atherton CA 94025 Office: 464 California St San Francisco CA 94070

KEMPER, RUFUS CROSBY, Jr., banker; b. Kansas City, Mo., Feb. 22, 1927; s. Rufus Crosby and Enid (Jackson) K.; grad. Phillips Acad., Andover, Mass., 1942; student U. Mo.; m. Cynthia Ann Warrick, June 24, 1949; children-Rufus Crosby III, Pamela Warrick, Sheila Smith. Pres., chief exec. officer, dir., Mo. Bancshares, Inc., Kansas City, Mo., City Nat. Bank & Trust Co., Kansas City, Mo.; chmn. bd. Grand Av. Bank & Trust Co., Kansas City, Mo.; pres., dir. Kemper Realty Co., Kansas City, Mo., Pioneer Service Corp., Kansas City, Mo.; v.p., dir. Kemper Investment Co., Kansas City, Mo.; dir., mem. exec. com. Interstate Securities Co., Kansas City, Mo.; dir., chmn. finance com. Gateway Sporting Goods Co., Kansas City, Mo.; dir. Bookfield Banking Co. (Mo.), Gen. Telephone Co. Midwest, City Bond & Mortgage Co., Commonwealth Treatres, Inc.; dir. mfrs. adv. bd. Lumbermens Mut. Ins. Co., Chgo. Mem. adv. com. United Funds Kansas City, Research Hosp., Kansas City; hon. dir. Rockhurst Coll.; trustee Kansas City Art Inst.; bd. dirs. Kansas City Indsl. Found., Kansas City area council Boy Scouts Am.; trustee Freedoms Found. at Valley Forge; mem. estate planning com. Christian Coll. Served with USNR, World War II. Recipient Distinguished Service award Kansas City Jr. C. of C., 1964, Key Man award, 1952. Mem. Assn. Res. City Bankers, Beta Theta Pi. Republican. Episcopalian. Clubs: River, Kansas City Country, Kansas City, 1021, 711 Kansas City, Mo. Home: 5700 Oakwood Rd Shawne Mission KS 66208 Office: Mo Bancshares Inc 10th and Grand Av Kansas City MO 64141

KEMPER, WALLACE CLEGG, sugar co. exec.; b. Franklin, La., July 11, 1904; s. Charles Delaware and Emma (Frer) K.; B.B.A., Tulane U., 1925; m. Clara B. Bush, May 29, 1928; children—Frances Buckner, Wallace Clegg, Clara Boise. Exec. v.p., treas. Sterling Sugar, Inc., Franklin, La., 1930-44; pres. Sterling Sugars Sales Corp., 1933-44; exec. v.p South Porto Rico Sugar Co. of P.R., N.Y.C., 1945-50; v.p. Ingenio Santa Fe, Dominican Republic 1948-50; v.p. Mar Ancha Corp., N.Y.C., 1947-50; pres. Southdown, Inc., New Orleans, 1950-66, chmn. bd., chief exec. officer, 1966-69; pres. Avoca, Inc.; dir. La.-So. Life Ins. Co., Delta Capital Corp. Dir. Bur. Governmental Research; trustee Pub. Affairs Council. Dir. Met. Area Com. Mem. Sugar Assn. (v.p.), Sugar Cane League. Clubs: Pickwick, La., Boston (New Orleans). Home: 1654 Valmont St New Orleans LA 70115 Office: Commerce Bldg New Orleans LA 70112

KEMPERMAN, JOHANNES HENRICUS BERNARDUS, educator, mathematician; b. Amsterdam, Netherlands, July 16, 1924; s. Albert J. and Gerarda (Jeurissen) K.; B.A., U. Amsterdam, 1945, M.A., 1948, Ph.D., 1950; m. Wilhelmina J.M. Ypma, Aug. 20, 1953; children—Steven Richard, Bruce Allen, Hubert John, Ingrid Maria, Eric Ypma. Research asso. Math. Centre, Amsterdam, 1948-51; vis. prof. Purdue U., 1951-53, asst. prof., 1953-55, asso. prof., 1955-59, prof., 1959-61; prof. math. U. Rochester (N.Y.), 1961—, chmn. dept., 1969-70, Fayerweather prof. math., 1970—; on leave to U. Amsterdam, 1958-59, U. Wis., 1960-61, Stanford, 1966-67. Fellow Inst. Math Statistics; mem. Am. Math. Soc., Math. Assn. Am., A.A.A.S., Soc. Indsl. and Applied Math., Dutch Math. Soc. Author: The Passage Problem For a Stationary Markov Chain, 1961. Asso. editor: Annals Math. Statistics, 1964-67, 70—. Contbr. articles profl. jours. Home: 99 Bastian Rd Rochester NY 14623

KEMPF, JOHN EMERSON, educator; b. Pittsfield, Mich., Sept. 14, 1912; s. Julius V. and Wanda (Laubengayer) K.; A.B., U. Mich., 1934, M.D., 1937; m. Alice Cornelia Hayes, June 8, 1937; 1 son, Mark Francis. Intern U. Mich. Hosp., 1937-38, resident asst. virology, 1938-41, instr. bacteriology, 1941-46; dir. Pasteur Inst., U. Mich., 1946; asso. prof. U. Ill. Coll. Medicine, Chgo., 1946-52, prof., 1952—, acting head dept. microbiology, 1964-65; cons. Coronet Films, 1966-67. Diplomate Am. Bd. Microbiology. Fellow Am. Acad. Microbiology, N.Y. Acad. Scis., Am. Pub. Health Assn., A.A.A.S.; mem. Am. Soc. Microbiology. Home: 303 Oak St Elmhurst IL 60126 Office: 835 S Wolcott St Chicago IL 60680

KEMPF, PAUL STUART, optics co. exec.; b. Dubuque, Ia., Apr. 25, 1918; s. Fred Ferdinand and Vera Content (Smith) K.; student Ia. State Coll., 1936-37; B.A. cum laude, U. Ia., 1941; M.B.A. with distinction, Harvard, 1947; m. Dorothea Ruth Guenther, Dec. 16, 1943 (div. June 1966); 1 son, Karlton Guenther. Asst. to mgr. indsl. relations Inland Steel Co., 1947-51; mgr. indsl. relations Inland Steel Products Co., 1951-54; dir. indsl. relations Pacific Mercury Electronics, 1954- 56, Hoffman Electronics, 1956-57; v.p. personnel and indsl. relations Crane Co., 1957-59; dir. corp. indsl. relations Hughes Aircraft Co., 1959-64; pres. chmn. Western Optics, Inc., 1964—; instr. U. Cal. at Los Angeles, 1957. Served to lt. USNR, 1942-45. Recipient award for unusual and valuable contbn. to personnel adminstrn. Los Angeles Mchts. and Mfrs. Assn., 1956. Mem. Am. Mgmt. Assn., Am. Soc. Personnel Adminstrn., Harvard Bus. Sch. Assn., Phi Beta Kappa, Theta Xi. Republican. Methodist. Office: 531 Stevens St Solana Beach CA 92075

KEMPFER, HOMER HADLEY, educator; b. Prairie Home, Mo., Mar. 9, 1911; s. John J. and Anna Elizabeth (Hertzig) K.; B.S., Central Mo. State Tchrs. Coll., 1933; M.A., U. Mo., 1935; Ed.D., Columbia Tchrs. Coll., 1941; m. Maurine Lyon, June 5, 1932; children—Margaret Deane, Norma Bernadine; m. 2d, Helen Friend Allion, Dec. 31, 1955. Rural tchr., Jamestown, Mo., 1929-30, high school prin., High Hill, Mo., 1931-35; supt. schs. Bellflower, Mo., 1935- 37, Rothville, Mo., 1937-38; prin. high sch., Sweet Springs, Mo., 1938- 40; asst. secondary edn. Tchrs. Coll. Columbia, 1940-41; supr. adult edn. Office Edn., Washington, 1947-52; exec. dir. Nat. Home Study Council, Washington, 1952-58; adult edn. adviser Ministry of Edn., Govt. of India, ICA, 1958-60; dep. chief edn. adviser ICA Mission to India, 1960-63; chief Eastern So. Africa br. edn. div. Agy. Internat. Devel., Wash., 1963-66; chief literacy div. UNESCO, Paris, France, 1966- 67; dir. U.S. Armed Forces Inst., Madison, Wis., 1967-69; exec. dir. Nat. Assn. Trade and Tech. Schs., 1965-66; dir. Inst. for Ind. Study, Washington, 1969—; dir. Va. Tech/Reston Program Grad. Studies, 1970—. Cons. to nat. commn. on adult education finance, 1953-54. Recipient distinguished service citation Nat. Home Study Council, 1958. Mem. Adult Edn. Assn. U.S. (v.p. 1952-53), Indian Adult Edn. Assn., N.E.A., Am. Sociol. Soc. Author: Adult Education, 1955; How to Choose a Correspondence School, 1959. Contbr. articles to ednl. mags. Address: 12100 Sunset Hills Dr Reston VA 22070

KEMPFF, WILHELM WALTER FRIEDRICH, pianist, composer; b. Berlin, Germany, Nov. 25, 1895; educated Berlin U. and Conservatoire. Prof., dir. Stuttgart Staatliche Hochschule für Musik, 1924-29; concert tours as pianist throughout the world, 1929—. Recipient Mendelssohn prize; Artibus et Litteris medal (Sweden). Mem. Prussian Acad. Arts. Composer 2 symphonies, 4 operas, piano concertos, also chamber, vocal and choral music. Author: Unter dem Zimbelstern; (autobiography) Das Werden eines Musikers. Address: care Ibbs & Tillett 124 Wigmore St London W1 England

KEMPLE, JOSEPH NEPHI, excavating equipment mfg. co. exec.; b. Marion, O., Mar. 14, 1921; s. William H. and Eva (Kaminar) K.; B.S. in Engring., Stanford, 1948; m. Roberta Williams, June 17, 1945; children—Kathleen, Steven. With Columbia-Geneca div. (now Western operations) U.S. Steel Corp., San Francisco, 1947-57, product mgr., 1952-57; with Page Steel & Wire div. Am. Chain & Cable Co., Inc., Monessen, Pa., 57-62, gen. mgr., 1959-62; exec. v.p. Warner Co., Phila., 1962-63; pres. Guiberson div. Dresser Industries, Inc., Dallas, 1963-66; exec. v.p. marketing Dresser Oil Tool div., Dallas, 1966-68; pres., dir. Marion Power and Shovel Co., Inc., 1968—; dir. Fahey Bank, Marion. Mem. exec. bd. Harding Area council Boy Scouts Am., 1971—. Bd. dirs. Marion Gen. Hosp., Marion United Community Services, Indsl. Med. Found., Marion; trustee Blue Cross Central Ohio. Mem. Symposiarchs, Tau Beta Pi. Home: 1140 Kingwood Dr Marion OH 43302 Office: 617 W Center St Marion OH 43302

KEMPNER, HARRIS LEON, business exec.; b. Galveston, Tex., Oct. 6, 1903; s. I.H. and Henrietta (Blum) K.; B.A. cum laude, Harvard, 1923; m. Ruth Alma Levy, Apr 24, 1939; children—Harris Leon, Marion Lee (killed in action.). Chmn. bd., dir. Imperial Sugar Co., 1954—; chmn. bd. U.S. Nat. Bank, Galveston, Schwaback Kempner & Perutz, N.Y.C., Dallas, Galveston; trustee H. Kempner, Sugar Land Industry. Mem., past dir. New Orleans Cotton Exchange; mem. N.Y. Cotton Exchange. Served to comdr. USNR, 1942-45. Decorated Legion of Merit. Mem. Galveston C. of C. (past v.p., dir.), Texas Cotton Assn. (past pres.), Am. Cotton Shippers Assn. (past pres.) Clubs: Artillery, Quarterdeck (Galveston); Harvard (N.Y.C.); Army Navy (Washington). Home: 4810 Denver Dr Galveston TX 77550 Office: US Nat Bank Bldg Galveston TX 77550

KEMPNER, ISAAC HERBERT, III, sugar co. exec.; b. Houston, Aug. 28, 1932; s. Isaac Herbert, Jr. and Mary (Carroll) K.; grad Choate Sch., 1951; B.A. Stanford U., 1955, M.B.A., 1959; m. Helen Hill, July 1, 1967. Asst. v.p., Tex. Nat. Bank, Houston, 1959-64; v.p., sec.-treas., mgr. raw sugar Imperial Sugar Co., Sugarland, Tex., 1964-71, chmn. bd., 1971—; dir. Capital Nat. Bank, Houston, Sugarland State Bank; chmn. exec. com. Sugarland Industries, 1968—; trustee H. Kempner Jr. Trust Assn., Meth. Hosp., Houston, Assn. Community TV, Houston. Served to 1st lt. USMCR, 1955-57. Clubs: Bayou, Ramada, Houston Country (Houston); Camden Ale and Quail (Camden, Tex.). Office: Box 9 Sugarland TX 77478

KEMPNER, JACK JULIAN, educator; b. Ridgefield Park, N.J., Jan. 5, 1917; s. Emanuel and Sylvia (Wald) K.; B.S., N.Y.U., 1947; M.S., U. Colo., 1953; Ph.D., Ohio State U., 1956; m. Marjorie H. Vale, Sept. 17, 1941; children-Kenneth, Roger, Clifford. Chief accountant, office mgr. Columbia Lithographing Corp., N.Y.C., 1939-41; asst. prof. naval sci. Columbia, 1944-45; asso. prof. accounting Cal. Western U., San Diego, 1947-51; asst. prof. naval sci. U. Colo., 1951-53; grad. instr. accounting Ohio State U., 1953-56; prof., chmn. dept. accounting U. Mont., Missoula, 1956—; vis. prof. Mich. State U. at Sao Paulo, Brazil, 1962-64; pvt. practice auditor, tax adviser. Treas., bd. dirs. Missoula Crippled Childrens Assn. Served to comdr. USNR, 1941-46. Named CPA of Year, Mont., 1970. C.P.A., Mont. Mem. Am. Inst. C.P.A.'s Mont. Soc. C.P.A.'s (past pres.), Am. Accounting Assn., Nat. Assn. Accountants, Beta Gamma Sigam, Alpha Kappa Psi, Beta Alpha Psi. Conglist. (dir.). Rotarian, Elk. Contbr. articles profl. jours. Home: 440 King St Missoula MT 59801

KEMPNER, ROBERT MAX WASILII, internat. lawyer, polit. scientist; b. Freiburg, Germany, Oct. 17, 1899; s. Walter K. and Lydia (Rabinowitsch) K.; student of law, polit. sci., pub. adminstrn., criminol. univs. of Berlin, Breslau, Freiburg, (Dr. of Law and Pub. Adminstrn.); student U. Pa.; m. Ruth Lydia Hahn; children—Lucian Walter, André Franklin. Came to U.S., 1939, naturalized U.S. citizen. Asst. to state atty., Berlin, 1926; judge municipal court, Berlin, 1927; superior govt. counselor Ministry of Interior, Berlin (chief legal adviser of Prussian police system of 76,000 men; recommended suppression of Nazi party and prosecution of Hitler for high treason and perjury, 1930, later expatriated by Hitler); judge civil service tribunal, 1928-33; lectr. German Acad. Politics Sch. Social Work, prof. polit. sci. and criminology, Police Inst., Berlin, 1926-33; counselor internat. law and migration problems, 1934- 35. Pres. and prof. polit. sci., Fiorenza Coll., Florence, Italy, and Nice, France, 1936-39; research asso. and asst. Inst. Local and State Govt., U. Pa. (research on machinery of European dictatorships under Carnegie and Carl Schurz grants), 1939-42; expert to Fed. courts, espionage and fgn. agent trials; expert cons., Dept. of Justice, OSS and to sec. of War on legal, polit., police and intelligence techniques of European dictatorships and fgn. orgns. in U.S., 1942-45; U.S. staff prosecutuor in Nuremberg trials against Goering, Frick et al, research dir. U.S. prosecution, 1945-46; dep. U.S. chief of counsel for war crimes, chief prosecutor of German Reich cabinet mems., state secs. and diplomats Nuremberg, 1946-49; expert cons. in internat. law, indemnification matters, and prosecution of war criminals, 1951—; cons. to Israel Govt. in Eichmann case, 1961; vis. prof. U. Erlangen; lectr. before numerous schs., colls., univs. and pvt. orgns. Mem. Am. Polit. Sci. Assn., Am. Acad. Polit. and Social Sci. Am. Soc. for Internat. Law, German Bar. Author several books, primarily on Germany, 1931—; The Judgment in The Wilhelmstrassen Case, 1950; German Police Administration, 1953; Eichmann and Accomplices, 1961; SS Under Crossexamination, 1964; The Warren Report in German Language, 1964; Edith Stein and Anne Frank-Two of Hundred thousand, 1968; The Third Reich under Crossexamination, 1969. Contbr. profl. jours. Home: 112 Lansdowne Ct Lansdowne PA 19050 ☆

KEMPNER, WALTER, physician; b. Berlin, Germany, Jan. 25, 1903; s. Walter and Lydia (Rabinowitsch) K.; M.D., U. Heidelberg, Germany, 1926. Came to U.S., 1934, naturalized, 1941. Intern medicine U. Heidelberg, 1926-27; research asst. and asso. to Dr. Otto Warburg, Kaiser Wilhelm Inst. for Cellular Physiology, 1927-28, 33-34; asst. physician dept. medicine Berlin U. Sch. Medicine, 1928-33; with Duke Sch. Medicine 1934—, asso., asst. prof., asso. prof., 1934-51, prof., 1952—. Trustee Walter Kempner Found. Fellow A.C.P.; mem. Am. Physiol. Soc., A.M.A., Am. Geriatrics Soc., World Med. Assn. Contbr. articles to articles to profl. jours. Originator rice diet in treatment hypertensive and arteriosclerotic vascular disease, heart and kidney disease, vascular retinopathy, diabetes mellitus and obesity. Home: 1505 Virginia Av Durham NC 27705

KEMPTON, JAMES MURRAY, editor; b. Balt., Dec. 16, 1918; s. James Branson and Sally (Ambler) K.; B.A., Johns Hopkins, 1939; m. Mina Bluethenthal, June 11, 1942; children—Sally Ambler, James Murray, Arthur Herbert, David Llewellyn; m. 2d Beverly Gary; 1 son, Christopher. Publicity dir. Am. Labor Party, 1941-42; reporter N.Y. Post, 1942-43, asst. to labor columnist, 1947-49, labor columnist, 1949-63; reporter Wilmington (N.C.) Morning Star, 1946-47; editor New Republic, 1963-64; columnist N.Y. World Telegram, 1964-66, N.Y. Post, 1965-69, N.Y. Rev. Books, 1969- -; commentator CBS, 1970—. Served as cpl. AUS, 1943-45. Recipient Sydney Hillman Found. award for reporting, 1950; Page One award Newspaper Guild, 1958, 60; George Polk Meml. award, 1966. Democrat (del. nat. conv. 1968). Author: Part of Our Time, 1955; America Comes of Middle Age, 1962. Address: 800 West End Av New York City NY 10025

KEMPTON, RUDOLF THEODORE, retired educator; b. Haverhill, Mass., May 30, 1902; s. Eugene Judson and Laura Emma (Sanborn) K.; B.S., Bates Coll., 1924; M.A., Columbia, 1925; Ph.D., N.Y.U., 1932; m. Elizabeth Thomas Leader, Dec. 25, 1926; 1 dau., Laura Estelle. Student asst. Bates Coll., 1922; asst. in biology N.Y.U., 1924-26, instr. 1926-32; research asso. pharmacology U. Pa., 1932-35; asst. prof. biology Princeton, 1935-37; prof. zoology and curator Natural History Museum, Vassar Coll., 1937-67, chmn. dept. zoology, 1940-62, prof. emeritus biology, 1967—; teaching staff in physiology Marine Biol. Lab., 1941- 47; on leave, 1945-46; tchr. physiology Army U. Center, Shrivenham, Eng.; researcher Marineland of Fla., 1964-65. Trustee Marine Biol. Lab., Woods Hole, Mass., 1948. Mem. Am. Soc. Zoologists (sec. 1954-58), Physiol. Soc. Phila., Soc. Gen. Physiol., Phi Beta Kappa, Sigma Xi. Methodist. Club: University (Poughkeepsie). Author: Laboratory Manual for Comparative Anatomy (with M. E. Little), 1926; (with Fred Brown) Sex Questions and Answers, 1948. Home: Rural Route 3 Box 351 St Augustine FL 32084

KENAN, THOMAS AUGUSTINE, army officer; b. Atlanta, Oct. 10, 1917; s. Samuel W. and Josephine (Richardson) K.; B.S., The Citadel, 1939; M.S., Ohio State U., 1947, Ph.D., 1948; grad. Inf. Sch., 1941-42, Command and Gen. Staff Coll., 1943, Army War Coll., 1954; m. Lucette M. Rollett, Sept. 18, 1954; 1 dau., Dominique. Commd. 2d lt. U.S. Army, 1939, advanced through grades to maj. gen., 1966; company comdr., battalion comdr., regtl. S3 and Div. G3, 22 Inf. Regt., 4th Inf. Div., 1942-46; personnel staff officer Office Asst. Chief Staff, G1, Dept. Army, 1946-48; chief mgmt. officer AG div. SHAPE, Paris, France, 1951-53; br. chief and div. exec officer asst. chief staff, G1, Dept. Army (DA), 1954-58; battle group comdr. 11th Inf., 2d Inf. Div., Ft. Benning, Ga., 1958-59, asst. chief staff, 1959-60; chief staff G1, Hdqrs. 8th U.S. Army, USARPAC, Korea, 1960-61; chief manpower and tng. div. office Sec. Def., Washington, 1961-62, dir. adminstrn. and mgmt. Office Mil. Assistance, 1962-63, dep. chief Office Res. Components, 1963-67; comdg. gen. U.S. Army Tgn. Center, inf., Ft. Ord, Cal., 1967—. Decorated D.S.M., Silver Star, Bronze Star with oak leaf cluster, Purple Heart, Combat Inf. badge, Army Commendation ribbon; Criox de Guerre with palm (France); Fourragere (Belgium). Mem. Sigma Xi, Tau Beta Pi. Rotarian (hon.). Home: Quarters 327 Presidio of Monterey CA 93940 Office: Hdqrs USATC Inf Fort Ord CA 92941

KENDALL, BRUCE EDWARD, retired army officer; b. Alabam, Ark., Nov. 12, 1910; s. Lemuel B. and Julia (Price) K.; B.S., U. Ark., 1933; grad Command and Gen. Staff Coll., Indsl. Coll. Armed Forces, 1950, Advanced Mgmt. Program, Harvard; m. Betty Jane Billingsley, June 2, 1934; 1 dau., Ann (Mrs. James R. Monteith, Jr.). Commd. 2d lt., inf., U.S. Army, 1933, advanced through grades to maj. gen., 1964; comdr. CCC Camp, then staff dist. hdqrs., Little Rock, 1933-40; various assignments q.m. depots, 1941; chief depot operations Office Q.M. Gen., q.m. 8th Army, 1941-49; q.m. U.S. Forces Austria, dep. q.m. U.S. Army, Europe, 1950-57; dep. comdr. Army Logistics Mgmt. Center. Ft. Lee, Va., 1957-58; comdg. officer Schenectady Gen. Depot, then asst. dir. supply Dept. Army, Washington, 1958-60; dir. adminstrn., dir. operations, Office Q.M. Gen., 1960-62; dir. supply U.S. Army Supply and Maintenance Command, 1962-64; dir. logistics services Hdqrs. Def. Supply Agy., 1964- 65, exec. dir. supply operations, 1965-66; dep. comdg. gen. U.S. Army, Ryukyu Islands, 1966; comdg. gen. U.S. Army Japan, 1967-68; assigned Indsl. Coll. Armed Forces, Ft. L.J. McNair, Washington, 1969-70; retired, 1970. Decorated D.S.M. with oak leaf cluster, Legion Merit with 3 oak leaf clusters. Home: Route 2 Fayetteville AR 72701

KENDALL, CHARLES SHILLING, clergyman; b. Fredericksburg, Ind., Apr. 12, 1905; s. Landy Haven and Pearl (Shilling) K.; A.B., DePauw U., 1927, D.D., 1945; S.T.B., Boston U., 1930, S.T.M., 1930-32, Th.D., 1942; student Harvard, 1929-30; D.H., So. Cal. Coll. Osteopathy, 1957; LL.D., Lincoln U., 1965; m. Mary Lous Travis, Jan. 1, 1930; children—Charles Travis, Margaret Ann, Philip Wesley. Ordained to ministry Methodist Ch., 1925; pastor in Maywood, Ind., 1925-28, Gloucester, Mass., 1928-33, Los Angeles, 1933-38, 38-42, Somerville, Mass., 1938, Phoenix, 1942-56, First Meth. Ch., Hollywood, Cal., 1956-70; supt. Tucson dist. So. Cal.- Ariz. Conf., United Meth. Ch., 1970—, trustee, 1954-68. Mem. council world service Meth. Ch., 1952-64; pres. Hollywood Ministerial Assn., 1967, Los Angeles Council Chs., 1964-65, Los Angeles United Ministers Assn., 1968-70. Mem. Ariz. Gov. Com. Youth Prison Reform, 1942-44; mem. Coodinating Council Hollywood, 1958-62. Recipient Goodwill Industries 30 Year award, 1968; Distinguished Alumnus award Boston U., 1964. Mem. Hollywood C. of C., Phi Beta Kappa, Delta Sigma Rho. Optimist, Lion, Mason (32). Recording artist for Dot, Word records; player chimes and vibra harp. Home: 5935 E 4th St Tucson AZ 85711

KENDALL, CURTIS, banker; b. Mayfield, Ky., May 5, 1903; s. James Porter and Clara Ann (Wagoner) K.; B.A., Vanderbilt U., 1925; m. Marion Douglas, Feb. 24, 1936; children—Ann Douglas (Mrs. Morris W. Ray). Tchr., U. Mil. Sch., Mobile, Ala., 1925-29; salesman Foreman & Meador, real estate, Mobile, 1929-34; with Am. Nat. Bank & Trust Co., Mobile, 1934-61, sr. v.p., 1936-61, dir., 1946-61; with Birmingham Trust Nat. Bank (Ala.), 1961—, sr. v.p., 1963—; mem. faculty Sch. Banking of South, La. State U., 1957-69, Sch. Consumer Banking, U. Va., 1958-59. Mem. exec. com. Mobile Arts Council, 1959-60; trustee Birmingham Symphony Assn.; hon. vice chmn. bd. trustees Julius T. Wright Sch. Girls, Mobile. Named Outstanding Installment Banker in Ala., Ala. Banker's Assn., 1961. Mem. Am. Bankers Assn. (installment credit commn. 1956-58), Relay House, Phi Beta Kappa, Chi Phi. Republican. Baptist. Home: 212 Cross Ridge Rd Birmingham AL 35213 Office: PO Box 2554 Birmingham AL 35302

KENDALL, DAVID WALBRIDGE, lawyer; b. Indpls., Feb. 11, 1903; s. Calvin Noyes and Alla Perkins (Field) K.; student Phillips Acad., 1918-20; A.B., Princeton, 1924; LL.B., U. Mich., 1931; LL.D., Ind. Central Coll., 1964; m. Elizabeth Way, Dec. 17, 1934; 1 son, David Walbridge. Newspaper reporter, editorial writer, 1925-28; admitted to Mich. bar. 1931, since practiced in Jackson; mem. firm McKone, Badley, Kendall & Domke; gen. counsel U.S. Treasury, 1954-55; asst. sec. of Treasury, 1955-57; mem. firm Cummings, Sellers, Reeves, Conner & Kendall, 1957-58, Cummings & Sellers, 1961-62; v.p. legal affairs Chrysler Corp., 1962-68; now of counsel Butzel, Eaman, Long, Gust & Kennedy; chmn. bd. incorporators Nat. R.R. Passenger Corp., 1971; spl. counsel to Pres. of U.S., 1958-61; dir. Acacia Mut. Life Ins. Co., Washington. Mem. Lawyers Com. for Civil Rights Under Law. Trustee Fed. City Council, 1961—; chmn. Jackson Housing Authority; past pres. bd. edn. Union Sch. Dist., Jackson. Past v.p. United Givers Fund, Washington. pres. Grosse Pointe War Meml.; mem. nat. council, gen. div. laymen's work P.E. Ch.; trustee Episcopal Diocese of Mich. Mem. Republican Nat. Com., 1952-56. Mem. adv. com. U.S. Coast Guard Acad.; trustee Kenyon Coll., Gambier, O.; mem. bd. Hutzel Hosp., Med. Center Devel. Corp., Detroit. Served as combat intelligence officer, USAAF, 1942-45. Mem. Am., Fed. bar assns., Am. Judicature Soc., Am. Law Inst., Newcomen Soc., Mil. Order World Wars, Am. Legion, V.F.W., Res. Officers Assn. (judge advocate Mich. dept.), Assn. Gen. Counsel, Bar Assn. N.Y. (congl. ethics com.), Alumni Council Phillips Acad. (v.p.) Phi Delta Phi. Episcopalian (vestryman 1961-62). Mason, Elk. Clubs: Metropolitan, Chevy Chase (Washington); Detroit, Detroit Athletic, Yondotega (Detroit); Town (Jackson); Princeton, University (N.Y.C.). Contbr. articles to mil. publs. Home: 75 Lake Shore Rd Grosse Pointe Farms MI 48236 Office: First Nat Bldg Detroit MI 48226

KENDALL, DAVIDSON TIMOTHY educator; b. Chicago, 1928; B.S. in Physics, Yale, 1950; Ph.D. in Chemistry, Harvard, 1956; m. Sally Ann Jones, July 5, 1957; children--Kenneth J., Nancy A. Chemist, Acme Chem. Co., Blue Island, Ill., 1950-51; director of Research Lab., Indsl. Chemicals Corp., Cambridge, Mass., 1956-60; project coordinator environmental sect. Steinmetz Assos., Chgo., 1960-61; v.p. for research Bauer Bros. Chem. Co., Inc., Memphis, 1961-64; asst. prof. chemistry Washington U., St. Louis, 1964-66, asso. prof., 1966-70, prof., 1970-, head of chemistry dept., 1970-71. Vis. prof. So. Ill. U., summer 1967, U. of Ore., 1969. Scoutmaster, Boy Scouts America, University City, Mo., 1968-70. Bd. dirs. Rest Haven Home for Elderly, 1960-61; trustee of the Lutheran Hosp., 1965-71. Served from lt. to capt., AUS, 1951-53. Mem. Am. Chem. Soc., Sci. Research Soc. Am. (chpt. treas. 1967), Sigma Xi. Author: (with others) Basic Inorganic Chemistry, 1971. Home: Fairfax Apts 7291 Windermere Dr University City MO 63105 Office: Dept Chemistry Washington University St Louis MO 63130

KENDALL, EDWARD CALVIN, educator, biochemist; b. S. Norwalk, Conn., Mar. 8, 1886; s. George Stanley and Eva Frances (Abbott) K.; B.S., Columbia, 1908, M.S., 1909, Ph.D., 1910, D.Sc., 1951; D.Sc., U. Cin., 1922, Yale, Western Res. U., Williams Coll., Nat. U. Ireland, Columbia, 1951, Gustavus Adolphus Coll., 1963; m. Rebecca Kennedy, Dec. 30, 1915; children—Hugh, Roy, Norman, Elizabeth (Mrs. J.J. Steve). Research chemist Parke, Davis & Co., Detroit, 1910-11; investigations on thyroid gland St. Luke's Hosp., N.Y.C., 1911-14; head sect. biochemistry Mayo Clinic, 1914, prof. physiologic chemistry Mayo Found., U. Minn., 1921-51; vis. prof. chemistry James Forrestal Research Center, Princeton, 1952—. Recipient John Scott prize and premium City of Phila., 1921 (researches in thyroxin); Chandler medal Columbia, 1925; Squibb award for outstanding research in endocrinology, 1945; Lasker award (jointly with Dr. Hench) Am. Pub. Health Assn., 1949; Page One award (jointly with Dr. Hench) Newspaper Guild N.Y., 1950; John Phillips Meml. award A.C.P. in Boston, 1950; Research Corp. N.Y. award, 1950; Research award Am. Pharm. Mfrs. Assn., 1950; Passano Found. award (with Dr. Hench) San Francisco, 1950; Medal of Honour, Canadian Pharm. Mfrs. Assn., 1950; Nobel prize in physiology and medicine (with Dr. Philip S. Hench and Dr. Tadeus Reichstein), 1950; Dr. C.C. Criss award (jointly with Dr. Hench), 1951; Award of Merit (with Dr. Hench), Masonic Found. Med. Research and Humane Welfare, 1951; Cameron award (with Prof. Reichstein) U. Edinburgh, 1951; Heberden Soc. award, London, 1951; Alexander Hamilton medal Alumni Columbia Coll., 1961; Sci. Achievement award A.M.A., 1965. Mem. Am. Philos. Soc., Am. Acad. Arts and Scis., Am. Soc. Biol. Chemists (pres. 1925-26), Am. Physiol. Soc., Am. Soc. Exptl. Pathology, Am. Soc. Exptl. Biology and Medicine, Am. Chem. Soc. (Remsen Meml. award Md. sect. 1950), Harvey Soc., A.A.A.S., Assn. Am. Physicians (Kober award 1952), Endocrine Soc. (pres. 1930-31), Nat. Acad. Scis., N.Y. Acad. Scis., Swedish Soc. Republican. Conglist. Contbns. include isolation of thyroxine, crystallization of glutathione and establishment of its chem. structure, separation and identification of a series of compounds from adrenal cortex; prepared cortisone by partial synthesis (with Merck & Co., Inc.), investigated effects of cortisone and ACTH on rheumatoid arthritis and in rheumatic fever (with Drs. Hench, Slocumb, Polley). Home: 3 Queenston Pl Princeton NJ 08540

KENDALL, GEORGE HAYWOOD, mech. engring. cons.; b. Worcester, Mass., Apr. 18, 1894; s. Frank Pierson and Florence (Cheney) K.; M.E., Internat. Corr. Schs., 1917; spl. physics course Worcester Poly. Inst., 1917; student econs. and finance Babson Inst., 1933-34; m. Mabel Christine Peterson, June 18, 1918; 1 son, George Haywood. Machine tool designer Norton Co., 1913-20; chief draftsman Jefferies-Norton Co., 1920-26; chief engr. Bearium Metals Corp., 1926-33; co-ordinating engr. Chrysler-Revere Copper & Brass Co., 1933-36; comml., service engr. Norma Hoffman Bearings Corp., 1936-42; chief engr. Sargent & Co., 1942-43; propr. George Kendall, mech. engrs. and cons., New London and Darien, Conn., 1923—; dir., chief engr. Multra Corp.; pres., dir. Kenhos Corp.; co- owner, exec. dir. Kenbos Patent Devel. Co.; spl. cons. on design, charge Eastern dist. div. Design & Devel., Inc., New London, 1969—; pres. Kendall-Russell, Inc., owners Kendo automatic process clothing mfg., 1971—; tchr., speaker in field, 1956—. Mem. Am. Soc. Tool and Mfg. Engrs., Nat. Soc. Profl. Engrs., Am. Soc. Indsl. Engrs., Am. Mgmt. Assn. Mason. Author: Automatic Machine Assembly, 1958; Instant Estimating Guide, 1948. Contbr. articles to profl. jours. Patentee in field; inventor original 1st fully automatic high speed process of clothing manufacture, garments at 10 to 30 per minute. Home: 342 Plant St Groton CT 06340 Office: 231 State St New London CT 06320 also PO Box 2 Noroton Heights Sta Darien CT 06823

KENDALL, GEORGE PRESTON, ins. co. exec.; b. Seattle, Aug. 11, 1909; s. George R. and Edna (Woods) K.; B.S., U. Ill., 1931; m. Helen A. Hilliard, Sept. 30, 1933; children—Goerge Preston, Thomas C., Helen R. With Washington Nat. Ins. Co., Evanston, Ill., 1931—, sec., 1950-56, exec. v.p., 1956-68, dir., 1948—, pres., 1962-67, chmn. bd., chief exec. officer, 1968- -: chmn. bd., chief exec. officer, dir. Washington Nat. Corp., 1969—; dir. Anchor Corp., State Nat. Bank Evanston. Dir., treas. C.P. Kendall Found., Evanston. Served from 2d lt. to 1st lt., inf., AUS, 1942-45. Decorated Purple Heart. Mem. Newcomen Soc. N. Am., Am. Life Conv., Ill., Evanston chambers commerce, Theta Chi. Mason (K.T., Shriner). Clubs: Optimist (pres. 1947), University (Evanston); Westmoreland Country (Wilmette); Bankers, Executives (Chgo.). Home: 70 Indian Hill Rd Winnetka IL 60093 Office: 1630 Chicago Av Evanston IL 60201

KENDALL, GLENN ROBERT, Jr. mfg. exec.; b. Lima, O., Apr. 1, 1932; B.S., U. San Francisco, 1954; M.S., Stanford University, 1956; m. Rosemarie Lois Brown, May 15, 1955; 1 son, Anthony Robinson. Sales rep. Ames-Brockton Fabricated Products, Akron, O., 1956-58, sales mgr. Coshocton, Ohio, 1959-61, gen. manager plant, 1961-68, v.p. sales, 1968--. Instr. bus. Coshocton Jr. College, 1968-69. Mem. Coshocton C. of C. (vice president 1967-68, pres. 1969-70), Sales Executives Institute, Phi Beta Kappa, Sigma Chi, Phi Mu. Democrat. Mem. Christian Ch. (lay leader). Mason (32, Shriner). Clubs: Coshocton Country, Coshocton City, Running Deer Country. Home: 2d Av Coshocton OH Office: 3d Av Coshocton OH

KENDALL, HARRY T., Jr., paper co. exec.; b. Houston, 1912. Exec. v.p. operations, dir. Potlatch Forests, Inc.; dir. Globe Box Co., Houston, United Cal. Bank, Los Angeles, Minn. Power & Light Co., Duluth. Home: 60 McLaren Av San Francisco CA 94121 Office: PO Box 3591 San Francisco CA 94119

KENDALL, JAMES CLARKE, oil co. exec.; b. Nowata, Okla., Apr. 28, 1915; s. Frost Clarke and Ola (Hawkins) K.; student Okla. State U., 1933-35; B.S. in Bus. Adminstrn., U. Tulsa, 1938; m. Betty LeNoir Steinson, Dec. 20, 1940; children—James Clarke II, Katherine Elizabeth. Cost accountant Mid West Printing Co., 1938-42; with Amoco Prodn. Co., and predecessor, 1942—, comptroller, 1963—. Served with USNR, 1943-46. Mem. Financial Execs. Inst., Am. Petroleum Inst., Sigma Alpha Epsilon. Republican. Club: Tulsa Petroleum. Home: 2871 E 36th Pl Tulsa OK 74105 Office: PO Box 591 Tulsa OK 74102

KENDALL, JOHN PLIMPTON, mfg. co. exec.; b. Boston, June 26, 1928; s. Henry Plimpton and Evelyn (Way) K.; grad. Deerfield (Mass.) Acad., 1946; student Amherst Coll., 1951; B.A., Harvard, 1953; LL.D. (hon.), Washington and Jefferson Coll., 1971; m. Nancy Nichols Feick, Oct. 8, 1955; children—Andrew Way, Sarah Louise, David Feick. With Kendall Co., Boston, 1956—, mgr. European operations, 1966-68, v.p., 1968-70, chmn. bd., 1970—, also dir.; dir. Nat. Shawmut Bank, Boston. Pres. Henry P. Kendall Found.; nat. adv. council Hampshire Coll., Amherst, Mass.; trustee Andover Newton Theol. Sch., Kendall Whaling Museum, Franklin Found., Children's Hosp. Med. Center, Boston. Served with USNR, 1946-47, USMCR, 1953-55. Home: 293 Moose Hill Pky Sharon MA 02067 Office: 225 Franklin St Boston MA 02110

KENDALL, JOHN W., lawyer; b. Marshfield, Ore., Oct. 6, 1911; s. John C. and Gertrude (Walrath) K.; LL.B., U. Ore., 1935; LL.M., Georgetown U.; m. Jean Stitt, Aug. 15, 1935; children—Barbara, John. Atty. with Ben S. Fisher, Washington, 1935-41, Black & Kendall, Portland, Ore., 1941-46; partner in law firm Black, Kendall, Tremaine, Booth & Higgins, and predecessor, Portland, 1946—. Bd. dirs. Ore. Heart Assn., 1959—. Mem. Am. Bar Assn. (chmn. com. radio and TV 1959). Club: Multnomah Athletic (past sec., dir.) (Portland). Home: 2628 SW Patton Ct Portland OR 97201 Office: Cascade Bldg Portland OR 97204

KENDALL, KATHERINE ANNE, social worker; b. Muir-of-Ord, Scotland, Sept. 8, 1910; d. Roderick and Annie Scott (Walker) Tuach; came to U.S., 1920, naturalized, 1940; B.A., U. Ill., 1933; M.A., La. State U., 1939; Ph.D., U. Chgo., 1950; m. Willmoore Kendall, June 22, 1935 (div. Apr. 1950). Asst. prof. Richmond Sch. Social Work, 1941-42; asst. dir. home service A.R.C., 1942-44; lectr. U. Chgo. Sch. Social Service Adminstrn., 1944-45; asst. dir., tng. supr. Inter-Am. and Internat. Tng. units U.S. Children's Bur., 1945- 47; social affairs officer UN Secretariat, 1947-50; exec. sec. Am. Assn. Schs. Social Work, 1950-52; ednl. sec. Council on Social Work Edn., 1952- 58, asso. dir., 1958-63, exec. dir., 1963-66, dir. internat. edn., 1966- 71; Carnegie vis. prof. U. Hawaii, 1960-61. Mem. exec. bd. Internat. Assn. Schs. Social Work, 1954-66, sec.-gen., 1966—, ofcl. non-govtl. rep. UN, 1954—; dir. Internat. Conf. on Social Work Edn., Population and Family Planning, East-West Center, Hawaii, 1970; mem. Un Internat. meeting experts on social work tng., Munich, 1956; faculty mem. UN Seminar, Keeru, Finland, 1952; assignment by UN, U.S. govt., pvt. orgns. on spl. mission social work edn., Guatemala, 1949, Brazil, 1952, Paraguay, 1954; dir. 1st seminar Schs. Social Work in Central Am., 1963. Mem. Mortar Bd., Nat. Assn. Social Workers, Nat. Conf. Social Welfare, Internat. Council on Social Welfare, Phi Beta Kappa, Chi Omega. Author: (UN reports) International Exchange of Social Welfare Personnel, 1949; Training for Social Work: First International Survey, 1950. Editor: Social work values in an Age of Discontent, 1970; Population Dynamics and Family Planning: A New Responsibility for Social Work Education, 1971; co-editor: Internat. Social Work. Home: 350 First Av New York City NY 10010 Office: 345 E 46th St New York City NY 10017

KENDALL, LACE, see Stoutenburg, Adrien.

KENDALL, MAURICE WESLEY, army officer; b. Lincoln City, Ind., Oct. 20, 1921; s. Noah Wesley and Martha (Meriwether) K.; B.S., Ind. U., 1942; grad. Command and Gen. Staff Coll., 1953, Armed Forces Staff Coll., 1956, Army War Coll., 1961; M.A., George Washington U., 1961; m. Charlene Gross, Aug. 28, 1942; children—Karen Rae (Mrs. Vernon Parker), John Michael. Commd. 2d lt. U.S. Army, 1943, advanced through grades to brig. gen., 1969; chief plans br. J-5, Hdqrs. UNC USFK, Seoul, Korea, 1961-62; sr. instr. tactics, chmn. attack com., brigade and bn. operations dept. Inf. Sch., Ft. Benning, Ga., 1962-64, asst. chief of staff Gl, dir. personnel U.S. Army Inf. Center, 1965-66; comdr. 1st Brigade, 9th Inf. Div., Ft. Riley, Kan. and S. Vietnam, 1966-67; chief of staff 9th Inf. Div., Camp Bearcat and S. Vietnam, 1967; operations officer Pacific Div., Office Joint Chiefs of Staff, Washington, 1968; dep. dir. for operations (NMCC), Operations Directorate, J-3, Office Joint Chiefs of Staff, Washington, 1968-69, dep. dir. for commands areas, 1969-70, dep. dir. for strategic and gen. operations, 1970; asst. div. comdr. 4th Inf. Div., Camp Radcliffe, S.Vietnam, 1970; comdg. gen., 1970; dep. comdg. gen., chief of staff Hdqrs. I Field Force, Vietnam, USARV, Nha Trang, Vietnam, 1971; dir. interam. region, internat. security affairs Office Sec. Def., 1971—. Decorated D.S.M., Silver Star with oak leaf cluster, Legion of Merit with 3 oak leaf clusters, Bronze Star medal with 3 oak leaf clusters, Air medal with 17 oak leaf clusters, Commendation medal, Purple Heart, Combat Inf. badge; French Fourragere; Gallantry Cross with gold star (Vietnam), Army Distinguished Service Order 2d Class, Nat. Def. Order 5th class (Vietnam). Home: 5727 Dupree Ct Alexandria VA 22303 Office: Asst Sec Defense The Pentagon Washington DC 20301

KENDALL, PAUL MURRAY, educator, author; b. Phila., Mar. 1, 1911; s. Oscar Benjamin and Helen (Murray) K.; A.B., U. Va., 1932, M.A., 1933, Ph.D., 1939; m. Carol Seeger, June 15, 1939; children—Carol Seeger, Gillian Murray. Mem. faculty English dept. Ohio U., 1937-70, Distinguished prof. English, 1959-70, Regents prof. English 1966-70; vis. prof. U. Kan., Lawrence, 1970—. Ford Found. fellow, 1952-53; Guggenheim fellow, 1957-58, 61-61. Mem. Renaissance Soc. Am., Am. Hist. Assn., Nat. Assn. Standard Med. Vocabulary. Author: Richard the Third, 1955; Warwick the Kingmaker, 1957; The Yorkist Age, 1962; The Art of Biography, 1965; Louis XI, 1971. Home: 928 Holiday Dr Lawrence KS 66044

KENDALL, RICHARD CHARLES, adj. gen. Mont.; b. Moab, Utah, July 7, 1917; s. Charles T. and Marselda (Rassmussen) K.; ed. Mont. State U., 1938; grad. Command and Gen. Staff Coll., 1960; m. Jane B. Brown, Jan. 11, 1942; children—Richard J., Charles D., Anthony W., Rex T. With U.S. Forest Service, 1936-40, Dept. Justice, 1940-47; automobile dealer, Deerlodge, Mont., 1948-60; served with 1st Army, ETO, 1943-45; mem. Mont. N.G., 1947-, maj. gen., 1964; adj. gen. Mont., 1962—; dir. Mont. S.S.S., 1964—; exec. dir. Mont. Civil Def., 1962—. Decorated Air medal with 2 oak leaf clusters, Bronze Star. Mem. N.G. Assn. U.S. Mason (Shriner), Kiwanian, Elk. Home: 512 Milwaukee St Deer Lodge MT 59722 Office: Hdgrs Mont National Guard Helena MT 59601

KENDALL, ROBERT REAM, oil co. exec.; b. Aberdeen, S.D., Mar. 9, 1917; s. Glenn Warren and Florence (Baker) K.; B.S. in Commerce, Drake U., 1939; m. Noma Georgia Schroeder, Oct. 22, 1944; children—Mildred Marian (Mrs. Wilfred R. DeLorge), Roberta Noma, Charles Ream. With Standard-Vacuum Oil Co., 1939- 62, asst. treas., 1959-62; treas. Mobil Petroleum Co. Inc., 1962-65; asst. treas. Mobil Oil Corp., 1964-65; mng. dir. Mei Foo Investments Ltd., Hong Kong, 1965—. Mem. Alpha Tau Omega, Delta Sigma Pi. Republican. Presbyn. Clubs: Hong Kong, Royal Hong Kong Jockey; Sind (Pakistan); Royal Bombay (India) Yacht; Willingdon (India). Home: 46 Inverness Rd Scarsdale NY 010583 Office: Mei Foo Sun Cheun Hong Kong

KENDALL, T.H., Jr., banker; b. Crystal Springs, Miss., 1905; grad. Miss. Coll., 1926. Sr. v.p., exec. officer First Nat. Bank, Jackson, Miss.; pres., dir. Merchants & Planters Bank, Gaddis Farms, Gaddis Motor Co.; v.p., dir. Gaddis & McLaurin, Inc.; chmn. Merchants Bank, Bolton. Home: 343 Glen Way Jackson MS 39216 Office: 248 E Captiol St Jackson MS 39205*

KENDALL, WALTER SELLEW, clergyman; b. Barron, Wis., Nov. 23, 1904; s. James Wilbur and Olive Bell (Cook) K.; D.D. (hon.), Greenville (Ill.) Coll., 1967; m. Ruth Johnson, Sept. 12, 1924; children—Richard S., Walter B., Elmer M., Olive (Mrs. Robert Hodson). Ordained deacon Free Meth. Ch., 1926, elder, 1928; pastor in Minn., 1924-29; evangelist, 1929-32, 35-50; dist. supt., Wis., 1932-35; gen. conf. evangelist, 1951-53; conf. supt., Ore., 1953-58, bishop, 1958-69, bishop emeritus, 1969—. Chmn. commn. missions Free Meth. Ch., 1958-64, chmn. adminstrv. commn., 1964-69, pres. bd. adminstrn., 1964-69, chmn. bd. bishops, 1964-69; chmn. bd. Free Meth. Pub. House, 1964-69; pres. World Fellowship Free Meth. Chs., 1964-69; mem. bd. adminstrn. Nat. Assn. Evangelicals, 1964-65. Home: 204 Cascade Dr Box 36 Lebanon OR 97355

KENDALL, WILLIAM HERSEY, r.r. exec.; b. Somerville, Mass., Mar. 24, 1910; s. Warren C. and Helen (Hodgkins) K.; A.B., Dartmouth, 1932; C.E., Thayer Sch. Civil Engring, 1933; m. Lucile W. Hayworth, Oct. 31, 1935; children—Roberta, William Thomas, James (dec.). Maintenance engr. Pa. R.R., 1933-48; exec. officer A.C.L. R.R., 1948-50, Clinchfield R.R., 1950-54 (now dir., mem. exec. com.); exec. officer L. & N. R.R., 1954—; v.p., gen. mgr., 1957-59, pres., 1959—, also dir.; dir., mem. exec. com. Ga. R.R.; dir. Atlanta & West Point R.R., Western Ry. of Ala., Commonwealth Life Ins. Co., Louisville, Capital Holding Co., Louisville, Hillerich & Bradsby Co., Louisville, Hercules, Inc., Wilmington, Del., Third Nat. Bank Nashville, Citizens Fidelity Bank & Trust Co., Louisville. Bd. dirs. Meth. Hosp., Louisville; trustee U. Louisville, Mem. Assn. Am. R.R.'s (dir.), Assn. So. R.R.'s (dir.), Am. Soc. Traffic and Transp., Alpha Tau Omega. Clubs: Louisville Country, Pendenhis (Louisville). Home: 6602 Deep Creek Dr Prospect KY 40059 Office: 908 W Broadway Louisville KY 40202

KENDALL, WILLIAM RAYMOND, orgn. adminstr.; b. Pasedena, Cal., Mar. 21, 1910; s. F. Arthur Cox and Myrtle Selby (Miles) K.; A.B., Occidental Coll., 1932, Mus.D. (hon.), 1947; A.M., Stanford, 1937; postgrad. U. Basel (Switzerland), 1938-39; Ph.D., Cornell U., 1940; m. Elizabeth Holman McClelland, June 26, 1936 (dec. Sept. 1946); children—Robert Arthur, Peter Holman; m. 2d, Marjorie Ann Schubring, Nov. 4, 1948 (div. 1957); 1 son, Richard Raymond; m. 3d, Nancy N. Scott, Sept. 26, 1958. Instr. Whittier Coll., 1933-34, Stanford, 1934-38; asst. prof. music Dartmouth, 1940-43; prof. music U. Mich., 1946-48; prof. music U. So. Cal., 1948—, dean Sch. Music, 1948-65, Sch. Performing Arts, 1965-67; pres. Performing Arts Acad. Music Center, 1967-69; music editor Los Angeles Mirror, 1948-62; music columnist Los Angeles Times, 1962-65; asso. music editor Time-Life History U.S., 1961-64; exec. dir. Young Musicians Found., Los Angeles, 1969—. Music coordinator Nat. U.S.O., 1942-45; spl. cons. music to sec. war, 1944-46; mem. music adv. panel Dept. State for Internat. Intercultural Exchange Program, 1958—; exec. dir. Rachmaninoff Fund, 1945-48. Mem. Nat. Assn. Schs. Music (v.p. 1949-50, 52-55), Music Tchrs. Nat. Assn. (treas. 1943-46, 49-51, pres. 1946-48), Am. Mus. Soc. (v.p. 1946-47, treas. 1947-48), Phi Beta Kappa, Pi Kappa Lambda, Phi Kappa Phi, Sigma Alpha Epsilon, Phi Mu Alpha Sinfonia. Democrat. Methodist. Clubs: Lotos (N.Y.C.); Dena Strand Beach and Tennis (Dana Point, Cal.). Contbr. articles to music jours. Home: 1014 Buena Vista St South Pasadena CA 91030 Office: 135 N Grand Av Los Angeles CA 90012

KENDEIGH, SAMUEL CHARLES, biologist; b. S. Amherst, O., Dec. 18, 1904, s. Milo Cornelius and Clara King (Gilman) K.; A.B., Oberlin Coll., 1926, M.A., 1927; postgrad. U. Neb., 1927-28; Ph.D., U. Ill., 1930; m. Dorothy Elizabeth Sutton, Sept. 6, 1930; children—Katherine Jane, Donald Charles. Instr. biology Western Res. U., 1930-36; asst. prof. zoology U. Ill., 1936- 43, asso. prof., 1943-48, prof., 1948—. Chmn. Ill. Nature Preserves Commn., 1964-71. Mem. Am. Ornithol. Union (Brewster award 1951), v.p. 1969, 70, Wilson Ornithol. Soc., (past pres.), Cooper Ornithol. Club, Nat. Audubon Soc., Ecol. Soc. Am. (past pres.), Brit. Ecol. Soc., Am. Soc. Zoologists, Wildlife Soc., Genetics Assn., Am. Soc. Mammalogists, Ohio, Ill., acads. sci., Phi Beta Kappa, Sigma Xi, Phi Kappa Phi. Author: Animal Ecology, 1961; also articles. Home: 1116 W Healey St Champaign IL 61820

KENDELL, HERBERT WORLEY, physician; b. Covington, O., Mar. 26, 1907; s. Herbert Weaver and Llora Agnes (Worley) K.; student Ohio State U., 1925-27; B.M., U. Cin., 1932, M.D., 1933; postgrad. phys. medicine Mayo Clinic, 1946-47, Mass. Inst. Tech., 1947; m. Bernice Lacy Loyd, Dec. 8, 1945; children—Chris (dec.), Craig Lynn: children by previous marriage—James Robert, Thomas W., William M. Intern Miami Valley Hosp., Dayton, O., 1932-33, resident pathology, 1933-35; head dept. phys. medicine, asso. dir. Kettering Inst. Med. Research. 1935- 42; clin. prof. phys. medicine and rehab. U. Ill. Coll. Medicine, 1951—, also med. dir. Inst. Phys. Medicine and Rehab.; mem. staff St. Francis, Meth. hosps., Peoria, Ill., 1951-58, dir. edn. and research, 1958-60, med. dir., 1960, sr. cons., 1960-65; pvt. practice, 1965—; staff Proctor Hosp., Peoria; cons. Peoria State Hosp. Supervising editor Med. Abstract Service, Physician's Record Co.; command surgeon (maj.), USPHS, 1942, med. officer charge Chgo. Intensive Treatment Center and State Fever Therapy Unit, Brookhaven (Miss.) Med. Center, 1942-46; mem. profl. adv. com. div. services for crippled children U. Ill.; mem. Commn. to Investigate Hospitalization of Paraplegics Ill.; chmn. liaison com. Am. Acad. and Congress Phys. Medicine and Rehab.-Am. Hosp. Assn. Diplomate Am. Bd. Phys. Medicine and Rehab. Fellow A.C.P.; mem. A.M.A., Am. Acad. Phys. Medicine and Rehab., Am. Congress Phys. Medicine and Rehab. (pres. 1947-48), Am. Acad. Neurology, Am. Geriatric Soc., Am. Assn. Study Headache, Am. Rheumatism Assn., Am. Acad. Electrodiagnosis and Electromyography, other med. socs. Contbr. articles profl. jours. Home: 3512 N California Av Peoria IL 61603

KENDERDINE, JOHN MARSHALL, ret. army officer, petroleum engr.; b. Ft. Worth, Dec. 6, 1912; s. Robert Leonard and Caroline (Raab) K.; B.S. in Petroleum Engring., Tex. A. and M. Coll., 1934; graduate Army War Coll., 1953; grad. Advanced Mgmt. Program, Harvard, 1959, Exec. Decision Inst., 1961; m. Su Ann Carroll, Feb. 26, 1937; children—James Marshall, Su Carroll (Mrs. H. Franklin Hain III). Petroleum engr. Gulf Oil Corp., 1934-37; br. mgr. Norvell-Wilder Supply Co., Midland. Tex., 1938-41; commd. 1st ltd. AUS 1941, advanced through grades to brig. gen., 1962; mil. logistician in France, Germany and U.S., World War II; spl. asst. to administr. War Assets Adminstrn., 1946; mil. staff and command assignments, 1947-60; joint petroleum officer Europe, 1961; exec. dir. supply operations Def. Supply Agy., 1962-65; comdr. Def. Indsl. Supply Center, Phila., 1965-66, Def. Personnel Support Center, Phila., 1966-67, ret.; v.p. Scott Paper Co., 1967-70; pres. C.F. Adams, Inc., Ft. Worth, 1970—. Decorated Legion of Merit, Joint Service Commendation medal, Commendation ribbon with 3 oak leaf clusters, D.S.M. Registered profl. engr., Tex. Mem. Def. Supply Assn., Assn. U.S. Army, Flight Safety Found., Armed Forces Communications and Electronics Assn. (bd. dirs. 1965), Commerce and Industry Council Phila., Phila. C. of C. (dir. 1966), Airline Passengers Assn. (adv. bd.). Clubs: Union League, Airways. Contbr. articles to profl. jours. Home: 3212 Chapparral Lane Fort Worth TX 76109 Office: C F Adams Inc PO Box 253 Fort Worth TX 76101

KENDIG, EDWIN LAWRENCE, Jr., physician; b. Victoria, Va., Nov. 12, 1911; s. Edwin Lawrence and Mary McGuire (Yates) K.; B.A. magna cum laude, Hampden-Sydney Coll., 1932, B.S. magna cum laude, 1933; M.D., U. Va., 1936; m. Emily Virginia Parker, Mar. 22, 1941; children—Anne Randolph (Mrs. Ronald F. Young), Mary Emily Corbin. Successively house officer Med. Coll. Va. Hosp., Bellevue Hosp., N.Y.C., Babies Hosp., Wilmington, N.C., Johns Hopkins Hosp., 1936-40; instr. pediatrics Johns Hopkins Sch. Medicine, 1944; practice of medicine specializing pediatrics, Richmond, 1940-; cons. diseases of chest in children; prof. pediatrics Med. Coll. Va., 1958- 70, clin. prof. pediatrics, 1970—, dir. Child Chest Clinic, 1944—; former chief staff St. Mary's Hosp. dir. Met. Nat. Bank, Richmond. Mem. Va. exec. com. White House Conf. on Children and Youth, 1960; chmn. bd. health City of Richmond, 1961-69. Bd. visitors U. Va., past mem. med. alumni bd.; past mem. bd. dirs. Va. Hosp. Service Assn. Member Am. Thoracic Soc., A.M.A., So. Med. Assn., So. Soc. Pediatric Research, Am. Acad. Pediatrics (past pres. Va. sect., founding mem., past chmn. sect. diseases chest), Va. (past pres.), Richmond (past pres.) pediatrics socs., Richmond Acad. Medicine (past pres., past chmn. bd. of trustees), Soc. Cin., Omicron Delta Kappa, Tau Kappa Alpha, Kappa Sigma, Phi Beta Kappa. Episcopalian. Clubs: Commonwealth, Country Club of Va.; Farmington Country (Charlottesville); Princess Anne Country (Virginia Beach); Commonwealth (Richmond). Author articles on Tb, diseases of chest in children. Contbg. editor: Current Pediatric Therapy (Gellis and Kagan); Antimicrobral Therapy (Kagan). Editor: Disorders of the Respiratory Tract in Children. Home: 5008 Cary Street Rd Richmond VA 23226 Office: 3603 Grove Av Richmond VA 23221

KENDIG, MARJORIE MERCER, educator; b. N.Y.C., 1896; d. Philip M. and Jane M. (Mercer) Kendig; A.B., Vassar Coll., 1915; grad. study U. Geneva (Switzerland), 1931-32; M.A., Columbia, 1934; m. D. F. Krueger, 1933 (div. 1939); m. 2d, Edward Lindley Gates, Dec. 22, 1951. Editor Charles Scribners Sons, George H. Doran, others, 1918-30; asst. dir. Progressive Coll., Geneva, 1930-31; prin. Barstow Sch., Kansas City, 1934-38; asso. Alfred Korzybski, 1934-49; founder, 1949, since editor Gen. Semantics Bull.; ednl. dir. Inst. Gen. Semantics, 1938-50, dir., 1950-64, consulting dir., 1965—; organizing chmn. Korzybski Centennial Congress, 1971—; vis. lectr. U. Denver, 1943, 44, 65, N.Y.U., 1947. Author: Alfred Korzybski and His Work: A Memoir, 1950; Linguistic and Semantic Dimensions of Man's Environment: A Key to Korzybski, 1955. Editor papers from 2d Congress on Gen. Semantics, 1943; Collected Papers of Alfred Korzybksi, 1955; Selected Papers on General Semantics, 1959; Korzybaski's Teachings Today, 1966. Author articles. Address: RD Lakeville CT 06039

KENDIG, PERRY FRIDY, coll. pres.; b. Mountville, Pa., July 7, 1910; s. Calvin Miles and Blanche (Fridy) K.; A.B., Franklin and Marshall Coll., 1932; A.M., U. Pa., 1936, Ph.D., 1947; m. Virginia Gantt, Apr. 17, 1947; children—Beth Roberts, John Gantt, William Calvin. Prin. East Drumore Twp. High Sch., Lancaster County, Pa., 1932-34; asst. instr. English, U. Pa., 1936-38; spl. instr. English, Drexel Inst. Tech., 1937-38; from instr. to prof., head dept. English, dean students Muhlenberg Coll., 1938-52; dean coll., prof. English, Roanoke Coll., 1952-63, pres., 1963—. Dir. Salem br. First Nat. Exchange Bank Va. Bd. advisers Roanoke YWCA; bd. dirs. Roanoke Fine Arts Center, Roanoke Symphony Soc. Served to lt. comdr. USNR, 1942-46. Mem. Modern Lang Assn. Am., Hawk Mountain Sanctuary Assn., Am. Assn. U. Profs., Va. Soc. Ornithology. Roanoke Valley Bird Club, English Speaking Union (dir. Roanoke Valley br.), Newcomen Soc., Phi Beta Kappa, Blue Key, Phi Sigma Kappa, Omicron Delta Kappa, Delta Sigma Rho, Tau Kappa Alpha, Eta Sigma Phi, Alpha Kappa Alpha, Alpha Psi Omega. Lutheran. Clubs: University (Washington); Commonwealth (Richmond, Va.); Shenandoah (Roanoke); Town (Salem); University (N.Y.C.); Roanoke Valley Torch (past pres.); Faculty (U. Pa.). Author: Trinity Reformed Church: An Historical Sketch, 1938; The Poems of St. Columban Translated into English Verse, 1949; Some Notes on a Little Known American Novel: The Prisoners of Niagara or Errors of Education (by Jesse Lynch Holman, 1810), 1956. Home: 535 Market St Salem VA 24153

KENDLER, BERNHARD, editor; b. Cin., Jan. 28, 1934; s. Harry Harlan and Mildred (Black) K.; B.A. in English, N.Y. U., 1955; M.A. in Comparative Lit., U. Mich., 1956. Research asst. Cal. Tchrs. Assn., 1958-60; editor A.S. Barnes & Co., Inc., N.Y.C., 1960-62; copy editor J.B. Lippincott Co., Phila., 1962- 63; mng. editor, editor Cornell U. Press, Ithaca, N.Y., 1963—. Mem. Am. Hist. Assn., Phi Beta Kappa. Home: 503 N Tioga St Ithaca NY 14850 Office: 124 Roberts Pl Ithaca NY 14850

KENDLER, HOWARD HARVARD, educator, psychologist; b. N.Y.C., June 9, 1919; s. Harry H. and Sylvia (Rosenberg) K.; A.B., Bklyn. Coll., 1940; M.A., U. Ia., 1941, Ph.D., 1943; m. Tracy Seedman, Sept. 20, 1941; children—Joel Harlan, Kenneth Seedman. Instr. U. Ia., 1943; research psychologist OSRD, 1944; asst. prof. U. Colo., 1946-48; asso. prof. N.Y.U. 1948-51, prof., 1951-63, chmn. dept. Univ. Coll., 1951-61; prof. U. Cal. at Santa Barbara, 1963—, chmn. dept. psychology, 1965-66; project dir. Office Naval Research, 1950—, USAAF, 1951-53. Mem. adv. panel psycholobiology, NSF, 1960-62; tng. com. Nat. Inst. Child Health and Human Devel., 1963-66; cons. Dept. Def., Smithsonian Instn., 1959-60, Human Resources Research Office, George Washington U., 1960. Served as first lt., AUS, chief clin. psychologist Walter Reed Gen. Hosp., 1945-46. Fellow Center for Advanced Studies in Behaviorial Scis., Stanford, Cal., 1969-70; NSF grantee, 1954—. Mem. Am. (pres. div. exptl. psychology 1964-65, pres. div. gen. psychology 1967-68), Western (pres. 1970-71) psychol. assns., Soc. Exptl. Psychologists (exec. com. 1971—), Psychonomic Soc. (gov. bd. 1963-69, chmn. 1968-69), Sigma Xi. Author: Basic Psychology, rev. edit., 1968; co-author: Basic Psychology: Brief Edition, 1970. Co-editor: Essays in Neobehaviorism: A Memorial Volume to Kenneth W. Spence; asso. editor Jour. Exptl. Psychology, 1963-65. Contbr. profl. jours. Home: 4596 Camino Molinero Santa Barbara CA 93105

KENDREW, ALBERT EDWIN, former architect; b. Compton County, Que., Can., June 24, 1903; s. Albert and Minnie (Bowen) K.; came to U.S., 1917, naturalized, 1935; student Northeastern U., 1920-22, D. Fine Arts, 1969; certificate archtl. constrn. Wentworth Inst., Boston, 1924; student Boston Archtl. Club-Atelier, 1926-29; m. Melinda R. Ide, June 23, 1928; children—Nancy Hale (Mrs. Herbert E. Bell), Lois Rockwood (Mrs. L.A. Caporal). With F.A. Norcross, architect, Boston 1923-26, Perry, Shaw & Hepburn, architects, Boston, 1926-34; resident architect Colonial Williamsburg (Va.), 1934-43, v.p., 1943-57, sr. v.p., dir. archtl. constrn. and maintenance, 1957-65, sr. v.p., dir. long- range planning, 1965-68; ret.; dir. Strawberry Banke, Inc., archtl. adviser Nauvoo Restoration, Inc. Mem. Williamsburg Planning Commn.; past chmn. Va. Art Commn. Bd. dirs. Chesapeake Maritime Museum. Fellow A.I.A.; mem. Thornton Soc., Newcomen Soc. Home: 9 Bayberry Lane Williamsburg VA 23185

KENDREW, JOHN COWDERY, scientist; b. Oxford, Eng., Mar. 24, 1917; s. Wilfrid Goerge and Evelyn May Graham (Sandberg) K.; B.A., Trinity Coll., Cambridge U., 1939, M.A., 1943. Ph.D., 1949, Sc.D., 1962. With Ministry Aircraft Prodn., 1940-45; sci. adviser allied air comdr. in chief South East Asia, 1944; dep. chmn. Med. Research Council Lab. for Molecular Biology, Cambridge U., 1947—, also fellow of Peterhouse; reader Davy-Faraday Lab., Royal Instn., London, 1954-68; sci. adv. Ministry Def., 1960- 64; editor-in-chief Jour. Molecular Biology. 1959—. Decorated comdr. Order Brit. Empire; recipient Nobel prize in chemistry, 1962. Fellow Royal Soc.; fgn. hon. mem. Am. Acad. Arts and Scis.; hon. mem. Am. Soc. Biol. Chemists; mem. Brit., Am. biophys. socs., Internat. Orgn. Pure and Applied Biophysics (v.p. 1964). Home: Guildhall 4 Church Lane Linton Cambridgeshire England Office: Peterhouse Cambridge England

KENDRICK, BAYNARD HARDWICK, author: b. Phila., Apr. 8, 1894; s. John Ryland and Julia (Lawton) K.; ed. Tome School, Port Deposit, Md. and Episcopal Acad., Phila.; m. Edythe Stevens, 1919; children—Baynard, Edythe, Julia. Sec. Selden Cypress Door Co., Palatka, Fla., 1921-27; pres. Trades Pub. Co. Phila., 1928; gen. mgr. Peter Clark, Inc., N.Y. City, 1929; gen. mgr. Bing & Bing's Hotels, N.Y.C., 1930-31; free lance writer 1932—. Enlisted in Can. Army within one hour after Can. declared war, Aug. 1914; served in C.E.F., 1914-18. Awarded 1914-15 Star, Canadian War medal, Brit. War medal; Robert Meltzer Award, 1951, Spearhead Medal from 3d Armored Div. Club, 1951. Cons. to staff, Old Farms Convalescent Hosp. for Blinded Veterans, U.S. Army, Avon, Conn., during World War II; sighted adviser and hon. life mem. Blinded Vets. Assn. Recipient plaque from Gen. Omar N. Bradley for service to blinded veterans of World War II. Mem. Authors League, Mystery Writers Am., Inc. (1st pres.; grand master 1967), Washington Sq. Assn., Florida Hist. Soc. (dir., regional v.p.), Democrat. Episcopalian. Mason. Clubs: Carolina Yacht (Charleston, S.C.); Marshall Chess (N.Y. City). Author: Blood on Lake Louisa, 1934; The Iron Spiders, 1936; The Eleven of Diamonds, 1936; The Last Express, 1937; The Whistling Hangman, 1937; Death Beyond the Go- thru, 1938; The Odor of Violets, 1941; Blind Man's Bluff, 1943; Death Knell, 1945; Out of Control, 1945; Lights Out, 1945; Flames of Time, (Lit. Guild selection), 1948; The Tunnel, 1949; You Die Today, 1952; They Never Talk Back (with Heinrich Trefflich), 1953; Blind Allies, 1954; Reservations for Death, 1957; Clear and Present Danger, 1958; Hot Red Money, 1959; The Aluminum Turtle, 1960; Frankincense and Murder, 1961; Florida Trails to Turnpikes, 1915-65; Flight From A Firing Wall, 1966; motion pictures include; The Last Express, 1938; Eyes in the Night (starring Edward Arnold and Ann Harding), 1942; The Hidden Eye (Edward Arnold), 1945; Bright Victory (starring Arthur Kennedy and Peggy Dow). Contbr. to mags. Books have been transcribed into Braille. Address: care Paul R Reynolds Inc 599 Fifth Av New York City NY 10017

KENDRICK, CALDWELL CHAPPELEAR, lawyer; b. Arlington, Va., Mar. 27, 1910; s. Luther Garland and Mary Eula (Chappelear) K.; A.B., George Washington U., 1932; LL.B., Harvard, 1935; m. Ellen Spanjer, Sept. 17, 1935; children—Pamela (Mrs. Kenneth N. Baker), Eric Caldwell. Admitted to Va. bar, 1935, since practiced in Arlington; sr. partner firm Phillips, Kendrick, Gearhart & Aylor, 1940- -. Vice chmn. bd. First Va. Bankshares Corp., 1957—, vice chmn., dir., Trust Co. of First Va.; dir., counsel, mem. exec. and trust coms., chmn. audit com. First Va. Bank; also dir., mem. exec. and bonus incentive cons.; dir. Arlington Mortgage Co., First Va. Life Ins. Co., First Va. Bank Bldg., Inc.; co-owner, dir., v.p., gen. mgr. Real Title Corp.; owner, dir. Upton Corp.; co-owner, dir. Old Dominion Warehouse Corp. President Arlington Rotary Ednl. Found., 1959—. Mem. Am., Arlington (past pres.) bar assns., Va. State Bar. Presbyn. (elder, trustee). Rotarian (past pres. Arlington). Club: Washington Golf and Country (past pres.) (Arlington). Home: 5019 N 30th St Arlington VA 22207 Office: 1427 N Courthouse Rd Arlington VA 22216

KENDRICK, DOUGLAS BLAIR, Jr., retired army med. officer, educator; b. Atlanta, July 21, 1907; s. Douglas Blair and Callie (Cason) K.; B.S., Emory U., 1928, M.D., 1931; grad. Army Med. Sch., 1937, Med. Field Service Sch. (Skinner medal), 1938, Command and Gen. Staff Coll., 1947, Army Med. Dept. Research and Grad. Sch., 1950, Spl. Weapons Project, 1952, Navy Med. Center Hosp. Adminstrv. Course, 1954, Arty. Sch. Spl. Weapons Course, 1955, Walter Reed Army Inst. Research, 1956; postgrad. Mayo Found., 1938-39, 48-49, U. Vienna (Austria), 1960; m. Dorothea Belle Reynolds, Nov. 17, 1934. Commd. 1st lt. M.C., U.S. Army, 1934, advanced through grades to maj. gen., 1964; various assignments army hosps., U.S., 1934-44; asst. surgeon staff Hdqrs. USAF PC, Hawaii, 1944-45; with Hdqrs. 10th Army, Okinawa, 1945; comdg. officer 31st Field Hosp., Okinawa, 1945; plans and operations officer, med. sect. Hdqrs. 10th Army, Okinawa, 1945; med. officer to comdr.-in-chief, Hdqrs. FEC, Tokyo, Japan, 1945-48, also physician to Gen. MacArthur; asst. chief surg. service Walter Reed Army Hosp., 1949-50; chmn. blood and blood derivatives group Office Surgeon Gen., 1950-52; post surgeon, comdg. officer Army Hosp., West Point, N.Y., 1952-55; exec. officer to surgeon gen. U.S. Army, 1955-57, chief surg. cons., 1957-58; surg. cons. Hdqrs. USAREUR, Heidelberg, Germany, 1958-61; dir. staff health and med. Office Asst. Sec. Def. Manpower, 1961-62; comdg. gen. 549th Hosp. Center, Heidelberg, 1962, 9th Hosp. Center, 1962-64; surgeon USAREUR, Heidelberg, 1964-65; comdg. gen. Walter Reed Army Med. Center, Washington, 1965-67; retired, 1967; med. dir. Grady Meml. Hosp., Atlanta, 1967—; prof. surgery Emory U. Sch. Medicine, 1967—, asso. dean, 1968—. Decorated D.S.M., Legion of Merit with oak leaf cluster, Bronze Star; recipient Gorgas medal Assn. Mil. Surgeons, 1952. Diplomate Am. Bd. Surgery. Fellow A.C.S., Am. Assn. Surgery Trauma, So. Surg. Assn.; mem. A.M.A., Phi Beta Kappa, Sigma Nu, Alpha Omega Alpha, Omicron Delta Kappa. Author: Blood Program in World War II, 1964; also articles. Home: 3217 Teton Dr NW Atlanta GA 30339 Office: Grady Meml Hosp Atlanta GA 30303

KENDRICK, JAMES BLAIR, Jr., ednl. adminstr., research scientist; b. Lafayette, Ind., Oct. 21, 1920; s. James Blair and Violet (McDonald) K.; B.A., U. Cal. at Berkeley, 1942; Ph.D., U. Wis., 1947; m. Evelyn May Henle, May 17, 1942; children—Janet Blair, Douglas Henle. Mem. staff, faculty U. Cal. at Riverside, 1947- 68, prof. plant pathology and plant pathologist, 1961-68, chmn. dept., 1963-68; v.p. agrl. scis. U. Cal., 1968—. Spl. research diseases vegetable crops. Participant 10th Internat. Bot. Congress, Edinburgh, Scotland, 1964; mem. Cal. Bd. Agr., 1968—. Served with AUS, 1944-46. NSF sr. postdoctoral fellow U. Cambridge (Eng.) and Rothamsted (Eng.) Exptl. Sta., 1961-62. Fellow A.A.A.S.; mem. Am. Phytopath. Soc. (bd. editors jour. 1965-68, councilor at large 1968-70), Internat. Soc. Plant Pathology (council), Am. Inst. Biol. Scis., Cal. C. of C. (agrl. com. 1968—), Phi Beta Kappa, Sigma Xi. Presbyn. (elder). Club: Commonwealth of Cal. (San Francisco). Contbr. articles profl. jours. Home: 615 Spruce St Berkeley CA 94707 Office: University Hall 2200 University Av Berkeley CA 94720

KENDRICK, JAMES GIVENS, mcht.; b. Mpls., Aug. 26, 1913; s. Harry Lee and Mae E. (Ring) K.; student U. Minn., 1931-35; postgrad. N.Y.U., 1939, Columbia, 1941, advanced mgmt. program Harvard, 1949; m. Margaret H. Bushnell, July 23, 1938; children—Anne Lee (Mrs. J. Michael Edwards), Joan Curry (Mrs. Michael L. Bond), Mary Elizabeth (Mrs. Jerry D. Peterson). With W.T. Grant Co., 1935—, Western regional mgr., 1954-58, dir., 1964—, pres. Zeller's Ltd. (Can.) subsidiary, Montreal, Que., 1958-63, dir., 1958—; v.p. sales W.T. Grant Co., N.Y.C., 1963—, now pres., chief exec. officer, dir. Zeller's, Ltd.; dir. Niagara Finance Co., Ltd., Montreal. Bd. dirs. Retail Council Can.; pres. Montreal Bd. Trade. Active YMCA, 1946—; exec. mem. World Alliance, 1962—, also bd. dirs. Mem. Alpha Tau Omega. Presbyn. Clubs: Montreal Athletic St. James (Montreal); Shawbridge (Que.) Country. Home: 250 Clarke Av Westmount Montreal 215 Quebec Canada Office: Zeller's Ltd 5250 Decarle Blvd Montreal 248 Quebec Canada

KENDRICK, JOHN JOSEPH, lawyer; b. Brookline, Mass., Sept. 6, 1898; s. William and Margaret (Spillane) K.; B.A., Cath. U. Am., 1920; LL.B., St. John's U., 1925; m. Margaret Mary Lane, Aug. 14, 1947; children—Margaret Mary, Helen Madaline, Kathleen Ellyn, John Thomas, Jean Louise. Auditor, Internal Revenue Service, 1920-25; admitted to Ohio bar, 1925, since practiced in Toledo; partner firm Shumaker, Loop and Kendrick, 1930—. Dir. Commodore Perry Co., Nat. Lime and Stone Co, Haas-Jordan Co. Mem. spl. finance com., Toledo, 1933; co-founder Toledo Estate Planning Council, 1955, pres., 1955-56. Mem. endowment com. Toledo Art Mus., 1962—. Served with U.S. Army, 1918. C.P.A., Ohio. Mem. Am., Ohio (past chmn. taxation com.), Toledo bar assns., Ohio (bd. govs. 1935), Toledo Dist. (pres. 1933-34) golf assns. Republican. Roman Cath. Club: Inverness (pres. 1945-47) (Toledo). Home: 2507 Edgehill Rd Toledo OH 43615 Office: 811 Madison Av Toledo OH 43624

KENDRICK, THOMAS DOWNING, art historian; b. 1895; Litt.D. (hon.), univs. Durham and Oxford, also U. Dublin; m. Helen Kiek, 1922 (dec. 1955); m. 2d, Katharine Elizabeth Wrigley, 1957. Keeper of British antiquities British Museum, 1938-50, dir., prin. librarian, 1951-59; retired, 1959. Mem. Royal Commn. of 1851. Created knight, 1951; hon. fellow Oriel Coll., Oxford U.; hon. asso. Royal Inst. British Architects. Fellow British Acad., Soc. Antiquaries; fgn. mem. Royal Swedish Acad. Letters, History and Antiquities; mem. German Archaeol. Inst. Club: Athenaeum. Author: The Lisbon Earthquake, 1956; Saint James in Spain; 1960, Great Love for Icarus, 1962; Mary of Agreda, 1967

KENDZIERSKI, LOTTIE HENRYKA, educator; b. Milw., July 23, 1917; d. Stanislaus and Leocadia (Cywinski) Kendzierski; B.A., Marquette U., 1937, M.A., 1938; Ph.D., Fordham U., 1944. Instr. Mt. St. Mary Coll., Hooksett, N.H., 1940-41, Coll. New Rochelle (N.Y.), 1941-42; instr. Marquette U., 1946-51, asst. prof. philosophy, 1951-54, asso. prof., 1954-64, prof., 1964—. Mem. Am. Cath. Philos. Assn. Author: (with G. Smith) The Philosophy of Being, 1961; (with F.C. Wade) Cajetan: Commentary on Being and Essence, 1964; St. Thomas Aquinas: On Charity, 1960. Home: 3038 S 60th St Milwaukee WI 53219

KENEALY, THOMAS LAWRENCE, investment co. exec.; b. Chgo., Apr. 30, 1913; s. Thomas Francis and Lillian (Grattan) K.; student Loyola U., Chgo.; m. Adele Doyle, Nov. 10, 1943; children—Roger D., Mary A. Pres. Investors Syndicate Am., Inc.; v.p. Investors Diversified Service, Inc., Mpls. Roman Catholic. Clubs: Minneapolis Golf, Minneapolis Athletic. Home: 4800 Sunnyside Rd Minneapolis MN 55424 Office: Investors Bldg Minneapolis MN 55402

KENEALY, WILLIAM JAMES, clergyman; b. Boston, July 30, 1904; s. William Edward and Mary Ann (Fay) K.; ascetical studies in novitiate, Yonkers, N.Y., 1922-23, Shadowbrook, Lenox, Mass., 1923-24; A.B., Boston Coll., 1928, A.M., 1929; Ph.D., Gregorian U., 1932; S.T.L., Weston Coll., 1935; LL.B., Georgetown U., 1939. Joined Soc. of Jesus, 1922, ordained priest Roman Catholic Ch., 1934; prof. classical Latin, Boston Coll., 1929-31, asst. prof. philosophy, 1929-31; admitted to D.C. and Mass. bars; dean, prof. law Boston Coll. Law Sch., 1939-56; prof. law Loyola U., New Orleans, 1956-58, acting dean, 1957; prof. law Loyola U., Chgo., 1958-63, Boston Coll. Law Sch., 1963-68; dir. nat. office Jesuit Social Apostalate, Washington, 1968-71; mem. U.S. Bishop's Campaign for Human Devel., 1970—. Trustee of Boston Coll., 1946-56, trustee, dir., 1970—; trustee Wheeling (W.Va.) Coll., 1970—. Served as lt. comdr., Chaplain Corps, USNR, 1943-46. Fellow Am. Acad. Arts Scis.; mem. Am. Bar Assn., Am. Law Inst., Am. Judicature Soc., Am. Jesuit Ednl. Assn., Conf. Jesuit Law Schs. (chmn. 1959). Home: Boston Coll Chestnut Hill MA 02167

KENEFICK, EDWARD R., former broadcasting co. exec.; grad. U. Notre Dame. Formerly spl. agt. FBI, then ednl. adviser Alexander Hamilton Inst., N.Y.C. and head football coach Mt. Carmel (Pa.) Township High Sch.; mem. sales staff WCBS-TV, N.Y.C., 1957-59; with WBBM-TV, Chgo., 1960-70, v.p., gen. mgr., 1965-70. Bd. dirs. Chgo. Better Bus. Bur. Formerly dist. 7 chmn. Ill. div. Cancer Crusade; mem. leadership council Met. Open Communities, Chgo.; mem. Northwestern U. Assos.; mem. bus. adv. council Chgo. Urban League; communications adv. com. Mayor Chgo. Com. Econ. and Cultural Devel. Chgo.; adv. com. Chgo. Civic Fedn.; mem. adv. bd. Citizenship Council Met. Chgo. Bd. dirs. Chgo. Chamber Orch., Jr. Achievement, Nat. Conf. Christians and Jews, Chgo. Council Fgn. Relations. Named Regional Coach of Year in Pa., 1948. Address: 630 N McClurg Ct Chicago IL 60611

KENEFICK, JOHN COOPER, r.r. exec.; b. Buffalo, Dec. 26, 1921; s. John L. and Charlotte (Cooper) K.; B.S., Princeton, 1943; m. Catherine Lynch, 1950; 1 dau., Mary. With U.P. R.R., 1947-52, N.Y.C. R.R., 1946, 54-68, D. & R.G.W. R.R. Co., 1952-54; v.p. transp. Pa. N.Y. Central Transp. Co., N.Y.C., 1968; v.p. U.P. R.R., Omaha, 1968-69, exec. v.p., 1969-70, chief exec. officer, 1970—. Served to lt. (j.g.) USNR, 1943-46. Roman Catholic. Home: 410 Fairacres Rd Omaha NB 68132 Office: 1416 Dodge St Omaha NB 68102

KENELLY, JOHN WILLIS, Jr., educator; b. Bogalusa, La., Nov. 22, 1935; s. John Willis and Erma (Whittom) K.; B.S., Southeastern La. U., 1957; M.S., U. Miss., 1957; Ph.D., U. Fla., 1961; m. Charmaine Voss, Aug. 12, 1956; children—Deidre, Ammie, John Trent. Instr., U. Fla., 1959-61; asst. prof. U. Southwestern La., 1961-63; asso. prof. Clemson (S.C.) U., 1962-68, prof. math., head dept., 1969—; prof. math., chmn. dept. La. State U., New Orleans, 1968-69. Research investigator NASA; cons. in field. Mem. com. undergrad. programs Math. Consultant's Bur., 1968—. Mem. Math. Assn. Am. (vis. lectr. 1969—), Am. Math. Soc., Nat. Council Tchrs. Math., A.A.A.S., Am. Assn. U. Profs., Sigma Xi. Author: Informal Logic, 1967. Contbr. articles to profl. jours. Referee: Pacific Jour. Math., also procs. Am. Math. Soc. Home: 327 Woodland Way Clemson SC 29631

KENEN, PETER BALN, educator, economist; b. Cleve., Nov. 30, 1932; s. Isaiah Leo and Beatrice (Bain) K.; A.B., Columbia, 1954; M.A., Harvard, 1956, Ph.D., 1958; m. Regina Horowitz, Aug. 21, 1955; children—Joanne Lisa, Marc David, Stephenie Hope, Judith Rebecca. Mem. faculty Columbia, 1957-71, prof. econs., 1964-71, chmn. dept., 1967-69, provost univ., 1969-70, adviser to pres., 1970-71; prof. econs. and internat. finance, dir. internat. finance sect. Princeton, 1971—; cons. U.S. Treasury, 1962-68, Bur. Budget, 1964-68. Recipient David A. Wells prize Harvard, 1958-59; fellow Center Advanced Study Behavioral Scis., 1971-72. Mem. Am. Econ. Assn., Royal Econ. Soc., Econometric Soc., Acad. Polit. Sci., Council Fgn. Relations. Author: British Monetary Policy and the Balance of Payments, (1951-57), 1960; Giant Among Nations, 1960; Money, Debt and Economic Activity (with A.G. Hart and A. Entine), 1969; (with R. Lubitz) International Economics, 3d edit., 1971. Co-editor: The Open Economy, 1968. Contbr. articles profl. jours. Research on econ. basis for internat. trade, internat. financial theory and policy. Home: 715 Forester Dr Princeton NJ 08640

KENISON, FRANK ROWE, judge; b. Conway, N.H., Nov. 1, 1907; s. Arthur Edson and Isadore Gertrude (Rowe) K.; A.B., Dartmouth, 1929, LL.D., 1954; LL.B., Boston U., 1932, LL.D., 1955; Dr.Juristic Sci., Suffolk U., 1959; LL.D., U. N.H., 1966, Franklin Pierce Coll., 1966; m. Loretta M. Landry, Apr. 8, 1939; children—Thomas, Mary Ann, Frank. Admitted to N.H. bar, 1932; Carroll County solicitor, 1935-37; asst. atty. gen., 1937-40, atty. gen., 1940-42, 45-46; asso. justice N.H. Supreme Ct., Concord, 1946-52, chief justice, 1952—. Served with USNR, 1942-45. Mem. Am., N.H. bar assns., Am. Judicature Soc., Am. Law Inst., Delta Upsilon. Republican. Home: 176 Centrest Concord NH 03301 Office: Supreme Court Bldg Concord NH 03301

KENISTON, KENNETH, educator, psychologist; b. Chgo., Jan. 6, 1930; s. Hayward and Roberta (Cannell) K.; B.A., Harvard, 1951; D.Phil. Oxford (Eng.) U., 1956; m. Ellen Uviller, June 6, 1960; children—Ann Rogers, Sarah Hayward. Jr. fellow Harvard Soc. Fellows, 1953-56; research asso. Lab. Human Relations, dept. social relations Harvard, 1956-62, lectr. clin. psychology, 1960-62; mem. faculty Yale Med. Sch., 1962—, asso. prof., asso. dir. social and community psychiatry tng. program, 1966-69, prof. psychology (psychiatry), dir. Behavioral Scis. Study Center, 1969—. Mem. Carnegie Commn. Higher Edn. Mem. Am. Acad. Arts and Scis., Council Fgn. Relations, Phi Beta Kappa, Sigma Xi, Author: The Uncommitted: Alienated Youth in American Society, 1965; Young Radicals; Notes on Committed Youth, 1968; Youth and Dissent, 1971. Office: 333 Cedar St New Haven CT 06510

KENLY, GRANGER FARWELL, pharm. co. exec.; b. Portland, Ore., Feb. 15, 1919; s. F. Corning and Ruth (Farwell) K.; A.B. cum laude, Harvard, 1941; m. Suzanne Warner, Feb. 7, 1948; children-Margaret Farwell, Granger Farwell. Adminstrv. asst. to v.p. Poole Bros., Inc., Cho., 1941-42; asst. advt. mgr. Sunset Mag., San Francisco, 1946-47; pub. relations, sales promotion mgr. Pabco Products, Inc., San Francisco, 1947-51; v.p. mgmt., supr. Needham, Louis & Brorby, Inc., Chgo., 1951-60; mgr. marketing plans dept. Pure Oil Co., Palatine, Ill., 1961-62, v.p. pub. relations, personnel, 1962-66; v.p. pub. relations Abbott Labs., North Chicago, Ill., 1966—. Bd. dirs. Evanston Hosp. Served to maj. USAAF, 1942-46; ETO. Mem. Pub. Relations Soc. Am., New Eng. Soc. in City N.Y., Pharm. Mfrs. Am., Chgo. Assn. Commerce, Newcomen Soc. N. Am. Republican. Conglist. Clubs: Chicago; Glen View (Ill.) Golf; Lagunitas Country (Ross, Cal.); Harvard (N.Y.C.). Home: 631 Briar Lane Northfield IL 60093 Office: Abbott Park North Chicago IL 60064

KENMORE, ROBERT HENRY, retail co. exec.; b. N.Y.C., Mar. 24, 1930; s. Herbert and Noemi (Rice) K.; grad cum laude, Choate Sch., 1946; B.A., U. Cal., Los Angeles, 1953; m. Rose-Marie Palmade, Oct. 11, 1954; children—Robert, Christine. Analyst, J.R. Williston & Co., N.Y.C., 1954-58; sr. analyst Wellington Fund, Phila., 1958-62; partner Roth, Gerard & Co., N.Y.C., 1962-63; v.p. Internat. Tel. & Tel. Co., N.Y.C., 1963-68; chmn., chief exec. Kenton Corp., N.Y.C., 1968—; dir. Cartier, Inc., Mark Cross, Ltd., FBC Stores, Inc., Handy Assos., Ben Kahn Furs Corp., Georges Kaplan, Inc., Kenneth Jay Lane, Inc., Republic-Cellini Corp., Valentino Couture, Kenmore Galleries, Inc. Chmn., Childrens Asthma Research Inst. and Hosp., 1970-71. Home: 245 E 61st St New York City NY 10021 Office: 919 3d Av New York City NY 10017

KENN, EDWARD JOHN LITTLEJOHN, packaging co. exec.; b. N.Y.C., June 1, 1918; s. Edward and Dorothea L. (Miller) K.; B.S. in Social Sci., Coll. City N.Y., 1939; LL.B., Columbia, 1942; postgrad. N.Y.U. Law Sch., 1944-50; m. Alison Bartlett, May 14, 1955 (div. 1963); 1 dau., Dana Lauren. Admitted to N.Y. bar, 1942, Ill. bar, 1961; asso. firm White & Case, N.Y.C., 1942- 60; gen. counsel Packaging Corp. Am., Evanston, Ill., 1960—, sec., 1964- -, v.p., 1965—. Served to 2d lt. AUS, 1942. Mem. Am., Ill., Chgo. bar assns., St. Andrew Soc., Phi Beta Kappa. Episcopalian. Elk. Club: North Shore Country (Glenview, Ill). Home: 220 Woodland Av Winnetka IL 60093 Office: 1603 Orrington Av Evanston IL 60204

KENNA, FRANCIS REGIS, hosp. adminstr.; b. Pitts., July 28, 1932; s. Walter J. and Wilma (Blattner) K.; B.S., Duquesne U., 1954; M.B.A., U. Chgo., 1966; student John Marshall Law Sch., 1967; m. Mary R. Miller, Apr. 24, 1954; children—Regina Mary, Francis Regis, Richard Aloysius, Kathleen Ann, Matthew Scott. Chief pharmacist Homestead Hosp., Pa., 1957; dir. pharmacy Southside Hosp., Pitts., 1957-60; dir. pharmacy U. Chgo. Hosps. and Clinics, 1960-65, adminstrv. asst. pharmacy-central material service, 1965-67, asst. dir., 1967-69, acting dir., 1969, dir., 1969—; asst. prof. grad. program hosp. adminstrn. U. Chgo., 1969—. Pharmacy cons. Am. Hosp. Assn., Chgo., 1961-65. Bd. dirs. Chgo. Hosp. Council, Home Destitute Crippled Children, Ill. Regional Med. Program; trustee Chgo. Home for Incurables. Served with U.S. Army, 1955-57. Mem. Am. (past pres.), Ill. (past pres.) socs. hosp. pharmacists, Am. Pharm. Assn. (past 1st v.p. Chgo. br.), Drug Information Assn. Pharmacy editor Hosp. Topics nat. monthly publ. Contbr. articles profl. jours. Home: 2623 W 84th Pl Chicago IL 60652 Office: 950 E 59th St Chicago IL 60637

KENNA, HOWARD JAMES, ch. adminstr.; b. Clontarf, Minn., Oct. 16, 1901; s. John Edward and Ursula Mary (McShane) K.; A.B., U. Notre Dame, 1926, M.S., 1932, Litt.D., 1953; S.T.B., Cath. U. Am., 1929; Sc.D., Cath. U. Chile, 1956; LL.D., (hon.) U. Portland, 1963. Joined Congregation of Holy Cross, 1922; ordained priest Roman Cath. Ch., 1930; rector Moreau Sem., South Bend, Ind., 1937-43; dir. studies U. Notre Dame, 1944-49, v.p. acad. affairs, 1949-50; asst. gen., gen. sec. congregation Holy Cross, N.Y.C., 1950-53; rector Holy Cross Coll., Washington, 1952-55; pres. U. Portland, 1955-62; provincial superior Ind. Province of Priests of Holy Cross, 1962—. Bd. regents U. Portland; trustee U. Notre Dame. Mem. Assn. Symbolic Logic. K.C. (4), Elk. Home: 1304 E Jefferson Blvd South Bend IN 46617

KENNALLY, VINCENT IGNATIUS, bishop; b. Boston, June 11, 1895; s. Willam J. and Mary Ann (Murphy) K.; A.B., Woodstock (Md.) Coll., 1921, M.A., 1922. Joined Soc. of Jesus, 1915, ordained priest Roman Cath. Ch., 1928; tchr. Ateneo de Manila, 1922-25; asst. editor Jesuit Missions, 1930-31; prof. philosophy Boston Coll., 1929-30; superior Mission Cagayan de Oro, P.I., 1933-39; rector, master novices, Novaliches, P.I., 1940-45; adminstr. apostoltic and religious superior Caroline and Marshall Islands, 1946-51; vice provincial Jesuit Vice Province of Philippines, 1952-56; bishop of Caroline and Marshall Islands, also aux. chaplain, 1957—. Mem. U.S. Cath. Conf., Nat. Conf. Cath. Bishops Conferentia Episcopal Pacific. Address: Bishop's Residence Truk Caroline Islands 96942

KENNAMER, LORRIN GARFIELD, Jr., univ. dean; b. Abilene, Tex., Dec. 20, 1924; s. Lorrin Garfield and Ruie Lee (Hart) K.; A.B., Eastern Ky. State Coll., 1947; M.S., U. Tenn., 1949; Ph.D., George Peabody Coll., 1952; m. Laura Helen Durham, Dec. 22, 1948. Tchr., Oak Ridge High Sch., 1947-49; from instr. to asso. prof., chmn. dept. geography and geology E. Tex. State Coll., Commerce, 1952-56; mem. faculty U. Tex., 1956-67, prof. geography, 1961-67, chmn. dept., 1961-67, asso. dean arts and scis., 1961-67; dean arts and scis. Tex. Tech. U., 1967-70; dean U. Tex. Coll. Edn., Austin, 1970—; vis. summer prof. U. Vt., 1959, Mich. State U., 1961, U. Wash., 1967. Bd. examiners Tex. Edn. Agy., 1964-71; com. exams. Coll. Entrance Exam. Bd., 1965-71, trustee, 1970-74. Served to lt. (j.g.) USNR, World War II. Hon. life fellow Tex. Acad. Sci.; mem. Nat. Council Geog. Edn. (exec. bd. 1958-65, sec. 1958-64, pres. 1967), Assn. Am. Geographers (exec. council 1962-64, 68-71), Am. Geog. Soc., Southwestern Social Sci. Assn. (pres. elect 1971), Sigma Xi, Omicron Delta Kappa, Pi Gamma Mu, Phi Delta Kappa, Phi Kappa Phi. Unitarian. Author: (with Bowden, Hoffman) Geography Worktext Series, 2d edit., 1967; (with S. Arbingast) Atlas of Texas, rev. edit., 1967; (with W. Chambers) Texans and Their Land, 1964; (with James Reese) Texas-Land of Contrast, 1971. Home: 5902B Mountain Climb Dr Austin TX 78731

KENNAN, GEORGE FROST, former ambassador, educator; b. Milw., Feb. 16, 1904; A.B., Princeton, 1925; m.; children—Grace, Joan E., Christopher, Wendy. Vice consul, Hamburg, 1927, Tallinn, Finland, 1928; 3d sec., Riga, Kovno, and Tallinn, 1929; lang. officer, Berlin, 1929; 3d sec., Riga, 1931; accompanied Ambassador Bullitt to Moscow, 1933, 3d sec., 1934; consul, Vienna, 1935, 2d sec., Moscow, 1935; 2d sec., Praha, 1938; consul, Prague, 1939; 2d sec., Berlin, 1939, 1st sec., 1940; counselor legation, Lisbon, 1942; counsellor Am. delegation European Adv. Commn., London, 1944; minister-counselor, Moscow, 1945; dep. for fgn. affairs Nat. War Coll., Washington, 1946; dir. policy planning staff Dept. State, 1947; dept. counselor, chief long range adviser to sec. state, 1949-50; mem. Inst. for Advanced Study, 1950-52; U.S. ambassador to Soviet Union, 1952; ret. from Fgn. Service, 1953; mem. Inst. for Advanced Study, Princeton, 1953, permanent prof., 1956—, Stafford Little lectr., 1954; George Eastman vis. prof. Oxford U., 1957-58; ambassador to Yugoslavia, 1961-63; U. fellow Harvard, 1965-70. Fellow All Souls Coll., Oxford U., 1969. Mem. Nat. Inst. Arts and Letters (pres. 1964-67, dir.), Am. Acad. Arts and Letters (pres. 1967- -), Am. Philos. Soc., Royal Soc. Arts (Benjamin Franklin fellow 1968). Club: Century (N.Y.C.). Author: American Diplomacy 1900-1950 (1951 Freedom House award); Realities of American Foreign Policy, 1954; Das Amerikanisch Russische Verhältnis 1954; Russia Leaves the War, vol. I of Soviet-American Relations 1917-20, 1956 (Bancroft prize 1956, Nat. Book award, Francis Parkman prize, Pulitzer prize 1957); Decision to Intervene, vol. 2, 1958; Russia, The Atom and The West, 1958: Russia and the West Under Lenin and Stalin, 1961; On Dealing with the Communist World, 1964; Memoirs, 1925-1950, 1967 (Pulitzer prize 1968, Nat. Book award); From Prague after Munich, 1968; Democracy and the Student Left, 1968; The Marquis de Custine and His Russia in 1839, 1971. Address: Inst for Advanced Study Princeton NJ 08540

KENNAN, KENT WHEELER, educator, composer; b. Milw., Apr. 18, 1913; s. Kossuth Kent and Sara Louise (Wheeler) K.; student U. Mich., 1930-32; B.Mus. in Composition and Theory, Eastman Sch. of Music, U. Rochester, 1934, M.Mus. in Composition, 1936; student Royal Acad. of Santa Cecilia, Rome, 1938. Mem. faculty Kent (O.) State U., 1939-40; tchr. composition, orchestration, counterpoint and theory U. Tex., 1940-42, 45- 46, 1949—; tchr. theory Ohio State U., 1947-49; tchr. composition, orchestration Eastman Sch. of Music, summers 1954, 56. Served with USAAF, 1942-46. Recipient Prix de Rome in Music, 1936. Mem. A.S.C.A.P., Am. Assn. U. Profs., Delta Tau Delta, Phi Mu Alpha, Pi Kappa Lambda. Composer: Night Soliloguy; 5 Preludes for Piano; other compositions. Orchestral works have been performed under Toscanini, Ormandy, Hanson, others, by N.Y. Philharmonic Symphony, Phila. Orch., Rochester Philharmonic and Civic orchs., NBC Symphony, Los Angeles Philharmonic, Houston, Detroit, Chgo., San Antonio, Oklahoma City symphonies, others. Author: Technique of Orchestration, rev. edit., 1970; Counterpoint, rev. edit., 1972. Address: U Tex Music Dept Austin TX 78712

KENNARD, CHARLES W., investment banker; b. London, Eng., Oct. 1, 1907; s. Walter and Louise (Brazier) K.; B.A., Magdalene Coll., Cambridge (Eng.) U., 1930; B.Sc., U. London, 1929; m. Ruth C. Foley, Aug. 19, 1935 (dec. 1965); children—Susan (Mrs. Richard M. Clark), Bruce D., Peter L. Came to U.S., 1930, naturalized, 1942. With Mellon Securities Corp., Pitts., 1944-46; with Smith, Barney & Co., Inc., and predecessor, 1934-44, 47—, exec. v.p., 1965-66, vice chmn., 1966-67, chmn. bd., 1968-70, hon. chmn., 1970—; dir. Shulton, Inc., Chgo. Musical Instrument Co., U.S. Industries, Inc. Home: 19 Circle Crest Manhasset NY 11030 Office: 20 Broad St New York City NY 10005

KENNARD, EDWARD A, educator, anthropologist; b. N.Y.C., Oct. 24, 1907; s. Edward Thomas and Reina (Gans) K.; A.B., Dartmouth, 1929; Ph.D., Columbia, 1936; m. Helen Quammen, Jan. 26, 1935. Editor, Am. Ethnology and Archeology, Fed. Writers Project, 1936-38; specialist Indian lang. Office Indian Affairs, 1939-47; prof. anthropology Fgn. Service Inst., State Dept., 1947-54; chief anthrop. service VA hosps., Downey, Ill. and Perry Point, Md., 1954-60; prof. anthropology U. Pitts., 1960—, chmn. dept., 1960-63. Fellow Am. Anthrop. Assn., A.A.A.S.; mem. Linguistic Soc. Am., Soc. Applied Anthropology (exec. bd. 1950-52), Am. Ethnol. Soc. Author: Hopi Kachinas, 1938. Editor: Bilingual Education Texts in Navaho, Dakota, Hopi, 1940-47. Home: 6605 Woodwell St Pittsburgh PA 15217

KENNARD, FRANK L., banker; b. Montclair, N.J., 1922; B.S., Yale, 1943; married. Salesman, Union Ball Paper Co., 1946-51; mgr. Standard & Poor's Corp., 1951-52; exec. asst. N.Y. Trust Co., 1952-56; with Union Commerce Bank, Cleve., 1956—, asst. cashier, 1957-59, asst. v.p., 1959-62, v.p., 1962-70, sr. v.p., 1970—; dir.

Harmon-Slocum Pub. Co. Inc. Served as 1st lt. AUS, 1943-46. Home: 6308 Sunset Av Independence OH 44131 Office: 917 Euclid Av Cleveland OH 44101*

KENNARD, WILLIAM JEFFERS, physician, assn. cons.; b. Havana, Cuba, Sept. 26, 1906; s. William Jeffers and Mary Elizabeth (Rutherford) K.; B.S., U. Pitts., 1928, M.D., 1930; grad. Med. Field Service Sch., 1933, Sch. Aviation Medicine, 1934, Nat. War Coll., 1947; m. Marian Robinson Brown, June 20, 1930; children—Anne Eloise (Mrs. David D. Johnson), Beverly Jeffers (Mrs. John C. Wren), Marian Elizabeth (Mrs. Jack G. Sarver). Commd. 1st lt. M.C., U.S. Army, 1930, advanced through grades to brig. gen. USAF, 1952; intern Walter Reed Gen. Hosp., Washington, 1930-31, resident internal medicine, 1931-32; student Army Med. Sch., 1932-33; surg. and med. insp. Air Forces and Army troops, Philippines, 1940-42; command surgeon Far East Air Force, 1941-42, N.E. Australia, 1942, 2d Bomber Command, 1943-44; comdg. officer Regional and Convalescent Hosp., Ft. George Wright, Spokane, 1944-46; chief aviation medicine and care flyer div. Office Air Surgeon, Hdqrs. USAF, Washington, 1947-49, dir. plans and hospitalization Office Surgeon Gen., 1949-51; sr. med. officer SHAPE, NATO, 1951-54; command surgeon Mil. Air Trans. Service, 1954-55; ret., 1955; asso. dir., later dir. Washington office A.M.A., 1955-58; exec. v.p. Aerospace Med. Assn., Washington, 1959-67, cons. 1967—. Mem. med. adv. com. to fed. air surgeon FAA, Dept. Transp., 1966-70. Decorated D.S.M., Silver Star, Legion Merit with oak leaf cluster, Purple Heart; Philippine Presdl. distinguished citation; Medaille d'Honneur du Service de Santé de l'Air (France); recipient Theodore C. Lyster award, 1965. Diplomate Am. Bd. Preventive Medicine (vice chmn. aviation medicine). Fellow Internat. Acad. Aviation and Space Medicine; mem. Soc. Med. Consultants to Armed Forces, A.M.A. (mem. com. on aerospace medicine, sec. sect. preventive medicine), D.C. Med. Soc., Am. Pub. Health Assn., Am. Soc. Assn. Execs., Am. Med. Execs. Assn., Am. Coll. Preventive Medicine, Air Force Assn., Aerospace Med. Assn., Flying Physicians Assn., Am. Med. Writers Assn. Baptist. Home: 1312 24th St S Arlington VA 22202

KENNEALLY, JOSEPH THOMAS, corp. exec.; b. Mpls., July 31, 1926; s. Joseph Thomas and Olga Loraine (Halverson) K.; B.A. in Econs., U. Minn., 1949, M.A. in Internat. Law and Internat. Econs., 1950; m. Patricia Jane Steele, May 14, 1955; children—Joseph Thomas III, Timothy, Stephen, Patricia, Matthew, Michael. With No. Trust Co., Chgo., 1952-54; asst. to sr. partner E. F. Hutton & Co., N.Y.C., 1954-57; v.p. F. W. Richmond & Co., N.Y.C., 1957- 59; exec. v.p. Houston Oil Field Material Co., Inc., (co. name now Internat. Systems & Controls Corp.), 1959-60, pres., 1960-62, chmn. bd., 1964—. also dir.; chmn. Pritchard-Rhodes Ltd., London, Eng., Mix-Mill, Inc., Bluffton, Ind., Pemar Engring., Miami, Investors Counsel, Inc., Houston; chmn. bd., chief exec. officer Black, Sivalls and Bryson, Kansas City, Mo.; chmn., dir. Oil Equipment Ltd., Calgary, Alta., Can.; gen. partner Kenro & Co., N.Y.C.; dir. Houston Citizens Bank & Trust Co., Petroleum Equipment Suppliers Assn., J.F. Pritchard & Co., Kansas City, Mo., Atlantic Gulf & Pacific Co., Manila, P.I. Served to capt. AUS, 1944-48, 50-52. Mem. Phi Beta Kappa. Roman Cath. Home: 2208 Brentwood St Houston TX 77019 Office: 2727 Allen Pkwy Houston TX 77019

KENNEDY, A. MACGREGOR, accounting co. exec.; b. Glengarry County, Ont., Can., Feb. 13, 1907; s. William and Annabella (McKillop) K.; ed. Cornwall Coll. Inst., Queen's U.; m. Marjorie Jean Henley, Aug. 29, 1936; one dau. With John MacKay & Co., Toronto, Ont., 1924, Wilton C. Edd's & Sons, Toronto, 1926; with Ernst & Ernst, Toronto, 1935—, now partner in charge. Mem. Bd. of Trade Met. Toronto. Clubs: Royal Canadian Yacht. Thornhill Golf (Toronto). Home: 10 Lamport Av Toronto Ontario Canada Office: 7 King St E Toronto Ontario Canada*

KENNEDY, ARTHUR, actor; b. Worcester, Mass., Feb. 17, 1914; s. John Timothy and Helen (Thompson) K.; student Carnegie Inst. Tech.; m. Mary Cheffey, 1938; children—Terence Gordon, Laurie Ewing. Broadway debut in Maurice Evans' King Richard II, 1937; on tour with group presenting vignettes of Shakespeare, also at Globe Theatre, N.Y.C.; appeared WPA prodn. Life and Death of an American, 1939; appeared opposite Ethel Barrymore in motion picture International Incident; other films include High Sierra, Air Force, The Glass Menagerie, Lawrence of Arabia, City for Conquest, 1940, Devotion, 1946, Champion, 1949. Bright Victory, 1952. Trial, 1955, Deperate Hours, 1955, Peyton Place, 1958, Elmer Gantry, 1960, Home Is the Hero, 1962, Adventures of the Young Man, Cheyenne Autumn, 1964; also in Westerns; on Broadway in Arthur Miller dramatizations, All My Sons, 1947, Death of a Salesman, 1949, The Crucible, 1953. Recipient Antoinette Perry award for best supporting actor in Death of a Salesman, 1949; nominated Acad. Award. Address: care Phil Gersh Agy 232 N Canon Dr Beverly Hills CA 90210

KENNEDY, BERNARD JOSEPH, utility exec.; b. Niagara Falls, N.Y., Aug. 16, 1931; s. Edward J. and Frances (Coyle) K.; B.A., Niagara U., 1953; LL.B., U. Mich., 1958; m. Geraldine Drexelius, Sept. 20, 1958; children—Mary Kathleen, Maureen Jean, Patricia, Colleen, Joseph B. Admitted to N.Y. bar, 1960; legal asst. Iroquois Gas Corp., Buffalo, 1958-63, gen. atty., 1963-67, sec., gen. counsel, 1967—; dir. Producers Gas Co. (Olean, N.Y.). Pres. Assn. Retarded Children, Erie County, 1970-71. Mem. Erie County Rep. Com., 1963—. Served to 1st lt. AUS, 1953-55. Mem. Am., Erie County N.Y. bar assns., Def. Research Inst., Am. Gas Assn., Buffalo Area C. of C. Home: 33 Ruskin Rd Eggertsville NY 14226 Office: 10 Lafayette Sq Buffalo NY 14203

KENNEDY, CHARLES FRANCIS, mfg. exec.; b. Elmira, N.Y., Feb. 10, 1915; s. Daniel J. and Katherine (Landy) K.; B.S., U. Mich., 1936; m. Roselynn Cook, Oct. 29, 1938; children—Charles C., Kathryn L., Kevin, Thomas M., Carol A. Sales engr. Eastman Kodak Co., Rochester, N.Y., 1937; with Kennedy Valve Mfg. Co., Inc., Elmira, 1937—, v.p., works mgr., pres., 1948—; v.p. Grinnell Corp.; chmn. bd. Swift Lubricator Co.; pres. Alba-Trans, Inc.; dir. N.Y.State Electric & Gas Corp., Security Mut. Life Ins. Co. N.Y., Marine Midland Bank-Southern, Watkins Salt Co.; trustee Elmira Savs. Bank. Trustee Elmira Coll.; chmn. bd. trustees St. Joseph's Hosp. Mem. Valve Mfrs. Assn. (pres. 1962-63), Newcomen Soc. K.C. Clubs: Marco Polo (N.Y.C.); Seaview Country; Corning Country; Elmira City, Elmira Country; Stone Harbor Yacht. Home: West Rd Strathmont Park Elmira NY 14905 (summer) 1-110th St Stone Harbor NJ 08247 Office: 01021 E Water St Elmira NY 14901

KENNEDY, CHESTER ROTHWELL, steel co. exec.; b. Blairsville, Pa., Aug. 28, 1919; s. Thomas L. and Leighfy (Sebring) K.; grad. Robert Morris Coll., 1941; m. Dorothy Larue McIlwain, Sept. 12, 1946. Staff accountant Lybrand, Ross Bros. & Montgomery, Pitts., 1945-59; controller Washington Steel Corp. (Pa.), 1959-68, treas., 1968-70, sec., treas., 1970—, also dir.; dir. Calstrip Steel Corp. Bd. dirs. Robert Morris Coll. Served with AUS, 1941-45. Recipient Heritage award Robert Morris Coll., 1965. Mem. Nat. Assn. Accountants (pres. Pitts. chpt., nat. dir.), Robert Morris Coll. Alumni Assn. (pres.). Home: 5631 Marilynn Dr Pittsburgh PA 15236 Office: Woodland and Griffith Avs Washington PA 15301

KENNEDY, CLEPHANE ARNOT, univ. pres.; b. N.Y.C., Feb. 20, 1897; d. Frank Clephane and Martha (Smith) Arnot; student Northfield Sem., N.Y.U., George Washington U.; B.C.S., Benjamin Franklin U., 1934; m. John Thomas Kennedy III, 1921 (dec. July 1958); 1 dau., Marthajane. Founding mem. bd. Benjamin Franklin U., 1925, sec., 1943-58, pres. 1958—. Organizer, mem. bd. Friday Morning Music Club Nat. Found., 1946—; mem. Commrs. Adv. Council on Higher Edn. Recipient citation for war service Pres. U.S., 1946. Mem. League Republican Women (v.p. 1947-49), Am. Judicature Soc., Acad. Polit. Sci., Am. Assn. Accounting, Soc. Four Arts (Palm Beach. Fla.), N.E.A. (life), D.C. Council Adminstrv. Women Edn., Am. Assn. Specialized Colls. (charter; trustee). Republican. Presbyn. Clubs: Sesamee Imperial (London); Washington, Univ. Arts (Washington); Soroptimist. Home: Arkenderry 3820 Reno Rd Washington DC 20008

KENNEDY, DAVID M., former sec. treasury; b. Randolph, Utah, July 21, 1905; s. George and Katherine (Johnson) K.; B.A., Weber Coll., Utah, 1928; A.M., George Washington U., 1935, LL.B., 1937; grad. Rutgers U., Grad. Sch. Banking, 1939; m. Lenora Bingham, Nov. 4, 1925; children—Marilyn, Barbara Ann, Carol Joyce, Patricia Lenore. Mem. staff bd. govs. Fed. Res. System, successively as tech. asst., div. bank operations, economist div. research and statistics, spl. asst. to chmn. bd. govs., 1930-46; v.p. bond dept. Continental Ill. Nat. Bank & Trust Co., Chgo., 1946, v.p., 1954-56, dir., pres., 1956-59, chmn. bd., chief exec. officer, 1959-69; spl. asst. to sec. treasury, Washington, 1953-54, sec. of treasury, 1969-71; ambassador-at-large, mem. President's Cabinet, 1971—; Mem. Fed. Adv. Com. on Financial Assets; nat. pub. adv. com. Regional Econ. Devel.; fed. adv. council Fed. Res. Bd.; chmn. Pres.'s Commn. on Budgetary Concepts, Joint Commn. on the Coinage; chmn. nat. adv. council Internat. Monetary and Financial Policies; chmn. exec. bd. Com. Econ. and Cultural Devel. Chgo.; chmn. exec. com. citizens Bond Com. Greater Chgo. Mem. citizens com. U. Ill.; bd. assos. Depaul U. Chmn New Chgo. Found., Library of Congress Trust Fund Bd.; bd. dirs. Chgo. Found. Cultural Devel.; mng. trustee Fed. Old Age and Survivors Ins. Trust Fund; trustee Presbyn.-St. Luke's Hosp., Chgo., U. Chgo., Com. Econ. Devel., George Washington U.; chmn. exec. com. devel. council Brigham Young U. Mem. Am. Bankers Assn., Council Latin Am. (trustee), Assn. Res. City Bankers, Pi Gamma Mu. Mem. Ch. Jesus Christ of Latter-day Saints (1st councilor Chgo. stake, bishop Washington). Clubs: Bankers, University, Union League, Chicago, Mid-Am., Commercial, Executives (Chgo.); Old Elm Country (Fort Sheridan, Ill.); Glenview (Ill.) Country. Home: 1701 N Kent St Arlington VA 22209

KENNEDY, DAVIS LEE, journalist; b. Elkin, W. Va., Aug. 21, 1938; s. John A. and Bruce (Lee) K.; B.A. magna cum laude, Harvard, 1960, M.B.A., 1966. Bus. writer Va. Pilot, Norfolk-Portsmouth Newspapers, 1966-67; with advt. dept. Norfolk Norfolk Newspapers, 1967-69; marketing and promotion mgr. Balt. Sun papers, 1970—. Served to 1st lt. AUS, 1960-62. Clubs: Chevy Chase (Washington); Harbor (Norfolk); Harvard (N.Y.C.). Home: 6003 Lakehurst Dr Baltimore MD 21210 Office: Centre and Calvert Sts Baltimore MD 21203

KENNEDY, DONALD, educator; b. N.Y.C., Aug. 18, 1931; s. William Dorsey and Barbara (Bean) K.; A.B., Harvard, 1952, A.M., 1954, Ph.D., 1956; m. Barbara Jeannette Dewey, June 11, 1953; children—Laura Page, Julia Hale. Mem. faculty Syracuse U., 1956-60; mem. faculty Stanford, 1960—, prof. biol. scis., chmn. dept., 1965—; biology editor W. H. Freeman Co., pubs., San Francisco, 1962—. Bd. overseers Harvard. Fellow Am. Acad. Arts and Scis., A.A.A.S.; mem. Am. Physiol. Soc., Soc. Gen. Physiologists, Am. Soc. Zoologists, Soc. Exptl. Biology (U.K.). Author: (with W. H. Telfer) The Biology of Organisms, 1965; also articles. Editor: The Living Cell, 1966; From Cell to Organism, 1967; editorial bd. Jour. Exptl. Zoology, 1965-71, Zeitschrift für vergleichende Physiologie, 1965—, Jour. Neurophysiology, 1969—. Home: 680 Lowell Av Palo Alto CA 94301 Office: Dept Biol Sci Stanford U Stanford CA 94301

KENNEDY, DONALD SIPE, electric utility exec.; b. Rushville, Ind., Jan. 5, 1902; s. Jesse Barnes and Florence (Sipe) K.; student Butler U., 1919-21, LL.D., 1960; A.B., U. Ariz., 1923, LL.D., 1960; LL.D., Oklahoma City U., 1958; D.Sc., Bethany Coll. of Nazarene, 1967; H.H.D., Okla., Christian Coll., 1971; m. Gertrude Hacker, Aug. 17, 1927; 1 dau., Donna Lee (Mrs. Thomas E. Vogel), Clk., Okla. Gas & Electric Co., 1923, various positions, 1923-28, Eastern div. auditor, 1928-40, asst. treas., main office, 1940-42, treas., v.p., dir., 1942, exec. v.p., 1948, pres., chmn., 1949-66, chmn. bd., chief exec. officer, 1966—; pres. Okla. Industries, Inc., 1951-53; dir. 1st Okla. Bank Corp., Oklahoma City, Village Bank (Okla.), M-K-T R.R., Katy Industries. Chmn. U.S. nat. com. World Power Conf., 1963—. Chmn. Okla. Bd. Regents Higher Edn.; pres. Oklahoma City Community Chest, 1946-48, Oklahoma City C. of C., 1954; mem. Nat. Adv. Research Resources Council; Okla. civilian aide to sec. army. Bd. dirs. YMCA. Mem. N.A.M., Electric Inst. (dir., pres. 1956-57), Assn. Edison Illuminating Cos. (pres.), Phi Delta Theta. Mason (32). Episcopalian (sr. warden). Clubs: Oklahoma City Golf and Country; Rolling Rock (Ligonier, Pa.). Home: 6616 Hillcrest Oklahoma City OK 73116 Office: 321 N Harvey Oklahoma City OK 73101

KENNEDY, DOUGLAS STROTHER, magazine editor; b. Worcester, Mass., Aug. 1, 1919; s. George Henry and Margaret (Smith) K.; A.B., Brown U., 1941; m. Ann Elizabeth Newdick, Oct. 24, 1944 (dec.); m. 2d, Trude E. Bohner, June 26, 1966. Reporter Worcester Eve. Gazette, 1945; sportswriter N.Y. Herald Tribune, 1945-50; sport editor Time Magazine, 1950-54; editor in chief True Magazine, 1954—. Served as lt. on PT boats, USNR, 1941-45. Decorated Purple Heart, Presidential Unit Citation; E. P. Dutton award for best mag. sport story, 1952. Mem. Alpha Delta Phi (nat. exec. council 1951-52). Clubs: Lambs, Artists and Writers, Overseas Press, Sports Car of Am., Sakonnet Golf, Adventures Unlimited (v.p.). Writer- photographer for films. Writer-narrator of radio sports show. Writer- producer-narrator of TV films. Contbr. nat. mags. Home: 150 W 67th St New York City NY 10023 Office: 67 W 44th St New York City NY 10036

KENNEDY, EDWARD EUGENE, economist, statistician; b. Grand Junction, Ia., Apr. 12, 1894; s. James M. and Mary N. (Ryan) K.; student pub. and parochial schs. Ia.; m. Edna Mae Crandell, May 1, 1919 (dec. 1938); children—Gertrude Elizabeth (dec.), Regene Maxine (Mrs. Paul F. J. LePore), Edward Charles (dec.), Edward Louis (dec.), Paul Eugene, Mary Darlene (Mrs. William W. Schmidt); m. 2d. Marie C. Puncke, Oct. 3, 1939 (dec. 1964); m. 3d, Elizabeth G. Haney, Feb. 12, 1966. Livestock and grain farmer, Grand Junction, Ia. and St. James, Minn., 1915-26; sec.-treas. Nat. Farmers Union, 1931-37, legislative agt., 1933-41; research dir. and economist, dist. 50 United Mine Workers of Am., 1942-70; v.p. Nationwide Com. Import-Export Policy, 1971—; asso. judge Orphan's Ct. Howard County, Md., 1971—. Mem. chems., paper and paperboard and coal tar labor adv. coms. WPB, World War II; mem. roster tech. reps. consulting with Office Spl. Rep. for Trade Negotiations, Exec. Office Pres.; mem. adv. council Employee Welfare and Pension Benefit Plans, Dept. Labor, 1962-64. Mem. Md. Democratic Central Com., 1966-70; Mem. county council Howard Country, 1971—. Roman Catholic. K.C. Home: Illiowa 9309 Whiskey Bottom Rd RFD 1 Laurel MD 20810 Office: 815 15th St Washington DC 20005

KENNEDY, EDWARD MOORE, U.S. senator; b. Boston, Mass., Feb. 22, 1932; s. Joseph Patrick and Rose (Fitzgerald) K.; A.B., Harvard, 1954; LL.B., U. Va., 1959; hon. degree Am. Internat. Coll. 1969; m. Virginia Joan Bennett, Nov. 29, 1958; children—Kara Ann, Edward Moore, Patrick Joseph. Admitted to Mass. bar, 1959; asst. dist. atty., Suffolk County, Mass., 1961-62; U.S. senator from Mass., 1962—, former asst. majority leader U.S. Senate. Pres. Joseph P. Kennedy, Jr. Found., 1961—; adv. bd. Emmanuel Coll.; trustee Boston U., Lahey Clinic, Boston, Children's Hosp. Med. Center, Boston, John F. Kennedy Library, Boston Symphony, John F. Kennedy Center for Performing Arts, Robert F. Kennedy Meml. Found.; bd. vistors Fletcher Sch.; bd. advisers Dunbarton Oaks Research Library and Collections; mem. corp. Northeastern U., Mass. Gen. Hosp. Served with AUS, 1951-53. Decorated Order of Merit (Italy); named one of 10 outstanding young men of 1967 U.S. Jr. C. of C. Author: Decisions for a Decade. Home: 3 Charles River Sq Boston MA 02114 Office: Senate Office Bldg Washington DC 20510

KENNEDY, EDWIN L., investment banker; b. Marion, O., May 25, 1904; s. Edwin Clarence and Emma Clara (Lust) K.; A.B., Ohio U., 1926; grad. student finance Ohio State U., 1928-29; spl. session Harvard, summer 1930; LL.D., Ohio U., 1965; D.B.A., Findlay Coll., 1968; L.H.D., Juniata Coll., 1968; m. Ruth Zimmerman, May 25, 1932; 1 son, Edwin DeWeese. With Standard & Poor's financial publishing, N.Y.C., 1929-32; bank liquidation Pa. Dept. Banking, 1932-36; investment counsel, pvt. financial work for Du Pont family, 1936-41; mng. dir., head oil dept. Lehman Brothers, Inc., N.Y.C., 1941—; dir. Kerr-McGee Corp., Oil Shale Corp., Sunlite Oil Co. Ltd., Ingram Corp. Bd. dirs. Ohio U. Fund; trustee Hiram (O.) Coll., Ohio U., Athens, Juniata (Pa.) Coll., Morristown (N.J.) Meml. Hosp. Mem. Ind. Petroleum Assn. Am., Am. Petroleum Inst., Ohio U. Alumni Assn. (past pres.), Am. Inst. Mining, Metall. and Petroleum Engrs., Theta Chi, Phi Delta Gamma, Tau Kappa Alpha. Beta Gamma Sigma, Phi Beta Kappa. Clubs: Economic, University (N.Y.C.); Baltusrol Country. Home: Glen Alpine Rd New Vernon NJ (summer) Calabogie Ontario Canada Office: 1 William St New York City NY 10004

KENNEDY, EUGENE F., Jr., architect; b. Bklyn., Jan. 31, 1904; s. Eugene F. and Anna (Lee) K.; grad. Boston Archtl. Center, 1924; Rotch traveling scholar, Rome and Paris, 1924-26; m. Carol Fox, Apr. 10, 1928; children—Rosalyn, Peter, Michael, Maura. Partner firm Kennedy, Kennedy and Keefe (formerly Maginnis and Walsh and Kennedy), Boston, 1922—, chief designer, 1926-41, mem. firm, 1941—; prin. works include Carney Hosp., Boston Coll. Law Sch., Boston Coll. Sch. Edn. (all Boston), Moors Hall, Radcliffe Coll. (Cambridge, Mass.), Nazareth Home for Children (Harleston Parker gold medal 1954) (Jamaica Plain, Mass.), Cath. Most Holy Redeemer (Corner Brook, Newfoundland), Ch. Our Lady Queen of Martyrs (Queensboro prize 1954) (Forest Hills, N.Y.), Cath. Mary Our Queen (Balt.), Nat. Shrine of Immaculate Conception (Washington). Fellow A.I.A.; mem. Boston Soc. Architects, Mass. Assn. Architects. Home: 101 Chestnut St Boston MA 02108 Office: 126 Newbury St Boston MA 02106

KENNEDY, EUGENE PATRICK, educator; b. Chgo., Sept. 4, 1919; s. Michael and Catherine (Frawley) K.; B.Sc., De Paul U., 1941; Ph.D. (Nutrition Found. fellow), U. Chgo., 1949; A.M. (hon.), Harvard, 1960; m. Adelaide Majewski, Oct. 27, 1943; children—Lisa, Sheila, Kathy. Research chemist chem. research dept. Armour & Co., 1941-47; postdoctoral fellow Am. Cancer Soc., U. Cal. at Berkeley, 1949-50; with Ben May Lab. Cancer Research, dept. biochemistry U. Chgo., 1950-56, prof. biochemistry, 1956-60; sr. postdoctoral fellow NSF, Oxford (Eng.) U., 1959-60; Hamilton Kuhn prof. biol. chemistry Harvard Med. Sch., 1960—, head dept., 1960-65. Recipient Glycerine research award, 1955; Am. Oil Chemist Soc. Lipid Research award, 1970. Mem. Am. Chem. Soc. (Paul Lewis award 1958), Nat. Acad. Sci., Am. Soc. Biol. Chemists (pres. 1970-71), Am. Acad. Arts and Scis. Home: 63 Buckminster Rd Brookline MA 02146 Office: Dept Biol Chemistry Harvard Med Sch Boston MA 02115

KENNEDY, FRANCES, librarian; b. St. Louis, Dec. 2, 1907; d. William John and Maud (Gilhart) K.; student Oklahoma City U., 1924-26; A.B., U. Okla., 1928; B.L.S., U. Ill., 1931, M.S., 1948. Br. librarian Muskogee (Okla.) Pub. Library, 1928-29; staff State U. Ia., summer 1931; reference librarian Oklahoma City Pub. Library, 1931-47; librarian Oklahoma City U. Library, 1947—, prof. library sci.; instr. U. Okla. Library Sch., summer 1958, 59. Bd. dirs. Okla. County Health Assn., 1956-61; pres., dir. Variety Health Center. Mem. Am. (council 1956- 60, 69-72), Southwestern (dir. 1955-56, editor 1958-64), Okla. (pres. 1945-47, editor jour. 1954-57; distinguished service award 1965) library assns., Am. Assn. U. Women, Assn. Coll. and Research Libraries, Alpha Omicron Pi, Beta Phi Mu. Democrat, Episcopalian. Home: 1629 Camden Way Oklahoma City OK 73116

KENNEDY, FRANK BRITTAIN, investment banker; b. Medford, Mass., May 29, 1904; s. Frank Alexander and Sadie (Brittain) K.; student Boston U., 1924-30; m. Kathryn James, June 12, 1926; children—Frank Brittain, Martha Burrage Fitch. New Eng. mgr. C.F. Childs & Co., 1925-31; treas., dir. Webster, Kennedy & Co., 1932-37; pres., dir. Kennedy, Spence & Co., 1937-39; propr. F. Brittain Kennedy & Co., Boston, 1940—. Mem. exec. bd. Old Colony council, mem. exec. com. nat. council Boy Scouts Am. Vice chmn. bd. trustees Lahey Clinic Found. Episcopalian. Clubs: Boston Municipal Bond, Down Town (Boston); Cohasset (Mass.) Golf. Home: 384 Jerusalem Rd Cohasset MA 02025 Office: 75 Federal St Boston MA 02110

KENNEDY, FRANK ROBERT, govt. ofcl., educator, lawyer; b. Strafford, Mo., July 27, 1914; s. David Rolland and Maida Mary (Appleby) K.; A.B., S.W. Mo. State Coll., 1935; LL.B., Washington U., 1939; J.S.D., Yale, 1953, Sterling fellow, 1939-40; m. Patricia Harvey, Aug. 26, 1939; children—Candace (Mrs. V.P. Gottschall), Robert Mitchell, Diane, David Harold. Tchr., forensic coach Lebanon (Mo.) High Sch., 1935-36; admitted to Mo. bar, 1939, Ia. bar, 1961; instr. law State U. Ia., 1940-41, asst. prof. law, 1941-46, asso. prof., 1946-49, prof., 1949-61; prof. law U. Mich., Ann Arbor, 1961—; on leave as exec. dir. Commn. to Study Bankruptcy Laws U.S., Washington, 1971—. Acting chief counsel to indsl. user unit, rationing div. OPA, Washington, 1942-43; vis. prof. U. Mich., 1958-59, U. Tex., 1963; U. Pa., 1966. Reporter adv. com. bankruptcy rules Jud. Conf. U.S. Served from ensign to lt. comdr. USNR, 1943-46. Mem. Am. Bar Assn., Am. Assn. U. Profs., Nat. Bankruptcy Conf., Am. Law Inst., Order of Coif, Order of Artus, Delta Theta Phi, Omicron Delta Kappa, Pi Sigma Alpha. Republican. Unitarian. Co-author: Collier on Bankruptcy, vol. 4, 1942, 54, 59. Contbr. articles to legal, tech. jours. Home: 4501 Connecticut Av NW Washington DC 20008 Office: 1016 16th St NW Washington DC 20036

KENNEDY, GAIL, educator, editor; b. Cadott, Wis., Sept. 17, 1900; s. Herbert Daniel and Jessie (Young) K.; B.A., U. Minn., 1922; M.A., Columbia, 1923, Ph.D., 1928; m. Joy E. Peterson, May 28, 1925; children—Miriam Gove (Mrs. Arnold Modell), Margaret Gall (Mrs.

Joseph L. Gornick), Jesse Ward. Fellow Columbia, 1923-24, lectr. philosophy, 1924-25; asst. dir. New Sch. Social Research, 1925-26; instr. philosophy Amherst Coll., 1926-30, asst. prof., 1930-36, asso. prof., 1936-39, prof., 1939—, on Henry C. Folger Found., 1953—. Price officer Western Mass. office OPA, 1943. Guggenheim fellow, 1929-30. Mem. Am. Philos. Assn., Am. Assn. U. Profs. Editor, author: (with others) Education at Amherst: The New Program, 1955. Editor: Bacon, Hobbes, Locke: Selected Writings, 1937; Democracy and the Gospel of Wealth, 1949; Pragmatism and American Culture, 1950; Education for Democracy, 1952; (with Max H. Fisch, others) The Classic American Philosophers, 1951; Evolution and Religion, 1957; (with Milton R. Konvitz) The American Pragmatists: Selected Writings, 1960; (with Joseph Epstein) The Process of Philosophy, 1966; Transcendentalist Revolt, 1968; (with Lewis E. Hahn, others) A Guide to the Works of John Dewey, 1970. Contbr.: Sidney Hook and The Contemporary World, 1968; articles, revs. profl. jours. Home: 148 Lincoln Av Amherst MA 01002

KENNEDY, GEORGE, actor; b. Feb. 1926. Films include Jolly Pink Jungle; The Ballad of Josie; Cool Hand Luke (Oscar award); Bandolero; Boston Strangler; Guns of the magnificent Seven; Gaily Gaily; The Good Guys and The Bad Guys; Airport. Tick. . . tick. . . tick; False Witness. Served with U.S. Army sixteen years. Address: care CMA, 9255 Sunset Blvd., Los Angeles, CA.*

KENNEDY, GEORGE CLAYTON, geologist, educator; b. Dillon, Mont., Sept. 22, 1919; s. Clayton Tierney and Maude (Coley) K.; B.A., Harvard, 1940, M.A., 1941, Ph.D., 1947; m. Sally Slocum, Oct. 1, 1951; children—Clayton S., Deborah E., Jennifer A.; m. 2d, Ruth Porter, May 11, 1968. Mem. faculty Harvard, 1946-52; mem. faculty U. Cal. at Los Angeles, 1952—, prof. geology, 1953—. Vice pres. Los Angeles County Museum Alliance, 1955—; chmn. Los Angeles Ethnic Arts Council, 1970. Recipient award Minerol. Soc. Am., 1956. Fellow Am. Acad. Arts and Scis. Contbr. profl. jours. Club: Explorers (vice chmn. 1967-68) (N.Y.C.). Home: 3131 Antelo Rd Los Angeles CA 90024

KENNEDY, GEORGE D., business exec.; b. 1926; student Williams Coll.; m. With Scott Paper Co., 1947-52, Champion Paper Co., 1952-65; exec. v.p. Brown Co., 1965-71, also dir.; exec. v.p. Internat. Minerals & Chem. Corp., Skokie, Ill., 1971—. Office: 5401 Old Orchard Rd Skokie IL 60076

KENNEDY, GEORGE W., mfg. exec. Past chief exec. officer, chmn. exec. com. Kelsey-Hayes Co., Romulus, Mich., now chmn. bd. dir. Mfrs. Nat. Bank (Detroit), Kelsey Wheel Co., Ltd. (Windsor, Ont.). Home: 32055 Bingham Rd Southfield MI 48010 Office: 38471 Huron River Dr Romulus MI 48174*

KENNEDY, GERALD HAMILTON, bishop; b. Benzonia, Mich., Aug. 30, 1907; s. Herbert Grant and Marian (Phelps) K.; A.B., Coll. of Pacific, 1929, D.S.T., 1952; A.M., Pacific Sch. Religion, 1931, B.D., 1932; D.D., 1952; S.T.M., Hartford Theol. Sem., 1933, Ph.D., 1934; LL.D., Coll. of Puget Sound, 1949; Litt.D., Neb. Wesleyan U., 1950; L. H.D., Beliot Coll., 1952; LL.D., Ohio Wesleyan U., 1952; D.D., Redlands U., 1954, Bucknell U., 1959; H. H.D., Bradley U., 1956; L.H.D., Cal. Western U., 1967; m. Mary Grace Leeper, June 2, 1928. Ordained ministry Methodist Church 1932; pastor, First Congregational Church, Collinsville, Conn., 1932-36, Calvary Meth. Ch., San Jose, Calif., 1936-40, First Meth. Ch., Palo Alto, Calif., 1940-42; acting prof. homiletics, Pacific Sch. Religion, 1938-42; pastor, St. Paul Meth. Ch., Lincoln, Neb., 1942-48; bishop of Methodist Ch., Portland area, 1948; bishop of Methodist Ch., Los Angeles area, 1952; dir. Wesley Foundation, Stanford U., 1940-42; lecturer in religion, Nebraska Wesleyan U., 1942; radio preacher, KFAB and KFOR, Lincoln, Neb., Sundays, 1945-48; book program, KEX, Portland, Ore., Tuesday, 1949; Pilgrimage in World of Books, ABC, 1954; Earl lecturer, Pacific School Religion, 1946; Peyton lecturer, Southern Meth. U., 1949; Slover lecturer Southwestern U., 1950; Quillian lectr. Emory U., 1951; Mendenhall lectr., Depauw U., 1954; Beecher lecturer, Yale U., 1954; Ayer lecturer, Colgate-Rochester, 1955; Grey lectr. Duke, 1957; Auburn lectr. Union Theol. Sem., 1957; Willson lectr. Southwestern Coll., 1964; sr. minister First Meth. Chr., Pasadena, Cal., 1969—. Denman lectr. Perkins Sch. Theology, Dallas; Voigt lecturer McKendree Coll., 1968. Member of the exec. co. Community Chest, Lincoln, Neb., 1945-48; pres. Council Social Agys., Lincoln, 1946-48; pres. Council of Bishops of Meth. Ch., 1960-61; mem. bd. trustees U. of Pacific, Pasadena Playhouse, Pacific Sch. Religion, Cal. Western U., So. Cal. Sch. Theology; pres. Gen. Bd. Evangelism, Methodist Church, 1964-68; executive bd. Nat. Council Churches. Mem. Cal. State Bd. Edn. Clubs: Rotary, Bel Air Country, Jonathan, University, Lakeside (Los Angeles). Author: His Word Through Preaching, 1947; Have This Mind, 1948; The Best of John Henry Jowett (edited), 1948; The Lion and the Lamb, 1950; With Singleness of Heart, 1951; Go Inquire of the Lord, 1952; A Reader's Notebook, 1953; Who Speaks for God?, 1954; God's Good News, 1955; The Christian and His America, 1956; The Methodist Way of Life, 1958; I Believe, 1958; Readers Notebook, 2, 1959; The Parables, 1960; While I'm On My Feet, 1963; For Preachers and Other Sinners, 1964; Fresh Every Morning, 1966. Seven Words of the Minister, 1968; For Laymen and Other Martyrs, 1969. Home: 1530 Pegfair Estates Dr Pasadena CA 91103 Office: 5250 Santa Monica Blvd Los Angeles CA 90029

KENNEDY, HAROLD THOMAS, cons. engr.; b. Bklyn., June 9, 1908; s. Thomas H. and Claudine L. (Swift) K.; student U. Detroit, 1928-31, N.Y.U., 1933; m. E. Dorothy Young, Nov. 22, 1947; children—Marilyn, Judith, Sheila, Laurie. Pres. H.T. Kennedy Co., Inc., N.Y.C., 1945-68, also dir.; pres. G.K.N. Internat., Inc. 1968-69; cons. engr. Design & Devel. Assos., Glen Ridge, N.J., 1969—; dir. CKNI (Can.) Ltd., Toronto. Pres. Am. Importers Assn., 1959-61, sr. councillor, 1961-69. Address: 96 Douglas Rd Glen Ridge NJ 07028

KENNEDY, HARRY SHERBOURNE, bishop; b. Bklyn., Aug. 21, 1901; s. David K. and Ida (Hargreaves) K.; student Colo. State Coll., 1922-26; A.B., St. John's Theol. Sem., 1926; postgrad. U. So. Cal., 1931; D.D., Seabury-Western Theol. Sem., 1943; S.T.D., Ch. Div. Sch. Pacific, 1944; D.D., Trinity Coll., 1957; L.H.D., Colo. Coll., 1967; m. Katharine Kittle, July 27, 1927; children—Bruce H., David K., Paul S., Joel and Mark (twins). Ordained to ministry Episcopal Ch., 1926; clergyman P.E. Ch., 1926-44, bishop of Honolulu, 1944—. Served to capt. as chaplain AUS, 1942-43. Decorated comdr. Order Brit. Empire, 1964. Address: 1001 Wilder Av Honolulu HI 96822

KENNEDY, J. RUSSELL, corp. exec.; b. Tex., Apr. 15, 1906; s. James W. and Sophie (Noble) K.; B.S., Tex. A. and M. U., 1928; m. Ailee Marie Crehan, Dec. 20, 1931; children—J.R., Kay, Marie, Ailee. Economist U.S. Dept. Agr., 1928-44; successively gen. mgr., exec. v.p., pres. Calcot, Ltd., Bakersfield, Cal., 1944—. Mem. various agrl. adv. commns. U.S. Dept. Agr., 1950, 60-68. Bd. Dirs. Bakersfield Meml. Hosp. Mem. Cotton Council Internat. (pres. 1970-71). Democrat. Episcopalian. Home: 2493 Beech St Bakersfield CA 93301 Office: Box 259 Bakersfield CA 93302

KENNEDY, JACQUELINE LEE BOUVIER (Mrs. John F. Kennedy) see Onassis, Jacquelin Lee Bouvier Kennedy.

KENNEDY, JAMES ALOYSIUS CHARLES, lawyer; b. Omaha, Oct. 31, 1875; s. Thomas and Anna M. (Kennedy) K.; student Creighton Prep. Sch., 1888; night sch. Omaha U., 1896-97; law sch. U. Ia., 1898; LL.B., Neb. U., 1900; m. Caroline Purvis, June 1, 1905; children—Ann Marie (Mrs. James S. Hauck), Jean (Mrs. John George Jones), James Aloyoius Charles. Messenger boy, bookkeeper First Nat. Bank of Omaha, 1891-98; admitted to Neb. bar, 1900; elected mem. Neb. Legislature, 1903; dep. co. atty. Douglas Co., Neb., 1903-04; apptd. U.S. referee bankruptcy, 1908-18; sr. mem. Kennedy, Holland, DeLacy & Svoboda, 1917—; dir. Mut. Benefit Health & Accident Assn., Kennedy Co., Inc. Mem. Draft Bd. Appeals, Omaha, World War I. Served with 2d Neb. Vol. Inf., AUS, Spanish War; pvt. to 1st lt. judge adv., ordnance officer regt. Co. G. Mem. Phi Delta Phi, Phi Delta Theta. Clubs: Omaha, Country (Omaha). Home: 521 N 38th St Omaha NB 68131 Office: City National Bank Bldg Omaha NB 68102

KENNEDY, JAMES FRANCIS, Jr., lawyer; b. Pitts., June 21, 1924; s. James Francis and Marie (Hardiman) K.; B.A., U. Pitts., 1947, J.D., 1949; m. Anne K. Griffin, June 10, 1950; children-Brian Eileen, Jane Frances, Mary, Stephen, Claire. Admitted to Pa. bar, 1950, Ohio bar, 1950; practiced in Scranton, 1950- 51, Toledo, 1956—; instr. Bus. Adminstrn. Sch., U. Scranton, 1949-51; trial atty. Chief Counsel's Office, Internal Revenue Service, 1951-56; partner Marshall, Melhorn, Bloch & Belt, 1956—; lectr. Cleve. Bar Assn. Tax Insts., 1964-68. Dir. Caisson, Inc. Legal counsel The Bridge, Inc. Served to lt. (j.g.) USNR, 1943-46. Mem. Am., Ohio, Toledo bar assns., Order of Coif, Beta Gamma Sigma. Home: 3161 Hopewell Pl Toledo OH 43606 Office: Nat Bank Bldg Toledo OH 43604

KENNEDY, JAMES PAUL, educator; b. Barnes City, Ia., Apr. 25, 1911; s. Thomas Clifford and Elsie (Lowry) K.; B.A., William Penn Coll., 1932; Mus.B. in Edn., Northwestern U., 1933, Mus.M., 1934; Ph.D., State U. Ia., 1940; student Matthay Pianoforte Sch., London, Eng., 1941; m. Frances Theodore Moor, June 10, 1937; children—Dennisse, Thomas, James Paul, John, Mary. Instr. music Hiram (O.) Coll., 1934-36; instr., asst. and asso. prof. music Bowling Green (O.) State U., 1937-62, prof. music, dir. Sch. Music, 1962—, dir. choral activities, 1940-58, chmn. dept., 1956-58. Mem. Music Tchrs. Nat. Assn. (v.p.), Music Educators Nat. Conf. Home: 611 S Main St Bowling Green OH 43402

KENNEDY, JAMES ROSS, chem. mfr.; b. Kearny, N.J., July 31, 1911; s. James Ruddick and Mary (Ross) K.; B.A., U. Wis., 1935; m. Doris Ritti, Jan. 15, 1947; children—James R., John, Karen. With Home Fire Ins. Co., 1935-40, Peat, Marwick, Mitchell & Co., 1940-44; with Celanese Corp., 1944—, exec. v.p. 1960-66, vice chmn., 1966—, also dir.; dir. Continental Coffee Co., Prudential Gibraltar Fund, ARA Services, Inc. Vice Pres., trustee Nat. Urban League; mem. Conf. Bd. Trustee Com. Econ. Devel. Mem. Internat. C. of C. (trustee U.S. council), Psi Upsilon. Club: Essex Fells (N.J.) Country. Home: Old Chester Rd Essex Fells NJ 07021 Office: 522 Fifth Av New York City NY 10036

KENNEDY, JAMES WALTER, profl. sports orgn. exec.; b. Stamford, Conn., June 8, 1912; s. Michael James and Lottie (Hofman) K.; B.A. in Edn. and Journalism, U. Notre Dame, 1934; m. Marion McRedmond, Nov. 28, 1940; children—David Michael, Robert Francis, Kathleen Marie. Social worker Cath. Charities, Stamford, 1934-37; athletic coach St. Basil's Prep. Sch., Stamford, 1937- 39; head Cath. textbook dept. Macmillan Pub. Co., 1939-41, Loyola U. Press, Chgo., 1941-43; dir. pub. relations U. Notre Dame, 1943-46; propr. pub. relations firm, N.Y.C., Stamford, 1946-59; mayor Stamford, 1959-63; commr. Nat. Basketball Assn., 1963—. Mem. Stamford Bd. Edn., 1948-51, Stamford Park Commn., 1955-59; mem. Conn. Commn. Higher Edn., 1966-67, Conn. Devel. Commn. Campaign mgr. for U.S. Senator Ribicoff, 1962. Chmn. trustees State Colls. Conn., 1966-67. Named knight of St. Gregory, 1966. Democrat. Home: 68 3d St Stamford CT 06905 Office: 2 Pennsylvania Plaza New York City NY 10001

KENNEDY, JAMES WILLIAM, clergyman; b. Denison, Tex., Aug. 22, 1905; s. Sydney Carr and Addie Myrtle (Francis) K.; student Tex. A. and M. Coll., 1923-24, U. Colo., 1927- 29, Northwestern, 1929-32; S.T.B., Western Theol. Sem., 1932; A.B., Stephen F. Austin Coll., 1934; S.T.M., U. South, 1946; D.D. (hon.), Seabury Western Theol. Sem., 1948; m. Frances Pleasants Campbell, Aug. 19, 1935; children—Stephen Campbell, Jane Pleasants. Ordained to ministry P.E. Ch., 1932; asst. rector St. John's Ch., West Hartford, Conn., 1932-33; priest-in-charge 4 missions Diocese of Tex., 1933-37; rector Ch. of Epiphany, Atlanta, 1937-39, All Saints, Richmond, Va., 1939-45, Christ Ch., Lexington, Ky., 1945-55; rector Ch. of Ascension, N.Y.C., 1955-64; dir., editor Forward Movement Publs., 1964—; condr. radio programs Haven, WMBG, Richmond, 1940-46, Parson Jim, WMBG, Richmond, WLAP, Lexington, 1946-49, Bible Reading Cambridge U. Press, WLAP, Lexington, 1950, Miniature Ch. of Air, WMBG, 1940-41; preacher Mut. Radio Chapel, 1944, Episcopal Ch. of Air, 1948-49. Chmn. dept. Christian edn. Diocese Va., 1943-45, Diocese Lexington, 1945- 53; chmn. dept. Christian social relations Diocese Atlanta, 1937-39; dep. to Gen. Gonv. P.E. Ch., 1946, 49, 52, sec. ecumenical relations, mem. joint commn. ecumenical relations, 1949—; accredited visitor 1st assembly World Council Chs., Amsterdam, Netherlands, 1948, del. 2d assembly, 1954 (chmn. radio and TV com.); exchange preacher to Great Britain under Fed. Council Chs., Ch. Peace Union and World World, 1956; A World on Film, 1966; Figures of Light, 1971. Found. Sermon award, 1950, 51. Mem. Omicron Delta Kappa. Club: Torch (past internat. pres.). Author: Haven, 1942; Haven House, 1944; The Man Who Wanted to Know, 1944; Hey Buddy, 1946; Advance Into Light, 1947; Parson's Sampler, 1948; Venture of Faith, 1948; A Lenten Query, 1950; Exploring Paths of Church Unity, 1951; Henry Drummond; an Anthology, 1953; He That Gathereth, 1953; Evanston Notebook, 1953; Meditations in His Presence, 1954; Evanston Scrapbook, 1954; Holy Island, 1957, paper back edit., 1969; The Most Comfortable Sacrament, 1961; No Darkness At All, 1962; The Unknown Worshipper, 1964; Minister's Shop-Talk, 1965. Home: 3333 Mannington Av Cincinnati OH 45226 Office: 412 Sycamore St Cincinnati OH 45202

KENNEDY, JOHN A., editor, pub., broadcasting exec.; b. St. Paul, Dec. 21, 1898; s. Charles C. and Mary M. (Sullivan) K.; grad. Trinity Coll., Sioux City, Ia., 1918; B.S., Coe Coll., 1922, D.Litt., 1958; B.C.L., Georgetown U., 1928; m. Viera Hines, Nov. 19, 1924 (div. 1932); 1 son, John Hines; m. 2d, Ellen Bruce Lee, Nov. 21, 1932; children—Patricia Henry (Mrs. David Allen Grimsted), Davis Lee; stepchildren—Stoddard P. Johnston, Mrs. Peter M. Norton. Mem. staff Sioux City Tribune, 1918, Cedar Rapids Rep. and Cedar Rapids Gazette, 1919-22, Washington Herald, 1922; exec. Hearst Newspapers; conducted several investigations of widespread abuses in various fed. govt. agys. resulting in conviction of offenders; purchased control Exponent, Clarksburg, W.Va., 1935 (sold 1940); owner W.Va. Network Charleston, Clarksburg, Huntington, Parkersburg, 1936-50; former chmn. bd. Kennedy Broadcasting Co. (KFMB- KFMB-TV) San Diego; now chmn. bd. Kenco Enterprises, Inc., Sioux Falls, S.D.; editor, pub. Sioux Falls Argus-Leader, Sioux Falls, S.D., 1954-63. Mem. bars of Ia., D.C. Trustee Coe Coll. Served with U.S. Army, World War I; capt. USNR, World War II. Recipient Pugsley prize of $1,000 for most noteworthy work by a Washington corr., 1929. Clubs: Metropolitan, National Press, Chevy Chase (Washington); Racquet and Tennis (N.Y.); LaJolla (Cal.) Beach and Tennis; Gulf Stream Golf; Gulf Stream Bath and Tennis; Palm Beach Bath and Tennis. Home: 3250 Polo Dr Gulf Stream Box 1896 Delray Beach FL 33444 (summer) 939 Coast Blvd LaJolla CA 92037 Office: Kenco Enterprises Inc 1045 Bldg Delray Beach FL 33444

KENNEDY, JOHN EDWARD, pub. health physician; b. Lawrence, Mass., May 4, 1917; s. Henry Joseph and Elizabeth (Cronin) K.; B.S., U. Vt., 1939. M.D. cum laude, 1942; M.P.H. cum laude, Harvard, 1957; m. Olga Sommer, June 12, 1943; children —Kathy, Jack, Karen, Gretchen, Clytie, Robert, Jeffrey. Intern St. Mary's Hosp., Bklyn., 1942-43; pvt. practice, Bloomfield, Conn., 1946- 52; asso. mem. med. staff St. Francis Hosp., Hartford, Conn., 1946-52; med. officer, then dist. chief pub. health, Palau Islands, 1952-54; dir. med. services Terr. Guam, 1954-56, Terr. Am. Samoa, 1957-59; chief pub. health adviser U.S. mission to Cambodia, ICA, 1959-64, Djakarta, Indonesia, 1964-65; pub. health adviser AID, Vientiane, Laos, 1965-66; chief public health adv. USOM, AID, Bangkok, Thailand, 1966—. U.S. mem. Research Council South Pacific Commn., Noumea, New Caledonia, 1954-59; chmn. 1st joint Pacific Is. Conf. on Tb. 1959; instituted 1st civilian filariasis research and control program, Am. Samoa, 1958; organizer woman's health coms. system for health improvement remote villages, Am. Samoa, 1958-59; U.S. del. 12th WHO Western Pacific regional com. meeting, Wellington, New Zealand, 1961. Served to major, M.C., AUS, 1943-46; ETO. Mem. Phi Delta Theta, Nu Sigma Nu. Catholic. Author treatises. Home: RFD 1 Kent CT 06757 Office: Office Pub Health USOM Bangkok Thailand

KENNEDY, JOHN HENRY, financial exec.; b. Phila., Feb. 28, 1930; s. John J. and Catherine (Ward) K.; B.S, LaSalle Coll., 1951; m. Marjorie A. Walters, Nov. 17, 1951; children-John Henry, Sarah Anne, Paul J., Ward W., Grace Maria, Joseph W. Account mgr. Price Waterhouse & Co., Phila., 1953-61; controller Alco Oil & Chem. Corp., Phila., 1962-65; controller Alco Standard Corp., Valley Forge, P., 966—, v.p., 1969—, also dir. Served to 1st lt. USMCR, 1951-53. C.P.A., Pa. Mem. Am. Inst. C.P.A.'s, Pa. Soc. C.P.A.'s,, Financial Execs. Inst., Nat. Assn. Accountants. Clubs: Overbrook Golf (Bryn Maar, Pa.); Seaview Country (Absecon, N.J.). Home: 619 College Av Haverford PA 19041 Office: Valley Forge PA 19481

KENNEDY, JOHN JOSEPH, educator, author; b. E. Orange, N.J., Mar. 28, 1933; s. George T. and Rosemary (Ferris) K.; B.S. in Mech. Engring., Newark Coll. Engring., 1955; M.B.A., Ohio State U., 1959, Ph.D., 1962; m. Margaret Teresa Coyle, July 21, 1956; children—John Joseph, Eileen Mary, Margaret Teresa, Rosemary Margaret, Cathleen Ann. With Standard Oil-Esso Research and Engring., 1955-56; research asso. Def. Mgmt. Center, Ohio State U., 1959-62; mem. faculty U. Notre Dame, 1962—, now prof. marketing, chmn. dept. Sch. Bus.; prin. partner Contract Mgmt. Inst., Washington, 1962- 67; partner Corriden, Dow, Marks, Kennedy, cons.; cons. in field. Served with USAF, 1956-59. Mem. Nat. Contract Mgmt. Assn. (bd. advisers), Tau Beta Pi, Omicron Delta Kappa, Pi Tau Sigma, Eta Kappa Nu. Author: Marketing Principles; Incentive Contracting; also articles. Home: 17812 Woodthowsn Lane South Bend IN 46624

KENNEDY, JOHN LYON, psychologist; b. Saginaw, Mich., May 26, 1913; s. James Sheldon and Elizabeth (Lyon) K.; certificate Sacramento Jr. Coll., 1932; A.B., Stanford, 1934; A.M., Brown U., 1936, Ph.D., 1937; m. Nancy Elliott Kidd, Aug. 27, 1938; children—James Walden, Marianna Elliott, Katherine Ann. Research asst. Yerkes Labs. Primate Biology, Yale, 1936-37; Thomas Welton Stanford fellow psychical research Stanford, 1937-39; asst. prof. psychology Tufts U., 1939-42, asso. prof., chmn. dept., 1945-46, prof., chmn. dept., 1946-51, also dir. Inst. Applied Exptl. Psychology; tech. asst. to exec. sec. com. on service personnel NRC, 1942-43; tech. aide OSRD, 1943-45; psychologist RAND Corp., 1951-57; Dorman T. Warren prof. psychology Princeton, 1957-67, chmn. dept. psychology, 1958-66, vis. prof., 1966-67; v.p. Inst. Ednl. Devel., 1966-69; vis. prof. U. So. Cal. Grad. Sch. Bus. Adminstrn., 1969-71; lectr. mgmt. Sch. Bus. Adminstrn. and Econs., San Fernando Valley State Coll., Northridge, Cal., 1971—. Cons. psychologist govt. agys., bus. firms. Fellow Center Advanced Study in Behavioral Scis., 1954-55. Mem. A.A.A.S., Am., Western, Cal. psychol. assns., Am. Assn. U. Profs., Soc. Exptl. Psychologists, Phi Beta Kappa, Sigma Xi. Club: Cosmos (Washington). Editor: Handbook of Human Engineering Data for Design Engineers, 1949. Contbr. articles to profl. jours. Home; 1127A 22d St Santa Monica CA 90403 Office: Sch Bus Adminstrn and Econs San Fernando Valley State Coll Northridge CA 91324

KENNEDY, JOHN RAYMOND, mfg. exec.; b. N.Y.C., 1900; s. Patrick and Margaret (Denne) K.; B.C. S., N.Y.U., 1924; m. Ethel Rose Leavy, June 27, 1928; children—Ethel (Mrs. William R. Marran), John, Quentin. Cashier Colgate Parker Co., Banking house N.Y.C., 1918; with Copper Export Assn., 1921; mgr., treas. Copper Inst., copper exporter, 1921; with Fed. Paper Board Co., Bogota, N.J., 1935—, successively, asst. to pres., treas., 1935- 42, pres., dir., 1942-65, chmn. bd., 1965—; dir. James Talcott, Inc., N.Y.C., First Nat. State Bank, Newark. Board trustees Seton Hall U., Orange, N.J.; past pres. N. Bergen council Boy Scouts Am.; adv. bd. Holy Name Hosp., Teaneck, N.J. Knight of Equestrian Order of Holy Sepulchre of Jerusalem, Knight of Malta, Knight of St. Gregory. Recipient Madden Meml. award, N.Y.U. Mem. Am. Paper Inst. (dir., past chmn. bd., mem. exec. com.), Nat. Paperboard Assn. (past pres., dir., mem. exec. com.), Lambda Sigma Phi, Beta Gamma Sigma. Clubs: New York Athletic, University (N.Y.C.); Ridgewood (N.J.) Country; Knickerbocker Country (Tenafly, N.J.), Everglades, Bath and Tennis (Palm Beach, Fla.); Maidstone, Nat. Golf (L.I., N.Y.); Lambs, Union League (N.Y.C.). Home: 16 Woodland Park Dr Tenafly NJ 07670 Office: 75 Chestnut Ridge Rd Montvale NJ 07645

KENNEDY, JOHN RAYMOND, Jr., paper board co. exec.; b. N.Y.C., Sept. 21, 1930; s. John Raymond and Ethel (Leavy) K.; B.S., Georgetown U., 1952; m. Joyce Willis, June 30, 1952; children—John John Raymond III, James Willis, Andrew, Paula. Pres., dir. Fed. Paper Board Co., Inc., Montvale, N.J. Home: 4 Boulder Rd Tenafly, NJ 07670. Office: 75 Chestnut Ridge Rd Montvale NJ 07645

KENNEDY, JOHN WESLEY, coll. ofcl.; b. Spencer, N.C., Oct. 9, 1920; s. John Quincy and Willie (Huffman) K.; A.B., Duke, 1942, A.M., 1947; Ph.D., U. N.C. at Chapel Hill, 1951; m. Melva Pearce Dail, Aug. 21, 1942; children—John Wesley, Marcia Frances, Melva Ann. Asst. prof. econs., bus. adminstrn. U. Fla., 1949-52; asso. prof., prof. Auburn U., 1952-56; faculty U. N.C., Greensboro, 1956—, dean Grad. Sch., 1964-71, prof. econs., 1964—, vice chancellor for grad. studies, 1971—. Labor arbitrator, 1954—. Pres., Greensboro Assn. Retarded Children, 1958-60. Served to lt. USNR, 1942-45. Mem. Am., So. econ. assns., Indsl. Relations and Research Assn. Baptist (deacon 1966-70). Author: (with others) Applied Economics, 7th edit., 1967; A Problem Manual in Economic Theory, 5th edit., 1968. Contbr. articles to profl. jours. Home: 2505 Fairway Dr Greensboro NC 27408

KENNEDY, JOSEPH, see Kennedy, X. J.

KENNEDY, JOSEPH BRADY, Jr., oil co. exec.; b. N.Y.C., Apr. 29, 1912; s. Joseph Brady and Louise (Eckstein) K.; student Johns Hopkins, 1930-32; E.M., Colo. Sch. Mines, 1935; postgrad. in bus. Harvard, 1960; m. Edna Joyce Andrews, July 15, 1948; children—Stuart Allen, Judith (Mrs. John Elias), Joseph Brady III, Joanne Joyce. With Sinclair Oil & Gas Co., 1935-65, various positions in geol. and prodn. depts., Tulsa, Midland, Tex., also Casper, Wyo., 1935-54, v.p., div. mgr. Houston, 1954-57, exec. v.p. for operations, Tulsa, 1957-64, pres., 1964-65; dir. sinclair Oil Corp., 1964—, exec. v.p., 1965—; Bd. dirs. Internat. Petroleum Expn., Tulsa, 1964-65. Served to lt. comdr. USNR, 1942-46. Registered profl. engr., Tex. Mem. Am. Petroleum Inst., Alpha Tau Omega, Tau Beta Phi. Episcopalian. Clubs: Houston, Tejas (Houston); Palm Bay (Miami); Sky (N.Y.C.). Home: 2100 S Ocean Lane Ft Lauderdale FL 33316

KENNEDY, KEITH FURNIVAL, paper co. exec., lawyer; b. New London, Conn., Nov. 1, 1925; s. Joseph Reilly and Madeleine (Mason) K.; B.S., Yale, 1949; LL.B., Harvard, 1953; m. Joan Ruth Canfield, Feb. 11, 1956; children—Joseph Keith, Austin Robert, Thomas Canfield, Richard Furnival. Admitted to N.Y. bar, 1955; atty. Vick Chem. Co., 1953-54, 58- 60; sec., dir. personnel J.T. Baker Chem. Co., 1955-58; with Riegel Paper Corp., 1960—, sec., 1961-69, gen., atty., 1964-69, v.p. finance and law, counsel, 1969—; dir. Mohawk Paper Mills, Inc., Laminex, Inc., Techbilt, Inc., Community Concepts Corp., Britain-Riegel Indsl., Ltd., Capt., Scarsdale Vol. Fire Co. 3, 1966—. Bd. dirs., sec. Adoption service Westchester, 1966—, pres., 1971—. Served to 1st lt. AUS, 1943-46, 51-52. Mem. Assn. Bar City N.Y., Am. Soc. Corporate Secs., St. Andrews Soc. N.Y., Chi Phi. Roman Catholic. Clubs: Economic of N.Y., Yale (N.Y.C.); Larchmont (N.Y.) Yacht; Niantic Bay (Conn.) Yacht. Home: 16 Innes Rd Scarsdale NY 10583 Office: 260 Madison Av New York City NY 10016

KENNEDY, KENNETH WADE, army officer; b. Nacogdoches, Tex., Sept. 3, 1918; s. Joseph William and Mattie (Wade) K.; B.S., U.S. Mil. Acad., 1941; M.S. in Civil Engring., Mass. Inst. Tech., 1947; grad. Army War Coll., 1962; m. Audrey Ruth Smith, June 17, 1944; children—Kenneth W., Debra Lynn, Susan B. Commd. 2d lt. U.S. Army, 1941, advanced through grades to brig. gen., 1968; chief constrn. and maintenance SAC, 1947-49; comdr. 159th Engr. Constrn. Group, Ft. Bragg, N.C., 1960-61; engr. Mil. Assistance Command, Vietnam, 1964-65; chief engr. career br. Army Dept., 1966-67; comdg. gen. Army Eng. Command, Europe, Frankfurt, Germany, 1967—. Mem. exec. bd. Transatlantic council Boy Scouts Am., 1971. Decorated D.S.M., Legion Merit with oak leaf cluster, Air medal, Army Commendation medal with oak leaf cluster. Registered profl. engr., Tex. Mem. Soc. Am. Mil. Engrs. Home: Quarters 216 Bad Vilbel Frankfurt Germany Office: Army Engr Command Europe APO New York City NY 09757

KENNEDY, LEO RAYMOND, educator; b. Alexandria, S.D., Aug. 25, 1903; s. Daniel and Katherine (McGuire) K.; student Columbus Coll., Chamberlain, S.D., 1917- 20, Columbus Coll., Sioux Falls, S.D., 1920-21; A.B., Creighton U., 1924, A.M., 1925; postgrad. U. Minn., 1926-28; Ph.D., U. Neb., 1930; m. Grace Harlan, June 8, 1933; 1 child, Paula Leo. Instr., St. Mary's Coll., Winona, Minn., 1925-27, Creighton U., Omaha, 1930-37; prof. edn., dean Univ. Coll., St. Louis U., 1937- 44; prof. edn. and dir. vets. counseling Marquette U., Milw., 1944-47; prof. edn., chmn. dept. Creighton U., 1947-71. Chmn., Met. Bur. for War-Time Child Welfare. Mem. N.E.A., Am. Psychol. Assn., Sigma Xi, Psi Chi, Phi Delta Kappa. Address: 9119 Hickory St Omaha NB 68124

KENNEDY, MATTHEW WASHINGTON, educator, pianist; b. Americus, Ga., Mar. 10, 1921; s. Royal Clement and Mary (Dowdell) K.; diploma Juilliard Inst. Mus. Art, 1940; A.B., Fisk U., 1946 M.S., Juilliard Sch. Music, 1950; postgrad. George Peabody Coll. for Tchrs.; m. Anne Lucille Gamble, May 23, 1956; 1 dau., Nina Gamble. Faculty, Fisk U., Nashville, 1947-48, 54—, asso. prof., 1967—, dir. univ. Jubilee Singers, 1957-68. Pianist-accompanist throughout world, 1946-47, 50-54; solo pianist, 1958—. Served with AUS, World War II; ETO. Gabriel scholar, 1941. Mem. Sigma Upsilon Pi, Omega Psi Phi. Baptist (deacon). Club: Nashville Fine Arts. Home: 2417 Gardner Lane Nashville TN 37207.

KENNEDY, MAYNARD THOMAS, educator; b. Altoona, Pa., June 20, 1912; s. Thomas Joseph and Helen (Wilkins) K.; A.B., Swarthmore Coll., 1934; M.A., U. Pa., 1938, Ph.D., 1947; m. Ruth Janet Corbin, Oct. 23, 1937; children—Patricia (Mrs. George A. Vare, Jr.), Thomas Corbin. Instr. econs. Muhlenberg Coll., 1938-41; impartial chmn. Full Fashioned Hosiery Industry, 1941-43; instr. econs. U. Pa., 1943-47, asst. prof., then asso. prof. indsl. relations, 1947-50; dir. indsl. and pub. relations Atlas Powder Co., 1950-56; prof. bus. adminstrn. Harvard Bus. Sch., 1956—; mem. labor arbitration panels Am. Arbitration Assn., Fed. Mediation and Conciliation Service. Mem. Indsl. Relations Research Assn., Nat. Acad. Arbitrators. Mem. Soc. of Friends. Author: Effective Labor Arbitration, 1948; The Significance of Wage Uniformity in Industry- Wide Bargaining, 1949; Automation Funds and Displaced Workers, 1962. Home: 14 Hundreds Circle Wellesley Hills MA 02181 Office: Harvard Bus School Soldiers Field Boston MA 02163

KENNEDY, MERVILLE T., educator. Prof. polit. sci. Bryn Mawr Coll. Office: Dept Polit Sci Bryn Mawr Coll Bryn Mawr PA 19010*

KENNEDY, ORISON GLEN, pharm. co. exec.; b. Lost Creek, W.Va., Apr. 19, 1917; s. Charles Emory and Nora (Radcliffe) K.; B.A. in Bus. Adminstrn., Salem Coll., 1939; postgrad. student, Harvard, 1955; m. Betty Jane Ash, Feb. 18, 1943; children—Katherine, Orison Glen. With Johnson and Johnson, 1945-51, regional sales mgr., Phila., 1950-51; with Lehn & Fink Products Corp., 1951-58, mgr. proprietary div., dir. co., 1954-58; v.p. planning Miles Labs., Inc., 1958-62, pres. Miles products div., 1962-64, dir., 1960-64; chmn., pres. Nationwide Papers, Inc., Chgo., 1964-66; pres. Market Planning Corp., N.Y.C., 1966-69; pres. and chief exec. officer of Norwich Pharmacal Co. (N.Y.), 1969-71; v.p. Morton-Norwich Products Co., Chgo., 1971—; dir. C.G. Conn. Ltd. Chmn. trustees Salem Coll., 1963—. Served with USAAF 1943-45. Mem. Nat. Assn. Sales Execs., Am. Mgmt. Assn. Clubs: Chicago Athletic; Elcona Country (pres. 1962) (Elkhart, Ind.). Office: 110 N Wacker Dr Chicago IL 60606

KENNEDY, QUENTIN J., paper co. exec.; b. 1933; grad. Georgetown U.; m. Admitted to N.Y. bar; with Federal Paper Board Co. Inc., 1959—, sec., 1963—. Address: 24 River Rd Bogota, NJ 07603.*

KENNEDY, RALPH EUGENE, govt. ofcl.; b. Springfield, Mo., Nov. 20, 1919; s. David Rolland and Mary (Appleby) K.; B.S., S.W. Mo. State Coll., 1942; LL.B. (J.D.), Washington U., 1944; m. Elizabeth Lyle Fenton, Jan. 14, 1950 (dec. Feb. 1959); m. 2d, Blanche Noe Crane, Aug. 18, 1962; children—Kenneth Crane, Jean Crane, Joan Crane, Mary Elizabeth. Admitted to Mo. bar, 1944; pvt. practice, St. Louis, 1944-48; field atty. NLRB, St. Louis, Buffalo, Atlanta, Ft. Worth, Tex. regional offices, 1948-55, regional dir., St. Louis, 1955-58, regional dir., Los Angeles, 1958-70, mem. bd., Washington, 1970—; guest lectr. U. Cal., Los Angeles, 1963, U. So. Cal., 1965. Mem. Am., Mo., St. Louis, Fed. bar assns. Home: 1550 Bonita Ct Ontario CA 91762 Office: 1717 Pennsylvania Av NW Washington DC 20570

KENNEDY, ROBERT EDWIN, coll. pres.; b. Portland, Ore., Oct. 31, 1915; s. Edwin R. and Hazel (Powell) K.; A.B., San Diego State Coll., 1938; M.A., Stanford, 1950; Ph.D., Claremont Grad. Sch. and U. Center, 1966; m. Mary Paxton, June 12, 1938; children—Robert Edwin, Maridel (Mrs. John Salisbury), Stephen, Susan (Mrs. Robert Lattanzio). Reporter, San Diego Sun, 1937-38; exec. sec. Civic Affairs Conf., San Diego, 1938-39; advt. mgr. Hamilton's, Ltd., San Diego, 1939-40; mem. pub. relations staff, head journalism dept. Cal. State Poly. Coll., San Luis Obispo, 1940-48, dir. pub. relations, 1948-54, asst. to pres., 1954-57, dean arts and scis., 1957-59, v.p., 1959-67, pres., 1967—. Bd. dirs. Santa Lucia council Boy Scouts Am. Mem. Am. Assn. State Colls. and Univs. (dir.), Am. Coll. Pub. Relations Assn. (past dir., pres. 12th Dist.), San Luis Obispo C. of C. (past dir.), Blue Key, Sigma Delta Chi. Contbr. articles profl. jours. Home: 1385 Cazadero St San Luis Obispo CA 93401

KENNEDY, ROBERT EMMET, newspaperman; b. Cincinnati, O., June 7, 1910; s. Robert Emmet and Amelia (Garnier) K.; student DePaul U., 1928; m. Rosetta Vinson, Oct. 27, 1933; children—Jeanne Colleen (Mrs. Theodore Lamb), Robert Emmet. Police reporter, later asst. city editor, City News Bureau, 1929-35; asst. city editor, political editor, Washington correspondent, editorial page editor Chicago Times, 1935-48; editorial writer Chicago Suntimes, Chicago, Ill., 1948-50, chief editorial writer, 1950-65, asso. editor, 1965—. Mem. Am. Soc. Newspaper Editors, Nat. Conf. Editorial Writers (chairman 1958), Sigma Delta Chi. Club: Chicago Press (President 1963). Home: 2321 Bryant Av Evanston, IL 60201. Office: 401 N Wabash Av Chicago IL 60611

KENNEDY, ROSE FITZGERALD, (Mrs. Joseph P. Kennedy), b. Boston, 1890; m. Joseph P. Kennedy, 1914 (dec. 1969); children—Joseph (dec.) John Fitzgerald, (Pres. U.S. 1961-63; dec.) Rosemary, Kathleen (dec.), Eunice (Mrs. Robert Sargent Shriver), Patricia (Mrs. Patricia Lawford), Robert Francis (dec.), Jean (Mrs. Stephen Smith), Edward M. Address: Hyannis MA*

KENNEDY, RUTH LEE, educator; b. Centerville, Tex., Oct. 15, 1895; d. Oliver W. and Carrie Lee (McWaters) Kennedy; A.B., U. Tex., 1916, A.M., 1917; postgrad. U. Cal., 1924-25; Ph.D., U. Pa., 1931. Tchr. Spanish, San Benito (Tex.) High Sch., 1917-18, Temple High Sch., 1918-19; instr. English, Okla. Coll. for Women, 1919-20; tchr. Spanish, Sam Houston State Normal Coll., 1920-21; instr. English, U. P.R., 1921-22; head Spanish dept. S.W. Tex. State Tchrs. Coll., 1922-24, 1925-26; head Spanish dept. San Antonio Jr. Coll., 1926-28, 1929-30; asst. prof. Smith Coll., 1930-34, asso. prof., 1935-44, prof. Spanish lang. and lit., 1944-61, emeritus, 1961—; prof. Romance langs. U. Ariz., 1961-70, emeritus, 1970—; dir. Smith Coll. Jrs. in Spain, 1956-58. Vis. lectr. Oxford and Cambridge Univs., 1946, U. Mich., summer 1949, U. Ariz., 1950-51, U. Cal., summer 1951. Fellow Am. Assn. U. Women, 1937-38, 45-46, U. Pa., 1945-46; John S. Guggenheim fellow, 1950-51. Mem. Modern Lang. Assn., Am. Assn. Tchrs. Spanish, Hispanic Soc. Am., Internat. Inst. for Girls in Spain, Am. Assn. U. Women, Phi Beta Kappa. Republican. Author: The Dramatic Art of Moreto, 1931-32; La prudencia en la mujer and the Ambient that Brought It Forth (PMLA rated most influential article pub. by them in field of Spanish or Hispanic Culture and Lang. between 1885 and 1958), 1948. Contbr. articles on Golden Age lit. culture of Spain to profl. jours. Home: 1201 E Helen St Tucson AZ 85719

KENNEDY, SABE MCCLAIN, Jr., coll. ofcl.; b. Wootton, Colo., May 1, 1923; s. Sabe McClain and Margaret (Heathington) K.; B.A., Tex. Tech. Coll., 1943, M.A., 1946; postgrad. U. Nancy (France), 1945; Ph.D., U. Colo., 1952; m. Mary Frances Peak, Dec. 21, 1946; children—Marta, Lori. With Tex. Tech. Coll., 1946—, successively instr., asst. prof., 1949-53, asso. prof., 1953-57, prof., 1957—, acting asst. dean Coll. Arts and Scis., 1952-53, asst. dean, 1955-59, acting dean, 1959-61, dean, 1961-66, v.p. for academic affairs, 1966—; part-time instr. polit. sci. U. Colo., 1950. Council Deans Arts and Scis. State Univs. and Land Grant Colls. 2d v.p. Tex. Tb Assn. Served from pvt. to 2d lt., AUS, 1943-46; ETO; lt. col. Res. Mem. Assn. Tex. Colls. (chmn. conf. acad. deans 1966-67), So. Conf. Acad. Deans, Internat. Studies Assn., Southwestern Polit. Sci. Assn., Mil. Govt. Assn., S.W. Social Sci. Assn. (chmn. govt. sect. 1953, gen. program chmn. 1958), Res. Officers Assn. (pres. S. Plains chpt. 1953-57), Am., Western polit. sci. assns., W. Tex. Tb assn. (pres. 1968-69), Tex. Tb and Respiratory Diseases Assn. (pres. elect), Pi Sigma Alpha, Pi Gamma Mu, Sigma Delta Pi (hon.). Mem. Church of Christ. Home: 3705 67th St Lubbock TX 79413

KENNEDY, SARGENT, ednl. adminstr.; b. Cambridge, Mass., Apr. 5, 1907; s. Frank Lowell and Grace Lowell (Forbes) K.; A.B., Harvard, 1928, M.S., 1930, M.B.A., 1937; m. Elisabeth Morgan Pratt, Apr. 6, 1929; children—Frank Lowell II, Cynthia Pratt, Elisabeth Morgan, Nathaniel Forbes. Plant dept. N.J. Bell Telephone Co., 1930-35; research staff Harvard Bus. Sch., 1937-39; asst. dean Harvard, 1939-45, registrar, sec. faculty arts and scis., 1945-65, sec. corp., sec. bd. overseers, 1965-71. Home: 4 Kennedy Rd Cambridge MA 02138

KENNEDY, THOMAS JAMES, Jr., govt. ofcl; b. Washington, June 24, 1920; s. Thomas James and Ruth Elizabeth (Norris) K.; B.S. Cath. U. Am., 1940; M.D., Johns Hopkins, 1943; m. F. Elaine Godtfring, Sept. 30, 1950; children—Thomas James III, Ann Elizabeth, Joan Frances, Paul Edward, Christopher Alan. Intern med. service Peter Bent Brigham Hosp., Boston, 1944; research fellow, research service 3d med. div. Goldwater Meml. Hosp., N.Y.C., 1945-47, resident physician, research service 1st med. div., 1947-50; research fellow N.Y. U. Coll. Medicine, 1945-47; asst. medicine Columbia Coll. Phys. and Surg., 1948-50; joined USPHS, 1950, asst. surgeon gen.; asso. medicine George Washington U. Sch. Medicine, 1951-65; investigator lab. kidney and electrolyte metabolism Nat. Heart Inst., 1950-60, attending physician, responsible physician, 1953-60; asst. to dir. labs. and clinics Office Dir., NIH, 1960-62, spl. asst. to dir. for sci. communications, 1962-65, dir. div. research facilities and resources, 1965-68, asso. dir. for program planning and evaluation, office of dir. 1968—. Served to capt. AUS, 1944-47. Diplomate Am. Bd. Internal Medicine. Mem. Am. Fedn. Clin. Research, Am. Physiol. Soc. Home: 10703 Weymouth St Garrett Park MD 20766 Office: OPPE OD NIH Bldg 1 Bethesda MD 20014

KENNEDY, TOLBERT HALL, educator; b. Martin, Tenn., May 21, 1906; s. James G. and Bernice Elva (Hall) E.; student Freedman-Hardeman Coll., 1923-25, Abilene Christian Coll., 1925-28; A.B., U. of Tenn., 1929; A.M., Peabody Inst., 1940; student Peabody Inst. and Vanderbilt U., 1940-42; Ph.D., Peabody Inst., 1942; m. Edna Ruth Hogan, Dec. 1929; children—Larry, Jerry. Supt. of schs., Obion County, Tenn., 1925-29; athletic coach, Bradford (Tenn.) high sch., 1930-35; supt., Lafayette (Tenn.) schs., 1935-39; prof. social sci., Middle Tenn. State Coll., 1942-44; prof. sociology, State Coll. of Wash Pullman. since 1944, chmn. div. of social sciences since 1947, asso. dean coll. scis. and arts, 1953-64, sr. dean College Sciences and Arts, 1964—; Fulbright-Hays lectr. U. Capetown, S. Africa, 1966. Member A.A.A.S., Am. Sociol. Soc., Pacific Sociol. Soc., Am. Assn. Social Workers, Alpha Kappa Delta, Phi Delta Kappa, Phi Kappa Phi. Mem. Church of Christ. Democrat. Author of monographs and contbr. articles on race relations, etc., to profl. publs. Home: 415 Crestview Pullman Washington WA 99163

KENNEDY, VERNE CORNELIUS, Jr., engring. co. exec.; b. Mitchell, S.D., Sept. 15, 1919; s. Verne and Ella Ruth (Whitlow) K.; B.S. E. Metall. Engring., U. Mich., 1942, M.S. in Physics, 1950. Instr. metal processing U. Mich., 1946-47; dir. sales and engring. Streeter-Amet. Co., Grayslake, Ill., 1947-52, v.p., 1952-58; exec. dir. U. Okla. Research Inst., 1958-62, 65-68; exec. v.p. Streeter Amet div. Mangood Co., Grayslake, Ill., 1962-65; asso. prof. metall. engring. U. Okla., 1958-60, prof., 1960-70, v.p. contract research, 1966-68, v.p. for operations, 1967-70; pres. Hayek Engring. Co., Inc., Chgo., 1970—; nat. councillor U. Okla. Plan for Excellence Exec. bd., dist. chmn. N. Shore Area council Boy Scouts Am., 1963-65; chmn. State Adv. Com. Sci., Engring. and Specialized Personnel SSS, 1966-70. Trustee George Washington Carver Found. of Tuskegee Inst., 1964—; bd. dirs. Indsl. Mgmt. Inst. Lake Forest (Ill.) Coll., 1965, U. Okla. Research Inst., 1962-65, Condell Meml. Hosp., Libertyville, Ill., 1963-65, So. Regional Edn. Bd., 1966-70, Okla. Econ. Devel. Found., Inc., 1966-68, Ozarks Unlimited, Inc. U. Okla., 1966-70; dir. Okla. Bur. Standards, 1958-62, 65-70. Served to capt., 3d Marine Div., USMC, 1942-46; col. Res. Decorated Bronze Star. Registered profl. engr., Ill., Okla. Mem. Am. Soc. M.E., Am. Soc. Testing Materials, Nat. Soc. Profl. Engrs., Instrument Soc. Am., Am. Soc. Metals, Sci. Apparatus Makers Assn. (chmn. phys. testing div. 1955-58), Mid-Am. State Univs. Assn., Am. Soc. Engring. Edn., Am. Ordnance Assn., A.A.A.S., Okla. State (bd. of dirs. 1968-70), Oklahoma City, Norman (dir.) chambers commerce, Frontiers Sci. Found., Nat. Scalemen's Assn., Scale Mfrs. Assn. (dir., v.p. 1964-66), Sigma Xi, Sigma Tau, Tau Beta Pi, Sigma Chi. Mason (32, Shriner), Rotarian. Clubs: Racquet (Chgo.); Petroleum (Oklahoma City); Globe and Anchor Soc., Union League (Chgo.). Home: 505 N Lake Shore Dr Chicago IL 60611 Office: 69 W Washington St Chicago IL 60602

KENNEDY, WALTER WALLACE, banker; b. Birmingham, Dec. 20, 1898; s. Hughes Benjamin and Katherine (Hausman) K.; LL.B., U. Ala., 1921; student Grad. Sch. Banking, Rutgers U., 1945-47; m. Myra Belle Pope, Sept. 28, 1926; children—Walter, Ann Carter, Carol Pope. Admitted to Ala. bar, 1921; practiced in Birmingham, 1921-26; asst. to pres. Birmingham Electric Co., 1926-29; asst. trust officer First Nat. Bank Birmingham, 1929-35; trust officer First Nat. Bank Montgomery, 1935-43, exec. v.p., 1943-48, pres., 1948-64, chmn. bd., 1964-69, hon. chmn. bd., 1969—, also dir.; v.p. 1st Ala. Bancshares, Inc., 1970—. Chmn. bd. regents Grad. Sch. Banking, Rutgers U., 1963-67. Treas., Community Chest Montgomery, 1947-49, v.p., 1953; Montgomery Tb Sanitorium, 1948-49; pres. Montgomery Area council Boy Scouts Am., 1937-40; dir. Montgomery County A.R.C., v.p., 1952-53. Served lt., inf. U.S. Army, 1918-19; lt. col. USAAF, 1942-45. Mem. Am. Amateur Artists Assn., U. Ala. Alumni Assn. (pres. 1949), Am. Bar Assn., Ala. (past pres.), Am. (pres. trust div. 1957-58) bankers assns., Omicron Delta Kappa, Phi Delta Phi, Phi Gamma Delta. Episcopalian. Rotarian. Clubs: Montgomery Country; Redstone (Birmingham). Author textbooks. Contbr. articles to legal, banking jours. Home: 2092 Myrtlewood Dr Montgomery AL 36111 Office: First Nat Bank of Montgomery Montgomery AL 36101

KENNEDY, WILBERT KEITH, educator; b. Vancouver, Wash., Jan. 4, 1919; s. Wilbert Parsons and Gracie Evelyn (Woolf) K.; B.S., Wash. State U., 1940; M.S. in Agr., Cornell U., 1941, Ph.D., 1947; m. Barbara Josephine Barber, Dec. 9, 1941; children—Wilbert Keith, James Clayton. Asst. prof., asst. agronomist Wash. State Coll., 1947-48, asso. prof., asso. agronomist, 1948-49; prof. agronomy Cornell U., Ithaca, N.Y., 1949—, asso. dir. research N.Y. State Coll. Agr., Cornell U., also asso. dir. Cornell U. Agr. Exptl. Sta., 1959, dir. research and dir. expt. sta., 1959-65, asso. dean N.Y. State Coll. Agr., 1965-67, vice provost univ., 1967—. Cons., Kasetsart U., Thailand, 1968, Ford Found., Malaysia, 1970. Mem. sch. bd., Dryden, N.Y., 1953-55; exec. com. Louis Agassiz council Boy Scouts Am., 1955—; active local Community Chest. Served to maj. AUS, 1942-46. Guggenheim fellow, Fulbright scholar, 1956-57. Recipient N.Y. Farmers award, 1958; Merit Certificate award Am. Grassland Council, 1964. Fellow Am. Soc. Agronomy, A.A.A.S.; mem. Sigma Xi, Phi Kappa Phi, Alpha Zeta. Rotarian. Contbr. articles to profl. jours. Home: Route 2 Freeville NY 13068 Office: Day Hall Cornell U Ithaca NY 14850

KENNEDY, WILLIAM BLAIR, physician, educator; b. Bridgeport, O., Jan. 2, 1914; s. Philip Aiken and Lucy Ada (Clark) K.; B.S., Allegheny Coll., 1935; M.D., U. Pa., 1940; m. Edna Marsh, Oct. 4, 1941; children—William B., Philip M., Dorothy A., Kathryn L. Intern Geisinger Meml. Hosp., 1940-41, resident medicine, 1941-42; faculty mem., sch. medicine U. Pa. since 1942, fellowship medicine, 1942-45, asst. to dean, 1946-51, vice dean, 1951-58, asso. dean, 1958-67; asso. dir. Nat. Bd. of Med. Examiners, 1967—. Dir. Phila. Met. Assn., Phila. div. Am. Cancer Soc. Mem. Am. Diabetes Assn. Presbyn. (ruling elder). Home: 11 Chestnut Lane Stafford Wayne PA 19087 Office: 3930 Chestnut St Philadelphia PA 19104

KENNEDY, WILLIAM FRITZ, lawyer; b. Phila., July 11, 1906; s. William John and Bertha (Vurpillot) K.; B.A., U. Pa., 1926, LL.B., 1929, Gowen fellow, 1930; m. Ruth Bennett Maris, June 30, 1928; 1 son, William John. Admitted to Pa. bar, 1929, N.Y. bar, 1931; asso. Sullivan & Cromwell, N.Y.C., 1930-45; gen. solicitor, asst. sec. Internat. Nickel Co. of Can., Ltd., 1945-53, sec., 1953—; gen. solicitor, asst. sec. Internat. Nickel Co., Inc., N.Y.C., 1945-57, sec., 1957—, also dir. Mem. Am., N.Y. bar assns., Assn. Bar City N.Y., Mining and Metall. Soc. N.Y. Am., Phi Beta Kappa, Delta Sigma Rho, Order of Coif. Clubs: University, Lunch (N.Y.C.). Home: 200 E 66th St New York City, NY 10021. Office: 67 Wall St New York City NY 10005

KENNEDY, WILLIAM JAMES, home furnishing co. exec.; b. New Haven, Nov. 28, 1915; s. William D. and Cecelia (MacCormac) K.; B.S., Yale, 1938; M.B.A., N.Y. U., 1952; m. Mary Ellen Fogarty, Sept. 11, 1948; children—Mary Ellen, Ann Elizabeth, Robert William. Sec., asst. treas. Alexander Smith, Inc., Yonkers, N.Y., 1946-55; sec. Mohasco Industries, Amsterdam, N.Y., 1955—; dir. Barcalo Mfg. Corp. Sec., bd. dirs. Mohasco Meml. Fund; trustee Regional Hosp. Planning and Rev. Council, Northeast N.Y.; Mem. Yale Alumni Bd. Mem. Trade Relations Council (trustee), Carpet Inst. Am. (chmn. tariff com.), Phi Beta Kappa, Sigma Xi, Beta Gamma Sigma. Home: 6 Park Lane Scotia NY 12302 Office: 57 Lyon St Amsterdam NY 12010

KENNEDY, X.J. JOSEPH, educator, poet; b. Dover, N.J., Aug. 21, 1929; s. Joseph Francis and Agnes (Rauter) K.; B.Sc., Seton Hall U., 1950; M.A., Columbia, 1951; certificate U. Paris (France), 1956; m. Dorothy Mintzlaff, 1962; children—Kathleen, David, Matthew, Daniel. Teaching fellow U. Mich., Ann Arbor, 1956-60, instr. English, 1960-62; faculty English dept. Woman's Coll., U. N.C., Greensboro, 1962-63; asst. prof. English Tufts U., Medford, Mass., 1963-67, asso. prof., 1967—. Vis. lectr. Wellesley Coll., 1964, U. Cal. Irvine, 1966-67. Judge, Nat. Council on Arts poetry book selections, 1969, 70. Served with USNR, 1951-55. Recipient Lamont Poetry award

Acad. Am. Poets, Bess Hokin prize Poetry Mag., 1961; grant Nat. Council Arts and Humanities, 1967-68; Shelley Meml. award, 1970. Bread Loaf fellow in poetry Middlebury Coll., 1960. Mem. John Barton Wolgamot Soc., P.E.N., Author's Guild, Phi Beta Kappa. Author: Nude Descending a Staircase, 1961; Introduction To Poetry, 1966, 2d edit., 1971; Growing into Love, 1969. Poetry editor: Paris Rev., 1961-64. Editor (with J.E. Camp) Mark Twain's Frontier, 1963; (with J.E. Camp, Keith Waldrop) Pegasus Descending, 1971. Editor, pub. Countermeasures mag., 1971—. Contbr. New Yorker, Poetry, Paris Rev., N.Y. Times Book Rev., Dissent, Hudson Rev., others. Home: 4 Fern Way Bedford MA 01730 Office: Tufts U Medford MA 02155

KENNELLY, ROBERT ANDREW, educator, geographer; b. Jamestown, N.D., Oct. 6, 1919; s. Patrick James and Helena (Rotering) K.; student N.D. State Sch. Sci., 1936-38; B.A., State U. Ia., 1948, M.A., 1950, Ph.D., 1952; student Nat. U. Mexico, summer 1950; m. Martha Mullan, Sept. 7, 1946; children—Robert Andrew, Barbara Jane, Donald James. Grad. asst. State U. Ia., 1948-51, part-time instr., 1951; faculty Long Beach (Cal.) State Coll., 1952-71, prof. geography, 1961-71, coordinator dept. social scis., 1957-58, chmn. div. social scis., 1958-64; cons. chancellor's office, asso. dean acad. planning, trustees Cal. State Colls., 1964-67; v.p. adminstrn. Cal. State Coll., Hayward, 1967—. Vis. summer prof. Central Wash. State Coll., Ellensburg, 1962, 63, U. Ida., 1964. Served as pilot USAAF, World War II; ETO; lt. col. Res. (ret.). Decorated D.F.C. Mem. Assn. Am. Geographers, Pacific Coast Geographers, Pacific Coast Council Latin Am. Studies, Cal. Council Geog. Tchrs., Los Angeles Geog. Soc., Sigma Nu. Editor: Cal. Geographer, 1959-69. Contbr. articles to profl. jours. Home: 17869 Almond Rd Castro Valley CA 94546

KENNELTY, JOHN EARL, assn. exec.; b. Irwin, Pa., Apr. 25, 1922; s. John D. and Irene (Wolf) K.; B.S., St. Vincent Coll., 1949; m. Mildred Johnson, Sept. 15, 1950; children—Pamela J., Timothy J. Reporter Tribune Rev., Greensburg, Pa., 1949-56, mgr. Greensburg-Central Westmoreland C. of C., 1956-67; exec. v.p. Utica (N.Y.) C. of C., 1967—; mem. bd. regents Insts. Orgn. Mgmt., U.S. C. of C., 1970-71. Mem. Mayor's Adv. Com. Devel., Utica, 1968-71. Served with AUS, 1942-45. Mem. N.Y. State Chamber Execs. (bd. dirs.), Am. C. of C. Execs. Mem. United Ch. of Christ (chmn. trustees). Clubs: Fort Schuyler; Yahnundasis Golf (Utica). Home: 23 Clarion Dr Whitesboro NY 13492 Office: 1401 First Nat Bank Bldg Utica NY 13501

KENNER, RALPH EUGENE, banker; b. Columbia City, Ind., Aug. 29, 1908; s. John Clarence and Mable (Bills) K.; B.B.A., Internat. Coll., Fort Wayne, Ind., 1928; certificate Am. Inst. Banking, 1939; grad. Rutgers U. Grad. Sch. Banking, 1940; m. Lorraine Thomas, Dec. 12, 1942; 1 son, Phillip Lee. With Lincoln Nat. Bank & Trust Co., Fort Wayne, 1929—, v.p., 1958—, cashier, 1962—. Treas., dir. Opportunities, Inc., 1958—; bd. dirs. Parkview Meml. Hosp., 1969—. Mem. Am. Inst. Banking (past pres.), No. Ill. Conf. Bank Auditors and Comptrollers (past pres.), Round Table Internat. (past pres.), C. of C. Methodist. Mason (32). Club: Fort Wayne Country. Home: 8931 Stellhorn Rd Fort Wayne IN 46805 Office: 116 E Berry St Fort Wayne IN 46802

KENNEY, EDWARD CHRISTOPHER, former navy med. officer; b. Corning, O., Feb. 19, 1904; s. James and Carrie (Heckenhauer) K.; B.S., Denison U., 1926, D.Sc., 1958; M.D., U. Cin., 1929, LL.D., 1963; m. Helen R. Dern, Dec. 12, 1925; children—Joan (Mrs. Robert C. Diamond), James Warren. Commd. lt. (j.g.) M.C., USN, 1929, advanced through grades to rear adm., 1957; intern Naval Hosp., Phila., then assigned as jr. med. officer shore stas. and on ships; assigned U.S.S. Boise, 1942-43; then served overseas as exec. officer fleet hosps., and as chief medicine Corona (Cal.) Navy Hosp. and Camp Lejeune (N.C.) Naval Hosp.; chief medicine, exec. officer Phila. Naval Hosp., 1952-55; comdg. officer Jacksonville (Fla.) Naval Hosp., 1955, Bethesda (Md.) Naval Hosp., 1955-58; rep. to Bur. Medicine as asst. chief personnel and profl. operations, Navy Dept., 1958-59; dep., asst. chief Bur. Medicine and Surgery, Navy Dept., 1959-61; surgeon gen. Navy, Washington, 1961-65, rear adm. ret. Dir. med. edn. N. Broward Hosp. Dist., 1965-71. Decorated D.S.M., Navy Cross, Bronze Star medal. Diplomate Am. Bd. Internal Medicine. Fellow A.C.P.; mem. A.M.A., Sigma Alpha Epsilon, Alpha Kappa Kappa. Office: 935 Intracoastal Dr Fort Lauderdale FL 33316

KENNEY, GEORGE CHURCHILL, former air force officer; b. Yarmouth, N.S., Can., Aug. 6, 1889 (parents Am. citizens); s. Joseph Atwood and Louise (Churchill) K.; student Mass. Inst. Tech., 1907-11; LL.D., U. Notre Dame, 1947; m. Hazel Dell Richardson; 1 son, William Richardson; m. 2d, Alice Steward Maxey, June 5, 1922; 1 dau., Julia (Mrs. Edward C. Hoagland); m. 3d, Sarah Schermerhorn, Dec. 13, 1955. Railroad surveyor, engr., 1911-14; pres. Beaver Contracting & Engring. Corp., Boston, 1914-17; commd. lt. AS, U.S. Army, 1917, advanced through grades to gen., 1945; comdr. 4th Air Force, 1942, Allied Air Force, S.W. Pacific, 1942-45, Pacific, 1945; sr. U.S. rep. mil. staff com. UN, 1946; comdg. gen. SAC, 1946-48, Air U., 1948-51; ret. 1951. Pres., Nat. Arthritis and Rheumatism Found., 1951-63. Decorated D.S.C. with oak leaf cluster, D.S.M. with two clusters, Silver Star, D.F.C., Legion Merit, Purple Heart, Bronze Star; knight comdr. Order Brit. Empire; Legion Honor, Croix de Guerre (France); Order Leopold, Croix de Guerre (Belgium); Order of Orange-Nassau with Swords (Netherlands); Order Mil. Merit (Guatemala); Philippine Star. Mem. Am. Legion, Mil. Order World Wars N.Y., V.F.W. Mason. Club: Lotus (N.Y.C.). Author: General Kenney Reports, 1948; The MacArthur I Know, 1951; The Saga of Pappy Gunn, 1959; Dick BongAce of Aces, 1960. Home: 111 E 56th St New York City NY 10022

KENNEY, HAROLD D., mfg. co. exec.; b. Lowell, Ind., Nov. 21, 1919; s. Denzil H. and Ruth Ann (Turner) K.; A.B., Valparaiso U., 1941; student Western Res. U., 1948-49; m. Georgia Daisy Simmons, Feb. 11, 1943; children—Stephen C., Philip S. With U.S. Steel Corp., 1946-53; with Babcock & Wilcox Co., 1953, asst. comptroller, 1962-65, comptroller, 1965—. Served to 1st lt. AUS, 1942-46. Mem. Financial Execs. Inst., Nat. Assn. Accountants. Lutheran. Clubs: Canadian (N.Y.C.); Patterson (Fairfield, Conn.). Home: 478 Mariomi Rd New Canaan CT 06840 Office: 161 E 42d St New York City NY 10017

KENNEY, HARRY WILMOT, life ins. co. exec.; b. Kansas City, Mo., Jan. 30, 1914; s. Matthew A. and Lillian (Stemmons) K.; student Kansas City Jr. Coll., 1932, Wentworth Mil. Acad., 1933-34; A.A., Rockburst Coll., 1936; m. Thelma Jo Holt, Mar. 9, 1965; children—Michael C., Sharon E., Dana Ross (Mrs. J. B. Warren), B. Kay Ross, Pamela Jo Ross. With Kansas City Life Ins. Co., 1934—, controller, 1952-60, v.p. controller, 1960-64, administrv. v.p., 1964-65, exec. v.p., 1965—, dir., 1965—. Bd. dirs. St. Lukes Episcopal Hosp., Jackson County (Mo.) Sports Commn., Area Council of Nat. Council on Alcoholism; adv. trustees Research Hosp. Served to maj. AUS, 1943-46; ETO. Decorated Silver Star, Bronze Star, Purple Heart with two oak leaf clusters; Belgian Fourrager. Mem. Life Office Mgmt. Assn. (nat. director), Advertising and Sales Executives Club, Administrative Mgmt. Assn. (dir. chpt.), Controllers Inst. Republican. Episcopalian (sr. warden). Contbr. articles profl. publs. Home: 6316 W 101st Terrace Overland Park KS 66212 Office: 3520 Broadway Kansas City MO 64141

KENNEY, HOWARD WASHINGTON, physician; b. Tuskegee Institute, Ala., Oct. 4, 1917; s. John A. and Frieda (Armstrong) K.; B.S., Bates Coll., 1940; M.D., Meharry Med. Coll., 1944; m. Gwendolyn Persley, July 31, 1943; children—Diane Elizabeth, Linda Harper, Phyllis Armstrong, Howard Washington. Intern, Syndenham Hosp., N.Y.C., 1944; resident internal medicine Freedmen's Hosp., Washington, 1945-46; fellow internal medicine Howard U. Med. Sch., 1946-47, research fellow cardiovascular disease, 1947-48; staff physician VA Hosp., Tuskegee, 1948-49; pvt. practice, Newark, 1949-51, Tuskegee, 1953-55; mem. staff Tuskegee VA Hosp., 1955-62, hosp. dir., 1959-62, cons., 1953-55; dir. VA Hosp., East Orange, N.J., 1962-65; med. dir. Tuskegee Inst., 1965-69; regional med. dir., region I, VA, 1969—; cons. internal medicine Community Hosp., Newark, 1949-51, John A. Andrew Meml. Hosp., Tuskegee Institute., 1953-55. Mem. NIH Rev. Com. for Div. Regional Med. Programs for Heart Disease, Cancer, Stroke and Related Diseases, 1967-70; chmn. med. adv. com. Macon County chpt. Nat. Found., 1953-55. Mem. Bd. Police Commrs., East Orange, 1963-65. Bd. dirs. Albert Schweitzer Fellowship, 1970—. Served to capt. M.C., AUS, 1943-44, 51-53. Diplomate Am. Bd. Internal Medicine. Fellow A.C.P.; mem. Am., Nat. med. assns., John A. Andrew Clin. Soc. (pres. 1958, sec. 1965-69), Alpha Omega Alpha, Kappa Pi. Episcopalian (past vestryman). Contbr. articles to profl. jours. Home: 8201 16th St Silver Spring MD 20910 Office: VA Central Office Region 1 Vermont and H Sts Washington DC 20420

KENNEY, JOHN ANDREW, Jr., physician; b. Tuskegee Inst., Ala., Oct. 8, 1914; s. John Andrew and Frieda (Armstrong) K.; B.S. (William F. Manuel award 1942), Bates Coll., 1942; M.D., Howard U., 1945; m. Larcenia Ferne Wood, June 5, 1943; children—Frances Wood, John Andrew III, Anne Kathleen. Instr. biochemistry Howard Med. Sch., 1946-48; intern Cleve. City Hosp., 1948-49; grad. tng. dermatology and syphilology U. Pa., Grad. Sch. Medicine, 1949-50; resident physician dermatology U. Mich. Hosp., 1950-52; research asso. U. Mich. Med. Sch., 1952-53; pvt. practice dermatology and syphilology, Cleve., 1953-61; pres. med. staff Forest City Hosp., 1958-59; asso. dir. dermatology St. Vincent Charity Hosp., 1959-61; staff Freedmen's, D.C. Gen., Children's, Washington VA hosps., Washington Hosp. Center ; asst. clin. prof. dermatology Western Res. U. Sch. Medicine, 1956-61; prof., chmn. div. dermatology Howard U. Coll. Medicine, 1961—; cons. dermatology to med. dir. U.S. Dept. State and Walter Reed Army Med. Center. Chmn. Health Planning Adv. Council D.C., 1969-71. vice chmn. Met. Washington Diplomate Am. Bd. Dermatology and Syphilology. Fellow A.C.P., Am. Acad. Dermatology; mem. Social Hygiene Soc. Met. Washington (pres.), Nat. Med. Assn. (asst. editor jour. 1947-52, mem. jr. publ. com. 1952-62, pres. 1962-63, chmn. med. legis. com. bd. trustees), A.M.A., Washington Dermat. Soc. (pres. 1969-70), Acad. Medicine Cleve., D.C. Med. Soc., Soc. Investigative Dermatology, A.A.A.S., Am. Venereal Disease Assn., Nat. Commn. on Venereal Disease, Am. Dermatol. ASSN., Sigma Xi (pres. Howard U. Chpt. 1970-71). Contbr. articles to profl. jours. Home: 1442 Iris St NW Washington DC 20012 Office: Freedmen's Hosp Washington DC 20001

KENNEY, JOHN EDWARD, ret. business exec., engr.; b. Havre De Grace, Md., Apr. 27, 1900; s. Daniel Cyril and Catherine (Brown) K.; student U. Notre Dame, 1917-19; B.S., Carnegie Inst. Tech., 1922; m. Caroline Green, June 16, 1926; 1 dau., Katherine. Engring., sales work Foster Wheeler Corp., Chgo., v.p., 1945-58, exec. v.p., dir., 1958-59, pres., chief exec. officer, 1960-65, chmn. bd., chief exec. officer, 1965-68, chmn. bd., 1968-71; dir. Liberty Mut. Ins. Co., Foster Wheeler Corp., Manhattan Refrigerating Co., Peoples Bank of W. Pa., Newcastle, Oxy-Dry Sprayer Corp., Chgo., Electrographic Corp. Served in SATC, 1918. Decorated knight of Holy Sepulchre. Registered profl. engr., Ill., N.Y., Fla. Mem. Am. Soc. M.E., Am. Petroleum Inst., Am. Inst. Chem. Engrs., Newcomen Soc., Tau Beta Pi, Phi Kappa Psi. Roman Catholic. Clubs: University, Canadian, Economic (N.Y.C.); Baltusrol Golf (Springfield, N.J.); Royal and Ancient Golf of St. Andrews (Fife, Scotland). Home: 50 Sutton Pl S New York City NY 10022 Office: 666 Fifth Av New York City NY 10019

KENNEY, JOHN JAMES, corp. ofcl.; b. Bklyn., Aug. 28, 1898; s. John J. and Freida (Keller) K.; student pub. schs.; m. Helen E. Huneke, Sept. 9, 1917; children—John James, Donald. With IBM Corp., N.Y.C., 1917-, clerical worker, sales rep., br. mgr., dist. mgr., mgr. postwar planning dept., field operations exec., dir. sales promotion, gen. service mgr., 1917-54, v.p., 1954-63. Mem. Nat. Accountants Assn. Clubs: Sales Executives, New York Athletic (N.Y.C.); Royal Palm Yacht and Country. Home: 232 Royal Palm Way Boca Raton FL 33432 also 200 E 66th St New York City NY 10021

KENNEY, JOHN WILLIAM, banker; b. Redwood Falls, Minn., Oct. 6, 1918; s. Charles H. and Mary Ellen (Peavoy) K.; B.S., U. So. Cal., 1941; postgrad. U. Wash., 1954; m. Kathryn Dodds, Jan. 3, 1942; children—Nancy D. (Mrs. Stanley Evans), Janice L. Vice pres. United Cal. Bank, Los Angeles, 1945-65, exec. v.p., 1968—; pres., chief exec. officer So. Ariz. Bank & Trust Co., Tucson, 1966-68; exec. v.p., chief adminstrv. officer United Cal. Bank, San Francisco, 1969—. Pres., Devel. Authority for Tucson's Expansion, 1966-68. Served with USMCR, 1940-42; to lt. comdr. USNR, 1942-45; ETO, PTO. Mem. Tucson C. of C. (dir.) Kappa Sigma, Alpha Kappa Psi. Clubs: Cal. Golf, Bankers (San Francisco); Beverly Hills Stock Exchange; Los Angeles Country. Home: 1170 Sacramento St San Francisco CA 94108 Office: 405 Montgomery St San Francisco CA 94104

KENNEY, LAWRENCE W., mfg. co. exec.; b. 1926; married. With Nat. Union Electric Corp., Stamford, Conn., 1947—, controller Durham Mfg. Co. subsidiary, 1960-64, controller parent co., 1964-70, treas., 1970—. Served with USNR, 1943-46. Office: Nat Union Electric Corp Cummings Point Stamford CT 06904*

KENNEY, LOUIS AUGUSTINE, librarian; b. Dorchester, Neb., Feb. 28, 1917; s. Frank J. and Amelia (Peter) K.; A.B., Neb. State Tchrs. Coll., 1939; B.L.S., U. Ill., 1940, M.S., 1947; postgrad. U. Zurich (Switzerland), 1949-50; Ph.D., U. Md., 1960; m. Josephine Signer, July 17, 1950; children—Martin, Bonita, Philip, Douglas. Asst. librarian Engring. Library, U. Ill., 1940-41, 46, bibliographer acquisition dept., 1947-48, serials cataloger, 1955-57; acquisition librarian U. Notre Dame, 1948- 54; chief tech. services Ill. State Library, 1957-59; chief librarian Air Force Inst. Tech., 1959-60; dir. libraries San Diego State Coll. Mem. San Diego Opera Guild, San Diego Symphony Assn. Mem. A.L.A., Am. Hist. Soc., Spl. Libraries Assn., Cal. Library Assn. (dist. pres. 1965), Am. Assn. U. Profs., Phi Alpha Theta. Home: 5026 Yerba Anita Way San Diego CA 92115

KENNEY, MALCOLM EDWARD, educator, chemist; b. Berkeley, Cal., Oct. 7, 1928; s. James T. and Elizabeth (Whyte) K.; B.S., U. Redlands, 1950; Ph.D., Cornell U., 1954; m. Betty Cutting, June 22, 1951. Mem. faculty Case Inst. Tech. (now Case Western Reserve), 1956—, asso. prof., 1962-67, prof. of chemistry, since 1967, James Teagle Professorial fellow, 1964—. Served with AUS, 1954-56. Recipient Charles J. Strosacher Teaching award Case Inst. Tech., 1964. Mem. Am. Chem. Soc. Author: (with others) Programmed Supplements for General Chemistry, 1963; also articles. Home: 1203 Hereford Rd Cleveland Heights OH 44118

KENNEY, RICHARD LAWRENCE, retail chain exec.; b. Waltham, Mass., July 21, 1927; s. Francis John, Sr., and Margaret Veronica (Mahon) K.; B.B.A. with high honors, Northeastern U., 1958; m. Margaret Mary Donahue, June 5, 1954; children—Leona A., Richard Lawrence, Margaret-Mary D., Michael L. Tax mgr., internal auditor Warren Bros. Co., Cambridge, Mass., 1951-62; mgr. finance and taxation Stop and Shop, Inc., Boston, 1962-69; asst. treas., tax mgr. 1st Nat. Stores, Inc., Somerville, Mass., 1969-70, controller, 1970—; tax cons. Served with USAAF, 1945-47. Mem. Tax Execs. Inst. (dir. New Eng. chpt.), Nat. Assn. Pub. Accountants, Sigma Epsilon Rho. Home: 20 Mill Lane Hingham MA 02043 Office: 5 Middlesex Av Somerville MA 02143

KENNEY, THOMAS JAMES, lawyer; b. Balt., Oct. 9, 1909; s. John Henry and Bridget Catherine (McHale) K.; A.B., Loyola Coll., Balt., 1932; LL.B., U. Md., 1935; m. Agnes V. Urbus, June 20, 1940; children—Thomas James, Michael Paul, Kathleen Agnes, Geraldine Ann, John Timothy, Brigid Eileen, Mary Louise. Admitted to Md. bar, 1935; since practiced in Balt.; partner firm Kenney & Kaiser, 1937-41, 46-56, Kenney, Gallagher & Ricciuti, 1959-61; asst. U.S. atty. Md., 1941-46, U.S. atty. Md., 1963-67; asso. judge Supreme Bench of Baltimore City, 1967-68; counsel law firm Burke, Gerber & Wilen, Balt., 1969—. Instr. law Mt. Vernon Law Sch., 1937-40; instr. comml. law Md. Sch. Accounting, 1936-40; mem. character com. Md. Ct. Appeals, 1963—. Chmn., Balt. Off-Street Parking Co., 1957-63. Fellow Am. Bar Found.; mem. Am., Md., Balt. bar assns., Hibernian Soc. (dir.), Holy Name Soc. (past pres. Balt. Archdiocese), Laymen's Retreat League (past v.p.), Gamma Eta Gamma. Club: Center (Balt.). Home: 2500 Erdman Av Baltimore MD 21213 Office: 326 St Paul Pl Baltimore MD 21202

KENNEY, VINCENT PAUL, physicist, educator; b. N.Y.C., Sept. 15, 1927; s. Vincent Thomas and Marguerite Claire (Cox) K.; A.B., Iona Coll., 1948; M.S., Fordham U., 1950, Ph.D., 1956; m. Margaret Campbell Dennison, Oct. 16, 1954; children—Ann Marguerite, Charles Dennison, John Belden, Mary Elizabeth. Jr. research asso. Brookhaven Nat. Lab, Upton, N.Y., 1953-55; faculty U. Ky., 1955-63; faculty U. Notre Dame, South Bend, Ind., 1963—, prof. physics, 1966—; vis. research staff, cons. Oak Ridge Nat. Lab., 1955-63, Lawrence Radiation Lab., 1959-61, Cern, 1961-63, Brookhaven Nat. Lab., 1957—, Argonne (Ill.) Nat. Lab., 1963—, Nat. Accelerator Lab., 1969—. Served to 1st lt. USAF, 1951-53. Mex Planck fellow Inst. for Physics and Astrophysics, Munich, Germany, 1961-62. Recipient Alumni Achievement award Iona Coll., 1966. Fellow Am. Phys. Soc.; mem. A.A.A.S., Sigma Xi. Roman Catholic. Club: Odd Couples. Research boson spectroscopy, high energy multiparticle interactions. Home: 1329 N St Joseph South Bend IN 46617

KENNEY, W. JOHN, lawyer; b. Oklahoma City, June 16, 1904; s. Franklin R. and Nelle (Torrence) K.; student Lawrenceville (N.J.) Sch., 1919-22; A.B., Stanford, 1926; LL.B., Harvard, 1929; m. Elinor Craig, Jan. 17, 1931; children—Elinor (Mrs. Philip B. Brown), John F., Priscilla (Mrs. Edward J. Streator, Jr.), David T. Practiced law, San Francisco, 1929-36; chief oil and gas unit SEC, 1936-38; practice law, Los Angeles, 1938-41; spl. asst. to under sec. Navy, chmn. Navy Price Adjustment Bd., gen. counsel, 1941-46; asst. sec. Navy, 1946-47; undersec. Navy, 1947-49, head ECA, Eng., 1949-50; dep. dir. for Mut. Security, 1952; mem. firm Sullivan, Shea & Kenney, Washington, 1950-70; counsel law firm Cox, Langford & Brown, Washington, 1971—. Dir. Riggs Nat. Bank, Mchts. Transfer & Storage Co. (both Washington). Chmn. bd. D.C. chpt. A.R.C.; trustee Meridian House Found. Chmn., Democratic Central Com. D.C., 1960-64. Adv. council Johns Hopkins Sch. Advanced Internat. Study. Mem. Am. Bar Assn., English Speaking Union. Democrat. Clubs: Pacific Union (San Francisco); California (Los Angeles); Metropolitan. Chevy Chase, Burning Tree (Washington). Home: 78 Kalorama Circle NW Washington DC 20008 Office: 1521 New Hampshire Av NW Washington DC 20036

KENNEY, WILLIAM F., dept. store exec.; b. 1910; married. With Enterprise Stores Inc., Boston, 1945-55; with King's Dept. Stores Inc., and predecessor, 1955-, exec. v.p., 1961—, also gen. mgr., dir. Served to col AUS, World War II. Address: 150 California St Newton MA 02158*

KENNICK, WILLIAM ELMER, educator; b. Lebanon, Ill., May 28, 1923; s. Samuel Arthur and Dorothy (Campbell) K.; B.A., Oberlin Coll., 1945; M.A., (hon.), Amherst Coll., 1962; Ph.D., Cornell U., 1952; m. Anna Perkins Howes, June 25, 1949; children—Christopher Campbell, Justin Howes, Sylvia Bowditch. Instr. philosophy Oberlin Coll., 1947-48, Boston U., 1950-51; faculty Oberlin Coll., 1951-56, asst. prof. philosophy, head dept., 1953-56; mem. faculty Amherst (Mass.) Coll., 1956—, prof. philosophy, 1962—. Served with M.C., AUS, 1946-47. Mem. Am. Philos. Assn., Phi Beta Kappa. Author: Art and Philosophy, 1964; (with Morris Lazerowitz) Metaphysics: Readings and Reappraisals, 1966. Mem. editorial bd. Mass. Rev., 1962—. Contbr. articles to profl. jours. Home: 96 Northampton Rd Amherst MA 01002

KENNISON, HUGH F., corp. exec.; b. Providence, Mass., 1916; grad. Mass. Inst. Tech., 1939. Pres., chief exec. officer, dir. Interpace Corp., Parsippany, N.J. Home: 111 Avon Dr Essex Fell NJ 07021 Office: Cherry Hill Rd Parsippany NJ 07054

KENNON, ALBERT WILSON, Jr., lawyer; b. St. Clairsville, O., Apr. 21, 1909; s. Albert Wilson and Ida Bell (Updegraff) K.; A.B., Lafayette Coll., 1932; LL.B., Duke, 1935. m. Margaret Wannamaker, Aug. 24, 1935; 1 son, Albert William. Admitted to N.C. bar, 1934; since in pvt. practice law, Durham; mem. firm Kennon & Kennon. Served as lt. USNR, 1942-45; PTO. Fellow Am. Coll. Probate Counsel; mem. Am., N.C. (pres. 1955-56), bar assns., N.C. State Bar (counselor 1967-70), Del. Soc. Cin., 14th Jud. Bar N.C. (pres. 1961-62), Duke Law Sch. Alumni Assn. (pres. 1961-62), Order of Coif, Zeta Psi, Phi Delta Phi. Episcopalian. Home: 3801 Hope Valley Rd Durham NC 27707 Office: Home Savings and Loan Bldg Durham NC 27701

KENNY, CHARLES FRANCIS, savs. and loan assn. exec.; b. Midland Park, N.J., Aug. 12, 1910; s. Charles Francis and Theresa (Monley) K.; B.S., Rutgers U., 1931, M.A., 1937; m. Anastasia M. Wall, Aug. 19, 1939; children—Phyllis, Charles F., Steven, Robert, Jean. Jr. civil engr. engring. div. N.J. Tax Dept., Trenton, 1930-35, resettlement, div., 1936; auditor Byers & Co., Rutherford, N.J., 1937; with Island Fed. Savs. & Loan Assn., Hempstead, N.Y., 1937—, head mortgage dept., asst. treas., treas., v.p., 1937-59, dir., 1952—, exec. v.p., 1959-60, pres., 1960—. Director Fed. Home Loan Bank of N.Y. Instr. extension div. Coll. City N.Y., 1946—, Hofstra Coll., 1950-54, Ind. U., 1958—. Mem. Soc. Residential Appraisers (asso.), Am. Savs. and Loan Inst. (trustee, 1952-59, nat. pres., 1958-59), U.S. Savs. and Loan League (exec. com., dir.), Savs. Assn. League N.Y. State (dir.). Tau Beta Pi, Sigma Phi Epsilon, Republican. Roman Catholic. Clubs:

Kiwanis (past pres.), Hempstead Golf, Hempstead Golf and Country (Hempstead); Southward Ho Country (gov.). Home: 70 West Lane Bay Shore NY 11706 Office: 196 Fulton Av Hempstead NY 11550

KENNY, DUMONT FRANCIS, coll. pres.; b. N.Y.C., Dec. 3, 1914; s. Paul T. and Gertrude (Bandilla) K.; B.S., Fordham U., 1940; Ph.D., U. Chgo., 1953; L.H.D., Ia. Wesleyan U., 1967; m. Esther Mary Greenwood, Aug. 10, 1944; children—Marshall Francis, Jeremy Durbin, Pamela Anne, Terrence Paul, Rebecca Olive. Head dept. edn. P. K. Kenedy & Sons, publishers, N.Y.C., 1940-41; asst. prof., chmn. dept. philosophy Lewis Coll., Lockport, Ill., 1949-52; v.p. program devel. Nat. Conf. Christians and Jews, 1953-63; pres. Queensborough Community Coll. of City U. N.Y., Bayside, N.Y., 1963-66, York Coll., Flushing, N.Y., 1966-70, Temple Buell Coll., Denver, 1970—. Mem. adv. council higher edn. N.Y. State Dept. Edn. and Bd. Regents, 1965-69. Chmn. community appeal N. Shore (L.I.) chpt. A.R.C., 1966-67. Bd. dirs. Queens chpts. Nat. Conf. Christians and Jews, 1963-70, Rocky Mountain region, 1970—; chmn. bd. dirs. LaFarge Inst., N.Y.C., 1964—; trustee Buckley Country Day Sch., Roslyn, N.Y., 1968-70. Served to capt. AUS, 1942-46; ETO. Mem. N.Y. Historical Soc., English Speaking Union, N.Y. Acad. Scis., Alpha Beta Kappa. Clubs: Denver, Cherry Hills Country, Rotary (Denver). Contbr. books, jours. Home: 1714 Poplar St Denver CO 80220 Office: Temple Buell Coll Denver CO 80220

KENNY, HERBERT ANDREW, editor, author; b. Roxbury, Mass., Dec. 22, 1912; s. Herbert A. and Mary (Conroy) K.; A.B., Boston Coll., 1934; m. Teresa E. Flaherty, Sept. 16, 1939; children—Ann Herbert A. P., Susan R. Mem. staff Boston Post, 1933-56, night city editor, 1953-56; editorial writer Boston Globe, 1956- 62, editor for arts and books, 1962—; lectr. Suffolk U., 1947-50. Mem. Gov. Mass. Arts Council, 1965-66. Mem. appeals bd., Manchester, Mass., 1950—, chmn. 1960—. Robert Frost fellow poetry Bread Loaf Writers Conf., 1956. Mem. Harvard Musical Assn., Eire Soc., Poetry Soc. Am., New Eng. Poetry Club, Catholic Poetry Soc. Catholic. Clubs: St Botolph, Tavern. Author; (with G. P. Keane) A Catholic Quiz Book, 1947; Sonnets to the Virgin Mary, 1955; (poetry) Twelve Birds, 1964; (poetry) Suburban Man, 1965; Dear Dolphin, 1967; Alistare Owl, 1969; Cape Ann: Cape America, 1971. Home: 804 Summer St Manchester-by-the-Sea MA 01944 Office: Boston Globe Boston MA 01944

KENNY, JAMES DONALD, lawyer; b. San Francisco, Aug. 20, 1938; s. James B. and Claire (McDonald) K.; B.A., U. Santa Clara, 1960; J.D., U. San Francisco, 1965; m. Christine Carlson, Feb. 1, 1964; children—James Francis, John Joseph. Traffic rep. States Marine Lines, Inc., San Francisco, 1960-65, legal counsel, N.Y.C., 1965-67; admitted to Cal. bar, 1966; practiced in San Francisco, 1967—; resident partner Galland, Kharasch, Calkins & Lippmann, 1967-69; asso. Loughran, Berol & Hagerty, 1969-70; corporate sec., legal counsel Am. Pres. Lines, San Francisco, 1970—. Bd. dirs. San Francisco Better Bus. Bur. Served with Transp. Corps, AUS, 1960- 61. Mem. Am. Inst. Mcht. Shipping (mem. exec. com. Pacific area), Maritime Law Assn. U.S., Maritime Aminstrv. Bar Assn., Am., San Francisco bar assns., State Bar Cal., Am. Soc. Corporate Secs. Clubs: Olympic, World Trade (San Francisco). Home: 917 Edgewood Rd Redwood City CA 94062 Office: 601 California St San Francisco CA 94108

KENNY, NICHOLAS NAPOLEON, (Nick Kenny), newspaper columnist; b. Astoria, L.I. City, N.Y., Feb. 3, 1895; s. Richard Joseph and Josephine (Duval) K.; student short story and scenario writing Columbia, 1922; m. Kathryn Judge, Oct. 2, 1927; children—Patricia Patricia (Mrs. Pat Goebel), Joy (Mrs. Robert Kern). Sports writer, writer column Getting an Earful, and rewrite man Bayonne (N.J.) Times, 1920-23; sports editor, rewriteman Boston Am., 1923-24; rewrite man N.Y. Jour., 1924-27, N.Y. Daily News, 1927-30; radio columnist N.Y. Daily Mirror, 1930—; writer syndicated column Nick Kenny Speaking (poetry, news about radio TV, stage and screen personalities), 1930—, pres. Goldmine Music, Inc., music pubs., 1946—. Served with USN, 1911-18; Mcht. Marine, 1918-20. Decorated by Cardinal Spellman for canteen work, entertaining servicemen, World War II; received awards from Army and Navy depts. for similar work. Mem. Songwriters Protective Assn., Newspaper Guild, Am. Fedn. Radio Artists, Am. Guild Variety Artists, Profl. Music Men's Contact Assn., Am. Soc. Composers, Authors and Pubs. Roman Catholic. Club: Winged Foot Golf. Writer lyrics of songs including: There's a Gold-mine in the Sky, Love Letters in the Sand, Carelessly, In My Cabin of Dreams, Little Old Cathedral in the Pines, Makebelieve Island, While a Cigarette Was Burning, Beyond the Purple Hills, Scattered Toys, Gone Fishin', It's Funny But It's True, Undertow. Author: Collected Poems of Nick Kenny; Poems To Inspire; others. Lectr. newspaper bus., poetry. Home: 2932 Greenbrier St Sarasota FL 33580

KENNY, ROBERT WALKER, judge; b. Los Angeles, Aug. 21, 1901; s. Robert Wolfenden and Minnie (Carleton) K.; ed. A.B., Stanford, 1921; m. Sara McCann, Oct. 14, 1922. Corr., United Press Assn., San Francisco, London (Eng.), Los Angeles, 1920-23; on staff Chgo. Tribune, Paris, France, 1923, Los Angeles Evening Herald, 1924-27; admitted to Cal., bar, 1926; since in practiced law at Los Angeles; municipal judge Los Angeles County, 1931-32, superior judge, 1932-38; mem. Cal. State Senate, Los Angeles County, 1939-42; atty. gen. Cal., 1943-47; superior ct. judge, 1966—. Mem. Lawyers Guild (nat. pres. 1940-48), Phi Gamma Delta. Democrat. Clubs: California, Los Angeles Athletic (Los Angeles); Press (San Francisco). Home: 8358 Ridpath Dr Los Angeles CA 90046 Office: County Courthouse 111 N Hill St Los Angeles CA 90012

KENNY, ROBERT WEBB, educator; b. Somerville, Mass., Feb. 10, 1902; s. John and Jane (Webb) K.; Ph.B., Brown U., 1925, M.A., 1926, Ph.D., 1933; m. Gertrude Frances Brady, Mar. 24, 1928; children—Robert Webb, Susan Fitz Randolph. Asst. prof. Northeastern U., 1926-28; with Brown U., 1928— prof. English lit. 1950—; dean of coll. 1947-51. Trustee, v.p. Providence Pub. Library; trustee R.I. Sch. Design; exec. dir., sec. R.I. Found. Served as lt. col. AUS, 1941-46, 51-53; PTO; brig. gen. Mem. Phi Beta Kappa, Beta Theta Pi. Contbr. articles profl. jours. Home: 80 Power St Providence RI 02906

KENNY, THOMAS JAMES, investment banker; b. West Bend, Wis., Nov. 19, 1921; s. Delbert James and Olive (Kauffung) K.; student St. Norbert Coll., 1940-42; B.S., U.S. Naval Acad., 1945; LL.B., Marquette U., 1950; m. Roberta Therese Morris, Oct. 11, 1947; children—John P., Kathleen J., Daniel J., Mary J., Colleen F. With underwriting dept. B.C. Ziegler & Co., West Bend, 1950, 52-58, mgr. underwriting dept., v.p., dir., 1958-65, pres., 1965- -, chmn., 1966—; pres. 1st Ch. Financing Corp., 1965—; chmn. Security Co.; pres. Ziegler Financing Corp., Ziegler Fund, Ziegler Select Fund, Inc.; dir. Newton Fund. Dir., clk. West Bend Sch. Bd., 1959-65. Trustee St. John's Mil. Acad., Delafield, Wis. Served with USNR, 1945-47, 51-52. Mem. Am. Legion. Rotarian (pres. 1965), K.C. Clubs: West Bend Country; Union League (Chgo); University (Milw.); Bankers (N.Y.C.). Home: 1321 Evergreen St West Bend WI Office: 215 N Main St West Bend WI 53095

KENT, ALLEGRA, ballerina; b. Los Angeles, Aug. 11: ed. pub. schs.; m. Bert Stern, Feb. 28, 1959; children—Trista, Susannah, Bret. Mem. N.Y.C. Ballet Co., 1953—; prin. ballets include Seven Deadly Sins, 1958. Swan Lake, also Bugaku, 1964, Afternoon of a Swan, also Night Shadows, 1962, also Episodes. Address: 200 E 62d St New York City NY 10021

KENT, CARLETON VOLNEY, Jr., newspaperman; b. Northfield, Minn., June 13, 1909; s. Carleton Volney and Cecilia (Loizeaux) K.; A.B., U. of Kansas, 1932; m. Janet Hurd, Oct. 19, 1935; 1 son, Carleton Hurd. Newspaper reporter Lawrence (Kan.) Daily Journal-World, Daily Oklahoman, Okla. City, Kansas City Times. Okla. City Times; with Chicago Times (now Sun-Times) since 1939; war corr., Pacific and European theaters, 1942-4, Washington corr. since 1945. Mem. White House Corrs. Assn. (pres. 1950-51). Clubs: National Press, Overseas Writers (Washington, D.C.), Gridiron, Burning Tree (Bethesda, Md.). Home: 227 N Royal St Alexandria VA 22314 Office: National Press Bldg Washington DC 20004

KENT, CHARLES HADLEY, ins. co. exec.; b. Wright City, Mo., June 25, 1933; s. Miller H. and Emma (Becker) K.; B.S., U. Mo., Columbia, 1960; postgrad. U. Mo. at Kansas City, 1969; m. Ida Twitchell, Jan. 29, 1956; 1 dau., Linda L. Ins. and credit investigator, supr. Retail Credit Co., Kirksville and Columbia, Mo., 1956-58, 61-62; office and credit mgr. Firestone Stores, Columbia, 1960-61; investigator U.S. Civil Service Commn. and Dept. Labor, Kansas City, St. Louis, Washington, 1962-63; budget and fiscal technician U.S. Forest Service, Harrisonburg, Va., Winchester, Ky., 1963-66; budget analyst FAA, 1966-67; dir. budget and cost Kansas City Life Ins. Co., 1967-69, controller, 1969—. Served with U.S. Army, 1953-55; Korea. Recipient award FAA, 1967. Mem. Nat. Assn. Accountants, Life Office Mgmt. Assn., Planning Exec. Inst. Lutheran. Home: 6432 Freeman Av Kansas City KS 66102 Office: 3520 Broadway Kansas City MO 64141

KENT, DONALD PETERSON, educator, gerontologist; b. Phila., June 4, 1916; s. Ralph and Ida (Peterson) K.; B.S., Pa. State Coll., 1940; M.A., Temple U., 1945; Ph.D., U. Pa., 1950; m. Marion H. Clime, Aug. 30, 1941; children—Marion H., Martha H. Instr. sociology U. Pa., 1945-50; asso. prof. sociology U. Conn., 1950-57; dir. Inst. Gerontology, 1957-61; spl. asst. to sec. health, edn. and welfare, Washington, 1961-63; dir. U.S. Office Aging, Washington, 1963-65; prof., head dpet. sociology and anthropology Pa. State U., University Park, 1965—. Chmn., Conn. Commn. on Services for Elderly Persons, 1957-61; vice chmn. Pres.'s Council on Aging, 1961-63. Recipient Distinguished Service award Inst. for Ret. Profls. Fellow Gerontological Soc. (pres. psychol. and social sect. 1966-67), Am. Sociol. Soc. Author: The Refugee Intellectual, 1953. Editor-in-chief: Gerontologist, 1967-70. Contbr. articles profl. jours. Home: 926 Outer Dr State College PA 16801 Office: Pa State U Coll Liberal Arts University Park PA 16802

KENT, ERNEST DARYL, educator; b. Woonsocket, R.I., Dec. 28, 1912; s. William I. and Verl (Hoskins) K.; B.A., Guilford (N.C.) Coll., 1936; B.D., Hartford Theol. Sem., 1939; Ph.D. in Philosophy, Columbia, 1954; m. Mary Elizabeth Osgood, July 8, 1940; children—Peter, Robert, Louise. Recorded Friends minister, 1936; asst. minister in New Britain, Conn., 1937-39; youth work supr. Hartford County YMCA, 1937-39; mem. faculty Guilford Coll., 1939—, dean students, 1959-62, dean coll., 1962-68, prof. of philosophy and religion, 1968—. Served as chaplain, USNR, 1943-46. Mem. N.C. Philos. Assn., N.C. Assn. Tchrs. Religion, Am. Acad. Religion. Home: 1201 Nathan Hunt Rd Greensboro NC 27410

KENT, FRANK W., fine arts appraiser; b. Salt Lake City, Feb. 16, 1912; s. Frank T. and Florence W. (Wardrup) K.; scholarship with honors in Music, U. Utah, 1930; student Chgo. Art Inst., 1931, Art Students League, N.Y.C., 1931-32; pvt. study in Paris, France, 1934, Mexico, 1946, 52; B.F.A., Syracuse U., 1937, M.F.A., 1938; m. Helen Allred, June 12, 1935; children—Sharon F., Randall N. Prof. art Bradley U., Peoria, Ill., 1938-44, Syracuse U., 1944-58; ednl. dir. Mexican Art Workshop, 1949-55; lectr. Postiano (Italy) Art Workshop, 1956; dir. Crocker Art Gallery, Sacramento, 1958-68; now fine arts appraiser, researcher, restorer Hunter Gallery, San Francisco; dir. pub. programs and exhbns. Syracuse U., 1950—; work rep. permanent collections Ia. State U., Bradley U., U. Ill., Chgo. Art Inst., Syracuse U., Syracuse Mus. Fine Arts. Mem. Syracuse Commn. Fine Arts, 1948-50. Sr. mem. Am. Soc. Appraisers. Home: 5600A Fulton St San Francisco CA 94121 Office: Hunter Gallery 284 Post St San Francisco CA 94102

KENT, FREDERICK HEBER, lawyer; b. Fitzgerald, Ga., Apr. 26, 1905; s. Heber and Juanita (McDuffie) K.; J.D., U. Ga., 1926; m. Norma C. Futch, Apr. 25, 1929; children—Frederick Heber. Norma Futch, John Bradford, James Cleveland. Admitted to Ga., Fla. bars, 1926, since practiced in Jacksonville; sr. partner Kent, Durden & Kent. Chmn. bd. Kent Theatres, Inc.; v.p., dir. Fla. State Theatres, Inc., 1936-50; dir. Fla. Nat. Bank of Jacksonville. Mem. city council, Jacksonville, 1933-37; chmn. local A.R.C., 1934, 1950; pres. Jacksonville's 50 Years of Progress Assn., 1951; bd. YMCA, Jacksonville Community Chest-United Fund, 1958-59. Chmn. Fla. State Plant Bd., 1955-56; mem. Bd. Control Fla. Instns. of Higher Learning (chmn. 1955-56); pres. Riverside Hosp. Assn., 1964-65; chmn. State Jr. Coll. Council, 1962—; chmn. bd. trustees Fla. Jr. Coll., Jacksonville, 1965—; trustee Bolles Sch. 1954-65; chmn. Fla. Quadricentennial Commn., 1962-65. Served as lt., USNR, 1942-45. Recipient Distinguished Service award U.S. Jr. C. of C., 1933, Ted Arnold award, 1961. Mem. Am., Florida and Jacksonville bar assns., Jacksonville and Fla. C,s. of C., Am. Judicature Soc., Newcomen Soc. N.A., Am. Legion, Sigma Alpha Epsilon, Delta Sigma Pi. Democrat. (chmn. state exec. com. 1938-40, chmn. finance com., 1937-40). Clubs: Timuquana Country, Florida Yacht. Seminole, Friars. Ye Mystic Revellers Highlands Country, Ponte Vedra, Rotary (pres. 1958-59), River. Home: 4961 Morven Rd Jacksonville FL 32210 Office: Fla Nat Bank Bldg Jacksonville FL 32202

KENT, GEORGE CANTINE, Jr., educator; b. Kingston, N.Y., July 25, 1914; s. George Cantine and Charlotte (Delamater) K.; B.A., Maryville (Tenn.) Coll., 1937; M.A., Vanderbilt U., 1938, Ph.D., 1942; m. Lila Carringer, June 8, 1937: 1 dau., Susan Carolyn. Asst. biology Maryville Coll., 1935-37; teaching fellow Vanderbilt U., 1937-42; research asso. Cornell U., summer 1941; instr. embryology Vanderbilt U., summer 1942; vis. prof. zoology Northwestern State Coll., Natchitoches, La., summer 1955; faculty La. State U., 1942—, prof. zoology, 1956—, alumni prof., 1967—, chmn. of dept. zoology, physiology and entomology, 1960-64; cons. bur. Commn. Undergrad. Edn. Biol. Scis.; vis. lectr. sci. insts. Vice chmn. bd. govs. Center Research in Coll. Instrn. Sci. and Math., Fla. State U., 1966-70. Pres. Young Men's Bus. Club Baton Rouge, 1948. Mem. La. State Guard, 1942-46. Recipient Nat. Council Scholarship medal Phi Sigma, 1970. Fellow A.A.A.S.; mem. Am. Inst. Biol. Scis., Am. Soc. Zoologists, Soc. Exptl. Biology and Medicine, Endocrine Soc., N.Y. Acad. Scis., La. Acad. Sci. (pres. 1959, editor proc. 1945-55), Assn. S.E. Biologists (v.p. 1950, pres. 1956), Soc. for Study Reproduction, Sigma Xi, Alpha Epsilon Delta (life), Omicron Delta Kappa, Phi Sigma (hon.). Author: Comparative Anatomy of the Vertebrates, 1954, rev. edits., 1965, 69; Practical Anatomy of the Dogfish, Necturus and Cat, 4th edit., 1962; Anatomy of the Vertebrates, 1967; also numerous articles in field. Home: 482 Stanford Av Baton Rouge LA 70808

KENT, GEORGE CLARENCE, plant pathologist; b. Keene, N.H., July 28, 1910; s. Harry Llewellyn and Ursula (Dickinson) K.; student N.M. A. and M., 1927-30; A.B., Oxford U., Eng., 1933; Ph.D., Ia. State Coll., 1936; m. Ruth Victoria Olson, July 30, 1938; children—Ann Elizabeth, George Alan, Thomas Richard. Grad. asst. Ia. State Coll., 1933-36, instr., 1937-39, asst. prof., 1939-44, asso. prof., 1944, prof. botany, plant pathology, 1944-45; prof. plant pathology Cornell U., Ithaca, N.Y., 1945—, head dept., 1950-70, acting head botany dept., 1961-63, prof. and head botany dept. 1963-64, coordinator planning and devel. Coll. Agr., 1970—; prof. plant pathology Cornell project U. Philippines Coll. Agr., 1952-54, 65. Editor, Phytopathology, 1949-51. Fellow Am. Phytopath. Soc.; mem. Bot. Soc. Am., Am. Assn. Rhodes Scholars, Sigma Xi, Phi Kappa Phi. Home: 408 Klinewoods Rd Ithaca NY 14850

KENT, GLENN ALTRAN, air force officer; b. Red Cloud, Neb., June 25, 1915; s. Louis F. and Sadie V. (Gilmore) K.; A.B., Western State Coll., Colo., 1936; M.S., Cal. Inst. Tech., 1942; grad. Naval Postgrad. Sch., 1948; M.S., U. Cal. at Berkeley, 1950; grad. Air War Coll., 1957; fellow Center for Internat. Affairs, Harvard, 1961-62; m. Phyllis Horton, June 27, 1953; children—Kimberly S., Glenn Cameron. Commd. 2d lt. U.S. Army, 1941, advanced through grades to maj. gen., 1966; weather officer overseas and U.S., 1942-45; assigned atomic warfare Hdqrs. USAF, 1950- 53, spl. weapons, Kirtland AFB, N.M., 1953-56, weapons planning Hdqrs. USAF, 1957-61; mil. asst. to dep. dir. def. research and engring., Washington, 1962-65; assigned research and devel. planning and analysis Hdqrs. USAF, 1965-66; devel. plans, Hdqrs. AFSC, 1966-68, asst. chief staff, studies and analysis, 1968—. Decorated D.S.M., Legion of Merit with oak leaf cluster, Commendation medal with oak leaf cluster. Mem. Air Force Assn., Contbr. articles to profl. jours. Home: 8300 Wagon Wheel Rd Alexandria VA 22309 Office: Pentagon Washington DC 20330

KENT, HAROLD WINFIELD, sch. adminstr.; b. Oskaloosa, Ia., Mar. 29, 1900; s. Charles Almet and Lena (Brown) B.S. in Commerce, Northwestern U., 1921, M.S. in Edn., 1936; m. Ethel Ida Elmer, Dec. 21, 1929; 1 son, Thomas Richard. Tchr., Garfield Sch., Chgo., 1921-23, Lake View High Sch., 1923-25; prin. Prussing Sch., 1925-37; dir. Prussing Community Center, 1932-37; prin. Camp Roosevelt High Sch. Camp, 1925-30, Lane Tech. High Sch., 1938; dir. radio council Chgo. Pub. Schs., 1938-41; edn. dir. radio br., bur. pub. relations War Dept., 1941-42; pres. Kamehameha Schs., Honolulu, 1946-62, pres. emeritus, 1962—. Cons. to trustees Bernice P. Bishop Estate, 1962—. Mem. Hawaii adv. com. Fed. Civil Rights Commn.; chmn. Honolulu YMCA Centennial, 1969; pres. Hawaii Soc. for Crippled Children and Adults; Trustee Hawaii Econ. Council; bd. dirs. Honolulu YMCA: dir. fund campaign Hawaii Cancer Soc.; mem. bd. govs. Shriners Hops., Honolulu; life regent Northwestern U.; incorporator, dir. Lahalna Restoration Found. Served from maj. to col. AUS, 1942-46. Mem. N.E.A., Assn. for Edn. by Radio (pres. 1941-44), Hawaiian Hist. Soc. (pres. 1960-63), Res. Officers Assn., Social Sci. Assn. Honolulu (sec.), Am. Legion, S.A.R., Phi Delta Kappa, Lambda Chi Alpha. Conglist. (moderator Hawaiian Evang. Assn. Congl. Christian Chs. 1952-54, trustee Hawaii Conf. United Ch. of Christ). Rotarian, Mason (Shriner), Red Cross of Constantine (grand chamberlain). Clubs: University (Evanston, Ill.); Northwestern University (pres. Honolulu 1946), Oahu Country. Author: Charles Reed Bishop, Man of Hawaii; Album of Likenesses: Charles Reed Bishop and Bernice Pauahi Bishop; Charles M. Hyde, Robert Louis Stevenson, Father Damien. Home: 1451 Ohialoke St Honolulu HI 96821

KENT, HARRY CHRISTISON, educator; b. Los Angeles, May 20, 1930; s. Harry and Florence (Christison) K.; Geol. engr., Colo. Sch. Mines, 1952; M.S., Stanford, 1953; Ph.D., U. Colo., 1965; m. Sheila Marie Kelly, Aug. 18, 1956; children—Colleen Marie, Bruce Kelly. Geologist, The California Co., Fla. and La., 1953-56; mem. faculty Colo. Sch. Mines, Golden, 1956—, asso. prof., 1967-69, prof., head geology dept., 1969—. Bd. mgrs. Jeffco br. YMCA, Denver. Fellow Geol. Soc. Am.; mem. Am. Assn. Petroleum Geologists, Paleontological Soc., Soc. Econ. Paleontologists and Mineralogists, Sigma Xi. Home: 5131 Jellison Ct Arvada CO 80002 Office: Geology Dept Colo Sch Mines Golden CO 80401

KENT, HOLLISTER, regional planner; b. Brookline, Mass., Mar. 1, 1916; s. Ira Rich and Louise (Andrews) K.; grad. Milton Acad., 1935; S.B., Harvard, 1939; M.Regional Planning, Cornell U., 1952, Ph.D., 1956; m. Edith Rairden Rudd, June 7, 1947; children—Margaret Ann (Mrs. Alvin Patscheck, Jr.), Bruce Rairden, Polly Curtiss, Timothy Rich. Nicholas Coburn. Instr., Fountain Valley Sch., Colorado Springs, Colo., 1939-42; asst. dean admissions, instr. fine arts Hofstra Coll., 1947-50; gen. mgr. charge site selection for Brasilia, Brazil, 1954-56, cons., 1956; dir. town planning, Kitimat, B.C., Can., 1956-58; dir. regional planning Sargent-Webster-Crenshaw & Folley, Syracuse, N.Y., 1958-61; sr. partner Planners Collaborative, Syracuse and Norwich, Vt., 1962—; pres. Western Australia Devel. Corp., Appleyard Corp.; dir. Intergroup, Planning and Devel. Collaborative Intern.; vis. prof. schs. architecture Columbia, Cornell U., Dartmouth; adj. prof. Syracuse U. Mem. diocesan council Episcopal Diocese Central N.Y., 1965-69; v.p. Old West Ch. Assn. Mem. Kent Tavern Com; chmn. Champlain Corridor Com. Trustee Lakco, Vt. Hist. Soc. Served with AUS, 1942-47. Decorated Bronze Star, Purple Heart. Mem. Am. Inst. Planners (pres. N.Y. State chpt. 1960), Phi Kappa Phi, Gargoyle (pres. 1956). Democat. Episcopalian. Clubs: D.U., Hasty Pudding (Harvard); Harvard (N.Y.C. and Vt.). Author articles. Home: Mechanic St Norwich VT 05055 Office: House of Seven Nations Mechanic St Norwich VT 05055

KENT, JACK, (John Wellington), cartoonist; b. Burlington, Ia., Mar. 10, 1920; s. Ralph Arthur and Marguerite Judith (Bruhl) K.; student pub. and pvt. schs.; m. June Kilstofte, June 9, 1954; 1 son, John. Comml. artist, 1935-41; free-lance cartoons various mags., 1945-50; created comic strip King Aroo, 1950-65; free lance cartoons and humor to mags. Served to 1st lt. F.A., AUS, 1941-45. Mem. Nat. Cartoonists Soc., Authors Guild, Authors League Am. Author: King Aroo, 1952. Author-illustrator: (juveniles) Just Only John, 1968; Clotilda, 1969; Mr. Elephant's Birthday Party, 1969; Fly Away Home, 1969; The Grown-Up Day, 1969; The Blah, 1970; Mr. Meebles, 1970; Jack Kent's Book of Nursery Tales, 1970; The Fat Cat, 1971; The Wizard of Wallaby Wallow, 1971. Home: 103 W Johnson St San Antonio TX 78204

KENT, JACK ALVIN, clergyman; b. Dombey, Okla., Oct. 22, 1921; s. Uriah William and Mary (Smith) K.; student U. Chgo., 1942-43; B.A., U. Cal. at Berkeley, 1948, B.D., 1950; m. Dorothy Myser, Apr. 23, 1949; children—Carolyn Lee, Jack Andrew, Dorothy Allison. Ordained to ministry Unitarian Ch., 1950; minister Grafton (Mass.) Unitarian Ch., 1950-53, minister 1st Unitarian Ch., Long Beach, Cal., 1953-60; asso. regional dir. Middle Atlantic States Council Chs., N.Y.C., 1960-63; minister First Unitarian Ch., Chgo., 1963-68; minister N. Shore Unitarian Ch., W. Vancouver, B.C., 1968—; adviser students Columbia, 1960-62; chaplain students U. Chgo., 1962-63, Lions Gate Hosp., North Vancouver, B.C., 1970—; organizer Joseph

Priestly, Met. N.Y.C. and St. Lawrence dists., 1963; mem. bd. Chgo. Area Council Liberal Chs.; bd. dirs. Unitarian Universalist Service Com. Mem. Head Start Child Devel. Adv. Com., 1967-68, Chgo. Com. on Urban Opportunity, 1967-68, Chgo. Commn. on Human Relations, 1966-68; adviser North Shore Youth Council, West Vancouver, 1971—. Bd. dirs. Starr King Sch. for Ministry, Berkeley, Cal., Vancouver Soc. for Pollution and Environmental Control. Served with AUS, 1943-47. Home: 2586 Nelson Av West Vancouver British Columbia Canada Office: P O Box 133 West Vancouver British Columbia Canada

KENT, JAMES A., educator, engineer; b. New Britain, Conn., Feb. 10, 1922; B.A. in Chem. Engring., W.Va. U., 1943, Ph.D., 1950; m. Anita C. Barbe, Feb. 20, 1943 children-James, David, Nicholas, Edward, JOseph. Research engr. Dow Chem. Co., Midland, Mich., 1950-52; research group leader, Mansanto Chem. Co., Nitro, W. Va., 1952-54; prof.f. chem. and nuclear engring. W. Va. U., 1954-67, asso. dean engring., 1963-67; dean coll. engring. Mich. Tech Chmn., Gov's Adv. Com. on State Tech. Services, W. Va., 1966-67; mem. Artificial Heart Com., Nat. Heart and Lung Inst., 1970-71; Cons. Ho. Interstate Nuclear Bd. Served to 1st H.,C.E., Aus, 1943-46. Recipient MEritorious Achievement award, Pitts. sect. Am. Nuclear Soc., 1966; numerous awards engring. and sci. hon. socs. Mem. Am. Inst. Chem. Engrs., Sigma Xi, Tau Beta Pi. Rotariann Author: Industiral Chemistry, 1962. Contbr. articles to profl. jours. Prin. developer radiation- processed wood-plastic combinations. Home: 1008 E 6th St Houghton MI 49931

KENT, LEONARD J., ednl. adminstr. Dean Sch. Grad. Studies Chico State Coll. Office: Chico State Coll Chico CA*

KENT, NORMAN, artist; b. Pitts., Oct. 24, 1903; s. Carl Hayes and Nella Louise (Howe) K.; grad. Sch. Fine and Applied Art, Rochester Inst. Tech., 1925; student Art Students League N.Y., 1925-26, studio in Italy, 1933-34; m. Diana Grace Whittinghill, Nov. 9, 1933; children—Mary Argyle, Diana Suzanne Howe. Free-lance illustrator, Buffalo, 1926-28, Rochester, N.Y., 1928-33, Geneva, N.Y., 1934-43; instr. art William Smith Coll., Geneva, N.Y., 1934-36, asst. prof. art Hobart and William Smith colls., Geneva, 1936-43, prof. art, on leave, 1943-45; mng. editor Am. Artist (mag.) 1943-48; art dir. Internat. Edits., Reader's Digest, 1948-51; art editor True mag., 1952-55; editor Am. Artist, 1956-69, sr. editor, 1970—, editor emeritus, 1971—. One man shows maj. cities and museums, U.S., abroad, 1930—; exhibited regional and nat. shows U.S., 1927—; represented many permanent collections, including Balt., Phila. museums of art, Library of Congress, Carnegie Inst., others. Recipient numerous awards including: Lillian Fairchild award (woodcuts), U. Rochester, 1929, Mildred Boericke prize Print Club of Phila., 1941, Library of Congress, 1951, O'Hara and Osborne prizes Am. Watercolor Soc., 1954-59, gold medal of honor Nat. Arts Club, 1967, others. Elected Academician, N.A.D., 1949. Mem. Art Student League N.Y. (life), Print Club of Rochester, other profl. orgns. Episcopalian. Clubs: Century, Salmagundi (hon.). Author several items in field: Watercolor Methods. 1955; Seascapes and Landscapes in Watercolor, 1956; 100 Watercolor Techniques, 1968; Drawings by American Artists, 1968. Home: 437 Carroll Av Mamaroneck NY 10543

KENT, RICHARD HAROLD, accountant; b. Kalamazoo, June 9, 1918; s. Harold S. and Alice (Budd) K.; A.B., Western Mich. U., 1939; M.B.A. with distinction, U. Mich., 1941; m. Virginia Duewel, Sept. 23, 1944; 1 dau., Susan Kay. With Ernst & Ernst, Detroit, 1941-42, San Francisco, 1946-57, Oakland, Cal., 1957—, partner, 1961—. Served to lt. comdr. Supply Corps, USNR, 1942-46. C.P.A., Cal. Mem. Am. Inst. C.P.A.'s, Cal. Soc. C.P.A.'s, Am. Accounting Assn., Beta Gamma Sigma. Mason. Rotarian. Club: Athenian- Nile (Oakland, Cal.) Home: 1166 Camino Vallecito Lafayette CA 94549 Office: 1330 Broadway Oakland CA 94612

KENT, WILLIAM WALLACE, U.S. circuit judge; b. Galesburg, Mich., May 1, 1916; s. Harold S. and Alice W. (Budd) K.; B.A., Western Mich. Coll., 1937; J.D., U. Mich., 1940; LL.D., Western Mich. U., 1956; m. LaVerne Fredlund, July 7, 1940; children—W. Wallace, Virginia Louise, Eric H., Robert J., E. Ann, Martha. Admitted to Mich. bar, 1940; asst. pros. atty., friend of ct. Kalamazoo County, 1941-44, pros. atty., 1945-46; practice law, Kalamazoo, 1944-54; U.S. dist. judge, 1954-71; judge U.S. Court of Appeals, 6th Circuit, 1971—. Affiliate, Legal Aid Bur., Family Service Center. Mem. Am., Mich., Kalamazoo County bar assns., Am. Judicature Soc. Mason (grand master Mich. 1960-61). Clubs: Optimist, Kalamazoo (past pres.), Gull Lake Country; University (Cin.). Home: 812 Wilshire Blvd Kalamazoo MI 49001 Office: 410 W Michigan Av Kalamazoo MI 49006

KENTERA, GEORGE RICHARD, newspaperman; b. Humboldt, Tenn., July 15, 1922; s. Chris William and Clara Belle (Williams) K.; B.J., U. Mo., 1943; m. Eileen Ruth Kohler, Dec. 18, 1945; children—Gale Lynn, Jean Anne. Mem. staff Newark Evening News, 1947—, Washington corr., 1959-65, mng. editor, 1965-70, exec. editor, 1970—. Club: National Press (Washington); Orange Lawn Tennis. Home: 18 Claremont Dr Maplewood NJ 07040 Office: Newark News Newark NJ 07101

KENTNER, LOUIS PHILIP, pianist; b. Karvin, Silesia, July 19, 1905; s. Julius and Gisella (Buchsbaum) K.; masters diploma in composition Royal Acad. Music, Budapest, Hungary; pvt. study with Arnold Szekeley, Leo Weiner, Zoltan Kodaly; m. Griselda Gould, May 29, 1946. Became British citizen, 1946. Began concert career, 1924; recitals in London, India, Ceylon, Indonesia, Israel, New Zealand, Australia, South Africa, U.S., Can.; toured USSR, 1963, 64, 65, 66, India, Wales, Iceland, 1969, also toured in Hungary; played in trios with Menuhin and Cassado, Edinburgh and Bath festivals, Italy, Spain. Composer sonatinas, chamber music, orchestral work. Mem. Inc. Soc. Musicians, Am. Guild Musical Artists, Royal Acad. Music (hon.), Liszt Soc. (founder, pres. U.K.). Address: 1 Mallord St Chelsea London SW3 England

KENTON, STANLEY NEWCOMB, musician; b. Wichita, Kan., Feb. 19, 1912; s. Thomas Floyd and Stella E. (Newcomb) K.; grad. high sch.; m. Violet R. Peters, July 31, 1935 (div. Feb. 1950); one dau., Leslie B.; m. 2d, Margaret Ann Richards, Oct. 18, 1955 (div.); children—Dana Lynn, Lance N. Kenton. Organized band Artistry in Rhythm, 1941; leader Stan Kenton Orch. Hollywood, Cal., 1941—; worldwide concert appearances, billed as artistry in rhythm, progressive jazz, innovations in modern music; condr. Los Angeles Neophonic Orch. Organizer Stan Kenton Clinics Teenage Musicians, 1965. Recipient popularity poll recognition and awards U.S. and abroad. Office: 1012 S Robertson Blvd Los Angeles CA 90035

KENWAY, HERBERT PHIPPS, lawyer; b. Newton, Mass., June 8, 1912; s. Herbert W. and Elsie V. (Tucker) K.; grad. Phillips Acad., Andover, Mass. 1930; B.A., Yale, 1934; postgrad. N.Y. U. Law Sch., 1934-35, George Washington U., 1937; m. Ursula Poor, Nov. 30, 1935; children—Herbert Winthrop II, Geoffrey Tucker; m. 2d, Kari Petersen, Mar. 23, 1951; 1 son, Kimball Leif. Law clk. E.F. Wenderoth, Washington, 1935-37; admitted to D.C. bar, 1937, Mass. bar, 1946; asso. firm Kenway & Witter, Boston, 1937-42, partner, 1946-48; partner firm Kenway, Jenney & Heldreth, Boston, 1948—. Served with USNR, 1942-46. Fellow Am. Coll. Trial Lawyers; mem. Am., Boston bar assns., Am. (past pres.), Boston (past pres.) patent law assns. Club: Union (Boston); Eastern Yacht (Marblehead). Home: 15 Arthur Av Marblehead MA 01945 Office: 24 School St Boston MA 02108

KENWAY, HERBERT WINTHROP, lawyer; b. Boston, Dec. 1, 1881; s. Herbert Phipps and Alice (Kimball) K.; student Mass. Inst. Tech.; m. Elose V. Tucker, Oct. 10, 1906 (dec.); children—Herbert P., Margaret K. (Mrs. Haydon); m. 2d, Helen M. Marcy, Jan. 29, 1959. With U.S. Patent Office, 1906-08, U.S. Shoe Machinery Co., 1908-27; sr. partner firm Kenway, Jenney & Hildieth, Boston, 1948—. Mem. Boston Patent Law Assn. (pres. 1952-54). Home: 30 Valentine Park West Newton MA 02165 Office: 24 School St Boston MA 02108

KENWORTHY, CARROLL H., newspaperman; b. Kokomo, Ind., May 10, 1904; s. Murray S. and Ida Lenora (Holloway) K.; A.B., Earlham Coll., Richmond, Ind., 1925; student Hartford (Conn.) Sem., 1926; A.M., Columbia, 1927; m. Mary Lowes, Jan. 1, 1932; children-Thomas L., David K. (dec.), Lee Hadley. Reporter Hartford Courant, 1926, Japan Advertiser, Tokyo, 1927-29; corr. for newspapers in U.S. and China from Tokyo, 1927-29; with Washington Bur. of Wall Street Jour., 1929; diplomatic reporter for Washington Bur. of United Press, 1930-40, editor fgn. dept., Washington, D.C., 1941-67. Trustee, Earlham Coll., 1954-63. Mem. of Overseas Writers (twice pres.), Nat. Press Club. Home: 1425 44th St Washington DC 20007 Office: Nat Press Bldg Washington DC 20007

KENWORTHY, WALTER, educator, zoologist; b. Phila., Jan. 19, 1922; s. James H. and Anna (Goldmann) K.; B.A., Temple U., 1943; Ph.D., U. Pa., 1953; m. Regina Dombrowski, Aug. 5, 1944; children—James, Paul. Faculty, Brown U., 1952-64, asso. prof. biology, 1958-64; dean coll., prof. biology Wheaton Coll., Norton, Mass., 1964—. Fellow A.A.A.S.; mem. Genetics Soc. Am., Soc. for Study Evolution, Am. Soc. Mammalogists, Am. Soc. for Cell Biology. Home: 28 Elm St Norton MA 02766

KENYATTA, JOMO, pres. Republic of Kenya; b. circa 1889; ed. Ch. of Scotland Mission Kikuyu, Kenya, London (Eng.) Sch. Econs.; m., 4 sons, 4 daus. Gen. sec. Kikuyu Central Assn., 1922; founder 1st African-owned pour., Mwigwithania, 1928; sent to Eng. by Kenya Africans to press case for independence; traveled in Europe; briefly represented Ethiopia at League of Nations; pres. 1st Pan-African Congress, Manchester, Eng., 1945, Kenya Africa Union, 1947-52; imprisoned and detained by Brit., 1952-61; elected in absentia as pres. Kenya African Nat. Union, 1960; mem. Legislative Council, 1962; minister of state for constl. affairs and econ. planning, 1962; pres. Republic of Kenya, 1964—, prime minister, also minister for internal security and def., and fgn. affairs, 1963—. Author: Facing Mt. Kenya; Kenya, The Land of Conflict, My People of Kikuyu. Address: P O Box 30510 Nairobi Kenya*

KENYATTA, ROHN, alto saxophonist. Address: care Afro-Am Cultural Center 139 W 125th St New York City NY 10027*

KENYON, ALLEN, accountant; b. Gilmanton, Wis., Oct. 19, 1908; s. Allen and Margaret (Armour) K.; student U. Wis., 1925-28; m. Magda Fedas, Aug. 25, 1945; children—Allen T. Scott, Barry W. Armour, Dorry Mann. Pub. accountant Price Waterhouse & Co., Milw. and Chgo., 1929-41; asst. dir. Gen. Accounting Office, Washington, 1947-51; comptroller Allegheny Power System, Inc., N.Y.C., 1951—. Mem. Mayor's Adv. Com. on Govtl. Operations, New Rochelle; mem. Council for Unity, New Rochelle, Bd. dirs. Larchmont Woods Assn., New Rochelle. Served to lt. comdr. USNR, 1942-46. Mem. Am. Inst. C.P.A.'s, N.Y. Soc. C.P.A.'s, Financial Execs. Inst., Phi Kappa Tau. Club: Marco Polo (N.Y.C.). Home: 80 Ridge Rd New Rochelle NY 10804 Office: 320 Park Av New York City NY 10022

KENYON, CHARLES MOIR, pub. co. exec.; b. Pawtucket, R.I., Nov. 6, 1916; s. Archibald and Jessie Maria (Griffiths) K.; A.B., Brown U., 1937, M.A., 1939, postgrad., 1939-41; postgrad. U. Mich., 1940-41; m. Muriel Vanderbilt, Feb. 5, 1943; children—Richard, Ann (Mrs. Charles Griffiths), Barbara (Mrs. Ferdinand Engel), Robert, Elizabeth. Instr. English, Brown U., 1939-41, 45-46; mng. editor Chilton Co., Phila., 1946-53; pub. relations exec. Gray & Rogers, Phila., 1953-56; accounts supr., mgr. direct mail advt. J. Walter Thompson Co., N.Y.C., 1956-67; dir. marketing Am. Edn. Publs., Middletown, Conn., 1967, pres., 1967—; v.p. Xerox Edn. Group, 1967—; chmn. bd. Everyweek Ednl. Press, Rickmansworth, Eng., 1968—; asso. dir. Conn. Bank & Trust Co.; dir. Ginn & Co., Boston. Corporator, Middlesex Meml. Hosp. Served to capt. USNR, 1941-45. Clubs: Old Lyme (Conn.) Country, Pettipaug Yacht (Essex, Conn.). Author: First Voyage Out, 1967. Home: River Rd Essex CT 06426 Office: 245 Long Hill Rd Middletown CT 06457

KENYON, DORA, business exec.; b. 1910. With Gaylords Nat. Corp., N.Y.C., 1939—, sec., 1955—. Office: 306 W 37th St New York City NY 10018*

KENYON, DOROTHY, lawyer; b. New York, N.Y. Feb. 17, 1888; d. William Houston and Maria Wellington (Stanwood) Kenyon; A.B., Smith Coll., 1908; J.D., N.Y.U. Law Schl., 1917; LL.D., Keuka Coll., 1939; LL.D. (hon.) Smith Coll., Wilson Coll. 1948; Oberlin Coll., 1950; L.H.D., Beaver Coll. 1949; LL.D., Western Coll. for Women, 1966. Admitted to the N.Y. bar, 1917; in general practice of law, N.Y., 1919-39; mem. Straus and Kenyon, 1930-39; justice Municipal Court, City of N.Y., 1939-40; resumed gen. practice, 1940; 1st dept. commr. of licenses, City of N.Y., 1936-38. Mem. League of Nations Com. on Legal Status of Women, 1938-43; mem. exec. com., Citizens Union of N.Y.; Womanpower Commn., apptd. by N.Y. State Idsl. Commr. to advise on wartime employment problems of women, 1942; nat. dir. Am. Civil Liberties Union, vice chmn., sec., chmn. equality com.; bat. bd. Am. Middle East Rehab.; v.p. League Mut. Aid; adv. council Urban League, N.Y.C.; bd. dirs. Com. Civil Rights Met. N.Y.; former v.p. Am. Assn. U. Women; dir. Pioneer Youth Am., Assn. for Aid of Crippled Children, Consumers Coop. Services, Inc., Internat. Alliance of Women for Suffrage and Equal Citizenship (past v.p.); mem. com. to draft model state law on consumer cooperative corp., 1937; past pres. Our Cooperative House, 433 W. 21st St., Inc.; past pres. Consumer's League of N.Y.; past v.p. Alumnae Assn. Smith Coll., U.S. del. to U.N. Commn. on the Status of Women, 1946-49; dir. N.Y. chapter, Mem. nat. bd. Ams. for Dem. Action; mem. nat. bd. YWCA; bd. dirs. Lower W. Side Anti-Poverty Bd., Inc. mem. adv. council for Christian Action, Am. Friends of Middle East; adv. com. League for Mut. Aid, Greater N.Y. Urban League; administrv. and exec. com. Intergroup Com. for Integration of N.Y.C. Schools. Exec. com., past chmn. patronage com. New Chelsea Reform Democratic Club; N.Y. County Dem. committeewoman. Mem. Am., N.Y. City and N.Y. State bar assns., N.Y. County Lawyers Assn., Internat. Law Assn., Am. Med. Women's Assn. (hon.), N.Y. State (hon.), N.Y.C. (hon.) Women's med. assns., Am. Assn. U. Women, League Women Voters, Nat. Assn. Women Lawyers, N.Y.U. Law Sch. Alumni Assn. (mem. bd.), Phi Beta Kappa (senator united chpts. 1940-58). Clubs: Cosmopolitan, Smith College, Women's University, Women's City (N.Y.C.). Contbr. to Equality, 1965. Home: 433 W 21st St New York City NY 10011 Office: 433 W 21st St New York City NY 10011

KENYON, HEWITT, educator, mathematician; b. Marysville, Cal., Aug. 31, 1920; s. Frederick Newcomb and Inez (Hewitt) K.; B.S. in Chemistry, U. Cal. at Berkeley, 1942, Ph.D. in Math., 1954; m. Barbara Elise Vernon, July 19, 1947; children—Charity, Emily; m. 2d, Linda Root, July 17, 1961; children—Amos, Rachel, Leah. Instr., U. Rochester (N.Y.), 1952-55, asst. prof., 1955-61; asst. prof. George Washington U., Washington, 1961-63, asso. prof., 1963-66, prof., chmn. math. dept., 1967—; vis. asso. prof. U. Cal. at Berkeley, 1966-67. Served with USNR, 1942-46. Mem. Am. Math. Soc., Math. Assn. Am., Am. Assn. U. Profs., Sigma Xi. Home: 1611 Kennedy Pl NW Washington DC 20011

KENYON, KATHLEEN MARY, archaeologist; b. London, Eng., Jan. 5, 1906; d. Frederic George and Amy (Hunt) Kenyon; B.A., Somerville Coll., 1928, M.A., 1933, D.Litt., 1964; D.Litt., U. London, 1951, Exeter U., 1969; L.H.D. (hon.), Kenyon (O.) Coll., 1959. Asst. archeal. expdns., 1930-35; sec. Inst. Archaeology, U. London, 1935-48; dir. archaeol. expdns., 1936—; lectr. Palestinian archaeology London Inst. Archaeology, 1948-62; dir. Brit. Sch. Archeology in Jerusalem, 1951-66; prin. St. Hugh's Coll., Oxford U., 1962—. Divisional comdt. Brit. Red Cross Soc., 1939-43, dir. youth dept., 1942-45. Trustee Brit. Museum. Comdr. Order Brit. Empire. Fellow Soc. Antiquaries (v.p. 1957-61), Brit. Acad. (v.p. 1965-71), Surry Archaeol. Soc. (pres. 1961-69). Author books. Home: Old Brands Lodge Terriers High Wycomb Bucks England Office: St Hugh's Coll Oxford U Oxford England

KENYON, RICHARD ALBERT, educator; b. Syracuse, N.Y., Apr. 8, 1933; s. Albert Rees and Marjorie Ellen (Robinson) K.; B.M.E., Clarkson Coll., 1954; M.S., Cornell U., 1956; Ph.D., Syracuse U., 1965; m. Barbara Louise Kibbe, June 12, 1954; children—Alan Richard, David Lewis, Steven Arthur. Instr. mech. engring. Cornell U., 1954-56; instr. Clarkson Coll. Tech., Potsdam, N.Y., 1956-58, asst. prof., 1958-62, asso. prof., 1962-70, head dept. mech. engring., 1968-69, asso. dean Grad. Sch., 1966-68, asso. dir. div. research, 1966-68; prof., head dept. mech. engring. Rochester (N.Y.) Inst. Tech., 1970-71, dean Coll. Engring., 1971—. Exec. council St. Lawrence council Boy Scouts Am., 1967-68. Treas., sec. Potsdam Village Republican Com., 1966-70. Bd. dirs. Potsdam Wesley Found., Potsdam Parents Nursery Sch. NSF sci. faculty fellow Syracuse U., 1962-64. Mem. Rochester Engring. Soc., Am. Soc. M.E., Am. Soc. Engring. Edn., Am. Assn. U. Profs., Tau Beta Pi, Pi Tau Sigma. Club: Clayton Yacht (N.Y.). Author: Priniciples of Fluid Mechanics, 1960; Fundamentals of Thermodynamics, 1962. Home: 57 Old Forge Lane Pittsford NY 14534 Office: 1 Lomb Meml Dr Rochester NY 14623

KENYON, ROBERT EDWIN, Jr., publisher; b. Chgo., Sept. 23, 1908; s. Robert E. and Edith L. (Ahrens) K.; A.B., Kenyon Coll., 1930; postgrad Princeton, 1930-31; m. Doris M. Bokum, Sept. 23, 1937; children—Robert Edwin III, Pamela. With Lloyd's of London, 1931-32; engaged in ins. business, Chgo., 1932-40; Western mgr. Ahrens Pub. Co., Chgo., 1941-45; with Printers' Ink Pub. Co., N.Y.C., 1945-46, advt. sales mgr., 1946-50, advt. dir., 1950-54, dir., 1952-56, v.p. pub., 1954-56; vice chmn. adv. com. Dept. Commerce, 1959-61; with Mag. Pubs. Assn., Inc., 1956—, exec. v.p., 1961-; exec. v.p. Pubs. Information Bur., 1961—; Periodical Pub. Assn., 1961—; sec. Am. Soc. Mag. Editors, 1963—; pres., pub. Episcopalian mag., 1961—. Bd. dirs. Advt. Council, Brand Names Found. Mem. Advt. Fedn. Am. (dir.), Phi Beta Kappa, Beta Theta Pi, Alpha Delta Sigma, Alpha Pi Kappa. Episcopalian. Clubs: Union League, Princeton, Church (N.Y.C.); Rocky Point (Old Greenwich); Riverside (Conn.) Yacht. Home: Putnam Park Greenwich CT Office: 575 Lexington Av New York City NY 10022

KENYON, THEODORE STANWOOD, patent lawyer; b. N.Y. City, Jan. 17, 1890; s. William Houston and Maria Wellington (Stanwood) K.; A.B. cum laude Harvard, 1911; LL.B., Columbia, 1914 (editor Columbia Law Review 1912-14); m. Martha Tipton, July 2, 1919 (dec. 1935); children—Stanwood, Madge (Mrs. John W. Fisher), Edward Tipton; m. 2d, Helen Ward (dec. 1963); m. 3d, Sarah Whitney, 1969. Asso. Kenyon & Kenyon, N.Y.C., 1914-19, mem. 1919. Mem. Common Council, Summit, 1928-31. Pres. Overlook Hosp., 1951; trustee Kent Pl. Sch. for Girls, Summit, 1928-43, Pingry Sch, for Boys (Elizabeth, N.J.), 1935-48; adv. council Patent Trademarke and Copyright Foundation of George Washington U., 1950-62. Served with N.Y. N.G., 1912-17; capt. 306th inf. 77th Div., U.S. Army, 1918-19. Decorated D.S.C. (U.S.); Legion of Honor, Croix de Guerre (France). Mem. N.Y. Patent Law Assn. (pres. 1940-41), Am. Bar Assn., Am. Patent Law Assn. Clubs: Baltusrol Country, Monday Night (Summit, N.J.); Harvard of N.Y. Home: 24 Campbell Rd Short Hills NJ 07078 Office: 59 Maiden Lane New York City NY 10038

KENYON, WILLIAM HOUSTON, Jr., lawyer; b. Lakeville, Conn., Aug. 23, 1899; s. William Houston and Maria Wellington (Stanwood) K.; A.B., Harvard, 1921, LL.B., 1924; m. Mildred Adams, Jan. 2, 1935. Admitted to N.Y. bar, 1925; with firm Kenyon & Kenyon Reilly Carr & Chapin, patent attys., N.Y.C., 1924-25, partner, 1929-43, 46—; asst. U.S. atty. So. Dist. N.Y., 1925-27; spl. asst. U.S. atty. gen., chief antitrust div., N.Y.C., 1927-29. Lectr. law N.Y. U. Law Sch., 1928-36; chief patent counsel procurement War Dept., 1943-45; counsel Pres. Truman's Com. Survey Patent System, 1945-46; vis. lectr. Yale Law Sch., 1948-62. N.Y. area agt. Harvard Law Sch. Fund, 1947-70, Harvard Coll. Fund, 1961—; mem. Harvard Fund Council, 1965-66, 70-71; chmn. Harvard Class 1921 45th Reunion gift com., 1965-66, 50th Reunion gift com., 1970-71, mem. Class 1921 Com., 1971—. Trustee Kenyon Prize Fund, Coll. City N.Y., 1934—. Served with A.R.C., 1918; Italy. Recipient Sec. War commendation and medal exceptional civilian service, 1945. Mem. Am., N.Y. (bd. govs. 1949-58, v.p. 1954-56, pres. 1956-57, chmn. com. profl. ethics and grievances 1969—) patent law assns., Am. Law Inst., Am. Bar Assn., N.Y. County Lawyers Assn. (chmn. com. fed. legislation 1946-49), Assn. Bar City N.Y. (chmn. com. on patents 1968-71). Clubs: Harvard, Lawyers, Bankers (N.Y.C.); Metropolitan (Washington). Contbr. articles to legal jours. Home: 340 E 72d St New York City NY 10021 also Sunset Hill Rd Redding CT 06896 Office: 59 Maiden Lane New York City NY 10038

KEOGH, BROOKS JAMES, rancher; b. Williston, N.D., Aug. 4, 1914; s. Frank Patrick and Elizabeth (Carney) K.; student St. John's, Collegeville, Minn., U. N.D.; B.A., Coll. St. Thomas, St. Paul, 1938; m. Kathleen Mary Hyland, Jan. 5, 1944; children—Kathleen Patricia, Mary Elizabeth, Francis Patrick. Dist. supr. Westland Oil Co., Minot, N.D., 1939-42; propr. Keogh Land & Cattle Co., Keene, N.D., 1944—; dir. Northwestern Bell Telephone Co. Co-chmn. McKenzie County Republican party. Bd. regents Mary Coll., Bismarck, N.D.; trustee Nat. Cowboy Hall of Fame, Oklahoma City. Served with USMCR, World War II. Mem. Am. Nat. Cattlemen's Assn. (past pres.), N.D. Stockmen's Assn. (past pres.), N.D. Grazing Assn. (past pres.), N.D. Farm Bur. (dir.), Kappa Sigma. K.C., Elk. Address: Keogh Ranch Keene ND 58847

KEOGH, EUGENE JAMES, former congressman; b. Bklyn., Aug. 30, 1907; s. James Preston and Elizabeth (Kehoe) K.; B.C.S., N.Y. U., 1927; LL.B., Fordham U., 1930; m. Virginia Fitzgerald; children—Susan, E. Preston. Tchr. pub schs., N.Y.C., 1927-28; clk. N.Y.C. Bd. Transp., 1928-30; law clk., 1930-31; admitted to N.Y. Bar,

1932; since practiced in N.Y.C.; mem. firm Halpin Keogh & St. John; mem. N.Y. State Assembly 1936; mem. 75th to 87th Congresses from 9th N.Y. Dist, 88th to 89th Congresses, 11th N.Y. Dist. Trustee, counsel East N.Y. Savs. Bank; dir. City Title Ins. Co. N.Y. World's Fair 1964-65 Corp., Am. Chemosol Corp., Athlone Industries, Inc.; mem. adv. com. Nat. Bank N. Am. Chmn., Franklin Delano Roosevelt Meml. Commn. Mem. Assn. Bar City N.Y., N.Y. State Bklyn., Am. bar assns., Am. Irish Hist. Assn., Theta Chi, Delta Theta Phi. Democrat. Roman Catholic. Club: Brooklyn. Home: 333 E 57th St New York City NY 10022 Office: 630 Fifth Av New York City NY 10020

KEOGH, JAMES, journalist; b. Platte County, Neb., Oct. 29, 1916; s. David James and Edith (Dwyer) K.; Ph.B., Creighton U., 1938; m. Verna Pedersen, May 17, 1940; children—Kevin, Katherine Ann. Reporter, Omaha World-Herald, 1938-48, city editor, 1948-51; contbg. editor Time mag., 1951-52, asso. editor, 1952-56, sr. editor, 1956-61, asst. mng. editor, 1961-68, exec. editor, 1968; chief writing and research Nixon for Pres. campaign, 1968; spl. asst. Pres. U.S., 1969-70. Clubs: Belle Haven (pres.-commodore 1967-68) (Greenwich, Conn.); Federal City (Washington). Author: This is Nixon, 1956. Home: Harbor Dr Greenwich CT 06830

KEOSIAN, JOHN, educator, scientist; b. Armenia, Mar. 28, 1906; s. Hagop and Paris (Boyajian) K.; came to U.S., 1912, naturalized, 1932; B.S., N.Y. U., 1927, Ph.D., 1936; m. Jessie S. Levey, Nov. 4, 1933; 1 dau., Julie. Asst. instr. N.Y.U., 1927-33; instr. U. Newark, 1933-37, asst. prof., 1937-42, asso. prof., 1942-46; asso. prof. Rutgers U., 1946-47, prof. biology, 1947—, chmn. dept., 1952-57, dir. div. of natural sci., 1957-64. Fulbright scholar to Greece, 1969-70. Mem. Am. Soc. of Naturalists, Corp. Marine Biol. Lab., Woods Hole, Mass. Fellow N.Y. Acad. Sci.; mem. Genetics Soc. Am., A.A.A.S. Contbr. articles on cell physiology, biochemical genetics to scientific jours. Author: The Origin of Life. Home: 57 5th Av New York City NY 10003 Office: 195 University Av Newark NJ 07102

KEOUGH, FRANCIS PAUL, librarian; b. Brookline, Mass., Apr. 2, 1917; s. John Joseph and Annie (O'Malley) K.; Adj. in Arts, Havard, 1940; B.S. in L.S., Columbia, 1947; m. Helen C. Drews, May 13, 1954; children—David D., Ann, Jeffrey. With Boston Pub. Library, 1934-39; asst. Harvard Archives, 1939-42, reference asst. Coll. Library, 1947-51; archivist radiation lab. Mass. Inst. Tech., 1945-46; library dir. Framingham (Mass.) City Library, 1951-64; dir. Springfield (Mass.) Pub. Library, 1964—; exec. dir. Springfield Library and Museums Assn., 1971—. Lectr. communications Simmons Coll. Sch. Library Sci., 1958, 60, on reference methods, 1961-62; lectr. information resources and techniques Mass. Dept. Edn., 1958; library cons. Chmn. adv. com. certification, mem. spl. adv. com. personnel standards for regional personnel Adv. Com. Title III and IV, L.S.C.A.; mem. planning com. Mass. Library Assn., Springfield Adult Edn. Council; exec. bd. Western Mass. Regional Adv. Council. Served with AUS, 1942-45. Mem. Am., Mass. (past pres., chmn. coms.), New Eng. library assns., Western Mass. Library Club, Men's Librarian Club. Club: Harvard (Springfield). Home: 16 Oxford St Springfield MA 01108 Office: 220 State St Springfield MA 01103

KEOWN, KENNETH K., physician; b. Independence, Mo., May 25, 1917; s. Charles and Sibyl Ellen (Richards) K.; M.D., Hahnemann Med Coll. and Hosp., Phila., 1941; m. Helen Jane Mooney, Nov. 23, 1941; children—Kenneth K., Linda Jane. Intern, Huron Rd. Hosp., East Cleveland, O., 1941-42; resident anesthesiology Hahnemann Med. Coll. and Hosp., 1946-48; practice medicine, Phila., 1948—; asso. prof. anesthesiology Hahnemann Med. Coll. and Hosp., 1948-57, U. Mo. Sch. Medicine and Anesthesiology to Med. Center Hosp., 1957—; prof. anethesiology, chmn. dept. U. Mo. Med. Center, also med. dir., 1969—. Served as maj. M.C., AUS, 1942-46. Diplomate Am. Bd. Anesthesiology. Fellow Am. Coll. Anesthesiologists (bd. govs.); mem. Internat. Anesthesia Research Soc. (chmn. bd. trustees), A.M.A. (chmn. sect. anesthesiology), Boone County Med. Soc., Mo. Soc. Anesthesiology, A.A.A.S., Am. Med. Writers Assn. Rotarian (pres.). Author: Anesthesia for Surgery of the Heart, 1956, rev. 1963. Home: 402 Westmount St Columbia MO 65201 Office: Med Center U Mo 807 Stadium Rd Columbia MO 65201

KEOWN, WILLIAM HAMILTON, educator; b. Madison, Wis., Dec. 24, 1914; s. Robert McArdle and Frances (Burnham) K.; B.A., U. Wis., 1936, M.B.A., 1947, Ph.D., 1954; m. Elizabeth Belle Seward, July 7, 1943; children—Allan Hamilton, David Wortham. Asst. exec. Four Lakes council Boy Scouts Am., Madison, Wis., 1936-38, exec. State Line council, Beloit, 1938-41; instr. commerce U. Wis., 1947-48; dir. indsl. relations Ry. Co., Louisville, 1948-49; faculty U. Okla., Norman, 1949—, asst. prof., asso. prof., 1949-56, David Ross Boyd prof. bus. mgmt., 1958—, chmn. dept. bus. mgmt., 1953-59. Served from pvt. to capt. AUS, 1941-46. Mem. Acad. Mgmt., Am. Econ. Assn., Indsl. Relations Research Assn., Am. Assn. U. Profs., Am. Acad. Polit. and Social Sci., Southwestern Mgmt. Assn. Episcopalian. Home: 536 S Lahoma Av Norman OK 73069

KEPECS, JOSEPH GOODMAN, physician, educator; b. Phila., Oct. 8, 1912; s. Jacob and Mary (Goodman) K.; B.S., U. Chgo., 1935, M.D., 1937; grad. Inst. for Psychoanalysis, Chgo., 1949; m. Joan A. Epstein, Oct. 17, 1944; children—Susan, Jonathan. Intern Cook County Hosp., Chgo., 1938-39; resident St. Elizabeths' Hosp., Washington, 1940-41; practice medicine, specializing in psychiatry, Madison, Wis., 1965—; attending physician dept. psychiatry Michael Reese Hosp., Chgo., 1950-65; prof. psychiatry U. Wis., 1965—; lectr. Chgo. Inst. for Psychoanalysis, 1957-60; professorial lectr. dept. psychiatry U. Chgo., 1960-65. Served with AUS, 1941-46. Mem. Am. Psychoanalytic Assn., Am. Psychosomatic Soc., Am. Psychiat. Assn., Chgo. Psychoanalytic Soc. (pres. 1964-65). Home: 3580 Lake Mendota Dr Madison WI 53705 Office: 1300 University Av Madison WI 53706

KEPES, GYORGY, author, painter, educator; b. Selyp, Hungary, Oct. 4, 1906; s. Ferene and Ilona (Fai) K.; M.A., Royal Acad. Fine Art, 1928; m. Juliet Appleby, Nov. 3, 1937; children—Juliet, Imre. Came to U.S., 1937. Pub. in collaboration with Dan Gyorgy, Tul a Valon, 1929; exhbn. paintings, Budapest, Berlin, N.Y. City, 1930-32, London, 1935-37; head light and color dept. New Bauhaus, 1937-38, Inst. of Design, 1938-43; designed exhbn. Arts of U.N., Art Inst., 1944 (all Chicago); designed introduction room Expn. Dest Techniques Americaines de l'Habitation et de L'Urbanisme, Paris, 1945; prof. visual design Mass. Inst. Tech., since 1946, dir. Center Advanced Visual Studies, 1967—, Inst. prof., 1970; designer section of Triennale de Milano, 1968; exhbns. Art Inst., Chicago, Katherine Kuh Gallery, San Francisco Mus. Art, Mus. Modern Art, N.Y.C., Cleveland, Phila., Mus. Fine Arts, Houston, Dallas Mus. Fine Arts, Rome. Boston, London, and other cities. Recipient Guggenheim fellow, 1960-61. Awards: Am. Inst. Graphic Arts, Soc. Typog. Arts; Silver medal, Architectural League, 1961; Fine Arts award Am. Inst. of Architects, 1968. Fellow Am. Acad. of Arts and Scis.; mem. National Inst. of Arts and Letters. Author: Language of Vision, 1944; The New Landscape, 1956; articles-profl. jours. Editor: Visual Arts Today, 1960; Vision and Value Series, 6 vols., 1965. Home: 90 Larchwood Dr Cambridge MA 02138

KEPHART, A. EVANS, lawyer; b. Ebensburg, Pa. Dec. 21, 1905; s. John William and Florence M. (Evans) K.; grad. Lawrenceville (N.J.) Sch., 1923; A.B., Princeton, 1927; LL.B., Harvard, 1930; m. Ruth Bond Hill, 1929; children—Susan Hill (Mrs. Howard K. Simpson), Katherine Evans (Mrs. Christopher Barnes); m. 2d, Marie Elizabeth Kenny, June 16, 1949; children—Samuel Robinson,, James William. Admitted to Pa. bar, 1930, since practiced in Phila.; legal sec. Supreme Ct. Pa., 1930-32; asst. city solicitor Phila., 1930-37; examiner Pa. Bd. Law Examiners, 1932-54; mem. Pa. Senate, 1939-54; partner firm Stassen & Kephart, 1959-68; state ct. adminstr. Supreme Ct. Pa., 1968—. Recipient Good Citizenship award S.A.R. Mem. Am., Pa., Phila. bar assns., Mil. Order Loyal Legion. Clubs: Union League (Phila.); Philadelphia Country (Gladwyne, Pa.), Mason. Home: 615 Old Gulph Rd Bryn Mawr PA 19010 Office: City Hall Philadelphia PA 19107

KEPLINGER, LIVINGSTON BOND, mgmt. cons., steel co. exec.; b. Grand Rapids, Mich., Jan. 6, 1891; s. Frank Edward and Clara Douglas (Bond) K.; grad. Culver Mil. Acad., 1908, U. Wis., 1912; m. Martha Rachel Quiggle, June 16, 1914; 1 son, Livingston Bond. Exec. v.p. Peters Cartridge Co., Cin., 1910-25; exec. Dillon Read & Co., N.Y.C., 1926-30; cons. engr., reorgn. specialist, San Francisco, 1930-40 (assisted reorgn. Cal. irrigation dists.); v.p., dir., gen. mgr. Rheem Mfg. Co., 1940-45; pres. Steel Shipping Container Inst., Inc., N.Y.C., 1945-66, now chmn. bd.; pres. Bankam. Co., 1930-40, Gen. Metals Corp., 1930-40, Pacific Coast Mortgage Co., 1930-40, Overseas Steel Shipping Container Corp., 1940-50; steel cons., chmn. adv. com. WPB, 1940-50; pres., dir. Synthetasine Protective Coatings, Inc. 1946-66; chmn. Prentice Electronic Corp., 1970—; pres. Spelman Prentice Corp., 1970—; chmn. exec. com., dir. Lynch Communication Systems Inc., 1965—; dir. emeritus Copperweld Steel Co. Cons. steel div. WPB, 1942-44. Trustee Am. Econ. Found. Mem. Newcomen Soc. Eng., S.A.R., Phi Delta Theta. Clubs: University (San Francisco); Sky (N.Y.C.); Thunderbird Country (Palm Springs, Cal.). Home: 71359 Cypress Rd Thunderbird Country Club Palm Springs CA 92262 Office: 1075 California St San Francisco CA 94108

KEPPEL, FRANCIS, ednl. exec.; b. N.Y.C., Apr. 16, 1916; s. Frederick Paul and Helen Tracy (Brown) K.; A.B., Harvard Coll., 1938; LL.D., Hamline U., 1957, Oakland U., U. Pa., Tufts, Boston U., 1963, Middlebury Coll., 1964; L.H.D., Cal. State Coll., Hamilton Coll., 1964, Carnegie Inst. Tech., Bates Coll., Bucknell U.; LL.D., Yeshiva U., Clark U., Providence Coll., Brandeis U., U. State N.Y.; Pd.D., Baldwin-Wallace Coll.; m. Edith Moulton Swain, July 19, 1941; children—Edith Tracy, Susan Moulton. With Harvard Coll., 1939-41; sec. of Joint Army and Navy Com. on Welfare and Recreation, Washington, 1941-44; asst. to provost Harvard, 1946-48, dean faculty edn., 1948-62; U.S. commr. edn., 1962-65; asst. sec. edn. Dept. Health, Edn. and Welfare, 1965-66; chmn. bd. Gen. Learning Corp., N.Y.C., 1966—. Vice chmn. bd. higher edn. City U. N.Y., 1967-71; bd. overseers Harvard; trustee Carnegie Corp., Russell Sage Found. Served to 1st lt. AUS, 1944-46. Fellow Am. Acad. Arts and Scis.; mem. Phi Beta Kappa. Clubs. Cosmos (Washington); Century Assn. (N.Y.C.). Author: The Necessary Revolution in American Education, 1966. Home: 1100 Park Av New York City NY 10028 Office: 1 E 54th St New York City NY 10022

KEPPEL, JOHN, fgn. service officer; b. Quogue, L.I., N.Y., Aug. 21, 1917; s. David and Dorothy (Vickery) K.; grad. with honors Milton Acad., 1936; A.B. cum laude, Harvard, 1940; spl. student Johns Hopkins U., 1967-68; m. Grace Marjorie Wood, June 7, 1952; 1 son, David. Fgn. service officer, 1947—; tng. Russian lang., Fgn. Service Inst., 3rd sec., vice consul, Moscow, 1947-50, 2d sec., Consul, 1953-55; assigned Frankfurt, 1950; 2d sec., vice consul, Seoul, Korea, 1950-52, consul, 1952; assigned Regensberg, 1952; 2d sec., Rome, 1955-56, 1st sec., 1957; dep. chief div. research and analysis, USSR, Eastern Europe, Dept. of State, Washington, 1958, chief bloc internat. polit. activities div., 1959-62; dep. dir. office of research and analysis for Sino-Soviet bloc, 1961; fellow Center for Internat. Affairs, Harvard, 1961-62; counsellor of embassy for political affairs, Rio de Janeiro, 1962-64; sr. tng. officer Fgn. Service Inst., Dept. of State, Washington, 1965-66, chmn. div. polit. studies, 1966-67; special student Johns Hopkins U., 1967-68; deputy special asst. to Sec. State, 1968-69; chief operations staff UN Fund for Population Activities, 1969—. Served from pvt. to capt., inf., AUS, 1941-46. Decorated Bronze Star medal with clusters: Croix de Guerre (France). Home: 45 E 89th St New York City NY 10028 Office: UN Fund for Population Activities 485 Lexington Av New York City NY 10017

KEPPERS, GEORGE LEONARD, educator; b. Avon, Minn., Feb. 10, 1915; s. Bernard J. and Marie (Fischer) K.; B.A., St. Cloud State Coll., 1937; M.A., Colo. State Coll., 1946; postgrad. U. Minn., summers 1947-49; Ed.D., U. Colo., 1953; m. Lois Fae Zittleman, June 9, 1941; children—Kathleen Marie (Mrs. Thomas Ortega), Steven George, Bruce John, Barbara Lois. Tchr. pub. schs., Minn., 1937-42, 46-47; instr. math. Ia. State Tchrs. Coll., Cedar Falls, 1942-51; dir. guidance Albuquerque Pub. Schs., 1953-56; faculty U. N.M., Albuquerque, 1956—, prof. guiding and counseling, 1961—, chmn. dept. guidance and spl. edn., 1966—, dir. Manzanita Center, U. N.M., 1965—. asst. dean Coll. Edn., 1968—. Vis. lectr. summers U. Colo., 1956, U. Hawaii, 1962, 66. Served with USAAF, 1942-46. Recipient Nat. award for teaching guidance via TV, 1962. Mem. Am. Psychol. Assn., Am. Personnel and Guidance Assn. (life, nat. rec. com. 1961), Nat. Vocational Guidance Assn., Assn. Counselor Educators and Suprs., Phi Kappa Phi. Kiwanian. Contbr. articles to profl. jours. Home: 824 Truman St N E Albuquerque NM 87110

KEPPLER, HERBERT, mag. editor; b. N.Y.C., Apr. 21, 1925; s. Victor and Josephine T. (Windmann) K.; B.A., Harvard, 1945; m. Louise M. Lyman, July 7, 1956; children—Kathryn Louise, Thomas Victor. Reporter, N.Y. Sun, 1948-49; with Modern Photography, N.Y.C., 1950—, editorial dir., publisher, 1967—. Served to ensign USNR, 1945-46. Mem. Rolls-Royce Owners Club. Author: Official 35mm Camera Rating Guide, 1957; Keppler on the Eye-Level Reflex, 1960; How to Make Better Pictures in Your Home, 1962; 124 Ways to Test Cameras, Lenses and Equipment, 1962; The Pentax Way, 1966. Home: 119 N Highland Pl Croton-on-Hudson NY 10520 Office: 165 W 46th St New York City NY 10036

KER, CHARLES H., mfg. exec.; b. Chgo., July 28, 1903; s. Charles H. and Ethelyn L. (Hoskins) K.; A.B., Wabash Coll., 1924; m. Jessie M. Anglin, Sept 2, 1933; 1 son, Charles A. With Dalton Foundries, Inc., Warsaw, 1927—, cost clk., supt., gen. supt., v.p., 1927-52, pres., 1952-59, chmn. bd., 1959-68, hon. chmn., 1968—; dir. Lake City Bank (Warsaw). Mem. Ind. Mfrs. Assn., Gray Iron Founders Soc. (pres. 1955). Presbyn. Mason. Club: Union League (Chgo.). Home: 1202 E Main St Warsaw IN 46580 Office: Dalton Foundries Inc Warsaw IN 46580

KERBY, WILLIAM FREDERICK, bus. exec.; b. Washington, July 28, 1908; s. Frederick Monroe and Helen Frances (Hunter) K.; A.B., U. Mich., 1930; Frances Justina Douglass, June 8, 1935; children—Jean Frances, Judith Ann. Staff corr. U.P.I., Washington, 1930-32. Wall St. Jour., Washington, 1933-35, copy editor, N.Y.C., 1938, news, editor, 1938-40, asst. mng. editor, 1941-42, mng. editor, 1943-44, exec. editor, 1945-51, v.p. Dow Jones & Co., Inc., pubs. Wall Street Jour., 1951-60, exec. v.p., 1961-66, pres., chief exec. officer, 1966—, editorial dir., 1958-66, also dir.; in pub. relations, 1936-37. Trustee Williamsburgh Savs. Bank, Bklyn. Pres. Newspaper Fund; regent L.I. Coll. Hosp.; bd. dirs. Beekman-Downtown Hosp., N.Y.C. Mem. Phi Beta Kappa, Sigma Delta Chi, Phi Kappa Tau. Episcopalian. Clubs: National Press (Wash.); Heights Casino, Brooklyn (Bklyn.): Union, Recess (N.Y.C.). Home: 253 Hicks St Brooklyn NY 11261 also Buck Hill Falls PA Office: 30 Broad St New York City NY 10004

KERCHER, JOHN WESLEY, Jr., accountant; b. Columbus, O., Jan. 26, 1915; s. John Wesley and Gudrun C. (Carston) K.; student U. Cin., 1932-34; Antioch Coll., 1934-36; m. Flora Elizabeth Blakeslee, Mar. 26, 1938; children—John Wesley III, William Henry. With Ernst & Ernst, C.P.A.'s, 1942—, partner in charge South Central dist., Atlanta, 1957—. C.P.A. in 10 states. Trustee Atlanta Arts Alliance. Pres., Atlanta Symphony Orch. Mem. Am. Inst. C.P.A.'s, Nat. Assn. Accountants, Ga. Soc. C.P.A.'s. Club: Capital City, Cheroke Town and Country (Atlanta). Home: 145 Valley Rd NW Atlanta GA 30305 Office: First Nat Bank Tower Atlanta GA 30303

KERCHER, LEONARD CLAYTON, sociologist; b. Bridgewater, O., Dec. 15, 1901; s. Albertus Clayton and Emma (Roost) K.; student Western Mich. Coll., 1922-24; U. of London, summer 1934; A.B., U. Mich. 1927, A.M., 1928, Ph.D., 1939; m. Dorotha Carter, Aug. 6, 1938; 1 dau., Ann Carolyn (dec.). Sch. teacher, Camden, Mich., 1919-20, Waldron, 1920-22, Kalamazoo, 1924-26; prof. sociology, Western Mich. Coll., 1928—, head dept. sociology and anthropology, 1945—, chmn. div. of social sci., 1948-52; lectr. sociology Horace Rackham Sch. Grad. Studies, U. Mich., 1939-51; vis. prof. summers, U. Redlands (Cal.), 1950. Ashridge Coll., England, 1952-54-57. U. Vt., 1953. Oxford (Eng.), U., 1960, 63, 66; dir. East Africa Seminar summer, 1965, 68. Study in Europe, Africa under Carnegie grant, 1960-61. Mem. commn. social work Am. Council Social Work Edn. Mem. Am. Sociol. Soc., Nat. Geog. Soc., Am. Acad. of Polit. and Social Sci., Mich. Sociol. Soc., Mich. Acad. of Arts and Scis., Kalamazoo Council Social Agencies (pres. 1957-58), Mental Hygiene Soc. (pres. local chpt.), Alpha Kappa Delta, Phi Gamma Mu, Kappa Delta Pi. Presbyn. (elder). Clubs: Rotary, Torch (internat. pres. 1957-58). Author: Consumers Cooperatives (with Kebker and Leland), 1941; Sociological Foundations of Education (with others), 1942; contbr. to sociol. jours. Home: 2148 Sheffield Dr Kalamazoo MI 49008

KERKER, MILTON, coll. dean; b. Utica, N.Y., Sept. 25, 1920; s. Samuel and Sarah (Cohen) K.; A.B., Columbia, 1941 M.A., 1947, Ph.D., 1949; m. Revaa Stemerman, June 16, 1946; children-Ruth Ann, Martin Joseph, Susan Lee, Joel Leon. Mem. faculty Clarkson Coll. Tech., Potsdam, N.Y., 1949—, prof. chemistry, 1956—, chmn. dept., 1960—, dean Sch. Arts and Sci., 1964—; Unilevr vis. prof. U. Bristol (Eng.), 1967-68; Welch Found. lectr., 1964. Ford Found. fellow, 1952-53. Fellow Optical Soc. Am.; mem. Am. Chem. Soc. (chmn. div. colloid and surface chemistry 1965-66; Kendall award 1971), History Sci. Soc., Soc. History Tech., A.A.A.S. Author: Electromagnetic Scattering, 1963; The Scattering of Light and Other Electromagnetic Radiation 1969; also articles. Editor-in-chief Jour. Colloid and Interface Sci., 1965—. Home: 4 Hillcrest Dr Potsdam NY 13676

KERLAN, ROBERT KEITH, orthopedic surgeon; b. Bowlus, Minn., May 13, 1922; s. Samuel Zack and Flora (Rose) K.. B.A., So. Cal., 1942, M.D., 1945; m. Rachel Frauenfelder, June 25, 1949; children—Kimberly, Robert Keith, Kerry. Intern Los Angeles County Hosp., 1945-47, resident, 1947-50; pvt. practice orthopedic surgery, Los Angeles, 1950—; mem. staff Daniel Freeman Centinela Valley Community, Los Angeles County-U. So. Cal. Med. Center hosps.; asst. clin. prof. orthopaedic surgery U. So. Cal. Sch. Medicine; cons. Los Angeles Lakers Basketball Club, Los Angeles Kings Hockey Club, Cal. Angels Baseball Club, San Diego Padres Baseball Club. Dir. San Diego Padres Nat. League Baseball Club. Served with AUS, 1942-45. Diplomate Am. Bd. Orthopaedic Surgery. Mem. Western Harness Racing Assn. (bd. dirs.), Alpha Chi Delta, Phi Chi. Home: 301 S Rockingham St Los Angeles CA 90049 Office: 3701 Stocker St Los Angeles CA 90008

KERLEY, JAMES JOSEPH, chem. co. exec.; b. Phila., Nov. 20, 1922; s. Philip William and Jane Veronica (Touey) K.; B.S. magna cum laude, Temple U., 1944; M.A., U. Pa., 1949, postgrad., 1949-51; LL.D., Temple U., 1969; m. Dorothea Long Ickler, Oct. 24, 1944; children—Janet, James, Doris Ann, Suzanne. Trainee, Smith, Barney & Co., Phila., 1946-47; instr. finance Temple U., 1947-51; with Ford Motor Co., 1951-58; v.p., div. controller Crosley div. Avco Co., 1958-60; v.p. controller Ling-Temco-Vought Co., Dallas, 1960-62; v.p. finance Trans World Airlines, N.Y.C., 1962-65, sr. v.p., 1965-68, mem. exec. com., 1964-68, also dir.; financial v.p. Internat. Utilities Corp., 1968-69; sr. v.p. finance Lone Star Cement Corp., 1969-70; v.p. finance Monsanto Co., 1970—, also dir.; dir. Merc. Trust Co., St. Louis. Mem. pres.'s council St. Louis U. Served to 1st lt. USMCR, 1943-46; PTO. Mem. Beta Gamma Sigma. Home: 33 Briarcliff St Louis MO 63124 Office: 800 N Lindbergh Blvd St Louis MO 63166

KERLIKOWSKE, ALBERT CARL, former hosp. exec.; b. St. Joseph, Mich., Jan. 7, 1900; s. Albert R. and Caroline (Kling) K.; M.D., U. Mich., 1923; m. Aline Cake, Nov. 14, 1922; children-Aline (Mrs. Harold M. Hultquist), Carolyn (Mrs. M.R. Chase), Mary Ann (Mrs. Thomas K. Pope). Intern, U. Mich. Hosp., 1923-24, resident ophthalmology, 1924-25, adminstrv. medicine as chief resident physician, 1924-28, asst. dir., 1928-45, dir., 1945-70. Regent, Coll. Hosp. Adminstrs.; dir. Mich. Med. Service. Pres. Tri-State Assembly, 1957-58. Fellow Am. Coll. Hosp. Adminstrs. (pres. 1954-55); mem. Mich. Hosp. Assn. (pres. 1956—), Phi Chi. Home: 7111 S Riverside Dr Marine City MI 48039

KERLINGER, FRED NICHOLS, educator; b. N.Y.C., July 4, 1910; s. George Edward and Lotte (Fisher) K.; B.S., N.Y.U., 1942; M.A., U. Mich., 1951, Ph.D., 1953; m. Betty Jane McCue, Dec. 16, 1946; children—Paul Nichols, Stephen Charles. Regional civil edn. officer, Shikoku, Japan, 1947-50; asst. prof. ednl. sociology and psychology Wayne State U., 1953-55; mem. faculty N.Y.U., 1955—, prof. ednl. psychology, 1960—, head div. behavioral scis., 1968—; vis. prof. Columbia, summer 1955, U. Cal. at Berkeley, summer 1968. Mem. Hartsdale (N.Y.) Bd. Edn., 1960-63; chmn. Citizens Com. Racial Disturbances, 1968-69. Served to 2d lt. AUS, 1942-46. Fellow Am. Psychol. Assn.; mem. A.A.A.S., Am. Assn. U. Profs. Author: Foundations of Behavioral Research, 1964; also articles. Rev. editor Am. Ednl. Research Jour., 1967-69; editor Rev. Research in Edn., 1970—. Home: 60 Charlotte Pl Hartsdale NY 10530 Office: New York Univ New York City NY 10003

KERMAN, JOSEPH WILFRED, educator, musicologist, critic; b. London, Eng., Apr. 3, 1924 (parents Am. citizens); A.B., N.Y. U., 1943; Ph.D., Princeton, 1950; D.H.L., Fairfield U., 1970; m. Vivian Shaviro, Sept. 12, 1945; children—Jonathan, Peter, Lucy. Instr. music Princeton, 1947; dir. grad. studies Westminster Choir Coll., 1949-51; faculty U. Cal. at Berkeley, 1951—, prof. music, 1960—, chmn. dept., 1961-64. Hodder jr. fellow Princeton, 1957-58; Guggenheim fellow, 1960; grantee Nat. Inst. Arts and Letters, 1956; Fulbright fellow, vis. fellow All Souls Coll., Oxford, 1966-67; sr. fellow Soc. for Humanities, Cornell, 1970; fellow Clare Hall, Cambridge, 1971. Mem. Am.

Musicological Soc. Author: Opera as Drama, 1956; The Elizabethan Madrigal, 1962; The Beethoven Quartets, 1967; (with H.W. Janson) History of Art and Music, 1968. Editor: Beethoven Autograph Miscellany, 1970. Contbr. numerous articles, criticism to profl. jours. Home: 1530 La Loma Av Berkeley CA 94708

KERMODE, JOHN FRANK, critic; b. Douglas, Isle of Man, Nov. 29, 1919; s. John Pritchard and Doris (Kennedy) K.; B.A., Liverpool U., 1940, M.A., 1947; m. Maureen Eccles, Dec. 20, 1947 (div. 1970); children—Mark, Deborah. Lectr. King's Coll. Newcastle, U. Durham, 1947-49, Reading U., 1949-58; John Edward Taylor prof. English, Manchester U., 1958-65; fellow Center Advanced Studies, Wesleyan U., Conn., 1963-64; Winterstoke prof. English, Bristol U., 1965- 67; Lord Northcliffe prof. of English lit. U. Coll., London, England, 1967—; Mary Flexner lecturer, Bryn Mawr, 1965. Mem. Arts Council Gt. Britain, 1968—. Served with Royal Navy, 1940-46. Fellow Royal Soc. Lit.; mem. Poetry Book Soc. (chmn. 1968—). Author: Romantic Image, 1957; The Living Milton, 1960; Wallace Stevens, 1960; Puzzles and Epiphanies, 1963; The Sense of an Ending, 1967; Continuities, 1968; Shakespeare, Spenser, Donne, 1971; Modern Essays, 1971. Gen. editor Modern Masters, 1970—. Office: Univ Coll Gower St London WC 1 England

KERN, BERNARD DONALD, educator, physicist; b. New Castle, Ind., Oct. 31, 1919; s. William Bernard and Cecile (Hudson) K.; B.S., Ind. U., 1942, M.S., 1947, Ph.D., 1949; m. Nedda Wisler Burdsall, Aug. 20, 1946; children-Richard B., Jonathan K., Arthur R. Physicist, Signal Corps and Manhattan Project, Chgo., 1942-43; sr. physicist Oak Ridge Nat. Lab., 1949-50; mem. faculty U. Ky., 1950—, prof. physics, 1958—, chmn. dept. physics and astronomy, 1967-69; physicist U.S. Naval Radiol. Def. Lab., San Francisco, 1957-58, cons., 1957-69; prof. Inst. Teknologi Bandung, Bandung, Indonesia, U. Ky., State Dept. Ednl. Assistance Program, 1961- 62. Served to lt. (j.g.) USNR, 1943-46. Fellow Am. Phys. Soc.; mem. Am. Inst. Physics, Sigma Xi. Author articles on nuclear physics. Office: Dept Physics and Astronomy U Ky Lexington KY 40506

KERN, BYRON MEHL, chem. co. exec.; b. Leavenworth, Kan., Jan. 26, 1921; s. Leo John and Florence (Mehl) K.; B.S. in Chem. Engring., U. Kan., 1943; m. Mary Ann Green, Oct. 1, 1943; children—Rebecca, Jeffrey. With gen. chems. div. Allied Chem. Corp., 1943-46; with Spencer Chem. Co., Kansas City, Mo., 1946-66, v.p., 1959-66; asst. to pres. Chemplex Co., Rolling Meadows, Ill., 1966—, v.p., 1966-68, sr. v.p., 1968—. Mem. Am. Inst. Chem. Engrs., Tau Beta Pi, Sigma Tau, Phi Delta Theta. Home: 1017 N Blackburn Dr Palatine, IL 60067 Office: Chemplex Co Rolling Meadows IL 60008

KERN, CHARLES JAMES, home products co. exec.; b. Schenectady, Mar. 17, 1913; s. Joseph J. and Magdalen (Yaeger) K.; B.S., U. N.M. Union Coll., 1935; M.S., Poly. Inst. Bklyn., 1942; Ph.D., N.Y. U., 1954; m. Bess Heinbuch, Sept. 10, 1937; children—Charles Douglas, Linda Anne. Chief chemist supremacy prod. R.H. Macy & Co., 1935-42; v.p. Ives Labs. div. Am. Home Products Corp., 1942-49, v.p. Wyeth Labs., 1949-67, v.p. Am. Home Products Corp., 1968-69, exec. v.p. Wyeth Labs., Radnor, Pa., 1969-70, pres., 1971—. Trustee Phila. Coll. Pharmacy and Sci.; bd. dirs. J.S. Sharpe Research Found. Mem. Greater Phila. C. of C., Am. Chem. Soc., Am. Pharm. Assn., A.A.A.S., N.Y. Acad. Sci., Franklin Inst., Sigma Xi. Home: 310 S Roberts Rd Rosemont PA 19312 Office: Wyeth Labs Radnor PA 19088

KERN, FRANKLIN LORENZ, banker; b. Frankenmuth Mich., Aug. 22, 1932; s. Ruben William and Regina (Bernthal) K.; B.A., Mich. State U., 1954; diploma, Bank Adminstrn. Inst. and Northwestern U., 1963, Bank Adminstrn. Inst. and U. Wis., 1971; m. Loretta Lee Gehrke, Apr. 22, 1962; children—Andrew James, Sara Beth. Asst. to controller Second Nat. Bank, Saginaw, Mich., 1963-65, auditor, 1965—. Sec.-treas. Frankenmuth Community Band, 1967—; chmn. Student Aid Fund St Lorenz Lutheran Congregation, 1964—; sec. 125th anniversary com., Frankenmuth, Mich., 1969. Bd. dirs. Saginaw Civic Symphony Assn. Mem. Bank Adminstrn. Inst. (pres. Eastern Mich. chpt.), Mich. State U., Frankenmuth High Sch. (past sec.-treas.) alumni assns. Address: 2d Nat Bank of Saginaw 101 N Washington Saginaw MI 48607

KERN, HARRY FREDERICK, editor; b. Denver, July 7, 1911; s. Harry F. and Alice (Robertson) K.; student Harvard, 1930-35; m. Janet Campbell Mackenzie, Dec. 27, 1939; children—Rosemary Annand, Nathaniel Robertson. Joined Newsweek, 1935, became asst. editor, 1937, asso. editor, 1941, war editor, 1942; sr. editor internat. affairs Newsweek mag., N.Y.C. 1950-56, also editor-in-chief internat. edits., 1950-56; dir. Fgn. Reports, 1956. Decorated Order Sacred Treasure (Japan); Order of Merit (Lebanon). Mem. Council Fgn. Relations, Japan Soc. Clubs: Harvard, Knickerbocker (N.Y.C.); National Press, Metropolitan (Washington); Travellers (Paris). Home: Lloyd Lane Huntington NY 11743 Office: 4 W 58th St New York City NY 10019

KERN, IRVING JOHN, food co. exec.; b. N.Y.C. Feb. 10, 1914; s. John and Min (Weitzner) Kleinberger; B.S., N.Y.U., 1934, student Grad. Sch. Art and Sci., 1960-65; m. Beatrice Rubenfeld, June 22, 1941; childrenJohn A., Arthur H., Robert M. Asst. buyer Bloomingdale's Dept. Store, N.Y.C., 1934-40; with Deltown Foods, Inc., Yonkers, N.Y., pres., 1966—. Mem. Community Mental Health Services Board of Westchester County, 1954-59; mem. bd. dirs., sec. Westchester County Assn., 1950-57; exec. bd. Westchester County Better Bus. Bur. Served to lt. col. AUS, 1940-45. Decorated Bronze Star. Mem. N.Y. Milk Bottlers Fedn. (pres. dir.), Met. Dairy Inst. (exec. v.p. dir.), Phi Beta Kappa, Tau Epsilon Phi. Home: 6 White Birch Lane Scarsdale NY 10583 Office: 1170 Sawmill River Rd Yonkers NY 10701

KERN, RICHARD ARMINIUS, physician; b. Columbia, Pa., Feb. 20, 1891; s. Rev. George and Wilhelmine (Maurer) K.; A.B., U. Pa., 1910, M.D., 1914; LL.D., Lebanon Valley Coll., 1947; Sc. D., Franklin and Marshall Coll., 1947, Temple U., 1958, and Bucknell U., 1959; m. Donna A. Couch, Aug. 19, 1927; children—Richard Bradford, Donna Natalie. Interne and sr. med. resident Univ. Hosp., 1914-17; instr. in medicine, U. Pa., 1919-23, asso, 1923-28, asst. prof., 1928-34, prof. clin. medicine, 1934-46, Louis A. Godey fellow in med., 1927-31; prof. clin. medicine, grad. Sch. of Med. U. Pa., 1934, vis. phys. Hosp. of U. Pa., also chief med. outpatient dept. and allergy sec.; prof. med. and head Dept. of Med. Temple U. Sch. of Med. and Hosp., 1946-56, prof. emeritus, 1956-. Vice pres. Bd. of Health, Lower Merion Twp., 1934-54, pres., 1955-58; v.p. Phila. Bd. Health, 1960-61. Trustee Temple U., 1958—. Served as lt. M.C., U.S. Navy, World War I; capt., Medical Corps, USNR; organizer N.R. Specialist Unit at U. Pa.; on active duty South Pacific Mar. 1942 to Mar., 1944, U.S.S. Solace and Halsey Staff; Chief of Med. and Rehabilitation Officer, Naval Hosp., Phila., 1944-46, rank rear adm., 1952, ret., 1955; med. officer in command, volunteer Res. Div. 4-3. Chief, div. gen. med., Vets. Adminstrn., 1946-47; cons. Surg. Gen. Army, 1947—; mem. Armed Forces Epidemiology Bd., 1956-68; mem. Naval Research adv. com., 1957—; cons. Surgeon Gen. Navy, 1949—; cons. Armed Forces Inst. Pathology, 1962; mem. def. sci. bd. Dept. of Def., 1956-64; mem. nat. health resources adv. com. Office Emergency Preparedness; mem. nat. adv. com. to SSS, 1969—; dir., trustee Research Found. Nat. Assn. Mental Health, 1962. Chmn. com. naval med. research, Div. Med. Scis., NRC, 1951-69. Master A.C.P. (sec. general 1951-55, pres. 1957-58, regent 1958-61); mem. Internat. Soc. Internal Medicine (pres. 1970—), Pa. Med. Soc. (pres. 1964-65), A.M.A. (chmn. sect. military medicine 1952-53), Soc. U.S. Med. Cons. (pres. 1954), Am. Assn. Advancement Sci., Assn. Am. Physicians, Soc. for Clin. Investigation, Am. Clin. and Climatol. Assn., Assn., for study of Allergy (ex-pres.), Soc. for Study of Asthma and Allied Conditions (ex-pres.), Assn. Mil. Surgeons (pres. 1960), Phila. Medico-Legal Inst., Coll. of Physicians of Phila. (pres. 1952), Am. Acad. Allergy, Sigma Xi, Alpha Omega Alpha, Phi Chi, Phi Gamma Delta. Grand Master of Masons in Pa., 1945-46; active mem. Supreme Council (33). Republican. Mem. United Ch. of Christ. Clubs: Union League (Phila.); Philadelphia Country (Bala-Cynwyd, Pa.); Army and Navy (Washington). Contbr. many papers to med. jours. Asso. editor Am. Jour. of Med. Sciences, 1925-50, editor 1951-67. Home: 1239 Remington Road Wynnewood PA 19096 Office: Temple U Hosp 3401 North Broad St Philadelphia PA 19140

KERN, ROBERT BRADFORD, clothing mfg. co. exec.; b. San Francisco, Apr. 27, 1920; s. Reuben W. and Grace (Bradford) K.; B.S., U. San Francisco, 1948; m. Beverly Janis Bennetts, Apr. 17, 1946; children—Stanley Robert, Reynold Bradford. Pub. accountant Benjamin H. Hicklin, C.P.A., San Francisco, 1947-50; with Levi Strauss & Co., San Francisco, 1951—, sec.-treas., 1964—, also dir., mem. exec. com., 1971—; dir. Levi Strauss & Co.-Europe S.A., Levi Strauss (Far East), Levi Strauss Pan Am., Levi Strauss Can; Ltd. Sec.-treas. Levi Strauss Found. Served with AUS, 1941-45. Mem. Financial Exec. Inst. Rotarian. Home: 3404 Black Hawk Rd Lafayette CA 94549 Office: 98 Battery St San Francisco CA 94106

KERNAGHAN, KENNETH WATT, dept. store exec.; b. Toronto, Can., Mar. 6, 1916; s. Hugh and Lucy (Watt) K.; B.A., U. Toronto, 1937; grad. Osgoode Hall Law Sch., 1940; m. Edna Mortley Button, Oct. 4, 1941. Read law with John S. Macfarlane, 1937-40; called to Ont. bar, 1940, created Queen's counsel, 1958; trust officer London & Western Trust Co. Ltd., 1940-44, mgr. Toronto officer, 1945; with Simpsons Ltd., 1945—; v.p., sec., 1968—; sec. Simpsons Acceptance Co. Ltd., Simpsons Profit Sharing Retirement Fund, Burton Charitable Found.; sec., dir. Greenridge Investments Ltd., Pinerocks Ltd., Van Holme Investments Ltd., Limestone Hall Farms Ltd., Robert Simpson Co. Ltd. and subsidiaries; dir. Lakeshore Shopping Plaza Ltd., Les Galeries D'Anjou Ltd., Woodbine-Sheppard Shopping Center Ltd., Pape Investments Ltd., Anjou Holdings Ltd., Micmac Shopping Center Ltd. Mem. Bd. Trade Met. Toronto. Mem. County York Law Assn., Canadian Bar Assn., Canadian Mfrs. Assn., Am. Mgmt. Assn., Chartered Inst. Secs., Toronto Assn. Canadian Gen. Counsel, Phi Delta Phi. Clubs: Toronto Cricket Skating and Curling, Lawyers, Empire, Canadian, Granite (Toronto). Home: 4 Deer Park Crescent Toronto 7 Ontario Canada Office: 401 Bay St Toronto 1 Ontario Canada

KERNAN, ALVIN BERNARD, educator; b. Manchester, Ga., June 13, 1923; s. Alvin Berbanks and Jimmie Katherine (Fletcher) P.; B.A., Williams Coll., 1949; B.A., Oxford U., 1951; Ph.D., Yale, 1954; m. Suzanne Scoble, Dec. 13, 1949; children—Geoffrey, Katherine, Marjorie, Alvin. Instr. English, Rensselaer Poly. Inst., Troy, N.Y., 1953-54; instr. Yale, 1954-59, asst. prof. English, 1959-63, asso. prof., 1963-66, prof., 1966—, asso. provost, 1965-68, acting provost, 1970, dir. div. humanities, 1970—. Served with USN, 1941-45. Decorated Navy cross, D.F.C., Air medal. Moody fellow, 1949-51, Morse fellow, 1957-58; Am. Council Learned Socs. fellow, 1961-62; Nat. Endowment Humanities sr. scholar fellow, 1968-69. Mem. Phi Beta Kappa. Author: The Cankered Muse, 1959; The Plot of Satire, 1965; The English Drama, 1576-1613, 1973. Home: 280 Mill Rd North Haven CT 06473

KERNAN, FRANCIS, investment banker; b. Buffalo, June 29, 1903; s. Francis K. and Mary (Spratt) K.; A.B., Harvard, 1924, LL.B., 1927; m. Maud Tilton, July 20, 1934; children—Francis, Ann (Mrs. Patrick F.J. Macrory), Benjamin. Admitted to (N.Y. bar, 1927; atty. Simpson, Thacher & Barlett, N.Y.C., 1927-36; partner White, Weld & Co., investment bankers, 1936—; dir. Can. Export Gas & Oil, Ltd., Liberian Iron Ore Ltd. Mem. Cardinal's Com. of Laity for N.Y. Cath. Charities. Trustee United Hosp.-Fund, N.Y.C.; gov. New York Hosp. Served as lt. comdr. USNR, 1941-45. Office: 300 Park Av New York City NY 10016

KERNAN, RICHARD D., life ins. co. exec.; b. Utica, N.Y., 1909; ed. Harvard, 1931; m. Mathilde Manly Shea, 1965. Vice pres., treas. Equitable Life Assurance Soc. U.S.; dir. Fiduciary Trust Co. N.Y. Served to lt. comdr. USNR, 1942-46. Roman Catholic. Clubs: Harvard, River, Southampton; Jupiter Island, Sadaquada Golf. Home: 765 Park Av New York City NY 10021 Office: 1285 Av Americas New York City NY 10019 *

KERNAN, THOMAS F., b. 1911; B.B.A., City Coll. N.Y.; with Orlin & Luther, accounting firm, 1946-48; pvt. accounting practice, 1948-49; with U.S. AEC, 1948-59; with Aerojet-Gen. Corp., El Monte, Cal., 1959-70, asst. to v.p., asst. treas., treas., 1966-70; treas. Republic Corp., 1970—. Address: 9190 E Flair Dr El Monte CA 91731 *

KERNAN, WALTER AVERY, lawyer; b. Utica, N.Y., Dec. 1, 1913; s. Francis K. and Mary (Spratt) K.; grad. Milton Acad., 1932; A.B., Harvard, 1936, LL.B., 1939; m. Leslie Hadden, May 10, 1942; children—Anita, Mary (Mrs. Winthrop Rutherford, Jr.), Emily, Nancy, Beatrice, Charles. Admitted to N.Y. bar, 1940, since practiced in N.Y.C.; asso. firm Carter, Ledyard & Milburn, 1939-41, 46-51, mem. firm, 1951—. Trustee Helen Huntington Hull Fund; hon. trustee Fordham U.; bd. govs. N.Y. Hosp., Real Estate Bd.; bd. dirs. Fresh Air Fund. Served from pvt. to capt., AUS, 1941-46, PTO. Mem. Am. Bar Assn., Assn. Bar City N.Y., also mem. N.Y. State Bar Assn. Clubs: Piping Rock (Long Island, N.Y.); Links, Harvard, Down Town (N.Y.C.). Home: 830 Park Av New York City NY 10021 Office: 2 Wall St New York City NY 10005

KERNAN, WARNICK J., lawyer; b. Utica, N.Y., July 24, 1880; s. William and Frances (Warnick) K.; A.B., Georgetown U., 1901; special course Cornell Law Sch., 1902-04; LL.D., Hamilton Coll., 1934; unmarried. Admitted to N.Y. bar, 1904, and since practiced in Utica; mem. Kernan and Kernan; spl. dist. atty., Oneida Co., 1915-16; trustee Savs. Bank of Utica, 1916-55. Mem. Bd. Sch. Commrs., Utica, 1907-14; mem. Law Revision Commn. of State of N.Y., 1934-47, chmn., 1940-47; referee in railroad reorganization proceedings by appointment of U.S. Circuit Court of Appeals, 2d Circuit, 1935; chmn. Alien Enemy Hearing Bd. Northern Dist. of N.Y., 1941-45, by appointment U.S. atty. general. Chmn. Spl. Com. of N.Y. State Bar Assn. to investigate jud. conditions in Albany Co., 1944-45. Counsel to Temp. Commn. on Need for a State U., 1947-48. Pres. bd. of trustees Utica Pub. Library, 1929-62. Temporary chmn. Dem. State Conv., 1927. Pres. N.Y. State Bar Assn., 1940. Charter mem. Am. Law Inst.; mem. Am. Judicature Soc., Am., N.Y. and Oneida County bar assns. Roman Catholic. Clubs: University (N.Y. City): Fort Schuyler, Sadaquada Golf (Utica). Home: 210 Rutger St Utica NY 13501 Office: First National Bank Bldg Utica NY 12101

KERNAN, WILLIAM JOHN, Jr., educator, physicist; b. Balt., Oct. 18, 1933; s. William John and Helen (Burgess) K.; B.S., Loyola Coll., Balt., 1955; M.S., U. Chgo., 1956, Ph.D., 1960; m. Delma Loane, Sept. 1, 1956; children—Lauren, Andrea, Mark. Asst. physicist Argonne Nat. Lab., 1960-61; asst. prof. N.Y.U., 1961-63; guest staff mem. Brookhaven Nat. Lab., 1960—; asso. prof. physics Ia. State U., Ames, 1963-66, prof. physics, 1966—; physicist Ames Lab. U.S. AEC, 1963-66, sr. physicist, 1966-69, asst. div. chief, 1969—. Trustee, mem. sci. com. Univs. Research Assn., Inc. Fellow Am. Phys. Soc.; mem. Sigma Xi. Contbr. articles profl. jours. Home: 2524 Eisenhower Av Ames IA 50010

KERNER, FRED, book pub., author; b. Montreal, Can., Feb. 15, 1921; s. Sam and Vera (Goldman) K.; B.A., Sir George Williams U., Montreal, 1942; m. Jean Elizabeth Somerville, July 17, 1945 (div. Apr. 1951); 1 son. Jon Fredrik; m. 2d, Sally Dee Stouten, May 18, 1959; children—David, Diane. Asst. sports editor Montreal Gazette, 1942-44; news editor Canadian Press, Montreal, Toronto, N.Y.C., 1944-50; asst. night city editor A.P., N.Y.C., 1950-57; editor Hawthorn Books, Inc., N.Y.C., 1957-58, pres., editor-in-chief, 1965-67; exec. editor Crest-Premier Books, N.Y.C., 1958-63, editor-in-chief, 1963-64; pres. Centaur House, Inc., pubs., 1964-; pub. Fred Kerner/Pub Projects, 1967—; dir. book and ednl. divs. Reader's Digest (Can.), 1969—; v.p. Publitex Internat. Corp., pubs., 1968—; dir. Nat. Mint, Inc. Panelist various profl. confs. Mem. local sch. bd., N.Y.C., 1968-69. Chmn. pubs. com. Edward R. Murrow Meml. Fund. Mem. Canadian Authors Assn., Mystery Writers Am., Canadian Soc. Profl. Journalists, Authors Guild, Authors League Am., Am. Acad. Polit. and Social Sci., Internat. Platform Assn., Alumni Assn. Sir George Williams U. (exec. com. 197O—), Sigma Delta Chi. Clubs: Advertising, Deadline., Overseas Press, Dutch Treat (N.Y.C.); Toronto Men's Press; Author's (London, Eng.). Author: (with Leonid Kotkin) Eat, Think and be Slender, 1954; (with Walter M. Germain) The Magic Power of Your Mind, 1956; (with Joyce Brothers) Ten Days to a Successful Memory, 1957; Stress and Your Heart, 1961; (pseudonym Frederick Kerr) Watch Your Weight Go Down, 1962; (with Walter M. Germain) Secrets of Your Supraconscious, 1965; (with David Goodman) What's Best for Your ChildAnd You, 1966; (with Jesse Reid) Buy High, Sell Higher, 1966; (pseudonym M.N. Thaler) It's Fun to Fondue, 1968. Contbg. author: Successful Writers and How They Work, 1958; Words on Paper, 1960; Overseas Press Club Cookbook, 1964; Chambers Encyclopedia. Editor: Love is a Man's Affair, 1958; Treasury of Lincoln Quotations, 1965. Home: 400 Landsdowne Av Westmount Quebec Canada Office: 215 Redfern Westmount Quebec Canada

KERNER, GEORGE C., educator. Prof. philosophy Mich State U. Office: Dept Philosophy Mich State U East Lansing MI 48824*

KERNER, OTTO, judge; b. Chgo., Aug. 15, 1908; s. Otto and Rose Barbara (Chmelik) K.; A.B., Brown U., 1930; postgrad. Trinity Coll., Cambridge U., Eng., 1930-31; J.D., Northwestern U., 1934; hon. degrees, Brown U., Northwestern U., St. Procopius Coll., Lincoln Coll., Quincy Coll., McKendree Coll., Culver-Stockton Coll., So. Ill. U., Ill. Inst. Tech., Bradley U., Chgo.-Kent Coll. Law, Mundelein Coll., Drake U., Ill. State Coll.; m. Helena I. Cermak, Oct. 20, 1934; children—Anton J.C., Helene C. Admitted to Ill. bar, 1934; asso. with Cooke, Sullivan, & Ricks, 1934; became partner Kerner, Jaros & Tittle, law firm, 1935; U.S. dist atty. No. Dist. ill., 1947-54; county judge Cook County, 1954-61; gov. Ill., 1961-68; judge U.S. Ct. Appeals, Chgo., 1968—. Vice pres. Chgo. council, mem. 7th regional exec. council Boy Scouts Am., hon. commr. Chgo. council; dir. Bohemian Charitable Assn., Glenview United Fund, Cancer and Red Cross funds; mem. Chgo. Crime Prevention Council, 1950-53; chmn. Pres.'s Commn. on Civil Disorders, 1968. Trustee Brown U. Mem. Ill. N.G., 106th Cav., 1934-36; trans. to F.A., 1936, advancing from pvt. to capt., 1941, served to maj. gen., inf., 1941-46; PTO. Decorated Soldier's medal, Bronze Star. Recipient Silver Beaver, Silver Antelope, Silver Buffalo awards Boy Scouts Am. Mem. Am. (alternate del. 1948), Fed., Ill., Chgo., West Suburban bar assns., Bohemian Lawyers, Am. Judicature Soc., Mil. Order World Wars (1st vice comdr. 1946-47), Alpha Delta Phi, Phi Delta Phi. Democrat. Mason (33), Nat. Soujourner, Red Cross of Constantine, Moose, Odd Fellow, Royal Arcanum. Clubs: Commonwealth, Brown, Wayfarers, Legal, Law, Economic, Commercial, Saddle and Cycle (Chgo.). Home: 233 E Walton Chicago IL 60611 Office: 219 S Dearborn St Chicago IL 60604

KERNEY, JAMES, Jr., newspaper publisher; b. Trenton, N.J., Dec. 17, 1910; s. James and Sarah (Mullen) K.; student Lawrenceville Sch., 1925-29, Princeton, 1929-30; m. 2d, Betty Taylor Barrow; children (by previous marriage)—Ellen Regan, Mary, Regan, Lincoln. Reporter, Fall River (Mass.) Herald-News, 1929; with Wash. Bur., U.P.I., 1930-31, Newark Evening News, 1932; v.p., editor Trenton Times Corp. (pub. Trenton Times, Sunday Times-Advertiser), 1933-58; exec. v.p. Water Research Found., 1958-61; pub. Trenton Times Newspapers, 1962—, also editor; v.p., Manistique Pulp & Paper Co.; dir. Del. & Bound Brook R.R., Trenton-Princeton Traction Co. State dir. OPA, 1942-43; mem. Delaware River Port Authority, 1966-70, N.J. Constnl. Revision Com., 1941-42, 46-47; pres. Trenton Opera Assn., 1935-40, Mercer County Meml. Bldg. Com.; chmn. adv. com. Rutgers Sch. Journalism, 1938-48; v.p. Navy League, 1943-45, Sec. N.J. Econ. Devel. Council, 1944-48, State Dept. Edn., 1946-47; mem. N.J. Tax Policy Com., 1955-67; vice chmn. Interstate Com. on Del.; pres. exec. com. Trenton Coalition, 1968—; dir. Phila. 1976 Bicentennial Corp., 1968-70, Middlesex-Somerset-Mercer Regional Study Council, 1969—; mem. Tri-State Transp. Commn., 1970—. Dir. Nat. Conf. Christians and Jews, 1947-51; Am. Civil Liberties Union, 1952-55; vice chmn. Gov. Com. Civil Rights, 1949; Pulitzer Prize juror, 1948. Mem. Internat. Press Inst. (chmn. Am. com. 1954-58), Am. Liberal Assn. (pres. 1954-58), N.J. Jud. Council (chmn. com. on traffic rules and regulations 1947-49), Inst. Jud. Adminstrn. (fellow 1951-61), N.J. Jud. Conf., Am. Newspaper Pubs. Assn. (com. on journalism edn. 1969—), Nat. Alliance Businessmen (adv. bd. 1970—), Trenton-Mercer County C. of C. (pres. 1970—). Roman Catholic. Clubs: Trenton; Essex (Newark); Century, Racquet (Phila.). Home: 34 Fackler Rd R D 1 Trenton NJ 08648 Office: Trenton Times Newspapers Trenton NJ 08605

KERNKAMP, MILTON FREDRICK, educator, plant pathologist; b. St. Paul, Sept. 16, 1911; s. John Henry and Laura (Mahle) K.; B.S., U. Minn., 1934, M.S., 1938, Ph.D., 1941; m. Kathryn Griffith, June 27, 1936 (dec. May 1962); m. 2d, Marjorie Gerlich, Dec. 19, 1962. Faculty, U. Minn., 1936-41, 46— prof. plant pathology, 1956—, asst. dir. agrl. expt. sta., 1956-61, head dept. plant pathology, 1961—; plant pathologist Dept. Agr., Meridian, Miss., 1941-42, charge Coop. Rust Lab., St. Paul, 1961-67; collaborator U.S. Dept. Agr., 1961—. Served to capt. AUS, 1942-46; MTO. Mem. Am. Phytopath. Soc. (asso. editor jour. 1947-49, sec.-treas. 1948-51, v.p. 1952, pres. N. Central div. 1953, asst. bus. mgr.-treas. 1966-67, treas.-bus. mgr. 1967-70), A.A.A.S., Am. Assn. U. Profs., Minn. Acad. Sci., Am. Soc. Agronomy, Am. Inst. Biol. Scis., Sigma Xi, Gamma Alpha, Gamma Sigma Delta. Mem. editorial bd. Minn. Farm and Home Sci., 1949-52, chmn., 1957-61. Contbr. articles to profl. jours. Home: 2466 N Albert St St Paul MN 55113

KERNODLE, RIGDON WAYNE, sociologist, educator; b. Greensboro, N.C., 1919; s. William Edgar and Lena Florence (McClain) K.; A.A., Brevard Jr. Coll., 1941; B.A., U. N.C., 1943, M.A., 1945, Ph.D., 1949; m. Ruth Granbery Lynch, Feb. 22, 1945; children—Michael Wayne, Kathryn Ruth. Instr. sociology Coll. William and Mary, 1945-47, chmn., prof. dept. sociology, 1952—, Heritage prof., 1968. Teaching staff residency tng. program in psychiatry Eastern State Hosp. Mem. Am., So. (2d v.p.) sociol. socs., Nat. Council Family Relations, Internat. Congress on Social Psychiatry. Author: (with C.F. Marsh) Hampton Roads Communities in World War II, 1951; Last of Rugged Individualist, 1960; Unsolved Issues in American Society, 1960. Editor: The Sixth Decade of Our Century, 1959; Values, Decisions and the American Economy, 1961; Nonmedical Leaves From a Mental Hospital, 1966; The Aegelic Tennis Stroke, 1968. Home: 108 Governors Dr Williamsburg VA 23185

KERNS, ROLLAND EDWARD, electric utility exec.; b. Lincoln, Neb., Apr. 13, 1904; s. Charles Edward and Myrta (Hugg) K.; student Bard Coll., Annandale-on-Hudson, N.Y., 1923-26; m. Lilian Theo Looper, Sept. 23, 1926; 1 son, Richard R. With Okla. Gas and Electric Co., 1926—, sec., 1960—, treas., -, financial v.p., became 1968; now ret.; Assos., 1937—. Sec., Okla. Jr. C. of C., 1937-38. Chmn. investment com. Okla. Gas and Electric Retirement Plan, 1961—. Bd. dirs. Okla. Gas and Electric Found. Recipient Accounting award Edison Electric Inst., 1935; Brochure award Financial World Analysts, 1964. Mem. Inst. Internal Auditors Oklahoma City (charter), Internat. Accountants Soc. (life), Am. Soc. Corp. Secs., Okla. Soc. Financial Analysts, Oklahoma City, Okla. chambers commerce. Episcopalian (vestryman, treas., lay reader). Clubs: Economic, Exchange, Beacon, Quail Creek Country, Men's Dinner, Sooner Dinner (Oklahoma City). Home: 5817 N Barnes Av Oklahoma City OK 73112 Office: 321 N Harvey Av Oklahoma City OK 73101

KERR, ALBERT LOUIS, Jr., headmaster; b. Lawrence, Mass., Sept. 9, 1916; s. Albert Louis and Jennie (Burford) K.; grad. Phillips Andover Acad., 1935; A.B., Yale, 1939; Ed.M., Harvard, 1952; H.H.D., Bucknell U., 1969; m. Pamela Rae Morgan, Sept. 6, 1952; children—Stuart Hamilton, Jean Elizabeth. Tchr., Gilman Sch., Balt., 1939-40, 47-51, Cooperstown (N.Y.) Acad., 1940-42, Gov. Dummer Acad., South Byfield, Mass., 1953-57; headmaster Berwick Acad., South Berwick, Me., 1957-64, Peddie Sch., Hightstown, N.J., 1964—. Trustee Princeton Area United Fund, 1967—, Columbus Boychoir Sch., Princeton, 1969—; bd. dirs. Hightstown YMCA. Served as lt. USNR, 1942-46. Mem. Middle Atlantic States Assn. Colls. and Secondary Schs., N.J. Ind. Schs. Headmasters Assn., English-Speaking Union, Phi Delta Kappa. Club: Yale (N.Y.C.). Home: 321 S Main St Hightstown NJ 08520

KERR, ALEXANDER TAYLOR, labor union exec.; b. Weaver, Ill., Dec. 11, 1920; s. Robert and Isabella (Lang) K.; student N.Y. U., 1947-48; m. Mildred Agnes Kluber, Kluber, Oct. 6, 1945; children—Elaine Margaret, Robert Anthony, Susan Amy. Mem. Seafarers Internat. Union N.Am., AFL-CIO, 1943—, fiscal officer, officer, 1961-65, sec.-treas. Atlantic, Gulf, Lakes and Inland Waters div., 1962- 1962—; sec.-treas. Seafarers Port O'Call Club, Seafarers Balt. Port O'Call Corp., Seafarers Bldg. Corp., Seafarers Balt. Bldg. Corp., Seafarers Phila. Bldg. Corp., Seafarers La. Bldg. Corp., Seafarers Ill. Bldg. Corp., Log Press, Inc., Seafarers Washington Bldg. Corp., Seafarers Mich. Bldg. Corp., Seafarers Ala. Bldg. Corp., Seafarers Cal. Bldg. Corp., Welfare N.Y. Bldg. Corp., Welfare Phila. Bldg. Corp., Welfare Balt. Corp., Welfare Mobile Bldg. Corp., Welfare New Orleans Bldg. Corp., M.A.P. Norfolk Bldg. Corp., Welfare N.Y. Restaurant Corp., Welfare Balt. Restaurant Corp.; Seafarers Welfare Plan, Seafarers Vacation Plan, Seafarers Pension Plan, Seafarers Hiring Hall Fund Trust, United Indsl. Workers N.Am. Pension Plan, United Indsl. Workers N.Am. Welfare Plan. N.Y. Bldg. Corp., Welfare Phila. Bldg. Corp., Welfare Balt. Corp., Welfare Mobile Bldg. Corp., Welfare New Orleans Bldg. Corp., M.A.P. Norfolk Bldg. Corp., Welfare N.Y. Restaurant Corp. Welfare Balt Restaurant Corp.; Seafarers Welfare Plan, Seafarers Vacation Plan, Seafarers Pension Plan, Seafarers Hiring Hall Fund Trust, United Indsl. Workers N.Am. Pension Plan, United Indsl. Workers N.Am. Welfare Plan. Served with USNR, 1942- 44. Decorated Purple Heart. Mem. Am. Numis. Assn. Eagle, Moose. Home: 689 Oakley Pl Oradell NJ 07649 Office: 675 4th Av Brooklyn NY 11232

KERR, BARBARA, magazine editor; b. Boston; d. Barrett and Barbara (Higginson) Wendell; grad. Milton (Mass.) Acad., 1928; student Sorbonne, Paris, France, 1928-29; m. Horace H. Soule, Dec. 29, 1934 (div. 1938); 1 son, Christopher W.; m. 2d, Chester B. Kerr, July 8, 1944 (div. 1949); 1 son, Alexander. With publs. div. OWI, 1941-44, historian, 1944; editorial writer Boston Traveler, 1948-50; pub. affairs editor Woman's Home Companion mag., 1955-57; asso. producer WCBS-TV Views the Press, 1961-62; mng. editor Mademoiselle mag., 1962-68; asso. editor Seventeen magazine, 1968—. Mem. pub. affairs com. Nat. Bd. YWCA. Clubs: Cosmopolitan, Overseas Press (N.Y.C.). Contbr. articles nat. mags., free-lance writer. Editor: Ventures in Diplomacy (William Phillips), 1950. Home: 127 E 92d St New York City NY 10028 Office: Seventeen Mag 320 Park Av New York City NY 10022

KERR, BEN J., Jr., banker; b. Denison, Tex., June 14, 1918; s. Ben J. Kerr; B.S. in Bus., U. Okla., 1939; M.B.A., Harvard, 1941; m. Marrian Grace Hardie, Sept. 16, 1941; children—Ben J., III, Janet Lynn (Mrs. Norman W. Smith), Guy Hardie. Exec. sec. Richard Gill Co., San Antonio, 1951-53; wholesale rep. Nat. Securities and Research Corp., 1953—; with Mercantile Nat. Bank Dallas, 1953—, now sr. v.p., exec. trust officer; dir. Horn Blueprint Co., Beverly Hills, Inc., King Ranch Oil & Lignite Co.; thesis adviser Southwestern Grad. Sch. Banking. Pres. Dallas Estate Council, 1961-62. Exec. com. Dallas County Heart Assn. Served to lt. comdr. USNR, 1941-48. Mem. Am. Soc. Corp. Secretaries (pres. Dallas regional group, 1966-67), Dallas Assn. Security Dealers. Presbyn. Mason (Shriner). Club: Okla. Univ. (Dallas). Home: 444 Larchmont St Dallas TX 75205 Office: P O Box 5415 Dallas TX 75222

KERR, BREENE MITCHELL, geologist; b. Ada, Okla., Jan. 27, 1929; s. Robert Samuel and Grayce (Breene) K.; B.S. in Geology, Mass. Inst. Tech., 1951; spl. student U. Okla., 1950-51; m. Frances Shaffer McMillin, Mar. 24, 1951; children—Breene Mitchell, Katherine McMillin, Bradley Emerson. With Kerr-McGee Oil Industries, Inc., 1951-64, 67-69, mgr. land dept. oil and gas div., 1961-64, dir., 1957—; dep. asst. adminstr. NASA, 1964, asst. adminstr. for technology utilization, 1964-66, asst. adminstr. for policy analysis, 1966-67; v.p. Kerr McGee Chem. Corp., 1967-69; sr. partner Resource Analysis and Mgmt. Group, 1969—. Mem. corp. Mass. Inst. Tech., 1969—, mem. vis. com. dept. earth scis., 1963—, chmn. vis. com. dept. civil engring., 1970—, mem. corp. devel. com. chmn. bd. trustees Kerr Found. Served to 1st lt. AUS, 1951-53. Mem. Am. Assn. Petroleum Geologists, Am. Soc. Pub. Adminstrn. (council 1965-68), Mass. Inst. Tech. Alumni Assn. (v.p. 1968-70). Unitarian. Clubs: Mass. Inst. Tech. Okla. (past pres.); University (Washington). Home: Oklahoma City OK Office: First Nat Center Oklahoma City OK 73102

KERR, CHESTER BROOKS, publisher; b. Norwalk, Conn., Aug. 5, 1913; s. Chester M. and Mary (Seymour) K.; B.A., Yale, 1936, asso. fellow Berkeley Coll., Yale, 1950; children by previous marriages—John Seymour II, Philip, Alexander, and Chester Brooks; m. Joan Paterson Mills, 1964; step-children—Edwin S. Mills, Hilary Paterson Mills, Alison Mills. Editor, Harcourt, Brace & Co., 1936-40; dir. Atlantic Monthly Press, 1940-41; acting dir. U.S. Internat. Book Assn., 1946; v.p. Reynal & Hitchcock, 1947; dir. Survey of Am. U. Presses, 1948-49; sec. Yale U. Press, 1949-59, dir., 1959—; mem. adminstrv. bd. Papers of Benjamin Franklin, 1954-70; cons. Ford Found. univ. presses pub. program, 1956-63, 65-67. Chief book div. OWI, 1942-45; cons. asst. sec. state for information, 1951. Exec. com. Nat. Book Com., 1968—. Vice chmn. Conn. Vols. for Stevenson, 1952, co-chmn. New Haven McCarthy for Pres. Com., 1968. Trustee New Haven Free Pub. Library, 1953-70. Mem. Assn. Am. Univ. Presses (pres. 1965-67, dir. 1967-68). Am. Book Pubs. Council (dir. 1966-69), Clubs: Yale, Publishers Lunch, Grolier (N.Y.C.); Yale, Graduate, Elizabethan (New Haven). Home: 421 Humphrey St New Haven CT 06511 Office: Yale U Press New Haven CT 06520

KERR, CLARK, educator; b. Stony Creek, Pa., May 17, 1911; s. Samuel William and Caroline (Clark) K.; B.A., Swarthmore Coll., 1932, LL.D., 1952; M.A., Stanford, 1933; postgrad. London Sch. Econs., 1936, 39, Ph.D., U. Cal., 1939; LL.D., Harvard, 1958, Princeton, 1959, others; m. Catherine Spaulding, Dec. 25, 1934; children—Clark E., Alexander W., Caroline M. Traveling fellow Am. Friends Service Com., 1935-36; instr. econs. Antioch Coll., 1936-37; teaching fellow U. Cal., 1937-38; Newton Booth fellow, 1938-39; acting asst. prof. labor econs. Stanford, 1939-40; asst., later asso. prof., U. Wash., 1940-45; asso. prof., dir. Inst. Indsl. Relations, U. Cal. at Berkeley, 1945-52, chancellor, 1952-58, pres., 1958-67; chmn. Carnegie Commn. on Higher Edn., 1967—. Vice chmn. divs. War Labor Bd., 1943-45; nat. arbitrator Armour Co. and United Packing House Workers, 1945-52; impartial chmn. Waterfront Employers, Pacific Coast and Internat. Longshoremen's and Warehousemen's Union, 1946-47; pub. mem. Nat. WSB, 1950-51; various arbitrations in pub. utilities, newspaper, aircraft, canning, oil, local transport and other industries, 1942—. First vice chmn. Am. Council Edn., 1953-54; bd. dirs. Center for Advanced Study in Behavioral Sci. of Ford Found., 1953-61; adv. panel, Soc. Sci. Research, NSF, 1953-57; chmn. Armour Automation Commn., 1959—. Trustee Rockefeller Found. Mem. Am., Royal, Western econ. assns., Am. Acad. Arts and Scis., Indsl. Relations Research Assn., Nat. Acad. Arbitrators, Am. Assn. U. Profs., Kappa Sigma, Phi Beta Kappa. Mem. Soc. of Friends. Clubs: Bohemian, Pacific Union (San Francisco); California (Los Angeles); Cosmos (Washington); Century (N.Y.C.). Author: (with E. Wight Bakke), Unions, Management and the Public, 1948, rev. edit. 1960; (with Dunlop, Harrison, Myers) Industrialism and Industrial Man, 1960, rev. edit., 1964; The Uses of the University, 1963; Labor and Management in Industrial Society, 1964; Marshall, Marx and Modern Times, 1968. Contbr. Am. Jour. Sociology, Quar. Jour. Econs., Fortune, Atlantic Monthly, Harvard Bus. Rev., Am. Econ. Rev., Rev. Econs. and Statistics. Home: 8300 Buckingham Dr El Cerrito CA 94530

KERR, DEBORAH, actress; b. Helensburgh, Scotland, Sept. 30, 1921; d. Arthur Kerr-Trimmer; student Helensburgh schs., Northumberland House Sch., Bristol; m. Anthony C. Bartley, Nov. 28, 1945 (div. 1959); children—Melanie, Jane, Francesca; m. 2d, Peter Viertel, July 23, 1960. Began motion picture career in England in Major Barbara, 1940; has appeared in Love on the Dole, Hatter's Castle, The Day Will Dawn, The Avengers, Perfect Strangers, Colonel Blimp, I See a Dark Stranger; came to U.S. 1947; has appeared in Black Narcissus, The Hucksters, Edward, My Son, King Solomon's Mines, Quo Vadis, Thunder in the East, Prisoner of Zenda, Julius Caesar, Dream Wife, Young Bess, From Here to Eternity, The End of the Affair, 1955. Appeared on stage in Heartbreak House, 1943. Gaslight (for Brit. troops in Europe), 1945, Tea and Sympathy, 1954-55, Proud and Profane, 1956; The King and I, 1956; Heaven Knows Mr. Alison, 1956; Bonjour Tristesse, 1958; Count Your Blessings, 1959; The Journey, 1959; Beloved Infidel, 1959; The Grass Is Greener, 1960; The Sundowners, 1960 (recipient Don N.Y. Critics Award 1960); The Naked Edge, 1961; Chalk Garden, 1964; Night of the Iguana, 1964; Marriage on the Rocks, 1965; Casino Royale, 1967; The Gypsy Moths; The Arrangement. Recipient of the Sarah Siddons award as Chgos. actress of the year. Home: Pacific Palisades CA 90210 Office: 20th Century Fox Ltd Beverly Hills CA 90210

KERR, EDMUND H., lawyer; b. Pitts., Nov. 27, 1924; s. Edmund H. and F. Josephine (Collins) K.; A.B., Stanford, 1949, LL.B. (mng. editor Law Rev. 1950-51), 1951; m. Jane Richard, Oct. 30, 1954; children—Susan, Daniel; m. 2d. Loretta Silano, May 1, 1968; children—Richard, Jill, Susan, Jennifer. Admitted to N.Y. bar, 1951, since practiced in N.Y.C.; partner firm Cleary, Gottlieb, Steen & Hamilton, 1962—. Sec., Abacus Fund, Inc.; dir. Franklin Custodian Funds. Inc., Holmes Protection, Inc., Express Fund. Bd. visitors Stanford Law Sch. Served with inf. AUS, World War II. Decorated Purple Heart with oak leaf cluster. Mem. Am., N.Y. bar assns., N.Y. County Lawyers Assn., Order of Coif. Contbr. articles to profl jours. Home: 27 Prospect Park W Brooklyn NY 11215 Office: 1 State Street Plaza New York City NY 10004

KERR, ELIZABETH MARGARET, educator; b. Sault Ste. Marie, Mich., Jan. 25, 1905; d. John Arthur and Katherine (Hirth) Kerr; B.A., U. Minn., 1926, M.A., 1927, Ph.D., 1941. Instr. English, Tabor Coll., 1929-30, U. Minn., 1930-37, 38-43, Coll. St. Catherine, 1937-38; asst. prof. Rockford (Ill.) Coll., 1943-45; instr., then asso. prof. Wis. State Coll., Milw., 1945-56; mem. faculty U. Wis.-Milw., 1956-70, prof. English, 1959-70, prof. emeritus, 1970—. Mem. Modern Lang. Assn., Midwest Modern Lang. Assn., Sigma Tau Delta, Phi Kappa Phi. Author: Bibliography of the Sequence Novel, 1950; Yoknapatawpha: Faulkner's Little Postage Stamp of Native Soil, 1969; also articles. Co-editor: Aspects of American English, 2d edit., 1971. Address: 4259 N Sercombe Rd Milwaukee WI 63216

KERR, ELMORE COE, Jr., art dealer; b. N.Y., Sept. 3, 1914; s. E. Coe and Marian (Myth) K.; grad. St. Paul's Sch., 1933; B.A., Yale, 1937; student Command and Gen. Staff Coll., 1944; m. Sarah Nichols, Sept. 27, 1947 (dec. 1965); 1 son, E. Coe III; m. 2d, Anne Wright Baxter, Aug. 19, 1966. With Knoedler & Co., N.Y.C., 1937—, beginning as asst. print dept., dir., 1948, pres., 1957-69; pres. Coe Kerr Gallery Inc. (art dealers), 1969—; Uptown adv. bd. Chem. Bank Bd. dirs. Fedn. des Alliances Francaise. Served from pvt. to lt. col. AUS, 1941-46. Decorated Bronze Star with cluster; Croix de Guerre (France). Home: 68 Woods Lane East Hampton NY 11937 Office: 49 E 82d St New York City NY 10028

KERR, EWING THOMAS, U.S. dist. judge; b. Bowie, Tex., Jan. 21, 1900; s. George N. and Ellen H. (Wisdom) K.; B.A., U. Okla., 1923; B.S., Central Coll., Okla., 1923; postgrad. U. Colo., 1925; m. Ellen Irene Peterson, Feb. 22, 1933; children—Hugh Neal, Judith Ann. Prin. Jr. High Sch., Hominy, Okla., 1923-25, Cheyenne Pub. Schs. 1925-27; admitted to Wyo. bar, 1927; practice at Cheyenne, 1927-29; asst. U.S. dist. atty. for Wyo., 1930-33; apptd. atty. gen. for Wyo. 1939-43; atty. for Wyo. Senate, 1943; U.S. dist. judge Dist. Wyo., Cheyenne, 1955—. Served as maj. AUS, with Allied Commn. in Italy; head Legal Div. in area; reorganized civilian cts. in Austria, 1945. Mem. Wyo. State Bar Assn., Cheyenne C. of C. Republican. Presbyn. Mason (past master lodge, past grand master lodge, 33), Rotarian. Home: 2951 Spruce Dr Cheyenne WY 82001 Office: P O Bldg Cheyenne WY 82001

KERR, GRAHAM, TV entertainer; b. London, Eng., 1934; m. Treena Van Doorne; 3 children. Past mgr. Royal Ascot Hotel, London; chief catering adviser to Royal New Zealand Air Force; star TV series The Galloping Gourmet. Author: Graham Kerr Cookbook by the Galloping Gourmet, 1970. Address: care Dir Pub Relations Fremantle of Can Ltd 257 Jarvis St Toronto Ontario Canada*

KERR, HARRISON, composer; b. Cleveland, O., Oct. 13, 1897; s. Harrison and Elizabeth (Rettig) K.; grad. Cleveland (O.) high schs., 1916; student Conservatoirie Americain de Fontainebleau, France, 1921; m. Jeanne McHugh, Aug. 30, 1928. Dir. music, Greenbrier Coll., Lewisburg, W.Va., 1927-28, Chase Sch., Brooklyn, N.Y., 1928-35; editor of Trend, illustrated bi-monthly of the arts, 1932-35; sec. Am. Composers Alliance, since 1937; exec. sec. Am. Music Center, 1940-47; chief Music, Art and Exhibit Sect., Reorientation Br., Civil Affairs Div., Dept. of Army, 1946-49; dean Coll. Fine Arts, U. Okla., 1949-64, prof., composer in residence, 1960-68, emeritus, 1968—. Mem. exec. bd. Nat. Music Council; mem. bd. dirs. Am. Music Center; mem. Music Adv. Com. U.N.E.S.C.O.; formerly sec. and mem. bd. dirs. Nat. Music League. Recent performances of larger compositions in Austria, Hungary, Germany, Japan, Korea, Thailand, various South Am. Countries and U.S. Compositions include 3 symphonies and other orchestral works, chamber music and many shorter pieces. Home: 1014 E Louisiana St Norman OK 73069

KERR, HAWLEY COE, former oil co. exec.; b. Tulsa, Nov. 12, 1901; s. Charles William and Annie Elizabeth (Coe) K.; A.B., U. Tulsa, 1922; LL.B., U. Okla., 1925; m. Marguerite Carmen Baca, Dec. 30, 1939; children—Stephen Pendaries, Michael Hawley. Admitted to Okla. bar, 1925, U.S. Supreme Ct. bar, 1949; gen. practice, Tulsa, 1925-37; mem. legal staff Skelly Oil Co., Tulsa, 1937-70, gen. counsel, 1960-66, corp. sec., 1961-66, cons. atty., 1967-70, corp. sec., 1967-70; sec., dir. Skelly Pipe Line Co.; sec.-treas., dir. Skelly Internat. Oil Co.; sec. Skelly Oil Co. of Iran, 1964-70; dir. Hawkeye Chem. Co., Clinton, Ia. Adv. bd. Internat. Oil & Gas Ednl. Center. Served to lt. col. USAAF, 1942-45. Mem. Am., Okla., Tulsa County bar assns., Ind. Producers Assn., Am. Petroleum Inst., Mid-Continent Oil and Gas Assn., Tulsa C. of C., Sigma Alpha Epsilon. Presbyn. Club: Tulsa. Author treatise. Home: 3153 S Utica St Tulsa OK 74105

KERR, HERBERT T., corp. exec.; b. Dobbs Ferry, N.Y., Aug. 1, 1921; s. James and Annie (Allen) K.; B.S. in Commerce, Rider Coll.; m. June Marilyn Zamek, May 25, 1957; children—Pamela Judith, Thomas Mason. Sr. mem. tax audit and services staff Ernst & Ernst, N.Y.C., 1949-55; with U.S. Industries, Inc., N.Y.C., 1955—, v.p., controller, v.p., treas., 1962-69, sr. v.p., 1969-70, exec. v.p., 1970—, also dir.; dir. Health Industries, Inc. Served with USAAF, 1942-45. Episcopalian (sr. warden). Home: Hudson Rd W Ardley-on-Hudson NY 10503 Office: 529 Fifth Av New York City NY 10017

KERR, HUGH THOMSON, editor, educator; b. Chgo., July 1, 1909; s. Hugh Thomson and Olive May (Boggs) K.; A.B., Princeton, 1931; B.D., Western Theol. Sem., Pitts., 1934; M.A., U. Pitts., 1934; Ph.D., U. Edinburgh (Scotland), 1936; m. Dorothy DePree, Dec. 28, 1938; 1 son, Stephen T. Ordained to ministry Presbyn. Ch., 1934; from instr. to prof. doctrinal theology Louisville Presbyn. Theol. Sem., 1936-40; prof. systematic theology Princeton Theol. Sem., 1940—, chmn. dept. theology, 1949-56, chmn. grad. study com., 1957—, adv. council dept. religion, 1954—, dir. Westminster Found. of univ., 1954—; asso. editor Theology Today quar., 1944-50, editor, 1950—. Del. for N.Am., World Alliance Reformed Chs., 1954—; mem. commn. on women World Council Chs., 1950-54, del. faith and order conf., 1957; chmn. com. curriculum Council Theol. Edn., 1949-53; mem. coms. marriage and divorce, ordination of women Presbyn. Ch., 1955-57. Guggenheim fellow, 1960. Mem. Am. Theol. Soc., Soc. Bibl. Lit. and Exegesis, Nat. Assn. Bib. Instrs., Am. Ch. History Soc., Duodecim (Hazen Found.). Author: A Compend of Calvin's Institutes, 1938 (in Japanese 1958); A Compend of Luther's Theology, 1943; Positive Protestantism: An Interpretation of the Gospel, 1950 (in Japanese 1954); Mystery and Meaning in the Christian Faith, 1958; What Divides Protestants Today, 1958; By John Calvin, 1960; Readings in Christian Thought, 1966. Editor: Sons of the Prophets, 1963. Contbr. numerous articles to profl. jours., chpts. to books. Home: 707 Rosedale Rd Princeton NJ 08540

KERR, JAMES ROBERT, mfr.; b. Las Vegas, N.M., Sept. 23, 1917; s. Louis Alexander and Mary Louise (Lynch) K.; student Pasadena City Coll.; m. Colleen Warrick, Sept. 18, 1943; children—Mary Lou, Cathy S., James R., William L. Commd. 2d lt. USAF, 1942, advanced through grades to col., 1954, now col. res.; dir. West Coast office Avco Corp., 1954-56, v.p. charge def. planning N.Y. office, 1956-57, pres. Lycoming div., 1957-60, pres. research and advanced devel. div., 1958-6O, dir. corp., 1959—, exec. v.p., 1960-61, pres., 1961—, chief operating officer, 1961-70, chief exec. officer, 1970—; chmn. bd., dir. Avco Bradcasting Corp., 1964; dir. Avco Financial Services, Republic Steel Corp., Corp., Paul Revere Life Ins. Co., Paul Revere Variable Annuity Ins. Co., Carte Blanche Corp., Rancho Bernardo. Bd. dirs. Sacred Heart U., trustee Nat. Safety Council; chmn. bd. advisers Merrimack Coll.; trustee Nat. Security Indsl. Assn. Decorated knight of St. Gregory. Mem. Aerospace Industries Assn. (dir.). Clubs: Metropolitan (N.Y.C.); LaJolla Country; Blind Brook (Port Chester, N.Y.); George Town (Washington); Economic N.Y., New York Yacht. Home: 1175 Muirlands Dr LaJolla CA 92037 Office: 1275 King St Greenwich CT 06830

KERR, JAMES W., pipe line co. exec.; b. Hamilton, Ont., Can., Mar. 11, 1914; s. George Robert and Helen Robertson (Bews) K.; B.Sc., U. Toronto; m. Ruth Eleanor Marrs, Oct. 5, 1940; children—David, Barbara. Various positions with Canadian Westinghouse Co., 1937-58, v.p., gen. mgr. apparatus products group, 1956-58; pres., chief exec. officer Trans Can. PipeLines, Toronto, 1958-61, chmn. bd., pres., 1961-68, chmn., chief exec. officer, 1968—; pres., dir. Banner Petroleums, Internat. Pipeline Engring; Ltd., TransCanada Gas Products, Western PipeLines; dir. Mfrs. Life Ins., Gt. Lakes Gas Transmission Co., Canadian Imperial Bank Commerce, Bell Canada. Former pres. Bd. Trade Met. Toronto. Bd. govs., v.p. trustee Queen Elizabeth Hosp., Toronto; bd. govs. Ont. Research Found. Served as squadron leader RCAF, 1942-45. Mem. Bd. Trade Met. Toronto (past pres.), Canadian (past pres.), Am. (dir.) gas assns., Assn. Profl. Engrs. Province of Ont. Clubs: York, Toronto, Hamilton, Rosedale Golf. Home: 5 Old Forest Hill Rd Toronto 7 Ontario Canada Office: 150 Eglinton Av E Toronto 12 Ontario Canada

KERR, JEAN, writer; b. Scranton, Pa., July 1923; d. Thomas J. and Kitty (O'Neill) Collins; M.F.A., Cath. U. Am., 1945; L.H.D., Northwestern U., 1962; L.H.D., Fordham U., 1965; m. Walter Kerr, Aug. 16, 1943; children—Christopher, John and Colin (twins), Gilbert, Gregory, Katharine. Author: (play) Jenny Kissed Me, 1949; Touch and Go, 1950; (play) King of Hearts (with Eleanor Brooke), 1954; Please Don't Eat the Daisies, 1957; The Snake Has All The Lines, 1960; (play) Mary, Mary, 1961; (play) Poor Richard, 1964;

Penny Candy, 1970. Recipient Campion award, 1971; Laetare medal, 1971. Democrat. Roman Catholic. Home: 1 Beach Av Larchmont NY 10538

KERR, JOHN, actor; lawyer; b. N.Y.C., Nov. 15, 1931; s. Geoffrey and June (Walker) K.; B.A., Harvard; J.D., U. Cal. at Los Angeles; m. Priscilla Smith; 3 children. Appeared in summer stock and on TV; Broadway performances include Bernardine, South Pacific, Tea and Sympathy, All Summer Long; films include The Cobweb, Gaby, Tea and Sympathy, The Vintage, South Pacific, Girl of The Night, Pit and the Pendulum, Seven Women from Hell; appeared in TV serial Peyton Place; asso. law firm Tyre & Kamins, Los Angeles. Office: 1800 Century Park E Los Angeles CA 90067

KERR, JOHN HARLAN, lawyer, business exec.; b. Cleve., July 27, 1908; s. Clarence Vincent and Myrtle (Harlan) K; A.B., Princeton, 1930; LL.B., Western Res. U., 1933; m. Betty Jeffries, Sept. 3, 1938 (dec.); children—Catharine E., Jacqueline J.; m. 2d, Mildred Knouff, Nov. 18, 1963. Admitted to Ohio bar, 1933; asso. Squire, Sanders & Dempsey, Cleve. 1933-40; atty. Am. Steel & Wire Co., 1940-44, gen. atty., sec., 1944-46; sec. Lake Superior & Ishpeming R.R. Co., 1946-50; counsel, sec. Cleve. Cliffs Iron Co., 1946-59, v.p., 1952-59, also officer or dir. various subsidiaries; sec. Thompson Ramo Wooldridge, Inc., 1959-60, v.p., gen. counsel, 1960-68; counsel TRW, Inc., 1968—. Republican precinct committeeman, Cleve. Trustee Goodrich Social Settlement, 1949-55; trustee Western Reserve U., 1953-57, vice chmn. bd. govs., 1957-60; trustee Cleve. Play House Found. Mem. Am., Ohio State, Cleve. bar assns., Am. Judicature Soc., Am. Iron and Steel Inst., Cleve. C. of C., U. Sch. Alumni Assn. (pres. 1950-51), Am. Soc. Corp. Secs. (pres. Cleve. group 1957-58), Phi Delta Phi. Republican. Presbyn. Clubs: Kirtland (O.); Union (Cleve.); Princeton (N.Y.C.); Mid-Ocean (Bermuda). Home: Sherwin Rd Willoughby OH 44094 summer Ambleside Camden North Paget East Bermuda

KERR, MALCOLM HOOPER, educator, polit. scientist; b. Beirut, Lebanon, Oct. 8, 1931 (parents Am. citizens); s. Stanley E. and Elsa (Reckman) K.; A.B., Princeton, 1953; M.A., Am. U. Beirut, 1955; Ph.D., Johns Hopkins, 1958; m. Ann C. Zwicker, Aug. 18, 1956; children—Susan Elizabeth, John Malcolm, Stephen Douglas, Andrew Stanley. Asst. prof. Am. U. Beirut, 1958-61; faculty U. Cal. at Los Angeles, 1961—, prof. polit. sci., 1967—, chmn. dept., 1967-70; vis. prof. Am. U. Beirut, 1965-66. Bd. dirs. Am. Friends of Middle East, 1969—. Rockefeller fellow St. Antony's Coll., Oxford U. (Eng.), 1961-62; fellow Am. Research Center Egypt, 1964-65. Mem. Am. Polit. Sci. Assn., Middle East Studies Assn. (v.p. 1968-69). Author: Lebanon in the Last Years of Feudalism, 1840-1868, 1959; Islamic Reform, 1965; The Arab Cold War, 3d edit., 1971. Home: 1421 Chautaugua Blvd Pacific Palisades CA 90272 Office: Dept Polit Sci U Cal Los Angeles CA 90024

KERR, PAUL FRANCIS, univ. prof.; b. Hemet, Calif., Jan. 12, 1897; s. Joseph and Emma (Fowler) K.; B.S., Occidental Coll., 1919, D.Sc., 1960; Ph.D., Stanford U., 1923; m. Helen Richardson Squire, Sept. 2, 1924; children—Paul Squire, Ruth (Mrs. William Jakoby), Nancy (Mrs. Peter Del Grande). Instr. mineralogy and geology, Stanford, 1923-24, acting asst. prof., summer sessions, 1924-31; instr. Columbia, 1924-26, asst. prof., 1926-32, asso. prof., 1932-40, prof. mineralogy, 1940—, Newberry prof., 1952—, prof. emeritus, 1965—, acting exec. officer dept. of geology, spring 1942, exec. officer, 1944-50, research coordinator, 1950—; vis. Carnegie prof. S.A., 1941; guest prof. U. Oslo (Norway), 1960; cons. Manhattan Project, 1944; panel on geology, Research Devel. Bd., 1947-49; Clay Mineral Standards Project, Am. Petroleum Inst., 1948-50. Served in U.S. Army, 1918. Tech. cons. Army-Navy Munitions Bd., 1942-43. Chmn. com. on Internat. Inspection Radioactive Minerals, Carnegie Endowment for Internat. peace, 1946; UN cons. to review uranium occurrences at Geneva Conf. on Peaceful Uses of Atomic Energy, 1955. Recipient K.C. Li award outstanding work field of tungsten, 1957. Fellow Geol. Soc. Am. (v.p. 1947), Am. Geog. Soc., Mineral. Soc. Am. (sec. 1933-43, pres. 1946); mem. Soc. Econ. Geology, Am. Inst. Mining Engrs., N.Y. Acad. Science, A.A.A.S. (chmn. geol. and geog. div. 1956) Clay Minerals Soc. (distinguished mem.), Mineral Soc. Great Britain, Geol. Soc. Belgium (corr.), Bavarian Acad. Sci., Sigma Xi, Phi Beta Kappa. Methodist. Mason. Club: Men's Faculty (Columbia U.); N.Y. Mineralogical (pres. 1926-27). Author: Thin Section Mineralogy, 1933; Optical Mineralogy, 1941; Tungsten Mineralization in U.S., 1946; Natural Occurrence of Uranium and Thorium, 1955; Uranium Alteration and Mineralization, Marysvale, Utah, 1957. Co-author: Mineral Recognition, 1967. Contbr. articles to tech. jours. and publs. Cons. on applications of geology and mineralogy; Orton Lectr. Am. Ceramic Soc., 1938. Study of Uranium-bearing veins AEC. Home: 501 W 120th St New York City NY 10027

KERR, ROBERT AIRDRIE, banker; b. Haverstraw, N.Y., May 15, 1920; s. William Ambercrombie and Edna (Cooper) K.; B.A., Hamilton Coll., 1940; m. Twyliah Hamstreet, Dec. 21, 1956; children—William Abercrombie, Robert Airdrie, Alexander Knight. With Irving Trust Co., N.Y.C., 1947-71, sr. v.p., 1965-71, head nat. div., 1966-68; pres. Winters Nat. Bank and Trust Co., 1968—; dir. American Transp. Enterprises, Inc., N.Y.C. Trustee, Inc. Village of Tuxedo Park, N.Y., 1960-64, Trustee Hamilton Coll., 1958—, chmn. budget and finance com., 1964—; trustee Tuxedo Park Sch., 1961—. Served to lt. comdr. USNR, 1941-45, 51-52. Mem. Delta Upsilon Clubs: Tuxedo; Sky (N.Y.C.); Moraine Country (Kettering, O.). Home: 449 Glenridge Rd Kettering OH 45429 Office: 40 N Main St Dayton OH 45402

KERR, THOMAS, flour milling exec.; b. Portland, Ore., May 1, 1910; s. Thomas and Mabel (Macleay) K.; B.A., Yale, 1932; m. Barbare Pooley, Jan. 26, 1948; children—Edmund Edmund Randolph Labbe, Thomas, Josephine Sheldon. Pres. Kerr Gifford Co., Portland, 1932-55, Kerr Grain Corp., Portland, 1955—, Hawaiian Flour Mills, Inc., Honolulu, 1963—, Helix Milling Co., Portland, 1942—; v.p., dir. Port San Francisco Grain Terminal, Inc., 1958—; pres., owner Kerr-Peters Inc., 1967—; partner Plateau Farms; pres. Kerr Land & Livestock Co., 1968—; dir. Stockmens Life Ins. Co., U.P. R.R., Oregon Bank, Fidelity Savs & Loan, San Francisco, Penninsula Savs & Loan, Umatilla Palletti Container Co. Pres. Portland Grain Exchange, 1940, 48; chmn. Pacific Internat. Livestock Assn., 1964—; mem. White House Conference Export Expansion, 1963-64; dir. Portland Met. Futures, Unlimited, 1963—. Trustee Reed Coll., Thacher Sch.; bd. dirs. Portland Symphony Soc., Ore. Roadside Council, Ore. Museum Sci. and Industry. Maj. AUS, 1942-45; PTO. Decorated Bronze Star. Mem. Portland (dir.), British-Am. (dir.) chambers commerce, Portland Freight Traffic Assn. (dir., past chmn.), Pacific Millers Assn. (past pres.), Japan Soc. Ore. (past pres., dir.), Yale Alumni Assn. Ore. (past pres.). Clubs: Merchants Exchange (Portland and San Francisco); Rotary, Arlington, University, Waverly Country, Racquet, Oswego Hunt (Portland); Pacific Union, Burlingame Country (San Francisco); Rainier (Seattle); Vancouver, Capilano Golf and Country (Vancouver, B.C., Can.). Home: 11648 SW Military Lane Portland OR 97219 Office: World Trade Bldg Portland OR 97204

KERR, THOMAS JEFFERSON, IV, coll. pres.; b. Columbus, O., Oct. 8, 1933; s. Thomas Jefferson and Ruth Glenora (Powell) K.; B.S., Cornell U., 1956; M.A., U. Buffalo, 1959; Ph.D. (univ. fellow), Syracuse U., 1965; m. Donna Jean Lawton, June 11, 1955; children—Thomas Jefferson V, Cheryl Lee, Kathleen Anne. Asst. prof. then prof. history Otterbein Coll., Westerville, O., 1963-71, acting acad. dean, 1969-70, pres., 1971—. Mem. Franklin County Draft Bd., 1969-71. Recipient Cokesbury Grad. Coll. Teaching award, 1963. Mem. Am. Hist. Assn., Orgn. Am. Historians, Am. Assn. Univ. Profs., Labor Historians, Ohio Acad. History, Phi Kappa Phi, Kappa Phi Kappa, Omicron Chi Epsilon, Phi Eta Sigma. Republican. Methodist. Mason, Rotarian. Home: 111 N West St Westerville OH 43081

KERR, WALTER F., drama critic, author; b. Evanston, Ill., July 8, 1913; s. Walter Sylvester and Esther (Daugherty) K.; B.S. in Speech, Northwestern U., 1937, M.A., 1938, L.H.D., 1962; LL.D., St. Mary's, Notre Dame, D.Litt., LaSalle, 1956; D.Litt., Fordham U., 1965, Notre Dame U., 1968; m. Jean Collins, Aug. 16, 1943; children—Christopher, Colin, John, Gilbert, Gregory, Katharine. Instr. speech and drama Cath. U., Washington, 1938-45, asso. prof. drama, 1945-49; dir. in profl. theatre Sing Out, Sweet Land, 1944 (Theatre Guild); Touch and Go (George Abbott), King of Hearts (Elaine Perry); drama critic Commonweal, 1950-52, N.Y. Herald Tribune, 1951-66; drama critic N.Y. Times, 1966—; specialism drama theory, criticism; drama cons. Saudek Assos., in television. Recipient George Jean Nathan award, 1964; Dineen award Nat. Cath. Theatre Conf., 1966; Iona award, 1970; Campion award, 1971; Laetare medal, 1971. Mem. N.Y. Critics' Circle (pres. 1955-57). Author: (plays) Sing Out, Sweet Land; Touch and Go; (books) How Not to Write a Play, 1955; Criticism and Censorship, 1957; Pieces at Eight, 1958; The Decline of Pleasure, 1962; The Theatre in Spite of Itself, 1963; Tragedy and Comedy, 1967; Thirty Plays Hath November, 1969. Contbr. articles to profl. publs. Home: 1 Beach Av Larchmont Manor NY 10538 Office: 230 W 41st St New York City NY 10018

KERR, WILLIAM, educator; b. Sawyer, Kan., Aug. 19, 1919; s. William and Maria Louise (Gill) K.; B.S. in Elec. Engring., U. Tenn., 1942, M.S., 1947; Ph.D., U. Mich., 1954; m. Ruth Duncan, Apr. 28, 1945; children—William Duncan, John Gill, Scott Winston. Instr., asst. prof. U. Tenn., 1942-44, 46-48; faculty U. Mich., Ann Arbor, 1948—, prof. nuclear engring., 1958—, chmn. dept., 1961—, acting dir. Mich. Meml.-Phoenix Project, 1961-65, dir., 1965—, project supr. AID-Nuclear Nuclear Energy Project, 1956-65. Cons. Atomic Power Devel. Assos., 1954—, Argonne Nat. Lab., Colo. Commn. on Higher Edn.; chmn. nuclear engring. edn. com. Asso. Midwest Univs., 1961-62, pres., 1966-67, bd. dirs., 1965-67; trustee Argonne Univs. Assn., 1965—. Mem. Am. Soc. Engring. Edn., I.E.E.E., Am. Nuclear Soc., Sigma Xi, Eta Kappa Nu, Phi Kappa Phi, Tau Beta Pi. Home: 2009 Hall St Ann Arbor MI 48104

KERR, WILLIAM ALEXANDER, glass co. exec.; b. Pasadena, Cal., Jan. 5, 1915; s. Alexander Hewitt and Ruth (Kalbus) K.; B.S. in Bus. Adminstrn., U. So. Cal., 1936, postgrad. in chem. engring., 1936-37; m. Beverly Lucille Kendall, Apr. 30, 1944; children—Constance (Mrs. John A. McDonald), William Bruce, David Alexander. Capt., check pilot Trans World Airlines, 1941-51; asst. dir. flight dept. Northrop Aircraft, Inc., 1952-57; with Kerr Glass Mfg. Corp., Los Angeles, 1937-41, 57—, v.p. prodn. and finance, 1957-67, pres., 1967—, also chmn. bd.; dir. Kerr Sport Shop Inc., Olympic Wholesale Sporting Goods Inc. Bd. dirs. Valley Cathedral Inc., Northridge, Cal. (v.p. 1968—), Canary Island Gospel Mission, A.H. Kerr Benevolent Assn. Mem. Glass Container Mfrs. Inst. (trustee). Republican. Presbyn. (elder). Home: 16183 Royal Oak Rd Encino CA 91316 Office: 611 S Shatto Pl Los Angeles CA 90005

KERR, WILLIAM D., investment banker. With firm Bacon, Whipple & Co., Chgo., 1927-60, partner, 1930-60; gen. partner Wertheim & Co., N.Y.C., 1960—. Mem. Investment Bankers Assn. Am. (chmn. central states 1954-55; nat. gov. 1955-57, v.p., 1958-59 pres. 1959-60); dir. Alterman Foods, Inc., Atlanta. Gov. Assn. Stock Exchange Firms. Clubs: Bond (pres. 1956), Chicago (Chgo.); Bond, Blind Brook (N.Y.C.); Augusta Nat. Golf. Home: 35 E 75th St New York City NY 10021 Office: One Chase Manhattan Plaza New York City NY 10005

KERR, WILLIAM LEVINSON, lawyer; b. Van Horn, Tex., June 5, 1904; s. Monroe T. and Mattie (King) K.; student Tex. Christian U., 1922-24, U. Tex., 1924-25; LL.B., Cumberland U., 1927; m. Frances Hubbard, Feb. 28, 1929; children—William Monroe, Theodore Morris. Admitted to Tex. bar, 1927; practiced in Pecos, 1927-42, Midland, 1944-; dist. atty., 109th Judical Dist. Tex., 1933-41, dist. judge, 1942-44; partner Kerr, Fitz-Gerald & Kerr. Dir. Midland Savs. Assn. Past chmn. bd. State Tchrs. Colls. Tex. Fellow Am. Coll. Trial Lawyers, Am. Coll. Probate Counsel; mem. Am. Bar Assn., State Bar Tex. (pres. 1961-62), Am., Tex. bar founds. Rotarian. Home: 1200 Country Club Dr. Midland TX 79701 Office: Midland Tower Bldg Midland TX 79701

KERR, WILLIAM SLEIGH, coll. ofcl.; b. Portland, Ore., Dec. 11, 1911; s. Duncan John and Elizabeth (Muir) K.; student St. Paul Acad., U. Minn., 1932-36; m. Nan Netsch, Mar. 5, 1949; children—Andrew D., William Sleigh III, Elizabeth Nan. With the C.B. & Q. R.R. Co., 1936-54, exec. asst. to pres., 1949-54; v.p., bus. mgr. Northwestern U., Evanston, Ill., 1954—; dir. 1st Fed. Savs. & Loan Assn. Chgo., State Nat. Bank of Evanston, Chgo. & Eastern Ill. R.R., No. Ill. Gas. Bd. dirs. James C. King Home. Mem. Joint Brazil-U.S. Econ. Devel. Commn., 1952-53. Served as lt. col. AUS, 1942-45; CBI. Mem. Am. Ry. Engrs. Assn., Am. Soc. Mil. Engrs., Newcomen Soc., Chi Psi, Tau Beta Pi, Omicron Kappa Upsilon. Republican. Presbyn. Clubs: Chicago, Lake Shore, Commercial, Economic, Tavern, Executives (Chgo.); Glenview (Ill.); University (Evanston). Home: 2437 Sheridan Rd Evanston IL 60436

KERR, H. C., lawyer; b. Toronto, Ont., Can., Oct. 29, 1927; B.A., U. Toronto; LL.B., Osgoode Hall. Admitted to Ont. bar, 1955; now partner firm McLean, Lyons & Kerr, Toronto. Mem. Canadian Bar Assn., County of York Law Assn. Office: 372 Bay St Toronto 1 Ontario Canada*

KERREBROCK, JACK LEO, educator; b. Los Angeles, Feb. 6, 1928; s. Oscar A. and Florence (Hoy) K.; student U. Ore., 1946-47; B.S., Ore. State Coll., 1950; M.S., Yale, 1951; Ph.D., Cal. Inst. Tech., 1956; m. Bernice Veverka, Apr. 11, 1953; children—Christopher, Nancy, Peter. Aero. research scientist Lewis Lab., NASA, Cleve., 1951-53; research fellow Cal. Inst. Tech., 1955-56; engring. leader Oak Ridge Nat. Lab., 1956-58; sr. research fellow Cal. Inst. Tech., 1958-60; faculty Mass. Inst. Tech., 1960—, prof. aeros. and astronautics, dir. Space Propulsion Lab., 1965—, dir. Gas Turbine Lab., 1969—. Cons. to govt., industry, 1957—. Mem. steering com. symposium engring. aspects of magnetohydrodynamics, 1962—. Asso. fellow Am. Inst. Aeros., and Astronautics; mem. Am. Phys. Soc. Home: Tower Rd Lincoln MA 01773 Office: Mass Inst Tech Cambridge MA 02139

KERRIDGE, ROBERT LOUIS, trade assn. exec.; b. New London, Conn., July 7, 1910; s. Philip Markham and Agnes (Briggs) K.; A.B., Dickinson Coll., 1932; m. Margaret Green, Sept. 3, 1938; children—David Tate, James Gordon, Julie Thorburn. With Riegel Paper Corp., 1934-68, dir. marketing, 1960-68, v.p., 1953-68, also dir., mgr. Pulp, Paper and Paper board Export Assn. U.S., N.Y. C., 1969—. Home: R D 1 Riegelsville PA 18077 Office: 90 Park Av New York City NY 10016

KERRIGAN, GERALD AUSTIN, physician, educator; b. N.Y.C., Sept. 4, 1920; s. James Joseph and Laura (White) K.; B.S. cum laude, Harvard, 1943, M.D., 1946; m. Mary Patricia O'Connor, June 21, 1947; children—Laura, Catherine, Michael, Anne. Intern, Childrens Hosp., Boston, 1946-47; house officer Childrens Med. Service, Mass. Gen. Hosp., Boston, 1949-50, asst. resident, 1950-51, chief resident, 1951-52, asst. to Childrens Med. Service, 1954-55, asst. physician, 1955-56; practice in Milwaukee, 1956—; clin. and research fellow pediatrics Harvard Med. Sch. and Mass. Gen. Hosp., 1952-54; attending physician Milw. Childrens Hosp., 1956—; instr. pediatrics Harvard Med. Sch., 1954-56; asst. prof. pediatrics Sch. Medicine, Marquette U., 1956-59, asso. prof., 1959-64, prof., dean, 1965—; mem. adv. com. Wis. Regional med. Program, 1967—; mem. Gov.'s Task Force for Med. Edn. in Wis., 1967—. Mem. corp. United Community Services Greater Milw., 1967—. Served to lt. (j.g.), M.C., USNR, 1947-49. Recipient research grants NIH, 1959-60, 60-61. Diplomate Am. Bd. Pediatrics. Mem. Am. Acad. Pediatrics, A.M.A., Assn. Am. Med. Colls., Midwest Soc. Pediatrics, A.M.A., Assn. Am. Med. Colls., Midwest Soc. Pediatric Research, Milw. Acad. Medicine, Am., New Eng., Milw. pediatric socs., Soc. for Pediatric Research, Am. Cancer Soc. (dir. Milw. chpt.). Cons. editor Medical Aspects of Human Sexuality, 1967—. Conbr. articles profl. jours. Home: 1081 E Circle Dr Milwaukee WI 53217 Office: 561 N 15th St Milwaukee WI 53203

KERRIGAN, JAMES LEO, transp. co. exec.; b. Boston, Oct. 13, 1929; s. James Leo and Katherine M. (O'Brien) K.; student Boston U., 1952-53; m. Patricia Alice Kerrigan, June 13, 1953; children—Mary Jane, Billie, Paula, Peter, Susan, Maureen, James Jr. With Greyhound Lines, Phoenix, 1947—, mem. sales amd marketing depts., 1950-67, pres. Central Greyhound div., 1967-68, pres. combined Eastern and So. divs., 1969, pres., chief exec. officer corp., 1970—; group v.p. transp. Greyhound Corp., 1970—, also dir.; dir. Jefferson Lines, Inc., Tex., N.M., and Okla. Coaches, So. Kan. Greyhound Lines, Inc., N.M. Transp. Co. Served with USMC, 1950-52. Mem. Nat. Assn. Motor Bus Owners (bd. dirs.). Home: 5129 Desert Jewel Dr Phoenix AZ 85253 Office: Greyhound Tower Phoenix AZ 85077

KERRIGAN, THOMAS M., lawyer; b. N.Y.C., July 7, 1906; s. Thomas Michael and Gertrude (Bush) K.; B.A., Columbia, 1928, postgrad. Law Sch., 1931; postgrad. St. John's Coll., 1933; m. Floyd Young Penn, Apr. 9, 1936; 1 son, Thomas M. Admitted to N.Y. bar, practiced in N.Y.C.; asso. Phillip, Mahoney, Leibell & Fielding, 1934-37; partner Lyons & Kerrigan, 1937-44; with Putney, Twombly, Hall & Hirson and predecessor firms, 1942—, partner, 1947—; labor counsel Columbia, Weston Instruments Co., Inc., NCR Adding Machine Div., U.S. Freight Co., Smith Research & Devel. Co. Chmn. adv. com. football Columbia. Recipient Alumni Athletic award, 1959, Columbia U. Alumni medal, 1954; Adm. of Chesapeake Bay, 1967. Mem. Assn. Bar City N.Y., Zeta Psi. Roman Catholic. Clubs: Columbia University, University (N.Y.C.); Mantoloking Yacht, Stamford Yacht, Varsity C. Columbia (past pres.). Home: 66 Ocean Dr E Stamford CT 06902 Office: 250 Park Av New York City NY 10017

KERSCH, ROBERT STANLEY, corp. exec; b. Mpls., 1928; LL.B., U. Minn., 1952. Sec. DeSoto. Inc., Sonneborn Bldg. Products, Inc. Mason. Home: 435 Beverly Dr Wilmette IL 60091 Office: 1700 S Mt Prospect Rd Des Plains IL 60018*

KERSCHNER, HAROLD BENNER, clergyman; b. Trappe, Pa., June 10, 1895; s. James George and Pruella Elizabeth (Benner) K.; A.B., Ursinus Coll., Collegeville, Pa., 1916, B.D., 1920, D.D., 1936; student Central Theol. Sem., Dayton, O., 1916-19; S.T.B., Union Theol. Sem., N.Y., 1920; A.M., Columbia, 1921; m. Mabel Clare Gardner, June 29, 1921. Ordained to ministry Ref. Ch., 1918; pastor Kent St. Ref. Ch., Bklyn., 1919-21, Old First Ref. Ch., Phila., 1921-31, First Presbyn. Ch., Poughkeepsie, N.Y., 1931-52; research in ch. music 1952—. Dir. Phila. Fedn. Chs., 1922-31; dir. Christian Assn., U. Pa., 1924-31; chmn. Lenten Services, Poughkeepsie, 1935-48; mem. adv. bd. Beaver Coll., Jenkintown, Pa., 1941-61; mem. exec. com. Community Chest, Poughkeepsie, 1940-42; mem. com. on united promotion Presbyn. Ch. U.S.A., 1936-42, chmn. com. spiritual life, 1936-42 (as such sponsored 1st World Communion Sunday 1936), chmn. standing com. Christian edn., 1944, mem. bd. pensions, 1946-52. Mem. Youth Adminstrn., N.Y. State, 1937-42; mem. exec. com. Weekday Schs. of Religion, 1941-48; adv. bd. Colored Community Center, 1942-48; mem. Def. Council, 1942-45; chmn. Brotherhood Week Observance, 1942-43. (all Poughkeepsie), Wartime Service Commn., N. River Presbytery, 1941-45; civilian chaplain Presbyn. Ch., Miami area, 1943. Mason. Club: Wranglers (Phila.). Editor: (with Rufus W. Miller) The Church School Hymnal, 1922. Contbr. to Best Sermons, 1926, Reformed Church Pulpit, 1928; The Communion Service, 1937; Successful Leters for Churches (Abingdon-Cokesbury), 1946. Home: 2949 Berkely Rd Ardmore PA 19003

KERSHAW, CHARLES J., business exec.; b. Ravenswood, Ill., 1907. Former partner Reynolds & Co., N.Y.C.; dir. Clearing Corp.; mem. N.Y. Stock Exchange. Home: 66 The Oaks Roslyn Estates NY 11576 Office: 120 Broadway New York City NY 10005

KERSHAW, JOSEPH ALEXANDER, educator, economist; b. Bala-Cynwyd, Pa., Apr. 21, 1913; s. Isaac and Caroline (Alexander) F.; A.B., Princeton, 1935; A.M., N.Y. U., 1938; Ph.D., Columbia, 1947; m. Mary Anna Nettleton, Oct. 8, 1936; children—David N., Stephen A. Asst. prof. econs. Hofstra Coll., 1936-42; dir. ration banking br. OPA, 1942-47; asst., also head econs. dept. Rand Corp., 1948-62; prof. econs., provost Williams Coll., Williamstown, Mass., 1962-68, prof. econs., 1970—; asst. dir. Office Econ. Opportunity, 1965-66; program officer Ford Found., 1968-70, cons., 1970—; Mem. commn. adminstrn. Am. Council for Edn., 1964-68; bd. advisers Inst. for Research on Poverty, U. Wis., 1966-68. Author: History of Ration Banking, 1947; (with R. McKean) Teacher Shortages and Salary Schedules, 1962; Government Against Poverty, 1970. Home: Jerome Dr Williamstown MA 01267

KERSHAW, WILLIAM JOHN, Jr., banker; b. Milford, Del., Sept. 30, 1933; s. William John and Julia (King) K.; asso. degree in accounting Goldey-Beacon Jr. Coll., 1952; m. Joyce E. Cordrey, Apr. 4, 1953; children-Andrea, Lynn, Kimberly Joyce, Mark Cordrey. Teller, Peoples Nat. Bank, Laurel, Del., 1956-59; with Farmers Bank, Laurel, 1959-66, asst. auditor, Dover, Del., 1966-69, auditor, 1969—. Treas. United Community Fund Central Del., 1970, now mem. bd. Served with AUS, 1954-56. Mem. Am. Inst. Banking (chpt. pres. 1968-69). Home: 877 Schoolhouse Lane Dover DE 19401 Office: 18 Luockerman St Dover DE 19401

KERSHNER, HOWARD ELDRED, author, found. exec.; b. Tescott, Kan., Nov. 17, 1891; s. Isaiah and Cora (Lett) K.; grad. Fowler Friends' Acad., Fowler, Kan., 1910; A.B. Friends' Univ.,

Wichita, Kan., 1914; grad. student, Harvard U., 1923-24; hon. Dr. of Humane Letters, Washington and Jefferson Coll., 1941; LL.D. (hon.) Friends Univ., Wichita, Kan., 1948; Litt.D., Grove City College, Pa., 1957; D.D., George Fox Coll., 1969; H.H.D., Northwood Inst., 1970; married Gertrude Elizabeth Townsend, July 6, 1915; children—Wendell Townsend, Margaret Lynette (Mrs. Stephen C. Weber), Mary Linaford (Mrs. Glenn C. Bassett, Jr.). Boston real estate office, 1914- 16, editor pub. Dodge City Daily Jour., Kansas, 1917-18, asst. to chief of newspaper section War Industries Bd., Washington, D.C., 1918; real estate operator in Boston, Kansas and Florida, 1919-27, publisher, Nat. Am. Soc., N.Y., 1927-38; dir. relief in Europe for American Friends Com., 1939-42; exec. vice pres. and dir. of the Internat. Commn. for Child refugees 1939-52. Dir. child feeding, Spanish Civil War, 1939-40, in unoccupied France, 1940-42; obtained funds from grants by 24 govts.; vice chmn. Save the Children Fedn., sec., 1950-; mem. bd. Americanism Ednl. League; mem. Am.-African Affairs Assn.; Nat. Tax Reform Com.; Am. Emergency Com. Panama Canal adv. bd. Supreme Ct. Amendment League; Am. Conservative Union; member executive committee National Committee on Food for Small Democracies; former dir. CARE. Founder and chmn. Temp. Council on Food for European Children, 1943-45; diplomatic mission to principal Latin-Am. capitals, seeking grants for Internat. Children's Fund of U.N., 1947-48. One of founders Christian Freedom Found., Incorporated (president 1950-69, now chmn. bd.), N.Y. Bd. directors Community Development Fund. Mem. Mont Pelerin Soc. Mem. Soc. of Friends (Quakers). Clk. N.Y. yearly meeting of Friends (1945-51). Republican. Author: The Menace of Roosevelt and his Policies, 1936; William Squire Kenyon, 1931; One Humanity, 1943, British edition, 1944; Quaker Service in Modern War, 1950; God, Gold and Government, 1956; Diamonds, Persimmons and Stars, 1964. "Dividing the Wealth Are you Getting a Fair Share?". Edited and arranged: Air Pioneering in the Arctic, 1928; James W. Ellsworth, a biography, 1929; Lincoln Ellsworth, 1930. Editor of fortnightly journal Christian Economics. Narrator for film "Children of Tragedy" and "Reconstruction Begins;" made more than 300 radio addresses about condition of children in Europe; also weekly news commentator on 325 radio stas., called Howard Kershners Commentary on the News, 1958-. Author five hundred papers. Author of syndicated column Its Up to You; Sermonettes pub. semimonthly in Christian Economics and used in church calendars of 1600 chs. Decorated Chevalier, Order of Leopold (Belgium); Medaille d'Honneur d'Argent des Affaires Etrangers (France); Ordre de Merité, Union Internationale de Protection de l'Enfants, Geneva, Switzerland; Chevalier Legion of Honor (France), Freedom Found. Medal, 1952-57, 59. Home: 390 S Hauser Blvd Los Angeles, CA 90036. Office: 17960 Crescent Av Buena Park CA

KERSHNER, IRVIN, film dir.; b. Phila., Apr. 29, 1923; ed. in fine arts Temple U., U. Cal. Documentary film maker USIS, Middle East, 1950-52; dir., cameraman TV documentary Confidential File, 1953-55; dir. Roth-Kershner Prodns., Inc. Dir. movies including: Stakeout on Dope Street, Young Captives, Hoodlum Priest; TV films including The Rebel. Office: care 20th Century Fox 444 W 56th St New York City NY 10019*

KERST, DONALD WILLIAM, physicist; b. Galena, Ill., Nov. 1, 1911; s. Herman Samuel and Lilian (Wetz) K.; B.A., U. Wis., 1934, Ph.D., 1937, D. Sc., 1961; D.Sc., Lawrence Coll., 1942; Dr. Honoris Causa, U. São Paulo (Brazil); m. Dorothy Birkett, Aug. 1940; children—Marilyn Elizabeth, Stephen Marshall. Instr. physics U. Ill., 1938, asst. prof., 1940, asso. prof., 1942, prof., 1943; war work Los Alamos, N.M., 1943-45; tech. dir. Midwestern Univs. Research Assn., 1953-57; with John Jay Hopkins Lab. for pure and applied sci. atomic div. Gen. Dynamics Corp., 1957-62; E. M. Terry prof. physics U. Wis. 1962—. Winner Comstock prize Nat. Acad. Scis. for devel. betatron, 1945, John Scott award, 1946, John Price Wetherill medal Franklin Inst. for devel. of betatron, 1950. Mem. Nat. Acad. Scis. Home: 1506 Wood Lane Madison, WI

KERSTEN, MILES STOKES, educator; b. St. Paul, Aug. 12, 1913; s. Louie John and Mabel (Stokes) K.; B.C.E., U. Minn., 1934, M.S., 1936, Ph.D., 1945; m. Eveline Carlsen, June 10, 1938; children—Cynthia (Mrs. John H. Doran), Thomas Louie. Soils engr. Minn. Dept. Hwys., 1934-37; instr. civil engring. U. Minn., Mpls., 1937-43, asst. prof., 1946-47, asso. prof., 1947-53, prof., 1953- ; spl. investigator Hwy. Research Bd., Washington, 1944-45, chmn. dept. soils, geology and founds., 1958-63. Fellow Am. Soc. C.E. (past pres. N.W. sect.); mem. Nat. Soc. Profl. Engrs., Am. Soc. Engring. Edn., Sigma Xi, Chi Epsilon, Tau Beta Pi, Theta Tau. Contbr. articles to profl. jours. Home: 3716 47th Av S Minneapolis MN 55406 Office: Exptl Engring Bldg U Minn Minneapolis MN 55455

KERSTEN, RICHARD SIEGMANN, telephone co. exec.; b. Mpls., July 22, 1907; s. George Albert and Adeline Louise (Siegmann) K.; B.S. in Engring. magna cum laude, Harvard, 1928; m. Lois Holliday, July 21, 1934; children—Richard Holliday, Katherine Louise (Mrs. Wallman). Instr. engring. Harvard, 1928-30; with N.J. Bell Telephone Co., 1930—, asst. v.p., 1962-65, v.p., 1965—. Registered profl. engr., N.J. Mem. Harvard Soc. Engrs. and Scientists, Nat. Soc. Profl. Engrs., I.E.E.E., Am. Soc. Engring. Edn., Tau Beta Pi, Delta Upsilon. Club: Essex (Newark). Home: 107 Chatham St Chatham NJ 07928 Office: 540 Broad St Newark NJ 07101

KERSTETTER, WILLIAM EDWARD, univ. pres., clergyman; b. Lykens, Pa., Apr. 25, 1913; s. William and Susan (Rudisill) K.; grad. Girard Coll., 1930; A.B., Dickinson Coll., 1936; LL.D., 1954; S.T.B. magna cum laude, Boston U., 1939, Ph.D., 1943; postgrad. Harvard, Emory U., 1939-43; L.H.D., Simpson Coll., 1963; LL.D., Butler U., 1967, Ind. State U., 1971; m. Leona Bateman, Dec. 25, 1941; children—William Edward, Laura Lamson. Ordained to ministry Meth. Ch., 1938; plant accounting office Bell Telephone Co. of Pa., 1930-32; dir. religious edn. United Ch., Norwood, Mass., 1937-41; minister Hull (Mass.) Meth. Ch., 1941-42; asso. prof., chmn. dept. philosophy Baldwin-Wallace Coll., 1946-51, prof., chmn. dept., 1949-51, dir. religious activities, 1947-50; prof., chmn. dept. philosophy and religion Hamline U., 1951-53; interim minister First Meth. Ch., St. Paul, 1952; faculty Garrett Theol. Sem., Northwestern, summer 1952; pres. Simpson Coll., Indianola, Ia., 1953-63, DePauw U., Greencastle, Ind., 1963—. Mem commn. on religion higher edn. Assn. Am. Colls., 1965-67; mem. Univ. senate Meth. Ch., 1964—, v.p., 1971—; v.p. Ia. Coll. Found. Mem. pres.'s adv. council Assn. Governing Bds.; pres. Independent Colls. and Univs. Ind., 1965-66, Ind. Conf. Higher Edn., 1967-68. Trustee Religious Heritage of Am. Served as capt., chaplain USAAF, 1943-46. Jacob Sleeper fellow, 1939-40; Kent fellow, 1939-42; Borden Parker Bowne fellow philosophy, 1941-42. Fellow Soc. Religion in Higher Edn.; mem. Am. Philos. Assn., Am. Acad. Religion, Am. Assn. U. Profs., Ind. Ann. Conf. Meth. Ch., Ia. Assn. UN (pres. 1960-61), Gt. Lakes Colls. Assn. (chmn. bd. 1969—), Omicron Delta Kappa (hon.), Phi Kappa Sigma. Rotarian. Clubs: Columbia (Indpls.); Windy Hill (Greencastle); University (N.Y.C.); Mokus (Boston). Author numerous articles, book revs., book chpt.; co-author An Experiment in General Education, 1957. Bd. adv. editors Outstanding Young Men Am. Home: 125 Wood St Greencastle IN 46135

KERTESZ, ANDRE, photographer; b. Budapest, Hungary, July 2, 1894; s. Leopold and Ernestine (Hoffman) K.; grad. Hungarian Acad. Commerce, Budapest, 1912; m. Elizabeth Sali, June 17, 1933. Came to U.S., 1936, naturalized, 1944. One-man shows include Sacre du Printemps, Paris, France, 1927, Art Inst. Chgo., 1946, Bibliotheque Nationale, Paris, France, 1963, IV Mostra Biennale Internazionale della Fotografia, Venice, Italy, Museum Modern Art, N.Y.C., 1964; published books Paris Vu Par Andre Kertesz, 1934, Enfants, 1933, Nos Amies Les Betes, 1936, Les Cathedrales Du Vin, 1937, Day of Paris, 1945, André Kertész, Photographer, 1964. Mem. Am. Soc. Mag. Photographers, 1964. Mem. Am. Soc. Mag. Photographers. Contbr. photographs to Am., European mags. Home: 2 Fifth Av New York City NY 10011

KERTESZ, ISTVAN, conductor; b. Budapest, Hungary, Aug. 28, 1929; s. Miklos and Margot (Muresian) K.; M.Conducting, Franz Liszt Acad. Music, Budapest, 1953; M.Conducting cum laude, Accademia di Santa Cecilia, Rome, Italy, 1958; m. Edith Gabry, Sept. 10, 1951; children—Gabor, Peter, Kathrin. Prin. condr. Philharmonia in Györ (Hungary), 1953-55, States Opera, Budapest, 1955-57; gen. music dir., Augsburg, Germany, 1958-63; prof. Acad. Music, Budapest, 1952-57; guest condr. throughout world, 1959- -; gen. music dir. Operahaus Köln, Cologne, Germany, 1964—; prin. condr. London (Eng.) Symphony Orch., 1965-68; Prin. conductor Ravinia Festival, Ill., 1970—; prof. Mozarteum Salzburg for Condrs., summer 1964; condr. Salzburg Festival, 1961-64; rec. artist London Records. Recipient Arnold Bax medal from Germany, 1966; Edison prize (Holland) for Bluebeard, 1966, for Mozart, 1967. Author: Premio D'Atri for Conducting, 1958. Home: Franz Seiwertstrasse 15 Köln Germany Office: Opernhause Köln Germany

KERTESZ, STEPHEN DENIS, educator, diplomat, author; b. Putnok, Hungary, Apr. 8, 1904; s. Lajos and Maria (Stolcz) K.; LL.D., U. Budapest, 1926; diploma internat. relations U. Paris, 1928; Rockefeller fellow Yale, Oxford, Geneva univs., 1935-37; m. Margaret Cornelia de Fulop, Oct. 7, 1931; children— Marianne (Mrs. Endre Sipos), Agnes (Mrs. Peter Serenyi). With Hungarian Fgn. Ministry, 1931-47, head peace prep. div., 1945-46, sec.-gen. Hungarian Peace Delegation, 1946; Hungarian minister to Italy, 1947; vis. asso. prof. Yale Law Sch., 1948-50; prof. polit. sci. Notre Dame U., 1950—, mem. Grad. Council, 1961-64, cons. Fgn. Area Fellowship program, 1961-64, acting head dept. polit. sci., 1962-64, Franklin Miles prof. polit. sci., 1963, also dir. Soviet and East Central European Center, 1954-69, chmn. com. internat. relations, 1955—, dir. Western European studies program, 1965—, dir. Inst. on Internat. Studies, 1968—, Cardinal O'Hara prof. gqvt. and internat. studies, 1969. Guggenheim fellow, 1958-59; Rockefeller grantee Europe, N.Am., 1965-66. Mem. Am., Internat. polit. sci. assns., Internat. Free Acad. Sci. and Letters, Am. Acad. Polit. and Social Sci., Am. Assn. for Advancement Slavic Studies, Am. Soc. Internat. Law, Cath. Commn. Intellectual and Cultural Affairs, Internat. Studies Assn. Author: The International Responsibility of the State, Budapest, 1938; Diplomacy in a Whirlpool: Hungary Between Nazi Germany and Soviet Russia, 1953; Quest for Peace Through Diplomacy, 1967. Editor, contbr.: The Fate of East Central Europe: Hopes and Failures of American Foreign Policy, 1956; American Diplomacy in a New Era, 1961; East Central Europe and the World: Developments in the Post-Stalin Era, 1962; Nuclear Non Proliferation in A World of Nuclear Powers, 1967; The Task of Universities in a Changing World, 1971; (with M.A. Fitzsimons) Diplomacy in a Changing World, 1959, What America Stands For, 1959. Home: 1246 Woodlawn Blvd South Bend IN

KERTH, LEROY T., educator; b. Visalia, Cal., Nov. 23, 1928; s. Lewis John and Frances (Niccolls) K.; A.B. in Physics, U. Cal. at Berkeley, 1950, Ph.D., 1957; m. Ruth Lorraine Littlefield, Nov. 19, 1950; children—Norman Lewis, Randall Thomas, Christine Jane, Bradley Niccolls. Mem. staff Lawrence Berkeley Lab, U. Cal. at Berkeley, 1950-59, sr. scientist, 1959-61; asso. prof. physics U. Cal. at Berkeley, 1961-65, prof., 1965—, asso. dean Coll. Letters and Scis., 1966—, spl. asst. to chancellor, 1970—. Fellow Am. Phys. Soc. Home: 5 Los Conejos St Orinda CA 94563 Office: Physics Dept U Cal Berkeley CA 94701

KERTZ, HUBERT LEONARD, telephone co. exec.; b. San Francisco, July 11, 1910; s. Hubert J. and Laura V. (Seavey) K.; A.B., Stanford, 1934, E.E., 1936; m. Justine Jankowsky, July 28, 1934; children—Brenda L., Pamela. With Pacific Tel. & Tel. Co., 1926-42, 46-61, asst. v.p., 1953-58, v.p., 1958-61; asst. v.p. Am.Tel.&Tel. Co., 1961-64, v.p., 1964—; dir. Mich. Bell Telephone Co., Ill. Bell Telephone Co. Served from lt. (j.g.) to comdr. USNR, 1942-46; PTO. Decorated Bronze Star medal. Fellow I.E.E.E.; mem. Armed Forces Communication Assn., Am. Mgmt. Assn., Cal. C. of C., Soc. Cal. Pioneers. Club: Economic (N.Y.C.). Home: 1385 York Av New York City NY 10021 Office: 195 Broadway New York City NY 10007

KERVICK, JOHN A., ednl. adminstr., b. Elizabeth, N.J., May 6, 1906; s. John A. and Johanna (Dillon) K.; A.B., Fordham U., 1927; LL.B., Mercer Beasley Sch. Law, 1931; m. Catherine B. Burke, Jan. 2, 1932; children—Joan, Catherine, Eileen, Margaret, Mary. Tchr. social studies Elizabeth pub. schs., 1927- 34; dep. mayor Elizabeth, 1935-38; exec. dir. Housing Authority, Elizabeth, 1938-42; mgmt. dir. Fed. Pub. Housing Authority, N.Y.C., 1942- 44, dir. region II, 1944-63; treas. , of N.J., Trenton, 1958-70; v.p. Coll. Medicine and Dentistry N.J., Newark, 1970—. Chmn. bd. Nat. Housing Conf.; past commr. Delaware River Port Authority; mem. N.Y. Bd. Realtors. Bd. dirs. St. Barnabas Med. Center. Mem. Nat. Assn. Housing Ofcls. (dir.). Democrat. Roman Catholic. Elk. Clubs: N.Y. Athletic (N.Y.C.); Deal Golf and Country. Home: 102 Fairfield Dr Short Hills NJ 07078 Office: 100 Bergan St Newark NJ 07103

KERWIN, CHARLES CORNELIUS, investment exec.; b. Chgo., Feb. 5, 1892; s. Michael William and Catherine Camilla (Quinlan) K.; student pvt., pub. schs.; LL.D. (hon.), U. Chgo., 1960; m. Mary Allen Gray, Sept. 4, 1926; children—Mary Catherine (Mrs. George J. Murphy), Elizabeth Anne (Mrs. Oren Taft Pollock), Margaret Agnes (Mrs. William A. Crane). Real estate sales Ballard, Rowe & Whitman, 1915-18; salesman Halsey, Stuart & Co., Inc., 1919-26, 30-66, v.p., 1966- 68, sr. v.p., 1968-; pres. Kerwin & Co., 1929-30, Blackfoot Coal & Land Corp. 1942—, Western Comml. Co. of Del. 1926—; v.p. Locust Street Co., 1927-52, pres., 1952—. Dir. Community Fund of Chgo., 1934-45, exec. com., 1939-45, v.p., 1941-45, dir., v.p., exec. com. war fund, 1945-46; treas. Cath. Ch. Extension Soc. U.S., 1926-64, v.p., 1944-64; pres. Cath. Charities, Archidiocese Chgo., 1939-44, dir., mem. exec. com. Chmn. bd. lay trustees Loyola U., Chgo., 1960-66, mem. bd. lay trustees, 1948—; treas. St. Vincent's Crib Soc. Governing life mem. Art Inst. Chgo.; bd. dirs. Lyric Opera. Served with Ordnance Dept. U.S. Army, 1918. Decorated knight comdr. Order of Pius IX, Pro Eclesia et Pontifice (Pope Pius XI), knight comdr. Order of Pius IX (Pope Pius XII); recipient Damen award Loyola U., 1968. Clubs: Chicago, Chicago Athletic, Attic (Chgo.); Onwentsia, Old Old Elm (Lake Forest, Ill.); Evansville (Ind.) Country. Home: 994 Meadow Lane Lake Forest IL 60045 Office: 123 S La Salle St Chicago IL 60603

KERWIN, JEROME GREGORY, ret. educator, polit. scientist; b. Albany, N.Y., Feb. 25, 1896; s. Timothy Edward and Alice (McCarthy) K.; A.B., Dartmouth, 1919; A.M., Columbia, 1921, Ph.D., 1926; LL.D., Holy Cross Coll., Mass., 1947; Litt.D., U. Notre Dame, 1953. Instr. polit. sci. Dartmouth, 1921-23, instr. U. Chgo., 1921-26, asst. prof. polit. sci., 1926-29, asso. prof., 1929-41, dean students social sci. div., 1935-41, 57-61, prof. polit. sci., 1941-61, emeritus prof.; dir. honors div. and prof. polit. sci. U. Santa Clara, Cal., 1961-66; chmn. Walgreen Found., 1945-56. Fenwick lectr. Holy Cross Coll., Worcester, Mass., 1947; chmn. Chgo. Inst. Social and Religious Studies, 1944-53; v.p. Cath. Assn. Internat. Peace, 1958—. Bd. lay advisers Rosary Coll.; bd. dirs. Inst. European Studies, Chgo. Cath. Interracial Council; exec. com. Stanford-Santa Clara Colloquium on Ecumenium. Mem. Religious Edn. Assn. U.S. and Can. (pres. 1957-62), Am. Acad. Polit. Sci., Am. Polit. Sci. Assn., Am. Acad. Polit. and Social Sci., Serra Internat., Nat. Conf. Christians and Jews, Fedn. Religious Action in Social and Civil Order (adv. council), Ind. Voters Ill., Thomas More Assn. (dir.), Phi Beta Kappa. Democrat. Roman Catholic. Clubs: Quadrangle, University. Author: Federal Water Power Legislation, 1926; Schools and City Government, 1938; The Great Tradition, 1947; Catholic Viewpoint on Church and State, 1960; Government, Politics and Catholics, 1961. Editor: Civil-Military Relations, 1946; polit. sci. contbr. Cath. Ency. Contbr. Ency. Brit., Commonweal America, also polit. sci. revs. Home: 911 Camino Dr Santa Clara CA 95050

KERWIN, LARKIN, educator; b. Quebec, Que., Can., June 22, 1924; s. Timothy and Catherine (Longeren) K.; B.S., St. Francis Xavier U., 1944; M.S., Mass. Inst. Tech., 1946; D.Sc., Laval U., 1949; LL.D., 1970; m. Marie G. Turcot, June 10, 1950; children—Nene, Alan, Larkin Jr., Terry, Rosa Marie, Gregory, Timothy, Guillermina. Asst. prof. prof. physics Laval U., 1948-51, asso. prof., 1951-56, prof., 1956—, chmn. dept., 1961-67, vice-dean faculty scis., 1967-69, vice-rector, 1969—; research physicist Geotech. Corp., Cambridge, 1945-46. Mem. Def. Research Bd. Bd. govs. St. Lawrence Coll. Decorated Lt. Gov.'s medal, 1941; Gov. Gen. medal, 1944; Pariseau medal, 1965; Centenary medal, 1967; Prix David, 1951; knight Equestrian Order Holy Secpulchre Jerusalem. Fellow Royal Soc. Can.; mem. Internat. Union Pure and Applied Physics (asso. sec.-gen.), Assn. Canadienne-Francaise pour l'avancement des sciences, Am. Phys. Soc., Corp. Profl. Engrs. Quebec, Sociedad Mexicana Fisica, Canadian Assn. Physicists (medal 1969), Quebec C. of C. Club: Cercle Universitaire (Quebec). Author: Atomic Physics, an Introduction, 1963; also articles. Home: 2166 Parc Bourbonniere Sillery Quebec 6 Canada

KERWIN, RICHARD EKMAN, banker; b. Worcester, Mass., Sept. 24, 1926; s. Charles Carlin and Lillian Maria (Ekman) K.; A.B., Dartmouth, 1950; m. Mary Luhman, Sept. 8, 1950; children—John, Peter, Kimberly Dee. Self-employed food broker, 1950-53; with United Cal. Bank, Los Angeles, 1953-71, asst. v.p., 1960, v.p., 1961-70, sr. v.p., 1970-71; exec. v.p. Western Bancorp., Los Angeles, 1971—. Area vice chmn. United Crusade, 1970—. Served with USNR, 1944-46. Republican. Mason. Club: South Hills Country (Covina, Cal.). Home: 12612 Woodley Av Granada Hills CA 91344 Office: 600 S Spring St Los Angeles CA 90054

KERWIN, WALTER THOMAS, Jr., army officer; b. West Chester, Pa., June 14, 1917; s. Walter Thomas and Mary (Farra) K.; B.S., U.S. Mil. Acad., 1939; grad. Command Gen. Staff Coll., 1948, Armed Forces Staff Coll., 1953, Army War Coll., 1957, Nat. War Coll., 1960; m. Barbara Walker Connell, July 10, 1940; children—Bruce Richard, Margaret Ann. Commd. 2d lt. F.A., AUS, 1939, advanced through grades to lt. gen. U.S. Army, 1968; arty. plans and operations officer 3d Inf. Div., Africa-Mediterranean Area-Europe, World War II; theatre operations officer War Dept. Gen. Staff, Washington, 1945-47; instr. Command and Gen. Staff Coll., 1948-51; asst. plans officer, dir. Turkish Arty. Sch., Joint Mil. Mission Aid to Turkey, 1951-53; plans and operations officer, asso. group leader Los Alamos Sci. Lab., 1953-56; comdg. officer 56th Arty. Group, Ft. Bragg, N.C., 1957- 59; dep. dir. spl. weapons, research and devel. div. Dept. Army Gen. Staff, 1960-61; comdg. gen. 3d Armored Div. Arty., Hanau, Germany, 1961- 63; chief nuclear activities br. SHAPE, Paris, France, 1963-65; comdg. gen. 3d Armored Div., Frankfurt, Germany, 1965-66; asst. dep. chief staff mil. operations Dept. Army, Washington, 1966-67, chief staff mil. assistance command Vietnam, 1967-68, comdg. gen. II field force, Vietnam, 1968-69; dir. Civil Disturbance Planning and Operations, 1969; dep. chief staff personnel Dept. Army, 1969—. Mem.-at-large Nat. council Boy Scouts Am. Decorated Legion of Merit with oak leaf cluster, Bronze Star, Purple Heart, Army Commendation medal, Air medal, Legion of Valor, D.S.M. with oak leaf cluster. Office: Dep Chief Staff for Personnel Dept Army Washington DC 20310

KESEY, KEN, writer; b. La Hunta, Colo., Sept. 17, 1935; s. Fred and Geneva (Smith) K.; B.S., U. Ore., 1957; postgrad. Stanford, 1958-59; m. Norma Faye Haxby, May 20, 1956; children—Shannon, Zane, Jed, Sunshine. Pres., Intrepid Trips, Inc., motion picture producers, 1964-. Author: One Flew Over the Cuckoos Nest, 1962; Sometimes A Great Notion, 1964. Address: 819 Eddy St San Francisco CA 94109

KESICKE, FRANCIS E., banker; b. Yonkers, N.Y., Apr., 17, 1917; s. Frank E. and Constance (Anderson), K.; B.S. in Mech. Engring., U. Notre Dame, 1938; m. Ruth C. Hohl, Nov, 28, 1942; children—Kenneth, Eugene, Christopher. Field engr. Wright Aero Corp., 1940-47; with Ninth Fed. Savs. & Loan Assn., N.Y.C., 1947—, pres., 1967—. Home: 20 Wingate Rd Yonkers NY 10705 Office: 1457 Broadway New York City NY 10036

KESLER, ALONZO PRATT, lawyer; b. Salt Lake City, Apr. 26, 1905; s. Alonzo Pratt and Donnette (Smith) K.; student U. Liege (Belgium), 1926-27; A.B., U. Utah, 1930, J.D., 1933; m. Ellen Tourssen, June 30, 1939; children— Pamela, John Tourssen. Admitted to Utah bar, 1933, since practiced in Salt Lake City; mem. firm Callister, Kessler & Callister; city pros. atty. Salt Lake City, 1935-40, asst. city atty., 1940-52. Republican candidate for atty. gen. Utah, 1944-48; chmn. Rep. State Com., 1950-53, mem. Rep. Nat. Com., 1952-53; chmn. state delegation Rep. Nat. Conv., 1952; former atty. gen. State of Utah; U.S. atty. Dist. Utah, 1953-61; commr. Utah State Tax Commn. Mem. Nat. Conf. Commrs. Uniform State Laws, 1957—; chmn. Utah Commn. on Uniform State Laws; mem. exec. com. Community Welfare Council, 1957-59; pres. emigration league Western Baseball Assn.; chmn. speakers com. A.R.C., 1945, Nat. Found. Infantile Paralysis campaign, 1950; chmn. state, county campaigns Am. Cancer Soc. Pres., Young Republicans, 1937-38. Bd. dirs. Legal aid Soc., Salt Lake City, 1934-71, pres., 1964-66. Mem. Utah State Bar (pres. 1959-60), Am. (mem. jr. bar council 1937-39, vice chmn. 1940, mem. council gen. practice sect., mem. ho. of dels.), Fed. (pres. Utah chpt. 1970-71), Salt Lake County (pres. 1945-46) bar assns., Pi Kappa Alpha. Kiwanian. Club: Salt Lake Country (Salt Lake City). Home: 875 Donner Way Salt Lake City UT 84108 Office: Kennecott Bldg Salt Lake City UT 84101

KESLER, ARCHIE BOWMAN, Jr., banker; b. Salt Lake City, Mar. 18, 1911; s. Archie Bowman and Frances (Hackard) K.; student pub. schs., Salt Lake City; m. Phyllis Evans, Feb. 7, 1951; 1 dau., Susannah Evans. With Walker Bank & Trust Co., Salt Lake City, 1929-, now chmn. bd., pres., chief exec. officer, dir.; dir. Skaggs Drug Centers, Inc. Trustee Westminster Coll. Served to lt. col., Finance Dept., AUS, 1942-46. Mem. Greater Salt Lake C. of C. (dir.). Clubs: Reserve City Bankers, Rotary, Alta. Home: 3157 Louise Av Salt Lake City UT 84109 Office: 175 S Main St Salt Lake City UT 84110

KESNER, BERNARD, physician. Asst. commr. City Hosp. Center at Elmhurst. Office: 79-01 Broadway Elmhurst Sta Flushing NY 11373*

KESSEL, BARNEY, musician; b. Muskogee, Okla., Oct. 17, 1923; s. Abraham and Ruth (Raisher) K.; student pub. schs., Muskogee; m. Betty Jane Rase, Aug. 15, 1961; children (by previous marriage)—Dan Alan, David Brian. Began career as jazz guitarist Chico Marx Orch., Blackhawk Restaurant, Chgo., 1942-43; played with Benny Goodman, Artie Shaw, Charlie Barnet; free lance musician in TV, radio, motion pictures, recordings; music cons., 1945-. Recipient awards Downbeat, Metronome, Playboy, Melody Maker. Mem. A.S.C.A.P., Am. Fedn. Musicians. Author: The Guitar, 1967. Address: 1727 Las Flores Dr Glendale CA 91207

KESSEL, BRINA, ornithologist; b. Ithaca, Nov. 20, 1925; d. Marcel and Quinta (Cattell) Kessel; B.S. (Albert R. Brand Bird Song Found. scholar), Cornell U., 1947, Ph.D., 1951; M.S. (Wis. Alumni Research Found. fellow), U. Wis., 1949; m. Raymond B. Roof, June 19, 1957 (dec. 1968). Student asst. Patuxent Research Refuge, 1946; student teaching asst. Cornell U., 1945- 47, grad. asst., 1947-48, 49-51; instr. biol. sci. U. Alaska, summer 1951, asst. prof. biol. sci., 1951-54, asso. prof. zoology, 1954-59, prof. zoology, 1959—, head dept. biol. scis., 1957-66, dean Coll. Biol. Scis. and Renewable Resources, 1961—, project dir. U. Alaska ecol. investigation for AEC Project Chariot, 1959-63. Fellow A.A.A.S.; elective mem. Am. Ornithologists Union; mem. Alaska, Wilson, Cooper ornith. socs., Animal Behavior Soc., Am. Inst. Biol. Scis., Am. Soc. Zoologists, Ecol. Soc. Am., Arctic Inst. N.Am., Pacific Northwest Bird and Mammal Soc., Sigma Xi (pres. U. Alaska 1957), Phi Kappa Phi, Sigma Delta Epsilon. Contbr. articles to profl. jours. Home: Box 211 College AK 99735

KESSEL, EDWARD LUTHER, zoologist, educator; b. Osborne, Kan., Apr. 27, 1904; s. George Grant and Harriet Lavon (Flenniken) K.; student U. Cal. at Berkeley, 1921-22, B.S., 1925, M.S., 1928, Ph.D., 1936; student Greenville (Ill.) Coll., 1922-24; m. Marguerite Berta Baldwin, Apr. 19, 1935; children—Margaret Mary (Mrs. Claude E. Hunter), Leonard Joseph. Instr. zoology, entomology Marquette U., 1928-30; asst. prof. biology U. San Francisco, 1930-36, asso. prof., 1936-38, prof., 1938—, chmn. dept., 1938-69; asst. curator insects Cal. Acad. Scis., 1945-50, asso. curator diptera, 1950—. Mem. Commn. on Racial and Cultural Relations, No. Cal.-Nev. Council Chs., 1961-64; chmn. Christian citizenship and social action com. Marin County (Cal.) Council Chs., 1962-65; chmn. Protestant Interracial Fellowship, 1962-65; mem. exec. bd. Marin County br. N.A.A.C.P., Marin Com. for Fair Play in Housing, No. Cal. chpt. Presbyn. Interracial Council. Recipient Distinguished Teaching award U. San Francisco, 1970. Fellow A.A.A.S., Cal. Acad. Scis.; mem. Pacific Coast (past pres.), Kan. entomol. socs., Soc. Systematic Zoology (past sect. councilor), Biosystematists, Wilderness Soc., Nature Conservancy, Animal Behavior Soc., Sigma Xi, Phi Sigma. Author: Embryology of Fleas, 1936; Mating Habits of Balloon Flies, 1955; Mating Behavior and Activity-Rest Periodicity in Protoclythia, 1962; Revision of The Genera of Platypezidae, 1968; Platypezidae of the Oriental Zoogeographic Region, 1969; Platypezidae of the Ethiopian Zoogeographic Region, 1970. Editor: Wasmann Jour. Biology, 1939—. Procs. Occasional Papers and Memoirs of the Cal. Acad. Scis., 1950—; A Century of Progress in the Natural Sciences 1853-1953, 1955. Home: P O Box 265 Novato CA 94947 Office: Dept Biology U San Francisco San Francisco CA 94117

KESSEL, JOHN FLENNIKEN, univ. prof.; b. Medicine Lodge, Kan., Feb. 28, 1894; s. George Grant and Harriet Levon (Flenniken) K.; ed. Natal Govt. Tchrs. Coll., South Africa, 1913-14 A.B., Greenville (Ill.) Coll., 1919; A.M., U. Calif., 1921, Ph.D., 1923; m. Ruth Elizabeth Brodhead, June 19, 1918; children—Margaret Lucene (Mikkelsen), John Delbert. Teaching fellow U. Calif., 1919-22, Univ. fellow, 1922-25; asso. in parasitology Peking (China) Union Med. Coll., 1923-27; asso. prof. parasitology U. Calif. at Los Angeles, 1927-29; prof. tropical diseases Coll. Medical Evangelists, 1928-31; prof. bacteriology and parasitology Sch. of Medicine, U. So. Calif., 1931-51; prof. infectious diseases (parasitology and tropic diseases). head div., med. sch. U. Cal., Los Angeles, 1951-63, emeritus prof. infectious and tropical diseases School Public Health, U. Cal. at Los Angeles, 1963—; chief microbiologist at Los Angeles County Hosp., 1928-50. Chmn. Filariasis Found., U. So. Calif., 1947-51; asso. Institut de Recherches Medicales de la Polynesie Française; mem. typing com. Nat. Found. Infantile Paralysis, 1948-51; dir. Tropic Diseases Project, U. Calif. at Los Angeles, 1951—. Cons. Calif. State Health Dept., 1940-52, USPHS, 1943-61, and Microbiology, Los Angeles Co. Hosp., 1950—, Filariasis South Pacific Commn., 1951—, Parasitology World Health Organization, 1951—, Pacific Science Board, NRA, 1953—, Estelle Doheny Eve Foundation, 1956-64. Fellow A.A.A.S., Am. Pub. Health Assn., Cal. Acad. Scis., Royal Soc. Tropical Medicine and Hygiene, Am. Acad. Microbiology :mem. Am. Bd. Microbiology (diplomate), Internat. Filariasis Assn. (pres. 1963-70), Am. Soc. Tropical Medicine (councillor 1942-47; editorial bd. 1946-52), Soc. Parasitologists (councillor 1938-41; editorial b a 1941-43), Soc. Exptl. Biology and Medicine (councillor 1934; pres. So. Calif. br. 1931), Soc. Am. Bacteriologists, Am. Acad. Tropical Medicine (councilor 1951), Western Soc. of Naturalists (pres. 1937), Nat. Malaria Soc., Sigma Xi, Phi Sigma, Phi Kappa Phi. Chevalier de la Legion d'Honneur. Research includes tropical diseases, especially intestional bacteria and protozoa of man and lab. animals; fungus infections of man, including coccidioidomycosis and cryptococcosis; virus infections, including poliomyelitis and infectious myxomatosis, helminth infections, including filariasis and hookworm. Address: Sch of Pub Health U of California Los Angeles CA 90024

KESSEL, JOHN HOWARD, polit. scientist, educator; b. Dayton, O., Oct. 13, 1928; s. Arthur V. and Helen (Hopkins) K.; student Purdue U., 1946-48; B.A., Ohio State U., 1950; Ph.D., Columbia, 1958; m. Margaret Sarah Wagner, Aug. 22, 1954; children—Robert Arthur, Thomas John. Instr., Amherst and Mt. Holyoke colls., 1957-58; instr., asst. prof. Amherst Coll., 1958-61; asst. prof. U. Wash., 1961-65; Arthur E. Braun prof. polit. sci. Allegheny Coll., Meadville, Pa., 1965-70; prof. polit. sci. Ohio State U., Columbus, 1970—. Mem. exec. council Inter-Univ. Consortium for Polit. Research, 1964-65, 67-68. Exec. dir. Nixon-Lodge Vols. Mass., 1960; dir. arts, scis. div. Republican Nat. Com., 1963-64. Served with USNR, 1950-53. Nat. Center Edn. in Politics nat. conv. fellow, 1960, nat. com. fellow, 1963-64, Govt. Affairs Inst. nat. com. fellow, 1964. Mem. Am. Polit Sci. Assn. (exec. council 1969-71). Author: The Goldwater Coalition: Republican Strategies in 1964, 1968. Co-editor: Micropolitics-Individual and Group Level Concepts, 1970. Contbr. articles to profl. jours. Home: 516 E Schreyer Pl Columbus OH 43214

KESSEL, LAWRENCE REEFER, corp. exec., investor; b. Kansas City, Mo., Nov. 1, 1903; s. Paul and Laura (Reefer) K.; B.S. magna cum laude, Harvard, 1925; spl. work Univs. Goettingen, Sorbonne, Munich, Berlin, Columbia, Harvard Bus. Sch.; m. Marie Adler, Mar. 25, 1933; 1 dau., Laura. Operated mining, farming and retail store enterprises as entrepreneur or cons., hdqrs. Kansas City, Mo., 1925-48; asso. with investment fund Graham- Newman Corp., hdqrs. N.Y.C., 1949-54; pres., chmn. bd. Adam Hat Stores, Inc.; dir. Nathan Straus-Duparquet, Utica Knitting Co., Dean Phipps Stores, Inc., United Cities Realty Corp., Studio Apts. Co. Inc., Greater N.Y. Devel. Co., Sidney Blumenthal & Co., Inc., Wood Harmon Corp., Curtis Pub. Co., Thew Shovel Co., Ogdensburg Terminal Corp., C.K.P. Devels. Ltd.; mem. exec. com., dir. A.S. Beck Shoe Corp., Arrow Machinery Co., Brantford Coach & Body, Ltd., Rutland Corp.; v.p., dir. Landis Machine Co.; dir. Am. Type Founders Co. Inc., Saturday Evening Post Co., Norwich & Worcester R.R. Co., Pibly Fund, Inc.; gen. partner Lawrence Kessel & Assos., Alden Industries, indsl. finance; v.p., chmn. exec. com., dir. Cockshutt Farm Equipment, Ltd.; dir., mem. finance com. Del. & Hudson Co., Champlain Nat. Securities, Inc.; bd. mgrs. Champlain Nat. Corp. Trustee United Service for New Ams. Mem. Am. Finance Assn., N.Y. Soc. Security Analysts, Harvard-Yale-Princeton '25 Assn. (sec.). Club: Harvard (N.Y.C., Kansas City, Mo.). Home: 4 E 78th St New York City NY 10021

KESSEL, REUBEN A., educator, economist; b. Chgo., Apr. 2, 1923; s. A.J. and Blossom (Naiman) K.; M.B.A., U. Chgo., 1948, Ph.D., 1954; m. Shirley Kerner, Sept. 16, 1952; 1 dau., Catherine B. Economist, RAND Corp., Santa Monica, Cal., 1952-56; asst. prof. Sch. Bus., U. Cal. at Los Angeles, 1956-57; faculty U. Chgo. Sch. Bus., 1957—, prof. econs., 1964—, dir. research, 1969—. With Nat. Bur. Econ. Research, N.Y.C., 1961-62; cons., dir., Bell Fed. Savs. & Loan Assn., Chgo., 1956—. Impartial econ. expert Judge Robeson, Fed. Ct. Chgo., 1966-. Served with AUS, 1943-46. Mem. Am. Econ. Assn. Author: Cyclical Behavior of the Term Structure of Interest Rates, 1965; also articles. Home: 2235 Hutchison Rd Flossmoor IL 60422 Office: Sch Business U Chicago Chicago IL 60637

KESSELMAN, LOUIS COLERIDGE, educator; b. Columbus, O., Nov. 12, 1919; s. Max and Pearl (Miller) K.; A.B., Ohio State U., 1940, M.A., 1941, Ph.D., 1947; m. Jennie Stregevsky, Jan. 3, 1942; children—Penny Lou, Jonathan Rhys. Instr. polit. sci. Ohio State U., 1941-47; asst. prof. U. Louisville, 1947-51, asso. prof., 1951-53, prof., 1953—, chmn. dept. polit sci., 1953-70. Fulbright lectr. U. Oslo, 1953-54, U. Helsinki, Finnish Sch. Social Scis., 1960-61. Economist regional War Labor Bd., Cleve., 1943; pub. panel mem., hearing ofcr. and arbitrator Nat. War Labor Bd., 1943-45; mem. enforcement commn. regional WSB, Cleve., 1951-53; labor arbitrator Fed. Mediation and Conciliation Service, Am. Arbitration Assn., Louisville Labor-Mgmt. Commn. Dir. Scandinavian Inst. on Am. Trade Unionism, 1954; cons. Ky. Com. Human Relations, 1954-57, So. Regional Council, 1957; mem. Ky. Personnel Merit System Council, 1955-57. Mem. Nat. Acad. Arbitrators, Am., Ky. (exec. bd.) civil liberties unions, Am. Assn. U. Profs., Midwest Polit. Sci. Conf., Ky. Conf. Polit. Scientists (pres. 1963-64), Am., Finnish polit. sci. assns., Pi Sigma Alpha, Phi Kappa Phi. Author: The Social Politics of F.E.P.C., 1948. Mem. editorial bd. Midwest Jour. Polit. Sci., 1957-60. Contbr. articles to profl. jours. Home: 502 Brookview Rd Louisville KY 40207

KESSEN, WILLIAM, psychologist; b. Key West, Fla., Jan. 18, 1925; s. Herman Lowry and Maria Angela (Lord) K.; B.S., U. Fla., 1948; Sc.M., Brown U., 1950; Ph.D., Yale, 1952; m. Marion Lord, June 10, 1950; children—Judith, Deborah, Anne, Peter Christopher, Andrew Lord, John Michael. Postdoctoral fellow Child Study Center, Yale, 1952-54, faculty dept. psychology and Child Study Center, 1954-65, prof. psychology and research asso. pediatrics, 1965—; fellow Center Advanced Study Behavioral Sciences, 1959-60. Mem. intellective processes research com. Social Sci. Research Council, 1959-63, chmn., 1961-63. Recipient aux. research award Social Sci. Research Council, 1958. Guggenheim fellow, 1970-71. Fellow A.A.A.S.; mem. Am. Assn. U. Profs., Am. Psychol. Assn., Soc. Research Child Devel., Soc. Exptl. Psychologists. Author: (with G. Mandler) The Language of Psychology, 1959; The Child, 1965. Co-editor: Perspectives in Psychology, 1964. Contbr. articles to profl. jours. Home: 3 Halstead Lane Branford CT 06405 Office: 333 Cedar St New Haven CT 06519

KESSIE, JACK JOEL, editor; b. Chgo., July 7, 1927; s. Sam and Esther (Schuffman) K.; student Loyola U., Chgo., 1945-46, Roosevelt Coll., 1946-47; B.C.S., Drake U., 1949; m. Carole Craig, Dec. 11, 1964. Adv. dir. Coronet Instructional Films, Chgo., 1949-50; mng. editor playboy mag., Chgo., 1955—. Served with AUS, 1950-52. Club: Chicago Press. Home: 1 E Schiller St Chicago IL 60610 Office: 919 N Michigan Av Chicago IL 60611

KESSINGER, DON EULON, profl. baseball player; b. Forrest City, Ark., July 17, 1942; s. Howard and Ida (Bannister) K.; B.S. in Bus. Adminstrn., U. Miss.; m. Carolyn Crawley, Feb. 20, 1965; children-Keith, Kevin, Mem. Chgo. Cubs Nat. League Profl. Baseball Team, since 1964—; leading shortstop in assists. Bd. dirs. Chgo. Met. Area YMCA, Chgo. chpt. Fellowship Christian Athletes. Served with AUS. Named All Star Shortstop, 1958, 69, 70; recipient Golden Glove award, 1969. Mem. Sigma Nu. Home: 1314 Adirondack St Northbrook IL 60062 Office: Wrigley Field Chicago IL

KESSLER, BERNARD, retail exec.; b. N.Y.C., Jan. 2, 1922; s. Morris and Kate (Harrison) K.; B.S. in Bus., N.Y. U., 1946; student Amos Tuck Sch., Dartmouth. 1942; m. Debra Dubin, Feb. 14, 1951; childen—Peter, Susan, Matthew, David. Founder, pres. Knighthood Shirt Corp., 1947-50; mdsg. v.p. men's haberdashery chain, 1951-56; founder Unishops, Inc., 1957—, chmn.. bd., chief exec. officer, 1962—. Pres. Mass Mdsg. Research Found. Mem. pace setters com. United Jewish Appeal, 1968-69. Trustee Daus. Israel. Pleasant Valley Home Aged, Jewish Community Council. Daniel I. Kessler Meml. Found. Served with USMCR, 1941-45. Recipient Mass. Mdsg. Hall of Fame award U. Mass., 1965. Mem. Sales Execs. Club N.Y.C., A.I.M. (pres. council). Clubs: Green Brook Country (N. Caldwell, N.J.); Brentwood Country (Los Angeles); City Athletic, Manhattan, Marco Polo (N.Y.C.); Palm Beach (Fla.) Country. Home: 98 Minnisink Rd Short Hills NJ 07078 Office: 21 Caven Point Av Jersey City NJ 07305

KESSLER, CLAY JACKSON, holding co. exec.; b. Oklahoma City, Aug. 13, 1916; s. James Marshall and Trula (Worley) K.; B.S., U. Okla., 1939; m. Nell Connellee, June 17, 1936; children—Jean C. (Mrs. Fred Hallman), Anne E. Publisher, Research Reports, 1949-59; with Doric Corp., 1959—, sr. v.p., 1961-63, exec. v.p., 1963-71, pres., 1971—, also dir. corp. and subsidiaries. Mem. Am. Mgmt. Assn., Phi Gamma Delta. Home: 425 N W 34th St Oklahoma City OK 73118

KESSLER, FRIEDRICH, educator; b. Hechingen, Germany, Aug. 25, 1901; s. Wilhelm and Helene (Krueger) K.; student univs. Tuebingen, Munich, Marburg, 1919-22; J.U.D., U. Berlin, 1928; A.M. (hon.), Yale, 1947; LL.D., Boston U., 1970; m. Eva Ionas, July 30, 1930. Came to U.S., 1934, naturalized, 1942. Research mem. Kaiser Wilhelm Inst. Fgn. and Internat. Law, Berlin, Germany, 1926-33; privatdozent Handelshochschule, Berlin, 1931-34; instr., asst. prof. Yale Law Sch., 1935-38; asso. prof., prof. U. Chgo. Law Sch., 1938-47; prof. law Yale, 1947-58, Justus S. Hotchkiss prof. law, 1958-64, Sterling prof. law, 1964-70. Vis. prof. law Harvard Law Sch., 1960-61, U. Cal. at Berkeley, 1964, 70—. Mem. Ill. Bar, Am. Law Inst., Order of Coif. Home: 7 Briar Lane Hamden CT 06511

KESSLER, GEORGE WILLIAM, mfg. co. exec.; b. St. Louis, Mar. 1, 1908; s. William Henry and Blanche M. (Pougher) K.; B.S. in Mech. Engring., U. Ill., 1930; m. Alice May Maxwell, July 28, 1951; children—Judith Ann Green, William Clarkson. With Babcock & Wilcox Co., Barberton, O., 1930—, v.p. engring. power generation div., 1961—. Fellow Am. Soc. M.E.; mem. Am. Standards Assn. (dir.), Soc. Naval Architects and Marine Engrs. (Joseph H. Linard award 1949), Am. Soc. Naval Engrs., Franklin Inst., Nat. Acad. Engring., Welding Research Council, Tau Beta Pi, Phi Eta Sigma, Sigma Tau, Pi Tau Sigma, Alpha Sigma Phi. Clubs: Propeller, Cornell (N.Y.C.). Contbr. articles to profl. jours. Patentee in field. Home: 2515 Shade Park Dr Akron OH 44313 Office: Babcock & Wilcox Co Barberton OH 44203

KESSLER, HENRY H., physician; b. Newark, N.J., Apr. 10, 1896; s. Simon and Bertha (Portugese) K.; A.B., Cornell U., Ithaca N.Y., 1916, M.D., Cornell U. Med. Sch., New York, N.Y., 1919; A.M., Columbia, 1932, Ph.D., 1934; m. Jessie Winnick, Dec. 25, 1918; children—Sanford, Jerome, Joan. In practice as orthopedic surgeon, Newark, N.J., since 1920; attending orthopedic physician, Newark City Hosp., Newark Beth Israel and Hosp. for Crippled Children, Hasbrouck (N.J.) Hosp. Cons. to UN on rehabilitation facilities in Yugoslavia, 1951, Indonesia, 1954, Phillippines, 1955-56; cons. to Internat. Soc. for Welfare of Cripples on rehabilitation facilities in S. Africa, 1955; survey on rehabilitation needs and facilities in foreign countries, 1947-53; del. by Pres. of U.S. to Internat. Congress of Industrial Accidents in Budapest, 1928, Geneva, 1931, Brussels, 1935, Frankfurt, 1938. Mem. N.J. Rehabilitation Commn. Diplomate Am. Bd. Orthopedic Surgery. Fellow Am. Coll. Surgeons, Am. Acad. Orthopedic Surgeons, Am. Pub. Health Assn., Am. Med. Assn. Commd. lt. comdr., USNR, 1936; on active duty since 1941; in South Pacific, 1943; formerly served as capt. USNR serving as chief, amputation center, U.S. Naval Hosp., Mare Island, Calif., Hunterian lecturer, London, Eng., 1935. Recipient gold medal Am. Acad. Orthopedic Surgeons, 1936; Am. Design award, 1944; Advertising Club award, Newark, 1945; recipient E. J. Ill award, 1951; Physicians award Pres. Com. on Employment Physically Handicapped, 1952; award Nat. Conf. Christians and Jews, 1953; Lasker Award, 1954; Gold Medal award by Holland Soc. of N.Y., 1956; Speidel award by Internat. Coll. of Surgeons, 1956; World Vets. Fed. award, 1956; Philippine Legion of Honor, 1956; William G. Anderson award, 1956; Order Phoenix Citation (Greece), 1962; Red Cross award (Madrid) 1964. Fellow Internat. Coll. Surgeons; past pres. Internat. Soc. for Welfare of Cripples; dir. Kessler Inst. for Rehabilitation. Mason. Author: Accidental Injuries, 1931; Occupational Disability Legislation, 1932; The Crippled and Disabled, 1934; Cineplasty, 1947; Rehabilitation of the Physically Handicapped, 1947; The Principles and Practices of Rehabilitation, 1950; Low Back Pain in Industry, 1955; Peter Stuyvesant and His New York, 1959; The Knife Is Not Enough, 1968. Home: 53 Lincoln Park Newark NJ 07102

KESSLER, IRVING KENNETH, mfg. co. exec.; b. Phila., Feb. 14, 1919; s. Jack and Regina (Berkowitz) K.; B.S., Temple U., 1939; postgrad. U. Pa., 1944-46; m. Betinna Chertcoff, May 31, 1942; children—Jeffrey Theodore, John Allen. Wage and salary adminstr. Victor div. RCA, 1941-46; v.p. John B. Stetson Co., 1946-57; mgr. mgmt. engring. RCA, 1957-59, div. v.p., gen. mgr. airborne systems div., Camden, N.J., 1959-61, div. v.p., gen. mgr. Aerospace Communications and Controls Div., 1961-63; div. v.p., gen. mgr. RCA Aerospace Systems Div., 1963-67, v.p. def. electronic products, 1968-69, exec. v.p. def. electronic products, 1969-70, exec. v.p. govt. and comml. systems, 1970—; chmn bd., pres RCA Def. Electronics Corp., 1968—. Mem. panel arbitrators Fed. Mediation and Conciliation Service, 1948—. Chmn. bd. Phila. Survey Group, 1951-52; chmn. indsl. com. North br. YMCA, Phila., 1947-56; area indsl. chmn. Phila. County Savs. Bond Com., 1954-57; indsl. chmn. Jr. Baseball Fedn., 1956-58; dist. chmn. Philenape dist. Boy Scouts Am.; adv. com., chmn. awards com. Phila. United Fund; v.p. Stetson Hosp., Phila.; mem. policy com. devel. program, chmn. fund raising campaign Temple U. Bd. dirs. Demonstration Industries Physically Handicapped; bd. govs. Rydal-Meadowbrook Civic Assn.; trustee NSIA. Recipient merit award Research Inst. Am., 1953. Mem. Armed Forces Communications and Electronics Assn., N.A.M., Am. Arbitration Assn. (nat. panel arbitrators), Indsl. Relations Assn. Phila. (pres. 1956-57), Phila. C of C. (chmn indsl. relations com.), Am. Soc. Naval Engrs., Assn. U.S. Army, Pa. Soc., Nat. Space Club, Am. Inst. Aeros. and Astronautics, Am. Ordnance Assn., Air Force Assn. Club: Keystone Collie (pres. Phila. 1957). Contbr. articles to profl. jours. Home: 2 North Close Moorestown Mews Moorestown NJ 08057 Office: RCA Marne Hwy Moorestown NJ 08057

KESSLER, JOHN OTTO, educator; b. Vienna, Austria, Nov. 26, 1928; s. Jacques and Alice Blanca (Neuhűt) K.; came to U.S., 1940, naturalized, 1946; A.B., Columbia, 1949, Ph.D., 1953; m. Eva M. Bondy, Sept. 9, 1950; children—Helen J., Steven J. With RCA Corp., Princeton, N.J., 1952-66, sr. mem. tech. staff, 1960-66, mgr. grad. recruiting, 1964-66; prof. physics U. Ariz., Tucson, 1966—. Vis. research asso. Princeton, 1962-64. Fellow A.A.A.S.; mem. Am. Phys. Soc., Phi Beta Kappa. Contbr. articles to tech. jours. Patentee in field. Home: 2740 E Camino La Zorrela Tucson AZ 85718

KESSLER, KARL GUNTHER, physicist; b. Hamburg, Germany, Aug. 21, 1919; s. Gunther and Anna (Schneider) K.; came to U.S., 1926, naturalized, 1933; A.B., U. Mich., 1941, B.S., 1942, Ph.D. in Physics, 1947; m. Elizabeth Louise Kefgen, June 28, 1944; children—Heidi Ann, Susan Mary. Asst., instr., research physicist U. Mich., 1942-48; physicist Nat. Bur. Standards, 1948-, chief spectroscopy sect., 1959-62, chief atomic physics div., 1962-70, chief optical physics div., 1970—. Recipient Exceptional Service award Dept. Commerce, 1962. Fellow Am. Phys. Soc., Optical Soc. Am. (pres. 1969); mem. Am. Astron. Soc., Internat. Astron. Union, A.A.A.S., Acad. Sci. Washington, Philos. Soc. Washington, Phi Beta Kappa, Sigma Xi. Home: 5927 Anniston Rd Bethesda MD 20034 Office: Nat Bur Standards Washington DC 20234

KESSLER, LEO, JR., grocery chain exec.; b. Cleve., Dec. 2, 1924; s. Leo and Helen (Maley) K.; B.S., U. Dayton, 1950; m. Mary Alma Schmall, Oct. 21, 1950; children-Marie Elizabeth, Kathleen Ann, Leo III, Joseph Michael. Mgr. mgmt. services dept. Ernst & Ernst, C.P.A.'s, Dayton, O., 1950-60; v.p., treas. Toulmin Enterprises, Dayton, 1960-63; v.p., treas. Wood Shovel & Tool Co., Piqua, O., 1963-65; corporate controller Bissell, Inc., Grand Rapids, Mich., 1965-66; v.p., treas. Am. Community Stores Corp. & Supermarkets Interstate, Inc., Omaha, 1966—; prof. accounting U. Dayton, 1958-63. Served with AUS, 1943-46. Decorated Bronze Star medal. C.P.A., Ohio. Mem. Am. Inst. C.P.A.'s, Nat. Assn. Accountants, Nat. Assn. Internal Auditors. Republican. K.C. Home: 204 S 88th St Omaha NB 68114 Office: 2708 S 84th St Omaha NB 68124

KESSLER, MELVIN EGBERT, architect; b. N.Y.C., Mar. 22, 1913; s. Samuel J. and Rose (Greenfield) K.; student Lehigh U., 1930-31, Columbia, 1932-33; B.Arch., N.Y. U., 1938; m. Mildred Jacobson, Nov. 28, 1934; children—Barbara (Mrs. Donald Lasky), Stuart,

Nancy (Mrs. Frederick Knauer). Designer, L.M. Rothman, N.Y.C., 1932-33, 38-40; chief archtl. designer George Provot, N.Y.C., 1932-35; archtl. designer N.Y.C. Bd. Edn., 1935-37, M.W. Kellogg & Co., 1943-45; asso. architect N.Y. State Div. Housing, 1945-47; partner S.J. Kessler & Sons, architects and engrs., N.Y.C. 1948—. Vis. lectr. Pratt U. and Mechanics Inst., N.Y.C., 1960-; prin. works include Washington Sq. Village, N.Y.C.; developed concept redevel. slums without tenant relocation, 1966. Cons. N.Y.C. Slum Clearance Com., 1954-58; mem. Mayor N.Y.C. Panel Architects, 1942-. Bd. dirs. Shield David Home for Retarded Children, Bronx. Recipient Honor award FHA, 1964, Honor award Urban Renewal Assn., 1964, Albert S. Bard award Bard Found., 1965, Honor award N.Y.C. C. of C., 1958, 61, 63, Philanthropic award Shield of David, 1960. Mem. A.I.A. (v.p. Bronx chpt. 1953-54), N.Y. Soc. Architects, N.Y. Bldg. Congress, Am. Soc. Mil. Engrs., Bronx C. of C., Am. Soc. Testing Materials. Lion. Clubs: University (N.Y. U.); Lehigh. Home: Navarro Central Park S New York City NY 10019 Office: 598 Madison Av New York City NY 10022

KESSLER, NATHAN, mfg. co. exec.; b. St. Louis, Aug. 19, 1923; s. Isadore Harry and Esther (Becker) K.; B.S., M.S., in Chem. Engring. (White-Rodgers fellow), Washington U., St. Louis, 1944; m. Sara Ellen Potashnick, June 21, 1947; children—Joy Sandra, Gail Sue, Margie Ann. With A.E. Staley Mfg. Co., Decatur Ill., 1944—, plant supt., 1962-63, gen. supt., 1963-67, v.p., 1967—, group v.p. tech., 1970—, also dir., mem. exec. com.; dir. Wastech Inc., Houston. Mem. exec. com. of steering com. for formation Jr. Coll. Central Ill.; dir., past pres. bd. United Fund Decatur; bd. dirs. Planned Parenthood of Decatur, Registered profl. engr., Ill. Mem. Am. Inst. Chem. Engrs., Am. Oil Chemists Soc., Nat. Soybean Processors Assn. (chmn. plant operations symposium 1964), Corn Refiners Assn. (chmn. pollution control com.), Decatur Assn. Commerce. Mem. B'nai B'rith (past pres. Decatur). Home: 1405 W Sunset St Decatur IL 60018 Office: A E Staley Mfg Co Decatur IL 62525

KESSLER, PAUL THOMAS, Jr., food co. exec.; b. Zion, Ill., Aug. 18, 1918; s. Paul Thomas and Mary (Leech) K.; B.S., Northwestern U., 1939, M.B.A., 1940; J.D., Loyola U., Chgo., 1940; m. Shuda G. Reighard, Nov. 14, 1947; children—John Richard, Mary Kathern, George Paul, Paul Thomas III. Auditor, David Himmelblau & Co., 1940-42, alien property custodian, asst. chief accountant, 1942-43; mgr. Arthur Andersen & Co., C.P.A.'s, Chgo., 1943-47; admitted to Ill. bar; partner firm Winston, Strawn, Smith & Patterson, Chgo., 1947-66; exec. v.p., dir. Beatrice Foods Co., Chgo., 1966—; dir. Chamberlain Mfg. Corp., Central Nat. Chgo. Corp., Central Nat. Bank in Chgo. Bd. dirs. Found. Fgn. Affairs. C.P.A., Ill. Mem. Law Club Chgo., Am., Chgo. bar assns. Clubs: Chicago, Mid Day (Chgo.); Knollwood (Lake Forest); Bath and Tennis (Lake Bluff, Ill.). Home: 893 E Westleigh Rd Lake Forest IL 60045 Office: 120 S LaSalle St Chicago IL 60603

KESSLER, SAMUEL J., architect; b. N.Y.C., Aug. 10, 1886; B.S. in Engring., Cooper Union, 1910; LL.B., N.Y. Law Sch., 1932. Previously propr. firm S. J. Kessler, now S. J. Kessler & Sons. Mem. A.I.A. (pres. Bronx chpt. 1945-47). Address: 598 Madison Av New York City NY 10022*

KESSLER, SILAS GEORGE, clergyman; b. St. Louis, Aug. 29, 1911; s. Jacob G. and Lena (Hoffman) K.; B.A., U. Dubuque, 1932, B.D., 1934, LL.D., 1964; D.D., Dubuque Theol. Sem., 1941; LL.D., Huron Coll., 1966; m. Ruth Margaret Schap, July 3, 1935; children—Eleanor (Mrs. William A. Wilson), Stanley. Ordained to ministry Presbyn. Ch., 1934; pastor in Farmington, Ia., 1934- 37, Fullerton, Neb., 1937-40, 1st Presbyn. Ch. Hastings, Neb., 1940—. Mem. bd. Christian edn. U.P. Ch. U.S.A., 1951-65, moderator Gen. Assembly, 1963-64, mem. gen. council, 1963-66; pres. Neb. Council Chs., 1966-68. Co-chmn. fund raising com. Chapel All Faiths, Hastings State Hosp., Ingleside, Neb., 1957. Trustee Hastings Coll.; bd. dirs. U. Dubuque. Home: 1223 Pershing Rd Hastings NB 68901 Office: 621 N Lincoln Av Hastings NB 68901

KESSLER, WAYNE, state ofcl.; b. Jamestown, Ind., Apr. 8, 1911; s. William Harry and Helen D. (Spencer) K.; B.S.A., U. Ariz., 1934; m. E. Irleen Cardin, Nov. 12, 1938; children—Elaine D., Alan W. Range conservationist U.S. Bur. Indian Affairs, Sells, Ariz., 1934-35; with U.S. Soil Conservation Service, N.M., Ariz., 1935-45, 48-50, Ariz. Dept. Vocational Agr., Phoenix, 1948; soil conservationist U.S. Bur. Land Mgmt., Phoenix, 1946- 48; dir. Ariz. Div. Soil Conservation, Phoenix, 1950—. State chmn. Ariz. Conservation Edn. Adv. Council. Trustee Nat. Assn. State Soil Conservation Adminstrn. Officers. Served with C.E., AUS, 1942-44. Recipient Star Farmer degree Future Farmers Am., 1960. Mem. Am. Soc. Range Mgmt. (pres. 1964), Soil Conservation Soc. Am., Ariz. Acad. Sci., Ariz. Assn. Soil Conservation Dists., Ariz. Cattle Growers Assn., Ariz. Reclamation Assn. Home: 6710 N 10th Av Phoenix AZ 85014 Office: Arizona State Office Bldg Phoenix AZ 85003

KESTEN, HARRY, educator. Prof. math. Cornell U., Ithaca, N.Y. Office: 35 Turkey Hill Rd Ithaca NY 14850*

KESTER, LENARD, artist; b. N.Y.C., May 10, 1917; s. Human and Yetta (Kalfus) K.; student pub. schs. Exhibited one-man shows, art galleries and museums U.S., maj. nat. exhbns.; paintings in permanent collections Bklyn., Toledo, Boston, Denver, Balt., Springfield, Mo. museums, U. Miami; also pvt. collections. Designer stained glass window Billy Rose Mausoleum. Recipient numerous prizes, awards; awarded Life mag. commn., 1947; executed Mayo Clinic mural, 1953; Tiffany Found. fellow, 1949. Mem. Am. Watercolor Soc. (Windsor and Newton award 1959), Soc. Western Artists; asso. N.A.D. (Obrig prize 1959, Saltus gold medal). Studio: 1117 N Genesee Av Los Angeles CA 90046

KESTER, RANDALL BLAIR, lawyer; b. Vale, Ore., Oct. 20, 1916; s. Bruce R. and Mabel M. (Judd) K.; A.B., Willamette U., 1937; J.D., Columbia, 1940; m. Rachael L. Woodhouse, Oct. 20, 1940; children—Laura, Sylvia, Lynne. Admitted to Ore. bar, 1940; asso., then partner Maguire, Shields, Morrison & Bailey, Portland, 1940-57; partner Maguire, Shields, Morrison, Bailey & Kester, 1958-66; partner Maguire, Kester & Cosgrave, 1966—; instr. Northwestern Coll. Law, 1947-56; justice Ore. Supreme Ct., 1957-58; gen. solicitor northwestern dist. U.P. R.R., 1958—, Yakima Valley Transportation Co., 1958—, Spokane Internat. R.R. Co., 1959—; v.p., dir. Deschutes R.R. Co.; dir. Portland Traction Co., Mount Hood Railway Co., Portland Terminal R.R. Co., Camas Prairie R.R. Co. Trustee Willamette U. Recipient Silver Beaver award Boy Scouts Am. Past v.p. Portland area council Boy Scouts of Am.; past pres. Mountain Rescue and Safety Council Ore. Mem. Am., Multnomah (past pres.) bar assns., Ore. R.R. Assn. (chmn.), Ore. State Bar, Am. Law Inst., Inst. Jud. Adminstrn., Nat., Mt. Hood (past pres.) ski patrols, Mazamas (past pres., climbing chmn.), Wy'east Climbers, Phi Delta Phi, Beta Theta Pi, Tau Kappa Alpha. Clubs: Arlington, City, University, Multnomah Athletic, Portland Yacht (Portland). Home: 10075 S W Hawthorne Lane Portland OR 97225 Office: 727 Pittock Block Portland OR 97205

KESTER, WILLIAM, business and financial editor St. Louis Post Dispatch. Address: 1133 Franklin Av St Louis MO 63102*

KESTING, THEODORE, mag. editor; b. Mont Clare, Pa., Aug. 27, 1918; s. Theodore F. and Pauline (Hechler) K.; student Girard Coll., 1928-36, Pa. Sch. Indsl. Arts, 1937-39, Charles Morrice Price Sch., 1940-41; m. Jean M. Hoffman, Jan. 6, 1945 (dec.); children—Virginia Joan, Frederic, Kristin, David; m. 2d. Lorraine Williams, Mar. 4, 1968. Editor, Curtis Pub. Co., 1936-45; editor, v.p. Sports Afield Pub. Co., Mpls., 1945-53; editor, pub. Am. Boy, 1950-53; editor Sports Afield, Hearst mags., 1956-70, editor Rod and Gun, 1969-70, editor at large Sports Afield, 1971—. Author: The Outdoor Encyclopedia, 1957. Home: Beaver Dam Farm Hume VA 22639 Office: 250 W 55th St New York City NY 10019

KESTLER, MAXIMILANO, ambassador, permanent rep. Guatemala to UN. Address: 205 E 42d St New York City NY 10017*

KESTON, HERMANN, author Copernicus and His World; Ferdinand and Isabella; Casanova; editor (Heinrich Heine) Works of Prose.*

KETCHAM, ALBERT RAVENSWOOD, III, lawyer; b. Phila., Oct. 22, 1925; s. Albert Ravenswood, Jr. and Margaret (Lincoln) K.; B.A. cum laude, U. Vt., 1949; LL.B. cum laude, Harvard, 1952; m. Miriam T. Peterson, Oct. 21, 1950; children—William L., Nancy A., Jonathan M., Susan L., Richard A. Admitted to N.Y. bar, 1954, since practiced in N.Y.C.; asso. atty. Winthrop, Stimson, Putnam & Roberts, 1953-56; asst. sec. Bristol-Myers Co., 1956-66, sec., 1966-71. Mem. Planning and Zoning Commn., Wilton, Conn., 1963-65; mem. Bd. Finance, Wilton, 1967—, chmn., 1968—. Mem. Assn. Bar City N.Y., Phi Beta Kappa, Alpha Tau Omega. Republican. Episcopalian. Home: 131 Millstone Rd Wilton CT 06897 Office: 345 Park Av NC 10022

KETCHAM, ALFRED SCHUTT, surgeon; b. Newark, N.Y., Oct. 7, 1924; s. Colston Esty and Ellen (Schutt) K.; B.S., Hobart Coll., 1945, Sc.D. (hon.); M.D., U. Rochester, 1949; m. Elsie Jane Chase, July 13, 1946; children—Sue Ellen, Wendy Jane, Sally Lin, Jill Ann, Jeff Terry, Dana Kay. Intern, U.S. Naval Med. Center, Bethesda, Md., 1949-50; surg. resident USPHS Hosp., San Francisco, 1950- 52, Seattle, 1952-55; chief surgery USPHS Indian Hosp., Talihina, Okla., 1955-57; investigator, asso. surgeon Nat. Cancer Inst., NIH, Bethesda, Md., 1957-62, chief surgery, 1962—, asso. sci. dir. for clin. research, 1971—. Diplomate Am. Bd. Surgery. Mem. A.M.A., USPHS Clin. Soc., European Soc. Cancer Research, Soc. Head and Neck Surgeons, James Ewing Soc., A.C.S., Am. Radium Soc., Am. Assn. Cancer Research, Theta Delta Chi. Contbr. articles to profl. publs. Home: 1006 Brice Rd Rockville MD 20852 Office: Nat Cancer Inst Bethesda MD 20014

KETCHAM, BRUCE VALENLINE, educator; b. Wilmington, Del., Mar. 17, 1918; s. Valenline O. and Grace (Hendrie) K.; B.Engring., Yale, 1940; M. Aero. Engring., Okla. U., 1956; m. Emily Harter Wilcox, Apr. 8, 1944; children—Elaine, Anne, Bruce Valenline, Jayne. Design engr. Pratt & Whitney Aircraft Corp., 1940-47; faculty U. Okla., 1947-64, prof. propulsion, 1959-64; head aerospace dept. U. Tulsa, 1964—, dir. research and devel., 1966—, also prof. of aerospace engring. Cons., Todd Engring. Co.; mng. editor Rocket and Space Sci. Series, Howard W. Sams, pub. Dir. Holland Aircraft Co., Inc., Motion Products, Inc. Bd. dirs. Tulsa Sci. Found., Tulsa Safety Council. Registered profl. engr., Okla. Mem. Amateur Rocket Assn. (chmn. bd. dirs.), Okla. Soc. Profl. Engrs., Am. Inst. Aeros. and Astronautics, Sigma Xi, Sigma Gamma Tau. Home: 2956 E 47th St Tulsa OK 74105

KETCHAM, CHARLES BROWN, educator; b. Oberlin, O., Mar. 5, 1926; s. Charles Burgess and Lucile (Brown) K.; B.A. magna cum laude, Mt. Union Coll., Alliance, O., 1949; Fulbright scholar philosophy U. Edinburgh (Scotland), 1949-50, div. student New Coll., 1950-51; div. student U. Zurich (Switzerland), 1951; B.D. magna cum laude, Drew U., 1953; Ezra Squire Tipple fellow St. Mary's Coll., U. St. Andrews (Scotland), 1953, Ph.D., 1956; Postdoctoral fellow Harvard Div. Sch., 1970; m. Joyce Alene Parker, June 29, 1950; 1 son, Merrick Scott. Ordained to ministry Methodist Ch., 1952; minister Rockaway Valley, N.J., 1955-57; lectr. philosophy Drew U., 1957; chaplain Allegheny Coll., 1957-63, faculty, 1957—, James M. Thoburn prof. religion, chmn. dept. religion and philosophy, 1966—; vis. scholar Union Theol. Sem., N.Y.C., 1963-64. Chmn. com. higher edn. Western Pa. conf. Meth. Ch., 1962-67; del World Meth. Ecumenical Conf., Oxford, Eng., 1962 Div. vice chmn. local United Fund, 1965-70. Bd. dirs. Meadville Multiracial Com., 1966-70, Meadville chpt. N.A.A.C.P., 1963—. Served with AUS, 1944-46. Mem. Nat. Assn. Coll. and Univ. Chaplains, Am. Acad. Religion, Psi Kappa Omega. Author: The Search for Meaningful Existence, 1968; Co-author, editor; Faith and Freedom, 1969. Contbr. jours. Home: 369 Henry St Meadville PA 16335

KETCHAM, HENRY KING, cartoonist; b. Seattle, Mar. 14, 1920; s. Weaver Vinson and Virginia Emma (King) K.; student U. Wash., 1938; m. Alice Louise Mahar, June 13, 1942 (dec.); 1 son, Dennis L.; m. 2d, Jo Anne Stevens, July 1, 1959 (div.); m. 3d, Rolande Praeprost, June 9, 1970. Animator, Walter Lantz Prodns., Universal Studios, Hollywood, Cal., 1938-39, Walt Disney Prodns., 1939-42; free lance cartoonist 1945-51; creator Dennis the Menace, 1951—, distributed by Pubs.-Hall Syndicate, Inc. Served as chief photographer specialist, USNR, 1941-45, creative work Navy War Bond, Tng. Film Program, 1942-45. Recipeint Billy de Beck Award for outstanding cartoonist, 1952. Mem. Phi Delta Theta, Nat. Cartoonists Soc. Clubs: Mill Reef (Antigua); Golf Club de Geneva; Old Baldy (Saratoga, Wyo.); American International Club Geneva (v.p.). Author: Dennis the Menace cartoon book collections, 1954- -; I Wanna Go Home, 1965. Co-designer Dennis The Menace Playground. Home: P O Box BB Carmal Valley CA 93924 also 14 Parc du Chateau Banquet Geneva Switzerland

KETCHAM, HOWARD, color, design and illumination engr.; b. N.Y.C., Sept. 4, 1902; s. Charles Belden and Suzanne (Brightson) K.; A.B., M.Sc., Amherst, 1925; student N.Y. Sch. Design, 1926-27, Columbia, 1939-40; m. Lois R. Barrett (div. 1942); m. 2d, Mary L. Sauerbrun, Mar. 14, 1944 (div.); children—Suzanne, Marsha, Mary Louise. Art dir. H. K. McCann Co., advt., 1925-27; dir. color adv. service E. I. duPont de Nemours, 1927-34; originated profession color-engring., 1935; chmn. Howard Ketcham, Inc. Colorstyled, created lighting for or designed more than 500 products, establishments and packages for Am. business; works include: re-styled coaches for railroads, supermarkets, chains of gasoline stations; interior and exterior styling jet airplanes; developed color styling for all automobile mfrs., grading color lines for paints, fabrics; for USAF developed optimum lighting for all aircraft; color-coordinator Am. Enka Corp. Pioneer in transmission of colors from Europe to Am. by wireless, Aug. 5, 1936; developed telephone colors for Bell Telephone Labs. Instigator of pioneer nationwide consumer surveys to predetermine color, texture and design preferences for manufactured articles; color cons. House & Garden mag., developing color palette annually for use by mfrs. of house furnishings; cons. U.S. Steel Homes Inc., 1954—, Goodrich Rubber Co. 1954—, Standard- Vacuum Oil Co. Kroger Co., 1960, Am. Airlines, Inc., Volkswagon, Walgreen Drug Co., Am. Cyanamid, Scripto, Inc., Grand Union Co., 1963—; Ford Div., R. J. Reynolds Tobacco Co., S.S. Kresge, 1964—, Borden Co., Nat. Homes, McCrory Stores, Ford Motor Co., Coca-Cola Co., Asbestos & Vinyl. Asbestos Tile Inst. Lecturer, Harvard Ohio State, Northwestern and Minn. U.'s Recipient Wolf award for package design ingenuity; design awards Kidskin Guild, Art Dirs. League, and others; $10,000 prize for Color Schemers in Readers Digest, 1936. Served as commd. officer in sec. of navy's Office Research and Inventions, World War II. Mem. Nat. Paint, Varnish and Lacquer Assn. (chnn. com. on color surveys), Nat. Retail Dry Goods Assn., Illuminating Engring. Soc., Soc. Automotive Engrs., Soc. War 1812, Vet. Corps Arty., Soc. Am. Wars, Indsl. Designers Soc. Am. (dir.), Intersoc. Color Council, Am. Arbitration Assn. St. Georges Soc. N.Y., Chi Psi. Republican. Episcopalian. Clubs: University, Architectural League (New York City); Lake Placid (N.Y.); Interrallie (Paris); Echo Lake Country; Seawanhaka Corinthian (Yacht; Madison Beach (Connecticut). Author: How to Use Color and Design in the Home, 1949 (Book of Month Club selection); Color-It's Theory and Application, 1952; Paint It Yourself; Color Planning In Business and Industry; articles in periodicals. Cons. and/or editor: American Fabrics, Television, Fleetowner, Color Engring. mags., Life, Newsweek. Home: 1150 Fifth Av New York City NY 10022 Office: 101 Park Av New York City NY 10017 also Cold Spring Harbor NY 10516

KETCHUM, ALTON HARRINGTON, advt. exec.; b. Cleve., Oct. 8, 1904; s. Wesley H. and Velma M. (Davis) K.; B.A., Western Res. U., 1926; m. Robyna Neilson, Apr. 27, 1940; 1 dau., Deborah (Mrs. Harvey Lambert). Began his career as special corr. United Press, 1926-27; editorial, advt. work Penton Pub. Co., Powers- House Co., Nesbitt Service Co., 1927-33; with McCann-Erickson, Inc., 1934-62, beginning as copy writer, successively copy group head, v.p., creative supr. internat. div., 1948-62; v.p. Infoplan div. Interpublic, Inc., 1962-64; corporate adminstrv. staff Interpublic, 1964-69; mng. dir. Harrington's Hist. Resources, 1970—. Spl. asst. Petroleum Adminstrn. for War, 1943-44; supr. nat. campaign to explain Am. econ. system sponsored by Advt. Council, 1948-51; spl. rep. U.S. Information Agy., India, 1954, cons., 1956—, mem. exec. res., 1957-60; designed People's Capitalism exhibit for U.S. Information Agy., 1956, Golden Key Exhibit for Dept. of Commerce, 1956. Organizer Westchester- Fairfield (Conn.) Com. of Am. Assn. for UN, 1946; gave original designs for baton and badge of marshals of France to French people, 1953. Mem. Greenwich (Conn.) Auxiliary Police. Recipient award Freedoms Found., 1949, award of merit U.S. Information Agy., 1956; medal for outstanding service to advt., Advt. Fedn. Am., 1961; Gov.'s award for achievement, State Ohio, 1965. Mem. Assn. Am. Geographers, Am. Acad. Polit. and Social Sci., Am., Greenwich hist. socs., India-Am. League (president 1960-64), Hist. Assn. Gt. Britain, Nat. Planning Assn. Author: Follow the Sun, 1930; The Miracle of America, 1948; The March of Freedom, 1951; Let Freedom Ring, 1952; Uncle Sam: The Man and The Legend, 1959. Editor: Bull. Inst. Marketing Communications, 1965-69; Principles and Practices of Marketing Communications, 1966. Mem. internat. editorial bd. World Govt. News, 1949-52. Home: Cognewaug Road Cos Cob CT 06807 Office: 485 Lexington Av New York City NY 10017

KETCHUM, CARLTON GRISWOLD, fund raising counsel; b. Yankton, S.D., Feb. 17, 1892; s. Lester and Luna L. (Beard) K.; student Oberlin Coll., 1910-11; B.S. in Econs., U. Pitts., 1916; m. Mildred Caroline Storey, Oct. 8, 1914; 1 son, David Storey. Various positions, 1900-12; asst. to dir. univ. extension U. Pitts., 1912-14, asst. registrar, 1914-16, publicity, asso. campaign dir., campaign dir., 1916—; pres., dir. Ketchum, Inc., campaign direction, pub. relations, Pitts., 1919-66, chmn., 1966—. Bd. dirs. YMCA; v.p., bd. dirs. Assn. for Improvement the Poor; v.p. 100,000 Pennsylvanians. Finance dir. Republican Nat. Com., 1937-41, 49-57; mem. Rep. finance coms. Served from pvt. to 2d lt. U.S. Army, 1917-19; from lt. col. to col. USAAF, 1942-45. Mem. Am. Legion, Omicron Delta Kappa. Presbyn. (nat. exec. com. Lay Com.), Mason. Clubs: Duquesne, University (Pitts.). Home: 530 Glen Arden Dr Pittsburgh PA 15208 Office: 314 Chatham Center Pittsburgh PA 15219

KETCHUM, DAVID STOREY, fund raising counsel; b. Pitts., Sept. 28, 1920; s. Carlton G. and Mildred (Storey) K.; grad. Shady Side Acad., 1937; A.B., Cornell U., 1941; m. Sally Louise Doerschuk, Jan. 14, 1950; children—Louise Anne, Laura Jean. Sales rep. IBM Corp., 1941-42; pres., dir. Ketchum, Inc., Pitts., 1945- -. Trustee Childrens Home Pitts.; past v.p. Council Chs. Pitts.; pres. Am. Assn. Fund Raising Counsel, 1969-70, now mem. exec. com., bd. dirs; mem. Cornell U. Council; bd. dirs. Animal Rescue League of Pitts. Served to capt. USAAF, 1942-45. Decorated Bronze Star medal. Mem. Pitts. Bibliophiles, Sigma Alpha Epsilon. Republican. Presbyn. Club: Union League (N.Y.C.); Duquesne, University, Fox Chapel Racquet (Pitts.). Home: 131 Yorkshire Rd Pittsburgh PA 15208 Office: Chatham Center Pittsburgh PA 15219

KETCHUM, GARDNER MASON, educator; b. Phila., Oct. 20 1919; s. Harold Bostwick and Bertha (Mason) K.; S.B., Mass. Inst. Tech., 1941, S.M., 1944, Sc.D., 1949; m. Marion Stanford, Mar. 19, 1949; 1 son, Richard Gardner. Asst., then instr. Mass. Inst. Tech., 1941-48; devel. engr. Gen. Electric Co., 1948-53; faculty Union Coll., Schenectady, 1953—, prof. mech. engring., 1956—, chmn. dept., 1962—. cons. indsl. cos., U.S. Army. Registered profl. engr., N.Y. Fellow Am. Soc. M.E.; mem. Am. Soc. Engring. Edn., Am. Assn. U. Profs., Sigma Xi, Tau Beta Pi. Home: 1307 Glenwood Blvd Schenectady NY 12308

KETCHUM, HARRY WILBUR, govt. ofcl.; b. Colorado Springs, Colo., May 10, 1910; s. John Henry and Arial (Harkrader) K.; A.B., U. Denver, 1933; M.B.A., Harvard Grad. Sch. Bus. Adminstrn., 1935; m. Sybil Mae Leuty, June 8, 1935; children—Harry Wilbur, Lynne Anne. Instr. econs. U. Conn., 1935-36; asst. prof. bus. adminstrn. Judson Coll., Marion, Ala., 1936-39; chmn. dept. statistics, prof. econs., dean undergrad. div., dir. Sch. Social Sci. and Pub. Affairs, Am. U., 1939-47; asst. chief marketing div., chief distbn. cost sect. Office Industry and Commerce, U.S. Dept. Commerce, 1947-50; charge alumnium task force, light metals div. NPA, 1950-51, dir. program rev. staff and dir. program coordination and review div. Office Civilian Requirements, 1951-52, chief emergency flood mission, Mo.-Miss. river basins, 1952, dep. asst. adminstr. for civilian requirements, 1952; dep. to asst. dir., and dir. distbn. costs div., 1952-53, dir. of office distbn. Bus. and Def. Services Adminstrn., 1952-62, dir. marketing information div., 1962-64, economist Office Chems, and Consumer Products, 1965—, dir. marketing information staff div. Bus. and Def. Services Adminstrn. cons. OPA, 1943; Mem. Pi Kappa Alpha. Mason. Contbr. articles to profl. jours. Home: 906 La Grande Rd Silver Spring MD 20903 Office: US Dept Commerce Washington DC 20230

KETCHUM, MARSHALL DANA, educator; b. Buffalo, Dec. 16, 1905; s. Dorr Mason and Maude (Moore) K.; B.S., Syracuse U., 1928, M.S., 1929; Ph.D., U. Chgo., 1937; m. Clara Louise Whitten, Sept. 1, 1931; children—Marshall Dorr, Richard Jennings. Registrar, Syracuse U., 1929-30; instr. Duke, 1931-32; asst. prof., asso. prof., prof. Utah State U., 1932-38, U. Ky., 1938-46; professorial lectr. Grad. Sch. Bus., U. Chgo., 1945, mem. faculty, 1946—, asso. prof., 1946-51, prof., 1951—; lectr. exec. devel. program U. Mich., 1954-63. Dir., bd. regents Life Officers Investment Seminar, 1948—, Financial Analysts

Seminar, 1956—; dir., chmn. exec. com. Conf. Savs. and Residential Financing, 1958-67; editoral adv. in finance Houghton Mifflin Co., 1960—. Mem. Am. Econ. Assn., Am. Finance Assn. (past pres., editor Jour. Finance, 1946-55, chmn. bd. dirs., chmn. adv. com., chmn. editorial bd., mem. adv. com. 1957-61), Am. Real Estate and Urban Econs. Assn., Am. Assn. U. Profs. Clubs: Quadrangle, Economic (Chgo.) Author: The Fixed Investment Trust, 1937; (with Ralph R. Pickett) Investment Principles and Policy, 1954. Co-editor: Readings in Financial Institutions, 1965. Contbr. articles profl. jours. Home: 5805 Dorchester Av Chicago IL 60637

KETCHUM, MORRIS, Jr., architect; b. N.Y.C., May 5, 1904; s. Morris and Jane (Gillet) K.; A.B., Columbia, 1926, B.Arch., 1928; diploma architecture Sch. Fine Arts, Fontainbleau, France, 1928; m. Isabella Taylor Stiger, Apr. 28, 1934. Instr. archtl. design, sch. architecture and allied arts N.Y. U., 1942-43; asst. prof. archtl. design Yale, 1943-45; lectr., vis. critic in design Cooper Union Art Sch., 1943-45, 56-58; faculty grad. sch. arch. Pratt Inst., 1954-56; partner Morris Ketchum Jr. & Assos., N.Y.C., work included ednl., comml., instl. design, especially coll. bldgs., pub. and zool. bldgs., schs., dept. stores, shopping centers; projects include State U. Agrl. and Tech. Coll. Campus, Morrisville, N.Y., Queens Coll. Campus, N.Y.C., Bronx Zoo World of Darkness, N.Y.C., Bronx Zoo World of Birds, Intermediate Sch. 29, N.Y.C., May D&F, Denver, U.S. embassy and ambassador's residence, Rabat, Morocco, Nordiska Kompaniet, Stockholm, Sweden. Decorated chevalier Ordre des Arts et Lettres. Fellow A.I.A. (pres. 1965-66); mem. Archtl. League N.Y. (past pres.), Municipal Art Soc. N.Y. (past pres.). Episcopalian. Author: Shops and Stores. Contbr. articles to mags. Home: 200 E 62d St New York City NY 10021 Office: 919 3d Av New York City NY 10022

KETCHUM, PAUL ALLISON, glass mfg. co. exec.; b. Quincy, Mass., May 3, 1908; s. Woodford and Eleanor (Ross) K.; A.B., Harvard, 1931; m. Elizabeth Sargent, Oct. 15, 1932 (dec. Dec. 1938); children—Ezekiel, Elizabeth; m. 2d, Frances Blaser, June 19, 1941; children—John, Susan. With PPG Industries (formerly Pitts. Plate Glass Co.), 1931—, v.p. glass sales, 1959—. Clubs: Harvard-Yale-Princeton, Duquesne, Harvard of Western Pa. (Pitts.). Home: 195 Vernon Dr Pittsburgh PA 15228 Office: 1 Gateway Center Pittsburgh PA 15222

KETCHUM, PHILLIPS, lawyer; b. Portland, Me., Dec. 16, 1884; s. Charles John and Rebekah Kimball (Phillips) K.; A.B., Harvard, 1906, LL.B., 1908; m. Margery S. Amory, May 22, 1928 (dec. Oct. 1948); children—Phillips, Jonathan, Rebekah; m. 2d, Amey P. Amory, Apr. 18, 1953. Partner firm Herrick, Smith, Donald, Farley & Ketchum, Boston; dir. Wyman Gordon Co., Samuel Cabot, Inc. Home: Glen St Natick MA 01760 Office: 294 Washington St Boston MA 02108

KETCHUM, RICHARD MALCOLM, editor, writer; b. Pitts., Mar. 15, 1922; s. George and Thelma (Patton) K.; grad. Shady Side Acad., Pitts., 1939; B.A., Yale, 1943; m. Barbara Jane Bray, Apr. 24, 1943; children—Liza (Mrs. Murrow), Thomas Bray. Asst. to pres. Charles F. Orvis Co., Manchester, Vt., 1946-48; owner advt. agy., partner Vermonters, Ltd., Manchester, 1948-51; with USIA, 1951-56, chief visual materials div., 1956; editor book div. Am. Heritage Pub. Co., Inc., 1956-64; editorial dir. book div., 1964-67, mng. dir. book div., 1967—, also v.p., dir., asso. editor Am. Heritage mag., mem. adv. bd. Horizon mag. Trustee Vt. Hist. Soc.; mem. New Eng. Forestry Found. Served to lt. (j.g.) USNR, 1943-46. Clubs: Yale, Coffee House (N.Y.C.); Metropolitan (Washington). Author: Male Husbandry, 1956; American Heritage Book of Great Historic Places, 1957; The Battle for Bunker Hill, 1962; Faces from the Past, 1970; The Secret Life of the Forest, 1970. Editor: What is Communism?, 1955; What is Democracy?, 1955; American Heritage Book of the Revolution, 1958; American Heritage Book of the Pioneer Spirit, 1959; American Heritage Picture History of the Civil War (spl. Pulitzer prize citation 1961), 1960; The Horizon Book of the Renaissance, 1961; Four Days, 1964; The Original Water-Color Paintings by John James Audubon for the Birds of America. Home: Dorset VT 05251 Office: American Heritage 551 Fifth Av New York City NY 10017

KETELSEN, JAMES LEE, constrn. and farm equipment co. exec.; b. Davenport, Ia., Nov. 14, 1930; s. Ernest Henry and Helen (Schumann) K.; B.S. in Bus. Adminstrn., Northwestern U., 1952; m. Joan Velde, Feb. 22, 1953; children—James V., Lee. Accountant, Price Waterhouse & Co., C.P.A.'s, Chgo., 1955-59; with J.I. Case Co., Racine, Wis., 1959—, v.p. finance, treas., 1962-67, V.P. operations, 1967-68, pres., chief exec. officer, 1968—. also dir. Served to lt. USNR, 1952-55. C.P.A., Ill. Mem. Financial Execs. Inst., Young Pres. Orgn., Chi Psi. Home: 110 Raven Turn E Racine WI 53402 Office: 700 State St Racine WI 53404

KETNER, WAYNE MITCHELL, glass co. exec.; b. Toboso, O., Dec. 10, 1920; s. George A. and Nellie (Irwin) K.; B.S., Ohio U., 1942; postgrad. Harvard Grad. Sch. Bus. Adminstrn., 1942-43; m. Frances Elizabeth Berry, Sept. 3, 1944; children—Gary Wayne, Pamela Ann. With Owens- Corning Fiberglas Corp., Toledo, 1943—, asst. comptroller, 1964-65, comptroller, 1965-68, v.p., controller, 1969—. Mem. Financial Execs. Inst., Delta Tau Delta. Methodist. Mason. Club: Inverness (Toledo). Home: 4614 Penridge Rd Toledo OH 43615 Office: Fiberglas Tower Toledo OH 43601

KETO, JOHN EDWIN, cons. engr.; b. Maynard, Mass., June 9, 1909; s. Wayne and Tynne Jameson (Stein) K.; E.E., U. Cin., 1932, M.S., 1935; D.Sc., Bradley U. Peoria, Ill., 1961; m. Evelyn Camburn, Apr. 29, 1936; children—Martha Sharron, John Wayne. Teaching fellow elec. engring. U. Cin., 1933-35; research physicist propagation and high frequency phenomena Signal Corps. U.S. Army and Air Force, Wright Field, Dayton, O., 1935-41, br. chief and chief engr. Radar Lab., 1941-46, chief Aircraft Radiation Lab., 1946-51, tech. dir. Weapons Components div., 1951-52, became tech. dir. Wright air devel. div. Air Research and Devel. Command, 1952, now chief scientist aero. systems div. Air Force Systems Command, 1957-69; cons., 1969—. Mem. exec. com. Ohio Research and Devel. Found. 1963-65. Mem. radar panel, research and development bd. Nat. Mil. Establishment, 1947-51; U.S. Air Force mem. Dept. Def. Com., Sr. Sci. and Engring. Service, 1957, Air Force mem. exec. com. U.S. Nat. Com. Internat. Sci. Radio Union, 1957-69. Trustee Wright State U., Dayton, O. Recipient Presidential Medal for Merit, 1946; scholarship Am. Mgmt. Assn., 1956. Fellow Inst. Radio Engrs. (chmn. Dayton sect. 1946-47); mem. Profl. Group Aero and Navigational Electronics, Profl. Group Mil. Electronics, Armed Forces Communications and Electronics Assn. (dir. Dayton sect. 1954-56), Sigma Xi, Tau Beta Pi, Eta Kappa Nu, American Assn. Common Clubs. Home: 829 Laurelwood Rd Dayton OH 45419

KETRING, VERNON VIVIAN, lawyer; b. Tahyer, Kan., Oct. 9, 1904; s. Herman Feaster and Elva Pearl (Riggs) K.; A.B., U. Neb., 1929; student U. Colo., 1925; J.D., U. Denver, 1940; m. Daisy Cones; 1 dau., Sally Lou (Mrs. Martin L. Merritt). Admitted to Colo. bar, 1940, since practiced in Denver; asst. U.S. atty. for Dist. of Colo., 1957-61. Mem. Inter-Am. Bar Assn., Am. Judicature Soc., Am., Fed., Colo. (treas. 1942-52, award of merit 1951), Denver (chmn. membership com. 1941) bar assns., Phi Gamma Delta, Phi Delta Phi. Clubs: Denver Country; Garden of the Gods (Colorado Springs, Colo.). Address: 5375 S Clarkson St Littleton CO 80121

KETTENEH, FRANCIS ANTHONY BERNARD, business exec.; b. Beirut Lebanon, Nov. 7, 1897; s. Anthony and Ellen (Salameh) K.; student Kaiserswerther Disconissen Schule, Coll. Francais du Sacré Coeur; B.S., Am. U. Beirut, 1914, C.E., 1916; m. Mary Shoucair, Apr. 23, 1934; children—Joyce, Anthony, Lorna, Edward. Came to U.S., 1941, naturalized, 1946. Founder, Eastern Transport Co., Ltd. (now merged with Nairn Transport Co.), 1924; partner Kettaneh Freres, distbrs. in Near East products of Gen. Electric, Siemens, Am. Laundry Machinery Industries, Harnischfeger Corp., Taylor Instruments, Transaires, Co., Allies Chem. Internat., Curtis div. Tramsaores, Inc., Nat. Presto Industries, Inc., United Aircraft Internat., A.J. Alsdorf Corp.; made 1st cross-desert trip by car from Beirut to Baghdad, Apr. 1923. Decorated officer Order Cedars (Republic Lebanon); Legion Honor (France). Fellow Morgan Library (N.Y.C.); mem. Soc. Automotive Engrs., Auto. Importers Assn. for Lebanon and Syria (hon. life pres.), Council Fgn. Relations, Acad. Polit. Sci., Econ. Council N.Y., Am Acad. Polit. and Social Sci., Alumni Assn. Am. U. Beyrouth. Clubs: Grolier, Metropolitan (N.Y.C.). Home: 888 Park Av New York City NY 10021 Office: 745 Fifth Av New York City NY 10022

KETTER, ROBERT LEWIS, univ. pres.; b. Welch, W. Va., Dec. 7, 1928; s. E. F. and Ella Louise (Drummn) K.; B.S. in Civil Engring., U. Mo., 1950; M.S. in Civil Engring., Lehigh U., 1952, Ph.D., 1956; m. Lorelei Zimmerman, Dec. 22, 1948; children—Katharyn, Susannah, Mary, Michael. From research asst. to research asst prof. civil engring. Lehigh U., 1950-58; prof. civil engring., chmn. dept. U. Buffalo, 1958; acting dean Grad. Sch. State U. N.Y. at Buffalo, 1965-66, dean grad. sch., 1966-67, vice president of university, 1967-69, pres., 1970—. Chmn. bd. trustees Western N.Y. Nuclear Research Center, Inc.; chmn. Comprehensive Health Planning Council of Western N.Y., Inc. Chmn. Bach Choir of Bethlehem, Pa., 1953-56. Bd. mgrs. Buffalo and Erie County Hist. Soc.; music adv. com. Buffalo Philharmonic Orch. Soc. Recipient Adams Memorial award Am. Welding Soc., 1968. Mem. Am. Soc. C.E. (bd. dirs. Niagara Frontier sect., chmn. serveral nat. (coms.), Column Research Council of Engring. Found. (chmn. tech. coms.), Internat. Inst. Welding (ofcl. expert rep. U.S. on commn. X), Internat. Assn. Bridge and Structural Engrs., Am. Welding Soc., Buffalo Fine Arts Acad., Buffalo Soc. Natural Scis., Sigma Xi, Tau Beta Pi, Phi Eta Sigma, Omicron Delta Kappa, Pi Mu Epsilon, Chi Epsilon. Author: (with S.P. Prawel, Jr.) Modern Methods of Engineering Computation, 1969; also articles in field. Home: 48 Highgate Av Buffalo NY 14214

KETTLE, JAMES WILLIAM, chem. co. exec.; b. Gary, Ind., May 10, 1915; s. James R.P. and Hazel (Bunce) K.; B.S. in Mech. Engring., Purdue U., 1937; m. Laura Wilkins, Nov. 8, 1941; children—Judith Ann, Barbara, Robert, Nancy. With U.S. Steel Corp., 1937-54; controller Stauffer Chem. Co., N.Y.C., 1954-58, treas., controller, 1958-59, v.p. finance, 1959-61, dir., 1962—, v.p., asst. gen. mgr. Victor Chem. div., Chgo., 1961-62, v.p., gen mgr. Victor Chem. div., 1962-65, v.p. adminstrn., 1965-68, sr. v.p. finance, 1968-69, sr. v.p. adminstrn., 1969—. Mem. financial Execs. Inst. Clubs: Chicago; University, Economic, Canadian (N.Y.C.). Home: 5 Pilot Rock Lane Riverside CT 06878 Office: 299 Park Av New York City NY 10017

KETTLE, JOHN JOSEPH, bank exec.; b. Dallas, 1895; s. James and Martha (Wallace K.; student Bryan High Sch., Met. Bus. Sch.; m. Pauline Wood, Mar. 23, 1916; children—Pauline (Mrs. Chas A. Haynes), Dorothy (dec.). With 1st Nat. Bank, Dallas since 1913, asst. cashier, asst. v.p. and v.p., sr. v.p., 1950-60, vice chmn., 1960-67; vice chmn. bd., dir. Kan. State Bank & Trust Co., Wichita, 1967—; dir. City Nat. Bank, Plainview, Exchange 1967—; dir. City Nat. Bank, Plainview, Exchange Savings and Loan Assn., Dallas, Tex. v.p., dir. State Fair of Tex.; dir. State Fair Musicals. Mem. Ind. Petroleum Assn., Mid-Continent Oil and Gas Assn., Ind. Producers and Royalty Owners Assn., Am. Inst. Banking, Am., Res. City, Tex. bankers assns. Presbyn. Mason (Shriner, past master). Clubs: Petroleum, Gun, Cipango, Brook Hollow Country, Dallas Country, Dinner Dance (Dallas) Home: 4504 Westway Dallas TX 75205 Office: 1401 Elm St Dallas TX 75202

KETTLER, RAYMOND WILLIAM, ednl. adminstr.; b. Riceville, Ia., June 26, 1912; s. Henry and Elsie (Abraham) K.; B.A., State Coll. Ia., 1936; M.A., U. Ill., 1940, student, 1940-41; m. Phylis Staples; children (by previous marriage)—Bruce Raymond, Robert Warren. Asst. bus. mgr. Ia. State Tchrs. Coll., 1936-38, 1941; accountant U. Ill., 1938-41; budget and adminstrv. officer Okla. State Regents for Higher Edn., 1941-42; bus. mgr. Purdue U., 1942-55; controller U. Cal., 1955-59, vice president finance, 1959-63; v.p., treas. Devel. and Resources Corp., 1963-64; asst. v.p., controller State U. N.Y., now vice chancellor for finance, management and bus.; instructor institutes for college and univ. bus. officers U. Omaha, U. Ky., Santa Barbara Coll., U. Cal.; lecturer Sch. Bus. Adinstrn., U. Cal., Berkeley; dir. Midwest Library Corp. Cons. Legislative Workshop on Financing Higher Edn., N.M. State Bd. Edn. Finance, National Sci. Found., others; regional workshop for Pres. Com. on Edn. beyond High Sch. Trustee Inst. for Ednl. Mgmt. Mem. Am. Soc Pub. Adminstrn., Financial Execs. Inst. Am., Eastern Assn. Coll. and U. Bus. Officers, Beta Alpha Psi, Phi Delta Kappa, Kappa Delta Pi, Alpha Chi Rho. Member editorial board Coll. and Univ. Business mag., 1952-65; editorial com. Vol. I Coll. and Univ. Business Adminstrn., 1952. Contbr. articles profls. mags. Home: 200 Pine Ridge Dr Guilderland NY 12084 Office: 9 Thurlow Terrace Albany NY 12203

KETTLER, STANTON PETER, broadcasting co. exec.; b. Wheeling, W.Va., Nov. 18, 1907; s. Charles Louis and Mary Ellen (Stanton) K.; B.S., Washington and Jefferson Coll., 1929; m. Virginia Pennington, Jan. 19, 1935; children—Sally Pennington (Mrs. Walter G. Evans), Peter Stanton. Salesman, Dillon Reed & Co., Reliance Life Ins. Co., Sun Life Assurance Co., Re-Ly-On Products, 1929-37; with Storer Broadcasting Co., Miami Beach, Fla., 1937—, v.p. charge operations, 1955-58, exec. v.p. operations, 1958-61, exec. v.p., 1961-65, pres., 1965- 67, vice chmn. bd., 1967—, dir.; dir. N.E. Airlines, Inc. Mem. Orange Bowl Com. Bd. dirs. Miami Heart Inst., Miami Beach, 1951; bd. dirs., exec. com. Community TV Found. So. Fla., 1970—; trustee Washington and Jefferson Coll., Washington, Pa. Mem. Broadcast Pioneers (mem. bd. directors 1966—), Internat. Radio and TV Soc., Miami Beach, Miami Shores chambers commerce, Kappa Sigma. Elk, Mason, Kiwanian. Mem. Community Ch. Clubs: Indian Creek Country (Indian Creek Village, Fla.); LaGorce Country (Miami Beach); Miami, Palm Bay, Country of Miami, Variety of Greater Miami; Old Baldy (Saratoga, Wyo.); Jockey (Miami). Home: 1301 N E 101st St Miami Shores FL 33138 Office: 1177 Kane Concourse Miami Beach FL 33154

KETY, SEYMOUR SOLOMON, physiologist; b. Phila., Aug. 25, 1915; s. Louis and Ethel (Snyderman) K.; A.B., U. Pa., 1936, M.D., 1940, Sc.D., 1965; M.A. (hon.), Harvard, 1967; Sc.D., Loyola U., 1969; m. Josephine R. Cross, June 18, 1940; children—Lawrence Philip, Roberta Frances. Intern, Phila. Gen. Hosp., 1940-42; NRC fellow Harvard, 1943-44; instr. pharmacology U. Pa. Sch. Medicine, 1943-44, asso. pharmacology, 1944-46, asst. prof., 1946-48, prof. clin. physiology Grad. Sch. Medicine, 1948- 51; Thomas Dent Mütter lectr., 1951; NIH lectr., 1960; Henry Phipps prof., dir. dept. psychiatry Johns Hopkins Sch. Medicine, 1961-62; Thomas William Salmon lectr., 1961; Alvarenga Prize lectr., 1961; Acad. lectr. Am. Psychiat. Assn., 1961; James Arthur lectr., 1966; 3d Mental Health Research Fund. lectr., London, 1965; Benjamin Musser lectr., 1970; chmn. biosci. com. NASA, 1959-60 . Asso. dir. in charge research Nat. Insts. Mental Health and Neurol. Diseases and Blindness, 1951-56, chief Lab. Clin. Sci., Nat. Insts. Mental Health, 1956-61, 62-67; prof. psychiatry Harvard Med. Sch., 1967—, dir. psychiat. research labs. Mass. Gen. Hosp., Boston, 1967—. Organizing com. Internat. Neuro-chem. Symposia, 1952-60; sci. adv. com. Mass. Gen. Hosp., 1956-60; Found.'s Fund Research in Psychiatry, 1962-65, asso. Neuroscis. Research Found., 1962—. Recipient Theobold Smith award, 1949, Max Weinstein award, 1954; Distinguished Service award Dept. Health, Edn. and Welfare, 1958; Stanley Dean award, 1962. Distinguished fellow Am. Psychiat. Assn.; mem. Nat. Acad. Scis., Am. Acad. Arts and Scis., Assn. Research Nervous and Mental Disease (trustee, pres. 1965), Am. Psychopath. Assn. (pres. 1965), Soc. for Psychiat. Research, Am. Soc. Clin. Investigation, Am. Physiol. Soc., Am. Neurol. Assn. Am. Soc. Pharmacology and Exptl. Therapeutics, Sigma Xi, Phi Beta Kappa, Alpha Omega Alpha. Mem. editorial bd. Jour. Neurochemistry, 1955-67, Psychopharmacologia, 1958—, Exptl. Neurology, 1958—, Pharmacological Revs., 1960-63. Editor-in-chief Jour. Psychiat. Research, 1959—. Contbr. sci. articles to profl. publs. Office: Dept Psychiatry Mass Gen Hosp Boston MA 02114

KEUFFEL, JACK WARREN, educator, physicist; b. Montclair, N.J., May 10, 1919; s. Adolf W. and Alice (Jaeggli) K.; A.B., Princeton, 1941; Ph.D., Cal. Inst. Tech., 1948; m. Elizabeth M. Higgins, July 6, 1946; 1 son, Warren P. OSRD Liaison officer, Admiralty Signals Establishment for Mass. Inst. Tech., Eng., 1942-43; with Radar Countermeasures Field Lab. of Harvard, Malvern, Eng., 1943-45; instr. Princeton, 1948-53; asso. prof. physics U. Utah, 1953-60, prof., 1960—, prin. investigator Cosmic Ray Research Project, 1954—. Recipient Willard Gardner prize, Utah Acad. Scis., 1969. Mem. Phi Beta Kappa, Sigma Xi. Research on muon capture and discovery of Utah effect in ultra-high-energy cosmic ray muons, cosmic ray neutrino studies. Home: 5432 Cottonwood Lane Salt Lake City UT 84117

KEULER, ROLAND LEO, shoe co. exec.; b. Kiel, Wis., Aug. 28, 1933; s. Joseph N. and Christina (Woelfel) K.; B.A., Marquette U., 1959; m. Shirley A. Johst, June 22, 1957; children— Suzanne Marie, Catherine Ann, David Richard, Carolyn Marie, Brian John and Barbara Jean (twins). Accountant, Arthur Andersen & Co., C.P.A.'s, Milw., 1959-65; sec.-treas. Napco Graphic Arts, Inc., Milw., 1965-70; controller Weyenberg Shoe Mfg. Co., Milw., 1970—. Active local United Fund. Served with AUS, 1954-56. C.P.A., Wis. Mem. Am. Inst. C.P.A.'s, Wis. Soc. C.P.A.'s, Accounting Research Assn., Holy Name Soc. (past local pres.), Beta Gamma Sigma, Beta Alpha Psi. Home: 720 W Fairfield Ct Glendale WI 53217 Office: 234 E Reservoir Av Milwaukee WI 53212

KEVAN, DOUGLAS KEITH MCEWAN, educator, entomologist; b. Helsinki, Finland, Oct. 31, 1920; s. Douglas K. and Gwynneth M. (Paine) K.; B.Sc. with 1st class honours in Zoology, U. Edinburgh (Scotland), 1941; Associateship, Imperial Coll. Tropical Agr., U. W.I., Trinidad, 1943; Ph.D., U. Nottingham (Eng.), 1956; m. Kathleen Edith Luckin, Sept. 11, 1943; children—Peter G., Martin K., Simon M. Entomologist, H.M. Colonial Service, Trinidad, 1941-43, Kenya Dept. Agr., 1943-48; acting sr. entomologist Uganda Dept. Agr., 1945; Brit. mil. adminstr., civilian locust-liaison officer, Somalia, 1946-47; 1st head zoology sect. U. Nottingham Sch. Agr., 1948-58; prof. entomology Macdonald Coll., McGill U., 1958—, chmn. dept. entomology and plant pathology, 1958-64, chmn. entomology, 1964—, chmn. Lyman Entomol. Mus., 1960—. Fellow Royal Soc. Edinburgh, Royal Entomol. Soc. London; mem. Inst. Biology, Entomol. Soc. Can., entomol. socs. Am., Que., Ont., Canadian Soc. Zoologists, Am. Entomol. Soc., Assn. Brit. Zoologists, Systematics Assn., Soc. Systematic Zoology, Assn. Applied Biologists, Brit. Trust for Entomology, Sigma Xi, numerous others. Author: Soil Animals, 2d edit., 1968; also numerous articles. Editor, contbg. author: Soil Zoology, 1955. Research on Orthoptera, especially taxonomy of Pyrgomorphidae and Gryllidae, soil fauna especially smaller arthropods. Home: 20 Woodridge Crescent Beaconsfield Quebec Canada Office: Dept Entomology Macdonald Campus of McGill U Ste Anne de Bellevue Quebec Canada

KEVENACKOWSKI, STANISLAV mfg. co. exec.; b. Cin., May 21, 1910; grad. Phillips Acad., Andover, Mass., 1927; B.S., Princeton, 1931; postgrad. Mass. Inst. Tech., 1931-33; m. Jean R. Holland, June 16, 1935; children--Lois A., Andrew M., James. Salesman, Brown Mfg. Co., Boston, 1932-33; jr. engr. Ball Metals Co., Carson City, Nev., 1933-36, engr., 1936-37, sr. engr., 1937-40; project engr. Kingston Engring. Co., Los Angeles, 1940-43; with dept. engring. City of Denver, 1946-50, dep. head, 1950-52; 2d v.p. Johnson Mfg. Co., Kansas City, Kansas, 1952-54, v.p. for engring., 1954-57; v.p. research Consol. Industries, Inc., South Bend, Ind., 1957-60, exec. v.p., 1960-65, pres., 1965-70, chmn. bd., chief exec. officer, 1970--, also dir.; dir. ABC Chem. Co., 2d Nat. Bank, Country Food Storage Co., Providence Indsl. Corp. Pres., Dewey High Sch., Kansas City, Mo., 1953-54; fund chmn. local div. Salvation Army, 1959-60. Mem. South Bend Republican Com., 1964-68. Bd. dirs. Ind. council Boy Scouts Am., 1969-71; trustee Lovell Found. Served to lt., Corps Engrs., AUS, 1943-45. Decorated Bronze Star medal. Member N.A.M., South Bend C. of C. (v.p. 1963-65, dir. 1965-70), Am. Mgmt. Assn., Ind. Engrs. Soc. (program com. 1961-62), Princeton Alumni Assn. Episcopalian. Home: 6823 Broad Terrace Av South Bend IN 46505 Office: PO Box 1019 South Bend IN 46501

KEVENEY, ROBERT ANTHONY, journalist b. Detroit, May 17, 1937; s. William Gerald and Romelda (Oberliesen) K.; B.A. in Journalism, Wayne State U., 1962; student Eastern Mich. U., 1955-57; m. Sally Anne Urbanski, Feb. 3, 1962; children—Matthew William, Timothy John, Molly Ann. With Ypsilanti (Mich.) Press, 1961-63. Dayton (O.) Daily News, 1963—. Served with AUS, 1957-60. Recipient Sidney Hillman Found. award, 1967; Am. Polit. sci. Assn. award, 1967; profl. award for newspaper series I Joined The Far Right. Home: 185 Weller Av Centerville OH 45459

KEVILL, DENNIS NEIL, educator; b. Walton-Le-Dale, Eng., May 27, 1935; s. Henry and Freda Margaret (Cater) K.; B.Sc., Univ. Coll., London, 1956, Ph.D., 1960; m. Jadwiga Bronislawa Kaleta, July 15, 1965; 1 son, Peter Andrew. Came to U.S., 1960, naturalized, 1966. Asst. lectr. Univ. Coll., 1959-60; research asso. U. Neb., 1960-63; faculty No. Ill. U., DeKalb, 1963—, prof. chemistry, 1970—. Cons. to industry. Mem. Am. Chem. Soc., Chem. Soc. (London), Sigma Xi, Phi Lambda Upsilon. Contbr. articles to profl. jours. Home: 595 Normal Rd DeKalb IL 60115

KEWER, ELEANOR DOBSON, former editor; b. Kensington Md., Mar. 17, 1904; d. Alle Nelson and Carolie C. (Robinette) Dobson; student George Washington U., 1922-24; A.B., U. Wis., 1926; m. Leslie John Kewer, Dec. 22, 1951 (dec. 1966). Research asst. Dictionary of Am. Biography, Washington, 1926-29, asst. editor, 1929-36; asst. editor Harvard Press, 1936-43, chief editor, 1943-65, chief editor for spl. projects, 1966-70. Lectr. summer course in pub. procedures Radcliffe Coll., 1947-61. Trustee Bedford Free Pub.

Library. Mem. Mass. Women's Corps, 1941-46, capt., 1943-46. Mem. League Women Voters. Episcopalian. Home: 262 Old Billerica Rd Bedford MA 01730

KEY, DAVID MCKENDREE, former fgn. service officer; b. Tokyo, Japan, Feb. 4, 1900; (parents Am. citizens); s. Albert Lenoir and Grace (Condit-Smith) K.; student Groton Mass., Sch., 1912-18; A.B., Harvard, 1922; postgrad. Gonville and Caius Coll., Cambridge, Eng., 1922-23, Georgetown Sch. Fgn. Service, Washington, 1923-24; m. Marjorie Wright, Feb. 7, 1925; children—Albert Lenoir II, David McKendree, Marjorie. Detailed to Dept. State, 1925; vice consul of career at Antwerp, 1926; 3d sec. embassy, Berlin, 1927, London, 1929; attended Disarmament Conf., Geneva, 1932, London Econ. Conf., 1933; asst. chief Div Current Information, 1934; consul, 2d sec., Ottawa, 1936; 1st sec. embassy, Rome, 1940; asst. liaison officer Dept. State, 1941-44; consul gen., Barcelona, 1944-45; counselor of embassy, Rome, 1945-46, Rio do Janeiro, 1947-49; ambassador to Burma, 1950- 52; Far Eastern adviser U.S. delegation 6th, 7th, 8th gen. assemblies UN, 1952-53; asst. sec. state internat. orgn. affairs, 1953-55; gen. mgr. Am. Fgn. Service Assn., 1957-61; pres., Diplomatic and Consular Officers Ret. Inc., 1957-58. Chmn. nat. com. An. Med. Center for Burma, 1959-64. Pvt. USMC, World War I. Decorated World War Victory medal. Clubs: Metropolitan, Alibi, Dacor House (D.C.); Black Hall, Old Lyme Country. Home: Old Lyme CT 06371

KEY, DONALD, art critic; b. Iowa City, Jan. 30, 1923; s. Philip R. and Lola (Diehl) Lola (Diehl) K.; B.A. in Journalism, U. Ia., 1950; m. Patricia Anne Miller, May 11, 1947; 1 son, Theodore Allen. Asst to editor, fine arts columnist Cedar Rapids (Ia.) Gazette, 1950-59; art editor Milw. Jour., 1959—. Served with AUS, 1942-46; ETO. Mem. Theta Xi, Sigma Delta Chi. Club: Milwaukee Press. Author articles, revs. Home: 7519 N Crossway Rd Milwaukee WI 53217 Office: Milw Jour Jour Sq Milwaukee WI 53201

KEY, RICHARD MICHAEL, fgn. service officer; b. Poland, Sept. 4, 1922; s. Stanislaw and Hedwig (Trzaska) Mikulski; came to U.S., 1923, naturalized, 1929; B.A., Queens Coll., 1945; M.A., Columbia, 1948; Ph.D. in Romance Langs. and Lits., U. Kan., 1956; m. Pearl Amalia Frasco, Apr. 4, 1944; children—Richard Ralph, Kristen Hedwig. Instr. Spanish, U. Kan., 1948-52, Rutgers U., 1951-53; asst. prof. Purdue U., 1955-56; joined USIA, 1956; assigned Argentina, 1956-60, Panama, 1963; dep. chief and acting chief English teaching div., 1963-65; information specialist Office Pub. Affairs Latin Am., State Dept., 1965-66, spl. asst. to dir. Office Panamanian Affairs, 1966-67; regional book officer, Mexico City, 1967-68; cultural attache, Caracas, Venezuela, 1968-70; dep. pub. affairs officer, Rio de Janeiro. Served with AUS, 1943-46. Office: American Embassy (USIS-Rio) APO New York City NY 09676

KEY, TED, cartoonist; b. Fresno, Cal., Aug. 25, 1912; s. Simon Leon and Fanny (Kahn) K.; A.B., U. Cal. at Berkeley, 1933; m. Anne Elizabeth Wilkinson, Sept. 30, 1937; children—Stephen Lewis, David, Peter. Asso. editor Judge, 1937; writer, cartoonist Sat.Eve.Post, Look, New Yorker, This Week, others; radio script writer J. Walter Thompson Co., for CBS, NBC; radio play The Clinic, pub in anthology Best Broadcasts of 1939-40; creator cartoon features Diz and Liz, Jack and Jill mag., 1961; Mem. Nat. Cartoonist Soc. Author, creator of Hazel appearing in Sat. Eve. Post, 1943-69, King Features Syndicate, 1969—, (book) Hazel, 1946; Here's Hazel!, 1949; Many Happy Returns, 1950, If You Like Hazel, 1952; So'm I, 1953; Hazel Rides Again, 1955; Fasten Your Seat Belts, 1956; Phyllis, 1957; All Hazel, 1958; The Hazel Jubilee, 1959; The Biggest Dog in the World, 1960; Hazel Time, 1962; Life With Hazel, 1965, 1965; Diz and Liz, 1965; Squirrels in the Feeding Station, 1967; Hazel Power, 1971; (screenplay) Showdown at Ulcer Gulch, Million Dollar Duck. Creator Hazel TV Show, NBC-TV. Served with Signal Corps, AUS, 1944-46. Jewish religion. Club: Players (N.Y.C.). Address: 1964 Glenhardie Rd Wayne PA 19087

KEYE, WILLIAM R., corp. exec.; b. 1921; B.S. in Elec. Engring., U. Minn., 1943; married. Entire career with Control Data Corp., sr. v.p. operations, 1967—, also dir. Address: 3112 Wendhurst Av SE Minneapolis MN 54400*

KEYES, DANIEL, actor; m. Sasha von Scherler; appeared in Broadway shows including Take Her She's Mine, First Love, Christine, Only in America, Remarkable Mr. Pennypacker, Six Characters in Search of an Author; played in nat. company of Inherit The Wind, Mr. Roberts, off-Broadway in Plays for Blecker Street, Epitaph For George Dillon, Our Town, The Man Who Never Died.*

KEYES, DONALD BABCOCK, consultant; b. Westerly, R.I., Feb. 8, 1891; s. Austin Herbert and Charlotte (Babcock) K.; B.S., U. of N.H., 1913; A.M., Columbia, 1914; Ph.D., U. of Calif., 1917; hon. D.Sc., U. of N.H., 1946; D. Eng. (hon.) Stevens Institute Technology, 1947; m. Stella Margarete Liss; 1 dau., Nancy Chloe. Research chem. engr. Beckman & Linden Engring. Corp., San Francisco, 1917-18, U.S. Industrial Alcohol Co. and U.S. Industrial Chem. Co., N.Y. City, 1918-24; dir. research and patent adviser, U.S. Industrial Alcohol Co., Baltimore, 1924-26; prof. chem. engring. and head of chem. engring. div., also mem. exec. staff Engring. Experiment Station U. of Ill., 1926-45; cons. for War Prodn. Bd., Sept. 1941-Dec. 1942; chief of chemical industries branch. Office of Production Research and Development. WPB, Jan. 1943-June 1944; cons. Hevden Chem. Co., 1951- 56; Nat. Assn. Mfrs. Research com. 1951-64; cons. Arthur D. Little, Inc., 1952-58; director O.P.R.D. July 1944-Oct. 1945; W.P.B. mem. of T.I.I.C. Special War Missions to England Oct. 1943 and Apr. 1945; vice pres. Heyden Corp. in N.Y., 1945-50; asso. James G. Bronson & Assos., N.Y.C. Dir. Am. Plastics Corp., Mar. 1946-Jan. 1948, Heyden Cehmical Corporation 1946-52, American Potash & Chemical Company, Oct. 1946-50. Fellow A.A.A.S., Am. Inst. Chemists (pres. 1954-55, chmn. board dirs. 1955-56); mem. Am. Chemical Society, Am. Institute of Chemical Engineers, Society Chemical Industry (France), Society Chemical Industry (London), Assn. Research Dirs., Sigma Xi, Omega Chi Epsilon, Alpha Chi Sigma, Phi Lambda Upsilon, Tau Beta Pi. Clubs: University, Chemists (N.Y.); Cosmos (Washington). Author: (with Deem) Chemical Engineers Manual, 1942; (with Faith and Clark), Industrial Chemicals, 1950, 2d edit., 1957, 3d edit., 1965. Office: care James G Bronson Assos 437 Fifth Av New York City NY 10016

KEYES, FENTON, inst. adminstr.; b. N.Y.C., Jan. 26, 1915; s. Harold Brown and Elsie Louise (Fenton) K.; B.A., Yale, 1937, Ph.D., 1942; m. Elizabeth Dortch Dix, Nov. 18, 1944; children—Charles Fenton, Janet Bayard. Instr. sociology Colgate U, 1940-42; supervisor records Hdqrs. 2d Service Command M.I., Governors Island, N.Y., 1942-43; analyst Dept. Justice, Washington, 1943; asst. prof. sociology, asst. to pres. Skidmore Coll., 1946-47, bus. mgr., 1947-53, v.p., 1953-56; dean of college, dean of graduate school, Texas State College for Women, 1956-57, Tex. Woman's U., dean of faculty and grad. studies, 1957-60; pres. Coker College Hartsville, S.C., 1960-68; lab. mgr. behavioral and social scis. lab. Franklin Inst. Research Labs., Phila., 1968-70; dir. academic af- fairs Coll. Allied Health Scis. Thomas Jefferson U., 1970—. Member of adv. com. Pringle Memorial Funds, N.Y. Community Trust; sec., treas., chmn. S.C. Found. Ind. Colls.; pres. S.C. Assn. Colls. Bd. dirs. S.C. div. Am. Cancer Soc. Served from pvt. to capt. AUS, 1943-46, chief historian Staff Comdg. Gen. China Theater, 1944-46. Decorated Bronze Star (with Oak-Leaf Cluster). Fellow Am. Sociol. Assn.; mem. Central States Anthrop. Soc., Am. Anthrop. Assn., Am. Assn. U. Profs., So., Southwestern sociol. socs., Am. Coll. Pub. Relations Assn., Republican. Episcopalian (vestryman). Clubs: University (N.Y.C.); Mory's Assn. Contbr. profl. jours. Home: 643 Addison St Philadelphia PA 19147 (summer) Chelmsford North Litchfield Beach Box 221 Pawley's Island SC 29585 Office: 1025 Walnut St Philadelphia PA 19107

KEYES, FRANCIS, ednl. adminstr.; b. Boston, Dec. 4, 1912; s. Henry Wilder and Frances (Wheeler) K.; grad. Milton (Mass.) Acad., 1932; B.S., Harvard, 1936; m. Louise Burleigh McNeil, June 16, 1937; children—Peter Bowen, John Parkinson 2d, David Johnson, Virginia Bowen, Frances and Louise (twins). Faculty, Ridgefield (Conn.) Sch., 1936-37, Harvard Sch. Edn., 1937-38; faculty Westminister Sch., Simsbury, Conn., 1938—, became headmaster, 1956, now pres., also dir. Chmn., Simsbury Community Fund; mem. founders com. U. Hart- ford. Trustee Walks Found., Renbrook Sch.; bd. dirs. Mt. Sinai Hosp.; bd. dirs., founding pres. Simsbury War Meml. Pool. Mem. Conn. Assn. Ind. Schs. (exec. com., pres.), Headmaster Assn. Rotarian (pres. Simsbury). Clubs: Harvard No. Conn.; West Hartford (Conn.) Tennis; Hopbrook Gold; Hartford (Conn.) Golf; Harvard (N.Y.C.). Address: 995 Hopmeadow St Simsbury, CT 06070

KEYES, FREDERICK GEORGE, physical chemist; b. Kingston, Can., June 24, 1885; s. John George and Margaret (Williams) K.; B.S., R.I. Coll., 1906; M.S., Brown Univ., 1907, Ph.D., 1909; D.Sc., Yale, 1934, D.Sc., R.I. Coll, 1942, Brown U., 1963; m. Gabrielle Alice Bowers, Dec. 27, 1923. Asst. in chemistry, Brown U., 1906-07, instr., 1908-09, G.A.R. research fellow, 1909; research asso. in physical chemistry, Mass. Inst. tech., 1910- 13; chief engr. Cooper-Hewitt Electric Co., 1913-16; asso. prof. phys. chemistry research, 1916-19, prof., 1920-50, dir. research lab. phys. chemistry, 1920-1945, in charge dept. chemistry, 1922-1945, prof. emeritus and lecturer since 1950, all at Mass. Inst. Tech.; pres., gen. mgr. Keyes Sci. Corp., Cambridge, Mass. Chmn. U.S. commn. Internat. Stean Properties Com. Commd. capt. U.S. Army, Dec. 1917, major, Sept., 1918; dir. Sci. and Control Lab., A.E.F., at Puteaux, France, 1918-19; citation by comdr.-in-chief A.E.F., June 1919; lt. col. Chem Warfare R.C. Recipient Theodore William Richards Medal Award, 1942; American Society Mech. Engrs. Am. Soc. Mech. Engrs. Award, 1948. Fellow Am. Acad. Arts and Sci. Am. Physical Soc., A.A.A.S.; mem. Am. Chem. Soc., Nat. Acad. Sci., An. Soc. Refrigerating Engrs. (hon.), Phi Sigma Kappa, Sigma Xi. Author: The Thermodynamic Properties of Ammonia, 1916; Thermodynamic Properties of Steam (with J.H. Keepan), 1936. contbr. numerous papers on investigations of the thermodynamic properties of matter, kinetic theory of matter and applications of thermodynamics to chemical equilibria problems, etc. Home: 15 Berkeley St Cambridge MA 02138

KEYES, FREEMAN, advertising exec.; b. Gunter, Tex., June 20, 1902; s. Perch Clark and Olive Leska (Freeman) K.; B.S., Tex. A. M. Coll., 1925; student U. of S. Calif., 1927-28; m. Delores King, Feb. 12, 1931; Engr. Paramount Pictures Corp., 1928-30; production engr. Nat Broadcasting Co., 1930-32; v.p. Philip O. Palmer., Co., 1933-34; account exec. Baggaley, Horton & Hoyt. Inc. 1934-35; pres., accounts exec. Russel M. Seeds Co., Inc.; chmn. chief exec. officer, pres. Keyes, Madden & Jones, Chgo.; now hon. chmn. finance com., dir. Post-Keyes-Gardner. Republican. Mem. Ch. of Christ. Club: Lake Shore Athletic (Chicago). Home: 1120 Lake Shore Drive Chicago IL 60611 Office: 875 N Michigan Av Chicago IL 60611

KEYES, HAROLD FRANCIS, Jr., mfg. co. exec.; b. Leominster, Mass., July 19, 1912; s. Harold Francis and Evelyn (Canning) K.; student Northeastern U., 1931-37; m. Helen Bowker, Dec. 11, 1937; 1 dau., Judith (Mrs. Richard K. Jette). Staff mem. pub. accountant Hitchcock & Co., C.P.A.'s, 1938-42; treas. Flax Processing & Linen Co., 1942-43, 45-50; sec., asst. treas. Brown & Sharpe Mfg. Co., N. Kingstown, R.I., 1951—. Mem. Navy-Civilian Council, Naval Air Sta., Quonset Point, R.I., 1963—. Trustee Eastern States Exposition. Served with USNR, 1943-45. Fellow Mass., R.I. socs. C.P.A.'s; mem. Am. Inst. C.P.A.'s, North Kingstown C. of C. (dir. 1968—). Home: PO Box 115 Harmony RI 02829 Office: PO Box 456 North Kingstown RI 02852

KEYES, JIMMY WARREN, banker; b. Goliad, Tex., Jan. 5, 1934; s. Marion B. and Helen (Hyatt) K.; B.B.A.., 1956; m. Anita E. Anderson, Sept. 9, 1961; children-Brian Alan, Shelley Elizabeth. Jr. auditor Ernst & Ernst, San Antonio, 1958- 60; accountant W.E. Bakke & Son, San Antonio, 1960-61; with Frost Nat. Bank, San Antonio, 1961—, asst. v.p., auditor, 1968—. Trustee Teen Acres, Inc., San Antonio. Served with AUS, 1956-58. Mem. Bank Adminstrn. Inst. (sec.-treas. San Antonio chpt., 1970-71). Optimist (pres. Tower Club, 1969-70, sec.-treas. S. Central Tex. dist. 1970-71). Home: 3622 Electra Dr San Antonio TX 78218 Office: Frost National Bank P O Drawer 1600 San Antonio TX 78206

KEYES, LEROY, profl. football player; b. Newport News, Va., Feb. 18, 1947; s. Henry Paul and Doris Mae (Keyes) Huggins; B.P.E., Purdue U., 1969. All-state in football, basketball and track George Washington Carver High Sch., 1963-65; All-Am. at Purdue U., 1967-68; played in East-West Shrine Game-Hula Bowl, 2d in Heisman Trophy balleting, 1969; mem. team Phila. Eagles, 1969—. Mem. Omega Psi Phi. Home: 7701 Lindbergh Blvd Philadelphia PA 19153

KEYES, PAUL WILLIAM, TV writer, producer; b. Dorchester, Mass., Mar. 18, 1924; s. Frank J. and Marion T. (Bailey) K.; grad. high sch.; m. Miriam E. Kelleher, Nov. 19, 1949. Producer, dir. Yankee Network, 1946-52; freelance TV writer, producer, 1952-54; mem. comedy devel. program NBC, N.Y.C., 1955; writer Steve Allen TV Show and Tonight Show, 1956; head writer Jack Paar Tonight Show, 1957-62; head writer, co- producer Jack Paar Program, Jack Paar Presents Spl., Square World of Jack Paar Spl., head writer Wonderful World of Jack Paar Spl., 1962- 65; head writer, co-producer Dean Martin Show, 1965-68; head writer Laugh-In Spl., Ice Capades Spl., 1967, Laugh-In Series, 1968; producer, writer Laugh-In Series, 1968-69, producer, head writer, 1971—; producer, writer John Wayne Spl., 1970; pres. Paul W. Keyes Prodns., Inc., 1968—. Served with inf. AUS, 1942-46; ETO. Recipient Emmy awards as Laugh-In writer, 1968, 69, as Laugh-In producer, 1969-70. Mem. Writers Guild Am., Nat. Acad. TV Arts and Scis. Republican. Roman Catholic. Home: 7674 Woodrow Wilson Dr Hollywood CA 90046 Office: 10000 Riverside Dr North Hollywood CA 91602

KEYES, WILLIAM FRANCIS, govt. ofcl.; b. N.Y.C., Jan. 15, 1917; s. William Francis and Eunice Henrietta (Warnken) K.; B.S., Manhattan Coll., 1939; postgrad. Mass. Inst. Tech., 1941-42; M.S., Columbia, 1950; m. Helen Erika Wellmann, Dec. 21, 1947; children—Anne, William, Alice. Chemist, metallurgist, Minas de Matahambre, Cuba, 1939-41; dep. chief U.S. Census sect. Office Mil. Govt., Berlin, Germany, 1946-47; area specialist, projects engr. Bur. Mines, Washington, 1952-56; regional minerals officer Am. Consulate Gen., Johannesburg, South Africa, 1960-67; minerals attache Am. Embassy, Mexico, 1968—. Served with AUS, 1943-46. Mem. Am. Inst. Mining, Metall. and Petroleum Engrs. Home: 205 Aconcagua Mexico DF Mexico Office: 305 Reforma Mexico DF Mexico

KEYFITZ, NATHAN, educator, sociologist; b. Montreal, Que., Can., June 29, 1913; s. Arthur and Anna (Gerstein) K.; B.Sc., McGill U., Montreal, 1934; Ph.D., U. Chgo., 1952; m. Beatrice Orkin, Oct. 8, 1939; children—Barbara Lee, Robert Norman. Census clk., statistician, sr. research statistician Dominion Bur. Statistics. Govt. Can., 1936-59; dir. Colombo Plan Bur., Colombo, 1956-57; prof. sociology U. Toronto, 1959-63; prof. U. Chgo., 1963-68, Chmn. sociology dept., 1965-68; prof. demography U. Cal. at Berkeley, 1968—. Tech. assistance assignments for UN, Burma, 1951, Indonesia, 1953-54, Argentina, 1960, Santiago, Chile, 1963. Fellow Royal Soc. Can., Royal Statis. Soc., Am. Statis. Assn. (chmn. social statistics sect. 1961); mem. Canadian Polit. Sci. Assn. (chmn. sociology and anthropology sect. 1961), Inter-Am., Internat. statis. insts., Population Assn. Am. (pres. 1969-70). Author: Introduction to the Mathematics of Population, 1968. Contbr. articles to profl. jours. Home: 500 The Alameda Berkeley CA 94707

KEYNES, GEOFFREY LANGDON, former, surgeon, author; b. Cambridge, Eng., Mar. 25, 1887; s. John Neville and Florence (Brown) K.; ed. Pembroke Coll., Cambridge U., 1910; M.A., St. Bartholomew's Hosp., London, Eng., 1913; M.D., Cambridge U., 1918, Litt. (hon.), 1965; m. Margaret Elizabeth Darwin, May 12, 1917; children—Richard Darwin, Quentin George, William Milo, Stephen John. Surgeon staff st. Bartholomew's Hosp., 1930-52; ret., 1952; Harveian orator Royal Coll. Physicians, 1958; Osler orator, also gold medal, 1960; Moynihan lectr. Royal Coll. Surgeons, 1963; Wilkins lectr. Royal Soc., 1966. Trustee Nat. Portrait Gallery, 1942-66, chmn., 1958-66; hon. librarian Royal Coll. Surgeons; founder, trustee William Blake Trust, 1949; trustee Rupert Brooke, 1933. Served with BEF, 1914-19, RAF, 1939- 45. Created knight bachelor, 1955; recipient James Tait Black award, 1966. Hon. fellow Pembroke Coll., Cambridge U.; fellow Royal Coll. Surgeons (Cecil Joll prize 1953), Royal Coll. Surgeons Can., Royal Coll. Physicians, Royal Coll. Obstetricians and Gynecolgists; hon. fellow Am. Surg. Assn., Royal Soc. Medicine, Modern Lang. Assn. Author: Life of William Harvey, 1966; Bibliographies of Blake, 2d edit., 1969, Donne, 3d edit., 1958; Sir Thomas Browne, 2d edit., 1968; Evelyn, 2d edit., 1968. Editor: Writings of William Blake, 1925-71; Sir Thomas Browne, 1920-32, 1964. Address: Lammas House Brinkley Newmarket Suffolk England

KEYS, ANCEL, physiologist; b. Colorado Springs, Colo., Jan. 26, 1904; s. Benjamin Pious and Caroline Emma (Chaney) K.; B.A., U. Cal., 1925, M.A., 1928; Ph.D., 1930; D.Phil., King's Coll., Cambridge U., Eng., 1936; m. Margaret Edith Haney, Sept. 20, 1939; children—Caroline Ann, Henry, Martha. NRC fellow, Copenhagen, Denmark, 1930-31, Cambridge, Eng., 1931-32; lectr., demonstrator in physiology, Cambridge, 1932-33; instr. biochem. scis. Harvard, 1933-36; asst. prof. biochemistry Mayo Found., Rochester, Minn., 1936-37, asso. prof., 1937; asso. prof. physiology and phys. edn. U. Minn., 1937-39, prof., 1939-46, prof. Sch. Pub. Health 1946—. Research asso. Woods Hole Oceonographic Inst., 1933-34; organizer, mgr. Internat. High Altitude Expdn. to Chile, 1935; dir. lab. physiol. hygiene U. Minn.; dir. fgn. research programs on heart disease and nutrition. Mem. OSRD and responsible investigator, 1942-46; spl. cons. on foods to sec. war, 1940-43; chmn. Joint FAO/WHO Expert Com. on Nutrition, 1951; now expert cons. WHO, FAO, and UNESCO, chmn. FAO calorie com.; spl. sr. research fellow USPHS, 1963-64; coordinator Internat. Coop. Research Epidemiol. Heart Disease in Finland, Yugoslavia, Holland, Italy, Greece. Sr. Fulbright scholar Oxford U., 1951-52. Decorated comdr. Order of Lion (Finland). Recipient McCollum award Am. Soc. Clin. Nutrition, 1967. Fellow Am. Pub. Health Assn., A.A.A.S., Am. Coll. Cardiology; mem. Am. Soc. for Study Arteriosclerosis, Minn. Acad. Sci., Am. Heart Assn., Am. Soc. Biol. Chemists, Soc. Exptl. Biology and Medicine, Am. Physiol. Soc., Gerontology Soc., Brit. Nutrition Soc., Internat. Soc. Cardiology (chmn. research com. 1963-66), Am. Epidemiol. Soc., Pi Kappa Alpha, Sigma Xi; corr. mem. Acad. Medicine Chirurg Piceno (hon.), Soc. Geografica Americana (Buenos Aires, Argentina); hon. mem. Cardiol. Soc. India, Soc. Endocrinology, Acad. Medicine Rome. Sr. author: Biology of Human Starvation (2 vols.); author: Eat Well and Stay Well, 1959, 63; The Benevolent Bean, 1967. Editor: Cardiovascular Epidemiology, 1967; Coronary Heart Disease in Seven Countries, 1970; mem. editorial bds. many sci., med. jours. Contbr. monographs, articles to tech. lit. Home: 3270 Lake Owasso Heights Saint Paul MN 55112 also Minnelea Pioppi Salerno Italy 84060

KEYS, SAMUEL ROBERT, univ. dean; b. New Castle, Ind., July 11, 1922; s. John B. and Pearl (Smith) K.; student Earlham Coll., 1942-44; B.A., Olivet Nazarene Coll., 1948; M.A., U. Mo. at Kansas City, 1950; Ph.D., U. Minn., 1958; m. Martha Elizabeth Ludwig, May 28, 1949; children—Carol, Bryan, Dana, Scott. Tchr., counselor Kansas City (Mo.) pub. schs., 1949-53; asst. prof. No. Ill. U., 1958-60; asso. curriculum coordinator State of Ill., 1960-61; asso. prof. N.Y.U., 1961-67; asso. dean Coll. Edn. of U. Mo., 1967-69; prof., dean Coll. Edn., Kansas State U., 1969—. Mem. bd. Mid-Continent Regional Ednl. Lab.; mem. standards adv. bd. Kan. Dept. Edn. Served with USNR, 1942-45. Fellow Fund Advancement Edn., 1953-54. Mem. Am. Assn. Univ. Profs., Assn. Supervision and Curriculum Devel., Assn. Higher Edn., Phi Delta Kappa. Club: Rotary (Manhattan). Home: 2339 Chris Dr Manhattan KS 66502

KEYS, THOMAS EDWARD, med. library cons.; b. Greenville, Miss., Dec. 2, 1908; s. Thomas Napoleon and Margaret (Boothroyd) K.; A.B., Beloit Coll., 1931; Carnegie fellow U. Chgo. Grad. Library Sch., 1932-33, M.A., 1934; postgrad. U. Mich. Library Sch., summer 1933; m. Elizabeth Schaack, Nov. 2, 1934; children—Thomas Frederick, Charles Edward. Order asst. Newberry Library, Chgo., 1931-32; asst. librarian Mayo Clinic, Rochester, Minn., 1934-35, reference librarian, 1935-42, librarian, 1946-69, sr. library cons., 1969—; asso. prof. hist. medicine Mayo Found. Library at U. Minn., 1957-69, prof. history medicine Mayo Grad. Sch., 1969—. Bd. regents Nat. Library of Medicine, 1950-62; hon. cons. Army Med. Library, 1946-50. Chmn. reading com. Gamehaven area Boy Scouts Am., Rochester, 1936-42. Served from 1st lt. to lt. col., Med. Adminstrv. Corps, AUS, 1942-46. Awarded Army Commendation Ribbon (surgeon gen.) 1946; Distinguished Service citation Beloit Coll. Alumni, 1956. Mem. Internat. Soc. for History of Medicine, Med. Library Assn. (editor bull. 1942-45, pres. 1957-58, Noyes award 1966), Mayo Found. Soc. History Medicine (pres. 1965-66), Spl. Libraries Assn., Am. Soc. Anesethesiologists (hon.), Am. Osler Soc. (hon.), Am. Assn. History of Medicine, Phi Beta Kappa, Beta Phi Mu, Pi Kappa Alpha. Episcopalian. Rotarian. Author: (with F.A. Willius) Cardiac Classics 1941, 61; The Development of Anesthesia, 1943; A History of Surgical Anesthesia, 1945, rev., 1963 (Japanese edit. 1966, German edit. Die Geschichte der Chirurischen Anaesthesia 1968); Applied Medical Library Practice, 1958; (with A. Faulconer, Jr.) Foundations of Anesthesiology, 2 vols., 1965. Contbr. numerous articles pertaining library sci. to sci. publs. Mem. editorial bd. Blakiston's New Gould Medical Dictionary, 1949. Dir.: (with L.A. Julin) An Introduction to the Use of the Mayo Clinic Library (motion picture in color with sound track), 1948, rev. 1953. Home: 130 Skyline Dr Rochester MN 55901 Office: Mayo Clinic Library Rochester MN 55901

KEYSER, FRANK RAY, judge; b. Woodsville, N.H., Sept. 29, 1898; s. Winifield Scott and Harriet E. (Bailey) K.; student Tufts Coll., 1918, Norwich U., 1919-20; pvt. study law; m. Ellen Eula Larkin, July 2, 1921; children—Natalie (Mrs. David A Niles), Frank Ray. Office work banks, Wells River, Chelsea, Vt., 1918-19, Lyndonville, Northfield, 1920-24; sch. tchr., 1924-26; student in law office, 1926-29; admitted to Vt. bar, 1929, practiced in Chelsea; mem. Wilson, Adams & Keyser, 1929-31, Wilson & Keyser, 1931-36, Wilson, Carver, Davis & Keyser, 1936-40, Wilson & Keyser, 1940-56; superior ct. judge Vt., 1956-64; asso. justice Vt. Supreme Ct., 1964—. Auditor, Town of Chelsea, 1926- 35, agt., 1934-38, chmn. sch. bd., 1935-43, grand juror, 1939-43, moderator, 1948—; dep. probation officer Orange County, 1929-32, dep. clk., 1929-38, moderator, 1932-33, state's atty., 1931-35, clk., 1938- 42. Mem. Vt. Ho. of Reps., 1937-41; sec. Civil and Mil. Affairs, Vt., 1953. Mem. Am., Vt. (pres. 1952-53) bar assns., Am. Legion. Republican. Conglist. Mason (Shriner); mem. Order Eastern Star. Address: Chelsea VT 05038

KEYSER, FRANK RAY, Jr., former gov. Vt.; b. Chelsea, Vt. Aug. 17, 1927; s. Frank Ray and Ellen L. (Larkin) K.; student Tufts Coll., 1946-49, LL.D. 1961; L.B., Boston U., 1952; LL.D., Norwich U., 1962; m. Joan Friedgen, July 15, 1950; children—Christopher Scott, Carol Ellen, Frank Ray III. Admitted to Vt. bar, 1952, practiced in Chelsea, 1952-65; mem. Vt. Ho. of Reps. from Chelsea Dist., 1955-59, speaker, 1959-60; gov. Vt., 1961-63; mem. law firm Wilson & Keyser, 1952-65: now pres., dir. Vt. Marble Co.; dir. Fed. Res. Bank Boston, Union Mut. Ins. Co. Served with USNR, World War II. Named Outstanding Young Vermonter, Vt. Jr. C. of C., 1959; One of 10 Outstanding Young Men in Nation, 1961, Nat Jr. C. of C. Mem. Am., Vt. bar assns., Vt. Jr. Bar Assn. (past chmn.), Farm Bur., Am. Legion. Republican. Mason. Address: Proctor VT 05765

KEYSER, MARIAN BARBARA, headmistress; b. Washington, Oct. 31, 1918; d. Paul Victor and Marian (Speare) Keyser; B.A., Vassar Coll., 1940; M.A., Columbia, 1941. Tchr., Hunter Coll. High Sch., 1946-64; Fulbright tchr., The Netherlands, 1955- 56; ednl. adviser Am. sponsored schs. overseas, State Dept., 1964-65; headmistress Madeira Sch., Greenway. Va., 1965—. Bd. visitors Va. Commonwealth U. Mem. Nat. Assn. Secondary Sch. Prins., Nat. Assn. Ind. Schs., Headmistresses Assn. East, Nat. Assn. Prins. Secondary Schs. Girls. Address: Madeira Sch Greenway VA 22067 also Shelter Island Heights NY 11965

KEYSER, PAUL VICTOR, Jr., petroleum exec.; b. Washington, Nov. 12, 1906; s. Paul Victor and Marian (Speare) K.; B.S., Mass. Inst. Tech., 1929, M.S., 1930; m. Aslaug Brekke, Sept. 9, 1932; one dau., Kari (Mrs. Jay H. McDowell). With Mobil Oil Corp. (formerly Socony Mobil Oil Co., Inc., 1930- -, successively asst. mgr. tech. service dept., acting asst. gen. mgr. labs., dir. research and development labs., mgr. lubricating dept., marketing mgr., domestic, v.p., dir. charge fgn. trade, 1955-59, sr. v.p. planning, 1959-60, exec. v.p. charge chemicals, since 1960—. Mem. Am. Mgmt. Assn., Mfg. Chemists' Assn., Am. Chem. Soc., Council Fgn. Relations, A.A.A.S., Am. Petroleum Inst. Home: 40 Fifth Av New York City NY 10011 Office: 150 E 42d St New York City NY 10017

KEYSERLING, LEON H., economist, lawyer; b. Charleston, S.C., Jan. 22, 1908; s. William and Jennie (Hyman) K.; A.B., Columbia, 1928, postgrad. in econs., 1931-33; LL.B., Harvard, 1931; D.Bus. Sci., Bryant Coll., 1965; m. Mary Dublin, Oct. 4, 1940. Admitted to N.Y., D.C., U.S. Supreme Ct. bars; asst. dept. econs. Columbia, 1932-33; atty. A.A.A., 1933; sec. and legislative asst. to Senator Robert F. Wagner, 1933-37; gen. counsel U.S. Housing Authority, 1937-38, dep. adminstr. and gen. counsel, 1938-42; acting adminstr., 1941-42; acting commr. Fed. Pub. Housing Authority, 1942; gen. counsel Nat. Housing Agy., 1942- 46; vice chmn. Pres.'s Council Econ. Advisers (Employment Act 1946) 1946- 50, chmn., 1950-53; now cons. economist and practicing atty.; hon. mem. faculty Indsl. Coll. Armed Forces, 1966—. Cons. Senate coms., on legislation relating to banking and currency, indsl. recovery and pub. works, housing, social security, labor relations and employment, taxation and monetary policy, 1933-46, 53—; cons. economist working with various nat. orgns., govts., firms and individuals. Founder, pres. Cong. Econ. Progress, 1954- -. Dir. Park Elec. Corp., Giant Food Co. Mem. Am. Econ. Assn., Am. Polit. Sci. Assn., Phi Beta Kappa. Author various monographs, articles and studies; book-length studies include: Inflation-Cause and Cure, 1959; The Federal Budget and the General Welfare, 1959; Key Policies For Full Employment, 1960; The Peace by Investment Corporation, 1961; Poverty and Deprivation in the U.S., 1962; Taxes and the Public Interest, 1963; Two Top Priority Programs to Reduce Unemployment, 1963; The Toll of Rising Interest Rates, 1964; Progress or Poverty, 1964; Agriculture and the Public Interest, 1965; The Role of Wages in a Great Society, 1966; Goals for Teachers Salaries in our Public Schools, 1967; Achieving Nationwide Educational Excellence, 1968; Israel's Economic Progress, 1968; Taxation of Whom and for What?, 1969; More Growth with Less Inflation or More Inflation Without Growth?, 1970; won $10,000 2d prize 1944 Pabst Postwar Employment Awards for essay "The Am. Economic Goal; A Practical Start Towards Postwar Full Employment "Co- author numerous pub. reports of Council Econ. Advisers, 1946-53; prin. author A Freedom Budget for All Americans, 1966. Home: 2610 Upton St NW Washington DC 20008 Office: 1001 Connecticut Av NW Washington DC 20036

KEYSERLING, MARY DUBLIN, economist; b. N.Y.C., May 25, 1910; d. Louis I. and Augusta (Salik) Dublin; A.B., Barnard Coll., 1930; postgrad. London Sch. Econs., Geneva Sch. Internat. Studies, Columbia, 1931-33; research grantee Columbia, 1933-34; LL.D., Bryant Coll., 1964; L.H.D., Woman's Med. Coll. Pa., 1968; m. Leon H. Keyserling, Oct. 4, 1940. Staff mem. Com. Costs Med. Care, Washington, 1930, State Charities Aid Assn., N.Y.C., 1931; tchr. econs., statistics Sarah Lawrence Coll., 1933-38; exec. sec. Nat. Consumers League, N.Y.C., 1938-40; coordinator hearings com. nat. def. migration Ho. of Reps., Washington, 1941; chief research and statis. div. Office Civilian Def., 1942; economist Fgn. Econs. Adminstrn., 1943, chief liberated areas div. bur. supplies, 1944-45; chief spl. program div. Office Internat. Trade, Dept. Commerce, 1946-49, dir. internat. econ. analysis div., 1950-53; asso. dir. Conf. Econ. Progress, also econ. cons., 1953-64; dir. womans bur. U.S. Dept. Labor, 1964-69; Am. Specialist lectr. in Africa for U.S. State Dept., 1969; econ. cons., lectr., 1969—. Mem. child devel. com. NSF. Pres., Women's Nat. Democratic Club 1963-64. Mem. bd. Friendship House, Washington, Day Care and Child Devel. Council Am. Nat. Com. on Household Employment. Mem. Am. Econ. Assn., Nat. Consumers League (bd.), Nat. Fedn. Settlements and Neighborhoods Houses (bd.), Nat. Assembly for Social Policy and Devel. (trustee), Nat. Capital Day Care Assn. (bd.), Phi Beta Kappa. Address: 2610 Upton St N W Washington DC 20008

KEZIOS, STOTHE PETER, educator. Prof. mech. engring., dir. dept. mech. engring. Ga. Inst. Tech., Atlanta Office: Dept Mech Engring Ga Inst Tech Atlanta GA 30332*

KHADDURI, MAJID, educator; b. Mosul, Iraq, Sept. 27, 1909; s. Khadduri Q. and Latifa (Saati) K.; B.A., Am. U., Beirut, 1932; Ph.D., U. Chgo., 1938; m. Majdia Dawaff, Dec. 9, 1942; children—Farid, Shirin. Came to U.S., 1947, naturalized, 1954. Prof. higher tchrs. and law colls., Baghdad, 1938-47; vis. prof. Ind. U., 1947-48, U. Chgo., 1948-49; prof. sch. advanced internat. studies Johns Hopkins, 1949—, Distinguished research prof., 1970—; dir. research and edn. Middle East Inst., Washington, 1950—, bd. governors. Recipient of Rockefeller research grant for a book on Islamic Law of Nations, 1963. Member Iraq delegation UN Conf., San Francisco, 1945. Decorated Order of Rafidian (Iraq). Mem. Am. Polit. Sci. Assn., Am. Soc. Internat. Law, Shaybani Soc. Internat. Law of Washington (pres.), P.E.N. (sec. Baghdad Center 1940-47, sec. N.Y. Center 1968—). Club: Cosmos (Washington, D.C.) Author: (book) War and and Peace in the Law of Islam, 1955; Independent Iraq, 1951; Islamic Jurisprodence, 1961; Modern Libya, 1963; others. Home: 4454 Tindall St Washington DC 20016 Office: 1740 Massachusetts Av Washington DC 20036

KHALID, MANSOUR, Sudanese diplomat, UN ofcl.; b. Sudan, Jan. 17, 1931; ed. U. Khartoum, U. Pa., U. Paris. Atty., Khartoum, 1957-59; legal officer UN, N.Y.C., 1962-63; dep. UN resident rep., Algeria, 1964-65; with Bur. Relations with Mem. States, UNESCO, Paris, 1965-69; minister youth and social affairs, Sudan, 1969-71; chmn. Sudan delegation gen. assembly UN, now permanent rep., 1971—. Vis. prof. internat. law U. Colo., 1968; spl. cons. personal rep. UNESCO Dir.-Gen. for UNWRA fundraising mission, 1970. Office: Permanent Mission Democratic Republic of Sudan to UN 757 3d Av New York City NY 10017*

KHAMA, SERETSE, Botswana govt. ofcl.; b. July 1, 1921; s. Sekgoma II; ed. Fort Hare U., Witwatersrand U. (S. Africa), Balliol Coll., Oxford (Eng.) U.; LL.D. (hon.), LL.B. (hon.); m. Ruth Williams, 1948; 4 children. Pres., Bechuanaland Dem. Party; mem. Legislative Council and Exec. Council, 1961-65; mem. Legislative Assembly, prime minister of Bechuanaland, 1965-66; mem. Parl., pres. Republic of Botswana, 1966—. Address: Pvt Bag 1 Gaborone Botswana*

KHAN, AGHA MUHOMMAD YAHYA, Pres. of Pakistan; b. Peshawar (formerly part of India), Feb. 4, 1917; s. Agha Saadat Ali Khan; grad. Govt. coll., Lahore (now Pakistan), 1936; m. Fakhira Khan, Apr. 4, 1945; children—Ali Yahya, Yasmeen. Commd. officer, 1938, advanced through grades to gen.; service in ETO, NATOUSA, World War II; comdr. div. in inf., Pakistani Army, during Pakistan-India war, 1965; comdr.-in-chief, Pakistan, 1966—; Pres. of Pakistan, 1969—. Decorated Hilal-i-Pakistan, Hilal-i-Jurat. Islamic religion. Address: President's House Rawalpindi Pakistan

KHAN, FAZLUR RAHMAN, structural engr.; b. Dacca, Pakistan, Apr. 3, 1929; s. Abdur Rahman and Khadija (Khanum) K.; B.S., U. Dacca, 1950, Structural Engr., U. Ill., 1952, M.S. in Civil Engring., 1953, M.S. in Theoretical and Applied Mechanics 1955, Ph.D., 1955; m. Liselotte A. Turba, Aug. 3, 1959; 1 dau., Yasmin Sabina. Came to U.S., 1952, naturalized, 1967. Lectr., U. Dacca, 1950-59; Fulbright scholar, 1952-53; project engr. Skidmore, Owings & Merrill, Chgo., 1955-57, sr. project engr., 1960-65, asso. partner, 1965-70, gen. partner, 1970—; exec. engr. Karachi Devel. Authority, Pakistan, 1958-60. Adj. prof. architecture Ill. Inst. Tech., 1966—; designer structural system for 100 story John Hancock Center, Chgo., 110 story Sears Hdgrs. Bldg., Chgo., 52 story Shell Plaza Bldg., Houston. Chmn., Chgo. Com. High Rise Bldgs., 1970. Named among Constrn. Men of Year, Engring. News Record, 1966, 68, 70; Chicagoan of Year in Architecture and Engring., 1970. Mem. Am. Inst. Steel Constrn., Am. Concrete Inst., Am. Welding Soc., Reinforced Concrete Research Council, Am. Soc. C.E. Home: 5201 S Cornell Av Chicago IL 60615 Office: 30 W Monroe St Chicago IL 60603

KHAN, MUHAMMAD ZAFRULLA, judge of Pakistan, Internat. Court Justice. Address: Internat Court Justice United Nations New York City NY 10017 NY 10017

KHARASCH, ROBERT NELSON, lawyer; b. Washington, Dec. 13, 1926; s. Morris S. and Ethel (Nelson) K.; Ph.B., U. Chgo., 1946, B.S., 1948, J.D., 1951; m. Shari Barton, Dec. 26, 1966; children-Mark Robert, Frank William. Admitted to D.C. bar, 1952, since practiced in Washington; pvt. practice, 1952-54; partner Galland, Kharasch, Calkins & Brown, 1955—; cons. Dept. Transp., 1967- 68; mem. study group on legal impediments to intermodel transp. Nat. Acad. Scis. Dir. RDA, Inc. Chmn. Campaign for Chgo., D.C., 1968-69. Mem. Am. Bar Assn. (past com. chmn.), Order of Coif, Phi Beta Kappa. Contbr. articles profl. jours. Inventor Teachall Teaching Machine. Home: 2914 Fessenden St N W Washington DC 20008 Office: 054 31st N W Washington DC 200007

KHARMAWAN, BYANTI, govt. ofcl.; b. Tegal, Indonesia, June 1, 1906; s. Khouw and Liem Kharmawan; grad. cum laude, U. Rotterdam Sch. Econs., 1932. Engaged in pvt. business, 1942; research Netherlands Econ. Inst., Rotterdam, 1949; financial journalist, Amsterdam, 1966; Indonesian civil servant, 1953; econ. adviser Central Bank, 1963; exec. dir. Asain Devel. Bank, 1968; exec. dir. Internat. Monetary Fund, 1968—. Author: Willem Kloos en de dichtkunst, 1931; also articles. Home: 4501 Connecticut Av NW Washington DC Office: Internat Monetary Fund 19th and H Sts Washington DC 20431

KHATCHATURIAN, ARAM, composer; b. Tiflis, Armenia, May 6, 1904; student Gnesin Sch. Music, Moscow, Moscow Conservatory; m. Nina Makarova. Compositions include Dance (violin and piano), 1926, Dance Suite (orchestra), 1933, Symphony No. 1934, Concerto for Piano and Orchestra, 1936; Poem About Stalin, 1938, Concerto for Violin and Orchestra, 1940, Symphony No. 2, 1943, Russian Fantasy, 1945. Cello Concerto, 1946; Overture—Poems, 1950; ballets include Happiness, 1940, Gayané (orchestral suite includes Sabre Dance), 1941, Spartak, 1951; incidental music for Lermontor play Masquerade, 1944; music for films Battle for Stalingrad, Othello. Composer three suites from ballet, Spartak, 1959, three suites-pictures from ballet, Spartak, 1959, overture for symphony orchestra, 1959, three aires for high voice with orch., lyrics based on verses Armenian classic poets, 1947, music for comedy, The Widows of Valencia (by Lope de Vega), 1955, Ode to Joy for symphony orch., chorus, mezzo soprano, ensemble of violins and harps, 1957, sonatina in 3 parts for piano, 1958, music for Macbeth, 1958, for King Lear, 1958, rhapsody for violin and piano, 1959. Awarded Stalin prize, 1942, Order of Lenin for outstanding services in development of music.

KHATRI, PADMA BAHADUR, maj. gen., former ambassador of Nepal to U.S. Address: 2730 34th Pl NW Washington DC 20007

KHAURY, HERBERT BUCKINGHAM, (Tiny Tim), entertainer; b. N.Y.C.; s. Butrus H. and Tillie (Staff) K.; ed. pub. schs., N.Y.C.; m. Vicki Budinger, Dec. 17, 1969. Appearances include Caesars Palace, Las Vegas, 1968, Albert Hall, London, Eng., 1968, Johnny Carson TV show, 1968, Ed Sullivan TV show, 1968; mem. guest staff Laugh-In-TV show, 1968; also appeared on Jackie Gleason show, 1969, Hollywood Palace TV show, 1969, and at Fontainebleau Hotel, Miami Beach, Fla., 1968, Latin Casino, Cherry Hill, N.J., 1969, Sherman House, Chgo., 1969, Steel Pier, N.J., 1969, Sahara Hotel, Tahoe, Nev., 1969. Address: 359 N Canon Dr Beverly Hills CA 90210

KHEEL, THEODORE WOODROW, lawyer, arbitrator and mediator of labor disputes; b. New York City, N.Y., May 9, 1914; s. Samuel and Kate (Herzenstein) K.; A.B., Cornell U., 1935, LL.B., 1937; m. Ann Sunstein, July 1, 1937; children—Ellen Margaret, Robert Jeffrey, Constance Elizabeth, Martha Louise, Jane Meredith, Katherine Emily. Admitted to New York bar, 1937; partner firm Battle, Fowler, Stokes & Kheel, 1949—. Chmn. bd. dirs. Republic Nat. Bank of N.Y.; dir. Athlone Industries, Inc., Combustion Equipment Assos., Inc., Jessop Steel Co., Stirling Homex Corp., U.S. Smelting, Refining & Mining Co., Western Union Telegraph Co.; trustee Manhattan Savs. Bank. Pres., Am. Found. Automation and Employment, Inc.; adviser Inst. Collective Bargaining and Group Relations Inc.; mem. Presdl. bds. various labor disputes, 1962-66; spl. cons. Pres.'s Com. Equal Employment Opportunity, 1962-63; mem. Pres.'s Maritime Adv. Com., 1964-66, Pres.'s Nat. Citizens Com. for Community Relations, 1964-68 Pres., Nat. Urban League, 1956-60; chmn. Mayor's Com. Job Advancement, 1962-65. Chmn. bd. Met. Applied Research Center, Inc.; bd. dirs. Acad. Ednl. Devel., Inc.; trustee N.Y.C.-Rand Inst.; chmn. exec. bd. Corsi Labor-Mgmt. Relations Inst. of Pace Coll. Author: Transit and Arbitration, 1960; Pros and Cons of Compulsory Arbitration, 1961; How Race Relations Affect Your Business, 1963; Guide to Fair Employment Practices, 1964. Home: 407 W 246th St Bronx NY 10471 Office: 280 Park Av New York City NY 10017

KHOMAN, THANAT, Thailand diplomat; b. Bangkok, Thailand, May 9, 1914; s. Phya Pipakasa Satyathipatai and Khunying Thanom Laoha-Sethi; student Assumption Coll. Thailand, U. Bordeaux; LL.D., U. Paris, France, 1940; diploma Ecole des Sciences Politiques, Paris, also Institut des Hautes Etudes Internationales, Paris; m. Molee Virangkura, Apr. 28, 1914; children—Thavida, Monthira, Thirawudh. Joined Thai Fgn. Office, 1941; 2d. sec. Thai embassy, Tokyo, Japan, 1942-43; charge d'affaires Thai embassy, Washington, 1946-47, ambassador, 1957-59; charge d'affaires Thai legation, New Delhi, India, 1947-49; dir.-gen. dept. econ. affairs UN, 1950-52, dir.-gen. dept. UN affairs, 1950-51; dep., acting permanent rep. of Thailand to UN, 1952- 57; mem. UN Internat. Law Commn., 1957; chmn. UN Com. on S.W. Africa; chmn. UN Gen. Assembly Trusteeship Com., 1957; Thai minister fgn. affairs, 1959—. Lectr. Chulalongkorn and Moral Sci. univs., Bangkok, Thailand. Decorated knight grand cross Order of Crown, Order of Crown, Order of Chula Chom Klao (Thailand). Mem. Am. Soc. Internat. Law. Home: 123 Petchaburi Rd Bangkok Thailand Office: Ministry Fgn Affairs Bangkok Thailand

KHORANA, HAR GOBIND, chemist, b. Raipur, India, Jan. 9, 1922; s. Shri Ganpat Rai and Shrimati Krishna (Devi) K.; B.S., Punjab U., 1943, M.S., 1945; Ph.D., Liverpool (Eng.) U., 1948; D.Sc., U. Chgo., 1967; m. Esther Elizabeth Sibler, 1952; children—Julia, Emilie, Dave Roy. Head organic chemistry group B.C. Research Council, 1952-60; vis. prof. Rockefeller Inst., N.Y.C., 1958—; prof. co-dir. Inst. Enzyme Research, U. Wis., Madison, 1960-70, prof. dept. biochemistry, 1962-70, Conrad A. Elvehjem prof. life scis., 1964-70; vis. prof. Stanford, 1964. Mem. adv. bd. Biopolymers. Recipient Merck award Chem. Inst. Can., 1958, Gold medal Profl. Inst. Pub. Service Can., 1960, Dannie-Heinneman Preiz, Göttingen, Germany, 1967, Remsen award Johns Hopkins, 1968, Am. Chem. Soc. award for creative work in synthetic organic chemistry, 1968, Louisa Gross Horwitz prize, 1968, Lasker Found. award for basic med. research, 1968, Nobel prize in medicine, 1968; elected to Deutsche Akademie der Naturforscher Leopoldina, HalleSaale, Germany, 1968. Overseas fellow Churchill Coll., Cambridge, Eng., 1967. Fellow Chem. Inst. Can., Am. Acad. Arts and Scis.; mem. Nat. Acad. Sci. Author: Some Recent Developments in the Chemistry of Phosphate Esters of Biological Interests, 1961. Mem. editorial bd. Jour. Am. Chem. Soc., 1963—. Research and numerous publs. on chem. methods for synthesis of nucleotides, coenzymes and nucleic acids; elucidation on the genetic code. Home: Thorstrand Rd Madison WI 53705 Office: 1702 University Av Madison WI 53706

KHOSROVANI, KHOSRO, Iranian diplomat; b. Mahallat, Iran, June 14, 1914; s. Mohamad Hashim and Marhamat Khosrovani; Ph.D., U. Birmingham (Eng.); m. Farah Karimi- Zand, Apr. 4, 1927; children—Laben, Bahman. First sec. Imperial Embassy Iran, Washington, 1946, minister, 1960-61; advisor, del. Iranian Permanent Mission to UN, 1947-59; under sec. Ministry Fgn. Affairs, 1959- 60; Iranian ambassador to Turkey, 1963-65; Iranian ambassador to U.S., Washington, 1965-67; Iranian ambassador to UAR, 1971—; Supreme inspector Foreign Ministry; under-sec. National Economy, 1952-53. Mng. dir. Fgn. Transaction Co.; chmn. bd. inspectorate Nat. Iranian Oil Co. Chmn. bd. Policy and Polit. Programs. Decorated Order Homayoun Iranian Govt. Home: 41 Darband Av Teheran Iran Office: care Ministry Fgn Affairs Teheran Iran

KHRENNIKOV, TIKHON NIKOLAEVICH composer; b. Yelets, USSR, 1913; student Moscow Musical Technicum; grad. with distinction Moscow Conservatory, 1936. Composer opera In the Storm, based on Virta's novel Solitude; songs for voice and piano include The Best Lad, Drinking Song; music for Ostrovsky's play Guilty Through Guiltless, Katav's play A Soldier Came from the Front; composer music for films The Swineherd and the Shepherd, At Six P.M., After the War, The Train goes to East, opera Frol Skobiev, opera Mother. Recipient Stalin prizes, also various other medals, awards; named People's Artist of Russian Soviet Federated Socialist Republic. Mem. USSR Union Soviet Composers (1st sec.), All Union Soc. for Cultural Relations Fgn. Countries (chmn. music sect.). Composer: Symphony in B-Minor, Do Not Sing Beautiful One, Winter Road, I am Here Inesilia, Concert for Violin and Orchestra, 100 Devils and One Girl, White Nights, Concerto for Cello, Concerto for Piano. Composer music for play It was Long, Long Time Ago. Address: USSR Union Soviet Composers Moscow USSR

KHRUNOV, LT. COL. YEVGENY, Russian Cosmonaut who transferred from Soyuz 5 to Soyuz 4, Jan. 1969. Jan. 1969. Address: care Sci Research Inst Petrovsky Park Moscow USSR*

KHURI, NICOLA NAJIB, educator, physicist; b. Beirut, Lebanon, May 27, 1933; s. Najib N. and Odette (Joujou) K.; came to U.S., 1959, naturalized, 1970; B.A with high distinction, Am. U. Beirut, 1952; Ph.D., Princeton, 1957; m. Elizabeth Anne Tyson, Dec. 9, 1955; children—Suzanne Odette, Najib Nicholas. Asst. prof. Am. U. Beirut, 1957-58, 60-61, asso. prof., 1961-62; mem. Inst. Advanced Study, Princeton, 1959-60, 62-63; vis. asso. prof. Columbia, 1963-64; asso. prof. Rockefeller U., 1964-68, prof., 1968—. Cons. Brookhaven Nat. Lab., 1963—. Trustee Am. U. Beirut, Brearley Sch., N.Y.C. Fellow Am. Phys. Soc. Contbr. articles to profl. jours. Home: 4715 Iselin Av Riverdale NY 10471 Office: Rockefeller U New York City NY 10021

KI, ZAO WOU, artist; b. Peking, China, 1921; student Nat. Sch. Fine Arts, Hanchow. Prof. Nat. Sch. Fine Arts, 1941-47; participant Salon de Mai, 1950—; one-man exhbns. Galerie Pierre and Galerie de

France, Paris, also abroad; graphic artist rep. museums modern art throughout world. Address: care Soc. des Artistes Independants Grand Palais des Champs-Elysees Cour La Reine Paris 83 France

KIAM, VICTOR KERMIT, II, watch mfg. co. exec.; b. New Orleans, Dec. 7, 1926; s. Victor Kermit and Nanon (Newman) K.; grad. Phillips Acad., 1944; B.S., B.A., Yale, 1948; student Sorbonne, Paris, 1949; M.B.A., Harvard, 1951; m. Ellen Lipscher, Nov. 26, 1956; children—Lisa, Victor Kermit, Robin. Salesman, dist. mgr., product mgr. cosmetics div. Lever Bros., 1951-53, supr., dist. mgr. Pepsodent div., 1954-55; marketing dir. woman's ware div. Internat. Latex Corp., 1955-58, v.p. marketing, 1958-60, v.p., gen. mgr. div. Sarong, Inc., 1960-64, pres., 1964-68, v.p. parent co., 1960-68; pres. Benrus Corp., 1968—, chief exec. officer, 1971—; chmn. bd. PIC Design Corp., 1968—. Mem. adv. com. Norwalk Community Coll. Trustee Hillside Hosp.; bd. dirs. Child Welfare League Am. Served with USNR, 1944-47. Mem. Young Pres. Orgn., U.S. Tennis Assn. Clubs: Century Country, Regency Whist. Home: 630 Park Av New York City NY 10021 Office: Benrus Center Route 7 Ridgefield CT 06877

KIAMIE, MITCHELL, engring. co. exec.; b. 1921; B.S., N.Y.U., 1942; married. Accountant, O.F. Taylor & Co., 1942-45; with Arthur Andersen & Co., 1945-53; asst. comptroller Gen. Dynamics Corp., 1953-60; controller Combustion Engring. Inc., N.Y.C., 1961-67, v.p., controller, 1967—. Served with AUS, 1942-43. C.P.A., N.Y. Office: 277 Park Av New York City NY 10017*

KIBBE, ALBERT PAYNE, uranium co. exec.; b. Abbeville, La., Aug. 9, 1917; s. Joseph Everrard and Estelle (Laundry) K.; B.S., Southwestern La. Inst., 1937; student Tulane U., 1936-38, La. State U., 1938-40; m. Evelyn Ryberg, Dec. 23, 1940; children—A. Payne, Marie Estelle, Nanette Ryberg, Gail Ryberg. Gen. supt. W. Ryberg Co., 1941-44; sales rep. investments Blyth & Co., 1946-48; pres. A. P. Kibbe & Co., 1948-57; treas., dir. Utah Sand & Gravel Products Corp., 1948—, pres., 1969—; pres., dir. Lisbon Uranium Corp., Salt Lake City, 1954-59, Hidden Splendor Mining Co., 1957-62; v.p. Atlas Corp., 1962-64, pres., 1965-66, president Atlas Minerals, Division Atlas Corp., 1962-66; pres. Kibbe & Asso., 1966—; chmn. bd. Nuclear Exchange Corp., 1968—; director Surety Life Insurance Company, First Security Bank of Utah. Served as ensign USNR, 1944-46. Mem. Utah Mining Assn., Salt Lake City C. of C., Am. Inst. Mining, Metall. and Petroleum Engrs., U.S. C. of C. Atomic Indsl. Forum Inc. (dir.), Indsl. Relations Council (dir.). Clubs: Alta, Salt Lake Country (Salt Lake City); Wall Street, Mining, Metropolitan (N.Y.C.); Alta; Eldorado (Palm Desert, Cal.). Home: Salt Lake City UT Office: First Security Bldg Salt Lake UT 84111

KIBBE, MILTON HOMER, physician, hosp. adminstr.; b. West Stafford, Conn., Aug. 14, 1911; s. Harlow Lawton and Queerie (Avery) K.; B.S., U. Mass., 1934; M.D., Tufts U., 1938; postgrad. Columbia, Harvard, Yale; m. Elizabeth Alderman, June 11, 1935; children—Jill (Mrs. Joseph McNamara), Barry, Dennis, Karen, Vickie. Intern, Muhlenberg Hosp., 1938-39, Somerset Hosp., 1939-40; pvt. practice neurology and neurosurgery, Plainfield, N.J., 1940- 41, psychiatry and neurology, Springfield, Mass., 1946-58; clin. dir. Lynchburg (Va.) Tng. Sch. Hosp., 1958-60; supt. Peterburg (Va.) Tng. Sch. and Hosp., Central State Hosp.; asso. clin. prof. psychiatry Med. Coll. Va.; spl. research brain injuries, electorencephalography. Bd. dirs. Chesapeake dist. Found. Mentally Retarded and Physically Handicapped. Served to maj. M.C., AUS, 1941-46. Recipient Christian P. Sorensen award Civitan Internat., 1963. Diplomate Am. Bd. Neurology and Psychiatry. Fellow Am. Psychiat. Assn. Club: Civitan (pres. Peterburg 1966-67). Address: Petersburg Tng Sch and Hosp Box 4110 Petersburg VA 23803

KIBBEE, CHANDLER HOEGH, corp. exec.; b. Mpls., Dec. 7, 1907; s. E.Channing and Helen (Hoegh) K.; student Yale, 1926- 29; m. Jane Bartley, Aug. 27, 1932; children—Sharon, Peter; m. Mercedes Kellough, Apr. 29, 1947. Bond Trader, contract man for financial instns. Solomon Bros. & Hutzler, 1929-38; mgr. Chgo. office Wood Struthers & Co., 1938-41; asst. to compliance chief WPB, 1941-42; asst. treas., financial officer Am. Airlines, Inc., N.Y.C., 1946-50; sec., asst. treas. Philip Morris, Inc., N.Y.C., 1950-55, sec., treas., 1955-57, chief financial officer, 1957, v.p., treas., dir., 1957-59, exec. v.p. finance 1959-67, exec. v.p. strategic planning, 1967—, mem. exec. com., 1962—; dir. Christiania Gen. Ins. Corp. N.Y., L.S. Ayres & Co., Indpls. Bd. dirs. Nat. Travelers Aid Assn.; trustee Mus. Am. Indian-Heye Found. Served to lt. USNR, 1943-45, Mem. Fgn. Policy Assn. Clubs: Pinnacle, Yale (N.Y.C.); Sleepy Hollow Country (Briarcliffe, N.Y.). Home: 47 E 87th St New York City NY 10028 Office: 100 Park Av New York City NY 10017

KIBBEY, DONALD EUGENE, mathematician, educator; b. Junction City, Kan., Feb. 19, 1912; s. Frank Preble and Maude (Pierce) K.; A.B., U. Ill., 1935, A.M., 1936, Ph.D., 1942; m. Mary Elizabeth Lichliter, Nov. 26, 1938; children—Hal Stephen, David Lawrence, Ann Marilyn. Grad. asst. U. Ill., 1936-39; instr. U. Kansas City, 1939-42, Mich. State U., 1942; asst. prof. math. Syracuse (N.Y.) U., 1946-48, asso. prof., 1948-51, prof., 1951—, chmn. dept., 1950-71, v.p. research and grad. affairs, 1971—. Served from 1st lt. to maj. AUS, 1942-46. Mem. Am. Math. Soc., Math Assn. Am. (gov. 1964-67), Soc. Indsl. and Applied Math., Am. Assn. U. Profs. Author: (with H.W. Reddick) Differential Equations, 1956. Home: 3 Erregger Terrace Syracuse NY 13224

KIBBEY, HAL PIERCE, mfg. co. exec.; b. Junction City, Kan., Feb. 18, 1914; s. Frank Prebble and Maude (Pierce) K.; B.C.E., U. Ill., 1936; m. Marie Elizabeth Mesch, May 1, 1940; children—Mark Henry, Hames Pierce, Susan. Salesman, Carnegie Ill. Steel Corp., Chgo., 1936-49; asst. v.p. United Steel Supply div. U.S. Steel Corp., Chgo., 1949-57; pres. Gate City Steel Corp., Omaha, 1957-63; v.p. Stanray Corp., Chgo., 1963-66, pres., chief exec. officer, 1966-71; pres. E.W. Bliss Co., Salem, O., 1971—. Served with USNR, 1942-46. Mem. Am. Soc. C.E. Clubs: Chicago, University (Chgo.); Glenview. Home: 200 Garwood Dr Canfield OH 44406 Office: 530 S Ellsworth Av Salem OH 44460

KIBBY, LEO PAUL, educator; b. Iola, Kan., Feb., 20, 1906; s. Milo Edwin and Merty (Simpson) K.; A.B., Stanford, 1929; A.M., N.M. State Tchrs. Coll., 1933; Ph.D., U. So. Cal., 1942; m. Jean Eleanor McGovney, June 27, 1938; children—Byron Paul, Norman Lloyd. Tchr. history N.M. State Tchrs. Coll., 1929-33; headmaster Flintridge Sch. Boys, Pasadena, Cal., 1933- 35; dean men, dean guidance Ventura (Cal.) Jr. Coll., 1935-42, vice prin., 1940-42, 46; teaching fellow U. So. Cal., 1939-40; mem. faculty San Jose (Cal.) State Coll., 1946—, prof. history 1948-70, prof. emeritus, 1970—; chmn. social sci. dept., 1952-65, dean ednl. services and summer sessions, 1965-70. Lectr. ednl. bus. and profl. orgns., local and state hist. socs. Mem. adv. planning com., Saratoga, Cal., 1959-60; adv. council Civil War Centennial Commn., 1958—. Served to lt. comdr. USNR, 1942-45. Mem. So. Hist. Assn., Theta Delta Chi, Alpha Psi Omega, Phi Alpha Theta, Phi Delta Kappa. Author: Book Review Reference for a Decade of Civil War Books, 1950-60, also 1960 supplement; California, the Civil War and the Indian Problem; also articles and revs. Home: 15230 Pepper Lane Saratoga CA 95070

KIBINGE, LEONARD OLIVER, diplomat of Kenya; b. Kabete, Kenya, Mar. 10, 1934; s. Oliver Warui and Judith (Nini) K.; B.A. with honors, Makerere U. (London), 1960; Dipl. P.A. University Coll. Nairobi, 1962; certificate diplomacy Am. U., 1963; m. Jane Nyambura Kibera, Aug. 7, 1965; children—Michael Warui, Judith Nini, James Kibera. Mem. mgmt. staff Brit. Am. Tobacco Co., E. Africa, 1960-61; asst. sec. Kenya Govt., 1961-64; sr. asst. sec. Fgn. Affairs, Nairobi, 1964-67, dep. sec., 1967-68; sec. E. African Community, Common Market and Econ. Affairs Secretariat, 1968; mem. Ministry Agr., Nairobi, 1968; ambassador to U.S., 1969—. Address: Embassy of the Republic of Kenya 1875 Connecticut Av Washington DC 20009

KIBLER, DAVID BURKE, III, lawyer; b. Lakeland, Fla., Feb. 5, 1924; s. David Burke, Jr. and Bessie (Dew) K.; B.A. cum laude, U. Fla., 1947, J.D., 1949; m. Nell Idalene Bryant, Sept. 26, 1945; children—David Burke IV, Thomas Bryant, Jacquelyn, Nancy Dew. Admitted to Fla. bar, 1949; since practiced in Lakeland; partner firm Holland & Knight and predecessors, 1964—. Dir., v.p. Kibler Agrl. Corp.; dir. Fla. Nat. Bank, Fla. Tile Industries, Inc. (both Lakeland), Chris McGuire, Inc., Ft. Lauderdale, Fla.; sec., dir. Lakeland Fed. Savs. & Loan Assn. Past pres., bd. dirs., exec. com. Lakeland United Fund; mem. Fla. Bd. Regents, 1967—, chmn., 1969—; ex-officio mem. Fla. Council 100. Served to 1st lt. AUS, 1943-46; ETO. Decorated Bronze Star with V, Purple Heart with oak leaf cluster. Mem. Am., 10th Jud. Circuit bar assns., Am. Judicature Soc., Fla. Bar, Am. Legion, Alpha Tau Omega, Phi Delta Phi. Democrat. Presbyn. Rotarian, Elk. Clubs: Lakeland Yacht and Country, Lone Palm Golf (Lakeland); University (Tampa, Fla.). Home: 2113 Fairmont Av Lakeland FL 33802 Office: 92 Lake Wire Dr Lakeland FL 33802

KIBRE, PEARL, educator, historian; b. Phila.; d. Kenneth and Jane (du Plone) Kibre; student U. Cal. at Los Angeles, 1920-22, A.B., at Berkeley, 1924, M.A., 1925; Ph.D., Columbia, 1936. Instr. history Pasadena (Cal.) Jr. Coll., 1925-28; research asst. Columbia, 1929-37; instr. history Bklyn., 1937- 38; faculty Hunter Coll., City U N.Y., 1938—, prof. history, 1957—. Research fellow N.Y. Acad. Medicine, Nyon, Switzerland, 1938-39; Guggenheim fellow, 1950-51. Fellow Mediaeval Acad. Am. (third vice president 1964-67; member History Sci. Soc., Am. Assn. U. Profs., Medieval Club N.Y.C., Am. Hist. Assn., Phi Beta Kappa; mem. corr. Acad. Internationale d'Histoire des Sciences. Author: The Library of Pico della Mirandola, 1936; (with Lynn Thorndike) A Catalogue of Incipits of Mediaeval Scientific Writings in Latin, 2d edit., 1963; The Nations in the Mediaeval Universities, 1948; Scholarly Privileges in the Middle Ages (Haskins gold medal 1964), 1962. Co-editor: Osiris, vol. XI, 1954. Contbr. books, profl. jours. Home: 1100 Madison Av New York City NY 10028

KIBRICK, ANNE, nursing educator; b. Palmer, Mass., June 1, 1919; d. Martin and Christine (Grigas) Karlon; R.N., Worcester (Mass.) Hahnemann Hosp., 1941; B.S., Boston U., 1945; M.A., Columbia Tchrs. Coll., 1948; Ed.D., Harvard, 1958; m. Sidney Kibrick, June 16, 1949; children—Joan, John. Asst. edn. dir. Cushing VA Hosp., Framingham, Mass., 1948-49; asst. prof. nursing Simmons Coll., Boston, 1949-55; dir. grad. div. Boston U. Sch. Nursing, 1958-63, dean, 1963-68, prof., 1968-70; chmn. dept. nursing Boston Coll. Grad. Sch. Arts and Sci., 1970—. Cons. div. nursing USPHS, 1964-68; nat adv. council Nurse Tng. USPHS, NIH, 1968—. Mem. Gov.'s Com. and Area Bd. Mental Health and Mental Retardation, Nat. Commn. for Study Nursing and Nursing Edn., 1970—. Bd. mem. Brookline Mental Health Assn., Met. Chpt. A.R.C. Mem. Nat. (pres. 1971—), Mass. leagues nursing, Am., Mass. nurses assns., Sigma Theta Tau, Pi Lambda Theta. Home: 381 Clinton Rd Brookline MA 02146

KIDD, ALAN REYNOLDS, banker; b. Buffalo, Apr. 17, 1905; s. Fred J. and Harriet (Maltby) K.; B.S., U. Ala., 1927; m. Alice Taft Bradley, June 12, 1932; children—John B., Alan Reynolds, James N. With No. Trust Co., Chgo., 1928—, v.p., 1947-64, sr. v.p., 1964—. Dir., treas. Chicagoland Internat. Trade Fair, 1957-63; dir., mem. investment com. Hosp. Service Corp., Chgo., 1961—. Mem. guarantors com. Ravinia Festival Assn., 1963—, vice chmn. com., 1965-68; acting pres. Highland Park Hosp., 1958, 1st v.p., 1954- 60, bd. mgrs., 1952-63, bd. trustees, 1952— mem. investment com., 1960-; chmn. Highland Park Community Fund, 1954, pres., 1952, chmn. spl. gifts, 1951. Mem. citizens bd. U. Chgo., 1958—. Co-chmn. banking sect. United Settlement Appeal. Mem. Am. Bankers Assn. (chmn. exec. com. conv. 1958), Chgo. Assn. Commerce and Industry (bd. dirs. 1955—, treas. 1955-57), Ill., Nat. assns. mfrs., Ill. C. of C. (bd. dirs. 1961—, treas. 1964—), Western Golf Assn. (bd. dirs., v.p., treas.), Ill. Sr. Golf Assn., U. Ala. Alumni Assn. Episcopalian (vestryman 1957—, chmn. finance com. 1957-58, sr. warden 1969-70). Clubs: Bankers, Chicago, Economic, Executives, Mid-Am. (Chgo.); Exmoor Country (pres. 1962-63). Home: 1104 Skokie Ridge Dr Glencoe IL 60022 Office: 50 S La Salle St Chicago IL 60690

KIDD, AUBREY VIVIAN, banker; b. Richmond, Va., Aug. 1, 1908; s. Robert Henry and Lucy (Warriner) K.; B.S. in Bus. Adminstrn., U. Richmond, 1930; m. Audrey Elizabeth Murray, Sept. 15, 1933; children—Suzanne Murray, Robert Cabell. With The Bank of Va., also Va. Commonwealth Bankshares, Inc., Richmond, 1927—, part-time bookkeeper, auditor, asst. v.p., cashier, 1927-52, v.p., sec. 1952-66, sr. v.p., sec., 1966—. Lectr., U. Richmond Evening Sch. Bus. Adminstrn., 1936-53; lectr. Sch. Consumer Banking, U. Va., 1953-71, trustee, 1960—. Council pres. Boy Scouts Am., 1954-55, mem. exec. bd., 1951-65; chmn. Richmond Local Milk Bd., 1960-62. Trustee Bapt. Ministers' Relief Fund Va., 1959- 65. Pres. Consumers Bankers Assn., 1968-69. Mem. Am. Inst. Banking. Home: 7308 Normandy Dr Richmond VA 23229 Office: 800 E Main St Richmond VA 23260

KIDD, CHARLES VINCENT, assn. exec.; b. Paulsboro, N.J. Jan. 22, 1914; s. Walter Stephen and Nettie (Sparks) K.; A.B., Princeton, 1935, M.A., 1937; Dr. Pub. Adminstrn., Harvard, 1957; m. Blanche Facer Hoover, Aug. 27, 1938; children—David, Stephen. Economist war Manpower Commn., Office War Moblzn. and Reconversion, Council Econ. Advisers, 1944-46; exec. sec. Pres.'s Sci. Research Bd., 1947; chief research planning Nat. Insts. Health, Bethesda, Maryland, 1948-60, asso. dir., 1960-64; exec. sec. fed. council sci. and technology. Office Sci. and Technology, 1964-69; exec. sec., dir. council on fed. relations Assn. Am. Univs., 1970—. Cons. Pan-Am. Health Orgn., 1964—, WHO 1958—, Ford Found., 1960—, Education and World Affairs, 1965-70, State Dept., 1970—; mem. U.S. del. to UN Conf. Sci. and Tech., 1964, to UNESCO Conf. Sci. Policy, Karlovy Vary, 1966, to OAS Conf. Edn., Sci. and Culture, Maracay, 1968; head U.S. delegation to Castasia Conf., New Delhi, 1968; adv. com. Woodrow Wilson Sch. Princeton, 1965- 67. Recipient Rockefeller Pub. Service award, 1955; Distinguished Service award, Dept. HEW, 1964. Served at lt. (j.g.), USNR, 1944-46. Fellow Am. Assn. Advancement Sci.; mem. Am. Pub. Health Assn., Am. Soc. for Pub. Adminstrn. Clubs: Princeton (Washington); Cosmos; Hajji Baba. Author: American Universities and Federal Research 1959, also articles on sci. and ednl. policy. Home: 3900 Connecticut Av Washington DC 20008 Office: Assn. Am. Univs 1 Dupont Circle Washington DC 20036

KIDD, GLENN O., business exec.; b. Lawrenceburgh, Tenn., Aug. 24, 1915; s. Joe Pullen and Gertrude (Smallwood) K.; B.S., Washington U., 1936; LL.B., George Washington U., 1940; m. Elise Clark, Nov. 19, 1939; children—Glenn Clark, Gary Wilmot, Pamela Elise, Christopher Warren. Atty.-examiner ICC, 1936-41; asst. sec. Lehigh Coal and Navigation Co., 1942, sec. and asst. treas., 1945, v.p. sales, 1950, pres., 1953-54; v.p. Fundamental Investors, Inc., Diversified Growth Stock Fund, Inc., Hugh W. Long and Co., Inc. Diversified Investment Fund, Inc., Manhattan Bond Fund, Inc., 1954-57; v.p., dir. Dyson-Kissner Corp.; dir. Esterline Angus Instrument Co., Colonial Natural Gas Co., Kearney-Nat Inc., Wallace-Murray Corp. Esterline Angus Instrument Co. Mem. D.C. Bar Assn., Am. Mgmt. Assn., Newcomen Soc. N.A. Clubs: Racquet, Midday (Phila.); Union League (N.Y.C.). Home: Arrowhead Way Darien CT 06820 Office: 230 Park Av New York City NY 10017

KIDD, HENRY M., corp. exec.; b. Spencerville, O., 1909. Exec. v.p. DeVilviss Co., Toledo, 1963-67, pres., 1967—. Home: 3503 Kenwood Blvd Toledo OH 43606 Office: 300 Phillips Av Toledo OH 43601*

KIDD, ISAAC CAMPBELL, naval officer; b. Cleve., Aug. 14, 1919; s. Isaac Campbell and Inez Nellie (Gilmore) K.; student St. Albans Sch., Washington, 1932-36, St. George's Sch., Newport, R.I., 1936-37, Columbian Prep. Sch., Washington, 1937-38; B.S., U.S. Naval Acad., 1942; m. Marie Angelique deGolian, July 11, 1942; children—Isaac Campbell III, Keven G., Marie A.D., Christopher A., Regina I., Mary Corrinne. Commd. ensign, 1941, advanced through grades to adm., 1971; posts include U.S.S. Cowie, 1942-44, U.S.S. Putnam, 1944-46; staff comdr. destroyers Atlantic Fleet, 1946-48; bur. Naval Personnel, 1948-51; with U.S.S. Salem, 1951-52; comdr. U.S.S. Ellyson, 1952-53; mem. staff Supt. Naval Acad., 1953-56; comdr. U.S.S. Barry, 1956-58, Destroyer Div. 322, 1961, Destroyer Squadron 32, 1961, Squadron 18, 1961-62; exec. to chief naval operations, 1962-66; asst. chief of staff for logistics for comdr. in chief Allied Forces, 1966-68; comdr. cruiser-destroyer Flotilla 12, 1968-69, 1st Fleet, 1969-70, 6th Fleet, 1970-71; chief naval material, 1971—. Decorated D.S.M., Legion of Merit with two gold stars, Bronze Star medal with combat V. Mem. Internat. Scuba Assn. (pres. 1966-68), Soc. Mil. Engrs. Italy (pres. 1967-68). Address: c/o Am Nat Bank Jacksonville FL

KIDD, JOHN BURNS, air force officer; b. Cleve., Apr. 15, 1919; s. Caughey Cleveland and Hazel (Maskey) K.; student Oberlin Coll., 1937-40, U. Md., 1951, 1964, U. N.M., 1958; grad. Air War Coll., 1957; m. Mary Jane Johnson, Aug. 29, 1942; children—John Burns, Laurie Christine. Comd. 2d lt. USAAF, 1940, advanced through grades to maj. gen. USAF, 1970; squadron comdr., group operations officer 100th Bomb Group, 8th Air Force, Eng., World War II; chief flight operations Berlin airlift, 1949-50; war planner Hdqrs. USAF, 1952-56; staff officer Joint Staff, Pacific div., operations Joint Chiefs Staff, 1963-66, chief Pacific div., 1965-66; dep. operations officer comdr.-in-chief Pacific staff, Hawaii, 1966-69; dep. dir. personnel planning Hdqrs. USAF, 1969-70, dir. personnel planning, 1970—. Decorated D.S.M., Silver Star, Legion of Merit, D.F.C. with oak leaf cluster, Air medal with 2 oak leaf clusters, Air Force Commendation medal; Croix de Guerre with palm (France). Mem. Daedalian Soc., Air Force Assn., Air Force Hist. Soc. Innovator air force macro personnel plan. Home: 9112 Coronado Terrace Fairfax VA 22030 Office: Headquarters US Air Force Dir Personnel Planning Washington DC 20330

KIDD, JOHN GRAYDON, exptl. pathologist, educator; b. Edgewood, Tex., July 20, 1908; s. John F. and Rose (Steed) K.; A.B., Duke, 1928; M.D., Johns Hopkins, 1932; m. Maudine Adams, July 23, 1939; children—Maudanne, Graydon, Elizabeth, Robert. Intern, asst. resident physician Henry Ford Hosp., Detroit, 1932- 34; asst., asso., asso. mem. pathology and bacteriology Rockefeller Inst. Med. Research, 1934-44; prof. pathology Cornell U. Med. Coll., pathologist-in-chief N.Y. Hosp., 1944-64; mem. research council, bd. dirs. Pub. Health Research Inst., N.Y.C., 1948-57; bd. sci. dirs., trustee Roscoe B. Jackson Meml. Lab., Bar Harbor, 1955—, pres. bd. trustees, 1960-64, Found. Trustee Trudeau hon. chmn, 1964—; cons. Rockefeller U., 1956—. Recipient Eli Lilly award, 1939, Leland Fikes Research award, 1968. Fellow A.A.A.S, N.Y. Acad. Medicine (chmn. sect. microbiology 1952-53); mem. A.M.A., Am. Soc. Exptl. Pathology (pres. 1949-50), Am. Assn. Pathologists and Bacteriologists (council 1957-62, pres. 1961), Am. Assn. Immunologists, Soc. Am. Bacteriologists, Soc. for Exptl. Biology and Medicine, Soc. Gen. Microbiology (Gt. Britain), Am. Assn. Cancer Research, Harvey Soc., N.Y. Path. Soc. (v.p. 1957-58, pres. 1958-59), Royal Soc. Medicine (Gt. Britain), Phi Beta Kappa, Sigma Xi. Methodist. Clubs: Cosmos, Century. Editor: The Pathogenesis and Pathology of Viral Diseases; The Dynamics of Virus and Rickettsial Infections. Home: 229 Pondfield Rd Bronxville NY 10708 also 322 San Augustine St Center TX 75935 Office: 1300 York Av New York City NY 10021

KIDD, MICHAEL, choreographer; student Coll. City of N.Y.; scholarship Sch. of Am. Ballet. Choreography includes: On Stage, for Ballet Theatre, Seven Brides for Seven Brothers; Finian's Rainbow; Can-Can; Li'l Abner; Merry Andrew; Destry Rides Again. Produced (with N. Richard Nash) Wildcat, 1960; Subways are for Sleeping, 1962; Here's Love, 1963; Ben Franklin in Paris, 1964. Recipient Antoinette award for scene design, Li'l Abner, 1957.

KIDD, PAUL JAMES GARLAND, lawyer, corp. exec.; Kingston, Ont., Can., June 25, 1913; s. Charles Edward and Mary (Youngson) K.; B.A., Queens U., 1932; barrister- at-law Osgoode Hall Law Sch., 1936; spl. course Columbia, 1955; m. Elizabeth Dixon, May 23, 1940; children—Virginia E., Ruth M. Called to Ont. bar, 1936; created Queen's counsel, 1954; v.p., dir. Hiram Walker- Gooderham & Worts, Ltd.; officer, dir. various subsidiary cos.; dir. Corby Distilleries Ltd., Liquid Carbonic Canadian Corp Ltd. Mem. Delta Chi. Presbyn. Home: 7080 Riverside Dr East Windsor 16 Ontario Canada Office: 2072 Riverside Dr E Walkerville 15 Ontario Canada

KIDD, ROY WALTER, banker; b. Rockhold, Ky., June 8, 1922; s. Arthur and Effie (Steele) K.; student Eastern Ky. State U., 1940-43; LL.B., U. Memphis, 1949; grad. Central States Sch. Banking, 1959; m. Tommie Elizabeth Fuller, Sept. 13, 1943; children—Lynda (Mrs. Bernard L. Greer, Jr.), Elaine (Mrs. Phillip B. Powell), Roy Walter. Admitted to Tenn. bar, 1949; with First Nat. Bank, Memphis, 1946—, v.p. mortgage loan, 1959-68, sr. v.p., 1968—, also mgr. mortgage loan div., 1961—; dir. Investors Mortgage Service, Inc. subsidiary First Nat. Holding Corp., Memphis; trustee First Memphis Realty Trust, Boston. Pres. Civitan Club, East Memphis, 1960-61. Served to lt. (j.g.) USNR, 1943-46; ETO. Mem. Am. Bankers Assn. (mortgage adv. council 1966—). Mem. Christian Ch. Club: University (Memphis). Home: 211 Alexander St Memphis TN 38111 Office: 165 Madison Av Memphis TN 38103

KIDD, SAMUEL EBERTS, clergyman; b. Allentown, Pa., Feb. 20, 1914; s. Harvey Samuel and Anna Florence (Kramer) K.; A.B., Muhlenberg Coll., 1935, D.D., 1959; grad. Luth. Theol. Sem., Phila., 1938; m. Elizabeth Gehman, July 1, 1939; children—Suzanne E. (Mrs. Fred C. Damarin, Jr.), Elizabeth G. (Mrs. Wendell C. Ehinger), Margaret L. (Mrs. Donald R. Jacoby), John S. Ordained to ministry Luth. Ch., 1938; asst. pastor Lancaster, Pa., 1938-40; pastor Easton,

Pa., 1941-43, Norristown, Pa., 1943-53; stewardship sec. Evang. Luth. Ministerium Pa., adjacent states, 1953-61, pres., 1961-62; pres. Eastern Pa. Synod Luth. Ch. Am., 1963-68; exec. dir. Mich. Council Chs., 1969—. Mem. exec. council Luth. Ch. Am.; vice chmn. commn. on world missions Luth. World Fedn. Author: Texts for Church School. Contbr. articles to profl. jours. Home: 1050 Glenhaven Av East Lansing MI 48823 Office: 205 W Saginaw Lansing MI 48901

KIDD, WILLIAM CAUGHEY, publishing co. exec.; b. Cleve., July 5, 1914; s. Caughey C. and Hazel (Maskey) K.; A.B., Oberlin Coll., 1936; M.B.A., Harvard, 1938; m. Elaine Lacroix, Apr. 24, 1943; children—Sally C., Susan G. Mem. staff Arthur Andersen & Co., C.P.A.'s Chgo., 1938-41; with S.C. Johnson & Son, Inc., Racine, Wis., 1946-65, treas., 1955-62, v.p., regional dir. Europe, 1962-65; with Western Pub. Co., Racine, 1965—, pres., 1967-71, chmn., 1971—. Mem. region VII com. Boy Scouts Am., 1958—; chmn. Racine Environment Commn., 1967-69. Served as aviator USNR, 1941-45. Clubs: University (Chgo.); Racine Country, Somerset (Racine); Boston (New Orleans); American (London, Eng.); Sunningdale Golf (Ascot, Eng.). Home: 3063 Michigan Blvd Racine WI 53402 Office: 1220 Mound Av Racine WI 53404

KIDDE, JOHN FREDERICK, mfg. co. exec; b. Montclair, N.J., Oct. 21, 1905; s. Walter and Louise (Carter) K.; A.B., Princeton, 1926; M.E., Stevens Inst. Tech., 1928; LL.D, (hon.) Upsala Coll., 1957; m. Katharine Lyon, Apr. 19, 1929; children—John Lyon, Katharine; m. 2d, Mary Taylor MacKenzie, Mar. 24, 1942. With Cities Service Co., N.Y.C., 1928- 29, J.R. Williston & Co., N.Y.C., 1929-34; advt. mgr. Walter Kidde & Co., Inc., N.Y.C., 1934-37; treas. Walter Kidde & Co., also Walter Kidde Constructors, Inc., 1937-42; pres. Walter Kidde & Co., Inc., Belleville, N.J., 1943-61, chmn., 1961-66, chmn. exec. com., 1966—, also dir.; dir. Walter Kidde Co., Ltd. (Eng.), Firemen's Ins. Co. Newark, Nat. Newark and Essex Bank. Chmn., dir. Clara Maass Meml. Hosp., Belleville; vice chmn. bd. Stevens Inst. Tech.; trustee Bellville Found., Episcopal Found.-Diocese of Newark; dir. N.J. Safety Council. Republican. Episcopalian. Clubs: Montclair (N.J.) Golf; Nat. Golf Links of Am. (Southhampton, N.Y.); Country of Fla.; Ocean, Gulf Stream Bath and Tennis, Little (Delray Beach, Fla.), Westhampton Beach (N.Y.) Country; Quantuck Beach (N.Y.); Essex (Newark); Links (N.Y.C.). Home: 12 S Mountain Av Montclair NJ 07307 also Country Club of Fla Delray Beach FL 33444 Office: 9 Brighton Rd Clifton NJ 07012

KIDDE, WALTER LAWRENCE, former corp. exec.; b. Montclair, N.J., Sept. 20, 1903; s. Walter and Louise (Carter) K.; A.B., Dartmouth, 1924; m. Ervin Hence, Oct. 1, 1927 (div. 1960); children—Walter II, Kyle B. (dec.), Richard M.; m. 2d, Beatrice M. Werner, Oct. 28, 1960. With Bell Telephone Labs., 1924-37, Western Electric Co., 1937-43; treas. Walter Kidde Constructors, Inc., 1943-63, dir., 1943-69; with Walter Kidde & Co., Inc., 1943-69, treas., 1950-69, sec., 1962-69, now dir. Pres. Adult Sch. Montclair, 1938-39; chmn. N.J. Legislative Commn. Study Adminstrn. Welfare, 1950-52; v.p. N.J. Bd. Child Welfare, 1957-63; chmn. N.J. Bd. Pub. Welfare, 1963—. Bd. dirs. Bonnie Brae Farm Boys, 1948—. Episcopalian. Clubs: Montclair Golf; Westhampton Country (Westhampton Beach, N.Y.). Home: 415 Claremont Av Montclair NJ 07042

KIDDER, BRADLEY PAIGE, architect; b. Denver, July 22, 1901; s. Frank Eugene and Katherine Emory (Newhall) K.; A.B., colo. Coll., 1924; student architecture, U. Pa., 1924-26; m. Harriet W. Brumstead, Apr. 5, 1928; children—Katherine Alice, Bradley Paige. Mem. Historic Am. Bldgs. Survey, N.M., 1934; with firm John Gaw Meem & Assos., architects, Santa Fe, 1934-42; pvt. practice, Santa Fe, 1947-57; partner firm McHugh & Hooker, Bradley P. Kidder & Assos., Santa Fe, 1957-65, now partner firm McHugh & Kidder, Architects; prin.works include Santa Fe Pavillion, 1957, Methodist Ch., Farmington, N.M., 1959, St. James Ch., Taos, N.M., 1960, Immaculate Heart of Mary Sen., Santa Fe, 1961, also pvt. residences. Trustee Am. Archtl. Found., 1957-59; pres. A.I.A. Found., 1960-61; chmn. N.M. Bd. Examiners for Architects, 1951-57; chmn. N.M. Constrn. Industries Commn., 1967—. Served with USNR, 1942-45. Fellow A.I.A (pres. N.M. 1950- 51, regional dir. 1955-58; Edward C. Kemper award 1959); mem. New Mexico Society Architects (pres. 1965), Phi Delta Theta, Theta Alpha Phi. Episcopalian. Lion (dist. gov. 1954-55). Home 900 E Garcia Rd 87501 Office: 717 Canyon Rd Santa Fe NM 87501

KIDDER, GEORGE HOWELL, lawyer; b. Boston, June 14, 1925; s. Henry Purkitt and Julia Edwards (Howell) K.; grad. St. Mark's Sch., Southborough, Mass., 1943; student Williams Coll., 1943-44; B.Naval Sci., Tufts Coll., 1945; LL.B., Harvard, 1950; m. Ellen Windom Warren, Aug. 17, 1946 (dec. May 1956); children—Susan Warren, George Howell, Stephen Wells; m. 2d, Priscilla Peele Hunnewell, Sept. 3, 1958; children—Priscilla Hunnewell, Timothy Hurd, Peter Arnold. Admitted to Mass. bar. 1951; with Office Gen. Counsel, CIA, 1952-54; practice in Boston, 1951-52, 54—; mem. firm Hemenway & Barnes, 1956—. Dir. State St. Boston Financial Corp., State St. Bank & Trust Co. Pres. bd. trustees Concord Acad., Fenn Sch., Concord; trustee Wellesley Coll., St. Mark's Sch.; v.p. bd. trustees Episcopal Theol. Sch., Cambridge, Mass.; bd. overseers Boston Symphony Orch. Mem. Tau Beta Pi. Home: Spencer Brook Rd Concord MA 01742 Office: 73 Tremont St Boston MA 02108

KIDDER, GEORGE WALLACE, Jr., former educator; b. Oregon City, Ore., Dec. 29, 1902; s. George W. and Jennie (Moulton) K.; A.B., U. Ore., 1926; A.M., U. Calif., 1929; Ph.D., Columbia, 1932; M.S. (hon.), Amherst Coll. 1949; Sc.D. (hon.), Wesleyan U., 1950; m. Ruth Rushworth, Aug. 1930; children—George Wallace III, Beverly Ruth, Rushworth Moulton. Instr. biology Coll. City of N.Y. 1929-37; asst. prof. biology Brown U., 1937-46; asso. prof. biology Amherst (Mass.) Coll., 1946-49, Stone prof. biology, 1949-70, prof. emeritus, 1970—; instr. protozoology Marine Biol. Lab., Woods Hole, Mass., 1935-41. Vis. prof. biochemistry U. Cal. Santa Cruz, 1968; exec. bd. Inst. Animal Resources. Chmn. Gordon Research Conf. Vitamins and Metabolism, 1957; Asso. mem. Armed Forces Epidemiological Bd., 1958-63. Fellow Am. Acad. Arts and Sci., A.A.A.S., Am. Acad. Microbiology; mem. Soc. for Exptl. Biology and Medicine, Am. Soc. Zoologists, Am. Soc. Biol. Chemists, Soc. Devel. and Growth, Sigma Xi. Editor: Internat. Jour. Microbiology, 1958—, Protozoa in Chem. Zoology, vol. I; co-editor Biochemistry and Physiology of Nutrition. Home: Amherst Rd Leverett MA 01054

KIDDER, JAMES HUGH, surgeon; b. N.Y.C., Jan. 7, 1902; s. Hugh and Ann Elizabeth (Jordan) K.; student Columbia, 1919-20; A.B., Fordham U., 1924; M.D., Cornell U., 1928. Intern, Peck Meml. Hosp., Bklyn., 1928, French Hosp., N.Y.C., 1929- 1930; surgeon French Hosp., N.Y., instr. surgery, 1931-32; cons. surgeon Elmhurst Gen., St. Barnabas hosps.; clin. prof. surgery N.Y. Med. Coll.; dean Fordham U. Coll. Pharmacy, 1932, now emeritus. Ordered to active duty as Res. Officer, capt. M.C., U.S. Army, 1941; advanced to brig. gen.; past exec. officer 7th Evacuation Hosp., So. Pacific; comdg. officer 134th Evacuation Hosp., E.T.O. Cons. to Army Surgeon Gen., spl. asst. to Surgeon Gen. Fellow A.A.A.S., A.M.A., A.C.S.; mem. Am. Pharm. Assn., N.Y. State Pharm. Assn., N.Y. Acad. Medicine, N.Y. Acad. Pharmacy, N.Y. Acad. Sci., Assn. U.S. Army, Res. Officers Assn. (pres. D.C. Army chpt.), V.F.W., Am. Legion (comdr. Caduceus post), Mil. Order World Wars, Soc. Cons. to Armed Forces, Assn. Mil. Surgeons U.S. (nat. pres. 1967), Chi Gamma Iota, Phi Chi, Alpha Sigma Phi. Home: 5031 Fieldston Rd New York City NY 10471 Office: Office Surgeon Gen Dept Army Washington DC 20314

KIDENEY, JAMES WILLIAMS, architect; b. Pitts., Apr. 25, 1899; s. William W. and Ada J. (Porter) K.; B.S., U. Mich., 1921; m. Isabel Houck, Aug. 15, 1930. With archtl. office, Buffalo, 1921-22; student, Europe, 1922-23; pvt. practice medicine, 1926; partner Paul Hyde Harbach, 1929-42; pvt. practice, specializing in design schs., instnl. bldgs. and housing, Buffalo, 1942-50, as James Wm. Kideney, Smith & Fitzgerald (now firm Kideney, Smith & Fitzgerald). Mem. adv. council on sch. bldgs., grounds N.Y. State Edn. Dept. 1941-43, panel community planning cons., 1945-47; cons. architect N.Y. Joint Legislative Com. on Investigation Sch. Costs, 1941; chmn. com. architects, engrs. and landscape architects of Buffalo for post war constrn.; mem. N.Y. Gov.'s vol. com. on housing and constrn.; mem. airport adv. bd. Buffalo, 1950-52; mem. N.Y. State Bd. Examiners for Architects, 1949-56, chmn. 1953. Recipient awards of merit N.Y. State Assn. Architects for design dormitory and student Union bldg., N.Y. State Tchrs. Coll., Buffalo, 1949, Lockport, Tonawanda and Syracuse Central Office bldg. for N.Y. Telephone Co., mention for design other instnl. bldgs., 1950. Licensed architect, N.Y., Fla., N.J. certificate Nat. Council. Fellow A.I.A. chmn. com. state and municipal pub. works 1942-46, chmn. com. local pub. bldgs. 1947-49); mem. Am. Soc. Planning Ofcls., C. of C., Buffalo Fine Arts Acad. (life), Buffalo Pub. Library (life), N.Y. State Assn. Architects (pres. 1938-42), Alpha Rho Chi. Rotarian. Clubs: Buffalo; University (Albany). Home: 56 Soldiers Pl Buffalo, NY 14222. Office: 374 Deleware Av Buffalo NY 14202

KIDERA, GEORGE J., surgeon; b. Chgo., Apr. 29, 1913; s. Edward J. and Marie (Nadherny) K.; student Northwestern U., 1930-31, Crane Jr. Coll., 1931-33; B.S., U. Ill., 1935, M.D., 1937; postgrad. Sch. Aviation Medicine, 1942, Cook County Hosp. Post Grad. Sch., 1948; m. Marie A. Cuchna, Aug. 1938; children—George Peter, Kristina Alice. Intern, resident W. Suburban Hosp., Oak Park, Ill., 1937-38, surg. staff mem.; pres. West Suburban Hosp. Interns Alumni Assn., 1949-51; regional med. dir. United Air Lines, Chgo., 1938, 46-51, med. dir., 1951—. Served to lt. col., flight surgeon USAAF, 1942-46. Recipient Pres. award United Air Lines, 1950. Diplomate Am. Bd. Preventive Medicine. Fellow Aerospace Med. Assn. (pres. 1960, Howard D. Edwards award 1960, mem. exec. council 1963, Theodore C. Lyster award 1970, Am. Coll. Preventive Medicine; mem. A.M.A., Airline Med. Dirs. Assn. (mem. exec. council, 1950-51, pres. 1955), Ill. Med. Soc., Am. Assn. Indsl. Physicians and Surgeons, Chgo., Des Plaines (sec.) med. socs., Am. Med. Writers Assn., Internat. Air Transport Assn., Am. Coll. Preventive Medicine. Contbr. articles to med. jours. Home: 21 Northgate Rd Riverside IL 60546 Office: United Air Lines Exec Office O'Hare Field IL 60666

KIDNEIGH, JOHN CHRISTOPHER social work educator; b. Nyssa, Ore., Apr. 28, 1907; s. John C. and Alma Mary (Forbes) K.; A.B., U. Utah, 1939, certificate Social Work, M.A., 1941; postgrad. U. Denver, 1942; m. Clara Mae Howell, Jan. 12, 1928; children—Jeannette Claire, Evelyn Alma. Various positions in case and group work, 1928-34; supr. Salt Lake (City) Community Services, 1934-39; supt. Lytton Home and Sch. for Children, 1939-40; supr. state merit system Utah Dept. Pub. Welfare, 1940-41, Colo. Dept. Pub. Welfare, 1941-43; regional personnel cons. Social Security Adminstrn., FSA, 1943-45, asst. regional dir., 1945-46; asso. prof., asso. dir. U. Minn. Sch. Social Work, 1946-49, prof., dir. Sch. Social Work, 1949—. Chmn. adv. council on child welfare services U.S. Dept. Health Edn. and Welfare, also chmn. tng. grants com. U.S. Childrens Bur.; v.p., mem. exec. com. Hennepin County Health and Welfare Council, 1968—; mem. bd., pres. Group Health Plan, Inc. Recipient spl. award Nat. Assn. Social Workers. Mem. bd. Community Chest, Council Social Agys. Hennepin County, Minn. Welfare Conf. (past chmn. pub. welfare adminstrn. div., Social Service Adv. Council VA (past chmn.). Mem. Nat. Conf. Social Work, Am. Soc. Pub. Adminstrn. (past pres. Minn. chpt.) Am. Assn. Social Workers (past pres. Twin City chpt., nat. bd.), Am. Assn. Schs. Social Work (past pres. nat.), Family and Children's Service Soc. Hennepin County (bd. mem.), Council Social Work Edn. (past bd. mem., past chmn. commn. on accreditation), Nat. Assn. Social Workers (nat. pres.), Humanist Credit Union (past pres.), Nat. Insts. Mental Health USPHS Tng. Com. (past chmn. psychiat. social work), Am. Assn. U. Profs., Urban League (bd. mem.). Unitarian. Clubs: Citizens of Minneapolis (bd. mem.), University of Minn. Campus. Contbr. articles to profl. publs. Home: 1925 E River Rd Minneapolis MN 55414

KIDNER, FRANK LEROY, univ. ofcl., b. Detroit, Jan. 7, 1910; s. Frank Leon and Lila Rae (Hannan) K.; A.B., U. Cal. at Berkeley, 1936; Ph.D., Columbia, 1944; m. Ann Elizabeth Lawrence, June 15, 1942; children—Frank LeRoy, Jane Norman, Elizabeth Ann. Mem. faculty U. Cal. at Berkeley, 1939—, prof. econs., 1949—, dir. Bur. Bus. and Econ. Research, 1941-59, dean ednl. relations, 1960-66, v.p. for ednl. relations, 1966—; guest prof. U. Leiden (Netherlands), 1950-51. Asst. regional price exec. OPA, 1943-44; chmn. trucking panel WLB, 1944-45; asst. exec. officer UN Conf. Internat. Orgn., 1945. Pres. Asso. Univ. Burs. Bus. and Econ. Research, 1949-50. Trustee Newhouse Found., San Francisco; bd. dirs, Berkeley chpt. A.R.C., 1956-58. Mem. Am., Western (pres. 1950-54) econ. assns., Athletic Assn. Western Univs. (pres. 1959-60), Phi Beta Kappa. Episcopalian. Clubs: Faculty (pres. 1953-59) (Berkeley); Bohemian (San Francisco). Author monographs, articles. Home: 1025 Creston Rd Berkeley, CA 94708

KIDSTON, A. I., savs. and trust co. exec.; b. Youngstown, O., 1901; grad. Grad. Sch. Banking, Rutgers U., 1941. Pres., dir. Dollar Savs. & Trust Co., Youngstown. Pres., dir. Mahoning Valley San. Dist. Mason. Home: 1555 Brantford Blvd Youngstown OH 44509 Office: Central Sq Box 450 Youngstown OH 44501

KIDSTON, DONALD ERNEST, fgn. service officer; b. Hudson, Mass., Apr. 10, 1913; s. Ernest Archibald George and Bessie Maud (Grant) K.; law student Suffolk U., 1933, Nat. U., 1935; m. Geraldine Barrett, Apr. 17, 1942; children—Deborah, William Barrett. Contracts specialist Soil Conservation Service, 1935-36; adminstrv. asst. Social Security Bd., 1936-37; adminstrv. officer, certifying officer R.R. Retirement Bd., 1937-41; adminstrv. officer WPB, 1941-45; spl. asst. to adminstr. War Assets Adminstrn., 1946-48; chief office adminstrn. mgmt. Office Sec. Def., 1948-54; exec. officer ICA, Manila, P.I., 1954-57, Karachi, 1957- 59, Kabul, Afghanistan, 1959-62; asst. dir. mgmt. AID, Ankara, Turkey, 1962-65, asso. dir., Saigon, Vietnam, 1967-68, asso. asst. adminstr. AID, Dept. State, Washington, 1968-70, asst. dir., New Delhi, 1970—. Served to comdr. USNR, World War II; capt. Res. Decorated Bronze Star medal, Purple Heart. Mem. Am. Legion, Mil. Order Purple Heart. Clubs: Saigon Golf, Saigon Circle Sportief, Manila, Polo; Foreign Service, Internat., Army and Navy City (Washington); New Delhi Golf; Congressional Country (Md.). Home: New Baltimore VA Office: US Dept State AID Washington DC 20520

KIDWELL, HOMER BAIRD, lawyer; b. Maricpa, Cal., Oct. 20, 1911; s. Homer and Mabel M. (Baird) K.; A.B., Stanford, 1932, LL.B., 1935; m. Margaret E. Greenwell, Jan. 4, 1940; children—Alan B., Frances J. Admitted to Cal. bar, 1935, Hawaii bar, 1937; practice law with Anderson, Wrenn & Jenks, Honolulu, 1939-68, Jenks, Kidwell, Goodsill & Anderson, 1969—. Mem. Hawaii Uniform Laws Commn., 1951-59, 65—. Bd. visitors Stanford Law Sch., 1959. Mem. Am. Bar Assn. (ho. of dels. 1958-59, 65-71, bd. govs. 1971—), Bar Assn. Hawaii (pres. 1958), State Bar Cal. Home: 2140 Puualii Pl Honolulu HI 96822 Office: Castle & Cooke Bldg Honolulu HI 96813

KIDWELL, JAMES BEIDIEMAN, savs. and loan assn. exec.; b. San Francisco, Aug. 17, 1906; s. John Leonard and Annie (Kenny) K.; student St. Mary's Coll., Moraga, Cal., 1924; m. Mary Elizabeth Tucker, Apr. 22, 1931; children—Kenneth L., Robert E. Teller, Hibernia Bank, San Francisco, 1925-27; with Eureka Fed. Savs. & Loan Assn., San Francisco, 1927—, pres., 1951-66, chmn. bd., 1966—; pres., dir. Eureka Aux. Corp., 1948—; v.p., dir. Ins. & Bonding Services, Inc., 1968—. Clubs: Commonwealth, Olympic (San Francisco). Home: 1625 Valparaiso Av Menlo Park CA 94026 Office: 4610 Mission St San Francisco CA 94112

KIDWELL, KENNETH LEONARD, savs. and loan assn. exec.; b. San Francisco, Jan. 30, 1934; s. James B. and Elizabeth (Tucker) K.; student San Mateo (Cal.) Jr. Coll.; m. Hazel Eckert, Nov. 18, 1961; children—Kendell Kathryn, Kathleen Karen. With Eureka Fed. Savs. & Loan Assn., San Francisco, 1953—, exec. v.p., 1962- 66, pres., 1966—, also dir. Mem. San Francisco Real Estate Bd. Mem. U.S. Savs. and Loan League Federally Chartered Assns. Bd. dirs. Psoriasis Research Assn. Mem. Cal. Savs. and Loan League, Peninsula Gen. Contractors Assn. Republican. Roman Catholic. Clubs: Sharon Heights Golf; Spyglass Hill Golf; Olympic. Home: 17 Robert S Dr Menlo Park CA 94025 Office: 4610 Mission St San Francisco CA 94114

KIEB, ORMONDE ANTON, corp. exec.; b. Springfield, Mass., Aug. 17, 1901; s. August Anton and Harriet Augusta (Livingston) K.; student Franklin and Marshall Coll., Lancaster, Pa., 1920-23; m. Gladys Chandler, Nov. 14, 1928; 1 dau., Elizabeth Livingston (Mrs. Albert L. Diano). With real estate bus., E.J. Maier Corp., 1925-27; pres., sec. Kieb- Pasbjerg, Inc and Kieb-Pasbjerg Agy., Inc., 1946-50; pres. The Kieb Co., Newark, 1933—; dir. Clinton Title & Mortgage Guaranty Co., 1945- 48; asst. postmaster gen., 1953-59; pvt. cons., pres. First Marketing Corp., 1959—; pres. Kieb, Turnbull & Jewett Corp., Princeton, N.J., 1967—; pres. Property Marketing Corp., 1963—, gen. mgr., 1970—; gen. mgr. Homestead Enterprise, 1970—, Aladco, Inc., 1970—. Hon. mem. planning bd., Maplewood, N.J.; land use adv. com. Dept. Econ. Devel. State of N.J., 1945-48, mem. adv. com. on roadside improvement Highway Dept., 1944-47, mem. Gov.'s com. on housing, 1948; chmn. Commn. Efficiency and Economy in State Govt., 1964-68. Dir. Newark YMCA 1950- 54, v.p., 1951-53; v.p. Realtors' Nat. Found. Inc. 1962, dir., 1962-68, pres., 1969; v.p. YM-YWCA Newark and vicinity, 1959-62; mem. Newark adv. bd. Salvation Army. Recipient Distinguished Service award by Govt. Mem. Am. Soc. Real Estate Counselors, Monmouth County Bd. Realtors, N.Y. Inst. Real Estate Mgmt. (governing council 1943-55; pres. 1951; editorial bd. The Jour. Property Management 1944-45), Nat. Assn. Real Estate Bds. (v.p. 1946-52, 60-61, 63-68), Nat. Inst. Land and Farm Brokers, Internat. Real Estate Fedn., Soc. Indsl. Realtors (charter), Phi Sigma Kappa. Mason, Rotarian. Episcopalian. Clubs: Manasquan River Golf; Downtown; National Aviation (Washington); Executive. Home: 606 Rankin Rd Brielle NJ 08730 Office: 19 Chambers St Princeton NJ 08450 also 1000 Warren Av Spring Lake Heights NJ 07762

KIECHLIN, ROBERT JEROME, coal co. exec.; b. N.Y.C., Nov. 2, 1919; s. Henry, Jr. and Lydia C. (Bergmann) K.; B.S. in Accounting, N.Y.U., 1940; m. Regina W. Kolakowski, Oct. 6, 1951; children—Robert Jerome, Regina, William. With Paisley & Conroy, C.P.A.'s, N.Y.C., 1945-52; with N.J. Zinc Co., 1952—, asst. comptroller, 1957-61, comptroller, 1961-66, treas. and comptroller, 1966-71; controller Peabody Coal Co., St. Louis, 1971—. Served with USNR, 1942-45; PTO. Decorated Navy Cross. C.P.A., N.Y. Mem. N.Y. State Soc. C.P.A.'s, Am. Inst. C.P.A.'s Financial Execs. Inst. Home: 12886 Whitehorse Lane St Louis MO 63131 Office: 301 N Memorial Dr St Louis MO 63102

KIECKHEFER, JAMES FERDINAND, investment banker; b. Milw., Mar. 2, 1918; s. Alfred John and Allison (More) K.; B.A., Princeton, 1939; M.B.A., Harvard, 1941; m. Judith Ridgway, May 8, 1943; children—Judith Carroll, James Ferdinand, Robert Allison, Elizabeth Ann, Constance Louise, Thomas Ridgway. Asst. to v.p. mfg. Nat. Enameling and Stamping Co., 1946-52; new bus. dept. Goldman, Sachs & Co., 1952-59; v.p. Loewi & Co., Inc., Milw., 1959—; dir. Granite City Steel Co. Bd. dirs. Milw. Boys' Club. Served to 1st lt. AUS, 1942-45. Clubs: Milwaukee, Milwaukee Country, Milwaukee University. Home: 8250 N River Rd Milwaukee WI 53217 Office: 225 E Mason St Milwaukee WI 53202

KIEFER, CHARLES FREDERICK, mgmt. cons.; b. Hamilton, N.Y., July 1, 1911; s. Charles F. and Belle (Palmer) K.; A.B., George Washington U., 1940; student U. Pitts., 1932- 34; M.P.A., Harvard, 1941; m. Helen Maxine Enlow, Dec. 21, 1941; 1 son, Charles Frederick. With Dept. Agr., 1934-66, dir. Office Mgmt. Appraisal and Systems Devel., 1965, 66; exec. dir. CAB, 1966-70; cons. Moshman Assos., Washington, 1970—; cons. Ford Found. Served to capt. USAAF, 1942-46. Littauer fellow, 1941-42; recipient Certificate of Merit, Dept. Agr. Mem. Am. Polit. Sci. Assn., Am. Soc. Pub. Adminstrn., Omicron Delta Kappa, Pi Gamma Mu. Democrat. Conglist. Clubs: Harvard (Washington); International, Aero. Home: 5302 18th St N Arlington VA 22205 Office: 6400 Goldsboro Rd Washington DC 20034

KIEFER, FRANK XAVIER, assn. exec.; b. Bklyn., Oct. 14, 1911; s. Frank X. and Elizabeth (Heninger) K.; extension student Rutgers U., 1933; m. Aug. 7, 1942; children—Robert J., Christine Louise. Mgr. retail sales promotion Bakelite Corp., 1940-51; editor, pub. Dept. Store Economist, 1951-66; exec. v.p. Nat. Assn. Textile and Apparel Wholesalers, 1966—. Served with AUS, 1942-46. Mem. Am. Soc. Assn. Execs., N.Y. State Soc. Assn. Execs., Nat. Assn. Wholesalers, Eta Mu Pi. Home: 58 Wardell Circle Oceanport NJ 07757 Office: 350 Fifth Av New York City NY 10001

KIEFER, HOWARD EVAN, educator; b. West Seneca, N.Y., July 4, 1917; s. Charles A. and Edith (Witzig) K.; B.Ed., N.Y. State U. Coll. at Fredonia, 1947, M.S., 1950; Ed.D., U. Buffalo, 1956; postgrad. Oxford U. (Eng.), 1961; m. Mildred Crabtree, June 29, 1955; 1 son, Howard Evan II. Prof. philosophy, head dept. State U. N.Y. at Brockport, 1950-69, dean humanities, 1969—. Dir. Internat. Philosophy Year, 1967-68. Served to capt. M.I., AUS, 1942-46, 50-51. Decorated Bronze Star medal. Co-editor: Contemporary Philosophic Thought, 4 vols., 1969. Home: 4033 N Lake Rd Brockport NY 14420

KIEFER, JACK CARL, mathematician; b. Cin., Jan. 25, 1924; s. Carl J. and Marguerite (Rosenau) K.; B.S., M.S., Mass. Inst. Tech., 1948; Ph.D., Columbia, 1952; m. Dooley Sciple, Sept. 15, 1957; children-Sarah Elisabeth, Daniel Jonathan Baird. Instr. Cornell U., Ithaca, N.Y., 1951-52, asst. prof., 1952-55, asso. prof., 1955-59, prof. math., 1959—; vis. prof. Oxford (Eng.) U., 1958-59; Guggenheim fellow Stanford, 1962-63. Vice Chmn. Tompkins County (N.Y.)

Liberal Party, 1967—. Served to 1st lt. USAAF, 1943-46. Fellow Inst. Math. Statistics (Wald Meml. lectr. 1962, pres. 1969-70); mem. Am. Math. Soc., Mycol. Soc. Am., N. Am. Mycol. Assn. Author: (with others) Sequential Banking Procedures, 1968. Asso. editor Zeitschrift Für Warscheinlichkeitstheorie. Contbr. articles on math. statistics and probability theory to profl. jours. Home: 629 Highland Rd Ithaca NY 14850

KIEFER, NORVIN CHARLES, physician; b. Lorain, O., Mar. 28, 1905; s. Charles Norvin and Maude Ann (Hodgins) K.; student Western Res. U., 1923-26; M.D., U. Mich., 1930; M.Pub. Health, Johns Hopkins, 1947; m. Annetta Elizabeth Singler, Feb. 3, 1928; children—Elizabeth (Mrs. Arthur Wimsatt), Norma (Mrs. William J. Brandle), Colet (Mrs. Lloyd Boothby), Eva (Mrs. Rocco Yervasi). Practiced medicine, Geneva, O., 1931-45; spl. asst. to pres. Leonard Wood Meml., N.Y.C., 1943-45; asst. to chief div. Tb, USPHS, 1945-48, in charge health emergency planning Office Surgeon Gen., 1948-49; also acting chief med. and health div. Office Civil Def. Planning in Office Sec. Def., 1948-49; dir. health resources office Nat. Security Resources Bd., 1949- 51; dir. health and spl. weapons def. div. Fed. Civil Def. Adminstrn., 1951-53; v.p., chief med. dir. Equitable Life Assurance Soc. of U.S., N.Y.C., 1953-70. Vice pres. research Nat. Safety Council, 1962-68, chmn. research com., 1962-68, chmn. med. and health com., dir.; U.S. del. Internat. Assn. Accident and Traffic Medicine; dir., chmn. med. and health com. Nat. Council on Aging, 1962-66; chmn. allied health services com. Health Ins. Council, 1961-66; med. adv. com. bur. disability ins. Social Security Adminstrn.; mem. Nat. Hwy. Safety Adv. Com., 1967-70. Trustee Automotive Safety Found.; bd. dirs. Nat. Fedn. Hwy. Users. Resigned commn. as officer USPHS, 1953, officer inactive Res., 1953-70. Recipient first Distinguished Service award Fed. Civil Def. Adminstrn., 1953. Diplomate Am. Bd. Preventive Medicine and Pub. Health. Fellow Am. Coll. Allergists, Indsl. Med. Assn., N.Y. Acad. Medicine (chmn. occupational medicine sect. 1967-69), Am. Coll. Preventive Medicine; mem. A.M.A., Am. Pub. Health Assn., Am. Heart Assn., A.A.A.S., Am. Soc. Tropical Medicine, Am. Trudeau Soc., Nat. Tb Assn., Am. Assn. Mil. Surgeons, Greater N.Y. Safety Council (pres. 1956-62), Am. Med. Writers Assn., Nat. Council Alcoholism (dir. 1958-63, 70—, chmn. com. on accidents 1970—), N.Y. Indsl. Med. Assn. (dir.), Nat. Health Council (pres. 1958-59), Assn. Life Ins. Med. Dirs., N.Y. County and N.Y. State Med. Socs., Med. Dirs. Forum, Am. Acad. Occupational Medicine. Episcopalian. Author: Present Concepts of Rehabilitation in Tuberculosis, 1948; also health and med. articles in profl. jours. Address: 2440 Sedgwick Av Bronx NY 10468

KIEFFER, JAMES MILTON, lawyer; b. Newark, May 22, 1921; s. Alonzo Michael and Mae (St. Germaine) K.; A.B., Hamilton Coll., 1946; LL.B., Cornell U., 1949; m. Eleanor Jane Van Atta, Sept. 7, 1946; children—Michael J., Laura J., Andrew V., Elizabeth A. Admitted to N.Y. bar, 1949, since practiced in Rochester; asso., then partner Remington, Gifford, Willy & Williams, 1949-60; staff asst. to pres. Pfaudler Permutit, Inc., 1960-61, house counsel, 1961-63, sec., counsel, 1963-65; sec., counsel Ritter Pfaudler Corp. (now Sybron Corp.), 1965-68, v.p., sec., counsel, 1968—; dir. Degna (Australia) Pty. Ltd., Aero Chem. Research Labs., Inc., Patterson Dental Co., Thermolyne Corp., Pfaudler Permutit S.A. de C.V. (Mexico), Pfaudler Devel. Corp. (Panama), Sybron (Asia) Ltd. Bd. dirs. Park Av. Hosp., Rochester, N.Y. Served to 1st lt. USAAF, 1943-46. Mem. Am., Monroe County bar assns., Am. Soc. Corporate Secs., Rochester C. of C., Order of Coif. Psi Upsilon, Phi Delta Phi. Republican. Roman Catholic. Club: University (Rochester). Home: 52 Green Valley Rd Pittsford NY 14534 Office: Midtown Tower Rochester NY 14604

KIEFFER, JAROLD ALAN, govt. ofcl.; b. Mpls., May 5, 1923; s. Charles O. and Edith (Feinberg) K.; B.A., U. Minn., 1947, Ph.D., 1950; m. Frances Clarfield, Aug. 13, 1949; children—Edith Charlotte, Charles Edward, Philip William. Teaching asst. polit. sci. dept. U. Minn., 1949, social sci. program, 1950-51; research asst., world affairs program Mpls. Star, 1949-50; exec. sec. def. moblzn. manpower coms., staff asst. to exec. sec. ODM, 1951-52, staff sec., 1952, asst. to exec. officer, exec. sec. borrowing authority review bd., 1953, spl. asst. to dir., 1955-56, acting dep. asst. dir. nat. security affairs, 1956-57, cons., 1958; exec. asst. to dir. orgn. and personnel, exec. sec. personnel adv. com. AEC, 1952-53; asst. Pres.'s Adv. Com. on Govt. Orgn., 1953-58, cons., 1958, asst. to chmn. com., 1959-61; asst. to Arthur S. Flemming mem. 2d Hoover Commn., liaison to task force on personnel and civil service Hoover Commn., 1953-55, asst. to Meyer Kestnbaum, spl. asst. to Pres. for Hoover Commn. matters, 1955-56, adviser to Kestnbaum, 1956-57; asst. to Nelson Rockefeller, 1957-58; cons. Dept. Health, Edn. and Welfare, Washington, 1958, asst. to sec., 1958-59, asst. to sec. for program analysis, 1959-61; sec. bd. trustees Nat. Cultural Center, 1959-63, exec. dir., 1961-63; asso. prof. polit. sci. U. Ore., 1963-67, prof. pub. affairs and adminstrn., 1967-69, asst. to pres., 1963-67, chmn. pub. affairs and adminstrn. programs Sch. Community Service and Pub. Affairs, 1967-69; dir. Macalester Found. for Higher Edn., 1969-71; exec. officer bd. trustees Macalester Coll., 1970-71, also adj. prof. polit. sci., 1969-71; dir. Office Internat. Tng., AID, State Dept., 1971—. Vice chmn. Gov.'s Planning Council on the Arts and Humanities, State Ore., 1965-67; chmn. Project 70's Task Force On State Govt. Reorgn., Ore., 1968-69; cons. Office High Speed Ground Transp., U.S. Dept. Transp., 1968-69, U.S. Office Edn., 1971. Officer, mem. exec. com. Lane County Auditorium Assn., 1963-69. Served with AUS, 1942-46. Mem. Am. Polit. Sci. Assn., Am. Soc. Pub. Adminstrn. Home: 9019 Hamilton Dr Fairfax VA 22030

KIEFFER, JOHN SPANGLER, ret. coll. dean; b. Hagerstown, Md., Aug. 6, 1904; s. John Brainerd and Alice Venable Bourne (Hays) K.; A.B., Harvard, 1926, A.M., 1929; Ph.D., Johns Hopkins, 1962; m. Roxana Byrd White, Nov. 26, 1929. Master in French and English, Litchfield (Conn.) Sch., 1927-28; instr. classical langs. St. John's Coll. Annapolis, Md., 1929-34, asst. prof., 1934-39, tutor, 1939—, mem. bd. visitors and govs., 1943-51, pres., 1947-49, dir. adult edn., 1951-57, dean, 1962-69. Mem. Am. Philol. Assn., Classical Assn. Atlantic States. Democrat. Episcopalian. Clubs: Harvard Club of Maryland; 14 W. Hamilton St. (Balt.). Author: Galen's introduction to Logic: translation and commentary, 1964. Home: 2 Cumberland Ct Annapolis MD 21401

KIEFFER, WILLIAM BRETT, pulp and paper industry exec.; b. Hawaii, Nov. 11, 1914; s. Philip Joseph and Beatrice (Brett) K.; B.S., U.S. Mil. Acad., 1938; grad. Air War Coll., 1950, Nat. War Coll., 1954; m. Margaret McDonald, Apr. 26, 1940; children—John Brett, Kathleen (Mrs. David S. Sullivan), William Rice. Enlisted in U.S. Army, 1932, commd. 2d lt., 1938, advanced through grade to lt. gen. USAF, 1967; comdr. 2d Bomb Wing, SAC, 1959-60, 45th Air Div., 1960-61, dir. personnel, 1961-64; asst. dep. chief staff personnel Hdqrs. USAF, 1964-67; comdr. 8th Air Force, SAC, 1967-70, ret., 1970; with Fraser Cos., Ltd., Edmundston, N.B., Can., 1970—. Decorated Legion of Merit, D.S.M., D.F.C., Air medal; Croix de Guerre (France). Home: Madawaska ME Office: Fraser Cos., Ltd Edmundston New Brunswick Canada

KIEFFER, WILLIAM FRANKLINN, educator; b. Trenton, N.J., Mar. 16, 1915; s. William Miles and Carrie Jeanette (Halfpenny) K.; B.A., Wooster Coll. 1936; M.Sc., Ohio State U., 1938; Ph.D. (Jesse Metcalf fellow 1939-40), Brown U., 1940; m. Elaine Steele, June 22, 1940; children—Richard William, Lois Jeanette. Instr. chemistry Coll. Wooster, (O.), 1940-42, Pa. State U. extension, summers 1941, 42; asst. prof. chemistry Western Res. U., 1942-46; prof. chemistry Coll. Wooster, 1946—, chmn. dept. chemistry, 1968—. Vis. prof. U. Wash., summer 1955; research participant radiation chemistry Oak Ridge Nat. Lab., 1951-52; vis. scientist in chemistry NSF, 1957—; Sci. Faculty fellow Mass. Inst. Tech., 1963-64; vis. scholar Stanford U., 1969-70; chmn. adv. com. for NBC prodn. Continental Classroom of Am. Chem. Soc, (counseller 1956—; chmn. local sect. 1949; recipient award in chem. edn. 1968), N.Y., Ohio acads. sci., A.A.A.S., Am. Assn. U. Profs., Phi Beta Kappa, Sigma Xi. Presbyn. (elder, trustee). Rotarian. Author: The Mole Concept in Chemistry, 1961; Chemistry, A cultural Approach, 1971. Editor: Selected Readings in General Chemistry, 1958; Selected Readings for Chemical Bond, 1960; Selected Readings in Inorganic Chemistry, 1962; Selected Readings in History of Chemistry, 1965. Editor Jour. Chem. Edn., 1955-67. Contbr. numerous articles profl. jours. Home: 1586 Bellevue Dr Wooster OH 44691

KIEFT, LESTER, chemist; b. Grand Haven, Mich., Sept. 18, 1912; s. Martin and Dena (Rossien) K.; A.B., Hope Coll., 1934; M.S., Pa. State Coll., 1936, Ph.D., 1939; m. Norma Elaine Richenbacher, June 28, 1941; children—John Martin, Richard, James. Asst., Pa. State Coll., 1934-37; asst. prof. chemistry Pa. State Jr. Coll., 1937-42; asst. prof. chemistry Bucknell U., 1942-44, prof. and head chemistry dept., 1944—; summer lectr., engring., sci. and mgmt. war tng. program, 1941; dir. Inst. High Sch. Sci. Tchrs., Bucknell U., 1957—, dir. Inst. for Hign Ability Secondary Students. Pres. Lewisburgh Borough Council, 1962-65. In charge Lewisburg (Pa.) Youth Activities, 1944-51. Mem. Am. Chem. Soc. (analytical subcom. on exams. and tests for soc. coop. chemistry test, vice chmn. central Pa. sect. 1954, chmn. 1955, chmn. Susquehanna Valley sect. 1958-59), A.A.A.S., Pa. Sci. Tchrs. (dir. 1958—). Nat. Sci. Tchrs. Assn., Blue Key, Alpha Chi Sigma, Phi Eta Sigma, Sigma Xi, Phi Lambda Upsilon. Republican Mem. Evang. and Ref. Ch. (mem. ch. council 1944—). Club: Lions (dist. gov. 1956-57; chmn. Sight Conservation and Eye Research Found. 1957—). Home: 319 Buffalo Rd Lewisburg PA 17837

KIEHL, ELMER RUDOLPH, educator; b. Malta Bend, Mo., July 2, 1916; s. Ben William and Emilie (Hill) K.; B.S., U. Mo., 1942, M.A., 1950; student Ia. State Coll., 1948; Ph.D., Harvard, 1958; m. Helen Coral Meals, Sept. 24, 1942; children—Kathleen, Kathleen, Frederick, Marlene, Nancy. Asst. country extension agt., 1946-47; extension marketing specialist Columbia, 1947-49; instr. U. Mo., 1949-51, asst. prof., 1951-53, asso prof., 1953-55, prof. 1955- -, chmn. dept. agr. econs., 1957-60, dean faculty Coll. Agr., dir. Agrl. Expt. Sta., 1960—; cons. U.S. Dept. Agr., Bur. Census U.S. Dept. Commerce, 1964; mem. Nat. Agrl. Adv. Commn., 1936-65, Nat. Commn. Food Marketing, 1964-66; chmn. Council U.S. Univs. for Rural Devil. 1966-68; bd. govs. Am. Royal, Kansas City, 1967—. Mem. Gov. Mo. Adv. Com. on Water, Gov.'s Adv. Council Agr.; state chmn. Mo. Rural Areas Devel. Com.; mem. Mo. Soils Dist. Com. Served from 2d lt. to maj., AUS, 1942-46. Mem. Am. Econ. Assn., Am. Farm Econ. Assn., Econometric Soc., Mo. Conservation Fedn., Blue Key. Gamma Sigma Delta, Alpha Pi Zeta (past pres.), Alpha Gamma Sigma (past pres. nat. chpt.), Alpha Zeta, Gamma Alpha. Lutheran. Rotarian. Contbr. articles to profl. jours. Home: 603 Edgewood Columbia MO 65201

KIEHN, CLIFFORD LAVERNE, plastic surgeon; b. Detroit, Apr. 7, 1907; s. Adolph H. and Eleanor C. (Horne) K.; D.D.S., U. Mich., 1930, M.D. 1941; D.Sc. (honorary), Ferris State College, 1966; m. Margaret Ann MacNab, June 11, 1932; 1 dau. Frances Ann (Mrs. William Browne). Intern U. Mich. Hosp., 1938-42, intern maxillofacial surgery. 1942, asst. surgeon plastic surgery, surgeon-in-charge plastic and maxillofacial surgery, staff plastic surgery St. Vincent's Charity Hosp., 1950—; attending maxillofacial surgery Crile VA Hosp., 1948; asso. vis. surgeon Cleve. City Hosp., 1948; asst. surgeon plastic and maxillofacial surgery St. Luke's Hosp., Cleve., 1948; cons. Highland View, Cleve. State hosps.; cons., asst. plastic surgeon Good Samaritan Hosp., Sandusky, O.; cons., vis. surgeon St. Alexis, Huron Rd., St. Ann's hosps.; asso. plastic surgeon Marymount Hosp.; prof. oral and maxillofacial surgery, clin. prof. plastic surgery Western Res. Sch. Medicine, 1964—. Served to lt. col., M.C., AUS, World War II. Diplomate Am. Bd. Plastic Surgery (v.p. 1949—). Fellow A.C.S., American Surgical Association; member American Society Maxillofacial Surgery (past pres.), A.M.A., Am. Assn. Surgery Trauma, Indsl. Med. Assn., American Society of Plastic and Reconstructive Surgery (past president of foundation), American Assn. Cleft Rehab., Am. Assn. Plastic Surgeons (past pres.), Am. Soc. Oral Surgeons, Am. Dental Soc., British Assn. Plastic Surgeons, Internat. Soc. Surgeons, Soc. Head and Neck Surgeons, Canadian Soc. Plastic Surgeons, Ohio Valley Soc. Plastic Surgeons (past pres.), Soc. Cons. to Armed Forces, Am. Soc. Esthetic Surgeons. Home: 2024 Mt Vernon Blvd East Cleveland OH 44112 Office: 10605 Chester Av Cleveland OH

KIEKHAEFER, E.C., mfg. co. exec.; b. Wis., June 4, 1906; s. Arno C. and Clara M. (Wessel) K.; student Milw. Sch. Engring., 1925, U. Wis. at Milw., 1928-31; m. Freda L. Greenfield, June 25, 1932; children—Helen Jean (Mrs. R. Thomas Wimberly), Anita Rac, Frederick Carl. Detailer, Nash Motors Co., Milw., 1925-28; machine designer, chief engr. Stearns Magnetic Mfg. Co., Milw., 1928-39; founder Kiekhaefer Corp., Fond du Lac, Wis., 1939, pres., 1939-70; chmn. bd. Kiekhaefer Mercury of Australia Pty. Ltd., 1961-70, Internat. Mercury Outboards, Ltd., 1958-70, Recreational Products Mart, Inc., Fond du Lac, 1971—; pres. Kiekhaefer Mercury of Can., Ltd., 1960-70, Lake X Corp., St. Cloud, Fla., 1961—, Kiekhaefer Aeromarine Motors Inc., Fond du Lac, 1964—, Kiekhaefer Enterprises, Inc., Fond du Lac, 1970—; v.p., dir. Brunswick Corp., 1961-70; dir. Marshall & Isley Bank, Milw., MHV Enterprises, Ottawa. Trustee Fond du Lac YMCA; bd. dirs. Big Bros., Inc., Fond du Lac; adv. bd. Cape Haze Marine Labs., Sarasota, Fla. Named Boating Man of Year, Marine Trades Assn., 1969; recipient certificate of appreciation U.S. Power Squadron, 1969. Mem. Am. Soc. M.E., Soc. Automotive Engrs., I.E.E.E., Milw. Assn. Engrs. and Scientists, Am. Power Boat Assn. (chmn. indsl. adv. com.; mem. honor squadron; named outboard man of year), Offshore Power Boat Racing Assn. (dir.), Canadian Boating Fedn. (hon. vice commodore). Patentee magnetic separators, engines, marine propulsion devices. Office: 1970 Aeromarine Dr Fond du Lac WI 54935

KIEL, FRED OTTO, banker; b. Kansas City, Mo., Apr. 18, 1912; s. Fred H. and Anna (Berndt) K.; B.S., U. Kan., 1933, M.B.A., 1936; postgrad. Ohio State U., 1941-42; m. Helen Baird, Oct. 29, 1937; children-Frederick, Kathy, James. Asst. prof. econs. U. N.M., 1936-43; indsl. economist Fed. Res. Bank, Cleve., 1945-50, sr. economist, 1950-55, sr. economist, adminstrv. officer, 1955- 61, v.p., Cin., 1961-70, sr. v.p. charge Cin. br., 1970—. Mem. Am. Statis. Assn. (past pres. bus. statistics sect.), Cin. C. of C., Bankers Club Cin. (past gov.), Robert Morris Assos., Beta Gamma Sigma. Presbyn. (trustee, elder). Club: Queen City (Cin.). Home: 6127 Shadowslope Lane Cincinnati OH 45244 Office: 101 W 4th St Cincinnati OH 45201

KIELAN-JAWOROWSKA, ZOFIA EMILIA, paleontologist; b. Sokolow, Poland, Apr. 25, 1925; d. Franciszek and Maria (Osinska) Kielan; grad. in Zoology and Paleontology, U. Warsaw (Poland) 1949, Doctor's degree, 1954; m. Zbigniew Jaworowski, May 8, 1958; 1 son, Mariusz. Asst., later asst. prof. paleontology U. Warsaw, 1948-52; asst. prof. Inst. Paleontology, Polish Acad. Scis., 1952-60, prof., dir. Inst., 1961—; organizer, leader Polish-Mongolian Paleontol. Expdns. to Mongolia, 1963-71. Decorated Polonia Restituta, 1966. Fellow. Polish Geol. Soc., Polish Zool. Soc., Soc. Vetebrate Paleontology, Paleontol. Soc.; mem. Polish Acad. Scis. Spl. research paleozoic invertebrates from Europe, mesozoic veterbrates from Mongolia. Home: 141 Bonifacego Warsaw 34 Poland Office: Zaklad Paleozoologii Zwirki i Wigury 93 Warsaw 22 Poland

KIELY, JOHN A., lawyer; b. Covington, Ky., Oct. 10, 1900; LL.B., Salmon P. Chase Coll. Law, 1926. Admitted to Ohio bar, 1926, Ky. bar, 1926; now partner firm Rendigs, Fry, Kiely & Dennis, Cin. Fellow Am. Coll. Trial Lawyers; mem. Ky., Ohio State, Cin., Kenton County bar assns. Office: Central Trust Tower Cincinnati OH 45202*

KIELY, JOHN ROCHE, corp. exec.; b. Berkeley, Cal., Nov. 8, 1906; s. John R. and Isabelle (MacLean) K.; B.S. in Civil Engring., U. Wash., 1931; m. Margaret Lee Hughes, Jan. 20, 1940; children—John Roche III, Margaret Isobel, Michael Hughes, Kathryn Emily, Mary MacLean. Constrn. engr. Rainier Pulp and Paper Co., 1924-31, supt., 1931-36; resident engr. Rayonier, Inc., 1937- 40, asst. gen. supt., 1940-42; mgr. outfitting, subassembly, also transport Cal. Shipbldg. Corp., 1942-45; project mgr. Bechtel Bros. McCone Co., 1945-48; mgr. Bechtel Corp., San Francisco, 1948-51, v.p., 1951-54, dir., 1954, sr. v.p., 1957-67, exec. v.p., 1967—; exec. v.p., dir. Bechtel, Inc.; dir. Canadian Bechtel Ltd. Registered profl. engr., Wash., Ariz., Cal., Ohio, Md., Va., Fla., N.Y., Mich., D.C., Alaska, Nfld. Mem. Atomic Indsl. Forum, Nat. Acad. Engring., Engrs. Joint Council, Am. Soc. C.E., Am. Soc. M.E., Phi Beta Kappa, Sigma Xi, Tau Beta Pi. Clubs: California (Los Angeles); Stock Exchange, Engineers Pacific- Union (San Francisco); Union (Cleve.). Home: 206 Manzanita Way Woodside CA 94062 Office: 50 Beale St San Francisco CA 94111

KIELY, MARGARET, educator; b. Bridgeport, Conn.; d. Daniel and Margaret (Collins) Kiely; B.S., Columbia, 1916, A.M., 1924, Ph.D., 1930; LL.D., Fairfield U., 1953, U. Bridgeport, 1967, Queens Coll., 1968. Dean Queens Coll., Flushing, N.Y., 1937-60, now dean emeritus, was acting pres., 1947-49; adv. bd. Albertus Magnus Coll., New Haven. Secretary Nat. Council Edn.; sch. nursing com. Queens Hosp. Center. Mayor's Com. Unity, 1949-55; mem. Conn. State Bd. Edn., 1950—, Conn. Commn. Higher Edn., 1964—; mem. N.Y. Assn. for Blind (Queens Council); exec. bd. Queens North Shore chpt. A.R.C. Mem. Ecumenical Commn., Diocese of Bridgeport. Mem. Nat. Council Women of U.S., Internat. Council of Women. Mediaeval Acad. of Am., Flushing Interfaith Soc. (v.p.). Catholic Commn. on Intellectual and Cultural Affairs. Am. Assn. U. Women, Nat. Assn. Acad. Deans (hon.). Am. Com. for Irish Studies, Am. Com. Preservation Historic Ireland, Cath. Assn. Internat. Peace Kappa Delta Pi. Catholic. Club: Soroptomist. Home: 250 Myrtle Av Bridgeport CT 06604 Office: 144-80 Sanford Av Flushing NY 11355

KIELY, MARY FRANCES, librarian; b. Dorchester, Mass., Feb. 19, 1965; d. Daniel B. and Frances Ellen (Carten) Kiely; B.Ed. in L.S., R.I. Coll. Edn., 1926. Mem. childrens library staff Providence Pub. Library, 1926-35; editor in chief Pro Parvulis Book Club, N.Y.C., 1935-53; head librarian Providence Central High Sch., 1955-58; catalog librarian Bryant Coll. Bus. Adminstrn., Providence, 1958-64, coll. librarian, 1964—, vis. lectr. Grad. Library Sch., Cath. U. Am., 1944-45. Mem. R.I. Commn. Study Pulps and Comics, 1953. Recipient Anthony medal Providence pub. schs., 1918. Mem. R.I. Sch. Library Assn. (pres. 1956-58), R.I. Hist. Soc., Am., New Eng., R.I. library assns., Spl. Libraries Assn., Am. Mgmt. Assn., Am. Assn. U. Women. Roman Cath. Author: O'Donel of Destiny, 1939; Traffic Lights: Safe Highways in to Children's New Literature. 1940: also articles, essays. Compiler: New Worlds to Live, rev. edit., lit., 1945. Home: 125 Hope St Providence RI 02906

KIENBUSCH, WILLIAM, artist; b. N.Y.C., Apr. 13, 1914; s. Carl Otto and Mildred (Pressinger) von K.; grad. Hotchkiss Prep. Sch., 1932; B.A., Princeton, 1936; student Art Students League, 1936-37, Colorado Springs Fine Arts Center, Colarossi's, Paris, France, also with Anton Refregier and Stuart Davis, N.Y.C. Exhbns. Bklyn. Mus., Albright Art Gallery, Buffalo, Chgo. Art Inst., Des Moines Art Center, Walker Art Center, Mpls., Carnegie Art Inst., Pitts., Va. Mus. Arts, Richmond; former instr. Bklyn. Mus. Art Sch.; works represented permanent collections Mus. of Art U. Mich., Toledo Mus. Art, Munson-Williams-Proctor Inst., Utica, N.Y., W.R. Nelson Gallery Art, Kansas City, Mo., Ft. Worth Art Mus., U. Neb., Met. Mus. Art, Mus. Modern Art, Whitney Mus. Am. Art (N.Y.C.), Newark Mus., Albright Art Gallery, Buffalo, Toronto Art Gallery, Phila. Mus. Art, Pa. Acad. Art, Detroit Mus. Art, Boston Mus. Art, others; purchase Ford Found.; representative exhbn. Am. Art, Brussels World Fair, 1958. Served as sgt. AUS, 1942-45; instr. camouflage 936th Engrs.; constrn. target charts B-29 bombing raids, 949th Engrs. Recipient 1st prize for drawing Bklyn. Artists Biennial, 1952; prize for drawing Met. Mus., N.Y.C., 1952; Guggenheim Fellow, 1958. Mem. Phi Beta Kappa. Home: Kraushaar Galleries 1055 Madison Av New York City NY 10028

KIENDL, ARTHUR HERBERT, Jr., ednl. adminstr.; b. Glen Rock, N.J., May 26, 1922; s. Arthur Herbert and Mary (Moneypenny) K.; A.B., Dartmouth, 1947; M.A., Columbia, 1951; m. Jean Margaret Sprague, June 18, 1944; children—Deborah Jean, Arthur Herbert III. Tchr., Coopertown (N.Y.) Acad., 1947-48; asst. to dean coll. Dartmouth, 1948-51, asst. dean coll., 1951-53, dir. counselling, 1953-54, asso. dean coll. Dartmouth, 1954-58; dir. housing, also dir. student activities U. Chgo., 1954-55; dean students U. Colo., 1958-63; headmaster Mt. Hermon (Mass.) Sch., 1963-71; pres. Cranbrook Schs., Bloomfield Hills, Mich., 1971—. Trustee Dublin Sch., Hinckley Sch., Ulysses S. Grant Found., Bennett Coll., Nat. Rowing Found. Served to capt. USAAF, 1942-46. Mem. Phi Delta Kappa, Tau Sigma. Club: Economic (Detroit). Home: 4989 Stoneleigh Dr Bloomfield Hills MI 48013

KIENDL, THEODORE, lawyer; b. N.Y.C., May 5, 1890; s. Theodore and Louisa B. (Hearn) K.; A.B., Columbia, 1910, LL.B., 1913; m. Frances G. Vaughan, June 17, 1916; children—Helen (Mrs. Alvin F. Lindsay), Theodore, Jr., Philip Randolph. Admitted to N.Y. bar, 1913, since practiced in N.Y.C.; mem. firm Davis Polk & Wardwell, and predecessor firms, 1921—, now of counsel. Spl. trial examiner Bd. Edn. City N.Y.; spl. asst. atty. gen. N.Y., 1952-53. Mem. Am., N.Y. State, N.Y. Co., N.Y.C. bar assns. Home: 35 Durham Rd Bronxville NY 10708 Office: 1 Chase Manhattan Plaza New York City NY 10005

KIENE, TOM LEE, editor; b. Topeka, Mar. 19, 1906; s. Llewellyn and Martha (Jaqueth) K.; student Washburn U., 1924-25; B.J., U. Mo., 1927; m. Lorette Josephine Letourneau, Dec. 4, 1931; 1 dau., Llewellyn (Mrs. Roger Bartholow). City editor Concordia (Kan.) Blade-Empire, 1927-42; reporter Topeka State Jour., 1942-45, city editor, 1945-52, mng. editor, 1952-58; exec. editor Topeka Capital-Jour., 1958—; Chmn. Kan. A.P., 1964-65. Dir. Topeka Flood Control Assn., 1960—. Served with AUS, 1942-43. Mem. Topeka C. of C. (dir. 1965- 67), Am. Soc. Newspaper Editors, Asso. Press Mng.

Editors Assn., Kappa Sigma, Sigma Delta Chi, Kappa Tau Alpha. Rotarian (pres. Topeka 1968- 69). Home: 617 Warren St Topeka KS 66607 Office: 616 Jefferson St Topeka KS 66607

KIENZLE, CHARLES ARLINGTON, lawyer; b. Painesville, O., Mar. 11, 1921; s. Charles John and Luella (Reynolds) K.; B.A., Ohio State U., 1942, J.D. summa cum laude, 1947; m. Jane Wright, June 5, 1943; children—Barbara Jeanne, Nancy Lea, David Wright. Admitted to Ohio bar, 1947, since practiced in Columbus, partner firm Dunbar, Kienzle & Murphey, and predecessor, 1952—; lectr. Coll. Commerce, Ohio State U., 1948-49. Moderator weekly TV and radio program Columbus Town Meeting, 1951—. Bd. dirs. Franklin County chpt. A.R.C., 1956-60. Recipient Distinguished Service award U.S. Jr. C. of C., 1951. Served with USNR, 1943-46. Mem. Am., Ohio (council dels. 1963-67), Columbus (bd. govs. 1956- 58, 59-63, pres. 1961-62) bar assns. Am. Judicature Soc., Columbus Area (bd. dirs. 1970—), Ohio (bd. dirs. 1968-70) chambers commerce, Order of Coif, Phi Gamma Delta, Phi Delta Phi. Clubs: Columbus Athletic, Executives (pres. 1961-62), Scioto Country (Columbus). Home: 2367 Southway Dr Columbus OH 43221 Office: 250 E Broad Columbus OH 43215

KIENZLE, WILLIAM XAVIER, clergyman, editor; b. Detroit, Sept. 11, 1928; s. Alphonso and Mary Louise (Boyle) K.; B.A., Sacred Heart Sem., Detroit, 1950; postgrad. U. Detroit, 1960-61. Ordained priest Roman Catholic Ch., 1954; served three Detroit parishes, 1954-62; editor Mich. Cath. Newspaper, 1962—; sec.- treas. Mich. Cath. Co., 1962—, Fed. Composition Co., 1962—. Recipient Journalism award Mich. K.C., 1963. Mem. Cath. Press Assn. Club: Detroit Press. Composer book and lyrics for musical comedy, Campaign Capers, 1961. Home: 2701 W Chicago Blvd Detroit MI 48206 Office: 644 Selden St Detroit MI 48201

KIEPPER, ALAN FREDERICK, city mgr.; b. Syracuse, N.Y., July 3, 1928; s. John Carl and Sarah (McFadden) K.; A.B. cum laude, U. N.H., 1950; M.P.A., Wayne State U., 1960; m. Edith Harper, June 28, 1953; children—Patricia Ellen, Jane Elizabeth, Paul Frederick, Nancy Diana (dec.). Adminstrv. intern City of Richmond, Va., 1953, budget and mgmt. officer, 1953-59, asst. city mgr., Richmond, 1967, city mgr., 1967—; asst. to county mgr. Montgomery County, Rockville, Md., 1959-63; county mgr. Fulton County, Atlanta, 1963-67. Chmn. Twin Trailer Study Commn. Bd. dirs. Nat. Assn. County Adminstrs., 1965-67; mem. pub. ofcls. adv. council Office Econ. Opportunity. Bd. dirs. Richmond chpt. Nat. Conf. Christians and Jews, 1967—, Atlanta Assn. Retarded Children, 1964-67: bd. dirs. Richmond Area Assn. Retarded Children, 1967—, pres., 1969-70. Served to 1st lt. AUS, 1951-53. Mem. Internat. City Mgrs. Assn., Am. Soc. for Pub. Adminstrn. (pres. Va. chpt. 1970-71), Municipal Finance Officers Assn., Alpha Tau Omega, Tau Kappa Alpha, Phi Kappa Phi, Pi Gamma Mu. Episcopalian. Home: 409 Henri Rd Richmond VA 23226 Office: City Hall Richmond VA 23219

KIER, HOUSTON CLEVELAND, glass mfg. co. exec.; b. Oakland, Cal., July 28, 1918; s. Houston C. and Liola Estelle (Phelps) K.; student Santa Ana (Cal.) Jr. Coll., 1937, Fullerton (Cal.) Jr. Coll., 1938; m. Mary Lou Pearson Oct. 19, 1940; children—Pamela Ann, Janet Louise. Tech. sales mgr. Goodyear Tire and Rubber Co., 1939-42; engaged in pvt. bus., 1946-49; pres. Vita Paket Citrus Products Co., Covina, Cal., 1949-66, Thatcher Glass Mfg. Co. N.Y.C., 1966—; past dir. Weber Showcase, Weber Aircraft, Pepsi-Cola Santa Ana. Molecular Engring. Co. Founder Nat. Orange Juice Assn., 1957, pres., 1958, chmn. bd., 1960. Pres. Orange County (Cal.) Fine Arts Assn., 1965. Served with USAAF, 1942-46; PTO. Mem. Wine and Food Soc. (past pres.), Am. Legion, U.S. Power Squadron. Mason (Shriner), Elk. Clubs: Jonathan (Los Angeles); Hacienda Country (Whittler, Cal.); Yorba Linda Country (Yorba Linda, Cal.); Balboa (Cal.) Angling. Home: 715 Park Av New York City NY 10021 Office: 375 Park Av New York City NY 10022

KIER, PORTER MARTIN, paleontologist; b. Pitts., Oct. 22, 1927; s. Samuel Martin and Mary (Kebler) K.; B.S., U. Mich., 1950, M.S., 1951; Ph.D., U. Cambridge (Eng.), 1954; m. Mary Ellen Laverly, Sept. 9, 1950; children—William McKee, Elizabeth Lavely. Asst. prof. U. Houston, 1956-57; curator Smithsonian Instn., Washington, 1957-67, chmn. dept. paleobiology, 1967- -. Fulbright scholar, 1951-52; Guggenheim fellow, 1968. Fellow A.A.A.S., Geol. Soc. Am., Geol. Soc. London; mem. Paleontol. Soc. (pres. elect). Research and publs. in systematics of fossil enchinoids and living habits of recent echinoids. Home: 5104 Bradford Dr Annandale VA 22003 Office: Smithsonian Instn Washington DC 20560

KIERAN, JAMES, physician; b. Yonkers, N.Y., Feb. 9, 1920; s. John and Alma (Boldtmann) K.; A.B., Yale, 1941; M.D., Columbia, 1944; divorced; children—Anne, James, Margaret (Mrs. Jack Goldwasser), Jane, John, Robert. Intern and resident Bellevue Hosp., N.Y.C., 1944-49; pvt. practice medicine Oakland, Cal., 1950-59, Berkeley, Cal., 1959-70; asso. clin. prof. medicine U. Cal. Sch. Medicine, San Francisco, 1959—; dir. pulmonary disease service Stanford Sch. Medicine, 1957-60. Served to capt., M.C., USAAF, 1945-47. Mem. Am. (pres. elect 1970-71), Cal. (pres. 1961-62) thoracic socs., Tb and Respiratory Disease Assn. Cal. (pres. 1969-70). Rotarian. Address: 2340 Ward St Berkeley CA 94705

KIERAN, JOHN FRANCIS, writer; b. N.Y.C., Aug. 2, 1892; s. James Michael and Kate (Donohue) K.; ed. Coll. City N.Y., 3 years; B.S. cum laude, Fordham U., 1912; D.Sc., Clarkson Coll., 1941; M.A., Wesleyan U., 1942; m. Alma Boldtmann, May 14, 1919; (dec. June 1944); children—James Michael, John Francis, Beatrice; m. 2d, Margaret Ford, Sept. 5, 1947. With N.Y. Times sports dept., 1915-43; columnist on N.Y. Sun, 1943-44. Elector, Hall of Fame for Gt. Americans, N.Y.C., 1945—. Recipient John Burroughs medal, 1960. Author: Story of Olympic Games, 1936; Nature Notes, 1941; American Sporting Scene, 1941; Footnotes on Nature, 1947; Not Under Oath: Recollections and Reflections, 1964. Contbr. chpts. on sports to We Saw It Happen, 1938; America Now, 1938; Introduction to Nature, 1957; Natural History of New York City, 1959; contbr. articles to many mags., also articles on philology and natural history. Mem. "bd. of experts" of radio program, "Information, Please" Home: Rockport MA 01966

KIERANS, ERIC WILLIAM, Canadian govt. ofcl.; b. Montreal, Que., Can., Feb. 2, 1914; s. Hugh and Lena S. Kerans; ed. Loyola Coll., McGill U.; B.A. in Sales; m. Catherine Whelan, Nov. 12, 1938; children—Thomas Edward, Catherine Anne. Sales promotion E.S. & A. Robinson Ltd. nd Planned Sales Ltd., Montreal, 1943-45; pres. Canadian Adhesives Ltd., 1946—, Hygiene Products Ltd., 1952-60; former minister of health, minister of revenue Province of Que.; postmaster gen., minister of communications, 1968—. Prof. commerce, dir. Sch. Commerce, McGill U., 1953-60; former pres. Montreal Stock Exchange Canadian Stock Exchange. Served to lt. Canadian Army, 1942-45. Home: 5631 Queen Mary Rd Hampstead Quebec Canada*

KIERLAND, ROBERT RICHARD, physician; b. Mahnomen, Minn., June 13, 1910; s. Peter E. and Elsie (Oschner) K.; B.S., U. Minn., 1932, B.M., 1932, M.D., 1933; M.S., Mayo Found., 1939; m. Margaret Lytle, Nov. 2, 1934; children—Marcia (Mrs. John F. McCally), Peter L. Fellow dermatology and syphilology Mayo Found., 1937-40, prof. dermatology, 1957—; cons. physician Mayo Clinic, 1940—, head sect. dermatology, 1962-70, sr. cons., 1970—. Cons. surgeon 5th Army, USPHS. Chmn. bd. Dermatology Found. Served with M.C., AUS, World War II; col. Res. Mem. Am. Acad. Dermatology (past sec.-treas.; pres. 1963) A.M.A. (past mem. ho. of dels.; chmn. sect. dermatology 1966), Am. Dermatol. Assn. (pres. 1968), Soc. Investigative Dermatology, A.A.A.S., Internat. Assn. Tropical Dermatology (asso. editor), Minn. Dermatol. Soc. (past pres.), Sigma Xi, Chi Psi; hon. mem. Assn. Mil. Dermatologists, Dallas Soc., Clin. Soc., Pacific Dermatologic Assn.; hon. and corr. mem. many fgn. dermatol. socs. Club: Rochester Golf and Country. Chief editor: Archives of Dermatology. Home: Mounted Route 72 Rochester MN 55901 Office: 200 1st St SW Rochester MN 55901

KIERNAN, EDWIN A., Jr., lawyer; b. N.Y.C., Aug. 2, 1926; s. Edwin A. and Helen M. (Clarke) K.; A.B., Columbia, 1947, LL.B., 1950, J.D., 1969; LL.M., N.Y.U., 1957; m. Ellen Mary Irving, Feb. 18, 1952; children—Robert Clarke, Katherine Waters. Admitted to N.Y. bar, 1950; asso. Simpson, Thacher & Bartlett, N.Y.C., 1950-52, 54-55; asso. Wickes, Riddell, Bloomer, Jacobi & McGuire, N.Y.C., 1956-59; atty. Western Electric Co., Inc., 1959-60; atty. Interpublic Group of Cos., Inc., N.Y.C., 1960-64, mng. atty., 1964-68, asst. gen. counsel, 1968—; sec. McCann-Erickson, Inc., N.Y.C., 1962—. Served with USNR, 1944-46, 52-54. Mem. Am. Bar Assn., Assn. Bar City N.Y., Phi Beta Kappa. Home: 544 1st St Brooklyn NY 11215 Office: 1271 Av Americas New York City NY 10020

KIERNAN, LOYD JULIAN, ret. r.r. ofcl.; b. Vicksburg, Miss., Sept. 12, 1895; s. Thomas and Margaret Elizabeth (Hartman) K.; Master of Accounts, Holy Cross Coll., New Orleans, 1909; m. Jennie P. Howard, June 29, 1921; children— Loyd J., Frances Margaret (Mrs. Wm. A. Ries). With I.C. R.R., 1911-37; with Equitable Life Assurance Soc., 1938-42, Assn. Am. R.R.'s, Washington, 1942-55; exec. v.p., chief exec. officer B. & M. R.R., 1955; cons. transportation U.S. Govt., other countries, 1956-61. Sec.-gen. 8th Pan- Am. Ry. Congress, Washington, 1953. Served from pvt. to 1st lt. 155th Inf., U.S. Army, 1916-19; capt. O.R.C. ret. Episcopalian. Club: Army and Navy (Washington). Contbr. profl. publs. Home: 301 W Enid Dr Key Biscayne Miami FL 33149

KIERNAN, OWEN BURNS, ednl. adminstr.; b. Randolph, Mass., Mar. 9, 1914; s. Thomas Francis and Elizabeth (Burns) K.; B.S., Bridgewater (Mass.) State Tchrs. Coll., 1935; M.Ed., Boston U., 1940; Ed.D. Harvard, 1950; L.H.D. (hon.), Lesley Coll., 1956; LL.D., Northeastern U., 1961; Litt.D., (hon.) Stonehill Coll., 1965; Ped.D., (hon.) R.I. Coll., 1966; Sc.D., (hon.) Boston U., 1968; m. Esther Harriet Thorley, July 13, 1940; children—Joan Ann, Nancy Elizabeth, John Albert. Prin. Henry T. Wing High Sch., Sandwich, Mass., 1938-44; supt. schs., Wayland and Sudbury, Mass., 1944-51, Milton, 1951-57; commr. edn. State of Mass., 1957-68; exec. sec. Nat. Assn. Secondary Sch. Prins., 1969—. Past chmn. Mass. Bd. Edn., Mass. Bd. Vocational Edn.; corp. mem. Mass. Inst. Tech.; trustee U. Mass., Lowell Tech. Inst., Mus. Fine Arts, Mus. Sci. Boston, Boston U. Mem. Am. Assn. Sch. Adminstrs., New Eng., Mass. supts. assns., Council Chief State Sch. Officers (pres. 1967), Phi Delta Kappa. Home: 4000 Massachusetts Av NW Washington DC 20016 Office: 1201 16th St NW Washington DC 20036

KIERNAN, WALTER, ret. news commentator; b. New Haven, Jan. 24, 1902; s. Daniel Harry and Alice M. (Rowen) K.; ed. New Haven High Sch.; m. Helen Hastings, Sept. 3, 1924; children—David, Richard, Jerome. Reporter and feature writer New Haven Union, 1924-26; writer and editor New Haven Register, 1926-28; mem. A.P. staff, 1928-29; dir. publicity and editor K.C. News, New Haven, 1929-31; pub. and editor West Haven Town Crier, 1930-37; Conn. state mgr. Internat. News Service, Hartford, 1937; feature writer, columnist and roving corr., N.Y.C., 1937-43; radio commentator ABC network, N.Y.C., 1943-52; commentator NBC, 1952-60, WOR, 1961-69, One Man's Opinion, WOR-TV, 1964-69. Mem. Acad. TV Arts and Scis., Cath. Actors Guild (past pres.). Roman Catholic. Clubs: The Lambs; Circus Saints and Sinners (N.Y.C. and Washington). Author: One Man's Opinion. Home: 9 Oakmont Circle Ormond Beach FL 32074

KIERSCH, GEORGE ALFRED, educator, geologist; b. Lodi, Cal., Apr. 15, 1918; s. A.T. and Viola E. (Bahmeier) K.; student Jr. Coll. and San Jose State Coll., 1936-38; Geol. Engr., Colo. Sch. Mines, 1942; Ph.D., U. Ariz., 1947; m. Jane Keith, Nov. 29, 1942; children—Dana Elizabeth, Mary Annan, George Keith, Nancy McCandless. Teaching fellow dept. geology U. Ariz., 1945-47, asst. prof., 1951-55; geologist 79 Mining Co., 1946-47, underground exploration tests U.S. Corps Engrs., 1948, Folsom Dam project, 1949-50; supervising geologist Internat. Boundary and Water Commn., 1950-51; dir. mineral resources survey Navajo-Hopi Indian Reservations, 1952-55; asst. chief exploration So. Pacific Co., San Francisco, 1956-60; asso. prof. geology Cornell U., Ithaca, N.Y., 1960-63, prof. 1963—, chmn. dept. geol. scis., 1965—; cons. engring. geologist U.S.A., fgn. projects, 1953—; pres. Geo. Sci. & Resources Corp., Phoenix, 1962—. Mem. adv. bd. to trustees Colo. Sch. Mines, 1962—. Served to capt., C.E., AUS, 1942- 45. Sr. postdoctoral fellow NSF, Vienna, Austria, 1963-64; recipient Holdredge award Assn. Engring. Geologists, 1965. Fellow Geol. Soc. Am., Am. Soc. C.E., Soc. Econ. Geologists; mem. U.S. commn. Large Dams, Sigma Xi, Tau Beta Pi, Theta Tau, Sigma Phi Epsilon. Mason. Club: Country (Ithaca). Author: Engineering Geology, 1955; Mineral Resources of Navajo- Hopi Indian Reservations Ariz-Utah, 1955-56; Geothermal Steam, 1964. Contbr. numerous articles tech. jours., bulls. Home: 119 Warwick Pl Ithaca NY 14850

KIERSTEAD, WILSON HOPPER, advt. exec.; b. Nutley, N.J., Mar. 6, 1918; s. Wilson Hopper and Harte (Marvin) K.; A.B., Wesleyan U., Middletown, Conn., 1940; m. Mary Devereux Rudd, Apr. 9, 1962; children—Cornelius Rudd, Nicholas Edward. With R.H. Macy & Co., N.Y.C., 1940-42, asst. buyer, 1941-42; mdsg. exec. R.H. Macy-Bamberger's, N.Y.C. and N.J., 1945-48; with Young & Rubicam, Inc., N.Y.C., 1948—, v.p., supr., 1953-60, mem. plans bd., 1960—, dir. merchandising, 1960-61, sr. v.p., div. mgr., 1961-62; mng. dir. Young & Rubicam, Ltd., London, 1962-65, sr. v.p., N.Y.C., 1965-68, exec. v.p., 1968—, asso. mgr., N.Y.C., 1971—. Served to lt. (s.g.) USNR, 1942-45. Mem. Alpha Delta Phi. Club: Union League. Home: 901 Lexington Av New York City NY 10021 Office: 285 Madison Av New York City NY 10017

KIESINGER, KURT GEORG, hon. chmn. Christian Democratic Union; b. Ebingen, Germany, Apr. 6, 1904; s. Christian and Dominika (Grimm) K.; ed. univs. Tübingen and Berlin; m. Marie Luise Schneider, Dec. 24, 1932; children—Peter, Viola (Mrs. Volkmar Wentzel). Lawyer in Berlin, 1934-45, in Tübingen, 1948; mem. Bundestag, 1949-58, 69—, chmn. joint com., 1949-57, chmn. fgn. affairs com., 1954-58; v.p. consulative assembly of Council of Europe, 1955-58, chmn. Christian Democratic group, 1957-58; mem. bd. Christian Democratic Union Germany, now hon. chmn.; prime minister of Land Baden-Württemberg, 1958-66; pres. Bundesrat, 1962-63; chancellor of West Germany, 1966-69. Decorated grand cross merit 1st class Fed. Republic Germany; Order of Merit (Bavaria); grand cross Order Merit Italian Republic; grand office Legion of Honor (France); Pius Orden, 1968; Grand Silver decoration with ribbon (Austria); Grand Cross Order Isabel the Catholic (Spain); 1st class Author: Ideen vom Ganzen; Reden und Betrachtungen, 1964; Stationen, 1969; also articles on fgn. politics. Home: Engel friedshalde 48 Tuebingen West Germany Office: Bundeshaus Bonn West Germany

KIESTER, EDWIN HAMMITT, Jr., editor; b. Turtle Creek, Pa., Dec. 30, 1927; s. Edwin H. and Lila (Plowden) K.; B.A., U. Pitts., 1950; m. Elizabeth Ann Wimsatt, Oct. 10, 1953; children—Philip, Army, Elizabeth, Ann. Reporter Pitts. Sun- Telegraph, 1944-53; asso. editor Parade Mag., N.Y.C., 1954-63, managing editor, 1963-68, exec. editor True Magazine, 1968—. Served with AUS, 1945-47. Recipient Ted V. Rodgers award 1957. Mem. Edn. Writers Assn., Soc. Am. Travel Writers. Author: How and Where to Vacation with Children: and Enjoy It, 1963; (with Alice Miel) The Shortchanged Children of Suburbia, The Case of the Missing Executive. Home: 1 Blind Brook Rd S Westport CT 08880 Office: 67 W 44th St New York City NY 10036

KIEV, ISAAC EDWARD, clergyman; b. N.Y.C., Mar. 21, 1905; s. Nathan and Anna (Radin) K.; student Columbia, 1924-26; M.H.L., Rabbi, Jewish Inst. Religion, 1927; D.D., Hebrew Union Coll., 1956; m. Mary B. Nover, Dec. 20, 1930 (dec. June 1964); children—Ari, Aviva (Mrs. Avigdor Warsha). Research asst. Jewish Inst. Relgion, 1927-28; asst. librarian Hebrew Bibliographer, 1928-43; librarian Hebrew Union Coll.-Jewish Inst. Religion, 1943—; chaplain Dept. Hosps., N.Y.C., 1927—, Sea View Hosp. Synagogue, 1930—; acting rabbi Free Synagogue Westchester, 1957; asso. rabbi Congregation Habonim, N.Y.C., 1968—. Sec. Jewish Cultural Reconstrn. N.Y., 1949-51; chmn. Jewish Book Council Am., 1970. Trustee Alexander Kohut Found., Nissan Touroff Found., Israel Matz Found. Mem. Assn. Bibl. Instrs., Soc. Bibl. Lit., Hebrew Lang. Acad., Am. Acad. Jewish Research, Am. Jewish Hist. Soc., Am. Oriental Soc., Israel Exploration Soc., Soc. Jewish Bibliophies, Mekize Nirdamin Soc. Asso. editor Jewish Book Ann., 1952—, Studies in Bibliography and Booklore, 1953—. Translation Kafra Haggadah, 1949. Contbr. articles mags., anns. Home: 4 S Pinehurst Av New York City NY 10033 Office: 40 W 68th St New York City NY 10023

KIEWEL, FRANK DONALD, brewery exec.; b. Little Falls, Minn., May 5, 1905; s. Frank A. and Alice C. (Green) K.; B.B.A., U. Minn., 1930; m. Gladys E. Bethke, Jan. 14, 1939; children—James, Carolyn. With Mpls. Brewing Co., 1933-, pres., 1951—, also gen. mgr. and dir. Mem. Delta Tau Delta. Episcopalian (sr. warden). Home: 4106 Cedarwood Rd Minneapolis MN 55416 Office: 1215 Marshall St N E MInneapolis MN 55413

KIEWIT, PETER, contractor; b. Omaha, Sept. 12, 1900; s. Peter and Anna (Schleicker) K.; student Dartmouth, LL.D., 1960; LL.D., U. Omaha, 1958, Hastings Coll., 1964, U. Neb., 1964, Creighton U., 1968; m. Mary Drake, Jan. 22, 1922; 1 son, Peter; m. 2d, Evelyn Stotts Newton, July 2, 1952. Apprentice mason, foreman and supt. bldg. constrn. Peter Kiewit Sons' Co., 1920-31, pres. Peter Kiewit Sons' Inc., 1931—, now chmn. bd., chief exec. officer; v.p., dir. Herald Corp., Omaha; acting chmn., dir. C., R.I. & P. Ry.; dir. World Pub. Co., Omaha, No. Natural Gas Co., Omaha Nat. Bank, Northwestern Bell Telephone Co., Omaha. Trustee Hastings Coll., Omaha Indsl. Found., Joslyn Liberal Arts Soc., Omaha, Eisenhower Med. Center, U. Neb. Found.; bd. dirs. Jr. Achievement Omaha, Girls Town, Omaha, Eugene C. Eppley Found, Omaha Redevel. Corp., Creighton U.; pres. Bishop Clarkson Meml. Hosp. Recipient Moles non-mem. award, 1953. Mem. C. of C. (dir.). Clubs: Omaha, Omaha Country, Plaza (Omaha); Thunderbird Country (Palm Springs, Cal.); Eldorado Country (Palm Desert, Cal.). Presbyn. (trustee). Home Penthouse Apt 1 Kiewit Plaza Omaha NB 68131 Office:: 1000 Kiewit Plaza Omaha NB 68131

KIEWIT, PETER, Jr., lawyer; b. Omaha, May 11, 1926; s. Peter and Mary (Drake) K.; B.A., U. Ariz., 1950, J.D., 1953; m. Barbara MacIsaac, Aug. 7, 1966; children—Peter IV, Drake, Tod. Admitted to Ariz. bar, 1953, since practiced in Phoenix; asso. Rawlins, Ellis, Burrus & Kiewit, 1953-56, partner, 1956-63, sr. partner, 1963—. Sec., Union Rock & Materials Corp.; dir. Peter Kiewit Sons, Inc., Cal. Health Care, Inc. Pres., Neurol. Scis. Found. Trustee Barrow Neurol. Found. Served with AUS, 1944-46. Mem. Phi Delta Phi, Sigma Alpha Epsilon. Republican. Clubs: Phoenix Lawyers; Paradise Valley Country (Scottsdale, Ariz.). Home: 2210 Encanto Dr NW Phoenix AZ 85007 Office: Security Bldg Phoenix AZ 85004

KIGER, JOSEPH CHARLES, educator; b. Kenton County, Ky. Aug. 19, 1920; s. Carl C. and Genevieve (Hoelscher) K.; A.B., Birmingham-So. Coll., 1943; M.A., U. Ala., 1947; Ph.D., Vanderbilt U., 1950; m. Jean Myrick Moore, Mar. 27, 1947; children—Carl A., John J. Teaching fellow Vanderbilt U., 1948-50; instr. history U. Ala., summer 1950, Washington U., St. Louis, 1950-51; dir. research select com. to investigate founds. U.S. Ho. of Reps., 1952; staff asso. Am. Council Edn., Washington, 1953-55; asst. dir. So. Fellowships Fund, Chapel Hill, N.C., 1955-58; asso. prof. history U. Ala., 1958-61; prof. history U. Miss., 1961—, chmn. dept. history, 1969—; cons. non-profit orgns., also govt., 1954—. Served to capt. USMCR, 1942-46. Guggenheim fellow, 1960; grantee Russell Sage Found., 1953, Rockefeller Found., 1961, Am. Philos. Soc., 1964. Mem. Am., So. (life) hist. assns., Am. Studies Assn. Author: Operating Principles of the Larger Foundations, 1954; (with others) Sponsored Research Policy of Colleges and Universities, 1954; American Learned Societies, 1963. Home: Country Club Rd Oxford MS 38655 Office: Dept History Univ Miss University MS 38677

KIGHT, ALONZO BARNARD, mfg. co. exec.; b. N.Y.C. Apr. 24, 1915; s. Alonzo Barnard and Florence (Cox) K.; A.B., Harvard, 1936; LL.B., Columbia, 1940; M.B.A., U. Chgo., 1954; m. Audrey Anne, Mar. 13, 1971; 1 dau., Jean Pirie. Admitted to D.C. bar, 1941, Ill. bar, 1944, U.S. Supreme Ct., 1944, others; patent atty. fgn. patent dept. Western Electric Co., 1946-48; with Borg-Warner Corp., 1949-69, v.p. Borg-Warner Internat., 1955-61, pres., dir., 1961- 69, v.p. parent corp., 1962-69; now v.p.-internat. N. Am. Rockwell Corp., Pitts.; pres. N.Am. Rockwell Internat. Served with USNR, 1944-46. Mem. Beta Gamma Sigma, Phi Delta Phi. Clubs: Duquesne (Pitts.); Fox Chapel Racquet; Harvard (N.Y.C.). Home: Gateway Towers Gateway Center Pittsburgh PA 15222 Office: N Am Rockwell Bldg Pittsburgh PA 15222

KILBORNE, ROBERT STEWART, state official; b. New York City, Aug. 1, 1905; s. Robert Stewart and Katharine (Skinner) K.; grad. Groton (Mass.) Sch., 1923; Yale, 1923-25; m. Barbara Briggs, Nov. 28, 1925 (dec. 1968); children—Belle (Mrs. Kilborne Waterman), Robert Stewart III (deceased), George Briggs; m. 2d, Jane Lowes Houk, May 2, 1969. Joined William Skinner & Sons (Mass. Common Law Trust), N.Y.C., 1925, president Truhu Fabrics Corp. (a subsidiary), 1933, vice pres. William Skinner & Sons, 1941, trustee, 1945-61, pres., 1947-61; dir. The Equitable Life Assurance Soc. U.S. Commr. of conservation N.Y. State Conservation Dept., 1966-70; spl. asst. to Gov. on Conservation affairs, 1970—. Member Industry adv. com. OPA, Washington, 1943-46, OPS, 1951-53; member adv. com. Research & Development br. Mil. Planning Div. Office Q.M. Gen., Washington 1943-49, Synthetic Branch, Broad Woven Fabrics Division, Quarter master Association, Washington, 1951-61;

chairman Saratoga Springs Commission, 1966—; alternate to gov. N.Y. State for Delaware River Basin Commn., 1966—; mem. bd. Saratoga Performing Arts Center, 1966—, Gt. Lakes Commn., Hudson River Valley Commn., 1966—; commr. N.Y. State Taconic Park Commn., 1963—; temporary study commn. for future Adirondacks. Trustee Arthur Butler Meml. Sanctuary, 1967—; dir. Union Theol. Sem., 1950-66. Mem. Am. Cotton Mfrs. Inst., Inc. (dir. 1958-62), Nat. Fedn. Textiles, Inc. (dir. 1949-58, pres. 1954-55), Am. Arbitration Assn., Am. Textile Mfrs. Inst. (hon. dir. 1962—), C. of C. of N.Y.C., Soc. Mayflower Descs., New Eng. Soc. of N.Y., Delta Kappa Epsilon. Republican. Presbyn. (elder). Clubs: Wings: Redford (N.Y.) Golf and Tennis; Yale (N.Y.C.); University (Albany, N.Y.). Home: The Hook Road Katonah NY 10536 Office: 105 White Plains Rd Tarrytown NY 10591

KILBORNE, WILLIAM SKINNER, bus. cons.; b. Stockbridge, Mass., Sept. 1, 1912; s. Robert Stewart and Katherine (Skinner) K.; grad. Groton Sch., 1931; B.A., Yale, 1935; M.B.A., Harvard, 1937; m. Elizabeth Briggs, June 25, 1935; children—William Skinner, Bejamin Briggs, Allerton Wright, Katharine Skinner. With William Skinner & Sons, 1937-53, v.p., 1942-53, trustee, 1947-61; dir. Lexington Lumber Co., 1938-43; dir. Internat. Silk Assn., 1948-53, v.p., 1951-53; spl. asst. to Sec. of Commerce, 1953-57; business research B. F. Goodrich Co., 1958-60; v.p. Casey & Kilborne, Inc., N.Y. City, 1960-62; pres. William S. Kilborne, Inc., 1962—; vice pres. John Moynahan & Co., Inc., 1963-66; chmn. Harkil Corp., 1969—. Mem. Nat. Def. Exec. Res., 1958-70. Vice pres. 15th Assembly District Republican Club, N.Y.C., 1939-41. mem. N.Y. County Rep. Com. 1940-41. Dir. Nat. Fedn. Settlements, 1941-42, 44-46; trustee N.Y. Sch. Social Work, 1952-53, hon. trustee, 1953-59; dir. Lenox Hill Neighborhood Assn., 1939-50, pres. 1941-46; dir. Morningside Community Center, 1945-53, hon. dir., 1953-60; dir. Union Settlement, 1966—. Mem. Maryflower Soc., Assn. Corp. Growth. Presbyn. Clubs: Yale, University (N.Y.C.). Home: 400 E 56th St New York City NY 10022 Office: 41 E 42d St New York City NY 10017

KILBOURNE, EDWIN DENNIS, educator, virologist; b. Buffalo, July 10, 1920; s. Edwin I. and Elizabethh (Alward) K.; A.B., Cornell U., 1942, M.D., 1944; m. Joy Schmid, Dec. 20, 1952; children—Edwin Michael, Richard Schmid, Christopher Norton, Paul Alward. Asst., Rockefeller Inst., 1948-51; mem. faculty Tulane U., 1951-55; mem. faculty Cornell U. Med. Coll., N.Y.C., 1955-68, prof. pub. health, dir. div. virus research, 1961-68; prof., chmn. dept. microbiology Mt. Sinai Sch. Medicine, City U. New York, 1968—; mem. staff N.Y. Hosp., 1955-68. Mem. commn. on influenza Armed Forces Epidemiological Bd., 1965—; mem. Health Research Council N.Y.C., 1968—; mem. adv. com. infectious diseases, chmn. subcom. influenza Nat. Inst. Allergy and Infectious Diseases. Mem. Harvey Soc., So., Central (emeritus) socs. clin. research, A.A.A.S., Am. Assn. Immunologists, Am. Acad. Microbiology, Soc. Exptl. Biology and Medicine, Am. Soc. Clin. Investigation (emeritus), N.Y. Acad. Sci., N.Y. Acad. Medicine, Am. Pub. Health Assn., Am. Thoracic Soc., Assn. Am. Physicians, Am. Soc. Microbiology, Infectious Diseases Soc. Am. Author: (with Wilson G. Smillie) Preventive Medicine and Public Health, 3d edit., 1963. Research and publs. on hormonal influences, genetic studies and exptl. transmission of viruses, recombiant virus vaccines especially influenza. Home: 446 Hillcrest Rd Ridgewood NJ 07450 Office: City U New York Mt Sinai Sch Medicine Dept Microbiology Fifth Av at 100th St New York City NY 10029

KILBOURNE, JAMES H., lawyer; b. Minneapolis, Kan., Dec. 3, 1912; B.S., N.D. State Coll., 1935; J.D., U. Mich., 1938. Admitted to Mont. bar, 1938; mem. firm Crowley, Kilbourne, Haughey, Hanson and Gallagher, Billings, Mont. Mem. Am., Mont., Yellowstone County bar assns., Order of Coif. Office: 500 Electric Bldg Billings MT 59101*

KILBRIDE, BERNARD JAMES, educator; b. Portland, Me., Jan. 24, 1928; s. Gabriel Patrick and Josephine (Reardon) K.; A.B., St. Francis Xavier U., 1950; M.S., Columbia, 1955; Ph.D., U. Tex., 1961; m. Avis Chamberlain, Jan. 29, 1955; children—Bernard James II, Sean Paul, Sioban Anne, Darach Padraic, Liam Michael. Chmn. dept. bus. St. Fracis Xavier U., 1957-60; lectr. finance U. Tex. at Austin, 1960-61; asst. prof. finance U. Ill. at Urbana, 1961-63; mem. faculuty U. Notre Dame, 1963—, asso. prof., 1963- 69, prof., 1969—, chmn. dept., 1963—; asso. Kirschner Research Assos., Albuquerque, 1964—. C.P.A., Tex. Mem. Chgo. Investment Analysts Soc., Financial Execs. Inst., Am. Inst. C.P.A.'s. Home: 2804 Corpus Christi Dr South Bend IN 46628 Office: PO Box 161 U Notre Dame Notre Dame IN 46556

KILBRIDE, THOMAS BERNARD, advt. exec.; b. Mpls., Mar. 9, 1919; s. Thomas Bernard and Jeanne (Froberg) K.; grad. Advanced Mgmt. program, Harvard, 1966; m. Carol Hanson, May 9, 1937; children—Thomas Bernard, Larry A., Marcia (Mrs. Theodore J. Glaros), Stephen J., Jan. C., Jill L. With advt. dept. Pillsbury Mills, Mpls., 1937-38; salesman Western Grocer Co., Albert Lea, Minn., 1938-43; v.p., dir. Red & White Stores, Mpls., 1946-57; account exec. Knox Reeves Advt., Inc., Mpls. 1957-60, v.p., dir., 1960- 66, pres., 1966-70, chmn. bd., 1970—; dir. N.W. 4A. Served to 1st lt., inf. AUS, 1943-46. Recipient Man of Year award Mpls. Sales Exec., 1958. Mem. Mpls. Sales Execs. Club (past pres.), Mpls. Advt. Club (past pres.), Alpha Delta Sigma. Club: Minneapolis, Minneapolis Athletic. Home: 20 E Elmwood Pl Minneapolis MN 55419 Office: 400 2d Av S Minneapolis MN 55401

KILBRIDGE, JAMES XAVIER, lawyer, corp. exec.; b. Chgo., Jan. 18, 1926; s. Joseph T. and Lillian (Volker) K.; LL.B., Loyola U., Chgo., 1950; m. Ethel Bristol, Aug. 28, 1954; children—Nancy, Sally, James Xavier, John. Admitted to Ill. bar, 1949, D.C. bar, 1952, N.Y. bar, 1968; atty. Dept. Justice, also spl. asst. to atty. gen., 1950-56; atty. Office Chief Counsel, Internal Revenue Service, 1956-60; tax counsel, asst. gen. counsel Litton Industries, Inc.,1960-64, corp. sec., 1964- 66; v.p., gen. counsel Walter Kidde & Co., Bellville, N.J., 1966-69, sr. v.p., dir., 1969—. Served with USNR, 1944-46. Mem. Am. Bar Assn. Home: 227 Gregory Rd Franklin Lakes NJ 07417 Office: 9 Brighton Rd Clifton NJ 07012

KILBRIDGE, MAURICE D., educator; b. Chgo., June 2, 1920; s. Joseph T. and Lillian (Volker) K.; B.S. in Mathematics, Loyola U., Chgo., 1942, M.S., 1947; M.S. in Indsl. Engring., Ill. Inst. Tech. 1950; Ph.D., State U. Ia., 1953; M.A. (hon.), Harvard U., 1967; m. Helen R. Herley; children—Peter, Anthony, Christopher. Asst. prof. mathematics Loyola U., Chgo, 1947- 48; exec. tng. dir. Spiegel, Inc. Chgo., 1948-51; asst. prof., asso. prof., prof. indsl. engring. Ill. Inst. Techn., 1951-57, dir. dept. indsl. engring, 1953-58, coordinator research, 1956-58; prof. mgmt. Grad. Sch. Bus. U. Chgo., 1958-63; asst. dir. U.S. AID Mission to India, 1963-65; faculty research fellow dept, social relations Harvard, 1960- 61, prof. bus. adminstrn. Grad. Sch. Bus. Adminstrn., 1965-69, acting dean, prof. urban systems Grad. Sch. Design; mem. Harvard adv. mission to Nat. Planning Rd., Govt. of Pakistan, 1954-56. Served as lt. USNR, World War II. Profl. engr., Ia. Mem. Inst. Mgmt. Sci., Am. Soc. Planning Ofcls., Internat. Acad. Law and Sci., Am. Sociol. Assn. Author: Productive Uses of Nuclear Energy, 1958; Productivity and the Work-Pay Exchange, 1959; An Economic Analysis of the Housing and Urban Development Act of 1968, 1969; Urban Analysis, 1969. Home: 7 Juniper Pl Lexington MA 02173

KILBURN, LANE DIXON, coll. pres.; b. Norton, Mass., Apr. 6, 1923; s. Winford Almon and Mary Elizabeth (Sampson) K.; Ph.B., Laval U., Que., Can., 1948, Ph.L., 1950. Entered Congregation of Holy Cross, 1950, ordained priest Roman Catholic Ch., 1955; instr. philosophy King's Coll., Wilkes-Barre, Pa., 1955-56, 57-58, dean coll., 1958-64, pres. coll., 1964—. Bd. dirs. Boy Scouts, Community Concert Assn., Wilkes-Barre Philharmonic Soc. Mem. Am. Soc. Aesthetics, N.E.A., Nat. Cath. Edn. Assn., Am. Assn. Colls. Tchrs. Edn. (instl. rep.), New Eng. Historic and Geneal. Soc., Am. Students of Laval (pres.), Quebec Little Art Theatre, Am. Colony Quebec, C. of C. (chmn. edn. com.), Pa. Soc., Wyoming Valley Hist. and Geol. Soc. K.C. (4). Author: The Role and Moral Value of Music, 1951; also articles. Home: 133 N Franklin St Wilkes-Barre PA 18702

KILCARR, J. KENNETH, airlines co. exec.; b. N.Y.C., Feb. 2, 1918; s. Joseph Kenneth and Anne Loretta (McFarland) K.; B.B.A., Manhattan Coll., 1938; grad. Harvard Bus. Sch. Advanced Mgmt. Program, 1966; m. Janet Rita Wallum, May 7, 1949; children—Joan, Barbara, John, Clare. With Eastern Air Lines, 1940- 57, asst. treas., 1954-57; with Am. Airlines, Inc., 1957—, asst. v.p., asst. treas., 1959-63, controller, now v.p. and controller. Clubs: Wings (N.Y.); Hackensack (N.J.) Golf. Home: 50 Heritage Ct Hillsdale NJ 07642 Office: 633 3d Av New York City NY 10017

KILDAY, RALPH, utility exec.; b. Portland, Me., Nov. 4, 1903; s. John Coleman and Sarah (Greeley) K.; grad. Hebron Acad., 1922; student Bentley Sch. Accounting and Bus. 1922-27, Northeastern Law Sch., evenings 1928-29; m. Ruth K. Walker, Aug. 9, 1930; children—Jean Coleman (Mrs. Robert A. Fabish), Barbara Ellen (Mrs. Richard C. Belden). With Stone & Webster Service Corp., Boston, 1922-30, corporate specialist, N.Y.C., 1930-47; asst. sec. Va. Electric & Power Co., Richmond, 1947-57, sec., 1957—. Mem. Am. Soc. Corporate Secs., Newcomen Soc. Ind. Republican. Home: 49 Malvan Av Richmond VA 23221 Office: 700 E Franklin St Richmond VA 23209

KILDEGAARD, INGRID C., advt. exec.; b. N.Y.C.; d. Avel C. and Ellen (Hansen) Kildegaard; A.B., Central Mich. U., 1939; M.A., U. Minn., 1950. High sch. tchrs. in Muskegon Heights and Grand Rapids, Mich., 1939-44; asst. to chief physicist, research lab. Air Reduction Co., 1944-46; statician Ted Bates Advt., N.Y.C., 1950; dir. research Assn. Jr. Leagues Am., 1951-56; with Advt. Research Found., N.Y.C., 1956—, asst. tech. dir., 1964-66, dir. tech. services 1965-68, tech. dir., 1968—, v.p., 1969—, mem. editorial staff jours., 1960—. Chmn. bd. Fed. Statistics Users Conf., 1965-67. Bd. dirs. Luth Found. Religious Drama, 1960—. Fellow A.A.A.S., Am. Statis. Assn. (chmn. com. statistics in marketing 1964—); mem. Am. Marketing Assn. Lutheran (trustee 1959-65). Author: Federal Statistics in Advertising. Home: 420 E 23d St New York City NY 10010 Office: 3 E 54th St New York City NY 10022

KILEY, DANIEL URBAN, landscape architect; b. Boston, Sept. 2, 1912; s. Louis James and Louise (Baxter) K.: student Harvard Grad. Sch. Design, 1936-38; m. Anne Lothrop Sturges, June 11, 1942; children—Kathleen, Kor, Christopher, Antonia, Timothy, Christina, Aaron Alcott, Caleb. From apprentice to asso. Warren Manning, landscape design and regional planning, Cambridge, Mass., 1932- 38; planning technician Concord (N.H.) City Plan Bd., 1938; architect Nat. Park Service, 1939, U.S. Housing Authority, 1940, Asso. Town Planning, Washington, 1940; pvt. practice as landscape architect, site planner, architect, 1940—; lectr., critic Balt. Mus., 1949, Worcester (Mass.) Mus., 1950, La. State U., 1950, Cornell U., 1957, Met. Mus., 1959, N.C. State Coll., 1958, Rensselaer Poly. Inst., 1960, Harvard, 1962-63, Clemson Coll., 1963, also univs. Ill., Minn., Pa., Syracuse, Va., Wash., Yale, U. Cal. at Berkeley, U. Utah, Salt Lake City; prin. works include: Kitimat, B.C., Can. new city, 1951, Rockefeller Inst., N.Y., 1956, Union Carbide & Carbon, Westchester, N.Y., 1957, Reynolds Metals Co., Richmond, Va., 1958, Independence Mall, 3d block, Phila., 1959-60, U. Minn., Mpls., 1960, Lincoln Center, N.Y., 1960, Yale U., 1961, Dulles Internat. Airport, Washington, 1961-63, Nat. Acad. Sci., Washington, 1961, Richmond Civic Center, Cummins Engine Plant, Columbus, Ind., 1962, Burr-McManus Plaza, Hartford, Conn., 1962, Rochester Inst. Tech., 1962, Armstrong Cork Co., Lancaster Pa., 1963, U.S. Air Force Acad., Colorado Springs, Colo., Nat. Center Atmospheric Research, Boulder, Colo., 1963, New Eng. States Worlds Fair, 1963, Fredonia (N.Y.) State Coll., 1963, Potstam (N.Y.) State Coll., E.M. Willard Sch., Troy, N.Y., Central Filtration Plant, Chgo., Chgo. Art Inst., 1963, Chgo. Bright New City—Ellensburg State Coll., 1968. Mem. design rev. panel Redevel. Land Agy., Washington. Mem. BiState Planning Commn., Lake Champlain Basin Region, 1959-63, Pres.'s Adv. Council Planning Pennsylvania Av., Washington, 1962—, Vt. Bd. Architects Registration, 1963, jury S.W. Redevel. Area, Washington, Boston Redevel. Authority, 1963, Nat. Honor Awards, Urban Redevel. Authority, also FHA, Washington, 1964. Served to capt. AUS, World War II. Decorated Legion of Merit; co-recipient 1st prize Jefferson Nat. Expansion Meml. Competition, 1947; U. N.H. Student Union Bldg. Competition, 1951; A.I.A. honor award Concordia State Coll., Ft. Wayne, Ind., 1960, A.I.A. honor award Stiles and Morse Colls., Yale, 1963, A.I.A. honor award Dulles Airport, Washington, 1963; hon. mention Chgo. Tribune Better Homes for Family Living, 1947; award of merit House and Home mag., 1957; 1st prize Progressive Architecture mag., 1961; award of merit Am. Soc. Landscape Architects, 1962, gold medal Phila. chpt. A.I.A., Gov.'s Design award State Cal., 1966; Bard awards, N.Y.C. Ford Found. Ct., 1968, N.Y.C. Lincoln Center North Ct., 1967. Mem. N.A.D., Nat. Council Arts and Govt. Club: Century. Author articles. Address: Wings Point Charlotte VT 05445

KILEY, LEO AUSTIN, ret. air force officer; b. Boston, May 22, 1918; s. Leo A. and Pauline (Barnett) K.; S.B. in Chem. Engring., Mass. Inst. Tech., 1939, student Grad. Sch. Meteorology, 1940; Ph.D. in Nuclear Chemistry, Ohio State U., 1952; LL.D. (hon.) N.M. State U., 1967; m. Luna D. Hamilton, Apr. 16, 1944; children—Michael John, Karen Lee (Mrs. Kenneth W. Hardy), Thomas Leo. Commd. 2d lt. USAAF, 1939, advanced through grades to brig. gen. USAF, 1965; various assignments, U.S., 1941-47; comdr. 15th Weather Squadron, Philippine Islands and Okinawa, 1947, Hickam (Hawaii) Weather Central, 1948-49; student Air Force Command and Staff Sch., 1949; chief plans and operations div. 2059th Air Weather Wing, Tinker AFB, Okla., 1950; chief programs br. and dep. dir., atomic warfare directorate Air Force Cambridge (Mass.) Research Center, 1953-54; dep. chief, then chief biophysics div. Air Force Weapons Center, Kirtland AFB, N.M., 1954-59; asst. dep. chief staff, later dep. chief staff, weapons effects tests, field command, Def. Atomic Support Agy., also mil. dep. test mgr. Nev. test site and comdr. joint task unit 813 Joint Task Force 8, Pacific Proving Ground, 1959-63; vice comdr., later comdr. Air Force Cambridge Research Labs., 1963-65; comdr. Air Force Missile Devel. Center, Holloman AFB, N.M., 1965-67; dep. dir. devel., dep. chief staff research and devel. Hdqrs. USAF, 1967-68; comdr. Office Aerospace Research, Arlington, Va., 1968-69; gen. mgr. neutron devices dept. Gen. Electric, St. Petersburg, Fla., 1969—. Decorated D.S.M., Legion of Merit with oak leaf cluster, Army Commendation medal, various unit and area ribbons. Mem. Am. Geophys. Union, Research Soc. Am., Sigma Xi. Home: 12 Harbor View Lane Largo FL 33540 Office: P O Box 11508 St Petersburg FL 33733

KILEY, RICHARD PAUL, actor; b. Chgo., Mar. 31, 1922; s. Leo Joseph and Leonore (McKenna) K.; student Loyola U., 1940, Barnum Dramatic Sch., Chgo., 1941-42; m. Mary Bell Wood, May 5, 1948; children—David, Michael, Kathleen, Dorothea, Erin, Dierdre. Actor, radio, Chicago, Illinois, 1941; stage appearance, touring co. of Street Car Named Desire; TV appearances in Patterns, Just and Unjust, P.O.W., other shows; appeared Broadway plays, including Misalliance, Kismet, Time Limit, Redhead, Advise and Consent, I Had a Ball (musical), Her First Roman (based on Shaw's Caesar & Cleopatra) 1968; No strings (musical), 1962-63; motion picture appearances include Blackboard Jungle, Phenix City Story, also Spanish Affair, The Mob, Pickup on South Street; played Don Quixote in music-drama, Man of La Mancha (Drama Critics award, Drama Guild award, Antoinette Perry award), 1966. Served with USNR, World War II. Recipient Antoinette Perry award as best actor in a musical, 1958. Club: Players (N.Y.C.). Address: care Arthur Kennard Assos Inc 8776 Sunset Blvd Hollywood CA 90069

KILEY, ROGER JOSEPH, judge; b. Chgo., Oct. 23, 1900; s. Roger and Maria (Quinlan) K.; LL.B., U. Notre Dame, 1923; m. Helen Burke, June 20, 1933; children—Kathleen, Deirdre (Mrs. LeFevour) and Roger Joseph, Maura, Gillian (Mrs. Carey), John. Asst. football coach U. Notre Dame, 1922, Loyola U., 1923-27, Auburn U., 1930-32; admitted to Ill. bar, 1924; judge Superior Ct. of Cook County, 1940, Appellate Ct. of Ill., 1st Dist., 1941-61; judge U.S. Ct. Appeals for 7th Circuit, 1961— Alderman 37th Ward, Chgo., 1933-40. Adv. council U. Notre Dame Law Sch.; dir. Great books Found., Inc., St. Thomas More Assn., Inc., Catholic Charities. Mem. Am., Ill., Chgo. bar assns., Cath. Lawyers Guild. Clubs: University (Chgo.); Butterfield Country (Hinsdale, Ill.). Home: 169 N Grove Av Oak Park IL 60301 Office: 219 S Deaborn St Chicago IL 60604

KILEY, THOMAS HAROLD, banker; b. Kansas, Ill., Mar. 4, 1908; s. James P. and Lois (Fairchild) K.; A.B., U. Ill., 1930; m. Mary Elizabeth Hooper; children—Linda, Sharon, Ann. Credit corr. 1st Nat. City Bank of N.Y., 1930-38; credit mgr. Latin Am. and Caribbean div. U.S. Steel Export Co., 1938-42; v.p., trust officer Ohio Citizens Trust Co., 1942-56; pres., dir. 1st Nat. Bank of Eastern Pa., Wilkes-Barre; dir. Wilkes-Barre Transit Corp., Liberty Throning Co., Inc., Nationwide Tire Co., Inc. (all Wilkes-Barre), UGI Corp., Phila., E.W. Industries, Inc., Stroudsburg, Pa.; lectr. Grad. Sch. Banking, Rutgers U., 1957-58. Dir., Pa. Higher Edn. Assistance Agy., Harrisburg, 1963-67; treas. dir. Econ. Devel. Council N.E. Pa. Active civic, welfare groups; chmn. Greater Wilkes-Barre Indsl. Fund, 1965. Trustee, vice chmn. bd. Wilkes Coll.; trustee Found. Ind. Colls. Inc. Pa., U. Ill. Found. Mem. Pa. (dir.), Greater Wilkes-Barre (pres. 1963-64) chambers commerce, Delta Sigma Rho. Presbyn. Mason. Home: 39 Reynolds St Kingston PA 18704 Office: 11 W Market St Wilkes-Barre PA 18701

KILFEATHER, MICHAEL JOSEPH, news co. exec.; b. N.Y.C., June 14, 1906; s. Michael Joseph and Mary (Mullaney) K.; student Columbia, 1927-29; m. Dorothy Perry, June 1, 1929; children—Paul Edward, Michael Joseph, Robert Francis, Kathleen Marie (Mrs. Ronald Kusky). With Am. News Co., Inc., N.Y.C., 1921—, cashier, 1949-59, asst. treas., 1959-60, treas., 1960-69, v.p., treas., 1969—, dir., 1966—. K.C. Home: Collins St Hillsdale NY 12529 Office: 131 Varick St New York City NY 10013

KILGORE, AL, cartoonist; b. Newark, Dec. 19, 1927; s. Alfred R. and Ruth (Helwig) K.; grad. Art Career Sch., N.Y.C., 1951; m. Dolores M. Preusch, June 7, 1958. Illustrator children's books Pageant Press, 1952-55, gag cartoons for weekly trade paper, 1952-62; author Bullwinkle Comic Books, Western Pub. Co., 1960-62; author, illustrator Bullwinkle newspaper comic strip Bell-McClure Syndicate, 1962-65; advt. comics for Quaker Oats Co., 1965, storyboards for Underdog, TV show, 1966-67; illustrator Pink Panther books Lion Press, 1968; weekly caricature-puzzle feature TV Star-Screen, 1969—; co-producer, dir., author script and lyrics for animated cartoon The World of Hans Christian Andersen, 1970-71. Served with USAAF, 1946-47. Mem. Nat. Cartoonists Soc., Sons of the Desert (a founder), Nat. Orgn. Laurel and Hardy Buffs. Address: 216-55 113th Dr Queens Village NY 11429

KILGORE, JOE MADISON, former congressman, and lawyer; b. Brown County, Texas, Dec. 10, 1918; s. William Henry and Myrtle (Armstrong) K.; student Trinity U., 1935-36, U. Tex., 1936-41; m. Jane Redman, July 28, 1945; children—Mark, Dean, Bill, Shannon. Admitted to Tex. bar, 1946; practiced Edinburg, Texas, 1946-54; mem. Tex. Ho. of Reps., 1946-55; mem. 84th to 88th Congresses, 15th Dist. Tex.; now mem. firm McGinnis, Lochridge & Kilgore, Austin, Tex.; dir. First State Bank & Trust Co., Mission, Tex.; chmn. bd. Tex. State Bank, Austin. Regent U. Tex.; dir. Mission Valley Mills. Served as lt. col. USAAF. World War II; maj. gen. Res. Decorated Silver Star. Distinguished Flying Cross, Air Medal with 2 oak leaf clusters, 2 unit citations, 4 personal citations. Mem. Am., Travis County bar assns., State Bar of Texas, Austin C. of C. (dir.), Delta Theta Phi. Methodist (ofcl. bd.). Democrat. Home: 3311 River Rd Austin TX 78703 Office: Texas State Bank Bldg 900 Congress St Austin TX 78701

KILGORE, JOHN EDWARD, Jr., private investor; b. Wichita Falls, Tex., Jan. 12, 1921; s. John Edward and Lillian (Amery) K.; A.B., Amherst Coll., 1941; LL.B., Harvard, 1944; m. 2d, Emilie Smith Gilbreath, Nov. 27, 1965; children—John Edward III, Constance Pritchett, Ralph, Robert, Alexander. Admitted to Tex. bar, 1948; partner Kilgore & Kilgore, Dallas, 1948-57, J. H. Whitney & Co., N.Y.C., 1957-68, John E. Kilgore & Co., 1968—. Dir. various corps. Served as a naval aviator, 1942-45. Mem. Phi Beta Kappa. Clubs: Links, Union (N.Y.C.); Maidstone (East Hampton, N.Y.). Home: 1407 Kirby Dr Houston, TX 77019. Office: Tenneco Bldg Houston TX 77002

KILGORE, ROBERT JOHN, lawyer; b. Erie, Pa., May 12, 1925; s. Charles D. and Mary Jane (Lee) K.; B.S., Grove City Coll., 1951; LL.B., U. Mich., 1954; m. Betty Baker, Dec. 21, 1946; children—Deborah Jean, Nancy Loulida, Susan Ann. Admitted to Mich. bar, 1955, Pa. bar, 1957; partner Marsh. Spaeder, Baur, Spaeder & Schapf, Erie, 1957-63; gen. counsel, sec. Hammermill Paper Co., Erie, 1964—, v.p., 1971—. Served with USNR, 1943-48. Mem. Am., Pa., Erie County bar assns., Mason. Republican. Home: 2612 Lakeside Dr Erie PA 16511 Office: Hammermill Paper Co 1453 E Lake Rd Erie PA 16507

KILGORE, THOMAS, Jr., clergyman; b. Woodruff, S.C., Feb. 20, 1913; s. Thomas and Eugenia (Langston) K.; A.B., Morehouse Coll., 1935; postgrad. Howard U., 1944- 45; B.D., Union Theol. Sem., 1957; D.D., Shaw U., 1956, Morehouse Coll., 1963, Morris Coll., 1967; m. Jeannetta Miriam Scott, Dec. 28, 1936; children—Lynn Elda, Jini Medina. Ordained to ministry Baptist Ch.; pastor New Bethel Bapt. Ch., Asheville, N.C., 1936-38, Friendship Bapt. Ch., Winston-Salem, N.C., 1938-47, Rising Star Bapt. Ch., Walnut Cove, N.C., 1941-47, Friendship Bapt. Ch., N.Y.C., 1947-63, 2d Bapt. Ch., Los Angeles,

1963—; chaplain Winston-Salem State Tchrs. Coll., 1941-44. Dir. The Bank of Finance, Los Angeles. Exec. sec. Gen. Bapt. State Conv. N.C., 1945-47; pres. Am. Bapt. Conv., 1969; west coast dir. So. Christian Leadership Conf., 1963, nat. bd. dirs., 1959; chmn. Concerned Clergy Los Angeles, 1968; v.p. Los Angeles Council Chrs. 1969; 1st v.p. Progressive Nat. Bapt. Conv., 1966. Trustee Morehouse Coll., Am. Bapt. Sem. of West. Recipient Service award N.Y. YMCA, 1963. Mem. Omega Psi Phi, Chi Alpha. Mason. Co-author: Four Minute Talks for Laymen, 1966. Home: 1238 Westchester Pl Los Angeles CA 90019 Office: 2412 Griffith Av Los Angeles CA 90011

KILGORE, WILLIAM JACKSON, educator; b. Dallas, Apr. 30, 1917; s. Rather Bowlin and Clara (Cole) K.; A.B., Baylor U., 1938; Th.M., So. Bapt. Theol. Sem., 1941. Th.D. (fellow 1941-43), 1943; Ph.D., U. Tex., 1958; student Columbia, 1949; m. Barbara Schmickle, Dec. 4, 1943; 1 dau., Barbara Sullivan. Interim prof. philosophy and religion Georgetown (Ky.) Coll., 1943; prof. philosophy and Greek, Buenos Aires (Argentina) Internat. Sem., 1944-49; prof. philosophy Baylor U., 1949—, chmn. dept., 1959—; asst. prof. philosophy U. Tex., summer 1958. Grantee Danforth Found., 1957-58, Am. Council Learned Socs., 1961. Mem. Am., Southwestern (council 1961, pres. 1963- 64) philos. assns., Am. Assn. U. Profs. (2d v.p.; nat. council 1962-65, 68—; pres. Tex. conf. 1965; chmn. nat. com. on acad. freedom in ch. related instns.), Tex. Philos. Soc., Interam. Soc. Psychology, Alpha Chi. Author: Alejandro Korn's Interpretation of Creative Freedom, 1958; Una evaluación crítica de la philosofía de Alejandro Korn, 1961; One America, Two Cultures, 1965; An Introductory Logic, 1968; also articles in English and Spanish. Home: 305 Guittard Av Waco TX 76706

KILGOUR, BAYARD LIVINGSTON, Jr., telephone exec.; b. Cin. Feb. 27, 1904; s. Bayard Livingston and Virginia Morton (Ernst) K.; B.S., Harvard, 1927; m. Kate E. Gray, Apr. 25, 1931; children—David Gray, Bayard Livingston III. Comml. and statis. work Am. Tel. & Tel. Co., N.Y.C., 1927-30; plant dept., asst. to pres. Cin. Bell, Inc. (formerly Cin. and Suburban Bell Telephone Co.), 1930-31, became v.p. 1931, former chmn. bd., now dir.; dir. Union Central Life Ins. Co., Central Trust Co., Central Bancorp., Inc. Trustee, Herman Schneider Found.; Cin. Mus. Assn. hon. curator Slavic Collections in Harvard Coll. Library. Mem. I.E.E.E., Caledonian Soc., Harvard Engring. Soc. (N.Y.), Newcomen Soc. Presbyn. Clubs: Harvard; The Brook Twenty-Nine (N.Y.C.); Bobemian (San Francisco); Queen City, Harvard, Camargo, Commonwealth, Commercial, Cincinnati Country (Cin.); Fly (Cambridge, Mass.). Home: 4500 Drake Rd Cincinnati OH 45243 Office: 225 E 4th St Cincinnati OH 45202

KILGOUR, DAVID ECKFORD, life ins. exec.; b. Brandon, Man., Can., Dec. 26, 1912; s. Justice J.F. and Geills (McCrae) K.; student St. Andrew's Coll., Aurora, Ont., Can.; B.A., U. Man., 1933; m. Mary Sophia Russell, 1936; children—Geills McCrae (Mrs. John N. Turner), David William, Donald Alexander. With Great-West Life Assurance Co. of Winnipeg, Can., 1933-71, beginning as mem. agy. dept., sec., supt. agys., asst. gen. mgr. and supt. agys., asst. gen. mgr. and dir. agys., gen. mgr., dir., 1933-58, v.p., mng. dir., 1958-59, pres., 1959-71. Past mem. exec. com. Am. Life Conv. Past chmn. Canadian council Nat. Indsl. Conf. Bd.; dir. Nat. Indsl. Conf. Bd. U.S. Office: 201 Drumore Av Winnipeg 9 Manitoba Canada

KILGOUR, FREDERICK GRIDLEY, librarian; b. Springfield, Mass., Jan. 6, 1914; s. Edward Francis and Lillian Bess (Piper) K.; A.B., Harvard, 1935; student Columbia Sch. Library Service, summers, 1939-41; m. Eleanor Margaret Beach, Sept. 3, 1940; children—Christopher Beach, Martha, Alison, Meredith. Staff, Harvard Coll. Library, 1935-42, OSS, 1942-45; dept. dir. office of intelligence collection and dissemination, U.S. Dept. State, 1946-48; librarian Yale Med. Library, 1948-65, asso. librarian for research and devel. Yale U. Library, 1965-67, mng. editor Yale Jour. Biology and Medicine 1949-65, lectr. in history of sci. Yale 1950-59, lectr. history of tech., 1961-67, fellow Davenport Coll., 1950-67; dir. Ohio Coll. Library Center, Columbus, 1967—. Served as lt. (j.g.) USNR, 1943-46; overseas duty, 1944-45. Decorated Legion of Merit. Mem. A.L.A., Med. Library Assn., Am. Soc. Information Sci. Author: Library of the Medical Institution of Yale College and Its Catalogue of 1865, 1960. Co-author: Engineering in History, 1956. Editor: Cristobal Mendez, Book of Bodily Exercises, 1960; Jour. Library Automation. Contbr. to scholarly jours. Home: 1415 Kirkley Rd Columbus OH 43221 Office: 1314 Kinnear Rd Columbus OH 43212

KILHAM, LAWRENCE, educator, virologist; b. Brookline, Mass., Aug. 10, 1910; s. Walter H. and Jane (Houston) K.; A.B., Harvard, 1932, M.A., 1935, M.D., 1940; m. Jane Kaufholz, May 10, 1941; children—Peter, Michael, Joshua, Benjamin, Phoebe. Intern medicine Lakeside Hosp., Cleve., 1940-41; physician Harvard-Red Cross Hosp., Salisbury, Eng., 1941-42; with dept. epidemiology Harvard Sch. Pub. Health, 1946-49, NIH, 1949-53, 56-61, Virus Research Inst., Entebbe, Uganda, 1954-55, Rocky Mountain Lab., Hamilton, Mont., 1955-56; prof. microbiology Dartmouth Med. Sch., 1961- -. Served with M.C., AUS, 1942-46; ETO. Research Carrer award, Nat. Cancer Inst., 1964. Mem. Soc. Exptl. Biology and Medicine, A.A.A.S., Am. Ornothologists Union. Discoverer K-virus of mice, Kilham rat virus, squirrel fibroma virus. Home: Lyme NH 03768 Office: Dartmouth Med Sch Hanover NH 03755

KILHAM, WALTHER H., Jr., architect; b. Brookline, Mass., Apr. 29, 1904; s. Walter Harrington and Jane (Houston) K.; A.B., Harvard, 1925, M.Arch., 1928; postgrad. N.Y. U. Sch. Architecture, 1929-30, Grad. Sch. Bus. Adminstrn., 1931; m. Louise Collins, Jan. 23, 1943; children—Leslie (Mrs. Jeffrey Johnson), Timothy, Eleanor, Amy Edna. With Rockefeller Center Architects, 1929-32; partner Van der Gracht & Kilham, asso. architects, 1937-42, O'Connor & Kilham, N.Y.C., 1943-68, Kilham, Beder & Chu, 1969—. Principal architect, Zone Constructing Quartermaster, Zone Two, 1941; chief, site planning sect., U.S. Engrs. N.Y. Dist. 1942-43; architect-engr. for war projects, 1944-45; prin. works include Hinton House (Putney, Vt.), Lincoln Hall Sch. (Westchester), Carroll (Wis.) Coll. Library, Firestone Library, Princeton U.; restoration 'Old Kenyon', Ohio; home office bldg. Phoenix Ins. Co., Hartford; library U. Louisville, Tokeneke Sch., Darien, Nat. Library of Medicine, cadet barracks West Point, Robert Frost Library, Amherst; architect-engr. for def. projects, 1951-57; partner joint venture O'Connor & Kilham with Clarke & Rapuano, James Mongitore & Assos., and Weiskopf & Pickworth on expansion plan of U.S. Mil. Acad., West Point; asso. prof. architecture Va. Poly. Inst., 1954; vis. lectr. Princeton, 1953-56; mem. vis. com. Nat. Architect Accrediting Bd., 1945-60. Mem. Mass. N.G., 4 years, F.A. Res., 10 years. Wheelwright fellow Harvard, 1938. Trustee Beaux Arts Inst. Design, 1947-49, Putney Sch., Putney Grad. Sch. Tchr. Edn., 1951-54. Fellow A.I.A. (past pres. N.Y. chpt.; mem. survey commn. archtl. edn. and registration (Carnegie Funds), 1950-54; Arnold Brunner scholarship N.Y. chpt. 1969) N.A.D.; mem. Fine Arts Fedn. N.Y. (pres. 1955-57), Nat. Sculpture Soc., Am. Craftsmens Council (trustee 1960—), Soc. Am. Mil. Engrs. Clubs: Harvard Travelers (Boston); Coffee House, Century Association, Explorers (N.Y.C.). Home: 314 N Maple Av Greenwich CT 06830 Office: 101 Park Av New York City NY 10017

KILKENNY, JOHN FRANCIS, U.S. judge; b. Heppner, Ore., Oct. 26, 1901; s. John Sheridan and Rose Ann (Curran) K.; LL.B. cum laude, U. Notre Dame, 1925; m. Virginia Brannock, Oct. 14, 1931; children—John Michael, Karen Margaret. Admitted to Ore. bar, 1926, and practiced in Pendleton; partner Kilkenny & Fabre and predecessors, 1926-59; judge, U.S. Dist. Ct. of Ore., 1959-69, U.S. Ct. Appeals, 1969—. Pres., dir. Happy Canyon Co., 1939-40. Mem. Ore. Bd. Bar Examiners, 1951, 52. Trustee Ore. State Library, Umatilia County Library; mem. bd. trustees U. Portland. Fellow Am. Bar Found., Am. Coll. Trial Lawyers; mem. Am. Oregon (president 1943-44) bar assns., American Judicature Society, American Irish Historical Soc. (vice president), Ore. Geographic Names Bd., Knight Malta. Republican. Roman Catholic. Clubs: University; Arlington. Author: Shamrocks and Shepherds. Home: 821 S W Davenport Portland OR 97201 Office: U S Courthouse Portland OR 97205

KILKER, CLARENCE CHRISTIAN, investment banker b. Le Mars, Ia., July 13, 1905; s. Chris A. and Lena (Hinz) K.; B.A., Westmar Coll., 1927; B.S., Morningside Coll., 1931; M.A., U. Neb., 1938; postgrad. U. So. Cal., summer 1934, Columbia, 1941, U. Kan., 1942; m. Edna D. Spiecker, July 10, 1932; children—Wallace Jay, Karen Kay (Mrs. Harold G. Brown). Tchr., Onslow (Ia.) High Sch., 1927-28; prin. Newburg (Mo.) High Sch., 1928-30; tchr., prin. South Sioux City (Neb.) Jr. High Sch., 1931-37; prin. South Sioux City High Sch., 1937- 39, Manhattan (Kan.) Jr. High Sch., 1939-44; summer instr. U. Kan., 1942, Kan. State U., 1943; mgr. Manhattan C. of C. and Credit Bur., 1944-48; exec. v.p. Kan. C. of C., Topeka, 1949-70; registered rep. Seltsam, Hanni & Co., Topeka, 1970—. Summer instr. S.W. Inst. Orgn. Mgmt., 1947-48, U. Colo., 1948, 64. Sec. Manhattan Viking Co., Inc., 1945-48; pres. Lil' Duffer of Neb., Inc., 1966—; lectr. coll., univ. workshops on econ. edn. for tchrs., summers 1959—; profl. speaker community devel., mgmt., pvt. enterprise econs. Mem. Council of State C. of C.'s (exec. com. 1953; sec. 1961), Kan Assn. Orgn. Mgrs. (past pres.), Asso. Credit Burs. Kan. (past pres.), U.S., Kan., Topeka chambers commerce, Alpha Kappa Psi, Phi Kappa Delta. Presbyn. (trustee, deacon). Home: 1316 Campbell Av Topeka KS 66604 Office: First National Bank Tower Topeka KS 66603

KILLE, FRANK RALPH educator, zoologist; b. Salem, O., Aug. 2, 1904; s. Ellsworth and Retta (Vogel) K.; B.S., Coll. Wooster, 1926, LL.D., 1954; S.M., U. Chgo., 1929, Ph.D., 1934; m. Frances Kerby, Aug. 24, 1929; 1 son, J. Frank. Tchr. biology and chemistry, Hubbard (O.) High Sch., 1926-28; asst. prof. zoology, Birmingham-So. Coll., 1929-30, asso. prof., 1930-31; asst. in zoology U. Chgo., 1931-33, U. Rochester, 1933; instr. zoology, Swarthmore Coll., 1934-36, asst. prof., 1936-43; asso. prof. zool., 1943-45, acting dean, summer 1944; part-time lecturer in biol., Bryn Mawr Coll., 1943; dean of men and prof. zoology, Carleton Coll., Northfield, Minn., 1945-46, dean of coll. and prof. zoology, 1946-57; asso. commr. for higher and profl. edn. N.Y., 1958-67, dir. Office Sci. and Tech., 1967-69; asso. commr. sci., tech. and professions, N.Y. State Edn. Dept., 1969—; mem. zoology staff, Marine Biol. Lab., Woods Hole, Mass., summers 1935-39; guest investigator Carnegie Instn., Marine Biology Sta., Tortugas, summers 1936, 37; Served as coordinator Navy V-12 premed. program, Swarthmore Coll., World War II. Fellow A.A.A.S.; mem. Am. Soc. Zoologists, Am. Conf. Acad. Deans (chmn. 1953), Am. Assn. Anatomists, Marine Biol. Lab. Corp., Sigma Xi, Phi Beta Kappa. Home: 340 Albany Shaker Rd Loudonville NY 12211 Office: NY State Edn Dept Albany NY 12210

KILLEBREW, GWENDOLYN, mezzo-soprano; grad. Temple U.; with Met. Opera, 1966—; appeared in Die Walkure, Carmen, Masked Ball, Martha. Address: Met Opera Co Lincoln Center New York City NY*

KILLEBREW, HARMON, mem. Minnesota Twins Profl. Baseball Team. Named Most Valuable Player in Am. League. 1969. Address: care Metropolitan Stadium 8001 Cedar Av Bloomington MN 55402 *

KILLEEN, SYLVESTER MICHAEL, clergyman; b. Rice Lake, Wis., Jan. 6, 1905; s. Thomas Michael and Bridget (McLeod) K.; A.B., St. Norbert Coll., 1927, L.H.D., 1969; student St. Norbert Abbey Sem., 1927-31; A.M., Cath. U. Am., 1936, Ph.D., 1939. Entered Order of Norbertines, 1925; ordained priest Roman Catholic Ch., 1930; instr. St. Norbert High Sch., 1930-32; asst. dir. Columbus Community Club, Green Bay, Wis., 1932-35; prin. Central Cath. High Sch., 1941-47; coadjutor abbot at St. Norbert Abbey, De Pere, 1947-55, abbot, 1955-70, also exec. v.p. St. Norbert Coll., 1947-55, chancellor, 1955—, trustee, 1970—. Mem. Nat. Cath. Philos. Assn., Wis. Hist. Soc. Address: St Norbert Abbey De Pere WI 54115

KILLEFER, TOM, corp. exec., lawyer; b. Los Angeles, Jan. 7, 1917; s. Wade and Dorothy (Parks) K.; A.B. cum laude, Stanford; J.D., Harvard, 1942; B.C.L., Oxford U., 1947; m. Carolyn Clothier, Apr. 17, 1948; children—Wade II, Caroline, Gail, Anne. Admitted to Cal. bar, 1946, D.C. bar, 1954, Mich. bar, 1966; with Lillick, Geary, Wheat, Adams & Charles, Cal. and Washington, 1947-49, partner, 1956-59; staff U.S. High Commn. for Germany, 1951-52; exec. dir. Com. Am. Steamship Lines, 1959-60; 1st v.p., vice chmn., dir. Export-Import Bank of Washington, 1960-62; U.S. exec. dir. Inter-Am. Devel. Bank, spl. asst. to Sec. of Treasury, 1962- 66; exec. asst. to v.p. legal affairs Chrysler Corp., Detroit, 1966-67, v.p. finance, 1967, v.p. finance, gen. counsel, 1968—, also dir.; dir. Chrysler Leasing Corp., Chrysler Financial Corp., Chrysler Realty Corp., Chrysler Overseas Capital Corp., Chrysler France, Chrysler U.K., Chrysler Spain, Big Sky of Mont., Car City Ins. Co., Adela Investment Co., S.A., Luxembourg. Sr. adviser, mem. U.S. delegation 1st and 2d ann. meetings Inter-Am. Econ. and Social Council. Bd. dirs. Detroit Symphony Orch.; exec. com., bd. dirs., finance com. Fgn. Policy Assn., Overseas Devel. Council, United Found. Atlantic Council U.S.; trustee Merrill-Palmer Inst., Detroit Area Council World Affairs, Pine Manor Jr. Coll. Served to lt. (s.g.) USNR, 1941- 46. Decorated D.F.C. (Navy), Air medal, Purple Heart. Mem. Am. Soc. Internat. Law, State Bar Cal., Am., Inter-Am. bar assns., State Bar Mich., Am. Assn. Rhodes Scholars, Assn. Gen. Counsel, Phi Beta Kappa, Zeta Psi. Episcopalian (vestryman 1960-65). Clubs: Alibi, Alfalfa, Chevy Chase, Metropolitan (Washington); University, Country Detroit, Detroit, Yondotega (Detroit); Pacific Union (San Francisco); Links (N.Y.). Home: 350 Provencal Rd Grosse Pointe Farms MI 48236 Office: 341 Massachusetts Av Detroit MI 48231

KILLELEA, JOSEPH RICHARD, univ. adminstr.; b. N.Y.C., July 14, 1917; s.Charles Joseph and Margaret (McSherry) K.; B.S., Manhattan Coll., 1940; Ph.D., N.Y.U., 1949; m. Lillian Ruth Smith, Nov. 18, 1950; 1 dau., Ellen Marie. Instr. chemistry Manhattan Coll., 1940-44; teaching fellow N.Y.U., 1944-48; prof. chemistry, head dept. Iona Coll., New Rochelle, N.Y., 1948-52; sr. engr. Westinghouse Electric Co., 1952-53; tech. dir. Mineral Boneficiation Lab., Columbia, 1953-58, mgr. tech. services Indsl. Reactor Lab., 1958-63; dir. Nuclear Center, Lowell (Mass.) Tech. Inst., 1963—. Mem. Am. Nuclear Soc., Am. Chem. Soc., Sigma Xi. Home: 25 Berkeley Dr Chelmsford MA 01824 Office: 1 Textile Av Lowell MA 01854

KILLEN, JAMES S., fgn. service officer; b. Jan. 13, 1904. Gen. rep., then 1st v.p. labor unions, 1937-52; asst. to dir. of bur. WPB, 1944-45; chief labor div. SCAP, 1947-48, ECA, London, 1949-50; chief MSA mission to Yugoslavia, 1952-53; with FOA, 1953-55, ICA, 1955-56; dir. USOM, Karachi, 1957-59, Seoul, 1961-62, Saigon, 1964-65; dir. AID mission to Turkey, 1967—. Address: Am Embassy AID Ankara Turkey*

KILLEN, ROBERT BURTON, utility exec.; b. Dayton, O., July 13, 1913; s. Leo C. and E. Myrle (Clark) K.; E.E., U. Cin., 1936; m. Amber Heintzelman, June 24, 1939; children—Kathleen (Mrs. Robert H. Blank), Timothy, Constance, Calvin. With Dayton Power & Light Co. (O.), 1933—, group v.p., 1968-70, exec. v.p., 1970-71, pres., 1971—; dir. Winters Nat. Bank & Trust Co. Mem. Ohio Elec. Utility Inst. (dir.), Dayton Area C. of C. (dir.), I.E.E.E., Engrs. Club Dayton (bd. govs. 1966-68). Home: 93 W Ridgeway Rd Centerville OH 45459 Office: 25 N Main St Dayton OH 45401

KILLENBERG, GEORGE ANDREW, newspaper editor; b. St. Clair County, Ill., Mar. 17, 1917; s. George W. and Lavina (Ruhl) K.; B.S., St. Louis U., 1954, M.A., 1958; m. Therese Murphy, June 3, 1943; children—George M., Mary C., John A., Terry M., Susan M. Engaged in pub. relations, 1935-41; mem. staff St. Louis Globe- Democrat, 1941—, city editor, 1956-66, mng. editor, 1966—. Bd. dirs. Boys Town Mo., 1960—, St. Louis div. Mo. Assn. for Social Welfare. Chmn. Mid-Am. Press Inst. Served with AUS, 1942-46. Mem. Sigma Delta Chi. Roman Catholic. Clubs: Press (pres. 1964), Media (St. Louis). Home: 3042 Hatherly Dr Bel-Nor MO 63121 Office: 710 N 12th St St Louis MO 63101

KILLENS, JOHN OLIVER, author; b. Macon, Ga.; ed. Edward Waters Coll., Morris Brown Coll., Howard U., Terrell Law Sch., Columbia, N.Y. U.; married; 2 children. Founder, chmn. Harlem Writers' Guild Workshop; writer-in-residence Fisk U.; tchr. creative writing New Sch. Social Research; now adjunct prof. Columbia, also head Creative Writer's Workshop, Black Culture Seminar. Formerly staff NLRB. Served with armed forces World War II; PTO. Author: Youngblood; And Then We Heard the Thunder, 1963; Black Man's Burden (essays), 1966; 'sippi, 1967; Odds Against Tomorrow (screenplay). Editor: The Trial Record of Denmark Vesey, 1970; The Cotillion, 1971. Home: Brooklyn NY Office: care Trident Press Inc 630 Fifth Av New York City NY 10020

KILLGORE, ANDREW IVY, fgn. service officer; b. Greensboro, Ala., Nov. 7, 1919; s. Robert Morris and Mary Elmae (Wimberly) K.; B.S., Livingston (Ala.) State Tchrs. Coll., 1943; LL.B., U. Ala., 1949; m. Marjorie Elizabeth Davis, Dec. 10, 1948; children—Elizabeth Nicholls, Andrew Nicholls, Jane Grace, Roberta Morris. Admitted to Ala. bar, 1949; joined U.S. Fgn. Service, 1950; consul. Jerusalem, 1957-59; head polit. sect. Am. embassy, Amman, Jordan, 1959-61; officer-in-charge Iraq-Jordan affairs Dept. State, 1962- 65; pub. affairs officer Am. embassy, Baghdad, Iraq, 1965-67; polit. officer (consul), Dacca, East Pakistan, 1967—. Served to lt. (j.g.) USNR, 1943-46. Mem. Phi Alpha Delta. Address: Am Consulate Gen APO New York City NY 09683

KILLIAN, JAMES R., Jr., coll. adminstr.; b. Blacksburg, S.C., July 24, 1904; s. James Robert and Jeannette (Rhyne) K.; student Trinity Coll. Duke U., 1921-23, LL.D., 1949; B.S., Mass. Inst. Tech., 1926; hon. Sc.D., Middlebury Coll., 1945, Bates Coll., 1950, U. Havana, Cuba, 1953, Notre Dame U., 1954, Lowell Tech. Inst., 1954, Columbia, Coll. Wooster, Oberlin Coll., 1958, U. Akron, 1959, Worcester Poly. Inst., 1960, U. Me., 1963; LL.D., Union Coll., 1947, Bowdoin Coll., Northeastern U., 1949, Boston U., Harvard, 1950, Williams Coll., Lehigh U., U. Pa., 1951, U. Chattanooga, 1954, Tufts U., 1955, U. Cal., Amherst Coll., 1956. Coll. William and Mary, 1957, Brandeis U., 1958, Johns Hopkins, N.Y.U., 1959, Providence Coll., Temple U., 1960, U. S.C., 1961, Meadville Theol. Sch., 1962; D.Applied Sci., U. Montreal, 1958; D.Eng., Drexel Inst. Tech., 1948, U. Ill., 1960, U. Mass., 1961; Ed.D. (hon.), R.I. Coll., 1962; H.H.D., Rollins Coll., 1964; m. Elizabeth Parks, Aug. 21, 1929; children—Carolyn (Mrs. Paul Staley), Rhyne Meredith. Asst. mng. editor Technology Rev., 1926-27, mng. editor, 1927-30, editor, 1930-39; exec. asst. to pres. Mass. Inst. Tech., 1939-43, exec. v.p., 1943-45, v.p., 1945-48, pres., 1948-59, chmn. corp., 1959-70; dir. Am. Tel. & Tel. Co., Cabot Corp., Polaroid Corp., Gen. Motors Corp., Corp. for Pub. Broadcasting. Chmn. Carnegie Commn. on Ednl. TV, 1965-67. Mem. Pres.' Communication Policy Bd., 1950-51, President's Com. on Mgmt., 1950-52; mem. sci. adv. com. ODM, 1951-57; chmn. Army Sci. Adv. Panel, 1951-56; chmn. Pres.' Bd. Cons. on Fgn. Intelligence Activities, 1956- 57; spl. asst. to Pres. U.S. for sci. and tech., 1957-59; chmn. Pres.' Sci. Adv. Com., 1957-59, mem., 1957-61, cons., 1961—; mem. Adv. Council on State Depts. Edn., U.S. Office Edn., 1965-68; chmn. President's Fgn. Intelligence Adv. Bd., 1961-63; mem. gen. adv. bd. U.S. Arms Control and Disarmament Agy., 1969—. Recipient President's Certificate of Merit, 1948, Certificate of Appreciation, Dept. of Army, 1953; Exceptional Civilian Service award Dept. of Army; Pub. Welfare medal Nat. Acad. Scis., 1957; George Foster Peabody Broadcasting Spl. Edn. award, 1968; decorated Croix d'officer, Legion of Honor (France), 1957; Hoover medal, 1963, others. Bd. visitors U.S. Naval Acad., 1953-55; moderator Am. Unitarian Assn., 1960-61. Trustee Nutrition Found., 1954-70, Washington U., 1966-70, Mt. Holyoke Coll., Alfred P. Sloan Found., Boston Mus. Fine Arts, Mitre Corp. (chmn. 1967-69); bd. dirs. Nat. Merit Scholarship Corp., 1960-63; mem. Mass. Bd. Edn., 1962-65. Fellow Am. Acad. Arts and Scis.; mem. Nat. Acad. Engring., Am. Soc. Engring. Edn. (hon.), Sigma Chi, Phi Beta Kappa (hon.), Tau Beta Pi (hon.). Clubs: Metropolitan (Washington); Odd Volumes, St. Botolph Union, Algonquin (Boston); Century, University (N.Y.C.). Address: care Mass Inst Technology Cambridge MA 02139

KILLIAN, LEWIS MARTIN, educator; b. Darien, Ga., Feb. 15, 1919; s. Lewis Martin and Edith (Robinson) K.; A.B., U. Ga., 1940, M.A., 1941; Ph.D., U. Chgo., 1949; m. Katharine Newbold Goold, Apr. 11, 1942; children—Katharine Newbold, Lewis Martin, John Calhoun. Asst. prof. sociology U. Okla., 1949-52; asso. prof. sociology Fla. State U., 1952-57, prof., 1957-68, chmn. dept. sociology, 1966-68; prof., head dept. sociology U. Conn., 1968-69; prof. U. Mass., Amherst, 1969—; vis. prof. U. Cal. at Los Angeles, 1965-66; cons. com. disaster studies NRC, 1952-57; cons. to atty. gen. of Fla., 1954-55. Col. USAR Mem. Am., So. (v.p.) sociol. socs., Phi Beta Kappa, Omicron Delta Kappa, Kappa Alpha. Author: (with Ralph H. Turner) Collective Behavior, 1957; (with Charles M. Grigg) Racial Crisis in America, 1963; The Impossible Revolution, 1968; White Southerners, 1970. Home: 19 Hickory Lane Amherst MA 01002

KILLIAN, ROBERT KENNETH, atty. gen. Conn.; b. Hartford, Conn., Sept. 15, 1919; s. Edward Francis and Annie (Nemser) K.; B.A., Union Coll., Schenectady, 1942; LL.B., U. Conn., 1948; m. Mildred Evelyn Farnan, Dec. 7, 1942; children—Robert Kenneth, Cynthia Elaine. Admitted to Conn. bar, 1948, since practiced in Hartford; partner firm Gould Killian & Krechevsky, 1948—; asst. corp. counsel, Hartford, 1951-54; atty. gen. Conn., 1967—. Chmn. Conn. com. Nat. Jewish Hosp. and Research Center, Denver, 1968—. Chmn. Hartford Democratic Town Com., 1963-67. Trustee Hartford div. Conn. Cancer Soc., 1959—; bd. dirs. Hartford Legal Aid Soc., 1967—. Served to 1st lt., inf., AUS, 1942-46. Decorated Purple Heart.

Mem. Am., Conn., Hartford bar assns., Am. Judicature Soc., Am. Trial Lawyers Soc. K.C., Elk. Home: 234 Terry Rd Hartford CT 06105 Office: 37 Lewis St Hartford CT 06103

KILLIAN, THOMAS JOSEPH, physicist; b. Schenectady, Aug. 4, 1904; s. Edwin Albert and Abigail (Fitzgerald) K.; B.S. and M.S. in Elec. Engring., Mass. Inst. Tech., 1926; A.M., Princeton, 1927, Ph.D., 1929; m. Ilona Elizabeth Bucko, Sept. 12, 1938; 1 son, Thomas J. Instr. elec. engring. Mass. Inst. Tech., 1929-30, physics, 1930-32; physicist Barkon Tube Lighting Corp., Seattle, 1932-33, dir. research and v.p., 1933-39; dir. research Frink Corp., Barkon-Frink Corp., 1939-41; dir. Frink Corp., L.I. City, N.Y., since 1948. Dean maths. Seattle U., 1933-36; dean engring. and architecture Cath. U., Washington, 1954-56; dean engring. U. Portland, 1965-69; prof. applied sci. Portland State U., 1969—; Ore., 1970—. Head of sci. br. Office of Naval Research, 1946-47, sci. dir., research div., 1947-52. Served from lt. to capt. USNR, 1941-46, rear adm., 1961—; head physics br. Naval Postgrad. Sch., 1942-44; radar and guided missile coordinator Office of Chief of Naval Operations, 1944-46; on inactive duty since 1946; tng. officer Vol. Research Res. since 1949; weapons systems evaluation group under Joint Chiefs of Staff 1950-51; sci. dir. Office of Ordnance Research, U.S. Army, 1952-54, cons. Office Operations Research 1954—; dep. chief, and chief sci., Office Naval Research, 1955-61; dir. research and asst. to pres. for sci. and engring. Seattle U., 1962- 64; sci. dir. Scientic Research Labs., Inc., Seattle, 1964-65. Registered profl. engr., Wash., D.C. Fellow A.A.A.S., I.E.E.E.; mem. Am. Geophys. Union, Nat. Soc. Profl. Engrs., Am. Soc. Engring. Edn., Naval Res. Assn., Res. Officers Assn., Illuminating Engring. Soc., Am. Phys. Soc., Operation Research Soc., Albertus Magnus Guild (pres. 1965—), Phi Kappa, Tau Beta Pi, Sigma Xi. Roman Catholic. Clubs: Technology (N.Y.C.); Cosmos (Washington); City (chmn. noise control com.), University (Portland). Holder patents on pressure control devices and electronic developments. Author publs. on thermionics, discharges in gases, electronics, illumination, artifical day-lighting, statistics, research planning and adminstrn. Home: 4409 N Willamette Blvd Portland OR 97203

KILLIN, CHARLES CLARK, lawyer; b. Peoria, Ill., June 12, 1923; s. Thomas James and Marie (Clark) K.; A.B., U. Mich., 1947, LL.B., 1950. Admitted to Okla. bar, 1950, since practiced in Tulsa; partner firm Conner, Winters, Ballaine, Barry & McGowen and predecessor firm, 1958—. Served with AUS, 1943-46. Mem. Am., Okla., Tulsa County bar assns., Theta Chi, Phi Alpha Delta. Republican. Presbyn. Rotarian. Home: 2130 E 59th St Tulsa OK 74105 Office: First Nat Bldg Tulsa OK 74103

KILLIN, RICHARD C., advt. agy. exec. Sr. v.p. Young and Rubicam, Inc., N.Y.C. Office: 285 Madison Av New York City NY 10017*

KILLINGER, GEORGE GLENN, psychologist, criminologist; b. Marion, Va., Mar. 13, 1908; s. James Peter and Lena (Kelly) K.; A.B., Wittenberg Coll., 1930; Ph.D., U. of N.C., 1933; LL.D., Wittenberg Coll., 1953; m. Grace Davis, June 29, 1935; children—Robert Peter, Evangeline, George Evan. Research asst., Mooseheart Lab. for Child Research, summers, 1929-31; instr. psychology, U. of N.C., 1930-33; asst. personnel dir., Mathieson Alkali Works, 1933-34; psychologist and spl. asst. to personnel dir., Tenn. Valley Authority, Knoxville, 1934-36; dir., out-patient and social service, Southwestern State Hosp., Marion, Va., 1936-37; psychologist USPHS, Fed. Reformatory, Chillicothe, O., 1937-38; supervisor of edn., U.S. Penitentiary, Atlanta, 1938-40, asst. asso. warden, 1940-41; supervisor of edn., U.S. Bur. of Prisons, Washington, 1941-43; chief, psychobiol. activites, War Shipping Adminstrn., 1943-47; chmn. clemency and parole bd., Office of Sec. of Army, Washington, 1947-48; chmn. U.S. bd. of parole, Dept. of Justice, Washington, 1948-53, mem., 1953-60. Lectr. George Washington U., 1953- 54; prof. dept. criminology and corrections Fla. State U., 1960-65; dir. Inst. Contemporary Corrections and Behavioral Sciences, Sam Houston State Coll., Huntsville, 1965—. Mem. Tex. Commn. on Law Enforcement Standards and Edn. Served as lt. comdr., commd. officer USPHS, 1943-47; scientist dir. U.S. Public Health Service Reserve. Recipient research grant U.S. Dept. Labor, 1966. Diplomate in clinical psychology Am. Bd. Examiners in Profl. Psychology, Am. Psychol. Assn. Fellow, Am. Psychol. Assn., A.A.A.S.; mem. Am. Prison Assn. Am. Assn. Adult Edn., U.S.P.H.S. Res. Officers Assn., Ednl. Found., Inc., Nat. Probation Parole Assn. (adv. council, 1952-54), Wittenberg Alumni Assn. (Washington, p.p.). Am. Legion, Alpha Psi Delta, Phi Mu Delta, Psi Chi, Pi Kappa Alpha. Democrat. Lutheran. Clubs: Kiwanis, Advt. (N.Y.). Kenwood Golf and Country, Touchdown, Univ. (Washington); Warwick (Houston); Huntsville (Huntsville, Tex.). Author: The Psychobiological Program of the War Shipping Administration, 1947; Personality Disorders, 1946; Prison Work as a Post-War Career, 1946. Contbr. numerous sci. articles to tech. and professional publs. Home: 2209 Avenue S Huntsville TX 77340

KILLINGSWORTH, CHARLES CLINTON, economist; b. Webb City, Mo., Jan. 1, 1917; s. James Ray and Genevieve Theresa (Beahan) K.; A.B., Mo. State Coll., 1938; A.M., Okla. State U., 1939; Ph.D., U. Wis., 1946; m. Beverly Hannah Kritzman, Feb. 6, 1943 (dec. Aug. 1970); children—Mark Robert, Charlotte Eve; m. 2d, Jacquelyn Brown Schrecengost, June 19, 1971. Instr. polit. economy Johns Hopkins, 1941-45; chief, analytical studies unit Social Security Adminstrn., 1945-46; panel chmn. and spl. hearing officer Nat. War Labor Bd., 1943-46; mem. faculty Mich. State U., 1947—, prof. and head dept. econs., 1949-57, dir. Labor and Indsl. Relations Center, 1956-59, Univ. prof., 1960—. Arbitrator labor-mgmt., disputes since 1943; permanent umpire Bethlehem Steel Co. and United Steel Workers Am. 1947- 52; nat. umpire U.S. Rubber Co., Rubber Workers Union, 1953-55, Ford Motor Co. and UAW, 1955-58; nat. umpire Goodyear Tire & Rubber Co. and United Rubber Workers, 1959-61; acting chmn. Bd. Conciliation and Arbitration U.S. Steel Corp., United Steelworkers Am. (CIO), 1950-51; cons. to WSB, 1951 (chmn. 1952-53); permanent umpire Youngstown Sheet & Tube Co. and Steelworkers, 1963-67; permanent arbitrator Firestone Tire & Rubber Co. and Rubber Workers, 1971—, Crucible Steel Co. and Steelworkers, 1971—. Mem. panel arbitrators Am. Arbitration Assn., Fed. Mediation and Conciliation Service; mem. Nat. Manpower Policy Task Force, 1965—. Mem. Nat. Acad. of Arbitrators (v.p. 1958-60; bd. govs. 1952-55; pres. 1968), Indsl. Relations Research Assn. (exec. bd. 1956-58), Am. Econ. Assn., Am. Assn. U. Profs., Delta Sigma Pi. Author: State Labor Relations Acts, 1948; co-author: Trade Union Publns. 1851-1941 (3 vols.), 1944-45; Jobs and Income for Negroes, 1968; also articles in field of econs. Home: 4584 Sequoia Trail Okemos MI 48864

KILLION, FREDERICK WILLIAM, Jr., lawyer; b. Mobile, Oct. 11, 1934; s. Frederick William and Mildred (McKinney) K.; A.B., U. Ala., 1955, LL.B., 1956; m. Peggy Ann Boyd, June 4, 1952; children-Kimberly Dianne, Frederick William III, James Willard, John Timothy. Admitted to Ala. bar, 199, since practiced in Mobil; partner firm Pillans, Reams, Tappan Wood & Roberts, 1963—; Bd. dirs. Mobile Jr. Co. of C, 1960-68, pres., 1966-67; bd. dirs. Am. Jr. Miss Pagenat, 1965-67, Ala. Deep Sea Fishing Rodio, 1960-62, Mobile Azalea Trail, 1960-62. Bd. dirs. Child Day Care Center, 1968-70; adv. bd. Youthpower, 1966-67. Served with AUS, 1956-58. Named Outstanding Man of Year, 1968. Mem. Ala., Mobile, Mobile County (pres. jr. bar sect. 1964- 65) bar assns., Phi Alpha Delta. Home: 2772 Graffhill Dr Mobile AL 36601 Office: PO Box 2245 Mobile AL 36601

KILLION, GEORGE LEONARD, steamship exec.; b. Steamboat Springs, Colo., Apr. 15, 1901; s. James Abraham and Lydia Jane (Harris) K.; student U. So. Cal., 1920-21, U. Cal., 1921-22; m. Grace Ludora Harris, Dec. 25, 1922 (dec.); 1 son, James L.; m. 2d, Margaretha Rhaneberg. Mem. editorial staff various West Coast newspapers, 1925-30; pub. relations, financial cons., Oakland, Cal., 1930-35; pub. relations, legislative cons. Safeway Stores, Oakland, 1935-39; commr. Golden Gate Internat. Expdn., 1939; dir. of finance, State Cal., 1940-43; asst. to petroleum adminstrn. for war, Washington, 1943; chmn. bd. Metro-Goldwyn-Mayer, 1957-63, 63-69, 70—, vice chmn., 1969- 70, dir., mem. exec. com., 1963—; past pres. Am. President Lines, Ltd., San Francisco, now dir., cons.; chmn. Prentice Electronics, 1967—; dir. World Airways, Communications Satellite Corp.; dir. First Western Bank. Ambassador U.S. Mission to UN, 1966-67. Asst. to treas., Dem. Nat. Com., 1944, treas., 1945-47; Bd. dirs. San Francisco Internat. Film Festival, San Francisco chpt. Am. Cancer Soc., Japan Inter-Christian U. Fund, Cal. Council Meals for Millions; trustee San Francisco Maritime Mus., John F. Kennedy Library Corp., Eleanor Roosevelt Cancer Found., Am. Freedom from Hunger Found., United Seamen's Service; mem. adv. bd., dir. Pacific Am. S.S. Assn.; mem. San Francisco World Trade Center Authority; chmn. 11 western states March of Dimes, National Found.; mem. nat. council Eleanor Roosevelt Meml. Found.; adv. council Am. Korean Found.; sponsor, nat. council United Negro Coll. Fund. Served as maj. AUS, Staff of Allied Mil. Gov't., 1943. Mem. Am. Bur. Shipping (bd. mgrs.), Nat. Def. Transp. Assn. (life), Nat. Conf. Christians and Jews (bd. advisers), Greater San Francisco C. of C. (dir.). Democrat. Clubs: Bohemian, Olympic, World Trade (pres. 1957-66), Stock Exchange (San Francisco); Eldorado Country (Palm Desert, Cal.). Home: 1090 Chestnut St San Francisco CA 94104 Office: Bank of America Center San Francisco CA 94104

KILLION, RAYMOND FRANCIS, life ins. co. exec.; b. Boston, Jan. 2, 1909; s. Francis M. and Sarah (Knox) K.; B.S. cum laude, Tufts U., 1931; m. Helene Weldon, June 13, 1936; children—Roger, Raymond. With Met. Life Ins. Co., N.Y.C., 1932—, sr. v.p. ins. relations, 1969-71, sr. v.p. corp. and govt. relations, 1971—. Fellow Actuarial Soc. Am.; mem. Tau Beta Pi. Home: 5 High Ridge Rd Wilton CT 06897 Office: 1 Madison Av New York City NY 10010

KILLIPS, DANFORTH, investment adviser; b. Chgo., Oct. 22, 1918; s. Andrew F. and Ruth D. (Patrick) K.; B.S.L., Northwestern U., 1941, LL.B., 1947; m. Leslie Parker, Apr. 5, 1947; children—Bruce Danforth, John Mitchell. Admitted to Ill. bar, 1947; with firm Seago, Pipin, Bradley & Vetter, Chgo., 1946- 48, Parker & Carter, Chgo., 1948-52; v.p., dir. Looart Press, Inc., Colorado Springs, Colo., 1952-60, dir., 1968—; with Growth Research, Inc., Chgo., 1960-69, v.p., 1961, pres., 1961-69, also dir.; with Growth Industry Shares, Inc., Chgo., 1960—, v.p. 1962—, also dir.; investment mgr. William Blair & Co., Chgo., 1969—. Bd. dirs. Colorado Springs chpt. A.R.C., 1958-60, Colorado Springs YMCA, 1958-60, Vascular Disease Research Found., Chgo., 1964—; adv. bd. Chgo. Salvation Army, 1966—. Served to capt. USAAF, 1941-45. Mem. Newcomen Soc. North Am., Sigma Chi, Phi Delta Phi. Conglist. Clubs: Chicago Athletic Assn., Cliff Dwellers, Literary (Chgo.). Home: 1866 Sherman Av Evanston IL 60201 Office: 135 S LaSalle St Chicago IL 60603

KILLORAN, CLAIR JOHN, lawyer; b. Weiser, Ida., Apr. 12, 1905; s. Charles J. and Ada (Percifield) K.; A.B., Univ. of Ida. 1928; LL.B., Georgetown Univ., 1932; m. Anne Regina Biggs, Nov. 30, 1935; 1 dau., Claire Joanne. Admitted to D.C. bar, 1933, Del. bar, 1934; mem. firm Borton, Melson & Killoran, Wilmington, Del., 1934, Melson & Killoran, 1935-41, Clair John Killoran, 1941-45, Killoran and Van Brunt since 1946. Dep. atty.-gen. State of Del., 1937-39, chief dep. atty.-gen., 1940-43, atty.-gen., 1943- 47. Dir. and gen. counsel Del. Mutual Life Ins. Co., Foster Park Housing Corp. Del. state bd. Accountants 1947-51, bd. Governors Georgetown U. Alumni Assn., Senate mem.; dir. Del. Trust Co. Keynoter Rep. State Conv., 1944-46; Rep. state chmn., 1950-56; chmn. Del. del. Nat. Conv., 1952; delegate to National Republican Convention, 1956. Fellow Am. Coll. Trial Lawyers; mem. Am. Del. State (pres. 1959-61) bar assns., Kappa Sigma, Elk. Clubs: Wilmington, Biderman Golf, Wilmington Country (dir. 1959—) (Wilmington); Lambs (N.Y.C.); Seaview Country (Absecon, N.Y.). Home: 1103 Franklin St Wilmington DE 19808 Office: Market Tower Wilmington DE 19801

KILLORAN, ROLLIN H., b. 1907; B.A., U. Ore., married. With Montgomery Ward & Co.; with Fred Meyer. Inc., 1940—, v.p. marketing, sec., 1959-68, 1st v.p., dir. marketing, 1968—, also dir. Address: 3740 NE Klickitat St Portland OR 97212*

KILLORIN, EDWARD WYLLY, lawyer; b. Savannah, Ga., Oct. 16, 1928; s. Joseph Ignatius and Myrtle (Bell) K.; B.S., Spring Hill Coll., Mobile, 1952; LL.B. magna cum laude, U. Ga., 1957; m. Virginia Melson Ware, June 15, 1957; children—Robert Ware, Edward Wylly, Joseph Rigdon. Admitted to Ga. bar, 1956; practice in Atlanta, 1957—; partner firm Gambrell, Russell, Killorin, Wade & Forbes, 1964—; lectr. Inst. Continuing Legal Edn. Ga., 1967—. Tree farmer, 1961—; dir. Ga. Bus. and Realty Brokers, Inc. Served with AUS, 1946-47, 52-54. Mem. Am., Internat. Ga., Atlanta (editor Atlanta Lawyer 1967-70, exec. com. 1971—) bar assns., Am. Judicature Soc., Lawyers Club Atlanta, Atlanta Legal Aid Soc. (adv. com. 1966-70, dir. 1971—), Nat. Legal Aid and Defender Assn., Internat. Assn. Ins. Counsel, Atlanta Lawyers Found., Ga. Def. Lawyers Assn., Ga. C. of C. (chmn. govtl. dept. 1970—), Def. Research Inst. (Ga. chmn. 1970—), Spring Hill Coll. Alumni Assn. (nat. pres.-elect 1970-71), High Mus. Art, Ga. Forestry Assn. (bd. dirs. 1969—), Am. Forestry Assn., Demosthenian Lit. Soc. (pres. 1957), Phi Beta Kappa, Phi Beta Kappa Assos., Phi Kappa Phi, Phi Delta Phi, Phi Omega, Sphinx, Blue Key, Gridiron. Clubs: Capital City, Peachtree Golf, Commerce (Atlanta). Roman Cath. Contbr. legal jours. Home: 436 Blackland Rd NW Atlanta GA 30342 Office: First Nat Bank Tower Atlanta GA 30303

KILLOUGH, ROBERT SLEEPER, aircraft co. exec.; b. Waco, Tex., Aug. 26, 1913; s. Robert McMullen, and Ione (Yinger) K.; A.B., Baylor U., 1934, J.D., 1936; m. Mildred Painter, Oct. 4, 1946; children—Donna K. (Mrs. Samuel C. Hayer), Regina (Mrs. Harold C. Bennett), Vicki L. Admitted to Cal. bar, 1946, Tex. bar, 1936; practice in Houston, 1936-41; counsel AEC, 1946-51; with Hughes Aircraft Co., 1951—, sec., 1963—, gen. atty., 1963—; dir. Hughes Aircraft Internat. Service Co., Emilhus Microcomponents Ltd. Bd. dirs. Santa Barbara Research Center. Served to 1st lt. AUS, 1945-46. Mem. Am., Cal., Tex., Los Angeles County bar assns. Home: 800 Linda Flora Dr Los Angeles CA 90049. Office: Hughes Aircraft Co Culver City CA 90230

KILLY, JEAN-CLAUDE, French skier; b. St. Cloud, France, Aug. 30, 1943; s. Robert and Elaine (Fidelaire) K. Mem. French Nat. Jr. Ski Team, 1960-62; mem. French Nat. Ski Team 1964—; winner internat. downhill and combined championships, 1966; winner World Cup, 1966-67, 67-68; winner triple Olympic crown (downhill, slalom, giant slalom), 1968 Winter Olympics; named European champion by Fedn. Internat. des Ski, 1965; winner men's slalom, Sun Valley, Ida., 1966; recipient High Sierra cup, 1966, Hahnenkamm trophy, Kitzbuehel, Austria, 1967. Served with French Army, Algeria, 1962-64. Address: La Bergerie Val'd'Isere France *

KILMARTIN, EDWARD JOHN, educator; b. Portland, Me., Aug. 31, 1923; s. Patrick Joseph and Elizabeth Gertrude (Sullivan) K.; A.B., Boston Coll., 1947, M.A. in Philosophy, 1948, S.T.L., 1955; M.S. in Chemistry, Holy Cross Coll., 1950; S.T.D., Gregorian U., Rome, Italy, 1958. Joined Soc. of Jesus, 1941, ordained priest Roman Cath. Ch., 1954; tchr. chemistry Fairfield (Conn.) Prep. Sch., 1950-51; prof. sacramental theology Weston Coll., Sch. Theology of Boston Coll., 1958—, dean sch. 1960-62. Mem. Cath. Theol. Soc. Am., Cath. Bibl. Assn. Editor: New Testament Abstracts, 1959-67. Author: The Eucharist in the Primitive Church, 1965; also articles on N.T. Address: 40 Kirkland St Cambridge MA 02138

KILMER, FOREST, newspaper editor. Exec. editor Davenport (Ia.) Times-Democrat. Office: Davenport Newspapers 124 E 42d St Davenport IA 52808*

KILMER, NED ARNTZ, Jr., banker; b. Detroit, Nov. 1, 1917; s. Ned Arntz and Jessie (Johnstone) K.; A.B., U. Mich., 1938, postgrad., 1951-52; grad. Rutgers U., 1957; m. Jane Quirk, Aug. 6, 1949; children—Ned Arntz III, John Q. Auditor, RFC, Washington, 1938-47, chief fiscal div., Detroit, 1947-50; operations examiner Detroit Bank & Trust Co., 1950-53; asst. v.p., auditor City Bank & Trust Co., Jackson, Mich., 1953-56, cashier, 1956-59, exec. v.p., 1959-62, pres., 1962—; dir. Knickerbocker Co., Gen. Products Corp., Civic Center Hotel Corp. Treas., Mercy Hosp. Bldg. Fund, 1955; chmn. County Tb Drive, 1956; pres. Jackson Meml. Camp for Children, 1958-59; co-chmn. Jackson Torch Drive, 1959; treas. United Community Services, 1961, v.p., 1964-65, pres., 1966-67; treas. Area Indsl. Devel. Corp., 1964-65; v.p. Central Area Improvement Corp., 1966-67. Bd. dirs. Goodwill Industries; trustee County Sanitorium. Served to capt. USAAF, 1942-46; PTO. Mem. Am. Inst. Banking, Robert Morris Assos., Mich. Bankers Assn. (past com. chmn.), Jackson C. of C. (pres., dir.), Phi Sigma Kappa. Presbyn. (trustee). Kiwanian. Clubs: Jackson Country (pres.), Town. Home: 3961 Fayette Ct Jackson MI 49203. Office: 161 W Michigan Av Jackson MI 49201

KILMNICK, MAURIE LOUIS, mfg. co. exec.; b. Kansas City, Mo., May 25, 1918; s. Samuel and Sarah (Eagles) K.; student Northwestern U., 1942, Inst. Personal Devel., Wabash Coll., 1961-65; m. Rose Zwerling, Aug. 10, 1947; children—Jamy H., Brian C. Accountant, John E. Burke & Co., then S.D. Leidesdorf & Co., 1942-48; with Signode Corp., Chgo., 1948—, asst. sec., 1955-68, treas., 1961—; treas. Signode Internat. Ltd., 1961—, Addison-Semmes Corp., 1961—, Signode S.A. de C.V., 1961—; treas., asst. sec. Signode Internat. (W.H.), Signode Overseas Co.; dir, Reichel& Drews, Inc. Home: 6704 N Francisco Av Chicago IL 60645 Office: 2600 N Western Av Chicago IL 60647

KILPATRICK, ARNOLD ROY, coll. pres.; b. Eros, La., Aug. 5, 1920; s. Luther Lonnie and Blanche (Burkett) K., student N.E., Jr. Coll., 1938-41, Northwestern state Coll., 1943; M.Ed., La. State U., 1953, Ed.D., 1964; m. Juanita Cardozier, July 8, 1950; children—Lael Alexis, Joel Young. Tchr., coach Jonesboro-Hodge high sch., 1946-51; asst. prof., coach N.E. La. State Coll., 1951- 52, athletic dir., head basketball coach, 1952-57, asst. prof. edn., 1957-65, head elementary and secondary edn. dept. 1965-66; dean of Coll., Northwestern State Coll. La., Natchitoches, 1966, pres., 1966—. Dir. Savs. Life Ins. Co. Served with USAAF, 1943-46. Named Outstanding Young Man of Monroe-West Monroe Jr. C. of C., 1954. Mem. N.E.A., Nat. Soc. Study Edn., Nat. Assn. Intercollegiate Athletics (mem. exec. com.). Mason (Shriner), Rotarian. Club: Breakfast Civitan (past pres. lt. gov. N.W. La. dist.) (Monroe). Home: 631 College Av Natchitoches LA 71457

KILPATRICK, CARROLL, newspaper writer; b. Montgomery, Ala., Sept. 2, 1913; s. Andrew Carroll and Mary (Anderson) K.; A.B., Ala. U., 1935; Nieman fellow Harvard, 1939-40; m. Frances Talbot Williams, Mar. 6, 1941; children—Andrew Carroll, Frank Williams. Editorial writer, Birmingham News, 1935-37, European assignment, 1937; asso. editor, Montgomery Advertiser, 1937-39; nat. affairs writer on Newsweek, 1940; Washington corr. for Birmingham News and Age-Herald, Raleigh (N.C.) News and Observer, Yorkshire (Eng.) Post, 1940-43; Washington corr. The Chgo. Sun, 1943-46; Washington corr. for San Francisco Chronicle 1946-51; asst. chief State Dept. press sect., 1951-52; staff writer Washington Post, 1952—, now White House corr. Mem. Phi Delta Theta, Omicron Delta Kappa. Clubs: Cosmos, Overseas Writers (pres. 1967), Federal City (Washington). Co-author: The Kennedy Circle, 1961. Editor: Roosevelt and Daniels, A Friendship in Politics, 1952. Contbr. mags. Home: 4238 43d St Washington DC 20016 Address: The Washington Post Washington DC 20005

KILPATRICK, CHARLES OTIS, newspaper editor; b. Fairview, Okla., June 16, 1922; s. John E. and Myrtle (Arant) K.; B.A., Stephen F. Austin State Coll., 1942; m. Margie Ada Partin, June 3, 1944; children—Kent Fairles, Millicent Kye, Mark Kevin. With daily newspapers, Nacogdoches, Tex., 1940-42, with Daily Sentinel, Nacogdoches, 1946-48, Courier-Times, Tyler, Tex., 1948-49; regional editor Tyler Morning Telegraph, 1949, mng. editor, 1949-50; mem. staff Evening News, San Antonio, 1950-51; Sunday Editor San Antonio Express, 1951-54; asst. mng. editor Evening News, 1954-55, mng. editor, 1955-65; asst. exec. editor San Antonio Express and San Antonio News, 1957-58, exec. editor, 1958, v.p., 1967; pub. San Antonio Express, 1971—. Mem. adv. council Sch. Communications, U. Tex. Pulitzer prize journalism juror, 1963, 64, 67, 71. Served as comdg. ofcr. 14th Inf. Bn., USMCR; lt. col. Res. Mem. Tex. A.P. Mng. Editors Assn. (pres. 1963), C. of C. (dir.), Am. Soc. Newspaper Editors. Episcopalian (bd. vestry, bishop's com. pub. relations Diocese W. Tex.). Home: 2019 E Lawndale St San Antonio TX 78209 Office: Express Pub Co Av E at 3d St San Antonio TX 78206

KILPATRICK, FRANKLIN PEIRCE, edueator; b. Okanogan, Wash., Apr. 30, 1920; s. Wilbur C. and Alberta (Peirce) K.; B.A., U. Wash., 1942, M.S., 1947; M.A., Ph.D., Princeton, 1950; m. Mary Frances Reynolds, Oct. 30, 1943; children—Dean James, Karen Mary, Joan Terese, Carol Anne. Instr., asst. prof. psychology Princeton, 1950-55; head consumer research and research devel. Nat. Analysts, Inc., Phila., 1955-59; sr. staff mem. Brookings Instn., 1959-67; dean Coll. Grad. Studies, prof. psychology U. Del., Newark, 1967—. Cons., lectr. IBM, Gen. Electric Co., Motorola Co., Nat. Acad. Pub. Adminstrn. Mem. Del. Adv. Council on Tchr. Edn. and Profl. Standards, 1968—; mem. Am. Bar Assn. Task Force on Ct. Adminstrn., 1969; mem. adv. panel Inst. for Ct. Mgmt., 1969—; bd. advisers Inst. for Internat. Social Research. Served to 1st lt. AUS, 1942-46. Decorated Bronze Star medal, Purple Heart. Fellow Am. Psychol. Assn.; mem. Phi Beta Kappa, Sigma Xi. Author: The Image of the Federal Service, 1964; Explorations in Transactional Psychology, 1961. Contbr. articles to profl. jours. Home: 900 Baylor Dr Newark DE 19711

KILPATRICK, GEORGE HARRINGTON II, banker; b. Denver, Apr. 20, 1936; s. George Harrington and Margaret M. (Wall) K.; B.S. in Finance with honors, U. Colo., 1959; m. Dorothy Ray Winter, June 13, 1959; children—Robin, Jeffrey. Credit analyst, gen. banking officer 1st Nat. Bank, Dallas, 1960-70, asst. cashier, 1962-64, asst. v.p., 1964-67, v.p., 1967-70, sr. v.p., 1970—, div. head loan adminstrn., 1970-71, group head, gen. banking services (responsible for 6 gen. banking divs.,), 1971—. Div. chmn. United Fund, 1970—, Park Cities-N. Dallas YMCA, 1971—. Mem. Robert Morris Assos., Sigma Chi. Methodist. Club: Dallas Athletic. Home: 3800 Wentwood Dallas TX 75225 Office: PO Box 6031 Dallas TX 75222

KILPATRICK, JAMES JACKSON, Jr., newspaperman; b. Oklahoma City, Nov. 1, 1920; s. James Jackson and Alma Mia (Hawley) K.; B.J., U. Mo., 1941; m. Marie Louise Pietri, Sept. 21, 1942; children—Michael Sean, Christopher Hawley, Kevin Pietri. Reporter, Richmond (Va.) News Leader, 1941-49, chief editorial writer, 1949-51, editor, 1951-67; writer nat. syndicated column; asso. Nat. Rev., 1964-68, contbg. editor, 1968—. TV commentator. Vice chmn. Va. Com. on Constl. Govt., 1962-68; chmn. Va. Magna Carta Com., 1965. Pres. Beadle Bumble Fund, 1954—. Recipient medal of honor for distinguished service in journalism, U. Mo., 1953; ann. award for editorial writing, Sigma Delta Chi, 1954. Mem. Nat. Conf. of Editorial Writers (chmn. 1955-56). Va. Ornithology Soc., Black-Eyed Pea Soc. Am. (No. 1 Pea, pro-tem. 1965—). Whig. Episcopalian. Author: The Sovereign States, 1957; The Smut Peddlers, 1960; The Southern Case for School Segregation, 1962. Editor: We the States, 1964. Co-editor; The Lasting South, 1957. Home: White Walnut Hill Woodville VA 22749 Office: 412 Princess St Alexandria VA 22314

KILPATRICK, MARTIN EDWARD, lawyer; b. Athens, Ga., Aug. 1, 1905; s. Irby T. and Eva Pauline (Richter) K.; B.S., U. Ga., 1926. LL.B., 1928; m. Mary Hurt Clayton, Dec. 28, 1946; children—Mary, Martin, Melissa, Sally, Nancy. Admitted to Ga. bar, 1928, since practiced in Atlanta; now sr. partner Kilpatrick, Cody, Rogers, McClatchey & Regenstein. Chmn. exec. com., dir. Fulton Nat. Bank; dir. Provident Life Accident Ins. Co., Scripto, Inc.; dir. Scientific-Atlanta, Inc., M.A. Ferst, Ltd., Keystone Coca-Cola Bottling Co., So. Cross Industries Inc. Mem. Am., Georgia and Atlanta bar assns., Phi Beta Kappa. Episcopalian. Clubs: Atlanta Lawyers, Peidmont Driving, Capital City. Home: 400 W Paces Ferry Rd Atlanta GA 30327 Office: Hurt Bldg Atlanta GA 30303

KILPATRICK, SAMUEL JAMES, Jr., educator, biometrician; b. Belfast, North Ireland, Apr. 24, 1931; s. Samuel James and Mary (Maginnis) K.; B.Sc. with honours, Queens U., Belfast, 1954, M.Sc., 1957, Ph.D., 1960; m. Mary Coyne Brown, Feb. 6, 1957; children—Mark Duncan, Sara Ellen. Came to U.S., 1965. Asst. lectr. social preventive medicine Queens U., 1954-58, lectr., 1958-61; postdoctoral fellow statistics USPHS, Ia. State U., 1960-61; lectr. statistics Aberdeen (Scotland) U., 1961-65; prof. biometry, chmn. dept. Med. Coll. Va., Va. Commonwealth U., 1965—. Fellow Royal Statis. Soc.; mem. Biometrics Soc., Am. Statis. Soc., Assn. Computing Machinery, Inst. Biol. Scis. Home: 7808 Ardendale Rd Richmond VA 23225

KILROY, JOHN MUIR, lawyer; b. Kansas City, Mo., Apr. 12, 1918; s. James L. and Jane Alice (Scurry) K.; student Kansas City Jr. Coll., 1935-37; A.B., U. Kansas City, 1940; LL.B., U. Mo., 1942; m. Lorraine K. Butler, Jan. 26, 1946; children—John Muir, William Terence. Admitted to Mo. bar, 1942; practice in Kansas City, 1946—; partner firm Shughart, Thomson & Kilroy, 1946—. Panelist numerous med.-legal groups A.C.S., Mo. Med. Assn., Kan. U. Med. Sch., S.W. Clin. Soc. Chmn. bd. dirs. Kansas City Heart Assn. Served to capt. AUS, 1942-46. Fellow Am. Coll. Trial Lawyers; mem. Internat. Assn. Barristers, Internat. Assn. Ins. Counsel, Lawyers Assn. Kansas City (pres.), Fedn. Ins. Counsel. Am., Mo. bar assns., Mo. Bar (chmn. med. legal com.), Kansas City C. of C. Contbr. articles profl. jours. Home: 6860 Tomahawk Rd Shawnee Mission KS 66208 Office: Commerce Bank Bldg 922 Walnut St Kansas City MO 64106

KILSON, MARTIN LUTHER, educator. Prof. govt. Harvard. Office: Dept Govt Harvard Cambridge MA*

KILTY, JEROME TIMOTHY, playwright, stage dir., actor; b. Balt., June 24, 1922; s. Harold Joseph and Irene (Zellinger) K.; B.A., Harvard, 1949; m. Cavada Humphrey, May 11, 1956. Co-founder, dir., actor Brattle Theatre Co., Cambridge, Mass., 1948-52; actor N.Y.C. stage and TV, 1952-57, including Relapse, 1951, Quadrille, 1952, Misalliance, 1953; played Falstaff, Iago, City Centre, 1954; writer, actor Dear Liar, Chgo. and London, 1957; writer, dir. Ides of March, London, 1963, Long Live Life, San Francisco, 1967; dir. Marie Bell, Elisabeth Bergner, Maria Casares, Pierre Brasseur in French, German, Italian Prodn., 1962-65; asso. dir. Am. Conservatory Theatre, San Francisco, 1966-68, Am. Shakespeare Co., Stratford, Conn., 1965-68; dir. Possibilities, N.Y.C., 1968; writer, dir. Don't Shoot Mable It's Your Husband, 1968; writer-actor: Dear Love, Boston, 1969. Served to capt. USAAF, 1942-46; ETO. Decorated D.F.C., Air medal with five clusters. Mem. Signet Soc. Club: Players (N.Y.C.). Home: 7 W 16th St New York City NY 10011

KIM, CHONG KYU, Korean diplomat; b. Korea, Dec. 11, 1927; s. Duk Oh and Myongsun (Chung) K.; ed. Yonsei U. (Seoul, Korea), 1949; grad. U. Mo., 1957; m. Jisung Park, June 1, 1950; children—Young-hee, Chin-chul, Chin-hyun, Yoo-hee. With Bank of Korea, Seoul, 1949-51; editor Hankook Ilbo, Seoul, 1952-63, pres., pub., 1964-67; ambassador, dep. chief Korean embassy, Saigon, Republic of Vietnam, 1968-69; consul gen. Korean consulate, Honolulu, 1969-70; ambassador Korean embassy Tehran, Iran, 1970—. Address: Korean Embassy Kh Kakh 427 Tehran Iran

KIM, DONG JO, Korean diplomat; b. Pusan, Korea, Aug. 14, 1918; s. Byung Woo and Won Tong (Cho) K.; grad. Seoul Comml. Jr. Coll., 1940, Kyushu Imperial U. Japan, 1943; m. Duman Song, May 24, 1943; children—Young Ai, Young Sook, Dae-Young, Young-Ja, Min-Young, Young-Myoung. Sec. gen. Ministry of Communications. 1949-51, dir. Audit and Budget Bur., 1951; dir. Polit. Affairs Bur., Ministry Fgn. Affairs, 1951-52, 54-56; counselor Korean embassy in Republic China, 1952-54; mem. Korean Delegation to 12th UN Gen. Assembly, 1956—; vice minister fgn. affairs, 1957-59; spl. envoy of pres. heading goodwill mission to Philippines, Fedn. Malaya, Thailand, Republic Vietnam and Republic China, 1960; chief del. Asian Peoples Anti- Communist League Conf., Saigon, 1963; chmn. third com., sec.-gen. Freedom Center; pres. Korea Trade Promotion Corp., 1964; ambassador to Japan, chief Korean Delegation to Korea-Japan Overall Talks, 1964; ambassador at large, 1965; ambassador E. And P. to Japan, 1966; spl. envoy of Pres. heading goodwill and econ. cooperation mission to Hong Kong, Taiwan, Fed. Malaysia, Thailand, India, Pakistan, Ceylon, South Vietnam, 1967-; ambassador E. and P. to U.S. Office: 2320 Massachusetts Av NW Washington DC 20008

KIM, IL SUNG, premier of N. Korea: b. Pyongyang, Korea, Apr. 15, 1912. Founder, leader Communist Youth League, from 1927; founder Assn. for Restoration of the Fatherland, chmn., 1936; founder Communist Party of Korea, chief sec., 1945—; founder, chmn. N. Korean Provisional People's Com., 1946-47; chmn. successor N. Korean People's Com., 1947—; founder, premier Democratic People's Republic of Korea, 1958—. Mem. Workers Party Korea (chmn. central com. 1949-66, gen. sec. 1966—). Organized, led Korean Revolutionary Army, 1930; founder predecessor to Korean People's Revolutionary Army, 1932. Created marshal Democratic People's Republic Korea, 1953; Hero of Labor; decorated 3 orders Nat. Flag 1st class, Order of freedom and Independence 1st class. Author numerous works on revolution and reconstrn. Address: care of Ency Pub Ho Acad Social Scis Democratic People's Republic of Korea

KIM, JAI SOO, physicist, educator; b. Taegu, Korea, Nov. 1, 1925; s. Wan Sup and Chanam (Whang) K.; B.Sc. in Physics, Seoul Nat. U. (Korea), 1949; M.S. in Physics U. Sask. (Can.), 1957, Ph.D., 1958; m. Hai Kyou Kim, Nov. 2, 1952; children-Kami, Tomi, Kihyun, Himi. Came to U.S., 1958, naturalized, 1963. Asst. prof. physics Clarkson Coll. Tech., Potsdam, N.Y., 1958-59; asst. prof. physics U. Ida., Moscow, 1959-62, asso. prof., 1962-65, prof., 1965-67; prof. atmospheric sci. and physics State U.N.Y. at Albany, 1967—, chmn. dept. atmospheric sci., 1969—. Mem. Am. Inst. Physics, Am. Geophys. Union, Sigma Xi. Contbr. articles profl. jours. Home: 33 Folmsbee Dr Menands NY 12204 Office: 1400 Washington St Albany NY 12203

KIM, RICHARD E., author, educator; b. Hamhung City, Korea, Mar. 13, 1932; s. Chan-Doh and Ok-Hyun (Rhee) K.; student Middlebury (Vt.) Coll., 1955-59; M.A., Johns Hopkins, 1960; M.F.A., State U. Ia., 1962; M.A., Harvard, 1963; m. Penelope Ann Groll, Feb. 1960; children—David, Melissa. Instr. English, Long Beach (Cal.) State Coll., 1963-64; asst. prof. English, U. Mass. at Amherst, 1964-68, asso. prof., 1968—; vis. prof. Syracuse U., 1970—. Served to 1st lt. Republic of Korea Army, 1950-54. Author: The Martyred, 1964; The Innocent, 1968; Lost Names, 1970. Address: Leverett Rd Shutesbury MA 01072

KIM, SUNG KWOO, Korean diplomat; b. Seoul, Korea, Nov, 5, 1934; s. Duk Yang and Kyung (Chung) K.; B.A., Hanyang Engring. Coll., 1956; M.A., Sch. Pub. Adminstrn. Seoul Nat. U., 1967; m. Soo Jin Lee, Dec. 10, 1968; children—Han Soo, Han Joon. Sec. to Pres. of Korea, 1963-68; sr. research Inst. Fgn. Affairs, Ministry Fgn. Affairs, 1968-69; counselor, consul gen. Korean embassy, Washington, 1969—; tchr. English and chem. engring. Inst. Hong-myoung, Seoul, 1953-55. Pres. Kai-mi Philanthropies Assn., Korea, 1967-70. Served to capt., Arty., Korean Army, 1957-63. Mem. Consular Corps Washington. Home: 6174 Edsall Rd Alexandria VA 22304 Office: 2320 Massachusetts Av Washington DC 20008

KIM, WAN HEE, educator; b. Osan Korea, May 24, 1926; s. Sang Chul and Cuck Hyung (Chong) K.; B.E., Seoul Nat. U., 1950; M.S. in Elec. Engring., U. Utah, 1954, Ph.D., 1956; m. Chung Sook Noh, Jan. 23, 1960; children—Millie, Richard K. Came to U.S., 1953, naturalized, 1962. Research asst. U. Ill. at Urbana, 1955-56; research staff IBM Research Center, Poughkeepsie, N.Y., 1956-57; asst. prof. Columbia U., N.Y.C., 1957-59, asso. prof., 1957-63, prof. elec. engring., 1963-70. Chmn. Tech. Cons., Inc., N.Y.C., 1962-69; chmn. KOMKOR Am., Inc., N.Y.C., 1970—; dir. Newko Electronics Corp., Los Angeles, Korea Keyboard Corp., Seoul, Korea. Spl. cons. for Govt. Korea, 1967—; U.S. rep. on U.S.-Japan Scientists Coop. Program. Served with Korean Army, 1950-53. Decorated Bronze Star; Guggenheim grantee, 1964; 8 NSF research grants, 1958-. Fellow I.E.E.E., Union Radio Scientifique International (Mem. U.S. nat. com. Commn. 6, 1963-). Sigma Xi, Tau Beta Pi. Author: (with R.T. chien) Topological Analysis and Synthesis of Communication Networks, 1962; (with M. Kawakami) Active Networks-Theory and Applications, 1969; (with H.E. Meadows) Modern Network Analysis, 1970; also numerous articles. Home: 282 Woodland St Tenafly NJ 07670 Office: 120th St and Broadway New York City NY 10027

KIM, YONGJEUNG, inst. exec.; b. Kum-San, Korea, Apr. 2, 1898; s. Iltak and Madam (Park) K.; student Harvard, Columbia, U. So. Cal., George Washington U.; m. Mary Ann Kim, July 2, 1934; children—Marilyn Annette, Diane Claire. Mgr., K. & S. Jobbers, Los Angeles, 1934-43; Founder, pres. Korean Affairs Inst., Washington, 1943. Former mem. Korean Nat. Assn. N.A. (exec. mem., dir. pub. relations 1939-43); formerly English lang. editor New Korea Weekly; mem. exec. com., dir. pub. relations United Korean Com. Am., 1941-43; observed UNRRA Conf., Montreal, 1944; contbr. broadcasts OWI, World War II; made observation trip to So. Korea, summer, 1947; observed 3d session of UN Gen. Assembly, Paris, 1948; pub. Voice of Korea; contbr. feature articles to periodicals. Address: 3900 Watson Pl NW Washington DC 20016

KIMBALL, ALLYN WINTHROP, educator; b. Buffalo, Oct. 2, 1921; s. Allyn Winthrop and Ethel (Manson) K.; B.S., U. Buffalo, 1943; postgrad. Mass. Inst. Tech., 1943; Ph.D., N.C. State Coll., 1950; m. Evelyn Marie Lay, June 16, 1944; children—Keith Allan, Lynn Ellen. Exptl. statistician USAF Sch. Aviation Medicine, Randolph Field, Tex., 1948-50; chief statistics sect., mathematics panel Oak Ridge Nat. Lab., 1950-60; prof. statistics and biostatistics Johns Hopkins, 1960—, chmn. dept. biostatistics, 1960-66, dean faculty arts and scis., 1966-70. Trustee Asso. Univ., Inc., 1962—. Served from ensign to lt., USNR, 1943-46. Fellow A.A.A.S., Am. Statis. Assn.; mem. Biometric Soc., Am. Math. Soc., Inst. Math. Statistics. Contbr. papers sci. lit. Home: 1106 Hampton Garth Towson MD 21204 Office: Johns Hopkins U Baltimore MD 21205

KIMBALL, ARTHUR ALDEN, govt. ofcl; b. Washington, Aug. 22, 1908; s. Dr. Arthur Herbert and Helena Maria (Kimball) K.; A.B., George Washington U., 1931, LL.B., 1933; m. Betty Virginia Little, May 7, 1962; 1 dau., Laurie Alden; stepchildren—Catherine, Jeannie Ann, Lise Margaret. Admitted to D.C. bar, 1933, Md. bar, 1934; economist Bur. Fgn. and Domestic Commerce, Dept. of Commerce, 1928-34; asst. dep. adminstr. N.R.A., 1934- 36; chief fiscal standards sect. Bur. Employment Security, Social Security Bd., Fed. Security Agy., 1936-42; indsl. relations cons. VA, 1946-47; spl. asst. to asst. sec. of state for adminstrn., 1947-49; exec. dir. Bur. German Affairs, Dept. State, 1949-52, asst. adminstrs. later dept. adminstr. U.S. Internat. Information Adminstrn., 1952- 53, interim dir. to activate new U.S. Information Agy., 1953; staff dir. Pres.'s Adv. Com. on Govt. Orgn., 1953-60; mem. NLRB, 1960-61; partner in law firm Boykin and DeFrancis, 1961-66; asst. dir. for profl. relations Bur. Health Ins. (Medicare), Social Security Adminstrn., Dept. of Health, Edn., Welfare, Washington, 1966-68; dept. regulations officer Office Sec. Health, Edn., Welfare, 1968-70; chief Office Fed.-State Agreements, Family Assistance Planning Staff, Dept. Health, Edn., Welfare, 1970-71; staff asst. for welfare reform The White House, 1971—. Exec. officer Army Budget Office, mem. Army Procurement Assignment Bd., War Dept., 1942-45; chief adminstrn. Internat. Mil. Trials, Nuremberg, Germany, 1945-46; dir. legislative planning for adminstrn. Marshall Plan (ECA), 1947; dir. planning for establishment of embassy to replace mil. occupation in Korea, 1948; dir. planning for establishment of Office U.S. High Commr. to replace mil. occupation in Germany, 1949; dir. planning for establishment U.S. Internat. Information Adminstrn. operating Voice of Am. and other information media, 1951. Bd. dirs. Internat. Youth Achievement Awards Found., Found. for Prevention Addictive Diseases, 1965-68. Served from capt. to col., AUS, Gen. Staff, War Dept., 1943-45, overseas Germany, 1945-46; civil affairs U.S. Army Res. ret. Decorated Legion of Merit, Army Commendation Ribbon with oak leaf cluster; Legion of Honor (France); Order of St. Olaf (Norway); Order of White Lion (Free Czechoslovakia under Pres. Benes); Order of Polona Restituta (Poland). Mem. Sigma Phi Epsilon, Delta Phi Epsilon. Home: 2104 Military Rd N Arlington VA 22207 Office: The White House Washington DC 20500

KIMBALL, CHARLES HENRY GALLWEY, lawyer; b. Chg., Jan. 26, 1909; s. Ralph Rigg and Eva (Hetherington) K.; grad. Phillips Acad., Andover, Mass, 1927; A.B., Amherst Coll., 1931; J.D., Northwestern, U., 1934; m. Ruth Landrum, Jan. 12, 1946. Admitted to Ill. bar, 1934, since practiced in Chgo.; partner firm Ashcraft & Ashcraft and predecessors, 1934—. Dir. Sethness Products Co., Werner, Kennelly Co., Armored Express Corp. of Chgo., Garfield Ridge State Bank & Trust Co., 1st State Bank & Trust Co. of Park Ridge, 1st State Bank & Trust Co. of Hanover Park, 1st State Bank & Trust Co. of Franklin Park, Dempster Plaza State Bank & Trust Co., Northpoint State Bank & Trust Co., Joanna Western Mills Co., Scarborough & Co. Bd. dirs. Inst. Am. Strategy. Served with USNR, 1942-46. Mem. Phi Beta Kappa. Order of Coif, Psi Upsilon. Clubs: University, Mid America, Tavern, Saddle and Cycle, Mid-Day, Anglers (Chgo.). Editor Ill. Law Rev., 1933-34. Home: 1360 Lake Shore Dr Chicago IL 60610 Office: 105 S LaSalle St Chicago IL 60603

KIMBALL, CHARLES NEWTON, sci. research adminstr.; b. Boston, Apr. 21, 1911; s. Charles Newton and Josephine Marie (Riley) K.; B.S. in Elec. Engring., Northeastern U., 1931, D.Eng., (hon.), 1955; M.S., Harvard, 1932, Sc.D., 1934; Sc.D. (hon.), Park College, 1958; LL.D., Parsons College Fairfield, Ia., 1959; married Mary Louise Theis, Oct. 3, 1951; children—John Theis, Susanne Louise. Research engr. RCA, 1937-41; instr. Grad. Sch. Engring, N.Y.U., 1940-41; v.p., dir. Aircraft Accessories Corp., 1941-46, C.J. Patterson Co., 1946-48; tech. dir. research labs. div. Bendix Aviation Corp., 1948- 50; pres. Midwest Research Inst., Kansas City. 1950-; dir. Trans World Airlines, Inc., Hallmark Cards, Inc. Mem. Army Scientific Adv. Panel; trustee Citizens Conf. on State Legislatures. Bd. regents Rockhurst Coll.; trustee Hallmark Foundation, University of Kansas City, Committee Econ. Development, Menninger Found. Fellow I.E.E.E.; mem. Sci. Research Soc. Am., A.A.A.S., Mo. Squires, Tau Beta Pi, Eta Kappa Nu. Clubs: Kansas City, University, Mission Hills (Kansas City, Mo.). Home: 5550 Mission Dr Shawnee Mission KS 66208 Office: 425 Volker Blvd Kansas City MO 64110

KIMBALL, DAVID TENNEY, mfr.; b. Williams, Ariz., July 31, 1927; s. George W. and Marguerite (Vadeboncoeur) K.; B.S., U. N.M., 1950; student exec. program U. Cal. at Los Angeles, 1961-62; m. Patricia Louise Brown, Sept. 8, 1948; children—Mary Lynette, Lori Ann, Leslie Sue, Caryn Louise. Supervisory engr. N. Am. Aviation, Downey, Cal., 1950-59; v.p., gen. mgr. Telecomputing Corp., Los Angeles, 1959; v.p., group exec. Whittaker Corp., Los Angeles, 1966-68; pres. Tasker Industries, Los Angeles, 1968—, also dir.; chmn. bd. dirs. Courier Communications, Inc., 1967-68. Served with USN, 1944-46. Recipient Balfour nat. award Sigma Chi, 1950. Mem. Van Nuys C. of C. (dir. 1961-62), Phi Kappa Phi, Sigma Tau, Kappa Mu Epsilon, Sigma Chi. Republican. Roman Catholic. Home: 6006 Clear Valley Rd Calabasas CA 91302 Office: 4561 Colorado Blvd Los Angeles CA 90039

KIMBALL, EDWARD LAWRENCE, educator; b. Safford, Ariz., Sept. 23, 1930; s. Speer Woolley and Camilla (Eyring) K.; B.S., U. Utah, 1953; LL.B., 1955; LL.M., U. Pa., 1959, S.J.D., 1962; m. Evelyn Bee Madsen, June 9, 1954; children—Christian Edward, Paula, Mary, Miles Spencer, Jordan Andrew, Joseph Ellsworth, Sarah Camilla. Admitted to Utah bar, 1955; law clk. Utah Supreme Ct., 1955; mem. faculty U. Mont., 1956-62, asso. prof. law, 1960-62; mem. faculty U. Wis. at Madison, 1962—, prof. law, 1967—; mem. spl. review bd. Wis. Dept. Health and Social Services, 1970—. Dist. committeeman Four Lakes council Boy Scouts Am., 1965—. Bicentennial fellow, U. Pa., 1955-56; Rockefeller fellow, U. Wis., 1961-62. Mem. Utah Bar Assn., Phi Beta Kappa, Order of Coif, Phi Kappa Phi, Lambda Delta Sigma, Delta Phi Kappa, Phi Delta Phi. Mem. Ch. Jesus Christ Latter-day Saints (bishop). Author: (with others) Criminal Justice Administration, 1969. Editorial bd. Brigham Young U. Studies, 1970—, The Carpenter, 1969—. Home: 4149 Mandan Crescent Madison WI 53711

KIMBALL, FRED MERRILL, utility exec.; b. Hartington, Neb., Feb. 8, 1909; s. Fred M. and Minnie Leila (Jones) K.; student U. N.M., 1926-28; m. Anita Josephine Bazer, June 19, 1959; children—Sandra D., Lawrence K., K. Leigh. Asst. comml. mgr. Kan. Elec. Power Co., Leavenworth and Lawrence, 1929-39; gen. comml. mgr. Mo. Pub. Service Co., Warrensburg, 1939-42; chief allocation sect. Office War Utilities of W.P.B., Washington, 1942-45; promotion mgr. Portland Gas & Coke Co. (Ore.), 1945-49; successively gen. sales mgr., v.p. sales, v.p., sr. v.p. and dir. Kan. Gas & Elec. Co., Wichita, 1949—; dir. Kan. State Bank & Trust Co. Chmn. exec. com. Kan. Council Electricity and the Environment; mem. exec. com. Mo. Valley Elec. Assn.; mem. Assn. Edison Illuminating Cos.; chmn. Kan. Farm Electrification Council; mem. exec. com. Kan. Com. on Relation of Electricity to Agr.; chmn. Sales Execs. Conf. Chmn. bd. dirs. Wichita Area Devel., 1963-65; chmn. S. Central Kan. Econ. Devel. Council, 1956-59; pres. United Fund, 1960-61; active Boy Scouts Am., YMCA, Mental Health Assn.; bd. dirs. Mid-Ark. Valley Devl. Assn. Mem. exec. com., Trustee Wesley Hosp., 1959—; dir. Wichita State U. Athletic Corp., 1966—; trustee KG & E Charitable Found., 1967—. Mem. Edison Elec. Inst., Newcomen Soc., Sales and Marketing Execs. (pres.), Wichita C. of C. (pres.), U.S., Kan. C.'s of C., N.A.M., Sigma Chi. Methodist. Clubs: Wichita Rotary (pres.), Wichita Century (dir.), Wichita, Wichita Country. Home: 550 N Armour Dr Wichita KS Office: 120 E 1st St Wichita KS 67202

KIMBALL, GEORGE ALLEN, lawyer; b. Clio, La., Sept. 28, 1903; s. Louis Rownd and Elisabeth (Sibley) K.; LL.B., La. State U., 1928; m. Aimee de Graffenried, June 8, 1934; children—George Allen, Elaine. Admitted to La. bar, 1928; practice in Monroe, 1929-44, Lake Charles, 1944—; partner Jones, Kimball, Harper, Tete & Wetherill, 1954—. Vice pres., dir. Tidelands Life Ins. Co., Bunkie, La., 1956, Tidelands Capital Corp., New Orleans, 1963—. Mem. La. Ins. Commn., 1941-48, chmn., 1945-48. Mem. Gov.'s Legal Reform Com., 1964—. Bd. regents U. of South, 1961-67, chmn., 1965-67. Mem. La. C. of C. (pres.), Am., La. bar assns., Phi Delta Phi, Alpha Tau Omega. Episcopalian. Clubs: Boston (New Orleans); Pioneer (Lake Charles). Home: 117 Pithon St Lake Charles LA 70601 Office: Gulf Nat Bank Bldg Lake Charles LA 70601

KIMBALL, JOHN THOMAS, corp. exec.; b. Bayou Current, La., Nov. 5, 1910; s. Thomas W. and Nora (Kimball) K.; B.S., Millsaps Coll., 1934; m. Louise Day, May 20, 1932; children—John Thomas, Bethanne, Mary Sue. Residential salesmen to dist. mgr. Miss. Power & Light Co., Jackson, 1934-46; asst. to pres. Central Ariz. Light & Power Co., 1946-48, v.p., 1948-52; exec. v.p. Ariz. Pub. Service Co., Phoenix, 1953-54; v.p., gen. mgr. Idaho Power Co., 1954-59; exec. v.p. Am. & Fgn. Power Co., Inc., 1959-64, mem. bd., 1959-68; sr. v.p., bd. mem. Electric Bond & Share Co., 1963-68; chmn. Ebasco Services, Inc., 1963-68; chmn. bd. EBS Management, Cons., Inc., 1964-68, Walter Kidde Constrs., Inc., Chem. Constrn. Corp., 1965-68; pres., chief adminstrv. officer Freeport Power Co., Grand Bahama Airport Co., Freeport Oil Co., Harobor Div. and Indsl. Devel. Bd. dirs., mgmt. com. Grand Bahama Port Authority, 1968-70, pres., 1970—. Past pres. Roosevelt council (Phoenix), Andrew Jackson council (Jaxon, Miss.), Mountainview council (Boise, Ia.) of Boy Scouts Am.; past regional v. chmn. nat. mem. campaign A.R.C., past dir. Boise chpt.; past v.p. Boise United Fund ; past dir. Phoenix Community Chest. Past mem. bad. St. Luke's Hosp., past chmn. bldg. com. Past mem. exec. bd. Western Idaho Eastern Ore. Inds. Devel. Council. Exec. dir. Miss. Agrl. and Indsl. Bd., 1945-46. Named Outstanding young man of Miss., 1945; recipient Silver Beaver, Silver Antelope, Silver Buffalo awards, Boy Scouts of Am. Mem. Nat. Assn. Electric Cos. N.A.M., N.W. Electric Light & Power Assn. (past pres.), I.E.E.E., U.S. C. of C., Newcomen Soc. Methodist (chmn. ofcl. bd.). Clubs: Metropolitan, Recess (N.Y.C.). Home: 548 Inagna Av Freeport Grand Bahama Island Office: PO Box F 2666 Freeport Grand Bahama Island

KIMBALL, LINDSLEY FISKE, found. exec.; b. Bklyn., N.Y., Nov. 27, 1894; s. Francis Tappan and Susie (Williams) K.; A.B., Columbia, 1917; Ph.D., N.Y. U., 1930; LL.D., Hobart and William Smith Colls., 1959; LL.D., Xavier U., 1968; m. Maude Ryder Kouwenhoven, Sept. 9, 1926; children—Richard T., Dean F. Inventor mathematical device used by USN; asst. to v.p., Underwood Typewriter, 1919-24; Boy Scouts of Am., 1924-38; dir. corps and spl. gifts Greater N.Y. Fund, 1938-42, cons. to pres., United Service Orgn., 1942-43, adminstrv. v.p., 1943-45, pres., 1945-49, 51-52, v.p. Rockefeller Found., 1949-53, exec. v.p., 1953-60; trustee Rockefeller U., 1947-, treas., 1959-65; v.p., dir. Gen. Edn. Board, 1959-60; mem. distbn. com. N.Y. Community Trust. Cons. Nat. Indsl. Conf. Bd. Mem. War-time Joint Army and Navy Com. on Welfare and Recreation. Asso. with Rockefeller Bros. Fund; trustee Nat. Urban League, Inc., Sealantic Fund; mem. exec. bd. A.R.C. Greater N.Y.; v.p., mem. exec. com. Community Blood Council of Greater N.Y.; chmn. devel. com. N.Y. Blood Center and Research Inst.; dir., mem. exec. com., United Negro Coll. Fund. Vice chmn. N. Am. Adminstrv. Com., World Council of Christian Edn. Bd. dirs. Vets. Hosp. Camp Shows; trustee Sleepy Hollow Restoration; chmn. civilian com. on welfare and recreation, Dept. Def., 1948; vice chmn. dirs., finance com. Council on Founds.; trustee, treas. States Urban Action Center; mem. adv. com. Urban America. Mem. Pres.'s Com. Religion Welfare in Armed Forces. Awarded Joint Army and Navy Citation, Presdl. award of Medal for Merit, 1946. Republican. Conglist. Clubs: Century Association, Rockefeller Center Luncheon, Hemisphere (bd. gov.) (N.Y.C.); Sands Point and Bath and Tennis. Home: 132 Revere Rd Manhasset NY 11030 Office: 30 Rockefeller Plaza New York City NY 10020

KIMBALL, PENN TOWNSEND II, state ofcl., educator, journalist; b. New Britain, Conn., Oct 12, 1915; s. Arthur G. and Effie (Smallen) K.; grad. Lawrenceville Sch., 1933; B.A., Princeton, 1937; B.A., M.A., Balliol Coll., Oxford (Eng.) U., 1939; postgrad. Yale, 1950-51, Columbia, 1951-58; m. Janet Evelyn Fraser, Apr. 8, 1947; 1 dau., Elisabeth. Reporter U.S. News and World Report, 1939-40, PM Newspaper, 1940-41; contbg. editor Time mag., 1945-46; sr. editor New Republic, 1947; adminstrv. asst. to Gov. Bowles of Conn., 1948-49; exec. sec. U.S. Senator Benton, 1949-50; asst. to Sunday editor N.Y. Times, 1951-54; with TV Radio Workshop, Ford Found., 1954-55; sr. editor Colliers, 1955-56; partner Louis Harris & Assos., N.Y.C., 1957-58; adminstrv. asst. to Gov. Harriman of N.Y., 1958; prof. Columbia Grad. Sch. Journalism, 1959-, mem. adminstrv. bd. Bur. Applied Social Research, 1963-67, cons. editor Harris Survey, 1963-; faculty Salzburg (Austria) Seminar in Am. Studies, 1967; vis. lectr. Dartmouth, U. Cal. at Berkeley, U. Conn. Sec. com. on appropriations Conn. Gen. Assembly, 1949, mem. citizens commn., 1968-69; mem. bd. finance, Westport, Conn., 1953-55, mem. charter commn., 1957, justice of peace, 1959-60, rep. town meeting, 1959-63; mem. Conn. Constl. Conv., 1965; dir. pub. affairs Urban Devel. Corp., State N.Y., 1971—. Served to capt. USMCR, 1941-45; PTO. Rhodes Scholar, 1937-39. Mem. Am. Assn. Pub. Opinion Research, Phi Beta Kappa. Democrat. Conglist. Club: National Press (Washington). Author: Bobby Kennedy and The New Politics, 1968; also articles in nat. magazines. Bd. editors Columbia Journalism Rev., 1963—. Home: 23 Meeker Rd Westport CT 06880 Office: Columbia Sch Journalism 116th and Broadway New York City NY

KIMBALL, RAYMOND ALONZO, assn. exec.; b. Kanosh, Utah, Apr. 1918; s. Abraham A. and Mary Jan (Gardner) K.; B.S. Utah State U., 1941; M.S. (Sloan fellow), U. Denver, 1946; postgrad, Stanford, 1951-52; m. Adrus Hansen, Sept. 30, 1943; children—Kristine, Diane, Treo, Colette, Melanie, Sr. researcher Utah Found., Salt Lake City, 1946-47; dir. research Colo. Pub. Expenditure Council, Denver, 1948-53, exec. dir., 1954-58; tax agt. C F & I Steel Corp., Denver, 1959-62; asst. to pres. Denver Dry Goods Co., 1963-65. Trustee Govtl. Research Assn.; pres. elect, dir. Vis, Nurses Assn. of Colo. Served to lt. USNR, 1942-45. Mem. Colo. Assn. Commerce and Industry (exec. v.p. 1966-71, pres. 1971—), Colo. Soc. Assn. Execs. (past pres.), Mfrs. Assn. Colo. (dir.). Rotarian (sec., dir.). Clubs: City Dinner (past pres., dir.), Denver Athletic (Denver) Home: 3228 E Fremont Dr Littleton CO 80122 Office: 1390 Logan St Denver CO 80203

KIMBALL, RICHARD ARTHUR, architect; b. Oberlin, O., June 30, 1899; s. Arthur Smith and Cyvelia (Winship) K.; A.B., Yale, 1922, B.F.A., 1927; student Columbia, 1923-25; m. Josephine Dodge, May 3, 1928; children—Richard Arthur, Geoffrey Dodge. Draftsman, job capt., jr. partner James Gamble Rogers, N.Y.C., 1927-34; partner Kimball and Husted, 1934-42, Gugler, Kimball and Husted, 1944—; cons. architect to Oberlin Coll., 1938-41; occasional cons. to Yale, Cornell, The Taft Sch., Bennett Coll., and pvt. schs. Chmn. Historic Dist. Commn., Salisbury. Trustee Saint-Guadens Meml., Brooks Sch., North Andover, Mass., Miss Porter's Sch., Farmington, Conn.; dir. Edward MacDowell Assn.; dir. Am. Acad. in Rome, 1960-66, now cons.; council Yale U.; mem. Thomas and Helen Hastings Fund. Served as dep. dir. facilities bur. WPB, 1942-44. Asso. fellow Calhoun Coll., Yale. Nat. Academician. Fellow A.I.A.; mem. N.A.D. (academician). Club: Century Association. Address: Salisbury CT 06068

KIMBALL, ROLAND BALDWIN, educator; b. Manchester, N.H., Apr. 12, 1921; s. Richard Henry and Frieda Clara (Obst) K.; B.S. in Math., U. N.H., 1942, M.Ed., 1949; Ed.D. (Charles Eliot scholar 1952-53), Harvard, 1958; John Hay fellow humanities, Williams Coll., 1960; m. Charlotte Buecher, Apr. 12, 1943; children—Thomas Lloyd, Keneth David, Scott Roland. Meteorologist, Am. Airlines, Inc., 1946-47; tchr. math. Concord (N.H.) High Sch., 1947-54; dir. secondary sch. services N.H. Dept. Edn., 1955-58, chief div. instrn., 1959-62; asso. prof. Stanford Sch. Edn., 1962-63; prof. edn., chmn. dept. U. N.H., 1963—. Cons. Nat. Endowment for Humanities, 1968, U.S. Dep. Schs., European Theater, 1968-70; adv. com. on tchr. edn. New Eng. Regional Commn., 1968-69. Chmn. N.H. Comm. Maths. and Sci., 1957-60, N.H. Com. Improvement Instrn. in English, 1960-62; bd. govs. New Eng. Ednl. Data System, 1961-69; trustee N.H. Higher Edn. Assistance Found., 1963-68; bd. dirs. N.H. Council Better Schs., 1962-69, Eastern Ednl. TV Network, 1961; chmn. N.H. Council for Tchr. Edn., 1965-68; mem. adv. com. on edn. N.H. Charitable Fund, 1966-70; mem. Gov.'s Com. on Econ. Opportunity, 1965-69. Served with USAAF, 1942-46; Res. ret. Decorated Air Force Commendation ribbon. Mem. Assn. Supervision and Curriculum Devel., Am. Ednl. Research Assn., Phi Kappa Phi, Kappa Delta Pi, Phi Delta Kappa. Contbr. profl. jours. Co- author: Education for Effective Thinking, 1960. Home: Riverview Rd Durham NH 03824 Office: Dept Edn Univ New Hampshire Durham NH 03824

KIMBALL, SOLON TOOTHAKER, educator, anthropologist; b. Manhattan, Kan., Aug. 12, 1909; s. Charles Augustus and Matie (Toothaker) K.; B.S., Kan. State U., 1930, Sc.D., 1963; A.M., Harvard, 1933, Ph.D., 1936; m. Hannah Jackson Price, Dec. 24, 1935; children—Sally Makielski, John Price. Sheldon fellow Harvard, 1933; head socio-economic surveys. Navajo Reservation, Dept. Interior, 1936-42; vis. prof. anthropology and sociology Okla. U., summer 1940; head community orgn. War Relocation Authority, 1942-45; asso. prof. sociology and anthropology Mich. State Coll., 1945-48; head dept., prof. of sociology and anthropology U. Ala., 1948-53; vis. prof. sociology U. Chicago, summer 1947, anthropology U. Cal., summer 1957; social anthropol. research in Ireland, 1932-33, Navajo Indians, 1936-42, summer 1949, rural communities in Michigan, 1945-48; prof. anthropology and edn. Columbia Tchrs. College, 1953-66; grad, research prof. anthropology U. Fla., 1966—; vis. prof. Univ. P.R., summer 1954; UNESCO specialist Brazilian Center Ednl. Research, 1958-59. Social Science Research Council fellow, 1961-62; Guggenheim fellow, 1966-67. Fellow Am. Anthrop. Assn., Soc. Applied Anthropology (pres. 1953), Am. Sociol. Soc.; mem. So. Anthrop. Soc., Am. Ethnol. Soc. (pres. 1970-71), Alpha Kappa Delta, Sigma Delta Chi, Reta Theta Pi. Author: Family and Community in Ireland (with C.M. Arensberg), rev. 2d edit., 1968; Community Government in War Relocation Centers, 1946; The Talladega Story (with Marion Pearsall), 1954; Readings in the Science of Human Relations (editor), 1949; (with J.E. McClellan) Education and the New America, 1962; (with C.M. Arensberg) Culture and Community, 1965; Crossing Cultural Boundaries (with James B. Watson), 1971. Home: 531 S W 26th Pl Gainesville FL 32601

KIMBALL, SPENCER LEVAN, univ. dean; b. Thatcher, Ariz., Aug. 26, 1918; s. Spencer Woolley and Camilla (Evring) K.; B.S., U. Ariz., 1940; postgrad. U. Utah, 1946-47; B.C.L., Oxford (Eng.) U., 1949; S.J.D., U. Wis., 1958; m. Kathryn Ann Murphy, June 12, 1939; children—Barbara Jean (Mrs. Thomas Sherman), Judith Ann (Mrs. William Stillion), Kathleen Louise, Spencer David, Kent Douglas, Timothy Jay. Asso. prof. U. Utah, 1949-50, dean, 1950-54, prof., 1954-57; prof. U. Mich., 1957-68, dir. legal research Law Sch., 1962-67, dir. legal research Law Sch., 1962-67; staff dir. Wis. Ins. Law Revision Project, 1966-; dean, prof. law U. Wis. Law Sch., 1968—. Pres., bd. dirs. Ann Arbor br. Am. Civil Liberties Union, 1959-63. Served to lt. USNR, 1943-46. Fellow Am. Bar Found.; Mem. Am., Mich., Utah, Wis. bar assns., Internat. Assn. Ins. Lawyers (past pres.), Am. Assn. U. Profs., Phi Beta Kappa, Phi Kappa Phi. Democrat. Author: Insurance and Public Policy (Elizur Wright award), 1960; Introduction to the Legal System, 1966; Essays in Insurance Regulation, 1966. Co-editor: Insurance, Government and Social Policy, 1969. Contbr. profl. jours. Home: 6413 Landfall Dr Madison WI 53705

KIMBALL, SPENCER WOOLLEY, clergyman; b. Salt Lake City, Mar. 28, 1895; s. Andrew and Olive (Woolley) K.; student Gila Jr. Coll., 1910-14, Brigham Young U., 1917, U. of Ariz., 1917; LL.D. (hon.), Brigham Young U., 1969; m. Camilla Eyring, Nov. 17, 1917; children—Spencer LeVan, Olive Beth (Mrs. Grant M. Mack), Andrew Eyring, Edward Lawrence. Mem. Council of Twelve Apostles of the Ch. of Jesus Christ of Latter-day Saints, 1943—, on mission, Mo., 1914-16; pres. Seventies Quorum, stake clk., Thatcher, Ariz., 1918-38; counselor St. Joseph Stake Presidency, 1924-36; pres. Mt. Graham Stake, 1938-43; teller, clk. later asst. cashier Ariz. Trust & Sav. Bank, Safford, 1918-23. Bank of Safford, 1923-26; pres., mgr. Kimball Greenhalgh Ins. & Realty Co., Safford. Ariz., 1927-43; sec. Gila Valley Irrigation Co., 1935-43; organizer, part owner Gila Broadcasting Co., Safford, 1935—. Mem. Ariz. Assn. Teachers Retirement Bd., Thatcher and Safford (Ariz.) city councils; bd. dirs. A.R.C., Safford; chmn. war fund drives. Trustee Gila Coll. Mem. Boy Scouts Am. Clubs: Rotary Internat. (dist. gov.); Rotary (pres.) (Safford, Ariz.). Home: 2028 Laird Dr Salt Lake City UT 84108 Office: 47 E South Temple St Salt Lake CIty UT 84108

KIMBALL, THOMAS LLOYD, conservationist; b. Los Angeles, Feb. 21, 1918; s. David Patton and Nellie (Nash) K.; student Phoenix Jr. Coll., 1937; B.S., Brigham Young U., 1939; m. Arvella Allen, Sept. 25, 1940; children—Patricia (Mrs. John N. Clark), Pamela (Mrs. Merrill R. Hunt), Kay (Mrs. Stephen Lafleur), Thomas S., Andrea, Allen Kent. With Ariz. Game and Fish Commn., 1939-52; dir. 1947-52; dir. Colo. Game and Fish Commn., 1952-60; exec. dir. nat. Wildlife Fedn., Washington, 1960—; sec. Interior's Adv. Bd. Wildlife Mgmt., 1962—; chmn. Natural Resources Council Am., 1962-64, now mem. exec. com.; cons. wildlife planning study Cal. Dept. Game and Fish; biologist cons. wildlife affairs Legislative Interim Com. on Wildlife Ore. Mem. Citizens Com. Outdoor Recreation Resources Review Commn. Report; trustee Ding Darling Found.; mem. Pres.'s Air Quality Adv. Bd., 1970-73; mem. adv. bd. Dept. Health, Edn. and Welfare Water Quality Criteria Study, Keep Am. Beautiful; del. Internat. Union for Conservation of Nature and Natural Resources. Served with USAAF, World War II. Recipient Certificate of Merit Nash Motor Co., 1953. Outstanding Service award Game and Fish Commn. Colo., 1961, Conservation Service award U.S. Dept. Interior, 1964, Distinguished Citizen award U. Ariz., 1964. Fellow A.A.A.S.; mem. Western (pres.), Midwest (pres.) assns. game and fish commrs., Wildlife Soc., Am. Forestry Assn., Am. Fisheries Soc., Soc. for Range Mgmt. Home: 825 Mackall Av McLean VA 22101 Office: 1412 16th St NW Washington DC 20036

KIMBALL, VERA F., editor, writer; b. Seward, Alaska, Feb. 8, 1903; d. Irving L. and Della (Carpenter) Kimball; A.B., Columbia, 1929; m. William T. Castles, Jr., Dec. 2, 1942. On clerical staff Legislature of Ty. of Alaska, 1923; with Alaska R.R., Anchorage, 1923-24, N.A. Newspaper Alliance, Met. Mus. Art, Gen. Foods Corp., Todd-Robertson & Todd (all N.Y. City), part time 1924- 29; asst. to sec. Am. Inst. Chemists, 1929-35; editor The Chemist, N.Y. C., 1935-68, associate editor, 1968-69; sec. S.C. Inst. Chemists, 1969—. Mem. N.Y. Acad. Scis., Am. Inst. Chemists (hon. life), A.A.A.S., Cook Inlet Hist. Soc., Alaska (charter mem.), Chester County hist. socs. Club: Barnard College (N.Y. City). Author: Firearms and Their Use (with W.T. Castles), 1942; Your Future in Chemistry (with M.R. Bhagwat), 1943. Contbr. World Scope Ency., The Ency. of Chemistry, year books, profl. and popular mags. Home: Magnolia Apts Chester SC 29706 Office: Route 2 Chester SC 29706

KIMBARK, EDWARD WILSON, elec. engr.; b. Chgo., Sept. 21, 1902; s. Edward Hall and Maude (Wilson) K.; B.S., Northwestern U., 1924, E.E., 1925; S.M., Mass. Inst. Tech., 1933, Sc.D., 1937; m. Ruth Elizabeth Merrick, July 19, 1930. Substa. operator Pub. Ser. Co. No. Ill., Evanston, 1925-26; asst. testing lab., 1926-26; asst. prof. elec. engring. Northwestern U., 1939-41, asso. prof., 1941-45, prof., 1945-50, acting chmn., 1941-42; dean Sch. Engring. Seattle U., 1955-62; elec. engr. Br. of System Engring. Bonneville Power Adminstrn. Fellow I.E.E.E., Am. Inst. Elec. Engring. Author: Power System Stability, 3 vols., 1948-56; Elec. Transmission of Power and Signals, 1949; Direct Current Transmission, 1971. Editor: Principles of Radar, 1944. Contbr. articles profl. jours. Home: 3233 N E Thompson St Portland OR 97212 Office: P O Box 3621 Portland OR 97208*

KIMBEL, WILLIAM ANTHONY, govt. cons., corp. exec.; b. N.Y.C., Jan. 5, 1888; s. Anthony and Eleanor (Haubner) K.; B.S., Columbia, 1909; m. L. Maud Windeler, Jan. 17, 1920; children—Frances Joyce K. Gunnels, Richard ANthony. Asst. mil attache Am. embassy, London, 1916; pres. A. Kimbel & Son, archtl. and decorative contractors and mfrs., N.Y.C., 1922-41; asst. to dir. OSS, 1941-45; owner, pub. Myrtle Beach (S.C.) News, 1946-48; adminstrv. dir. Anglo-Am. Council on Productivity, 1948-50; pres. Midcoast Investment, Myrtle Beach, 1950—; dir. pub. relations Hi-Q div. Aerorox Corp., 1948-65. U.S. rep. Econ. Commn. for Europe, 1954, 55; adviser delegation UNESCO, 1954; cons. Dept. State, 1963—. Pres., Am. Inst. Decorators, 1938-40; pres. Coastal Ednl. Found. S.C. Served with U.S. Army, World War I; AEF Recipient Medal of Merit, Columbia. Mem. Pilgrims Soc. Am., Am. Camellia Soc., U.S. Srs. Golf Assn., S.C. Hist. Soc., Winyah Indigo Soc. Clubs: Metropolitan, Chevy Chase (Washington); University, Racquet and Tennis (N.Y.C.); Dunes Golf and Beach (Myrtle Beach). Home: Wachesaw Plantation Murrells Inlet SC 29576 Office: P O Box 1526 Myrtle Beach SC 29577

KIMBELL, JOHN TIMOTHY, pharm. co. exec.; b. LaGrange, Ga., June 19, 1925; s. John Timothy and Irma Mae (Milam) K.; B.S., U. So. Cal., 1950; m. Dorothy Haller, Feb. 14, 1962; children—Stacy, Kent, Jeffrey. Sales rep. Ethicon, Inc. (Johnson & Johnson), Somerville, N.J., 1950-57, field asst., 1957, field coordinator Fenwal Labs., Ethicon, 1958, sales mgr., 1959; dir. marketing Fenwal Labs., Baxter Labs., Inc., 1960-65, dir. marketing Fenwal Labs., Flint Labs., 1962-65, v.p. marketing Baxter Labs., Inc., Morton Grove, Ill., 1965-68, exec. v.p., 1968-71, pres., 1971—, also dir.; dir. Bresnahan Computer Leasing Corp. Pres., Midwest Alumni Club, U. So. Cal. Served with USAAF, 1943-46. Decorated D.F.C., Air medal, Purple Heart. Mem. Assn. for Advancement Med. Instrumentation (v.p.), Med., Surg. Mfrs. Assn. (dir.), Health Industries Assn. (dir.), Midwest Pharm. Advt. Club, Pharm. Mfrs. Assn., A.M.A., N.A.M. Club: Executive (Chgo.). Home: 333 E Foster Pl Lake Forest IL 60045 Office: 6301 Lincoln Av Morton Grove IL 60053

KIMBER, HARRY HUBERT, educator; b. Indpls., May 12, 1903; s. Arthur Smith and Carrie (Echols) K.; A.B., U. Mich., 1925. M.A. 1928, Ph.D., 1932; m. Daisy Schulz, Mar. 3, 1928; children—Rebecca Cope, Caroline Echols, Katherine Spangler. Inst. history U. Mich., 1927-28; asst. prof. history and polit. sci. Bradley Coll., 1928-31; prof. history Mich. State Coll., 1932—, head of dept. humanities, dir. div. social sci., 1943-62, prof., head dept. religion, dir. residence instrn. Coll. Arts and Letters, 1964-70, prof. emeritus, 1970—. Mem. Patriarchal Order St. Vladimir, Mich. Acad. Sci. and Arts, Mich. Coll. Assn. (pres. 1950-51, chmn. com. legislation 1952-55), All-Coll. Ednl. Research Com. (chmn. 1952-56), Phi Beta Kappa, Phi Alpha Theta, Pi Gamma Mu. Episcopalian. Mason (32). Co-author: The Teaching of Religion in State Universities, 1960. Co-editor: Readings in the History of Civilization. 1939. Contbr. ednl. publs. Home: 474 Butterfield Dr East Lansing MI 48823

KIMBERLIN, ROBERT TOWNE, mfg. co. exec.; b. Terre Haute, Ind., Nov. 6, 1908; s. Robert O'Brien and Elizabeth Perle (Towne) K.; B.A., DePauw U., 1930; M.A., Harvard, 1932, LL.B., 1934; m. Naomi Ruth Hall June 7, 1935; children—Elizabeth Ann, Robert Hall, Jane Vernon. Admitted to N.Y. bar, 1935; asso. firm Sullivan & Cromwell, N.Y.C., 1934-38; asst. to pres. Crown Zellerbach Corp., 1938-51, sec., 1951-54, 60—, v.p., 1954—, treas., 1961—. Trustee Pacific Sch. Religion, Berkeley, Cal. Mem. Am. Soc. Corporate Secs. (past pres.), Phi Beta Kappa, Phi Kappa Psi. Club: Commonwealth Cal., Commercial (San Francisco). Home: 59 Park Way Piedmont CA 94611 Office: 1 Bush St San Francisco CA 94119

KIMBERLY, JOHN ROBBINS, ret. pulp and paper mfr.; b. Neenah, Wis., Apr. 13, 1903; s. James Cheney and Geraldine (Hardin) K.; grad. Phillips Andover Acad., 1922; Mass. Inst. Tech., 1926; m. Elizabeth Essick, Nov. 12, 1927; children—Josephine C. (Mrs. Douglas Peterson), John R., William E., Richard H. With Kimberly Clark Corp., Neenah, Wis., 1924—, v.p. charge sales, 1943-53, pres., 1953-67, chmn., 1967-70, now dir.; ret.; dir. Spruce Falls Power & Paper Company, Limited; dir. Wis. Telephone Co., First Nat. City Bank of New York, First Nat. Bank (Neenah), Corning Glass Works. Trustee Northwestern Mutual Life Ins. Co. Trustee Lawrence U., Episcopal Ch. Foundation; chmn. bd. trustees Theda Clark Meml. Hosp. Mem. Bus. Council. Address: Route 1 Box 17C Queenstown MD 21658

KIMBERLY, ROBERT CLYATT, surgeon; b. Catonsville, Md., July 20, 1909; s. George Maney and Alice (Roberts) K.; A.B., Yale, 1930; M.D., Johns Hopkins, 1934; m. Helen Marion, June 30, 1937; children—William Robert, James Clyatt; m. 2d, Joanne Lawrence Leonard, Apr. 14, 1956; 1 stepson, John B. Leonard. Intern, then resident surgery Royal Victoria Hosp., Montreal, Can., 1934-37; pvt. practice surgery, Balt., 1937—; surgeon Johns Hopkins, Union Meml. Hosp., also Greater Balt. Med. Center; instr. surgery Johns Hopkins Med. Sch., 1940-; cons. surgeon gen. U.S. Army, Anne Arundel Gen. Hosp., Annapolis, Md.; dir. Eudowood Sanatorium, Balt., 1947—. Vice chmn. Mayor Balt. Coordinating Council Fund Raising Activities, 1962-65. Served to lt. col., M.C., AUS. 1941-46; ETO, PTO; col. Md. N.G., 1958-67. Fellow A.M. A., A.C.S., So. Surg. Assn., Southeastern Surg. congress; mem. Balt. City Med. Soc. (treas., 1954-61). Assn. Mil. Surgeons U.S. (pres. 1964; founders medal 1956), Soc. Med. Cons. Armed Forces (sec. 1963-67, pres. 1968). Medical and Chirurgical Faculty Maryland (v.p. 1965), St. George's Soc., 29th Div. Assn. N.G. Episcopalian (vestryman). Clubs: Baltimore Country, University, Johns Hopkins, Paint and Powder (Balt.). Contbr. med. jours. Home: 1120 Bellemore Rd Baltimore MD 21210 Office: 103 E Chase St Baltimore MD 21202

KIMBLE, GREGORY ADAMS, educator; b. Mason City, Ia., Oct. 21, 1917; s. Howard and Iola (Adams) K.; A.B., Carleton Coll., 1940; M.A., Northwestern U., 1942; Ph.D., State U. Ia., 1945; m. Lucille Laird, Dec. 30, 1943; childen—Jeffrey Laird, Judith Elisabeth. Instr. to asst. prof. psychology Brown U., 1945-50; asst. prof. psychology Yale, 1950-52; asso. prof. to prof. psychology Duke, 1952-68; prof., chmn. dept. psychology U. Colo., 1968—. Psychology editor Ronald Press Co.; chmn. exptl. psychology research review com. Nat. Inst. Mental Health, 1968-71. Fellow A.A.A.S., Am. Psychol. Assn. (past pres. div. exptl. psychology, past chmn. policy and planning bd.); mem. Psychonomic Soc. (governing bd. 1963-67), Eastern, Midwestern, Rocky Mountain psychol. assns. Author: (with Dr. Norman Garmezy) Principles of General Psychology, 1968; Conditioning and Learning, 1961; Foundations of Conditioning and Learning, 1967. Home: 443 Wewoka Dr Boulder CO 80303

KIMBLE, JOSEPH CHANSLOR, lawyer; b. Hanford, Cal., Jan, 3, 1910; s. Robert and Laura (Wiley) K.; A.B., U. Cal. at Berkeley, 1931; LL.B., Harvard, 1934; m. Betty Minturn, Mar. 19, 1937 (div. July 1960); children—Ward Minturn, Betsy Kennedy; m. 2d, Sally S. Waldo, July 25, 1961; children—Steven Waldo, Wendy Waldo, Carolyn. Admitted to N.Y. State bar, 1935, Cal. Bar, 1937; practice in Fresno, 1939—; partner Kimble MacMichael & Jackson; lectr. law U. Cal. at Berkeley, 1952—. Mng. partner Caldarko Gas co., 1958-, K.A.L. Oil Co., 1957-; v.p., dir. McCarthy Tank & Steel Co., Bakersfield, Cal., 1949—; mgr., dir. Kennedy Co., 1957-66. Mem. Gov. Cal. Com. Agrl. Labor Resources, 1951. Mem. Fresno County Republican Central Com. 1943-49. Pres. Fresno City and County Children's Hosp. and Guidance Clinic, 1950-51. Mem. Am. Bar Assn., State Bar Cal. (chmn. com. taxation 1946-48, Central Valley Empire Assn. (pres. 1948-49), Fresno City and County C. of C. (pres. 1946-48), Phi Gamma Delta. Conglist. Clubs: Rotary (pres. 1948-49), Harvard (pres. 1959-60), University-Sequoia-Sunnyside (Fresno); Lincolns Inn (Harvard Law Sch.); Family, Commonwealth (San Francisco). Author articles taxes. Home: 1261 San Ramon St Fresno CA 93705 Office: Guarantee Sav Bldg Fresno CA 93721

KIMBLE, KENNETH LEROY, lawyer, ins. co. exec.; b. Mankato, Minn., July 13, 1910; s. Fred Adam and Effie Jane (Smith) K.; B.A., U. Minn., 1932, LL.B., 1934; m. Martha Louise Smith, Sept. 2, 1939; children—James Lawson, William Beldon. Admitted to Minn. bar, 1934, D.C. bar, 1947, also U.S. Supreme Ct.; spl. atty. antitrust div. Dept. Justice, 1934-37, spl. asst. to atty. gen. antitrust div., 1938-41, chief appellate sect. antitrust div., 1942-43, 1st asst. antitrust div., 1946-47; pvt. practice, Washington, 1948-54; with Life Ins. Assn. Am., Washington, 1955-, asso. gen. counsel, 1958- 64, v.p., gen. counsel, 1965—. Mem. Atty. Gen.'s Nat. Com. Study Antitrust Laws, 1953-55. Served to 1st lt. AUS, 1943-45. Mem. Am., Fed., D.C. bar assn., Assn. Life Ins. Counsel, Met. Washington Bd. Trade, Tau Kappa Epsilon, Phi Alpha Delta. Clubs: Columbia Country (Chevy Chase); University (Washington). Home: 3800 Club Dr Chevy Chase MD 20015 Office 1701 K St NW Washington DC 20006

KIMBLE, WILLIAM EARL, lawyer; b. Denver, May 4, 1926; s. George Wilbur and Grace (Fick) K.; LL.B., U. Ariz., 1951; m. Jean M. Cayia, Dec. 27, 1950; children—Mark, Cary, Timothy, Stephen, Philip, Peter, Michael. Spl. agt. FBI, 1951-52; admitted to Ariz. bar, 1951; practice in Bisbee, 1952-60, Tucson, 1962- -; partner Gentry, McNulty & Kimble, 1952-60; judge Superior Ct. Ariz., 1960-62; partner Lesher & Scruggs, 1962—. Commr., Ariz. Oil and Gas Commn., 1958-60; lectr. Law U. Ariz. Coll. Law, 1962—; spl. asst. atty. gen. Ariz., 1963—; spl. counsel U. Ariz.; counsel Ariz. Regional Med. Program. Republican nominee Ariz. atty. gen., 1956, U.S. Congress, 1964. Served with USNR, 1944-46. Mem. Sigma Chi, Phi Alpha Delta. Home: 95 Camino Miramonte Tucson AZ 85716 Office: 3773 E Broadway Tucson AZ 85716

KIMBREL, MONROE, banker: b. Miller County, Ga., Aug. 4, 1916; s. Charlie C. and Effie (Folds) K.; B.S., U. Ga., 1936; grad. Stonier Grad., Sch. Banking, Rutgers U., 1949; m. Nita Matlock, Apr. 17, 1941; children-Jenny Wood (Mrs. James Bunn III), Charles Daniel. With Farm Credit Adminstrn., Columbia, S.C., 1936-46; with First Nat. Bank, Thomson, Ga., 1946-65, chmn. bd., 1961-65; chmn. bd. Bank Fort Valley (Ga.), 1963-65; dir. Fed. Res. Bank Atlanta, 1960-65, sr. v.p., 1965, 1st v.p., 1965-68, pres., 1968—. Mem. Am. (pres. 1962-63), Ga. (pres. 1956-57) bankers assns. Rotarian (past dist. gov.). Home: 620 Peachtree St Atlanta GA 30308 Office: Fed Res Bank Atlanta GA 30303

KIMBRELL, CHARLES A., lawyer; b. Augusta, Ga., Mar. 15, 1921; A.B., U. Ga., 1942, LL.B., 1947. Admitted to Fla. bar, 1948; now mem. firm Dixon, Bradford, Williams, McKay & Kimbrell, Miami. Mem. Fla. Jud. Qualification Commn., 1968—. Fellow Am. Coll. Trial Lawyers, Am. Bar Found.; mem. Am., Dade County (pres. 1963-64) bar assns., Fla. Bar (gov. 1965-67), Internat. Assn. Ins. Counsel, Fedn. Ins. Counsel. Office: Dade Fed Office Bldg 101 E Flagler St Miami FL*

KIMBRELL, HORACE WARREN, lawyer; b. Lees Summit, Mo., Apr. 19, 1916; s. Raymond Benefiel and Ruberta Katherine (Magers) K., A.B., U. Kansas City (Mo.), 1936, LL.B., 1939; m. Ethel Young, Aug. 5, 1956. Admitted to Mo. bar. 1939, since practiced in Kansas City; first asst. U.S. atty. Western Dist. Mo., 1953- 61; asst. general counsel Kansas City Life Ins. Co., 1961—. Pres. Goodwill Industries Greater Kansas City, 1952-66, chmn. bd., 1966-; pres. Goodwill Industries Am., Inc., 1961-66, chmn. bd., 1966-68, nat. ambassador, 1968—; secretary trustees U. Kansas City, 1949-; trustee, chmn. finance com. St. Paul Sch. Theology Methodist, Kansas City, 1958—. Served USNR, 1942-46. Mem. Am., Fed. (pres. Kansas City 1958), 8th circuit nat. v.p. 1965-67, member of the national council since 1967—, Kansas City, Inter-Am. bar assns., Kansas City Lawyers Assn., Mo. Bar, Am. Judicature Soc., Nat. Lawyers Club (charter), Am. Soc. Internat. Law, Internat. Platform Assn., Navy League, State Hist. Soc. Mo. (life), World Order Through Law Center (charter). Republican. Methodist (ofel. bd., Sunday sch.(tchr.). Home: 5900 E 129th St Grandview MO 64030 Office: 3520 Broadway Kansas City MO 64111

KIMBROUGH, EMILY (Emily Kimbrough Wrench), writer; b. Muncie., Ind., Oct. 23, 1899; d. Hal Curry and Charlotte Emily (Wiles) Kimbrough; B.A., Bryn Mawr Coll., 1921; student The Sorbonne, Paris, 1922; m. John Wrench. Dec. 31. 1926; children—Margaret Achsah and Alis Emily (twins). Editor Fashions of the Hour, Marshall Field & Co., Chgo., 1922-27; fashion editor Ladies' Home Jour., 1927, mng. editor, 1927-29; writer, 1932—. Author: Our Hearts Were Young and Gay (with Cornelia Otis Skinner), 1942; We Followed Our Hearts to Hollywood. 1943; How Dear to My Hearts, 1944; It Gives Me Great Pleasure, 1948; The Innocents from Indiana, 1950; Through Charley's Door, 1952; Forty Plus and Fancy Free, 1954; So Near and Yet So Far, 1955; Water, Water Everywhere, 1956; And a Right Good Crew, 1958; Pleasure by the Busload, 1961; Forever Old, Forever New, 1964; Floating Island, 1968. Home: 11 E 73d St New York City NY 10021

KIMBROUGH, EMORY CALLOWAY LANDON, Jr., educator, sociologist; b. Clarksville, Tenn., Nov. 15, 1934; s. Emory Calloway Landon and Martha (Beaumont) K.; A.B., Davidson Coll., 1957; M.A. (Nat. Woodrow Wilson fellow), U. N.C., 1959, Ph.D. (So. fellow), 1963. Teaching fellow U. N.C, 1960-62; instr. sociology Washington and Lee U., Lexington, Va., 1962-63, asst. prof., 1963-66, asso. prof., 1966-69, prof., 1969—, chmn. dept. sociology and anthropology, 1967—. Fellow Am. Sociol. Assn.; mem. So. Sociol. Soc., Phi Beta Kappa, Alpha Tau Omega. Episcopalian. Home: 710 Thorn Hill Rd Lexington VA 24450

KIMBROUGH, RALPH BRADLEY, educator; b. Rhea Springs, Tenn., Mar. 12, 1922; s. Robert Bradley and Elizabeth (Crosby) K.; B.S., U. Tenn., 1948, M.S., 1949, Ed.D., 1953: m. Gladys King, Dec. 21, 1946; 1 son, Ralph Bradley. Tchr., Knoxville (Tenn.) High Sch, 1948-49; prin. Nichols Sch., Lenoir City, Tenn., 1950- 51; mem. staff So. States Coop. Program in Ednl. Adminstrn., 1953-54; prof. U. Tenn., 1954-58; prof. U. Fla., 1958-65, chmn. dept. ednl. adminstrn. and supervision, 1966—. Served with AUS, 1943-45; ETO. Mem. Am. Edn. Research Assn., Am. Assn. U. Profs., N.E.A., Am. Assn. Sch. Adminstrs., Fla. Edn. Assn., Phi Delta Kappa. Author: (with others) Community Leadership for Public Education, 1955; Political Power and Educational Decision Making, 1964; (with others) Philosophic Theory and Practice in Educational Administration, 1966; Administering Elementary Schools: Concepts and Practices, 1968. Contbr. articles profl. jours. Home: 917 N W 40th Dr Gainesville FL 32601

KIMBROUGH, VERMAN, coll. pres. emeritus; b. Rockford, Ala., Apr. 6, 1902; s. James Robert and Bertie (Newman) K.; A.B., Birmingham-So. Coll., 1925, grad, student 1928-29; m. Edith Rebecca Averyt, July 15, 1929; 1 son, Robert Averyt. Instr. history, Birmingham-So. Coll., 1925-26; instr. sociology and history, So. Coll., 1929-31; asst. to pres. Ringling Sch. of Art, 1931-33, pres., 1933-71, pres. emeritus, 1971—; dir. First Fed. Savs. & Loan Assn., Ednl. TV Sta. WEDU, Tampa, Fla. Mayor City of Sarasota, Fla., 1938-39. Supt. Pub. Instrn., Sarasota County, Fla., 1945-53. Fellow Nat. Coll of Toronto, Can. 1938. Mem. Alpha Tau Omega. Pi Gamma Mu. Omicron Delta Kappa, Democrat. Club: Field. Home: 1874 Wisteria St Sarasota FL 33579

KIMBROUGH, WILLIAM JOSEPH, librarian; b. Bowling Green, Ky., Apr. 21, 1930; s. William Joseph and Mary Alice (Sexton) K.; A.B., Western Ky. U., 1952; M.A., Ind. U., 1956; m. Ann Cecil Cornett, Nov. 25, 1954; children—Charles Madison, Howard David. Reference asst. Gross Pointe (Mich.) Pub. Library, 1956- 58; head librarian Sturgis (Mich.) Pub. Libary, 1958-60; supr. adult services Lansing (Mich.) Pub. Library, 1960-65, chief librarian, 1965-69; asst. librarian, dir. pub. service Denver Pub. Library, 1969—. Served to 1st lt. AUS, 1952-54. Mem. Am., Mich. (past pres.), Colo. library assns. Home: 2111 S St Paul St Denver CO 80210 Office: 1357 Broadway Denver CO 80203

KIMEL, WILLIAM ROBERT, educator; b. Cunningham, Kan., May 2, 1922; s. Chester LeRoy and Llonda Florence (Hart) K.; B.S., Kan. State U., 1944, M.S., 1949; Ph.D., U. Wis., 1956; m. Mila D. Brown, Aug. 14, 1952. Research asso. Argonne (Ill.) Nat. Lab., 1957-58; engr. Boeing Airplane Co., summer 1953, Westinghouse Electric Co., summer 1954, U.S. Forest Products Lab., 1955- 56; from instr. to asso. prof. mech. engring. Kan. State U., Manhattan, 1946-58; prof., head nuclear engring. dept., 1958-68; dean, dir. engring. expt. sta., prof. nuclear engring., U. Mo., Columbia, 1968—. Mem. Kan. Gov.'s Adv. Com. on Atomic Energy, 1961-68, chmn., 1966-68; mem. Asso. Midwest Univs. Nuclear Engring. Edn. Com., 1959—. chmn., 1966-67; mem. Columbia Indsl. Commn.; mem. adv. com. to Office of Civil Def., 1964-69. Registered profl. engr., Kan., Mo. Fellow Am. Nuclear Soc. (chmn. edn. devel. com. 1967-69, chmn. edn. com. 1963-66, mem. exec. com. for tech. group edn. 1964-66, mem. planning com. 1966—, exec. com. edn. div. 1968, vice chmn. edn. div., 1969-70); mem. Am. Soc. for Engring. Edn. (chmn. nuclear engring. div. 1963-64, mem. steering com. council of tech. divs. 1964-65, mem. com. on relations with AEC 1964, 67—, chmn. nuclear engring. Brochure com. 1966-68), Columbia C. of C. (bd. dirs.). Contbr. articles to profl. jours. Home: 900 Yale St Columbia MO 65201

KIMMEL, DONALD LORAINE, educator; b. Juniata, Pa., July 12, 1906; s. Jesse Melvin and Clara Alberta (Cutshall) K.; B.S., Gettysburg Coll., 1929; M.S., U. Mich., 1935, Ph.D., 1938; m. Jessie Elizabeth Brown, June 16, 1934; children—Donald Loraine, Charles B., Richard O. High sch. sci. tchr., 1929-36; food chemist, 1935-36; demonstrator fellow anatomy U. Mich., 1936-38; instr. La. State U. Sch. Medicine, 1938-42, asst. prof. anatomy, 1942; asso. prof. Baylor U. Med. Coll., 1943; asso. prof. Temple U. Sch. Medicine, 1943-50, prof., 1950-57; prof., chmn. dept. anatomy Chgo. Med. Sch., 1957-66, W.Va. U. Med. Center, 1966—. Active local Boy Scouts Am., YMCA, Community Chest, A.R.C. Recipient award for demonstration bladder innervation A.M.A., 1955. Mem. Am. Assn. Anatomists, Acad. Neurologists, Cajal Club, Phi Beta Kappa, Sigma Xi, Beta Beta Beta. Author: Structure and Function of the Human Body, 1945. Home: 609 Valley View St Morganton WV 26505

KIMMEL, JOE ROBERT, biochemist, educator; b. DuQuoin, Ill., May 3, 1922; s. Maurice Edward and Roberta (Pyatt) K.; A.B., DePauw U., 1943; M.D., Johns Hoplins, 1947; Ph.D., U. Utah, 1954; m. Jean Howell, Apr. 3, 1947; children-Philip H., Lynn, Ellen, Bruce E. Intern, Salt Lake City Gen. Hosp., 1947-49; resident U.S. Naval Hosp., Oakland, Cal. 1950-52; research instr. biochemistry U. Utah Coll. Medicine, 1954-55, asst. research prof. biochemistry, 1955-59, asso. research prof. biochemistry, 1959-60, asso. prof. biochemistry, 1960-62, asso. prof. biochemistry and pediatrics, 1962-64; prof. biochemistry and medicine, dir. McIlvain Labs., Kan. U. Med. Center, 1964—. Served with USNR, 1950-52. Recipient Career Devel. award USPHS, 1960. Henry Strong Denison scholar Johns Hopkins, 1946-47. Mem. Am. Soc. Biol. Chemists, Am. Assn. U. Profs., A.A.A.S., Alpha Omega Alpha. Home: 6219 W 61st Terrace Shawnee Mission KS 66202 Office: Rainbow Blvd at 39th St Kansas Ciy KS 66103

KIMMEL, ROBERT MARION, ret. corp. exec., lawyer; b. Kendallville, Ind., June 10, 1905; s. Charles W. and Hortense (Abrams) K.; A.B., Case Western Res. U., 1926, J.D., 1928; m. Evelyn Lane Eastman, Oct. 26, 1929; children—Sarah Jean (Mrs. James Allen Young), Susan Lane (Mrs. Gordon Evans Wood). Admitted to Ohio bar, 1928; staff legal dept. Firestone Tire & Rubber Co., Akron, O., 1929-40; with Cleveland Cliffs Iron Co., Cleve., 1940-70, sec., 1953-70; past sec. affiliated cos. Mem. YMCA. Mem. Am. Soc. Corporate Secretaries, Ohio, Cleve., Am. bar assns., Greater Cleve. Growth Assn., Delta Kappa Epsilon, Phi Delta Phi. Republican. Presbyn. Club: Midday. Kiwanian. Home: 1756 Oakmount Rd South Euclid OH 44121 Office: Terminal Towers Cleveland OH 44113

KIMPEL, BENJAMIN FRANKLIN, educator; b. Racine, Wis., May 9, 1905; s. Benjamin F. and Agnes (Beltz) K.; B.A., U. Wis., 1926; fellow anthropology U. Neb., 1927-28; Ph.D. (Tew fellow), Yale, 1932. Ordained to ministry Am. Unitarian Assn., 1937; mem. faculty Kan. Wesleyan U., 1933-36, prof. philosophy, 1935-36; prof. philosophy Drew U., 1938—. Mem. Am. Assn. U. Profs., Am. Philos. Assn. Author: Religious Faith, Language, and Knowledge, 1952; Faith and Moral Authority, 1953; Symbols of Religious Faith, 1954; Moral Principles in the Bible, 1956; Language and Religion, 1957; Principles of Moral Philosophy, 1960; Kant's Critical Philosophy, 1964; Hegel's Philosophy of History, 1964; Nietzsche's Beyond Good and Evil, 1964; Schopenhauer's Philosophy, 1965; Philosophy of Zen Buddhism, 1966. Home: North Bennington VT 05257 Office: Draw Univ Madison NJ 07940

KIMPTON, LAWRENCE A., ret. oil co. exec.; b. Kansas City, Mo., Oct. 7, 1910; s. Carl Edward and Lynn (Kennedy) K.; A.B., Stanford, 1931, M.A., 1932; Ph.D., Cornell U., 1935; D.Sc., Beloit Coll., 1952; LL.D., Lake Forest Coll., 1955, Knox Coll., 1956, Northwestern U., 1958, U. Mo., 1960, U. Ill., 1961, U. Alaska, 1966; L.H.D., U. Chgo., 1961; m. Marcia Drennon, Oct. 2, 1943 (dec. Mar. 1963). Tchr. Deep Springs (Cal.) Coll., 1935, dean, dir., 1936-41; operator, part owner cattle ranch in Nev., 1941-42; prof. math. and philosophy, dean Coll. Liberal Arts, U. Kansas City, 1942-43; chief adminstrv., officer metall. lab., atomic bomb project, U. Chgo., 1943-44, dean students, sec. faculties, prof. philosophy, and edn., 1944-46, v.p., dean faculties, prof. philosophy and edn., 1946-47; dean students, prof. philosophy Stanford, 1947-50; v.p. devel. U. Chgo., 1950-51, chancellor, prof. philosophy, 1951-60; gen. mgr. planning Standard Oil Ind., 1960-63, v.p., 1963-68, asst. to chmn. bd., 1968-71 also dir.; now cons. Standard Oil Ind.; dir. Quacker Oats Co., C. & O. Ry. Stanford Fellow, 1959. Trustee Museum Sci. and Industry, Chgo., Newberry Library, Chgo., Robert A. Taft Inst. Govt.; bd. visitors Tulane U. Decorated officier de la Legion d'Honneur (France). Mem. Phi Beta Kappa, Phi Kappa Phi, Delta Sigma Rho. Clubs: Tavern, Chicago, Commercial, Chicago Yacht, Commonwealth, Economic, Wayfarers (Chgo.); Bohemian (San Francisco). Office: 910 S Michigan Av Chicago IL 60680

KINARD, HARGETT YINGLING, ret. banker; b. York, Pa., May 29, 1912; s. Henry B. and Edith R. (Yingling) K.; student Drexel Inst., Phila., 1928-29; grad. Rider Coll., Trenton, N.J., 1933; m. Pearl E. Greenhill, Aug, 20, 1932; children—Joan S. (Mrs. Edward J. Mercado), Lois E. (Mrs. Hugh T. Bower), Gail E. (Mrs. Joseph R. Eastburn). Asso. firm Lybrand, Ross Bros. & Montgomery, Phila., 1933-51; with Electric Storage Battery Co., Phila., 1951-55, comptroller, 1952-55; v.p., treas. Maule Industries, Inc., 1955-58; v.p. finance, 1958-59; financial cons. to various internat. firms, 1959-60; v.p., comptroller First Union Nat. Bank of N.C., Charlotte, 1960-63, sr. v.p., comptroller, 1963-65, exec. v.p., comptroller, 1965-71; sr. v.p., treas. 1st Union Nat. Bank Corp., 1968-71; now cons. C.P.A., Pa. Mem. Am., Pa. insts. C.P.A.'s, N.C. Assn. C.P.A.'s, Financial Execs. Inst, Bank Adminstrn. Inst., Charlotte C. of C. Presbyn. Clubs: Carmel Country; Charlotte Executives; Kiwanis. Home: 5825 Lansing Dr Charlotte NC 28211

KINARIWALA, BHARAT, educator, elec. engr.; b. Ahmedabad, India, Oct. 14, 1926; s. Jamnadas and Hiralaxmi (Shodhan) K.; came to U.S., 1951, naturalized, 1963; B.S., Bernares Hindu U., 1950; M.S., U. Cal. at Berkeley, 1954, Ph.D., 1957; m. Marva Schor, Apr. 23, 1953; children—Neela, Maya. Elec. engr. Cosmos India Rubber Works, Ltd., Bombay, India, 1950-51; acting asst. prof. U. Cal. at Berkeley, 1956-57; mem. tech. staff Bell Telephone Lab., N.J., 1957-66; prof. U. Hawaii, 1966—, chmn. dept. elec. engring., 1969—. Mem. I.E.E.E. (chmn. symposium on circuit theory 1969, adminstrv. com. 1968, 69), Sigma Xi. Research synthesis active RC networks, 1959; timing problem in high speed digital communication, 1961-64; theory distributed networks, 1964-66; computing algorithms, 1966—. Asso. editor IEEE Trans. Circuit Theory, 1967-69. Home: 729 Elepaio St Honolulu HI 96816

KINCADE, ARTHUR WARREN, banker; b. Chillicothe, Mo., Aug. 14, 1896; s. John Albert and Flora (Dilley) K.; ed. high sch. and coll., 1 year; m. Mary Josephine Igou, Aug. 22, 1917; children—Arthur Warren, Imogene, Patricia Josephine. Officer varous banks in Okla. and Tex., 1915-31; pres. W. Tex. Mortgage Loan Co. and its subsidiaries, Amarillo, also v.p. First Nat. Bank, Amarillo, 1931-37; exec. v.p. Fourth Nat. Bank, Wichita, Kan., 1937-40, pres., 1940-69, chmn. bd., chief exec. officer, 1969—; chmn. bd., chief exec. officer Fourth Financial Corp., Wichita, Mem. Am. Petroleum Inst., Newcomen Soc., Alpha Kappa Psi (hon.). Mason (K.T.; 32; Shriner). Author articles. Home: PO Box 1090 Wichita KS 67202 Office: Fourth Nat Bank Wichita KS 67202

KINCAID, ARON, actor; b. Los Angeles, June 15, 1943; s. Norman Neale and Neva Ferne (Baker) Williams; B.A., U. Cal. at Los Angeles, 1962. Actor appearing in motion pictures, television, and stage; television debut in Bachelor Father, 1962; has appeared in over 100 television shows; motion picture credits include Girls on the Beach, Beach Ball, Ski Party, Ghost in the Invisible Bikini, Happiest Millionaire, Proud, Damned and Dead, Black Water Gold; numerous stage appearances on West Coast. Served with USCGR, 1963-71. Recipient award for most promising player, Screen World, 1966, Louella Parson's nomination for stardom, 1966. Mem. Delta Tau Delta. Home: 9861 Easton Dr Beverly Hills CA 90210 Office: care Arthur Kennard Assos Inc 8776 Sunset Blvd Los Angeles CA 90069

KINCAID, GARVICE DELMAR, banker, ins. co. exec.; b. Lee County, Ky., Aug. 9, 1912; s. Douglas and Minnie (Johnson) K.; student Eastern Tchr. Coll., 1930-33; A.B., U. Ky. 1934. LL.B., 1937; Litt. D., Ky. Wesleyan Coll., 1961; LL.D., Eastern Ky. State Coll., Richmond, 1965; m. Nelle Wilson, Oct. 4, 1940; children—Jane and Joan (twins). Admitted to Ky. bar, 1937, since practiced in Lexington; senior partner Kincaid, Wilson, Schaefer, Trimble & Hembree; chairman board Central Bank, Lexington, 1945—, chmn. board Marathon (Florida) Bank, Dania chmn. board (Fla.) Bank, Dania Bank (Fla.), 1959—, First Nat. Bank Carlisle, Ky., 1st Nat. Bank, Nicholasville, Ky., 1st Nat. Bank, Georgetown, Ky., Peoples-Comml. Bank, Winchester Ky., Comml. Bank, Middlesboro, Kentucky, also chairman of board Traders, Nat. Bank, Mt. Sterling, Ky., Bank of Danville, Ky., Powell County Bank, Stanton, Ky.; chmn. Ky. Central Life Ins. Co., Lexington; pres. Ky. Finance Co., Lexington, 1946—, Cardinal Corp., Lexington, Ky., 1958—, Central Realty Co., Lexington; dir. Nat. Bank & Trust Co., Paris, Ky., 1st Farmers Nat. Bank, Owenton, Ky., Corbin Deposit Bank, Corbin, Ky., Peoples Bank & Trust Co., Berea, Ky., Bank Williamsburg (Ky.); owner radio stations WINN, Louisville, WFFG, Marathon, Florida, WHOO, Orlando, Fla., WVLK, Lexington, Founder, chmn. bd. Lexington Boys Club, Kincaid Found; chmn. Muscular Dystrophy Assn., Nat. Library Week; bd. dirs. Lexington YMCA. Co-recipient Horatio Alger award, 1960; named Ky. Col., 1953, Outstanding Citizen of Ky., Ky. Press Assn., 1966; named to Nat. Newspaper boy Hall of Fame, 1965. Mem. Christian Ch. Mason (Shriner), Moose. Elk. Clubs: Lexington Country; Surf (Miami, Fla.). Home: 1800 Richmond Rd Lexington KY 40502 Office: Central Bank Bldg Lexington KY 40507

KINCAID, HARRY GROVE, lawyer; b. Clifton Forge, Va., Jan. 5, 1920; s. John A. and Lelia B. (Grove) K.; A.B., Washington and Lee U., 1941. LL.B., 1946; m. Anne L. Walton, May 17, 1944; children—Sally, Anne, Elizabeth, John. Admitted to Fla. bar, 1946, since practiced in Jacksonville; mem. firm Knight, Kincaid, Poucher & Harris, 1956—. Dir., sec. Jacksonville Fed. Savs. & Loan Assn., 1953—. Mem. Bd. Pub. Instrn., 1965-67. Gov. A.R.C., 1956-59, dir., past chmn. Duval County chpt.; past pres. Duval County Legal Aid Assn. Served from ensign to lt., USNR, 1943-45; capt. Res. Mem. Am., Fla. (past chmn. legal aid com.), Jacksonville bar assn. C. of C. of U.S., Jacksonville Area C. of C., Order of Coif, Phi Beta Kapps, Delta Upsilon. Democrat. Episcopalian (chancellor Diocese of Fla.). Clubs: Timuquana Country; Florida Yacht (commodore 1960-61) Home: 4344 Mcgirts Boulevard Jacksonville FL 32210 Office: AM Heritage Bldg Jacksonville FL 32202

KINCAID, HUGH REID, lawyer; b. Fayetteville, Ark., Sept. 30, 1934; s. Hugh Z. and Mary (Gose) K.; B.S., U. Ark., 1956, J.D., 1959; m. Diane Frances Divers, June 4, 1961; children-William Reid, Kathryn Lea. Admitted to Ark. bar, 1959; practice in Fayetteville, 1963—; trial atty. U.S. Dept. Justice, 1961-63; city atty., Fayetteville, 1965-69; mem. firm Kincaid & Horne, 1968—; instr. bus. law Coll. Bus. Adminstrn., U. Ark., 1963—. Pres. N.W. Ark. Community Concert Assn.; bd. dirs. Fayetteville Pub. Schs., Washington County chpt. A.R.C. Served to 1st lt., Judge Adv. Gen. Corps, U.S. Army, 1956-61. Mem. Am., Ark., Washington County (past pres.) bar assns., Am. Judicature Soc. Methodist. Lion. Home: 520 Lakeridge St Fayetteville AR 72701 Office: First Nat Bank Bldg Fayetteville AR 72701

KINCAID, JAMES LESLIE, hotel corp. exec. b. Syracuse, N.Y., Nov. 28, 1884; s. James and Carrie (Dennis) K.; LL.B., Syracuse U., 1908; Ph.D. (hon.) U. Santo Domingo, 1946; m. Ada C. Shinaman, Nov. 23, 1914 (div. 1927); children—Jane (Mrs. Frederick Taylor, Jr.), Dorothy (Mrs. William O. Kopel) (dec.); m. 2d, Mary Grant, May 23, 1940. Admitted to N.Y. bar, 1909; practice in Syracuse; asst. to pres. United Hotels Co. Am., 1919-20, v.p., 1921-26; chmn. bd. Am. Hotels Corp, (co. directing operation of 70 hotels in U.S.); now retired. Mem. Assembly N.Y. State, 1915-16. Served from pvt. to maj., N.Y. N.G. Cav., 1904-16; maj. judge adv., N.Y.G. Div. U.S. Army, Mexican border service; dir. Fed. Registration Bur., N.Y., 1917; maj. and lt. col. judge adv. AEF, 1917-19; adj. gen. N.Y., 1921-22; apptd. maj. gen. N.Y. Nat. Guard by Gov. Smith, 1923; res. brig. gen. N.Y. N.G.; called to U.S. Army, May 1943, served in Sch. Mil. Govt., U. Va.; Algiers, Africa., Aug. 1943; landed Salerno beach, D-plus-5, Sept. 1943; sr. civil affairs officer, Province Naples, Italy (Mil. Govt.) Sept. 1943-July 1944; comdr. Vesuvius Emergency Operation, Mar. 1944; staff So. line of communications supplying 7th Army, July 1944-Jan. 1945; inactive status Apr. 1945; brig. general AUS ret. Decorated D.S.C. (U.S.); Distinguished Service Order (Brit.); chevalier Legion of Honor (French); officer of the Crown (Belgium); officer Order Knights of Malta; Order of St. Maurice and St. Lazarus (Italy): hon. citizen of Naples, Italy; comdr. Order of Crown (Italian). Republican. Roman Catholic. Home: South Seas Plantation Captiva Island FL 33924

KINCAID, JAMES LEWIS, lawyer; b. Carthage, Mo., Oct. 3, 1936; s. Joseph Lewis and Kathryn (Stein) K.; A.B., Harvard, 1958, J.D., 1961; m. Aloah Ann Burke, Aug. 24, 1958; children—Kathryn Burke, James Lewis, Joseph Robert. Admitted to Okla. bar, 1961, since practiced in Tulsa; partner firm Huffman, Arrington, Scheurich & Kincaid, 1967—. Coach of debate Holland Hall Sch., Tulsa, 1969—. Mem. Am., Okla., Tulsa County bar assns., Harvard Alumni Assn., Harvard Law Sch. Assn. Okla. (pres. 1969—). Clubs: Tulsa, Southern Hills (Tulsa). Author: Techniques of Successful Debating, 1960. Home: 1346 E 26th St Tulsa OK 74114 Office: Okla Natural Bldg Tulsa OK 74119

KINCAID, JOHN FRANKLIN, ret. govt. ofcl.; b. Blackwell, Mo., Feb. 27, 1912; s. John Randall and Rose (Rich) K.; A.B., Central Coll., Fayette, Mo., 1934; M.A., George Washington U., 1936; Ph.D., Princeton, 1938; m. Nancy Virginia Ange, June 28, 1938; children—James Randall, John Peter, Thomas Franklin. Instr. chemistry U. Rochester, 1938-42; group leader explosives research lab. Carnegie Inst. Tech., 1942-45; research scientist Gen. Electric Co., 1945-46; head high pressure research dept. Rohm & Haas Co., 1946-49, research supr., 1949-58; head gen. sci. br., adv. research project div. Inst. Def. Analysis, 1958-59, dep. dir. advanced research projects div., 1959-60, dir. research and engring. support div., 1960-62; ind. cons., 1962-63; v.p. research and devel. Internat. Minerals and Chem. Corp., 1963-67; asst. sec. Dept. Commerce, 1967-69; now cons. Recipient Naval Ordnance Devel. award, 1945, Presdl. certificate merit, 1948. Mem. Am. Chem. Soc. Clubs: Cosmos (Washington); Princeton (N.Y.C.). Author articles. Inventor or co-inventor mil. and indsl. processes and products. Home: 1415 Rhode Island Av NW Washington DC 20024

KINCANNON, JACK F., dept. store exec.; b. Waco, Tex., Dec. 3, 1918; s. Byron N. and Lucille (Farris) K.; student So. Meth. U., Harvard Bus. Sch.; m. Mildred Neeley, June 7, 1941; 1 dau., Judith. With Sears Roebuck & Co., 1939—, retail comptroller, Chgo., 1960-62, sr. asst. comptroller, 1962-64, divisional v.p., 1964-67, v.p., comptroller, 1967—; dir. Universal Rundle Corp., Sears Roebuck Acceptance Corp., Homart Devel. Co., Sears, Roebuck de P.R., DeSoto, Inc. Served to maj. AUS, 1943-45; ETO. Decorated Bronze Star medal. Mem. Chicago Retail Controllers (dir.), Ill. C. of C. (dir.). Home: 1000 Lake Shore Plaza Chicago IL 60611 Office: 925 S Homan St Chicago IL 60607

KINCANNON, LAYTON ELDON, petroleum refining co. exec.; b. Bruceville, Tex., Feb. 12, 1906; s. John Ragsdale Joel Thomas and Jennie Belle (Mixson) K.; A.B., Southwestern U., 1926; m. Hazel Glee Saunders, Feb. 24, 1929; 1 son, Louis Eldon. Teacher Conoroe (Tex.) High Sch., 1926-28, prin., 1928-29; with Rock Island Oil Co., Duncan, Okla., 1929-41, v.p., 1936-41; v.p., gen. mgr. Rock Island Refining Corp., Indpls., 1941-68, exec. v.p., 1968-70, chmn. bd. dirs., 1971—; dir. Am. Fletcher Nat. Bank & Trust Co. Bd. dirs. University Heights Hosp.; Goodwill Industries, Inc.; Crossroads Rehabilitation Center. Mem. Indpls. C. of C. (pres. 1969-70, dir. 1960—), Nat. Petroleum Refiners Assn. (pres. 1964-65), Am. Petroleum Inst., Chgo. Oil Men's Club. Republican. Presbyn. Kiwanian. Clubs: Highland Golf and Country (dir. 1952-53, 61-63, v.p., sec.-treas. 1962-63, pres. 1970); Junto (pres. 1970) (Indpls.). Home: 7480 Holliday Dr E Indianapolis IN 46260 Office: PO Box 68007 Indianapolis IN 46268

KINCH, JOHN WILLARD, educator; b. Bklyn., May 4, 1931; s. Francis M. and Carrie (Alger) K.; B.A., U. Wash., 1955, M.A., 1957, Ph.D., 1959; m. Honor T. Denney, Aug. 24, 1968; children—Sally Jo, Linda Kay; step daughter, Cathy Lennig. Instr. sociology U. Wash., 1957-59; asst. prof. to prof. sociology San Francisco State Coll., 1959—, chmn. dept. sociology, 1968—; vis. prof. Stanford, 1964, U. Hawaii, 1969. Trustee San Francisco Suicide Prevention, Inc. Served with U.S. Army, 1951-54. Mem. Am., Pacific sociol. assns., Alpha Kappa Delta. Author: Sociology in the World Today, 1971. Home: 609 Arballo Dr San Francisco CA 94132

KINCHELOE, JAMES BENJAMIN, educator; b. Church Hill, Tenn., May 26, 1916; s. Enos E. and Ada (Smith) K.; student Emory and Henry Coll., 1935, E. Tenn. State U., 1936; B.S., U. Tenn., 1948, M.S., 1949; Ph.D., George Peabody Coll., 1954; m. Blanche Booher, Nov. 21, 1941; 1 dau., Deborah Ann. Tchr., Tenn. pub. schs., 1936-39, adminstr., 1949-52; supt. schs., Tucumcari, N.M., 1955-57, Fayette County, Ky., 1957-61; prof. edn. U. Ky., 1961—, chmn. dept. ednl. adminstrn., 1964-70; cons. in field, 1952—. Pres. So. Regional Council Ednl. Adminstrn., 1966; Sec.-treas. Ky. Assn. Colls., Secondary and Elementary Schs., 1961-66. Counseling Service, 1966-68, bd. dirs., 1964—. Served with USAAF, 1944-46. Mem. Am. Assn. Sch. Adminstrs., Nat. Soc. Study Edn., Phi Delta Kappa. Democrat. Methodist. Author: (with others) Public White and Negro Schools in the South, 1955. Home: 3440 Belvoir Dr Lexington KY 40502

KINCHELOE, SAMUEL CLARENCE, writer and educator; b. Georgetown, O., Nov. 20, 1890; s. Robert Stone and Elizabeth Olive (Kimball) K.; A.B., Drake U., Des Moines, Ia., 1916; A.M., U. of Chicago, 1919, Ph.D., 1929; Litt.D, Pacific U., 1949; D.D., Chgo. Theol. Sem., 1957, Drake U., 1959; m. Alma Beulah Elifrits, June 16, 1916 (dec. Mar. 1949); children—Beulah Jean (Mrs. Fletcher Taylor), Robert Stone; m. 2d, Evah Irene Ostrander, Oct. 20, 1950. Ordained to the ministry of the Christian Ch., 1916, and served as pastor, Lake City, Ia., 1917-18; asst., dept. sociology, U. of Chicago, 1921-23; head dept. sociology, George Williams Coll., 1923-28; research asso. and lecturer, sociology of religion. Chicago Theol. Sem., and dir. of research and survey Chicago Congregational Union, 1928-31; asst. prof. of sociology of religion, Chicago Theol. Sem., 1931-39; became prof. Chicago Theol. Sem, 1939. and Federated Theol. Faculty, Univ. of Chgo., 1943; pres. Tougaloo Southern Christian Coll., 1956-60; prof. sociology of religion Interdenominational Theological Center, Atlanta, Georgia, 1960-64. Served with U.S. Army, World War I. Mem. bd. trustees LeMoyne Coll., 1948-54. Recipient Citation Distinguished Service, Bd. of Home Missions, Congregational Christian denomination, 1949. Chmn. Am. Missionary Assn. Bd. Home Missions (dean, internat. seminar, 1949); mem. Council Chs. of Christ in U.S.A. Constituting Convention; mem. Bd. Home Missions, Congl. Christian Chs. (exec. com. 1946-54); dir. research and survey Chgo. Congl. Union, 1928-44. Ch. Fedn. of Greater Chgo., 1944-49; chmn. bd. U. Chgo. Settlement 1946-49; Mem. Phi Beta Kappa. Club: Quadrangle. Author: Religion in the Depression, 1937; The American City and Its Church, 1938. Contbr. articles in religious publs. Home: Stony Hollow Rd Rural Route 2 Box 173 A Georgetown OH 45121

KINCHLA, RONALD ARTHUR, educator; b. Newton, Mass., July 4, 1935; s. Joseph T. and Alice (Chandler) K.; B.A., U. Cal., 1958, Ph.D., 1962; children—Kendall, Chandler. NSF postdoctoral fellow NASA-Ames Research Center, Mountain View, Cal., 1962-64; asst. prof. psychology N.Y. U., N.Y.C., 1964-67; asso. prof. MacMaster U., Hamilton, Ont., Can., 1967-69; prof. Princeton, U., 1969—. Mem. adv.com. psychology Nat. Research Council Can., 1967-69. Mem. Western Psychol. Assn., Sigma Xi. Author: Statistics for Introductory Psychology, 1964. Home: 85 Hartley Av Princeton NJ 08540

KINDAHL, JAMES KEITH, educator, economist; b. Chgo., Dec. 3, 1931; s. Walter and Ruth (Boers) K.; A.B., U. Chgo., 1958, M.B.A., 1953, Ph.D., 1958; m. Connie Albright, June 7, 1957; children—Carolyn, Kelvin. Asst. prof. polit. economy Johns Hopkins, 1958-63; asso. prof. econs. Amherst Coll., 1963-65; Lilly faculty fellow U. Chgo., 1965-66, vis. asso. prof., 1966-67; mem. faculty U. Mass., 1967—, prof. econs., 1968—, head dept., 1968-71. Served with AUS, 1953-55. Mem. Am. Econ. Assn., Am. Statis. Assn., Econometric Soc. Author: (with G.J. Stigler) The Behavior of Industrial Prices, 1970. Home: RR 2 Pelham Hill Amherst MA 01002

KINDALL, ALVA FREDERICK, educator; b. Pueblo, Colo., Sept, 27 1906; s. Axel F. and Mathilda (Allstrom) K.; A.B., U. Cal. at Berkeley, 1930; M.B.A. with distinction, Harvard, 1932; m. Frances W. Clayton, Sept. 19, 1936; 1 dau., Nan Clayton (Mrs. Peter A. Holmes). With Standard Oil Co. Cal., 1932-35; mem. staff Indsl. Relations Counselors, Inc., N.Y.C., 1935-36; asst. dir. indsl. relations Gen. Foods Corp., N.Y.C., 1937-40; personnel dir. H. P. Hood & Sons Co., Boston, 1940-45; dir. indsl. relations Castle & Cooke. Ltd., Honolulu, 1945-46; personnel adminstr. Rexall Drug Co., Los Angeles, 1946-47; personnel dir. Wm. Filene's Sons Co., Boston, 1947-55; prof. bus. adminstrn. Harvard Grad. Sch. Bus. Adminstrn., 1955—. Dir. Window shop, Cambridge, Mass. Mem. Indsl. Relations Research Assn., Am. Mgmt. Assn. Author: Personnel Administration-Principles and Cases, 3d edit., 1969. Home: 2300 Ptarmigan Dr Walnut Creek CA 94595 Office: Soldiers Field Rd Boston MA 02163

KINDELSBERGER, GLENDON L. chemist, educator; b. Chicago, 1928; B.S. in Physics, Yale, 1950; Ph.D. in Chemistry, Harvard, 1956; m. Sally Ann Jones, July 5, 1957; children--Kenneth J., Nancy A. Chemist, Acme Chem. Co., Blue Island, Ill., 1950-51; director of Reseach Lab., Indsl. Chemicals Corp., Cambridge, Mass., 1956-60; project coordinator environmental sect. Steinmetz Assos., Chgo., 1960-61; v.p. for reseach Bauer Bros. Chem. Co., Inc., Memphis, 1961-64; asst. prof. chemistry Washington U., St. Louis, 1964-66, asso. prof., 1966-70, prof., 1970--, head of chemistry dept., 1970-71. Vis. prof. So. Ill. U., summer 1967, U. of Ore., 1969. Scoutmaster, Boy Scouts America, University City, Mo., 1968-70. Bd. dirs. Rest Haven Home for Elderly, 1960-61; trustee of the Lutheran Hosp., 1965-71. Served from lt. to capt., AUS, 1951-53. Mem. Am. Chem. Soc., Sci. Research Soc. Am. (chpt. treas. 1967), Sigma Xi. Author: (with others) Basic Inorganic Chemistry, 1971. Contbr. articles to profl. jours., encys., also chpts. to books. Home: Fairfax Apts 7291 Windermere Dr University City MO 63105 Office: Dept Chemistry Washington University St Louis MO 63130

KINDELSPERGER, WALTER LEWIS, univ. dean; b. Viola, Ill., Aug 3, 1906; s. Everett and Nellie (Smith) K.; A.B., U. Chgo., 1939, M.A., 1941, Ph.D., 1958; m. Adrienne Stoppelman, June 17 1936. Engaged in settlement work, Peoria, Ill., 1927- 31; program work, head resident Eli Bates Settlement, Chgo., 1931-41; research asso. Social Planning Council, Atlanta, 1941-42; group work, recreation sec. Council Social Agencies, New Orleans, also part-time tchr. Tulane U. Sch. Social Work, 1942-44; prof. group work Tulane U. Sch. Group Work, 1944-58, W. R. Irby prof. social welfare policy, dean sch., 1958-65, now dean of Sch. of Social Work. Mem. planning com. and conf. research So. Regional Edn. Bd.; evaluation com. bd. dirs. planning council Council Social Agencies; mem. commn. accreditation Council Social Work Edn., 1958-61; adv. com. Juvenile Ct. Orleans Parish, 1959-60; del. of La. to White House Conf. Children and Youth, 1960. Mem. Nat. Conf. Social Work (chmn. group work sect. 1948- 49), Am. Assn. Social Workers (vice chmn. New Orleans 1951, Am. Assn. Group Workers (bd. dirs.), Am. Assn. U. Profs., Nat. Assn. Social Workers. Author: (with Gladys Ryland) New Developments in the Theory and Practice of Social Group Work, 1956; also reports, proceedings. Home: 2939 Esplanade Av New Orleans LA 70119

KINDER, HAROLD M., corp. ofcl.; b. Pittsburgh, Feb. 22, 1911; s. O. W. and Mary (Parsons) K.; student pub. schs. of Flint, Mich., Northwestern Traffic Inst., 1940; m. Eva C. Korocz, Apr. 3, 1948. Transportation supt. Kirby-Butler Co., Flint, 1928-36; police exec., Flint, 1936-42, traffic engr., 1946-47, police chief, 1947-48; city mgr., City of Flint, 1948-52; bus. mgr. Mich. Liquor Control Commn., 1952-54; Ohio mgr. Nat. Distillers Products Co., 1954-61, v.p., 1961-68, control states div. mgr., v.p., mgr. nat. brands div., N.Y.C., 1968-. Industry com. Nat. Alcoholic Beverage Control Assn. Commd. 2d lt. U.S. Army, adv. to maj., 1946; service in N. Africa, Sicily, Italy, France, Germany, Greece; disch. as major, Corps. Mil. Police, O.R.C., 1946. Mem. Red Feather Fund of Flint. Recipient gold medal, Nat. Distillers, 1962. Decorated: Order Brit. Empire, 1945; Legion of Merit, Bronze star medal, Army Commendation ribbon, Corono de Italy, Morocco-Sultan's medal, E.A.M.E. campaign ribbon with 5 battle stars. Internat. Assn. Chiefs Police, Nat. Safety Council (mem. program com.) Elk. Fraternal Order Police. Author: Circumstantial Evidence-Bah. Home: 35 E 38th St New York City NY 10016 Office: 99 Park Av New York City NY 10016

KINDER, JAMES S., educator, author; b. Millersville, Mo., Oct. 19, 1895; s. Robert F. and Emily (Runnels) K.; B.S., Southeast Mo. State Coll., 1921; student Univ. Coll. of (Aberystwyth) Wales, 1919; U. Mo., 1922; A.M., Columbia Tchrs. Coll., 1923, Ph.D., 1934; m. Mary Clare Lett, Sept. 11, 1919. Pub. sch. tchr. and adminstr., Bertrand, Mo., Oak Ridge, Mo., Marysvale, Utah. Sullivan, Mo.; mem. faculty, Chatham Coll. 1923-53, prof. edn., head dept. edn., and dir. film service, 1938—; prof. edn. San Diego State Coll., 1953—. Vis. prof. summers Geneva Coll., U. Pitts., U. Wyo., Mich. State U., Southwestern La. Inst., San Diego State Coll., 1950, U. Va., 1951, Pa. State U. 1952. Served with AEF, France. 1917-18; instr. A.S.T.P., 1944; asst. adminstr., engring. sci. mgmt. War Tng. Program, Western Pa. area, 1941-45. Mem. Dept. Audio-Visual Instrn. of N.E.A., Ednl. Film Library Assn. (an organizer and mem. first bd. dirs., Phi Delta Kappa (pres. Xi chpt., 1945-47). Mason. Author: The Internal Administration of the Liberal Arts College, 1934; Audio-Visual Materials and Techniques, 1950, 1959; Educational Tests for Use in Institutions of Higher Learning (with C.W. Odell), 1930; Audio-Visual Reader (with F. Dean McClusky), 1954; Using Audio-Visual Material in Education, 1965; co-author: (with M.D. Alcorn and J.R. Schunert) Better Teaching in Secondary Schs., 1964, rev. edit., 1970. Contbr. to Sociological Foundation of Education, 1942. Contbr. articles in various jours. Home: 6124 Pontiac St San Diego CA 92115

KINDER, KATHARINE LOUISE, librarian; b. Rockford, O., Mar. 21, 1912; d. George R. and Nelle O. Kinder; B.A., Miami U., 1936; B.L.S., Columbia, 1936. Head circulation dept. Mt. Holyoke Coll. Library, 1938-43; chief librarian Johns-Manville Research and Engring. Center, Manville, N.J., 1946—. Served with USNR, 1943-46. Mem. Spl. Libraries Assn. (pres. 1956-57), A.L.A., Am. Documentation Inst., Soc. Am. Archivists. Home: 1025 Plainfield Av Plainfield NJ 07060 Office: Johns Manville Research and Engring Center Manville NJ 08835

KINDERMAN, ROBERT HENRY, pharm. co. exec.; b. Chgo., Jan 9, 1913; s. Fred and Laura (Zuehr) K.; B.S., U. Ill., 1935, LL.B., 1937; m. Loraine E. Loewe, Apr. 5, 1941; children—Robert Henry, Nancy, Carol. Admitted to Ill. bar, 1937; with firm Hinshaw & Culbertson, Chgo., 1937-44; trial atty. Office Chief Counsel, Bur. Internal Revenue, 1944-51; with firm Sidley, Austin, Burgess & Smith, Chgo., 1951-55; with Mead Johnson & Co., Evansville, Ind., 1955-68, sec., 1955-59, v.p. finance, 1959-61, v.p., treas., 1961-63, v.p. adminstrn., 1963-65, exec. v.p., 1965-68, also dir.; v.p. operations control div. Allied Chem. Corp., 1968-71. Trustee Mead Johnson & Co. Found., 1961-68. Mem. Am., Ind., Ill., Cal. bar assns., Beta Gamma Sigma, Phi Delta Phi, Phi Kappa Phi, Delta Phi. Home: 6 Reed Rd Morristown NJ 07960 Office: 61 Broadway New York City NY 10006

KINDIG, CARL HAROLD, educator; b. New Columbus, Pa., May 29, 1905; s. Charles Daniel and Ella Nora (Beishline) K.; B.S. in Civil Engring., Gettysburg Coll., 1929; M.C.E., Rensselaer Poly. Inst., 1933, D.Civil Engring., 1935; m. Lucille Marion Gilchrist, Nov. 7, 1936; children—Robert Allen, Richard Carl. Instr., Rensselaer Poly. Inst., 1930-33, 35-39; prof., chmn. dept. civil engring. Southwestern La. Inst., 1939-43; faculty Bucknell U., Lewisburg, Pa., 1943—, prof. civil engring., 1947—, dir. materials testing lab., 1945—. Cons., design engr. to industry. Grantee NSF, 1945, Pa. Dept. Transp. and Fed. Hwy. Adminstrn., 1968—. Registered profl. engr., Pa., N.Y. Mem. Am. Soc. Testing Materials, Soc. Exptl. Stress Analysis, Am. Soc. Engring. Edn., Sigma Xi, Pi Mu Epsilon. Methodist. (pres. trustees 1970-72). Lion, Mason. Co-author reports. Home: Campus Lane Lewisburg PA 17837

KINDLEBERGER, CHARLES P., II, economist; b. N.Y.C., Oct. 12, 1910; s. E. Crosby and Elizabeth Randall (McIlvaine) K.; student Kent (Conn.) Sch., 1924-28; A.B., U. Pa., 1932; A.M., Columbia, 1934, Ph.D., 1937; m. Sarah Bache Miles, May 1, 1937; children — Charles P., Richard S., Sarah, Elizabeth. Research in internat. trade and finance, Fed. Reserve Bank of N.Y., 1936-39, Bank for Internat. Settlements, 1939-40, bd. of govs. Fed. Reserve System, 1940-42; Am. sec. Joint Econ. Com. of U.S. and Can., 1941-42; served in Office of Strategic Services, Washington, 1942-44, 45; chief div. German and Austrian Econ. Affairs. Dept. of State, Washington, 1945-48; asso. prof. econ. Mass. Inst. of Tech., 1948-51, prof., 1951—, chmn. faculty, 1965-67. Intelligence Officer 12th army group, 1944-45; disch. rank of maj., Gen. Staff Corps. Decorated Legion of Merit, Bronze Star. Mem. Am. Acad. Arts and Sci., Am. Econ. Assn. (v.p. 1966), Phi Beta Kappa, Delta Psi. Episcopalian. Club: St. Anthony (Boston). Author: International Short-Term Capital Movements, 1937; The Dollar Shortage, 1950; International Economics, 1953, rev., 1968; The Terms of Trade, 1956; Economic Development, 1958, rev. 1965; Foreign Trade and the National Economy, 1962; Economic Growth of France and Britain, 1851-1950, 1964; Europe and the Dollar, 1966; Postwar European Growth, 1967; American Business Abroad, 1969; Power and Money, 1970. Editor: The International Corporation, 1970. Home: Bedford Rd Lincoln MA 01773

KINDLER, HERBERT SEYMOUR, assn. exec.; b. N.Y.C., Feb. 16, 1928; s. Samuel and Alice (Yanklowitz) K.; B.S., Mass. Inst. Tech., 1948; m. Phyllis Fay Pitegoff, May 25, 1952; children—Alex Michael, David John, Peggy Blanche. Design engr. Honeywell, Inc., Phila., 1949-51; project engr. Catalytic Constrn. Co., Phila., 1951-55; mgr. gasoline plant engring. Black Sivalls & Bryson, Inc., Oklahoma City, 1955-56; exec. dir. Instrument Soc. Am., Pitts., 1956—. Registered profl. engr., N.Y. Mem. A.A.A.S., Council of Engring. and Sci. Soc. Execs. (dir.), Instrument Soc. Am., Am. Soc. M.E., I.E.E.E. Author: Organizing the Technical Conference, 1960. Patentee electronic potentiometer mechanisms, instrument mass fluid flow measurement. Home: 128 Elatan Dr Pittsburgh PA 15243 Office: 400 Stanwix St Pittsburgh PA 15222

KINDRED, LESLIE WITHROW, educator; b. Boston, Dec. 27, 1905; s. Leslie Withrow and Veronica (Vater) K.; student Clark U., 1924-26; A.B., U. Mich., 1928, A.M., 1934, Ph.D., 1938; m. Helen F. Parmenter, Dec. 24, 1932: children—James W., Robert H. Tchr. pub. schs., Ann Arbor, Mich., 1928-34; critic, demonstration tchr. U. High Sch., U. Mich., 1934-38; dir. Marsh Found., Van Wert, O., 1938-39; cons. Mich. Dept. Pub. Instrn., 1939-40; asst. prof. edn. Temple U., 1940-43, asso. prof. edn., 1943-44, prof. edn., 1945-, dir. dept. ednl. adminstrn., 1953-58, prof. ednl. adminstrn., 1958-; instr. comparative edn. course in Europe, summers, 1958, 59, South Am., summers, 1961, 62, 66, 69. Mng. dir. Pub. Edn. and Child Labor Assn. Pa., 1943-45. Mem. Nat. Sch. Pub. Relations Assn. (editorial adv. bd. 1953), Middle Atlantic States Assn. Colls. and Secondary Schs. (chmn. evaluation com. 1940-50), Pa. Edn. Assn. (sec. div. higher edn. 1949-51), Am. Assn. Sch. Adminstrs., Nat. Assn. Secondary Sch. Prins., Nat. Soc. Study Edn., Pa. Schoolmen's Club, Phi Delta Kappa, Phi Kappa Phi, Tau Kappa Alpha, Kappa Phi Kappa. Author: (with Leo M. Chamberlain) The Teacher and School Organization, latest rev. edit., 1966; The Intermediate Schools, 1968. Compiler, editor: Public Relations in Secondary Schools, 1948; Supervisory Problems on Secondary Schools, 1950; School Public Relations, 1957; How to Tell the School Story, 1960; Staff Welfare Practices in the Public Schools, 1963; Communication Research and School Community Relations, 1965. Contbr. Critical Incidents in Teaching, 1964; Preparation Programs for School Administrators, 1963. Home: 81 Brennan Dr Bryn Mawr PA 19010 Office: Temple U Philadelphia PA 19122

KINDSVATER, CARL EDWARD, water resources engr.; b. Hoisington, Kan. Aug. 1, 1913; s. John Alexander and Katherine Elizabeth (Michel) K.; B.S. in Civil Engring., U. Kan., 1935; M.S. in Hydraulic Engring., State U. Ia.; m. Ruth Margaret Goodwin, Dec. 8, 1935; children—Kenneth Carl, Carol Ruth, Paul Edward. Hydraulic engr. T.V.A., 1937-43, U.S. Engrs., 1943-45; asso. prof. Ga. Inst. Tech., 1945-49, prof., 1949-55, Regents' prof., 1955-, dir. Water Resources Center, 1963-70, dir. Environmental Resources Center, 1970—; cons. water resources engr., 1946—. Registered profl. engr., Ga. Fellow Am. Soc. C.E. (Collingswood prize 1945, Rickey medal 1955, Norman medal 1956, 60; dir. 1963-66); mem. Am. Geophys.

Union, Am. Soc. Engring. Edn. Internat. Assn. Hydraulic Research, Sigma Xi, Tau Beta Pi, Phi Kappa Phi, Chi Epsilon, Omicron Delta Kappa. Author tech. research papers. Home: 4850 Carol Lane NW Atlanta GA 30327

KINDWALL, NILS A., sulphur co. exec.; b. 1923; A.B., Princeton, 1943; M.B.A., Columbia, 1948; married. Asst. mgr. market surgeys Johns Manville Corp., 1948-58; with William E. Hill & Co., 1958; with Freeport Sulphur Co., 1958—, treas., 1968—. Address: 161 E 42d St New York City NY 10017*

KINERSON, KENDALL SCOTT, educator; b. Peacham, Vt., Mar. 8, 1921; s. Charles Raymond and Elizabeth (Scott) K.; B.S., U. N.H., 1943; M.S., Rensselaer Poly. Inst., 1953; Ph.D., Mich. State U., 1957; m. Shirley Laighton, May 25, 1943; children—Nancy (Mrs. Dennis M. Dwyer), Linda (Mrs. Peter S. Stewart), Margaret, Louise, Katherine, Scott. Instr. physics U. Mass., Ft. Devens, 1946-48; instr. physics and math. to prof. physics and math., chmn. dept. math. Russell Sage Coll., Troy, N.Y., 1948—; cons. N.Y. State Dept. Edn., Bur. Secondary Curriculum Devel., Div. Evaluation of Higher Edn., Rensselaer Poly, Inst. Served to capt. AUS, 1943-46. Danforth tchr., 1955. Mem. Am. Assn. Physics Tchrs., Math. Assn. Am. Presbyn. (elder, trustee). Author: (with Parsegian, Meltzer and Luchins) Introduction to Natural Science, 1968; Laboratory and Mathematics Supplement to Introduction to Natural Science, 1968. Home: 451 Pinewoods Av Extension Troy NY 12180

KING, ALAN, entertainer; b. Bklyn., Dec. 26, 1927; s. Bernard and Minnie (Solomon) K.; ed. pub. schs., Bklyn.; m. Jeannette Sprung, Feb. 1, 1947; children—Bobby, Andrew. Appeared Catskill Mountains and burlesque, also U.S. Army camps; cafes and vaudeville, U.S. and Eng.; Dominion Theatre, London, 1957, Palace Theatre, London, 1959, Palace Theatre (with Judy Garland), N.Y.C., 1958, Met. Opera House (with Judy Garland), 1960, also Waldorf Astoria Hotel; TV appearances include Garry Moore Show, Ed Sullivan Show, Perry Como Show, also panel shows; royal command performance for Queen Elizabeth II, Glasgow, Scotland, 1958; appeared in play The Lion in Winter, 1966; appeared in film Bye, Bye Braverman. Club: The Friars (monitor) (New York City, N.Y). Co-author of: Anybody Who Owns His Own Home Deserves It, 1962; Help! I'm a Prisoner in a Chinese Bakery, 1964; also mag. articles. Home: 40 Shore Dr Kings Point Great Neck NY 11024 Office: 165 W 46th St New York City NY 10036

KING, ALGIN BRADDY, coll. dean; b. Latta, S.C., Jan. 19, 1926; s. Dewey Algin and Elizabeth (Braddy) K.; B.A. in Retailing and Polit. Sci. (W.T. Grant Retailing scholar) cum laude, U. S.C., 1947; M.S., N.Y.U., 1953; Ph.D., Ohio State U., 1966; m. Drucilla Ratcliff, Jan. 17, 1948; children—Drucilla Ratcliff, Martha Louise. Exec. trainee Sears, Roebuck & Co., 1948-48; instr. retailing U. S.C., 1948-51; chief econ. analysis br. dist. OPS, 1951-53; exec. dir. Columbia (S.C.) Mchts. Assn., 1953-54; asst. prof. Tex. A. and M. Coll., 1954-55; mem. faculty Coll. William and Mary, 1955—, prof. bus. adminstrn., 1959—, dir. Bur. Bus. Research, 1959-63, asso. dean Sch. Bus. Adminstrn., 1968—; teaching asst. Ohio State U., 1963-64; professorial lectr. George Washington U.; mgmt. cons. U.S. Army. Mem. U.S. Jr. C. of C., Am. Marketing Assn., Acad. Mgmt., Phi Beta Kappa. Republican. Methodist. Mason, Rotarian. Author: (with others) Hampton Watergront Economic Study, 1967; also chpts. in books, articles. Home: 141K Lake Powell Rd Williamsburg VA 23185

KING, ALLEN LEWIS, physicist; b. Rochester, N.Y., Mar. 27, 1910; s. Lewis Allen and Elizabeth Wilhemina (Neitzke) K; B.A., U. Rochester, 1932, M.A., 1933, Ph.D., 1937; postgrad. U. Mich. summer 1934; M.A. (hon.), Dartmouth, 1948; m. Nancy Tessiene Form, June 30, 1937; children—Nancy Maribeth, Allen Anthron, Fern Tessiene. Instr. physics, Rochester, 1936-37, Rensselaer Poly. Inst., 1937-42, Dartmouth, 1942-43; asst. prof. Dartmouth, 1943-48, prof., 1948—; cons., 1941—; vis. lectr., cons. Tougaloo So. Christian Coll., 1957; vis. lectr. St. Andrews Presbyn. Coll., 1968. Fellow A.A.A.S.; mem. Biophys. Soc., Am. Phys. Soc. (chmn. N.E. sect. 1969-70), Am. Assn. Physics Tchrs. (chmn. N.E. sect. 1957-59), N.H. Acad. Sci. (pres. 1959-60), Optical Soc. Am., Phi Beta Kappa, Sigma Xi. Author sci. articles and books. Home: 10 Conant Rd Hanover NH 03755

KING, ALLEN STEWART, pub. utility exec.; b. Mpls., Aug. 20, 1900; s. George Alexander Newton and Anna Louise (Cotton) K.; B.S., Mass. Inst. Tech., 1922; m. Ann E. Quigley, Apr. 18, 1925; children—Ann Louise (dec.), George Stewart. Engr. Fargo (N.D.) div. No. States Power Co., 1923-25, gen. supt., 1925- 30, mgr. Minot (N.D.) div., 1930-34, Grand Forks (N.D.) div., 1934-45, mgr. Fargo div., N.D. agt., 1945-51, exec. v.p., Mpls., 1951-54, president, 1954-64, chmn. bd., prin. exec. officer, 1964-65, chmn. bd., chmn. emeritus and dir.; dir. Northwest Bancorp., St. Croix Falls Wis. Improvement Co., other cos. Chmn. Community Chest, 1931-32; dir., v.p. N.D. War Chest, 1941-45, N.D. War Bond State Com., 1941-45, N.D.-Minn. Resources Development Commn., 1945-51. Mem. bd. trustees St. Lukes Hosp. Fargo, 1948-51. Pres. Grand Forks council Boy Scouts Am., 1937-39. Fargo council, 1946, v. chmn. region X since 1942, mem. nat. council; awarded Silver Beaver and Silver Antelope. Mem. Grand Forks C. of C. (dir. 1935- 45, pres. 1942). Edison Electric Inst. (pres. 1959-60), Am. Legion. Episcopalian (treas. Province of N.W.P.E. Ch., 1936-49). Elk. Clubs: Minneapolis, Rotary, Minneapolis Athletic, Minikahda (Mpls.); Metropolitan (N.Y.C.). Home: 3540 James Av S Minneapolis MN 55408 Office: 414 Nicollet Mall Minneapolis MN 55401

KING, ANNIE GREENE, (Mrs. Jay Bernard King), librarian; b. Trenton, N.C., Jan. 19, 1922; d. Lott Thomas and Annie (Williams) Greene; A.B., N.C. Central U., 1942, B.L.S., 1947; M.L.S., U. Ill., 1952; m. Jay Bernard King, Mar. 19, 1950; children—Margaret Denise, Cheryl Louise, Jay Bernard, Wayne Maurice. Tchr. pub. schs. Jones County, N.C., 1942-46; librarian Jones High Sch., Washington, N.C., 1946-47; librarian Fla. Meml. Coll., St. Augustine, 1948-50; reference librarian Tuskegee Inst., Ala., 1951-66, librarian, 1966—. Mem. Am., Southeastern, Ala. library assns., Jack and Jill of Am., Delta Sigma Theta. Methodist. Home: 207 Johnson St Tuskegee Institute AL 36088

KING, ARNOLD KIMSEY, educator; b. Hendersonville, N.C., Dec. 3, 1901; s. William Fanning Pinckney and Julia (Anderson) K.; A.B., U. N.C., 1925; A.M., U. Chgo., 1927, Ph.D., U. 1951; m. Edna Coates, Aug. 31, 1929; children—Arnold Kimsey, William Dennis, Mary Ann. Instr. edn. U. N.C., 1925-26, asst. prof. teaching history, 1927-39, asso. prof. edn., 1939-43, prof. edn., 1943—, adviser Gen. Coll., 1942-45, asso. dean Grad, Sch., 1945-68, dir. summer session, 1958-64; v.p. inst. research Consol. U. N.C., 1964—; chmn. edni. adv. com. NASA Ednl. Programs Br. 1963—. Local coordinator U. N.C. participation in Coop. Study Teacher Edn. of Commn. on Tchr. Edn., 1939-43; chmn. region 6 Woodrow Wilson fellowship program Assn. Am. Univs., 1952-55. Trustee, N.C. Wesleyan Coll., Meth. Home for Children, Raleigh. Gen. Edn. Bd. fellow U. Chgo., 1933-34; Henry Milton Wolf fellow history, 1935-36. Mem. N.E.A., Assn. for Instl. Research, Phi Beta Kappa, Phi Delta Kappa, Lambda Chi Alpha, Democrat. Methodist (del. to gen. conf. Dallas 1968, St. Louis 1970). Kiwanian. Editor: Secondary Education in the South (with W. Carson Ryan and J. Minor Gwynn), 1946; Research in Progress, vols. 27-35 in U. N.C. Record Series, 1949-57; Planning for the Future, 1958; Long Range Planning, 1969. Home: 512 Dogwood Drive Chapel Hill NC 27514

KING, AUGUST ALLEN, educator; b. Trousdale, Okla., Aug. 8, 1910; s. Homer and May (Graham) K.; B.S., U. Tulsa, 1934, LL.B., 1941; LL.M., U. Mich., 1947; m. Lillian S. Knollenberg, Mar. 23, 1944; children—Ronald Allen, Virginia May. With Stanolind Oil & Gas Co., 1937-46; admitted to Okla. bar. 1941; legal dept. Pub. Service Co. of Okla., 1947-48; instr. U. Tulsa Sch. Law, 1948- 52, adminstrv. dean, 1949-58, dean, 1958-63, asso. prof., 1952, prof., 1953-65; prof. law Am. U. Coll. of Law, Washington, 1965—, dir. admission, 1968-69, asso. dean, 1969-70. Asst. treas., trustee Tulsa County Legal Aid Soc., 1954-55. Served as pvt. USAAF, 1942-44. Mem. Am., Okla., Tulsa County bar assns., Nat. Lawyers Club, Delta Theta Phi, Lambda Chi Alpha, Phi Mu Alpha. Home: 3601 Faircastle Dr Chevy Chase MD 20015 Office: Am U Massachusetts and Nebraska Avs NW Washington DC 20016

KING, BARRY GRIFFITH, physiologist; b. Pitts., Dec. 19, 1904; s. Samuel Victor and Annie M. (Jones) K.; A.B., U. Cal. at Berkeley, 1924, M.A., 1925; postgrad. Pasteur Inst., 1926, Cambridge Inst., 1927; Ph.D., Columbia, 1935; m. Estelle Marie Jochumsen, July 6, 1926; children—Aloysia Fahnestock (Mrs. Edward W. Hard, Jr.), Barry Griffith. Asst. instr. physiology U. Cal. at Berkeley Med. Sch., 1924-26; instr. physiology, then asst. prof. Coll. Phy. & Surg., Columbia, 1927-43; cons. physiol. med. sci. div. Office Naval Research, 1947; chief aeromed. design, div. med. service CAA, 1947-52, research exec., 1952-57; v.p. life sci. Operations Research Inc., Silver Spring, Md., 1958-61; chief research br. injury control USPHS, Dept. Health, Edn. and Welfare, 1961-64, sci. adviser, 1965—, sci. adviser USPHS, 1967—. Mem. Pres.'s Conf. Indsl. Safety. 1948—; dep. dir. com. accidental traumas Armed Forces Epidemiol. Bd., 1951-; adv. panel Hwy. Traffic Safety Research, Nat. Acad. Scis.-NRC. 1965—; also mem. spl. com. long range planning Hwy. Research Bd.; adv. panel Nat. Coop. Hwy. Research Program, 1965—; research rev. bd. Am. Soc. Safety Engrs., 1964—. mem. vehicle spltys. com. Govt. Services Adminstrn., 1964—; cons. surgeon gen. Dept. Army, 1956—. Served to capt. USNR, 1943-47. Recipient Flight Safety award, 1955; Gold medal Dept. Commerce, 1955 Fellow Aerospace Med. Assn.; A.A.A.S., Am. Physiol. Soc., Harvey Soc., Soc. Exptl. Biology and Medicine, Indsl. Hygiene Assn. Contbr. numerous texts, articles. Spl. research environmental and aviation physiology, exptl. surgery, stress, effect elec. shock on heart action, accidental injury research. Home: 5300 Hamilton Av Cincinnati OH 45224 Office: Federal Office Bldg Cincinnati OH 45202

KING, BENJAMIN CHAMBERLIN, lawyer; b. New Iberia, La., May 14, 1915; s. Henry Allen and Sue (Chamberlin) K.; B.A., Tulane U., 1935, J.D., 1938; m. Luise Haessler, July 26, 1947; children—Katherine, Margaret, Ben, Sue. Admitted to La. bar, 1938; practice in New Iberia, 1938-41, Shreveport, 1946—; sr. partner Cook, Clark, Egan, Yancey & King, 1946-. Served to lt. col. USAAF, 1941-46. Decorated D.F.C., Air medal with 2 oak leaf clusters. Mem. Am., La., Shreveport bar assns., Delta Kappa Epsilon, Phi Delta Phi. Episcopalian. Home: 4524 Fairfield Av Shreveport LA 71106 Office: Commercial Bank Bldg Shreveport LA 71107

KING, BENTON DAVIS, physician, educator; b. Hackensack, N.J., Oct. 20, 1919; s. Louis Reimer and Edna (Davis) K.; grad. Peddie Sch., 1937; B.S., Haverford Coll., 1941; M.D., U. Pa., 1944; m. Josephine Yager, July 5, 1945; children—Garrett Davis, Loring Brooke. Intern Pa. Hosp., Phila., 1944-45; tng. anesthesiology Presbyn. Hosp., Phila., U. Pa. Hosp., Phila., 1945-48; asso. surgery U. Pa. Sch. Medicine, 1948-52, research asso. anesthesiology Grad. Sch. Medicine, 1949-52; asso. prof. anesthesiology State U. N.Y., Downstate Med. Center, 1954-57, prof., chmn. anesthesiology dept., 1969—; prof. anesthesiology, chmn. dept. State U. N.Y. at Buffalo Sch. Medicine, 1957-69, prof. anesthesiology Sch. of Dentistry, 1964-69; head dept. anesthesiology Meyer Memorial Hosp. Buffalo, 1957-69, Buffalo Childrens Hosp., 1964-69; head dept. anesthesiology State U. Hosp., Bklyn., 1969—, Kings County Hosp., 1969—; cons. Malmonides Hosp. Med. Center, Bklyn., VA Hosp., Bklyn. Diplomate Am. Board Anesthesiology. Fellow Am. Coll. Anesthesiologists; mem. Assn. U. Anesthetists, Assn. Am. Med. Colls., Am. Soc. Anesthesiologists, A.M.A., Soc. Acad. Anesthesia Chairmen. Home: 3 Bonnie Heights Flower Hill Manhasset NY 11030 Office: State U NY Downstate Medical Center Brooklyn NY 11203

KING, BRUCE, gov. of N.M.; b. Stanley, N.M., Apr. 6, 1924; s. William and Molly (Schooler) K.; student U. N.M., 1943-44; m. Alice Marie Martin, June 1, 1947; children—Bill, Gary. Rancher, farmer, Stanley, N.M.; mem. Santa Fe County Commn., 1955-58, chmn., 1957-58; mem. N.M. Ho. of Reps., 1959-68, speaker, 1963-68; pres. N.M. Constl. Conv., 1969; gov. of N.M., 1971—. Co-owner King's Butane Co., Stanley. Mem. Gov.'s Task Force on Edn., 1968; mem., v.p. N.M. Soil and Water Conservation Commn. Democratic state chmn., 1966. Bd. dirs. Edgewood Soil Conversation Commn. Served with F.A., AUS, 1944-46; PTO. Mem. Nat. Conf. State Legis. Leaders (exec. com.), Western Conf. Council State Govs. (exec. com.), N.M. Farm and Livestock Bur. (bd. dirs.) N.M. Cattle Growers (dir.) Am. Cattle Growers (nat. feeder com.), Am. Legion. Elk. Home: Stanley NM also Gov's Mansion Santa Fe NM 87501 Office: Gov's Office State Capitol Santa Fe NM 87501

KING, CARLETON JAMES, congressman; b. Saratoga Springs, N.Y., June 15, 1904; s. James H. and Anna L. (Rose) K.; LL.B., Union U., Albany, N.Y., 1926; m. Constance M. Roddy, Aug. 16, 1933; children—Carleton James, Constance M. (Mrs. James A. Murphy). Admitted to N.Y. bar, 1926, since practiced in Saratoga Springs; mem. firm King, Duval & Murphy; acting city judge, Saratoga Springs, 1934-40; asst. dist. atty. Saratoga County, 1940-50, dist. atty., 1950-61; mem. 87th Congress 31st Dist. N.Y.; mem. 88th-92d Congresses, 30th Dist. N.Y., former mem. judiciary com., former mem. pub. works com., mem. com. armed services. Pres. N.Y. State Dist. Attys. Assn., 1955. Republican. Elk (past exalted ruler Saratoga). Clubs: Army-Navy, Touchdown (Washington). Home: 126 Nelson Av Saratoga Springs NY 12866 Office: Rayburn House Office Building Washington DC 20525

KING, CHARLES ERWIN, architect; b. Cynthiana, Ky., Oct. 10, 1919; s. Lawrence Garnett and Laura (Spencer) K.; B.S., U. Ill., 1946; m. Constance Goldman, Feb. 18, 1967; 1 son by previous marriage—James Marsh. Practicing architect, Belleville, Ill., 1950-60, St. Louis, 1962-67; mgr. architecture and interior design Westinghouse Corporate Design Center, Pitts., 1967-70; asst. to dir. Westinghouse Corporate Design Center, Pitts., 1970—; asst. prof. architecture U. Ill., 1958-59. Dir. Craig House, Technoma; founder So. Ill. region Sports Car Club Am., 1955. Served to 1st lt. USAAF, 1942-45. Francis J. Plym fellow, U. Ill., 1951. Fellow A.I.A. Home: 612 S Linden Av Pittsburgh PA 15208 Office: Westinghouse Bldg Pittsburgh PA 15222

KING, CHARLES GLEN, chemist; b. Entiat, Wash., Oct. 22, 1896; s. Charles Clement and Mary (Bookwalter) K.; B.S., Wash. State Coll., 1918; M.S., U. Pitts. 1920, Ph.D., 1923; postgrad. Columbia, 1926-27, Cambridge (Eng.) U., 1929-30; D. Sci., Wash. State Coll., 1950, U. Pitts., 1950, Drexel Inst., 1955; Dr. of Pub. Service, Denison U., 1961; m. Hilda Bainton, Sept. 11, 1919; children—Dorothy, Robert Bainton, Kendall Willard. By-products specialist, State of Wash., 1918-19; instr. chemistry U. Pitts., 1920-26, asst. prof., 1926-30, prof. 1930-43; research asst. Columbia, 1926-27, vis. prof. chem., 1942-46, prof., 1946-62, emeritus; asso. dir. Inst. Nutrition Sci., 1963-66; spl. lectr., 1967—; dir. grants mgmt. St. Luke's Hosp. Center, 1966-67; sci. dir. Nutrition Found., 1942-55, exec. dir., 1955-61, pres., 1961-63, trustee, 1963-; cons. Rockefeller Found., 1963-66; mem. sci. adv. bd. Robert A. Welch Found., 1954-63, isolated vitamin C, 1932. Agrl. Research Policy Com., U.S. Dept. Agr., 1950-57; mem. exec. bd. U.S. com. UNICEF. Cons. Office of Surgeon Gen., AUS, 1940-66; NIH Study Sect. Chmn., 1946-51; Office Surg. Gen., USPHS, 1940-66. Trustee Boyce Thompson Inst., Food Law Inst.; pres. 5th Internat. Congress on Nutrition, 1960. Served as pvt. 12th Inf. Machine Gun Co., 1918. Recipient Pa. Award of Merit 1938, Pa. Pub. Health Assn. award, 1939, Pitts. award, 1943, G.M.A. award, 1944, John Scott award, 1949; Nicholas Appert award Inst. Food Technologists Chgo. sect., 1955; Charles Spencer award Am. Chem. Soc., 1963; Conrad A. Elvehjem award Am. Inst. Nutrition, 1966; Purkinje Gold medal Acad. Scis., Czechoslovakia, 1969. Mem. Food and Nutrition Bd., 1940-70. Mem. Internat. Union Nutritional Scis. (pres. 1966-69), N.Y. Acad. Medicine, Am. Chem. Soc., Am. Soc. Biol. Chemists (pres. 1954-55), Inst. Food Technologists, Nat. Acad. Scis. (exec. com. internat. council sci. unions 1966-69), Am. Forestry Assn., A.A.A.S., Am. Inst. Nutrition (pres. 1949-50), Am. Pub. Health Assn. (treas. 1949-60, pres. 1961-62), Royal Soc. Health (Eng.), Harvey Soc., Nutrition Soc. (Eng.), Phi Beta Kappa, Sigma Xi, Omicron Delta Kappa. Baptist. Clubs: Century (N.Y.C.); Cosmos (Washington). Home: 39 Devon Road Bronxville NY 10708 Office: Inst Human Nutrition Columbia U 511 W 166th St New York City NY 10032

KING, CHARLES HENRY, lawyer, educator; b. Gulfport, Miss., Aug. 8, 1906; s. William A. and Gertrude A. (Cody) K.; A.B., Detroit Inst. Tech., 1940; LL.B., Detroit Coll. Law, 1933; LL.M., U. Mich., 1941; m. Ouida A. Jolls, June 8, 1933; 1 son, Charles Henry. Admitted to Mich. bar, 1933, practiced in Detroit, 1933-37; prof. law Detroit Coll. Law, 1937-44, dean since 1944; civil service commr. City of Highland Park, Mich., 1951-53; mem. FCC, 1960-61. Chmn. Mich. Taft-for-Pres. Com., 1952; Republican candidate Justice of Mich. Supreme Ct., 1952. Mem. Am., Detroit bar assns., State Bar Mich., Am. Law Inst., Am. Judicature Soc., Harmonie Soc. Author: Michigan Circuit Court Practice, 1963. Home: 67640 Eight Mile Road South Lyon MI 48178 Office: 130 East Elizabeth Detroit MI 48201

KING, CHARLES HORACE, ret. automotive mfr., mink rancher; b. Ypsilanti, Mich., Nov. 5, 1899; s. Horace Clinton and Clarissa Minnie (Monfort) K.; B.S. in Mech. Engring., U. Mich., 1921, M.E., 1946; m. Verne Cartwright, June 28, 1930; children—Thomas (dec.), Patricia, Brian, Sharon. With Clark Equipment Co., Buchanan, Mich., 1925-65, successively pattern maker, machinist, assembler, draftsman, tool designer, foreman, supt., plant mgr. mfg., 1925-46, v.p. mfg., 1946-54, v.p. automotive div., 1954-65, dir., 1955-65; owner King Mink Ranch, Marcellus, Mich.; v.p. Diamond Harber Inn, Cassopolis, Mich.; pres. Cartwright Shoe Co., Albion, Mich.; dir. Inter City Bank, Beacon Water Resources. Republican. Presbyn. Mason, Elk, Moose, Author: Supervisory Development Techniques, 1946. Home: RD 3 Diamond Lake Cassopolis MI 49031 Office: King Mink Ranch RFD 1 Marcellus MI 49067

KING, CHESTER HARDING, lawyer; b. Syracuse, N.Y., Mar. 30, 1913; s. Chester Harding and Kathleen (Comstock) K.; grad. Kent (Conn.) Sch., 1930; A.B., Harvard, 1934, LL.B., 1937; m. Mary Ellen Crapon de Caprona, Dec. 18, 1948; children—Chester Harding III, Eleanor Mather, Charles Noel, Peter Denys Sedgwick. Admitted to N.Y. bar, 1937, since practiced in Syracuse; partner firm Bond, Schoeneck & King, 1952—. Served to capt., inf., AUS, 1941-45. Decorated Bronze Star with oak leaf cluster. Mem. Am., N.Y. State (chmn. com. estate gift taxation 1968-70), Onondaga County bar assns., Am. Judicature Soc., Am. Coll. Probate Counsel. Home: 32 Albany Street Cazenovia NY 13035 Office: State Tower Syracuse NY 13202

KING, CLINTON, artist; b. Ft. Worth, Oct. 3, 1901; s. John Porter and Lorena (Blair) K.; student Princeton, 1924, Nat. Acad. Design Grand Central Sch. Art, Broadmoor Art Acad., 1924-25; studied engraving with Hayter, Paris, 1969-70; m. Duff Stirling Twysden, Aug. 1928 (dec.); m. 2d, Narcissa Swift, Apr. 12, 1941. Numerous one-man shows U.S. and fgn. countries, 1932-, latest being Ohana Gallery, London, Eng., 1959, Galleries Marigny, Paris, France, 1959, 61, Galleries Jeanne Castel, Paris, 1963, William Findlay Gallery, Chgo., 1964, 65, Univ. Club, Chgo., 1965, Brinken Galleries, Stockholm, Sweden, 1966, Gallerie Transposition, Paris, 1966, Lakeview Center Arts and Scis., Peoria, Ill., 1968, Cathedral of Christ the King, Kalamazoo, 1971; exhibited group shows large cities U.S. and fgn. countries, including Carnegie Inst., Chgo. Art Inst. (Clyde M. Carr prize 1944), Phila. Annual, Nat. Acad. Design, Toledo Mus. Art, Phila. Watercolor Soc., Corcoran Biennial, St. Louis Art Mus., Salon D'Automne, Paris, France, Santa Fe Art Mus.; rep. permanent collections City of Paris, Ft. Worth Art Assn., Santa Fe Art Mus. Club: Chicago Arts. Home: 1235 Astor St Chicago IL 60610 Studio: Main St Lakeside MI 49116

KING, CORETTA SCOTT, (Mrs. Martin Luther King, Jr.), lectr., writer, concert singer; b. Marion, Ala., Apr. 27, 1927; d. Obidiah and Bernice (McMurray) Scott; A.B., Antioch Coll., 1951; Mus.B., New Eng. Conservatory Music, 1954, L.H.D., 1971; L.H.D., Boston U., 1969, Marymount-Manhattan Coll., 1969, Brandeis U., 1969, Wilberforce U., 1970, Bethune-Cookman Coll., 1970, Morehouse Coll., 1970, Princeton, 1970, Keuka Coll., 1970; LL.D., U. Bridgeport, 1970, Morgan State Coll., 1970, Northeastern U., 1971, Bates Coll., 1971; m. Martin Luther King, Jr., June 18, 1953 (dec. Apr. 1968); children—Yolanda Denise, Martin Luther II, Dexter Scott, Bernice Albertine. Concert debut, Springfield, O., 1948, numerous concerts throughout U.S.; concerts India, 1959; performances Freedom Concert; voice instr. Morris Brown Coll., Atlanta, 1962; lectr., writer. Del. White House Conf. Children and Youth, 1960; sponsor Sane Nuclear Policy, Com. on Responsibility, Mobilization to End War in Viet Nam, 1966, 67, Margaret Sanger Meml. Found.; pres. Martin Luther King, Jr. Meml. Center, Martin Luther King, Jr. Found.; chmn. Commn. on Econ. Justice for Women; mem. exec. com. Nat. Com. of Inquiry; sponsor So. Rural Action Project, Inc., co-chmn. Clergy and Laymen concerned about Vietnam; active YWCA. Bds. dirs. So. Christian Leadership Conf., Martin Luther King, Jr. Found. Gt. Britain; trustee Robert F. Kennedy Meml. Recipient Outstanding Citizenship award Montgomery (Ala.) Improvement Assn., 1959, Merit award St. Louis Argus, 1960, Distinguished Achievement award Nat. Orgn. Colored Women's Clubs, 1962, Louise Waterman Wise award Am. Jewish Congress Women's Aux., 1963, Myrtle Wreath award Cleve. Hadassah, 1965, Wateler Peace prize, 1968, Dag Hammarskjold award, 1969, Pacem in Terris award Internat. Overseas Service Found., 1969, Leadership for Freedom award Roosevelt U., 1971, Martin Luther King Meml. medal Coll. City N.Y., 1971, numerous others; named Woman of Year, Utility Club N.Y.C., 1962, Woman of Year, Nat. Assn. Radio and TV Announcers, 1968.

Mem. Nat. Council Negro Women (Ann. Brotherhood award, 1957), Women Strike for Peace (del. disarmament conf. Geneva, Switzerland 1962, citation for work in peace and freedom 1963), Women's Orgn. Internat. League for Peace and Freedom, United Church Women (bd. mgrs.), Alpha Kappa Alpha (hon.). Baptist (mem. choir, trustee ch., guild adviser). Club: Links (Human Dignity and Human Rights award Norfolk chpt. 1964). Author: My Life With Martin Luther King, Jr., 1969. Contbr. articles to mags. Address: 234 Sunset Av N W Atlanta GA 30314

KING, CYRIL BERNARD, newspaper editor; b. Tidioute, Pa., Aug. 10, 1905; s. Bernard Christy and Gertrude (Thomson) K.; m. Dorothea L. Brower, Nov. 29, 1934; children—Dorothy (Mrs. Daniel McCormick), Barbara Ann. With Oil City (Pa.) Derrick, 1925-29; city editor Altoona (Pa.) Tribune, 1929-30; mem. staff Pitts. Press, 1930-34; 1930-34; news broadcaster radio sta. KDKA, Pitts., 1932-34; gen. mgr. radio sta. WEBR, Buffalo, 1942-52, v.p., 1942—; editor Courier-Express Buffalo, 1952—; v.p. Courier-Cable Co., 1965—. Bd. dirs. Buffalo chpt. Am. Cancer Soc. Chmn. Buffalo and Ft. Erie Pub. Bridge Authority. Mem. N.Y. State (past pres.), Am. Socs. newspaper editors. Mason (hon. 33), Kiwanian. Home: 36 Columbia Drive Williamsville NY 14221 Office: Courier-Express Buffalo NY 14240

KING, DAMON DEE, hosp. adminstr.; b. Huntingdon, Tenn., Sept. 9, 1934; s. V. L. and Quicnye (Smith) K.; B.S., U. Tenn., 1957; certificate, Ga. State Coll., 1960; m. Janet Hudson, Dec. 31, 1959; children—David G., DeAnn, Robin. Asst. adminstr. Coahoma County Hosp., Clarksdale, Miss., 1957; adminstr. Walton County Hosp., Monroe, Ga., 1961-65; adminstr. Hall County Hosp., Gainesville, Ga., 1965-68; adminstr. Macon (Ga.) Hosp., 1968—. Chmn. Walton County (Ga.) Blood drive, 1962-65; sec.-treas. Macon-Bibb County Hosp. Authority; bd. dirs. Gainesville Mental Health Assn., Tng. Union; trustee, mem. exec. com. Blue Cross-Blue Shield Ga. Served to 1st lt., Med. Service Corps, U.S. Army, 1957-61. Recipient Distinguished Service award as Outstanding Young Man of Year, Monroe Jr. C. of C., 1965, Distinguished Service awards Monroe and Walton County, 1964, Ga. Hosp. Assn., 1969. Mem. Am., Southeastern, Ga. (pres., trustee) hosp. assns., N.E. Ga. Hosp. Council (pres. 1964), Am. Coll. Hosp. Adminstrs., Macon C. of C. Baptist (deacon, bd. dirs.). Rotarian, Kiwanian, Elk. Home: 745 Captain Kell Dr Macon GA 31204 Office: 777 Hemlock St Macon GA 31201

KING, DAVID JOSEPH, educator; b. Ellsworth, Me., Mar. 15, 1931; s. Leslie Stanwood and Julia Ann (Smith) K.; B.A., Boston U., 1951; M.A., U. Me., 1952; Ph.D., U. Md., 1958; m. Nancy Jean Moulton, Nov. 29, 1952; children—Vernon Gregory, Christine Ann. Asst. to asso. prof. Am. U., Washington, 1958-63; asso. prof. to prof., chmn. psychology dept., Albion (Mich.) Coll., 1963-68; prof., dept. chmn. State U. N.Y. At Oswego, 1968—; research asso. Sibley Meml. Hosp., Washington. Served with AUS, 1953-55. Research grantee NSF, Nat. Inst. Mental Health, Office Edn. Mem. Am., Eastern, Midwestern psychol. assns., A.A.A.S. Contr. articles human memory profl. jours. Home: RD 3 Broadview Oswego NY 13126

KING, DAVID SIODAHL, lawyer; b. Salt Lake City, June 20, 1917; s. William H. and Vera (Sjodahl) K.; B.A. in Econs., U. Utah, 1937; LL.B., Georgetown U., 1942; m. Rosalie Helene Lehner, Mar. 10, 1949; children—Jody (Mrs. Robert Y. Olsen), David Sjodahl, Franklin Lawrence, Stephen Edward, Matthew Thomas, Elliot West, Christine, Christopher Henry. Missionary, Ch. of Jesus Christ of Latter-Day Saints, Great Britain, 1937-39; admitted to Utah bar, 1942, D.C. bar, 1944; law clk. to U.S. judge Stephens, 1942- 43; counsel Utah Tax Commn., 1945-46; pvt. practice, Salt Lake City, 1945-60, Washington, 1971—; asst. gen. supt. Mut. Improvement Assn., Latter-Day Saints Ch., 1949-58; tchr. law Stevens Henegar Coll., Salt Lake City; 1950-58; mem. 86th-87th, 89th Congress 2d Dist. Utah; U.S. ambassador to Malagasy Republic, until 1971. Democratic candidate for U.S. Senate, 1962. Address: 1730 K St Washington DC 20006

KING, DAVID V., retail exec.; b. Hutchinson, Kan., 1924; ed. Kan. State U. Pres., dir. Retail Centers of the Americas, Inc. Home: 124 Country Club Dr Port Washington NY 11050 Office: 605 Rockaway Turnpike Lawrence NY 11559

KING, DONALD BERNARD, coll. dean; b. Bristol, Conn., Sept. 3, 1913; s. John and Kathryn (Jones) K.; B.A., Dartmouth, 1935; Ph.D., Princeton, 1938; m. Louise F. Dupraz, June 11, 1938; children—Judith, John, Peter, Jeremy, Robert, Kathryn. Instr. classics Dartmouth, 1938-39; mem. Soc. of Fellows of Harvard, 1939-41; asst. prof. English composition Pa. State U., 1941-43; asso. prof. classics and history Beloit (Wis.) Coll., 1946-51; prof. classics and English, Coll. Mt. St. Joseph on-the-Ohio, 1961-67; dean of the coll. St. Norbert Coll., West DePere, Wis., 1967—. Examiner, cons. North Central Assn., 1959—, commr. colls. and univs., 1968—. Served to lt. USNR, 1943-46. Mem. Am. Assn. Univ. Profs., Am. Assn. Higher Edn., Classical Assn. Middle West and South, Conf. Acad. Deans. Author: Erasmus' On Copia of Words and Ideas, 1963. Contbr. articles profl. jours. Home: 2080 W Vista Circle West DePere WI 54178

KING, DONALD ELIOT, physician; b. Porterville, Cal., Mar. 13, 1903; s. Thomas Jefferson and Ellen (Lynn) K.; M.D., Stanford, 1927; m. Eva Schwartz, Dec. 7, 1926; children—Donald, Sharon, Steven, Douglas. Interne Stanford U. Hosp., 1926-28; instr. surgery, U. Mich. Med. Sch., 1930-32, asst. prof. (bone- joint), 1932-34; asso. prof. surgery Stanford Medical School, 1934-48, prof., 1948-59, clinical prof. surgery, 1959-67; clin. prof. orthopedic surgery U. Cal., 1967—, Diplomate Am. Board Orthopedic Surgery. Mem. A.M.A., San Francisco County, Cal. med. socs., Am. Acad. Orthopedics Surgery, Am. Orthopedic Assn. Office: 2351 Clay Street San Francisco CA 94115

KING, ED REUBEN, naval officer; b. Memphis, Jan. 2, 1913; s. Ed R. and Betty (New) K.; B.S. in Engring., U.S. Naval Acad., 1936; grad. Nat. War Coll., 1956; M.A. in Polit. Sci. George Washington U., 1961; m. Bula Gentry Lee, Dec. 10, 1938; children—Bettye Lee (Mis. John Ferguson), Robbye Lee, Edward Lee. Commd. ensign U.S. Navy, 1936, advanced through grades to rear adm., 1964; comdr. destroyers in Pacific, World War II and Korean War; comdr. cruiser destroyer flotilla, Mediterranean, 1965; mem. staff to chief naval operations, 1967; now chmn. Ship Characteristics Bd. Decorated Legion of Merit, Bronze Star. Club: Army Navy Country (chmn. bd. govs. 1966-) (Washington). Author: (D. Van Nostrand) Shiphandling, 1953. Home: 4501 Arlington Blvd Arlington VA 22203 Office: The Pentagon Washington DC 20301

KING, EDGAR IRWIN, educator, lawyer; b. Logan, Kan., Nov. 18, 1913; s. Edgar Irwin and Frances Emmaline (Brown) K.; student Hays State Coll., 1930-32; A.B., U. Kan., 1934, LL.B., 1937; LL.D., (hon.), Temple U., 1959; m. Anna Grace Vander Velde, Aug. 19, 1937. Admitted to Kan. bar, 1937, Ohio, 1947; practice of law, Logan, Kan., 1937; asst. prof. law U. Kansas City, 1937-41; asso. prof. law U. Louisville, 1941-46; asso. prof. law Western Res. U., 1946-50, prof., 1950-62, asst. dean, 1951-58, dir. grad. law program, 1953-58, dean, 1958-62; prof. law Dickinson Sch. Law, Carlisle, Pa., 1962—, asst. dean, 1967—; vis. prof. Hastings Coll. Law, U. Cal., 1971-72. Chmn. regional enforcement commn. WSB, 1952-53. Served as comdr., USNR, 1943-46. Mem. Am. Bar Assn., Am. Law Inst., Am. Legal History Soc., Order of Coif, Phi Alpha Delta. Co-author: Notes and Annotations to Kentucky Revised Statues, 1944; also articles legal periodicals. Editor: Juvenile Court Handbook. Home: 625 Belvedere Carlisle PA 17013

KING, EDMUND LUDWIG, educator; b. St. Louis, Jan. 10, 1914; s. William F.B. and Lydia (Ludwig) Seifert; B.A., U. Tex., 1933, M.A., 1934, Ph.D., 1949; m. Willard Fahrenkamp, Jan. 29, 1951. Instr. Miss. State Coll., Starkville, 1936-38, asst. prof. modern languages, 1938-41; instr. English, U. Tex., Austin, 1946; instr. Spanish, Princeton, 1946-50, asst. prof., 1950-57, asso. prof., 1957-60, prof. chmn., dept. Romance langs., 1966—. Vice pres. Internat. Inst. Madrid, 1969—. Served to maj. AUS, 1941-46. Decorated Bronze Star; Golden Cross of Merit (Polish Republic). Mem. Modern Language Assn. Democrat. Author: Bécquer: From Painter to Poet, 1953. Translator: The Structure of Spanish History (A. Castro), 1953. Editor: El Humo Dormido (G. Miró), 1967. Home: 171 Western Way Princeton NJ 08540

KING, EDWARD CALDWELL, lawyer; b. Delta, Colo., Aug. 14, 1896; s. Alfred Rufus and Annie Rachel (Caldwell) K.; ed. Warren Acad., Denver; A.B., U. Denver, 1919, LL.B., 1922, LL.D., 1952; LL.D., U. Colo., 1965; m. Mary- Jess Hedrick, Aug. 15, 1925; children—Nancy Jane, Neil Caldwell. Admitted to Colo. bar 1922, in gen. practice, Denver, 1922-29; mem. Twitchell, Clark, Burkhardt and King, 1923-27, Gould and King, 1927-29; trust officer Internat. Trust Co., 1929-38, exec. v.p., 1939-40; prof., dean Sch. of Law, U. Colo., 1940-63; counsel law firm Hollenbeck, King, French & Miller, Boulder, Colo., 1965—. Vice chmn. War Labor Bd., 9th Region, 1943; publ. mem. Regional WSB, 1951. Co-dir. Legal research Inst. N.Y.U., Ankara, Turkey, 1957-58. Served as 2d lt., F.A., World War I; commd. maj., Special Res. AUS, May 13, 1943; lt. col., Jan. 1945; served Africa and Italy, Sept. 1943-Oct. 1945; chief, property control div., Allied Com. for Italy. Decorated Legion of Merit; knight officer Order of Crown of Italy. Mem. Colo. Ho. of Reps., 1927-30, Denver Planning Commn., 1938-40, Civic League of Denver, 1930-40. Fellow Am. Coll. Probate Counsel; mem. Am. (chmn. real property, probate and trust law sect., 1956-57), Boulder County, Colo. (pres. 1963-64) bar assns., Law Club, Sigma Alpha Epsilon, Phi Delta Phi, Sigma Delta Chi, Order of Coif. Club: University (Denver). Author: Future Interests in Colorado; Colorado Practice Methods (2 vols.), 1956, 2d edit. (3 vols.), 1970. Home: 1850 Folsom St Boulder CO 80302 Office: 1966 13th St Boulder CO 80302

KING, EDWARD FRANCIS, textile co. exec.; b. Montreal, Can., Aug. 22, 1904; s. William Patrick and Sarah (Horan) K.; m. Hilda Bradley, Oct. 10, 1932. With Dominion Textile Co. Ltd., Montreal, 1920-45, 53—, v.p. sales, 1953-62, exec. v.p., 1966, pres., now chmn., also dir.; chmn., dir. Caldwell Linen Mills, Penmans, Ltd.; dir. Esmond Mills Ltd., Bd. dirs. Canadian Textiles Inst., Loyola Coll. Home: 1700 McGregor Montreal 25 Quebec Canada Office: 1950 Sherbrooke St W Montreal Quebec Canada

KING, EDWARD J., ret. govt. ofcl.; b. Lawrence, Mass., Nov. 8, 1904; s. James and Mary Ellen (Ward) K.; ed. pub. schs.; m. June C. Barton, Sept 1, 1930; children—Almeda C., James B. Sec., I.U.E. local 278, AFL-CIO, 1943-61; legislative agt. Western Mass. council CIO, 1946-61; commnr. U.S. sect. Internat. Boundary Commn. U.S. and Can., 1961-69. Mem. Ludlow (Mass.) Sch. Comm. 1954—; chmn. Draft Bd. 78, 1950—. Bd. dirs. Urban League, 1960-61. K.C. Club: Italian (Ludlow). Home: 21 Birch Street Ludlow MA 01056

KING, EDWARD JASPER, educator; b. Iowa City, June 4, 1916; s. Irving and Alta (Burke) K.; B.A., State U. Ia., 1937; Ph.D., Yale, 1942; m. Grace E. Wentworth, Feb. 23, 1946; 1 son, Andrew W. Analyst, Dow Chem. Co., 1937-39; instr. chemistry Yale, 1942-46; mem. faculty Barnard Coll., 1946-, prof. chemistry, 1959-; vis. reader phys. chemistry U. New Eng., Armidale, N.S. W., Australia, 1966-67. NSF Faculty fellow, 1959-6O. Fellow A.A.A.S.; mem. Am. Chem. Soc. (vis. asso. com. profl. tng.), Am. Phys. Soc., Faraday Soc. Author: Qualitative Analysis and Electrolytic Solutions, 1959; Acid-Base Equilibria, 1965; (with Paul and Farinholt) General Chemistry, 1967. Home: 54 Morningside Dr New York City NY 10025

KING, EDWARD LOUIS, educator; b. Grand Forks, N.D., Mar. 15, 1920; s. Edward Louis and Beatrice (Nicholson) K.; student Long Beach (Cal.) Jr. Coll., 1938-41; B.S., U. Cal., Berkeley, 1942, Ph.D., 1945; m. Joy Kerler, Dec. 20, 1952; children—Paul, Marcia. Research chemist Manhattan Project, U. Cal., Berkeley, 1942-46; mem. chemistry faculty Harvard, 1946-48, U. Wis., 1948-62; mem. chemistry faculty U. Colo., Boulder, 1963—, chmn. dept. chemistry, 1970—. Guggenheim fellow, 1957-58. Mem. Am. Chem. Soc., Chem. Soc. London, Faraday Soc., A.A.A.S., Phi Beta Kappa, Sigma Xi. Author: How Chemical Reactions Occur, 1963. Editor: Inorganic Chemistry, 1964-68. Home: 3820 Barr Ct Boulder CO 80303

KING, EDWARD WARD, transp. co. exec.; b. Surgoinsville, Tenn., Jan. 12, 1896; s. John Rutledge and Margaret (Collup) K.; grad. high sch.; m. Myrtle Charlton, Mar. 27, 1922; children—E. William, John. R., Margaret (Mrs. Edwin O. Norris). Founder, King Motor Co., Kingsport, Tenn., 1925-32; founder, pres. Mason & Dixon Lines, Inc., Kingsport, 1932-57, chmn. bd. 1957—; chmn. bd. Mason & Dixon Tank Lines, Inc., Kingsport, Crown Enterprises, Inc., Kingsport; pres. 10 affiliated cos.; past pres., dir. Kingsport Properties; past chmn. bd. Kingsport Nat. Bank. Dist. chmn. Am. Cancer Soc., 1962-63; gen. chmn. Appalachia Heart Assn., 1961-62; mem. President's Club, U. Tenn., 1968—; mem. Tenn. Tax Study Commn., 1967. Past dirs. Community Chest; trustee Holston Conf. Colls. Served with U.S. Army, World War I; France, Germany. Recipient Legion of Honor award Kiwanis Kingsport, 1937, also Appreciation certificate Am. Cancer Soc., Pioneer Future award Tenn. Jr. C. of C., Appreciation certificate Am. Heart Assn. Mem. Transp. Ins. Co. (bd. dirs.), Tenn. Motor Transp. Assn. (past pres.), Am. Trucking Assn. (bd. dirs., past v.p.), So. Motor Carriers Rate Conf. (founder, past bd. govs.), Am. Soc. Traffic and Transp. (founder) N.A.M., Transp. Assn. Am., A.I.M., U.S., Kingsport (past bd. dirs.) chambers commerce, Am. Legion, Am. Hereford Assn., Am. Angus Assn. Methodist. Democrat. Kiwanian, Moose. Club: Ridgefields Country. Home: 1349 Linville St Kingsport TN 37660 Office: 1311 Eastman Rd Kingsport TN 37664

KING, ELBERT GLENWOOD, banker; b. nr. Appalachia, Va., Sept. 17, 1906; s. Maynard E. and Minnie (Morton) K.; student Miller Sch. Bus., 1925-26; m. Charlotte Adams, Apr. 6, 1947; 1 son, Edward Lee. Sec., asst. cashier, cashier, v.p., pres. First Nat. Bank of Appalachia, 1961-65; sr. v.p. First Nat. Exchange Bank, Appalachia, 1965—; dir. Interstate R.R. Co., Big Stone Gap Land Co., Appalachia Ins. Co., Lonesome Pine Hosp., Lonesome Pine Doctors Bldg. Chmn. Appalachia Planning Commn., 1970—. Founder Edward Lee King Meml. Scholarship Fund; adv. bd. Mountain Empire Community Coll.; bd. dirs. Clinch Valley Coll. Served with AUS, 1943-44. Mem. Am. Legion (comdr.), Appalachia C. of C. (pres.). Baptist (deacon, treas.). Lion, Odd Fellow. Home: 608 Spruce St Appalachia VA 24216 Office: 102 Main St Appalachia VA 24216

KING, ELMER RICHARD, physician, educator; b. Logan County, O., May 15, 1916; s. John Oliver and Clara (Yoder) K.; B.A., Ohio State U., 1939, M.D., 1941; AEC fellow Duke, 1948-49; postgrad. tng. Oak Ridge Inst. Nuclear Studies, 1949-50, Mayo Found., 1953; m. Marie Hutchings Pace, Mar. 29, 1941; children—Elmer Richard, Marsha Ann, John Michael, Suzanne. Commd. lt. (j.g.), M.C., U.S. Navy, 1941, advanced through grades to capt., 1961; intern U.S. Naval Hosp., Pensacola, Fla.; with atomic def. div. Bur. Medicine and Surgery, 1946-47; sr. scientist Operation Sandstone, Eniwetok Atoll, 1947; resident radiology U.S. Naval Hosp., Bethesda, Md., 1950-53; dir. div. nuclear medicine U.S. Naval Med. Center, Bethesda, 1954-61, chief radiology, 1958-61; ret., 1961; mem. faculty Med. Coll. Va., 1961—, prof. radiology, chmn. dept., 1965-; chief radiol. service VA Hosp., Richmond, 1965—. Bd. dirs. James F. Aicken Found. Recipient certificate of merit Sec. Navy, 1947, Surgeon Gen. U.S., 1961; Alumni Achievement award Ohio State U., 1966. Diplomate Am. Bd. Radiology (board of trustees). Fellow Am. Coll. Radiology (bd. of chancellors); mem. A.A.A.S., Radiol. Soc. North Am., Am. Radium Soc. (2d v.p. 1966-), Am. Roentgen Ray Soc., Assn. Univ. Radiologists, Soc. Nuclear Medicine (bd. of trustees), Am. Assn. Univ. Profs., Am. Assn. Med. Colls., Brit. Inst. Radiology, Am. Soc. Therapy Radiology, A.M.A., Va Med. Soc., Va. Radiol. Soc., Nu Sigma Nu. Republican Methodist Episcopalian. Clubs: Willow Oaks, Bull and Bear (Richmond). Author: (with T. G. Mitchell) Laboratory Guide to Nuclear Medicine, 1960; also numerous papers. Editor: (with Charles Behrens) Atomic Medicine, 1969. Home: 10300 Cherokee Road Richmond VA 23235

KING, FRANCIS WALTER, educator, clin. psychologist; b. Washington, Dec. 13, 1918; s. Francis Walter and Ellen (Lockwood) K.; B.S., Bowdoin Coll., 1940; M.A., Boston U., 1941; Ph.D., Harvard, 1952; m. Dorothy Jay Cushman, July 3, 1943; children—Marilyn Jay (Mrs. Raymond Carroll Dickinson, Jr.), Michael Bruce. Psychologist, head social service dept. State Farm, Bridgewater, Mass., 1941-42; part-time instr. social sci. Boston U., 1946-48; mem. faculty Dartmouth, 1949-, clin. psychologist Coll. Health Service, prof. psychology and med. psychology Med. Sch., 1960—, adminstv. dir. mental health div., Coll. Health Service, 1967-; cons. VA Hosp., White River Junction, Vt., 1963-. Chmn. N.H. Bd. Examiners Psychologists, 1963-70; mem. adv. com. N.H. Dept. Health, and Welfare, 1966-69. Served to capt. AUS, 1942-46. Diplomate clin. psychology Am. Bd. Profl. Psychology. Fellow Soc. Projective Techniques, Am. Coll. Health Assn.; mem. Am., Eastern, New Eng., N.H. (pres. 1959-60) psychol. assns., Am. Group Psychotherapy Assn., Northeastern Soc. Group Psychotherapy, Am. Assn. U. Profs., Sigma Xi. Contbr. profl. jours. Home: 4 Kingsford Rd Hanover NH 03755

KING, FRANK LESTER, banker; b. Sparta, Ill., Aug. 5, 1897; s. John L. and Anna (Syar) K.; ed. Northwestern Sch. of Commerce; m. Lucille Alhime, Aug. 30, 1924; children—Frank Lester, John Frederick, Robert Alexander. Asst. cashier 1st Nat. Bank, Sparta, 1916-18; nat. bank examiner, 1920-25; asst. cashier Mut. Nat. Bank, Chgo., 1926- 27; joined Continental Nat. Bank and Trust Co. (now Continental Ill. Nat. Bank and Trust Co.), Chgo., 1928, comptroller, 1930; exec. v.p., dir. United Cal. Bank, Los Angeles, 1943, pres., dir., 1945-59, chmn. bd., 1959; chmn. Western Bancorp., 1959—; dir. United Cal. Bank Internat., 1962—; dir. U.S. Borax and Chem. Co., Pacific Indemnity Co., Pacific Mut. Life Ins. Co., Cyprus Mines Corp., El Paso Natural Gas Co. Dir. Assn. Registered Bank Holding Cos. Trustee U. So. Cal. Mem. Assn. Res. City Bankers. Clubs: Los Angeles Country, Cal., Automobile of Southern Cal. (dir.), Stock Exchange (Los Angeles); Pacific Union (San Francisco); The Links (N.Y.C.). Home: 10375 Wilshire Blvd Los Angeles CA 90024 Office: 600 S Spring Street Los Angeles CA 90054

KING, FREDERIC RHINELANDER, architect; b. N.Y.C., Apr. 13, 1887; s. LeRoy and Ethel (Rhinelander) K.; A.B. cum laude, Harvard, 1908, Columbia Archtl. Sch., 1908-11, Ecole des Beaux Arts, Paris, France, 1912-14; m. Edith P. Morgan, Feb. 9, 1924; children—David Rhinelander, Jonathan LeRoy. With McKim, Mead and White, 1914-17; with Carrere and Hastings, 1919-20; asso. Marion S. Wyeth, 1920-32; partner Wyeth & King, 1932-64. Mem. A.R.C. Commn., 1917; constrn. div. W.P.B., N.Y.C. and Washington, 1942-43. Trustee Barnard Coll., 1933-57; former chmn. (bd. of trustees of N. Y. Soc. Library; trustee St. Luke's Hosp. (hon.). Served as 1st lt., U.S. Army, G2 AEF, 1918-19, Am. Commn. to Negotiate Peace; mem. Coolidge's Mission to Austria, 1919. Academician N.A.D. Fellow A.I.A.; mem. Soc. Beaux Arts. Republican. Clubs: Century Association, Harvard, Pilgrims of U.S. Church. Address: 340 East 72d Street New York City NY 10021

KING, FREDERICK HERBERT, educator; b. Leeds, Eng., Jan. 26, 1905; s. Philip and Sarah (Lascot) K.; came to U.S., 1908, naturalized, 1915; A.B., Columbia, 1926, M.D., 1929; m. Lucile Menz, Nov. 4, 1936; children—Barbara, Morton Litt. Intern, Jewish Hosp. Bklyn., 1929-31; fellow pathology Mt. Sinai Hosp., N.Y.C., 1931-33, fellow cardiovascular research, 1933-35, adj. physician, 1936-48, asso. attending physician, 1953—; asso. clin. prof. medicine Mt. Sinai Sch. Medicine, 1968-69, instr. medicine Columbia Coll. Physicians and Surgeons, 1944-48, lectr., 1948-61, asso. in medicine, 1961—; clin. prof. medicine, 1969—. Fellow N.Y. Acad. Medicine, A.C.P.; mem. A.M.A., N.Y. County Med. Soc., Alpha Omega Alpha. Research cardiovascular dynamics, velocity of blood flow, congenital heart disease. Home: 15 W 81st St New York City NY 10023 Office: 55 E 66th St New York City NY 10020

KING, GEORGE HAROLD, lumberman; b. Mt. Lebanon, La., Nov. 11, 1896; s. William L. and Julia C. (Baker) K.; ed. Gibsland High Sch.; m. French Freeman, Aug. 25, 1917; 1 son, George Harold. With Long Bell Lumber Co., Ludington, La., 1913-17; shipping clk. Forrest Lumber Co., Oakdale, La., 1917-21; supt. pine lumber operations Hillyer-Deutsch-Edwards, Oakdale, 1921-24; gen. mgr. Hillyer-Edwards-Fuller, Glenmora, La., 1924-36, v.p., 1936-41; organizer King-Edwards-Fuller, St. Francisville, La., mng. partner, 1941-45; pres. King Lumber Industries, Canton, 1946-58, chmn., 1958—; pres. Canton & Carthage R.R. Co., 1946-; dir. Am. Bank & Trust Co. Mem. La. Mineral Bd., 1952. Mem. So. Hardwood Producers (pres. 1951-52), N.A.M. (dir.), Nat. Hardwood Lumber Assn. (dir.). Home: 1465 Ted Dunham Drive Baton Rouge LA 70802 Office: King Lumber Industries Fidelity Nat Bank Bldg Baton Rouge LA 70801

KING, GEORGE HAROLD, Jr., lumberman, former gov. Fed. Res. System; b. Oakdale, La., Aug. 18, 1920; s. George Harold and French (Freeman) D.; B.S., La. State U., 1941; student summer sch. U. Colo., 1939-41; m. Daudrille Elaine Hollaway, May 15, 1942; children—Linda Elaine, George Harold III, Lisa Hollaway; m. 2d, Shirley Lynn Goss, Sept. 5, 1964; children—Teresa Lynn, Christopher Baker. Treas., King Lumber Industries, 1946-49, exec. v.p., 1950-58, pres., 1958-59, exec. v.p., now pres.; breeder purebred Hereford cattle, 1949-62; dir. New Orleans br. Fed. Res. Bank of Atlanta, 1956-59, chmn. 1958, bd. govs. Fed. Res. System, 1959- 63; dir. Canton & Carthage R.R., 1946-56, Am. Bank & Trust Co., Baton Rouge, La. Dir. Miss. Econ. Council, 1958. Served as lt. USNR, 1942-46. Commendation for accomplishments cattle breeding, Miss. Legislature, 1956. Mem. Am. (dir. 1956-59), Miss. (dir. 1949—, pres.

1951) Hereford assns., Newcomen Soc., Sigma Chi, Beta Gamma Sigma (hon.). Presbyn. Clubs: Baton Rouge (La.) Country; Burning Tree (Bethesda, Md.). Home: 2710 Fairway Dr Baton Rouge LA 70809 Office: PO Box 2307 Baton Rouge LA 70821

KING, HARRY ALBERT, coll. dean; b. Washington, Aug. 26, 1901; s. Frank Arlington and Nellie Agatha (Werres) K.; Mus.B., U. Rochester, 1927; M.A., N.Y.U., 1928, Ph.D., 1939; m. Marjorie Francis Topliffe, Aug. 15, 1932; children—Kathryn Johnston, Charles Johnston, Francis A. Profl. musician Washington and Rochester symphony orchestras, 1920-25, Erie (Pa.) Philharmonic Orchestra, 1950-58; faculty State Normal Sch., Fredonia, N.Y., 1928—, asso. dir. Tchrs. Coll., 1948-58, dean, 1958—; acad. dean State University College of Education, Fredonia, 1960-66, dean emeritus, 1966—; dir. Semester in Antwerp Program (Belgium), 1966-69. Mem. Am. Fedn. Musicians (v.p. Local 108), Am. String Tchrs. Assn. (past sec.), N.Y. State Music Assn. (v.p., exec. com. 1950-56), Music Tchrs. Nat. Assn., Music Educators Nat. Conf., Phi Delta Kappa, Phi Mu Alpha Sinfonia. K.C., Kiwanian. Home: Box 416 Ripley NY 14775 Office: State University Coll Fredonia NY 14063

KING, HARRY O., investment exec.; b. Chgo., Mar. 6, 1890; s. William James and Caroline King; ed. high school; m. Mildred L. Holmes, Dec. 11, 1915; children—Barbara (Mrs. Alexander Hawley), Harry O., Saranne (Mrs. Charles P. Neumann); m. 2d, Isabella Selmes Greenway, Apr. 22, 1939. Salesman A. M. Castle & Co., Chgo., 1908-15; pres. King Pressed Steel Co., Chgo., 1915-23; v.p. and gen. mgr. Bassick Co., Bridgeport, Conn., 1923-27; pres., dir. Sahaba, Inc., (N.Y.C. Div. adminstr. NRA, Washington, 1933-34; mng. dir. Copper Code Authority, N.Y. C., 1934-35; dir. Copper Div. W.P.B., Washington, 1942-44; chmn. Combined Allied Copper Com., Combined Raw Materials Bd., Washington, 1942-44; spl. asst. chief of staff USAF, Washington, 1950-52; spl. cons. USAF Comdr. Air Materiel Command, Wright-Patterson AFB, Dayton, O., 1953—. Recipient USAF award for meritorious service, 1953, also the USAF exceptional service medal, 1960. Episcopalian. Clubs: Racquet and Tennis, Links, Turf and Field, United Hunts Cloud (N.Y.C.); Piping Rock (Locust Valley, N.Y.); Chicago; Lyford Cay (Nassau, Bahamas). Address: 132 East 92d Street New York City NY 10028

KING, HARVEY MARINUS, ch. architect, engr.; b. Byron, Minn., June 5, 1894; s. David Francis and Mary Eva Lena (Craig) K.; B.S., U. Minn., 1918; M. Arch., Mass. Inst. Tech., 1923; spl. course edn. U. Louisville, 1932; m. Margaret Elizabeth Farley, Dec. 28, 1921; children—David Farley, Richard Harding. Draftsman Croft & Boerner, Duluth, Mpls., C. H. Johnston, St. Paul, Stuart M. French, Weiser, Ida., Frank Irving Cooper Corp., Boston, 1919- 22; draftsman, instr. engring. div. coll. agr. U. Minn., 1917; asso. prof. architecture and allied arts U. Ore., 1920-22; prof. architecture, head dept. N.D. Agr. Coll., 1923-24; instr. Louisville Inst. Tech., 1934- 36; pvt. practice architecture, Louisville, 1937-54, specialist ch. architecture, 1924—; architect-sec. bd. ch. extension Methodist Ch. South, 1924-36; dir. architecture, div. home missions and ch. extension Meth. Ch., 1946-54; asso. sec. and dir. dept. of architecture, sect. ch. extension, div. nat. missions of bd. missions, Meth. Ch., 1954-61; tchr. spl. short courses, pastor's tng. schs. various colls. Served with USNR, 1918-22, to lt. to comdr., 1942- 46. Licensed architect 22 states; certified by Nat. Council of Archtl. Registration Bds. Mem. Soc. Archtl. Historians, A.I.A. (past pres. Ky.), Ch. Archtl. Guild Am. (past dir. at large), Nat. Council Chs. of Christ in U.S.A. (dept. ch. bldg. and architecture), Soc. Am. Mil Engrs., Res. Officers Assn., Am. Assn. Engrs., Ky. Assn. Architects, Naval Res. Assn., Alpha Rho Chi, Sigma Phi Delta, Phi Tau Theta. Author: Board of Church Extension-History, 1882-1932; A Guide to Church Planning-The Small Church, Sect. I, Sect. II; The Suburban Church (3 vols.), 1952. Contbr. articles on ch. architecture to ch. mags. Home: 227 Bayou Woods Dr Fort Walton Beach FL 32548

KING, HENRY, motion picture dir.; b. Christiansburg, Va., Jan. 24, 1896. With Norfolk & Western R.R., then toured in stock, circuses, vaudeville and burlesque; appeared N.Y. stage in Top O'the Morning; motion picture actor for Pathe Studios; exec. head Inspiration Co.; with Fox Film Co., remaining after merger with 20th Century Pictures Co.; producer motion pictures 23/ Hours Leave, Tol'able David, Fury, White Sister; motion pictures directed include Stella Dallas, Romola, Winning of Barbara Worth, Woman Disputed, Over the Hill, Carolina, State Fair, Country Doctor, Ramona, Lloyds of London, In Old Chicago, Alexander's Ragtime Band, Jesse James, Little Old New York, Stanley and Livingstone, Maryland, Chad Hanna, Yank in the R.A.F., Black Swan, Song of Bernadette, Wilson, Bell for Adano, Margie, Captain from Castile, Deep Waters, Twelve O'Clock High, The Gun Fighter, I'd Climb the Highest Mountain, David and Bathsheba, Wait 'till the Sun Shines Nellie, Snows of Kilmanjaro, O. Henry's Full House, King of the Khyber Rifles, Untamed, Love is a Many Splendored Thing, Carousel, The Sun Also Rises, This Earth is Mine, Tender is the Night. Address: 1474 Carla Ridge Beverly Hills CA 90210 *

KING, HUGER SINKLER, corp. exec.; b. Darlington, S.C., June 15, 1907; s. C. Coker and Mary Simons (Sinkler) K.; student The Citadel, 1923-25; J.D., U. S.C., 1928; m. Mary Lynn Carlson, May 21, 1932; children—Huger S., L. Richardson, Laurinda C., Michael Lowndes. Admitted to N.C. bar, 1928, practiced in Greensboro, 1928-58, sr. partner King, Adams, Kleemeier & Hagan, 1955- 58; pres. Richardson Corp.; chmn. Piedmont Financial Co. Inc. of N.Y.; dir., chmn. exec. com. Reins. Corp. of N.Y.; dir., chmn. exec. com. Piedmont Life Ins. Co., Lexington Mgmt. Co.; pres. Piedmont Mgmt. Co., Inc.; dir. Richardson- Merrell, Inc., Piedmont Adv. Corp., N.C. Nat. Bank. Trustee, v.p. Richardson Found. Past pres. Greensboro Community Chest; chmn. Empty Stocking Fund. Mayor, Greensboro, 1940-42. Bd. trustees Davidson Coll., 1963-68. Served as lt. comdr. USNR, 1942-45. Mem. Greensboro C. of C. (past pres.). Presbyn. (elder). Clubs: University (N.Y.C.); Merchants and Manufacturers, Greensboro Country (past pres.) (Greensboro). Home: 610 Woodland Dr Greensboro NC 27408 Office: Piedmont Bldg Greensboro NC 27401 also 1515 Summer St Stamford CT 06905

KING, IVAN ROBERT, astronomer; b. Far Rockaway, N.Y., June 25, 1927; s. Myram and Anne (Franzblau) K.; A.B., Hamilton Coll., 1946; A.M., Harvard, 1947, Ph.D., 1952; m. Alice Greene, Nov. 21, 1952; children—David, Lucy, Adam, Jane. Instr. astronomy Harvard, 1951-52; mathematician Perkin-Elmer Corp., Norwalk, Conn., 1951-52; methods analyst U.S. Dept. Def., Washington, 1954-56; with U. Ill., 1956-64; asso. prof. astronomy U. Cal. at Berkeley, 1964-66, prof., 1966—, chmn. astronomy dept., 1967-70. Mem. Soc. of Fellows, Harvard, 1947-51. Mem. Am. Astron. Soc. (councillor 1963-66), Internat. Astron. Union. Contbr. numerous articles in field to sci. jours. Study of stellar systems. Office: Dept Astronomy U Cal Berkeley CA 94720

KING, JACKSON FREDRICK, banker; b. Columbus, O., May 17, 1905; s. Hugo Herman and Jessie (Huffman) K.; B.A., Colo. Coll., 1927; m. Fanchon Norton, Feb. 12, 1947. With Halsey Stuart & Co., Inc., 1927-37, Brown, Schlessman, Owen & Co., Denver, 1937-42; with First Nat. Bank Casper (Wyo.), 1946—, pres., 1957- 68, chmn. bd., chief exec. officer, 1968—, also dir. Mem. regional adv. com. to comptroller currency, 1965-69. Trustee Paul Stock Found., Casper Coll., Found.; nat. adv. com. U.S.O. Served to maj. AUS, 1942-46. Named Boss of Year, Casper C. of C., 1957. Mem. Am. Bankers Assn. (exec. com. nat. bank div. 1964-67, adv. com. savs. div. 1963—), Phi Beta Kappa, Beta Theta Pi, Alpha Kappa Psi. Republican. Episcopalian. Rotarian (past pres. Casper). Home: 2001 Lynwood Pl Casper WY 82601 Office: P O Box 40 Casper WY 82602

KING, JAMES AMBROS, tenor; b. Dodge City, Kan., May 22. 1925; s. Howard Willis and Hettie (Shaffer) K.; B.Mus., La. State U., 1950; M.A., U. Kansas City (Mo.), 1952; m. 2d, Marieluise Nagel, Nov. 5, 1964; children-David Howard, Daniel Morris, Ardis Ruth, Thomas Richard. Mem. Deutsche Oper, Berlin, Germany, 1962—; guest appearences in Vienna, Bayreuth, Salzburg Festival, Munich, Covent Garden; debut Met. Opera, 1966; repertoire includes Lohengrin, Fidelio, Carmen, Pagliacci, Die Walkuere, Ariadne auf Naxos., Die Frau ohne Schatten, Daphne, Turandot, Tosca, Parsifal; spl. work in field of German opera; recording artist London Records. Served with USNR, 1943-45. Baptist. Address: Gabriel-Max-Strasse 27 Munich West Germany

KING, JAMES F., b. 1920; B.S. in Accounting, M.B.A. in Mgmt., N.Y.U.; married. Asst. comptroller Burroughs, Welcome & Co., 1944-53; treas., asst. to pres. Nat. Selected Prods. Inc., 1953-56; with Collins & Alkman Corp., 1956—, asst. sec., sec., comptroller, 1959-66, v.p. adminstrn., sec., 1966-70, group v.p., 1970—. Address: P O Box 1599 Charlotte NC 28201

KING, JAMES M., Jr., investment banker; b. Joliet, Ill., Jan. 22, 1910; s. James M. and Sallie (Tobey) K.; student Amherst Coll., 1929-31, Northeastern U., 1941, Am. Inst. Banking, 1931-40; m. Helen Lucette Prichard, Oct. 27, 1929; children—Celeste (dec.), Helen Justine, Deborah Angell, Timothy Winans. Asst. treas. Newport (R.I.) Trust Co., 1931-47; sec. to Robert R. Young, 1947-49; spl. asst. C. & O. Ry., N.Y.C., 1947-52; spl. asst. America Corp. (formerly Chesapeake Industries, Inc.), 1949-50, treas. 1950-52; pres. Television Center, 1951-52; sr. partner Francis I. duPont & Co., 1952-71; v.p. duPont Glore Forgan, Inc., N.Y.C., 1971—. Mem. Alpha Delta Phi. Episcopalian. Club: The Brook (N.Y.C.). Home: Hook Rd Bedford NY 10506 Office: 1 Wall St New York City NY 10005

KING, JEROME HENRY, Jr., naval officer; b. Youngstown, O., July 14, 1919; s. Jerome Henry and Florence Ethel (Taylor) K.; B.Metall. Engring., Yale, 1941; postgrad. U.S. Naval Postgrad. Sch., Annapolis, Md., 1948-49, U.S. Naval War Coll., Newport, R.I., 1957-58; M.S., Mass. Inst. Tec., 1951; m. Jane Dustin Bellows, July 13, 1945; children—Judith (Mrs. Joe L. Griggs), Nancy (Mrs. Jon A. Harris), Sally. Commd. ensign USN, 1941, advanced through grades to vice adm., 1970; comdr. Destroyer Bache, 1953-55, Destroyer Div. 601, 1960-61, Nuclear Weapons Tng. Center, Atlantic, 1961-62, Destroyer Tender Yellowstone, 1962-63, Destroyer Squadron One, 1965-66, Antisubmarine Warfare Group One, 1968-69, U.S. Naval Forces, Vietnam, 1970-71; staff Carrier Div. Six, 1958-60; asst. chief of staff for plans 7th Fleet, 1963-65; exec. asst. to chief naval operations, 1966-68; chmn. ship characteristics bd. Office of Chief Naval Operations, 1969-70; dep. chief naval operations, 1971—. Decorated D.S.M., Legion of Merit with gold star, Bronze Star with combat V, Navy Commendation medal with combat V and gold star, Vietnamese Gallantry Cross. Mem. Sigma Xi, Tau Beta Pi. Home: Quarters B Naval Observatory Washington DC 20390 Office: Dep Chief Naval Operations The Pentagon Washington DC 20350

KING, JOHN ETHELBERT, Jr., univ. adminstr.; b. Oklahoma City, Okla., July 29, 1913; s.John Ethelbert and Iosa Wynetka (Koontz) K., Sr.; A.B., N. Tex. State Coll., 1932; M.S., U. of Ark., 1937; Ph.D., Cornell, 1941; LL.D., Coll. of Ozarks, Clarksville, Ark. 1966; L.H.D., No. Mich. U. 1966; m. Glennie Beanland, Dec. 25, 1936; children—Wynetka Ann (Mrs. Rex Reynolds), Rebecca Ferris (Mrs. Jon Shutt). Tchr. of langs., coach Frisco (Tex.) High School, 1933-35; camp educational adv., Co. 1708, C.C.C. (forest service), Ozone, Arkansas, 1935-37; regents fellow rural education, Cornell, 1937-38; principal Dwight Indian Sch., Vian, Okla., 1938-40; supt. Tucson (Ariz.) Indian Sch., 1941-43; asst. prof. of rural edn. and dir. extra mural studies, Cornell, 1945-47; academic dean and prof. of rural edn. U. of Minn., Duluth br., 1947. acting provost, 1950-51, provost, 1951-53; pres. Kan. State Tchrs. Coll., Emporia, 1953-66, U. Wyo., 1966-67; prof., chmn. dept. higher edn. So. Ill. U., Carbondale. Served as lt. (s.g.) USNR, 1943-45; deck officer U.S.S. Hyde A.P.A. 173. Bd. dirs. nat. missions Presbyn. Ch. U.S.A., Mem. A.A.A.S., Am. Assn. Coll. Tchrs. Edn. (pres. 1966), N.E.A., S.A.R, Phi Delta Kappa, Phi Kappa Phi, Lanbda Chi Alpha, Kappa Delta Pi. Home: 207 Colonial Dr Carbondale IL 62901

KING, JOHN GORDON, educator, physicist; b. London, Eng., Aug. 13, 1925; s. Gordon Allan and Sara (Merrick) K.; brought to U.S., 1928, naturalized, 1931; B.S., Mass. Inst. Tech., 1950, Ph.D., 1953; m. Elisabeth Sleck, June 11, 1949; children—Alan, Andrew, James, Charles, Martha, David, Benjamin, Matthew. Technician underwater sound lab. Harvard, 1943-45; mem. faculty dept. physics Mass. Inst. Tech., 1953—, prof., 1965—; cons. Avco Corp., 1955-58. Served with AUS, 1944, USNR, 1944-46. Recipient Sloan award Sloan Found., 1956. Mem. Am. Phys. Soc., Am. Assn. Physics Tchrs. (Millikan award 1965). Author papers in field. Home: 51 Upland Rd Brookline MA 02146 Office: Mass Inst Tech Cambridge MA 02139

KING, JOHN HAMILTON, judge; b. Willimantic, Conn., Apr. 21, 1900; s. William Albert and Jennie Stella (Cady) K.; A.B., Yale, 1923, LL.B., 1925. Admitted to Conn. bar, 1925; gen. practice law, Willimantic, 1925-40; law clk. com. on judiciary Conn. Gen. Assembly, 1927-37; sec. law clk. Commn. to Revise Gen. Statutes of Conn., 1927-30; mem. examining bd. Conn. State Bar, 1928-42; asst. atty. gen. Conn., 1929-31; mem. Jud. Council of Conn. 1931-47 county health officer, Windham County, 1934-39; mem. Spl. Commn. to Study Pauper Laws of Conn., 1935-37; judge Superior Ct., 1940-57; justice Conn. Supreme Ct., 1957- 63, chief justice, 1963-70, ret.; state referce, 1970—. Fellow Am. Bar Assn.; mem. Windham County Law Library Assn., Am. Judicature Soc., Conn., Windham County bar assns., S.A.R., American Legion, Alpha Chi Rho. Republican. Conglist. Clubs: Graduate, Mory's (New Haven); University (Hartford). Home: 89 Windham Rd Willimantic CT 06226 Office: Court House Willimantic CT 06226

KING, JOHN HARRY, Jr., ophthalmologist; b. Washington, Sept. 28, 1910; s. John Harry and Mary (Ganley) K.; B.S., Georgetown U., 1932, M.D., 1934; m. Helen Davis Tewksbury, Mar. 28, 1936; children—Suzanne Tewksbury (Mrs. William Doran Clark), John Harry III. Intern, Letterman Gen. Hosp., San Francisco, 1934-35; served to col., M.C., U.S. Army, 1935-55, chief ophthalmology Tripler Gen. Hosp., Honolulu, 1948-51, Walter Reed Gen. Hosp., Washington, 1951-55, dir. ocular research, 1951-55; ret., 1955; practice medicine specializing in ophthalmology, Washington, 1955—; sr. surgeon Washington Hosp. Center; clin. prof. ophthalmology George Washington U. Med. Sch.; clin. prof. surgery (ophthalmology) Georgetown U.; med. dir., 1st pres. Internat. Eye Found. Nat. cons. emeritus to surgeon gen. of Air Force; cons. to surgeon gen. of U.S. Army; organizer, 1st med. dir. Washington Eye Bank; organizer, bd. dirs. Eye Bank Assn. Am.; vis. prof. U. P.R. Decorated Air medal, asso. comdr. Most Venerable Order Hosp. St. John of Jerusalem (Eng.); recipient citation for distinguished service rendered to eye banks, 1963. Diplomate Am. Bd. Ophthalmology. Fellow A.C.S., Am. Acad. Ophthalmology and Otolarynogology (certificate of award for distinguished services 1964, 65); mem. A.M.A., Am. Ophthal. Soc. (award 1958), Soc. Mil. Ophthalmology (past pres.), Pan Am. Assn. Ophthalmology (dir.; Gradle medal for teaching 1968), Mil. Order Caraboa; hon. mem. ophthal. socs. Peru, Guatemala, Dominican Republic, Turkey, Barraquer Eye Bank of Spain. Lion. Clubs: Chevy Chase Country, Army-Navy. Author 4 textbooks on eye surgery. Mem. editorial bd. E.E.N.T. Digest Jours. Contbr. numerous articles to sci. publs. Developer 1st successful method of preserving human eye tissues, 1954; inventor eye surg. instruments; research in eye preservation, surg. techniques, cornea transplantation. Home: 101 E Lenox St Chevy Chase MD 20015 Office: 6000 Wisconsin Av Chevy Chase MD 20015

KING, JOHN LAWRENCE, indsl. relations cons.; b. Claremont, Minn., June 1, 1904; s. John and Mary (Tierney) K.; A.B., U. Wash., 1925, A.M., 1941; m. Barbara A. Strodhoff, Oct. 9, 1938; 1 son, Ronald L. (dec.). Tchr., coach pub. schs., 1926-37; state high sch. supr., Wash., 1937-41; dir. radio and research Wash. State Grange, 1942-50; pres. R. K. Printing & Splty. Co.; v.p., chmn. bd. Innova Corp.; sec.-treas., dir. Western Sawdust Products, Inc.; sec.-treas., dir. KIRO-AM FM and TV, 1951-65. Cons. Community Devel., China, Japan, P.I., Hong Kong, Hawaii; cons. communications and pub. relations West Germany; exec. com. Seattle-Kobe Sister City Affiliation, Seattle chpt. People to People; bd. dirs. Seattle Urban Renewal Com.; mem. Farm Lab. Adv. Com. mem. Seattle Adminstrv. Survey Com.; past pres. King County Safety Council; mem. Wage Stablzn. Commn., 1950-52. Bd. dirs. Group Health Coop., 1948-50, Council of Planning Affiliates, Washington Internat. Trade Fair, Found. Internat. Understanding Through Students, Woessner Art Center; bd. regents U. Wash., pres., 1946-67; exec. com. Ryther Child Center. Mem. Assn. Governing Bds. of Univs. and Colls. (v.p.), C. of C., Pub. Relations Round Table (past pres. Seattle), Washington State Grange (mem. coms.), Fgn Affairs Council, Pub. Relations Soc., Phi Delta Kappa, Alpha Kappa Delta (past pres.), Tau Kappa Alpha. Clubs: Seattle China (dir., past pres.); India Commerce and Cultural (dir.); Metropolitan Dinner (v.p.). Author: Teenage Drinking. Home: 6533 Beach Dr SW Seattle WA 98116 Office: 444 Ravenna Blvd Seattle WA 98115

KING, JOHN PORTER, Jr., candy mfg. co. exec.; b. Ft. Worth, Aug. 18, 1898; s. John Porter and Lorena (Blair) K.; A.B., U. Tex., 1920. Pres., King Candy Co., Ft. Worth, 1946- -; dir. Ft. Worth Nat. Bank, Tex. Electric Service Co. Served with USMCR, World War I, World War II. Mem. Beta Theta Pi. Presbyn. (trustee). Clubs: Fort Worth, River Crest Country. Office: PO Box 2080 Fort Worth TX 76101

KING, JOHN Q. TAYLOR, coll. pres.; b. Memphis, Sept. 25, 1921; s. John Q. Taylor and Alice (Woodson) Johnson; B.A., Fisk U., 1941; grad. Landig Coll. Mortuary Sci., 1942; B.S., Huston-Tillotson Coll., 1947; M.S., DePaul U., 1950; Ph.D., U. Tex., 1957; LL.D., Southwestern U., 1970; m. Marcet Hines, June 28, 1942; children—John Q., Clinton Allen, Marjon Alicia, Stuart Hines. Mortician, King-Tears Mortuary, Austin, Tex., 1946—; with Huston-Tillotson Coll., 1947—, prof. math., 1952-65, dean, 1960-65, pres., 1965—, vis. sci. Tex. Acad. Sci., 1960-67; mem. coop. writing com. Pitman Pub. Corp., 1956, 58, 60, 62. Div. officer Boy Scouts Am., 1956-60; peace edn. com. Am. Friends Service Com., 1959-66; mem. Austin com. USO, 1960-. Mem. gen. bd. edn. United Meth. Ch., mem. Tex. Conf. Chs., 1963—, exec. com. South Central Jurisdictional Bd. Christian Social Concerns; del. Meth. Gen. and Jurisdictional Confs., 1956, 60, 64, 66, 67, 68, 70. Bd. dirs. Wesley Found., U. Tex., 1953-69, Texas So. U., 1960—, Tex. Conf. Chs., 1963—, Child and Family Service, 1964-70, Tex. Mental Health Assn., 1955-67, Austin chpt. Nat. Conf. Christian and Jews, Tex. Meth. Student Movement, Community Council of Austin and Travis County, Eden Home for the Aged, Travis County unit Am. Cancer Society, 1963-69, United Fund of Austin and Travis County, 1965-70; mem. Gov.'s Com. Aging; adv. com. Regional Med. Program Tex.; trustee Fisk U. Served to capt. AUS, 1942-46; col. Res. Recipient Carl Bredt award U. Tex. Coll. Edn., 1970. Mem. Am. Statis. Assn., Nat. Inst. Sci., Austin C. of C. (v.p., dir. 1967-70), Sigma Pi Phi, Delta Pi Epsilon, Alpha Phi Alpha, Phi Delta Kappa, Alpha Kappa Mu. United Methodist. Mason (33), Kiwanian. Author: (with wife) The Story of Twenty-Three Famous Negro Americans, 1967. Contbr. numerous articles religious and profl. jours. Home: 2400 Givens Av Austin TX 78722

KING, JOHN WILLIAM, judge; b. Manchester, N.H., Oct. 10, 1918; s. Michael J. and Anna (Lydon) K.; A.B., Harvard, 1938; M.A., Columbia, 1941, LL.B., 1943, LL.D.; M.A. (hon.), Dartmouth Coll.; LL.D., St. Anselm's Coll., U. N.H., Columbia U.; Dr. Civil Laws (hon.) New England Coll.; Dr. Pub. Adminstrn., Franklin Pierce Coll., Suffolk U.; m. Anna MaLaughlin, Oct. 13, 1945. Admitted to N.Y. bar, 1942, N.H. bar, 1945; pvt. practice, N.Y.C., 1943- 48; sr. partner King, Nixon, Christy & Tessier, attys.; now asso. justice Superior Ct. of N.H.; instr. bus. law St. Anselm's Coll., Manchester, 1948—; mem. N.H. Constl. Conv., 1956; chmn. Manchester delegation N.H. Legislature, 1957; mem. sub-com. legislative counsel, 1957, minority leader, 1959-62; gov. N.H., 1963-69. Mem. N.H. ballot law commn., 1952-54; sec. charter revision commn., Manchester, 1954-55, mem. salary adjustment commn., 1957—, chmn. ward line commn., 1957—. Past pres. J.F. McElwain Manchester Employees' Credit Union, 1956—; bd. dirs. N.H. Tb. Soc., trustee St. Anselm's Coll. Mem. Am., N.Y. State, N.H., Manchester bar assns., Bar Assn. City N.Y., Am. Judicature Society (dir. N.H.). Elk. Eagle, K.C. Clubs: Canadian, Raphael, Manchester Press, Belgium, Manchester Turnverein (Manchester). Home: Connemdra Farm Kennedy Hill Rd Goffstown NH 03045 Office: 489 Canal St Manchester NH 03101

KING, JONATHAN, architect; b. N.Y.C., Dec. 31, 1925; s. Gordon Congdon and Carol Therese (Weiss) K.; B.A., Columbia, 1949; m. Cynthia Bregman. Asso. editor G.P. Putnam's Sons, N.Y.C., 1949-52; staff asso. Fund Advancement Edn. Ford Found., 1952-58; sec. treas. Ednl. Facilities Labs., Inc., N.Y.C., 1958-67, v.p., treas., 1967-70; sr. v.p. in charge systems bldg. Caudill Rowlett Scott, architects, engrs., planners, Houston, 1970—. Mem. tech. panel to adv. com. HUD. Served with AUS, 1943-46; PTO. Recipient Am. Builder Mag. award for innovations in bldg., 1965. Mem. Soc. Coll. and U. Planning, Bldg. Research Inst., Council Ednl. Facilities Planners, A.I.A. (hon.) Nat. Acad. Scis. Club: Columbia University, Horseshoe Harbor Yacht. Contbr. articles Archtl. Record, Sat. Rev. Archtl. Design, others. Home: 680 Flintdale Rd Houston TX 77024 Office: 1111 W Loop S Houston TX 77027

KING, JOSEPH BERTRAM, architect; b. Greenville, S.C., Sept. 14, 1924; s. Joseph A. and Bertram (Kerns) K.; student Memphis State Coll., 1943; B.Arch. with honors, N.C. State U., 1949; m. Julia Nelson Hipps, Aug. 2, 1945; children—Allen, David, Thomas. Prin., J. Bertram King, Asheville, N.C., 1952—. Chmn., Planning and Zoning Commn., Asheville, 1966—; vice chmn. Met. Planning Bd., 1966—. Bd. dirs. United Fund, N.C. Design Found., mem. exec. com., 1969—; trustee Aston Park Hosp. Served with USAAF, 1942-45; ETO.

Decorated Air medal with 2 oak leaf clusters. Recipient various honor awards. Fellow A.I.A. (pres. elect N.C., mem. nat. com. on licensing); mem. N.C. Bd. Architecture, Asheville C. of C. (pres. elect). Home: 222 Country Club Rd Asheville NC 28804 Office: 351 Merrimon Av Asheville NC 28804

KING, JOSEPH H., banker; b. Fort Worth, Feb. 17, 1902; s. Silas Lee and Mary (Rayner) K.; student Columbia, 1921-23; m. Rosalee Speaker, Oct. 13, 1923 (div. Apr. 1960); children—Susan, Anthony S.; m. 2d, Gioconda Castro, Apr. 27, 1960. With Guardian Trust Co., N.Y., 1925-26, J. and W. Seligman & Co., N.Y. City, 1927-38. Union Securities Corp., 1938-56, pres.; merged with Eastman Dillon & Co., 1956; sr. partner Eastman Dillon, Union Securities & Co., 1956-71, chmn. bd., 1971—; dir., mem. finance com. Am. Express Co.; dir. Am. Express Internat. Banking Corp., Colo. Interstate Corp., Sperry Rand Corp., Union Camp Corp., M. Lowenstein & Sons, Inc.; trustee MONY Mortgage Investors. Clubs: Blind Brook, Links (N.Y.C.). Home: 800 Park Av New York City NY 10021 Office: 1 Chase Manhattan Plaza New York City NY 10005

KING, JOSEPH LEONARD, Jr., educator; b. Mappsville, Va., Aug. 12, 1892; s. Joseph Leonard and Annie (Hubbard) K.; A.B., U. Richmond, 1913, LL.D., 1958; A.M., Columbia, 1922, Ph.D., 1927; m. Dora Evelyn Connor, Mar. 10, 1920; 1 son, William Connor. Asst., then asso. prof. English, Miss. Agrl. Coll., 1918-21; mem. faculty Denison U., 1924—, prof. English, 1924-, L.W. Burke prof., 1938—; lectr U. Ariz., summer 1962; prof. Howard Coll., 1962—. Served to 2d lt. U.S. Army, World War I; AEF in France. Mem. Modern Lang. Assn., Am. Assn. U. Profs., Phi Beta Kappa, Phi Gamma Delta, Omicron Delta Kappa. Baptist. Address: Samford U Birmingham AL 35209

KING, KENDALL WILLARD, educator, biochemist; b. Pitts., Feb. 20, 1926; s. Charles Glen and Hilda (Bainton) K.; B.S., Va. Poly. Inst., 1949, M.S., 1950; Ph.D., U. Wis., 1952; m. Kathleen Elva Abbitt, Sept. 13, 1947; children— Virginia Lee, Russell Glen. Mem. faculty Va. Poly. Inst., 1953-68, prof. biochemistry, 1959-68, head dept. biochemistry and nutrition, 1966-68; asst. v.p.-grants Research Corp., program dir. Williams Waterman Program, 1968—; research asso. Columbia, 1959-60. Adviser protein adv. group WHO/FAO/UNICEF/Pan Am. Health Orgn.; indsl. cons. enzymes; mem. coms. Nat. Acad. Sci. NRC, also mem. com. internat. nutrition programs. Served with AUS, 1944-46. Awarded Ordre de Travaux (Republic Haiti). Mem. Am. Inst. Nutrition, Am. Soc. Biol. Chemists, Am. Chem. Soc., A.A.A.S., Inst. Food Tech., Am. Inst. Chemists, Am. Assn. Cereal Chemists, Soc. Nutrition Edn., Sigma Xi (pres. elect 1967), Phi Lambda Upsilon, Phi Sigma. Baptist. Spl. research mode of action of cellulases, intermediary metabolism amino acids, nutrition edn. in emerging soc's. Home: 20 Westminster Dr Scarsdale NY 10583 Office: 405 Lexington Av New York City NY 10017

KING, KENNARD, banker; b. Indpls., May 20, 1917; s. Lucien and Anna 'Margaret (Wiley() K.; A.B. (Rector scholar), DePauw U., 1939; grad. Am. Inst. Banking, 1956; postgrad. U. Wis., Sch. Banking, 1959-61; m. Margaret Rose Zapf, Oct. 23, 1948; children-Margaret Rose, Kennard Zapf. Pres., owner King Coffee Co., 1945-54; with Mchts. Nat. Bank & Trust Co., Indpls., 1954—, v.p., mgr. comml. loan dept., 1965-66, mem. mgmt. com., v.p., sr. loan officer, 1966-68, sr. v.p., 1968—. Bd. dirs. Indpls. Electrotype Foundry. Served to lt. S.G. USNR, 1941-45. Decorated D.F.C., Air Medal (7) Mem. Ind. Assn.Credit Men (pres., dir.), Robert Morris Assos., (bd. dirs. Ohio valley), Newcomen Soc. N.Am., Phi Kappa Psi. Republican. Methodist. Clubs: Army-Navy (past treas.), Contemporary Literary (past treas.), Optimist, Meridian Hills Country, Columbia, DePau Alumni. Home: 8890 Pickwick Dr Indianapolis IN 46260 Office: 11 S Meridian St Indianapolis IN 46204

KING, KERRYN, corp. exec.; b. Dallas, Oct. 15, 1917; s. Oswin Kerryn and Naiad Isobel (Keedy) K; B.S., So. Meth. U., 1939, LL.D., 1966; m. Carol Fritz, Nov. 11, 1939 (div.); children—Steven, Valerie (Mrs. Peter Riker Beaven), Wyldon, Zoe; m. 2d, Mrs. Shirley L. Maytag, Dec. 16, 1967. Asst. to v.p. Tex. Power & Light Co., 1939-42; publns. editor Consol. Vultee Aircraft Corp., 1942-43; with Hill & Knowlton, Inc., 1943-52, v.p., 1947-52; dir. pub. relations dept. Texaco, Inc., 1953-57, asst. gen. mgr. 1957, gen. mgr., 1957-58, v.p., 1958-60, v.p., asst. to chmn. bd., 1960- 63, v.p. charge operations (Latin Am.), 1963-65, v.p. pub. relations and personnel, 1965-71, sr. v.p. world wide sales, 1971—; chmn. bd. Texaco Trinidad, Inc. Civilian pub. relations adv. com. U.S. Mil. Acad.; hon. trustee Horace Mann Sch.; bd. dirs. Nat. Hwy. Users Fedn. Safety and Mobility. Mem. U.S. C. of C. (bd. dirs. transp. and communication com.), Pub. Relations Soc. Am., Sigma Delta Chi. Clubs: Metropolitan, River, Cloud. Editorial adviser to Pub. Relations News. Home: 834 Fifth Av New York City NY 10021 Office: 135 E 42d St New York City NY 10017

KING, LAFAYETTE CARROLL, educator; b. Marysvale, Utah, Sept. 9, 1914; s. W. Lafayette and E. Blanch (Bleak) K.; B.S., Utah State U., 1936; Ph.D., Mich. State U., 1942; m. Vencie Yergensen, Aug. 27, 1937; children—William C., Kathryn Ann (Mrs. Bruce Gordon), Barbara (Mrs. Michael G. Scott), John Robert, Richard Allen. Mem. faculty Northwestern U., 1942—, asso. prof. chemistry, 1949-55, prof., 1955—; cons. food chemistry Nat. Dairy Products Corp., 1953-68; dir. chemistry studies project NSF, Chgo., 1961-62. Mem. U.S.-Japanese Conf. Chem. Edn., 1964, Intern Am. Conf. Chem. Edn., 1965; organizer, Indo-U.S. Nat. Conf. Chem. Edn., 1969. Fellow A.A.A.S.; mem. Am. Chem. Soc. (chmn. adv. council coll. chemistry, 1966; Chem. Edn. award, 1969), Nat. Sci. Tchrs. Assn., Chem. Soc. London, Am. Inst. Chemistry, Sigma Xi, Phi Lambda Upsilon, Sigma Pi Sigma. Contbr. profl. jours. Home: 2724 Central Park Evanston IL 60201

KING, LAWRENCE SCHMIDT, lawyer; b. Preston, Ia., Sept. 9, 1903; s. Fred S. and Augusta (Schmidt) K.; student Grinnell Coll., 1923-25; LL.B., U. Mich., 1927; m. Elizabeth McDowell, Oct. 1, 1927; children—Lawrence Albert, Roger William, Ruth Ann (Mrs. Jeffry D. Ballard). Admitted to Mich. bar, 1927, since practiced in Detroit; with firm Miller, Canfield, Paddock & Stone, 1927- -, mem., 1936—, sr. mem. 1940—. Commr., City Pleasant Ridge, 1944-50. Pres., trustee John Scudder Found. for Old People, Luella Hannan Meml. Home. Sec., trustee David M. Whitney Fund; trustee William Beaumont Hosp., Mich. Cancer Found. Mem. Am., Mich., Detroit bar assns., Am. Judicature Soc., Mich. Editor Trusts and Estates, Delta Theta Phi. Republican. Conglist. Clubs: Detroit; Pine Lake Country (Orchard Lake, Mich.). Home: 102 Endicott Rd Bloomfield Hills MI 48013 Office: Detroit Bank & Trust Bldg Detroit MI 48226

KING, LELAND W., architect; b. Battle Creek, Mich., Dec. 17, 1907; s. Leland Wiggins and Elizabeth Gale (Arnold) K.; student Ga. Sch. Tech., 1927; Armour Inst. Tech. (Chgo. Art Inst., Beaux Arts Design), 1928-29; m. Hametia Fielder, Nov. 29, 1934; children—Sheryl Letia, Louisa Sands. Archtl. draftsman, designer indsl., sch., hosp. and residential projects, Ga., Ill., Mich., Wis., 1925-32; registered architect, Ariz., N.Y., Cal.; supr architect's office U.S. Treasury, 1935-37; field inspector, diplomatic and consular bldgs., Dept. State, 1937-40, in Scandinavia, Balkans, Europe, Middle East, Central and S.A., asst. and asso. chief Fgn. Bldg. Operations, 1941-51; dir. and supervising architect, 1952-54, in charge U.S. diplomatic and consular bldg. design and constrn., Worldwide. Cons. to Bd. Edn., White Fish Bay, Milw., 1931- 32; tech. adviser to U.S. delegation UNESCO Hdqrs. Bldg., Paris, 1952- 53; exec. sec. Fgn. Service Bldgs., Com. of Congress, 1952-54; gen. archtl. and indsl. design as asso. Norman Bel Geddes, 1954-55; asso. with James Gordon Carr, Architect, 1956; v.p., dir. architecture Pereira and Luckman, 1956-59; supervising archl. Ampex Corp., 1959-62; pvt. archtl. practice, 1961—. Chmn. architectural and constrn. engring. panel research, engring. adv. council to postmaster gen., 1967, 68. Works exhibited Mus. Modern Art, N.Y.C., 1953 and at Octagon 1954. Supervising architect U.S. Embassy projects, Stockholm, Paris, 1953, receiving honor award A.I.A., 1955, 56. Fellow A.I.A.; mem. Cal. C. of C. Clubs: Cosmos (Washington); Stanford University Golf. Address: 68 Euclid Av Atherton CA 94025

KING, LEON, banker; b. Phila., June 4, 1921; s. Abraham and Ethel (Walton) K.; B.S., U. Pa., 1945; m. Diane Averbach, Nov. 30, 1946; children—Cheryl G. (Mrs. Robert Salz), Elliot W., Louis E. Practice pub. accounting, Phila., 1946-52; controller Hotel div. Bankers Securities Corp., 1952-58; controller Sun Ray Drug Co., 1958-60; controller Bellevue Stratford Hotel, 1960-64; sr. v.p. Indsl. Valley Bank, Phila., 1964—. Lectr., Sch. Banking Bucknell U. Bd. dirs. Phila.-N.J. Area chpt. Nat. Conf. on Christians and Jews, Central Valley Found., Indsl. Valley Bank Golf Classic. C.P.A., Pa. Mem. Phila. C. of C., Bank Adminstrn. Inst., Am., Pa. insts. C.P.A.'s, U. Pa. Alumni Assn., Beta Gamma Sigma. Office: Indsl Valley Bank Bldg Philadelphia PA 19103

KING, LESLIE JOHN, educator; b. Christchurch, New Zealand, Nov. 10, 1934; s. Lawrence Charles and Phyllis Ivy (Walter) K.; B.A., U. New Zealand, 1955, M.A., 1957; Ph.D., U. Ia., 1960; m. Doreen Mercia Brown, Oct. 22, 1960; children—Loren A., Andrew Brett. Lectr. U. New Zealand, 1960-62; asst. prof. McGill U., Montreal, Que., 1962-65; prof. geography Ohio State U., 1964-70, McMaster U., Hamilton, Ont., Can., 1970—. Mem. Hamilton Urban Renewal Com., 1970—. Recipient Fulbright travel award, 1957. Mem. Assn. Am. Geographers, Am. Statis. Soc., Regional Sci. Assn. Author: Readings in Economic Geography, 1968; Statistical Analysis in Geography, 1969. Home: 117 Mansfield Dr Ancaster Ontario Canada Office: McMaster U Hamilton Ontario Canada

KING, LOUIS DELWIN, coll. dean; b. Walhalla, S.C., July 31, 1917; s. Henry Louis and Zoie (Bond) K.; B.S. magna cum laude, U. S.C., 1949; M.S., U. Fla., 1951; Ph.D., 1953. Drug clk., Walhalla, 1935-42; registered pharmacist Bells Drug Store, Walhalla, 1949-50; teaching asst. U. Fla., 1950-51; mem. faculty Rutgers U., 1953—, prof. pharmacy, asso. dean Coll. Pharmacy, 1966—. Served with AUS, 1942-46. Fellow A.A.A.S.; mem. Am. Pharm. Assn., N.Y., N.J. acads. sci., Sigma Xi, Rho Chi, Kappa Psi. Contbr. profl. and sci. jours. Home: 10 Landing Lane New Brunswick NJ 08903

KING, MARIAN, author; b. Washington; d. Joseph and Jeannette (Michel) King; student Miss Maderia's Sch., Greenway, Va.; studied abroad. Author: ABC Game Book, 1928; The Mirror of Youth, 1928; ABC Game Cards, 1930; Kees (Jr. Lit. Guild selection), 1930; The Story of Athletics, 1931; The Dutch Mother Goose, 1931; Amnon, A Lad of Palestine, 1932; Skeeta, 1933; The Golden Cat Head, 1933; Kees and Kleintje (Jr. Lit. Guild Selection), 1934; A Boy of Poland, 1934; Sean and Sheela, 1937; It Happened in England, 1939; Piccolino, 1939; Elizabeth: The Tudor Princess, 1940; Young King David, 1948; The Coat of Many Colors, 1951; Young Mary Stuart: Queen of Scots, 1954; Portraits of Children in the National Gallery Art (Life of Christ), 1950, (Portraits of Children in the National Gallery of Art), 1953, (filmed and won 2 emmy awards) A Gallery of Children, 1955, rev. edit., 1967; Portrait of Jesus (King James version and Douay version, separate vols.), 1956, rev. edit., 1970; A Gallery of Mothers and their Children, 1958; What Would You Do; Mary Baker Eddy Child of Promise, 1968; The Star of Bethlehem, 1968. Children's book editor The National Observer. Selected Bible Text (King James Version) for Paintings Depicting the Life of Christ for the Nat. Gallery of Art Folder No. 2. Contbr. to books of several sch. book pubs.; also various periodicals. Served with Brit. Supply Missions, Washington, 1940-45; mem. White House Conf. Children, 1970, Hospitality Information Services, Washington. Mem. Authors Guild, Nat. Council Women, Childrens Book Guild, Authors Book Guild Am. Researcher TV film U.S. One. Home: 4501 Connecticut Av Washington DC 20008

KING, MATTHEW WAKEFIELD, banker; b. Louisville, May 13, 1910; s. John Campbell and Susan Speed (Wakefield) K.; student U. Louisville, 1927-29; grad. Am. Inst. Banking, 1932; m. Helen Sullivan, Feb. 26, 1944 (dec. Apr. 1970); 1 son, Vincent Davis. Engaged in banking, 1926—; with Liberty Nat. Bank and Trust Co., Louisville, 1961—, sr. v.p., 1967—; treas. K & I R.R., 1955-61. Past bd. dirs. St. Anthony's Hosp., Louisville. Mem. Am., Ky. bankers assns., Robert Morris Assos., Louisville C. of C., Newcomen Soc. N.Am., Ky. C. of C., Assn. Res. City Bankers, R.R. Treas. Assn., Louisville Credit Mens Assn. (pres., dir.). Clubs: Pendennis, Filson, Boat (Louisville). Home: Weissinger-Gaulbert Apts 709 S 3d St Louisville KY 40203 Office: 416 W Jefferson St Louisville KY 40202

KING, MORRIS KENTON, dean med. sch.; b. Oklahoma City, Nov. 13, 1924; s. C. Willard and Lenore (Miesse) K.; B.A., U. Okla., 1947; M.D., Vanderbilt U., 1951; m. June Ellen Greenfield, June 21, 1953; children—Michael, Douglas, John, David, Thomas. Intern Barnes Hosp., St. Louis, 1951-52, resident, 1954- 55; resident Vanderbilt U. Hosp., 1953-54; mem. faculty preventive medicine Washington U., St. Louis, 1958—, prof. 1967—, dean, Sch. Medicine, 1965—. Served with USNR, 1943-46, Mem. Central Soc. Clin. Research, Infectious Diseases Soc. Am. Home: 7017 Kingsbury St Saint Louis, MO 63130 Office: 660 S Euclid St Saint Louis MO 63110

KING, MORTON BRANDON, sociologist; b. Shelbyville, Tenn., Mar. 24, 1913; s. Morton Brandon and Margaret (Moody) K.; student Webb Sch., Bell Buckle, Tenn., 1927-30; A.B., Vanderbilt U., 1934, A.M., 1936; Ph.D., U. Wis., (Julius Rosenwald Fund fellow, 1938-39), 1940; postdoctoral study, U. N.C., U. Mich.; m. Joan Smith. Case visitor Davidson County (Tenn.) Welfare Commn., Nashville, 1934-35; asst. prof. sociology U. Miss., 1939-41; asso. prof. sociology Miss. State Coll., 1941-43; prof. sociology and chmn. dept. U. Miss., 1946-56; vis. prof. sociology So. Meth. U., 1956-57, prof. sociology, 1958—, chmn. dept. sociology, 1960-64, 69-71; fellow Grad. Council Humanities, 1964-65; vis. lectr. Northwestern U., 1957-58. Chmn. Tex. Com. Population Study, 1960- 62, Southwest Faculty Conf., 1960-61; mem. Council on Ch.-Related Colls. of Meth. Ch., 1966—. Served as 2d lt. AUS, 1943-46. Mem. Am. (council 1966-67), Southwestern, So. (pres. 1954-55) Sociol. socs., Am. Assn. U. Profs. A.A.A.S., Soc. Sci. Study Religion, Sigma Alpha Epsilon, Phi Beta Kappa, Alpha Kappa Delta. Methodist. Address: PO Box 192 So Meth U Dallas TX 75222

KING, ORDIE HERBERT, Jr., oral pathologist; b. Memphis, Aug. 11, 1933; s. Ordie Herbert and Hazel (Eaton) K.; B.S., Memphis State U., 1957; D.D.S., U. Tenn., 1959, Ph.D., 1965; m. Harriet Huffman, June 8, 1963; children—Anna LaVelle, Ordie Herbert III. USPHS postdoctoral fellow U. Tenn., 1960-62; resident oral pathology U. Tenn. and City of Memphis Hosps., 1962-63; research asso. dept. pathology U. Tenn., 1963-65, asst. prof. pathology, 1965; asst. prof. pathology Northwestern U., 1966; asso. prof., chmn. dept. oral pathology St. Louis U., 1967-69, prof., chmn. dept. oral pathology, 1969-70; acting chmn., vis. asso. prof. dept. oral pathology Washington U., St. Louis, 1969-70; prof. oral pathology, asso. prof. pathology W.Va. U., Morgantown, 1970—; dental cons. to chief med. examiner State of Tenn., 1963-65; mem. med. staff W.Tenn. Cancer Clinic, 1962-65; chmn. dept. dentistry St. Louis U. Hosps.,1967-70; cons. cancer control program Nat. Center for Chronic Disease Control, USPHS, 1967-70. Diplomate Am. Bd. Oral Pathology. Fellow Am. Acad. Oral Pathology; mem. Am. Soc. Cytology, Am. Assn. for Cancer Edn., Am. Dental Assn., Delta Sigma Delta, Kappa Alpha, Phi Rho Sigma, Omicron Kappa Upsilon. Contbr. articles profl. jours. Home: Route 5 Box 85 Morgantown WV 26505

KING, PETER, chemist; b. Boston, Dec. 12, 1910; s. Peter and Isabella (Rodgers) K.; student U. Notre Dame, 1930-31; A.B., U. Cal. at Los Angeles, 1936; Ph.D., Cath. U. Am. 1942; m. Elizabeth Louise Toole, Apr. 25, 1942; children—Peter, Pamela M., Stephen J., Elizabeth A., John R., Victoria L. Chemist, asso. dir. research for materials Naval Research Lab., Washington, 1939-64; sci. dir. Office Naval Reseach br. office, London, Eng., 1964-66, dep. chief, chief scientist, Washington, 1966—. Recipient Navy Distinguished Civilian Service award, 1960. Mem. Am. Chem. Soc., Washington Acad. Scis., Philos. Soc., A.A.A.S. Contbr. articles profl. jours. Patentee in field. Home: 1120 Cameron Rd Alexandria VA 22308 Office: Ballston Tower 800 N Quincy St Arlington VA 22217

KING, PETER COTTERILL, govt. ofcl.; b. White Plains, N.Y., Aug. 23, 1930; s. Robert Cotterill and Ruth (McKeown) K.; B.S., U.S. Mil. Acad., 1952; M.B.A., U. Pa., 1958; seminar certificate, Harvard, 1968; m. Nancy English, June 28, 1958; children-Margot E., Philip M. Commd. 2d lt. U.S. Army, 1952, advanced through grades to 1st lt., 1956; resigned, 1956; maj. Res.; systems engr. IBM Corp. Research Center, Yorktown Heights, N.Y., 1958- 62; v.p. Security Bank & Trust Co., Lawton, Okla., 1962-69; pres. Security Broadcasting Co., Lawton, 1964-69; adminstr. Southwestern Power Adminstrn., Dept. Interior, 1969—. Chmn. United Fund campaign, Lawton, 1968; chmn. Okla. Arts and Humanities Council, 1970—. Mem. Lawton City Council, 1968-69. Bd. dirs. Tulsa County Assn. Mem. N.A.M., U.S. C. of C., Tulsa C. of C. Republican. Episcopalian. Home: 1120 E 24th Pl Tulsa OK 74114 Office: 333 W 4th St Tulsa OK 74101

KING, PRESTON CLOUD, Jr., lawyer; b. Washington, July 30, 1904; s. Preston C. and Sally (Myers) K.; LL.D., Georgetown U., 1927; m. Kathryn M. Larcombe, Aug. 15, 1929; 1 dau., Barbara (Mrs. Bruce Allan Reichelderfer). Admitted to D.C. bar, 1927, Md. bar, 1933, Ill. bar, 1940; asso. law firm Adkins & Nesbit, Washington, 1927-29; partner Pope, Ballard & Loos, Washington and Chgo., 1929—. Mem. admission and grievance committee United States District Courts for D.C. Past president Potomac Democratic Club. Mem. Am. (fed. judiciary com.), D.C. (pres. 1952-53), Md. bar assns., Md. Hist. Soc. Methodist (trustee). Clubs: Lawyers, Barristers (past pres.), Metropolitan (Washington); Potomac (Md.) Hunt; Chevy Chase (Md.). Home: Rexholm Farm 12630 Travilah Rd Gaithersburg MD 20760 Office: 888 17th St N W Washington DC 20006

KING, RICHARD ADAMS, educator, agrl. economist; b. Worcester, Mass., July 2, 1922; s. Philip and Eleanor Foster (Adams) K.; B.S., U. Conn., 1946; M.S., U. Cal. at Berkeley, 1947; M.P.A. (Littauer fellow 1947-48), Harvard, 1948, Ph.D., 1951; postdoctoral fellow polit. economy, U. Chgo., 1955-56; m. Alfreda May Smedberg, June 10, 1944; children—Philip Austin, Sara Foster, Deborah Shattuck, Susan Chamberlain. Field asst. farm mgmt. and statis. clk. U. Conn., 1943-46; grad. asst. Giannini Found. Agrl. Econos., U. Cal. at Berkeley, 1946-47; asst. prof. agrl. econs. U. Conn., 1948-50; mem. faculty N.C. State U. of Raleigh, 1951—, asso. prof. agrl. econs., 1951-55, prof. agrl. econs., 1956—, M.G. Mann prof., 1957—; coordinator agrl. econs. N.C. agrl. research mission to Peru, also vis. prof. faculty social scis. U. Agraria, La Molina, Lima, Peru, 1964-65; vis. prof. agrl. econs. U. Cal. at Berkeley, 1969. Vis. lectr. Grad. Sch. Bus. Adminstrn., U. Va., 1961-63. Cons. Ford Found., Research Triangle Inst. Bd. dirs. Franklinton Center, 1960—, chmn., 1968. Served with USAAF, 1943. Mem. Am. Econ. Assn., Am. Agrl. Econs. Assn., Econometric Soc. Author: Interregional Competition Research Methods, 1965; (with A.J. Couto) The Agricultural Development of Peru, 1969; (with R.G. Bressler, Jr.) Markets, Prices and Interregional Trade, 1970. Home: 2108 Buckingham Rd Raleigh NC 27607

KING, RICHARD HARDING, food processing co. exec.; b. Louisville, Oct. 19, 1925; s. Harvey M. and Margaret (Farley) K.; B.B.A., Tulane U., 1946; M.B.A., Northwestern U., 1948; m. Marjorie R. Jones, Feb. 19, 1959; children—Ronald Craig, David Malcolm. With Winchester div. Olin-Mathieson Chem. Corp., New Haven, 1947-53; instr. evenings New Haven Jr. Coll., 1948-53; with Ford div. Ford Motor Co., 1953-59; mgr. profit analysis and control Chrysler Internat., S.A., Geneva, Switzerland, 1959-61; financial cons. corp. controllers dept. Raytheon Co., 1961-62; with Glidden Co., 1962-67 (co. merged with SCM Corp., 1967), v.p. corp. planning, 1967-68; controller Internat. Milling Co., 1968-69; v.p. finance Internat. Multifoods Corp. (name changed 1970), 1970—; speaker in planning field, 1965—; dir. Selective Search, Inc. Mem. Nat. Soc. Corp. Planning, Am. Mgmt. Assn., Nat. Indsl. Conf. Bd., Financial Execs. Inst., World Future Soc., Beta Gamma Sigma, Omicron Delta Kappa. Methodist. Club: Minneapolis Athletic. Home: 4705 Annaway Dr Edina MN 55436 Office: Investors Bldg Minneapolis MN 55415

KING, ROBERT BRUCE, educator; b. Rochester, N.H., Feb. 27, 1938; s. Samuel Joshua and Frances Katherine (Shelly) K.; B.A., Oberlin Coll., 1957; Ph.D., Harvard, 1961; m. Jane Hermine Kempner, June 20, 1960; children—Robert Bruce, David Samuel. Research chemist E.I. duPont de Nemours, Wilmington, Del., 1961-62; fellow Mellon Inst., Pitts., 1962-64, sr. fellow, 1964-66; research asso. prof. chemistry U. Ga., 1966-68, research prof., 1968—; cons. in field. Alfred P. Sloan Found. fellow, 1967-69. Mem. Am. Chem. Soc. (recipient award 1971), Chem. Soc. (London), Sigma Xi. Unitarian Universalist. Clubs: Athens Country; Tanglewood Pool Assn. Author: Organometallic Syntheses, 1965; Transition Metal Organometallic Chemistry: An Introduction, 1969. Editorial bd. Chem. Revs., 1970-72, Jour. Organometallic Chemistry, 1966—, Organometallics in Chem. Syntheses, 1969—. Home: 185 Holly Falls Dr Athens GA 30601

KING, ROBERT BURNETT, educator, physicist; b. Pasadena, Cal., June 6, 1908; s. Arthur Scott and Louise (Burnett) K.; B.A., Pomona Coll., 1930; Ph.D., Princeton, 1933; m. Helen Frances Leonard, Aug. 8, 1931; children—Margaret Louise (Mrs. Peter Kip Norvell), Janet (Mrs. Daniel Lloyd Crotty). NRC fellow Mt. Wilson Obs., 1933-34, mem. staff, 1938-48; instr. Mass. Inst. Tech., 1935-38; with OSRD, Cal. Inst. Tech., 1942-45, mem. faculty, 1948-68, prof. physics, 1952-68. Recipient Presdl. Certificate of Merit, 1948. Mem. Am. Astron. Soc., Internat. Astron. Union, Astron. Soc. Pacific Optical Soc. Am., Sigma Xi, Nu Alpha Phi. Republican. Spl. research atomic and molecular spectroscopy, solar physics. Author articles in field. Home: P O Box 725 Mendocino CA 95460

KING, ROBERT CHARLES, educator, scientist; b. N.Y.C., June 3, 1928; s. Charles James and Amanda (McCutchen) K.; B.S., Yale, 1948, Ph.D., 1952; m. Violet Mejia de Leon, Feb. 20, 1953; children—Vaughan, Archie, Amanda. Scientist biology dept. Brookhaven Nat. Lab., 1951-55; mem. faculty Northwestern U., 1956—, prof. biology, 1964—; chmn. 8th Brookhaven Symposium in Biology, 1955; vis. investigator, fellow Rockefeller U., 1959; NSF sr. postdoctoral fellow, Edinburgh, Scotland, 1958, div. entomology Commonwealth Sci. and Indsl. Research Orgn., Canberra, Australia, 1963, Sericultural Expt. Sta., Tokyo, Japan, 1970. Fellow A.A.A.S.; mem. Am. Soc. Zoologists, Histochem. Soc., Am. Soc. Cell Biology, Electron Microscopy Soc. Am., Genetics Soc. Am., Am. Naturalists, Soc. Devel. Biology, Sigma Xi (pres. Northwestern U. chpt. 1966-67). Author: Genetics 2d edit., 1965; A Dictionary of Genetics, 2d edit., 1972; Ovarian Development in Drosophila Melanogaster, 1970; also numerous papers. Home: 2104 Evert Ct Northbrook IL 60062 Office: Dept Biology Northwestern Univ Evanston IL 60201

KING, ROBERT COTTON, newspaper editor; b. Mpls., Jan. 8, 1931; s. George Herbert and Helen (Morse) K.; B.A., U. Minn., 1954; m. Arlene Catherine Wortman, May 23, 1955; children-Robert Cotton, Mary Louise, Catharine Ann. Mgr. Morris (Minn.) C. of C., 1957-59, Fergus Falls (Minn.) C. of C., 1959-62; editor Fergus Falls Daily Jour., 1962-65; editorial writer Mpls. Tribune, 1965-67; asst. mng. editor Mpls. Star, 1967-68, mng. editor, 1969—. Bd. dirs. Edina (Minn.) Little League Baseball, 1969—. Served to 1st lt. AUS, 1955-57. Profl. Journalism fellow Stanford, 1968. Mem. Am. Soc. Newspaper Editors, A.P. Mng. Editors Assn., Sigma Delta Chi. Episcopalian. Kiwanian. Club: St. Anthony (Mpls.). Home: 5809 Oaklawn Av Edina MN 55424 Office: 425 Portland Av Minneapolis MN 55415

KING, ROBERT DOAN, corp. exec.; b. East Cleveland, O., Feb. 27, 1914; s. Herbert D. and Lillian A. (Jenks) K.; A.B., Yale, 1937; m. Elinor C. Guy, Sept. 2, 1939; children—Sarah C., Robert Doan. Accountant Travelers Ins. Co., 1937-41; spl. rep. of pres., Internat. Tel. & Tel. Corp., Germany, 1945-46; asst. to asst. v.p., tech. dir., Fed. Tel. & Radio Corp., 1946; spl. asst., sr. logistical tech. adviser Gen. Staff, Dept. of Army, 1946-51; spl. asst. to under sec. Office Sec. Army, 1951-53, dir. program rev. and analysis, 1953-54, dep. asst. sec. army, 1954-59; mgr. tech. operations Fed. Systems div. IBM, 1959-61, dir. joint def. program, 1961-67, cons. on govt. relations, 1967—. Army rep. Hoover Commn., 1954-55; alternate mem. Pres.'s Air Coordinating Com., 1952-53. Exec. v.p., dir. Southwestern Okla. Oil Co., Inc., 1957-59. Chmn. budget com., dir. Nat. Bd. Promotion Rifle Practice, 1954-59. Served from 2d lt. to lt. col., AUS, 1941-45; col. Res. Decorated Legion of Merit; recipient Exceptional Civilian Service award. Mem. Nat. Security Indsl. Assn. (past chpt. pres.), Def. Supply Assn. (past chpt. pres.), Alpha Chi Rho. Episcopalian. Club: Belle Haven Country (Alexandria, Va.). Home: 1702 Hollinwood Dr Alexandria VA 22307 Office: 1801 K St NW Washington DC 20006

KING, ROBERT LEONARD, physician; b. Pearisburg, Va., Feb. 4, 1904; s. Clarence L. and Katharine (Oglesby) K.; student Washington and Lee U., 1920-22; M.D., U. Va., 1928, BS., 1931; m. Phoebe E. Edmunds, Dec. 29, 1936; children—Robert Leonard, Phoebe Ann (Mrs. Malcolm A. Moore), John Edmunds, Margaret C. (Mrs. F. Christian Killien), George R., Henry E. Intern U. Va. Hosp., 1928-29, resident, 1929-31; instr., 1926-31; partner Mason Clinic, Seattle, 1939-69, chief sect. cardiology, 1946-67, chief internal medicine, 1958-69, emeritus chief medicine, 1969—; chief med. service Virginia Mason Hosp., 1950-65, emeritus, 1969—, chief profl. services, 1966-69, also trustee; clin. asst. prof. U. Wash., 1947-53, clin. asso. prof. medicine, 1948—, mem. cardiac sub-com. regional med. program, 1967; honoree Robert L. King chair of cardiovascular research, U. Wash., 1957; cons. internal medicine and cardiology Seattle Med. Surg. Clinic, 1969—, cons. U.S. VA Hosp.; Sr. Cons. Harborview Hosp.; mem. staff Drs. Hosp., Providence Hosp., Overlake Meml. Hosp., St. Frances Xavier Cabrini Hosp., Swedish Hosp. Mem. Sommer Meml. Lectures Avd. Com., 1966—. Bd. trustees Virginia Mason Research Center, Seattle. Mem. Seattle Found. Served to lt. col., AUS, 1942-46. Diplomate Am. Bd. Internal Medicine, Nat. Bd. Med. Examiners. Fellow A.C.P., Am. Fedn. Clin. Research, Am. Med. Authors (hon.), Am. Coll. Cardiology (gov. Wash. 1966-69); mem. King County Med. Soc., A.M.A., Am. (pres. 1952-53; chmn. policy com. 1965—, bd. trustees, hon. mem. council clin. cardiology), Wash. (trustee; chmn. research policy com.) heart assns., Seattle Acad. Internal Medicine, North Pacific Soc. Internal Medicine, Am. Rheumatism Assn., Wash. Med. Assn., S.A.R., Pacific Interurban Clin. Club (chmn. 1967-69), Sigma Phi Epsilon, Iota Sigma, Nu Sigma Nu, Alpha Omega Alpha, Raven Soc. Clubs: University, Seattle Golf, Rotary, Overlake Golf and Country. Editor-in-chief Cardiology Digest. Contbr. articles med. jours. Home: 834 Hillside Dr E Seattle WA 98102 Office: 700 Broadway Av Seattle WA 98101

KING, ROBERT LEROY, univ. dean; b. Decatur, Ga., Jan. 22, 1931; s. John Todd and Charlotte (Stringer) K.; B.B.A., U. Ga., 1952; M.A., Mich. State U., 1953, Ph.D., 1960; m. Helen Butler Leaptrott, Mar. 25, 1956; children-Robert Todd, Keith Alan, John Christopher. Asst. instr. Mich. State U., 1955-57; asst. prof., then asso. prof. U. S.C., 1957-65; mem. faculty Va. Poly. Inst. and State U., 1965—, prof. bus. adminstrn., 1965—, head dept., 1969—, asso. dean Grad. Sch., 1968-69; cons. in field. Served with AUS, 1953-55; maj. Res. Ford fellow, 1956-57, 64-65; fellow Found. Econ. Edn., 1963. Mem. Am. (editor bibliographies series 1968—, chmn. collegiate chpt. and student activites com. 1967—), So. (2d v.p. 1970) marketing assns., Am. Sociol. Assn., Am. Acad. Advt., Am. Assn. U. Profs., Delta Sigma Pi, Omicron Delta Kappa, Beta Gamma Sigma. Editor: Marketing and the New Science of Planning, 1968; An Annotated Index of the Proceedings of American Marketing Association Conferences, 1955-65, 1966; also articles. Home: 1400 Hillcrest Dr Blacksburg VA 24060

KING, ROBERT LLOYD, hosp. cons.; b. Burkburnett, Tex., July 5, 1918; s. James Arvil and Willie Ivy (Williamson) K.; student Midwestern U., Wichita Falls, Tex., 1935-36, Hardin-Simmons U., 1936-37; B.S. in Archtl. Engring., U. Okla., 1941; m. Louise Roberson, April 31, 1941 (dec. 1946); m. 2d, Hazel Marie Mitchell, Sept. 20, 1947; children—Robert Lloyd, James Frank, Ruth Angela, Cynthia Carol, Janet Cornelia. Arthitect design div. Bur. Yards and Docks, Navy Dept., 1941-43; hosp. architect Inst. Inter Am. Affairs in Latin Am., 1943-46; chief architect tech. dir. Colombian Nat. Housing Authority, Bogota, 1946-48; pvt. practice as hosp. and planning cons., Austin, Tex., 1948-52; architect, planning cons. for ICA in Latin Am., 1952-59; pvt. practice hosp. and planning cons., Austin, 1959—; pvt. cons. Ghana, W. Africa, 1960; Latin Am., 1961-62. M em. Inter Am. Planning Soc., Internat. Fedn. Housing and Planning, Colombian Architects Soc., Am. Hosp. Assn., Am. Pub. Health Assn., Tau Beta Pi, Sigma Tau. Presbyn. Author: Rural Housing in Colombia, 1946; Hospital Program for the Nat. Integrated Health Plan of Peru, 1958; 10,000 House of Social Interest, Peru, 1958; Hospital Architecture and Planning, 1959; Housing, Urban Planning and Recreation Facilities, S. Peru, 1959; Medical Sch. and Teaching Hosp., Ghana, 1960; Regional Integrated Health Facilities for Panama, 1962; Health Facilities Design and Construction, 15th Annual Caribbean Conference, 1964; The Caribbean: Its Health Problems. Home: 1801 Vance Circle Austin TX 78701 Office: 504 W 24th St Austin TX 78705

KING, RONOLD WYETH PERCIVAL, educator; b. Williamstown, Mass., Sept. 19, 1905; s. James Percival and Edith Marianne Beate (Seyerlen) K.; A.B., U. Rochester, 1927, S.M., 1929; Ph.D., U. Wis., 1932; student U. Munich, Germany, 1928-29, Cornell U., 1929-30; m. Justine Merrell, June 22, 1937; 1 son, Christopher Merrell. Asst. in physics U. Rochester, 1927-28; Am.-German exchange student, 1929-30; White fellow in physics Cornell U., 1929-30; U. fellow in elec. engring. U. Wis., 1930-32, research asst., 1932-34; instr. physics Lafayette Coll., 1934-36, asst. prof., 1936-37; Guggenheim fellow, Berlin, Germany, 1937-38; with Harvard U., 1938—, successively instr., asst. prof., asso. prof., 1938-46, prof. applied physics, 1946—. Guggenheim fellow, Europe, 1958. Fellow Am. Acad. Arts and Scis., Am. Phys. Soc., A.A.A.S., I.E.E.E.; mem. Modern Lang. Assn., Internat. Sci. Radio Union, Am. Assn. Univ. Profs., Bavarian Acad. Sci. (contbg. mem.), Phi Beta Kappa, Sigma Xi. Author: Electromagnetic Engineering, Vol. 1, 1945, 2d edit. Fundamental Electromagnetic Theory, 1963; Transmission Lines, Antennas and Wave Guides (with A.H. Wing and H.R. Mimmo) 1945, 2d edit., 1965; Transmission-Line Theory, 1955, 2d edit., 1965; Theory of Linear Antennas, 1956; (with T.T. Wu) Scattering and Diffraction of Waves, 1959; (with R.B. Mack and S.S. Sandler) Arrays of Cylindrical Dipoles, 1968; (with C.W. Harrison, Jr.) Antennas and Waves: A Modern Approach, 1969; Tables of Antenna Characteristics, 1971; also articles in field. Home: 92 Hillcrest Pkwy Winchester MA 01890 Office: Gordon McKay Lab Harvard U Cambridge MA 02138

KING, RUFUS, lawyer; b. Seattle, Mar. 25, 1917; s. Rufus Gunn and Marian (Towle) K.; A.B., Princeton, 1938; postgrad. Stanford, 1940-41; LL.B., Yale, 1943; m. Janice L. Chase, June 15, 1941 (div. June 1951); children—Rufus, Agnes S.; m. 2d, Anita Siegel, 1967. Instr. Princeton, 1938-39; admitted to N.Y. bar, 1944, D.C. bar, 1948, Md. bar, 1953; partner Rice & King, Washington, 1953-64; pvt. practice, Washington, since 1964—; counsel Senate Crime Com., 1951, also other congl. coms.; cons. Nat. Commn. Law Enforcement and Adminstrn. Justice. Chmn. joint com. on narcotic drugs Am. Bar Assn. and A.M.A., 1956—, Pres. Montgomery County Community Psychiat. Clinic. Mem. Am. (chmn. criminal law sect. 1957-60, sec. 1954-57, mem. ho. of dels. 1960—, chmn. spl. com. atomic attack 1962—, del. sect. individual rights), N.Y. State, Md. bar assns., Bar Assn. D.C. Episcopalian. Clubs: Princeton (N.Y.C.); Metropolitan (Washington); American (Miami). Author: Gambling and Organized Crime, 1968; The Drug Hangup, 1971. Contbr. articles profl. jours. Home: 3524 Williamsburg Lane NW Washington DC 20008 Office: Woodward Bldg Washington DC 20005

KING, SAMUEL PAILTHORPE, lawyer; b. Hankow, China, Apr. 13, 1916 (parents Am. citizens); s. Samuel W. and Pauline (Evans) K.; B.S., Yale, 1937, LL.B., 1940; m. Anne Van Patten Grilk, July 8, 1944; children—Samuel Pailthorpe, Louise Van Patten, Charlotte Lelepoki. Admitted to D.C., Hawaii bars, 1940; practiced law, Honolulu, 1941-42, 46—, Washington, 1942; atty. King & McGregor, 1947-53, King & Myhre, 1957-61; judge, first circuit ct., Hawaii, 1961-66; judge Family Ct., 1st Circuit, State Hawaii, 1966-70. Served with USNR, 1941-46; capt. Res. ret. Fellow Am. Bar Found.; mem. Hawaii Bar Assn. (pres. 1953). Republican (chmn. Hawaiian Central com. 1953-55). Co-translator, co-editor: The Theory and Practice of GO (O. Korschelt), 1965. Episcopalian. Home: 3964 B Old Pali Rd Honolulu HI 96817 Office: 470 Alexander Young Bldg Honolulu HI 96813

KING, SETH S., journalist. Reporter, Oklahoma City Times; polit. reporter, Albany corr. N.Y. World Telegram and Sun; regional corr. N.Y. Times, Des Moines, 1953-56; first fgn. assignment to Israel, 1956, several assignments in Middle East, 1957-59; joined Times Bur., London, 1960, resident corr. Sigapore, Kuala Lumpur, Malaysia, 1963-66. Address: NY Times Co 229 W 43d St New York City NY 10036

KING, SHELDON SELIG, hosp. adminstr.; b. N.Y.C., Aug. 28, 1931; s. Benjamin and Jeanne (Fritz) K.; A.B., N.Y.U., 1952; M.S., Yale, 1957; m. Ruth Arden Zeller, June 26, 1955; children—Tracy Elizabeth, Meredith Ellen, Adam Bradley. Adminstrv. intern Montefiore Hosp., N.Y.C., 1952-53, 55; adminstrv. asst. Mt. Sinai Hosp., N.Y.C., 1957-60, asst. dir., 1960-66, dir. planning, 1966-68; exec. dir. Albert Einstein Coll. Medicine-Bronx Municipal Hosp. Center, Bronx, N.Y., 1968—; asst. prof. Albert Einstein Coll. Medicine, N.Y.C., 1968—; preceptor George Washington U., Ithaca Coll., Yale, U. Mo., City U. N.Y. Bd. dirs. Brith Milah Bd. Served with AUS, 1953-55. Fellow Am. Coll. Hosp. Adminstrs., Am. Pub. Health Assn., Royal Soc. Health; mem. Am. Hosp. Assn., Am. Soc. Pub. Adminstrn. Home: 37 Buckingham Rd Cresskill NJ 07626 Office: Pelham Pkwy S and Eastchester Rd Bronx NY 10461

KING, SOL, architect; b. Poland, July 19, 1909; s. Lester and Celia (Sarna) K.; came to U.S., 1923; naturalized, 1925; student U. Detroit, 1929-31; B.S. in Archt., U. Mich., 1934; m. Jennie Lifshitz, Apr. 14, 1935; children—Phyllis D. (dec.), (Mrs. Samuel P. Weiner), Susan M. (Mrs. Gary M. Roggin). With Albert Kahn Assos., archts. and engrs., Detroit, 1935—, dir. architecture, 1956—, pres., 1958—; propr. Sol King, architect, Detroit, 1958—; prin. works include Willow Run (Mich.) Bomber Plant, 1942, assembly plant Ford Motor Co., St. Louis, 1948, main office bldg. Ford div. Ford Motor Co., Dearborn, Mich., 1957, Nat. Bank Detroit hdqrs. bldg., 1959, physics and astronomy bldg. U. Mich., 1963, Gen. Motors Futurama Bldg., N.Y. World's Fair, 1964, lab. and office bldg. Avon Products, Inc., Springdale, O., 1965, Woodhaven (Mich.) Stamping plant, 1965, Ford-Avon-Atlanta (Ga.) Southeastern br. facilities, 1969, Houston Chronicle printing plant, 1970. Pub. adv. panel archtl. services Gen. Services Adminstrn., 1967-69. Mem. founders Soc. Detroit Inst. Arts, 1950—; bd. dirs. sec., treas., v.p. Jewish Community Center, Detroit, 1946-56; trustee Thomas Alva Edison Found.; mem. grad. scholarship com. Coll. Architecture and Design, U. Mich., 1956—, chmn. alumni adv. com., semi-centennial celebration, 1956; sponsor fgn. student exchange Program Assn. Collegiate Schs. Architecture, 1963-64, 65-67; sponsor grad. scholarship Albert Kahn Assos., 1956—. Recipient Sesquicentennial award U. Mich., 1967; Sol King award for excellent teaching in architecture U. Mich, 1969; Wisdom award of honor Wisdom Hall of Fame, 1970. Fellow A.I.A. (pres. Detroit chpt. 1969-70), Mich. Soc. Architects (Gold medal award 1967, mem. various nat. coms. 1962—, bd. dirs. 1951-56, chmn. task force on a uniform fed. archtl.-engring. contract com. 1969), Engring. Soc. Detroit (vice pres. 1968, pres. 1969-70, bd. dirs.); mem. Newcomen Soc. N.Am. (dir.), Soc. Archtl. Historians (dir.), Technion Soc., Bldg. Ofcls. Conf. Am., Bldg. Research Inst., Greater Detroit Board Commerce, O.R.T. Jewish religion (bd. govs. Congregation Shaarey Zedek 1966—). Clubs: Standard City, Economic (Detroit); President's (U. Mich.); Franklin Hills (Mich.) Country. Home: North Park Towers East North Park Dr Southfield MI 48075 Office: New Center Bldg Detroit MI 48202

KING, SPENCER BIDWELL, Jr., educator; b. Birmingham, Ala., Feb. 19, 1904; s. Spencer Bidwell and Lizzie Emma (Dodson) K.; A.B., Mercer U., 1929; M.A., Peabody Coll., 1936; Ph.D., U. N.C., 1950; student Vanderbilt U., U. Mich.; m. Caroline Janet Paul, Dec. 26, 1934; children—Spencer Bidwell III, Janet Paul, Margaret Caroline (Mrs. Robert J. Edenfield). Prin. Fruitland Inst., Hendersonville, N.C., 1930-33; instr. history Mars Hill Coll., 1933-46, asst. dean, 1942-46; vis. prof. Furman U., summers 1940, 43, 44; asso. prof. history Mercer U., 1946-48, prof., 1948—, chmn. dept., 1946-70; vis. prof. history Emory U., summer 1960, U. Ga., summer 1963; columnist Macon Telegraph, 1960-65. Research asst. Inst. Research Social Sci. U. N.C., 1945; chmn. bd. editors Ardivan Press, Macon, 1960-62; trustee Macon Youth Mus., 1956-65. Mem. hist. commn. So. Baptist Conv. Recipient Carnegie grant for hist. research, 1950-51. Named An Outstanding Educator of America, 1971. Mem. So. Hist. Assn., Ga. Soc. Hist. Research (pres. 1953), So. Bapt. (pres. 1970), Ga. (curator), Ga. Bapt. (curator) hist. socs., Kappa Phi Kappa, Pi Gamma Mu. Baptist. Club: Palaver. Author: Selective Service in North Carolina in World War II, 1949; (with Coulter and Saye) History of Georgia, 1954; Ebb Tide as Seen Through the Diary of Josephine Clay Habersham, 1863, 1958; Georgia Voices: a documentary history to 1872, 1966. Editor: J.C. Butler's Historical Record of Macon and Central Georgia, 1958,69, Eliza Frances Andrews' Wartime Journal of a Georgia Girl, 1960; Rebel Lawyer; Letters of Theodorick W. Montfort, 1861-1862, 1965. Ga. editor: Ency. of So. Baptists, 2 vols., Ency. Brit., Collier's Ency.; contbr. articles and book reviews in hist., lit. jours. Home: 570 El Dorado Dr Macon GA 31204

KING, SPENCER MATHEWS, diplomat; b. San Juan, P.R., Aug. 11, 1917; s. Amos J. and Cora S. (Morison) K.; grad. Kent Sch., 1936; B.A., Yale, 1940; student Sch. Fgn. Service, Georgetown U., summer 1940, Civil Affairs Tng. Sch., U. Mich., 1944-45, U. Chgo., 1951; grad. Nat. War Coll., 1958; m. Josephine Montes Smith, Nov. 19, 1966. Mem. U.S. Fgn. Service, 1945—; 3d sec., vice consul, La Paz, Bolivia, 1946-48; assigned Dept. of State, 1948-51; 1st sec., consul, Prague, Czechoslovakia, 1951-54; chief E. European br. Voice of Am., 1954-55; spl. asst. to asst. sec. of state for Interam. affairs, 1955-57; fgn. service insp., 1958-62; dep. chief mission, consul gen., Quito, Ecuador, 1962, Santo Domingo, Dominican Republic, 1962-64; dep. insp. gen. Dept. State, 1964-69; now U.S. ambassador to Guyana, 1969—. Served to maj., AUS, 1941-46; PTO. Mem. Alpha Signa Phi, Cum Laude Soc., Canon and Castle. clubs: Yale (N.Y.C. and Washington); Manor Country (Rockville, Md.); University (Washington). Home: 21 Pearl St Belfast ME 04915 Office: Dept of State Washington DC 20525

KING, T. EUGENE, banker. Cashier, First Security Bank Utah. Office: PO Box 478 Salt Lake City UT 84110*

KING, THOMAS BARRETT, airlines exec.; b. Chgo., Jan. 13, 1926; s. William Barrett and Martha Clark (Bennett) K.; B.S. in Math., U. N.M., 1945; m. Helen Haley Chapman, Dec. 27, 1964. Pub. relations dir. Studebacker-Packard Corp., S. Bend, Ind., 1953-57; v.p. marketing Kiekhaefer Corp., Fond du Lac, Wis., 1957-64; exec. v.p. U.S. Execs., Inc., Milw., 1964-65; v.p. promotion Braniff Internat., Dallas, 1964—; pres. Tourism Investments, S.A., 1968—; pres., dir. Hotel Assos., 1967-70. Served to lt. (s.g.) USNR, 1943-46, 50-53. Office: Braniff Bldg Exchange Park Dallas TX 75235

KING, THOMAS BROWN, glass co. exec.; b. Hamilton, Ont., Can., June 6, 1913; s. James Watt and Hannah Brewster (Brown) K.; grad. Trinity Coll. Sch., Port Hope, Ont., 1931; student McGill U. (Can.), 1931-32; m. Mary Helen Campbell, Sept. 9, 1939; children—Diana (Mrs. L. Brian Timmins), Cynthia. With corporate sec.'s dept. Dominion Glass Co., Ltd., Montreal, Que., Can., 1932—, asst. sec., 1945-56, corporate sec., 1956—; dir., 1966-67. Served to capt. Canadian Army, 1939-44, Brit. Army, 1945. Fellow Chartered Inst. Secs.; mem. Systems and Procedures Assn. (pres. Montreal chpt. 1959-66), Kappa Alpha. Presbyn. (ruling elder, ch. trustee). Clubs: Kinsman of Montreal, St. James's and Montreal Badminton and Squash (Montreal). Home: 65 Holton Av Westmount 217 Quebec Canada Office: Dominion Glass Co Ltd 1080 Beaver Hall Hill Montreal 128 Quebec Canada

KING, THOMAS BURNESS, educator; b. Motherwell, Scotland, Apr. 27, 1923; s. Robert Dick and Mary Ann Forbes (Burness) K.; B.Sc., Glasgow U., 1945, Ph.D., 1950; m. Helen Z. Scott, Apr. 3, 1950; children—Lesley Helen, Anne Scott, Robert Alan, Edith Burness. Came to U.S., 1953, naturalized, 1959. Metallurgist, Clyde Alloy Steel Co., Scotland, 1940-41, research metallurgist, 1945-46; asso. lectr. metallurgy Royal Coll. Sci. and Tech., Glasgow, 1948-50, lectr., 1950-52; mem. faculty Mass. Inst. Tech., 1953—, prof. metallurgy, 1961—, head dept., 1962—. Fellow Am. Acad. Arts and Scis.; mem. Am. Inst. Mining, Metall. and Petroleum Engrs., Am. Soc. Metals, Iron and Steel Inst., Sigma Xi. Home: 23 Jefferson Rd Winchester MA 01890 Office: Mass Inst Tech Cambridge MA 02139

KING, THOMAS CLAIR, educator; b. Seneca, Kan., July 24, 1910; s. James Grover and Mary Ellen (Turner) K.; B.A., Ft. Hays (Kan.) State Coll., 1940, M.S., 1941; Ed.D., Harvard, 1950; m. Alta Marie Litton, Feb. 27, 1932; children—Lois Caroline (Mrs. Robert Fitzgerald), Gladys Kay (Mrs. Sidney Baker). Classroom tchr., prin. elementary schs., Gove County, Kan., 1930-36; supt. schs., Stockton, Kan., 1941-42; instr. edn. Bethany Coll., Lindsborg, Kan., 1947-48; asso. prof. edn. U. Me., 1948-51; dean Coll. Edn. and Nursing, U. Vt., 1951-68; prof. edn. U. Miami, Coral Gables, 1968—; lectr. history Seminole Jr. Coll., Sanford, Fla., 1971—. Mem. Vt. Gov.'s Commn. on Status of Women, 1966-68. State Mem. Adv. Com. Nursing Edn., 1965-68, Vt. Adminstrv. Council Tchr. Edn., 1955-65; bd. dirs. Nat. League Nursing, 1960-68. Served as lt. USNR, 1944-46. Mem. New Eng. Council Econ. Edn. (trustee 1961-68), Soc. Study Edn. Kappa Delta Pi, Pi Gamma Mu, Phi Kappa Phi, Kappa Phi Kappa. Home: 5112 Dorian Av Orlando FL 32809

KING, THOMAS CREIGHTON, physician, univ. provost; b. Salt Lake City, Apr. 10, 1928; s. Creighton G. and Alice (Edwards) K.; B.S., U. Utah, 1952, M.D., 1954; M.A. in Ednl. Psychology, U. Mo., Kansas City, 1963; m. Joan Peters, Aug. 23, 1952; children—John Creighton, Elizabeth, Patrick Edward. Intern, Columbia-Presbyn. Hosp., N.Y.C., 1954-55; resident U. Utah Hosps., 1955-59; practice medicine, specializing in thoracic surgery, Kansas City, Mo., 1960-64, Chgo., 1964-66, Salt Lake City, 1966—; asst. prof. surgery U. Kan., 1960-64; asso. chief staff, dir. research labs. Kansas City Vets. Hosp., 1962-64; asso. prof. surgery U. Ill., 1964-66, chief of tng. Center for Study Med. Edn., 1964-66, asso. prof. ednl. psychology, 1964-66; attending surgeon U. Ill. Research and Edn. Hosp., 1964-66; asso. attending surgeon Cook County Hosp., Chgo., 1964-66; asso. prof. surgery, asso. dean Coll. Medicine, U. Utah, Salt Lake City, 1966-68, acad. v.p., 1968-69, provost, 1969—, prof. surgery, 1969—; staff surgeon U. Utah Med. Center, 1966—; chief thoracic surgery VA Hosp., Salt Lake City, 1968—. Cons. med. edn. WHO; chmn. surg. tng. com. VA. Mem. Gov.'s Task Force Comprehensive Health Planning Program, 1969—; mem. Utah Bd. Health, 1967—, mem. regional adv. group Intermountain Regional Med. Program, 1969—. Bd. dirs. Community Services Council, United Health Found. Served with USNR, 1945-46. Mem. A.C.S., Am. Ednl. Research Assn., Am. Fedn. Clin. Research, Soc. U. Surgeons, Western Surg. Assn., Assn. Am. Med. Colls. Contbr. articles profl. jours. Home: 2863 Oquirrh Dr Salt Lake City UT 84108

KING, THOMAS STARR, Jr., transp. exec., ret. naval officer; b. Wilmington, Del., Dec. 7, 1914; s. Thomas Starr and Anne (Winchester) K.; B.S. in Mech. Engring., U.S. Naval Acad., 1936; M.S. in Elec. Engring., Mass. Inst. Tech., 1945; m. Jeanne Sanford Everett, Aug. 10, 1938; children—Thomas Starr IV, William Kimberly, Anne Stuart. Commd. ensign U.S. Navy, 1936, advanced through grades to rear adm., 1965; comdr. exptl. destroyer U.S.S. Winslow, 1948-49, Destroyer Div. 212, 1954-55, Destroyer Squadron 5, 1961-62, Destroyer Flotillas 5 and 11, 1962-63, 65-66; mem. staff comdr. Seventh Fleet, Korean War; comdr. U.S.S. Observation Island, Polaris exptl. test ship, 1960-61; grad. Naval War Coll. 1952; asst. chief Bur. Naval Weapons, 1964-65; mfg. officer Naval Gun Factory, 1955-58; comdr. joint navy-airforce task group that recovered Astronaut Shirra, 1962, Astronaut Cooper, 1963; comdr. Cruiser Destroyer Flotilla 11, 1965-66; asst. chief naval operations (tng.), Washington, 1966-70, ret.; gen. mgr. Tri Country Met. Transp. Dist. Ore., Portland, 1970—. Decorated Legion of Merit, Bronze Star with combat V. Mem. U.S. Naval Inst., Am. Ordnance Assn. Presbyn. Home: 6230 Kellogg Dr McLean VA 22101 Office: Gen Mgr Tri Country Met Transp Dist Ore Portland OR 97202

KING, WARREN THOMAS, editorial cartoonist; b. Queens, L.I., N.Y., Jan. 3, 1916; s. Thomas Joseph and Rose (Beck) K.; B.S., Fordham U., 1938; student Grand Central Sch. Art, 1938, Phoenix Art Inst., 1938-41; m. Nadine Sensabaugh, Mar. 11, 1950; children—Dennis, Patricia, Suzanne. Free lance illustrator for books, advt., mags., movies, N.Y.C., 1940-61; editorial cartoonist Nat. Assn. Mfrs., N.Y.C., 1951—, Daily News, N.Y.C., 1955—. Paintings permanently rep. at The Pentagon, Air Force Acad., Colorado Springs, Colo.; paintings exhibited internationally. Recipient Freedom Found. medals of honor, 1953, 59, certificate merit, 1960, Newspaper Guild award, 1959, 61, Soc. Silurians award, 1960, 61, 64, George Washington Honor medal Freedoms Found., 1963, Brotherhood award Nat. Conf. Christians and Jews, 1963, Freedoms Found. Medal of Honor, 1965, Soc. Silurians Honorable Mention, 1965, Page One award, 1967, Nat. Headliners Club award, 1968, Nat. Art Dirs. Club award, 1968, Overseas Press Club citation, 1968. Mem. Soc. Illustrators, Nat. Cartoonist Soc., Soc. Silurians, Am. Assn. Editorial Cartoonists. Club: Dutch Treat. Home: Captain's Lane Wilton CT Office: care News Syndicate Co Inc 220 E 42nd St New York City NY 10017

KING, WILLARD FAHRENKAMP, (Mrs. Edmund Ludwig King), educator; b. Roswell, N.M., July 13, 1924; d. W. F. and Willard (Pickerill) Fahrenkamp; student Tex. Christian U., 1939-40; B.A., U. Tex., 1943, M.A., 1946; Ph.D., Brown U., 1957; m. Edmund Ludwig King, Jan. 29, 1951. Instr. Spanish, U. Tex., 1946-47, 49-50; instr. Spanish, Brown U., 1950-51; instr. Spanish, Bryn Mawr (Pa.) Coll., 1958-60, asst. prof., 1960-64, asso. prof., 1964-70, prof. Spanish, 1970—, chmn. dept. Spanish, 1964—. Bd. dirs. Internat. Inst. in Spain. Guggenheim fellow, 1965-66. Mem. Modern Lang. Assn., Renaissance Soc. Am., Phi Beta Kappa. Democrat. Author: Prosa novelística y academias literarias en el siglo XVII, 1963; also article. Home: 171 Western Way Princeton NJ 08540 Office: Thomas Library Bryn Mawr Coll Bryn Mawr PA 19010

KING, WILLARD LEROY, lawyer; b. Batavia, Ill., Dec. 9, 1893; s. Willard E. and Ellen (White) K.; student Knox Coll., 1912-14; Ph.B., Chicago U., 1916, J.D., 1917; D.C.L. (honorary), Bowdoin College, 1951; LL.D., Knox College, 1954; married to Margaret A. Erickson, December 15, 1930; 1 daughter, Margaret (Mrs. Thomas R. Moore). Admitted to Ill. bar, 1917; began practice in Peoria; draftsman of Com. of Phraseology and Style (Ill. Constl. Conv.), 1919-20; began Chgo. practice with Rosenthal, Hamill & Wormser, became mem. 1926; now King, Robin, Gale & Pillinger. Mem. Loyalty Rev. Bd., Civil Service Commission, 1951-53. Served as second lieutenant Infantry, 1918. Trustee Museum Science and Industry, Menninger Found. Member American Bar Assn., Ill. State Bar Assn., Chicago Bar Assn. (bd. mgrs. 1929-38), Chicago Law Inst. (pres. 1938), Ill. State, Chgo. (trustee) hist. socs., Delta Sigma Rho, Phi Gamma Delta, Order of the Coif. Clubs: University, Chicago Literary (president 1941-42), Caxton (pres. 1954-55), Law (pres. 1953-54), South Shore Country, Grolier (New York). Co-author: Law of Opinion Evidence in Illinois, 1942; author Melville Weston Fuller, 1950; Lincoln's Manager David Davis, 1960. Contbr. to legal mags. Home: 5801 Dorchester Av Chicago IL 60637 Office: 135 S LaSalle St Chicago IL 60603

KING, WILLIAM DICKEY, sculptor; b. Jacksonville, Fla., Feb. 25, 1925; s. Walter Blake and Florence Elizabeth (Dickey) K.; student U. Fla., 1942-44, Cooper Union Art Sch., N.Y.C., 1945-48, Bklyn. Museum Art Sch., 1949, Skowhegan Sch. Painting and Sculpture, 1948; m. Lois Dodd, Oct. 12, 1948 (div. 1952); 1 son, Eli; m. 2d, Shirley Bowman, June 6, 1955 (div. 1967); 1 dau., Amy; m. 3d, Anne Kobin, Apr. 20, 1968. Exhbns. include Roko Gallery, N.Y.C., 1947-52, Downtown Gallery, N.Y.C., 1952, Alan Gallery, N.Y.C., 1953-60, Terry Dinternfass Inc., N.Y.C., 1960, Whitney Mus. Art, 1952-57, Mus. Modern Art, 1950-59, Guggenheim Mus., 1966, Phila. Mus., 1949, Los Angeles County Mus., 1966, Brandeis U. Art Gallery, 1965, U. Cal. at Berkeley Gallery, 1966, U. Ill., 1959-65. Address: care Terry Dintetnfass Inc E 67th St New York City NY 10021

KING, WILLIAM EMERY, ins. exec.; b. Glendive, Mont., Aug. 13, 1912; s. William S. and Gertrude L. (Emery) K.; B.S., Hamline U., 1934; LL.B., St. Paul Coll. Law, 1939; m. Florence Tousley, Dec. 26, 1936; children—Judith, Winifred, Robert. Ins. claim adjuster Employers Liability Assurance Corp. 1935-41; admitted to Minn. bar, 1939; practice of law, St. Paul, 1939-45; claim atty. St. Paul Fire & Marine Ins. Co., 1941-48, asst. sec., 1948-52, sec., 1952-54, v.p., 1954—, also dir.; dir. St. Paul Fire & Marine Ins. Co., St. Paul Mercury Indemnity Co., St. Paul Mercury Ins. Co. Mem. bd. St. Paul chpt. A.R.C. Bd. trustees Hamline U. Mem. Hamline U. Alumni Assn. (pres. 1956-57), St. Paul C. of C. (bd. 1963-66). Clubs: Minnesota, Somerset (St. Paul). Home: 2365 Delaware Av St Paul MN 55118 Office: 385 Washington St St Paul MN 55102

KING, WILLIAM HAVEN, lawyer; b. Huntington, W. Va., Oct. 1911, s. James Edward and Princess (Turner) K.; A.B., Dartmouth, 1933; LL.B., U. Richmond, 1936; m. Suzanne Davis, Aug. 30, 1935; children—Susan (Mrs. W. Hammond Hunt), William Haven. Admitted to Va. bar, 1935, since practiced in Richmond Virginia; partner firm McGuire, Woods and Battle, 1941—. Mem. Va. Board Law Examiners, 1951—. Vice pres., gen. counsel William P. Poythress & Co., Inc., Citizens Home Ins. Co.; dir., gen. Counsel Blue Cross Va., Blue Shield Va. (pres. 1963-66). Chmn. parking bd. City Richmond, 1958-64. Pres. Richmond chpt. A.R.C., 1956-58, bd. dirs. 1949—; bd. dirs. Richmond YMCA, 1957-64, Westbrook Sanatorium, Inc., 1957-70; pres. Va. League Planned Parenthood, Inc., 1965-66. Mem. bd. mgrs. Nat. Conf. Bar Examiners, 1962-68, chmn. 1966-67. Served to lt. (s.g.) USNR, World War II; PTO. Fellow Am. Bar Found., Am. College of Trial Lawyers; mem. American (ho. dels. 1967-68), Richmond (pres. 1957-58) bar assns., Va. State Bar (pres. 1960-61, chmn. com. legal ethics 1958-60), Va. Bar Assn. (exec. com. 1946-49), Am. Judicature Soc., Va. Soc. S.R. (pres. 1968-70), Newcomen Society, Omicron Delta Kappa, Psi Upsilon, Casque and Gauntlet. Clubs: Country of Virginia, Rotunda, Bull and Bear. Home: 6126 St Andrews Circle Richmond VA 23216 Office: Ross Bldg Richmond VA 23219

KING, WILLIAM JOSEPH, banker; b. Phila., Mar. 13, 1929; s. Mahlon H. and Louise (Swindells) K.; A.B., U. Pa., 1960; m. Jean L. Dale, Sept. 2, 1950; children—William Joseph, Pamela J., Gregory P. Asst. treas. Fidelity Bank, Phila., 1958- 60, asst. v.p., 1960-63, v.p., 1963-66, sr. v.p., 1966-69, exec. v.p., 1969—; chmn. bd. Fidelity Optimation Services, Inc.; pres. Fidelity Computer Services, Inc.; sec.-treas. Phila. Clearing House Assn. Mem. Gov.'s Tech. Adv. Com. on Electronic Data Processing, 1964. Mem. adv. bd. Pa. Sch. Banking. Served to maj. AUS, 1947-66. Mason. Clubs: Union League, Midday (Phila.). Home: Pine Rd North of Moredon Rd Philadelphia PA 19115 Office: Fidelity Bank Broad and Walnut Sts Philadelphia PA 19109

KING, WILLIAM JULIAN, cons. engr.; b. Baton Rouge, Apr. 27, 1902; s. William Thomas and Mary Fredonia (Cross) K.; B. Chem. Engring., Tulane U., 1925, M.E., 1933; student advanced course in engring., Gen. Electric Co., Schenectady, 1926-29; m. Helen Kendall Ross, June 22, 1929; children—Kendall C., Robert J., Alan R., Stuart E. Radio operator around the world tour, 1926; test engr., Gen. Electric Co., Schenectady, 1926-28, refrigerator engring., 1928-30, research and cons. in heat transmission, 1930-33, in charge devel. and design air conditioning and heating equipment, 1933-40, charge research and field applications of aircraft turbosuperchargers and jet propulsion engines, 1940-45; research engr. in charge combustion and gas turbine research, Battelle Meml. Inst., Columbus, O., 1945-46; dir. Sibley Sch. M.E., Cornell U., 1946-49; prof. engring. U. of Cal. at Los Angeles, 1949-69, now emeritus. Mem. div. indsl. and engring. research NRC, 1930-33; mem. subcom. on superchargers Nat. Advisory Com. for Aeronautics, 1941-44. Profl. engr., Cal. Mem. Soc. Automotive Engrs., Am. Soc. M.E., Air Pollution Control Assn., Tau Beta Pi. Presbyn. Kiwanian. Club: Faculty. Author: (Series of articles) The Basic Laws and Data of Heat Transmission, Mechanical Engineering, 1932; (series of 3 articles) The Unwritten Laws of Engineering, Mechanical Engineering, 1944 (awarded Melville medal by Am. Soc. M.E. for series, 1945). Home: 26684 Sun City Blvd Sun City CA 92381 Office: Engring Dept U Cal Los Angeles CA 90024

KING, WILLIAM TRAVERS, III, educator, chemist; b. Denver, Aug. 6, 1928; s. William Travers, Jr. and Evelyn (Seal) K.; B.S., U. Wash., 1952; Ph.D., U. Minn., 1956; m. Helen Ann Smick, July 19, 1952; children—Zoe Ann, Philip Travers, Steven Adam. Postdoctoral fellow Yale, 1957; instr. Brown U., Providence, 1957-59, asst. prof., 1959-63, asso. prof., 1963-68, prof. chemistry, 1968—. Served with USMC, 1946-49. Mem. Am. Phys. Soc. Home: 71 Roger Williams Av Rumford RI 02916 Office: Chemistry Dept Brown U Providence RI 02912

KING, WILLIS JEFFERSON, ret. bishop; b. Rose Hill, Tex., Oct. 1, 1886; s. Anderson William and Emma (Blackshear) K.; A.B. at Wiley College, Marshall, Tex., 1910; S.T.B., Boston U. Sch. of Theol. 1913, Ph.D., 1921; hon. D.D., Boston U., 1933; student Harvard Divinity Sch.; m. Permella J. Kelly, June 4, 1913, (died Feb. 23, 1943); children—Velma Norine, Eloise Aurora, Grace Evangeline; married 2d, Emma Clarissa Arnold, June 28, 1944. Entered ministry M.E. Ch., 1908; pastor Greenville, Tex., 1908-10; asso. pastor St. Mark's Ch., N.Y.C., 1911; pastor Fourth Ch., Boston, St. Paul Ch., Galveston, Tex., Trinity Ch., Houston, until 1918; prof. O.T. and Christian sociology, Gammon Theol. Sem. Atlanta, 1918-30, pres., 1932-48, lectr, 1952; elected bishop, 1944, assigned to Liberia, W. Africa; reassigned, 1948; assigned to La., Miss. and Upper Miss. Confs., 1953; resident bishop New Orleans area, central jurisdiction The Methodist Church, 1956-60. President of Samuel Houston College 1930-32. Fellow Julius Rosenwald Fund, for resrch. in Oxford U. and Palestine, under auspices Am. Sch. of Oriental Research (on leave of absence from Gammon Theol. Seminary), 1929-30. Represented Negro students at World's Student Christian Federation, Peking, China, 1922. Recipient of the Great Band of the Humane Order of African Redemption, Liberia, 1956; Knight Commander of the Order of African Pioneers. Member General Conf., M.E. Ch., 1924, 28, 32, 40, 44; del. to Conf. on Life and Work, Oxford, Eng., 1937; del. to World Council Meth. Ch., Oxford, 4951; rep. Bishop's council to Africa Central Conf., Belgian Congo, 1952; mem. Nat. Preaching Mission Staff, 1936-37; mem. Commn. of Unification of Meth. Chs. in Am.; mem. Atlanta Sch. of Social Work; member Commn. on Interracial Cooperation since 1940. Mem. Am. Oriental Soc., Southern Sociol. Soc., Am. Acad. Polit. and Social Science, Am. Schs. Oriental Research. Nat. Geographic Soc., Omega Psi Phi, Democrat. Author: The Negro in American Life, 1926. Collaborator: Personalism in Theology and Christian Bases of World Order, 1943. Home: 4834 Prentiss Av New Orleans LA 70126

KING, WINSTON LEE, clergyman, educator; b. Avilla, Ind., Aug. 30, 1907; s. Alfred H. and Alberta (Bodenhafer) K.; A.B., Asbury Coll., 1929; B.D., Andover Newton Theol. Sch., 1936; S.T.M., Harvard, 1938, Ph.D., 1940; m. Jocelyn A. Brownlee, June 2, 1931; children—Carroll (Mrs. Carroll A. Heideman), Christopher R., Jonathan B. Ordained to ministry Methodist Ch., later Congl. Ch., 1935; minister in New England, 1930-43, 45-49; dean chapel, prof. philosophy and religion Grinnell Coll., 1949-64, Rand prof. applied Christianity, 1961-64; prof. history of religions Vanderbilt U., 1964—; research in Japan, 1970-71; Fulbright lectr. history and philosophy of religion Kyoto (Japan) U., 1965-66; vis. prof. Internat. Inst. Advanced Buddhistic Studies, Rangoon, Burma, 1958-60. Served as chaplain AUS, 1943-45; ETO. Decorated Bronze Star with oak leaf cluster. Mem. Am. Acad. Religion, Am. Soc. Study Religion, Am. Assn. of U. Profs. Author: The Holy Imperative, 1949; Introduction to Religion, 1954; Buddhism and Christianity, 1962; In the Hope of Nibbana, 1964; A Thousand Lives Away, 1964; Introduction to Religion: A Phemenological Approach, 1968. Lit. editor: Jour. Am. Acad. Religion, 1967—. Contbr. to books. Home: 2001 21st Av S Nashville TN 37212

KING, WOODY, Jr., playwright, actor, dir.; a founder Concept-East Theatre. Bd. dirs. cultural arts program mblzn. for Youth in N.Y. Author: Problems Facing Negro Actors. Address: 250 River Dr New York City NY 10038*

KING, B. B., singer, guitarist; b. Itta Bern, Miss., Sept. 16, 1925; began teaching self guitar, 1945, later studied Schillinger System. Formerly disc jockey and singer Memphis radio; recording artist for RPM, Crown, Bullet, Kent, ABC-Paramount records. Address: care ABC Records 1330 Av of Americas New York City NY 10019*

KINGERY, DWANE, univ. dean; b. Winchester, Ida., Jan. 27, 1927; s. Burrell Thomas and Allie (Chowning) K.; B.S. in Edn., S.W. Mo. State Coll., 1949; M.Ed., U. Mo., 1953, Ed.D., 1956; m. Frances Jean Duff, Apr. 16, 1949; children—Karen, Kent, David. High sch. tchr. English and Spanish, Mountain Grove, Mo., 1946-49, Crystal City, Mo., 1952-54; teaching fellow U. Mo., 1954-56; mem. faculty N. Tex. State U., 1956—, prof. edn., 1962—, dean Sch. Edn., 1966-. Served with USNR, 1945-46. Gregory fellow U. Mo., 1954-56. Mem. Tex. Tchrs. Assn., N.E.A., Assn. Higher Edn., Assn. Supervision and Curriculum Devel., Phi Delta Kappa, Denton C. of C. Kiwanian. Home: 2021 Mistywood St Denton TX 76201

KINGERY, REDVERS WRAY, savs. and loan assn. exec.; b. B.C., Can., Jan. 30, 1926; s. Wray Thornton and Aida (Davidson) K.; brought to U.S., 1926, naturalized, 1947; C.E., U. So. Cal., 1954; m. Loretta Ryan, Jan. 3, 1953; children—Redvers Scott, Heather Ann. Field engr. C.F. Braun Co., Alhambra, Cal., 1949; constrn. engr. Wilputte Coke Oven Co., N.Y.C., 1950; pres. B-K Engr.-Bldrs., Glendale, Cal., 1960; with Imperial Savs. of Newport-Pasadena, Pasadena, Cal., 1965—, pres., 1967—, also dir.; dir. Imperial Savs. of the South, San Diego. Chmn. Navy League Sea Cadets, Pasadena, 1969; com. mem. Tournament of Roses, Pasadena, 1963, Bd. dirs. Pasadena Boys Club. Served with USAAF, 1944-46. Republican Episcopalian. Clubs: California (Los Angeles); Valley Hunt, Annandale Golf (Pasadena); (La Glulla Baja, Cal., Mexico). Home: 820 Oak Knoll Circle Pasadena CA 91106 Office: 61 S Lake Av Pasadena CA 91101

KINGERY, WILLIAM DAVID, educator, ceramist; b. N.Y.C., July 7, 1926; s. Lisle B. and Margaret (Reynolds) K.; grad. Taft Sch., Watertown, Conn., 1943; S.B., Mass. Inst. Tech., 1950, Sc.D., 1952; m. Gertrude Phillips, Nov. 22, 1965; children—William David, Peter (dec.), Rebekah, Andrew. Mem. faculty Mass. Inst. Tech., 1951—, prof. ceramics, 1960—. Mem. materials adv. bd. Nat. Acad. Sci., 1960-68. Fellow Am. Ceramic Soc (Ross Coffin Purdy award 1952; John Jeppson award 1958; outstanding service award New Eng. sect. 1957); hon. mem. Keramos; mem. Am. Chem. Soc., Glaciological Soc. Author: Property Measurements at High Temperatures, 1959; Introduction to Ceramics, 1960. Editor: Ceramic Fabrication Process, 1958; Kinetics of High-Temperature Process, 1959; Ice and Snow, 1963. Contbr. profl. jours. Home: Allens Point Rd Marion MA 02738 Office: 77 Massachusetts Av Cambridge MA 02139

KINGHAN, CHARLES ROSS, artist; b. Anthony, Kan., Jan. 18, 1895; s. Robert E. and Sarah Frances (Edwards) K; student Acad. Fine Arts, Am. Acad. Art, Art Inst, Audubon Sch. Art (all Chgo.); m. Ruth F. Weidler, Sept. 13, 1927; children—Donald Earl, Charles Bruce. Asso. Stevens, Sundblom & Henry Studios, Chgo., 1926-30; free-lance, 1950-51; tchr. Am. Acad. Art, 1933-35; co-owner Huguenot Sch. Art, 1949-53; with Maxon Advt. Agy., 1952-53; art work Batten, Barton, Durstine & Osborn Advt. Agy., N.Y.C., 1954; now tchr. pvt. class in water color, mem. juries of award and selection Am. Water-color Soc., Allied Artists; represented permanent collections Smithsonian Instn., Washington, Phila. Mus. Art, U. Me., also pvt. collections. Recipient gold medal All Ill. Soc. Arts, 1933, Ernest Quantrel award Hudson Valley Art Assn., 1951; 1st prize New Rochelle Woman's Club, 1951, 53, Westchester Woman's Club, Bronxville, N.Y., 1954; 1st prize watercolor Westchester Fedn. Women's Clubs, 1956; Emily Lowe award Am. Watercolor Soc., 1957; Hebrew Vets. Assn. (John Newton Howitt award, 1959, Rudolph Lesch award 1965; v. p. 1969), others. A.N.A. Mem. Am. Watercolor Soc. (v.p. 1969, 71), Phila. Watercolor Club, Allied Artists Hudson Valley Art Assn. (dir.), New Rochelle Art Assn. (past pres.). Club: Salmagundi. Author: Rendering Techniques, for Commercial Art and Advertising, 1957; Ted Kautzky and How He Painted, 1959; also contbr. articles art mags. Home: 7 Lomond Pl New Rochelle NY 10804

KINGMAN, DONG, artist, educator; b. Oakland, Cal., Apr. 1, 1911; s. Dong Kwong and Lew Shee K.; student Lin-Nom, Hong Kong, 1924-26; m. Wong Shee, Sept. 1929 (dec. June 1954); children—Eddie, Don Kingman Jr., m. 2d, Helena Kuo, Oct., 1956. Tchr. art, San Diego Art Gallery, 1941-43; now tchr. Famous Artists Schs., Westport, Conn. Lectr. tour around world sponsored by internat. cultural exchange program, State Dept., 1954. Awarded Guggenheim fellowships 1942, 43. Recipient award, Chgo. Internat. Watercolor Exhbn., 1944; gold medal of honor, Audubon Artist Exbn., Nov. 1946; winner $300 prize award, Am. award Metropolitan Special Watercolor Exhibit, 1952. Permanent Collections: Whitney Mus. Am. Art, Am. Acad. Arts and Letters, Bklyn. Mus., Toledo Mus. Art, Joslyn Art Museum, Omaha, Mus. of Fine Arts, Boston, Met. Mus. of Art, Mus. of Modern Art, N.Y.; U. Neb., Wadsworth Atheneum, Bloomington (Ill.) Art Assn. San Francisco Museum, Mills Coll. De Young Museum, Albert Bender Collection, Eleanor Roosevelt Collection, Chicago Art Inst., N.Y. State Teachers Coll., Springfield (Ill.) Art Assn., Cranbrook Acad. of Art, Butler Art Inst., Ft. Wayne Museum, Addison Gallery, U.S. Dept. of State, and many others. Served U.S. Army. Illustrator: The Bamboo Gate (Vanya Oakes), 1946; China's Story (Enid LaMonte Meadowcroft), 1946; Nightingale (Andersen), 1948; Johnny Hong in Chinatown (Clyde Robert Bulla), 1952, Caen's and Kingman's San Francisco (Herb Caen), 1964; City on the Golden Hill (Herb Caen), 1967. Painted title paintings for Flower Drum Song and 55 Days at Peking. Home: 21 W 58th St New York City NY 10019 Office: care Hammer Galleries 51 E 57th St New York City NY 10022

KINGMAN, EUGENE, museum ofcl.; b. Providence, Nov. 10, 1909; s. Eugene Allerton and Celia Arnold (Spicer) K.; B.A., Yale, 1932, B.F.A., 1935; D.F.A. (hon.), Creighton U., 1968; m. Mary Elizabeth Yelm, June 10, 1939; children—Mary Martha, Elizabeth Anne. Instr. mural painting R.I. Sch. Design, 1935-39; dir. Philbrook Art Center, Tulsa 1939-42; asst. dir. Joslyn Art Mus., Omaha, Neb., 1946-47, dir., 1947-69, also trustee; dir. exhibits and programs Tex. Tech. U. Mus., Lubbock, 1969—; works exhibited Nat. Park Service Exhibit, Paris Expn., 1931; executed mural Post Office, Hyattsville, Md., 1937, Kemmerer, Wyo., 1938, East Providence, R.I., 1939, N.Y. Times Bldg., N.Y.C., 1948; lithograph in permanent collection Library of Congress. U.S. del. Conf. Regional Museums, Schaffhausen, Switzerland, 1954; cons. on exhbns. Smithsonian Instn., 1957-58, 60-61. Mem. Neb. Arts Council, v.p., 1966—; mem. Gov.'s Mural Commn., 1949—; mem. Gov. Neb. Hall of Fame Commn., Omaha, 1968—; bd. regents Coll. of St. Mary, Omaha, 1968-69. Recipient 1st prize graphic art Okla. Artists Ann., 1940; 1st purchase prize in painting Mulvane Art Mus. Ann. Exhbn., Topeka, Kan., 1951; 1st prize; mems. exhbn., Providence Art Club, 1956; Myrtle award Hadassah, 1965; KMTV television, 1968, many others. Mem. Am. Assn. Museums, A. Assn. Art Mus. Dirs. (v.p. 1967-68), Audubon Artists Group N.Y., Asso. Artists Omaha. Clubs: Professional men's of Omaha (pres. 1951); Providence Art. Home: 3714 68th St Lubbock TX 79413 Office: Mus Tex Tech U Lubbock TX

KINGMAN, HARRY ELLIS, Jr., veterinarian, assn. exec.; b. Ft. Collins, Colo., Sept. 4, 1911; s. Harry Ellis and Edna E. (Garbutt) K.; D.V.M., Colo. State U., 1933; m. Helen P. Allen, Aug. 3, 1936; 1 dau., Kay Allene. With Dept. Agr., 1934- 39; chief vet. Wilson & Co., Inc., 1939-53; dir. profl. relations Am. Vet. Med. Assn., 1953-58, treas., 1952-58, exec. sec., 1958-66; exec. dir. Nat. Soc. Med. Research, 1966—; pres. Livestock Conservation, Inc., 1960-62, Livestock adv. com. Dept. Agr., 1955-62; mem. nat. food and drug council FDA. Mem. Phi Delta Theta. Club: University (Chgo.). Home: 6171 Leesburg Pike Falls Church VA 22047 Office: 1330 Massachusetts Av Washington DC 20005

KINGMAN, HENRY SELDEN, Jr., banker; b. Mpls., Feb. 23, 1922; s. Henry Selden and Josephine (Woodward) K.; B.A., Amherst Coll., 1943; m. Marilyn Eastman, Apr. 26, 1947; children—Katharine, Sally, David, Woodward. With Gen. Mills, 1946-57; pres. Farmers & Mechanics Savs. Bank, Mpls., 1969—. Office: 90 S 6th St Minneapolis MN 55402

KINGMAN, JOSEPH RANSDELL, III, banker; b. Mpls., Dec. 8, 1927; s. Joseph R. and Margaret (Morris) K.; B.A., Amherst Coll., 1949; m. Polly Penney, Sept. 26, 1951; children—J. Brantley, Kate Perry. Asst. v.p. 1st Nat. Bank Mpls., 1950-62; with Imperial Financial Sers., Inc., Mpls., 1962-69, v.p., sr. marketing officer, 1967-69; sr. v.p. 1st Nat. Bank Mpls., 1969—; dir. Shedd Brown, Inc. Mem. Minn. Republican Central Com., 1961—, treas. finance com., 1961—. Bd. dirs. YMCA, Minn. Theatre Found., Nat. Jewish Hosp., Denver. Served with U.S. Army, 1950-52. Club: Minneapolis. Home: Route 7 Box 314 Wayzata MN 55391 Office: PO Box 512 Minneapolis MN 55440

KINGMAN, WILLIAM LOCKWOOD, financial cons.; b. Medford, Mass., Aug. 21, 1930; s. Henry Eugene and Helen Elizabeth (Crandell) K.; grad. Middlesex Sch., Concord, Mass., 1949; B.A. in Econs., Yale, 1953; m. Nancy Barbara Dean, Mar. 27, 1954; children—Lawrence Eugene, Celena Elizabeth. With Franklin Mgmt. Corp., Boston, 1956—, v.p., 1960-66, exec. v.p., 1966-68, vice chmn., 1968-71, chmn., 1971—, also dir.; with Franklin Mgmt. Corp., N.Y.C., 1959-71, v.p., dir., 1960-71; corporator Middlesex Instn. Savs., 1959—, trustee, 1961—; trustee New Eng. Fund (now Sigma Trust), 1961—; dir. Archtl. Ceiling, Inc., 1959-62, Sigma Capital, 1969—. Mem. Acton Republican Com. Mem. corp. Emerson Hosp., Concord, Mass., 1960—, Trustee, 1961—; treas. The Fenn Sch., Concord, Mass. Served to lt. (j.g.) USNR, 1953-56; lt. (s.g.) Res. Mem. Navy League U.S. Clubs: Down Town, Union (Boston); Cumberland (Portland, Me.); Concord Country. Home: 65 Esterbrook Rd RFD 1 Acton MA 01720 Office: 10 Post Office Sq Boston MA 02109

KINGMAN, WOODWARD, govt. ofcl.; b. Mpls., Sept. 5, 1925; s. Henry Selden and Josephine (Woodward) K.; B.A. cum laude, Amherst Coll., 1949; M.B.A., Harvard, 1951. Budget analyst Cowles Mags., Inc., N.Y.C., 1951-56; loan officer First Nat. City Bank, N.Y.C., 1956-66; asst. to exec. v.p. finance Internat. Tel. & Tel. Corp., 1967-69; dep. asst. sec. for housing prodn. and mortgage credit, pres. Govt. Nat. Mortgage Assn., dep. commr. FHA, Dept. Housing and Urban Devel., Washington, 1969—. Research asst. N.Y. State Joint Legislative Com. on Housing and Urban Devel., 1964. Pres. N.Y. Young Republican Club, 1955-56; mem. City Council, N.Y.C., 1966. Pres. Forest Neighborhood House, N.Y.C., 1968-69; pres., bd. dirs. Louis Braille Found. for Blind Musicians, N.Y.C., 1967-69. Served to 2d lt., inf., AUS, 1943-46. Conglist. Clubs: Knickerbocker, Racquet and Tennis, American Alpine, Harvard, (N.Y.C.). Home: 2715 Dumbarton Av Washington DC 20007 Office: Dept Housing and Urban Devel 451 7th St SW Washington DC 20410

KINGREY, BURNELL WAYNE, coll. dean; b. Worthington, Minn., Sept. 12, 1912; s. Harold Raymond and Iva (Goodrich) K.; A.A., Worthington Jr. Coll., 1941; D.V.M., Ia. State U., 1944, M.S., 1955; m. Patricia Abbott, June 3, 1945; children—Michael, Jean, Karel. Pvt. practice vet. medicine, Lena, Ill., 1944-53; faculty Ia. State U., 1953-63, prof., head dept. vet. medicine and surgery, 1955-63, dir. clinics Vet. Research Council, 1958-63; dean Sch. of Veterinary medicine, U. Mo., 1963—. Mem. Lena Sch. Bd., 1952- 63. ICA cons. to Argentina and Chile, 1961: Agy. Internat. Devel. cons. to San Carlos U., Guatemala, 1962, India, 1968. Mem. A.A.A.S., Am. Pub. Health Assn., Am. Ia., Central Ia. vet. med. assns., Am. Assn. Vet. Clincians, Am. Acad. Sci., Am. Legion, Phi Kappa Phi, Delta Psi Omega. Gamma Sigma Delta, Phi Beta, Sigma Xi. Rotarian, Mason. Home: 104 S Ann St Columbia MO 65201

KINGSBURY, FREDERICK HUTCHINSON, Jr., banker; b. Scranton, Pa., May 21, 1907; s. Frederick H. and Hope (MacIntosh) K.; student The Hill Sch., 1923-25; A.B., Princeton, 1929; m. Charlotte Meyer Beresford, Apr. 27, 1934 (div. May 1962); children—Hope MacIntosh (Mrs. Kent Ransom Costikyan, Jr.), Frederick H. III; m. 2d, Eleanor Bried O'Donnell, Oct. 3, 1962. With Brown Bros. Harriman & Co., 1929—, partner, 1949—; mem. bd. dirs. Providentia Ltd.; chmn. bd. Prudential Ins. Co. Gt. Britain (N.Y.), Hudson Ins. Co.; dir. Interpace Corp., Bangor Punta Corp.; chmn. U.S. exec. com. Skandia Ins. Co., Stockholm; dir. Instoria, Inc., Fleming- Suez Brown Bros. Ltd., London. Mem. alumni council Princeton, 1949-54. Decorated Officer Order Orange-Nassau (Netherlands). Mem. Netherlands C. of C. in U.S., Inc. (dir.). Clubs: University, Links (N.Y.C.); University Cottage (Princeton): Montclair (N.J.) Golf; Pine Valley Golf (Clementon, N.J.); Blooming Grove Hunting and Fishing (Hawley, Pa.); India House (N.Y.C.). Presbyn. (trustee). Home: 655 Park Av New York City NY 10021 Office: 59 Wall St New York City NY 10005

KINGSBURY, GILBERT WILLIAM, Sr., assn. exec.; b. Covington, Ky., Apr. 27, 1909 s. William P. and Naoma (Runge) K.; A.B. in Econs., U. Ky., 1933; m. Sylvia Irene Phillips, Nov. 21, 1936; 1 son, Gilber William. Reporter, asst. city editor Ky Post, 1933-39; asst. dean U. Cin., 1939-41; adminstrv. asst. Senators G. Withers, Earle Clements, 1949-51; news editor Crosley Broadcasting Corp., 1941-45, Washington corr., 1945-49, dir., v.p., 1951—; v.p. Star-Fed. Bldg. & Loan; asst. v.p. (U. Ky., Lexington); exec. v.p. Ohio Valley Improvement Assn., Cons. Ky. Turnpike Authority; dep. hwy. commnr. Ky. Past pres. Covington YMCA. Mem. Ky. Ho. Reps., 1958-60. Bd. dirs. Greater Cin. chpt. A.R.C., Dan Beard council Boy Scouts Am., Blue Ridge Assembly; adv. bd. St. Elizabeth Hosp., Covington, Ky.; bd. trustees, mem. exec. com. U. Ky. Recipient Award of Merit, Am. Pub. Relations Assn., 1953-55. Mem. Radio Corrs. Assn., Christopher Gist Hist. Soc. (past pres.), U.S. Savs. and Loan League, Ky. Council Chs. (exec. com.) Democrat. Mem. Ch. of Christ. Clubs: Nat. Press; Optimist, Ft Mitchell Country. Home: 210 Edgwood Rd Fort Mitchell KY 41017 Office: 4017 Carew Tower Cincinnati OH 45202

KINGSBURY, JAMES MARTIN, investment banker; b. Paterson, N.J., May 25, 1934; s. Oliver Addison and Margaret (Smith) K.; B.S., Yale, 1956; M.B.A., N.Y.U., 1965; m. Marguerite Snow MacPherson, Sept. 30, 1961; children—Anne Howard, Heather Snow, James Merwin. With Dominick & Dominick, Inc., N.Y.C., 1959-70, v.p., 1966-70; partner Edwards & Hanly, 1970—; pres. Air Lease Arroyo, N.Y.C., 1967—. Mem. exec. com. Class 1956, Yale, 1961—. Trustee, treas. L.I. Coll. Hosp., 1965- -. Served to lt. USNR, 1956-59. Mem. Investment Assn. N.Y. (bd. dirs. 1966-68; pres. 1968), Kappa Beta Phi. Clubs: Bond, Lunch (N.Y.C.); Fox Meadows Tennis (Scarsdale, N.Y.); Montauk, Heights Casino (Bklyn.); Point O'Wood Assn. (Fire Island, N.Y.). Home: 228 Lincoln Pl Brooklyn NY 11217 Office: One Whitehall St New York City NY 10004

KINGSBURY-SMITH, JOSEPH, journalist; b. N.Y.C., Feb. 20, 1908; s. William Barstow and Maria (Jordan) S.; educated privately and at St Francis Xavier, N.Y.C., 1918, St. Joseph's Sch., 1923, Friend's Prep. Sch., Poughkeepsie, N.Y., 1926, U. London, 1928; m. Eileen King, July 20, 1940; children—Eileen Jordan, Diane. Copy boy, cub reporter, Internat. News Service, 1924-26; fgn. cable desk, United Press, 1926-27; reporter London Bur., Internat. News Service, 1927-31, covered U.S. Senate, 1931- 32, State, War, Navy Depts. 1932-36, mgr. London Bur., 1936, exec. asst. dir. fgn. service, 1940, State Dept., 1941-44; became European gen. mgr. Internat. News Service and Internat. News Photos; v.p., dir. Hearst Corp., gen. mgr. Internat. News Service, Internat. News Photos, 1955-58, now v.p., European dir. Hearst Corp., chief fgn. writer Hearst Newspapers and King Features Syndicate, 1966—; became v.p., dir. Hearst Consol. Pubs., Inc., 1958; pub. N.Y. Jour.-Am. Trustee Fordham U., Hearst Estate. Recipient George R. Holmes Meml. award, 1941-49, Nat. Headliners' Club award, 1941, 47, 50; Sigma Delta Chi Distinguished Service award, 1949; L.I.U. George Polk award, 1950; Chevalier Legion of Honor, 1950; Pulitzer prize for distinguished internat. reporting, 1956; Knight of Malta; knight comdr. Order St. Denis of Zante; U.S. Govt.'s Distinguished Service award, 1961. Club: Brook. Home: Via Dei Foraggi 88-A Rome Italy

KINGSLEY, DANIEL THAIN, govt. ofcl.; b. Portland, Ore., Oct. 1, 1932; s. George Archibald and Jane (Powers) K.; grad. Phillips Acad., 1950; A.B. cum laude, Princeton, 1954; m. Eleanor Lamar Bate, Jan. 26, 1955; children—Daniel Thain, Blake, Christopher, Elizabeth. Sales mgr. Kingsley Lumber Co., Portland, 1959-62, pres., 1962-68; commr. Gen. Services Adminstrn., Washington, 1969-71; spl. asst. to Pres., White House Offfice, Exec. Office of Pres., 1971—. Vice pres. Parry Center for Children, Portland, 1966—68. Trustee Bishop Dagwell Hall, Episcopal Boys Sch., Portland. Served with AUS, 1954-56. Republican. Episcopalian. Clubs: Multnomah Athletic (trustee), Racquet (Portland); Bethesda (Md.) Country. Home: 8000 Herb Farm Dr Bethesda MD 20034 Office: White House Washington DC*

KINGSLEY, FRANCIS GERARD, mcht.; b. St. Albans, Vt., Oct. 31, 1895; s. Edward C. and Mary E. Kingsley; A.B., Syracuse U., 1919; student London Sch. Econs., Eng., 1919-20; m. Ora Rimes, Jan. 6, 1925; 1 dau., Ora. Jr. officer, fgn. service, Nat. City Bank, N.Y.C., 1920-25; buyer, John Wanamaker, N.Y., 1925-32; v.p. Mercantile Stores, Inc., N.Y.C., 1932-34, pres., 1934-41, chmn. bd., 1941-60, chmn. exec. com., 1960—; pres., dir. King Mill Oil Co., D.M. Trucking Co., Excelsior Housing Corp., Johnston Housing Corp., McCormick Housing Corp.; v.p. Milliken Inc.; dir. Grace Petroleum Corp., W. R. Grace & Co., Lockhart R.R. Co., Pacolet Mfg. Co., Drayton Mills, Laurens Mills. Mem. New Eng. Soc. Clubs: India House, Union League, University (N.Y.C.); New Canaan Country; Lake Placid (N.Y.) Skating. Home: Canoe Hill Rd New Canaan CT 06840 Office: 1045 6th Av New York City NY 10009

KINGSLEY, JOHN DONALD, orgn. exec.; b. Cambridge, N.Y., Mar. 25, 1908; s. John Henry and Carolyn (Donaldson) K.; A.B., Syracuse U., 1929, M.A., Maxwell Grad. Sch. of Pub. Affairs, 1930, Ph.D., 1933; grad. work London Sch. of Economics, U. London, 1936-38; LL.D., U. Louisville, 1950; m. Alice W. Boyd, June 1930 (div.); 1 dau., Jennifer Anne; m. 2d, Ruth Caplan, June 1946; children—Peter, Christine. Began career as instr. of government Antioch Coll., 1933-35, post doctoral European fellow Social Science Research Council, 1936-38; prof. govt. Antioch Coll., 1938-42; dir. Middle East and Africa, The Ford Found., 1963—, spl. rep. for Middle East Affairs, 1968—. Asst. regional dir. War Manpower Commn., 1942-44. dep. exec. dir., 1944-45; dep. dir. Office of War Mobilization, 1945-46; program coordinator The White House Office, 1946-47; exec. sec. President's Sci. Research Bd., 1946-47; White House liaison President's Commn. on Higher Edn., 1946-47; prin. chief of sections Internat. Labor Office, Geneva, Switzerland, 1947-48; chief of mission to Greece, 1947; asst. Fed. Security Adminstr., 1948-49, dir. gen. Internat. Refugee Orgn., 1949-51; U.N. agt. gen. Korean reconstruction, 1951-53; adminstr., trustee Paris Refugee Reparations Fund 1949-57; exec. dir. Community Council of Greater N.Y., 1953-59. Mem. U.S. delegation to U.N. Econ. and Social Council, 1948. Mem. Nat. Conf. Christians and Jews (dir.), Nat. Health and Welfare Retirement Assn., Tolstoy Found. dir.), Brit. Inst. Pub. Adminstrn., American Polit. Science Assn., Phi Beta Kappa. Democrat. Author: (with W.E. Mosher) Public Personnel Administration, 1936, 2d edit., 1940; Representative Bureaucracy, 1942. Home: 611 Lake Av Greenwich CT 06830 Office: P O Box 2379 Beirut Lebanon

KINGSLEY, JOHN M., business exec.; b. Riverdale, N.Y., Feb. 28, 1903; s. Darwin P. and Josephine (McCall) K.; A.B., Yale, 1925; M.B.A., Harvard, 1928; m. Elizabeth Curry, Nov. 26, 1930; children—John M., Elizabeth C. With Nat. City Bank, 1930-36; with Henry Phipps Estates since 1939; pres., Ressemer Trust Co., Ressemer Securities Corp.; dir. Am. Smelting & Refining Co., Internat. Paper Co., Am. Natural Gas Co. Clubs: River (N.Y.C.); Round Hill (Greenwich, Conn.). Home: 599 Round Hill Rd Greenwich CT 06830

KINGSLEY, JOHN MCCALL, Jr., food co. exec.; b. Berlin, Germany, Dec. 1, 1931; s. John McCall and Elizabeth (Curry) K.; B.A., Yale, 1953; M.B.A., Harvard, 1955; C.P.A., N.Y., 1961; m. Ines Hinckeldeyn, 1967; children—John M. III, Kate Alexandra. Sr. staff accountant Price Waterhouse & Co., C.P.A.'s, N.Y.C., 1957-62; asso. Dillon, Read & Co., Inc., N.Y.C., 1962-65; v.p. finance Gen. Host Corp., N.Y.C., 1966-69; v.p. corporate finance F.S. Smithers & Co., Inc., 1970-71; exec. v.p. Sturm, Ruger & Co., Inc., 1971—. Served with AUS, 1955-57. Mem. Am. Inst. C.P.A.'s, N.Y. State Soc., C.P.A.'s. Republican. Episcopalian. Clubs: University (N.Y.C.); Round Hill (Greenwich, Conn.). Home: Will Merry Lane Greenwich CT 06830 Office: Lacey Pl Southport CT 06490

KINGSLEY, JOSEPH THEODORE, Jr., air force officer; b. Pitts., May 4, 1916; s. Joseph Theodore Amos (Tumlin) K.; B.A., U.S. Mil. Acad., 1939; grad. Flying Sch., Randolph AFB, Tex., 1940, Indsl. Coll. Armed Forces, 1956; grad. Advanced Mgmt. Program, Harvard, 1957; m. Jane Gray, Aug. 26, 1942; children—Joseph Theodore III, Gail Gray. Commd. 2d lt. AUS, 1939, advanced through grades to maj. gen. USAF, 1963; mem. B-17 patrol with anti-submarine operations, Atlantic, 1942-43; assigned Guam, Tinian and Okinawa, 1944-46, War Dept. Gen. Staff, 1497-49, U.S. Munitions Bd., 1949-51, Ankara, Turkey, 1951-53; chief staff Air Material Comnand, 1957-60; assigned legislative liaison Hdqrs. USAF, 1960-61, U.S. Fgn. Aid program, 1961-63; spl. asst. mil. assistance affairs Joint Chief Staff, 1963-65; v.p. Loving Helicopter Co., Silver Springs, 1965-67; chief tech. asst. div. Office Internat. Aviation Affairs, Fed. Aviation Adminstrn., 1968—. Mem. Inter-Am. Def. Bd., 1962-63, Mexican Commn., 1962-63, Joint Brazil Mil. Commn., 1962-63. Pres. Chantilly Small Loan Co., Herndon, Va., 1960-65. Decorated Legion of Merit, Bronze Star; Medal of Stars (Chile). Mem. Nat. Aeros. Assn. Mason (32, Shriner, Jester). Clubs: Columbia Country (officer, bd. dirs.) (Chevy Chase, Md.); Army-Navy. Home: 1421 29th St NW Washington DC 20007 Office: Fed Aviation Adminstrn Washington DC 20590

KINGSLEY, ROBERT, judge; b. Cedar Falls, Ia., Oct. 8, 1903; s. Frank Amos and Angeline (Van Niman) K.; A.B., U. Minn., 1923, A.M., 1923, LL.B., 1926; S.J.D., Harvard, 1928; m. Doris Field Forbes-Manson, June 12, 1937. Admitted to Minn. Bar, 1926, Cal. bar, 1934; instr. law U. Minn., 1926-27; Thayer teaching fellow sch. law, Harvard, 1927-28; asst. prof. law U. So. Cal., 1928-30, prof. law, 1930-63, vice dean sch. law, 1947-51, asso. dean, 1951-52, dean, 1952-63; vis. prof. law U. Chgo., 1930, U. N.C., 1955, Hastings Coll. Law, 1956; vis. lectr. U. Witwatersrand, Cape Town, South Africa, 1958; justice Cal. Dist. Ct. of Appeal, 2d Appellate dist., Div. 4, 1963—. Mem. Am., Los Angeles County bar assns., Los Angeles Civic Light Opera Assn. (sec.), Order of Coif, Phi Beta Kappa, Delta Sigma Rho, Delta Theta Phi. Clubs: National Lawyers (Washington); University (Los Angeles). Home: 236 S Citrus Av Los Angeles CA 90036 Office: 217 W 1st St Los Angeles CA 90012

KINGSLEY, ROBERT IRVING, lawyer; b. Pittsburgh, Aug. 2, 1925; s. Silas E., Jr. and Sara C. (Scott) K.; B.S. with honors, U. Pitts., 1949, LL.B. (Samuel T. Owens fellow), 1952; m. Mary M. Reilly, Feb. 14, 1948 (div. 1965); children—Richard, Barbara Patricia, Brian, Robert; m. 2d, Mary Ricks, July 30, 1966; dau., Sara. Land and tax agt. Jones & Laughlin Steel Co., 1952-54; admitted to Pa. bar, 1953; tax atty. Pitts. Plate Glass Co., 1954-57; with Crucible Steel Co. Am., 1957-66, sec., 1963-66, gen. counsel, 1965-66; admitted to the Texas bar, 1967; mem. of the law firm Keeney and Miller, attys., Texarkana, Texas, 1967-71; with law dept. Dresser Industries Inc., 1971—. Pres. Whitehall (Pa.) Pub. Library, 1962-63, bd. dirs., 1962—. Served with USNR, 1942-46; PTO. Mem. Am., Allegheny County bar assns., Am. Soc. Corp. Secretaries Am. Iron and Steel Inst., Omicron Delta Kappa, Sigma Chi, Delta Theta Phi. Club: University (Pitts.). Home: 9216 Northpoint Dr Dallas TX 75238 Office: Republic Nat Bank Bldg Dallas TX 75201

KINGSLEY, SIDNEY, playwright; b. N.Y.C., Oct. 22, 1906; s. Dr. Robert and Sonia (Kirshner) K.; student Townsend Harris Hall, 1920-24; B.A., Cornell, 1928; m. Madge Evans, July 25, 1939. Author: (plays) Men in White, 1934, The Patriots, 1943; author, dir.; (plays) Dead End, 1936, Ten Million Ghosts, 1937, The World We Make, 1939, Detective Story, 1949, Darkness at Noon, 1951, Lunatics and Lovers, 1954; Night Life, 1962. Awarded Pulitzer prize for best American play, 1934; Theater Club medal for best play, 1934, 36, 43; Drama Critics Circle award for best play, 1943, 51; N.Y. Newspaper Guild front page award, 1943, Page One Citation, 1949; Federated Women's Club award, Cath. Dial award, 1943; Edgar Allen Poe award for play, film, 1949; Donaldson award for outstanding achievement in theater, Am. Acad. Arts and Letters award of merit medal for outstanding drama, 1951.*

KINGSLEY, THOMAS DROWNE, economist; b. Rutland, Vt., Oct. 12, 1916; s. Percy Morgan and Fanny (Drowne) K.; grad. Mercersburg Acad., 1936; A.B., Yale, 1940; student Fletcher Sch. Law and Diplomacy, 1940-41, Universidad Nacional De Buenos Aires (Argentina), 1942, Grad. Sch. Pub. Adminstrn., Harvard, 1955-56; m. Martha Bush Clark, Nov. 8, 1943; children—Martha Clark (Mrs. Goshen), Mary Lee. Joined U.S. Fgn. Service, 1943; assigned successively Montevideo, Uruguay, Caracas, Venezuela, Asuncion, Paraguay, Dusseldorf, Germany, 1943-55; staff Operations Coordinating Bd., Exec. Office Pres., Washington, 1956-58; 1st sec. embassy, Lisbon, Portugal, 1958-62; chief air transport relations, Aviation Div., Dept. of State, 1962-63, chief econ. affairs Office Brazil Affairs, 1963-66; chief econ. affairs and consul Am. Consulate Gen., Sao Paulo, Brazil, 1966-69; sr. economist for Latin Am., Export-Import Bank of U.S., Washington, 1969—. Mem. Am. Fgn. Service Assn., Diplomatic and Consular Officers Ret. Clubs: Harvard, Yale (Washington). Home: 5105 Battery Lane Bethesda MD 20014 Office: 811 Vermont Av Washington DC 20005

KINGSLEY, WALTER INGALLS, TV exec.; b. N.Y.C., Oct. 20, 1923; s. Samuel and Esther (Schenker) K.; grad. Phillips Andover Acad., 1942; B.A., Amherst Coll., 1947; m. Betty Jane Bower, Oct. 14, 1944; children—Samuel John, James Oliver, Thomas Andrew; m. 2d, Patricia Ann Ratchford, Apr. 1, 1966; 1 dau., Janis Susan. Salees exec. Cowles Broadcasting Co., Boston, 1948-50; gen. sales mgr. United Artists, N.Y.C. and Los Angeles, 1950-58; pres. Independent Television Corp., N.Y.C., 1958-61; v.p. Metromedia Producers Corp. div. Metromedia, N.Y.C., 1966—; faculty Interracial Council for Bus. Opportunity, N.Y.C. Co-founder Big Bros. Greater Los Angeles, 1955; v.p., bd. dirs. Big Bros. Am. Served with AUS, 1943-46. Home: 400 E 56th St New York City NY 10022 Office: 485 Lexington Av New York City NY 10017

KINGSNORTH, NEIL GEORGE, ret. can co. exec.; b. Grand Rapids, Mich., July 28, 1907; s. John Billings and Margarite (Fortuin) K.; student U. Chgo., 1923-24; B.S. in Mech. Engring., U. Ill., 1930; m. Louise Harlow Thompson, Jan. 14, 1939; children—Susan Louise, Robert Craig. Mech. engr. Ingersoll-Rand Co., 1930-31; with Dixie Cup Co., 1931-57, v.p., 1955-58; v.p. mfr. Dixie Cup div. Am. Can Co., 1957-60, v.p., gen. mgr. milk container div., 1960-66. Mem. phys. fitness council Greenwich YMCA, 1967—. Bd. dirs. Ft. Smith (Ark.) chpt. A.R.C., 1952-55, Easton (Pa.) chpt., 1959-60; bd. dirs. Ft. Smith Boys Club, 1949-55, v.p., 1953-54; bd. dirs. Ft. Smith Community Chest, 1953-54, chmn. fund drive, 1954; bd. curators Stephens Coll., Columbia, Mo., 1962—. Served to lt. col. AUS, 1942-46; PTO. Decorated Air medal, Bronze Star. Registered profl. engr., Ill. Mem. Am. Mgmt. Assn. (mem. mfg. div. planning council 1964-69). Presbyn. (ruling elder). Club: Union League (N.Y.C.). Home: 18 Terrace West Woodbury CT 06798

KINIERY, GLADYS, govt. ofcl.; b. Footville, Wis., Nov. 14, 1904; d. William J. and Julia (Murphy) Kiniery; R.N., Mercy Hosp. Sch. Nursing, Janesville, Wis., 1925; Ph.B., Loyola U., Chicago, 1936; M.S. in Pub. Health, U. of Mich., 1940, In pvt. practice and gen. staff nursing, Madison, Wis., 1925-29; head nurse, supervisor, Cook County Hosp., Chicago, 1930-36, supervisor U. of Chicago Clinics, Chicago Lying-In Hosp., 1936-38, supervisor. Max Epstein Clinics, 4939-41; staff nurse, Branch County health dept., W.K. Kellogg Foundn., Battle Creek, Mich., 1941-43; instr. coll. nursing Wayne Univ., 1943-44, asst. prof. of nursing, 1944-45; supervisor Detroit Visiting Nurse Assn., 1945-47; dean School of Nursing, Loyola U., Chgo., 1947-66; chief program rev. unit div. nursing USPHS, Dept. Health, Edn. and Welfare, Arlington, Va., 1966—. Pres. Detroit Dist. Mich. State Nurses Assn., 1946-47. Mem. Am. Nurses Assn., Nat. League for Nursing, Washington Nurses Assn., Alpha Tau Delta, Sigma Theta Tau. Home: 1701 N Kent St Arlington VA 22209 Office: Div Nursing USPHS Dept Health Edn and Welfare 900 Rockville Pike Bethesda MD 20014

KINIERY, PAUL, coll. prof.; b. Footville, Wis., Jan. 15, 1900; s. William John and Julia (Murphy) K.; A.B., St. Francis (Wis.) Sem., 1924; A.M., U. of Wis., 1926; Ph.D., 1930; unmarried. with Loyola U., 1929—, asst. prof. history, 1929-31, prof. hist., 1935-70, emeritus, 1970—. Mem. Am. Hist. Assn., Am. Assn. Univ. Profs., Am. Catholic Hist. Assn. K.C. Home: 1211 N La Salle St Chicago IL 60610

KINIGSTEIN, JONAH, painter; b. N.Y.C., June 26, 1923; s. Jacob and Yetta (Zelman) K.; student Cooper Union Art Sch., 1941-43, La Grande Chaumiere, Paris, France, 1947-51, Belle Arte, Rome, Italy, 1953-54; m. Barbara Stein, May 17, 1952; children—Noah, Lisa. One man shows include Les Impressions D'Art, Paris, 1948; Galleries Breteau, Paris, 1950, Alan Gallery, N.Y.C., 1954, 55, Stembab Gallery, Boston, 1959, Werbin Gallery, Detroit, 1957, ACA Gallery, N.Y., 1959, Grippi Gallery, New York City, 1962, Kinematic art at Nordness Gallery, 1964; group shows include Salon d'Automn, Paris, 1949, 50, Salon De Mai, Paris, 1949-50, Salon de Moine de Trente, Paris, 1949, 50, Whitney Mus. Young Am. exhbn., 1957, Bklyn. Mus., 1956, Nat. Acad. Arts and Letters, 1958, Butler Art Inst., 1956; rep. premanent collections Whitney Mus., Mus. Modern Art, Albright Art Gallery, Butler Art Inst., Nelson Gallery Art, Washington Mus., Brandeis Coll., U. Ill., U. Ariz., Ain Herod Mus. in Tel Aviv, also pvt.

collections. Fulbright scholar, Italy, 1953-54; grantee Nat. Acad. Arts and Letters, 1958; recipient 2d prize Butler Art Inst., 1956, purchase prize U. Ill., 1959, Louis Comfort Tiffany Found. award, 1962; recipient 1st prize Silvermine Guild, 1959, Perkins-Elmer prize, 1962. Address: 134 2d Av New York City NY 10003

KINKAID, THOMAS CASSIN naval officer; b. Hanover, N.H., Apr. 3, 1888; s. Thomas Wright and Virginia Lee (Cassin) K.; grad. U.S. Naval Academy, 1908; m. Helen Sherburne Ross, Apr. 25, 1911. Promoted through grades to admiral. Tech. advisor to Am. del., Gen. Disarmament Conf., Geneva, Switzerland, Jan.- July 1932; naval attaché Am. Embassy, Rome (Italy), Nov. 1938-Mar. 1941; additional duty naval attaché Belgrade, Yugoslavia, 1939-41; promoted rear adm., 1941; now adm.; comd. cruiser group action off Bougainville, Feb. 20, 1942; Salamaua-Lae raid, Mar. 10, 1942; Battle of Coral Sea, May 4-8, 1942; Battle of Midway, June 3-6, 1942; comd. Enterprise carrier group, Guadalcanal-Tulagi landings, Aug. 7-9, 1942; battle of Eastern Solomons, Aug. 25, 1942, Santa Cruz Islands, Oct. 26, 1942; Guadalcanal, Nov. 15, 1942; comdr. North Pacific Force in Aleutian campaign, Jan.-Oct. 1943; promoted vice adm., June 1943; comdr. 7th Fleet, and comdr. Allied Naval Forces, Southwest Pacific Area, Nov. 1943- Sept. 1945, New Guinea and Philippine campaigns, including battle for Leyte Gulf, Oct. 25, 1944; promoted admiral, Apr. 1945; landed 24th Corps in Korea, Sept. 1945, and with Lt. Gen. Hodge, took surrender of Japanese Army and Navy in Seoul; landed Am. Marines under Maj. Gen. Rockey at Taku and at Tsingtao, China; transported 5 Chinese armies from Haiphong, Kowloon and Ningpo, landed them at Formosa, Chingwantao and Tsingtao; detached 7th Fleet Nov. 19, 1945; took comd. Eastern Sea Frontier and Atlantic Res., Jan. 16, 1946; retired from active duty May 1, 1950. Vice chmn. Am. Battle Monuments Commn. Mem. Nat. Security Training Commn. Decorations: Navy D.S.M. with 3 gold stars, Army Legion of Merit, Army D.S.M. Presidential Citation, Victory Medal, Atlantic Clasp, American Defense Service Medal, Asiatic-Pacific Campaign Medal (10 battle stars), W.W. II Victory Medal; Companion Order of the Bath (British); Grand Officer Order Orange Nassau with Swords (Netherlands); Order Al Merito, Gran Oficial (Chilean); Grand Officer Order of Leopold with Palm, Croix de Guerre with Palm (Belgian). Mem. Soc. Cincinnatus in State N.H. Clubs: Chevy Chase, Army-Navy, Aibi (Washington), Union (N.Y.). Home: 2134 R St NW Washington DC 20008

KINNAIRD, CLARK, writer; b. Louisville, Ky., May 4, 1901; s. Charles Beck and Nellie (Wright) K.; m. Marian Gosnell, 1925; children—Kenneth, Laird. Employed on various papers and corr. in Europe, 1921-24; mng. editor (Central Press Assn., 1924-28; editor-pub. Edenton (N.C.) Daily News 1928-30; asso. editor King Features Syndicate, 1930-37, 1939-70; Your America Day-by-Day and Daybook Am., syndicated columns, 1949—. Broadcaster and book reviewer. Served with USN, 1918-19. Author: 500 Americans, 1939; War Comes to Us, 1942; The Real F.D.R., 1945; This Must Not Happen Again, 1945; It Happened in 1945, 1946; It Happened in 1946, 1947; The Last Defense (with J.H. Heinz and J. Iorgy), 1947; George Washington: The Pictorial Biography, 1967; Editor: Runyon Short Takes, 1947; Runyon Poems for Men, 1948; Runyon First and Last, 1949, A Treasury of Damon Runyon, 1959; First Century and Forward, 1966; Rube Goldberg vs. The Machine Age, 1968. Recipient awards from Freedoms Found., 1949, 50, 53, 62, Children Am. Revolution, 1960, Dept. Def., 1966, Am. Legion, 1968. Club: Dutch Treat (N.Y.C.). Home: 76 Mine St Flemington NJ 08822 Office: 235 E 45th St New York City NY 10017

KINNAIRD, LAWRENCE, educator; b. Williamstown, W.Va., July 9, 1893; s. John Asher and Virginia May (Hall) K.; A.B., U. Mich., 1915; postgrad. U. Grenoble, France, 1919; M.A., U. Cal., 1927, Ph.D., 1928; m. Lucia Fuller Burk, Aug. 3, 1929. Asst. and asso. prof. history San Francisco State Coll., 1932-36; asst. prof., U. Cal., Coll. Agr., 1936-37; asst. and asso. prof. history, U. Cal., 1937-48, prof. history, 1948-60; vis. prof. Chatham Coll., 1962-63, U. Cal. at Santa Barbara, 1960-62, 63-66. Acting dir. Bancroft Library, 1954-55. Served as 1st lt., U.S. Army, 1917-20 with Air Service. Cultural attaché, U.S. Embassy, Santiago, Chile, 1942-45; chmn. U.S. delegation to 4th Inter-Am. Congress Tchrs., Santiago, 1943. Mem. Alpha Sigma Phi. Editor and author: Spain in the Mississippi Valley, 1945; The Frontiers of New Spain, 1766-1768, 1958. Author: History of the Golden Gate (for Nat. Park Service), 1962; History of the Greater San Francisco Bay Region, 1966. Mem. bd. editors Pacific Hist. Rev., 1956-59. Contbr. to hist. pubs. Office: Dept History U California Berkeley CA 94720

KINNARD, HARRY WILLIAM OSBORN, aircraft com. exec., ret. army officer; b. Dallas, May 7, 1915; s. Harry William Osborn and Cynthia Anne (Peabody) K.; B.S., U.S. Mil. Acad., 1939; grad. Inf. Sch., 1942, Air Command and Staff Coll., 1949, Armed Forces Staff Coll., 1955, Army War Coll., 1956, Nat. War Coll., 1959; m. Mikelle Carey, Sept. 9, 1940; children—Bruce, Robert, Susan, Kathleen, Harry, Cynthia. Commd. 2d lt., inf., U.S. Army, 1939, advanced through grades to lt. gen., 1967; assigned U.S. and Hawaii, 1939-44; comdr. 1st Btn., 501st Parachute Regt., 1944; G-3, 101st Airborne Div., 1944-45; comdr. airborne test sect. Army Field Forces Bd., Ft. Bragg, N.C., 1946-49; tech. adviser motion picture Battleground, 1949; airborne mem. Officers Group I, Tripartite Standardization, 1950-52; instr. airborne operations, Staff Coll., 1952-55; comdr. 1st Airborne Battle Group, 501st Inf., 101st Airborne Div., Ft. Campbell, Ky., 1956-58; assigned Office Dep. Chief Staff Operations, 1958, Office Dep. Dir. Def. Research and Engring., Office Sec. Def., 1959-61; exec. to sec. of army, 1961-62; asst. div. comdr. 101st Airborne Div., Ft. Campbell, 1962-63; comdr. 11th Air Assault Div., Ft. Benning, 1963-65; comdr. 1st Cav. Div. Air Mobile, Ft. Benning and Vietnam, 1965-66; dep. asst. chief staff for force devel. Dept. Army, 1966-67; comdg. gen. Combat Devels. Command, 1969, ret., 1969; v.p. McCulloch Aircraft Corp., 1970—. Decorated D.S.C., Distinguished Service medal with two oak leaf clusters, Silver Star, Legion of Merit with oak leaf cluster, Bronze Star, Air medal with eight oak leaf clusters, Commendation ribbon with medal pendant, Purple Heart; Knight Mil. Order William (Netherlands); Officer Crown Order Leopold, Croix de Guerre with palm, Fourragere (Belgium); Croix de Guerre with palm (France); Orange Lanyard (Holland); Gallantry Cross with palm (Vietnam). Mem. Assn. Grads. U.S. Mil. Acad., 101st Airborne Div. Assn., Airborne Assn., Army Athletic Assn., Parachute Club Am., Assn. U.S. Army, Army Aviation Assn. (pres.), Am. Helicopter Assn., 1st Cav. Div. Assn. Roman Catholic. Home: 815 Arroyo Dr Prescott AZ 86301

KINNARD, JOHN GRISWOLD, banking exec; b. Mpls., June 10, 1911; s. Chester Haines and Agnes (Griswold) K.; student U. Minn., 1928-30; m. Betty Miller, Jan. 4, 1936; children—Sally Stevenson, John Griswold. Partner Kinnard, McLaughlin Accounting, 1936-39; investment analyst Investor Syndicate, 1939-44; chmn. bd. John G. Kinnard & Co., Inc., Mpls., Kinnard Cos. Inc.; past exec. v.p., dir. Craig-Hallum, Kinnard, Inc.; past pres., dir. Gen. Securities, Inc., Venture Fund, Inc., Kinnco., Inc.; dir. United Petroleum & Mining Corp.; lectr. Wharton Sch. Finance, 1963, St. John U. Exec. com. Midwest Stock Exchange. Mem. budget and distbn. com. United Fund; pres., chmn. finance com. Wells Meml. Inc.; mem. investment com. Childrens Hosp. Bd. dirs. Boys Club Mpls.; active local YMCA, Salvation Army, A.R.C. Mem. Nat. Security Traders Assn., Investment Bankers Assn., Nat. Assn. Security Dealers, Delta Upsilon. Clubs: Minikanda; Minneapolis; Wayzata; Twin City Bond; Automobile. Home: 325-D Narcissus Lane Wayzata MN 55391 Office: 740 Northstar Center Minneapolis MN 55402 also 110 S 7th St Minneapolis MN 55402

KINNARD, LEO DOUGLAS, army officer; b. Morristown, N.J., Sept. 13, 1921; s. Frederick Henry and Mary (Toomey) K.; B.S., U.S. Mil. Acad., 1944; M.S., Princeton, 1948; M.A., George Washington U., 1961; grad. Army War Coll., 1961; m. Wade Tyree, July 6, 1951; 1 son, Frederick Douglas. Commd. 2d lt. U.S. Army, 1944, advanced through grades to brig. gen., 1968; asst sec. Army Gen. Staff, 1957-59; spl. asst. chief staff to Supreme Hdqrs. Allied Powers, Europe, Paris, 1961-64; comdr. 24th Div. Arty., Germany, 1964-65; dir. communist Chinese studies Army War Coll., 1965-66; chief operation analysis U.S. Mil. Assistance Command, Vietnam, 1966-67; asst. or nuclear planning affairs Office Asst. Sec. Def., Washington, 1967-68; dir. plans, operations Continental U.S. Army, Command, 1968-69; comdg. gen. II Field Force Arty., Vietnam, 1969; chief off staff II Field Force, Vietnam, 1969-70; fellow dept. politics Princeton, cons. nat. security affairs. Decorated D.S.M., Legion Merit, D.F.C.; Nat. Order Vietnam 5th class with Gallantry Cross (Republic S. Vietnam), 1970. Mem. Am. Polit. Sci. Assn., Assn. Grads. U.S. Mil. Acad., Princeton Alumni Assn., Assn. U.S. Army. Club: Nassau (Princeton). Home: 364 Jefferson Rd Princeton NJ 08540

KINNARD, WILLIAM JAMES, Jr., univ. dean; b. Wilmington, Del., Apr. 18, 1932; s. William J. and Helen F. (Ossenkemper) K.; B.S., U. Pitts., 1953, M.S., 1955; Ph.D., Purdue U., 1957; m. Dolores F. Malia, July 18, 1959. From instr. to prof. U. Pitts., 1957-68; prof. pharmacology, dean Sch. Pharmacy, U. Md., 1968—. Fellow Am. Fed. Pharm. Edn., 1954-57; recipient Honors Achievement award Angiology Research Fedn., 1960-65. Mem. Am. Soc. Pharmacology and Exptl. Therapy, Am. Pharm. Assn., Am. Pub. Health Assn., Drug Information Assn., Acad. Pharm. Scis., Am. Acad. Clin. Toxicology, Sigma Xi, Rho Chi. Lutheran. Contbr. jours. in field. Home: 4000 N Charles St Baltimore MD 21218

KINNE, FRANCES BARTLETT, univ. dean; b. Story City, Ia., May 23, 1917; d. Charles Morton and Bertha (Olson) Bartlett; student edn. U. No. Ia., 1936; B. Mus. Edn., Drake U., 1940, M. Mus. Edn., 1944; Ph.D. cum laude, U. Frankfurt (Germany), 1957; m. Harry L. Kinne, Jr., June 24, 1948. Tchr. music Kelley (Ia.) Consol. Sch., 1936-37; music supr. Boxholm (Ia.) Consol. Sch., 1937-40, Des Moines pub. schs., 1940-43; sr. hostess Camp Crowder, Mo., 1943-46; recreation dir. VA, Wadsworth, Kan., 1946-48; lectr. music, English, also Western culture Tsuda Coll., Tokyo, Japan, 1949-50; music cons. U.S. Army Gen. Hdqrs., Tokyo, 1950-51; mem. faculty Jacksonville U., 1958—, prof. music and humanities, 1963—, also dean Coll. of Fine Arts, 1961—, Distinguished Univ. prof., 1961-62. Bd. dirs. Arts Force Mayor's Adv. Com., Delius Assn., Jacksonville Sesquicentennial Commn., Jacksonville Civic Music Assn., Jacksonville Art Mus., Jacksonville Council Arts, Jacksonville Symphony Assn., Jacksonville Symphony Women's Guild. Recipient hon. awards Bus. and Profl. Womens Clubs, 1962; Distinguished Service award, Drake U., 1966. Mem. Am. Assn. U. Women, Nat., Fla., Jacksonville music tchrs. assns., Music Educators Nat. Conf., Fla. Music Edn. Assn. (dir.), Friday Musicale, Fla. Coll. Music Edn. Assn. (past pres., v.p.), Delius Assn. of Fla., Fla. Council of Arts, Nat. Assn. Schs. Music, Civic Music Assn., Jacksonville C. of C. (dir., chmn. fine arts com.), Internat. Council Fine Arts Deans, Alpha Xi Delta, Mu Phi Epsilon; hon. mem. 3d Armored Div. Clubs: P.E.O.; St. John's; Women's Jacksonville. Author: A Comparative Study of British Traditional and American Indigenous Ballads, 1958; Dilemma of the Arts in Our Contemporary Society, 1962; Music, Moon and Man, 1970; also numerous papers and articles. Home: 5341 Selton Av Jacksonville FL 32211

KINNE, MORRIS Y., Jr., meat co. exec.; b. Webster City, Ia., Dec. 18, 1928; s. Morris T. and Gladys (Shirley) K.; student Ia. State U., 1947-49; B.A. in Gen. Sci., State U. Ia., 1955; J.D., 1958; m. Katherine Ann Spencer, June 6, 1957; children—Michael, Douglas, Cathryn, Patricia. Admitted to Ia. bar, 1958; mem. tax dept. Peat, Marwick, Mitchell & Co., C.P.A.'s, Des Moines, Ia. 1958-59; with law firm Dickinson, Throckmorton, Parker, Mannheimer & Raife, Des Moines, 1959-64; sec. Rath Packing Co., Waterloo, Ia., 1964—. Served with USAF, 1951-54. Mem. Am., Ia., Black Hawk County bar Assns., Am. Soc. Corp. Secretaries, Am. Meat Inst. Home: 2772 Crestline St Waterloo IA 50702 Office: P O Box 330 Waterloo IA 50703

KINNEAR, JAMES WESLEY, III, petroleum co. exec.; b. Pitts., Mar. 21, 1928; s. James Wesley and Susan (Jenkins) K.; B.S., U.S. Naval Acad., 1950; m. Mary Tullis, June 17, 1950; children—Robin Wood, Susan, James Wesley IV, William M. With Texaco, Inc., 1954—, mgr., Hawaii, 1959-63, div. sales mgr., Los Angeles, 1963-64, asst. to vice chmn. bd., N.Y.C., 1964-65, asst. to chmn. bd., gen. mgr. marine dept., 1965, v.p. supply and distbn., 1966-70, sr. v.p., 1970—; dir. Caltex Petroleum Corp., Jefferson Chem. Co., Tex.-U.S. Chem. Co. Served to lt. (j.g.) USNR, 1950-54. Mem. U.S. Naval Inst. Episcopalian. Home: Clubs: Round Hill; Verbank Hunting; Iron City Fishing. Home: Taconic Rd Greenwich CT 06830 Office: 135 E 42d St New York City NY 10017

KINNEARY, JOSEPH PETER, U.S. judge; b. Cin., Sept. 19, 1905; s. Joseph and Anne (Mulvihill) K.; B.A., U. Notre Dame, 1928; LL.B., U. Cin., 1935; m. Byrnece Camille Rogers, June 26, 1950. Admitted to Ohio bar, 1935; U.S. Supreme Ct., 1960; pvt. practice in Cin. and Columbus, 1935-61; asst. atty. gen. Ohio, 1937-39, 1st asst. atty. gen., 1949-51, spl. counsel to atty. gen., 1959-61; U.S. atty. So Dist. Ohio, 1961-66; judge U.S. Dist. Ct., So. Dist. Ohio, 1966—; lectr. law trusts Coll. Law, U. Cin., 1948. Delegate Democratic Nat. Conv., 1952. Served to capt. AUS, World War II. Decorated Army Commendation ribbon. Mem. Phi Delta Phi. Roman Catholic. Home: 2208 Arlington Av Columbus OH 43221 Office: 85 Marconi Blvd Columbus OH 43216

KINNELL, GALWAY, writer; b. Providence, Feb. 1, 1927; s. James Scot and Elizabeth (Mills) K.; A.B., Princeton, 1948; M.A., U. Rochester, 1949; children—Maud Natasha, Fergus. Guggenheim fellow, 1963-64; recipient award Nat. Inst. Arts and Letters, 1962, Longview Found. award, 1962, Rockefeller Found. grant, 1968, Amy Lowell traveling scholarship, 1969, Cecil Hemley poetry prize, 1969, Brandeis U. creative arts award, 1969. Author: (poems) What a Kingdom It Was, 1960; Flower Herding on Mount Monadnock, 1964; (translation) The Poems of Francois Villon, 1965; Black Light (novel), 1966; (poems) Body Rags, 1968; (translation) On The Motion and Immobility of Douve, 1968; (translation) The Lackawanna Elegy, 1970; (poems) First Poems, 1971; (poems) The Book of Nightmares, 1971. Address: Sheffield VT 05866

KINNEY, ANDREW JOHN, Air Force officer; b. Macon, Ga., Sept. 19, 1914; s. Emory Jackson and Mayme (Andrew) K.; S.B., U.S. Mil. Acad., 1939; grad. Army War Coll., 1946, Air War Coll., 1953; m. Lois Lang, Sept. 6, 1939; children—Lois Andrea, Jackson Lang; m. 2d, Joyce Fox, Feb. 9, 1953; children—Diaane Fox, Andrew John. Commd. 2d lt. U.S. Army, 1939, trans. Air Force, 1940, advanced through grades to maj. gen., 1963; comdg. officer Biggs AFB, El Paso, Tex., 1944; exec. officer to dep. supreme Allied comdr., S.E. Asia, and comdr. U.S. troops, Ceylon, 1945; sr. pilot's rating, 1946; assigned to plans div., hdqrs. USAF, 1947-50; assigned joint strategic plans and operations group Gen. Hdqrs., Tokyo, 1950; air staff adviser NSC, Hdqrs. USAF, 1953-54; exec. asst. to sec. Air Force, 1955- 56; dir. information Hdqrs. USAF, 1956-57; former comdg. gen. Chanute AFB, Ill.; dir. devel. planning USAF, 1963, asst. dep. chief staff Research and Devel., 1964-66; comdg. gen. Armament Devel. and Test Center, Eglin AFB, Fla. Decorated Bronze Star medal. Mem. Air Force Assn. Club: Army-Navy Country (Washington). Home: Route 1 RFD 78 Fort Walton Beach FL Office: Hdqrs Armament Devel and Test Center Eglin AFB FL

KINNEY, DONALD RICHARD educator; b. E. Sparta, O., June 21, 1923; s. Hobart Harry and Hope (Rice) K.; B.A. summa cum laude, Mt. Union Coll., Alliance, O., 1954; L.H.D., 1966; m. Dora Evelyn Davis, June 16, 1962 (dec. 1965) ; 1 son, Allan Clark. With Hadley Sch. for Blind, Winnetka, Ill., 1954—, exec. v.p., 1969—; cons. adv. com. Nat. Center Deaf-Blind Youths and Adults. Mem. com. services for deaf-blind World Council Welfare of Blind. Recipient Anne Sullivan Macy centennial award, 1966, citation Dwight Eisenhower, 1959, citation Midland Authors Soc., 1968, Helen Keller gold medal, 1948. Mem. Am. Assn. Workers for Blind, U.S. Cheese Fedn., Pi Gamma Mu, Sigma Alpha Epsilon. Lion. Author: Independent Living Without Sight and Hearing, 1967; Harp of Silence, 1967; Flutes Beyond the Day, 1953; Encore, 1954; Flight of Arrows, 1950. Home: 896 Elm St Winnetka IL 60093

KINNEY, EARL ROBERT, food co. exec.; b. Burnham, Me., Apr. 12, 1917; s. Harry E. and Ethel (Vose) K.; A.B., Bates Coll., 1939; postgrad., Harvard Grad. Sch., 1940; m. Mary Reid, Dec. 14, 1940; children—Jeanie Elizabeth, Earl Robert, Isabella Alice. Founder, N. Atlantic Pack Co., Bar Harbor, Me., 1941, pres., 1941-42, treas., dir., 1941-64; with Gorton Corp. (became subsidiary Gen. Mills, Inc. 1968), 1954-68, pres., 1958-68; v.p. Gen. Mills, Inc., 1968-69, exec. v.p., 1969—, chief financial officer, 1970—; dir. Bond Industries, Inc., Putnam Investors Fund, Putnam Income Fund; trustee George Putnam Fund, Putnam Growth Fund. Trustee, Seacoast Missionary Soc., Central Inst.; trustee Bates Coll., also chmn. alumni drives, 1960-64; bd. dirs., exec. com. Tyrone Guthrie Theatre; trustee Me. Central Inst. Office: 9200 Wayzata Blvd Minneapolis MN 55440

KINNEY, EUGENE MCDONALD, mfg. exec.; b. Buffalo, Apr. 20, 1921; s. John McInerny and Mary Loretta (McDonald) K.; B.A., Dartmouth, 1944; m. Barbara Humbird Dickason, Nov. 26, 1949; children—Catherine, John, Elizabeth, Robert. With Zenith Radio Corp., 1946—, now dir., sr. v.p. charge of Zenith's spl. products. Mem. bd. govs. Henrotin Hosp.; trustee Vt. Acad.; v.p. Nat. Assn. Hearing and Speech Agys. Served as lt. USNR, World War II. Mem. Delta Tau Delta. Clubs: Chicago Yacht, Racquet (Chgo.); Westmoreland Country; Michigan Shores. Home: 123 Kenilworth Av Kenilworth IL 60093 Office: 6501 W Grand Av Chicago IL 60635

KINNEY, FRANCIS LAWRENCE, utility exec.; b. Waterbury, Conn., Dec. 15, 1932; s. John Patrick and Flavian (Brennan) K.; B.S., Coll. Holy Cross, 1954; J.D., U. Conn., 1963; m. Maureen Helen Maroney, May 14, 1955; children—Lisa, Mary Lynn, Maureen, Tricia, Michael. Admitted to Conn. bar, 1963; sec. N.E. Utilities, Hartford, Conn., N.E. Utilities Service Co., Conn. Light & Power Co., Hartford Electric Light Co., Western Mass. Electric Co., Hoyoke Water Power Co., Conn. Yankee Atomic Power Co., 1969—. Served from ensign to lt. (j.g.) USNR, 1954-57. Mem. Conn., Hartford County bar assns., Am. Soc. Corporate Secs. Home: 76 Pheasant Run Newington CT 06111 Office: PO Box 270 Hartford CT 06101

KINNEY, GILBERT FORD, educator, chem. engr.; b. Judsonia, Ark., Dec. 29, 1907; s. Gilbert Earle and Mabel (Ford) K.; A.B., Ark. Coll., 1928; M.S., U. Tenn., 1930; Ph.D., N.Y. U., 1935; student Mass. Inst. Tech., 1938; m. Martha Turquand Stinson, Sept. 6, 1934; children—Abbott Hart (Mrs. Robert Hall), Gilbert Ford. Operator radio sta. WNBZ, 1930-32; head inst. chemistry Pratt Inst., 1935-42; monitor Operation Crossroads, 1946; prof. chem. engring. Naval Postgrad. Sch., 1946—, chmn. material sci. and chemistry dept., 1963—, cons. in field, 1952—. Served to lt. comdr. USNR, 1942-46. Recipient Distinguished Prof. Medallion Naval Postgrad. Sch., 1967. Fellow Am. Insts. Chemists; mem. Am. Chem. Soc., Am. Assn. U. Profs., Ret. Officers Assn., Sigma Xi, Alpha Chi Sigma, Alpha Lambda Tau. Author: Engineering Thermodynamics, 1953; Plastics, 1958; Explosive Shocks, 1962. Home: 1116 Sylvan Rd Monterey CA 93940

KINNEY, JOHN MARTIN, educator, surgeon, research; b. Evanston, Ill., May 24, 1921; s. Edwin Hamilton and Mary (Martin) K.; A.B., Denison U., 1943; M.D., Harvard, 1946; m. Joyce Patnoe, Dec. 26, 1944; children—Walter Keith, Paul Thurman, Katherine Sue. Surg. intern Peter Bent Brigham Hosp., Boston, 1946-47, surg. resident, 1952-57, Am. Cancer Soc., USNR clin. trainee 1955, jr. asso. surgery, 1958-62, asso. surgery, 1960-63; asso. attending surgeon Presbyn. Hosp., N.Y.C., 1963-67, attending surgeon, 1967—, dir. surg. metabolism unit, 1963—; cons. surgery Harlem Hosp., N.Y.C., 1964—; AEC post-doctoral fellow NRC in biophysics and biochemistry, 1949-52; instr. surgery, Arthur Tracy Cabot fellow, Henry E. Warren fellow, tutor med. scis. Harvard Med. Sch., 1957-60, asso. in surgery, 1958-60, asst. prof. surgery, 1960-63; asso. prof. surgery Columbia Coll. Phys. and Surg., 1963-67, prof. surgery, 1967—; dir. surg. trainee program NIH, 1966—; mem. adv. com. metabolism in trauma U.S. Army Med. Research and Devel. Command. Served to lt. (j.g.) USNR at Naval Radiol. Def. Lab., 1947-49. Named Career Scientist Health Research Council N.Y.C., 1965; recipient citation Denison U. Alumni, 1968. Mem. NRC (mem. coms. on shock chmn. 1969, emergency med. services), A.C.S. (mem. cons. pre-and postoperative care; liaison mem. for A.C.S. to sect. clin. care Am. Soc. Anesthesiologists; chmn. editorial com.; editor manual pre-and postoperative care; recipient Mead Johnson award, 1956-59), N.Y. Acad. Scis. (mem. com. publs. and awards), Nat. Insts. Gen. Med. Scis. (mem. surgery tng. com.), Nat. Acad. Engring. (mem. adv. panel to com. on interplay of engring. with biology and medicine), Soc. Univ. Surgeons, Am. Surg. Assn., Kansas City, N. Y. State, Boston surg. socs., A.A.A.S., Allen O. Whipple Surg. Soc., Royal Soc. Medicine (London), Internat. Soc. Burn Injuries (Edinburgh), Am. Assn. for Surgery of Trauma, A.M.A., N.Y. Acad. Medicine, N.Y. County Med. Soc., Am. Burn Assn. Contbr. numerous articles, chpts. in books Home: 20 Kensington Rd Ardsley NY 10502 Office: 630 W 168th St New York City NY 10032

KINNEY, KNOX BAIRD, lawyer; b. Memphis, July 22 1924; s. Kenneth Hays and Ruby Lucille (Baird) K.; B.S., Vanderbilt U., 1947, J.D., 1949; m. Patsy Lee Patrick, Apr. 15, 1951; children-Knox Baird, Patsy June. Admitted to Ark. bar, 1949, also Supreme Ct. Ark., Supreme Ct. Tenn., U.S. Supreme Ct.; practiced in Forrest City, 1949—; mem. Ark. Bd. Law Examiners, 1961-67; city atty., Forrest City, 1969—. Mem. Ark. Ho. of Reps., 1951-58. Served to 2d lt., M.I., AUS, World War II; ETO. Recipient Young Man of Year award Ark. Jr. C. of C., 1955. Mem. Am., Ark., St. Francis County (past pres.) bar assns., Forrest City C. of C. (past pres.), V.F.W., Phi Delta Theta,

Phi Alpha Delta. Baptist (trustee). Rotarian (past pres.). Home: 329 Virginia Circle Forrest City AR 72335 Office: Kinney Bldg Forest City AR 72335

KINNEY, SAMUEL MARKS, Jr., bus. exec., lawyer; b. Jenkintown, Pa., July 10, 1925; s. Samuel Marks and Margaret R. (Rennie) K.; grad. Lawrenceville Sch., 1942; student Allegheny Coll., 1942-43; B.A., Pa. State Coll., 1946; LL.B., Rutgers U., 1948; m. Kathryn Clouser, Sept. 21, 1946; children—Kathryn Lee, Samuel Marks III, Brian Scott. Admitted to N.J. bar, 1949; asso. atty. Martin & Reiley, Newark, 1949-51; counsel, mgr. army contracts Daystrom Instrument div. Daystrom, Inc., 1951-54; asst. sec., counsel Daystrom, Inc., Murray Hill, N.J., 1954-57, sec., counsel, 1957-59, asst. v.p. finance, 1959-61, v.p., gen. counsel, 1961-62; v.p., sec., dir. Union Camp Corp., sr. v.p. 1969-70, exec. v.p., 1970—; dir. Allied Container Corp., N.J. Life Ins. Co., Lafarge Emballage, S.A. (France), Cartonajes Union, S.A. (Spain). Chmn. Union County (N.J.) Young Republican Club, Inc., 1951-52; mem. Westfield Town Council, 1961-67, chmn. finance and laws and rules coms. Mem. bus. exec. research com. Bus. Execs. Research Center, Rutgers U., 1957-58. Served with USMCR, 1943-45. Mem. Am. Mgmt. Assn., Am. Soc. Corporate Secs., Am. Judicature Soc., Am. Ordnance Assn., Am. Legion, Am. Bar Assn., Stockholder Relations Soc. N.Y. Episcopalian (vestryman). Clubs: Echo Lake Country (Westfield); Merchants (N.Y.). Contbr. papers to profl. jours. Home: 355 Wychwood Rd Westfield NJ Office: 1600 Valley Rd Wayne NJ 07470

KINNEY, SHELDON HOARD, naval officer; b. Pasadena, Cal., Aug. 27, 1918; s. Harold S. and Gladys (Hoard) K.; B.S., U.S. Naval Acad., 1941; M.A., George Washington U., 1965, J.D., 1960; grad. Nat. War Coll., 1960; m. Elizabeth Mercier Douglas, Dec. 27, 1941; children—Douglas Sheldon, Bruce Harold. Commd. ensign U.S. Navy, 1941, advanced through grades to rear adm., 1967; comdr. U.S.S. Edsall, 1943-44, U.S.S. Bronstein, 1944-45, U.S.S. Taylor, 1952-53, U.S.S. Mitscher, 1956-58, U.S.S. Missisinewa, 1962-63, Amphibious Force, 6th Fleet, 1963-64; assigned U.S. Naval Acad., 1954- 56, Office Naval Operations, 1958-69; staff duty Cincusnaveur, 1960-62; comdt. of midshipmen U.S. Naval Acad., 1964-67; comdr. Cruiser- Destroyer Flotilla 11 and comdr. Operation Sea Dragon, Vietnam, 1967-69; head edn. and tng. Navy Dept., 1969-70, dep. chief naval personnel, 1970-71; comdr. cruiser destroyers Pacific Fleet, 1971—. Bd. dirs. U.S. Naval Inst. Decorated Navy Cross, Legion of Merit (2), Navy and Marine Corps Medal of heroism, Bronze Star medal (2), Commendation medal, also fgn. decorations. Home: 661 S Los Robles Pasadena CA 91106 Office: COMCRUDESPAC FPO San Francisco CA 96601

KINNEY, STERLING EDWARD, lawyer; b. Miami, Tex., Nov. 3, 1916; s. John E. and Bena (Carter) K.; student Amarillo Jr. Coll., 1934-36, West Tex. U., 1937-38; LL.B., U. Tex., 1942; m. Dorothy Ann Adams, Dec. 26, 1942; children—Anne Leigh, Leslie Elaine, Julie Lynn. Admitted to Tex. bar, 1941; mem. firm Gibson, Ochsner, Adkins, Harlan & Hankins and predecessor, Amarillo, Tex., 1945- -. Pres. Amarillo Symphony, 1967-69. Vice chmn. Presbyteries Coop. Com., United Presbyn. Ch. U.S.A., 1968-70. Served with AUS, 1942-45. Decorated Bronze Star. Mem. Am., Amarillo (past pres.) bar assns., State Bar Tex. Home: Route 1 Box 336 Amarillo TX 79106 Office: Fisk Bldg Amarillo TX 79101

KINNEY, THOMAS DEARMAN, physician; b. Franklin, Pa., Mar. 19, 1909; s. Thomas Andrew and Minnie (DeArman) K.; A.B., U. Pa., 1931; M.D., Duke, 1936; m. Elanor Shepard Roberts, July 9, 1939; children—Thomas Roberts, Eleanor DeArman, Hannah Chase, Janet Shepard. Intern, Johns Hopkins Hosp., Balt., 1936- 38; asst. pathologist Malory Inst. Pathology, Boston City Hosp., 1943-44; asso. pathologist Peter Bent Brigham Hosp., Boston, 1944-47; pathologist in chief Cleve. Met. Gen. Hosp., 1947-50, dir. pathology, 1950-60; sr. cons. Crile VA Hosp., Cleve., 1947-60; asst. pathology Yale, 1938-39; instr. pathology Boston U., 1940-41; asst. prof. pathology Tufts Coll. Med. Sch., 1943-44; instr. pathology Harvard Med. Sch., 1944-47; asso. prof. pathology Western Res. U. Med. Sch., 1947-50, prof. pathology, 1950-60; prof. chmn. dept. pathology Duke Med. Center, 1960—; cons. Armed Forces Inst. Pathology, Washington, 1960- -, mem. sci. adv. bd. cons., 1964—. Mem. pathology study sect. USPHS, 1956-63, chmn., 1959-62; mem. council Inst. Gen. Med. Scis., 1963-66; prin. cons. pathology Nat. Inst. Gen. Med. Scis., 1967- -, chmn. automation med. lab. scis. rev. com., 1969; mem. sci. adv. bd. Armed Forces Inst. Pathology; adv. council pathology Allied Scis. Service Am.; mem. spl. med. adv. group VA, 1966—; com. div. med. scis. Nat. Acad. of Sci., NRC. Sec.-treas. dir. Univs. Asso. for Research and Edn. in Pathology, 1966—. Trustee, Cleve. Center Alcoholism, Cleve. Health Mus., Cleve. Zoo, Cleve. Med. Library Assn., Cuyahoga unit Am. Cancer Soc.; v.p., trustee Cleve. Chamber Music Soc. Fellow A.A.A.S., Coll. Am. Pathologists; mem. Cleve. Acad. Medicine (pres. 1957-58, trustee), Cleve. Area Heart Soc. (trustee), Council Internat. Acad. Pathology, Soc. Exptl. Biology and Medicine (council 1955-56), Am. Assn. Pathologists and Bacteriologists (pres. 1965-66), Am. Soc. Exptl. Pathology (mem. council 1964—), Ohio Med. Assn., A.M.A., Am. Soc. Clin. Nutrition, Inter-soc. Com. Research in Pathology (sec.-treas. 1962—), Inter-soc. Com. Pathology Information (sec.-treas. 1964-65), Mass. Med. Soc., Soc. Exptl. Pathologists and Bacteriologists, N.C. Soc. Pathologists, So. Med. Soc., Am. Soc. Cell Biology, Am. Soc. Clin. Nutrition, Tissue Culture Assn., Am. Assn. Cancer Research, Am. Heart Soc., Diabetes Assn. Greater Cleve. (trustee), Inter-soc. Cytology Council, Am. Soc. Human Genetics, Soc. Geog. Pathology, Sigma Xi, Nu Sigma Nu, Theta Delta Chi, Alpha Omega Alpha. Editor: Laboratory Investigation, 1952-66, Am. Jour. Pathology, 1967—. Home: 3120 Devon Rd Durham NC 27706 Office: Duke U Med Center Durham NC 27706

KINNEY, WILLIAM SLOANE, Jr., advt. exec.; b. Canton, O., July 6, 1916; s. William S. and Beulah (Batchelor) K.; B.A., Haverford Coll., 1938; m. Catherine Cullom, Aug. 14, 1943; children—Carol, Josephine, Daniel. Asst. account exec. Donohue & Coe, Inc., N.Y.C., 1939-40; circulation and promotion N.J. Jour.-Am., 1940-41; account exec., copywriter H.M. Klingensmith Co., Canton, 1946-47; with Gray & Rogers, Inc., Phila., 1947—, exec. v.p., 1967—. also dir.; dir. Metered Parking Corp., William S. Kinney, Inc. Communications coordinator Mayor Phila. Council Youth Opportunity, 1968- 69. Served to capt. USAAF, 1941-45. Mem. Phi Beta Kappa. Episcopalian. Clubs: Whitford (Pa.) Country; Midday (Phila.). Home: 414 King Rd West Chester, PA 19380 Office: 12 S 12th St Philadelphia PA 19301

KINO, GORDON STANLEY, educator; b. Melbourne, Australia, June 15, 1928; s. William Hector and Sybil (Cohen) K.; B.Sc. with 1st class honours in Math., London (Eng.) U., 1948, M.Sc. in Math., 1950; Ph.D. in Elec. Engring., Stanford, 1955; m. Dorothy Beryl Lovelace, Oct. 30, 1955; 1 dau., Carol Ann. Came to U.S., 1951, naturalized, 1967. Jr. scientist Mullard Research Lab., Salford, Surrey, Eng., 1947-51; research asst., then research asso. Stanford, 1951-55; mem. tech. staff Bell Telephone Labs., 1955-57; research asso. Stanford, 1957-61, mem. faculty, 1961—, prof. elec. engring. 1965—; cons. to industry, 1957—. Guggenheim fellow, 1967-68. Fellow I.E.E.E., Am. Phys. Soc. Author: (with Kirstein, Waters) Space Charge Flow, 1968; also papers microwave tubes; electron optics, plasma physics, bulk effects in semiconductors, acoustics. Inventor Kino electron gun, 1959. Home: 867 Cedro Way Stanford CA 94305

KINOSHITA, TOICHIRO, physicist, educator; b. Tokyo, Japan, Jan. 23, 1925; s. Tsutomu and Fumi (Ueda) K.; B.S., Tokyo U., 1947, Ph.D., 1952; m. Masako Matsuoka, Oct. 14, 1951; children—Kay, June, Ray. Came to U.S., 1952, naturalized, 1965. Mem. Inst. for Advanced Study, Princeton, N.J., 1952-54; postdoctoral fellow Columbia, 1954-55; faculty Cornell U., Ithaca, N.Y., 1955—, prof. physics and nuclear studies, 1964—. Mem. Am. Phys. Soc. Contbr. articles profl. jours. Home: 5 Winthrop Pl Ithaca NY 14850

KINOSITA, RIOJUN, scientist; b. Japan, Sept. 17, 1893; s. Yukimichi and Nui (Tanabe) K.; M.D., Tokyo U., 1921; postgrad. U. Coll., London, also Cambridge (Eng.) U., 1924-26; Ph.D., Hokkaido U., 1926; m. Florence M. Ritson, Nov. 6, 1925; 1 dau., Akiko (Mrs. Denis Lotspeich). Came to U.S., 1949. Research asso. Freiburg (Germany) U., 1922-24; prof. pathology Hokkaido U., 1922-32; prof. pathology, dir. cancer research Osaka U., 1932-52; pres. Osaka City U., 1946-48; vis. prof. pathology and infectious diseases U. Cal. at Los Angeles, 1949—; research dir., then chmn. dept. exptl. pathology City of Hope Med. Center, 1952-62, research dir. emeritus, 1962—, head, cancer research lab. spl. research carcinogenesis. Recipient Outstanding Research award City of Hope, 1962, Med. Research Contbn. award Takeda Sci. Advancement Found., 1965. Home: 3350 Fish Canyon Rd Duarte CA 91010

KINSELLA, JOHN JOSEPH, educator; b. Newburgh, N.Y., Sept. 3, 1907; s. John P. and Rose Anna (Dillon) K.; A.B., N.Y. State Coll. for Tchrs. at Albany, 1928; M.A., Columbia, 1931, Ed.D., 1943; m. Helen T. Dowd, Apr. 30, 1938; children—John, William. High sch. math. tchr., Piermont, N.Y., 1928- 29, Monticello, 1929-30, Free Acad., Newburgh, 1930-42; tchr. Univ. Sch., Ohio State U., 1942-44, acting asst. dir., 1946-47, asso. prof. dept. edn. 1947-49; chmn. dept. math. edn., sch. edn. N.Y.U., 1949-59, prof. edn., dept. sci. and maths. edn., 1949-65; chmn. grad. programs Newark State Coll., 1965—, prof. math., 1967—. Served as lt. (j.g.), USNR, 1944- 46; communications officer Communications in Hawaii, 1944-46. Mem. N.E.A., Nat. Council Tchrs. Math., Am. Assn. U. Profs., Math. Assn. Am., Assn. Math. Tchrs. N.J. (pres. 1968-69). Author: Wartime Applications of Elementary Mathematics (pamphlet), Ohio State Univ., 1945; Secondary School Mathematics, 1965. Co-author: Algebra, Its Structure and Applications, 1967; Geometry, A Dimensional Approach, 1968. Contbr. articles to profl. jours. Home: 1060 Prospect Av Mountainside NJ 07092 Office: Newark State Coll Union NJ 07083

KINSEY, BERNARD BRUNO, educator; b. London, Eng., June 15, 1910; s. Rudolf Julius and Marie (Voss) K.; B.A., Cambridge (Eng.) U., 1932, Ph.D., 1937; m. Freda M. Oldham, July 19, 1943 (div. Sept. 1961); children—Jennifer, Nicholas, Peter; m. 2d, Marian Hall, Jan. 26, 1968; Came to U.S., 1958. Commonwealth fellow, U. Cal. at Berkeley, 1933-36; lectr. U. Liverpool (Eng.), 1936-39; with Ministry Aircraft Prodn., Eng., 1939-42; research scientist, Cambridge, Eng., 1942-44; research physicist Atomic Energy Can., Monreal, guest researcher U. Cal. at Berkeley, 1954-55; research scientist Atomic Energy Research Establishment, Harwell, Eng., 1955-58; prof. physics U. Tex., Austin 1958—. Home: 102 Skyline Dr Austin TX 78746

KINSEY, VICTOR EVERETT, ophthalmic chemist; b. Pitts., Aug. 4, 1909; s. William L. and Grace (Everett) K.; student Carnegie Inst. Tech., 1927-28; B.A., U. Pitts., 1931, Ph.D., 1935; m. Irene Mackey, Aug. 22, 1935. Research asso. Grad. Sch. Medicine U. Pa., biochemist Sharp and Dohme Biol. labs., 1936-38; research asso. Med. Sch. U. Pitts., 1938-40; research asso. Howe Lab., Harvard Med. Sch., 1941-43, instr., 1944-46, asst. prof., 1946 -50; asst. dir. research Kresge Eye Inst., Detroit, 1950-68; prof. ophthalmic chemistry Wayne State U. Med. Sch., 1950-68; prof., dir. Inst. Biol. Scis., Oakland U., Rochester, Mich., 1968—. Mem. research exec. council Nat. Soc. Prevention Blindness; mem. com. ophthalmology and radiation cataracts Nat. Acad. Scis., NRC, 1951- -. Dir. Nat. Found. for Eye Research; mem. sci. adv. com. Nat. Council to Combat Blindness, Inc.; mem. nat. adv. neurol. diseases and blindness council USPHS, 1962-66, nat. adv. eye inst. council, 1967-68. Dir. Detroit Opera Theatre, Inc. Co-recipient of the Warren Triennial award Mass. Gen. Hosp., 1943; recipient Proctor award, 1952, Lasker award, 1956; Modern medicine Distinguished award, 1959. Mem. Fedn. Am. Socs. for Exptl. Biology, Assn. Research Ophthalmology (mem. bd. trustees; chmn. 1960), New Eng. (hon.) Detroit (hon.) ophthalmology socs., Am. Chem. Soc., Am. Soc. Biol. Chemists, Sigma Xi. Club: Torch (dir. Detroit). Author: Index to Iron and Steel Patents, 2d edit., 1931; also numerous articles on ocular physiology and biochemistry. Home: 6916 Dublin Fair Rd Troy MI 48084 Office: Inst Biol Scis Oakland U Rochester MI 48063

KINSEY, WILLIAM H., lawyer; b. Cleve., Oct. 16, 1918; A.B., Wayne U., 1940; J.D., U. Mich., 1942. Admitted to Mich. bar, 1942, N.Y. bar, 1947, Ore. bar, 1948; now partner firm Mautz, Souther, Spaulding, Kinsey & Williamson, Portland, Ore. Mem. Am., Multnomah County bar assns., Ore. State Bar. Office: 1100 SW 6th Av Portland OR 97204*

KINSINGER, JACK BURL, educator, chemist; b. Akron, O., June 23, 1925; s. William Franklin and Idelle (Althaus) K.; B.A., Hiram Coll., 1948; M.S., Cornell U., 1951; Ph.D., U. Pa., 1958; m. Addie Jean Parker, Sept. 2, 1946; children—Paul Craig, Amy Jo. Group leader research Rohm & Haas Co., Phila., 1951-56; asst. prof. Mich. State U., East Lansing, 1957-61, asso. prof., 1961-66, prof. chemistry, 1966—, asso. chmn. dept. chemistry, 1965-69, chmn., 1969—; cons. Union Carbide Co., 1958—, vice chmn. div. polymer chemistry, 1966-68, chmn., 1969. Served to 2d lt. USAAF, 1943-45. Mem. Am. Chem. Soc., Am. Phys. Soc., Optical Soc. Am., A.A.A.S., N.Y. Acad. Sci., I.E.E.E., Sigma Xi. Editor: Computer Symposium, 1968. Contbr. chpt. Ency. Polymer Chemistry, 1971. Home: 4432 Greenwood St Okemos MI 48823 Office: Dept Chemistry Mich State U East Lansing MI 48823

KINSMAN, GEORGE, utility exec.; b. Decatur, Ill., Feb. 7, 1902; s. Charles Collins and Bertha (Lee) K.; B.S. in Mech. Enging., Armour Inst. Tech., 1924; m. Jeannette Buice, Aug. 7, 1928; 1 son, Charles R. Engr. various firms, 1924-27; with Fla. Power & Light, 1928-42, v.p., 1950-67, sr. v.p., 1967—; with Pacific Gas & Elec. Co., 1945-48, Cal. Mfr. Assn., 1948-50. Vice chmn. So. Interstate Nuclear Bd., 1970—. Served with USNR, 1942-45. Fellow Fla. Engring. Soc. (pres. 1961-62), Am. Soc. M.E.; mem. Atomic Indsl. Forum (dir.), Am. Nuclear Soc. (dir.). Home: 4235 Douglas Rd Coconut Grove Miami FL 33133 Office: 4200 Flagler St P O Box 3100 Miami FL 33101

KINSOLVING, ARTHUR LEE, clergyman; b. Huntington, L.I., N.Y., Aug. 24, 1899; s. Arthur Barksdale and Sally Archer (Bruce) K.; B.A., U. Va., 1920; Rhodes scholar from Va., Christ Ch., Oxford U., 1920-23, B.A., 1923, M.A., 1925; B.D., Va. Theol. Sem., 1924; D.D., Amherst Coll., 1931, U. Vt., 1937, Boston U., 1939; Princeton, 1945; L.H.D., Rollins Coll., 1938; m. Mary Kemp Blagden, Sept. 4, 1937. Deacon, 1923, priest, 1924, P.E. Ch.; rector Grace Ch., Amherst, Mass., 1924-30, Trinity Ch., Boston, 1930-40, Trinity Ch., Princeton, N.J., 1940-47, St. James Ch., N.Y.C., 1947-69; dean Convocation of Manhattan, 1959—. Mem. dept. evangelism Nat. Council Chs. Trustee, Cathedral St. John the Divine. Pres. N.Y. P.E. City Mission; chmn. Nat. Commn. on Coll. Work. Trustee, The Chapin Sch. Former chmn. U. Christian Mission. Mem. Phi Beta Kappa, Delta Kappa Epsilon. Mason. Clubs: Century Association, Hay Harbor, Fisher Island Yacht. Home: 6001 Hunt Ridge Rd Baltimore MD 21210 Office: 865 Madison Av New York City NY

KINSOLVING, CHARLES JAMES, III, bishop; b. Bklyn., Jan 14, 1904; s. Charles James Jr. and Edith (Lewis) K.; student Mass. Inst. Tech., 1921-22; B.A., U. of South, 1925, B.D., 1928, D.D., 1954; m. Mary Robinson, Aug. 2, 1932; children—Charles James IV, John Armistead. Ordained to ministry P.E. Ch. as deacon, 1928, priest in charge St. Barabas, Denton, Tex., 1929-36; rector Ch. of Holy Faith, Santa Fe, 1936-53; consecrated bishop P.E. Ch., 1953, bishop coadjutor Diocese of N.M. and Southwest Tex., 1953-56, bishop, 1956—. Address: PO Box 2003 Santa Fe NM 87501

KINSTLER, EVERETT RAYMOND, artist; b. N.Y.C., Aug. 5, 1926; s. Joseph E. and Essie Kinstler; ed. Art Students League, N.Y.C., 1943-45; m. Lea C. Nation, June 23, 1958; children—Katherine Katherine G., Dana C. Started career as illustrator, N.Y.C., 1943, began specializing in portraiture, 1955; portraits include Mrs. Irenee duPont, Jr., Herbert Lehman, Gen. Mark W. Clark, Alan B. Shepard, Jr., Scott Carpenter, Admiral David McDonald, Orville Freeman, W. Willard Wirtz, David Kennedy, also numerous others; exhibited works in one man shows at Grand Central Art Galleries, N.Y.C., 1960; rep. permanent collections Cal. Hist. Soc., Mus. City N.Y., Met. Mus. Art, N.Y.C., The Pentagon, FAA, Mystic Seaport Mus., U.S. Navy Art Collection, Smithsonian Instn., numerous colls., univs., bus. firms. Instr. Art Students League, N.Y.C. Recipient Gold medal Nat. Arts Club, 1956; Salmagundi Club prize Allied Artists, 1968; hon. mention Am. Watercolor Soc. 100th Anniversary Exhbn.; Salmagundi first prize, 1969; Painting award Allied Artist Annual, 1969. Mem. of Allied Artists Am. (dir. 1958-60), Artists Fellowships, Inc. (pres. 1967-70), Art Students League (life), Portraits Inc., Am. Watercolor Soc., Audubon Artists (pres.), Nat. Acad. Design (asso.). Clubs: Century Assn. (trustee), Dutch Treat, Salamagundi, Nat. Arts (v.p.) (N.Y.C.); Rembrandt; Players. Author: Painting Portraits, 1971. Illustrator books including: The Opera Companion (George Martin), 1962; Our Federal Government (Patricia Acheson), 1962; Verdi (George Martin), 1963. Address: National Arts Club 15 Gramercy Park New York City NY 10003

KINTNER, EARL WILSON, lawyer; b. Corydon, Ind., Nov. 6, 1912; s. Lee and Lillie Florence (Chanley) K.; A.B., De Pauw U., 1936; J.D., Ind. U., 1938; LL.D., De Pauw U., 1970; m. Valerie Patricia Wildy, May 28, 1948; 1 son Christopher Earl Mackelean; children by previous marriage—Anna Victoria, Jonathan M., Rosemary Jane (dec.). Admitted to Ind. bar, 1938, U.S. Supreme Ct. bar, 1945, D.C. bar, 1953; practice in Princeton, Ind., 1938-44; city atty., Princeton, 1939-42; pros. atty. 6th Ind. Jud. Circuit, 1943-48; dep. U.S. Commr. UN War Crimes Commn., 1945-48; sr. trial atty. FTC. 1948-50, legal adviser, 1950-53, gen. counsel, 1953-59, chmn., 1959-61; pres. Fed. Bar Bldg. Corp. Del., chmn. com. hearing officers Pres.'s Conf. on Adminstrv. Procedure, 1953-54; mem. panel on invention and innovation U.S. Dept. Commerce, 1965-66; mem. U.S. Adminstrv. Conf., 1970. Served from ensign to lt. USNR, 1944-46. Recipient Distinguished Service award Ind. U., 1960, Distinguished Alumni award DePauw U., 1965. Mem. Fed. (pres. 1956-57, 58-59), Am. (chmn. adminstrv. law sect. 1959- 60, council antitrust law sect. 1958-61), N.Y. (exec. com antitrust sect.) bar assns. Fed. Bar Found, (pres.), Am. Judicature Soc. (dir. 1961-64), Am. Legion, D.A.V., Sigma Delta Chi, Phi Delta Phi (pres. Province II 1962-67), Pi Sigma Alpha, Delta Sigma Rho, Lambda Chi Alpha. Republican. Episcopalian. Clubs: Cosmos, National Lawyers (pres), National Press, Capitol Hill (Washington); Union League (N.Y.); Coral Beach and Tennis. Mason (32 Shriner). Author: An Antitrust Primer, 1964; A Robinson-Patman Primer, 1970; A Business Practice Primer, 1971. Editor: The United Nations War Crimes Commission and Development of the Laws of War, 1948; The Hadamar Trial, 1948; FTC staff legal manual, 1952. Home: 3210 34th St NW washington DC 20008 Office: Fed Bar Bldg Washington DC 20006

KINTNER, ROBERT CHESTER, chem. engr.; b. Milford Center, O., Mar. 3, 1900; s. John Christian and Frances Elizabeth (Campbell) K.; B.Chem. Engring., Ohio State U., 1923, M.S., 1929, Ph.D., 1931; m. LeEvelyn Gillam, Mar. 2, 1929. Chem. engr. Drackett Chem. Co., 1923-24, Crystal Carbonic Labs., 1925, Swift & Co., 1926-27; asst. dept. chem. engring. Ohio State U., 1928-29; asst. prof. Rose Poly. Inst., 1929-30, Bucknell U., 1933-37; asso. prof. Ill. Inst. Tech., 1937-42, prof., 1942-69, emeritus, 1969—, asst. dean Grad. Sch., 1944-50; sr. vis. fellow U. Aston, Birmingham, Eng., 1969. Registered profl. engr., Ill. Mem. Am. Inst. Chem. Engrs. (chmn. chem. engring. edn. project com. 1954- 58), Am. Chem. Soc., Scabbard and Blade, Sigma Xi, Alpha Chi Sigma, Phi Lambda Upsilon, Pi Mu Epsilon. Author articles bubble and drop phenomena. Home: 8107 Roberts Rd Bridgeview IL 60455

KINZEL, AUGUSTUS BRAUN, tech. exec.; b. N.Y.C., July 26, 1900; s. Otto and Josephine (Braun) K.; A.B., Columbia, 1919; B.S., Mass. Inst. Tech., 1921, D. Met., Eng. 1922; D.Sc., U. Nancy (France) D.hon. causa, 1963; D. Eng., N.Y.U., 1955; D.Sc., Clarkson Coll. Tech., 1957; D. Eng., Rensselaer Inst., 1965, Worcester Poly. Inst., 1965, U. Mich., 1967; LL.D., Queens U., 1966; D.Sc., Northwestern U., 1969; m. 1927 (div.); children—Carol (Mrs. Charles Uht), Doris (Mrs. Richard Campbell), August F., Angela (Mrs. John W. Talbot), Helen (Mrs. William Murray Hawkins, Jr.); m. 2d, Marie MacClymont, May 3, 1945. Metallurigist Gen. Electric Co., Pittsfield, Mass., 1919-20, 22-23, Henry Disston & Sons, Inc., Phila., 1923-26; lectr., instr. extension courses in advanced metallurgy Temple U., 1925-26; research metallurgist Union Carbide & Carbon Research Labs., Inc., N.Y.C., 1926-28, group leader, 1928-31, chief metallurgist, 1931-45, v.p., 1945-48, pres., 1948-65, v.p. Electro Metall. Co. a div., 1944-54; dir. research Union Carbide Corp., 1954-55, v.p. research, 1955-65; pres., chief exec. officer Salk Inst. Biol. Scis., LaJolla, Cal., 1965- 67; chmn. bd. Cybertek, Inc.; trustee System Devel. Found., Santa Monica, Cal., Menasco-Am. Optical Co., Southbridge, Mass.; dir. Kalvar Corp., Sprague Electric Co., Gen. Am. Investors Co., Inc., N.Y.C., Beckman Instruments, Inc., Fullerton, Cal. Chmn. governing council Courant Inst. Math. Scis. N.Y.U.; trustee Cal. Inst. Tech.; chmn. The Engring. Found. Bd., N.Y.C., 1945-48; bd. dirs. Riverside Research Inst., Scripps Meml. Hosp.; v.p., dir. Berkshire Farm Research Inst. Recipient Howe Meml. Lectr., Am. Inst. Mining and Metall. Engrs., 1952; Sauveur Lectr., Am. Soc. Metals, 1952; Morehead medal, Internat. Acetylene Assn., 1955; Stevens Inst. Tech. Powder Metallurgy Medal award, 1959; Indsl. Research Inst. medal, 1960; James Douglas Gold Medal award, Am. Inst. Mining, Metall and Petroleum Engrs., 1960. Men. Mass. Inst. Tech. Corp., 1956-61. Fellow N.Y. Acad. Scis., Royal Soc. Arts, Am. Inst. Chemists, Metall. Soc., Am. Soc. Metals (Campbell lectr. 1947, Burgess Meml. lectr. 1956, past chmn. N.Y. sect.), Metall. Soc.; mem. Eurospace (hon.), Engrs. Joint Council (hon., pres. 1960-61), Am. Philos. Soc., Soc. Chem. Industry, Nat. Acad. Engring. (founding pres.), Nat. Acad. Scis., Am. Inst. Mining, Metallurgy and Petroleum

Engrs. (hon. mem., past pres.), Am. Welding Soc. (dir., Adams lectr. 1944), Internat. Inst. Med. Electronics and Biomed. Engring., Am. Soc. Testing Materials, Soc. Automotive Engrs., Am. Iron and Steel Inst., Internat. Inst. Welding (v.p.; elector Hall of Fame). Clubs: La Jolla (Cal.) Beach and Tennis; Cosmos (Washington), University Chemists, Racquet and Tennis (N.Y.C.); San Diego Cuyamaca. Sr. author: Alloys of Iron and Chromium, vols. 1 and 2, 1937, 40. Contbr. articles on metallurgy and engring. to tech. pubs. Patentee metallurgy and engring. Address: 1738 Castellane Rd LaJolla CA 92037

KINZER, JOHN MARVIN, army officer; b. Jenkins, Ky., May 25, 1918; s. JOhn Marvin and Julia (Crutchfield) K.; B.S. in Agr., U. Fla., 1940; M.A. in Internat. Affairs, George Washington U., 1962; m. Marie Elizabeth Boucher, Dec. 1, 1945; children—Jeanne Marie, John Francis, Daniel Marvin. Commd. 2d lt. U.S. Army, 1940, advanced through grades to brig. gen., 1967; comdr. Airborne Arty., Japan, 1946, Germany, 1956, Ft. Campbell, Ky., 1962; mem. faculty Command and Staff Coll., 1952-55, Army War Coll., 1959-62; asst. chief staff plans/policy Hdqrs. MACV, Saigon, 1964-65, Allied Forces So. Europe, Naples, 1967-70; comdr. Civil Affairs Group, Ft. Gordon, Ga., 1965-67; doctoral candidate, asst. to v.p. for student affairs U. Fla., 1970—. Supr. religious edn. in stas. in Japan, 1948-49, Germany, 1956-58, U.S., 1959-64; commnr. Tranatlantic counil Boy Scouts Am., 1967-70. Bd. dirs. Episcopal Day Sch., Augusta, Ga. Decorated D.S.M., Legion of Merit, Bronze Star, Air medal, Army Commendation medal. Mem. Alpha Zeta, Phi Kappa Phi. Republican. Episcopalian. Rotarian. Home: 4909 NW 16th Pl Gainesville FL 32601

KIP, ARTHUR FREDERIC, educator; b. Los Angeles, Sept. 27, 1910; s. Frederic F. and Alice (Gump) K.; A.B., U. Cal. at Berkeley, 1935, Ph.D., 1939; m. Joan Hill, Mar. 24, 1944; children—Jonathan, Jennifer (Mrs. Ronald Bier). Research asst. Mass. Inst. Tech., Cambridge, 1939-41, asst. prof., 1945-51; mem. faculty dept. physics U. Cal. at Berkeley, 1951—, asso. prof., 1952-55, prof., 1956—; operations research scientist U.S. Navy, 1941-45. Guggenheim fellow, 1958-59. Mem. Am. Phys. Soc., A.A.A.S., Am. Assn. U. Profs. Author: Fundamentals of Electricity and Magnetism, 2d rev. edit., 1969. Home: 775 San Diego Rd Berkeley CA 94707

KIPHUTH, DELANEY, univ. dir. athletics; b. New Haven, Mar. 6, 1918; s. Robert J.H. and Louise (DeLaney) K.; grad. Phillips Acad., 1937; B.A., Yale, 1941, M.A., 1947; m. Janet E. Baillie, Sept. 18, 1944; children—Margaret Allan, Louise DeLaney (dec.). Instr. history, asst. athletics Hotchkiss Sch., 1941-42, instr. history, dir. athletics, 1948-54; dir. athletics, lectr. history Yale, 1954—. Pres. bd. dirs. Ulysses Grant Found., Inc. Bd. dirs. New Haven YMCA; bd. trustees Hopkins Grammar Sch. Served to maj. USAAF, 1943-45. Decorated Bronze Star medal (U.S.); Croix de Guerre (France). Home: 4 Carleton St Hamden CT 06517 Office: Ray Tompkins House Yale U New Haven CT 06520

KIPLINGER, AUSTIN HUNTINGTON, editor, pub.; b. Washington, Sept. 19, 1918; s. Willard Monroe and Irene (Austin) K.; A.B., Cornell U., 1939; student Harvard Grad. Sch., 1939- 40; m. Mary Louise Cobb, Dec. 11, 1944; children—Todd Lawrence, Knight Austin. Reporter Kiplinger Washington Letter, 1939, San Francisco Chronicle, 1940-41; exec. editor Kiplinger mag., Changing Times, 1945- 48; columnist Chgo. Jour. of Commerce, 1949-50; news commentator ABC, Chgo., 1951-55, NBC, Chgo., 1955-56; exec. v.p. The Kiplinger Washington Editors, 1956-59, pres., 1959—; editor Kiplinger Washington Letter, 1961—; pub. Changing Times Mag., 1959—. Trustee of Landon Sch., 1960-63. Pres. Juvenile Protective Assn. Chgo., 1955-56; chmn. Mayor's Adv. Com. on Youth Welfare, Chgo., 1956; vice chmn. Nat. Capital Health and Welfare Council, 1960-67. Trustee Cornell U., 1960—, chmn. U. council, 1965-68. Served as naval aviator aboard carriers PTO, 1942-45. Mem. Telluride Assn., Assn. Radio and TV News Analysts, Phi Beta Kappa, Delta Upsilon, Sigma Delta Chi. Unitarian. Clubs: Metropolitan, National Press, Overseas Writers (Washington); Commonwealth (Chgo.); Cornell (N.Y.); Potomac Hunt; Chevy Chase. Author: (with W. M. Kiplinger) Boom and Inflation Ahead, 1958. Home: Montevideo Poolesville, MD 20837 Office: 1729 H St Washington DC 20006

KIPNIS, ALEXANDER, Russian basso; b. Ukraine, Russia, Feb. 1, 1891; grad. Warsaw Conservatory as condr., 1912; studied voice, Berlin, Germany 1912-15; m. Mildred Levy, Apr. 7, 1925; 1 son, Igor. Debut, Wiesbaden Opera, 1917; first U.S. appearance, Manhattan Opera House, N.Y., 1923; concert appearances, Buenos Aires, Paris, London, Germany, Scandinavia, Australia, 1925-35, including Beyreuth Festival, 1927-33, Salzburg Festival, 1932-37, Chgo. Civic Opera, 1924-32; recitals throughout U.S., 1938-48; mem. Met. Opera since 1939. Extensive recordings include vocal compositions from Mozart to present day composers, opera, including Wagnerian basso roles, Hugo Wolf and Schubert Lieder; also 2 vols. Brahms records, Russian operatic arias, and Boris Godounoff. Mem. Juilliard Sch. Music. Mem. Am. Acad. Singing Tchrs. Home: Berkeley Rd Westport CT 06880 Address: Berkeley Rd Westport CT 06880

KIPNIS, IGOR, harpsichordist; b. Berlin, Germany, Sept. 27, 1930; s. Alexander and Mildred (Levy) K.; student Westport (Conn.) Sch. Music, 1941-48; A.B., Harvard, 1952; m. Judith Robison, Jan. 6, 1953; 1 son, Jeremy Robison. Deriviative citizenship. Debut, radio sta. WNYC, 1959; solo debut, N.Y.C. Hist. Soc., 1962; concerts recitals throughout U.S. and Can., 1962—; tours Europe, 1967, 69, 70, S.Am., 1968, Israel, 1969, Australia and Hawaii, 1971; tchr. baroque performance practice Berkshire Music Center, Tanglewood, Mass., summers 1964-67, chmn. baroque dept., 1965-67; asso. prof. fine arts Fairfield (Conn.) U., 1971—; rec. artist Golden Crest, Kapp, Vanguard, Decca, Epic, Columbia, Odyssey records; music critic, 1957—; record reviewer Stereo Review, 1961—; host of weekly radio program Age of Baroque, WQXR, N.Y., 1966-68. Served with AUS, 1952-54. Recipient nominations Nat. Acad. Recording Arts and Scis., 1964; Martha Baird Rockefeller Fund for Music, Inc. grants, 1966; 68; Deutsche Schallplatten Preis, 1969. Mem. Am. Musicol. Soc., Dolmetsch Found., Galpin Soc. Club: Bohemians (N.Y.C.). Editor: A First Harpsichord Book, 1970. Home: Drummer Lane RFD 2 West Redding CT 06896

KIPP, DEAN CARL, educator, physician; b. Manhattan, Kan., Apr. 27, 1918; s. Carl Louis and Ethel (McKean) K.; student St. Benedict's Coll., 1935-37; B.S., Kan. State U., 1939; M.D., Kan.U., 1943; m. Mary Elizabeth Davis, May 28, 1943; children—Karen Dean (Mrs. Donald R. McCann, Jr.), Jan Kendree (Mrs. Larry McElwain); Crane Davis. Intern Ohio State U. Hosp., 1943-44, resident surgery, 1947-49; resident pathology Barnes Hosp., St. Louis, 1946-47; clin. asso. prof. surgery Southwestern br. U. Tex. Med. Sch., Dallas, 1962—; chief dept. plastic surgery Baylor U. Med. Center, 1965—. Served with M.C., USNR, World War II: PTO. Diplomate Am. Bd. Plastic Surgery. Fellow A.C.S.; mem. Am., Tex., Dallas med. assns., Am. Soc. Plastic Surgeons, Internat. Fedn. Plastic Surgeons, Tex. Surg. Soc., Tex. Soc. Plastic Surgeons. Home: 3717 Villanova St Dallas TX 95225

KIPP, DONALD BOGART, lawyer; b. Passaic, N.J., Nov. 15, 1905; s. Reuben Eugene and Bessie W. (Bogart) K.; B.S., Princeton, 1928; LL.B., Harvard, 1931; m. Beatrice V. Behr, May 14, 1937; children—Beatrice Nelson, Peter John, Kathie Howell (dec.), Donald Bogart, Frederic Howell. Admitted to N.J. bar, 1932, since practiced in Newark; now mem. firm Pitney, Hardin & Kipp; dir. Fund Am. Cos., Fireman's Fund Ins. Co., Am. Can Co., N.Y.C.; dir. Nat. Newark & Essex Bank, United N.J. R.R. & Canal Co., Am. Ins. Co., Pub. Service Electric & Gas Co., N.J. Bell Telephone Co., Nat. Surety Corp. Mem. N.J. Corp. Law Revision Commn. Trustee, Morristown (N.J.). Meml. Hosp.; charter trustee Princeton. Served as lt. and lt. comdr., USNR 1942-44. Mem. Am., N.J., Essex County bar assns., St. Nicholas Soc., Holland Soc. of N.Y., N.J. Hist. Soc. (trustee; sec.), Am. Law Inst. Clubs: Essex (Newark); Morristown, Edgartown Yacht; Metropolitan (Washington); N.Y. Yacht, Somerset Hills Country. Home: Spring Valley Rd Morristown NJ 07960 Office: 57O Broad St Newark NJ 07102

KIPP, HAROLD C., banker; b. 1922; student U. Mich.; married. With Crocker-Citizens Nat. Bank, Los Angeles, 1950—, regional v.p., 1967-69, sr. v.p., regional v.p., 1969—. Served with USAF, 1942-45. Office: 611 W 6th St Los Angeles CA 90054*

KIPP, RAYMOND JOSEPH, coll. dean; b. Ossian, Ia., Dec. 7, 1922; s. William and Pauline T. (Giesing) K.; B.S. in Civil Engring., Marquette U., 1951; M.S., U. Wis., 1957, Ph.D., 1965; m. Margaret D. Bradley, Aug. 27, 1949; children—Jerry S., Carole J. Asst. city engr., Los Angeles, 1951-52; mem. faculty Marquette U., Milw., 1953—, acting dean Coll. Engring., 1971—. Served with USNR, 1942-47. Decorated Air medal with oak leaf cluster. Mem. Am. Soc. C.E., Am. Soc. Engring. Edn., Nat. Soc. Profl. Engrs., Water Pollution Control Fedn., Am. Water Works Assn. Home: 628 Elmspring Wauwatosa WI 53226 Office: 1515 W Wisconsin Av Milwaukee WI 53233

KIPPENHAN, CHARLES JACOB, educator, mech. engr.; b. Middle Amana, Ia., Nov. 8, 1919; s. Adam John and Emilie (Heinemann) K.; B.S. in Mech. Engring., State U. Ia., 1940, M.S., 1946, Ph.D., 1948; m. Jane Elizabeth Munsinger, Dec. 18, 1941; children—Judith Evans (Mrs. James R. Halstead II), Kurt Alfred. Instr. mech. engring. State U. Ia., 1941-42; from asst. prof. mech. engring. to prof., head dept. Washington U., St. Louis, 1948-64; prof. mech. engring., chmn. dept. U. Wash., 1964—; cons. to industry, 1949—. Served to lt. USN, 1942-46. AEC-Am. Soc. Engring. Edn. fellow nuclear energy seminar Cornell U., summer 1959, direct energy conversion U. Ill., summer 1963; NSF sci. tchr. fellow TH Munich, Germany, 1960-61. Mem. Am. Inst. Aeros. and Astronautics, Am. Soc. Engring. Edn., Am. Soc. M.E., Sigma Xi, Theta Tau, Pi Tau Sigma, Tau Beta Pi. Unitarian. Club: St. Louis Engineers. Contbr. profl. jours. Home: 3908 NE 38th St Seattle WA 98105

KIRACOFE, CLIFFORD ATTICK, lawyer, ins. co. exec.; b. Harrisburg, Pa., Oct. 31, 1907; s. Clifford Owen and Grace (Attick) K.; B.A., Susquehanna U., 1930; student Harvard Law Sch., 1930-31, Dickenson Law Sch., 1932-33; LL.B., John Marshall Law Sch., 1936; student Northwestern U. Law Sch., 1938-39; m. Elizabeth A. James, June 29, 1940; children—Clifford Attick, James B. Admitted to I11. bar, 1937, since practiced in Chgo.; partner firm Smith, Barker, Kiracofe, Allan & O'Brien, 1950—; sec., corp. counsel Lumbermens Mut. Casualty Co., Am. Motorists Ins. Co., Am. Mfrs. Mut. Ins. Co., Fed. Kemper Life Assurance Co., Fed. Mut. Ins. Co., Fidelity Life Assn., Ia. Kemper Mut. Ins. Co., Kemperco, Inc., Sequoia Ins. Co.; v.p., dir., corp. counsel Nat. Agts. Service Co., Inc.; sec., dir., corp. counsel Kemper Securities Sales Co.; sec., dir. Kemper Life Agy., Am. Underwriting Corp., Atlantic Consumer Discount Co., Nat. Eastern Corp., Tower Finance Corp., Mercury Acceptance Corp., Hogan & Farwell, Inc., Nat. Loss Control Service Corp.; sec. Economy Fire & Casualty Co., Central Mortgage Co., Twenty North Wacker Corp., Kemperco Reins. Co.; asst. sec. Kemper County Mut. Ins. Co.; asst. sec., dir. Extel Corp.; dir. Asso. Mutuals, Inc. (La.). Mem. adv. com. Taxpayers Fedn. I11., 1964—. Sec. James S. Kemper Found.; bd. dirs. St. Leonard's House, Chgo., 1959-64; trustee Village of Lake Bluff, Ill., 1947-54. Mem. Ill. C. of C., Chgo. Assn. Commerce and Industry, Am. (vice chmn. com. on ins. cos. sect. taxation), Ill., Chgo., Lake County bar assns., Internat. Assn. Ins. Law, Nat. Consumer Finance Assn., Nat. Tax Assn., Am. Soc. Corp. Secs., Mut. Ins. Com. on Fed. Taxation, N.A.M. (taxation com.). Clubs: Bath and Tennis (Lake Forest and Lake Bluff, Ill.); Farmington Country (Charlottesville, Va.). Home: Bath and Tennis Club PO Box 653 Lake Forest IL 60045 Office: 4750 Sheridan Rd Chicago IL 60640

KIRBY, ALLAN PRICE, corp. exec.; b. Wilkes-Barre, Pa., July 31, 1892; s. Fred Morgan and Jessie (Owen) K.; student Wyoming Sem., 1906-08, Lawrenceville (N. J.) Sch.; 1908-10, Lafayette Coll., Easton, Pa., 1910-12, D.H.L., 1946; LL.D. (hon.), St. Joseph's Coll., Phila., 1964; m. Marian G. Sutherland, Feb. 14, 1918; children—Grace Jessie, Fred Morgan II, Ann Sutherland, Allan P. Office mgr. Bathurst (New Brunswick) Lumber Co., 1914-15; treas. Jenkins-Kirby Packing Co., 1915-22; 22; pres. Kirby-Davis Co., 1922-34; v.p. 2d Nat. Bank, Wilkes-Barre, 1924-34; pres. Imperial Motor Corp., 1934-46; Pres. Alleghany Corp. 1939-61, chmn. bd. and chief exec. officer, 1963-67, chmn. emeritus, 1967—. Mem. Zeta Psi. Republican. Episcopalian. Mason (32d). Home: Harding Twp Morristown NJ 07960 Office: 17 DeHart St Morristown NJ 07960

KIRBY, ALLAN PRICE, Jr., investment co. exec.; b. Wilkes Barre, Pa., June 18, 1931; s. Allan Price and Marian (Sutherland) K.; grad. Morristown Sch., 1949; B.A., Lafayette Coll., 1953; m. Shelby Baran, Aug. 20, 1953; children—Jessie Ann, Allan Price III, Slater Baran, Coray Sutherland, Milan Stanton. Pres. Liberty Sq., Inc., Morristown, N.J.; dir., chmn. exec. com. Investors Diversified Services, Inc.; dir., mem. exec. com. Alleghany Corp.; dir. Bonwit Teller Co., I.S.L. Variable Annuity Fund, I.D.S. New Dimensions Fund, Inc., I.D.S. Progressive Fund, Inc., I.D.S. Growth Fund, Inc.; mem. Midtown adv. bd. Chem. Bank, Pres. bd. trustees Fred M. and Jessie A. Kirby Episcopal House; trustee, treas. Angeline Elizabeth Kirby Meml. Health Center. Served as lt. (j.g.), USNR, 1953-55. Mem. Delta Kappa Epsilon. Clubs: Morris County Golf (Convent, N.J.); Black River Fish and Game (Pottersville, N.J.). Office: 17 DeHart St Morristown NJ 07960

KIRBY, DONALD BEACH, architect; b. Denver, Feb. 25, 1905; s. Clarence Valentine and Florence (Beach) K.; B.Arch., U. Pa., 1926; m. Edith Dance; children—Donald Dance, Barbara Beach; m. Eleanor Wobber Wells, Feb. 11, 1962. Travels included Eng., France and Italy with Bur. U. Travel, Newton, Mass., 1926, 28, 29; with firms James W. O'Connor, also Godwin, Thompson & Patterson, N.Y.C., 1926-29, Gordon Kaufmann, also Reginald Johnson, Los Angeles, 1929-32; individual practice, San Francisco, 1933—; regional home use dir. Nat. Housing Agy., 1942-45; prin. works include two residences for Maharajah of Indore, 1939, Players Cafe, Hollywood, 1941, Miss Burke's Sch., San Francisco (A.I.A. and Sch. Adminstrs. award 1953), Castle AFB, Merced, Cal., 1953, Post Library Presidio of San Francisco, 1958; remodel housing project Naval Postgrad. Sch., 1962. Mem. San Francisco Planning Commn., 1957-59; pres. Cal. Builders Exchange, 1941-42; chmn. Bldg. Industry Conf. Bd. San Francisco, 1965-66. Recipient House Beautiful residential award, 1935. Fellow A.I.A. (bd. dirs., exec. com. 1954-57, pres. No. Cal. chpt. 1949-50); mem. Soc. Am. Mil. Engrs. (dir. San Francisco 1965, pres. 1966). Mason. Clubs: St. Francis Yacht, San Francisco Engineers. Address: 875 Chestnut St San Francisco CA 94133

KIRBY, DURWARD, entertainer; b. Covington, Ky., Aug. 24: s. Homer Cleveland and Alma Katherine (Haglage) K.; M.E., Purdue U.; m. Mary Paxton, June 7, 1941; children—Randall, Randall, Dennis. Engaged in radio, 1934-48, in TV, 1948- -; network newscaster, actor, comedian and spl. events reporter, 1934—; starred in tour of play Take Her, She's Mine, 1964, Impossible Years, 1966, Generation, 1967, Critic's Choice, 1968; also starred on Broadway in comedy, Me and Thee, 1965. Served with USNR; World War II. Recipient H. P. David nat. announcers award NBC, 1941; named one of three most popular TV comml. announcers Broadcasting Publs. and Advt. Agy. Publs., 1950-63; named Ky. col., 1964; named to Council Sagamores, Ind., 1966. Mem. A.F.T.R.A., Screen Actors Guild, Actors Equity Assn.‡ Address: Bronxville NY 10708

KIRBY, FRED MORGAN, II, investment co. exec.; b. Wilkes Barre, Pa., Nov. 23, 1919; s. Allan P. and Marian G. (Sutherland) K.; grad. Lawrenceville Sch., 1938, A.B., Lafayette Coll., Easton, Pa., 1942; student Harvard Grad. Sch. Bus. Adminstrn., 1947; m. A. Walker Dillard, Apr. 30, 1949; children—Alice, Fred Morgan III, Dillard, Jefferson. Vice pres., then pres., dir. Allan Corp., 1953—; pres., chmn. Filtration Engrs., Inc., 1951-56; exec. v.p., then pres., chmn. Alleghany Corp., 1961-67, chmn., 1967—; dir. mem. exec. com. Pittston Co., U.S. Industries, Inc.; chmn., mem. exec. com. Investors Diversified Services, Inc.; dir. F.W. Woolworth Co., Dillard Paper Co., Alpha Portland Cement Co., Hotel Waldorf Astoria Corp. Bd. trustees Fred M. and Jessie A. Kirby Episcopal House, Inc.; pres., bd. dirs. F.M. Kirby Found. Served as lt. (s.g.) USNR, 1942-46. Mem. Zeta Psi. Clubs: Westmoreland (Wilkes Barre, Pa.); Morris County (N.J.) Golf: Racquet and Tennis (N.Y.C.); Spring Valley Hounds.

KIRBY, GEORGE FRANCIS, petroleum co. exec.; b. Cheneyville, La., Dec. 7, 1916; s. George Francis and Vesta (Mason) K.; A.B., La. Coll., 1936; M.S., La. State U., 1938, Ph.D., 1940; postgrad. Harvard, 1952; m. Nannette Dutsch, Dec. 12, 1941; children-Michael E., John M. With Ethyl Corp., N.Y.C., 1940-69, v.p. research and devel., 1955-62, exec. v.p., 1963-64, pres., 1964-69, also dir.; dir., mem. exec. com. Tex. Eastern Transmission Corp., Houston, 1969—, exec. v.p., 1970—; dir. La. Nat. Bank; cons. prof. La. State U. Mem. Presidents Air Quality Adv. Bd., 1968-71. Bd. dirs. La. State U. Found. Mem. Am. Chem. Soc., Am. Inst. Chem. Engrs., A.A.A.S., Am. Petroleum Inst., Environmental Scis. Inst. (mem. adv. council for bd.), Gulf Research Inst. (trustee), Soc. Automotive Engrs. Clubs: Chemists, Pinnacle, Twenty-Nine, Economic (N.Y.C.), Baton Rouge Country, Camelot (Baton Rouge); Houston Petroleum (Houston). Home: 6821 Highland Rd Baton Rouge LA70808 Office: 921 Main at McKinney Houston TX 77001

KIRBY, JAMES CORDELL, Jr., legal educator; b. Macon County, Tenn., June 19, 1928; s. James Cordell and Belulah (Russell) K.; B.A., Vanderbilt U., 1950; student Law Sch., 1950- 51; LL.B., LL.M., N.Y.U., 1954; m. Barbara Glenn Eggleston, Mar. 22, 1955. Admitted to Tenn. bar, 1954, Ill. bar, 1966, Ohio bar, 1971; also U.S. Supreme Ct.; with firm Waller, Davis & Lansden, Nashville, 1954-55, 57-61; chief counsel judiciary subcom. constl. amendments U.S. Senate , 1961-63; asso. prof., then prof. law Vandebilt U. Law Sch., 1963-65; prof. law Northwestern U. Law Sch., 1965-68; prof. law N.Y.U., 1968-70; dean coll. law Ohio State U., 1970—; mem. panels Am. Arbitration Assn., also Fed. Mediation and Conciliation Service; research dir. spl. study congl. ethical standards Assn. Bar City N.Y., 1967—; vis. prof. N.Y.U. Sch. Law, 1968-69. Bd. dirs. Nashville Jr. C. of C., 1960-61; v.p. Nasvhille UN Assn., 1961. Served as 1st lt. AUS, 1956-57. Mem. Am. (spl. commn. presdl. inability and vice presdl. vacancy 1964; spl. comm. electoral coll. reform 1966), Order of Coif, Phi Beta Kappa, Phi Kappa Sigma, Omicron Delta Kappa. Democrat. Episcopalian. Home: 1509 LaFayette Dr Columbus OH 43220

KIRBY, JOHN PENDY educator; b. Hoosick Falls, N.Y., Jan. 20, 1905; s. William James and Kathleen Mary K.; A.B., Hamilton Coll., Clinton; N.Y., 1927; student Columbia, 1928-29; Ph. D., Yale, (Donald Grant Mitchell fellow in English 1936-37); 1937; m. Frances Wallace Allen, June 18, 1932. Instr. English, Pa. State Coll., 1929-34; asst. asso. prof. English, Lake Forest (Ill.) Coll., 1937-41; prof. English, Mary Washington Coll. U. Va., 1941-47, vis. prof. U. Va.; 1964-65, also summers 1945—; prof.; chmn. dept. English Randolph-Macon Woman's Coll. since 1947; vis. prof. Sweet Briar Coll., 1950; vis. prof. English, U. Va.; 1964-65. Mem. Modern Lang. Assn., Coll. English Assn.; Nat. Council Tchrs. English, South Atlantic Modern Lang. Assn.; Soc. for Theatre Research (London); Am. Soc. for Eighteenth Century Studies, Assn. Depts. English; English-Speaking Union. Editor: Index to the Private Papers of James Boswell from Malahide Castle (with Frederick A. Pottle), 1937; Literature of Western Civilization (with L. G. Locke and M. E. Porter, 2 vols), 1952. Co- editor of The Explicator since 1942. Contbr. articles profl. jours. Home: 1130 Rugby Rd Lynchburg VA 24503

KIRBY, ROBERT EMORY, mfg. co. exec.; b. Ames, Ia., Nov. 8, 1918; s. Robert Stearns and Ora (Walker) K.; B.S., Pa. State U., 1939; M.B.A., Harvard, 1956; m. Barbara Anne McClintock, July 11, 1942; children—Mary Linda, Donna Susan (dec.). With W.Va. Pulp & Paper Co., 1939-43; with Westinghouse Elec. Corp., 1946—, gen. mgr. electronics div., 1958-63, v.p. engring., 1963-64, group v.p. indsl. group, 1964-66, exec. v.p., dir., 1966- 69, pres. Industry and Def. Co., 1969—; dir. Canadian Westinghouse Co., Ltd., Deane & Deane, Inc., Home Capital Funds, Inc., Pitts. br. Fed. Res. Bank. Bd. dirs. Pitts. Symphony; trustee U. Pitts. Served with USNR, 1943-46. Mem. Pitts. C. of C., I.E.E.E., Am. Soc. Naval Engrs., Kappa Gamma Psi, Beta Theta Pi. Clubs: Chartiers Country, Duquesne (dir.) (Pitts.); Bay Hill; Cotton Bay; Rolling Rock; Laurel Valley (Ligonier, Pa.); Sky (N.Y.C.). Home: 250 Tech Rd Pittsburgh PA 15205 Office: Westinghouse Bldg Pittsburgh PA 15222

KIRBY, ROBERT STEPHEN, corp. exec.; b. Rochelle, Ill., Aug. 4, 1925; s. Stephen F. and Eulalia E. (Coleman) K.; B.S., U. Ill., 1948; student U. Wis., 1948; J.D., U. Ill., 1950; m. Carolyn C. Clark, June 10, 1950; children—Kathleen, Robert, James, Thomas, Julie. Admitted to Ill. bar, 1950; partner firm Frisch & Fox, Chgo., 1950-52; atty. to asst. gen. solicitor I.C. R.R. Co., Chgo., 1952-69; asst. gen. counsel, asst. sec. Ill. Central Industries, Inc., Chgo., 1969-70, v.p., sec., dir. manpower resources, 1970—; dir. Perfect Plus Hosiery, Inc. Gov. Henrotin Hosp. (Chgo.). Served with USMC, 1943-45. Mem. Soc. Trial Lawyers, Chgo. Bar Assn., Delta Kappa Epsilon, Phi Delta Phi. Club: Skokie Country (Glencoe, Ill.). Home: 432 Washington Av Glencoe IL 60022 Office: 135 E 11th Pl Chicago IL 60605

KIRBY, ROBION CROMWELL, educator, mathematician; b. Chgo., Feb. 25, 1938; s. Bernard Cromwell and Pauline (Robion) K.; B.S., U. Chgo., 1959, M.S., 1960, Ph.D., 1965; student Rice U., 1964-65; m. Ingrid Renate Pagalys, Sept. 7, 1962; children—Rolf Edward, Katharine Anne. Asst. prof. math. U. Cal. at Los Angeles, 1965-69, prof., 1969-71; prof. math. U. Cal. at Berkeley, 1971—; vis. asst. prof. U. Wis., 1967; mem. Inst. for Advanced Study, 1968, 69; vis. prof. Cambridge U., 1970, Harvard, 1971. Mem. Am. Math. Soc. (Veblen prize 1971). Office: Math Dept U Cal Berkeley CA 94720

KIRBY, THOMAS AUSTIN, univ. prof. b. Albion N.Y., Sept. 7, 1904; s. Thomas Austin and Emma Marie (Griffin) K.; student Hamilton Coll., 1922-24; A.B., Cath. U. Am., 1927, A.M. 1928; student U. Heidelberg 1929, U. Munich 1929-30; Ph.D., Johns Hopkins U., 1933; m. Josie Warren Dyson, May 31, 1937; children—Thomas Austin (dec.), Albert Charles, David Kirk. Prof. English, St. Thomas Coll. (now U. Scranton), 1933-34, Manhattan Coll., 1934-35; asst. prof. La. State U. 1935-39, asso. prof. 1939-43, prof. English, 1943—, acting chmn., dept. English 1940-42, head dept. , 1942—. Mem. Am. Assn. U. Profs. (past. pres., v.p., sec. local chpt., S. Central Modern Lang. Assn. (v.p., mem. exec. com., 1947-48), Modern Lang. Assn. Am., Medieval Acad. Am., Modern Humanities Research Assn., Internat. Arthurian Soc., Am. Dialect Soc., Nat. Council Tchrs. English, Soc. Study Mediaeval Lang. and Lit., Internat. Assn. U. Profs. English, Nat. Cath. Com. Intellectual and Cultural Affairs, Psi Upsilon. Roman Catholic. Author: Chaucer's Troilus: A Study in Courtly Love, 1940; False Gallop (verse), 1956. Editor: Studies for William A. Read (with N.M. Caffee), 1940; Philolgica (with H. B. Woolf), 1949; (with W.J. Olive) Essays in Honor of Esmond Linworth Marilla, 1970. Contbr. numerous articles, notes and revs. in Profl. publs.: splty. medieval lit. (especially Chaucer). Editorial bd. The Chaucer Rev.; adv. com. Variorum Chaucer. Home: 6347 Moss Side Lane Baton Rouge LA 70808

KIRBY, THOMAS MALCOLM, lawyer; b. Jacksonville, Fla., Jan. 19, 1923; s. Claudius C. and Lucy (Greenwood) K.; A.A., U. Fla., 1946, J.D., 1948; m. Fleta Charme Benson, Aug. 2, 1967; children—Claudia Anne, Kimberly Ann. Admitted to Fla. bar, 1948, since practiced in Jacksonville; partner firm Howell, Kirby, Montgomery & D'Aiuto, 1951—. Bd. dirs. YMCA Opportunity House, Jacksonville, 1950-53, Boys Service Council and Big Bros. Am., 1949-55. Served as pilot USMCR, 1944-45. Decorated Air medal with oak leaf cluster, D.F.C. Mem. Am., Fla. bar assns., Internat. Assn. Ins. Counsel, Fla. Def. Counsel Assn., Phi Delta Phi, Sigma Alpha Epsilon. Home: 2717 Forest Circle Jacksonville FL 32217 Office: Gulf Life Tower Jacksonville FL 32207

KIRBY, VANCE NATHANIEL, legal educator; b. Bronxville, N.Y., Aug. 23, 1912; s. Harry N. and Elsa (Greene) K.; A.B., Dartmouth, 1934; LL.B., Harvard, 1937; m. Harriet A. Geary, Dec. 5, 1942; children—Kate P. (Mrs. William P. Docken) John L., David V. Admitted to Mass. bar, 1938, Conn. bar, 1939, Ill. bar, 1953; with Treasury Dept., 1942-53, tax legislative counsel, 1948-53; mem. faculty Northwestern U. Law Sch., 1953—, prof. law, 1957—; cons. firm Chadwell, Keck, Kayser, Ruggles & McLaren, Chgo., 1957—. Trustee, Winnetka Pub. Library, 1961-67, pres., 1965-66. Mem. Ill. (chmn. fed. tax com. 1960-62), Chgo. (chmn. fed. tax com. 1959-61) bar assns. Home: 864 Burr Av Winnetka IL 60093 Office: 357 E Chicago Av Chicago IL 60603

KIRBY, WILLIAM THOMAS, lawyer; b. Chicago, Jan. 2, 1911; s. William T. and Margaret (Durkin) K.; A.B., U. Notre Dame, 1932, J.D., 1934; m. Evelyn McAdams, Apr. 6, 1940 (dec. May 1967); children-Catherine, James, Mary, Judith. Admitted to Ill. bar, 1934, also U.S. Supreme Ct.; practice in Chgo., 1945; partner firm Hubachek, Kelly, Rauch & Kirby, 1965—; gen. counsel Bankers Life & Casualty Co., Chgo., Citizens Bank & Trust Co., Park Ridge, Ill.; asst. atty. gen. Ill., 1949-53; fed. referee in bankruptcy, 1936-40. Mem. Ill.-Ind. Bi-State Devel. and Study Commn., 1957-59; bd. dirs. Waukegan Port Dist., 1960-70; zone real estate dir. War Assets Adminstrn., 1946-47. Served to capt., C.E., AUS, World War II. Fellow Am. Coll. Trial Lawyers; mem. Soc. Trial Lawyers, Am., Ill., Chgo., Lake County, 7th Circuit bar assns. Catholic. Club: Glen Flora Country (Waukegan, Ill.). Home: 303 Douglas St Waukegan IL 60085 Office: Hubachek, Kelly, Rauch & Kirby Prudential Plaza Chicago IL 60601

KIRCHEN, ALEXANDER WALT chemist, educator; b. Chicago, 1928; B.S. in Physics, Yale, 1950; Ph.D. in Chemistry, Harvard, 1956; m. Sally Ann Jones, July 5, 1957; children--Kenneth J., Nancy A. Chemist, Acme Chem. Co., Blue Island, Ill., 1950-51; director of Research Lab., Indsl. Chemicals Corp., Cambrige, Mass., 1956-60; project coordinator environmental sect. Steinmetz Assos., Chgo., 1960-61; v.p. for research Bauer Bros. Chem. Co., Inc., Memphis, 1961-64; asst. prof. chemistry Washington U., St. Louis, 1964-66, asso. prof., 1966-70, prof., 1970--, head of chemistry dept., 1970-71. Vis. prof. So. Ill. U., summer 1967, U. of Ore., 1969. Bd. dirs. Rest Haven Home for Elderly, 1960-61; trustee of the Lutheran Hosp., 1965-71. Served from lt. to capt., AUS, 1951-53. Mem. Am. Chem. Soc., Sci. Research Soc. Am. (chpt. treas. 1967), Sigma Xi. Author: (with others) Basic Inorganic Chemistry, 1971. Home: Fairfax Apts 7291 Windermere Dr University City MO 63105 Office: Dept Chemistry Washington University St Louis MO 63130

KIRCHER, DONALD PETER, bus. exec.; b. St. Paul, Apr. 28, 1915; s. Frank Joseph and Alma (Peterson) K.; student U. Minn., 1932-36; LL.B., Columbia, 1939; LL.D., Monmouth Coll.; m. Ghilan Hall, Aug. 24, 1942 (dec.); children—Linda Anne (dec.), Peter Hall; m. 2d. Lois Moeller, Jan. 19, 1965; 1 dau., Lois Amaryllis. Admitted to N.Y. State bar, 1939, individual practice law, 1939-48, with Winthrop, Stimson, Putnam & Roberts, 1939- 41, 46-48; asst. to pres. Singer Co., 1948-49, asst. v.p., 1949-52, v.p., 1952-58, pres., chief exec. officer, 1958-68, pres., chmn. 1968—, also dir.; pres. chief exec. officer Singer Sewing Machine Co.; dir. Bristol-Myers Co., Morgan Guaranty Trust Co. N.Y. also Gen. Cable Corp., The Lehman Corp., Met. Life Ins. Co. Mem. State Dept.'s Adv. Com. on Internat. Bus. Problems, Citizens Com. Higher Edn. N.J. Trustee, Matheny Sch., Morristown (N.J.) Meml. Hosp., N.J. Coll. Fund Assn., Inc.; bd. dirs. Seniven Found., Inc., Clark Found; bd. overseers Found. Advancement Grad. Study in Engrng.; trustees Tax Found., U.S. Council Internat. C. of C. Served from pvt. to capt.; AUS, 1941-45; ETO. Decorated Silver star with 2 oak leaf clusters, Bronze Star medal, Purple Heart with oak leaf cluster, Presdl. Unit Citation, Chevalier Order of Leopold and Croix de Guerre (Belgium); recipient Gold medal of Achievement Poor Richard Club Phila., 1967. Mem. Pilgrims U.S. Center for Inter-Am. Relations, Phi Delta Theta, Phi Delta Phi. Clubs: University (N.Y.C.); Essex Hunt. Home: 230 E 62d St New York City NY 10021 Office: 30 Rockefeller Plaza New York City NY 10020

KIRCHER, JOHN EDWIN, oil co. exec.; b. Wayland, Mo., Dec. 7, 1917; s. Henry Frederick and Anna (Porter) K.; B.A., Culver-Stockton Coll., 1939; Ph.D., U. Mo., 1942; m. Dorothy June Eaton, Jan. 19, 1946; children—Mark Henry, Gary John, Elizabeth Jessica. Research chemist, dir. sales Sharples Chem. Co., Phila., 1942-45; dir. devel. Stephan Chem. Co., Chgo., 1945-51; with petrochem. dept. Continental Oil Co., Houston, 1951-60, regional gen. mgr., Ft. Worth, 1960-62, exec. asst. to pres., Houston, 1962-63, v.p. marketing, 1963-65, v.p., world-wide coordinator mfg. and marketing, N.Y.C., 1965, exec. v.p., dir., 1966-71, pres. Eastern Hemisphere Petroleum div., 1971—. Mem. Am. Chem. Soc., Am. Petroleum Inst., Lambda Chi Alpha. Methodist. Mason. Clubs: Houston; Fifth Ave. (N.Y.C.); Greenwich Country. Home: Highland Farm Rd Greenwich CT 06830 Office: 30 Rockefeller Plaza New York City NY 10020

KIRCHER, RALF CHARLES, advt. exec.; b. Pitts., May 22, 1907; s. William Charles and Marthe (Osborn) K.; B.B.A., Ohio U., 1929; m. Virginia Paul, Oct. 7, 1933; children—Dudley Paul, Christine (Mrs. Donald Jones); m. 2d, Susanne Rike McConnaughey, Nov. 22, 1962. Copywriter, Hugo Wagensteil & Assos., 1929- 38; pres. Ralf Kircher Co., 1938-42, Kircher, Lytle, Helton & Collett, 1942-47; chmn. bd., creative dir. Kircher, Helton & Collett, Inc., Dayton, O., 1947—. Pres., Dayton Mus. Natural History, 1968-70, chmn., 1971. Mem. Dayton Advt. Club: (pres. 1960), Gamma Gamma Gamma, Sigma Alpha Epsilon, Omicron Delta Kappa, Alpha Delta Sigma. Episcopalian. Author: There's a Fly in This Room, 1946; Wrap as a Gift, 1948; also articles. Home: 4405 Dello Dell Rd Dayton OH 45429 Office: Grant-Deneau Tower Dayton OH 45402

KIRCHER, WILLIAM L., labor union exec.; b. Athens, O., Mar. 2, 1915; s. Charles P. and Josephine (McCoy) K.; A.B. In Journalism, Ohio U., 1936; m. Hilda B. Espel, Jan. 20, 1940; children—Thomas J., Mary Jo (Mrs. D. J. Huck). Internat. rep. UAW-CIO, 1942-51, dir. Wage Stblzn. Office, Washington, 1951-53, asst. to v.p., Detroit, 1952-55; asst. dir. orgn. AFL-CIO, 1955- 56, asst. regional dir., Ohio and W.Va., 1956-64, asst. nat. orgn. dir., 1964-65, dir., 1965—. Cons., Nat. Conf. Catholic Men; exec. bd. Nat. Cath. Social Action Conf. Named Alumni of Year, Ohio U., 1968. Home: 3444 Chiswick Ct Silver Spring MD Office: 815 16th St NW Washington DC 20006

KIRCHHOFER, ALFRED HENRY, broadcasting exec.; b. Buffalo, May 25, 1892; s. Robert and Elizabeth (Boldt) K.; ed. high school, Buffalo Litt. D. (hon.), St. Bonaventure U., 1963, D'Youville Coll., 1964; m. Emma M. Schugardt; Jan. 27, 1914; 1 son, Robert A. Boys' work sec. Genesee YMCA Buffalo, 1909-10; with Buffalo Com.; Buffalo Times, Buffalo Courier until 1913; editor Western N. Y. Post, 1913-14; with Buffalo Evening News since 1915, Washington corr., 1921-27, mng. editor 1927-56, editor; 1956-66; exec. v.p. Buffalo Evening News, Inc. 1956-66, dir., 1956- -; v.p. WBEN, Inc., 1930-56, pres.; 1956-67; vis. prof. U. Mo. Sch. Journalism, 1967—. Dir. Trico Products Corp. Publicity dir. U. Buffalo $5,000,000 endowment fund campaign, 1920-29. Bd. dirs. Roswell Park Meml. Inst.-U. Mo. Sc. Writing Seminar. Active in Liberty Loan and Red Cross campaigns, World War I. Asso. dir. publicity. Republican Nat. Com., 1928, dir. publicity, 1936. Dir. Millard Filmore Hosp.; past dir. Internat. Inst.; past mem. adv. bd. Am. Press Inst.; pres. Am. Council Edn. Journalism, 1950-52; apptd. to Syracuse U. Sch. Journalism council of editors and pubs., 1958; dir. Crippled Children Camps, Inc., 1946-66; sec. bd. visitors Roswell Park Meml. Inst. dir. ANRC (Buffalo chpt.), Buffalo Philharmonic Orch.; trustee U. Buffalo Found.; 1962-65; chmn. journalism adv. council St. Bonaventure U.; 1965-69, now mem. journalism adv. council; adv. bd. Children's Hosp.; dir. Buffalo Fine Arts Acad., Health Research, Inc., Fresh Air Mission, N.Y. Def. Council; trustee United Fund Buffalo and Erie County: exec. bd. Nat. Council Christians and Jews. Recipient of journalism medal, U. Mo.; Syracuse U. Sch. Journalism Distinguished Service medal, 1958; Distinguished Citizen Achievement award Canisus Coll. Bd. of Regent, 1960; U. Buffalo Sch. Bus. Alumni award, 1961; award for Distinguished Service to Journalism, Frontier Press Club, 1962; award Nat. Council Christians & Jews, 1964; Buffalo and Erie County Hist. Soc. Red Jacket award, 1966; Liberty Bell award, Erie County Bar Assn., 1967; Law Day Citizenship award, N.Y. State Bar Assn., 1967; Medal in recognition Community service Buffalo Club, 1968; Nat. Brotherhood citation Buffalo, Lockport chpts. NCCI, 1968. Trustee Sci. Service, 1940-54; mem. bd. trustees Buffalo YMCA Mem. adv. council Erie County Civil Defense, dir. Buffalo & Erie City Tb Assn. Mem. Am. Soc. Newspaper Editors (dir. 1930; sec., 1931; v.p. 1934-36; pres. 1937), N.Y. Soc. Newspaper Editors (dir. 1961-63); Am. Press Ins. founder), Soc. TV Pioneers (charter mem., Cult of the White Buffalo, Newcomen Soc., Sigma Delta Chi; life mem. Buffalo Library. Presbyn. Mason (33, Shriner). Clubs: Gridiron, National Press (pres. 1927), Capitol Hill (Washington); Rotary (hon.), Buffalo, Buffalo Country; Saturn. Home: 925 Delaware Av Buffalo NY 14209 Address: 218 Main St Buffalo NY 14203

KIRCHHOFF, DONALD JOSEPH, bus. exec.; b. Richmond Heights, Mo., June 29, 1925; s. Joseph V. and Freida (Kruger) K.; B.S., Miami U., Oxford, O., 1946; M.B.A., Harvard, 1949; m. Bluette Hartman, May 24, 1947; children—Susan Lee, Barbara Ann, Karen Mari. Accountant, Kroger Co., 1949-51; controller Nat. Food Stores Mich., 1953-56; with Standard Fruit & S.S. Co., 1956-69, v.p., 1961-62, exec. v.p., 1962-64, pres., dir., 1964-69; exec. v.p., dir. Castle & Cooke, Inc., 1970—. Served to lt. USNR, 1943-48, 51-53. Mem. Honolulu C. of C. Club: Pacific (Honolulu). Home: 3635 Diamond Head Rd Honolulu HI 96816 Office: Financial Plaza of Pacific Honolulu HI 96813

KIRCHMAN, ROBERT LESTER, coll. dean; b. Ft. Smith, Ark., May 6, 1926; s. Lester Herman and Desirene (Wilson) K.; B.Mus., Hendrix (Ark.) Coll., 1949; M.Ed., U. Mo., 1961; m. Mary Margaret Holmes, June 2, 1950; children—Carrie Ann, Christopher Robert, Catherine Margaret. Band dir. Harrison (Ark.) pub. schs., 1949-61; counselor Ark. A. and M. Coll., College Heights, 1961- 62, acad. dean, 1962—. Mem. Ark. Fulbright Com., 1962—; mem. Ark. State Commn. on Econ. Edn., 1968—. Served with USAAF, 1944-45. Mem. Nat., Ark. edn. assns., Assn. Higher Education, Ark. Dean's Assn. (pres. 1965-66). Methodist. Kiwanian (sec. Monticello club 1963, pres. 1964, lt. gov. div. 20, 1965). Home: PO Box 3052 Monticello AR 71655

KIRCHNER, EDWIN JAMES, food co. exec.; b. Keokuk, Ia., July 4, 1924; s. Edwin William and Gertrude Ann (Breheny) K.; grad. high sch.; m. Wilma Bernice Johnson, Apr. 21, 1944; children—Linda (Mrs. R.J. Hurley, Jr.), Karen Ann, Patrick Adam. Accounting, Union Electric Power Co., Keokuk, 1942-48; with Hubinger Co., Keokuk, 1948—, adminstrv. asst. to v.p. finance, 1960-67, asst. v.p., asst. treas., asst. sec., 1967-69, treas., asst. sec., dir., 1969—; dir., sec.-treas. Keokuk Grain Inspection Service, 1970—. Bd. dirs. South Lee County (Ia.) chpt. A.R.C., 1965—, chpt. chmn., 1969—. Served with USAAF, 1943-46; ETO, MTO. K.C. (treas. 1965—), Elk. Home: 2 Wahkonsa Heights Keokuk IA 52632 Office: 601 Main St Keokuk IA 52632

KIRCHNER, JOHN ALBERT, educator; b. Waynesboro, Pa., Mar. 27, 1915; s. Francis Edward and Jessie Cecilia (Cameron) K.; M.D., U. Va., 1940; M.S. (hon.), Yale, 1952; m. Aline Legault, Oct. 11, 1947; children—John C., Thomas L., Paul E., Marie Cecile, Christine A. Intern Charity Hosp., New Orleans, 1940- 41; resident otolaryngology Johns Hopkins Hosp., 1946-50; mem. faculty Yale Sch. Medicine, 1951—, prof. otolaryngology, 1962—; cons. in research NIH, 1966—; spl. research pathology and physiology of larynx and pharynx. Served to capt. AUS, 1942-46. Decorated Bronze Star. Recipient Harris P. Mosher award research Am. Trilogical Soc., 1958. Fellow A.C.S.; mem. Am. Laryngol. Assn. (Casselberry award 1966, also Newcomb award in 1969), New Eng. Otolaryngol. Soc. (pres. 1965-66), Am. Assn. Head and Neck Surgery, Collegium Oto-Rhino-Laryngologicum Amicitae Sacrum, Sigma Xi. Editor: Yearbook Ear, Nose and Throat, 1969—. Home: Rimmon Hill Rd Woodbridge CT 06525 Office: 333 Cedar St New Haven CT 06510

KIRCHNER, LEON, composer, pianist; b. Bklyn., Jan. 24, 1919; s. Samuel and Pauline K.; A.B., U. Cal. at Berkeley, 1940; m. Gertrude Schoenberg, July 8, 1949; children—Paul, Lisa. Faculty, Mills Coll., Oakland, Cal., 1952-61, Luther B. Marchant prof. music, 1954-61; prof. music Harvard, 1961-66, Walter B. Rosen Prof. music, 1966—. Recipient Prix de Paris, 1942; N.Y. Music Critics award, 1950, 60, Naumburg award for composition, Library Congress, 1954, award Am. Acad. Arts and Letters. Guggenheim 1948-50; 1948-5O; Mem. A.S.C.A.P., Internat. Soc. Contemporary Music, League Am. Composers, Nat. Inst. Arts and Letters, Am. Acad. Arts & Scis., Am. Assn. U. Profs. Composer Piano Sonata, 1948; Piano Suite 49, 1949; Sinfonia, 1951; Sonata Concertante, 1952; Piano Concerto, 1953; Trio for Piano, Violin and Cello, 1954; Toccata for Strings, Solo Winds and Percussion, 1955; String Quartet 2, 1958; Concerto for Violin, Cello, 10 Winds and Percussion, 1960, Piano Concerto No. 2, 1962; Words from Wordsworth for chorus, 1966; String Quartet No. 3, 1966 (Pulitizer prize 1967), Music for Orch., 1969. Address: Harvard U Cambridge MA 02138

KIRCHNER, WALTHER, educator, historian; b. Berlin, Germany, May 18, 1905; s. Paul K. and Alice K.; came to U.S., 1926, naturalized, 1944; A.B., U. Cal. at Los Angeles, 1941, M.A., 1942, Ph.D., 1944; m. Frederica Mosher, Jan. 10, 1944. Lectr., U. Cal. at Los Angeles, 1943-45; mem. faculty U. Del., 1945-70, H. Rodney Sharp prof., 1965-70; vis. prof. U. Pa., 1946-50, Lehigh U., 1947, U. Munster (Germany), 1964, U. Munich, (Germany), 1967-68; mem. Inst. Advanced Study, Princeton, 1955-56. Mem. Am. Hist. Assn., Am. Soc. Reformation Research (pres. 1958), Am. Assn. Advancement Slavic Studies, Am. Econ. History Soc., Hansischer Geschichtsverein. Author: Rise of the Baltic Question, 1954; History of Russia, 1948; Western Civilization, 2 vols., 1958-60; Jacob Fries, 1955; Economic Relations Between Russia and the West, 1966; The Middle Ages, 1968; Alba, 1963; also articles. Am. editor Jahrbücher für Geschichte Osteuropas. Home: Cranbury Rd Princeton Junction NJ 08550

KIRCHWEY, FREDA, editor, writer; d. George W. and Dora (Wendell) Kirchwey; grad. Horace Mann Sch., N.Y.C., 1911; A.B., Barnard Coll. (Columbia), 1915; L.H.D., Rollins Coll., 1944; m. Evans Clark, Nov. 9, 1915; children—Brewster (dec.), Michael Kirchwey, Jeffrey (dec.). Reporter, Morning Telegraph, N.Y.C., 1915-16; editorial staff Every Week, N.Y.C., 1917-18; staff Sunday Tribune, 1918; with The Nation, 1918—, mng. editor, 1922-28, became v.p., 1922, literary editor, 1928-29, editor, 1932—, editor and pub., 1937-55. Decorated chevalier French Legion of Honor, 1946. Mem. Commn. World Devel. and World Disarmament, Womens Internat. League Peace and Freedom, Am. Civil Liberties Union, Internat. League Rights Man, N.A.A.C.P., Com. Democratic Spain (vice chmn.), League Women Voters, Mus. Modern Art. Club: Cosmopolitan (N.Y.C.). Address: 390 1st Av New York City NY 10010

KIRGIS, FREDERIC L., lawyer; b. Chicago Heights, Ill., Sept 25, 1907; s. Frederic and Anne (Smith) K.; A.B., U. Ill., 1929, J.D., 1931; J.S.D. Yale, 1936; m. Kathryn Burrows, June 30, 1933; children—Frederic L., Jerry B., Ann Patricia. Admitted to Colo. bar, 1941; instr. law U. Ill., 1931-32; Sterling teaching fellow in law Yale, 1932-33; asst. solicitor U.S. Dept. Interior, 1933-36, first asst. solicitor, 1936-40; spl. asst. to U.S. Atty. Gen., 1941-45; partner Gorsuch, Kirgis, Campbell, Walker & Grover, Denver, 1945—. Mem. adv. council U.S. Pub. Land Law Rev. Commn., 1965-7O. Mem. Am. (chmn. sect. of adminstv. law 1965-66), Colo., Denver bar assns., Order of Coif, Phi Beta Kappa Clubs: Denver Country; Law, Denver. Home: 220 S Eudora St Denver CO 80222 Office: Security Life Bldg Denver CO 80202

KIRIACON, ARTHUR JACK, drug mfr.; b. N.Y.C., Aug. 15, 1925; s. Jack Arthur and Corinne (Drowne) K.; B.B.A., Iona Coll., 1948; M.B.A., N.Y. U., 1950; m. Dolores Marie Venditti, Feb. 13, 1968; children—Jane, John. Tax accountant Am. Tobacco Co., 1948-57; treas. Caster-Wallace, Inc., 1957-70, exec. v.p., 1970—. Served with USNR, 1943-45. Home: 340 E 64th St New York City NY 10021 Office: 767 Fifth Av New York City NY 10022

KIRILENKO, ANDREI PAVOLICH, govt. ofcl. USSR; b. 1906; ed. Higher Tech. Sch. Engaged as fitter, 1925- 29; mem. Young Communist League, 1929-30; engr., 1936-38; sec. dist., later regional com. Zaporozhe regional com. C.T.S.U., 1938-41, 43; 1st sec. Nicolaev City and Regional Com., S.P.S.U., 1947-50, Dnepropetrovsk Regional Com., 1950-51, Sverdlovsk Regional Com., 1955-63; candidate mem. Presidium Central Com. Communist Party USSR, 1957-61, mem. 1962-66, sec., 1966—; mem. Politburo, 1966—; 1st vice chmn. bur. for R.S.F.S.R., 1962—. Address: Politburo of Central Com Communist Party Moscow USSR*

KIRK, ARTHUR SHERMAN, banker, realtor; b. Hiawatha, Kan., June 25, 1891; s. Sherman and Harriot (White) K.; A.B., Drake U., 1914, LL.B., 1923; A.M., Harvard, 1915; m. Elizabeth Leland Chamberlain, Sept. 9, 1919; children—Joseph C., Catherine (Mrs. Edwin Tim Elliot). Admitted to Ia. bar, 1923; propr. Chamberlain, Kirk & Cline, realtors, Des Moines, 1923—; pres. Home Fed. Savs & Loan Assn., Des Moines, 1936-57, chmn. bd., 1957—; mem. exec. com., dir. Valley Bank & Trust Co., Des Moines, 1934—. Mem. Des Moines Planning and Zoning Com., 1935-45. Chmn. trustees Drake U., 1964-66, chmn. relay com., 1959. Served with U.S. Army, 1917-19, Mem. Des Moines Real Estate Bd. (pres. 1926, 39); Ia. Assn. Real Estate Bds. (pres. 1934-35), Am. Inst. Real Estate Brokers (pres. 1945), Am. Inst. Real Estate Appraisers (gov. council 1935-38), Am. Soc. Real Estate Counselors (gov. council 1966-69, Order of Coif, Phi Beta Kappa; Sigma Alpha Epsilon. Mason (32). Clubs: Des Moines, Wakonda (Des Moines). Home: 3807 Grand Av Des Moines IA 50312 Office: 507 9th St Des Moines IA 50309

KIRK, CAMERON, steel co. exec.; b. Pueblo, Colo., May 22, 1925; s. George M. and Georgia (Tucker) K.; LL.B., U. Colo., 1950; m. Barbara Lewis, June 10, 1947; children—Nancy Lynn, Georgia Lee, Cameron, Kristen Ann, George Edward. With CF & I Steel Corp., 1953—, asst. sec., 1955-62, sec., 1962—. Served with USNR, World War II, Korea. Home: 57 Morehead Dr Rye NY 10580 Office: 300 Park Av New York City NY 10022

KIRK, CHARLES FREDERICK, educator; b. Steubenville, O., June 12, 1916; s. Robert Carey and Helen (Hall) K.; B.A., Coll. of Wooster, 1939; M.A., Ohio State U., 1940, Ph.D., 1957; m. Leona May Dickerman, Apr. 11, 1942; children—Charla Jeanne (Mrs. William V. Paulus), Bruce Martin. Mem. faculty Kent State U., 1941—, prof., chmn. dept. Romance langs. and Classics, 1964—. Served with AUS, 1942-45. Mem. Am. Assn. Tchrs. Spanish and Portuguese, Ohio Modern Lang. Tchrs. Assn., Am. Assn. U. Profs., Modern Lang. Assn. Mem. United Ch. Christ (chmn. bd. deacons 1962-65, bd. Christian edn. 1957-61). Author: Successful Devices in Teaching Spanish, 1958. Home: 962 Middlebury Rd Kent OH 44240

KIRK, CLAUDE ROY, Jr., former gov. of Fla.; b. San Bernardino, Cal., Jan 7, 1926; s. Claude Roy and Sarah (McLure) K.; B.S., Duke, 1945; LL.B., U. Ala., 1949; m. Erika Mattfeld, Feb. 18, 1967; children by previous marriage—Sarah Stokes, Katherine Gilmer, Franklin, William; children—by present marriage— Claudia Mattfeld, Erik. Engaged as salesman of ins. and bus. supplies, 1949-54; vice chmn. Am. Heritage Life Ins. Co., 1954-60; partner Hayden, Stone, Inc., investment bankers, 1960-64; founder Kirk Investment Co., 1964;

gov. of Fla., 1967-7O. Bd. trustees Am. U., Monaco. Served to 1st lt. USMCR, 1943-46, 5O-52. Decorated Air medal. Mem. Financial Analysis Soc. Republican. Episcopalian (trustee). Clubs: Saints and Sinners, 21 (N.Y.C.). Address: PO Box 668 Palm Beach FL 33480

KIRK, DANIEL LEE, physician; b. Alliance, O., Aug. 1, 1919; s. John Lee and Olive (Strine) K.; student Gettysburg Coll., 1940; M.D., George Washington U., 1943; certificate in Clin. Psychiatry, U. Pa., 1955; certificate, U. Wis., 1963; m. Betty Kathryn Blair, Sept. 9, 1942; children—Daniel Lee, Nancy Jayne. Intern Harrisburg (Pa.) Hosp., 1943-44; resident psychiatry Harrisburg State Hosp., 1944-45; practice medicine, specializing in psychiatry, Waynesboro, Pa., 1945-50; staff physician Elwyn (Pa.) Sch., 1950-52, clin. dir. 1952-57; asst. supt. Pennhurst State Sch. and Hosp. Spring City, Pa., 1957-59; supt. Selinsgrove (Pa.) State Sch. and Hosp., 1959-68 now med. dir., research chmn. South Mountain (Pa.) Restoration Center; adj. prof. dept. spl. edn. Pa. State U., 1965—; adviser Smith Kline & French film Toymakers; cons. Comprehensive Mental Health/Mental Retardation Program Region IV. Served with M.C., AUS, 1945. Fellow Am. Geriatrics Soc.; Am. Assn. Mental Deficiency; N.Y. Acad. Scis.; mem. A.M.A., Pa. Med. Soc., Med. Club Phila., Assn. Med. Supts. Mental Hosps., Nat., Pa. assns. retarded children. Mason, Rotarian. Contbr. articles med. jours. Home: 201 N Church St Waynesboro PA 17268 Office: South Mountain Restoration Center South Mountain PA 17261

KIRK, DUDLEY, sociologist; b. Rochester, N.Y., Oct. 6, 1913; s. William and Margaret Louise (Dudley) K.; A.B., Pomona Coll., 1934; M.A., Fletcher Sch. Law and Diplomacy, 1935; M.A., Harvard, 1938, Ph.D., 1946; student U. Mexico, 1930, London Sch. Econ. and Polit. Sci., 1936; m. Ruth Louise Avelar, Nov. 21, 1947; children—Margaret Louise, John Dudley, Deborah Avelar. Tutor sociology Harvard, 1937-39; research asst., later research asso. Office Population Research, Princeton, 1939-47, asst. prof. sociology at univ., 1945-47; demographer Office Intelligence Research, State Dept., 1947-51, chief, div. research Near East, S. Asia and Africa, 1952, chief planning staff for research and intelligence, 1952-54; staff mem. Pres.'s Com. Immigration and Naturalization, 1951; demographic dir. Population Council, N.Y.C., 1954-67, sr. cons., 1967—; prof. demography Food Research Inst. and dept. sociology Stanford, 1967—, Morrison prof. population studies, 1971—. Mem. research adv. com. AID, 1968—. Fellow Center Advanced Study in the Behavioral Scis., 1964-65. Fellow A.A.A.S., Am. Pub. Health Assn., Am. Sociol. Assn., Am. Statis. Assn., Inter-Am. Statis. Inst.; mem. Am. Eugenics Soc. (dir., chmn. editorial bd. Social Biology, pres. 1969—); Am. Acad. Polit. and Social Sci., Internat. Union Sci. Study Population, Population Assn. Am. (pres. 1959-60). Sociol. Research Assn. Club: Harvard (N.Y.C.). Author: (with others) The Future Population of Europe and the Soviet Union, 1944; Europe's Population in the Interwar Years, 1946; (with others) The Principles of Political Geography, 1957. Home: 854 Lathrop Dr Stanford CA

KIRK, GEOFFREY STEPHEN, educator, author; b. Nottingham, Eng., Dec. 3, 1921; s. Frederick Tilzey and Enid (Pentecost) K.; M.A., Clare Coll., Cambridge (Eng.) U., 1947, Litt. D., 1964; M.A., Yale, 1964; m. Barbara Helen Traill, Jan. 8, 1950; 1 dau., Lydia. Research fellow Trinity Hall, Cambridge U., 1946-49, fellow, 1950; Commonwealth Fund fellow Harvard, 1949-50; successively asst. lectr., lectr., reader Cambridge U., 1951-64; prof. classics Yale, 1964-71; prof. Classics, Bristol (Eng.) U., 1971—; Sather prof. classical lit. U. Cal. at Berkeley, 1968-69. Served with Royal Navy, 1941-45. Decorated D.S.C. Fellow Brit. Acad. Author: Heraclitus, the Cosmic Fragments, 1954; (with J.E. Raven) The Presocratic Philosophers, 1957; The Songs of Homer, 1962; Myth, It's Meaning and Function, 1970. Editor: Language and Background of Homer, 1964. Office: The University Bristol England

KIRK, GRAYSON LOUIS, educator; b. Jeffersonville, O., Oct. 12, 1903; s. Traine C. and Nora (Eichelberger) K.; B.A., Miami (O.) U., 1924, LL.D., 1950; M.A., Clark U., 1925; Ph.D., U. Wis., 193O; postgrad., Ecole Libre des Sciences Politiques. Paris, 1928-29; hon. degrees from over 35 U.S. and fgn. colls. and univs., 195O—; m. Marion Louise Sands. Aug. 17, 1925; 1 son, John. Mem. faculties U. Wis., Columbia, 1929-40; prof. govt. Columbia, 1943-47, provost, 1949-50, v.p., provost 1950-51, pres., trustee univ., 1953-68, pres., trustee emeritus, 1968—, Bryce prof. history internat. relations, 1959—; dir. Mobil oil Co., IBM, Nation-Wide Securities Co., Dividend Shares, Inc., Consol. Edison Co. N.Y., Inc.; trustee Greenwich Savs. Bank. Trustee Asia Found., Nutrition Found., Inc., Inst. Internat. Edn., French Inst.; bd. dir's. Belgium Am. Edn. Found., Inc. Fellow Social Sci. Research Council, 1936-37; mem. secretariat staff Dumbarton Oaks Conf., 1944; exec. officer, 3d Commn., San Francisco Conf., 1945. Named Comdr. Order Orange-Nassau (Netherlands); 1952; Hon. Knight Comdr. Most Excellent Order Brit. Empire, 1955; Comdr. French Nat. Order Legion Honor, 1956; Grand Ufficialato dell- Ordíne al Merito della Repubblica (Italy), 1956; Asso. Knight Order of Hosp. of St. John Jerusalem, 1959; Medal of the Order of Taj. Iran; 1961; Cross of Grand Officer Order George 1 (Greece); Order Sacred Treasure, 1st class (Japan): commandeur de 1' Order des Palmes Academiques (France). Mem. several profl. learned socs., Phi Kappa Tau. Clubs: Athenaeum (London); Union, Columbia University, Links N.Y.; Bohemian (San Francisco); University, Cosmos. Author of several works in internat. relations field. Editor: (with R. P. Stebbins) War and National Policy a Syllabus, 1942. Contbr. to Fgn. Affairs, Polit. Sci. Quar., Am. Polit. Sci. Rev, Yale Law Re. Home: 680 W 246th St Riverdale NY 10471 Office: Columbia U Law Sch 435 W 116th St New York City NY 10027

KIRK, JOHN ESBEN, physician; b. Kallundborg, Denmark, Nov. 8, 1905; s. Ole Christian Mathias and Augusta Dorthea (Bang) K.; M.D., U. Copenhagen, 1929, Ph.D., 1936; m. Irma Muser, May 28, 1934; children—Ermalynn, Peter, Lillian, Thomas Esben, Paul Albert. Came to U.S., 1947, naturalized, 1949. Asst. Rockefeller Inst. Med. Research, N.Y.C., 1931-34; asst. resident physician Bispebjerg Municipal Hosp., Copenhagen, 1934-36; resident med. dept. U. Hosp., U. Copenhagen, 1936-39; dir. City Health Labs., Copenhagen, 1936- 39; chief physician med. dept. Holstebro Co. Hosp. Denmark, 1939-47; dir. research div. gerontology sch. medicine Washington U., St. Louis, since 1947, asst. prof. medicine, 1947-50, asso. prof. of medicine, 1950-64, prof. medicine, 1964—. Recipient Wisdom Award of Honor, 1970. Fellow A.C.P.; mem. Internat. Acad. Pathology. Am. Soc. Study of Premortal Condition (pres. 1960-65), Am. Soc. Biol. Chemists, Gerontological Soc., Central Soc. Clin. Research, Am. Soc. Study Arteriosclerosis, Soc. Exptl. Biology and Medicine, Harvey Soc., Royal Soc. Medicine (London), Alpha Omega Alpha (hon.). Author: Enzymes of the Arterial Wall, 1969. Editor Jour. of Gerontology, 1948-62. Home: 7320 B Fernbrook Dr St Louis MO 63123

KIRK, JOHN KENNETH, former govt. ofcl.; b. Manchester, N.H., Sept. 7, 1908; s. John and Lillian (Partridge) K.; B.S. in Chemistry. U. N.H., 1930; m. Florence Agon Meng, July 3, 1934. With FDA, Dept. Health, Edn. and Welfare, 1930-70, asso. commnr. for compliance, 1966-70. Recipient merit citation Civil Service League, 1955,; Superior Service award Dept. Health, Edn. and Welfare, 1956. Mem. Alpha Chi Sigma. Home: 1552 Lake Av Clearwater FL 33516

KIRK, KENNETH B., bus. exec.; b. Forest Grove, Pa., July 19, 1901; s. Pierson Vasey and Eva (Burson) K.; M.E., Pa. State Coll., 1920; m. Helen White, Oct. 20, 1926; children—Cynthia Grace, Helen Cecilia. Asst. marketing mgr. Standard Oil Co. of Brazil, S.A., 1921-23; prodn. mgr. Sociedade Anonyma Marvin, Rio de Janeiro, Brazil, 1923-25; founder Kirk-Dail Corp., Los Angeles, 1926, pres., gen. mgr. offices in Los Angeles, Seattle, Chgo., Pitts., Atlanta; dir. Radelin-Kirk Ltd.; owner, directing mgr. Kirk Dial Co., Dallas; chmn. bd. Coachella Valley Savs. & Loan, Palm Springs; securities broker, Beverly Hills and Palm Springs; pres. Helken Engring. Co., v.p. S and K Devel. Corp.; treas. Palm Desert Country Club Estates, Inc. Chmn. bus. adv. com., Beverly Hills, Cal. Pres. Desert Hosp. Dist.; past chmn., dir. Annual Desert Circus, Palm Springs. Cal.; dir. Desert Mus., Palm Springs Community Chest; past pres. Cal. State Assn. Dist. Hosps. Vice Mayor of Palm Springs. Mem. Los Angeles Press Club, Phi Gamma Delta. Republican. Episcopalian. Mason (Shriner) Rotarian (gov.). Clubs: Bel-Air Bay (Los Angeles); O'Donnell Golf, Tennis and Racquet, Committee of Twenty Five (Palm Springs); Royal Canadian Yacht (Toronto, Ont.); Beverly Hills (Cal.); Mount Kenya Safari (Africa). Home: (summer) 702 N Bedford Dr Beverly Hills CA (winter) 155 S Belardo Palm Springs FL 33460 Office: Kirk Bldg 140 S Beverly Dr Beverly Hills CA 90212

KIRK, LAWRENCE MARRON, investment counsel; b. Boston, Aug. 21, 1909; s. John and Maud (Johnson) K.; grad. Advanced Mgmt. Program, Harvard, 1946; m. Mary E. Curran, Jan. 12, 1946; children-Elizabeth M. (Mrs. Norman J. Praught), Sarah G. (Mrs. Patrick D. Henry), Kathleen E., Lawrence Marron, Marie B., Susan A. Mgr. Harriman Ripley, Inc., 1950-55; pres. Chase Distbrs. Corp., 1955-67, chmn. bd., 1967—; vice chmn. John P. Chase, Inc., Boston, 1967—, also dir.; dir. Income & Capital Shares, Chase Investment Services (both Boston). Bd. dirs. Rebecca Pomroy House Found. Served to col., inf., AUS, 1941-46; ETO. Decorated Bronze Star, Purple Heart. Club: Wianno (Osterville, Mass.). Home: 232 Franklin St Newton MA 02158 Office: 535 Boylston St Boston MA 02116

KIRK, LISA, mus. comedy entertainer; b. Brownsville, Pa.; d. George and Elsie (Furlong) Kirk; m. Robert Wells, Apr. 17, 1949. Theatrical debut in Good Night Ladies, 1945; other Broadway appearances include Windy City, 1946, Are You With It, 1946, Allergo, 1947, Kiss Me Kate, 1948; night-club appearances, 1946—; has appeared at Persian Room and Waldorf Astoria Hotel, N.Y.C., also Coconut Grove and Ciro's, Hollywood, Fairmont, San Francisco, Caribé Hilton Hotel, San Juan, P.R., Shoreham Hotel, Washington, Palmer House, Chgo., Americana, Miami Beach, Shamrock Hotel, Houston, Monteleone Hotel, New Orleans: television appearances include Ed Sullivan Show, Dinah Shore Show, G.E. Theatre, Studio One, Music from Schubert Alley, A Salute to Cole Porter, Tribute to Richard Rodgers, Salute to Rodgers and Hammerstein, Toast to Jerome Kern, Pontiac Star Parade, numerous others; recs. for RCA-Victor. Address: Hiller Agency 9220 Sunset Blvd Los Angeles CA 90069

KIRK, LUCILE DVORAK, editor; b. Cleve., Mar. 25, 1898; d. Joseph and Ada M. (Ackley) Dvorak; student Miami U., 1917-18; A.B., Case Western Res. U., 1919; M.A., Tchrs. Coll. Columbia, 1944: m. George W. Kirk, Mar. 5, 1927 (dec. 1962); children—Catherine Ada (Mrs. Richard Lee Stauffer), Mary Daler (Mrs. Ray Smith). Advt. copywriter for Allen Brett Assos., Cleve., 1919-20; asst. dir. publs. Cleve. Bd. Edn., 1920-22; reporter, feature writer, sch. page editor Cleve. Press, 1922-24; Chautauqua supt. with Radcliffe of Washington, 1924; advt. copywriter McCann Erickson, Cleve., 1925-27; co-owner Chelsea Book Shop, Greenwich Village, N.Y., 1927-35; mng., then exec. editor Sch. and Coll. Mgmt. (formerly Sch. Mgmt.), N.Y.C., 1935-51; Met. N.Y. editor Parents Mag., 1936-67, beauty editor and Pacific Coast editor, 1951-67, also N.E. edit. of Parents Mag., 1962- 67, Canadian editor, 1954-56. Mem. Tchrs. Coll. Alumni Fellowship Fund Com., 1954-68. One of ten Am. dels. to 1st Asian-Am. Women Journalists Conf., Honolulu, 1965. Mem. nat. publicity com. Camp Fire Girls, 1968—. Mem. Am. Inst. Graphic Arts (mag. Clinic com. Certificate of Merit, 1956), Case Western Reserve U. Alumni in New York (former pres., exec. com., 1940—, recipient of certificate of honor 1963; fund bd. 1965-69), Cosmetic Career Women, Soc. Am. Travel Writers (dir. 1962-65), Pan Pacific S.E. Asia Women's Assn., Theta Sigma Phi (pres. N.Y. chpt. 1956-58; nat. v.p. 1958- 60; distinguished service award 1963, v.p. 1966-69), Gamma Delta Tau, Alpha Omicron Pi (distinguished service award 1967). Club: Manor (chmn. travel sect.) (Pelham, N.Y.). Republican. Conglist. Home: 1 Hillside Av Pelham NY 10803

KIRK, PAUL GRATTAN, state justice; b. East Boston, Mass., Sept. 25, 1904; s. John and Maud Anne (Johnson) K.; A.B., Harvard, 1926, LL.B., 1929; S.J.D. (hon.), Suffolk U., 1969; m. Josephine O'Connell, Sept. 19, 1934; children—Kathleen, Josephine (Mrs. William J. Cleary, Jr.), Paul Grattan, Maud Anne (Mrs. Brian McDermott), Edward W. Admitted to Mass. bar, 1929; gen. practice, 1929-34; commnr. pub. safety, Mass., 1934-37; justice Superior Ct. Mass., 1937-60, Supreme Jud. Ct. Mass., 1960-71. Trustee Edward Scholarship Fund, 1935—, Yankee Div. Meml. Fund. Served to col., inf., AUS, 1940-45. Recipient St. Thomas More medal Diocese Worcester. Home: 455 Phinney's Lane Centerville MA 02632 Office: Court House Boston MA 02108

KIRK, PAUL HAYDEN, architect; b. Salt Lake City, Nov. 18, 1914; s. Spencer B. and Melvina (Blair) K.; B.A., U. Wash., 1937; m. Helen C. Richardson, Feb. 16, 1939; children—Christopher Paul, Hannah Jo. Individual archtl. practice, 1939-45, 1950-55; partner Chiareli & Kirk, Seattle, 1946-49; Paul Hayden Kirk & Assos., 1956-60; Kirk, Wallace, McKinley & Assos., 1960—. Mem. design adv. council Portland (Ore.) Devel. Commn., cons., to U.S. Pub. Housing Adminstrn. Recipient Gold medal 7th Pan Am. Congress Architects, Cuba, 1949; award of merit for architecture Boys Internat. Camp, San Juan, P.R., Progressive Architecture mag., 1949; grand prize for clinics and office bldgs. Unit Masonry, 1954; award of merit for residential design and constrn. House and Home mag., 1957, 58; 1st, 2d, 3d prizes for residence House and Garden, 1957; numerous other awards for residences, office bldgs. Research and design tech. devel. wood products Weyerhaeuser Timber Co., Andersen Corp., 1958. Fellow A.I.A. (chmn. profl. practices com. local chpt.); mem. Wash. State Cattlemen's Assn. Author: (with Eugene Sternberg) Doctor's Offices and Clinics: Medical and Dental 1955. Office: 2000 Fairview Av E Seattle WA 98102

KIRK, PHYLLIS, actress; b. Plainfield, N.J., Sept. 18, 1930; d. Theodore and Adele (Kroohs) Kirkegaard; student Neighborhood Playhouse, N.Y.C., 1950-59; m. Warren V. Bush, Dec. 28, 1966; 2 step-daughters. Debut in Theatre Guild prodn. of play My Name is Aquilon, 1949; starring roles in numerous films, including Our Very Own, 1950, Two Weeks With Love, 1950, Iron Mistress, 1952, About Face, 1952, Mrs. O'Malley and Mr. Malone, 1950, House of Wax, 1953, Thunder Over the Plains, 1953, Sad Sack, 1957, Three Guys Named Mike, 1951, Back from Eternity, 1956, Johnny Concho, 1956, A Life of Her Own, 1950; guest starring roles on numerous TV shows, including Philco-Goodyear Playhouse, 1951, Zane Gray Theater, 1955, Robert Montgomery Presents, 1953-55, Climax, 1953, Chrysler Playhouse, 1955, Studio One, 1953, U.S. Steel Hour, 1951-52, George Gobel Show, 1957, Playhouse Ninety, 1954-55, Tennessee Ernie Ford Show, 1958, Armstrong Circle Theatre, 1951; co-starred with Red Buttons in Red Buttons Series, 1953-54, with Peter Lawford in NBC series The Thin Man (Emmy nomination), 1957-59; appeared as guest star on all maj. talk and panel shows, including Dick Cavett Show, 1967—, Virginia Graham Show, 1964-65, Mike Douglas Show, 1967, Password, 1966-67, To Tell The Truth, 1966—; hosted, wrote own ABC Network discussion program Young Set, 1965; co-hosted ABC-TV A.M. Show, Los Angeles, 1970; spl. news corr. WBKB-TV, Chgo., 1964; guest appearances on TV shows Name of the Game, 1970, F.B.I., 1970; star nat. tour of play Wait Until Dark, 1966. Active various orgns. to abolish capital punishment. Bd. dirs. NOW (Neighbors of Watts), Los Angeles. Democrat. Home: Los Angeles CA 90069

KIRK, REGINALD HALLING lawyer, corp. exec.; b. Kent, O., 1922; B.A., Yale, 1943, LL.B., 1944; m. Mae Reed, May 2, 1949; 1 son. Admitted to Massachusetts bar, 1944; practiced in Boston, 1947--; gen. counsel Acme Mfg. Co., Boston, 1966--; dir. 1st Nat. Bank. Home: 23 Beacon St Boston MA 02107

KIRK, RONALD T., (Roland), musician, music publishing exec.; b. Columbus, O., Aug. 7, 1937; s. Theodore and Gertrude (Broaddus) K.; ed Columbus Sch. for Blind; m. Edith Hasking, Feb. 6, 1962; 1 son, Rory. Performer tenor sax, manzello, flute, U.S., Europe, Japan, 1949—; leader Roland Kirk Quartet, 1954—; writer Broadcast Music, Inc., 1962—; pres. Rokir Music Corp., N.Y.C., 1964—. Recipient 1st place award Downbeat Mag., 1962, 63, 64, 65, Melody Maker Mag., 1963, 64, 66; named Musician of Yr., Melody Maker, 1964, 66, World New Star in German Jazz Poll. 1964, 65. Mem. Am. Fedn. Musicians. Composer: You Dig It, 1961; Three in One Without the Oil, 1962; Reeds and Deeds, Lonesome August Child, 1963; April Morning, Abstract Improvisations, Gifts and Messages, Hipchops, 1964; Ruined Castles, Serenade to a Cuckoo, Mystical Dream, 1965; RipRig and Panic; For Bechet, Byas and Fats; Hippery Slippery, Flippery; Jurez; Shakey Money; Nothin' But the Truth, 1966. Address: 415 Central Park W New York City NY 10025*

KIRK, RUDOLF, educator; b. Washington, Jan. 20, 1898; s. Charles Farquhar and Annie (Brooke) K.; grad. Sidwell Friends Sch., Washington, 1918; A.B. with honors in English, Princeton, 1922, A.M. (Charles Scribner fellow in English lit. 1927-28), 1928, Ph.D., 1932; M.A., U. Ia., 1925; m. Clara Marburg, Sept. 8, 1930; children—Frances Jeffries (dec.), Susanne, Geoffrey (dec.), Donald. Instr. English, State U. Ia., 1922-25; mem. faculty Rutgers U., 1928-63, successively instr., asst. prof., asso. prof., 1928-45, prof. dept. English, 1945-63, acting chmn., 1956-57, chmn. dept. English, 1960- 63; Distinguished prof. English, Southwest Tex. State U., 1963-67; vis. prof. U. Wis., 1964; vis. prof. English, Un. Ill. at Chgo. Circle, 1967-69; vis. prof. English summer sessions U. N.M., 1948, N.Y.U., 1949, U. Mo., 1950, 53; Fulbright prof. Am lit. and civilization U. Liege, Belgium, 1955-56; Fulbright lectr. U. Ghent, 1955, Rome, 1956. Chmn. Coll. Conf. on English, Central Atlantic States, 1933; founder (with Carleton Brown) English Inst., 1939, sec., 1939-45, chmn., 1949, editor ann., 1940-43; bd. dirs. Community Chest New Brunswick area, 1942-45; trustee William Alexander Procter Found., 1951- 63. Served with U.S. Army, 1918. Recipient medal U. of Ghent, 1956, Silver medal, U. Liege, 1956; named Hon. citizen Tex., 1967. Mem. Modern Lang. Assn. (chmn. 17th Century group 1944, Howells group 1950), Am. Assn. U. Profs., Guild Scholars, Phi Beta Kappa. Episcopalian. Author: Mr. Pepys Upon the State of Christ-Hosp., 1935; (with Clara M. Kirk) The Church of St. John the Evangelist; a Parish History, 1961; also articles and revs.; (with Clara M. Kirk) William Dean Howells, 1962. Editor: The City-Madam (Philip Massinger), 1934; Heaven Upon Earth and Characters of Vertues and Vices (Joseph Hall), 1948; Moral Philosophie of the Stoicks (G. DuVair), 1951; (with Clara M. Kirk) Types of English Poetry, 1940, Representative Selections of W. D. Howells, 1950; (with C. M. Hall) Two Bookes of Constancie (J. Lipsius), 1939; Animadversions (J. Milton), 1953; (with Clara M. Kirk) Criticism and Fiction and Other Essays by W. D. Howells, 1959; (with C. F. Main) Essays in Literary Hist., 1960; (with C. M. Kirk), Letters of an Altrurian Traveller 1893-1894, 1961. Rise of Silas Lapham (by W. D. Howells), 1962; (with Clara M. Kirk) European and American Masters, 1963; (with C. M. Kirk) Charlotte Temple, 1964; (with Clara M. Kirk) Altrurian Romances (W.D. Howells), 1968. Founder, editor Jour. Rutgers U. Library, 1937-48. Address: 402 Balcones Apts San Marcos TX 78666

KIRK, RUSSELL AMOS, author, columnist; b. Plymouth, Mich., Oct. 19, 1918; s. Russell Andrew and Marjorie (Pierce) K.; B.A., Mich. State U., 1940; M.A., Duke, 1941; D. Litt., St. Andrews U., Scotland, 1952; hon. degrees include Litt. D., Boston Coll., St. John's U., Loyola Coll., Balt., LL.D., Park Coll.; L.H.D., Le Moyne Coll., 1963, m. Annette Yvonne Courtemanche, Sept. 19, 1964. Asst. prof., history civilization Mich. State Coll., 1946-53; Daly lectr. U. Detroit, 1954; mem. faculty politics New Sch. for Social Research, 1959-61; research prof. politics C. W. Post Coll., 1957-69; univ. prof. L.I. U., 1960-69; vis. prof. various univs. Contbr. to scholarly and popular publs., U.S., Can., Gt. Britain, Australia, Norway, Austria, including Sewanee Rev., New English Rev., Dublin Rev., Yale Rev., Jour. History of Ideas, Annals of Am. Acad., N.Y. Times mag., Fortune, Wall St. Jour., History Today, The Critic, Kenyon Rev., Nat. Rev., The Month, S.W. Rev., Commonweal, Christianity Today, Queen's Quar., America, Contemporary Rev., History Today, 1935—; founder quar. jour. Modern Age; editor quar. Univ. Bookman; writer syndicated daily newspaper column To the Point in over 100 U.S. Newspapers. Guggenheim fellow. Sr. fellow Am. Council Learned Socs. Author: John Randolph of Roanoke, 1951, 64; The Conservative Mind, 1953, 60; St. Andrews, 1954; A Program for Conservatives, 1954; Academic Freedom, 1955; Beyond the Dreams of Avarice, 1956; The Intelligent Woman's Guide to Conservatism, 1957; The American Cause, 1957; Old House of Fear, 1961; The Surly Sullen Bell, 1962; Confessions of a Bohemian Tory, 1963; The Intemperate Professor, 1965; A Creature of the Twilight 1966; Edmund Burke, 1967; Political Principles of Robert A. Taft, 1967; Enemies of the Permanent Things, 1969; also critical intros. and prefaces to reprints standard scholarly works. Address: Mecosta MI 49332

KIRK, SAMUEL ALEXANDER, psychologist, educator; b. Rugby, N.D., Sept. 1, 1904; s. Richard B. and Nellie (Boussard) K.; Ph.B., U. Chgo., 1929, M.S., 1931; Ph.D., U. Mich., 1935; L.H.D., Lesley Coll., 1969; m. Winifred Eloise Day, June 25, 1933; children—Jerome Richard, Nancy Lorraine. Research psychologist Wayne Country Tng. Sch., Northville, Mich., 1931-34, mental hygienist, 1934-35; dir. div. edn. for exceptional children State Tchrs. Coll., Milw., 1935-42, 46; chmn. grad. sch. vis. lectr. U. Mich, 1942; prof. edn. and psychology U. Ill., 1947-68, prof. emeritus, 1968—; dir. Inst. Research Exceptional Children, 1952-68; prof. spl. edn. U. Ariz., Tucson, 1968—. Served as maj. with AUS, 1942-46. Recipient 1st internat. award for profl. service in mental retardation Joseph P. Kennedy Jr. Found., 1962, J.E. Wallace Wallin ann. award Council for Exceptional Children, 1966; ann. award Assn. Children with Hearing Disabilities, 1966; ann. award Caritas Soc., 1966. Fellow Am. Psychol. Assn., Am. Assn. for Mental Deficiency; mem. Internat. Council Exceptional Children (pres. 1941-43), Nat. Soc. Study Edn. (chmn. 1950 yearbook com.), Brit. Assn. Spl. Edn. (hon. v.p. 1962), Sigma Xi. Author: (with Hegge and Kirk) Remedial Reading Drills, 1936; Teaching Reading to Slow- Learning Children, 1940; (with Johnson) Educating the

Retarded Child, 1951; (with Karnes and Kirk) You and Your Retarded Child, 1955; Early Education of the Mentally Retarded, 1958; Educating Exceptional Children, 1962; (with Wiener) Behavior Research on Exceptional Children, 1964; (with McCarthy and Kirk) The Illinois Test of Psycholinguistic Abilities, 1968; (with Kirk) Psycholinguistic Learning Disabilities, 1971. Contbr. articles profl. publs. Home: 9500 Morrill Way Tucson AZ 85715

KIRK, SHERWOOD, librarian; b. Kermit, W.Va., July 12, 1924; s. James Douglas and Magdalene (Elkins) K.; student Mich. State U., 1944; A.B., U. Ky., 1949; postgrad. U. Ill., 1949-50; m. Ora Ward, Jan. 9, 1958; children—Diana, James Sherwood, Philip Lindsey. Student asst. U. Ky., 1946-49; circulation asst. U. Ill., 1949-51; head reference and circulation Marshall U., 1951-52; sr. library asst. to librarian U. Neb., 1952-54; spl. project asst. Nat. Agr. Library, Washington, 1954-55; reference asst., liaison loan div. Library of Congress, 1955-56, catalog asst., 1956-57; coordinator pub. library services Ky. Dept. Libraries, Frankfort, 1957-63, asst. state librarian, 1963-69; state librarian Fla., 1969-71; asso. dir. library operations Ill. State Library, Springfield, 1971—; planning cons. Perry County (Ky.) Pub. Library, 1966-69. Mem. Ky. Gov.'s Planning Com. on Libraries, 1968; chmn. Fla. Sec. of State's Com. Library Service to State Govt., 1970; adv. com. library services and constrn. Fla. State Library. Recipient plaque for outstanding librarian Ky. Library Trustee Assn., 1968. Mem. A.L.A. (council 1967-69), Ky. (pres. 1965-66), Fla., Ill. library assns., Assn. State Library Agencies. Mason. Club: Optimist (Frankfort). Home: 2341 Westchester Blvd Springfield IL 62704 Office: Centennial Bldg Springfield IL 62706

KIRK, STANLEY, steel co. exec.; b. Portsmouth, Va., Feb. 28, 1906; s. Less and Mae (Weston) K.; student Morris-Harvey Coll.; m. Lucille Viola Kirk, May 3, 1925. Sales mgr. Longines-Wittnauer Watch Co., 1944-55; with Phoenix Steel Corp., 1955-68, chmn., chief exec. officer until 1968. Adv. bd. bus. econs. U. Del. Chmn. No. Del. Savs. Bond and Freedom Shares dr., 1968. Served with AUS, World War II. Mason.*

KIRK, STEPHEN S., librarian; b. 1926; B.A., Okla. U., 1948, M.A., 1950; M.A. in L.S., La. State U.; m. Charlotte Wornall; 1 dau., Julia. Formerly tchr. English, Lamar Coll., Beaumont, Tex., then with D.C. Heath Pub. Co.; now head Kansas City (Mo.) pub. library system. Address: 5065 Clark Dr Roeland Park MO *

KIRK, WILFRED BERNARD, banker; b. Narrowsburg, N.Y., Oct. 12, 1913; s. James H. and Laura (Gebhart) K.; grad. Notre Dame U., 1937, Harvard Bus. Sch., 1948; postgrad. Columbia, 1937-38; m. Eleanor Schnell, Apr. 17, 1939; children-Peter, J.P., Mark, Anne, Camille. With First Nat. City Bank, N.Y.C., 1937-52; adminstrv. v.p. Emigrant Savs. Bank, N.Y.C., 1952-54; sr. v.p. charge nat. accounts Tex. Bank & Trust Co., Dallas, 1954—. Trustee Catholic Charity Found. Mem. N.Y. State Savs. Bank Assn. (past chmn. commerce financial pub. relations), Master Knighs Sovereign Mil. Order Malta, East Side C. of C. (past chmn. Bowery improvement com.). Home: 6238 Woodland Dr Dallas TX 75235 Office: PO Box 50688 Dallas TX 75250

KIRK, WILLIAM JOHNSON, investment counsel; b. Boston, Sept. 9, 1907; s. John and Maud Annie (Johnson) K.; S.B., Mass. Inst. Tech., 1928; M.B.A. with high distinction, Harvard, 1930; LL.B., Boston Coll., 1942; m. Alice Guertin, Aug. 19, 1937; children—George Lorimer, William Johnson, David Guertin, Mary Parker, Anne Williams, Joseph Peter. Student editor Harvard Bus. Review; asst. dir. research Lee Higginson Trust Co., 1930-32; with John P. Chase, Inc., 1932—, exec. v.p., 1954-59, pres., 1959-68, vice chmn. bd. for adminstrn. and planning, 1968—, also dir.; pres., dir., chmn. exec. com. Boston Terminal Co., 1961-69; pres., dir. Providence Produce Warehouse Co., 1961-69, Income & Capital Shares, Inc., Chase Frontier Fund, Inc., Chase Spl. Fund Boston, Inc., Chase Capital Fund Boston, Inc., trustee, v.p. Chase Fiduciary Assos.; dir., mem. exec. com. N.E. Transp. Co., 1961-69; incorporator Newton Savs. Bank, 1960-70, dir. Chase Distbrs. Corp. Unified Funds. Inc., 1953-69, Unified Mut. Shares, Inc., 1964-69, Boston Capital Corp. Realty Hotels, Inc., 1961-69, Chase Investment Services, Union Freight R.R. Co., 1961-69, AutEx Service Corp., 1968-69; trustee of N.Y. N.H. & R.R. Co., 1961-69, Shareholders' Trust of Boston, The Chase Fund of Boston. Mem. corp., v.p., dir. Josiah Willard Hayden Recreation Center, Inc. Served from lt. (s.g.) to comdr., USNR, 1942-46. Mem. Tau Beta Pi, Chi Epsilon. Home: Box 383 North Falmouth MA 02556 Office: Chase Bldg 535 Boylston St Boston MA 02116

KIRK, WILLIAM TALBOT, assn. exec.; b. Columbus, O., Mar. 24, 1918; s. Emmet Lyle and Katherine (Talbot) K.; B.S., Ohio State U., 1932; grad. N.Y. Sch. Social Work, Columbia, 1936, Harvard U. Sch. for Overseas Adminstrn., 1943; m. Ruth Van Voorhis, Sept. 15, 1934; 1 son, David G. Exec. sec. Protestant Family Welfare, Inc., Albany, N.Y., 1938-41; exec. dir. Provident Family & Children's Service, Kansas City, Mo., 1941-43; dir. spl. services div. Community Service Soc. of N.Y., 1945-50; dir. Am. br., Internat. Social Service, N.Y.C., 1950-62, internat. dir., Geneva, Switzerland, 1950-62; exec. dir. Motion Picture and TV Fund, Inc., Los Angeles, until 1971, cons., 1971—. Past pres. sch. bd., Hartsdale, N.Y. Served capt. to maj., AUS, 1943-45. Decorated Bronze Star medal. Mem. Alumni Assn. N.Y. Sch. Social Work (past pres.), Nat. Assn. Social Workers, Nat. Conf. Social Work (exec. com.), U.S. Com. for Refugees, Internat. Inst. Los Angeles (past pres.), Pres., Acad. Motion Picture Arts and Scis., Beta Theta Pi. Home: 430 S Burnside Av Los Angeles CA 90036 Office: 335 N LaBrea Av Los Angeles CA 90036

KIRKBRIDE, CHALMER GATIN, cons. engr.; b. nr. Tyrone, Okla., Dec. 27, 1906; s. Zachariah Martin and Georgia Anna (Gatlin) K.; B.S.E., U. Mich., 1930, M.S.E., 1930; Sc.D., Beaver Coll., 1959; Eng. D., Drexel U., 1960, PMC Colls., 1970; m. Billie Lucille Skains, Apr. 13, 1939; 1 son, Chalmer Gatlin. Chem. engr. research dept. Standard Oil Co., Whiting, Ind., 1930-34; asst. chief chemist Am. Oil Co., Texas City, Tex., 1934-38, asst. dir. of research, 1938- 41; chief chem. engring. devel. Magnolia Petroleum Co. (now part Mobile Oil Co.), Dallas, 1942-44; distinguished prof. dept. chem. engring., Tex. A. and M. U., 1944-47, cons. chem. engr., 1944-47; sci. cons. to sec. of War, Bikini atomic bomb tests, 1946; mgr. research and devel. Houdry Process Corp., Marcus Hook, Pa., 1947-48, v.p. charge research and devel., 1948-52, pres. and chmn. bd., Phila., 1952-56, dir., 1948-62; exec. dir. research, engring. depts. Sun Oil Co., Phila., 1956-60, v.p. research, engring., 1960-70, dir., 1963-70; pres. Avisun, Phila., 1959-60, dir., 1959-68; dir. Sun Olin Chem. Co., 1958-70, P.R. Sun Oil Co., 1968-70 Dir. Co-ordinating Research Council, 1958-70, pres., 1965-67. Mem. Pres. Nixon's Task Force on Oceanography, 1969; mem. adv. panel on sea grant programs N.O.A.A. Dept. Commerce, 1970—; indsl. and profl. adv. council Pa. State U., 1965—. Served as 2d lt. Chem. Warfare Res., 1935-40. Mem. bd. trustees PMC Colls., Chester, Pa., 1956—; vice chmn. bd. trustees 1959-71; chmn. bd. dirs. Riddle Meml. Hosp., 1965-67, dir., 1965-71; trustee U.S. Naval Acad. Found. Recipient Distinguished Pub. Service award, U.S. Navy, 1968; Engring. Centennial medal PMC Colls., 1970. Fellow Am. Inst. Chem. Engrs. (pres. 1954, profl. progress award 1951, founders award 1967); mem. Am. Chem. Soc., Am. Petroleum Inst., Nat. Acad. of Engring., Alpha Chi Sigma, Phi Lambda Upsilon, Tau Beta Pi. Clubs: Chemists (N.Y.C.); Union League (Phila.); Greenville (Del.) Country; Delaware Turf. Author: Chemical Engineering Fundamentals, 1947. Contbr. articles profl. jours. and bulls. Patentee in field of catalysis and petroleum refining. Home: La Casa Del Rio RD 2 Elkton MD 21921

KIRKBY, ARTHUR MARTIN, librarian; b. Didsbury, Alta., Can., Sept. 22, 1911; s. Edgar Martin and Anna (Blow) K.; A.B., U. B.C., 1944; B.S., Columbia, 1946; m. Carolyn Elizabeth Pullman, July 24, 1950; children—Arthur Martin, Kevin Reid. Came to U.S., 1945, naturalized, 1952. Asst. Calgary (Alta.) Pub. Library, 1932-40; adminstrv. asst., dir. central adult services Enoch Pratt Free Library, Balt., 1946-49, adminstrv. asst., asst. dir., 1949-52; librarian Norfolk (Va.) Pub. Library, 1952—. Mem. Am. (council 1957-60), Southeastern, Va. (pres. 1967) library assns., Norfolk Hist. Soc. (bd.). Rotarian.Club: Torch (pres. 1959-60) (Norfolk). Home: 1519 Morris Av Norfolk VA 23509 Office: 301 City Hall Av Norfolk VA 23510

KIRKCONNELL, WATSON, educator; b. Port Hope, Ont., Can., May 16, 1895; s. Thomas and Bertha (Watson) K.; M.A., Queen's U., 1916; student Oxford U., 1921-22; Ph.D., Debrecen U., Hungary, 1938; LL.D., U. Ottawa, 1944; U. N.B., 1949; Dr. Polit. Econ., Ukraine Free U., 1950; D.Litt., McMaster U., 1953, Assumption U., 1955, U. Man., 1957; L.H.D., Alliance Coll., 1958; D.ès L., Laval U., 1962; Litt. D., Acadia U., 1964, St. Francis Xavier U., 1966; D.C.L., St. Mary's U., 1964; m. Isabel Peel, 1924 (dec. 1925); children—James, Thomas; m. 2d, Hope Kitchener, Aug. 6, 1930; children—Helen, Janet, Susan. Lectr., asst. prof., asso. prof., prof. English Wesley Coll., Winnipeg, 1922-32; prof. Latin United Coll., Winnipeg, 1932-40; prof., head dept English McMaster U., 1940-48; pres. Acadia U., Wolfville 1948-64, pres. emeritus, 1964, prof. English, 1964-68. Mem. fed. adv. com. fgn. lang. groups, 1940-45. Served as capt. Canadian Army, 1916-19. Named laureate Polish Acad. Letters; decorated Knight Order of Polonia Restituta, 1936; Pierce gold medal, Royal Soc. Can., 1941; knight comdr. Order of Falcon (Iceland); Shevchenko medal, 1964; Gold Medal Freedom, Hungary, 1964; Centennial Medal (Can.), 1967; Medal of Service, Order of Can., 1968. Fellow Royal Soc. Can. (sect. pres. 1967-68), Icelandic Soc. Letters, Petöfi Soc. Hungary, Kisfaludy Soc. Hungary; mem. Candian Authors Assn. (nat. pres. 1942-44, 56-58), Writers' War Com. Can. (chmn. 1942-44), Humanities Research Council Can. (chmn. 1944-47), Bapt. Union Western Can. (pres. 1938-40), Bapt. Fedn. Can. (nat. pres. 1953-56). Mason. Author: European Elegies, 1928; Icelandic Verse, 1930; The Magyar Muse, 1933; Golden Treasury of Polish Lyrics, 1936; The Flying Bull and Other Tales, 1940; Twilight of Liberty, 1941; Seven Pillars of Freedom, 1944; Little Treasury of Hungarian Verse, 1946; The Celestial Cycle, 1952; Pan Tadeusz in English Verse, 1960; (with C. H. Andrusyshen) The Ukrainian Poets, 1963; Complete Works of Shevchenko, 1963; That Invincible Samson, 1964; Centennial Tales and Other Poems, 1965; A Slice of Canada, Memoirs, 1967; The Fifth Quarter-Century, 1968; A Psalter for Everyman, 1969; Knight of Mark Twain, 1970. Home: 101 Main St Woifville Nova Scotia Canada

KIRKEBY, EDWIN OLIVER, bus. exec.; b. Chgo., May 5, 1903; s. Marius and Signe (Hansen) K.; student U. Ill., 1923-24; m. Melba Bartlett, Feb. 27, 1935; 1 dau., Jane. Partner, Hilgard Westwood Co., Edgewater Towers; gen. partner Kirkeby Center. Bd. dirs., officer Kirkeby Found.; trustee Kirkeby Trust. Mason (Shriner). Club: Bel Air Country. Home: 656 Siena Way Bel Air CA 90024 Office: 10889 Wilshire Blvd Los Angeles CA 90024

KIRKENDALL, ERNEST OLIVER, metall. engr., assn. exec.; b. East Jordan, Mich., July 6, 1914; s. George Oliver and Rachel (Geck) K.; B.S., Wayne U., 1934; M.S., U. Mich., 1935, D.Sc., 1938; m. Maxine Mae Marrs, Feb. 2, 1938 (dec. June 1969); children—Carol (Mrs. J. G. Leunk, Jr.), Howard Ernest, Barbara (Mrs. T. K. Davis). Instr., Wayne U., 1937-41, asst. prof., 1941- 46; sec. metals div. Am. Inst. Mining, Metall. and Petroleum Engrs., 1946-55, assn. gen. sec., 1955-63; sec., gen. mgr. United Engring. Trustees, Inc., N.Y.C., 1963-65; metall. engr. Am. Iron and Steel Inst., 1965-66, asst. v.p., 1966-68, v.p., 1968-. Sec. Engring. Found., 1963-65. Hon. mem. Iron and Steel Inst. (London), Verein Deutscher Eisenhuttenleute (Dusseldorf), Assn. des Igenieurs Sortis de l'Ecole Liege; mem. Sigma Xi, Tau Beta Pi. Club: Presbyterian Men's (New Rochelle, N.Y.). Contbr. articles trade jours. Home: 15 Lord Kitchener Rd New Rochelle NY 10804 Office: 150 E 42d St New York City NY 10017

KIRKENDALL, JAMES FREDERICK, air force officer; b. Omaha, Feb. 19, 1920; s. Oren Frederick and Bessie (Evernham) K.; student San Mateo Jr. Coll., 1937-38; B.S., U. Neb., 1941; M.B.A., George Washington U., 1963; m. Elizabeth Keville, Nov. 20, 1942 (dec. Feb. 1968); 1 son, James Frederick. Commd. 2d lt. USAAF, 1942, advanced through grades to maj. gen., 1969; air force mem. Weapons Systems Evaluation Group, Office Dir. Def. for Research and Engring., Def. Dept., Washington, 1959-61; chief command plans, also dep. dir. plans for war plans Hdqrs. USAF, Washington, 1961-62, exec. to chief of staff, 1963-66; comdr. 47th Air Div., Castle AFB, Cal., 1966; asst. dep. chief staff for ops. Hdqrs. Tactical Air Command, Langley AFB, Va., 1966-69; dep. chief staff for operations Hdqrs. 7th Air Force, Tan Son Nhut, Vietnam, 1969-70; dep. comdr. 7/13th Air Force Udorn Royal Thai AFB, Thailand, 1970; comdt. Armed Forces Staff Coll., Norfolk, Va., 1970—. Decorated D.S.M., Silver Star, Legion of Merit with 3 oak leaf clusters, D.F.C. with 2 oak leaf clusters, Bronze Star, Air medal with 13 oak leaf clusters, Purple Heart with oak leaf clusters (U.S.); Croix de Guerre with palm, Croix de Guerre with Etoile de Bronze (France); Vietnam Air Force Distinguished Service Order 1st Class (Vietnam). Mem. Sigma Nu. Baptist. Home: 478 Powhatan St US Naval Station Norfolk VA 23511

KIRKENDALL, LESTER ALLEN, educator; b. Oberlin, Kan., Nov. 15, 1903; s. Charles Francis and Alva Jennie (Hudson) K.; student Washington Coll., 1924-25; B.S., Kan. State Coll., 1928; M.A., Tchrs. Coll. Columbia, 1931, Ph.D., 1937; m. Laura Marguerite Williams, June 18, 1936; children—Karen, Karl. Tchr., adminstr. Oberlin (Kan.) pub. schs., 1927-33; prof. edn. Tchrs. Coll. Conn., New Britain, 1935-41; prof. edn., head div. ednl. guidance, U. Okla., 1941-43; with USPHS, 1943-45; assigned U.S. Office Edn., specialist in sex edn., 1944-45; instr. U.S. Army U., Florence, Italy, 1945; dir. Assn. for Family Living, Chgo., 1946-48; prof. Ore. State Univ., Corvallis, 1948-69; vis. prof. U. Kansas Med. Center, 1966; on summer session faculties various colls. and univs.; lectr. in colls. and univs. Mem. bd. trustees Am. Inst. Family Relations, 1959, del. World Family Congress, Paris, 1958, Rome 1965; dir. of Nat. Council Family Relations, 1952-56, 65- 68; mem. bd. dirs. Pacific Northwest Council Family Relations, 1954-60, pres., 1954; founding and bd. mem. Sex Edn. and Information Council U.S. Recipient research grants E.C. Brown Trust and Nat. Acad. Sci. for research in adolescent sex behavior. Mem. of Internat. Soc. Gen. Semantics, Soc. Sci. Study of Sex, Am. Humanist Assn. (dir. (1966-68, 71—), Am. Assn. Sex Educators and Counselors (v.p.), Phi Kappa Phi, Phi Delta Kappa, Kappa Delta Pi. Author: Changes in Adjustments of High School Pupils, 1937; Sex Adjustments of Young Men, 1940; Understanding Sex, 1947, rev. edit., 1971; Goals for American Education, 1948; Dating Tips for Teens, 1962; Sex Education as Human Relations, 1950; Student Council in Action, 1953; Understanding The Other Sex, 1955; The Oregon Developmental Center, 1955; Too Young to Marry?, 1956; Premarital Intercourse and Interpersonal Relationships, 1961; Sex and Our Society, 1964; You're Maturing Now, 1968; Understanding Love, 1968; Helping Children Understand Sex, 1969; Teachers Question and Answers About Sex; also numerous articles Am. and fgn. mags. and jours. Co-editor Sex in the Adolescent Years, 1968; Sex in the Childhood Years, 1970; The New Sexual Revolution, 1971; A Student's Guide to Marriage and Family Life Literature, 1971. Home: 12601 SE River Rd Portland OR 97222

KIRKENDALL, RICHARD STEWART, educator, historian; b. Spokane, Wash., Apr. 11, 1928; s. Roland P. and Marjorie (Monfort) K.; B.A. magna cum laude, Gonzaga U., 1950; M.S., U. Wis., 1953, Ph.D., 1958; m. Joan Carol Nelson, Aug. 19, 1950; children—Thomas Reed, Andrew John, Theodore Nelson. Research asst. U. Wis. at Madison, 1952-55; instr. Wesleyan U., Middletown, Conn., 1955- 58; asst. prof. U. Mo. at Columbia, 1958-61, asso. prof., 1961-67, prof. history, 1967—, chmn. dept., 1968-71. Served with USNR, 1950-52. Grantee Am. Philos. Soc., 1958, 61, The Truman Library Inst. Nat. and Internat. Affairs, 1964, 67. Mem. Orgn. Am. Historians (nominating com. 1968-70, Turner award com. 1968—, editorial bd. 1970—), Am. Hist. Assn., Agrl. History Soc. (exec. com. 1963-66), Alpha Sigma Nu, QEBH. Author: Social Scientists and Farm Politics in the Age of Roosevelt, 1966; The Truman Period as a Research Field, 1967. Home: 4101 Faurot Dr Columbia MO 65201

KIRKENDOLL, CHESTER ARTHUR, Jr., bishop; b. Searcy, Ark., June 3, 1914; s. Chester Arthur and Mattie (Wyatt) K.; A.B., Lane Coll., 1938; A.M., Northwestern, 1941; Litt. D., Tex. Coll., 1957; m. Alice Elizabeth Singleton, June 3, 1940; children—Chester, Loretta Jean, Kapel. Dir. leadership edn., also asso. editor ch. sch. publs. Gen. Bd. Christian Edn. Colored M.E. Ch., 1940-50; pres. Lane Coll. 1950-70; bishop Christian Meth. Episcopal Ch., 1970—. Dir. United Negro Coll. Fund; mem. commn. on higher edn. Nat. Council Chs. of Christ in Am. Mem. N.A.A.C.P., Alpha Phi Alpha. Author: Improving the Educational Program of the Local Church, 1949. Home: 308 10th Av W Birmingham AL 35204

KIRKHAM, DON, soil physicist, educator; b. Provo, Utah, Feb. 11, 1908; s. Francis Washinton and Martha Alzina (Robison) K.; clarinetist diploma, McCune Sch. Music and Art, Salt Lake City, 1926; student U. Utah, 1925-27; A.B. with honors in physics, Columbia, 1933, A.M. in Physics, 1934, Ph.D. in Physics, 1938; Erediplom, U. Ghent (Belgium), 1958; D. Agrl. Scis. (hon.), Royal Agrl. U., Ghent, 1963; m. Mary Elizabeth Erwin, Sept. 2, 1939; children—Victoria, Mary Beth, Don Collier. Asst., physics Columbia, 1934-38; instr., asst. prof. math. and physics, also asso. Agrl. Expt. Sta., Utah State U., 1937-40; hydraulic engr. Soil Conversation Service, Dept. Agr., 1940; civilian physicist Bur. Ordnance, U.S. Navy, 1940-46; asso. physics, George Washington U., 1946; faculty Ia. State U., 1946—, Curtiss Distinguished prof. agr., prof. agronomy and physics, 1959—. Fulbright prof. The Netherlands, 1950-51; Fulbright prof., Guggenheim fellow, Belgium, 1957-58; lectr. U. Vienna (Austria), 1958, Ireland, 1960; land reclamation adviser Turkish Govt., 1959; Ford Found, land reclamation cons. UAR, also lectr. Alexandria (Egypt) U., 1961; sect. chmn. Internat. Soil Structure Symposium, Belgium, 1958; panelist Internat. Atomic Energy Vienna, 1960; lectr. Yugoslavia, Bulgaria, 1964; mem. U.S. AID Univ. Study Team, Argentina, summer 1965. Council mem. Internat. Sodic Soil Symposium, Budapest, 1964; dir. Ia. Water Resources Research Council. Active Boy Scouts Am. Mem. Utah N.G., 1925-27. Fellow Am. Phys. Soc., Am. Soc. Agronomy; mem. Am. Geophysics Union (award most meritorious paper sci. hydrology 1952), Soil Sci. Soc. Am. (chmn. soil physics 1950; Stevenson award 1951, 25th anniversary honor lect. 1961, del. to internat. meetings in Bucharest 1964), Am. Math. Assn., Netherlands Soc. Agrl. Research, Internat. Soil Sci. Soc. (U.S. v.p. 1957-59), Ia. Acad. Soc. (most meritorious paper math. 1948, physics 1949). S.A.R. (v.p. Ia. 1966), Sigma Xi (honor lectr. U. Ia. chpt. 1959), Phi Kappa Phi, Gamma Sigma Delta. Republican. Mem. Ch. of Jesus Christ of Latter-Day Saints (missionary Germany 1927-30, pres. Hamburg dist. 1930). Contbr. numerous articles in books, sci. jours. Asso. editor Jour. Water Resources Research. Patentee. Home: 2109 Clark Av Ames IA 50010

KIRKHAM, FRANCIS ROBISON, lawyer; b. Fillmore, Utah, Aug. 23, 1904; s. Francis W. and Alzina (Robison) K.; A.B., George Washington U., 1930, LL.B., 1931; m. Ellis Musser, July 9, 1929; children—James F., Elizabeth (Mrs. James Stillman, Jr.), Katherine (Mrs. Geoffrey Hallam Movius), Eugene R. Admitted to D.C. bar, 1931, Cal. bar, 1936; law clk. Chief Justice Charles E. Hughes, 1933-35; with firm Pillsbury, Madison & Sutro, San Francisco, 1936—, partner, 1940—; gen. counsel Standard Oil Co. Cal., 1960-70. Mem. atty. gen.'s nat. com. to study antitrust laws, 1953-55. Recipient Alumni Achievement award, 1970. Fellow Am. Coll. Trial Lawyers, Am. Bar Found.; mem. Am. (chmn. anti-trust law sect. 1961), San Francisco bar assns., State Bar Cal., Am. Law Inst., Am. Judicature Soc., Am. Soc. Internat. Law, Order of Coif, Delta Theta Phi. Clubs: Pacific Union, Bohemian, San Francisco Golf, Stock Exchange (San Francisco). Author: (with Reynolds Robertson) Jurisdiction of the Supreme Court of the U.S. Drafted for Supreme Court Revision of General Orders in Bankruptcy, 1936, 39. Home: 3245 Pacific Av San Francisco CA 94118 Office: Standard Oil Bldg San Francisco CA 94104

KIRKLAND, ALFRED YOUNGES, lawyer; b. Elgin, Ill., Oct. 6, 1917; s. Alfred H. and Elizabeth (Younges) K.; B.A., U. Ill., 1941, J.D., 1943; m. Gwendolyn E. Muntz, June 14, 1941; children—Pamela E. (Mrs. Wayne M. Jensen), Alfred Younges II, James Muntz. Admitted to Ill. bar, 1943; asso. firm Mayer, Meyer, Austrian & Platt, Chgo., 1943; sr. partner firm Kirkland, Brady, McQueen, Martin & Callahan, and predecessors, Elgin, 1951—; spl. asst. atty. gen. Ill., 1969—. Dir. Larkin Bank Elgin. Mem. council practicing lawyers U. Ill. Law Forum, 1969—, mem. adv. bd., 1962-65, adv. council continuing legal edn., 1959-62; Ill. chmn. Def. Research Inst., 1965-66. Pres., Elgin YMCA, 1963. Served to 2d lt. AUS, 1943-46. Fellow Am. Coll. Trial Lawyers, Am. Bar Found.; mem. Am. (ho. dels. 1967-70), Ill. (pres. 1968-69), Kane County (pres. 1961-62), Elgin (pres. 1951-52), Chgo. bar assns., Am. Judicature Soc. (bd. dirs. 1967- -), Ill. Bar Found. (bd. dirs. 1961-69), Ill. Def. Counsel (bd. dirs. 1966-69), Soc. Trial Lawyers, Legal Club Chgo., Internat. Assn. Ins. Counsel, Fed. Ins. Counsel, Assn. Ins. Counsel, Outdoor Writers Assn. Am., Assn. Great Lakes Outdoor Writers (dir.), Nat. Writers Club, Ill. C. of C. (dir. 1969-70), Phi Delta Phi, Sigma Nu. Republican. Conglist. Elk, Moose. Clubs: Elgin Country (pres. 1956); Cosmopolitan (judge adv. internat.) Outdoor editor Elgin Daily Courier- News; fishing editor Midwest Outdoors Mag. Home: 246 Leith Ct Elgin IL 60120 Office: 80 S Grove St Elgin IL 60120

KIRKLAND, BRYANT MAYS, clergyman; b. Essex, Conn., May 2, 1914; s. Henry Burnham and Helen Josephine (Mays) K.; A.B., Wheaton Coll., 1935; Th.B., Princeton Theol. Sem., 1938; Th.M., Eastern Bapt. Theol. Sem., Phila., 1946; D.D. (hon.), Beaver Coll., 1949, Lafayette Coll., 1962, Denison U., 1964; LL.D., U. Tulsa, 1962; S.T.D., Parson Coll., 1966; Litt.D., Washington and Jefferson Coll., 1968; m. Bernice Eleanor Tanis, Aug. 19, 1937; children—Nancy Tanis (Mrs. Tom L. Thompson), Elinor Ann (Mrs. Anthony Landrum Hite), Virginia Lee (Mrs. Laird James Stuart). Ordained to ministry Presbyn. Ch., 1938; pastor, Pa., 38-46, N.J., 1946-57, Tulsa, 1957-62, Fifth Av. Presbyn. Ch., N.Y.C., 1962—. Vis. lectr. homiletics

Princeton Theol. Sem., 1951- 56, 64—; overseas guest lectr. U.S. Armed Forces, U.S. Army Chaplain Sch., 1965, 68, 71; mem. Commn. Ecumenical Mission and Relations, Presbyn. Ch., 1949-62, mem. Commn. on Continuing Edn., 1967; mem. council Nat. Presbyn. Ch. Center, Washington, 1962-65. Trustee Beaver Coll., U. Tulsa; v.p. bd. trustees Princeton Theol. Sem. Mem. Am. Bible Soc. (trustee). Rotarian. Clubs: Tulsa; Westchester Country; University Princeton (N.Y.C.). Author: Growing in Christian Faith, 1963; Home Before Dark, 1965. Contb. author: Evangelical Sermons of Our Day, 1959; Year of Evangelism in Local Church, 196O. Home: 1158 Fifth Av New York City NY 10029 Office: 7 W 55th St New York City NY 10019

KIRKLAND, EDWARD CHASE, educator; b. Bellows Falls, Vt., May 24, 1894; s. Edward and Mary (Chase) K.; A.B., Dartmouth, 1916, Litt.D., 1948; A.M. Harvard, 1921, Ph.D., 1924; M.A., Cambridge U., 1956; Litt.D., Princeton, 1957, Bowdoin Coll., 1961; m. Ruth Stevens Babson, Sept. 4, 1924; 1 son, Edward. Instr. in citizenship, Dartmouth Coll., 1920-21; instr. in history Mass. Inst. Tech., 1922-24; asst. prof. Am. history Brown U., 1924-30; asso. prof. Bowdoin Coll., 1930-31, prof., 1931-55, prof. emeritus, 1955—; Pitt prof. Am. history, Cambridge U., 1956-57; Commonwealth lectr. U. Coll., London, 1952. Served as pvt. 1st class Ambulance Service, U.S. Army, with the French Army, 1917-19. Decorated Croix de Guerre (France). Mem. Am. Hist. Assn., Orgn. of Am. Historians (pres. 1955-56); Econ. History Assn. (pres. 1953-54), Am. Newcomen Soc., Mass. Hist. Soc., Colonial Soc. Mass., Am. Antiquarian Soc., Am. Friends of Lafayette, Am. Assn. U. Profs. (pres. 1946-48), Am. Acad. Arts and Scis., Phi Beta Kappa (senator 1950-70). Author: Peacemakers of 1864, 1927; A History of American Economic Life, 1932, 39, 52, 69; Brunswick's Golden Age, 1942; Men, Cities and Transportation, a Study in New England History 1520-1920, 1948; Business in the Gilded Age: The Conservatives' Balance Sheet, 1952; Dream and Thought in the Business Community, 1860- 1900, 1956; Industry Comes of Age: Business, Labor and Public Policy 1860-1897, 1961. Editor: Andrew Carnegie, Gospel of Wealth, 1962; Charles Francis Adams, Jr., 1835-1915; The Patrician at Bay, 1965. Home: Thetford Center VT 05075

KIRKLAND, JAMES BRYANT, univ. dean; b. Lewisburg, Tenn., June 17, 1904; s. James Alexander and Pearl (Bryant) K.; B.S., U. Tenn., 1926; M.S., 1936; Ph.D., Ohio State U., 1947; m. Eileen Griffis, June 14, 1932; 1 son, James Bryant. Tchr. vocational agr. Hixson (Tenn.) High Sch., 1926-29; tchr., part time instr., dept. agrl. edn. U. Tenn., 1928-36, asso. prof. agrl. edn., 1936-45, prof. and head dept. agrl. edn., 1945-48; dean Sch. Edn., N.C. State U., 1948-69. Gov's Commn. on Study Pub. Schs., 1967-68. Mem. Am. Vocational Assn. (chmn. research com. in agrl. edn. So. Region, 1946-53, resolutions com., 1946-54, adv. council, 1951-52), N.E.A., Nat. Soc. Study Edn., So. Regional Conf., Phi Sigma Kappa, Alpha Zeta, Phi Delta Kappa, Phi Kappa Phi, Kappa Phi Kappa. Lion (pres. Raleigh 1960-61, zone chmn. 1962- 63, dep. dist. gov. 1963-64, dist. gov. 1964-65). Home: 2621 Grant Av Raleigh NC 27608

KIRKLAND, JOSEPH LANE, labor union ofcl.; b. Camden, S.C., Mar. 12, 1922; s. Randolph Withers and Louise (Richardson) K.; student Newberry (S.C.) Coll., 1940; grad. U.S. Merchant Marine Acad., 1942; B.S., Georgetown U. Sch. Fgn. Service, 1948; m. Edith Draper Hollyday, June 10, 1944; children—Blair Hollyday (Mrs. John F. Horton), Lucy Alexander, Louise Richardson (Mrs. Michael Condon), Edith Hollyday, Katharine. Deck officer U.S. Merchant Marine, 1941-46; nautical scientist Hydrographic Office, Navy Dept., 1947-48; mem. research staff AFL, 1948-53; asst. dir. dept. social security AFL CIO, 1953-58; dir. research and edn. Internat. Union Operating Engrs., 1958-60; exec. asst. to pres. AFL-CIO, 1961-69, sec.-treas., 1969—. Pres. Inst. Collective Bargaining and Group Relations bd. mem. Found. Automation and Employment, Am. Inst. Free Labor Devel.; mem. Commn. Founds. and Pvt. Philanthropies; mem. Commn. on Financial Structure; mem. Blue Ribbon Def. Panel. Bd. dirs. Am. Council Arts, Nat. Corp. for Housing Partnerships, Experiments in Art and Tech. Fellow Am. Pub. Health Assn., A.A.A.S.; mem. Internat. Orgn. Masters, Mates and Pilots. Home: 12000 Old Georgetown Rd Rockville MD 20852 Office: 815 16th St NW Washington DC 20006

KIRKLAND, VANCE HALL, artist, educator; b. Convoy, O., Nov. 3, 1904; s. Charles Frederick and Lulu (Hall) K.; B.E.A., Cleve. Sch. Art, 1928; student Western Res. U.; m. Anne Oliphant Olson, July 26, 1941. An organizer art dept. U. Denver, 1929, dir. dept., 1929- 31; founded Kirkland Sch. Art, Denver, 1932, dir., 1932-46 when sch. became an affiliate Sch. Art, U. Denver, dir. Sch. Art, 1946-69; lectr., 1956-57. Paintings in collections of Chgo. Art Inst., William Rockhill Nelson Gallery, Kansas City, Norton Gallery, West Palm Beach, Colorado Springs Fine Arts Center, Denver Art Mus., Santa Barbara Mus., Oakland Art Mus., San Diego Mus., Columbus Gallery Fine Arts. Club: University (Denver). Home: 817 Pearl St Denver CO 80203 Office: 1311 Pearl St Denver CO 80203

KIRKLIN, JOHN WEBSTER, surgeon; b. Muncie, Ind., Aug. 5, 1917; s. Byrl R. and Gladys (Webster) K.; B.A., U. Minn., 1938; M.D., Harvard, 1942; m. Margaret K. Hair, Dec. 5, 1943; children—John, James, Helen. Intern, U. Pa. Hosp., 1942-43; fellow surgery Mayo Clinic, Rochester, Minn., 1943-44, 46-48, 49-50, surgeon, 1950-66; asst. resident surgery Children's Hosp., Boston, 1948-49; asst. prof. surgery Mayo Found., U. Minn., 1953-57, asso. prof., 1957-60, prof. surgery, 1960-66; prof., chmn. dept. surgery Sch. Medicine and Med. Center, U. Ala., Birmingham, 1966—; surgeon-in-chief U. Ala. Hosps. and Clinics. Served to capt. M.C., AUS, 1944-46. Home: 2564 Altadena Rd Birmingham AL 35233 Office: 1919 7th Av S Birmingham AL 35233

KIRKMAN, ELWOOD F., lawyer, banker; b. Phila., 1904; LL.B., Georgetown U., 1925; LL.D., Dickinson Sch. Law, 1964. Sr. mem. Kirkman, Mulligan, Bell & Armstrong; pres., dir. 1st Nat. Bank of South Jersey, Atlantic City, Flanders Hotel Co.; chmn. bd., dir. Cape May County Nat. Bank, Ocean City, N.J.; pres. Chelsea Title & Guaranty Co.; dir. S. Jersey Gas Co., Lenox, Inc. Past chmn. Atlantic City Expressway Authority. Trustee, Dickinson Law Sch. Fellow Am. Bar Found., Am. Coll. Probate Counsel; mem. Am. Bankers Assn. Mason. Home: Flanders Hotel Ocean City NJ Office: 1st Nat Bank Bldg 1301 Atlantic Av Atlantic City NJ 08401

KIRKMAN, OSCAR ARTHUR, ry. ofcl.; b. High Point, N.C., Apr. 16, 1900; s. Oscar Arthur and Lulu Blanche (Hammer) K.; student Havana, Cuba, 1919-20; B.S., M.S., U. Va., 1924; studied law U. Va., 1924-25, Oxford U., Eng., 1926-28; m. Katharine Morgan, Mar. 11, 1933; children— Alvin Larkin, Caroline Elizabeth, John, Susan. Mem. faculty, U. Va., 1922-25; news editor High Point (N.C.) Enterprise, 1925-26; admitted to N.C. bar, 1929; dir., sec., treas., exec. v.p. High Point, Thomasville & Denton R.R. Co., 1930-65; on leave as cons., Office of Def. Transp. in P.R., as Fed. operating mgr. Am. R.R. Co. P.R., 1943-44; Distinguished lectr. polit. sci. High Point Coll., 1965—; mem. Klein & Saks econ. and financial mission, Chile, 1956; mem. bd. dirs. Wachovia Bank & Trust Co.; dir. So. Furniture Expn. Bldg., Inc.; mem. regional bd. Liberty Mut. Ins. Co., Boston; v.p., mem. bd. dirs. Am. Short Line R.R. Assn., 193O-65; pres. Atlantic Savs. and Loan Assn. since 1937. Mayor, High Point, 1939-43; mem. N.C. House of Reps., 1949-52; mem. N.C. Senate, 1953-61, mem. adv. budget commn. N.C. 1959-61; mem. of city council, High Point 1969—. Chmn. bd. dirs. N.C. Sanatoria for Tb, 1951—; mem. Inter-Racial Commn., 1938—; chmn. Human Relations Commn., High Point, 1966-67. Served in U.S. Army, 1918. Mem. Am. Legion, Delta Sigma Rho, Omicron Delta Kappa, Alpha Kappa Psi (nat. pres. 1929- 33), Beta Gamma Sigma. Democrat. Methodist. Mason. Clubs: Country; Royal Aero (London). Address: 501 W High St High Point NC 27260

KIRKMAN, RALPH EVERETT, clergyman, coll. dean; b. Energy, Ill., Nov. 16, 1928; s. William Cecil and Madge (Kirby) K.; A.B., Baylor U., 1950, M.A., 1951; postgrad. Southwestern Bapt. Theol. Sem., 1955; Ed.D., North Tex. State Coll., 1957; postgrad. U. Minn., summer 1958, Harvard, 1959; m. Loisteen Pool, Aug. 17, 1948; children—Kathy Lynne, Jody Ann, Abby. Ordained to ministry Bapt. Ch., 1946; pastor First Bapt. Ch., Valier, Ill., 1946, Abbott (Tex.) Bapt. Ch., 1947-50; English fellow Baylor U., 1951-52; pastor 2d Bapt. Ch., West Frankfort, Ill., 1952-55, 1st Bapt. Ch., Justin, Tex., 1955-56; dean students Ouachita Bapt. Coll., 1956-58, dean faculty, 1958-61; registrar, dir. instl. research Concord Coll., Athens, W.Va., 1961-62, dean Mobile (Ala.) College, 1962-65, acad. v.p., dean coll., 1963-65; dean grad. sch. Middle Tenn. State U., Murfreesboro; now prof. higher edn. George Peabody Coll. Tchrs. Mem. Am. Assn. U. Profs., Nat. Soc. Study Edn., Am. Acad. Polit. and Social Sci., Am. Guidance and Personnel Assn., Am. Assn. Collegiate Registrars and Admissions Officers, Nat., Tenn. edn. assns., Assn. Higher Edn., Nat. Vocational Guidance Assn., Alpha Kappa Delta, Phi Delta Kappa, Sigma Tau Delta. Editor: Peabody Jour. Edn., 1970—. Home: Route 4 Murfreesboro TN 37130 Office: George Peabody Coll Tchrs Box 7 Nashville TN 37203

KIRKNESS, ARNOLD GODFRED, merchandising exec.; b. Lake Park, Minn., June 17, 1904; s. Severin A. and Hansina (Verstaf) K.; B.S., U. N.D., 1928; m. Nettie L. Blecken, Nov. 29, 1928; children—Richard A., Joan (Mrs. Donald W. Perlich), Jean (Mrs. Ralph Hohenstein), Faye (Mrs. Judson P. Jasmin). Instr. high sch., N.D., 1925-26; with Gamble-Skogmo, Inc., Mpls., 1928-69, dir.; pres., dir. Gamble Macleod, Ltd., Macleod Stedman, Ltd., Gamble Macleod, Ltd.; former pres., chmn. board, dir. Macleod Stedman, Ltd.; pres., dir. Claude Neon Advt., Ltd.; sec.-treas. Universal Signs, Ltd.; dir. E. L. Ruddy Co., Ltd., Gamble-Stogmo, Inc., Clark's-Gamble of Can., Ltd., Gamble Drugs, Ltd. Macleod's Store Properties, Ltd. Mode O'Day Corp., Ltd., Marshall Wells Ltd.; mem. council Winnipeg office Can. Permanent Trust Co. Bd. trustees United Way of Greater Winnipeg. Mem. Sigma Alpha Epsilon. Clubs: Blue Key (Manitoba); Winnipeg Winter; St. Charles Country (Winnipeg). Home: Ste 6 230 Hugo Winnipeg Manitoba Canada Office: 1530 Gamble Pl Winnipeg Manitoba Canada

KIRKPATRICK, CHARLES EUGENE, elec. co. exec.; b. Stone Canon, Cal., Jan. 11, 1909; s. Raymond R. and Edna (Oxley) K.; B.S., U.S. Naval Acad., 1931; m. Margaret Armstrong, Jan. 2, 1932; children—Mary Griffin, Robert A. With Pacific Gas & Elec. Co., 1935; with Graybar Elec. Co., 1938—, successively salesman, dept. mgr., br. mgr., 1936-50, dist. mgr., Cleve., 1950-58, Central dist. mgr., Chgo., 1958—70, v.p., regional mgr., 1970—, dir., 1956- -, voting trustee, 1969. Served to ensign USN, 1931-34, lt. comdr. USNR, 1942-45. Decorated Navy Cross. Republican. Presbyn. Clubs: Union League (Chgo.); Chicago Golf (Wheaton, Ill.). Home: 345 Hillcrest Av Hinsdale IL 60521 Office: 2045 N Cornell Av Melrose Park IL 60160

KIRKPATRICK, CHARLES LINCOLN, paper co. exec.; b. Braintree, Mass., Jan. 27, 1912; s. Arthur Wells and Maude Winthrop (Lincoln) K.; B.S., Bowdoin Coll., 1933; LL.B., Harvard, 1936; m. Ruth Frances Garrod, Sept. 19, 1936; children—Richard A., Janice R. (Mrs. J. H. Galloway), Dana A. Was admitted to Mass. bar, 1936; with Am. Writing Paper Corp., Holyoke, Mass., 1938-62, pres., 1958-62, co. now known as Eagle-A Linweave div. Brown Co., v.p. Brown Co., 1963—; dir. Mass. Blue Cross. Home: 41 East St South Hadley MA 01075 Office: 10 Eagle-A Av Holyoke MA

KIRKPATRICK, CHARLES VERNE, educator, petroleum engr.; b. Jacksonville, Tex., Sept. 27, 1916; s. Charles Leslie and Lenora (Morris) K.; B.S., Tex. A. and M. Coll., 1940; M.E., U. Houston, 1952; m. Lois Morrow, Feb. 15, 1941; children—Jean, Kathleen. Design engr. Emsco Derrick Co., Houston, 1945-47; dir. petroleum engring. U. Houston, 1947—, prof., 1953—, chmn. div. chem.- petroleum engring., 1959—, asso. dean Cullen Coll. Engring., 1962- 63, chmn. petroleum engring. dept. Cullen Coll. of Engring., 1963-, acting dean, 1963-65, dean, 1965—; spl. lectr. on oil prodn. by gas lift, fgn. and domestic; active cons. oil and gas. Served as maj., A.A.A., AUS, 1940-45. Mem. Soc. Petroleum Engrs. (bd. dirs. 1964—), Engrs.' Council Profl. Devel. (chmn. region IV, 1962- -; AIME rep. to bd. dirs. 1967-69; vice chmn. engring. edn. and accreditation com. 1969—), Am. Inst. Mining, Metall. and Petroleum Engrs. (chmn. council of edn., 1961-62), Am. Petroleum Inst. (dir. nuclear logging calibration facility 1959—), Am. Soc. Engring Edn., Nat., Texas (pres. San Jacinto chpt. 1967-68) socs. profl. engrs. Author: Power of Gas, rev. edit., 1958; also tech. papers on petroleum prodn. engring., also monograph. Home: 3611 Wood Valley Dr Houston TX 77025

KIRKPATRICK, CLAYTON, newspaper editor; b. Waterman, Ill., Jan. 8, 1915; s. Clayton Matteson and Mable Rose (Swift) K.; A.B., U. Ill., 1937; m. Thelma Marie De Mott, Feb. 13, 1943; children—Pamela Marie (Mrs. Foy), Bruce, Eileen Bea, James Walter. Reporter, City News Bur., Chgo., 1938; men. staff Chgo. Tribune, 1938—, day city editor, 1950- 61, city editor, 1961-63, asst. mng. editor, 1963-65, mng. editor, 1965-67, exec. editor, 1967-69, editor, 1969—; v.p. Chgo. Tribune Co., 1967—; pres. Chgo. Tribune Press Service. Served with USAAF. 1942-45. Decorated Bronze Star Medal. Mem. Phi Beta Kappa, Sigma Delta Chi. Republican. Methodist. Clubs: Chicago, Tavern, Chicago Press, Commercial, Glen Oak Country. Home: 861 Crescent Blvd Glen Ellyn IL 60137 Office: 435 N Michigan Av Chicago IL 60611

KIRKPATRICK, DOW NAPIER, clergyman; b. Sesser, Ill., Jan. 3, 1917; s. Hiram Singleton and Effie (Dycus) K.; student Ill. Wesleyan U., 1933-34; A.B., Asbury Coll., 1938; B.D., Emory U., 1940; Ph.D., Drew U., 1945; postgrad. Oxford (Eng.) U., 1946-47; m. Marjorie Savage, June 1, 1938; children—Dow II, David Earl. Ordained to ministry Methodist Ch., 1940; asso. pastor St. Mark Ch., Atlanta, 1939-40; supply pastor, Milford, Pa., 1941-45; pastor Young Harris, Ga., 1947-51, 1st Meth. Ch., Athens, 1951-57, St. Mark Ch., Atlanta, 1957-62, 1st. Meth. Ch., Evanston, Ill., 1962—. Del., Gen. Conf. Meth. Ch., 1956, 60, 68, World Meth. Conf., 1951, 56, 61, 66; mem. World Meth. Council; co-chmn. Oxford Inst. on Meth. Theol. Studies, 1958, 62, 65, 69; chmn. structure study commn. United Meth. Ch. Served as chaplain USNR, 1945-46. Author: Six Days and Sunday, 1968. Editor: The Doctrine of the Church, 1964; The Finality of Christ, 1966, The Living God, 1971. Home: 310 Church St Evanston IL 60201 Office: 1630 Hinman Av Evanston IL 60201

KIRKPATRICK, EDWARD THOMSON, coll. dean; b. Cranbrook, B.C., Can., Jan. 15, 1925; s. John Thomson and Mary P. (Jones) K.; came to U.S., 1954; B.A.Sc., U. B.C., 1947; M. S., Carnegie Inst. Tech., 1956, Ph.D., 1958; m. Barbara Jane Kelsberg, May 22, 1948; children—Allan Thomson, Karen Amie, Barbara Ann, Keith Edward. Test engr. Canadian Gen. Electric Co., Peterboro, Ont., 1947-48; sales engr., sales mgr. F. D. Bolton Ltd., Vancouver, B.C., 1948-54; asst. prof. Carnegie Inst. Tech., 1954-58; prof. U. Pitts., 1958-59; prof., chmn. dept. mech. engring., also dir. computing center U. Toledo, 1959-64; dean Coll. Engring., Rochester Inst. Tech., 1964-71; pres. Wentworth Inst., 1971—; cons. to industry, 1958—. Mem. Am. Soc. M.E., Am. Soc. Engring. Edn., Am. Assn. U. Profs., Rochester Engring. Soc. (bd. dirs. 1965—). Author: (with H. J. Wilhelm) 1620 Fortran H-D Programming, 1963. Home: 40 Radcliffe Rd Weston MA 02193 Office: 550 Huntington Av Boston MA 02115

KIRKPATRICK, EVRON MAURICE, assn. exec.; b. nr. Raub, Ind., Aug. 15, 1911; s. Omer and Lenna Mae (Hain) K.; B.A. with high honors, U. Ill., 1932, A.M. 1933; Ph.D. (Cowles Fellow in govt. 1933-35), Yale 1939; m. Jeane D. Jordan, Feb. 20, 1955; children—Thomas Reed (dec.), Mary Ellen, Ann Maureen, Douglas J., John E., Stuart A. Instr. polit. ci. U. Minn., 1935-39, asst. prof., 1939-43, asso. prof., 1943-48, prof., 1948, chmn. social sci. div., 1944-48; asst. research dir. research and analysis br. O.S.S., 1945; asst. research dir. and projects control officer research and intelligence Dept. State, 1946, intelligence program adviser, 1947, chief, external research staff, 1948-52, chief, psychol., intelligence and research staff, 1952-54, dep. dir. Office of Intelligence Research, 1954; exec. dir. Am. Polit. Sci. Assn., 1954—; editorial adviser in polit. sci. Henry Holt & Co., 1952-60, Holt Rinehart, and Winston, 1960-68; chmn. bd. trustees Operations and Policy Research Inc., 1955—; lectr. Howard U., 1957-61; cons. Nat. Ednl. Television, 1963-65; professorial lectr. Georgetown U., 1959—; mem. Presdl. Task Force on Career Advancement, 1966. Trustee, Nat. Center Edn. Politics; trustee Helen Dwight Reid Ednl. Found., 1960—, treas. 1964—; dir. Govtl. Affairs Inst., 1954-64; mem. adv. com. on fgn. affairs So. Regional Edn. Bd., 1952-56; chmn. trustees Inst. Am. Univs., France, 1958—. Mem. Nat. Arbitration Assn. (bd. arbitrators 1943-47), Internat. (mem. council 1955—, exec. com. 1958-64), Am. polit. sci. assns., Nat. Acad. Scis. (mem. div. behavioral scis. NRC 1963-66, mem. com. internat. relations in behavioral NRC 1966—), Am. Peace Soc. (sec.), Phi Beta Kappa, Pi Sigma Alpha (mem. exec. com. 1958—). Author: The People, Politics, and the Politician, 1941, American Government, 1942, Survey of American Government, 1943; Running the Country, (with A. N. Christensen), 1946; Target: The World Communist Propaganda Activities in 1955, 1956; Elections - USA (with Jeane Kirkpatrick), 1956: Year of Crisis: An analysis of Communist Propaganda Activities in 1956, 1957; articles in profl. jours. Contbr. Man and Society, 1938; Essays on the Behavioral Study of Politics, 1962; Perspectives, 1963. Home: 6812 Granby St Bethesda MD 20034 Office: 1527 New Hampshire Av NW Washington DC 20036

KIRKPATRICK, FORREST HUNTER, corp. exec.; b. Galion, O., Sept. 4, 1905; s. Arch M. and Mildred (Hunter) K.; student U. Dijon, 1926; A.B., Bethany Coll., 1927, LL.D., 1949; A.M., Columbia, 1931, profl. diploma, 1931, 36; postgrad. U. London, U. Pitts.; LL.D., Coll. Steubenville, 1958, Drury Coll., 1968. Dean, Bethany Coll., 1927-40; gen. mgr. personnel RCA, 1941-46; adj. prof., vis. prof. Bethany Coll., N.Y.U., U. Pitts., Columbia U., U. Akron, 1946-52; asst. to chmn. Wheeling Steel Corp., 1952-64, v.p., 1964-70; chmn. W.Va. Hosp. Service, Inc.; dir. Wheeling- Pitts. Steel Corp., First Nat. Bank & Trust Co., Steubenville, O., Sharon Tube Co., 1st Steuben Bancorp. Vis. prof. W.Va. U., 1970—. Cons. War Manpower Com., 1942-44, Dept. State, 1944, U.S. Civil Service, 1945, Post Office Dept., 1953, Health, Edn. and Welfare, 1970, fgn. trade mission Dept. Commerce, 1962. Mem. W.Va. Commn. Higher Edn., 1963-70; bd. govs. W.Va. U., 1957-69; bd. dirs. Wheeling Symphony Soc., Inc., 1950—; trustee Ohio Valley Gen. Hosp., Wheeling, 1954—. Mem. Am. Iron and Steel Inst., W.Va. Mfrs. Assn. (bd. dirs. 1955—), Am. Econs. Assn., Indsl. Relations Research Assn. (life), Nat. Assn. Mfrs., Am. Acad. Polit. Sci. (life), Am. Personnel and Guidance Assn. (life), Am. Statis. Assn., Beta Gamma Sigma, Beta Theta Pi, Alpha Kappa Psi, Kappa Delta i, Phi Delta Kappa. Clubs: University (N.Y.C.; Pitts.); Fort Henry (Wheeling); Economic, Duquesne (Pitts.); Lakeview Country (Morgantown, W.Va.), Contbr. Personnel Administration and Labor RelationsA Book of Readings, 1952; author research reports and articles. Home: TallyHo Apts 931 National Rd Wheeling WV 26003 Office: Box 268 Wheeling WV 26003

KIRKPATRICK, JOHN ELSON, oil co. exec.; b. Oklahoma City, Feb. 13, 1908; s. Elmer Elsworth and Claudia (Spencer) K.; student U.S. Mil. Acad., 1925-26; B.S., U.S. Naval Acad., 1931; student Harvard Grad. Sch. Bus. Adminstrn., 1935-36; LL.D., Oklahoma City U., 1963; Dr. Humanities, Bethany Nazarene Coll., 1966; m. Eleanor Blake, June 20, 1932; 1 dau., Joan Elson Keesee. Founder, v.p., treas. of Allied Steel Products Corp., Tulsa, 1936-41; v.p., treas. Kirkpatrick & Bale Oil Co., Oklahoma City, 1945-50; owner Kirkpatrick Oil Co., Oklahoma City, 1950—; hon. vice chmn. bd., dir. mem. exec. com. Liberty Nat. Bank and Trust Co.; adv. bd. Liberty Mut. Ins. Co.; sr. partner Kirkpatrick Supply Co., Kirkpatrick Pipeline Co., Jennings Engine Supply Co., Kirkpatrick Oil & Gas Co., Kirkpatrick Drilling Co., Kirkpatrick Trucking Co.; dir. Nat. Gas & Oil Corp., May Av. Bank & Trust Co. Oklahoma City; adv. dir. Stockyards Bank Oklahoma City. Pres. Okla. Zool. Soc.; trustee Okla. City U.; trustee, also donor bldg. Okla. Art Center; bd. dirs. Okla U. Found., Okla. State Fair, Oklahoma City YMCA, Oklahoma City Opera Assn., Oklahoma City Symphony Orch., also Nat. Conf. Christians and Jews; exec. com. Frontiers of Sci. Found., Mercy Hosp., Oklahoma City; trustee Okla. Sci. and Arts Found.; past pres. Presbyn. Homes; chmn. Santa Claus Commn., Oklahoma City; mem. Maritime Adv. Bd.; pres. Oklahoma City Community Found., Lyric Theatre Okla.; trustee Nat. Cowboy Hall Fame and Western Heritage Center, Presbyn. Hosp.; bd. dirs. Okla. Med. Research Found.; mem. pres.' bd. Okla. Christian Coll.; mem. adv. com. Okla. U. Med. Sch. Served from ensign to capt. USN, 1931- 35, 41-45; rear adm. ret. Decorated Bronze Star with V; recipient Distinguished Service award Okla. U., 1959; Nat. Brotherhood citation, Nat. Conf. of Christians and Jews, 1962; named to Okla. Hall of Fame, 1962. Mem. Ind. Petroleum Assn. (past dir.), Oklahoma City C. of C. (life dir.), Oklahoma Petroleum council (dir.), Okla. Hist. Soc. (life). Clubs: Rotary, Oklahoma City Petroleum (pres. 1959-60). Home: 1800 Wilshire Blvd Oklahoma City OK 73116 Office: 1300 N Broadway Oklahoma City OK 73103

KIRKPATRICK, JOHN GILDERSLEEVE, lawyer; b. Toronto, Can., Jan. 28, 1917; s. Herbert Rutherfoord and Edna (Nelles) K.; B.Sc., McGill U., 1939, B.C.L., 1942; m. Irena Groten, June 24, 1944; children—Xenia, Kathleen, Patricia, Joseph. Admitted to Que. bar, 1943, created Queen's counsel, 1961; partner in firm of Ogilvy, Cope, Porteous, Hansard, Marler, Montgomery & Renault and predecessors, Montreal, 1942—. Chmn., dir. L. M. Ericsson Ltd.; dir. Domtar Ltd., Volvo (Can.) Ltd., Mokta (Can.) Ltd., Royfund Ltd., Deram Ltd., Canron Ltd. Gov. Trinity Coll. Sch. Anglican. Home: 634 Victoria Av Westmount 217 Quebec Canada Office: 1 Place Ville Marie Montreal 113 Quebec Canada

KIRKPATRICK, LAURENCE VERNON, clergyman; b. Chickasha, Okla., Apr. 20, 1930; s. Robert Royce and Hallie Blanche (Garner) K.; A.B., Phillips U., Enid, Okla., 1952; B.D., Yale, 1955; Ed.D., Columbia, 1962; S.T.D. (hon.), Milligan Coll., 1967. Ordained to ministry Christian Ch., 1952; minister in Tulsa, 1953, Cin., 1955-56,

Wellington, Kan., 1956-59; asso. sec. World Council Christian Edn., 1959-63; gen. sec. World Conv. Chs. of Christ, 1963—; cons. to meetings Nat. and World councils chs. Home: 220 E 60th St New York City NY 10022 Office: 475 Riverside Dr New York City NY 10027

KIRKPATRICK, LYMAN BICKFORD, Jr., educator; b. Rochester, N.Y., July 15, 1916; s. Lyman Bickford and Lyde (Paull) K.; B.A., Princeton, 1938; m. Jeanne Courtney, Feb. 21, 1939 (div.); children—Lyman Bickford III, Jeanne Barclay, Paull Timothy, Helen Paull; m. 2d, Rita Meade, Sept. 3, 1965. Asst. mng. dir. Bur. Nat. Affairs, Washington, 1938-40; editor, personnel dir. U.S. News Publ. Corp., Washington, 1940-42; editorial staff World Report, Washington, 1945-47; div. chief CIA, Washington, 1947-50, asst. dir., 1950-53, insp. gen., 1953-61, exec. dir., 1962-65; prof. polit. sci., univ. prof. Brown U., 1967—; Nimitz prof. Navy War Coll., 1966—, Nimitz chair, 1971-72. Served from 1st lt. to maj., OSS, AUS, 1942- 45; ETO. Decorated Bronze Star nedal, Legion of Merit (U.S.); Croix de Guerre (France, Belgium); recipient ann. Career Service award Nat. Civil Service League, 1960; ann. award Princeton Class of 1938, 1960; Pres.'s award Distinguished Fed. Civilian Service, 1964. Episcopalian. Author: The Real CIA, 1968; American Security Policy, 1968; Captains Without Eyes: Major Intelligence Failures in World War II, 1969. Ann. contbr.: Ency. Brit. Book of the Year, 1947-60. Home: Anawan Cliffs Dr RD 2 Box 9A Narragansett RI 02882

KIRKPATRICK, MILES WELLS, govt. ofcl.; b. Easton, Pa., June 1, 1918; s. William H. and Mary Stewart (Wells) K.; A.B., Princeton, 1940; LL.B., U. Pa., 1943; m. Anna Paddock Skerrett, Feb. 9, 1945; children—William, Nancy, Mary. Admitted to Pa. bar, 1943; asso., then partner Morgan, Lewis & Bockius, Phila., 1944-70; chmn. FTC, Washington, 1970—. Served with Armored Div., A.C., AUS, 1942-44. Mem. Am. (chmn. antitrust sect. 1968-69), Pa., Phila. bar assns., Nat. Lawyers Club. Clubs: Princeton (Washington); Union League, Midday (Phila.). Home: 40 Hillside Rd Philadelphia PA 19087 Office: FTC 6th and Pennsylvania Av NW Washington DC 20580

KIRKPATRICK, RALPH, harpsichordist; b. Leominster, Mass., June 10, 1911; s. Edwin Asbury and Florence May (Clifford) K.; A.B., Harvard, 1931; Harvard fellow, Paris, Berlin, Eng., 1931-33; Guggenheim fellow for study 17th and 18th century music, 1937; Mus. D. (hon.), Oberlin, 1957; studied with Nadia Boulanger, Wanda Landowska, Arnold Dolmetsch, Gunther Ranin, Heinz Tiessen. Pub. concert, Berlin, 1933, other cities Germany and Italy; faculty Salzburg Mozarteum Acad., summers 1933, 34; pub. concerts U.S., 1934—; dir. festivals 18th century music, Williamsburg, Va., 1938-46; harpsichord, clavicord solo and chamber music concerts throughout U.S., 1939—; soloist with major orchs. in U.S. and Europe, ann. transcontinental trips, 1944—, European tours, 1947—; vis. lectr. Yale, 1940, asso. prof., 1956-65, prof. music, 1965- -; Ernest Bloch prof. music U. Cal., Berkeley, 1964. Decorated Knight Cross Order Al merito della Republica (Italy). Mem. Am. Acad. Arts and Scis., Am. Philos. Soc. Recorded albums Scarlatti sonatas, 1948, 53, 55, Bach Clavier Ubung, 1952, Bach's Complete Keyboard Works, 1956-67, Mozart concertos, 1951, 56, sonatas, 1945-52. Author: Biography of Domenico Scarlatti, 1953. Editor: Bach's Goldberg Variations, Scarlatti sonatas. Address: Old Quarry Guilford CT 06437

KIRKPATRICK, RICHARD BOGUE, newspaperman, lawyer; b. Van Buren, Ind., Dec. 16, 1912; s. Otto L. and Magnolia (Bogue) K.; J.D., U. Cin., 1952; m. Carolyn Ann Hawkins, Dec. 12, 1943 (dec. Sept. 1960); 1 son, Thomas Hawkins; m. 2d, Kay Poch Lynch, Aug. 26, 1971; 1 stepdau., Vicki Leigh Lynch. With editorial dept. Cin. Enquirer, 1934-68, polit. columnist, 1948-68, head bur., Frankfort, Ky., 1948-56, Columbus, O., 1956-61, bur. chief, Washington, 1961-68. Admitted to Ohio bar, 1952, Ky. bar 1952, U.S. Supreme Ct., 1963, D.C., bar, 1968; partner Ansary, Kirkpatrick & Rosse, Washington, 1968-69; sec. dir. Campbell Music Co., Inc., 1968-69. Cons. NASA, 1968-69; asst. minority counsel U.S. House Ways and Means Com., 1969- 70; aide U.S. Paul J. Fannin, 1970; staff asst. criminal div. Justice Dept., Washington, 1970—. Mem. scholarships adv. com. Am. Polit. Sci. Assn. Served to lt. col. AUS, 1941-45, 46-47. Mem. Am., Ohio, Ky., D.C. bar assns., Sigma Delta Chi. Methodist (trustee 1953-55). Clubs: National Press (Washington). Home: 5006 Westport Rd Chevy Chase MD 20015 Office: Justice Dept Washington DC 20530

KIRKPATRICK, ROBERT LEWIS, lawyer; b. Renfrew, Pa., Dec. 31, 1906; s. John L. and Ella Z. (White) K.; A.B., Allegheny Coll., 1931; LL.D., Allegheny Coll., 1965; m. Harriet Louise Wildey, Aug. 27, 1930; children—Judith (Mrs. Richard E. Sigler), Harriet Louise (Mrs. George N. Forker), Robert Lewis, James Wildey Kirkpatrick. Admtted to Pa. bar, 1931; partner Kirkpatrick, Lockhart, Johnson & Hutchison, 1946—; asst. sec., dir. Shenango Furnace Co.; dir. Monongahela Connecting R.R. Co., Aliquippa & So. R.R. Co., Cuyahoga Valley Ry., Shenango, Inc., Farm Coal Co.; trustee W.P. Snyder Estate. Trustee Allegheny Coll.; dir. Western Pa. Conservancy; bd. governance Pa. Bar. Served to lt. col. AUS, 1942-45. Decorated Legion of Merit. Mem. Am. Bar Assn., Am. Law Inst., Phi Beta Kappa, Delta Tau Delta. Presbyn. Mason. Club: Duquesne (Pitts.); Rolling Rock. Home: 1420 Centre Av Pittsburgh PA 15219 Office: Oliver Bldg Pittsburgh PA 15222

KIRKPATRICK, THOMAS HERBERT, actuary; b. London, Ont., Can., May 3, 1909; s. Robert M. and Ada (Taylor) K.; B.A., U. Western Ont., 1932; m. Margaret C. Richardson, Feb. 17, 1933; children—Robert T., John F., Janet E. Came to U.S., 1948, naturalized 1953. Asst. actuary London Life Ins. Co., 1932-48; supt. group dept. Paul Revere Life Ins. Co., Worcester, Mass., 1948-52, v.p. actuary, 1952-68, sr. actuary, 1968—, also dir.; asst. treas. Paul Revere Corp.; dir. Paul Revere Variable Annuity Ins. Co., Paul Revere Equity Mgmt. Co., Paul Revere Equity Sales Co. Vice pres., asst. treas. Paul Revere Fund, Inc.; v.p. bd. dirs. U. Western Ont. Found.; bd. dirs. Worcester chpt. A.R.C.; bd. mgrs. Contract Accumulation Fund; mem. adv. council Northeastern U. Grad. Sch. Actuarial Sci. Served to lt. col. Canadian Army, 1940-46. Fellow Soc. Actuaries; mem. Am. Acad. Actuaries, actuaries club Boston, Hartford, Am. Math. Soc., Mass. Golfers Assn. Episcopalian. Mason (Shriner). Club: Worcester Country. Home: 10 Brookshire Rd Worcester MA 01609 Office: 18 Chestnut St Worcester MA 01608

KIRKPATRICK, WILLIAM, mining co. exec.; b. Butte, Mont., May 18, 1911; s. Joseph A. and Rufina (Tremblay) K.; LL.B., Georgtown U., 1936; m. Mary Pat Kirkpatrick, Nov. 18, 1957; five children. Vice pres. Anaconda Co.; dir. Internat. Smelting & Refining Co. Bd. dirs., chmn. antitrust and trade regulations com. U.S. C. of C. Served with USNR, World War II. Mem. Am., D.C., Ill., Mont. bar assns., N.Y.C. C. of C., Am. Inst. M.E., Am. Mining Congress, N.W. Mining Assn., N.Y.C. Mining Club, Am. Legion, Newcomen Soc. N.Am. Elk. Clubs: Butte Country, Town (Butte); Canoe Brook Country (Summit). Home: 49 Druid Hill Rd Summit NJ 07450 Office: 25 Broadway New York City NY 10004

KIRKPATRICK, WILLIAM ALEXANDER, steel co. exec.; b. Pitts., May 11, 1923; s. Harlow Barton and Elizabeth (Hillman) K.; A.B., Yale, 1944; m. Jo Anne McCollough, Aug. 20, 1945; children—Carolin Gaylord, William Alexander. With Allegheny Ludlum Industries, Inc., Pitts., 1946—, statistician, 1950-51, asst. to controller, 1951- 54, mgr. budgets and statistics, 1954-55, asst. controller, 1955-60, controller, 1960—, v.p. finance, 1968—. Mem. exec. bd. Allegheny Housing Rehab. Corp. Served to 2d lt., inv., AUS, 1943-46. Mem. Am. Iron and Steel Inst., Financial Execs. Inst., Pitts. Soc. of Financial Analysts. Clubs: Duquesne, Harvard-Yale-Princeton, Chartiers Country (Pitts.). Home: Winthrop Rd Rosslyn Farms Carnegie PA 15106 Office: Oliver Bldg Pittsburgh PA 15222

KIRKSEY, HOWARD GRADEN, coll. dean; b. Perryville, Tenn., Feb. 12, 1910; s. Oliver Columbus and Jennie Jane (Johnson) K.; A.B., Union U., 1934; M.A., George Peabody Coll., 1937, Ph.D., 1950; m. Elizabeth Campbell, May 14, 1936; 1 son, Howard Graden. High sch. tchr., prin., regional supr. Tenn. Dept. Edn., 1945-49; with Middle Tenn. State U., 1949—, head dept. edn., 1949-54, dir. Grad. Sch., 1951-65, dean faculties, 1954-71, v.p. for acad. affairs, 1971—. Bd. dirs. Rutherford Hosp. Mem. N.E.A., Tenn. Coll. Assn. (exec. sec.), Tenn. Edn. Assn. (chmn. profl. rights and responsibility com.), Phi Delta Kappa, Sigma Alpha Epsilon, Pi Kappa Delta. Mason, Rotarian. Home: 1015 E Bell St Murfreesboro TN 37130

KIRKWOOD, GORDON MACDONALD, educator; b. Toronto, Ont., Can., May 7, 1916; s. George Leslie MacKay and Gertrude Erie (Marlatt) K.; came to U.S., 1946, naturalized, 1961; B.A., Trinity Coll., U. Toronto, 1938; M.A., Cornell U., 1939; Ph.D., Johns Hopkins, 1942; m. Patricia Marie Frueh, Sept. 16, 1940; children—Michael John, David Hoyt. Sr. Latin master Lower Can. Coll., Montreal, 1945-46; lectr. Latin, U. Sask., summer 1946; mem. faculty Cornell U., 1946—, prof. classics, 1959—, chmn. dept., 1963—. Served to lt. Royal Canadian Naval Vol. Service, 1943-45. Mem. Am. Philol. Assn., Classical Assn. Atlantic States, Am. Assn. U. Profs., Phi Beta Kappa. Author: A Study of Sophoclean Drama (award of merit Am. Philol. Assn. 1959), 1958; A Short Guide to Classical Mythology, 1959; also numerous articles. Co-editor: Cornell Studies in Classical Philology, 1959—. Home: 516 Cayuga Heights Rd Ithaca NY 14850

KIRKWOOD, MAURICE RICHARD, banker; b. Tipton, Ind., Dec. 24, 1920; s. Walter Bryan and Lettie (Cooper) K.; B.S. with distinction, Ind. U., 1942, M.S., 1943; m. Anne Elizabeth Smith, Aug. 30, 1942; children—Candace Lynn, Susan Kay. Instr., Ind. U., 1942-43; gen. mgr. Stars & Stripes, Darmstadt, Germany, 1946-52; v.p. Fidelity Bank & Trust Co., Indpls., 1952-59; v.p., sec. to bd. Am. Fletcher Nat. Bank and Trust Co., Indpls., 1959—; sec., dir. 101 Monument Corp., 1966-70; guest lectr. Ind. U. Bus. Sch., 1954—; sec. Indpls. Clearing House, 1956-57; dir. instr., Am. Inst. Banking, 1959-61. Sec., dir. Ind. Dept. Financial Instns., 1965—; sec. to adv. com. of banking comptroller of the currency. Treas. Muscular Dysthrophy Assn., 1959-64; treas. P.T.A., 1958-60; dist. chmn. United Fund, 1957; mem. regional adv. com. to Comptroller Currency, 1970-72. Bd. dirs. Meth. Home for Aged, Franklin, Ind. Served to 1st lt. AUS, 1943-46. Recipient Meritorious Civilian Service award Dept. Army, 1952; award of appreciation Office Comptroller of Currency, 1962. Mem. Robert Morris Assos. (bd. dirs. 1965-69; chmn. bd. regents Comml. Lending Sch., 1968- -; pres. Ohio Valley chpt. 1963-64), Ind. U. Sch. Bus. Alumni Assn. (bd. dirs. 1965-69), Nat. Assn., Accountants, Indpls. C. of C., Ind. Traffic Safety Found., Indpls. Civic Progress Assn., Ind. Credit Men's Assn., Sigma Nu, Beta Gamma Sigma, Phi Eta Sigma, Delta Sigma Pi. Methodist. Clubs: Hillcrest Country, Indiana University Men's, Columbia (Indpls.). Author: National Bank and the Future, 1962. Home: 4545 Dickson Rd Indianapolis IN 46226 Office: 101 Monument Circle Indianapolis IN 46204

KIRKWOOD, ROBERT CAMPBELL, former chain store exec.; b. Provo, Utah, Nov. 19, 1904; s. Thomas Matthew and Sarah Jane (Whitehead) K.; student pub. schs. of Provo; D.C.S. (hon.), Suffolk U.; LL.D., Simpson Coll.; m. Virginia Viola Bates, Jan. 1, 1924; children—Robert Campbell, Mary Jane. With F.W. Woolworth Co., 1923—, successively trainee, Provo and Salt Lake City, store mgr., Denver, Sheridan, Wyo., Mitchell, S.D., Bismarck, Grand Forks, (N.D.), Des Moines, Ia., supt. Mpls. dist., personnel dir., mdse. supr., asst. dist. mgr. San Francisco, exec. office rep. N.Y.C., dist. mgr. Boston, then to exec. office in charge devel. self-service stores, v.p. and dir., exec. v.p., 1955- 58, exec. officer, pres., 1958-65, chmn. bd., chief exec. officer, 1965-69; former pres., dir. F.W. Woolworth Co., Ltd.-Can., F.W. Woolworth Co., Mexico; dir. Irving Trust Co., N.Y.C., Charter N.Y. Corp., Richman Clothing Co. N.Y.C. Trustee, Simpson Coll. Clubs: Lost Tree (North Palm Beach, Fla.); Country (Greenwich). Address: 806 Village Rd Lost Tree Village North Palm Beach FL 33408

KIRKWOOD, SAMUEL BROWN, univ. pres.; b. Seattle, May 2, 1907; s. Samuel Kennedy and Edith Alice (Brown) K.; A.B., Macalester Coll., 1928, D.Sc. (hon.), 1951; M.D., Harvard, 1931; LL.D., Amherst Coll., 1966; m. Grace Hight, May 2, 1934; children—Douglas, Diana. Intern pathology Boston City Hosp., 1931; intern surgery Mass. Gen. Hosp., 1932; epidemiologist Mass. Dept. Health, 1934; intern obstetrics Boston Lying-in-Hosp., 1935, resident obstetrics, 1938; resident gynecology Free Hosp. Women, Brookline, Mass., 1936; mem. faculty Harvard Med. Sch., 1939-53, clin. prof. maternal health, 1953; commr. Mass. Dept. Pub. Health, 1953-58; chief pub. health div. ICA, Iran, 1959-61; dean faculties med. scis., prof. obstetrics Am. U. Beirut (Lebanon), 1962-65, pres., 1965—; lectr. internat. health Harvard, 1965. Mem. adv. com. maternal and child health, subcom. care premature infant Mass. Dept. Health, 1940; cons. gynecology VA, 1946-49; adviser Pakistan Ministry Health, 1953-58; cons. cancer control USPHS, 1959. Pres. Winchester Art Assn., 1955-56; chmn. music group Winchester Coll. Club, 1948-58. Trustee Pahlavi U. Shiraz, Iran, 1961. Served to lt. col., M.C., AUS, 1942-46; PTO. Founding fellow Am. Coll. Obstetrics and Gynecology; fellow Am. Pub. Health Assn.; mem. Assn. Mil. Surgeons, Mass. Pub. Health Assn., Mass. Heart Assn., Assn. State and Terr. Health Officers, Am. Assn. Pub. Health Physicians, Royal Soc. Health, Assn. Maternal and Infant Health, Mass., Roxbury Crossing med. socs., Civil Affairs Med. Assn., Boston Obstet. Soc., Aesculapian Club, Assn. Am. Med. Colls., Alpha Omega Alpha, Delta Omega. Presbyn. Address: Am U of Beirut Beirut Lebanon

KIRKWOOD, WILLIAM, Jr., oil co. exec.; b. Petroleum, Ind., Aug. 8, 1911; s. William and Bernice (Miller) K.; student LaSalle Extension U., 1930-35, Cornell U., 1955, Harvard, 1961; m. Maxine Ullman, Mar. 31, 1939; children—William Quentin, Diane Kay. With Marathon Oil Co., Findlay, O., 1933—, asst. mgr. gen. accounting div., 1959-62, mgr. domestic accounting div., 1962-64, controller, 1964—; controller Marathon Pipe Line Co. Mem. Findlay Area C. of C. (treas.), Financial Execs. Inst., Am. Petroleum Inst., Beta Alpha Psi. Republican. Presbyn. Clubs: Findlay Country (treas.), Elks. Home: 2428 S Main St Findlay OH 45840 Office: 539 S Main St Findlay OH 45840

KIRMSER, PHILIP GEORGE, educator; b. St. Paul, Dec. 17, 1919; s. Philip and Helen Juliana (Mendler) K.; B.Chem. Engring., U. Minn., 1939, M.S. in Math., 1944, Ph.D., 1958; m. Jeune Ethel Blomquist, June 12, 1942; children—Lawrence Philip, Sandra Jeune. Instr., Kan. State U., 1942-44; mech. engr. U.S. Naval Ordnance Lab., 1946-48; instr. U. Minn., 1948-54; asso. prof. Kan. State U., 1954-58, prof., 1958—, head applied mechanics dept., 1962—. Vis. scientist Institut Battelle, Geneva, Switzerland, 1970; cons. Phillips Petroleum Co., 1961-64, Boeing Co., 1966, J.B. Ehrsam Co., 1964, Bayer McElrath, mgmt. consultants, 1965—. Served to lt. (j.g.) USNR, 1944-46. Fulbright scholar to Netherlands, 1951-52; cited by USN for work at Bikini atomic tests, 1946. Registered profl. engr., Kan. Mem. Am. Soc. for Engring. Edn. (pres. Kan.-Neb. sect. 1961-62), Am. Math. Assn., Am. Math. Soc., Soc. het Koninklijk Instituut van Ingenieurs, Sigma Xi, Phi Lambda Upsilon, Phi Kappa Phi, Pi Mu Epsilon. Contbr. articles to tech. jours. Patentee heated melt recyle responsive to temperative differential of crystal mass. Home: 1009 Michael Rd Manhattan KS 66502

KIRN, LOUIS JOSEPH, ret. naval officer; b. Milw., June 8, 1908; s. Michael and Frances (Androjna) K.; B.S., U.S. Naval Acad., 1932; grad. Armed Forces Staff Coll., 1948, Naval War Coll., 1951, Imperial Def. Coll., London, Eng., 1956; m. Ray Reynoir, Mar. 17, 1959. Commd. ensign U.S. Navy, 1932, advanced through grades to rear adm., 1959; designated naval aviator, 1936; comdg. officer Scouting Squadron 3, Solomon Islands, 1942-43; staff operations officer, staff comdr. Air Force S. Pacific, Quadalcanal, 1943-44; operations officer, staff comdr. Carrier Div. 2, 1944-45; asst. tng. officer, staff chief Naval Air Tng., Pensacola, Fla., 1945-48; exec. officer U.S.S. Leyte, 1948-49; chief field liaison br. Office Information, Navy Dept., 1952-55; comdr. seaplane tender U.S.S. Currituck, 1957; comdg. officer aircraft carrier U.S.S. Randolph, 1957- 58; chief staff to comdr. Carrier Div. 4, 1958-59; comdr. Carrier Div. 19, 1959-60; chief Naval Air Advanced Tng., Corpus Christi, Tex., 1960- 62; comdr. Carrier Div. 5, 1926-63, Key West Force, 1963-64; dep. dir. Joint Staff, Washington, 1964-65, vice dir., 1966; U.S. Def. attache, U.S. Naval attache, U.S. Naval attache for air, Am. embassy, London, 1967-70; exec. sec. Episcopal Diocese S.E. Fla., Miami, 1970—. Decorated Navy Cross, D.F.C., Legion of Merit (2), D.S.M., Bronze Star, Air medal. Mem. U.S. Naval Inst., Mil. Order World Wars. Clubs: N.Y. Yacht; Army-Navy (Washington); Key West Country; Calusa Country (Miami); Whispering Pines Country Club of North Carolina. Address: 525 NE 15th St Miami FL 33132

KIRRMANN, ERNEST NESTOR, educator; b. Strasbourg, France, Feb. 28, 1905; s. Edouard and Louise (Schaeffer) K.; came to U.S., 1924, naturalized, 1931; B.S., Coll. City N.Y., 1930; certificate U Strasbourg, 1932; M.A., Columbia, 1933; postgrad. Middlebury Coll., summers 1937-39; Ph.D. (Univ. fellow), Northwestern U., 1946; m. Dorothy May Jones, July 19, 1934 (dec. 1966); m. 2d, Winnie Sculthorp, Nov. 5, 1968. Optician 1924-31; instr., sr. master French, German, Mt. Hermon Sch. Boys, Northfield Sch. Girls, 1931- 59; asso. prof. German, French, Sweet Briar (Va.) Coll., 1959-64, prof. German, 1964-70, prof. emeritus, 1970—, chmn. modern lang. dept., 1961-64; Fulbright Exchange tchr. English, French, Schadow Schule, Berlin, Germany, 1953- 54; vis. lectr. German, Sweet Briar (Va.) Coll., 1958-59; vis. prof. French, Randolph Macon Woman's Coll., 1959. Mem. Modern Lang. Assn. Am., Am. Assn. Tchrs. French, Am. Assn. Tchrs. German (pres. Va. chpt.), Va. Modern Lang. Assn., Am. Assn. U. Profs. Translator: Death and the Plowman, 1958. Home: PO Box 3 Sweet Briar VA 24595 also 3 Rue Oberlin Strasbourg France

KIRSCH, CHARLES EDWARD, mfg. co. exec.; b. Sturgis, Mich., Sept. 21, 1927; s. Guy W. and Flora (Callender) K.; student DePauw U., 1946-48, Western Mich. U., 1948-49; m. Barbara Jean Carls, June 22, 1957; children—Kathy Lynn, Lauri Beth, Amy, Charles. With Kirsch Co., 1949—, sec., 1956-57, exec. v.p. marketing, 1957-60, exec. v.p., 1960-65, pres., 1965—, also dir.; pres. Scotscraft, Inc., Scottsville, Ky., 1960—; mem. bd. dirs. Sturgis Savs. & Loan Assn. (Mich.), Union Bank & Trust Co., Grand Rapids, Mich. Trustee Sturgis Found. Mason (Shriner). Clubs: Klinger Lake Country (pres. 1956) (Sturgis); Lake Mich. Yachting Assn. (dir.); Chicago Yacht; Macatawa Bay Yacht; Rotary (past pres. Sturgis). Home: 1108 S Lakeview St Sturgis MI 49091 Office: Kirsch Co Sturgis MI 49091

KIRSCH, EDWARD, hosp. adminstr.; b. Montreal, Que., Can., May 21, 1911; s. Simon and Malca (Cossman) K.; B.Sc., McGill U., 1934, M.D., 1937; m. Alice Elizabeth Gartley, Apr. 26, 1941; children—Robert Alan, Peter Leigh. Came to U.S., 1939, naturalized, 1944. Intern Jewish Gen. Hosp., Montreal, 1937-39; resident pvt. pavilion Montefiore Hosp., N.Y.C., 1939-40, div. pulmonary diseases, 1940-42; asst. dir. Jewish Hosp., Bklyn., 1942-44; dir. Menorah Hosp., Kansas City, Mo., 1945; exec. dir. Lebanon Hosp., N.Y.C., 1946-63, Bronx-Lebanon Hosp. Center, N.Y.C., 1963—. Spl. examiner N.Y.C., 1956-65. Mem. regional adv. group N.Y. Met. Regional Med. Program. Bd. dirs. Hosp. Credit Exchange, 1970-71. Recipient awards Fedn. Jewish Philanthropies N.Y.C., United Jewish Appeal Greater N.Y., State Israel Bonds. Fellow Am. Coll. Hosp. Adminstrs.; mem. Am. Hosp. Assn., A.M.A., Bronx County Med. Soc., Greater N.Y. Hosp. Assn. (bd. govs. 1962-64, 70—), Hosp. Assn. N.Y. State (ho. dels. 1961—), N.Y.C. Blood Transfusion Assn. (bd. dirs. 1963-66), Hosp. Adminstrs. Club N.Y.C. (pres. 1967-68). Home: 3 Hamilton Rd Scarsdale NY 10583 Office: 1276 Fulton Av Bronx NY 10456

KIRSCH, EDWIN JOSEPH, educator, microbiologist; b. Hoboken, N.J., Aug. 25, 1924; s. Max and Lena (Lessing) K.; B.S., Mich. State U., 1949; M.S., Purdue U., 1955, Ph.D., 1958; m. Kathleen Marie Willington, Aug. 10, 1945; children—Glenn Edward, Lee Edwin, Paul Willington. Research biologist Lederle Labs., Am. Cyanamid Co., 1950-53, sr. scientist, 1957-63; asso. prof. Purdue U., 1963-69, prof., 1969—; cons. NASA Apollo project, 1968-69; cons. biol. waste-treatment and waste-reuse, 1965—. Served with M.C. USAAF, 1943-45. Mem. Am. Soc. Microbiology, Soc. Indsl. Microbiology, Water Pollution Control Fedn., Ind. Water Pollution Control Assn., Sigma Xi. Club: Fortnightly Literary (Lafayette). Contbr. articles profl. jours. Home: 1616 Sheridan Dr West Lafayette IN 47906

KIRSCH, JOHN WENDELL, mfg. co. exec.; b. Sturgis, Mich., Aug. 1, 1927; s. John Nicholas and Evelyn (McLauchlin) K.; ed. Albion Coll., 1949; M.B.A., U. Ind., 1950; m. Genevieve E. Moodey, June 25, 1949; children—Christopher J., Nicholas R., Mark M. With Kirsch Co., Sturgis, 1951—, exec. v.p. operations, 1957-60, pres., 1960-65, chmn. bd., 1965—, also dir.; v.p. dir. Kirsch of Can., Ltd.; mem. bd. dirs. Scottscraft, Inc. Citizens State Bank, Ideal Mfg. Co. Mem. bd. trustees Tri-State Coll., Angola, Ind. Mem. Sturgis C. of C. (dir.). Mason (K.T.), National Association of Manufacturers (dir.). Clubs: Rotary (past pres.), Klinger Lake Country (past pres.) (Sturgis). Home: 902 S Lakeview St Sturgis MI 49091 Office: Kirsch Co Sturgis MI 49091

KIRSCH, ROBERT, author, critic; b. Coney Island, N.Y., Oct. 18, 1922; s. Abraham and Pauline (Alterwein) K.; B.A., U. Ca. at Los Angeles, 1949, M.A., 1951, C.Phil., 1970; Litt.D., U. Redlands, 1970; m. Nancy Harris; children—Paul, Randal, Eric, Jonathan. Marya. Reporter, Sun Star, Merced, Cal., 1940, U.P., 1946; reporter, feature writer Hollywood (Cal.) Citizen-News, 1947-52; lit. editor, book columnist Los Angeles Times, 1952—; lectr. journalism U. Cal. at Los Angeles, 1953, 59- 60, 61—. Served with USNR, 1941-45. Mem. Phi Beta Kappa, Sigma Delta Chi, Kappa Tau Alpha. Democrat. Jewish religion. Author: Do Not Go Gentle, 1958; In the Wrong Rain, 1959; Madeleine Austrian, 1960; The Wars of Pardon, 1965; (pseud. Robert

Dundee) The Restless Lovers, 1960, Pandora's Box, 1961, Inferno, 1962; (pseud. Robert Bancroft) The Castilian Rose, 1961; Knight of the Scimitar, 1965; West of the West: Witness to the California Experience (with William F. Murphy), 1968. Office: Los Angeles Times Times-Mirror Sq Los Angeles CA 90053

KIRSCHENBAUM, JULES, artist; b. N.Y.C., Mar. 25, 1930; s. Louis and Anna B. (Gitlitz) K.; student Bklyn. Mus. Art Sch., 1948-51; m. Cornelis Ruhtenberg, July 18, 1956; 1 son, Matthew. Exhibited Met. Mus., Chgo. Art Inst., Corcoran Gallery, Mus. Modern Art, Whitney Mus., Pa. Acad., Acad. Arts and Letters, Nat. Acad. Design, also in Rome, Florence and Spoleto, Italy; represented in permanent collections Whitney Mus., Everhart Mus., Scranton, Pa.; asso. prof. art Drake U. Recipient Dana medal Pa. Acad., 1953, 1st prize Butler Art Inst., Youngstown, O., 1957, Hallgarten prize Nat. Acad. Design, 1953, I. Maynard award, 1954, Wallace Truman prize, 1955, 1st prize figure painting, 1960. Fulbright scholar, 1956. A.N.A. Address: 3908 Grand Av Des Moines IA

KIRSHEN, HIMY BENJAMIN, coll. dean; b. London, Eng., July 26, 1903; s. Solomon and Leah Rachel (Gordon) K.; B.S., Whitman Coll., Walla Walla, Wash., 1926; postgrad., Columbia Law Sch., 1926-28, M.A., 1929; Ph.D., U. Wis., 1937; m. Verona Ethel Bishop, Sept. 2, 1926; 1 dau., Joan Elizabeth. Instr. econs. Coll. City N.Y., 1927-29; asst. prof. U. Me., 1929-36, head dept. of econs. and sociology, prof. econs., 1937-57; fellow U. Wis. 1932-33, asst., 1937; dean Sch. Bus. Adminstrn., U. Mass., 1957-67; prof. of Santa Clara, 1967—. Mem. of Me. Mediation Bd., 1951-57. Mem. Am. Econ. Assn., Am. Assn. U. Profs., Am. Arbitration Assn., Phi Beta Kappa, Beta Gamma Sigma (nat. exec. com. 1966-68, nat. treas. 1968-70), Pi Kappa Delta, Delta Sigma, Rho Phi, Kappa Phi. Author: Essay in Legal Economics, 1932; chpt. on Economic Control, in Social Control, (edited by Joseph Roucek), 1947; The Ideology of American Labor, 1960. Home: 5469 St Catherine Ct San Jose CA 95127 Office: Sch Bus U Santa Clara Santa Clara CA 95053

KIRSHEN, PHILIP HOWARD, textile exec.; b. N.Y.C., Apr. 2, 1907; s. Joseph and Helen (Berestisky) K.; B.C.S., N.Y. U., 1928; m. Irene Norans, Sept. 16, 1944; children—Nina Karen, Janice Sue. Pub. accounting, N.Y., N.J., 1926-32; asst. comptroller United Mchts. & Mfrs., Inc. and subsidiaries, N.Y.C., 1932-45, comptroller, 1945-67, exec. v.p., 1967—; treas. Clearwater Finishing Co., Statistics, Inc.; sec. United Internat. Corp.; dir. Asso. Textiles Can., Brit. Silk Dyeing Co., Ltd., United Mchts. and Mfrs. (U.K.), Ltd., C.P.A., N.Y. Mem. Am. Mgmt. Assn., Nat. Assn. Cost Accountants, Delta Mu Delta. Home: 10 Hillside Rd Bronxville NY 10708 Office: 1407 Broadway New York City NY 10018

KIRSNER, JOSEPH BARNETT, physician, educator; b. Boston, Sept. 21, 1909; s. Harris and Ida (Waiser) K.; M.D., Tufts, U., 1933; Ph.D. in Biol. Scis., U. Chgo., 1942; m. Minnie Schneider, Jan. 6, 1934; 1 son, Robert S. Intern Woodlawn Hosp., Chgo., 1933-34, resident, 1934-35; asst. in medicine U. Chgo., 1935-37, mem. faculty, 1937—, asso prof., 1946-51, prof., 1951—, Louis Block prof. medicine, 1968—, chief of staff, also dep. dean for med. affairs, 1971—. Cons. NIH, 1956—; hon. pres. Gastrointestinal Research Found., 1961—. Mem. drug efficacy adv. com. to NRC. Served with M.C., AUS, 1943-46; ETO; PTO. Mem. Am. Assn. Physicians, A.C.P., Am. Gastroenterol. Assn. (governing bd.), Am. Gastroscopic Soc. (past pres.), Am. Soc. Clin. Investigation, Central Soc. Clin. Research, Chgo. Soc. Internal Medicine (past pres.), Inst. Medicine Chgo. Research in gastrointestinal disorders, inflammatory disease of gastrointestinal tract. Editorial bd. Annals Internal Medicine, Clin. Pharmacology and Therapeutics. Home: 5805 Dorchester Av Chicago IL 60637

KIRSNER, ROBERT, educator; b. nr. Ukmerge, Lithuania, July 9, 1921; s. Samuel and Anna (Levine) K.; came to U.S., 1935, naturalized, 1943; A.B., U. Cin., 1943, M.A., 1945; M.A., Princeton, 1947, Ph.D., 1949; m. Mildred Dorothy Warshofsky, Apr. 11, 1947; children—Steven and David (twins), Barbara, Kenneth, Tamara. Instr., Princeton, 1945-49; from asst. prof. to prof. Romance langs. and lit. U. Cin., 1949-64; prof. Spanish, U. Miami (Fla.), 1964—, chmn. dept. fgn. langs., 1965—; vis. prof. Johns Hopkins, summer 1948, Nat. U. Guatamala, summer 1951, Tulane U., summer 1957, Nat. Def. Edn. Act Lang. Inst., San Francisco State Coll., summer 1959, Nat. Def. Edn. Act. Lang. Inst., Mich. State U., 1961, U. Ariz., summer 1964, U. Cal. at Berkeley, summer 1966; resident dir. Rollins Coll. in Bogota, 1963-64. Mem. Princeton Admissions Com. Mem. Jewish Community Relations Council Cin., 1954-64. Bd. dirs. Hillel Found., U. Cin., 1953-59. Served with AUS, 1943-44. Mem. Am. Assn. Tchrs. Spanish and Portuguese (chmn. Lit. sect. 1951, exec. com. 1959- 61, pres. So. Ohio chpt. 1950-52), Modern Lang. Assn. Am. (chmn. bibliog. com. Spanish contemporary lit. sect. 1951-54, chmn. 18th-19th centuries sect. 1962), Am. Assn. U. Profs. (pres. U. Cin. chpt. 1962- 63), Central States, So. Atlantic modern lang. assns., Ohio Modern Lang. Tchrs. Assn. (pres. 1960-61), Inst. de Lit. Iberoamericana. Mem. B'nai B'rith (v.p. Cin. 1953-54). Club: Princeton (v.p.) (So. Fla.). Author: (with Brent) Cuentos espanoles, 1950; (with Irving) Paisajes del Sur, 1954; (with Kinne) A Repasar!, 1954; (with Brent) Bibliography of America Castro's Writings, 1956; (with Brent) New Bibliography of Castro's Writings, 1964; The Novels and Travels of Camilo Jose Cela, 1964; La Catira, novela américo- hispano, 1965; Historia de Una Escalera: A Play in Search of Characters, 1965; also articles. Home: 500 Alminar St Coral Gables FL 33146

KIRST, HANS HELLMUT, author; b. Osterode, Dec. 5, 1914; s. Johannes and Gertrud (Golldack) K.; ed. Volkschule/ Gymnasium, Osterode; m. Ruth Mueller, Dec. 14, 1962. Mem. P.E.N., Bundesrepublic Deutschland, Authors Guild U.S. Author: Wir nannten ihn Galgenstrick, 1950; 08/15, 1954; Febrik der Offiziere, 1960; Kameraden, 1961; Die Nacht der Generale, 1962; Aufstand der Soldaten, 1965; Die Wölfe, 1967; Kein Vaterland, 1968. Home: Caslano b Lugano San Michele Switzerland and 8133 Feldafing b München Moorweg 5 West Germany

KIRSTEIN, GEORGE GARLAND, ins. co. exec., author; b. Rochester, N.Y., Dec. 10, 1909; s. Louis E. and Rose (Stein) K.; grad. Berkshire Sch., 1928; A.B., Harvard, 1932: m. Jane Stolle Cianfarra, Sept. 26, 1957 (dec.). Asst. dir. RKO Radio Pictures, Hollywood, Cal., 1932-33; v.p. Bloomingdale Bros., Inc., 1933-41; exec. sec. Nat War Labor Bd., 1941-43; dir. Mgmt.-Employee Relations, Inc., 1946-50; exec. v.p. Health Ins. plan of Greater N.Y., 1950-55; pub. The Nation, 1955-65; exec. v.p. Montefiore Hosp. and Med. Center, 1966-69. Vis. com. Harvard Sch. Pub. Health, 1968—. Served as lt. USNR, 1943-45. Club: Sheldrake Yacht (Mamaroneck). Author: The Rich. Home: Taylor's Lane Mamaroneck NY 10543

KIRSTEIN, LINCOLN, promoter Am. ballet; b. Rochester, N.Y., May 4, 1907; s. Louis E. and Rose (Stein) K.; B.S., Harvard, 1930; m. Fidelma Cadmus, Apr. 1941. Founder, Hound and Horn (lit. Periodical, 1927, editor, 1927-34; established Sch. Am. Ballet, N.Y.C., 1933, now dir.; dir. N.Y. City Ballet Co.; dir. gen. Am. Ballet. Vice pres. Am. Dressage Inst. Author: Dance: A short History of Theatrical Dancing, 1935; Blast at Ballet, 1938; Low Ceiling (poems), 1935; Ballet Alphabet, 1939; pub. Pavel Tchelitchew Drawings, 1947; Elle Nadelman Drawings, 1949; The Classic Ballet, 1952; Rhymes & More Rhymes of a Pfc., 1965; Movement and Metaphore: Four Centuries of Ballet, 1969. Address: State Theater Lincoln Center New York City NY 10023

KIRSTEN, DOROTHY, opera singer; b. Montclair, N.J., July 6, 1919; d. George W. and Margaret (Beggs) Kirsten; mus. tng. U.S., France and Italy; Mus.D., Ithaca Coll.; m. John D. French, July 18, 1955. Debut as Musetta in La Boheme, Chgo. Opera Co., Nov. 1940; debut Met. Opera Co., Dec., 1945; has sung roles of Violetta, Cho Cho San, Juliet, Marguerite, Manon Lescaut, Nedda, Micaela, Louise, Fiora, Tosca, Mimi, Massanet Manon, Cressida, Girl of Golden West, and many operettas. Episcopalian. Address: care Metropolitan Opera Co Lincoln Center New York City NY 10023

KIRTLAND, LYNN, educator; b. Exeter, N.H., May 17, 1913; s. John Copeland and May (Durham) K.; grad. Phillips Exeter Acad., 1931; B.A., Williams Coll., 1935; M.A., Princeton, 1937, Ph.D., 1938; m. Monika Hornsteiner, Jan. 11, 1963; children—Sarah W., Joseph, Julia, Alexander. Master, St. Paul's Sch., Concord, N.H., 1938-40; instr., Phillips Exeter (N.H.) Acad., 1940-49; asst. prof. Classics, U. Tex. at Austin, 1949-53; mem. faculty Wells Coll., Aurora, N.Y., 1953—, prof. Classics, 1960—, asst. to pres. acad. affairs, 1967-69. Served with USNR, 1942-45, 51-53. Mem. Am. Philol. Assn., Archeol. Inst. Am. Home: Box 25 Aurora NY 13026

KIRWAN, ALBERT DENNIS, educator; b. Louisville, Dec. 22, 1904; s. Martin John and Margaret (O'Sullivan) K.; A.B., U. Ky., 1926; LL.B., U. Louisville, 1929, M.A., 1945; Ph.D., Duke, 1947; m. Elizabeth Lewis Heil, Aug. 14, 1931; children—Albert Dennis, William English II. Tchr., coach, pub. schs. of Louisville, 1927-37: coach U. Ky., 1938-45, asso. prof. history, dean of men, 1947-49, dean of students, 1949-54, prof. history, 1954—, pres., 1968-69, dean Grad. Sch., 1960-66, Distinguished prof. Coll. Arts and Scis., 1967. Guggenheim fellow, 1960-61; Fulbright fellow, of U. Vienna, 1966-67. Mem. Am., So. (recipient Charles Sydnor Book award 1964), Miss. Valley hist. assns., Nat. Collegiate Athletics Assn. (chmn. rules infractions com. 1955-61, Phi Beta Kappa, Phi Alpha Theta, Phi Delta Phi. Author: The Revolt of the Rednecks, 1951; Johnny Green of the Orphan Brigade, 1956; The Confederacy, A Documentary History, 1959; The Life of John Jordan Crittenden, 1962; (with T.D. Clark) The South Since Appomattox, 1966. Editor: The Civilization of the Old South: Writings of Clement Eaton, 1968. Home: 535 Russell Av Lexington KY 40508

KIRWAN, JAMES ALEXANDER, govt. ofcl.; b. Drogheda, Ireland, May 9, 1928; s. James and Gertrude (McKelvey) K.; student Irish Christian Bros., Drogheda until 1946. Officer, Irish Revenue Commrs., 1946-50; 3d sec. Dept. External Affairs, Dublin, 1950-54; 3d sec. Irish Embassy, London, 1954-56; vice consul, dep. consul gen., N.Y.C., 1956-62; sec., The Hague, 1963-45; consul gen. San Francisco, 1965-70; counsellor press and imformation, Embassy of Ireland, Washington, 1970—; mem. delegation Gen. Assembly UN, 1961, 62, 65, 69. Mem. County Louth Archaeol. Soc. Ireland. Clubs: National (Washington);Nat. University of Ireland (London). Home: 2801 New Mexico Av NW Washington DC 20007 Office: Embassy Ireland 2334 Massachusetts Av NW Washington

KISELEWSKI, JOSEPH, sculptor; b. Browerville, Minn., Feb. 16, 1901; s. Blasius and Sophie (Wollney), K.; ed. Mpls. Sch. Art, 1918-21, N.A.D., 1921-23, Beaux Arts Inst. Design, 1923-25; m. Adeline Peters, June 20, 1931. Works: statue of Gen. Pulaski, Milwa.; fishery pediment for the U.S. Dept. of Commerce Bldg., Washington; exterior and interior work on George Rogers Clark Meml., Vincennes, Ind.; groups at entrance of Bronx County Courthouse, N.Y.C.; figure of John Wesley, Winston-Salem, N.C.; Katherine Ely Tiffany sun dial, Bryn Mawr (Pa.) Coll.; Madonna and Child, Rosary Coll. River Forest, Ill.; Sea horse fountain, Huntington Mus., Brookgreen, S.C.; 3 medallions for Lyman Ellyn Mus., New London, Conn.; meml. to Jessir L. Eddy, Tarrytown, N.Y.; two life size statues for garden at St. Joseph's Ch., Browerville, Minn.; giant sundial, Bus. Systems Bldg., and four fountains for RCA Bldg., New York World's Fair, 1939; 11 works for Met. Housing Project, N.Y.C.; heroic figure of S24Christ" for Bishop's Monument, Fargo, N.D.; Good Conduct Medal for U.S. War Dept.; World Peace Medal for Soc. of Medalists, N.Y.C.; bronze statue of Our Lady of the Mountains, Covington, Ky.; 4 plaques for House Chamber of Capitol Bldg., 2 reliefs for Gen. Accounting Bldg., Washington; heroic statue of John Peter Zenger, Bronx, N.Y.; World War II meml. Vets. Cemetary Holland; Justice, large limestone panel N.Y.C. Cts. Bldg., Moses for Syracuse U. Law Sch., 1966, Harold Vanderbilt bronze statue U. Nashville, 1965, Sylvanus Thayer bronze bust for Hall of Fame for Great Ams., N.Y.U., 1966, others. Awarded Prix de Rome, 1926-29; Beaux Arts Paris prize, 1925-26; Elizabeth N. Watrous gold medal, 1937; silver medal, Archtl. League, N.Y.C. Asso. fellow Am. Acad. in Rome. Mem. N.A.D., Archtl. League of N.Y., Nat. Sculpture Soc. Roman Catholic. Club: Century Assn. Home: 433 E 82nd St New York City NY 10028

KISER, CLYDE VERNON, demographer; b. Bessemer City, N.C., July 22, 1904; s. Augustus Burton and Minnie May (Carpenter) K.; A.B. (Mangum medal 1925), U. N.C., 1925, A.M., 1927; Ph.D. (Richard W. Gilder fellow 1930-31), Columbia, 1932; m. Louise Venable Kennedy, Feb. 24, 1934 (dec. Mar. 1954). Research fellow Milbank Meml. Fund, N.Y.C., 1931-33, research asso., mem. tech. staff, 1933-62, sr. mem. tech. staff, 1962-69, v.p. for tech. affairs, 1969-70; statis. cons. USPHS, 1936; vis. research asso., sr. research demographer Office Population Research, Princeton, 1942—; adj. prof. sociology N.Y. U., 1945-56. Cons., Pan Am. Health 1967. Mem. census adv. com.Nat. Com. on Vital and Health, 1966-69; Statistics; 1966-69; chmn. local arrangements com. N.Y.C., Internat. Population Conf., 1961; mem. standing com. Pub. Health Conf. Records and Statistics, Div. Vital Statistics, Dept. Health, Edn. and Welfare, 1958-64, chmn. subcom. fertility measurement, 1963, chmn. subcom. on population dynamics, 1968-69. Bd. dirs. Gallaudet Coll. Recipient Grant Squires prize Columbia, 1940. Fellow Am. Statis. Assn.; mem. Am. Eugenics Soc., (pres. 1963-69), Population Assn. Am. (pres. 1952- 53), Eastern Sociol. Soc. (v.p. 1959-60, chmn. com. social statistics, 1960-68), Internat. Union Sci. Study Population (chmn. U.S. nat. com. 1958-61), Am. Pub. Health Assn., Am. Sociol. Assn. (com. on govt. statistics). Democrat. Lutheran. Author: Sea Island to City: A Study of St. Helena Islanders in Harlem and Other Urban Centers, 1932; Group Difference in Urban Fertility, 1942; (with Grabill and Whelpton) The Fertility of American Women, 1958; (with Grabill and Campbell) Trends and Variations in Fertility in the United States, 1968. Editor:Research in Family Planning, 1962; (with Whelpton) Social and Psychological Factors Affecting Fertility, vols. I- V, 1946-58; Estudios de Demografia, 1967. Home: 261 Hawthorne Av Princeton NJ Office: Milbank Meml Fund 40 Wall St New York City NY 10005

KISER, JAMES WEBB, banker, lawyer; b. Belmont, N.C., Aug. 16, 1934 s. Walter Webb and Lottie (Bumgardner) K.; B.S., Davidson Coll., 1956; J.D., U. N.C., 1959; m. Nancy Lee Howard, Feb. 9, 1963; children—James Leland, Robert Howard. Admitted to N.C. bar, also U.S. Supreme Ct., asso. firm Ervin, Horack, Snepp & McArtha, Charlotte, N.C., 1962-64; asst. city atty., Charlotte, 1964-65, acting city atty., 1965-66, city atty., 1966-68; v.p., counsel, corp. sec. N.C. Nat. Bank, Charlotte, 1968—; v.p., sec., counsel NCNB Corp., 1968—; sec. NCNB Properties, 1968—, NCNB Mortgage Corp., 1969. Served to capt. AUS, 1959-62. Decorated Commendation medal. Mem. Am., N.C., 26th Jud. Dist. bar assns., N.C. State Bar, Am. Soc. Corp. Secs., Am. Judicature Soc., Order of Coif. Methodist. Lion. Club: Olde Providence Racquet and Swim (Charlotte). Home: 1316 Biltmore Dr Charlotte NC 28207 Office: 200 S Tryon St Charlotte NC 28207

KISH, ALEXANDER JOHN, assn. exec.; b. Ithaca, N.Y., Oct. 6, 1916; s. John M. and Regina (Takacs) K.; B.S. in Hotel Adminstrn., Cornell U., 1939; m. Marion Valentine Owen, Sept. 26, 1942; children—Karen R. (Mrs. Victor M. Hodson), David O., Jacqueline M. Asst. to dean Sch. Hotel Adminstrn., Cornell U., 1939-42; with Coop. GLF Exchange, Ithaca, 1946-67; v.p., treas. merged company Agway, Inc., Syracuse, N.Y., 1967—; dir. Marine Midland Bank Central N.Y., Syracuse, Texas City Refining Co. (Tex.), Curtice-Burns Inc., Rochester, N.Y. Mem. Syracuse Met. Devel. Authority, 1967—. Mem. exec. devel. program Cornell U., 1960; mem. advanced mgmt. program Harvard U., 1970. Served with USNR, 1942-46. Mem. Syracuse C. of C. Home: 108 Longmeadow Circle Syracuse NY 13205 Office: Box 1333 Syracuse NY 13201

KISH, LESLIE, educator, research statistician; b. Poprad, Hungary, July 27, 1910; s. Albert and Serena (Spiegel) Kiss; came to U.S., 1926, naturalized, 1936; B.S., Coll. City N.Y., 1939; M.A., U. Mich., 1948, Ph.D., 1952; m. Rhea Helen Kuleske, Mar. 3, 1947; children—Carla Elene, Andrea Stefanie. Sect. head U.S. Bur. of Census, 1940-41; statistician Dept. Agr., 1941- 47; mem. faculty U. Mich., 1951—, prof. sociology, 1960—, sampling head of the Survey Research Center, 1951—, also program dir. Inst. of Social Research, 1963—, research asso. Population Studies Center, 1961—, dir. sampling program fgn. statisticians, 1962- -; vis. prof. in statistics London Sch. Econs. Served with USAAF, 1942-45. Fellow Am. Statis. Assn. (sect. chmn.), Am. Sociol. Assn. (sect. chmn.), Royal Statis. Soc.; mem. Population Assn. of America, Inter-America Statis. Inst., Internat. Union Sci. Study Population. Author: Survey Sampling, 1965; also articles, chpts. in books. Home: 702 Sunset Rd Ann Arbor MI 48103

KISLIK, RICHARD WILLIAM, corp. exec.; b. N.Y.C., Oct. 31, 1927; s. Louis K. and Isabelle (Deutelbaum) K.; A.B., Harvard, 1948, M.B.A., 1949; m. Audrey Gerber, June 19, 1949; children—Nancy J., Andrew R., Laurie S., Wendy J. Research asst. Harvard Bus. Sch., 1949-50; asst. controller Maidenform Brassiere Co., 1950-54; controller Doubleday & Co., Inc., 1954-60; treas., dir. Ziff-Davis Pub. Co., 1960-61; v.p. finance, dir. Random House, Inc., 1961-68; cons., 1968; v.p. Intext Ednl. Pubs., Inc., 1968-69, pres., 1969—; exec. v.p. Intext, Inc., 1970-71, pres., 1971—; dir. Lin Broadcasting Corp., Learning Resources, Inc. Home: 8 Meadow Lane Freeport NY 11520 Office: 257 Park Av New York City NY 10010

KISPERT, MALCOLM GORDON, ednl. adminstr.; b. Fall River, Mass., Jan. 15, 1923; s. Edwin P. and Margaret E. (MacIntyre) K.; S.B., Mass. Inst. Tech., 1944, M.S., 1946; m. Janice McCreery, Aug. 6, 1944; children—Robert G., Nancy D., Pamela J., Richard M. Exec. asst. to pres. Mass. Inst. Tech., 1946-56, asst. chancellor, 1956-57, adminstrv. vice chancellor, 1957-61, v.p. acad. adminstrn., 1961-71, inst. sec., 1971—. Dir. Cambridge Trust Co., Baird-Atomic Corp., Harbridge House, Inc. Bd. trustees Hampton Inst., Dana Hall Schs., Wellesley, Mass. Vice pres. Harvard Coop. Soc., 1959—. Served to lt. (j.g.) USNR, 1944-46; Mem. Inst. Aero. Scis., Tau Beta Pi. Clubs: Commercial, St. Botolph (Boston). Home: 5 Sterling Dr Dover MA 02030 Office: Mass Inst Tech Cambridge MA 02147

KISSEL, LESTER, lawyer; b. Hartford, Wis., June 14, 1903; s. Adolph P. and Lillian (Schuppert) K.; B.A., U. Wis., 1925; postgrad. U. Geneva (Switzerland), 1925-26; J.D., Harvard, 1931; m. Alice MacRae, Oct. 4, 1934; 1 son, Stephen. Admitted to N.Y. bar, 1932; partner firm Seward & Kissel, N.Y.C., 1949—; gen. and mng. partner A.W. Jones and Co., N.Y.C., 1965—. Trustee Found. for Vol. Service, N.Y.C. Mem. Am. (found. fellow), N.Y. bar assns., Bar Assn. City N.Y. Clubs: Union, River, Down Town Assn. (N.Y.C.); Mid Ocean (Bermuda). Home: 1170 Fifth Av New York City NY 10029 Office: 63 Wall St New York City NY 10005

KISSELL, CARTER, lawyer; b. West Unity, O., Mar. 20, 1901; s. Jeremiah Wilson and Gertrude (Coslet) K.; A.B., Ohio State U., 1925, LL.B., J.D., 1927; m. Ann Huntington, Sept. 9, 1929; children—Sarah, Sollace, Judith. Admitted to Ohio bar, 1927; asso. Tolles, Hogsett & Ginn, Cleve., 1927-36, partner, 1936-58; partner Jones, Day, Cockley & Reavis: pres., chief exec. officer Nat. Castings Co., 1958-64, chmn., chief exec. officer, 1964-65; vice chmn. bd. Midland-Ross Corp., 1965-; dir. Bell Intercontinental Corp., Interlake Steel Corp., Equity Corp., United Bd. & Carton Co.; chmn. Med. Mut. Cleve., Inc. Mem. MSA Evaluation Team, Italy, 1953; chmn. Little Hoover Commn., Cleve., 1965-67, Trustee Cleve. Inst. Music; chmn. mem. exec. com. Cleve. Devel. Found., 1966-68. Mem. bd. Overseers Case-Western Res. U., chmn. bd. overseers, trustee, 1967; chmn. trustee Bexley Hall Episcopal Sem.; vice chmn., trustee Rochester Center Theol. Studies; trustee, mem. exec. com. Colgate-Rochester Divinity Sch. Mem. Trans. Assn. Am. (hon. life), C. of C., Am., Cleve. bar assns. Episcopalian. Clubs: Union, Chagrin Valley Hunt (Cleve.); Castalia Trout; Pepper Pike Country. Author: The Old War Horse (play), 1942; West Unity, Ohio, 1971. Home: Woodstock Rd Gates Mills Cleveland OH 44040 Office: Union Commerce Bldg Cleveland OH 44114

KISSICK, HAROLD G., investment analyst; b. Chillicothe, Mo., Dec. 2, 1910; s. Orrin W. and Nellie M. (Colton) K.; LL.B., Wash. Coll. Law, 1934; student George Washington U., 1942-43; m. Clara G. Doll, Nov. 27, 1935; childrenJean M., Ralph L., John H. With John Morrell & Co., Sioux Falls, S.D., 1929- 30; Bur. Immigration and Naturalization, U.S. Dept. Labor, 1930-31; adminstrv., budget and personnel duties U.S. Dept. State, 1931-45, internat. conf. adminstrn. and planning, 1945-52, dir. Office Internat. Confs., 1952-59; counselor of Embassy, Ankara, Turkey, 1959-62; cons. A.I.D., 1963-64; asso. Jones, Kreeger & Co., investments, 1965-68; with Paine, Webber, Jackson & Curtis, 1968-69; asst. adminstrv. officer inaugural meetings of Bds. of Govs. of IMF and Internat. Bank of for Reconstrn. and Devel., Savannah, Ga., 1946; asst. sec. gen. 4th Internat. Congresses on Tropical Medicine and Malaria, Washington, 1948; exec. sec. Inter- Am. Conf. on Conservation of Renewable Natural Resources, Denver, 1948; dep. sec. gen. Internat. Wheat Conf., Washington, 1949; exec. sec. U.S. delegate Tripartite Discussions and Sessions of N. Atlantic Council, 1950, 9th session, Lisbon, 1952; dept. sec. gen Conf. for Conclusion and Signature of Treaty of Peace with Japan, San Francisco, 1951; exec. sec. 3d session of Provisional Intergovtl. Com. for Movement of Migrants from Europe, Washington, 1952; exec. sec. U.S. delegation conf. heads of govt., Geneva, 1955; sec. U.S. delegation meeting fgn. ministers, Geneva, 1955; sec. U.S. delegation U.S.-United Kingdom Bermuda meeting, 1957. Home: 6310 Stratford Rd Chevy Chase MD 20015

KISSINGER, HAROLD ARTHUR, army officer; b. Elkhart Lake, Wis., Apr. 7, 1922; s. Arthur Philip and Lillian (Becker) K.; B.S., U. Wis., 1956, M.B.A., 1958; grad. Command and Gen. Staff Coll., 1961, Indsl. Coll. Armed Forces, 1964; m. Marilyn Hope Lueke, July 26,

1944; children—Mark Donald, Greg W. Commd. 2d lt. U.S. Army, 1944, advanced through grades to brig. gen., 1969; staff officer Office Chief of Staff of U.S. Army, 1962-63; politico-mil. adviser Office Asst. Sec. of Def., Washington, 1965-68; dep. comdg. gen. U.S. Army Electronics Command, Ft. Monmouth, N.J., 1968-70; comdg. gen. Cam Ranh Bay Support Command, Vietnam, 1970—; prof. mil. sci. and tactics Wash. State U., 1946-49. Pres., dir. The Kiscan Corp. (Wis.). Decorated Legion of Merit, Army Commemdation medal. Mem. Assn. U.S. Army, Armed Forces Communications and Electronics Assn., Wis. Alumni Assn., Pi Kappa Alpha. Mason. Author: Automation in Manufacturing and Supply Management Systems, 1958; The Computer Comes of Age, 1964. Home: 151 N Lincoln St Elkhart Lake WI 53020 Office: Commanding General US Army Support Command Cam Ranh Bay Vietnam APO San Francisco CA 96312

KISSINGER, HENRY ALFRED, govt. ofcl.; b. Fuerth, Germany, May 27, 1923; s. Louis and Paula (Stern) K.; A.B. summa cum laude, Harvard, 1950, M.A., 1952, Ph.D., 1954; m. Ann Fleischer, Feb. 6, 1949 (div. 1964); children—Elizabeth, David. Came to U.S. in 1938, naturalized, 1943. Exec. director Harvard internat. seminar, 1951-69, lectr. dept. govt., 1957-59, dir. def. studies program, 1958-69, asso. prof. govt., 1959-62, prof., 1962-69, faculty Center Internat. Affairs, Harvard, 1960-69; asst. Pres. Nixon nat. security affairs, 1969—; study dir. nuclear weapons and fgn. policy Council Fgn. Relations, 1955-56; dir. spl. studies project Rockefeller Bros. Fund, Inc., 1956-58. Cons. operations research office, 1950-61, cons. to dir. Psychol. strategy bd., 1952, cons. operations coordinating bd., 1955, cons. weapons systems evaluation group, 1959- 60; cons. Nat. Security Council, 1961-62, U.S. Arms Control and Disarmament Agy., 1961-68; cons. Dept. State, 1965-69. Served with AUS, 1943-46. Recipient of citation Overseas Press Club, 1958; Woodrow Wilson prize for best book fields of govt., politics, internat. affairs 1958. Mem. Am. Polit. Sci. Assn., Council Fgn. Relations, Am. Acad. Arts and Scis., Phi Beta Kappa. Clubs: Cosmos, Federal City (Washington); St. Botolph (Boston); Century (N.Y.C.). Author: Nuclear Weapons and Foreign Policy, 1957; A World Restored: Castlereagh, Metternich and the Restoration of Peace, 1812-22, 1957; The Necessity for Choice: Prospects of American Foreign Policy, 1961; The Troubled Partnership: A Reappraisal of the Atlantic Alliance, 1965. Editor: Problems of National Strategy: A Book of Readings, 1965. Confluence, An. Internat. Forum, 1951-58. Contbr. profl. jours. Office: The White House Washington DC 20500

KISSINGER, WALTER BERNHARD, automotive, aircraft mfg. co. exec.; b. Furth, Germany, June 21, 1924; s. Louis and Paula (Stern) K.; came to U.S., 1938, naturalized, 1939; B.E., Princeton, 1951; M.B.A., Harvard, 1953; m. Eugenie Van Drooge, July 4, 1958; children—William, Thomas, Dana Marie, John Frans. Asst. to v.p. fgn. operations Gen. Tire & Rubber Co., Akron, O., 1953-56; pres. Advanced Vacuun Products Co., Stamford, Conn., 1957-62; exec. v.p., dir. Glass-tite Industries, Providence, 1960-62; v.p., gen. mgr. Harman- Kardon, Inc., Plainview, N.Y., asst. to pres. Jerrold Corp., 1963-64; exec. v.p., dir. Jervis Corp., Hicksville, N.Y., 1964-68; pres., chief exec. officer Allen Electric & Equipment Co., Chgo., 1969-. Served to capt. AUS, 1943-46, 50. Decorated Commendation medal. Club: Princeton of New York. Home: Lower Dr Huntington Bay Sands Point NY 11743 Office: 534 Broad Hollow Rd Melville Sands Point NY 11746

KISSLINGER, CARL, educator, geophysicist; b. St. Louis, Aug. 30, 1926; s. Fred and Emma (Tobias) K.; B.S., St. Louis U., 1947, M.S., 1949. Ph.D., 1952; m. Millicent Ann Thorson, Mar. 27, 1948; children—Susan, Karen, Ellen, Pamela, Jerome. Faculty, St. Louis U., 1949—, prof. geophysics, geophys. engring., 1961—, chmn. dept. earth nd atmostpheric scis., 1963—. UNESCO expert in seismology, chief tech. adviser Internat. Inst. Seismology and Earthquake Engring., Tokyo, Japan, 1966-67; chmn. com. seismology NRC-Nat. Acad. Scis., 1970—; U.S. nat. corr. Internat. Assn. Seismology and Physics of Earth's Interior, 1970-72. Fellow Am. Geophys. Union (bd. dirs. sect. seismology, 1970-72); mem. Soc. Exploration Geophysicists, Seismol. Soc. Am. (bd. dirs. 1968—), Am. Soc. Engring. Edn., Phi Beta Kappa, Sigma Xi. Home: 7434 Melrose Av St Louis MO 63130

KISSLINGER, LEONARD SOL, educator, physicist; b. St. Louis, Aug. 15, 1930; s. Fred and Emma (Tobias) K.; B.S., St. Louis U., 1951; M.A., Ind. U., 1952, Ph.D. (NSF fellow), 1956; m. Margaret V. Hampton, Sept. 1, 1956; children—Stephen A., Benjamin L., Paul W. Faculty, Case Western Res. U., 1956-69, asso. prof., 1960-63, prof. physics, 1963-69; prof. physics Carnegie-Mellon U., Pitts., 1969—; Researcher, Niels Bohr Inst., Copenhagen, Denmark, 1958-59, Weizmann Inst. Sci., Rehovoth, Isreal, 1962-63, Mass. Inst. Tech., 1966-67. Research Corp. fellow, 1958-59; Weizmann Meml. fellow, 1962-63. Fellow Am. Phys. Soc.; mem. A.A.A.S., Am. Assn. U. Profs., Sigma Xi, Pi Mu Epsilon. Contbr. articles to profl. jours. Home: 4785 Wallingford St Pittsburgh PA 15213

KISSNER, FRANKLIN H., bus. exec.; b. Pa., 1909; grad. Harvard, 1930. Chmn. Wallace-Murray Corp., N.Y.C.; pres., dir. Dyson-Kissner Corp., N.Y.; dir. Electronic Communications, Inc., Kearney-Nat., Inc. Office: 500 5th Av New York City NY 10020*

KIST, LEROY EMERSON, accountant; b. Chgo., July 22, 1912; s. Clarence B. and Phoebe (Coleman) K.; student Crane Coll., 1930-32, Northwestern U., 1935-40, Loyola U., Chgo., 1941; m. Ruth M. Pierce, Apr. 19, 1941; children-Robert E., Patricia L., William J., David J., Deborah S. Sr. Assessment record clk. Cook County (Ill.) Assessor, 1935-41; partner Ernst & Ernst, C.P.A.'s, Chgo., 1941—, now partner charge tech. accounting and auditing services Northwestern Dist.; instr. accounting DePaul U. Grad. Sch., 1968—. Pres. Cook County Sch. Dist. No. 23 Bd. Edn., Prospect Heights, 1963-64. Mem. Am. Inst. C.P.A.'s, Ill. Soc. C.P.A.'s (chmn. accounting prins. com.). Clubs: Union League, Tower (Chgo.); Park Ridge Country. Home: 848 N Merrill Av Park Ridge IL 60068 Office: 150 S Wacker Dr Chicago IL 60604

KISTIAKOWSKY, GEORGE BOGDAN educator; b. Kiev, Russia, Nov. 18, 1900; s. Bogdan and Mary (Berenstam) K.; came to U.S., 1926, naturalized, 1933; student Kiev pub. sch., and high sch., to 1918; Ph.D., U. of Berlin, 1925; D.Sc., Harvard, 1955, Williams Coll., 1958, Oxford, 1959, U. Pa., 1960, U. Rochester, Carnegie Tech., 1961, Princeton U., Case Inst. Tech., 1962; m. Hildegard Moebius, 1926; 1 dau., Vera; m. 2d, Irma E. Shuler, 1945; m. 3d, Elaine Mahoney, 1962. Internat. research fellow, Princeton, 1926-28, research asso., 1928-30; asst. prof. chemistry, Harvard, 1930-33, asso. prof., 1933-37, prof. chemistry, 1937-59, 61—; spl. asst. to The Pres. for sci. and tech., 1959-61; chmn. sci. bd., dir. Itek Corp., 1961—. Mem. Pres.' Sci. Adv. Com., 1957-63. Recipient Medal for Merit, 1946; Nichols medal, 1947; Brit. Medal for Service in Cause of Freedom, 1948; Priestly award, 1958; Willard Gibbs medal, 1960; Medal Freedom, 1961; Ledlie prize, 1961, Parsons medal, 1963; Nat. Medal of Sci. 1967; Peter Debye award in phys. chemistry, 1968. Hon. fellow Chem. Soc. (London); fgn. mem. Royal Soc.; mem. Nat. Acad. Scis. (v.p. 1965—), Am. Acad. Scis., Am. Chem. Soc., Am. Philos. Soc., Am.Phys. Soc. Address: 12 Oxford St Cambridge MA 02138

KISTING, ANDREW JAMES, packing co. exec.; b. Benton, Wis., Mar. 1, 1909; s. Joseph B. and Elizabeth (Hying) K.; m. Blanche Genz, Dec. 27, 1966; children by previous marriage—Judith, (Mrs. Leo Schluetir), Jane (Mrs. Glen Callahan), Andrew W., James R., Kathleen M., William A. Partner, M.E. Brooks, C.P.A., Dubuque, Ia., 1936-38; admitted to Ia. bar, 1940; individual practice accounting, Dubuque, 1938-43; sec. Dubuque Packing Co., 1943—, v.p., 1966—, 1943—, also dir.; exec. v.p. Dubuque Life Ins. Co.; dir. Krey Packing Co., St. Louis. Sec. Wahlert Found. C.P.A., Ia., Wis., Cal.; Mem. Am. Inst. C.P.A.'s, Am., Ia. bar assns., Dubuque C. of C. K.C., Elk. Club: Dubuque Golf and Country. Home: 2525 St Anne Dr Dubuque IA 52001 Office: Dubuque Life Insurance Co 1766 Central St Dubuque IA 52001

KISTLER, ALAN ANTHONY, union ofcl.; b. Pitts., Oct. 1, 1920; s. Alan A. and Margaret (Ward) K.; M.A., U. Chgo., 1951; m. Marie Connolly, Sept. 14, 1948; children—Kevin, Mary Anne, Margaret Mary. Elevator operator William Penn Hotel, Pitts., 1939- 40; reporter Internat. News Service, Pitts., 1940-42; med. typist U. Chgo. Clinics, 1947-50; exec. sec.-organizer CIO Local 1657, Chgo., 1950-51; laborer Jones & Laughlin Steel Corp., Pitts., 1952; field rep. dept. orgn. CIO, Washington, 1952-55, asst. to AFL-CIO dir. orgn., 1955-63, asst. nat. dir. orgn., 1963—. City councilman, Greenbelt, Md., 1955-59; mayor, Greenbelt, 1959-61. Served with Med. Dept., AUS, 1942-46; ETO. Mem. United Steelworkers Am. Home: 5358 28th St NW Washington DC 20015 Office: 815 16th St NW Washington DC 20006

KISTLER, JOY WILLIAM, educator; b. Sedalia, Mo., Jan. 5, 1898; s. John and Frances (Stuart) K.; student Central Coll., Fayette, Mo., 1916-19; A.B., Culver-Stockton Coll., Canton, Mo., 1925; A.M., U. Ia., 1932, Ph.D., 1935; H.H.D. (hon.), Central Meth. Coll., 1970; m. Elizabeth Bothwell, Aug. 29, 1923; children—Jean Joy (Mrs. Phillip Kendall), Judith (Mrs. J.P. Callaghan), James B. Dir. athletics, No. Mil. Acad., Mexico, Mo., 1920-25, 1928-31; dir. phys. edn. and athletics, Culver-Stockton Coll., 1925-28; dir. phys. edn., Univ. High Sch., Iowa City, 1931-35; asso. prof. phys. edn., State U. of Ia., 1935-41; head dept. of health and phys. edn. La. State U., 1941-68; vis. lectr. Sch. Phys. Edn. U. Conn., 1968-69; acting head dept. phys. edn. and athletics Central Meth. Coll., 1969-70. Recipient honor award Am. Assn. Health Phys. Edn. and Recreation, 1954, La. State Assn. Health, Phys. Edn. and Recreation, 1958; distinguished alumni citation Central Coll., 1959; Nat. Phys. Fitness Leadership award winner, U.S. Jaycee, Met. Life Ins. Co., 1969. Mem. Am. Acad. Phys. Edn., N.E.A., mem. Am. (pres. 1967-68; chmn. of phys. edn. div. 1964-65), So. Dist. (pres. 1947-48), Ia. (pres. 1940-41), La. (pres. 1944-45) assns. for health, phys. edn. and recreation, Am. Coll. Phys. Edn. Assn. (pres. 1961). Home: 1205 Stephens Av Baton Rouge LA 70808

KIT, SAUL, educator, biochemist; b. Passaic, N.J., Nov. 25, 1920; s. Isadore and Minnie (Darvick) K.; A.B., U. Cal. at Berkeley, 1948, Ph.D., 1951; m. Dorothy Anken, Sept. 28, 1945; children—Sally, Malon, Gordon. Post-doctoral fellow U. Chgo., 1951-52; research chemist, asst. biochemist U. Tex. M. D. Anderson Hosp. and Tumor Inst., Houston, 1952-57, asso. biochemist, 1957-60, biochemist, chief sect. nucleo protein metabolism, 1961-62; prof. biochemistry, head div. biochem. virology Baylor U. Coll. Medicine, Houston, 1962—. Served with AUS, 1942-46. Mem. Am. Soc. Cell Biology (treas. 1965-68, pres. 1971), Am. Assn. Cancer Research, Am. Soc. Biol. Chemists, Am. Chem. Soc., Am. Soc. Microbiology. Contbr. articles profl. jours. Home: 11935 Wink St Houston TX 77024

KITAGAWA, JOSEPH MITSUO, educator; b. Osaka, Japan, Mar. 8, 1915; s. Chiyokichi and Kumi (Nozaki) K.; B.A., Rikkyo U., Tokyo, Japan, 1937; Ph.D., U. Chgo., 1951; m. Evelyn Mae Rose, July 22, 1946; 1 dau., Anne Rose. Came to U.S., 1941, naturalized, 1955. Mem. faculty U. Chgo., 1951—, asso. prof. history of religions, 1959-64, prof., 1964—, dean Divinity Sch., 1970—. Editorial adviser history of religions sect. Ency. Brit., 1956-. Recipient Distinguished Citizen of Fgn. Birth award Immigrant Service League, 1958. Mem. Am. Soc. for the Study Religions (pres. 1967—). Author: Religions of the East, 1960; Gibt es ein Verstehen Fremder Religionen, 1963; Religion in Japanese History, 1966; co-author: The Great Asian Religions, 1969. Editor: The Comparative Study of Religions (J. Wach), 1958; Modern Trends in World Religions, 1959; The History of Religions: Essays on the Problem of Understanding, 1967; Understanding and Believing (J. Wach), 1968; Understanding Modern China, 1969; co-editor The History of Religions: Essays in Methodology, 1959; Folk Religion in Japan (I. Hori), 1968; Myths and Symbols: Studies in Honor of M. Eliade, 1969. Home: 5512 Woodlawn Av Chicago IL 60637

KITAJ, R.B., artist; b. Chagrin Falls, O., 1932; s. Jeanne Brooks; diploma Ruskin Sch., U. Oxford, 1960; grad. Royal Coll. Art, London, 1962; children—Lemuel, Dominie Lee. Exhibited one man shows at Marlborough Fine Art, London, 1963, N.Y.C., 1965, Los Angeles County Mus., 1965, Stedelijk Mus., Amsterdam. 1967, Cleve. Mus., 1967, U. Cal. at Berkeley, 1968; rep. in permanent collections in museums in U.S. and Europe; vis. lectr. Slade Sch., U. London; vis. prof. U. Cal. at Berkeley, U. Cal. Los Angeles. Home: care Marlborough Fine Art Ltd 17 Old Bond St London W1 England

KITCH, PAUL RICHARD, lawyer; b. Marion, Kan., June 18, 1911; s. Charles A. and Anna (Haun) K.; A.B., Southwestern Coll., Winfield, Kan., 1932; J.D., U. Chgo., 1935; m. Josephine Pridmore, Jan. 25, 1936; children-Edmund, Paul Richard, Thomas, James, David. Admitted to Kan. bar, 1935; asso. firm Brooks, Brooks & Fleeson, Witchita, 1935-42, mem. firm, 1942; with firm Fleeson, Gooing, Coulson & Kitch, Wichita, Kan., 1942—, sr. partner, since 1957—. Dir. Wichita Eagle & Beacon Pub. Co., Kan. State Bank & Trust Co., Wichita. Pres. Wichita Bd. Edn., 1947. Mem. Wichita Area C. of C. (pres. 1961). Home: 10801 E 21st St Wichita KS 67201 Office: Wichita Plaza Bldg Wichita KS 67206

KITCHEL, DENISON, lawyer; b. Bronxville, N.Y., Mar. 1, 1908; s. William Lloyd and Grace (Wheeler) K.; A.B., Yale, 1930; LL.B., Harvard, 1933; m. Naomi Margaret Douglas, Apr. 22, 1941; children—James Douglas, Harvey Denison. Admitted to Ariz. bar, 1934; asso. Ellinwood & Ross, Phoenix, also Bisbee, 1934- 38, mem. firm, 1938-46; mem. firm Evans, Kitchel & Jenckes, Phoenix, 1946-70, of counsel, 1970—; former counsel Phelps Dodge Corp., Am. Smelting & Refining Co., So. Pacific Co., Motorola, Am. Airlines, Borden Co. Chmn. com. labor relations Am. Mining Congress, 1957-63; spokesman mining industry Congl. Com. on Labor Legislation, 1953-63; vice chairman Ariz. Copper Tariff Bd., 1967—. Gen. counsel Ariz. Republican State Com., 1957-63; gen. dir. Goldwater for Pres. Com., 1963, Rep. presdl. Campaign, 1963. Mem. U.S. delegation tripartite tech. meeting on mines ILO Geneva, Switzerland, 1957; mem. adv. panel on labor-mgmt., U.S. Senate, 1959-60. Served from 1st lt. to lt. col. USAAF, 1942-45. Mem. Am., Maricopa County bar assns., State Bar Ariz., Am. Inst. Mining, Metall. and Petroleum Engrs., Free Soc. Assn. (pres. 1965-69), Mont Pelerin Soc. Episcopalian. Author: Too Grave a Risk-The Connally Amendment Issue, 1963. Home: 2912 Sherran Lane Phoenix AZ 85003 Office: 363 N 1st Av Phoenix AZ 85003

KITCHEL, GEORGE BEHRMAN, oilwell drilling co. exec.; b. Alta Loma, Tex., June 29, 1909; s. James Roderick and Mary Graham (Behrman) K.; B.S. in Mech. Engring., Rice U., 1931; m. Mariann Adkins, June 9, 1934. With McEvoy Co., Houston, 1931- 32, Halliburton Oilwell Cementing Co., 1932, Humble Oil & Refining Co., 1932-35, 36-49, Broderick Boiler Co., Muncie, Ind., 1935-36; with Kerr- McGee Corp., Oklahoma City, 1949—, v.p. contracts, Houston, 1955—; v.p. Transworld Drilling Co., Transworld Drilling Co. Ltd., Kerr-McGee Ltd. Registered profl. engr., Tex. Mem. Am. Petroleum Inst. (citation of service 1956, certificate of appreciation 1958), Am. Assn. Oilwell Drilling Contractors (dir.), Ind. Petroleum Assn. Am., Baronial Order Magna Charta, Tau Beta Pi. Clubs: Houston, International Petroleum (Houston). Home: 5519 Tupper Lake Houston TX 77027 Office: 3801 Kirby Dr Houston TX 77006

KITCHELL, RALPH LLOYD, veterinarian, educator; b. Waukee, Ia., July 9, 1919; s. John J. and Josephine (Gutshall) K.; D.V.M., Ia. State Coll., 1943; Ph.D., U. Minn., 1951; m. Mary Clare Murray, Mar. 27, 1947; children—Margaret Anne, Michael John, Martha Marie. Instr. bacteriology Kan. State Coll., 1943; research fellow Animal Diagnostic Lab., U. Minn., 1946-47; instr. sect. vet. anatomy, 1947-51, asso. prof., 1951-54, acting head sect., 1948-51, head div. vet. anatomy, 1951-54, asst. dean Coll. Vet. Medicine, 1960- 63, asso. dean. 1963-64; dean, Coll. Vet. Medicine, Kan. State Coll., 1964-65, Coll. Vet. Medicine, Ia. State U., Ames, 1966-71; vis. prof. anatomy Sch. Vet. Medicine, U. Cal. at Davis, 1971—. Served to maj. AUS, 1943-46; CBI. Recipient Faculty Recognition award U. Minn., 1952, 54; USPHS spl. research fellow, Stockholm, London, 1957-58. Mem. Am. Assn. Anatomists, Am. Assn. Vet. Anatomists (past pres.), Conf. Research Workers Animal Diseases, Am. Vet. Med. Assn. Contbr. articles on vet. neurology to sci. jours. Home: 1918 Apple Lane Davis CA 95616

KITCHEN, DELMAS KENDALL, physician; b. Ark., Nov. 16, 1906; B.A., Little Rock Coll., 1928; B.S., U. Ark., 1932, M.D., 1932; m. 1934. Intern Gorgas Hosp., Panama, C.Z., 1932-33; resident Polyclinic Hosp., N.Y.C., 1934; pvt. practice of medicine, Ark., 1935-36; successively sales and promotion, asst. to sci. dir. lab. research, asst. to v.p. research and product devel. Parke, Davis & Co., 1936-45; med. dir. Bristol Labs., 1945-49, v.p. Bristol- Myers Co., chief med. counsel asso. cos., 1949-52; cons. USPHS, 1949-55; asst. clin. prof. dermatology and syphilology Bellevue Med. Center, N.Y.U. Postgrad. Sch., 1949-56; v.p. Cortez F. Enloe, Inc., advt. agy., 1952-56; v.p., cons. Perma-chem Corp., 1953-54, cons. promotion, research mgmt. corporate operations, 1954-57; asso. Emerson Cook Co., underwriting and security investments, 1955-57; with Chattem Drug & Chem. Co. and affiliates, 1959-, now chmn. product devel. com., asst. advt. and sales, also med. dir.; med. dir. subsidiary, Brayten Pharm. Co., Chattanooga; spl. med. cons. Warner-Lambert Research Inst., Morris Plains, N.J., 1967—. Mem. nat. exec. com. chmn. disaster com. Hamilton County chpt. A.R.C. Decorated Medal of Honor (Haiti), 1948. Mem. Assn. Med. Dirs. N.Y. (pres. 1951), Pharm. Mfrs. Assn., Pharm. Advt. Club, Proprietary Assn., A.I.M., Am. Acad. Dermatology and Syphilology, A.A.A.S., Am. Chem. Soc., Am. Found. Tropical Medicine, A.M.A., Am. Pub. Health Assn., Soc. Tropical Medicine and Hygiene, Am. Vènereal Disease Assn., Endocrine Soc., N.Y. Acad. Medicine, N.Y. Acad. Scis. Soc. Investigative Dermatology, World Med. Assn. (founder mem. U.S. com.); Internat. Acad. Law and Sci. (mem. council 1963-), Aeorspace Med. Assn., hon. mem. of fgn. sci. socs. Episcopalian (mem. vestry). Mason (32, Shriner), Kiwanian (bd. dirs.). Clubs: Explorers; Torch (Chattanooga Author numerous bus., research publs. Home: 4715 Fairwood Lane Chattanooga TN 37416 Office: Chattem Drug and Chem Co Chattanooga TN 37409

KITCHEN, HERBERT NORD, banker; b. Cranston, R.I., Oct. 30, 1915; s. Arthur H. and Laura (Nordstrom) K.; grad. Rutgers U. Stonier Grad. Sch. Banking, 1964, Sch. Bank Pub. Relations, Northwestern U., 1953; m. Judith Clarke, Mar. 18, 1939; children—Martha E. (Mrs. Lawrence Casazza), Stephen N. With Indsl. Nat. Bank R.I., Providence, 1933—, sr. v.p., 1969—. Pres. Greater Providence YMCA, 1959-61, Rogers Williams Gen. Hosp., Providence, 1967—, Home for Aged, Providence, 1957—; trustee, past chmn. Methodist Health and Welfare Bd. So. New Eng. Served with AUS, 1943-46. Mason (hon. 33). Home: 617 Namquid Dr Warwick RI 02888 Office: 111 Westminster St Providence RI 02903

KITCHEN, JEFFREY COLEMAN, bus. exec.; b. Bend, Ore., Jan. 25, 1921; s. Alfred G. and Mina Louise (Coleman) K.; B.S., U. Ore., 1943; m. Helen Angell, Aug. 12, 1944; children—Jeffrey Coleman, Lynn Wallace, Erik Lloyd. Intern for Lend- Lease Adminstrn., Nat. Inst. Pub. Affairs, also asst. to dep. chief Brit. Empire div., 1943-44; asst. to prin. lend-lease rep. Am. Econ. Mission to Middle East, Cairo, Egypt, 1944-46; spl. financial cons., dir. lend-lease div. Office Fgn. Liquidation Commr., Cairo, 1946-47; asst. to country specialist, then country specialist Iranian desk, State Dept., 1947-48; intern UN, Paris, France, 1948; acting chief policy reports staff, exec. secretariat State Dept., 1948-51, spl. asst. to sec. state, 1952-53, dep. dir. exec. secretariat, 1953-54; dep. dir. for Greek, Turkish, Iranian affairs State Dept., 1954-56; mem. sr. staff RAND Corp., 1956-61; dep. asst. sec. politico-mil. affairs State Dept., 1961-67; mem. sr. seminar fgn. policy State Dept., 1967-68; v.p. nat. devel. programs, also corp. exec. Iran, Northrop Corp., 1968—. Recipient William A. Jump Meml. award for outstanding pub. service, 1956. Mem. Council Fgn. Relations, Am. Fgn. Service Assn., Sigma Delta Chi. Clubs: Imperial Country (Tehran, Iran); International (Washington). Home: 10401 Riverwood Dr Potomac MD 20854 also 28 Ehteshamieh Tehran Iran Office: P O Box 3380 Tehran Iran

KITCHEN, JOHN MILTON, lawyer; b. Indpls., Apr. 15, 1912; s. William Burrette and Edith (Scott) K.; grad. Wabash Coll., 1933; J.D., Harvard, 1937; m. Jane Rauch, Apr. 8, 1939; children—Jeanne, Marjorie, John, Louise. Partner firm Chase & Kitchen, Indpls., 1949—. Pres. Rauch, Kitchen, Reynolds Corp., 1954—, John M. Kitchen Agy., Inc., 1955—. Chmn. Gov. Ind. Commn. Jud. Reform, 1969—; gen. counsel U.S. Auto Club, 1959—; sec., gen. counsel, mem. exec. com. U.S. Auto Club Benevolent Assn., 1959—; gen. counsel, exec. com. Nat. Clay Cts. Championship, 1969—. Western Clay Cts. Championship, 194668. Staff contbr. sports Indpls. Newspapers, Inc., 1959—. Pres. Tudor Hall Sch., Inc.,1962-65. Green Hill Found., 1954-58. Served to capt. AUS, 194246. Mem. Am. (ho. dels.), Ind. (ho. dels.), Indpls. (pres. 1969-70) bar assns., Indpls. Assn. Wabash (pres. 1950-52), Phi Beta Kappa. Clubs: Univty; Dramatic; Woodstock; Trader's Point Hunt; Little Harbor. Author: Legal Aspects of Procurement Terminations and Renegotiation, 1952; Capital Gain v. Ordinary Income, 1958; A Lawyer's Life, 1969. Home: 6130 Crow's Nest Dr Indianapolis IN 46208 Office: Fletcher Trust Bldg Indianapolis IN 46204

KITCHENS, ALTON WALTER, pub. co. exec.; b. Atlanta, June 24, 1918; s. Walter Russell and Camilla Ross (Clark) K.; student Ga. Evening Coll., 1937-40; m. Mary Elizabeth Breedlove, May 28, 1941; children—T. Russell, Janis. With F.W. Dodge div. McGraw-Hill, Inc., 1939—, group v.p., 1964—. Clubs: Castle View Town and Country (Atlanta); Burning Tree Country (Greenwich); Engineers (N.Y.C.). Home: 10 Wyngate Rd Greenwich CT 06830 Office: 330 W 42d St New York City NY 10036

KITCHIN, ALVIN PAUL, lawyer; b. Scotland Neck, N.C., Sept. 13, 1908; s. Alvin Paul and Carrie (Lawrence) K.; student Wake Forest Coll., 1931; m. Dora Little, Oct. 13, 1934; children—Alvin Paul, Henry L. Admitted to N.C. bar, 1930; pvt. practice, Scotland Neck, 1930-33; atty. FBI 1933-45; mem. firm Taylor, Kitchin & Taylor, Wadesboro, N.C., 1945-56; mem. 85th-87th Congresses, 8th Dist. of N.C.; counsel subcom. on revision and codification, Senate Com. on the Judiciary, 1963-64; now in pvt. practice of law, Wadesboro, N.C. Mem. N.C., Anson County bar assns. Democrat. Baptist. Mason, Rotarian. Home: Country Club Rd Wadesboro NC 28170 Office: 103 N Greene St Wadesboro NC 28170

KITCHIN, LEE COLEMAN, broadcasting exec.; b. Newport News, Va., July 14, 1934; s. James David and Margaret Lee (Coleman) K.; student U. Va., 1959, LL.B., 1962; P.M.D., Harvard, 1966; m. Virginia Lord MacKethan, Aug. 15, 1959; children—Lee Coleman, Alexander Heard, Lewis Camern. Admitted to Va. bar, 1962; asso. Kaufman, Oberndorfer & Spainhour, Norfolk, Va., 1962-64; sec. Landmark Communications, Inc., 1964-67; pres. WTAR Radio-TV Corp., Norfolk, 1967—; dir. Tidewater Better Bus. Bur. Dir. Tidewater area Boy Scouts Am., Norfolk Symphony Orch. Dir. Landmark Charitable Found. Served with AUS, 1955-57. Mem. Am., Va., Norfolk-Portsmouth bar assns., Internat. Radio and TV Soc., Va., Norfolk, Portsmouth, Virginia Beach, Peninsula C.'s of C., Phi Alpha Delta. Clubs: Norfolk Yacht and Country, Harbour, Norfolk Sports (Norfolk). Home: 1025 Baldwin Av Norfolk VA 23507 Office: 720 Boush St Norfolk VA 23510

KITE, ORAN H., banker; Former chmn. exec. com., chmn. sr. loan com. Republic Nat. Bank of Dallas; dir. Stratoflex, Inc., Ft. Worth, Gt. S.W. Corp., Arlington, Tex., Mo.-Kan.-Tex. R.R. Co., St. Louis. Office: Republic Nat Bank Ervay St Dallas TX 75202

KITELEY, MURRAY JAMES, educator; b. Saskatoon, Sask., Can., Jan. 11, 1929; s. Eric James and Elsie (Oles) K.; came to U.S., 1947, naturalized, 1953; B.A., U. Minn., 1950, M.A., 1958, Ph.D., 1959; postgrad. Princeton Theol. Sem., 1951-52; m. Jean Louise Vettel, Aug. 18, 1951; children—Geoffrey James, Brian Alan, Barbara Jean. Instr., U. Minn., 1958-59; asst. prof. San Jose State Coll., 1959-62; asst. prof. Smith Coll., Northampton, Mass., 1962- 65, asso. prof., 1965-67, prof., 1968—. Served with AUS, 1954-56. Nat. Found. for Humanities grantee, 1969—. Am. Council Learned Socs. fellow, 1965-66. Mem. Anstotelian Soc., Am. Philos. Assn. Home: 25 Harrison Av Northampton MA 01060

KITMAN, MARVIN, journalist; b. Pitts., Nov. 24, 1929; s. Myer and Rose (Kaufman) K.; B.A., Coll. City N.Y., 1953; m. Carol Sibushnick, Oct. 28, 1951; children—Jamie Lincoln, Suzy, Andrea Jordana. Columnist, Armstrong Daily, N.Y.C., 1956-66; cons. Al Capp Enterprises, 1961-63; staff writer Sat. Eve. Post, 1965-66; news.-mng. editor Monocle mag., N.Y.C., 1963—; TV critic New Leader mag., N.Y.C., 1967—; asst. to treas. Monocle Periodicals, 1965—, bd. dirs., 1966—, founding partner Monocle Book div., 1968; lectr. colls. and univs., 1963—; humorist-in-residence Solow/Wexton, Inc., N.Y.C., 1966-67; sr. writer Carl Ally Inc., advt., 1967-68; v.p. urban affairs Pub. Relations Analysts, 1968; TV critic, columnist Newday and Los Angeles Times Syndicate, 1969—; exec. dir.. Spanish Civil War Roundtable No. N. J. Mem. Leonia (N.J.) Pub. Library, 1961—. Republican candidate for presdl. nomination, 1964. Served with AUS, 1953-55. Author: The Number-One Best Seller, 1966; (pseudonym William Randolph Hirsch with Richard Lingeman) The RCAF (Red Chinese Air Force) Exercise, Diet and Sex Book, 1967; You Can't Judge A Book By It's Cover, 1970; George Washington's Expense Account, 1970; also articles, book revs. Office: care Newsday Garden City NY 11530

KITT, EARTHA MAE, actress, singer; b. North, S.C., Jan. 26, 1928; d. John and Anna Kitt; grad. high sch.; m. William McDonald, June 1960 (div.) 1 dau. Soloist with Katherine Dunham Dance Group, 1948; night club singer, 1949—, appearing in France, Turkey, Greece, Egypt, N.Y.C., Hollywood, Las Vegas, London, Stockholm; stage appearances in Dr. Faustus, Paris, 1951, New Faces of 1952, N.Y.C., Mrs. Patterson, N.Y.C., 1954, Shinbone Alley, N.Y.C., 1957; motion pictures include New Faces, 1953, Accused, 1957, Anna Lucasta, 1958, Mark of the Hawk, St. Louis Blues; also 2 French films; rec. artist for RCA Victor; numerous television appearances. Named Woman of Year, Nat. Assn. Negro Musicians, 1968. Author: Thursday's Child, 1956; A Tart Is Not a Sweet.

KITTAY, SOL, apparel co. exec.; b. London, Eng., Nov. 6, 1910; s. Abraham Isaac and Rose (Darer) K.; came to U.S., 1926, naturalized, 1926; student N.Y.U., 1926-29; m. Frieda Strauss, Nov. 6, 1938; children—Arlyne (Mrs. Jeremy Zimmermann), Jeffrey. Chmn. bd. NCC Industries, Inc., N.Y.C., La Preparacion Textil, Barcelona, Spain, 1965—; dir. Franklin Nat. Bank, N.Y.C., Hutchison- Sabre Textiles London (Eng.). Bd. dirs. Beth Israel Hosp., Hillside Hosp., Westchester Urban League; trustee Horace Mann. Sch.; Mem. Confrerie des Chevaliers du Tastevin, Commanderie de Bordeaux, Physicians Wine Appreciation Soc. (bd. dirs.). Clubs: Harmonie (N.Y.C.), Old Oaks Country (Purchase, N.Y.). Home: Red Roof Farm N Ridge St Port Chester NY 10573 also Ritz Towers New York City NY 10022 Office: 299 Park Av New York City NY 10017

KITTEL, CHARLES, physicist; b. N.Y.C., July 18, 1916; s. George Paul and Helen (Lemler) K.; student Mass. Inst. Tech., 1934-36; B.A., Cambridge U., 1938; Ph.D., U. Wis., 1941; m. Muriel A. Lister, June 23, 1938. Guggenheim fellow, 1946, 57, 64; research physicist Bell Telephone Labs., 1947-51; prof. physics U. Cal. at Berkeley, 1951—. Governing bd. Am. Inst. Physics, 1956- 59. Recipient Oliver Buckley Solid State Physics prize, 1957. Fellow Am. Phys. Soc. (chmn. div. solid state physics 1957; council 1958-62), Am. Acad. Arts and Scis.; mem. Nat. Acad. Scis. Author: Introduction to Solid State Physics, 1953; Quantum Theory of Solids, 1963. Home: 89 San Mateo Rd Berkeley CA 94707

KITTIKACHORN, THANOM, prime minister of Thailand; b. 1911; ed. Mil. Acad., Bangkok; m.; 2 sons, 3 daughters. Entered Mil. Survey Dept. as student officer, 1931, advanced through grades to gen.; assigned planning sect., 1934-35; instr. mil. edn. dept., 1936- 38, 39-41, 44-46; active service in Shan State, 1941; instr. tech. br. Mil. Acad., 1946-47; comdr. 21st Inf. Regt., 1947-48, 11th Inf. Regt., 1948-49; dep. comdr. 1st Inf. Div., 1949-50, comdr., 1950-51; dep. comdr. 1st Army, 1951-54, comdr., 1954-55; mem. Def. Coll., 1955; dep. minister coops., 1955-57; asst. comdr.-in-chief Army, 1957; dep. minister def., 1957, minister, 1957-58; prime minister, minister def., 1958-59; dep. prime minister, minister def., 1959-63; prime minister Thailand, 1963—; field marshal, 1963—, also spl. aide de camp to King; minister of def.; supreme comdr. Royal Thai Armed Forces; polit. leader United Thai Armed Forces. Address: 99 Soi Ranong 2 Dusit Bangkok Office: Supreme Command Hdqrs Ministry of Def Bangkok Thailand

KITTLE, CHARLES FREDERICK, surgeon; b. Athens, O., Oct. 24, 1921; s. Frederick F. and Ida (Falls) K.; A.B. with honors, Ohio U., Athens, O., 1944, LL.D., 1967; M.D. with honors, U. Chgo., 1945; M.S. in Surgery, U. Kan., 1950; m. Jeane Mignon Groenier, Mar. 23, 1945; children— Candace Mignon, Bradley Dean, Leslie Jeane, Brian David. Intern U. Chgo. Clinics, 1945-46; resident gen. and thoracic surgery U. Kan. Med. Center, 1948-52; spl. tng. radio-isotopes for med. use Oak Ridge Inst. Nuclear Studies, 1950, cons. med. div., 1950-55; mem. faculty U. Kan. Sch. Medicine, 1950-66; asso. prof. surgery, lectr. history medicine, 1959-66; cons. thoracic surgery VA Hosp., Wadsworth, Kan., 1954-57, cons. gen. surgery, 1957-60; attending gen. surgery VA Hosp., Kansas City, Mo., 1954-66, VA Hosp., Wichita, Kan., 1955-62; prof. surgery, head sect. thoracic and cardiovascular surgery U. Chgo. Clinics, 1966- -; attending surgery Cook County Hosp., 1966—; cons. Municipal Tb Sanatorium, Chicago, 1968—; spl. research cardiovascular surgery, control of blood flow. Served as lt. (j.g.) USNR, 1946-48. Clin. fellow Am. Cancer Soc., 1950-52; Markle scholar med. scis., 1953-58. Diplomate Am. Bd. Surgery, Am. Bd. Thoracic Surgery (mem. bd. 1967—). Mem. A.A.A.S., Am. Assn. History Medicine, Am. Assn. Thoracic Surgery, Am. Coll. Cardiology (bd. govs. Kan. 1963-66, Illinois 1968—), Chgo. Surg. Soc., A.C.S. (bd. govs. vascular surgery 1965-68), Am. Heart Assn. (chmn. program com. cardiovascular surgery, 1965-68, exec. com. cardiovascular surgery council, 1962—, asso. editor bull. 1964-66), A.M.A., Am. Physiol. Assn., Central Surg. Soc., Chgo. Med. Soc., Am. Surg. Assn., Internat. Cardiovascular Soc. (sec. 1965—), Internat. Soc. Surgery, Soc. Clin. Surgery, Soc. Vascular Surgery, Soc. Univ. Surgeons (pres. 1966-67), Soc. Thoracic Surgery, Phi Beta Kappa, Sigma Xi, Alpha Omega Alpha. Home: 4950 Chicago Beach Dr Chicago IL 60615 Office: 950 E 59th St Chicago IL 60637

KITTLESON, HENRY MARSHALL, lawyer; b. Tampa, Fla., May 13, 1929; s. Edgar O. and Ardath (Ayers) K.; (Ayers) K.; B.S., U. Fla., 1951, LL.B., 1953; m. Barbara Clark, Mar. 20, 1954; 1 dau., Laura Helen. Admitted to Fla. bar, 1953; partner Holland & Knight, Lakeland and Bartow, Fla., 1955—. Vice chmn. Fla. Law Revision Commn. Dir. Dir. Bartow Fed. Savs. & Loan Assn. Mem. Bartow Zoning Bd. Adjustment, 1963-64. Served to maj. USAF, 1953-55. Mem. Am. Law Inst., Bartow C. of C. (dir.), Am. Bar Assn., Fla. Bar, Sigma Phi Epsilon, Phi Delta Phi. Democrat. Presbyn. Clubs: Peace River; University; Lakeland Yacht and Country. Home: 715 Soledad Av Bartow FL 33830 Office: 92 Lake Wire Dr Lakeland FL 33802 Office: 92 Lake Wire Dr Lakeland FL 33802

KITTO, PAUL W., pres. Pacific Nat. Bank, Seattle. Address: 900 2d Av Seattle WA 98111*

KITTO, RICHARD CHARLES JACKSON, lawyer; b. Pen Argyl, Pa., Jan. 9, 1919; s. Charles W. and Dina (Jackson) K.; A.B., Princeton, 1940; LL.B., U. Pa., 1943; m. Ruth B. Dennis, Sept. 26, 1946; children—Richard, Jr., William D. Admitted to Pa. bar, 1943; asso. MacCoy, Evans & Lewis, Phila., 1947-52; pvt. practice, Pen Argyl, 1952-58; legal specialist indsl. relations Standard Pressed Steel Co., Jenkintown, Pa., 1958-59, corporate counsel, 1959-62, asst. sec., 1962-63, sec., 1963-66; v.p., counsel Stephens-Jackson Co., Pen Argyl, 1959—, also dir. Dir. Olney Fed. Savs. & Loan, Phila., 1967—. Chmn. parents adv. council Abington Twp. Sr. High Sch., 1963-64. Served with CIC, AUS, 1943-46; ETO. Mem. Am. Legion. Republican. Methodist. Clubs: Princeton (N.Y.C.); Nassau (Princeton, N.J.). Home: 1086 Rd Jenkintown PA 19046 Office: 1086 Kingsley Rd Jenkintown PA 19046 also Stephens-Jackson Co Pen Argyl PA 18072

KITTREDGE, JOHN KENDALL, ins. co. exec.; b. Pitts., July 7, 1927; s. Richard Carlyle and Velma (Null) K.; B.A., Williams Coll., 1948; m. Elizabeth Delo, May 26, 1951; children—Amy, Carol. With Prudential Ins. Co. Am., 1948—, v.p., 1965. Treas. Prospect House, Orange, N.J., 1964-68. Bd. dirs. Mental Health Assn. Essex County, 1968—; trustee Coll. Medicine and Dentistry N.J., 1970—, chmn., 1971—. Fellow Soc. Actuaries; mem. Am. Acad. Actuaries, Phi Beta Kappa. Home: 90 Druid Hill Rd Summit NJ 07901 Office: Prudential Plaza Newark NJ 07101

KITTRELL, FLEMMIE PANSY, educator; b. Henderson, N.C., Dec. 25, 1904; d. James Lee and Alice (Mills) Kittrell; B.S., Hampton Inst., 1928; Ph.D., Cornell U., 1936. Dean students, dir. home econs. Bennett Coll., Greensboro, N.C., 1928-40; dean women, dir. div. home econs. Hampton Inst., 1940-44; prof. home econs., head dept. Howard U., 1944—; Fulbright lectr. Baroda (India) U., 1950-51; mem. ICA mission to India, 1953-55 Condr. nutrition survey in Liberia, W. Africa for State Dept., 1947; nutrition of India Survey in edn. for FOA UNICEF, 1960; cons. home econs. program to Congo, 1961- 62. Taustee, Freedom from Hunger Found., Inc., Sibly Hosp., Washington, Hampton Inst., Palmer Meml. Inst., Sedelia, N.C.; men. home econs. coll. council Cornell U. Recipient Liberian award, Alumni award Hampton Inst., Internat. Club. award Howard U., Meritorious award OPA, 1st Internat. award Century Club, 1965, Alumni award Coll. Home Econ. Cornell U. for contbn. to human devel. and quality environment, 1968. Fellow A.A.A.S.; mem. Am. Assn. U. Women, N.E.A. (life), Am. Dietetics Assn., Am. Home Econs. Assn., Am. Tchrs. Assn., Assn. Child Edn., Soc. Prodigal Son, Sigma Xi, Omicron Nu, Pi Lambda Theta, Phi Kappa Phi, Sigma Delta Epsilon, Beta Kappa Chi. Home: 3200 Warder St NW Washington DC 20010

KITTSLEY, SCOTT LOREN, educator; b. Port Washington, Wis., Feb. 17, 1921; s. Harry Martin and Irene Rebecca (Scott) K.; B.S., U. Wis., 1942; M.S., Western Res. U., 1944, Ph.D., 1945; m. Helen Ruth Jung, Aug. 23, 1946. Instr. chemistry Marquette U., Milw., 1945-50, asst. prof. chemistry, 1950-56, asso. prof. chemistry, 1956-61, prof. chemistry, 1961—, chmn. dept., 1957-62. Fellow A.A.A.S., Am. Inst. Chemists; mem. Am. Chem. Soc., Wis. Acad. Scis., Arts and Letters, Soc. Sigma Xi. Author: Physical Chemistry, 3d edit., 1969. Contbr. to Jour. American Chem. Soc., Jour. Chem. Edn., other profl. jours. Home: 839 N Marshall Milwaukee WI 53202

KITZINGER, ERNST, educator; b. Munich, Germany, Dec. 27, 1912; s. Wilhelm and Elisabeth (Merzbacher) K.; student U. Rome, 1931-32; Ph.D., U. Munich, 1934; D. Litt. (hon.), Swarthmore Coll.; m. Margaret Susan Theobald, July 22, 1944; children—Stephen Anthony, Margaret Rachel, Adrian Nicholas. Came to U.S., 1941, naturalized, 1948. Asst., Brit. Museum, London, Eng., 1935-40; with Dumbarton Oaks Center for Byzantine Studies (Trustees for Harvard), Washington, 1941-67, successively jr. fellow, fellow, asst. prof. Byzantine art and archeology, asso. prof., 1941-56, prof., 1956-67, dir. studies, 1955-66, A. Kingsley Porter U. prof. Harvard, 1967—; research analyst OSS, 1943-45. Mem. Inst. Advanced Study, Princeton, 1966-67. Fellow Am. Acad. Arts and Scis., Medieval Acad. Am., Brit. Acad. (corr.), Bavarian Acad. Scis. (corr. fellow); mem. of Coll. Art Assn. Am., Archeol. Inst. of Am., German Archaeol. Inst., Am. Philos. Soc. Author: Early Medieval Art in the British Museum, 1940; The Mosaics of Monreale, 1960. Home: 7 Waterhouse St Cambridge MA 02138

KITZMILLER, FRANCIS RODERICK, oil co. exec.; b. Winchester, Ind., Jan. 5, 1932; s. Francis J., and Leona (Heaston) K.; B.S., Ball State U., 1954; m. Patricia L. Harbour, July 27, 1952; children—Jill Ann, Jon Roderick, Janie Louise. With Shell Oil Co., 1954, D.C. Baldwin, C.P.A., Midland, Tex., 1955-56; joined Permian Corp., Midland, 1957, former sec. Presbyn. (deacon 1961). Home: 2403 Stanolind St Midland TX 79701 Office: 1509 W Wall St Midland TX 79701

KITZMILLER, JAMES BLAINE, educator; b. Toledo, June 30, 1918; s. James B. and Ella (Halpin) K.; B.S., DeSales Coll., 1939; M.S., U. Mich., 1942, Ph.D., 1948; m. Mary Elizabeth Kiel, Oct. 9, 1943; children—Kathleen, James, Christine, John. Entomologist, Toledo Mus., 1939-41; asst. zoology U. Mich., 1941-42; with U. Ill., 1948—, successively instr. zoology, asst. prof., asso. prof., 1948-59, prof., 1959—, chmn. dept., 1957-64. Cons., WHO, Pan Am. San. Bur., N.I.H., also pub. cos. Served to 1st lt. AUS, 1943-46. Fulbright fellow, Pavia, Italy, 1953. Mem. Am. Soc. Zoologists, Am. Inst. Biol. Scis., Genetics Soc., Entomol. Soc. Am., Soc. Study Evolution, Am. Mosquito Control Assn., Grand Rapids (Minn.) C. of C. Contbr. numerous articles to med. and sci. jours. Home: 1406 Mayfair St Champaign IL 61820

KIVELSON, DANIEL, educator, chemist; b. N.Y.C., July 11, 1929; s. Harvey E. and Eva (Kivelson) K., A.B., Harvard, 1949, M.S., 1950, Ph.D., 1953; m. Margaret Galland, Aug. 15, 1949; children—Steven Allan, Valerie Ann. Instr. physics Mass. Inst. Tech., 1953-55; mem. faculty U. Cal. at Los Angeles, 1955—, prof. chemistry, 1962—; cons. to govt., 1965—. Guggenheim fellow, 1959; Sloan fellow, 1961-66; NSF sr. posdoctoral fellow, 1965- 66. Recipient Cal. sect. award Am. Chem. Soc. Asso. editor Jour. Chem. Physics, 1968. Home: 1280 Monument St Pacific Palisades CA 90272 Office: Dept Chemistry U Cal at Los Angeles Los Angeles CA 90024

KIXMILLER, EDGAR BYRON, lawyer; b. Bicknell, Ind., Dec. 19, 1885; s. Frederick and Ellen (Mason) K.; student DePauw U., 1904-07, U. Chgo., 1908-09; LL.B., Yale, 1913; m. Claire Willis, Dec. 24, 1913; 1 dau., Betty (Mrs. John S. Russell, Jr.). Admitted to Ind. bar, 1912, Ill. bar, 1913, asst. pros. atty. Ind., 1913-14; atty. Swift & Co. 1914—, gen. atty. 1931-42, gen. counsel, 1942-52. Mem. Civic Fedn. (Chgo. adv. com.), Am., N.Y. State, Ill., Chgo. bar assns., Law Inst. Chgo., Judicature Soc., Phi Gamma Gelta, Chi Tau Kappa. Clubs: Chicago Tax, South Shore Country, Mid-Day, Yale, Law, University (Chgo.). Author: Treatise on Federal Food Control Law, 1918; contbr. articles to jours.; former editor Yale Law Jour. Home: 7059 South Shore Dr Chicago IL 60649

KIXMILLER, RICHARD WOOD, chem. industry exec.; b. Evanston, Ill., May 13, 1920; s. William and May (Wood) KixM.; A.B.; Princeton, 1942; m. Josephine Wallace, May 15, 1943; children—Richard Farwell, John William, Daniel Walter. Research chemist Standard Oil of Ind., 1942-43; with Office of Rubber Dir., W.P.B., 1943-44; dir. product devel. Celanese Corp. Am., 1946-49, asst. to gen. mgr., 1949-52, gen. mgr., 1952-55, v.p., gen. mgr. chem. div., 1955-59, exec. v.p., 1960-65, vice chmn., 1965-66, dir., 1956-; pres. Celanese Chem. Co., Celanese Plastics Co., 1959-60, in charge internat. operations, 1960-64; chmn. Wiltek, Inc., 1968—; dir. Keuffel and Esser Co., Am. Metal Market Co., Wallace Bus. Forms, Seaboard Surety Co., Summit & Elizabeth Trust Co. Inst. Sci. and Tech. Trustee, Drew U. Pringy Sch., Lillia Babbit Hyde Found. Served to lt. (j.g.) USNR, 1944-46. Mem. Mfg. Chemists Assn. (dir. 1960-63), Comml. Chem. Devel. Assn., Am. Chem. Soc., Am. Inst. Chem. Engrs., Chem. Market Research Assn., A.A.A.S., Phi Beta Kappa, Sigma Xi. Methodist. Clubs: Chemists, Princeton, New York Yacht. Pinnacle (N.Y.C.); Beacon Hill (trustee 1962-65 Summit, N.J.); Baltusrol (Springfield, N.J.). Home: 114 Prospect St Summit NJ 07901 Office: 522 Fifth Av New York City NY 10036

KIZER, BENJAMIN HAMILTON, lawyer; b. Champaign County, O., Oct. 29, 1878; s. Benjamin Franklin and Mary Louise (Hamilton) K.; LL.B., U. Mich., 1902; LL.D., Linfield Coll., McMinville, Ore., Reed Coll., Portland, Ore.; m. Helen Bullis, May 19, 1915 (dec. Sept. 21, 1919); m. 2d, Mabel Ashley, Mar. 12, 1921; 1 dau., Carolyn Ashley (Mrs. Stimson Bulliet). Admitted to Mich. bar, 1902, Wash. bar, 1902, and since practiced in Spokane. Pres., Spokane City Plan Commn., 1928-44; former chmn. Wash. State Planning Council, 1933-44; chmn. Pacific N.W. Regional Planning Commn.; former pres. Am. Soc. Planning Ofcls. Bd. regents Reed Coll., Portland, chmn. World Affairs Council of Inland Empire. Asso., Nat. War Labor Bd. (chmn. West Coast Lumber Commn.). Spl. master U.S. Circuit Ct. Appeals, 9th Circuit, 1942-44; dir. China Office, UNRRA, 1944-46. Walker-Ames prof. internat. relations U. Wash., 1946-47, Wash. State chmn. Crusade for Freedom, 1950; chmn. Rhodes Scholars Exam. Com. for 6 Pacific N.W. States 1932—. Recipient Auspicious Star, Grand Cordon (China). Mem. Am., Wash. State (past pres.), Spokane County (past pres.) assns., assns, Order of Coif, Phi Beta Kappa, Author: The U.S. Canadian Northwest. Home: Culmstock Arms Apt Hotel Spokane WA 99204 Office: Paulsen Bldg Spokane WA 99201

KIZER, JOHN OSCAR, lawyer; b. Wheeling, W.Va., Mar. 6, 1913; s. Edwin O. and Laura E. (Dennis) K.; A.B., W. Va. U., 1934, LL.B., 1936; m. Lillian Taylor Cart, Sept. 15, 1934; children—Nora (Mrs. William Meriwether Bowen), Stephen. Dir. safety responsibility dept. W.Va. Rd. Commn., 1936-39; admitted to W. Va. bar, 1936; asso. mem. firm Clark, Woodroe & Butts, Charleston, 1939; partner Campbell, Love, Woodroe & Kizer, and predecessors, Charleston, 1939-; gen. receiver Circuit Ct. Kanawha County, 1940—. Mem. com. legal ethics W.Va. State Bar, 1965-71, vice chmn. 1970-71, chmn. com. legislation, 1960-71. Bd. dirs., past pres. Children's Mus., Charleston. Am., mem. W.Va. bar assns., W. Va. State Bar, Delta Tau Delta. Presbyn. (trustee). Clubs: Berry Hills Country; Army-Navy. Home: 2506 Kanawha Av SE Charleston WV 25304 Office: 1200 Charleston Nat Plaza Charleston WV 25301

KJARTANSSON, HANNES, Icelandic ambassador; b. Reykjavik, Iceland, Feb. 27, 1917; s. Kjartan Gunnlaugsson and Margret (Berndsen) K.; grad. Menntaskoli, Reykjavik; engrng. student Technische Hochschule der Freien Stadt Danzig; econ. student. U. of Iceland, Reykjavik, m. Elin G. G. Sigurdsson, Mar. 13, 1941; children—Kiartan Jonas, Stefania Margret, Anna Elin. In charge N.Y.C. office of Icelandic firm, 1940-45; established own firm and served as pres. since 1945; Icelandic consul in charge consulate gen. N.Y., 1948-50, consul gen. Iceland since 1950; rep. Icelandic Herringboard and other Icelandic govt. export- import agys. in U.S.; Icelandic alternat. delegate 9th UN Assembly. N.Y., 1954; Icelandic delegate 12th, 14th-19th UN assembly; Icelandic ambassador to UN, 1965—, to Lima, Peru, 1970—; v.p. 22d Gen. Assembly, 1967-68. Decorated grand cross Icelandic Order of Falcon. Pres. Icelandic Soc. N.Y., 1945-47. Lutheran. Home: 46 Sunnybrook Rd Bronxville NY 10708 Office: 420 Lexington Av New York City NY 10017

KJELSON, LEE, music educator; b. Stromsburg, Neb., Aug. 27, 1926; s. Albert V. and Marjorie (Hedbloom) K.; B.M.E., U. Neb., 1948, Mus.M., 1951; Ph.D., U. Ia., 1957; m. Betty Lorraine Aasen, July 31, 1949; children—Lee Richard 11, John A. (Jay). Music tchr. pub. schs., Neb. and Ia., 1948-54; grad. asst. Exptl. Sch. Univ. High, U. Ia., 1955-57; asst. prof. music Western State Coll., Gunnison, Colo., 1957-60; prof. music Cal. State Coll., Hayward, 1960-67; prof. music, chmn. dept. music edn. U. Miami (Fla.), 1967—; choral condr. and clinician for state and nat. music edn. assns.; vis. prof. colls. and univs. Mem. Music Educators Nat. Conf. Democrat. Mem. United Ch. Christ. Editor, composer, arranger choral music, Co-author: Basic Series, 1969. Home: 631 Tibidabo St Coral Gables FL 33143

KLABER, EUGENE HENRY, architect; b. N.Y.C., Oct. 1, 1883; s. Maurice and Dora (Frankfeld) K.; B.S. in Arch., Columbia, 1906; architet diplome par le gouvernement, Ecole des Beaux Arts, Paris, 1910; m. Doretta Oppenheim, Aug. 31, 1913; children—Joseph (dec.), Susan. Archtl. designer, 1910; architect N.Y.C., 1914-24, Chgo., 1924-33; chief tech. staff Housing div. PWA, Washington, 1933-34; dir. architecture for rental housing FHA, 1934-42; practicing architect Washington, 1942-44, dir. div. planning and housing Sch. Architecture, Columbia, N.Y.C., 1944-46; housing and planning, cons., Quakertown, Pa., 1946—. Served as 1st lt., C.E., U.S. Army, 1918. Fellow A.I.A. (past pres. Chgo. chpt.); mem. Am. Inst. Planners, Am. Soc. Planning Ofcls. (hon. life). Author: Housing Design, 1954. Home: Route 1 Quakertown PA 18951

KLAERNER, CURTIS MAURICE, oil co. exec.; b. Fredericksburg, Tex., Sept. 7, 1920; s. Elgin and Irene (Wagner) K.; B.S. in Chem. Engring., U. Tex., 1942; grad. program sr. execs., Mass. Inst. Tech., 1956; m. Aileen E. Eitt, Sept. 4, 1942; children—Sherilyn Kay, Curtis Elgin. Process engr., then chief process engr. Magnolia Petroleum Co., 1942-53; refinery mgr., then mgr. Eastern region mfg. Socony Mobil Oil Co., 1953-59; regional exec., then regional v.p. Mobil Internat. Oil Co., 1959-61; pres. Mobil Inner Europe, Geneva, Switzerland, 1962-65; corp. v.p. charge marine transp. and internat. sales Socony Mobil Oil Co., 1965-69; exec. v.p. internat. div. Mobil Oil Corp., 1969—. Mem. Phi Eta Sigma, Omega Chi Epsilon, Phi Kappa Sigma. Republican. Episcopalian. Clubs: Union League, Circumnavigators (N.Y.C.); Woodway Country (Darien. Conn.); International (Washington). Home: 37 Holly La Darien CT 06820 Office: 150 E 42d St New York City NY 10017

KLAG, EDWIN JAMES, hosp. adminstr.; b. Toledo, Feb. 9, 1915; s. John Christian and Florence (Wolff) K.; Ph.B., U. Toledo, 1936, J.D., 1941; m. Marjorie Ruth McDermott, Sept. 5, 1942; children—Nancy A. (Mrs. Norman T. Shawver), Kathryn Ann (Mrs. James Haymaker), Thomas E., John R. Admitted to Ohio bar, 1941; with Owens-Illinois, Toledo, 1937-42; with VA, St. Louis, 1946-48, Springfield Mo., 1948-49; dir. VA Center, Wichita, Kan., 1949-68, Wood, Wis., 1968—. Chmn. Midway Kan. chpt. A.R.C., 1961-62, bd. dirs. Greater Milw. chpt., 1968—; bd. dirs. Med. Center Southeastern Wis., Milw. Regional Med. TV Milw. Cancer Soc. Served to capt. AUS, 1942-46; col. Res. Fellow Am. Coll. Hosp. Adminstrs.; mem. Hosp. Council Greater Milw., Ohio Bar Assn., Fed. Ofcls. Assn. (pres. Milw. 1969-70), Am. Legion, Delta Theat Phi, Pi Kappa Delta. Rotarian. Address: 5000 W National St Wood Milwaukee WI 53193

KLAGES, ROY ARTHUR, educator; b. Cape Girardeau, Mo., Aug. 31, 1916; s. Arthur F. and Mary (Ulrich) K.; B.S., Mo. State Coll., 1938; postgrad. Northwestern U., 1939; M.B.A., U. Tex., Austin, 1945; postgrad. Miss. State U., 1950, Washington U., St. Louis, 1953; Ph.D., St. Louis U., 1959; m. Dorothy M. Cole, Dec. 1, 1941 (dec. 1952); 1 dau., Mary Frances (Mrs. Dale S. Sass); m. 2d, Ida Cook Parr, Dec. 23, 1955; stepchildren—Frances V. Parr (Mrs. Edward Duffield), Lawrence L. Parr. With S.E. Missourian Newspaper, Cape Girardeau, 1932-38; bookstore mgr. Mo. State Coll., 1934-38; supt., instr. Belgrade (Mo.) Consol. Schs., 1938-42; instr. Cape Girardeau Pub. Schs., 1942-43; asst. prof. Southwestern Coll., Winfield, Kan., 1943-45; asso. prof., div. head marketing Miss. State U., 1945-55; grad. asst., instr. St. Louis U., 1955-59; asso. prof. marketing U. Detroit, 1959-64; prof., chmn. marketing Sch. Bus., State U. N.Y. at Albany, 1964—; bus. cons.; dir. Advt. Inst., St. Louis, 1957-58. Mem. Am. Marketing Assn., Nat. Fgn. Trade Council, Am. Collegiate Retail Assn., Sales and Marketing Execs. Assn. Eastern N.Y. (pres., 1970-71, dir. 1964-70), Sales and Marketings Execs. Internat. (vice chmn. coll. relations com.), Nat. Retail Merchants Assn., Am. Econ. Assn. Methodist. Mason, Kiwanian. Home: 20 Hillcrest Dr Jonesville NY 12098 Office: 1400 Washington Av Albany NY 12203

KLAGSBRUNN, HANS ALEXANDER, lawyer; b. Vienna, Austria, Apr. 28, 1909; came to U.S., 1912; s. Hugo and Lili (Brandt) K.; student Vienna Gymnasium, 1922-25; B.A., Yale, 1929, LL.B., 1932; postgrad. Harvard Law Sch., 1932-33; m. Elizabeth Mapelsden Ramsey, January 27, 1934. Admitted to D.C. bar, bar U.S. Supreme Ct., 1935; asso. Reconstrn. Finance Corp. and affiliates, 1933-45; exec. v.p., gen. counsel, dir. and mem. exec. com. Def. Plant Corp.; surplus property dir. and asst. gen. counsel RFC; RFC mem. Hancock Contract Settlement Bd. and Clayton Surplus Property Bd. in Office War Mobilization; dep. dir. Office War Mobilization and Reconversion, The White House, 1945-46; mem. Army Chem. Corps Reorgn. Com., 1955-56; Sr. mem. Klagsbrunn & Hanes, attys., 1946-68; counsel to successor firm, 1969—. Mem. Health and Welfare Council, bd. dirs., 1958—, pres., 1961-63; mem. Loudoun County Sanitation Authority, 1959-68, vice chmn., 1965-68. Bd. dirs. Friendship House, 1957-68, pres., 1959-68; bd. dirs. Columbia Hosp. for Women, 1964—, sec., 1966-67, 1st v.p., 1967-68. Recipient Community Service awards, 1961, 63. Mem. Am. Bar. Found., Fed. Bar Assn., Am. Arbitration Assn. (nat. panel), Bar Assn. D.C. (council mem. adminstrv. law sect. 1952-55, chmn. U.S. Ct. Appeals com. 1966-67). Am. Bar Assn. (past chmn. coms.), U.S. Ct. Appeals Com. on admissions and grievances 1967—), Nat. Planning Assn., A.I.M., Am. Judicature Soc., Newcomen Soc., Phi Beta Kappa, Order of Coif, Phi Beta Kappa Assos., Nat. Symphony Orch. Assn. Clubs: Metropolitan, Yale, National Press, City Tavern. Home: 3420 Q St N W Washington DC 20007 also Salem Farm R F D 1 Purcellville VA 22132 Office: Ring Bldg Washington DC 20036

KLAGSTAD, ROBERT EDGAR, banker; b. Detroit, Mar. 10, 1923; s. Harold L. and Ione (Hatch) K.; student Mass. Inst. Tech., 1941-42; B.B.A. in Accounting, U. Mich., 1949; m. Shirley E. Weemhoff, Apr. 3, 1948; children—Karen Ione, Robert J., Richard H. With Price, Waterhouse & Co., C.P.A.'s, Chgo., 1949-53; v.p., comptroller Lake Shore Nat. Bank, Chgo., 1953-63; v.p., controller Marine Corp., Milw., 1963—; v.p., controller Plaza Bldg. Mgmt. Corp., 1964—; pres. One Eleven East Corp., 1967—. Served to 1st lt. USAAF, 1942-45; ETO. C.P.A., Wis. Mem. Am. Inst. C.P.A's, Wis. Soc. C.P.A.'s, Exptl. Aircraft Assn., Internat. Aerobatic Club, Delta Kappa Epsilon. Republican, Mem. Reformed Ch. Address: 1021 1021 W Duchess Ct Milwaukee WI 53217

KLAMON, LAWRENCE PAINE, diversified co. exec.; b. St. Louis, Mar. 17, 1937; s. Joseph Martin and Rose (Schimel) K.; A.B., Washington U., 1958; LL.B., Yale, 1961; m. Jo Ann Karen Beatty, Nov. 8, 1957; children—Stephen Robert, Karen Jean, Lawrence Paine. Confidential asst. Office Sec. Def., Washington, 1961-62, spl. asst. to gen. counsel, 1962-63; admitted to N.Y. bar, 1964; asso. Cravath, Swaine & Moore, N.Y.C., 1963-67; v.p., gen. counsel Fuqua Industries, Inc., Atlanta, 1967—. Mem. Am. Bar Assn., Assn. Bar City N.Y., Am. Soc. Corporate Secs., Order of Coif, Phi Beta Kappa, Omicron Delta Kappa. Bd. editors Yale Law Jour., 1959-61. Home: 4032 McClatchey Circle NE Atlanta GA 30342 Office: First Nat Bank Tower Atlanta GA 30303

KLAPPER, JOSEPH THOMAS, sociologist; b. N.Y.C., Jan. 11, 1917; s. Paul and Flora (Eydenberg) K.; B.S. cum laude, Harvard, 1936; M.A., U. Chgo., 1938; Ph.D. in Sociology, Columbia, 1960; m. Hope Lunin, July 15, 1949. Instr. English, Bklyn. Polytech. Inst., 1939-40; teaching tutor English, Coll. City N.Y., 1939-41; research asst., then research asso. Bur. Applied Social Research, Columbia, 1946-49; acting asst. prof. sociology U. Wash., 1949- 50, also editor Wash. State Pub. Opinion Lab.; project dir., then chief media evaluation sect. Voice of Am., USIA, 1951-54; research asso., project dir. Bur. Applied Social Research, Columbia, 1954-58; cons. communications research, behavioral research service Gen. Elec. Co., 1958-62; dir. social research CBS, N.Y.C., 1962—. Vis. asst. prof. sociology and anthropology Stanford, summer 1950; cons. communications research Am.-Jewish Com., also broadcasting and film commn. Nat. Council Chs. of Christ, 1957-64; asso. Columbia Seminar on Pub. Communication, 1952—. Columbia Seminar on Basic and Applied Research. Mem. Pres. Commn. on Obscenity and Pornography, 1968-70, Surgeon Gen.'s Sci. Adv. Com., 1969-71. Served to capt. AUS, 1941- 46. Rockefeller fellow, 1946-47. Fellow Am. Sociol. Assn.; mem. Am. Assn. Pub. Opinion Research (exec. council 1954—, counsellor-at- large 1956-57, 66—, sec.-treas. 1957-61, pres. 1962-63), World Assn. Pub. Opinion Research, Radio-Television Research Council. Author: The Effects of Mass Communication, 1960, monographs, and numerous articles. Editorial staff Pub. Opinion Quar. Home: 340 E 57th St New York City NY 10022 Office: CBS 51 W 52d St New York City NY 10019

KLAPPERICH, FRANK LAWRENCE, Jr., investment banker; b. Oak Park, Ill., Oct. 11, 1934; s. Frank Lawrence and Marjorie (Doan) K.; A.B., Princeton, 1956; M.B.A., Harvard, 1961; m. Margaret Monroe Touborg, Mar. 9, 1957; children—Margaret Friis, Susan Doane, Frank Lawrence III, Elizabeth Monroe. With Kidder, Peabody & Co., Inc., Chgo., 1961—, v.p., 1965—; chmn. bd. Wheaton Bancorp., Diversified Ins. Service Co., Northfield Bancorp., Inc. Chgo. Served with USN, 1956-59; comdr. Res. Mem. Investment Analysts Soc. Chgo., Investment Bankers Assn. Am., Harvard Bus. Sch. Assn. Chgo. Clubs: Princeton (N.J.) Charter; Princeton (N.Y.C.); Tavern, University, Mid Day, Bond, Economic, Chicago, Executives, Princeton (pres. 1970-71), Harvard (Chgo.); Glen View (Golf, Ill.); La Coquille (Palm Beach, Fla.); Indian Hill (Winnetka, Ill.). Home: 345 Woodley Rd Winnetka IL 60093 Office: 1 First Nat Plaza Chicago IL 60670

KLAPPERT, PETER, poet, educator; b. Rockville Center, N.Y., Nov. 14, 1942; s. Herman Emil and Grace Barbara (Rupp) K.; B.A., Cornell U., 1964; M.A., U. Ia., 1967, M.F.A., 1968. Instr. English, Rollins Coll., Winter Park, Fla., 1968-71; Briggs-Copeland lectr. English, Harvard, Cambridge, Mass., 1971—. Winner Yale Series of Younger Poets Competition, 1970. Mem. Coll. English Assn., Asso. Writing Programs. Democrat. Author: (poems) Lugging Vegetables to Nantucket, 1971; After The Rhymers Guild, 1971. Home: 351 Harvard St Cambridge MA 02138

KLAPRAT, ELMER EARL, ins. co. exec.; b. Wausau, Wis., Mar. 11, 1919; s. Gustav and Pauline (Will) K.; Ph.B., U. Wis., 1942, LL.B., 1946; m. Jean Schoenherr, Mar. 23, 1941; children—Nancy Leigh, Carol Ann (Mrs. Raymond Giles). Admitted to Wis. bar, 1946, U.S. Supreme Ct. bar, 1971; practiced in Wausau, Wis., 1946—; claims adjuster Employers Ins. of Wausau, 1942-46, atty., 1946-48, br. legal mgr., 1948- 54, asst. counsel, 1954-56, asst. gen. counsel, 1956-60, v.p., gen. counsel, 1960-70, sr. counsel, 1970—. Mem. Am., Wis., Marathon County bar assns., Internat. Assn. Ins. Counsel. Home: 815 Broadway Wausau WI 54401 Office: 2000 Westwood Dr Wausau WI 54401

KLARE, GEORGE ROGER, educator; b. Mpls., Apr. 17, 1922; s. George C. and Lee (Launer) K.; student U. Neb., 1940-41, U. Minn., 1941-43, U. Mo., 1943; B.A., U. Minn., 1946, M.A., 1947, Ph.D., 1950; m. Julia Marie Price Matson, Dec. 24, 1946; children—Deborah, Roger, Barbara. Instr., U. Minn., 1948-50; staff psychologist Psychol. Corp., N.Y.C., 1950-51; research asso. U. Ill., 1952-54; asst. prof. dept. psychology Ohio U., Athens, 1954-57, asso. prof., 1957-62, prof. 1962, chmn. dept., 1959-63, acting dean Coll. Arts and Sci., 1965, dean, 1966—; on leave as research asso. Harvard, 1968-69; vis. prof. State U. N.Y. at Stony Brook, 1971—. Staff mem. N.Y.C. Writers Conf., 1956-57; cons., lectr. Nat. Project Agr. Communication, 1957-59, Com. on World Literacy and Christian Lit., 1958-62; exec. asst., sr. research engr. Autonetics, 1960-61; cons. Resources Devel. Corp., 1962-65, Boston Pub. Sch., 1968, D.C. Heath, 1971—. Liaison rep. Internat. Communication Assn. to Nat. Reading Council, 1970—. Served to 1st lt. USAAF, 1943-45. Decorated Air Medal, Purple Heart. Mem. Am. Psychol. Assn., Nat. Soc. for Program Instr., Internat. Communication Assn., Am. Ednl. Research Assn., Delta Phi Lambda, Psi Chi, Phi Delta Kappa. Author: (with Byron Buck) Know Your Reader, 1954; The Measurement of Readability, 1963; (with Paul A. Games) Elementary Statistics: Data Analysis for the Behavioral Sciences, 1967. Home: 42 Elmwood Pl Athens OH 45701

KLARMAN, HERBERT ELIAS, educator, economist; b. Chmielnik, Poland, Dec. 21, 1916; s. Morris Louis and Helen (Klarman) K.; came to U.S. 1929, naturalized, 1929; A.B., Columbia. 1939; M.A., U. Wis., 1941, Ph.D., 1946; m. Mary A. Monk, 1967; children—Seth Andrew, Joseph Michael. Asst., then asso. dir. Hosp. Council Greater N.Y., 1949-51, 52-62; asst. dir. N.Y. State Hosp. Study, Columbia, 1948-49; asst. prof. econs. Bklyn., 1947-48; economist nat. income div. Dept. Commerce, 1946-47; med. economist Nat. Security Resources Bd., 1951-52; mem. faculty Johns Hopkins, 1962-69, prof. pub. health adminstrn. and polit. economy, 1965-69; prof. environmental medicine and community health Downstate Med. Center, State U. N.Y., 1969- 70; prof. econs. Grad. Sch. Pub. Adminstrn. N.Y. U., 1970—. Mem. Health services research study sect. NIH, 1962-66; chmn. planning com. 2d Conf. on Econs. Health, 1967-69; chmn. med. care and med. econs. adv. com. 3rd Nat. Cancer Survey, 1967—; mem. U.S. Nat. Com. on Vital and Health Statistics, 1967-71. Served to capt. AUS, 1942-46. Recipient first Norman A. Welch Meml. award Nat. Assn. Blue Shield Plans, 1965. Fellow Am. Pub. Health Assn.; mem. Am. Econ. Assn., Am. Statis. Assn., A.A.A.S., Royal Econ. Soc., Phi Beta Kappa. Author: Hospital Care in New York City, 1963; Economics of Health, 1965; also articles, chpts. in books. Editor: Empirical Studies in Health Economics, 1970. Home: 100 Bleecker St New York City NY 10012

KLARMANN, ADOLF D., educator; b. Austria, Sept. 18, 1904; s. Oscar and Regina (Trompeter) K.; Came to U.S., 1923, naturalized, 1929; student Berlin U., 1922-23; A.B., N.Y. U., 1926, M.A., 1927; postgrad. Munich U., 1927-28; Ph.D., U. Pa., 1930; Litt.D., Lebanon Valley Coll., 1967; m. Isolde Doernenburg, Aug. 12, 1939. Instr., N.Y. U., 1926-28, U. Rochester, 1928-29, 30-31; faculty U. Pa., 1929—, prof. German and gen. lit., 1955—. Vis. prof. U. Cal. at Los Angeles, U. Cal. at Berkeley, U. Colo., Johns Hopkins. Jusserand fellow, 1936, 52; Fulbright research fellow to Vienna, 1952-53; Guggenheim fellow, 1966-67; hon. mem. Phi Beta Kappa, 1967; recipient cross honor 1st class Letters and Arts (Austria). Mem. Internat. Assn. Germanists, Internat. Fedn. Modern Langs. and Lits., Modern Humanities Assn., Modern Lang. Assn., Am. Assn. U. Profs., Am. Assn. Tchrs. German, Am. Council Study Austrian Lit. (pres. 1969—). Contbr. articles to profl. jours. Editor lit. estate of Franz Werfel, 1945—; editor German Quar., 1963-65. Home: E610 Garden Ct 47th and Pine Sts Philadelphia PA 19143

KLASEN, PETER, artist; b. Lubeck, Germany, 1935; student Sch. Fine Arts, Berlin. 1956- 59. One man shows Munich, 1964, Paris, 1966; participant internat. exhbns. Mythologies Quotidiennes at Municipal Mus. Modern Art, Paris, 1964, Bande Dessinee et Figuration Narrative at Mus. Decorative Arts Paris, 1967. Address: 143 Rue Clignancourt Paris France*

KLASS, SIDNEY, publisher, editor; b. Bklyn., Mar. 18, 1916; s. Morris and Helen (Epstein) K.; student Mesifta Theol. Sem., 1928-34; m. Irene Schrieber, Aug. 31, 1940; children—Naomi, Linda. Editor., pub. Bklyn. Daily Newspaper, 1950- -, now pres., gen. mgr. and purchasing agt.; pub. Bklyn. Weekly, Shorefront News. Jewish Press; pres. Surf Realty Corp., 1940—, Surf Publs., Inc. Office: 2427 Surf Av Brooklyn NY 11224

KLASSEN, ELMER THEODORE, govt. ofcl.; b. Hillsboro, Kan., Nov. 6, 1908; student Harvard Bus. Sch., 1952; m. Bessie Crooks, May 19,1929; 1 dau., Joan Marie, m. 2d, Marie Callahan, June 8, 1963. With Am. Can Co., N.Y.C., 1925-68, gen. mgr. indsl. relations, 1955-58, v.p. indsl. relations, 1958-61, v.p., asst. gen. mgr. Canco Div., 1961-62, v.p., gen. mgr. Canco Div., 1962- 64, exec. v.p. div. operations, 1964, exec. v.p. corporated operations, 1964-65, pres., 1965-68; dep. postmaster gen. P.O. Dept., Washington 1969-71. Chmn. bd. Inst. for Collective Bargaining and Group Relations, N.Y.C.; trustee Postgrad Inst. Osteo. Medicine and Surgery, N.Y.C.; adv. council Business College, Pa. State Univ.; bd. govs. U.S. Postal Service, 1971—. Mem. Newcomen Soc. North Am. Republican. Methodist, Elk. Clubs: Sky, Economic, Elks, Harvard Business School (N.Y.C.); Capitol Hill (Washington). Home: Reeds Bridge Rd Conway MA 01341

KLASSEN, KARL PETER, educator, physician; b. Spat, Crimea, USSR, Oct. 25, 1908; s. Peter and Anna Maria (Warkentin) K.; B.S., Wheaton (Ill.) Coll., 1941; M.D., U. Chgo., 1936; m. Elvera Ann Hertz, May 28, 1938; children—Peter, Kristina Ann (Mrs. Edwin Owen). Intern, Billings Hosp., Chgo., 1927; fellow surg. research Ohio State U. Coll. Medicine, Columbus, O., 1938, resident surgery, 1938-41, mem. faculty, 1941—, prof., dir. div. thoracic surgery, 1960—; chmn. thoracic surgery Children's Hosp., Columbus, 1967—. Trustee Center Sci. and Industry, Columbus. Mem. pres.'s club Ohio State U. Diplomate Am. Bd. Surgery, Am. Bd. Thoracic Sugery. Fellow A.M.A., A.C.S., Am. Coll. Chest Physicians; mem. Internat., Columbus surg. socs., Central Ohio Heart Assn. (trustee, past pres.), Am. Assn. Thoracic Surgery, Soc. Thoracic Surgery, Central Surg. Assn. (past pres.). Contbr. articles to med. jours. Home: 2375 Oxford Rd Columbus OH 43221

KLASSEN, PETER PIERRE, educator; b. Simferopol, Crimea, Russia, Oct. 17, 1904; s. Peter P. and Anna (Warkentin) K.; came to U.S., 1925, naturalized, 1941; B.A., Denison U., 1931; M.A., U. Chgo., 1938, Ph.D., 1949; m. Elsie May Woodward, Dec. 27, 1939; children—Peter Thomas, Ruth Ann (Mrs. George Jackson), Richard William. Instr. sociology Coll. of Ozarks, 1938-39; mem. faculty Pa. State U., 1939-41; social sci. analyst U.S. Govt., 1942-46; asst. prof. U. Fla., 1947-48; asst. prof. U. Ill., Chgo., 1948-51, asso. prof., 1951-54, prof., 1954—, head, dept. sociology and anthropology, 1964-68, dir. Office Demographic Studies, 1968—; lectr. Sch. Financial Pub. Relations, Northwestern U., 1954-70; lectr. Sch. Bank Marketing, U. Colo., 1970—; pvt. cons., 1960—; profl. lectr. Mem. tech. staff Higher Edn. Commn. Ill., 1955-57; cons. Bd. Higher Edn. Ill., 1958-62. Fellow Am. Sociol. Assn.; mem. Am. Statis. Assn., A.A.A.S., Am. Population Assn., Chgo. Statis. Assn. Club: American Commoner (Granville, O.). Author: (with D.C. Poole) Handbook of Foreign Nationalities, 1943; (with Alden Cuttshall) World Patterns and World Problems, 1949; (with James McKenzie) Illinois Looks to the Future in Higher Education, 1957; also monographs. Home: 425 N Scoville Oak Park IL 60302

KLATELL, JACK, dentist; b. N.Y.C., July 15, 1918; s. Meyer and Jennie (Merin) Klatsky; B.S., Coll. City N.Y., 1938; D.D.S., Columbia, 1941; m. Arline Bragin, Aug. 9, 1944: children—Robert E., David A. Dental intern Mt. Sinai Hosp., N.Y. C., 1941-42; sr. resident dental and oral surgery Seaview Hosp., S.I., N.Y., 1942-43; pvt. practice dentistry, N.Y.C., 1943- -; dir. dept. dentistry, dentist-in-chief Mt. Sinai Hosp., 1965—; asso. clin. prof. N.Y.U. Coll. Dentistry, 1967—; prof. dentistry Mt. Sinai Sch. Medicine, 1966—, also chmn. dept. Served to capt., Dental Corps, AUS, 1943-46. Fellow Am. Coll. of Dentists; mem. Am. Dental Assn., Am. Acad. Oral Pathology, N.Y. Inst. Clin. Oral Pathology, Met. Conf. Hosp. Dental Chiefs, Am. Assn. Hosp. Dental Chiefs, Phi Beta Kappa, Omicron Kappa Upsilon, Alpha Omega. Contbr. profl. jours. Home: 8 E 3d St New York City NY 10028 Office: 59 E 54th St New York City NY 10022

KLATSKIN, GERALD, physician; b. N.Y.C., May 14, 1910; s. Archibald and Celia (Golubowski) K.; A.B., Cornell U., 1929, M.D., 1933; M.A. (hon.), Yale, 1957; m. Ethelyn Henry, Dec. 10, 1949; children—Jane, Robert P., Ann Henry. Intern, asst. resident medicine New Haven Hosp., 1933-35, resident medicine, 1937-38; intern surgery Strong Meml. Hosp., Rochester, N.Y., 1935-36, asso. resident medicine, 1936-37; instr. medicine U. Rochester, 1936-37; from instr. to prof. medicine Yale Sch. Medicine, 1937-64, David Paige Smith prof. medicine, 1964—; asso. physician Yale-New Haven Med. Center; cons. West Haven VA Hosp. Served from capt. to lt. col., M.C., AUS, 1942-46. Diplomate Am. Bd. Internal Medicine. Fellow A.C.P.; mem. Assn. Am. Physicians, Interurban Clin. Club, Soc. Exptl. Biology and Medicine, Am. Assn. Study Liver Diseases (pres. 1957), Phi Beta Kappa, Sigma Xi, Alpha Omega Alpha. Author articles in field, contbr. books. Home: 37 Woodlawn St Hamden CT 06517 Office: Dept Internal Medicine Yale Sch Medicine 333 Cedar St New Haven CT 06510

KLATTE, ERNEST WILLIAM, psychiatrist; b. Indpls., Jan. 11, 1926; s. Ernest William and Catherine May (Ladd) K.; M.D., Ind. U., 1948; m. Jane Krider, June 19, 1948; children—Neva Renee, Ernest William III. Intern, Long Beach Naval Hosp., 1948-49; resident psychiatry John Seeley Hosp., Galveston, Tex., 1950- 51, Langley Porter Neuropsychiat. Inst., San Francisco, 1951-52; practice medicine, specializing in psychiatry, Yokosuka, Japan, 1952-54, Imola, Cal., 1954-56, Talmage, Cal., 1956—; asst. chief psychiatry Inpatient and Outpatient Psychiat. Services, Yokosuka Naval Hosp., 1952- 54; staff psychiatrist Napa State Hosp., 1954-56; sr. psychiatrist Mendocino State Hosp., 1956-57, dir. clin. services, 1957-59, asso. supt., 1959, supt., med. dir., 1960-69; program chief Orange County Mental Health Services, 1969-71, dir., 1971—; asso. clin. prof. psychiatry U. Cal. at Irvine, 1969—. Mem. A.M.A., Am., No. Cal. (mem. council) psychiat. socs. Address: 2215 N Broadway Santa Ana CA 92706

KLATTE, EUGENE CARL, physician, educator; b. Indpls., Mar. 19, 1928; s. Ernest William and Catherine May (Ladd) K.; student Purdue U., 1945-47; A. B., Ind. U., 1949, M.D., 1952; m. Barbara Ann Lyntton, Aug. 26, 1950; children—Susan Lynn. Constance Leah, Kathryn Jean, Jeannette Ann. Rotating intern U. Mich. Hosp., 1952-53; resident radiology U. Cal. at San Francisco, 1955- 57; Picker scholar radiol. research Ind. U. Sch. Medicine, 1957-59, mem. faculty, 1957-62, asso. prof. radiology, 1960-62; prof. radiology, chmn. dept.

Vanderbilt U. Sch. Medicine, 1962—. Served to capt. USAF, 1953-55. Mem. A.M.A. Radiol. Soc. N. Am., Am. Coll. Radiology, Assn. Univ. Radiologists, Pediatric Radiol. Soc., Phi Beta Kappa, Alpha Omega Alpha. Home: 6006 Hickory Valley Rd Nashville TN 37205

KLATZ, HAROLD DAVID, violist; b. Milw., Nov. 24, 1914; s. Morris and Ada (Pollack) K.; Mus.B. in Music Edn., U. Wis., 1940; m. Esther Grunsfield, Dec. 31, 1952; children—Susan, Judith, Daniel. Prin. violist Nat. Symphony, Washington, 1944, Chgo. Opera Co., 1946, NBC, Chgo., 1946-61; mem. Chgo Symphony Orch., 1948-49; asso. prof. viola Northwestern U., 1961-70; mem. Sheridan String Quartet, 1960—; mem. Casals Festival Orch., San Juan, P.R., 1960-63. Founder, Chamber Music Guild Chgo., 1959—. Mem. Chgo. Fedn. Musicians (bd. dirs.), Am. String Tchrs. Assn., (v.p. Ill.). Clubs: Arts, Literary (Chgo.). Home: 424 Oakdale Av Chicago IL 60614

KLAUS, ELMER ERWIN, chem. engr., educator; b. Neffsville, Pa., Apr. 19, 1921; s. Elmer Ernest and Esther (Graver) K.; B.S., Franklin and Marshall Coll., 1943; M.S., Pa. State U., 1946, Ph.D., 1952; m. Jean Rebecca Hartswick, Sept. 22, 1945; children—Dennis Richard, Diane Gail. Researh asst. Pa. State U., 1943-46, instr., 1946-52, asst. prof., 1952-56, asso. research prof., 1956-66, prof. chem. engring., 1966—. Chmn. Am. Soc. Lubrication Engrs.-Am. Soc. M.E. Lubrication Conf., 1967. Exec. bd. Juniata Valley council Boy Scouts Am., 1965—. Recipient Pentathalon award Franklin and Marshall Coll., 1943. Fellow Am. Inst. Chemists; mem. Am. Chem. Soc., Am. Inst. Chem. Engrs., Am. Soc. Lubrication Engrs. (dir.), Sigma Xi, Alpha Chi Sigma, Phi Lambda Upsilon, Sigma Pi Sigma. Mem. United Ch. of Christ. Mason (Shriner). Co-editor Boundary Lubrication—An Appraisal of World Literature, 1969. Asso. editor Jour. of Lubrication Technology, 1968—. Contbr. articles profl. jours. Home: 221 Nimitz Av State College PA 16801 Office: Chem Engring Bldg PA State U University Park PA 16802

KLAUS, JOSEF, former chancellor of Austria; b. Mauthen, Carinthia, Austria Aug. 15, 1910; s. Matthias and Theresia (Pfliegl) K.; LL.B., U. Vienna, 1934; m. Erna Seywald, 1936; children—Michael, Uta-Maria, Norbert, Bernard. Engaged in practice of law, Vienna, 1934—; with econ. sect. Vienna Chamber Workers and Employees, 1934-38; provincial gov. Salzburg, 1949; chmn. Salzburg sect. Austrian's People's Party, 1952, nat. chmn., 1963—; mem. Austrian Parliament, 1962—; fed . minister finance, 1961-63; fed. chancellor Austria, 1964—. Decorated grand cross gold with ribbon Austrian Order Merit, 1964, grand cross silver with ribbon, 1960, grand cross gold with star, 1954, hon. mem. Vienna Philharmonic Orch., Internat. Mozarteum Found. Address: Wien 1 Ballhauspl 2 Austria

KLAUS, LESTER ANTHONY, lawyer; b. St. Louis, Apr. 15, 1936; s. Justin Anthony and Dorothy (Larkin) K.; B.S., U. Mo., 1958; LL.B. cum laude, St. Louis U., 1961; LL.M. summa cum laude, Georgetown U., 1963; M.B.A., Oklahoma City U., 1967; m. Janet Hoef, Sept. 6, 1958; 1 dau., Karen Marie. Admitted to Mo. bar, 1961, Okla. bar, 1966; practice in Washington, 1961-65, Oklahoma City, 1966—; trial atty. FTC, 1961-65; atty. Hines, Klaus & Wilsey, 1966—; asso. prof. law U. Okla. Coll. Law; adj. prof. law Oklahoma City U.; adj. prof. econs. Oklahoma City U. Grad. Sch. Bus., Mass. Inst. Tech. Program. Decorated Order of Woolsack. Mem. Am., Mo., Okla., Fed. bar assns., Oklahoma City C. of C., Alpha Tau Omega, Phi Delta Phi, Delta Sigma Pi. Asst. editor St. Louis U. Law Jour., 1961. Contbr. articles profl. jours. Home: 2513 NW 66th St Oklahoma City OK 73116 Office: 2000 Classen Center Oklahoma City OK

KLAUS, ROBERT ADOLF, printing co. exec.; b. Freiburg, Germany; Feb. 22, 1905; s. Paul and Margaret (Budde) K.; student London (Eng.) Sch. Econs., 1924, N.Y. U., 1931; grad. Am. Mgmt. Assn. 1958; m. Gladys L. Welters, Apr. 20, 1935; children—Robin B., Margaret. Engaged in banking and fgn. exchange, N.Y.C. 1928-31; with Price Waterhouse & Co., C.P.A.'s, N.Y.C., 1931-33; graphic arts survey, Milw., 1933-34; with W.A. Krueger Co., Brookfield, Wis., 1934—, now chmn.; pres. Tyler Printing Co., Phoenix, 1961—. Active local YMCA, Boy Scouts Am. Mem. Am. Mgmt. Assn., Pres.'s Profl. Assn., Milw. C. of C., Book Mfrs. Inst. Club: Milwaukee Athletic. Home: Route 3 39903 Cedar La Oconomowoc WI 53006 Office: 12821 W Blue Mound Rd Brookfield WI 53005*

KLAUSLER, ALFRED PAUL, clergyman, journalist; b. Hankinson, N.D., Feb. 22, 1910; s. Joseph Paul and Amanda (Hunziker) K.; diploma Concordia Coll., St. Paul, 1929, Concordia Sem., St. Louis, 1932; student Columbia, U. Chgo.; M.A., Loyola U., Chgo., 1961; Litt.D., Valparaiso U.; m. Signe Fox, June 28, 1934; children—Peter M., Paula S., Thomas A. Ordained to the ministry Luth. Ch., 1934; pastor Our Savior's Luth. Ch., Glendive, Mont., 1934-42; exec. sec. dept. comnunications Walther League, 1946-66, Asso. Ch. Press, 1961—; religion editor Westinghouse Broadcasting, 1969—; instr. Valparaiso U., 1950- 52, Concordia Tchrs. Coll., River Forest, Ill., 1954; lectr. Wartburg Sem., Kent State U., Concordia Sem.; asst. pastor St. Philip Luth. Ch. Served as chaplain AUS, 1942-46; col. Res.; staff command chaplain, 322d Logis, Command, Fort Lee, 1961-62. Decorated Army Commendation Medal, Oak Leaf Cluster. Mem. Nat. Religious Publicity Council (pres. Chgo. 1958-59), Chgo. Bible Soc. (bd. mgrs. 1961-63), Luth. Human Relations Assn. Am. (dir.), Alpha Lambda Phi, Pi Gamma Mu, Sigma Delta Chi. Clubs: Chicago Headline, Chicago Press (Chicago). Author: (fiction) Midnight Lion, 1957; Growth in Worship, 1957; Christ, and Your Job, 1958; Meditations for Youth, 1959; Censorship and Obscenity, 1966; also mag. articles. Home: 2520 S 60th Ct Chicago IL 60650 Office: 343 N Dearborn St Chicago IL 60604

KLAUSMEYER, ROBERT OSCAR, lawyer; b. Cin., Nov. 17, 1917; s. Oscar A. and Marion (Kuhn) K.; A.B., Cornell U., 1938, LL.B., 1940; m. Ruth Ballard, July 6, 1940; children—Peter B., William C. Admitted to Ohio bar, 1940, since practiced in Cin.; partner firm Frost & Jacobs, 1952—. Served to Lt. USNR, 1942-46. Home: 8950 Hopewell Rd Cincinnati OH 45242 Office: Central Trust Tower Cincinnati OH 45202

KLAUSNER, NEAL WILLIAM, educator; b. Neenah, Wis., May 22, 1907; s. Oscar Karl and Emma (Larson) K.; A.B., Lawrence Coll., Appleton, Wis., 1931; B.D., Colgate-Rochester Divinity Sch., 1934; Ph.D., Yale 1941; student U. Chgo., summer 1936; m. Mary Harriet Ellis, June 10, 1936; children—David Neal, Richard Ellis. Asso. prof. philosophy and psychology U. of Redlands, Cal., 1936-44; acting dean of chapel and asso. prof. philosophy Grinnell (Ia.) Coll., 1944-45, prof. philosophy and chmn. dept. philosophy and religion, 1946, chmn. div. social scis., 1951; vis. prof. philosophy Am. Coll., Paris, spring 1966, Selected as trustee honor prof., Grinnell, 1948. Ford Found. fellow Cambridge and Oxford, 1952- 53; mem. regional com. for selection of Woodrow Wilson fellowships. Mem. Am. Philos. Assn. Am. Assn. U. Profs., Am. Council Learned Socs. (regional asso. 1957), Phi Beta Kappa (mem. com. on qualifications united chpts.). Sigma Phi Epsilon, Blue Key. Author: (with P. G Kuntz) Philosophy: The Study of Alternative Beliefs, 1961. Contbr. articles and revs. to various jours. Home: 913 7th Av Grinnell IA 50112

KLAVAN, ISRAEL, clergyman; b. Zaskevitch, Lithuania, June 9, 1915; s. Joshua and Fannie (Sheifer) K.; came to U.S., 1924, naturalized, 1927; B.A., Yeshiva Coll., 1937; rabbi. Rabbi Isaac Elchanan Theol. Sem., 1940; student Bernard Revel Grad. Sch., Yeshiva U., 1938-40; D.D. (honoris causa), Yeshiva U., 1970; m. Sadie Rabinowitz, Feb. 22, 1942; children—Avram Macy, Judith Rachelle. Ordained rabbi, 1940; rabbi in Fitchburg, Mass., 1940-42, Williamsport, Pa., 1942-46, Mt. Vernon, N.Y., 1946-53; exec. v.p. Rabbinical council Am., 1953—. Recipient Bernard Revel Meml. award Yeshiva Coll. Alumni Assn., 1963; award Fedn. Jewish Philanthropies, 1967. Mem. commn. Jewish chaplaincy Nat. Jewish Welfare Bd. Home: 108 22 64th Rd Forest Hills NY 11375 Office: 220 Park Av S New York City NY 10003

KLAWANS, ARTHUR HERMAN, physician, educator; b. Chgo., Aug. 14, 1902; s. Israel and Fannie Klawans; B.S., U. Chgo., 1924; M.D., Rush Med. Sch., Chgo., 1928; m. Hannah M. Stein, Mar. 14, 1927; children—Dorothy (Mrs. Hubert Rosenblum), Arthur Herman. Mem. faculty U. Ill. Med. Sch., 1941-71, clin. prof. obstetrics and gynecology, 1961-71; clin. prof. obstetrics and gynecology Rush Med. Coll., 1970—; cons. obstetrics and gynecologist Presbyn.-St. Luke's Hosp., Chgo., 1970—. Diplomate Am. Bd. Obstetricians and Gynecologists. Mem. A.M.A., Ill., Chgo. med. socs., Am. Coll. Obstetricians and Gynecologists, Central Assn. Obstetricians and Gynecologists, Chgo. Gynecol. Soc. Home: 777 N Michigan Av Chicago IL 60611 Office: 30 N Michigan Av Chicago IL 60602

KLAY, ANDOR C., fgn. service officer; b. Hungary, June 27, 1912; s. Alexander C. and Eva (Varga) K.; B. Mus., Liszt (Hungary) Conservatory Music, 1931; LL.D., Royal Hungarian U., Budapest, 1935; m. Gerda Herz, Apr. 7, 1947; 1 son, Laurence Dennis. Naturalized 1927. Editor U.S. fgn. lang. dailies, Cleve., 1935-42; polit. sect. chief U.S. Office Censorship, 1942-43; intelligence specialist State Dept., 1945-51, chief Hungary sect., div. research for USSR and Eastern Europe, 1951-56; apptd. U.S. Fgn. Service, 1956, consul, 2d sec. embassy, Belgrade, 1958-59, 1st sec., 1959-61; consul, chief polit. officer, Frankfurt am Main, 1962-67; chief Eastern Affairs div. U.S. Mission Berlin, 1968-70; spl. fgn. service asst. legal div. State Dept., 1970—. Served with OSS, AUS, 1943-45. Mem. Am. Fgn. Service Assn. Author: Daring Diplomacy, 1957; The Visitor Speaks, 1950; also books in Hungarian, articles, essay. Home: 3402 Garfield St N W Washington DC 20007

KLAYF, BERNARD SPENCER, dept. store exec.; b. N.Y.C., Apr. 9, 1921; s. Abraham and Ella (Davis) K.; Ph.B., U. Wis., 1942; m. Betty Louise Buchbinder, Aug. 15, 1945 (dec. Nov. 1950); 1 dau., Barbara Lynn; m. 2d, Aurelia Dixon McIntyre, Nov. 30, 1951; 1 dau., Martha Spencer. With WPB, Washington, 1942-43; with Federated Dept. Stores, Inc., 1946—, v.p. for personnel and operations Shillito div., Cin., 1947-55, v.p., gen. mdse. mgr., 1956-62, exec. v.p. Burdine div., Miami, Fla., 1962-65, v.p. parent co., Cin., 1965-69, sr. v.p., 1970—; dir. Asso. Merchandising Corp., N.Y.C. Bd. dirs. Goodwill Industries, Cin. Community Chest. Served to capt. USAAF, 1943-46. Clubs: Bankers, Whist, Losantiville County (Cin.). Home: 1 Grandin Pl Cincinnati OH 45208 Office: 222 W 7th St Cincinnati OH 45202

KLEBE, GISELHER, composer; b. June 28, 1925; s. Frantz K. and Gertrud (Michaelis) K.; ed. Berlin (Germany) Conservatory; pupil of Boris Blacher for composition; m. Lore Schiller, 1946; children—Sonja, Annette. Prof. Detmold (Germany) Music Acad. Recipient Art prize City Berlin, 1952, Composition prize Internat. Music Conv. on Music of 20th Century, Rome, Italy, 1954, Grand Art prize Northhine-Westphalia, 1959. Composer: Deux Nocturnes pour Grand Orchestre: Römische Elegien; Messe für Blaser; Messe Gebet einer armen Seele; Stabat Mater; 3d Symphony; Die Räuber (opera); Die tödlichen Wünsche (opera); Die Ermordung Casars (opera); Alkmene; Figaro lässt sich scheiden (opera); Jacobowsky und der Oberst (opera); Das Märchen von der schönen Lilie (opera). Address: 168 Guellenstr Kr Detmold West Germany*

KLEBERG, JACK CARL, automotive parts marketing co. exec.; b. Chgo., July 22, 1930; s. Carl W. and Margaret (Johnson) K.; B.S., U.S. Mil. Acad., 1952; student Xavier U., Cin., 1962-63; M.B.A., Wayne State U., 1966; m. Bonnie Seidel, June 14, 1952; children—Bonnie Beth, Wendy, Kathleen, Craig Charles, Jacquelyn Suzanne. Commd. 2d lt. U.S. Army, 1952, advanced through grades to 1st lt., 1956, resigned 1956; with Gen. Motors Corp., 1958-64, Master Consol., Inc., 1964-67; spl. asst. to pres. Dunhill Internat., 1967-68; v.p. marketing Goerlich's, Inc., Toledo, 1968-69, pres., 1969—, also dir. Mem. West Point Grad. Assn. Home: 5300 Bristol Ct Toledo OH 43624 Office: 3539 Glendale Av Toledo OH 43601

KLEBERG, ROBERT JUSTUS, Jr. ranchman; b. Corpus Christi, Tex., Mar, 29, 1896; s. Robert Justus and Alice Gertrudis (King) K.; ed. pub. schs. and U. of Wis.; hon. Dr. Agrl. Sci., Tex. A & M U., 1941; D. Sc., U. Wis., 1967; m. Helen Campbell, Mar. 2, 1926 (dec. 1963); l dau., Helen King (Mrs. Lloyd L. Groves). Engaged in ranching since 1916; pres. King Ranch, Inc.; served as trustee Henrietta King Estate, holding large investment in land and cattle; largely responsible for the devel. of the Santa Gertrudis breed of cattle; pres. John B. Ragland Mercantile Co.; dir. Mo. Pacific R.R., Corpus Christi State Nat. Bank, Asphalt Belt Ry. Co., King Ranch (Australia) Pty. Ltd., King Ranch Pastoral Co., Pty., Ltd. (Australia) King Ranch Argentina, S.A., King Ranch do Brazil, Ranch Adarouch, Morocco, King Ranch Espaa, Spain. Pres. Buck & Doe Run Valley Farms Co., Coatesville, Pa., King Ranch Farm, Lexington, Ky. Mem. Tex. and Southwestern Cattle Raisers Assn. (exec. com.) , N.Y. Racing Assn., Inc. (trustee), Nat. Indsl. Conf. Bd., Com. Econ. Devel., Thoroughbred Club of Am., Sigma Chi. Clubs: Country; Turf and Field, Jockey, River, Racquet and Tennis (N.Y.C.). Home: King Ranch Kingsville TX 78363

KLECKNER, ALBERT LOUIS, educator; b. Allentown, Pa., Oct. 23, 1909; s. Claude Robert and Lottie (Clymer) K.; Ph.D., D.V.M., B.S., Franklin and Marshall Coll., 1931; M.S. (George B. Wood fellow bacteriology 1931-32), 1932, Ph.D. (T.A. Scott research fellow 1932-35), 1935; D.V.M., U. Ga., 1953; m. Emily Jane Snyder, Nov. 13, 1943; children—Richard Louis, Barbara Jane. Instr. bacteriology U. Pa., 1932-35, research asso. Sch. Animal Pathology, 1938- 42; instr. bacteriology U. Kan., 1936-37; research bacteriologist Pitman-Moore Co., Indpls., 1943-47, tech. adviser vet., 1947-49; prof., head dept. microbiology and preventive medicine, Sch. Vet. Medicine, U. Ga., 1949-66, dir. of veterinary research, 1951-64, asso. dir. inst. of comparative medicine, 1965-67, dir., 1967-68, asso. dean, 1967-68; asst. v.p. for instrn. U. Ga., 1969—. Diplomate Am. Bd. Microbiology, Am. Bd. Vet. Spltys. (exec. com. 1969—); charter diplomate Am. Coll. Vet Microbiologists (chmn. bd. govs. 1964-69). Fellow Am. Acad. Microbiology; mem. Am. Vet. Med. Assn. (sect. officer 1961 and 1962, rep. on Am. Bd. Microbiology 1964-70), Am. Assn. Avian Pathologists (dir. 1961-66), S.E. Soc. Am. Bacteriologists (pres. 1951-53, counsellor 1953-54), Animal Disease Research Workers So. States (dir. 1953-55, pres. 1961-62), Am. Soc. Microbiology, Conf. Research Workers in Animal Diseases in North Am. (mem. bd. of dirs. 1968—), Sigma Xi, Phi Kappa Tau, Omega Tau Sigma, Phi Kappa Phi, Phi Zeta, Gamma Sigma Delta. Presbyn. Club: Athens City. Asso editor Jour. Avian Diseases, 1960-68. Home: 315 W Lake Dr Athens GA 30601

KLECKNER, DONALD CHARLES, coll. pres.; b. Clyde, O., Feb. 13, 1920; s. Max LeRoy and Esther Olivia (Wright) K.; A.B., Heidelberg Coll., 1942; M.A., U. Mich. 1947, Ph.D., 1953; postdoctoral certificate, U. Birmingham (Eng.), 1954; m. Mary Elizabeth Coons, Feb. 4, 1945; children—Celeste, Charlotte, Dan Charles. Teaching fellow, coach debate U. Mich., 1946-48; chmn. dept. speech Heidelberg Coll., 1948-51; dir. forensics Bowling Green State U., 1952- 55, chmn. dept. speech, 1955-62, mng. dir. Huron Summer Playhouse, 1956, exec. head, 1955-62; dean Elmhurst (Ill.) Coll., 1962- 65, pres., 1965-71; pres. Chapman Coll., 1971—; profl. dramatic reader, pub. speaker. Served to lt. USNR, 1942-45. Recipient incentive grant for outstanding teaching Heidelberg Coll., 1950; named faculty man of year Omicron Delta Kappa, 1956. Mem. Ohio Assn. Coll. Tchrs. Speech (pres. 1954-55), Ohio Community Theatre Assn. (pres. 1955-57, dir. 1955-61), Assn. Higher Edn., Phi Eta Sigma, Omicron Delta Kappa, Alpha Tau Omega, Pi Kappa Delta, Kappa Delta Pi, Alpha Psi Omega. Rotarian. Home: 9602 James Circle Villa Park CA 92667

KLEE, VICTOR LA RUE, Jr., mathematician, educator; b. San Francisco, Sept. 18, 1925; s. Victor La Rue and Mildred (Muller) K.; B.A., Pomona Coll., 1945, D.Sc., 1965; Ph.D., U. Va., 1949; m. Elizabeth Bliss, June 10, 1945; children—Wendy Pamela (Mrs. Paul James Wehrenberg), Barbara Christine, Susan Lisette, Heidi Elizabeth. Asst. prof. U. Va., 1949-53; NRC fellow Inst. for Advanced Study, 1951-52; asst. prof. U. Wash., Seattle, 1953-54, asso. prof., 1954-57, prof. math., 1957—; vis. asso. prof. U. Cal. at Los Angeles, 1955-56; NSF sr. postdoctoral fellow, Sloan Found. fellow U. Copenhagen, 1958-60; cons. to industry. Mem. Am. Math. Soc. (asso. sec. 1955-58, mem. exec. com. 1969-70), Math. Assn. Am. (pres. 1971—), Soc. for Indsl. and Applied Math., Assn. Computing Machinery, Operations Research Soc. Am., Inst. Mgmt. Sci., Nat. Council Tchrs. Math., A.A.A.S., Phi Beta Kappa, Sigma Xi (nat. lectr. 1969). Contbr. articles profl. jours. Home: 13706 39th Av NE Seattle WA 98125

KLEENE, STEPHEN COLE, educator, mathematician; b. Hartford, Conn., Jan. 5, 1909; s. Gustav Adolph and Alice Lena (Cole) K.; A.B., Summa cum laude, Amherst Coll., 1930, Sc.D. (hon.), 1970, Ph.D., Princeton, 1934; m. Nancy Elliott, Sept. 21, 1942 (dec. Jan. 1970); children—Paul Elliott, Kenneth Cole, Bruce Metcalf, Pamela Lee. Teaching and research math. Princeton, 1930-35; mem. Inst. Advanced Study, 1939-40, 65-66; vis. prof. Princeton, 1956-57; asso. prof. Amherst Coll., 1941-42; instr. math. U. Wis., 1935-37, asst. prof., 1937-41, asso. prof., 1946- 48, prof., 1948-64, Cyrus C. MacDuffee prof. of math., 1964—, chmn. of dept., 1957-58, 60-62, chmn. dept. numerical analysis, 1962-63, acting dir. of Math. Research Center U. S. Army, 1966 -67, dean Coll. Letters and Sci., 1969—. Mem. div. math. NRC, 1956-58, chmn. designate div. math. sci., 1969-71; pres. Internat. Union History and Philosophy Sci., 1961. Guggenheim fellow U. Amsterdam, 195O; NSF grantee U. Marburg, 1958-59. Served from lt. (j.g.) to lt. comdr., NSNR, 1942- 46. Fellow A.A.A.S.; mem. Audubon Soc., Nature Conservancy, Am. Math. Soc., Math. Assn. Am., Assn. Symbolic Logic (mem. exec. com. 1939-41, v.p. 1942, 47-49, pres. 1956-58), Nat. Acad. Sci., Phi Beta Kappa, Sigma Xi (pres. Wis. chpt. 1951-52). Club: Sierra. Democrat. Author: Introduction to Metamathematics, 1952; (with Richard E. Vesley) The Foundations of Intuitionistic Mathematics, 1965; Mathematical Logic, 1967. Cons. editor Jour. Symbolic Logic, 1936- 42, 46-49, editor, 1950-62. Author articles on math. logic and founds. Home: 1514 Wood La Madison WI 53705

KLEFFNER, FRANK ROY, educator; b. Twin Falls, Ida., Oct. 22, 1925; s. Frank G. and Dorothy (Roy) K.; student Ida. State Coll., 1946-48; B.S., U. Wis., 1949, M.S., 1951, Ph.D., 1952; m. Charlotte Peterson, Aug. 2, 1948; children-Gregory William, Douglas Charles, Kristine Ann. Mem. faculty Washington U., St. Louis, 1952—, prof. speech pathology, 1960—; dir. div. speech pathology Central Inst. for Deaf, 1960—; cons., lectr. in field. Pres. Citizens Com. for Univ. City Schs., 1968, Better Edn. Through Sensible Taxation, 1969. Served with AUS, 1944-46. Decorated Bronze Star. Fellow, Am. S Hearing Assn. (pres. 1970); mem. Mo. Speech and Hearing Assn., Speech and Hearing Assn. Greater St. Louis (Pres. 1956), Alexander G. Bell Assn. for Deaf, Author numerous articles in field. Home: 818 S Euclid St St Louis MO 63110

KLEHR, HAROLD, coll. dean; b. Chgo., June 8, 1921; s. Samuel and Bessie (Brenes) K.; B.S., Northwestern U., 1946, M.S. (USPHS fellow), 1948, Ph.D., 1950; m. Helen Cohen, Aug. 6, 1944; 1 dau., Katherine Bess. Head, psychology sect. Great Lakes (Ill.) Naval Hosp., 1950-53; asst. chief psychologist West Side VA Hosp., Chgo., 1953-57; asst. dir., asso. prof. psychology student counseling service U. Ill., Chgo., 1957-64, dir. student counseling, 1964—, prof. psychology, 1966—, asso. dean student affairs, 1970—. Served with USNR, 1942. Mem. Am., Ill. psychol. assns., Ill. Group Psychotherapy Soc., Am. Personnel and Guidance Assn., Am. Assn. U. Profs., Chgo. Psychol. Club, Sigma Xi. Home: 4435 Kirk St Skokie IL 60076

KLEILER, FRANK MUNRO, govt. ofcl.; b. Green Bay, Wis., Apr. 17, 1914; s. Frank Andrew and Addie (Munro) K.; A.B., Antioch Coll., Yellow Springs, O., 1938; student Am. U., Washington, 1937-38; m. Frances Pauline Brezon, Apr. 10, 1939; children—David Allen, James Robert. Reporter, The Evening Star, Washington, 1935-36, The Boston Herald, 1936-37; clk. to bd. mem. Nat. Mediation Bd., 1937-39; asst. to bd. mem. NLRB, 1939- 41, field examiner, Cleve., 1941-42, Indpls., 1942-43, Chgo., 1943-44, regional dir., Pitts., 1944-47, exec. sec. Washington, 1947-5l; disputes dir. W.S.B., 1951-52, pub. mem. review and appeals com. 1952-53; exec. sec. NLRB 1953-6O; dep. commr. Bur. Labor- Mgmt. Reports, Dept. Labor, 1960-62, dir. Office Welfare and Pension Plans, 1962-63, dir. Office Labor-Mgmt. and Welfare Pension Reports, 1963-70, dep. asst. sec. for planning and evaluation, 1970—. Mem. Acad. Polit. Sci., Indsl. Relations Research Assn. Home: 9100 Warren St Silver Spring MD 20910 Office: US Dept Labor Washington DC 20210

KLEIMAN, JOSEPH, materials co. exec.; b. Grand Rapids, Mich., Oct. 1, 1919; s. Jacob and Bessie (Targowitch) K.; B.S. in Engring., U. Mich., 1941, M.S., 1942; m. Shirley Ruth Present. Aug. 30, 1942; children—Richard Neil, Robert, William, Engr., Reeves Instrument Corp., N.Y.C., 1946-51; v.p., gen. mgr. Belock Instrument Corp., College Point, N.Y., 1951-58; v.p., gen. mgr. Whittaker Gyro Div. Telecomputing Corp., Los Angeles,1958-59, exec. v.p. corp., 1959-64; v.p. corporate devel. Whittaker Corp., 1964-67, sr. v.p., 1967—, also dir.; mem. dir. Space Scis., Inc., Crown Aluminum Industries, Inc., Aaron Ferer & Sons, Yardney Electric Corp., Terrax Inc., Tasker Industries, Whittaker Leasing Corp. Bd. dirs. Israel Inst. Tech.; trustee Union Am. Hebrew Congregations. Mem. Am. Soc. for Technion (dir.), Nat., Cal. socs. profl. engrs., Sigma Xi, Phi Lambda Upsilon, Iota Alpha. Jewish religion. Home: 11240 Chalon Rd Los Angeles CA 90049 Office: 9229 Sunset Blvd Los Angeles CA 90069

KLEIN, ADOLPH F., banker; b. Detroit, 1900. Chmn. bd. Wayne Oakland Bank, Royal Oak, Mich. Home: 4128 Amherst Rd Royal Oak MI 48072 Office: 400 S Main St PO Box 231 Royal Oak MI 48068

KLEIN, ARTHUR LUCE, theatrical co. exec.; b. Carbondale, Pa., Mar. 31, 1916; s. Joseph and Jennie (Kallish) K.; B.A., U. Mich., 1939, M.A., 1940, Ph.D., 1948; postgrad. Sorbonne, Paris, 1947; m. Luce Weill-Kinsbourg, Oct. 8, 1946; children—Judith, Florence, Joel, Rosine. Asst. prof. dept. dramatic art U. Cal. at Berkeley, 1948-50; producer Royal Acad. Dramatic Art, London, Eng., 1950-52; dir. Our Town, Bruno and Sidney at Watergate, Phoenix Theatres, London, 1952; tour Glass Menagerie, on Continent and throughout Scandinavia, 1953, Skits & Sketches, in Europe, 1954-55; founder Spoken Arts, Inc., New Rochelle, N.Y., 1956, pres., 1956—; lectr. Am. theatre for Dept. State in Europe, 1954. Bd. dirs. Boys Clubs of New Rochelle. Served as capt., Signal Corps, AUS, 1942-45; ETO. Democrat. Jewish religion. Co- translator: Anouih's Medea, 1949; The Rendezvous at Senlis, 1949, Cecile or School for Fathers; translator Puss in Boots, 1970. Home: 95 Valley Rd New Rochelle NY 10801 Office: Spoken Arts Bldg 310 North Av New Rochelle NY 10801

KLEIN, CHARLES, judge, b. Atlantic City, Sept. 16, 1900; s. Samuel and Esther (Grun) K.; LL.B., Temple U., 1921, LL.D. 1949: postgrad. Villanova U. Extension Sch., 1922; LL.D., Franklin and Marshall Coll., 1959, U. Pa., 1967, La Salle Coll., 1968; L.H.D., Dickinson Coll., 1960; J.D., St. Joseph's Coll., 1961; D.C.L., Bucknell U., 1963; m. Rosalie S. Benson, June 3O, 1933; 1 son, Richard Benson. Admitted to Pa. bar. 1921, since practiced in Phila.; spl. counsel Pa. Dept. Banking, 1927-31; spl. dep. atty. gen., 1931-34; judge Orphans Ct., Phila., 1934-52, pres. judge, 1952—; North lectr. Franklin and Marshall Coll., 1940; acting dean Temple U. Sch. Law, 1941-42. Served as Gov.'s counsel Pub. Service Commn. Investigation, counsel Joint Legislative Com. investigating milk industry in Pa.; spl. asst. OPA; spl. adviser Republic of Cuba. Past pres. Jewish Hosp., Am. Jewish Com., Jewish Family Welfare Council; past v.p. Albert Einstein Med. Center; former dir. many philanthropic and civic orgns.; bd. trustees Conwell Sch. Theology; trustee, hon. chancellor Temple U. Recipient U. Distinguished Alumni award, Robert L. Johnson award, Lucien Moss Home award, Clair Post Am. Legion Honor award, B'nai B'rith Mid-City Lodge Civic Award; law library Temple U. named in his honor. Clubs: Caveat, Socialegal, Midday (Phila.). Home: 6408 Overbrook Av Philadelphia PA 19154 Office: City Hall Philadelphia PA 19107

KLEIN, CHARLES CONRAD, lawyer; b. Ironton, O., Oct. 21, 1917; s. John Alfred and Rose Gertrude (Callahan) K.; B.A., George Washington U., 1942; J.D., U. Cin., 1949; m. Ruth Wiehoff, June 7, 1947; children-Dennis, Roger, Thomas. Admitted to Ohio bar, 1949, also U.S. Supreme Ct.; with treaty division State Dept., 1939-43; regional claims atty. mut. of Omaha, 1951-55; practiced in Ironton, O mem. firm Edwards, Klien, Compton & Allen, 1955—. Mem. Lawrence County Family Counseling Service, 1955—; committeeman Boy Scouts Am., 1960. Mem. exec. com. Lawrence County Republican Party, 1956- -. Served with AUS, 1943-46; PTO. Decorated Bronze Star medal. Mem. Am., Ohio, Lawrence County bar assns., Internat. Assn. Ins. Counsel, Am, Coll. Probate Counsel, Elk, Kiwanian (pres. 1960). Home: 520 Center St Ironton OH 45638 Office: First Nat Bank Bldg Ironton OH 45638

KLEIN, DAVID, fgn. service officer; b. N.Y.C., Sept. 2, 1919; s. Sam and Fannie H. (Falk) K.; B.A., Bklyn. Coll., 1939; M.B.A., Harvard, 1947; M.A., Columbia, 1952; postgrad. U. Md., 1964-66; grad. Nat. War Coll., 1966; m. Anne L. Cochran, Mar. 14, 1953; children—Peter S., Steven C., John W., Barbara J., Richard L., Suzanne G. Fgn. service officer, 1947—; vice consul, Lourenco Marques, 1947-49; 3d sec., econ. officer, Rangoon, Burma, 1949-51; Russian lang. and area studies Dept. State, 1951-52; 2d sec., consular/econ. officer, Moscow, 1952-54; Regensburg-Soviet studies, 1954-55; polit./econ. officer, Berlin, 1955-57; 1st sec., polit. officer, Bonn, Germany, 1957-60; Soviet desk Dept. State, 1960-62; sr. mem. for European affairs staff Nat. Security Council, 1962-65; counselor econ. affairs, Moscow, 1966-67, counselor polit. affairs, 1967-68; polit. advisor, Berlin, 1968-71; U.S. minister to Berlin, 1971—; instr. govt. and politics U. Md., 1969-71. Served as maj. AUS, 1941-46. Decorated Legion of Merit; recipient superior service award Dept. State, 1964. Mem. Harvard Bus. Club (v.p. Washington 1965-66), Am. Fgn. Service Assn. Unitarian. Clubs: Rotary, Blau/Weiss (Berlin). Author: The Basmachi, a Study in Soviet Nationalities, 1952. Home: 14728 Magnolia Blvd Sherman Oaks CA Office: USBER APO New York City NY 09742

KLEIN, EDMUND, shoe co. exec.; b. Stryi, Poland, Nov. 15 1919; s. Morris and Annie K.; B.B.A., Coll. City N.Y., 1943; m. Norma Shapiro, Nov. 6, 1948; children—Michael, Alan, Nancy. Asst. controller, asst. treas. A. S. Beck Shoe Corp., N.Y.C., 1945-60; with Shoe Corp. Am., Columbus, O., 1960—, now v.p. finance, treas., dir. Served with AUS, 1943-45; ETO. Mem. N.Y. State Soc. C.P.A.'s. Financial Execs. Inst. Home: 1597 Peace Pl Columbus OH 43209 Office: 35 N 4th st Columbus OH 43215

KLEIN, EDWARD ELKAN, clergyman; b. Newark, May 25, 1913; s. Benjamin and Elsa (Elkan) K.; B.A. magna cum laude, N.Y.U., 1934; M.H.L., Rabbi, Hebrew Union Coll.-Jewish Inst. Religion, 1940, D.D., 1965; m. Ruth Anne Strauss, Sept. ll, 1940; children—Barbara Anne (Mrs. Peter Hillman), Stephen Alan. Rabbi, 1940; asst. rabbi Stephen Wise Free Synagogue, N.Y.C., 1940-42, rabbi, 1943—; dir. Hillel Found., U. Cal. at Berkeley, 1942-43. Vis. lectr. homiletics Hebrew Union Coll.-Jewish Inst. Relgion, N.Y.C., 1966—. Co-chmn. League of West Side Orgns., 1952—; mem. N.Y.C. Mayor's Appeal Bd. for Fair Housing Practices. 1958-62, N.Y.C. Mayor's Adv. Com. on Higher Edn., 1966-68; mem. nat. adv. com. Religious Action Center, Washington, chmn. clergy adv. com. Planned Parenthood Assn. Manhattan and Bronx; mem. social action commn. Union Am. Hebrew Congregations, 1960—; past chmn. ch. and state com. Central Conf. Am. Rabbis; chmn. bd. Lincoln Sq. Community Council. Bd. dirs. Am. Found. on Nonviolence. Fellow Nat. Council on Religion in Higher Edn.; mem. Phi Beta Kappa. Home: 240 W 98th St New York City NY 10025 Office: 30 W 68th st New York City NY 10023

KLEIN, ERNEST LEOPOLD, pub. relations counsel; b. chgo., Dec. 29, 1898; s. Leopold and Regina (Schick) K.; studied European coll. and univs.; m. Elsie Offenberg, Jan. 6, 1920 (dec. Dec. 1928); 1 dau., Juliet Florence (Mrs. Stanley Garver); m. 2d, Emmy Holstein, May 23, 193O; l dau., Regina Lene (Mrs. Leo Charvat). Former pub. Chgo. newspapers, Nat. and internat. weeklies; nat. adv. bd. WPA; 1934- 36; resigned to resume pvt. bus.; pres. Planet Products Corp. Mem. U.S. Reparations Mission, and spl. asst. to Ambassador Edwin W. Pauley, 1946; personal rep. U.S. Pres. for reparations. Pres., chmn. bd. Leopold and Regina Klein Found.; bd. govs. Menninger Found.; exec. com. Nat. Jewish Hosp., Denver, Brandeis U. Mem. Am. Legion, Jewish War Vets. U.S. (hon.). Jewish. Mason; mem. B'nai B'rith. Clubs: National Press, National Republican (Washington); Town, City (Chgo.). Author: How to Stay Rich, 195O; What of the Night, 1951; Our Appointment with Destiny (trilogy), 1952. Address: 1000 Lake Shore Dr Chicago IL 60611

KLEIN, EUGENE VICTOR, television exec.; b. N.Y.C., Jan. 29, 1921; s. Benjamin and Sadie (Olsen) K.; student RCA Insts., Inc., 1939-41; m. Frances L. Fisher, June 20, 1943; children—Randee, Mike. Automobile Dealer in Cal., 1946—, automobile distbr., 1955—; pres., dir. Nat. Theatres & Television, Inc. (now Nat. Gen. Corp.) Beverly Hills, Cal., 1961-69, chmn. bd., until 1969, chmn. bd., chief exec. officer, 1969—; chmn. bd. Columbia Savs. & Loan; dir. Dymo Industries, Inc. Trustee, City of Hope, Montclair Coll. Prep. Sch. Served to capt. USAAF, 1941-46. Clubs: Friars (Beverly Hills). Home: 410 Trousdale Pl Beverly Hills CA 90210 Office: 9570 Wilshire Blvd Beverly Hills CA 90212

KLEIN, HAROLD PETER, banker; b. Templeton, Ia., Oct. 29, 1905; s. William E. and Rose Mary (Schwaller) K.; B.S.C., U. Notre Dame, 1926; m. Winifred L. Coakley, Oct. 12, 1931; children—Jo-Ann, Robert J., William E., Katherine E. Dir., ret. officer Ia.- Des Moines Nat. Bank. Chmn., Des Moines Urban Renewal Bd., 1969—; mem. bd. Mercy Hosp., 1947—, pres., 1957-58; mem. bd. edn. St. Joseph Acad., 1964—. Trustee Clarke Coll., Dubuque, Ia.; bd. dirs. Greater Des Moines Community Found. Named Des Moines Man of Year, Notre Dame Club, 1960; recipient award Ia.-Quad Cities region Nat. Conf. Christians and Jews, 1967. Mem. Des Moines C. of C. (dir., pres. 1945). Roman Catholic. Clubs: Des Moines, Wakonda (Des Moines). Home: 3100 Grand Av Des Moines IA 50312

KLEIN, HARRIS J., lawyer, truck co. exec.; b. N.Y.C., June 18, 1906; LL.B., St. Lawrence U. 1927; m. 2d, Cecilia Klein, April 2, 1945; children—Joan (Mrs. Norman Taucher), Barbara (Mrs. Melvin Goldfeder), Carol (Mrs. Thomas Hall), Mitchell P. Chmn. bd., pres. N.Y. Equities, Inc.; pres., dir. Carmic Transp. Co. Inc.; dir., gen. counsel I.O.A. Data Corp.; pres. Interstate Motor Carriers Agy. Inc., Allen Bruce & Mitchell, Inc. Mem. N.Y.C. Transit Authority, 1953-55; pres. N.Y. Civic League. Chmn. finance com. N.Y. State Democratic Com., 1950-55; del. Dem. Nat. Conv., 1954; Mem. N.Y. State Constl. Conv., 1967. Mem. N. Y. State Bar Assn., Bar Assn. City N.Y., Motor Carriers Counsel U.S. (past pres.). Home: 215 Beaumont St Brooklyn NY 11235 Office: 280 Broadway New York City NY 10007

KLEIN, HERBERT GEORGE, govt. ofcl.; b. Los Angeles, Apr. 1, 1918; s. George and Amy (Cordes) K.; A.B., U. So. Cal., 1940; m. Marjorie G. Galbraith, Nov. 1, 1941; children—Joanne L. (Mrs. Robert Mayne), Patricia A. (Mrs. H. Thomas Howell). Reporter, Alhambra (Cal.) Post-Advocate, 1940-42, news editor, 1946-50; spl. corr. Copley Newspapers, 1946-50, Wash. corr., 1950; with San Diego Union, 1950-68, editorial writer, 1950-52, editorial page editor, 1952-56, asso. editor, 1956-57, exec. editor, 1957-58, editor, 1959- 68; mgr. communications Nixon for Pres. Campaign, 1968-69; dir. communications Exec. Br., U.S. Govt., 1969—. Mem. Commn. of Californias. Bd. dirs. San Diego chpt. A.R.C. Publicity dir. Eisenhower-Nixon campaign in Cal., 1952; asst. press sec. Vice Pres. Nixon Campaign, 1956; press sec. Nixon inqugural, 1957, Nixon campaign, 1958; spl. asst., press sec. to Nixon, 1959-61; press sec. Nixon Gov. Canpaign, 1962; dir. communications Nixon presdl. campaign 1968. Served with USNR, 1942-46; comdr. Res. Mem. La Jolla (Cal.) Lamplighters, Am. Soc. Newspaper Editors, Am. Legion, Cal. (Am. del. internat. conv., Manila, P.I. 1950), Alhambra (past pres.) jr. chambers commerce, San Diego Conv. and Visitors Bur. (bd. dirs.), San Diego-Yokohama Friendship Soc. (bd. dirs.), Sigma Delta Chi (nat. com. chmn., gen. activities chmn. nat. conv., 1958), Delta Chi. Presbyn. (elder; bd. Nat. Presbyn. Center). Kiwanian (hon.), Rotarian (hon.). Home: 4917 Crescent St Chevy Chase MD 20015 Office: 1600 Pennsylvania Av Washington DC 20002

KLEIN, ISAAC, rabbi; b. Hungary, Sept. 5, 1905; s. Samuel and Ilka (Hershkowitz) K.; came to U.S., 1921, naturalized, 1923; B.A., Coll. City N.Y., 1931; M.S., U. Mass., 1937; Ph.D., Harvard, 1948; student Yeshivah, 1921-26; M.H.L., Rabbi, Jewish Theol. Sem., 1934. Hattarat Horäah, 1937, D.D., 1960; m. Henriette Levine, June 26, 1932; children—Hannah (Mrs. Paul Katz), Miriam (Mrs. Saul Shapiro), Ruth (Mrs. Gerald Berkowitz). Ordained rabbi, 1934; rabbi Kodimoh Congregation, Springfield, 1934-53; rep. staff Synagogue Council Am. on staff High Commr. of Germany, 1949-50; rabbi Temple Shaarey Zedek, Buffalo, 1953-69, sr. rabbi, 1969—. Lectr. culture and thought of Middle East and Medieval Jewish Philosophy, U. Buffalo; vis. asso. prof. Jewish life and practice Jewish Theol. Sem. Am.; chaplain on 1st boat load Hungarian refugees, 1956. Pres. Rabbinical Assembly of Am., 1958- 60, chmn. Kashruth com., 1960—. Served as chaplain AUS, 1942-45. Author: The Ten Commandments in a Changing World, 1944; also translations, intro. and commentary Book XII of Code of Maimonides. 1951; also articles on Jewish law and on med. ethics in learned jours. Home: 40 Hardt Lane Buffalo NY 14226 Office: Temple Sharrey Zedek Getzville and Hartford Rds Buffalo NY 14226

KLEIN, JOSEPH, mus. dir.; b. Sharon, Mass., July 16, 1936; grad. Columbia; pvt. studies, Tanglewood, Mass.; pupil of Nadia Boulanger, Paris, France; married; 2 sons. Formerly chmn. music dept. Horace Mann Sch., N.Y.C.; condr. 1st N.Y. revival of Kismet, then road of Flower Drum Song and nat. co. of The Boys From Syracuse; formerly arranger- pianist for CBS radio and television; mus. coach for Crosby family for Hollywood Palace Television Show, and mus. dir. Seagram Liquor Indsl., Miami, Fla.; active in star-system theatres including Ben Kapen's Melodyland, Hyatt Music Theatre, Circle Star Theatre, Carousel Theatre, also Los Angeles Civic Light Opera; now mus. dir. nat. co. The Man of La Mancha. Mem. Am. Fedn. Musicans, Actors Equity, Soc. Stage Dirs. and Choreographers. Address: care Actors Equity Assn 165 W 46th St New York City NY 10036*

KLEIN, JOSEPH J., bus. exec.; b. 1916; chem. engring, degrees, Northwestern U., 1937; LL.B., Duke, 1940; married Vice pres., sec. Chgo. Pump Co., 1940-45; pres. Fiberbond Co., 1952-62; v.p. Union Carbide Corp., also v.p., gen. mgr. fibers and fabrics div. 1962-67; exec. v.p. MSL Industries, Inc., 1967-70; chmn. bd. U.S. Lighting Systems, Inc., 1970—. Office: 8600 Melrose St Los Angeles CA 90069

KLEIN, JULIUS, army officer, journalist, pub. relations counsel, vets. leader; b. Chgo., Sept. 5, 1901; s. Leopold and Regina (Schick) K.; ed. Sophien Coll., Berlin, Germany, 1919; Grad. Sch. Mil. Govt., U. Va.; m. Helen Holstein, May 11, 1928. War Corr., World War I; editor, Hearst Newspapers, 1926-33; exec. R.K.O., Universal Pictures, Hollywood, Cal., 1934-39; nat. comdr. Jewish War Vets. of U.S.A., 1947-48, chmn. exec. com., 1952. Chmn. Julius Klein Pub. Relations, Inc., 1947—. Hon. dir. Hebrew Theol. Coll., Chgo. Served as field clk., U.S. Mil. Commn., U.S. Army, 1918-19; joined Ill. N.G., 1933, head, investigation of subversive activities in middle west, 1933-34, lt. col., 1941; active service, 33rd div., Ill. N.G., 1941; comd. 23d q.m. truck regt., 1943, service in South Pacific, Philippines; in charge of 10,000 troops in active theater of South Pacific and Phillippine Islands, 1943; advanced to col., 1944, spl. asst. to sec. of war, 1946, separated from service, 1946; continued assn. with Ill. N.G. as comdg. officer, 623d q.m. group and attached service troops; brig. gen., 109th anti-aircraft arty. brig., 1948-51, nominated brig. gen. of line (N.G. U.S.), 1949, confirmed 1950; maj. gen. U.S. Army Res.; transferred U.S. Army Res., ret. maj. gen. Ill. N.G.; made fact finding mission to Europe for Armed Services sub-com. U.S. Senate Appropriations Com., 1954; nat. def. cons. to U.S. Senate; mem. Ill. armory bd., 1954; Republican candidate for U.S. senate, 1954. Nat. pres. Nat. Shrine to Jewish War Dead, until 1970. Decorated Soldier's Medal for Heroism, Citation for Heroism, Philippine Distinguished Service Star, Legion of Merit (2 clusters), Bronze star, ribbon of French Legion of Honor, Nat. Comdrs. Citation Catholic War Vets U.S.; 1950 award Am. Jewish Lt. Found. Mem. Chgo. Council Fgn. Relations, Pub. Relations Soc. Am., N.A.M. (internat. econ. affairs com.), Am. Ordanance Assn., Assn. U.S. Army, Am. Legion, D.A.V., Amvets, Jewish War Vets., Fgn. Policy Assn. (nat. council). Republican (del. nat. conv. 1940, 48, 56, 60). Mason; mem. B'nai B'rith. Clubs: Overseas Pres, Army and Navy, National Press. Author: Windy City, Black Cargo, General Delivery, American Spy. Home: 1040 Lake Shore Dr Chicago IL 60611 Office: 1 E Wacker Dr Chicago IL 60601

KLEIN, LAWRENCE ROBERT, economist, educator; b. Omaha, Sept. 14, 1920; s. Leo Byron and Blanch (Monheit) K.; B.A., U. Cal. at Berkeley, 1942; Ph.D., Mass. Inst. Tech., 1944; M.A., Lincoln Coll., Oxford U., 1957; m. Sonia Adelson, Feb. 15, 1947; children—Hannah, Rebecca, Rachel, Jonathan. Faculty, U. Chgo., 1944-47; research asso. Nat. Bur. Econ. Research, 1948-50; faculty U. Mich., 1949-54; research asso. Survey Research Center, 1949-54, Oxford Inst. Statistics, 1954-58; faculty U. Pa., Phila., 1958—, prof., 1958—, Univ. prof., 1964—, Benjamin Franklin prof., 1968—. Vis. prof. Osaka U., 1960, U. Colo., 1962, City U. N.Y., 1962-63, Hebrew U., 1964, Princeton, 1966, Stanford U., summer 1968; Ford vis. prof. U. Cal. at Berkeley, 1968, Inst. for Advanced Studies, Vienna, 1970 ; cons. UNCTAD, 1966, 67, McMilan Co., E. I. du Pont de Nemours, 1966-68, State of N. Y., 1969, Am. Tel. & Tel. Co., 1969; chmn. bd. trustees Wharton Econometric Forecasting Assos., Inc., 1969—; trustee Maurice Falk Inst. for Econ. Research, Israel, 1969—; mem. Com. on Prices Fed. Res. Bd.; prin. investigator econometric model project Brookings Instn., 1963—; sr. adviser Brookings Panel on Econ. Activity, 1970—. cons. Canadian Govt., 1947. Fellow Econometric Soc. (past pres.), Am. Acad. Arts and Scis.; mem. Am. Philos. Soc., Social Sci. Research Council (fellow 1945-46, 47-48, com. econ. stability, dir. 1971), Am. Econ. Assn. (John Bates Clark medalist 1959, exec. com. 1966-68), Am. Assn. U. Profs. Author: The Keynesian Revolution, 1947; Textbook of Econometrics, 1953; An Econometric Model of the United States, 1929-1952, 1955; Wharton Econometric Forecasting Model, 1967; Essay on the Theory of Economic Prediction, 1968. Author-editor: Brookings Quar. Econometric Model of U.S. Editor: Internat. Econ. Rev., 1959-65, asso. editor, 1965—. Home: 1317 Medford Rd Wynnewood PA 19096 Office: U Pa Philadelphia PA 19104

KLEIN, LOUIS, former chem. co. exec.; b. Brockton, Mass., Mar. 24, 1907; s. Morris and Clara (Goldin) K.; A.B., Harvard, 1927; m. Josephine Seibert, Aug. 6, 1948; children—Lois, Jeffrey. Research asst. Harvard Engring. Sch., 1927-28; with Rohm and Haas Co. and related firm Resinous Products and Chem. Co. (exec. v.p. and dir., 1943-49), Phila., 1928—, v.p., vice chmn. exec. com. and dir. Rohm and Haas Co., 1949-70, now dir. Mem. Am. Chem. Soc., Am. Inst. Chem. Engrs., A.A.A.S. Home: 968 Idlewild Rd Gladwyne PA 19035

KLEIN, MARCUS, educator; b. Cleve., Apr. 19, 1928; s. Nelson and Lena (Miller) K.; B.A., Western Reserve U., 1950; M.A., Columbia U., 1952, Ph.D., 1962; m. Marian Weitzman, Nov. 20, 1960; children—Jennifer, Eric. Mem. faculty Barnard Coll., N.Y.C., 1952-65, instr. English, 1957-62, asst. prof., 1962-65; asso. prof. State U. N. Y. at Buffalo, 1965-68, prof., chmn. dept. English, 1968—; vis. prof. U. Toulouse (France), 1966-67. Served to sgt. AUS, 1946-47. Mem. Modern Language Assn., Phi Beta Kappa. Author: After Alienation: American Novels in Mid-Century, 1964, 65; (with Robert Pack), Innocence and Experience, 1966, Short Stories: Classic Modern, Contemporary, 1967; The American Novel since World War II, 1969. Home: 130 Jewett Pkwy Buffalo NY 14214

KLEIN, MARTIN JESSE, physicist, educator; b. N.Y.C., June 25, 1924; s. Adolph and Mary (Neuman) K.; A.B., Columbia, 1942, M.A., 1944; Ph.D., Mass. Inst. Tech., 1948; m. Miriam June Levin, Oct. 28, 1945; children—Rona F. (Mrs. Andrew Glass), Sarah M., Nancy R. With OSRD for USN, 1944-45; research asso. physics Mass. Inst. Tech., 1946-49; instr. dept. physics Case Inst. Tech., 1949-51, asst. prof., 1951-55, asso. prof., 1955-60, prof., 1960-67, acting dept. head, 1966-67; prof. history of physics Yale, 1967—; NRC fellow Dublin (Ireland) Inst. Advanced Studies, 1952-53; John Simon Guggenheim Meml. fellow, Leyden, Netherlands, 1958-59, Yale, 1967-68. Fellow Am. Phys. Soc., A.A.A.S.; mem. History of Sci. Soc., Am. Assn. Physics Tchrs., Am. Assn. U. Profs., Phi Beta Kappa, Sigma Xi. Author: Paul Ehrenfest, Vol. I: The Making of a Theoretical Physicist, 1970. Editor: Collected Scientific Papers of Paul Ehrenfest, 1959. Editorial adviser Ency. Brit., 1956—. Translator: Letters on Wave Mechanics, 1967. Contbr. articles profl. jours. Address: 244 Lawrence St New Haven CT 06511

KLEIN, MAURICE J., lawyer; b. Phila., Aug. 23, 1908; s. Joseph A. and Raye (Blum) K.; LL.B., Temple U., 1932; m. Fay Clearfield, Jan. 7, 1934; children—Raymond, Jerome. Admitted to Pa. bar, 1932, since practiced in Phila.; sr. partner Abrahams & Loewenstein 1944—; dir. officer in cos., Phila, N.Y.C., Fla., officer, dir. chain of nursing homes; Nat. vice chmn. bd. trustees Union of Am. Hebrew Congregations, 1967—, nat. bd. mem., 1961—; pres. Council Reform Synagogues of Pa., 1964-68; pres. Phila. Fedn. Reform Synagogues, 1961-63; pres. Congregation Judea, Philadelphia, 1955-57, hon. life trustee, 1957—; trustee Jewish Community Relations Council, 1961-65. Named Man of the Year Northeast High Sch., Phila., 1969. Mem. Phila. Bar Assn., Alumni Assn. Northeast High Sch., Phila., (pres. 1965-67, hon. life trustee 1967—), Lambda Sigma Kappa. Home: Coventry House Coventry and Valley Rds Melrose Park PA 19126 Office: Land Title Bldg Philadelphia PA 19110

KLEIN, MILES VINCENT, educator, physicist; b. Cleve., Mar. 9, 1953; s. Max Ralph and Isabelle (Benjamin) K.; B.S., Northwestern U., 1954; Ph.D., Cornell U., 1961; m. Barbara J. Pincus, Sept. 2, 1956; children-Cynthia, Gail. NSF postdoctoral fellow, Stuttgart, Germany, 1961; mem. faculty U. Ill. at Urbana, 1962—, prof. physics, 1969—. Fellow Am. Phys. Soc.; mem. Optical Soc. Am. Author: Optics, 1970. Home: 403 Vermont Av Urbana IL 61801

KLEIN, MILTON MARTIN, educator; b. N.Y.C., Aug. 15, 1917; s. Edward and Margaret (Greenfield) K.; B.S.S., Coll. City N.Y., 1937, M.S. in Edn., 1939; Ph.D., Columbia, 1954; m. 2d, Margaret Gordon, Aug. 25, 1963; children—Edward Gordon, Peter Gordon. Historian, USAAF, 1944-47; tchr. N.Y. City pub. schs., 1947-57; vis. prof. Columbia, summers 1959, 60, lectr. history, winters, 1954-58; prof. history, chmn. dept. L.I. U., 1958-62, dean Coll. Liberal Arts and Sci., 1962-66; dean grad. studies and research State U. N.Y., Fredonia, 1966-69; prof. history U. Tenn., 1969—. Fulbright lectr. U. Canterbury, Christchurch, New Zealand, 1962; Ford Found. travelling fellow, 1955-56; Lilly Found.-Clements Library fellow, 1961; chmn. Columbia U. Faculty Seminar on Early Am. History and Culture, 1971-72. Served to lt. col. USAF Res. Mem. Am. Hist. Assn., Conf. on Brit. Studies, Orgn. Am. Historians, Am. Soc. for Legal History (chmn. membership com. 1969—, dir. 1971—), Phi Beta Kappa, Sigma Alpha Mu, Phi Alpha Theta. Author: Social Studies for the Academically Talented Student, 1960; also numerous articles.

Editor: Independent Reflector (William Livingston), 1963; mem. editorial bd. Am. Jour. Legal History, 1971—. Home: 8124 Kingsdale Dr Knoxville TN 37919

KLEIN, MORTON JOSEPH, chemist; b. Chgo., Feb. 26, 1928; s. Isador J. and Rose (Tiger) K.; student Ill. Inst. Tech., 1945-46, Ph.D., 1953; B.S., U. Ill., 1948; m. Ruth Blum, June 16, 1953; children—Gayle Susan, Mitchell Jay, Ronald David. Mem. staff IIT Research Inst., Chgo., 1953—, asst. dir. chemistry, 1962-65, dir. applied chemistry, 1965-67, dir. chemistry research, 1967—. Mem. Ill. com. CARE, 1962-64. Recipient award sci. merit IIT Research Inst., 1957. Mem. Am. Chem. Soc., Am. Inst. Chemists, Am. Inst. Aero. and Astronautics, Sigma Xi, Phi Lambda Upsilon. Club: Chemists (N.Y.C.). Home: 9021 Sleeping Bear Rd Skokie IL 60076 Office: 10 W 35th St Chicago IL 60616

KLEIN, PHILIP, educator; b. Phila., Dec. 20, 1906; s. Sigmund and Rosa (Jacoby) K.; student U. Pa., 1924-28, U. London, 1954; Mus. D., Coombs Coll. Music, 1961; H.H.D., Moore Coll. Art, 1962; m. Esther Moyerman, Apr. 26, 1930; children—Arthur, Karen Louise. Reporter, Phila. Inquirer, 1924-30; pres. Philip Klein Advt., Inc., 1930- 40, past chmn.; pub. Phila. Jewish Times, 1947-50; pres. Rittenhouse Press, 1948-52, Hercum Jr. Coll., 1951—, chmn. bd. trustees, 1962—; pres. The Junto, 1954—, Phila. All-Star Forum Series; chief purser Mathiasen's Tanker Industries, Inc., 1951; chmn. Greenmount Co., Phila. Pub. Co., Inc.; treas. Met. Ednl. Television Corp. Co-chmn. Internat. Seminar on World Politics. Pres., Phila. Meml. Park; exec. dir. Phila. Civil Def. Council, 1956-61, pres. U.S. Council, 1959-60; chmn. Nat. Commn. Adult Edn. Finance; mem. exec. com. Big Bros. Am.; former mem. exec. bd. Boy Scouts Am. Vice chmn. Phila. City Planning Commn., 1958—; commr. Dept. Pub. Property of Phila., 1961; pres. Phila. Marina, 1959—; chmn. Phila. br. ANTA; chmn. United Seamen's Service. Hon. chmn. Long Beach Island Found. Arts and Scis.; mem. exec. com. Mary Bailey Found.; trustee Charles Morris Price Sch.; chmn. bd. trustees Pathway Sch. Served as staff officer U.S. Mcht. Marine, 1942-46. Decorated by Brazilian Govt. Fellow Internat. Gerontol. Soc., Royal Soc. Arts; mem. Pa. Acad. Fine Arts, Internat. House of Phila. (pres.), Fedn. Community Councils (dir.), Jr. Coll. Assn. Middle Atlantic States (exec. com.), Internat. Semantics Soc., Pan Am. Assn., English Speaking Union, Am. Assn. Sch. Adminstrs., Pa. Welfare Forum (v.p.), Adult Edn. Assn. (pres. 1958-59), U.S. Coast Guard League, Alliance Francaise, also numerous other profl. orgns. and assns. Clubs: Contemporary, Art Alliance, Poor Richard (Phila.); University (N.Y.C.); National Press (Washington). Home: 1520 Spruce St Philadelphia PA 19102 Office: 1530 Spruce St Philadelphia PA 19102

KLEIN, ROBERT, foundry exec.; b. Phila., Dec. 3, 1924; s. Julius and Eleanor (Arons) K.; B.A., Pa. State U., 1948; m. Judith Auritt, June 30, 1946; children—William J., Sally G., Anne L. From indsl. engr. to pres. Caloric Corp., Topton, Pa., 1948-69; pres. Samuel Klein Corp., Alburtis, Pa., 1969—, Alliance Wall Corp., Alliance, O., 1965—; chmn. bd. Eichler Wood Products Co., Laury's Station, Pa., 1971—; mng. dir. Alliance Europe, Genk, Belgium, 1971—; dir., v.p. Nat. Bank Topton, 1960-67. Chmn. adv. com. Good Shepherd Home Workshop, 1967—; pres. bd. assos. Muhlenberg Coll., 1969- 70, trustee, 1970—; trustee Jewish Fedn. Allentown, Porcelain Enamel Inst., Nat. Foundry Assn. Served with USMCR, 1943-45. Decorated Purple Heart. Home: 2720 Allen St Allentown PA 18104 Office: Box 444 Alburtis PA 18011

KLEIN, RONALD P., lawyer; b. San Francisco, Nov. 28, 1927; s. Milton A. and Annette (Platt) K.; A.B. in Psychology, Stanford, 1949; LL.B. magna cum laude, Harvard, 1952; m. Elizabeth Burns, Nov. 29, 1960; children—Lisa Jill, Jonathan. Admitted to Cal. bar, 1953, Ariz. bar, 1959; law clk. to Judge William E. Orr, U.S. Ct. Appeals, 9th Jud. Circuit, San Francisco, 1952-53; pvt. practice law, San Francisco, 1953-58; with Del E. Webb Corp., Phoenix, 1958-66, dir. legal dept., 1961-64, v.p., gen. counsel, 1964-66, sec., 1966; v.p., gen. counsel Hunt Foods & Industries, Inc., Fullerton, Cal., 1966-68; v.p., gen. counsel Occidental Petroleum Corp., Los Angeles, 1968—. Served with AUS, 1946-47. Mem. Am., Ariz., Los Angeles bar assns., State Bar Cal. Home: 490 Tigertail Rd Los Angeles CA 90049 Office: 10889 Wilshire Blvd Los Angeles CA 90024

KLEIN, SEYMOUR MILLER, lawyer, business exec.; b. N.Y.C., Mar. 14, 1909; s. Emanuel and Sadie (Miller) K.; B.S.S. cum laude, Coll. City N.Y., 1929; J.D. cum laude, Harvard, 1932; m. Ruth Liberman, Oct. 29, 1939; children-Jeffrey Peter, Donald Stuart. Admitted to N.Y. bar, 1933, also U.S. Dist. Ct., So. Dist. N.Y., U.S. Ct. of Appeals 2d and 3d circuits, U.S. Tax Ct., U.S. Supreme Ct.; asst. U.S. atty. So. Dist. N.Y., 1932-39; spl. asst. to atty. gen.. U.S., 1934-36; partner Lynton, Klein, Opton & Saslow and predecessor firms, N.Y.C., 1939—; lectr. Practising Law Inst., 1946—. Pres. 100 Park Av., Inc., Louis Adler Realty Co., Inc.; dir. Arnold Constable Corp., Midtown Realty Owners Assn., Inc.; prof. dir. Essex House Hote, Inc. Referee appellate div. N.Y. State Supreme Ct. to examine accounts of coms. of incompetent persons, 1963—; mem. departmental com. for ct. adminstrn. First Judicial Dept., 1966—; mem. judicial relatioons Com. appellate div. Supreme Ct. N.Y., 1968—; chmn. sub-com. on scope, procedure and program of departmental com. for ct. adminstrn. First Judicial Dept., 1969—; hon. commr. Pub. Events City N.Y., 1969—; mem. N.Y.C. Cultural Council, 1969—. Pres. Louis and Bessie Adler Found., Ruth and Seymour Klein Found.; v.p., gen. counsel, bd. dirs. 92d St YM-YWHA; bd. dirs. Citizen Tax Council; alternate trustee Fedn. Jewish Philanthropies N.Y. Recipient Friend of Lehigh award Lehigh U. Alumni Assn., 1970. Mem. Assn. Bar City N.Y. (past mem. exec., grievance and judiaciary com.)., Am. Arbitration Assn. (nat. panel arbitrators), N.Y. County Lawyers Assn., N.Y. State Bar Assn., Phi Beta Kappa, Zeta Beta Tau. Clubs: Harmonie (bd. govs., mem. exec. com.) (N.Y.C.); Sunningdale Country (past pres., mem. exec. com., bd. govs.) (Scarsdale, N.Y.). Bd. editors: Harvard Law Rev., 1932. Home: 480 Park Av New York NY 10022 Office: 100 Park Av New York NY 10017

KLEIN, WALTER CONRAD, clergyman; b. Bklyn., May 28, 1904; s. Louis William and Lillian (Sommer) K.; B.A., Lehigh U., 1924; B.D., Gen. Theol. Sem., 1929, S.T.M., 1932, S.T.D., 1933; Ph.D., Columbia, 1940; S.T.D., Seabury- Western Theol. Sem., 1957; D.C.L., Nashotah House, 1964; m. Helene M. Rosentreter, Apr. 24, 1935; children—Katherine Katherine Joanna, John Conrad. Asst., St. Mary the Virgin Ch., N.Y.C., 1930-33; curate Grace Episcopal Ch., Newark, 1934-35; vicar St. Paul's Ch., Morris Plains, N.J., 1935- 37, St. Augustine's Chapel, Norristown, Pa., 1937-38; lectr. Phila. Div. Sch., 1937-38, chmn. grad. dept., 1938-42; rector St. Barnabas' Ch., Haddington, Phila., 1942-43; spl. preacher St. Mark's Episcopal Ch., Phila., 1946; Am. rep. on staff Anglican bishop of Jerusalem, 1946-50; canon residentiary St. George's Cathedral, Jerusalem, 1948-50; prof. O.T., Seabury-Western Theol. Sem., 1950-59, asst. dean, 1952-59; pres., dean Nashotah House, 1959-63, trustee, 1959-67; bishop coadjutor No. Ind., bishop, 1963—. Pres. bd. trustees Howe Sch.; mem. corp. Seabury-Western Theol. Sem. Served to lt. comdr., chaplain USNR, 1943-46. Mem. Phi Beta Kapp. Author: The Elucidation of Islam's Foundation, 1940; Johann Conrad Beissel; Mystic and Martinet, 1942; Clothed With Salvation, 1953; The Psychological Pattern of Old Testament Prophecy, 1956; Jeremiah, 1963; The Dying Lord, 1963; A Priest Forever, 1964; also popular and sci. articles. Home: 1319 E Wayne St N South Bend IN 46615 Office: 117 N Lafayette Blvd South Bend IN 46601

KLEIN, WELLS CAMPBELL, internat. agy. exec.; b. N.Y.C., Oct. 10, 1926; s. Philip and Alice (Campbell) K.; B.A., Sarah Lawrence Coll., 1949; grad. student Cornell U., 1956-58. Staff asst. CARE, Yugoslavia, 1951, dir. research unit, N.Y.C., 1951-52, mission chief Yugoslavia, 1952-53, Japan, 1954, Vietnam, 1954-55, acting Far East regional dir., 1955, dir. program devel. div., N.Y.C., 1959-6O, mem. African survey team, 1961; dir. CARE medico div., N.Y.C. and Algeria, 1962-63; adminstr. Robert P. Gersin Assos., indsl. design, 1964-65; survey Internat. Rescue Com., Vietnam, 1965; asst. dir. Office Refugee Coordination, AID, Vietnam, 1965-66, dir. refugee and social welfare div. Vietnam Bur., AID, Washington, 1966- 67; gen. dir. Am. br. Internat. Social Service, 1967—; instr. sociology and anthropology Cornell U., 1956-58. Mem. exec. com. Am. Immigration and Citizenship Conf., 1967—. Served with USNR, 1944-46. Far Eastern studies fellow Cornell U., 1956; Ford Found. fellow, 1957-58. Author: (with M. Weiner) "Vietnam" Government and Politics of Southeast Asia, 1959. Home: 152 Hillair Circle White Plains NY 10605 Office: 345 E 46th St New York City NY 10017

KLEIN, WILLIAM, Jr., chocolate co. exec.; b. Elizabethtown, Pa., Jan. 10, 1917; s. William and Ray (Treichler) K.; student Franklin and Marshall Acad., 1930-31; m. Elizabeth Ann Fisher, Dec. 29, 1951; 1 son, William III. With Klein Chocolate Co., Elizabethtown, 1933—, treas., gen. mgr., 1954-, pres., 1962—; pres. Kleins Kars. antique cars, 1956—; v.p. Strasbury R.R. Co. (Pa.), also dir. Bd. dirs. Elizabethtown Library. Mem. N.A.M., Pa. Assn. Mfrs., Chocolate Mfg. Assn., N.Y. Cocoa Exchange, Antique Auto Club Am., Bentley Drivers Club, Brit. Racing Drivers Club, Rolls Royce Owners Club, Lancaster Aero. Club, Royal Photog. Soc., Classical Car Club Am. Home: Stone Gables Elizabethtown PA 17022 Office: Klein Chocolate Co Brown St Elizabethtown PA 17022

KLEIN, WILLIAM HERBERT, radiation biologist; b. Mt. Healthy, O., Nov. 6, 1920; s. William Frederick and Louisa (Urmston) K.; B.A., Miami U., Oxford, O., 1942; Ph.D. (research fellow), Purdue U., 1951; m. Winifred Smith, Dec. 25, 1942; children—Elaine Louise (Mrs. Louis H. Knapp), Carla Jeanne. Chemist, Hilton-Davis Chem. Co., Cin., 1945-56; instr. botany Miami U., 1946-47; research instr. Purdue U., 1950-51; plant physiologist Smithsonian Instn., Washington, 1951-58, chief div. radiation and organisms Astrophys. Obs., 1958-65, dir. radiation biology lab., 1965—; on loan to U.S. AEC, biology div., 1966-67; vis. lectr. biophysics U. Md. Grad. Sch. 1956; cons. AEC, 1960—; mem. NRC, 1966—. Exec. sec.-treas. Am. Soc. Plant Physiologists, 1960—; hon. adv. editor Photochemistry and Photobiology, 1962—. Served with USAAF, 1942-45. Mem. Radiation Research Soc., Am. Inst. Biol. Scis., A.A.A.S., Solar Energy Soc. (dir., editorial bd. 1969—), Scandinavian Soc. Plant Physiology, Japanese Soc. Plant Physiologists, Sigma Xi, Phi Eta Sigma. Lutheran (lay chmn. council and congregation). Contbr. sci. papers to various sci. jours. and symposia. Home: 7901 Kentbury Dr Bethesda MD 20014 Office: Smithsonian Radiation Biology Lab 12441 Parklawn Dr Rockville MD 20852

KLEIN, WILLIAM KENNETH, hosp. dir.; b. Mpls., Sept. 9. 1916; s. Kenneth O. and Lenora (Bye) K.; B.B.A., U. Minn., 1938; m. Mariam Ott, May 18, 1940; children—Kenneth William, Henry Alexander, Marianne. Dir. services and supplies, also asst. dir. U. Minn. Hosps., 1942-47; dir. Hurley Hosp., Flint, Mich., 1947-53; dir. L.I. Coll. Hosp., 1953-66, exec. dir., 1966—. Dir. Group Health Hosp. Ins., Inc., Medici Fund, Med. Centers Asso., L.I. Coll. Hosp. Nursing Home Co. Fellow Am. Coll. Hosp. Adminstrs.; mem. Am. Hosp. Assn., Hosp. Assn. N.Y. State (trustee), Greater N.Y. Hosp. Assn. (past pres.), Alpha Delta Phi (chmn. nat. exec. council). Home: 9 Plum Beach Point Dr Port Washington NY 11050 Office: 340 Henry St Brooklyn NY 11201

KLEIN, WILLIE, newspaperman; b. Newark, June 24, 1913; s. Max and Lena (Rettig) K.; Student N.Y.U., 1931-34; m. Sandra C. Tolchinsky, June 22, 1933; children-David, Barry, Moss. With Newark Star-Ledger, 1932—, sports editor, 1962—. Mem. Baseball Writers Assn. Am., Nat. Profl. Football Writers Assn. Am., Nat. Bd. Sports Editors. Home: 15 Dorset Dr Clarrk NJ 07066 Office: Star-Ledger Plaza Newark NJ 07101

KLEINBERG, JACOB, educator, chemist; b. Passaic, N.J., Feb. 14, 1914; s. William and Rebecca (Sirota) K.; B.S., Randolph-Macon Coll., 1934; M.S., U. Ill., 1937, Ph.D., 1939; m. Jane L. Crawford, June 11, 1942; children—Judith Ann, Mary Jill. Asst. prof. James Millikin U., 1940-43, U. Ill. Coll. Pharmacy, 1943-46; mem. faculty U. Kan., 1946—, prof. chemistry, 1951—, chmn. dept., 1963-70. Mem. Am. Chem. Soc., Phi Beta Kappa, Sigma Xi. Author: Unfamiliar Oxidation States, 1950; (with L.F. Audrieth) Non- Agueous Solvents, 1953; (with W.J. Argersinger, Jr. and E. Griswold) Inogranic Chemistry, 1960; (with J.C. Bailar, Jr. and T. Moeller) University Chemistry, 1965. Mem. editorial bd. Chem. Revs., 1951-53, Inorganic Chemistry, 1961-64, Jour. Inorganic and Nuclear Chemistry, 1955—. Spl. research unfamiliar oxidation states of metals, non-aqueous solvents. Home: 9 Winona St Lawrence KS 66044

KLEINDIENST, RICHARD GORDON, govt. ofcl.; b. Winslow, Ariz., Aug. 1923; s. Alfred and Gladys (Love) K.; A.B. magna cum laude, Harvard, 1947, LL.B., 195O; m. Margaret Dunbar, Sept. 3, 1948; children—Alfred Dunbar, Wallace Heath, Anne Lucile, Carolyn Love. Admitted to Ariz. bar, 1950; law clk. firm Ropes & Grey, Boston, 1949-50; asso., then partner firm Jennings, Strouss, Salmon & Trask, Phoenix, 1950-57; sr. partner firm Shimmel, Hill, Kleindienst & Bishop, Phoenix, 1958-69; dep. atty. gen. Dept. Justice, 1969—. Past mem. bd. Small Bus. Devel. Center, Office Econ. Opportunity. Mem. Ariz. Ho. of Reps. from Maricopa County, 1953-54; chmn. Ariz. Young Republican League, 1955, Ariz. Rep. Com., 1956-60, 61- 63; mem. Rep. Nat. Com., 1956-60, 6l, 63; nat. dir. field operations Goldwater Pres. com., 1964; candidate for gov. Ariz., 1964; nat. dir. field operations Nixon for Pres. Com., 1968; gen. counsel Rep. Nat. Com., 1968. Past bd. dirs. local Am. Legion, V.F.W., Urban League, Goodwill Industries, Ariz., Am. heart assns., Phoenix Day Nursery, Phoenix Symphony Assn. Served to lt. USAAF, World War II. Mem. Fed. Bar Assn. (pres. 1970—), Phi Beta Kappa, Sigma Alpha Epsilon. Clubs: Thunderbirds, Arizona (Phoenix). Home: 8464 Portland Pl McLean VA 22101 Office: Dept Justice Washington DC 20530

KLEINE, HERMAN, fgn. service officer; b. N.Y.C., Mar. 6, 1920; s. Max and Fannie (Schechter) K.; B.S., N.Y. State Coll. for Tchrs., Albany, 1941; M.A., Clark U., 1942, Ph.D., 1951; m. Paula Stein, June 16, 1962; 1 son, Joseph. Researcher for Nat. Indsl. Conf. Bd., 1946; instr. to asst. prof. Worcester Poly tech. Inst., 1946-49; economist ECA, Mut. Security Agy., The Hague, Netherlands, 1949-53; internat. relations and econs. FOA, ICA, Washington, 1955-57; dir. U.S. Operations Mission to Ethiopia, ICA, 1957-59, asst. dep. dir. for operations 1959-61; Nat. War Coll., 1961-62; AID adviser UN Mission, U.S., N.Y.C., 1962- 64; dep. asst. adminstr. for Africa AID, Washington, 1964-67; dep. dir. U.S. AID mission to Brazil, 1967, now with Bur. Latin Am., Bur. Inter-Am. Affairs. Mem. U.S. delegation UN Gen. Assembly, 1962, 63. Served from pvt. to capt. USAAF, 1942-46. duPont fellow, 1948. Mem. Am. Econ. Assn., Am. Soc. Engring. Edn., Kappa Phi Kappa. Jewish religion. Home: 412 Vieira Souto Ipanema Rio de Janeiro Brazil Office: USAID/DD APO New York City NY 09676

KLEINERMAN, ISAAC, television exec.; b. N.Y.C. July 21, 1916; s. Aaron and Clara (Lieberson) K.; student Coll. City N.Y., 1935-36; m. Evelyn Bloch, May 31, 1941 (div. Nov. 1962); children—Laura, Judith; m. 2d, Alida Livingston Carey, Dec. 31, 1962 (div. Aug. 1967); m. 3d, Rita Gethner, Dec. 22, 1967. With Seiden Motion Picture Co., 1936-37, Modern Talking Picture Co., 1938-39, Twentieth Century Fox, N.Y.C., 1940-43; film editor, dir. RKO, N.Y.C., 1945-51; film editor, dir. NBC, 1951-57; asso. producer Twentieth Century series CBS, N.Y.C., 1957-60, producer, 1960—; co-producer World War 1 series, 1964-65, producer The 21st Century Series, 1967-. Trustee of Flaherty Film Found. Served with AUS, 1943-44. Recipient Emmy award Nat. Acad. Television Arts and Scis., 1968. Mem. Screen Dirs. Guild. Home: 8 East 76th St New York City NY 10021 Office: CBS News 524 W 57th St New York City NY 10019

KLEINERT, NORMAN E., banker; b. Phila., Aug. 14. 1919; s. Edward and Eleanor (Achterman) K.; B.S. in Econs., LaSalle Coll., Phila., 1954; student real estate, Swathmore Coll., 1947; m. Helen Boyd Davis, Feb. 24, 1945; children-Norma Elaine, Edward Lewis, Nancy Jean, William Boyd. Real estate appraiser First Mortgage Corp., Phila., 1946-48, Equitable Life Ins. Co. Phila., 1948-50; mortgage loan mgr. N.Y. Life Ins. Co., Detroit, 1950-64; exec. v.p. Bank of Commonwealth, Detroit, 1964—; lectr. Sch. State Bank Examining Personnel, U. Ill. Served to 1st lt. AUS, 1944-46. Mem. Am. Inst. Real Estate Appraisers (pres. Mich. chpt. 1959, sec. 1957, v.p. 1958), Econ. Club Detroit, Mortgage Bankers Assn., Mich. Real Estate Assn., Detroit Real Estate Bd. Home: 869 Lake Shore Rd Grosse Pointe Shores MI 48236 Office: 719 Groswold St Detroit MI 48231

KLEINERT, ROBERT WILLIAM, telephone co. exec.; b. Phila., Apr. 6, 1923; s. Edward and Eleanor (Achtermann) K.; B.S. in Elec. Engring., Drexel U., 1951; m. E. Jane Bass, June 24, 1950; children—Richard W., Robert A., John C. Messenger, installer Bell Telephone Co. of Pa., 1940-42; plant, engr., sales, marketing to gen. mgr. long lines dept. Am. Tel. & Tel. Co., 1942-63, asst. v.p., 1963-65, dir. operations long lines dept., 1966-70; pres. N.J. Bell Telephone Co., Newark, 1970—, also dir.; dir. Fidelity Union Trust Co., Bamberger's. Bd. dirs. Better Bus. Bur. Greater Newark; trustee Newark Mus., United Hosps. of Newark, Greater Newark Urban Coalition. Served with AUS, 1943-46. Mem. I.E.E.E., Armed Forces Communication Electronics Assn., N.J. Tax Policy Com., N.J. (dir.), Greater Newark (dir.) chambers commerce. Clubs: Downtown, Essex (Newark). Home: 856 Apache Rd Franklin Lakes NJ 07417 Office: 540 Broad St Newark NJ 07101

KLEINFELD, ERWIN, educator; b. Vienna, Austria, Apr. 19, 1927; s. Lazar and Gina (Schönbach) K.; B.S., City Coll., N.Y., 1948; M.A., U. Pa., 1949; Ph.D., U. Wis., 1951; m. Margaret Morgan, July 2, 1968; children—Barbara, David. Came to U.S., 1940. Instr. U. Chgo., 1951-53; asst. pro. Ohio State U., 1953-56, asso. prof., 1957-60, prof., 1960-62; prof. math. Syracuse U., 1962-67, U. Hawaii, 1967-68, U. Ia., 1968—; vis. lectr. Yale, 1956-57; cons. Nat. Bur. Standards, summer 1953; research specialist U. Conn., summer 1955; research mathematician Bowdoin Coll., summer 1957; research asso. Cornell U., summer 1958, U. Cal. at Los Angeles, summer 1959, Stanford, summer 1960, Inst. Def. Analysis, summer 1961, 62, AID-India, summer 1964, 65. Served with AUS, 1945-46. Recipient Wis. Alumni Research Found. fellowship, 1949-51; U.S. Army Research Office grantee, 1955-70; NSF grantee, 1970—. Mem. Am. Math. Soc., Sigma Xi. Editorial bd. Jour. Algebra-Academic Press; cons. editor Merrill Pub. Co.-Div. Bell & Howell. Contbr. articles research jours. Home: 1205 Franklin Iowa City IA 52240

KLEINHOLZ, FRANK, artist; b. Bklyn., Feb. 17, 1901; s. Herman and Bessie Kleinholz; ed. pub. schs. and high sch., Bklyn.; student Bedford YMCA Prep Sch., 1916-18, Colby Coll., Waterville, Me., 1918-19, Fordham Law Sch., N.Y.C., 1920-23; studied art with Alex Dobkin, 1938, with Sol Wilson, Am. Artists Sch., N.Y.C., 1939; m. Leah Schwartz, June 18, 1927 (dec. Oct. 2, 1945); m. 2d, Lidia Brestovan, Apr. 22, 1946; children—Lisa, Marco, Anna. Practicing Lawyer, 1924-36; attention to painting 1936—. Exhibited Am. Artists Sch., 1940; painting "Abstractionists," Directions in Am. Painting Exhbn., Carnegie Inst., Pitts., 1941, purchased by Carnegie acting dir., John O'Connor, Pa. Acad. of Fine Art, Phila., 1942; Va. Biennial, Richmond, 1942; 2 paintings "Back Street" and "Bargain Counter," Artists for Victory Exhbn., Met. Mus., N.Y.C., 1942, "Back Street" awarded 6th purchase prize, also rep. Bklyn., Newark and other large mus. One-man show Asso. Am. Artists Galleries, N.Y.C., 1942-43, also shows, 1944—; exhibited Akron (O.) Art Inst., 1965, ACA Gallery, Rome, Italy, 1965. Represented in Met. Mus. and pvt. collections of Mr. and Mrs. Otto Spaeth and Mr. John O'Connor. Author: Frank Kleinholz, a Self Portrait, 1965. Home: 18 Prospect Av Port Washington NY 11050 Office: care ACA Gallery 63 E 57th St New York City NY 10022

KLEINHOLZ, LEWIS HERMANN, educator; b. N.Y.C., May 18, 1910; s. Jacob Karl and Fannie (Geller) K.; B.S., Colby Coll., 1930, Sc.D., 1963; M.A., Harvard, 1935, Ph.D., 1937; diploma Army Sch. Aviation Medicine, 1942, R.A.F. Sch. Air-Sea Rescue, 1944. Instr. Colby Coll., 1930-33; teaching fellow Harvard, 1934-35, instr., tutor, 1940-4l; research investigator Marine Biol. Lab., Woods Hole, Mass., 1935-68, summer instr. 1948-66, dir. invertebrate zool. staff, 1949-53; asst. Radcliffe Coll., 1936-37; research investigator Marine Biol. Lab., St. George's, Bermuda, 1936, Plymouth, Eng., 1937, Naples, Italy, 1937, 51- 52; lectr. Am. U., Beirut, also Egyptian U., 1938; instr. Cambridge Jr. Coll., 1938-42; research investigator Marine Biol. Lab., Cold Spring Harbor, N.Y., 1940; project engr. Aero-Med. Research Lab., Wright Field, O., 1945; asst. prof. Reed Coll., 1946-47, asso. prof., 1947-50, prof. 1950—, chmn. dept. biology 1955-61; research investigator Marine Biol. Lab., Plymouth, Eng., 1960, Kristinebergs Zoologiska Sta., Sweden, 1960, 61, Stazione Zoologica, Naples, 1960, Station Biologique de Roscoff, France, 1962; vis. research prof. Med.-Kem. Inst., U. Lund, Sweden, 1961-62; U.S. rep. Internat. Sci. Symposium, Paris, 1947, Naples, 1953: NRC Adv. Com. on Naples, Italy, Research Station; NSF Symposium; Selection of Sci. Personnel, 1954; Biol. Research in Liberal Arts Coll., 1954; Ford Found. Fund for Advancement of Edn., Western Selection Com., 1954; mem. internat. symposium on recent advances in physiology invertebrates, U. Ore., 1955; mem. examining com. basic sci., Ore. Bd. Higher Edn., 1949-60; mem. cell biology sect., div. research grants NIH. Dir. Portland Jr. Symphony Soc., 1950-58; trustee Marine Biol. Lab., Woods Hole, 1950. Served as observer RAF, 1944, capt. USAAF, 1945. Guggenheim Found. fellow, 1945-46; State Dept. Fulbright fellow, 1951- 52; sci. faculty fellow NSF, 1958-59; fellow N.Y. Acad. Sci., 1958—. Mem. Am. Inst. Biol. Scis. (steering com. for biol. scis. curriculum study 1958-60), Marine Biol. Assn. of U.K., Marine Biol. Assn. India, Am. Soc. Zoologists (exec. com. 1959-62), Ore., N.Y. acads. sci., Nat. Conf. Pre-Med. Edn., Internat. Soc. Cell Biology, Soc. Gen Physiologists, Phi Beta Kappa, Sigma Xi, Gamma Alpha. Author: Selected Invertebrate Types (with Brown et al), 1950; Recent

Advances in the Physiology of Invertebrates (with Scheer et al), 1957; Physiology of Crustacea (with Waterman et al). 1959; The Functional Organization of the Compound Eye (with Bernhard et al). 1966. Contbr. profl. jours. Mem. internat. bd. editors Pubblicazioni della Stazione Zoologica di Napoli, 1959; bd. editors Biol. Bull., 1962-66. Address: Reed Coll Portland OR 97202

KLEINJANS, EVERETT, ednl. adminstr.; b. Zeeland, Mich., Sept. 6, 1919; s. George and Cornelia (van Koevering) K.; A.B., Hope Coll., Holland, Mich., 1943; M.A., U. Mich., 1948, Ph.D., 1958; L.H.D. (hon.), George Williams Coll., 1969; m. Edith Ellen Klaaren, May 4, 1946; children—Brian, David, John, Monica, Constance, Instr., English Lang. Inst., U. Mich., 1948; instr. English, Talmadge Coll., China, 1948-50; prin. Am. Sch. in Japan, 1952; prof. English, Meiji Gakuin U., Tokyo, Japan 1952-56; prof. English lang. and linguistics Internat. Christian U., Tokyo, 1958-67, v.p. acad. affairs, 1962-67, dean Coll. Liberal Arts, 1965-67, chmn. div. langs., 1965-67, dir. Inter Univ. Center Japanese Studies, 1965-67, dep. chancellor acad. affairs East-West Center, 1967-68, chancellor East-West Center, 1968—; cons. in field. Vice chmn. Commn. Coop. English in Japan; English orientation dir. Exchange Persons Br., Tokyo; mem. Commn. Advancement Christian Higher Edn. in East Asia. Trustee Center Applied Linguistics, Ferris Girls Sch., Yokoyama, Am. Sch. Japan; bd. dirs. Inst. Religion and Social Change. Served with AUS, 1943-46. Mem. Linguistic Soc. Am., Internat. House Japan, Assn. Asian Studies, Japan Am. Soc. Mem. Reformed Ch. Am. (deacon). Author numerous articles.. Home: 4366 Aukai Av Honolulu HI 96815

KLEINKAUF, HENRY Y., mech. contracting exec., banker; b. Joplin, Mo., Feb. 4, 1908; s. Henry D. and Grace (Yund) K.; B.S. in Archtl. Engring., U. Neb., 1930; m. Mary Louise Nesbit, Dec. 27, 1931; children-James Henry, Kenneth Robert, Thomas Paul, William John. With Natkin Engring. Co., Kansas City, Mo., 1930-32; with Natkin & Co., Omaha, 1932—, partner 1933-47, v.p., dir., 1947-50, pres., 1950-59, 65—, chmn. bd., 1960-65; chmn. bd. Omaha br. Fed. Res. Bank of Kansas City; dir. Hillcrest Center, The Center, Inc., Scott Publishing Co., Omaha, Woodmen Accident & Life Co., Lincoln, Neb. Trustee Doane Coll. Registered profl. engr., Neb. Mem. Mech. Contractors Assn. Am. Inc. (pres. 1965-66), Newcomen Soc. Home: Skyline Rd Elkhorn NB Office: 4001 Leavenworth St Omaha NB 68105

KLEINMAN, ABRAHAM MORRIS, physician, hosp. adminstr.; b. N.Y.C., May 30, 1907; s. Sam and Sima (Reich) K.; B.S., Coll. City N.Y., 1926; M.D., U. Md., 1930; m. Lillian Doris Rabinowitz, June 24, 1934; children—Leonard I., Sylvia (Mrs. Bernard Grossfeld). Intern Beth David Hosp., N.Y.C., 1930-31; asst. pathologist Cumberland Hosp., Bklyn., 1932-46, asso. attending in medicine, 1939-46; dir. profl. services VA br. office 2, N.Y.C., 1946- 48; chief med. service VA Hosp., S.I., N.Y., 1948-49; dir. profl. services VA Hosp. Bklyn., 1949-57; hosp. dir. VA Hosp., Bronx, N.Y., 1957—; clin. asso. prof. internal medicine N.Y. Downstate Med. Center, Bklyn., 1950-57; lectr. pub. health and adminstrv. medicine Columbia, N.Y.C., 1961—; prof. adminstrv. medicine Mt. Sinai Sch. Medicine, 1969—. Adv. Com. Bronx chpt. A.R.C.; hon. pres. Kingsbridge Heights Jewish Center. Served from 1st. lt. to maj. M.C., AUS, 1942-46. Fellow A.C.P., N.Y. Acad. Medicine; mem. A.M.A., N.Y. Acad. Scis., Harvey Soc., Am. Fellowship of Israeli Med. Assn., Am. Friends Hebrew U., Zionist Orgn. Am. Home: 130 W Kingsbridge Rd Bronx NY 10468 Office: VA Hospital Bronx NY 10468

KLEINODER, JACK, stampings mfr., assn. ofcl.; b. Nuremberg, Germany, Apr. 11, 1906; s. Jakob and B. (Lehner) K.; student tech. courses, Germany, U.S.; m. Bertha Singler. Apprentice tool and die maker, Germany; tool and die maker, Germany, also U.S., 1926—; pres. Volkert Stampings, Inc., 1954-68; subsidiary The Stanley Works, L.I., N.Y., 1966; pres. Kleinoder Corp., Albertson, N.Y., 1968—. Mem. Nat. Tool, Die and Precision Machining Assn. (pres. 1959), Queens C. of C. Home: 31 Boxwood La East Hills Roslyn Heights NY 12123 Office: 983 Willis Av Albertson NY 11507

KLEINPELL, ROBERT MINSSEN, educator, paleontologist, geologist; b. Chgo., Sept. 13, 1905; s. William Ernst and Alma Louise (Wilke) K.; A.B., Occidental Coll., Los Angeles, 1926; A.M., Stanford, 1928, Ph.D., 1934; m. Dariel Shively, Dec. 29, 1934. Field geologist Richfield Oil Co., 1928-31; asst. geologist U.S. Geol. Survey, 1931-33; cons. geologist and paleontologist Cal. petroleum industry, 1933-39; stratigrapher petroleum survey Nat. Devel. Co., P.I. 1939-45; instr. systematic biology and hist. geology, coll. curriculum Santo Tomas and Los Banos Internment Camps, P.I., 1942-45; mem. faculty U. Cal. at Berkeley, 1946—, prof. paleontology, 1947—; cons. paleontologist geologist, 1945—; vis. prof. micropaleontology Cal. Inst. Tech., 1939-41; acting dir. Mus. Paleontology, U. Cal. at Berkeley, 1958-60; mem. bd. adv. editors geol. sci. U. Cal. Press, 1964—; editor Cushman Found. for Foraminiferal Research, 1962-65, asst. editor, 1965-70. Fellow Geol. Soc. Am., Am. Geog. Soc., A.A.A.S., Cal. Acad. Sci., Paleontol. Soc. (chmn. Pacific Coast sect., councilor 1963-64, nat. v.p., councilor 1964-65); mem. Am. Assn. Petroleum Geologists (Distinguished lectr. 1960; hon. life), Soc. Econ. Paleontologists and Mineralogists (hon. life mem. Pacific sect. nat. v.p., councilor 1961-62, councilor for paleontology 1967-68), Am. Mus. Natural History (bd. adviser dept. micropaleontology 1945-48), Am. Acad. Polit. Scis., Far Eastern Assn., Biosystematists, LeConte Soc., Phi Beta Kappa, Sigma Xi, Theta Tau, Alpha Tau Omega. Republican. Lutheran. Author: Miocene Stratigraphy of California, 1955; also articles. Home: 5959 Margarido Dr Oakland CA 94618 Office: Dept and Museum Paleontology Univ California Berkeley CA 94720

KLEINSCHMIDT, C. CARL, business exec.; b. 1911; grad. U. Pitts.; married. Mgr., Williams & Co. Inc., Pitts., 1934-51, asst. gen. mgr. warehouse operations, 1951-53, exec. v.p., 1953-68, pres., 1968—, also dir. Office: 901 Pennsylvania Av Pittsburgh PA 15233*

KLEIS, ROBERT WILLIAM, engring. educator; b. Martin, Mich., Nov. 30, 1925; s. Roy Harry and Marguerite E. (Montieth) K.; B.S. in Agr. Engring., Mich. State Coll., 1949, M.S., 1951; Ph.D., Mich. State U., 1957; m. Beatrice M. Heinze, Dec. 26, 1948; children—Cinthia Lee, Pamela Sue. Instr. agrl. engring. Mich. State Coll., 1949-51; from instr. to asst. prof. agrl. engring., also head electrification and processing sect. U. Ill., 1951-56; prof. agrl. engring., head dept. U. Mass., 1957-66; prof., chmn. dept. agrl. engring. U. Neb., 1966-67, asso. dir. agrl. expt. sta., 1967—; spl. appointments U. Cal., 1963, U. Md., 1965. Chmn. Amherst 4-H Council; dir. Hampshire County Youth Council; mem. New Eng. Council Econ. Devel. Served with AUS, 1944-46. Registered profl. engr., Ill., Mass. Fellow Am. Soc. Agrl. Engrs. (mem. cabinet, chmn. electric power and processing div. 1963-64); mem. Am. Soc. Engring. Edn., Engrs. Joint Council (nat. planning com. 1961), Engrs. Council Profl. Devel., Engring Alumni Assn. Mich. State U. (bd. dirs.), Farmhouse, Sigma Xi, Tau Beta Pi, Phi Lambda Tau, Pi Mu Epilon, Gamma Sigma Delta, Alpha Epsilon. Conglist. Mason (Shriner), Rotarian. Contbr. profl. jours., books. Home: 6520 Sumner Lincoln NB 68522

KLEISNER, GEORGE HARRY merchandising exec.; b. Chgo., Apr. 20, 1909; s. John and Marie (Frey) K.; B.S., Northwestern U., 1930; m. Mary Cecilia Wetzel, Aug. 28, 1937; children—Particia, Pamela, Kerry, Kim. Mng. editor W. L. Johnson Pub. Co., 1930-33; with Montgomery Ward & Co., 1933-64, beginning as mdse. trainee, Chgo., successively asst. div. mgr., N.Y.C., buyer, div. mgr. hosiery and accessories, asst. soft lines mdse. mgr., soft lines mdse. mgr., 1933-52, charge N.Y. office, 1952-64, v.p., 1955-57, mdse. mgr., 1958-64; asso. mgmt. cons. Wendell C. Walker & Assos., 1964-65; v.p. charge N.Y. office Bear Brand Hosiery Co., 1965—. 2nd lt. Q.M.C., U.S. Army Res., 1938-43. Mem. Northwestern U. Alumni Assn. (dir. 1931-33), Holy Name Soc., Wool Club N.Y.C., Theta Xi, Sigma Delta Chi. Republican. Roman Catholic. Home: 52 Barry Rd Scarsdale NY 10583 Office: 609 Fifth Av New York City NY 10017

KLEM, CHARLES, ret. stock exchange exec.; b. N.Y.C., Jan. 28, 1906; s. John and Hannah (Moen) K.; student pub. schs. of East Rutherford, N.J.; m. Grace Neubauer, Feb. 19, 1931; children—Charles, John Joseph. With N.Y. Stock Exchange 1922-71, v.p. 1946-71. Home: 151 Lake Dr Mountain Lakes NJ 07046

KLEM, WALTER, ret. actuary; b. N.Y.C., Apr. 26, 1904; s. John and Hannah (Moen) K.; ed. pub. schs., East Rutherford, N.J.; m. Edith Dodd, May 1930 (div. Dec. 1935); 1 dau., Laura; m. 2d, Mary E. Jacoby, June 1949; children—Susan, Christopher. Began with Mut. Life Ins. Co. of N.Y., 1918, became asso. actuary, 1941-47; 2d v.p., asso. actuary Equitable Life Assurance Soc. of U.S. 1947-51, v.p. asso. actuary, 1951-53, sr. v.p., actuary, 1953-68; chmn. actuarial sci. div. Coll. of Ins., N.Y.C., 1968-70; mem. bd. actuaries U.S. pub. law 239, 1954-68; v.p. for U.S., Internat. Congresses Actuaries, 1957-68; dir. Can. Life Ins. Co. of N.Y. Served USN, 1942-45; comdr. USNR ret. Fellow Soc. Actuaries (pres. 1954-55), Canadian Inst. Actuaries; mem. Am. Acad. Actuaries, Ins. Soc. N.Y. (trustee), Coll. of Ins. (chmn. 1961-62), Inst. Actuaries Gt. Britain (hon. overseas mem.), Internat. Actuarial Assn., Instituto de Actuaries Espanoles (corr.). Home: 30 Western Dr Short Hills NJ 07078

KLEMA, ERNEST DONALD, educator, nuclear physicist; b. Wilson, Kan., Oct. 4, 1920; s. William W. and Mary Bess (Vopat) K.; A.B. in Chemistry, U. Kan., 1941; M.A. in Physics, 1942; postgrad. Princeton, 1942, U. Ill., 1946-49; Ph.D. in Physics, Rice U., 1951; m. Virginia Clyde Carlock, May 23, 1953; children—Donald David, Catherine Marion. Staff scientist Los Alamos Sci. Lab., 1943-46; sr. physicist Oak Ridge Nat. Lab., 1950-56, prin. physicist, 1958; asso. prof. nuclear engring. U. Mich., 1956-58; prof. nuclear engring. Northwestern U., 1959-68, chmn. dept. engring. scis., 1960-66; prof. engring. sci. Tufts U., 1968—, dean Coll. Engring., 1968—. Chmn. subcom. on neutron standards and measurements NRC, 1958-62; del. Internat. Atomic Energy Agy. symposium neutron detection, dosimetry and standardiazation, Harwell, Eng., 1962; cons. Oak Ridge Nat. Lab., Argonne Nat. Lab. Fellow Am. Phys. Soc., Am Nuclear Soc.; mem. Am. Soc. Engring. Edn., Phi Beta Kappa, Sigma Xi, Pi Mu Epsilon, Alpha Chi Sigma. Clubs: Harbor (Seal Harbor, Me.); Princeton (N.Y.). Author articles fision cross-sects., gamma-gamma angular correlations, empirical nuclear models, thermal neutron measurements, semi-conductor radiation detectors. Patentee purification hydrogen-argon mixtures. Home 11 Talbot Av Somerville MA 02155 Office: Tufts U Medford MA 02155

KLEMENS, PAUL GUSTAV, physicist, educator; b. Vienna, Austria, May 24, 1925; s. Walter and Ida (Klug) K.; B.S., U. Sydney, 1946; M.S., 1948; D.Phil., Oxford U., 1950; m. Ruth H. Wiener, July 30, 1950; children-Michael W., Susan M. Came to U.S., 1959, naturalized, 1968. Prin. research officer div. physics Nat. Standards Lab., Sydney, Australia, 1950-59; with Westinghouse Research Labs., Pitts., 1959-67; prof., chmn. dept. physics U. Conn., 1967—; vis. prof. U. Leiden, Netherlands, 1963-64. Fellow Inst. Physics, Am., Gt. Britain phys. socs. Home: 232 Ferguson Rd Manchester CT 06040 Office: Dept Physics U Conn Storrs CT 06268

KLEMENS, RONEY WALTER, steel co. exec.; b. Duquesne, Pa., Feb. 19, 1938; s. Walter and Frieda (Brunner) K.; B.S., U. Detroit, 1959; m. Barbara Badarak, Jan. 30, 1960; children—Roney, Jerome, Thomas, Robert. From staff accountant to audit mgr. Price Waterhouse & Co., C.P.A.'s, Pitts., 1959-70; controller Cyclops Corp., Pitts., 1970—. Am. inst. C.P.A.'s. Republican. Catholic. Home: 450 Miranda Rd Pittsburgh PA 15241 Office: 650 Washington Rd Pittsburgh PA 15228

KLEMKE, ELMER DANIEL, educator; b. St. Paul, July 29, 1926; s. Daniel and Matilda (Gutsche) K.; B.A. magna cum laude, Hamline U., 1950; postgrad. U. Minn., 1953-55; M.A., Northwestern U., 1958, Ph.D., 1960. Faculty, Kendall Coll., Evanston, Ill., 1957-59, DePauw U., Greencastle, Ind., 1959-64; mem. faculty Roosevelt U., Chgo., 1964—, chmn. dept. philosophy, 1965—. Named Best Tchr., DePauw U., 1962, Top Prof., Roosevelt U., 1965. Scholar, assistantship Hamline U., 1947-50, assistantship U. Minn., 1953-55, assistantship, fellow Northwestern U., 1957-59. Mem. Am. Philos. Assn. (sec.-treas. Western div. 1969—), Am. Assn. U. Profs. Author: The Epistemology of G.E. Moore, 1969. Editor: Essays on Frege, 1968; Studies in the Philosophy of G.E. Moore, 1969; Essays on Bertrand Russell, 1970; Essays on Wittgenstein, 1971. Contbr. articles profl. jours. Home: 2311 Central St Evanston IL 60201

KLEMM, FREDERICK ALVIN, educator; b. Harrisburg, Pa., Dec. 29, 1912; s. Charles Augustus and Frieda (Ahlefeld) K.; A.B., Dickinson Coll., 1933; postgrad U. Goettingen, Germany, 1933-34; M.A., Duke, 1935; Ph.D., U. Pa., 1939; m. Eleanor Gansloser, Aug. 10, 1940; children—Virginia A., R. Christopher, William Jeffrey. Faculty, U. Pa., 1935-47; faculty Union Coll., Schenectady, 1947—, prof. German, 1955-, dir. evening div., 1952-55, dir. Union Coll.-Gen. Elec. Co. apprentice tng. program, 1956—, chmn. dept. modern Angs., 1959—, chmn. div. humanities, 1961—; mem. Carnegie Found. Com. Ednl. Inquiry, 1952-55; research U. Innsbruck, Austria, 1956; vis. specialist Nat. Security Agy., Washington, summer 1957. Served to 1st lt. AUS. 1943-46. Jusserand travel fellow, 1938. Mem. N.Y. State Fedn. Fgn. Lang. Tchrs. (treas. 1958—), Am. Assn. U. Profs., Modern Lang. Assn., Am. Assn. Tchrs. German, Alpha Chi Rho, Delta Phi Alpha. Presbyn. Author: The Death Problem in Gerhart Hauptmann, 1939. Co-author: Europe for the Thoughtful American, 1962. Contbr. articles profl., hist. jours. Home: 1566 Regent St Schenectady NY

KLEMPERER, OTTO, conductor; b. Breslau, Germany, 1885; ed. Frankfurt Conservatory; LL.D., Occidental Coll., also U. Cal. at Los Angeles; widower; childrenWerner, Lotte. Condr. various European opera Cos., also guest condr. N.Y. Philharmonic Orch.; later condr. Los Angeles Philharmonic Orch.; prin. condr. for life and hon. pres. New Philharmonia Orch. and Chorus, London; appeared as condr. of concerts and operas Russia, Europe, N.Am., S.Am., Can., Israel, Australia. Composer operas, symphonies, chambers mus. songs. Author: Minor Recollections, 1964. Home: Dufourstrasse 104 8008 Zurich Switzerland

KLEMPERER, WERNER, actor. Address: care Ashley Famous Agy Inc 9255 Sunset Blvd Los Angeles CA 90069*

KLEMPERER, WILLIAM ALOYS, educator; b. N.Y.C., Oct. 6, 1927; s. Paul and Margit (Freund) K.; A.B., Harvard, 1950; Ph.D., U. Cal. at Berkeley, 1954; m. Elizabeth Cole, Jan. 12, 1949; children—Joyce Hillary, Paul, Wendy Judith. Instr., U. Cal. at Berkeley, 1954; mem. faculty Harvard, 1954—, prof. chemistry, 1965—. Served with USNR, 1944-46. Fellow Am. Phys. Soc.; mem. Nat. Acad. Scis. Office: 12 Oxford St Cambridge MA 02138

KLEMT, CALVIN CARL, sem. librarian; b. Louisville, Aug. 19, 1925; s. William Walter and Emma (Bach) K.; student U. Ky., 1946-49; B.A., Heidelberg Coll., 1950; B.D., Union Theol. Sem., N.Y.C., 1953; A.M. in L.S., U. Mich., 1962; m. Bette Mae Bartlett, June 7, 1951; children—Kristin Elizabeth, Paul William. Ordained to ministry Evang. and Ref. Ch., 1953; pastor Suffield (O.) Evang. and Ref. Ch., 1953-58, Big Rapids (Mich.) United Ch. of Christ, 1959-61; librarian Central Luth. Theol. Sem., Fremont, Neb., 1962-66, Austin (Tex.) Presbyn. Theol. Sem., 1966—. Served with AUS, 1943-46. Mem. Am. Theol. Library Assn. Home: 4804 Broken Bow Pass Austin TX 78745

KLENDSHOJ, NIELS CHRISTIAN, physician, biochemist; b. Denmark, Feb. 1, 1902; s. Niels Christian and Ane Marie (Jensen) K.; B.A., Borgerdydskolen, Copenhagen, 1921; postgrad., Royal Polytech. Inst., U. Copenhagen, 1926; M.D., U. Buffalo, 1937; m. Annette Roberta Heinz, Feb. 24, 1933; children—Ole, John, Arne; m. 2d, June Esther Davis, Feb. 4, 1963. Came to U.S., 1927, naturalized, 1935. With Arner Co., Inc., Buffalo, 1927—, successively control chemist, prodn. engr., med. and tech. dir., exec. v.p., 1927-52, pres., 1952-59; chmn. bd. Strong Cobb Arner, Inc. (merger Arner Co. and Strong Cobb and Co.), 1959-67, pres., chief exec. officer, 1963-65; biochemist Buffalo Gen. Hosp., 1937—, now cons. biochemist and physician, clin. prof. toxicology. Past mem. joint legislative com. on narcotics State N.Y. Republican. Clubs: Buffalo, Country of Buffalo. Author: Fundamentals of Biochemistry in Clinical Medicine, 1953; also numerous articles on medicine, toxicology. Co-discoverer blood substances B and O.; practical application of specific blood factors in transfusions. Home: 80 Elmhurst Rd Buffalo NY 14226 Office: 2900 Main St Buffalo NY 14214

KLENK, ERNST, chemist, educator; b. Pfalzgrafenweiler, Germany, Oct. 14, 1896; s. Johannes and Katharina (Grossmann) K.; Abitur, Oberrealschule Tubingen, 1914; Dr. rer. nat., U. Tübingen. 1923; m. Margarete Aldinger, July 9, 1937; children—Hans-Dietar, Fritz, Wolfgang. Dozent physiol. chemistry U. Tübingen, 1926; prof. physiol. chemistry U. Cologne (Germany), 1936—, dir. Inst. Physiol. Chemistry, 1936-65, prof. emeritus, 1965—, dean med. faculty, 1947-48, rector, 1961-62. Recipient Norman medal Deutsche Gesellschaft für Fettforschung, 1953, Heinrich Wieland prize, 1964, award Am. Oil Chemists Soc., 1965, Stouffer prize, 1966. Mem. Deutsche Akademie der Naturforscher Leopoldina, Am. Soc. Biol. Chemists (hon.), Gesellschaft für Biologische Chemie (hon.). Research on metabolism of polyenoic fatty acids, lipids of brain and other tissues. Home: 18 Kermeterstrasse 5 Cologne 41 (Lindenthal) Germany

KLENSCH, CHARLES HUGH, banker; b. Akron, O., Oct. 27, 1923; s. Charles Frederick and Bernice Lee (Green) K.; B.A., Williams Coll., 1948; m. Jean Elisabeth Burnaford- Davey, Sept. 2, 1951 (div. Nov. 1963); children—Elizabeth Gabriele, Charles John Burnaford; m. 2d, Elsa Aeschbacher, Apr. 23, 1966. Sports editor Rome (Italy) Daily Am., 1949; city editor Durango (Colo.) Herald-Democrat; telegraph editor Colorado Springs (Colo.) Free Press, 1951; Internat. News Service, Denver, 1951-53, Madrid, 1953-54, Moscow, 1954-57, Berlin, 1957, diplomatic corr., London, 1957-58, Parade, 1959; propr. Underground Press, 1960—; news corr. ABC-News, 1961-66, bur. mgr. Saigon, 1965-66; asst. v.p. pub. relations 1st Nat. City Bank, N.Y.C. 1966-70, asst. v.p. operating group, 1970—. Mem. Pub. Relations Soc. Am., Internat. Assn. Indsl. Communication. Club: Overseas Press (N.Y.C.). Home: 35 E 9th St New York City NY 10003 Office: 399 Park Av New York City NY 10022

KLEPP, AMELIA LOIS, univ. dean; b. Elizabeth, N.J., Aug. 27, 1911; d. John Charles and Amelia (Klem) Fischer; B.A., Coll. St. Elizabeth, 1946; M.S., N.Y. U., 1948, M.B.A., 1960; m. Henry P. Klepp, June 12, 1938 (dec.). Dir. tng. Hahne & Co., Newark, 1934-43; mem. faculty N.Y. U., 1948-57, Coll. St. Elizabeth, 1960; dean of women Seton Hall U., 1960—. Fellow Case Inst. Tech., 1960, N.Y. U., 1948-50. Mem. Zonta Internat. Author articles, tng. manuals. Home 60 Fairmount Av Morristown NJ 07960 Office: Seton Hall Univ South Orange NJ 07979

KLEPPE, THOMAS S., govt. ofcl.; b. Kintyre, N.D., July 1, 1919; s. Lars O. and Hannah (Savig) K.; student Valley City (N.D.) State Tchrs. Coll., 1937; m. Glendora Loew Gompf, Dec. 18, 1958; children—Janis Eileen, Thomas Stewart, Jane Paula, Jill Marie, Bookkeeper, Stock Growers Bank, Napoleon, N.D., 1941; asst. cashier Dakota Nat. Bank, Bismarck, N.D., 1941-42, also dir.; bookkeeper Gold Seal Co., Bismarck, 1946-48, v.p., treas., 1948-58, pres., treas., 1958-64; v.p. dir. J.M. Dain & Co., Inc., Mpls., 1965-66; mem. 90th-91st Congresses 2d Dist. N.D.; adminstr. U.S. Small Bus. Adminstrn., 1971—. Mayor, Bismarck, 1950-54; Republican finance chmn. Burleigh County, 1962; treas. N.D., 1963. Served with AUS, 1942-46. Recipient Outstanding Young Man of Year award Bismarck Jr. C. of C., 1950. Mem. Am. Legion. Lutheran. Elk, Lion. Home: 9609 Hillridge Dr Kensington MD 20795 Office: 1441 L St NW Washington DC 20416

KLEPSER, HARRY JOHN, educator, geologist; b. Buffalo, Mar. 10, 1908; s. Frederick and Effie (Woods) K.; A.B., Syracuse U., 1932, M.S., 1933; Ph.D., Ohio State U., 1936; m. Pearl E. Phelps, Dec. 22, 1936; children—Virginia (Mrs. Gilbert Jacobs), Barbara (Mrs. William Phelps), Carol (Mrs. Frank McKenzie). Asst. prof. Capital U., 1936-43; asst. prof. S.D. State Coll., 1943-44; geologist U.S. Geol. Survey, 1944-45; asst. prof. U. Tenn., Knoxville, 1946-47, asso. prof., 1947-50, prof., 1950—, head dept. geology, 1961—; geol. cons. AEC. Fellow Geol. Soc. Am., A.A.A.S.; mem. Am. Assn. Petroleum Geologists, Nat. Assn. Geology Tchrs., Tenn. Acad. Sci., Scientists and Engrs. for Appalachia, Sigma Xi. Home: 5610 Pinellas Dr Knoxville TN 37919

KLERMAN, GERALD LAWRENCE, physician; b. N.Y.C., Dec. 29, 1928; s. Philip and Rose (Duxom) K.; A.B., Cornell U., 1950; M.D., N.Y. Coll. Medicine, 1954; M.A., Harvard, 1970; m. Lorraine Vogel, Nov. 28, 1954; children—Jacob Alex, Karen Paula, Elizabeth Beryl, Daniel Marc. Intern, asst. resident Bellevue Hosp. Center, N.Y.C., 1954-56; resident psychiatry, chief of service Mass. Mental Health Center, 1956-59, asst. dir. psychiatry, 1962-65; research psychiatrist Nat. Inst. Mental Health, 1959-61, cons., 1961-70; asso. prof. pychiatry Yale, 1965-70; dir. Conn. Mental Health Center, 1967-70; prof. psychiatry Harvard Med. Sch., Boston, 1970—; supt. Erich Lindemann Mental Health Center, 1970—; cons. WHO, 1966, VA Psychiatrics, 1966-70. Charter fellow Am. Coll. Psychopharmacology; mem. Collegium Internat. on Psychopharmacology, Am. Psychiat. Assn. (chmn. Task Force on Research Aspects of Community Mental Health Centers, Hofheimer prize for research 1969). Home: 21 Hammond St Chestnut Hill MA 02167 Office: Mass Gen Hosp 2 Fruit St Boston MA 02114

KLESSIG, ERNST HUGO, electronics co. exec.; b. Waubeka, Wis., Mar. 27, 1926; s. Ernst J. and Cinderella (Maurer) K.; B.B.A., U. Wis., 1952, LL.B., 1952; m. Rosemarie Gates, Sept. 10, 1949; children—Richard, Constance. Admitted to Wis. bar, 1952; with Gen. Elec. Co., 1952-65, mgr. information systems, Bloomington, Ill., 1961-65; with Warwick Electronics Inc., Chgo., 1965- -, controller, sec. 1967—; dir. Thomas Organ Co., Midwest Cabinet Corp., Saginaw Furniture Shops, Inc. Served with USNR, 1944-46. Presbyn. (deacon 1965-68). Mason (Shriner).

KLESTIL, THOMAS, Austrian diplomat; b. Vienna, Austria, Nov. 4, 1932; s. Thomas and Maria (Maier) K.; M. Econs. and Internat. Trade, U. Vienna, 1955, D. Econs. and Internat. Trade, 1957; m. Edith Wielander, June 5, 1957; children—Ursula, Thomas, Stefan. In Austrian govt. service, 1955—; mem. Office Econ. Coordination, Fed. Chancellery, 1955-59; mem. permanent Austrian delegation to OEEC, Paris, 1959-62; head econ. office Austrian Embassy, Washington, 1962-66; personal asst. to Austrian Fedn. Chancellor, Vienna, 1966-69; Austrian consul gen., Los Angeles, 1969—. Decorated comdr. Order King Leopold (Belgium); comdr. Holy Shrine of Emperor Japan; knight Order of King Norway. Office: 3440 Wilshire Blvd Los Angeles CA 90010

KLETZKI, PAUL, condr; b. Lodz, Poland, Mar. 21, 1900; ed. Warsaw U. and Conservatory, also Hochschule, Berlin, Germany; m. Celine Hildegard Woodtli. Mem. Lodz Philharmonic, 1914-19; conducting debut, 1927; on tour Europe, Australia, S.Am., Central Am., 1948; U.S. debut, 1958; prof. Lausanne Conservatory, also Milan Superior Sch. Music; regular condr. Lucerne Festival; condr. concerts Israel Philharmonic, 1953; mus. dir. Orch. Suisse Romand, Geneva, 1967—. Composer: 3 Symphonies, Concerti for Violin and Pianoforte; 4 String Quartets, other works. Address: Orch Suisse Romand Geneva Switzerland also care Hurock Concerts Inc 730 Fifth Av New York City NY 10019

KLEY, JOHN ARTHUR, banker; b. Jericho, N.Y., Oct. 24, 1921; s. John and Annie (Upton) K.; grad. Rutgers U. Sch. Banking. 1952; m. Florence Elizabeth Cannon, Sept. 1, 1945; 1 dau., Martha Anne. With Washington Irving Trust Co. and successor County Trust Co., White Plains, N.Y., 1937—, asst. treas., asst. v.p., v.p., 1951-57, exec. v.p., 1957-60., pres., 1960—; v.p., dir. Bank New York County 1968—. Chmn. bd. trustees Westchester Community Coll; past pres. Legal Aid Soc. West County. Served from pvt. to lt. col. USAAF. 1942-46. Recipient Leffinqwell medal, 1960. Mem. N. Y. State Bankers Assn. (pres. 1969-70. Episcopalian. Clubs: Westchester Country (Harrison, N.Y.); Whippoorwill (Armonk, N.Y.). Home: 4 Old Farm Rd 5 Pleasantville NY 10570 Office: 235 Main St White Plains NY 10601

KLIEFORTH, ALEXANDER ALFRED, govt. ofcl.; b. Archangel, Russia, Dec. 31, 1918 (parents Am. citizens); s. Alfred W. and Barbara A. (Leslie) K.; student U. Louvain (Belgium), 1938-39, U. Geneva (Switzerland), 1938; A.B., St. Norbert Coll., 1940, LL.D., 1961; postgrad., George Washington U., 1950-52; A.M., Fletcher Sch. Law and Diplomacy, 1941; m. Jane A. Courtney, Aug. 1, 1944 (dec.); children—Alexander, William; m. 2d, Gloria P. Fiora, Jan. 20, 1968. Teaching fellow St. Norbert Coll., 1939-40; jr. econ. analyst Am. embassy, Bogota, Colombia, 1941-43; vice consul, Cali, Colombia, 1943-44; supr. fgn. lang. dept. Sch. Advanced Internat. Studies, Washington, 1946-49; pub. information officer, dep. exec. dir. War Claims Commn., 1951-54; successively chief, French service, chief, E. Europe br., chief W. and N. Europe br., chief European div., Voice of Am., USIA, 1955-58; dir. Radio in Am. Sector, U.S. Mission, Berlin, Germany, 1959- 61; program dir. Voice of Am., 1961-66; Sr. Seminar in Fgn. Policy, Dept. State, 1966-67; counsellor of embassy, Rome, Italy, 1967—. Served with AUS, 1944-46. Home: Lemon Grove CA 92045 Office: Am Embassy Rome Italy

KLIGERMAN, MORTON M., radiologist; b. Phila., Dec. 26, 1917; s. Samuel and Dorothy (Medvene) K.; B.S., Temple U., 1938, M.D., 1941, M.S., 1948; m. Barbara B. Coleman, Mar. 14, 1956; children—Hilary, Thomas A., Valiá C. Intern, resident Temple U. Hosp., 1941-44, instr. radiology Temple U. Med. Sch. and Hosp., 1947-48; asst. radiologist Presbyn. Hosp., N.Y.C., 1948-49, asso. attending radiologist, 1956-58; instr. radiology Columbia, 1948-49, asst. prof., 1950-53, asso. prof., 1953-58; Robert E. Hunter prof. radiology, chmn. dept. radiology Yale Sch. Medicine, 1958—; radiologist-in-chief Yale-New Haven Hosp., 1958—. Served from lt. to capt. M.C., AUS, 1944-47. Fellow Royal Soc. Medicine (London), Am. Coll. Radiology; mem. Assn. U. Radiologists (sec.-treas. 1965-66; pres. 1967-68), Am. Soc. Therapeutic Radiology (pres. 1969), Am. Roentgen Ray Soc., Babcock Hon. Surg. Soc., Am. Radium Soc. (v.p. 1971), Conn., New Haven County Med. Socs., Radiol. Soc. N.Am., Radiation Research Soc., A.A.A.S. Contbr. articles in field. Co-editor: Yearbook of Radiology, 1954-64. Home: 274 Ogden St New Haven CT 06511 Office: 333 Cedar St New Haven CT 06510

KLIMCZAK, ERNEST JOSEPH, mfg. co. exec.; b. Chgo., Aug. 3, 1924; s. John and Angeline (Niadek) K.; B.S., Ill. Inst. Tech., 1945; M.B.A., U. Chgo., 1958; m. Bernice Klimezak. Employed with Ahlberg Bearning Co., Chgo., 1943- 58, v.p., gen. mgr., dir., 1955-58; exec. v.p., dir. Braden Winch Co., Tulsa, 1958-61; gen. mgr. Arrow Gear Co., Tulsa, 1958-61; v.p. Motor Products Corp., Detroit, 1959-61; pres., dir. Allied/Egry Bus. Systems, Inc., Dayton, O., 1959-65, Egry Continuous Forms, Ltd., Toronto, Can., 1960-65, Allied Paper Inc., Kalamazoo, 1964—. Registered profl. engr., Ill. Mem. Pi Tau Sigma. Home: 2624 Brookhaven Dr Portage MI 49008 Office: 1608 Lake St Kalamazoo MI 49003

KLIMPL, EMANUEL, business exec.; b. 1915; B.S., Coll. City N.Y.; LL.B., Columbia U., 1938. Admitted to N.Y. bar, 1939; partner Parker, Chapin & Flattau, N.Y.C.; v.p., dir., sec. Spartans Industries, Inc.*

KLINE, ARTHUR F., educator: b. Anderson, Ind., Oct. 13, 1919; s. Auzro and Mable (McCarty) K.; A.B., Ball State U., 1946; Ph.D., Ind. U., 1962; m. Margaret Sue Venable, May 7, 1943; children—Cheryl Ann, Gerald Wesley. Asst. prof. sociology Western State Coll., Gunnison, Colo., 1951-55, Ind. State Coll., Terre Haute, 1955-59, U. Fla., 1959-60; mem. faculty Ind. State U., 1960—, prof. sociology, chmn. dept., 1963—. Chmn. citizens adv. council Vigo County Circuit Ct., Terre Haute, 1962-63; pres. bd. Wesley Found., Terre Haute, 1965-68; mem. citizens adv. council Gov. Ind. Youth Commn., 1962-63. Served to capt. AUS, 1942-46. Mem. Am. Sociol. Assn., Nat. Council Family Relations, Nat. Council Crime and Delinquency, Am. Soc. Criminology, Soc. Study Social Problems, Ohio Valley, Midwest sociol socs., Blue Key, Alpha Kappa Delta, Sigma Zeta, Kappa Delta Pi. Home: 76 Judith La Terre Haute IN 47802

KLINE, CHARLES EDWIN, bldg. and loan assn. exec.; b. Boonsboro, Md., June 12, 1907; s. Stanley Pefov Fahrney and Julia Catherine (Mullendove) K.; B.S. in Econs., Wharton Sch. Finance U. Pa., 1929; m. Dorotha E. Eldridge, July 12, 1940 (separated). Teller, Boonsboro (Md.) Bank, 1929-31; examiner Md. Bank Dept., 1933; nat. bank examiner Comptroller of Currency, 1933-38; asst. mgr. First Fed. Savs. and Loan Assn., Washington, 1938-42; asst. to pres. Fed. Home Loan Bank, Greensboro, N.C., 1942-43; sec., 1946-50; exec. v.p., dir. Citizens Bldg. & Loan Assn., Silver Spring, Md., 1950-53, pres., dir., 1953—; v.p. Potomac Apts., Hagerstown, Md., 1950—; pres., dir. Kline Bros., Inc., Boonsboro, 1961-64; pres. Am. Savs. and Loan Inst., Washington chpt., 1940; dir. Security Title & Guarentee Corp., Balt., 1952—, Md. Mortgage Co., Balt., 1953—, Md Savs.-Share Ins. Corp., 1962-66, Met. Nat. Bank, Silver Spring. Mem. com. mgmt. Silver Spring br. Met. YMCA, 1951-63, chmn. com. mgmt., 1955-56, dir., 1956-60, gen. chmn. Capital Fund Dr., 1960, asst. to pres., 1962, v.p., 1964; pres. Met. Washington YMCA, 1965; mem. Nat. Council YMCAs, v.p. Central Atlantic area YMCA, 1958-62, sec., 1962-64; dir. Health and Welfare Council Met. Washington, 1951-54; campaign chmn. Montgomery County Community Chest and Council, 1955, v.p., 1956; bd. dirs. Montgomery County Assn. Retarded Children, 1955-56; treas. Montgomery County chpt. A.R.C., 1956-68; dir. Silver Spring Progress Com., 1962, Md. Council Crime and Delinquency, 1962—; dist. com. mem. at large Capital Area Council Boy Scouts Am., 1965; pres., dir. Friends of Clara Barton, Inc., 1964—. Bd. dirs. Montgomery County Retarded Children's Day Center, Montgomery County Arts Center. Served to lt. col. AUS, 1943-45. Recipient ann. award outstanding leadership Montgomery County Community Chest, 1957, Charles G. Scott award outstanding service, 1960; named YMCA Man of Year, 1964. Mem. Md. (dir. 1956—), Met. Washington (dir. 1968) savs. and loan leagues. Rotarian. Clubs; Columbia Country. Home: 1011 Arlington Blvd Arlington VA 22209 Office: 8485 Fenton St Silver Spring MD 20910

KLINE, CHARLES TALCOTT, newspaper exec.; b. Chgo., Jan. 18, 1911; s. William Shinn and Elma Erwin (Talcott) K.; A.B., U. Mich., 1932; m. Velma Helene Case, Apr. 20, 1935 (dec. July 1955); children—Marion Suzanne, Charles Talcott; m. 2d. Janet Poulsen, July 3, 1956; childrenNan, Sue. George. Began career in the advt. dept. Chgo. Tribune, 1934-35, Chgo. Times, 1935-37; nat. newspaper rep., 1937-43; sales dept. Met. Sunday Newspapers, Inc., 1943-50, Western mgr., 1950-53, v.p. 1953-54, pres., 1954—; dir. Standard of Am. Life Ins. Co. Pres. Newspaper Comics Council. Mem. Sigma Delta Chi, Theta Delta Chi. Clubs: University (Chgo.); Union League (Mich.), Overseas Press (N.Y.C.); Patterson, Saugatuck Shores (Westport, Conn.). Home: Twin Bridge Acres Rd Westport CT 06880 Office: 260 Madison Av New York City NY 10016

KLINE, CLAIRE BENTON, Jr., sem. pres. b. Pitts., May 13, 1925; s. Claire Benton and Wilma S. (Huot) K.; B.A., Coll. Wooster. 1944; B.D., Princeton Theol. Sem., 1948, Th. M., 1949; Ph.D., Yale, 1961; m. Mary C. Hicks, June 6, 1950; children—John B., Mary M. Ordained to ministry Presbyn. Ch. U.S.A., 1948; asst. instr. philosophy Yale, 1950- 51; interim supply pastor, Bklyn., 1950-51; asst. prof. philosophy Agnes Scott Coll., 1951-61, asso. prof., 1961-62, prof., 1962-68, chmn. dept., 1957-63, dean faculty, 1957-68; vis. prof. theology Columbia Theol. Sem., 1964-65, prof. theology, dean faculty, 1969-71, pres., 1971—; vis. asst. prof. philosophy Emory U., summers 1952-54, 56. Mem. UN Assn. U.S.A. (v.p. Atlanta Chpt.), Phi Beta Kappa. Democrat. Home: 320 Inman Dr Decatur GA 30030

KLINE, DANIEL L., educator; b. Phila., Dec. 25, 1917; s. Emanuel and Hettie (Salkowe) K.; B.S., Purdue U., 1942; Ph.D. in Physiology, Columbia Coll. Phys. and Surg., 1946; m. Vivian Bass. Apr. 25, 1945; children—Katherine, Elizabeth, Emily. Instr. physiology Columbia Coll. Phys. and Surg., 1945; from asst. prof. to asso. prof. physiology Yale Med. Sch., 1949- 66; prof. physiology, chmn. dept. Cin. Coll. Medicine, 1966—. Guggenheim fellow, 1957-58. Mem. Am. Physiol. Soc., Am. Assn. U. Profs., Assn. Am. Med. Colls., Am. Fedn. Scientists, A.A.A.S., Sigma Xi. Mem. editorial bd. Am. Jour. Physiology, 1965-70, Jour. Applied Physiology; cons. editor Science. Home: 933 Avondale Av Cincinnati OH 45229

KLINE, GEORGE H., ins. co. exec.; b. Leonia, N.J., Sept. 15, 1916; B.A., M.A. in Pub. Adminstrn., LL.B., Syracuse U. With N.Y. State Ins. Dept. 1948-53, dep. supt., 1950-53; with Allstate Ins. Co., 1954—, v.p., sec. gen. counsel, 1957—. Mem. N.Y., Ill. bar Assns., Phi Beta Kappa, Phi Delta Phi. Pi Gamma Mu. Home: 727 Forest Av Wilmette IL Office: Allstate Plaza Northbrook IL 60062

KLINE, GEORGE LOUIS, educator, author; b. galesburg, Ill., Mar. 3, 1921; s. Allen Sides and Wahneta (Burner) K.; student Boston U., 1938-41; A.B. with honors, Columbia Coll., 1947; M.A., Columbia, 1948, Ph.D., 1950; m. Virginia Harrington Hardy, Apr. 17, 1943; children—Brenda Marie, Jeffrey Allen, Christina Hardy. Instr. philosophy Columbia, 1950-52, 53-54, asst. prof., 1954-60, vis. asst. prof. U. Chgo., 1952-53; asso. prof. philosophy and Russian, Bryn Mawr Coll., 1960-66, prof. philosophy, 1966- -. Served with USAAF. 1942-45. Decorated D.F.C; recipient Cutting Traveling fellowship to Paris, 1949-50; Fulbright fellowship, 1950; Ford fellowship to Paris, 1954-55; Rockefeller fellowship to USSR and E. Europe, 1960; Sr. fellowship Nat. Endowment for the Humanities, 1970-71. Mem. Am. Philos. Assn., Soc. Ancient Greek Philosophy, Metaphys. Soc. Am. (councillor 1969-71), Philosophy Edn. Soc. (pub. Rev. Metaphys.; dir. 1966—), Soc. Phenomenology and Existential Philosophy, Am. Assn. Advancement Slavic Studies, Hegel Soc. Am. (councillor 1968-70, v.p. 1971—), Phi Beta Kappa. Author: Spinoza in Soviet Philosophy, 1952; Religious and Anti- Religious Thought in Russia, 1968; co-author Continuity and Change in Russian and Soviet Thought, 1955; Marx and the Western World, 1967; Phenomenology and Existentialism, 1967, rev. edit., 1969; Hegel and The Philosophy of Religion, 1970. Translator: History of Russian Philosophy (V.V. Zenkovsky), 2 vols., 1953. Editor: Soviet Education, 1957; Alfred North Whitehead: Essays on his Philosophy, 1963. Editor, contbr.; European Philosophy Today, 1965. Co-editor, contbr.: Russian Philosophy, 3 vols., 1965, 2d edit., 1969. Co-editor: Jour. Philosophy, 1959-64, cons. editor, 1964—; cons. editor Ency. Philosophy, 1962-67, Studies in Soviet Thought, 1962—, Jour. Value Inquiry, 1967—, Process Studies, 1970—; cons. editor philosophy Current Digest of Soviet Press, 1961-64. Home: 632 Valley View Rd Ardmore PA 19003 Office: Thomas Library Bryn Mawr Coll Bryn Mawr PA 19010

KLINE, GORDON MABEY, chemist, editor; b. Trenton, N.J., Feb. 9, 1903; s. Manuel Kuhl and Florence (Campbell) K.; A.B., Colgate U., 1925; M.S., George Washington U., 1926; Ph.D., U. Md., 1934; m. Dorothy Beard, Mar. 15, 1926; 1 dau. Ann Linthicum (Mrs. Robert True Cook). Research chemist N.Y. State Dept. Health, 1926-27; research chemist Picatinny Arsenal, 1928-29; chemist, phys. sci. adminstr. Nat. Bur. Standards, Washington, 1929-69, chief organic plastics sect., 1935-51, chief div. polymers, 1951-63, cons. 1964-69; tech. editor Modern Plastics Mag., editorial dir., cons. Modern Plastics Ency., 1936—; tech. investigator with U.S. Army, ETO, 1945. Chmn. tech. com. on plastics Internat. Standardization Orgn., ann. meetings N.Y.C., 1951, Turin, Italy, 1952, Stockholm, Sweden, 1953, Brighton, Eng., 1954. Paris, France, 1955, The Hague, Netherlands, 1956, Burgenstock, Switzerland, 1957, Washington, 1958, U.S. del., Munich, 1959, Prague, 1960, Turin, 1961, Warsaw, 1962, London, 1963, Budapest, 1964, Bucharest, 1965, Stockholm, Sweden, 1966, Phila., 1968, Prague, 1969, Paris, 1970; sec. div. plastics and polymers Internat. Union Pure and Applied Chemistry 1951- 59, vice chmn., 1959-63, chmn., 1963-67, mem. macro-molecules div., 1967- -; plastics adv. council Princeton, 1957-65. Recipient Honor award Am. Inst. Chemists, Washington sect., 1952, Exceptional Service Gold medal Dept. Commerce, 1953, award Standards Engrs. Soc., 1964, Rosa award Nat. Bur. Standards, 1965. Mem. Am. Soc. Testing Materials (award of merit 1954), Am. Chem. Soc., Am. Inst. Chemists, Soc. Plastics Engrs., Soc. Plastics Industry, Phi Beta Kappa, Sigma Xi. Clubs: Cosmos (Washington); Chemists (N.Y.C.). Editor: Analytical Chemistry of Polymers, Part 1, 1959, Parts 11 and 111, 1961. Contbr. articles profl. jours. Home: 331 S Palmway Lake Worth FL 33460 Office: 1301 Av Americas New York City NY 10019

KLINE, HAROLD BENNET, mining co. exec.; b. Columbia, Mo., Aug. 10, 1910; s. Harold Bennett and Florence Rollins (Gray) K.; A.B., U. Mo., 1932; LL.B. (editor Law Rev.), Harvard, 1935. Admitted to N.Y. bar, 1937, Mo. bar, 1947, Wis. bar, 1953; with firm Root, Clark, Buckner & Ballantine, N.Y.C., 1935-41; pvt. practice, St. Louis, 1947-49; counsel Fed. Res. Bank, St. Louis, 1950-52; atty. Gen. Electric Co., 1953-57; with Tex. Gulf Sulphur Co., N.Y.C., 1958—, sec., 1961-63, v.p., sec., 1963-64, v.p. adminstrv. affairs, gen. counsel, 1964—. Served with AUS, 1942-46. Mem. Phi Beta Kappa, Phi Delta Theta. Episcopalian. Home: 860 UN Plaza New York City NY 10017 Office: 200 Park Av New York City NY 10017

KLINE, HIBBERD VAN BUREN, Jr., geographer, educator; b. Leonia, N.J., Oct. 16, 1913; s. Hibberd Van Buren and Helen (Howard) K.; A.B. magna cum laude, Syracuse U., 1936; M.A., U. Wis., 1938, Ph.D., 1941; m. Caryl Morse, Aug. 5, 1939; children—Hibberd Van Buren III, Wayne Morse. Research analyst Library of Congress, 1941; geographer, chief cartographer OSS, 1941-43, chief map div., Algiers, 1943-44, chief map div., London, 1944-45; chief map intelligence sect. State Dept., 1945-46, chief cartographic br., 1946- 47; vis. lectr. U. Wis., 1947; vis. prof. Grad. Sch. Bus., Columbia, 1952; asst., then asso. prof. geography, Syracuse U., 1946-59; sr. lectr. Fourah Bay Coll., Sierra Leone, 1954-55; prof. geography, chmn. dept., also chmn. African studies program, U. Pitts., 1959—, acting dean grad. div. social Scis., 1966-67, sec. univ. senate, 1969—; cons. ECA and MSA, 1950-53, 20th Century Fund, 1954-59, African misson ICA, 1961; mem. com. geography NRC, 1948-52; co-ordinator tng. project for Liberia, Peace Corps, 1962. Pres. Pitt Resources Devel. Inst., Pitts., 1966—; v.p. U. Sci. Center, Pitts., 1968—. Mem. Assn. Am. Geographers, African Studies Assn. (founder), Phi Beta Kappa, Sigma Xi, Phi Kappa Phi. Home: 210 Tennyson Av Pittsburgh PA 15213 Office: U Pittsburgh Pittsburgh PA 15213

KLINE, JOHN WILLIAM, air force officer; b. Zanesville, O., June 26, 1919; s. Gerry William and Lillian Elizabeth (Scheider) K.; student Ohio U., 1937-40; grad. Primary, Basic and Advanced Flying Schs., 1941, Air Command and Staff Sch., 1949, Air War Coll., 1959; m. Katherine Edmond Winton, Oct. 24, 1942; children—Susan Isabel (Mrs. John Farris Morehead), Flora Edmond (Mrs. Richard Grandall Creighton), Elizabeth Gerry. Commd. 2d lt. USAAF, 1941, advanced through grades to maj. gen. USAF, 1969; comdr. 2d Bomb Wing, Hunter AFB, Ga., 1961-63, 397th Bomb Wing, Dow AFB, Me., 1963-64; dir. operations, chief staff Hdqrs. 8th Air Force, Westover AFB, Mass., 964-66; vice comdr. 3rd Air Div., Andersen AFB, Guam, 1966-68; asst. dep. chief staff operations Hdqrs. SAC, Offutt AFB, Neb., 1968-69; vice-comdr. 2d Air Force, Barksdale AFB, La., 1969—. Decorated Legion of Merit with 3 oak leaf clusters, Air medal with oak leaf cluster, Air Force Commendation medal; Air Force Distinguished Service Order (Republic Vietnam). Mem. Beta Theta Pi. Presbyn. Club: Shreveport Country. Home: 205 Av B W Barksdale AFB LA 71110 Office: Vice Commander 2d Air Force Barksdale AFB LA 71110

KLINE, LEE B., architect; b. Renton, Wash., Feb. 2, 1914; s. Abraham McCubbin and Pearl (Davidson) K.; B.Arch., U. So. Cal., 1937; m. Martha Stiglmeier, Aug. 29, 1936; children—Patricia (Mrs. Patricia Lemon), Joanne Louise. Draftsman, designer, 1937-43; pvt. archtl. practice, Los Angeles, 1943—; instr. engring. extension U. Cal., 1947-53; mem. panel arbitrators Am. Arbitration Assn., 1964—. Dir. LaCanada br. A.R.C., 1959—. Pres. LaCanada Irrigation Dist., 1966—, dir., 1963—. Recipient distinguished service citation, Cal. council A.I.A., 1960, honor awards, A.I.A., 1957, 59, School of the Month awards, Nation's Schools, 1964, 71. Fellow A.I.A. (pres. Pasadena chpt. 1957, pres. Cal. council 1959). Home: 5160 Oakwood Av LaCanada CA 91011 Office: 963 W Colorado Blvd Los Angeles CA 90041

KLINE, MORRIS, educator; b. Bklyn., May 1, 1908; s. Bernard and Sarah (Spatt) K.; B.Sc., N.Y. U., 1930, M.Sc., 1932, Ph.D., 1936; m. Helen Mann, Sept. 4, 1939; children—Elizabeth Mann, Judith Mann, Douglas Mann. Asst., Inst. Advanced Study, Princeton, 1936-38; faculty N.Y. U., 1938-42, 45—, prof. math., 1952—, dir. div. electromagnetic research, 1946-66, chmn. dept. math. Washington Sq. Coll., 1959-70; Physicist Signal Corps Engring. Labs., Ft. Monmouth, N.J., 1942-45. Guggenheim fellow, 1958-59; Fulbright lectr. in Germany, 1958-59. Mem. Am. Math. Soc., Math. Assn. Am., I.E.E.E. Author: Mathematics in Western Culture, 1953; Mathematics and the Physical World. 1959; Mathematics, A Cultural Approach, 1962; Electromagnetic Theory and Geometrical Optics, 1965; Calculus, An Intuitive and Physical Approach, 2 vols., 1967; Mathematics for Liberal Arts, 1967. Editor: The Theory of Electromagnetic Waves, 1951; Mathematics in the Modern World, 1968. Home: 1024 E 26th St Brooklyn NY 10010 Office: N Y U Washington Square New York City NY 10003

KLINE, MURRAY ROBERT Jr. diversified mfg. co. exec.; b. Cin., May 21, 1910; grad. Phillips Acad., Andover, Mass., 1927; B.S., Princeton, 1931; postgrad. Mass. Inst. Tech., 1931-33; m. Jean R. Holland, June 16, 1935; children--Lois A., Andrew M., James. Salesman, Brown Mfg. Co., Boston, 1932-33; jr. engr. Ball Metals Co., Carson City, Nev., 1933-36, engr., 1936-37, sr. engr., 1937-40; project engr. Kingston Engring. Co., Los Angeles, 1940-43; with dept. engring. City of Denver, 1946-50, dep. head, 1950-52; 2d v.p. Johnson Mfg. Co., Kansas City, Kansas, 1952-54, v.p. for engring., 1954-57; v.p. research Consol. Industries, Inc., South Bend, Ind., 1957-60, exec. v.p., 1960-65, pres., 1965-70, chmn. bd., chief exec. officer, 1970--, also dir.; dir. ABC Chem. Co., 2d Nat. Bank, Country Food Storage Co., Providence Indsl. Corp. (Ind.), Wilson Investment Co., Inc., Hammond Life Ins. Co., Inc. (Ind.), Prudential Ins. Co., Haverford Mfg. Co., Leader Pub. Co. Pres., Dewey High Sch., Kansas City, Mo., 1953-54; fund chmn. local div. Salvation Army, 1959-60. Mem. South Bend Republican Com., 1964-68. Bd. dirs. Ind. council Boy Scouts Am., 1969-71; trustee Lovell Found. Served to lt., Corps Engrs., AUS, 1943-45. Decorated Bronze Star medal. Member N.A.M., South Bend C. of C. (v.p. 1963-65, dir. 1965-70), Am. Mgmt. Assn., Ind. Engrs. Soc. (program com. 1961-62), Princeton Alumni Assn. Episcopalian. Rotarian, Optimist. Clubs: South Bend Golf; Links (N.Y.C.). Home: 6823 Broad Terrace Av South Bend IN 46505 Office: PO Box 1019 South Bend IN 46501

KLINE, NICHOLAS FREDERICK chemist, educator; b. Chicago, 1928; B.S. in Physics, Yale, 1950; Ph.D. in Chemistry, Harvard, 1956; m. Sally Ann Jones, July 5, 1957; children--Kenneth J., Nancy A. Chemist, Acme Chem. Co., Blue Island, Ill., 1950-51; director of Research Lab., Indsl. Chemicals Corp., Cambridge, Mass., 1956-60; project coordinator environmental sect. Steinmetz Assos., Chgo., 1960-61; v.p. for research Bauer Bros. Chem. Co., Inc., Memphis,

1961-64; asst. prof. chemistry Washington U., St. Louis, 1964-66, asso. prof., 1966-70, prof., 1970--, head of chemistry dept., 1970-71. Vis. prof. So. Ill. U., summer 1967, U. of Ore., 1969. Scoutmaster, Boy Scouts America, University City, Mo., 1968-70. Bd. dirs. Rest Haven Home for Elderly, 1960-61; trustee of the Lutheran Hosp., 1965-71. Served from lt. to capt., AUS, 1951-53. Mem. Am. Chem. Soc., Sci. Research Soc. Am. (chpt. treas. 1967), Sigma Xi. Author: (with others) Basic Inorganic Chemistry, 1971. Home: Fairfax Apts 7291 Windermere Dr University City MO 63105 Office: Dept Chemistry Washington University St Louis MO 63130

KLINE, ORAL LEE, biochemist; b. Reynolds, Ind., Sept. 12, 1905; s. Aaron and Mary A. (Green) K.; B.S., U. Wis., 1929, M.S., 1931, Ph.D., 1934; m. Susan White, July 10, 1929; children—Peter L., Michael J., Thomas J. Mem. dept. biochemistry U. Wis., 1934-35; biochemist div. nutrition FDA, 1936-47, dir. research div. nutrition, 1947-58, dir. div. food, 1958-59, dir. div. nutrition, 1959-62, asst. commr. sci., 1962-66; dir. Office Nutrition Sci. Services, Am. Inst. Nutrition, 1966—, exec. officer, 1971—. Mem. adv. coms. for NRC U.S. Pharmacopia and Nat. Formulary; chmn. Nat. Acad. Scis. Nat. Com. for the Internat. Union of Nutrition Scis., 1964-67; mem. coms. arrangements Internat. Nutrition Congress, 1960, Internat. Congress Antibiotics, 1953. Recipient Distinguished Service award Dept. Health, Edn. and Welfare, 1956; C.A. Elvehjem Pub. Service in Nutrition award, Am. Inst. Nutrition, 1971. Fellow A.A.A.S.; mem. Am. Inst. Nutrition (council 1953-56; asso. editor jour.; pres. 1965-66), Am. Chem. Soc., Soc. Exptl. Biology and Medicine (chmn. D.C. 1949), Animal Nutrition Research Council (chmn. 1952), Assn. Ofcl. Agrl. Chemists (referee nutritional adjuncts 1950-58), Am. Pub. Health Assn. Club: Cosmos (Washington). Author numerous articles in field, contbr. jours., encys. Home: 9416 Holland Ct Bethesda MD 20014 Office: 9650 Rockville Pike Bethesda MD 20014

KLINE, REAMER, coll. pres.; b. San Jose, Cal., Dec. 2, 1910; s. Allen Marshall and Florence (Reamer) K.; B.A., Middlebury (Vt.) Coll., 1932, D.D. (hon.), 1955; M.A., U. Mich. 1936; B.D., Episcopal Theol. Sch. Cambridge, Mass., 1938; D.D. Middlebury Coll., 1955., S.T.D. Gen. Theol. Sem., 1963; m. Louise E. Brayton, June 17, 1933; children—Florence (Mrs. David Britton), Penelope (Mrs. William Bardel), Marcia. Asst. editor Lydonville (Vt.) Union Jour., Colebroke (N.H.) News and Sentinel, 1933-34; ordained to ministry Episcopal Ch., 1938; curate, Fitchburg, Mass., 1938; rector, Nashua, N.H., 1938-44, St. Mark's Ch., New Britain, Conn. 1944-60; pres. Bard Coll. Annandale-on- Hudson, 1960—. Pres. standing com. Diocese Comm., 1955-56, chmn. dept. Christian edn., 1945-60; del. gen. convs. Episcopal Ch., 1943, 55, 58; convenor nat. confs. ch. and city Episcopal Ch., 1958-61. Chmn., New Britain Civil Rights Commn., 1957-60; mem. New Britain Commn. Urban Redevel., 1951-57. Bd. dirs. Empire State Found. Liberal Arts Coll., Union for Experimenting Colls.; founding mem. Assn. Episcopal Colls. Address: Bard Coll Annandale-on-Hudson NY 12504

KLINE, RICHARD ERIC mfg. exec.; b. Lima, O., Apr. 1, 1932; B.S., U. San Francisco, 1954; M.S., Stanford University, 1956; m. Rosemarie Lois Brown, May 15, 1955; 1 son, Anthony Robinson. Sales rep. Ames-Brockton Fabricated Products, Akron, O., 1956-58, sales mgr. Coshocton, Ohio, 1959-61, gen. manager plant, 1961-68, v.p. · sales, 1968--. Instr. bus. Coshocton Jr. College, 1968-69. Secretary Coshocton YMCA, 1960-61; active Boy Scouts of America. Named Man of Year, Coshocton Junior Chamber of Commerce, 1968. Mem. Coshocton C. of C. (vice president 1967-68, pres. 1969-70), English Speaking Union, Coshocton Sertoma Club, Nat. Assn. Mfrs., Sales Executives Institute, Phi Beta Kappa, Sigma Chi, Phi Mu. Democrat. Mem. Christian Ch. (lay leader). Mason (32, Shriner). Clubs: Coshocton Country, Coshocton City, Running Deer Country. Home: 2d Av Coshocton OH Office: 3d Av Coshocton OH

KLINE, ROBERT REEVES, clergyman, educator; b. Williamsport, Pa., Dec. 27, 1918; s. Feorge F. and Gertrude (Thibodeau) K.; B.A., Mt. St. Mary's Coll., Emmitsburg, Md., 1941; student Mt. St. Mary's Sem., Emmitsburg, 1941-45; M.A., Georgetown U., 1951, Ph.D., 1959. Ordained priest Roman Catholic Ch., 1945, created domestic prelate, 1962; parish priest Diocese of Scranton, Pa., 1945-47; asst. dean mem. Mt. St. Mary's Coll., 1947-53, chaplain, 1953- 57; chaplain St. Joseph Coll. Women, Emmitsburg, 1957-61, lectr., 1947- -; chmn. dept. philosophy Mt. St. Mary's Coll. and Sem., 1952-62, pres., 1961-67, chmn. dept. psychology and sociology, 1969—, trustee, 1951-68, chmn. bd. trustees, 1961-67. Prosynodal judge Matrimonial Tribunal, Archdiocese of Balt., 1971—. Mem. Am. Cath. Philos. Assn., Acad. Religion and Mental Health, Monsignor Tierney Honor Soc., Delta Epsilon Sigma. Author: The Present State of Axiology in the United States, 1959. Address: Mt St Mary's Coll and Sem Emmitsburg MD 21727

KLINE, SIDNEY DELONG, banker; b. West Reading, Pa., June 15, 1902; s. Simon S. and Elda M. (DeLong) K.; A.B., Dickinson Coll., Carlisle, Pa., 1924, M.A., 1926, LL.B., 1926, LL.D., 1956; LL.D., Albright Coll., 1955; m. Leona C. Barkalow, Aug. 4, 1928; children—Joan Clarice (Mrs. Ralph M. Gingrich), Sidney DeLong, Robert Cornelius, Elinor Susan (Mrs. Charles R. Hart). Admitted to Pa. bar, 1926; clk. Mut. Trust Co., Phila., 1926-27; jr. officer Union Bank & Trust Co., 1927-28, Corn Exchange Nat. Bank & Trust Co., 1928-29; trust officer Colonial Trust Co., Reading, Pa., 1929-33; v.p. Am. Bank & Trust Co. Pa. (formerly Berks County Trust Co.), 1933-44, pres., dir., 1944-68, chmn. bd., 1960—, chief exec. officer, 1968—; chmn. Berks Title Ins. Co., Reading; dir.Bell Telephone Co. Pa., Am. Casualty Co., Reading; Valley Forge Ins. Co., Valley Forge Life Ins. Co. (Reading), Reading Co. (Phila.). Trustee, Dickinson Coll., Dickinson Sch. Law, Albright Coll., Reading; pres. Greater Berks Devel. Fund. Mem. Pa. Bankers Assn. (past pres.), Am., Pa. bar assns. Clubs: Berkshire Country, Wyomissing (Reading). Home: 62 Grandview Blvd Wyomissing Hills Reading PA 19610 Office: 35 N 6th St Reading PA 19601

KLINEFELTER, JAMES LOUIS, lawyer; b. Los Angeles, Oct. 8, 1925; s. Theron Albert and Anna Marie (Coffey) K.; B.A., U. Ala., 1949, LL.B., 1951; m. Joanne Wright, Dec. 26, 1957 (div.); children-Patricia Anne, Jeanne Marie, Christopher Wright. Admitted to Ala. bar, 1951; regional claims rep. State Far Mut. Auto Ins. Co., Anniston, Ala., 1951-54; partner firm Burnham, Klinefelter and Halsey, Anniston, 1954—, Dir. So. Plating and Mfg. Co. Mem. Ala. and Calhoun County Democratic Exec. Com., 1964—. Served to lt. (j.g.) USNR, 1943-46. Mem. Am., Ala. (sec.-treas. practice and prodecure sect.), Calhoun County bar assns., Phi Kappa Sigma, Phi Alpha Theta. Clubs: Kiwanis (past pres.), Anniston Country (Anniston). Home: 713 Oak St Anniston AL 36201 Office: Comml Nat Bank Bldg P O Box 1618 Anniston AL 36202

KLING, JOHN F., banker; b. 1928; student Wharton Sch. U. Pa., Temple U.; married. Mgr. electronic data processing dept. Penn Mut. Life Ins. Co., 1960-64; sr. v.p. operations div. Continental Bank & Trust Co., Norristown, Pa., 1964-68; v.p. corporate planning Provident Nat. Bank subsidiary Provident Nat. Corp., Phila., 1968-69, sr. v.p. operations div. and corporate planning, 1969, treas., asst. sec. Provident Nat. Corp., 1969—. Served as 1st lt. AUS, 1946-47, 51-52. Office: Broad and Chestnut Sts Philadelphia PA 19101*

KLING, JULIUS WILLIAM, psychologist, educator; b. Bklyn., Dec. 22, 1922; s. Julius Eugene and Eva (Berger) K.; B.A., U. Ill., 1948, M.A., 1949, Ph.D., 195l; M.A., Brown U., 1958; m. Jane Ella Stewart, July 22, 1945; children—Katherine Louise (Mrs. Winter), Patricia Ellen, William Stewart, Andrew Arthur. Asst., U. Ill., 1948-51; instr. to prof. Brown U., Providence, 1951—, chmn. psychology Dept., 1964—; mem. study sect., Nat. Inst. Mental Health, 1964-68. USPHS spl. research fellow, Eng., 1968-69. Served to 1st lt., cav., AUS, 1942-47, Fellow Am. Psychol. Assn., A.A.A.S.; mem. Eastern, R.I. psychol. assns., Psychonomic Soc., Sigma Xi. Contbr. profl. jours. Home: 124 Morris Av Providence RI 02906

KLING, MERLE, educator; b. Russia, June 15, 1919: s. Saul and Dina (Hoffman) K.; came to U.S. 1921, naturalized, 1927; A.B., Washington U., St. Louis, 1940, M.A., 1941, Ph.D., 1949; m. Ann Ruth Yasgur, Jan. 1, 1948; 1 son, Arnold Saul. Mem. faculty Washington U., St. Louis, 1946—, prof. polit. sci., 1961—, dean faculty arts and scis., 1966-69, acting chmn. dept. polit. sci., 1970-71; vis. prof. U. Ill., 1961; research asso. Center Internat. Studies, Princeton, 1964-65. Served with AUS, 1942-45. Mem. Am. (council 1967-1969), Midwest (pres. 1969-70) polit. sci. assns., Midwest Conf. Polit. Scientists, Am. Assn. U. Profs., Phi Beta Kappa, Alpha Kappa Delta, Omicron Delta Kappa. Author: The Soviet Theory of Internationalism, 1952; A Mexican Interest Group in Action, 1961; also articles. Editor Midwest Jour. Polit. Sci., 1965-66. Home: 8166 Whitburn Dr St Louis MO 63105

KLING, SAMUEL GROVER, lawyer, author; b. N.Y.C., Feb. 4, 1910; s. Morris and Mary (Schilling) K.; student Balt. City Coll., U. Balt. Law Sch.; m. Esther C. Beierfeld, June 26, 1936 (dec. 1953); m. 2d, Rena Levine, Jan. 1, 1964. Feature article writer Balt. Sunday Sun, 1929-31; admitted to Md. bar, 1933, Fed. bar, 1940; began practice at Balt., 1933; book reviewer N.Y. Herald Tribune, Harvard Law Rev., N.Y. Times, Sat. Rev. of Lit.; lectr. marriage and divorce, 1940- -; nat. syndicated columnist Your Marriage, 1948-56; marriage cons. daily radio program Your Marriage, MBS, 1949. Mem. Am., Md. Balt. bar assns. Author: Your Legal Rights, 1945; The Marriage Reader, 1947; For Better, For Worse, 1947; Adventures in Love, 1948; The Art of Being Happy, 1948; Your Marriage Counselor. 1949; Handy Legal Adviser, 1949; The Marriage Guide, 1950; Your Legal Adviser, 1955; How to Win and Hold a Mate, 1957; Popular Legal Encyclopedia, 1957; The Legal Encyclopedia for Home and Business, 1959; The Complete Guide to Divorce, 1963; Complete Guide to Everyday Law, 1965; Sexual Behavior and the Law, 1965; Legal Encyclopedia and Dictionary, 1970; Your Will and What to do About It, 1971; contbr. legal articles Ency. Americana. Contbr. to nat. mags. Address: 4000 N Charles St Baltimore MD 21218

KLING, THEODORE, Jr., banker; b. Woobury, N.J., Aug. 18, 1925; s. Theodore and Catherine (O'Neill) K.; A.B., Lafayette Coll., 1948; LL.B., Temple U., 1952; m. Mary M. Clinton, Apr. 14, 1952; children—Catherine V., Jacqueline M., Theodore, Neill C., Bernard G. Pvt. legal practice, 1952-55; trust officer Fidelity Bank, Phila., 1965-66; v.p. Continental Bank, Norristown, Pa., 1966-69, adminstrv. v.p., 1969, sr. v.p., 1970—; dir. Billy Penn Corp., Phila. Mem. adv. bd. St. Joseph's Hosp., Phila., 1968—. Served with AUS, 1943-45. Rotarian. Club: Manufacturers Golf and Country (Oreland, Pa.). Home: 1909 Sycamore Lane Flourtown PA 19031 Office: Continental Bank Main and Swede Sts Norristown PA 19404

KLING, VINCENT GEORGE, architect; b. East Orange, N.J., May 9, 1916; s. G. Nelson and Pauline (Geiger) K.; B.Arch., Columbia, 1940; M. Arch., Mass. Inst. Tech., 1942; m. Caperton Booth, June 20, 1942; childrenVincent George, Robert Booth. Pvt. archtl. practice, Phila., 1946-; designer bldgs. U.S. and abroad. Mem. pub. adv. panel on archtl. services U.S. Govt. Gen. Services Adminstrn. Mem. Phila. Art Comn., Phila., Citizens' Council on City Planning. Trustee Columbia U., also Fountainebleu Fine Arts and Music Schs. Assn., Episcopal Acad., Overbrook, Pa.; asso. trustee U. Pa. Served to lt. USNR, 1941-46. Recipient 1st honor award A.I.A., 1954, Phila. Arts Festival award, 1959, Gold medal and diploma of Honor, City of Quito, Ecuador for design of U.S. Embassy office bldg.; Samuel Finley Breese Morse medal for arch. (Sharples Dining Hall, Swarthmore Coll.), N.A.D., 1968, others. Fellow A.I.A.; mem. N.J., Pa. socs. architects, C. of C. Greater Phila., Nat. Inst. Archtl. Edn., Am. Hosp. Assn., Am. Soc. Testing Materials, U.S. Naval Inst., Columbia U., Mass. Inst. Tech. alumni assns., S.A.R., Sigma Alpha Epsilon. Clubs: Union League; Golf; Bala (Pa.) Golf. Exec. architect Penn Center, Phila.; other prin. works included: Municipal Services Bldg., U.S. Mint, Jefferson Med. Coll. Hosp. and Sci. Center (all Phila.), Lankenau Hosp., Overbrook, U. Conn. Health Center, Swarthmore Coll. Library and Dining Hall. Home: 715 Righters Mill Rd Penn Valley PA 15675 Office: 1401 Arch St Philadelphia PA 19102

KLING, WILLIAM, bus. exec., ret. fgn. service officer; b. N.Y.C., May 8, 1915; s. Irving and Sophie (Kling) K.; B.S., Coll. City N.Y., 1937; M.S., Mass. State Coll., 1938; Ph.D., Clark U., 1943; m. Suzanne Kaufman (M.D.), June 28, 1940; children—Robert Irving, Michael Paul, Virginia Airini Susan. Grad. asst. Mass. State Coll., 1937-38, Clark U., 1938-39; instr. Coll. City N.Y., 1939-40; agrl. economist Dept. Agr., also War Foods Adminstrn., 1940-45; agrl. attache, Bucharest, Rumania, Budapest, Hungary, Belgrade, Yugoslavia, Sofia, Bulgeria, Tirana, Albania, 1945- 47; first sec., consul Am. embassy, London, 1948-54; 1st sec. consul Am. embassy, Wellington, New Zealand, 1954-60; assigned Dept. of State, Washington, 1960-68, chief div. of functional intelligence, 1961-63, dep. dir. and acting dir. Office of Functional and External Research, 1962-63; econ. adviser to Bur. African Affairs, U.S. Dept. State, 1963-66, dep. dir. econ. affairs Office Inter African Affairs, 1966-68; dir. govt. and econ. affairs Uniroyal, Inc., Washington, 1968—. Mem. Nat. Def. Exec. Res., 1970—; cons. to Office Emergency Preparedness Exec. Office of Pres., 1970—. Recipient Meritorious Honor award, State Dept., 1968. Mem. Am. Fgn. Service Assn., Soc. Internat. Devel., Air Force Assn., Navy League, Assn. U.S. Army, Washington Urban League, Am. Ordnance Assn., Am. Chem. Soc. Club: National Economic. Contbr. profl. jours. Home: 6434 Lakeview Dr Lake Barcroft Falls Church VA 22041 Office: Uniroyal Inc 1700 K St N W Washington DC 20006

KLINGBERG, FRANK WYSOR, educator; b. Los Angeles, May 24, 1919; s. Frank J. and Elizabeth (Wysor) K.; B.A., U. Cal. at Los Angeles, 1941, Ph.D., 1948; student Stanford, 1941-42, U. N.C., 1942; m. Katherine Stuart Moore, Mar. 3, 1945; children-Anne Elizabeth, Frank Moore, Mem. faculty U. N.C. at Chapel Hill, 1948—, prof. Am. history, 1955—, chmn. social sci. div., 1964-70, mem. chancellor's adv. com., 1970—. Grant-in-aid Carnegie Found., 1949, Huntington Library, 1954; grantee Social Sci. Research Council, 1954; Ford Found. fellow, 1954- 55. Mem. Am. Hist. Assn., So., Miss. Valley hist. socs., Delta Tau Delta. Author: Correspondence Between Henry Stephens Randall and Hugh Blair Grigsby; Southern Claims Commission, A Study in Unionism; Documentary History of the United States from 1965. Home: Hawthorne Lane Chapel Hill NC 27514

KLINGBERG, WILLIAM GENE, physician, educator; b. Wichita, Kan., Sept. 17, 1916; s. Harry Richard and Ethel (Martin) K.; A.B., Municipal U. Wichita, 1939; M.D. cum laude, Washington U., St. Louis, 1943; m. Barbara Jean Hendrickson, June 18, 1941 children-William Gene, Judith Jean, Susan Jane, John David. Intern, St. Louis Children's Hosp., 1943-44, 1944-45; asso. prof. pediatrics Washington U. Sch. Medicine, 1947-60; prof. pediatrics, head and chmn. dept. U. W.Va. Sch. Medicine, 1960-. Served to capt. AUS, 1945-47. Diplomate Am. Bd. Pediatrics. Mem. Am. Acad. Pediatrics, Alpha Omega Alpha, Sigma Chi. Home: 636 Bellaire Dr Morgantown WV

KLINGBIEL, RAY I., judge; b. 1901; student U. Notre Dame and Augustana Coll.; LL.B., U. Ill.; LL.D., Chgo. Kent Coll. of Law, 1964; m. Julia Stone; children—Donna, Tom. Admitted to Ill. bar, 1924; practiced in East Moline, Ill.; city atty., 1925-39; judge Ill. Circuit Ct., 1945-53; became justice Supreme Ct. Ill., 1953, chief justice, 1956-57, 63-66. Mayor, East Moline, 1939-45. Named Citizen of Year East Moline, 1957. Past pres. Ill. Municipal League. Mason (33). Contbr. articles law jours. Home: 4801 Coaltown Rd Moline IL 61265

KLINGEL, THOMAS RALPH, railroad ofcl.; b. St. Paul, Apr. 21, 1915; s. Edward L. and Jessie (Odor) K.; B.S. in Civil Engring., U. Minn., 1937; m. Natalja Hurley, Mar. 1, 1948; children—Jon Thomas, Louise. With engring. dept. Soo Line R.R. Co., 1937-38; insp. engring. Grad. Sch., U. Minn., 1938-39, asst. prof., then asso. prof. civil engring. Inst. Tech., 1947-51; with Soo Line R.R. Co., 1940-47, 51—, v.p. operations and maintenance, 1961-65, now exec. v.p. Mem. Am. Soc. Civil Engineers, Am. Ry. Engring. Assn. Home: 4106 Highwood Rd Minneapolis MN Office: Soo Line Bldg Minneapolis MN 55402

KLINGENSTEIN, JOSEPH, investment banker; b. N.Y.C., June 4, 1891; s. Jacob and Clara (Buttenwieser) K.; A.B., Columbia, 1933; m. Esther Helen Adler, Nov. 14, 1922; children—John, Frederick A. With Hallgarten & Co., N.Y.C., 1911- 20; mem. stock exchange firm Arthur E. Frank, 1920-27; with Wertheim & Co. 1927—, sr. partner 1950—; dir. Bond Stores, Inc., Continental Baking Co., Erlangen Corp., Gen. Realty & Utilities Corp., Abacus Fund. Gov., N.Y. Stock Exchange, 1938-44, 1947-55. Vice pres. Mount Sinai Hosp., 1944, now chmn. bd. Home: 1120 Park Av New York City NY 10028 Office: 1 Chase Manhattan Plaza New York City NY

KLINGER, WALLACE RICHARD, educator; b. Steubenville, O., Dec. 6, 1905; s. Richard Eugene and Wilhelmina (Gustafson) K.; B.S., Gettyburg Coll., 1929; M.S., U. Pa., 1937, Ph.D., 1944; m. Brunhilde Ingeborg Wolff, Jan. 26, 1929; childrenChristine Ingeborg (Mrs. Richard L. Paul), Sigrid Brunhilde (Mrs Bernard Bensen). Social studies tchr., baseball coach Lower Moreland High Sch., Huntington Valley, Pa., 1929-31, Frenchtown (N.J.) High Sch., 1931-36; social studies tchr., dir. camp Tonawanda, Ellis Coll., Newtown Square, Pa., 1944-45; information specialist OWI, 1944- 45; dean faculty Hartwick Coll., Oneonta, N.Y., 1945-67, acting pres., 1967- 69, sr. prof. history, museum curator, 1969-. Served to lt. col. AUS, 1958. Mem. Eastern Assn. Coll. Deans and Advisers Students (sec.- treas.), Am., N.Y. hist. assns., Res. Officer Assn., Am. Assn. Museums, Northeast Mus. Conf., Phi Beta Kappa, Phi Gamma Delta, Kappa Phi Kappa. Republican. Lutheran. Mason. Home: 12 Jackson Av Oneonta NY 13820

KLINGLER, EUGENE HERMAN, elec. engr., educator; b. Ft. Wayne, Ind., Sept. 3, 1932; s. Herman and Helen (Gerhardstein) K.; B.S., Ind. Inst. Tech., 1953; M.S., N.M. State U., 1957; Ph.D., Carnegie Inst. Tech., 1961; m. Rosemary Racht, Dec. 27, 1954; children-Eugenie Marie, Theodore, Roxane, Sidney Ann, Georgia Kay, Fritz James. Eng., Servomechanisms Lab., Wheatfield Plant, Bell Aircraft Corp., Buffalo, 1953-55; faculty N.M. State U., 1957; weapons systems analyst Westinghouse Air Arm div., Balt., 1957; instr. Ind. Inst. Tech., Ft. Wayne, 1958, chmn. dept. elec. engring., 1965-69; project engr. dept. elec. engring. Carnegie Inst. Tech., 1957-61; staff engr. inertial equipment lab. Space Tech. Labs., Redondo Beach, Cal., 1961-62 ; chief electronics engr. spl. products div. Fairchild Camera & Instrument Corp., Los Angeles, 1962; sr. mem. tech. staff, staff to dir. space systems lab. Northrop Space Labs., Hawthorne, Cal., 1962-63; mgr. hide research lab. N.Am., Aviation, Inc., Tulsa, 1963-65; prof., chmn. dept. elec. engring. U. Detroit, 1969—; tchr. U. So. Cal., 1961-62, U. Tulsa, 1964. Pres., chmn. bd. Power-Tech., Inc., Ft. Wayne. Served with U.S. Army, 1955-57. Ford fellow Carnegie Inst. Tech., 1959-61. Registered profl. engr., Mich., Ind. Mem. I.E.E.E. (group vice chmn.), Engring. Soc. Detroit, Sigma Xi, Sigma Pi Sigma. Patentee in field. Home: 18603 Wildemere Detroit MI 48221

KLINGMAN, HERBERT FREDERICK, educator; b. Watertown, Wis., July 14, 1906; B.A., U. Wis., 1929, M.A., 1930, Ph.D. in Econs., 1949; M.B.A., Harvard, 1932; married. Statistician, analyst Gt. Atlantic & Pacific Tea Co., 1932-34, dir. analyst, head of research, midwest div., 1934-38; prof. finance Coll. of Commerce, U. Notre Dame, 1938-42; asst. dir. gen. statis. staff, chief program and statistics br., gen. indsl. equipment div. War Prodn. Bd., 1942-45; prof. bus. adminstrn. U. Ark., 1947-50, head dept. marketing, 1948-59; research projects supr., bus. information div. Dun & Broadstreet, Inc., 1950-52; dir. research Controllership Found., Inc., 1953-59; prof. bus. adminstrn. U. Wis.-Milw., 1966—. Cons. Nat. Inst. Devel. Adminstrn., Bangkok, Thailand, 1966-68. Mem. Am. Econ. Assn. , Am. Mgmt. Assn., Am. Soc. Adv. Mgmt., Financial Execs. Inst., Investment Analysts Soc. Am. Office: Dept Bus Administrn U Wis-Milw Milwaukee WI 53201*

KLINK, RICHARD KARL, mfg. co. exec.; b. Milw., Feb. 11, 1922; s. Karl F. and Loretta (Toussaint) K.; B.S., State U. Ia., 1948; M.B.A., U. Chgo., 1960; m. Maurine Kersten, July 17, 1946; children-Richard, Steven, Donald. Staff accountant Ernst & Ernst, Chgo., 1948-55; asst. treas. Bliss & Laughlin Industries, Inc., Oak Brook, Ill., 1955-58, sec., treas., 1958-66, v.p., sec., treas., 1966—. Mem. Am. Inst. C.P.A.'s, Ill. Soc. C.P.A.'s, Nat. Assn. Accountants, Am. Soc. Corporate Secs. Home: 3506 Spring Rd Oak Brook IL 60521 Office: 122 W 22d St Oak Brook IL 60521

KLIP, WILLEM, educator, physician; b. Rotterdam, Netherlands, Nov. 26, 1917; s. Willem and Maria Cornelia (Koopman) K.; M.D., U. Utrecht, Netherlands, 1945, Ph.D., 1951, Ph.D. in theoretical physics, 1955, D.Sc., 1962; m. Dorothea Augusta Bueno, Sept. 15, 1955; children—Maria Helena, Emmy Josine, Johanna Dorothea, Dorothy Elizabeth. Came to U.S., 1958, naturalized, 1964. Gen. practice medicine, Netherlands, 1946-47; with Lab. of Bacteriology of U. Utrecht for Nat. Research Council, 1946-51, Lab. of Physics of Dept. Med. Physics, 1952-58; prof. physics U. Ala. in Birmingham, 1958—; vis. prof. physiology and biophysics U. P.R. Author: Velocity and Damping of the Pulse Wave, 1962; Theoretical Foundations of Medical Physics, 2 vols., 1969. Home: 3137 Dolly Ridge Dr Birmingham AL 35243

KLITGAARD, GEORGINA, artist; b. N.Y.C., July 3, 1893; d. John Austen and Georgina (Berrian) Berrain; B.A., Barnard Coll., 1912; m. Kaj. Klitgaard, 1919; children—Peter, Wallace. Gave first 1-man exhbn. of paintings, N.Y.C., 1927. Prin. works; Vertical Landscape, Girl and Child Under Pine Tree, Landscape with Blooming Tree, Clear and Cold, Winter in Bearsville, View of Kingston. Exhibited at Pitts. Internat., Chgo., San Francisco and N.Y. world's fairs, Corcoran Gallery (Washington); mural decorations for Goshen, N.Y.,

Poughkeepsie, N.Y. and Pelham, Ga. One-man exhbn., Concoran Gallery, Washington, 1941, Rehn Galleries (6 shows), 1930—. St. Goudens Meml., 1948, Woodstock, N.Y., 1955, 64. Represented in Met. Mus. Art, Whitney Mus. Am. Art, Newark Mus., Dayton Art Inst., New Brit. Art Inst., Bklyn. Mus. Recipient awards Carnegie Internat. Exhbn., Pa. Acad., Art Inst. Chgo., Pan Am. Exhbn., San Francisco, others. Fellow Huntington Hartford Found., 1965-65, Guggenheim Found.; Helene Wurlitzer Found. N.M. grantee, 1967-69. Mem. Am. Soc. Painters, Sculptors and Gravers, Audubon Artists, Am. Recorders Soc. Home: Bearsville NY Address: Rehn Galleries 655 Madison Av New York City NY

KLITZKE, THEODORE ELMER, coll. dean; b. Chgo., Nov. 4, 1915; s. John Frederick and Edith (Bachman) K.; B.F.A., Chgo. Art Inst., 1940; B.A., U. Chgo., 1941, Ph.D., 1953; m. Margaret Bridget Gaughan, Feb. 23, 1946; children—Annetta, Margaret. Instr. art history U. Chgo., 1946-47; edn. adviser U.S. Armed Forces in Germany, Nurnberg, 1948-51; asst. prof. art history N.Y. State Coll. Ceramics, State U. N.Y. at Alfred, 1953-59; prof. art history, chmn. dept. U. Ala., 1959-68; v.p. acad. affairs, dean Coll. Art, Md. Inst., 1968—. Bd. dirs. Ala. chpt. Am. Civil Liberties Union, 1965-68, v.p. Tuscaloosa chpt., 1967-68; bd. dirs. S.W. Ala. Self-Help Housing, 1966-68. Served with AUS, 1942-46. Recipient First Annual Peace and Freedom award Democratic Student Orgn., U. Ala., 1968; citation Civil Liberties Union Ala. Mem. Southeastern Coll. Art Conf. (pres. 1961-62), Am. Assn. U. Profs., Coll. Art Assn. Contbr. articles in field. Home: 7918 Sherwood Av Baltimore MD 21204

KLOB, RAYMOND CHARLES, banker; b. London, Eng., July 1920; s. Raymond E. and Florence B. (Cox) K.; student Dulwich Coll., London, 1938, London Sch. Econs., 1940; m. Gloria G. Grant, Nov. 15, 1942; 1 son, Grant. Came to U.S., 1940. With Nat. Bur. Econ. Research, N.Y.C., 1940-43; with Fed. Res. Bd., Washington, 1946-53; sr. v.p., cashier Mellon Nat. Bank & Trust Co., Pitts., 1953-. Bd. dirs., chmn. Blue Cross Western Pa. Served to maj. USAAF, 1943-46. Mem. Systems and Procedures Assn. Am., Am. Bankers Assn. (com. chmn.). Clubs: Duquesne, Pittsburgh Athletic. Home: 118 S Dallas Av Pittsburgh PA 15208 Office: Mellon Nat Bank & Trust Co Mellon Sq Pittsburgh PA 15230

KLOBUCAR, BERISLAV, conductor; b. Zagreb, Yugoslavia, Aug. 28, 1924; s. Franio and Maria (Cernousek) K.; ed. Musik Acad. Zagreb, 1948, Mozarteum Salzburg, 1950- 51; m. Natalie Savic, Nov. 11, 1954; 1 dau., Marina. Corepetitor, Opera House Zagreb, 1939-41, conductor, 1941-51; emigrated to Austria, 1951; permanent conductor Vienna State Opera, 1953-; artistic dir. Graz Opera, 1963-; guest conductor, Brussels, 1954, Torino, 1959, Palermo, 1960, Berlin, 1958-59, Hamburg, 1960, Buenos Aires (Colon), 1961-63, Bayreuth, 1964-67, 68, Stockholm, 1965, 68, Milano, 1967, N.Y., 1968. Hon. Title of prof., 1967. Lyon. Home: Argentinierstrasse 20 Vienna Austria Office: State Opera Vienna Austria

KLOCK, CHARLES GLEASON, sales finance co. exec.; b. Oil City, Pa., Aug. 2, 1912; s. Charles G. and Marion (Brown) K.; grad. in Econs. with honors Oberlin Cell., 1934; m. Grace Marion Ranch, Sept. 28, 1940; children—Lawrence S., Roger R. With Gen. Elec. Co., 1934-60, mgr. sales and distbn. planning, 1958-60; pres. Gen. Elec. Credit Corp., N.Y.C., 1960—, also dir.; chmn. bd. GECC Leasing Corp.; dir. Elect. Mut. Liability Ins. Co. Served to lt. USNR, 1943-46. Mem. Am. Mgmt. Assn. Home: 480 Middlesex Rd Darien CT Office: 570 Lexington Av New York City NY 10021

KLOCKO, RICHARD PHILLIP, air force officer; b. Dunkirk, N.Y., Feb. 26, 1915; s. Frank Nicholas and Julia Beatrice (Renswick) K.; B.S., U.S. Mil. Acad., 1937; grad. Air Force Flying Sch., 1938, Air War Coll., 1950; m. Madelyn Norine Ahern, Oct. 15, 1938; children—Mary Julia (Mrs. William T. King), Kerry Ann (Mrs. Alexander V. McDermont), Susan Ellen (Mrs. Richard J. Cabaniss), Richard Phillip, Nancy Jane. Commd. 2d lt. USAAF, 1937, advanced through grades to lt. gen. USAF, 1967; with various fighter-pilot units., 1938-43; prisoner of war ETO, 1943-45; staff positions, Washington, 1945-49; student, instr. Air War Coll., Maxwell AFB, Ala., 1949-54; with Air Force Security Service, 1954-65, comdr., 1962-65; comdr. Air Force Communications Service, 1965- 67; dir. Def. Communications Agy., Washington, 1967—. Decorated D.S.M., Silver Star, Legion of Merit with 2 oak leaf clusters, Bronze Star medal, Air Medal with 3 clusters. Home: Quarters 25 Bolling AFB Washington DC 20332 Office: Dir Def Communications Agy Washington DC 20305

KLOEB, FRANK LE BLOND, U.S. judge; b. Celina, O., June 16, 1890; s. Charles A. and Emma (Le Blond) K.; student Ohio State U., 1908-09; law study Ohio State U., U. of Wis., 1915-17; LL.D. (hon.), U. Toledo; m. Florence Root, Sept. 2, 1930; 1 dau., Carol Le Blond. Began law practice at Celina, 1919; mem. Loree & Kloeb, 1921; pros. atty. Mercer County, Ohio, 1921- 24; mem. 73d, 74th and 75th Congresses (1933-38), 4th Ohio Dist.; judge U.S. Dist. Ct., No. Dist. Ohio, 1937-64, sr. dist. judge, 1964—. Served as ensign, U.S. Navy, World War 1. Mem. Am., Ohio, Lucas County, Toledo bar assns., Am. Legion, Sigma Alpha Epsilon, Phi Delta Phi. Democrat. K.C. Home: 3156 Kylemore Rd Toledo OH 43606 Address: US District Court Federal Bldg Toledo OH 43624

KLOEFFLER, ROYCE GERALD, educator, engineer, and author; b. Armada, Michigan, on June 18, 1890; s. Galenus W. and Dora (Powell) K.; student Mich. State Coll., 1908-09; B.S., U. Mich., 1913; student Columbia, summer 1927; M.S., Mass. Inst. Tech., 1930; m. Hazel Marguerite Davis, Oct. 14, 1915; children—Doris May (Mrs. William Braden), Gale Davis. Engring trainee Gen. Elec. Co., 1913-15; instr. elec. engring, U. Ida., 1915-16; asst. prof. elec. engring. Kan. State U., 1916-22, asso. prof., 1922-25, prof., 1925-60, emeritus 1960, head, dept. elec. engring., 1927-55; prof. Mass. Inst. Tech., summers 1933, 35; br. chief and engr. Nat. Security Agy., 1955-62, Fellow I.E.E.E.; mem. Am. Soc. Engring. Edn., Nat. Soc. Profl. Engrs., Sigma Xi, Phi Kappa Phi, Eta Kappa Nu, Sigma Tau. Author: Telephone Communication Systems, 1925; Direct Current Machinery (with Kerchner and Brenneman), 1934; Principles of Electronics, 1942; Industrial Electronics and Control, 1949; Basic Electronics (with Horrell), 1949; Electric Engring. Economics and Practice, 1952; Basic Theory in Electrical Engineering (with Sitz), 1955; Basic Electronics (with Hargrave), 1963; Electron Tubes, 1966; Americanism versus International Communism, 1967. Home: 729 Lakeside Park Clearwater FL 33515

KLOETZEL, MILTON CARL, univ. ofcl.; b. Detroit, Aug. 28, 1913; s. Arthur G. and Hildegard (Maak) K.; B.S., U. Mich., 1934, Ph.D., 1937, post-doctoral fellow, 1937-38; m. Elizabeth Gorder, July 9, 1938; childrenJohn Arthur, James Erling, Paul Milton, Mark Edward. Instr. chemistry, Harvard, 1938-41; asst., then asso. prof. DePauw U., 1941-45; mem. faculty U. So. Cal., 1945-, prof. chemistry, 1950—, dean Grad. School, 1958-68, interim v.p. acad. affairs, 1967-69, v.p. research and grad. affairs, 1967- 70, acad. v.p., 1970—. Responsible investigator com. med. research OSRD, 1943-45. Cal. Coordinating Council Higher Edn., 1965-67; Grad. Rec. Exams. Bd., 1966-70. Bd. dirs. Good Hope Med. Found. Mem. Assn. Ind. Cal. Colls. and Univs., (trustee) Am. Chem. Soc., Western Assn. Grad. Schs. (chmn. 1962), Am. Inst. Chemists, A.A.A.S., Phi Beta Kappa, Sigma Xi, Phi Kappa Phi, Phi Lambda Upsilon. Contbr. research papers organic chemistry. Asso. editor Organic Reactions, 1948. Home: 7386 Via Lorado Palos Verdes Peninsula, CA 90274.

KLONIS, STEWART, artist, educator; b. Naughatuck, Conn., Dec. 24, 1901; s. Michael and Constance (Wren) K.; student N.Y. U., 1924-26, Art Students League N.Y., 1927-31; m. Charlotte O. Leal, June 26, 1931 (div. 1959); m. 2d, Laura Palumbo, Oct. 1959; 1 dau., Laura Maddalena. Mem. of Artists Aid Com., 1932-36; acting treas. Artists, Coop. Market, 1933; mem. bd. control Art Students League N.Y., 1934, treas., 1935-36, pres., 1937-45, exec. dir. 1946—, hon. mem., 1952—; v.p. Am. Fine Art Soc. N.Y., 1939- 41, pres. 1941—; trustee Edward MacDowell traveling Scholarship Fund, 1934-45; instr. Queens Coll., 1940-45; mem. adv. council N.Y.C. Center Gallery, 1954— chmn., 1954; mem. arts com. Fulbright Awards, 1949-57, chmn., 1953-55, 57; mem. adv. com. for arts Inst. Internat. Edn., 1961—. Bd. dirs. MacDowell Colony, 1970; trustee Nat. Arts Mus. of Sports, 1963—. Benjamin Franklin fellow Royal Soc. Arts; mem. Municipal Art Soc. Democrat. Club: Century Association. Office: 215 W 57th St New York City NY 10019

KLONOWSKI, HENRY THEOPHILUS THOMAS, clergyman; b. Scranton, Pa., Mar. 8, 1893; s. Ladislaus and Apolonia (Kurzydlowska) K.; A.B., St. Thomas Coll., 1916; student St. Francis Sem., 1916-17, Cyril and Methodius Sem., 1917-19; S.T.B., Collegio Capranica and Gregorian U., 1920; S.T.L., Angelico U., 1923, S.T.D., 1924. Ordained priest Roman Catholic Ch., 1920; adminstr. Parish of St. Mary, Wilkes-Barre, Pa., 1921; mng. editor Angelicum, Rome, 1923-24; asst. pastor, Dickson City, Pa., 1925; chaplain Maloney Home, Scranton, 1928-38, also prof. religion Marywood Coll.; past prof., head, dept. Latin, U. Scranton; pastor Sacred Hearts of Jesus and Mary, Scranton, 1938—. Sec., Diocesan Tribunal, 1928-37, vicar ofcl., 1937-46, officialis 1947—; consecrated titular bishop of Daldis and aux. bishop of Scranton, 1947, vicar gen., 1954. Sec., Diocesan Bd. Examiners of Junior Clergy and Seminarians 1928-46, moderator 1947—; dep. visitor for Religious (Nuns) 1937—. Mem. bd. examiners Dept. Pub. Assistance, 1938. Asso. editor Cath. Light, 1934-43. Home: 1213 Prospect Av Scranton PA 18505

KLOPFER, DONALD SIMON, publisher; b. N.Y.C., Jan. 23, 1902; s. Simon and Stella (Danziger) K.; student Phillips Acad., Andover, Mass., 1916-18, Williams Coll., 1918- 20; m. Marian Ansbacher, Sept. 14, 1925 (div. 1933); 1 dau., Lois; m. 2d, Florence Selwyn, June 30, 1937. Treas. United Diamond Works, Inc., 1921- 25; v.p. Modern Library, Inc., 1925—; sec., treas. Random House, Inc., 1927, vice chmn. bd., 1965-70, chmn. bd., 1970—, also chmn. exec. com., dir.; chmn. bd. Grossett Dunlap, Inc. 1956-57. Dir. New Sch. Social Research, N.Y.C. Served as maj. USAAF, 1942-45. Mem. Am. Inst. Graphic Arts (pres. 1949-50), Book Pubs. Council (v.p. 1952; pres. 1954- 56). Clubs: Harmonie, Century, Grolier (N.Y.C.); Country (Harrison, N.Y.). Home: 575 Park Av New York City NY 10021 Office: 201 E 50th St New York City NY 10022

KLOPP, CALVIN TREXLER, surgeon; b. Atlantic City, Dec. 7, 1912; s. Ray C. and Sally (Trexler) K.; A.B., Swarthmore Coll., 1934; M.D. cum laude, Harvard, 1938; m. Ellen Spangler, May 30, 1936; childrenBenjamin, Cynthia, Spangler. Surg. intern Boston City, New Eng. Deaconess and Reading hosps., 1938-41; surg. resident Meml. Hosp., N.Y.C., 1941-44; dir. Warwick Cancer Clinic, Washington, 1946-48; faculty George Washington U., 1948—, dir. cancer service, 1948—, Warwick prof. surgery, 1960—, med. dir. univ. clinic, 1969—. Served with M.C. USNR, 1944-46. Mem. A.M.A, A.C.S., James Ewing Soc., Soc. Head and Neck Surgeons, Am. Goiter Assn., Am. Assn. Cancer Research, Am. Radium Soc., So. Surg. Soc. Home: R F D 1 Olney MD Office: 2150 Pennsylvania Av NW Washington DC 20037

KLOPP, RICHARD PACKARD, constrn. co. exec.; b. Reading, Pa., Mar. 11, 1921; s. A. V. and Dorothy (Packard) K.; grad. Mercersburg Acad., 1939; B.S. in Chem. Engring., Cornell U., 1943; m. Louise Henry, Jan. 6, 1945; children—Deborah A., John R. Chem. engr. Texas Co., 1946-52; with Catalytic Constrn. Co., Phila., 1952—, now pres. Served to 1st lt. AUS, 1943-46. Registered profl. engr., La. Pa. Mem. Am. Inst. Chem. Engrs. Am. Petroleum Inst., Nat. Soc. Profl. Engrs., Nat. Petroleum Refiners Assn., Mercantile Lit. Assn., Newcomen Soc., Mercersburg Acad. Alumni Assn. (mem. council 1965—), Phi Gamma Delta, Republican. Clubs: Philadelphia Country; Seaview Country (Absecon, N.J.). Home: 1201 Waverly Rd Gladwyne PA 19035 Office: 1628 Walnut St Philadelphia PA 19102

KLOPPENBURG, RALPH H., architect; b. Davenport, Ia., Nov. 9, 1903; s. Louis and Alvina (Haase) K.; B.Arch., U. Ill., 1926; m. Bernyce Schlichting, 1926; childrenJack Ralph, Robert K., Jerry King, Sally (Mrs. David F. Conley). Instr., U Ill., 1926-28; practice as Ralph Kloppenburg, 1931-59, Kloppenburg & Kloppenburg, Milw., 1959—; prin. works include schs., Menomonee Falls, Wis., 1948-68, West Bend Mut. Ins. Co. (Wis.), Milw. Downer Sem., River Hills, 1961. Zoology Research Bldg., U. Wis., Madison, 1961, Badger Meter Mfg. Co., Milw., Phys. Edn. and Bus. Econs. bldgs. Whitewater U., 1966-67, Univ. Sch., Milw., 1970, others. Mem. Wis. Registration Bd. Architects and Engrs., 1946-65. Fellow A.I.A. (pres. Wis. chpt. 1945-47). Republican. Episcopalian. Rotarian. Clubs: Milwaukee, University, Milwaukee Country. Home: 708 E Green Tree Rd Milwaukee WI Office: 5856 Port Washington Rd Milwaukee WI 53217

KLOPSTEG, PAUL ERNEST, edn., research cons.; b. Henderson, Minn., May 30, 1889; s. Julius and Magdelene (Kuesthardt) K.; B.S. in Elec. Engring., U. Minn., 1911, M.A., 1913, Ph.D., 1916, Sc.D., Northwestern U., 1942; Sc.D., Wesleyan U., 1948; m. Amanda Marie Toedt, June 11, 1914; children-Marie, Irma Louise (dec.), Ruth Helen. Asst. in physics U. Minn. 1911-13, instr., 1913-17, asst. prof., 1917; devel. engr. Ordnance Dept., U.S. Army, 1917-18; in charge tech. advt. Leeds & Northrup Co., Phil., 1918- 21; in charge devel. and mfg. Central Sci. Co., 1921-30, dir., 1922-55, pres., 1930-44; prof. applied sci. Northwestern U., dir. research Northwestern Tech. Inst., 1944-54, prof. emeritus, 1954—, spl. cons. to Univ. pres., 1961-63. Spl. research cons. nat. research orgns.; bd. govs. Argonne Nat. Lab., 1947-50, chmn., 1949-50; asso. dir. NSF, 1951-58, spl. cons., 1958-62; chmn. com. atmospheric scis. Nat. Acad. Scis.—NRC, 1958-60, mem., 1957- 64; trustee, mem. exec. com. U. Corp. Atmospheric Research, 1963-66. chmn. vis. com. John Crerar Library, 1963-66. Mem. Personnel Security Rev. Bd., AEC, 1953-62. Recipient Modern Pioneers' award, N.A.M., 1939, medal for Merit with Presdl. citation, 1948; Outstanding Achievement medal U. Minn., 1950; Maurice Thompson medal of honor Nat. Archery Assn.; Compton medal of Honor, Nat. Field Archery Assn.; Whiffen Meml. award Archery Inst. Fellow A.A.A.S. (dir. 1948-69, pres., 1959, chmn. 1960, treas. 1961-69, bd. govs.); hon. mem. Am. Meteorol. Soc.; mem. several prof. assns. and orgns. Clubs: University (Evanston, Ill.); Cosmos (Washington). Contbr. many papers in sci. jours. and archery mags.; books on archery. Contbr. Ency. Britannica. Inventor many scientific instruments. Home: 828 Apple Tree Lane Glenview IL 60025 ☆

KLORES, WALTER, advt. exec.; b. Bklyn., Mar. 7, 1940; s. Samuel Charles and Francine (Brown) K.; B.A., Brandeis U., 1961; M.B.A., U. Chgo., 1963; m. Sandra Silk, June 24, 1962; children—Jill Diane, Pamela Beth. Asst. account exec. Benton & Bowles, N.Y.C., 1964-66; account exec. Pritchard Wood, Inc., N.Y.C., 1966-68; v.p., dir. accounts McCann-Erickson, Inc., N.Y.C., 1968—. Mem. Citizens for Clean Air Assn., N.Y.C. Mem. Brandeis U. Alumni Assn. (exec. com.). Home: 501 E 79th St New York City NY 10021 Office: 485 Lexington Av New York City NY 10017

KLOS, ELMAR, film writer, dir; b. Brno, Czechoslovakia, Jan. 26, 1910; s. Rudolf and Mary (Horicova) K.; student Charl's U. Pragye (Czechoslovakia), 1933; m. Anne Vopalka, Dec. 23, 1935; children-Elen, Elmar. Documentary film dir., 1934-37; chief, film dept. Bata Shoe Co., Zlin, 1937-45; artistic documentary film unit Czechoslovak Film Corp., Prague, 1945-49; chief prodn., scenario writer, dir. with Jan Kadar, 1952, 54, 57, 58, 60, 62, 63, 65; 8 films for Studio Barrandov, Prague, latest being Shop on Main Street (Acad. award 1965); prof. Film Acad. Prague, 1948-. Recipient award for best film of year Czechoslovak Govt., 1953, 63, 65. Mem. Assn. Czechoslovakian Film Artists (pres. 1961-65, v.p. 1966-). Home: 58 Barandovska St Prague Czechoslovakia Office: Film Studio Barrandov Prague Czechoslovakia

KLOSE, JEROME B., lawyer; b. Chgo., Feb. 7, 1923; B.S., U. Ill., 1947, J.D., 1949. Admitted to Ill. bar, 1950; mem. firm Merriam, Marshall, Shapiro and Klose, Chgo. Mem. Am., Chgo. bar assns., Patent Law Assn. Chgo. Office: 30 W Monroe St Chicago IL 60603*

KLOSINSKI, STANLEY JOSEPH, accountant; b. LaSalle, Ill., June 5, 1920; s. Joseph John and Charlotte (Swiderski) K.; B.S., U. Ill., 1943; m. Catherine Karos, Apr. 24, 1954; children—Patricia Irene, Earlene Anne, James. With Laventhol, Krekstein, Horwath & Horwath, and predecessor, C.P.A.'s 1946—, gen. partner, Tampa, Fla., 1959—. Fla. Hotel and Motel Assn. mem. ways and means com. 1964. Served with AUS, World War II; ETO. C.P.A., Ill., Mo., La., Ga., Fla. Asso. mem. Am. Assn. Hosp. Accountants, Greater Tampa C. of C. (conv. com. 1965), Contbr. articles to jours. Home: 841 Bayshore Blvd Tampa FL 33606 Office: First Nat Bank Bldg Tampa FL 33602

KLOSKA, RONALD FRANK, financial exec.; b. Grand Rapids, Mich., Oct. 24, 1933; s. Frank B. and Catherine (Hilaski) K.; student St. Joseph Sem., Grand Rapids, Mich., 1947-53; Ph.B., U. Montreal, Que., Can., 1955; M.B.A., U. Mich., 1957; m. Mary E. Minick, Sept. 7, 1957; children—Kathleen Ann, Elizabeth Marie, Ronald Francis, Mary Josephine. Staff accountant Lybrand Ross Bros. & Montgomery, Niles, Mich., 1957, staff to sr. accountant 1960-63; treas., v.p., Skyline Corp., Elkhart, In., 196367, exec. v.p. finance, treas., 1967—, also dir. Served to 1st lt. AUS, 1957-60. Mem. Am. Inst. C.P.A.'s, Mich., Ind. assns. C.P.A.'s, Nat. Assn. Accountants, Elkhart C. of C., Roman Catholic. Club: Elcona Country. Home: 1518 Springbrook Dr Elkhart IN Office: 2520 By Pass Rd Elkhart IN 46514

KLOSNER, JEROME MARTIN, educator; b. N.Y.C., Mar. 23, 1928; s. Morris and Minnie (Rosenblum) K.; B.C.E., Coll. City N.Y., 1948; M.S., Columbia, 1950; Ph.D., Poly. Inst. Bklyn., 1959; m. Naomi Beth Certner, May 31, 1965; children—Michael Robert, Lise Helaine, Marc Alexander. Sr. structures engr. Republic Aviation Corp., Farmingdale, N.Y., 1952-56; sr. scientist Avco Research & Advanced Devel. Div., Wilmington, Mass., 1956, cons., 1956-67; research asso. Poly. Inst. Bklyn., 1956-59, asst. prof., 1959-62, asso. prof., 1962-67, prof. applied mechanics, 1967—; cons. Gen. Applied Sci. Labs., Inc., L.I., N.Y., 1959, FTC, Washington, 1963, Ingersoll-Rand Corp. Research Center, Princeton, N.J., 1966, Technautics Corp., N.Y.C., 1968-69; vis. mem. Courant Inst. Math. Scis., N.Y.U., 1966-67. Asso. fellow Am. Inst. Aeros. and Astronautics; mem. Am. Soc. C.E., Am. Soc. M.E., Soc. of Rheology, Am. Assn. U. Profs., Sigma Xi, Sigma Gamma Tau. Reviewer, contbr. articles profl. jours. Office: 333 Jay St Brooklyn NY 11201

KLOSS, GENE, (Mrs. Phillips Kloss, nee Alice Geneva Glasier), artist; b. Oakland, Cal., July 27, 1903; d. Herbert P. and Carrie (Hefty) Glasier; A.B., U. Cal., 1924; student Cal. Sch. Fine Arts, 1924-25; m. Phillips Kloss, May 19, 1925. One-man shows Sandzen Meml. Gallery, Lindsborg, Kan. Albany Inst. History and Art, 1953, Tulsa, Scottsdale, Arix., Albuquerque, 1956, Findlay Galleries, Chgo., 1957, Mus. N.M. 1960, W. Tex. Mus., 1964, Mus. Arts and Scis., Grand Junction, Colo., 1967, Mus. Okla., 1970; exhibited in Three Centuries Art U.S., Paris, 1938; represented in collections Library Congress, Carnegie Inst., Smithsonian Instn., N.Y. Pub. Library, Met. Mus., Pa. Acad. Fine Arts, Chgo., Art Inst., San Francisco Mus., Honolulu Acad. Fine Arts, Dallas Mus., Mus. N.M., Tulsa U., Kan. State Coll., Pa. U. John Taylor Arms Meml., Met. Mus., Peabody Mus., Mus. Tokyo, Auchenback Found. for Graphic Arts, San Francisco, Nat. Gallery, U. N.M. Mus., Copley Library, La Jolla, Cal., others; executed 1953 membership prints for Albany Print Club and for Soc. Am. Graphic Artists; executed gift plate for Print Makers of Cal., 1956; exhibited with Audubon Soc., 1955; etcher, painter in oil, watercolor. Recipient Eyre Gold medal Pa. Acad. Fine Arts, 1936; asso. mem. award Cal. Soc. Etchers, 1934; honorarium Cal. Soc. Etchers, 1940, 41, 44; 3d award oils Oakland Art Gallery Ann., 1939; Purchase prize Chgo. Soc. Etchers, 1940; Best Black and White, Tucson Fine Arts Assn., 1941; 1st prize Print Club, Phila., 1944; Purchase prize Library Congress, 1946; 1st prize prints N.M. State Fair, 1946, Ann. Exhibit, Meriden, Conn., 1947; Open award Cal. Soc. Etchers, 1949-51; Henry B. Shope prize Soc. Am. Etchers, 1951, hon. mention, 1953; 1st prize prints Arts and Crafts Assn., Meriden, Conn., 1951; 1st prize Chgo. Soc. Etchers, 1952; Phila. Sketch Club prize, 1957; Fowler purchase prize Albany Print Club, 1959, purchase prize, 1961; Annoymous prize N.A.D., 1961. Mem. N.A.D., Soc. Am. Graphic Artists, Print Club of Albany, Phila. Water Color Club, M.B.L.S. (adv.). Home: Taos NM 87571

KLOSSON, BORIS HANSEN, fgn. service officer; b. Buffalo, Jan. 21, 1919; s. Michael M. and Kenena (Hansen) K.; student Inst. Universitaire de Hautes Etudes Internationales, Geneva, 1938-39; B.S., Hamilton Coll., 1940; M.A., Fletcher Sch. Law and Diplomacy, 1941; m. Harriet F. Cheston, May 3, 1947; children—Michael, Harriet, Christopher, Charles. With Dept. of State, 1945—. with div. research on USSR and Eastern Europe, 1945—, dep. chief, 1951-55, chief, 1955-57; mem. faculty Nat. War Coll. 1957-59; counselor for polit. affairs Am. embassy, Moscow, USSR, 1959- 62; counselor Am. embassy, Kingston, Jamaica, 1962-65; dir. Soviet and E. European exchanges Dept. State, Washington, 1965-69; dep. chief mission Am. embassy, Moscow, USSR, 1969-. Served with AUS, 1943- 45. Mem. Phi Beta Kappa, Psi Upsilon. Address: Am Embassy APO New York City NY 09862

KLOSTERMAN, DON, football team adminstr.; b. Los Angeles; ed. Loyola U., Cal.; m. Clare; children—Kurt, Katie. Former player Cleve. Browns, Dallas Texans, Los Angeles Rams, Calgary Stampeders of Canadian Football League; gen. mgr. Houston Oilers, until 1970; gen. mgr. Balt. Colts., 1970—. Mem. Am. Football League, 1960—. Office: 600 N Howard St Baltimore MD 21201*

KLOSTERMEYER, HOWARD RANDOLPH, lawyer; b. Charleston, W.Va., Jan. 29, 1904; s. Frederick George and Carrie (Wooten) K.; D.J., U. W.Va., 1926; m. Katherine Louise Smith, Feb.

6, 1927; children—Frederick H., William H., Alice Ann (Mrs. Reid H. Erwin). Admitted to W.Va. bar, 1926, also U.S. Supreme Ct.; practice in Charleston, 1926—; partner firm Spilman, Thomas, Battle & Klostermeyer, 1954—. Dir. Charleston Transit Co., Kanawha Drug Co., Peerless Eagle Coal Co. Chmn. W.Va. Citizens Com. Adoption Sch. Bldg. Constl. Amendment, 1951; mem. W.Va. Jud. Council, 1970; past legal adviser, mem. adv. council Kanawha County council Girl Scouts Am.; past mem. Citizens Adv. Com. to Kanawha County Ct. in extensive remodeling courthouse; mem. Citizens Adv. Com. to Kanawha County Bd. edn. in County-Wide Sch. Bldg. program; past mem. Citizens Adv. Com. to Charleston in selecting location S. Side Bridge across Kanawha River; past chmn. adv. com. local troop Boy Scouts Am.; mem. Kanawha Bd. Edn., 1942-49. Republican nominee Ho. of Dels., Kanawha County, 1934; treas. W.Va. Rep. Finance Com., 1952-53. Bd. dirs. Herscher Found. Inc. Mem. Am., W.Va., Kanawha County (pres. 1943) bar assns., W.Va. State Bar (chmn. dist. no. 8 com. grievances 1955, spl. com. group ins. 1954-56), Phi Kappa Psi, Phi Alpha Delta. Presbyn. (deacon 1943—, trustee 1950—). Club: Army-Navy (asso.) (Charleston). Home: 4609 Kanawha Av SE Charleston WV 25304 Office: Kanawha Banking & Trust Bldg Charleston WV 25301

KLOTSCHE, J. MARTIN, Univ. chancellor; b. Scribner, Neb., Nov. 28, 1907; s. Ernest Heinrich and Marie (Kluge) K.; A.B., Midland Coll., Fremont, Neb., 1925, D.Sc., 1965; M.A., U. Neb., 1928, LL.D., 1967; Ph.D., U. Wis. 1931; LL.D, Carthage Coll., 1955; D. Hum., U. Mo., 1970; m. Roberta Roberts, June 13, 1936; children—Allan John, Charles Martin, John Chester. Instr. Dorchester (Neb.) high sch., 1924-27; asst. U. Wis., 1928-30; Pres. Adams fellow U. Wis., 1930-31; prof. history Wis. State Coll., Milw., 1931-44, dean of instrn., 1944-46, pres., 1946- 56; chancellor U. Wis.-Milw., 1956—; vis. lectr. U. Wis., 1944; dir. Inst. of World Affairs, Salisbury, Conn., summer, 1943; faculty chmn. Inst. for Social Progress, Wellesley, Mass., summers, 1947, 48, 49, 52; mem. nat. exec. com. Nat. Conf. of Christians and Jews, 1951—, chmn. nat. edn. commn., 1951-57; dir. Inst. World Affairs, summer 1948, 50; ednl. cons. in Germany for U.S. Office Edn., spring 1953; chief of party, study higher edn. in Brazil, 1967-68. Lectr. throughout U.S. Mem. Wis. Edn. Assn., Assn. Urban Univs. (pres. 1967-68), N.E.A., Phi Beta Kappa, Phi Delta Kappa, Phi Kappa Phi, Phi Mu Sigma, Alpha Phi Omega. Lutheran. Author: The Urban University and the Future of Our Cities, 1966. Contbr. ednl. jours. Home: 4430 N Lake Dr Milwaukee WI 53211

KLOTZ, ARTHUR PAUL, educator, physician; b. Milw., Sept. 28, 1913; s. Paul Oscar and Christine (Kratt) K.; student Marguette U., 1931-33; B.S., U. Chgo., 1938, M.D., 1938; m. Margaret Pollar, Mar. 16, 1941; children—Stephen Arthur, Suzanne Ruth, John Haven, Peter Paul. Intern Cin. Gen. Hosp., 1938-39; resident Aspinwall VA Hosp., Pitts., 1946-49; asst., instr. U. Chgo., 1949-54; chief sect. gastroenterology U. Kan. Med. Center, Kansas City, 1954—, prof. medicine, 1962—;. Served to capt., M.C., U.S. Army, 1942-45. Decorated Bronze Star Mem. A.M.A. (rep. sci. exhibits in gastroenterology). Editorial bd. Am. Jour. Digestive Diseases, 1963-67. Contbr. articles profl. jours. Home: RFD 2 Box 246 Olathe KS 66061 Office: U Kan Med Center 39th and Rainbow Blvd Kansas City KS 66103

KLOTZ, HERBERT WERNER, mgmt. cons.; b. Berlin, Germany, Feb. 24, 1917; s. Herbert and Gertrud Klotz; B.A., Zuoz (Switzerland) Coll., 1935; postgrad., U. Zurich (Switzerland) 1935-36; m. Patricia Radford Hopkins, Apr. 3, 1954; childrenRadford Werner, Leslie Ritchie, James Taylor. Came to U.S., 1937, naturalized, 1944. With Smith, Barney & Co., and predecessor, N.Y.C., 1937-42, W.E. Hutton & Co., N.Y.C., 1946-48; engaged in mgmt. personal investments, 1949-52; with Winslow, Douglas & McEvoy, N.Y.C., 1953-54; pres., treas. Tex. Securities Corp., N.Y.C., 1954-57, S.W. Adv. Services, Inc., N.Y.C., 1954-57; with Alex Brown & Sons, Washington, 1957-60; spl. asst. to sec. commerce, 1961, dep. to sec. commerce, 1961-62; asst. sec. commerce adminstrn., 1962-65; pres., dir. Potomac Packaging Corp., 1966; exec. v. p. Am. Growth Investment Co. 1966-67; dir. Govt. Systems Center, Kurt Salmon Assos., Inc., 1968-69; pres., dir. Quest Research Corp., 1970—. Asso. dir. Nat. Com. Bus. and Profl. Men and Women for Kennedy- Johnson, 1960. Served to 1st lt. AUS, 1942-45. Democrat. Episcopalian. Clubs: National Press, 1925 F Street, Metropolitan, Federal City (Washington); Millbrook (N.Y.) Hunt; Warrenton (Va.) Hunt. Home: 1404 Langley Pl McLean, VA 22101 Office: 6825 Redmond Dr McLean VA 22101

KLOTZ, IRVING MYRON, scientist, educator; b. Chgo., Jan. 22, 1916; s. Frank and Mollie (Nasatir) K.; B.S., U. Chgo., 1937, Ph.D., 1940; m. Mary Sue Hanlon, Aug. 7, 1966; children—Edward, Audie Jeanne, David. Research asso. in chemistry Northwestern U., 1940-42, instr., 1942- 46, asst. prof., 1946-47, asso. prof., 1947-50, prof., 1950-63, Morrison prof. chemistry, 1963—; Lalor fellow Marine Biol. Lab., Woods Hole, Mass., 1947-48, corp. mem., 1947—. Trustee, Marine Biol. Lab., Woods Hole, 1957-65. Recipient Army-Navy certificate of appreciation for wartime research, 1948. Fellow Royal Soc. Medicine, Am. Acad. Arts and Scis.; mem. Nat. Acad. Scis., Am. Soc. Biol. Chemists, Am. Chem. Soc. (Eli Lilly award 1949, Midwest award 1970), A.A.A.S., Phi Beta Kappa, Sigma Xi, Phi Lambda Upsilon, Alpha Chi Sigma. Author: Chemical Thermodynamics, 1950, rev. edit., 1964, Energies in Biochemical Reactions, 1957, rev. edit., 1967; articles sci. jours. Home: 2400 N Lakeview Av Chicago IL 60614

KLOTZ, JOHN WESLEY, govt. ofcl.; b. Pitts., May 2, 1919; s. E. I. and Lydia (Banse) K.; student Capital U., 1937-39; B.S. in Physics, Ohio State U., 1942, student Grad. Sch., 1942; m. Norma E. Faust, June 27, 1964; children—Donald, Cheryl. Research engr. Naval Research Lab., 1942-47; adminstrv. engr. Research and Devel. Bd., Office Sec. Def., 1948-53, dir. electronics, 1954-57, dir. defensive missiles Office Dir. Guided Missiles, 1957-59, dep. asst. dir. def. research and engring., 1959-63, chmn. research group on fed. aviation, 1963—, asst. dir., tactical command and surveillance systems, 1965-69, asst. dir. combat support, 1970—. Adv. mem. exec. com. Radio Tech. Com. for Aeros., 1971—. Mem. I.E.E.E., Am. Ordnance Assn., Springfield (Va.) Civic Assn. (v.p. 1955), Sigma Pi Sigma. Presbyn. Club: Springfield Swimming (pres. 1956). Home: 3401 Saylor Pl Alexandria VA 22304 Office: Office of Dir Def Research and Engring The Pentagon Washington DC 20301

KLOTZ, ROY E., business exec. Pres., Anadite, Inc., South Gate, Cal. Office: 10647 Garfield Av South Gate CA 90280*

KLOUCEK, JEROME WENSEL, educator; b. Milw., Sept. 25, 1913; s. Joseph and Anna (Kolafa) K.; B.A., U. Chgo., 1935, M.A., 1940; Ph.D., Northwestern U., 1958. Tchr., Elgin (Ill.) Acad., 1938-40, Morgan Park Mil. Acad., Chgo., 1940-43; instr. English, registrar Montgomery Jr. Coll., Takoma Park, Md., 1946- 50, instr. English, 1953-56; mem. faculty U. Toledo, 1957-, prof. English, 1962—, acting dean Coll. Arts and Scis., 1961-62, dean, 1962- 67. Served with C.E. AUS, 1943-46. Mem. Modern Lang. Assn., Am. Studies Assn., Nat. Council Tchrs. English, Am. Assn. U. Profs. Contbr. articles to profl. jours. Office: Dept English Univ Toledo Toledo OH 43606

KLUBERG, JOHN WILLIAM, pub. utility exec.; b. Geneva, Ill., Aug. 31, 1913; s. William F. and Jennie (Strom) K.; B.S. in Accounting, U. Ill., 1937; m. Beverly B. Belyea, Oct. 22, 1938; childrenLynn (Mrs. William J. Cunningham), Karen Lee. With Arthur Andersen & Co., C.P.A.'s Chgo., 1937-46, Detroit, 1946- 51; with Consumers Power Co., Jackson, Mich., 1951—, v.p., controller, 1964—. C.P.A., Ill., Mich. Mem. Am. Inst. C.P.A.'s, Financial Execs. Inst. Home: 1990 Shoemaker Dr Jackson MI 49203 Office: 212 W Michigan Av Jackson MI 49201

KLUBERTANZ, GEORGE PETER, clergyman, coll. dean; b. nr. Columbus, Wis., June 29, 1912; s. Joseph and Clara V. (Belda) K.; student Salvatorian Sem., St. Nazianz, Wis., 1926-31; A.B., St. Louis U., 1935, M.A., 1938; Ph.D., U. Toronto, 1947. Mem. Soc. of Jesus, 1931—; ordained priest Roman Catholic Ch., 1944; instr. classics and philosophy Creighton U., 1939-40; instr. philosophy St. Louis U., 1948-51, asst. prof., 1951-54, asso. prof., 1954-59, prof., 1959—, acting dean Coll. Philosophy and Letters, 1952-53, dean, 1953-70, chmn. dept. philosophy, 1965-68, acting dean Sch. Div., 1970—. Mem. Am. Cath. Philos. Assn. (past pres.), Psychologists Interested in Religious Issues, Metaphys. Soc. Am. (pres. 1956-57, exec. council 1958-62). Societe philosophique de Louvain. Author: The Discursive Power, 1952; The Philosophy of Human Nature, 1953; Introduction to the Philosophy of Being, 1955; St. Thomas Aquinas on Analogy, 1960; (with Maurice R. Holloway) Being and God, 1963; The Habits and Virtues, 1965. Editor: Avicenna' De Anima', 1949; editor The Modern Schoolman, 1937-38, 50-59, 64—, mem. editorial bd., 1959—. Home: 3700 W Pine Blvd St Louis MO 63108

KLUCKMAN, REVONE W., mfg. co. exec.; b. Mound City, S.D., 1929, B.S., U. S.D., 1952; married; children—Paul, Jeffrey, Jane. With Arthur Anderson & Co., C.P.A.'s, 1952- 67, partner, 1961-67; controller Zenith Radio Corp., 1967-68, v.p., controller, 1968—. Home: 2905 Shannon Rd Northbrook IL 60062 Office: 1900 N Austin Av Chicago IL 60639

KLUCZYNSKI, JOHN C., congressman; b. Chgo., Feb. 15, 1896; s. Thomas and Mary (Sulaski) K.; student pub. and parochial schs.; m. Mary Zapart, Apr. 15, 1936 (dec.); m. 2d, Estelle Plowy, Nov. 15, 1939. Caterer 1920—, partner Syrena Restaurants, Chgo. Elected to Ill. Ho. of Reps., 1932, and re- elected for 7 terms. Mem. 82d to 91st congresses, 5th Ill. Dist., mem. Pub. Works Com., House Select Com. Small Bus. Served with 8th F.A., AEF, 1918-19. Mem. Polish Nat. Alliance, Polish Roman Catholic Union. Democrat. Roman Catholic. Club: Travelers (Chgo.). Home: 1754 W Garfield Blvd Chicago IL 60609

KLUGE, ALEXANDER, author (short stories) Attendance List for A Funeral; (novel) The Battle. Address: care McGraw-Hill Book Co 330 W 42d St New York City NY 10036

KLUGE, JOHN WERNER, broadcasting and advt. exec.; b. Chemnitz, Germany, Sept. 21, 1914; s. Fritz and Gertrude (Donj) K.; student Wayne U.; B.A. (4 year honor scholar), Columbia, 1937; m. Yolanda Zucco, Apr. 28, 1969; children—Samantha Kluge, Joseph B. Zucco. Vice pres., sales mgr. Otten Bros., Inc., Detroit, 1937-41; pres., dir. radio sta. WGAY, Silver Spring, Md., 1946-59, St. Louis Broadcasting Corp., Brentwood, Mo., 1953-58, Pitts. Broadcasting Co., 1954-59; pres., treas., dir. Capitol Broadcasting Co., Nashville, 1954-59, Asso. Broadcasters, Inc., Ft. Worth-Dallas, 1957-59; partner Western N.Y. Broadcasting Co., Buffalo, 1957-60; pres., dir. Washington Planagraph Co., 1956-60, Mid.-Fla. Radio Corp., Orlando, 1952- 59; treas., dir. Mid-Fla. Television Corp., 1957-60; owner Kluge Investment Co., Washington, 1956-60; partner Nashton Properties, Nashville, 1954- 60, Texworth Investment Co., Ft. Worth, 1957-60; chmn. bd. Seaboard Service System, Inc., 1957-58; pres. New Eng. Fritos, Boston, 1947-55, N.Y. Inst. Dietetics, N.Y.C., 1953-60; chmn. bd., pres., dir. Metromedia, Inc., N.Y.C., including met. broadcasting div., world wide broadcasting div. and Foster & Kleiser div., outdoor advt.; chmn. bd., treas., dir. Kluge, Finkelstein & Co., food brokers, Balt.; chmn. bd., treas. Tri-Suburban Broadcasting Corp., Washington, Kluge & Co., Washington, Silver City Sales Co., Washington; dir. Marriott-Hot Shoppes, Inc., Nat. Bank Md., Waldorf Astoria Corp., Just One Break, Inc.; mem. adv. council Mfrs. Hanover Trust Co. Mem. Washington Bd. Trade. Bd. dirs., Brand Names Found., Inc.; trustee Strang Clinic Miliken U. Served to capt. AUS, 1941-45. Mem. Nat., Washington (pres. 1958) food brokers assns., Grocery Wheels Washington, Grocery Mfrs. Reps. Washington, Advt. Club Washington, Nat. Assn. Radio and Television Broadcasters, Advt. Council N.Y.C., Nat. Sugar Brokers Assn. Clubs: Army and Navy, University, Figure Skating, National Capital Skeet and Trap, Broadcasters (Washington); Metropolitan, Columbia Associates, University (N.Y.C.); Olympic (San Francisco); Marco Polo. (N.H. gov.). Office: 277 Park Av New York City NY 10017

KLUGE, RALPH WENDEL, educator; b. Chgo., Oct. 8, 1905; s. Edward E. and Alma (Wirth) K.; B.S. in Civil Engring., U. Ill., 1928, M.S. in Structural Engring., 1930; m. Mercedes Wittenfeld, June 7, 1929; children—Donald, Paul. From research asst. to research asst. prof. U. Ill., 1931-41; research engr. Nat. Bur. Standards, 1941-48; asso. prof. structural engring. Purdue U., 1948-51; chmn. civil engring. dept. U. Fla., 1951-69. Mem. North Central Fla. Regional Planning Council. Mem. Am. Concrete Inst. (co-recipicnt Wason medal 1938), Prestressed Concrete Inst. (hon.), Am. Soc. C.E., Am. Soc. Engring. Edn., Sigma Xi, Tau Beta Pi, Sigma Tau. Contbr. articles engring. jours. Home: 2211 N W 3d Pl Gainesville FL 32601

KLUGER, RICHARD, editor; b. Paterson, N.J., Sept. 18, 1934; s. David and Ida (Abramson) K.; A.B. cum laude, Princeton, 1956; m. Phyllis Schlain, Mar. 23, 1957; children—Matthew Harold, Leonard Theodore. Copy editor Wall St. Jour., 1956-57; editor, pub. County Citizen, New City, N.Y., 1958-60; staff writer N.Y. Post, 1960-61; asso. editor Forbes mag., 1962; gen. books editor N.Y. Herald Tribune, 1962-63, book editor, 1963—, editor Book Week, 1963-66; sr. editor Simon and Schuster, 1966-68, mng. editor, 1968, exec. editor, 1968-70; editor-in-chief Atheneum Pubs., 1970—. Club: Princeton (N.Y.C.). Author: When the Bough Breaks, 1964; National Anthem, 1969. Home: 17 Main St Ridgefield CT 06877 Office: 122 E 42d St New York City NY 10017

KLUMPP, EUGENE P., pres. Nat. Assn. Broadcaster Employees and Technicians. Address: 80 E Jackson Blvd Chicago IL 60604

KLUMPP, THEODORE GEORGE, bus. exec.; b. N.Y.C. May 15, 1903; s. Charles and Marie (Hayo) K.; B.S., Princeton, 1924; M.D., Harvard, 1928; D.Sc. (hon.) Phila. Coll. Pharmacy and Sci., 1943; LL.D., U. of Chattanooga, 1960; D.Sc., New Eng. Coll. Pharmacy, 1961; D.Sc., Albany Med. Coll. 1964; m. Virginia R. Morgan, Aug. 3, 1934; children—Virginia-Ann, Karla-Marie, Kathleen Morgan, Maralys, Russell Allen, Theodore George. Intern, Peter Bent Brigham Hosp., Boston, 1929-30; asst. resident physician Lakeside Hosp., Cleve., 1930- 32; instr. and asst. clinic prof. Yale U Med. Sch., 1932-36; chief Drug Div., FDA, Washington, 1936-41; adj. clin. prof. medicine George Washington U., Washington, 1940-41; dir. drugs, food and phys. therapy and sec. council on pharmacy and chemistry A.M.A., Chgo., 1941-42; chmn. dir. Winthrop Labs. div. Sterling Drug. Inc.; v.p., dir. Sterling Drug Inc., N.Y.C.; pres., dir. Winthrop Products, Inc., of N.J., 1947-51; cons. surgeon C. & O. Ry.; dir. Sterwin Chem., Inc., 1949—, Breon Labs., Inc., 1952—. Vice pres. U.S. Pharmacopoeia, 1950-70; chmn. Task Force on Handicapped, O.D.M., 1951. Bd. dirs. World Med. Assn., N.Y. Heart Assn.; bd. of govs. Sterling-Winthrop Research Inst. chmn. bd. govs. Nat. Vitamin Found., 1947- 49, mem. exec. com. and chmn. finance com.; chmn. med. service task force Hoover Commn. on Orgn. Exec. Br. Gov.; mem. Nat. Adv. Council Vocational Rehab.; mem. Gov's. Council on Rehab., 1959-61, N.Y. Vocational Rehab. Planning Council, 1967-; mem. planning bd. Village Sands Point, 1958—. Mem. vis. com. Harvard Sch. Public Health, 1958-64, Harvard Med. Sch. and Sch. Dental Medicine, 1964-70; sec. Nat. Fund Med. Edn., 1968- 69, pres., 1969—. Trustee Bklyn. Coll. Pharmacy, L.I. U. First recipient Spl. award for Distinguished Service Am. Pharm. Mfrs. Assn., 1955. Fellow A.C.P., N.Y. Acad. Medicine, A.A.A.S., Am. Soc. Clin. Investigation; mem. Pharm. Mfrs. Assn. (pres. 1948-50; dir.; v.p. 1958), Am. Hosp. Assn. (hon.), A.M.A., Am. Pharm. Assn., New Haven County Med. Soc., Academia de Ciencias Medicas, Fisicas y Naturales de La Habana, Nat. Health Assembly, Chemists Club, Sigma Xi, Alpha Kappa Alpha. Methodist. Clubs: Princeton (N.Y.C.); Manhasset Bay Yacht. Contbr. articles on therapeutics, food, drug, and cosmetic act, also various med. subjects. Home: Messenger Lane Sands Point NY 11050 Office: 90 Park Av New York City NY 10016

KLUNE, RAYMOND A., former motion picture prodn. exec.; b. N.Y.C., Apr. 10, 1904; s. Frederick C. and Katherine (Kolb) K.; B.S., N.Y. U., 1927; m. Lillian Becker Jan. 7, 1928 (dec.); childrenDonald C., Carol (Mrs. Willard L. Cummings, Jr.); m. 2d, Hillary Brooke, Mar. 12, 1960. Asst. gen. mgr., prodn. mgr. Selznick Internat. Pictures, Culver City, Cal., 1936-43; exec. prodn. mgr., exec. producer charge low budget pictures 2Oth Century- Fox Film Corp., Beverly Hills, Cal., 1943-55; v.p. charge studio operations RKO Teleradio Pictures, Inc., also officer subsidiaries, 1956-58; gen. mgr. Metro-Goldwyn-Mayer Studios, Culver City, 1958-69; v.p. Metro-Goldwyn- Mayer, Inc., N.Y.C., 1959-69. Office: 10202 W Washington Blvd Culver City CA 90230

KLUTTZ, JERRY, former news columnist; b. Clinton, Mo., May 27, 1907; s. Lawson Milo and Adelia (McKinney) K.; student Central Coll., Fayette, Mo., 1925-26, U. Mo., 1927-28; B.S., George Washington U., 1931; m. Electa Tassin, Mar. 19, 1935; childrenGerald Eugene, John Lawson, James Edward. Reporter, Washington Herald, 1931, Washington Daily News, 1932-40; editor Fed. Diary column Washington Post, 1940-70; founder Fed. Employee Newsletter, 1948, editor, 1948-70; conducted radio news programs, 1934- 46. Recipient awards Washington Newspaper Guild, 1947, 53, Clapper-Edson award, 1949. Mem. Nat. Press Club, Fed. (pres.), White House corrs. assns., Internat. Platform Assn., Sigma Delta Chi, Sigma Chi. Club: Washington Golf and country. Home: 3705 Lorcom Lane Arlington VA 22207

KLUTZNICK, PHILIP M. ret. ambassador; b. Kansas City, Mo., July 9, 1907; s. Morris and Minnie (Spindler) K.; student U. Kan., 1924-25, U. Neb., 1925-26; LL.B., Creighton U., Omaha, Neb., 1929, LL.D., 1957; D.H.L. (hon.), Dropsie Coll., 1954, Hebrew Union Coll. Jewish Inst. Religion, 1957, LL.D., Wilberforce (O.) U., 1959; LL.D., Chgo. Med. Sch., 1968; D.H.L., Coll. Jewish Studies, 1968; m. Ethel Riekes, June 8, 1930; children-Bettylu, Richard (dec.), Thomas Joseph, James Benjamin, Robert, Samuel. Admitted to bar, 1930; U.S. commr. Fed. Pub. Housing Authority, 1944-46. Chmn. bd. Urban Investment and Devel. Co.; Am. Bank & Trust Co. N.Y., Swiss Israel Trade Bank, Geneva, Switzerland; pres. Oak Brook Utility Co.; dir. Mortgage Guaranty Ins. Corp., Milw. Mem. U.S. delegations to UN, 1957, 61, 62; U.S. rep., rank of ambassador, to ECOSOC, 1961-63. Mem. bd. Nat. Jewish Welfare Bd.; exec. com. United Jewish Appeal; nat. council Boy Scouts Am. Bd. govs. Met. Housing and Planning Council. Trustee, treas. Eleanor Roosevelt Meml. Found.; mem. bd. Ednl. Facilities Labs., Creighton U., Roosevelt U.; co-chmn. research and planning com., trustee com. for Econ. Devel.; trustee Adlai Stevenson Inst. Internat. Affairs. Mem. UN Assn. U.S.A. (exec. com., mem. bd.), Nat. Assembly for Social Policy and Devel. (mem. bd.), Council on Religion and Internat. Affairs (trustee, vice chmn.), Chgo. Assn. Commerce and Industry (dir.), Lambda Alpha, Phi Epsilon Pi (hon.). Mem. B'nai B'rith (hon. internat. pres.) Clubs: Highland (Omaha); Cosmos (Washington); Standard, Northmoor Country (Chgo.). Home: 175 E Delaware Pl Chicago IL 60611 Office: 401 N Michigan Av Chicago IL 60611

KLUVER, HEINRICH, psychologist; b. Holstein, Germany, May 25, 1897; s. Wilhelm and Dorothea (Wbbers) K.; student U. Hamburg (Germany) and U. Berlin, 1920-23; Ph.D., Stanford, 1924; M.D. (hon.), U. Basel, 1965; Ph.D. (hon.), U. Hamburg; 1969; m. Cessa Feyerabend, Feb. 4, 1927. Came to U.S., 1923, naturalized, 1934. Instr. psychology U. Minn., 1924-26; Social Science Research Council Fellow, 1926-28; research psychologist Behavior Research Fund, Chgo., 1928-33, asso. mem. Otho S.A. Sprague Meml. Inst., 1933-38, mem. Otho S.A. Sprague Meml. Inst., 1938- 46, prof. exptl. psychology, div. biol. sci., 1938-57, Sewell L. Avery distinguished service prof. biol. psychology, 1957-62, emeritus, 1963—; mem. Armed Forces-NRC Com. on Vision, 1960-65; mem. program project com. Nat. Inst. Gen. Med. Scis., NIH, 1963-66; prin. investigator Nat. Inst. Mental Health, 1963-. Recipient Karl Spencer Lashley award in neurobiology Am. Philos. Soc., 1960; Samuel W. Hamilton award Am. Psychopath. Assn., 1963; Gold medal award Am. Psychol. Found., 1965; Modern Medicine Distinguished Achievement award; 1969; Gold Medal award Eastern Psychiat. Research Assn., 1969. Mem. Nat. Acad. Scis., Am. Acad. Arts and Scis., Am. Psychol. Assn., A.A.A.S., Am. Physiol. Soc., Am. Neurol. Assn. (hon.), Soc. Exptl. Psychologists, Midwestern Psychol. Assn., Neuroscis. Research Program, Chgo. Psychol. Club, Optical Soc. Am., Soc. Biol. Psychiatry, Am. Soc. Human Genetics, N.Y. Acad. Sci., Assn. Research Nervous and Mental Disease, Am. Philos. Soc., Am. Soc. for Cybernetics, Internat. Brain Research Orgn., Royal Soc. Medicine, Pavlovian Soc. N. Am., Am. Acad. Neurology, Internat. Primatol. Soc., Am. Coll. Neuropsychopharmacology (hon.), Soc. Exptl. Biology and Medicine, Inst. Medicine Chgo.; Psychonomic Soc., Eastern Psychiat. Research Assn., Animal Behavior Soc. Am. Club: Quadrangle (Chgo.) Author: An Experimental Study of the Eidetic Type, 1926; Mescal, 1928; Behavior Mechanisms in Monkeys, 1933; Mescal and Mechanism of Hallucinations, 1966. Asso. editor: Jour. of Psychology, 1935—, Jour. Comporative Physiol. Psychology, 1947-50, Exptl. Neurology, Psychopharmacologia, 1959-68, Jour. Genetic Psychology, Perspectives in Biology and Medicine, Genetic Psychology Monographs, 1960—, Neuropsychologia, others. Contbr. articles to sci. jours. Home: 5312 Blackstone Av Chicago IL 60615 Office: U Chgo Chicago IL 60637

KLUWIN, JOHN A., lawyer; b. Oshkosh, Wis., Sept. 16, 1907; s. Fred R. and Nellie (McCarthy) K.; LL.B., Marquette U., 1930; m. Noreta Roemer, Sept. 29, 1934; children Mary Ann, John A., Robert J., William J., Thomas N., Michael G. Admitted to Wis. bar, 1930, since practiced in Milw.; lectr. in law Marquette U. Law Sch., part time 1945-51. Pub. panel mem. WLB, 1944-45. Fellow Am. Bar Found. mem. Internat. Assn. Ins. Counsel (past pres.), Am. (state del.), Wis. (past pres.), Milw. (past pres.) bar assns., Am. Arbitration Assn., Am. Coll. Trial Lawyers (regent 1964-68), Marquette U.

Alumni Assn. (pres. 1964-65). Roman Catholic. Clubs: Milwaukee Athletic; "M", Marquette University. Contbr. to Marquette Law Rev. Home: 9325 Hickory Dr Kewaskum WI 53040 Office: 1100 W Wells St Milwaukee WI 53233

KMENTT, WALDEMAR, lyric tenor; b. Vienna, Austria, Feb 2, 1929; s. Maximilian and Grete (Montandon) K.; student Hochschule für Musik and Darstellende Krunst (Vienna), 1949-51; m. Rosemarie Rainer, Nov. 4, 1959; 1 dau., Marina. Mem. Vienna State Opera, 1951-; performed Salzburg festivals, 1956-; guest performances Europe, S. Am., Far East; recs. Decca Records. Austrian Kammersänger, 1962-. Home: 36 Johnann Straussgasse Vienna 4, Austria

KNABE, GEORGE WILLIAM, Jr., med. educator; b. Grand Rapids, Mich., June 29, 1924; s. George William and Dorothy Emma (Fischofer) K.; student Mich. State Coll., 1942-43. The Citadel, 1943-44. Johns Hopkins, 1944-45; M.D., U. Md., 1949; m. Lorine J. Moffit, Jan. 16, 1954; children—Katharine, Elizabeth, Ann, Dorothy. Intern Balt. City Hosps., 1949-50; resident pathology Cleve. Clinic Found., 1950-51. Henry Ford Hosp., Detroit, 1953-54; chief, lab. service VA Center, Dayton, O., also clin. asst. prof. pathology Ohio State U., 1955-57; med. edn. adviser pathology ICA, El Salvador, also vis. prof. pathology U. El Salvador Sch. Medicine, 1957- 59; asst. prof. pathology U. P.R. Sch. Medicine, 1959-60; prof., chmn. dept. pathology, Sch. Medicine U. S. D., 1960-68, dean Sch. Medicine, 1967—. Served from 1st lt. to capt. M.C., USAF, 1951-53. Diplomate Am. Bd. Pathology. Mem. A.M.A., Am. Soc. Clin. Pathologists, Coll. Am. Pathologists, Internat. Acad. Pathology, Pan Am. Med. Assn. Home: Park Lane Vermillion SD 57069

KNAEBEL, JOHN BALLANTINE mining exec.; b. Denver, Jan. 1, 1906; s. Ernest and Cornelia (Park) K.; student Cornell U., 1924-28; field geology Northwestern U., summer 1928; B.S. in Engring., Stanford, 1929. E.M., 1930; m. Joy James, 1931 (div. May 1956); children-Jeffrey James, Stephen Park; m. 2d. Nelle M. McNulty, Mar. 14, 1958; 1 stepson, Terrence Patrick McNulty. Mining engr. Cananea Consol. Copper Co., Mexico, 1929; with U.S. Bur. Mines, 1931-33; mgr. East Mindanao Mining Co., P.I., 1934-36; cons. engr., Western U.S., Can., C.A.M., 1937-38; mng. dir. Amparo Mining Co., Ltd., Can., 1938-40; successively supt., asst. mgr., asst. to v.p., asst. mgr. Western Mines, U.S. Smelting, Refining & Mining Co., N.M., Utah, Western U.S., 1940-46; engr. in charge Anaconda Brit. Guiana Mines, Ltd., also mng. dir. Mineracao Gurupi. S.A., Brasil (Anaconda Copper Mining Co. subsidiaries), 1946-50, mgr. N.M. operations Anaconda Copper Mining Co., 1951-56, Anaconda Co., 1955-, asst. to v.p. in charge mining operations, N.Y.C., 1956-58; cons. engr., 1958; pres., mng. dir. Anaconda Iron Ore (Ont). Ltd., Can., 1959-; v.p., gen. mgr. Anaconda Co. (Can.), Ltd., Western div., 1962-; v.p. Anaconda Am. Brass, Ltd., Western Exploration div., 1963-; gen mgr. new mines dept. Anaconda Co., N.Y.C., 1963—, v.p., 1964—. Named Mining Man of Year Mining World mag., 1956; recipient William Lawrence Saunders Gold medal for distinguished achievement in mining Am. Inst. Mining Metall. and Petroleum Engrs., 1959. Mem. N.M. (dir. 1952-57, pres. 1956), Colo., Ariz. mining assns., Am. Mining Congress (Western bd. govs. 1955-57). Geol. and Mining Soc., Am. Inst. Mining, Metall. and Petroleum Engrs., Soc. Econ. Geologists, Tucson C. of C. (dir., mem. exec. com. 1964), Ariz. Acad., Canadian Inst. Mining and Metallurgy, Assn. Profl. Engrs. Assn. Profl. Engrs. Ont., Aircraft Owners and Pilots Assn., Sigma Xi, Sigma Gamma Epsilon, Quiet Birdmen. Clubs: Old Pueblo (Tucson); Mining (N.Y.C.). Contbr. articles, tech. papers on mining. Home: PO Box L Winston OR 97496 Office: P O Box 127 Sahuarita AZ 85629

KNANE, CHARLES JOSEPH, banker; b. Louisville, Jan. 2, 1920; s. Henry and Lillian (Berger) K.; student U. Louisville, 1951; grad. Rutgers U. Grad. Sch. Banking, 1954, Columbia Comml. Banks Sr. Mgmt. Sch., 1959; m. Rosemary Wilder, Oct. 4, 1941; children—Charles Joseph, Michael. With Citizens Fidelity Bank, Louisville, 1940—, v.p. charge banking, 1961-62, 1st v.p., 1962-67, exec. v.p., 1967-70, pres., 1970—, also dir., past instr. U. Louisville. Mem. Louisville Municipal Athletic Com.; past pres. bd. dirs., chmn. finance com. Children's Hosp., Louisville; past chmn. fund Pub. Parks Tennis Tournament; past bd. dirs. Louisville drive Cerebral Palsy Assn.; past chmn. for Ky., Crusade for Freedom, 1957-58; mem. Nat. Pub. Parks Tennis Tournament. Bd. dirs. Louisville Theatre Assn., U. Louisville Assos. Served with AUS, 1942-45. Recipient Crusade for Freedom award, 1957; President's citation for outstanding service U. Louisville, 1959. Mem. Louisville Credit Mens Assn., Robert Morris Assos., Newcomen Soc., Louisville Hist. Soc. Republican. Clubs: Harvard Business, Filson. Pendennis, Louisville Country (Louisville). Author: Bank Financing of Small Loan Companies, 1954. Home: 5838 Brittany Woods Circle Louisville KY 40207 Office: 437 W Jefferson St Louisville KY 40202

KNAPHEIDE, OLIVER CHARLES, Jr., bus. exec.; b. Winner, S.D., Apr. 28, 1914; s. Oliver Charles and Mary (Brown) K.; student S.D. State Coll., 1931-34; m. Phyllis Ray, Aug. 4, 1944; 1 dau., Linda F. (Mrs. Thomas K. Calhoun). With Gardner Denver Co., Quincy, Ill., 1934—, now sec. Served with USNR, 1941-45. Mem. N.A.M., Quincy C. of C. Presbyn. (trustee). Clubs: Quincy Boat, Quincy Country. Home: Rural Route 2 N 24th St Quincy IL 62301 Office: Gardner Denver Co Gardner Expressway Quincy IL 62301

KNAPLUND, PAUL WILLIAM, bus. machines co. exec.; b. Madison, Wis., Aug. 19, 1928; s. Paul Alexander and Dorothy Alice (King) K.; A.B., Harvard, 1949; M.A., U. Wis., 1950; m. Virginia Joan Samp, Sept. 27, 1951; children-Paul Alexander, Kristine Samp, Justin King, Eric Colbert. With IBM, 1950—, v.p. 1964—. Bd. dirs. Westchester Mental Health Assn.; trustee Nat. Rowing Found. Mem. Am. Math. Soc. Club: American Yacht. Home: 5 Pinecrest Rd Scarsdale, NY 10585. Office: Old Orchard Rd Armonk NY 10504

KNAPP, DANIEL C., govt. ofcl.; b. Peoria, Ill., June 19, 1915; s. Christian and Nina (Fernsler) K.; B.A., Bradley U., 1937; M.A., U. Ill., 1938; postgrad., Ohio State U., 1944-45; grad. Advanced Mgmt. Program, Harvard, 1962; m. Ruth Weinberger, Dec. 18, 1948; children-Theresa L., Karen D. Govt. intern Nat. Inst. Pub. Affairs, Washington, 1938-39; adminstrv. aide Social Security Bd., 1939-42; chief, dept. recruitment and placement VA, 1946-51; exec. officer Dept. Army, Washington and Okinawa, 1951-62; joined U.S. Fgn. Service, 1962, dep. chief career devel. staff State Dept., 1962-64, chief manpower resources staff, 1964-66; dir. manpower planning program, 1966-68; dir. personnel environmental health service HEW, Washington, 1968—. Served to 1st lt. AUS, 1942-46. Mem. Am. Soc. Pub. Adminstrn., Soc. Personnel Adminstrn., Pub. Personnel Assn., Pi Gamma Mu. Contbr. articles profl. jours. Home: 15421 Carrolton Rd Rockville, MD 20853. Office: Dept Health Edn and Welfare Washington DC 20204

KNAPP, FORREST LAMAR, clergyman, cons.; b. Rio Grande County, Colo., Dec. 12, 1899; s. Melvin Smith and Olive (Rosebrough) K.; B.S. in Elec. Engring., Colo. State Coll., 1921; B.D., Yale, 1924, Ph.D., 1927; m. Helen Florence Klein, June 30, 1928; 1 son, Burt Lovell (dec.). Ordained to ministry Congl. Ch., 1924; asst. pastor United Ch., Bridgeport, Conn., 1924-27; supt. religious edn. Cleve. Ch. Fedn., 1927-28; dir. leadership edn., mem. bd. editors Internat. Jour. Religious Edn., Internat. Council Religious Edn., 1929-39, dir. ch. sch. adminstrn., 1931-37, dir. research, 1931-32, chmn. Bur. Research, 1933-34, dir. field adminstrn., 1937-39, mem. ednl. commn. 1929-45; exec. sec. program com. Internat. Conv. on Christian Edn., 1930, exec. sec. gen. conv. com., 1938, mem. exec. com., trustee, 1940-50; mem. Council of Ch. Bds. of Edn., 1935-39; mem. div. Christian edn. and div. fgn. missions Nat. Council Chs. of Christ in U.S.; v.p. John Milton Soc. for Blind, 1942-54; asso. gen. sec. World Council Christian Edn. N.Y.C., 1939-40, gen. sec., 1940-53; gen. sec. Mass. Council Chs., 1954-69; cons. New Eng. Consultation of Ch. Leaders, 1969—. Lectr. religious edn. Northwestern U., 1932-33; visited various countries of Asia, The Americas, Africa, Near East to aid interdenominational work in Christian edn.; frat. del. 1st assembly World Council Chs., Amsterdam, 1948. Mem. Pi Kappa Delta, Lambda Chi Alpha. Author: Leadership Education in the Church, 1933; Next Steps in Latin-America, 1942; Handbook for Local Councils of Churches, 1955. Editor: The Christian Challenge to the Modern World, 1938, Christian Education and World Evangelization, 1941, Relations Between Church and State, 1960, Church Cooperation: Dead-End Street or Highway to Unity?, 1966. Home: Spectacle Rd Lakewood Hills East Sandwich MA 02537

KNAPP, GEORGE C., savs. and loan exec.; b. Salt Lake City, 1895. Chmn. bd., pres. Honolulu Savs. & Loan Co. Home: 999 Wilder St Honolulu HI 96822 Office: 182 Merchant St PO Box 539 Honolulu HI 96809*

KNAPP, GEORGE EDWARD III, banker; b. N.Y.C., Nov. 1, 1912; s. George Edward, Jr. and Nellie Ethel (Ernst) K.; student Am. Inst. Banking, 1932-36, Pace Coll., 1939-42, Grad. Sch. Banking, Rutgers U., 1954-57; m. Mary Elizabeth Horner, Aug. 31, 1941; 1 son, Paul Dennis. With East N.Y. Savs. Bank, Bklyn., 1931—, accountant, 1934-50, mortgage mgr., 1950-53, auditor, 1953—. Mem. Savs. Bank Auditors and Controllers Forum. Served with AUS, 1942-46; CBI. Baptist (trustee). Home: 9 Waverly St Huntington Station NY 11746 Office: 2644 Atlantic Av Brooklyn NY 11207

KNAPP, GEORGE FRANCIS, telephone co. exec.; b. N.Y.C., Sept. 6, 1931; s. George F. and Annette (McCabe) K.; B.E.E., Manhattan Coll., 1953; M.B.A., N.Y. U., 1964; m. Ann Eileen Stanley, Jan. 9, 1954; children—Eileen, Kathleen, George, Margaret, Richard. With Westinghouse Corp., 1953; engr. N.Y. Telephone Co., 1956-57, Bell Telephone Labs., 1958-59; mgmt. positions N.Y. Telephone Co., 1960-66; dir. operations Compania de Telefonos de Chile (ITT), Santiago, 1966-68; exec. v.p. P.R. Telephone Co., San Juan, 1969, pres., 1970—, also dir.; dir. V.I. Telephone Co. Bd. dirs. A.R.C., Puerto Rico council Boy Scouts Am. Served with Signal Corps, AUS, 1954-56. Registered profl. engr., N.Y., Chile. Mem. Nat. Assn. Businessmen P.R. (bd. dirs.), Young Pres.'s Orgn., ITT Exec. Assn. (pres.), Manhattan Coll. Alumni (pres. P.R.). Rotarian. Home: 1687 Gardenia St Urbanizacion San Francisco Rio Piedras PR 00927 Office: 1500 FD Roosevelt ave Caparra San Juan PR 00936

KNAPP, GEORGE LAWRENCE, Jr., outdoor advt. exec.; b. Shawnee, Okla., Sept. 10, 1915; s. George Lawrence and Edna Lois (Chitty) K.; grad. Okla. Mil. Acad., 1935; B.A., Okla. U., 1937; m. Mary Elizabeth Lambert, Feb. 18, 1939; children—Nancy Gail, Dorothy Jeanne. Partner, Knapp Advt. Co., 1951—; pres. Knapp Outdoor Advt. Corp., 1961-69, Knapp Neon & Plastic Sign Co., 1969—; dir. Farmers & Mchts. Bank & Trust co., Tulsa. Mem. Pres's adv. council for traffic safety; past chmn. Okla. Wild Life Commn. Bd. dirs. Asso. Industries Okla., Better Bus. Bur. Tulsa, Advt. Council, Tulsa Cancer Soc., Goodwill Industries. Served to lt. (j.g.) USNR, 1943-46. Mem. Outdoor Advt. Assn. Am. (dir. at large), Advt. Fedn. Am. (past pres., dir.), Execs. Assn. (past pres.), Izaak Walton League of Tulsa, Izaak Walton League of Okla. (past pres.), Tulsa C. of C., Beta Theta Pi. Rotarian. Clubs: Tulsa, Southern Hills Country, Oklahoma University Alumni (adv. bd. dirs.), Okla. Green Country. Home: 3145 E 42d St Tulsa OK Office: 6702 E 11th St Tulsa OK 74112

KNAPP, JAMES BARCLAY, Air Force officer; b. Macomb, Ill., Aug. 13, 1915; s. Porter and Minta Pearl (Barclay) k.; student Transylvania Coll., 1932-33, Western Ill. State Tchrs. Coll., 1933-35; B.S. in Engring., U.S. Mil. Acad., 1939; grad. Air War Coll., 1953; D.Sc. (hon.), Parsons Coll., 1959; m. Mary Emma Finger, Nov. 23, 1940; children-Gail Eugenia (Mrs. LeRoy Greene), Meta Sue (Mrs. Kenneth Fouts), Mary Elizabeth, Barbara, James Barclay. Commd. 2d lt. U.S. Army, 1939, advanced through grades to maj. gen. USAF, 1961; pilot, 1940; comdr. Goose Air Base, Labrador, 1953-57; dir. civil engring. Hdqrs. SAC, Offutt AFB, Neb., 1957-63; comdr. 16th Air Force, Spain 1963-64; dir. personnel Hdqrs. SAC, 1964-66, chief of staff, 1966-69; comdr. Chanute TTC, Ill. 1969— Decorated Silver Star, D.S.M., Legion of Merit with 2 oak leaf clusters, D.F.C. with oak leaf cluster, Air medal with 4 oak leaf clusters; Croix de Guerre (France). Registered profl. engr., Neb., Colo. Mem. Nat. Soc. Profl. Engrs. Home: 134 Vinson Circle Rantoul IL 61866

KNAPP, JOHN ANDREW, Jr., food co. exec.; b. St. Paul, Feb. 5, 1931; s. John Andrew and Kathryn M. (Rost) K.; student U. Minn., 1952-53; m. Katherine M. Brunner, Jan. 27, 1951; children—Mary, Deborah, Margaret, John G., Mark, Patricia, Michael, Steven. Accountant, Dan Bartz & Assos., Milw., 1953-58; controller Golden Dawn Foods, Sharon, Pa., 1958-63; treas. Super Foods Service, Chgo., 1963-64; gen. mgr. Bozzuto's, Inc., Cheshire, Conn., 1964-67; exec. v.p. Elm Farm Foods Co., Boston, 1968—. Served with USAF, Korean War. Home: 32 Meadowbrook Rd Sherborn MA 01770 Office: 600 Columbia Rd Boston MA 02125

KNAPP, JOHN MERRILL, educator; b. N.Y.C., May 9, 1914; s. John Harold and Lillian (Merrill) K.; A.B., Yale, 1936; M.A., Columbia, 1941; Mus.D., Westminster Choir Coll., 1970; m. Elizabeth-Ann Campbell, Feb. 21, 1944; children Joan, Phoebe. Tchr. history Thacher Sch., Ojai, Cal., 1936-38; asst. dir. Yale Glee Club, 1938-39; faculty Princeton, 1941-42, 46—, prof. music, 1961—, dir. Glee Club, 1941-42, 46-52, asst. dean Coll., 1955-58, dean, 1961-66. Trustee Hun Sch., Westminster Choir Coll., Hotchkiss Sch. Served with USNR, 1942-46. Mem. Am. Conf. Acad. Deans, Internat. Am. musicol. socs., Coll. Music Soc., Am. Assn. U. Profs., Halle Händel Soc. (exec. bd.), Göttingen Handel Soc. (exec. com.). Editor: Selected List of Music for Mens Voices, 1952. Home: Rosedale Lane Princeton NJ 08540

KNAPP, JOHN WILLIAMS, educator; B.S., Va. Mil. Inst.; M.S., Ph.D., Johns Hopkins. Prof. civil engring., head civil engring. curriculum Va. Mil. Inst., Lexington. Office: Dept Civil Engring Va Mil Inst Lexington VA*

KNAPP, JOSEPH BURKE, banker; b. Portland, Ore., Jan. 25, 1913; s. Joseph Burke and Cornelia Ann (Pinkham) K.; A.B., Stanford, 1933; B.A. (Rhodes scholar) Oxford U., 1935, B.Litt., 1936; m. Hilary Eaves, April 4, 1939; children—Louis, Rosalind, Elise, Michael. Spl. asst. to mng. dir. Brown Harriman Ltd., London, 1936-40; economist Fed Res. Bd., 1940- 44; adviser on German econ. affairs U.S. Dept. State and German Mil. Govt., 1944- 45; spl. asst. to chmn. Fed. Res. Bd., 1945-48; dir. Office Financial and Devel. Policy, Dept. State, 1948-49; asst. dir. econ. dept. Internat. Bank for Reconstrn. and Devel., 1950-52, dir. Western Hemisphere dept., 1952-56, v.p., 1956—; econ. adviser U.S. delegation NATO, 1950-51; U.S. pres. Joint Brazil U.S. Econ. Devel. Commn., 1951-52. Pres., Washington Drama Soc., 1959-70. Trustee Mt. Vernon Coll. Clubs: Columbia Country (Chevy Chase, Md.); Metropolitan, International (Washington). Home: 3701 Curtis Ct Chevy Chase MD 20015 Office: Internat Bank 1818 H St Washington DC 20006

KNAPP, JOSEPH GRANT, economist; b. Loveland, Colo., Nov. 22, 1900; s. Mason E. and Florence Amy (White) K.; student Colo. A. and M. Coll., 1918-19, U. Ill., 1921-21, U. Chgo., 1923-24; B.S., U. Neb., 1922, M.A. (H.E. Sidles scholar), 1923, D.Sc., 1967; Ph.D., Stanford, 1929; D.Sc., N.C. State U., 1967; m. Carol Maud Freston West, Feb. 13, 1929; childrenSheila Margaret (Mrs. Woodard), John Laurence. Research asst. U. Chgo., 1923-24; fellow Food Research Inst., Stanford, 1924-25, teaching asst., 1925-26; mem. staff Inst. Econs., Brookings Instn., 1926- 29, 44-46, asso. prof. charge agrl. marketing, asso. agrl. economist N.C. State Coll. 1929-34; sr. agrl. economist FCA, 1934-36, prin. agrl. economist, 1936-48, asso. and acting chief coop. research and service div., 1948-53; adminstr. farmer coop. service, U.S. Dept. Agr., Washington, 1954-66; ind. writer, cons., 1966-. Recipient Pioneer award Am. Inst. Cooperation, 1964. Mem. Am. Econ. Assn., Am. Farm Econs. Assn., Am. Marketing Assn. (pres. Washington chpt. 1956-57), Phi Kappa Phi, Sigma Nu, Alpha Kappa Psi. Club: Cosmos (Washington). Author: (with Edwin Griswold Nourse) The Cooperative Marketing of Livestock, 1931; The Hard Winter Wheat Pools, 1933; E.A. Stokdyk-Architect of Cooperation, 1953; Seeds That Grew-A History of The Cooperative Grange League Federation Exchange, 1960; Farmers in Business-Studies in Cooperative Enterprise, 1963; An Appraisement of Agricultural Cooperation in Ireland, 1964; An Analysis of Agricultural Cooperation in England, 1965; (with others) Great American Cooperators, 1967; The Glen Haven Story, 1967; The Rise of American Cooperative Enterprise, 1969. Contbr. articles to various profl. jours. Home: 7119 Fairfax Rd Bethesda, MD 20014

KNAPP, LEONARD DAYTON, labor union ofcl.; b. Lowell, Mich., Aug. 4, 1914; s. Floyd Clark and Emma Amelia (Swanson) K.; student pub. schs., Marne, Mich.; Chief mechanic Consumers Power Co., Grand Rapids, Mich., 1937-61; nat. rep. Utility Workers Union, 1961-63; pres. Mich. Utility Workers Council, Jackson, 1963-67., nat. sec.-treas., Washington, 1967—. Scoutmaster, Boy Scouts of Am., Marne, 1930-41. Served with USAAF, 1941-45; CBI. Democrat. Methodist. Home: 4701 Willard Av Chevy Chase MD 20015 Office: 1875 Connecticut Av Washington DC 20009

KNAPP, ROBERT HAMPDEN, educator, psychologist; b. Portland, Ore., Apr. 16, 1915; s. Joseph Burke and Cornelia (Pinkham) K.; B.A., U. Ore., 1938, M.A., 1939; M.A., Harvard, 1940, Ph.D., 1948; M.A. (hon.), Wesleyan U., Middletown, Conn., 1956; m. Johnsia Nelson, Mar. 19, 1945; children—Robert Hampden, Abigail Pinkham, Hiatt Jefferson, Sarah Elizabeth. Mem. faculty Wesleyan U., 1946—, now prof. psychology, also chmn. dept. Dep dir., Ford Found., 1953-54; dir. sci. faculty fellowship panel NSF, 1957—; mem. Gov. Conn. Bd. Certification Psychologists, 1959—. Chmn. Planning and Zoning Commn., Haddam, Conn., 1957-59. Democratic candidate for Conn. Legislature, 1956. Served with OSS, AUS, 1942-45. Mem. Am. Psychol. Assn. (pres. div. psychology and the arts 1967-68), Am. Ortho- Psychiat. Assn., Am. Soc. Aesthetics, Am. Assn. Humanistic Psychology, Phi Beta Kappa, Sigma Xi, Sigma Nu. Club: Harvard (N.Y.C.). Author: (with H.B. Goodrich) The Origins of American Scientists, 1954; (with J.J. Greenbaum) The Younger American Scholar, 1954; Origins of the American Humanistic Scholar, 1964; also numerous papers. Home: 20 Lawn Av Middletown CT 06457

KNAPP, SHERMAN RICHMOND, ret. utility exec.; b. Danbury, Conn., June 17, 1905; s. Frederick Abijah and Julia (Richmond) K.; E.E. Cornell, 1928; m. Eleanor Tracy, June 23, 1928; children—Sherman R., Barbara, Duncan Tracy. With Conn. Light & Power Co., Berlin, 1928—, cadet engr., 1928-31, sales engr., 1931-37, mgr. New Milford dist., 1937-41, asst. to sales v.p., 1941-48, asst. to pres., 1948-50, exec. v.p., 1950-52, pres., dir., 1952-64, chmn., dir., 1964-70; pres., chief exec. officer N.E. Utilities, Wethersfield, Conn., 1966-67, chmn. bd., chief exec. officer 1967-69, chmn. exec. com.; 1970—; chmn., dir. Conn. Yankee Atomic Power Co.; dir. Atomic Indsl. Forum, Inc., Hartford Ins. Group, Conn. Bank and Trust Co., Emhart Mfg Co., Hartford Steam Boiler Ins. and Inspection Co., Scovill Mfg. Co. Mem. Nat. Indsl. Conf. Bd.; past pres. Edison Elec. Inst., Elec. Council New Eng.; chmn. Conn. Flood Recovery Com., 1955; mem. Conn. Research Commn. (emeritus). Trustee, Conn. Coll., Inst. Living. Mem. New Eng. Gas Assn. (past pres.), Lambda Chi Alpha. Clubs: The Hartford; Shuttle Meadow Country (New Britain, Conn.); Sky (N.Y.C.); Metropolitan (Washington). Home: 1210 Kensington Rd Kensington CT 06037 Office: 176 Cumberland Av Wethersfield CT 06109

KNAPP, WHITMAN, lawyer; b. N.Y.C., Feb. 24, 1909; s. Wallace Percy and Carolina Morgan (Miller) K.; grad. Choate Sch., 1927; B.A., Yale 1931; LL.B., Harvard, 1934; m. Ann Fallert, May 17, 1962; 1 son, Gregory Wallace; children by previous marriage—Whitman Everett, Caroline (Mrs. Edward M. W. Hines), Marion Elizabeth. Admitted to N.Y. bar, 1935; with firm Cadwalader, Wickersham & Taft, N.Y.C., 1935-37; dep. asst. dist. atty., N.Y.C., 1937- 41; with firm Donovan, Leisure, Newton & Lumbard, N.Y.C., 1941; mem. staff dist. atty. N.Y.C., 1942-50, chief, appeal bur., 1944-50; partner firm Barrett Knapp Smith Schapiro & Simon, and predecessors, 1950—. Spl. counsel N.Y. State Youth Commn., 1950-53, Waterfront Commn. N.Y. Harbor, 1953-54; mem. temporary commn. revision N.Y. State penal law and criminal code, 1964-69; chmn. Knapp Commn. to Investigate Allegations of Police Corruption in N.Y.C., 1969—. gen. counsel Urban League Greater N.Y., 1962—. Sec., Community Council Greater N.Y., 1952-58; pres. Dalton Schs., N.Y.C., 1950-53, Youth House, 1967-68. Trustee Univ. Settlement, 1945-64, Moblzn. for Youth, 1965-70. Mem. Am. Law Inst., Am. Bar Found., Am. Coll. Trial Lawyers, Assn. Bar City N.Y. (sec. 1946-49, chmn. exec. com. 1971—), N.Y. County Lawyers Assn., Am., N.Y. State bar assns. Editor, Harvard Law Rev., 1933- 34. Home: 79 W 12th St New York City NY 10011 Office: 26 Broadway New York City NY 10004

KNAPPSTEIN, HEINRICH, German diplomat; b. Bochum, Germany, Apr. 14, 1906; s. Joseph and Clara (Herbst) K.; ed. univs. Cologne, Berlin and Bonn, (Germany), also U. Cin.; m. Adelheid Löhr, Dec. 23, 1933; childrenMechthild (Mrs. Armin Frank), Ursula. Mem. editorial staff Frankfurter Zeitung, 1936- 43; dep. state minister reconstrn. and liberation Govt. Hesse, 1945-49; consul. gen., Chgo., 1951-56; ambassador to Spain, 1956-58; dep. under sec. Fgn. Ministry, Bonn, 1958-60; German observer to UN, 1960-62; ambassador to U.S., 1962-68. Home: 638 Bad Homburg V d H Tannenwaldallee 19 Germany

KNAUER, VIRGINIA HARRINGTON WRIGHT, (Mrs. Wilhelm F. Knauer), govt. ofcl.; b. Phila., Mar. 28, 1915; d. Herman Winfield and Helen (Harrington) Wright; B.F.A., U. Pa., 1937; postgrad. Pa. Acad. Fine Arts; Royal Acad. Fine Arts, Florence, Italy, 1938-39; L.H.D., Russell Sage Coll., Pa. Coll. Podiatric Medicine; m. Wilhelm

F. Knauer, Jan. 27, 1940; children—Wilhelm F., Valerie H. (Mrs. I. Townsend Burden III). Dir., Pa., Bur. Consumer Protection, 1968-69; spl. asst. consumer affairs to Pres. Richard M. Nixon 1969—. U.S. rep., vice chmn. consumer policy com. OECD. Councilman-at-large, Phila., 1959- 68; vice-chmn. Phila. County Republican Com., 1958—; pres. Phila. Congress Rep. Councils, 1958—; dir. Pa. Council Rep. Women, 1963; founder N.E. Council Rep. Women, pres., 1956-64. Bd. dirs. Hannah Penn House, v.p., 1971; co-founder Knauer Found. Historic Preservation. Named Distinguished Dau. Pa., 1969. Trustee Pa. Coll., Podiatric Medicine. Mem. Zeta Tau Alpha, Kappa Delta Epsilon (hon.). Episcopalian. Club: Doberman Pinscher (nat. pres. 1957-58). Home: Morelton Riverbank at Fitler St Philadelphia PA 19114 Office: White House Washington DC

KNAUSS, JOHN ATKINSON, univ. dean, oceanographer; b. Detroit, Sept. 1, 1925; s. Karl Ernst and Loise (Atkinson) K.; B.S., Mass. Inst. Tech., 1946; M.A., U. Mich., 1949; Ph.D., Scripps Instn. Oceanography, U. Cal., 1959; m. Marilyn Mattson, Sept. 6, 1954; childrenKarl, William. Oceangrapher, Navy Electronics Lab., San Diego, 1947, Office Naval Research, 1949-51, Scripps Instn. Oceanography, 1951-52, 55-62; dean Grad. Sch. Oceanography, U. R.I. 1962—, provost for marine affairs, 1969—. Leader 10 oceanographic expdns. to study oceanic circulation, 1955-65; chmn. U.S. phys.-chem. panel Internat. Indian Ocean Expdn., 1959-62, mem. internat. com. for planning, 1960; mem. com. on oceanography Nat. Acad. Scis., 1966-70; mem. Pres's. Commn. on Marine Scis., Engring and Resources. 1967-68. Served with USNR, 1943-46, 53-54. Mem. Am. Geophys. Union (pres. oceanographic sect. 1965-67), Nat. Oceanography Assn. (dir. 1969—), Am. Soc. for Oceanography (dir. 1970—), Assn. Sea Grant Instns. (pres. 1970-71), Nat. Acad. Sci. (mem. ocean sci. affairs bd. 1971—, chmn. ocean sci. com. 1971—). Home: Willett Rd Saunderstown RI 02874 Office: U R I Kingston RI

KNEBEL, FLETCHER, writer; b. Dayton, O., Oct. 1, 1911; s. A.G. and Mary (Lewis) K.; A.B., Miami U., Oxford, O., 1934; m. Laura Bergquist, 1965; children by previous marriageJack G., Mary L. With Coatesville (Pa.) Record, 1934, Chattanooga (Tenn.) News, 1934-35, Toledo News Bee, 1936; with Cleve. Plain Dealer, 1936-50; Washington corr., 1937-50; corr. Washington bur. Cowles Publs., 1950-64; syndicated columnist Potomac Fever, 1951-64. Served to lt. USNR, 1942-45. Mem. Phi Beta Kappa, Sigma Chi. Clubs: Gridiron, National Press, Nassau. Author: Night of Camp David. 1965, The Zinzin Road, 1966; Vanished, 1968; Trespass, 1969. Co-author: No High Ground, 1960; Seven Days in May, 1962; Convention, 1964. Address: 208 Edgerstoune Rd Princeton NJ 08540

KNECHT, ANDREW WILSON, cons. engr.; b. Phila., May 4, 1907; s. George G. and Sylvia (Organ) K.; M.E., Stevens Inst. Tech., 1928; m. Hilda M. Birch, Sept. 6, 1930; children—Andrew Wilson (dec.), Brian B. Engr., Clyde R. Place, cons. engr., 1929-35, asso., 1937-46; office mgr. Tag Mfrs. Inst., 1935-37; chief mech., elec. engr., asst. chief engr. Walter Kidde Constructors, 1946-51; mng. partner Seelye, Stevenson, Value & Knecht, N.Y.C., 1951—; pres. Seelye, Stevenson, Value & Knecht, Inc. Mem. War Manpower Bd., 1945-46; cons. on fuels and conservation program Dept. Commerce, 1946. Mem. Bd. Edn., Yonkers, N.Y., 1946-51. Trustee Yonkers Gen. Hosp. Registered profl. engr., 16 states and D.C. Fellow Am. Soc. M.E. (exec. com. of com. profl. practice cons. engrs. 1956-59), Am. Soc. C.E.; mem. Am. Soc. Heating, Refrigerating and Air Conditioning Engrs., I.E.E.E., Am. Inst. Cons. Engrs. (past mem. council), N.Y. Assn. Cons. Engrs., Soc. Am. Mil. Engrs. (dir., past pres. N.Y. post), N.Y. Bldg. Congress (pres., dir.), Nat. Soc. Profl. Engrs., Cons. Engrs. Council, Am. Mgmt. Assn., Am. Soc. Testing Materials, N.Y. Soc. Profl. Engrs. Clubs: Ardsley Country; Seaview Country, Union League (N.Y.C.); Ponte Vedra Country (Jacksonville, Fla.). Home: 39 Brace Terrace Dobbs Ferry NY 10522 Office: 99 Park Av New York City NY 10016

KNEDLER, JOHN WARREN, Jr., Sch. adminstr. b. Elmhurst, Pa., Apr. 29, 1901; s. John Warren and Sally Kate (Greiss) K.; A.B., Harvard, 1924, M.A., 1927, Ph. D., 1937. Prof. English, Manhattan Sch. of Music 1945-56, lectr. in English, 1956- 60, dir. humanities, 1957-62, adminstrv. head 1969—; instr. English, N.Y.U., 1929-34, 35-37, asst. prof., 1937-42, asst. prof. physics, 1942-45, asso. prof. English, 1945-51, prof. English, 1951—, asst. dean, 1946-57, asso. dean, 1957-60, dean Univ. Coll. 1960-67; Chmn., Intercollegiate YMCA of N.Y.C., 1964-65. Mem. Renaissance Soc. N.Y.C., Modern Humanities Assn., Coll. Assn. English Tchrs., Modern Lang. Assn. Am., Assn. Higher Edn., Assn. Coll. Deans and Advisers, Phi Beta Kappa, Phi Gamma Delta. Club: Harvard, New York University (N.Y.C.), Editor: Masterworks of Science, 1947. Home: Moscow PA 18444 and Webb Av Bronx New York City NY 10468

KNEEBONE, E.J., mining co. exec.; b. San Francisco, Sept. 11, 1913; s. Joseph Russell and Rose (Green) K.; student, U. Nev., 1934; m. Mary Elizabeth Washburn, Feb. 8, 1936; children—Kathryn (Mrs. Raymond Willard Pearson), Terrence Holmes. With various mining cos., various locations, 1933-40; office mgr. Atok-Big Wedge Mining Co., Baguio, Philippines, 1940-42, 46-51; with Benguet Consol., Inc., Baguio and Manila, Philippines, 1951—, asst. v.p., 1966-69, v.p., 1969—; dir. Engring. Equipment Inc.; v.p., dir. Wire Rope Corp.; chmn. bd., treas. Arrow Forwarding Corp. Mem. Am. Assn. Philippines, Am.-Philippines Guardian Assn., Mackay Sch. Mines Alumni Assn., Baguio Jr. C. of C. (past pres.), Alpha Tau Omega. Mason (Scottish Rite, 32). Clubs: Manila, University (Manila). Home: 10 Rocha Makati Rizal Philippines Office: 2756 Pasong Tamo Ext Makato Rizal Philippines

KNEIP, FREDERICK EVOY, paper co. exec.; b. Fashington, Apr. 17, 1917; s. Frederick E. and Anita (Dieterich) K.; A.B., Dartmouth, 1936; grad. advanced mgmt. program Harvard, 1960; m. Loraine Condit, May 4, 1940; children—Frederick C., Loraine DeRonde, Edward Arthur. With E.A. Pierce & Co., N.Y.C., 1936-38; sales engr. Nichols Engring. & Research, N.Y.C., 1938-41; with Union-Camp Corp., Savannah Ga., Trenton, N.J., 1941-57, gen. mgr., Lakeland, Fla., 1957-58, div. sales and gen. mgr., N.Y.C., 1958-65; sr. v.p., dir. Stone Container Corp., Chgo., 1965—. Served with USMC, 1942-46. Home: 69 Indian Hill Rd Winnetka IL 60093 Office: 360 N Michigan Av Chicago IL 60601

KNEIP, RICHARD FRANCIS, gov. S.D.; b. Tyler, Minn., Jan. 7, 1933; s. Frank J. and Bernice D. (Pederson) K.; student S.D. State U., Brookings, 1955, St. John's U., Collegeville, Minn., 1956; Nancy Pankey, Apr. 19, 1957; 8 sons. Owner, operator Kneip Sales, dairy equipment firm, Salem, S.D., 1962—; gov. S.D., 1971—. Mem. S.D. Constl. Revision Commn., 1969-71; mem. S.D. Senate, 1965-71. Served with USAAF, 1951-55; ETO. Democrat. Roman Catholic. Elk. Address: Exec Office Pierre SD 57501

KNEISLY, NATHANIEL MCKAY, pub. co. exec.; b. Omaha, Apr. 5, 1892; s. Charles Christian and Harriet Augusta (McKay) K.; student U. Ill., 1914; m. Mary Eleanor Simpson, June 5, 1923, Vice pres., gen. mgr. Mut. Motor Stores, Chgo., 1914-16; sales mgr. Equipment Co., Kansas City, Mo., 1919-21, pres., 1921-23; with Irving-Cloud Pub. Co., Chgo., 1926-, v.p., gen. mgr., 1941-50, pres., 1950-65, vice chmn. bd., 1965—. Chmn., Nat. Bus. Publs., 1956-57. Active U. Ill. Found. Served with U.S. Army, 1917-18. Mem. Theta Delta Chi. Club: President's of University of Illinois. Home: 1456 Wesley Av Evanston IL 60201 Office: 7300 N Cicero Av Lincolnwood CA 60646

KNELLER, JOHN WILLIAM, coll. pres.; b. Oldham, Eng., Oct. 15, 1916; s. John William and Margaret Ann (Truslove) K.; A.B., Clark U., 1938, Litt.D., 1970; A.M., Yale, 1948, Ph.D., 1950; student U. Paris (France), 1949-50; m. Alice Bowerman Hart, Apr. 30, 1943; 1 dau., Linda Hart. Mem. faculty Oberlin Coll., 1950-69, prof. French, 1959-69, chmn. dept. Romance languages, 1959-65, provost, 1965-69; pres. Bklyn. Coll., 1969—; mng. editor French Review, 1963-65, editor, 1965-68. Mem. N.Y. State Commr.'s Adv. Council on Higher Edn. Adv. com. for Congressman Bertram L. Podell. Bd. dirs. G.F. Kneller Found.; bd. trustees Clark U., Bklyn. Inst. Arts and Scis.; mem. alumni bd. Yale. Served with AUS, 1942-46. Mem. Am. Assn. Tchrs. French (pres. Ohio chpt. 1964-65, exec. council 1963-68), Modern Lang. Assn. (exec. council), Am. Assn. U. Profs., Yale Grad. Sch. Assn. (exec. com.), Kappa Delta Pi (hon.), Alpha Sigma Lambda (hon.). Co-author: Initiation au francais, 1963; Introduction a la poesie francaise, 1962. Contbr. articles jours. in field. Home: 115 Westminster Rd Brooklyn NY 11218

KNELLER, WILLIAM ARTHUR, educator, geologist; b. Cleve., Apr. 7, 1929; s. John Jacob and Cora (Schilke) K.; A.B., Miami U., Oxford, O., 1951; M.S., 1955; Ph.D. (William Herbert Hobbs fellow, NSF fellow), U. Mich., 1964; m. Olga Tihonovna Kanareff, July 14, 1951; children—Karinlee, Gregory John, Ellen Kay, Kurt Tihon. Asst. prof. geology Eastern Mich. U., Ypsilanti, 1959-60; mem. faculty U. Toledo, 1961—, asso. prof., 1964-67, prof., chmn. dept. geology, 1967—; prof. field geology U. Mich., Jackson Hole, Wyo., summer 1966; various engring. positions, summers 1948-56; cons. constrn., mining, engring. and other companies. Served with 2d Marine Div., USMCR, 1951-53. Rackham U. Fellow (declined), 1956; NSF vis. prof. Miami U., Oxford, summer 1965. Fellow Geol. Soc. Am.; mem. Mineral. Soc. Am. Soc. Econ. Paleontologists and Mineraologists, A.A.A.S., Electron Microscopy Soc. Am., Sigma Xi, Sigma Gamma Epsilon, Phi Sigma. Home : 1761 Cherry Lawn Dr Toledo OH 43614

KNEPLER, HENRY WILLIAM, educator; b. Vienna, Austria, May 8, 1922; s. Hugo and Hedwig (Moser) K.; B.A., Queen's U., Kingston, Can., 1942-46, B.A., 1945, M.A., 1946; Ph.D., U. Chgo., 1950; m. Myrna Cohn, Apr. 23, 1961; children— Elizabeth, Elinor, Anne. Came to U.S., 1946, naturalized, 1955. Mem. faculty Ill. Inst. Tech., 1947—, prof. English, 1962—, chmn. dept. humanities, 1961—; vis. prof. Sorbonne-U. Paris, 1971—. Author: (with S.K. Workman) A Range of Writing, 1959; (with R. S. Cassell) What is the Play?, 1967; The Gilded Stage, 1968; Man About Paris, 1970. Home: 1344 E Madison Park Chicago IL 60615

KNEPPER, GEORGE W., educator; b. Akron, O., Jan. 15, 1926; s. George W. and Grace (Darling) K.; B.A., U. Akron, 1948; M.A., U. Mich., 1950, Ph.D., 1954; m. Phyllis Watkins, Aug. 21, 1949; children—Susan Lynne, John Arthur. Mem. faculty U. Akron, 1948-49, 54—, asso. prof. history, head dept., 1959-62, dean Coll. Liberal Arts, 1962-67, prof. history, 1964—. Served to ensign USNR, 1943-46. Fulbright fellow U. London (Eng.), 1953-54. Mem. Am., So. hist. assns., Orgn. Am. Historians, Ohio Acad. History, Omicron Delta Kappa, Alpha Tau Omega, Phi Alpha Theta, Alpha Sigma Lambda. Author: New Lamps for Old, One Hundred Years of Urban Higher Education at the University of Akron, 1970. Editor: Travels in the Southland; The Journal of Lucius Verus Bierce 1822-23, 1966. Home: 2317 19th St Cuyahoga Falls OH 44223 Office: Univ Akron Akron OH 44304

KNEPPER, WILLIAM EDWARD, lawyer; b. Tiffin, O., Oct. 25, 1909; s. Russell Monroe and Mamie (Corn) K.; A.B., Ohio State U., 1931; postgrad., Columbus Coll. Law, 1931-32; m. Lucille Witten, Jan. 13, 1933; children-Richard Scott, Bonne Lee (Mrs. Cookston); m. 2d, Mary Morrill Lichtenberg, Mar. 30, 1964; step-children- Mary L. (Mrs. Daum), James W., John M. Admitted to Ohio bar, 1933, since practiced in Columbus; partner firm Knepper, White & Dempsey, 1933-54, now firm of Knepper, White, Richards & Miller. Mem. Ohio Bar Examining Com., 1945-50, chmn., 1950. Pres., Def. Research Inst., Inc., 1965-66. Chmn, Franklin County Court House Annex Bldg. Commn., 1946-54, State Underground Parking Commn., 1955-58, 61-69. Fellow Am. Coll. Trial Lawyers; mem. Am., Ohio (exec. commn. 1951-54), Columbus (pres. 1947-48) bar assns., Internat. Assn. Ins. Counsel (pres. 1962- 63), Am. Judicature Soc., Columbus Area C. of C. (chmn. 1963-65), Ohio State U. Assn. (pres. 1967-69), Columbus Players Club (pres. 1943), Pi Kappa Alpha, Kappa Kappa Psi. Democrat. Episcopalian Mason (33, K.T., Shriner). Clubs: Athletic, Young Business Men's (Columbus). Author: Liability of Corprorate Officers and Directors, 1969; Ohio Civil Practice, 1970. Co-Author: The Ohio Manual of General Practice, 1956; Judicial Conveyances and Eminent Domain (Ohio), 1960. Editor: Insurance Counsel Jour., 1955-61. Contbr. numerous articles to profl. jours. and law revs. Home: 2625 York Rd Columbus OH 43221 Office: 150 E Broad St Columbus OH 43215

KNEZEVICH, STEPHEN JOSEPH, educator; b. Milw., Mar. 16, 1920; s. Thomas and Eva (Bukovac) K.; B.S., U. Wis., Milw., 1941; M.S., U. Wis., Madison, 1945, Ph.D., 1951; m. Doris Lorraine Boggs, June 9, 1943; children—Michael Thomas, Mark Paul, Mary Ruth. High sch. tchr. sci. and math., Algoma, Wis., 1941-44; supt. schs., Spencer, Wis., 1944-47, Port Edwards, Wis., 1947-50; asso. prof. edn. adminstrn. U. Tulsa, 1951-54; asso. and prof. edn. U. Ia., 1954-61; prof., head dept. Fla. State U., 1961-65; asso. sec. Am. Assn. Sch. Adminstrs., Washington, 1965-70, sec. ethics com., 1966-70, sec. com. for advancement of sch. adminstrn., 1966-70; dir. Nat. Acad. Sch. Execs., 1968-70; prof. edn. adminstrn. U. Wis., Madison, 1970—; vis. prof. summers U. Colo., 1965, U. Mich., 1967, U. Ida., 1968, U. Nev., 1969; prin. investigator, dir. dissemination project Wis. Research and Devel. Center on Cognitive Learning, 1970—; cons. to Rand Corp., 1970—. Mem. adv. com. Washington Internships in Edn., 1968—. All-Univ fellow U. Wis., 1950-51. Mem. Am. Assn. Sch. Adminstrs. (life), N.E.A. Author books, articles profl. jours., chpts. in books. Home: 318 N Yellowstone Dr Madison WI 53705

KNICKERBOCKER, KENNETH LESLIE, coll. ofcl., editor; b. Dallas, May 19, 1905; s. Hubert DeLancy and Julia (Opdenweyer) K.; A.B., So. Meth. U., 1925, A.M., 1927; Ph.D., Yale, 1933; m. Dorothy McDonald, June 30, 1928; children—Robert Keats, Alzada Jean. Instr. English, Tex. Tech. Coll., 1926-29, 1932-34; asst. prof. English, R.I. State Coll., 1934-36, asso. prof., 1936-38, prof. English, head dept., 1938-46; prof., chmn. freshman English, U. Tenn., 1946-57, asso. dean Coll. Liberal Arts, 1957-58, dean, 1958-63, head dept. English, 1962-71, acad. v.p., 1971—, Distinguished Service prof. English, 1964—. Chmn. state com. survey role and needs higher edn., 1956-57; exec. com. Assn. Depts. English, 1968-71. Served as lt. USNR, 1943-46. Am. Council Learned Socs. grantee, 1934. Mem. Modern Lang. Assn. Am., So. Atlantic Modern Lang. Assn., Nat. Council Tchrs. English, Coll. English Assn. (dir. 1956-58), Tenn. Coll English Assn. (pres. 1956-57), Am. Assn. U. Profs., Tenn. Edn. Assn., Conf. Coll. Composition and Communication (exec. com., nominating com.), Assn. Am. Univs. and Land-Grant Colls. (exec. com. 1959-62), So. Atlantic Assn. Depts. English (pres.), Phi Beta Kappa, Kappa Alpha (So.), Phi Kappa Phi. Editor: New letters of Robert Browning (with William C. DeVane), 1950; Selections from the Poetry of Robert Browning, 1951; compiler, editor Ideas for Writing, 1951; Interpreting Literature (with H.W. Reninger), 1955; Readings and Assignments in Freshman English (with B. Stewart), 1961; Instructors Manual (with H. Reninger), 1965; The Browning Critics (with Boyd Litzinger), 1966; Writing About Poetry, 1967. Contbr. articles learned jours. on 19th century lit. figures. Home: 3524 Bluff Point Dr Knoxville TN 37920

KNICKERBOCKER, PAINE, drama and film critic; b. N.Y.C., Mar. 16, 1912; s. Reginald Canning and Mary (Paine) K.; A.B., Dartmouth, 1933; M.A., U. Cal. at Berkeley, 1939; m. Nancy Burt, June 12, 1940; children-Peggy (Mrs. John H. Hanan III), Anthony Paine. With advt. agys., N.Y.C., 1933-37; asst. to pres. Mills Coll., 1940-42; with Oakland (Cal.) Tribune, 1946-52; with San Francisco Chronicle, 1952-, drama critic, 1955-. Served to lt. USNR, 1942-46. Recipient Critics award Dirs. Guild Am., 1963. Mem. San Francisco Zool. Soc., Beta Theta Pi. Home: 2600 Union St San Francisco CA 94123

KNIERIEM, FREDERICK MORTIMER, banker; b. Balt., Aug. 9, 1911; s. Charles and Catherine (Knoop) K.; student Johns Hopkins, 1931-35; LL.B., U. Balt., 1941; postgrad. Rutgers U., 1943-46; m. Dorotha Lee Ford, June 7, 1937. With Union Trust Co. of Md., Balt., 1935—, trust officer, 1945-61, v.p., 1961-68, sr. v.p., 1968—; dir. Gen. Supply & Equipment Co., Cable Co., Balt., Wolverine Porcelain & Enameling Co., Detroit; faculty U. Balt., 1959-67. Mem. Real Estate Bd. Greater Balt. Mem. Md. Bar Assn., Am. Judicature Soc., Md. Bankers Assn., Trust Assn. Md., Balt. Estate Panning Council, U. Balt. Alumni Assn. (bd. govs.), Sigma Delta Kappa. Democrat. Presbyn. Club: Center (Balt.). Home: 2116 Arlonne Dr Baltimore MD 21228 Office: 1 N Charles St Blaustein Dr Baltimore MD 21228 Office: 1 N Charles St Blaustein Bldg Baltimore MD 21203

KNIES, PAUL HENRY, life ins. co. exec.; b. Colunbus, O., Jan. 28, 1918; s. Daniel and Eva (Schneider) K.; B.A., Ohio State U., 1940; m. Evadna Johnson, Mar. 16, 1941; children—Barbara Ann (Mrs. H. Michael Sell), Philip L., Paul R. With Met. Life Ins. Co., 1940—, controller, 1964—. Trustee Valley Hosp., Ridgewood. Served with arty. AUS, 1942-45. Fellow Soc. Actuaries; mem. Financial Execs. Inst., Inst. Internal Auditors. Home: 650 Westbrook Rd Ridgewood NJ 07450 Office 1 Madison Av New York City NY 10010

KNIETER, GERARD LEONARD, educator; b. Bklyn., June 2, 1931; s. Jack and Shirley (Lezinsky) K.; B.S., N.Y. U., 1953, M.A., 1954; Ed.D., Columbia, 1961; m. Barbara Cashetta, Dec. 5, 1953; Asst. prof. music edn. San Jose (Cal.) State Coll., 1962-65; acting dean, asst. to dean, asso. prof. music Duquesne U., 1965-67; prof. Temple U., 1967—, also chmn. dept. music edn.; cons. state depts. edn., sch. systems, univs. for interdisciplinary programs in arts; speaker nat. arts orgns., nat. profl. orgns. Served with AUS, 1954-56. Recipient Arch award N.Y. U., 1953. Mem. Am. Assn. U. Profs., Soc. for Ethnomusicology, Music Educators Nat. Conf., Phi Mu Alpha Sinfonia, Kappa Phi Kappa. Research applying psychology of creativity to tchr. edn. in arts. Developer interdisciplinary arts programs, applications of psychology of learning to tchr. edn. in arts. Home: 853 Goshen Rd Newtown Sq PA 19073 Office: College of Music Temple Univ Philadelphia PA 19122

KNIGHT, ALAN T., constrn. co. exec.; b. Phila., 1902; ed. Drexel Inst. Tech., 1930. Chmn. bd. dirs. Catalytic Constrn. Co., Phila.; chmn. Catalytic Constrn. Can. Ltd.; dir. Catalytic Caribe, Inc. Home: Rose Valley Rd Wallingford PA 19086

KNIGHT, ALFRED BISHOP, lawyer; b. Dill City, Okla., Jan. 6, 1920; s. Earl M. and Minnie Belle (Bishop) K.; A.B., Washington, 1941; LL.B. (editor Law Rev.), George Washington U., 1946; divorced; children-Grover Earl, Alfred B Knight, Jr. Dane S Knight, Dannelle (Mrs. Jeff Weaver), Mary Beth, James P Knight. Admitted to Okla. bar, 1946; practice in Tulsa, 1946—, partner firm Knight, Wilburn & Wagner, 1954—; tchr. ins. law, 1951-54. Pres. Tulsa Jaycees, 1948-49; bd. dirs. Tulsa C. of C., 1949-50; charter mem. bd. Tulsa Livestock and Fair; pres. Okla. Cutting Horse Assn., 1966; exec. com. Nat. Cutting Horse Assn., 1965—; pres. Palomino Assn., 1964. Served to lt. USNR, 1941-46. Mem. Am., Okla., Tulsa bar assns., Insternat. Assn. Inst. Attys. Democrat. Home: Route 1 Box 26 Sperry OK Office: Beacon Bldg 406 S Boulder St Tulsa OK 74103

KNIGHT, ARTHUR, educator, author. Past mem. faculty Inst. Film Techniques at City Coll. N.Y., Columbia, Hunter Coll., New Sch. Social Research; now prof. cinema dept. U. So. Cal., also film critic Sat. Rev. Author: The Liveliest Art; The Hollywood Style; (with Hollis Alpert) History of Sex in the Movies; also 50 documentary scripts. Home: 2653 Hollyridge Dr Los Angeles CA 90028 Address: care Saturday Review 380 Madison Av New York City NY 10017

KNIGHT, ARTHUR W., fibre and textile mfr.; b. London, Eng., Mar. 29, 1917; s. Arthur Frederick and Emily (Scott) K.; B.Commerce with 1st class honours (Leverhulme scholar 1938-39), London Sch. Econs., 1938; m. Joan Osborne, June 2, 1945 (dec. 1968). With J. Sainsbury, provision mchts., 1933-38; with Courtaulds Ltd., London, 1939—, dir., 1958—, dep. chmn., 1970—. Mem. council Manchester Bus. Sch.; mem. Commn. Third London Airport, 1968-70. Served to lt. colonel Brit. Army, 1940-46. Club: Reform (London). Home: 9 Radnor Pl London W2 England Office: Courtaulds Ltd 18 Hanover Sq London W1 England

KNIGHT, DEWEY, lawyer; b. Nashville, Ga.; July 3, 1898; s. Jonathan Perry and Ada (Parrish) K.; B.A., U Ga., 1918, student Law Sch. 1917-18; postgrad., Columbia, 1919-20; m. Laura Frasuer, Aug. 31, 1924; children George Dewey, Charles Frasuer. Admitted to Ga. bar, 1920, Fla. bar, 1925; practice law. Nashville, Ga., 1920-25, Miami, Fla. 1925—; with Knight, Smith, Underwood & Peters, 1926-65, Knight, Underwood, Peters, Hoeveler & Pickle, attys., 1965—; pros. atty., Nashville, 1923- 25. Pres. Fla. Tb Assn., 1949, 50. Served to ensign USNRF, World War I. Mem. Am., Dade County bar Assns., Am. Judicature Soc., Fla. Bar. Kiwanian. Home: 1828 SW Espanola Dr Miami FL 33133 Office: Ingraham Bldg Miami FL 33131

KNIGHT, DOUGLAS MALTLAND, ednl. adminstr. b. Cambridge, Mass., June 8, 1921; s. Claude Rupert and Fanny Sarah Douglas (Brown) K.; A.B., Yale, 1942, M.A., 1944, Ph.D., 1946; LL.D. Ripon Coll., Knox Coll.; Litt. D., St. Norbert Coll.; LL.D., Davidson Coll., 1963; L.H.D., Lawrence U., 1964, Carleton Coll., 1966; Litt.D., Wake Forest Coll., 1964; LL.D., U. of N.C., 1965, Emory U., 1965, Ohio Wesleyan U., 1970; m. Grace Wallace Nichols, Oct. 31, 1942; children—Christopher, Douglas Maitland, Thomas, Stephen. Instr. English, Yale, 1946-47, asst. prof., 1947-53; vis. asst. prof. English, U. Cal. at Berkeley, summer 1949; Morse Research fellow, 1951- 52; pres. Lawrence Coll., Appleton, Wis., 1954-63, Duke, Durham, N.C., 1963-69; div. v.p. ednl. devel. RCA, N.Y.C., 1969-71, div. v.p. edn. services, 1971—; pres. RCA Iran, 1971—. U.S. del. SEATO Conf. Asian Univ. Pres.'s Pakistan, 1961; nat. commn. UNESCO, 1965- 67; chmn. Nat. Adv. Commn. Libraries, 1966-68. Former mem. corp. Mass. Inst. Tech.; trustee Woodrow Wilson Nat. Fellowship Found., bd. dirs. Council for Financial 156 to Edn.; mem. Yale Alumni Bd.; mem. Mem. Modern Lang. Assn., Soc. Soc. Religion in Higher Edn.

(dir.), Phi Beta Kappa. Clubs: Century Association (N.Y.C.); Cosmos (Washington); Elizabethan, Berzelius (New Haven). Author: Pope and the Heroic Tradition, 1951; (poetry) The Dark Gate, 1971. Editor, contbr. Iliad and Odyssey, Twickenham edit., 1967, Libraries at Large, Tradition, Innovation and the National Interest, 1970, Medical Ventures and the University, 1967. Home: R F D 1 Box 156 Stockton NJ 08559 Office: 30 Rockfeller Plaza New York City NY 10020

KNIGHT, ELLIOT PRESTON, silverware mfg. co exec.; b. Newburyport, Mass., Jan. 5, 1900; s. Franklin Pierce and Annie (Horrocks) K.; B.S., Mass. Inst. Tech., 1923; m. Ethel Lucinda Landford, June 27,1925. Asst. chief engr. Eddystone Mfg. Co. (Pa.), 1923-24; mgr. engring. Employers Group Ins. Cos., Boston, 1924-58; chmn. bd., dir. Towle Mfg. Co., Newburyport, 1958—; dir. Charles D. Briddell Co., Cristfield, Md. Mem. Newburyport Sch. Com., 1930-33, Newbury Planning Bd., 1960-63; pres., Wheelwright Sci. Sch., Newburyport. Trustee, Anna Jaques Hosp., Newburyport. Served with U.S. Navy, World War I; served to comdr. UNSR, World War II. Recipient Commendation award. Registered profl. engr., Mass. Mem. Am. Legion. Republican. Presbyn. Mason. Home: 59 High Rd Newbury MA 01950 Office: 260 Merrimac St Newburyport MA 01950

KNIGHT, FRANCES GLADYS, govt. ofcl.; b. Newport, R.I., July 22, 1905; d. Frederick and Fanni (Smolik) Knight; ed. in France, Czechoslovakia, Monaco; student N.Y. U., Columbia, Hunter Coll., N.Y.C.; L.H.D., Mo. Valley Coll., Marshall, Mo., 1963; m. Wayne W. Parrish, Sept. 15, 1935. Div. chief Nat. Indsl Recovery Adminstrn., 1934-36; dep. dir. information program WPA, 1936-39; pub. relations cons. White House Conf. on Children, 1940; spl. asst. to commr. Nat. Def. Adv. Com., 1941- 42; pub. relations dir. U.S. Office Civilian Def., 1942-45; dir. pub. relations Am. Retail Fedn., 1945-47; Congl. cons., 1947-48; information specialist; dep. adminstr. security and consular affairs, Dept. State, 1948-55, dir. Passport Office, 1955—. Home: 2221 3Oth St N W Washington DC 20008 Office: Dept of State Washington DC 20525

KNIGHT, FRANK BARDSLEY, educator; b. Chgo., Oct. 11, 1933; s. Frank Hyneman and Ethel Unus (Verry) K.; B.A., Cornell U., 1955; Ph.D., Princeton, 1959; m. Ingeborg Gertrud Belz, July 30, 1970; 1 dau., Marion Anita. Asst. prof. U. Minn., 1959-62; mem. faculty U. Ill., Champaign, 1963—, prof. math., 1968—. A.P. Sloan Found. Postdoctoral fellow, 1968-70. Mem. Math. Assn. Am., Am. Math. Soc. Club: American Alpine (N.Y.C.). Home: 1212 W University St Champaign IL 61820

KNIGHT, FRANK HYNEMAN, educator; b. White Oak Twp., McLean County, Ill., Nov. 7, 1885; s. Winton Cyrus and Julia Ann (Hynerman) K.; student Am. U., Harriman, Tenn., 1905-07; Ph.B., Milligan (Tenn.) Coll., 1911; B.S., A.M., U. Tenn., 1913; Ph. D., Cornell U., 1916; D.Litt., Princeton. 1946; LL.D., Northwestern U., U. Glasgow, 1951, U. Rochester; L.H.D., Columbia, 1954; H.H.D., U. Ill., 1967; m. Minerva O. Shelburne, May 23, 1911 (div. 1928); children—Laura Eleanor, Alice Louise, Horace Shelbourne, Gladys Susan; m. 2d. Ethel Verry, Sept. 3, 1929; children—Frank Bardsley, Charles Alfred. Instr. econs. Cornell U., 1916-17, U. of Chgo., 1917-19; asso. prof. econs. U. of Ia., 1919-22, prof. 1922-28; prof. econs. U. Chgo., 1928—. Center for Behavioral Studies fellow 1957. Recipient Walker medal, 1957, Great Living Am. award U.S. C. of C., 1959. Fellow Am. Acad. Arts and Sci.; mem. Am. Econ. Assn. (pres. 1950), Royal Econ. Soc., Accademia Nazionale dei Lincei, Rome, Phi Beta Kappa (hon. Upsilon chpt. U. Tenn.). Club: Quadrangle. Translator: General Econmic History (Max Weber), 1927. Author: Risk, Uncertainty and Profit, 1921; The Ethics of Competition and Other Essays, 1935; (with Thornton W. Merriam) The Economic Order and Religion, 1945; Freedom and Reform, 1947; The Economic Organization, 1951; Essays on History and Method of Economics, 1956; Intelligence and Democratic Action, 1960. Contbr. to econ. jours. Home: 1321 E 56th St Chicago IL 60637

KNIGHT, FREDERICK HAWLEY, lawyer, bus. exec.; b. Brattleboro, Vt., Sept. 29, 1906; s. Fred Samuel and Susan (Hawley) K.; B.S., Worcester Poly tech. Inst. 1928; LL.B., George Washington U., 1933; m. Mary Lake Cox, July 7,1936. Test engr. Gen. Elec. Co., Schenectady, 1928-29; patent examiner U.S. Patent Office, Washington, 1929-37; admitted to D.C. bar, 1933; patent atty. Corning Glass Works, (N.Y.) 1937-45, asst. sec., 1945-53, sec., 1953—, corporate counsel, 1961—, v.p., 1969—; sec. Corning Glass Works of Can., Ltd., 1946—; sec. Corning Mus. Glass, 1952—; sec., dir. Corning Glass Internat. S.A., 1960—, Corhart Refractories Co., Louisville, 1966. Bd. dirs. Asso. Industries N.Y. State. Sec., Corning Glass Works Found., 1953—. Mem. Am. Bar Assn., Am. Group Internat. Assn. Protection Indsl. Property. Presbyn. Clubs: University. (N.Y.C.); Corning Country. Home: 257 Delevan Av Corning NY 14830 Office: Corning Glass Works Corning NY 14830

KNIGHT, GEORGE BLANCHARD, lawyer; b. Baraboo, Wis., July 14, 1923; s. George H. and Florence (Dunham) K.; B.B.A., U. Wis., 1948, LL.B., J.D., 1950; m. Virginia A. Whitty, Apr. 17, 1948; childrenPatricia Jo, Julienne Whitty. Admitted to Wis. bar, 1950; atty. Northwestern Mut. Life Ins. Co., Milw., 1950- 56; asst. counsel H. K. Porter Co., Inc., Pitts., 1956-60; corporate atty. Mead Johnson & Co., Evansville, Ind., 1960-65; sec., gen. counsel Harnischfeger Corp., Milw., 1965-. Served to 1st lt. USAAF, 1943-46. Mem. Am., Wis., MIlw. bar assns. Home; 7119 N Barnett Lane Fox Point WI 53246 Office: 4400 W National Av Milwaukee WI

KNIGHT, GUY WILFRED, r.r. exec.; b. Port Deposit, Md., July 28, 1906; s. William J. and Mary E. (Hall) K; A.B., Pa. State Coll., 1930; LL.B., U. Pa., 1933; m. Athene D. Wessel, June 10, 1950; 1 dau., Mary Ellen. Admitted to Pa. bar, 1933; pvt. practice of law, 1933; with Pa. R.R. Co., 1934-69, successively asst. gen. solicitor, asst. gen. counsel, gen. atty., 1934- 55, dir. labor relations, 1955-62, v.p., 1962-64, v.p. labor relations and personnel, 1964-68; sr. v.p. Penn Central Co., 1968-69, ret., 1969. Mem. Eastern R.R. Carriers' Conf. Com.; exec. com. Bur. Information Eastern Railways; Eastern com. Nat. R.R. Adjustment Bd.; indsl. relations com. N.A.M. Served as lt. USNR, 1944-45. Mem. U.S. C. of C., Am. Bar Assn., Am. Judicature Soc., Md. Soc. Pa., Am. Acad. Polit. and Social Sci., Theta Chi. Clubs: Lawyers (Phila.); Chester River Yacht and Country (Chestertown, Md.); Little Egg Harbor Yacht (Beach Haven, N.J.). Home: 514 Gulph Rd Wayne PA 19087

KNIGHT, HARLAND LEE, ins. co. exec.; b. Portland, Me., May 24, 1908; s. Lewis P. and Ethel (Johnson) L.; B.S., U. Me., 1930; m. Ruth L. Barker, June 16, 1934; 1 son, Peter Alden. Auditor, Union Mut. Life Ins. Co., 1932-36, traveling auditor, 1936-39, in charge Boston office, 1936-39, asst. to pres., 1939-43, supt. agys., 1944-45, agy. v.p., 1945; field supr. Mass. Protective and Paul Revere, Worcester, Mass., 1948-49, supt. agys., 1949-50, agy. v.p., 1950-57; supt. agys. Security Mut. Life Ins. Co., 1957, agy. v.p., 1957-61, v.p. pub. relations, 1961; pres. S.W. Indemnity & Life Ins. Co., Dallas, 1961-65, Lamar Life Ins. Co., 1965—, Lamar Life Broadcasting Co., 1965—; dir., exec. com. First Nat. Bank Jackson. Exec. com. Andrew Jackson council Boy Scouts Am.; mem. bd. Miss. Econ. Council; 2d vice chmn. Miss. 4-H Clubs; mem. Citizens Adv. Com.; mem. Industrial-Distribution Com. Bd. dirs. United Givers Fund, Indsl. Devel. Corp., Miss. Indsl. and Spl. Services; trustee Miss. Found. Independent Colls.; adv. com. St. Dominic-Jackson Meml. Hosp. Mem. Nat. Life Underwriters, Health Ins. Assn. Am., Jackson C. of C., Phi Mu Delta. Mason. Clubs: Newcomen, Country of Jackson (treas.), Rotary, Capital City, Petroleum. Home: 5116 Saratoga Dr Jackson MS 39205 Office: 317 S Capitol St Jackson MS 39205

KNIGHT, HAROLD MURRAY, banker; b. Melbourne, Australia, Aug. 13, 1919; s. Walter H.P. and Agnes (Hughes) K.; ed. Scotch Coll., Hawthorn, Victoria; M. Comm., U. Melbourne, 1961; m. Gwenuth Catherine Pennington, Apr. 7, 1951; children—John F., Richard H.O., Susan G., Andrew W., Paul H. With Commonwealth Bank Australia, 1930-40, 46-55; mem. stats. div., research and stats. dept. IMF, Washington, 1955-59, asst. chief, 1957-59; with Reserve Bank Australia, Sydney, 1960—, mgr. investment dept., 1964-68, dep. gov. and dep. chmn. bd., 1968—. Served with Australian Imperial Forces and Royal Australian Navy, 1940-46. Decorated D.S.C. Home: 39 Hull Rd Beecroft New South Wales 2119 Australia Office: 65 Martin Pl Sydney New South Wales 2000 Australia

KNIGHT, HARRY W., mgmt. cons.; b. Sedalia, Mo., Apr. 20, 1909; s. Harry William and Florence (Lay) K.; A.B., Amherst Coll., 1931; postgrad. Harvard Grad. Sch. Bus. Adminstrn., 1931-32; M.A. Northwestern U., 1940; m. Agnes Berger, Sept. 15, 1934; children—Kirk Lay, Harry William. With Harris Trust co., Chgo., 1932-33; sales adminstr. Bauer & Black, 1934-36; finance dir. City of Winnetka (Ill.), 1937-40; city mgr., Two Rivers, Wis., 1941; chief budget sec. WPB, Washington, 1942; asst. chief program control div., munitions assignment bd. Combined Chiefs of Staff, Washington, 1942-43; finance dir. UNRRA, 1945, sec. finance com. 3d Council Meeting London, 1945; v.p. Booz, Allen & Hamilton, Inc., 1945-66; chmn. bd. Knight, Gladieux & Smith, 1966—; dir. Scott Capitol Devel. Corp., Internat. Farm Systems, Burlington Industries, Inc., INA Life Ins. Co. of N.Y., Waldorf Astoria Hotel, Foxboro Co., Shearson Capitol Fund, Shearson Appreciation Fund. Chmn. Darien Community Fund dr., 1954; chmn. career conf. Amherst Coll., 1951-54, nat. chmn. capital program, 1962-65, life trustee, 1964—; pres. Harvard Bus. Sch. Assn., 1960; chmn. golden anniversary Harvard Bus. Sch., 1958. Chmn., Republican finance campaign, Darien, Conn., 1952. Trustee Com. for Econ. Devel., 1968—, Hampshire Coll., 1968—. Served to lt. USNR, 1943-45. Recipient medal for eminent service Amherst Coll. Mem. Fgn. Policy Assn. (dir. 1955-70) UN Assn. (gov. 1970), Delta Kappa Epsilon. Presbyn. Clubs: Downtown, Economic, Harvard Business School (pres. 1970-71), University, Sky (N.Y.C.) Wee Burn Country (Darien, Conn.); Hobe Sound Yacht, Jupiter Island (Hobe Sound, Fla.); Pine Valley Golf. Home: 107 Long Neck Point Rd Darien CT 06820 Office: 299 Park Av New York City NY 10017

KNIGHT, HOMER LOUIS, educator; b. Esther, Mo., May 31, 1907; s. Aubrey J. and Edna Lucretia (Humphrey) K.; B.S., N.E. Mo. State Tchrs. Coll., 1933; postgrad. U. Hawaii, 1935; A.M., U. Tex., 1938; Ph. D., U. Mo., 1945; m. Alma Naomi McFarland, July 7, 1928. Pub. sch. tchr., Mo., 1927-41; grad. asst. history U. Mo., 1941-42, instr. history, 1942-45; asso. prof. English history N.E. Mo. State Tchrs. Coll., 1945-47; prof. history, head dept. history Westminster Coll., Fulton, Mo., 1947-50, coll. dean, 1950-54; now prof. history, head dept. Okla. State Univ. Mem. Am., Miss. Valley hist. socs., So. Hist. Assn., Omicron Delta Kappa, Phi Alpha Theta. Home: 84 University Circle Stillwater OK 74074

KNIGHT, JAMES ALBERT, Jr., educator; b. LaGrange, Ga., Oct. 16, 1920; s. James Albert and Evelyn (Brooks) K.; B.S., Wofford Coll., 1942; M.S., Ga. Inst. Tech., 1944; Ph.D., Pa. State U., 1950; m. Marian Kemper Krape, Oct. 2, 1948; children—Marcia Krape, James Kent, John Craig. Asst. prof. chemistry Ga. Inst. Tech., Atlanta, 1950-53, asso. prof., 1953-57, research asso. prof., 1957-62, research prof., 1962—. Served with AUS, 1944-46. Mem. Am. Chem. Soc., A.A.A.S., Phi Beta Kappa, Sigma Xi, Phi Lambda Upsilon. Lutheran. Home: 2117 Kodiak Dr NE Atlanta GA 30345

KNIGHT, JAMES ALLEN, univ. dean, physician; b. St. George, S.C., Oct. 20, 1918; s. Thomas Samuel and Carolyn (Carn) K.; A.B., Wofford Coll., 1941; B.D., Duke, 1944; M.D., Vanderbilt U., 1952; M.P.H., Tulane U., 1962; m. Sally Templeman, June 8, 1963; 1 son, Steven Allen. Intern, Grady Meml. Hosp., Atlanta, 1952-53; asst. resident pediatrics Duke U. Hosp., 1953-54; resident psychiatry Tulane U. Service Charity Hosp., 1955-58; mem. faculty Baylor U. Coll. Medicine, 1958-61, asso. prof. psychiatry, 1961, asst. dean, 1960-61; asso. prof. psychiatry, dir. sect. community psychiatry Tulane U. Sch. Medicine, 1961-63, prof. psychiatry, asso. dean, 1964—; Harkness prof. psychiatry and religion, dir. program psychiatry and religion Union Theol. Sem., N.Y.C., 1963-64. Served as chaplain USNR, 1944-46. Travelling fellow WHO at C. G. Jung Inst., Zurich, Switzerland, 1961. Mem. Am. Psychiat. Assn., Am. Acad. Psychoanalysis, Am. Pub. Health Assn., Acad. Religion and Mental Health, Phi Beta Kappa. Author: Counselling the Dying, 1964; A Manual for the Comprehensive Community Mental Health Clinic, 1964; A Psychiatrist Looks at Religion and Health, 1964; Allergy and Human Emotions, 1967; Motivations in Play, Games and Sports, 1967; For the Love of Money, 1968; Conscience and Guilt, 1969. Home: 7450 Pearl St New Orleans LA 70118

KNIGHT, JAMES L., newspaperman; b. Akron, O., 1909. Chmn. bd., chief exec. officer Knight Newspapers, Inc.; pres. Knight Pub. Co., Charlotte, N.C.; pub. Charlotte Observer, Charlotte News; chmn. bd. Miami (Fla.) Herald Pub. Co.; dir. Keynoter Pub. Co., Gables Pub. Co.; pres., dir. Tallahasee Democrat, Macon Telegraph Pub. Co.; dir. So. Prodn. Program, Inc. Dir. A.P. Mem. So. Newspaper Pubs. Assn. (pres. 1957; chmn. bd. 1958), Am. Newspapers Pubs. Assn. (dir.). Clubs: Portage Country (Akron); Bath, LaGorce, Indian Creek, Surf (Miami); Detroit; Chicago; Key Largo Anglers, Crown Colony, Hatteras Marlin, National Press; Lyford Cay (New Providence, Bahamas). Home: 8995 Collins Av Miami Beach FL 33154 Office: care Miami Herald 1 Herald Plaza Miami FL 33101

KNIGHT, JOHN LOWDEN, clergyman; b. Beverly, N.J., Nov. 2, 1915; s. John Lowden and Elizabeth (MacBurney) K.; A.B., Drew U., 1939; A.M. Boston U., 1941, S.T.B., 1942; M.A., Vanderbilt U., 1943; D.D., Kan. Wesleyan U., 1947; LL.D., Willamette U., 1949; m. Alice Olivia Kingston, Aug. 9, 1941; children—Merrie Elizabeth, Wendy. Pastor Lake Shore Park Meth. Ch., Lynn, Mass., 1940-42, Belleview (Tenn.) Meth. Ch., 1942-43; prof. and asst. to pres., Willamette U., Salem, Ore., 1943-46; chancellor Neb. Wesleyan U., Lincoln, 1946-49; pres. Baldwin-Wallace Coll., 1949-54; pastor Trinity Meth. Ch., Columbus, O., 1954-61, First Meth. Ch., Syracuse, N.Y., 1961-67; pres. Wesley Theol. Sem., Washington, 1967—. Mem. Religious Edn. Assn., Phi Kappa Phi, Phi Delta Kappa, Pi Gamma Mu, Pi Kappa Delta. Republican. Contbr. ednl. and religious articles to periodicals and mags. Religious lectr. Home: 3825 University Av NW Washington DC 20016 Office: Wesley Theol Sem 4400 Massachusetts Av NW Washington DC 20016

KNIGHT, JOHN ROBERT, YMCA exec.; b. Knoxville, Tenn., Aug. 19, 1906; s. John Melvin and Lelia (Coile) K.; A.B., Otterbein Coll., 1928; M.A. in Social Adminstrn., Ohio State U., 1939; M. Gertrude Reid, Dec. 31, 1930; children—Robert Melvin, Douglas Reid. Asst. young men's sec. Dayton (O.) YMCA, 1928-34; adult program sec. Columbus (O.) YMCA, 1934-41, Toledo YMCA, 1941-45; exec. sec. Central YMCA, Toledo, 1945-48; asso. area exec. Ohio-W.Va. Area Council YMCA, 1948-66; dir. exptl. film-discussion project under grant Fund Adult Edn., YMCA Nat. Council, 1952-53. Sec. North Am. Assn. Secs. YMCA, 1954-57, v.p., 1960-63, pres., 1963-66, exec. dir., 1967—; mem. gov. bd. World Fedn. Assn. Secs. YMCA, 1963-66; mem. program leadership team Centennial World Conf. YMCA's, Paris, France, 1955; U.S. del. World Council YMCA's, Tokyo, Japan, 1965; U.S. del. World Conf. Tng., YMCA, Mainau, Germany, 1963; U.S. rep. to governing bd. World Fedn. YMCA Secs., Mainau, 1969, Nottingham, Eng., 1969. Mem. program leadership team White House Conf. Children and Youth, 1960. Mem. Nat. Alumni Assn. Otterbein Coll. (pres. 1960-61), Pi Kappa Delta. Methodist (mem. bd.). Author and/or editor YMCA publs. Home: 350 Brevoort Rd Columbus OH 43214 Office: 50 W Broad St Columbus OH 43215

KNIGHT, JOHN SHIVELY, newspaper publisher; b. Bluefield, W.Va., Oct. 26, 1894; s. Charles Landon and Clara Irene (Scheifly) K.; student Tome Sch., Md., 1911-14, Cornell U., 1914-17; LL.D., U. Akron, 1945, Northwestern U., 1947, Kent State U., 1958, Ohio State U., 1961, U. Mich. 1969, Oberlin Coll., 1969, Colby Coll., 1969; m. Katharine McLain, Nov. 21, 1921 (dec. 1929); children—John Shively (dec. Mar. 1945), Charles Landon, Frank McLain (dec.); m. 2d, Beryl Zoller Comstock, Jan. 24, 1932; 1 dau., Mrs. Kenneth Hewitt. Newspaper reporter and exec., 1920-25; mng. editor Akron (O.) Beacon Jour., 1925-33, editor 1933—; editorial dir. Springfield (O.) Sun, 1925-27; editorial dir. Massilion (O.) Ind., 1927-33, pres., 1933-37; chmn. bd., pub. Miami (Fla.) Herald, 1937-61, now editorial chmn.; pres. Beacon Jour. Pub. Co., Knight Newspapers, Inc., to 1966, now editorial chmn.; purchased and discontinued Miami (Fla.) Tribune, Nov. 30, 1937; purchased Detroit Free Press, 1940, pres. and editor, 1940-67, now editorial chmn.; owner, editor and pub. Chgo. Daily News, 1944-59; v.p. Charlotte (N.C.) Observer, 1954, Charlotte News, 1959—, also Tallahassee Democrat. Chief liaison officer between U.S. and Brit. censorship, London, Eng., 1943-44, Trustee Cornell U., U. Miami, Nat. Jewish Hosp.; bd. dirs., N.Y. World's Fair. Served with 113th Inf., AAC and AEF, 1917-19. Recipient Frank M. Hawks Meml. trophy, 1947, citation of merit from Poor Richard Club, 1946, Honor award distinguished service journalism U. Mo. 1949, Brotherhood of Children award, 1946; medal for achievement in journalism Syracuse U., 1946, La Prensa award, 1954, Am.'s Found. award, 1959, John Peter Zenger award, 1967, Pultizer prize for distinguished editorial writing, 1968. Carr Van Anda award Ohio U., 1970; others; cited Outstanding Chicagoan in Inter- Am. relations U.S.-Uruguay alliance, 1952. Established Knight Meml. Fund commemorating his father; La Prensa Scholarship furthering Inter-Am. understanding. Mem. Am. Soc. Newspaper Editors (past Pres.), V.F.W., Am. Legion, A.P. (past dir., chmn. finance com., mem. exec. com.), 40 and 8, Phi Sigma Kappa, Sigma Delta Chi. Episcopalian. Clubs: Portage Country (Akron, O.); Tin Whistles (Pinehurst, N.C.); Bath, Indian Creek (Miami); Union (Cleve.); Detroit, Detroit Athletic, Detroit Economic, Country Grosse Pointe (Detroit); Burning Tree Golf (Washington); Racquet, Chicago, Tavern, Casino, Commercial, Saddle and Cycle (Chgo.); Old Elm (Ft. Sheridan, Ill.) Glenview (Golf, Ill.). Home: 255 N Portage Path Akron OH 44303 Office: 44 E Exchange St Akron OH 44309 also Miami Herald Miami FL and Free Press Detroit MI

KNIGHT, JOHN W., life ins. co. exec.; b. Neame, La., June 3, 1924; s. William Jennings and Mabel (Patterson) K.; student Kan. State Coll., 1943; B.A., U. Tex., Austin, 1949, M.A., 1951; m. Marian Rose Menn, June 3, 1949; children—John Michael, Marsha Lynn, Jeffrey Alan, Stephen Edward. Asst. v.p. Rio Grande Nat. Life Ins. Co., Dallas, 1950-59; v.p., controller Am. Gen. Life Ins. Co., Houston, 1959—, also dir.; dir. Am. Gen. Life Ins. Co. Del., Houston. Served with AUS, 1943-46; ETO, Japan. Mem. Ins. Accounting and Statis. Assn., Financial Execs. Inst. Republican. Lutheran. Home: 6143 Ella Lee Lane Houston TX 77027 Office: 2727 Allen Pky Houston TX 77019

KNIGHT, LESTER BENJAMIN, cons. engr.; b. Albany, N.Y., June 29, 1907 s. Lester B. and Louise (Vaast) K.; M.E., Cornell U., 1929; student Chgo. Kent Coll. Law, 1932- 34; m. Elizabeth Anne Field, Mar. 5, 1935; children—Charles Field, Leslie Knight. Vice pres. Nat. Engring. Co., Chgo., 1930-43; chmn. Lester B. Knight & Assos., Inc., mgmt. and cons. engrs., Chgo., 1945-69, chmn., 1969—; chmn. Universal Castings Corp., Chgo., 1950—, Lester B. Knight Internat. Corp., Chgo., 1952—; A.B. Knight, Stockholm, Sweden, 1962—; dir. Knight Wegenstein, Zurich, Switzerland, Kinght-Wegenstein Ltd., London, Eng.; spl. research foundry mgmt., operation, design, automation and mechanization. Pres., adminstrv. dir. Travelers Aid Soc. Chgo., 1958-60, pres. sponsoring bd., exec. com., 1960—. Served to lt. comdr. USNR, 1943-45. Mem. Am. Foundrymens Soc., Am. Soc. M.E., Am. Mgmt. Assn., Assn. Cons. Mgmt. Engrs., Chgo. C. of C. (dir., v.p. indsl. devel. and policy com.), Ill. Engr. Council (1st v.p., dir., exec. com.), Alpha Tau Omega. Clubs: University, Mid-America, Chicago, Economic (bd. dirs.) (Chgo.); Delray Dunes (Delray Beach, Fla.); Glenview Golf (Golf, Ill.); Army-Navy (Washington); Country of Florida (Golf, Fla.). Home: Glenview Club Golf IL 60029 Office: 549 W Randolph St Chicago IL 60606

KNIGHT, NATHANIEL BUTLER, Jr., lawyer; b. Gretna, La., Apr. 10, 1909; s. Nathaniel Butler and Josephine Hilda (Hock) K.; LL.B., Tulane U., 1932, B.A., 1943, B. in Elec. Engring., 1944; postgrad., Harvard Bus. Sch., 1945; m. Ada Brunies, Oct. 8, 1938; children—Karen Linda, Kathleen Constance. Admitted to La. bar, 1932; law asso. firm Milling, Godchaux, Saal & Milling, New Orleans, 1932-35; individual practice, Gretna, La.; mem. La. Pub. Service Commn., 1940- -, chmn., 1948, 57-64; mem. firm Knight, D'Angelo & Knight. Chmn. Guaranty Bank & Trust Co., Gretna, 1951—; pres. Jefferson Savs. & Loan Assn., Metairie, La., 1955—. Vice pres. United Fund Greater New Orleans, 1962—. Trustee, Isaac Delgado Mus. Art; bd. dirs. W. Jefferson Gen. Hosp. Served to lt. USNR, 1944-46. Mem. Am., La., Jefferson Parish (pres. 1961) bar assns., Am. Judicature Soc., New Orleans Area C. of C. (past dir.), La. Engring. Soc., I.E.E.E., V.F.W., Am. Legion, Nat. Assn. R.R. and Utilities Commrs. (pres. 1963-64), Order of Coif, Phi Alpha Delta, Delta Sigma Phi. Lion K.C. Asso., Tulane Law Rev., 1930-32. Home: 11 Willow Dr Gretna LA Office: 1011 4th St Gretna LA

KNIGHT, NORMAN, radio-TV exec.; b. July 24, 1924; m. Susannah Howard Andre, Aug. 26, 1914; children-Norman Scott, Randolph Howard, Jeffrey Bryant, Robert Andre. Announcer, salesman sta. WTMV, 1942; announcer, promotion mgr., continuity dir. sta. KTHS, 1943; announcer sta. WMC, 1943; announcer, salesman sta. WMMN, 1944; gen. mgr. sta. WAJR, 1944-46; Eastern dir. sta. relations MBS, 1946-49; v.p. sales and advt., and promotion Sponsor Publs., Inc., 1950-53; gen. mgr. sta. WABD, 1953-54; exec. v.p., gen. mgr. Yankee Network div. RKO Teleradio Pictures, Inc. (operating Yankee Network WNAC, WRKO, WNAC-TV), also dir. Yankee Network, v.p. RKO Teleradio Pictures, 1954-60, pres. Yankee div. RKO Teleradio Pictures, Inc., 1957-60; pres. Yankee div. RKO Gen., Inc., 1958-60; pres., treas. Knight Mgmt. Corp., 1960-69, Knight Sales, inc., 1960—, Knight Radio, Inc. (WGIR and WNHS), Knight Broadcasting N.H., Inc. (WHEB and WPFM), Radio Claremont, Inc.

(WTSV and WTSV-FM), Radio Fitchburg, Inc. (WEIM and WSRS), Knight Sales Inc., Quality Radio Corp. (WSAR), 1960—, Palm Beach, Broadcasting corp. (WQXT, WMOM), WCKS, Cocoa Beach, Fla.; pres. Caribbean Communications Corp. established complete TV sta. pub. affairs film unit which produced River of Life, Weltschmerz (film document Hungarian Revolt), Noel New England and Brotherhood Series, others. Radio-TV chmn. United Fund Greater Boston, Mass. Cancer Soc., A.R.C. chpt. Met. Boston, Mass. Cancer Soc., A.R.C. chpt. Met. Boston; radio chmn. Salvation Army; dir. Stawbery Banke: dir. Mayor's Com. Youth Week. Bd. dirs. New Eng. Nephrosis Found.; pres. New Eng. Kidney Disease Found., Norman Knight Charitable Found.; trustee Mass. Bd. Regional Community Colls.; trustee Agassiz Village Camps, Crippled Children's Non-Sectarian Fund, Boys and Girls Camps, Inc.; exec. com., dir. Rescue, Inc.; exec. com. The Jimmy Fund; exec. com., trustee Children's Cancer Research Found.; mem. finance com. Com. Econ. Devel. Fellow Brandeis U. Mem. Devel. council Boston U. Bd. dirs. Freedoms Found., also nat. co-chmn. Am. Freedom Center. Recipient Americanism award Am. Heritage Com., 1959. Named one of ten outstanding young men Boston Jr. C. of C., 1956; recipient award for contbns. radio and TV industry Alpha Epsilon Rho, 1957; several Americanism awards from various vets. orgn., 1959-60. Mem. Radio-TV Execs. Sec., Young Presidents Orgn., Broadcast Pioneers, Am. Inst. Mgmt., Nat. Conf. Christians and Jews (N.E. chmn. com. communications), Alpha Epsilon Rho. Clubs: Variety (Boston); Broadcasting Executives of New Eng. Author: Sales Techniques for Radio and TV; Management and Sales Correlation in Broadcasting; Film and the TV Station; Awake America; The Cause of All Mankind, others. Home: 100 Country Dr Weston MA 02193 Office: 400 Commonwealth Av Boston MA 02215

KNIGHT, PETER OLLPHANT, Jr., banker; b. Tampa, Fla., 1902; m. Rhoda Fraleigh; children Rhoda K. Martorell, Peter Oliphant IV. Chmn. emeritus Exchange Nat. Bank, Tampa, dir.; chmn., exec. com., dir. Tampa Elec. Co. mem. firm Holland & Knight. Home: 224 Blanca Av Davis Islands Tampa FL 33606 Office: Exchange Nat Bldg Tampa FL 33601

KNIGHT, RALPH MERTON, consumer products and chem. co. exec.; b. Limestone, Me., Apr. 19, 1915; s. Perley B. and Gladys (Carver) K.; B.S. in Chem. Engring. cum laude, Newark Coll. Engring., 1939; postgrad. U. Del., 1940-41; m. Margaret White, May 2, 1941 (div.); 1 son, Calvin L.; m. 2d, Nancy Green, Aug. 1964; children— Marie Elizabeth, Deborah Angella. From chem. engr. to asst. div. supt. E. I. duPont de Nemours & Co., Inc. 1940-52; research asso. Ind.-Whiting Research Labs., Standard Oil Co. (Ind.), 1952-53; with U.S. Indsl. Chems. Co., 1953-59, mgr. polymer planning and application, 1957- 58, v.p. plastics, 1958-59; v.p. Dart Industries Inc. (formerly Rexall Drug & Chem. Co.), 1960—, dir., 1961—, also pres., chief exec. officer chem. group.; dir. CT Film Co., Estireno del Zulia. Mem. Soc. Plastics Industry, Am. Inst. Chem. Engring., Tau Beta Pi. Club: Eldorado Country (Palm Desert, Cal.); Bel Air Bay, Bel Air Country. Home: 433 S Beverly Glen Blvd Los Angeles CA 90024 Office: 8480 Beverly Blvd Los Angeles CA 90054

KNIGHT, RICHARD BENNETT, educator, cons. engr.; b. Cin., Oct. 11, 1914; s. Harry C. and Helen (Van Horn) K.; B.S., U. Md., 1935; M.S., U. Ill., 1939; m. Sara Kelso Wooten, May 27, 1944; children—Barbara Ann, Richard Bennett. Grad. research asst., Am. Soc. Heating and Ventilating Engrs.; fellow in mech. engring. U. Ill., Urbana, 1937-39; air conditioning engr. Md. Refrigeration Co., Balt., 1940, York-Shipley, Inc., York, Pa., 1946; mech. engr. Army Chem. Center, War Dept., Md., 1940-42; vibrations engr. Glenn L. Martin Co., Middle River, Md., 1942-45; asso. prof. heating and ventilating U. Ky., Lexington, 1946-52; L.L. Vaughan prof. mech. engring. N.C. State U., Raleigh, 1952—; Fulbright vis. lectr. Alexandria (Egypt) U., 1951; UNESCO lectr., Lebanon, Syria, Iraq, 1951; heating and air conditioning cons. to architects and engrs., 1952—; heat transfer and air conditioning cons. Convair, Ft. Worth, Martin Co., Balt., 1953-57; research participant Oak Ridge Inst. Nuclear Studies, 1958-59; heat transfer cons. Oak Ridge Nat. Lab., 1958—; chief scientist P.R. Nuclear Center, Mayaquez, 1961-62, heat transfer cons., 1962; AEC lectr. in univs. and atomic energy labs., Brazil, Argentina, Bolivia, Peru, Colombia, 1962. Mem. N.C. Bd. Refrigeration Examiners, 1968—, chmn. bd., 1970—. Bd. dirs. N.C. State Coll., YMCA. Recipient Outstanding Tchr. award N.C. State U., 1969-70. Registered profl. engr., N.C., Ky. Mem. Am. Soc. Engring. Edn., Am. Soc. Heating, Refrigerating and Air Conditioning Engrs., Pi Tau Sigma. Presbyn. Lion. Club: Raleigh Engineers. Home: 3005 Eton Rd Raleigh NC 27608

KNIGHT, RICHARD BRAYTON, printing co. exec.; b. Providence, July 19, 1917; s. Howard and Elisabeth (Braman) K.; grad. Phillips Exeter Acad., 1934; A.B., Princeton, 1938; m. Louise Atwood, Dec. 2, 1939; childrenHoward Atwood, Richard Dexter, James Atwood; m. 2d, Clarice W. Legget, June 29, 1961. With Livermore and Knight Co., Pawtucket, R.I., 1938-69, exec. v.p., 1945- 52, pres., 1952-69, also dir.; v.p., dir. Bank Lithograph Co., Pawtucket, 1941-69; pres., dir. Stamps, Inc., Pawtucket, 1954-69, Printing Corp. Am., N.Y.C., 1962-69; with Knights, Hoagland & Co., Greenwich, Conn., 1969—; cons. Am. Can Co., dir. R.I. Hosp. Trust Co., Providence. Served to lt. (s.g.) USNR, 1941-45. Mason. Clubs: Augusta (Ga.) Nat. Golf; Lake Placid (N.Y.); Union League (N.Y.C.); Hope (Providence); Agawam Hunt, Squantum (East Providence, R.I.); Winged Foot Golf (Mamaroneck, N.Y.); Country Club of Fla. (Delray Beach, Fla.). Home: 1 Inlet Cay Dr Ocean Ridge Delray Beach FL Office: Knight Hoagland & Co 2 Greenwich Plaza Greenwich CT 06830

KNIGHT, RICHARD LLOYD, airline exec.; b. Coatesville, Ind., Oct. 29, 1912; s. Chauncey D. and Daisy M. (Job) K.; A.B. in Econs., De Pauw U., 1934; postgrad. Columbia, 1936; m. Margaret Barclay, Dec. 12, 1935; children—Judith, Nancy. Vice pres. Gen. Electric Credit Corp., N.Y.C., 1948-52; div. mgr. finance transformer div. Gen. Electric Co., Pittsfield, Mass., 1952-54, mgr. financial personnel and adminstrv. service, N.Y.C., 1954-60; v.p., treas. Gen. Dynamics Corp., N.Y.C., 1960-61, v.p. finance, 1961-62; exec. v.p., dir. James Talcott, Inc., N.Y.C., 1962-64, pres., dir., 1964-65; exec. v.p. finance Federated Dept. Stores, Cin., 1965-70; group v.p. Pan Am. World Airways, N.Y.C., 1970—. Mem. Nat. Assn. Accountants, Am. Accounting Assn., Am. Finance Assn., Am. Mgmt. Assn., Financial Execs. Inst., Phi Kappa Psi. Club: Metropolitan (N.Y.C.). Home: 870 United Nations Plaza New York City NY 10017 Office: 200 Park Av New York City NY 10017

KNIGHT, RIDGWAY BREWSTER, U.S. ambassador; b. Paris, France (parents U.S. citizens), June 12, 1911; s. Aston and Caroline Ridgway (Brewster) K.; B.S., U. Paris, 1928, Ph.B., 1929; M.B.A., Harvard, 1931; m. Betty R. Spalding, Oct. 1, 1932 (div. July 5, 1945); children—Eliot, Brewster, Louis; m. 2d, Colette Lalier, Aug. 26, 1946; 1 son, Christopher. Asst. to pres. Cartier, Inc., 1931-35; v.p., treas. Bellows & Co., Inc., 1936-41; vice consul, tech. advisor Murphy Mission to N. Africa, 1941-42; U.S. mem. Allied Commn. for Investigating Possible Rectification of Franco-Italian Border,1946; 2d sec., spl. asst. to ambassador, Paris, 1945-50; officer in charge European polit.-mil. Affairs, Dept. State, 1950, acting dep. dir. European Regional Affairs, 1951, coordinator Internat. Conf., 1951-52, dep. dir. Western European Affairs, 1952, acting dir., 1953; dep. asst. high commr. for Germany, 1954-55; polit. adviser to Supreme Allied Comdr. Europe, 1955-57; dep. chief mission minister plenipotentiary Am. embassy, Karachi, Pakistan, 1957-59; dep. dir. Operations Coordinating Rd., The White House, 1960; minister consul gen., Damascus, Syria, 1960-61; ambassador to Syria, 1961-65, Belgium, 1965-69, Portugal, 1969—. Served to maj. AUS, 1943-1945. Decorated Medal of Merit, Bronze Star Medal with 2 oak leaf clusters, Legion of Honor (U.S.); Croix de Guerre with 3 clusters (France); medal of Merit of Knights of Malta, medal for Valor, Order of Vols. of Liberty (Italy); Comdr. Ouissam Alaouite (Morocco); Comdr. Nicham Iftikar (Tunis); Grand Cross of Order of Crown (Belgium). Mem. Acad. French Wines. Clubs: The Brook (N.Y.C.); Metropolitan (Washington). Home: 120 E 81st St New York City NY

KNIGHT, ROBERT HUNTINGTON, lawyer; b. New Haven, Feb. 27, 1919; s. Earl Wall and Frances Pierpont (Whitney) K.; grad. Phillips Acad., Andover, Mass., 1936; B.A., Yale, 1940; LL.B., U. Va., 1947; m. Alice Isabel Valle, Dec. 14, 1940; children—Robert Huntington, Jessie Valle, Patricia Whitney, Alice Isabel, Eli Whitney. With John Orr Young, Inc., advt. agy., 1940-41; asst. prof. U. Va. Law Sch., 1947-49; admitted to N.Y. bar, 1950; asso. firm Shearman & Sterling & Wright, N.Y.C., 1949-55, partner, 1955-58; dep. asst. sec. def. for internat. security affairs Dept. Def., 1958-61; gen. consel Treasury Dept., 1961-62; partner Shearman & Sterling, N.Y.C., 1961—. Dir. Owens-Corning Fiberglas Corp., Brit. Steel Corp., Inc., Gen. Adjustment Bur., Inc. Mem. Intelsat Arbitration Panel, 1971—. Bd. dirs. U. Va. Law Sch. Found. Asia Found., Inst. for Internat. Order. Served to lt. col. USAAF, 1941-45. Mem. Am., Fed., Internat., Inter-Am. bar assns., Bar Assn. City N.Y., N.Y. County Lawyers Assn., Internat. Law Assn., Washington Inst. Fgn. Affairs, Council Fgn. Relations. Clubs: Down Town Association, Pilgrims, Lunch, The Links (N.Y.C.); Army and Navy, Metropolitan City Tavern (Washington); Fifth Avenue (N.Y.C.). Home: 548 Stanwich Rd Greenwich CT 06830 Office: 53 Wall St New York City NY 10005

KNIGHT, RODGER D., Jr., banker; b. Denver, 1913; ed. U. Colo. Chmn. bd. United Bank of Denver; pres., dir. Denver U.S. Nat. Center; mem. fed. adv. council Fed. Res. System. Home: 6 Lynn Rd Englewood CO 80110 Office: Denver U S Bank U S Nat Center Denver CO 90217

KNIGHT, THOMAS STANLEY, educator, philosopher; b. Sharon, Pa., Dec. 21, 1921; s. Thomas S. and Mary (McCarthy) K.; A.B., W. Liberty (W.Va.) State Coll., 1951; M.A., Syracuse U., 1953, Ph.D., 1956; m. Betty A. Roller, Apr. 18, 1942; children—Thomas Stanley, Irvin R. Chmn. Sch. Arts and Scis., Russell Sage Coll., Troy, N.Y., 1957-58; mem. exec. com. Utica Coll. of Syracuse U., 1959-63, mem. sr. seminart planning bd., 1961-63, chmn. behavioral studies div., 1960-62; prof., chmn. dept. philosophy Adelphi U., 1965—. Served with AUS, 1942-45. Mem. Am. Assn. U. Profs., Am. Philos. Assn., L.I. Philos. Soc., Chi Beta Phi, Phi Beta Chi. Author: Charles Sanders Peirce: The Man and His Philosophy, 2d edit., 1970; also numerous articles, revs. Gen. editor Great American Thinkers Series. Home: 132 E 35th St New York City NY 10016 Office: Adelphi Univ Garden City NY 11530

KNIGHT, VERNON, physician; b. Osceola, Mo., Sept. 6, 1917; s. Iven Robert and Myrtle (Andrews) K.; A.B., William Jewell Coll., 1939; M.D., Harvard, 1943; m. Elizabeth Gordon, Sept. 21, 1946; children-Hunter, Caroline, James, John. Intern medicine Mass. Meml. Hosps., Boston, 1943; house officer N.Y. Hosp.-Cornell Med. Center, 1945-46, research fellow dept. medicine, 1946-52; asst. prof. medicine Cornell Med. Coll., 1953-54; attending physician Cornell Med. Service Bellevue Hosp. and Meml. Center for Cancer, N.Y.C., 1953-54; asso. prof. medicine Vanderbilt U. Med. Sch., 1954-59; clin. dir. Inst. Allergy and Infectious Diseases, NIH, Bethesda, Md., 1959-66, Gen. Clin. Research Centers Com., bd. sci. counselors Div. Biologics Standards; prof., chmn. dept. microbiology, prof. medicine Baylor U. Coll. of Medicine, Houston, 1966- -. Mem. commn. epidemiological survey, commn. influenza Armed Forces Epidemiological Bd. Com. for tng. in infectious diseases in Va. U. Med. Centers, VA. Served to lt. (s.g.), M.C., USNR, 1944-46. Diplomate Am. Bd. Internal Medicine. Mem. A.C.P., Assn. Am. Physicians, Am. Soc. Clin. Investigation, Am. Clin. and Climatol. Assn., Soc. Exptl. Biology and Medicine. Home: 11735 Green Bay Dr Houston TX 77024 Office: 1200 Moursund Av Houston TX 77025

KNIGHT, WALKER LEIGH, clergyman, editor; b. Henderson, Ky., Feb. 6, 1924; s. Cooksey Bennett and Rowena (Henderson) K.; B.A., Baylor U., 1949; m. Iva Nell Moseley, Nov. 10, 1943; children—Walker Leigh, Kenneth Wayne, Nelda Denise, Emily Jill. Reporter, Henderson Gleanor and Jour., 1942; ordained to ministry Bapt. Ch., 1948; pastor in Dale, Tex., 1948-49; editor Falls County Record, Marlin, Tex., 1948-49; asso. editor Bapt. Standard, Dallas, 1950- 59; editorial sec. So. Bapt. Home Mission Bd., Atlanta, also editor Home Missions mag. and Atlanta bur. chief Bapt. Press News Service, 1959—. Served with USAAF, 1943-45. Mem. Asso. Church Press, So. Bapt. Press Assn., Bapt. Pub. Relations Assn. Author: Panama, The Land Between, 1965; Struggle for Integrity, 1969; See How Love Works, 1971. Home: 1008 Forrest Blvd Decatur GA 30030 Office: 1350 Spring St NW Atlanta GA 30309

KNIGHT, WALTER DAVID, coll. dean, physicist; b. N.Y.C., Oct. 14, 1919; s. Walter David and Ruth (Hubbard) K.; A.B., Middlebury (Vt.) Coll., 1941; M.A., Duke, 1943, Ph.D., 1950; m. Elizabeth Lewis Wiggins, Apr. 7, 1945; childrenMargaret Benton, Jonathan Goodnow. Instr. physics Duke, 1943-44, Trinity Coll., Hartford, Conn., 1946-50; mem. faculty U. Cal. at Berkeley, 1950-, prof. physics, 1961-, dean Coll. Letters and Sci., 1967-; cons. Brookhaven Nat. Lab., 1948-50. Served to lt. (j.g.) USNR, 1944-46. Sloan fellow, 1956-59; Guggenheim fellow, 1961. Fellow Am. Phys. Soc.; mem. Am. Assn. Physics Tchrs., A.A.A.S., Am. Assn. U. Profs., Sigma Xi. Author: (with others) The Berkeley Physics Course-Mechanics, 1965, also articles. Home: 800 Cragmont Av Berkeley CA 94708

KNIGHT, WALTER EARLY, c. of c. exec.; b. Dayton, Ky., Oct. 15, 1911; s. Noel B. and Nelle (Early) K.; A.B. in Econs., Western Ky. U., 1933; M.A. in Econs., Peabody Coll., 1940; m. Lina Baldauf, Dec. 24, 1940; children—Carol (Mrs. Ellard V. Nunnaly), Susan. Asst. prof. U. Louisville, 1947-50; asso. orgainzer Louisville C. of C., 1950-57; organizer indsl. devel. function Boston C. of C., 1957-65; exec. v.p. Jersey City C. of C., 1965—; tobacco industry cons. Business Week mag., 1947-67. Chmn., dir. town personnel dept., Cohasset, Mass., 1962-65. Recipient Annual award New Boston Com., 1964. Fellow Am. Indsl. Devel. Council; mem. Am. Marketing Assn., Am., N.J. (pres. 1968) assns. chamber commerce execs. Home: 478 Riverside Dr E Princeton NJ 05840 Office: 911 Bergen Av Jersey City NJ 07306

KNIGHT, WAYNE HENINGER, lawyer; b. Salt Lake City, Apr. 17, 1908; s. Oscar Raymond and Lottie (Heninger) K.; B.A., U. Utah, 1933; J.D., George Washington U., 1937; m. Pauline Pingree, Mar. 6, 1936; children—Roger Wayne, Carol Jean (Mrs. Douglas Lee Miner). Admitted to D.C. bar, 1936, Cal. bar, 1944, also Supreme Ct. U.S.; practice in Washington, 1937-38, Chgo., 1939-42, San Francisco, 1943-45, Los Angeles, 1946—; atty. office gen. counsel SEC, 1938-42; atty.-in-charge San Francisco office Alien Property Custodian, 1943-45; mem. firm Overton, Lyman & Prince, 1945—. Chmn. Com. Bar Examiners Cal., 1962-63. Trustee Claremont Men's Coll. Mem. Am., Los Angeles County bar assns., State Bar Cal. Republican. Mem. Ch. of Jesus Christ of Latter-day Saints. Clubs: Chancery (Los Angeles); Pauma Valley (Cal.) Country. Home: 885 Winston Av San Marino CA 91108 Office: 550 S Flower St Los Angeles CA 90017

KNIGHT, WILLIAM EDWARDS, fgn. service officer; b. Tarrytown, N.Y., Feb. 1, 1922; s. Arthur Octavius and Mabel (Jenkins) K.; B.A. in Internat. Relations, Yale, 1943, M.A., 1946; m. Ruth Lee, Aug. 14, 1946; children—Jeffrey William, Peter Edwards. Fgn. service officer State Dept., 1946—; vice consul, Genoa, Italy, 1946-48; 3d sec., then 2d sec., Rome, Italy, 1948-51; Italian desk officer, Washington, 1951-55; 1st sec., consul, head econ. sect. Am. embassy, Reykjavik, Iceland, 1955-57; consul, 1st sec., head econ. sect. Am. embassy, Canberra, Australia, 1957-61; officer charge Italian-Austrian affairs, Washington, 1961; dep. dir. Western European affairs, 1961-62; student Indsl. Coll. Armed Forces, Washington, 1962-63; asst. chief negotiations div. Office of Internat. Aviation Affairs, Dept. State, 1963-67; counselor for econ. affairs Am. embassy, Manila, 1967-71, dep. chief mission, 1971—. Trustee Brent Sch., Baguio, P.I., 1969—. Served to 1st lt. USAAF, 1943- 45. Lion. Clubs: International Aviation (pres. Washington 1964-65); Army-Navy (dir., treas. 1971—) (Manila); Commonwealth (Canberra). Address: American Embassy Manila Philippines

KNIGHT, WILLIAM WESLEY, publisher; b. Winnebago, Minn., Feb. 8, 1909; s. Fred A. and Edith (Bartholomew) K.; LL.B., U. Ore., 1932; m. Lota Hatfield, Mar. 4, 1937; children—Phillip, Jeanne and Joanne (twins). Admitted to Ore. bar, 1932; practiced in Roseburg and Portland, 1932-39; exec. sec. Pacific N.W. Newspaper Assn., 1939-46; mem. staff Ore. Jour., 1946—. pres., pub. 1953—. Mem. Ore. Legislature, 1935. Episcopalian. Home: 3650 SE Claybourne Portland OR 97202 Office: 1320 SW Broadway Portland OR 97201

KNIGHT, WILLIAM WINDUS, Jr., investment co. exec.; b. Toledo, Jan. 27, 1905; s. William Windus and Edna (Ford) K.; A.B., Yale, 1927; M.B.A., Harvard, 1962-66; pres., dir. Knight hand Co., Inc., 1963—, Biminis Blue 1929; m. Elsie Stranahan, Sept. 12, 1931; children—John Lord, Diana (Mrs. Lawrence T. Foster). Asst. gen. mgr., dir. Wyandotte Chems. Corp., 1929-40; pres. Ford Bldg. Co., Detroit, 1934-42; chief, tank and combat vehicle sect. OPM, Washington, 1940-42; asst. to exec. v.p. Libbey-Owens- Ford Glass Co., 1945-47, pres. Plaskon div., 1947-53; v.p., sec.-treas. TAG Airlines, Inc., Toledo, 1955-57; pres., dir. Nicholas Corp., Toledo, 1954-67, chmn. bd., dir., 1968-71, now dir.; treas., dir. W. Bingham Co., Toledo, 1962-66; pres., dir. Knight Land Co., Inc., 1963—, Biminis Blue Water, Inc., Ltd., 1963—; mem. St. Lawrence Seaway Devel. Corp., 1969—; dir. Toledo Scale Corp., Toledo Trust Co., Belmont Devel. Co., Dana Corp. Chmn. bd. dirs. Toledo-Lucas County Port Authority, 1956—. Vice chmn. bd. trustees Inst. Med. Research of Toledo Hosp.; v.p., trustee Research Found., U. Toledo, 1963-71; trustee, chmn. finance com. Toledo State Coll. Medicine, 1964-70; vice-chmn., trustee Toledo Hosp. Endowment Fund, 1958—; adv. com. Hosp. Planning Assn. of Greater Toledo. Trustee Cancer Cytology Found. Served to lt. col. ordance dept. AUS, 1942-45. Decorated Legion of Merit; Royal Order of Vasa (Sweden). Mem. Nat. Def. Transp. Assn., Am. Ordnance Assn., Am. Legion. Episcopalian. Clubs: Toledo Country, Toledo, Propeller, Belmont Country (Toledo); Yale (N.Y.C.); Detroit; Country of Florida (Delray Beach). Home: Glen Eagles Rd Perrysburg OH 43551 Office: Nat Bank Bldg Toledo OH 43604

KNIGHTON, HOLMES TUTT, bacteriologist; b. Bellamy, Ala., Sept. 15, 1902; s. Thomas Abraham and Nettie Eugenia (Cannady) K.; student Marion (Ala.) Mil. Inst., 1920- 21; D.D.S., Tulane U. of La., 1926; m. Madeline Nichols, Aug. 6, 1936; children—Shirley Nichols, Carole Ann. Pvt. practice of dentistry, York, Ala., 1926-29; pub. health dentist, Lauderdale County, Florence, Ala., 1929-30; intern Forsyth Dental Infirmary, Boston, 1930-31; Rockefeller fellow in dental research U. Rochester, 1931-33; instr. in bacteriology, U. Ga. Med. Sch., 1933-34; instr. in operative dentistry, Med. Coll. of Va., 1934-36, prof. dentistry and bacteriology, 1951—, dir. dental research, 1956—, asst. dean Med. Coll. Va. Sch. Dentistry, 1964-68, asso. dean, 1968-71; asst. prof. bacteriology, U. Louisville Med. Sch., 1936-40, asso. prof., 1940-46; prof. dental medicine Washington U. Sch. Dentistry, 1946-47, prof. bacteriology, chmn. dept. bacteriology pathology, 1947-50; prof. dentistry U. Ala., 1950-51. Fellow Am. Acad. Microbiology, Am. Coll. Dentists; mem. Internat. Assn. for Dental Research (pres. 1960-61), Am. Dental Assn., Soc. Am. Bacteriologists, Sigma Xi, Omicron Kappa Upsilon, Xi Psi Phi. Democrat. Methodist. Home: 1101 Normandy Dr Richmond VA 23229

KNIGHTS, NORMAN JAMES, univ. adminstr.; b. Winnipeg, Man., Can., Dec. 31, 1922; s. Coby William and Ida (Waters) K.; brought to U.S., 1923, naturalized, 1951; A.B., DePauw U., 1946; M.B.A., Harvard, 1948; m. Merilyn Louise Smythe, Sept. 7, 1946; children-Laurie, Norman James, Holly and Heidi (twins). Adminstrv. asst. Booz, Allen & Hamilton, N.Y.C., 1948; sales rep. Marathon Corp., 1948-57; dir. pub. relations and devel. DePauw U., Greencastle, Inc., 1957-66, asst. to pres., 1966-69âv.p. 1969—. Dir. Greencastle Savs. and Loan Assn., 1968—. Greencastle Devel. Corp., 1969- -. Pres. Greencastle Plan C?1960-65; mem. Clay-Owen-Putnam County Community Action Program, 1962—, pres., 1965—. Bd. dirs. Community Action Program. Served with RCAF, 1943-45. Wilton Park fellow, 1966. Mem. Am. (dist. dir., trustee 1968-69, trustee 1970—), Ind. (pres. 1967) coll. pub. relations assn., Ind. Colls. and Univs. Indiana (exec- com; sec.-treas. 1966—), Greencastle C. of C. (pres. 1960), Phi Kappa Psi. Christian Scientist (chmn. bd. 1967-70). Rotarian (v.p. Greencastle 1967). Home: Rural Route 2 Greencastle IN 46135

KNIPE, JAMES LAUNCELOT, econ. cons.; b. Marshall, Ill., Mar. 31, 1904; s. Henry Hedges and Mabel (Graham) K.; Ph.B., Yale, 1926, M.A., 1934; Ph.D., 1940; m. Danielle Rolin, June 14, 1930; children—James Graham, Peter Rolin. Organizer, financier telephone utilities, Chicago, 1926-32; own investment counsel firm, New Haven, 1932-41; research dir. Hawaii Employers' Council, Honolulu, 1946-47; asst. to pres. to v.p., dir. Union Bag & Paper Corp., N.Y.C., 1947-51; v.p., gen. sales mgr., dir. Ball Bros. Co., Inc., Muncie, Ind., 1952; exec. v.p., dir. C.E. Hooper, Inc., 1953, pres., chmn. bd., 1954-57; cons. to chmn. bd. govs. Fed. Res. System, 1959-62; financial and econ. cons., 1962—; vis. prof. finance U. N.C., Chapel Hill, 1965- 67; prof. econs. East Carolina U., Greenville, 1967—. Served to comdr. USNR, 1941-46. Rotarian. Clubs: University (N.Y.C.); Chevy Chase (Md.); Hillsboro (Pompano Beach, Fla.). Author: The Guaranteed Annual Wage (with Alexander Calder), 1948; The Federal Reserve and the American Dollar, 1965. Contbr. weekly financial commentary to local TV. Home: Box 2066 Greenville NC 27834

KNIPLING, EDWARD FRED, entomologist, govt. ofcl.; b. Port Lavaca, Tex., Mar. 20, 1909; s. Henry J. and Hulda (Rasch) K.; B.S., Tex. A. and M. Coll., 1930; M.S., Ia. State Coll., 1932, Ph.D., 1947; D.Sc., Catawba Coll., 1962, N.D. State U., 1967, Clemson U., 1970; m. Phoebe R. Hall, July 21, 1934; children—Edwina H., Anita A., Edward B., Gray D., Ronald R. With Dept. Agr., 1931—, beginning as jr. entomologist, successively asst. entomologist, asso. entomologist, sr. entomologist, prin., chief insects affecting man and animal research br., 1931-53, dir. entomology research div. Agrl. Research Service, 1953- 70, sci. adviser, 1970—; dir. entomology research Orlando Lab., Fla., 1943-46. Recipient U.S. Typhus Commn. medal, Pres.'s Medal for Merit, King's Medal for cause of freedom, alumni centennial award Ia. State Coll., 1958; Hoblitzelle nat. award in agrl. scis., 1960; Rockefeller Pub. Service award, 1966; Nat. Medal of Sci., 1966; Pres.'s Civilian Ser. award, 1971; several distinguished service awards. Mem. A.A.A.S., Am. Soc. Tropical Medicine and Hygiene, Entomol. Soc. Am., Washington Acad. Sci., Nat. Mosquito Assn., Nat. Pest Control Assn., Am. Assn. Econ. Entomologists (pres. 1952), Nat. Acad. Scis., Sigma Xi. Club: Cosmos. Contbr. articles on entomology research. Home: 2623 Military Rd Arlington VA 22207 Office: Nat Agrl Library Beltsville MD 20705

KNIPP, JULIAN KNAUSE, physicist; b. Champaign, Ill., Jan. 18, 1910; s. Charles Tobias and Frances (Knause) K.; B.A. with high honors in Math., U. Ill., 1931; A.M., Harvard, 1932, Ph.D., 1935; m. Christine Simmons, Apr. 6, 1943; children—Julia Simmons Harris, Barbara Lynell, Pauline Evelyn Knipper. Instr. to asst. prof. physics Purdue U., 1936-46; asso. prof. to prof. Ia. State Coll., 1946-55; prof. physics Tufts U., 1955—, chmn. dept., 1955-68, asso. dean of liberal arts, 1967-68, dean faculty arts and scis., 1968-69; staff Mass. Inst. Tech. Radiation Lab., 1942- 45. John Tyndall fellow Harvard, 1932-35; Sheldon traveling fellow to Utrecht and Leipzig, 1935-36; John Simon Guggenheim Meml. fellow, Copenhagen, 1948-49; sr. physicist Ames Lab. AEC, 1948-55; NSF fellow to Rome, 1961-62; vis. philosopher, Beirut, Lebanon, 1970. Fellow Am. Acad. Arts and Scis. Republican. Episcopalian. Author: (with D. Hamilton, J.B.H. Kuper) Klystrons and Microwave Triodes. Home: South Mowing Shoreham VT 05774 Office: Tufts U Medford MA 02155

KNIPSCHILD, ROBERT, educator, artist; b. Freeport, Ill., Aug. 17, 1927; s. Leon Francis and Alice (Walsh) K.; B.A., U. Wis., 1950; M.F.A., Cranbrook Acad. Art, 1951; m. Patricia Ann O'Connor, Sept. 1, 1949; childrenAbby Clare, Amy Louise, John Eliot, Jill Anne, Sarah Kate. Tchr., Balt. Mus. Art, 1951-52, Am. U., 1952, U. Conn., 1954-56, U. Wis., 1956-60, U. Ia., 1960- 66; prof. art, chmn. div. art, dir. grad. studies fine arts U. Cin., 1966—; exhbns. include Mus. Modern Art, Whitney Mus., Met. Mus., Corcoran Mus., Boston Mus., Carnegie, Inst., also in Europe, Japan and Australia. Served with AUS, 1945-47. Home: 3346 Jefferson Av Cincinnati OH 45220

KNISEL, RUSSELL H., banker; b. Englewood, N.J., June 18, 1933; s. Adolph C. and Elsa (Vieght) K.; B.A., Wesleyan U., Middletown, Conn., 1955; postgrad. Harvard Grad. Sch. Bus., 1963; m. Diane Taylor, June 18, 1955; children—Susan, Kimberly, Sally, Russell H. Pension mgr. Conn. Gen. Life Ins. Co., 1955-56; with Marine Midland Bank, N.Y.C., 1956—, sr. v.p., 1968—. Mem. Am. Pensions Conf., N.Y. State Bankers Assn., Wesleyan Alumni Assn. Clubs: Manhattan, Williams (N.Y.C.); Park Country (Buffalo); Wee Burn Country (Darien). Home: 27 Beach Dr Darien CT 06820 Office: 250 Park Av New York City NY 10017

KNISELY, WILLIAM HAGERMAN, educator; b. Houghton, Mich., Feb. 3, 1922; s. Samuel Henry and Flora (Hagerman) K.; Ph.B., U. Chgo., 1947, B.S., 1950; postgrad. U. Brussels (Belgium), 1950; M.S., Med. Coll. S.C., 1952, Ph.D., 1954; m. Marguerite Marie Labasse, Jan. 18, 1947; children—Chantal, Marc, Paul, Colette, Philip. Instr. anatomy, teaching fellow medicine Duke, 1954-56, instr. medicine, 1956-57, asst. prof. anatomy, 1957-58, asso. prof. anatomy, also asst. prof. medicine, 1958-59; prof., chmn. dept. anatomy U. Ky. Coll. Medicine, 1959-63; dir. Inst. Biology and Medicine, Mich. State U., 1963-70; vice-chancellor health affairs U. Tex. System, 1970—. Mem. Nat. Adv. Council Edn. for Health Professions Served with AUS, 1943-46. Am. Heart Assn. reseach fellow, 1955-57; sr. research fellow USPHS, 1957-59. Fellow Royal Micros. Soc. London; mem. Am. Heart Assn., Gerontol. Soc., Am. Cancer Soc., Am. Assn. Anatomists, Microcirculatory Conf. (exec. council 1959; pres. 1961-62), N.Y. Acad. Sci., Tex. Thoracic Soc., Human Biology Soc., Oxford, Eng., Am. Pub. Health Assn., Am. Assn. History Medicine, A.M.A. (affiliate), Sigma Xi. Home: 4015 Sierra Dr Austin TX 78731

KNISKERN, MAYNARD, editor, writer; b. Schenectady, Nov. 5, 1912; s. Henry Parsons and Hermia Loraine (Maynard) K.; student U. of Miami (Fla.), 1932-33; L.H.D., Wittenberg U., 1970; m. Ora Lazenby, Oct. 11, 1945. Free-lance writer, 1933-36; newspaper and mag. editorial writer, 1936-39; editor Cranston (R.I.) Herald, 1939-42, Springfield (O.) Sun, 1946—. Served as air operations officer and combat corr. with USNR, 1942-46. Recipient Am. citizenship medal, for journalistic activities, V.F.W. 1940. Mem. Pi Delta Epsilon. Episcopalian. Home: 2775 S Limestone St Springfield OH 45505 Office: Springfield Newspapers Inc Springfield OH 45501

KNISPEL, MERLIN DEAN, pharm. co. exec.; b. Ft. Wayne, Ind., June 19, 1931; s. Otto F. and Hilda (Springer) K.; B.A., Ind. U., 1953; m. Carol Circle, June 21, 1953; children—Shannon Jane, Shelly Jo, Sheryl Jean, Stacy Jill, Sandra Jaye. Jr., then sr. accountant Price Waterhouse & Co., 1953-60; with Miles Labs., Inc., 1960—, asst. corp. controller, 1967, treas., 1967—. Served with AUS, 1954-56. C.P.A., Ind. Mem. Am. Inst. C.P.A.'s, Ind. Assn. C.P.A.'s. Presbyn. (trustee). Home: Box 193 RR3 Edwardsburg MI 49112 Office: 1127 Myrtle St Elkhart IN 46514

KNOBEL, FRANKLIN E., supermarket exec.; b. N.Y.C., Dec. 19, 1926; s. Benjamin and Mildred (Furst) K.; B.S., N.Y. U., 1950; m. Norma Kass, May 29, 1956; children—Peter, John, Steven. Realtor, N.Y.C., 1950-68; chmn. H.C. Bohack Co., Inc., Bklyn., 1968—. Trustee LeRoy Hosp., N.Y.C. Served with USNR, 1944-46. Mem. Tau Epsilon Phi. Club: Inwood (N.Y.) Country. Home: 105 Everit Av Hewlett Bay Park NY 11557 Office: 48-25 Metropolitan Av Brooklyn NY 11237

KNOBIL, ERNST, physiologist; b. Berlin, Germany, Sept. 20, 1926; s. Jakob and Regina (Seidmann) K.; came to U.S., 1940, naturalized, 1945; B.S., Cornell U., 1948, Ph.D. (Schering fellow endocrinology, 1949-51), 1951; m. Julane Hotchkiss, July 11, 1959; children—Erich Richard, Mark, Nicholas, Katharine. Asst., zoology Cornell U., 1948-49; Milton Research fellow Harvard, 1951-53, from instr. to asst. prof. physiology Med. Sch., 1953-61; spl. research pituitary gland, endocrinology reprodn. John and Mary R. Markle Found. scholar med. scis., 1956-61; Richard Beatty Mellon prof. physiology, chmn. dept. U. Pitts. Sch. Medicine, 1961—; Bowditch lectr. Am. Physiol. Soc., 1965; cons. USPHS (surgeon gen. U.S.), Ford Found; mem. adv. council Inst. Lab. Animal Resources, NRC-Nat. Acad. Sci., 1966-69; mem. nat. sci. adv. bd. Growth, Inc., 1969. Served with AUS, 1944-46. Fellow A.A.A.S; mem. Am. Soc. Zoologists, Soc. Exptl. Biology and Medicine, Am. Physiol. Soc. (mem. council 1969—), Endocrine Soc. (Ciba award 1961; council 1968-71), Soc. Endocrinology (Gt. Britain), Assn. Chairmen Depts. Physiology (pres. 1969), Am. Assn. Med. Colls. (adminstrv. bd. council acad. socs.), Nat. Bd. Med. Examiners, Sigma Xi. Mem. editorial bd. Am. jour. Physiology, 1959-68, Am. Jour. Endocrinology, 1959—; editorial com. Ann. Rev. Physiology, 1968—. Home: W Waldheim Rd Pittsburgh PA 15215

KNOBLAUCH, ARTHUR LEWIS, univ. pres.; b. Riga. Mich., Nov. 17, 1906; s. Ferdinand and Wilhelmina (Kolz) K.; B.S., Mich. State U., 1929; M.A., U. Mich., 1933; Ed.D. (McGregor scholar), Harvard, 1942; m. Muriel Marguerite Clemes, Aug. 12, 1929; children-Jane Harriet (Mrs. Mann), Nancy Carolyn (Mrs. Sonnenberg), Muriel Ann (Mrs. Fanning). Tchr. high sch., Buchanan, Mich., 1929-31, dir. athletics, prin., 1931-35; supt. schs., Cassopolis, Mich., 1935-39; exec. sec. Conn. Tchrs. Assn., 1940-41; asso. prof. edn. U. Conn., 1941-43, prof. edn., dir. div. univ. extension, summer session and continuing edn., 1943-55; vis. prof. U. Mich., 1950; pres. State Coll., Moorhead, Minn., 1955-58; pres. Western Ill. U., 1959-68, pres. emeritus, 1969—, prof. emeritus polit. sci., pres. U. Found., 1960-69; vis. prof. U. Ariz., 1971; cons. Saga Found. Pres. Prairie council Boy Scouts, Am., 1960-65, now mem. nat. council; pres. United Fund, 1960-62; mem. Gov's Adv. Council Ill., 1968—. Dir. Positive Attitude, Inc., Galesburg. Regent Lincoln Acad. Ill., Ill. State U., Regency Univs. Ill., 1969—; interim Sec. Ill. Community Coll. Trustees Assn., 1970-71. Recipient Silver Beaver award Boy Scouts Am., 1955, Silver Antelope award, 1964; Fulbright lectureship, Burma, 1952-53, Russia, 1959; Danforth grant seminar in higher edn., Wash., 1960; Distinguished Alumni award Mich. State U., 1960; Legion of Honor award Internat. Order of DeMolay, 1961. Mem. Am. Soc. for Pub. Adminstrn. (pres. Conn. chpt. 1946-47, 49-50), Conn. Schoolmasters Assn., N.E.A., Sch. Pub. Relations Assn., A.A.A.S., Soc. Adult Edn. (internat. understanding com. 1956-61), Soc. for Acad. Achievement (pres. 1968—), Alpha Gamma Rho, Alpha Zeta, Pi Kappa Delta, Phi Delta Kappa, Alpha Phi Omega, Phi Sigma. Presbyn. Mason (32, Shriner), Rotarian. Author articles profl. jours. Home: Rural Rt 1 Roseville IL 61473

KNOBLAUCH, HAROLD CARL, agrl. sci. cons.; b. Riga, Mich., Oct. 9, 1908; s. Ferdinand and Wilhelmina (Kolz) K.; B.S., Mich. State Coll., 1931; M.S., R.I. State Coll., 1933; Ph.D., Rutgers U., 1942; D.Sc., U.R.I., 1958; m. Willeta Johnson, Mar. 25, 1939; children—Harold, Richard, Carol. Research and teaching agronomy U. R.I., 1931-35; with soil and land use surveys Soil Conservation Service, N.Y., Ga., 1935-37, research supr., New Brunswick, N.J., 1937-50; soil technologist at Office Experiment Stas., Dept. Agr., 1940-48, asst. chief, 1948-53, dir. state expt. stas. div., 1954-61; dep. adminstr. of Coop. State Expt. Sta. Service 1962-63; asso. adminstr. Coop. State Research Service, 1963-70; agrl. sci. cons., author, 1970—. Fulbright-Hays advanced research scholar U. Queensland, Brisbane, Australia, 1967-68. Chmn. Nat. Soil Research Com., 1948-50; mem. U.S. del. 4th Internat. Congress Soil Sci., 1950; mem. organizing and exec. com. 6th Internat. Grassland Congress, 1952; mem. Hobitzelle Nat. Agrl. Sci. Award Com., 1953; mem. joint com. Dept. Agr. and Nat. Assn. State Univs. and Land-Grant Colls. Edn. for Govt. Service, 1962-67; Research and Edn. Panel on World Food Supply, 1966-67; joint panel Fed.-State Relations in Agrl. Research, 1968-69. Fellow A.A.A.S., Am. Soc. Agronomy; mem. Am., Internat. soil sci. socs., Inst. Biol. Scis., Am. Forestry Assn., Sigma Xi, Phi Kappa Phi, Alpha Zeta, Alpha Gamma Rho. Mason. Club: Cosmos. Author articles in field. Address: Route 1 Box 247G Front Royal VA 22630

KNOBLOCH, CARL WILLIAM, Jr., holding co. exec.; b. N.Y.C., Apr. 16, 1930; s. Carl William and Lilly Louise (Smith) K.; B.A., Yale, 1951; M.B.A., Harvard, 1953; m. Emily Champion, Nov. 30, 1957; children—Carla, Emily Jean, Eleanor Louise. With Lehman Bros., N.Y.C., 1954-57, Kidder, Peabody & Co., N.Y.C., 1957-61; pres. Uni Capital Corp., Atlanta, 1961—; dir. Gen. Instrument Corp. (N.Y.C.), Am. Bankers Life Assurance Co. (Miami). Mem. exec. com. bd. visitors Emory U. Clubs: Yale, Anglers (N.Y.C.); Piedmont Driving (Atlanta). Home: 2575 Arden Rd NW Atlanta GA 30327 Office: First National Bank Tower Atlanta GA 30303

KNOBLOCH, IRVING WILLIAM, educator; b. Buffalo, Mar. 1, 1907; s. Philip and Henrietta (Linke) K.; B.A. magna cum laude, U. Buffalo, 1930, M.A., 1932; postgrad., Harvard, 1930-31; Ph.D., Ia. State Coll., 1942; m. Natalie Mueller, Dec. 28, 1934; children—Karen Gail, Keith Rickard, Craig Geoffrey. Wildlife technician Dept. Interior, 1933-37; dir. Buffalo Botanic Garden, 1931- 33; collector plants, animals, Mexico, 1937-40; instr. botany Ia. State Coll., 1942-43; asst. prof. biology U. Buffalo, 1943-45; asst. prof. biol. scis. Mich. State U., 1945-47, asso. prof., 1947-51, prof. natural scis., 1951-59, prof. botany, 1959—. Recipient award for sci. work NSF; award for research Sigma Xi. Mem. Bot. Soc. Am. (chmn. and sec. teaching sect.); Am. Assn. U. Profs., Am. Civil Liberties Union, Mich. Acad. Arts, Sci. and Letters, Am. Sci. Affiliation (biology editor), Am. Fern Soc. (v.p. 1965-67, pres. 1967- 69), Nature Conservancy, Sigma Xi. Author: Readings in Biological Science, 1967; Selected Botanical Papers, 1963; (with D. Correll) Ferns and Fern Allies of Chihuahua, Mexico, 1962. Contbr. articles profl. jours. Home: 336 University Dr East Lansing MI 48933

KNOCH, WIN G., judge; b. Naperville, Ill., May 24, 1895; s. William and Adolphine C. (Boecker) K.; LL.B., DePaul U., 1917; LL.D. North Central Coll., St. Procopius Coll., Lisle, Ill. DePaul U., 1968; m. Irene Mae Fauth, June 30, 1926; children—Marjorie Ann (Mrs. Kenneth Schaller), Marion (Mrs. Donald Wehrill), Doris Marie (Mrs. Warren Wood), Joanne (Mrs. James Strong). Admitted to Ill. bar, 1917, since practiced in Naperville; partner Reed, Knoch & Keeney, 1922-30; asst. state's atty., DuPage County, 1922-30, county judge, 1930-39; circuit judge 16th Jud. Circuit Ill., 1939-53; U.S. dist. judge, 1953-58; judge U.S. Ct. Appeals, 1958-67; sr. circuit judge U.S. Ct. Appeals, 1967- -. Gen. chmn. Naperville Centennial Celebration, 1931. Served to lt. inf. U.S. Army, AEF, 1917-19. Recipient Silver Beaver Boy Scouts Am. Mem. Am., Ill., DuPage County (past Pres.) bar assns., Ill. County and Probate Judges Assn. (past Pres.), Ill. Circuit and Superior Judges Assn. (past pres.), Am. Legion (past comdr. city, county, dist.), 40 and 8. Republican. Roman Catholic. K.C. Elk, Moose. Club: Naperville Country. Home: 501 N Main St Naperville IL Office: 219 S Dearborn St Chicago IL 60604

KNOCHEL, JOHN CLIFFORD, flat glass mfr.; b. Newark, Nov. 2, 1909; s. John A. and Frances E. (Watts) K.; B.S., Newark Coll. Engring., 1932; m. Frances E. Bridges, May 29, 1942; children—Gail W., Cheryl Bridges, William C. Chemist, prodn. and sales staff E. I. DuPont de Nemours & Co., 1932-47; v.p., dir. DeVoe & Reynolds Co., 1947-58; v.p., dir. Am. Marietta Co., 1959-62; pres. Am. Saint Gobain Corp., 1962—; dir. 1st Nat. Bank Sullivan County, also mem. trust inv. com. Mem. industry adv. bd. resins and chems, 1950-52. Mem. devel. council U. Tenn. Bd. dirs. Holston Valley Community Hosp., Kingsport Community Chest, Jr. Achievement. Mem. Nat. Paint, Varnish and Lacquer Assn. (dir., exec. com. 1954-58), Am. Ordnance Assn. Clubs: Audubon Country (Louisville). Home: 2137 Bon Aire Dr Kingsport TN 37662 Office: P O Box 929 Lincoln St Kingsport TN 37662

KNODEL, ARTHUR JULIUS, educator; b. St. Louis, May 21, 1916; s. Karl A. and Mina (Glueckin) K.; M.A. in French, U. Cal. at Berkeley, 1942, Ph.D. in Romance langs., 1948. Teaching asst., St. Germain-en-Laye, France, 1938-39; mem. faculty U. So. Cal., 1948-, prof. French, 1959-, chmn. dept., 1960-67. Decorated Palmes Academiques Mem. Modern Lang. Assn., Phi Beta Kappa. Author: Saint-John Perse, 1966; also articles, trans. ‡

KNOEDLER, ELMER L., chem. engr.; b. Gloucester, N.J., Feb. 12, 1912; s. Elmer L. and Carolyn (Belle) K.; M.E., Cornell U., 1934, M.S., 1936; Ph.D., Columbia, 1952; m. Ruth Timanus, Oct. 1960 (dec. Dec. 1964); m. 2d, Mabel Dyer Todd, Jan. 15, 1966; children—Dianne, Homer. With Atlantic Mfg. Co., 1934-35; asst. supt. charge Davis Emergency Equipment Co., 1937-38; charge research and devel. metal power process Metals Disintegrating Co., 1939-41; cons. chem. engr., sr. field engr. Sheppard T. Powell, 1941-, now partner Sheppard T. Powell & Assos., Balt. Mem. Md. Bd. for Registration Engrs. and Land Surveyors. Registered profl. engr. 19 states. Fellow Am. Soc. M.E. (chmn. com. water conditioning and indsl. waste); mem. A Inst. Chem. Engrs. (chmn. Balt. sect. 1953), Am. Chem. Soc., Am. Water Works Assn., Am. Inst. Cons. Engrs. Club N.Y., Sigma Xi, Phi Lambda Upsilon. Clubs: Cornell (Md.; N.Y.); Maryland; Annapolis and Venice Yacht. Contbr. numerous articles tech., profl. jours. Home: 225 Nottingham Hill Sherwood Forest MD 21405 Office: 305 N Charles St Baltimore MD 21201

KNOEFEL, PETER KLERNER, pharmacologist, educator; b. New Albany, Ind., Aug. 4, 1906; s. August and Wilhelmina (Kerner) K.; B.A., U. Wis., 1927, M.A., 1928; M.D., Harvard, 1931; m. Francesca Spina, Oct. 2, 1953. NRC fellow U. Cal. at San Francisco, 1931-33; research asso. pharmacology Vanderbilt U. Med. Sch., 1933-35; mem. faculty U. Louisville, 1935—, prof. pharmacology, 1939-68, prof. emeritus, 1970—, chmn. dept., 1941-66. Mem. Am. Soc. Pharmacology, Am. Chem. Soc., Phi Kappa Phi. Author: Radiopaque Diagnostic Agents, 1961; Radiocontrast Agents, 1971; also papers. Home: 425 W Ormsby Av Louisville KY 40203

KNOELL, W.H., steel co. exec.; b. Pitts., Aug. 1, 1924; s. William F. and Hazel (Holverstott) K.; student Cornell U., 1942; B.S. in Mech. Engring., Carnegie Mellon U., 1947; J.D., U. Pitts., 1950; m. E. Anne Kirkland, Jan. 26, 1952; children—Kristin Anne, Susan Elizabeth, Amy Lynn, Gretchen. Practice law with firm Shoemaker-Knoell, 1949-50; asst. to exec. v.p. Pitts. Corning Corp., 1950-55; asst. sec. Crucible Steel Co. Am., 1955-57, sec., 1957-63, v.p., 1963-67; v.p. Cyclops Corp., 1967-68, exec. v.p., 1968—; dir. Dickerson Enterprises, Inc., Cyclops Corp. Bd. dirs. Sch. Dist. Upper St. Clair Twp., Pitts. Regional Planning Assn.; bd. visitors U. Pitts. Law Sch. Served with USAAF, 1943-45. Mem. Am., Allegheny County bar assns., Am. Iron and Steel Inst., Pi Tau Sigma, Theta Tau, Beta Theta Pi, Phi Alpha Delta. Clubs: University, Duquesne, St. Clair Country (Pitts.). Home: 1802 Murdstone Rd Pittsburgh PA 15241 Office: 650 Washington Rd Pittsburgh PA 15228

KNOEPFLMACHER, U.C., educator; b. Munich, Germany, June 26, 1931; s. George Alexander and Hilde (Welsz) K.; came to U.S., 1951, naturalized, 1963; A.B., U. Cal. at Berkeley, 1955, M.A. in English, 1957; Ph.D., Princton, 1961; m. Cecilia Mandzuch, June 11, 1959; children-Julie, Paul. Instr. U. Cal. at Berkeley, 1961-62, asst. prof. English lit., 1962-66, asso. prof., 1966- 69, prof., 1969—, asst. dean Coll. Letters and Scis., 1967-71; cons. in field. Fellow Am. Council Learned Scos., 1965; Humanities Research prof., 1966-67; Guggenheim fellow, 1969-70. Mem. Nat. Council Tchrs. English, Central Cal. Council Tchrs. English, Modern Lang. Assn. Democrat. Jewish religion. Author: Religious Humanism and the Victorian Novel, 1965, 70; George Eliot's Early Novels; The Limits of Realism, 1968; Laughter and Despair: Readings in Ten Novels of the Victorian Era, 1971. Editor Phases of Faith, 1970. Editorial bd. Victorian Studies, 1965—. Contbr. articles profl. jours. Home: 1329 Walnut St Berkeley CA 94709

KNOERICH, VOKER FELIX, German diplomat; b. Waldenburg, Silesia, Oct. 11, 1932; s. Otto Paul and Margarete (Schierenberg) K.; M.A., U. Gottingen (Germany), 1958; m. Dagmar Maria Korte, May 29, 1965. Lawyer, Lower Saxony, Germany, 1959-63; assessor Govt-Braunschweg, 1963-65, German Fed. Parliament, 1965; personal asst. to fed. sci. minister, 1966-69; 1st sec., acting sci. attache German embassy, Washington, 1969—. Mem. Christian Democratic Union. Home: 6927 Whitehall Pl McLean VA 22101 Office: 4645 Reservoir Rd Washington DC 20007

KNOFF, GERALD EVERETT, clergyman; b. Madison Lake, Minn., May 6, 1907; s. Frank Berthold and Winnie Ethel (Thayer) K.; A.B., Fla. So. Coll., 1930; B.D., Yale, 1933, Ph.D., 1936; H.H.D., St. Paul's U., Tokyo, Japan, 1958; LL.D., Westmar Coll., 1964; m. Dorothy Mann Cooper, Sept. 1, 1931; children—Elizabeth Ann, William Cooper, Sara Louise. Ordained to ministry Methodist Ch., 1935; exec. sec. New Haven Council Chs., 1933-34; minister South Meriden Meth. Ch., 1934- 36, Clinton (Conn.) Meth. Ch., 1936-38; dir. bur. religious activities Ia. State Tchrs. Coll., Cedar Falls, 1938-44; dir. ednl. program Internat. Council Religious Edn., Chgo., 1944-45, asso. gen. sec., 1945-51; gen. dir. Commn. of Gen. Christian Edn., Nat. Council Chs., Chgo., 1951-52; exec. sec. div. Christian edn. Nat. Council Chs. Christ in U.S., 1952-64, asso. gen. sec. Christian edn., 1965—; chmn. program com. World Council Christian Edn., 1951-58, also mem. bd. mgrs. vice chmn. World Council Christian Edn., 1967—; com. div. ecumenical action World Council Chs., 1969—; mem. curriculum com. Meth. Ch., 1948-52; exec. sec. The Study of Christian Edn., 1944-1947; mem. Preacher Exchange, Gt. Britain, 1954, 56. Mem. Am. Acad. Religion, Religious Edn. Assn., Soc. Mayflower Descs., Assn. Council Secs., Pi Gamma Mu. Contbr. articles on Christian edn. in ch. press. Home: 34 Pine Grove Av Summit NJ 07901 Office: 475 Riverside Dr New York City NY 10027

KNOLES, GEORGE HARMON, educator; b. Los Angeles, Feb. 20, 1907; s. Tully Cleon and Emily (Walline) K.; A.B., Coll. Pacific, 1928, A.M., 1930, Ph.D., Stanford, 1939; m. Amandalee Barker, June 12, 1930; children—Ann Barker, Alice Laurane. Instr. history Union High Sch., Lodi, Cal., 1930-35; asst. in history Stanford, 1935-36, instr. history, 1937-41, asst. prof., 1942- 46, asso. prof., 1946-51, prof. history, 1951—, Margaret Byrne prof. Am. history, 1968—, chmn. dept. history, 1968—; dir. Inst. Am. History. Prof. history, chmn. div. social sci. State Coll. Edn., Greeley, Colo., 1941-42; summer tchr. Central Wash. Coll. Edn., Ellenburgh, 1939, State Coll., Flagstaff, Ariz, 1940, 1941, U. Cal. at Los Angeles, 1947; Stanford-Tokyo Us., Am. Studies Seminars, Tokyo, 1950-52, 56, U. Wyo., 1955; Fulbright distinguished lectr., Japan, 1971. Served to lt. USNR, 1944-46. Mem. Am., So. hist. assns., Orgn. Am. Historians (exec. com. 1950-54, bd. editors review 1955-58), Am. Studies Assn. (council 1952-54), Soc. of Am. Historians. Methodist. Rotarian. Club: Commonwealth. Author: The Presidential Campaign and Election of 1892, 1942; Readings in Western Civilization (with Rixford K. Snyder), 1951; The Jazz Age Revisited, 1955; The New United States, 1959. Editor: The Crisis of The Union, 1860-61, 1965; Sources in American History, 10 vols., 1965-66; The Responsibilities of Power, 1900-1929, 1967. Contbr. articles. Home: P O Box 3284 Stanford CA 94305

KNOLL, DENYS WILLIAM, ret. naval officer; b. Erie, Pa., Mar. 7, 1907; s. Edmund Amandus and Ida Mary (Illig) K.; B.S., U.S. Naval Acad., 1930, postgrad. 1936-38; M.S., Mass. Inst. Tech., 1939; LL.D., Gannon Coll., Erie, 1959; m. Genevieve Parker Hawkins, Feb. 29, 1940 (dec. Aug. 1963); m. 2d, Audrey Gallagher Schultz, Apr. 5, 1968. Commd. ensign U.S. Navy, 1930, advanced to rear adm., 1957; various assignments in ships, 1930-41; staff comdr. naval forces Philippines, also with comdg. gen. U.S. forces in Philippines, 1941-42;

mem. staff of Adm. King, 1942-44; naval mem. U.S. Mil. Mission to Russia, 1944-45; naval adviser organizing meeting UN in London, later organized, served as 1st sec., mil. staff com. UN, 1945-46; comdg. officer U.S.S. Severn, 1946-48; with strategic plans div. office Chicf Naval Operations, 1948-52, 53-54; comdg. officer U.S.S. Menard, 1952-53, U.S.S. Roanoke, 1954-55; chief staff 7th Fleet, 1955-57; chmn. ship characteristics bd. Navy Dept., 1957-59; comdr. Destroyer Flotila 4, 1959-60; mem. staff Office Chief Naval Operations, Navy Dept., 1960-61; comdr. Service Force, Atlantic Fleet, 1961-62; oceanographer Navy Office Chief Naval Operations, 1963-65; dep. comdr. Mil. Sea Transp. Service, Navy Dept., Washington, 1965-67; ret. 1967; asst. to gen. mgr. Erie Marine, div. Litton Industries 1967—. Decorated Legion of Merit with Gold Star for 2d decoration, Navy Letter Commendation with 2 stars, Bronze Star (Army), Distinguished Unit emblem with oak leaf cluster (Army), numerous service ribbons. Clubs: Propeller, Army and Navy (Washington); Kahkwa, Erie, Aviation Country, Maennerchor (Erie, Pa.). Home: 4760 Wolf Rd Erie PA 16505 Office: Erie Marine PO Box 4022 Holland St Erie PA 16512

KNOLL, JERRY, govt. ofcl., b. Cin., Mar. 29, 1924; s. Adolph and Hilda (Schuman) K.; B.A., U. Chgo., 1947, M.B.A., 1947; student U. Mich., 1943. With U.S. Mil. Govt., Frankfurt and Berlin, Germany, 1948-49; U.S. sec. econs. and fgn. trade and exchange coms. Allied High Commn., Bonn, Germany, 1949-51, asst. to dep. econ. adviser, spl. asst. to dir. Mut. Security Adminstrn. Mission, Bonn, 1951-52; asst. div. dir. Office Dep. Dir. for Mut. Def. Assistance Control, ICA, Washington, 1952-55, internat. economist Dept. State, 1955-59, ICA, 1959-61, dep. dir. Office Devel. Planning, AID, 1961-64, dir. Office West African Affairs, 1964-68, dir. Office Eastern and S. African Affairs, 1968—. Served to capt. AUS, 1943-45. Recipient meritorious service award FOA, 1955. Home: 4000 Massachusetts Av Washington DC 20016 Office: AID Washington DC 20523

KNOLL, RUDOLF, bass-baritone; b. Herzberg-Pfalz, Germany, Singer leading theatres throughout Europe; debut with Met. Opera, 1968. Address: care Met Opera Assn Inc Lincoln Plaza New York City NY *

KNOLLENBERG, BERNHARD, writer; b. Richmond, Ind., Nov. 26, 1892; s. George H. and Agnes (Steen) K.; A.B., Earlham Coll., 1912, LL.D., 1944; A.M., Harvard, 1914, LL.B., 1916; A.M. (hon.), Yale, 1938; m. Mary McClennen, 1920; 1 son, Walter; m. 2d, Mary Lightfoot Tarleton, 1934. Admitted to bar, 1916; practiced law, 1916-38; mem. firm Lord, Day & Lord, N.Y.C., 1929-38; librarian Yale, 1938-44; cons. expert U.S. Treasury, 1939-40; sr. dep. adminstr. Lend Lease Adminstrn., 1943-44; div. dep. OSS, 1944- 45; U.S. commr. Internat. Commn. for N.W. Atlantic Fisheries, 1950-58. Mem. Conn. Hist. Commn. Served with Naval Intelligence USN., 1917-18. Hon trustee, Conn. Coll; asso. fellow Saybrook Coll., Yale. Mem. Am. Antiquarian Soc., Colonial Soc. Mass., Mass. Hist. Soc., Soc. Cin. Clubs: Century Assn. (N.Y.C.); Elizabethan (New Haven). Author: Washington and the Revolution: A Re-Appraisal, 1940; Whitewater Valley, 1946; Samuel Ward, 1952; Origin of the American Revolution, 1960; George Washington: The Virginia Period, 1964. Contbr. Atlantic Monthly, Harpers, law and hist. jours. Home: Parker's Point Chester CT 06412

KNOOPS, JONATHON WEST chemist, educator; b. Chicago, 1928; B.S. in Physics, Yale, 1950; Ph.D. in Chemistry, Harvard, 1956; m. Sally Ann Jones, July 5, 1957; children--Kenneth J., Nancy A. Chemist, Acme Chem. Co., Blue Island, Ill., 1950-51; director of Research Lab., Indsl. Chemicals Corp., Cambridge, Mass., 1956-60; project coordinator environmental sect. Steinmetz Assos., Chgo., 1960-61; v.p. for research Bauer Bros. Chem. Co., Inc., Memphis, 1961-64; asst. prof. chemistry Washington U., St. Louis, 1964-66, asso. prof., 1966-70, prof., 1970--, head of chemistry dept., 1970-71. Vis. prof. So. Ill. U., summer 1967, U. of Ore., 1969. Scoutmaster, Boy Scouts America, University City, Mo., 1968-70. Bd. dirs. Rest Haven Home for Elderly, 1960-61; trustee of the Lutheran Hosp., 1965-71. Served from lt. to capt., AUS, 1951-53. Mem. Am. Chem. Soc., Sci. Research Soc. Am. (chpt. treas. 1967), Sigma Xi. Author: (with others) Basic Inorganic Chemistry, 1971. Home: Fairfax Apts 7291 Windermere Dr University City MO 63105 Office: Dept Chemistry Washington University St Louis MO 63130

KNOPF, ALEXANDER BENJAMIN mfg. exec.; b. Lima, O., Apr. 1, 1932; B.S., U. San Francisco, 1954; M.S., Stanford University, 1956; m. Rosemarie Lois Brown, May 15, 1955; 1 son, Anthony Robinson. Sales rep. Ames-Brockton Fabricated Products, Akron, O., 1956-58, sales mgr. Coshocton, Ohio, 1959-61, gen. manager plant, 1961-68, v.p. sales, 1968--. Instr. bus. Coshocton Jr. College, 1968-69. Mem. Coshocton C. of C. (vice president 1967-68, pres. 1969-70), English Speaking Union, Coshocton Sertoma Club, Nat. Assn. Mfrs., Sales Executives Institute, Phi Beta Kappa, Sigma Chi, Phi Mu. Democrat. Mem. Christian Ch. (lay reader). Mason (32, Shriner). Clubs: Coshocton Country, Coshocton City, Running Deer Country. Home: 2d Av Coshocton OH Office: 3d Av Coshocton OH

KNOPF, ALFRED, Jr., publisher; b. White Plains, N.Y., June 17, 1918; s. Alfred A. and Blanche (Wolf) K.; grad. Phillips Exeter Acad., 1937; A.B., Union Coll., Schenectady, 1942; m. Alice Laine, July 27, 1952; childrenAlison, Susan, David. With Atheneum Pubs., N.Y.C., 1959-, chmn. bd., 1964-. Served to capt. USAAF, 1941-45. Mem. Delta Upsilon. Clubs: Players, Dutch Treat (N.Y.C.); Tavern (Chgo.); Odd Volumes (Boston); Nassau (Princeton, N.J.). Home: Bayberry Ridge Westport CT 06880 Office: 122 E 42d St New York City NY 10017

KNOPF, ALFRED A. publisher; b. N.Y.C., Sept. 12, 1892; s. Samuel and Ida (Japhe) K.; grad. Mackenzie Sch., 1908; A.B., Columbia, 1912; L.H.D., Yale, 1958, Columbia, Bucknell U., 1959, Lehigh U., 1960, William and Mary; LL.D., Brandeis U., 1963; D.Litt., Adelphi U., 1966, U. Chattanooga, 1966; m. Blanche Wolfe, 1916 (dec.); 1 son, Alfred; m. 2d, Helen Norcross Hedrick, 1967. Founded pub. firm, 1915, pres. Alfred A. Knopf, Inc., N.Y.C., 1918-57, chmn. bd., 1957- -; dir. Random House Inc. Decorated Comendador Ordem Nacional do Cruzeiro do Sul (Brazil); recipient Cornelius Amory Pugsley gold medal for conservation and preservation, 1960; Alexander Hamilton medal Assn. Alumni Columbia, 1966. Clubs: Cosmos (Washington); Century Country (Harrison, N.Y.); Lotos (N.Y.C.). Home: Purchase NY 10577 Office: 201 E 50th St New York City NY 10022

KNOPF, IRWIN JAY, educator; b. N.Y.C., June 14, 1924; s. Joseph and Esther (Inselman) K.; A.B., N.Y.U., 1948; M.A., Northwestern U., 1949, Ph.D., 1952; m. Roberta Iris Olin, Dec. 29, 1951; children-William Douglas, David Richard, Judith Ann. Asst. prof. clin. psychology, then asso. prof. clin. psychology, then asso. prof., head div. psychology, dept. psychiatry State U. Ia., 1952-58; asso. prof., chief div. psychology, dept. psychiatry U. Tex., 1958-62, prof., chmn. div. psychology, 1962-64; prof. psychology chmn. dept. Emory U., 1964—; cons. in field. Field selection officer Peace Corps; mem. Profl. adv. panel, div. mental health Ga. Dept. Pub. Health. Served with inf. AUS, 1944-45. Decorated Purple Heart. Fellow Am. Psychol. Assn., Am. Orthopsychiat. Assn.; mem. Midwestern, Southwestern, Southeastern, Tex., Ga. psychol. assns. Author articles in field. Cons. editor: Contemporary Psychology, 1961—. Home: 4256 Exeter Close N W Altanta GA 30325

KNOPF, KENYON ALFRED, economist, educator; b. Cleve., Nov. 24, 1921; s. Harold C. and Emma A. (Underwood) K.; A.B. magna cum laude with high honors in Econs., Kenyon Coll., 1942; M.A. in Econs., Ph.D., Harvard, 1949; m. Madelyn Lee Trebilcock, Mar. 28, 1953; children-Kristin Lee, Mary George. Mem. faculty Grinnell Coll., 1949-67, prof. econs., 1960-67, Jentzen prof., 1961-67, chmn. dept., 1958-60, chmn. div. social studies, 1962-64, chmn. faculty, 1964-67; prof. econs., dean coll., Whitman Coll., Walla Walla, Wash., 1967-70, prof. econs., provost, dean faculty, 1970—. Mem. youth council, City Grinnell, 1957-59; bd. Walla Walla United Fund; mem. Walla Walla County Mental Health Bd., 1968—. Councilman, City Grinnell, 1964-67. Mem. Ia. adv. council Small Business Adminstrn. Served with USAAF, 1943-46. Grantee Social Sci. Research Council, 1951-52. Mem. Am. Conf. Acad. Deans (exec. com.), Econ. History Assn., Am., Midwest econ. assns., Phi Beta Kappa, Delta Tau Delta. Author: (with Robert H. Haveman) The Market System, 1966, 2d edit., 1970. Editor: (with James H. Stauss) The Teaching of Elementary Economics, 1960; Introduction to Economics Series (9 vols.), 1966, 2d edit., 1970-71. Office: Whitman Coll Walla Walla WA 99362

KNOPF, LEONARD HENRY, lithographic exec.; b. Chgo., June 18, 1900; s. Andrew Jackson and Genevieve (Dickhut) K.; student U. Ill., 1919-21; m. Dorothy Abbott, June 26, 1922; children—Leonard Abbott, Dorothy (Mrs. James Kirst); m. 2d, Muriel Carpenter, Nov. 25, 1950; children—Reynold F., Jennifer M. With Meyercord Co., Chgo., 1923—, successively press boy, office boy, salesman, sales mgr., 1923-35, now chmn. bd.; chmn. Can. Decalcomania Co., Ltd., Toronto, Meyercord Co. de Mexico, Mexico City, Calcomanias Meyercord de Cuba, Havana; dir. Nat. Bank Austin. Past pres. Lithographic Tech. Fund. Mem. Phi Kappa Tau. Conglist. Mason (32, Shriner). Home: 4 Woodley Manor Winnetka IL 60093 Office: 365 E North Av Carol Stream IL 60187

KNOPF, MAURICE JAY, constrn. co. exec.; b. Wilmington Del., Oct. 8, 1918; s. Samuel J. and Eva (Millman) K.; student U. Del., 1940; m. Kathryn E. Richardson, Aug. 17, 1946; childrenSusan M., Sally D., Stacy A. Mem. engring. staff E.I. duPont DeNemours & Co., 1941-55; gen. mgr. John A. Robbins Co., Inc., Phila., 1956-57; with F.H. McGraw & Co., 1957-, asst. to pres., 1960, v.p., 1960-62, exec. v.p., 1962, pres., chief exec. officer, 1962-, also dir.; pres., dir. F.H. McGraw & Co. of Conn., Inc., McGraw Industries, Inc., F.H. McGraw & Co. of So. Conn., McGraw Terminal, Inc., Nat. Automatic Pipeline Operators, Inc., Nat. Pipeline Co., Inc., No. Mich. Pipeline Co., Unamco Corp.; dir. Paulsboro Chem. Corp N.J., Action, Inc., Constn. Plaza, Inc. Served with USAAF, 1943-45. Home: 78 Ledyard Rd West Hartford CT Office: 780 Windsor St Hartford CT

KNOPOFF, LEON, educator; b. Los Angeles, July 1, 1925; s. Max and Ray (Singer) K.; student Los Angeles City Coll., 1941-42; B.S. in Elec Engring., Cal. Inst. Tech., 1944, M.S. in Physics, 1946, Ph.D. in Physics, 1949; m. Joanne Van Cleef, Apr. 9, 1961; children—Katherine Alexandra, Rachel Anne, Michael Van Cleef. Asst., then asso. prof. physics Miami U., Oxford, O., 1948-50; mem. faculty U. Cal. at Los Angeles, 1950—, prof. physics, 1961—, prof. geophysics, 1959—, research musicologist, 1963—; prof. geophysics Cal. Inst. Tech., 1962-63, research asso. seismology, 1963-64; vis. prof. Technische Hochschule, Karlsruhe, Germany, 1966. Chmn. U.S. Nat. Upper Mantle Com., 1963-71; sec. Internat. Upper Mantle Com., 1963-71. NSF sr. postdoctoral fellow Cambridge (Eng.) U., 1960-61. Fellow Am. Acad. Arts and Scis.; mem. Nat. Acad. Scis., Am. Phys. Soc., Am. Geophys. Union, Seismol. Soc., Acoustical Soc. Am., Royal Astron. Soc., A.A.A.S. Office: U Cal Los Angeles CA 90024

KNOPP, MARVIN ISADORE, educator; b. Chgo., Jan. 4, 1933; s. Mitshel and Minnie (Israel) K.; B.S., U. Ill., 1954, A.M., 1955, Ph.D., 1958; m. Josephine Zadovsky, June 9, 1957; children—Seth David, Abby Alissa, Elana Elaine. Research mathematician Space Tech. Labs., Los Angeles, 1958-59; NSF postdoctoral fellow Inst. Advanced Study, Princeton, N.J., 1959-60; asst. prof. U. Wis., 1960-62, asso. prof., 1962-67, prof., 1967—; mathematician Nat. Bur. Standards, Washington, 1963-64; vis. prof. U. Basel (Switzerland), 1968-69; prof. U. Ill. at Chgo. Circle, 1970—. NSF grantee, 1960—. Author: Theory of Area, 1970; Modular Functions in Analytic Number Theory, 1971. Home: 5433 Eastview Park Chicago IL 60615 Office: 613 Van Vleck U Wi Madison WI 53706 also Univ Ill at Chicago Circle 311 SEO Bldg Chicago IL 60680

KNOPPERS, ANTONIE THEODOOR, chem. mfr.; b. Kapelle, Netherlands, Feb. 27, 1915; s. Bastiaan A. and Annetje (Valkenier) K.; M.D., U. Amsterdam, 1939; Dr. Pharmocology, U. Leyde, 1941; D.Sc. (hon.), Worcester Polytech. Inst.; m. Maria J. Willemsen, June 1, 1939; children—Bastiaan A., Maria H., Anneke C., Elizabeth E. Came to U.S., 1953; naturalized, 1958. Research asst. Pharmacol. Inst., U. Amsterdam, 1940-43; dir. pharmacology Amsterdam Chininefabriek, 1943- 52; prof. Free U. of Amsterdam 1950-53; mng. dir. Nederlandsche Kininefabriek, 1950-53; med. dir. Merck Sharp & Dohme Internat., 1953-55; v.p., gen. mgr. Merck Sharp & Dohme Internat. div. Merck & Co., Inc., N.Y.C., 1955-57, pres., sr. v.p.; pres. Merck & Co., Inc., 1971—, also dir. John Wiley & Sons, Inc., Scott Paper Co. Trustee Drew U., Salk Inst. Mem. Internat. C. of C. (chmn. U.S. council), Fgn. Policy Assn. (dir.), Council of Fgn. Relations, Netherlands C. of C. (exec. com., v.p.), N.Y. Acad. Scis., Asia Soc. (trustee), Presbyn. Clubs: Echo Lake Country, Recess, Netherlands (N.Y.C.); Baltusrol Golf. Contbr. sci. papers. Mem. therapy com. Netherlands Med. Jour., 1950-53; cofounder Documenta Tropica Neerlandica et Indonesica. Home: 38 Lenox Rd Summit NJ 07901 Office: Merck & Co Inc Rahway NJ 07065

KNORPP, WALTER WESLEY, pub., bank dir.; b. Chgo., May 19, 1891; s. John Walter and Eda Clara (Young) K.; grad. Phoenix High Sch., 1909; m. Anna Pearl Stauffer, Nov. 19, 1920; children-Betty Ann (dec.), Mary Jane (Mrs. Courtlandt Van Voorhis), Margaret Eda (Mrs Elbert Haven Neese). With Ariz. Republic successively as carrier, mailer and circulation mgr., 1905-09; circulation mgr. San Bernardino Free Press, 1909-10; advt. mgr. Tribune, San Diego, 1910-17; asst. bus. mgr. and bus. mgr. Ariz. Republic, 1917-29; negotiated purchase Phoenix Gazette, 1930; gen. mgr., pub. Republic and Gazette, 1930-46; pres. Ariz. Pub. Co.; v.p., dir. Republic and Gazette Engraving Co.; organized Ariz. Broadcasting Co. radio network, 1930-46; dir. First Nat. Bank Ariz., 1956-65. Sect. Sargt. Q.M.C., AEF, U.S. Army, 1918-19. Chmn. Phoenix Civilian Def. Com., 1941-44. Vice pres., dir. Ariz. State U. Found.; adv. bd. St. Lukes Hosp., Phoenix YMCA; hon. curator Heard Mus.; hon. trustee Good Samaritan Hosp.; bd. dirs. Neurol. Scis. Found. Past dir. Nat. Assn. Better Bus. Burs. Mem. A.P., 1940-46, instrumental in municipal, civic and polit. cleanup. Chmn. Phoenix U.S. Army Adv. com., 1948- 50; civilian aide to sec. U.S. Army, 1950-64; bd. advisers Indsl. Coll. Armed Forces. Recipient Outstanding Civilian medal, U.S.A., 1964. Mem. Def. Orientation Conf. Assn., Am. Legion, English Speaking Union (past dir.), Navy League, Fraternal Order Police, Ariz. Newspaper Assn. Democrat. Methodist. Mason (Shriner), Kiwanian. Clubs: Hiram (past pres.), Executives (dir.), Phoenix Country, de Concho, Symphony, Fine Arts, Civic Opera, (Phoenix); Arizona Automobile, Paradise Valley Country. Address: Hotel Westward Ho Phoenix AZ 85036

KNORR, DONALD ROBERT, architect; b. Chgo., Dec. 25, 1922; s. Arthur Herman and Esther Gertrude (Sternbeck) K.; B.S., U. Ill., 1947; postgrad. Cranbrook Acad. Art, 1948; m. Anne Hall, May 14, 1949; children—Torin Jon, Kipp D., Guy Douglass. Designer Eero Saarinen & Assos., 1947-49; designer, project mgr. Skidmore, Owings & Merrill, San Francisco, 1949-51; prin. Knorr Assos., San Francisco, 1951-56; partner Knorr-Elliott & Assos., San Francisco, 1956—; vis. critic Cal. State Poly. Coll. Sch. Architecture, 1969, 71. Served to lt. (j.g.) USNR, 1943-46. Fellow A.I.A. Home: 14 Entrata St San Anselmo CA 94960 Office: 631 Clay St San Francisco CA 94111

KNORR, KLAUS EUGENE, educator; b. Essen, West Germany, May 16, 1911; s. Eugene and Bertha (Brill) K.; LL.B., U. Tuebingen, Germany, 1935; Ph.D., U. Chgo., 1941; m. Marianne Uhlman, July 6, 1937; childrenMonica, Annette, Nicholas. Came to U.S., 1937, naturalized, 1940. Research asso. Food Research Inst., Stanford, 1941-45; asso. prof. Yale, 1942-52; prof. econs. Princeton, 1952-68, prof. internat. affairs, 1968—, dir. Center Internat. Studies, 1961-68; cons. The Rand Corp., Dept. State, Dept. Def., other govtl. depts. Mem. Am. Econ. Assn. Unitarian. Author: British Colonial Theories, 1944; The War Potential of Nations, 1956; NATO and American Security, 1959; Limited Strategic War, 1962; On the Uses of Military Power in the Nuclear Age, 1966; Military Power and Potential, 1970. Contbr. profl. jours. Home: 23 Laurel Rd Princeton NJ 08540

KNORR, LESTER, artist; b. Wilder, Ida., May 1, 1916; s. Martin Luther and Pauline (Lehman) K.; student Univ. Center, Florence, Italy, 1945; A.B., San Jose State Coll., 1948; M.A., Ohio State U., 1951, Ph.D., 1954; m. Jeanne Boardman, Dec. 18, 1955, children-Kim Lesley, Todd Loring. Asst. prof. philosophy and art S.W. Tex. State Coll., 1956-59; dir. Sch. Art, Bradley U., 1959-69; one man shows Regional Arts Gallery, N.Y.C., 1956, 58, Devorah Shormar Gallery, Chgo., 1965; shows with wife Laguna Goloria Gallery, Austin, Tex., 1957, Witte Mus., San Antonio, 1957. Served with AUS, 1942-45. Home: 2012 E Reservoir Blvd Peoria IL

KNORR, NATHAN HOMER, clergyman; b. Bethlehem, Pa., April 23, 1905; s. Donel Ellsworth and Estella (Bloss) K.; grad. Allentown, Pa., High Sch., 1923; m. Jan. 31, 1953. Began with Watch Tower Bible and Tract Soc., Bklyn., 1923, gen. mgr. pub. office, 1932; dir. People's Pulpit Assn. (now Watchtower Bible and Tract Soc. Inc.), 1934, dir., v.p., 1940, pres., 1942-. Pres. Internat. Bible Students Assn., London, 1942-. Mem. Jehovah's Witness. Home: 124 Columbia Heights Brooklyn NY 11201

KNORR, WALTER HERBERT, metals co. exec.; b. Newark, Dec. 29, 1908; s. Fred and Marie (Rebman) K.; grad. Am. Inst. Banking; m. Bernice I. Steiert, Sept. 24, 1936; children— Roger B., Richard B., Robert J. With Continental Copper & Steel Industries, Inc., N.Y.C., 1940—, treas., 1948—, v.p., 1962—; mem. finance com., pres. Condominio Insurgentes, S.A.-Mexico City, Mexico, 1950—; treas. Continental Rubber Works, Erie, 1962—; dir. Asceras Anglo S.A. de C.V., Mexico City. Mem. N.Y. Commodity Exchange, Nat. Assn. Accountants. Club: Colonia (N.J.) Country (dir.). Home: 1715 Westover Rd Clark NJ 07066 Office: 100 E 42d St New York City NY 10017

KNORTZ, HERBERT CHARLES, communications co. exec.; b. Bklyn., Mar 31, 1921; s. John Walter and Elizabeth (Grotyohann) K.; B.B.A., St. Johns U., 1946; M.B.A., N.Y. U., 1949; m. Lorraine Marion Kraut, Aug. 12, 1949; children—Steven Holbrook, Elizabeth Alyn, David Cartwright. Supervising clk. Bklyn. Trust Co., 1938-43; with Price Waterhouse & Co., C.P.A.'s, N.Y.C., 1945-51; supr. standard costs Lever Bros. Co., 1951-55; mgr. cost dept. Crown Cork & Seal Co., 1955-56; asst. comptroller Royal McBee Corp., 1956-60; controller Mack Trucks, Inc., Plainfield, N.J., 1960-61; dep. comptroller Internat. Tel. & Tel. Corp., 1961-63, v.p., controller, 1963- 65, sr. v.p., comptroller, 1965—; dir., officer several subsidiaries; v.p. Cortina Shops, Ridgefield, 1961-71; pres., partner Lewisboro Tennis Club, 1971—. Lectr. profl. meetings. Served with USAAF, 1943-45. C.P.A., N.Y. Mem. Financial Execs. Inst. (v.p. research found., nat. chmn. balance of payments com.), Am. Mgmt. Assn., Am. Contract Bridge League, Am. Inst. C.P.A.'s, Nat. Assn. Accountants, The Board Room, Internat. Assn. Financial Exec. Insts. (pres.), Delta Mu Delta, Beta Gamma Sigma. Clubs: Armonk Tennis, International Golf: Accountants. Contbg. author Handbook of International Management, Financial Executives Handbook. Editor: Food for Thought. Home: 4 Manor Rd Ridgefield CT 06877 Office: Internat Tel & Tel Corp 51st St and Park Av New York City NY 10022

KNOTHE, ADOLF HEINRICH, space scientist, govt. ofcl.; b. Traisa, Germany, Sept. 17, 1921; s. Max Louis and Elisabeth Magdalene (Weingärtner) K.; M.S. in Applied Math., Darmstadt (Germany) Tech. U., 1947, Ph.D., 1952; m. Johanna Krauter, Oct. 18, 1947 (div. 1963); children—Hennelore, Ralph Peter; m. 2d, Hilda Marian Arnold, Nov. 14, 1964. Came to U.S., 1953, naturalized, 1958. Mathematician, Peenemuende (Germany) Rocket Center, 1943-45; asst. prof. Inst. Practical Math., Darmstadt Tech. U., 1947-51; mathematician Farbwerke Hoechst, Germany, 1951-52; chief guidance theory sect. U.S. Army Ordnance Guided Missile Devel. Div., 1953-58; asst. to dir., systems analysis and reliability lab., Army Ballistic Missile Agy., 1958- 59, sci. asst. to dir., missile firing lab., 1959-60; chief tech. staff, Launch Operations Center, NASA, 1960-64; sr. scientist Kennedy Space Center, 1964—; part-time adj. prof. math. Fla. Inst. Tech., Melbourne. Mem. Am. Inst. Aeros. and Astronautics. Home: 102 N Indian Circle Cocoa FL 32022 Office: Kennedy Space Center FL 32899

KNOTT, AUBREY KIRK, educator; b. Blue Ridge, Tex., July 19, 1903; s. John Alvin and Bettie Louise (Perry) K.; A.B., Baylor U., 1924, M.A., 1925; Ed.D., U. Ore., 1941; m. Velma E. James, Sept. 14, 1924 (dec.); children-James Kirk, Marijo (Mrs. Richard Rianda); m. 2d, Margaret B. Aven, Sept. 6, 1969. Tchr. pub. schs., supr. lang. arts, Boulder, Colo., 1926-40; with West Tex. State U., 1940—, successively dean lower div., prof. English, chmn. div. humanities, 1950—. Mem. Coll. Tchrs. English Tex., Phi Delta Kappa, Alpha Kappa Delta. Presbyn. Home: 3403-B Jane Dr Amarillo TX 79109

KNOTT, FREDERICK, playwright; s. Cyril Wakefield and Margaret Caroline (Paull) K.; M.A. with honors, Cambridge (Eng.) U.; m. Ann Hillary, Nov. 10, 1953; 1 son. Served to maj., Royal Arty., 1939-46. Recipient Edgar Allen Poe awards for plays Dial M for Murder, 1952, Write Me a Murder, 1961, Mem. Dramatists Guild.

KNOTT, HENRY JOSEPH, constrn. co. exec.; b. Balt., Nov. 2, 1906; s. Henry A. and Martha (Doyle) K.; student Loyola Coll., Balt.; LL.D., Coll. Notre Dame of Md., 1963, Mt. St. Mary's Coll., Emmitsburg, Md., 1971; m. Marion I. Burk, Aug. 2, 1928; children—Mary Patricia (Mrs. J. Walter Smith), Marion Isabel (Mrs. Frederick S. Beckman), Martha Alice (Mrs. Robert Emmet Voelkel, Jr.), Margaret Celeste (Mrs. John Henry Riehl, III), Henry Joseph, Catherine Philomen (Mrs. Richard A. Weis), Rose Marie (Mrs.

George A. Porter), Sara Lindsey (Mrs. Edward B. Harris, Jr.), Francis Xavier, James Frederick, Mary Stuart. With Arundel Corp., Balt., chmn. bd., pres., 1967—, also dir.; dir., mem. exec. com. Md. Nat. Bank; dir. Easco Corp. Mem. bldg. com., trustee Johns Hopkins Hosp.; mem. appellate jud. selection commn. 2d Appellate Circuit Md.; mem. Balt. Archdiocesan Ins. Com., Cardinal's Finance Com. Bd. govs. Bon Secours Hosp.; trustee Good Samaritan Hosp., Notre Dame Coll., Loyola-Notre Dame Joint Library, United Fund Md.; mem. joint bd. trustees Children's Rehab. Inst., Johns Hopkins U. and Hosp. Named comdr. Knights St. Gregory. Club: Balt. Engineers. Home: 6101 Gentry Lane Baltimore MD 21210 Office: 501 St Paul Pl Baltimore MD 21202 also 2 W University Pl Baltimore MD 21210

KNOTT, LAURENCE THOMPSON, ret. newspaper exec.; b. Jamaica Plain, Mass., Aug. 14, 1904; s. James Edward and Ellen (Thompson) K.; student Boston U., 1922-23; m. Bethany Crowe, Feb. 14, 1931; children—Susanne (Mrs. Panayotis Stylianos Komonthouros) (dec.), Laurence Thompson. Employee, Boston Advertiser, 1923, Boston Herald Traveler 1924-25, Chgo. Tribune, 1926-43, asst. advt. dir. Chgo Sun, 1943-46, advt. dir., 1946-47; asst. advt. dir. Chgo. Sun-Times, 1947-50, advt. dir. 1950-54, v.p., advt. dir. newspaper div. Field Enterprises, Inc., 1954-63, v.p., gen. sales mgr. Chgo. Sun-Times and Chgo. Daily News, 1963—, mem. newspaper div. exec. com. and mgmt. bd., chmn. marketing bd.; mem. conf. bd. This Week mag. Mem. Am. Newspaper Pubs. Assn. (past chmn. plans com.; dir; Bur. Advt.), Internat. Newspaper Advt. Execs. Assn. (past pres., hon. life mem., past chmn. advt. agy. relations com.), Alpha Delta Sigma. Clubs: Tavern, Mid-America (Chgo.) Home: 4242 Cresta Av Santa Barbara CA 93110

KNOTTS, DON, actor; b. Morgantown, W.Va., July 21, 1924; s. William Jesse and Elsie (Moore) K.; B.A., W.Va. U., 1948; m. Kathryn Metz, Dec. 27, 1947; children—Karen Ann, Thomas Allen. Appeared on Broadway in No Time for Sergeants, 1955-56; with Steve Allen television shows, 1956-60; role of Barney Fife in Andy Griffith television series, 1960—; starred in movies the Ghost and Mr. Chicken, 1966; appeared on TV as star of Don Knotts Show, 1970. Recipient Emmy award for outstanding performance in supporting role, 1961, 62, 63. Home: 760 N LaCienega Blvd Los Angeles CA 90069

KNOTTS, GLENN RICHARD, assn. exec.; b. E. Chicago, Ind., May 16, 1934; s. V. Raymond and Opal Ione (Alexander) K.; B.S., Purdue U., 1956, M.S., 1960, Ph.D., 1968; M.S., Ind. U., 1964. Mem. profl. staff Baptist Meml. Hosp., San Antonio, 1957-60; instr. chemistry San Antonio Coll., 1958-60; admintrv. A.M.A., 1960-61, research asso., 1961-62, dir. advt. evaluation, div. sci. activites, 1963-69; vis. prof. health edn. Madison (Va.) Coll., summer 1965, Union (Ky.) Coll., summers 1965, 66, 69, Utah State U., 1965; vis. lectr., con. health Ind. U., 1965—; vis. distinguished prof. health sci. Kent State U., 1969—; vis. prof. Pahlavi U. Med. Sch., Iran, summer 1970; exec. dir. Am. Sch. Health Assn., 1969—. Cons. in field, 1964—; mem. sci. cons. bd. Assn. de Saude Escolar, Brazil, 1969—; exec. com. Internat. Union Sch. and Univ. Health and Medicine,1969—. Served with AUS, 1956-58. Fellow Am. Pub. Health Assn., Am. Sch. Health Assn., Am. Inst. Chemists; mem. Am. Pharm. Assn., Am. Chem. Assn., Am. Assn. U. Profs., A.A.A.S., Am. Acad. Pharm. Scis., A.M.A., Royal Soc. Health, Purdue U., Ind. U. alumni assns, Sigma Xi, Rho Chi, Sigma Delta Chi, Phi Delta Kappa, Kappa Psi. Republican. Presbyn. Clubs: Purdue Chemists; Purdue, Press, Triangle, Internat. Whitehall (Chgo.). Co- author textbooks, film strips. Contbr. articles profl. jours. Home: 2010 Hastings Dr Kent OH 44240 Office: 107 S Depeyster St Kent OH 44240

KNOTTS, WALTER E., educator; B.A., U. B.C. (Can.); M.A., Ph.D., Harvard. Prof., chmn. dept. English, State U. N.Y. at Albany. Office: Dept English State U NY at Albany Albany NY 12203*

KNOWLAND, JOSEPH WILLIAM, newspaper exec.; b. Oakland, Cal., July 26, 1930; s. William Fife and Helen (Herrick) K.; B.A., U. Cal. at Berkeley, 1953; m. Dolores Faye Beall, June 24, 1950; children—Deanne Christian, William Fife, Rebecca Beall. With Oakland Tribune, 1953—, reporter, 1955-60, asst. city editor, 1960-61, asst. editor, 1961, asst. gen. mgr., 1962-66, asst. pub., 1966-69, gen. mgr., 1969—; v.p. Tribune Pub. Co.; v.p., sec. Tribune Bldg Co.; v.p. Franklin Investment Co. Mem. exec. com. State Bar Cal. U. Cal. Law Ednl. Project, 1970-71. Trustee Mills Coll., Oakland, 1968-69, Cal. Coll. Arts and Crafts, Oakland, 1968-69. Mem. Oakland C. of C. (dir. 1968-69), Sigma Alpha Epsilon. Club: The Bohemian (San Francisco). Office: 401 13th St Oakland CA 94512

KNOWLAND, WILLIAM FIFE, publisher; b. Alameda, Cal., June 26, 1908; s. Joseph Russell and Ellie (Fife) K.; A.B., U. Cal., 1929; m. Helen Davis Herrick, Dec. 31, 1926; children-Emelyn Jewett, Joseph William, Helen Estelle. Pres. Franklin Investment Co.; pub., editor Oakland Tribune; pres., pub. Tribune Pub. Co. Mem. Cal. Assembly, 1933-35, Senate, 1935-39. Mem. Republican Nat. Com., 1938, chmn. Rep. Exec. Com., 1941-42. Served in AUS, 1942-45; in service overseas when apptd. U.S. senator to fill the unexpired term of Hiram W. Johnson, dec., elected full term, 1946, re-elected 1952, majority leader, 1953-54, minority leader, 1955-58; mem. U.S. delegation to 11th session UN Gen. Assembly. Mem. U.S., Cal. State (dir.), Oakland (dir.) chambers commerce, Zeta Psi, Sigma Delta Chi. Republican. Methodist. Mason (33, Shriner), Native Sons of the Golden West, Eagles, Moose, Elk. Clubs: Bohemian (San Francisco); Athenian-Nile (Oakland). Home: 290 Lee St Oakland CA 94610 Office: Tribune Bldg Oakland CA 94612

KNOWLER, LLOYD A., educator; b. Hedrick, Ia., Jan. 30, 1908; s. C.C. and Louise (Wood) K.; B.A., State U. Ia., 1932, M.S., 1934, Ph.D., 1937; m. Faith M. Stamler, June 30, 1935; children—Mary Louise, William C. Grad. asst. math., astronomy State U. Ia., 1932-34, 1935-37, mem. faculty 1939—, prof., chmn. dept. math. and astronomy, 1946-59, prof. dept. math., 1959- 65, prof. div. math. scis., 1965—; statis. quality control adviser with ICA, Bur. Census in India, 1960-61; inst. math. Hunter Coll., 1937-39; staff short courses, quality control by statis. methods Northwestern U., 1945, Purdue U., 1946-59, 62-65, 68-71, U. Ill., 1948- 59, 62-65, 68-71, U. Colo., 1950, 51, 53, U. Cal. at Los Angeles, 1956-59, 62-64, U. Mich., 1966; actuary State Old Age Assistance Commn. Ia., 1934-35; cons. actuary, cons. statis. quality control indsl. firms, govt. agys. Bd. dirs. Ia. Med. Service, 1966—, exec. com., 1968—. Treas., Clk. Town of University Heights, 1951-53, clk., 1954-60, 62—. Fellow Am. Soc. Quality Control (mem. editorial bd. 1946-54, 60- 65; chmn. examining com., 1949-52; Shewhart medal co., 1950-53, 1956-59, chmn. 1964-66;, reporter panel 1967—, bio-med. steering com. 1967—, publs. mgmt. bd. 1968—; recipient Shewhart medal 1962); mem. Operations Research, Am. Math Soc., Math. Assn. Am. (chmn. Ia. sect. 1952- 53), Operations Research Assn. Quad Cities, Midwestern Actuarial Forum, Am. Acad. Actuaries, Inst. of Math. Statistics, Am. Soc. of Engring. Edn., Biometric Soc., Am. Assn. U. Profs. (sec., treas. U. Ia. 1946-47, pres., 1952-53), Am. Statis. Assn., Am. Pension Conf., Central Assn. Sci., Math. Tchrs., Ia. Acad. Sci., Am. Soc. Engring. Edn., Soc. Advancement Edn., Phi Beta Kappa (sec., treas. Hunter Coll., 1938-39, pres. U. Ia., 1948-49), Sigma Xi, Phi Mu Upsilon, Theta Xi. Rotarian. Club: Triangle (Iowa City). Co-author: Basic Skills in Mathematics, 1952; Quality Control by Statistical Methods, 1969. Contbr. articles actuarial sci. and statistics, profl. jours., reports, pamphlets, manuals. Home: 207 Golfview Av Iowa City IA 52240

KNOWLES, ALISON, artist; b. N.Y., 1933; student Middlebury Coll., Pratt Inst., Manhattan Sch. Printing. Executed large canvas Mother using massive blow-ups and enlargements, 1959-60, series of canvases using silkscreen, photog. and chem. transfers, 1960, environmental printed works on plastic, 1961, 62; active in starting Fluxus Movement in Europe, 1962; directed own Happenings, performed in those of William Meyer, Dick Higgins, Emmet Williams, George Brecht, Nam June Paik, others; began T Dictionary, also The Big Book, 1964; exhibited one man shows Nonagon Gallery, N.Y.C., 1962, Phase 11 Gallery, Toronto, Ont., Can., 1967; exhibited group shows including Studio Spichernstrasse 28, Cologne, Germany, 1962, Rolf Nelson Gallery, Los Angeles, 1963, Fluxhall, N.Y.C., 1964, Phila. Mus. Art, 1966, Something Else Gallery, N.Y.C., 1966. Stedelijk van Abbemuseum, Eindhoven, Netherlands, 1967, Chgo. Mus. Contemporary Art, 1967. Home: New York City NY *

KNOWLES, ASA SMALIDGE, univ. pres.; b. Northeast Harbor, Me., Jan. 15, 1909; s. Jerome Henry and Lilla Belle (Smallidge) K.: student Thayer Acad., South Braintree, Mass. 1925-26; A.B., Bowdoin Coll., 1930, LL.D., 1951; A.M., Boston U., 1935; LL.D., Northeastern U., 1957, Emerson Coll., 1960, U. Toledo, 1960; Litt.D., Western New Eng. Coll., 1961; Sc.D., New Eng. Coll. Pharmacy, 1962, Lowell Tech. Inst., 1966; D.B.A., U. R.I., 1967; Sc.D. Bus. Edn., Bryant Coll., 1967; LL.D., Brandeis U., 1968; m. Edna Irene Worsnop, Mar. 24, 1930; children-Asa Worsnop, Margaret Anne. Prof. indsl. engring., head dept. Northeastern U., Boston, 1936-39, dean Coll. Bus Adminstrn., dir. Bur. Bus. Research and prof. indsl. adminstrn., 1939-42; dean Sch. Bus. Adminstrn., dir. div. of gem. coll. extension and prof. indsl. adminstrn., U. of R.I., 1942-46; pres. Asso. Colls. Upper N.Y., 1946-48, v.p. devel. Cornell U., Ithaca, N.Y., 1948-51; pres. U. Toledo, 1951-58; pres. Northeastern U., 1959-. Corporator Provident Instn. Savs.; dir. Nat. Shawmut Bank Boston, Shawmut Assn., Inc. Mem. joint com. on grad. work Fedn. Regional Com. Higher Edn., 1967-70, chmn., 1970—. Dir. Boston Council Navy League, 1969-. Army adv. panel on R.O.T.C., 1961-. Recipient Internat. Order DeMolay, Legion of Honor; U.S. Army Outstanding Civilian Service medal, 1962; Albert S. Bard award, Chi Psi, 1964; Distinguished Civilian Service medal, citation, 1966; Outstanding Son of Me. award, 1970. Fellow Am. Acad. Arts and Scis.; mem. Am. Inst. Indsl. Engrs. (hon.), New Eng. Assn. Colls. and Secondary Schs. (v.p. 1969—), Assn. Am. Colls. (com. coll. adminstrn.), Am. Council Edn. (com. on higher adult edn.), Pershing Rifles (hon.), Scabbard and Blade (hon.), Tau Blue Key. Beta Pi, Beta Gamma Sigma, Chi Psi, Alpha Kappa Psi, Phi Kappa Phi, Pi Delta Phi, Delta Sigma Teta (hon.), Alpha Pi Mu (hon.). Republican. Episcopalian. Author: Job Evaluation for Hourly and Salaried Workers, 1943. Co-author: Industrial Management, 1944; Production Control 1944; Management of Manpower. Editor-in-chief: Handbook of College and University Administration, 1970. Contbg. editor Prodn. Handbook. Home: 388 Beacon St Boston MA 02115

KNOWLES, EDWARD F., architect; b. Bklyn., Aug. 12, 1929; s. Frank W. and Isabel (Leudesdorff) K.; B. Arch., Pratt Inst., 1951; m. Barbara Lee Dupree, Mar. 14, 1953; children—Christopher, Sarah, Mary, Emily. Pvt. practice architecture, N.Y.C., 1960—; partner Macfadyen & Knowles, architects, N.Y.C., 1965-68. Tchr., Pratt Inst., 1959-60, Cooper Union, 1960-64, Columbia, 1965-66; cons. N.Y. State Council Arts, Bklyn. Inst., Inst. Man and Sci., San Francisco Arts Resources Devel. Com., Richmond Found., N.Y.C. Dept. Parks Mem. A.I.A., N.Y. Soc. Architects. Prin. works include: IBM World Trade Corp., Wolf Trap Farm Park, City Center Music and Drama, Bklyn. Acad. Music, N.Y.C. Bd. Higher Edn., Manhattan Sch. Music, Litton Ednl. Pub. Co., New Boston City Hall. Office: 130 W 56th St New York City NY 10019

KNOWLES, EDWARD GILLETT, lawyer; b. Denver, Nov. 13, 1892; s. Charles Nelson and Florence (Reily) K.; A.B.; U. Colo., 1914, LL.B., 1916; m. Helen Montgomery Dorsey, Sept. 28, 1920; childrenHelen Dorsey (Mrs. Thomas E. Buchanan, Jr.), Clayton Dorsey. Admitted to Colo. bar, since practiced in Denver; now mem. firm Knowles, Hooper & Molen; gen. atty. Colo. Union Pacific R.R. Co., 1937- -. Del. to Internat. Bar Assn. conf.. Salzburg, 1960, chmn. com. scope and corr., 1960; chmn. nat. conf. bar pres. Am. Bar Assn., 1960. Served to 1st cav. U.S. Army, 1917- 19. Mem. Am. (mem. ho. dels. 1955-63, bd. govs. 1963-66), Colo. (pres. 1951-51), Denver (pres. 1948-49) bar assns., Beta Theta Phi, Phi Delta Phi. Clubs: Denver, Denver Country, University (Denver). Home: 426 Gilpin St Denver CO Office: Denver Club Bldg Denver CO

KNOWLES, ENOCH O., Jr., savs. and loan exec.; b. Weleetka, Okla., Feb. 7, 1920; s. Enoch O. and Margaret (Kelly) K.; student pub. schs.; m. Ada Powell, Apr. 14, 1943; childrenBetty Ann, Enoch O. III, Robert O. Clk., Brown Trading Co., Weleetka, 1938-41; investigator, dept. head Retail Credit Co., Tulsa, 1946-48; chief mortgage credit examiner FHA, Tulsa, 1949-52; resident asst. mgr. Farm & Home Savs., Kansas City, Mo., 1952-56, v.p., resident mgr., 1957-59; pres. Peoples Savs. Assn., Toledo, 1960—, People's Service Co., Inc. Trustee Community Improvement Corp., Toledo, Toledo Growth Council; bd. dirs. Toledo Community Chest, Girl Scouts of Maumee Valley, O., Community Planning Council, Toledo Small Bus. Assn. Served to capt. AUS, 1942-46. Mem. U.S., Ohio savs. & loan leagues (exec. com.), Savs. Instns. Marketing Soc. Am. (trustee), Toledo Real Estate Bd., Toledo Home Builders, Toledo C. of C . (trustee 1966-67). Club: Toledo. Home: 6261 Sylvania Av Toledo OH 43623 Office: Peoples Savs Assn 337 Huron St Toledo OH 43604

KNOWLES, HAROLD LORAINE, educator: b. Chgo., Aug. 21, 1905; s. Frank Elwood and Josie (Gage) K.; A.B., Phillips U., 1926; Ph.D., U. Kan., 1932; m. Dorothy Ruth White, Sept. 9, 1931; 1 dau., Carolyn (Mrs. Lee E. Eubank). Grad. asst., fellow physics U. Kan., 1926-31; instr. physics U. Fla., 1931-36, asst. prof., 1937-42, asso. prof., 1943, 46-48, research engr. Fla. Engring. and Indsl. Expt. Sta., 1944-45, prof. physics, 1949-52, prof. phys. scis., 1953—, head dept., 1955-67. Mem. Am. Assn. U. Profs., Am. Phys. Soc., Am. Assn. Physics Tchrs., Assn. Higher Edn., Phi Beta Kappa, Sigma Xi. Author: (with L. W. Gaddum) Our Physical Environment, 1953; (with G. C. Omer, B. W. Mundy, W.H. Yoho) Physical Science: Men and Concepts, 1962. Home: 1424 NW 12th Rd Gainesville FL 32601

KNOWLES, HUGH SHALER, cons. engr.; b. Hynes, Ia., Sept. 23, 1904; s. Harry Holmes and Margaret (Heacock) K.; student Ala. Polytech. Inst., 1920-21; A.B., Columbia, 1928; postgrad., U. Chgo., 1930-34; m. Josephine Knotts, Aug. 5, 1928; children—James, Margaret (Mrs. Schink), Katherine (Mrs. Strasberg). Radio operator on various s.s. U.S. Mcht. Marine, 1921-23; dept. editor Popular Radio, N.Y.C., 1924-25; asso. radio editor N.Y. Herald Tribune, 1927-28; engr. Hammarlund Mfg. Co., N.Y.C., 1927-28; gen. mgr. parts div. Silver Marshall, Inc., Chgo. 1928-30; chief engr. Jensen Mfg. Co., Chgo., 1931-50, v.p., 1940-50; lectr. in grad. physics, U. Chgo., 1935-36; cons. engr. 1936—; pres., dir. research Indsl. Research Products, Inc., Elk Grove Vill., Ill., 1946—, Knowles Electronics, Inc., Franklin Park, Ill., 1954—; pres. Knotts Edward Corp., Franklin Park, 1965—, Synchro-Start Products, Inc., 1968—, Financial Corp. Ill., 1969—; chmn. bd. Knowles Electronics, Ltd., Burgess Hill, Eng., 1961—; Mem. U.S. delegation Electrotech. Commn. TC29, 1953, 54, head del., 1955, 57; head del. U.S. Internat. Orgn. for Standardization TC43, 1955. Mem. Acoustical Standards Bd., 1958-60. Fellow I.E.E.E. (nat. chmn. PGA 1960-61, chmn. standards com. on electroacoustics, 1938-41), Acoustical Soc. Am. (exec. council 1942- 44, pres. 1945-47), Chgo. Radio Engrs. (past pres.) Radio Mfrs. Assn. (chmn. standards com. on sound equipment 1931-41, chmn. sound equipment sect., 1945-47), NRC (mem. exec. com. sci. div. 1950-51), Research and Devel. Bd. Dept. Def., (chmn. acoustics panel, 1948-50), Am. Inst. Physics, (gov. bd. 1951-58: mem. exec. com., 1954-58), Nat. Acad. Engrs., Audio Engring. Soc. (pres. 1965-66) Conglist. Club: River Forest Tennis. Author: Acoustics, Loudspeakers, Telephone Receivers and Microphones, Wiley Engineering Handbook Series, 1936 and 1950; Loudspeakers and Room Acoustics, Henney's Radio Engineering Handbook, 1941, 50, 59. Contbr. numerous tech. articles. Inventor in field of acoustics and electronics. Home: 1119 Duncan Av Elgin IL 60120

KNOWLES, JACK OLIVER, veterinarian; b. Cheyenne, Wyo., June 12, 1916; s. Adam T. and Mable B. (Behymer) K.; V.M.D., U. Pa., 1938; m. Connie Fisher, Nov. 28, 1939; children—Donna L., Jane A. Owner, Knowles Animal Clinic, Miami, Fla., 1946—; research asso. prof. U. Miami Sch. Medicine, 1955—. Served with Vet. Corps AUS, World War II. Recipient Mills award for outstanding contbn. to vet. medicine U. Ga. chpt. Alpha Psi, 1971. Mem. Am. Vet. Med. Assn. (past pres.). Mason (32), Rotarian (pres. Miami 1970-71). Clubs: Coral Gables Country; Riviera Country; Coral Gables Century (pres.). Contbr. numerous articles, also chpt. in books. Editor: Canine Filariasis. Home: 1240 Mariola Ct Coral Gables FL Office: 1000 N W 27th Av Miami FL 33125

KNOWLES, JOHN, author; b. Fairmont, W.Va., Sept. 16, 1926; s. James Myron and Mary Beatrice (Shea) K.; grad. Phillips Exeter Acad., 1945; B.A., Yale, 1949. Reporter, Hartford (Conn.) Courant, 1950-52; free-lance writer, 1952-56; asso. editor Holiday mag., 1956-60. Author: (novel) A Separate Peace (Rosenthal award Nat. Inst. Arts and Letters 1960, William Faulkner Found. award 1960), 1960; Morning in Antibes, 1962; Double Vision, 1964; Phineas System, 1968; Paragon, 1970; also articles, short stories. Home: 575 Madison Av New York City NY 10022

KNOWLES, JOHN HILTON, physician, med. adminstr.; b. Chgo., May 23, 1926; s. James and Jean Laurence (Turnbull) K.; A.B., Harvard, 1947; M.D. cum laude, Washington U., 1951; LL.D., (hon.), Northeastern U., 1969, Babson Coll., 1971; Sc.D. (hon.), Washington U., St. Louis, 1970, Hahnemann Med. Coll., 1971; D.C.L. (hon.), Union Coll., 1970, D.H.L., Ithaca Coll., 1971; m. Edith Morris LaCroix, June 13, 1953; children—Edith LaCroix, John Charles Paine, James Turnbull, Jean Laurence, Robert Munro. Intern medicine Mass. Gen. Hosp., 1951-52, asst. resident medicine, 1952-53, resident medicine, 1955-56, chief resident medicine, 1958-59, asst. medicine, chief pulmonary disease unit, 1959-61, asst. physician, dir. med. affairs, 1961-62, asso. physician, 1962-64, gen. dir., 1962—, physician, 1964—; teaching fellow medicine Harvard Med. Sch., 1952-53, asst. medicine, 1958-59, instr. medicine, 1959-60, asso. in medicine, 1960-63, lectr. medicine, 1963—, prof. medicine, 1969—; USPHS postdoctoral fellow dept. physiology U. Rochester Med. Sch., also dept. physiology U. Buffalo, 1956-57. Limited partner Paine, Webber, Jackson & Curtis. Mem. Pub. Health Council Commonwealth Mass. Mem. gen. assembly Boston YMCA. Trustee Mus. Sci., Belmont Hill Sch., James Jackson Putnam Children's Center, Edn. Devel. Corp., Dept. Health and Hosps. City Boston; dir. Boston Garden Arena Corp., Boston Patriots, Boston Bruins, Chase Frontier Fund. Served at lt. M.C., USNR, 1953-55. Fellow A.C.P., Am. Acad. Arts and Scis.; mem. Am. Pub. Health Assn., Assn. Am. Med. Colls., Am. Hosp. Assn., Soc. Med. Adminstrs., A.M.A., Am. Fedn. Clin. Research, Nat. Acad. Scis. Inst. Medicine, Harvard Alumni Assn. (dir.), Boston Library Soc., Kappa Pi Eta, Alpha Omega Alpha. Clubs: Commercial-Merchants, Tavern, Tennis and Racquet, Harvard, Aesculapian (Boston); Country (Brookline); Myopia Hunt (Mass.); Somerset. Author: Respiratory Physiology and its Clinical Application, 1959. Editor: Hospitals, Doctors and Public Interest, 1965; The Teaching HOspital, 1966; Views of Medical Education and Medical Care, 1967. Home: 28 Fernwood Rd Chestnut Hill MA 02167 Office: Mass Gen Hosp Boston MA 02114

KNOWLES, PATRIC, actor; b. Yorkshire, Eng., Nov. 11, 1911; s. Laurence and Nell (Mitchell) K.; student various schools at Oxford U., 1916-26; m. Gladys Enid Percival, Oct. 5, 1935; children—Michael Patric, Antonia Wendy. Came to U.S., 1936. Actor, Am. debut in Charge of the Light Brigade, 1936; motion picture credits include Honours Easy, Mister Hobo, Two's Company, Give Me Your Heart, It's Love I'm After, Expensive Husbands, Adventures of Robin Hood, How Green Was My Valley, Forever and a Day, Of Human Bondage, Bride Wore Boots, Ivy, Kitty, Monsieur Beaucaire, Dream Girl, Big Steal, Quebec, Three Came Home, Mutiny, Tarzan's Savage Fury, Jamaica Run, Flame of Calcutta, World Ramsom, Khyber Patrol, No Man's Woman, Band of Angels, Auntie Mame, The Way West, In Enemy Country, The Devil's Brigade, Chisum. Hon. mayor City of Tarzana, Cal., 1952-54. Served with R.C.A.F., 1941-43, USAAF, 1943-45. Mason. Club: Woodland Hills (Cal.) Country (pres. 1953). Author: Even Steven, 1961.‡

KNOWLES, RICHARD THOMAS, army officer; b. Chgo., Dec. 20, 1916; s. John T. and Signe (Almcrantz) K.; student U. Ill., 1939-42, Command and Gen. Staff Coll., 1952, Armed Forces Staff Coll., 1956, U.S. Army War Coll., 1959; m. Barbara Jane Smaus, May 24, 1942; children-Diane T. (Mrs. James Buchwald), Katherine T. (Mrs. Gordon Lidbetter), Rebecca J. (Mrs. Stanley Crosby), Richard J. Commd. 2d lt. U.S. Army, 1942; advanced through grades to lt. gen., 1970; exec., bn. comdr. 96th F.S. Bn., Far East Command, 1950-51; student, then instr. Command and Gen. Staff Coll., Ft. Leavenworth, Kan., 1951-55; chief budget and plans br. Office Dep. Chief of Staff, Personnel, U.S. Army, Washington, 1956-58, chief Establishments Bur., Hdqrs. U.S. Army Element, SHAPE, 1959-60, mil. asst. Office CChief of Staff, Hdqrs. SHAPE, 1960-62; comdg. officer 3d U.S. Army Missile Command, Ft. Bragg, N.C., 1962-63; div. arty. comdr., asst. div. comdr. 11th Air Assault Div., Ft. Benning, Ga., 1963-65; asst. div. comdr. 1st Cav. Div., (airmobile), Ft. Benning, 1965-66; chief of staff II Field Force, Vietnam, 1966; comdg. gen. 196th Light Inf. Brigade, Vietnam, 1966-67; comdr. gen. Task Force Oregon, Vietnam, 1967; asst. dep. chief of staff for mil. operations U.S. Army, Washington, 1968-70; asst. to chmn. Joint Chiefs of Staff, Washington, 1970—. Decorated D.S.M. with oak leaf cluster, Silver Star medal, Legion of Merit with bronze oak leaf cluster, D.F.C.. with bronze oak leaf cluster, Bronze Star medal with V device and oak leaf cluster, Air medal with 25 oak leaf clusters, Vietnam Nat. Order 5th Class, Vietnam Gallantry Cross with 2 bronze palms, Vietnam Armed Forces Honor medal 1st Class. Office: Pentagon Washington DC 20301

KNOWLES, WARREN PERLEY, former gov. Wis., financial corp. exec; b. River Falls, Wis., Aug. 19, 1908; s. Warren P. and Anna Theresa (Deneen) K.; B.A., carleton Coll., 1930; LL.B., U. Wis., 1933; LL.D., Marquette U., 1965, Northland Coll., 1965, Ripon Coll.;

L.H.D., Carroll Coll.; hon. degree Milton Coll., 1970, Lakeland Coll.; m. Dorothy C. Guidry, Apr. 17, 1943 (div. 1968). Admitted to Wis. bar, 1933, partner Deor & Knowles, New Richmond, 1935—; admitted to practice ICC, U.S. Treas. Dept.; lt. gov. of Wis., 1954-63; gov. of Wis., 1964-71. Chmn. bd. Inland Financial Corp., Milw., 1971—; vice chmn. bd. Heritage Bank of Whitefish Bay, Heritage Bank of Milw., 1971—; dir. Newton & Co., Goetz-Haessler-James Agy., Inc. Mem. Pres.'s Commn. on Sch. Finance, 1971—; chmn. Wis. Land Use and Devel. Soc. Mem. Wis. Senate 1940-53, majority floor leader, 1943-53, chmn. legislative council, 1947, jud. council, 1951-53. Del. Republican Nat. Conv., 1948, 56, 60, 64, 68, chmn. Wis. delegation, 1968. Bd. dirs. Greater Milw. Commn.; trustee Mt. Mary Coll., Milw. Boys Club. Served as lt. USNR, 1942-46. Mem. Met. Milw. C. of C., Mil. Order World Wars, Am., Wis., St. Croix-Pierce County bar assns., Assn. Ins. Counsel, Wis. Alumni Assn. (pres. 1952-53), Nat. Conf. Christians and Jews (chmn. Wis. chpt., 1957- 58), V.F.W., Am. Legion, 40 and 8. Republican. Elk. Clubs: Milwaukee Athletic, Milwaukee, University; Madison (Wis.). Office: 435 E Mason St P O Box 339 Milwaukee WI 53201

KNOWLTON, EDGAR COLBY, Jr., educator; b. Delaware, O., Sept. 14, 1921; s. Edgar Colby and Mildred (Hunt) K.; A.B., Harvard, 1941, A.M., 1942; Ph.D., Stanford, 1959. Instr., U. Hawaii, Honolulu, 1948-53, asst. prof. European langs., 1954-59, asso. prof., 1959-65, prof., 1965—; vis. prof. linguistics U. Malaya, Kuala Lumpur, 1962-64; music reviewer Honolulu Advertiser, 1957-61. Mem. program com. Hawaiian Hist. Soc., 1961-62. Served with USNR, 1944-46, 51-52. Mem. Siam Soc., Am. Assn. Tchrs. Spanish and Portuguese, Linguistic Soc. Am., Modern Lang. Assn., Royal Asiatic Soc. (Malaysian br.), Am. Assn. Tchrs. Spanish (pres. Hawaii chpt. 1964-65) Phi Beta Kappa, Sigma Delta Pi. Translator of Francisco de Sa de Meneses, The Conquest of Malacca, 1970. Contbr. articles profl. jours. Home: 1026 Kalo Pl Honolulu HI 96814

KNOWLTON, HUGH, investment banker; b. Brookline, Mass., July 27, 1893; s. Daniel S. and Alice M. (Joyce) K.; A.B., Yale, 1914; LL.B., Harvard, 1921; m. Christine Stanley, Dec. 6, 1917; children—Mary Christine (Mrs. John Sulzer), Hugh, Stanley, Winthrop; m. 2d, Delores Anderson, Aug. 14, 1956. Admitted to N.Y. bar, 1921; practiced with Appleton, Butler & Rice (now Appleton, Rice & Perrin), N.Y., 1921-26; v.p. Internat. Acceptance Bank, Inc., 1926-29; v.p. Internat. Manhattan Co., Inc., 1929- 31; partner Kuhn, Loeb & Co., 1933-42, 46—; govt. service in charge of communications div. U.S. Comml. Co., 1942-43; dir. research and planning Eastern Air Lines, Inc., 1943-45, dir., 1938-63. Served to 1st lt. F.A., U.S. Army, AEF, World War I. Bd. dirs., past pres. Jackson Lab.; bd. dirs. N.Y. Travelers Aid Soc. Asso. mem. Am. Inst. Aeros. and Astronautics. Clubs: Down Town Association, Racquet and Tennis, University (N.Y.C.). Author: Air Transportation in the United States, 1942. Home: Palisades NY 10964 Office: 40 Wall St New York City NY 10005

KNOWLTON, HUGH, Jr., bus. cons.; b. N.Y.C., Feb. 1, 1923; s. Hugh and Christine (Stanley) K.; A.B., Yale, 1945; LL.B., Harvard, 1949. Dir. Addressograph Multigraph Corp., Internat. Flavors & Fragrances, Schieffelin & Co., Richton Internat. Corp.; adv. bd. Chem. Bank; trustee Providence Loan Soc. N.Y. Trustee Lenox Hill Hosp., Groton Sch. (Mass.). Mem. Aspen Soc. Fellows, Am. Soc. Internat. Law, State Bar Cal., Bar Assn. San Francisco, Nat. Council Fgn. Policy Assn., French C. of C. in U.S. Clubs: Bond, Recess, Economic, N.Y. Athletic, University (N.Y.C.); Nat. Golf Links Am. (Southampton, L.I); Blind Brook (Port Chester, N.Y.) Address: 1345 Av of the Americas New York City NY 10019

KNOWLTON, JOHN MACLEAR, pharm. co. exec.; b. Peoria, Ill., Oct. 20, 1912; s. James Albert and Ethel May (Maclear) K.; A.B., Grinnell (Ia.) Coll., 1934; J.D., U. Chgo., 1936; m. Lucy Helen Harnden, Oct. 11, 1940; children—Lucy Alma (Mrs Gary Hovis), Eva May, Jacqueline. Admitted to Ill. bar, 1937; with firm Righeimer & Righeimer, Chgo., 1938-49; with Baxter Labs., Inc., Morton Grove, Ill., 1949—, sec., gen. counsel, 1949—, v.p., 1962—, also dir. Served to lt. comdr. USNR, 1942-46. Mem. Am., Chgo. bar assns., Am. Soc. Corp. Secs. Home: 656 Ardsley Rd Winnetka IL 60093 Office: 6301 Lincoln Av Morton Grove IL 60053

KNOWLTON, PERRY HOSMER, literary agy. exec.; b. N.Y.C., Mar. 25, 1927; s. Henry Randolph and Gladys (Perry) K.; grad. Philips Exeter Acad., N.H., 1945; A.B., Princeton, 1949; m. Louisa Carver Tripp, Sept. 24, 1954; (div.); children—Timothy Frederick, Elizabeth Perry, Virginia Tripp. Asst. dir. admissions Lawrenceville (N.J.) Sch., 1950-53; editor Charles Scribners Sons, N.Y., 1953-60; v.p. Curtis Brown, Ltd., N.Y.C., 1960-68, pres., 1968—; v.p. Collins-Knowlton-Wing, N.Y.C., 1965-68, pres., 1968—. Vice pres., bd. dirs. Friends of the Earth, 1969—. Served with AUS, 1945-47. Mem. Soc. Authors' Reps. (head lit. br. 1969—). Clubs: Players, Coffee House (N.Y.C.); Royal Ocean Racing (London). Home: 29 Bethune St New York City NY 10014 also Calhoun Hill Rd Andes NY 13713 Office: 60 E 56th St New York City NY 10022

KNOWLTON, WILLIAM ALLEN, army officer; b. Weston, Mass., June 19, 1920; s. Frank Warren and Isabelle (Riese) K.; B.S., U.S. Mil. Acad., 1943; M.A., Columbia U., 1957; grad. Nat. War Coll., 1960; m. Marjorie Adams Downey, Nov. 27, 1943; children—William Allen, Davis Downey, Timothy Riese, Hollister. Commd. 2d lt., U.S. Army, 1943, advanced through grades to Lt. gen., 1971; assigned 7th Armored Div., World War II, Army General Staff, 1947-49, SHAPE, France, 1951-54; asso. prof. social scis. U.S. Mil. Acad., 1955-58; bn. comdr. 3d Armored Cav. Regt., 1958-59; mil. attache, Tunisia, 1961-63; brig. comdr., Ft. Knox, Ky., 1963-64; Office Chief Staff, U.S. Army, 1964-65; mil. asst. to spl. asst. to sec. and dep. sec. def. Office Sec. Def., 1965-66; sec. Joint Staff, dir. pacification support, also dep. asst. chief staff for civil operations and revolutionary devel. support U.S. Mil. Assistance Comd., Vietnam, 1966-67; asst. div. comdr. 9th Inf. Div., Vietnam, 1968; sec. gen. staff Office Chief Staff U.S. Army, 1968-70; supt. U.S. Mil. Acad., 1970—. Decorated D.S.M., Silver Star 2 oak leaf clusters, Legion of Merit with oak leaf cluster, D.F.C., Bronze Star with V device, Air medal with 9 oak leaf clusters, Army Commendation medal with oak leaf cluster, Belgian and Vietnamese decorations; recipient George Washington honor medal Freedoms Found. at Valley Forge, 1957, 58. Mem. Am. Econs. Assn., Am. Mil. Inst., Council Fgn. Relations, Am. Acad. Polit. nd Social Sci., Acad. Polit. Sci. Clubs: University (N.Y.C.); Army and Navy (Washington). Contbr. Ency. Americana and nat. mags. Home: West Springfield NH 03284 Office: U S Mil Acad West Point NY 10996

KNOWLTON, WINTHROP, pub. co. exec.; b. N.Y.C., Sept. 1, 1930; s. Hugh and Christine (Stanley) K.; grad. Lawrenceville Sch., 1948; B.A., Harvard, 1953, M.B.A., 1955; m. Mina Elizabeth Minnerly, June 23, 1951 (div. 1960); children—Winthrop, Christopher, Oliver; m. 2d, Grace Daniels Farrar, July 8, 1960; children—Eliza Courtney, Samantha Farrar. With White, Weld & Co., Inc., N.Y.C., 1955—, v.p., 1961, gen. partner, 1962-65, ltd. partner, 1965—; with Office Edn., Washington, 1965; dep. asst. sec. treasury for internat. affairs, 1965-66, asst. sec., 1966-68; exec. v.p., dir. Harper & Row 1968-70, pres., 1970—; pub. Harper's Mag. Press; dir. Abacus Fund, Systems Applications, Inc. Bd. dirs., trustee Jackson Lab., Bar Harbor, Me.; trustee Tchrs. Coll. Mem. Council on Fgn. Relations. Clubs: Century, Harvard, Union. Co-author: A Killing in the Market, 1958; author Growth Opportunities in Common Stocks, 1965. Home: Sneden's Landing Palisades NY 10960 Office: 49 E 33d St New York City NY 10016

KNOX, ALEXANDER, actor; b. Strathroy, Ont., Can., Jan. 16, 1907; ed. Western Ont. U. Appeared on N.Y. stage in Romeo and Juliet, The Three Sisters, Jupiter Laughs, Jason, The Closing Door; London stage appearances include The Jealous God, Winter Journey, Henry VIII, Geneva, King of Nowhere; movies include The Sea Wolf, This Above All, Commandos Strike at Dawn, None Shall Escape, I'd Climb the Highest Mountain, Sleeping Tiger, Crack in the Mirror, Reach for the Sky, The Longest Day, Wreck of the Mary Deare, Woman of Straw, Mr. Moses; frequent television appearances. Author: (novel) Bride of Quietness; (plays) Old Master, The Closing Door, Red On White. Address: care United Artists Corp 1729 7th Av New York City NY 10019*

KNOX, BERNARD MACGREGOR WALKER, educator; b. Bradford, Eng., Nov. 24, 1914; s. Bernard and Rowena (Walker) K.; B.A., St. John's Coll., U. Cambridge (Eng.), 1936; Ph.D., Yale, 1948; M. A. (hon.), Harvard, 1962; LL.D., Princeton, 1964; m. Betty Baur, Apr. 12, 1939; 1 son, Bernard MacGregor Baur. Came to U.S., 1939, naturalized, 1943. Mem. faculty Yale, 1947-61, prof. classics, 1959-61; dir. Center Hellenic Studies, Washington, 1961—; Sather lectr. U. Cal. at Berkeley, 1963. Served to capt. AUS, 1942-45; ETO. Decorated Bronze Star with Cluster; Croix de Guerre (France); Guggenheim fellow 1956-57; award for lit. Nat. Inst. Arts and Letters, 1967. Mem. Am. Philol. Assn. Author: Oedipus at Thebes, 1957; (acting version) Oedipus the King, 1958; The Heroic Temper, 1964; also articles. Author, actor ednl. films on Oedipus of Sophocles. Address: Center Hellenic Studies 3100 Whitehaven St Washington DC 20008

KNOX, CARL WARNER, univ. ofcl.; b. Bow, N.H., June 15, 1916; s. Roy Layton and Alice Emma (Small) K.; A.B., U. Ill., 1938, M.S., 1941, Ph.D., 1953; student Ohio State U., 1941-42; m. Elizabeth Jane Phillips, May 26, 1939; 1 son, Enos Phillips. Asst. dean of men Ohio U., Athens, 1941-42; supr. temporary housing U. Ill., 1946-49; asst. dean men No. Ill. State Coll., 1950-52; dean men Miami U., 1952-59, U. Ill., 1959-67; dean, v.p. student affairs, prof. Fla. Atlantic U. 1967—. Mem. Fla. Bd. Regents Council Student Affairs. Bd. dirs. U. Ill. YMCA; mem. personnel com. nat. YMCA. Served as lt. USNR, 1942-46. Mem. Nat. Assn. Student Personnel Adminstrs. (exec. com., sec.- treas. 1958-66; pres. 1967-68; editorial bd. assn. jour.), Delta Sigma Pi, Phi Delta Kappa, Omicron Delta Kappa, Phi Eta Sigma, Delta Phi, Alpha Phi Omega, Phi Kappa Phi. Rotarian. Home: 3205 NE 6th Dr Boca Raton FL 33432

KNOX, CLINTON EVERETT, fgn. service officer; b. New Bedford, Mass., May 6, 1908; s. William Jacob and Estella Jane (Briggs) K.; B.A., Williams Coll., 1930; M.A., Brown U., 1931; Ph.D., Harvard, 1939; m. Clementine Elizabeth Murphy, Nov. 24, 1934; children—William Everett, Karen Louise. Instr. history Morgan State Coll., Balt., 1931-43; with State Dept., 1945—; dep. chief Western European sect., div. research, 1945-46, chief No. and Western European br., 1947-52, asst. chief div. research for Western Europe, 1952-55, chief div., 1955-57; 1st sec., consul Am. embassy, Paris, France, 1957-63; counselor exec. sect. in Tegucigalpa, Honduras, 1963-65; A. E. and P., Dahomey, Contonov, 1964-69, Port-au-Prince, Haiti, 1969—. Served with AUS, 1943-45. Mem. Phi Beta Kappa. Home: 21 Woodman Park Rochester NY Office: Dept of State Washington DC

KNOX, HUBBARD ALLEN, Jr., broker; b. Mayesville, S.C., July 31, 1908; s. Hubbard A. and Eunice (Ballenger) K.; A.B., Davidson Coll., 1929; m. Clare L. Hargrove, Nov. 1, 1935; children—Hubbard Allen III, James H., Susan B. Salesman F. Eberstadt & Co., N.Y.C., 1937-38; broker Fahnestock & Co., mems. N.Y. Stock Exchange, Summit, N.J., 1938—; dir. Gen. Portland Cement Co., Dallas. Republican. Episcopalian. Clubs: Beacon Hill (Summit, N.J.); Tuscarora (Millbrook, N.Y.). Home: 20 Little Wolf Rd Summit NJ 07901 Office: 18 Bank St Summit NJ 07901

KNOX, JOHN, clergyman, educator; b. Frankfort, Ky., Dec. 30, 1900; s. Absalom and Emma Belle (Mann) K.; A.B., Randolph-Macon Coll., 1919, Litt.D., 1948; B.D., Emory U., 1925, S.T.D., 1956; Ph.D., U. Chgo., 1935; D.D., Phila. Div. Sch., 1963, Glasgow U., 1963; S.T.D., Gen. Theol. Sem., Berkeley Divinity Div. Sch.; m. Lois Adelaide Bolles, June 14, 1930; children—John, Hamilton Bolles. Ordained to ministry Meth. Ch., 1924, served pastorates Balt., 1923-24, Bethesda, Md., 1928-29; asst. prof. Bible Emory U., 1924-27; minister Fisk U., 1929-36; mng. editor Christendom, 1936-38; mem. editorial staff Christian Century, 1936-38; asso. prof. N.T. Hartford Theol. Sem., 1938- 39; asso. prof. homiletics, N.T. U. Chgo., 1939-42, prof., 1942-43; prof. sacred lit. Union Theol. Sem., 1943-66, emeritus, 1966—, dir. studies 1945-57; ordained to the ministry Episcopal Ch., 1962; prof. N.T. Episcopal Theol. Sem. S.W., 1966-71, emeritus, 1971—, lectr., 1971-72; Ayer lectr. Colgate Rochester Div. Sch., 1944; William Belden Noble lectr. Harvard, 1946-47; Jackson lectr. So. Meth. U., 1950; McFadin lectr. Tex. Christian U., 1952; Fulbright lectr. U. Cambridge, 1952-53; Hoover lectr., U. Chgo., 1955; Shaffer lectr., Yale, 1956; Gray lectr. Duke, 1956; Carew lectr. Hartford Theol. Sem., 1957; Ingersoll lectr. Harvard, 1960; Richard lectr. U. Va., 1963; Page lectr. Berkeley Div. Sch., 1968. Mem. Soc. Bibl. Lit. (pres. 1963), Am. Theol. Soc. (pres. 1961), Nat. Council Religion Higher Edn., Phi Beta Kappa. Author: He Whom a Dream Hath Possessed, 1932; Philemon Among the Letters of Paul, 1935; The Man Christ Jesus, 1941; Marcion and the New Testament, 1942; Christ the Lord, 1945; The Fourth Gospel and the Later Epistles, 1945; On the Meaning of Christ, 1947; Chapters in a Life of Paul, 1950; Criticism and Faith, 1952; Commentary on Romans in Interpreter's Bible, 1953; The Early Church and the Coming Great Church, 1955; The Integrity of Preaching, 1957; Death of Christ, 1958; Jesus Lord and Christ, 1958; Christ and the Hope of Glory, 1960; The Ethic of Jesus in the Teaching of the Church, 1961; Life in Christ Jesus, 1961; The Church and the Reality of Christ, 1962; A Guide for the Reader of the New Testament, 1963; Myth and Truth, 1964; The Humanity and Divinity of Christ, 1967; Limits of Unbelief, 1970. Editor: Religion and the Present Crisis, 1942; Jour. Religion, 1939-43. Asso. editor The Interpreter's Bible, 12 vols., 1951-57; The Interpreter's Dictionary of the Bible, 4 vols., 1962. Contbr. Oxford Annotated Bible; also various theol. jours. Home: Medford Leas Medford NJ 08055 Office: 606 Rathervue Pl Austin TX 78705

KNOX, JOHN, Jr., educator; b. Nashville, Tenn., Mar. 5, 1932; s. John and Lois Adelaide (Bolles) K.; student Cambridge U., 1952; B.A., Emory U., 1953; Ph.D., Yale, 1961; m. Alida Sanford van Bronkhorst, June 30, 1962; children—Trever McTaggart, Amethy Alida. Instr. philosophy C.W. Post Coll., L.I.U., 1960, asst. prof. philosophy, 1961-67; asso. prof. philosophy Drew U., Madison, N.J., 1967-71, prof., chmn. dept., 1971—. Served from ensign to lt. (j.g.), USNR, 1953-56. Mem. Am. Philos. Assn., Phi Beta Kappa, Phi Sigma Tau. Contbr. articles philos. publs. Home: 28 Broadview Av Madison NJ 07940 Office: Drew U Madison NJ 07940

KNOX, JOHN BROOKS, food mfg. co. exec.; b. Gloversville, N.Y., July 22, 1918; s. James E. and Eleanor (Williams) K.; grad. Manlius Sch., 1936; m. Irene Baez, Aug. 9, 1961; children—Anne (Mrs. Hallock), Rose, Kimberly, Amy, John, James. Salesman, W.K. Kellogg Co., N.Y.C., 1937-38; treas. C.B. Knox Co., Johnstown, N.Y., 1938-39; prodn. test pilot Ryan Aero. Co., 1940-41; with Knox Gelatin Co., Johnstown, 1946—; pres., 1955—; pres. Knox Gelatin Ltd. (Can.), 1952—; chmn. bd. Kind & Knox Gelatin Co., 1966—. Served with USAAF, World War II. Home: RFD Lake Pleasant NY 12108 Office: 1 Knox Av Johnstown NY 12095

KNOX, JOHN MARSHALL, dermatologist; b. Dallas, Apr. 11, 1925; s. John Marshall and Katie (Dickie) K.; B.S., Tex. A. and M. U., 1944; M.D., Baylor U., 1949; m. Lullene Powell, Dec. 18, 1948; children—Lynda Lee, Jane Ann, John Marshall, Byron Powell. Intern New Orleans Charity Hosp., 1949-50; resident Univ. Hosp., Ann Arbor, Mich., 1950, 54-55, U. Okla. Hosp., 1953-54; mem. faculty Baylor U. Coll. Medicine, 1955—, prof., chmn. dept. dermatology and syphilology, 1963—; chief dermatology VA Hosp., Houston, 1963-69, cons., 1969—; chief dermatology Ben Taub Gen. Hosp., Houston, 1963—, Tex. Childrens Hosp., Houston, 1967—; sr. attending physician Meth. Hosp., Houston, 1964—. Mem. Commn. cutaneous diseases Armed Forces Eipdemiol. Bd., 1968—; chmn. council, dir. Nat. Porgram for Dermatology; mem. Nat. Commn. Venereal Disease, 1971. Served as capt., M.C., USAF, 1951-52. Diplomate Am. Bd. Dermatology. Mem. Soc. Investigative Dermatology (bd. dirs. 1960-65), Am. Social Health Assn. (bd. dirs. 1962—), Am. Dermatol. Assn., A.M.A., Houston (pres. 1965-66), Tex. (v.p. 1965-66) dermatol. socs., Am. Venereal Disease Assn. (pres. 1968), So. Med. Assn. (chmn. sect. dermatology 1965-66), Alpha Omega Alpha. Author numerous articles in field. Mem. editorial bds. jours. in field. Home: 419 Blalock St Houston TX 77024

KNOX, KATHARINE MCCOOK, art historian; b. Washington; d. Anson G. and Hettie Beatty McCook; grad. Miss Spence's Sch., N.Y.C., 1908; m. Hugh S. Knox, Dec. 14, 1911; 1 dau., Kathleen (Mrs. Richard Austin Smith). Chmn. loan exhbn. in D.C., Mus. Modern Art, 1938; chmn. exhbns. Corcoran Gallery Art, 1932, 37, 52, 57; spl. cons. Am. Processional, 1950, Our Town, Alexandria, Va., 1956; chmn. loan exhbn. Robert E. Lee memorabilia in Textile Mus., Washington, 1931, Primarily Am., 1954; spl. cons. Profiles of the Time of James Monroe, Smithsonian Instn., 1958; chmn. art critics com. D.A.R., 1959-61, chmn. D.A.R. Mus. exhbn. A Century of Am. Needlecraft, 1959; numerous talks on Am. art; hon. mem. Lincoln Sesquicentennial Commn. (recipient bronze medallion, 1960); adv. council Civil War Centennial Commn., others; mem. Pres.'s Adv. Com. on Arts, John F. Kennedy Center for Performing Arts. Gen. chmn. Flower Mart, Washington Cathedral, 1946, treas. garden com., 1948; cons. We the People, pub. U.S. Capitol Hist. Soc., 1964. Mem. Republican Com. for D.C.; alt. del. Rep. Nat. Conv., 1960, del., mem. credentials com., 1964. Exec. com. D.C. bd. R.E. Lee Meml. Found.; bd. dirs. Historic Georgetown, Inc.; trustee Frick Art Ref. Library, N.Y.; mem. council, fellow Corcoran Gallery Art (recipient Bronze medal of Merit 1966). Mem. League Republican Women D.C. (program chmn. 1959-61), Nat. Soc. Colonial Dames, Dames Loyal Legion, Daus. Union Vets., Soc. Descendants Found. of Hartford (Conn.), Jr. Army-Navy Guild Orgn. (founder mem. 1943). Presbyn. Clubs: Colony (N.Y.C.); Golf (Pitts.); American Newspaper Women (asso.), Sulgrave, Capitol Hill (past gov.) (Washington); Chevy Chase (Md.). Author: The Sharples, Their Portraits of George Washington and His Contemporaries 1930; The Portraits of the Adams-Clement Collection and Their Painters, 1951; Surprise Personalities in Georgetown, D.C., 1958; Healy's Lincoln No. 1, 1959. Contbr. articles various publs. Home: 3259 N St NW Washington DC 20007

KNOX, NORTHRUP RAND, investment banker; b. Buffalo, Dec. 24, 1928; s. Seymour and Helen (Northrup) K.; grad. St. Paul's Sch., 1946; B.A., Yale, 1950; student Cornell U., 1952; m. Lucetta Crisp, June 21, 1950; children—Linda Gilbert, Northrup Rand. Pres., dir. Seykay Corp., Buffalo, 1961—; dir., chmn. exec. com. Marine Midland Bank-Western; dir. Midland Capital Corp., Niagara Share Corp. Chmn. bd. trustees Aiken Prep. Sch.; v.p. Hitchcock Found.; treas. Buffalo Fine Arts Acad.; trustee Buffalo Mus. Sci.; v.p., dir. Seymour H. Knox Found. World ct. tennis champion, 1959-69. Home: Buffalo Rd East Aurora NY 14052 Office: Marine Trust Bldg Buffalo NY 14203

KNOX, RICHARD MELVIN, oil co. exec.; b. Covington, Okla., Mar. 15, 1923; s. Charles and Vivian Marguerite (Slichter) K.; student U. Okla., 1940-43; m. Mary Jo Miller, May 5, 1943; children—Mary Lynn, Richard Melvin, Kimie Marie and Karie Louise (twins). Formed Knox Industries Corp., Enid., Okla., 1949, pres., 1957-63; co. acquired by Kerr-McGee Corp., 1961, v.p. marketing-pipeline-refining, 1963-68; pres. Knox Corp., Rock Island, Ill.; pres. Knox Hi Octane Corp., 1957—; dir. Western Investors Corp. Mem. Okla. Personnel Bd., 1960-61. Served to 1st lt. AUS, 1943-46. Mem. Enid C. of C. (pres. 1961), Am. Petroleum Inst., Soc. Ind. Gasoline Marketers Am. (bd. dirs.), Young Pres. Orgn. Presbyn. Home: 15 Robert Av Davenport IA 52803 Office: Knox Corp PO Box 910 Rock Island IL 61201

KNOX, ROBERT S., printing co. exec.; b. 1916; married. With Price Waterhouse & Co., C.P.A.'s 1939-52; with W.F. Hall Printing Co., 1952—, chmn. bd., pres., chief exec. officer, 1966—, also dir. Address: 4600 Diversey Av Chicago IL 60639*

KNOX, ROBERT SEIPLE, educator, physicist; b. Franklin, N.J., July 13, 1931; s. Harvey Stoll and Laura (Seiple) K.; B.S. in Engring. Physics, Lehigh U., 1953; Ph.D. in Physics and Optics, U. Rochester, 1958; m. Mirta I. Borges, Sept. 1, 1954; children—Bruce Robert, Wayne Harvey, Lee Benjamin. Research asso. U. Ill., 1958-59; research asst. prof., 1959-60; mem. faculty U. Rochester (N.Y.), 1960—, asso. prof. dept. physics, 1963-68, prof., 1968—, chmn. dept. physics and astronomy, 1969—; cons. Argonne Nat. Lab., 1959-69, Naval Research Lab., 1960—, Xerox Corp., 1963—. Fellow Am. Phys. Soc.; mem. A.A.A.S. Author: Theory of Excitons, 1963; (with A. Gold) Symmetry in the Solid State, 1964; (with D. L. Dexter) Excitons, 1965; also articles. Research on atomic spectra and structure, absorption and luminescence spectra ionic and molecular crystals, band structure of nonmetallic solids. Office: Dept Physics and Astronomy U Rochester Rochester NY 14627

KNOX, SEYMOUR H., corp. exec.; b. Buffalo, Sept. 1, 1898; s. Seymour Horace and Grace (Millard) K.; student, Hotchkiss Prep. Sch., 1914-16, B.A., Yale, 1920; m. Helen Northrup, Nov. 20, 1923; children—Seymour Horace, III, Northrup. Banker, 1920; became v.p. Marine Trust Co., 1927, chmn. bd., 1943-70; dir. Marine Midland Bank N.Y., F.W. Woolworth Co., Niagara Share Corp. Trustee, Aiken Prep. Sch. Pres., dir. Buffalo Fine Arts Acad.; chmn. N.Y. State Council on the Arts. Mem. Scroll and Key Soc. (Yale), Delta Kappa Epsilon. Clubs: Buffalo, Country, Saturn, Tennis and Squash (Buffalo); Racquet and Tennis, River (N.Y.C.); Bucks (London); Travellers (Paris). Home: 57 Oakland Pl Buffalo NY 14222 Office: Marine Trust Bldg Buffalo NY 14203

KNOX, SEYMOUR H., III, profl. hockey exec.; Chmn., pres. Buffalo Sabres hockey team, Nat. Hockey League. Regional v.p. Dominick & Dominick. Address: 70 Niagara St Buffalo NY 14202*

KNOX, WALTER EUGENE III, educator, physician; b. Norcatur, Kan., July 21, 1918; s. Walter Eugene and Lucy (Frewen) K.; A.B., U. Neb., 1939; M.D., Harvard, 1943; m. Olga Halpert, Oct. 6, 1967; children-Phebe Lee (Mrs. William B. Whitehead), Tamsin Ann, Walter Eugene IV. Itern, then asst. physician Presbyn. Hosp., N.Y.C., 1943-48; spl. research fellow USPHS, U. Cambridge (Eng.) and Nat. Inst. Med. Research, London, 1949-52; asso. prof. biochemistry Tufts U. Med. Sch., 1953; prof. biochemistry Am. U., Beirut, 1961-62; mem. faculty Harvard Med. Sch. and New Eng. Deaconess Hosp., Boston, 1953—, prof. biol. chemistry, 1969—. Chmn. metabolism study sect. NIH, 1962-65. Served to capt., M.C., AUS, 1944-47. Recipient Claude Bernard medal U. Montreal, 1970. Mellow N.Y. Acad. Sci.; mem. Am. Assn. Cancer Research, Am. Chem. Soc., Am. Soc. Biol. Chemistry, Am. Soc. Human Genetics, Biochem. Soc., Harvey Soc., Japanese Biochem. Soc. (hon.). Author papers in field. Co-editor: Research in Medical Science. Editor: Enzymologia Biologica et Clinica. Home: 63 Powell St Brookline MA 02146 Office: 185 Pilgrim Rd Boston MA 02215

KNOX, WARREN BARR, coll. pres.; b. Whittier, Cal., Aug. 22, 1925; s. Lavern V. and Bertha (Barr) K.; B.A., Whittier Coll., 1949; M.A., 1951, LL.D., 1965; student Claremount Grad. Sch., 1951-52; m. Nancy Sears Chambers, June 20, 1945; children—Charles Warren, John Warren. Tchr., Montebello (Cal.) High Sch., 1950-52; asst. to pres. Pomona Coll., 1952-59; v.p. Whitman Coll., 1959-64; pres. Coll. of Ida., Caldwell, 1964—. Chmn. Rhodes Scholarship Selection for Ida., 1965-69; mem. Ida. delagation Nat. Compact for Edn. of Am.; mem. nexus com. Presbyn. Coll. Union, 1970—; mem. Ida. Higher Edn. Adv. Council. Mem. Boise Art Assos., 1965—; vice chmn. Ore-Ida. council Boy Scouts Am., 1964—, hon. mem. nat. council, 1960—. Served with USNR, 1942-45. Mem. Am. Alumni Council, Am. Coll. Pub. Relations Assn., Am., Western hist. assns., Wisdom Soc., Intercollegiate Knights (hon.). Republican. Presbyn. Kiwanian. Contbr. profl. jours. Home: 1923 Everett St Caldwell ID 83605

KNOX, WILLIAM EDWARD, bus. exec.; b. Somerville, Mass., June 24, 1901; s. Willian H. and Elizabeth E. (Berry) K.; B.S. in E.E., U. N.H., 1921, D.Eng., 1954; Dr. Honoris Causa, U. Uruguay, 1946; m. Ella C. Griffin, June 10, 1927; 1 son, William Edward. Entered grad. student tng. course, Westinghouse Electric & Mfg. Corp., East Pittsburgh, Pa., 1921; became sales clk. Westinghouse Electric Internat. Co., N.Y.C., 1922, salesman, 1925-32, asst. to gen. mgr., 1932- 36, asst. gen. mgr., 1937-44, v.p., 1944-46, pres., 1946-63, chmn., 1963- 66; v.p. Westinghouse Elec. Corp., 1959-65; pres. William E. Knox Assos., Inc., internat. cons. N.Y.C., 1966—; bd. dirs. European-Am. Banking Corp., N.Y.C., European- Am. Bank & Trust Co., N.Y.C. Reistan, Inc., Techint Inc., N.Y.C., U.S. Banknote Corp., Decorated comdr. Order Al Merito, Chile, 1942; Knight Comdr., Order of Sun, Peru, 1947; Officer Legion of Honor (France); Knight of Magistral Grace, Soverign Mil. Order of Malta, 1949; Knight Order of St. Olav (Norway), 1947; Comdr. Order Al Merito della Repubblica (Italy), 1954; Comdr. Order of Isabel la Catolica, Spain, Order of the Sacred Treasure, Japan, 1956; Order of the Brilliant Star, Rep. China, 1956; Officer Order of Cruzeiro do Sul, Brazil, 1958, comdr. Order of Leopold (Belgium), 1962, comdr. Nat. Order Ivory Coast, 1962, comdr. Phillippine Legion Honor, 1963; recipient Westinghouse Order of Merit for Outstanding Accomplishments, 1940, Capt. Robert Dollar Meml. award, 1962. Mem. Regional Export Expansion Council, Far East- Am. Council of Commerce and Industry (vice chmn.), S.R. in State of N.Y., Pi Kappa Alpha. Republican. Clubs: Sky (gov.), Wall Street (N.Y.C.); Cedar Grove Beach (gov.); Wypagyl Country (New Rochelle, N.Y.). Home: 30 Vernon Rd Scarsdale NY 10583 Office: 200 Park Av New York City NY 10017

KNOX, WILLIAM FRANCIS, lawyer; b. Connellsville, Pa., Jan. 29, 1885; s. Alfred C. and Annie Ewing (Wilson) K.; A.B., Yale, 1907; LL.B., U. Pitts., 1910; m. Ruth Thoburn, June 29, 1916 (dec. Apr. 1950); children—William F. (dec.), James Thoburn; m. 2d, Margaret Thoburn, June 21, 1951 (dec. Sept. 1969). Admitted to Pa. bar, 1910; mem. firm Moorhead & Knox, Pitts., 1917—, now sr. partner. Vice pres., dir. Homewood Cemetery; trustee YMCA. Mem. Am., Pa., Allegheny County bar assns. Methodist. Clubs: Duquesne, Fox Chapel, Harvard-Yale-Princeton. Home: 8 Robin Rd Pittsburgh PA 15217 Office: Oliver Bldg Pittsburgh PA 15222

KNOX, WILLIAM WALLACE U.S. judge; b. Erie, Pa., June 18, 1911; s. Wallace John and Edna (Wallace) K.; A.B., U. Mich., 1932, J.D., 1935; m. Agnes Ruth Graham, Sept. 5, 1936; children-Virginia M., Wallace John, Charles Graham, Katherine Elizabeth. Admitted to Pa. bar, 1935, since practiced in Erie; partner Knox, Graham, Pearson & McLaughlin; judge U.S. Dist. Co. No. Dist. Pa., 1970—. Pres. Erie. County Lawyers Title Co.; sec., dir. Lyons Transp. Co.; dir. Worster Motor Lines, Inc. Solicitor Erie Sch. Dist., 1943-46, Harborcreek Twp. Sch. Dist., 1955—, Millcreek Sch. Dist., 1959—, Millcreek Sch. Dist., 1959—, Erie County Sch. Bd., 1961- -, Union City Sch. Bd., Erie Met. Transit Authority, 1966—. Mem. bd. pub. assistance Erie County, 1955. Bd. dirs. Family and Child Service of Erie. Served to 1st lt. Pa. State Guard, 1941-46. Recipient Certificate of Merit, Family and Child Service, 1956. Mem. Am., Pa., Erie County (pres.) bar assns., Am.. Judicature Soc., Erie C. of C. (dir.), Pa. Citizens Assn. (dir. 1955-64, v.p., 1957-61), Order of Coif, Phi Beta Kappa. Republican. Presbyn. (trustee). Mason. Home: 5602 Bonaventure Dr Erie P A 16505 Office: 23 W 10th St Erie PA 16501

KNUDSEN, CONRAD CALVERT, mfg. co. exec.; b. Tacoma, Oct. 3, 1923; s. Conrad D. and Annabelle (Callison) K.; B.A., U. Wash., 1948, LL.B., 1950; fellow law, Columbia, 1951; m. Julia Lee Roderick, Nov. 22, 1950; childrenConrad Calvert, Elizabeth Page, Colin Roderick, David Callison. Admitted to Wash. bar, 1950; asso., then partner Bogle, Bogle & Gates, Seattle, 1951-60; exec. v.p., dir. Aberdeen Plywood & Veneers, Inc., 1960-63; v.p., dir. Evans Products Co., 1963, exec. v.p., dir., 1963-64, pres., dir., 1964-68, vice chmn., dir., 1968; sr. v.p. Weyerhaeuser Co., 1969—; dir. Nat. Bank of Commerce Seattle. Trustee Weyerhaeuser Co. Found. Mem. Am., Wash. bar assns. Home: 1015 Evergreen Point Rd Medina WA 98039 Office: Tacoma Bldg Tacoma WA 98401

KNUDSEN, JOHANNES HENRIK VILSTRUP, educator, clergyman; b. Nysted, Neb., Oct. 10, 1902; s. R. Thorvald and Thora (Vilstrup) K.; cand. mag. U. Copenhagen (Denmark), 1927; S.T.M., Hartford Sem. Found., 1941, Ph.D., 1943; m. Ellen Catherine Paulsen, July 19, 1934; childrenSonja, Lois Vilstrup (Mrs. Gordon Lund). Tchr., Grand View Coll., Des Moines, 1927-35; ordained to ministry Luth. Ch., 1935; pastor in Askov, Minn. and Hartford, Conn., 1935-42; pres. Grand View Coll., 1942-52; dean Grand View Sem., 1942-54; prof. Luth. Sch. Theology at Chgo., 1954-, dean grad. studies, 1955-68. Del. Luth. World Assembly, Hanover, Germany, 1952, Faith and Order meeting World Council Chs., Lund, Sweden, 1952, Montreal, Can., 1963; mem. Joint Commn. Luth. Unity, 1955-62. Chmn. Maywood (Ill.) Council Human Relations, 1965-66, Maywood Commn. Human Relations, 1966-67. Decorated knight Order Dannebrog, 1958. Mem. Ch. History Soc., Am. Theol. Soc. Author: Introduction to the Danish Language, 1935; Danish Rebel, 1955; Frikirkedannelse (in Danish), 1965. Home: 1366 E 57th St Chicago IL 60637

KNUDSEN, ORAN MILTON, educator; b. Provo, Utah, Nov. 14, 1909; s. Milton Herman and Vivian Etta (Cram) K.; B.S. in Chemistry, U. Wis., 1933; Ph.D., N.Y. U., 1938; m. Marie Lillian Eccles, May 26, 1936; children—Dorothy (Mrs. Larry D. Lilly), Margaret Ann. Teaching fellow N.Y. U., 1933-38, L.I. U., 1938-39; Alfred U. Extension, Jamestown, N.Y., 1939-42; asst. prof. Mich. State U., 1942-46; faculty Rose-Hulman Inst. Tech., Terre Haute, Ind., 1946—. Fellow A.A.A.S.; mem. Am. Chem. Soc. (ednl. com.), Sigma XI. Mem. Ch. of Jesus Christ of Latter-day Saints (dist. pres. 1957-64). Home: 124 Bluebird Dr Terre Haute IN 47803

KNUDSEN, SEMON EMIL, automotive mfr.; b. Buffalo, Oct. 2, 1912; s. William S. and Clara (Euler) K.; student Dartmouth, 1931-32, engring., Mass. Inst. Tech., 1936; m. Florence Anne McConnell, June 16, 1938; children Judy, Peter, Lisa, Kristina. With Gen. Motors Corp., 1939-, successively chief insp. def. Pontiac Motor div., supt. car assembly, asst. master mechanic, dir. process devel. sect. Gen. Motors, asst. mfg. mgr. Allison div. aircraft engine operations, mfg. mgr., 1939-55, gen. mgr. Detroit Diesel Engine div., 1955—, gen. mgr. Pontiac Motor div., 1956-61, group v.p. in charge overseas and Canadian group Gen. Motors Corp., 1965-66, exec. v.p. Dayton household appliance, 1966-68, past dir., mem. exec. com.; pres. Ford Co., 1968-69. Bd. dirs. Boys' Clubs of Detroit; mem. nat. bd. Boys' Blubs Am., 1959—, also chmn. Michigan state com.; mem. Mass. Inst. Tech. Corp.; pres. Mich. United Fund; trustee, Oakland U. Found. Mem. Am. Ordnance Assn., Soc. Automotive Engrs., Am. Soc. Tool Engrs., Delta Upsilon. Clubs: Yondotega, Detroit, Detroit Athletic; Bloomfield Hills (Mich.) Country; Old (Algonac, Mich.); Woodstock Country (Indpls). Home: 31500 Bingham Rd Birmingham MI Office: Gen Motors Bldg Detroit MI 48202

KNUDSEN, VERN O., physicist, univ. chancellor emeritus; b. Provo, Utah, Dec. 27, 1893; s. Andrew and Chesty (Sward) K.; A.B., Brigham Young U., 1915; Ph.D., U. Chgo., 1922; LL.D., U. Cal. at Los Angeles, 1960; m. Florence Telford, Dec. 19, 1919; children—Marilyn (dec.), Robert Telford Andrew, Vern Oliver Morris, Margaret Constance. Research engr., 1918-19; instr. physics, U. Cal. at Los Angeles, 1922-23, asst. prof., 1923-27, asso. prof., 1927-34, prof., 1934—, dean grad. div. 1934-58, vice chancellor, 1956-59, chancellor, 1959—, chancellor emeritus, cons. on acoustics, 1960—, chmn. dept. physics, 1932-38; cons. acoustics to univs., colls., music bldgs., civic auditoriums, theaters, chs. Dir. Statham Instruments. Vice pres. Los Angeles Bldg. and Safety Commn., 1940-41; pres. Hollywood Bowl, Los Angeles, 1960-61, chmn., 1961-62; pres. Cal. Inst. Cancer Research, 1963-65; bd. dirs. Chamber Symphony Soc. Cal. (v.p. 1965—), So. Cal. Choral Music Assn.; war research, Nat. Def. Research Com., 1941-44; Nat. Research Counsel, 1942-45; invented instruments for measuring and correcting impaired hearing, 1924-25; ear defenders, 1938-39. Awarded A.A.A.S. prize, 1934; Wallace C. Sabine medal for original contbns. to archtl. acoustics, 1958; John H. Potts Meml. award Audio-Engring. Soc., 1964; gold medal Acoustical Soc. Am., 1967; physics bldg. U. Cal. at Los Angeles named Knudsen Hall, 1964; Wisdom award of honor Wisdom Soc., 1970; Tchr. of Yr., Cal. Tchr. Remembrance Day Found., 1970; Distinguished Alumnus award U. Chgo. Club Greater Los Angeles, 1971. Fellow A.A.A.S., Am. Phys. Soc., Acoustical Soc. Am. (pres. 1933-35). Mem. Ch. of Jesus Christ of Latter Day Saints. Author: Architectural Acoustics, 1932; Audiometry, 1937; Acoustical Designing in Architecture (with Cyril Harris), 1950. Contbr. Sci. articles. Home: 13181 Rivera Ranch Rd Los Angeles CA 90049

KNUDSON, ALVIN BERNT CLIFFORD, physician; b. Waubay, S.D., June 28, 1910; s. Alfred Henry and Anna Berentina Lorraine (Erickson) K.; B.S., U. Minn., 1937, B.M., 1938, M.D., 1939; fellow phys. medicine and rehab. Mayo Clinic, 1943; Baruch fellow Mass. Inst. Tech., 1945; m. Florence Josephine Rusche, July 1, 1933; children—Alvin Richard, Arthur Bernard Charles. Temporary clk. U.S. P.O., Mpls., 1930-35, permanent clk., 1935-39; physician VA, 1939—, beginning in hosps., Mpls., St. Cloud, Minn., Ft. Custer, Mich., Dwight, Ill., then asst. chief phys. medicine and rehab. div. VA Central Office, 1939-48, dir. phys. medicine and rehab. service, dept. medicine and surgery Central Office, Washington, 1948—; asso., phys. medicine and rehab. George Washington U. Sch. Medicine, 1949—; asst. clin. prof. phys. medicine and rehab. Georgetown U. Sch. Medicine, 1954—. Rep. VA to 1st Internat. Congress Phys. Medicine, London, 1952; mem. Baruch Com. on Phys. Medicine and Rehab. 1948-53; tech. adviser Commn. on Chronic Illness, 1949-56; chmn. com. on rehab. Nat. Conf. on Aging, 1951; cons. med. com. Pres.'s Com. for Employment Handicapped, 1954—; co-chmn., mem. med. com. Davis Meml., Goodwill Industries Rehab. Center, Washington, 1956—. Served to lt. col. M.C., AUS, 1944-46. Recipient John Eisele Davis award Assn. Phys. and Mental Rehab., 1953. Diplomate Am. Bd. Phys. Medicine and Rehab. (examining mem. bd. 1949—). Fellow Am. Psychiat. Assn., A.C.P., A.M.A. (cons. council phys. medicine and rehab. 1951-54), Indsl. Medicine Assn., Am. Acad. Phys. Medicine and Rehab. (gov. 1949-52), Am. Occupational Therapy Assn.; mem. Am. Congress Phys. Medicine and Rehab. (gov. 1951—, pres. 1956-57, chmn. exec. council 1957—), So. Med. Assn. (chmn. sect. phys. medicine and rehab.), Pan Am. Med. Assn. (sec. sect. phys. medicine and rehab. 1952-54), Am. Hosp. Assn., Assn. Mil. Surgeons, D.C. Med. Soc., Met. Washington Soc. Phys. Medicine and Rehab., Springfield Civic Assn., Am. Legion, Holy Name Soc., Internat. Soc. Welfare of Cripples (founder mem.), Assn. Phys. and Mental Rehab., Am. Assn. Rehab. Therapists, Assn. Med. Rehab. Dirs. and Coordinators, Internat. Congress Phys. Medicine and Rehab. Asso. editor Gerialtrics Med. Jour., 1952—. Contbr. articles med., profl. jours. and publs. Home: 7000 Sylvan Glen Lane Fairfax Station VA 22039 Office: VA Central Office Vermont and H Sts Washington DC 20025

KNUDSON, CHARLES ANTHONY, educator; b. Sheboygan, Wis., Nov. 23, 1903; s, Charles Anthony Caroline (Hanson) K.; B.S. summa cum laude, Dartmouth, 1924; A.M., Harvard, 1925, Ph.D., 1929; student Sorbonne, 1926-28; m. Donna D. Finger, Jan. 28, 1960. Instr. Romance langs. U. Buffalo, 1928- 29; asst. prof. French, U. Mich., 1929-37, prof., 1937-40; prof., head dept. romance langs. Hamilton Coll., 1940-46, dir. mil. programs, 1943- 44; prof. French, U. Ill., 1946—, head dept., 1954-65. Served with O.W.I., Gt. Britain, France, 1944-46, regional dir. S.W. France, 1945. Decorated Legion of Honor, 1951, Officer, 1959. Mem. Modern Lang. Canadian Assn., Medieval Acad., Am. Assn. Tchrs. French, Assn. Internationale d'Etudes Francaises, Phi Beta Kappa, Delta Upsilon. Author: (with Louis Chapard) Introduction to French Pronunciation, 1934. Editor: (with Jean Misrahi) Jehan de Saintré, 1965. Contbr. articles French, Am., Canadian periodicals. Home: 907 McHenry St Urbana IL 61801

KNUDSON, HARRY EDWARD, Jr., elec. mfg. co. exec.; b. N.Y.C., Dec. 30, 1921; s. Harry Edward and Helen (Jones) K.; B.S. in Elec. Engring., Bucknell U., 1947; m. Anne Howland, Sept. 21, 1944; children—Anne, Erik. Cadet engr. Phila. Electric Co., 1947; with Fed. Pacific Electric Co., Newark, 1947—, exec. v.p., 1970—, also dir. Bd. dirs. Frost Valley YMCA. Served with USNR, 1943-46. Mem. Nat. Elec. Mfrs. Assn. (bd. dirs. power equipment div.), I.E.E.E., Newcomen Soc. N.Am., Phi Kappa Psi, Kappa Eta Nu. Methodist. Home: 608 Johnston Dr Watchung NJ 07060 Office: 150 Av L Newark NJ 07101

KNUDSON, HARVEY BORNEMANN, judge; b. Finley, N.D., June 26, 1903; s. Enoch Bornemann and Josephine Emelia (Hanson) K.; LL.B., U. N.D., 1931; m. Pearl Irene Pederson, June 17, 1933; children—Harvey Bornemann, Duane Arthur, Marion Jeanette (Mrs. Roy D. Rud), Kay Eileen (Mrs. Jerome Jacobs). Admitted to N.D. bar, 1931; sec-treas. Nat. Farm Loan Assns., Finley and Mayville, N.D., 1933-43; individual practice in Finley and Mayville, 1931-65; judge N.D. Supreme Ct., 1965—. Mem. Traill County War Bd., 1942-44; chmn. Traill County Savs. Bond Com., 1944-65, Gov. N.D. Com. Children and Youth, 1960-62. Sch. treas., Finley, 1934-38; mem. N.D. Legislature from Steele-Griggs County, 1937-38; mem. N.D. Senate from Traill County, 1951-58, chmn. senate jud. com., 1957; alderman, Mayville City Council, 1942-48; city atty., Mayville, 1958-65. Mem. Am., 1st Dist. (pres. 1951-53), N.D. (exec. com. 1951-53) bar assns., Farm Bur., Phi Alpha Delta. Lutheran (pres. congregation, chmn. bd. trustees 1961-64). Mason (Shriner), Modern Woodman. Club: Apple Creek Country. Home: 2124 2d St N Bismarck ND 58501 Office: Supreme Court Chambers State Capitol Bldg Bismarck ND 58501

KNUDSON, WILLIAM, librarian; b. Racine, Wis., Nov. 27, 1911; s. Hans and Anne Marie (Tobiasson) K.; A.B., U. Wis., 1933, J.D., 1938. Admitted to Wis. bar, 1938; law fellow Wis. Atty. Gen.'s Dept., 1938; individual practice law, Madison, Wis., 1939-42, 46-47; atty. State Farm Mut. Ins. Co., Madison, 1947-56; asst. librarian Wis. State Library, 1957-68, head librarian, 1969—. Served with AUS, 1942-46. Mem. State Bar Wis., Dane County Bar Assn., Am. Assn. Law Libraries. Author: Wisconsin Legal Research Guide, 1962, 2d edit., 1971. Home: 4817 Sheboygan Av Madison WI 53705 Office: Wis State Library Wis State Capitol Madison WI 53702

KNUDTEN, EDWIN HERMAN, clergyman, ch. ofcl.; b. Chgo., June 9, 1902; s. Christian and Anna (Siewert) K.; A.B., Carthage Coll., 1923; B.D., Hamma Div. Sch., Springfield, O., 1926; D.D., Wittenberg U., 1948, Upsala College, East Orange, N.J., 1965; LL.D., Wagner Coll., 1951; m. Josephine Huckins, Aug. 9, 1930; 1 dau., Anne Josephine. Ordained to ministry Luth. Ch., 1926; pastor Ascension Ch., 1926-27, St. John Ch., Rutherford, N.J., 1927-50: pres. N.J. Conf. United Luth. Synod of N.Y., 1943-45; chmn. com. for orgn. Evang. Luth. Synod N.J., 1948-50; pres. Evang. Luth. Synod N.J., United Luth. Ch. Am., 1950-62; mem. bd. fgn. missions United Luth. Ch. Am., 1954-62, mem. bd. world missions, 1964-69; co-chmn. of com. orgn. N.J. Synod of Luth, Ch. An., 1961-62; pres. N.J. Synod. of Luth. Ch, Am., 1962-70, ret. 1970; Luth. Ch, in Am. councilor to Nat. Luth. Council, 1962-64. Bd. trustees Upsala Coll., East Orange, N.J., Clara Maass Hosp., Belleville, N.J.; bd. dirs. Luth. Theol. Sem. at Phila. Mem. N.J. Council Chs. (v.p. 1959-61; pres. 1961- 62). Home: 672B Newcastle Ct Lakewood NJ 08701

KNUTSON, HERBERT CLAUS, entomologist, zoologist, educator: b. Crawfordsville, Ia., Sept. 6, 1915; s. Frank John and Alta Pearl (Hough) K.; A.B., Ia. Wesleyan Coll., 1936; M.S., So. Meth. U., 1937; Ph.D., U. Minn., 1941: m. Helen Lambley, Sept. 14, 1939; 1 son, Kevin Thomas. Instr. biology So. Meth. U., 1939-40; instr, zoology U, R.I., 1942-43, asst. prof. zoology, 1946-48, asso. prof., head dept. zoology, 1948-51, prof., head dept., 1951-53; adminstr. R.I. Div. Entomology and Plant Industry, 1946-48; prof., head dept. entomology, chief entomologist Kan. Agrl. Expt. Sta., Kan. State U., 1953—; entomologist Kan. Entomol. Commn., 1953-63; mem. Nat. Plant Bd., 1956-59; spl. cons. USPHS. Examiner Ednl. Testing Service, Coll. Entrance Examining Bd., Princeton, 1949-54. Served to lt. comdr. USPHS, 1943-46. Recipient Alumni Merit award Ia. Wesleyan Coll., 1961. Mem. Entomol. Soc. Am. (governing bd. 1962-65, pres. North Central br. 1970-71), Kan. Entomol. Soc. (pres.), Lambda Chi Alpha, Sigma Xi, Phi Kappa Phi, Phi Sigma, Gamma Sigma Delta. Mason (Shriner), Rotarian. Contbr. tech. jours. Home: 2016 Hunting Av Manhattan KS 66502

KNUTSON, HOWARD THOMAS, coll. dean; b. Whalan, Minn., Feb. 8, 1916; s. Martin Bernard and Julia (Fredrikson) K.; B.A., Luther Coll., 1937; M.A., U. Wyo., 1950, Ed.D., 1953; m. Eunice Lenore King, Aug. 14, 1939; children—Kristin (Mrs. D. Rodney Bluhm), Karl Martin, Katherine Jane. Tchr. Lincoln-Lee Consolidated Sch., Albert City, Ia., 1937-39, supt., 1939-42; supt. schs. Rembrandt (Ia.) Consolidated Sch., 1946-52; grad. asst., part-time instr. U. Wyo., 1952-53; asst. prof. Ia. State Tchrs. Coll., 1953-56, asso. prof., 1956-59; asst. dean instrn. State Coll. Ia., 1960-64, asso. dean instrn., 1964-68; prof. edn., dean Coll. Edn., dir. summer session U. No. Ia., 1968—; dir. Cedar Falls Trust & Savs. Bank. Served with USAAF, World War II. Mem. Cedar Falls C. of C., Am. Assn. Sch. Adminstrs., Nat., Ia. State edn. assns., Ia. Assn. Sch. Adminstrs., Council Ednl. Facility Planners, Phi Delta Kappa. Democrat. Home: 269 Clark Dr Cedar Falls IA 50613

KNUTSON, JOHN WILLIAM, dental educator; b. Minnesota, Minn., Nov. 3, 1907; s. John and Marie (Swennes) K.; D.D.S., U. Minn., 1931; M.P.H., Johns Hopkins, 1939, Dr. P.H., 1940; D.Sc. (hon.), U. Pa., 1960; m. Ethel Lawrence Trask, Apr. 27, 1935; childrenKaren Ann, Kristin Joan, John William, Paul Allen. Intern Marine Hosp., Chgo., 1931-34; commd. dental officer, USPHS, 1934-61, child hygiene investigations, NIH, Hagerstown Dental Studies, 1937-39, research, Minn. Dept. of Health, 1940-44; dental dir., chief div. of dental pub. health, 1948- 52, asst. surgeon gen., chief dental officer, 1952-61, also asso. chief of bur. of state services; instr. dentistry in pub, health, Georgetown U. Sch. Dentistry, 1947-61; prof. preventive dentistry, pub. health U. Cal. at Los Angeles, 1961—, acting dean Sch. Dentristry, 1969-70. Dental health officer WHO, 1955, cons., 1970-71; cons. Dept. State AID, Adv. Com. Internat, Edn, Health Manpower; mem. NIH-HIDR Caries Task Force. Chmn. San Francisco forum Nat. Conf. Community Health Services, 1965; pres. Nat. Health Council, 1966. Recipient Henry Spenadel award, 1959; Distinguished Service medal USPHS, 1961; H. Trendley Dean award, 1966; outstanding Achievement medal, award U, Minn., 1951. Diplomate, founding mem. Am. Bd. Dental Pub. Health. Hon. fellow Internat. Coll. Dentists, Royal Soc. Health, Fedn. Dentaire Internationale; mem. Am. Dental Assn., Am. Pub. Health Assn. (pres. 1956-57), Am. Assn. Pub. Health Dentists, A.A.A.S., Internat. Assn. Dental Research, Omicron Kappa Upsilon, Delta Omega, Pi Kappa Alpha. Club: Cosmos (Washington). Editor: Year Book of Dentistry, 1948-66. Contbr. Dentistry in Public Health, 1949. Contbr. articles in dental, pub, health and other sci. publs. Home: 15312 Longbow Dr Sherman Oaks CA 91403 Office: Center Health Scis U Cal Los Angeles CA 90024

KNUTSON, JOSEPH LEONARD, clergyman, coll. pres.; b. Grafton, N.D., Feb. 14, 1906; s. Thomas J. and Linda (Knudson) K.; A.B., St. Olaf Coll., 1927, LL.D., 1952; B.Th., Luther Sem., 1930; m. Beatrice H. Olson, Aug. 1, 1930; childrenPaul, Solveig, Fredrik. Ordained to ministry Luth. Ch., 1930; pastor, DeKalb, Ill., 1930-32, Peterson, Minn., 1932-37, Lake Mills, Ia., 1937-43, Ames, Ia., 1943-48, Mpls., 1948-51; pres. Concordia Coll., Moorhead, Minn.,

1951—. Mem. Evang. Luth. Ch. com. on ch. union. Decorated Order of St. Olaf (Norway). Author: With Hands Uplifted, 1947. Home: 709 S 8th St Moorhead MN 56560

KNUTSON, KENT SIGUART, ch. ofcl.; b. Goldfield, Ia., Aug. 7, 1924; s. Gunner and Gertrude (Thorsheim) K.; B.A., Ia. State U., 1947; B.Th., Luther Theol. Sem., St. Paul, 1951; Ph.D., Columbia, 1961; m. Norma E. Arnesen, Sept. 5, 1951; children—Kirsten, Kristofer, Kent, Kaia, Kimberly, Karl. Chem. engr. Standard Oil of Ind., 1948; ordained to ministry Lutheran Ch., 1954; pastor Our Saviour Luth. Ch., S.I. N.Y., 1954-58; prof. theology Luth. Sem., St. Paul, 1958-68; pres. Wartburg Theol. Sem., Dubuque, Ia., 1968-70; pres. Am. Luth. Ch., Mpls., 1971—. Served with USNR, 1944-46. Author: His Only Son Our Lord, 1964; The Struggle for Middle America, 1965; God's Drama-Seven Acts, 1969. Editor: Dialog, A Jour. of Theology, 1965-68. Home: 1566 Sumter Av N Minneapolis MN 55427 Office: 422 S 5th St Minneapolis MN 55415

KNUTSON, OSCAR RUDOLPH, judge; b. Superior, Wis., Oct. 9, 1899; s. Bottolf and Rachel (Satren) K.; grad. Northwest Sch. Agr., Crookston, Minn., 1919; student St. Olaf Coll., 1920; LL.B., U. of Minn., 1927; LL.D., William Mitchell Coll. Law, 1966; m. Louise M. Halvorson, June 20, 1934 (dec. Jan. 28, 1955); children—Richard and Robert (twins), Anne Joyce; m. 2d, Katherine M. Anderson, July 9, 1968. Admitted to Minn. bar, 1927, practiced at Warren, 1927-40; judge Dist. Ct. of 14th Dist., 1941-48; asso. justice Minn. Supreme Ct., 1948-62, chief justice, 1962—. Sec., treas., mgr. Warren Telephone Co., 1939-49. Mayor, Warren, 1936-41, resigning to take post as Dist. Ct. judge. Recipient Outstanding Alumnus award St. Olaf Coll., 1962, Outstanding Achievement awards, U. Minn., 1963, U. Minn. Law Sch., 1966. Mem. Am., Minn., 14th Jud. Dist. bar assns., Am. Judicature Soc., A.R.C. (chnn. country chpt., 1930-40). Mason (Shriner). Clubs: St. Paul Athletic; 6 O'clock, Torske Klubben (Mpls). Home: 751 Upper Colonial Dr St Paul MN 55118 Office: State Capitol St Paul MN 55118

KNUTTI, RALPH EDDY, med. administr.; b. Palo Alto, Cal., July 24, 1901; s. John Gottlieb and Eleanor (Eddy) K.; A.B., W.Va. U., 1923, B,S., 1926; M.D., Yale, 1928; m. Dorothy Weedon Kaiser, Aug. 15, 1946 (div. Sept. 1955); m. 2d, Sara Hooker Hardwicke, Aug. 17, 1957. Tchr., Grafton (W.Va.) High Sch., 1923- 24; asst. in pathology Vanderbilt U., 1928-29; intern Lakeside Hosp., Cleve., 1929-30; asst. pathology and bacteriology Rockefeller Inst. Med. Research, N.Y.C., 1930-32; instr. pathology U. Rochester, 1932-35, asst. prof., 1935-42; asst. prof. pathology U. So. Cal., 1942-48, asso. prof., 1948-51; dir. labs. Los Angeles Childrens Hosp., 1942-51; med. dir. USPHS, 1951-65; chief extramural programs Nat. Inst. Arthritis and Metabolic Diseases NIH, Bethesda, Md., 1951-60, asso. dir., 1960-61, dir. Nat. Heart Inst,, 1961-65; mem. directing council Pakistan-SEATO Cholera Lab., 1962-65, chmn., 1963-65; exec. officer Am. Soc. Exptl. Pathology, 1965—, Univs. Asso. for Research and Edn. in Pathology, Inc., 1965—. Bd. dirs. Los Angeles Child Guidance Clinic, 1949-51. Hon. fellow Am. Coll. Cardiology (trustee); mem. Am. Heart Assn. (past dir.), Am. Assn. Pathologists and Bacteriologists, Am. Soc. Exptl. Pathology, A.A.A.S., A.M.A., Am. Rheumatism Assn., Sigma Xi, Alpha Kappa Kappa, Sigma Chi. Home: 9212 Aldershot Dr Bethesda MD 20034 Office: 9650 Rockville Pike Bethesda MD 20014

KNUTZEN, VICTOR FRANCIS, accountant; b. Burlington, Wash., Dec. 11, 1914; s. William J. and Helena (Anenson) K.; student Pacific Luth. Coll., 1932-33, Wash. State Coll., 1933-34; B.A., U. Wash., 1936; m. Margaret Elizabeth Carlson, Aug. 31, 1940; children—John A., James V., Gerald C., Ingrid M. With Boeing Co., Seattle, 1941—, successively exec. accounting positions, controller Seattle div., asst. corporate controller, 1941-61, corporate controller, 1961—. Mem. Washington Soc. C.P.A.'s, Seattle C. of C., Financial Execs. Inst., Beta Gamma Sigma, Beta Alpha Psi. Presbyn. Mason. Home: 2649 S 304th St Federal Way WA 98002 Office: Washington 7755 E Marginal Way Seattle WA 98108

KO, WEN-HSIUNG, educator; b. Shang-Hong, Fukien, China, Apr. 12, 1923; s. Sing-Ming and Sou-Ye (Kao) K.; B.S. in E.E. (Tan-Ka-Kee fellow), Nat. Amoy U., Fukien, China, 1946; M.S., Case Inst. Tech., 1956, Ph.D., 1959; m. Christina Chen, Oct. 12, 1957; children—Kathleen, Janet, Linda, Alexander. Came to U.S., 1954, naturalized, 1963. Engr., then sr. engr. Taiwan Telecommunication Adminstrn., 1946-54; mem. faculty Case Inst. Tech., Cleve., 1954—, prof. elec. engring., dir. solid state electronics lab., 1967—, acting dir., engring. design center, 1969—; cons. Conoflow Corp., IBM, Diamond Alkali, NIH, 1966-70; mem. study of rev. NASA life sci. program Nat. Acad. Sci./NRC, summer 1970. Mem. I.E.E.E., Instrument Soc. Am., Am. Inst. Biol. Sci. (bioinstrumentation adv. council 1965-68), Sigma Xi, Eta Kappa Nu. Home: 1634 Compton Rd Cleveland Heights OH 44118 Office: Engring Design Center Case Western Res U Cleveland OH 44106

KOBAYASHI, BERT TAKAAKI, judge; b. Honolulu, July 8, 1916; s. Zengoro and Kiyo (Yamasaki) K.; A.B., Gettysburg Coll., 1938, J.D. (hon.), 1966; J.D., Harvard, 1943; m. Victoria Tsuchiya, Nov. 25, 1938; children—Bert Takaaki, Josephine Leilani, Victoria Puanani, Lincoln Kalani. Admitted to Hawaii bar, 1946; law clk. to atty. gen., Hawaii, 1945; dep. city and county atty., Honolulu, 1946, dep. pub. prosecutor, 1947-48; pvt. practice of law, Honolulu, 1948-62; atty.-gen., Hawaii, 1962-69; asso. justice Supreme Ct. Hawaii, 1969—; magistrate Waialua Ct., Oahu, 1952-59. Mem. Hawaii Subversive Activities Commn., 1958-62; mem. Gov.'s Com. Sex Offenders, 1959-60. Mem. bd. Nuuanu YMCA, 1952-53. Mem. Bar Assn. Hawaii (pres. 1959). Democrat. Home: 4738 Analii St Honolulu HI 96821 Office: Jud Bldg Honolulu HI 96809

KOBAYASHI, RIKI educator, chem. engr.; b. Webster, Tex., May 13, 1924; s. Mitsutaro and Moto (Shigeta) K.; B.S. in Chem. Engring., Rice U., 1944; M.S., U. Mich., 1947, Ph.D. in Chem. Engring., 1951; m. Barbara Joan Stevens, June 1, 1957; children-James Brock, Alec Stevens. Mem. Faculty Rice U., 1951—, prof. chem. engring., 1965—, Calder prof. of chem. engring., 1967—; cons. chem. engr., 1952-. Served with AUS, 1945-46. Mem. Am. Inst. Chem. Engrs., Am Inst. Physics, Am. Chem. Soc., Am. Inst. Mining and Metall. Engrs., Signa Xi, Alpha Chi Sigma, Tau Beta Pi, Phi Lambda Upsilon, Phi Kappa Phi. Unitarian. Author: (with others) Handbook of Natural Gas Engineering, 1959, also numerous articles. Home: 844 Oak Valley Dr Houston TX 77024

KOBAYASHI, SHOSHICHI, mathematician, educator; b. Kofu, Japan, Jan. 4, 1932; s. Kyuzo and Yoshie (Obi) K.; B.S., U. Tokyo, 1953; postgrad. U. Paris, 1953, U. Strasbourg, 1954; Ph.D. in Math., U. Wash., 1956; m. Yukiko Ashizawa, May 11, 1957; children—Sumire, Mei. Came to U.S., 1954. Mem. Inst. Advanced Study, Princeton, N.J., 1956-58; research asso. Mass. Inst. Tech., 1958-60; asst. prof. U. B.C., Vancouver, 1960-62; asst. prof. U. Cal. at Berkeley, 1962-63, asso. prof., 1963-66, prof. math., 1966—; vis. prof. U. Mainz (Germany), 1966, U. Bonn, (Germany), 1969, Mass. Inst. Tech., 1970. Sloan fellow, 1964-66. Mem. Am. Swiss math. socs., Canadian Math. Congress, Société Mathématique de France, Math. Soc. Japan. Author: (with K. Nomizu) Foundations of Differential Geometry, Vol. I, 1963, Vol. II, 1969; Hyperbolic Manifolds and Holomorphic Mappings, 1970. Editor: Pure and Applied Mathematics, 1969—; asso. editor Duke Math. Jour., 1970—. Home: 421 Michigan Av Berkeley CA 94707

KOBER, ARTHUR, writer; b. Austria-Hungary, Aug. 25, 1900; s. Adolph Mayer and Tillie (Ballison) K.; brought to U.S. 1904; ed. Pub. high schools, N.Y.C.; m. Lillian Hellman, Dec. 25, 1925 (div. 1932); m. 2d. Margaret Frohnknecht, Jan. 11, 1941 (dec. 1951); 1 dau., Cathy. Theatrical press agt. Lee & J. J. Shubert, Edgar Selwyn, Jed Harris, Herman Shumlin, Ruth Draper, 1923-30; produced "Me" by Henry Myers, Princess Theatre, 1925; contbr. to N.Y. World, Evening Sun: wrote N.Y. and Hollywood columns on Morning Telegraph, 1930; screen writer (30 motion pictures), 1930-37 and 1941-46, including work on The Little Foxes, Wintertime, In the Meantime, Darling, Don Juan Quilligan, My Own True Love. Mem. Dramatists Guild (N.Y.), P.E.N. Author: Thunder Over the Bronx, 1935; Having Wonderful Time, 1937; Pardon Me for Pointing, 1939; My Dear Bella, 1941; That Man Is Here Again, 1946; Bella, Bella Kissed a Fella, 1951; Wish You Were Here (with Joshua Logan and Harold Rome), 1952; Ooh, What You Said!, 1958; A Mighty Man Is He (with George Oppenheimer), 1959. Mem. faculty New Sch. Social Research, N.Y., 1953. Mem. Authors Guild. Contbr. to The New Yorker. Home: 271 Central Park W New York City NY 10024

KOBER, CARL L., radio and missile engr.; b. Vienna, Austria, Nov. 22, 1913; s. Leopold and Maria (Cremer) K.; Ph.D., U. Vienna, 1935; Dr. phil. habil., Tech. U. Vienna, 1938; m. Christiana Futschig, Mar. 26, 1942; children—Wolfgang, Peter C. Came to U.S., 1949, naturalized, 1958. Project engr. Elin A.G., Vienna, Austria, 1936-39; chief, radar lab. GEMA, Berlin, Germany, 1940-45; mgr. automotive accessories Proschwitz Industrie Works, Kufstein, Austria, 1945-48; asso. prof. applied physics Tech. U., Vienna, 1948-49; mgr. automotive accessories Secowerk, Vienna, 1948-49; cons. Aircraft Radiation Lab., Wright Air Devel. Center, 1949-53, cons. Armament Lab., 1953-55; dir. devel., mech. div. Gen. Mills, Inc., 1955-57; v.p. missiles and ordnance AVCO/Crosley, 1958-61; dir. advanced program div. Martin Co., Denver, 1961-62, dir. advanced tech., 1962-67, dir. Apollo applications sci. program, 1968- -; affiliate prof. mech. engring. Colo. State U.; pioneered radar in Germany; devel. work high resolution radars for reconnaissance and precision bombing, also radar inertial systems. Fellow I.E.E.E., Am. Geophys. Soc., Am. Inst. Aeros. and Astronautics; mem. Am. Phys. Soc., Am. Ordnance Assn. Address: care Martin Marietta Corp Denver CO

KOBLER, JOHN, writer; b. Mt. Vernon, N.Y., Jan. 7, 1910; s. Albert John and Mignon (Sommers) K.; B.A., Williams Coll., 1931; m. Adele Palmer, Jan. 7, 1932 (div. 1945); children—Albert John III, Lynn (Mrs. James Hannon, Jr.); m. 2d, Ruth Margaret Low, Apr. 5, 1945 (div. 1963); children—Karen, Andrea m. 3d, Evelyn Cummins, Feb. 10, 1966. Newspaper reporter N.Y. Evening Jour., fgn. corr. INS, Universal Syndicate, reporter-feature writer King Features, N.Y. Daily Mirror, 1931-39; editor PM, 1940-42; civilian intelligence officer North Africa, Italy, France, 1943-44; attached Am. embassy, Paris, 1945-46; asso. editor Life, 1946-47; free lance contbr. New Yorker, Life, Sat. Eve Post, Colliers, others, 1947-57; contbg. editor Sat. Eve. Post, 1957-64, editor-at-large, 1965—. Author: Trial of Ruth Snyder and Judd Gray, 1938; Some Like it Gory, 1940; Afternoon in the Attic, 1950; The Reluctant Surgeon, A Biography of John Hunter, 1960; Luce: His Time, Life and Fortune, 1968; Capone, 1971. Home: 165 W 66th St New York City NY 10023

KOBRICK, A. MORRIS, lawyer; b. Bklyn., June 2, 1909; s. Jacob and Minnie (Rich) K.; A.B. cum laude, Harvard, 1932, LL.B., 1935, LL.M., 1938; m. Dorothy Sarah Witten, Mar. 30, 1941; children—Jeffrey Witten, Frederick Robert. Washington atty. for U.S. R.R. Retirement Bd.; head atty. Dept. Justice; spl. asst. to U.S. atty. gen.; individual practice law, Boston, 1946—; partner firm Mintz, Levin, Cohn and Glovsky, 1952—; lectr. Past pres. local P.T.A.; past troop chmn. local council Boy Scouts Am. Past mem. Newton City Democratic Com. Mem. Am., Fed., Boston bar assns. Home: 199 Otis St West Newton MA 02165 Office: 1 Center Plaza Boston MA 02108

KOBRICK, HENRY ROBERT, paper co. exec.; b. N.Y.C., Sept. 30, 1918; s. Arthur and Dorothy (Artenberg) K.; B.A. in Econs., N.Y. U., 1940; M.A., Pa. State Coll., 1941; m. Florence E. Held, Jan. 1, 1942; 1 son, Ronald Merritt. Economist, WPB, Washington, 1941-44; with Lily-Tulip Corp., 1944-, v.p. Lily Cups Ltd., Toronto, Ont., Can., 1950-62, v.p. planning Lily-Tulip Cup Corp., N.Y.C., 1962-; now exec. v.p. Home: 136 E 56th St New York City NY 10022 Office: 122 E 42d St New York City NY 10017

KOCH, ADOLPH MEYER, educator, psychologist; b. Austria, Poland, June 18 1908; s. Harry and Dora (Roth) K.; A.B., George Washington U., 1930; A.M., Columbia, 1931, Ph.D., 1935; LL.B., St. John's U., 1937; J.S.D., St. Lawrence U., 1939; m. Evelyn Friedberg, June 25, 1939; children—Marlene Harriet, Bruce Steuert. Research, Rockefeller Inst., 1931-32; instr. psychology Essex County Jr. Coll., Newark, 1933-36, prof. psychology, asst. dean, 1937- 38, dean, 1938-39, pres., 1939-44; pres. Essex Coll. Medicine and Surgery, 1944-46; instr. psychology Yonkers Coll., 1936-37; instr. Broward County Adult Edn. Div., 1955-58; instr. psychology U. Miami Extension Div., 1958-60; instr. psychology Jr. Coll. Broward County, 1960-62, dir. instl. research, 1966—; lectr. psychology Broward Jr. Coll., 1968—; practicing psychologist, 1946—; newspaper columnist. Fellow A.A.A.S., Am. Psychol. Assn.; mem. Fla. Psychol. Assn., Fla. Acad. Scis., Broward County Psychol. Assn. (pres.), Fla. Ednl. Research Assn., George Washington U. Alumni Orgn., Sigma Xi. Club: Fort Lauderdale Country. Contbr. articles to profl. jours. Address: 2319 N E 15th Terrace Ft Lauderdale FL 33305

KOCH, ARNOLD THEODOR, lawyer; b. Bklyn., Mar. 30, 1900; s. Otto and Adele F. (Eschen) K.; A.B., Columbia, 1921, LL.B., 1923; m. Jean Von der Lancken, June 1, 1929 (dec. Apr. 1969); 1 son, Arnold Theodor; m. Marye-Stuart Gress, June 5, 1971. Admitted to N.Y. bar, 1924, Mass. bar, 1955; asso. Haight, Smith, Griffen & Deming, 1923-25; asso., trial counsel Roosevelt & O'Connor, 1925-32; asso., trial counsel O'Connor & Farber, 1932-37, mem. firm, 1937-50; trial counsel, mem. Myles, Wornser & Koch, 1950-60, Wormser, Koch, Kiely & Alessandroni, 1960—; lectr. trial practice Practising Law Inst.; dir. Beneficial Corp. Past chmn. fair rents com., chmn. planning bd., Montclair; chmn. Montclair com. for revision N.J. constn.; mem. Montclair Housing Authority; past pres. Montclair Assn. Trustee Montclair Art Mus.; chmn. Columbia Coll. Fund, 1951. Served as cadet Coast Arty. Sch., Fortress Monroe, Va., 1918. Mem. Assn. Bar City of N.Y., Am., N.Y. bar assns., Soc. Older Grads. Columbia, Delta Upsilon. Conglist. Author: Depositions and Discovery Under the Federal Rules, 1951. Home: 319 Andrews Av Delray Beach FL 33444 summer Brigadoon South Harwich MA 02645 Office: 100 Park Av New York City NY 10017

KOCH, CARL, architect; b. Milw., May 11, 1912; s. Albert Carl and Ruth (Chamberlain) K.; B.A. cum laude, Harvard, 1934, M.Arch., 1937; Bacon travelling fellow, 1938-39; m. Persis White, Dec. 23, 1934; children—Cyrus, Otto, Molly, Carl; m. 2d. Jean Emery, Dec. 24, 1951; children—David, Samuel, Elizabeth. With Sven Markelius, Sweden, 1937, Gropius and Breuer, 1938; sr. architect Nat. Housing Agy., 1942-44; prin. Carl Koch & Assos., Inc., Boston, 1939—; pres. Techcrete Inc., 1971—; prin. works include Acorn House, Fitchburg (Mass.) Youth Library, series houses for Techbuilt, Inc., motor lodges Howard Johnson Co., portable housing USAF, research and devel. project Armco Corp., Ferro Corp., Reynolds Metals, Nat. Steel, Lockheed Aircraft; master planner USAF; concrete bldg. systems design; urban renewal and town planning projects in N.Y.C., Detroit, Boston, Balt., Me.; former lectr. Mass. Inst. Tech. Bd. dirs. Citizens Housing and Planning Assn. Met. Boston; pres. Techcrete, Inc. Served as lt. USNR, 1944-46. Recipient honor award for Acorn House, A.I.A., 1949, Bronze medal, Phila. chpt. A.I.A., 1951, and Gold medal, N.Y. Archtl. League, 1953, 3 awards for Techbuilt House, Parents Mag., 1954, award of merit for Techbuilt House, 1956; Am. Library Assn. A.I.A. Nat. Book Com. 1st honor award, 1963; Honor award Boston Arts Festival, 1963; Frank P. Brown medal Franklin Inst., 1967; Indsl. Arts medal A.I.A., 1969. Fellow A.I.A.; mem. Mass. State Assn. Architects, Boston Soc. Architects, Bldg. Research Inst. Author: (with Andy Lewis) At Home with Tomorrow, 1958. Contbr. articles in field to mags. and jours. Home: 52 Holden Lane Concord MA 01742 Office: 35-36 Lewis Wharf Boston MA 02110

KOCH, CARL GALLAND, lawyer; b. Seattle, May 26, 1916; s. Samuel and Cora (Dinkelspiel) K.; B.A., U. Wash., 1938, J.D., 1940; m. Joan R. Smith, Nov. 26, 1944; children—Carlyn Joan, Robert B. Admitted to Wash. bar, 1940, since practiced in Seattle; partner firm Karr, Tuttle, Koch, Campbell, Mawer & Morrow and predecessors, 1950—; lectr. 7th Ann. Tax Forum U. Puget Sound, 1961. Mem. candidates investigating com. Seattle Municipal League, 1958-70; mem. child study div. Health and Welfare Council Seattle, United Good Neighbors, Seattle, 1951-52; chmn. Seattle chpt. Am. Jewish Com., 1954-55, mem. exec. com., 1950—, mem. Western regional adv. com., 1964- -, mem. nat. exec. bd., 1966—; v.p. Federated Jewish Fund and Council Seattle, 1964, bd. dirs., 1950—; mem. regional bd. Nat. Conf. Christians and Jews, 1954—. Trustee Jewish Publ. Soc. Am. Served to 1st lt. AUS, 1942-46. Life master Am. Contract Bridge League; mem. Am., Wash., Seattle-King County bar assns., Seattle Estate Planning Council, Western Pension Conf., Nat. Found. Health, Welfare and Pensions Plans, Zeta Beta Tau (pres. Alpha Mu chpt. 1937-38), Pi Tau (pres. Seattle 1935), Phi Alpha Delta. Club: Glendale Country (pres. 1965, bd. dirs. 1957-60, 63-66) (Bellevue). Home: 5183 N E Laurelcrest Lane Seattle WA 98105 Office: Seattle First Nat Bank Bldg 1001 4th Av Seattle WA 98104

KOCH, CHARLES DEGANAHL, corp. exec.; b. Wichita, Kan., Nov. 1, 1935; s. Fred Chase and Mary (Robinson) K.; B.S. in Gen. Engring., Mass. Inst. Tech., 1957, M.S. in Mech. Engring., 1958, M.S. in Chem. Engring., 1959. Engr., Arthur D. Little, Inc., Cambridge, Mass., 1959-61; v.p. Koch Engring Co., Inc., Wichita, 1961-63, pres., 63-, also chmn., 1967-; pres. Koch Industries, Wichita, 1966-, also chmn., 1967-; chmn. Koch Internat., SpA, Bergamo, Italy, 1962-, Muirhead Engring., Ltd., Toronto, Ont., Can., 1966-, Koch Venture Capital, Inc., Cambridge, 1968-; pres. Koch. Devel. Corp., Wichita, 1968—; dir. Gr. No. Oil Co., St. Paul, Matador Chem. Co., Inc., Houston, The Matador Cattle Co., Wichita, ABCOR, Inc., Cambridge, Walden Research Corp., Cambridge, IMLAC Corp., Cambridge, First Nat. Bank Wichita, The Coleman Co., Inc., Wichita. Pres. Fred C. Koch Found., Inc.; chmn. Inst. for Humane Studies, Inc; bd. dirs. Center for Ind. Edn. Mem. Am. Inst. Chem. Engrs., Am. Chem. Soc., Sigma Xi. Clubs: Wichita Country; New York Athletic; Chicago; Longwood Cricket (Boston). Home: 1400 N Woodlawn St Wichita KS 67208 Office: 4111 E 37th St N Wichita KS 67201

KOCH, CHARLES JOSEPH, savings and loan assn. exec.; b. Cleve., Oct. 29, 1919; s. Charles Frank and Mary (Cunat) K.; B.S., Case Inst. of Technology, 1941; m. Elizabeth Rusch, May 7, 1945; children—Charles John, John David. Dir. space div. Martin Marietta Corp., Balt., 1941-67; mgr. advanced program McDonnell Douglas Corp., St. Louis, 1967-68; pres. The First Fed. Savings & Loan Assn. Cleve., 1968—, also dir. Mem. NASA Adv. Com., 1956-67; instr. Johns Hopkins U., U. Md., 1943-47. Mem. Greater Cleve. Growth Assn. Bd. dirs. Am. Cancer Soc. Mem. Sigma Xi, Phi Kappa Theta, Tau Beta Pi. Office: 5733 Broadway Cleveland OH 44127

KOCH, EDWARD I., congressman; b. N.Y.C., Dec. 12, 1924; student Coll. City N.Y. LL.B., N.Y.U., 1948. Admitted to N.Y. bar, 1949; former sr. partner firm Koch, Lankenau, Schwartz & Kovner; mem. N.Y.C. Council, 1966; mem. 91st-92d congresses from 17th Dist. N.Y. Founder, MacDougal Area Neighborhood Assn., also N.Y. Citizens for an Ind. Office of Pub. Complaints. Democratic dist. leader Greenwich Village, 1963-65; mem. Village Ind. Dems. Served with AUS, World War II. Mem. N.Y. Civil Liberties Union, Lawyers Constl. Def. Com. Mem. Democratic Liberal Party. Address: House Office Bldg Washington DC 20515

KOCH, EDWIN GEORGE coll. pres.; b. Butte, Mont., Sept. 8, 1905; s. Edwin and Della (Hendrickson) K.; B.A., Mont. State U., 1928; Ph.D., U. Ill., 1932; m. Ruth Mae Smith, Oct. 12, 1930. Chemist, Shell Oil Co., 1932-33, Amalgamated Sugar Co., 1933-34; camp comdr. Civilian Conservation Corps, Ft. Missoula, Mont., 1934-36; research chemist Atlas Powder Co., 1936- 37; instr. chemistry U. Tenn., 1937-41; asst. prof. chemistry U. Tex., 1946; prof. of chemistry and head dept. Mont. Coll. Mineral Sci. and Tech., Butte, 1946-57, pres., 1957—. Dir., Prudential Fed. Savs. & Loan Assn., Helena br. Fed. Res, Bank Mpls. Chmn. Council on Natural Resources and Devel. for Mont., 1966-67; mem. edn. adv. com. Upper Midwest Research and Devel. Council. Mem. Com. 100 for 50th Anniversary Am. Legion, 1968. Bd. dirs. Butte Civic Concert Orch., Butte chpt. A.R.C., World Mus. Mining. Served to lt. col. Ordnance Corps AUS, 1941-46. Mem. N.W. Mining Assn., Am. Chem. Soc., Am. Soc. Engring. Edn., Am. Inst. Mining, Metall. and Petroleum Engrs., Mont. Mining Assn., Res. Officers Assn., Butte C. of C. (pres. 1966), Sigma Xi, Kiwanian (pres. 1961). Home: 1315 W Platinum St Butte MT 59701

KOCH, GEORGE PRICE, Naval officer; b. Cresson, Pa., June 21, 1910; s. Edward Louis and Mary (Price) K.; B.S., U.S. Naval Acad., 1933; m. Virginia Vredenburgh, June 5, 1937; children—George Price, James Peter, Alexander Richard, Virginia Cabell. Commd. ensign U.S.N., 1934, advanced through grades to rear adm., 1961; designated naval aviator, 1934; various assignments in ships and ashore, 1934-42; comdg. officer Hdqrs. Squadron 5, 1942-43; mem. staff comdr. in chief U.S. Fleet, 1943-44; comdg. officer U.S.S. Humboldt, 1944-45; navigator, operations officer U.S.S. Leyte, 1945-47; grad. Naval War Coll., 1948; exec. officer Naval Air Tech. Tng. Center, Memphis, 1948-50. Naval Sta., Kodiak, Alaska, 1950-52; operations officer, then chief staff on staff comdr. Fleet Air Wings, Atlantic, 1952-53; head, war plans br. Office Chief Naval Operations, 1953-55; comdr. Naval Air Sta., Barbers Point, Hawaii, 1955-57; chief staff to comdr. Fleet Air, Quonset Point, R.I., 1957-58; comdr. Fleet Air Wing 3, 1958-59; comdg. officer Naval Air Sta., Norfolk, Va., 1959-61; comdr. Carrier Div. 18, 1961-62, Fleet Air Wings Atlantic, 1962-63; chief, Naval Air Res. Tng., 1963-65; comdr. Carrier Task Force, Mediterranean, 1965-67; comdr. Naval forces So. Command, comdt. 15th Naval Dist., Canal Zone, 1967-69; comdt. Naval Dist., Washington, 1969—. Decorated numerous unit, battle and area ribbons. Home: Tingey House Navy Yard Washington DC 20390 Office: Comdt Naval Dist Navy Yard Washington DC 20390

KOCH, GRAHAM ROBINSON ELLSWORTH, lawyer; b. Pulaski, Va., Oct. 11, 1926; s. Arthur Ellsworth and Julia (Robinson) K.; B.A., U. Va., 1950, LL.B., 1952; m. Jane McNaughton, Oct. 20, 1951; children—Elizabeth, Graham Robinson. Admitted to Va. bar, 1952, Tex. bar, 1956; spl. atty. Internal Revenue Service, 1953-60; partner Akin, Vial, Hamilton, Koch, & Tubb, Dallas, 1961—. Dir. Owen Labs., Inc., Dallas, Semiconductor Component Substrates Corp., Dallas. Served with USAAF, 1945-47. Mem. Sigma Alpha Epsilon. Republican. Home: 13720 Sprucewood St Dallas TX 75240 Office: Republic Bank Tower Dallas TX 75201

KOCH, H. WILLIAM, physicist; b. N.Y.C., Sept. 28, 1920; s. John William and Elizabeth (Hirsch) K.; B.S., Queens Coll., 1941; M.S., U. Ill., 1942, Ph.D., 1944; m. Margaret Giles, Feb. 3, 1945; children—John, Kathleen, Donald, Robert, Russell. Asst. prof. physics U. Ill., 1944-49; research physicist, Oak Ridge, Tenn., 1945-46; chief high energy radiation sect. Nat. Bur. Standards, Washington, 1949-62, chief div. radiation physics 1962-66; dir. Am. Inst. Physics, 1966—. Mem. Numerical Data Adv. Bd., physics survey com. Nat. Acad. Scis. Named Alumnus of Year, Queens Coll., 1960. Fellow Am. Phys. Soc.; mem. Acoustical Soc. Am., Soc. Rheology, Am. Astron. Soc., Am. Crystallographic Assn., Internat. Union Pure and Applied Physics (UN com.), Nat. Acad. Scis. (exec. com. div. phys. scis.), Sigma Xi, Sigma Pi Sigma, Phi Kappa Phi, Gamma Alpha. Club: Cosmos (Washington). Home: 3 Church Lane Scarsdale NY 10583

KOCH, HANS HENRIK, Danish govt. ofcl.; b. Copenhagen, Apr. 17, 1905; s. Harald and Gerda Wienberg (Andersen) K.; LL.B., U. Copenhagen, 1930; m. Agnete Christensen, Jan. 2, 1932; children—Jorgen, Christian, Niels. Acting asst. prin. officer Ministry Social Affairs, 1930-37, asst. prin. officer, 1937-41, chief, employment dept., 1941; permanent sec. state Ministry Labour and Social Affairs, 1942-57; del. Internat. Labour Conf., mem. governing body Internat. Labour Office, 1948-51; mem. Danish Atomic Energy Commn., 1955, chmn. exec. com., 1956—; chmn. Greenland Commn., 1949-50; mem. Nordic Coop. Com. Peaceful Uses Atomic Energy, 1957. Chmn., Danish delegation Internat. Atomic Energy Conf., 1957, gov., 1959, 63, 67; mem. steering com. European Nuclear Energy Agy., 1958—; mem. Govt. Disarmament Com., 1961—, chmn., 1968. mem. Govt. Com. Civil Service Orgn., 1960-65; chmn. Greenland Council, 1964; mem. Danish delegation to negotiate for Danish membership of European Communities, 1970—. Home: Esplanaden 7 Copenhagen Denmark Office: Danish Atomic Energy Commn Strangade 29 Copenhagen K Denmark

KOCH, JOHN, artist, painter; b. Toledo, Aug. 18, 1909; s. Edward John and Marion (O'Hara) K.; ed. pub. schs. and high sch., Ann Arbor, Mich.; m. Dora Zaslavsky, Dec. 23, 1935. Resident in Paris, 1929-33, N.Y.C., 1933—. Entirely self-taught as artist. Exhibited Salon de Printemps (hon. mention) and Salon de Tuilleries, 1929, and in all leading exhbns. of Am. painting since 1939; one-man show, Valentine Gallery, N.Y. C., 1935, Kraushaar Gallery, N.Y. C., 1939, 41, 43, 46, 49, 51, 61, 65, Nelson Rockhill Found., Kansas City, Mo., 1940, Hudson Gallery, Detroit, 1941, Whyte Gallery, Washington, 1944, Art Alliance, Phila., 1945, Portraits, Inc., N.Y.C., Courie Galleries, Los Angeles, Provo, Utah, Suffolk Mus., Stonybrook, N.Y., Syracuse (N.Y.) Mus., 1951, Kraushaar Gallery, 1958, 69, Speed Mus., Louisville, 1971. Represented Bklyn. Mus. Art, Boston Inst. of Arts, William Rockhill Nelson Gallery, Kansas City, Mo., museums of Canajoharie, N.Y., Bennington, Vt., New Britain, Conn., Springfield, Mass., Newark, N.J., Parrish Mus., South Hampton, N.Y., U. of Ga. Received 1st hon. mention Carnegie Inst., 1943; hon. mention Audubon Artists, 1950; mus. purchases Omaha, Neb., Toledo, Mus.; Met. Mus., 1954, 57; Des Moines, Art Center purchase, 1954, Legion of Honor, San Francisco, 1952; Grumbacher award, Audubon Artists, 1958; Ranger Fund purchase prize, Nat. Acad., 1951, Altman prize, 1959, Gold Medal award, 1962; 1st award in oils and John J. McDonough M.D. award, 27th Ann. Butler Inst.; Lotus Club award of Merits, 1964; Artists Fellowship medal, 1964; Century Club medal, 1967; Sammuel Finley Breese Morse Medal in oil painting, 1968. Academician Nat. Acad. Design. Mem. Allied Artists Am. (dir.), Nat. Inst. Arts and Letters. Club: Century (medal 1967). Home: 300 Central Park W New York City NY 10024 Office: care Kraushaar Galleries 1005 Madison Av New York City NY 10021

KOCH, KENNETH, poet; b. Cin., Feb. 27, 1925; s. Stuart J. and Lillian Amy (Loth) K.; A.B., Harvard, 1948; M.A., Columbia, 1953, Ph.D., 1959; m. Mary Janice Elwood, June 12, 1954; 1 dau., Katherine. Mem. faculty Columbia, 1959—, asst. prof. English and comparative lit., 1962-66, asso. prof. English and comparative lit., 1966-71, prof. English and comparative lit., 1971—; bd. editors lit. mag., Locus Solus, 1960-62. Fulbright fellow, 1950-51; Guggenheim fellow, 1961-62. Author: (poems) Poems, 1953, Ko, or A Season on Earth, 1959, Permanently, 1961, Thank You and Other Poems, 1962; When the Sun Tries to Go On, 1969, The Pleasures of Peace, 1970; Bertha and Other Plays, 1966; (plays produced) Little Red Riding Hood, 1953, Bertha, 1959, The Election, 1960, Pericles, 1960, George Washington Crossing the Delaware, 1962, Guinevere or the Death of the Kangaroo, 1964, The Love Suicides at Kaluka, 1965, The Moon Balloon, 1969; (edn.) Wishes, Lies and Dreams: Teaching Children to Write Poetry, 1970. Home: 278 W 4th St New York City NY 10014

KOCH, MELVIN A., instrument mfg. co. exec. Treas., controller Weston Instruments, Inc., Newark. Office: 614 Frelinghuysen Av Newark NJ 07114*

KOCH, PHILIP, educator; b. N.Y.C., Dec. 31, 1927; s. Samuel and Esther (Goldstein) K.; A.B. Magna cum laude, Harvard, 1949, A.M., 1951, Ph.D., 1955; m. Frances A. Bonanno, June 15, 1952; children-Philip Samuel, Erec Russell. Substitute instr. Phillips Exeter Acad., 1950; teaching fellow Harvard, 1950-53, 54-55; instr. Northwestern U., 1955-56; instr., then asst. prof. Bryn Mawr Coll., 1956-61; mem. faculty U. Pitts., 1961—, prof. French and Italian, chmn. dept., 1966—. Bd. dirs. French Cultural Center Western Pa., 1968—. Predoctoral Fulbright fellow, Italy, 1953- 54; Fulbright research travel grantee, Paris, 1965-66; sr. research fellow Am. Council Learned Socs., Paris, 1969-70. Mem. Modern Lang. Assn., Am.. Assn. Tchrs. French, Am. Assn. U. Profs., Alliance Francaise de Pittsburgh (v.p. 1962-63), Phi Beta Kappa. Club: Harvard (Phila. and Pitts.). Author, editor in field. Home: 5525 Avondale Pl Pittsburgh PA 15206

KOCH, RALPH RICHARD, architect; b. Omaha, Nov. 1, 1928; s. Ralph Ruben and Agnes (Janda) K.; B.Arch., U. Neb., 1951; m. Jane Lee Goeres, Dec. 27, 1950; children—Sharon Lee, Richard Joohn, Barbara Jo. Designer, draftsman Hugill, Blatherwick, Fritzel & Kroeger, Sioux Falls, S.D., 1953-57; asso. Howard Parezo & Assos., Sioux Falls, 1957-61; prin. Ralph Koch & Assos., Sioux Falls, 1961-69; partner Koch, Hazard & Assos., Sious Falls, 1969-71. Mem. Sioux Falls Zool. Soc., 1966-71, Civic Fine Arts Assn., 1967-71, Sioux Falls Symphony Assn., 1965-71, Assn. for Retarded Children, 1966-71. Bd. dirs. Sioux Vocational Sch. for Handicapped, Sioux Falls Symphony Assn. Served to capt., C.E., AUS, 1951-53. Mem. Archtl. Forum, Sioux Falls Indl. Found., C. of C., Cosmopolitan Internat. (v.p.), A.I.A. (state pres. 1969), Am. Legion, V.F.W., Kappa Sigma. Republican. Roman Catholic. K.C. (4), Elk (exalted ruler 1970-71). Architect Karl E. Mundt Library, Dakota State Coll., Madison, S.D., 1968, dedicated by Pres. Nixon, June 3, 1969, named Outstanding State Bldg. at S.D. Engr.'s Office, 1968. Home: 728 Woodlawn Dr Sioux Falls SD 57102 Office: 100 N Phillips Av Sioux Falls SD 57102

KOCH, RAYMOND FELT, mfg. corp. exec.: b. Chgo., Sept. 27, 1919; s. Raymond Joseph and Virginia (Felt) K.; B.S., Mass. Inst. Tech., 1941; m. Helen Huling, Sept. 20, 1947; children—Helen M., Raymond W., Margaret Ann. With Comptometer Corp., 1946-61, asst. to pres., 1950-56, asst. sec., 1954- 57, sec., 1957-61; sec. Victor Comptometer Corp., Chgo., 1961—. Trustee Hadley Sch. for Blind, Winnetka, Ill. Served from 2d lt. to maj., Ordnance Dept., AUS, 1941-46. Mem. S.A.R., Am. Soc. Corporate Secs., Field Mus. Natural History Chgo., Chgo. Hist. Soc., Delta Tau Delta. Roman Catholic. Clubs: Economic, Executives, Union League (Chgo.); Indian Hill (Winnetka). Home: 38 Essex Rd Winnetka IL 60093 Office: 3900 N Rockwell St Chicago IL 60618

KOCH, RAYMOND JOSEPH , bus. exec.: b. Chgo., Apr. 19, 1892; s. Nicholas and Annie Virginia (Finkler) K.; B.S. in C.E., Armour Inst. of Tech., 1913, C.E., 1918; LL.D., Ill. Inst. Tech., 1968; m. H. Virginia Felt, Apr. 30, 1918 (dec. Jan. 1955); children-Major Raymond Felt, Mary Elizabeth (Mrs. Alfred C. Schmidt), Virginia (Mrs. Allen C. Senear), Ruth (Mrs. Ronald E. Allen). Designer of concrete structures Bridge Dept., C.M., St. P. & P.R.R., 1913-16; sales engr. Ilg Electric Ventilating Co., Chgo., 1917-20, credit mgr., 1920-29, asst. treas., 1925-29; treas., dir. Comptometer Corp. (formerly Felt and Tarrant Mfg. Co.), Chgo., 1930-34, pres., 1934-55, dir., 1934-, chmn. bd., 1955-61; vice chmn. bd. Victor-Comptometer Corp., 1961-70. Pres. Employers' Assn. Chgo., 1938-40, dir., 1938-58; sec. Ill. Inst. Tech., 1948—, also trustee, mem. exec. com.; trustee ITT Research Inst. Dir., 1st v.p., later pres. Ill. Mfrs. Assn., 1947; industry panel men., region 10 War Labor Bd., 1944-45. Trustee Hadley Sch. for Blind, Winnetka, Ill. Mem. Am. Ordnance Assn., Tau Beta Pi, Delta Tau Delta. Republican. Roman Catholic. Clubs: Executives, Union League (past treas.; v.p.) (Chgo.) Indian Hill (Winnetka); Skokie Country (Glencoe, Ill.). Home: 285 White Oak Lane Winnetka IL 60093 Office: 3900 N Rockwell St Chicago IL 60618

KOCH, RICHARD, architect; b. New Orleans, June 9, 1889; s. Julius and Anna (Frotscher) K.; B.A., Tulane U., 1910; student Atelier Bernier, Paris, 1911-12: Architect since 1916; mem. firm Armstrong & Koch, New Orleans, 1916-35; individual practice, 1935-55, mem. firm Richard Koch & Samuel Wilson Jr., 1955—. Dist. officer Historic Am. Bldgs. Survey in La.; past dir. Gulf States Dist., A.I.A.; pres. La. State Bd. Archtl. Examiners; pres. Nat. Archtl. Accrediting Bd.; chmn. Zoning Bd. of Appeals and Adustment, New Orleans. Past 2d v.p. Isaac Delgado Museum Art. Served as 1st lt. Air Service, U.S. Army, 1916-18. Recipient silver medal Archtl. League N.Y., 1938. Fellow A.I.A.; mem. N.A.D. Home: 1550 2d St New Orleans LA 70130 Office: Masonic Temple Bldg New Orleans LA 70130

KOCH, RICHARD, pediatrician; b. N.D., Nov. 24, 1921; s. Valentine and Barbara (Fisher) K.; A.B., U. Cal. at Berkeley, 1958; M.D., U. Rochester, 1951; m. Kathryn Jean Holt, Oct. 2, 1943; children—Jill, Thomas, Christine, Martin, Leslie. Mem. staff Children's Hosp. Los Angeles, 1952—, dir. mental retardation program, 1955—; faculty U. So. Cal., 1955—, prof. pediatrics. Mem. Project Hope, Trujillo, Peru, 1970. Mem. A.M.A., Am. Assn. on Mental Deficiency (pres. 1968-69), Am. Acad. Pediatrics, Nat. Assn. Retarded Children, Western Soc. Pediatric Research. Author: (with James Dobson) The Mentally Retarded Child and his Family, 1971. Research, numerous publs. on mental retardation and relation to pediatrics. Home: 6334 W 80th St Los Angeles CA 90045 Office: 4650 W Sunset Blvd Los Angeles CA 90027

KOCH, ROBERT, engr., cement co. exec; b. Zurich, Switzerland, Feb. 17, 1909; s. Ernest C. and Emmy (de Vigier) K.; M.E., Inst. Tech., Zurich, 1933; children—Beat, Fernand, Janine, Thomas. Asst. to mgr. Société Anonyme des Ciments Libanais, Chekka, Liban, 1935-36; tech. mgr. Société Egyptienne des Ciments Portland Tourah, Tourah Le Caire, 1936-37; asst. to sales mgr. Climents d'Obourg S.A., Brussels, Belgium, 1938-39; tech. mgr. Vigier Cement, Ltd., Luterbach, Switzerland, pres. 1943—; pres. St. Lawrence Cement Co., Montreal, Que., 1952—, chmn. bd., 1963—; exec. bd. Holderbank Financiere Glaris S.A., Glaris, Switzerland, S.A.F.A.A. Société Anonyme Francaise des Appareils Automatiques, Paris, AVAG Automatenverpflegungs AG Zurich, Switzerland, Dufferin Materials & Constrns. Ltd., Toronto, Ont., Can.; chmn. A Bangerter & Co., Ltd. (Lyss); vice chmn. bd. Eerste Nederlandsche Cement Industrie (Holland); dir. ARFA Tube Mill Ltd. Basel CH, Bank Leu Ltd., Zurich, Ciments d'Obourg SA, Brussels, Construvit SA, Lyss CH, Schoeller Textile SA Schaffhausen, CH, Wasserngrat SA, Gstaad, Switzerland. Mem. Swiss Engr. and Architect Soc. Club: Golf of Basel. Office: Vigler Cement Ltd 4700 Luterbach Soleure Switzerland

KOCH, ROBERT ALAN, educator; b. Durham, N.C., Nov. 23, 1919; s. Frederick Henry and Loretta Jean (Hannigan) K.; B.A., U. N.C., 1940, M.A., 1942; M.F.A. (Woodrow Wilson fellow, Procter fellow), Princeton, 1948, Ph.D., 1954. Instr., asst. dir. Art Museum, Princeton, asst. prof., 1955-57, asso, prof., 1958-64, prof. curator prints, 1965—; viss. prif. Princeton Theol. Sem., 1954-56, Inst. Fine Arts, N.Y.U., summer 1962. Served to 1st lt. AUS, 1942-46. Recipient FUlbright research award for Belgium, 1956-57; Am. Council Learned Socs. grantee, 1961-62. Mem. Coll. Art Assn. Am. (bd. dirs. 1961-63), Mediaeval Acad. Am. (councillor 1964-66), Renaiaissance Soc. Am., Archaeol. Inst. Phi Beta Kappa, Author: Joachim Patinir, 1968. Home: 10 Mercer St Princeton NJ 08540

KOCH, ROBERT JOSEPH, bus. exec.; b. Chester, Pa., Apr. 2, 1921; s. Edward Lewis and Mary (Price) K.; B.S. in Indsl. Engring., Pa. State U., 1942; m. May Dulaney Belt, Sept. 15, 1945; children—Marietta, Rebecca, Price, Catherine. With Arundel Corp., Balt., 1937—, v.p., 1962-63, pres., 1963-71, chief exec. officer, 1965-67, now vice chmn., sec.; dir. Md. Slag Co.; adv. dir. Md. Nat. Bank. Served to lt. USNR, World War II. Mem. Balt. Assn. Commerce, Soc. Am. Mil. Engrs., Engrs. Club Balt., Beavers, Sigma Nu. Roman Catholic. Club: Maryland (Balt.). Home: 207 Hawthorne Rd Baltimore MD 21210 Office: 501 St Paul Pl Baltimore MD 21202

KOCH, ROY SWARTZ, clergyman; b. Ont., Can., Sept. 6, 1913; s. Charles S. and Minerva (Swartz) K.; student Waterloo (Ont.) Coll., 1944; B.A., Goshen Coll. Bib. Sem., 1945, B.D., 1959; m. Martha Horst, Aug. 8, 1942; childrenRobert Laverne, Arlene Elizabeth, Richard Daniel, Rodney James, Helen Jane, Sheila Ann. Came to U.S., 1957. Ordained to ministry Mennonite Ch., 1936, created bishop, 1951; prin. Ont. Mennonite Bible Sch., Kitchener, 1952-57; pastor S. Union Mennonite Ch., West Liberty, O., 1957-70; bishop S.W. Ohio Mennonite chs., 1959-70; conf. minister Ind.- Mich. Conf. of Mennonite Ch., 1971—. Moderator Ohio and Eastern Mennonite Conf., 1962-66, pres., 1969-70; moderator Mennonit Gen. Conf., 1963-65. Author: Zestful Living for Older Adults, 1963. Editor minister's sect. Builder mag., 1964-. Address: 204 S 6th St Goshen IN 46526

KOCH, SIGMUND, educator, author; b. N.Y.C., Apr. 18, 1917; s. John D. and Helen (Karman) K.; B.A., N.Y.U., 1938; M.A., State U. Ia., 1939; Ph.D., Duke, 1942; m. Rosemary Lys Dunlap, June 18, 1955; children—John L., Katherine E. Mem. faculty Duke, 1942-47, 48-64, prof. psychology, 1953-64; asso. prof. Clark U., 1947-48; Fulbright prof. Univ. Coll., London, Eng., 1952-53; project dir. study of status of psychology Am. Psychol. Assn., 1953—; dir. program humanities and arts Ford Found., 1964-67; Univ. prof. arts and letters, Stiles prof. comparative studies, prof. psychology and philosophy U. Tex. at Austin, 1967—; vis. asso. rof. U. Wash., 1949, U. Colo., 1951; vis. prof. U. N.C., 1959; Stevens vis. fellow Western Behavioral Scis. Inst., 1961; Morrison lectr. Scripps Inst., 1961; Elliott lectr. U. Minn., 1961, 67. Mem. Dartmouth Conf. Learning Theory, 1950; mem. stand-by unit U. N.C., Operations Analysis Br., Hdqrs. USAF, 1952; occasionnal cons. Ford Found., 1953—; mem. Conf. Behaviorism, Minn. Center Philosophy of Sci., 1954; mem. conf. Research re Thinking NSF, 1954; mem. Colo. Coll. Conf. Relations between Sci. and Humanities, 1961; mem. Conf. Behaviorism vs Phenomenology Rice U., 1963, Conf. Psychology and Humanities Great Lakes Coll. Assn., 1968; adviser Nat. Acad. Sci., 1964. Fellow Am. Psychol. Assn. (pres. div. philos. psychology 1966-67, div. psychology and arts 1968-69, rep. to council, 1968-71), A.A.A.S., Psychonomic Soc.; mem. Study Group Unity and Knowledge (exec. com. 1967-70). Phi Beta Kappa, Sigma Xi. Author: Psychology: A Study of a Science, Vol. 7, 1971, editor vos. 1-6; co-author: Modern Learning Theory, 1954; Behaviorism and Phenomenology, 1964; Science and Human Affairs, 1965; The Anatomy of Knowledge, 1969; also articles. Contbr. Ency. Britannica. Home: 5809 Westslope Dr Austin TX 78731

KOCH, WALTER KARL, lawyer; b. Denver, Nov. 8, 1901; s. Karl and Wanda Otellia (Tischler) K.; A.B., U. Colo., 1923; J.D., U. Denver, 1925, postgrad, 1929-31; Eng.D., Colo. Sch. Mines, 1958; LL.D., Colo. Coll., 1962; m. Lillian E. Lind, Sept. 23, 1925 (dec. July 1940); childrenWanda Elizabeth (Mrs. James M. Wilson), Ellen Janet (Mrs. K. William Buchholz); m. 2d, Ruth Brooks Reid, Aug. 11, 1945. Student Mountain States Tel. & Tel. Co., 1923-25, dist. traffic supt., Pueblo, Colo., 1925-28, traffic chief, Denver, 1928-30, gen. sales mgr., 1930-33, comml. supervisor, Salt Lake City, 1933-35, Denver, 1939-45, gen. comml. mgr., 1945-49, v.p., 1949-52, bd. dirs., 1949-70, pres., 1952-66; dir. Silver State Savs. & Loan Assn., Wheat Ridge Found., Denver Dry Goods Co. Capitol Life Ins. Co., Assoc. Corp. N. Am.; adviser Denver U.S. Nat. Bank. Partner Holme Roberts & Owen. Former dir. Mountain States Employers Council. Pres. Mile High United Fund, 1961; dir. Central City House Opera Assn., Nat. West Stock Show; trustee YMCA, former dir. Council Religion and Internat. Affairs; dir. Luth. Hosp. and Med. Center; past dir., v.p. Nat. Safety Council; trustee Denver Mus. Natural History; dir. Children's Hosp.; mem. Denver com. Fgn. Relations. Dir. Air Force Acad. Found.; past trustee Denver Zool. Found.; trustee, U. Denver, Denver Symphony Soc.; dir. Met. Safety Council, Colo. Assn. Commerce and Industry; civilian aide Sec. Army for Colo., 1956. Past trustee Aspen Inst. Humanistic Studies, Boettcher Found.; past dir. Luth. Ch.-Mo. Synod. Recipient Distinguished Service award U. Colo., 1953; Brotherhood award Nat. Conf. Christians and Jews, 1963; Marquis award Am. Inst. Mgmt., 1965; certificate achievement Assn. U.S. Army, 1965; U.S. Savs. Bond Patriots medal, 1965; Evans award U. Denver, 1966; Distinguished Alumni award Delta Sigma Rho-Tau Kappa Alpha Forensic Soc., 1966; Liberty Bell award Luth. Brotherhood, 1966; Distinguished Service to Safety award, Nat. Safety Council. Mem. Denver Real Estate Investment Assn. (trustee), Telephone Pioneers Am. (past pres.), Colo., Denver (past pres.) chambers commerce, Res. Officers Assn. U.S. (hon. life), Colo. Assn. Ind. Colls. and Univs. (past pres.), Am., Colo., Denver bar assns., U.S., Colo. sr. golfers assns., Alpha Kappa Psi (hon.), Delta Sigma Rho, Phi Alpha Delta, Pi Kappa Alpha, Beta Gamma Sigma. Clubs: Tower, Denver, Athletic, Rotary (pres. 1966-67, dir.), Country, Mile High, University, Cherry Hills Country, Lion (past pres., dir.). Home: 33 Sunset Dr Englewood CO 80110 Office: 1700 Broadway Denver CO 80202

KOCHAKIAN, CHARLES DANIEL, endocrinologist, educator; b. Haverhill, Mass., Nov. 18, 1908; s. Daniel S. and Haigoohee (Nalbandian) K.; A.B., Boston U., 1930, M.A., 1931; Ph.D., U. Rochester, 1936; m. Beatrice Irene Armstrong, July 27, 1940; 1 son, Charles Pedlar. Fellow, dept. vital econs. U. Rochester, 1933-36, mem. faculty, 1936-51; prof. research biochemistry, head dept. biochemistry and endocrinology, 1951-57; asso. dir. Med. Research Found. Okla., 1951-53, coordinator research, 1953-55; prof. physiology U. Ala. Med. Center, 1957—, prof. biochemistry, 1961—, dir. exptl. endocrinology, 1961—, acting coordinator research, 1960-61; mem. com. growth NRC, 1949-51; cons. Fels Research Inst., 1956, M.D. Anderson Hosp. and Tumor Inst., 1956; vis. Claude Bernard prof. Inst. Exptl. Biology and Medicine, U. Montreal, 1950; mem. panel drugs for metabolic disturbance of drug efficacy study Nat. Acad. Scis.-NRC, 1966—; cons. dental sch. com. Okla. Dental Assn., 1954-57. Mem. adv. council Jefferson County (Ala.) div. Am. Cancer Soc., 1960-62. Recipient Claude Bernard medal, 1950; medal Osaka Endocrine Soc., 1962. Fellow A.A.A.S.; mem. Am. Soc. Biol. Chemists, Am. Physiol. Soc., Endocrine Soc., Soc. Exptl. Biology and Medicine, Am. Chem. Soc., A.M.A. (chmn. screening group com. steroids and hormones 1952-57), Sigma Xi (past pres., sec.-treas. chpt.). Presbyn. (elder). Spl. research on metabolic effect hormones, mechanisms of hormone action, metabolism of steroid hormones by tissue enzymes, hormone-enzyme relationships. Discoverer protein anabolic action of androgens. Home: 3617 Oakdale Rd Birmingham AL 35223

KOCHANSKI, ADRIAN JOSEPH, educator; b. Milw., July 29, 1918; s. Alois S. and Antionette (Czerwinski) K.: A.B., St. Louis U., 1941, M.A. 1942, Ph.L., 1943, S.T.L., 1949; Ph.D., U. Chgo., 1955. Tchr., head prefect Campion High Sch., Prairie du Chien, Wis., 1942-46; asst. prof. edn. Marquette U., 1954-60, dean Coll. Liberal Arts, 1954-60; regional dir. edn. Wis. Province Soc. of Jesus, 1960-68; founder Sogang U., Seoul, Korea, 1960, The Cath. U. of Salta (Argentina), 1964; vis. scholar Stanford U., 1968-69; exec. asst. v.p. acad. affairs San Diego State Coll., 1969-70, dean acad. planning, 1970—. Mem. N.E.A., Nat. Edn. Am. Assn. U. Profs., Phi Delta Kappa. Address: 14770 Caminito Orense Oeste San Diego CA 92129

KOCHEN, SIMON BERNARD, educator, mathematician; b. Antwerp, Belgium, Aug. 14, 1934; s. Solomon and Rose (Goldfarb) K.; B.Sc., McGill U., 1954, M.Sc., 1955; M.A., Princeton, 1956, Ph.D., 1958; m. Beth Susan Forsheit, June 11, 1961; children—Eve Judith, David Ian, Karen Rose. Came to U.S., 1959. Research asst. prof. U. Montreal, 1958-59; from asst. prof. to prof. Cornell U., 1959-67; mem. Inst. Advanced Study, Princeton, 1966-67; Guggenheim fellow, vis. prof. Fed. Polt. Inst., Zurich (Switzerland), 1962-63; prof. math. Princeton, 1967—. Recipient Cole prize in number theory Am. Math. Soc., 1967. Home: 114 FitzRandolph Rd Princeton NJ 08540

KOCHER, ERIC, univ. dean; b. Trinidad, B.W.I., June 29, 1912; brought to U.S., 1919, naturalized, 1925; s. Paul William and Frieda Marie (Schwabe) K.; A.B., Princeton, 1932; M.B.A., Harvard, 1934; student drama sch. Yale, 1940- 41; m. Margaret Helburn, Apr. 26, 1947; childrenEric Glenn, Terry, Christopher, Debra. Asst. economist FHA, Washington, 1934-36; asso. social sci. analyst Social Security Bd., 1936-40; dir. displaced persons camps, Austria, UNRRA

1945-46; New Eng. organizer Citizens Com. on Displaced Persons, 1947; labor attache Am. embassy, Brussels, Belgium, 1947-52; Nat. War Coll., 1952-53; U.S. consul gen., Kuala Lumpur, Malaya, 1953-55; dep. dir. Office S.E. Asian Affairs, 1956-58, dir., 1958-59; dep. chief mission, counselor embassy, Amman, Jordan, 1959-61, Belgrade, Yugoslavia, 1962-65; diplomat in residence U. Tex., Austin, 1965-66; chief profl. placement service Dept. of State, 1966-68; State Dept. Rep. Job Corps, 1968-69; asso. dean Columbia U. Sch. Internat. Affairs, 1969-. Served with AUS, 1942-45; chief civilian labor br. Mil. Labor Service in France, Belgium, Germany, 1944-45; released to Res. as maj. Decorated Bronze star; recipient Am. Theatre Wing award for best original play, 1957; Baton Rouge Little Theatre award Best Original Play of 1959. Mem. Princeton Alumni Assn., Diplomatic and Consular Officers Ret. Author: Apocalypse (included Yale Vol. Best Radio Plays), 1941; In Shadow of Cathedral (included in Best One Act Plays 1951-52); Karma (included in Best Short Plays, 1952-53); Medal for Julien (included in best short plays 1954-55). Home: 102 Shore Rd Douglaston NY 11363

KOCHER, PAUL HAROLD, educator; b. Trinidad, B.W.I., Apr. 23, 1907; s. Paul William and Freida (Schwabe) K.; A.B., Columbia, 1926; J.D., Stanford, 1929, M.A., 1932, Ph.D., 1936; m. Annis Cox, Aug. 31,1936; children—Paul Dana, Carl Alvin. Instr., Stanford, 1936-38; instr., then asst. prof. U. Wash., 1938-46; prof. U. Neb., 1948-49, Claremont Grad. Sch., 1949-58; prof. English and humanities Stanford, 1960—. Fellow Folger Shakespeare Library, 1939-40; Guggenheim fellow, 1946-47, 55-56; Huntingdon Library fellow, 1952-53. Mem. Modern Lang. Assn., Renaissance Soc. Am., San Luis Obispo County Hist. Soc., Wilderness Soc., Order of Coif. Author: Christopher Marlowe, 1946; Science and Religion in Elizabethan England, 1953. Editor: (Marlowe) Doctor Faustus, 1950. Editor Huntington Library Quar., 1952-53; editorial bd. Jour. History of Ideas, 1951-59. Contbr. profl. jours. Home: 867 Mission St San Luis Obispo CA 93401

KOCHI, JAY KAZUO, chemist, educator; b. Los Angeles, May 17, 1927; s. Tsuruzo and Shizuko (Moriya) K.; student Cornell U., 1945; B.S., U. Cal. at Los Angeles, 1949; Ph.D., Ia. State U., 1952; m. Marion Kiyono, Mar. 1, 1959; children—Sims, Ariel, Julia. Faculty Harvard, 1952-55; NIH fellow Cambridge (Eng.) U., 1956; mem. faculty Ia. State U., 1956; with Shell Devel. Co., 1957-61; mem. faculty dept. chemistry Case Western Res. U., 1962-69, prof., 1966-69; prof. chemistry Ins. U., Bloomington, 1969—; cons. chemist, 1964—. Mem. Am. Chem. Soc., Chem. Soc. (London), Sigma Xi. Research on mechanism of catalysis of organic reactions, organometallics, photochemistry. Home: 217 S Hillsdale Dr Bloomington IN 47401

KOCHMAN, MOHAMED NASSIM, Mauritanian lawyer, diplomatist, internat. banker; b. Oct. 25, 1932; ed. Van Vollenhoven Lycee, Dakar, Senegal, Marcel Gambier Coll., Lisieux, France, Caen U. and Inst. Polit. Studies, also faculty law and econ. scis., Grenoble, France. Lawyer, Ct. of Appeal, Dakar, 1958-61; 1st sec. embassy, Washington, also Mauritanian permanent mission to UN, 1961; 1st counsellor, later charge d'affaires, Washington, 1962-64; charge d'affaires permanent mission of Mauritania to UN, 1964; alt. del. Internat. Bank Reconstrn. and Devel., Internat. Finance Corp., also Internat. Devel. Assn., 1962-64; exec. dir. for Cameroon, Central African Republic, Chad, Democratic Republic of Congo, Mali, Mauritius, Dahomey, Gabon, Ivory Coast, Malagasy Republic, Mauritania, Niger, Rwanda, Senegal, Somalia, Togo and Upper Volta, 1964—. Address: 5180 Linnean Terrace N W Washington DC 20008

KOCHS, HERBERT WILLIAM, indsl. chem. mfr.; b. Chgo., Mar. 28, 1903; s. August and Adelaide (Petersen) K.; student Mass. Inst. Tech., 1920-23, Northwestern U., 1923- 24; m. Elizabeth Kennedy, 1924; 1 dau., Nancy (Mrs. E. K. Shaw); m. 2d, Mildred Swift, Dec. 2, 1928; childrenSusan M. (Mrs. W. E. Judevine) (dec.), Herbert William, Judith Anne (Mrs. Nelson Shaw); m. 3d, Phyllis Anderson, Nov. 10, 1955; m. 4th, Paula Leggett, Dec. 28, 1959; childrenJustin and Martin (twins). Sec., Diversey Corp., Chgo., 1927- 32, v.p., 1932-35, pres., 1935-43, now chmn.; dir. Nat. Council on Crime and Delinquency, pres., 1959-64, hon. v.p., 1964-67; former dir. Grant Hosp.; chmn. bd. mgrs. Uhlich Childrens Home, 1956-58. Clubs: M.I.T. (past pres.), Chicago Athletic (Chgo.); Indian Hill (Winnetka, Ill.); American (London, Eng.). Office: 212 W Monroe St Chicago IL 60606

KOCISKO, STEPHEN JOHN, clergyman; b. Mpls., June 11, 1915; s. John Z. and Anna (Somosz) K.; Ph.B., Propaganda Fide U., 1937, S.T.L., 1941. Ordained priest Roman Cath. Ch., 1941; chancellor Byzantine Cath. Diocese of Pitts., 1956, consecrated bishop, 1956; rector Byzantine Cath. Sem., Pitts., 1958-63; 1st bishop Byzantine Eparchy (diocese) of Passaic, 1963-69; met. archbishop of Munhall, 1969—. Address: 50 Riverview Ave Pittsburgh PA 15214

KOCIVAR, BEN, mag. editor; b. Jamaica, L.I., N.Y., Apr. 13, 1916; s. Isidor and Rebecca (Ladman) K.; B.S. in Social Sci., Coll. City N.Y., 1938; grad. cons. editor Popular Sci. mag., 1970—; v.p. Jamaica Wholesale Meat Co. student U. Mo., 1939-40; m. Thelma Levine, Aug. 31, 1941; childrenKarl, Carol, Jane. Reporter, Chgo. City News Bur., 1940-41; information specialist bur. pub. relations, War Dept., 1941-42; editor U.S. Army Newsmap of Orientation Program, 1942-44; sr. editor Look mag., 1944-; cons. editor Popular Sci. mag., 1970—; v.p. Jamaica Wholesale Meat Co., 1956—; propr. Air Pixies, aerial photography, N.Y.C., 1948—; cons. Pan Am. World Airways, N.Y.C., 1969- . Mem. Collier Trophy com. Nat. Aero. Assn., 1959-65. Democratic committeeman, North Castle, N.Y., 1958—; candidate North Castle Town Bd., 1958. Bd. dirs. Banksville Community House, Greenwich, Conn. Recipient TWA aviation writing award, 1958; co-recipient TWA picture award, 1957. Mem. Aviation-Space Writers Assn., N.Y. Travel Writers Assn., Internat. Motor Press Assn., Am. Inst. Aeros. and Astronautics. Home: RFD 2 Bedford NY 10506 Office: 575 Madison Av New York City NY 10022

KOCK, WINSTON EDWARD scientist, corp. exec.; b. Cin., Dec. 5, 1909; s. Henry Edward and Olivia (Hoffman) K.; E.E., U. Cin., 1932, M.S., 1933, D. Sc. (hon.), 1952; Ph.D., U. Berlin, 1934; postgrad. Inst. Advanced Study, Princeton, 1935-36; fellow Indian Inst. Sci. Bangalore, India, summer 1936; m. Kathleen Redmond, June 24, 1939; childrenWinston Edward, Robert Marshall, Kathleen Redmond. Teaching fellow U. Cin., 1934-35; research engr. Baldwin Piano Co., 1936-38, dir. electronic research, 1938-42; research engr. microwaves Bell Telephone Labs., 1942-51, dir. acoustics research, 1951-55, dir. audio and video systems research, 1955-56; chief sci. systems div. Bendix Corp., 1956-57, dir., gen. mgr. Bendix research labs. div., Southfield, Mich., 1958-62, v.p. corp., Detroit, 1962-64; v.p., chief scientist Bendix Corp., Detroit, 1966—; dir. Electronics Research Center, NASA, Cambridge, Mass., 1964-66: Mem. Hartwell com. Nat. Acad. Sci., summer 1950, Teota com., 1952, Lamplight com., 1953, Nobska com., 1956, ARDC-Nat. Acad. Sci. com., 1957, Atlantis com., 1960; cons. Sec. Def., 1958-, U.S. Def. Dept. adv. panel on electronics, 1959—; mem. reactor devel. Com., bd. dirs. Argonne Univs. Assn., 1967—; bd. dirs. Atomic Indsl. Forum, chmn. space nuclear com.; mem. com. on undersea warfare Nat. Acad. Scis.; mem. research and devel. task group Def. Sci. Bd. Mem. U.S. delegation NSF, Holography Seminar. 1967, 69. Trustee Western Coll. for Women, 1962—, chmn., 1968-70; adv. com. U. Cin., 1957—. Recipient Outstanding Young Engr. award Eta Kappa Nu, 1938, award of merit, 1959; Naval Ordnance award, 1946; U.S. Navy Distinguished Pub. Service medal, 1964; George Washington medal Engrs. Club, 1966; Confere award, Worcestor Jr. Coll., 1965. Fellow I.E.E.E. (chmn. of profl. group on audio), Am. Phys. Soc., Am. Acoustical Soc., A.A.A.S., Am. Inst. Aeros. & Astronautics (asso); hon. fellow Indian Acad. Scis.; mem. Am. Inst. Physics, N.A.M., Indsl. Research Inst., Am. Ordnance Assn., Nat. Security Indsl. Assn., Am. Orchid Soc., Sigma Xi, Tau Beta Pi, Eta Kappa Nu (nat. chmn. 1946, bd. dirs. 1960-63). Presbyn. (ruling elder 1960—). Club: Cosmos. Author: Sound Waves and Light Waves, 1965; Lasers and Holography, 1969; numerous papers. Inventions and research Baldwin Electronic organ, waveguide microwave lens, underwater sound, speech analysis, narrow band TV. Home: 903 Oakdale Rd Barton Hills Ann Arbor MI 48105 Office: Bendix Corp Exec Offices Southfield MI 48202

KOCKELMANS, JOSEPH J., philosopher, educator; Meerssen L., Netherlands, Dec. 1, 1923; s. Alphons Hubert and Philomena (Raeven) K.; Ph.D., Angelico, Rome, 1951; postdoctoral studies in math. with Prof. H. Busard, Venlo, physics with Prof. A. Fokker, Leyden, phenomenology with Prof. H. Van Breda, Louvain, 1951-63; m. Dorothy H. Greiner, Oct. 26, 1964; 1 son, Joseph Martin. Came to U.S., 1964, naturalized, 1968. Prof. philosophy Agrl. U., Wageningen, Netherlands, 1963-64; prof. philosophy New Sch. for Social Research, N.Y.C., 1964-65; prof. philosophy U. Pitts., 1965-68, Pa. State U., University Park, 1968—. Recipient Gold medal Teyler's Tweede Genootschap, Haarlem, 1958. Mem. Am. Philos. Assn., Soc. for Phenomenology and Existential Philosphy, Am. Assn. U. Profs. Author: Phenomenology and Physicial Science, 1966; Husserl's Phenomenological Psychology, 1967; The World in Science and Philosophy, 1969; Martin Heidegger: A First Introduction to his Philosophy, 1965; Edmund Husserl: A First Introduction to his Phenomenology, 1967. Editor: (with John M. Anderson and Calvin O. Schrag) Man and World: An Internat. Philos. Rev., 1968; (with Jan Aler and M. vanNierop) Dutch Heidegger Library, 1970. Home: 903 Willard Circle State College PA 16801

KOCUREK ,LOUIS JOE, investment co. exec.; b. Dime Box, Tex., Dec. 31, 1906; s. Joe L. and Adela (Bordovsky) K.; B.B.A., U. Tex., 1929; m. Millie Matcek, Nov. 19, 1932; childrenLouis Joe, David Carl, Richard John, Mary Ann, Thomas Michael. With Mercantile Securities Co., Dallas, 1929-31; with Rauscher, Pierce Securities Corp., Dallas, 1931-, v.p., mgr., San Antonio, 1934- -, vice chmn., 1969—; dir. Alleghany Corp., 1961- 63. Pres. San Antonio Symphony, 1957-59, chmn. bd., 1961-62, now dir.; bd. govs. Our Lady of Lake Coll. Decorated Knight of Malta, 1966. Clubs: San Antonio Country, San Antonio, St. Anthony, Oak Hills Country (San Antonio). Home: 720 Ivy Lane San Antonio TX 78209 Office: Milam Bldg San Antonio TX 78205

KODAIRA, KUNIHIKO, mathematician; b. Tokyo, Japan, Mar. 16, 1915; s. Gonichi and Ichi (Kanai) K.; M.S., Tokyo U., 1938, Ph.D., 1949; m. Sei Iyanaga, May 30, 1943. Came to U.S., 1949. Asst. prof. Tokyo U., 1943-51, prof., 1951-55; mem. Inst. for Advanced Study, Princeton, 1949-50, 51-52, 55-61; vis. asst. prof. Johns Hopkins, 1950-51, prof. 1962—; vis. prof. Princeton, 1952-53, research asso., 1953—, prof., 1956-62; prof. math. Stanford, 1965—. Recipient Fields medal and prize Internat. Congress Mathematicians, 1954; Order of Culture, Tokyo, 1957. Mem. Am. Math. Soc. Home: 4301 Norwood Rd Baltimore MD 21218

KOEB, RICHARD WILLIAM, banker; b. Rochester, N.Y., Jan. 21, 1911; s. Joseph Andrew and Olga (Uebel) K.; student Los Angeles Poly. Inst., 1924-28, Stock Exchange Inst., 1931, Am. Inst. Banking, 1928-35, U. Cal. at Los Angeles, 1942; m. Kathleen Shields, Apr. 28, 1948; children—Christopher J., Barry J., Kenneth S. With Cal. Bank, Los Angeles, 1928-41; asst. treas. Menasco Mfg. Co., Burbank, Cal., 1941-47; v.p. Farmers & Stockmens Bank, Phoenix, 1954-56; v.p. Bank of Douglas, Phoenix, 1956-60; v.p. Ariz. Bank, Phoenix, 1960-64, sr. v.p., 1964—; pres., dir. Aracadia Water Co., Scottsdale, Ariz., 1959—. Pres., bd. dirs. Goodwill Industries Ariz.; adv. bd. Roosevelt council Boy Scouts Am., Mem. Ariz. Mortgage Bankers Assn. (pres. 1965). Republican. Presbyn. (elder 1956—). Home: 5335 Calle del Norte Phoenix AZ 85018 Office: 44 W Monroe Phoenix AZ 85003

KOEDEL, JOHN GILBERT, Jr., forge co. exec.; b. Pitts., June 25, 1937; s. John Gilbert and Elizabeth Marie (Kramer) K.; B.S. in Commerce, Washington and Lee U., 1959; m. Fay Birren, Dec. 21, 1963; 1 son, John III. Asst. v.p. Pitts. Nat. Bank, 1960-68; treas. Nat. Forge Co., Irvine, Pa., 1968—; asst. treas. Nat. Forge Export Corp., Irvine, 1968—.Served with AUS, 1960. Mason. Clubs: Erie (Pa.) Yacht; Conewango (Warren, Pa.). Home: 118 East St Warren PA 16365 Office: Nat Forge Co Irvine PA 16329

KOEGEL, OTTO ERWIN, lawyer; b. Boonville, Ind., Nov. 23, 1891; s. Henry and Laura Carolyn (Coe) K.; J.D., George Washington U., 1915, LL.M., 1916 (first honors highest average during course); D.C.L., Am. U., 1921; m. Rae Fisher, Sept. 30, 1916; children—James Erwin, Ruth Ann, William Fisher. Practiced law, Washington, 1916—, also Chgo., 1924-31; mem. Matthews & Koegel, Chgo., 1926-31; mem. Hughes, Schurman & Dwight, 1931-37; now mem. Royall, Koegel and Wells, N.Y.C.; chief counsel Twentieth Century-Fox Film Corp.; asso. counsel Bur. War Risk Ins., Treasury Dept., 1918-23; asst. gen. counsel U.S. Vets.' Bur. 1923; asst. U.S. atty. for D.C., 1924; prof. law of domestic relations, torts and criminal law, Nat. U., 1920-24; dir. and counsel several corps. associated with motion picture and ins.; propr. Kaywood Farm. Active in civic affairs of Westchester County; former chmn. Citizens Com. for Fusion, Bronxville, and for Twp. of Somers; chmn. War Meat Com., World War II; legal mem. of Com. on Hereditary Defectives in U.S. of 2d Internat. Congress Eugenics, N.Y., 1922; mem. com. on marriage laws, Am. Assn. for Family Social Work (allied with Russell Sage Found.); mem. N.Y. State Am. Revolution Bicentennial Commn. Trustee, Am. U., Washington. Recipient 1st Bishop's medal N.Y. Episcopal diocese, 1957. Mem. Am., N.Y., Chgo. bar assns., Am. Judicature Soc., Am. Scenic and Hist. Preservation Soc. (exec. com.), John Jay Homestead Assn. (pres.), Sigma Nu Phi, Pi Gamma Mu (hon.). Methodist. Mason (32). Clubs: University (Washington); Siwanoy Country (Mt. Vernon, N.Y.). Author: Common Law Marriage and Its Development in the United States, 1922; Walter S. Carter, Collector of Young Masters, 1952; articles in legal periodicals. Home: Granite Springs NY 10527 also 720 Park Av New York City NY 10021 Office: 200 Park Av New York City NY 10017

KOEHL, GEORGE MARTIN, educator; b. College Point, N.Y., July 24, 1909; s. Robert Curt and Katherine (Bauer) K.; A.B., U. N.C., 1931; A.M., George Washington U., 1933; m. Alma Schlotheuber, June 22, 1935; children—Robert Henry, Alma Ruth. Tchr. physics N.Y. State pub. schs., 1934-37, D.C. pub. schs., 1937-42, 46; physicist Carnegie Instn., Washington, 1942-45; asst. prof. physics George Washington U., 1946, asso. prof., 1947-52, prof., 1952—, dean jr. coll., 1954-61; asso. dean Columbian Coll. Arts and Scis., 1962- 71. Recipient Naval Ordnance Devel. award, 1945; Washington Acad. Sci. award. 1964. Mem. Am. Phys. Soc., Am. Assn. Physics Tchrs. (pres. Chesapeake sect. 1950; exec. com. 1951), Fed. Schoolmen's Club. Home: 515 Mansfield Rd Silver Spring MD 20910 Office: George Washington U Washington DC 20006

KOEHLER, FULTON, educator; b. Mpls., Feb. 22, 1915; s. Frank Oliver and Mary Belle (Fulton) K.; student Oberlin Coll., 1932-35; B.A., U. Minn., 1936, M.A., 1937, Ph.D., 1939; m. Mary Jane Confer, Mar. 26, 1940; children—George F., Ruth (Mrs. John F. Bergerson), James F.C., Thomas E. Asst. prof. to prof. math. U. Minn., Mpls., 1942—; founder Seismic Computing Corp., Houston, 1964, cons., v.p., dir., 1964—. Cons. Honeywell Corp. Mem. Am. Math. Soc., Math. Assn. Am., Soc. Exploration Geophysicists, Phi Beta Kappa, Sigma Xi. Presbyn. (deacon). Home: 4726 Girard Av S Minneapolis MN 55409

KOEHLER, GEORGE APPLEGATE, broadcasting co. exec.; b. Phila., July 23, 1921; s. Herbert Jacques and Mildred Warrington (Applegate) K.; B.A., U. Pa., 1942; m. Jane Marie Caputi, Feb. 20, 1944; children—Eric George, Gary Stephen. Various positions WFIL Stas., Phila., 1945-55, sta. mgr. WFIL Radio and Television, 1955-68; gen. mgr. radio and television div. Triangle Pubs., Inc., Phila., 1968—; pres. Gateway Communications, Inc., Phila., 1970—. Mem. planning com. Phila. Commn. on Human Relations, 1957; mem. Adv. Com. on Naval Affairs, 1968—; pub. relations chmn. United Fund, 1965. Trustee Meth. Hosp., Simpson House for Aged, Phila.; bd. dirs. Hero Scholarship Fund, Better Bus. Bur., Salvation Army, Crime Commn. Phila. Served to capt., USAAF, 1942-45. Decorated D.F.C., Air medal with 3 oak leaf clusters. Recipient Distinguished Service award Chapel of 4 Chaplains, 1969; named Man of Year, Television and Radio Advt. Club Phila., 1971. Mem. Pa. Assn. Broadcasters (pres. 1958-59), ABC-TV Affiliates Assn. (adv. bd. 1967-71, chmn. 1970-71), Alpha Delta Sigma. Republican. Methodist. Rotarian (pres. 1960). Club: Union League (Phila.). Home: 710 S Park Dr Westmont NJ 08108 Office: 4100 City Line Av Philadelphia PA 19131

KOEHLER, JOHN THEODORE, lawyer; b. North Braddock, Pa., Mar. 14, 1904; s. William Ernest and Mathilde (Hackbart) K.; student Grove City (Pa.) Coll., 1921- 23; A.B. highest honors, dept. Politics, Princeton, 1924-26; LL.B., Harvard, 1930; m. Eleanor Rust Peirce, 1949; children—John T., Mathilde R., Elizabeth P. Asso. with law firms of Miller, Otis & Farr (Willkie, Owen, Otis, Farr & Gallagher), N.Y.C. 1930-31; Smith, Buchanan and Ingersoll, Pitts. 1931-33; Semmes, Bowen & Semmes, Balt. 1937-41; spl. atty. Treasury Dept., 1933-34; spl. asst. to atty. gen. U.S., 1934-35; tax counsel Md. Casualty Co., Balt., 1935-37; counsel Bur. Ships, Navy Dept., 1946, asst. gen. counsel dept., 1947-49; asst. sec. Navy, 1949-51; chmn. Fed. Maritime Bd., Maritime Adminstr., 1950; chmn. Renegotiation Bd., 1951-53; dir. Woodward and Lothrop, Washington; lectr. corporate tax problems Practicing Law Inst., various banking and ins. execs. assns. Organized and trained Navy's Underwater Demolition Teams, World War 11, released as comdr., 1945. Decorated Silver Star Medal, 1944. Mem. Am., (sect. on taxation), Md., D.C. bar assns., Phi Beta Kappa. United Lutheran. Club: Metropolitan (Washington); Chevy Chase (Md.). Home: 5806 Cedar Pkwy Chevy Chase MD 20015 Office: Wire Bldg Washington DC 20005

KOEHLER, MARK LOWELL, clergyman; b. Brownsville, Ore., Mar. 12, 1915; s. Charles Frederick and Grace (Griffith) K.; B.A. in Econs., Whitworth Coll., Spokane, 1937; M.A., San Francisco Theol. Sem., 1938, B.D., 1939; Th.M., Princeton Theol. Sem., 1941; D.D., U. Dubuque, 1959; LL.D., Hastings Coll., 1964; m. Clara Belle Braden, May 19, 1939; 1 dau., Michal Ann. Ordained to ministry Presbyn. Ch., 1939; student pastor, Winters, Cal., 1937-40; pastor 1st Presbyn. Ch., Port Townsend, Cal., 1940-43; head, dept. Bible and Christian edn., also chaplain Whitworth Coll., 1943-49, exec. v.p. 1962-64, pres., 1964-69; sr. pastor 1st Presbyn. Ch., Yakima, Wash., 1950-62; sr. pastor 1st Presbyn. Ch., Las Vegas, 1969- -. Chmn. gen. council Synod Wash.-Alaska, 1963-69, moderator, 1960. Temporary adv. council Pub. Higher Edn. Wash. Trustee, San Francisco Theol. Sem.; bd. dirs. Spokane United Good Neighbors, Wash. Alcohol Problems Assn. Mem. N.E.A., Wash. Edn. Assn., Am. Assn. Sch. Adminstrs., Am. Council Edn., Assn. Am. Colls., Phi Kappa Delta. Rotarian. Clubs: Spokane, Spokane Country. Address: First Presbyterian Church 1515 W Charleston Blvd Las Vegas NV 89102

KOEHLER, PETER HUBER, forest products co. exec.; b. Portland, Ore., Apr. 11, 1929; s. Kurt H. and Dorothy (Huber) K.; A.B. in Econs., Stanford U. 1951; m. Alice S. Malar children-Richard, Kurt, Peter Huber, Neil, Paul, Thomas. Prodn. coordinator M & M Woodworking Co., Portland, Ore., 1952-56; v.p., gen. mgr. Coastal Veneers Inc., Crescent City, Cal., 1956-61; gen. mgr. Multnomah Plywood Corp., Portland, 1961-63; exec. v.p., gen. mgr. forest products group Evans Products Co., 1963—. Bd. dirs. Portland Opera Assn., 1969—. Portland Family Counseling Service, 1969—. Mem. Am. Plywood Assn. (trustee 1970—), Western Wood Products Assn. (bd. dirs. 1969—), Timber Operators Council (pres., dir. 1968—). Home: 717 N E E 43d St Portland OR 97213 Office: 1121 S W Salmon St Portland OR 97208

KOEHLER, ROBERT EARL, editor; b. Oconomowoc, Wis., July 6, 1924; s. George John and Ida Mae (Watterson) K.; B.A., U. Wis., 1948. Editorial asst. Pacific Builder & Engr., Inc., 1953-56; editor Architecture/West, 1956-62; asso. editor A.I.A. Jour., Washington, 1962-65, editor, 1965—; contbr. to Parents Mag. Press Yearbook, 1966-70. Recipient award for outstanding publ., Western Soc. Bus. Publs., 1959. Mem. A.I.A. (hon.), Wis. Alumni Assn., Sigma Delta Chi. Roman Catholic. Editor: 50th Anniversary Annual of The Mountaineers, Inc., 1956. Office: 1785 Massachusetts Av NW Washington DC 20036

KOEHLER, ROBERT EARL, corp. exec.; b. Geneva, Ill., Aug. 8, 1920; s. Earl Lawrence and Martha (Wartman) K.; B.A., N. Central Coll., Nashville, Ill., 1940; M.S., U. Ill., 1941; m. Norma Hubrig, Aug. 20, 1942; children-Diane (Mrs. Larry M. Rich), Robert Earl, Steven, Alan, Barbara. Audit mgr. Arthur Andersen & Co., Chgo., 1941-55; controller, asst. treas. Nat. Tea Co., Chgo., 1955-62; v.p. finance Marriott Corp., Bethesda, Md., 1962—. Mem. Mayor's Econ Devel. Com., Washington, 1970—. Served to lt. (j.g.) USNR, 1944-46. C.P.A., Ill. Mem. Financial Execs. Inst., Am. Inst. C.P.A.'s. Home: 7301 Marbury Rd Bethesda MD 20034 Office: 5161 River Rd Bethesda MD 20016

KOEHN, CHARLES WILLIAM, bass; b. Milw., Feb. 11; s. Albert J. and Ida (Wasch) K.; student Marquette U., 1937-41, Am. Theatre Wing, N.Y.C., 1946-51; m. Joanne Pruitt, Nov. 2, 1956. Leading bass Florentine Opera Co., Milw., 1958-, Kiel (Germany) Stadt theatre, 1964-65, Boston Opera Co., 1968, Am. Nat. Opera Co. on tour, 1967-68, Skylight Comic Opera Ltd., Milw., 1960-67; mem. Lyric Opera Co. Chgo., 1969—, Nev. Opera Co., Birmingham Opera Co., 1969—; also guest artist Bielefeld (Germany) Opera, Pforzheim (Germany) Opera 1964-65. Served to lt. comdr. USNR, World War 11 and Korea. Home: 2712 N Maryland Av Milwaukee WI 53211 Office: 1501 N Hawley Rd Milwaukee WI 53208

KOEHNEKE, MARTIN LUTHER, coll. pres.; b. Dodge Center, Minn., Apr. 11, 1916; s. Paul Frederick and Louise (Burandt) K.; student Concordia Coll., 1933-35, Concordia Sem., 1935-37, 38, 39;

M.Ed., U. Tex., 1956; m. Irma Ann Knippa, 1940; childrenBarbara Ann, Richard, Janice, Kathleen. Ordained to ministry Luth. Ch., 1940; vicar Trinity Luth. Ch., Cape Girardeau, Mo., 1937-38; pastor Mt. Calvary Luth. Ch., Raymondville. Tex., 1940-43, Mt. Olive Luth. Ch., San Antonio, 1943-50; counselor parish edn. Tex. dist. Luth. Ch. Missouri Synod, 1950-54; pres. Concordia Tchrs. Coll., 1954—. Mem. Luth. Edn. Assn., N.E.A., Am. Assn. Sch. Adminstrs., Assn. Student Teaching. Rotarian. Author: God and I, 1956. Editor Lone Star Observer, 1950-54, Concordia Pulpit, 1958. Co- translator: The Victor Speaks, 1958. Home: 946 Clinton Place River Forest IL

KOELB, CLAYTON TALMADGE, ins. co. exec.; b. Mystic, Conn., May 9, 1920; s. Ralph Hammond and Gladys (Clayton) K.; A.B., Dartmouth, 1941; m. Janice Miller, Aug. 30, 1941; children—Clayton T., Albert M., Susan H. Staff accountant tax dept. Ernst & Ernst, C.P.A.'s, Providence, 1943-47; asst. treas. New Eng. Butt Co., Proidence, 1947-49; with Automobile Mut. Ins. Co. Am. and Factory Mut. Liability Ins. Co. Am., Providence, 1949—, asst. treas., 1951-55, treas., 1955—. Trustee Providence Country Day Sch. C.P.A., R.I. Mem. Phi Beta Kappa. Clubs: Atlantic Tune, Turks Head, University (Providence). Home. Matunuck Beach Rd Wakefield RI 02879 Office: 10 Weybosett St Providence RI 02904

KOELLA, GEORGE BRAMPTON pharmacologist; b. Phila., Oct. 8, 1918; s. Frederick Christian and Emily Mary (Brampton) K.; B.Sc., Phila. Coll. Pharmacy and Sci., 1939, D.Sc., 1965; Ph.D., U. Pa., 1946; M.D., Johns Hopkins, 1950; m. Winnifred Jean Angenent, Feb. 6, 1954; children-Peter Brampton, William Angenent, Jonathan, Stuart. Bio-assayist, LaWall & Harrisson, 1939-42; instr. Phila. Coll. Pharmacy and Sci., 1939-42; Chalfont fellow ophthalmology Wilmer Inst., Johns Hopkins, 1946-50; asst. prof. pharmacology Columbia Coll. Phys. and Surg., 1950-52; prof. pharmacology Grad. Sch. Medicine, U. Pa., 1952-, chmn. dept. psysiology and pharmacology, 1957-59, dean Grad. Sch. Medicine, 1957-59, chmn. dept. pharmacology Schs. Medicine, 1959-; Hachmeister lectr. Georgetown U. Med. Sch., 1952; Merck lectr. McGill U. Med. Sch., 1955; spl. lectr. U. London, 1961; vis. lectr. U. Brazil, 1962. Cons., McNeil Labs., 1959- 66, Phila. Gen. Hosp., 1953—, Valley Forge Army Hosp., 1954—, Army Chem. Corps, 1956-, Phila. Naval Hosp., 1957-; vis. lectr. pharmacology Phila. Coll. Pharmacy and Sci., 1955-57; mem. pharmacology study sect. USPHS, 1958-62, chmn. pharmacology study sect. 1965-68; vis. prof., Guggenheim fellow U. Lausanne, 1963-64; vis. prof. pharmacology, chmn. dept. Paklavi U., Shiraz, Iran, 1969-70. Sec. gen. Internat. Union of Pharmacology, 1966-69. Mem. bd. sci. counselors Nat. Heart Inst. NIH, USPHS, 1960-64, mem. nat. adv. neurol. diseases and stroke council, 1970—. Trustee Phila. Coll. Pharmacy and Sci.; bd. mgrs. Wistar Inst., Served to 1st lt. Med. Adminstrn. Corps, AUS, 1942-46. Recipient Abel prize in pharmacology Am. Soc. Pharmacology and Exptl. Therapeutics, 1950; Travel award XVIIIth Internat. Physiol. Congress, Copenhagen, Federated Socs., 1950; Borden undergrad. research award, 1950. Fellow A.A.A.S. (v.p. 1971), N.Y. Acad. Scis.; mem. Am. Soc. Pharmacology and Exptl. Therapeutics (pres. 1965-66), Histochem. Soc., Harvey Soc., Soc. Biol. Psychiatry, John Morgan Soc., Sydenham Coterie, Sons Copper Beeches, Internat. Union Pharmacology (v.p. 1969—), Brit. Pharmacol. Soc., Biol. Soc. Chile (hon.), Internat. Neurochem. Soc., Soc. for Neurosci., Sigma Xi. Asso. editor Remington's Practice of Pharmacy, 1951. Mem. editorial bd. Pharmacol. Revs., 1955-63, chmn., 1959-62; hon. editorial adv. bd. Biochem. Pharmacology, 1958—, editorial adv. bd. Internat. Jour. Neurosci., 1970—; editorial com. Ann. Rev. Pharmacology, 1959-65; editor: Cholinesterases and Anticholinesterase Agents, 1963; contbr. articles on pharmacology. Home: 205 College Av Swarthmore PA 19081 Office: U Pa Philadelphia PA 19104

KOELSCH, CHARLES FREDERICK, chemist; b. Boise, Ida., Jan. 31,1907; s. Charles F. and Katherine Clyde (Oliver) K.; B.S., U. Wis., 1928, Ph.D., 1931; m. Helen Hermanson, June 14, 1938; childrenKaren Lucile, Charles F., John Marshall. Instr. chemistry U. Ill. summer 1931; NRC fellow Harvard, 1931-32; instr. organic chemistry U. Minn., 1932-34, asst. prof., 1934-37, asso. prof., 1937-46, prof. chemistry, 1946—. Mem. Am. Chem. Soc., Brit. Chem. Soc., Alpha Chi Sigma, Phi Lambda Upsilon. Recipient Langmuir award in chemistry for investigations on chemistry of condensed ring systems, 1934. Home: 2303 Folwell St St Paul MN 55108 Office: U Minn St Paul MN 55455

KOELSCH, MONTGOMERY OLIVER, judge; b. Boise, Ida., Mar. 5, 1912; s. Charles F. and Katherine (Oliver) K.; B.A., U. Wash., 1932, LL.B., 1935; m. Virginia L. Daley, Oct. 30, 1937; children—Katherine, John, Jane. Admitted to Ida. bar, 1936, Wash. bar, 1936; with firm Davison & Davison, Boise, 1936-39, Oleary & Koelsch, Boise, 1939-50; dist. judge 3d Dist. of Ida., 1951-59; circuit judge U.S. Ct. Appeals, 9th Circuit, 1959—. Mem. Am. Judicature Soc. Episcopalian. Home: 715 N 9th St Boise ID 83702 Office: U S Post Office and Courthouse San Francisco CA 94103

KOEMPEL, LESLIE ALICE, educator; b. San Francisco, Jan. 22, 1907; d. Herman Charles and Edna (Luyster) Koempel; A.B., U. Cal. at Berkeley, 1929; social work certificate Bryn Mawr Coll., 1932, Ph.D., 1937. Instr., then asst. prof. sociology Skidmore Coll., 1936-38; asso. prof. sociology Rockford Coll., 1938-43; adult edn. expt. Henry Street Settlement, N.Y.C., 1943-44; asst. prof. Mt. Holyoke Coll., 1944-46; asst., asso. prof. then prof. sociology Vassar Coll., 1946-, Margaret Sites Halleck Found. prof., 1959-, past chmn. dept. econs., sociology and anthropology. Active local orgns., Poughkeepsie. Mem. Am. Sociol. Assn., Eastern Sociol. Soc., Am. Assn. U. Profs. Home: 4 W Haight Av Poughkeepsie NY 12603

KOENEMUND, PAUL WILLIAM, steel co. cons.; b. Moundsville, W.Va., Aug. 16, 1911; s. August William and Jessie Mae (Hendrix) K.; student Carnegie Inst. Tech., 1930- 35; m. Virginia Rae Dotson, June 17, 1937; 1 son, William Charles. Asst. master mechanic Wheeling Steel Corp. (W.Va.), 1936-40, fuel engr., 1940- 41, estimator, 1941-46, plant engr., 1946-50, asst. gen. mgr., 1950, gen. mgr., 1950-55, chief corp. engr., 1955-57, v.p. operations, 1957-64, v.p. engring., 1964-66, adminstrv. v.p., 1967-68; exec. v.p. adminstrn. and planning Wheeling Pitts. Steel, 1968-69, exec. v.p. research, 1969-70, cons., 1971—. Mem. Nat. Mgmt. Assn., Am. Inst. Mining, Metall. and Petroleum Engrs., Am. Iron and Steel Inst., W.Va. Soc. Profl. Engrs., Am. Soc. Metals, Am. Iron and Steel Engrs. Methodist. Home: 502 Washington Av Glen Dale WV 26038

KOENIG, CHARLES LOUIS chemist; b. Yonkers, N.Y., Oct. 11, 1911; s. Henry and Gertrude Marie (Holste) K.; B.S., N.Y.U., 1932, Ph.D. (Inman fellow 1932-33), 1936; m. 2d, Janie Ray Shofner; children-Livy, Charlou, Arthur, Friedrich. Stack chief N.Y. Pub. Library, 1928-32; sr. chemist Solvay Process Co., Syracuse, N.Y., 1936-45; chemist Lithaloys Corp., N.Y.C., 1945-46; chem. cons. N.Y.C., 1945-47; chief, research branch, N.Y. directed operations AEC, 1946-47; chmn. chemistry and chem. engring. research Armour Research Found., 1947-49; asst. dir. research Stanford Research Inst., 1950-51; v.p. S.W. Research Inst., 1951-56, Louis Koenig Research, 1956—; cons. USPHS. Pres. Alamo Dist. Science Fair, Inc.; mem. U.S. Com. Large Dams. Lectr., writer numerous publs. on water resources and econs., including syndicated newspaper column. Mem. A.A.A.S., Am. Chem. Soc. (nat. councilor), Am. Inst. Chemists, Am. Waterworks Assn., Am. Water Resources Assn., Am. Geophys. Union, Nat. Water Well Assn., Am. Inst. Chem. Engrs., Am. Assn. Cost Engrs., Water Pollution Control Fedn., Sci. Research Soc. Am., Sigma Xi. Asst. editor Chem. Abstracts, 1949—. Genealogist. Address: Route 10 Box 108 San Antonio TX 78216

KOENIG, FREDERICK GILMAN, Jr., mfg. exec.; b. Birmingham, Ala., Oct. 1, 1915; s. Frederick Gilman and Myra (Browne) K.; A.B., Birmingham-So. Coll., 1935; LL.B., Harvard, 1938; m. Mary Anne Geisking, June 30, 1946; 1 son, Donald C. Admitted to Ala. bar, 1938; pvt. practice, Birmingham, 1938-41; atty. TVA, 1941-42, 18 Beechmont St Worcester MA 01609 1948-54, v.p., 1953-54, exec. v.p., mem. exec. com., dir., 1954-68, pres. 1968—; pres. Ketona Chem. Corp. (Ala.) Dir. Asso. Industries Ala.; mem. Ala. Water Improvement Commn., 1962-65; mem. adv. bd. Salvation Army, Birmingham; v.p. Ala. Mining Inst.; dir. Jefferson County Comm. Chest. Dir. Am. Coke and Chems. Inst.; dir. So. States Indsl. Council. Served from pvt. to capt., inf., AUS, 1942-46; ETO. Decorated Bronze Star Medal. Mem. Am., Ala., Birmingham bar assns., Soc. Mayflower Desc., Soc. Colonial Wars, S.A.R., S.R., Birmingham Better Bus. Bur. (dir., exec. com.), Ala., Birmingham (dir. 1968-70)chambers commerce, Newcomen Soc. Omicron Delta Kappa, Tau Kappa Alpha, Sigma Alpha Epsilon. Presbyn. Kiwanian (dir. Birmingham 1966-67). Clubs: Birmingham Country, Mountain Brook, The Club, Downtown. Home: 3401 E Briarcliff Rd Birmingham AL 35223 Office: P O Box 354 First Nat Bldg Birmingham AL35202

KOENIG, HAROLD, physician, scientist; b. N.Y.C., Mar. 16, 1921; s. David and Anna (Burg) K.; B.S., Rutgers U., 1942; M.B., Chgo. Med. Sch., 1946, M.D., 1947; M.S., Northwestern U., 1945; Ph.D., U. Pa., 1948; m. Ruth Steinman, Feb. 11, 1945; childrenSusan, Leslie. Intern Walther Meml. Hosp., Chgo., 1946-47; resident U. Chgo. Clinics, 1955, Northwestern U. Med. Center, 1956-57; research fellow Northwestern U., 1944-46; practice medicine, specializing in neurology, Chgo., 1955-; instr. anatomy U. Pa., 1947- 48, asst. prof., 1948-49; asst. prof. anatomy Chgo. Med. Sch., 1949-53, asso. prof. neuroanatomy, 1953-54; asst. prof. neurol. and psychiatry Northwestern U., 1957-59, asso. prof., 1959-63, prof., 1963—; chief neurology service VA Research Hosp., Chgo., 1956-. Mem. Am. Neurol. Assn., Am. Acad. Neurology (sec. neurochem. sect., 1961-63, chmn. 1963-65, councillor 1963—), Am. Soc. Neurochemistry, Am. Assn. Neuropathologists, Am. Soc. Cell Biology, Histochem. Soc., Internat. Neurochem. Soc., Soc. Exptl. Biology and Medicine. Author articles in field. Home: 45 E Elm St Chicago IL 60611 Office: 333 E Huron St Chicago IL 60611

KOENIG, HERMAN EDWARD, educator; b. Marissa, Ill., Dec. 12, 1924; s. Herman Christopher and Clara (Spleth) K.; B.S., U. Ill., 1947, M.S., 1949, Ph.D., 1953; m. Ruth Janet Parett, June 12, 1949; children—Bruce, Roger, Steven. Asst. prof. U. Ill., 1953-56; mem. faculty Mich. State U., 1956—, prof. elec. engring., 1959—, chmn. dept., 1968—, dir. system sci. program Coll. Engring., 1966-68; vis. asst. prof. Mass. Inst. Tech., 1954-55; cons. in field. Bd. advisers Center Environmental Study, Grand Rapids Environmental Study Center. Recipient Distinguished Faculty award Mich. State U., 1968. Mem. I.E.E.E. (Dist. First Prize award 1959), Am. Soc. Engring. Edn., Sigma Xi, Tau Beta Pi, Phi Kappa Phi, Eta Kappa Nu. Home: 4733 Mohican Lane Okemos MI 48864 Office: Engring Bldg Mich State Univ East Lansing MI 48823

KOENIG, IRVIN H., mfg. co. exec.; b. Streator, Ill., July 22, 1918; s. Alex and Augusta K.; ed. pub. schs., Streator; m. Opal D. Graffis, Dec. 26, 1939; childrenWilliam, Linda Sue. Exec. v.p. Diamond Internat. Corp. Served with USNR, 1944-46. Home: 208 Hickok Rd New Canaan CT 06840 Office: 733 3d Av New York City NY 10017

KOENIG, JOHN HENRY, educator; b. St. Marys, O., Apr. 9, 1909; s. John Henry and Clara Elizabeth (Boesel) K.; B. Chem. Engring., Ohio State U., 1931, Chem. Engr., 1935, M.S., 1936, Ph.D., 1938; m. Shirley Ann Smith, Jan. 4, 1941; childrenClara E., Belva M., Shirley A., Sarah K., John Richard. Chemist, Gen. Electric Co., Pittsfield, Mass., 1931-35; research fellow Ohio Engring. Expt. Sta., Columbus, 1935-38; research engr. Hall China Co., East Liverpool, O., 1938-42; prof., head dept. of ceramics Rutgers U., New Brunswick, N.J., also dir. N.J. State Ceramic Research Inst., 1945-70, ret. Pres. 6th Internat. Congress on Glass, 1962-65. Mem. Am. Ceramic Soc. (pres. 1962-63), Am. Soc. Testing Materials (past dir.), Nat. Ceramic Ednl. Council (past pres.), Keramos (past nat. pres.). Address: Route 1 Box 105 Delta CO 81416

KOENIG, KARL FRED, educator; b. Hartford, Conn., Aug. 21, 1906; s. William J. and Emma (Feil) K.; B.S., Trinity Coll., Hartford, 1929, Litt.D., 1966; fellow Inst. Internat. Edn., U. Leipzig (Germany), 1932-33; Ph.D., Yale, 1935; m. Ruth Fleming Vanderpoel, Nov. 24, 1933; children—William V., Karl Peter, Julia Ward (Mrs. William H. Mitchell), Maria Renata. Part-time tchr. Trinity Coll., 1933-34; mem. faculty Colgate U., 1935—, prof. German, 1954—; tchr. adult edn. Ham High Sch., Hamilton, N.Y., 1955-56. Mem. Sherburne Art Soc. Fulbright fellow, Austria, 1953-54; guest Fed. Republic Germany, 1958; Carnegie research grantee, 1958, 71—. Mem. Am. Assn. Tchrs. German (pres regional chpt. 1946-48), Am. Assn. U. Profs., Modern Lang. Assn., N.Y. State Assn. Fgn. Lang. Tchrs., Phi Kappa Tau, Delta Phi Alpha. Republican. Lutheran. Author: (with J.S. Termper) Kohlhaas, 1949; also articles in field. Home: Johnny Cake Hill Hamilton NY 13346

KOENIG, PAUL THIES, mfg. co. exec.; b. Cleve., Apr. 5, 1910; s. Frank D. and Johanna M. (Thies) K.; B.B.A., Western Res. U., 1942; m. Marjorie Holzschuer, June 17, 1939; children—Jean (Mrs. Richard W. Linn), Paul Frank. Jr. accountant, Dale W. Black, C.P.A.'s, Cleve., 1929-30; cost and gen. accountant Indsl. Rayon Corp., 1930-37; chief accountant Rayon Machinery Corp., 1937-41; treas. Park-Ohio Industries, Inc., mfr. diesel engine parts and elec. heat treat equipment, Cleve., 1941—; dir. Morco, Inc. Mem. Nat. Assn. Accountants, Treasurers Club Cleve., Financial Execs. Inst. Home: 19379 Westover Av Rocky River OH 44116 Office: 3800 Harvard Av Cleveland OH 44105

KOENIG, ROBERT P mining co. exec.; b. N.Y.C., Apr. 26, 1904; s. F. Otto and Margarette (Purington) K.; A.B. magna cum laude, Harvard, 1924; D. Eng. (hon.), Sch. Mines, Mont. U., 1958; m. 2d, Angela Pow, Feb., 16, 1946; childrenRobert Julian, Harold Otto, Margarette Whittemore, Rosalie Angela, John Lauriston. Asst. geologist Cerro de Pasco Copper Corp. (now Cerro Corp.), 1925-27; engr. New Verde Mines Corp., 1927-30, Internat. Mining Corp., 1930-32, Lehman Bros., 1935-36; v.p., gen. mgr. Montezuma Corp., 1933-35; v.p., pres., dir. Elec. Shovel Coal Corp., 1936-39; pres., dir. Ayrshire-Patoka Collieries Corp., 1939-50; pres., dir. Cerro Corp., 1950-70, chmn., 1970—; Compãnia Minera Andina, S.A., 1960-70, dir., 1960—; dir. Atlantic Cement Co., Inc., So. Peru Copper Corp.; trustee Mut. Life Ins. Co. N.Y. Mem. Nat. Bituminous Coal Adv. Council, 1948-50; chmn., 1948, acting dir. industry div. ECA, 1948. Served to col. C.E., AUS; staff Gen. Eisenhower, SHAEF. 1942-45. Decorated Order Brit. Empire; Croix de Guerre with Palms (Belgium); Croix de Guerre, Legion Honor (France); Legion of Merit (U.S.); recipient Rand award An. Inst. Mining, Metall, and Petroleum Engrs., 1962. Mem. Am. Inst. Mining and Metall. Engrs., Canadian Inst. Mining and Metallurgy, Instn. Mining and Metallurgy (London), Mining and Metall. Soc. Am., Harvard Engring. Soc., Soc. Econ. Geologists, Council Fgn. Relations, Marine Hist. Assn. (trustee), Zinc Devel. Assn. Lead Devel. Assn. (chmn. 1969-71). Clubs: Harvard, India House (hon.), Links (N.Y.); Scawanaka Corinthian Yacht (Oyster Bay, N.Y.); Winter; Cold Spring Harbor (N.Y.) Beach; Marco Polo; Mining; Metropolitan (Washington). Author: An American Engineer Looks at British Coal (Foreign Affairs), 1948; Ore, Avalanches and Water, 1968. Home: 340 Cove Neck Rd Oyster Bay NY 11771 Office: 300 Park Av New York City NY 70022

KOENIG, VIRGIL, educator, biochemist; b. Kansas City, Mo., Oct. 10, 1913; s. John William and Hilah Ethel (Ward) K.; A.B., U. Mo. at Kansas City, 1936; M.S., Okla. State U., 1938; Ph.D., U. Colo., 1940; m. Hildegard Zerne, Feb. 26, 1949; children-LeRoy William, Lawrence Nils, Cynthia Sonsie, Patrick Christopher. With Armour & Co., Chgo., 1941-48; staff mem. Los Alamos Sci. Lab., 1948-54; prin. scientist VA Research Hosp., Chgo., 1954-56; asst. prof., then asso. prof. biochemistry Northwestern U., 1954-60; prin. scientist Gen. Mills Co., Mpls., 1960-63; prof. biochemistry, chmn. dept. U. Tex. Med. Br., Galveston, 1963—. Trustee, Village of Brookfield, Ill., 1957-60. Elk. Mem. Seventh Day Adventist Ch. Author papers in field. Home: 1913 Carter Lane LaMarque TX 77568 Office: U Tex Med Branch Galveston TX 77550

KOENIGSBERG, MARVIN LEE, lawyer; b. Chgo., Dec. 10, 1918; s. Isadore and Minnie (Oliff) K.; B.S.L., Northwestern U., 1942, J.D., 1942. Admitted to Ill. Bar, 1942, since practiced in Chgo.; asso. Legal Aid Bur. Chgo., 1942-44; partner firm Friednan, Koven, Salzman, Koenigsberg, Specks & Homer, and predecessors, 1951—. Asst. sec. Hilton Hotels Corp. Bd. dirs. Jewish Home for Aged, Chgo. Mem. Am., Ill., Chgo. bar assns., Decalogue Soc., Praetorians, Tau Epsilon Rho. Mem. B'nai B'rith (lodge pres. 1952). Club: Covenant (Chgo.). Home: 5630 N Sheridan Rd Chicago IL 60626 Office: 208 S LaSalle St Chicago IL 60604

KOENIGSMARK, HARRY CONRAD, mfg. co. exec.; b. Waterloo, Ill., Jan. 23, 1912; s. Morris A. and Florence (Feldmeier) K.; B.S., U. Ill., 1933; m. Martha Pettitt, May 29, 1959; children by previous marriage—Barbara L. (Mrs. John C. Osborne), Joyce A. With Ernst & Ernst, C.P.A.'s, Chgo., 1933-35; with Bendix Corp., 1935—, controller, 1966-70, v.p. finance, 1970—. Home: 18840 San Jose St Lathrop Village MI 48075 Office: Fisher Bldg Detroit MI 48202

KOENKER, ROBERT HENRY, educator; b. Mankato, Minn., Mar. 4, 1913; s. Frank H. and Hattie (Roos) K.; B.E., Mankato State Tchrs. Coll., 1935; M.A., U. Minn., 1937, Ph.D., 1941; m. Jeanette Bandelin, June 7, 1943; children—Susan, Frank, Jeffrey. Dir. grad. studies, prof. edn. Ball State Tchrs. Coll., 1946-64, dean grad. program, 1964-66, prof. edn., psychology, 1964-, dean Grad. Sch., 1966—. Examiner, cons. North Central Assn. Colls. and Secondary schs.; cons., mem. com. preparation coll. tchrs. Council Grad. Schs. U.S.; cons.-expert Bur. Higher Edn. U.S. Office Edn.; examiner Nat. Council Accreditation Tchr. Edn. Chmn. Delaware County (Ind.) Selective Service Bd., 1950-. Served with USCG, 1941-45. Mem. Nat. Council Tchrs. Math., Am., Ind. psychol. assns., Midwest Conf. Grad. Study and Research, Am. Assn. State Colls. and Univs. (grad. studies com.), Ind. Tchrs. Assn., N.E.A., Phi Delta Kappa, Kappa Delta Pi, Blue Key. Methodist. Author: Row Peterson Arithmetic Books, Grades 3-8, 2d edit., 1959. Contbr. articles profl. jours. Home: 3000 Riverside Av Muncie IN 47304

KOENKER, WILLIAM ERNEST, educator; b. Regent, N.D., Jan. 6, 1911; s. Ernest and Caroline (Libbe) K.; B.A., Dickinson State Tchrs. Coll., 1934; M.A., U. N.D., 1939; Ph.D., Ohio State U., 1949; m. Margaret Fries, 1940 (dec. 1952); 1 son, Roger; m. 2d, Winifred Finlay Daly, June 9, 1953; 1 stepson, Denis. Prin. Walsh County High Sch., 1939-42; instr. U. N.D., 1946, prof., chmn. econs. dept., 1954-62, dir. Bur. Bus. and Econ. Research, 1957-62 v.p. acad. affairs, 1962—; asso. dir. case analysis div., regional WSB, Dallas, 1951-52, pub. mem., Mpls., 1952; program economist ICA, Baghdad, Iraq, 1958-59, acting program officer, 1959. Dir. tax equity study, N.D. Legislative Research Com. Served as sgt. AUS, 1942- 46. Mem. Am. Econ. Assn., Am. Finance Assn., Am. Assn. U. Profs. Home: 427 Campbell Dr Grand Forks ND 58201

KOEPER, H.F., educator. Prof. history of architecture and art U. Ill. Chgo. Circle. Home: 910 Lake Shore Dr Chicago IL 60610*

KOEPFLI, JOSEPH BLAKE, chemist; b. Los Angeles, Feb. 5, 1904; s. Joseph Otto and Juliette Morse (Blake) K.; A.B., Stanford, 1924, A.M., 1925; D.Phil., Oxford, 1928; m. Margaret Campbell, June 12, 1935 (div.); children—David, Daphne; m. 2d, Ann Shields Brown, Feb. 23, 1962. Research fellow Cal. Inst. Tech., 1928-29, research asso. in chemistry 1932—; instr. pharmacology Johns Hopkins Sch. Medicine 1929-31; sr. sci. officer Am. embassy, London, 1947-48. Served as spl. asst. to chmn. div. chemistry and chem. tech., NRC, 1942-45, mem. panel on synthesis antimalarial drugs, 1943-46; sci. adviser to Dept. of State, 1951-53; U.S. chmn. sci. and tech. NATO Task Force, 1957; mem. panel Pres.' sci. adv. com., 1957-64; adv. com. internat. sci. activities NSF, 1960-63; mem. U.S. delegation Atlantic Congress, 1959; mem. U.S. nat. commn. UNESCO, 1964-68; mem. com. sci. and tech. Nat. Citizens Commn. Internat. Coop., 1965. Trustee Barlow Sanatorium Assn., So. Cal. Symphony-Hollywood Bowl Assn. (pres. 1964-67), Los Angeles County Mus. Art. Recipient War-Navy certificate of Appreciation 1947. Fellow A.A.A.S., Chem. Soc. London; mem. Am. Chem. Soc., Sigma Xi, Alpha Tau Omega. Clubs: California (Los Angeles); Bohemian (San Francisco); Cosmos (Washington). Office: Calif Inst Tech Pasadena CA 91109

KOEPKE, GEORGE HENRY, medical educator; b. Toledo, Jan. 1, 1916; s. George Herman and Louise Florence (Kutz) K.; B.S., U. Toledo, 1945; M.D., U. Cin., 1949; m. Helen LaBoiteaux, Oct. 6, 1940; children—Susan (Mrs. David Healy), Sandra (Mrs. Bradley Hitt). Intern Toledo Hosp., 1949-50; resident Univ. Hosp., Ann Arbor, Mich., 1950-53; pvt. practice specializing phys. medicine and rehab., Toledo, 1954; prof. U. Mich. Med. Sch., 1954—. Chmn. Am. Bd. Phys. Medicine and Rehab., 1969. Mem. A.M.A., Am. Acad. Phys. Medicine and Rehab., Am. Congress Rehab. Medicine, Assn. Acad. Physiatrists, United Cerebral Palsy Assn., Mich., Washtenaw County (past pres.) med. socs. Home: 1429 Kearney Av Ann Arbor MI 48104

KOEPPE, ROGER ERDMAN, educator, biochemist; b. Amoy, China, May 2, 1922 (parents Am. citizens); s. Edwin Walter and Elizabeth (Renskers) K.; A.B. in Chemistry, Hope Coll., 1944; M.S., U. Ill., 1947, Ph.D., 1950; m. Norma Winifred Lemmer, 1947; children—Roger E. II, Mary E., Sarah C., Edwin C., Peter V. Teaching asst., then Univ. fellow U. Ill., 1946-49, AEC predoctoral fellow, 1949-50, research asst., then research asso., 1951-52; from instr. to asso. prof. U. Tenn., 1952-59; mem. faculty Okla. State U., 1959-, prof. biochemistry, 1960-, head dept., 1963—; vis. prof. U. Pa., 1966-67. Pres. Stillwater Jr.-Sr. High P.T.A., 1964-65. Served with AUS, 1944-46. Mem. A.A.A.S., Am. Chem. Soc. (chmn. Okla. 1965), Am. Soc. Biol. Chemists, Okla. Acad. Sci., Stillwater C. of C.,

Biochem. Soc., Sigma Xi, Phi Lambda Upsilon, Alpha Chi Sigma. Presbyn. (elder). Contbr. profl. jours. Home: 1724 W 3d St Stillwater OK 74074

KOEPSEL, WELLINGTON WESLEY, educator; b. McQueeney, Tex., Dec. 1921; s. Wesley Wellington and Hulda (Nagel) K.; B.S. in Elec. Engring., U. Tex., 1944, M.S., 1951; Ph.D., Okla. State U., 1960; m. Dorothy Helen Adams, June 25, 1950; children—Kirsten Marta, Gretchen Lisa, Wellington Lief. Engr., City Pub. Service Bd., San Antonio, 1946-47; research sci. Mil. Physics Research Lab., U. Tex., 1948-51; research engr. North Am. Aviation, Downey, Cal. 1951; asst. prof. So. Methodist U., 1951-59; asso. prof. U. N.M., Alburquerque, 1960-63; asso. prof. Duke, 1963-64; prof., head dept. elec. engring. Kan. State U., Manhattan, 1964-. Served from ensign to lt. (j.g.), USNR, 1944-46. Mem. Am. Soc. Engring. Edn., I.E.E.E., Sigma Xi, Eta Kappa Nu. Contbr. articles profl. jours. Home: 2815 Illinois Lane Manhattan KS 66502

KOERBLE, CHARLES EDWARD, educator; b. Milw., Dec. 18, 1914; s. Edward Ludwig and Georgia Alberta (Wilhelm) K.; B.A., Lawrence Coll., 1941; M.A., U. Wis., 1951, Ph.D., 1954; m. Betty Jean Bevis, June 15, 1951; children—Brian Edward, Barbara Lee. Machinist apprentice, 1934-37; high sch. tchr., 1941-43; social service worker, 1946-48; dir. counseling, guidance N.W. Mo. State Coll., 1954-56, dean faculty, 1956-60, dean students, 1960-70, prof. guidance, counseling, 1970—. City councilman, Maryville, 1957-60, mayor, 1960-65. Served with AUS, 1943- 46. Mem. A.A.A.S., N.E.A., Am. Personal and Guidance Assn., Internat. Council Exceptional Children, Nat. Assn. Student Personnel Adminstrs., Phi Delta Kappa, Delta Tau Delta. Mason, Rotarian (pres. 1959-60). Home 965 S Walnut St Maryville MO 64468

KOERNER, HENRY, painter; b. Vienna, Austria, Aug. 28, 1915; s. Leo and Fanny (Mager) K.; student Acad. Applied Art, 1935-37; m. Joan Frasher, Aug. 15, 1953; children—Stephanie Beth, Joseph Leo. Came to U.S., 1939, naturalized, 1944, Works exhibited: Berlin, 1947, Midtown Galleries, N.Y.C., 1947, 1948, ann. exhbn. Whitney Mus., 1947; permanent mem. Midtown Galleries group 1947—; paintings include: Vanity Fair, The Skin of Our Teeth, The Prophet, My Parents, Monkey Bars, A Winter Journey, Life Guard, The Rose Arbor, The Beach, Subway, Fence Between Us, Frozen, Looking, June Night, The Lot, Barber Shop, The Bride, Fire on the Beach, also gouaches and drawings; cover portraits for Time Mag.; artist in residence Chatham Coll., 1952-53; vis. artist Cal. Coll. Arts, Crafts summer, 1955; resident vis. artist Munson-Williams-Proctor Inst., 1956-57. Served with AUS, 1943-46. Author, illustrator: Unfinished Sentence. Address: 1055 S Nesley Av Pittsburgh PA 15217

KOERNER, JAMES DAVID, author, found. exec.; b. Cedar Rapids, Ia., Feb. 3, 1923; s. John A. and May K. (Watson) K.; B.A., Washington U., St. Louis, 1947, M.A., 1949, Ph.D. in Am. Studies, 1952. Mem. faculty Kan. State U., 1952-54; mem. faculty humanities Mass. Inst. Tech., 1956-58; exec. dir Council Basic Edn., Washington, 1959-61, pres., 1962; editor-in-chief Edn. Devel. Center, Inc., 1967-70; program officer Alfred P. Sloan Found., 1970—. Served as pilot USAAF, 1942-45. Grantee Lilly Endowment and Council Basic Edn., 1964-66; Ford postdoctoral fellowship, 1954 55. Author: The Miseducation of American Teachers, 1963; Reform In EducationEngland And The United States, 1968; Who Controls American Education?, 1968. Editor: The Case for Basic Education, 1959; (with D. Colville) The Craft of Writing, 1961; The Parsons College Bubble: A Tale of Higher Education in America, 1970. Contbr. nat. periodicals. Home: 60 S Maple Av Westport CT 06880 Office: Alfred P Sloan Found 630 Fifth Av New York City NY 10020

KOERNER, VICTOR FREDERICK, machinery co. exec.; b. Pitts., July 30, 1911; s. Albert Jacob and Frieda (Dennis) K.; student Carnegie-Mellon U., 1929-32; B.S., Duquesne U., 1937; m. Martha Reed Potter, Oct. 8, 1938; children—Theresa Jane, Albert Frederick, James Potter. Jr. accountant Price-Waterhouse & Co., 1935-36; with Mesta Machine Co., Pitts., 1936—, asst. treas., 1963, treas., 1963—. Active local Boy Scouts Am., Little League Baseball. Bd. dirs. Homestead (Pa.) Hosp., 1955—, treas., 1966-70, pres., 1970—. Served with USNR, 1943-45. Mem. Financial Execs. Inst., Kappa Sigma. Presbyn. Mason. Club: Valley Brook Country (Mt. Lebanon, Pa.). Home: 2210 Country Club Dr Pittsburgh PA 15241 Office: Box 1466 Pittsburgh PA 15230

KOESTER, CHARLES W., banker; b. Marysville, Kan., 1910; grad. U. Neb., 1931, Harvard Grad. Sch. Bus. Adminstrn., 1933; LL.B., George Washington U., 1937. Sr. v.p. City Nat. Bank & Trust Co., Kansas City, Mo.; dir. Planters State Bank, Exchange Bank Schmidt & Koester. Home: 2235 W 63d St Mission Hills KS 66206 Office: 10th and Grand Sts Kansas City MO 64141*

KOESTER, GEORGE ARTHUR, educator; b. Allen, Neb., Oct. 15, 1912; s. Gerhardt F. and Mathilda (Wessel) K.; B.A., Midland Coll., 1937; M.S., U. Colo., 1941; Ph.D., U. Minn., 1951; m. Alice M. Ringstrom, June 6, 1943; 1 son, George Thomas. Tchr. high schs., 1937-42; with San Diego State Coll., 1950-, prof. edn., adminstrv. chmn. div. edn., 1958—, exec. dean, 1964- -. Bd. dirs. Luth. Assn. Retarded Children and Home Guiding Hands. Served to capt. AUS, 1942-46; group leader Crossroads A-bomb Project, Marshall Islands, 1946. Mem. Am. Psychol. Assn., Phi Delta Kappa. Rotarian. Home: 5001 Rockford Dr San Diego CA 92115

KOESTER, HELMUT HEINRICH, educator; b. Hamburg, Germany, Dec. 18, 1926; s. Karl and Marie-Luise (Eitz) K.; Dr. Theol., U. Marburg (Germany), 1954; Privatdozent, U. Heidelberg (Germany), 1956; m. Gisela G. Harrassowitz, July 8, 1953; children—Reinhild, Almut, Ulrich, Heiko. Came to U.S., 1958. Ordained to ministry Luth. Ch., 1956; asst. pastor, Hannover, Germany, 1951-54; teaching asst., then asst. prof. U. Heidelberg, 1954-56, 56-58, 59; mem. faculty Harvard Div. Sch., 1958-, John H. Morison prof. N.T. studies, 1964—, Winn prof. ecclesiastical studies, 1968—; vis. prof. U. Heidelberg, 1963, Drew U., 1966. Served with German Navy, 1944-45. Guggenheim fellow, 1964-65. Fellow Am. Acad. Arts and Scis.; mem. Soc. Bib. Lit., Soc. Novi Testamenti Studiorum. Author: Synoptische Ueberlieferung bei den Apostolischen Vaetern, in Texte und Untersuchungen, 1957; Trajectories through Early Christianity (with James M. Robinson), 1971. Home: 12 Flintlock Rd Lexington MA 02173 Office: 45 Francis Av Cambridge MA 02138

KOESTER, ROBERT GREGG, record co. exec.; b. Wichita, Kan., Oct. 30, 1932; s. Edward Albert and Mary (Frank) K.; student St. Louis U., 1951-54; m. Susan Buescher. Organizer, propr. Blue Note Record Shop, St. Louis, 1952-58, Delmark Records, St. Louis, 1952-; founder Jazz Report mag., 1953, pub., 1953-60; owner Seynour's Jazz Mart, 1959-61; founder- owner Jazz Record Mart, 1961—; pub., editor Blues News Bull., 1961—. Recipient Grand Prix du Disque Hot Club France, 1963; Jay award for best blues LP, 1966, Internat. Critics Poll award Jazz mag. Mem. Jazz Inst. Chgo, (charter). Contbr. numerous articles, chpt. in book. Home: 5953 N Winthrop Av Chicago IL 60626 Office: 7 W Grand Av Chicago IL 60610

KOESTLER, ARTHUR, author; b. Budapest, Hungary, 1905; s. Henry and Adele Koestler; student Univ. and Polytech., Vienna, Austria, 1922-26; LL.D., Queens U. (Kingston, Ont.); m. Mamaine Paget, 1950; m. 3d, Cynthia Jefferies, 1965. Fgn. corr., Middle East, Paris, Berlin, 1926-31; mem. Graf Zeppelin Arctic Expdn., 1931; travels in Russia, Soviet Central Asia, 1932-33; covered Spanish Civil War for News Chronicle, London, 1936-37, imprisoned by Gen. Franco; served in French Fgn. Legion, 1939-40, Brit. Pioneer Corps, 1941-42, discharged, worked for Ministry Information and as night ambulance driver; spl. corr. in Palestine for The Times, London, 1945; Manchester Guardian and N.Y. Herald Tribune, 1948; vis. Chubb fellow Yale, 1950; fellow Centre for Advanced Study in Behavioral Scis., Stanford, 1964-65. Recipient Sonning prize U. Copenhagen, 1968. Fellow Royal Soc. Lit. Author: Spanish Testament, 1938; The Gladiators, 1939; Darkness at Noon (Book of the Month Club selection), 1941; Scum of the Earth, 1941; Arrival and Departure, 1943; The Yogi and the Commissar, 1945; Twilight Bar, 1945; Thieves in the Night, 1946; Insight and Outlook, 1949; Promise and Fulfillment, 1949; The God That Failed (with others), 1950; Arrow in the Blue, 1950; The Age of Longing, 1951; The Invisible Writing, 1952; The Trail of the Dinosaur, 1955; Reflections on Hanging, 1957; The Sleepwalkers, 1959; The Lotus and the Robot, 1960; Suicide of a Nation? (ed.), 1963; The Act of Creation, 1964; The Ghost in the Machine, 1968; Drinkers of Infinity, 1968; Beyond Reductionism: New Perspectives in the Life Sciences—The Alpbach Symposium (ed. with J.R. Smythies), 1969; The Case of the Midwife Toad, 1971; The Roots of Coincidence, 1971. Address: care A D Peters 10 Buckingham St London W C 2 England

KOESUN RUTH ANN ballerina; b. Chgo., May 15, 1928; d. Paul Z. and Mary M. (Mondulick) Koesun; student of Edna L. Baum, Swoboda, Stone-Camryn, Anthony Tudor. Mem. Am. Ballet Theatre, 1946-; prin. roles include Les Sylphides, Giselle, La Sylphide, Nutcracker Pas de Deux, Caprichos, Billy the Kid; numerous appearances in summer stock, nightclubs, also television. Co-dir. dance dept. Hull House, Chgo. Office: 1790 Broadway New York City NY 10019

KOFF, ROBERT LINCOLN, violinist; b. Los Angeles, Feb. 12, 1919; s. George and Bessie (Wolf) K.; B. Mus., Oberlin Coll., 1941; postgrad., Juilliard Grad. Sch. Music, 1942, 45-46; m. Rosalind Mann, Jan. 19, 1947; children—Daniel, Stephen, Jeremy. Founding mem. Julliard String Quartet, 1946-58, also mem. faculty Juilliard Sch. Music; guest artist, mem. faculty Tanglewood (Mass.) Music Festival, 1948-50, Aspen (Colo.) Festival, 1951-53; asso. prof., artist-in-residence, dir. performing activities in music Brandeis U., 1958—; rec. artist for Columbia, RCA, MGM, Cambridge rec. cos; 10 concert tours U.S. and Can., 3 in Europe. Served with AUS, 1942-45. Home: 18 Demar Rd Lexington MA 02173 Office: Dept Music Brandeis U Waltham MA 02154

KOFFLER, HENRY, scientist; b. Vienna, Austria, Sept. 17, 1922; s. Wilhelm and Louise (Nagler) K.; came to U.S., 1939, naturalized, 1945; B.S., U. Ariz., 1943; M.S., (Wis. Alumni Research Found. fellow 1943-46), U. Wis., 1944, Ph.D. (NRC predoctoral fellow 1946-47), 1947; student Oak Ridge Inst. Nuclear Studies, summer 1949; m. Phyllis Pierson, June 21, 1946. Faculty Purdue U., 1947—, prof. bacteriology, 1952-59, asst. dean Grad. Sch., 1959-60, prof. biology, 1952—, head, dept. biol. scis., 1959—; guest investigator, Guggenheim fellow Sch. Medicine, Western Res. U., 1953-54. Vice pres. sect. microbial chemistry 7th Internat. Congress Microbiology, Stockholm, 1958; prin. investigator research programs supported by NIH, Office Naval Research, AEC, NSF, Dept. Def., Rockefeller Found., Am. Cancer Soc., Ind. Elks Assn., others; mem. com. selection postdoctoral fellows, div. biology and agr., NRC-Nat. Acad. Scis., 1956- 58; mem. grad. fellowship evaluation panel NSF 1958-60, grad. bd., 1959-60; cons. U.S. Govt., 1951-57, also industry; chmn. Commn. on Undergrad. Edn. in Biol. Scis., 1967-69; mem. numerous internat. biochem., microbiol., bot. congresses. Recipient Eli Lilly Co. award in bacteriology and immunology, 1957. Fellow Am. Acad. Microbiology (charter), A.A.A.S., Ind. Acad. Sci. (chmn. bacteriology div. 1949-50); mem. Am. Assn. U. Profs. (councilor Purdue, 1950-52), Am. Chem. Soc. (vice chmn. Purdue 1958-59), Am. Soc. Biol. Chemists, Am. Soc. Cell Biology, Biophys. Soc., Rocky Mountain Biol. Lab., Bot. Soc. Am. (sec. microbiology 1950-53), Deutsche Gesellschaft für Hygiene und Mikrobiologie, Am. Soc. Microbiologists, Soc. Exptl. Biology and Medicine, Soc. Gen. Microbiology (Gt. Britain). Sigma Xi (ann. research award Purdue 1952). Phi Kappa Phi, Phi Sigma, Sigma Pi Sigma, Alpha Zeta, Gamma Alpha, Phi Lambda Upsilon. Contbr. numerous articles. Home: 1310 Sunset Lane West Lafayette IN 47906

KOFFSKY, NATHAN MORRIS, ret. govt. ofcl.; b. Albany, N.Y., Feb. 14, 1911; s. Samuel Paul and Rose Esther (Sutin) K.; B.A., Cornell U., 1931; M.A., Am. U., 1939; m. Ruth Esther Langer, Jan. 23, 1946; 1 son, Peter Langer. With Bur. Agrl. Econs., and successor agys., Dept. Agr., 1934-66, dep. administr. econs. and statistics Agrl. Marketing Service, 1959-61, adminstr. Econ. Research Service, 1961-65, dir. agrl. econs., 1965-66; agrl. econ. adviser Ford Found., India, 1966-68; cons. econ. planning, 1968—. Served to capt. USAAF, 1942-46. Fellow Am. Statis. Assn., Am. Agrl. Econ. Assn. (v.p. 1960); mem. Am. Econ. Assn., Internat. Assn. Agrl. Economists. Contbr. articles in field. Home: 5515 Greystone St Chevy Chase MD 20015

KOFI, ABRAHAM BENJAMIN BAH, diplomat of Ghana; b. Akuse, Ghana, Dec. 3, 1917; s.Godfried Ashalaey and Dedeyo (Abade) K.; B.A., U. London (Eng.), 1949; m. Irene Essumanda Quansah, Aug. 30, 1942; children—Wilhemina, Margaret, Ashalley, Mamle, Tetteh. Served with Gold Coast Civil Service; dist. controller posts and telegrams, Acora, 1953-55; joined Ghana Fgn. Service, 1955; assigned Monrovia, then Australia and London; prin. sec. Ministry External Affairs, 1961-62; high commnr. of Ghana to Pakistan, 1962-66; ambassador to Pakistan, 1962-66, to U.S., 1966-68.

KOGA, TOYOKI, physicist; b. Hanaishi, Japan, Apr. 1, 1912; s. Tamejiro and Kiku (Tabuchi) K.; M.A. in Physics, Tokyo U., 1937, D.Sc., 1948; m. Emiko Shinra, 1942, (div. 1946); children—Rokutaro Koga, Akiya Koga. Came to U.S., 1958, naturalized, 1968. Research fellow Toyko U., 1937-41; asst. prof. Nagoya (Japan) U., 1941-48, prof., 1948-59; sr. research fellow Cal. Inst. Tech., 1955- 56; vis. prof. U. Cal. at Berkeley, 1956, 58; research scientist U. So. Cal., 1959-63; prof. N.C. State U., Raleigh, 1963-64; vis. prof. Bklyn. Poly. Inst., 1964-67; mem. profl. staff TRW Systems, Inc., 1967-69. Fulbright scholar, 1955. Mem. Am. Phys. Soc. Author: Stochastic Process in Gaseous Systems, 1970. Contbr. articles profl. jours. Research on prins. and methods of kinetic theory, plasma physics. Home: 1907 Carnegie Lane Redondo Beach CA 90278

KOGAN, BERNARD ROBERT, educator; b. Chgo., May 16, 1920; A.B., U. Chgo., 1941, A.M., 1946, Ph.D., 1953; married, 1962; four children. Instr. English, Ind. U., 1946- 48; instr. humanities U. Chgo., 1949-51; mem. faculty U. Ill. at Chgo. Circle Campus, 1953—, now prof. English. Author, editor: The Chicago Haymarket Riot: Anarchy on Trial; Darwin and His Critics; Narrative Techniques in the Later Novels of Charles Dickens. Mem. Modern Lang. Assn. Am. Address: 9034 N Bennett Av Skokie IL 60203

KOGAN, HERMAN, author, editor; b. Chgo., Nov. 6, 1914; s. Isaac and Ida (Periman) K.; student Crane Jr. Coll., 1932-33; A.B., U. Chgo., 1936, postgrad. 1936; studied violin with Isidor Braus, harmony and composition with Walter Dellers, 1919-34; m. Alice Marie Schutt, Dec. 28, 1940 (div. 1946); m. 2d, Marilew C. Lowry, Oct. 1, 1950; children—Rick Isaac, Mark Shalom. High school corr. Chgo. Daily News and Chgo. Eve. Post, 1930-32; reporter, rewrite man Chgo. City News Bur., 1935-37; reporter, feature writer, re-write man Chgo. Tribune, 1937-42; with Chgo. Sun, 1942-47, editorial writer, 1943; book editor, drama critic Chgo. Sun-Times, 1951-58; dir. co. relations Ency. Britannica, Inc., 1958-61; asst. to exec. editor Chgo. Daily News, 1962- 65; asst. gen. mgr. news and newspapers Field Communications Corp., 1965- 68; editor Chgo. Sun Times Book Week, 1968-70, Chgo. Sun Times Showcase, 1970—. Served with USMC, 1943-46. Decorated Presdl. Unit citation. Recipient pub. award, Geog. Soc. Chgo.; contbns. to journalism award Am. Newspaper Guild; Adult Edn. Council award Panorama; Book Week award Soc. Midland Authors; 2 Emmy awards Chgo. chpt. Television Acad. Arts and Scis. Mem. Phi Beta Kappa. Jewish religion. Clubs: Arts, Tavern, Chicago Press (past pres.), Chicago Press Veterans Assn., Headline (v.p.). Author: (with Lloyd Wendt) Lords of the Levee, 1943; Uncommon Valor, 1947; (with Lloyd Wendt) Bet A Million!, 1948; (with Lloyd Wendt) Give the Lady What She Wants, 1952; (with Lloyd Wendt) Big Bill of Chicago, 1953; The Great EB, 1958; (with Lloyd Wendt) Chicago: A Pictorial History, 1959; The Long White Line, 1963; Lending is Our Business, 1966; The Great Fire: Chicago 1871 (with Robert Cromie), 1971. Contbr. articles Nation, New Republic, Liberty, Am. mag., United Nations World, Am. Lawn Tennis, Esquire, Fortune. Home: 1715 N North Park Chicago IL 60614 Office: 401 N Wabash Av Chicago IL 60611

KOGAN, LEONID BORISOVICH, violinist; b. Dnepropetrovsk, Ukraine, Oct. 14, 1924; ed. Moscow Conservatory. Concert tours Europe, U.S.A., Canada, China; prof. Moscow Conservatory, 1952—. Recipient 1st prize Internat. Youth Festival, Prague, 1947, internat. music competition, Brussels, 1951; Lenin prize, 1965. Address: State Concert Assn USSR 15 Neglinnaya Moscow USSR*

KOGEL, MARCUS DAVID, coll. ofcl., physician; b. Austria, Sept. 28, 1903; s. Abraham I. and Rose (Jacobowitz) K.; brought to U.S., 1913, naturalized, 1914; student Coll. City N.Y., 1921-22, Columbia, 1922-23; M.D., N.Y. Med. Coll., 1927, D.H.D., 1953; D.H.L., Yeshiva U., 1952; m. Fannie Irene Tomson, June 24, 1930; childrenIsobel (Mrs. Simeon Pollack), Joan (Mrs. Gerard Roskin). Intern, ass. resident, chief resident physician Met. Hosp., N.Y.C., 1927-29; dep. med. supt., then med. supt. Cumberland Hosp., Bklyn., 1930-35; med. supt. Queens Gen. Hosp., N.Y.C., 1935-41; gen. med. supt., dir. bur. medicine and hosp. services Dept. Hosps., N.Y.C., 1946-49; commr. hosps., N.Y.C., 1949-54; dean Albert Einstein Coll. Medicine, Yeshiva U., 1954-67, dean emeritus, 1967—, prof., chmn. dept. preventive and environmental medicine, 1954-60, Atran prof. social medicine, 1960-67, dean Sue Golding Grad. Div. Med. Sci., 1957-67, v.p. med. affairs and sci., 1967-69. Chief med. officer Civil Def., N.Y.C., 1949-53. Bd. dirs. Atran Found. Served as col. M.C. AUS, 1941- 46; dir. dept. mil. sanitation Med. Field Service Sch., Carlisle, Pa., then theater med. insp. and chief preventive medicine China Theater. Diplomate Am. Bd. Preventive Medicine. Fellow Am. Pub. Health Assn., N.Y. Acad. Medicine, Am. Acad. Preventive Medicine. Home: North Wading River Rd Wading River NY 11792

KOGSTAD, ARTHUR WOODROW, army officer; b. Chgo., Nov. 5, 1918; s. Casper Arthur and May (Brady) K.; B.S. in Commerce, Loyola U. at Chgo., 1940; grad. Nat. War Coll., 1960; M.A. in Internat. Affairs, George Washington U., 1964; m. Mary Lou Bell, Mar. 4, 1946; children—Marylou Michele, Marsha Anne. Commd. 2d lt., U.S. Army, 1942, advanced through grades to brig. gen., 1967; various troop assignments, 1942; asst. chief staff XIX Corps, 2d Armored Div., ETO, 1948-49; battalion comdr. 3d Armored Div., 1948-49; mem. armistice team Far East Command, 1951-54; tactics chief Armored Sch., Ft. Knox, Ky., 1954-56; prof. mil. sci. Pa. State U., 1956-59; dep. chief staff personnel Hdqrs. U.S. Army, Europe, 1960-61; brigade comdr. 4th Armored Div. 1962-63, asst. div. comdr., 1968; dep. dir. personnel Joint Chiefs Staff 1963-65; chief staff Area Command, Saigon, Vietnam, 1966; dir. personnel Hdqrs. European Command, 1967; dir. maintenance Army Material Command, Washington, 1969-70, dir. Internat. logistics, 1970—. Decorated Legion of Merit with 2 oak leaf clusters, Bronze Star with 2 oak leaf clusters, Joint Service medal, Army Commendatin medal; Croix de Guerre with gold and silver stars (France). Mem. Assn. U.S. Army, Armor Assn., Beta Pi, Blue Key, Alpha Sigma Nu. Club: University (Chgo.). Home: 3915 Terrace Dr Annandale VA 22003 Office: Headquarters Army Materiel Command Washington DC 20315

KOH, T.T.B., diplomat of Singapore; b. Singapore, Nov. 12, 1937; s. Han Kok and Tsai- Ying (Tsi) K.; LL.B., U. Malaya; LL.M., Harvard; diploma criminology, Cambridge (Eng.) U.; m. Siew-Aing, Aug. 5, 1967. Pvt. practice law, Singapore, 1961-62; tchr. law U. Singapore, 1962-67; joined Singapore Fgn. Service, 1967; later permanent rep. Singapore to UN, also high commr. to Can. Vice pres. Singapore sect. Internat. Commn. Jurists. Author legal articles. Home: 155 E 76th St New York City NY 10021

KOHL, BENEDICT M., lawyer; b. 1931; A.B., Brown U., 1952; LL.B. cum laude, Harvard, 1955. Admitted to D.C. bar, 1955, U.S. Supreme Ct. bar, 1962, N.J. bar, 1963; partner firm Lowenstein, Sandler, Brochin, Kohl and Fisher, Newark; atty. interpretative div. Office Chief Counsel, 1957-60, Office of Tax Legislative Counsel, U.S. Treasury Dept., 1960-62. Mem. Am., N.J. State, Essex County bar assns. Office: 744 Broad St Newark NJ 07102*

KOHL HERBERT v.p., treas. Kohl Corp. Address: 11100 W Burleigh St Milwaukee WI 53281

KOHL JOHN CLAYTON, state ofcl.; b. N.Y.C., June 22, 1908; s. Clayton C. and Margaret (Williams) K.; student Oberlin Coll., 1925-27; B.S.E., U. Mich., 1929; m. Gladys B. Mitchell, July 10, 1935; childrenJohn Clayton, Atlee Mitchell. With Cin. Union Terminal Co., 1929-30; mem. faculty Carnegie Inst. Tech., 1930-37; with Pitts. Plate Glass Co. and subsidiary Pitts. Corning Corp., 1937-46, prof. civil engring., dir. Transp. Inst., U. Mich., 1946-66; on leave as asst. adminstr. HHFA, 1961-66; exec. v.p. Am. Transit Assn., Washington, 1966; exec. sec., div. engring. Nat. Acad. Scis.-NRC, 1966-68; sr. asso. Wilbur Smith & Assos., Washington, 1968-70; commr. N.J. Dept. Transp., 1970—. Mem. Mich. Commn. Intergovtl. Relations, 1954-58; vice chmn. truck adv. bd. Mich. Pub. Service Commn., 1957-61; mem. Tristate Transp. Commn. N.Y., 1961-66, chmn., 1970-71; mem., vice chmn. Delaware Valley Regional Planning Commn., Phila., 1971; chmn. Govs. Transp. Com., 1970—; mem. transp. research adv. com. Dept. Agr., 1957- 61; mem. Pres.' Policy Adv. Com., 1963-66. Served to lt. USNR, 1944- 45. Recipient Distinguished Faculty award U. Mich., 1961. Registered profl. engr., Pa. Mem. Am. Soc. C.E. (pres. Mich. 1956), Am. Soc. Traffic and Transp. (founder mem.), Transp. Research Forum, Hwy. Research Bd. (asso.). Contbr. profl. jours. Home: 777 W State St Trenton NJ 08618 Office: NJ Dept Transp Trenton NJ 08625

KOHLBRENNER, BERNARD JOHN, educator; b. Syracuse, N.Y., Nov. 20, 1904; s. George and Catherine (Coman) K.; A.B., Syracuse U., 1927, A.M., 1928; Ed.D., Harvard, 1942; m. Elizabeth McFarland, Aug. 28, 1929; childrenAnne, Philip, Margaret, Mary. Instr. edn. St. Mary's Coll., Winona, Minn., 1928-29; instr. edn. St. Louis U., 1933-38, asst. prof. edn., 1939-40; prof. edn. Coll. New Rochelle (N.Y.), 1940-45; instr. edn. U. Notre Dame, 1929-33, asso. prof. edn., 1945-49, prof. edn., 1949-70, prof. emeritus, 1970—, head dept., 1949-58; specialist Ford Found. project Phillipines at U. San Carlos, Cebu City, P.I., 1968- 69; cons. editor McGraw Hill Book Co. Adv. mem. Marquis Biographical Library Soc., 1970. Nominated for Wisdom award Honor and Wisdom Hall Fame, 1970. Mem. Nat. Cath. Edn. Assn., Am. Assn. U. Profs., Phi Beta Kappa, Phi Kappa Phi, Kappa Phi Kappa, Delta Sigma Rho, Phi Delta Kappa. Author: (with James A. Burns) A History of Catholic Education in the United States, 1937. Home: 717 W Angela Blvd South Bend IN 46617 Office: U Notre Dame Notre Dame IN 46556

KOHLER, CHARLOTTE, editor; b. Richmond, Va., Sept. 16, 1908; d. Edwin Charles and Augusta F. (Bromm) Kohler,; B.A., Vassar, 1929; M.A., U. Va., 1933, Ph.D., 1936; Litt.D., Smith Coll., 1971. Instr. English, Woman's Coll. of U. N.C., 1936-41, asst. prof., 1941-42, mgn. editor Va. Quar. Rev., 1942-46, editor, 1946—; asso. prof. English, U. Va., 1965-71, prof. English, 1971—. Mem. Am. Assn. U. Women, Phi Beta Kappa. Episcopalian. Home: 1900 Edgewood Lane Charlottesville VA 22903 Office: One W Range Charlottesville VA 22903

KOHLER, ERIC LOUIS, accountant; b. Owosso, Mich., July 9, 1892; s. F. Edwin and Kate Evelyn (Bentley) K.; A.B., U. Mich., 1914; M.A., Northwestern U., 1915; C.P.A., Ill., 1916. With Arthur Andersen & Co., pub. accountants, Chgo., 1915-17, 19-20, 33-37, Kohler, Pettengill & Co. (later E.L. Kohler & Co.), 1922-33; prof. accounting, Northwestern Sch. Commerce, 1922-28; mem. State Bd. C.P.A. Examiners, 1928-31; comptroller TVA, 1938-41; with Office of Emergency Mgmt. and WPB, 1941-42; exec. officer, Petroleum Adminstn for War, 1942-44; cons. accountant, 1945-48, 1949—; controller E.C.A., 1948-49; financial advisor U.S. Sec. Agr., 1946; vis prof. Ohio State U., 1955-60; U. Minn., 1955, U. Chgo., 1958, U. Ill., 1966. Controller, Auditorium Theater Council, 1960-. Mem. adv. panel U.S. Comptroller Gen., 1967—. Mem. Excess-Profits Tax Council, U.S. Treasury, 1946-47; Capt. Q.M.C., U.S. Army, 1917-18. Recipient Alpha Kappa Psi award, 1958; elected to Accounting Hall of Fame, 1962. Mem. Ill. Soc. C.P.A.'s, Am. Inst. of C.P.A.'s, Am Accounting Assn. (pres. 1936, 1946), Nat. Assn. Accountants, Phi Mu Alpha, Beta Gamma Sigma, Beta Alpha Psi. Club: City (pres. 1934-35) (Chgo.). Author: Accounting Principles Underlying Federal Income Taxes, 1924, 3d edit., 1927; Accounting for Business Executives, 1927; Advanced Accounting Problems, 1939, 47, 59; Principles of Auditing, 1947, 54, 63; A Dictionary for Accountants, 1952, 4th edit., 1969; Accounting for Management, 1965. Co- author: Principles of Auditing, 1924, 26, 32, 37; Principles of Accounting, 1927-31; Accounting in the Federal Government, 1956. Contbr. to mags. on accounting and mgmt. Editor The Accounting Review, 1928-44. Home: 1421 E 58th St Chicago IL 60637 Office: 8 S Michigan Av Chicago IL 60603

KOHLER, FOY DAVID, ambassador, education; b. Oakwood, O., Feb. 15, 1908; s. Leander David and Myrtle (McClure) K.; student Toledo U., 1924-27, LL.D., 1964; B.S., Ohio State U., 1931, L.H.D., 1962; LL.D., U. Akron, 1967, Fendlay Coll 1967; m. Phyllis Penn, Aug. 7, 1935. Fgn. service officer since 1931; vice consul, Windsor, Ont., Can., 1932, Bucharest, Rumania, 1933-35, Belgrade, 1935 legation sec. and vice consul, Bucharest, 1935-36, Athens, Greece (also vice consul for Dodecanese Islands), 1936-41, Cairo, Egypt, 1941; country specialist, Dept. State, Washington, 1941-44, asst. chief. div. of Near Eastern Affairs, 1944-45; with Am. Embassy, London, 1944; adviser to U.S. mem. 2d session Council UN Relief and Rehab. Adminstr., Montreal, Can., 1944; polit. and liaison officer, U.S. delegation, UN Conf. on Internat. Orgn., San Francisco, 1945; sec. gen. U.S. Mission to Observe Greek Elections, 1945-46; spl. studies Cornell U., 1946; student Nat. War Coll., 1946; 1st Sec. Am. Embassy, Moscow, Jan. 1947, counsellor, June 1948, minister plenipotentiary, 1948; chief Internat. Broadcasting Div., Dept. State, 1949; dir. Voice of Am. broadcasts, 1949; asst. adminstr. Internat. Information Adminstrn., Feb. 1952; policy planning staff Dept. State, 1952; counselor of embassy, Ankara, Turkey 1953-56; detailed to ICA 1956-58; dep. asst. sec. of state for European affairs, 1958-59; asst. sec. state European Affairs, 1959-62; ambassador to USSR, 1962-66; dep. under sec. of state for polit. affairs Dept. State, 1966-67; prof. Center Advanced Internat. Studies U. Miami, 1968—; cons. Dept. State, Marine Scis. Council, NASA, 1968—. Mem. Phi Beta Kappa, Beta Gamma Sigma, Delta Upsilon. Author: Understanding the Russians: A Citizens' Primer, 1970. Home: 215 Golf Club Circle Village Tequesta Jupiter FL 33458 Office: Center Advanced Internat Studies U Miami PO Box 8123 Coral Gables FL 33124

KOHLER, HEINZ, educator; b. Berlin, Germany, Aug. 19, 1934; s. Arthur Oskar and Gertrud (Förster) K.; student Free U., Berlin, 1953-54, 55-57; M.A., U. Mich., 1958, Ph.D., 1961; M.A., Amherst Coll., 1969; m. Mary Elaine Schmiege, June 4, 1955; children—Marjorie Ann, Victoria Rose. Came to U.S., 1957, naturalized, 1960. Teaching fellow U. Mich., 1958-59, lectr., 1961; asst. prof. Amherst (Mass.) Coll., 1961-64, asso. prof., 1964-69, prof. econs., 1969—, chmn. dept. econs., 1963-64, 70-71; vis. prof. econs. Smith Coll., U. Mass., Mt. Holyoke Coll., 1963—. Mem. Am. Econ. Assn., Aircraft Owners and Pilots Assn. Author: Economic Integration in the Soviet Bloc, 1965; Welfare and Planning, 1966; Scarcity Challenged, incl. Study Guide and Instructor's Manual, 1968; Readings in Economics, 1968, 2d edit., 1969; Economics, the Science of Scarcity, incl. Programmed Study Guide and Instructor's Manual, 1970. Home: 278 Middle St Amherst MA 01002

KOHLER, KARL OTTO, Jr., cons. engr.; b. Ellensburg, Wash., June 20, 11905; s. Karl Otto and Anna Rose (Stauffer) K.; B.S. in Mining and Metall. Engring., Wash. State U., 1926; m. 2d, Shirley Edwards, Aug. 12, 1955; childrenJoanne Carlotta (Mrs. Edward Reiger), Karyl Susan, Thomas Steven. Mining engr. Western U.S. and Mexico, 1926-30; cons. mining engr., also engaged cadastral survey Kittitas County, Wash., 1930-35; with U.S. Soil Conservation Service, 1935-55, chief engr., Washington, 1952-55; investment engr. Export-Import Bank, Washington, 1950-52; cons. engr. Govt. Afghanistan for devel. Helmand Valley, 1955-60; asst. chief engr. Devel. Loan Fund, Washington, 1960-62; chief engr. Alliance for Progress, AID, Washington, 1962-69; cons. engr., 1969—; irrigation engr. for FAO in Thailand and India, 1947, 50. Fellow Am. Soc. C.E. Home: 2254 Old Military Rd Medford OR 97501

KOHLER, PAUL WHISTLER, advt. exec.; b. Mansfield, O., July 13, 1909; s. Emerson Daniel and Harriet (Whistler) K.; B.A., Ohio Wesleyan U., 1932; M.A., Ohio State U., 1940; grad. Am. Advt. Fedn. Marketing Seminar, Harvard, 1968; m. Geraldine Raney, Aug. 29, 1937; childrenMelinda (Mrs. Walter G. Andrews, Jr.), Bruce Raney, Ted Raney. Tchr. English and journalism Ohio high schs., 1932-36; sales and advt. supr. appliance div. Westinghouse Electric Corp., 1936-46; with Howard Swink Advt. Agy., Inc., Marion, O., 1946-, chmn. bd., 1968-, also dir. Pres. Marion Bd. Edn., 1955-67; v.p., dir. Marion County unit Am. Cancer Soc., 1965-, chmn. anti- smoking com., 1965—. Mem. Marketing Club North Central Ohio, Omicron Delta Kappa, Tau Kappa Epsilon, Phi Delta Kappa, Pi Delta Upsilon, Kappa Delta Pi. Unitarian-Universalist. Rotarian. Club: Marion Country (past pres.). Home: 666 King Av Marion OH 43302 Office: 372 E Center St Marion OH 43302

KOHLER, WALTER JODOK, Jr., mfg. exec.; b. Sheboygan, Wis., Apr. 4 1904 s. Walter Jodok and Charlotte (Schroeder) K.; grad. Philips-Andover Acad., 1921; Ph.B., Yale, 1925; LL.D. (hon.), Beloit (Wis.) Coll., 1951, Northland Coll.; D.C.L., Ripon Coll., 1953; L.H.D., Lakeland Coll., 1961; m. Charlotte McAleer, Nov. 8, 1948; children-Terry Jodok, Charlotte Nicolette. Employed Kohler Co. (Wis.), 1925-47; pres. The Vollrath Co., Sheboygan, 1947-68, chmn., 1959—; dir. Sq. D Co., Security First Nat. Bank, E. J. McAleer Co., Phila. Gov. Wis. 1951-56. Chmn. Am. Cancer Soc., 1952-59, dir., 1949-63. Served as lt. comdr. USNR, 1942-45. Republican. Clubs: University, Tavern, River (N.Y.C.); Mill Reef (Antigua). Home: Windway Kohler WI 53044 Office: 1236 N 18th St Sheboygan WI 53081

KOHLMAN, DAVID LESLIE, educator; b. Houston, Oct. 13, 1937; s. Leslie W. and Aarona (Booker) K.; B.S., U. Kan., 1959; M.S., U. Kan., 1960; Ph.D., Mass. Inst. Tech., 1963; m. Linda Marie Norris, Sept. 11, 1959; children—Bradley David, Jeffrey Andrew. Research engr. Boeing Co., Renton, Wash., 1963-64; asst. prof. aero. engring. U. Kan., 1964-67, asso. prof., 1967-70, prof., 1970—, chmn. dept., 1967—; cons. aircraft industry, F.A.A. Asso. fellow Am. Inst. Aeros. and Astronautics; mem. Am. Soc. Engring. Edn., Aerospace Dept. Chmn.'s Assn. (sec. 1971-72), Lawrence C. of C., Aircraft Owners and Pilots Assn., Sigma Xi, Tau Beta Pi, Sigma Tau, Sigma Gamma Tau. Mem. Reorgn. Ch. of Jesus Christ of Latter-Day Saints (elder). Research in aerodynamics, fluid mechanics, stability and control, light airplane design. Home: 103 Providence St Lawrence KS 66044

KOHLMEIER, LOUIS MARTIN, Jr., newspaper reporter; b. St. Louis, Feb. 17, 1926; s. Louis Martin and Anita (Werling) K.; B.Journalism, U. Mo., 1950; m. Barbara Anne Wilson, Nov. 15, 1958; childrenDaniel Kimbrell, Ann Werling. Staff writer Wall St. Jour., St. Louis and Chgo., 1952-57, Washington, 1960—, staff writer St. Louis Globe-Democrat, 1958-59. Served with AUS, 1950-52. Recipient Nat. Headliners Club award nat. reporting, 1959, Sigma Delta Chi award Washington corr., 1964, Pulitzer prize nat. reporting, 1964. Author: The RegulatorsWatchdog Agencies and the Public Interest, 1969. Home: 5902 Madawaska Rd Washington DC 20016 Office: Nat Press Bldg Washington DC 20005

KOHLMEYER, CHARLES, Jr., lawyer; b. New Orleans, Oct. 14, 1909; A.B., Tulane U., 1929, LL.B., 1932. Admitted to La. bar, 1932; mem. firm Lemle, Kelleher, Kohlmeyer, Matthews & Schumacher, New Orleans. Mem. Am., La. New Orleans bar assns., Maritime Law Assn. Office: 1800 Nat Bank Commerce Bldg New Orleans LA 70112*

KOHLMEYER, HERMAN STANFORD, broker; b. New Orleans, Aug. 24, 1906; s. Charles and Isa Josephine (Brown) K. B.A., Tulane U., 1927; m. Isabel Minette Well. May 5, 1931; children—Herman Stanford, Marie Emily. With L. F. Rothschild & Co., 1927- 31, Fenner & Beane, 1931-35; organizer Kohlmeyer & Co., New Orleans, 1935—, now partner; pres. Carondelet Safe Deposit Co. Past Pres. New Orleans Cotton Exchange; mem. of N.Y. Stock Exchange, N.Y. Cotton Exchange, Chicago Board Trade. Mem. cotton Export adv. com. U.S. Dept. Agr. Served as maj. USAAF, World War II. Home: 1931 State St New Orleans LA 70118 Office: 147 Carondelet St New Orleans LA 70112

KOHLS, RICHARD LOUIS, ednl. adminstr.; b. Kentland, Ind., Apr. 19, 1921; s. Clarence E. and Helen (Littlejohn) K.; B.S., Purdue U., 1942, Ph.D., 1950; M.A., U. Mo., 1947; m. Irene Elizabeth Shuster, Apr. 20, 1944; children—Michael E., Kathryn Ann. Instr. marketing and prices U. Mo. at Columbia, 1946-48; prof. agrl. marketing Purdue U., Lafayette, Ind., 1948-64, asst. head dept. agrl. econs., 1965-66, asst. acad. v.p., 1966-68, dean of agr., 1968—. Mem. adv. com. on econs. research Dept. Agr., 1958-62; vis. prof. U. Exeter (Eng.), 1964; mem. Ind. Health Facilities Planning Council, 1968—. Bd. dirs. Ind. 4-H Found., Purdue Research Found. Served to capt. mil. intelligence, 1942-46. Named Outstanding Tchr., Am. Assn. Argl. Econs.; recipient Outstanding Tchr. award Purdue U., 1967. Mem. Greater Lafayette C. of C., Purdue Agrl. Alumni Assn. (dir.), Internat., Am. assns. agrl. econs., Am. Marketing Assn., Am. Assn. Higher Edn., Alpha Gamma Rho. Mem. Christian Ch. (pres. ch. 1967, gov. bd. 1964-68). Author: Marketing Argicultural Products, 3d edit., 1965. Home: 1520 Woodland St West Lafayette IN 47906

KOHLSTEDT, DONALD WINSTON, library dir.; b. Milwaukee, Apr. 16, 1909; s. Edward Delor and Hannah Carrie (Sandmeir) K.; stud. Dakota Wesleyan U., 1925-28, LL.D. (hon.) 1953; A.B., U. of Ill., 1929, B. S. in Library Sci., with honors, 1930. A.M., 1935; m. Ethelyn Adelia Dunn, Feb. 22, 1930; children—Roger Winston, Carolyn Sue, Linda Rae. Stack supervisor, Univ. of Ill. Library, 1929-30; 1st asst. St. Louis Municipal Reference Library, 1930-34; instr. in public library adminstrn., U. of Ill. Library Sch., summer 1935; librarian Kansas City (Kan.) Pub. Library, 1935-44; became librarian Grand Rapids (Mich.) Pub. Library, 1941, now library dir.; bus. mgr. Pub. Libraries, a periodical, 1952-54; lectr. Library Sci., U. Mich., extension service, 1956-57, 59-60, 64-65, 67-68. Mem. Kansas State Planning Board, 1939-40; mem. Mich. State Bd. for Libraries, 1949-54, chmn., 1952-54; bd. dirs. Grand Rapids Council on World Affairs, Family Service Assn. (pres. 1955-57); chmn. steering com. Liberal Adult Edn. Program, Grand Rapids; chmn. Grand Rapids com. for rev. lit.; secretary Grand Rapids Historical Society; mem. exec. board Grand Rapid Adult Edn. Council, Friends of Library; mem. Mich. Council Better Libraries, Grand Rapids Cultural Devel. Com.; mem. Governor's Nat. Library Week Com., 1966. Mem. A.L.A. (council, 1949-52; chmn. library radio broadcasts com. 1939-40; chmn. audio-visual com. 1941-43, vice chmn., 1944-46; mem. fin. com. 1942-44, chmn. Constitution, Bylaws Com., 1954-56, exhibits round table exec. bd. 1954-56, chmn. standards com.; exibits cons. since 1969), Kansas Library Assn. (N.E. district chmn. 1935-36), Mich. Library Assn. (legis. com.; chmn. planning com. 1944-45, pres. 1946-47); v.p. U. Ill. Library Sch. Alumni Assn., 1935, 1942. Mem. Y.M.C.A. Edn. Com.; mem. bd. of dirs. Friends of Am. Art (1941-45). Better Films Council (pres. 1945-46), (both of Grand Rapids). Mem. Grand Rapids Furniture Designers Assn., Alpha Kappa Delta, Sigma Tau Delta, Beta Phi Mu. Republican. Methodist (bd. stewards First Ch., Grand Rapids, since 1941). Rotarian. Club: Torch (Grand Rapids). Home: 858 Iroquois Dr S E Grand Rapids MI 49502 Address: Grand Rapids Public Library Grand Rapids MI 49502

KOHMAN, TRUMAN PAUL, educator, chemist; b. Champaign, Ill., Mar. 8, 1916; s. Edward F. and Marguerite (Villepigue) K.; A.B. cum laude, Harvard, 1938; Ph.D., U. Wis., 1943; m. Jane Sievers, Oct. 13, 1945; children—Leslie Jane (Mrs. Sweetser), Paulette Lynn, Steven Truman. Teaching, research asst. U. Wis., 1938-42; research staff U. Chgo., 1942-44; chemist Hanford Engr. Works, DuPont Co., Richland, Wash., 1944-45; staff Argonne Nat. Lab., 1945-46; fellow Inst. Nuclear Studes, U. Chgo., 1946-48; mem. faculty Carnegie Inst. Tech. (now Carnegie-Mellon U.), Pitts., 1948—, prof. chemistry, 1957—, program chmn. earth and astron. scis., 1963-67; vis. prof. Indian Inst. Tech., Kanpur, India, 1962-63; cons. various corps. and instns. NSF fellow, 1957-58. Fellow Am. Phys. Soc., A.A.A.S.; mem. Am. Chem. Soc., Am. Geophys. Union, Am. Astron. Soc., Geochem. Soc., Meteoritical Soc., Fedn. Am. Scientists, Sigma Xi, Alpha Chi Sigma, Gamma Alpha. Research, publs. on theory and techniques of radioactivity, radioactive and radiogenic nuclides in meteorites, meteorite craters, nuclear phenomena in geochemistry. Home: 440 Greenhurst Dr Pittsburgh PA 15243

KOHN, BERNHARD L., tobacco co. exec.; b. 1920; student Lafayette Coll.; married. With Kohn Bros. Tobacco Co. Inc., Hartford, Conn., 1946-54; v.p. Cullman Bros. Inc., 1954-63; sr. v.p., dir. Gen. Cigar Co. Inc., N.Y.C., 1963—. Served with USMCR, World War II. Office: 605 3d Av New York City NY 10016*

KOHN, CLYDE FREDERICK, geographer; b. Mohawk, Mich., Apr. 10, 1911; s. George Ferdinand and Cora Frances (Saam) K.; A.B., No. Mich. Coll. Edn., 1935; A.M., U. Mich., 1936, Ph.D., 1940; m. Doris Venton Merker, Jan. 17, 1942; children—Susan, George. Tchr. rural sch., Marquette County, Mich., 1929- 30, pub. schs., Gwinn, Mich., 1930-34, Miss. State Coll. for Women, Columbus, 1940-42; instr., lectr. Harvard, 1942-45; asst. prof. geography and edn. Northwestern U., 1945-47, asso. prof., 1947- 58; prof. geography U. Ia., 1958—, dept. chmn., 1966—; cons. author Scott, Foresman & Co. Mem. U.S. Nat. Commn. for UNESCO, 1960-66. Mem. Nat. Council Accreditation Tchr. Edn., Assn. Am. Geographers (pres. 1967-68), Nat. Council Geographic Edn. (pres. 1951-53), Nat. Council Social Studies, Phi Beta Kappa, Phi Kappa Phi, Kappa Delta Pi. Episcopalian. Author: Cross Country, 1951. Co-author: City Town and Country, 1959; In All Our States, 1960; In The Americas, 1962; The World Today-Its Patterns and Cultures, 1963, rev. edit., 1970; Beyond The Americas, 1964; Family Studies, 1970; Local Studies, 1970; Metropolitan Studies, 1970; Regional Studies, 1970; United States and Canada, 1970; Inter-American Studies, 1970; also profl. papers in geographic and ednl. jours. Editor 19th yearbook, Nat. Council Social Studies; Geographic Approaches to Social Education; co-editor Readings in Urban Geography, 1959. Home: 934 Highwood Dr Iowa City IA 52240

KOHN, GABRIEL, sculptor; b. Phila., June 12, 1910; s. Asher and Minnie (Hoffman) K.; student Cooper Union, N.Y.C., 1929, Beaux Art Inst., N.Y.C., 1930-39, Atelier Zadkine, Paris, France, 1946. Rep. permanent collections Mus. Modern Art, Ringling Mus. Art, Sarasota, Fla., Whitney Mus., N.Y.C., Albright-Knox Gallery, Cranbrook Mus.; also pvt. collections; tchr. Bklyn. Mus. Art Sch., La Jolla (Cal.) Art Center, 1962, San Francisco Art Inst., 1963, U. Wash., 1964, U. Cal. at Santa Barbara, 1967, Cal. Inst. Fine Arts, 1968; participant Internat. Sculpture Symposium, Cal. State Coll. at Long Beach. Served with USAAF, 1942-45; ETO. Decorated French Medal Liberation; recipient Ford Found. fellowship, 1960; Tamarind Litho Workshop fellowship, 1963; Guggenheim Found. fellowship, 1967-68. Address: 10806 Ventura Blvd Studio City CA 91604

KOHN, HAROLD ELIAS, lawyer; b. Phila., Apr. 5, 1914; s. Joseph C. and Mayme (Rumm) K.; A.B., U. Pa., 1934, LL.B., 1937; m. Edith Anderson, Dec. 30, 1946; childrenAmy, Ellen, Joseph Carl. Admitted to Pa. bar, 1937, since practiced in Phila. Sec. treas., dir. Kohn Found.; bd. dirs., Arronson Found., Phila. Fedn. Jewish Agys., Phila. Psychiat. Center. v.p., bd. dirs. Phila. chpt. Am. Civil Liberties Union. Mem. Am., Pa., Phila. bar assns., Internat. Acad. Trial Lawyers, Jud. Conf. 3d Circuit, Phi Beta Kappa, Order of Coif. Club: Midday (Phila.). Home: Devon PA 19333 Office: 123 S Broad St Philadelphia PA 19109

KOHN, HENRY, lawyer; b. St. Louis, May 2, 1917; s. Henry and Hannah (Lederer) K.; B.A., Yale, 1939, LL.B., 1942; m. Anne Frankenthaler, Sept. 23, 1945; children—Margaret, Barbara, Alice. Admitted to Mo. bar, 1942, N.Y. bar, 1946; with Bd. Econ. Warfare, 1942; practice with George Frankenthaler, N.Y.C., 1946-48; pvt. practice, N.Y.C., 1949-56; sr. partner Frankenthaler and Kohn, N.Y.C., 1957—. Former pres., dir. Fiduciary Mut. Investing Co., Mercer Fund Inc.; dir. Edison Bros. Stores, Inc., Graphic Scis., Inc., HIDOC Internat., Inc., Information Sci., Inc. Chmn. bd., founder Am. Jewish Soc. for Service; dir. Nat. Jewish Welfare Bd. Bd. dirs. USO, Muscular Dystrophy Assn. Am., Commn. on Youth Service Projects, 92d St. YM-YWHA, Lavanburg Corner House Found.; v.p. Jewish Conciliation Bd. Am.; pres. Ed. Lee and Jean Campe Found., Sam and Louise Campe Found. Am. Served to capt. AUS, 1942-46. Mem. Am. Bar Assn., N.Y. County Lawyers Assn., Assn. Bar City N.Y., Phi Beta Kappa, Order of Coif. Jewish religion. Clubs: New York Lawn Bowling, Lawyers, Harmonie (N.Y.C.). Home: 155 E 72d St New York City NY 10021 also Strawberry Hill Ackert Hook Rd Rhinebeck NY 12572 Office: 120 Broadway New York City NY 10005

KOHN, HENRY IRVING, educator, radiologist; b. N.Y.C., Aug. 19, 1909; s. Washington Irving and Fanny (Brownstein) K.; A.B., Dartmouth, 1930; Ph.D. in Gen. Physiology, Harvard, 1935, M.D., 1946; m. Linda Hansen, Oct. 22, 1961; children—Mari Annabel, Lars Sebastian. Traveling fellow Gen. Edn. Bd. at univs. Stockholm (Sweden) and Cambridge (Eng.), 1935-37; instr., then asst. prof. physiology and Pharmacology Duke Med. Sch., 1937-43; intern Bellvue Hosp., N.Y.C., 1946-47; commd. officer USPHS serving successively in Balt., Oak Ridge Nat. Lab. and U. Cal. at San Francisco, 1947-53; clin. prof. exptl. radiology, also research radiologist in radiol. lab. U. Cal. at San Francisco, 1953-63; Alvan T. and Viola D. Fuller-Am. Cancer Soc. prof. radiology Harvard Med. Sch., 1963-68, David W. Gaiser prof. radiation biology, 1968—; dir. Center for Human Genetics, 1971—; dir. Shields Warren Radiation Lab., New Eng. Deaconess Hosp., 1964—. Sci. sec. adv. com. biology and med. AEC, 1958-62; cons. UN Sci. Commn. Effects Atomic Radiation, 1957; mem. RBE ad hoc com. Internat. Commn. Radiol. Protection, 1960-61; mem. radiation study sect. NIH, 1965-69. Mem. Brookline (Mass.) Town Meeting, 1971—. Diplomate Am. Bd. Radiology, 1952. Mem. Am. Physiol. Soc., Environmental Mutagen Soc., Radiation Research Soc. (council 1962-65). Asso. editor, Radiation Research, 1957-61. Home: 14 Monmouth Ct Brookline MA 02146 Office: 50 Binney St Boston MA 02115

KOHN, JAMES PAUL, educator; b. Dubuque, Ia., Oct. 31, 1924; s. Harry Theodore and Kathryn (Piepel) K.; B.S. in Chem. Engring., U. Notre Dame, 1951; M.S., U. Mich., 1952; Ph.D., U. Kan., 1956; m. Mary Louise McGovern, Aug. 30, 1958; children—Kathleen, Kevin, Mary Louise. Chem. engr. Reilly Tar & Chem. Corp., Indpls., 1946-51; mem. faculty U. Notre Dame, 1955—, prof., 1964—; cons. Am. Oil Co., summer 1958, Imagineering Interprises, 1957-65, Hills-Morrow, 1966-70. Served with AUS, 1943-46. Decorated Bronze Star, Purple Heart. Mem. Am. Chem. Soc., Am. Inst. Chem. Engrs., A.A.A.S., Sigma Xi. Republican. Roman Catholic. Patentee removal acific gaseous components from natural gas. Home: 17684 Waxwing Lane South Bend IN 46635 Office: Dept Chem Engring Notre Dame IN 46656

KOHN, JOHN PETER, Jr., lawyer; b. Montgomery, Ala., Dec. 27, 1902; s. John P. and Clementina R. (Cram) K.; ed. Starkes Univ. Sch., Montgomery, St. Louis U., Spring Hill Coll.; LL.B., U. Ala., 1925; m. Margaret Thorington, Mar. 6, 1937; 1 dau., Margaret T (Mrs. Doy McCall). Admitted to Ala. bar, 1925, since practiced in Montgomery; county atty., 1946—; spl. atty. for gov. Ala., 1964-65; asso. justice Spl. Supreme Ct. Ala., 1968; Capt. Ala. N.G., 1936; served with AUS, 1940-45. Mem. Am., Ala., Montgomery (pres. 1931) bar assns., S.A.R., Soc. Pioneers (trustee), Phi Delta Theta. Clubs: Beauvior Country (Montgomery); Young Democrats Ala. (pres. 1933-39). Author: The Voters Primer, 1939; The Cradle-Anatomy of a Town, 1969. Home: 2542 Woodly Rd Montgomery AL 36111 Office: 515 S Perry St Montgomery, AL 36104

KOHN, JOSEPH JOHN, educator, mathematician; b. Prague, Czechoslovakia, May 18, 1932; s. Otto and Emilie (Schwarz) K.; came to U.S., 1945, naturalized, 1953; S.B., Mass. Inst. Tech., 1953; M.A. Princeton, 1953, Ph.D., 1956; m. Anna DiCapua, Dec. 15, 1966; children—Edward, Emma. Instr. Princeton, 1956-57; mem. Inst. Advanced Study, 1957-58, 62-63; mem. faculty Brandeis U., 1958- 68, prof. math., 1965-68, chmn. dept., 1964-68; prof. math. Princeton, 1968—. NSF fellow, 1954; Sloan fellow, 1964. Mem. Am. Acad. Arts and Scis. Contbr. profl. jours. Home: 32 Sturges Way Princeton NJ 08540

KOHN, KARL, educator, composer; b. Vienna, Austria, Aug. 1, 1926; s. Frederick and Margit (Fisch) K.; came to U.S., 1939, naturalized, 1945; certificate, N.Y. Coll. Music, 1944; B.A. summa cum laude, Harvard, 1950, M.A., 1955; m. Margaret Case Sherman, June 23, 1950; children Susanna Margaret, Emily Elizabeth. Instr. music Pomona Coll., Claremont, Cal., 195O-54, asst. prof., 1954-59, asso. prof., 1959-65, prof., 1965—; teaching fellow Harvard, 1954-55; mem. faculty Berkshire Music Center, Tanglewood, summers 1954, 55, 57. Bd. dirs. Monday Evening Concerts (Los Angeles). Served with U.S. Army, 1945-46. Faculty Fulbright Research Scholar, Finland, 1955-56, Guggenheim fellow, grantee Howard Found., 1961-62. Mem. Coll. Music Soc. Composer; Castles and Kings, 1958; The Monk From Shu, 1959; Three Scenes For Orchestra, 1960; Serenade For Wind Quintet and Piano. 1961; Capriccios, 1962; Concerto Mutabile, 1962; Interludes, 1964; Sonata da Camera, 1965; Leisure and Other Songs, cantata for baritone and chamber ensemble, 1965; Encounters, for flute- piccolo and piano, 1966; Episodes for Piano and Orchestra, 1966; Introductions and Parodies, 1967; Encounters for Horn and Piano, 1967. Home: 674 W 10th St Claremont CA 91711

KOHN, LOUIS A., lawyer; b. Hayti, Mo., Mar. 8, 1907; s. Israel and Rachel (Falk) K.; A.B., U. Mo., 1927; LL.B., Harvard, 1930; m. Mary Jane Bunn, Oct. 30, 1947. Admitted to Ill. bar, 1931, since practiced in Chgo.; parnter Mayer, Brown & Platt, and predecessors, 1946—. Commr. Nat. Conf. Uniform State Laws, 1953—; mem. council U. Ill. Law Forum. 1956-58; vice-chmn. joint com. jud. article Ill. and Chgo. bar assns., 1951-57; gen. counsel Com. Modern Cts. Ill., 1958, vice chmn.; vice chmn. Citizens Com. Jud. Amendment, Ill., 1953- 55. Mem. nominating com. Chgo. Sch. Bd., 1950-52. Organizer Stevenson for Gov. Com., Ill., 1947; adminstrv. asst. Gov. Stevenson, 1949; incorporator Volunteers for Stevenson, 1952; del. Democratic Nat. Conv., 1952; chmn. Ill. Lawyers for Kennedy, 1960. Served as officer AUS, World War II; S.W. Pacific. Decorated Bronze Star; named Chicagoan of the Year for 1962. Fellow Am. Bar Found.; mem. Am. (chmn. spl. com. adminstrv. agy. appointments), Ill., Chgo. (Bd. mgrs. 1950-52) bar assns., Am. Judicature Soc., Assn. Bar City N.Y., Am. Law Inst., Inst. of judicial Adminstrn., Phi Beta Kappa. Clubs: Law, Tavern, Harvard (Chicago, Illinois). Author articles ct. reform, trusts, uniform commnl. code, Home: 900 N Michigan Av Chicago IL 60611 Office: 231 S LaSalle St Chicago IL 60604

KOHN, MARTIN BENNO, former dept. store exec.; b. Balt., Aug. 28, 1898; s. Benno and Clara (Strauss) K.; B.A., Johns Hopkins, 1918; m. Rosa Rosenthal, Aug. 14, 1924 (dec.); children—Eleanor C., Elizabeth (Mrs. M. Peter Moser). With Hochschild, Kohn & Co., Balt., 1923-69, pres., 1945-65, chmn. bd., 1965-69, ret., 1969; pres. Frederick Atkins, Inc., N.Y.C., 1948-51; dir. Md. Nat. Bank, Balt., Peck & Peck. Vice chmn. Lexington Market Commn., Balt., 1953-64; mem. Md. Commn. Govtl. Efficiency and Economy, 1948-51. Pres. Jewish Welfare Fedn. Balt., 1943-45; bd. dirs. Md. Tb Assn., 1932-51; bd. dirs. Balt. Symphony, 1943-64, v.p., 1947-48, 49-50; past bd. dirs. Children's Rehab. Inst., Balt., Asso. Jewish Charities, Balt. Served with U.S. Army, 1917-19. Mem. Nat. Retail Mchts. Assn. (chmn. exec. com. 1964-65; pres. 1966-67), Balt. Assn. Commerce (pres. 1958- 60). Home: 3513 Overbrook Rd Pikesville MD 21208

KOHN, MISCH HARRIS, artist; b. Kokomo, Ind., Mar. 26, 1916; s. Jacob and Anna (Kaplan) K.; B.F.A., John Herron Art Inst., Indpls., 1939; Student of Oroszco and Leopoldo Mendez, Mexico City, 1943; m. Lore Lise Traugott, May 19, 1945; children—Jessica, Tamara. Exhbns. include Art Inst. Chgo., 1951, 60, Los Angeles County Mus. Art, 1958, 60, Musee Nat. d'Art Moderne and Biblioteque Nat., Paris, 1959, Museu de Art Moderna, Rio de Janerio, 1954, Ljubliana, Yugoslavia, 1955, 57, 61, numerous others; works rep. permanent collections Mus. Modern Art, Bklyn. Mus., Met. Mus., Nat. Gallery, Library of Congress, Smithsonian Instn., Art Inst. Chgo., Bibliotheque Nat., Nat. Mus. Stockholm, Museo d'Art Moderna, Sao Paulo, Victoria Mus., Melbourne, Australia, Bezalel Nat. Mus., Jerusalem, U. London, Ministere des Arts et des Lettres, Paris, also 15 Am. embassies; asso. prof. art Ill. Inst. Tech., 1953-65, prof. art, 1965-70. Fellow Ford found., 1959, grantee, 1960; Guggenheim fellow, 1952, 54; recipient Alice McFadden Eyre gold medal Pa. Acad., 1949, Pennell medal, 1952; Burr Meml. gold medal Phila. Free Library, 1960; prize Bklyn. Mus. Nat. Print Exhibit, 1968; Internat. Graphic Arts Soc. prize Phila. Print Club, 1969. Mem. Soc. Am. Graphic Arts, Acad. of Florence, Print Council Am., Phila. Print Club. Address: 1200 E Madison Park Chicago IL 60615

KOHN, P. CORBIN, lawyer; b. Hartford, Conn., Apr. 11, 1909; s. George Eugene and Minnie Blakeslee (Corbin) K.; grad. Phillips Andover Acad., 1926; B.A., Yale, 1930, LL.B., 1933; m. Elizabeth Pontefract Childs, Oct. 3, 1936; children—Cynthia (Mrs. Albert N. Hobart III), George, Elizabeth; m. 2d, Marion Thompson Keser, Aug. 28, 1962. Admitted to Conn. Bar, 1933, since practiced in Hartford; with firm Butler, Howard, Volpe & Garrity, 1933- 41; legal adviser Conn. War Council, 1941-44; counsel Surplus Property Adminstrn. and War Assets Adminstrn., Washington, 1945-46; spl. asst. Commn. to Revise Gen. Statutes Conn., 1947-48; partner firm Howard, Kohn, Sprague & FitzGerald and predecessor firms, Hartford, 1947- -. Member West Hartford Town Council, 1951-55. Mem. Am., Conn., Hartford bar assns., Am. Judicature Soc. Universalist. Republican. Clubs: University (Hartford); Yale (N.Y.C.). Author (with William S. Locke) Connecticut Probate Practice, 3 vols., 1950-51. Home: 99 Walbridge Rd West Hartford CT 06119 Office: 229 Buckingham St Hartford CT 06106

KOHN, ROBERT, educator; b. Vienna, Austria, Jan. 19, 1908; s. Max and Serafine (Fehl) K.; J.D., U. Vienna, 1933; M.A., U. Toronto, 1945; m. Frances E.L. Holdom, Oct. 27, 1951; children—Peter Allan, Susan Patricia. Came to U.S., 1966. Chief pub. health sers. Dominion Bur. Stats., Ottawa, Can., 1947-59; cons. WHO and Pan Am. Health Orgn., Jamaica, 1959-61; asst. dir. research Royal Commn. on Health Sers., Ottawa, 1961-65; prof., Sch. Hygiene and Pub. Health, Johns Hopkins U., Balt., 1966—; cons. several internat. research projects. Bd. dirs. YMCA, 1954-56, Boy Scouts Am., 1952-59. Served with Canadian Army, 1945. Fellow Am. Pub. Health Assn.; mem. Am. Statis. Assn., Canadian Pub. Health Assn. Author: Emerging Patterns in Health Care, 1966; The Health of the Canadian People, 1967. Contbr. profl. jours. Home: 1815 Landrake Rd Baltimore MD 21204

KOHN, ROBERT ROTHENBERG, med. scientist; b. Cleve., June 14, 1925; s. Jacob Bertholdt and Carrie (Rothenberg) K.; B.S., U. Wis., 1949; Ph.D., U. Mich., 1953; M.D., Western Res. U., 1957; m. Vilma Lavetti, July 27, 1952; children—Deborah D., Justin M., Steven M., Peter L. NSF fellow, 1952-53; resident, USPHS fellow pathology, 1957-60; asso. prof. pathology Case Western Res. U. Sch. Medicine, 1964-70, prof. pathology, 1970—, prin. adminstr. program aging research and tng., 1962—; spl. research biochem. and pathol. aspects aging and degenerative processes. Served with USNR, 1943-46. Diplomate Am. Bd. Pathology. Mem. A.A.A.S., Am. Assn. Pathologists and Bacteriologists, Am. Soc. Exptl. Pathology, Soc. Exptl. Biology and Medicine, Gerontological Soc., Soc. Developmental Biology, Sigma Xi, Alpha Omega Alpha. Author numerous articles in field. Home: 2060 S Belvoir Blvd Cleveland OH 44121

KOHN, WALTER, educator, physicist; b. Vienna, Austria, Mar. 9, 1923; B.A., U. Toronto (Ont., Can.), 1945, M.A., 1946, LL.D., 1967; Ph.D. in Physics, Harvard, 1948. Indsl. physicist Sutton Horsley Co., Can., 1941-43; geophysicist Koulomzine, Que., 1944-46; instr. physics Harvard, 1948-50; asst. prof. Carnegie Inst. Tech., 1950-53, asso. prof., 1953-57, prof., 1957-60; prof. physics U. Cal. at San Diego, 1960—, chmn. dept., 1961-63. NRC fellow, 1951; NSF fellow, 1958; Guggenheim fellow, 1963; recipient Oliver Buckley prize, 1961; NSF sr. postdoctoral fellow, 1967. Fellow Am. Phys. Soc. (counselor-at-large 1968—), Am. Acad. Arts and Scis.; mem. Nat. Acad. Scis. Research on electron theory of solids. Office: U Cal at San Diego Revelle Coll PO Box 109 La Jolla CA 92037

KOHN, WILLIAM HENRY, clergyman; b. Winnipeg, Man., Can., Sept. 27, 1915 (parents Am. citizens); s. William Lewis and Christime (Obermowe) K.; student Concordia Coll., Milw., 1935, Concordia Theol. Sem., St Louis, 1939 D.D., 1964; postgrad. Johns Hopkins; m. Marian Ruth Luenser, June 1, 1941; childrenKathy, Carol, Marian. Ordained to ministry Luth. Ch., 1940; pastor in Wis. and Md., 1939-56, Redeemer Luth. Ch., Hyattsville, Md., 1956-63. Sec. Luth. Mission Soc. Md., 1946- 48, pres., 1948-50; chmn. mission bd. Southeastern dist. Luth. Ch. Mo. Synod, 1951-54, pres., 1954-59; bd. dirs. Luth. Ch. Mo. Synod, 1959-63; pres. Southeastern dist., 1963-67, exec. sec. missions, 1967—. Chmn. Luth. Immigration Service Com.; bd. dirs. Luth. World Relief. Served as chaplain AUS, 1943-46. Decorated Bronze Star. Home: 9018 Maple Grove Dr St Louis MO 63126 Office: 210 N Broadway St Louis MO 63102

KOHNLE, EDWARD LEROY, mfr. price-marking devices; b. Dayton, O., Feb. 26, 1892; s. Frederick and Laura Ophelia (Hildabolt) K.; student U. Pa., 1911-13; m. Esther Bridge, June 21, 1916; childrenJohn Edward, Phyllis Ann (Mrs. Richard C. Castor). With Monarch Marking System, 1912—, sec.-treas., dir., 1920-51, pres., 1951-63, chmn. bd., 1963-67, chmn, emeritus, 1967—; dir. emeritus Dayton Power & Light Co., Mchts. Nat. Bank; dir. State Fidelity, Fed. Savs. & Loan Assn. Mem. world's com. YMCA, 1937-42, pres. Dayton YMCA, 1936-40 (recipient leaders fellowship 1953); nat. exec. bd. Boy Scouts Am., 1953—, pres. Miami Valley council, 1953-55, 64-65, (recipient Silver Beaver award 1938, Silver Antelope award 1946, Silver Buffalo award 1958); dir. Jr. Achievement, pres., 1965-; trustee Miami Valley Hosp. Bd. trustees Wilmington Coll., 1957-60. Served as 1st lt., CAC, U.S. Army, 1918-25. Mem. C. of C. (pres. 1935-36), Ohio Soc. N.Y., Ch. Fedn. Dayton (v.p.), Dayton Philharmonic Assn. (dir.), Kappa Sigma, Baptist. Mason, Rotarian (past pres.). Club: Engineers (Dayton). Home: 2230 S Paterson Blvd Kettering OH 45409 Office: Dayton OH 45412

KOHNS, PAUL L., broker; b. N.Y.C., Sept. 26, 1900; s. Lee and Clare (Elfelt) K.; B.A., Williams Coll., 1921; m. Katharine E. Bach, June 12, 1931; children—Gail, Lee, Ann. Partner Hirsch & Co., N.Y.C., mems. N.Y. Stock Exchange, 1930—. Home: Kirby Lane Rye NY 10580 Office: 191 W Route 59 Nanuet NY 10954

KOHORN, HENRY, corp. exec.; b. Munich, Germany, June 15, 1914; s. Heinrich and Franciska (Leibenfrost) K.; came to U.S., 1937, naturalized, 1943; C.P.A., Northwestern U., 1946; m. Elizabeth Schneidt, May 30, 1937; 1 dau., June; m. 2d, Eleanor Laaker, Apr. 9, 1968. Pres., dir. Ocoma Foods Co., Omaha, 1957-62, Orchard Hill Farms, Red Hook, N.Y., 1959-62; pres. Omaha Cold Storage Co., 1957-62; v.p. Consol. Foods Corp., Chgo., 1956-62; now chmn. bd. Allen Electric & Equipment Co., Chgo. dir. Orion Industries, Inc. Home: 400 E Randolph St Chicago IL 60601 Office: 307 N Michigan Av Chicago IL 60601

KOHOUT, HOWARD CHARLES, railroad ofcl.; b. N.Y.C., Apr. 1, 1913; s. Charles and Ann (Pospisal) K.; B.S. in Civil Engring., Carnegie Inst. Tech., 1936; m. Ruth Millicent McClure, Apr. 10, 1937. With Pa. R.R., 1936-38, 40-43, 46-63, regional mgr., Phila., 1961-63; asso. with R.H. Clarke, engr. and architect, Bermuda, 1938-40; gen. mgr. Western region Pa. R.R.; now v.p., gen. mgr. Western region Penn Central R.R.; exec. com., dir. Belt Ry. Co. Chgo., Central Ind. Ry.; v.p., dir. Calumet Western Ry., Ft. Wayne Union Ry., Ill. No. Ry., Western Warehousing Co., Zanesville Terminal R.R.; dir., past v.p. Chgo. Union Sta. Co.; pres. Union Depot Co., Columbus, O.; pres., dir. Dayton Union Ry., Indpls. Union Ry., Mackinac Transp. Co.; dir. Cin. Union Terminal, Little Miami R.R., Pitts., Ft. Wayne & Chgo. Ry., Terminal R.R. Assn. St. Louis, Toledo Peoria & Western Ry., Excelsior Truck Leasing Co., Mchts. Trucking Co., Pa. Truck Lines, Penntruck Co., Inc. Served with USNR, 1943-46. Mem. Ohio R.R. Assn.(exec. com). Ill., Mich. railroads assns., Ill., Ohio (dir.) chambers commerce Chgo. Assn. Commerce and Industry. Republican. Episcopalian. Clubs: Duquesne (Pitts.); Union League (Phila); Chicago; Oak Park Country. Home: 1214 Astor St Chicago IL 60610 Office: Union Sta Chicago IL 60606

KOHRMAN, GEORGE E., coll. dean; B.S., M.A., Ed.D., U. Mo. Prof. indsl. edn., dean Coll. Applied Scis., Western Mich. U., Kalamazoo. Office: Coll Applied Scis Western Mich U Kalamazoo MI*

KOHUT, HEINZ, psychoanalyst, psychiatrist; b. Vienna, Austria, May 3, 1913; s. Felix and Else (Lampl) K.; grad Döblinger Gymnasium, Vienna, 1932; M.D., U. Vienna, 1938; m. Elizabeth Meyer, Oct. 9, 1948; 1 son, Thomas August. Came to U.S., 1940, naturalized, 1945. Resident neurology U. Chgo. Hosps., 1941- 42, asst. neurology, 1942-43, instr. neurology, 1943-44, instr. neurology and psychiatry, 1944-47, asst. prof. psychiatry, 1947-50, lectr. Sch. Social Service Adminstrn., 1952-53, professorial lectr. dept. psychiatry, 1957—; mem. Inst. Psychoanalysis, Chgo., 1953—. Diplomate in neurology and psychiatry Am. Bd. Psychiatry and Neurology. Mem. Internat. Psychoanalytic Assn. (v.p. 1965—), Am. Psychoanalytic Assn. (pres. 1964-65; editorial bd. jour. 1955-58, 60-63, 66-69, Chgo. Psychoanalytic Soc. (pres. 1963-64), Am. Psychiat. Assn., Chgo. Med. Soc., A.M.A., Sigmund Freud Archives, Inc. (v.p.). Contbr. profl. jours. Contbr. Concepts and Theories of Psychoanalysis (in Concepts of Personality), 1963; The Analysis of the Self, 1971. Home: 5805 S Dorchester Av Chicago IL 60637 Office: 180 N Michigan Av Chicago IL 60601

KOISCH, FRANCIS PAUL, army officer; b. Newburgh, N.Y., Oct. 7, 1919; s. Anthony Emil and Rose (Ladick) K.; B.S., U.S. Mil. Acad., 1942; M.S. in Civil Engring., U. Cal. at Berkeley, 1947; postgrad. Command and Gen. Staff Sch., 1954, Army War Coll., 1960; m. Emmaline M. Brunner, May 17, 1946; children—Mary Gail, Francis Paul, Robert C. Commd. 2d lt., C.E., U.S. Army, 1942, advanced through grades to maj. gen. 1969; served in S. Pacific, Europe, Viet Nam; dist. engr., Fort Worth, 1963-65; div. engr. N. Atlantic, 1966-69; dir. civil works Office Chief Engrs., Army Dept., Washington, 1969—. Mem. Marine Sci. Council, Engring. Joint Council, Internat. Com. Large Dams. Decorated D.S.M., Legion of Merit with 2 oak leaf clusters, Bronze Star, Air medal. Mem. Soc. Am. Mil. Engrs. (regional dir. 1966-69). Permanent Internat. Assn. Navigation Congresses (head Am. delegation 1969—). Contbr. papers on river hydraulics, coastal engring., dams, water resources planning. Home: Quarters 60 Ft Belvoir VA 22060 Office: Office Chief Engineers 1000 Independence Av Washington DC 20314

KOIVISTO, MAUNO HENRIK, Finnish banker, politician; b. Turku, Finalnd, Nov. 25, 1923; s. Juho and Hymni Sofia (Eskola) K.; Ph.D., U. Turku, 1956; m. Tellervo Kankaanranta, June 22, 1952; 1 dau., Assi Elina. Mng. dir. Helsinki Workers Savs. Bank (Finland), 1959-67; gov. Bank of Finland, Helsinki, 1968—; minister finance Finland, Helsinki, 1966-67, prime minister, 1968-70. Mem. bd. Post Savs. Bank, 1968—. Decorated Grand Cross Order of Finnish White Rose. Mem. Social Dem. party. Author: Social Relations in Turku Harbour, 1956. Home: 11 B 40 Pitkansillanranta Helsinki 53 00530 Finland Office: Bank of Finland P Box 10160 Helsinki 10 Finland

KOKE, RICHARD JOSEPH, exhibit designer, mus. curator; b. N.Y.C., Sept. 19, 1916; s. Joseph and Emily Josephine (Chevrolet) K.; student Art Students League, 1935, Cooper Union Art Inst., 1935-37; A.B., N.Y. U., 1941; M.A., Columbia, 1947; m. Mary A. Kimbley, Jan. 1, 1955. Historian, Bear Mountain (N.Y.) Trailside Hist. Mus., 1935-37; curator Stony Point (N.Y.) Battlefield Mus., summers 1937-41; research cons. Hudson Valley Survey, 1946-47; historian Saratoga Nat. Hist. Park, 1947; curator mus. N.Y. Hist. Soc., 1947—; conducted archaeol. investigations on Revolutionary War mil. sites in Highlands of the Hudson, N.Y., 1935-41. Served with AUS, 1942-45; art dir, in charge cartographic dept. M.C., 1942-44; battlefield history research analyst. hist. sect. Hdgrs. 1944-45; engaged in collection and editing of mil. data pertaining to tactical operations Am. forces, preparation ofcl. army histories of Services of Supply, 1st, 3d, 7th, 9th, 15th armies, Western European Front, World War 11. Recipient 1st prize hist. essay contest sponsored by Colonial Dames of N.Y., 1940. Mem. Am. Assn. Mus., Mus. Council. Club: Athenaeum (N.Y.C.). Editor: Scenic and Historic America, 1938. Contbr. mags. and revs. Home: 133 W 81st St New York City NY 10024 Office: 170 Central Park W New York City NY 10024

KOKE, WILLIAM LAWRENCE, former food co. exec.; b. Bronx, N.Y., Aug. 20, 1934; s. John Henry and Patricia (Gallagher) K.; B.S., U. Bridgeport, 1960; M.B.A., Harvard, 1962; m. Angela Bridgid Donovan, Oct. 26, 1963; children—Kathleen Ann, Christiane. Former treas. Ward Foods, Inc., N.Y.C.; dir. Pa. Mut. Fund.

KOKORIS, LOUIS A., mathematician, educator; b. Chgo., June 27, 1924; s. Tom and Helen (Georgoulis) K.; student Wright Jr. Coll., Chgo., 1942-43, U. Wis., 1943- 44; B.S., U. Chgo., 1947, M.S., 1948, Ph.D., 1952; m. Evangeline Antonopoulos, June 20, 1954; childrenEllen, Ann and Christine (twins). Instr., U. Wash., 1952-54, asst. prof., 1954-55; asst. prof. Washington U., St. Louis, 1955-56, 57-58; lectr. Yale, 1956-57; asso. prof. Ill. Inst. Tech., Chgo., 1958-63, prof., 1963-. Served with USAAF, 1943-46. Mem. Am. Math. Soc., Math. Assn. Am., Am. Assn. U. Profs. Home: 4844 N Nashville Av Chicago IL 60656

KOKOSCHKA, OSKAR, artist, writer; b. Pochlarn, Austria, March 1, 1886; student (scholar), Vienna Sch. Arts and Crafts; D.Litt., Oxford. Designer decorative cards and fans for Wiener Werkstatte; exhibited paintings, drawings and lithographs, also sculpture 1st Vienna Art Exhbn., 1908; went to Switzerland, 1909, then to Berlin; influenced by Expressionist movement; served with Austrian Army, World War I; prof. Dresden Acad., 1920; traveled in Eng., Switzerland, France, Spain, Italy, N. Africa, Near East, 1924-31, then returned to Vienna, Prague; went to Eng., 1938-58; vis. prof. Boston U., 1948; established Internat. Summer Sch., Salzburg, Austria, 1953; exhibited leading European cities, also N.Y.C., London. 1963; represented in permanent collections Albright Art Gallery, Buffalo Mus. Modern Art, Phillips Meml. Gallery, Washington, numerous others. Recipient Erasmus prize, 1960. Author plays: Mörder, Hoffnung der Franen, 1907; Der brennende Dornbusch, 1911; Hiob (music by Hindemith), 1911; Orpheus and Eurydice (music by Krenek), 1916; A Sea Ringed with Visions, 1962. Address: Villeuve Vaud Switzerland

KOLAKOWSKI, LESZEK, educator, philosopher; b. Radom, Poland, Oct. 23, 1927; s. Jerzy and Lucyna (Pietrusiewicz) K.; student U. Lodz (Poland), 1945-49; Dr. Degree, U. Warsaw, 1953; m. Tamara Dynenson, Nov. 19, 1949; 1 dau., Agnieszka. Asst., U. Lodz, 1947-49; mem. faculty U. Warsaw, 1950-68, prof. philosophy, 1964-68; expelled from univ. for polit. reasons, 1968; prof. Acad. Sci., Inst. of Philosophy, Warsaw, 1956—; vis. prof. McGill U., 1969, U. Cal. at Berkeley, 1970. Expelled from Communist party, 1966. Author: Toward a Marxist Humanism, 1968; The Alienation of Reason, 1968; also many others in Polish. Editor: Studia filozoficzne, 1957-59.

KOLAR, MILTON ANTON, corp. exec.; b. Chgo., Jan. 18, 1916; s. Frank J. and Josephine (Jaros) K.; B.S.C., Northwestern U., 1937, LL.B., 1939; m. Rae Solum, July 4, 1940; children—Caryn Rae, Britton Ward, Christine Edith. Admitted to Ill. bar, 1939; practice law, Chgo., 1939-54; atty. U.S. Gypsum Co., Chgo., 1940-42; atty. Butler Bros., Chgo., 1942-59; asst. sec., 1954-58, gen. devel. mgr., 1954-58, asst. to pres., 1958-59; gen. mgr. S.W. region Ben Franklin Stores div. City Products Corp. (acquired Butler Bros. 1959), Dallas, 1960-62, v.p., sec., City Products Corp., Des Plaines, Ill., 1962- 67; pres. Scott Stores div. City Products Corp., Des Plaines, 1967-69, pres. Herst-Allen div., 1969— sometimes lectr. Cons. OPS, Washington, 1951. Mem. Fed., Am., Ill., Chgo. bar assns., Am. Soc. Corporate Secs., Lambda Chi Alpha, Phi Delta Phi. Lutheran. Home: 326 Butler Dr Lake Forest IL 60045 Office: 1700 S Wolf Rd Des Plaines IL 60018

KOLASA, BLAIR JOHN, univ. dean; b. Barnesboro, Pa., Apr. 6, 1926; s. John Joseph and Mary Magdalene (Gunther) K.; B.S., Allegheny Coll., 1948; M.S., U. Pitts., 1950, Ph.D., 1954; J.D., Duquesne U., 1960; m. Susan D. Hubbell, Aug. 24, 1957 (div. Oct. 1969); 1 dau., Susan D.H. Indsl. fellow Psychol. Service of Pitts., 1954-55; adminstrv. asst. Superior Ct. of Pa., 1955-56; faculty Duquesne U., Pitts., 1956-66, 68—, prof., 1968—, dean Sch. Bus. and Adminstrn., 1971—; acting dean Kan. State U., Manhattan, 1966-68.

Legal counsel Republican Exec. Com., Allegheny County, 1965-66. Served with AUS, 1945-46, 51-53. Ford fellow, 1964. Mem. Am. Psychol. Assn., Allegheny County Bar Assn., Law Soc. Assn., Acad. Mgmt., Am. Psychology-Law Soc. Club: University (Pitts.). Author: Introduction to Behavioral Science for Business, 1969; Responsibility in Business: Issues and Problems, 1972. Home: 700 Forbes Av Pittsburgh PA 15219

KOLATCH, MYRON, mag. editor; b. Bklyn., Sept. 26, 1926; s. Philip S. and Rebecca (Langberg) K.; B.A , N.Y. U., 1950, postgrad in English, 1950-51; m. Francine Ruth Miller, Jan. 28, 1951; childrenBarry Steven, Jonathan Lee, Sari Elana. Mem. staff New Leader, 1953-, mng. editor, 1960-61, exec. editor, 1961-. Served with AUS, 1951-53. Home: 141-13 68th Dr Kew Gardens Hills NY 11367 Office: 212 Fifth Av New York City NY 10010

KOLB, GWIN JACKSON, educator; b. Aberdeen, Miss., Nov. 2, 1919; s. Roy Rolly and Nola Undine (Jackson) K.; B.A., Millsaps Coll., 1941; M.A., U. Chgo., 1946, Ph.D., 1949; m. Ruth Alma Godbold, Oct. 11, 1943, children-Gwin Jackson II, Alma Dean. Editorial asst. Modern Philology, 1946-56; mem. faculty U. Chgo., 1949—, prof. English, 1961—, chmn. dept., 1963—, chmn. coll. English staff, 1958-60, head humanities sect. in coll., 1960-62; vis. asso. prof. Northwestern U., winter 1958, Stanford, spring 1960; vis. prof. U. Washington, summer 1967. Served with USNR, 1942-45. Recipient Quantrell award U. Chgo., 1955; Guggenheim fellow, 1956-57; Alumni award, Millsaps Coll., 1967; grantee Am. Council Learned Socs., 1961-62. Mem. Midwest Modern Lang. Assn. (pres. 1964-65), Johnson Soc. Central Region (pres. 1965-66), Modern Lang. Assn., Nat. Council Tchrs. English (bd. dirs. coll. sect. 1966-68), Am. Assn. U. Profs., The Johnsonians, Assn. Depts. English (pres. 1968). Clubs: Caxton; Quadrangle (Chgo.). Co-author: Dr. Johnson's Dictionary, 1955; Reading Literature; A Workbook, 1955. Editor: (Samuel Johnson) Rasselas, 1962; co-editor: English Literature, 1660-1800; A Bibliography of Modern Studies Complied for Philological Quarterly, 1951-60, 2 vols., 1962. Home: 5819 Blackstone Av Chicago IL 60637

KOLB, LAWRENCE COLEMAN, physician, psychiatrist; b. Balt., June 16, 1911; s. Lawrence and Lillian Hess (Coleman) K.; B.A., Trinity Coll., Dublin U., Ireland, 1932; M.D., Johns Hopkins, 1934; m. Madeleine Currie, July 3, 1937; childrenPamela, Mary, Richards. Intern medicine, surgery Strong Meml. Hosp., Rochester, N.Y.; fellow neurology Johns Hopkins, 1936-38, instr., 1939-40; Markle fellow neurology Nat. Hosp. Queens Sq., Eng., 1938-39; psychiatrist Milw. Sanitorium, 1941; dir. research projects Nat. Inst. Mental Health, also pvt. practice psychiatry, 1946-49; research asso. Washington Sch. Psychiatry, 1946-49; cons. Mayo Clinic, also asso. prof. psychiatry U. Minn., 1949-54; dir. N.Y. State Psychiat. Inst., prof., chmn. dept. psychiatry, Columbia and dir. psychiat. service Presbyn. Hosp., N.Y.C., 1954—; pres. med. bd. Presbyn. Hosp., N.Y.C., 1962-64; cons. nat. adv. council USPHS, Dept. Health, Edn. and Welfare. Mem. panel med. scis. to asst. sec. of def., 1954-60. Diplomate Am. Bd. Psychiatry and Neurology (pres. 1968). Fellow Am. Psychiat. Assn. (pres. 1968), Am. Acad. Neurology, N.Y. Acad. Sci.; mem. Am. Neurol. Assn., Am. Psychoanalytic Assn., Assn. Research Nervous and Mental Diseases (pres. 1959), Sigma Xi, Alpha Omega Alpha. Clubs: Century Association, University (N.Y.C.); Vidonia Practitioners Author; (with O. R. Langworthy and L. G. Lewis) Physiology of Micturition, 1940; The Painful Phamtom, 1954; Modern Clinical Psychiatry, 1968. Home: 31 Old Smith Rd Tenafly NJ 07670 Office: 722 W 168th St New York City NY 10032

KOLB, NATHANIEL KEY, Jr., architect; b. Sherman, Tex., Aug. 17, 1933; s. Nathaniel Key and Nelcine (Dial) K.; B. Arch., Tex. A. and M. U., 1957; M.Arch., U. Pa., 1960; m. Catherine Conner, Nov. 23, 1958; children—Nathaniel Key III, Mary Catherine, Amy Monica, Peter Paul, John Conner, Elizabeth Dial. With Caudill, Rowlett & Scott, Houston, 1955-58, Vincent J. Kling, Architect, Phila., 1959-61, William B. Tabler, Architect, N.Y.C., 1961-63; pres., dir. OMNIPLAN Architects Harrell & Hamilton, Dallas, 1963—; dir. basic design program in architecture Tex. A. and M. U., 1957-59; adj. asst. prof. architecture Columbia, 1961-62; guest lectr. assns. and univs.; dir. OMNIPLAN, Inc. Dir. Save Open Space. Dir. Holy Trinity Sch. Mem. A.I.A. (commr. Dallas 1971), Tex. Soc. Architects, Dallas Mus. Fine Arts. Home: 4402 Rawlins St Dallas TX 75219 Office: Republic Bank Tower Dallas TX 75201

KOLB, WALTER E., bus. exec.; b. Bklyn., 1905. Hon. chmn. bd. Bank Commerce N.Y.; dir. Kentile, Inc., Bklyn. Home: 10 Dudley Lane Larchmont NY 10538 Office: 56 E 42d St New York City NY 10017

KOLB, WILLIAM LESTER, coll. dean, provost; b. Cin., Sept. 26, 1916; s. William Frederick and Lydia Marie (Atkins) K.; B.A. Magna cum laude with honors in Polit. Sci., Miami (O.) U., 1938; M.A., U. Wis., 1939, Ph.D., 1943; m. Helen Webster, June 15, 1940; children—Nina Marie, William Webster. Instr. sociology Okla. A. and M. Coll., 1941-43, 46; asst. prof. sociology Newcomb Coll. of Tulane U., 1946-48, asso. prof., then prof., head dept., also in Grad. Sch. Tulane U., 1948-59, univ. chmn. dept. sociology, 1955-57; Fred B. Hill prof. sociology, chmn. dept. sociology and anthropology Carleton Coll., 1959-64; dean, prof. sociology Beloit (Wis.) Coll., 1964- -, provost, 1970—. Mem. Edwin J. Beinecke Sr. Meml. scholarship com. S & H Found., Inc., 1971—. Mem. dept. Christian social realtions Episcopal Diocese La., 1957-58; vice chmn. Am. Conf. Academic Deans, 1968-69, chmn., 1969-70; chmn. Danforth Commn. on Study Campus Ministry, 1962-70; mem. exec., policy coms. Dept. Higher Edn. Nat. Council Chs. Christ, 1965-70, chmn. planning com. Coloquium on Religion and Higher Edn., 1966-67. Mem. La. chpt., bd. Am. Civil Liberties Union, 1956-59, bd. Minn. chpt., 1963-64, mem. Wis. chpt., 1964—. Served to lt. (j.g.) USNR, 1943-46. Post-doctoral fellow Soc. for Religion in Higher Edn., 1967. Mem. Am. Assn. U. Profs. (v.p. Minn. 1961-62, nat. council 1962-64), Am. Sociol. Assn. (council, exec. com. 1961-62, mem. MacIver award com. 1965-66, chmn. 1967), Midwestern Sociol. Soc. (council 1960-62, pres. 1966-67), Faculty Christian Fellowship (gen. com. 1960-62), Phi Beta Kappa (mem. Ralph Waldo Emerson award com. 1971—). Author: (with Logan Wilson) Sociological Analysis, 1949; (with J. Gould) A Dictionary of the Social Sciences, 1964; also articles, chpts. in books. Mem. editorial bd. Christian Scholar, 1960-62. Home: 821 Milwaukee Rd Beloit WI 53511

KOLBE, HENRY WALTER, hosp. adminstr.; b. N.Y.C., Sept. 22, 1904; s. Adam and Mary (Russell) K.; B.S., Coll. City N.Y., 1923; M.D., N.Y. U., 1927; m. Marion Spencer Anderson, Sept. 22, 1931; childrenHarry, George, Bruce. Intern City Hosp., N.Y.C., 1928-29, exec. physician, 1930-31; pvt. practice, N.Y.C., 1931-36; dep. med. supt. Municipal Sanatorium, N.Y.C., 1936-39, Met. Hosp., N.Y.C., 1939-42; med. supt. Lincoln Hosp., 1942-43, Coney Island (N.Y.) Hosp., 1947-48, Harlem Hosp., N.Y.C., 1949-52; gen. med. supt. N.Y.C. Dept. Hosps., 1952-55, dir. bur. medicine and hosp. services, 1955-59; exec. dir. Phila. Gen. Hosp., 1959-67, Pondville Hosp., Walpole, Mass., 1967—; cons. Govt. Guatemala, 1948-49, Hosp. Cons., Am. Coll. Hosp. projects in Burma, Columbia, Iran and U.S., 1949-. Med. officer Inst. Inter-Am. Affairs, 1945-47. Served as maj. AUS, 1943-45. Mem. Am. Assn. Hosp. Cons., Am. Coll. Hosp. Adminstrs., Am., Mass. pub. health assns., Am. Hosp. Assn. Author: Administrative Manual for Hospital System, Guatemala; Functional Administrative Organization of Hospital Service, Burma; Staffing Requirements for Hospitals, Burma; Hospital Plan for Guatemala. Office: Pondville Hosp Box 111 Walpole MA 02081

KOLCHIN, ELLIS ROBERT, educator, mathematician; b. N.Y.C., Apr. 18, 1916; s. Morris and Betty (Steinreich) K.; A.B., Columbia, 1937, Ph. D., 1941; m. Kate Weil, June 14, 1940; childrenPeter, Ellen. Mem. faculty Columbia, 1946-, prof. math., 1958-, chmn. dept., 1963-68. Mem. Am. Math. Soc. Home: 440 Riverside Dr New York City NY 10027

KOLEHMAINEN, JOHN ILMARI, educator; b. Conneaut, O., July 2, 1910; s. Matti and Julia (Tuomisto) K.; A.B., Western Res. U., 1933, M.A. in History, 1934, Ph.D., 1937; m. Astrid Irene Petrell, Aug. 6, 1939; children—Jan W., Joy K., Kay A. Mem. faculty Heidelberg Coll., Tiffin, O., 1938—, prof. polit. sci., 1940—. Vis. prof. Suomi Coll., Hancock, Mich., 1945-46, U. Minn., 1950-51; chief Finnish desk Voice of Am., 1951-52; Fulbright lectr. Helsinki U., 1956, Turku U., 1965. Decorated 1st class Order Finnish Lion. Corr. mem. Finnish Litt. Soc., Turku Hist. Soc., Porthan Soc. Author: The Finns in America: A Bibliographical Guide, 1947; Finns in America, 1968; (with Geoge Hill), Haven in the Woods: The Story of the Finns in Wisconsin 2d edit., 1965; Sow the Golden Seed, 1955; also articles. Home: 50 Parkview Dr Tiffin OH 44883

KOLEHMAINEN, WAINO MATHIAS, patent lawyer; b. Conneaut, O., July 25, 1906; s. Matti and Julia Karolina (Tuomisto) K.; B.S. in Elec. Engring., Union Coll., Schenectady, 1930; J.D., George Washington U., 1935; m. Katherine Kruse, July 17, 1935; children—Philip Michael, Richard Lyman, Julie Katherine. Various depts. Gen. Electric Co., 1923-31, staff patent dept., 1931-36; admitted to D.C. bar, 1935, Ill. bar, 1937; with Williams, Bradbury & Hinkle, Chgo., 1936-46, mem. firm, 1943-46; partner Hinkle, Horton, Ahlberg, Hansmann & Wupper, 1946-48; mem. firm Mason, Kolehmainen, Rathburn & Wyss, 1948-68, counsel, 1968—. Decorated Knight 1st Class, Order of Lion (Finland). Mem. Am. Patent Law Assn., Am.-Scandinavian Found., Finnish Am. C. of C. Midwest, Order Coif, Sigma Xi, Eta Kappa Nu, Lambda Chi Alpha, Phi Delta Phi. Republican. Lutheran. Club: Chicago Curling. Home: 1218 Oak St Winnetka IL 60093

KOLER, ROBERT DONALD, educator; b. Casper, Wyo., Feb. 14, 1924; s. Joseph Leonard and Nellie (Hayes) K.; B.A., U. Ore., 1945, M.D., 1947; hon. research asst. eugenics, biometry and genetics Univ. Coll. (London), 1960-61; m. June Rogers, June 23, 1945; children—Thomas E., Mary L. Intern U. Ore. Med. Sch., 1947-48, resident, 1948-49, 51-53; asst. prof. medicine U. Ore., 1956-59, asso. prof., 1959-64, prof. medicine, head hematology and exptl. medicine, 1964-69, prof. medicine, head med. genetics, 1967—. Mem. cancer research center com. Nat. Cancer Inst., 1968-72. Mem. Ore. Bd. Social Protection, 1967-70. Served to capt. M.C., AUS, 1949-51. Fellow A.C.P., Western Soc. Clin. Research (councilor 1964-66); mem. Am. Fedn. Clin. Research, Am. Soc. Hematology, Am. Soc. Human Genetics, Phi Beta Kappa, Alpha Omea Alpha. Contbr. articles profl. jours. Home: 2532 SW Hamilton Ct Portland OR 97201

KOLESNIK, WALTER BERNARD, educator; b. Rochester, N.Y., Dec. 18, 1923; s. Joseph F. and Martha (Kosmicki) K.; Ph.B., Marquette U., 1949, Ed.M., 1950; Ph.D., U. Wis., 1955; m. Kathryn Stallard, Aug. 7, 1948. Instr., Nazareth Coll., Rochester, 1950-54, U. Wis., 1954-55; mem. faculty U. Detroit, 1955-, prof. edn., 1963-, dir. div. tchr. edn., 1964-66. Served with USAAF, 1943-46. Mem. Am. Assn. U. Profs., Nat. Soc. Study Edn., Nat. Cath. Edn. Assn., Mich. Cath. Conf., Phi Delta Kappa. Author: Mental Discipline in Modern Education, 1958; Educational Psychology, 1963, 70; Catholic Education, 1965; Education and Acculturation in Modern Urban Society, 1965; Coeducation: Sex Differences and The Schools, 1969. Contbr. New Cath. Ency. Home: 16246 Fairfield Av Detroit MI 48221

KOLFF, WILLEM JOHAN, physician; b. Leiden, Holland, Feb. 14 1911; s. Jacob and Adriana (de Jonge) K.; student U. Leiden Med. Sch., 1930-38; M.D. summa cum laude, U. Groningen, 1946; m. Janke C. Huidekoper, Sept 4, 1937; children—Jacob, Adriana P., Albert C., Cornelis A., Gualtherus C.M. Came to U.S., 1950, naturalized, 1956. Internist, head med. dept. Municipal Hosp., Kampen, Holland; staff research div. Cleve. Clinic Found., 1950- 67; privaat docent, dept. medicine U. Leiden, Nether-Bunts Ednl. Inst., Cleve., 1950-67, head dept. artificial organs, 1958-67; prof. surgery, head div. artificial organs dept. surgery U. Utah Coll. Medicine, Salt Lake City, 1967—, research prof. engring. Inst. Biomed. Engring., 1967—; devel. artificial kidney for clin. use, 1943; oxygenator, 1956. Decorated commandeur Orde Van Oranje (Netherlands); recipient Landsteiner medal for establishment blood banks during war in Holland, Netherlands Red Cross, 1942; Cameron prize U. Edinburgh (Scotland), 1964; $5,000 award Gairdner Found., 1966; Valentine award N.Y. Acad. Medicine, 1969; 1st Gold medal Netherlands Surg. Soc., 1970. Mem. A.M.A., Am. Assn. U. Profs., Am. Physiol. Soc., Soc. for Exptl. Biology and Medicine, A.A.A.S., N.Y. Acad. Scis., Am. Soc. Artificial Internal Organs, Nat. Kidney Found., European Dialysis and Transplant Assn. Rotarian. Address: Div of Artificial Organs Univ of Utah Medical Center Salt Lake City UT 84112

KOLHOVEN, JOHN HENRY, transp. co. exec.; b. Covington, Ky., Apr. 9, 1927; s. Harry C. and Agnes V. (Bain) K.; Chase Coll., 1948-51, Xavier U., 1951-55. Asst. treas. Gruen Industries, Cin., 1954-58; treas. B. Kuppenheimer, Chgo., 1958-61; v.p. finance, treas. Gateway Transp. Co., LaCrosse, Wis., 1961—. Pres., LaCrosse Police and Fire Commn., 1966-71. Served with AUS, 1944-46. C.P.A., Ohio, Ill., Wis. Mem. Am. Inst. C.P.A.'s, Financial Execs. Inst. Elk. Home: 2251 Valley Rd LaCrosse WI 54601 Office: 2130 South Av LaCrosse WI 54601

KOLIN, ALEXANDER, educator, scientist; b. Odessa, Russia, Mar. 12, 1910; s. Rudolph and Luba (Gershberg) K.; student U. and Inst. Tech., Berlin, 1929-33; Doctorate in physics summa cum laude, German U. Prague, 1934; m. Renée Marie Laure Bourcier, Aug. 8, 1951. Research fellow in biophysics Michael Reese Hosp., Chgo., 1935-37; physicist Mt. Sinai Hosp., N.Y.C., 1938-41; instr. in physics Coll. City N.Y., 1941-44; instr. physics Columbia, 1944-45, research asso. Sch. Engring., 1941-46; asst. prof. N.Y.U., 1945-46; mem. faculty U. Chgo., 1947-56, asso. prof. physics, 1953-55; mem. faculty U. Cal. at Los Angeles, 1956—, prof. biophysics, 1961—. Recipient John Scott medal Phila., 1965; Albert F. Sperry medal Instrument Soc. Am., 1967. Mem. Am. Phys. Soc., Biophys. Soc., Physiol. Soc., Am. Assn. Physics Tchrs., A.A.A.S., Marine Biol. Lab., Dante Alighieri Soc., Internat. House Assn. Contbr. numerous articles sci. jours. Invented electromagnetic flow meter, 1935; devel. method for electromagnetic blood flow determination; devel. various electrophoretic methods. Author: Physics: Its Laws, Ideas and Methods, 1950. Home: 1298 Stradella Rd Los Angeles CA 90024

KOLIN, OSCAR, cosmetic co. exec.; b. 1908; m. With Helena Rubinstein. Inc., N.Y.C., 1928—, dir., 1947, v.p., 1964, exec. v.p., 1965, pres., 1966-70, chmn. bd., chief exec. officer, 1970—. Address: 767 Fifth Av New York City NY 10022

KOLKER, BERNDT LOTHAR, economist; b. Breslau, Germany, Aug. 16, 1916; s. Hubert E. and Rose (Basch) K.; Diplum Volkswirt, Friedrich Wilhelm U., Berlin, Germany, 1936; postgrad. Trinity Coll., Cambridge, Eng., 1936-37, Sorbonne, Paris, France, 1937-38; m. Eva Krevit, Nov. 17, 1941; 1 dau., Gale. Came to U.S., 1938, naturalized, 1942. Comml. adviser Brit. Govt. Bd. of Trade, 1947-50; chief economist Office Econ. Stblzn., Kansas City, Mo., 1951-52; dir. research Carter Corp., Kansas City, 1953-54; dir. indsl. econs. Midwest Research Inst., Kansas City, 1955-59; dir. research, v.p. U. Kansas City, 1959-63; dir. dept. applied econs. S.W. REsearch Inst., 1963-64; dir. dept. applied econs. Houston Research Inst., 1965-66; adj. prof. U. Houston, Rice U., 1965; provost Raymond Coll., U. of Pacific, Stockton, Cal., 1966—. Trustee Kansas City Med. Center, Civic Research Inst., Kansas City. Served to capt., M.I., AUS, 1941-46. Mem. Am. Econ. Assn., Regional Sci. Assn., A.A.A.S., Brit. Assn. for Advancement Sci., Nat. Planning Assn., Am. Acad. Polit. and Social Sci., Am. Acad. Arts and Scis. Home: 1148 Oxford Way Stockton CA 95204

KOLKEY, EUGENE LOUIS, advt. exec.; b. Chgo., Nov. 27, 1927; s. Samuel and Florence (Bernstein) K.; B.A. in Advt. Design, U. Ill., 1949; m. Gilda Cowan, Sept. 3, 1950; children—Daniel, Sandor, Eric. Art dir. Earle Ludgin, Chgo., 1949-51, Young & Rubicam, Chgo., 1951-53; sr. v.p., exec. creative dir. Leo Burnett, Chgo., 1953—, also dir. Recipient Clio TV award for best comml., 1967, 68; numerous awards from N.Y.C., Chgo. and Los Angeles Advt. and Art Directors Club, also Cannes Film Festival. Jewish religion. Club: Art Directors (pres. 1964), Arts (Chgo.). Created Tony the Tiger, 1953. Home: 822 Kimballwood Lane Highland Park IL 60035 Office: Leo Burnett Prudential Plaza Chicago IL 60601

KOLLEK, TEDDY (THEODORE), mayor Jerusalem; b. Vienna, Austria, May 27, 1911; s. Alfred and Margaret (Fleisher) K.; settled in Palestine, 1934; m. Tamar Schwarz, May 1937; children-Amos, Osnat. Founder mem. Kibbutz Ein Gev, Galilee, 1937; engaged in ednl. missions to Zionist youth groups, Europe, 1938- 40; staff mem. polit. dept. Jewish Agy., Jerusalem, 1940-47; in charge contacts with Jewish underground in Europe, 1942; mission to U.S. on behalf of Hagana, 1947-48; head U.S. div. Israel Fgn. Ministry, 1950; minister, Washington, 1951-52; dir. gen. Prime Minister's Office, Jerusalem, 1952-65; chmn. Israel Govt. Water Desalination Joint Project with U.S. Govt., 1964-65; chmn. bd. Africa-Israel Investment Co. Ltd., 1964-65; mayor Jerusalem, 1965-. Chmn. bd. Israel Mus., Jerusalem, 1964- -. Home: 6 Rashba St Rechavia Israel Office: City Hall Jerusalem Israel

KOLLER, E. FRED, economist; b. Turtle Lake, Wis., Apr. 3, 1907; s. Fred W. and Elizabeth (Prosser) K.; A.B. summa cum laude, Augustana Coll., 1929, LL.D., 1957; A.M., U. Minn., 1933, Ph.D., 1938; m. Ethel M. Eliker, Aug. 25, 1935. Asst. U. Minn., 1930-34, instr., 1934-38, asst. prof., 1938-42, asso. prof., 1942-46, prof., 1946-; sabbatical leave to head project for Nat. Bur. of Econ. Research entitled Financing of Farmer's Cooperatives in the U.S., 1946-47; tax analyst U.S. Treasury, Washington, 1934; bd. dirs. Experience, Inc., Mpls. Recipient Alumni Achievement award, Augustana Coll., 1969. Mem. Marketing Research Com. (chmn. 1959), North Central Dairy Marketing Research Com. (past chmn.), Am. Econ. Assn., Am. Agrl. Econ. Assn., Minn. Econ. Club (pres. 1944), Internat. Assn. Agrl. Economists, Am. Assn. U. Profs., Pi Kappa Delta, Gamma Sigma Delta (pres. Minn. chpt. 1959), Alpha Zeta. Mem. Evang. Luth. Ch. Author numerous bulls. Minn. Agr. Expt. Sta., numerous articles tech. and profl. jours. Home: 1466 Hythe St St Paul MN 55108 Office: Dept Agrl Econs U Minn St Paul MN 55101

KOLLER, HERBERT RICHARD, assn. exec.; b. Cleve., Sept. 5, 1921; s. Daniel D. and Frieda A. (Wiener) K.; B.S. in Chemistry, Western Res. U., 1942; J.D., Am. U., 1952; m. Shirley Ann Leavitt, Mar. 7, 1943; children—Donald Lee, Susan Lizbeth (Mrs. Willard C. VanHorne), Laura Frances. Chemist, Indsl. Rayon Co., 1942-43; patent examiner, information systems research and devel. U.S. Patent Office, 1943-66; dir. client services EBC Mgmt. Cons., Washington, 1966-68; sr. information scientist Leasco Systems & Research Corp., Bethesda, Md., 1968-69; exec. dir. Am. Soc. Information Sci., Washington, 1969—. Research asso. Patent, Trademark and Copyright Research Inst., George Washington U., 1968—; cons., lectr. in field. Sci. and tech. fellow Dept. Commerce, 1964-65. Mem. Am. Chem. Soc., Assn. Computing Machinery, Am. Soc. Information Sci., Am. Fedn. Information Processing Socs. (bd. dirs., exec. com.), Phi Epsilon Pi. Contbr. articles to profl. jours. Home: 2700 Virginia Av NW Washington DC 20037 Office: 1140 Connecticut Av NW Washington DC 20036

KOLLMANN, HILDA HANNA, banker; b. Tinley Park, Ill., Dec. 12, 1913; d. Ernest A. and Rosalie (Blume) Kollmann; ed. Bryant and Stratton Bus. Coll. Asst. cashier State Bank of Blue Island (Ill.) (became County Bank & Trust Co. 1962), 1945-53, cashier, 1953-60, asst. sec., 1953-54, sec., 1954-55, v.p., 1955-70, dir., 1956—, trust officer, 1959-66; v.p. Pullman Bank & Trust Co., Chgo., 1969-70, Standard Bank & Trust Co., Chgo., 1969-70 First Nat. Bank of Lockport 1969-70; v.p. investments Financial Mgmt. Assos., Inc., 1970—. Sec.-treas. Blue Island Pub. Welfare Assn., 1956-60, pres., 1961-63; chmn. indsl. and expansion com. Blue Island Planning Commn. Mem. Nat. Assn. Bank Women (pres. 1961-62), Assn. Chgo. Bank Women (pres. 1956-57). Home: 12761 S Gregory St Blue Island IL 60406 Office: 12015 S Western Av Blue Island IL 60406

KOLLMORGEN, WALTER MARTIN, geographer, educator; b. Bancroft, Neb., Feb. 10, 1907; s. Karl J. and Dorothea (Bendin) K.; B.S., U. Neb., 1931, M.A., 1933; Ph.D., Columbia, 1940. Social Sci. Research Council fellow, 1937-38; asso. agrl. economist Bur. Agrl. Econs. Dept. Agr., 1938-41, agrl. economist, 1943-46; economist War Labor Bd., 1941-42; research dir. Tenn. State Planning Commn., Nashville, 1942; asso. prof. geography U. Kan., 1946, prof., chmn. dept. geography, 1947-63, Distinguished prof. geography, 1963—; Fulbright research grant, Germany, 1954; Walker-Ames Distinguished prof. geography U. Washington, spring 1955. Mem. Am. Geog. Soc., Assn. Am. Geographers (editor Annals, 1955-61; v.p. 1965; pres. 1966-67), Kan. Acad. Scis., Sigma Xi. Author bulls. and monographs. Home: R F D 2 Lawrence KS 66044

KOLLROS, JERRY JOHN, zoologist; b. Vienna, Austria, Dec. 29, 1917; s. Jacob and Theresa (Hruby) K.; brought to U.S., 1920, naturalized, 1926; S.B., U. Chgo., 1938, Ph.D., 1942; m. Catharine Zenker Lutherman, Sept. 19, 1942; childrenJames Carl, Peter Richard. Research asst. neurosurgery U. Chgo., 1943-45, research asso. toxicity lab., 1945, instr. Zoology, 1945- 46; asso. State U. Ia., 1946-47, asst. prof., 1947-50, asso. prof., 1950- 57, prof., 1957—, chmn. dept. zoology, 1955-; vis. asst. prof. U. Cal. at Los Angeles, summer 1950; cons. Zoology Am. Coll. Dictionary. Fellow A.A.A.S. (regional cons. sci. teaching improvement program 1956- 57), Ia. Acad Sci.; mem. Am. Assn. U. Profs., Am. Assn. Anatomists (mem. exec. com. 1962-66), Am. Soc. Zoologists (past treas.), Internat. Inst.

Embryologists, N.Y. Acad. Scis., Am. Naturalists, Soc. Exptl. Biology and Medicine, Soc. Developmental Biology, Am. Soc. Cell Biology, Phi Beta Kappa, Sigma Xi. Author articles profl. jours. Home: 331 Melrose Ct Iowa City IA 52240

KOLODIN, IRVING music critic; b. New York. N.Y., Feb. 22, 1908; s. Benjamin and Leah (Geller) K.; ed. grammer and high sch., Newark. N.J.; student Inst. of Musical Art, N.Y. City, 1927-31; m. Irma Levy. June 19,1935 Instr. in harmony and theory, Inst. of Mus. Art, 1930-31; N.Y. Sun, 1932-50; asso. music critic and condr. of New Records Column, 1936-5O; lecturer on music criticism, Juilliard Summer Sch., 1938, 39; program annotator New York Philharmonic Orch. 1953—. Entered military service, 1943; mem. staff Official Guide to AAF and Air Force magazine. 1943-45. Music editor and critic to Sun, 1945-50; editor Recordings supplement of Sat. Rev. Lit. since 1947; music editor Saturday Review of Literature, 1950-52, asso. editor Sat. Rev. since 1952. Author: Metropolitan Opera, 1936, revised edit., 1939; The Kingdom of Swing (with Benny Goodman). 1939; The Critical Composer, 1940; Guide to Recorded Music, 1941, rev. edit., 1946, 49, 55; Story of the Metropolitan Opera, 1953; Composer as Listener, 1958; The Musical Life, 1958; Metropolitan Opera 1883-1966, 1966; The Continuity of Music, 1969. Contributing author Internat. Cyclopedia of Music and Musicians, Grove's Dictionary, various mags. Home: 1161 York Av New York City NY 10021 Office: 380 Madison Av New York City NY 10017

KOLODING, ALEXANDER GLEN chemist, educator; b. Chicago, 1928; B.S. in Physics, Yale, 1950; Ph.D. in Chemistry, Harvard, 1956; m. Sally Ann Jones, July 5, 1957; children--Kenneth J., Nancy A. Chemist, Acme Chem. Co., Blue Island, Ill., 1950-51; director of Research Lab., Indsl. Chemicals Corp., Cambridge, Mass., 1956-60; project coordinator environmental sect. Steinmetz Assos., Chgo., 1960-61; v.p. for research Bauer Bros. Chem. Co., Inc., Memphis, 1961-64; asst. prof. chemistry Washington U., St. Louis, 1964-66, asso. prof., 1966-70, prof., 1970--, head of chemistry dept., 1970-71. Vis. prof. So. Ill. U., summer 1967, U. of Ore., 1969. Scoutmaster, Boy Scouts America, University City, Mo., 1968-70. Bd. dirs. Rest Haven Home for Elderly, 1960-61; trustee of the Lutheran Hosp., 1965-71. Served from lt. to capt., AUS, 1951-53. Mem, Am. Chem. Soc., Sci. Research Soc. Am. (chpt. treas. 1967), Sigma Xi. Author: (with others) Basic Inorganic Chemistry, 1971. Home: Fairfax Apts 7291 Windermere Dr University City MO 63105 Office: Dept Chemistry Washington University St Louis MO 63130

KOLODY, JOHN THEODORE, hosp. adminstr.; b. Arnold, Pa., June 19, 1920; s. Theodore and Katherine (Krawec) K.; B.S. in Edn., Indiana (Pa.) U., 1942; M.S. in Hosp. Adminstrn., Columbia, 1947; m. Mildred Carolyn Secky, May 28, 1949; 1 son, John Theodore. With St. Barnabas Hosp., N.Y.C., 1946-, exec. dir., 1967-; lectr. hosp. adminstrn. Columbia, 1949-, St. John's U., 1960—. Bd. dirs. Bronx chpt. Nat. Multiple Sclerosis Soc., Nat. Conf. Christians and Jews, Bronx Soc. for Prevention Cruelty to Children, Bronx chpt. A.R.C. Bd. dirs. Bronx Westchester adv. bd. Mfrs. Hanover Trust Co. Bd. dirs. Bronx Bd. Trade. Served with USNR, 1942-46. Fellow Am. Coll. Hosp. Adminstrs., A.A.A.S., Am. Pub. Health Assn.; mem. Am. Hosp. Assn., Gerontological Soc., C. of C. (bd. dirs.), Council Hosp. Adminstrs. N.Y.C., N.Y. Adminstrs.' Conf. Group, Internat. Platform Assn. Mason. Club: Pelham (N.Y.) Country. Home: St Barnabas Hosp 183d St and 3d Av New York City NY 10457

KOLOWICH, RAYMUND FREDERICK, financier; b. Detroit, May 20, 1924; s. George J. and Irene (Acker) K.; A.B., St. Michael's Coll., 1945, L.H.D., 1966; m. Marilynn Convery, Oct. 13, 1951; children—Michael, Bradley, Brian, Sara, Thomas, James. Vice pres., dir. Detroit & Cleve. Navigation Co., 1948-60; pres. dir. Griswold Bldg., Inc., Detroit, 1950-65; sec., treas., v.p., dir. Whittier Corp., Detroit, 1950-60; v.p., treas., chmn., dir. DC Internat. (trucking), 1956-65; sec.-treas., dir. Superior Mfg. Co., 1962-66; v.p., dir. Mainstream Corp., 1965—; chmn., dir. Louisville Downs, Inc., 1965--; v.p., dir. Cadillac Coffee Co., Detroit, 1967—. Adviser, Voice of Youth, Free Enterprise Inst. Trustee, mem. exec. com. St. Michael's Coll. Served with U.S. Army, 1946-48. Clubs: Propeller U.S.; Grosse Pointe (Mich.) Yacht. Home: 135 Kenwood Rd Grosse Point Farms MI 48236

KOLSETH, J. HAROLD, mgmt. cons., corp. exec.; b. Schenectady, May 4, 1908; B.A., Union Coll., 1928; student Universite de Dijon (France), 1928; M.A. in Bus. Adminstrn., Harvard, 1931; m. Adele Rouyon Mackey, 1940; children—Sandra (Mrs. David F. Mawicke), Karen (Mrs. James P. Brossard). Faculty, Union Coll., 1928-29; with Atlas Supply Co., 1931-51, dir. research and devel., 1947-51; exec. v.p., dir. Devoe & Raynolds Co., N.Y.C., 1951-55; v.p. Anheuser Busch Inc., St. Louis, 1956-57; parnter, v.p. Barrington Assos., N.Y.C., 1957-58; prin. Kolseth & Partners, Greenwich, Conn., 1958-; mgmt. cons. Mem. WPB, 1942- 43; dir. operations Smaller War Plants Corp., 1944; cons. Dept. of State, Chile, 1957, Cuba, 1958, Ecuador, 1960, Brazil, 1961, Spain, 1961, Jamaica, 1962. V.p. Council Internat. Progress in Mgmt., 1966-67, also bd. directors. Served lt. comdr., USNR, 1944-45. Mem. Phi Beta Kappa; Pi Gamma Mu. Clubs: Indian Harbor Yacht, Harvard, Sky (N.Y.C.); Army and Navy (Washington); Greenwich Country. Contbr. articles to various mags. Home: Oakwood Lane Greenwich CT 06830 Office: P O Box 877 Greenwich CT 06830

KOLSTOE, RALPH HERTSQAARD, educator; b. Valley City, N.D., Sept. 10, 1926; s. Soren Olaf and Inger (Hertsgaard) K.; B.S. in Edn., State Coll., Valley City, 1948; M.S. in Psychology, U. N.D., 1959; Ph.D.in Psychology, Wash. State U., 1953; m. Carolyn Ruth Cockle, Oct. 11, 1947; childrenDavid, Mark, John, Paul. Elementary sch. prin., White Earth, Minn., 1948-49; research asso., then sr. research scientist Human Resources Research Office, Washington, 1953- 57; mem. faculty U. N.D., 1957-, prof. psychology, 1964-, chmn. dept., 1962—. Served with USNR, 1944- 46. Named an Outstanding Faculty Member students of U.N.D., 1965. Mem. Am. (council of reps. 1968-70), N.D. Cpres. 1963-64) Psychol. assns. Author: Introduction to Statistics for the Behavioral Sciences, 1969. Home: 2108 7th Av N Grand Forks ND 58201

KOLTHOFF, IZAAK MAURITS, prof. analytical chemistry; b. Almelo, Holland, Feb. 11, 1894; s. Moses and Rosetta (Wysenbeek) K.; Ph.D., U. Utrecht, (Holland), 1918; D.Sc. (hon.), U. Chgo.; Hon. Dr. Degree U. Groningen (Holland), 1964. Asst. in chem., U. of Utrecht, 1915-18, conservator, 1918-24, privatdocent, 1924-27; prof. analytical chem. and head dept. U. Minn., 1927-62, prof. emeritus, 1962- -. Chmn. com. analytical chem. NRC. Decorated comdr. Order of Oranje- Nassau, 1947; received William H. Nichols medal, N.Y. sect. Am. Chem. Soc.; Fisher award in analytical chemistry Am. Chem. Soc., also Minn. award; Anachem award 1961; Willard Gibbs Medal award Am. Chem. Soc., 1964; Polarographic Medal Polarographic Soc., Eng., 1964; Hanus medal Czechoslovak Chem. Soc., 1967; Kolthoff gold medal in analytical chemistry Acad. Pharm. Scis., 1967. Vice pres. Internat. Union of Pure and Applied Chemistry, pres. sect. analytical chem., chmn. commn. electroanalytical chemistry. Fgn. mem. Royal Flemish Acad. Belgium; corr. mem. Royal Soc. Sci. and Lettres of Bohemia; hon. mem. Finnish Chem. Soc., Czechoslav Chem. Soc., corr. of the Royal Acad. of Scis., Amsterdam; fellow A.A.A.S.; mem. Am. Pharm. Assn. (hon.), Israeli (hon.), Am. chem. socs., Am. Electrochem. Soc., Dutch Chem. Soc. (hon.), Dutch Pharm. Soc., Nat. Acad. Scis., Am. Acad. Arts and Scis., hon. mem. numerous profl. socs. and assns. Author: Konduktometrische Titrationen, 1923; The Theory of Indicators, 1926; Potentiometric Titrations, 1932; Volumetric Analysis (2 vols.), 1929. (3 vols), 1958; pH and Electrometric Titrations, 1941; Textbook on Quantitative Inorganic Analysis, 1935, 43, 52, 69; Acid-Base Indicators, 1936; Polarographic Analysis and Amperometric Titrations, 1941-52; Emulsion Polymerization 1955. Asso. editor Jour. Am. Chem. Soc. Co-editor: Treatise on Analysis Chemistry. Contbr. to tech. publs. Home: Campus Club U Minnesota Minneapolis MN 55455

KOLTON, PAUL, stock exchange exec.; b. N.Y.C., June 1, 1923; s. Sol and Rose (Naiman) Komisaruk; B.A. U. N.C., 1943; m. Edith B. Fromme, June 30, 1944; children—Robert Jay, Shelley. Editorial staff N.Y. Jour. Commerce, 1946- 47; account exec. Newell-Emmett Advt. Co., 1947-50, Cecil & Presbrey Advt., Inc., 1950-55; v.p. pub. information and press relations N.Y. Stock Exchange, 1955-62; exec. v.p. Am. Stock Exchange, 1962-71, pres., 1971—; dir. Am. Stock Exchange Clearing Corp., Am. Stock Exchange Realty Assos., Inc. Mem. Mayor's Conf. on Human Rights, Stamford, Conn.; mem. Banking and Securities Industry Com.; mem. bd. advisers N.Y. Inst. Finance. Dir. N.Y. Conv. and Visitors Bur. Served with USAAF, 1943-46. Mem. N.Y. C. of C. Soc. of Silurians. Club: Economic of N.Y. Author short stories, 1946-53. Home: 9 Hunting Ridge Rd Stamford CT 06903 Office: 86 Trinity Pl New York City NY 10006

KOMAR, ARTHUR B., educator; b. Bklyn., Mar. 26, 1931; s. Abraham and Mary (Baraway) K.; A.B., Princeton, 1952, Ph.D., 1956; m. Dolly Roth, Aug. 5, 1952; children—Arne, Tanya. Fellow, Niels Bohr Inst., Copenhagen, Denmark, 1956-57; research asso. Syracuse (N.Y.) U., 1957-59, vis. asst. prof., 1958-59, asst. prof., 1959-61, asso. prof., 1961-63; asso. prof. Belfer Grad. Sch., Yeshiva U., N.Y.C., 1963-66, prof. physicis, 1966—, dean, dir. Belfer Grad. Sch., 1968—. Fellow Am.-Scandinavian Soc.; mem. Am. Phys. Soc., Am. Assn. Physics Tchrs., Phi Beta Kappa. Asso. editor: Am. Jour. Physics, 1966—; editorial bd. Internat. Jour. Theoretical Physics, 1968—. Contbr. articles profl. jours. Home: 562 W 261st St Bronx NY 10471 Office: Yeshiva U Amsterdam Av and 186th St New York City NY 10033

KOMAROVSKY, MIRRA (Mrs. Marcus A. Heyman), educator; b. Russia; d. Manuel and Anna (Steinberg) Komarovsky; A.B., Barnard Coll., 1926; M.A., Columbia, 1927, Ph.D., 194O; m. Marcus A. Heyman, Oct. 2, 1940. Came to U.S., 1922, naturalized, 1933. Asst. prof. sociology Skidmore Coll., 1927-29; research asst., research asso. Yale Inst. Human Relations, Columbia, 1931-32; instr. sociology Barnard Coll., 1936-45, asst. prof., 1945- 47, asso. prof., 1948-53, prof., 1954—, chmn. dept., 1949-62, 65-68; Buell G. Gallagher prof. sociology Coll. City N.Y., spring 1965. Mem. Am. (council (1967-69, v.p. 1971-72), Eastern (pres. 1955-56) sociol. socs., Phi Beta Kappa. Author: (with Lundberg and McInerney), Leisure, A Suburban Study 1934; The Unemployed Man and His Family, 1940; Women in The Modern World: Their Education and Their Dilemmas, 1953; Blue-Collar Marriage, 1964. Asso. editor Am. Sociol. Review, 1957-60. Editor: Common Frontier of the Social Sciences, 1957. Contbr. articles profl. jours. Home: 340 Riverside Dr New York City NY 10025

KOMER, ROBERT WILLIAM, social scientist; b. Chgo., Feb. 23, 1922; s. Nathan A and Stella (Deiches) K.; S.B. magna cum laude, Harvard, 1942, M.B.A., 1947; student Nat. War Coll., 1956-57; m. Geraldine M. Peplin, Nov. 3, 1961; childrenDouglas Robert, Richard Donen, Anne Elizabeth. With CIA, 1947- 56; sr. staff mem. Nat. Security Council, 1961-65; dep. spl. asst. to Pres. for Nat. Security Council affairs, 1965-66; spl. asst. to Pres., 1966-67; dep. to comdr. USMACV for Cords, 1967-68; ambassador to Turkey, 1968-69; sr. social sci. researcher Rand Corp., Washington, 1969—. Served to 1st lt. AUS, 1943-46. Decorated Bronze Star; Nat. Order Vietnam, Vietnam Gold Economy medal, Revolutionary Devel. medal (Vietnam); Presdl. Medal of Freedom; distinguished honor award State Dept. Mem. Phi Beta Kappa. Club: Federal City (Washington). Home: 6359 Waterway Dr Fairfax County VA 22044 Office: Rand Corp 2100 MSt NW Washington DC 20037

KOMES, JEROME WILLIAM, engring. and constrn. co. exec.; b. Racine, Wis., June 23, 1911; s. John Frederick and Julia Mary (Meier) K.; ed. parochial schs., Fresno, Cal.; m. Flora Cabral, Feb. 16, 1935; children—Jerome Michael, John Anthony, Julia Mary. With Barrett & Hilp, constrn., San Francisco, 1928-38; part owner D. W. Nicholson Corp., constrn., Oakland, Cal., 1938-41; exec. positions Cal. Shipbldg. Corp., Los Angeles, 1941-46; with Bechtel Corp., San Francisco, 1946—, sr. v.p., mgr. internat. div., 1957-67, exec. v.p., 1967—, also dir.; pres. dir. subsidiary and affiliated corps. Mem. Am. Welding Soc. Clubs: Fifth Avenue (N.Y.C.); Commonwealth, Olympic, Presidio, Stock Exchange, World Trade, San Francisco Golf (San Francisco); Union Interalliee (Paris, France). Home: 2006 Washington St San Francisco CA 94109 Office: 50 Beale St San Francisco CA 94119

KOMIDAR, JOSEPH STANLEY, librarian; b. Chisholm, Minn., July 19, 1916; s. John and Jennie (Skrbec) K.; A.A., Hibbing Jr. Coll., 1936; B.L.S., U. Minn., 1938, B.A., 1941; M.A., U. Chgo., 1948; m. Mary Louise Watson, Aug. 16, 1957; children-Kathryn J., Joseph T. Reference asst. U. Minn. Library, 1938- 41; reference and loan librarian Carleton Coll., 1941-43; reference librarian Northwestern U., 1948-50, chief reference and spl. services div., 1950-56; univ. librarian Tufts U., 1956-; vis. lectr. U. Denver Sch. Librarianship, summer 1955. Served with USAAF, 1943-45. Mem. A.L.A., Assn. Coll. and Research Librarians, Am. Assn. U. Profs., Am. Soc. Information Sci., Beta Phi Mu. Contbr. articles profl. jours. and publs. Home: 8 Wells Rd Reading MA 01867 Office: Tufts U Medford MA 02155

KOMISAR, DAVID DANIEL, educator, psychologist; b. N.Y.C., July 20, 1917; s. Jacob and Yetta (Jacobson) K.; B.S.S., Coll. City N.Y., 1937, M.S., 1940; student Columbia, 1946-53, Sorbonne, 1946, U. Glasgow, 1945; m. Beatrice Liebman, Aug. 15, 1940; children—Jack Lloyd, June Diana. With Civil Service, N.Y.C., 1939-42; indsl. personnel work, 1943-44; counselor vocational rehab. U.S. Army, 1943-46; dir. guidance Mohawk Coll., 1946- 48; dir. guidance, chmn. dept. psychology Champlain Coll., State U. N.Y., Plattsburg, 1948-53; chmn. dept. psychology U. Hartford, 1953—, pres. univ. faculty senate, 1964-65, dean Sch. Arts and Scis., 1966-67, dean of faculties, 1967-70, v.p. acad. affairs, 1970—. Project dir. research in mental retardation Office of Vocational Rehab., Dept. Health, Edn. and Welfare, 1964-65, psycho-social com. social rehab. services, 1968—; head New Eng. Conf. on Mental Retardation, 1960, Conn. Task Force on Mental Retardation, 1960-61; Conn. rep. Nat. Def. Edn. Act, 1960-61; research fellow U.S. Office Vocational Rehab., 1962-63; Citizens Com. on State Welfare, Conn., 1967-69; mem. standing com. on accreditation Conn. Commn. on High Edn., 1969—. Co-chmn. Citizens Charter Com. of Hartford, 1959. Mem. bd. Hartford Jewish Community Center, 1955- 63, v.p., 1963—; mem. bd. Mental Health Assn., 1959-62. Recipient research grant for 3 yr. study residential care retarded children U. S. Dept. Health, Edn. and Welfare, 1965—. Mem. Conn. Valley Assn. Psychologists (past pres.), Am., Conn. (council; pres.) psychol. assns., Nat. Vocational Guidance Assn., Am. Personnel and Guidance Assn., Sigma Xi. Clubs: Connecticut Valley Torch (past pres.) Probus (nast pres.) (Hartford). Author articles on testing, therapy, vocational selection. Home: 88 Northbrook Dr West Hartford CT 06117

KOMMERS, ROBERT E., telephone co. exec.; b. Sheboygan, Wis., 1910; grad. U. Wis., 1932, LL.B., 1935. Sec., treas. Gen. Telephone Co. of Ill., Bloomington. Home: 1109 Elmwood Rd Bloomington IL 61701 Office: 1312 E Empire St Bloomington IL 61701*

KOMROFF, MANUEL, writer; b. N.Y. C., Sept. 7, 1890; s. Samuel and Belle (Borkes) K.; m. Elinor M. Barnard, Dec. 23, 1918 (dec.); m. 2d, Odette Steele, Oct. 19, 1938. Vice pres. Authors' Guild, 1941-43; mem. Council Authors Leaque, 1937- 47; gov. Overseas Press Club, 1942-44; adv. Council Writers' War Bd.; v.p. P.E.N. World Writers, Am. Center, 1945-47, sec., 1947-52. Author; The Grace of Lambs, 1925; Juggler's Kiss, 1927; The Voice of Fire, 1927; Coronet (2 vols.), 1929; The Fool and Death, 1930; Two Thieves, 1931; A New York Tempest, 1932; I, The Tiger, 1933; Waterloo, 1936; The March of the Hundred, 1939; The Magic Bow; A Romance of Paganini, 1940; What is a Miracle?, 1941; A Christmas Letter, 1941; In the Years of Our Lord, 1942; Don Quixote and Sancho (a play), 1942; All in Our Day, 1942; The Book of Tom Smith, A Biblio-Epitaph, 1942; The One Story: The Life of Christ, 1943; Feast of the Jesters, 1947; Echo of Evil, 1948; How to Write a Novel, 1950; Jade Star, 1951; Marco Polo, 1952; Jesus Through the Centuries, 1953; His Great Journey, 1953; Every Man's Bible, 1953; Napoleon, 1954; Gods and Demons, 1954; True Adventures of Spys, 1954; The Story of Jesus, 1955; Julius Caesar, 1955; Mozart, 1956; The Loves of Omar Khayyam, 1956; Abraham Lincoln, 1959; Men, Women and Children of the Bible, 1960; Thomas Jefferson, 1961; Beethoven and His Music, 1961; Mathew Brady, 1962; The Third Eye, 1962; Disraeli, 1963; Waterloo, 1963; Life in the Middle Ages, 1963; Charlemagne, 1964; Talleyrand, 1965; Marie Antionette, 1967; The Hudson River, 1967; The Whole World is Outside, 1968. Editor: Dostoyevsky's The Brothers Karamazov; Tolstoy's War and Peace, Travels of Marco Polo; Contemporaries of Marco Polo; The History of Herodotus; Tales of the Monks (Gesta Romanorum); The Romances of Voltaire; The Great Fables; Nietzsche's Zarathustra; The Apocrypha; Montesquieu's Persian Letters; Oriental Romances; Introductions to Balzac's Physiology of Marriage and Lafcadio Hearn's Some Chinese Ghosts, Reader's Digest Story of the Bible World. Editor of the Modern Library, 1921-26; The Library of Living Classics, 1928. Editor and founder of Black and Gold Library, 1926, Library of True Adventure, 1954. Del. UN for P.E.N. Internat. Writers, 1947. Spl. lectr. univs. on technique of novel. Contbr. to leading mags. Address: Hill 99 Woodstock NY 12498

KONDONASSIS, ALEXANDER JOHN, educator, economist; b. Greece, Feb. 8, 1928 s. John I. and Eve (Hatzistylianou) K.; came to U. S., 1948, naturalized, 1960; A.B. with distinction, DePauw Univ., 1952; M.A., Ind. U., 1953, Ph.D., 1961; m. Patricia Mundorff, Feb. 2, 1956; children—John, Yolanda. Teaching asso. Ind. U., 1954-56, lectr., 1956-58; mem. faculty U. Okla., 1958—, prof. econs., 1964—, David Ross Boyd prof. econs., 1970—, chmn. dept., 1961-71, chmn. com. world affairs, 1962-65, chmn. com. grad. Latin Am. affairs, 1964—, chmn. com. distinguished lecture series Coll. Bus., 1967-68, dir. advanced program in econs., 1971—; Fulbright prof. Athens (Greece) Sch. Econs. and Bus. Sci., 1965-66, vis. prof., 1971. Bd. dirs. Okla. Council Econ. Edn., 1961- 71; mem. Gov. Okla. Adv. Council Export Expansion, 1964-65; adv. council Inst. E. Mediterranean Affairs, 1967—. Bd. dirs. Am. Friends Wilton Park, N.Y., 1967—. Recipient U. Okla. Regents award excellence teaching, 1964; research grantee U. Okla. Research Inst. 1965-66. Mem. Am., So., Southwestern econ. assns., Midwest, Comparative econs. assns., Econ. History Assn., Am. Assn. U. Profs., Omicron Delta Epsilon, Beta Gamma Sigma. Author: Concepts of Economic Development with Special Reference to Underdeveloped Countries. 1963; Monetary Policies of the Bank of Greece, 1949-1951; Contributions to Monetary Stability and Economic Development, 1961; (with others) An Economic Base Study of Lawton, Okla., 1963; Economic Planning and Free Enterprise, 1966; The Greek Economy: The Old and the New, 1970. Home: 512 Manor Dr Norman OK 73069

KONDRASHIN, KIRILL PETROWICH, conductor; b. Moscow, USSR, Feb. 21, 1914; s. Petr Andreewich and Anna (Michailovna) K.; student Moscow Conservatory, 1936; m. Nina Leonzdowha Varlamorta, Dec. 18, 1931; children—Petr, Sergei, Andrej. Conductor, Mail Opera Theatre, Leningrad, 1937-43, Bolshoi Theatre, Moscow, 1943- 56, Moscow Philharmonic Orch., 1956—; appearances in Eng., France, Italy, Germany, Yugoslavia, Hungary, N. and S. Am. Named Nat. Artist of USSR; recipient Govt. prize. Mem. Communist Party. Home: Karetnij riad 5/10 Moscow K-6 USSR Office: Moscow Philharmonic Orchestra Moscow USSR

KONE, ELLIOTT H., educator; b. Hartford, Conn., Sept. 23, 1920; s. Samuel Charles and Anna Frances (Rosenberg) K.; B.A., Yale, 1949, M.A., 1953; postgrad. N.Y.U., 1957—; m. Grace Ann Hays, Dec. 29, 1962; childrenDavid, Stephen, Susanna. Founder, supr. photographic dept. Yale U. News Bur., 1948-50; fellow Branford Coll. Yale; co-founder Yale U. Audio Visual Center 1950, dir., 1952-66; film producer, founder Yale Film Series; founder Yale Series Recorded Poets; dir., pub. Readers Press, Inc.; pres. The Safe-Lite Co., Traffic Standard, Inc.; dir. Carillon Records, Inc., Group 9 Prodns., Inc.; co-founder, dir. Chester Electronic Labs., Inc. Rep. U.S. Office Edn. Bibl. Control Newer Edn. Media; co-chmn. N.E. Regional Audio Visual Leadership Conf. Active Boy Scouts; adv. council, sec., dir. Neighborhood Music Sch.; charter founder of Recording for the Blind, Inc., New Haven; mem. Yale Alumni Bd.; mem. com. New Haven Festival of the Arts; co-founder of Am. Film Festival; founder Long Wharf Theatre, New Haven; chmn. of com. performing arts Arts Council of Greater New Haven. Pres. Assn. For The Theatre Arts, Inc. Served with ord. dept., AUS, 1942-46. Mem. Yale Photog. Soc. (founder, past pres., chief faculty adviser), Conn. Audio Visual Edn. Assn. (past pres., dir.; editor annual bull.), Edn. Media Council, N.E.A., (dir. div. audio visual instrn.). Ednl. Film Library Assn. (pres., past v.p., dir.), Univ. Film Producers Assn., Am. Fedn. Film Socs., Nat. Assn. Ednl. Broadcasters, Assn. for Edn. Radio- Yale Glee Club Assos., Yale Sch. Drama Assos., Yale Friends of Music, Conn. Opera Assn., New Haven Symphony Assos., Alpha Phi Omega (past pres., nat. presidential rep.). Clubs: Yale (N.Y.C., New Haven); Yale Faculty. Author: Modern Teaching of Foreign Languages, 1959. Editor: Preparing for College Study, 1962; The Connecticut Story, 1962. Illustrator: Basic Swimming, 1953. publ., asso. editor, The Black People of America, 1970 Contbr. articles profl. publs. Patentee hwy. safety items. Home: Thimble Farms Rd Branford CT 06405

KONECCI, EUGENE B., educator; Ph.D. Now Alice K. Kleberg prof. mgmt. and aerospace engring., dir. research Coll. Bus. Adminstrn., U. Tex. Address: 6206 Highland Hills Dr Austin TX 78731

KONEN, JAMES CLIFFORD, chemist; b. Fargo, N.D., Aug. 11, 1909; s. Nick and Tilla (Evanson) K.; B.S., N.D. State Coll., 1933, M.S., 1935; D.Sc., N.D. State U., 1959; grad. advanced mgmt. program Harvard, 1955; m. Harriet Ruth Ayres, July 15, 1939;

childrenElizabeth Anne, John Ayre. Sales staff Firestone Co., 1934; with Archer-Daniels-Midland Co., 1935-70, dir. indsl. research, 1943-52, asst. v.p., 1952-55, v.p. in charge research devel., engring. and quality control, 1955-63, v.p. overseas operations, 1963-70; formerly v.p. internat. operations Ashland Chem. Co. div. Ashland Oil & Refining Co.; dir. Ashland Chems. Ltd. Birmingham, Eng., Admex, S.A., Mex. City, Oleochim S.A., Brussels, Belgium, Admicol, S.A., Bogota, Colombia, Belgolac, Brussels, Oleotecnica, Santander, Spain, Venezolanos de Resinas, S.A., Caracas, Venezuela, Nisshoku Aro Chems., Inc., Osaka, Japan. Mem. Minn. Nuclear Operations Com., U. Minn. Nat. Resources Com.; chmn. task group oilseeds and animal fats Pres.'s Commn. on Increased Use Agrl. Products, 1956-57. Mem. Am. Oil Chemist's Soc. (past pres.), A.A.A.S., Minn. Acad. Sci. (councilor), Fedn. Paint and Varnish Prodn. Clubs, Nat. Paint, Varnish and Lacquer Assn., Fatty Acid Assn., Am. Chem. Soc. Author tech. articles various publs. Patentee in field of glyceride oil processing, chem. modification. Home: 3521 Avignon Pl Columbus OH 43221 Office: 8 E Long St Columbus OH 43215

KONER, PAULINE, dancer, choreographer; b. N.Y.C.; d. Samuel and Ida (Ginsburg) Koner; student Columbia 1928-31; ballet student of Michel Fokine; student ethnic dance with Michio Ito, also Angel Cansino; m. Fritz Mahler, May 23, 1939. Solo concerts in N.Y.C., 1930—, Near East, 1932, Russia, 1935, U.S., 1930—; guest artist Jose Limon Co., 1945-60; guest artist, tchr. Jacob's Pillow Dance Festival, intermittently, 1945-70; dir. Pauline Koner Dance Co., 1947-64; guest choreographer Nat. Sch. Dance. Rome, Italy, 1960-63, Nat. Ballet Chile, 1961; performer, tchr. Conn. Coll. Sch. Dance, 1948-60; pioneer TV dance in CBS, 1945; established modern dance program in Japan under auspices Fulbright Com., 1965; State Dept. tour of India, Singapore and Korea, 1967; mem. faculty Sch. Performing Arts, N.Y.C., N.C. Sch. Arts, Winston-Salem; performed at White House, 1967; conducted choreography workshops Nat. Assn. Regional Ballets, 1968; staged ballet Dayton (O.) Civic Ballet, 1969, Alvin Ailey Co., 1969, Atlanta Ballet Co., 1969; guest tchr. modern dance Internat. Ballet Seminar, Copenhagen, 1971; lectr. and guest artist many leading univs. in U.S.; performed under auspices State Dept. in Mexico, S.Am., Europe. Recipient Grant Nat. Endowment of Arts, 1969; Dance Mag. award, 1963. Address: 340 W 72d St New York City NY 10023

KONIGSBURG, ELAINE LOBL, author; b. N.Y.C., Feb. 10, 1930; d. Adolph and Beulah (Klein) Lobl; B.S., Carnegie Inst. Tech., 1952; grad. student chemistry, U. Pitts., 1952-54; m. David Konigsburg, July 6, 1952; childrenPaul, Laruie, Ross. Author: (juveniles) Jennifer, Hecate, Macbeth, William McKinley and Me, Elizabeth, 1967; From The Mixed-Up Files of Mrs. Basil E. Frankweiler (Newbery medal 1968), 1967; About the B'nai Bagels, 1969.

KONINGSBERGER, HANS, author; b. Amsterdam, Holland, July 12, 1921; s. Daniel and Elizabeth (Van Collem) K.; student U. Amsterdam, 1939-41, 46, U. Zürich (Switzerland), 1941-43, Sorbonne, Paris, France, 1946; m. Henriette Waterland; 1 dau., Ellen; m. 2d, Elizabeth Sutherland Martinez; 1 dau., Tessa; m. 3d, Katherine Scanlon. Came to U.S., 1951. Editor, Amsterdam, weekly, 1947-50; radio dir., Indonesia, 1950-51. Active Am. Friends Service Com., 1955-60. Steering Com. Resist, 1967—. Served with Brit. Liberation Army, 1943-46. Author (some writings under name Hans Koning): Aquarel of Holland, 1950; The Golden Keys, 1956; The Affair, 1958; An American Romance, 1960; A Walk with Love and Death, 1961; I Know What I'm Doing, 1964; Love and Hate in China, 1966; The Revolutionary, 1967; Along the Roads of the New Russia, 1968; The Future of Che Guevara, 1971; The Almost World, 1972; (plays) The Blood-Red Cafe, 1958, Hermione, 1962; (films) Wind in the Pines, 1961, A Walk with Love and Death, 1968; The Revolutionary, 1970. Contributor essays, political articles to nat. magazines. Translator: (from Dutch) Maria Dermout, 2d edit., 1961. (from French) Carlo Coccioli, 1958, Heinrich, 1965. Home: 4 E 95th St New York City NY 10028 Office: care International Famous Agency 1301 Av of Americas New York City NY 10019

KONITZ, LEE, saxophonist; b. Chgo., Oct. 13, 1927; student Roosevelt Coll. With Gay Claridge, other comml. bands, chgo., later with Jerry Wald; toured with Claude Thornhill, 1947-48; recordings: Anthropology, Yardbird Suite, others; with Miles Davis Capitol recording group at Royal Roost, 1948, recorded with Davis, 1948-50; appeared with local groups in concerts Scandinavia, 1951; with Stan Kenton, 1952-53; formed own group, appearing N.Y.C., Boston, 1954-55; concerts with Hans Koller, Lars Gullin, in Germany, 1955; numerous performances Half Note Cafe, N.Y.C., 1957-58, 59. Recipient Metronome Poll award, 1954, Down Beat Critics Poll award, 1957-58.*

KONO, FUMIHIKO, corp. exec.; b. Japan, 1896; ed. Tokyo U. Formerly fuselage designer Mitsubishi Internal Combustion Engine Mfg. Co., now exec. v.p. Nagoya Airplane Factory, Mitsubishi Heavy Industries Ltd.; dir., gen. mgr. Kawasaki Engring. Works, East Japan Heavy Industries, Ltd. (now Mitsubishi Nippon Heavy Industries), 1952-62, became pres., 1961, now chmn.; dir. Mitsubishi Atomic Power Industries Inc. ‡

KONOPINSKI, EMIL JAN, physicist; b. Michigan City, Ind., Dec. 25, 1911; s. Joseph and Sophia (Sniegowski) K.; B.A. U. Mich., 1933, M.A., 1934. Ph. D., 1936. Nat. Research fellow Cornell U., 1936-38; became prof. physics Ind. U., 1938, now Distinguished Service prof. of physics; mem. research staff AEC Labs., Chgo., 1941, Berkeley, Cal., 1942, Los Alamos, 1943-46; cons. AEC, 1946-; Guggenhein fellow Harvard, 1950. Mem. fellowship bd. Nat. Research Council, 1951. Mem. Am. Phys. Soc., Phi Beta Kappa. Author articles beta decay, nuclear transmutations, elementary particles, spect rometers. Mem. bd. editors Physical Rev., 1946-49. Home: 1342 S Downs St Bloomington IN 47401

KONOPKA, GISELA PEIPER, (Mrs. Erhardt Paul Konopka), social worker, educator; b. Berlin, Germany, Feb. 11, 1910; d. Mendel and Bronia (Buttermann) Peiper; student Hamburg U. (Germany), 1929-33; M.S., U. Pitts., 1943; Dr. Social Welfare, Columbia, 1957; m. Erhardt Paul Konopka, June 23, 1941. Came to U.S. 1941, naturalized, 1944. Psychiat. group worker Child Guidence Clinic, Pitts., 1943-47; lectr. sch. social work U. Pitts., also Carnegie Inst. Tech., 1943-47; asso. prof. social work U. Minn., 1947-56, prof., 1956—, spl. asst. to v.p. for student affairs, 1969—, also dir. Center for Youth Devel. and Research, 1970—. Child welfare expert, group work U.S. High Commr. Med. Affairs, Germany, summers 1950, 51; tchr. social work in Germany, Dept. State. Summer 1956; Fulbright lectr., Netherlands, 1960-61; lectr. U. Cal. at Berkeley, 1961-62, in Near and Far East, 1970, Inst. for Social Services, Montrouge, France, 1971; dir. adolescent girl in conflict research project Nat. Inst. Mental Health grant, 1962-65; cons. VA Hosp., Mpls., standards for group homes State of Minn. Research and Evaluation Div., Office Child Devel., Dept. Health, Edn. and Welfare. Mem. Gov.'s Adv. Com. on Youth, Minn., nat. adv. com. Girl Scouts of Am. exec. com. group work recreation div., exec. com. Family and Children's Service, Hennepin County Welfare Council; former cons. Children's Treatment Center, Minn. Welfare Dept; internat. cons. in social group work by Internat. Conf. Schs. Social Work. Mem. bd. Mpls. Urban League, 1968. Named outstanding alumnus social work U. Pittsburgh, 1968; award for outstanding service Assn. for the Blind, 1966; Outstanding Alumnus award Sch. Social Work U. Pitts., 1968; citation U.S. Children's Bur., 1966, Vols. Am. Fellow Am. Orthopsychiat. Assn. (pres. 1963-64, dir.); mem. Nat. Assn. Social Workers (chmn. group work sect.), Nat. conf. Social Welfare (v.p., nat. chmn. history of social welfare group 1960, past dir.), Am. Assn. U. Profs., Urban League, Consumers League, United World Federalists. Author: Therapeutic Group Work with Children, 1940; Group Work in the Institution, 1954; Eduard Co. Lindeman and Social Work Philosophy, 1958; Social Group Work; A Helping Process, 1963; Adolescent Girls in Conflict, published in 1966. Co-author: Concepts and Methods of Social Work, edited Walter Friedlander, 1958. Contbr. numerous articles profl. jours. Home: 3809 Sheridan Av S Minneapolis MN 55410

KONRAD, JOHN F., ins. co. exec.; b. Oshkosh, Wis., Sept. 29, 1917; s. John F. and Alma (Below) K.; Ph.B., U. Wis., 1939, LL.B., 1942; m. June Ross, May 30, 1941; children—William R., Ann L. (Mrs. Russell J. Hynst), Barbara J. With Wis. Pub. Service Corp., 1946-54, Northwestern Mut. Life Ins. Co., 1954—, v.p., treas., 1967—. Vice pres. bd. Family Service of Milw. Served to capt. USAAF, 1942-46. Mem. Milw. Investment Analysts (past pres.), Financial Analysts Fedn. (past v.p.). Republican. Mem. United Ch. Christ. Clubs: University (Milw.), Town. Home: 3529 N Summit Av Milwaukee WI 53211 Office: 720 E Wisconsin Av Milwaukee WI 53202

KONTARSKY, ALOYS, pianist; b. Iserlohn, Westphalia, Germany, 1931. Address: care Dr R Goette 42 Worburgstrasse Hamburg Germany also care Time Records Inc 2 W 45th St New York City NY 10036

KONTISKY, STAFFORD EUGENE mfg. exec.; b. Lima, O., Apr. 1, 1932; B.S., U. San Francisco, 1954; M.S., Stanford University, 1956; m. Rosemarie Lois Brown, May 15, 1955; 1 son, Anthony Robinson. Sales rep. Ames-Brockton Fabricated Products, Akron, O., 1956-58, sales mgr. Coshocton, Ohio, 1959-61, gen. manager plant, 1961-68, v.p. sales, 1968--. Instr. bus. Coshocton Jr. College, 1968-69. Named Man of Year, Coshocton Junior Chamber of Commerce, 1968. Mem. Coshocton C. of C. (vice president 1967-68, pres. 1969-70), English Speaking Union, Coshocton Sertoma Club, Nat. Assn. Mfrs., Sales Executives Institute, Phi Beta Kappa, Sigma Chi, Phi Mu. Democrat. Mem. Christian Ch. (lay leader). Mason (32, Shriner). Clubs: Coshocton Country, Coshocton City, Running Deer Country. Home: 2d Av Coshocton OH Office: 3d Av Coshocton OH

KONTOS, EDWARD GEORGE, tobacco co. exec.; b. Bklyn., July 26, 1923; s. Peter G. and Dorothy C. (Hayden) K.; B.S., N.Y. U., 1949, M.B.A., 1954; m. Patricia A. Friedl, June 15, 1946. With P. Lorillard Co., 1950-, treas., 1961-. Office: 200 E 42d St New York City NY 10017

KONVITZ, MILTON RIDVAS, educator; b. Safad, Israel, Mar. 12, 1908; s. Rabbi Joseph and Welia (Ridvas-Wilowsky) K.; came to U.S., 1915; naturalized, 1926; B.S., N.Y. U.; 1928, A.M., 1930, J.D., 1930; Ph.D., Cornell (Sage fellow in philosophy 1932-33), 1933; Litt.D., Rutgers U., 1954; D.C.L., U. Liberia, 1962; L.H.D., Hebrew Union Coll-Jewish Inst. Religion, 1966; LL.D., Syracuse U., 1971; m. Mary Traub, June 18, 1942; 1 son, Josef. Admitted to N.J. bar, 1932, and practiced law Jersey City and Newark, 1933-46; lectr. on law and pub. adminstrn. N.Y.U., 1938-46; mem. faculty New Sch. for Social Research, 1944-46; prof. indsl. and labor relations N.Y. State Sch. of Indsl. and Labor Relations, Cornell U., 1946—; prof. law Cornell Law School 1956—; mem. Inst. for Advanced Study, Princeton, 1959-60; vis. prof., Hewbrew U., Jerusalem, 1970; dir. Liberian Codification of Laws project, 1952—. Gen. counsel Newark Housing Authority, 1938-43, N.J. Housing Authority, 1943-45; pub. rep., Nat. WLB, region 2, 1943-46; mem. enforcement commn. and hearing commr. Nat. WSB, region 2, 1952-53; chmn. nat. com. study of Jewish Edn. in U.S. 1958-59. Ford Found. Faculty fellowship, 1952-53; faculty Salzburg (Austria) Seminar in Am. Studies, 1952. Panel Fed. Mediation and Conciliation Service, N.Y. Mediation Bd., N.Y. State Pub. Employment Relations Bd. Pres. Hebrew Culture Found.; nat. bd. Histadrut Cultural Exchange Inst.; nat. commn. B'nai B'rith Hillel Found.; commn. reorgn. World Zionist Orgn.; bd. dirs. Am. Zionist Fedn.; trustee U. Liberia; Guggenheim fellow, 1953-54; Fund for the Republic fellow, 1955; Comdr. Order Star of Africa, Liberia, 1957, Grand Band, 1960; fellow Center Advanced Study Behavioral Scis., 1964-65; N.Y.U. Washington Sq. Coll. Distinguished Alumni award, 1964; Mordecai ben David distinguished award Yeshiva U., 1965; Morris J. Kaplun internat. prize Hebrew U., 1969. Fellow Am. Assn. Jewish Edn.; mem. Conf. Jewish Social Studies (dir.), Inst. for Unity of Sci. (treas. and sec.), Am. Jewish Congress (mem. adv. com.), Yivo Inst. (acad. council), Am. Philos. Assn., Am. Polit. Sci. Assn., Am. Assn. U. Profs. (council 1961-64), Am. Bar Assn., Internat. Soc. of Labor Law and Social Legislation, Indsl. Relations Research Assn., African Studies Assn., Am. Studies Assn., Am. Civil Liberties Union (nat. com.), N.A.A.C.P. (nat. legal com.), Jewish Publ. Soc. (mem. com. on publs.), Am. Jewish League for Israel (dir.), Workers Def. League (dir.), Order of Coif, Phi Beta Kappa, Phi Eta Sigma. Author: On the Nature of Value: Philosophy of Samuel Alexander, 1946; The Alien and the Asiatic in American Law, 1946; The Constitution and Civil Rights, 1947; Civil Rights in Immigration, 1953; Bill of Rights Reader, 1954; Fundamental Liberties of a Free People, 1957; A Century of Civil Rights, 1961; First Amendment Freedoms, 1963; Expanding Liberties: Freedom's Gains in Postwar America, 1966; Religious Liberty and Conscience, 1968; Judaism and Human Rights, 1972. Editor: Industrial and Labor Relations Review (vols. 1-5), 1947-52; Liberian Code of Laws (5 vols.), 1957-60; Liberian Law Reports (17 vols). Mem. editorial bds. of periodicals. Home: 16 The Byway Ithaca NY 14850 Office: Ives Hall Cornell U Ithaca NY 14850

KONYA, SANDOR, tenor; b. Sarkad, Hungary; Student Franz Liszt Acad., Budapest, also in Germany. Profl. debut, Bielefeld, 1951; leading tenor Berlin City Opera, 1955; Am. debut with San Francisco Opera, 1960; regular appearances with Met. Opera, Bayreuth Festival, operas of Covent Garden, La Scala, Rome, Vienna and San Francisco, Chgo. Symphony Orch.; recording artist for Deutsche-Grammophone, RCA, MGM records. Address: care Columbia Artists Mgmt Inc 165 W 57th St New York City NY 10019*

KOOKER, ARTHUR RAYMOND, historian; b. Matchwood, Mich., Feb. 25, 1907; s. David Arthur and Grace Agnes (Geroux) K.; A.B. in Edn., U. Mich., 1931, A.M., 1933, Ph.D., 1941; m. Miriam Jane Highley, Dec. 24, 1941; children-Jane Anne, Elizabeth Margaret, John Nelson. Tchr. social studies Forest Park Jr. High Sch., Crystal Falls, Mich., 1928-31; supt. McMillan Twp. schs., Ewen, Mich., 1932-33; univ. fellow U. Mich., 1935-36, teaching fellow history, 1938-41, resident adviser Chicago House, West Quadrangle, men's dormitories, 1939-41, vis. asso. prof. history, summer 1951; regional dir. for Mich., WPA sponsored survey Fed. Archives outside D.C., 1936-37, chief editor Inventories of Fed. Archives in the States, 1937-38; asst. prof. history U. So. Cal., 1941-46, asso. prof., 1947-55, prof., 1955—, chmn. dept. history, 1955-69. Expert cons. Air. U., Maxwell AFB, Montgomery, Ala., 1947-54. Served from 2d lt. to maj., USAAF, 1943-46. Mem. Am. (council Pacific Coast Br. 1949-5O, 59—), So. hist. assns., Orgn. Am. Historians, Los Angeles Civil War Round Table (exec. com. 1957-58, pres. 1959-60). Athletic Assn. Western Univs. (faculty athletic rep. 1959-65), Soc. Am. Archivists, Blue Key, Skull and Dagger, Phi Alpha Theta, Phi Kappa Phi. Democrat. Mason. Contbr. to Men and Planes, History of Army Air Forces in World War II (vol. 6), 1955. Home: 26430 via Desmonde Lomita CA 90717

KOONE, CARL DEWEY, govt. ofcl.; b. Little Rock, Aug. 26, 1922; s. Albert D. and Gertie M. (Bost) K.; student Ark. Poly. Coll., 1940-42; B.S.A., U. Ark., 1951, M.S., 1951; m. Verna Beatrice Knicannon, Nov. 7, 1947; children—Marsha, Donald. Instr. pub. schs., Ark., 1946-49; mem. faculty U. Ark., 1951-57; dep. food, agr. officer U.S.. Embassy, Nicaragua, 1957-60; agrl. officer, Costa Rica, 1960-66; rural devel. officer, Nicaragua, 1966—. Served with USAAF, 1942-45. Address: AID American Embassy Managua Nicaragua

KOONS, DONALDSON, educator, geologist; b. Seoul, Korea (parents Am. citizens), Aug. 23, 1917; s. Edwin Wade and Floy (Donaldson) K.; A.B., Columbia, 1939, M.A., 1941, Ph.D., 1945; m. Elizabeth Anne Ortquist, Nov. 18, 1944; children—Robert Wade, John Donaldson, Peter Ortquist, Linnea Louise. Tchr. geology Carleton Coll., Northfield, Minn., 1942-43, Columbia, 1946, W.Va. U. 1946-47; mem. faculty Colby Coll., Waterville, Me., 1947—, prof. geology, 1951—, chmn. dept., 1947—. Chmn. Me. Environmental Improvement Commn., 1968—, Gov. Me. Task Force Environment, 1969—, New Eng. Conf. Air Pollution, 1968. Faculty trustee Colby Coll., 1965-68, Coburn Classical Inst., 1963—. Served with USAAF, 1943-45. Fellow A.A.A.S., Geol. Soc. Am. Home: RFD 1 Pond Rd Oakland ME 04963 Office: Colby Coll Waterville ME 04901

KOONS, GEORGE RICHARD, mfg. co. exec.; b. Chgo., Jan. 1, 1917; s. George H. and Laura E. (Benton) K.; B.S., U. Chgo., 1938; m. Jean K. Weber, Oct. 21, 1939 (div. 1966); childrenGeorge B., Sheila J., Jeffrey L.; m. 2d, Katherine Hanson, 1966. Began career with Kimberly-Clark Corp., 1938-52, dir. manpower planning and orgn., 1951-52; dir. indsl. and pub. relations Bowaters So. Paper Corp., 1952-57; dir. indsl. relations Carter Carburetor Corp., div. ACF Industries, 1957-60; v.p. indsl. relations, Bunswick, Corp., 1960-67; v.p. employee relations Am. Can Co.; N.Y.C., 1967-. Lectr., seminar leader personnel adminstrn. and labor relations. Mem. Ill. Bd. Vocational Edn., 1964-66; chmn. Govtl. Manpower Policy Commn., 1966-67. Served to lt. col. AUS, 1952-46. Mem. Indsl. Relations Assn. Chgo. (bd. dirs. 1964-). Author articles profl. jours. Home: 230 E 48th St New York City NY 10017 Office: Am Can Co 100 Park Av New York City NY 10010

KOONTZ, CARL HENRY, educator, civil engr.; b. Portage, Pa., June 3, 1923; s. Henry and Clara (Rudnick) K.; B.S., U. Ill., 1948. M.S. in Structural Engring., 1950; m. Lillie Sue Judah, Sept. 14, 1946; childrenDeonna Louise, Gregory Kyle, Richard Henry. Instr. U. Ill., 1948-52; cons. blast resistant structures, 1950; bridge designer Ill. Div. Hwys., 1952; asst. prof. civil engring., mathematics Worcester Poly. Inst., 1952-56. asso. prof., 1956-57, prof., head dept. civil engring., 1957-; structural engring. cons. Chmn. bldg. code com., Worcester, Mass. Served as sgt., Signal Corps. AUS, 1943-46. Mem. Worcester Engring. Soc., Worcester Soc. C.E., Am. Soc. Engring. Edn., Internat. Assn. Bridge and Structural Engrs., Am. Concrete Inst., Am. Soc. C.E., Sigma Xi, Tau Beta Pi, Chi Epsilon, Sigma Phi Epsilon. Home: 19 Schussler Rd Worcester MA 01609

KOONTZ, ELIZABETH DUNCAN (Mrs. Harry Lee Koontz), govt. ofcl.; b. Salisbury, N.C., June 3, 1919; d. Samuel Edward and Lena (Jordan) Duncan; A.B., Livingstone Coll., 1938, L.H.D. (hon.), 1967; M.A., Atlanta U., 1941, Litt.D. (hon.); Ph.D. (hon.), Pacific U., Bryant Coll.; Ed.D. (hon.), Howard U.; LL.D., Am. U.; L.H.D. (hon.). Coppin State Coll.; H.H.D. (hon.), Eastern Mich. U.; Sc.D. in Edn. (hon.), Northeastern U.; m. Harry Lee Koontz, Nov. 26, 1947. Tchr., Harnett County Tng. Sch., Dunn, N.C., 1938-40, Aggrev Meml. Sch., Landis, N.C., 1940-41, 14th St. Sch., Winston-Salem, N.C., 1941-45, Price High Sch., Salisbury, 1945-49. Monroe Sch., 1949-65; tchr. spl. edn. Price Jr.-Sr. High Sch., 1965-68; dir. Women's Bur., Dept. Labor, Washington, 1969—. U.S. del. to UN Com. Status of Women, 1969—; mem. Youth Commn. Rowan (N.C.) County. 1955-57. Recipient Distinguished Alumni medallion for achievement Livingstone Coll., Distinguished Tchr. award Civitan Club Salisbury, Distinguished Citizenship award N.C. Dist. Civitan Internat. Mem. Rowan County Negro Civic League, N.C., Salisbury tchrs. assns., N.C. Assn. Classroom Tchrs. (pres. 1958-62), N.E.A. (pres. dept. classroom tchrs. 1965-66. nat. v.p. 1967-68, nat. pres. 1968-69), Zeta Phi Beta. Home: 418 S Caldwell St Salisbury NC 28144 Office: Dept of Labor Bldg 14th St and Constitution Av N W Washington DC 20210

KOONTZ, FORREST O., ret. refinery exec.; b. Sioux City, Ia., Jan. 7, 1899; s. Albert Weaver and Ida (Martin) K.; ed. pub. schs.; m. Josephine Messer, Aug. 28, 1927; children—Mrs. Jack Files, Mrs. R.E. Johnson. Successively salesman, asst. sales mgr., v.p. charge sales, exec. v.p., gen. sales mgr., pres., chmn. bd., now ret.; dir. Quaker State Oil Refining Corp., Oil City, Pa.; past v.p., dir. Quaker State Oil Refining Co. of Cal., Quaker State, S.A., TruckLite Co., Inc., Quaker State Oil Refining Co. of Can., Ltd.; dir. N.W. Pa. Bank and Trust Co. Mem. Pa. Crude Oil Assn. (dir.), Nat. Petroleum Refiners Assn., Oil City C. of C., Newcomen Soc. N.Am. Mason (32, Shriner). Home: 560 Bouquin Circle Oil City PA 16302

KOONTZ, HAROLD, educator, mgmt. cons.; b. Findlay, O., May 19, 1908; s. Joseph Darius and Harriett (Dillinger) K.; A.B., Oberlin Coll., 1930; M.B.A., Northwestern U., 1931; Ph.D., Yale, 1935; m. Mary Learey, June 16, 1935; childrenKaren Kathryn, Jean Carol. Asst. prof. econs. Colgate U., 1935- 41; chief traffic br. WPB, Washington, 1942-44; asst. to v.p. Assn. Am. R.R.'s, 1944-45; asst. to pres., dir. planning Trans-World Airlines, 1945-48; dir. comml. sales Consol. Vultee Aircraft Corp., 1948-50; prof. bus. policy and transp. Grad. Sch. Bus. Adminstrn., U. Cal. at Los Angeles, 1950-62, Mead Johnson prof. mgmt., 1962-; pres., dir. Inst. Adminstrv. Research, Inc., 1965-71; chmn. bd. Genisco Tech. Corp.; dir. Farr Corp., Dust Control. Inc., Roberts Cons. Ind., Planning Dynamics, Inc.; cons. several cos. Mem. Los Angeles Bd. Airport Commrs., 1961-65, Nat. Indsl. Conf. Bd. Fellow Acad. Mgmt. (pres. 1963), Internat. Acad. Mgmt. (bd. govs., chpt. chmn.); mem. Am. Mgmt Assn., Am. Soc. Traffic and Transp., Am. Econ. Assn., A.A.A.S., Inst. Mgmt. Scis. Author: Government Control of Business, 1941; (with Cyril O'Donnell) Principles of Management, 1968; (with R. W. Gable) Public Control of Private Enterprise, 1956; Readings in Management, 1959; Management; A Book of Readings, 1964, Toward a Unified Theory of Management, 1964; Board of Directors and Effective Management, 1967; Appraising Managers as Managers, 1971; also articles. Home: 4838 Gloria Av Encino CA 91316 Office: 405 Hilgard St Los Angeles CA 90024

KOONTZ, JOHN, state ofcl.; b. Goldfield, Nev., Oct. 19, 1906; s. Louis Kossuth and Ada May (Halstead) K.; grad. Goldfield High Sch., 1925; m. Margaret Elizabeth Bennett, Apr. 21, 1940. Office worker Nash Motor Co., Reno, 1925-26; in grocery bus., Goldfield, 1927-34; county recorder and auditor, Esmeralda County, Nev., 1935-42; dep. state bank examiner and auditor, Nev., 1943-46; sec. of State of Nev., 1946—. Served with Q.M.C., AUS, 1943. Mem. Nat. Assn. Secs. of

State (treas. 1956; pres. 1958). Democrat. Methodist. Elk, K.P. Compiled 3d and 4th edits. Political History of Nevada. Home 302 John St Carson City NV 89701 Office: State Capitol Carson City NV 89701

KOONTZ, PAUL GUTHRIE, lawyer; b. Seymour, Iowa, Nov. 19, 1894; s. James Alva and Jessie Annette (Smith) K.; student Henry Kendall Coll. (now Tulsa U.), 1912-13; A.B., U. Mo., 1916, LL.B., 1918; m. Mildred K. McBride, Oct. 1, 1924; children—Rosalie (Mrs. Charles K. Richmond), Jean (Mrs. Wm. H. Leedy), Paul Guthrie. Admitted to Mo. bar, 1917; pvt. practice law., Joplin. Mo., 1919-22, Kansas City, Mo., since 1923; partner Lathrop, Koontz, Righter, Clagett, Parker & Norquist; gen. counsel, dir. Butler Mfg. Co., 1939-65; chmn. bd. Swedish-Am. Savs. & Loan Assn.; dir. Kansas City Starlight Theatre Assn. Dem. mem. Kansas City cleanup bd. Election Commrs., 1938-41; leader citizens movement for non-partisan municipal govt., 1939-42; councilman-at-large, 1942-48; mem. exec. com. Citizens Assn.; mem. State Savs. and Loan Commn., 1961—, chmn. 1964—. Bd. regents Central Mo. State Coll., 1941-43, v.p., 1942-43; trustee Mo. Law Sch. Found., 1951-57; mem. adv. bd. Municipal Auditorium, 1958—, chmn. 1967-69. Served lt. F.A., U.S. Army, 1918-19. Recipient citation for outstanding achievement U. of Mo. Law Alumni Assn., 1966. Mem. Lawyers Assn. Kansas City, Am. Bar Assn., Am. Legion, 40 and 8, Mil. Order World Wars, S.R., Order Coif, Phi Alpha Delta. Sigma Phi Epsilon (past nat. pres.). Democrat. Mem. Christian Ch. (elder; trustee; chmn. ofcl. bd. 1954). Mason (Shriner, Jester) (dir. Kansas City Ct. 54, 1952). Clubs: Kansas City Country, Kansas City, University, Saddle and Sirloin (Kansas City); 40 Years Ago Column. Home: 834 W 64th Terrace Kansas CIty MO 64113 Office: Commerce Tower Kansas City MO 64199

KOONTZ, RAYMOND, bus. exec.; b. Asheville, N.C., 1912; m. Carol Hamlin; 1 son, Cary Hamlin. Pres., dir. Diebold, Inc.; dir. The Harter Bank and Trust Co. Mem. Newcomen Soc. North Am. Clubs: Canton, Brookside (Canton, O.); Minneapolis; Union (Cleve.); Congress Lake (Hartville, O.); Greenwich (Conn.) Country; Green Boundary (Aiken, S.C.). Home: 2601 Foxhills Dr N W Canton OH 44708 Office: 818 Mulberry Rd S E Canton OH 44702

KOOP, CHARLES EVERETT, surgeon; b. Bklyn., Oct. 14, 1916; s. John Everett and Helen (Apel) K.; A.B., Dartmouth Coll., 1937; M.D., Cornell U., 1941; Sc.D., U. Pa., 1947; m. Elizabeth Flanagan, Sept. 19, 1938; children—Allen vanBenschoten, Norman Apel, David Charles Everett, Elizabeth. Surgeon-in- chief Chilren's Hosp. of Phila, 1948—; prof. pediatriic surgery U. Pa. Sch. Medicine, 1959—; editor-in-chief Jour. Pediatric Surgery, 1965—; cons. U.S. Navy, 1964—. Mem. Am. Surg. Assn., Soc. U. Surgeons, Am. Acad. Pediatrics, Am. Coll. Surgeons, British Assn. Pediatric Surgeons, Internat. Soc. Surgery, Societe Francaise de Chirugie Infantile, A.M.A., Deutschen Gesselschaft für Kinderchirugi. Contbns. and publs. in surg. physiology, plasma substitutes, physiology of the surg. neonate, tech. advances in pediatric surgery. Home: 614 Righters Mill Rd Narberth PA 19072 Office: 1740 Bainbridge St Philadelphia PA 19146*

KOOP, THEODORE FREDERICK, broadcasting exec.; b. Monticello, Ia., Mar. 9, 1907; s. Frederick William and Laura Abby (Hicks) K.; A.B., Ia. U., 1928; L.H.D. (hon.), Ia. Wesleyan U., 1970. Reporter, editor A.P., Des Moines, New Haven, N.Y.C., Washington, 1928-41; mem. editorial staff Nat. Geog. Soc., Washington, 1941, 46-47; spl. asst. to U.S. Dir. Censorship, 1942-45, asst. dir. censorship, dept. dir., 1945; dir. news and pub. affairs CBS, Washington 1948-61, v.p. 1961- 71. Served as lt. USNR, 1942-45. Mem. Phi Beta Kappa, Delta Upsilon, Sigma Delta Chi. Clubs: University, National Press (pres. 1953) (Washington); Chevy Chase; Gridiron. Author: Weapon of Silence, 1946. Contbr. to Dateline: Washington, 1949. Home: 2737 Devonshire Pl N W Washington DC 20008

KOOPMAN, BERNARD OSGOOD, mathematician; b. Paris, France, Jan. 19, 1900 (parents Am. citizens); s. Augustus and Louise L. (Osgood) K.; A.B., Harvard, 1922, A.M., 1924. Ph.D., 1926; m. Louise Harvey, June 2, 1936; children—Philippa Heath, Winifred Sewall; m. 2d. Jane Bridgman, Mar. 21, 1948; children—Anne Osgood, Elizabeth Ware, Barbara Ward. Fellow (Harvard) U. of Paris, 1924-25; instr. math. Harvard, 1925-26; Nat. Research Fellow, Princeton, 1926-27; successively Instr. asst. prof., asso. prof., prof. math., Columbia. 1927-51, Adrian prof. math., 1951-68, emeritus, 1968—, chmn. dept., 1951-57; mem. staff E.D. Little Co., 1968—. Lectr., Harvard, 1936-37; mem. Weapons System Evaluation Group, office asst. sec. defense, 1956-57. Mem. Operations Research Group, Office of Comdr. in Chief, U.S. Navy, 1944-46 (on leave from Columbia); former cons. for Operations Evaluation Group (C.N.O.) U.S. Navy, U.S. operations researchh group liaison rep., U.K., 1959-61; dir. weapons systems evaluation div. Ins. Def. Analyses, 1964-65; adv. panel on operational research, NATO 1965-68. Served as pvt. U.S. Army, 1918. Fellow Operations Research Soc. Am. (v.p. 1956-57, pres. 1957- 58); mem. Am. Math. Soc. (council), Phi Beta Kappa, Sigma Xi. Clubs: Cosmos, Randolph Mountain (pres. 1968-70). Author: Search and Screening: numerous articles on operations research and math. and its applications in learned jours. in U.S. Address: Middle Rd Boxborough MA 01720

KOOPMAN, ERNEST THEODORE, ins. co. exec.; b. Flanagan, Ill., Jan. 12, 1911; s. Henry C. and Elizabeth (Hunsicker) K.; diploma bus. adminstrn., Wartburg Normal Coll., Waverly, Ia., 1931; m. Clara Milius, Sept. 6, 1935; children—Ronald, Elizabeth (Mrs. Richard M. Rausch), Joan (Mrs. William Block). With Lutheran Mut. Life ins. Co., Waverly, 1931—, pres., chmn. exec. com., 1965—, also dir. Chmn. Waverly United Fund campaign, 1968; county chmn. Radio Free Europe, 1969. Mem. bd., past pres. adv. bd. St. Joseph Mercy Hosp.; bd. dirs. treas. Cedar Valley Mental Health Center. Named Man of Year, Waverly Jr. C. of C., 1961; recipient award of distinction Burrill & Co., 1962. Mem. Waverly C. of C. (pres. 1958-59), Life Office Mgmt. Assn. (asso.). Republican. Lutheran. Clubs: Waverly Country, Rotary (past pres.) (Waverly). Home: 111 16th St SW Waverly IA 50677 Office: 201 1st St SE Waverly IA 50677

KOOPMAN, RICHARD JOHN WALTER, educator; b. St. Louis, June 24, 1905; s. Herman Henry Richard and Anna Cathrine (Heye) K.; B.S., U. Mo., 1928, Ph.D., 1942; M.S., Yale, 1933; m. Nellie Elkins Wisbrock, Sept. 7, 1934; 1 son, Richard Nelson. Test engr. Gen. Electric Co., Schenectady, 1928-31; instr. elec. engring. Yale, 1931-33, Mich. Coll. Mining and Tech., 1935-37; asst. prof. elec. engring. U. Kan., 1937-40. asso. prof., 1940-43; head elec. controls and electromechanics sect. Cornell Aero Lab., 1943-46; asso. prof. elec. engring. Washington U., St. Louis, 1946-49 prof. electronics and elec. sci., chmn. dept. 1949-65, prof. elec. engring., 1965—; cons. to corps. on automatic control and protection elec. circuits; research, devel. specialist and scientist Lockheed Aircraft corp., summers 1953-57; engr. Midwest Univs. Research Assn., summers 1960, 61; coll. faculty asso. Lockheed Cal. Corp., summers 1962, 63, 66; research elec. engr. U.S. Army Research and Devel. Labs., Ft. Belvoir, Va. summers 1964, 65, 67. Dir. of Bd. Edn., Brentwood, Mo., 1961—. Recipient nat. prize for paper (with H.R. Reed), Am. Inst. E.E., 1937. Registered profl. engr. Fellow I.E.E.E. (chmn. St. Louis sect. 1957); mem. Am. Soc. Engring. Edn. (pres. Mo.-Ark. sect. 1951), P.T.A. (pres. Frazier Sch. 1954), St. Louis Elec. Bd. Trade (dir. 1950-65), Sigma Xi, Tau Beta Pl, Acacia, Gamma Alpha, Eta Kappa Nu (nat. pres. 1964-65), Kappa Eta Kappa (past nat. pres.). Conglist. Mason (past master). Clubs: Circle, Engineers St. Louis (dir. 1953-55, treas. 1956, v.p. 1957-59, pres. 1960. Contbr. profl. jours., and profl. reports. Home: 2201 St Clair St Brentwood MO 63144 Office: Washington U St Louis MO 63130

KOOPMANS, LAMBERT HERMAN, educator; b. Chgo., July 23, 1930; s. John Otto and Pearl (Andrews) K.; A.B., San Diego State Coll., 1952; Ph.D., U. Cal., Berkeley, 1958; m. Sharon Iris Archibald, Dec. 24, 1955; children-Melissa, Vanessa, David, Andrew. Staff mem. Sandia Corp., Albuquerque, 1958-64, cons., 1964-68; asso. prof. dept. math. and statistics U. N.M., Albuquerque, 1964-68, prof., 1968—, chmn. dept. math. and statistics, 1969—; cons. Westinghouse Corp., 1965-66. Fellow Inst. Math. Statistics. Home: 7400 Dellwood Rd NE Albuquerque NM 87110

KOOPMANS, TJALLING CHARLES, economist; b. s'Graveland, Netherlands, Aug. 28, 1910; s. Sjoerd and Wijtske (van der Zee) K.; M.A., U. Utrecht (Netherlands) 1933; Ph.D., U. Leiden, (Netherlands) 1936; hon. doctorate econs. Netherlands Sch. Econs., 1963, Cath. U. Louvain, 1967; m. Truus Wanningen, Oct. 1936; children-Ann W., Henry S., Helen J. Came to U.S., 1940, naturalized, 1946. Lectr. Netherlands Econ. U., Rotterdam, 1936-38; specialist financial sect. League of Nations, 1938-40; research asso. Sch. Pub. and Internat. Affairs, Princeton, also spl. lectr., sch. bus. N.Y.U., 1940- 41; economist Penn Mutual Life Ins. Co., 1941-42; statistician Combined Shipping Adjustment Bd. and Brit. Mcht. Shipping Mission, 1942-44; research asso. Cowles Commn. Research Econs., U. Chgo., 1944-55, asso. prof. econs., 1946-48, prof. econs. 1948-55, dir. research Cowles Commn., 1948-54; prof. econs. Yale, 1955—, dir. Cowles Found. for Research in Economics, 1961-67, also fellow of Silliman College, Yale; Frank W. Taussig prof. econs. Harvard, 1960-61. Fellow Econometric Soc. (pres. 1950), Am. Statis. Assn.; mem. Am. Acad. Arts and Scis., Internat. Statis. Inst., Nat. Acad. Scis. Author: Three Essays on the State of Eonomic Science, 1957. Editor: Statistical Inference in Dynamic Economic Models, 1950; Activity Analysis of Production and Allocation, 1951; co-editor; Studies in Econometric Method, 1953. Contbr. profl. jours. Address: Cowles Found for Research in Economics Yale U Box 2125 Yale Station New Haven CT 06520

KOORENNY, RALPH LLOYD, univ. dean; b. Ryder, N.D., May 18, 1918; s. Abraham H. and Mary (Trihub) K.; B.A., Walla Walla Coll., 1946; M.A., Washington State U., 1948; Ph.D., U. Colo., 1957; m. Pauline Beeks, Dec. 24, 1942. Asst. prof. La Sierra Coll., Riverside, Cal., 1948-55; asso. prof. 1956-58, prof. econs., 1959—; asst. v.p. acad. affairs Haile Sellassie I U., Addis Ababa, Ethopia, 1965-67; acad. dean Coll. Arts and Scis., Loma Linda U., Riverside, Cal., 1967—. Served with AUS, 1942-46. Mem. Am. Assn. Higher Edn., Am. Econ. Assn. Republican. Mem. Seventh-day Adventist Ch. Home: 4948 Linn Dr Riverside CA 92505

KOOSMAN, JERRY MARTIN, profl. baseball player; b. Appleton, Minn., Dec. 23, 1942; s. Martin William and Lydia (Graese) K.; student U. Minn., Morris, 1960-61, State Sch. Sci., Whapeton, N.D., 1961-62; m. LaVonne Kathleen Sorum, Feb. 11, 1967; children-Michael Scott, Shawn Allen. Profl. baseball player with Greenville (S.C.) Mets, Williamsport (Pa.) Mets, 1965, Auburn (N.Y.) Mets, 1966, N.Y. Mets and Jacksonville (Fla.) Suns, 1967; pitcher N.Y. Mets, 1968—. Vice pres. Skyline Airfreight, Inc., Gen. Units, Inc., All Star Sports, N.Y.C.; dir. Midwest Empire, Inc., Anderson, Ind. Served with U.S. Army, 1962-64. Lutheran. Home: 2 Parkview Heights Morris MN 56267

KOOTZ, SAMUEL MELVIN, art dealer; b. Portsmouth, Va., Aug. 23, 1898; s. Louis and Ann (Persky) K.; LL.B., U. Va., 1921; m. Jane Ogden, Sept. 25, 1937. Owner Kootz Gallery, N.Y.C., specializing in modern American and European painting and sculpture, 1944—. Author: Modern American Painters, 1928; New Frontiers in American Painting, 1944; Puzzle in Paint, 1943; Puzzle in Petticoats, 1944; (play) Home is the Hunter, 1946. Address: 630 Park Av New York City NY 10021

KOPAC, MILAN JAMES, educator; b. Ravenna, Neb., Mar. 12, 1905; s. James and Mary B. (Skala) IK.; B.S., U. Neb., 1927, M.S., 1929, D.Sc. (hon.), 1962; Ph.D., U. Cal., 1934. Asst. in zoology U. Neb., 1927-29, vis. instr., 1934, vis. prof. biology, 1963; teaching fellow U. Cal., 1930- 33; Nat. Research fellow N.Y.U., 1934-35; reeseearch asso. biology Washington Square Coll., 1934-38, vis. asst. prof., 1938-43, asst. prof., 1944-46, asso. prof., 1947-49, prof. biology, N.Y.U., 1949—, head all univ. dept. biology, 1963-70, dir. Robert Chambers Lab. for Microsurgery, 1968—; investigator Tortugas Lab., Carnegie Inst., Washington, summers 1933-37; civilian investigator, O.S.R.D., U.S. Army and U.S. Navy, 1940-43; cons. Nat. Cancer Inst., USPHS, 1947-48; prin. investigator cancer research grants, USPHS, 1947—; mem. panel cell physiol. com. on growth NRC, 1949-54. Chairman of Gordon Research Conf. Cancer, 1964. Mem. Bermuda Biol. Sta., Inc.; mem. research adv. com. Cancer Inst. Miami; chmn. sci. adv. com. Damon Runyon Meml. Fund. for Cancer Research, 1966-69, sci. dir., 1967-69; physiology fellowships review panel NIH, 1963-66; adv. com. instnl. grants Am. Cancer Soc., 1963-66. Recipient Wisdom Soc. award, 1970. Fellow N.Y. Acad. Sci. (councilor, v.p., 1958, pres. 1960, trustee 1960- 62 Gold medal award 1969); mem. Am. Soc. Cytology (med. and founder mem.), Soc. Gen. Physiol., Internat. Soc. Cell Biology (founder mem.), Assn. Cancer Research, Inc., Harvey Soc. (hon. life), Inter-Soc. Cytology Council, Tissue Culture Assn., Sigma Xi (pres. N.Y.U. chpt. 1955-57). Cons. editor: Cancer Cytology and Cytochemistry; Mechanisms of Cell Division. Contbr. sci. articles tech. and med. jours.; specialist in microsurgery and its instrumentation. Address: 100 Washington Sq E New York City NY 10003

KOPF, KENNETH, govt. ofcl.; b. Farrar, Ia., May 28, 1904; s. John George and Melvilla Elvira (Kinney) K.; B.S. in Farm Crops and Soils, Ia. State Coll., 1930, Ph.D. in Plant Genetics, 1952; m. Sung Il Lee, Apr. 16, 1959; children—Kurt Lee, Nancy Lee. Plant breeder F.H. Woodruff & Sons, Milford, Conn., 1933-44; geneticist Dole Pineapple Co., Honolulu, 1944-49; research fellow Ia. State Coll., 1930-35, 49-52; chief mission, research adviser FAO, Iraq 1952-53; agriculturist Korean Civil Assistance Command, Seoul, 1954-55, chief agrl. tech., 1955-60; agronomist, agrl. diversification adviser, Bogota, Colombia, 1960-65; sr. agronomist AID, Lagos, 1965-70; chief agrl. research and devel. AID, Saigon, Vietnam, 1970—. Mem. A.A.A.S., Torrey Bot. Club, Am. Genetics Assn., Ia., N.Y., Hawaiian acads. sci., Trinidad, Am. philatelic socs., Crop Sci. Soc. Am., Soils Sci. Soc. Am., Nat. Geog. Soc., Smithsonian Instn., Nat. Wildlife Assn., Nat. Parks Assn., Am. Assn. India Affairs. Home: First Nat Bank Ames IA 50010 Office: USAID/ADFA Rd APO San Francisco CA 96243

KOPIT, ARTHUR, playwright; b. N.Y.C., May 10, 1937; s. George and Maxine (Dubin) K.; A.B. cum laude, Harvard, 1959. Author plays produced at Harvard: Questioning of Nick, 1957, On the Runway of Life You Never Know What's Coming Off Next, 1958, Sing to Me Through Open Windows, 1959, Aubade, 1959, Oh Dad, Poor Dad, Mamma's Hung You in the Closet and I'm Feelin' So Sad, 1960 (also prod. in London, Eng., 1961, off Broadway, 1962, on Broadway, 1963) released as a motion picture in 1967. Recipient of the Vernon Rice award, 1962, Outer Circle award, 1962. Mem. Writers Guild Am., Hasty Pudding Soc., Signet Soc., Phi Beta Kappa. Club: Harvard (N.Y.C.). Author: (6 one-act plays) The Day the Whores Came Out to Play Tennis, and Other Plays, 1965. Address: care Audrey Wood 555 Madison Av New York City NY 10022

KOPKIND, ANDREW DAVID, journalist; b. New Haven, Aug. 24,1935; s. Bernard Philip and Esther (Aaronson) K.; A.B., Cornell U., 1957; M.Sc. in Econs., London (Eng.) Sch. Econs., 1961. Reporter, Washington Post, 1958-59; corr. Time mag., 1961-65; asso. editor New Republic, 1965-67, contbg. editor, 1967-68; founder, editor Mayday and Hard Times Weeklies, Washington, 1968- -; Washington corr. New Statesman, London, 1965-69, Le Nouvel Observateur, Paris, 1967-69; pres. New Weekly Project, Inc. 1968-70. Author: America: The Mixed Curse, 1969. Address: 1065 31st St N W Washington DC 20007

KOPLAR, HAROLD, hotel exec.; b. St. Louis, Feb. 27, 1915; s. Sam and Jeannette (Grollnek) K.; U. Ill., 1938; m. Marie Lauer, Mar. 30, 1941; childrenRobert, Edward, Susan, Gen. mgr. Forest Park Hotel, St. Louis, 1940-43; asst. to pres. Chase and Park Plaza hotels, St. Louis, 1943-46; v.p., gen. mgr. Koplar Hotels (Chase and the Park Plaza), 1946; now pres.; mng. dir. Lodge of the 4 Seasons, Lake Ozark, Mo. 1961-, also pres.; pres. The Chase-Park Plaza, 1952—. Resort Corp. of Am., 1961—. Pres. York Investment Company, 1959-, KPLR-TV, St. Louis, 1959-; architect Starlight Roof, Khorassan Room, and the Exhibit Hall of the Chase-Park Plaza, Tiara Room of Park Plaza, Hi-way Theatre. Chmn. purveyors com. St. Louis Conv. Bur., 1957-59; dir. St. Louis Symphony Soc. 1958—. Trustee Jefferson Memorial, St. Louis. Consular Agent of France in St. Louis, 1956—. Mem. St. Louis C. of C. (dir., 1959-60), Am. (dir., 1954-55), St. Louis (pres. 1949-52) hotel assns., Zeta Beta Tau. Clubs: Westwood Country, Variety, Advertising, Hotel Assn. Ambassadors, Young Presidents, Lambs. Home: 500 S Warson Road Clayton MO 63105 Office: 212 N Kingshighway St Louis MO 63108

KOPP, CHARLES LEO, ins. co. exec.; b. Los Angeles, Jan. 10, 1922; s. Charles Leo and Katherine (Zirwes) K.; A.A., Los Angeles City Coll., 1943; postgrad. U. Redlands, 1943-45; J.D., U. So. Cal., 1949; m. Nancy Leonard, Oct. 28, 1944; children-Anne, Martha, Walter, James. Admitted to Cal. bar, 1950; practiced in Los Angeles, 1950-68, San Francisco, 1968—; asso. counsel Pacific Mut. Life Ins. Co., 1950-58; asst. gen. counsel Pacific Finance Corp., 1958-64; v.p., head law dept. United Cal. Bank, 1964-68; corporate sec. Indsl. Indemnity Co., 1968-69; asso. counsel West Coast Life Ins. Co., 1970—; tchr. U. So. Cal. Extension Div., 1954-57. Asso. mem. Republican Central Com. Cal., 1964—. Served to 1st lt. USMCR, 1943- 46. Mem. Am., Cal., San Francisco, Los Angeles bar assns., Cal. C. of C., Phi Alpha Delta. Club: San Francisco Commercial. Author: Life Insurance in Divorce Cases, 1956. Home: 190 Via Lerida Greenbrea CA 94904 Office: 605 Market St San Francisco CA 94105

KOPP, GEORGE ADAMS, educator; b. Montgomery City, Mo., Feb. 7, 1900; s. Philip R. and Mary E. (Smith) K.; A.B., Monmouth Coll., 1926; M.S., U. Wis., 1930, Ph.D., 1933; m. Julia R. Ball, June 22, 1924 (div. 1948); children—Joseph Blair, Kathleen Louise, Doris Helen; m. 2d Harriet C. Green, June 18, 1948. Chmn. speech dept. Jamestown (N.D.) Coll., 1926-28; instr., later asst. prof. U. Wis., 1928-36; instr. Columbia (on leàve Bell Telephone Lab., 1943-46), 1939-46; asso. prof. speech U. Mich., 1946-48; asst. prof. Wayne State U., 1936-39, prof. speech, 1948—. Mem. Nat. Soc. for Crippled Children and Adults, Inc., Nat. Assn. Tchrs. Speech, Am. Speech and Hearing Assn. (pres. 1959), Mich. Speech Correction Assn., Speech Assn. Am., Sigma Xi, Tau Kappa Alpha, Pi Kappa Delta, Delta Sigma Rho, Theta Alpha Phi. Author: Visible Speech (with R.K. Potter and H.C. Green), 1947, rev. edit. (with R.K. Potter and H.G. Kopp), 1966. Contbr. speech publs. Home: 6711 Golfcrest Dr San Diego CA 92119 Office: Wayne State U Detroit MI 48202

KOPP, GEORGE WILLIAM, univ. dean; b. Fredonia, N.Y., July 27, 1920; s. George William and Hazel (Smith) K.; B.S., State U. N.Y., Fredonia, 1951, M.S., 1953; Ed.D., Syracuse U., 1958; m. Earline Rae Ellis, Sept. 26, 1946; children—Thomas William, Timothy Raymond. Elementary sch. tchr. Westfield Central Sch., 1951-52; campus sch. tchr. State U. N.Y., Fredonia, 1952-55; grad. asst., instr., asst. prof. Syracuse U., 1955-60; dean grad. studies State U. N.Y., Oswego, 1960—, dir. summer session and continuing edn., 1960—. Served with USAAF, 1942-46. Mem. N.E.A., Kappa Delta Pi, Pi Delta Kappa. Republican. Presbyn. (elder). Mason, Rotarian. Home: Sleepy Hollow RD #3 Oswego NY 13126

KOPP, JOHN BARTON, bus. exec.; b. Plandome, N.Y., June 13, 1920; s. William A. J. and Anna (Stewart) K.; grad. Wilbraham Acad., 1936; B.S. in Naval Architecture and Marine Engring., Webb Inst. Naval Architecture, 1941; m. T. Lanelle Rogers, June 28, 1944; childrenSteven H., Jenny S., Martha L., Nancy B. Gen. supt. Cramp Shipbldg. Co., Phila., 1941-46; naval architect Jeffersonville Boat & Machine Co., 1946-49; gen. mgr. Ingalls Shipbldg. Corp., Decatur works, 1949-56, asst. v.p., 1956-60; asst. to v.p. operations Ingalls Iron Works Co., Birmingham, 1956-57, asst. v.p. operations, 1957-58, v.p. operations, 1959-61, pres., dir., 1961-63; asst. v.p. Ingalls Steel Constrn., 1957-61, pres., dir., 1961- 63; v.p., dir. Am. Shipbldg. Co., Lorain, O., 1963-66; sr. v.p., 1966-67; pres., chief exec. officer Cin. Sheet Metal & Roofing Co., 1967-69; pres., dir. Nashville Bridge Co., 1969—. Mem. Soc. Naval Architects and Marine Engrs., U.S., Nashville chambers commerce, S.A.R. Newcomen Soc. Clubs: Birmingham (Ala.) Country; Elyria (O.) Country; Hillwood Country, (Nashville). Home: 1247 Saxon Dr Nashville TN 37215 Office: Box 239 Nashville TN 37202

KOPP, W. BREWSTER, stock exchange exec.; b. Rochester, N.Y., Nov. 4 1925; s. Frederick J. and Bernice C. (Woodworth) K.; A.B. Harvard, 1946, M.B.A., 1949; m. Ruth S. Philpotts, June 18, 1949; children—Bradford, Jeffrey, Alexander. Investment analyst, N.Y., 1946-47, 49-51; with Standard Oil Co. (Ohio), 1951-53; with Am. Can Co., 1954-65, mgr. financial analysis, 1958-62, corp. mgr. financial planning and budgets, 1962- 64, div. controller, 1964-65; asst. sec. army for financial mgmt., 1965- 67; asst. to chmn. bd. First Nat. Bank, Boston, 1967, sr. v.p., 1967-69; v.p. finance and adminstrn. Digital Equipment Corp., Maynard, Mass., 1969-70; sr. v.p., mem. exec. com. Am. Stock Exchange, 1971—. Cons. to asst. sec. def., 1967-69. Mem. Financial Execs. Inst., Assn. U.S. Army. Republican. Clubs: Harvard (N.Y.C.); Norfolk (Conn.) Country. Home: Winchester Road Norfolk CT 06058 also 149 E 73d St New York City NY 10021 Office: American Stock Exchange 86 Trinity Pl New York City NY 10006

KOPPANG, HENRY OLIVER, banker; b. Starbuck, Minn.; s. Lars and Clara (Nedrud) K.; student Park Region Coll., Fergus Falls, Minn., 1916-17; Concordia Coll.-St. Olaf Coll., Northfield, Minn., 1917-19; m. Ruth Minor, Dec. 14, 1944. Comml. banking in N.D., 1919-20; with Fed. Res. Br. Bank, Helena, Mont., 1921-26; examiner Fed. Res. Bd., Washington, 1927-38, examiner in charge field staff, 1939-41; 1st v.p. Fed. Res. Bank of Kansas City (Mo.), 1941-66; vice chmn. bd., chmn. exec. com. Mid-Continent Nat. Bank Kansas City, Mo., 1966-68, chmn., 1968—. Pres. Greater Kansas City, nat. dir. Jr. Achievement Inc.; dir. Starlight Theatre Assn., Kansas City; dir., v.p., treas. Am. Royal Assn. Hon. dir. Rockhurst Coll., K.C. Served in S.A.T.C., Northfield, Minn., 1918. Mem. Kansas City C. of C. Presbyn. Clubs: Kansas City, Saddle and Sirloin (Kansas City); Montana, Green Meadow Country (Helena, Mont.), Home: 4618 Warwick Blvd Kansas City MO 64112 Office: Mid-Continent Nat Bank 4901 Main St Kansas City MO 64112

KOPPANYI, THEODORE educator; b. Gyöngyös, Hungary, Dec. 26, 1901; s. David and Gisella (Heller) K.; student Royal Hungarian Gymnasium, 1910-18, U. Budapest, 1918-20, U. of Vienna, 1920-23; Ph.D., U. of Vienna, 1923; m. Hermione Jane Bartels, May 27, 1928. Instr. in physiology, U. Chgo. Med. Sch., 1923-27; asst. prof. of pharmacology, Syracuse U., 1927-29; research asso. in pharmacology, Cornell U., 1929-30; prof. pharmacology, chmn. dept. pharmacology Georgetown U., 1930—; vis. prof. pharmacology Hebrew U., Jerusalem, 1959; cons. USAF; vis. scientist Nat. Heart Inst., NIH, Bethesda. Pres. II Latin-Am. Congress-Symposiun on Clin. Pharmacology. Recipient of Rask-ob award, 1957, Fulbright award, 1958. Fellow A.A.A.S. (council); mem. Washington Acad. Scis. Am. Soc. Zoölogists, Am. Physiol. Soc., Am. Soc. Pharmacology, Soc. for Exptl. Biology and Medicine, Argentine Med. Assn., Acad. Medicine (v.p. Washington 1956), Am. Assn. U. Profs. (mem. council). Sigma Xi, Alpha Omega Alpha. Democrat. Roman Catholic. Clubs: Quadrangle (Chgo.); Cosmos (Washington). Author: Modern Problems of Biology, 1925; Conquest of Life, 1930; Studies on Barbiturates, 1933- 54; Synergism and Antagonism of Drugs, 1938; co-author Experimental Pharmacodynamics, 1958. Reviser: Toxicology or the Effects of Poisons by Frank P. Underhill, 1936. Contbr. sci. jours. Home: 2712 Wisconsin Avenue Washington DC 20007

KOPPE, RICHARD, painter, sculptor; b. St. Paul, Mar. 4, 1916; s. Frederick Edward and Isabell Florence (Sandehn) K.; grad. (scholarship 1933-37), St. Paul Sch. Art, 1937; student (scholarship). New Bauhaus, Chgo., 1937-38; m. Catherine Louise Hinkle, June 25, 1955. Instr. aero. engring. U. Tex., 1944-45; mem. faculty Inst. Design, Ill. Inst. Tech., 1946-63, head visual design dept., 1949-61, asso. prof., 1953-63, head fine arts program, 1961-63; asso. prof. art U. Ill. at Chgo., 1963-65, prof. art, 1965—; numerous one man shows, 1936—, latest being Cliff Dwellers, Chgo., 1955, Gallery 4, Detroit, 1958, Feingarten Gallery, Chgo., 1957, Ill. Inst. Tech. (retrospective), 1961, Kalamazoo Inst. Arts, 1962, Main Street Gallery, Chgo., 1963, Mus. Contemporary Art, Chgo., 1970; group exhbns. include Art Inst. Chgo., Carnegie Inst., Met. Mus. Art, Whitney Mus. Art, Bklyn. Mus., U. Ill. at Urbana, Pa. Acad. Fine Arts, San Francisco Art Assn., Neb. Art Assn., Ill. State Fair, U. Minn., Denver Art Mus., Beaux Arts Palace, Paris, France, Nat. Acad. Design, Corcoran Gallery Art, St. Paul Sch. Art, Providence Art Club, St. Paul Art Center, Ill. State Mus., Springfield, Witte Meml. Mus., San Antonio. Wichita (Kan.) Art Mus., Tweed Gallery, Duluth, numerous travelling shows U. S. and Europe; rep. permanent collections Smith Coll., Ill. State Mus., U. Minn., Bklyn. Mus., Whitney Mus., Art Inst. Chgo., Ind. U., St. Paul Art Center, Kalamazoo Inst. Arts, Richard Koppe painting and manuscript collection Syracuse U., also high schs.; rep. numerous pvt. collections; commd. Hotel Sherman, Chgo., Robert Lederer, architect, Blanche Martin Assos., Chgo., Shaw, Metz & Dolio, architects, Andrew Toth, architect, also pvt. commns.; 50 Jahre Bauhaus exhibition Stuttgart, London, Amsterdam, Paris, Chgo., Toronto, Pasadena. Buenos Aires, Tokyo. Recipient Cahn prize Art Inst. of Chicago, 1948, Witkowsky prize, 1948, William and Bertha Clusnann prize, 1950, Pauline Palmer prize, 1960; 1st award Old Northwest Ty. Exhbn., 1950; Jule F. Brower prize Chgo. Artists Exhbn., 1958; Purchase award U. Minn., 1950, Bklyn. Mus., 1951; hon. mention Denver Art Mus., 1951, St. Paul Art Center, 1966; Merit award 21st N. Miss. Valley Artists Exhbn., 1968. Contbr. to publs in field. Home: 5256 North Rockwell Street Chicago IL 60625 Office; Dept Art Box 4348 Chicago IL 60680

KOPPELMANN, HERMAN HENRY, clergyman; b. Payette, Ida., Mar. 2, 1909; s. Henry H. and Elizabeth (Schlichting) K.; diploma Concordia Sem., St. Louis, 1932; D.D., Concordia Theol. Sem., Springfield, Ill., 1955; m. Lucille Marcella Pannier, July 14, 1935; children—David, Dal, William. Asst. pastor Trinity Luth. Ch., Springfield, 1932-37; pastor Salem Luth. Ch., Jacksonville, Ill., 1937-48; asst. exec. sec. Bd. World Missions, Luth. Ch.-Mo. Synod, 1948-60, exec. sec., 1960-66, asso. exec. sec. world areas, 1966—. Pres. Luth. Fgn. Missions Conf. N.Am., 1962-66; dir. Publicationes el Escudo and Stamps for Missions, 1967-70. Mem. Concordia Hist. Inst., Luth. Med. Missions Assn., Am. Bible Soc., Am. Topical Assn. Author: Our Obligation in the Christian Education of our Children, 1943; The Missouri Synod Enters Foreign Missions, 1953; The First Decade of Missouri Synod Missions in India, 1955. Contbr. various periodicals, mission encys. and resource books. Home: 2637 Winnebago St St Louis MO 63118 Office: 210 N Broadway St Louis MO 63102

KOPPER, ROBERT MARTIN, electric utility exec.; b. S. Bend, Ind., Sept. 16, 1908; s. August C. and Theresa (Lipetska) K.; B.C.S., Drake U., 1932; grad. utility exec. mgmt. course, U. Mich., 1953; m. Meredith Geyer, Oct. 14, 1934; childrenSandra (Mrs. Thomas Thrasher), Jocelyn (Mrs. Lloyd Mattock). With Ind. and Mich. Electric Co., 1926-, exec. v.p., 1968-; v.p., dir. Ind. Franklin Realty Co., Inc., S. Bend Mfg. Co., Inc., Twin Br. R.R. Co.; v.p. Franklin Real Estate Co.; dir. Am. Electric Power Service Corp., Ind. & Mich. Electric Co., Mich. Power Co., Mich. Gas Exploration Co., Three Rivers Devel. Corp. Mem. Ind. Electric Assn. (bd. dirs., past pres.), Ft. Wayne C. of C. (v.p., bd. dirs.), Ind. Soc. Chgo., Newcomen Soc., Chi Delta. Republican. Presbyn. Mason (Shriner), Elk. Clubs: Ft. Wayne Country; Hidden Valley (Graysburg, Mich.). Home: 2534 Ojibway Trail Fort Wayne IN 46807 Office: 2101 Spy Run Avenue Fort Wayne IN 46801

KOPPLE, ROBERT, lawyer; b. N.Y.C., Nov. 26, 1910; B.A., N.Y.U., 1932, J.D., 1934; m. Dorothy Stuhlbarg, July 22, 1944; childrenAnn Howard, Nancy Dunn. Admitted to N.Y. bar, 1934; practice of law, N.Y.C., 1934-39. Gen. mgr. Columbia Aircraft Products, Somerville, N.J., 1939-42; exec. v.p. Midtown Realty Owners Assn., Inc., N.Y.C., 1953-; pres. Exitolite Corp., N.Y.C., Quick Response Service, Inc., N.Y.C. Exec. v.p. Devel. Council, 1970—; Owners Com. on Electric Rates, N.Y.C., 1954—; mem. N.Y.C. Midtown Devel. Council, 1970—, organizer, 1st exec. v. p. N.Y. World's Fair Corp. 1958- 60; employer trustee Bldg. Service Welfare Fund, 1953—, Bldg. Service Pension N.Y. for Tercentenary Celebration, Fund, 1958—, Nat. BSEIU Pension Fund; 1968—; spl. adviser Mayor City N.Y. for Tercentenary Celebration, 1959-60; mem. N.Y. Am. Revolution Bicentennial Commn., 1968-. Mem. Nassau County Democratic Com., 1946-51, Nassau County candidate N.Y. State Senate, 1950. Served with Signal Corps, AUS, 1942-46; charge contract termination Gen. Electric Corp. Mem. Little Neck Bay Power Squadron (comdr.), U.S. Power Squadrons (rear comdr., nat. pub. relations officer), Am. Soc. Mil. Engrs., N.Y. State Bar Assn., Real Estate Bd. N.Y., Mutual Admiration Soc. N.Y. (pres.), Tau Delta Phi. Clubs: Sands Point Bath and Tennis, Luncheon, Rockefeller Center Luncheon, Penn Plaza Lunch, National Democratic. Home: 17 Greenway Roslyn NY 11576 Office: 450 7th Av New York City NY 10001

KOPROWSKI, HILARY, medical scientist; b. Warsaw, Poland, Dec. 5, 1916; s. Paul and Sarah (Berland) K.; B.A., Mikolaj Rej Gymnasium of Luth. Congregation, Warsaw, 1933; M.D., U. Warsaw, 1939; grad. Warsaw Conservatory Music and Santa Cecilia Acad., Rome; m. Dr. Irena Grasberg, July 14, 1938; childrenClaude Eugene, Christopher Dorian. Came to U.S., 1944, naturalized, 1950. Research asst. dept. gen. and exptl. pathology U. Warsaw, 1937-39; staff Yellow Fever Research Service, Rio de Janeiro, 1941-44; staff research div. Am. Cyanamid Co., 1944-46, asst. dir. viral and rickettsial research Lederle Lab., Pearl River, N.Y., 1946-57; dir. Wistar Inst., Phila., 1957-; prof. microbiology Grad. Sch. Arts and Scis., 1957; Wistar prof. of research medicine U. of Pa., 1957- -; research virus diseases, discover living virus vaccine against rabies, hog cholera, poliomyelitis; cons. WHO. Decorated Commandeur Ordre du Mérite pour la Recherche et l'Invention; Chevalier Order Royal De Lion, Belgium; Alvarenga prize. Coll. Physicians Phila., 1959; Alfred Jurzykowski Found Polish Millenium prize, 1966. Fellow N.Y. Acad. Medicine, N.Y. Acad. Scis. (pres. 1959; trustee 1960-), Am. Acad. Microbiology; mem. Am. Assn. Anatomists, Am. Soc. Microbiologists, Biochem. Soc. Eng., Am. Soc. Immunologists, Am. Soc. Tropical Medicine, Am. Assn. Cancer Research (dir. 1963-66), Am. Fedn. Clin. Research, Soc. Exptl. Biology and Medicine, Reticuloendothelial Soc. Asso. editor Virology, 1954-60, Jour. Bacteriology, 1955-59, Cancer Research, 1957- 62, Ergebnisse Der Mikrobiologie, 1965-, Folia Biologica, 1966-. Home: 334 Fairhill Road Wynnewood PA 19096 Office: Wistar Inst 36th and Spruce Streets Philadelphia PA 19104

KORANYI, ADAM, educator; b. Szeged, Hungary, July 13, 1932; s. Jeno and Vilma (Szigethy) K.; diploma U. Szeged, 1954; Ph.D., U. Chgo., 1959; m. Anna Eiben, Mar. 16, 1968; children—Peter, Daniel. Came to U.S., 1957, naturalized, 1963. Instr., Harvard, 1959-60; asst. prof. U. Cal., Berkeley, 1960-64; vis. asst. prof. Princeton, 1964-65; faculty Belfer Grad. Sch. Sci., Yeshiva U., N.Y.C., 1965—, prof. math., 1968—. Mem. Am. Math. Soc. Contbr. articles to profl. jours. Home: 517 Ridgeland Terrace Leonia NJ 07605 Office: Belfer Sch Yeshiva U New York City NY 10033

KORBEL, JOSEF, educator; b. Kysperk, Czechoslovakia, Sept. 20, 1909; s. Arnost and Olga (Ptackova) K.; J.D., Charles U., Prague, 1933; student Sorbonne, Paris 1928-29; m. Anna M. Spieglova, Apr. 20, 1935; childrenMadeleine Jana (Mrs. Joseph M.P. Albright), Anna Katherine (Mrs. G. Silva), John Joseph. Came to U.S., 1948, naturalized, 1957. With Czechoslovak Diplomatic Service, 1934-48, with Ministry Fgn. Affairs, Prague, 1934-36, press attache Legation, Belgrade, 1937-38, personal sec. to Jan Masaryk, London, 1939-40, head broadcasting dept. Czechoslovak Govt.-in-exile, London, 1940-45, chef de cabinet to Jan Masaryk, Prague, 1945, ambassador to Yugoslavia, Belgrade, 1945-48, mem. Czechoslovak Delegation to Paris Peace Conf., chmn. econ. com. for Balkan countries and Finland, 1946, mem., chmn. UN Commn. for Kashmir, 1948-49; prof. internat. relations, mem. staff Social Sci. Found., U. Denver, 1949-, dir. Social Sci. Found., 1959-, dean Grad. Sch. Internat, Studies, 1964-69, Andrew W. Mellon prof. internat. studies, 1969—; research fellow Russian Research Center, Harvard, 1957; sr. vis. fellow St. Anthony's Coll., Oxford, Eng., 1963; sr. research fellow European Inst., Columbia, 1968. Mem. Council Fgn. Relations, N.Y.C., Denver Com. Fgn. Relations. Served as lt. Czechoslovak Army, 1933-34. Recipient U. Denver Lectureship award for research, 1958. Mem. Am. Polit. Sci. Assn., Internat. Studies Assn., Am. Assn. Advancement Slavic Studies, Czechoslovak Soc. Arts and Scis. in Am., Phi Beta Kappa. Author: Tito's Communism, 1951; Danger in Kashmir, rev. edit., 1966; Communist Subversion of Czechoslovakia, 1959; Poland between East and West, 1963. Contbr. articles profl. jours. Home: 2314 South Madison Street Denver CO 80210

KORCHIN, SHELDON JEROME, educator; b. N.Y.C., Sept. 8, 1921; s. Solomon and Sally (Levine) K.; B.A. cum laude, Bklyn. Coll., 1943; M.A., Clark U., 1943; Ph.D., Harvard, 1946; m. Sylvia J. Brecher, June 16, 1942; childrenEllen, Jonathan, Marc. Research asst. N.Y. State Psychiat. Inst., 1940-42; teaching fellow Harvard, 1944-46; instr. Harvard, 1946-47; asst. chief clin. psychologist VA Mental Hygiene Clinic, Phila., 1947-50; instr. Princeton, 1947-48; dr. psychology lab. Michael Reese Hosp., also lectr. psychology U. Chgo., 1950-60; vis. scientist Nat. Inst. Mental Health, Bethesda, Md., 1959-60; Fulbright prof. U. Genoa, 1960-61; chief sect. stress Nat. Inst. Mental Health, 1961-63; prof., head psychology clinic U. Cal., 1963-. Cons. VA, Nat. Inst. Mental Health, State of Cal. Dept. Mental Health, U.S. Army Letterman Gen. Hosp. Mem. Am. Civil Liberties Union. Certified psychologist State of Cal. Diplomate Am. Bd. Examiners Profl. Psychology. Fellow Am. Psychol. Assn.; mem. Western Psychol. Assn., Am. Assn. U. Profs., A.A.A.S., Sigma Xi. Club: Sierra, Author: (with others) Anxiety and Stress, 1955. Contbr. articles profl. jours., chpts. in books. Home: 938 Santa Barbara Road Berkeley CA 94707

KORDA, REVA, (Mrs. William Korda), advt. exec.; b. N.Y.C., Dec. 24, 1926; d. Louis and Yetta (Sussman) Fine; B.A. magna cum laude, Hunter Coll., 1947; m. William Korda, Sept. 7, 1957; children—Joshua, Natasha. Copywriter Gimbels, N.Y.C., 1949-50, Macy's, N.Y.C., 1951-53; with Ogilvy & Mather, Inc., N.Y.C., 1953—, writer, 1953-62, sr. v.p., 1962—, creative dir., 1964—, also dir. Advt. dir. A.R.C. Fund Raising, N.Y.C., 1971. Mem. Phi Beta Kappa. Home: 271 Central Park West New York City NY 10024 Office: Ogilvy & Mather Inc 2 East 48th St New York City NY 10017

KOREE, JEAN ULYXES, indsl. engr.; b. Bucharest, Rumania, Mar. 12, 1894; ed. pvt. tutors, Bucharest and Berlin; m. Helen Moycah Brandow, Aug. 25, 1922; 1 dau., Moycah Bronson (Mrs. Antonio Poggi Cavaletti). Came to U.S., 1919, naturalized, 1943. Vice consul of Rumania, N.Y.C., 1919, consul, 1920, dep. high commr., 1921; pres. Glycerine Corp. of Am., Devel. Finance Corp. Pres. Jacques Loewe Research Found., 1945-59. Cofounder Soc. of Friends of Rumania; founder Mus. of City of N.Y. Decorated Knight Crown of Rumania, Knight Grand Cross of Charlemagne, Knight Grand Cross of St. Constantin and St. George, Knight Grand Cross of The Holy Sepulchre; Officer Carlos J. Finlay Nat. Order Merit (Cuba). Mem. Order of Red Cross of Constantine. Fellow N.Y. Acad. Scis.; mem. Acad. Polit. Sci., Nat. Inst. Social Scis. (life), Pan-Am. Soc. of U.S., Inc., Pilgrims of United States, Cuban C. of C. (life). Clubs: Church (N.Y.); Metropolitan; American (Havana), Mason (K.T.). Inventor numerous improvements on automatic firearms, airplanes, airplane equipment, other mech. devices; more recently invented and patented therapeutic preparations for intramuscular or subcutaneous injection and methods of making same. Home: 40 East 88th Street New York City NY 10028 Office: Bar Building 36 West 44th Street New York City NY 10036

KOREN, FINN, diplomat of Norway; b. Kristiansund, Norway, Sept. 13, 1918; s. Bjarne and Synnove (Lind) K.; Law Degree, U. Oslo, 1941; m. Synnove Onstad, Dec. 15, 1945; childrenElisabeth, Anita, Merete. Engaged in practice law, 1941-45; joined Norwegian Fgn. Service, 1945; vice consul, Shanghai, 1946-49; head Norwegian Govt. Representation, Peiping, 1950- 54; assigned Ministry Fgn. Affairs, 1955-59; chmn. Norwegian trade delegations to Israel, 1957, Germany, 1958, Denmark, 1958, 59, Sweden, 1958, 59; consul in Glasgow, Scotland, 1959-64; consul gen., Chgo., 1964- 69, San Francisco, 1969-. Decorated comdr. Royal Victorian Order (Great Britain); comdr. Order Maritime Merit (U.S.). Clubs: Norwegian Society, Norwegian Jockey, Oslo Golf (Oslo): Bohemian, World Trade (San Francisco). Home: 22 Normandie Terrace San Francisco CA 94115 Office: 244 California Street San Francisco CA 94111

KOREN, HENRY JOSEPH, educator, priest; b. Roermond, Netherlands, Dec. 30, 1912; s. Gerard Hubert and Anna Catherina (Smolenaers) K.; student Coll. Roermond, 1924- 30, Sem. of Gemert, 1932-35; S.T.B., Gregorian U., Rome, 1937, S.T.L., 1939; S.T.D., Cath. U. Am., 1941. Came to U.S., 1948, naturalized, 1954. Joined Holy Ghost Congregation, 1932; ordained priest Roman Cath. Ch., 1937; tchr. St. Mary's Coll., Trinidad, W.I., 1941-48; faculty Duquesne U., 1948-66, prof. philosophy, 1958-66, chmn. dept. philosophy, 1954- 65, chmn. dept. theology, 1962-66; prof. philosophy St. Leo (Fla.) Coll 1967—; ed. Duquesne Studies, 1951—. Author: Introduction to Science of Metaphysics, 1955; Introduction to Philosophy of Animate Nature, 1955; The Spiritans, 1958; Spiritual Writings of Claude Francis Poullart des Places, 1959; Introduction to Philosophy of Nature, 1960; Knaves or Knights?, 1962; Research in Philosophy, 1966; Marx and the Authentic Man, 1968; (with William A. Luijpen) A First Introduction to Existential Phenomenology, 1969, Religion and Atheism, 1971. Editor: Readings in Philosophy of Nature, 1959. Gen. editor: Spiritana Monumenta Historica, 1967. Address: P O Box 328 St Leo FL 33574

KOREN, HENRY LLOYD THORNELL, ret. fgn. service officer; b. Princeton, N.J., Mar. 13, 1911; s. William and Adelaide Louise (Thornell) K.; grad. Phillip Exeter Acad., 1929; A.B. cum laude, Princeton, 1933; m. Ely Virginia Cain, Aug. 30, 1941; children—Henry Lloyd Thornell, Anne Copeland Beale. With Ward Baking Co., 1933-35, Bank of N.Y., 1936-40; with CIA, 1947-48; joined U.S. Fgn. Service 1948, 2d sec., Port-au-Prince, Haiti, 1948-51. Bern, Switzerland, 1951- 52, counselor, Manila, P.I., 1958-61, dir. Office N.E. Asian Affairs, State Dept., 1961, Office S.E. Asian Affairs, 1962-64, A.E. and P. of U.S. to Republic of Congo, 1964-66, asst. dep. ambassador Am. embassy, Saigon, Vietnam, 1966-67, dep. for CORDS III Marine Amphibious Force Danang, Vietnam, 1967-68, fgn. service insp. Dept. State, Washington, 1968-69, polit. adviser to comdr. in chief Pacific, 1969-71; on leave to Army, Washington, 1953- 58, exec. asst. The White House, 1956-58. Served to col. F.A., AUS, 1940-46. Clubs: Chevy Chase (Md.); Army Navy Country (Arlington, Va.). Home: 4707 Reservoir Road N W Washington DC 20007

KOREVAAR, JACOB, educator; b. Netherlands, Jan. 25, 1923; s. Nijs and Cornelia Agatha (Wepster) K.; Ph.D. in Math., U. Leiden (Netherlands), 1949; m. Johanna Elzelina Ladestein, Aug. 4, 1950; children—Wilhelmina, Nicholas, Albert, Eric, David. Came to United States, 1953, naturalized, 1959. Research asso. Mathematics Center, Amsterdam, 1947-49; vis. lecturer Purdue U. 1949-51, U. Mich., summer 1950; prof. math. Inst. Tech., Delft, Netherlands, 1951-53; faculty U. Wis., 1953-64, prof. math., 1958-64, chmn. program applied math. and engring. physics, 1957-64; prof. math. U. Cal. San Diego at La Jolla, 1964—. Dir. research project in math. sponsored by Office Naval Research, Nat. Sci. Found. Mem. council Math. Center, Amsterdam, Recipient Reynolds award for excellence in teaching future engrs. U. Wis., 1958. Fellow A.A.A.S.; corr. Royal Netherlands Acad. Scis.; mem. Am. Math. Soc. (asso. editor proceedings 1957-59; chmn. summer inst. 1966), also Math. Assn. Am., Netherlands Math. Soc. Home: 1821 Torrey Pines Road La Jolla CA 92037

KORFF, SERGE ALEXANDER, physicist; b. Helsingfors, Finland, June 5, E1906; s. Baron Serge A. and Alletta (Van Reypen) K.; came to U.S., 1917; A.B., Princeton, 1928, A.M., 1929, Ph.D., 1931; m. Betty Hurd. Nat. Research fellow, Mt. Wilson Obs. and Cal. Inst. Tech., 1931-33; research fellow Cal. Inst. Tech., 1934-35; fellow Bartol Research Found., Swarthmore, Pa., 1937-40; research asso. Carnegie Instn., Washington, 1936-46, U. P.R., 1949-50; asst. prof. physics N.Y.U., 1941-44, asso. prof. 1944-46, prof. 1946-; nat. lectr. Sigma Xi, 1957; hon. prof. in cosmic radiation Universidad de San Andres, Bolivia, 1958; con. UN AEC, 1950-53; Sr. sci. adviser atomic energy div. UN, 1953-55. Leader cosmic ray expdn. to Mexico and Peru, 1934-36, to P. R. 1948-50; asso. astronomer Eclipse expdn. to Peru, 1937; adviser U.S. Antarctic Service expdn., 1939-41; wartime supr. physics research N.Y.U. Recipient O.S.R.D. citation; decorated Chevalier of the Legion of Honor, 1952; Commendatore Order of Cyprus and Jerusalem, 1952. Del. 5th South Am. Congress of Chemistry, Lima, Peru, 1951, 6th Congress of Chem., Caracas, Venezuela, 1955; vice chmn. Cosmic Ray Tech. Panel, U.S. Nat. Commn. for Internat. Geophys. Year, also U.S. del. to meetings in Rome, 1954, Mexico, 1955, Rio de Janeiro, 1956; mem. Comn. on High Altitude Research Stas. and editor of reports; hon. mem. faculty, U. Chile, 1951. Recipient Pregel prize N.Y. Acad. Scis., 1955; Curie medal Union Internat. Contre le Cancer, 1957; decorated Comdr. Order of Merit, 1957; Comdr. Order of St. Denis, 1968. Fellow Am. Phys. Soc., Royal Geog. Soc. (life), N.Y. Acad. Scis. (life; v.p. 1948-49 pres. elect. 1970—), A.A.A.S. (life), Am. Geog. Soc. (council mem. Lima (Peru) Geog. Soc. (hon.), Am. Astron. Soc., Peruvian Chem. Soc. (corr.), Am. Geophys. Union (life), Phi Beta Kappa, Sigma Xi (pres., v.p. N. Y. U. chpt. 1946-50), Sigma Pi Sigma (hon. mem.) Clubs: The Explorers (pres., 1955-58, dir., Century, Cosmos (Washington); Princeton (N.Y.). Author: Electron and Nuclear Counters, 1945; Electron and Nuclear Physics (with J. B. Hoag), 1947; also numerous articles in tech. jours. Editorial bd. Rev. of Sci. Instruments, 1945-51; Explorers Jour. since 1946. Home: 1088 Park Avenue New York City NY 10028

KORHOLZ, HERBERT FREDERICK, corp. exec.; b. Rees-Rhein, Holland, Apr. 9, 1913; s. Leo and Johanna (von Bering) K.; grad. Ecole Libre des Scis. Politiques U., Paris, France, 1931; post grad. student econs., Cambridge (Eng.) U., 1933; m. Martha Finneran, 1936; children—Anne (Mrs. Korholz Teel), Patricia (Mrs. Wedemeyer), Mary Lou (Mrs. Michael Kestler). Came to U.S., 1936, naturalized, 1941. Pres. Better Industries, Inc., Pueblo, Colo., 1951-63, Am. Gypsum Co., Albuquerque, 1963-65; chmn. bd. Treesdale Labs., Inc., Saxonburg, Pa., 1963-64; chmn. bd. chief exec. officer Susquehanna Corp., 1965-67, pres., chmn. exec. com., 1967-70, pres., chief exec. officer, chmn. exec. com., 1970—; pres., chief exec. officer, chmn. exec. com. Pan Am. Sulphur Co., Houston, 1970-71; dir. Azufrera Panamericana, S.A., Fertilizantes Fosfatados Mexicanos, S.A. Mem. Nat. Indsl. Conf. Bd. Clubs: Congressional Country (Washington); Garden of the Gods (Colorado Springs, Colo.); Acapulco (Mexico) Yacht. Home: 2510 Virginia Av NW Washington DC 20037 Office: Susquehanna Corp Shirley Hwy at Edsall Rd Alexandria VA 22314

KORLE, SINAN ARIF, UN officer; b. Istanbul, Turkey, Apr 4, 1914; s. Arif E. and Adile (Amir) K.; B.A., Robert Coll., Istanbul, 1936; M.A., U. Ia., 1939; m. Sara Ertugrul, July 23, 1949. Reporter, Tan, Istanbul, 1940-43; corr. Vatan, Istanbul, 1943-45, editor, 1945-51; information officer UN, 1951- 54; commentator Radio Istanbul, 1943-51; dir. UN Information Center, Athens, 1954-59, Teheran,

1959-60; UN Observer, Togo, 1960—; information officer, Congo, 1960-62; UN dep. chief protocol, 1962-68, chief protocol, 1968-. Res. officer Turkish Army. Author articles, short stories, poems, radio and film scripts, sketches. Home: 411 E 53d St New York City NY 10022 Office: United Nations New York City NY 10017

KORMAN, HARVEY HERSCHEL, actor; b. Chgo., Feb. 15, 1927; s. Cyril Raymond and Ellen (Blecher) K.; student Goodman Theatre, 1946-50; m. Donna Ehlert Aug. 27, 1960; children—Maria Ellen, Christopher Peter. Actor TV series The Danny Kaye Show, 1963-67, Carol Burnett Show, 1967—. Bd. dirs. Los Angeles Psychiat. Service. Served with USNR, 1945-46. Recipient 2 Emmy awards for Best Variety Performer. Home: 424 S Plymouth Blvd Los Angeles CA 90020 Office: 7800 Beverly Blvd Los Angeles CA

KORMANYOS, STEPHEN WILLIAM, physicist; b. Cleve., June 4, 1939; s. Stephen Frank and Rose (Szorady) K.; B.S., U. Toledo, 1962; M.S., U. Mich., 1963, Ph.D., 1966; m. Albina Joyce Macris, June 27, 1964; children—Stephen William, Brian Kenneth, Christopher Michael Kormanyos. With Aerospace Systems div. Bendix Corp., Ann Arbor, Mich., 1966—, now new product devel. mgr. Mem. Am. Phys. Soc. Home: 3221 Farmbrook Ct Ann Arbor MI 48104 Office: 3300 Plymouth Rd Ann Arbor MI 48107

KORN, BERTRAM WALLACE, rabbi, historian; b. Phila., Oct. 6, 1918; s. Manuel and Blanche (Bergman) K.; student U. Pa., 1935-36; A.B. with honors, U. Cin., 1939; rabbi, M.H.L., Hebrew Union Coll., 1943, fellow, 1946-49, D.H.L., 1949, D.D., 1968; LL.D., Temple U., 1957; D.Litt., Delaware Valley Coll., 1967; children—Judith Carole, Bertram Wallace; m. Rita Packman Dogole, Feb. 9, 1970. Ordained rabbi, 1943; rabbi, Govt. St. Temple, Mobile, 1943-44; asst. prof. Am. Jewish history Hebrew Union Coll., 1948-49; sr. rabbi Reform Congregation Keneseth Israel, Phila., 1949—; vis. prof. Am. Jewish history Hebrew Union Coll., Jewish Inst. Religion, N.Y.C., 1962—, Dropsie U., 1969—. Mem. Commn. Jewish Chaplaincy Jewish Welfare Bd.; v.p. Jewish Hist. Commn. of Civil War Centennial, 1961-65; adv. bd. Fed. Civil War Centennial Commn., 1961- 65; mem. Pres.'s Commn. on Observance of 25th Anniversary at UN, 1970-71; past mem. com. Jewish Americana, B'nai B'rith; past v.p. Phila Bd. Rabbis; past grand chaplain Pa. Grand Lodge Masons; chaplain Navy League of U.S., 1963-65; chmn. com. contemporaneous hist. Central Conf. Am. Rabbis, 1952-58, chmn. com. on chaplaincy, 1965-69, mem. exec. bd., 1969-71. Trustee Delaware Valley Coll., Pep Boys Ednl. Found.; bd. govs. Reconstructionist Rabbinical Coll., bd. dirs. Fedn. Jewish Agencies, Phila.; mem. bd. Chamber Symphony Phila. (past pres.). Served as chaplain USNR, 1944-46; capt. Res., 1963, Elected to Order of Anthony Wayne, Valley Forge Mil. Acad., 1969. Mem. Am.; Ill., Am. Jewish (past pres.) hist. assns., Orgn. Am. Historians, Jewish Publ. Soc. Am. (publ. com.), Chapel of Four Chaplains Phila. (life), Am. Legion (past dept. chaplain Pa.), Alumni Assn. Hebrew Union Coll. Jewish Inst. Religion (past pres.), Jewish Chaplains Assn. U.S. (pres. 1967-69), Am. Antiquarian Soc. (councillor 1969—). Author: American Jewry and the Civil War, 1951; Jewish Roots in Am., 1953; Eventful Years and Experiences, 1954; Carvalho's Incidents of Travel and Adventure, 1955; The American Reaction to the Mortara Case, 1957; Handbooks for Naval Reserve Chaplains, 1959; Benjamin Levy: New Orleans Printer & Publisher, 1961; Jews & Negro Slavery in the Old South, 1962. Editor Central Conf. Am. Rabbis Yearbook, 1953-54; 75th Anniversary History, Central Conf. Am. Rabbis, 1965 (exec. bd. 1969—) Early Jews of New Orleans, 1969 (Merit award Am. Assn. For State and Local History, 1970); The Jews of Mobile, Alabama, 1763-1841, 1970. Coeditor: Letters of Baron Corvo to Leonard Moore, 1960. Editorial adv. com. Civil War History, 1955-60, Jewish Digest, Jewish Social Studies; contbg. ed. Phila. Jewish Exponent, 1958-61. Office: Reform Congregation Keneseth Israel York Road and Township Line Elkins Park PA 19117

KORN, DAVID, educator; b. Kolbuszowa, Poland, Apr. 27, 1934; s. Joseph and Sunia (Neiss) K.; came to U.S., 1950, naturalized, 1954; student Bklyn. Coll., 1955-56; B.S. Georgetown U., 1958, M.S., 1960, Ph.D. (Nat. Def. Edn. Act fellow), 1964; m. Maria Orgel, June 25, 1961; children—Joseph Mark, Monique Diane. Asst. prof., dir. lang. labs. Coll. William and Mary, Norfolk, Va., 1959-61; research asso. Machine Translation Computer, Georgetown U., 1956-62; chmn. humanities div. Howard U., 1962—, prof., chmn. German-Russian dept., 1967—. Lectr., Fgn. Service Inst., Dept. State; cons. on Russian textbooks U.S. Armed Forces Inst.; asso. dir. Council on Internat. Student Ednl. Exchange in USSR, 1968. Bd. dirs. Jewish Social Service Agy. Served to 2d lt. AUS 1953-55. Recipient Key to City Norfolk. Mem. Modern Lang. Assn., Linguistic Soc. Am., Am. Assn. Tchrs. Slavic and East European Langs. (chpt. pres.), Georgetown U. Alumni Orgn. (gov., mem. exec. com., v.p. for Sch. Langs. and Linguistics). Mem. B'nai B'rith. Author various machine translations in field; contbr. articles and book revs. to profl. jours. Home: 2932 Davenport St N W Washington DC 20008

KORN, DAVID, pathologist; b. Providence, Mar. 5, 1933; s. Solomon and Claire (Liebman) K.; B.A., Harvard, 1954, M.D., 1959; m. Phoebe Richter, June 9, 1955; children-Michael Philip, Stephen James, Daniel Clair. Intern Mass. Gen. Hosp., Boston, 1959-60, 1960-61; research asso., 1961-63; mem. staff Lab. Biochem. Pharmacology, also asst. pathologist NIH, Bethesda, Md., 1963-68; prof., chmn. dept. pathology, also prof. Sch. Medicine, Stanford (Cal.), 1968—; physician-in-chief, pathology, Stanford U. Hosp., 1968—; cons. pathology Palo Alto VA Hosp., 1968—; sr. surgeon USPHS, 1961-66. Recipient Young Scientist award Md. Acad. Sci., 1967. Mem. Am. Soc. Biol. Chemists, Am. Soc. Exptl. Pathology, Am. Soc. Cell Biology, Internat. Acad. Pathology, Am. Soc. Microbiology, N.Y. Acad. Sci., A.A.A.S. Editorial bd. Human Pathology, 1969—. Home: 900 Lathrop Dr Stanford CA 94305

KORN, PETER GEORGE, ins. exec.; b. Kalispell, Mont., Mar. 7, 1903; s. Daniel and Theresa (Calary) K.; Ph.B., U. Chgo.; m. Mary Elizabeth Bulfer, Aug. 14, 1926; 1 dau., Elizabeth A. Chief claim adjuster Continental Casualty Co., 1924- 41; exec. v.p. Nat. Casualty Co., 1941-65, pres., 1965—, also dir. Home: 2615 Golfview Dr Troy MI 48084 Office: Griswold Bldg Detroit MI 40226

KORN, PHILIP A., food co. exec.; b. N.Y.C., Nov. 17, 1930; s. Morris and Sadie (Albrecht) K.; B.B.A., Coll. City N.Y., 1951; M.B.A., N.Y.U., 1956; m. Kay Susan Pollock, Dec. 24, 1950; children—Abner Paul, Ann Millicent. Mgr. financial analysis Gen. Foods Corp., White Plains, N.Y., 1961-62, asso. product mgr. Post div., 1965-67, sales devel. mgr. Post div., 1967-68, region mgr., ...-69, adminstv. asst. to pres., 1969, field sales mgr. Post. div., ... nat. sales mgr., 1970, v.p., 1970—, also exec. v.p. Burger ... Inc., Indpls., 1970-71, pres., 1971—. Served as cpl., ...US, 1952-54. Club: Woodland Country (Indpls.). ...t Dr Carmel IN 46032 Office: 1348 W 16th St ...

...ony condr.; b. N.Y.C.; A.B., Princeton, ...ent Juilliard Grad. Sch., 1937-39; m. ...Mrs. Peter G. Lehman), Nov. 14, ...ey Karp), Wendy (Mrs. Stephen ...Symphony Orch. (clarinet), Washington, 1939-40; asst. condr., Nat. Orchestral Assn., N.Y., 1940-42; founded Alumni Orch. of Nat. Orchestral Assn., conducted it in N.Y. concert and R.C.A. Victor record albums, 1941; fellowship in conducting with Serge Koussevitzky, 1941; asst. condr. N.Y. City (Center) Opera Co., 1945-46; condr. Original Ballet Russe, 1947; mus. dir. Orch. of Am., 1959-63; guest condr. Boston Pops Orch., Lewisohn Stadium Concerts, Czech. Philharmonic (Prague), philharmonic orchs. of Stockholm, Copenhagen and Oslo, Conservatoire Orch. of Paris, Carnegie Hall Pops London Symphony Orch., etc. 1945-50, New Orleans summer concerts 1949, NBC Symphony, Buffalo Philharmonic Orch., 1951-52, Lena concerts, also Montreal summer concerts; condr. Baton Rouge Symphony Orch. 1950-51; Cin. Symphony Orch., 1956, Asahi Broadcasting Symphony Orch. Japan, 1957, Phila. Dell Concerts, Kol Yisroel, Israel, Haifa Symphony, Israel, 1958, Carl Schurz Park concerts, 1962; condr. on records, notably Am. Music. Mem. faculty New York Coll; Music, 1965—. Mem. exec. com. Nat. Music Council; pres. Am. Council Judaism, 1966—. Chmn. Music School Com. Henry St. Settlement. Bd. dirs. Hosp. for Joint Diseases, N.Y.C., Musicians Found.; bd. govs. Bohemians; trustee Temple Emanu-El, N.Y. Served as lt., USCG, 1942-45. Author: Orchestral Accents. Clubs: Lotos; Princeton (N.Y.C.); Century Country; Harmonie. Address: 898 Park Avenue New York City NY 10021

KORN, ROY JOSEPH, educator, physician; b. Chgo., July 25, 1920; s. Isaac Emanuel and Anna Amanda (Anderson) K.; B.S., Northwestern U., 1942, M.D., 1946; m. Elsie Ann Kral, Jan. 15, 1955; children—Steven Arthur, Roy Joseph, Michael R., Patricia Ann. Intern, Wesley Meml. Hosp., Chgo., 1945-46; resident VA Hosp., Hines, Ill., 1949-51; chief med. service VA West Side Hosp., Chgo., 1958-62; adv. prof. faculty medicine Chiengmai (Thailand) U., 1962-64; asso. prof. U. Ill. Med. Sch., Chgo., 1959-64; prof. Chgo. Med. Sch., 1964; prof. medicine U. Ind. Med. Sch., 1965—; chief staff VA Hosp., Indpls., 1965—. Served to capt. M.C., AUS, 1946-48. Diplomate Am. Bd. Internal Medicine. Fellow A.C.P.; mem. Inst. Medicine Chgo., Chgo. Soc. Internal Medicine. Home: 6208 Spring Mill Rd Indianapolis IN 46260

KORNBERG, ARTHUR, biochemist; b. Bklyn., Mar. 3, 1918; s. Joseph and Lena (Katz) K.; B.S., Coll. City of N.Y. (N.Y. State scholarship), 1937; M.D., U. Rochester (Buswell scholarship), 1941; m. Sylvy R. Levy, Nov. 21, 1943; children—Roger, Thomas Bill, Kenneth Andrew. Intern medicine Strong Meml. Hosp., Rochester, N.Y., 1941-42; commd. officer, U.S.P.H.S., 1942, advanced through grades to med. dir., 1951; staff mem. Nat. Inst. Health, Bethesda, Md., 1942-52, nutrition sect., div. physiology, 1942- 45, chief sect. enzymes and metabolism, 1947-52; guest research worker depts. chemistry and pharmacology coll. medicine, N.Y.U., 1946, dept. biol. chemistry, med. sch., Washington U., 1947, dept. plant biochemistry U. Cal., 1951; formerly prof., head dept. microbiology, med. sch. Washington U.; formerly prof., head dept. biochemistry Stanford U. Served lt. (j.g.), med. officer, U.S. Coast Guard, 1942. Recipient Paul-Lewis award in enzyme chemistry, 1951; co-recipient of Nobel prize in medicine, 1959. Mem. Am. Soc. Biol. Chemists, Am. Chem. Soc., Harvey Soc., Am. Soc. Clin. Investigation, Nat. Inst. Health (Biochemistry study sect.), Nat. Acad. Scis., Am. Philos. Soc., Sigma Xi, Phi Beta Kappa, Alpha Omega Alpha. Author sci. articles. Home: 365 Golden Oak Dr Alpine Hills Portola Valley CA 94025

KORNBERG, WARREN STANLEY, journalist; b. N.Y.C., June 21, 1927; s. Murray and Helen (Blumberg) K.; B.A., Adelphi Coll., 1950; M.A., Columbia, 1952; postgrad. U. Mo., 1954- 55; m. Felice Sher, June 15, 1952; children-Lisa, Jena, Eva. Tchr. Hoffman Sch., Riverdale, N.Y., 1950-51, Bentley Sch., N.Y.C., 1951-52, Lynbrook, N.Y., 1952-54; reporter Fall River (Mass.) Herald News, 1955- 58; sci. editor Boston Herald, 1958-59; sci. reporter Washington Post, 1960-61; Washington corr.-sci. editor McGraw Hill Publs., Washington, 1962-66; editor Sci. News, Sci. News Yearbook, Sci. Service, Washington, 1966-70; dir. publns. Population Reference Bur., writer syndicated column Warren Kornberg of Science, 1969. Bd. dirs. Neighbors, Inc., Washington, 1967. Served with USNR, 1945-46. Recipient Jesse H. Neal editorial achievement award, 1965; Washington Newspaper Guild front page award, 1961. Mem. Nat. Assn. Sci. Writers, Nat. Press Club. Home: 11019 Kenilworth Av Garrett Park MD 20766 Office: 1755 Massachesetts Av NW Washington DC 20036

KORNEGAY, HORACE ROBINSON, orgn. exec., former congressman; b. Asheville, N.C., Mar 12, 1924; s. Marvin Earl and Blanche Person (Robinson) K.; B.S., Wake Forest Coll., 1947, LL.B., 1949; m. Annie Ben Beale, Mar. 25, 1950; childrenHorace Robinson, Kathryn Elder, Martha Beale. Admitted to N.C. bar, 1949, since practiced in Greensboro; admitted to U.S. Supreme Ct.; asst. solicitor Superior Ct. Guilford County, 1951-53; dist. solicitor 12th Solicitorial Dist., 1955-60; mem. 87th-90th Congresses 6th Dist. N.C.; v.p., counsel The Tobacco Inst., Washington, 1969-70, pres., exec. dir., 1970—. Mem. bd. visitors sch. of law Wake Forest U. Pres. Guilford Young Democratic Club, 1952, N.C. Young Dem. Clubs, 1953-54. Served with AUS, 1943-46. Decorated Purple Heart, Bronze Star medal, Combat Infantryman's Badge. Mem. Am., Fed., N.C., Greensboro bar assns., Am. Judicature Soc., Wake Forest Univ. Lawyers Alumni Assn. (past pres.), Am. Legion, V.F.W., Amvets, Brit. Legion (hon.), Alpha Sigma Phi, Phi Delta Phi, Omicron Delta Kappa. Methodist (past ofcl. bd.). Mason (Shriner). Clubs: Rotary, Congressional Country (Washington). Home: 7709 Charleston Dr Bethesda MD 20034 Office: 1776 K Street NW Washington DC 20006

KORNEL, LUDWIG, educator, physician; b. Jaslo, Poland, Feb. 27, 1923; s. Ezriel Edward and Ernestine (Karpf) K.; student U. Kazan Med. Inst., USSR, 1943-45; M.D., Wroclaw Med. Acad., Breslau, Poland, 1950; Ph.D., U. Birmingham, Eng., 1958; m. Esther Muller, May 27, 1952; children—Ezriel Edward, Amiel Mark. Came to U.S., 1958, naturalized, 1970. Intern, Univ. Hosp., Breslau, Poland, 1949-50, Hadassah-Hebrew U. Hosp., Jerusalem, 1950-51; resident medicine Hadassah-Hebrew U. Hosp., 1952-55; Brit. Council scholar, Univ. research fellow endocrinology U. Birmingham (Eng.), 1955-57, lectr. medicine, 1956-57; fellow endocrinology U. Ala. Med. Center, 1958-59, asst. prof., asso. prof., prof. medicine, 1961-67, dir. steroid sect., 1962-67, asso. prof. biochemistry, 1965-67; postdoctoral trainee in steroid biochemistry U. Utah, 1959-61; prof. medicine U. Ill. Coll. Medicine, Chgo., 1967—; attending physician, dir. steroid unit Presbyn.-St. Lukes Hosp., Chgo., 1967—, asso. biochemist, 1967-70, sr. biochemist on sci. staff, 1970—; prof. medicine and biochemistry Rush Med. Coll., Rush-Presbyn.-St. Lukes Med. Center, 1970—; hon. guest lectr. Polish Acad. Sci., Warsaw, 1965. Recipient Physicians Recognition award A.M.A., 1969, Outstanding New Citizen award Citizenship Council Met. Chgo., 1970. Fellow Am. Coll. Clin. Pharmacology and Chemotherapy; mem. A.M.A., Endocrine Soc., Am. Fedn. for Clin. Research, N.Y. Acad. Scis., Am. Physiol. Soc., Central Soc. for Clin. Research, A.A.A.S., Am. Acad. Polit. and Social Scis., Am. Assn. U. Profs., Sigma Xi. Contbr. articles profl. jours. Home: 6757 N LeRoy Av Lincolnwood IL 60646 Office: 1753 W Congress Pkwy Chicago IL 60612

KORNET, FRED, Jr., army officer; b. Wortendyke, N.J., Oct. 2, 1919; s. Fred and Adrianna (Roetman) K.; B.S. in Chem. Engring., Lehigh U., 1940; M.B.A., U. Chgo., 1957; m. Lois Jane Esau, June 20, 1942; children—Kathleen Jane (Mrs. Larry L. Johnson), Christine Anne. Textile mgr. Laros Textiles Corp., Bethlehem, Pa., 1945-50; commd. 2d lt. U.S. Army, 1941, advanced through grades to maj. gen., 1970; assigned U.S. and ETO, 1941-45; battalion S-3 and battalion exec. officer 2d Armored Cav. Regt., 1950-52; exec. officer 85th Ordnance Battalion, 1952-53; with prodn. dept. Watertown (Mass.) Arsenal, 1953-55; with indsl. div. Office Chief Ordnance, 1957-61; student Army War Coll., 1961-62; dep. asst. chief staff logistics 7th Logistical Command, Korea, 1962-63; assigned combat devel. command Inst. Advanced Studies, 1963-65; comdg. officer Watervliet (N.Y.) Arsenal, 1965-67; dir. ammunition Dept. Army, 1967-69, asst. dep. chief staff logistics (programs and budget), 1969—. Decorated Bronze Star, Army Commendation medal. Mem. Am. Ordnance Assn. Home: 2831 Beechwood Circle Arlington VA 22207 Office: The Pentagon Washington DC 20310

KORNFELD, JULIAN POTASH, lawyer; b. Dallas, May 1, 1934; s. Abraham L. and Abbie (Potash) K.; B.B.A., Tex. U., 1955, LL.B., 1957; LL.M. in Taxation, N.Y.U., 1962; m. Phyllis Eileen Mashbit, Aug. 16, 1959; children—Jill, Nancy. Admitted to Tex. bar, 1958, Okla. bar, 1963; practice in El Paso, 1959-61, Oklahoma City, 1962—; mem. firm Potash, Cameron, Bernat & Studdard, 1959-61, Andrews, Mosburg, Davis, Elam, Legg & Kornfeld, 1962—. Served to 1st lt., Q.M.C., AUS, 1957-59. Mem. Am., Okla., Tex. bar assns. Home: 3404 Partridge Rd Oklahoma City OK 73120 Office: United Founders Tower Oklahoma City OK 73112

KORNFELD, MURRAY, assn. exec.; m. Julia Hook; 1 son, Leonard Bertram. Founder, mng. editor, Diseases of the Chest since 1935, Diseases of the Nervous System, 1940-43, Diseases of the Eye, Ear, Nose and Throat, 1941-43. Founder, exec. trustee Am. Coll. of Chest Physicians, 1935-. Organized Internat. Congresses on Diseases of Chest. Recipient Am. Coll. Chest Physicians medal for meritorious achievement, 1959; medal Soviet Acad. Surgery, Moscow, 1966; medal, Nat. Order Merit, Republic Ecuador, 1967. Hon. fellow Am. Coll. Chest Physicians; mem. Asso. Editors of Tb Publs. (past presl; mem. exec. bd.), Med. Soc. Execs. Conf., Pan Am. Council, Counc Internat. Affairs, Am. Acad. Polit. and Social Sci. Certificates of merit Argentina, Brazil, Chile, Cuba, Ecuador, Germany, Greece, Italy, Mexico, Panama, Peru, Portugal, Spain, Uruguay, Korea, Japan, Thailand, Philippines, Hong Kong. Clubs: Horse Shoe (Eng.); Rotary. Home: 1350 Lake Shore Drive Chicago IL 60610 Office: 112 East Chestnut Street Chicago IL 60611

KORNYLJAK, PLATON, bishop; b. Stebni, Ukraine, Sept. 20, 1920; s. Volodyslau and Eugenia (Gribowsky) K.; D.Th., U. Rome (Italy), 1946, D. Ph., 1948. Ordained priest Roman Catholic Ch., 1945; asst. priest Olyphanot, Pa., 1948—, Ukranian Cathedral, Phila., 1948-52; sec. to bishop Ukranian Cath. Diocese U.S., Phila., 1949-52, also vice chancellor Ukranian Cath. Diocese U.S., 1949-52, chancellor, 1952-59; bishop for Ukranian Catholics in Germany, Munich, 1959—. Mem. theol. com. Vatican Council II, 1960—. Author: Sancti Augustini de efficacitate Sacramentorm doctrina contra Donastristas, 1953; La dialettica esistenziale del divino e dell'umano secondo Nicolo Berdiaeff, 1948. Address: Schönbergstrasse 9 Munich 86 Germany

KOROMZAY, DENES K., violist; b. Budapest, Hungary, May 18, 1913; s. Frederic and Elisabeth (Wittchen) K.; master diploma violin, Royal Franz Liszt Acad. Music, Budapest, 1930, degree composition and conducting 1931; masters course, Hockschule für Musik, Berlin, Germany, 1933-34; m. Eva Tormay, June 10, 1939; children—Dennis, Valentine. Naturalized U.S. citizen, 1960. Debut, Budapest Acad. Music, 1931; asst. concert-master Budapest Concert Orch., 1932-33; founder-mem. Hungarian String Quartet, 1935—; vis. prof., artist in residence U. So. Cal., 1950-52, Mills Coll., Oakland, Cal., 1950-52, U. Ore., 1956-57, U. Colo., 1961—. Home: 711 Lincoln Place Boulder CO 80302 Office: care Colbert Mgmt 850 7th Av New York City NY 10019

KORP, ANDREAS, coop. exec.; b. Graz, Austria, May 15, 1897; s. Andreas and Josephine (Froehlich) K.; ed. U. Graz, 1933. Sec., Coop. Union, 1923-26, mgr., 1926-33, dir., 1933-45; dir. gen. Coop. Wholesale Soc. Vienna, 1945-59; pres. Consumers Coop. Union of Austria, Vienna; minister of food, 1945; state sec. Ministry of Interior, 1952-53; mem. bd. Austrian Nat. Bank, 1946—, dep. gov., 1955—. Sr. vice chmn. Milk-Marketing Bd., 1945—. Home: 16 Matrasgasse 1130 Vienna Austria Office: 19 Theobaldgasse 1060 Vienna Austria

KORRY, EDWARD MALCOLM, U.S. ambassador; b. N.Y.C., Jan. 7, 1922; s. Samuel and Gertrude (Struhmeyer) K.; B.A., Washington and Lee U., 1942; grad. Advanced Mgmt. Program, Harvard, 1960; m. Patricia McCarthy, July 7, 1950; children—Patricia, Edward, Deborah, Alexandra. With NBC, 1941-43; fgn. corr. U.P., 1944-54; European editor Cowles Mags. and Broadcasting, Inc., 1954-60, asst. to pres., 1960-62; U.S. ambassador to Ethiopia, 1963-67, Chile, 1967—. Recipient citation distinguished fgn. reporting Overseas Press Club, 1958; Page One award mag. writing, 1958. Mem. Harvard Advanced Mgmt. Assn., Phi Beta Kappa. Rotarian. Club: Harvard Business (N.Y.C.). Author Korry Report on African devel. for Pres. Johnson. Address: American Embassy Santiago Chile

KORSAH-DICK, ANTHONY KOFI, diplomat of Ghana; b. Cape Coast, Ghana, Feb. 26, 1938; s. Augustus and Rosalind (Korsah) Dick; B.A., U. Ghana, 1962; diploma Inst. Pub. Adminstrn., London, 1963; m. Juliana Ashittey, Jan. 15, 1965; children—Tony Fifi, Augustus Jojo, David Yoku, James Edward, Ato Kwamena. Tchr. Adisadel Secondary Sch., 1959; asst. sec. Ministry of Fgn. Affairs, Accra, 1962-64; head chancery/charge d'affaires Ghana embassy, Havana, Cuba, 1965-66; charge d'affaires Ghana embassy, Algiers, 1966-67; desk officer for OAU and North Africa for Ministry of Fgn. Affairs, 1968-70; 1st sec. embassy Ghana, Washington, 1970—. Mem. sec. Ghana/Ivory Coast Border Demarcation Commn., 1968-70. Home: 6400 Redwing Rd Bethesda MD 20034 Office: 2460 16th St NW Washington DC 20009

KORSAN, PETER J., ins. co. exec.; b. Des Moines, 1915; LL.B., John Marshall Law Sch 1939. Sec., v.p. dir., gen. counsel Reliance Ins. Co., dir.; v.p., sec., gen. counsel, dir. Planet Ins. Co.; sec. Reliance Standard Life Ins. Co.; asst. sec. Gen. Casualty Co. Wis., Regent Ins. Co. Home: 32 Todmorden Dr Wallingford PA 19086 Office: 4 Penn Center Plaza Philadelphia PA 19103

KORSON, JAY HENRY, educator, sociologist; b. Phila., Jan. 9, 1910; s. Morris and Sophia (Jacobs) K.; B.S., Villanova U., 1931; M.A., Yale, 1942, Ph.D., 1947; m. Abigail Adams Scott, July 28, 1939; 1 son, Thomas Eliot. Instr., N.Y.U., 1941-42, Bowdoin Coll., 1942-44; mem. faculty U. Mass., 1944-, prof. sociology, 1948-, head dept. sociology and anthropology, 1950-66; vis. prof. sociology Mt. Holyoke Coll., 1950-51, 61; vis. prof. sociology Asia Found. fellow Kwansei Gakuin U., Japan, 1957; Fulbright lectr. U. Karachi (Pakistan), 1964-65. Fellow Am. Sociol. Assn., A.A.A.S.; mem. Eastern Sociol. Soc., Assn. Asian Studies. Clubs: Chocorua (N.H.) Mountain. Home: 55 Pokeberry Ridge Amherst MA 01002

KORSON, SELIG MORLEY, hosp. adminstr.; b. Bklyn., Nov. 28 1910; s. Joseph and Rose (Lieb) K.; A.B., Cornell U., 1932; M.D., Eclectic Med. Coll., 1936; m. Beatrice Gunner Goldman, Nov. 30, 1941; children—Eileen, Jane, Cathy. Intern Mercy Hosp., Wilkes-Barre, Pa., 1936-37; gen. practice medicine, Wilkes- Barre, 1937-42; asst. physician Grafton (Mass.) State Hosp., 1946, sr. physician, 1947, asst. supt., 1948; chief grade psychiatrist VA Hosp., Northampton, Mass., 1949-55, Bay Pines, Fla., 1955-58; supt. Mental Health Inst., Independence, Ia., 1958—; asst. clin. prof. psychiatry U. Ia. Med. Sch., 1971—; chmn. Ia. State Eugenics Bd. Pres. Buchanan County United Fund, 1963. Served to maj. AUS, 1942-46. Diplomate Am. Bd. Psychiatry and Neurology. Fellow Am. Psychiat. Assn. (certified mental hosp. adminstr., mem. task force in liaison with A.I.A. 1969-70), Am. Geriatric Soc.; mem. Ia. Psychiat. Soc. (mem. exec. com., past pres.), Buchanan County Med. Soc. (past pres.), Ia. Mental Health Assn. (profl. adv. bd.), Ia. Med. Soc., A.M.A., Am. Legion. Jewish religion. Mason (Shriner), Rotarian (past pres.); mem. B'nai B'rith. Contbr. articles field neurosis, psychiat. therapy, metabolism to med. jours. Address: Mental Health Inst Box 111 Independence IA 50644

KORST, HELMUT HANS, educator, engr.; b. Vienna, Austria, Jan. 4, 1916; s. Karl Otto and Blanche Ernestine (Desbalmes) K.; Dipl.-Ing., Technische Hochschule, Vienna, 1941, Dr. techn. Sc., 1947; m. Rudolfine Karoline Haslinger, July 25, 1942; childrenChristine Anne (Mrs. Gerald E. Kolar), Dorothea Maria, Peter Karl, Richard Helmut. Came to U.S., 1948, naturalized, 1954. Research engr. Maschinenfabrik Augsburg- N urnberg A.G. (Germany), 1941-45; asst. prof. mech. engring. Technische Hochschule, Vienna, 1945-48; mem. faculty U. Ill., 1948-, prof. mech. engring., 1951-, head dept., 1962-; vis. prof. Kan. State U., 1950, Va. Poly. Inst., 1954, Technische Hochschule, Vienna, 1957; design specialist Gen. Dynamics Convair, Ft. Worth, 1955; cons. Gen. Electric Co., 1959; propulsion specialist Rocketdyne div. North Am. Aviation In 1960, 65, 66, 67, 68; owner H. H. Korst Engrs. Cons., Urbana, Ill., 1956- ; cons. AGARD NATO, 1964. Sr. postdoctoral fellow NSF, 1957. Mem. Am. Inst. Indsl. Engrs., Am. Inst. Aeros. and Astronautics, Am. Soc. Engring. Edn., Am. Soc. M.E., Sigma Xi, Tau Beta Pi, Pi Tau Sigma, Sigma Tau. Author articles in field. Home: 3 Eton Court Champaign IL 61820 Office: Mech Engring Bldg University of Ill Urbana IL 61801

KORTENDICK, JAMES JOSEPH, clergyman, educator; b. Pecatonica, Ill., Mar. 19, 1907; s. Lawrence Valentine and Margaret (Dooley) K.; student St. Charles Coll., 1926-28; A.B., St Mary's Sem., Balt., 1930, M.A., 1932, S.T.B., 1933; student U. Wash., 1934-36, Marquette U., summer 1937; B.S. in L.S., Cath. Univ. America, 1940, M.A., 1942, Ph.D., 1963. Ordained priest Roman Cath. Ch., 1934; prof. English Lit. St. Edward's Sem., Seattle, 1934-36, St. Charles Coll., Catonsville, Md., 1936-37; prof. English and speech St. Mary's Sem., 1937-39, librarian and treas., 1937-39; reference and asst. librarian Cath. U. Am., 1941-46, asso. prof. library sci., 1946-70, prof., 1970—, head dept., 1947—; mem. staff of dirs. Theol. Coll., Cath. U. Am., 1941-69. Sec. of corp., chmn. bd. dirs. U.S. Book Exchange, 1948-50, pres., 1954-55, chmn. pub. relations com., 1956-58. Mem. Pres.'s Com. Employment Handicapped, 1965—. Mem. Soc. St. Sulpice. Mem. Cath. Library Assn. (hon. life; exec. council, 1943-58; chmn. coll. and univ. sect., 1942, 1946; chmn. com. Cath. Periodical Index 1952-60; pres. Wash.-Md.-Va. unit, 1941-43), Spl. Libraries Assn. (1st v.p. 1945-47), D.C. Library Assn. (exec. bd. mem. 1943-45, 50-52; pres. 1952-54), A.L.A. (chmn. planning com. library edn. div. 1958, mem. council 1950-54, library edn. div. 1st v.p. 1959-60, pres. 1960-61), Nat. Planning Commn. for Library Edn., Md. Library Assn., Am. Cath. Hist. Assn., Am. Assn. U. Profs., Gallery of Living Cath. Authors (exec. bd. 1941-43), Assn. Am. Library Schs. (sec.-treas. 1964-67; pres. 1969-70), Council Nat. Library Assn. (bd. trustees 1969—), Beta Phi Mu, Pi Gamma Mu. Author: The Library in the Catholic Theological Seminary in the United States, 1965 Post-Masters Education for Middle and Upper-level Personnel in Libraries and Information Centers, 1970. Editor: Studies in Library Sci., Cath. U. Am. Contbr. articles to mags. and jours. Home: 401 Michigan Av NE Washington DC 20017

KORTH, EUGENE HENRY, educator; b. Mankato, Minn., Nov. 23, 1917; TFs. Simon G. and Anna (Deglman) K.; A.B. in Classics, St. Louis U., 1941, in Philosophy, 1943, M.A. in History, 1946, S.T.L. in Theology, 1950; Ph.D. in History, U. Tex., 1956. Joined Soc. of Jesus, 1936, ordained priest Roman Cath. Ch., 1949; mem. faculty St. Louis U. High Sch., 1943-46; Doherty Found. fellow for research in Latin Am., 1953-54; mem. faculty Marquette U., 1956-68, chmn. dept. history, 1958-60, asso. prof., 1962-68, dean Coll. Liberal Arts, 1960-64; prof. history U. Detroit, 1969—; ednl. asst. Cath. U. Salta (Argentina), 1964—, acting dean, 1967-69. Mem. Am. Assn. for Higher Edn., Ass. Am. Colls., North Central Assn., N.E.A., Nat. Cath. Ednl. Assn., Jesuit Ednl. Assn., Am., Cath., Jesuit hist. assns., Conf. Latin Am. History, Wis. Assn. Pres. and Deans Ind. Colls., Wis. Acad. Arts and Scis., Phi Alpha Theta, Pi Gamma Mu, Sigma Delta Pi. Home: 4001 W McNichols Road Detroit, MI 48221

KORTH, FRED, lawyer; b. Yorktown, Tex. Sept. 9 1909 s. Fritz R. J. and Eleanor Marie (Stark) K.; A.B., U. Tex., 1932; LL.B., George Washington U., 1935, LL.D. (hon.), 1960; m. Vera Connell, Sept. 12, 1934 (div. Mar. 1966); children-Nina Maria, Fritz-Alan, Vera Sansom (dec.). Admitted to Tex., D.C. bars, 1935; practice of law, Ft. Worth, 1935-62; partner Wallace & Korth 1948-51; pvt. practice of law, Washington, 1964—; dep. counselor Dept. Army, 1951-52, asst. sec. of Army, 1952-53, cons. to sec. of Army, 1953-60; exec. v.p. Continental Nat. Bank, Ft. Worth, 1953-59, pres., 1959-61; sec. of Navy, Washington, 1962-63; 63; treas. Ft. Worth Air Terminal Corp., 1953-60; dir. Southwest Nat. Bank, El Paso, Tex., Fischbach & Moore, Inc., OKC Corp., Dallas, Panama Canal Co., 1961-64. Dir. Am. Air Filter. Pres. United Fund, Ft. Worth, Tarrant County, 1957-58; dir. Tex. & Southwestern Exposition & Fat Stock Show, Ft. Worth, 1953-63, treas., 1960-61. Served as lt. col., air transport command A.U.S., 1942-46. Recipient of exceptional civilian service award, Dept. Army, 1953. Mem. Am., Tex. bar. assns., Law Inst., Nat. Planning Assn. (nat. council), Tex. and Southwestern Cattle Raisers Assn. (treas. 1957-61), Phi Delta Phi, Sigma Phi Epsilon. Democrat. Clubs: Ft. Worth; International, George Town, Army-Navy (Washington); Ridglea; San Antonio Country. Office: Barr Bldg Farragut Sq Washington DC 20006

KORTMANN, LOUIS WILLIAM, former banker; b. West Point, N.Y., Nov. 4, 1904; s. Louis and Kate (Black) K.; grad. Am. Inst. Banking, 1933, Rutgers U. Grad. Sch. Banking, 1940; m. Helen Everett, Nov. 3, 1945. With Athens Nat. Bank (N.Y.), 1923-26, Chase Nat. Bank, N.Y.C., 1926-29; with Schenectady Trust Co., 1928—, sr. v.p., sec., 1952-63, pres., chmn. bd., 1963-70, now dir.; financial adv. to bd. dirs. Mech. Tech., Inc., 1963—. Sec.-treas. Schenectady County Clearing House Assn., 1949—. Treas. Schenectady Bur. Municipal Research, 1937-42. v.p., mem. bd. Schenectady Travelers Aid Soc., 1949—; treas., mem. bd. exec. com. Community Chest Schenectady 1943-44 51-53; adv. bd., chmn. finance com. St. Clare's Hosp. Mem. Am. (exec. com. 1955-58), N.Y. State (chmn. com. bank mgmt. and research 1959-60, chmn. govt. relations com. 1965, treas. 1958-59) bankers assns., Schenectady C. of C. (1st v.p. 1947-48), Am. Inst. Banking (pres. 1935-36). Mem. Reformed Ch. Clubs: Mohawk (pres. 1963, trustee 1960—), Mohawk Golf (chmn. audit com. 1939-44, comptroller 1948, chmn. bldg. com. 1960-61) (Schenectady); Lake George (Diamond Point, N.Y.). Home: 1811 Randolph Rd Schenectady NY 12308

KOS, CLAIR MICHAEL, otologist; b. Washington, Ia., Aug. 6, 1911; s. John Thomas and Philomena (Striegel) K.; B.S., U. Neb., 1933, M.D., 1937; postgrad. otolaryngology, Harvard Med. Sch., 1938-39; student Lempert Inst. Otology, N.Y.C., 1947; m. Dorothy Ellen McGinley, Sept. 3, 1936; childrenSusanne, Kathleen, Michael, Intern Bishop Clarkson Meml. Hosp., U. Neb., 1937-38; resident Mass. Eye and Ear Infirnary, Boston, 1939-41; asso. surgery, div. otolaryngology Duke Coll. Medicine, 1946-47; asst. prof., then prof. otolaryngology State U. Ia., 1947-60; dir. Otol. Med. Services, Iowa City, 1960-; otologist Mercy Hosp., Iowa City, 1961-. Cons. surgeon gen. USAF, 1951-, chmn. ad hoc com. hearing, 1951-60; mem. com. hearing and bioacoustics NRC, 1955-58; chmn. Ia. Conservation Hearing Com., 1958-68. Served to lt. col., M.C., AUS, 1941-46. Decorated Legion of Merit; co-recipient gold medal Am. Congress Phys. Medicine, 1951. Diplomate Am. Bd. Otolaryngology (examiner, dir. 1958-). Life fellow Am. Acad. Ophthalmology and Otolaryngology (lectr. grad. instl. courses 1945-67, sec. for otolaryngology 1959-, exec. sec.-treas. acad. 1969-; honor award services instrn. and research 1954); fellow Am., Internat. (vice regent 1959-64 colls. surgeons), American Laryngol., Rhinol. and Otol. Soc., A.M.A.; mem. Am. Otol. Soc., Am. Otosclerosis Study Group (pres. 1969), Ia. Acad. Ophthalmology and Otolaryngology (pres. 1958), Ia., Johnson med. socs., Kansas City (Mo.) Soc. Opthalmology-Otorhino Laryngology, (hon.), Miss. Valley Med. Soc., Pan- Am. Broncho-Esophagology Assn. (co-founder), Soc. Mil. Med. Cons., Central Am. Assn. Otolaryngology and Broncho-Esophagology Guatemala (hon.), La.-Miss. Ophthal. and Otolarvngol. Soc. (hon.), Dallas So. Med. Soc. (hon.), Phi Rho Sigma, Sigma Nu. Rotarian. Contbr. numerous articles profl. jours. Home: 1 Knollwood Lane Iowa City IA 55240 Office: 309 Iowa Avenue Iowa City IA 52240

KOSAKI, RICHARD HIROMICHI, ednl. adminstr.; b. Honolulu, Sept. 14, 1924; s. Kazuki and Kayo (Ozaki) K.; B.A., U. Hawaii, 1949; M.A., U. Minn., 1952, Ph.D., 1956; m. Mildred S. Doi, June 18, 1948; 1 son, Randall Keith. Adminstrv. asst. to speaker Hawaii Ho. of Reps., 1959; instr., researcher U. Hawaii, 1952-56, prof. polit. sci., 1957—, asst. to pres., 1963-65, v.p., 1965-71, chancellor, New Campus, 1971—. Mem. steering com. Edn. Commn. States, 1970—. Served to 1st lt. AUS, 1944-46. Mem. Western Assn. Schs. and Colls. (pres. 1970—). Home: 2549 Malama Pl Honolulu HI 96822

KOSCHMANN, ARNOLD HERMAN, educator, elec. engr.; b. Freeport, Ill., Nov. 30, 1926; s. H. Edward and Anna (Giessing) K.; A.B., Valparaiso U., 1948; B.S., Purdue U., 1950, M.S., 1951, Ph.D., 1954; m. Ellen Jean Buetow, Aug. 25, 1951; children—Julie Anna, Patti Jean, Nancy Ellen, James B. Asst. prof. elec. engring. U. Minn., 1954-57; asso. prof. elec. engring. U. N.M., Albuquerque, 1957-62, prof., chmn. dept. elec. engring., 1962-71; cons. Mpls.-Honeywell, 1954-57, Kirtland AFB, 1958-60, Dikewood Corp., Albuquerque, 1959-62. Chmn. Electronics Adv. Bd., Albuquerque, 1965. Bd. dirs. Multiple Sclerosis Albuquerque. Served with USNR, 1945-46. Mem. I.E.E.E., Am. Soc. Engring. Edn., Soc. Indsl. and Applied Math., Sigma Xi, Eta Kappa Nu, Sigma Tau. Lutheran (dir.). Home: 1212 Espanola St NE Albuquerque NM 87110

KOSCIUSKO-MORIZET, JACQUES, French diplomat; b. Paris, France, Jan. 31, 1913; s. Charles Kosciusko and Diane Milliaud; degree in ethics and sociology, Ecole Normale Superieure de Paris, 1934; agregation exam. in lit., 1937; m. Marianne Morizet, Aug. 25, 1939; children—Francois, Marie-Catherine (Mme. T. Postel-Vinay), Jacques-Antoine, Martine. Dir. of staff of Vincent Auriol, 1947-54, Felix Houphouet-Boigny, 1956-57; French del. UN Trusteeship Council, 1957-63; ambassador to Democratic Republic of Congo, Kinshasa, 1963-68; permanent rep. French to NATO, 1968-70, to UN, 1970—; tchr. faculty letters Sorbonne, 1941-46; lectr. lit. Columbia, 1946; spl. cons. UN Spl. Fund, 1963. Gen. del. World Fedn. War Vets., 1954-56; mem. High Com. for Youth and Sports for France and Overseas, 1956—. Municipal councillor, St. Nomla-Breteche, 1959—. Served with French Army and Resistance, World War II. Decorated officer Legion of Honor, Croix de Guerre, 1939-45, Medal of Resistance with rosette; knight comdr. Royal Victorian Order; grand officer Nat. Order Morocco, Ivory Coast and Senagal; recipient Gold medal of sports, 1951. Mem. French Record Acad. Club: Stade Francais (Paris). Home: 20 rue de Tournon Paris VIe 75 France Office: 4 E 79th St New York City NY 10021

KOSHEFF, MARTIN JOEL, electronics co. exec.; b. Queens, N.Y., Feb. 17, 1938; s. Nathan and Lilyan (Morgan) K.; student Mass. Inst. Tech., 1954-55; B.S., U. Pa., 1958; m. Janet Livingstone Haley, June 14, 1958; children—Jonathan, Andrew, Elizabeth, Charles. Staff cons. Scovell, Wellington & Co., Boston, 1958-61; financial v.p. Adv. Devel. Labs., Nashua, N.H., 1961- 65; treas. Sanders Assos., Inc., Nashua, 1965—; dir. Bank of N.H. Bd. dirs. United Fund of Greater Nashua. Mem. Financial Execs. Inst., Nat. Assn. Accountants, Am. Inst. C.P.A.'s, Mass. Soc. C.P.A.'s. Home: Dale St Wilton NH 03086 Office: DW Hwy S Nashua NH 03060

KOSHLAND, DANIEL EDWARD, ret. business exec.; b. San Francisco, Mar. 16, 1892; s. Marcus S. and Corinne (Schweitzer) K.; B.S., U. Cal., 1913; m. Eleanor Haas. Sept. 26, 1918; children—Daniel Edward, Frances C. (Mrs. Geballe). Phyllis R. (Mrs. Friedman). Asst. mgr. fgn. dept. Equitable Trust Co. of N.Y., 1914- 17; exec. Lazard Freres, bankers, N.Y.C., 1919-22; joined Levi Strauss & Co., San Francisco, 1922, v.p., treas., 1925, now dir.; dir. Am. Trust Co., Nat. Ice & Cold Storage Com. Mem. indsl. welfare commn., commr. State Cal. Served with U.S. Army, 1917-19. Mem. Congregation Emanu-el. Clubs: Family, Peninsula, Commercial, Argonaut. Home: 119 Reservoir Rd San Mateo CA 90207

KOSHLAND, STEPHEN ABRAHAM, stockbroker; b. Boston, Feb. 21, 1902; s. Abraham and Estelle (Wangeheim) K.; A.B., Harvard, 1925; m. Carol Falk, Apr. 14, 1938; childrenAnthony S., Kathryn. Wool buyer J. Koshland & Co., Boston, 1926- 30; trainee Hamershlag Borg & Co., stock brokers, 1930-31; partner Loeb, Rhoades & Co. (formerly known as Carl M. Loeb Rhoades & Co.), N.Y.C., 1931-. Mem. bd. govs. N.Y. Stock Exchange, 1960-66. Trustee of Harvard Advocate; mem. com. program for Harvard, 1960. Clubs: Harvard, Stock Exchange Luncheon (N.Y.C.). Home: 33 East Wall Street New York City NY 10005

KOSHLAND, WILLIAM A., pres. Alfred A. Knopf, Inc. Address: 52 East 64th Street New York City NY 10021*

KOSINSKI, ANTONI ALBERT, educator; b. Warsaw, Poland, May 25, 1930; s. Stanislaw and Walentyna (Kosinska) K.; M.A., U. Warsaw, 1952, Ph.D., 1956; m. Joan Burke, Sept. 23, 1961 (div.); 1 dau., Marta. Asst. prof. Inst. Math., Polish Acad. Scis., 1956-58; asst. prof. U. Cal., Berkeley, 1959-62, asso. prof., 1964-66; mem. Inst. for Advanced Study, Princeton, N.J., 1962-64; prof. Rutgers U., New Brunswick, N.J., 1966—. Recipient numerous NSF research grants. Mem. Am. Math. Soc. Contbr. articles to profl. jours. Home: R D 5 Cherrybrook Dr Princeton NJ 08540 Office: Dept Math Rutgers U New Brunswick NJ 08903

KOSINSKI, JERZY NIKODEM, author; b. Lodz, Poland, June 14, 1933; s. Mieczyslaw and Elzbieta (Liniecka) K.; M.A. in Polit. Sci., U. Lodz, 1953, M.A. in History, 1955; postgrad. Columbia, 1958-65, Ford Found. fellow, 1958-60; m. Mary H. Weir, Jan. 11, 1962 (div.). Came to U.S., 1957, naturalized, 1965. Asst. prof. Inst. Sociology and Cultural History, Polish Acad. Scis., Warsaw, 1955-57, Guggenheim Lit. fellow 1967; fellow Center for Advanced Studies Wesleyan U., 1968-69; sr. fellow Council Humanities Princeton U., 1969-70; vis. prof. English prose Sch. Drama Yale U., 1970-71; resident fellow Davenport Coll. Yale U., 1970-71. Recipient Nat. Book award for Steps, 1969; Award in Lit., Am. Acad. Arts and Letters, 1970. Mem. Authors Guild. Author: (pseudonym Joseph Novak) The Future is Ours, Comrade, 1960, No Third Path, 1962; The Painted Bird, 1965 (Best Fgn. book award 1966); Steps, 1968; Being There, 1971. Address: 440 East 79th St New York City NY 10021

KOSKI, WALTER S., scientist; b. Phila., Dec. 1, 1913; s. Bruno and Helen (Laskowska) Stankiewicz; Ph.D., Johns Hopkins, 1942; m. Helen Ireton Tag, May 11, 1940; children—Carol Lee, Ann Louise, Nancy Cheryl, Phyllis Ireton. Research chemist Hercules Powder Co., 1942-43; group leader Los Alamos Sci. Lab., 1944-47; physicist Brookhaven Nat. Lab., 1947-48; asso. prof. Johns Hopkins, 1947-55, prof. chemistry Grad. Sch., 1955—, chmn. dept., 1958-69. Recipient merit award Md. sect. Am. Chem. Soc. Fellow Am. Phys. Soc.; mem. Am. Chem. Soc., Phi Beta Kappa. Home: 809 East Seminary Av Towson MD 21204

KOSLOFF, IRVING S., pres. Phila. 76ers Profl. Basketball Team. Address: care Phila 76ers Sheraton Hotel Philadelphia PA 19103*

KOSMACH, FRANK P., savs. and loan assn. exec.; b. Selca, Yugoslavia, Nov. 19, 1893; s. Math Kosmac; came to U.S., 1901, naturalized, 1914; grad. Watson Bus. Coll., 1913; 3-year diploma Nat. League Savs. and Loan Sch., 1937; m. Clara L. Musolf, Oct. 8, 1924. With St. Paul Fed. Savs. & Loan Assn., Chgo., 1913- , sec., 1938-45, pres., 1945-68, now chmn.; dir. Fed. Home Loan Bank Chgo. Mem. Ill. Savs. Bond Com., 1963-; chmn. Community Victory Bond drs, World War II. Bd. govs. Gottlieb Meml. Hosp., Melrose Park, Ill.; bd. dirs. FuJen U. Found. Served with U.S. Army, World War I; AEF. Mem. Cook County Council Insured Assns., Cermak Rd. Bus. Men's Assn. (pres. 1945-47), U.S. Savs. and Loan League, Nat. Assn. Home Builders, Chgo. Mortgage Bankers Assn., Office Mgmt. Assn. Chgo., Chgo. Real Estate Bd., N. Side, W. Side real estate bds. Elk, Lion, Club: Olympia Field (Ill) Country. Home: 73 Longcommon Road Riverside, IL Office: 6700 West North Avenue Chicago IL 60635

KOSOK, MICHAEL, educator; b. N.Y.C., Apr. 12, 1931; s. Paul and Gretel (Tinti) K.; B.S., City Coll. N.Y., 1953; postgrad. N.Y. U., 1952-56; Ph.D., Columbia, 1964; m. Silvia Federici, Aug. 20, 1970. Lectr. Coll. City N.Y., 1955-56, Hunter Coll., N.Y.C., 1956-58; prof. physics, philosophy Fairleigh Dickinson U., Rutherford, N.J., 1958—. Symposium coordinator for Symposium on Non-Linear Research, A.A.A.S., 1971. Mem. Hegel Soc. Am. Contbr. articles profl. jours. Research philosophy of science. Home: 491 Pacific St Brooklyn NY 11217 Office: Fairleigh Dickinson U Rutherford NJ 07070

KOSOLAPOFF, GENNADY MICHAEL, chemist; b. Viatka, Russia, Sept. 2, 1909; s. Michael Paul and Alexandra Vasily (Shikhova) K.; came to U.S., 1924, naturalized, 1942; B.S. in Chem. Engring., Cooper Union, 1932; M.S. in Biochemistry, U. Mich., 1933, Sc.D. in Chemistry, 1936; m. Dorothea W. Bouton, July 20, 1934; childrenAlexandra, Michael, Patricia. Research chemist Libby-Owens-Ford Glass Co., 1936-38, Monsanto Chem. Co., 1938-48; asso. prof. Auburn U., 1948-53, research prof., 1953—; research cons. indsl. and govtl. agys., 1943—; dir. chem. research F.J. Seiler Research Lab. Office of Aerospace Research, Colo., 1963-64; cons. AEC; lectr. chemistry of phosphorus, 1949— Mem. Chem. Soc. London. Author: Organophosphorus Compounds, 1950; also sects. books and encys. Abstractor: Chem. Abstracts. Contbr. profl. jours. Home: 422 North College St. Auburn AL 36830 Office: PO Box 830 Auburn AL 36830

KOSS, LEOPOLD G., physician; b. Danzig, Poland, Oct. 2, 1920; s. Abram and Rose (Merenholc) K.; M.D., U. Berne (Switzerland), 1946; div.; children—Michael S., Andrew C., Richard P. Came to U.S., 1947, naturalized, 1952; m. Lydia Palla, 1965. Intern Lincoln Hosp., N.Y.C., 1947-48; tng. pathology St. Gallen, Switzerland, 1946-47, Kings County Hosp., Bklyn., 1949-51; instr. pathology L.I. Coll. Medicine, 1949-51; mem. staff Meml. Hosp. Cancer and Allied Diseases, N.Y.C., 1951-70, attending pathologist, 1961-70, chief cytology service, 1961-70; pathologist-in-chief Sinai Hosp. Balt., 1970—; asso. mem. Sloan-Kettering Inst. Cancer Research, N.Y.C., 1957-70; mem. staff Sloan-Kettering div. Postgrad. Sch. Med. Scis., Cornell U., 1952-70, asso. prof. pathology, 1957-70; vis. prof. pathology Jefferson Med. Coll., Phila., 1970—; vis. pathologist James Ewing Hosp., N.Y.C.; cons. pathologist N.Y. State Dept. Health, Hosp. Spl. Surgery, N.Y.C., USPHS Hosp., S.I., N.Y. Served to maj., M.C., AUS, 1955-57. Recipient Wien award Papanicolaou Cancer Inst., 1963, Alfred P. Sloan award cancer research, 1964; hon. prof. pathology Severance Med. Coll., Seoul, Korea, 1956. Fellow Am. Soc. Clin. Pathology, Coll. Am. Pathologists; mem. Am. Soc. Path. Bacteriologists, James Ewing Soc., A.M.A., Am. Soc. Cytology (pres. 1962; Papanicolaou award 1966), Internat. Acad. Pathology, Internat. Acad. Cytology (Goldblatt award 1962); corr. mem. Royal Acad. Medicine Spain; hon. mem. Brit. Soc. for Clin. Cytology, Korean Med. Assn., Mex., Argentinian socs. cytology, Japanese Soc. Pathology, Peruvian Soc. Obstetrics and Gynecology. Author: Diagnostic Cytology and It's Histopathologic Bases, 2d edit., 1968; also articles. Office: Sinai Hosp Balt Baltimore MD 21215

KOSSA, FRANK RAYMOND, army officer; b. Schulenberg, Tex., Nov. 1, 1897; s. John F. and Amelia (Klecka) K.; B.A., U. Louisville, 1936; m. Grace L. Lindley, Oct. 3, 1925; 1 son, David L. Brubeck. With U.S. Govt., 1919-27; engaged in business, 1927-42; served with U.S. Army, 1917-19; rejoined AUS, 1942- 46; engaged in business, 1946-48; rejoined U.S. Army, 1948, advanced through grades to col. 1963; dir. SSS, Ind. 1948-57; with nat. hdqrs. SSS, 1957-, asst. to dir., 1961-. Chmn. bd. Lindley Realty Co., Jeffersonville, Ind., 1948-. Mem. Def. Supply Assn., Mil. Order World Wars, Heroes of '76, World War I Vets. Assn., 40 and 8, Am. Legion (past comdr. Ind., vice chmn. security commn. 1946-), Vets. Fgn. Wars, AMVETS, Disable[illegible] Am. Vets., Regular Vets. Assn., Res. Officers Assn. (com. staff [illegible] Army, Navy and Air Force Vets. Can. (sec.-treas. U.S. [illegible] Assn., Jeffersonville C. of C. Republican. Lion, Elk. [illegible] Home: 317 East Riverside Drive Jeffersonville IN [illegible] F Street NW Washington DC 20006

KOSSAR, ARNOLD FRANKLYN, airc[illegible] Apr. 13, 1925; s. Hyman and Sonia (F[illegible] N.Y.U., 1945; Aero. Engr. Mass. Ins[illegible] Oct. 7, 1945; children—Enid Rae. [illegible] Vultee Aircraft Corp., San Di[illegible] Aircraft Corp., East Hartford [illegible]

Kaman Aircraft Corp., Bloomfield, Conn., 1951-55; mgr. advanced projects Wright Aero div. Curtiss-Wright Corp., Wood-Ridge, N.J., 1955-61, dir. corporate planning, tech. asst. to chmn. and pres., 1961-65, v.p., 1965—. Registered profl. engr., Conn. Mem. Inst. Aero. Scis., Am. Helicopter Soc., Am. Mgmt. Assn., A.A.A.S., N.Y. Acad. Scis., Sigma Xi, Tau Beta Pi, Gamma Alpha Pho. Home: 14-27 Mandon Place Fair Lawn NJ 07410 Office: Curtiss-Wright Corporation Wood-Ridge NJ 07075

KOSSEL, CLIFFORD GEORGE, univ. dean, clergyman; b. Omro, Wis., Apr. 22, 1916; s. George C. and Sarah (Haigh) K.; A.B., Gonzaga U., 1940, M.A., 1941; Ph.D., U. Toronto, 1945; Th.L., Alma Coll., 1949. Asso. prof. Gonzaga U., Spokane, 1950-63, prof. philosophy, 1963—, dean Sch. Philosophy and Letters, 1958-71, chmn. dept. philosophy, 1966-69; Sabbatical leave to Oxford, Eng. and Florence, Italy, 1969-70, Mem. Am. Cath., Jesuit (past pres.) philos. assns. Contbr. profl. jours. Home: Gonzaga U Spokane WA 99202

KOSSLER, HERMAN JOSEPH, naval officer; b. Portsmouth, Va., Dec. 8, 1911; s. Herman and Octavie (Barraud) K.; B.S., U.S. Naval Acad., 1934; grad. Submarine Sch., 1937, Nat. War Coll., 1955; m. Ursula Breher, July 16, 1947; childrenJudith, Mary, William, Gretchen, Jane, Katherine. Commd. ensign U.S. Navy, 1934, advanced through grades to rear adm., 1960; attached U.S.S. Idaho, 1934- 36, submarines Argonaut and Nautilus, prior World War II; exec. officer submarine Guardfish, comdg. officer Cavalla, World War II; assigned Bur. Naval Personnel, 1946-49; submarine service at sea, 1949-52; aide asst. sec. navy, 1952-54; with U.S.S. Sanborn, 1956; comdr. Submarine Squadron Two, 1957; office Chief Naval Operations, 1958, 59; comdr. Amphibious Squadron Ten, 1960; with Bur. Naval Weapons, 1961, office Chief Naval Operations, 1962-63; comdr. Mine Force Atlantic Fleet, 1963-66, U.S. Naval Forces Philippines, 1966-68, comdt. 6th Naval Dist., 1968-. Decorated Navy Cross, Silver Star medal (three), Presdl. Unit citation (twice), Legion Merit; Philippine Legion Honor (Comdr.); Korean Presdl. Unit citation. Home: Comdt's House (Qtrs A) Naval Base Charleston SC 29404 Office: Comdt 6th Naval Dist Charleston SC 29404

KOST, GUS R., retail stores exec. With Wieboldt Stores, Chgo., 1939—, controller, asst. sec., 1957—. Office: 1 N State St Chicago IL 60602*

KOSTANSKI, THADDEUS ANTHONY, electric utility co. exec.; b. Toledo, Feb. 11, 1925; s. John and Helen (Rogalski) K.; student John Carroll U., 1944-45; B.S. in Bus. Adminstrn., Miami U., Oxford, O., 1947; M.B.A., U. Toledo, 1963; m. Mildred Ann Plucher, Oct. 23, 1948; children—Kenneth, Charles, Jeanne Marie. With Toledo Edison Co., 1948—, asst. sec., 1952-58, dir. customer accounting, 1958-62, asst. controller, 1962-65, controller, 1965—, chief accounting officer, 1968—; instr. corporate finance U. Toledo, 1965-66. Sect. chmn. United Fund drives, Toledo, 1966-71. Bd. dirs. Jr. Achievement Northwestern Ohio. Served with USNR, 1943-46. Mem. Financial Execs. Inst., C. of C., Am. Legion, Exchange Club, Beta Alpha Psi. Home: 4834 Skelly Rd Toledo OH 43623 Office: Toledo Edison Co 420 Madison Av Toledo OH 43601

KOSTANT, BERTRAM, educator, mathematician; b. Bklyn., May 24, 1928; s. Abraham and Besse (Schantz) K.; B.S., Purdue U., 1950; Ph.D., U. Chgo., 1954; m. Ann Rebecca Siller, Feb. 16, 1968; children—Abbe, Steven, Shoshanna. Mem. Inst. Advanced Study, Princeton, 1953-55; Higgins lectr. Princeton, 1956-57; prof. mathematics U. Cal., 1957-62, Mass. Inst. Tech., 1962—; speaker Nice Internat. Congress, 1970. Guggenheim fellow; Sloan fellow; NSF fellow; AEC fellow. Mem. Am. Acad. Arts nd Scis., Am. Math. Soc. Jewish religion. Contbr. articles profl. jours. Home: 5 Merrill Rd Newton MA 02159 Office: Mass Inst Tech Cambridge MA 02139

KOSTECKE, B. WILLIAM, brewery exec.; b. Caro, Mich., Aug. 1, 1925; s. Steve and Srella (Telewiak) K.; B.S., U.S. Merchant Marine Acad., 1947, Mich. State U., 1951; m. LoRayne Smith, Mar. 25, 1950; children—Diane Marie, Keith William. Budget analyst Chrysler Corp., 1951-55; mgr. financial analysis Ford Motor Co., 1955-59; with Miller Brewing Co., Milw., 1959—, treas., 1966—, pres., chief exec. officer, dir., 1970—; v.p., dir. Containers Inc.; dir. Formosa Spring Brewery, Ltd. Bd. dirs. Greater Milw. Com., Met. Mils. Assn. Commerce, Mil. Vol. Equal Employment Opportunity Council, Milw. World Festival; vice chmn. Milw. Nat. Alliance Businessmen. Pres., treas., dir. Miller High Life Found.; bd. dirs. Milw. Boys Club, Milw. YMCA; trustee Citizens Govtl. Research Bur. Mem. U.S. Brewers Assn. (bd. dirs.), Financial Execs. Inst., Bier-Convent (W. Germany), Internat. Platform Assn. Clubs: Blue Mound Golf and Country (Wauwatosa, Wis.); North Shore Country (Mequon). Home: 11412 N Vega Av 79W Mequon WI 53092 Office: 4000 W State St Milwaukee WI 53208

KOSTELANETZ, ANDRE, orch. condr.; b. Leningrad, Russia; s. Nachman and Rosalie (Dimscha) K.; student St. Peter's Sch., 1911-18, St. Petersburg Conservatory of Music, 1920-22i hon. Mus. D., Albion (Mich.) Coll., 1939; Mus. D., Cin. Conservatory Music, 1945; m. Lily Pons, June 2, 1938 (div.); m. 2d, Sara Gene Orcutt, 1960 (div.). Came to U.S., 1922, naturalized, 1928. For many years conducted own shows over CBS; directed music for several motion pictures; selected by radio editors of U.S. and Can. for Fame Award as leading condr. for past several years. Made overseas tours conducting soldier orchrs. organized and trained by him, North Africa, Persian Gulf, Italian theatre, summer 1944, China-Burma-India and European theatres, winter 1944-45; Guest condr. N.Y. Philharmonic, also all leading orchs. in U.S. and abroad; prin. condr. N.Y. Philharmonic Promenades. Records with Columbia Records. Awarded Asiatic-Pacific ribbon by Army for overseas services. Commd. modern works by Copland, Thompson, Kern, Grofe, Creston, William Schuman, Hovhaness, Archibald MacLeish-Laderman. Address: CBS Building 51 West 52d St New York City NY 10019

KOSTELANETZ, BORIS, lawyer; b. Leningrad, Russia, June 16, 1911; s. Nachman and Rosalia (Dimschetz) K.; brought to U.S., 1920, naturalized, 1925; B.C.S., N.Y. U., 1933, B.S., 1936; J.D. magna cum laude, St. John's U., 1936; m. Ethel Cory, Dec. 18, 1938; children-Richard Cory, Lucy Cory. With Price, Waterhouse & Co., C.P.A.'s, N.Y.C., 1934-37; admitted to N.Y. bar, 1936; asst. U.S. atty. So. Dist. N.Y., also confidential asst. to U.S. atty, 1937-45; spl. asst. to atty. gen. U.S., 1943-46; chief, war frauds sect. Dept. Justice,
45-46; spl. counsel com. investigate crime in interstate commerce
196 nate, 1950-51; partner firm Kostelanzetz & Ritholz, and
1969- N.Y.C., 1946-; instr. accounting N.Y. U., 1937-47, adj.
Chef System 47—. Chmn., Kefauver for Pres. Com. N.Y. State,
Finance Corps, torious Service award N.Y. U., 1954; Pietas
Home: 11906 Fores 1; John T. Madden Meml. award N.Y. U.,
Indianapolis IN 4620 Am. Coll. Trial Lawyers, Am. Bar Found.;
N.Y. State bar assns., N.Y. County

KORN, RICHARD, symp Pres. 1969—, dir. 1958-64, 66-69,
1928; LL.B., Yale, 1931; stud ssn. Bar City N.Y., N.Y. State Soc.
Peggy Lashanska Rosenbaum (lumni Assn. (pres. 1951-52), St.
1945; childrenPenelope (Mrs. Stan 1955-57), N.Y. U. Men in
Lash), Lehman. Member Nat. awyers, New York Univ.
(N.Y.C.); Nat. Lawyers (Washington). Author: (with L. Bender) Criminal Aspects of Tax Fraud Cases, 1957, also articles. Home: 37 Washington Square West New York City NY 10011 Office: 52 Wall Street New York City NY 10005

KOSTELANETZ, RICHARD CORY, writer; b. N.Y.C., May 14, 1940; s. Boris and Ethel (Cory) K.; A.B. with honors Brown U., 1962; postgrad. Columbia, 1962-, (Fulbright scholar) King's Coll., U. London, 1964-65; m. Anne Louise Tidaback, Sept. 8, 1962. Woodrow Wilson fellow, 1962-63; Pulitzer fellow in critical writing, 1965-66. Editor and contbr. On Contemporary Literature, 1964; The New American Arts, 1965; editor Young American Writers. Contbr. articles to various mags. and revs. Address: care Curtis Brown Limited 575 Madison Avenue New York City NY 10022*

KOSTER, HENRY, motion picture dir.; b. Berlin, Germany, May 1, 1905; s. Albert and Emma (Salomon) Kosterlitz: student art schs. in Berlin and Vienna, 1921-23; m. Cathrin Kiraly, 1935; 1 son, Robert; m. 2d, Peggy Moran, Oct. 30, 1942; children—Nicolas, Peter. Came to U.S., 1936, naturalized, 1944 Author screenplays, dir. in Europe for Ufa, Terra, Aafa, European Universal, also Sascha-Tobis,; dir. for Universal Pictures, 1936-42 Goldwyn, Warner Bros., 1946-47, 20th Century Fox, 1947-65; Metro-Goldwyn- Mayer, 1943-45, 65—. Mem. Dirs. Guild Am. Home: 1216 Lachman Lane Pacific Palisades CA 90272

KOSTER, HENRY MILTON chem. co. exec.; b. Wood-Ridge, N.J., June 1907; s. John Frederick and Minna (Nibbe) K.; C.P.A., Pace Coll., 1929; m. Grace Gourley, Sept. 28, 1939; childrenKaren G., William H. Tax mgr. Air Reduction Co., Inc., N.Y.C., 1944-63, treas., 1963-. Mem. adv. bd. taxation Pace Coll., 1961- 68, consultor, 1968—. C.P.A., N.Y. Mem. Am. Inst. C.P.A.'s, N.Y. Soc. C.P.A.'s, Tax Execs. Inst. Club: Canadian (N.Y.C.). Home: 991 Richard Court Teaneck NJ 07666 Office: 150 E 42d St New York City NY 10017

KOSTER, RE, educator; b. Haarlem, Netherlands, July 14, 1900; d. Herman and Hendrika (Hagens) Koster; music student, Netherlands, Paris, France and Milan, Italy; m. David de Jong, May 27, 1937 (dec. 1953). Came to U.S., 1958. Debut, Paris, 1927; extensive concertizing in Italy, France, Holland, Belgium, Austria, Czechoslovakia and Eng., 1927-40, 45-53; lecture- recitals and masterclasses throughout U.S., 1958—; chmn. voice dept. New Eng. Conservatory Music, 1958-71; adjudicator contests. Men. Am. Soc. Musicology, Pi Kappa Lambda. Contbr. articles. Home: 28 I Av de la Motte Piquet Paris 7e France

KOSTER, SAMUEL WILLIAM army officer; b. West Liberty, Ia., Dec. 29, 1919; s. Samuel William and Maude (Smith) K.; student Grinnell (Ia.) Coll., 1937-38; B.S., U.S. Mil. Acad., 1942; grad. Command and Gen. Staff Coll., 1944, Armed Forces Staff Coll., 1952, Nat. War Coll., 1960; m. Cherie Kadgihn, Jan. 7, 1943; children—Samuel William, Susanne Louise, Nancy Kay, Robert Kadgihn, John Leo. Commd. 2d lt. U.S. Army, 1942, advanced through grades to maj. gen., 1968; assigned 104th Inf. Div., ETO, 1942-45, gen. hdqrs. Far East Command, Tokyo, 1946-49, U.S. Mil. Acad., 1949-50, 8th U.S. Army, Korea, 1951; G-3 Dept. Army, 1952-56; assigned SHAPE, Paris, 1956-59, Inf. Sch., 1960-64, 8th U.S. Army, Korea, 1964-66, Office Asst. Chief Staff for Force Devel., Dept. Army, 1966-67; comdg. gen. Americal Div., Vietnam, 1967-68; supt. U.S. Mil. Acad., 1968-70. Decorated D.S.M., Silver Star with oak leaf cluster, Legion of Merit with 2 oak leaf clusters, Bronze Star with oak leaf cluster, Purple Heart; Croix de Guerre (France). Elk, Lion, Rotarian. Address: Headquarters First US Army Ft Meade MD 20755

KOSTKA, WILLIAM JAMES, pub. relations, advt. exec.; b. Chgo., May 18, 1905; s. Matthew and Anna (Papacek) K.; B.A., Knox Coll., 1927; m. Dorothy Parmenter, June 15, 1928; children—Stefan, William. Formerly telegraph editor Chgo. Daily Drovers Jour.; central div. mgr. Internat. News Service; mng. editor Fawcett Publ.; editor Frank A. Munsey Publ., N.Y.C.; publicity dir. NBC; mng. editor Look mag.; v.p. Inst. Pub. Relations; pub. relations. advt. dir. U.S. Brewers Found., 1949; chmn. Wm. Kosika & Assos., Inc. 1949—. Mem. Pub. Relations Soc. Am., Phi Beta Kappa, Sigma Delta Chi, Tau Kappa Epsilon. Clubs: Nat. Press; Denver Press. Home: 1090 Lafayette St Denver CO 80218 Office: 1321 Bannock St Denver CO 80204

KOSTMAYER, JOHN HOUSTON, financial services exec.; b. New Orleans, June 12, 1915; s. Hiram Watkins and Carroll (Houston) K.; student Tulane U., 1932-34, 35-36, U. of South, 1934-35; m. Julia C., Sept. 10, 1940; children—John, Roger, Peter. Vice pres., dir. First Investors Corp., N.Y.C., 1953-67; v.p., group exec. ITT Financial Services, Internat. Tel. & Tel. Corp., N.Y.C., 1967- -; chmn. bd. Hamilton Funds, Inc., Hamilton Growth Fund, Inc., Hamilton Mgmt. Corp., ITT Family Security Sales Corp., ITT Life Ins. Co. of N.Y., ITT Variable Annuity Life Ins. Co.; pres., dir. Gt. Eastern Ins. Co., Monitor Underwriting Mgmt., Ltd.; dir. ITT Aetna Corp., Abbey Internat. Corp., Abbey Internat. Ins. Co., Ltd., Abbey Leven Nederland N.V., Abbey Life Assurance Co., Ltd., Abbey Life Ins. Co. of Can., Abbey Overseas Ins. Co., Ltd., ITT Midwestern Life Ins. Corp., ITT Thorp Corp., Intercontinentale S.p.A., London & Edinburgh Life Ins. Co., Ltd., London & Edinburgh Gen. Ins. Co., Ltd., N.V. Zwolsche Alegmeene Beleggings Maatschappij; bd. dirs., mem. exec. com. ITT Hamilton Life Ins. Co.; bd. govs. Investment Co. Inst. Chmn. Solebury Citizens Assn., 1966—. Trustee Solebury Sch., New Hope, Solebury Pub. Library, Vestry St. Philips Chapel. Home: Solebury Bucks County PA 18963 Office: 320 Park Av New York City NY 10022

KOSTNER, THEODORE, corporate exec.; b. Phila., July 4, 1912; s. Morris and Sarah (Curitz) K.; certificate of proficiency Wharton Evening Sch., U. Pa., 1933; m. Ruth Goldberg, Sept. 19, 1937; children—Gail Sylvia, Judith Starr, Melanie Susan. Jr. accountant Goldman, Turner & Co., N.Y.C., 1933-37; sr. accountant Max Bruckner, N.Y.C., 1937-41; self-employed C.P.A., N.Y.C., 1941-58; chmn. bd. Imperial Commodities Corp., 1968—; chmn. bd. Imperial Processing Corp., Sumatra Commodities Corp.; mng. dir. N.V. Deli Maatschappij; pres. Imperial Processing-P.R., Inc.; dir. Bridgforth Tobacco Co., Inc., Commonwealth Tobacco Co., Inc., Koch, Inc., DeHope-Goldschmidt Corp., Alan L. Grant Co., Inc., Imperial Processing Corp. Trustee Temple Gates of Zion, Valley Stream, N.Y. Mem. Am. Inst. C.P.A.'s, N.Y. State Soc. C.P.A.'s. Mason. Club: Wall Street. Home: 58 Park Dr North Valley Stream NY 11580 Office: 110 Wall St New York City NY 10005

KOSTUIK, JOHN, mining co. exec.; b. Poland, 1911; B.Sc., Queen's U., 1934, postgrad., 1935; married; children—John P., Paul S., David E., Margaret Rose. Pres., Denison Mines Ltd., Toronto, Ont., Can. Consol. Rexspar Minerals & Chms. Ltd., Argosy Mining, Ltd., Lakehead Mines, Ltd.; dir. Roman Corp., Molycorp. Am., Internat. Mogul Mines, Ltd., Black Hawk Mining, Ltd., Midepsa Industries, Ltd., Joy Mfg. Co. Chmn. research subcom. on mining Nat. Adv. Com. on Mining and Metall. Research. Mem. Ont. Mining Assn. (past pres.), Mining Assn. Can. (pres., dir.), Inst. Mining and Metall., Canadian Inst. Mining and Metallurgy, Am. Inst. Mining Engrs. Roman Catholic. Clubs: National; Engineers; York Downs Golf. Home: 14 Briancliff Dr Don Mills Ontario Canada Office: 4 Kings St W Toronto 1 Ontario Canada*

KOSTYO, JACK LAWRENCE, educator; b. Elyria, O., Oct. 1, 1931; s. Louis and Matilda (Thomasko) K.; A.B., Oberlin Coll., 1953; Ph.D., Cornell U., Ithaca, N.Y., 1957; m. Shirlianne Guth, June 10, 1953; children—Cecile A., Louis C. NRC fellow Harvard Med. Sch., Boston, 1957-59; asst. prof., prof. physiology Duke, 1959-68; prof., chmn. dept. physiology Emory U., Atlanta, 1968—. Mem. endocrinology study sect. NIH, USPHS, 1967—. Recipient Lederle Med. Faculty award, 1961; Ernst Oppenheimer Meml. award Endocrine Soc., 1969. Mem. Endocrine Soc. (mem. editorial bd.), Am. Physiol. Soc. (mem. editorial bd.), Soc. for Exptl. Biology and Medicine, Sigma Xi. Contbr. articles profl. jours. Home: 2065 Renault Lane NE Atlanta GA 30329

KOSYGIN, ALEXSAI N., premier of USSR; b. Leningrad, 1904; ed. Leningrad Coop. Tech. Inst., Leningrad Textile Inst., 1935. Worker in consumer cooperatives various dists. Siberia, 1924-49; foreman, dept. head Zhelyabov textile factory, Leningrad, 1935-37; dir. October Textile mill, Leningrad, 1937-38; chmn. exec. com. Leningrad City Council of Workers' Deputies, 1938-39; dep. of Supreme Soviet, 1938-; people's commissar Textile Industry of USSR, 1939-40; dep. chmn. Council People's Commissars of USSR, 1940-46; chmn. Council of People's Commissars of RSFSR, 1943-46; dep. chmn. Council of Ministers of USSR, 1946-60; minister of finance USSR, 1949-54, chmn. state planning comm., 1959-60, 1st dep. chmn. Council of Ministers, 1960-64, chmn. 1964-. Mem. Communist Party of Soviet Union, 1927-, mem. Central Com., 1939-; candidate mem., then mem. Politburo of Central Com., 1946-52, mem., 1966—, candidate mem., then mem. Presidium, 1952-53, 57-66. Decorated Hero of Socialist Labor, Qrder of Lenin (4), Gold Star Hammer and Sickle, Order of Red Flag, 9 medals. Address: The Kremlin Moscow USSR

KOTCH, ALEX, educator; b. Edwardsville, Pa., Aug. 18, 1926; s. Alex and Irene (Hazilla) K.; student Bucknell Jr. Coll., 1943-44; B.S. (Evan Pugh scholar), Pa. State U., 1946, M.S., 1947; Ph.D. (Monsanto Chem. Co. fellow), U. Ill., 1950; m. Anny Marie Brinkman, Mar. 5, 1952; children—Marianne (Mrs. Gerald L. Cassell), Axel, Robert, Jennifer. Research chemist central research dept. E.I. duPont de Nemours & Co., Wilmington, Del., 1952-54, chemist organic chems. dept., Deepwater Point, N.J., 1954-59; asso. program dir. for chemistry NSF, Washington, 1959-63, program dir. for organic chemistry, 1963-65; chief biosciences div. Office of Saline Water, Dept. Interior, Washington, 1965-66; staff asso. univ. sci. devel. sect. NSF, Washington, 1966-67; prof. chemistry, asso. chmn. U. Wis.-Madison, 1967—; cons.-examiner N.Central Assn. Colls. and Secondary Schs. U.S. Govt. Fulbright fellow Tech. U., Delft, Netherlands, 1950-51, Arthur D. Little Postdoctoral fellow Mass. Inst. Tech., 1951-52. Mem. Am. Chem. Soc., A.A.A.S., Am. Assn. U. Profs., Sigma Xi, Alpha Chi Sigma, Phi Kappa Phi, Phi Lambda Upsilon, Pi Mu Epsilon. Home: 6337 Piping Rock Rd Madison WI 53711

KOTCHIAN, A. CARL, aircraft co. exec.; b. Kermit, N.D., July 17, 1914; s. Adolphus C. and Mamie (Bonzer) K.; A.B., Stanford, 1935, M.B.A., 1938; m. Lucy Betty Carr, Nov. 8, 1940; 1 son, Robert Lawrence. Accountant Price, Waterhouse & Co., Los Angeles, 1936-40; budget mgr. Vega Airplane Co., Burbank, Cal., 1941-43; with Lockheed Aircraft Corp., Burbank, Cal., also Marietta, Ga., 1944-, seccessively budget mgr., chief cost accountant, dir. financial operations, dir. adminstrn., asst. mfg. mgr., asst. gen. mgr., 1944-56, v.p. gen. mgr. Ga. div. 1956-59, group v.p., 1959-65, exec. v.p., 1965-67, pres., 1967—, also dir.; dir. Rich's, Inc., Atlanta, Security Pacific Nat. Bank, Los Angeles. Past pres. Asso. Industries Ga. C.P.A., Cal. Clubs: Los Angeles Country, California (Los Angeles); Capital City (Atlanta). Home: 283 Bel Air Road Los Angeles CA 90024 Office: 2555 North Hollywood Way Burbank CA 91503

KOTHE, CHARLES ALOYSIUS, lawyer; b. Jersey City, Oct. 12, 1912; s. Charles A. and Lillian (Hansen) K.; student Bucknell U., 1930-33; A.B., U. Tulsa, 1934; scholarship U. Heidelberg (Germany); LL.B. With honors, U. Okla., 1938; m. Janet Fleming, Feb. 19, 1937; children—Diane, Charles F., James R., David J. Admitted to Okla. bar, 1938; with firm Smith & Kothe, Tulsa, 1938-39; staff counsel Mid-Continent Petroleum Co., Tulsa, 1939-41; gen. counsel Macnick Co., Tulsa, 1941-43; mem. firm Kulp, Pinson, Lupardus & Kothe, Tulsa, 1943-46; partner Kothe & Huff, Tulsa, 1946-57, Kothe, Hall & Sublett, 1957-59; of counsel Doerner, Stuart, Moreland, Campbell & Saunders, Tulsa, 1959-66, Kothe & Eagleton, 1966—; v.p. Neg. Institute, Labor Law, Tulsa Law School, 1939-59, v.p. indsl. relations N.A.M., N.Y.C., 1959- 65; v.p. Coburn Mfg. Co., 1966—. Faculty indsl. relations Okla. Sch. Accounting, 1957-58; atty., trustee Radio Inc., Tulsa; dir. T.D. Williamson Co. Panel Am. Arbitration Assn., Fed. Mediation and Conciliation Service; spl. cons. U.S. Dept. Labor, 1960—; dir. Protestant council 1964 N.Y. World's Fair; cofounder, 2d pres. Effective Citizens Orgn., 1957. Okla. chmn. Citizens for Eisenhower. Bd. dirs. Internat. Christian Leadership, Tulsa, Okla. Osteopathic Hosp. Named Citizen of the Year, Tulsa, 1946. Mem. Am. (10th Circuit councilman 1940), Okla. (chmn. labor law section) bar assns. U.S. Jr. (v.p. 1956), Okla. Junior (pres. 1955), Tulsa Jr. (pres. 1954), Tulsa (chmn. research div. 1955) chambers commerce, Jr. Bar Conf. Okla. (pres. 1946), U. Tulsa Alumni Assn. (pres. 1957), Order of Coif, Sigma Alpha Epsilon, Phi Delta Phi. Presbyn. (trustee Tulsa Presbytery; elder; state chmn. Presbyn. Restoration Fund). Mason (Shriner). Clubs: Tulsa; Southern Hills Country; Nat. Lawyers (Washington). Author: Industrial Relations in thc Non-Union Plant, 1960; NLRB and the Rights of Management, 1966. Editor: Tale of 22 Cities, 1964. Home: 4180 Oak Rd Tulsa OK 74105 Office: Philtower Bldg Tulsa OK 74103 also 1616 H St NW Washington DC 20006

KOTIN, PAUL pathologist, ednl. adminstr.; b. Chgo., Aug. 13, 1916; s. Elias and Rose (Spunt) K.; B.S., U. Ill., 1937, M.D., 1940; m. Helen Tepper, May 6, 1939; children—Joel Tepper, David Bernard. Intern Deaconess Hosp., Chgo., 1939- 40, resident pathology, 1940-41; pvt. practice pathology and internal medicine, San Luis Obispo, Cal., 1946-48; research pathology U. So. Cal., 1949-50; med. microbiologist Los Angeles County Hosp., 1950-51, attending staff pathologist, 1951-62; mem. faculty U. So. Cal., 1951-62, prof. pathology, 1959-60, Paul Pierce prof. pathology, 1960-62; chief carcinogenesis studies br. Nat. Cancer Inst., 1962-63, asso. dir. for field studies, 1963-64, scientific dir. for etiology, 1964-66; dir div. environmental health scis. NIH, 1966-71; v.p. for health scis. Temple U., Phila., 1971—; Edgar Allen Meml. lectr. Yale Sch. Medicine, 1957; vis. prof. oncology U. Wis., 1959- 60; vis. prof. pathology U. N.C., also Duke U.; Harry Shay Meml. lectr. Temple U., 1964; chmn. Gordon Research Conf. Cancer, 1965. Cons. air pollution med. program, div. spl. health service USPHS, 1958-62; mem. sci. adv. bd. Council Tobacco Research-U.S.A., 1962-65; adv. com. railroad diesel gases and dust Cal. Pub. Utilities Commn., 1956-62; adv. com. research pathogenesis cancer Am. Cancer Soc., 1962- 65; pathology study sect. NIH, 1962-66, lung cancer task force, 1967—; cancer prevention com. UICC, 1962-66, com. on exptl. design and methodology in carcinogenesis, 1967—; scientific com. Inst. Occupational and Environmental Health, Quebec. Asbestos Mining Assn., 1966—; member Fed. Com. Pest Control, 1964—; program com. Tenth Internat. Congress, 1967—. Expert panel on Carcinogenicity, 1962—, Nat. Environmental Health Scis. Center, 1965. Served with AUS, 1941-46. Sr. postdoctoral fellow NSF, 1959-60. Fellow Coll. Am.

Pathologists, N.Y. Acad. Scis.; mem. A.M.A. (com. for the research on tobacco an health 1966—), Am. Assn. Cancer Research (bd. dirs.), Am. Assn. Pathologists and Bacteriologists, A.A.A.S., Am. Soc. Exptl. Pathology, Internat. Acad. Pathology, Am. Inst. Biol. Scis., Am. Soc. Cell Biology, Sigma Xi. Corr. mem. permanent European com. Research Chronic Hazards, 1960—. Contbr. med. jours. Editorial adv. bd. Cancer Research, 1957-61, Internat. Review Experimental, Pathology; 1968—; editorial bd. A.M.A. Archives Pathology-asso. editor Environmental Research, 1966—. Home: Iris Lane Chapel Hill NC 27514 Office: Temple Univ Philadelphia PA 19122

KOTLER, PHILIP, educator; b. Chgo., May 27, 1931; s. Maurice and Betty (Bubar) K.; student DePaul U., 1948-50; M.A., U. Chgo., 1953; Ph.D., Mass. Inst. Tech., 1956; postgrad. U. Chgo., 1957, Harvard, 1960; m. Nancy Ruth Kellum, Jan. 30, 1955; children—Amy Elizabeth, Melissa Eve, Jessica Kellum. Research analyst Westinghouse Corp., Pitts., 1953; asst., asso. prof. Roosevelt U., Chgo., 1957-61; from asst. prof. to prof. econs. Northwestern U., 1962-69, A. Montgomery Ward prof. marketing, 1969—; adv. marketing editor Holt, Rinehart and Winston, 1965—. Chmn. Coll. on Marketing, Inst. Mgmt. Scis., 1968. Recipient Graham and Dodd award Financial Analysts Fedn., 1962, MacLaren Advt. Research award Canadian Advt. Research Found., 1964, Merit award Media/Scope, 1965, McKinsey award 1965, Alpha Kappa Psi Found. award, 1969. Mem. Am. Marketing Assn. (bd. dirs. 1970-72), Inst. Mgmt. Scis., Phi Beta Kappa. Author: Marketing Management: Analysis, Planning and Control, 1967; Marketing Decision Making: A Model- Building Approach 1971; Simulation in Social and Adminstrative Science, 1971; Creating Social Change, 1971. Home: 624 Central St Evanston IL 60201

KOTLOWITZ, ROBERT, editor, writer; b. Paterson, N.J., Nov. 21, 1924; s. Max and Debra (Kaplan) K.; B.A., Johns Hopkins, 1947; preparatory diploma Peabody Conservatory Music, 1941; m. Carol Naomi Leibowitz, Oct. 15, 1950; Books, children-Alexander William, Daniel Justin. Asso. editor Pocket Books, Inc., 1950-55, Discovery, 1952-55; mgr. press and information RCA Victor Records, 1955-60; sr. editor Show mag., 1960-64; sr. editor Harper's mag., 1965-67, mng. editor, 1967-; guest lectr. Queen's Coll., 1954-55; author monthly column Perforning Arts, 1966-. Mem. adv. bd. U. Minn. Drama Publs. Served with inf. AUS, 1943-46. Mem. N.A.A.C.P. (life). Club: Coffeehouse (N.Y.C.). Contbr. nat. publs. Home: 54 Riverside Dr New York City NY 10024 Office: 2 Park Av New York City NY 10016

KOTRADY, JOHN, assn. ofcl.; b. Duquesne, Pa., Feb. 5, 1911; s. John and Mary (Kollar) K.; B.S., Grove City (Pa.) Coll., 1933; m. Helen Beatrice Berndtson, May 31, 1936. Instr. chemistry and comml. law Mayville (N.Y.) High Sch., 1933-37; with Texaco, Inc., 1937-, sr. tech. librarian, 1959-, adminstrv. asst., 1968—. Pres. Dumont (N.J.) Community Chest Council, 1953-54; mem. Highland Hosp. Assn., Beacon, N.Y., 1959-. Served with AUS, World War II. Fellow Am. Inst. Chemists (chmn. N.Y. chpt. 1954-55; councilor 1956-57; chmn. annual meeting 1959; bd. dirs.; mem. nat. council 1959—; nat. sec., 1959—; Honor scroll N.Y. chpt. 1962); mem. Am. Chem. Soc. (treas., bd. dirs. N.Y. chpt. 1960-), Research Soc. Am., Pi Kappa Delta, Pi Gamma Mu. Presbyn. (supt. ch. sch.). Clubs: Chemists (N.Y.C.); Chelsea (N.Y.) Yacht. Home: 13 Wodenethe Dr Beacon NY 12508 Office: 60 E 42d St New York City NY 10017

KOTSCHNIG, WALTER MARIA, govt. ofcl., writer; b. Judenburg, Austria, Apr. 9, 1901 s. Ignaz and Therese (Huber) K.; student Univs. of Graz (Austria) and Kiel (Germany), 1920-24; Dr. Polit. Sci., Inst. of World Econs., Kiel, 1924; LL.D. (hon.), Rockford Coll. (Ill.), 1945; m. Elined Prys, Dec. 10, 1924; children Enid Maria Ileana, Christopher Hans Owen (dec.), John W. Came to U.S., 1936, naturalized, 1942. First asst., Inst. of World Econs., Kiel, 1924-25; sec. gen., Internat. Student Service, Geneva, Switzerland, 1925-34; dir., High Commn. for Refugees Coming from Germany, League of Nations, Geneva, 1934-36; prof. comparative edn., Smith Coll, and Mt. Holyoke Coll., 1937-44; asso. chief, Div. Internat. Orgn. Affairs, Dept. of State, Washington, 1944, in charge of specialized orgn. branch, 1945, acting chief, 1947-49; dir. Office UN Econ. and Social Affairs, 1949; dir. Office of Internat Econ. and Social Affairs, Dept. of State, 1954-62, spl. adviser Bur. Internat. Orgn. Affairs, 1962-65; minister, 1962; dep. asst. sec. state, 1965—; adviser of Ministry of Planning, Afghanistan, 1959; sec. U.S. delegation conf. to establish UNESCO, London, 1945, acting exec. sec. Prep. Commn. (on loan from State Dept.), 1946, adviser U.S. delegation, 1st gen. conf., Paris, 1946, 2d gen. conf., Mexico City, 1947; asso. exec. sec., cons. U.N. Subcommn. Econ. Reconstrn. Devastated Areas (on loan from State Dept.) 1946; asst. sec., U.S. Group, Dumbarton Oaks Conf. on Internat. Orgn. Washington, 1944; tech. expert, U.S. Delegation, San Francisco, 1945; adviser, Internat. Labor Conf., Paris, 1945, U.S. alt. del., Geneva, 1950; U.S. alt. del. governing body ILO, Mysore, India, 1951; adviser to U.S. reps. on UN econ. and social council, 2d to 6th sessions; dep. U.S. rep. Econ. and Social Council, 7th to 50th sessions, Lake Success, N.Y., Geneva, and Santiago, Chile; U.S. alternate delegate to UN conf. on tech. assistance, Lake Success, 1950, to 7th Gen. Conf. UNESCO, Paris, 1952, sr. advisor 8th Gen. Conf., Montevideo, 1954; adv., U.S. delegation to U.N. Gen. Assembly, N.Y., 1950; sr. adviser, U.S. delegation UN Gen. Assembly, 1955-56; dep. U.S. rep., U.N. Econ. Commn. for Asia and the Far East, Rangoon, Burma, 1952, Bangalore, India, 1956, Bangkok, 1957, Kuala Lumpur, 1958; U.S. observer at 1st session UN Econ. Commn. Africa, 1959, 3d session, 1961, 5th session, 1963; dep. U.S. rep. UN Econ. Commn. Latin Am., 1959; chmn. U.S. delegation Industry, Trade Com. ECAFE, Bangalore, 1956, Com. Industry and Resources, Bangkok, 1962; chmn. U.S. del., Wellington, New Zealand, 1965; chmn. U.S. delegation UN Econ. Com. for Europe, Geneva, 1962, 63, 64; vice chmn. U.S. delegation UN Conf. Trade and Devel., Geneva, 1964, 65; U.S. del. Gen. Conf. UNESCO, 1962, 64; U.S. dep. rep. UNESCO exec. bd., Istanbul, 1926; chmn. U. S. del. UNIDO Indsl. Symposium, Athens, 1967; spl. adviser, U.S. del. Internat. Middle Level Manpower Conf., P.R., 1962; U.S. del. UN Slavery Conf., Geneva, 1956; rapporteur UN Con. on Program Appraisal, 1959-60. Trustee Inst. Internat. Edn., 1946- 52. Awarded St. Sava Order, Yugoslavia, 1926, Officers Cross. Civil Service Order, Bulgaria, 1929. Mem. Council on Fgn. Relations. Mem. Soc. of Friends. Author: Unemployment in Learned Professions, 1937; Slaves Need No Leaders, 1943, co-author: Toward the General Welfare, 1957; The United Nations and Promotion of the General Welfare. Editor The University in a Changing World, 1932. Home: 3518 Bradley Lane Chevy Chase MD 20015 Office: Department of State Washington DC 20525

KOTT, JAN, educator; b. Warsaw, Poland, Oct. 27, 1914; s. Maurycy and Kazimiera (Wertenstein) K.; LL.N., U. Warsaw, 1936; Ph.D., U. Lodz (Poland), 1947; m. Lydia Steinhaus, June 17, 1939; children—Lydia Teresa, Michal Hugo. Came to U.S., 1966. Prof. Polish lit. U. Warsaw, 1952—; vis. prof. Polish lit. and drama Yale, 1966-67, vis. prof. drama, 1968-69; vis. prof. drama U. Cal. at Berkeleyy, 1967-68; prof. comparative drama State U. N.Y. at Stony Brook, 1969—. Served with Polish Army, 1939, Polish resistance movement, 1942-45. Recipient Herder award Vienna, Austria, 1964. Hon. mem. Modern Lang. Assn. Author: Shakespeare Our Contemporary, Polish edit., 1961, Am. edit., 1964; Theatre Notebook, 1968. Address: State U of NY Stony Brook NY 11790

KOTTKAMP, JOHN HARLAN, lawyer; b. Portland, Ore., Oct. 19, 1930; s. John Henry and Anne (Schnell) K.; B.S., U. Ore., 1952, LL.B., 1957; m. Elizabeth Ann Lawrence, July 10, 1954; children—Elizabeth, Andrew, Molly, Jennifer, Carrie. Admitted to Ore. bar, 1957, since practiced in Pendleton; asso. Kilkenny & Fabre, 1957-59; partner Fabre, Collins & Kottkamp, 1959-61; pvt. practice, 1961-64; partner Kottkamp & O'Rourke, 1964—. Chmn. bd. Umatilla County Heart Fund, 1958-59. Chmn. Umatilla County Republican Central Com., 1963-64. Served with AUS, 1952-54. Mem. Am., 6th Jud. (past pres.) bar assns., Am. Judicature Soc., Ore. Assn. Def. Counsel, Pendleton C. of C. (past dir.). Presbyn. (trustee). Rotarian (past pres.), Elk. Club: Pendleton Country (past pres.). Home: 910 NW 12th St Pendleton OR 97801 Office: 231 SE Byers Av Pendleton OR 97801

KOTTKE, FREDERIC JAMES physician, educator; b. Hayfield, Minn., May 26, 1917; s. George G. and Harriet Mae (Davidson) K.; B.S., U. Minn., 1939, M.S. in Physiology, 1941, Ph.D. in Physiology, 1944, M.D., 1945; m. Astrid Marie Erling, May 27, 1939; children—Jane, James, Mary, Thomas. Lab. asst. physiology U. Minn., 1939-40, instr., 1941-44, Baruch fellow phys. medicine, 1946-47 asst. prof. phys. medicine, 1947-49, asso. prof., 1949-53, head dept. phys. medicine and rehab., 1952—, prof., 1953—; cons. Mpls. VA Hosp., 1952—. Mem. Minn. State Bd. Health, 1964-67; mem. med. adv. bd. Office vocational rehab., 1961-67, mem. med. research study sect., 1961- 63; bd. dirs. Kenny Rehab. Found., 1960-64, v.p., 1960-63, sec., 1963-64; mem. bd. Am. Rehab. Found., 1964—, sec., 1964. Pres. Minn. Phys. Therapy Bd. Examiners, 1951-61. Diplomate Am. Bd. Phys. Medicine and Rehab. (mem. bd. 1955-69, chmn. bd. 1963-69). Mem. Am. Physiol. Soc., Soc. Exptl. Biology and Medicine, Am., Minn. med. assns., Am. Heart Assn., Am. Assn. U. Profs., Am. Physiol. Soc., Internat. Soc. for Rehab. of Disabled, Am. Congress Rehab. Medicine, Am. Congress Phys. Medicine and Rehab. (pres. 1959-60; chmn. program com. 3d internat. congress 1960), Am. Acad. Phys. Medicine and Rehab., Nat. Rehab. Assn., Minn. Acad. Medicine. Lutheran. Editorial board Archives Physical Medicine and Rehab., 1952—, Modern Medicine, 1955—. Home: 2741 Drew Av Minneapolis MN 55416 Office: University Medical Center U Minn Minneapolis MN 55455

KOTTMAN, ROY MILTON, educator; b. Thornton, Ia., Dec. 22, 1916; s. William D. and Millie J. (Christensen) K.; B.S. in Agr., Ia. State U., 1941, Ph.D., 1952; M.S. in Genetics, U. Wis., 1948; m. Wanda Loraine Moorman, Dec. 31, 1941; children—Gary Roy, Robert William, Wayne David, Janet Kay. Asst. prof. animal husbandry Ia. State U., 1946-47; grad. research asst. U. Wis., 1947-48; faculty Ia. State U., 1949-58, prof. animal husbandry, asso. dean agr., 1954-58; dean Coll. Agr., Forestry and Home Econs., dir. Agrl. Expt. Sta., W.Va. U., 1958-60; dean Coll. Agr. and Home Econs., Ohio State U., also dir. Agrl. Expt. Sta., 1960—, dir. Coop. Extension Service, 1964—; mem. Ohio Soil and Water Conservation Commn., 1960—; chmn. legislative subcom., expt. sta. com. on orgn. and policy div. agr. Nat. Assn. State Univs. and Land Grant Colls.; mem. governing bd. Agrl. Research Inst., Agr. Bd., Nat. Acad. Sci.-NRC, 1970—; bd. dirs. Agr. Careers, Inc., 1969—; mem. Pres.'s Task Force on Rural Devel., 1969—; mem. Gov.'s Task Force on Vocational and Tech. Edn. in Ohio, 1968. Bd. dirs. Am. Farm Bur. Research Found. Served to maj. AUS, 1941-46; col. Res. Mem. Am. Soc. Animal Sci. (chmn. teaching com. 1959), A.A.A.S., Exec. Order Ohio Commodores, Sigma Xi, Gamma Sigma Delta, Alpha Zeta, Phi Kappa Phi, Pi Kappa Phi, Phi Zeta (hon.). Rotarian. Clubs: Torch (Columbus, O.); National Dairy Shrine. Presbyn. Home: 1375 Kirkley Road Columbus OH 43221

KOTTMEYER, WILLIAM, supt. schs.; b. Dawn, Tex., Feb. 8, 1910; s. Henry and Anna (Frye) K.; B.S. in Edn., St. Louis U., 1935, A.M., 1939, Ph.D., 1954; m. Lucille Kirk, Oct. 17, 1936; childrenWilliam Kirk, Kirk Richard, Tchr., then prin. St. Louis pub. schs., 1935-42, asst. prof. Harris Tchrs. Coll., St. Louis, 1943-45; mem. staff St. Louis Bd., Edn., 1945—, dep. supt. 1961-64, superintendent of instruction, 1964-67, superintendent of schools, 1967-; founder reading clinics, 1943-. Mem. adv. bd. St. Louis council Boy Scouts Am., 1964-; trustee Parsons Blewett Meml. Fund Relief Distress Tchrs. and Advancement Profl. Tng., 1964-. Mem. N.E.A., Mo. Tchrs. Assn., Am., Mo. assns. sch. adminstrs., Phi Delta Kappa, Kappa Delta Pi. Author books on reading, textbooks for elementary edn. Home: 5751 Lindell Blvd Saint Louis MO 63112 Office: 911 Locust Street Saint Louis MO 63101

KOTULAK, RONALD, newspaperman; b. Detroit, July 31, 1935; s. John and Mary (Roman) K.; student Wayne State U., 1953-54; B.A. in Journalism, U. Mich., 1959; m. Jean Bond, May 6, 1961; children-Jeffrey, Kerry, Christopher. Mem. staff Chgo. Tribune, 1959-, sch. bd. reporter, 1961-63, sci. editor, 1965-. Recipient first place sci. writing award Am. Dental Assn., 1966; 1st place med. writing award A.M.A., 1968; 1st prize Russell L. Cecil award Arthritis Found., 1969. Mem. Nat. Assn. Sci. Writers. Home: 4116 Central Park Av Chicago IL 60618 Office: 435 N Michigan Av Chicago IL 60611

KOTZ, NATHAN KALLISON, (Nick), journalist; b. San Antonio, Tex., Sept. 16, 1932; s. Jacob and Tybe (Kallison) K.; grad. St. Albans Sch., 1951; A.B. magna cum laude with high honors in Internat. Relations, Dartmouth, 1955; student London (Eng.) Sch. Econs., 1955-56; m. Mary Lynn Booth, Aug. 7, 1960; 1 son, Jack Mitchell. Reporter Des Moines Register, 1958-64, Washington corr., 1964-70, also for other Cowles Publs. newspapers; nat. corr. Washington Post, 1970—. Bd. dirs. Ia. Bds. Internat. Edn., 1962-64, Suburban Md. Fair Housing, 1966—. Served to 1st lt. USMCR, 1956-58. Recipient Pulitzer prize for nat. reporting, 1968; Raymond Clapper Meml. award, 1966-68; Distinguished Service award Sigma Delta Chi, 1966; Robert F. Kennedy Journalism award, 1968. Mem. Phi Beta Kappa. Club: Nat. Press (Washington). Author: Let Them Eat Promises: The Politics of Hunger in America, 1969. Home: 5508 Montgomery St Chevy Chase MD 20015 Office: National Press Bldg Washington DC 20004

KOTZ, SAMUEL, educator, math. statistician; b. Harbin, China, Aug. 28, 1930 (parents Am. citizens) s. Boris and Guta (Kahana) K.; M.Sc., Hebrew U., Jerusalem, 1956; Ph.D., Cornell U., 1960; m. Roselyn Greenwald, Aug. 6, 1963; children—Tamar Ann, Harold David. Researcher, Israel Meterol. Service, 1954-58; lectr. Bar-Ilan U., Israel, 1960-62; postdoctoral fellow U. N.C., 1962-63; asso. prof. U. Toronto, 1963-67; prof. math. Temple U., 1967—. Served with Israeli Army, 1950-52. Fellow Am. Statis. Assn.; mem. Am. Math. Soc., London Math. Soc., Inst. Math. Statistics, Canadian Operations Research Soc., Author, editor 6 books, 2 Russian-English profl. dictionaries, numerous research papers. Home: 1618 Griffith St Philadelphia PA 19111

KOTZKY, ALEX SYLVESTER, syndicated cartoonist; b. N.Y.C., Sept. 11, 1923; s. Theodor and Helen (Owsieneoka) K.; student Art Students League, N.Y.C., 1941; m. Emma Matelli, Sept. 21, 1946; children—Brian, Bruce. Free-lance comml. artist, 1946-57; cartoonist syndicated strip Duke Hand, 1958-59, syndicated strip Apt. 3-G, 1961—. Served with inf. AUS, 1943-46. ETO. Decorated Combat Inf. badge. Mem. Nat. Cartoonist Soc. Address: 203-17 56th Av Bayside NY 11364

KOUCHAKJI, FAHIM JOSEPH art collector; b. Aleppo, Syria, Mar. 17, 1886; s. George A. and Emilia (Sharki) K.; student Ecole Grèque Episcopal St. Nicolas, Aleppo; studied banking, Credit Lyonnaise, Cairo, Egypt, 1904-09; m. Evelyn Curtis, 1930. Mgr. Kouchakji Frères, Paris, N.Y. and Aleppo, 1909-24; pres. Kouchakji Frères, N.Y., 1924-25. Naturalized citizen of U.S. Fellow in perpetuity Met. Mus. of Art. Mem. Met. Mus. of Art, Cleve. Museum of Art, Coll. Art Assn., Walter's Art Gallery, Friends Fogg Art Mus., Am. Italy Soc., Archaeol. Inst. Am., Asia Inst., Am. Acad. Polit. Sci., Iranian Inst. of Art and Archaeology, Nat. Geo. Soc., Iran-Am. Soc. Roman Catholic. Author: (with G.A. Eisen) Glass, 1927. Former owner Great Chalice of Antioch; pub. The Great Chalice of Antioch (2 vols.), 1925, popular edit. (1 vol.), 1933, and lectr. on that subject. Collaborator with G. A. Eisen: Portraits of Washington, 3 vol., 1933; Ancient Oriental Cylinder and other Seals, 1940. Collector of Greek, Egyptian Roman, Syrian, Persian and Arabic art, glass, Faience, etc. Home: 444 East 57th St New York City NY 10022 (summer) Shandaken NY 12480 Office: 30 East 60th St New York City NY 10022

KOUDELE, GORDON FREDERICK, utility exec.; b. Weston, Neb., June 9, 1912; s. Frank and Helen Henrietta (Jacobs) K.; B.S., U. Neb., 1936; student Luther Coll., 1932-34. Pub. accountant, 1936-44; with C.L. Paxson, Topeka, Kan., 1944-48, Arthur Young & Co., Kansas City, Mo., 1948-54; with Gas Service Co., Kansas City, 1954—, asst. sec., 1959—, asst. treas., 1962—, controller, 1970—. Dir. Downtown YMCA of Kansas City. C.P.A. Mem. Am. Inst. C.P.A.'s, Mo. Soc. C.P.A.'s, Nat. Assn. Accountants, Tax Execs. Inst., U. Neb. Alumni Assn. (pres. Kansas City 1958). Mason (Shriner). Home: 910 Pennsylvania Av Kansas City MO 64105 Office: Scarritt Bldg Kansas City MO 64142

KOUFAX, SANFORD, sportscaster; b. Bklyn., Dec. 30, 1935; student U. Cin. Pitcher, Bklyn . (now Los Angeles), Nat. League, 1955-66; sportscaster NBC, 1967—. With Los Angeles, World Series, 1959, 63, 65, 66. Named to All Star team Nat. League, 1963-66. Number one Major League Player of Year, 1963, 65, Nat. League Pitcher of Year, 1963-66, all Sporting News, Most Valuable Player, Nat. League, 1963; recipient Cy Young Meml. award, 1963, 65, 66. Address: care Dir Pub Relations NBC 30 Rockefeller Plaza New York City NY 10022*

KOUNTZ, AMBROSE EDWARD, lawyer; b. Pitts., June 18, 1892; s. Joseph L. and Mary (Rush) K.; LL.B., Dickinson Coll., 1913; m. Laura Marie Friday, May 14, 1919 (dec.); m. 2d, Carice N. Patterson, July 14, 1946. Admitted to Pa. bar, 1914; mem. law firm Kountz, Fry & Meyer, Pitts.; dir. West View Park Co., Pitts. Mem. Am., Pa., Allegheny County bar assns., Am. Judicature Soc., Sigma Chi. Club: Duquesne (Pitts.). Home: 129 Bellevue Road Pittsburgh PA 15229 Office: Frick Building Pittsburgh PA 15219

KOUNTZE, DENMAN, Jr., travel agt.; b. Omaha, June 10, 1929; s. Denman and Mary Mallory (Harris) K.; grad. Choate Sch., 1947; student U. Omaha, 1948-49; B.A., Yale, 1952; m. Elizabeth Jean Keebler, May 29, 1954; children—Charles Denman, Edward Harris. Reporter, feature writer Omaha World-Herald, 1953-56, entertainment editor, 1956-64; editor-in-chief, founder, co-owner Plainsman Mag., Omaha, 1964-67; entertainment mag. editor Omaha World-Herald, 1967-71; founder, owner Traveler's World, Inc., 1971—; dir. Easy Parking Co., Omaha Parking Mgmt. and Services, Inc., Omaha, Loop Parking Co. Trustee Hitchcock Found. of Omaha, Brownell-Talbot Sch. of Omaha. Mem. Omaha Press Club, Omaha C. of C. Republican. Episcopalian. Clubs: Yale (Omaha and N.Y.C.); Editor: Tested Collection Methods and Procedures, 1966. Home: 401 N 62d St Omaha NB 68132 Office: 1902 Howard St Omaha NB 68102

KOUNTZE, HAROLD, Jr., banker; b. Denver, Apr. 2, 1923; s. Harold and Louise (Bulkley) K.; grad. Hotchkiss Sch., Lakeville, Conn., 1941; B.A., Yale, 1944; postgrad. Grad. Sch. Banking, Rutgers U., 1953; m. Priscilla Van Tine, Feb. 3, 1945 (div. June 1957); children—Elizabeth (Mrs. James M. Idema, Jr.), Louise, Anne; m. 2d, Kay Howard, Feb. 7, 1959. With Chase Nat. Bank, N.Y.C., 1944- 45; with Colo. Nat. Bank, Denver, 1945—, asst. cashier, 1948-52, asst. v.p., 1952-55, v.p., 1955-68, v.p., cashier, 1968—, dir., 1966—, sec. bd., 1970—; sec. Colo. Nat. Bankshares, Inc.; dir. Miller-Vidor Land Co., Beaumont, Tex.; mem. adv. bd. S. Tex. Land Co. Treas. Mile High chpt. A.R.C., 1969—; treas. bd. dirs., Met. Denver chpt. Leukemia Soc. Am., 1967—; bd. regents Loan Mgmt. Seminar, Robert Morris Assos., 1969—. Mem. Robert Morris Assos. (dir. 1969—), Denver C. of C. Episcopalian (past treas. Diocese Colo.). Lion (dir., treas. Denver 1963-69). Home: 3281 S Krameria St Denver CO 80222 Office: Colo Nat Bank Denver CO 80217

KOURKENE, JACK, archtl. engr.; b. Saint-Brevin-l'Ocean, France, Apr. 14, 1927; s. Haig and Hermine (Artinoff) K.; came to U.S., 1947, naturalized, 1966; student Ecole Nationale des Ponts-et-Chaussées, Paris, 1946-47; B.S., Mass. Inst. Tech., 1948, postgrad., 1948-49. Research fellow U.S. Bur. Reclamation, Denver, 1950-51; cons. to Tex. Hwy. Dept., Dallas, 1953; cons. to owners, architects, structural engrs., gen. constrn. contractors, concrete products fabricators and steel products distbrs., 1953—; owner Prestress Service Internat., 1954—; instrumental in advent of Joseph T. Ryerson & Son, Inc. and others into mass prodn. and distbn. of standard steel posttensioning tendons and commodities, 1954—; prof. math. San Francisco Coll. for Women, 1958-59; structural engr. Skidmore, Owings & Merrill, San Francisco, 1961-63; prof. U. Cal. at Berkeley extension, 1968; project engr. San Francisco Bay Naval Shipyard, 1968; structural engr. Offshore Petroleum div. Brown & Root, Inc., Houston, 1969-70. Registered profl. engr., Cal. Fellow Am. Soc. C.E.; mem. Prestressed Concrete Inst., Structural Engrs. Assn. No. Cal., Mass. Inst. Tech. Alumni Assn., Société des Ingénieurs Civils de France, French Hosp. San Francisco, Carnegie Inst. Soc. Club: Lafayette (San Francisco). Author: Posttensioning Structures: Design and Techniques, 1968. Contbr. articles profl. jours. Inventor PSI open systems of posttensioning. Address: 3559 Jackson St San Francisco CA 94118

KOUSOULAS, DIMITRIOS GEORGE, educator, author: b. Khalkis, Greece, Dec. 22, 1923; s. George D. and Barbara (Lachnidakis) K.; LL.B., U. Athens (Greece), 1948; M.A. (Fulbright scholar) in Polit. Sci., Syracuse U., 1953, Ph.D., 1956; m. Mary Katris, Jan. 27, 1952; 1 son, George. Came to U.S., 1951; naturalized, 1958. Fgn. lang. specialist USIA, 1957-60; professional lectr. Nat. War Coll. George Washington U., 1961—; asst. prof. Howard U., 1961-64, asso. prof., 1965-67, prof. govt., chmn. dept., 1967—. Pres. Am. Com. on Cyprus Self-determination, 1964-66. Bd. trustees Ahepa Ednl. Found. 1968—. Served in Greek Armed Forces, 1948-50. Decorated Nat. Resistance medal, knight Royal Order of Phoenix, Golden Cross (Greece). Mem. Am. Acad. Polit. and Social Sci., Acad. Polit. Sci., Am., Internat. polit. sci. assns. Author: The Price of Freedom; Greece in World Affairs 1939-53, 1953; Key to Economic Progress, 1958; Revolution and Defeat; the Story of the Greek Communist Party,

1965; On Government; a Comparative Introduction, 1968. Home: 6252 Clearwood Rd Bethesda MD 20034 Office: Howard Univ Washington DC 20001

KOUTS, HERBERT JOHN CECIL, physicist; b. Bisbee, Ariz., Dec. 18, 1919; s. Oliver Allen and Lillian (Niemeyer) K.; B.S., La. State U., 1941, M.S., 1946; Ph.D., Princeton, 1952; m. Hertha Isla Pretorius, Feb. 2, 1942; children—Anne Elizabeth, Catherine Jennifer. Physicist, Brookhaven Nat. Lab., Upton, N.Y., 1950- -; spl. research elementary particle theory, nuclear reactor shielding, nuclear reactor physics, nuclear arms control, nuclear non-proliferation, nuclear reactor safety. Mem. adv. com. reactor physics AEC, 1956-62, mem. adv. com. reactor safeguards, 1962- 66, chmn. 1964; mem. European-Am. Adv. Com. Reactor Physics, 1962-68, Served with USAAF, 1942-45. Recipient Ernest O. Lawrence award AEC, 1963. Fellow Am. Nuclear Soc. (dir.). Editor: Advances in Nuclear Science and Technology, 1962-64. Home: South Country Road Bellport Brookhaven NY 11719 Office: Brookhaven Nat Lab Upton NY 11973

KOUVEL, JAMES SPYROS, educator, physicist; b. Jersey City, May 23, 1926; s. Spyros and Ifegenia (Cassianos) K.; B.Engring., Yale, 1946, Ph.D., 1951; m. Audrey Lumsden, June 26, 1953; children—Diana, Alexander. Research fellow U. Leeds (Eng.), 1951-53, Harvard, 1953-55; physicist Gen. Electric Co. Research and Devel. Center, 1955-69; prof. physics U. Ill. at Chgo. Circle, 1969—; vis. scientist Atomic Energy Research Establishment, Harwell, Eng., 1967-68; cons. Argonne Nat. Lab., 1969—, mem. rev. com., 1970—. Served with USNR, 1944-46. Guggenheim fellow, 1967-68. Fellow Am. Phys. Soc.; mem. Sigma Xi. Author papers in field. Editor Magnetism Conf. proc., 1965-67. Home: 223 N Euclid Av Oak Park IL 60302 Office: Box 4348 Chicago IL 60680

KOUWENHOVEN, JOHN ATLEE, educator, writer, mag. editor; b. Yonkers, N.Y., 1909; s. John Bennem and Grace (Atlee) K.; A.B., Wesleyan U., Middletown, Conn., 1931; A.M., Columbia, 1933, Ph.D., 1948; m. Eleanor W. Hayden, June 22, 1935 (div. 1959); children—Ann (dec.), Gerrit Wolphertsen; m. 2d, Joan Vatsek Arthur, June 12, 1960; stepchildren—Andrew Arthur, Elizabeth Arthur. Master in English, Harvey Sch., Hawthorne, N.Y., 1932-36; instr. English, Columbia Coll., 1936-38; mem. lit. faculty Bennington (Vt.) Coll., 1938-41; asst. editor Harper's Mag., 1941-44, asso. editor, 1944-46, contbg. editor, 1946-54; asso. in English and Am. studies Barnard Coll., Columbia, 1946-48, asso. prof. English, 1948-50, prof., 1950—; chmn. dept., 1950-54; dir. hist. files Brown Bros. Harriman & Co., 1964-68. Mem. vis. com. Costume Inst., Met. Mus. Art, 1971—; mem. adv. com. Archives Am. Art, 1967—. Trustee Merck Forest Found., 1950-70, past sec.; trustee R.I. Sch. Design, 1961-67, 68-70; trustee Vt. Council on Arts, 1968—, v.p., 1969—; trustee McCullough-Park Found., 1971—. Decorated Officer's Cross, Order of Orange-Nassau (Netherlands), 1954. Benjamin Franklin fellow, hon. corr. mem. Royal Soc. Arts (Great Britain); mem. Am. Studies Assn., Soc. Archtl. Historians, Soc. History Tech. (exec. council 1962-64, adv. council 1958-61, 65—). Author: Adventures of America 1857-1900, 1938; Made in America: The Arts in Modern Civilization, 1948; The Columbia Historical Portrait of New York, 1953; The Beer Can by the Highway, 1961; Partners in Banking, 1968; also articles in profl. jours. and popular mags. Co-author: American Studies in Transition, 1965. Editor New York Guide Book, 1964. Mem. editorial bd. Technology and Culture, 1958—. Home: Dorset VT 05251

KOUWENHOVEN, WILLIAM BENNETT elec. engr.; b. Brooklyn, N.Y., Jan. 13, 1886; s. Tunis Gerrit Bergen and Phebe Florence (Bennett) K.; E.E., Brooklyn Poly. Inst., 1906, M.E., 1907; Diplom Ingenieur, Karlsruhe Technische Hochschule, Baden, Germany, 1912, Doktor Ingenieur, 1913; LL.D., Johns Hopkins U., 1962; m. Abigail Baxter Remsen, June 22, 1910; 1 son, William Gerrit. Asst. in physics, Brooklyn Poly. Inst., 1906-07, instr. in physics and elec. engring., 1907-10; instr. in elec. engring., Washington U., 1913-14; same, Johns Hopkins, 1914-17, asso. in elec. engring., 1917-19; engring. supt. Winchester Repeating Arms Co. (leave of absence from Johns Hopkins), 1919-20; asso. prof. elec. engring., Johns Hopkins, 1919- 30, prof. and asst. dean Sch. of Engring., 1930-38, prof. and dean school of engring., 1938-54, prof. emeritus, 1954—; lectr. in surgery Johns Hopkins Sch. Medicine, 1956—; cons. engr. U.S. Bureau of Mines, U.S. Bureau Standards. Instr., rank of capt., R.O.T.C., World War. Recipient Ludwig Hekton Gold medal, A.M.A., 1961; Edison Medalist, Am. Inst. E.E., 1962. Fellow A.A.A.S., Am. Inst. E.E. (v.p. 1931-33; dir. 1935-39; chmn. Baltimore sect. 1922-31); mem. Am. Society for Testing Materials, Am. Welding Soc. Exec. Com. of Research Council, Nat. Acad. Sci., Am Heart Assn., Eta Kappa Nu. Tau Beta Pi, Sigma Xi, Pi Kappa Phi. Arbitrator, Nat. Assn. of Arbitration. Democrat. Presbyterian. Clubs: Johns Hopkins Baltimore Engineers, Gibson Island. Contributor of numerous articles and papers on electrical measurements, also on electric shock, magnetic analysis, electric welding, effect of electricity on heart, elec. defibrillation, closed chest cardiac massage, effects of high voltage electric fields on human beings, treatment of atrial fibrillation, etc., Trans. American Inst. Elec. Engring., Elec. World, Proc. Am. Soc. for Testing Materials, Welding Journal, med. and surg. jours., etc. Home: 334 Saint Dunstan's Road Baltimore MD 21212

KOVACH, EUGENE GEORGE, internat. orgn. ofcl.; b. Irvington, N.J., May 18, 1922; s. Eugene John and Hortense Marie (Telmany) K.; B.S., Wayne U., 1943, M.S., 1944; M.A., Harvard, 1948, Ph.D., 1949; m. Mary Eleanor Frenning, Apr. 11, 1950; children—George Eugene, Mary Edith, Katherine Eleanor, Christine Marie, John Peter. Mem. faculty, research organic chemistry Colgate U., 1950-51, U. Fla., 1949-54; sci. adviser to comdr. U.S. Naval Forces Germany, 1954-57; with NSF, 1958; with State Dept., Washington, 1959-70, accounting dir. Office Gen. Sci. Affairs, 1966-70; dep. asst. sec.-gen. for sci. affairs NATO, Brussels, Belgium, 1970—. Served with USNR, 1944-45. Recipient Wayne U. Distinguished Alumnus award, 1961. Mem. Am. Chem. Soc., A.A.A.S., Sigma Xi. Club: International (Brussels). Home: 12 Ave des Troenes 1950 Kraainem Belgium Office: Sci Affairs Div NATO 1110 Brussels Belgium

KOVACH, FRANCIS JOSEPH, educator; b. Budapest, Hungary, July 19, 1918; s. Joseph and Anna (Roch) K.; Ph.D. in Philosophy summa cum laude, U. Cologne (Germany), 1959; m. Elizabeth W. Thököly, July 19, 1942; children—Elizabeth (Mrs. James Cowan), Akos, Leslie, Agnes, Thomas. Came to U.S., 1951, naturalized, 1956. Instr., then asst. prof. philosophy Coll. St. Scholastica, Duluth, Minn., 1953-59; asst. prof. St. Benedict's Coll. and Mt. St. Scholastica, Atchison, Kan., 1959-62; Villanova U., 1962-64; mem. faculty Okla. U., 1964—, prof. philosophy, 1969—. Rep. Am. Council Learned Socs. 6th Internat. Congress Aesthetics, Amsterdam, Holland, 1964. Mem. Soc. Internat. pour l'etude de la philosophie medievale (Louvain, Belgium), Internat. Scotistic Soc., Brit. Soc. Aesthetics, Am. Cath. Philos. Assn. (pres. N. Central chpt. 1958), Am., Southwestern philos. socs. Author: Die Aesthetik des Thomas von Aquin, 1961; also articles. Home: 1126 Beverly Hills St Norman OK 73069

KOVACH, GEORGE PAUL, plastics co. exec.; b. Vienna, Austria, Dec. 29, 1912; s. Edmond and Paula (Dornhelm) Kovacs; Dipl. Eng., Technische Hochschule, Vienna, 1936; m. Madeline E. Besnyoe, Apr. 24, 1939; children—Peter J., Thomas A. Came to U.S., 1939, naturalized, 1945, Chief chemist Foster-Grant Co., Inc., Leominster, Mass., 1941-46, mgr. product devel., 1953-61; project mgr. Nixon Nitration Works (N.J.), 1946-47; mgr. plastics div. Atlantic Tubing & Rubber Co., R.I., 1947-51, Ciopay Corp., Cin., 1951- 53; pres. Koro Corp., Hudson, Mass., 1961—. Mem. Soc. Plastic Engrs. (nat. pres.), Soc. Plastics Industry (dir.). Contbr. Processing of Thermoplastics, 1959, Ency. Chem. Engring., 1961, Ency. Polymer Sci. and Tech., vols. 12, 13, 1970. Home: 770 Boylston St Boston MA 029199 Office: 560 Lower Main St Hudson MA 01749

KOVACIC, PETER, educator, chemist; b. Wylandville, Pa., Aug. 1, 1921; s. Marko and Barbara (Radinich) K.; A.B., Hanover (Ind.) Coll., 1943, D.Sc., 1964; Ph.D., U. Ill., 1946; postgrad. Mass. Inst. Tech., 1946-47; m. Dorothy Fehrenbacher, June 29, 1946; childrenLynn, Jan, Paul, Don, Eric, Ken. Instr., Columbia, 1947-48; research chemist E.I. du Pont de Nemours & Co., Inc., 1948-55; mem. faculty Case Western Res. U., Cleve., 1955-68, prof., 1965-68; prof. U. Wis. at Milw., 1968—. Cons. Sun Oil Co., 1965-67. Mem. Am. Chem. Soc., A.A.A.S., Am. Assn. U. Profs., Sigma Xi, Alpha Chi Sigma, Phi Gamma Delta. Author articles, revs. Mem. editorial bd. Macromolecular Synthesis, 1959-70. Home: 1506 E Dean Rd Milwaukee WI 53217 Office: U Of Wisconsin Milwaukee WI 53201

KOVACIK, LUDOVIT, banker. Gen. mgr. Comml. Bank of Czechoslovakia, Prague. Office: Na Prikope 14 Praha 1 Prague Czecholslovakia*

KOVALICK, WALTER W., bus. exec.; b. 1918; B.Mech. Engring., U. Akron, 1940; married. Various engring. and mfg. positions Borg Warner Corp., also Firestone Co., 1941-57; dir. mfg. Crane Co., Chgo., 1957-61; sr. v.p. operations Vendor Corp., 1961-65, exec. v.p., 1965; div. pres. Seeburg Corp., Chgo., 1966-67, exec. v.p., 1967—. Address: 1500 N Dayton St Chicago OH 60622*

KOVANOV, PAVEL VASILIEVICH, govt. ofcl. USSR; b. 1907; ed. Lenin State Pedagogical Inst. Chmn. collective farm Moscow region, 1930-31; with Commissariat of Edn., 1931- 42; 2d sec. central com. Communist Party Georgia, 1956-63; mem. permanent central com. Communist Party, 1944-56, dep. chmn. com. for party-state control and Council of Ministers USSR, 1963-65, dep. prime minister, chmn. com. people's control, 1965—, candidate mem. central com., 1961—. Served with Soviet Army, 1942-44. Address: USSR Committee of People's Control Ulitsa Kuibistseva 21 Moscow USSR*

KOVASZNAY, LESLIE STEPHEN GEORGE, scientist; b. Budapest, Hungary, Apr. 14, 1918; s. Laszlo Peter and Maria Anna (Mester) K.; Dipl. Ing., Royal Hungarian Inst., Budapest, 1941, Dr. Tech., 1943; postdoctoral study Cambridge U., 1946-47; Docteur h.c. U. d'Aix-Marseille, 1969; m. Anna Jolan Frenyo, Dec. 10, 1944; dau., Beatrice Mary. Came to U.S., 1947, naturalized, 1953. Asst. prof. Royal Hungarian U., 1941-44, adj. prof., 1944-46; asst. prof. Johns Hopkins, 1947-50, asso. prof., 1950-53, prof. aeros., 1953—, chmn. dept. mechanics, 1967-69; vis. prof. U. Mich., 1950, U. Tokyo, 1965-66; lectr. in Europe with adv. group aero. research and devel. NATO, 1953; cons. Nat. Bur. Standards, 1950-, NACA, 1952, Mass. Inst. Tech., 1953, USAF, 1954—. Guggenheim fellow, 1955; NSF sr. post-doctoral fellow U. Tokyo, 1956-66. Fellow Am. Acad. Arts and Scis., Am. Phys. Soc.; sr. mem. Inst. Radio Engrs.; mem. Inst. Aero. Scis., Sigma Xi, Tau Beta Pi. Contbr. profl. jours. Home: 5800 Stony Run Drive Baltimore MD 21210 Office: Johns Hopkins U Baltimore MD 21218

KOVEL, RALPH M., author, authority antiques; b. Milw., 1920; s. Lester and Dorothy (Bernstein) K.; student Ohio State U.; m. Terry Horvitz; childrenLee Ralph, Karen Jo. Owner, pres. Ralph M. Kovel and Asso. food broker; pres. Chgo. Sales Co., Antiques Inc., Celco Inc.; treas. Haven Enterprises Inc.; past tchr. course in antiques Western Res. U.; appeared radio and TV discussion programs, subject of antiques; with Terry Kovel, writer syndicated column, Know Your Antiques, 1955—, nat. non- comml. TV series about antiques, 1969—. Mem. rev. and allocations com. Welfare Fedn., Cleve. Past pres. E. End Neighnorhood Settlement House; past chmn. Woodhill Homes Adv. Com. Mem. bd. Soc. Collectors, Silver Mus. Religious Art. Recipient Lane Bryant award, 1966. Mem. Appraisers. Assn. Am., Cleve. Food Brokers,Nat. Food Brokers Assn., Asso. Grocery Mfrs. (rep.).Club: Oakwood. Author: (with Terry Kovel) Dictionary of Marks, Pottery and Porcelain, 1953; Directory of American Silver, Pewter and Silver Plate, 1961; American Country Furniture, 1780-1875, 1965; Know Your Antiques, 1967; The Complete Antiques Price List, 1968, 69, 70, 71. Contbr. articles on antiques, numerous publs. Home: 22000 Shaker Blvd Shaker Heights OH 44122 Office: care Crown Publishers 419 Park Avenue South New York City NY 10016 also 27621 Chagrin Blvd Cleveland OH 44122

KOVEL, TERRY HORVITZ (Mrs. Ralph Kovel), author, authority antiques; b. Cleve., 1928; d. Isadore and Rix (Osteryoung) Horvitz; B.A., Wellesley Coll., 1950; m. Ralph Kovel; children—Lee R., Karen. Tchr. math. Hawken Sch. for Boys, Shaker Heights, O., 1961-71; tchr. course in antiques Western Res. U.; radio and TV discussion programs on antiques; with Ralph Kovel, writer syndicated column, Know Your Antiques, 1955—; pub. TV series Know Your Antiques, 1969—. Past mem. bd. Soc. of Collectors, Silver Mus. Religious Art; mem. bd. Catholic DePaul Infant and Maternity Home, Council Jewish Women. Author: (with Ralph Kovel) Dictionary of Marks, Pottery and Porcelain, 1953, Directory of American Silver, Pewter and Silver Plate, 1961, American Country Furniture, 1780- 1875, 1965, Know Your Antiques, 1967, The Complete Antiques Price List, 1968, 4th edit., 1971, The Official Bottle Price List, 1971. Contbr. articles on antiques, numerous publs. Home: 22000 Shaker Blvd Shaker Heights OH 44122 Office: care Crown Publishers 419 Park Av S New York City NY 10016

KOVEN, HENRY HARRY, lawyer; b. Manchester, Eng., May 13, 1895; s. Harris and Sarah (Shaiman) K.; came to U.S., 1901, naturalized, 1919; LL.B., Chgo.-Kent Coll. Law, 1919; m. Pauline Klein, Dec. 28, 1919; children—Howard R., Lila (Mrs. Charles N. Salzman). Admitted to Ill. bar, 1920, since practiced in Chgo.; partner firm Friedman, Koven, Shapiro, Salzman, Koenigsberg, Specks & Homer, and predecessors, 1920—. Dir. Shapiro-Hamilton Co. Chmn. lawyers div. Chicago Met. Crusade of Mercy, 1965. Mem. Am., Ill., Chgo. bar assns., Decalogue Soc. Lawyers, S. Shore Fellowship, Phi Kappa Phi. Mem. B'nai B'rith. Club: Green Acres Country. Home: 200 E Chestnut St Chicago IL 60611 Office: 208 South LaSalle St Chicago IL 60604

KOVEN, HOWARD RICHARD, lawyer; b. Chgo., Apr. 20, 1921; s. Henry H. and Pauline (Klein) K.; A.B., U. Chgo., 1941, J.D., 1946; m. Eileen Shargel, Nov. 15, 1946; children—Maggie, Jane. Admitted to Ill. bar, 1946, D.C. bar, 1970; partner Friedman, Koven, Shapiro, Salzman, Koenigsberg, Specks & Homer, Chgo., also Fortas and Koven, Washington; atty., gen. counsel Chgo., Counsel Child Psychiatry, 1961—. Dir. Ronco Teleproducts. Nat. chmn. Nat. Epilepsy League, 1960-63. Sec., dir. Jupiter Oils, Ltd.; v.p., dir., gen. counsel Jupiter Corp., adv. bd. Amalgamated Trust & Savs. Bank, Met. Bank & Trust Co. Chgo. Pres. Epilepsy Assn. of Am. 1965-66; co-chmn. Epilepsy Found. of America, 1967-68. Served to lt. (s.g.) USNR, 1942-46. Mem. Am., Ill., Chgo. bar assns. Jewish religion. Home: 1616 Sheridan Rd Wilmette IL 60091 Office: 208 S LaSalle St Chicago IL 60604 also 1054 31st St NW Washington DC 20007

KOVNER, BENJAMIN, business exec.; b. N.Y.C., Nov. 27, 1901; s. Wolfe and Anna (Levin) K.; m. Kathleen Lane, June 20, 1936; children—Kathleen, Michael, Peter. Sec. Versailles Mgmt. Co., Inc., N.Y.C., 1935—; v.p. 450 7th Av., Inc. Kaufman Arcade Bldg., Inc.; dir. Kaufman 8th Av. Bldg., Inc. Home: 923 Fifth Av New York City NY 10021 Office: 450 7th Av New York City NY 10001

KOWALCZYK, LEON STANISLAW, educator; b. Motycz, Poland, May 3, 1908; s. Wojciech and Antonina (Obara) K.; diploma chem. engr., Warsaw Sch. Engring., 1931, D.Sc. in Engring., 1935; m. Badarski Bronislawa, Dec. 27, 1933. Came to U.S., 1950, naturalized, 1956. Part-time sr. asst. lectr. Warsaw Sch. Engring., 1932-39; asst. prof., vice chmn. chem. engring. dept., Polish Univ. Coll., London, Eng., 1947-50; faculty U. Detroit, 1950-, prof. chem. engring., 1955-, chmn. dept., 1959-. Served with Polish Army under British command, 1939-47. Decorated Virtuti Mil. (Poland); Croix de Guerre (France). Mem. Am. Inst. Chem. Engrs., Am. Chem. Soc., Instn. Chem. Engrs. (Great Britain), Tau Beta Pi, Gamma Eta Epsilon. Home: 20213 Archer St Detroit MI 48219

KOWALEWSKI, JOSEPH FRANCIS, educator; b. Higginsville, Mo., Dec. 31, 1899; s. Napoleon and Peggy (Murfchinski) K.; B.S., U. Chgo., 1927; M.S., U. Cin., 1931, Ph.D., 1938; m. Emma Christensen, Sept. 19, 1923; 1 son, Joseph W. Prof. chemistry Xavier U., Cin., 1929-36, Cin. Coll. Pharmacy, 1936-41, Our Lady of Cin. Coll., 1941-42; asst. dir. Institutum Divi Thomae, 1942-49; dir. applied research Sperti, Inc., 1942-49; dean Coll. Pharmacy U. Cin., 1949-71. Mem. Am., Ohio pharm. assns., Am. Chem. Soc., Sigma Xi, Rho Chi, Kappa Psi. Home: 3018 Golden Av Cincinnati OH 45226

KOWALSKI, FRANK, govt. ofcl.; b. Meriden, Conn., Oct. 18, 1907; s. Frank and Mary (Miller) K.; B.S., U.S. Mil. Acad., 1930; M.S., Mass. Inst. Tech., 1936; student Columbia, 1945; m. Helen Amelia Bober, Oct. 20, 1931; children—Carol Gelene, Barry Fran. Command. 2d lt., inf., U.S. Army, 1930, advanced through grades to col., 1944; various co., bdn., regt. assignments, 1930-44; chief tng. G-3 sect. Hdqrs. European Theater, 1944; dir. Disarmament Sch., London, Eng., 1944-45; dep. chief information and edn. div. Hdqrs. European Theater, 1945; chief mil. govt. of Kyoto, Osaka prefectures, Japan, 1948-49; dep. chief civil affairs, Japan, 1949-50; chief staff Mil. Adv. Group, Japan, 1950-52; comdt. U.S. Army Command Mgmt. Sch., 1954-58; ret., 1958; mem. 86th-87th Congresses, Conn.-at-Large; mem. Armed Service, Manpower Utilization coms.; mem. Subversive Activities Control Bd., 1963—. Decorated Legion of Merit with cluster, Bronze Star. Author articles on mil. mgmt. Holder patents for mil. items. Home: 7204 Regent Dr Alexandria VA 22307 Office: Subversive Activities Control Bd 811 Vermont Av Washington DC 20005

KOWALSKI, STEPHEN WESLEY, educator; b. Bayonne, N.J., June 24, 1931; s. Steve J. and Anna (Gillack) K.; B.S. Fairleigh Dickinson U., 1953; M.A., N.Y. U., 1954, Ph.D., 1964; m. Evelyn L. Geiger, Apr. 2, 1955 (div. Apr. 1971); children—Lillian Ann, Kathryn Lynn, Kristine Eve, Stephen Edward. Research chemist, cons. Shulton, Inc., Clifton, N.J., 1953-56; instr. chemistry Upsala Coll., East Orange, N.J., 1953-54, guest lectr., 1954-65; instr. sci. N.Y. U., N.Y.C., 1954-55; tchr. sci. Kearny (N.J.) High Sch., 1955-56; research chemist Hoffman LaRoche, Nutley, N.J., 1956-57; prof., chmn. physics-geosci. dept. Montclair State Coll., Upper Montclair, N.J., 1957—. Guest lectr. Fairleigh Dickinson U., 1955—; coordinator, supr. AID Summer Sci. Insts., India and Ohio State U., 1966; coordinator, supr. NSF-AID Summer Sci. Insts., India, 1967; sci. coordinator master of arts in teaching program Fairleigh Dickinson U., 1968. Bd. dirs. N.J. Consumers League, 1964-67, Montclair Athletic Commn.; sr. asso. Danforth Found., 1961—. Mem. Am. Chem. Soc. (nat. com. confs. and insts., div. chem. edn. 1968—), N.E.A., N.J. Edn. Assn. (chmn. higher edn. com. 1968—), Nat. (com. establishing goals sci. literacy), N.J. sci. tchrs. assns., Assn. N.J. Coll. and Univ. Profs. (founder 1969), A.A.A.S., Phi Delta Kappa (life). Elk. Author: Floridation of Polyethylenes, 1955; Chromotographic Separation of Xanthophylls, 1957; Laboratory Manual in Consumer Science, 1972; contbr. book Flavor Chemistry, 1959. Patentee permeability of polyethylene, floridation. Home: 23 Dwyer Rd Wayne NJ 07470 Office: Montclair State College Upper Montclair NJ 07043

KOYL, GEORGE SIMPSON, educator, architect; b. Evanston, Wyo., Feb. 8, 1885; s. Charles Henry and Caroline (Emigh) K.; B.Arch. (Univ. scholar), U. Pa., 1909, M.Arch. (Alumni fellow), 1911; D.F.A., 1942; m. Adelaide Wight Howard, Oct. 10, 1924. With Office of F.E. Edbrook, Architect, Denver, 1902-11; fellow Am. Acad. in Rome, 1911-14; instr. architecture Carnegie Inst. Tech., 1915; draftsman Office of Cass Gilbert, Architect, N.Y.C., 1915-19, McKim, Mead & White, N.Y.C., 1920-24; designer City and County Bldg., Denver, for Allied Architects, 1925-27; pvt. practice architecture, N.Y.C., 1928-29; mem. firm Rich, Mathesius & Koyl, 1929-32; critic in design Columbia, 1928, Princeton, 1928-30, N.Y.U., 1929-32; prof. architecture, dean Sch. Fine Arts, U. Pa., 1932-50, prof. emeritus, 1955—; dir. refresher courses Phila. chpt. A.I.A., 1940—. Mem. architects adv. om. Phila Housing Authority, 1937-38. Bd. dirs. House of Detention of Witnesses and Untried Prisoners, City and County of Phila., 1940. Served to 2d lt. A.C., U.S. Army, 1917-18. Fellow A.I.A.; mem. Century Assn. N.Y., Phila Art Alliance, Sigma Xi, Phi Sigma Kappa, Tau Sigma Delta. Club: Lenape (Phila.). Editor: American Architects Directory Vols. 1 and 2; American Architectural Drawings, 1969. Important works include City and County Bldgs., Denver, James Cardinal Gibbons Meml., Washington, canopy for residence of Mrs. Josiah H. Penniman,, Haverford, Pa. Address: 4400 Spruce St Philadelphia PA 19104

KOZAK, SAMUEL JOSEPH, educator; b. Peabody, Mass., Apr. 13, 1931; B.S., Bates Coll., 1954; M.S., Brown U., 1958; Ph.D. in Geology, U. Ia., 1961; married; 2 children. Asst. prof. geology Washington and Lee U., Lexington, Va., 1961-68, prof., 1968—. Served to lt. (j.g.) USNR, 1956-58. Mem. Am. Geol. Soc., Assn. Geology Tchrs. Office: Dept Geology Washington and Lee U Lexington VA 24450*

KOZELKA, ROBERT MARVIN, educator; b. Mpls., July 20, 1926; s. Richard L. and Winifred (Bradley) K.; B.A., U. Minn., 1947, M.A., 1948; Ph.D., Harvard, 1953; m. Carolyn Eckfeldt, Aug. 30, 1950; children—Paul, Thomas, James, Peter. Mem. faculty U. Minn., 1947-48, Tufts U., 1949-53, U. Neb., 1953-57; mem. faculty Williams Coll., 1957—, prof. math., 1966—, sec. faculty, 1965-70; vis. prof. U. N.C., 1963-64; vis. prof. anthropology and sociology U. Tex., 1970-71; research asso. anthropology Cornell U., 1960-63; cons. to industry, 1957-58. Served with USAAF, 1945. Mem. Inst. Math. Statistics, Am. Statis. Assn., Am. Anthrop. Assn. Author: Elements of Statistical Inference, 1961; Mathematical Anthropology, 1972. Home: 39 Belden St Williamstown MA 02167

KOZINSKI, ANDRZEJ WLADYSLAW, educator, biologist; b. Skierniewice, Poland, Oct. 1, 1925; s. Marian and Jozefina (Jasinski) K.; M.D., U. Warsaw, 1951, Ph.D. in Biochemistry, 1956; m. Patti Austin Barnes, Mar. 23, 1961; children—Catharine, Peter, Mark. Came to U.S., 1957, naturalized, 1963. Research asst. State Hygienic Inst., Warsaw, Poland, 1949-51; research asso. Inst. Biochemistry, Warsaw, 1951-53; asst. prof. dept. microbiology U. Warsaw, 1955-57; asst. prof. Inst. Microbiology, Rutgers U., 1959; NIH fellow dept. biology Johns Hopkins, 1962; asso. mem. Wistar Inst., 1962-66; asso. prof. dept. med. genetics U. Pa., Phila., 1966-70, prof. med. genetics and microbiology, 1970—. Mem. Soc. Biol. Chemistry, Biophys. Soc. Author: (with others) Wirusologia Ogolna, 1958. Publs. on first described the molecular mechanism of mating as a breaking and reunion of DNA molecules; recombination as an enzymatic process. Home: 6817 Cresheim Rd Philadelphia PA 19119

KOZLOFF, MAX, art critic; b. Chgo., June 21, 1933; s. Joseph and Rose (Hollobow) K.; B.A., U. Chgo., 1953, M.A., 1958; m. Joyce Blumberg, July 3, 1967. Art critic The Nation, 1961—; N.Y. corr. Art Internat., 1962-64; asso. editor Artforum, 1964—; instr. Cooper Union, 1960-61, Washington Sq. Coll., N.Y.U., 1961-62. Served with AUS, 1954-56. Pulitzer fellow critical writing, 1962; Frank Jewett Mather fellow art criticism; Guggenheim fellow, 1968-69. Author: Jasper Johns, 1969; Renderings Essays on a Century of Modern Art, 1968. Contbr. articles nat. mags. Home: 225 W 106th St New York City NY 10025

KOZLOWSKI, THEODORE THOMAS, educator; b. Buffalo, May 22, 1917; s. Theodore and Helen (Zamiara) K.; B.S., Syracuse U., 1939; M.A., Duke, 1941, Ph.D., 1947; postgrad. Mass. Inst. Tech., 1942-43; m. Maude Peters, June 29, 1954; Asst. prof. dept. botany U. Mass., 1947-48, asso. prof., 1948-50, prof., head dept. botany, 1950-58; prof. dept. forestry U. Wis., 1958—, chmn. dept., 1961-64; cons. NSF, Stanford Research Inst., FAO, Cornell Aeros., Malaysian Govt.; vis. biologist Am. Inst. Biol. Scis., 1969-71; vis. scientist Soc. Am. Foresters, 1963-71. Rapporteur World Consultation on Tree Improvement, 1963. Served to capt. USAAF, 1942-46. Mem. Soc. Plant Physiologists, Bot. Soc. Am., Ecol. Soc. Am., Soc. Am. Foresters, Societas Forestalis Fenniae (Finland), (hon.), Am. Inst. Biol. Scis., Sigma Xi, Phi Kappa Phi, Phi Sigma. Author: (with P.J. Kramer) Physiology of Trees, 1960; Water Metabolism in Plants, 1964; Growth and Development of Trees, 2 vols., 1971. Editor: Tree Growth, 1962; Water Deficits and Plant Growth, 3 vols., 1968; Seed Biology, 3 vols., 1971. Editorial bd. Forett Sci., Ecology; asso. editor Am. Midland Naturalist, Canadian Jour. Forest Research; editor physiol.-ecology book series Acad. Press., N.Y.C. Home: 10 S Rock Rd Madison WI 53705

KOZOL, JONATHAN, author; b. Boston, Sept. 5, 1936; s. Harry Leo and Ruth (Massell) K.; B.A., Harvard, 1958; Rhodes scholar, Magdalen Coll., Oxford, 1958-59. Writer in Paris, France and recipient Olympia Thousand Dollar award, 1962; Saxton fellow in creative writing from Harper & Row, 1964; tchr. Boston pub. schs., 1964-65, Newton pub. schs., 1966-68; cons. Store- front Learning Center, 1968—, also trustee. Trustee New Sch. for Children, Roxbury, Mass. Mem. Congress Racial Equality, Am. P.E.N. Center, Authors Guild. Author: Death At An Early Age, 1967 (Nat. Book award 1968). Home: 56 Linwood St Roxbury MA 02119

KOZY, JOHN, Jr., educator; b. Barnesville, Pa., May 26, 1931; s. John and Jennie (Koropatska) K.; B.A., Pa. State U., 1957, Ph.D., 1963; M.A., Cornell U., 1959; m. Ruth Sheen, Sept. 2, 1961. Instr. philosophy Pa. State U., 1961; asst. prof. philosophy U. Miss., 1961-63; prof. philosophy, chmn. dept. East Carolina U., Greenville, 1963—, dir. honors programs, 1964—, dir. div. undecided majs. 1965-67. Served with AUS, 1952-54. Mem. So. Assn. Philosphy and Psychology, Am. Philos. Assn., Metaphys. Soc. Am., Phi Sigma Tau (exec. council; editorial bd. mem. Dialogue Jour., nat. v.p. 1968-). Home: 1915 Sheerwood Dr Greenville, NC 27834

KRABACH, RICHARD LOWELL, city mgr.; b. Wapakoneta, O., May 25, 1913; s. Joseph A. and Eleanor (Tebben) K.; B.C.S., Xavier U., 1934; J.D., Ohio No. U., 1947; Dr. of Finance, Youngstown U., 1966; D. Pub. Finance, Ohio U., 1968; m. Henrietta Pete, Sept. 5, 1940; children—Joseph A. II, Kathryn (Mrs. James K. Long), Mary Constance. With Gen. Motors Acceptance Corp., Washington, 1935-41; budget dir. Westinghouse Corp., Lima, O., 1941-47; admitted to Ohio bar, 1947; pvt. practice, Lima, 1947-54; U.S. comptroller, V.I., 1954-57; chmn. bd. rev. Bur. Unemployment Compensation Ohio, 1959-63; state dir. finance, Columbus, O., 1963-68; city mgr., Cin., 1968-. Home: 2383 Observatory Rd Cincinnati OH 45208 Office: City Hall Cincinnati OH 45202

KRABLE, MONROE, union ofcl. Pres., Nat. Assn. Post Office and Gen. Services Maintenance Employees, AFL-CIO, Washington. Office: 724 9th St NW Washington DC 20001*

KRACKE, EDWARD AUGUSTUS, Jr., historian, educator; b. N.Y.C., Jan. 22, 1908; s. Edward Augustus and Leonora (Share) K.; A.B., Harvard, 1932, A.M., 1935, Ph.D., 1941; postgrad. U. Paris, 1935-36; m. Joan Hocking, June 8, 1935; children-Waud Hocking, Ernesta Henrietta. With OSS, 1942-45; with Dept. State, 1945-46; vis. asst. prof. Chinese, U. Chgo., 1946-47, asst. prof., 1947-53, asso. prof. Chinese lit. and instns., 1953-60, prof., 1960—, chmn. com. on Far Eastern civilizations, 1957-63, dir. Far Eastern Lang. and Area Center, 1959-63, 69—, mem. council of Senate, 1959-62, chmn. com. on Far Eastern studies, 1970—, chmn. Far Eastern Program in Coll., 1970—; mem. vis. com. for East Asian studies Harvard, 1960-66; mem. adv. com. on Chinese and Japanese studies Evanston Twp. High Sch., 1963-66; adviser East Asian Studies Program, U. Miami, 1966, Mich. State U., 1967. Mem. Far Eastern Assn. (past dir., editor monograph series), Comparative Studies in Soc. and History (past v.p., mem. editorial com.), Am. Council Learned Socs. (past sub-com. chmn.), Internat. Conf. on Instl. Change in China (past chmn.), Am. Oriental Soc. (past mem. exec. com.), Am. Hist. Assn., Assn. for Asian Studies, Societe Asiatique (Paris). Republican. Unitarian. Club: Chicago Literary. Author: Civil Service in Early Sung China, 960-1067, 1953, rev., 1968. Contbr. to Ency. Brit., 1962, 65. Contbr. articles profl. jours. Office: U Chgo Chicago IL 60637

KRAEGEL, NORBERT EDWARD, bus. exec.; b. Elmhurst, Ill., Dec. 22, 1930; s. Adolph C. and Hele (Thon) K.; B.S. in Bus. Adminstrn. and Accounting, 1953; m. Virginia Ann Robinson, Mar. 2, 1955; children-Charles, Cheryl, Scott, Sandra. Auditor, then. sr. auditor Author Anderson & Co., C.P.A.'s; formerly v.p. systems and information service C. & N. R.R.; v.p. finance Internat. Systems and Controls Corp., Kansas City, Mo.; formerly v.p. finance, dir. AAR Corp., Elk Grove, Ill.; now v.p., comptroller VAL, Inc. Home: 519 S Na-Wa-Ta St Mount Prospect IL 60056 Office: PO Box 66100 Chicago IL 60666

KRAEMER, PAUL WILHELM, utilities exec.; b. Mpls., Dec. 28, 1920; s. John C. and Rose (Schoenstuhl) K.; B.S. in Chem. Engring., U. Minn., 1942; B.S. in Law, William Mitchell Coll. Law, 1957; m. Doris Carter, Jan. 2, 1946; 1 son, Bruce. With Mpls. Gas Co., 1947—, v.p. operations, 1958- 66, exec. v.p., 1966-67, pres., 1967—, dir., 1965—, mem. exec. com., 1966—; chmn. bd. Bruest Industries Inc., Calcinator Corp.; dir. Northwestern Nat. Bank Mpls. Bd. dirs., exec. com. United Fund Mpls. Area; pres. Better Bus. Bur.; chmn. bd. trustees Inst. Gas Tech.; mem. pres.'s bd. advisers Augsburg Coll.; trustee William Mitchell Coll. Law, Dunwoody Indsl. Inst.; bd. govs. Meth. Hosp. Served to lt. USNR, 1942-46. Recipient Operating award of merit Am. Gas Assn., 1959; named Engr. of Year Mpls. Engrs. Club, 1968. Mem. Engrs. Club, Am. Gas Assn. Mason, Rotarian. Clubs: Minneapolis, Interlachen Country (Mpls.). Contbr. articles profl. jours. Home: 209 Farmdale Rd Hopkins MN 55343 Office: 733 Marquette Av Minneapolis MN 55402

KRAEMER, WILLIAM S., educator, philosopher; b. Newark, Sept. 3, 1909; s. Saul and Etta (Levy) K.; A.B. magna cum laude, Upsala Coll., 1932; M.A., N.Y.U., 1933, Ph.D., 1942; Wolfe fellow, U. Neb., 1933-35; m. Louise R. Russert, Mar. 4, 1950; children—Eric Russert, Robert Russert, Lisa Russert, Soren Russert. Instr., Essex Jr. Coll., Newark, 1935-37, dean, 1937-43; mem. faculty U. Ark., Fayetteville, 1947—, prof. philosophy, 1952—, chmn. dept., 1954—. Served to lt. USNR, 1943-47. Mem. Am., Ark. philos. assns., Am. Assn. U. Profs., Southwestern Philos. Conf., Mind Assn., Psi Chi. Author: L.T. Hobhouse's Theory of the Rational Good, 1945; The Naturalistic Foundations of Moore's Ethical Theory, 1969; also articles. Home: PO Box 631 Fayetteville AR 72701

KRAFFT, JULIA STEVEN, bus. exec.; b. Wheaton, Ill.; d. George Barnard and Rose (Austin) Clark; ed. bus. coll., Elgin, Ill., 1913-14; m. Walter A. Krafft, June 25, 1939; 1 dau. Virginia. Organized Steven's Candy Kitchens, Inc., 1921, pres. 1921-56, when sold; pres. succeeding corp. 611 N. Sacramento Corp.; pres. Honey Bear Farm, Genoa City, Wis., 1951-; owner The Little Traveler, Geneva, Ill., 1953—. Bd. dirs., v.p. Women's bd. Salvation Army, Chgo., mem. adv. bd.; dir. Women's Bds. Chgo. Boys Clubs , Passavant Meml. Hosp.; Lyric Opera; chmn. Chgo. Beautiful Com.; dir. Ch. League Am., Wheaton, Ill. Trustee Carthage Coll., Kenosha, Wis. Recipient Citizen's award V.F.W., 1944, various citations Am. Legion. Republican. Clubs: Business and Professional Women's, Chicago Woman's Fashion Group, Woman's Athletic, Arts, Lake Geneva Garden. Home: 199 Lake Shore Dr Chicago IL 60611

KRAFT, C. WILLIAM, Jr., judge; b. Phila., Dec. 14, 1903; s. C. William and Wilhelmina J. (Doerr) K.; A.B., U. Pa., 1924, LL.B., 1927; m. Frances M. McDevitt, June 27, 1942; 1 son, C. William lll. Admitted to Pa. bar, 1927; trial lawyer Kraft, Lipincott & Donaldson Media, Pa., 1928-55; dist. atty, Delaware County Pa., 1944-52; judge U.S. Dist. Court, Philadelphia, Pa., 1955-70, sr. judge, 1970—. Mem. Am. Pa., bar assns. Home: Brichouse Farm RD Glen Mills PA 19243 Office: US Court House Philadelphia PA 19107

KRAFT, CHARLES FRANKLIN, clergyman, educator; b. Kenton, O., Jan. 14, 1911; s. Frank D. and Emma L. (Dresbach) K.; student York Coll., 1928-29; B.A. summa cum laude, U. Colo., 1932; B.D. (Grad. fellow), U. Chgo., 1936, Ph.D. (Grad. fellow), 1937; m. Verna Louise Smith, June 3O, 1936; childrenRobert Draper, Laverna Lou. Supply pastor U.B. Ch., 1935; on trial So. Ill. Conf. Meth. Ch., 1938, ordained deacon, 1939, full connection, elder Mich. Conf., 1941; prof. philosophy and religion McKendree Coll., 1937-39; prof. Bible, Hamline U., 1939-40; head dept. religion Albion Coll. 1940-46; prof. O.T., DePauw U., 1946-47; asso. prof. Garrett Theol. Sem., Evanston, Ill., 1947, prof. O.T. interpretation, 1948-, dir. grad. studies, 1957- 66. Mem. Bd. Ministerial Tng., Mich. Conf., 1942-46; vis. prof. Illff Sch. Theology, summer 1940, Pacific Sch. Religion, summer 1945, Oberlin Grad. Sch. Theology, summer 1958, Leonard Theol. Coll., India, Am. Sch. Oriental Research, Jerusalem, Jordan, 1961-62. Mem. Soc. Bibl. Lit. (past nat. sec.), Am. Oriental Soc. (past pres. Middle West br.), Nat. Assn. Bibl. Instrs. (past pres. Midwest sect.), Chgo. Soc. Bibl. Research (past pres.), Am. Assn. Theol. Schs. (commn. on accrediting 1960-66, sec. 1964-66, Faculty fellow 1961-62), Phi Beta Kappa, Omicron Delta Kappa. Author: The Strophic Structure of Hebrew Poetry, 1938; Genesis: Beginnings of the Biblical Drama, 1964. Contbr. articles to Jour. Bible and Religion, Bibl. Research, Ency. Americana, Interpreter's Dictionary of the Bible, Hastings' Dictionary of the Bible, The Interpreter's One-Volume Commentary on the Bible, chpts. to A Stubborn Faith, The Bible and God's Mission; Illustrated Family Ency. of the Living Bible. Home: 2626 Isabella St Evanston IL 60201

KRAFT, CHARLES HENRY, metal products mfg. co. exec.; b. Cleve., Nov. 22, 1916; s. August W. and Helen (Doerge) K.; student Western Reserve U., 1936-37, Harvard Bus. Sch.; m. Bettejane Roth, May 14, 1942; children—Gregory C., Jeffrey J., Bradley J., Todd W. Office mgr. Lincoln Elec. Co., Cleve. also San Francisco, 1938-42; credit rep. Am. Steel & Wire Co., Cleve., 1947-52; asst. credit mgr. U.S. Steel Corp., Chgo., 1952-57; treas. U.S. Steel Supply Co., Chgo., 1957-59; asst. treas. corp. finance U.S. Steel Corp., N.Y.C., 1959-70; v.p., treas. The Anaconda Co., N.Y.C., 1970—; dir. Chile Exploration Co., N.Y.C. Served with USAAF, 1942-46. Mem. Am. Mining Congress, Am. Inst. Mining Engrs., Beta Theta Pi. Republican. Presbyn. Clubs: Downtown Athletic, Mining (N.Y.C.). Home: 32 Knob Hill Dr Summit NJ 07901 Office: 25 Broadway New York City NY 10004

KRAFT, CHRISTOPHER COLUMBUS, Jr., aero. engr.; b. Phoebus, Va., Feb. 28, 1924; s. Christopher Columbus and Vanda Olivia (Suddreth) K.; B.S. in Aero. Engring., Va. Poly. Inst., 1944; m. Elizabeth Anne Turnbull, Sept. 2, 1950; children—Gordon Turnbull, Kristi Anne. With NASA, and predecessor, 1945—, flying quality, stability and control measurements P47 Thunderbolt and P-51H Mustang, 1945-46, designed, supervised constrn. gust-alleviation system light transp. airplane, 1950-55, flight test measurements strength and persistence trailing vortices airplane, 1952, project engr. F8U-1 Crusader, 1957-58, mem. space task group for Project Mercury, 1956—, flight dir., 1959-70, dep. dir. Manned Spacecraft Center, 1970—. Mem. Inst. Aerospace Scis., Pi Tau Sigma. Episcopalian (lay reader). Home: 17 Southland Dr Hampton VA 23369 Office: Manned Spacecraft Center NASA 2101 Webster-Seabrook Rd Houston TX 77058

KRAFT, ERWIN OTTO, banker; b. Clifton, N.J., Nov. 4, 1909; s. Max O. and Frieda L. (Zschack) K.; student Rutgers U., 1946-48, Columbia Grad. Sch. Bus., 1961, N.Y. U. Grad. Sch. Bus. Adminstrn., 1960-64; m. Grace M. Atkins Apr. 29, 1933. Engaged in banking, 1926—; with 1st Nat. Bank Passaic County (N.J.), 1957-, pres., 1963-; dir. Windbeam Water Co., Cupsaw Plaza Inc. (both Ringwood, N.J.); lectr. Grad. Sch. Banking, Rutgers U., 1961. Co-chmn. Paterson (N.J.) United Fund, 1964-; mem. exec. bd. Alhtaha council Boy Scouts Am., 1962—, pres. 1967-69. Past councilman, mayor dir. bd. chosen freeholders, Passaic County. Trustee Paterson Salvation Army, Paterson State Coll. Devel. Fund, Inc. Served with USNR, 1942-46. Mem. Am. Inst. Banking (pres. Passaic County 1948-49), Am., N.J. (pres. 1970-71), Passaic County (pres. 1964) bankers assns., N.J. C. of C., Better Bus. Bur. (exec. bd.), Am. Legion. Mason. Contbr. articles profl. jours. Home: 231 Cupsaw Dr N Ringwood NJ 07456 Office: 515 Union Blvd Totowa Borough NJ 07512

KRAFT, JOSEPH, journalist; b. South Orange, N.J., Sept. 4, 1924; s. David Harry and Sophie (Surasky) K.; A.B., Columbia, 1947; postgrad., Princeton, 1948-49, inst. Advanced Study, 1950-51; m. Polly Winton, Jan. 6, 1960. Editorial writer Washington Post, 1951-52; staff writer N.Y. Times, 1953-57; Washington corr. Harper's mag., 1962-65; syndicated columnist Washington Post, Chgo. Daily News, others, 1963—. Served with AUS, 1943-46. Mem. Council Fgn. Relations, Phi Beta Kappa. Clubs: Century (N.Y.C.); Federal City (Washington). Author: The Struggle for Algeria, 1961; The Grand Design, 1962; Profiles in Power, 1966. Contbr. to publs. including New York, Atlantic Monthly. Home: 3021 N St NW Washington DC 20007

KRAFT, LEO, composer; b. N.Y.C., July 24, 1922; s. Nathan and Yetta (Kaplowitz) K.; B.A., Queens Coll., 1945; M.F.A., Princeton, 1947; m. Amy Lager, May 16, 1945, children-David, Evan. Prof. music Queens Coll., City U. N.Y., 1947-. Chmn. program com. Nat. Assn. Am. Composers and Condrs., 1963-65. Bd. dirs. Am. Music Center. Fulbright scholar, 1954-55. Mem. Coll. Music Soc. (2d v.p.), Am. Soc. Univ. Composers, A.S.C.A.P. Club: Bohemians (N.Y.C.). Composer: (for chorus and small orch.) A Proverb of Solomon, 1953; (piano solo) Partita 1, 1958; Variations for Orch., 1958; String Quartet 2, 1959; (for chorus) Psalm 114, 1961, Psalm 40, 1963; Four English Love Songs, 1961; Five Pieces for Clarinet and Piano, 1962; Three Pieces for Orchestra, 1963; Fantasy for Flute and Piano, 1963; (chorus and piano duet) To Night, 1963; (for winds) Partita 3, 1964; (orch.) Night Piece, 1965; Concerto for 13 Players, 1966; Dialogues for Flute and Tape, 1967 Concerto for Cello, Winds and Percussion, 1969; Spring in the Harbor, for soprano, cello, flute and piano, 1969. Author: (with Berkowitz and Fontrier) A New Approach to Sight Singing, 196O; A New Approach to Ear Training-Melody, 1967. Home: 9 Dunster Rd Great Neck NY 11021 Office: Queens Coll Flushing NY 11367

KRAFT, WILLIAM RUSSELL, Jr., army officer; b. Kingston, N.Y., Jan. 22, 1919; s. William R. and Florence (Gray) K.; B.S., U.S. Mil. Acad., 1942; M.A. in Internat. Affairs, George Washington U., 1963; m. Helen Frink, May 29, 1942; children—Elizabeth (Mrs. Jerry R. Rutherford), Alice (Mrs. Robert Middleton), William R. III. Commd. 2d lt. U.S. Army, 1942, advanced through grades to maj. gen., 1970; comdr. 1st Brigade, 3d Armored Div., Germany, 1963-64; asst. chief staff operations V Corps, Germany, 1964-67; dir. Western hemisphere region Office Sec. Def., 1967-68; asst. div. comdr. 9th Inf. Div., Vietnam, 1969; dep. J3 operations Mil. Assistance Command, Vietnam, 1969-70. commdr. gen. 7th Army Troops, Germany, 1970—. Decorated D.S.M., D.F.C., Legion of Merit, Bronze Star, Air medal; Croix de Guerre (France); Vietnamese Cross Gallantry. Home: 7 Burgevin St Kingston NY 12401 Office: Hdqrs US Army Europe and 7th Army Troops APO New York City NY 09102

KRAG, DONALD OTTO, lawyer; b. Alexander, Ia., Aug. 4, 1903; s. Otto Charles and Harriet (Keislich) K.; J.D., Southwestern U., 1933; m. Ethel Solvey Trygestad, June 6, 1936; children-Donald R., Donna Harriet (Mrs. Frank J. Reinhart), Nancy Ellen Hoover, Patricia Ann (Mrs. C. Lynn Carlson). Admitted to Cal. bar, 1933; U.S. Supreme Ct.; practice in Alhambra, 1933- -. Adv. dir. First Western Bank & Trust Co. City judge, Monterey Park, El Monte, West Covina, 1934-39. Pres. Alhambra Community Hosp.; past pres., sec., dir. Ingleside Psychiat. Hosp.; sec. Ingleside Mental Health Center; trustee Jean G. McCracken Trust. Mem. Am., San Gabriel Valley (past pres.). Los Angeles County (past trustee) bar assns., State Bar Cal., Am. Judicature Soc., Alhambra and Monterry Park C. of C. (past pres.). Home: 639 Arbolada Dr Arcadia CA 91006 Office: 100 S First St Alhambra CA 91802

KRAG, DONALD RICHARDS, lawyer; b. Pasadena, Cal., Feb. 7, 1927; s. Donald O. and Dorothy (Hibbard) K.; student U. Cal. at Los Angeles, 1946-48; J.D., Southwestern U., 1951; m. Merrilyn J. Waters, Oct. 18, 1947; children—Theodore R., Daniel R., William R., Thomas R., Charles R. Admitted to Cal. bar, 1952, since practiced in Alhambra; partner Krag & Krag, and predecessor firm, 1952—. Served with USNR, 1944-46: PTO. Mem. Los Angeles County Trial Lawyers Assn. (past pres.), San Gabriel Valley Bar Assn. (past pres.), Lawyer Pilots Bar Assn. (pres.). Conglist. Mason, Rotarian. Home: 935 Monte Verde Dr Arcadia CA 91006 Office: 100 S 1st St Alhambra CA 91801

KRAG, JENS OTTO, Danish govt. ofcl.; b. Randers, Denmark, Sept. 15 1914; s. Anders and Astrid (Marcussen) K.; cand. polit. Copenhagen U., 1940; m. Hel Virkner, July 31, 1959; children—Jens Christian, Astrid Helene. Minister commerce, shipping, Denmark, 1947-50; counsellor Danish embassy, Washington, 1950-52; minister economy and labor, 1953-57. fgn. econ. affairs, 1957-58. fgn. affairs, 1958-62, prime minister, Denmark, 1962- 66, prime minister and minister for fgn. affairs, 1966-68. Mem. Folketing, 1947—. Author: Kooperationen, Fremtiden og Plan økonomi 1945, co-author; Krigsøkonomi og Efterkrigs problemer, 1944; England bygger öp, 1947; Danmark besat og befriet, 1947; Tidehverv og Samfundsorden, 1954; Hans Hedtoft: Mandomsgerning, 1955; Wirtscharts- Politikund Socialdemokratie der Skandinavischen Länder, 1958; Ung mandi trediverne, 1969. Home: 61 Egernvej 2000 Copenhagen F Denmark Office: Folketinget Christiansborg 1218 Copenhagen KV Denmark

KRAGEN, ADRIAN ALBERT, educator; b. San Francisco, June 3, 1907; s. Simon and Minnie (Hables) K.; A.B., U. Cal. at Berkeley, 1931, LL.B., 1934; m. Billie Bercovich, June 4, 1933; childrenKenneth Allan, Robin Susan. Admitted to Cal. bar, 1934; individual practice, Oakland, 1934-39; dep. atty. gen. Cal., 1940-44; partner firm Loeb & Loeb, Los Angeles, 1945-52; Shannon Cecil Turner prof. law U. Cal. at Berkeley, 1952-, vice chancellor, 1960-63; gen. counsel Cal. Retailers, 1946-; tax cons. to industry, govt. Mem. Gov. Cal. Study Commn. Unemployment, 1950-53, Gov. Cal. Council Dept. Employment, 1954-66. Trustee, Alta Bates Community Hosp., Berkeley. Mem. Am. Bar Assn., Phi Beta Kappa, Order of Coif. Author: (with John McNulty) Cases and Materials Federal Income Taxation, 1970. Home: 426 Kentucky Av Berkeley, CA 94707

KRAHL, MAURICE EDWARD educator; b. Cambridge City, Ind., Sept. 17, 1908; s. Michael and Bertha (Hastings) K.; A.B. (Rector scholar), Depauw U., 1929; Ph.D. (Eli Lilly & Co. fellow), Johns Hopkins, 1932; m. Barbara Dodson, June 4, 1932 (dec. 1962); m. 2d, Ardis Lostroh, Feb. 4, 1967. Research chemist Eli Lilly & Co., Indpls., 1933-44; instr. pharmacology Coll. Phys. and Surg., Columbia, 1944-46; asst. prof. pharmacology, later asso. prof. biochemistry Washington U., St. Louis, 1946-53; prof. physiology U. Chgo., 1953-69; vis. prof. physiology Stanford, 1967-69, prof., 1969—; Banting lectr. English Diabetic Assn., 1950. Trustee, Marine Biol. Lab., Woods Hole, Mass. Mem. Am Assn. Cancer Research, Am. Soc. Biol. Chemists, Am. Soc. Pharmacology and Exptl. Therapeutics, Harvey Soc., Soc. Exptl. Biology and Medicine, Soc. Gen. Physiologists, Am. Diabetes Assn., Biochem. Soc. (Brit.), Phi Beta Kappa, Sigma Xi. Club: Quadrangle (Chgo.). Author: The Action of Insulin on Cells, 1961. Contrbr. articles sci. jours. Editorial bd. Biol. Bull., 1954-57, Diabetes, 1959-64, Endocrinology, 1964-67. Office: Dept Physiology Stanford U Stanford CA 94305

KRAINIS, BERNARD, musician; b. New Brunswick, N.J., Dec. 28, 1924; s. Abraham and Rose (Sachs) K.; student Denver U., 1946-48, N.Y.U., 1949-51; m. Betty Szold, June 16, 1957; 1 son, John Robert. Mus. dir. Am. Recorder Soc., 1949-61, pres., 1961-63; co-founder

N.Y. Pro Musica, 1953, asso. dir., recorder soloist, 1953-59; founder and dir. Recorder Inst.; recitals with Krainis Baroque Trio, Krainis Baroque Ensemble, Krainis Consort; soloist Phila. Orch., Festival Orch., N.Y. Chamber Orch.; performer recorder music for Classic, Esoteric. Columbia, Mercury, Decca, Kapp and Elan records. Served with USAAF, 1943-45. Mem. Music Library Assn., Galpin Soc. Author: Recorder Songbook, 1962. Address: 161 86th St New York City, NY 10024

KRAKOWER, CECIL ALEXANDER, physician; b. Montreal, Can., Sept. 4, 1907; s. Harry and Clara (Roth) K.; B.S., McGill U., 1928, M.D., 1932; m. Emma de la Rosa, Mar. 10, 1939; children-Daniel, Diana. Instr. pathology Harvard, 1934-36; asso., pathology Sch. Tropical Medicine, Columbia, 1936-39, asst. prof., 1939— 43; asso. prof. pathology U. Ill. Coll. Medicine, 1944-48, prof. pathology, 1948—, head dept., 1955; pathologist-in-chief U. Ill. Hosps., 1955—. Mem. Am. Assn. Pathologists and Bacteriologists, Am. Soc. Exptl. Pathology, Soc. Exptl. Biology and Medicine, Am. Coll. Pathologists, Internat. Assn. Med. Mus., Sigma Xi. Home: 949 Linden Av Oak Park IL 60302 Office: 1853 W Polk St Chicago IL 60612

KRAL, IRENE, singer, b. Chgo., Jan 18, 1932; m. Joe Burnett. Began with Woody Herman, Maynard Ferguson bands, later pop-jazz soloist several Steve Allen TV shows, also appeared with Stan Kenton, Herb Pomeroy bands; with Shelly Manne, 1962-63; recs. include Guitar from Ipanema (Laurindo Almeida). Address: 27 N East Av Oak Park IL 60302

KRALL, ANDERS ALBERT WALTER, advt. exec.; b. Bklyn., Dec. 20, 1925; s. Max and Emma (Larson) K.; A.B., Bates Coll., 1950; M.B.A., N.Y.U., 1954; m. Imogene Rollins, Dec. 1, 1951; children—Lisa, Phillip. Adminstrv. mgr. market research dept. Colgate Palmolive, N.Y.C., 1953-56; mgr. marketing and research Ruth Rauff & Ryan, N.Y.C., 1956-57; dir. market research Warner Bros., Bridgeport, Conn., 1957-62; sr. v.p., dir. research Cunningham & Walsh, 1962—; marketing instr. evenings Bridgeport U., 1958-62. Served with USNR, 1943-46, 51-52. Mem. Am. Mgmt. Assn., Market Research Council, Copy Research Council. Republican. Presbyn. Club: Manursing Island. Home: 33 Valleyview Av Rye NY 10580 Office: 260 Madison Av New York City NY 10016

KRAMER, ALEX, food vending co. exec.; b. Russia, May 1, 1912; s. Frank and Sarah (Gold) K.; came to U.S., 1912, naturalized, 1918; ed. pub. schs.; m. Rose Rosenthal, Feb. 6, 1944; children—Myra Ilene, Joel Herbert. Engaged in wholesale milk and dairy bus., 1938-62, food vending bus., 1948—; founder, 1954. Since pres. Autonatic Caterers Corp., Detroit; pres. Interstate Detroit Coffee Co., 1954—; became pres. Interstate United Corp., and predecessors, 1960, chmn. of board, 1966-68; dir. Petroleum Exploration & Devel. Funds, Abilene, Tex.; chmn. bd. Georgetown Assos., Denver; dir. Bally Case & Cooler Co. (Pa.). Active local fund raising drives. Bd. govs. Culinary Inst. Am. Served with USAAF, 1942-46; PTO. Mem. Nat. Automatic Merchandising Assn. (dir., mem. spl. com. vending problems). Home: 22343 LeRhone St Southfield MI 48075 Office: 16000 W Nine Mile Rd Southfield MI 48075

KRAMER, ARTHUR BENNETT, lawyer; b. N.Y.C., Jan. 10, 1927; s. George L. and Rea (Wishengrad) K.; B.S., Yale, 1949, M.A., 1951, LL.B., 1953; m. Alice J. Blumenfeld, Oct. 4, 1953; children—Elizabeth Brooks, Andrew Bennett, Rebecca Laurence. Admitted to N.Y. bar, 1953, since practiced in N.Y.C.; asso. Cole, Grimes, Friedman & Deitz, 1953-55; asst. U.S. atty. So. dist. N.Y., 1955-58, chief appellate atty., 1957-58; partner Nickerson, Kramer, Lowenstein, Nessen & Kamin and predecessor firms, 1958—; dir. Data Processing Financial & Gen. Corp., Bright Star Industries, Holtzer Cabot Corp. Adviser, President's Commn. on Law Enforcement and Adminstrn. of Justice, 1967-68. Trustee Jewish Bd. Guardians. Served with USNR, 1944- 46. Mem. Sigma Xi, Tau Beta Pi. Home: 5 Oakdale Rd Larchmont NY 10538 Office: 919 3d Av New York NY 10022

KRAMER, BERNARD, educator, physicist; b. N.Y.C., Nov. 12, 1922; s. Jack and Mollie (Miller) K.; Sc.B., City Coll. N.Y., 1942; Ph.D., N.Y.U., 1952; m. Miriam Adelman, Aug. 4, 1946; children—Matthew, Jesse. Physicist, Internat. Tel. & Tel. Corp., 1942-47; lectr. Bklyn. Coll., 1947-49; research asst., then research asso. N.Y.U., 1949-68; mem. faculty Hunter Coll., 1952—, prof. physics, 1966—, chmn. dept., 1960—. Mem. Am. Phys. Soc., Am. Assn. Physics Tchrs., Sigma Xi. Author articles luminescence and photoconductivity. Home: 115 Carnation St Bergenfield NJ 07621 Office: 695 Park Av New York City NY 10021

KRAMER, CHARLES RUSSELL, lawyer, univ. trustee; b. Newark, Aug. 17, 1910; s. Charles and Gertrude V. (Porter) K.; A.B., Rutgers U., 1931, LL.B., 1934; m. Mary A. Paxton Apr. 22, 1939; children-Carol B. (Mrs. William E. Britten, Jr.), Charles Russell. Admitted to N.J. bar, 1935, U.S. Supreme Ct., 1957; practice in Newark, 1935-; partner firm Smith, Kramer & Morrison, 1953—; judge Municipal Ct., Cedar Grove, N.J., 1947- 52. Mem. Bd. Edn., Cedar Grove, 1952-55. Trustee, Rutgers U., Served to capt. AUS, 1943-46. Mem. Am., N.J. Essex County bar assns., Phi Beta Kappa, Tau Kappa Alpha, Alpha Sigma Phi. Club: Down Town (Newark). Home: 55 Dale Dr Chatham NJ 07928 Office: 810 Broad St Newark NJ 07102

KRAMER, DONALD W., lawyer; b. Nicholson, Pa., Dec. 7, 1907; s. Charles and Anna (East) K.; A.B., Yale, 1929, LL.B., 1931; m. Gladys M. Dorion, July 1, 1935; children—Philip Joseph, Cecilie Ann, Nancy East, Susan Mary, Carole Jane, Charles E. Admitted to N.Y. bar, 1932, since practiced in Binghamton; asso. Lee, Levene & McAvoy and succeeding firms; sr. mem. firm Kramer, Wales, Robinson & McAvoy; asst. dist. attorney, Broome County, 1934-36. Commr. pub. safety, City of Binghamton, 1942-43, mayor, 1950- 57. Chmn. Binghamton City War Council 1943; 1st v.p. N.Y. Citizens Council Traffic Safety, Inc., 1968—. Del. Dem. Nat. Conv., 1952, 56. Chmn. council Harpun Coll. of U. State of N.Y., 1957-69, chmn. found., 1960-69. Mem. Internat. Assn. Ins. Counsel, Broome County and Am. bar assns., N.Y. State Bar Assn. (former chmn. ins. sect., chmn. com. hwy. safety and related matters), Am. Coll. Trial Lawyers, Phi Alpha Delta, Alpha Chi Rho. Democrat. (candiate for rep. in Congress, 37th Congl. Dist., 1940). Club: Binghamton. Home: 115 Chestnut St Binghamton NY 13905 Office: 59-61 Court St Binghamton NY 13901

KRAMER, FERDINAND, mortgage banker; b. Chgo., Aug. 10, 1901; s. Adolph F. and Ray (Friedberg) K.; Ph.B., U. Chgo., 1922; m. Stephanie Shambaugh, Dec. 22, 1932; childrenBarbara Shambaugh (Mrs. Forrest R. Bailey), Douglas, Anthony. Engaged in real estate bus. and mortgage banker, Chgo., 1922-; with Draper & Kramer, Inc., Chgo., 1922-, pres., 1944-. Program supr. Div. Def. Housing Coordination and successor Nat. Housing Agy., Washington, 1941-42; past pres. Met. Housing and Planning Council, Chgo.; past mem. Pres.'s Com. Equal Opportunity in Housing; past dir., past mem. exec. com. Urban Am., Inc. Past chmn. bd. U. Chgo. Alumni Fund; trustee U. Chgo. Recipient citation of merit U. Chgo. Alumni Assn., 1947, Individual Distinguished Housing and Redevel. Service award Nat. Assn. Housing Ofcls., 1952. Mem. Chgo. Mortgage Bankers Assn. (past pres.), Mortgage Bankers Assn. Am., Nat. Assn. Housing Ofcls., Chgo. Assn. Commerce and Industry, Fed. Nat. Mortgage Assn. (past dir.). Home: 2801 Martin Luther King Jr Dr Chicago IL 60616 Office: 30 W Monroe St Chicago IL 60603

KRAMER, FRANK RAYMOND, educator; b. Baraboo, Wis., Jan. 2, 1908; s. Chris Edward and Mabel (Shaw) K.; B. Humanities, U. Wis., 1929, M.A. in Greek and Latin, 1931, Ph.D., 1936; m. Hetty Louise Eising, Dec. 20, 1935; childrenBryce Allen, Anita Louise (Mrs. James Cyril Shew). Mem. faculty Heidelberg Coll., Tiffin, O., 1938—, prof. classics, 1944—; asso. in residence U. Wis., 1948-49, 51-52; vis. prof. Ohio State U., summer 1962; research Am. Sch. Classical Studies, Athens, 1965. Wis. Com. Study Am. Civilization grantee, 1948-49, 51-52, Social Sci. Research Council, 1951. Mem. Am. Philol. Assn., Classical Assn. Middle West and South, Ohio Classical Conf. (pres. 1948-49), Phi Alpha Theta, Eta Sigma Phi. Democrat. Mem. United Ch. Christ. Author: Voices in the Valley, Mythmaking and Folk Belief in the Shaping of the Middle West, 1964, also articles. Home: 25 Lincoln Rd Tiffin OH 44883

KRAMER, GEORGE NICHOLAS, writer; b. St. Mary's, Kan., Mar. 24, 1896; s. Mathias and Eva (Seitz) K.; A.B., St. Mary's Coll. (Kan.), 1918; student Marquette U., 1919-20; Cath. Univ. of Am., 1920-21, U. of Colo., 1927; Ph.D., U. So. Cal., 1936; m. Justina M. Kramer, June 20, 1922; children—Justin Anthony, Dolores Georgene (Mrs. Robert L. Waggoner), Regis Francis, Remigaemi Thomas. Instr. History and polit. sci. U. of Detroit, 1922-23; prof. history Regis Coll., Denver, 1925-28; with Loyola U. of Los Angeles, 1932-54, became Prof. history and dir. social studies, 1946; mem. editorial staff Daily Am. Tribune, Dubuque, Ia., 1921-22; mgr. and editor Walsenburg (Colo.) Independent, 1928-29; free-lance writer, 1923- 25, 29-32; mem. editorial staff The Tidings, Los Angeles, 1955-70, news analyst and columnist, 1957-70. Mem. Phi Beta Kappa. Author: Fundamentals of American Politics, 1948. Home: 3435 W 78th St Los Angeles CA 90043

KRAMER, GEORGE P., lawyer; b. Holyoke, Mass., Feb. 22, 1927; A.B., Harvard, 1950, LL.B., 1953; certificate Sorbonne, 1948. Admitted to N.Y. bar, 1954; asso. firm Watson, Leavenworth, Kelton & Taggart, N.Y.C., 1953-59, partner firm, 1960-65; partner Conboy, Hewitt, O'Brien & Boardman, N.Y.C., 1965- -. Lectr., Practicing Law Inst. Pres., Mergers Co., Inc., N.Y.C., River Valley Investment Co.; dir. Burleson Corp. Raymond & Whitcomb. Mem. N.Y. Cotton Exchange. Mng. trustee DeGroote Trust. Served to ensign USNR, 1945-46. Mem. Am., Internat. bar assns., Assn. Bar City N.Y. (sec. 1963-65, exec. com. 1970—), Am. Law Inst., U.S. Trademark Assn. Internationale Assn. pour la Protection de la Propriete Industrielle, Municipal Art Soc., Mass. Speleological Soc. (pres.). Club: Harvard (N.Y.C.). Author: Misleading Trademarks and Consumer Protection, 1954. Bd. editors Trademark Reporter. Home: 169 E 78th St New York City NY 10021 Office: 20 Exchange Pl New York City NY 10005

KRAMER, GERHARDT THEODORE, architect; b. New Orleans, Oct. 26, 1909; s. Gotthilf Mathias and Antonette (Smrck) K.; B.Arch., Tulane, 1930; M.Arch., Cornell, 1932; m. Ravenna Evelyn Ross, July 10, 1935; children—Gayle (Mrs. Gerald Grommet), Ross. Asso. in architecture Middle Am. Research Inst., Tulane, New Orleans, 1933-39; with Douglass V. Freret, New Orleans, 1939-42, Hugo K. Graf, St. Louis, 1946-53; prin. Kramer & Assos., St. Louis, 1953-56, Kramer & Harms, Inc., St. Louis, 1956—. Pres. Concordia Hist. Inst., St. Louis, 1969—, Landmarks Assn. St. Louis, Inc., 1960-62, 65-67, 68-71; pres., Heritage/St. Louis, 1970—. Bd. dirs. Chatillion-DeMenil House Found., St. Louis. Served with USNR, 1942-45. Fellow A.I.A. (Mo. preservation coordinator); mem. Soc. Archtl. Historians. Lutheran. Home: 243 E Jefferson Av Kirkwood MO 63122 Office: 9640 Clayton Rd St Louis MO 63124

KRAMER, HARRY SUMMERFIELD, Jr., lawyer; b. East St. Louis, Ill., Apr. 19, 1906; s. Harry Summerfield and Elizabeth C. (Daugherty) K.; student U. Ill., 1922-25; LL.B., Cumberland U., 1927; m. Ray Culler, June 20, 1931 (div. 1943); childrenCarol (Mrs. James S. Robertson), Beverley (Mrs. John C. Albertson); m. 2d, Jane Walker Parsons, June 30, 1944. Admitted to Mo. bar, 1927, since practiced in St. Louis; partner firm Armstrong, Teasdale, Kramer & Vaughan, attys., 1938—. Dir. Bank Bldg. & Equipment Corp. Mem. Am., St. Louis bar assns., Mo. Bar, Sigma Nu. Clubs: Racquet, University, N St. Louis bar assns., Mo. Bar, Sigma Nu. Clubs: Racquet, University, Noonday (St. Louis). Home: 4664 Pershing Pl St Louis MO 63108 Office: 611 Olive St St Louis MO 63101

KRAMER, HENRY THEODORE, reins. co. exec.; b. Chgo., Apr. 8, 1917; s. LeRoy and Margery (Hannegan) K.; grad. Lawrenceville (N.J.) Sch., 1936; B.S., Yale Sheffield Sci. Sch., 1940; m. Janet P. Bunyan, Oct. 4, 1941; children-Jean Hull, Ann Thomson. With Pa. R.R., 1940; asso. underwriter Am. Mut. Reins. Co., 1946-51; with Obrion Russell & Co., Boston, 1951- 56; v.p. Fire & Casualty Co. Conn., 1956-57; v.p. Allstate Ins. Co., 1957-65; asst. to pres. Swiss Re Corp., N.Y.C., 1965-66; pres., dir. N. Am. Reins. Co., N.Y.C., 1966-, Swiss Re Mgmt. Corp., N.Y.C., 1966—; dir. N. Am. Reassurance Co., Swiss Re Corp., Served to lt. comdr. USNR, 1941-46. Home: 101 Forest Av Rye NY 10580 Office: 245 Park Av New York City NY 10017

KRAMER, HERBERT HARVEY, research adminstr.; b. Brighton, Colo., Sept. 23, 1916; s. Jacob F. and Clara L. (Hiller) K.; B.Sc., Colo. State U., 1939; M.Sc., U. Minn., 1941, Ph.D., 1946; m. Rachelle L. Simonds, May 29, 1939; children—Carol A., James H. Grad. asst., instr., U. Minn., 1939-42, asso. Grad. Sch., 1945-46; geneticist Dept. Agr., 1942-45; from asst. prof. to prof. genetics Purdue U., 1946-61; dir. Neb. Agrl. Expt. Sta., 1961-67, Ind. Agrl. Expt. Sta., 1967—. Cons., United Fruit Co., 1957—, Rockefeller Found., 1963; State Dept. exchange del. to U.S.S.R., 1958. Recipient Distinguished Alumnus award U. Minn., 1968. Fellow Am. Soc. Agronomy (pres. 1966; Crop Sci. award 1953); mem. Crop Sci. Soc. Am. (pres. 1957), Sigma Xi, Alpha Zeta, Gamma Sigma Delta, Phi Kappa Phi, Sigma Chi. Elk. Contbr. Profl. jours. Office: Purdue U Agr Expt Sta Lafayette IN 47907

KRAMER, HERBERT JULIUS, pub. relations exec.; b. N.Y.C., July 22, 1922; s. Charles P. and Stella (Lewis) L.; B.A. magna cum laude, Harvard, 1942, M.A., 1946, Ph.D., 1949; LL.B., U. Conn., 1956; m. Karyl Kern, Dec. 2, 1942; children—Stephen, David, Jonathan, Katherine, Susan, Christina, Paul. Instr. English, Harvard, 1946-48, U. Cal. at Santa Clara, 1948-50; with Travelers Ins. Co., Hartford, Conn., 1951-65, asst. mgr. pub. information and advt. dept., 1952-59, dir. pub. information and advt. dept., 1959-64, 2d v.p., 1964-65; dir. pub. affairs Office Econ. Opportunity, 1965-69; sr. v.p. Daniel J. Edelman, Inc., Hartford, 1969—; vis. lectr. Pa. State U., 1969—, U. Conn., 1970-71. Co-founder, chmn. Greater Hartford People to People Council; mem. West Hartford Bd. Edn., 1957-63. Bd. dirs. YMCA World Service Com., Fgn. Policy Assn. Greater Hartford, Greater Hartford chpt. Nat. Conf. Christians and Jews, Urban League; trustee Hartt Coll., U. Hartford; mem. adv. com. Coll. Arts and Scis., Children's Services of Conn.; corporator Inst. for Living. Served to 1st lt. AUS, World War II; CBI. Named Father of Year, Hartford C. of C., 1959. Mem. pub. relations Soc. Am., Greater Hartford C. of C. Home: 26 Westland Av West Hartford CT 06107 Office: 266 Pearl St Hartford CT 06103

KRAMER, JACKSON CARLISLE, lawyer; b. Maryville, Tenn., Nov. 29, 1921; s. Russell Reed and Alice (Arnold) K.; A.B., Maryville Coll., 1942; LL.B., U. Mich., 1948; m. Margaret Ruth Clippinger, Aug. 14, 1943; children—Margaret Ann, Melinda Jane, Jackson Gillan. Admitted to Tenn. bar, 1948, since practiced in Knoxville; partner firm Kraner, Dye, Greenwood, JJohnson, Rayson & McVeigh, 1948- -. Chmn. bd. Blount Nat. Bank, Maryville; dir. Newman Pemberton Corp., Standard Knitting Mills Inc. Trustee Melrose Found., Holston Conf. Colls. Served to capt. USAAF, 1943-46. Mem. Am., Tenn., Knox County bar assns. Democrat. Methodist. Home: 3409 Old Settlers Trail Knoxville TN 37920 Office: Valley Fidelity Bank Bldg Knoxville TN 37901

KRAMER, JOHN HOWARD, educator; b. Canning, S.D., Nov. 12, 1902; s. John and Harriet (Purinton) K.; A.B., S.D. U., 1924i M.A., Ia. U., 193O; Ed.D., No. Colo. U., 1943; m. Lenette Dunlap, July 17, 1926; children-John Howard, Lenette Miriam. Speech tchr. Madison (S.D.) High Sch., 1924-27; instr. Dakota State Coll., Madison, S.D., 1925-27; supt. schs., Blunt, S.D., 1927-30, Miller, S.D., 1930-37, Spearfish, S.D., 1937-45; pres. So. State Coll., Springfield, S.D., 1945-54; head, dept. edn. S.D. State U., 1954-56; pres. No. State Coll., Aberdeen, S.D., 1956-68; prof. edn. S.D. State U., Brookings, 1968—; instr. Black Hills Tchrs. Coll., summers 1944, 45. Recipient Distinguished Service award U. S.D., 1966. Mem. S.D. Edn. Assn. (past pres.), N.E.A. Am. Assn. Sch. Adminstrs., Phi Delta Kappa, Alpha Tau Omega, Tau Kappa Alpha, Phi Delta Kappa, Kappa Delta Pi. Conglist. Mason (32, Shriner), Rotarian. Contbr. articles. Home: 1047 3d Av Brookings SD 57006

KRAMER, JOHN J., banker; b. Kansas City, Mo., 1920; ed. U. Wis., 1957. Exec. v.p. City Nat. Bank & Trust Co., Kansas City, Mo. Home: 2910 W 92d Pl Leawood KS 66206 Office: City Nat Bank & Trust Co 10th and Grand Sts Kansas City MO 64141*

KRAMER, KENNETH, editor; b. Batesville, Ind., Apr. 28, 1904; s. Henry H. and Anna (Bertrams) K.; B.A., DePauw U., 1927, LL.D., 1957; m. Bonita Vertrees Lester, Sept. 20, 1936. City editor Greensburg (Ind.) Daily News, 1924-25. Atascadero (Cal.) News, 1927-28; circulation mgr. Pacific Pub. Corp., San Francisco, 1928-30; circulation mgr. Pacific Coast edit. Wall Street Jour., 1930-34, news editor, Washington, 1935-44; pub. Rockford (Ill.) Daily News, 1934; advt. mgr. Ins. Broker, Chgo., 1935; copywriter Boxell & Jacobs, Chgo., 1935; Washington rep. Automotive Council War Prodn., 1944-45, Am. Iron and Steel Inst., 1945-46; exec. editor Bus. Week, N.Y.C., 1946-54, 63-65, mng. editor, 1954-63, editor-in-chief, 1966-69. Republican. Recipient Alumni citation Depauw U., 1952. Mem. Am. Soc. Mag. Writers, Soc. Bus. Writers, Sons of Ind. (pres. N.Y. 1959-60), Soc. of Silurians, Newcomen Soc., Sigma Delta Chi. Mason. Contbr. bus. articles mags. Home: 1435 La Linda Dr Lake San Marcos CA 92069

KRAMER, LAWRENCE, mayor of Paterson, N.J. Address: City Hall Paterson NJ 07505

KRAMER, MILTON JOSEPH, hotel cons.; b. N.Y.C., Aug. 6, 1904; s. Max J. and Yetty (Hauser) K.; grad. Peekskill Mil. Acad., Stamford Mil. Acad.; A.B., Rollins U., 1923. Builder hotels, 1923-30, theatres and office bldgs. 1931-46; ownership- management, 1946-69; former pres. Hotel Edison, Max J. Kramer and Sons Corp.; formerly pres. Monterey and Greystone hotels; engaged various bldg. enterprises; now hotel cons. Address: 680 Madison Av New York City NY 10021

KRAMER, MORTON, biostatistician; b. Balt., Mar. 20, 1914; s. David and Sarah (Valenstein) K.; A.B., Johns Hopkins, 1934, postgrad. Sch. Chemistry, 1934-35, Sc.D., Sch. of Hygiene and Pub. Health, 1939; m. Pauline Weinstein, Sept. 24, 1939; children—Barry Kenneth, James Lawrence, Nancy, Richard. Student asst. biostatistics Johns Hopkins Sch. Hygiene and Pub. Health, 1937-38; instr. preventive medicine N.Y.U. Med. Sch., 1938; statistician N.Y. State Dept. Health, Albany, 1939-40; asst. prof. biostatistics Sch. Tropical Medicine, also statistician, Insular Dept. Health, San Juan, P.R., 1940-42; econ. analyst Treasury Dept., Washington, 1942-43; tb. statistician, Cleve. and Cuyahoga County, 1943-46; asso. in biostatistics Western Res. U. Sch. Medicine, 1943-46; chief, information and research Office Internat. Health Relations, USPHS, 1946-49, chief, biometry br. Nat. Inst. Mental Health 1949—; commd. sr. scientist (res.), USPHS, 1949; cons. mental health WHO, 1959—, mem. expert panel health statistics, 1961—. Adviser, U.S. Delegation to 5th Session Interim Commn., WHO, Geneva, Switzerland, 1948, adviser U.S. Delegation to 6th Session, 1948; adviser U.S. Delegation to 1st World Health Assembly, Geneva, 1948; vis. scientist dept. pub. health London (Eng.) Sch. Hygiene and Tropical Medicine and Social Medicine Research Unit of Med. Research Council, 1968-69. Fellow Am. Statis. Assn., Am. Pub. Health Assn., Am. Psychiat. Assn. (hon.), Am. Orthopsychiat. Assn.; mem. Phi Beta Kappa, Phi Lambda Upsilon, Delta Omega. Club: Cosmos (Washington). Contbr. articles to sci. publs. Home: 9612 Sutherland Rd Silver Spring MD 20901 Office: Nat Inst of Health Health Services and Mental Health Adminstrn Dept Health Edn and Welfare Rockville MD 20852

KRAMER, PAUL JACKSON, educator, plant physiologist; b. Brookville, Ind., May 8, 1904; s. LeRoy and Minnie (Jackson) K.; A.B., Miami U., 1926; fellow botany U. Ida., 1926-27; M.S., Ohio State U., 1929, Ph.D., 1931; D.Sc., U. N.C., 1966; D.Litt., Miami U., 1966; m. Edith Vance, June 24, 1931; children—Jean (Mrs. A.F. Findeis, Jr.). Richard. Asst., botany Ohio State U., 1928-31; mem. faculty Duke, 1931—, successively instr., asst. prof., asso. prof., prof., 1931-54, James B. Duke prof., 1954—, former dir. grad. studies botany; on leave as program dir. in regulatory biology for NSF, 1960-61; dir. Sarah P. Duke Gardens; sr. vis. fellow Australian Acad. Sci., 1970. Vice pres. ecol. physiol. sect. 8th Internat. Bot. Congress, Paris, 1954. Trustee Biol. Abstracts, 1965-71, pres. bd., 1970; mem. vis. com. in biology Harvard, 1966-71. Recipient Merit award Bot. Soc. Am., 1956; award Soc. Am. Foresters, 1961. Fellow Am. Acad. Arts and Scis.; mem. Am. Inst. Biol. Scis. (organizing bd., pres. 1964), N.C. Acad. Scis. (pres. 1962), Nat. Acad. Scis. (chmn. bot. sect. 1968-70), Am. Soc. Plant Physicologists (pres. 1945, Charles Reid Barnes Life Membership award 1967) Bot. Soc. Am. (pres. 1964), A.A.A.S. (chmn. sect. G; v.p. 1956), Am. Philos. Soc., Phi Beta Kappa, Sigma Xi. Club: Cosmos (Washington). Author: Plant and Soil Water Relationships, 1949; The Physiology of Woody Plants (with T.T. Koslowski), 1959; Plant and Soil Water Relationships: A Modern Synthesis, 1969. Editorial bd. Ann. Rev. Plant Physiology, 1949-54, Plant Physiology. Home: 2251 Cranford Rd Durham NC 27706

KRAMER, PHILIP, petroleum refining exec.; b. N.Y.C., Jan. 27, 1921; s. Saul and Malvina (Kuttner) K.; B.B.A., Coll. City N.Y., 1940; M.B.A., Harvard, 1942; m. Sarah Greenberg, Dec. 27, 1942; childrenNoell M., Marilyn B., Glenn M. Mem. research staff Harvard Grad. Sch. Bus., 1942, 46; v.p. Paragon Oil Co., 1947-60; v.p. Pittston Co., 1960-69; pres. div. Met. Petroleum Co. 1960-69; exec. v.p., dir.

Amerada Hess Corp., 1969—. Served to lt. USNR, World War II. Home: 870 United Nations Plaza New York City NY 10017 Office: 51 W 51st St New York City NY 10019

KRAMER, REUBEN ROBERT, sculptor; b. Balt., Oct. 9, 1909; s. Israel and Bessie (Silver) K.; grad. Rinehart Sch. Sculpture, 1932, postgrad. (Traveling scholar), 1931-33, (fellow) Am. Acad. in Rome, 1936; m. Perna Krick, June 19, 1944. Exhibited Grand Central Galleries, N.Y.C., 1934. Balt. Mus. Art, 1939-58, Internat. Sculpture Show, Phila., 1940, 49, Pa. Acad. Fine Arts, 1949-53, 58, Corcoran Gallery, 1951-58, Am. Jewish Tercentenary Traveling Exhbn., 1954-55; one man shows Grand Central Galleries, N.Y.C., 1937, Md, Inst., Balt., 1937, Balt. Mus., 1939, 51, 59, Corcoran Gallery, 1960, Am. U., Washington, 1953; (with wife) Western Md. Coll., 1954, Hagerstown Mus., 1955; commd. to execute wood carving, P. O., St. Albans, W.Va., 1940; represented in collections Am. U., Corcoran Gallery, Balt. Mus. Art, also pvt. collections Martenet, IBM, Rosen, Horelick, others. Indsl. designer War Dept., 1942-45; founder Balt. Art Center Children, 1944, dir., 1944-55; instr. Md. Inst., 1957-58; pvt. instr. Recipient Am. Prix de Rome, 1934-36; 1st prize Balt. Mus. Art, 1940, 48, 51, 53, sculpture award, 1946, 49, 51, 52, 54; 1st prize for Md., Nat. Art Week, 1941; 1st prize Sculptors Guild of Md., 1948, Sculptors Guild of Washington, 1952, 54; 1st prize for artistry in craftsmanship Peale Mus., 1949, Drawing prize, 1954; Purchase prize IBM, 1941, Balt. Mus. Art, 1948, Corcoran Gallery Art, 1952; Nat. Inst. Arts and Letters sculpture grantee 1964; elected Balt. City Coll. Hall of Fame, 1962. Mem. Alumni Am. Acad. in Rome, Artists Equity Assn. Address: 121 Mosher St Baltimore MD 21217

KRAMER, ROBERT, univ. dean; b. Davenport, Ia., Aug. 17, 1913; s. Robert and Juanita (Mapes) K.; A.B. cum laude, Harvard, 1935, LL.B, Magna cum laude, 1938 m. Mary Rainey Gaston, Mar. 22, 1941; childrenMary Elizabeth (Mrs. Howard Helsinger), Lucy Mapes (Mrs. Dorsey Gardner), Robert Gaston. Admitted to D.C. bar, 1938, N.Y. bar, 1947; atty. NLRB, 1938-40, antitrust div. Dept. Justice, 1941-42; asso. firm Paul, Weiss, Wharton & Garrison, N.Y.C., 1946-47; prof. law Duke, 1947-59; vis. prof. law Stanford, 1950, U. Wis., 1956, U. N.C., 1957, N.Y. U., 1958, Northwestern U., 1959; asst. atty. gen. Office Legal Counsel, Dept. Justice, 1959-61; dean Nat. Law Center, George Washington U., Washington, 1961—. Served to lt. col. AUS, 1942-46; Decorated Legion of Merit. Mem. Am. Bar Assn., Am. Law Inst., Assn. Am. Law Schs. (exec. com. 1959). Democrat. Episcopalian. Author: (with C. L. B. Lowndes) Federal Gift and Estate Taxes, 1962. Editor: Law and Contemporary Problems, 1947-56, Jour. Legal Edn., 1948-55; Am. editor Business Law Rev., 1952-55. Home: 4326 36th ST NW Washington DC 20008 Office: 720 20th St Washington DC 20008

KRAMER, ROLAND LAIRD, educator, cons.; b. Phila., Feb. 26, 1898; s. John Howard and Agnes (Laird) K.; B.S., U. Pa., 1919, A.M., 1921, Ph.D., 1923; m. Mildred R. Cramer, June 9, 1920 (Dec. 1963) ; 1 dau., Jeanne. Instr. commerce and transp. U. Pa., 1919-23, asst. prof., 1923-31, prof. 1931-68; vis. scholar Tri-State coll., Angola. Ind., 1968-69; vis. prof. No. Ill. U. De Kalb, 1970-71; cons. to ss conf. and co. Spl. agt. U.S. Bur. Fgn. and Domestic Commerce, Washington, 1923, 1931; sr. econ. analyst Office Spl. Adviser to Pres on Fgn. Trade, Washington, 1935; bus. specialist Fgn. Trade Zones Bd., Washington, 1936; spl. expert U.S. Maritime Commn., Washington, 1938-39; con. Sec. Commerce, 1939-40; with war shipping adminstern. div. of statistics and research, 1942-45; con, Gov. of Panama Canal in charge of comml. traffic survey, 1946-47. Dir. Fgn. Trade Survey of mfrs. in Phila. area, 1955; mem. bd. World Affairs Council of Phila. Hon. Consul of Peru Phila., 1947-49. Chmn. 1st ward Democratic Party, Nether Providence Twp., Pa. Served with U.S. Army, S.A.T.C., 1918. Mem. Fgn. Traders Assn. Phila. (exec. sec. 1956-64), Am. Soc. Internat. Execs. (exec. v-p., sec. 1964), World Trade Council (adv. com.), Assn. Edn. Internat. Bus. (pres. 1962-64), C. of C. Greater Phila. Am. Legion, Sigma Phi Epsilon. Democrat. Presby, Rotarian. Club: Propeller of United States (nat. v.p., 1946-48. Author; History of Export and Import Railroad Freight Rates and their Effect upon the Foreign Trade of the U.S., 1924; Transportation in Relation to the Export Trade in Agricultural Products, 1924; (with G.G. Huebner) Foreign Trade- Principles and Practices, 1930; International Marketing, 1959; Economic Survey of Coastwise and Intercoastal Shipping, 1939, International Trade-Theory, Policy, Practice (with others), 1959; International Trade and Finance (with others), 1966. Home: 21 Cayuga Way Short Hills NJ 07078

KRAMER, RUSSELL ARNOLD, lawyer; b. Maryville, Tenn., Dec. 13, 1918; s. Russell Reed and Alice Gray (Arnold) K.; B.A., Maryville Coll., 1940; postgrad. U. Tex. Law Sch., 1941; J.D., U. Mich., 1946; m. Sara Lee Hellums, Mar. 8, 1942; children—John Reed, Sara Lynne, Randall A. Admitted to Tenn. bar, 1942; practice in Knoxville, 1946—; mem. firm Kramer, Dye, Greenwood, Johnson & Rayson and predecessor firm, 1947—. Dir. Vulcan Materials Co. Exec. sec. Tenn. Code Commn. Bd. dirs. Maryville Coll. Served from pvt. to capt. USAAF, 1942-46. Mem. Knoxville Bar Assn. Methodist. Home: 2201 Woodmere Dr Knoxville TN 37920 Office: Valley Fidelity Bank Bldg Knoxville TN 37902

KRAMER, SAMUAL NOAH, curator; b. Russia, Sept. 28, 1897; s. Benjamin and Yetta (Weinstein) K.; came to U.S., 1906, naturalized, 1919; student Sch. Pedagogy, 1915- 17; B.S., Temple U., 1921; student Dropsie Coll., 1926-27; Ph.D., U. Pa., 1929; fellow Am. Council Learned Socs., Am. Sch. Oriental Research, Bagdad, 1930-31; D.H.L. (hon.), Hebrew Union Coll., 1957; m. Mildred Tokarsky, Oct. 9, 1933; children—Daniel, Judith. Tchr. pub., pvt. schs., 1919-29; mem. excavating expdns. U. Pa., Billah, Gawra, also Fara, Iraw, 1930-31; research asst. specializing Sumerian Lang., Oriental Inst. U. Chgo., 1932-35, research asso., 1936-42; Guggenheim fellow, copied Sumerian Lit. tablets, Mus. Ancient Orient, Istanbul, 1937-39; study, copy of Sumerian lit. tablets, Mus. U. Pa., 1939—, research asso., 1942-43, asso. curator, 1943-49, curator tablet collections, and Clark Research prof. of Assyriology, 1950-68, emeritus, 1968—; ann. prof. Am. Schs. Oriental Research, travel to Istanbul, Bagdad, for archeol., epigraphic research, 1946-47; Fullbright Research prof. in Turkey, 1951-52; exchange prof. to Soviet Union, 1957; prof. Sorbonne, Paris, 1970-71. Mem. Am. Acad. Arts and Scis., Am. Philos. Soc., Am. Oriental Soc., Am. Anthrop. Assn., A.A.A.S., Archeol. Inst. Am. Soc. Bibl. Lit., Acad. Scis. in Finland, Academie des Inscriptions et Belles Lettres of Instit de France, Brit. Acad. Club: Oriental (Phila.). Author: Gilgamesh and the Huluppu Tree., 1938: Lamentation Over the Destruction of Ur, 1940; (with C.J. Gadd) Ur: Literary and Religious Texts, part one, pub. 1963, part two, pub. 1966. Editor: Sumerian Epics and Myths, and Sumerian Texts of Varied Contents, 1934; The Sumerian Mythology; A Study of Spiritual and Literary Achievement in the Third Millenium B.C.: Sumerian Literary Texts from Nippur, 1944; Biblical Paralles from Sumerian Literature, 1954; From the Tablets of Sumer, 1956, rev. as History Begins at Summer, 1959; The Sumerians: Their Character, History and Culture, 1963; Cradle of Civilization, 1967; The Sacred Marriage Rite, 1969; History of Mesopotamia (Times-Life series). Editor: Mythologies of the Ancient World, 1961. Contbr. articles profl. publs. Home: 5039 Schuyler St Philadelphia PA 19144

KRAMER, SIDNEY, publisher, lawyer; b. N.Y.C., 1915; s. Louis and Mildred (Hindin) K.; B.S., N.Y. U., 1936; J.D., Bklyn. Law Sch., St. Lawrence U., 1939; m. Esther Schansky, Oct. 21, 1939; childrenWendy Beth (Mrs. Michael K. Posner), Mark William. Admitted to N.Y. bar, 1940, Conn. bar, 1962; practice in N.Y.C., 1940-45, Westport, Conn., 1963—; sr. v.p., dir. Bantam Books, Inc., N.Y.C., 1945-67; pres., dir New Am. Library, N.Y.C., 1967— Chmn. Democratic Town Com., also justice peace. Westport, 1960-64. Mem. Nat. Assn. Pubs. (chmn.), Conn. Bar Assn., Assn. Am. Pubs. (chmn. paperback com. 1970-71). Club: Overseas Press. Home: 20 Bluewater Hill Westport CT 06880 Office: New Am Library 1301 Av of Americas New York City NY 10019 179 Main St Westport CT 06880

KRAMER, SIMON PAUL, author, cons.; b. Cin. Aug. 17, 1914; s. Simon Pendleton and Minnie (Halle) K.; B.A., Princeton, 1935; M.Litt., Trinity Coll., Cambridge U., 1938; m. Marie Louise Belden, Jan. 15, 1955 (div. 1968); 1 dau., Theresa. Co- ordinator Inter-Am. Affairs, 1940-43; staff CIA, 1947-51, Brookings Instn., 1952-53: partner Auerbach, Pollak & Richardson, mems. N.Y. Stock Exchange, 1954-57; pres. Corporacion Industrial, Panama, P.R.; pres. Panama Coop. Fisheries, Panama Shrimp, Inc., 1957-60. Mem. secretariat U.S. Nat. Com. IGY, Nat. Acad. Scis., 1956-57, cons. acad., 1960-62, Latin Am. cons., 1962—. Served to lt. USNR, 1943-46. Author: Lord Acton and the Present Crisis in Latin America, 1962; The Last Manchu, 1967; Latin American Panorama (with R.E. McNicoll), 1968, The City in American Life (with F.L. Holborn), 1970. Home: 3023 Dent Pl NW Washington DC 20007 Office: Dupont Circle Bldg 1346 Connecticut Av NW Washington DC 20036

KRAMER, STANLEY E., motion picture producer-director; b. N.Y.C., Sept. 29, 1913; B.S., N.Y. U., 1933; m. Ann Pearce, 1950 (div.); children—Casey, Larry; m. 2d, Karen Sharpe, 1966; children—Katharine, Jennifer. Producer of numerous motion pictures, including: So Ends Our Night, The Moon and Sixpence; with others formed Screen Plays, Inc., Hollywood, Cal., 1947; producer So This Is New York, Champion, 1949, Home of the Brave; organizer, pres. Stanley Kramer Prodns., Inc., 1949, producer The Men, Cyrano de Bergerac, 1950; set up Stanley Kramer Co., 1950, which joined Columbia Pictures, 1951, under arrangement permitting freedom in prodn. policies; producer High Noon (4 Acad. awards 1952), Caine Mutiny, 1953; formed Stanley Kramer Pictures Corp., 1954, producer, dir. Not as a Stranger, 1954; The Defiant Ones (N.Y. Film Critics award) 1958; On the Beach, 1959; Inherit the Wind, 1960; The Secret of Santa Vittoria, 1969; Bless the Beasts and the Children, 1971; prepared radio scripts for nat. network programs. Served to 1st lt. AUS, World War II Recipient One World award, San Remo, Italy, 1950; Look Achievement award as producer of year, 1950; N.Y. Film Critics award as best dir., 1958; Gallatin medal N.Y. U., 1968. Judgement at Nuremberg, 1961 (Irving Thalberg award 1962); It's a Mad, Mad, Mad, Mad World, 1963; Ship of Fools, 1965; Guess Who's Coming to Dinner, 1967; The Secret of Santa Vittoria, 1968; R.P.M., 1970; Bless the Beasts and the Children, 1971. Office: 1438 N Gower St Hollywood CA 90028

KRAMISH, ARNOLD, internat. orgn. exec.; b. Denver, June 6, 1923; s. John I. and Sara (Kaitz) K.; B.S., U. Denver, 1945; A.M., Harvard, 1947; m. Vivian Ruth Raker, Aug. 19, 1952; children—Pamela, Robert. With U.S. AEC, 1946-51; sr. staff mem. Rand Corp., Santa Monica, Cal., 1951-68; v.p. Inst. for the Future, Washington, 1968-70; sci. attache U.S. Mission to UNESCO, Paris, France, 1970—. Prof., U. Cal. at Los Angeles, 1965-66, London Sch. Econs., 1967-68; adj. prof. internat. studies U. Miami (Fla.), 1969. Served with AUS, 1943-46. Carnegie fellow Council in Fgn. Relations, 1958-59; John Simon Guggenheim fellow, 1966-67; research fellow Inst. for Strategic Studies, London, 1966-67. Mem. A.A.A.S. Author: Atomic Energy for our Business, 1959; Atomic Energy in the Soviet Union, 1959; The Peaceful Atom in Foreign Policy, 1963; The Future of Non-Nuclear Nations, 1970; also numerous articles, book chpts. Patentee nuclear radiometer. Home: 21 Chemin de la Grande Pelouse Le Vesinet 78 France Office: US Delegation 1 Rue Miollis Paris France

KRAMM, JOSEPH, playwright, actor, dir.; b. South Phila., Pa., grad. U. Pa., 1928; m. Isabel Bonner. Actor with Civic Repertory Theatre, N.Y.C., 1929-32; appeared on Broadway in L'Aiglon, 1934, Bury the Dead, 1936, Processional, 1937; in Golden Boy, London, 1938; again on Broadway in The Man Who Killed Lincoln, also in Liliom, and Journey to Jerusalem, 194O, Uncle Harry, 1942-43; dir. since 1947; first direction of Broadway play, Hope Is the Thing With Feathers, 1948; author of play, The Shrike (produced by Jose Ferrer), 1952, Giants Sons of Giants, 1962; also the teacher of acting Am. Theatre Wing Profl. Sch., 1952. Recipient Pulitzer prize in drama for The Shrike, 1952. Served with U.S. Army, 1943-46; participated in Battle of the Bulge. Office: 169 8th Av New York City NY 10011

KRAMPER, JAMES PETER, librarian; b. Omaha, Apr. 11, 1912; s. James L. and Cecilia (Mergen) K.; A.B., St. Louis U., 1936, Ph.L., 1938, M.A., 1942. Joined Soc. of Jesus, 1931, ordained priest Roman Catholic Ch., 1944; tchr. Campion High Sch., Prairie du Chien, Wis. 1938-41, 46-52; mem. faculty Creighton U., 1953—, dir. libraries, 1954—. Mem. A.L.A., Cath. Library Assn. Address: 2500 California St Omaha NB 68131

KRAMPF, CHARLES EDWARD, electronics co. exec.; b. Allegany, N.Y., May 7, 1908; s. Edward A. and Laura (Kaufman) K.; B.S. in Econs., Wharton Sch. of U. Pa., 1930; m. Judith C. Strempel, June 13, 1946; 1 son, John. Engaged in oil bus., 1930-44; with Electrical Reactance Corp., 1944-49; with Aerovox Corp., 1949-, exec. v.p., 1966-; pres. Micro Circuits Co., Los Angeles, 1967- ; v.p. Luther Mfg. Co., Olean, N.Y., 1956-; dir. Peoples Nat. Bank, Conway, N.C., Aerovox-can., Hamilton, Ont. Home: Briarcliffe Acres Myrtle Beach SC 29577 Office: Aerovox Corp Myrtle Beach SC 29577

KRAMPITZ, LESTER ORVILLE, microbiologist; b. Maple Lake, Minn., July 9, 1909; s. Henry Richard and Selma Amelia (Wolff) K.; A.B., Macalester Coll., St. Paul, 1931; Ph.D., Ia. State Coll., 1942; D.Sc. (hon.), Macalester Coll., 1958; m. Norma Cynthia Peterson, Oct. 17, 1931; 1 dau., Joyce Rita. Secondary sch. prin. Taunton, Minn., 1931-32, Sacred Heart, Minn., 1932-35, Lake Crystal, Minn., 1935-38; asst. Rockefeller Inst. for Med. Research, N.Y. C., 1942-43; instr. Bacteriol., Ia. State Coll., 1943-45, asst. prof., 1945-46; asso. prof. biochemistry, Med. Sch. Western Reserve, 1946-48, prof. microbiol., 1948—, dir. dept. microbiol., 1948—. Research fellow in bacteriol., Ia. State Coll., 1938-42, Fullbright research fellow U. Munich, 1955-56. Mem. Am. Soc. Bio. Chemists, Am. Acad. Microbiology, Am. Soc. Microbiologists, Am. Assn. Immunologist, Bayerische Akademie der Wissenschaften (corr.), Am. Chem. Soc., Soc. Exptl. Biology and Medicine, N.Y. Acad. Scis., Sigma Xi. Presbyn. Mason. Researcher in bacterial Metabolism. Home: 2476 Taylor Rd Cleveland Heights OH 44118 Office: Case Western Reserve Univ Cleveland OH 44106

KRANE, ROBERT ALAN, banker; b. Bloomfield, Ia., Nov. 17, 1933; s. Arnold and Ruth (Power) K.; B.S.C., State U. Ia., 1955; student Sch. Financial Pub. Relations, Northwestern U., 1964-65; m. Marcia Weicker Fry, June 12, 1954; children—Kristin, Alan, Kathrin, Andrew. With Ia.-Des Moines Nat. Bank 1959—, v.p. adminstrn., 1970—, Mem. community adv. com. econ. edn. Des Moines Pub. Schs., 1965—; div. chmn. Greater Des Moines United Campaign, 1971; mem. exec. com. Ia. Clergy Econs. Conf., 1966—; past pres. Des Moines Jaycees; past pres. Ia. Jaycees; v.p. 400 club U.S. Jaycees, 1965-66, chaplain, 1967-68. Bd. dirs. Boys Club Des Moines, Planned Parenthood of Ia.; bd. dirs., chmn. finance com. Big Bros. Des Moines, 1968—; co-chmn. Greater Des Moines Merit Employers Council, 1968-69; Served to 1st lt. AUS, 1956-59; ETO. Recipient Des Moines Distinguished Service award, 1968. Mem. Des Moines C. of C. (dir. 1964-65, chmn. program com. 1968-69). Presbyn. Home: 3109 Orchard Circle West Des Moines IA 50265 Office: Iowa-Des Moines Nat Bank 6th and Walnut Sts Des Moines IA 50309

KRANER, THOMAS E., machinery co. exec., b. Geneva, Ind.; s. Thomas E. and Gertrude (Keel) K.; B.S. in Mech. Engring., Purdue U., 1937; m. Elaine Teeple, Nov. 8, 1941; childrenMarsha, Thomas E. 111. With Cooper Bessemer, Mt. Vernon, O., 1937-, v.p., 1963-65, pres., 1965-; pres. C-B So., 1958-63; became v.p. Cooper Industries, Inc., 1965, now pres., also dir.; chmn. bd. Cooper Bessemer Can., Ltd., 1963-, dir. Cooper Mex. Me. Soc. Petroleum Engrs., Theta Chi. Mason. Home: 10915 Kirwich St Houston TX 77024 Office: First City Nat Bank Bldg Houston TX 77002

KRANICH, ROBERT HARRY, fgn. service officer; b. Bucyrus, O., Nov. 27, 1913; s. William and Bertha Elizabeth (Fritzinger) K.; A.B., Heidelberg Coll., 1934; postgrad. U. Chgo. Law Sch., 1935-38, Nat. War Coll., 1956-57; m. Chloris Maxine Coates, Aug. 8, 1940; children—William C., Robin C. Salesman, Crosley Corp., 1940; personnel officer SSB, WPB, 1941-43; v.p. Washington Assos., 1949-50; joined U.S. Fgn. Service, 1950; div. dir. Arms Control and Disarmament Agy., 1965-69; polit. adviser to comdr. in chief USAF Europe, 1969—. Lectr., Army War Coll., Navy War Coll. Served to capt. AUS, 1943-46. Mem. Am. Fgn. Service Assn., Nat. Rifle Assn., Acad. Polit. and Social Scis., Res. Officers Assn., Mil. Govt. Assn., Nu Sigma Alpha. Clubs: International, Ft. McNair Officers, American Foreign Service (Washington). Home: Rheinlandstrasse 23 Wiesbaden Germany Office: Hdqrs USAFE/POLAD Wiesbaden Germany

KRANICH, WILMER LEROY, educator; b. Phila., Nov. 20, 1919; s. Jacob H. and Elsie (Ernst) K.; B.S., U. Pa., 1940; Ph.D., Cornell U., 1944; m. Margaret Mansley, July 1, 1950; children—Laurence Wilmer, Deborah M., Gary R. McMullen fellow Cornell U., 1940-41, instr. chem. engring., 1941-44; asst. prof. chem. engring. Princeton, 1946-48; asso. prof. chem. engring. Worcester Polytech. Inst., 1948-49, prof. 1949-58, head, chem. engring. and chemistry, 1958- 67, George C. Gordon prof., head, dept. chem. engring., 1967—; staff cons. Arthur D. Little, Inc., 1949—. Served to lt. (j.g.) USNR, 1944-46. Mem. Am. Inst. Chem. Engrs., Am. Chem. Soc., Am. Soc. Engring. Edn., Sigma Xi, Tau Beta Pi, Alpha Chi Sigma. Baptist. Rotarian. Home: 18 Beechmont St Worcester MA 01609

KRANNERT, HERMAN CHARLES, business exec.; b. Chicago, Nov. 5, 1887; s. Charles and Louise (Jacob) K.; B.S. in Mech. Engring., U. Ill., 1912; LL.D., Ind. U., 1957, Butler U., 1960, Evansville Coll., 1963, DePauw U., 1964, U. Ill., 1965, Ind. Central Coll., 1967; D. Indsl. Adminstrn., Purdue U., 1962; m. Ellnora D. Decker, Oct. 1, 1919. Founder, chmn. bd., dir. Inland Container Corp., Anderson Box Co.; v.p., dir. Ga. Kraft Co.; dir. Ind. Nat. Bank, Morgan Packing Co., Inc., Austin, Ind. Past pres. bd. trustees Indpls.-Marion Bldg. Authority; chmn. bd. trustees Indpls. Mus. Art; bd. dirs. Herman Charles and Ellnora Decker Krannert Found.; trustee Ind. Central Coll., Butler U. (both Indpls.). Recipient Achievement award U. Ill., 1960, Law Day award Appellate Ct. Ind., 1964; Big Wheel award Ind. U. chpt. Sigma Delta Chi, 1965; Distinguished Alumni award U. Ill., 1967; named to Methodist Hall Fame in Philanthropy, 1966. Mem. N.A.M., Ind. Mfrs. Assn., Am. Soc. M.E., U.S., Ind., Indpls. chambers commerce, Chi Phi. Republican. Methodist. Mason (Shriner, K.T., 33), Sagamore of the Wabash. Clubs: Columbia, Athletic, University, Indianapolis Athletic (Indpls.); Woodstock; Meridian Hills Country. Home and office: Indianapolis IN 46206

KRANTZ, JOHN CHRISTIAN, Jr., educator; b. Balt. Oct. 8, 1899; s. John Christian and Johanna Fredericka (Steinmann) K.; Pharm. B., U. Md., 1923, M.S., 1924, Ph.D., 1928, Ph.M., hon. Sc.D., 1931; m. Helen King, June 15, 1921; 1 dau., Margaret Claire. Asso. prof. chemistry U. Md. Sch. Pharmacy and Dentistry, Balt., 1921-26, prof. chemistry, 1926-27; dir. pharm. research, Sharp & Dohme, Balt., 1927-30; chief Bur. Chemistry Md. Dept. Health, 1930-35; prof. pharmacology U. Md. Sch. Medicine, 1933-65, emeritus prof., 1965—. Mem. Revision Com. U.S. Pharmacopoeia (sec. 1940-50); cons. toxicologist U.S. Services Forces, 1943—; spl. cons. USPHS, 1949—; mem. NRC, 1959-62; chmn. adv. council environmental hygiene Md. Bd. Health, 1964-68; dir Scope, USP, 1968; med. sci cons. Huntingdon Research Center, 1965-69; dir. pharmacologic research Md. Psychiat. Research Center, 1969—. Served in S.A.T.C., 1918. Mem. Am. Coll. Cardiology (v.p.), Am. Therapeutic Soc., Am. Pharm. Assn., Am. Assn. Univ. Profs, Am. Soc. History Medicine, Am. Chem. Soc. (mem. council), Parmacol. Soc. (mem. council 1946—, v.p. 1949-50), Soc. for Exptl. Biology and Medicine A.A.A.S., Md. Acad. Sci., Md. Soc. for Med. Research (mem. exec. com.), N.Y. Acad. Sci., Soc. for Cancer Research, Sigma Xi, Awarded Simon medal, Ebert prize in chemistry, 1929; Rho Phi Honor award, 1955, U. Md. alumni award, 1958; distinguished service award Young Men's Christian 1958. Presbyn. Clubs: Gibson Island; Torch (pres. 1940-46); Grachur (Balt.); L'Hirondelle (Ruxton). Author: (textbook) Pharmacologic Principles of Medical Practice, 1949; The Art of Eloquence, 1951; A Portrait of Medical History and Current Medical Problems, 1962; Profiles of Medical Science and Inspired Moments, 1966. Home: Gibson Island MD 21056 Office: Box 3235 Baltimore MD 21228

KRANTZ, KERMIT EDWARD, educator, physician; b. Oak Park, Ill., June 4, 1923; s. Andrew Stanley and Beatrice H. (Cibrowski) K.; B.S., Northwestern U., 1945, B.M., 1947, M.S. in Anatomy, 1947, M.D., 1948; Litt.D. (hon.), William Woods Coll., 1971; m. Doris Cole Krantz, Sep. 7, 1946; children—Pamela (Mrs. Richard Huffstutter), Sarah Elizabeth, Kermit Tripler. Intern obstetrics and gynecology New York Lying-In Hosp., 1947-48; asst. resident, asst. obstetrics and gynecology Cornell U. Med. Coll., New York Lying-In Hosp., N.Y. Hosp., 1948-50; fellow, resident obstetrics and gynecology Mary Fletcher Hosp., Burlington, Vt., 1950-51, dir. Durfee Clinic, 1952-55; instr., then asst. prof. U. Vt. Coll. Medicine, 1951-55; asst. prof. U. Ark. Med. Sch., 1955-59; prof., chmn. dept. gynecology and obstetrics U. Kan. Med. Center, 1959—, lectr. history medicine, 1959—, prof. anatomy, 1963—; obstetrician and gynecologist in chief, 1959—; cons. in field. Bowen-Brooks fellow N.Y. Acad. Medicine, 1948-50; recipient Found. award S. Atlantic Assn. Obstetricians and Gynecologists, 1950, Am. Assn. Obstetricians and Gynecologists, 1950; named Outstanding Prof. in Coll. of Medicine, Nu Sigma Nu, 1955; Markle scholar med. sci., 1957-62. Diplomate Am. Bd. Obstetricians and Gynecologists. Founding fellow Am. Coll. Obstetricians and Gynecologists; fellow A.C.S.; mem. Am. Assn. Anatomists, Am. Fedn. Clin. Research, A.M.A., Am. Med. Writers Assn., Am. Fertility Soc., Am. Assn. U. Profs., Soc. Exptl. Biology and Medicine, Aerosopace Med. Assn. Endocrine Soc., Soc. Gynecologic

Investigation, Central Assn. Obstetricians and Gynecologists, N.Y. Acad. Medicine, N.Y. Acad. Sci., Kan. Med. Soc., Kan. Obstet. Soc., Kan. Obstet. Soc., Sigma Xi, Alpha Omega Alpha. Author numerous articles in field. Home: 6711 Overhill RD Shawnee Mission KS 66208 Office: Univ Kan Med Center Kansas City KS 66103

KRANZBERG, MELVIN, educator; b. St. Louis, Nov. 22, 1917; s. Samuel and Rose (Fitter) K.; A.B., Amherst Coll., 1938; M.A., Harvard, 1939, Ph.D., 1942; L.H.D., Denison U., 1967; Litt.D., Newark Coll. Engring., 1968; m. Nancy Lee Fox, 1943; children—Steven, John; m. 2d, Eva Mannering, 1955; m. 3d, Heido, Romo, 1962. Adminstrv. asst. service trades br. OPA, 1941-42; instr. history, tutor Harvard, 1946; instr. humanities Stevens Inst. Tech., 1946-47; asst. prof. history Amherst Coll., 1947-52; mem. faculty Case Western Res. U., 1952—, prof. history, 1959—, dir. grad. program history sci. and tech., 1963—; Harris Found. lectr. Northwestern U., 1970. Mem. tech. assessment panel Nat. Acad. Scis., 1968-69, mem. com. survey materials sci. and engring., 1971-72; chmn. hist. adv. com. NASA, 1967-69; vice chmn. U.S. Nat. Com. History and Philosophy Sci., 1970—, chmn., 1952-53; v.p. Internat. Coop. History Tech. Com., Internat. Union History Sci., 1968—; mem. Goddard prize essay com. Nat. Space Club, 1966—; history com. Am. Inst. Aero. and Astronautics, 1965-66. Served with AUS, 1943-46. Decorated Bronze Star, Combat Inf. badge; recipient Spl. Research Day citation Case Western Res. U., 1970; Apollo Achievement award NASA, 1969. Mem. Soc. History Technology (sec. 1958—; Leonardo da Vinci medal 1968), A.A.A.S., (v.p. 1966), Soc. French Hist. Studies (v.p. 1959), Sigma Xi, (nat. lectr. 1967, 68), Phi Beta Kappa, Epsilon Pi Tau. Author: The Seige of Paris, 1870-71, 1951; 1948—, A Turning Point?, 1959. Co-editor: Technology in Western Civilization, 2 vols., 1967; editor-in-chief Technology and Culture Quar. Jour., 1959—. Contbr. profl. jours. Home: 2440 Overlook Rd Cleveland Heights OH 44106 Office: Interdisciplinary Studies Case Western Res Univ Cleveland OH 44106

KRAPP, PHILIP VON SALTZA, editor; b. N.Y.C., June 6, 1919; s. George Philip and Elisabeth Christina (von Saltza) K.; B.A., Columbia, 1940; M.A., Yale, 1949, Ph.D., 1956; m. Anita Louise Scholz, Aug. 31, 1963. Dictionary editor Funk & Wagnalls Co., N.Y.C., 1942-46; sr. humanities editor Collier's Ency., N.Y.C., 1955-62; dictionary editor Scott, Foresman & Co., Chgo., 1962-66; editor U. Chgo. Press, 1966-67; sr. editor Ency. Britannica, Chgo., 1967-70; editor U. Mich. Press, Ann Arbor, 1970—. Mem. Modern Lang. Assn., Newberry Library Assos. Clubs Caxton, Grolier. Home: 754 Dellwood Dr Ann Arbor MI 48103 Office: 615 E University Ann Arbor MI 48106

KRASHEN, LEO, mfg. co. exec.; b. Chgo., June 11, 1912; s. Louis and Ida (Kapper) K.; J.D., John Marshall Law Sch., Chgo., 1939; night student Northwestern U., 1941-50, DePaul U., 1930-31; m. Julia Maller, Feb. 28, 1937; childrenGloria (Mrs. Ralph Schack), Stephen. Admitted to Ill. bar, 1939; partner Krashen, Pinzur, Bernstein, C.P.A.'s Chgo., 1950-51; comptroller, treas. Universal Screw Co., Chgo., 1951-60; with MSL Industries, 1960-70, comptroller, treas., 1960-66, treas., 1967-70; dir. Funding Corp. Mem. bus. mgmt. com. Jewish Centers Assn., Los Angeles. Trustee W. Coast Talmudical Sem. C.P.A., Ill., Cal. Mem. Am. Soc. for Technion, Am. Inst. C.P.A.s', Cal. Soc. C.P.A.'s, Financial Execs. Inst. Home: 1025 N Kings Rd Los Angeles CA 90069

KRASLOW, DAVID, newspaperman, author; b. N.Y.C., Apr. 16, 1926; s. Frank and Goldie (Sirota) K.; B.A., U. Miami (Fla.), 1948; m. Bernice Schonfeld, Sept. 18, 1949; children—Ellen Anne, Karen Leah, Susan Beth. Sports writer Miami News, 1947-48, successively sports writer, reporter, Washington corr. Miami Herald, 1948-63; with Los Angles Times, 1963—, Washington bur. chief, 1970—. Served with USAAF, 1944-46. Recipient George Polk award, 1969; Raymond Clapper award, 1969; Dumont award, 1969. Nieman fellow Harvard U., 1961-62. Mem. Sigma Delta Chi. Jewish-religion. Clubs: Gridiron, Federal City, Nat. Press (Washington). Co-author: A Certain Evil, 1965; The Secret Search for Peace in Vietnam, 1968. Home: 2316 N Gate Terrace Silver Spring MD 20906 Office: 1700 Pennsylvania Av N W Washington DC 20006

KRASNA, NORMAN, writer; b. N.Y.C., Nov. 7, 1909; s. Benjamin and Beatrice (Mannison) K.; student N.Y. U., Columbia, Law Sch. St. John's U.; m. Erle Galbraith, Dec. 7, 1951. Film critic N.Y. World, 1928; dramatic editor N.Y. Evening Graphic, 1929; writer screen plays for films, 1932—, including Richest Girl in the World, Fury, Bachelor Mother, Devil and Miss Jones, Princess O'Rourke (winner Academy award 1943), Ambassador's Daughter, Indiscreet; also writer-producer, dir., author stage plays, including Louder Please, 1931, Small Miracle, 1934, Dear Ruth, 1944, John Loves Mary, 1947, Time for Elizabeth (with Groucho Marx), 1948, Kind Sir, 1953, Who Was That Lady I Saw You With?, 1958; Sunday in New York, 1961; Love In E Flat, 1967. Office: 315 S Beverly Dr Beverly Hills CA 90212

KRASNER, LEE, painter; b. Bklyn.; ed. Cooper Union, City Coll. N.Y.; studied with Hans Hofmann; m. Jackson Pollock (dec.). Exhibited paintings at Palazzo Franeri, Turin, Italy, 1959, Galerie Beyeler, Basle, Switzerland, 1961, Laing Art Gallery, Newcastle-upon-Tyne. Eng., 1961, Marlborough Fine Art, London, Eng., 1961, Yale Art Gallery, 1961-62, Mt. Holyoke Coll., 1962. Wadsworth Atheneum, Hartford, Conn., 1962, Guild Hall, East Hampton, N.Y., 196264, Mary Washington Coll., U. Va., Fredericksburg 1962, Queens Coll., N.Y.C., 1962, Howard Wise Gallery, 1962, Guggenheim Mus., N.Y.C., 1964, Gallery of Modern Art, N.Y.C., 1965, Southampton Coll. of L.I. U., 1965, Jewish Mus., N.Y.C., 1967; exhibited with shows Hans Hofmann and His Studnts, 1963, 64, Abstract Watercolors by 14 Americans, 1963-65, White House traveling exhbn., 1967; exhibited in one man shows Betty Parsons Gallery, N.Y.C., 1951, Stable Gallery, N.Y.C., 1955, Martha Jackson Gallery, N.Y.C., 1958, Signa Gallery, East Hampton, 1959, Howard Wise Gallery, 1960, 62, Whitechapel Gallery, London, 1965, Arts Council of Gt. Britain, London, 1966, U. Ala. Gallery, 1967, Marlborough-Gerson Gallery, N.Y.C., 1968; represented in permanent collections. Address: The Springs East Hampton NY*

KRASNER, LOUIS, concert violinist; b. Cherkassy, Russia, June 21, 1903; s. Harry and Sara (Lechovetzky) K.; came to U.S., 1908, naturalized, 1914; diploma N.E. Conservatory Music, 1922; postgrad. study Berlin, Paris, Vienna; hon. prof. Accademia Filarmonica of Bologna, Italy; m. Adrienne Galimir, Oct. 10, 1936; children—Elsa, Vivien, Naomi. Concert appearances Europe and U.S.; soloist with orchs of Vienna, Rome, Berlin, Paris, London, B.B.C.; appeared with Boston Symphony, N.Y. Philharmonic, others; concertmaster Mpls. Symphony, 1944; prof. violin and chamber music Syracuse U., 1949—, condr. U. Symphony Orch., 1955—; faculty mem. Internat. String Congress, 1960-64; mus. dir. Syracuse Friends Chamber Music; participant ann. series chamber music concerts pub. schs., Syracuse; 1st performances of Alban Berg, Schoenberg, other violin concertos; chmn., editor 1964 string symposium Berkshire Music Center, Tanglewood, 1963-64. Mem. music panel Nat. Endowment for Arts, 1966—. Recipient R.I. Gov.'s award for excellence in arts, 1968. Mem. Am. String Tchrs. Assn. (founder, past pres. N.Y. chpt.). Editor: String Problems, Players and Paucity, 1965. Home: 521 Scott Av Syracuse NY 13224

KRASNEY, SAMUEL JOSEPH, metals co. exec.; b. Cleve., Mar. 26, 1925; s. Benjamin and Frieda (Palutsky) K.; B.B.A., Western Res. U., 1946; J.D., Cleve. Marshall Law Sch., 1950; m. Rosalind Friedman, Nov. 19, 1950; children—Nora, Paula, Sherry, Donna. Partner, Res. Audit Co., Cleve., 1946-61; partner Krasney, Polk & Friedman, accountants, Cleve., 1961—; chmn., chief exec. officer, treas. Banner Industries, Inc., Cleve., 1968—. Mem. cabinet Jewish Community Fedn. Bd. dirs. Menorah Park, Bur. Jewish Edn., Hebrew Acad. Mem. Am. Inst. C.P.A.'s, Ohio Soc. C.P.A.'s, Ohio, Cleve. bar assns. Mason. Home: 4286 Churchill Blvd University Heights OH 44118 Office: Superior Bldg Cleveland OH 44114

KRASNO, LOUIS RICHARD, physician; b. Chgo., Sept. 2, 1914; s. Morris and Anne (Kein) K.; B.S., Northwestern U., 1936, M.S., 1937, Ph.D., 1939, M.D., 1945; m. Elaine Ross, Apr. 20, 1940; 1 son, Richard Michael. Intern, Wesley Meml. Hosp., Chgo., 1944-45; resident N.Y. Orthopaedic Hosp., 1945-46; practice medicine, specializing in internal medicine, Chgo., 1946-51; asst. prof. U. Ill. Med. Sch., Chgo., 1947-51; research U.S. Naval Research Inst. Bethesda, Md., 1951-53; faculty, research U.S. Naval Sch. Aviation Medicine, Pensacola, Fla., 1953-56; dir. clin. research United Airlines, San Francisco, 1957-; asst. clin. prof. medicine Stanford Med. Sch. Served with USNR, 1951-57. Fellow Am. Coll. Pharmacology and Therapeutics, Am. Coll. Cardiology, Am. Coll. Angiology, Aerospace Med. Assn.; mem. A.M.A. (medal for original research in cardiovascular disease 1950), Cal. Med. Assn., Soc. for Exptl. Biology and Medicine, Assn. Mil. Surgeons, Am. Heart Assn., San Francisco C. of C., Sigma Xi. Clubs: Bohemian, Family, Olympic (San Francisco). Developer prototype present oxygen mask used in mil. and comml. aviation; method for adminstrn. aerosolized medication in respiratory diseases. Office: United Airlines Internat Airport San Francisco CA 94128

KRASNOFF, ALAN GERALD, educator; b. Somerville, Mass., Mar. 18, 1928; s. Morris and Anna (Romanow) K.; B.A., U. Bridgeport, 1950; M.A., U. Tex., Austin, 1954, Ph.D., 1956; m. Jane Harris, Sept. 6, 1959; children-Elizabeth, Susan, Mark, Daniel. Fellow, U. Tex., M.D. Anderson Hosp., 1954-58; instr. Washington U. Sch. Medicine, 1958-59; research psychologist VA Hosp., St. Louis, 1959-65; asso. prof. U. Mo., St. Louis, 1965-66, prof., chmn. dept. psychology, 1966-70, prof. psychology, 1970—; cons. psychologist Family and Childrens Service Greater St. Louis, 1959-65, Alton (Ill.) State Hosp., 1965—. Served with AUS, 19464-7. Rosalie B. Hite fellow, 1954-58., Hogg Found, fellow, 1957-58. Mem. Am., Midwestern, Mo. psychol. assns., Sigma Xi, Psi Chi. Contbr. articles profl. jours. Home: 533 Randy Dr St Louis MO 63141

KRASOVSKAYA, VERA, ballet historian; b. Petrograd (now Leningrad), Russia, Sept. 11, 1915; d. Michael and Maria (Zinovieva) Krasovsky; student Agrippina Vaganova, Choreographical Sch., Leningrad, 1924-33; student, post-grad. Inst. Theatre, Music and Cinematography, Leningrad, 1945-51; m. David Zolotnitsky, Nov. 15, 1949; 1 son (by previous marriage), Yuri. Dancer, Kirov's State Theatre of Opera and Ballet, 1933-41; evacuated to Belebei and Samarkand, 1942-44, tchr. ballet; entered Inst. Theatre, Music and Cinematography, Leningrad, 1945, sr. sciential collaborator, from 1953, candidate arts from 1954, doctor arts, 1965—, prof., 1971—. Mem. Councils on Choreography and on Coordination Sci. Research Work, Ministry of Culture USSR; mem. Arts Council Leningrad. Author: Vachtang Chabukiani, 1956, 2d edit., 1960; The Russian Ballet Theatre from its Origin to the Middle of the XIX Century, 1958; The Ballet in Leningrad, 1961; The Russian Ballet Theatre in the Second Half of the XIX Century, 1963; Anna Pavlova, 1964, 2d edit., 1965; Articles about Ballet, 1967; The Russian Ballet Theatre in the Beginning of the XX Century (1900-1917), 1971. Editor, author foreword: The ABC of the Classical Dance. Home: Povarskov pereulok 12 ap 12 Leningrad D-25 Russia Office: Inst of Theatre Music and Cinematography Isaakievskaya place 5 Leningrad USSR

KRASSNER, PAUL, editor; b. Bklyn., Apr. 9, 1932; s. Michael E. and Ida (Garlock) K.; student City Coll. N.Y.; m. Jeanne Johnson, June 30, 1963, (separated); dau. Holly. Mng. editor The Independent, 1954-58; editor The Realist, 1958-; founder Youth Internat. Party, 1967; film critic Cavalier mag.; society editor Ramparts mag.; active in both new left and psychedelic subculture. Bd. dirs. Am. Civil Liberties Union, Lower East Side Action Project, Parents Aid Soc. Ordained minister Universal Life Ch.; mem. faculty Free U. N.Y. Editor: (Lenny Bruce) How to Talk Dirty and Influence People. Address: 101 Av A New York City NY 10009

KRASSOWSKI, WITOLD, educator; b. Piesza Wola, Poland, Sept. 8, 1921; s. Grzmislaw and Janina (Krassowska) K.; came to U.S., 1948, naturalized, 1958; B.S., Purdue U., 1952, M.S., 1954; Ph.D., U. Cal. at Los Angeles, 1963; m. Elizabeth Therese Nolan, June 16, 1951; children—Frederick W., Thomas W., Daniel W. Teaching asst. Purue U. and U. Cal. at Los Angeles, 1952-56; instr. Occidental Coll., Los Angeles, 1956-57; instr. U. Santa Clara, Cal., 1957-59, asst. prof., 1959-63, asso. prof., 1964-69, prof. sociology, 1969—; adviser, ednl. cons. Civil Service Commn., FAA, Dept. Navy, Dept. Army, Dept. Coast Guard, VA, Internal Revenue Service, Cal. State Personnel Bd., Lockheed Co., FMC Corp., Jpjohn Co., Pacific Telephone Co., Sylvania Electric Co. Lectr., ednl. adviser YMCA San Jose, Boy Scouts Am. Trustee U. Santa Clara. Served with Polish Underground Army, 1939-44, Brit. Army, 1945-48. Decorated Cross of Valor, Cross of Merit. Fellow Kosciuszko Found., N.Y., 1953-54, Fulbright-Hayes fellow U. Madras, India, 1967-68. Fellow Am. Sociol. Assn.; mem. Pacific Sociol. Assn., A.A.A.S., Soc. for Study Social Problems, Alpha Kappa Delta. Roman Catholic. Author: (with others) The Impact of a Value-Oriented University on STudent Attitudes and Thinking, 1961; Sociology of Leadership, 1962. Home: 14360 Lutheria Way Saratoga CA 95070 Office: 820 Alviso St Santa Clara CA 95053

KRASTIN, KARL, coll. dean; b. Toledo, June 29, 1910; s. Arnold and Mella (Pollak) K.; A.B., Western Res. U., 1931, LL.B., 1934; J.S.D., Yale, 1955; m. Katherine Ott Raber, June 11, 1942; children—Frances Melanie, Charlotte Emily. Admitted to Ohio bar, 1934; practice in Cleve., 1934-40; Sterling fellow Yale Law Sch., 1946-48; mem. faculty U. Fla., 1948-63, prof. law, 1954-63; dean Coll. Law, U. Toledo, 1963—. Adviser, Fla. Nuclear Devel. Commn., 1961. Bd. dirs. Toledo Legal Aid Soc., Advocates Basic Legal Equality, Lucas County Ct. Served to maj. AUS, 1941-46. Mem. Ohio, Toledo bar assns., Am. Assn. U. Profs., Am. Law Inst., Assn. Am. Law Schs. (dir. student wave survey), Order of Coif. Contbr. legal publs. Home: 3314 Middlesex Dr Toledo OH 43606

KRATHWOHL, DAVID READING, educator; b. Chgo., May 14, 1921; s. William C. and Sarah (Reading) K.; adopted by Marie (Reimold) K.; B.S., U. Chgo., 1943, M.S., 1947, Ph.D., 1953; m. Helen Jean Abney, Dec. 20, 1943; children—James D. (dec. Nov. 1967), David A., Ruth Anne, and Kristin Jeanne. Asst. dir. unit on evaluation Bur. Ednl. Research Coll. Edn. U. Ill., 1949-55, instr., 1949-53 asst. prof., 1953- 55; asso. prof. Mich. State U., 1955-58, prof., 1958-65, research coordinator, 1955-63, chmn. Psychol. Found. Edn., 1960-63, dir. Bur. Ednl. Research, 1963-65; prof., dean Sch. Edn. Syracuse (N.Y.) U., 1965—; chmn. bd. trustees Eastern Regional Inst. for Edn., 1966-71. Served with USAAF, 1943-46. Fellow Am. Psychol. Assn.; mem. Am. Ednl. Research Assn. (president). Author: (with others) Taxonomy of Educational Objectives, The Classification of Educational Goals, Handbook 1; Cognitive Domain, 1956, (with others) Handbook 2; Affective Domain, 1964. Home: 9 Thornwood Lane Fayetteville NY 13066 Office: Slocum Hall Syracuse Univ Syracuse NY 13210

KRATKY, WARREN JOE, advt. exec.; b. St. Louis, June 13, 1924; s. Irwin Frank and Matilda (Wille) K.; B.A. magna cum laude, Harvard, 1946; m. Estel Ruth Heilig, Jan. 15, 1954; children—Bryan, Karen. With Gardner Advt. Co., St. Louis, 1948—, exec. v.p., 1965-67, pres., 1967—. Served with AUS, 1943-46. Home: 511 Tregaron Pl St Louis MO 63131 Office: 10 Broadway St Louis MO 63102

KRATT, EMIL JACOB, civil engr.; b. Portland, Ore., Nov. 9, 1899; s. Jacob and Antoinette (Koester) K.; C.E., U. Cin., 1923; m. Lucy Margaret Failing, Aug. 16, 1928; children—Henry, Emil, Theodore, Laura Antoinette. Vice chmn. bd. J.A. Jones Constrn. Co., Charlotte, N.C., 1935-68, now cons.; spl. lectr. to engring. Trustee Charlotte Community Coll. Mem. Am. Soc. C.E., Am. Soc. M.E., Alpha Tau Omega. Home: 7001 Sardis Rd Charlotte NC 28211 Office: 915 Olive St St Louis MO 63101 Office: 521 E Morehead St Charlotte NC 28211

KRATT, ROBERT ARTHUR, credit union exec.; b. Hancock, Mich., Nov. 1, 1924; s. Arthur Michael and Margaret (Finnegan) K.; B.A., St. Ambrose Coll., Ia., 1951; m. Elizabeth Jane Schmitt, Feb. 3, 1951; children—Claresa, John, Barbara, Susan, Katherine. Ill. rep. Newhouse Paper Co., Moline, Ill., 1951-53; treas., gen. mgr. Farmall Employees Credit Union Internat. Harvester Co., Rock Island, Ill., 1953—; dir. Cuna Mut. Ins. Soc., Madison, Wis., 1966—, chmn. bd., 1971—; chmn. Cumis Ins. Soc., Madison, 1969—; nat. dir. Cuna Internat., Inc.; dir. Ill. Credit Union League, Bensenville. Served with USNR, 1944-46; PTO. Roman Catholic. Kiwanian. Home: 2007 Elm St Davenport IA 52803 Office: PO Box 391 Mineral Point Rd Madison WI 53701

KRATT, WILLIAM E., former coll. pres.; b. Portland, Ore., June 11, 1906; s. Jacob and Antionette (Koester) K.; A.B., Linfield Coll., 1927, LL.D., 1946; A.M., U. Ore., 1932; m. Virginia Watson, June 11, 1938; children—Richard Edwin, Walter George. Supt. schs., North Powder, Ore., 1928-34; dean Menlo Jr. Coll., Menlo Park, Cal., 1934-43, pres. Menlo Sch. and Coll., 1945-71; exec. officer Navy V-12 unit, U. Redlands, Cal., 1943-45. Mem. adv. board of Wells Fargo Bank. Mem. adv. council Pacific area A.R.C., 1951-53. Mem. Cal. Assn. Ind. Secondary Schs. (past pres.), Northern Cal. Jr. Coll. Assn. (past pres.), Nat. Council Independent Schs. (vice chmn.), Am. Legion (vice comdr.), Phi Delta Kappa, Delta Tau Delta. Mason (32). Club: Rotary (past pres., dir.); Palo Alto; Menlo Country, Bohemian (San Francisco). Home: Atherton CA 94025

KRATZER, GUY LIVINGSTON, surgeon; b. Gratz, Pa., Apr. 24, 1911; s. Clarence U. and Carrie E. (Schwalm) K.; student Muhlenberg Coll., 1928-31; M.D., Temple U., 1935; M.S., U. Minn., 1945; m. Kathryn H. Miller, Jan. 27, 1940; 1 son, Guy Miller. Intern, Harrisburg Hosp., 1925-35; fellow proctology, surgery Mayo Clinic, 1942-46, fellow surgery, 1949-50; asso. surgeon Pottsville Hosp., 1936-41; asso. proctologist Allentown (Pa.) Hosp., 1946-, mem. tumor clinic, 1955—, chief, dept. proctology, 1958—; mem. C cons. staff Sacred Heart Hosp., 1946—; cons. proctologist Quakertown Community and Good Samaritan hosps. Active Civil Def.; mobile surg. unit Allentown Hosp., 1950—. Pres. Lehigh Valley chpt., bd. dirs. Am. Cancer Soc. Diplomate Am. Bd. Proctology. Fellow A.C.S. (pres. S.E. Pa. 1965-66), Am. Proctologic Soc., Internat. Coll. Surgeons; mem. Brazilian Proctologic Soc., A.A.A.S., Internat. Acad. Medicine, Shelter House Soc., Am. Med. Writers Assn., Pa. Proctologic Soc. (past pres.), Pa. Med. Soc., Am. Med. Authors, Lehigh Valley Med. Soc. (past pres.), Allentown C, of C. (gov.). Lion. Address: 1447 Hamilton St Allentown PA 18102

KRATZER, MYRON BERNARD, govt. ofcl.; b. N.Y.C., Feb. 21, 1925; s. Louis and Harriet (Lewin) K.; student Okla. U., 1941-43; B. Chem. Engring., Ohio State U., 1947; m. Rowena Susan Cole, June 18, 1948; children—Carl Gary, Steven Gregg. Chem. engr. Stanolind Oil & Gas Co., Tulsa, 1948-51; chem. Engr. AEC, 1951-58, asst. dir., then dep. dir., 1958-64, dir. div. internat. affairs, 1964-67, asst. gen. mgr. for internat. activities, 1967-71; sci. attaché Am. embassy, Buenos Aires, Argentina, 1971—. Served with C.E., AUS, 1943-46, Recipient William A. Jump award Dept. Agr., 1961, Distinguished Service medal AEC, 1969. Office: American Embassy Buenos Aires Argentina

KRAUS, EDWARD HENRY, educator, mineralogist; b. Syracuse, N.Y., Dec. 1, 1875; s. John Erhardt and Rosa Kocher (Knobel) K.; B.S., Syracuse U., 1896, M.S., 1897, Sc.D. (hon.), 1920, LL.D., 1934; Ph.D., U. Munich, 1901; Sc.D., U. Mich., 1967; m. Lena Margaret Hoffman, June 24, 1902; children—Margaret Anna (Mrs. Edward T. Ramsdell) (dec.), Edward Hoffman (dec.), John Daniel. Asst. in mineralogy and German, Syracuse U., 1896, instr., 1897-99, 1901- 02, asso. prof. mineralogy, 1902, prof. geology and chemistry, summers, 1903, 04; head, dept. sci. Central High Sch., Syracuse, 1902-04; asst. prof. mineralogy U. Mich., 1904-06, jr. prof., 1906-07, mineralogy and petrography, 1907-08, prof. and dir. mineral lab. 1908-19, prof. crystallography and mineralogy, and dir. Mineral Lab., 1919-33, prof. crystallography and mineralogy, 1933-46, sec., 1908-10, acting dean, 1911-15, dean summer session, 1915-33, acting dean, 1920-23, dean Coll. Pharmacy, 1923-33, and Coll. of Lit., Sci. and Arts, 1933-45, dean emeritus 1945—; Henry Russel lectr. U. Mich., 1945; Orton lectr. Am. Ceramic Soc., 1954. Recipient Roebling medal Mineral. Soc. Am., 1945. Fellow Geol. Soc. Am., A.A.A.S. Mineral Soc. Am. (pres. 1920, hon. pres. 1955—), Am. Coll. Dentists (hon.), Optical Soc. Am.; mem. Am. Gem Soc. (hon. certified gemologist 1954), German Mineral. Soc. (hon.), Am. Chem. Soc., Mich. Acad. Sci. (pres. 1920), Am. Inst. Mining and Metallurgy Engrs., Am. Pharmacy Assn., Mich. Schoolmasters Club (pres. 1943-44), Gemological Assn. Gt. Britain (hon., v.p. 1956—), German Gemological (hon.), Gemological Inst. Am. (pres. 1948-70), Phi Beta Kappa, Sigma Xi, Phi Kappa Phi. Author: Essentials of Crystallography, 1906; Descriptive Mineralogy, 1911; Tables for the Determination of Minerals (with W.F. Hunt) 1911; Mineralogy (with W.F. Hunt), 1920; Gems and Gem Materials (with E.F. Holden), 1925, 5th edit. (with C.B. Slawson), 1947; also numerous articles in scientific and ednl. jours., U.S. and abroad. Home: 1155 Arlington Blvd Ann Arbor MI 48104

KRAUS, HANS PETER, rare book dealer, pub.; b. Vienna, Austria, Oct. 12, 1907; s. Emil and Hilda (Rix) K.; student Acad. of Commerce. Vienna; Litt. D. (hon.); U. Bridgeport; m. Hanni Zucker Hale, Aug. 28, 1940; childrenMary Ann, Barbara, Evelyn, Susan, Hans Peter. Came to U.S., 1939, naturalized, 1945. Partner, H.P. Kraus Co., N.Y.C., 1940—70; pres. Kraus Periodicals, Inc., N.Y.C., 1948-68, Back Issues Corp., 1962-69, Kraus Reprint Corp., 1962-68; chmn. bd. Kraus Thomson Orgn. Ltd., 1968—. Trustee Yale Library

Assn. Decorated chevalier Legion of Honor (France). Mem. Bibliography Soc. Am., Bibliog. Soc. London, Gutenberg Soc. Clubs: Grolier (N.Y.C.); Golden!s Bridge Hounds (North Salem, N.Y.). Home: Sugar Hill Ridgefield CT 06877 Office: 16 E 46th St New York City NY 10017

KRAUS, JAMES ELLSWORTH, coll. dean; b. Rocky Ford, Colo., Nov. 19, 1909; s. Ernest W. and Grace V. (Helwick) K.; B.S., Colo. A.and M. Coll., 1932: M.S., U. Wis., 1934; Ph.D., Cornell U., 1940; m. Marion A. Strachan, Feb. 15, 1935 (dec.); 1 son, James R.; m. 2d, Barbara J. Branthoover, Sept. 30, 1961. Field asst. U.S. Dept. Agr., Cheyenne, Wyo., 1931-36, asst. physiologist, 1936-41; asst. Cornell U., 1939-40; asso. horticulturist, asso. prof. U. Ida., 1941-44, 45-47, prof. horticulture, also horticulturist, 1947-, head, dept. horticulture, 1948—, dean and dir. Coll. Agr., 1955—, asso. dir. Ida. Agrl. Expt. Sta., 1949-55, dir. Agrl. Expt. Sta. and Agr. Extension Service, 1955-; plant breeder Cal. Packing Corp., Rochelle, Ill., 1944-45. Mem. Am. Soc. Hort. Sci., Sigma Xi. Lion Contbr. articles in field. Home: 718 E 1st St Moscow ID 83843

KRAUS, JOE WALKER, librarian; b. Gorin, Mo., Aug. 31, 1917; s. Joseph M. and Rella Mae (Walker) K.; A.B., Culver-Stockton Coll., 1938; B.S. in L.S., U. Ill., 1939, M.A., 1941, Ph.D., 1960; m. Betsy Curtright, June 15, 1941; childrenRichard, David. Asst., U. Ill. Library, 1939-42, instr. Library Sch., 1946; librarian Westminster Coll., 1946-48; asst. librarian Tulane U., 1948-51; librarian Madison Coll., Harrisonburg, Va., 1951-62; dir. libraries Kan. State U., Manhattan, 1962-66; dir. libraries Ill. State U., Normal, 1966-; vis. lectr. U. Tex., summer 1958. Served with AUS, 1942-46. Mem. A.L.A., Assn. Coll. and Research Libraries, Am. Assn. U. Profs., Ill. Library Assn. (pres. 1970). Democrat. Presbyn. Home: 302 Mecherle Dr Bloomington IL 61701 Office: Milner Library Ill State U Normal IL 61761

KRAUS, JOHN DANIEL, elec. engr., astronomer; b. Ann Arbor, Mich., June 28, 1910; s. Edward Henry and Lena (Hoffman) K.; B.S., U. Mich., 1930, M.S., 1931, Ph.D., 1933; m. Alice Linnea Nelson, Dec. 20, 1941; children—John Daniel, Nelson Harward. Research indsl. noise reduction, 1934-35; research physicist cyclotron U. Mich., 1936-37; ind. research and cons. antennas, 1938-40; physicist degaussing ships Naval Ordnance Lab., Washington, 1940-43, div. head, 1942-43; research antennas Radio Research Lab., Harvard, 1943-45; asso. prof. elec. engring. Ohio State U., Columbus, 1946-49, prof. elec. engring., 1949-58, prof. elec. engring. and astronomy, 1958—, Taine G. McDougal prof., 1971—, also dir. radio obs. Recipient Sullivant medal Ohio State U., 1970. Fellow I.E.E.E.; mem. Am. Astron. Soc., Am. Phys. Soc. Author: Very High Frequency Technique (with Radio Research Lab. staff), 1947; Elements of Electromagnetics, 1949; Antennas, 1950; Electromagnetics, 1953; Radio Astronomy, 1966. Contbr. articles to profl. jours. Inventor corner reflector, helical beam, other antennas. Home: 1854 Home Rd Delaware OH 43015 Office: Ohio State University Columbus OH

KRAUS, KURT ADOLF, chemist; b. Windsheim, Germany, June 7, 1914; s. Emil and Hermine (Herz) K.; came to U.S., 1935, naturalized, 1941; B.S., Harvard, 1938; Ph.D., Johns Hopkins, 1941; m. Mary Elizabeth Campbell, July 25, 1945; children—Carolyn, Thomas, Katherine. Asst. chemist Johns Hopkins, 1938- 41, research fellow, 1941-42; instr. Tulane U., 1942-43; asso. chemist Metall. Lab., Chgo., 1943-45; group leader Clinton Labs., Oak Ridge, 1945-48, Oak Ridge Nat. Lab., 1949-62, dir. water research program, 1962- -. Mem. Am. Chem. Soc. (award chromatography and electrophoresis 1966), Research Soc. Am., Sigma Xi. Research inorganic chemistry, ion exchange, hydrous oxides, properties of solutions, inorganic polymers, desalination, pollution control. Home: 110 Ogontz Lane Oak Ridge TN 37830 Office: Oak Ridge Nat Lab Oak Ridge TN 37831

KRAUS, LILI, pianist, educator; b. Budapest. Mar. 4, 1908; d. Victor and Irene (Bak) Kraus; student of Zoltan Kodaly, Bela Bartok, Royal Acad. Music, Budapest, 1915-22, tchrs. diploma, 1925; student of Steuermann, New Acad., Vienna, Austria, 1925-27, M.A., 1927; student Artur Schnabel, Berlin, Germany, 1930-34; Mus.D. (hon.), Chgo. Mus. Coll.; m. Otto Mandl, Oct. 31, 1930 (dec. Aug. 26, 1956); children—Ruth Maria (Mrs. Fergus Pope), Michael Otto Patrick, Pianist with orchestras in Europe, 1926—, Dutch East Indies, 1940; Japanese prisoner-of-war, 1941-45; pianist in Australia and New Zealand, 1945-49, Europe, N. and S. Am., Asia, 1949—; world tours, 1925—; first to play all 25 Mozart piano conerti in N.Y., 1964-65; recorded all 25 Mozart piano concerti for CBS-Epic; now recording complete Schubert piano repertoire for Vanguard; lectr. various univs., U.S. and Europe; head piano dept. Cape Town U., S. Africa, 1949- 50; artist-in-residence Tex. Christian U., 1967—. Hon. mem. Music Tchrs. Assn. Cal., Sigma Alpha Iota. Office: care Alix Williamson 119 W 57th St New York City NY 10019

KRAUS, MENTOR A., lawyer; b. Columbia City, Ind., Aug. 11, 1905; s. Max and Julia (Wetstein) K.; A.B., U. Mich., 1927, LL.B., 1929; m. Wilma Bales, Mar. 9, 1940; children—Sarah Ann, Thomas Michael. Admitted to Ind. bar, 1929, since practiced in Ft. Wayne; partner Barrett, Barrett and McNagny, 1935- -; sec. O'Connor Industries, Inc.; dir. Franklin Elec. Co., Inc., Schafer Bakeries, Inc., Central States Seed Service, Inc., Perfection Biscuit Co. Mem. bd. visitors U. Mich. Law Sch., Ind. U. Law Sch. Bd. dirs., past pres. Family and Children's Service, Inc., Ft. Wayne: chmn. bd. trustees Ft. Wayne Fine Arts Sch. and Mus. Served to lt. comdr. USNR, 1943-46. Fellow Coll. of Probate Counsel, Am. Bar Found.; mem. Am., Ind. (pres. 1966-67), Allen County bar assns., Ft. Wayne C. of C. (pres.). Home: 11901 Covington Rd Fort Wayne IN 46804 Office: Lincoln Bank Tower Fort Wayne IN 46802

KRAUS, OLEN, educator; b. Berwick, Pa., Apr. 7, 1924; s. George N. and Mae (Sweppenheiser) K.; B.S., Pa. State U., 1950; M.S., Mich. State U., 1952, Ph.D., 1957; m. Violet V. Cragle, Apr. 26, 1946; children—Amy Marie, Stephanie Jane. Physicist Nat. Bur. Standards, Washington, 1956-62; chmn. dept. physics U. S.D., 1962-67, U. N.D., 1967—. Served with AUS, 1943-45. Standard Oil of Ind. fellow, 1954. Mem. Am. Phys. Soc., Am. Assn. Physics Tchrs., Am. Assn. Univ. Profs., Sigma Xi. Home: 2614 Olive St Grand Forks ND 58201

KRAUS, ROBERT, cartoonist, author, publisher; b. Milw., June 21, 1925; s. Jack and Esther (Rosen) K.; student Art Students League, N.Y.C.; m. Pamela Vivienne Evan Wong, Dec. 11, 1947; children—Bruce Robert, Charles William. Cartoonist, cover artist for New Yorker mag., 1952—; founder, 1966, since pres., editor-in-chief, pub. Windmill Books, Inc. Author: All the Mice Came, Ladybug, Ladybug, I, Mouse, Mouse at Sea, The Littlest Rabbit, The Trouble with Spider, Mirand's Beautiful Dream, Penguin's Pal, The Bunny Nutshell Library (4 vols.), Springfellow's Parade, The First Robin, Juniper, The Silver Dandelion, Amanda Remembers, My Son the Mouse, The Little Giant, Junior the Spoiled Cat, The Children Who Got Married, Lillian, Morgan and Teddy, The Tree that Stayed Up until Christmas, The Beautiful Princess, Pip Squeak, Mouse in Shining Armor, Ludwig the Dog Who Snored Symphonies; author, illustrator: Red Fox and the Hungry Tiger, Rabbit and Skunk and the Scary Rock, Rabbit and Skunk and the Big Fight, Rabbit and Skunk and Spooks, Whose Mouse Are You?, How Spider Saved Christmas, Bunya the Witch, Shaggy Fur Face, Daddy Long Ears, Hell. Hippopotamus, Leo the Late Bloomer, The Tail Who Wagged The Dog. Home: 212 Main St Ridgefield CT 06604 Office: 257 Park Av S New York City NY 10010

KRAUSE, CHARLES FREDERICK, lawyer; b. Chgoo., Aug. 28, 1931; s. Edgar H. and Edna L. (Pflug) K.; B.A., Va.paraso U., 1957; LL.B., Rutgers U., 1960; m. Joan Ames, Oct. 30, 1968; children-Kent C., Paul E., Jennifer A. Admitted to N.Y. bar, 1961; mem. firm Speisser,r, Shumate, Geoghan, Krause & Rheingold, N.Y.C. and Washington, 1961—. Vicice chmn. bd. Aerial Application Tech., Inc., N.Y.C., 1968; dir. Israel-Am. Tech., Inc., N.Y.C. Served to capt. USMCR, 1952-56. Mem. Am. Bar Assn., Am. Trial Lawyers Assn. Republican. Club: Wings N.Y.C., Home: Elm Rd Briarcliff Manor NY 10510 Office: 200 Park Av New York City NY 10017

KRAUSE, CLARENCE JOSEPH, banker; b. Hallettsville, Tex., Sept. 28, 1924; s. Joseph A. and Julia (Chromcak) K.; student Draughon's Bus. Coll., San Antonio, 1942, So. Meth. U., 1962; m. Maurice E. Barrett, Aug. 9, 1948; childrenEricka, Michael D. With Frost Nat. Bank, San Antonio, 1942-, asst. v.p., 1960, v.p., 1960-64, v.p., cashier, 1964-; tchr. Am. Inst. Banking. Served with USAAF, 1943-46. Mem. Am. Inst. Banking (past pres. San Antonio chpt.). Home: 450 McNeel Rd San Antonio TX 78228 Office: PO Box 1600 San Antonio TX 78206

KRAUSE, DONALD GUNTHER, lawyer; b. N.Y.C., July 4, 1921; s. Gunther Frederick and Hedwig (Haehlen) K.; B.A., Reed Coll., 1942; LL.B., U. Ore., 1949; m. Eugenie E. Hoppe, June 16, 1948 (dec., 1963); children-Janet (Mrs. David Vail), Joseph, David, Richard, Barbara, Susan; m. 2d, Patsy S. DeBernardis, June 25, 1966. Admitted to Ore. bar, 1949, since practiced in Portland; asso. Krause, Evans & Korn, 1949-55; partner Lindsay, Nahstoll, Hart, Duncan, Dafoe & Krause and predecessor firms, 1955—. Leader Portland Area council Boy Scouts Am., 1957-65. Pres., bd. dirs. Ore. Central chpt. Nat. Multiple Sclerosis Soc.; bd. dirs. Lutheran Homes and Hosps. Served with AUS, 1942-45. Fellow Am. Coll. Probate Counsel; mem. Ore. Bar Assn., Delta Theta Phi. Republican. Contbg. author: Oregon Probate Handbook, 1970. Home: 11525 S E 147th St Portland OR 97236 Office: Loyalty Bldg Portland OR 97204

KRAUSE, EDWARD WALTER, athletic dir., b. Chgo., Feb. 2, 1913; s. Walter and Thersa (Krauklis) K.; grad., U. Notre Dame, 1934; m. Elizabeth Linden, Aug. 27, 1938; childrenEdward Walter, Mary Elise, Philip Charles. Athletic dir., coach St. Mary's Coll., Winona, Minn., 1934-39; line coach Holy Cross Coll., 1939-42; line coach U. Notre Dame, 1942-44, 46-48, head basketball coach, 1942-44, 46-51, asst. athletic dir., 1948-49, athletic dir., 1949- -. Dir. 1st United Life Ins. Co. Pres. Community Chest; chmn. South Bend Recreation Bd.; vice chmn. Pan-Am. games. Bd. dirs. United Fund, Nat. Conf. Christians and Jews; Served to 1st lt. USMCR, 1944-46 Mem. C. of C. (dir.), Am. Legion. Catholic. K.C. (4) Eagle. Club: Country. Home: 309 Peashway St South Bend IN 46617 Office: U Notre Dame Notre Dame IN 46556

KRAUSE, ERNST HENRY, aerospace industry exec.; b. Milw., May 2, 1913; s. Ernst and Martha (Strege) K.; B.S. in Elec. Engring., U. Wis., 1934, M.S. in Physics, 1935, Ph.D. in Physics, 1938; m. Constance Fraser, June 29, 1939; children—Margaret Bird (Mrs. Keith McCormick), Katharine Louise, Carol Marjorie, Susan Fraser. With Naval Research Lab., Washington, 1938-54, dir. research Lockheed Aircraft Corp., Van Nuys, Cal., 1954-55; pres., chmn. Systems Research Corp., Van Nuys, 1955- 56; v.p., dir. Aeronutronic Systems, Inc., 1956-59; dir. tech. staff Aeronutronic div. Ford Motor Co., 1959-62; with Aerospace Corp., El Segundo, Cal., 1962—, sr. v.p. devel., 1968—. Pres., World Affairs Council of Inland So. Cal., 1968-69. Recipient Distinguished Civilian Service award USN, 1956. Fellow Am. Phys. Socl; asso. fellow Am. Inst. Aeros. and Astronautics; mem. Sigma Xi, Tau Beta Pi. Home: 1919 Glenwood Lane Newport Beach CA 92660 Office: 2350 E El Segundo Blvd El Segundo CA 90245

KRAUSE, FRANK BROOKS, banker; b. Mpls., Oct. 28, 1916; s. Claude G. and Ellen (Brooks) K.; B.A., Carleton Coll., Northfield Minn., 1938; B.S.L., U. Minn., 1940; LL.B., 1941; m. Katherine L. Nelson, Aug. 11, 1941; childrenMary, Jeanne, Nancy, Frank Brooks. Admitted to Minn. bar, 1941; with Nat. Bank Mpls., 1941—, v.p., sr. trust officer, 1963—; dir. Lindsay Bros. Co. Trustee, Breck Sch., Eitel Hosp. Mem. Minn., Hennepin County bar assns., Am. Inst. Banking. Conglist. (trustee). Rotarian. Home: 4882 W. Lake Harriet Blvd Minneapolis, MN 55410 Office: 120 S 6th St Minneapolis MN 55402

KRAUSE, HARRY DIETER, lawyer, educator; b. Görlitz, Germany, Apr. 23, 1932; s. Renatus and Ellen (Abel-Musgrave) K.; came to U.S., 1951, naturalized, 1954; student Freie Universett Berlin, 1950-51; B.A., U. Mich., 1954, J.D., 1958; m. Eva Maria Disselnkötter, Aug. 30, 1957; children-Philip Renatus, Thomas Walther, Peter Herbert. Admitted to Mich. bar, 1959, D.C. bar, 1959, Ill. bar, 1963, also U.S.Supreme Ct.; with firm Covington & Burling, 1958-60; with Ford Motor Co., Dearborn, Mich., 1960-63; asst. prof. Coll. Law, U. Ill. at Champaign, 1963-65, asso. prof., 1965-68, prof. law, 1968—; reporter com. on uniform legitimacy act Nat. Conf. Commrs. on Uniform State Laws; gen. reporter on kinship relations UNESCO sponsored Internat. Ency. Comparative Law; mem. adv. bd. Nat. Council on Illegitimacy; rapporteur VIIth Congress, Internat. Acad. Comparative Law, Uppsala, Sweden, 1966; cons. Family Study Commn. State of Ill., 1968-69. Served with U.S. Army, 1954-56. Guggenheim fellow, 1969-70; asso. center Advanced Study, U.Ill., 1970. Mem. Am. (com. chmn.), Ill. (past mem. council sect. on family law, internat. law) bar assns., Gesellschaft für Rechtsvergleichung, LAWASIA Assn., Order of Coif. Author: Illegitimacy: Law and Social Policy, 1971. Bd. editors Mich. Law Rev., 1957-58. Contbr. articles profl. jours. Home: 903 Silver St Urbana IL 61801 Office: Coll Law U Ill Champaign IL 61820

KRAUSE, LAVERNE ERICKSON, artist, painter, printmaker; b. Portland, Ore., July 21, 1924; d. James Martin and Hannah (Wrolstad) Erickson; B.S., U. Ore., 1946; student Portland Mus. Art Sch., 1951-58, Pratt Graphic Art Center, 1966; m. Lebrecht Gerhard Karuse, June 23, 1946 (div. June 1960); children—Max Martin, Darcia Elaine, Jay Gunnar. Painter, printmaker; one man exhbns. Portland Art Mus., 1952, 58, Portland State U., 1967, U. Ore. Mus. Art, 1968, Woodside Gallery, Seattle, 1965, Salt Lake Art Center, 1966, Fountain Gallery Portland, 1967, 69, La. State U., 1970; works rep. collections Portland Art Mus., Seattle Art Mus., Salt Lake Art Center, U. Ore., La. State U., Bank of Cal., 1st Nat. Bank of Ore., U.S. Nat. Bank of Ore., Haseltine Collection N.W. Art, U. Wash., Reed Coll., Portland State U.; instr. Mus. Art Sch., 1960-65; vis. printmaker Mt. Angel Coll., 1965; vis. asst. prof. U. Ore., 1966, asso. prof., 1969—; vis. asso. prof. La. State U., summer 1970. Mem. Gov. Ore. Planning Council for Arts and Humanities, 1965-67. Recipient purchase awards, N.W. Printmaker, 1954, Seattle Art Mus., 1960, Seattle Art Mus., 1964; recipient prize for painting, Ore. Centennial, 1959, Portland Art Mus., 1969. Mem. Artists Equity Assn. (pres. Ore. chpt. 1954-55, 66-68, nat. pres. 1969-70). Home: 3295 W 16th Av Eugene OR 97402

KRAUSE, RALPH ALVIN sci. cons.; b. San Francisco, Nov. 11, 1909; s. Alvin Christian and Maria Henrietta (Birth) K.; B.S., U. Cal., 1933; postgrad. Mass. Inst. Tech., 1946-47, Navy War Coll., 1952; m. Myrtise Eleanor Cavanaugh, June 30, 1934; childrenKaren Louise (Mrs. William A. Rafferty), Signe Ann (Mrs. Jeff Wheeler). Research and sales engr. Remler Radio Co., San Francisco, 1933-37; research engr. Standard Oil Co. Cal., 1937-41; asst. dir. lab. nuclear sci. Mass. Inst. Tech., 1946-47; asst. to pres. Raytheon Mfg. Co., Waltham, Mass., 1947-48; dir. research Stanford Research Inst., 1948-52, gen. mgr. research divs., 1952-54, asso. dir., 1954- 64; dir. Dept. Application Sci. Devel. UNESCO, 1964-68, cons., 1968-. Served to comdr. USNR 1941-46. Mem. A.A.A.S., I.E.E.E., Am. Nuclear Soc., Armed Forces Communications, Electronics Assn., Sci. Research Soc. Am., Assn. Applied Solar Energy (dir.). Clubs: Engineers, Commonwealth (San Francisco). Address: 550 Battery St San Francisco, CA 94111

KRAUSE, REGINALD FREDERICK, educator; b. Moyers, W.Va., July 4, 1912; s. Arthur Eugene and Minnie (Lawrence) K.; A.B., W.Va. U., 1936, M.S., 1939; Ph.D., U. Rochester, 1941; M.D., U. Vt., 1951; m. Oneita Talkington, Nov. 19, 1942; 1 son, Mark Allen. Asst. pharmacology and biochemistry U. Rochester, 1939-41; instr. pharmacology, then research asso. U. Vt., 1941, 46-51; prof. biochemistry, head, dept. Med. Sch., W.Va. U., 1951—; rotating intern Uniontown (Pa.) Hosp., 1953-54; spl. research vitamin A and carotene metabolism, lipid metabolism, atherosclerosis. Pres. bd. dirs. Monongalia Home for Aged, Morgantown. Served to maj. USAAF, 1941-46. Mem. Am. Soc. Clin. Nutrition (charter), Am. Soc. Clin. Pathology, Am. Soc. Biol. Chenists, Am. Chem. Soc., Soc. Exptl. Biology and Medicine, A.M.A., Am. Inst. Nutrition, Morgantown C. of C., Sigma Xi, Sigma Pi Sigma, Alpha Omega Alpha, Alpha Epsilon Delta, Kappa Delta Pi. Kiwanian (past pres. Morgantown). Contbg. editor: Modern Nutrition in Health and Disease, 1958. Home: 901 Hawthorne St Morgantown WV 26505

KRAUSE, RICHARD MICHAEL, immunologist; b. Marietta, Ohio, Jan. 4, 1925; s. Ellis L. and Jennie (Waterman) K.; B.A., Marietta Coll., 1947; M.D., Case Western Reserve U., 1952. Fellow preventive medicine dept. Case Western Reserve U., 1951-52; intern, asst. resident medicine Barnes Hosp., St. Louis, Mo., 1952-54; asst. Rockefeller U., 1954-57, asst. prof., 1957-61, asso. prof., 1961-62; prof. epidemiology Wash. U., 1962-66, asso. prof. medicine, 1962-65, prof. medicine, 1965-66; asso. prof., sr. physician to hosp. Rockefeller U., 1966-68, prof., sr. physician, 1968—; chmn. allergy and immunology study sect. NIH, 1966-70, mem. infectious diseases adv. com., 1970; mem. adv. council on research N.Y. Heart Assn., 1969—; bd. dirs., 1967; mem. commn. streptococcal and staphylococcal diseases Armed Forces Epidemiol. Bd., 1963—, dep. dir., 1968—. Bd. dirs. Royal Soc. Medicine Found. Served with AUS, 1944-46. Mem. Assn. Am. Physicians, Am. Soc. Clin. Investigation, Am. Assn. Immunologists, Am. Soc. Microbiology, The Harvey Soc. Research on the epidemiology of streptococcal diseases; immunochem. studies in streptococcal antigens; recognition of rabbit antibodies with molecular uniformity following streptococcal immunization. Home: 430 E 63d St New York City NY 10021 Office: Rockefeller U New York City NY 10021

KRAUSE, ROBERT FREDERICK, utility exec.; b. Cleve., Dec. 27, 1907; s. William John and Augusta (Grundman) K.; A.B., U. Ariz., 1931; J.D., U. Mich., 1936; m. Ann Woodward Verner, May 12, 1937; children—Robert Frederick, John Franklin. Admitted to Ohio bar, 1936; law clk. Tolles, Hogsett & Ginn, 1936-37; atty. SEC, also asso. dir. Pub. Utilities div., Washington, 1937-48; atty. New Eng. Power Service Co., Boston, 1948-50, pres., 1952-57; asst. to pres. New Eng. Elec. System, Boston, 1950-52, v.p., 1959-61, exec. v.p., 1961-63, pres., 1963-70, chief exec. officer, chmn., 1970—, also dir.; exec. v.p. New Eng. Power Service Co., 1962-63, pres., 1963-70, chmn., 1970—, dir., 1963—; exec. v.p. New Eng. Power Co., 1962-64, pres. 1964-70, chmn., 1970—, dir., 1964—; chmn., dir. Mass. Elec. Co., 1968—, v.p., dir. Vt. Yankee Nuclear Power Corp.; dir. Me. Yankee Atomic Power Co. Narragansett Elec. Co., Providence, Yankee Atomic Elec. Co., Conn. Yankee Atomic Power Co., Mass. Gas System, Mass. LNG Inc., First Nat. Bank Boston, First Nat. Boston Corp. Mem. corp. Mus. Sci., Boston, Wentworth Inst., Boston; turstee Newton-Wellesley Hosp., Newton, Mass., Thomas Alva Edison Found.; bd. dirs. Electric Council New Eng. Mem. Edison Elec. Inst. (dir.), Mass. Elec. and Gas Assn. (dir.), Mass., Ohio bar assns. Episcopalian. Home: 74 Avalon Rd Waban MA 02168 Office: 20 Turnpike Rd Westboro MA 01581

KRAUSE, WILLIAM AUSTIN, engring. co. exec.; b. Lennox, Cal., Nov. 16, 1930; s. William August and Grace Olive (Davies) K.; A.A., Pasadena City Coll., 1950; B.S. in Engring., U. Cal. at Berkeley, 1952; m. Patricia Marion McGookin, July 6, 1950; children—Kenneth R., Michael W., Richard R., William R. Supt. constrn. operations C.F. Braun Co., Alhambra, Cal., 1952-63; gen. mgr. Lummus Co., Bloomfield, N.J., 1963-69; pres., chief exec. officer J.F. Pritchard & Co., Kansas City, Mo., 1969—; dir. Pritchard-Rhodes, Ltd. (U.K.), London, Pritchard Canadian Ltd., Calgary, Alta., Can., KRD-Pritchard (Beirat), Cologne, Germany, Venfuel, Houston. Bd. dirs. Boys' Clubs Am., Jr. Achievement; hon. bd. dirs. Rockhurst Coll., Kansas City, Mo. Registered profl. engr., Cal., Del., Ky. Mem. Young Pres.'s Orgn. (sec. Kansas City chpt. 1971-72), Am. Soc. M.E., Am. Inst. Chem. Engrs., Am. Inst. Mining, Metall. and Petroleum Engrs., Nat. Soc. Profl. Engrs., Cal. Alumni Assn. Clubs: Kansas City; University (Houston). Home: 5100 W 83d St Prairie Village KS 66108 Office: 4625 Roanoke Pkwy Kansas City MO 64112

KRAUSHAAR, WILLIAM LESTER, educator, physicist; b. Newark, Apr. 1, 1920; s. Lester A. and Helen (Ousterhoudt) K.; B.S., Lafayette Coll., 1942; Ph.D., Cornell U., 1949; m. Margaret Freidinger, Feb. 27, 1943; children—Mark Jourdan, Susan, Andrew Woolman. Physicist, Nat. Bur. Standards, Washington, 1942-45; asso. prof. physics Mass. Inst. Tech., Cambridge, 1956-65, prof., 1962-65; prof. physics U. Wis., Madison, 1965—. Fellow Am. Phys. Soc., Am. Astron. Soc., Internat. Astron. Union, Am. Acad. Arts and Scis. Author: (with Uno Ingard) Introduction to Mechanics, Matter and Waves, 1960. Research and publs. on astrophysics; study of cosmic X and gamma radiation. Home: 1003 Oak Way Madison WI 53705

KRAUSKOPF, KONRAD BATES, geologist; b. Madison, Wis., Nov. 30, 1910; s. Francis Craig and Maude (Luvan) B.; student Whittier (Cal.) Coll., 1927-28; A.B., U. Wis., 1931; Ph.D. in Chemistry, U. Cal., 1934; Ph.D. in Geology, Stanford, 1939; D.Sc., U. Wis., Milw., 1971; m. Kathryn Isabel McCune, Jan. 1, 1936; children—Karen, Frances, Karl, Marion. Instr. chemistry U. Cal., 1934-35; instr. phys. scis. Stanford, 1935-39, asst. prof. geology, 1939-42, asso. prof., 1942-50, prof. geochemistry, 1950—, asso. dean Sch. Earth Scis., 1960—. Guggenheim fellow for geochem. research; Fulbright grantee for geochem. research in Norway, 1952-53; geologist U.S. Geol. Survey, 1943—. Served as chief, geog. sect. of C-2, U.S. Army, GHQ Tokyo, 1947-48. Awarded citation for Meritorious Civilian Service, Tokyo, 1948; recipient Day medal Geol. Soc. Am., 1960. Mem. A.A.A.S., Geol. Soc. Am. (pres. 1966-67), Nat. Acad. Scis., Am. Geophys. Union, Am. Geol. Inst. (pres. 1963-64), Geochem. Soc. (pres. 1970-71), Phi Beta Kappa, Sigma Xi, Sigma Nu, Alpha Chi Sigma, Phi Kappa Phi, Gamma Alpha. Author:

Fundamentals of Physical Science, 1941; (with Arthur Beiser) The Physical Universe; Introduction to Geochemistry, 1967. Home: 806 La Mesa Dr Menlo Park CA 94025

KRAUSS, ROBERT WALLFAR, educator, botanist; b. Cleve., Dec. 27, 1921; s. Wallfar Gradifer and Emma Eleanor (Mueller) K.; B.A., Oberlin Coll., 1947; M.S., U. Hawaii, 1949; Ph.D., U. Md., 1951; m. Wilberta Tucker Bunker, Aug. 29, 1947 (div. 1969); children—Robert Geoffrey, Douglas Andrew. Research fellow Carnegie Instn., also U. Md., 1951-54; mem. faculty U. Md., 1955—, prof. botany, 1959—, head dept., 1964—. Staff mem. Marine Biol. Lab., Woods Hole, Mass., 1955, 56, 57; cons. USAF Sch. Aviation Medicine, 1961—; spl. adviser on U.S./Soviet relations to adminstr. NASA, 1964—; sr. research affiliate Chesapeake Biol. Lab., 1968—. Served to 2d lt. AUS, 1943-46. Recipient achievement award in biology Washington Acad. Scis., 1961. Fellow A.A.A.S. (mem. council); mem. Am. Soc. Plant Physiologists (trustee 1964-70), Am. Inst. Biol. Scis. (sec.-treas. 1963-68), Bot. Soc. Am. (Darbaker award 1956), Bot. Soc. Washington (pres. 1964), Phycological Soc. Am. (pres. 1963—), Japanese Soc. Plant Physiologists, Phi Beta Kappa, Sigma Xi. Contbr. numerous articles to tech. jours. Home: Box 57 RD2 Denton MD 21629 Office: Dept Botany Univ Maryland College Park MD 20740

KRAUSS, SAMUEL GEORGE, musician, educator; b. Salem, O., Dec. 3, 1909; s. Samuel and Katerine (Wentzel) K.; diploma Curtis Inst. Music, 1935; m. Louise Thompson, Feb. 15, 1936; children—Samuel George, Sally Louise. Solo trumpeter Nat. Symphony, Washington, 1935-36, St. Louis Symphony, 1936-44, Phila. Orch., 1944-58, Robin Hood Dell, Phila., 1944-59, Bach Festival Orch., Bethlehem, Pa., 1944-64; co-first trumpet Phila. Orch., 1958—; instr. trumpet Peabody Conservatory, Balt., 1934-36, Nat. Music Camp, Interlochen, Mich., 1937-39, Curtis Inst. Music, 1946-69, Phila. Musical Acad., 1969—, Temple U., 1969—. Presbyn. Home: 107 Llandaff Rd Havertown PA 19083 Office: 30 S 15th St Philadelphia PA 19102

KRAUSSE, DANIEL MARSTON, oil co. exec.; b. Houston, Nov. 22, 1925; s. Louis Marston and Helen Sholes (Green) K.; B.S. in Chem. Engring., U. Tex., 1947; postgrad. U. Chgo., 1947-48. Advanced Mgmt. Program, Harvard, 1960; m. Barbara Jayne McEwen, Mar. 28, 1948; children—David Gearing, Helen Susan, Carolyn Russell. Asst. to mgr. research and devel. Sinclair Refining Co., Harvey, Ill., 1947-49; sr. v.p. Cosden Petroleum Corp., Big Spring, 1949-61; group v.p., dir. Dresser Industries, Inc., Dallas, 1961-65; pres. dir. Champlin Petroleum Co., Ft. Worth, 1965-67; pres., chief exec. officer Earth Resources Co., Dallas, 1967—; chmn. exec. com., dir. Bonanza Internat., Inc., 1967—; dir. Nat. Bank Commerce, Dallas. Mem. Southwest area council YMCA, 1960; trustee, exec. com. Howard County (Tex.) United Fund, 1955-61; adv. council Engring. Found., U. Tex., 1957-60; trustee-at-large Episcopal Funds, Inc. Served to lt. (j.g.) USNR, 1943-46. Named One of Five Outstanding Young Men in Tex., U.S. Jr. C. of C., 1958; named Distinguished Engring. Grad., U. Tex., 1962. Mem. U. Tex. Ex-Students Assn. (exec. council), Silver Spurs (pres. 1947), Delta Tau Delta, Tau Beta Pi, Phi Eta Sigma. Episcopalian (vestry, chmn. finance com.). Rotarian (past pres. Big Spring). Home: 5211 Meaders Lane Dallas TX 75229 Office: Expressway Tower 6116 N Central Expressway Dallas TX 75206

KRAUT, RALPH JOHN, machine tool exec.; b. Chgo., Nov. 24, 1908; s. Hans B. and Rosa (Buchs) K.; B.S. in Mech. Engring., U. Wis., 1930; children—Diane (Mrs. Matson), Karen (Mrs. Annis), Hans Beymer; m. 2d, Virginia Dunn Smith, Mar. 24, 1963. Prodn. engr. A.O. Smith Corp., Milw., 1931; successively student engr., advt., accounting and traveling auditor, Gen. Electric Co., Schenectady, 1931-35; asst. works mgr. and asst. to pres. Giddings & Lewis Machine Tool Co., Fond du Lac, Wis., 1935-39, dir., exec. v.p., 1939-42, pres., gen. mgr., dir., 1945-66, chmn. bd., chief exec. officer, 1966—; dir. Gt. No. Nekoosa Corp., N.Y.C., Twin Disc Clutch Co., Racine, Wis., Harnischfeger Corp., Milw., Employers Ins. Wausau (Wis.), Marshall & Ilsley Bank, Milw. Trustee, Wayland Acad., Beaver Dam, Wis. Registered profl. engr., Wis. Served to lt. col. Inf., AUS, 1942-45. Mem. Nat. Mgmt. Assn., U.S. Inf. Assn., Am. Legion, V.F.W., Am. Ordnance Assn., Am. Soc. M.E., Am. Soc. Tool and Mfg. Engrs., Am. Mgmt. Assn., Nat. Machine Tool Builders Assn. (past pres.), Tau Beta Pi, Theta Chi. Conglist. Elk, Rotarian. Clubs: South Hills Country, Milwaukee Athletic, Green Lake Yacht. Home: 545 Illinois Av Green Lake WI 54941 Office: Giddings & Lewis Inc Fond du Lac WI 54935

KRAUTGARTNER, KAREL, musician, composer; b. Miklulov, Czechoslovakia, July 20, 1922. Sideman in Czechoslovak dance orchs., 1940-55; soloist, leader own groups Czechoslovak Radio, 1955-; player festivals at Bled, 1962, Munich, 1964, Prague, 1964-65. Composer: The Students' Suite. Address: Prague 5 Zborovska 62, Czechoslovakia

KRAUTHEIMER, RICHARD, educator; b. Fuerth, Bavaria, July 6, 1897; s. Nathan and Martha (Landmann) K.; student univs. Munich, Berlin, Marburg; Ph.D., Halle- Wittenberg U., 1923; D.H.L., U. Louisville, 1959; hon. Dr., Frankfurt U., Germany, 1965, Christian Archeol., Rome Pontifical Inst. Christian Archeology, 1968; m. Trude Hess, Mar. 18, 1924. Came to U.S., 1935, naturalized, 1942. Privatdozent, Marburg U., 1928-35; asst. prof. U. Louisville, 1935-37; prof. history of art Vassar Coll., 1937-52; prof. history of art Inst. Fine Arts, N.Y. U., 1952-65, Jayne Wrightsman prof., 1965—. Sr. research analyst OSS, 1942-44. Guggenheim fellow, 1950, 63. Fellow Am., Jewish acads. arts and sci., Medieval Acad. Am., Brit. Acad. (corr.), Pontifical Acad. Archeology, Am. Philos. Soc.; mem. Max Planck Soc., German Archeol. Inst., Coll. Art Assn. Author: Corpus of the Early Christian Basilicas in Rome, 1937—; Lorenzo Ghiberti, 1956, 70; Early Christian and Byzantine Architecture, 1965; Collected Essays, 1969. Home: 28 Via Gregoriana Rome Italy

KRAUTTER, LOUIS MARTIN, advt. exec.; b. Phila., Nov. 3, 1906; s. Louis Christian and Estelle (Brockman) K.; student mech. engring., Washington U., 1924-30; m. Elisa Bialk, June 30, 1934; children—Elena Bialk, Elisabeth Ward. Copy writer Thomas M. Bowers Advt. Agy., Chgo., 1930-32, copy chief, 1932-33, v.p., 1933-34; account exec. Beaumont & Hohman, Inc., Chgo., 1934-36; creative dir. Cramer-Krasselt, Inc., Milw., 1936-40; dir. advt., sales promotion Crosley Corp., Cin., 1940-42; v.p. Stockton-West-Burkhart, Inc., 1942- 44; v.p., dir., account exec. Henri, Hurst & McDonald, Inc., Chgo., 1944- 49; advt. and merchandising cousel L. Martin Krauter & Assos., 1950, merged with Maxon, Inc., 1950, dir., v.p., gen. mgr., Chgo. office, 1950- 58; exec. v.p. Klau-Van Pietersom-Dunlap, Inc., Chgo., 1958-59; mgr. bus. devel. N.W. Ayer & Son, Inc., 1960-63; pres., treas. Wolf & Krautter, Inc., advt. and marketing agy., Chgo., 1963-. Mem. planning com. Family and Child Welfare div. Welfare Council Met. Chgo., 1958-63, vice chmn., 1964—; exec. dir. Episcopal Charities, Inc., 1970— Bd. dirs. Lawrence Hall, Inc., pres., 1955-60. Mem. Welfare Pub. Relations Forum Chgo., Chgo. Natural History Mus., Pi Kappa Alpha. Republican. Episcopalian. Contbr. articles advt. sales, indsl. trade publs. Home: 791 Bryant Av Winnetka IL 60093 Office: 520 N Michigan Av Chicago IL 60611

KRAVETZ, NATHAN, educator; b. N.Y.C., Feb. 11, 1921; s. Louis and Anna (Tau) K.; B.Ed., U. Cal. at Los Angeles, 1941, M.A., 1949, Ed.D., 1954; fellow edn. Harvard, 1951-52; m. Evelyn Cottan, Dec. 10, 1944; children—Deborah Ruth, Daniel. Tchr., Walnut Creek, Cal., 1941-42; tchr., vice prin., then prin. Los Angeles city schs., 1946-64; asso. prof. edn. Herbert H. Lehman Coll., City U. N.Y., 1964-69, prof., 1970—, dir. Nat. Tchr. Corps, Hunter Coll., 1966-68; cons. Day Care Council N.Y., 1967-69, div. tchr. edn. City U. N.Y., 1968-69; staff mem. Inst. for Edn. Planning, UNESCO, Paris, 1969—; vis. faculty San Diego State Coll., summers 1950, 53, Eastern Ore. Coll. Edn., summer 1955, Los Angeles State Coll., 1953, 54; faculty U. Cal. at Los Angeles, summer 1961, program coordinator Peace Corps, 1963; ednl. cons. Research Directorate, System Devel. Corp., Santa Monica, Cal., 1962-63; edn. adviser, tech. dir. edn. div. U.S. Operations Mission to Peru, ICA, 1958-60. Ednl. cons. Peruvian Ministry Edn., Faculty Edn. San Marcos U., Lima; mem. Peruvian Nat. Edn. Reform Commn., 1958-60; U.S. mem. joint scholarship commn. Am. embassy, Lima; Fulbright Commn., Lima; cons. Ford Found. Nat. Ednl. Planning Commn., Santiago, Chile, 1964; cons. UNESCO, U. Caracas (Venezuela), 1969; cons. chmn. evaluation panel; dir. evaluation research Center for Urban Edn., N.Y.C., 1965-69. Served with psychol. research unit USAAF, 1942-46. Mem. Harvard, U. Cal. at Los Angeles alumni assns., Am. Assn. U. Profs., N.E.A., Phi Delta Kappa, Kappa Delta Pi. Jewish religion. Mem. B'nai B'rith Anti Defamation League. Author: Two for a Walk, 1954; A Horse of Another Color, 1962; (with Ted Gordon) Tips to Teachers, 1962; A Monkeys Tale, 1964; (with Muriel Farrell) The Dog on the Ice, 1968; He Lost It! Let's Find It, 1969; (with Muriel Farrell) Is There a Lion in the House?, 1970; The Way of the Condor, 1970. Contbr. articles profl. publs. Chmn. editorial bd. The Kappa Delta Pi Record, 1968—. Office: Lehman Coll Bronx NY 10468

KRAVIS, IRVING BERNARD, educator, economist; b. Phila., Aug. 30, 1916; s. Nathan and Ethel (Gelgood) K.; B.S., U. Pa., 1938, M.A., 1939, Ph.D., 1947; m. Lillian Beatrice Panzer, June 22, 1941; children—Robert, Marcia, Ellen, Nathan. Instr. econs. Whitman Coll., 1941-42; economist Dept. Labor, 1946-48; asso. prof. U. Mass., 1948-49; mem. faculty U. Pa., 1949—, prof. econs., 1956—, chmn. dept., 1955-58, 62-67, asso. dean Wharton Sch. Finance and Commerce, 1958-60; cons. govtl. and internat. agys., 1949- -. Mem. sr. research staff Nat. Bur. Econ. Research, 1962—. Served to 1st lt. USAAF, 1942-46. Decorated Bronze Star medal. Ford Found. fellow, 1960- 61; Guggenheim fellow, 1966-67. Mem. Am. Econ. Assn., Royal Econ. Soc. Co-author: Price Competitiveness in World Trade, 1971; also articles. Home: 438 Warick Rd Wynnewood PA 19096 Office: Dept Economics Univ Pennsylvania Philadelphia PA 19104

KRAVITZ, EDWARD ARTHUR, educator; b. N.Y.C., Dec. 19, 1932; s. Isadore and Ada (Machlus) K.; B.S., Coll. City N.Y., 1954; Ph.D. in Biol. Chemistry, U. Mich., 1959; m. Kathryn A. Frakes, Oct. 11, 1958; children—David C., James F. Teaching asst. U. Mich., 1955; predoctoral research fellow Nat. Cancer Inst., 1955-58; postdoctoral research fellow Nat. Heart Inst., 1958-60; research fellow neurophysiology and neuropharmacology Harvard Med. Sch., 1960-61, instr. neurophysiology and neuropharmacology, 1961-63, asso., 1963-66, asst. prof., 1966, asst. prof. neurobiology, 1966-68, asso. prof. neurobiology, 1968-69, prof. neurobiology, 1969—. Mem. Am. Soc. Biol. Chemists. Contbr. articles profl. jours. Research chemistry of synaptic transmission. Home: 39 Robinson St Cambridge MA 02138 Office: Dept Neurobiology Harvard Med Sch Boston MA 02115

KRAYER, OTTO HERMANN, pharmacologist, educator; b. Koendringen, Germany, Oct. 22, 1899; s. Hermann and Frieds Berta (Wolfsperger) K.; student U. Freiberg, U. Munich, U. Berlin, 1919-25; M.D., U. Freiburg, 1926, M.D. (hon.), 1957; M.D. (hon.), U. Göttingen, 1962; M.A. (hon.), Harvard, 1942; m. Erna Ruth Philipp, July 27, 1939. Came to U.S., 1937, naturalized, 1944. Asst., pharmacology U. Freiburg, 1926-27; asst., pharmacology U. Berlin, 1927-29, privatdozent pharmacology, toxicology, 1929-32, acting head dept. pharmacology, 1930-32, prof. extraordinarius pharmacology, toxicology, 1932-33; Rockefeller fellow U. Coll., London, Eng., 1934; vis. prof., head, dept. pharmacology Am. U., Beirut, Lebanon, 1934-37; lectr. pharmacology Harvard Med. Sch., 1936, asso. prof. pharmacology, 1937-39, asso. prof. comparative pharmacology, 1939-51, head, dept. pharmacology, 1939-66, prof. pharmacology, 1951-54, Charles Wilder prof., 1954-64, Gustavus Adolphus Pfeiffer prof., 1964-66, Gustavus Adolphus Pfeiffer prof. emeritus, 1966—; Mayo Found. lectr. 1947, 52; univ. lectr. Aberdeen, 1955; Litchfield lectr. Oxford, 1955; spl. lectr. U. Coll., London, 1955; Fahr Lectr. U. Minn., 1956; univ. lectr. at Helsinki, Finland, 1961. Mem. USPHS Pharmacology Study Sect., 1950-54, U.S. Nat. Com. Internat. Union Physiol. Scis., 1959-65. Recipient Torald Sollmann award in pharmacology Am. Soc. Pharmacology and Exptl. Therapeutics, 1961. Mem. Finnish Pharmacol. Soc. (hon.), N.Y. Acad. Scis., Am. Soc. Pharmacology and Exptl. Therapeutics (pres. 1957-58), Nat. Acad. Scis., Swiss Acad. Med. Scis. (corrs.), Czechoslovakian Med. Soc. of J.E. Purkinje (hon.), Brit. Pharmacol. Soc. (hon.), Deutsche Pharmakologische Gesellschaft (hon.), A.A.A.S., Am. Acad. Arts and Scis., Soc. Exptl. Biology and Medicine, Soc. Pharmacology and Therapeutics of Argentine Med. Assn. (hon.), Alpha Omega Alpha (hon.). Editor Ergebnisse der Physiologie, 1950-70; asso. editor Pharmacol. Revs., 1948-52, editor-in-chief, 1953-59. Home: 431 S Alvernon Way Tucson AZ 85711

KREAGER, HENRY DEWAYNE, savs. and loan assn. officer; b. Alexandria, Minn., July 25, 1912; s. William Henry and Ida (Zimmerman) K.; A.B., Wash. State U., 1934, A.M., 1935; postgrad. Duke, 1935-36; Ph.D., Harvard, 1947; m. Lois Melville Schram, Oct. 19, 1941; children—William Henry, John Philip. Asst. to dir., spl. rep. in C.A., FEA, 1943-45; nat. dir. Community Action Programs, 1945-47; mem. staff Exec. Office of Pres., Washington, 1947-53; cons. indsl. economist, Washington, 1953-57, Seattle, 1960-70; Wash. dir. commerce and econ. devel., 1957-60; pres., chief exec. officer Pacific First Fed. Savs.and Loan Assn., Tacoma, Seattle, Portland and Eugene; dir. Pacific N.W. Bell Telephone Co., Washington Natural Gas Co., VWR United Corp., No. Life ins. Co., Rainier Cos., Seattle, Sci. Advances Inc., Columbus, O., URS systems Corp., San Mateo, Cal., Petroleum Exploration and Devel. Funds, Abilene, Tex. Commr. Seattle Worlds Fair Commn., 1960-63; pres. United Arts Council Puget Sound, 1970—; vice-chmn. Econ. Panel, Washington and N.Y.C., 1953—; trustee Seattle Area Indsl Council. Bd. regents Wash. State U.; trustee Lewis and Clark Coll. Littauer fellow, Harvard, 1938-39. Mem. Seattle C. of C. (trustee 1963—), Nat. Assn. Bus. Economists, Sigma Delta Chi, Kappa Sigma. Recipient Distinguished Service award Wash. Allied Daily Newspapers, 1960. Clubs: Rainier, Washington Athletic (Seattle); Nat. Press (Washington). Contbr. articles bus. and profl. jours. Home: 9250 NE 19th St Bellevue WA 98004 Office: Pacific First Fed Savs and Loan 11th and Pacific Sts Tacoma WA 98401

KREAMER, JOHN HARRISON, lawyer; b. Downs, Kan., Sept. 12, 1922; s. John Dean and Catherin (Harrison) K.; A.B., U. Kan., 1946; LL.B., Harvard, 1949; m. Marion Jane Enggas, July 28, 1951; children—Jane Caryle, Anne Enggas. Admitted to Mo. bar, 1949; mng. partner Gage, Tucker, Hodges, Kreamer, Kelly & Varner, Kansas City, 1959; instr. carriers U. Mo. at Kansas City Sch. Law, 1952-54. Sec., dir. U.S. Metal Container Co., 1967—, Plastic Ennterprises, Inc., 1967—, Delta-Chgo., Inc., 1961—, Anderson Corp., San Juan, P.R., 1964—; dir. Data Documents, Inc., Omaha, Jack Cooper Transp. Co., Cook Chem. Co., Kansas City. Mem. Jackson County Bond Adv. Com., 1969-70; chmn. adv. com. Sch. Bd., 1969; exec. com. Kansas City Citizens Assn., 1962—; dir., sec. Jr. Achievement Assn., 1962. Committeeman, Republican Party, 1952-53. Served to 1st lt., inf., AUS, 1942-45. Decorated Purple Heart, Bronze Star. Mem. Greater Kansas City C. of C. (dir., v.p. 1964-68), French Inst. Notre Dame de Sion (adv. bd. 1960-68), U. Kan. Meml. Assn. (pres. 1965-66), Lawyers Assn. K.C. (pres. 1964-65), Internat., Am. bar assns., Beta Theta Pi (pres. 1945), Pi Sigma Alpha. Conglist. Rotarian. Clubs: University (pres. 1963), Kansas City Country (dir. 1968-70). Home: 1246 W 59th St Kansas City MO 64113 Office: Bryant Bldg Kansas City MO 64106

KREBS, HANS ADOLF, scientist; b. Hildesheim, Germany, Aug. 25, 1900; s. Dr. Georg and Alma (Davidson) K.; ed. univs. Göttingen, Freiburg, Munich, Berlin; M.D., Hamburg U., 1925; M.A., Cambridge, U. 1934; Hon. doctorates U. Chgo., 1954, Freiburg U., 1955, U. Paris, 1956, Glasgow U., 1958, Sheffield U., 1959, London U., 1959, Jerusalem U., 1960, Humboldt U., Berlin, Germany, 1960, Leicester U., 1963, Granada Univ., 1964, Leeds U., 1964, U. Pa., 1965, U. Wales, 1965, also Bordeaux (France) U., 1966; m. Margaret C. Fieldhouse, 1938; 3 children. Asst. to prof. O.H. Warburg, Kaiser Wilhelm Inst., Berlin, 1926-30; instr. medicine Freiburg U., 1932; Rockefeller research student Cambridge U., 1933-34, demonstrator in biochem., 1934-35; lectr. pharmacology U. Sheffield, Eng., 1935-38, biochemistry, 1938-45, became prof., dir. research in cell metabolism. 1945; Whitley prof. biochemistry Oxford U., 1954-67, research scientist in Nuffield dept. of clinical medicine Radcliffe Infirmary, 1967—. Recipient Nobel Prize in Medicine for 1953; Lasker Award, Am. Pub. Health Assn. Fellow Royal Soc., London, Eng.; fgn. asso. Nat. Acad. Scis. U.S.A. Contbr. articles on biochemistry to jours. Home: 27 Abberbury Rd Iffley Oxford England

KREBS, HELMUT, opera and concert singer; b. Dortmund, Germany, Oct. 8, 1913; s. Friedrich and Lina (Sayn) K.; student Dortmund Conservatory, 1933, U. Berlin (Germany), 1934-37. Opera singer Volksoper, Berlin, 1937-41, Municipal Opera House, Berlin, 1947—; prof. vocal music U. Music, Berlin, 1957-63; prof. Hoch-Schule für Musik, Frankfurt, 1963—; concert singer, radio. recs; composer for orch., vocal groups, chamber music, songs, opera; editors Bote and Bock, Astoria Verlag. Recipient Music award city of Berlin, 1952, Salzburg, 1949-52, Glyndebourne, 1953, Edinborough, 1953; Kammersänger Berlin, 1963. Served with AUS, 1941-45. Address: 11 Im Dol Berlin 33 (Dahlem), Germany.

KREBS, MAX VANCE, fgn. service officer; b. Cin., June 26, 1916; s. August Leonidas and Katherine Louise (Vance) K.; A.B., Princeton, 1937; postgrad. U. Cin., 1938-39, U. Cal., 1946-47; m. Esther Willard Winn, Aug. 8, 1942; children—Marlyn Vance, Timothy Winn. Asst. to purchasing agt. Strietmann Biscuit Co., Mariemont, O., 1937-38, asst. credit mgr., 1938-41; asst. export mgr. Gantner & Mattern Co., San Francisco, 1946-47; 3d sec., vice consul Am. Embassy, Montevideo, 1947-49, 2nd sec., vice consul, Bogota, 1950-52, consul, Antwerp, 1952-55; tng. assignments officer Office of Personnel, Dept. of State, 1955-57, spl. asst. to Under Sec. State, 1957- 59, spl. asst. to Sec. State, 1959-60, polit. counselor, Manila, 1961- 64, Rio de Janeiro, 1964-67; dep. chief of mission, Guatemala, 1967-70; polit. adviser to comdr.-in-chief U.S. So. Command, C.Z., 1970-71; dep. chief mission (minister-counselor), Buenos Aires, Argentina, 1971—. Served as capt. AUS, 1941-46. Mem. Am. Fgn. Service Assn. (dir. 1957- 59). Mem. Am. Fgn. Service Assn. (dir. 1957-59). Presbyn. Office: Am Embassy Buenos Aires Argentina

KREBS, WALTER WINSTON, newspaper pub.; b. Johnstown, Pa., Mar. 8, 1894; s. Frederick and Margaret Winfred (Walters) K.; student Cornell U., 1913-17; LL.D., U. Pitts.; H.H.D., St. Francis Coll., Loretto, Pa., 1970; m. Cornelia Rogers, Jan. 18, 1939. Admitted to Pa. bar, 1920, and began practice in Johnstown; with Johnstown Tribune and Democrat 1925—, pub., 1927-63, now pres., editor; pres. Johnstown Tribune Pub. Co., WJAC, Inc. Chmn. adv. bd. U. Pitts. At Johnstown. Served to ensign U.S. Navy Flying Corps, 1918. Recipient Pa. awards for excellence for human relations and community service, 1969. Mem. Am. Soc. Newspaper Editors, Chi Phi, Phi Delta Phi, Sigma Delta Chi. Republican. Lutheran. Address: Tribune-Democrat Johnstown PA 15901

KRECH, DAVID, educator, psychologist; b. Russia, Mar. 27, 1909; s. Joseph and Sarah (Rabinowitz) Krechevsky; came to U.S., 1913, naturalized, 1925; B.S., N.Y. U., 1930, M.A., 1931; Ph.D., U. Cal. at Berkeley, 1933; m. Hilda Sidney Gruenberg, Sept. 17, 1943; 1 son, Richard Joseph. NRC fellow biol. scis. U. Chgo., 1933; research asso. Swarthmore Coll., 1937-38, asst. prof. psychology, 1945-47; instr. psychology U. Colo., 1938-39; mem. faculty U. Cal. at Berkeley, 1947—, prof. psychology, 1949-71, prof. emeritus, 1971—, Miller Research prof., 1960, 61; lectr. William Alanson White Sch. Psychiatry, Washington, 1945-46, Bryn Mawr Coll., 1945-46; vis. prof. Harvard, 1950-51, U. Oslo (Norway), 1949-50, U. Nijmegan (Holland), 1963; Fulbright prof., 1949-50, 63-64; Jacob Ziskind vis. prof. Brandeis U., 1968. Served with AUS, 1941-45. Recipient achievement citation N.Y. U. Alumni Assn., 1965, ann. award Internat. Forum Neurol. Orgn., 1969; certificate merit Math. and Sci. Center at Richmond (Va.), 1969; Distinguished Sci. Contbn. award Am. Psychol. Assn., 1970. Fellow Soc. Psychol. Study Social Issues (past pres.), Am. Psychol. Assn., Soc. Exptl. Psychology, Am. Coll. Neuropsychopharmacology, A.A.A.S.; mem. Western psychol. Assn. (past pres.), Internat. Brain Research Orgn., Soc. for Neuroscis., Internat. Soc. Psychoneuroendocrinology, Sigma Xi. Author: (with R.S. Crutchfield) Theory and Problems of Social Psychology, 1948; Elements of Psychology, 1958, 2d edit., 1969; (with Crutchfield and E. L. Ballachey) The Individual in Society, 1963; also numerous articles. Mem. adv. bd. Internat. Jour. Neuroscience. Home: 1496 Euclid Av Berkeley CA 94708

KREEGER, DAVID LLOYD, ins. co. exec.; b. N.Y. C., Jan. 4, 1909; s. Barnet and Laura (Bernen) K.; A.B. magna cum laude, Rutgers U., 1929; LL.B. magna cum laude, Harvard, 1932; m. Carmen Matanzo y Jaramillo, Jan. 12, 1938; children—Carolita Joy (Mrs. Robert B. Hoffman), Peter Laurens Harris. Admitted to N.J. bar, 1933, D.C. bar, 1941; individual practice in Newark, 1932-34; sr. atty. Dept. Agr., 1934-35; prin. atty. Dept. Interior, 1935-41; spl. asst. to atty. gen., also chief, Supreme Ct. sect., claims div. Dept. Justice, 1941-46; individual practice, Washington, 1946-49; sr. partner firm Kreeger, Ragland and Shapiro, Washington, 1949-57; with Govt. Employees Ins. Co., and affilates, Washington, 1957—, chmn. bd., chief exec. officer, 1970—; dir. Nat. Savs and Trust Co., Washington. Mem. Citizens Adv. Council D.C., 1961-64; spl. presdl. ambassador to inauguration Pres. Frei of Chile, 1964; U.S. del. to Econ. Council on Europe, 1967. Pres. Nat. Symphony Orch., 1970—; chmn. 5th Interam. Music Festival, 1971. Bd. trustees Am. U., Coll. V. I., Corcoran Gallery Art, Mt. Vernon Jr. Coll., Washington, Balt. Mus. Art, Opera Soc. Washington, Washington Ednl. Television Assn.; lay adv. bd. Dunbarton Coll. of Holy Cross; bd. dirs. Internat. Exhbns. Found.; mem. com. to visit Harvard Law Sch., 1967-70; bd. regents Georgetown U.; v.p., mem.

exec. bd. Am. Jewish Com.; pres. David Lloyd Kreeger Charitable Found. Recipient Meritorious Pub. Service award Govt. D.C., 1961, Bronze medal appreciation Corcoran Gallery Art, 1965, certificate Appreciation, N.Y. U. Grad. Sch. Bus. Adminstrn. Alumni Assn., 1965, Outstanding Service award Washington Jr. C. of C., 1966. Mem. Am., D.C. bar assns., alumni assns. Rutgers U., Harvard Law Sch., Phi Beta Kappa, Sigma Alpha Mu. Democrat. Jewish religion. Clubs: Metropolitan, National Press, Harvard, International, National Lawyers (Washington). Contbr. articles profl. jours. Editor Harvard Law Rev., 1930-32. Home: 2401 Foxhall Rd NW Washington DC 20007

KREEGER, JOSEPH PRYOR, investment broker; b. Balt., Aug. 31, 1911; s. Joseph Charles and Grace (Pryor) K.; student George Washington U., 1935; m. Jean Prince, Apr. 12, 1939; children—Deborah Lynn, Joseph Prince. Partner firm Robert C. Jones & Co. (name changed to Jones, Kreeger & Co.), 1939—; dir. Suburban Trust Co., Md., Allied Small Bus. Investments Corp., Washington. Mem. N.Y. Stock Exchange, also Washington Bd. of Trade. Kiwanian. Clubs: Congressional Country (Bethesda, Md.); Columbia Country (Chevy Chase, Md.); University (Washington). Home: 9011 Congressional Pkwy Bethesda MD 20014 Office: 1625 1 St NW Washington DC 20006

KREEGER, MORRIS HAROLD, hosp. cons.; b. N.Y., Aug. 17, 1910; s. Barnet and Laura (Betensky) K.; A.B., Rutgers U., 1931; M.D., Jefferson Med. Coll., 1935; postgrad., U. Pa., 1936-37; m. Naomi Mayor, 1935 (div. 1963); children—Charles, Lora; m. 2d, Reneé L. Gelman, Dec. 1964; one dau., Anne. Intern. Altoona (Pa.) Gen. Hosp., 1935-36; practice of medicine, 1937-39; med. resident Mt. Sinai Hosp., N.Y.C., 1940, asst. dir., 1941-46; exec. dir. Michael Reese Hosp., Chgo., 1946-60, hosp. cons., 1960—; mem. bd., Chgo. Hosp. Council 1950-59, pres., 1954. Bd. Dir. Blue Cross Plan for Hosp. Care, Francis W. Parker Sch. Recipient Chgo. Com. 100 Award Honor for outstanding civic and community Service, 1957. Mem. A.M.A., Ill., Chgo. med. socs., Ill. Hosp. Assn., Am. Coll. Hosp. Adminstrs., Am. Hosp. Assn., Am. Assn. Hosp. Cons., alumni assns. Rutgers U., Jefferson Med. Coll., U. Pa. Postgrad. Sch. Medicine, Sigma Alpha Mu, Phi Lambda Kappa. Home: 199 E Lake Shore Dr Chicago. IL 60611. Office: 111 N Wabash Av Chicago IL 60602

KREER, JOHN BELSHAW, educator; b. Bklyn., Sept. 25, 1927; s. John George, Jr. and Mabel (Belshaw) K.; B.S., Ia. State U., 1951; M.S., U. Ill., 1954, Ph.D., 1956; m. Vivienne Margaret Huffman, June 9, 1957; children—Carolyn Joan, Kenneth John. Instr., asst. prof. U. Ill., Urbana, 1955-59; asso. prof., prof. W.Va. U., Morgantown, 1959-64; asso. prof., prof. Mich. State U., East Lansing, 1964—; trustee Nat. Electronics Conf. Served with USN, 1946-48. Mem. I.E.E.E., Hwy. Research Bd., Simulation Council, Am. Soc. Engring. Edn., Assn. Internat. pour Caleal Analogique, Sigma Xi, Eta Kappa Nu, Tau Beta Pi, Pi Mu Epsilon, Phi Kappa Phi. Home: 1834 Pinecrest Dr East Lansing MI 48823

KREEVOY, MAURICE MORDECAI, chemist, educator; b. Boston, Aug. 28, 1928; s. Edward Phillip and Jennie (Gildesheim) K.; B.S., U. Cal. at Los Angeles, 1950; Ph.D. (Moore fellow), Mass. Inst. Tech., 1954; m. Raye Gladys Schwartz, Mar. 29, 1953; children—Edith Pamela, William Seth. Asst. prof. chemistry U. Minn., 1956-59, asso. prof., 1959-64, prof., 1964—; vis. prof. Inst. Ruder BoscoviÉ, Zagreb, Yugoslavia, 1969-70; cons. Gen. Mills. Inc., 1958—. NSF postdoctoral fellow, 1955-56; Sloan Found. fellow, 1960- 64; NSF Sr. postdoctoral fellow, 1962-63. Mem. Am. Chem. Soc., Chem. Soc. (London), Croatian Chem. Soc., Faraday Soc., Am. Assn. U. Profs., Sigma Psi. Patentee liquid ion exchange. Home: 2836 W River Rd Minneapolis,. MN 55406.

KREGER, ROD, govt. ofcl.; b. Clear Lake, S.D., Oct. 25, 1922; s. Fred Edward and Sarah (Anderson) K.; B.A., U. S.D., 1947; m. Elizabeth Ann Gregg, Jan. 31, 1955; children—Sarah Ann, Nancy Jo, Margo Elizabeth. Farm editor Aberdeen (S.D.) Am. News, 1947-48; asso. editor The Farmer Mag., St. Paul, 1948-50; congl. sec. Rep. H.O. Lovre, Rep., S.D., Washington, 1951-53; dir. farm activities Rep. Nat. Com., Washington, 1953-55; chief office congl. liaison and pub. information CAB, Washington, 1955- 56; congl. liaison officer Gen. Services Adminstrn., Washington, 1956- 59, spl. asst. to adminstr. congl. and pub. affairs, 1959-61, asst. adminstr., 1969-70, dep. adminstr., 1970—; appropriations asst. Senator Karl E. Mundt, Washington, 1961-69. Served with AUS, 1943-46. Recipient Distinguished Service award Gen. Services Adminstrn., 1961. Mem. Am. Legion. Home: 3556 N 36th Rd Arlington VA 22207 Office: 18th and F Sts NW Washington DC 20405

KREHBIEL, HARRY, ret. chem. co. exec.; b. Germany, Dec. 27, 1897; s. John and Elisabetha (Kirch) K.; ed. in Germany; m. Sigrid Reising, Sept. 24, 1927; children—Peter W., Harry E. Came to U.S., 1912, naturalized, 1922. Bank clk., 1917; with Catalin Corp. Am., N.Y.C., 1931-68, successively salesman, sales mgr., v.p., 1931-44, pres., 1944-68, chmn. bd., 1960-68, also dir. Mem. Searsdale Art Assn., Fed. Grand Jury Assn., Plastic Pioneers Assn., Mfg. Chemists Assn., Soc. Plastics Industry. Clubs: Union League (N.Y.C.); Westchester Country (Rye, N.Y.). Home: 4 Rutland Rd Scarsdale NY 10583

KREHBIEL, PETER W., mfg. co. exec.; b. 1929; A.B., Dartmouth, 1951; LL.B., N.Y. U., 1960; married. With firm Pennie, Edmonds, Morton, Taylor & Adams, N.Y.C., 1960- 64; with Am. Chain & Cable Co., 1964—, sec., 1967—, gen. counsel, 1970—. Served with USNR, 1951-55. Address: 929 Connecticut Av Bridgeport CT 06602

KREIDER, CARL, coll. provost; b. Wadsworth, O., Sept. 26, 1914; s. Lloyd S. and Adelia (Stover) K.; A.B., Goshen Coll., 1936; M.A., Princeton, 1938, Ph.D., 1941; postgrad. London Sch. Econs., 1938-39; m. Evelyn Burkholder, June 8, 1939; children—Alan Fetter, Rebecca Elizabeth (Mrs. Weldon Pries), Stephen Carl, Thomas Edmund. Field research fellow Brookings Instn., Washington, 1939-40; with Goshen Coll., 1940—, dean, 1944-70, pres., 1950-51, 70-71, provost, 1971—; dean Coll. Liberal Arts, Internat. Christian U., Tokyo, Japan, 1952-56. Coordinator com. on liberal arts N. Central Assn. Colls., 1948-51, 57-63, chmn. com. on liberal arts, 1965-69, editor news bull. com., 1960-62; Fulbright lectr. Hailie Selassie U., Ethiopia, 1963-64. Dir. Travel Equipment Corp. Mem. adv. council Danforth Found., 1958-61. Bd. dirs. Mennonite Aid, Inc. Mem. Am. Econ. Assn., Am. Assn. Higher Edn., Am. Assn. Acad. Deans. Mennonite (chmn. overseas com. bd. missions 1967—). Author: The Anglo-American Trade Agreement, 1943; Helping Developing Countries, 1968; Let My People Choose, 1969. Editor Mennonite Quar. Rev., 1950—. Home: 1121 S 8th St Goshen IN 46526

KREIDER, CHARLES MARR, forest products exec.; b. Chgo., Oct. 14, 1906; s. Charles Russel and Jennie (Marr) K.; B.S., U. Ill., 1927; m. Winifred Geissler, Dec. 26, 1932 (dec.); m. 2d, Mary Margaret Vaughan, 1964. From timekeeper to resident mgr. Starrett Bros., bldg. constrn., mgmt., 1927-37; mgr. Parkay flooring div. Wood Mosaic Co., Louisville, 1937-48; treas. Elmendorf Research, Inc., Chgo., 1948-56; asst. gen. mgr. Brooks- Scanlon, Inc., Bend, Ore., 1956-65, gen. mgr., 1965-68, dir., 1965-68, v.p., 1962-68; owner Charles M. Kreider, mgmt. counseling and cons., 1968—. Mem. Ore. Forest Products Research Adv. Com., 1961- 68, chmn., 1964-68. Active United Fund; mem. Gov.'s Long Range Wood Health Planning Com., 1967-69. Named Man of Month Wood and Wood Products Mag., 1965. Mem. Am. Soc. M.E., Am. Soc. Testing Materials (dir. Pacific N.W. sect.), Forest Products Research Soc. (pres. 1965), Western Wood Products Assn. (chmn. tech. com. 1966-68), Nat. Forest Products Assn., Theta Tau, Phi Kappa. Elk, Rotarian. Clubs: University, Arlington (Portland). Home: 7367 SW Eastmoor Terrace Portland OR 97225 Office: Century Bldg PO Box 25124 Portland OR 97225

KREIDER, DONALD LESTER, educator, mathematician; b. Lancaster, Pa., Dec. 5, 1931; s. Jacob Lester and Rosanna (Rittenhouse) K.; B.A., Lebanon Valley Coll., Annville, Pa., 1949-53; Ph.D., Mass. Inst. Tech., 1959; m. Mary Ellen Galebach, Nov. 23, 1952; children—John Richard, Paul Alan, David Kendall. Teaching asst., instr. Mass. Inst. Tech., 1953-58, instr., 1958-60, mathematician Dynamic Analysis and Control Lab., summer 1955; mem. faculty Dartmouth, 1960—, prof. math., 1967—, chmn. dept., 1967—. Mem. Norwich (Vt.) Bd. Sch. Dirs., 1965-68. Mem. Math. Assn. Am. (vice chmn. tchr. tng. panel com. undergrad. program math. 1968—; chmn. N.E. sect. 1970—), Am. Math. Soc., Assn. Symbolic Logic. Author: Introduction to Linear Analysis, 1966; Differential Equations,1968. Home: Box 156 Norwich VT 05055 Office: Dept Math Dartmouth Coll Hanover NH 03755

KREIDER, ORLANDO CLARK, educator; b. Lineville, Ia., Apr. 5, 1906; s. John Gilbert and Clara Mae (Clark) K.; B.A., Simpson Coll., 1928; M.S., Ia. State U., 1930, M.S., 1941, Ph.D., 1949; m. Julia Louise Ericsson, Aug. 6, 1934. Grad. asst. math. Ia. State U., 1928-30, prof. math., 1946—; with Western Electric Co., Chgo., summer 1929; prof. math., dean Ellsworth Jr. Coll., Iowa Falls, 1930-41; lectr. math., dir. NSF Summer Insts., Ia. State U., 1957-66; navigation instr. ROC Sch, USN, Treasure Island, summer 1951, Long Beach, summer 1952; mem.staff NSF Summer Inst., U. Ore., 1954. Sr. councilor Ia. Jr. Acad. Sci., 1937-39. Served to capt. USNR, 1942-46. Mem. Math. Assn. Am. (life mem., pres. Ia. sect. 1941), Ia. Acad. Sci. (life; pres. math. sect. 1941, chmn. sci. teaching sect. 1949), Natt. Council Tchrs. Math., Sch. Sci. and Math. Assn., Ia. Edn. Assn. (chmn. math. sect. 1936, 51), Am. Legion, V.F.W., Am. Numismatic Assn., Nat. Philatelic Soc., Phi Delta Kappa (life), Pi Mu Epsilon, Lambda Chi Alpha, Epsilon Sigma. Club: Toastmasters Internat. (area gov. 1943, pres. Ames 1953). Author: Mathematical Analysis, 1950. Contbr. articles profl. jours. Home: 1703 Bel Air Dr Ames IA 50010

KREIDLER, HOWARD EVERETT, retired air force officer; b. Tilden, Neb., Nov. 16, 1920; s. J. Everett and Grace (Edwards) K.; grad. Air Force Flying Sch., 1942; B.A., U. Md., 1958; grad. Air War Coll., 1959; m. LaVerne Fields, Dec. 28, 1942; children—Jerold Everett, Linda Lorene. Commd. 2d lt. USAAF, 1942, advanced through grades to brig. gen. USAF, 1963; instr. 34th Bombardment Group, Spokane, 1942-43; squadron comdr. 445th Bombardment Group, Eng., 1943-44; dir. operations 2d Combat Wing, Eng., 1944-45; chief pilot Air Transp. Command, 1945-46; dir. traffic Pacific div. Mil. Air Transp. Service, Hawaii, 1946-49; asst. dir. Hdqrs., Washington, 1949-51; student Command and Staff Sch., 1951; chief transp. operations div. Mil. Air Transp. Service, 1952; comdr. 1501 Air Transp. Group, Travis AFB, Cal., 1952-55; vice chief staff Mil. Air Transp. Service, 1955-56; comdr. 1254th Air Transp. Group, Washington, 1956-58; dep. comdr. Air Forces Ireland, 1959-60; chief air transp. div., dep. dir. operations Hdqrs. USAF, 1960-64; comdr. 437th Air Transp. Wing, Charleston, S.C., 1964-66; vice comdr. 21st Air Force, Mil. Airlift Command, McGuire AFB, N.J., 1966-67; dep. dir. operations Hdqrs. U.S. Strike Command, Tampa, Fla., 1967-70. Decorated Silver Star, D.S.M., Legion of Merit with oak leaf cluster, D.F.C. with oak leaf cluster, Air medal with 3 oak leaf cluster,; Vietnam Service medal with bronze star; Croix de Guerre with gold star (France). Home: Sea Pines Hilton Head Island SC 29928 Office: Hdqrs US Strike Command MacDill AFB FL 33608

KREIDLER, ROBERT NEIL, found. exec.; b. Detroit, Nov. 21, 1929 s. Albert Ardis and Jean (MacDougall) K.; B.A., Dartmouth, 1951; M.P.A., Harvard, 1953, M.A., 1954. With U.S. Govt., 1958-62, White House staff, 1958-61, Office Sci. and Tech., Exec. Office Pres., 1961-62; with Alfred P. Sloan Found., 1962—, v.p., 1965—, exec. v.p., 1968—. Served with USMCR, 1954-58. Fellow A.A.A.S.; mem. Nat. Acad. Scis. (mem. bd. on sci. and tech. for internat. devel.), Council on Fgn. Relations, Phi Beta Kappa, Delta Tau Delta. Clubs: New York Athletic, University (N.Y.C.). Office: 630 Fifth Av New York City NY 10020

KREILING, FREDERICK CHRISTIAN, educator; b. N.Y.C., May 5, 1922; s. Frederick Christian and Bertha Frances (Schneider) K.; A.B., Hofstra Coll., 1947; A.M., N.Y.U., 1951, Ph.D., 1959; m. Lenore A. Jacobs, Mar. 8, 1946; children—Susan Laura, Deborah Jane, Beth Ann. Faculty, Poly. Inst. Bklyn., 1948—, established History of Sci. Program, 1966, prof. history of sci., 1967—; adj. prof. history Bklyn. Coll., 1962, Beatman Found., 1965-68; Fulbright Exchange tchr., West Germany, 1955-56. Served with M.I., AUS, 1942-45. Mem. Am. Hist. Assn., History Sci. Soc. (past chmn. N.Y. chpt.), Soc. History Tech., Philosophy Sci. Assn. Unitarian. Contbr. articles profl. jours. Home: 64-64 229th St Bayside NY 11364 Office: 333 Jay St Brooklyn NY 11201

KREIS, RICHARD GEORGE, former banker; b. Dover, N.J., Oct. 6, 1904; s. Louis G. and Mary J. (Miller) K.; grad. Wharton Extension Sch., U. Pa., 1925; m. Mary M. Walsh, Sept. 10, 1930; children—Mary (Mrs. Michael Scanlon), Ann Marie (Mrs. John Kinnaman), Richard George. With Peoples Savs. & Dime Bank & Trust Co., Dime Bank Lincoln Trust Co., 1922-32; with auditing dept. 1st Nat. Bank, 1932-33, mgr. real estate owned by bank and Lincoln Realty Co., 1933-45, asst. v.p., 1945-51, v.p., 1951-56; v.p., cashier 1st Nat. Bank & Trust Co. (now Northeastern Nat. Bank Pa.), Scranton, 1956-69; pres. Lincoln Realty Co., 1945-46. Mgr., sec.-mgr. Scranton Clearing House Assn., 1958-69. Treas., bd. dirs. Community Med. Center, 1948—; bd. dirs. Scranton Catholic Youth Center. Home: 1027 Clay Av Scranton PA 18510

KREISEL, GEORGE educator; b. Graz, Austria, Sept. 15, 1923; s. Heinrich and Bertha (Wahrmann) K.; ScD., U. Cambridge (Eng.). Came to U.S. 1966. Formerly mem. faculty U. Reading (Eng.), Oxford (Eng.) U., also U. Paris (France); now prof. logic and foundations of math. Stanford. Past mem. Inst. Advanced Study, Princeton. Fellow Royal Soc. London. Author: (with J.L. Krivine) Elements of Mathematical Logic, 1967; also articles. Address: Dept Philosophy Stanford Univ Stanford CA 84305

KREISKY, BRUNO, Austrian fed. chancellor; b. Vienna, Austria, Jan. 22, 1911; s. Max and Irene (Felix) K.; LL.D., U. Vienna. 1938; m. Vera Furth, Apr. 23, 1942; children—Peter Steffan, Suzanne Christine. Active youth movement Social- Democratic Party to 1934, underground movement, imprisoned. 1935-36, 38, then escaped to Sweden; mem. sci. staff Stockholm Coop. Soc., 1939-46; with Austrian Fgn. Service, assigned Austrian Legation. Stockholm, 1946-51; asst. dir. Austrian Pres.'s Office, 1951-53; sec. state for fgn. affairs Fed. Chancellery, Fgn. Affairs Dept., 1953-59; mem. Parliament, 1956—; chief, Austrian delegation UN Gen. Assembly, 1957-65; fed. minister fgn. affairs, 1959-66; chmn. Socialist Pary Austria, 1967- -; fed. chancellor of Austria, 1970—. Pres., Vienna Inst. Devel.; v.p. Inst. for Advanced Studies, Theodor Körner Fund Promotion Arts and Scis. Decorated Gold Grand Cross of Honor (Austria); also numerous fgn. decorations. Author: The Challenge, Politics on the Threshhold of the Atomic Age. 1963; also speeches, articles on internat., econ. affairs. Home: Armbrustergasse 15 Vienna XIX Austria Office: Ballhausplatz 2 Vienna I Austria

KREISMAN, ARTHUR, coll. dean; b. Cambridge, Mass., June 7, 1918; s. Louis and Rose (Shechtell) K.; A.B., Brigham Young U., 1942; student Harvard, 1939; A.M., Boston U., 1943, Ph.D., 1952; m. B. Evelyn Goulston, Apr. 20, 1940; children—Peter Jon, Steven Alan, Richard Curt, James Bruce. Instr., So. Ore. Coll., Ashland, 1946, asst. prof., 1947-51, asso. prof., 1951-55, prof., 1955—, chmn. dept. English, 1951-63, chmn. humanities div., 1955-69, dir. gen. studies, 1959-66, dean arts and scis., 1966—; dir. Block Teaching Project, U.S. Office Edn., 1957-59, dir. Nat. Def. Edn. Act Inst. for Advanced Study in English, 1966. Mem. Gov.'s Adv. Com. on Arts and Humanities, 1966-69. Mem. Ashland City Council, 1950-54. Bd. dirs. Community Chest, Inst. Renaissance Studies, 1956-64; chmn. bd. trustees Ashland Community Hosp., 1960-62. Served with Signal Corps, AUS, 1943-45. Recipient prize for excellence in teaching, 1966. Ford Found. fellow in philosophy and religion Harvard, 1954. Mem. N.W. Assn. Schs. and Colls. (examiner 1968—), Am. Assn. U. Profs. (past pres. Ore. council), Nat. Council Tchrs. English (past pres. Ore. chpt.). Author: Correspondence Courses for State System, 1956; Contemporary Literature, 1961; Reader's Guide to the Classics, 1961. Editor: Oregon Centennial Anthology, 1959. Contbr. poetry and articles to periodicals. Office: So Ore Coll Ashland OR 97520

KREISSMAN, BERNARD, librarian; b. N.Y.C., June 17, 1919; s. Nathan and Sonia (Weisberg) K.; B.S.S., City Coll. N.Y., 1948; M.A., Columbia, 1949, M.S. in L.S., 1954; Ph.D., U. Neb., 1962; m. Shirley Fabian Relis, Aug. 29, 1942; children—Jane Starrett Jan, Judith Ann, Gregory George. Instr. remedial reading, 1937-38; mem. staff N.Y. Pub. library, 1946-54, supr. main reading room, 1951-54; asst. dir. libraries, asso. prof. U. Neb., 1954- 62; chief librarian, prof. City Coll. N.Y., 1962—. Mem. Council Higher Ednl. Instns., 1962—, chmn. library adv. bd., 1964—; rep. of A.L.A. on nat. commn. lit. of Nat. Council Tchrs. English, 1964—. Served with USAAF, 1943-46; PTO. Mem. A.L.A., Assn. Coll. and Research Libraries, Am. Assn. U. Profs. (exec. com. City Coll. N.Y. chpt. 1964—), N.Y. Library Club (exec. council 1962—, chmn. scholarship com. 1964—, pres. 1966-67), Bibliographical Soc. of Am., Archons of Colopbon. Grolier scholar Rutgers U. seminar advanced library adminstrn., 1955. Author: Pamela-Shamela, A Study of Criticisms, Burlesques, Parodies and Adaptations of Richardson's Pamela, 1960; also articles. Editor: (Sir Walter Scott) Life of John Dryden, 1963. Home: 21 Tappan Landing Rd Tarrytown, NY 10591. Office: City Coll NY Library New York City NY 10031

KREKELER, CARL H., educator, biologist; b. Leavenworth, Kan., Jan. 12, 1920; s. Carl and Louise (Wagner) K.; B.A., Concordia Sem., St. Louis, 1941; postgrad., Washington U., St. Louis, 1944-45; Ph.D., U. Chgo., 1955; m. June Lillian Paulson, Dec. 23, 1944; children—Nancy June, Barbara Sue. Instr. Bethany Coll., Mankato, Minn., 1942-44; ordained to ministry Lutheran Ch., 1945; pastor in Milw., 1945-47; mem. faculty Valparaiso U., 1947—, prof. biology, 1958—, chmn. dept., 1959—; naturalist Ind. State Park, summers 1951-52, chief naturalist, 1953-57. Mem. Soc. Study Evolution, Soc. Systemic Zoology, Ecol. Soc. Am., Nat. Speleological Soc., Ind. Acad. Scis., Sigma Xi. Author: (with William W. Bloom) General Biology: An Integrated Text Manual, 1963. Home: 360 McIntyre Ct Valparaiso, IN 46383.

KREMENLIEV, BORIS ANGELOFF, educator, author, composer; b. Razlog, Bulgaria, May 23, 1911; s. Angeles A. and Elena (Pashkuleva) K.; came to U.S., 1929, naturalized, 1944; B.Mus., DePaul U., 1935, M.Mus., 1937; Ph.D., U. Rochester, 1942; m. Elva Florence Baer, Sept. 20, 1945; children—Gregor, Elena. Mus. dir. S. German Network, War Dept., 1945-46; prof. music U. Cal. at Los Angeles, 1947—; Ford Found. Internat. and Comparative Studies grantee, 1962. Served psychol. warfare br. AUS, 1943-45. Recipient Penrose award research folklore Am. Philos. Soc., 1955; awards for contbn. to Am. music ASCAP, 1968, 69, 70, 71; U. Cal. fellow in Inst. Creative Arts, 1966-67. Mem. Internat. Soc. Folklore and Ethnology, Screen Composers Assn., A.S.C.A.P., Am. Fedn. Musicians, Am. Musicol. Soc., Am. Folklore Soc., Soc. for Ethnomusicology (chmn. So. Cal.; v.p.). Author: Music and Its Makers, 1938; Bulgarian-Macedonian Folk Music, 1952; Slavic Folklore, 1956; College and Adult Reading List, 1962. Contbr. to profl. jours. Compositions: Song Symphony, 1941; Stydy, 1947; Song for Parting (with E. Carson), 1949; Grapes, 1951; Crucifixion, 1952; Bulgarian Rhapsody, 1953; Facing West, 1954; Ghetto Story, 1959; Symphony No. 2, 1960; Cantata, Once to Every Man and Nation, 1961; Balkan Rhapsody, 1966; 2d String Quartet, 1966; Elegy for orch., 1968; Misa Juvenaliter, 1969; Sonata for String Bass, Piano, 1968-69; also music for radio, TV, motion pictures, chamber music, songs. Home: 10507 Troon Av Los Angeles CA 90064 Office: 405 Hilgard Av Los Angeles CA 90024

KREMENTZ, JILL, photographer. Work appeared in nat. mags., The Face of South Vietnam. Address: Saturday Review 380 Madison Av New York City NY 10017.*

KREMER, FRED, Jr., merchandising co. exec.; b. Chgo., July 24, 1926; s. Fred and Alice (Person) K.; B.S. in Bus. Adminstrn., Ill. Inst. Tech., 1950; m. Edna Berglund, Aug. 21, 1948; children—Gale, Kimberly, Lorna. With Ill. Inst. Tech. Research Inst., 1950-66, v.p. bus. operations, 1963-66; v.p. adminstrn. Asso. Merchandising Corp., 1966-68, v.p. administrn. and finance, sec.- treas., 1968—; v.p. ARF Devel. Corp., 1963-66. Mem. ad hoc. com. role patents in research Nat. Acad. Scis.-NRC, 1961-62. Served with USAAF, 1944-46. Mem. Am. Mgmt. Assn. Lutheran (past v.p., sec. bd., Sunday sch. supt.). Club: Economic of New York. Home: 14 Mayberry Rd Chappaqua, NY 10514. Office: Asso Merchandising Corp 1440 Broadway New York City NY 10018

KREMER, MERLE WILLIAM, electronic co. exec.; b. East Conneaut, O., Feb. 26, 1916; s. William Andrew and Alta (Baugher) K.; B.S., U. Mich., 1938, M.A., 1942; m. Ardis Rhinehart, Mar. 5, 1937; children—Richard, Ross. Began as asst. to parts gen. mgr. lamp div. Gen. Electric Co., Neia Park; asst. to pres. Allied Products Corp., Detroit, 1952-55; asst. gen. mgr. parts div. Sylvania Electric Products, Inc., Warren, Pa., 1956-57, gen. mgr. parts div., 1957, v.p., 1957-62, sr. v.p. charge Electronic Tube and Parts divs., 1962-64, head electronic components group, 1964-69, sr. v.p. lighting div., Danvers, Mass., 1969—. Home: 3 Harvard Ct Acton MA 01720 Office: 100 First Av Waltham MA 02154

KREML, FRANKLIN MARTIN, assn. exec.; b. Chgo., Jan. 11, 1907; s. Frank Joseph and Sophia Valeria (Dvorak) K.; student U. Wis., 1923-24, Northwestern U., 1925-29; J.D., John Marshall Law Sch., Chgo., 1932; m. Margaret Charlotte Parker, July 11, 1927; children—Franklin Parker, William Parker. With U.S. Bur. Rds., 1924-25; with Evanston Police Dept. while attending Northwestern

U., 1926-29, dir. Accident Prevention Bur., 1929-35; sec. City Council Commn. Traffic and Safety, Chgo., 1932; pub. safety specialist Purdue U., 1935-36; dir. traffic div. Internat. Assn. Chiefs of Police, 1936-55; dir. Traffic Officers Tng. Sch., (now known as Traffic Inst.) Northwestern U., 1932-55, dir. Transp. Center, 1955-62, v.p. univ., 1962-71; pres., chief exec. officer Automobile Mfrs. Assn., Detroit, 1971—. Mem. pres. Chgo. Police Bd. 1960—; chmn. Pres.'s Task Force Hwy. Safety, 1970. Served with AUS, World War II; ret. brig. gen. Decorated Legion of Merit, Bronze Star medal (U.S.); Order Brit. Empire; Italian Bronze Star, Italian Cross; recipient various civic service awards. Mem. Internat. Assn. Chiefs Police, Nat. Def. Transp. Assn., Theta Delta Phi, Delta Upsilon. Conglist. Clubs: University (Evanston, Ill.); Chicago, Tavern (Chgo.); Westmoreland Country (Wilmette, Ill.); Orchard Lake Country, Recess, Detroit Athletic (Detroit). Co-author several texts and manuals, numerous articles on traffic and traffic safety. Home: 2651 Sheridan Rd Evanston IL 60201 also 225 Barden Bloomfield Hills MI 48013 Office: New Center Bldg Detroit MI 48202 also 1619 Massachusetts Av NW Washington DC 20036

KRENEK, ERNST, composer; b. Vienna, Austria, Aug. 23, 1900; s. Ernst and Emanuela (Cizek) K.; student U. Vienna, State Acad. Music, Vienna, State Acad. Music, Berlin, Germany. Came to U.S., 1937, naturalized, 1945. Adviser to dir. State Opera House, Kassel, Germany, 1925-27; prof. music Vassar Coll., 1939-42; dean fine arts Hamline U., St. Paul, 1942-47; composer, Los Angeles, 1947—; compositions include sonatas, chamber music, concertos, orchestral, choral works, songs and operas. Mem. Am. Musicol. Soc., Acad. Arts (Berlin), Nat. Inst. Arts and Letters. Contributor books, articles mags., U.S. and Germany. Home: 10424 Pinyon Av Tujunga CA 91042

KRENITSKY, MICHAEL V., librarian; b. Duquesne, Pa., Nov. 15, 1915; s. Alexander and Anna (Beresnak) K.; B.S., Washington and Jefferson Coll., 1938; B.S. in L.S., Carnegie Inst. Tech., 1947; M.A., So. Meth. U., 1954; m. Jane Rook, June 15, 1941; children—Jane Ann (Mrs. Richard Williams), Michael V., John Rook. Librarian, Pa. Indsl. Sch., Camp Hill, 1941-43, Tex. Mil. Coll., Terrell, 1947-49; circulation librarian Tex. A. and M. Coll.; College Station, 1949-51, asso. librarian, 1951-61; library dir., prof. library sci. Mich. Tech. U., Houghton, 1961—; vis. prof. Library Sch., Tex. Woman's U., Denton, summer 1960; State Dept. ICA appointee to Indonesia to survey univ. library problems, 1959; mem. Mich Bd. for Libraries Adv. Com. on Mich.'s Reference and Research Resources, 1966- -. Treas. College Station United Fund, 1960. Served with AUS, 1943-46. Mem. A.L.A., Mich. (chmn. acad. library div. 1969—) Library Assn., Internat. Assns. Agrl. Librarians and Documentalists, Assn. Coll. and Research Libraries, Phi Delta Theta. Episcopalian. Contbr. articles profl. jours. Home: 1112 E 6th Av Houghton MI 49931 Office: Library Mich Tech U Houghton MI 49931

KRENKEL, PETER ASHTON, educator; b. San Francisco, Jan. 3, 1930; s. Harry Nichols and Daisy Genevieve (Ashton) K.; A.A., Coll. City San Francisco, 1952; B.S., U. Cal. at Berkeley, 1956, M.S., 1958, Ph.D., 1960; m. Norma Kay Williams, June 28, 1953. Instr., U. Cal., Berkeley, 1958-60; v.p. Asso. Water & Air Resources Engrs., Inc., Nashville, 1968—; chmn., prof. dept. environmental and water resources engring. Vanderbilt U., Nashville, 1960—. Cons. in field. Chmn. Thermal Pollution panel Nat. Water Commn., Washington, 1970—; chmn. Tenn. Air Conservation Commn., 1971—. Bd. dirs. Tenn. Tb and Respiratory Disease Assn. Served with AUS, 1953-55. Fellow USPHS, 1963 (award outstanding research san. engring. 1963). Mem. Am. Water Works Assn., Water Pollution Control Fedn., Air Pollution Control Assn., Am. Pub. Health Assn., Am. Inst. Chem. Engrs., Am. Soc. C.E., Sigma Xi, Tau Beta Pi, Chi Epsilon. Editor: (with F.L. Parker) Thermal Pollution, Biological Aspects, 1970; Thermal Pollution, Engineering Aspects, 1970. Contbr. articles to profl. jours. Home: 1304 Hildreth Dr Nashville TN 37215

KRENSKY, HAROLD, dept. store exec.; b. Boston, Apr. 7, 1912; s. Philip and Katherine (Bladd) K.; LL.B., Boston U., 1935; m. Adele Falk, July 5, 1936; 1 dau., Jane Paula. Admitted to Mass. bar, 1937; with Hearst Publs., 1935-42; with R. H. White's Boston, 1942-47; sr. v.p. charge merchandising and publicity Bloomingdale's, N.Y.C., 1947-59, chmn. bd. mng. dir., 1967-69; with William Filene's Sons Co., Boston, 1960-66, pres., 1963-65, chmn. bd., chief exec. officer, 1965-66; v.p. Federated Dept. Stores, Inc., 1965-69, group pres., 1969-71, vice chmn., 1971—, also dir.; dir. Liberty Mut. Ins. Co., Boston, Asso. Merchandising Corp. Asso., Merchandising Corp. Exec. com. Cambridge Sch., Weston, Mass.; trustee Boston U.; bd. dirs. Fashion Inst. Tech.; chmn. Edn. Found. of Fashion Inst. of Tech., adv. council Tobe Coburn Sch., also 1969 Tobe awardee; adv. bd. N.Y. Fashion Designers, Inc. Home: 860 UN Plaza New York City NY 10017 Office: Federated Dept Stores 104 W 40th St New York City NY 10018

KRENTZMAN, BEN, U.S. dist. judge; b. Milton, Fla., Mar. 21, 1914; s. Isaac B. and Juanita (Rogers) K.; B.S., LL.B., U. Fla., 1938; m. Wilma McMullen, Nov. 30, 1946; children—John Arthur, Mary Louise, Elizabeth Rogers. Admitted to Fla. bar, 1938; individual practice, Clearwater, 1938-41, 46-67; U.S. judge Tampa Div., Middle Dist. Fla., 1967-. Served to lt. col. AUS, 1941-46. Decorated Bronze Star medal. Home: 1541 Walnut St Clearwater, FL 33515. Office: PO Box 3209 Tampa FL 33601

KRENZ, DONALD A., business exec., lawyer; b. Buffalo, Apr. 24, 1936; s. Albert and Stella (Holls) K.; B.S., U. Buffalo, 1958; LL.B., Columbia, 1959; m. Darlene F. Hedin, May 26, 1962; children—Carolyn, Jeanne. Admitted to N.Y. bar, 1959; asso. atty. firm Royall, Koegel & Rogers, N.Y.C., 1959-66; with Ogden Corp., N.Y.C., 1966—, v.p., 1968-70, chief counsel, 1968—, sr. v.p., 1970—. Home: 240 Kelburne Av North Tarrytown NY 10591 Office: 161 E 42d St New York City NY 10017

KREPS, CLIFTON HOLLAND, Jr., educator; b. Augusta, Ga., May 12, 1920; s. Clifton Holland and Quincey Sarah (Blanchard) K.; B.A., Coll. William and Mary, 1941; A.M., U. N.C., 1942; Ph.D., Duke, 1948; m. Juanita Morris, Aug. 11, 1944; children—Sarah, Laura, Clifton Holland III. Instr., Pomona (Cal.) Coll., 1946-47; asst. prof. Denison U., 1947-49; from economist to chief statistician Fed. Res. Bank N.Y., 1949-55; Wachovia asso. prof. banking Grad. Sch. Bus. Administrn., U. N.C., 1955-60, Wachovia prof. banking, 1960—, also dir. Inst. Applied Bus. and Econ. Research, 1971—. Econ. cons. Fed. Res. Bank Richmond, 1962-64; sr. asso. Carter H. Golembe Assos., Washington; dir. Morgan Creek Land Co., Chapel Hill; econ. cons. Commn. Money and Credit, 1960, Allied Bankshares Corp., 1966- -, Coastal Plains Regional Commn., 1969—; ednl. cons. Am. Bankers Assn., 1962—; Ford Found. research fellow, 1965-66. Mem. U.S. C. of C., Am., So. econ. assns., A.A.A.S, Appalachian Finance Assn. (dir. 1968-70, pres. elect 1971), Am. (dir. 1968-70), So. (pres. 1963-64) finance assns., Financial Mgmt. Assn., Nat. Assn. Bus. Economists, Am. Assn. U. Profs., Phi Beta Kappa, Beta Gamma Sigma, Kappa Sigma. Democrat. Episcopalian. Clubs: Chapel Hill Country (pres. 1960-61, bd. govs. 1961- 62), Chapel Hill Tennis. Author: (with D.T. Lapkin) Improving the Competition for Funds Between Commercial Banks and Thrift Institutions, 1963; Money, Banking and Monetary Policy, 1962, rev. edit., 1967; Better Bank Relations with High Schools and Colleges, 1955; Character and Competitiveness of Local Banking, 1964; (with E.F. Gee) Analyzing Financial Statements, 1970. Editor: Federal Taxes, 1952; (with wife) Aid, Trade and Tariffs, 1953. Editorial bd. Jour. of Finance, 1965-68, So. Jour. of Bus., 1965—. Home: 1407 W Pettigrew St Durham NC 27514

KREPS, SAUL IAN, educator, chem. engr.; b. N.Y.C., Jan. 8, 1917; s. Harry and Ida.(Lapidus) K.; B.S., Coll. City N.Y., 1937; M.S., U. Ill., 1938; Ph.D., U. Pa., 1941; B.Chem. Engring., Poly. Inst. Bklyn., 1948; m. Sarah Kaskin, Dec. 24, 1944; children—Sipora (Mrs. Robert Lamb), David M., Matthew J., Michelle E. Research chemist Atlantic Refining Co., 1941-45; chief research chemist United Mchts. Labs., N.Y.C., 1945-48; tech. dir. Van Dyk & Co., Inc., Belleville, N.J., 1950-63; mem. faculty Newark Coll. Engring., 1948—, prof. chem. engring., 1960—; cons. to industry. Trustee Cedar Grove (N.J.) Pub. Library, 1958—. Mem. Am. Inst. Chem. Engring., Am. Chem. Soc., Am. Soc. Engring. Edn., A.L.A., Sigma Xi. Contbr. articles in field to profl. jours. Home: 40 Catherine Ct Cedar Grove NJ 07009 Office: 323 High St Newark NJ 07102

KRESGE, ALEXANDER JERRY, educator; b. Wilkes-Barre, Pa., July 17, 1926; B.A., Cornell U., 1949; Ph.D. (fellow) U. Ill., 1953; m. Yvonne Chiang, Dec. 6, 1963. Fulbright scholar Univ. Coll., London, 1953-54; research asso. Purdue U., Lafayette, Ind., 1954-55, Mass. Inst. Tech., Cambridge, 1955-57; asso. chemist Brookhaven Nat. Lab., Upton, L.I., N.Y., 1957-60; asst. prof. chemistry Ill. Inst. Tech., Chgo., 1960-63, asso. prof., 1964-68, prof., 1968—; vis. lectr. Bedford Coll., London, 1964-65; vis. prof. Oxford U., 1965, U. Toronto, 1970-71. Guggenheim fellow, 1964; NSF sr. fellow, 1964-65. Mem. Am. Chem. Soc., Brit. Chem. Soc. Office: Dept Chemistry Ill Inst Tech Chicago IL 60616

KRESGE, HOWARD SPERING, fgn. service officer; b. Oklahoma City, Dec. 23, 1914; s. Archer and Ruth (Sweet) S.; B.A., U. Wash., 1938; teaching certificate Seattle U., 1947; M.A., Gonzaga U., 1950; grad. student Wash. State Coll., 1951-52; m. Patricia Riley, July 26, 1941; children—Susan, Peter, John, Mary. Asso. prof., dir. audio-visual edn. Gonzaga U., 1948-51; dir. ECA film evaluation project Wash. State Coll., 1951-52; mem. U.S. delegation European Productivity Agy., Paris, 1952-59; chief orientation and counseling br. ICA, Washington, 1959-63; exec. dir. adv. com. on voluntary fgn. aid, and dir. voluntary fgn. aid service, AID, 1963—; head U.S. delegation Econ. Commn. for Africas Conf. on Rural Devel., 1971; U.S. rep. Internat. Council Ednl. Films, Paris, London, 1953-54; U.S. del. World Confedn. Orgns. Teaching Profession, Oxford, 1953. Served from 2d lt. to capt. AUS, 1941-45. Decorated Bronze Star; recipient Ch. World Service Christian Service award, 1971. Mem. Fgn. Service Assn., N.E.A., Alpha Delta Phi. Episcopalian. Home: 5011 46th St NW Washington DC 20016 Office: Dept of State Washington DC 20523

KRESH, PAUL, rec. exec., author, editor; b. N.Y.C., Dec. 3, 1919; s. Samuel and Jean (Feinsilver) K.; student Columbia, 1936-37; B.A., Coll. City N.Y., 1939. Scriptwriter radio sta. WNYC, 1940-42; publicist Nat. Jewish Welfare Bd., 1941-45; publicity dir. Am. ORT Fedn., 1945-46; asst. publicity dir. Council Jewish Fedns. and Welfare Funds, 1946-47; writer, publicist Nathan C. Belth Assos., 1947-50; motion picture dir., asst. publicity dir. United Jewish Appeal, 1950-59; pub. relations dir. Union Am. Hebrew Congs., 1959-67; editor Am. Judaism, 1960-67; dir., scriptwriter weekly CBS radio series Adventures in Judaism, 1961—; v.p., rec. dir. Spoken Arts Records, 1967-71; rec. exec. Caedmon Records, 1971—; contbg. editor Am. Record Guide, 1958-61, Stereo Rev., 1961—. Recipient Ohio State U. award for radio scripts Adventures in Music, 1940, 41, for Adventures in Judaism, 1965, 66, 68, 67; Golden Eagle award for film script The Days the Doors Closed, Council Internat. Nontheatrical Events, 1965; award Religious Heritage Found., 1968. Mem. Nat. Acad. Rec. Arts and Scis. (bd. govs.), Writers Guild Am. Author: The Power of the Unknown Citizen, 1969; also critical essays, revs., articles. Editor: American Judaism Reader, 1967; Spoken Arts Treasury of 100 Modern American Poets Reading Their Poems, 1969. Home: 2 Charlton St New York City NY 10014 Office: 505 8th Av New York City NY 10018

KRESHOVER, SEYMOUR JACOB, USPHS officer; b. N.Y.C., June 22, 1912; s. Jacob Siegfried and Rose (Herzenstein) K.; B.A., N.Y. U., 1934, M.D., 1949; D.D.S., U. Pa., 1938; Ph.D., Yale, 1942; D.Sc. (hon.), U. Buffalo, 1961, U. Pa., 1967, Boston U., 1969; m. Jacqueline Jean Baxter, Dec. 21, 1946; children—Karen L., Douglas W., Janis L., Lauren B. Prof. Oral pathology, dir. dental research, dir. postgrad. and grad. study Sch. Dentistry, Med. Coll. Va., 1949-56, vis. prof. dentistry research, 1956-67; sci. dir. Nat. Inst. Dental Research, 1956-66, dir. of inst., 1966—. Asso. trustee bd. med. edn. and research U. Pa., 1956-60; chmn. commn. on dental research Fedn. Dentaire Internat., 1962-67. Served with AUS, 1942-46. Recipient Meritorious Service medal USPHS, 1965. Diplomate Am. Bd. Oral Medicine. Fellow A.A.A.S. (sec. sect. on dentistry 1962-66), Am. Coll. Dentists (regent 1969—); mem. A.M.A., Am. Dental Assn., Internat. Assn. Dental Research (pres. 1962), Am. Pub. Health Assn. Home: 5206 W Cedar Lane Bethesda MD 20014 Office: Nat Institute of Dental Research National Insts Health Bethesda MD 20014

KRESS, JAMES F., mfg. co. exec.; b. Green Bay, Wis., June 11, 1929; s. George F. and Marguerite L. (Christensen) K.; B.B.A., U. Wis., 1951; m. Irene Gail Daniell, Apr. 4, 1953; children-William F., John F., Marguerite A., Virginia Louise. Vice pres., dir. Green Bay Box Co. and Green Bay Paper & Pulp Co., 1956-62; pres., dir. Green Bay Packing Corp., 1963—; pres., dir. Ark. Kraft Corp.; dir. Pioneer Container Corp., Twin Town Container Corp., Kalamazoo Container Corp., First Wis. Bank of Green Bay Shopko Stores, Inc. Finance chmn. 8th Dist. Republican Party of Wis. Bd. dirs. Am. Fedn. Religion and Psychology, YMCA, Bellin Meml. Hosp.; trustee Lakeland Coll. Served to lt. USNR, 1951-55. Named Outstanding Young Man of Green Bay, Jr. C. of C., 1963, One of Five Outstanding Young Men in Wis., 1964. Home: 300 W Mission Rd Green Bay WI 54301 Office: 831 Doblon St Green Bay WI 54305

KRESS, JOHN W., banker; b. Newark, November 26, 1904; s. John and Mary (Ruby) K.; B.C.S., N.Y. U., 1933; m. Rose Ruegg, June 16, 1931; children—John R., Donald G., Raymond P. With Howard Savs. Instn., Newark, 1921—, successively clk. asst. trust officer, asst. sec., asst. v.p., v.p. and trust officer, 1921-49, exec. v.p., 1949-61, pres., 1961-70, chmn. bd., 1970—. bd. mgrs., 1944—; dir. N.J. Realty Co., Central R.R. of Pa., Ragen Precision Industries, Reliance Ins. Co., Del. & Bound Brook R.R., Nat. Newark & Essex Bank, Lehigh & New Eng. Ry. Co., N.J. Nat. Gas Co., Asbury Park. Bd. dirs. Greater Newark Devel. Council; trustee United Community Fund and Council Essex and W. Hudson, Newark Mus., Symphony Hall, N.J. College Fund Assn., United Hosps. Newark. Mem. N.J. C. of C. (dir.), Nat. Assn. Mut. Savs. Banks, Am. Inst. Banking (hon. bd. govs. and bd. regents), N.Y. U. Alumni Assn., Newcomen Soc., N.J. Hist. Soc. Clubs: Bond, Essex (Newark); Montclair (N.J.) Golf. Home: 12 S Mountain Av Montclair NJ 07042 Office: 768 Broad St Newark NJ 07102

KRESS, ROY ALFRED, univ. dean; b. Elmira, N.Y., Oct. 4, 1916; s. Roy Alfred and Alice Elaine (Whitaker) K.; B.S. in Edn., Lock Haven State Coll., 1938; Ed.M., Temple U., 1949, Ph.D., 1956; m. Doris Ethel Parker, Mar. 29, 1940 (deceased July 1969); children—Keith Denton, Lance Whitaker, Gene Gordon; m. 2d, Eleanor Murphy Ladd, Dec. 4, 1969. Tchr., Woods Schs., Langhorne, Pa., 1938-43; tng. supr. VA, Phila., 1946-49; lectr. Temple U., Phila., 1949-55, prof. psychology, 1963-68, chmn. psychology of reading dept., 1968-70, asso. dean Grad. Sch., 1970—; ednl. dir. Shady Brook Schs., Richardson, Tex., 1955-58; asso. prof. Syracuse (N.Y.) U., 1958-63; vis. lectr. Tex. Women's U., 1956, So. State Coll. Ark., 1957, U. Ark., 1958, State U. N.Y., 1960, U. Colo., 1961; cons. edn. and psychology, U.S., Can., Australia. Instl. rep., scoutmaster Circle Ten council, the Onondaga Valley council Boy Scouts Am., 1955-63; faculty sponsor Alpha Phi Omega, Syracuse U., 1958-63. Served with USMCR, 1943-46. Research grantee Phila. Bd. Edn., 1965-68. Mem. Am. Psychol. Assn., Internat. Reading Assn. (mem. bd. 1964-67), Nat. Council Research in English (mem. bd. 1966-69), Coll. Reading Assn. (mem. bd. 1971-74), Nat. Soc. Study Edn., Am. Edn. Research Assn., A.A.A.S., Nat. Council Grad. Sch. Deans, Phi Delta Kappa, Sigma Pi, Alpha Phi Omega. Mason. Author: A Place to Start, 1963; (with Marjorie S. Johnson) Informal Reading Inventories, 1965; (with M.S. Johnson and J. McNiel) The Read System, rev. edit., 1971. 1969. Editor: That All May Learn to Read, 1959; (with M.S. Johnson) Corrective Reading in the Elementary Classroom, 1967 Outstanding Education Book of 1967, Pi Lambda Theta). Editor (with M.S. Johnson) proc. Ann. Reading Insts. Temple U., 1963-70, The Reading Teacher, 1967-71; editorial adv. bd. Reading Research Quar., 1965-70, Jour. Learning Disability, 1968—, The Reading Tchr., 1971—; adv. bd. ERIC/GRIER, 1968-71. Home: 800 Moredon Rd Meadowbrook PA 19046 Office: 1805 N Broad St Philadelphia PA 19122

KRESS, THOMAS GEORGE, mfg. co. exec.; b. Dubuque, Ia., May 11, 1931; s. Henry L. and Jane (Schadle) K.; B.A., Loras Coll., 1953; M.B.A., Northwestern U., 1961; grad. Advanced Mgmt. Program, Harvard, 1971; m. Lou Ann Kuehnle, Sept. 6, 1952; children—Kristine, Elizabeth, Kathleen,, Susan, Thomas George, Andrew, Julianna, Matthew. Cost analyst Gen. Electric Co., Chgo., 1956-62; div. controller Sheller Mfg. Corp., Keokuk, Ia., 1962-64, asst. corp. controller, Detroit, 1964-66; corp. controller Sheller Globe Corp., Toledo, 1967—. Served with U.S. Army, 1953-55. Mem. Financial Execs. Inst., Nat. Assn. Accountants. Clubs: Detroit Athletic; Sylvania (O.) Country. Home: 4731 Rose Glenn St Toledo OH 43615 Office: 1505 Jefferson Av Toledo OH 43624

KRETZ, ARVID LAMAR, paper co. exec.; b. Wyomissing, Pa., May 29, 1923; s. Francis W. and Laura A. (Welfly) K.; B.A., Muhlenberg Coll., 1950; m. Marie Eleanore Crosson, June 4, 1949; children—Arvid LaMar, Allan Lawrence. Field credit mgr. New Holland Machine Co. (Pa.), 1950-59; credit mgr. Airtemp div. Chrysler Corp., 1959-63; controller Fibreboard Corp., 1963—. Served with USMCR, 1942-46. Mem. Financial Exec. Inst. Home: 1285 Hillcrest Blvd Millbrae CA 94030 Office: 55 Francisco San Francisco CA 94133

KRETZMANN, ADALBERT RAPHAEL ALEXANDER, clergyman; b. Stamford, Conn., Apr. 15, 1903; s. Karl and Thekla (Hueschen) K.; Grad. Concordia Coll., Bronxville, N.Y., 1923; B.D., Concordia Sem., St. Louis, 1927, D.D. (hon.), 1967; Litt.D. (hon.), Concordia Coll., Seward, Neb., 1953; LL.D., Valparaiso U., 1959; D.D. (hon.), Wartburg Coll., Waverly, Ia., 1966; m. Josephine Heidelberg, Oct. 1, 1927; children—Norman, Joan (Mrs. Gerhard Krodel). Ordained to ministry Evang. Luth. Ch., 1927; asst. pastor Jersey City, 1924; prof. German, Concordia Coll., Ft. Wayne, Ind., 1925-26; vacancy pastor, Phila.. 1926; supply pastor, St. Louis, 1926-27; pastor St. Luke's Ch., Chgo., 1927—. Chmn. Synodical Young People's Bd.; pres. Ill. Dist. of Walther League, 1930- 32; sec. Luth. Hosp. Assn., 1929-31; sec. Chgo. Luth. Pastoral Conf., 1929-33; bd. dirs. Luther Inst., Chgo., 1931-33; pastoral adviser Internat. Luth. Walther League, 1929-54; chmn. North Side Forum Christian Edn., bd. dirs. Lakeview Community Council; lectr. on ch. art and liturgy Concordia Tchrs. Coll., River Forest, Ill., Concordia Sem., St. Louis Corr. Sch. Staff; lectr. on youth work Concordia Sem., St. Louis, Concordia Tchrs. Coll., Seward, Neb., Dr. Martin Luther Coll., New Ulm, Minn., Pacific Luth. U., Pacific Luth. Sem.; chmn. commn. worship Luth. Ch.-Missouri Synod; art editor The Cresset; asso. editor Sacred Music; asso. editor Luth. Witness. Lectr. Luther Laymen's League Seminars. Bd. dirs., Ministers Life and Casualty Co., Mpls., Luth. Sr. Citizens Found., Luth. Brotherhood (chmn. fine arts), Augustana Hosp., Luth. Gen. Hosp., Luth. Deaconess Hosp.; pres. Chgo. Bible Soc.; dir., v.p. Wheatridge Found., also chmn. social service. Bd. dirs. Tb Inst. Chgo. and Cook County. Recipient Gutenberg award, 1963. Mem. Am. Fedn. Art, Chgo. Art Inst. (life mem.), Concordia Hist. Inst., Am. Inst. Graphic Arts (adv. council religious teaching pictures), Met. Mus. (N.Y.), Walker Art Mus. (Minn.), Ch. Archtl. Guild Am., Guild for Religions Architecture, Am. Soc. Ch. Architecture (dir.). Author: History of Evangelical Lutheran Church of Saint Luke, 1884-1934; Liturgical Renaissance in the Lutheran Church, 1968; contbg. author Christmas Annual; also the author of prayers, "My Redeemer Liveth," "Wings of God," "Remember," Concordia Pulpit, "Motherhood Prayers and Meditations," "Festival and Occasional Sermons," "The Christian Way," "Service Prayer Book," "Loyalty," "Service Stars for Lutheran Youth," "Symbols. A Practical Handbook." "In Season, Out of Season," Concordia Pulpit, 1945, "Confirmation," "The Pastor at Work", 1960, "The Pastor at Prayer," 1959. Summer Speaker Internat. Luth. Hour, 1944, "Liturgy and Church Art", others and also numerous religious writings. Designer Coll. Synodical, also church seals; cons. in liturgical arts and design. Chmn. Chgo. Luth. Pastors Inst.; radio speaker Chgo. Luth. Hour, WGN Mid- day Devotions. Sec. Family Worship Hour (radio devotions). Home: 1501 W Melrose St Chicago IL 60657 Office: 1500 W Belmont Av Chicago IL 60657

KRETZMANN, JUSTUS PAUL, clergyman; b. N.Y.C., Feb. 27, 1913; s. Karl and Thekla (Hueschen) K.; student Concordia Coll., Bronxville, N.Y., 1933; B.D., Concordia Sem., St. Louis, 1938, D.D. (hon.) 1965; m. Norma Martha Kroehnke, Feb. 15, 1939; children—Karla (Mrs. Stanley Woell), Walter John. Ordained to ministry Lutheran Ch., 1939; asst. pastor in Buffalo, 1935-37, Bklyn., 1938-39; missionary, Nigeria, W. Africa, 1939-51; pastor Luth. Ch. Atonement, Florissant, Mo., 1952—; made world survey of missions, 1960, 61. Chmn. bd. parish edn. Luth. Ch. Mo. Synod, 1959—; chmn. Luth. Publicity Orgn., St. Louis, 1957-69; mem. Luth. Med. Mission Council, 1959-69. Bd. dirs. Luth. Hosp., St. Louis. Mem. Florissant Hist. Soc. Co-author: In Time...For Eternity, 1963. Contbg. editor Am. Luth.; mem. editorial com. St. Louis Luth. Contbr. religious publs. Home: 1090 Aubuchon St Florissant MO 63031 Office: 1285 N Florissant Rd Florissant MO 63031

KRETZMANN, OTTO PAUL, univ. ofcl.; b. Stamford, Conn., May 7, 1901; s. Karl and Thekla (Hueschen) K.; S.T.M., Concordia Sem., St. Louis, 1924; postgrad., Johns Hopkins, 1933; Litt.D. Concordia Sem., St. Louis, 1941; D.D., Thiel Coll., Greenville, Pa., 1947; LL.D., Capital U., 1950, Ind. U., 1959, Wabash Coll., 1962, Ind. State U., 1968; L.H.D., Pacific Luth. U., 1962, Cal. Luth. Coll., 1970; D.D., St. Joseph's Coll., 1967; m. Flora Ellen Rosenthal, Aug. 15, 1942; children—John Paul, Mark John, Stephen Paul. Instr., Concordia Sem., Springfield, Ill., 1924-34; exec. sec. Luth. Internat. Walther League, 1934-40; pres. Valparaiso (Ind.) U., 1940-68, chancellor,

1968—. Bd. dirs. Wheat-Ridge Sanatorium, Luth. Chgo. Med. Sch. sec. Bd. Edn. Mo. Synod.; pres. Hardt Found.; pres. Ind. Assn. Ind. and Ch. Related Colls.; bd. dirs. Ind. conf. Higher Edn., Mus. Youth of Am.; chmn. com. on pre-profl. edn. Assn. Am. Colls.; mem. Arbitration Bd. apptd. by Gov. Ind.; mem. Naval Res. adv. council 9th Naval Dist. Recipient Great Living Hoosier award, 1963. Fellow Royal Soc. Arts; mem. Ind. Hist. Commn., Acad. Polit. Sci., Tudor and Stuart Soc., Modern Lang. Assn., Am. Soc. Ch. History, Midwest Conf. Atomic Scientists and Religious Leaders. Author: The Road Back to God, 1934; Pilgrim, 1944; Sign of the Cross, 1959; Hosanna in the Whirlwind, 1969; co-author: Voices of the Passion, 1944; also articles. Editor emeritus, contbr. The Cresset (a rev. of lit., the arts and pub. affairs). Address: Valparaiso U Valparaiso, IN 46383.

KREUTZ, OSCAR R., savs. and loan assn. exec.; b. Sioux City, Ia.; ed. schs. in Sioux City, also Cambridge, Mass.; m. Marion Benton, 1926; children—Mary Ann (Mrs. J. C. Dodson), Barbara Jane (Mrs. M.H. Barrett). Organizer, First Fed. Savs. & Loan Assn., Sioux City, 1923, mng. officer, 1923-33; sec. Ia. Bldg. & Loan League, 1925-33; v.p. Fed. Home Loan Bank Chgo., 1934; chmn. rev. com. Fed. Home Loan Bank Bd., 1934-41; gen. mgr. Fed. Savs. & Loan Ins. Corp., 1941-44; exec. mgr. Nat. League of Insured Savs. Assn., 1944-53, exec. cons., 1953-54; exec. v.p. First Fed. Savs. & Loan Assn., St. Petersburg, Fla., 1953-54, pres., chmn. bd., 1954-68, chmn. bd., 1968—; dir. Milton Roy Co., Investors Mortgage Ins. Co. of Boston, CATV. Vice pres., mem. council, mem. exec. com. Internat. Union Bldg. Socs. and Savs. Assns.; cons. to Argentine Govt. for ICA, 1961, for AID, past mem. Fed. Home Loan Bank Bd. Task Force; pres. Fla. Savs. and Loan League, 1961. Mem. Fla. Council 100; past chmn. bd. dirs. Indsl. Devel. Commn. Fla.; past pres. Suncoasters of St. Petersburg, Inc., Producers of Sunshine Festival (chosen Mr. Sun 1962); past pres., bd. dirs. United Fund (gen. chmn. 1956- 57 campaign); mem., past pres. Com. of 100; pres. St. Petersburg Improvement Found.; mem. adv. bd. Abilities, Inc. of Fla. Hon. dir. Sci. Center; St. Petersburg Symphony Soc.; trustee Fla. Presbyn. Coll. Mem. Nat. League Insured Savs. Assns. (Pres. 1960), St. Petersburg C. of C. (dir., mem. exec. com.), Navy League U.S., Am. Legion, Newcomen Soc. N.Am. Presbyn. Mason (32). Clubs: Rotary: Bath; St. Petersburg Yacht; Lakewood Country; Quarterback; Commerce, Home: 2028 Brightwaters Blvd Snell Isle St Petersburg FL 33704 Office: First Fed Bldg St Petersburg FL 33731

KREUZER, BARTON, electronics co. exec.; b. N.Y.C., Feb. 18, 1909; s. Walter and Jeannette (Katz) K.; E.E., Bklyn. Polytech. Inst., 1928, postgrad., 1929-31; m. Virginia Brown, Feb. 16, 1935; children—Justin, Lloyd. With RCA, Camden, N.J., 1928—, mgr. theater and indsl. marketing dept., 1952-54, dir. product planning, 1954- 58, mgr. marketing Astro-Electronics Products div., 1958-60, div. v.p., gen. mgr., 1960-67, v.p., gen. mgr., 1967-68, exec. v.p. RCA, 1969, exec. v.p. Consumer Electronics, Indpls., 1970—; dir. RCA Sales Corp., RCA Distbg. Corp., RCA Taiwan, RCA Mexico, RCA Ltd. (Can.), Am. Fletcher Nat. Trust Bank & Trust Co., Indpls. Bd. dirs. Jr. Achievement Ind. Fellow Soc. Motion Pictures and Television Engrs. (exec. v.p. 1955-56, pres. 1957-58); mem. Ind. (dir.), Indpls. (dir.) chambers commerce, I.E.E.E. Club: Columbia (Indpls.). Home: 4000 N Meridian St Indianapolis IN 46208 Office: RCA Consumer Electronics Indianapolis IN 46204

KREVANS, JULIUS RICHARD, univ. dean, physician; b. N.Y.C., May 1, 1924; s. Sol and Anita (Makovetsky) K.; B.S. Arts and Scis., N.Y.U., 1943, M.D., 1946; m. Patricia N. Abrams, May 28, 1950; children—Mita, Julius R., Rachel, Sarah, Mora Kate. Intern, then resident Johns Hopkins Med. Sch., Balt., mem. faculty until 1971, dean acad. affairs, 1969-71; physician in chief Balt. City Hosp., 1963-69; prof. medicine U. Cal. at San Francisco, 1971—, also dean Sch. Medicine. Served with M.C., AUS, 1948-50. Diplomate Am. Bd. Internal Med. Mem. Assn. Am. Physicians. Contbr. articles on hematology, internal med. profl. jours. Office: U Cal Med Center San Francisco CA 94122

KREY, JOHN FREDERICK, business exec.; b. St. Louis, Aug. 18, 1905; s. Frederick and Anna (Strotjost) K.; student St. Louis U., 1922-24; m. K. Evelyn Dunsmoor, June 10, 1933; children—Jacquelyn Ann, John F. III. With Krey Packing Co., St. Louis, 1924—, successively as trainee, salesman, salesmgr., asst. gen. mgr., exec. v.p. and gen. mgr., pres., 1948—; v.p., dir. Pitchfork Land & Cattle Co.; asso. dir. Washington Fire & Marine Ins. Co., Ins. Co. of St. Louis; dir. Mound City Ice & Cold Storage, Bank of St. Louis, General Bankshares, St. Louis Union Trust Co., Baden Bank, Anheuser-Busch, Inc. Former chmn. bd., now dir., mem. exec. con. Am. Meat Inst., St. Louis County C. of C. (dir.), Automobile Club Mo. (bd. govs., mem. exec. com.). Roman Catholic. Clubs St. Louis Country, Racquet, Noonday, Mo. Athletic (St. Louis); Union League, Racquet (Chgo.); Rolling Rock (Ligonier, Pa.). Home: 10505 Ladue Rd St Louis MO 63141 Office: 3607 N Florissant Av St Louis MO 63107

KREYCHE, GERALD FRANCIS, educator; b. Kenosha, Wis., June 19, 1927; s. Harold Joseph and Henrietta Fredericka (Otemann) K.; A.B., DePaul U., 1949, A.M., 1950; Ph.D. cum laude, U. Ottawa (Can.), 1958; m. Eleanor Ann Okon, June 19, 1948. Mem. faculty De Paul U., 1950—, chmn. dept. philosophy, 1961—, prof., 1965—; now Danforth asso.; conducted radio programs, What Do You Think?, also What's the Big Idea?, 1960; frequent appearances ednl. and comml. television, also radio, 1958—; Aquinas lectr. Alverno Coll., Milw., 1963. Bd. dirs. Civitas Dei Found. Served with AUS, 1945-46. Mem. Nat. Conf. Christians and Jews, Am. Metaphys. Soc., Ill.-Ind. Am. Cath. Philos. Assn. (pres. 1960), Nat. Cath. Ednl. Assn., Am. Assn. U. Profs., Phi Kappa Theta, Phi Eta Sigma. Contbr. articles to religious publs. Book reviewer for New World. Co-editor Harbrace Philosophy series. Editorial bd. Jour. Existential Psychiatry. Home: 2551 Fontana Dr Glenview IL 60025 Office: DePaul U 25 E Jackson Blvd Chicago IL 60604

KREYCHE, ROBERT JOSEPH, author, educator; b. Racine, Wis., Aug. 26, 1920; s. Harold Joseph and Henrietta (Oteman) K.; B.A., M.A., Cath. U. Am.; Ph.D., U. Ottawa (Can.), 1952; m. Julianne Mangold, May 8, 1948 (dec. May 1969); children—Michael R., Thomas H., John A., Catharine A., Andrew J.; m. 2d, Dolores Ann Pritchard, Jan. 16, 1971. Mem. faculty Loyola U., Chgo., 1947-57, St. Joseph's Coll., Rensselaer, Ind., 1957-62, Rockhurst Coll., Kansas City, Mo., 1962-65; prof. philosophy U. Ariz., 1965—. Co-founder, pres. Thomas More Inst., Tucson. Mem. Am. Cath. Philos. Assn. (pres. 1967-68), Delta Epsilon Sigma (hon.). Author: Logic for Undergraduates; First Philosophy, God and Reality, 1965; God and Contemporary Man. Home: 2441 N Grannen Rd Tucson AZ 85705

KREYLING, EDWARD GEORGE, Jr., railroad ofcl.; b. St. Louis, June 1, 1923; s. Edward George and Mildred (Schroeder) K.; B.S. in Bus. Adminstrn., Washington U., St. Louis, 1947, M.B.A., 1954; m. Mary Emily Gronemeyer, Sept. 4, 1943; children—Carol (Mrs. Robert D. Knight), Deborah Ann (Mrs. Robert Glenn), Edward George III. Accountant Monsanto Chem. Co., 1947-50; chief statistician White Rodgers Elec. Co., St. Louis, 1950-54; dir. market research Laclede-Christy Co., St. Louis, 1954-55; with St. L.-S.F. Ry. 1955-69, dir. marketing, 1964- 65, v.p. traffic and indsl. devel., 1965-69; v.p. traffic I.C. R.R., Chgo., 1969-70; exec. v.p. Penn Central Transp. Co., Phila., 1970—. Active Boy Scouts Am. Served with AUS, 1943-45. Mem. Traffic Club N.Y.C., Nat. Def. Transp. Assn., Nat. Freight Traffic Assn., Ry. Systems and Mgmt. Assn., Delta Nu Alpha. Club: Union League (Chgo.). Home: 219 Glenmoor Rd Gladwyne PA 19035 Office: 6 Penn Center Philadelphia PA 19103

KRICK, IRVING PARKHURST, meteorologist; b. San Francisco, Dec. 20, 1906; s. H. I. and Mabel (Royal) K.; B.A., U. Cal., 1928; M.S., Cal. Inst. Tech., 1933, Ph.D., 1934; m. Jane Clark, May 23, 1930; 1 dau., Marllynn; m. 2d, Marie Spiro; 1 son, I. P. Krick, II. Asst. mgr. radio sta. KTAB, 1928- 29; pianist in concert and radio work, 1929-30; meteorologist, 1930—; set up 1st modern airline weather forecasting service for Western Air Express, 1932; became mem. staff Cal. Inst. Tech., 1933, asst. prof. meteorology, 1935-38, asso. prof., prof. and head dept., 1938-48; organized and pres. Am. Inst. Aerological Research and Water Resources Devel. Corp., 1950; pres. Irving P. Krick Assos., Inc., Irving P. Krick, Inc. (Tex.), Irving P. Krick Assos. Can. Ltd.; set up meteorology dept. for Am. Air Lines, Inc., 1935; cons., 1935-36; developed pvt. weather forecasting serv., supplying information to var. of cos.; has developed long-range weather forecasting method covering periods up to 25 years. Served as lt. Coast Arty. Corps, U.S. Army, 1928-36; commd. ensign USNR, 1938; maj. U.S. Army Air Corps, lt. col., 1943; Weather Directorate, Weather Central Div. unit comdr. of Long Range Forecast Unit A, 1942-43; chief weather information sect. SHAEF, 1944-45. Decorated Legion of Merit, Bronze Star with Oak leaf cluster (U.S.); Croix de Guerre (France); recipient Distinguished Service award Jr. C. of C.; chosen one of 10 outstanding men under age 35 by U.S. C. of C. Fellow Am. Inst. Aeros. and Astronautics (asso.), Royal Soc. Arts; mem. Royal Meteorol. Soc., A.A.A.S., Sigma Xi. Republican. Co-author: Sun, Sea and Sky, 1954. Writer numerous articles on Weather analysis, weather modification and forecasting and its application to agrl. and bus. industries. Pioneered applications rain increase and hail control; perfected comml. five year weather forecasts. Home: 328 Mountain View Pl Palm Springs CA 92262 Office: 611 S Palm Canyon Dr Palm Springs CA 92262

KRICKL, ANSON WOODING, engring. co. exec.; b. N.Y.C., Jan. 18, 1916; s. Maurice and Jane L. (Thompson) K.; B.E., Yale, 1937; m. Barbara Jane Smith, Nov. 27, 1937; children—Blaine S., Anson W., Richard T. Process and sales engr. E.B. Badger & Sons Co., Boston, 1937-51; asst. to v.p. sales Badger process div. Stone & Webster, Boston, 1951-53; asst. to pres. Catalytic Constrn. Co., Phila., 1953-57; v.p. mfg. Badger Co., Inc., Cambridge, Mass., 1957-59, sr. v.p. corporate planning, 1968—; mng. dir. Bader, Ltd., London, Eng., 1959-68; dir. Badger, Ltd. (London, Eng.). Dir. Emerson Hosp. (Concord, Mass.). Clubs: Concord Country; Yale (N.Y.C.); Wentworth, American (Eng.). Home: 80 Rollingwood Lane Concord MA 01742 Office: 1 Broadway Cambridge MA 02142

KRIDER, JAKE LUTHER, educator; b. Lewistown, Ill., Dec. 12, 1913; s. Reuben E. and Bessie A. (Beadles) K.; B.S., U. Ill., 1939, M.S., 1941; Ph.D., Cornell U., 1942; m. L. Louise Strode, Aug. 3, 1936. Asso., animal husbandry, asst. prof., then asso. prof. U. Ill., 1942-47, prof. animal sci., 1947- 50; dir. feed research and edn. McMillen Feed Mills div. Central Soya Co., Inc., 1950-51, v.p., dir. feed sales, 1951-56; v.p. pub. relations Central Soya Co., Inc., Ft. Wayne, Ind., 1956-63, mem. adv. bd. dirs., 1954- 57; prof., head dept. animal scis. Purdue U., Lafayette, Ind., 1963-71, prof. animal scis., 1971—. Recipient award for outstanding contbn. animal nutrition research Am. Feed Mfrs. Assn. and Am. Soc. for Animal Prodn., 1949; award of merit for service to agr. U. Ill., 1962; E. G. Cherbonnier award Grain and Feed Dealers Nat. Assn., 1966; Meritorious Service award Ind. Pork Producers Assn., 1967. Hon. fellow Am. Soc. Animal Sci. (pres. 1969, life mem.); mem. Poultry Sci. Assn., Am. Dairy Sci. Assn., A.A.A.S., Am. Feed Mfrs. Assn. (dir. 1957-63, exec. com. 1958-59), Farm House Frat., Sigma Xi. Methodist. Author: (with Dr. George P. Deyoe) Raising Swine, 1952; (with W.E. Carroll) Swine Production, 1971. Contbr. articles profl. jours., periodicals. Home: 1305 Ravinia Rd West Lafayette IN 47906

KRIEBEL, HENRY AUGUST, coll. pres.; b., Warren, Pa., Feb. 11, 1909; s. E. Wilbur and Augusta (Lesser) K.; B.S., Lehigh U., 1932, M.A., 1937; Ph.D., Columbia, 1951; m. Carrie E. S. Wahrmann, July 18, 1942; 1 son, J. Gifford. Instr., Cedar Crest Coll., 1932-37, Lehigh U., 1939-42; accounting officer Naval Air Material Center, Phila., 1942-45; chmn. accounting div. Babson Inst., Babson Park, Mass., 1946-61, dean faculty, 1957-61, pres., 1961- -. Trustee, Endicott Jr. Coll., Beverly, Mass., Bentley Coll. Served to lt. comdr. USNR, 1942-46. Mem. Nat. Assn. Accountants (pres. Boston 1960-61, nat. dir. 1961-62), Am. Accounting Assn., Mass. Soc. C.P.A.'s Delta Sigma Phi, Alpha Kappa Psi, Blue Key. Home: 56 Whiting Rd Wellesley Hills MA 02181

KRIEBEL, RICHARD THEODORE, ret. photog. co. exec.; b. Phila., Apr. 18, 1904; s. William S. and Annie (Wright) K.; B.S., Pa. State U., 1926; m. Ruth Comfort Miller, June 1, 1929; children—Nancy (Mrs. James V. Sciscent), Jill (Mrs. Donald R. Remington), Dorothy (Mrs. Ronald H. Lingren). Writer, N.W. Ayer & Son, Inc., Phila., 1928-29, Walter B. Snow & Staff, Inc., Boston, 1929-34, Sutherland-Abbott, Inc., Boston, 1934-36; sec., dir. pub. relations Polaroid Corp., Cambridge, Mass., 1936-66, cons., 1966-69. Home: 60 Snake Hill Rd Belmont MA 02178

KRIEBEL, WARREN WALTER, Jr., lawyer; b. Chicago, Jan. 14, 1905; s. Warren W. and Mathilde (LeGault) K.; A.B., U. Ill., 1927, J.D., 1929; m. Anne Hagen Nov. 2, 1929 (dec. 1960); 1 dau., Carol (Mrs. David Jorgenson); m. 2d, Lois Samuelson, Aug. 24, 1961. Admitted to N.Y. bar, 1931, Ill. bar, 1931; asso. Root, Clark, Buckner & Ballantine, N.Y. C., 1929-31, Kriebel & Hubbard, Chgo., 1931—, firm now is Kriebel & Jorgenson; atty. Berwyn Park Dist., 1931—; instr. in evidence John Marshall Law Sch., 1940-66. Mem. Am., Ill., Chgo. bar assns., Phi Beta Kappa, Order of Coif, Phi Delta Phi, Pi Mu Epsilon. Author articles in legal publs. Home: 67 Forest Av Riverside IL 60546 Office: 39 S LaSalle St Chicago IL 60603

KRIEG, LOWELL EDWIN, cons.; b. Marion, Ind., June 25, 1916; s. Charles M. and Ethel C. (Wolfe) K.; A.B. in Econs., U. Mich., 1937, postgrad. Sch. Bus. Adminstrn., 1938; m. Roberta J. Cole, Jan. 21, 1938; children—Peter, Stephanie, Michael, Melissa, Meredith, Christopher. Indsl. engr. King- Seeley Corp., 1939-40, Murray Corp. Am., 1941-45; mgmt. cons. Ernst & Ernst, 1945-46; with Ford Motor Co., 1946-61, gen. operations mgr. automotive electronic equipment operations, 1960-61; v.p. Olin Mathieson Chem. Corp., gen. mgr. Winchester-Western div., 1961-64, exec. v.p., dir., 1964-65; vice chmn. bd. FRIA, Compagnie Internationale pour la Prodn. de l'Alumine, 1964-71; chmn. Winchester-Western (Can.) Ltd., 1961-71; pres. Standard Packaging Corp., 1965-71, chief exec. officer, 1967-71; prin. Lowell E. Krieg Assos., Los Angeles, 1971—. Trustee, Conn. Pub. Expenditure Council; adv. com. New Haven Coll.; bd. dirs. United Fund Greater New Haven. Served with USNR, 1944-45. Mem. Am. Ordnance Assn., Am. Mgmt. Assn., Assn. U.S. Army, Wildlife Mgmt. Inst. (exec. com.), Sporting Arms and Ammunition Mfrs. Inst. (exec. com.). Clubs: Union League (N.Y.C.); Quinnipiac (New Haven); Saugatuck Harbor Yacht (Westport, Conn.). Home: 1372 Faren Dr Santa Ana CA Office: 1900 Av of Stars Los Angeles CA 90067

KRIEG, WENDELL JORDAN, educator, neuroanatomist; b. Lincoln, Neb., Apr. 13, 1906; s. Frank Wendell and Rosabelle (Jordan) K.; B.S., U. Neb., 1928; M.S., N.Y. U., 1931, Ph.D., 1935; m. Roberta Elaine Neill, June 28, 1952; 1 son, Rupert. High sch. tchr., 1924-25; instr., asst. prof. anatomy Coll. Medicine N.Y. U., 1929-44; asso. prof., dir. Inst. Neurology, Med. Sch. Northwestern U., 1944-48, prof. anatomy. 1948—; propr. Brain Books, 1955—. Mem. Am. Assn. Anatomists, Corp. Marine Biol. Lab. Woods Hole, Cajal Soc. (past pres.), Chgo. Lit. Soc. (past v.p.), Chgo. Neurol. Soc., Neurolec. Soc., Am. Neurol. Assn., Am. Acad. Neurology, Internat. Stereological Soc. Author: Atlas of Reconstructions of the Human Brain, 1941; Functional Neuroanatomy, 1966; Connections of the Frontal Cortex of the Monkey, 1954; Collected Papers of the Cerebrum, 1953; Brain Mechanisms in Diachrome, 1955; Polychrome Atlas of the Brain Stem, 1960; Letters to my Son, 1960; Atlas of Frontal Reconstructions of the Human Cerebrum, 1960; Connections of the Cerebral Cortex, 1963; It Takes A Thief, 1949. Contbr. articles profl. jours. Originator electroneuroprosthesis, 1949. Home: 1236 Hinman Av Evanston, IL 60202. Office: Northwestern U Med Sch 303 E Chicago Av Chicago IL 60612

KRIEG, WILLIAM HENRY, lawyer; b. Indpls., Jan. 13, 1907; s. August F. and Augusta (Beckmann) K.; A.B. cum laude, U. Notre Dame, 1929; J.D., Harvard, 1932; m. Virginia Ballweg, Oct. 28 1933; children—Peter Ballweg, Frederick William. Admitted to Ind. bar, 1932; individual practice, Indpls., 1932-40, 48—; mem. firm Krieg, DeVault, Alexander & Capehart. Pres., Packard Mfg. Co., Indpls., 1946-47; dir. Sargent Paint, Inc. Hook Drugs, Inc., Franklin Corp. (all Indpls.), Bell Fibre Products Corp., Marion, Ind., Steak N Shake, Inc., Bloomington, Ill.; dir., mem. exec. com. Mut. Hosp. Ins. Inc. (Blue Cross) Ind. Pres. Cornelia Cole Fairbanks Hosp. for Alcoholics, Indpls.; pres. bd. trustees Winona Meml. Hosp., Indpls., 1969-70; dir. emeritus Central Ind. council Boy Scouts; trustee Purdue U. Served from pvt. to lt. col. AUS, 1940-45; asst. gen. counsel nat. hdqrs. Selective Service System, 1943-45. Decorated Legion of Merit. Mem. Am., Ind., Indpls. bar assns. Republican. Roman Catholic. Clubs: Indianapolis Athletic, Indianapolis Sailing (commodore 1958); Wildwood Valley (pres.). Home: 6401 N Chester St Indianapolis IN 46220 Office: One Indiana Square Indianapolis IN 46204

KRIEG, WILLIAM LAURENCE, educator; b. Newark, O., Oct. 11, 1913; s. Laurence Montgomery and Helen (Crane) K.; A.B., Dartmouth, 1935; A.M., Fletcher Sch. Law and Diplomacy, 1936, grad. study, 1936-38; m. Laura Philinda Campbell, Feb. 6, 1943; children—Laurence John, Laura Campbell and Helen Middleton (twins). Apptd. fgn. service officer, vice consul, sec. Diplomatic Service, 1938; vice consul, Stuttgart, Germany, 1938, Milan, Italy, 1940, Lagos, Nigeria, 1941, Caaracas, Venezuela, 1944, 2d sec., 1945, consul, 1947; acting asst. chief div. North and West Coast affairs, Dept. State, 1948, officer in charge, 1950; 1st. sec., consul, dep. chief mission, Guatemala City, Guatemala, 1951; counselor of embassy, Guatemala, 1952; spl. asst. Bur. Inter-Am. affairs, Dept. State, 1954; detailed Nat. War Coll., 1955; dep. dir. office Inter-Am. Regional Polit. Affairs, 1956-58; counselor of embassy, Santiago, Chile, 1958-61; chief personnel policy council, Dept. State, 1961-62; chief career devel. and counseling staff, 1962-63, sr. fgn. service insp., 1964-65, 69-70; dir. Office Argentine-Paraguayan-Uruguayan Affairs, 1965-69; staff mem. Grad. Sch., Georgetown U., Washington, 1970—. Mem. Phi Beta Kappa. Home: 5208 Glenwood Rd Bethesda MD 20014 Office: Grad School Georgetown U Washington DC 20007

KRIEGER, CARL HENRY, biochemist, food co. exec.; b. Milw., Aug. 14, 1911; s. Alfred and Gretchen L. Thormaehlen) K.; B.S., U. Wis., 1933, M.S., 1938, Ph.D., 1940; m. Edna M. Balsley, Nov. 9, 1940; children—Nancy T. (Mrs. John E. Pace), John F., Elizabeth A. (Mrs. Thomas F. Patton). Research asso. Wis. Alumni Research Found., Madison, 1940-45, lab. mgr., 1945-50, dir. gen. labs., 1950-55; dir. basic research Campbell Soup Co., Camden, N.J., 1955-57, dir. basic research and product devel., 1957-61, v.p. product research, 1961—, pres. Campbell Soup Co. Research Inst., 1960- -, pres. Campbell Inst. for Food Research, 1966—. Past asso. referee Vitamin B12 Microbiol. Assn., Assn. Ofcl. Analytical Chemists, Inc.; past chmn. U.S. Pharmacopoeia Com. on Vitamin B12; treas. Research Mgmt. Group Phila., 1965-67; sec. Research Mgmt. Group of Phila., 1967-69; tech. adv. com. Inst. Nutrition Scis., Columbia U., 1966—; vice chmn. food industries adv. com. Nutrition Found., 1968-70, chmn., 1970—; nat. adv. com. Monell Chem. Senses Center, 1968—; mem. food and nutrition bd. NRC, 1969—. Sci. and tech. adv. com. AID, 1967—. Mem. U. Wis. Found. Fellow A.A.A.S.; mem. Am. Inst. Nutrition (finance com. 1967-69, chmn. com. on sustaining assos. 1966-68), Am. Chem. Soc. (exec. com. div. agrl. and food chemistry 1959-61), Nat. Canners Assn. (com. for studies on food preservation 1956—, sci. research com. 1960—), Am. Frozen Food Inst., Assn. Vitamin Chemists, Poultry Sci. Assn., Animal Nutrition Research Council, Inst. Food Technologists (com. on edn. 1961-64), Food Research Inst. (indls. adv. com. 1967-70), Franklin Inst., Pa. Soc., Wis. Alumni Assn. (dir. 1970—), Phi Tau Sigma, Phi Lambda Upsilon, Sigma Xi, Sigma Chi, Gamma Alpha. Clubs: Union League (Phila.), Wis. Alumni (pres. 1964-65) (Phila.). Contbr. articles profl. jours. Home: 722 Sussex Rd Wynnewood PA 19096 Office: Campbell Soup Co Camden NJ 08101

KRIEGER, IRVIN MITCHELL, educator; b. Cleve., May 14, 1923; s. William I. and Rose (Broosky) K.; B.S., Case Inst. Tech., 1944, M.S., 1948; Ph.D., Cornell, 1951; m. Theresa Melamed, June 9, 1965; 1 dau., Laura. Research asst. Case Inst. Tech., Cleve., 1946-47; teaching fellow Cornell U., Ithaca, N.Y., 1947-49; instr. Case Western Res. U., 1949-51, asst. prof., 1951-55, asso. prof., 1955-68, prof., 1968—; cons. for chem. firms. Served as ensign USNR, 1943-46. NSF fellow Université Libre De Bruxelles, 1959-60; sr. fellow, Weizmann Inst., 1970. Mem. Am. Chem. Soc., Am. Phys. Soc., Am. Inst. Chem. Engrs., Am. Assn. U. Profs., Soc. of Rheology. Contbr. articles profl. jours. Home: 2439 Kingston Rd Cleveland Heights OH 44118 Office: Case Western Res U Cleveland OH 44106

KRIEGER, KNUT AXEL, educator; b. Phila., Feb. 1, 1911; s. Bengt Eric Anshelm and Julia Maud (Popple) K.; B.S. in Chemistry, U. Pa., 1933, M.S., 1935, Ph.D., 1937; m. Miriam Rutherford Mick, Feb. 22, 1936; 1 son, Knut Rutherford. With U. Pa., 1933—, successively asst. instr., instr., asst. prof., asso. prof., prof., 1952—, acting dir. chemistry dept., 1952-54, supr. research contracts; cons. various corp. Mem. Am. Chem. Soc. (dir. Phila. sect. 1953-56), Catalysis Club Phila. (chmn. 1953), A.A.A.S., N.Y. Acad. Sci., Electrochem. Soc., Sigma Xi, Alpha Chi Sigma, Tau Beta Pi, Pi Mu Epsilon, Phi Lambda Upsilon. Contbr. articles sci. jours. Home: 4251 Regent Sq Philadelphia PA 19104 Office: U Pa Philadelphia PA 19104

KRIEGER, LEONARD, historian; b. Newark, Aug. 28, 1918; s. Isidore and Jennie (Glinn) K.; B.A., Rutgers U., 1938; M.A., Yale, 1942, Ph.D., 1949; m. Esther J. Smith, Aug. 13, 1949; children—Alan Davis, David Jonathan, Nathaniel Richard. Mem. faculty Yale, 1946-62, prof. history, 1961-62; Univ. prof. history U. Chgo., 1962-69; prof. history Columbia, N.Y.C., 1969—; vis. lectr. Northwestern U., 1950, Brandeis U., 1958, Columbia, 1960-61; vis. prof. Stanford, summer 1968, Johns Hopkins, 1971-72. Chmn. internat. conf. travel-grant com. Social Sci. Research Council, 1961-63; book prize com. Phi Beta Kappa, 1960-61; asso. Princeton

Council Humanities for Ford Humanities Project, 1959-64; fellow Center Advanced Study Behavioral Sci., 1956-57; mem. Inst. for Advanced Study, 1963, 69-70. Served to 1st lt. AUS, 1942-46. Mem. Am. Hist. Assn. (chmn. program com. 1960; exec. com. modern history sect. 1968-71), Am. Acad. Arts and Scis., Am. Soc. Polit. and Legal Philosophy. Author: The German Idea of Freedom, 1957; Politics of Discretion, 1965; Kings and Philosophers, 1970. Co-author: History, 1965. Series editor Classic European Historians, 1967—. Co-editor: The Responsibility of Power, 1967, 69; editor: Friedrich Engels, The German Revolutions, 1967. Mem. bd. editors Jour. History Ideas, 1963—. Office: Dept History Columbia U New York City NY 10027

KRIEGER, LEONARD HOBSON, bus. exec.; b. Pitts., May 14, 1905; s. Leon and Jennie (Fiengold) K.; A.B., Princeton, 1925; LL.B., U. Pitts., 1928; m. Rosalyn Sedler, June 13, 1929; children—Karl Frederick, Susan March. Admitted to Pa. bar, 1928; with firm Humes & Prather, Pitts., 1928-37; pres. S.W. Steel Corp., Pitts., 1937—; v.p. Luria Bros. & Co., N.Y.C., 1955—, Ogden Corp., N.Y.C., 1962—, Eimco Corp., Salt Lake City, 1962—; treas. Ringsdorff Corp., Pitts., 1950—. Mem. Inst. Scrap Iron and Steel (pres. 1956-57), Phi Beta Kappa. Clubs: Westmoreland Country (pres. 1950- 51), Concordia (Pitts.); Tamarisk Country (pres. 1970); Princeton, Harmonie (N.Y.C.). Home: Box 00 Palm Springs CA 92262 Office: 161 E 42d St New York City NY 10017

KRIEGER, MURRAY, educator, author; b. Newark, Nov. 27, 1923; s. Isidore and Jennie (Glinn) K.; student Rutgers U., 1940-42; M.A., U. Chgo., 1948; Ph.D. (Univ. fellow), Ohio State U., 1952; m. Joan Alice Stone, June 15, 1947; children—Catherine Leona, Eliot Franklin. Instr. English, Kenyon Coll., 1948-49, Ohio State U., 1951-52; asst. prof., then asso. prof. U. Minn., 1952-58; prof. English, U. Ill., 1958-63; M. F. Carpenter prof. lit. criticism U. Ia., 1963-66; prof. English, dir. program in criticism U. Cal. at Irvine, 1966—; asso. mem. Center Advanced Study, U. Ill., 1961-62. Served with AUS, 1942-46. Guggenheim fellow, 1956-57, 61-62; Am. Council Learned Socs. postdoctoral fellow, 1966-67; grantee Nat. Endowment for Humanities, 1971-72. Mem. Modern Lang. Assn., Am. Assn. U. Profs. Author: The New Apologists for Poetry, 1956; The Tragic Vision, 1960; A Window to Criticism; Shakespeare's Sonnets and Modern Poetics, 1964; The Play and Place of Criticism, 1967; The Classic Vision, 1971. Editor: (with Elisec Vivas) The Problems of Aesthetics, 1953; Northrop Frye in Modern Criticism, 1966. Home: 407 Pinecrest Dr Laguna Beach CA 92651 Office: Dept English Univ California Irvine CA 92664

KRIEGER, ROBERT LYMAN, mech. engr.; b. Louisville, Aug. 17, 1916; s. Robert N. and Ruth A. (Tuttle) K.; B.S. in Mech. Engring., Ga. Sch. Tech., 1943; m. Frances McLarty, Oct. 25, 1941; children—Robert Lyman, James, Karen, William, John, Richard, Mary Lynn. Engr. instrument research div. NACA, Langley Field, Va., 1943-48; engr.-in-charge Pilotless Aircraft Research Sta., N ASA, Wallops Island, Va., 1948-59, dir. Wallops Sta., 1959—. Mem. DelMarVa Adv. Council; chmn. adv. com. Eastern Shore br. U. Va.; chmn. Va. dist. DelMarVa council Boy Scouts. Dir. Eastern Shore Coll. Found. Mem. Eastern Shore C. of C. (dir.). Home: 1 Munson Circle Wallops Island VA 23337 Office: Wallops Station Wallops Island VA 23337

KRIEGER, ZANVYL, lawyer; b. Balt., Apr. 1, 1906; s. Herman and Bettie (Farber) K.; A.B., Johns Hopkins, 1928; LL.B., Harvard, 1931; m. Isabelle Loewenthal, Jan. 17, 1947; children—Bettie L., Jean L. Admitted to Md. bar. 1931; asso. firm Weinberg & Sweeten, Balt., 1931-37; partner firm Aiken & Krieger, Balt., 1937-41, Krieger & Sweeten, Balt., 1946—; asst. atty. gen. Md., 1939-42. Chmn. bd. U.S. Surg. Corp., Balt. Ice Sports, Inc.; chmn. exec. com., treas. Balt. Baseball Club, Balt. Bays, Inc.; founder, past v.p., dir. Balt. Football, Inc.; dir. First Federated Life Ins. Co., Churchill, Ltd. Bd. dirs. Nat. Conf. Christians and Jews; trustee Park Sch.; bd. dirs., treas. Krieger Fund, Inc. Served to maj. USAAF, 1942- 46. Mem. Am., Md., Balt. bar assns. Democrat. Jewish religion. Club: Suburban Country (bd. dirs.) (Baltimore Country).†

KRIEGHBAUM, HIRAM HILLIER, educator, writer; b. South Bend, Ind., Nov. 2, 1902; s. Hiram Cluro and Edith Emily (Hillier) K.; A.B., U. Wis., 1926; M.S. in Journalism, Northwestern U., 1939; m. Katherine Lancaster, June 6, 1945 (dec. Mar. 1959); 1 dau., Katherine (dec. Aug. 1969). Reporter, Reading (Pa.) Times, 1926-27; staff corr. United Press Assn., 1927-38, 42; asst., later asso. prof. journalism Kan. State Coll., 1938-42; information specialist dept. medicine and surgery VA, Washington, 1945-46; asso. prof. journalism U. Ore., 1946-47; pub. information officer WHO, N.Y.C., 1947-48; faculty N.Y. U., 1948—, chmn. dept. journalism, 1957-63, prof., 1960—. Sec.- treas. Council Advancement Sci. Writing, 1960-64, mem., 1960-68; dir. Gould House Seminars for Sci. Writers, 1960-62; supr. study of N.S.F.'s Insts. Programs, 1963-65; asso., univ. seminar on pub. communication Columbia, 1969—. Served to lt. comdr. USNR, 1942-45. Recipient Pioneer award Nat. Scholastic Press Assn., 1970. Mem. Nat. Assn. Sci. Writers, Nat. Conf. Editorial Writers, Internat. Press Inst., Assn. Edn. Journalism (council communications research 1958-66, pres. 1971-72), Journalism council Inc. (pres. 1970-71), A.A.A.S., Am. Soc. Journalism Sch. Adminstrs. (pres. 1961), Sigma Delta Chi, Kappa Tau Alpha. Methodist. Club: University (bd. govs. 1960-63; past pres.) (Mamaroneck). Author: American Newspaper Reporting Science News, 1941; Facts in Perspective, 1956; When Doctors Meet Reporters, 1957; Science, the News and the Public, 1958; (with Edmund C. Arnold) The Student Journalist: A Handbook for Staff and Adviser, 1963; Science and Mass Media, 1967; (with Hugh Rawson) To Improve Secondary School Science and Mathematics Teaching, 1968; (with Hugh Rawson) An Investment in Knowledge, 1969. Home: 731 River St Mamaroneck NY 10543 Office: Dept Journalism NY U Washington Sq New York City NY 10003

KRIENDLER, I. ROBERT, restaurant exec.; b. N.Y.C., Mar. 25, 1914; s. Carl and Sadie (Brenner) K.; B.A., Rutgers U., 1936; L.H.D., 1961; m. Florence Feller, Aug. 29, 1937; children—Karen Gale (Mrs. Stanley I. Nelson), Jeffrey Feller, John Carl. Asso., The "21 Club, N.Y.C. 1936—, successively apprentice asst., asst. to exec. staff, treas. and v.p., 1936-56, pres., 1956—; dir. Sonesta Internat. Hotels Corp., Iron Gate Products, Inc., Charles Luckman Assos.; adv. bd. Mfrs. Hanover Trust Co. Mem. Greater N.Y. council Boy Scouts Am., Girl Scouts. Bd. dirs. U.S. Naval Acad. Found., Damon Runyon Meml. Fund, Jack Kriendler-Charlie Berns Found., U.S. Com. for Refugees; bd. dirs., mem. exec. com. Nat. Football Hall Fame; trustee Fleming Coll., Zurich, Switzerland, Rutgers U., New Brunswick, N.J., Marine Mil. Acad., Harlingen, Tex., Mt. Sinai Hosp., N.Y.C. Served to lt. col. USMCR, 1940-46. Decorated Purple Heart, Bronze Star Medal, Legion of Merit; named Masonic War Vet. of Year, 1962; recipient Good Scout award N.Y. council Boy Scouts Am., 1966; Humanitarian award Anti-Defamation League, 1966; award Rutgers Alumni Fedn., 1969; Patriot award Congl. Medal of Honor Soc., 1969; Brotherhood award Nat. Conf. Christians and Jews, 1970. Mem. 3d Marine Div. Assn. (dir.), Marine Corps Res. Officers Assn. N.Y., Navy League (N.Y. council), Phi Epsilon Pi. Clubs: Soldiers, Sailors and Airmens (dir.), Rutgers (N.Y.C.); Army-Navy (Washington). Home: 390 West End Av New York City NY 10024 Office: 21 W 52d St New York City NY 10019

KRIENDLER, MAXWELL ARNOLD, beverage co. exec.; b. N.Y.C., Feb. 16, 1908; s. Karl and Sadie Miller (Brenner) K.; LL.B., St. John's U., 1929; m. Charlotte Campbell, Feb. 1967; children by previous marriage—John, Christopher, Jessica P., Maxwell C.C. With 21 Club, N.Y.C., 1946-57; v.p. 21 Brands, Inc., N.Y.C., 1955-70, cons., 1970—; dir. Iron Gate Products Co., Inc. Bd. dirs. Boys Town Italy, Joint Def. Appeal, Freedom House, George Jr. Republic, Aerospace Edn. Found., Air Force Museum, Found., Air Force Acad. Found., Air Force Assn. Fund; bd. govs. Long Island U.; regional fund chmn. Albert Einstein Coll. Medicine, Yeshiva U.; pres., dir. Jack Kriender Meml. Found. Served to col. USAAF, 1942-46; ETO; col. Res. ret. Decorated Legion of Merit, Commendation medal; recipient Exceptional Service award USAF, 1964, Man of Year award Air Force Assn., 1964, People to People Sports Com. award, 1964. Mem. Am. Legion (past post comdr.), Nat. Sojourners, Iota Theta. Mason. Club: Adventurers (N.Y.C.). Home: 1016 Fifth Av New York City NY 10028. Office: 23 W 52d St New York City NY 10019

KRIGBAUM, WILLIAM RICHARD, educator, chemist; b. Beardstown, Ill., Sept. 29, 1922; s. Daniel Dwight and Ella (Sutton) K.; B.S., James Millikin U., 1944, Sc.D., 1966; M.S., U. Ill., 1948, Ph.D., 1949; m. Esther Jean Wolfe, July 14, 1945; children—Mary Kathryn, Janet Ann, Lynn Carol. Faculty, Duke, 1950, prof., 1962—, James B. Duke prof. chemistry, 1969—; cons. E.I. duPont de Nemours & Co., 1955—. Alfred P. Sloan Research fellow, 1956-60; NSF Sr. Postdoctoral fellow Centre des Recherches sur les Macromolecules, Strasbourg, France, 1959-60, Institute fur physikalische Chemie, Graz, Austria, 1966-67. Fellow Am. Phys. Soc.; mem. Am. Chem. Soc., Am. Crystallographic Assn., Sigma Xi. Research, numerous publs. on characterization of high polymers by phys. chem. methods, such as x-ray diffraction, light scattering, osmotic pressure, solution thermodynamics; relation of molecular structure to phys. properties of elastomers and crystalline polymers. Home: 2504 Wilson St Durham NC 27706

KRIKORIAN, ROBERT VAHRAM, mfg. co. exec.; b. New Haven, Sept. 30, 1919; s. David K. and Rose L. (Constantian) K.; B.S. in Indsl. Adminstrn., Yale, 1950; m. Virginia Marie Edwards. May 22, 1943; children—Virginia Terrell, Gary Lee, Rand Jay, Stacy Jean. With Rex Chainbelt Inc., Milw., 1950—, v.p. constrn. machinery sec., 1962-63, exec. v.p., 1963-67, pres. 1967—, also dir. Served with USNR, 1944-46. Mem. Construction Industry Mfrs. Assn. (bd. dirs.), Nat. Ready Mixed Concrete Assn. (bd. dirs.), Yale Engring. Assn., Tau Belta Pi (pres. Alpha chpt. 1949). Conglist. Mason. Home: 5065 N Palisades Whitefish Bay WI 53217 Office: 2000 Marine Plaza Milwaukee WI 53201

KRILL, ALEX EUGENE, ophthalmologist, educator; b. Cleve., Oct. 20, 1928; s. Samuel and Bertha (Rosner) K.; B.S., Western Res. U., 1950; M.D., Ohio State U., 1954; m. Suzanne Altschul, May 31, 1964; 1 dau., Eileen. Intern, Phila. Gen. Hosp., 1954-55; resident ophthalmology U. Ill., 1958-60, USPHS spl. trainee ophthalmology, 1960-61; postgrad. fellow in visual physiology U. Mich., 1961; asst. prof., research asso. in ophthalmology U. Chgo., 1961- 65, asso. prof. 1965-68, prof., 1968—, mem. com. on genetics, 1967—. Served with USNR, 1955-57. Recipient award of merit Am. Acad. Ophthalmology and Otolaryngology, 1970; certificate of merit A.M.A., 1970. Diplomate Am. Bd. Ophthalmology. Mem. Am. Acad. Ophthalmology and Otolaryngology (sect. chmn.), A.C.S., Am. Ophthal. Soc., Internat. Congress Neuro-ophthalmology (sec. Western Hemisphere), Internat. Soc. Clin. Electroretinography (sec. Western Hemisphere), Phi Beta Kappa, Sigma Xi, Alpha Omega Alpha. Chief editor Ophthalmology Digest, 1970—; mem. editorial bd. Am. Jour. of Ophthalmology, 1966—, Investigative Ophthalmology, 1969—, Documenta Ophthalmologica, 1970—, Survey of Opthalmology, 1970—. Contbr. articles profl. jours. Home: 5648 S Harper Av Chicago IL 60637 Office: 950 E 59th St Chicago IL 60637

KRILL, KARL EMIL, univ. dean; b. St. Louis, Jan. 18, 1916; s. Emil and Mae Rose (Kohn) K.; student Washington U., St. Louis, 1933-34, U.S. Coast Guard Acad., 1936- 38; B.S. in Ceramic Engring., Mo. Sch. Mines and Metallurgy, 1941; M.S. in Geology, U. Colo., 1947; Ph.D., Ohio State U., 1951; m. Florence E. Mahoney, Feb. 22, 1943; children—Judith Ann, Karl Emil, Marybeth, Research asso. Nat. Clay Pipe Research Corp., 1947-51; chief, chem. engring. and materials br. Office Ordnance Research, 1952-53; asst. to dir. research found. Ohio State U., 1953-57, asst. to v.p., 1957-60, asso., 1960-63; spl. asst. to pres. U. Wis. at Madison, 1963-65, dean Grad. Sch. at Milw., 1965-71; dean Grad. Sch., prof. metallurgy and materials Youngstown (O.) State U., 1971—. Vice pres., vice chmn. bd. Nika Corp., Madison, 1967—. Mem. bd. supervisory cons. Denison Research Found., 1958-60. Served to comdr. USNR, 1941-45. Registered profl. engr., Ohio. Mem. A.A.A.S., Sigma Xi. Patentee forming methods for cementitious and clay pipe. Home: 6645 Placid Lake Dr Canfield OH 44406 Office: Youngstown State U Youngstown OH 44503

KRIM, ARTHUR B., lawyer; b. N.Y.C., Apr. 4, 1910; s. Morris and Rose (Ocko) K.; B.A., Columbia, 1930, LL.B., 1932; m. Mathilde Galland, Dec. 7, 1958. Admitted to N.Y. bar, 1933; asso., mem. firm Phillips, Nizer, Benjamin, Krim & Ballon; pres. United Artists Corp., 1951-69, now chmn. bd. Spl. cons. to U.S. pres., 1968-69. Dir. Transam. Corp. Chmn. Presidents Club for Presidents Kennedy, Johnson, 1962-68. Bd. dirs. African Am. Inst., Weizmann Inst. Sci., Lincoln U.; trustee Columbia, John F. Kennedy Library, Inc. Chmn., Democratic Nat. Finance Com., 1966-68. Served from 1st lt. to lt. col. AUS, 1942-45. Decorated cavaliere Ufficiale Della Republica Italiana; chevalier dans l'Ordre National de la Legion d'Honneur. Mem. N.Y. Bar Assn., UN Assn. U.S. (dir.), Columbia Law Sch. Alumni Assn. (dir. 1961-63), Phi Beta Kappa. Editor-in-chief Columbia Law Rev., 1931-32. Home: 33 E 69th St New York City NY 10021 Office: 729 7th Av New York City NY 10019

KRIM, SEYMOUR, writer; b. N.Y.C., May 11, 1922; s. Abraham and Ida (Goldberg) K.; student U. N.C., 1939-40; m. Eleanor Goff, 1946 (div. 1951). Reporter, New Yorker mag., 1941-42; writer OWI, 1943-45; publicity writer Paramount Pictures, 1952-54; scriptreader United Artists, 1955-61; editor Nugget mag., 1961-65; reporter N.Y. Herald Tribune, 1965-66; cons. editor Evergreen Rev., 1967. Tchr. non-fiction writing Columbia, 1964, St. Marks-on-Bowrie Writing Workshop, 1967-69, U. Ia. Writers Workshop, 1970-72. Author: Views of a Nearsighted Cannoneer, 1961; Shake it for the World, Smartass, 1970. Editor: Manhattan, An Anthology, 1954; The Beats, An Anthology, 1960. Contbr. revs. and articles to newspapers and mags. Home: 120 E 10th St New York City NY 10003

KRIMENDAHL, HERBERT FREDERICK, bus. exec.; b. Celina, O., 1896; s. Otto and Freda (Schanzlin) K.; ed. in pub. schs.; m. Mary Bess Christian Dec. 10, 1925; children—David Christian, Herbert Frederick, II. Began career with Crampton Canneries, Inc., Celina, O. 1919, pres. 1923-44; chmn. of bd., W. R. Roach & Co., Grand Rapids, Mich. 1941-46; v.p. Stokely Foods, Inc., Indianapolis, 1944-46; exec. v.p. Stokely-Van Camp, Inc., Indpls., 1946-48, pres., 1948-60, dir., 1946—, vice chmn. bd. dirs., 1956—; dir. 7 Kings Restaurants; dir. Young Industries, Lexington, Ky., Liberty Mut. Ins. Co., Boston; exec. bd. dirs. N.Y. & C.G.O.; trustee Am. Fletcher Mortgage Investors. Served with O.T.S., World War I; adminstr. tin order WPB, 1942. Mem. Nat. Canners Assn. (pres. 1940). Mason (Shriner). Clubs: Indpls. Athletic Columbia; Woodstock; Indian Creek Country; Trader Point Hunt. Home: 7020 E 116th St Noblesville IN 46060 Office: PO Box 40187 Indianapolis IN 46240

KRING, WALTER DONALD, clergyman; b. Lakewood; O., Mar. 10, 1916; s. Walter DeVaine and Rebecca Olive (Shumaker) K.; exchange student U. Hawaii, 1935-36; A.B., Occidental Coll., 1937, L.H.D., 1965; S.T.B., Harvard, 1940; LL.D., Emerson Coll., 1961; D.D., St. Lawrence U., 1968. Asst., Harvard Meml. Ch., 1939-41; asst. minister First Church, Boston, 1939-41; asst. dept. history Harvard, 1939-41; minister First Presbyn. Ch., Hoosick Falls, N.Y., 1941-43, First Unitarian Ch., Worcester, Mass. 1946-55, Unitarian Ch. of All Souls, N.Y.C., 1955—; pres. Beacon Press, Inc., 1955-59. Dir. Worcester Craft Center; dir., pres. Spence Chapin Adoption Agency; pres. Artist-Craftsmen, N.Y., 1960-63, 70—. Vis. com. Harvard Div. Sch., 1963-69; corporator Emerson Coll., 1960—, Worcester Art Mus., 1950-55. Served with Chaplains Corps, USNR, 1943-46. Recipient 1st prize high temperature stoneware Nat. Ceramic Show, 1954. Mem. Worcester (pres. 1954-55), East Midtown (pres. 1959-62, 68-69) ministers Assns., Am. Unitarian Assn. (sec. 1953-61); Harvard Divinity Sch. Alumni Assn. (past pres.; mem. council). Clubs: Worcester Economic (pres. 1954-55). Author: Religion is the Search for Meaning, 1955; Across the Abyss to God, 1966. Exhibitor ceramics, Worlds Fair, Brussels, 1958. Home: 401 E 88th St New York City NY 10028 Office: Unitarian Church of All Souls 1157 Lexington Av New York City NY 10021

KRINGEL, JOHN R., cement co. exec.; b. 1913; student mech. engring., U. Colo.; m. With engring. cons. firm prior to World War II; cons. aggregate and ready mix concrete producers, 1946-54; from plant supr. to exec. v.p. and pres. N.Y. Trap Rock Corp., 1954-65; with Lone Star Industries, 1965—, pres., chief exec. officer, 1969—, chmn. bd., 1970—, also dir. Served as officer USNR, 1942-45. Address: 1 Greenwich Plaza Greenwich CT 06830

KRINSKY, FRED, educator; b. Poland, Feb. 2, 1924; s. Jacob and Sarah (Rabinovitz) K.; came to U.S., 1927, naturalized, 1933; B.A., Bklyn. Coll., 1944; M.A., U. Pa., 1946, Ph.D., 1950; m. Marilyn Claire Seltzer, Aug. 3, 1947; children—David, Robert, Jeffrey, Glenn. Asst. instr. U. Cal., 1947; for, instr. to asso. prof. Syracuse U., 1948-61; mem. faculty U. So. Cal., 1960—, prof. polit. sci., chmn. dept., 1966—. Rabbi and educator Jewish communities Syracuse, N.Y. and Los Angeles, 1954—. Recipient award B'nai B'rith, 1958, Excellence in Teaching award U. So. Cal., 1963. Mem. Am., Western polit. sci. assns., Tau Epsilon Phi, Pi Sigma Alpha. Author: The Renacsent Jewish Nationalism, A Study of its Leading Concepts and Practices, 1950; Problems in Democratic Citizenship, 3d-6th rev. edits., 1956; (with Carol Fischer) The Middle East in Crisis, 1959; (with Gerald Rigby) The Theory and Practice of American Democracy, 1967; (with June Tapp) Ambivalent America, 1971. Editor: (with A.H. Cope) Franklin D. Roosevelt and the Supreme Court, 1952; (with E.E. Palmer) Yalta-Foundation for Peace of Dissension, 1952; (with A.H. Cope) The Current Defense of the Unitd States, 1954; (with Carl Vann) Summitry: 1960, 1960; (with Robert L. Piper) Algeria: Crisis in Conscience, 1964; (with Gerald Higby) Readings in Theory and Practice of American Democracy, 1965; (with Joseph Boskin) The Insight Series, 1968-70. Home: 4518 Fenwood Av Woodland Hills CA 91364 Office: Univ So Cal Univ Park Los Angeles CA 90007

KRINSLEY, DAVID HENRY, educator; b. Chgo., Jan. 9, 1927; s. Lazarus and Rose (Aaron) K.; Ph.B., U. Chgo., 1948, S.B., 1948, S.M., 1950, Ph.D., 1956; m. Ann L. Corrigan, Apr. 10, 1958; children—Karen, Jeanne, Brian. Micropaleontologist, Standard Oil Co., Los Angeles, 1951-52; asso. research petrologist research and devel. labs. Portland Cement Assn., Skokie, Ill., 1952-55; instr. phys. scis. U. Ill., Chgo., 1955-56; with Lamont Geol. Obs., Columbia, 1956-57; faculty Queens Coll. Coll. City N.Y., Flushing, 1957—, prof., 1966—, asso. dean faculty, 1966-70, acting dean faculty, 1970—. Served with AUS, 1945-46. Overseas fellow Churchill Coll. Cambridge U., 1970-71. Fellow Geol. Soc. Am.; mem. Sigma Xi. Home: 5 Cambridge Rd Great Neck NY 11023 Office: Dept Earth and Environmental Scis Queens Coll Flushing NY 11367

KRIPPAEHNE, WILLIAM WONN, physician, educator; b. Douglas, Alaska, 1917; M.D., U. Ore., 1946. Intern, U. Ore. Hosps. and Clinics, Portland, 1946-47, resident gen. surgery, 1949-53; mem. staff, instr. surgery U. Ore. Med. Sch., Portland, 1953-55, asst. prof., 1955-60, asso. prof., 1960-65, prof., chmn. dept. surgery, 1964—. Served to capt. MC, AUS, 1947-49. Address: U Ore Med Sch Portland OR 97201

KRIPS, HENRY JOSEF, conductor; b. Vienna, Austria, Apr. 8, 1902; s. Joseph and Linse (Seitz) K.; ed. Academy of Music, Vienna, Austria; pupil of Felix Weingartner, Prof. Mandyczewski; m. Mitzi Wilheim, 1947; m. 2d, Baroness Marietta Prochaska, Oct. 9, 1960. Music Coach, choirmaster; condr. Volsoper, Vienna, 1921-24; opera condr. Aussig/Elbe, 1924, Dortmund, 1925; gen. music dir. Karlsruhe, 1926-33; 1st condr. State Opera Vienna, 1933-38; prof. Acad. Music and Dramatic Art; guest condr. Opera, also Philharmonic Orch., Belgrade, 1938-39; reorganized Vienna State Opera, Hofmusikkapelle, Vienna, 1945; guest performances Salzburg Festival, 1946-48, Leningrad, Moscow, Nice, Paris, Marseille, Basle, London, Brussels, 1947; dir. Sch. for Conductors, Acad. Music and Dramatic Art, Vienna, 1949; chief condr. London Symphonic Orch., 1950; condr. Buffalo Philharmonic, 1954-63; condr., music dir. San Francisco Symphony Orch., 1963-64. Recipient Mozart Ring, Austria, 1965. Address: 78 Jerningham St North Adelaide South Australia*

KRISCH, ADOLPH OSCAR, hotel exec.; b. N.Y.C., June 3, 1916; s. Samuel J. and Miriam (Weinstein) K.; student Roanoke Coll., 1933-34, U. Va., 1934-37; m. Heidrun Ilsa Feller, June 16, 1966; children—Victoria (Mrs. David Salo), Juliana (Mrs. Martin L. Weiss). With various retail jewelers, 1936-57; chmn. bd. Am. Motor Inns, Inc., Roanoke, Va., 1957—; chmn., dir. Providers Benefit Ins. Co. Served with AUS, 1943-44. Mem. Internat. Assn. Holiday Inns (dir., pres. 1969). Home: 127 McClanahan St SW Roanoke VA 24014 Office: 103 W Campbell Av SW Roanoke VA 24007

KRISCH, ALAN DAVID, educator, physicist; b. Phila., Apr. 19, 1939; s. Kube and Jeanne (Freiberg) K.; A.B., U. Pa., 1960; Ph.D., Cornell U., 1964; m. Jean Peck, Aug. 27, 1961; 1 dau., Kathleen Susan. Instr., Cornell U., 1964; mem. faculty U. Mich., 1964—, asso. prof. high energy physics, 1966-68, prof., 1968—; discovered heaviest elementary particle, also structure within the proton, 1966. Mem. Am., Italian phys. socs., A.A.A.S. Office: Randall Lab U Mich Ann Arbor MI 48104 Mailing Address:

KRISHNAMURTI, JIDDU, author, philosopher; b. Madanapalle, S. India, 1895; ed. privately Eng. Formed World Order of Star 1911, dissolved, 1926; speaker, 1925—; founder Krishnamurti Found., Ojai, Cal., 1969. Author: Education and the Significance of Life, 1953; The

First and Last Freedom, 1954; Commentaries on Living; 1st series, 1956, 2d series, 1958, 3d series, 1960; Life Ahead, 1963; Think on These Things, 1964; Freedom from the Known, 1969; The Only Revolution, 1970; The Urgency of Change, 1971. Address: PO Box 216 Ojai CA 93023

KRISLOV, SAMUEL, educator; b. Cleve., Oct. 5, 1929; s. Isaak and Gertrude (Hutner) K.; student Western Res. U., 1947-48; B.A., N.Y. U., 1951, M.A., 1952; Ph.D., Princeton, 1955; m. Donna Carol Taylor, Sept. 15, 1951; children—Sharon Lee, Anne Beth, Daniel Robert, Melanie Bathsheba, Lee Shalom. Instr., U. Vt., 1955, Hunter Coll., 1955-56; asst. prof. U. Okla., 1956-60, asso. prof., 1960- 61; vis. lectr., asso. prof. Mich. State U., 1959-64; asso. prof. polit. sci. U. Minn., Mpls., 1964-65, prof., 1965—, chmn. dept., 1969—. Vis. prof. Columbia, 1966. Mem. Minn. Commn. on Jud. Standards, 1971—. Mem. exec. com. Democratic party Ingham County, Mich., 1962-64. Russell Sage fellow, 1966-67; NSF, Nat. Inst. Mental Health grantee, 1963, 67, 69, 71. Mem. Am., Midwest polit. sci. assns., Am. Assn. U. Profs., Phi Beta Kappa. Author: The Supreme Court in the Federal Process, 1965; The Negro in the Federal Bureaucracy, 1967; The Supreme Court and Political Freedom, 1968. Home: 1718 Oliver Av South Minneapolis MN 55405

KRISPYN, EGBERT, educator; b. Haarlem, Holland, June 14, 1930; s. Pieter Johan and Henriette (Lams) K.; B.A., U. Melbourne, Australia, 1957, M.A., 1958; postgrad. U. Tubingen, Germany, 1958-61; Ph.D., U. Pa., 1963; m. Joan Willings, Feb. 20, 1957; 1 son, Hugo Joost. Came to U.S., 1961, naturalized, 1970. Comml. employee Intternat. Trading Co., Europe, Sinapore, Thailand, Indonesia, 1947-51; lectr. U. Pa., 1961-63, asst. prof., 1964-66, asso. prof., 1966-68; asst. prof. U. Fla., Gainesville, 1963-64, prof., chmn. German and Russian dept., 1968—; editor Netherlandic sect. Twayne World Authors Series, 1966—, Library of Netherlandic Lit., Twayne Pub., Inc., 1970—; adv. editor Dimension, 1968—; co-editor Germanic Notes, 1970—. Recipient research grants Humboldt Found., 1965, Am. Philos. Soc., 1968, U. Pa., 1966. Mem. Modern Lang. Assn., Internat. Assn. for Germanic Studies, Modern Humanities Research Assn., Am. Assn. U. Profs. Author: Style and Society in German Literary Expressionism, 1964; George Heym: A Reluctant Rebel, 1968; Günter Eich, 1971. Contbr. articles profl. jours. Home: Route 3 Box 191U Gainesville FL 32601

KRISSMAN, MONTE ALAN, securities co. exec.; b. Memphis, Jan. 25, 1939; s. Michael M. and Celia (Katrovitz) K.; A.B., Emory U., 1960; postgrad. Harvard, 1960; LL.B., Stanford, 1964; m. Pauline B. Loomos, May 10, 1969. Admitted to Cal. bar, 1964; practice in Los Angeles, 1964-68; mem. firm Gibson, Dunn & Crutcher, 1964-68; exec. v.p. Jefferies & Co., Inc., Los Angeles, 1968- -, also dir.; dir. Standun, Inc., Horner, Walter & Co. Revision chmn. Stanford Moot Ct. Bd., 1963-64. Mem. Am., Cal., Los Angeles bar assns., Alpha Epsilon Pi, Phi Alpha Delta. Democrat. Clubs: University, Los Angeles Athletic (both Los Angeles). Home: 9595 Stuart Lane Beverly Hills CA 90210 Office: 445 S Figueroa St Los Angeles CA 90017

KRISTELLER, PAUL OSKAR, educator; b. Berlin, Germany, May 22, 1905; s. Heinrich and Alice (Magnus) K.; Dr. phil., U. Heidelberg, 1928; student U. Berlin, Freiburg U., Marburg U.; Dottore in filosofia, U. Pisa, 1937; Ph.D. (hon.), U. Padua, 1962; m. Edith Lewinnek, June 26, 1940. Came to U.S., 1939, naturalized, 1945. Fellow, Notgemeinshaft der Deutschen Wissenschaft, 1932-33; lectr. German, U. and Scuola Normale Superiore, Pisa, 1935-38; Fulbright vis. prof. Scuola Normale Superiore, 1952; asso., philosophy Columbia, 1939-48, asso. prof., 1948-56, prof., 1956-68, Frederick Woodbridge prof. philosophy, 1968—. Mem. Inst. for Advanced Study, Princeton, 1954-55, 61, 68-69. Recipient Serena medal for Italian studies Brit. Acad., 1958; Premio Internazionale Forte dei Marmi, 1968. Commendatore dell'Ordine el Merito della Repubblica Italiana. Guggenheim fellow, 1958-68-69. Fellow Mediaeval Acad. Am., Arcadia (corr. Rome, Italy), Am. Acad. Arts and Scis., Accademia dei Sepolti (Volterra, Italy); corr. fellow Académie des Inscriptions (Paris), Accademia Patavina (Padua), Monumenta Germaniae Historica (Munich), Istituto Veneto (Venice), Accademia degl. Intronati (Siena), Accademia Toscana 'La Colombaria' (Florence); mem. Am. Philos. Assn., Am. Soc. Ch. History, Medieval Acad. Am. (1st v.p. 1965-68), Am. Assn. Tchrs. Italian, Renaissance Soc. Am. (pes. 1957-59), Phi Beta Kappa. Author: The Philosophy of Marsilio Ficino, 1943; The Classics and Renaissance Thought, 1955; Studies in Renaissance Thought and Letters, 1956; Latin Manuscript Books before 1600, 1960, rev. edit., 1965; Renaissance Thought, 1961; Iter Italicum, vol. I, 1963, vol. II, 1967; Eight Philosophers of the Italian Renaissance, 1964; Renaissance Thought II, 1965; Renaissance Philosophy and the Medieval Tradition, 1966; Le thomisme et la pensée italienne de la Renaissance, 1967. Editor: Catalogus Translationum et Commentariorum, vol. I, 1960, vol. II, 1971; co-editor: Renaissance Philosophy of Man, 1948. Contbr. articles. Home: 423 W 120th St New York City NY 10035 Office: 1161 Amsterdam Av New York City NY 10027

KRISTOF, LADIS KRIS DONABED, polit. scientist, author; b. Cernauti, Rumania, Nov. 26, 1918; s. Witold and Maria (Zawadzki) Krzysztofowicz; student U. Paznan (Poland), 1937-39; B.A., Reed Coll., Portland, Ore., 1955; M.A., U. Chgo., 1956, Ph.D., 1969; m. Jane McWilliams, Dec. 29, 1956; 1 son, Nicholas. Came to U.S., 1952, naturalized, 1957. Regional exec. dir. Sovrom-Iemn, Rumania, 1948; mgr. Centre du Livre Suisse, Paris, France, 1951-52; lectr. U. Chgo., 1958-59; asso. dir. Inter-Univ. Project History Menshevism, N.Y.C., 1959-62; mem. faculty dept. polit. sci. Temple U., 1962-64; research fellow Hoover Instn., Stanford, 1964-67; faculty polit. sci. U. Santa Clara, 1967-68; asso. Studies Communist System, Stanford, 1968-69; mem. faculty polit. sci. U. Waterloo (Ont., Can.), 1969-71; asso. prof. polit. sci. Portland (Ore.) State U., 1971—. Active Internat. YMCA Center, Paris, 1950-52, N.A.A.C.P., Chgo., 1957-59. Served with Corps Engrs., Rumanian Army, 1942-43. Mem. Am. Polit. Sci. Assn., Assn. Am. Geographers, Am. Assn. Advancement Sci., Am. Geog. Soc. N.Y. Author: The Nature of Frontiers and Boundaries, 1959; The Origins and Evolution of Geopolitics, 1960; The Russian Image of Russia, 1967; also articles in Rumania, short story in Poland. Home: Rt 2 Box 430 Gaston OR 97119 Office: Portland State Univ Portland OR 97207

KRITCHEVSKY, DAVID, educator, biochemist; b. Kharkov, Russia, Jan. 25, 1920; s. Jacob and Leah (Kricewski) K.; came to U.S., 1923, naturalized, 1929; B.S., U. Chgo., 1939, M.S., 1942; Ph.D., Northwestern U., 1948; m. Evelyn Sholtes, Dec. 21, 1947; children—Barbara Ann, Janice Eileen, Stephen Bennett. Chemist, Ninol Labs., Chgo., 1939-46; postdoctoral fellow Fed. Inst. Tech., Zurich, Switzerland, 1948-49; biochemist Radiation Lab., U. Cal. at Berkeley, 1950-52, Lederle Lab., Pearl River, N.Y., 1952-57; biochemist Wistar Inst., Phila., 1957—; prof. biochemistry Sch. Vet. Medicine, U. Pa., Phila., 1965—. Mem. USPHS study sect. Nat. Heart Inst., 1964-68; chmn. research com. Spl. Dairy Industry Bd., 1963-70. Recipient Research Career award Nat. Heart Inst., 1962. Mem. Am. Soc. Biol. Chemists, A.A.A.S., Am., Swiss, Brit. chem. socs., Soc. Exptl. Biology and Medicine, Arteriosclerosis Council, Am. Heart Assn., Am. Soc. Oil Chemists (chmn. methods com. 1963-64), Internat. Soc. Fat Research. Author: Cholesterol, 1958; also numerous articles. Editor: (with G. Litwack) Actions of Hormones on Molecular Processes, 1964. Co-editor: Advances in Lipid Research, 1963—; editorial bd. Atherosclerosis, Archives Bio-chemistry and Biophysics, Jour. Nutrition, Lipids Nutrition Reports Internat., Exptl. and Molecular Pathology. Research on role vehicle when cholesterol and fat produces atherosclerosis in rabbits, effects saturated and unsaturated fat, deposition orally administered cholesterol in aorta man and rabbit; pioneered use radioactive cholesterol for metabolic expts. Home: 136 Lee Circle Bryn Mawr PA 19010 Office: Wistar Inst 36th and Spruce Sts Philadelphia PA 19104

KRITZER, HYMAN WILLIAM, librarian; b. N.Y.C., Nov. 9, 1918; s. George and Fannie (Hornick) K.; B.S., Am. U., 1952; student Inst. des Etudes Politiques, Paris, France, 1952-53; M.S. in L.S., Cath. U. Am., 1958; m. Simone Morali, Feb. 11, 1946; children—Matthew, Marie-Anne, Michele. Order clk. Am. U., 1954-57; head, acquisition dept U. Notre Dame, 1957-59, U. Md., 1959-60; head, acquisition dept. Ohio State U., 1960-62, asst. dir. libraries, 1962-66; dir. libraries Kent State U., 1966—, asst. provost, 1969—. Served with AUS, 1941-45. Mem. A.L.A., Ohio Library Assn., Ohio Coll. Assn. (pres. librarians sect. 1967-68), bibliog. socs. Am., Va., Am. Assn. U. Profs. Club: Rowfant. Rotarian. Home: 11182 Route 700 Hiram OH 44234 Office: Kent State U Library Kent OH 44240

KRIZA, JOHN, dancer; b. Berwyn, Ill., Jan. 15, 1919; s. John J. and Marie (Bily) K.; student Morton Jr. Coll., 1937-38. With WPA Ballet, Chgo., 1938-39, Chgo. Civic Opera Ballet, 1939-40, Am. Ballet Caravan, 1940, Am. Ballet Theatre, N.Y.C., 1940—, 1st dancer, 1955—; created original roles in Billy the Kid, Fancy Free, Interplay, Fall River Legend, Winter's Eve; danced classical roles in Giselle, Swan Lake, Les Sylphides; Broadway musicals include Folies Bergeres, 1940, Panama Hattie, 1941, Concert Varieties, 1944; summer stock singing dancing roles include Kiss Me Kate, Brigadoon, Song of Norway; also has appeared in night clubs and on TV. Home: Box 456 Wheaton IL 60187 Office: care Am Ballet Theatre 1790 Broadway New York City NY 10019

KRIZAY, JOHN, fgn. service officer; b. Washington, Pa., June 14, 1926; s. Stephen and Theresa (Gruden) K.; student Buena Vista Coll., 1947-48, U. Ala., 1948- 49; B.A., George Washington U., 1951; M.A., Yale, 1960; m. Jane Garland Isaacs, Aug. 18, 1950; 1 dau., Claudia Anne. Joined Dept. of State as intern, 1951; joined U.S. Fgn. Service, 1954, assigned Office German Affairs, State Dept., 1955-57; 2d sec. embassy, Bonn, Germany, 1957-59; 2d sec. embassy, Rio de Janeiro, 1960-64, 1st sec., 1964, 1st sec. embassy, Leopoldville, 1964-66, dep. dir. Office Regional Econ. Policy, Bur. Am. Republics Affairs, Dept. State, 1966-69, dir. Office Regional Econ. Policy, 1969-70; research dir., study on financing of med. costs in U.S., Twentieth Century Fund, 1970-71. Mem. Phi Beta Kappa. Home: 65 Observatory Circle NW Washington DC 20008 Office: Twentieth Century Fund 1755 Massachusetts Av NW Washington DC 20036

KROC, RAY A., restaurant co. exec.; b. 1903. With Lily Tulip Cup Co., 1923-41, sales mgr., until 1941; with Malt-A-Mixer Co., 1941-63; chmn. bd., pres. McDonald's Corp., Chgo., 1963—. Office: McDonald's Corp 221 N LaSalle St Chicago IL 60601

KROCH, ADOLPH, bus. exec.; b. Austria, Jan. 7, 1882; s. Rudolph and Dorothy (Pliple) K.; student U. Vienna, also L.H.D. (hon.); m. Gertrude Horn, June 1, 1909; children—Carl, Gretchen. Came to U.S., 1902, naturalized, 1908. Established Kroch's Bookstores, Inc., booksellers and pubs., Chgo., 1907, chmn. bd., 1949—; chmn. Kroch's & Brentano's Inc. Hon. fellow Am. Booksellers Assn.; mem. Art Inst. Chgo., Chgo. Hist. Soc., Chgo. Mus. Natural History. Republican. Mason. Author: A Great Bookstore in Action, 1939; Bookstores Can Be Saved, 1952. Home: 639 Pearl St Laguna Beach CA 92651 Office: 29 S Wabash Av Chicago IL 60603

KROCH, CARL ADOLPH, bookseller; b. Chgo., June 21, 1914; s. Adolph and Gertrude (Horn) K.; B.A., Cornell U., 1935; m. Jeanette Kennelly, Aug. 12, 1939. With Kroch's Bookstores, Inc., 1935-54, pres., dir., 1949-54; pres. Brentano's Bookstores, Inc., 1950-54; pres., dir. Kroch's & Brentano's, Inc., Chgo., 1954—; pres. Booksellers Catalog Service, Inc.; dir. Nat. Blvd. Bank Chgo. Bd. dirs. Passavant Meml. Hosp. Served to lt. USNR, 1942-45. Mem. Am. Booksellers Assn. (dir.), Wine and Food Soc., Beta Theta Pi. Clubs: North Shore Country (Glenview, Ill.); Caxton, Mid-America, Chicago Yacht, Tavern, University (Chicago); Tucson National Golf. Home: 3240 N Lake Shore Dr Chicago IL 60657 Office: 29 S Wabash Av Chicago IL 60603

KROCK, ARTHUR, newspaperman; b. Glasgow, Ky., Nov. 16, 1887; s. Joseph and Caroline (Morris) K.; A.A., Lewis Inst., Chgo.; A.M., Princeton; Litt.D., U. Louisville, U. Ky. (hon.), 1956, Centre Coll. Ky.; m. Marguerite Polleys, Apr. 22, 1911 (dec. 1938); 1 son, Thomas Polleys; m. 2d, Martha Granger Blair, 1939. Reporter, Louisville, 1907; became Washington corr. Louisville Times, 1910, also Louisville Courier-Journal, 1911; returned to Louisville, 1915, as editorial mgr. both papers; editor-in-chief Times, 1919-23; asst. to pres. N.Y. World, 1923-27; joined N.Y. Times Bd. Editors, 1927, Washington corr., 1932-53, Washington commentator, 1953-67. Mem. Pulitzer Prize Bd., Sch. Journalism, Columbia, 1940-53. Contbr. syndicated articles from Peace Conf., Paris, France, 1918-19; one of 3 Am. members of Inter-Allied Press Com. of Fourteen which induced open sessions of the Peace Conf.; asst. to chmn. Democratic Nat. Com., New York, campaign of 1920. Decorated comdr. Legion d'Honneur (France); Officer's Cross, Polonia Restituta; Knights' Cross in Order of St. Olav (Norway); recipient Pulitzer Prize for Washington Corrs., 1935, 38, nat. correspondence 1951 (declined); Presdl. Medal of Freedom, 1970; Freedom Found. at Valley Forge award, 1971. Democrat. Clubs: Metropolitan, Gridiron, 1925 F St. (Washington). Author: The Editorials of Henry Watterson, 1923; In The Nation, 1966; Memoirs: Sixty Years On The Firing Line, 1968; The Consent of the Governed and Other Deceits, 1971. Home: 2029 Connecticut Av NW Washington DC 20037 Office: 1920 L St Washington DC 20036

KROCK, EDWARD, business exec.; b. Old Boylston, Mass., Apr. 19, 1912; s. Max and Rose (Shain) K.; student pub. schs.; m. Miriam Alpert, July 30, 1937; children—Richard Alan, Nancy Ruth. Founder, Edward Krock Industries, 1949, pres., treas., 1949—; purchaser 17 Am. Woolen plants; sale Alcan Constrn. equipment; econ. adviser WPB, 1941-43. Alt. del. Democratic Nat. Conv., 1956, 60, 64. Trustee, Jewish Home for Aged. Recipient Free Enterprise Assn. award. Jewish religion. Mem. B'nai B'rith. Home: Rockinghorse Farm Brookfield MA 01506 Office: PO Box 456 Worcester MA 01613

KROEBER, CLIFTON BROWN, educator; b. Berkeley, Cal., Sept. 7, 1921; s. Clifton Spencer and Theodora (Kracaw) K.; A.B., U. Cal. at Berkeley, 1943, M.A., 1947, Ph.D., 1951; m. Elizabeth MacSwain Jones, Apr. 29, 1944; children—Jeffrey Alfred, Alan Matthew, Keith Elliot, Scott Clifton. Tchr., A-to-Zed Sch., Berkeley, 1940, extension div. U. Cal., 1950- 51; asst. prof. history U. Wis., 1951-55; mem. faculty Occidental Coll., 1955—, Norman Bridge prof. Hispanic Am. history, 1964—; prof. Guadalajara (Mexico) Summer Sch., 1957, 60. Heller Traveling fellow U. Cal., also fellow Social Sci. Research Council, 1949-50; Haynes Found. summer fellow, 1959; Am. Philos. Soc. grantee, 1966; Wenner-Gren Found. grantee anthrop. research, 1970. Mem. Am. Hist. Assn., Am. Assn. U. Profs., Conf. Latin Am. History, Latin Am. Studies Assn. Author: The Growth of the Shipping Industry in the Rio de la Plata Region, 1794-1860, 1957. Editor: (with W. D. Wyman) The Frontier in Perspective. 1957. Home: 1701 Linda Rosa Av Los Angeles CA 90041.

KROEGER, HAL A., bus. exec.; b. N.Y.C., July 31, 1910; s. Herbert F. and Catherine (Mulker) K.; A.B., Amherst Coll., 1931; m. Eleanor Marsh Rockwell, July 8, 1935; children—Keith, Hal, Lynn. Partner, A. & H. Kroeger Orgn., N.Y.C.; dir. Burndy Corp., Norwalk, Conn., Hudson Wire Co., Ossining, N.Y., Am. Hawaiian S.S. Co., N.Y.C., Journapak Corp., N.Y.C., Safety Elec. Co., New Haven, Burns Internat. Security Services Inc., N.Y.C., Lukens Steel Co., Coatesville, Pa., Pillar Corp., Milw. Home: Tower Hill Scarborough NY 10510 Office: 535 Fifth Av New York City NY 10017

KROEHLER, KENNETH, mfg. exec.; b. Oak Park, Ill., Oct. 21, 1917; s. Peter E. and Grace A. (Hubert) K.; B.S., U. Cal., 1939; m. June H. Staeker, May 9, 1941; 1 son, Peter K. With Kroehler Mfg. Co., 1939—, pres. 1963-67, chmn. bd., chief exec. officer, 1967—; dir., mem. exec. com. Protection Mut. Ins. Co.; adv. bd. Liberty Mut. Ins. Co. Chmn. bd. trustees North Central Coll., Naperville, Ill. Served to lt. USNR 1942-46. Mem. Furniture Club of Am. Clubs: Chicago Yacht; Hinsdale (Ill.) Golf; Lost Tree Golf (North Palm Beach, Fla.).

KROEPSCH, ROBERT HAYDEN, educator; b. Cambridge, Mass., Oct. 21, 1912; s. Robert Karl and Laura Melissa (Ringer) K.; A.B., Bates Coll., 1933, LL.D., 1971; Ed.M., Harvard, 1938, Ed.D., 1951; student Oxford U., summer 1939; m. Ruth Catherine Maurice Aug. 13, 1945. Instr. English, high sch., Melrose, Mass., 1933-37, Glens Falls, N.Y., 1938-41; demonstration tchr., instr. Harvard, summer 1941; prin. high sch., Pembroke, Mass., 1941-42; instr. English, U. Vt., 1946, registrar, 1946-48, dean adminstrn., 1948-56 (on leave 1949-50); exec. sec. N.E. Bd. Higher Edn., 1956-60; exec. dir. Western Interstate Commn. Higher Edn., Boulder, Colo., 1960—; lectr. Salzburg Seminar in Am. Studies, summer 1964. Mem. research adv. com. Western office Coll. Entrance Exam. Bd., 1965-67; mem. commn. on adminstrv. affairs Am. Council on Edn., 1966-70, dir., 1970-71, mem. commn. on acad. affairs, 1970—; mem. commn. of scholars Bd. of Higher Edn., State Ill., 1966—; mem. steering com. Colloquium on Higher Edn., 1966—, chmn., 1967-68. Mem. spl. edn. adv. com. United Cerebral Palsy Assn., 1966-69. Bd. govs. Ednl. Change, Inc. Served to capt. USAAF, 1942-46. Mem. N.E. Assn. Collegiate Registrars (v.p. 1948-50), Council Social Work Edn. (del.-at-large 1958-60), Council State Govts. (chmn. nat. conf. interstate compact 1964-65), Am. Assn. for Higher Edn. (mem. Mountain-Plains regional council 1970—), Nat. League Nursing (dir. 1963-71, mem. com. on perspectives 1967—), Nat. Commn. Community Health Services (task force on manpower 1963-65), N.E.A., Phi Delta Kappa, Tau Kappa Alpha. Home: 200 Brook Pl Boulder CO 80302 Office: Western Interstate Commn for Higher Edn PO Drawer P Boulder CO 80302

KROESEN, FREDERICK JAMES, Jr., army officer; b. Phillipsburg, N.J., Feb. 11, 1923; s. Frederick James and Jean (Shillinger) K.; student Rutgers, 1940-43; B.A. in Internat. Affairs, George Washington U., 1962, M.A., 1966; grad. Command and Gen. Staff Coll., 1956, Armed Forces Staff Coll., 1959, Army War Coll., 1962; m. Rowene Wilder McCray, Mar. 4, 1944; children—Karen McCray (Mrs. Stephen Warren Klare), Frederick James III, Gretchen McCray. Enlisted U.S. Army, 1942, commd. 2d lt., 1944, advanced through grades to brig. gen., 1969; various assignments U.S. and ETO, 1944-51; regtl. supply officer 504th Airborne Inf., 1951-53; exec. officer, comdg. officer 1st Battalion, 187th Airborne Regtl. Combat Team, Korea, 1953, comdg. officer 2d Battaltion, Beppu, Japan, 1953-55; 1955; intelligence staff officer Army Security Agy., 1956-59; adviser Royal Thai Army Logistics Coll., 1959-61; mem. faculty Army War Coll., 1962-65; dep. chief, then chief force programming div. Office Asst. Chief Staff. Force Devel., Dept. Army, 1965-68; comdg. officer 196th Light Inf. Brigade, Americal Div., Vietnam, 1968-69; dir. manpower and forces, Office Asst. Chief Staff Force Devel., Dept. Army, 1969—. Decorated Silver Star with oak leaf cluster, Legion of Merit with oak leaf cluster, D.F.C., Bronze Star with V device and 2 oak leaf clusters, Air medal with 15 oak leaf clusters, Army Commendation medal, Purple Heart, Combat Inf. badge with 2 stars; Vietnamese Nat. Order Merit and Cross Gallantry with palm. Mem. Assn. U.S. Army, Delta Upsilon. Home: 1515 N Highland St Arlington VA 22201 Office: Dept Army OACSFOR MF Washington DC 20310

KROG, KARIN, singer; b. Oslo, Norway, May 15, 1937; d. Eilif and Ragnhild (Naess) Krog; student of Anne Brown, 1962-68, Ivo Knesvic, 1968-71; m. Johannes Bergh, Sept. 21, 1957; children—Cathrine, Dot. Appearances at internat. jazz festivals at Antibes, 1964, Prague, 1966, Warsaw, 1966, Berlin, 1967, Molde, 1963, 64, 68-71, Kongsberg, 1966-67, 68, Stockholm, 1969, Frankfurt, 1970, World-Expo, Japan, 1970; internat. art festivals at Reckinghausen, 1967, Bergen, 1967, Harstad, 1968, Helsinki, 1970, Chateauvallen, 1970; concerts, TV appearances throughout Europe; State grant study tour USA, 1970; organized Norwegian Jazz musicians Norsk Jazzforum, 1965; recording artist for Philips, Sonet and MPS records. Recipient Downbeat Internat. Jazz Critic poll, 1965, 66, 67, 68, 69, 70. Address: Nobelsgt 35 Oslo 2 Norway

KROGENAS, GEORGE, orgn. exec.; b. N.Y.C., Aug. 3, 1909; s. Daniel and Mary Katherine (Danielsen) K.; B.B.A., Coll. City N.Y., 1939; m. Karen Elizabeth Malmquist, Oct. 2, 1948; 1 son, Robert John. Supr. gen. accounting dept. Borden's Farm Products, 1934-42; asst. comptroller Am. Cancer Soc., N.Y.C., 1946-56, comptroller, 1956-60, v.p., 1960—. Mem. com. for devel. uniform accounting procedures for vol. health agys. Nat. Health Council, 1960—. Committeeman, Boy Scouts Am. Served to lt. col. AUS, 1942-46; ETO. Mem. Am. Mgmt. Assn. Baptist (trustee). Home: 20 Harriet Lane Hungtington NY 11743 Office: 219 E 42d St New York City NY 10017

KROGER, SISTER MARY HONORA, coll. pres.; b. Kansas City, Mo.; A.B., Marygrove Coll., Monroe, Mich., 1922; A.M., U. Notre Dame, 1925; Ph.D., Forham U., 1928; D.Sc. Edn., Wayne U., 1952. Tchr., St. Thomas High Sch., Ann Arbor, Mich., 1916-24. prin., 1924-26; prof. Eglish, Marygrove Coll., Detroit, 1928-31, dean, 1930-37, pres., 1937; now pres. Our Lady of Cincinnati Coll.; speaker in field. Mem. N. Central Assn. Commn. Sch. Higher Edn., 1957-61, Mich. Commn. Tchr. Edn., 1959—. Mem. Sisters, Servants of the Immaculate Heart of Mary Adult Edn. Assn. Am. Am. Assn. Sch. Adminstrs. Contbr. to ednl. jours. Roman Catholic. Address: Our Lady of Cincinnati Coll Edgecliff Walnut Hills Cincinnatti OH 45206

KROGER, WILLIAM MEERS, mag. editor, writer; b. Washington, Oct. 24, 1913; s. Benjamin Joseph and Katherine (Meers) K.; student George Washington U., 1932-33; m. Margaret Elizabeth Hayden, Jan. 1, 1937; children—William Meers, Patricia Anne, Michael Joseph, Jay Paul. Newspaper feature writer Ind. Syndicate, 1933-44; free-lance Washington corr. bus. mags., 1944-45; prodn. editor Aviation News, 1945-47; asst. mng. editor Aviation Week, 1947-52; exec. editor Air Weapons Study Project, 1952-53. Great Lakes news bur. mgr. Bus. Week, 1953-61, marketing editor, 1961-67, asst. mng. editor, 1967-69, sr. editor, 1969—. Founder, treas. Detroit Press Club, 1958-59. Mem. Sigma Delta Chi. Roman Catholic. Contbr. articles mags. Home: 140 Baylor Av Hillsdale NJ 07642 Office: 330 W 42d St New York City NY 10036

KROGH-FLADMARK, WILHELM Norwegian diplomat; b. Oslo, Norway, Mar. 13, 1915; s. Wilhelm and Bergljot (Henricksen) K.-F.; law degree, U. Oslo, 1940; m. Ragnhild Margrethe Andersen, Aug. 21, 1948; children—Kristian, Hilde. Pvt. practice law, govt. service Ministry of Agr., 1942-45; mem. Norwegian Fgn. Service, 1945—; attache Norwegian Legation, Ottawa/Montreal, 1945-47; embassy sec., The Hague, 1947-50; mem. Ministry of Fgn. Affairs, 1950-53; consul, Hong Kong, 1954; 1st embassy sec., Copenhagen, 1955-57; consul, N.Y.C., 1957-62; civil dep. Norwegian Def. Coll., Oslo, 1963-65; head NATO div. and 3d adminstrv. div. Ministry of Fgn. Affairs, 1965-69; consul gen., Chgo., 1969—. Decorated Deltakermedaljen (Norway); officer Orange-Nassau (Netherlands); knight's cross 1st Class Dannebrog (Denmark). Home: 1125 Michigan Av Wilmette IL 60091 Office: 360 N Michigan Av Chicago IL 60601

KROGMAN, WILTON MARION, phys. anthropologist; b. Oak Park, Ill., June 28, 1903; s. Wilhelm Claus and Lydia Magdalena (Wriedt) K.; Ph.B., U. Chgo., 1926, A.M., 1927, Ph.D., 1929; Cleve. Found. fellow in anatomy, Western Res. U., 1928-29; NRC fellow Royal Coll. Surgeons, London, Eng., 1930-31; LL.D., Baylor U., 1955; D.Sc., U. Mich., 1969; m. Virginia Lane, Dec. 22, 1931 (div. 1944); children—Marian Knox, William Lane; m. 2d, Mary H. Winkley, Apr. 18, 1945; children—John Winkley, Mark Austin. Instr. phys. anthropology U. Chgo., 1929-30; asso. prof. anat. and phys. anthropology Western Res. U., 1931-38, U. Chgo., 1938-47; prof. phys. anthropology, div. grad. medicine U. Pa., 1947-71, emeritus, 1971—, former chmn. dept. phys. anthropology; dir. Phila. Center for Research in Child Growth, 1947-71; dir. research Lancaster (Pa.) Cleft Palate Clinic, 1971—; Walker Ames lectr. anthropology U. Wash., summer 1944. Fellow A.A.A.S. (sec., sect. H 1933-44, chmn. 1948-49); mem. Nat. Acad. Scis., Am. Assn. Phys. Anthropologists (past pres.), Soc. Research Child Devel. (past pres.), Phi Beta Kappa, Sigma Xi. Democrat. Specialist in skeletal identification in medico-legal problems; researcher in phys. growth and devel. infant and sch. child. Home: 1127 Spring Grove Av Lancaster PA 17603 Office: 24 N Lime St Lancaster PA 17602

KROL, EDWARD JOSEPH, surgeon; b. Chgo., Apr. 3, 1913; s. Alexander and Mary (Madalinski) K.; B.S., Central YMCA, Chgo., 1936; M.D., Loyola U., Chgo., 1939; m. Anne Estelle Shirvin, Feb. 1, 1942; children—Edwina Ann, Cynthia Lee, Edward Joseph, Gerald John. Extern, Holy Cross Hosp., Chgo., 1938-39, sr. attending surg. staff, 1948—, pres., chief staff, 1957-59, chmn. dept. surgery, 1959-60, co-chmn. dept. surgery, 1961-62, chmn. exec. bd., 1958-61, sec. bd. 1961-62, now mem. exec. bd.; intern St. Elizabeth's Hosp., Chgo., 1939-40; individual practice, Chgo., 1940-42, specializing surgery, 1945—; postgrad. surg. tng. Cook County Postgrad. Sch., Tufts U., U. Ill., Bunt's Inst. of Crile Clinic. Cleve., U. Minn., U. Kan.; clin. asst. surgery Rush Med. Sch., 1940-42; clin. asst. surgery Stritch Sch. Medicine, 1945-50, clin. instr. surgery, 1950—. Mem. Adv. Council to Gov. Ill. Chmn. adv. bd. Immaculata Coll., Chgo., 1955—; trustee Intestinal Research Inst., 1955—; mem. pres.'s council St. Xavier's Coll., Chgo., 1956—; chmn. bd. advisers Shelbourne Center, Valparaiso, Ind., 1960—. Served from lt. to capt. M.C., USAAF, 1942-45. Recipient certificate merit Internat. Acad. Proctology, award merit Dept. Cal. Mil. Order Purple Heart, meritorious service award Clin. Congress Abdominal Surgeons, also Gold medal Achievement, 1962. Diplomate Internat. Bd. Surgery, Am. Bd. Abdominal Surgery (chmn. bd.), Internat. Bd. Applied Nutrition. Fellow Internat. Coll. Surgeons, Am. Soc. Abdominal Surgery (pres. 1965-66), Internat. Acad. Proctology (trustee 1950-55, pres. 1953), Am. Coll. Gastroenterology (pres. 1962-63, bd. trustees 1950-64), Am. Coll. Nutrition, Royal Soc. Medicine, N.Y. Acad. Scis., A.A.A.S., Am. Geriatric Soc., Miss. Valley Med. Soc., A.M.A. (chmn. gen. surg. sect. 1962-63, exec. com. 1962-64), Acad. Psychosomatic Medicine, Internat. Coll. Applied Nutrition (v.p., bd. govs. 1961—), Soc. Acad. Achievement, Internat., Am. colls. angiology; mem. Am. Coll. Chest Physicians, World Med. Assn., Ill. (del.), Chgo. (counsellor) med. socs., Chgo. Path. Soc., Ill. Acad. Sci., Ill. Soc. Med. Research, Am. Nutrition Soc., Assn. Mil. Surgeons, Am. Thoracic Soc., Assn. Am. Med. Colls., Fedn. Am. Scis., Cath. Physicians Guild, Assn. Am. Phys. and Surg., Inst. Medicine Chgo. Clubs: American Sportsmens; Union League (Chgo.). Editorial staff Am. Jour. Abdominal Surgery, 1962; asso. editor Internat. Jour. Applied Nutrition, 1961; contbg. editor surg. sect. Am. Jour. Proctology, 1952—, Modern Nutrition Jour., 1961—. Contbr. numerons articles to med. jours. Office: 4255 W 63d St Chicago IL 60629

KROL, JOHN CARDINAL, archbishop; b. Cleve., Oct. 26, 1910; s. John and Anna (Pietruszka) K.; student St. Mary's Sem., Cleve., 1937; J.C.B., Gregorian U., Rome, 1939, J.C.L., 1940; J.C.D., Cath. U. Am., 1942; LL.D., John Carroll U., 1955; Ph.D., La Salle Coll., 1961; LL.D., St. Joseph Coll., 1961, St. John U., N.Y., 1964, Coll. Steubenville, 1967, Lycoming Meth. Coll., 1966, Temple U., 1964, Bellarmine- Ursuline Coll., 1968, Drexel U., 1970; D.S.T., Villanova U., 1961; L.H.D., Alliance Coll., 1967; D.D., Susquehanna U., 1970. Priest Roman Catholic Ch., 1937, pvt. chamberlain, 1945, domestic prelate 1951; parish asst., 1937-38; prof. Diocesan Sem., also chaplain Jennings Home for Aged, 1942- 43; vice chancellor Cleve. Diocese, 1943-51, chancellor of diocese, 1951- 53, promoter of justice, 1951-53; consecrated bishop, 1953; auxiliary bishop to bishop of Cleve., also vicar gen. Diocese of Cleve., 1953-61; archbishop of Phila., 1961—; elevated to Sacred Coll. fo Cardinals, 1967. Undersec., II Vatican Council, 1962-65; mem. Pontifical Commn. Communications Media, 1964; chmn. Nat. Cath. Office for Radio and Television, 1963-64, Nat. Cath. Office for Motion Pictures, Cath. Communications Found. 1965-70; chmn. Pa. Cath. Conf., 1961—; v.p. Nat. Conf. Cath. Bishops, 1966—; vice chmn. U.S. Cath. Conf., 1966—; mem. Pontifical Commn. for Mass Media Communications, 1966-70; mem. President's Nat. Citizens Com. Community Relations. Trustee Cath. U. Am., Washington, Nat. Shrine of Immaculate Conception, Washington, Cath. League for Religious Assistance to Poland; pres. Center for Applied Research in Apostolate, 1967-70. Decorated comdr. of cross Order of Merit (Italy), Nat. Order Republic of Chad; recipient gold medal Paderwski Found., 1961; Nat. Human Relations award Nat. Conf. Christians and Jews, 1967; Father Sourin award Cath. Philopatrian Inst., 1967; John Wesley Ecumenical award Old St. George's Meth. Ch., 1967. Mem. Canon Law Soc. Am. (pres. 1948-49). Home: 5700 City Av Philadelphia PA 19131 Office: 222 N 17th St Philadelphia PA 19103

KROLIKOWSKI, WALTER PHILIP, educator; b. Chgo., Sept. 9, 1923; s. Benjamin and Mary (Bennett) K.; B.E., Chgo. Tchrs. Coll., 1943; M.A., St. Louis U., 1953; Ph.D., U. Ill., 1965. Mem. Soc. of Jesus, 1946—; ordained priest Roman Catholic Ch., 1957; tchr. U. Detroit High Sch., 1953-54; asst. dean Xavier U., 1959-60; faculty Loyola U., Chgo., 1963—, dean Coll. Arts and Scis., 1964-70, now prof. edn. Address: 6525 N Sheridan Rd Chicago IL 60626

KROLL, BARRY LEWIS, lawyer; b. Chgo., June 8, 1934; s. Harry M. and Hannah (Lewis) K.; A.B. in Psychology with distinction, U. Mich., 1955, J.D. with distinction, 1958; m. Jayna Vivian Leibovitz, June 20, 1956; children—Steven Lee, Joan Lois, Nancy Maxine. Admitted to Ill. bar. 1958, since practiced in Chgo.; asso. firm Epstein, Manilow & Sachnoff. 1966-68, Schiff, Hardin, Waite Dorschel & Britton, 1968-69; partner Wolfberg & Kroll, 1970—; faculty John Marshall Law Sch., Chgo., 1969—; atty. for petitioner in U.S. Supreme Ct. decision Escobedo vs Ill., 1964; guest lectr. before groups, 1964-. Served to capt. AUS, 1959-62. Named Outstanding Young Man Park Forest (Ill.) Jr. C. of C., 1966. Mem. Ill., Chgo. bar assns., Bar Assn. 7th Fed. Circuit, Order of Coif, Tau Epsilon Rho, Alpha Epsilon Pi. Jewish religion (trustee cong. 1966-70, pres. men's club 1965-66). Asst. editor Mich. Law Rev., 1957-58. Home: 314 Gettysburg St Park Forest IL 60466 Office: 10 N Clark St Chicago IL 60602

KROLL, BORIS, textile designer, mfr., distbr.; b. Buffalo, Oct. 11, 1913; s. Nathan and Cecilla Kroll; ed. pub. schs.; m. Lynn Steyert, Mar. 7, 1941; children—Geoffrey, Eric David, Lisa. Pres. Cromwell Designs, Inc., 1938-61; pres. Boris Kroll Fabrics, Inc., 1946—; pres. Boris Kroll Fabrics of Los Angeles, Inc., 1955-64, Boris Kroll Fabrics of Miami, Inc., 1957-64, Boris Kroll Fabrics of Ill., Inc., 1959-64 (cos. merged with Boris Kroll Fabrics, Inc. 1961); pres. Inc., 1954—, Boris Kroll Indsl. Land Corp., 1966- Brois Kroll Fabrics, Inc., 1946—, Boris Kroll Jacquard Looms, Inc., 1954—, Boris Kroll Indsl. Land Corp., 1966- -, 220 East 51st Street Corp., 1950—; pres. Boris Kroll Prints, Inc. 1955-64, Boris Kroll Labs., Inc., 1957-64 (cos. merged with Boris Kroll Jacquard Looms, Inc. 1964). One-man show Seattle Art Mus., 1955, Detoit Inst. Arts, 1962, Purdue U., 1970, Ga. State U., 1970; exhibited World's Fair, N.Y.C., 1939, Good Design exhbn., Mus. Modern Art, 1953, Ford Found. and Govt. of India Handloom Fabrics Survey in India, 1956. Exhibits in permanent collection, Victoria and Albert Mus., London, Decorative Fabric Collection by Designer-Weavers of U.S., 1965, Detroit Inst. Arts, 1966. Vice pres. Resources Council of AID, 1963; mem. jury for Mich. Crafts Show, Detroit Inst. Arts, 1967; SONA adv. com. handicrafts and looms Export Corp. India, Ltd., 1967-70. Served with C.E., AUS, 1943-45. Mem. Decorative Design Assn. (pres. 1958), Am. Crafts Council, Am. Inst. Interior Designers, Nat. Home Fashions League, Nat. Soc. Interior Designers, Am. Assn. for Textile Tech., Color Assn. U.S. (dir. 1967—, chmn. home furnishings color card com. 1968—), Upholstery and Decorative Fabrics Assn. Am. Club: Arts of Chicago. Home: 200 E 57th St New York City NY 10022 Office: 979 3d Av New York City NY 10022

KROLL, LEON, artist; b. N.Y.C., Dec. 6, 1884; s. Marcus Nathaniel and Henrietta (Moss) K.; student Art Student's League, Nat. Acad. Design, N.Y.C.; with Jean Paul Laurens, Paris, France; m. Genevieve Domec, Oct. 18, 1923; 1 dau., Marie-Claude. Portrait, landscape, genre, still-life and mural artist; represented in permanent collections Met. Mus. Art, Detroit Mus., Los Angeles Mus., Art Inst. Chgo., Whitney Mus. Am. Art, Mus. Modern Art, and numerous other pub. and pvt. collections. Recipient over twenty four nat. and internat. awards including First Prize, Carnegie Internat., Pitts., 1936, several gold medals, 5 thousend dollar prizes, Benjamin Altman award landscape painting, 1965. Pres. U.S. Commn., Internat. Assn. Plastic Arts, 1954—. Executed murals in New Justice Bldg., Washington, and other major works in govt. bldgs. and monuments. A.N.A., 1920, N.A., 1927. Mem. several profl. assns., including, Nat. Inst. Arts and Letters, Am. Acad. Arts and Letters (dir. and chmn., art com.), Chevalier Legion of Honor (France). Clubs: Nat. Arts (life) (N.Y.C.); Boston Art (hon.); Friends of Art (hon.) (Balt.). Home: (summer and studio) Folly Cove Gloucester MA 01930 Address: 15 W 67th St New York City NY 10023

KROLL, NORMAN MYLES K., educator, physicist; b. Tulsa, Apr. 6, 1922; s. Cornelius and Grace (Aaronson) K.; student Rice Inst., 1938-40; A.B., Columbia, 1942, A.M., 1943, Ph.D., 1948; m. Sally Sharlot, Mar. 15, 1945; children—Linda Ruth, Cynthia Anne, Heather Roma, Ira Joseph. Mem. faculty of Columbia 1942-62, successively asst. in physics, asst. prof., asso. prof., prof., 1954-62, sci. staff Radiation Lab., 1943-62; prof. physics U. Cal. at San Diego, 1962—, chmn. physics dept., 1963-65; mem. Inst. Advanced Study, 1948-49; vis. scientist Brookhaven Nat. Lab., summers 1952-55. NRC fellow, 1948-50, Guggenheim fellow, 1955-56, Fulbright scholar, U. Rome, 1955-56; NSF sr. postdoctoral fellow, 1965-66. Fellow Am. Phys. Soc.; mem. Phi Beta Kappa, Sigma Xi. Author articles field. Bd. editors Jour. Math. Physics, 1966-68. Home: 2457 Calle del Oro La Jolla CA 92037

KROLL, ROBERT JAMES, educator; b. Cin., May 1, 1928; s. Joseph Henry and Mary Ann (Wefer) K.; B.S. in Aero. Engring., U. Cin., 1949, M.S., 1956; Ph.D., Mich. State U., 1962; m. Marilyn Ann Wolfer, Aug. 21, 1954; children—Stephen, Kenneth, Gregory, James, Thomas. Engr., Polak Steel Co., Cin., 1949-1951; sr. engr. Gen. Electric Co., 1952-57; faculty U. Cin., 1957—, prof. aerospace engring. dept., acting head, 1970—. Cons. to industry. Active local Boy Scouts Am. Served to ensign USNR, 1951-52. NSF sci. faculty fellow, 1961-62. Recipient Dolly Cohen award excellence univ. teaching U. Cin., 1968. Registered profl. engr., Ohio. Asso. fellow Am. Inst. Aeros. and Astronautics; Mem. Am. Soc. Engring. Edn., Soc. Exptl. Stress Analysis, Aircraft Owners and Pilots Assn., Sigma Xi, Phi Sigma Phi, Sigma Gamma Tau. Home: 6277 Oakcreek Dr Cincinnati OH 45239

KROLL, WILLIAM, violinist; b. N.Y.C., Jan. 30, 1901; s. Adolph and Fanny (Braham) K.; student Royal Acad., Berlin, Germany, 1911-14, Inst. Mus. Art, N.Y.C., 1917-22; m. Pearl Freeman, June 7, 1922; 1 dau., Barbara. Debut in N.Y.C., 1915; violinist with Elshuco Trio, 1923-29; 1st violinist with Coolidge Quartet, 1935-45; founder Kroll Quartet, 1945; tchr. violin and chamber music Mannes Coll. Music, N.Y.C., 1943—, Peabody Conservatory, Balt., 1947-65; co-head chamber music Tanglewood, Berkshire Music Center, 1949—; head string dept. Cleve. Conservatory Music, 1965-68; prof. violin Queens Coll., 1969—; soloist with orchs., U.S., Europe; soloist with Nat. Symphony Orch., White House, 1966. Recipient Coolidge medal Library of Congress, 1942. Club: Bohemians (N.Y.C.). Composer violin and chamber music. Address: 50 W 67th St New York City NY 10023

KROMBEIN, KARL VONVORSE, entomologist; b. Buffalo, May 26, 1912; s. Louis Henry and Gertrude (Hoeffler) K.; student Carnegie Inst. Tech., 1929-31, Canisius Coll., 1931-32; B.S., Cornell U., 1934, M.A., 1935, Ph.D., 1960; m. Dorothy Carpenter Buckingham, Dec. 11, 1942; childrn—Kristin, Kyra (Mrs. John W. Walker), Karlissa. Research entomologist Bur. Entomology and Plant Quarantine, Dept. Agr., 1941-51, investigations leader Insect Identification and Parasite Introduction Research br., 1951-65; chmn. dept. entomology Smithsonian Instn., Washington, 1965-71, sr. entomologist, 1971—; cons. to surgeon gen. USAF, 1959—. Served from 1st lt. to maj. AUS, 1942-46; PTO; col. USAF Res. Decorated Air Force Commendation medal; Chief Biomed. Scientist. Grantee Am. Philos. Soc., 1952, 55, 59, NSF, 1963. Fellow Entomol. Soc. Am. (governing bd. 1970—); mem. Societe Entomologigue d'Egypte (hon.), Washington Biologists Field Club (pres.), Entomol. Soc. Washington (past pres., past editor), A.A.A.S. (councillor 1970—), Biol. Soc. Washington, Sigma Xi, Sigma Phi Epsilon. Unitarian. Clubs: Cosmos (Washington); Explorers (N.Y.C.). Author, editor: (with others) Hymenoptera of America North of Mexico-Synoptic Catalog, 1951. Author: Trapnesting Wasps and Bees: Life Histories, Nests and Associates, 1967. Contbr. articles profl. jours. Home: 3026 John Marshall Dr Arlington VA 22207 Office: Smithsonian Instn Washington DC 20560

KROMHOUT, ROBERT ANDREW, educator; b. Elgin, Ill., Oct. 23, 1923; s. Andrew and Sarah (Tiffany) K.; B.S., Kan. State U., 1947; M.S., U. Ill., 1948, Ph.D., 1952; m. Ora Morlier, Dec. 21, 1950; children—Sharon, Brian, Ethan. Asst. prof. U. Ill., 1952-56; asst. prof. Fla. State U., Tallahassee, 1956-58, asso. prof., 1958-62, head dept. physics, 1959-62, prof. physics, 1962—; cons. Recon, Inc. Served with AUS, 1943-46. Mem. Am. Physics Soc., Am. Assn. Physics Tchrs., A.A.A.S., Sigma Xi, Phi Kappa Phi. Home: 206 Westminster Dr Tallahassee FL 32304

KROMM, FRANKLIN HERBERT, Jr., newspaper syndicate exec.; b. Ft. Wayne, Ind., Sept. 12, 1910; s. Franklin H. and Lena Bee (McKenzie) K.; grad. Central Cath. High, Internat. Accounting Sch.; m. Mildred C. Hershberger, Aug. 28, 1930; 1 son, Donald Eugene. Telephone maintenance Dudio Mfg. Co., 1928-29; salesman, 1930-33; pres. Kromm Trucking Co., 1933-36; gen. mgr. Frosty Cove Ice Cream Co., 1937-39; accountant, office mgr. McKinley Trucking Co., 1939-46; gen. mgr. Hopkins Syndicate, Inc., 1946—. Mem. Boy Scouts Am. (exec. local council), Hillsboro Bus. Men's Assn. and Civic Group; v.p., treas. Sci. Marriage Found., 1956—. Pres. trustees, Hillsboro, Ind., 1951—. Republican. Roman Catholic. K.C. Home: Coal Creek Av Hillsboro IN 47949 Office: Hopkins Bldg Mellott IN 47958

KRON, ARTHUR ADAM, advt. exec.; b. Union City, N.J., Feb. 7, 1901; s. Charles J. and Lillian (Wick) K.; A.A. in Bus. Adminstrn., N.Y. Inst., 1926; LL.D., Fairleigh Dickinson U., 1957; m. Ruth Mandeville Snyder, June 26, 1926; children—Arthur Adam, Constance Ruth (Mrs. Robert E. DeMott). With Gotham-Vladimir Advt., Inc., 1916-66, exec. v.p., mng. dir., 1950-58, pres., treas., 1958-60, chmn. bd., 1960-66; vice chmn. bd. Van Brunt & Co., Advt. Marketing, Inc., N.Y.C., 1966—; chmn. bd. Bus. Publs. Audit of Circulation, Inc., 1955-56; pres. Office Certified Circulation, Inc., 1957-62. Chmn. No. Valley chpt. A.R.C., 1950-57, mem. Eastern adv. council, 1955-58; pres. Englewood (N.J.) Hosp., 1957-66. Pres. N.J. Partners of Alliance. Trustee, Fairleigh Dickinson U., Rutherford, N.J.; bd. dirs. Am. Hosp., Istanbul, Turkey; chmn. Allied Services Orgn. Group Ins. Fund, 1957-60; chmn. bd. Bergen Jr. Coll.; bd. advisers Valparaiso (Ind.) U. Recipient Man of Year World-Wide award Internat. Advt. Assn., 1958. Mem. Internat. Advt. Conv. (founder), Internat. Advt. Assn. (pres. 1948- 49, chmn. N.Y. chpt. 1959-60, chmn. regional export expansion com. 1960- 61). Republican. Rotarian (pres. N.Y. 1969-70). Home: 581 Northumberland Rd Teaneck NJ 07666 Office: 711 3d Av New York City NY 10017

KRON, GERALD EDWARD, astronomer; b. Milw., Apr. 6, 1913; s. Edmund and Letty (Dietrich) K.; B.S., U. Wis., 1933, M.S., 1934; Ph.D., U. Cal., 1938; m. Katherine Carson Gordon, Apr. 22, 1946; children—Donald Gordon, Richard, Jenny, Virginia, Charles. Profl. astronomer Lick Obs., U. Cal., 1938-65; dir. U.S. Naval Obs., Flagstaff, Ariz., 1965- -; pure research in astrophysics, photoelec. photometry of eclipsing variable stars, devel. of improved methods of measuring faint radiation especially in infrared. Served with AUS, 1941-46. Mem. Am. Astron. Soc., Astron. Soc. Pacific. Developed astron. image tubes. Home: 416 N Bertrand St Flagstaff AZ 86001 Office: US Naval Obs PO Box 1149 Flagstaff AZ 86001

KRON, JOSEPH, food co. exec.; b. 1912; m. With Tom Borman interests, 1944—; treas. Lucky Stores, Inc. 1948-56; with subsidiaries Borman Food Stores, Inc., 1953-56, with Borman, Inc., 1956—, became v.p., 1963, exec. v.p., mgr. store operations, 1963, now chmn. bd., dir.; pres. Yankee Distbr., Inc., subsidiary. Office: 12300 Mark Twain Av Detroit MI 28227*

KRONAUER, CLIFFORD JOHN, Jr., air force officer; b. El Paso, Tex., Aug. 10, 1920; s. Clifford John and Linne Cox (Rhode) K.; grad. N.M. Mil Inst., 1940; S.B., Mass. Inst. Tech., 1951, S.M. in Aero. Engring., 1952; m. Charlotte Marie Quint, July 3, 1941; children—Donna (Mrs. Howard O. Sharpe, Jr.), Margaret, Mark, Laura, Carolyn, Brad. Commd. 2d lt. USAAF, 1941, advanced through grades to maj. gen., 1969; asst. dir. def. research and engring. Office Sec. Def., Washington, 1964-67; comdr. Air Force Western Test Range, Vanderberg AFB, Cal., 1967-70; chief staff Air Force Systems Command, Washington, 1970—. Decorated D.S.M., Legion of Merit, Air medal. Home: 8124 N Loop Dr El Paso TX 79907 Office: Hdqrs Air Force Systems Command Andrews AFB MD 20331

KRONE, GERALD SIDNEY, theatrical producer; b. Memphis, Feb. 25, 1933; s. Irving and Eva (Sauer) K.; A.B. cum laude, Washington U., St. Louis, 1954, A.M., 1958; student Oxford (Eng.) U., 1954; m. Dorothy Rhoda Olim, Apr. 4, 1965 (div. Feb. 1970). Mem. drama faculty Washington U., 1956-58; dir. St. Louis Opera Soc., 1956-58; actor in Blood Wedding, N.Y.C., 1958; TV dir., St. Louis, 1957- 58; dir. No Trifling with Love, N.Y.C., 1959, A Worm in Horseradish, 1961; gen. mgr. Saranac Lake (N.Y.) Summer Theatre, 1960; lectr. theatre mgmt., N.Y.C., 1963-65; asso. producer St. John Terrell's Music Circus, Lambertville, N.Y., 1964-68; asst. project dir. Title III Theatrical Demonstration Program, Hunterdon County, N.J., 1968-69; motion picture cons., N.Y.C., 1967—; theatrical producer in N.Y.C. with prodns. I Must Be Talking to My Friends, 1967, No Trifling with Love, 1959, A Worm in Horseradish, 1961, The Golden Apple, 1963, The Lion in Love, 1963, Pimpernel, 1965; pres. Krone-Olim Advt. Inc., 1968-70, Krone-Olim Mgmt., Inc., 1961-70; founder, adminstrv. dir. The Negro Ensemble Co., 1967-71; cons. in field, 1963—; motion picture producer The Inheritors, Rome, Italy, 1971. Served with AUS, 1954-56. Recipient Drama Desk award, 1968, Vernon Rice award, 1968, Obie award, 1968, Brandeis U. award, 1969, Tony award, 1969, Premio Roma, 1969. Mem. League Off- Broadway Theatres and Producers (sec.-treas. 1967-71), Assn. Theatrical Press Agts. and Mgrs. Home: 588 West End Av New York City NY 10024 Office: 1545 Broadway New York City NY 10036

KRONE, HELMUT, advt. exec.; b. N.Y.C., July 16, 1925; s. Otto and Emilie (Lohr) K.; student New Sch. Social Research, 1946-48; student graphic journalism with Alexi Brodovitch, 1946-48; m. Irene Beckmann, Nov. 14, 1970; children—Peter, Lisa, Eric, Mark. With Doyle Dane Bernbach, Inc., N.Y.C., 1954-69, sr. v.p., dir., spl. projects, 1966-69; partner Case and Krone, Inc., N.Y.C., 1969—; works included in Am. Inst. Graphic Arts 50 Best Advertisements in past 15 yrs; rep. in The 100 Best Advertisements, 1959; created Volkswagen and Avis campaigns. Served with USNR, 1943-46; PTO. Recipient 7 N.Y. Art Dirs. Club medals. Mem. Am. Inst. Graphic Arts, Irish Georgian Soc. Home: 1 E 62d St New York City NY 10021 Office: 4 W 58th St New York City NY 10019

KRONE, RALPH W., educator, physicist; b. Berlin, Germany, May 18, 1919; s. Oscar A. and Kate (Deutsch) K.; came to U.S., 1937; B.S., Antioch Coll., 1942; M.S., U. Ill., 1943; Ph.D., Johns Hopkins, 1949; m. Sara Jane Rasely, Dec. 26, 1942; children—Michael L., Royanna, Christopher A. Physicist, NACA, 1944-45; instr. U. Kan., Lawrence, 1948, asst. prof., 1949-54, asso. prof., 1955-60, prof., 1961—, acting chmn. dept. physics, 1965-66; prin. investigator AEC Research Project, 1957—. Fellow Am. Phys. Soc. Home: 501 Rockledge Rd Lawrence KS 66044

KRONEN, LEIF CHRISTIAN, metal co. exec., lawyer; b. Sioux City, Ia., Apr. 6, 1914; s. Lars C. and Anna (Running) K.; B.S., Neb. Wesleyan U., 1936; J.D. cum laude, U. Neb., 1968; m. Maxine Scott, June 13, 1939; children—Janet Kay (Mrs. Albert D. Bowers), Eric Scott, Linda Christine. Admitted to Neb. bar, 1940, N.Y. bar, 1967; law clk. to judge U.S. Ct. Appeals 8th Circuit, Kansas City, Mo., 1941; br. chief counsel OPA, Washington, 1942-46; individual practice law, Lexington, Neb., 1946-47; sec. Tanners Council Am., Inc., N.Y.C., 1947-62; atty. Gen. Elec. Co., Richland, Wash., 1962-65; sec., counsel Handy & Harman, N.Y.C., 1965—; sec., dir. Handy & Harman of Can., Ltd., Handy & Harman Tube Co., Inc. Mem. Am., N.Y., Neb. bar assns., Am. Soc. Corporate Secs., Order of Coif, Blue Key, Zeta Psi. Club: Scarsdale (N.Y.) Golf. Spl. cons. on leather Webster's 3d New Internat. Dictionary, 1961. Home: 5 Old Lane Scarsdale NY 10583 Office: 850 3d Av New York City NY 10022

KRONENBERG, HENRY HAROLD, educator; b. South Haven, Minn., Dec. 17, 1902; s. Joseph and Julia Augusta (Block) K.; A.B., Ill. Coll., Jacksonville, 1926; A.M., U. Ill. (fellow in edn. 1928-30), 1929; Ph.D., U. Minn. (Carnegie fellow 1931-34), 1935; m. Miriam Eloise Clark, Sept. 2, 1931; children—Henry Harold, Paula Elaine. Rural sch. teacher, Parshall, N.D., 1920-22; high sch. teacher, Kewanee, Ill., 1926-28; vis. prof. Neb. State Tchrs. Coll., Peru, 1930-31; mem. faculty U. Ark., 1934- -, prof. edn., 1944—, dean Coll. Edn., 1945-70, dean emeritus, 1970—, dir. summer sessions, 1945-70. Recipient Smith prize in math. Ill. Coll. 1924. Mem. Kappa Delta Pi, Phi Delta Kappa, Tau Kappa Alpha, Phi Alpha Theta. Presbyn. Lion. Author: Principles of Secondary Education, 1941, rev. edits., 1965, 70; Workbook and Manual to Accompany Beard and Beard's The Making of American Civilization, 1937. Editor Programs and Units in the Social Studies, 1941. Home: 1420 Rosemont St Route 9 Fayetteville AR 72701 Office: U of Ark Fayetteville AR 72701

KRONENBERGER, LOUIS, writer, critic; b. Cin., Dec. 9, 1904; s. Louis and Mabel (Newwitter) K.; student U. Cin., 3 years, Litt.D.; m. Emmy L. Plaut, Jan. 29, 1940; children—John, Elizabeth (Mrs. George A. Wanklyn). Editor, Boni & Liveright, 1926-33, Alfred A. Knopf, Inc., 1933- 35; editorial staff Fortune, 1936-38; drama critic Time, 1938-61; drama critic for PM, 1940-48; lectr. English, Columbia, 1950-51; Brandeis lectr., 1951-53, prof. theatre arts, librarian Brandeis U., Waltham, Mass., 1953-70; A. Lawrence Lowell vis. prof. Harvard, 1959; vis. lectr. Oxford U., Eng., 1959; Christian Gauss Seminar lectr. Princeton, 1961; adj. prof. English, Columbia, 1959; vis. prof. English, Stanford, 1963; Regents prof. U. Cal. at Berkeley, 1968; dir. Corp. Yaddo. Guggenheim fellow, 1969. Authors League Am. Fellow Am. Acad. Arts and Scis.; mem. Nat. Inst. Arts and Letters, Jewish religion. Clubs: Century Assn. (N.Y.C.); St. Botolph (Boston); Athenaeum (London). Author: The Grand Manner (novel), 1929; Kings and Desperate Men, 1942; Grand Right and Left (novel), 1952; The Thread of Laughter: Chapters on English Stage Comedy, 1952; Company Manners, 1954; The Republic of Letters, 1955; A Month of Sundays, 1961; The Cart and Horse, 1964; numerous articles in mags. Editor: An Anthology of Light Verse, 1934; An 18th Century Miscellany, 1936; The Viking Portable Reader's Companion, 1945; The Pleasure of Their Company, 1946; Portable Johnson and Boswell, 1947; G.B.S.: A Survey, 1953; The Maxims of La Rouchefoucauld, 1937. Contbr. to After the Genteel Tradition, 1937; Books that Changed Our Mind, 1939; Selected Works of Alexander Pope, 1948; Robinson Crusoe, 1948; Don Juan, 1949; Pride and Prejudice, 1950; Best Play Series, 1953-62; Marlborough's Duchess, 1958; Plays of G.B. Shaw, 1958; Novelists on Novelists, 1962; Plays of Oscar Wilde, 1962; Sense and Sensibility, 1962; Emma, 1963; The Great World (Greville's Memoirs 1814-1860), 1963; Hamlet, 1964; Quality: Its Image in the Arts, 1969; The Polished Surface, 1969; No Whippings, No Gold Watches, 1970; The Cutting Edge, 1970. Gen. editor: Great Letters Series: Masters of World Literature Series; co-editor: The Viking Book of Aphorisms, 1962; editor: Atlantic Brief Lives: A Biographical Companion to the Arts, 1971. Contbr. to The State of the Nation, 1965; staff contbr. Atlantic Monthly. Home: 1514 Beacon St Brookline MA 02146 also St Andrews New Brunswick Canada

KRONER, JOSEF, actor; b. Staskov, Czechoslovakia, Mar. 20, 1924; s. Ludvig and Maria (Matte) K.; ed. in Czechoslovakia; m. Teresia Hurbanova, June 2, 1950; 1 dau., Zuzanna. Appearances with Slovakian Town Theatre in Professor Poleshajev, Othello, Tartuffe, Phillip A. appearances with Slovak Nat. Theatre in Dr. Galen, White Illness, View of the Bridge, Dauphine, Saint Joan. Served with Czechosolovakian Army, 1945-47. Recipient State prize for acting. Mem. Slovak Actors Orgn. Home: 42 Kosicka St Bratislava Czechoslovakia Office: 21 Gorkeho St Bratislava Czechoslovakia

KRONER, LAWRENCE ROY, hosp. supt.; b. Watseka, Ill., July 19, 1921; s. Roy and Minnie (Trumble) K.; A.B., George Washington U., 1951, M.D., 1955; m. Virginia Louise Connon, Sept. 21, 1962; children—Lawrence Roy, Sharon Lynn, Eric Stephen, Amy Louise, Charles Clifford. Intern, George Washington U. Hosp., 1955-56; psychiatry and child psychiatry resident Western Psychiat. Insts. and Clinics, Pitts., 1956-60; staff psychiatrist Warren (Pa.) State Hosp., 1960-61; asst. supt. Murdoch Center, Butner, N.C., 1961-65; supt. Laurelton (Pa.) State Sch. and Hosp., 1965-70; instr. child psychiatry U. Pitts. Sch. Medicine, 1960-61, Duke Sch. Medicine, 1961-65; adj. prof. spl. edn. Pa. State U., 1965-70. Dir., SUNCOM Industries, Inc. Mem. adv. com. Child Welfare Services Union County, Lewisburg, Pa. Bd. dirs. Union County United Fund. Served with USNR, 1942-49. Mem. Am. Assn. Mental Deficiency, Am. Psychiat. Assn., Nu Sigma Nu. Presbyn. (elder). Address: 38 N 2d St Lewisburg PA 17837

KRONHEIM, MILTON STANLEY, corp., exec.; b. Washington, Oct. 2, 1888; s. Jacob and Judith (Benzinger) K.; ed. pub. schs., Washington; m. Meryl Goldsmith, Oct. 3, 1909; children—Milton Stanley, Judith E. Pres. Milton S. Kronheim & Co. Inc., Washington, The Kronheim Co., Balt.; dir. Madison Nat. Bank, Washington, Bd. dirs. Washington Better Bus. Bur. Bd. dirs. Boys Club, Big Brothers, Mt. St. Agnes Coll., Linwood Children's Center. Recipient Man of Year award Nat. Conf. Christians and Jews, 1960, Heart of Gold award Variety Club, 1962. Democrat. Mason (Shriner), Elk. Club: Optimist. Home: Mayflower Hotel Washington DC 20036 Office: 2900 V St NE Washington DC 20018

KRONKE, WALTER CHRISTIAN, utility exec.; b. Bklyn., Dec. 10, 1912; s. Christian and Anna (Dreves) K.; B.S. magna cum laude, N.Y. U., 1933. Accountant, Standard Oil Co., (N.J.), 1934-43; with Consol. Natural Gas Co., N.Y.C., 1943—, asst. treas., 1958-61, treas., 1962—, v.p., 1971—, also dir. Served to capt. AUS, 1943-46. C.P.A., N.Y. Mem. N.Y. State Soc. C.P.A.'s, Am. Gas Assn., Am. Finance Assn., Newcomen Soc. N.Am., Beta Gamma Sigma. Lutheran. Clubs: Economic Bankers (N.Y.C.): University (Pitts.). Home: 45 Hillpark Av Great Neck NY 11021 Office: 30 Rockefeller Plaza New York City NY 10020

KRONMAN, MARTIN JESSE, educator, biochemist, b. N.Y.C., Sept. 30, 1927; s. Abraham and Bertha (Spiegler) K.; B.S., Rutgers U., 1950; Ph.D., Temple U., 1955; m. Mary E. Whitney, Apr. 21, 1965; children—Betsy, Emlyn, David. Head Biochemistry lab., pioneering div. U.S. Army, Natick, Mass., 1961-68; asso. prof. biochemistry Upstate Med. Center, State U. N.Y., Syracuse, 1968—. Mem. Am. Chem. Soc. (award research milk proteins 1968), A.A.A.S., Am. Soc. Biol. Chemists, Sigma Xi. Home: 100 Dewitt Rd Syracuse NY 13210

KRONSTADT, ARNOLD MAYO, community and archtl. planner; b. Bklyn., July 28, 1919; s. Joseph and Sara (Golden) K.; student City Coll. N.Y., 1937-40; B. Mech. Engring., George Washington U., 1945; postgrad. in city and regional planning Cath. U. Am., 1966-71; m. Harriet Jullian Dearth, July 25, 1964; childrenby previous marriage—Janet Ellen (Mrs. Richard Rosen), Barbara Ann (Mrs. Paul Fourt), John Arnold. Engr., U.S. Naval Gun Factory, 1941-45, engr. charge Gage Labs., 1942-52; chief engr. and planner Carl M. Freeman Asso., Inc., Washington, 1952-56; cons. engr. and planner, Washington, 1956-57; sr. partner Collins & Kronstadt, architects, planners and engrs., Silver Spring, Md., 1957—; dir. Carl M. Freeman Assos., Inc., Mathews-Phillips, Inc., Pitts.; professorial lectr. Am. U. Sch. Bus. Adminstrn., Cath. U. Am. Sch. Architecture; cons. in field. Chmn. Montgomery County (Md.) Low and Middle Income Housing Commn., 1967- -, Montgomery County Tech. Adv. Com., 1954—, Bldg. Codes Com. Prince Georges County, Md., 1956—; mem. spl. constrn. standards com. schs., Montgomery County, 1959—; mem. Adv. Com. Planning and Zoning Law Study Commn. Md., 1968—; mem. Md. Planning Commn., 1969—; bldg. research adv. bd. Nat. Acad. Scis., 1955- -. Recipient award of merit A.I.A., 1965; award excellence architecture for Rossmoor Leisure World, Md., Met Washington Bd. Trade, 1965; award excellence architecture for Sursum Corda, Met. Washington Bd. Trade, 1969; Honor award for Sursum Corda, Dept. Housing and Urban Devel., 1970; A.I.P. Nat. award of merit for Columbia (Md.) Interfaith, 1970. Mem. Prince Georges, Montgomery County engring. socs., Suburban Md. Bldg. Assn., Met. Home Builders Washington. Unitarian. Clubs: Sycamore Island Canoe, Potomac Appalachian Trail (Washington); Plantation (Hilton, S.C.). Author: What Builders Should Know About Garden Apartments, 1959. Home: 3 Pooks Hill Rd Bethesda MD 20034 also 5 Lighthouse Rd Hilton Head SC 29928 Office: 1111 Spring St Silver Spring MD 20910

KRONZER, WALTER JAMES, lawyer; b. Mpls., Feb. 22, 1920; s. Walter James and Lillian (McLaughlin) K.; LL.B. with honors, U. Tex., 1943; m. Dorothy Barfield, Aug. 23, 1947; children—Walter James III, Kimberlee. Admitted to Tex. bar, 1943, since practiced in Houston; asso. firm Blades, Chiles, Moore & Kennerly, 1943-46, Helm & Jones, 1948-51; partner firm Brown, Kronzer, Abraham, Watkins & Steely, 1951—. Vis. lectr. U. Tex. Sch. Law, 1955—, U. Houston Sch. Law, 1960—; lectr. on tort and appellate law, 1955—. Adv. com. Tex. Supreme Ct., 1965—. Bd. dirs. Tex. Bill Rights Found.; bd. visitors Sch. Law, So. Meth. U. Research fellow Southwestern Legal Found. Fellow Am. Coll. Trial Lawyers; mem. Internat. Acad. Trial Lawyers, Houston Bar Assn. (pres. 1965-66), Houston Legal Found. (pres. 1966-67, trustee), Houston Trial Lawyers Assn. (pres. 1955-56), State Bar Tex. (grievance com. 1963-66), U. Tex. Law Sch. Assn. (pres. 1969-71), Order of Coif, Phi Delta Phi. Contbr. legal texts and jours. Home: 12 Gage Ct Houston, TX 77024 Office: Houston 1st Savs Bank Bldg Houston TX 77002

KROOTH, DAVID LOUIS lawyer; b. Chicago, Ill., July 15, 1907; s. Louis and Fannie (Wolf) K.; student Crane Jr. Coll., 1925-26; Ph.B., U. of Chicago, 1928, J.D., 1930; m. Molly Rand, April 8, 1933; children—Dorothy, John David. Admitted to Ill. Bar, 1930, Ct. Appeals for 7th Circuit, 1931, U.S. Supreme Ct., 1936, Ct. Appeals for D.C., 1947; in private practice, Chgo., 1930-33; counsel Fed. Emergency Adminstrn. of Pub. Works, Washington, D.C., 1933- 37; asso. gen. counsel U.S. Housing Authority, 1937-42; gen. counsel Fed. Pub. Housing Authority and Def. Homes Corp., 1942-46; gen. counsel Nat. Housing Agy. and Nat. Housing Expediter, 1946; mem. Washington law firm, Krooth and Altman; pres. Nat. Housing Conf., 1950, chmn. bd. dirs., 1951, chmn. legislative policy com.; mem. Consumer Interest Adv. Com. FHA, 1951-62; chmn. Housing Legislation Information Service, a pub. service clearing house for nat. orgns.; mem. Housing Finance Mission to Chile, ICA, 1958; head coop. housing team to Honduras, AID, 1963. Mem. Washington Bd. Trade, Am. (chmn. com. on housing and urban renewal sect. local govt. law 1962—, chmn. council sect. local govt. law 1970), D.C. bar assns., Nat. Assn. Housing and Redevel. Ofcls., Nat. Housing Conf., Nat. Assembly for Social Policy and Devel., Phi Beta Kappa, Order of Coif. Club: Woodmont Country. Contbg. editor on current decisions Jour. Housing. Home: 540 N St SW Washington DC 20024 Office: 1001 15th St NW Washington DC 20005

KROPF, ALLEN, educator; b. N.Y.C., Oct. 3, 1929; s. Samuel and Sophie (Hilowitz) K.; B.S., Queens Coll., 1951; Ph.D., U. Utah, 1954; m. Rita Berliner, Sept. 7, 1950; children—Noel, Julie, Aaron. Chemist, Applied Physics Lab., Johns Hopkins, Silver Springs, Md., 1954-56; research fellow Harvard, 1956-58; instr. Amherst Coll., 1958-59, asst. prof., 1959-62, asso. prof., 1962-67, prof., 1967—. Mem. A.A.A.S., Sigma Xi, Phi Beta Kappa. Research primary chem. processes of vision. Home: 50 Mt Pleasant St Amherst MA 01002

KROPF, RICHARD THOMAS, textile and chem. mfr.; b. Chgo., Oct. 12, 1909; s. Oscar A. and Edith A. (Anderson) K.; B.S., Mass. Inst. Tech., 1931; m. Marjorie K. Champlain, Oct. 21, 1937; children—Pamela M., Dana A., Christopher B. With Belding Heminway Co., Inc., N.Y.C., 1931—, dir. research, 1941-49, v.p., 1949-61, pres., 1961—, chief exec. officer, 1963—, also dir. Sci. cons. tech. indsl. intelligence com. Q.M. Gen.; chmn. Adv. Com. on Textiles, Apparel and Research. Recipient of Harold DeWitt Smith Medal. Mem. Textile Research Inst. (chmn., treas., trustee), Am. Soc. Testing Materials (pres.), Fiber Soc. (pres.), N.Y. Acad. Scis., Textile Inst., A.A.A.S., Am. Chem. Soc., Am. Phys., Soc., Am. Statis. Assn., Soc. Exptl. Stress Analysis, Am. Assn. Textile Tech. (recipient 1st Bronze medal), Tau Beta Pi. Sewing thread author and editor Textile Ency., 1959—. Home: Laurel Hill W Brother Dr Greenwich CT 06830 Office: 1407 Broadway New York City NY 10018

KROPOTKIN, IGOR NICHOLAS, pub. co. exec.; b. Russia, May 2, 1918; s. Nicholas and Tamara (Maximovitch) K.; came to U.S., 1927, naturalized, 1932; student Columbia, N.Y. U.; m. Marjorie Albohn, Feb. 16, 1947; children—Valerie, Michael. With Charles Scribner's Sons, N.Y.C., 1941—, dir., 1957—, v.p., 1960-67, sr. v.p., 1967—; pres. Scribner Book Stores, Inc., 1970—. Pres., Am. Booksellers Assn., 1962-64, chmn. bd., 1964—; adv. com. internat. book programs State Dept., 1962—; steering com. Nat. Library Week, 1962—; mem. Nat. Book Com., 1970—. Trustee, Princeton Store. Mem. Booksellers League N.Y. (pres.). Club: Columbia (N.Y.C.). Home: 20-15 Halstead Terrace Fair Lawn NJ 07410 Office: 597 Fifth Av New York City NY 10017

KROSBY, H. PETER, educator; b. Vollebekk, Norway, Mar. 3, 1929; s. Peter and Anna Elisabeth (Laganger) K.; B.A., U. B.C., 1955, M.A., 1958; Ph.D., Columbia, 1967; m. Maureen Elizabeth Phelan, Nov. 25, 1953; children—Peter J., Anne E., Kristin M., Karen S., Jane I. Came to U.S., 1958. Instr. Fairleigh Dickinson U., 1959-62; from instr. to asso. prof. history and Scandinavian studies U. Wis., 1962-68; prof. history State U. N.Y. at Albany, 1968—, chmn. dept., 1968-71; vis. lectr. Columbia, 1961; vis. prof. U. Md., 1968, U. Minn., 1970-71. Served with Norwegian Army, 1948-49. Ford Found. fgn. area tng. fellow Columbia, 1958-59; hon. fellow in Finland, Am.-Scandinavian Found., 1962, Luthgow Osborne lectr., 1966-67. Mem. Am. Hist. Assn., Soc. Advancement Scandinavian Studies (adv. com. 1968-72), Am-Scandinavian Found. Author: Nikkelidiplomatiaa Petsamossa 1940-41, 1966; Suomen valinta 1941, 1967; Finland, Germany and the Soviet Union, 1940-41; The Petsamo Dispute, 1968; Empire and Nations: Essays in Honour of Frederic H. Soward, 1969. Home: 1001 Red Pine Dr Schenectady NY 12303 Office: Dept History State Univ NY Albany NY 12203

KROSS, ANNA MOSCOWITZ, city ofcl.; b. Neshves, Russia; d. Mayer and Ester (Drazen) Moscowitz; student Columbia, 1907; LL.B., N.Y. U., 1910, LL.M. 1911; LL.D., Western Coll. for Women, 1954, N.Y. U., 1956; L.H.D., L.I. U., 1962; D. Hebrew Lit., Hebrew Union Coll., 1965; m. Isidor Kross, Apr. 15, 1917; children—Helen (Mrs. Howard Golden), Alice (Mrs. Marvin Frankel), Esther Lee (dec.). Admitted to N.Y. Bar, 1912; apptd. to Office of Corp. Counsel, assigned to family ct., N.Y.C., 1918-23; bench as magistrate, 1933-53, organized, presiding magistrate Home Term Ct., 1946. Commr. correction, N.Y.C., 1954-66; founded Wayward Minor Ct. now known as Girls' Term Ct. Recipient of many citations, awards, certificates, plaques from civic, bus. orgns., 1945—; citation USAF for great contbns. rehab.; 1st Ann. Eleanor Roosevelt Meml. award Women's Nat. Press Club, 1964. Mem. Am. Law Inst., Am. Bar Assn., Assn. Bar City N.Y., Nat. Assn. Women Lawyers, Nat. Fedn. Bus. and Profl. Women's Clubs. Inc., N.Y. County Lawyers Assn., Internat. Fedn. Women Lawyers, Am. Assn. U. Women, Nat. Jewish Welfare Bd., N.Y. League Bus. and Profl. Women, U.N. League Lawyers, Nat. Council on Family Relations, Am. Correctional Assn., Nat. Narcotic Enforcement Officers Assn., Nat. Jail Assn., Nat. Sheriffs Assn., Nat. Council on Crime and Delinquency, Nat. Assn. for Prevention of Narcotic Addiction, N.Y.C. Youth Bd. (ex- officio), N.Y.C. Correction Commn. (ex-officio), Lucy Stone League, Hadassah. Contbr. many works on jud. and correctional subjects. Home: 124 W 79th St New York City, NY 10024.

KROUT, JOHN ALLEN, ret. coll. dean; b. Tiffin, O., Oct. 3, 1896; s. Charles Allen and Eva Rinker (Bacher) K.; student Heidelberg Coll., 1914-17, L.H.D. (hon.), 1938; A.B., U. Mich., 1918; A.M., Columbia, 1920, Ph.D., 1925, LL.D., 1963; LL.D., Union Coll., 1952, Washington and Jefferson Coll., 1954, Trinity Coll., 1955, Hamilton Coll., 1957; m. Marion D. Good, Sept. 15, 1923; 1 dau., Eleanor Maria; m. 2d, Mary Pryseski, Oct. 1961. Pub. accountant A. S. Utter & Co., Chgo., 1919-20; instr. history Columbia, 1922-26, asst. prof., 1926-31, asso. prof., 1931-40, prof., 1940—; editor Polit. Sci. Quar., N.Y.C. and Proc. of Acad. Polit. Sci., 1937-49; acting dir. Sch. Gen. Studies, 1948-49; dean grad. faculty Columbia, 1949-53, asso. provost, 1950, now v.p. emeritus, provost; dean Heidelberg Coll., Tiffin, O., 1963-67; vis. prof. history Ariz. U., U. 1962-63. Cons., Hist. Office, AAF, 1945-46; dir. Empire City Savs. Bank. Mem. adv. bd. Nat. Pk. Service, Civil War Centennial Commn., 1958-65. Trustee, Mus. of City N.Y.; mem. bd. Atron Found. Decorated Order Liberator (Venezuela); Order Merit of Republic (Italy). Mem. Middle States Assn. History Tchrs. (pres. 1940-41), N.Y. State Hist. Assn. (trustee 1936—), Am. Hist. Assn., Acad. Polit. Sci., Soc. of Am. History (sec. 1944-45), Phi Beta Kappa (hon.), Delta Sigma Rho, Alpha Tau Omega. Baptist. Mason. Clubs: Cosmos (Washington); Century, Columbia Faculty (N.Y.) Author: The Origins of Prohibition, 1925; Annals of American Sport, 1929; American History for Colleges (with D. S. Muzzey), 1933; An Outline History of the U.S. (2 vols.), 1934; Approaches to American Social History (W.E. Lingelbach, editor), 1937; The Completion of Independence (with D.R. Fox), 1944; Great Expressions of Human Rights (R. M. MacIver, editor), 1951; The Adventure of the American People (with Henry F. Graff), 1959; Keepers of the Past. Editor: The Greater City (with Allen Nevins), 1948. Contbr. to Am. Mercury, Yale Rev., Hist. Outlook, Am. Hist. Rev., Outlook, etc. Home: 3422 N 60th St Phoenix AZ 85018

KROUT, JOHN EDWARD, banker, lawyer; b. Narberth, Pa., Jan. 5, 1920; s. Palled Bertram and Sara (Raffensperger) K.; grad. The Haverford Sch., 1937; A.B. with honors, Princeton, 1941; J.D. with high honors, Harvard, 1944; m. Patricia L. Swinehart, Aug. 15, 1942 (div. 1966); children-Joanne Lester (Mrs. George W. Phillips), John Alan, Robert Ellis. Admitted to Pa. bar, 1944; mem. firm Drinker, Biddle & Reath, Phila., 1944-59, partner, 1951- 59; sr. v.p. The Phila. Saving Fund Soc., 1959-70; pres. Germantown Savs. Bank, Phila., 1971—; dir. Fed.Nat. Mortgage Assn., Washington, 1970—. Bd. dirs. Crime Prevention Assn., Phila., 1961—; bd. corporators Med. Coll. Pa., Phila., 1963—. Mem. Mortgage Bankers Assn. Am. (bd. dirs.), Phila. Mortgage Bankers Assn. (pres. 1964), Pa. Soc. Sons of Revolution, Cloister Inn of Princeton, Lambda Alpha. Republican. Episcopalian. Clubs: Phila. Country, Merion Cricket, Princeton (Phila.). Home: 145 Fairview Rd Naberth PA 19072 Office: 5458 Germantown Av Philadelphia PA 19144

KRUEGEL, JAMES HENRY, financial exec.; b. Hackensack, N.J., June 19, 1923; s. Henry A. and Dorothy (Christensen) K.; B.B.A., Pace Coll., 1949; M.B.A., Rutgers U., 1956; m. Doris B. O'Donnell, Oct. 27, 1951; children—James H., Gary D. Controller Burroughs Supply Div., 1950-59; financial analyst ITT, 1960-64; exec. asst. to pres. ITT Export, 1964-66; asst. dir. adminstrn. ITT, 1966-67; sr. v.p., controller ITT Avis, Garden City, N.Y., 1967—. Mem. Beta Gamma Sigma. Home: 206 Merritt Dr Oradell NJ 07649 Office: 900 Old Country Rd Garden City NY 11530

KRUEGER, ERICH GOTTLIEB, neurosurgeon; b. Lemgo, Germany, Dec. 23, 1903; s. August Friedrich and Marie (Voltmann) K.; M.D., U. Heidelberg (Germany), 1929; m. Patricia A. Hanson, Nov. 2, 1961. Came to U.S., 1937, naturalized, 1944. Med.-surg. intern Sarepta Hosp., Bielefeld, Germany, 1929-30; resident gen. surgery Landeskrankenhaus, Detmold, Germany, 1930-33; asst. Physiol. Inst., U. Hamburg (Germany), 1933-37; research fellow, later attending physician internal medicine N.Y. Postgrad. Med. Sch., 1938-41; resident neurol. surgery N.Y. Neurol. Inst., 1942-45; chief, neurosurgery Bronx (N.Y.) VA Hosp., 1945-68, founder spinal cord injury center, 1945; dir. spinal cord injury service Central VA Office, Washington, 1968—; cons. spinal cord injury center Castle Point (N.Y.) Hosp., 1966-68; clin. prof. neurol. surgery Columbia Coll. Phys. and Surg., 1957; lectr. N.J. State Coll., 1968, VA postgrad courses, 1968—. Recipient hon. citation Paralyzed Vets. Assn. Am., 1948, highest award, 1971. Diplomate Am. Bd. Neurol. Surgery. Mem. Assn. Am. Neurol. Surgeons, N.Y. Acad. Medicine, N.Y. Soc. Neurosurgery (pres. 1963-64), Internat. Soc. Research Stereoencephalotomy, Am. Paraplegia Soc., Deutsche Gesellschaft für Neurochirurgie (corr.). Contbr. numerous articles, chpts. in books. Devised headrest for stereo-taxic brain operation, 1964. Home: 5007 Wyandot Ct Ft Sumner Hills Md Washington DC 20016 Office: 810 Vermont Av NW Washington DC 20420

KRUEGER, EVERETT HEATH, banker; b. Cleve., Apr. 19, 1919; s. Everette Henry and Marion (Heath) K.; A.B., Yale, 1941; LL.B., Western Res. U., 1947; m. Nancy A. Moore, June 10, 1944 (div. 1961); children—Kristin Anne, Everett Heath III, Thomas C., Kathleen E., Nancy K.; m. 2d, Shirle Cooke Wallingford, Nov. 1967. Admitted to Ohio bar, 1948; with firm Krueger, Gorman & Davis, Cleve., 1948-51; with Office Atty. Gen. Ohio, 1951-57, 1st asst. atty. gen., 1955-57; sec. to Gov. Ohio, 1957; mem. Pub. Utilities Commn. Ohio, 1957-62, chmn., 1957-60; v.p., counsel City Nat. Bank & Trust Co., Columbus, O., 1962—. Mem. alumni bd. Yale, 1967-71; Met. Park Bd., 1970—; v.p. Central Ohio council Boy Scouts Am., 1967-71; pres. Columbus Symphony Orch., 1971—. Trustee Ohio Dominican Coll. Served to capt. AUS, 1942-46. Mem. Am., Ohio, Cleve., Columbus bar assns., Zeta Psi, Phi Delta Phi. Republican. Episcopalian. Mason (32). Clubs: Yale (pres. Central Ohio 1971—); Columbus, Athletic, Scioto Country, Torch (Columbus). Home: 1960 Lytham Rd Columbus OH 43220 Office: 100 E Broad St Columbus OH 43215

KRUEGER, HILMAR CARL, univ. adminstr.; b. Milw., Apr. 19, 1904; s. Gustave August and Helen (Warner) K.; B.A., Northwestern Coll., 1925; Ph.D. (Charles K. Adams scholar), U. Wis., 1932; m. Mildred Clara Eggert, June 28, 1930; 1 son, Charles Robert. Fellow history U. Wis., 1926-27; instr. history at Milw., 1929-33, asst. prof., 1933-38, asso. prof., 1938-40, head, dept. history and polit. sci., 1935-40, dean men, 1937-40; asst. prof. history U. Cin., 1940-46, asso. prof., 1946-51, prof., 1951—, head dept., 1959- 63, dean founder, dean Univ. Coll., 1960-69, Raymond Walters Coll., 1967-69, vice provost for univ. brs. and community and tech. programs, 1969—; faculty summer sessions U. Mich. Fulbright research fellow, Italy, 1950-51. Mem. Am. Hist. Assn., Medieval Acad. Am., Societa Ligure di Storia Patria (Italy), Omicron Delta Kappa. dir. Pacific Western-Iran Ltd., Pacific Western Oil Corp., Tide Water-Iran Co-editor Genoese notarial cartularies. Contbr. articles to Am., European jours. Home: 2324 Madison Rd Cincinnati OH 45208

KRUEGER, JACK BURKE, editor; b. San Antonio, Sept. 26, 1908; s. August and Elizabeth (Hayden) K; student San Antonio Jr. Coll., U. Tex., 1929; m. Lucille Ann Leibe, Nov. 11, 1937; 1 dau., Kathryn Ann (Mrs. Fredric Seewald). Reporter, San Antonio Light, 1929-36; editor A.P., Dallas, San Francisco, 1936-44; city editor Dallas News, 1945-55, asst. mng. editor, 1955-57, mng. editor, 1957-68, exec. editor, 1968- -, v.p., 1970—; dir. A.H. Belo Corp. Mem. Am. Press Inst. (adv. bd.). A.P. Mng. Editors Assn. (pres. 1967-68), Am. Soc. Newspapers Editors, Sigma Delta Chi. Home: 5922 Joyce Way Dallas TX 75225 Office: Communications Center Dallas TX 75222

KRUEGER, KARL, orchestral condr.; b. Atchison, Kan., Jan. 19, 1894; s. Carl and Sophie (Sprick) K.; M.A., Kan. State U., 1913; studied law, U. Vienna, Heidelberg U.; studied composition under Robert Fuchs and Charles Skilton; studied conducting under Nikisch, Weingartner; m. Emita McCormick Jewett, Apr. 14, 1923; 1 dau., Theresa. Condr., Seattle Symphony Orch., 1926-32, Kansas City Philharmonic, 1933-43; Detroit Symphony Orch., 1943-49; guest condr. leading orchs., Europe, U.S., S.A. Founder, dir. Soc. Preservation Am. Mus. Heritage, 1957. Author: The Way of the Conductor, 1958. Home: 30 E 27th St New York City NY 10016 ☆

KRUEGER, MYRON WILLIAM, indsl. exec.; b. Green Bay, Wis., Nov. 15, 1910; s. Martin W. and Nellie (Mader) K.; A.B., U. Wis., 1935, A.M., 1935; m. Dorothy Raillie Sterrett, Apr. 25, 1936; children—Starry, William, Robert, Margaret. With Kimberly-Clark Corp., Neenah, Wis., 1936-39; asst. comptroller Carnegie-Ill. Steel Corp., Pitts., 1944-48; exec. v.p., treas., dir. Raymond Internat., N.Y.C., 1948-60; pres. M.W. Krueger Assos., 1960-68; v.p., dir. Hercules, Inc., Wilmington, Del., 1968—, chmn. finance com., 1969—; dir. Levinson Steel Co., Alliance Growth Fund. Trustee Wis. Alumni Research Found. Mem. Nat. Assn. Accountants (past nat. v.p.), Am. Arbitration Assn., Newcomen Soc., Phi Beta Kappa, Phi Kappa Phi, Artus, Delta Sigma Rho. Clubs: University (N.Y.C.); Essex County Country (West Orange, N.J.); Farmington Country (Charlottesville, Va.); Wilmington (Del.) Country. Home: 321 Hartshorn Dr Short Hills NJ 07078 also 2401 Pennsylvania Av Wilmington DE 19806 Office: 910 Market St Wilmington DE 19899

KRUEGER, PAUL G., mfg. co. exec.; b. Gary Ind., 1917; ed. Tulane U., 1940. Vice pres. United Carr Inc., now exec. v.p. Home: 31 Nobscot Rd Weston MA 02193 Office: Statler Office Bldg Boston MA 02116*

KRUEGER, ROBERT BLAIR, lawyer; b. Minot, N.D., Dec. 9, 1928; s. Paul Otto and Lila (Morse) K.; A.B., U. Kan., 1949; J.D., U. Mich., 1952; postgrad. U. So. Cal., 1960-65; m. Virginia Ruth Carmichael, June 3, 1956; children—Lisa Carmichael, Paula Leah, Robert Blair. Admitted to Kan. bar, 1952, Cal. bar, 1955; practice in Los Angeles, 1955—; asso. O'Melveny & Myers, 1955-59; partner Blair & Krueger, 1959-61; partner Nossaman, Waters, Scott, Krueger & Riodan, 1961—. Mem. Los Angeles Delegation to Cal. Bar Conf., 1961-69. Mem. Gov.'s Adv. Commn. on Ocean Resources, 1966-67, Cal. Adv. Commn. on Marine and Coastal Resources, 1967—, chmn., 1970—; mem. Adv. Council Inst. on Marine Resourses, U. Cal., 1966—. Mem. com. visitors U. Mich. Law Sch., 1967—, nat. com. of Law Sch., 1967—, Served to 1st lt. USMCR, 1952-54. Mem. Am. (chmn. com. marine resources liaison 1967-70, mem. council sect. natural resources law 1970—), Los Angeles County (chmn. real property sect. 1961-65) bar assns., Internat. Law Assn., Am. Soc. Internat. Law, Am. Soc. Oceanography (v.p. Pacific Western region), Barristers, Tau Kappa Epsilon, Phi Alpha Delta. Republican. Clubs: California, University (bd. dirs.), Chancery, Town Hall (chmn. oceanocraphy sect. 1971—) (Los Angeles); Valley Hunt (Pasadena). Asst. editor Mich. Law Rev., 1951-52; editor Los Angeles Bat Bull., 1961-63, Cal. Ba Jour., 1963-66, 67-72. Project dir., editor Study Outer Continental Shelf Lands of the United States, 1968. Home: 501 Vallombrosa Dr Pasadena CA 91107 also 9822 La Jolla Farms Rd La Jolla CA 92037 Office: 445 S Figueroa St Los Angeles CA 90017

KRUEGER, ROBERT JAMES, banker, accountant; b. Fargo, N.D., Dec. 7, 1930; s. James Frederick and Zelda Elizabeth (Resley) K.; B.S. in Bus. Adminstrn., U. S.D., 1956; m. Mary Macheak, June 1, 1957; children—Robert J., Julia A., John F., Rebecca E. Audit supr. Peat, Marwick, Mitchell & Co., C.P.A.'s, Chgo., 1956-66; controller Avis Indsl. Corp., Lansing, Mich., 1966-68; controller Lansing Gen. Hosp., 1968-70; gen. auditor Nat. Bank Detroit, 1970—; mem. faculty Colo. Sch. Banking, 1971. Served with USNR, 1952-54. C.P.A., Ill. Mem. Inst. Internal Auditors (gov. Detroit chpt.), Bank Adminstrn. Inst., Am. Inst. C.P.A.'s, Mich. Assn. C.P.A.'s, Nat., Am. Accounting assns. Home: 285 Kenwood Ct Grosse Pointe MI 48236 Office: 611 Woodward Av Detroit MI 48232

KRUEGER, ROBERT WILLIAM, profl. service co. exec.; b. Phila., Nov. 16, 1916; s. Robert Henry and Frieda (Lehmann) K.; m. Marjorie Evelyn Jones, July 26, 1941; children—Arlene R. (Mrs. Thomas Reher), Diane L. (Mrs. John Esser). Research engr. Douglas Aircraft Co., Santa Monica, Cal., 1942-46; asst. chief missiles div. RAND Corp., Santa Monica, 1946-53; missle systems cons., Los Angeles, 1953-54; pres. Planning Research Corp., Los Angeles, 1954—. Chmn. 59th Dist. Republican Central Com., 1960-61; pres. 59th Dist. Rep. Assembly, 1960-61; mem. Cal. Rep. Central Com., 1962—. Trustee U. Cal. Los Angeles Found. Mem. Am. Phys. Soc., Operations Research Soc. Am., Inst. Mgmt. Scis., Sigma Xi. Home: 1016 Moraga Dr Los Angeles CA 90049 Office: 1100 Glendon Av Los Angeles CA 90024

KRUEGER, ROY LAMBERT, corn refining exec.; b. Keokuk, Ia., May 14, 1906; s. Henry F. and Carrie (Fletcher) K.; B.A., State U. Ia., 1927, M.S., 1928; m. Ruth M. Snyder, Apr. 19, 1928; children—Diane (Mrs. William N. Hughes), Roy Lambert, Martha (Mrs. John W. Acer), Henry F., Sally S. (Mrs. Kenneth M. Dains). With Hubinger Co., Keokuk, 1928—, asst. chemist, chief chemist, tech. adviser, asst. bulk sales mgr., v.p. charge prodn., asst. to pres. and treas., exec. v.p., 1928-55, pres., 1955—, dir., 1939—; mem. Mo. adv. bd. Am. Mut. Liability Ins. Co. Mem. Keokuk Municipal Bridge Commn., Keokuk Grain Inspection Service; active local YMCA, Salvation Army, Community Chest. Trustee, Ia. Wesleyan Coll. Mem. Am. Chem. Soc., Keokuk C. of C., State U. Ia. Alumni Assn. Methodist, Rotarian, Elk, Clubs: Keokuk, Keokuk Country. Home: 1801 Grand Av Keokuk IA 52632 Office: 601 Main St Keokuk IA 52632

KRUENER, HARRY HOWARD, clergyman; b. Bklyn., Nov. 6, 1915; s. Henry and Florence (Edwards) K.; A.B., Haveford Coll., 1937; B.D., Andover Newton Theol. Sch., 1940; S.T.M., Boston U., 1954; D.D., Denison U., 1965; m. Martha Easton, Oct. 5, 1941 (dec. July 1959); 1 son, John Francis; m. 2d, Cheryl Woddell, June 20, 1961; 1 son, Philip C. Ordained to ministry Bapt. Ch., 1940; minister, Boston, 1940-48, Granville, O., 1948-55; dean of chapel Denison U., 1955-60; minister Plymouth Ch. of Pilgrims, Bklyn., 1960—; preacher, Chautauqua, 1970, Am. Ch., Athens, Greece, 1971. Bd. mgrs. Am. Bapt. Fgn. Mission Socs.; exec. bd., membership sec. Nat. Assn. Coll. and Univ. Chaplains; del. Nat. Council Chs.; mem. United Ch. of Christ; pres. Bklyn. Council Chs., Bklyn. Clerical Union, Bklyn. Meml. Soc. Trustee Andover Newton Theol. Sch., Denison U. Mem. Nat. Assn. Bibl. Instrs., Phi Beta Kappa, Omicron Delta Kappa. Mason (lodge chaplain). Club: Rembrandt (Bklyn.). Author: Specifically to Youth, 1959. Summer preacher Nat. Radio Pulpit, 1954. Home: 184 Columbia Heights Brooklyn NY 11201

KRUG, CHARLES F., oil co. exec.; b. Bklyn., 1909 grad. Lafayette Coll., 1930. Fordham Law Sch., 1934. Vice pres., sec., Getty Oil Co.; v.p., sec., dir. Pacific Western Iran Ltd., Pacific Western Oil Corp., Tide Water-Iran Ltd.; v.p., treas., dir. Getty Tankers Ltd., Hemisphere Transp. Corp., Transoceanic Shipping Corp., Gettymar Corp.; asst. sec., treas., dir. Iricon Agy. Ltd.; v.p., treas. Liberian Operations, Inc.; dir. Skelly Oil Co., Farmers Bank of State of Del. Home: Greenville DE 19807 Office: Getty Oil Co Pennsylvania Bldg Wilmington DE 19899*

KRUG, EDWARD AUGUST, educator; b. Chgo., Sept. 26, 1911; s. Rudolph Hugo and Anna (Wendt) K.; B.S. in Edn., Northwestern U., 1933, M.S., 1934; Ed.D., Stanford, 1941; m. Annie Ellen McDonald, Apr. 10, 1937; children—Elizabeth Anne, Margaret Jean, Peter. Tchr. social studies Evanston (Ill.) Twp. High Sch., 1935-38; evaluator motion picture project Am. Council Edn., 1938-39; research asso. Stanford, 1939-41, acting asst. prof. edn., 1941- 43, asso. prof., 1947-48; asst. prof. edn. Mont. State U., 1943-45; asso. prof. edn. U. Wis., 1945-47, 48-49, prof., 1949—. Mem. Am. Ednl. Studies Assn., History Edn. Soc. Episcopalian. Author: (with I.J. Quillen) Living in Our Communities, 1945, Living in Our America, 1951; Curriculum Planning, 1957; Secondary School Curriculum, 1960; Charles W. Eliot and Popular Education, 1961; The Shaping of the American High School, Vol. I, 1880-1920, 1964, 69, Vol. II, 1920-1941, 1972; Salient Dates in American Education, 1966. Home: 2339 W Lawn Av Madison WI 53711

KRUG, MARK M., historian, educator; b. Vienna, Austria, June 13, 1915; s. Daniel and Ann (Blumen) K.; came to U.S., 1940, naturalized, 1946; B.A., Tchrs. Coll., Jerusalem, Israel, 1938; M.A., Roosevelt U., Chgo., 1956; Ph.D. in History, U. Chgo., 1960; m. Ruth Kulwin, Dec. 19, 1943; children—Elyse, Orah. Tchr. social studies, chmn. dept. Lab High Sch., U. Chgo., 1958-61; mem. faculty U. Chgo., 1961—, prof. edn. in history, 1964—. Chmn. com. tchr. edn. and certification Nat. Council Social Edn., 1962—; adviser Nat. Ednl. Policies Commn., 1963—; mem. Ill. Task Force Edn., 1965—; ednl. dir. Council Study Mankind, 1962—. Mem. Am., Miss. Valley hist. assns., Nat. Council Social Studies, N.E.A. Author: Aneurin Bevan Cautious Rebel, 1961; Lyman Trumbull—Conservative Radical, 1965; History and the Social Sciences, 1967; The New Social Studies, 1971. Home: 3800 N Lake Shore Dr Chicago IL 60613

KRUG, RICHARD EUGENE, librarian; b. Milw., June 13, 1905; s. Richard E. and Katharina (Mertens) K.; B.A., U. Wis., 1927, J.D., 1929; m. Lucile Ransom, Sept. 1938. Admitted to Wis bar. 1929, practiced at Milw., 1929-30; municipal reference librarian Milwaukee Pub. Library, 1930-39, asst. librarian, 1939-41, librarian, 1941—. Bd. dirs. Milw. Repertory Theater. Mem. Spl. Libraries Assn., A.L.A., Civil War Round table, Milw. Art Center (trustee), Wis. Marine Hist. Soc., Milw. Council Adult Learning, Milw. Landmark Commn., Am. Assn. Adult Edn., State Hist. Soc. Wis. Clubs: Wisconsin, Milwaukee Press. Home: 2625 N Wahl Av Milwaukee WI 53211 Office: 814 W Wisconsin Av Milwaukee WI 53233

KRUG, ROBERT CHARLES, educator, chemist; b. Richmond, Va., July 23, 1918; s. Charles Frederick and Myra Uldine (Vaiden) K.; B.S., U. Richmond, 1940; M.S., Pa. State Coll., 1941; Ph.D., Ohio State U., 1944; m. Kathryn Rebecca Leviston, June 21, 1941; children—Charles Jeffrey, Robyn Irene. Research chemist Atlantic Refining Co., Phila., 1944-48; asst. prof. chemistry Washington and Lee U., 1948-49; faculty Va. Polytech. Inst., 1949-65, prof. chemistry, head dept., 1958-65; dean coll. George Mason Coll., U. Va., 1965-70, dean of faculty and grad. program, 1970—, also prof. chemistry; cons. chemistry, 1954—. Recipient W.E. Wine award for outstanding teaching Va. Polytech. Inst., 1957. Mem. Am. Chem. Soc. (chmn. Blue Ridge sect. 1956), Va. Acad. Scis. (past chmn. sec. chemistry sect.), Sigma Xi (pres. Va. Polytech. Inst. 1955), Phi Lambda Upsilon, Phi Kappa Phi (pres. Va. Polytech. Inst. 1959), Omicron Delta Kappa. Presbyn. (elder). Contbr. articles profl. jours. Home: 3716 Acosta Rd Fairfax VA 22030

KRUGER, FRED WALTER, mech. engr., univ. dean; b. Chgo., Dec. 17, 1921; s. Fred and Magdalen (Lotz) K.; student Valparaiso U., 1940-42; B.S. in Elec. Engring., Purdue U., 1942-43, B.S. in Mech. Engring., 1947; M.S. in Mech Engring., Notre Dame U., 1954; m. Esther Marie Foelber, Aug. 23, 1947; children—Paul Walter, John Robert, Thomas Herman. Mem. faculty Valparaiso (Ind.) U., 1947—, prof., 1959—, chmn. dept. mech. engring., 1955-65, dean Coll. Engring., 1965—. Cons., McDonnell Aircraft Co., Caterpillar Tractor Co., Argonne Lab., No. Ill. Gas Co.; mem. Ind. Bd. Registration for Profl. Engrs., 1957—. Served to lt. USNR, 1943-46. Registered profl. engr., Ind. Mem. Am. Soc. M.E., Am. Soc. for Engring. Edn., Tau Beta Pi. Lutheran. Home: 1058 Linwood Av Valparaiso, IN 46383.

KRUGER, FREDRICK CHRISTIAN, educator; b. St. Paul, Apr. 1, 1912; s. Rudolph Julius and Betty (Sandberg) K.; B.S., U. Minn., 1935, M.A., 1936; Ph.D., Harvard, 1941; Management course, Am. Mgmt. Assn., 1958; m. Helene Vivian Anderson, June 25, 1936; children-Kurn Frederick, Jan Christian (Mrs. Robert Steven Anderson). Grad. asst. U. Minn., 1935-36; asst. Minn. Geol. Survey, 1936; instr. Dartmouth, 1936-38; grad. asst., teaching fellow Harvard, 1938-41; grad. asst. Radcliffe Coll., 1948-41; geologist, asst. chief geologist Cerro de Pasco Corp., Peru, 1941-49; vis. lectr. Northwestern U., 1949; asso. prof., prof. U. Tenn., 1949-52; asst. chief geologist Reynolds Metals Co., Richmond, Va., 1952-57; chief geologist, dir. mining and exploration dept., v.p. mining and exploration div. Internat. Minerals & Chem. Corp., Skokie, Ill., 1957-66; dir. Internat. Minerals & Chems. Proprietary, Ltd. (ANZ), 1963-66; v.p., dir. I.M.C. Devel. Corp., 1964-66; prof., chmn. dept. mineral engring. Stanford, 1966—; cons. exploration and mining, 1949-52, 66—. Mem. mining study panel NRC, 1967—; organizer seminars for profl. geologists U. Tenn., 1949-52, seminar on continental drift, 1950, seminar on mining in Americas, Chgo. Internat. Trade Fair, 1961. Fellow Geol. Soc. Am.; mem. Soc. Econ. Geologists (past organizer symposium, mem. council), Am. Inst. Mining Engrs. (Henry Krumb lectr. 1967-69), Mining and Metall. Soc., Nat. Def. Exec. Res., A.A.A.S., Am. Geol. Inst. (past dir.), Soc. Mining Engrs. (past v.p., dir.), U.S. C. of C., Am. Mgmt. Assn., Sigma Xi, Sigma Gamma Epsilon. Home: 145 Wildwood Way Woodside CA 94062 Office: Stanford U Stanford CA 94305

KRUGER, GUSTAV OTTO, Jr., oral surgeon, educator; b. N.Y.C., Sept. 28, 1916; s. Gustav Otto and Anna Charlotte (Mellquist) K.; B.S., George Washington U., 1938, A.M., 1939; D.D.S., Georgetown U., 1939; m. Helyn E. Hollingsworth, Apr. 12, 1947; children—Deborah Ann (Mrs. M. Henry King III), Tristram Coffin, Abigail Hollingsworth. Intern, Johns Hopkins Hosp., 1939-40; fellow Mayo Found., 1940-42, 45-48; mem. faculty Georgetown U. Sch. Dentistry and Grad. Sch., 1948—, prof. oral surgery, chmn. dept., 1948—, asso. dean, 1966—; chief, dental dept. Georgetown U. Hosp., Washington, 1948—; cons. VA hosps. in Martinsburg, W.Va. and Washington, U.S. Naval Hosp., Bethesda, D.C. Gen. Hosp., Washington; cons. to Pres.'s physician, 1960-64; cons. Walter Reed Army Med. Center. Mem. cancer tng. com. Nat. Cancer Inst., USPHS, 1967-71, chmn., 1969-71. Served to capt. Dental Corps, AUS, 1942-45; CBI, PTO. Named Man of Year Georgetown U. Alumni Assn., 1961. Diplomate Am. Bd. Oral Surgery (pres. 1964). Fellow Am. (chmn. D.C. sect. 1969-71), Internat. (chmn. D.C. sect. 1967-70) colls. dentists; mem. Am. Dental Assn. (chmn. oral surgery sect. 1961, mem. rev. commn. on advanced edn. in oral surgery 1965-71, chmn. commn. 1969-71), D.C. Dental Soc. (pres. 1960), Am. (program chmn. 1961), Middle Atlantic (pres. 1952) socs. oral surgeons, Am. Acad. Oral Pathology, Am. Acad. Oral Roentgenology, Internat. Assn. Dental Research, Xi Psi Phi, Sigma Gamma Epsilon, Omicron Kappa Upsilon. Kiwanian. Author: Textbook of Oral Surgery, 1959. Home: 6806 Bradgrove Circle Bethesda MD 20034 Office: 3900 Reservoir Rd NW Washington DC 20007

KRUGER, HARDY, actor; b. Berlin, Germany, Apr. 12, 1928; s. Max and Auguste (Meier) K.; student Berlin High Sch., 1938-45; m. Francesca Marazzi, Dec. 31, 1965; children—Malaika, Hardy. Came to U.S., 1958. Actor in films, West Germany, 1949-56, England, 1956—; films include The One That Got Away, 1956, Sundays and Cybele, 1960, also films, USSR, Italy, Yugoslavia, France. Recipient Prix Femina, 1961, Grand Prix du Cinema Francais, 1960; named best actor in Yugoslavia 1970. Founder, part-owner Momella Game Lodge, Ltd., Momella Farm Ltd., Tanzania, East Africa, 1961—. Author: Eine Farm in Afrika, 1970; Sawimbulu, 1971. Address: Gandria Ticino 6978 Switzerland

KRUGER, JOSEPH, lawyer; b. Russia, July 16, 1901; s. Hyman and Fanny (Goodkin) K.; came to U.S., 1907, naturalized, 1914; A.B. cum laude, Harvard, 1922, LL.B., 1925; m. Alice Lewis, June 12, 1927; children—Frederick, Martin. Admitted to Mass. bar, 1926; individual practice, Boston, 1926-41; partner firm Widett & Kruger, Boston, 1942—; occasional lectr. continuing legal edn.; counsel New Boston Com., 1950-56. Trustee, Social Law Library, Combined Jewish Philanthropies; trustee Brookline Hosp., 1945—, pres., 1951-55. Club: New Century (past pres.) (Boston). Home: 209 Fuller St West Newton, MA 02165 Office: 1 Federal St Boston MA 02110

KRUGER, OTTO, actor, b. Toledo; ed. Mich. U., Columbia U.; m. Sue M. Druger; one dau., Ottilie. Engaged as dramatic actor on stage in Royal Family, Private Lives, Counsellor-at- law, others; screen debut in The Intruder, others include Beauty for Sale, Prizefighter and the Lady, Gallant Lady, Treasure Island, Chained, Men in White, Springtime for Henry, They Won't Forget, 711 Ocean Drive, Payment on Demand, High Noon, Magnificent Obsession, Black Widow, Last Command, many other plays, TV, motion pictures. Vice pres. Motion Picture Relief Fund. Mason. Club: The Lambs (N.Y.C.). Home: Roscomare Rd Bel-Air Los Angeles CA 90024 Office: Stewart Agy 9046 Sunset Blvd Los Angeles CA 90069

KRUGLAK, HAYM, educator, physicist; b. Dneprodzerzinsk, Ukraine, Mar. 24, 1909; s. Abram and Fanny (Schuster) K.; came to U.S., 1927, naturalized, 1934; B.A., U. Wis., 1934, M.A., 1936; Ph.D., U. Minn., 1951; student U. Chgo., 1942, 63-64; m. Mary Lee Stewart, May 2, 1941; children—Joyce, David. Instr. high sch., Sheboygan, Wis., 1936-38; instr. Tech. Coll., Milw., 1938-44; vis. asst. prof. physics Princeton, 1944-46; asst. prof. U. Minn., Mpls., 1946-54; prof. physics Western Mich. U., Kalamazoo, 1954—; curriculum supr. U.S. Army Signal Corps Repairmen Sch., Milw., 1942-44; dir. research project Office Naval Research, Mpls., 1951-54; dir. NSF Summer Inst., Kalamazoo, 1961, 67-69. Fellow A.A.A.S.; Mem. Am. Assn. Physics Tchrs., Am. Assn. U. Profs., Am. Technion Soc., Phi Beta Kappa. Jewish religion. Mem. B'nai B'rith. Author: Laboratory Performance Tests in General Physics, 1959; Basic Mathematics for the Physical Sciences, 1963. Home: 2127 Frederick Av Kalamazoo MI 49001

KRUGMAN, HERBERT ELLIS, psychologist; b. N.Y.C., May 3, 1921; s. Harry A. and Leah (Greenberg) K.; B Social Sci., Coll. City N.Y., 1942; Ph.D., Columbia, 1952; m. Dorothy Carol Coleman, Dec. 26, 1942; children—Edward Paul, Laura Nan. Project dir. Richardson, Bellows, Henry & Co., Inc., 1943-49, 53-58; research asso. Princeton Center Internat. Studies, also cons. Office Intelligence Research, State Dept., 1950-52; v.p. research Raymond Loewy/William Snaith, Inc., 1959-61; v.p. Ted Bates & Co., 1961-63; v.p. Marplan div. Communications Affiliates, Inc., N.Y.C., 1962-67; mgr. corporate pub. opinion research Gen. Electric Co., 1967—; evening lectr. Columbia 1957-62. Adv. bd. Found. Research Human Behavior; trustee Marketing Sci. Inst. Served with USAAF, 1942-45. Fellow Am. Psychol. Assn. (pres. div. consumer psychology 1966-67), Am. Sociol. Assn.; mem. Am. Assn. Pub. Opinion Research (pres. 1965-66). Contbr. articles profl. jours. Mem. editorial bd. Pub. Opinion Quar., 1966—, Jour. Profl. Psychology, 1968—. Home: 425 Riverside Dr New York City NY 10025 Office: Gen Electric Co 570 Lexington Av New York City NY

KRUGMAN, SAUL, physician, educator; b. N.Y.C., Apr. 7, 1911; s. Louis and Rachel (Cohen) K.; student Ohio State U., 1929-32; M.D., Med. Coll. Va., 1939; m. Sylvia Stern, Feb. 18, 1940; children—Richard David, Carol Lynn. Intern, then resident

Cumberland, Willard Parker and Bellevue hosps., N.Y.C., 1939-41, 46-48; teaching and med. research N.Y. U.-Bellevue Med. Center, 1948—, asso. prof. pediatrics, 1954-60, prof., chmn. dept., 1960—; dir. pediatric service Bellevue Hosp., 1960—, Univ. Hosp., 1960- -. Mem. commn. viral infections Nat. Bd. Med. Examiners; pediatric adv. com. N.Y.C. Dept. Health; mem. nat. adv. council Nat. Inst. Allergy and Infectious Diseases, 1965-69, chmn. infectious disease adv. com., 1971—. NIH research fellow, 1948-50. Fellow Am. Acad. Pediatrics; mem. Am. Pediatric Soc., Soc. Pediatric Research, N.Y. Acad. Medicine (chmn. pediatric sect. 1960-61), Am. Epidemiol. Soc., Harvey Soc., Assn. Am. Physicians. Co-author: Infectious Diseases of Children, 1968. Contbr. articles on infectious diseases to med. jours. Home: 300 E 33d St New York City NY 10016 Office: 550 1st Av New York City NY 10016

KRUH, ROBERT F., univ. dean; b. St. Louis, June 15, 1925; s. Frank O. and Nell (Dee) K.; A.B., Washington U., St. Louis 1948, Ph.D., 1951; m. Janet Jackson, Dec. 19, 1948; children—Lindsay, Nancy. Asst. prof. DePauw U., 1951-52; prof. chemistry U. Ark., 1962-67, chmn. dept., 1963-64, dean Coll. Arts and Scis., 1964-67; dean Grad. Sch., Kan. State U., 1967—. Sec. research council Nat. Assn. State Univs. and Land-Grant Colls., 1969—; v.p. Kan. State U. Research Found., 1969—; trustee Argonne Univs. Assn. Served with C.E., AUS, 1943-46; ETO. Fellow Am. Inst. Chemists; mem. Am. Chem. Soc., Am. Phys. Soc., A.A.A.S., Am. Assn. U. Profs., Blue Key, Phi Beta Kappa, Sigma Xi, Omicron Delta Kappa, Phi Kappa Phi. Contbr. profl. jours. Home: 2155 Blue Hills Rd Manhattan KS 66502

KRUIDENIER, DAVID, newspaper publisher; b. Des Moines, July 18, 1921; s. David S. and Florence (Cowles) K.; grad. Phillips Exeter Acad., 1940; B.A., Yale, 1946; M.B.A., Harvard, 1948; LL.D., Buena Vista Coll., 1960, Simpson Coll., 1963; m. Elizabeth Stuart, Dec. 29, 1948; 1 dau., Lisa. With Mpls. Star and Tribune, 1948-52, Des Moines Register and Tribune, 1952—, v.p., gen. mgr., 1960-70, pres., pub., 1971—; dir. Des Moines Register and Tribune Co., Ia.-Des Moines Nat. Bank, Nat. By-Products, Inc., Register and Tribune Syndicate, Inc., Ia. Kemper Mut. Ins. Co.; chmn. bd. Comml. Printing, Inc. Pres. Greater Des Moines Com.; mem. bus. com. Nat. Planning Assn. Pres. bd. Gardner Cowles Found.; chmn. bd. Drake U.; trustee Ia. Meth. Hosp., Des Moines Art Center, Menninger Found.; mem. Yale Devel. Bd. Served with USAAF, 1942-45. Decorated Air medal with three oak leaf clusters, D.F.C. Mem. Sigma Delta Chi, Beta Theta Pi. Club: Des Moines. Home: 3409 Southern Hills Dr Des Moines IA 50321 Office: 715 Locust St Des Moines IA 50304

KRUKOWSKI, LUCIAN, artist, educator; b. N.Y.C., Nov. 22, 1929; s. Stefan and Anna (Belcarz) K.; B.A., Bklyn. Coll., 1952; B.F.A., Yale, 1955; M.S., Pratt Inst., 1958; m. Marilyn Denmark, Jan. 14, 1955; 1 dau., Samantha. One-man exhbns. include Staempfli Gallery, N.Y.C., 1960, 63, Cee-je Gallery, N.Y.C., 1967, Loretto Hilton Gallery, St. Louis, 1970; group exhbns. include Mus. Modern Art, Bklyn. Mus., Frumkin Gallery, Tanager Gallery, numerous colls.; mem. faculty Pratt Inst., 1955-69, prof. art, 1964-69, chmn. dept. graphic art and design, 1968-69; dean Sch. Fine Arts, Washington U., St. Louis, 1969—; lectr. Dewey Centennial, Columbia, 1959, State U. N.Y. at Buffalo, 1967. Served with USMCR, 1952-54. Mem. Coll. Art Assn., Am. Soc. Aesthetics. Home: 24 Washington Terrace St Louis MO 63112 Office: Washington U St Louis MO 63130

KRULAK, VICTOR HAROLD, publisher; b. Denver, Jan. 7, 1913; s. Morris and Besse M. (Ball) K.; B.S., U.S. Naval Acad., 1934; LL.D., U. San Diego; m. Amy Chandler, June 1, 1936; children—Victor Harold, William Morris, Charles Chandler, Commd. 2d lt. USMC, 1934, advanced through grades to lt. gen.; service in China, at sea, with Fleet Marine Forces, 1935-39; staff officer, also bn. and regimental comdr., World War II; chief staff 1st Marine Div. Korea; formerly comdg. gen. Marine Corps Recruit Depot, San Diego; formerly spl asst. to dir., joint staff counterinsurgency and spl. activities Office Joint Chiefs Staff; comdr. gen. Fleet Marine Force, Pacific, 1964; now ret.; pres. Copley News Service, San Diego, 1969—. Decorated D.S.M., Navy Cross, Legion of Merit with 3 oak leaf clusters, Bronze Star medal, Air medal, Purple Heart (U.S.); Cross of Gallantry, Medal of Merit (Vietnam); Distinguished Service medal (Korea). Mem. U.S. Naval Inst., U.S. Marine Corps Assn., Am. Soc. Newspaper Editors. Home: 3665 Carleton St San Diego CA 92106 Office: The Copley Press Inc 940 3d Av San Diego CA 92101

KRUMBEIN, WILLIAM CHRISTIAN, geologist; b. Beaver Falls, Pa., Jan. 28, 1902; s. Charles J. and Hattie (Mauch) K.; Ph.B., U. Chgo., 1926, M.S., 1930, Ph.D., 1932; m. Margorie Kamm, Sept. 21, 1946. Auditor U.S. Nat. Adjustment Co., Chgo., 1924-26, comptroller, dir., 1926-30; research geologist Gulf Research and Devel. Co., Pitts., 1945-46; instr. geology U. Chgo., 1932-38, asst. prof., 1938-44, asso. prof., 1944-45; prof. geology Northwestern U., 1946-70, William Deering prof., 1960-70, Pres.'s fellow, 1965-66; geology cons. Brookhaven Nat. Lab., 1947-55; cons. Beach Erosion Bd., Corp. of Engrs., 1951—. John Simon Guggenheim fellow, 1941-42; Fulbright Lectr. Queen Mary Coll., U. London, 1960. Recipient War Dept. Commendation for meritorious civilian service, 1945. Fellow Am. Acad. Arts and Scis.; mem. Geol. Soc. Am., Am. Geophys. Union, Internat. Assn. for Math. Geology (exec. com. 1968—), Am. Assn. Petroleum Geologists (editor 1955-57), Soc. Econ. Paleontologists and Mineralogists, Sigma Xi, Phi Beta Kappa. Club: Cosmos. Author: (with Carey G. Croneis) Down to Earth, 1936; (with F.J. Pettijohn) Manual of Sedimentary Petrography, 1938; (with L.L. Sloss) Stratigraphy and Sedimentation; (with F.A. Graybill) Statistical Models in Geology, 1965. Author sci. articles. Home: 349 Sheridan Rd Winnetka IL 60093

KRUMBIEGEL, STANLEY E. physician; b. St. Paul, July 11, 1911; s. William Henry and Anna Lee (Barnum) K.; B.S., U. Minn., 1935, B.M., 1939, M.D., 1940; m. Lois Erna Marcouiller, June 16, 1939; children—Sandra Lois, William Ernest. Intern, U.S. Marine Hosp., Norfolk, Va., 1939-40; entered USPHS, served at U.S. Marine Hosp., Boston, 1940, U.S. Quarantine Sta., Boston, 1941; resident in neuropsychiatry N.Y. Psychiat. Inst., 1941, U.S. Marine Hosp., Ellis Island, N.Y., 1942; psychiatrist Fed. Reformatory, Chillicothe, O., 1942-44, U.S. Penitentiary, Leavenworth, Kan., 1944-45; chief med. officer and psychiatrist Fed. Correctional Instn., Sandstone, Minn., 1945-47; chief of assignment sect., div. of commd. officers USPHS, Washington, 1947-48; med. dir. Bur. Prisons, 1948-53; med. officer charge USPHS Outpatient Clinic, Washington, 1953- 57; program dir. Health Care Facilities Service, Dept. Health, Edn. and Welfare, 1957-68, acting health dir., 1968-69, asso. Region 6 program dir., 1969—. Med. dir. USPHS. Mem. A.M.A., Am. Psychiat. Assn., Assn. Mil. Surgeons U.S., USPHS Commd. Officers Assn., Am. Assn. Pub. Health Physicians, Kan. Pub. Health Assn. Roman Catholic. Home: 9216 Cherokee Lane Leawood KS 66206 Office: 601 E 12th St Kansas City MO 64106

KRUMBOLTZ, JOHN DWIGHT, psychologist; b. Cedar Rapids, Ia., Oct. 21, 1928; s. Dwight John and Margaret (Jones) K.; B.A., Coe Coll., Cedar Rapids, 1950; M.A., Columbia Tchrs. Coll., 1951; Ph.D., U. Minn., 1955; m. Helen Brandhorst, Aug. 22, 1954; children—Ann, Jennifer. Counselor, tchr. W. Waterloo (Ia.) High Sch., 1951-53; teaching asst., then instr. U. Minn., 1953-55; asst. prof. ednl. psychology, then asso. prof. Mich. State U., 1957-61; mem. faculty Stanford, 1961—, prof. edn. and psychology, 1966—. Served with USAF, 1955-57. Guggenheim fellow, 1967-68. Mem. Am. Psychol. Assn. (council of reps. 1968-71), Am. Ednl. Research Assn. (v.p. div. E., 1966-68), Am. Personnel and Guidance Assn. (Outstanding Research award 1959, 66, 68). Author: (with others) Learning to Study, 1960; (with Helen B. Krumboltz) Changing Children's Behavior, 1972; also articles, revs., monographs. Editor: Learning and the Educational Process, 1965; Revolution in Counseling, 1966; (with Carl E. Thoresen) Behavioral Counseling: Cases and Techniques, 1969. Home: 933 Valdez Pl Stanford CA 94305

KRUMHANSL, JAMES ARTHUR, physicist, educator; b. Cleve., Aug. 2, 1919; s. James and Marcella (Kelly) K.; B.S. in Elec. Engring., U. Dayton, 1939; M.S., Case Inst. Tech., 1940; Ph.D. in Physics, Cornell U., 1943; m. Barbara Dean Schminck, Dec. 26, 1944; children—James Lee, Carol Lynne, Peter Allen. Instr., Cornell U., 1943-44; physicist Stromberg-Carlson Co., 1944-46; mem. faculty Brown U., 1946-48, asso. prof., 1947-48; asst. prof., then asso. prof. Cornell U., 1948-55; asst. dir. research Nat. Carbon Co., 1955-57, asso. dir. research, 1957-58; prof. physics Cornell U., 1959—, dir. Lab. Atomic and Solid State Physics, 1960-64. Cons. to industry, 1946—; adv. com for AEC, Dept. Def., Nat. Acad. Sci., 1956—. Guggenheim fellow, 1959-60; NSF sr. postdoctoral fellow Oxford U., 1966-67. Fellow Am. Phys. Soc. (chmn. div. solid state physics 1968; councillor 1970—); mem. Am. Assn. U. Profs., A.A.A.S., Sigma Xi, Phi Kappa Phi. Republican. Presbyn. Club: Ithaca Yacht. Author articles. Editor Jour. Applied Physics, 1957-60; asso. editor Solid State Communications, 1963—, Rev. Modern Physics, 1968—. Home: 105 Berkshire Rd Ithaca NY 14850

KRUMHOLZ, LOUIS AUGUSTUS, educator; b. Harrington, Wash., Dec. 1, 1909; s. Frank Charles and Elizabeth (Griffin) K.; student St. Mary's Coll., Winona, Minn., 1927- 29, 30-31; B.S., Coll. St. Thomas, St. Paul, 1932; M.S., U. Ill., 1938; Ph.D., U. Mich., 1945; m. Edna Lorene Langhoff, Apr. 15, 1939. Asst. zoologist and draftsman Ill. Natural History Survey, Urbana, 1937-40; aquatic biologist Mich. Inst. Fisheries Research, Ann Arbor, 1940-45; instr. zoology Ind. U., also research asso. Ind. Lake and Stream Survey, Bloomington, 1945-50; aquatic biologist TVA, Oak Ridge 1950-54; resident biologist Lerner Marine Lab., Bimini, Bahamas, 1954-57; mem. faculty U. Louisville, 1957—, prof. biology, 1963—, dir. Water Resources Lab., 1967—. Mem. Am. Soc. Ichthyologists and Herpetologists (Best Student Paper award 1939, mng. editor Copeia 1963-65), Wildlife Soc. (Best Fisheries Paper award 1958, editor Wildlife Monographs 1958—), Ecol. Soc. Am., Am. Fisheries Soc., Brit. Ecol. Soc., Am. Soc. Zoologists, Am. Inst. Biol. Scis., A.A.A.S., Am. Soc. Fishery Research Biologists, Am. Soc. Limnology and Oceanography, Am. Water Resources Assn., Am. Assn. U. Profs. (pres. U. Louisville chpt. 1968-69), Ind., Ky. acads. sci., Sigma Xi. Home: 1214 Royal Av Louisville KY 40204

KRUMM, DANIEL JOHN, mfg. co. exec.; b. Sioux City, Ia., Oct. 15, 1926; s. Walter A. and Anna K. (Helmke) K.; B.A. in Commerce, U. Ia., 1950; postgrad. U. Mich., 1955; m. Ann L. Klingner, Feb. 28, 1953; children—David Jonathan, Timothy John. With Globe Office Furniture Co., Mpls., 1950-52; with Maytag Co., Newton, Ia., 1952—, v.p., 1970-71, exec. v.p., 1971—, also dir.; pres. Maytag Co. Ltd., Toronto, 1970—. Mem. Newton Citizens for Better Edn. Com., Newton Community Theatre. Served with USNR, 1944-46. Mem. Am. Marketing Assn. (past pres. Ia.), Newton C. of C. Maytag Mgmt. Club. Republican. Lutheran (council). Club: Newton Country. Home: 807 S 20th Av W Newton IA 50208 Office: 403 W 4th Av N Newton IA 50208

KRUMM, JOHN MCGILL, clergyman; b. South Bend, Ind., Mar. 15, 1913; s. William F. and Harriett Vincent (McGill) K.; A.A., Pasadena Jr. Coll., 1933; A.B., U. Cal., 1935; B.D., Va. Theol. Sem., 1938; Ph.D., Yale U., 1948; S.T.D., Kenyon, Gambier, Ohio, 1962; D.D., Berkeley Div. Sch. Ordained to ministry Episcopal Ch., 1938; vicar Episcopal chs., Compton Lynwood, Hawthorne, Cal., 1938-41; asst. rector St. Paul's Ch., New Haven, 1941-43; rector Ch. of St. Matthew, San Mateo, Cal., 1943-48; dean St. Paul's Cathedral, Los Angeles, 1948- 52; chaplain Columbia 1952-65; rector Church of Ascension, N.Y.C., 1965-71; bishop of So. Ohio, Episcopal Ch., 1971—. Vis. lectr. N.T., Berkeley Div. Sch., New Haven, 1942-43, ch. history Va. Theol., Sem., Alexandria, 1942; instr. Prospect Hill Sch., New Haven 1942-43; instr. religion U. So. Cal., 1950-52. Chmn. clergy div. U. Religious Conf., Los Angeles; pres. San Mateo-Burlingame (Cal.) Council Chs., 1947-48, Ch. Fedn. Los Angeles, 1951-52; chmn. nat. council Panel of Ams., 1953-61. Trustee Bexley Hall of Colgate-Rochester, Va. Theol. Sem., Kenyon Coll., Mt. Holyoke Coll. Democrat. Clubs: Century Assn., University. Author: Roadblocks of Faith (with J. A. Pike); What's In a Name: Why Am I an Episcopalian?; Modern Heresies, 1961; The Art of Being a Sinner, 1967. Home: 1273 Ida St Cincinnati OH 45202 Office: 412 Sycamore St Cincinnati OH 45202

KRUMME, ROBERT DARRELL, apparel co. exec.; b. St. Joseph, Mo., Oct. 13, 1938; s. Walter William and Etta (Hiner) K.; B.S., U. Neb., 1960; J.D. with honors, George Washington U., 1963; m. Judith Martha Sterner, Dec. 27, 1963; children—Dorothea, Robert, Ann. Admitted to N.Y. bar, 1964, also U.S. Supreme Ct.; with Covington & Burling, attys., Washington, 1962-63; asso. Sullivan & Cromwell, N.Y.C., 1963-69; sec., gen. counsel Cluett, Peabody & Co., Inc., N.Y.C., 1969—. Mem. N.Y. State, Am. bar assns., Assn. Bar City N.Y., Am. Soc. Corporate Secs., Sigma Chi, Ohi Delta Phi. Contbr. articles profl. jours. Home: 28 Stuyvesant Av Larchmont NY 10538 Office: 510 Fifth Av New York City NY 10036

KRUMRINE, CHARLES SIDNEY, banker; b. Bellefonte, Pa., June 29, 1897; s. Sidney and Mary Jane (Bubb) K.; grad. Pa. State U., 1918; m. Jane Brown Gilfillan, Sept. 20, 1924; 1 dau., Jane. With Liberty Real Estate Bank & Trust Co., Phila., 1923-57, v.p., dir., pres., 1940-56, chmn. exec. com., 1956-57; pres., dir. Central Pa. Gas Co., 1958-66; dir. investment com. Phila. Life Ins. Co. Bd. dirs. Better Bus. Bur. Greater Phila.; exec. com. finance com. Med. Service Assn. Pa.; treas. Meth. Hosp.; adv. bd. Holy Redeemer Hosp., Meadowbrook, Pa.; chmn. U.S. Savs. Bond Com. for Pa., 1956—. Served with AC, USN, World War I. Decorated Star of Solidarity (Italy), 1956. Mem. Pa. Soc. S.R., Pa. Bankers Assn. (chmn. group I, 1956). Navy League, Def. Orientation Conf. Assn. (regional dir. 1965—), Newcomen Soc. N. Am., Hist. Soc. Pa., Am. Legion, Sigma Alpha Epsilon. Republican. Episcopalian. Clubs: Bank Officers (past pres.), Sunday Breakfast, Philadelphia Country, Midday (Phila.); Seaview Country (Absecon, N.J). Home: 50 Raynham Rd Merion Station PA 19066 Office: Broad and Arch Sts Philadelphia PA 19107

KRUPA, GENE, musician; b. Chgo., Jan. 15, 1909; s. Bartley and Ann (Osloska) K.; student St. Joseph's Coll. (Ind.), 1926-27; m. Ethel Fawcett (dec.); m. 2d, Patricia Bowler, Apr. 22, 1959. Profl. drummer, 1927—; drummer Chgo. night clubs, later with Joe Kayser's band, dance orchestras of Red Nichols, Russ Columbo, Mal Hallett, Benny Goodman; formed dance orchestra, Gene Krupa and his orchestra, 1938-51; jazz player Philharmonic concert tours, recordings, TV; club appearances jazz trio and quartet, 1952—. Mem. Am. Fedn. Musicians. Author: Gene Krupa Drum Book. Address: 10 Ritchie Dr Yonkers NY 10705

KRUPANSKY, ROBERT BAZIL, US. judge; b. Cleve., Aug. 15, 1921; s. Frank A. and Anna (Lawrence) K.; B.A., Western Res. U., 1946, LL.B., 1948; J.D., Case Western Res. U., 1968; m. Marjorie Blaser, Nov. 13, 1952. Admitted to Ohio bar, 1948, also Supreme Ct. Ohio, Supreme Ct. U.S., U.S. Dist. Ct. No. Dist. Ohio, U.S. Circuit Ct. Appeals 6th Circuit, U.S. Ct. Customs and Patent Appeals, U.S. Customs Ct., ICC; pvt. practice, Cleve., 1948-52; asst. atty. gen. State of Ohio, 1951-57; mem. Gov. of Ohio cabinet and dir. Ohio Dept. Liquor Control, 1957-58; judge Common Pleas Ct. of Cuyahoga County, 1959-60; sr. partner Metzenbaum, Gaines, Krupansky, Finley & Stern, 1960-69; U.S. atty. No. Dist. Ohio, Cleve., 1969-70, U.S. judge, 1970—; adj. prof. law Case Western Res. U. Sch. Law, 1969-70. Served to 2d lt. AUS, 1942-46. Mem. Am., Fed., Ohio, Cleve., Cuyahoga County bar assns., Am. Judicature Soc., Assn. Asst. Attys. Gen. State Ohio. Home: 8303 Dalebrook Rd Independence OH 44131 Office: US Court House Cleveland OH 44114

KRUPAT, ARNOLD, educator; b. N.Y.C., Oct. 22, 1941; s. Milton and Ruth (Haberfeld) K.; B.A. summa cum laude, N.Y.U., 1962; postgrad. Universite de Strasbourg, 1962-63; M.A., Columbia, 1964, Ph.D., 1967; m. Cynthia Muser, Sept. 14, 1968; 1 dau., Tanya. Asst. prof. Rutgers U., 1966-68; prof. lit. Sarah Lawrence Coll., Bronxville, N.Y., 1968—; tchr. courses at State U. N.Y., Purchase, 1969-72. Mem. War Resisters League, 1969-72; mem. 9th Precinct Community Council, 1970-72. Fulbright fellow, 1962, Woodrow Wilson fellow, 1962, Nat. Endowment for Humanities fellow, 1970. Mem. Phi Beta Kappa. Contbr. book revs. to the Catholic World. Home: 305 E 10th St New York City NY 10009 Office: Bronxville NY 10708

KRUPSKA, DANIA (Mrs. Ted Thurston), choreographer; b. Fall River, Mass., Aug. 13, 1923; d. Bronislaw and Anna (Niementowska) Krupski; student Lankenau Sch. for Girls, Phila.; studied Ethel Phillips Dance Studio, Catherine Littlefield Ballet Studio, Mordkin Studio, Phila., Aubrey Hitchens Studio, N.Y., Egorova, Paris, Syvilla Fort, N.Y., Bobby Lewis Dir.'s Studio, N.Y.; m. Richard La Marr (div. 1953); 1 son, Brion LaMarr; m. 2d, Ted Thurston, May 27, 1954; 1 dau., Tina Lyn. Performed concerts, Phila., 1929-36, also toured Poland, Roumania, Balkan Countries, Hungary, Vienna, Palestine; joined Phila. Ballet (Littlefield) for European tour, 1937, Chgo. Opera Season, 1938; joined Am. Ballet (Ballanchine), N.Y.C., 1938; soloist Broadway prodn. Frank Fay Show, Radio City Music Hall Ballet; on nat. tour with Johnny Belinda; soloist in Chouve Souris, 1943; dancer in role of Dream Laurie, 1st nat. co. of Okla., later Broadway co., 1945; asst. to choreographer Agnes de Mille on Rodgers and Hammerstein prodn. Allegro, then in prodn. ballet Fall River Legend, opera Rape of Lucrece, Broadway prodns. Gentlemen Prefer Blonds, Paint Your Wagon, Girl in Pink Tights; assisted Michael Kidd in Broadway prodn. Can Can; choreographer Broadway prodn. Seventeen, 1st Shoestring Revue, Most Happy Fella, Carefree Heart, Happiest Girl in the World (Tony nominee), Her First Roman, 1968, Apollo and Miss Agnes, Met. Opera prodn. The Gypsy Baron; Italian mus. Rugantino, 1962, television Salute to the Peace Corps, 1965; guest choreographer Zorba for Nat. Theatre, Reykjavik, Iceland, 1971, Company for Stora Teatern, Gothenburg, Sweden, 1971, Fantastiks, Little Theatre, Gothenburg, 1971; dir. mus. prodns. N.Y. City Center, Most Happy Fella, 1959, Showboat, 1961, Fiorello, 1962 (also White House prodn. for gov.'s conf. 1968); television appearances include Buick Hour, 1952, Colgate Comedy Hour, 1953, Omnibus, U.S. Steel Theatre Guild Prodns. Mem. Actors Equity Assn., Soc. Stage Dirs and Choreographers (exec. bd. mem.). Ballets: Outlook for Three, Pointes on Jazz. Home: 43 Toilsome Lane East Hampton NY 11937 Office: 564 W 52d St New York City NY 10019

KRUS, DONALD M., educator; b. Paterson, N.J., Jan. 8, 1924; B.A., Drew U., 1949; M.A., Clark U., 1951, Ph.D. in Psychology, 1957; married; 1 child. Asst., Rockland Brain Research Project, Columbia-Greystone Assn., 1949-50; project dir. Am. Inst. Research, 1952-54; copywriter Union Switch & Signal Co., Westinghouse Air Brake Corp., 1954-55; asst. prof. psychology, co-dir. USPHS research grant Clark U., Worcester, Mass., 1957-62, asso. prof. psychology, 1962-69; prof., chmn. dept. psychology U. Mass., Boston. Served with USAAF, 1942-45. Mem. A.A.A.S., Am. Psychol. Assn. Office: Dept Psychology U Mass Boston MA 02116*

KRUSA, HANS ERNST, educator; b. Redwood, N.Y., Aug. 11, 1914; s. Henry B. and Johanna (Ebeling) K.; B.A., St. Olaf Coll., 1937; M.Sc. in Retailing, N.Y. U., 1938, Ph.D., 1955; M.S.P.H., U. of N.C., 1968; m. Renee Rontaine, Aug. 24, 1940 children—Paul F., Joan, Peter B. Formerly radio announcer sta. WCAL, Northfield, Minn.; with mgmt. div. Frederick Loeser and Co., Bklyn. and sales dept. R.H. Macy & Co.; mgmt. div. and treasurer's div., then supr. and merchandise control systems, James McCreery & Co., N.Y.C.; mem. faculty, Sears, Roebuck found. prof. retailing Sch. Retailing, N.Y.U., 1940-68; faculty Sch. Trade and Indsl. Edn., U. Fla., summer 1942; active planning, directing and presenting mgmt. seminars for bus. execs.; adv. to Govt. of Nigeria to organize bus. faculty U. Lagos, AID, 1962-64; project specialist bus. edn. Ford Found. U. Alexandria (U.A.R.), 1966-67; Ford Found. Mid-Career fellow Population Center U. N.C., 1967-68; project specialist population Ford Found., India, 1968-71; dep. dir. Carolina Population Center, U. N.C., Chapel Hill, 1971—. Mem. personnel com. Internat. House, N.Y.C.; past pres. bd. edn., Union Free Sch. Dist. 4, Northport, L.I., N.Y. Served to lt. USNR, 1943-46; mem. Res. Mem. Am. Marketing Assn., N.Y. State Sch. Bds. Assn., Population Assn. Am., Am. Pub. Health Assn., Soc. for Internat. Devel., Eta Mu Pi, Pi Kappa Delta. Clubs: N.Y.U. Faculty; Northport Yacht. Home: 703 Emory Dr Chapel Hill NC 27514

KRUSCHEN, JACK JOSEPH, actor; b. Winnipeg, Man., Can., Mar. 20, 1922; s. Morris and Sophie (Bogushevsky) K.; came to U.S., 1924; grad. high sch.; m. Violet Raphael Perruzzi, Feb. 23, 1963; children—Susan, Steven; stepson, Mark Mooring. Actor, KNX-Radio, 1938, since appeared on every leading radio dramatic and comedy show; appeared in TV on W6XAO, Los Angeles, 1939; motion pictures include Red Hot and Blue, 1948, The Apartment (Acad. award nomination for best actor), 1960; appeared in Broadway shows I Can Get It For You Wholesale, 1962, Promises, Promises (winner London Drama Critics award for best supporting actor), 1969-70; occasionally conduct acting seminars for univ., coll. students and tchrs. Served with AUS, 1942-45. Address: care CMA 8899 Beverly Blvd Los Angeles CA 90048

KRUSE, ALBERT, architect; b. Wilmington, Del., Dec. 22, 1897; s. Albert and Tilly Kruse; student Mass. Inst. Tech., 1916-18, 1920-22; m. Edith Gnann, Aug., 1940; children—William A., Elise D. Designer, Maginnis & Walsh, 1922-24, Charles Z. Klauder, 1924-34; with George E. Pope & Albert Kruse, Wilmington, 1935—; prin. works include restoration of Court House, and of New Castle (Del.) Presbyn. Church, Highlands Elementary Sch., Wilmington, Supreme Ct., Dover. Mem. Del. Art Center, chmn. exhibit commn., 1940—. Served with USN, World War I. Registered architect Del., Md., Pa. Fellow A.I.A. (pres. 1940-42). Club: Torch. Author: New Castle Sketches, 1932; Age of Confidence (illustrator), 1934. Home: 123 Edgewood Rd Alapocas Wilmington DE 19803 Office: 1116 West St Wilmington DE 19805

KRUSE, ARTHUR G., banker; b. Van Horn, Ia., 1898; ed. U. Ia. Formerly pres., mgr. First Fed. Savs. & Loan Assn., Alhambra, Cal.; now vice chmn. bd. Cal. Fed. Savs. & Loan Assn., Los Angeles; pres., dir. Alhambra Bond Co. Mason. Home: 904 W Huntington Dr Arcadia CA 91116 Office: 1 W Bay State Alhambra CA 91801

KRUSE, ARTHUR HENRY, social worker; b. Akron, O., Jan.7, 1910; s. Arthur E. and Mabel (Cramer) K.; A.B., U. Akron, 1930; A.M., Syracuse U., 1933; M.Sc., Western Res. U., 1940; m. Marianne Willis, Jan. 6, 1933; children—Gretchen, Stephen. Adminstr. pub. welfare activities N.Y. and Ohio, 1933-37; dir. pub. assistance, Summit County, O., 1937-40; asst. prof. pub. welfare Sch. Applied Social Sci., Western Res. U., Cleve., 1940-43; exec. sec. Council Social Agys., Akron, 1943-48; part time faculty mem. U. Akron, 1936-48; exec. dir. United Community Services, Washington, 1948-52; gen. sec. Family Service Assn., Cleve., 1952-62; exec. dir. Chgo. Community Fund and Met. Crusade of Mercy, 1962—; lectr. Mem. Nat. Assn. Social Workers (nat. pres. 1953- 55). Conglist. Rotarian. Clubs: Torch, University; Commercial (Chgo.). Home: 316 Forest St Winnetka IL 60093 Office: 72 W Adams St Chicago IL 60603

KRUSE, CORNELIUS WOLFRAM, sanitary engr., educator; b. College Station, Tex., Feb. 19, 1913; s. Samuel Andrew and Geraldine (Eilts), K.; B.S., Mo. Sch. Mines, 1934, C.E., 1939; M.S., Harvard, 1940; Dr.P.H., U. Pitts., 1961; m. Adele Reeburgh, Feb. 1, 1939; children—Judith Philippides, Carol Steil, Christina Ricklen, Cornelia. Resident san. engr. TVA, Health and Safety Dept., 1935-46; asso. prof. san. engring. Sch. Hygiene and Pub. Health Johns Hopkins, Balt., 1946-61, prof., head dept. environmental health, 1961—; vis. prof., head dept. pub. health engring. Inst. Hygiene U. Philippines, Manila, 1953-55; cons. TVA, WHO, Rockefeller Found., AID. Mem. Md. Bd. Health and Mental Hygiene. Chmn. subcom. animal reservoirs and vectors NRC San. Engring. and Environment, 1951-53; tech. mem. Md. Air Pollution Study Commn., 1950-51; mem. Commn. Environmental Hygiene Armed Forces Epidemiological Bd., 1963—. Mem. Am. Acad. Environmental Engrs., Am. Soc. C.E., Am. Water Works Assn., Am. Indsl. Hygiene Assn., Am. Pub. Health Assn., Am. Soc. Tropical Medicine and Hygiene. Contbr. articles profl. jours. Home: 2708 Beethoven Av Baltimore MD 21207 Office: 615 N Wolf St Baltimore MD 21205

KRUSE, EDGAR CHRIST, hosp. adminstr.; b. Ft. Wayne, Ind., June 15, 1912; s. Henry C. and Emma (Dreyer) K.; student Ind. U., 1930-33; m. Mildred Kramer, May 15, 1937; children—Dale Keith, Dennis Neal, Donald Edgar. Messenger, jr. exec. Home Tel. & Tel. Co., 1928-48; gen. auditor City Utilities, Ft. Wayne, 1948-52; asst. adminstr. Lutheran Hosp., Ft. Wayne, 1952-59, adminstr., 1959—. Mem. Ind. Bd. Health Regulating and Licensing Council, 1963-67; mem. adv. bd. Sch. Practical Nursing. Bd. dirs. A.R.C., Ft. Wayne chpt. Mem. Am. Assn. Hosp. Accountants (past pres. Ind. chpt.), Northeastern Ind. Hosp. Council (past pres.), Luth. Hosp. Assn. Am. (dir., past pres.), Tri-State Hosp. Assembly (dir., pres.), Ft. Wayne C. of C. Clubs: Junto Executive (dir., past pres.), 100 Per Cent (Ft. Wayne). Home: 6037 Ranger Trail Fort Wayne IN 46805 Office: 3024 Fairfield Av Fort Wayne IN 46807

KRUSE, HARRY DAYTON, med. researcher; b. Bridgeton, N.J., July 9, 1900; s. Charles and Emma Margaret (Woodruff) K.; A.B., Dickinson Coll., 1922, A.M., 1926, Dr. Chem., 1955; Sc.D., Johns Hopkins, 1926, M.D., 1932; m. Mary Helen Grayston, July 28, 1944; children—H. Dayton, Douglas, Duncan. NRC fellow in biochemistry, 1926-28; asso. in biochemistry Johns Hopkins, 1928-33, asso. prof., 1933-37; med. research with Milbank Meml. Fund, N.Y.C., 1937-52; exec. sec. Com. on Pub. Health, N.Y. Acad. Medicine, 1952-68; dir. div. of research and planning Med. Soc. State of N.Y., 1968- -; councilor Am. Inst. Nutrition, 1953-56. Mem. food and nutrition bd., chmn. com. on diagnosis and pathology of nutritional deficiencies NRC, 1942-48; mem. nutrition com. N.Y.C. chpt. A.R.C., 1940-53; v.p., mem. bd. dirs. Community Council of Greater N.Y., Inc. 1956-57. Bd. dirs. Goodwill Industries, Inc. v.p. Welfare and Health Council, N.Y.C., 1954-55; mem. Mayor's Commn. on Narcotics Addiction, 1965, Mayor's Task Force on Air Pollution, 1966. Served as cons. to Surgeon Gen. AUS, World War II. Fellow A.A.A.S., N.Y. Acad. Med., Am. Pub. Health Assn. Mem. Am. Soc. Biol. Chemists, Phi Beta Kappa, Sigma Xi, Alpha Chi Rho, Delta Omega. Contbr. articles on deficiency diseases and diagnosis of malnutrition. Editor books on alcoholism and mental disease. Author: Nutrition, Its Meaning, Scope and Significance. Home: 62 Tanglewylde Av Bronxville NY 10708 Office: 420 Lakeville Rd Lake Success NY 11040

KRUSE, HEEREN SAMUEL EILTS, architect; b. St. Louis, Oct. 20, 1911; s. Samuel Andrew and Geraldine (Eilts) K.; B.Arch., U. Ill., 1933, grad. study, 1934; student Beaux Arts Inst. Design, 1929-34, Bauhaus Sch. Design, 1935, seminar Taliesin, 1935; grad. Command and Gen. Staff Sch., 1945; m. Ada Juanita Meccalf, 1936 (div. 1942); m. 2d, Mary Ruth Owens, Dec. 21, 1945; children—Mary Katherine, David Samuel Owens, Candice Serena. Draftsman, George Fred Keck, Chgo., 1934-35; sec.-treas. Harford Field, Inc., architect, Hinsdale, Ill., 1935-36; master graphic arts Lake Forest (Ill.) Acad., 1936; architect E.A. Gruensfeld, Jr., Chgo., 1936-38; gen. practice, Chgo. and Centralia, Ill., 1939-42; architect William E. Kittle, Robert Law Weed & Assoc., also Nims, Inc., 1947-51; partner Watson & Deutschman, 1951-60; v.p. Watson, Deutschman & Kruse, architect and engrs., 1961—; instr. Miami Draftsmen's Club, 1959-62; lectr., adj. prof., prof. Clemson U., U. Miami, U. Waterloo, 1967—; projects include Young Sch., Salem Twp., Ill., 1941, Yoyogi Chapel, Tokyo, Japan, 1946, U.S. Post Office, Biscayne Annex, Miami, 1956, Cutler Ridge Jr. High Sch., 1960, U. Miami Library, 1961, Fla. Atlantic U., 1963, Miami Springs Sr. High Sch., 1964, Computing Center, U. Miami, 1965, Triton Towers, Miami Beach, 1967. Mem. Welfare Bldg. Council; chmn. edn. com. Interprofl. Council for Environmental Design, 1969—. Mem. bd. Children's Home Soc. of Florida, asst. treas., 1959; mem. Dade County Research Found., U. Miami Sustaining Found.; mem. adv. bd. League Women Voters. Bd. dirs. Douglas Village (Fla). Served to col., C.E., AUS 1942-46. Medalist, Beaux Inst. Design, 1933. Fellow A.I.A. (dir. Fla. region 1967-69, past exec. com.); mem. Fla. Assn. Architects (sec. 1957, pres. 1958, dir. bd. 1959-63), Soc. Am. Mil. Engrs., Miami Econ. Research Soc., Fla. Planning and Zoning Assn., Sch. Thermal Environment Council, Constrn. Specifications Inst., Alpha Rho Chi. Home: 14521 Memorial Hwy North Miami FL 33161 Office: 1600 NW LeJeune Rd Miami FL 33144

KRUSE, ROLAND ROBERT, lawyer; b. Wapakoneta, O., Apr. 7, 1917; s. August L. and Lelia (Pohl) K.; B.A., Miami U., 1937; J.D., U. Mich., 1940; m. Doyce R. Manning, May 6, 1967; children-James A., Bonnie Jean (Mrs. Richard E. Parker), Robert K. Admitted to Ohio bar, 1940, Ariz. bar, 1951; practice in Wapakoneta, 1940-42, Phoenix, 1952—; ind. ins. claim adjuster, Phoenix, 1947-52; mem. firm Snell & Wilmer, 1952—. Pres. North Congl. Homes, Phoexix. Served with USNR, 1943-46. Mem. Am. (com. vice chmn.), Ohio, Ariz. (sect. chmn.), Maricopa County bar assns., Am. Coll. Probate Counsel (Ariz. state chmn.). Mem. United Ch. of Christ. Mason. Home: 727 E Desert Park Lane Phoenix AZ 85020 Office: Security Bldg Phoenix AZ 85004

KRUSEN, EDWARD MONTGOMERY, educator, physician; b. Phila., Feb. 7, 1920; s. Edward M. and Gladys (Hopper) K.; B.A., U. Pa., 1941, M.D., 1944; M.S., U. Minn., 1950; m. Ursula Leden, Nov. 13, 1948; children—Richard Montgomery, Nancy Elizabeth. Intern, Phila. Gen. Hosp., 1944-45; resident phys. medicine and rehab. Mayo Clinic, 1945-46, 48-50, 1st asst., 1949-50; dir. dept., chief service, phys. medicine and rehab. Baylor U. Med. Center, 1950—, dir. Sch. Phys. Therapy, 1951—, prof. phys. therapy, 1958—; mem. faculty Southwestern Med. Sch., 1951—, prof. phys. medicine and rehab., 1961—, chmn. dept., 1951-55; VA area cons., 1954—; med. cons. Am. Rehab. Found., 1957—. Chmn. med. adv. bd., mem. exec. bd. United Cerebral Palsy Assn. Tex.; mem. Gov.'s Commn. on Vocational Rehab.; mem. med. adv. bd. Arthritis and Rheumatism Assn., Hemophilia Assn., Muscular Dystrophy Assn. Served to capt. M.C., AUS, 1946-48. Recipient Community Service award Goodwill Industries Dallas, 1955; award for service United Cerebral Palsy Assn. Tex., 1964, Muscular Dystrophy Assn., 1965, 67. Diplomate Am. Bd. Phys. Medicine and Rehab. (mem. bd.). Mem. A.M.A. (adv. com. phys. therapy edn.), So. (chmn. sect. phys. medicine and rehab. 1953), Tex. (chmn. rehab. com. 1964—), Dallas med. assns., Tex. Soc. Phys. Medicine and Rehab. (sec. 1957, chmn. 1959), Am., Tex. (bd. govs. 1964-68) rheumatism assns., Am. Congress Phys. Medicine and Rehab., Am. Acad. Phys. Medicine and Rehab., Med. Dirs. Phys. Therapy Schs. (chmn. 1960), Internat. Soc. Welfare Disabled, So. Clin. Soc., Am. Acad. Cerebral Palsy, Sigma Xi. Club: Dallas Gun. Contbr. numerous articles in field, also chpts. in books. Home: 3500 Colgate Av Dallas, TX 75225.

KRUSEN, FRANK HAMMOND, physician; b. Phila., June 26, 1898; s. Wilmer and Elizabeth Pearson (Gilbert) K.; grad. Wm. Penn Charter Prep. Sch., 1915; premed. student Jefferson Med. Coll. 1915-16, M.D., 1921, LL.D., (hon.) 1966; M.D. (hon.), Justus Liebig U., Giessen, Germany, 1962; m. Margaret Louise Borland, May 28, 1921; children—Joanne Elizabeth (Mrs. Robert M. Hart), Janice Alison. Intern, Jefferson Hosp., Phila., 1921-24, asst. surgeon, 1925-26; asst. surgeon Phila. Gen. Hosp., 1925-28; asso. in medicine and dir. dept. phys. medicine Temple U., 1929-35; asso. dean Temple Med. Sch., 1925- 35; head, sect. on phys. medicine and rehab. Mayo Clinic, 1935- 58, sr. cons., 1958-63; v.p. staff Mayo Clinic, 1957-58; asso. prof. phys. medicine and rehab. Mayo Found. U. Minn., 1935-41, prof., 1941-63, prof., emeritus, 1963—; pres. Sister Elizabeth Kenny Found., Inc.; dir. Kenny Rehab. Inst., 1960-63, prof., coordinator phys. medicine and rehab. Temple U. Sch. Medicine and Hosp., Phila., 1963-68, prof. emeritus, 1968—, dir. rehab. planning, 1965-68, project dir. research and tng. center phys. medicine and rehab., 1964-68; sr. cons. phys. medicine and rehab. Moss Rehab. Hosp., 1964-68; project dir. research and tng. center phys. medicine and rehab., prof. phys. medicine and rehab. Tufts U. Sch. Medicine, 1968-70; chief cons. phys. medicine Army surgeon gen., 1946-49, 51-68, VA, 1946- 49. Served with S.A.T.C., World War I. Dir., mem. adminstrv. bd., chmn. sci. adv. com. of Baruch Com. on Phys. Medicine, 1944-51, chmn. Baruch Com. on War and Post War Phys. Rehab., 1944-51; counselor Nat. Soc. for Crippled Children, 1947-59; chmn. Am. Bd. Phys. Medicine and Rehab., 1947-49; pres. Minn. Bd. Health, 1955-63; pres. Internat. Congress Phys. Medicine, 1960; mem. com. on rehab. Am. Heart Assn., 1957-58; chmn. Am. Rehab. Found.; chmn. Gov.'s Com. Vocational Rehab., 1955-60; co- chmn. ad hoc com. Pres.'s Com. on Employment of Handicapped, 1966; mem. exec. com., bd. dirs. Goodwill Industries, Inc., 1967—, v.p. bd. dirs., 1968-69. Trustee, Nat. Inst. on Rehab. and Health Services; bd. dirs. Elizabeth Kenny Inst. Recipient 1944 Ann. Gold Key award Am. Congress of Phys. Medicine and Rehab.; Physicians Award for services to handicapped Pres. U.S., 1953; award of Merit, State Pa., 1954; Modern Medicine Distinguished Service award, 1956; Distinguished Service award A.M.A., 1958; citation Minn. Gov., 1958; Gold medal award Conn. Soc. Phys. Medicine, 1960; Goodwill Industries award, 1961; Dignity of Man award Kessler Inst. Rehab., 1966; George G. Deaver award Inst. for Crippled and Disabled, N.Y.C., 1968; Dwight Eisenhower award, 1969; Speedy award Paralyzed Vets. Am., 1970; citation Nat. Industries for Blind, 1970. Fellow A.C.P., Royal Soc. Medicine (hon.); asso. fellow Am. Acad. Phys. Edn.; mem. Am. Acad. Phys. Medicine and Rehab. (past pres.), Am. Congress of Phys. Medicine and Rehab. (past pres.; treas. 1950-70), Soc. Phys. Medicine (past pres.), A.A.A.S., A.M.A. (chmn. council on med. physics, chmn. com. on rehab., del. from sect. on phys. medicine), World Med. Assn., Am. Assn. U. Profs., Internat. Fedn. Phys. Medicine (founder, 1st pres. 1952), Am. Med. Writers Assn., Minn. Med. Assn., Minn. Physiat. Soc (hon.), Brit. Assn. Phys. Medicine (hon.), Danish Soc. Phys. Medicine (hon.), Am. Rheumatism Assn., Liga Argentina contra el Rhumatisme (hon.), All-India Occupational Therapists Assn. (hon.), Brazilian Soc. Phys. Medicine (hon.), Pa. Soc. of S.R., Sigma Xi (pres. Mayo Found. chpt. 1958-59), Blue Key, Phi Alpha Sigma, Theta Nu Epsilon. Republican. Episcopalian. Mason. Club: University (Rochester, Minn.). Author: Light Therapy, 1933; Physical Therapy in Arthritis, 1937; Physical Medicine, 1941; Concepts in Rehabilitation of the Handicapped, 1964. Editor: Yearbook of Physical Medicine and Rehabilitation, 1949-51; Physical Medicine and Rehabilitation for the Clinican, 1951; Handbook of Physical Medicine and Rehabilitation, 1965; Iberia Jour. Editorial bd. Internat. Rev. of Phys. Medicine, Geriatrics, Geriatric Rev., Exerpta Medica. Contbr. med. jours. Home: Route 1 Box 301 Orleans, MA 02653

KRUSEN, HENRY STANLEY, investment banker; b. East Orange, N.J., Jan. 13, 1907; s. Henry Addis and Sallie (Scarborough) K.; A.B., Cornell U., 1928; postgrad., Sch. Bus., N.Y. U., 1930-52; m. Elizabeth Geary Hoopes, Oct. 24, 1941; children—Sallie (Mrs. Albert E. Riester), Richard T. With Nat. City Co., N.Y.C., 1928-34, Harriman, Ripley & Co., Inc., N.Y.C., 1934-42; with Shearson, Hammill & Co., Inc., and predecessor, 1946—, sr. v.p., 1964- 65, pres., 1966-70, also dir.; dir. Higbie Mfg. Co., Rochester, Mich., Russ Togs, Inc., N.Y.C., Wheeling Pitt. Steel Corp., Pitts., Kings Dept. Stores, Newton, Mass. Founder, Nat. Young Republicans, 1930; chmn. East Orange Rep. City Com., 1939-41; vice chmn. Essex County Rep. Com., 1940-41. Bd. dirs., chmn. exec. com. Beekman Downtown Hosp., N.Y.C., 1957—; trustee, chmn. finance com. Union Coll., Cranford, N.J.; past trustee treas., chmn. finance com. Overlook Hosp., Summit. Served to comdr. USNR, 1943-45. Decorated Legion of Merit. Mem. Phi Kappa Psi, Scabbard and Blade. Clubs: Baltusrol Golf (Springfield, N.J.); Gardiners's Bay Golf (Shelter Island, N.Y.); Bond (N.Y.C.). Home: 80 Prospect Hill Av Summit NJ 07901 Office: 14 Wall St New York City NY 10005

KRUSEN, LESLIE CONARD, lawyer; b. Phila., May 7, 1897; s. George Cornell and Lavinia (Conard) K.; grad. Farnum Prep. Sch., 1914; B.S., U. Pa., 1918, LL.B., 1922; m. Kathryn Malan, Jan. 27, 1923 (dec.); children—Leslie C., Gordon M.; 2d m. Leatha Davis, Nov. 25, 1949. Admitted to Pa. bar, 1922; asso. Biddle, Paul, Dawson & Yocum, Phila., 1922-30; partner Krusen, Evans & Byrne, specializing in maritime and corporate law, 1930—; counsel various steamship, oil, ins. cos. Served as ensign, USN, 1917-19. Mem. Am., Pa. State, Phila. bar assns., Maritime Law Assn. U.S., Lambda Chi Alpha. Clubs: Racquet (Phila.); Riverton Country; Downtown. Home: 110 Oakford Av Delanco NJ 08075 Office: 21 S 12th St Philadelphia PA 19107

KRUSHENICK, NICHOLAS, artist; b. N.Y.C., May 31, 1929; student Hofmann Sch., N.Y.C. Cofounder Brata Gallery, N.Y.C.; exhibited in one man shows at Camino Gallery, N.Y.C., 1956, Brata Gallery, N.Y.C., 1958, 60. Graham Gallery, 1962, 64, Cinema I and Cinema II, N.Y.C., 1964; exhibited in group shows at Wagner Coll., 1958, Howard Wise Gallery, Cleve., 1960, Barnard Coll., 1962, Galerie Creuze, Paris, 1958, Modern, Tokyo, 1959, Mus. Modern Art Contemporary Painters and Sculptors as Printmakers, 1964, De Cordova, Lincoln, Mass., 1962, Whitney Mus. Am. Art Ann., 1963, Los Angeles County Mus. Art, Post Painterly Abstraction, 1964; represented in permanent collections Kalamazoo Inst., Mus. Modern Art. Served with AUS, 1947-48. Longview Found. grantee. Address: 131 W 21st St New York City NY 10011*

KRUSKAL, MARTIN DAVID, math. physicist; b. N.Y.C., Sept. 28, 1925; s. Joseph Bernard and Lillian Rose (Vorhaus) K.; B.S., U. Chgo., 1945; M.S., N.Y. U., 1948, Ph.D., 1952; m. Laura Lovejoy Lashinsky, Oct. 8, 1950; children—Karen Lillian, Kerry David, Clyde Philip. Research asst., part-time instr. math. N.Y. U., to 1951; research asso. Princeton Plasma Physics Lab. (formerly Project Matterhorn), 1951-59, sr. research asso., 1959—, asso. head, theoretical div., 1956-64, now prof. astrophys. scis. Princeton, chmn. applied math. program, 1968—. Mem. U.S. contingent, 2d Internat. Conf. on Peaceful Uses Atomic Energy, Geneva, 1958, IAEA Conf., 1961; cons. Los Alamos Sci. Lab., Livermore Radiation Lab., Oak Ridge Nat. Lab., RCA, IBM; dir. Internat. Sch. Nonlinear Math. and Physics, summer 1966. NSF sr. postdoctoral fellow, 1959-60; Fulbright grantee U. Grenoble, Summer Sch. Theoretical Physics, Les Houches, France, 1959. Fellow Am. Phys. Soc.; mem. Am. Math. Soc., Math. Assn. Am., Soc. Indsl. and Applied Math., Phi Beta Kappa, Sigma Xi, Pi Lambda Phi. Author: (with others) La théorie des gaz neutres et ionisés, 1960. Home: 60 Littlebrook Rd N Princeton NJ 08540

KRUSKAL, WILLIAM HENRY, educator, statistician; b. N.Y.C., Oct. 10, 1919; s. Joseph Bernard and Lillian Rose (Vorhaus) K.; S.B., Harvard, 1940, M.S., 1941; Ph.D., Columbia, 1955; m. Norma Jane Evans, Aug. 23, 1942; children—Vincent Joseph, Thomas Evan, Jonas David. Mathematician, U.S. Naval Proving Ground, 1941-44; v.p. Kruskal and Kruskal, Inc., N.Y.C., 1946-48; mem. facutly U. Chgo., 1950—, prof. statistics, 1962—, chmn. dept., 1966—. Vis. prof. U. Cal. at Berkeley, 1955-56, Harvard, summer 1959; fellow Center Advanced Study Behavioral Scis., 1970-71. Served with USNR, 1944-46. Sr. postdoctoral fellow NSF, 1970-71. Fellow Inst. Math. Statistics (pres. 1970-71), Am. Statis. Assn., A.A.A.S.; mem. Internat. Statis. Inst., Royal Statis. Soc., Am. Math. Soc., Math. Assn. Am., Biometric Soc., Internat. Assn. Statistics in Phys. Scis., Phi Beta Kappa, Sigma Xi. Editor: Annals of Mathematical Statistics, 1958-61; Mathematical Sciences and Social Sciences, 1970; asso. editor for statistics Internat. Ency. Social Scis.; chmn. editorial bd. Statis. Research Monographs, 1953-58. Home: 1227 E 54th St Chicago IL 60615

KRUTZSCH, PHILIP HENRY, prof. anatomy, head dept. U. Ariz. Address: Dept of Anatomy Univ Ariz Tucson AZ 85721

KRUYER, CLETUS H., banker; b. Indpls., Feb. 4, 1921; s. Cletus H. and Frances (Sullivan) K.; A.B., Ind. U., 1948; M.A., U. Notre Dame, 1971; m. Laura Lindley, Sept. 30, 1950; children—Kathleen, Karen, Peter. With First Bank and Trust Co., S. Bend. Ind., 1948—, pres., 1965—. Bd. dirs. United Community Services, S. Bend, 1967—; exec. com. Ind. U. Alumni, 1967—. Served with USNR, 1943- 46; ETO. Mem. Ind. Bankers Assn. (past pres., mem. council), S. Bend C. of C. (chmn. govt. relations div. 1967). Episcopalian. Elk. Clubs: S. Bend Country; Indiana (bd. dirs. 1967—). Home: 1528 Hoover Av South Bend IN 46615 Office: 133 S Main St South Bend IN 46601

KRUZEL, JOSEPH JOHN, air force officer; b. Wilkes-Barre, Pa., Feb. 17, 1918; s. John Andrew and Mary (Wozniak) K.; B.S., U. Scranton, 1938; grad. Air Command and Staff Sch., 1949, Air War Coll., 1954, Nat. War Coll., 1961; m. Violet M. Clark, Aug. 1, 1944; children—Joseph John, Victoria L. (Mrs. Lawrence P. Farrell, Jr.), David C., Daniel P. Commd. 2d lt. USAAF, 1940, advanced through grade to maj. gen., USAF, 1968; fighter pilot P.I. and S.W. Pacific, 1941-42; dep. comdr., then comdr. 361st Fighter Group, Eng., 1943-44; dep. comdr. Seymour Johnson Air Base, 1945; staff officer, Korea and Japan, 1946-47; comdr. 18th Fighter Group, 1948; staff officr war plans div. hdqrs. USAF, 1949-53; mem. staff Air War Coll., 1954-57; staff officer USAFE and SHAPE, 1958-60; vice comdr., then comdr. 354th Tactical Fighter Wing, 1961-64; comdr. 832d Air Div., 1964 65; dep. chief staff operations Hdqrs. PACAF, 1965-68; vice comdr. 5th Air Force Japan, 1968-69; dep. dir. operations hdqrs. USAF, 1969-70. Decorated Silver Star with oak leaf cluster, D.S.M., Legion of Merit, D.F.C. with 2 oak leaf clusters, Bronze Star, Air medal with 5 oak leaf clusters, Army Commendation medal. Mem. Am. Legion, Fighter Aces Assn., Air Force Assn., Air Force Hist. Assn. Home: PO Box 117 Shalimar FL 32579

KRYTER, KARL DAVID, research engr.; b. Indpls., Oct. 13, 1914; s. George David and Mary Matilda (Christoph) K.; student Ind. U., 1935-37; A.B., Butler U., 1939; Ph.D., U. Rochester, 1942; m. Grace Irene Brown, June 21, 1946; children—Dianne, Victoria (Mrs. Myron I. Liebhaber), Kathryn. Research fellow Harvard, 1942-46; asst. prof. Washington U., 1946-48; dir. human resources research labs. Air Force Cambridge Research Center, 1948-57; head dept. psychoacoustics Bolt Beranek & Newman, Inc., Cambridge, Mass., 1957-65; dir. Sensory Scis. Research Center of Stanford Research Inst., Menlo Park, Cal., 1965—; chmn. bd. dirs. Acousis Co. (Los Altos, Cal.); tchr. Colby Coll., 1960-63, Mass. Inst. Tech., 1958-59. Advisor U.S. Pres.'s Office for Sci. and Tech., 1968-70; mem. SST environmental study com. Dept. Interior, 1969; chmn. exec. council com. hearing and bioacoustics Nat. Acad. Sci.-NRC, 1960. Recipient research grants NIH, 1965-72, Nat. Inst. Mental Health, 1970-72. Fellow Am. Psychol. Assn. (council reps. 1966-69), Soc. Engring. Psychologists (pres. 1965), Acoustical Soc. Am. (pres. 1972); mem. Brit. Acoustical Soc. Author: The Effects of Noise on Man, 1970. Contbr. articles profl. jours. Home: 13725 Robleda Rd Los Altos Hills CA 94022 Office: 333 Ravenswood Av Menlo Park CA 94025

KRYZA, ELMER GREGORY, fgn. service officer; b. Detroit, Mar. 12, 1922; s. Frank Theodore and Anna Frances (Chapp) K.; student Oberlin Coll., 1944-45; grad. U. Va., 1946, Air War Coll., 1968; m. Jeanne Marie Deniau, Apr. 7, 1949; children—Frank Theodore, Christopher Deniau. Products expediter Bohn Aluminum, Detroit, 1940-42; civilian staff USN, Tangier, Ciudad Trujillo, 1947-50; vice consul, Curacao, 1952-54; 3d sec. Am. embassy, Brussels, Belgium, 1954-57; 2d sec., Belgrade, Yugoslavia, 1957-59; supervisory adminstrv. officer Dept. State, 1959-63; 1st sec., Nairobi, Kenya, 1963-67; counselor, Kinshasa, 1968-70; counselor, Rio de Janeiro and Brasilia, Brazil, 1970—. Pres. Sch. Bd. Am. Sch., Kinshasa, 1968-70. Served to lt. USNR, 1942-47, 50-52; ETO, Korea. Recipient meritorious service award Dept. State, 1965. Mem. Fgn. Service Assn., Phi Delta Theta. Contbr. articles profl. jours. Home: Dept State Washington DC 20520 Office: Am Emasssy Rio de Janeiro APO New York City NY 09676

KRYZSKO, SYLVESTER JOSEPH, banker, coll. regent; b. Greenbush, Minn, Dec. 3, 1903; s. Francis and Katherine (Marciniak) K.; diploma Am. Inst. Banking, 1937, Rutgers U. Grad. Sch. Banking, 1941, Harvard Sr. Bank Officers Seminar, 1958; m. Vivian LaVone Bradley, May 6, 1934; children—Camilla Jane, Karen Ann. With Farmers & Mchts. State Bank, Greenbush, 1922-25, Minn. Banking Dept., 1925; with Winona Nat. & Savs. Bank (Minn.), 1925-70, pres., dir., 1949-70; pres., dir. Town & Country State Bank of Winona, 1971—; chmn. bd. First State Bank, Rollingstone, Minn., 1969—; pres. Winona Devel. Co., Owl Realty Improvement Co., Winona. Trustee Found. Comml. Banks, 1961-67, vice chmn., 1962- 67; vice chmn., trustee Found. for Full-Service Banks, 1963-69; instr. Winona chpt. Am. Inst. Banking, 1941-50. Mem. Minn. Coll. Bd., 1951-65, pres., 1957-61; adv. bd. St. Mary's Coll., Winona, Coll. St. Teresa, Winona. Mem. Minn. Orient Trade Tour Delegation, 1957; organizer Winona Indsl. Devel. Assn., 1950, dir., 1950-61; treas. Gamhaven area Boy Scouts Am. Found.; chmn. Ann. Steamboat Days Celebration, 1956; king Winona Winter Carnival, 1956; vice chmn. Devel. Council for Minn. State Colls., 1968-69, chmn., 1969-71. Chmn., Winona Young Republicans, 1935-37; chmn. Winona County Rep. Com., 1937-40, 46-51, treas., 1940-46; mem. Minn. Central Rep. Com., 1946-50. Bd. dirs. Winona YMCA, Newman Center at Winona State Coll. Decorated knight Order St. Gregory the Gt. (Pope Paul VI); recipient Bishop's Cath. Action medal Diocese Winona, 1962; Silver Beaver award Boy Scouts Am., 1957; Teresa of Avila award Coll. St Teresa 1968; Distinguished Service award U.S. Treasury Dept., 1969. Mem. Am. Bankers Assn. (exec. com. 1950-57, 63—, chmn. savs. bonds com. 1963-69), Am. Inst. Banking (exec. com. 1943-46), Minn. Bankers Assn. (pres. 1951-52), Financial Pub. Relations Assn. (Minn. chmn. 1958-59), Alpha Kappa Psi (hon. life). Elk (exalted ruler 1946-48), K.C. (4) Kiwanian (pres. Winona 1952, lt. gov. 1968-69). Contbr. articles profl. journals. Home: 566 S Baker St Winona MN 55987 Office: Town and Country State Bank Winona MN 55987

KRZYZANIAK, MARIAN, educator; b. Poland, Feb. 4, 1911; s. Walenty and Stanislawa (Baran) K.; M.Econs. and Polit. Sci., U. Poznan, 1932; M.A., U. Alta., 1954; Ph.D., Mass. Inst. Tech., 1959; m. Hylda-Lucy Roberta Baldwin, May 14, 959; children-Andrezej, Valentine Christopher Baldwin. Came to U.S., 1956, naturalized, 1964. With ins. company in Poland, 1934-36; civil servant Polish Govt., 1936-39; with company in Canadian oilfields, 1955-56; mem. faculty U. Mich., 1958-59, U. Mont., 1959-60, Johns Hopkins, 1960-61, Wayne State U., 1961-64; mem. faculty Rice U., 1964—, Henry Fox, Sr. prof. econs., 1969—; vis. prof. Tex. So. U., spring 1966, St. Thomas U., Houston, 1968-70, Mont. U., summer 1967. Served with Polish Army, 1939. Recipient Fund Research Recognition award Wayne State U., 1963. Mem. Internat. Inst. Pub. Finance, Internat. Platform Assn., Polish Social and Cultural Center. Author: (with Richard A. Musgrave) The Shifting of the Corporation Income Tax, 1963; also articles. Author, editor; Effects of Corporation Income Tax, 1966. Home: 4103 Durness St Houston TX 77025

KRZYZANOWSKI RICHARD LUCIEN, lawyer, cork and seal co. exec.; b. Warsaw, Poland, Mar. 25, 1932; s. Andrzej and Maria (Kowalczyk) K.; LL.B., U. Warsaw, 1956; M. Comparative Law, U. Pa., 1960; Ph.D., U. Paris (France), 1961; postgrad. The Hague (Netherlands) Acad. Internat. Law, 1959; m. Theresa Widzinski, Sept. 12, 1961; 1 dau., Suzanne. Came to U.S., 1966. Admitted to Pa. bar, 1969; legal adviser Polish Govt., Warsaw, 1961-65; house counsel, sec. Crown Cork & Seal Co., Inc., Phila., 1967—. Adviser Polish delegation Gen. Assembly UN 1963, Polish delegation Geneva (Switzerland) Disarmament Conf., 1963-64. Mem. Am. Soc. Internat. Law. Home: 3342 E Hollywood Circle Pennsauken NJ 08109 Office: 9300 Ashton Rd Philadelphia PA 19136

KU, Y. H., educator; b. Wusih, Kiangsu, China, Dec. 24, 1902; s. Ken Ming Ku and Ching-Su Wang; S.B., Mass. Inst. Tech., 1925, S.M., 1926, Sc.D., 1928; m. Wei-zing Wang, Apr. 1, 1929; children—Wei-Lien, Wei-Ching, Wei-Wen (Mrs. Chi-Liang Hsieh), Walter, Wei-Chung, Victor, Anna. Came to U.S., 1950. Prof. elec. engring., head dept. Chekiang U., China, 1929-30; dean engring. Central U., China, 1931-32, pres., 1944-45; dean engring. Tsing Hua U., China, 1932-37; vice minister Ministry Edn., Republic of China, 1938-44; edn. commr., Shanghai, 1945-47; vis. prof. Mass. Inst. Tech., 1950-52; prof. U. Pa., 1952—; cons. Gen. Elec. Co., RCA. Recipient Gold medal Ministry Edn., Republic of China. Fellow Academia Sinica, I.E.E.E., Instn. Elec. Engrs. (London); mem. Am. Soc. Engring. Edn., Internat. Union Theoretical and Applied Mechanics (mem. gen. assembly), U.S. Nat. Com. on Theoretical and Applied Mechanics, Sigma Xi, Eta Kappa Nu. Author: Analysis and Control of Nonlinear Systems, 1958; Electric Energy Conversion, 1959; Transient Circuit Analysis, 1961; Analysis and Control of Linear Systems, 1962; Collected Works (poems, plays, novels, essays in Chinese), 1961; Woodcutter's Song, 1963; Pine Wind, 1964; Lotus Song, 1966; Lofty Mountains, 1968; The Liang River, 1970; The Hui Spring, 1971. Home: 4947 Sansom St Philadelphia PA 19139 Office: 200 S 33d St Philadelphia PA 19104

KUBASOV, VALERY, Russian cosmonaut on Soyuz 7, 1969. Address: care Science Research Inst Petrovky Park Moscow, USSR.*

KUBELIK, RAFAEL, conductor, composer; b. Bychory, Czechoslovakia, June 29, 1914; s. Jan and Marianna (Szeel) K.; student Conservatory Music (Prague); m. Ludmila Bertlova, June 29, 1942 (dec. June 1961); 1 son, Martin; m. 2d, Elsie Morison, Jan. 4, 1963. Condr. Czech Philharmonic Soc., Prague, 1936-39; musical dir. Opera, Brno, Czechoslovakia, 1939-41; chief conductor Czech Philharmonic Orchestra, Prague, 1941-48; musical dir. Chgo. Symphony Orchestra, 1950-53; guest condr. Covent Garden Opera Co., London, June 1955, mus. dir., 1955-58; chief condr. Bavarian Radio Symphony Orch., 1961—, on tour, Japan, 1965; made concert tours with Vienna Philharmonic Orch. (latest, Germany 1956), with Concertgebouw Orchestra (latest throughout U.S.A. 1954); guest condr. all internat. festivals and major orchs. in Europe and U.S.; condr. The Trojans, first public, uncut performance in London, and with distinguished internat. cast, June 1957. Composer four operas, 2 symphonies with chorus, cello and violin concertos, string quartets, violin and piano music, sacred choral music, songs, music for string orch. Address: Kostanienbaum Hans Im Sand Switzerland

KUBERT, JOSEPH MANDEL, educator; b. Chgo., June 14, 1917; s. Nathan and Rose (Kohn) K.; B.S., Ill. Inst. Tech., 1937, M.S., 1940; m. Judith Korngold, July 7, 1951; children—David Emanuel, Anne Susan, Charles Nathan. Head, survey dept. Pullman Standard Car Mfg. Co., Chgo., 1937-40; with Booz, Allen & Hamilton, Inc., Chgo., 1940-70, partner, 1948-61, v.p., 1962-70; vis. prof. bus. policy Grad. Sch. Bus., U. Chgo., 1970—; dir. Unarco Industries, Inc., Mattel, Inc. Mem. commn. on orgn. Ill. Dept. Transp. Registered profl. engr., Ill. Mem. Inst. Mgmt. Consultants (charter), Chgo. Assn. Commerce and Industry (world trade com.), Newcomen Soc. Clubs: Economic, Executives, Standard (Chgo.); Briarwood Country (Deerfield, Ill.). Home: 589 Greenleaf Av Glencoe IL 60022 Office: 5836 S Greenwood Av Chicago IL 60637

KUBICEK, LILLIAN KATHERINE, lawyer; b. Chgo., Jan. 4, 1913; d. John and Katherine (Starankovic) Kubicek; B.A., U. Ill., 1933, LL.B., 1935, J.D., 1967; m. Stephen Osusky, Jan. 1939 (div. 1945). Admitted to Ill. bar, 1935; mem. firm Kirkland, Ellis, Hodson, Chafptz & Masters, Chgo., 1936-60, partner, 1950-60; gen. counsel Seeburg Corp., Chgo. 1960—, sec., 1960-64, v.p., 1964—, dir., 1960—, mem. exec. com., 1965—. Vol. worker campaigns for Senator Paul H. Douglas, Gov. Otto Kerner, active in groups to amend Ill. 8 Hour Day Law for Woman. Bd. dirs., mem. bldg. com. Slovak Am. Charitable Assn. Mem. Women's Bar Assn. of Ill. (officer, mem. various coms.), Am., Ill., Chgo. bar assns. Contbr. articles to legal jours. Home: 6475 Wabansia Av Chicago IL 60622 Office: 1500 N Dayton St Chicago IL 60622 60622

KUBIE, JOHN SAMUEL, corp. exec.; b. N.Y.C., Jan. 11, 1922; s. David S. and Amy (Levy) K.; grad. Horace Mann Sch., N.Y.C., 1939, Philips Acad., Andover, Mass., 1940; B.A., Yale, 1944; m. Marion Latz, Aug. 26, 1945; children—Nancy, John L., Kathryn E., Lisa A. Vice pres. Seligman & Latz, Inc., N.Y.C., 1945-62, pres., 1962—. Co-chmn. Scarsdale chpt. Nat. Conf. Christians and Jews; industry chmn. N.Y. Heart Fund; treas. Yale U. Class of 1944; mem. bd. edn. Union Free Sch. Dist. 11, Yorktown Heights, N.Y. Bd. dirs. Wiltwyck Sch. for Boys, Grand St. Settlement. Served with USAAF, World War II. Jewish religion. Club: Fairview Country (Elmsford, N.Y.) Home: 51 Greenacres Av Scarsdale NY 10583 also Hammond Rd Millbrook NY 12545 Office: 666 Fifth Av New York City NY 10019

KUBIK, GAIL, composer, condr., educator; b. South Coffeyville, Okla., Sept. 5, 1914; s. Henry H. and Eva O. (Thompson) K.; Mus.B. with distinction, Eastman Sch., U. Rochester, 1934; Mus.M. cum laude, Am. Conservatory, Chgo., 1935; grad. study Harvard, 1937-38; studied piano under Ida Smith, violin under Samuel Belov, Robert Reed, Alexander Baird, compostion under Edward Royce, Bernard Rogers, Leo Sowerby, Walter Piston, Nadia Boulanger, conducting under Harold Byrns, Igor Markevitch; Mus. D. (hon.), Monmouth Coll., 1955; m. Jessie Louise Mayer, Apr. 5, 1938; m. 2d, Joyce Mary Scott-Paine, Dec. 21, 1946; m. 3d, Mary Gibbs Tyler, Apr. 9, 1952; m. 4th, Joan Allred Sanders, Sept. 1, 1970. Composer music, 1930—; violin soloist Kubik Ensemble (Evalyn, Howard, Gail, Henry K.), 1930-37; N.Y. Civic Orch., 1937, Chgo., 1938, Rochester, 1939; tchr. Monmouth (Ill.) Coll., 1934-36, Dakota Wesleyan U., 1936-37, Columbia Tchrs. Coll., 1938-40; staff composer, music program advisor NBC, 1940- 41; concert, functional-music commns., 1940-71; dir. mus. OWI Bur. Motion Pictures, 1942-43; composer-condr. film, radio units USAAF, 1943-46; prof. music U. So. Cal., summer 1946; guest lectr. Accademia di Santa Cecilia, Rome, Italy, 1952, Oxford U., 1966; vis. prof. Kan. State U., 1969; prof. music, composer-in-residence Scripps Coll., Claremont, Cal., 1970—; lecture tours, U.S., 1968—; appeared guest condr. NBC, CBS, Denver, Columbus (O.) symphonies, Orch. Radio Italiana, Rome, Orch. Sinfonica Siciliana, Palermo, Orchestre Radio Symphonique, Paris, London Philharmonic Orch., BBC Concert Orch.; outstanding works include: Variations on a 13th Century Troubador Song, 1935; In Praise of Johnny Appleseed, 1938, rev. 1961; Stewball Variations (band), 1943; Memphis Belle; War-time Episode, 1944; Litany and Prayer (men's chorus, brass, percussion), 1943-45; Folk Song Suite, 1945; A Mirror for the Sky (folk opera), 1946; Spring Valley Overture, 1947; Piano Sonata, 1947; Symphony in E Flat, 1947-49; Profiles, Folk Song Sketches (chorus), 1948; Boston Baked Beans (opera piccola), 1950; Celebrations and Epilogue (piano), 1938-50; Symphony Concertante, 1952, rev., 1953; Thunderbolt Overture, 1953, Symphony No. 2 in F, 1955, Symphony No. 3, 1956, Scenario for Orchestra, 1957, Sonatinas for Piano, 1941, Violin and Piano, 1941, Clarinet and Piano, 1959; Two Divertimenti (small orch.), 1959, Scenes for Orch., 1964, A Christmas Set (chamber chorus, small orch.), 1968; Prayer and Toccata (organ, small orch.), 1968, A Record of Our Time (cantata for chorus, narration and orch.), 1970; Divertimento No. 3, 1971. Film scores include: The World at War, 1942; Memphis Belle, 1943 (N.Y. Film Critics award 1944); Gerald McBoing Boing 1950 (Academy award 1951); Two Gals and a Guy, 1951; Transatlantic, 1952: The Desperate Hours, 1955; Down to Earth, 1959. Golden Jubilee award (Scherzo for Large Orchestra), Chgo. Symphony, 1941; 1st prize (Violin Concerto), Jascha Heifetz competition, 1941; award (Sonatina for violin, piano), Soc. Pub. Am. Music, 1943; citation for documentary film score (World at War), Nat. Assn. Am. Composers and Condrs., 1943; Guggenheim fellow, 1944, 65; Prix de Rome award, 1950, 51; Pulitzer prize (Symphony Concertante), 1952. Am. del. Venice Film Festival, Internat. Conf. Music in Films, 1959; A.S.C.A.P. del. UNESCO Internat. Conf., Denver, 1959; Am. del. UNESCO, Paris, 1966, Budapest, 1966. Mem. A.S.C.A.P., Phi Mu Alpha Sinfonia (hon. life). Club: Century (N.Y.C.). Recorded works RCA Victor, Columbia, Capitol and Contemporary recording cos. Lectr., contbr. profl. publs. Home: care Scripps Coll Claremont CA 91711

KUBIS, JOSEPH FRANCIS, educator; b. N.Y.C., Mar. 13, 1911; s. John and Mary (Antosz) K.; B.A., St. John's U., 1932; M.A., Fordham U., 1935, Ph.D., 1937; m. Stella H. Rokitnicki, Aug. 16, 1937; children—Joseph John, Theresa Stella. Mem. faculty Fordham U., 1934—, prof. psychology, 1953—; cons. to govt., also city, state and fed. authorities on interrogation; cons. to NASA, VA. Mem. Am. Psychol. Assn., Am. Statis. Assn., Biometric Soc., Math. Assn. Am., Psychometric Soc., Sigma Xi. Home: 37-18 88th St Jackson Heights, NY 11372 Office: Grad Sch Fordham Univ Bronx NY 10458

KUBISCH, JACK BLOOM, govt. ofcl. b. Hannibal Mo., Nov. 5, 1921; s. Benjamin Harrison and Beatrice (Bloom) K.; student Central Meth. Coll., Fayette, Mo., 1938- 40; A.B., U. Mo., 1942; postgrad., Harvard Bus. Sch., 1946; m. Constance Linn Rippe, Dec. 28, 1944; children—David Benjamin, John Christopher, Anne Christine, Joan Elizabeth. With U.S. Fgn. Service in Rio de Janeiro, Brazil, 1947-49; econ. commnr. ECA, Paris, France, 1949-50; export mgr. Bendix Home Appliance Co., 1950, gen. mgr. Bendix Home Appliance Can., Ltd., 1951, dir. internat. operations Bendix Home Appliance Co., 1951-53; pres., chmn. bd. Great No. Distbrs., South Bend, Ind., 1953-61, J.B. Kubish & Assos., South Bend, 1954-61; dep. dir. USOM to Ceylon, 1961-62; dir. U.S. AID mission to Brazil, 1962-65; minister econ. affairs Am. embassy, Rio de Janeiro, 1962-65; dir. Office Brazil Affairs, Dept. State, Washington, 1965-69; dep. chief Am. embassy, Mexico, 1969—. Served to lt. USNR, 1942-45. Home: Sierra Paracaima 1065 Mexico DF Mexico Office: American Embassy Apartado Postal 88 bis Mexico DF Mexico

KUBLER, GEORGE ALEXANDER, educator; b. Los Angeles, July 26, 1912; s. Frederick William and Ellen Orloff-Beckmann K.; A.B., Yale, 1934, A.M., 1936, Ph.D., 1940; student univs. Berlin, Munich and N.Y.; m. Elizabeth Bushnell, Feb. 12, 1937; children—Alexandra, Cornelia, Edward, Elena. Mem. faculty Yale 1938—, prof. history of art, 1947-63, Robert Lehman prof. art history, 1963—; vis. prof. U. Chgo., 1946, U. San Marcos, Lima, Peru, 1948-49, U. Mexico, 1958, Harvard, 1966-67; chief UNESCO Mission to Cuzco, Peru, 1951. Guggenheim fellow Mexico, 1943-44, Spain, 1952-53, 56-57. Recipient Alice Davis Hitchcock award, 1962, Charles Rufus Morey prize, 1963. Mem. Am. Acad. Arts and Scis., Spanish Inst. (bd. dirs.), Hispanic Soc. (corr. mem.), Acad. Franciscan History, Conn. Acad. Arts and Scis., Soc. des Américanistes de Paris, Real Academia de San Fernando (corr. mem.). Author: Religious Architecture of New Mexico, 1940; Mexican Architecture of the Sixteenth Century, 1948; Arquitectura Espaola 1600-1800, 1957; Architecture in Spain and Portugal and Their American Dominions (with M. Soria); Art and Architecture of Ancient America, 1962; Shape of Time, 1962; the Antiquity of Painting by Felix da Costa, 1967; Studies of Classic Maya Iconography, 1969. Editor: Art Bull. (Coll. Art Assn.), 1945-47. Contbr. articles art publs. Home: 406 Humphrey St New Haven CT 06511

KUBLY, HERBERT, author, educator; b. New Glarus, Wis., Apr. 26, 1915; s. Nic H. and Alda (Ott) K.; B.A., U. Wis., 1937. City desk reporter Pitts. Sun-Telegraph, 1937-39, edn. editor, art critic, 1939-42; reporter, feature writer N.Y. Herald-Tribune, 1942-44; critic, editor Time mag., 1945-47; nat. sec. Dramatists Guild Am., 1947-49; asso. prof. speech, dir. Playwright's Workshop, U. Ill., 1949-53; lectr. Columbia U., N.Y.C., 1962-64, New Sch. Social Research, N.Y., 1962-64; prof. English, San Francisco State Coll., 1964-68; prof. English, U. Wis., Kenosha, 1969—. Recipient Rockefeller grant for creative writing, 1947-48; MacDowell Colony fellow, 1947-48, 56-62; Fulbright grant for study humanities in Italy, 1950-51; Nat. Book award for non-fiction, 1956; 1st award Wis. Council for Writers, 1970. Mem. Edward MacDowell Assn., Pi Epsilon Delta, Theta Chi. Democrat. Mem. United Church of Christ. Author: American in Italy, 1955; Easter in Sicily, 1956; Varieties of Love, 1958; Italy, 1961; The Whisling Zone, 1963; Switzerland, 1963; At Large, 1964; Gods and Heroes, 1969; The Workshop, 1969; (plays) Men to the Sea, 1944, Inherit the Wind, 1946, The Cocoon, 1954, Beautiful Dreamer, 1956, The Virus, 1969. Contbr. articles, stories nat. mags. Home: Wilhelm Tell Farm New Glarus WI Office: care William Morris Agy 1350 Av Americas New York City NY 10019

KUBRICK, STANLEY, producer, dir., writer; b. N.Y.C., July 26, 1928; ed. high sch. Staff photographer Look mag.; writer, producer, dir. documentaries, including Day of the Flight, Flying Padre, Dr. Strangelove (N.Y. Critic award), 1964; producer, dir. Fear and Desire, Killer's Kiss; dir. The Killing; writer, dir. Paths of Glory; dir. Spartacus, 1960, Lolita, 1962; producer, dir., writer 2001: A Space Odessey (Oscar award best spl. visual effects), 1968.*

KUBZANSKY, PHILIP EUGENE, univ. dean; b. Bklyn., Aug. 11, 1928; s. Joseph and Libby (Kolko) K.; B.S. in Social Sci., Coll. City N.Y. 1950; Ph.D., Duke, 1954; m. Judith Linda Sagarin, Apr. 15, 1962; children—Jessica Rose, Michael Samuel, Laura Diane. Postdoctoral fellow community mental health Mass. Gen. Hosp., 1956-57; chief psychologist Boston City Hosp., 1957-60; research asso. Harvard Med. Sch., 1957—; mem. faculty Boston U., 1960—, prof. psychology, 1967—, dean Grad. Sch., 1967—. Served with AUS, 1954-56. Mem. Am., Mass. psychol. assns., A.A.A.S., Sigma Xi. Contbr. sci. papers. Home: 41 Nobscot Rd Newton Centre, MA 02159. Office: Grad Sch Boston U Boston MA 02215

KUCERA, DANIEL WILLIAM, clergyman, coll. pres.; b. Chgo., May 7, 1923; s. Joseph F. and Lillian (Petrzelka) K.; B.A., St. Procopius Coll., 1945; M.A., Cath. U. Am., 1950, Ph.D., 1955. Registrar, St. Procopius Coll., 1945-49, 54-56, dean studies, 1956-64, pres., 1959-65, chancellor, 1964-71; pres. Ill. Benedictine Coll., Lisle, Ill., 1971—; ordained priest Roman Catholic Ch., 1949; elected abbot St. Procopius Abbey, 1964. Mem. Am. Benedictine Acad., Soc. for Advancement Edn., Nat. Cath. Ednl. Assn. Author: Church-State Relationships in Education in Illinois-Washington, 1955. Address: Ill Benedictine Coll Lisle IL 60532

KUCERA, HENRY, educator; b. Trebarov, Czechoslovakia, Feb. 15, 1925; s. Jindrich and Marie (Kral) K.; came to U.S., 1949, naturalized, 1953; M.A., Charles U., Prague, Czechoslovakia, 1947; Ph.D., Harvard, 1952; M.A. (hon.), Brown U., 1958; m. Jacqueline M. Fortin, Oct. 6, 1951; children—Thomas Henry, Edward James. Asst. prof. fgn. langs. U. Fla., 1952-55; mem. faculty Brown U., 1955—, prof. Slavic langs. and linguistics, 1963—, chmn. dept. Slavic langs., 1965-68, head resident fellow, 1956-66; research asso. Russian Research Center, Harvard, 1952, Mass. Inst. Tech., 1960-63; vis. prof. U. Mich., 1967, U. Cal. at Berkeley, 1969. Bd. dirs. Internat. Inst. Providence, 1960-67. Ford fellow, 1954-55; Howard Found. fellow, 1960-61: Guggenheim fellow, 1960-61; sr. fellow Nat. Endowment for Humanities. 1968-69. Mem. Am. Com. Slavists (exec. com. 1965-68), Linguistic Soc. Am., Modern Lang Assn., Internat. Linguistic Assn., Czechoslovak Soc. Arts & Scis. in Am., Am. Assn. Tchrs. Slavic and E. European Langs, Author: The Phonology of Czech, 1961; (with W.N. Francis) Computational Analysis of Present-Day American English, 1967; (with G. Monroe) A Comparative Quantitative Phonology of Russian, Czech and German, 1968; Some Quantitative Lexical Analyses of Russian, Czech and English, 1968; also linguistic and lit. articles. Editor: American Contributions to the Sixth International Congress of Slavists, 1968. Home: 196 Bowen St Providence RI 02906

KUCHAR, GEORGE ANDREW, Jr., motion picture dir.; b. N.Y.C., Aug. 31, 1942; s. George and Stella (Mateszow) K.; student Sch. Indsl. Art, N.Y.C., 1957-60. Prodns. include: I Was a Teenage Rumpot, The Naked and the Nude, A Town Called Tempest, Lust for Ecstasy, Anita Needs Me, Corruption of the Damned, Hold Me While I'm Naked, Eclipse of the Sun Virgin, Color Me Shameless. Address: 531 Vallejo St San Francisco CA 94133

KUCHAR, MIKE JOHN, ind. film maker; b. N.Y.C., Aug. 31, 1942; s. George and Stella (Mateszow) K.; grad. High Sch. Art and Design, 1960. Motion pictures include Sins of the Fleshapoids, 1965, Green Desire, 1966, The Secret of Wendell Samson, 1966; exhibited at Gallery Modern Art, Washington, Mus. Modern Art, N.Y.C. Address: 531 Vallejo St San Francisco CA 94133

KUCHEL, ELDRED RUSSEL, economist, univ. provost; b. Kingsley, Ia., Mar. 14, 1918; s. Philip and Minnie (Lage) K.; B.A., Westmar Coll., 1939; M.A., State U. Ia., 1942. Ph.D., 1954; m. Keith Hill, Aug. 26, 1937; children—Vicki Lee, Craig Russel, Gary Alan. High sch. social sci. tchr., 1940-42; prof. econs. U. Wyo., 1946-62, head dept. econs., sociology, anthropology and geography, 1957-62, acting asst. dean Coll. Arts and Scis., 1960-61; dean Bradley U., Peoria, Ill., 1962-63, v.p. for acad. affairs, 1963-71; provost South Acad. Center, No. Ariz. U., Flagstaff, 1971—. Cons., Examiner N. Central Assn. Colls. and Univs.; cons. for establishment Community Jr. Coll., Peoria, 1967-68. Past pres. bd. trustees Peoria Art Guild; past trustee, exec. com. Lakeview Center for Arts and Scis., Peoria. Served to lt. (s.g.) USNR, 1942-45. Mem. Rocky Mountain Social Sci. Assn. (v.p. 1959- 60, pres. 1960-61), Am., Midwest econ. assns., Nat. Platform Assn., Omicron Delta Kappa, Alpha Kappa Psi, Phi Delta Kappa, Phi Kappa Phi. Clubs: Kiwanis, Mt. Hawley Country. Home: 2799 Darleen Dr Flagstaff AZ 86001

KUCHEL, THOMAS HENRY, lawyer; b. Anaheim, Cal., Aug, 15, 1910; s. Henry and Lutetia (Bailey) K.; A.B. cum laude, U. So. Cal., 1932, LL.B., 1935; m. Betty Mellenthin, Mellenthin, June 2, 1942; 1 dau., Karen Christine (Mrs. Delman W. Smith). Admitted to Cal. bar, 1935, D.C. bar, 1968; practiced in Anaheim, 1935- 46, mem. Cal. State Assembly, 1937-40, Senate, 1940-46; controller State of Cal., 1946-53; U.S. senator from Cal., 1953-69, asst. Republican leader, 1959-69, mem. appropriations, interior and insular affairs coms.;

partner Wyman, Bautzer, Finell, Rothman & Kuchel, Beverly Hills, Cal. and Washington, 1969—. Served as lt. USNR, 1942-45. Mem. Am. Legion, Phi Delta Phi, Phi Kappa Psi, Phi Kappa Phi. Republican. Episcopalian. Mason, Elk. Office: 9601 Wilshire Blvd Beverly Hills CA 90212 also 1211 Connecticut Av NW Washington DC 20036 also 1211 Connecticut Av NW Washington DC 20036

KUCHEMAN, HENRY BERNARD, Jr., Air Force officer; b. Balt, June 8, 1919; s. Henry Bernard and Catherine A. (Quensen) K.; B.S., Va. Polytech. Inst., M.Chem Engring., 1949; grad. Command and Gen. Staff Coll., 1945, Indsl. Coll. Armed Forces, 1960; m. Frances Hall, Dec. 27, 1947; children—William Henry, James Quensen, David Brian. Commd. 2d lt. USAAF, 1942, advanced through grades to maj. gen. USAF, 1968; various assignments, U.S., 1941-43, 44-46; squad-comdr., operations officer 354th Fighter Squadron, 355th Fighter Group, Steeple Morden, Eng., 1943-44; operations officer, flying tng. officer 86th Fighter Group, Nordholtz, Germany, 1946; asst. A-3 64th Fighter wing, Bad Kissingen, Germany, 1946-47; flying safety officer Hdqrs. Tactical Air Command, 1947; research and devel. staff officer, Research and Devel. Directorate, Dep. Chief Staff/Devel., Hdqrs. USAF, 1949-53; asst. dir. test operations Air Force Armament Center, Eglin AFB, Fla., 1953-54, chief weapons and missiles br., 1954-55, dir. tech, support, 1955-57, dep. comdr. for test, 1957-58; dir. plans and programs Air Proving Ground Center, Elgin AFB, 1958, asst. dep. comdr. devel. and test, 1958-59; dir. air force space boosters, Ballistic Missle Div., Los Angeles, 1960, asst. dep. comdr. for space Space Systems Div., Los Angeles, 1960-61, dir. Agena D Program, 1961-62, dep. for communications satellite systems, 1962-64, dep. for unmanned systems, 1964-66; dep. for limited war, aero. systems div., Air Force Systems Command, Wright-Patterson AFB, O., 1966, vice comdr., 1966-68; dir. devel. Dep. Chief Staff/Research and Devel. Hq. USAF, Washington, 1968-70; asst. dep. chief staff/Research and Devel., Hdqrs. USAF, 1970—. Decorated Silver Star, Legion of Merit with 2 oak leaf clusters, various unit and area ribbons. Mem. Am. Ordnance Assn. (pres. Fla. 1959), Tau Beta Pi, Phi Lambda Upsilon. Home: 7801 Birnam Wood Dr McLean VA 22101 Office: Dep Chief Staff Research and Devel Hdqrs USAF Washington DC 20418

KUCK, KERMIT THEODORE, machine tool co. exec.; b. New Knoxville, O., Oct. 22, 1912; s. W. Theodore and L. Elizabeth (Eversman) K.; B. Mech. Engring., Ohio State U., 1934; m. Ella Hoge, Aug. 20, 1938; children—Joe A., W. Theodore, With Monarch Machine Co., Sidney, O., 1935-, pres., 1961—, also dir.; mem. bd. dirs. First Nat. Exchange Bank. Pres. Wilson Meml. Hosp., 1952-53, Sidney Civic Assn., 1956; sec.-treas. Sidney Community Found., 1957-61; pres. Monarch Machine Tool Co. Found. Mem. Nat. Machine Tool Builders Assn. (dir.). Republican. Club: Engineers (Dayton). Home: 1800 Pt Jefferson Rd Sidney OH 45365 Office: Monarch Machine Tool Co Oak St Sidney OH 45365

KUCKES, ARTHUR F., educator, physicist; b. N.Y.C., June 1, 1932; s. Herman F. and Marie (Borcherding) K.; student Mass. Inst. Tech., 1949-53, U. Goettingen (Germany), 1953-54, U. Paris (France), 1954-55, Harvard, 1955-59; m. Haralyn Dubin, Mar. 21, 1959; children—Niki, Laura, Dylan. Research physicist Princeton, 1959-66; physicist Culham Lab., Eng., 1966-68; prof. physics Cornell U., Ithaca, N.Y., 1968—. Cons., Lawrence Radiation Lab., U. Cal. Mem. Am. Phys. Soc. Home: 115 Kelvin Pl Ithaca NY 14850

KUEBLER, ERNEST WILLIAM, clergyman, educator; b. Kansas City, Mo., Oct. 29, 1903; s. Ernest Albrecht and Martha Regina (Spielberger) K.; student Kansas City (Mo.) Jr. Coll., 1921-23; Ph.B., Boston U., 1926, B.R.E., 1929; A.M., grad. study, Yale Divinity Sch., 1930-32; S.T.D., Starr King Theol. Sch., 1935; m. Naomi Abrams, May 17, 1930; children—Valerie, Christopher Charles, Cheryl. Gen. sec. Dauphine Co. (Pa.) Sabbath Sch. Assn., 1927-29; exec. sec. Harrisburg (Pa.) Council Religious Edn., 1929-30; dir. Bridgeport (Conn.) Weekday Religious Edn. System, 1930-32; dir. religious edn. Central Congl. Ch., Newtonville, Mass., 1932-35; sec. dept. religious edn. Am. Unitarian Assn., 1935-37; ordained Unitarian Ch., 1938; dir. div. edn. Am. Unitarian Assn., Boston, 1937-49, exec. v.p., 1949-54; adminstr., dir. div. edn. Council Liberal Chs. (Universalist-Unitarian), 1954-61; dir. edn. dept. Unitarian Universalist Assn., 1961-62; projects dir. Hugh Moore Fund, N.Y.C., 1962-64; exec. dir. St. Lawrence Unitarian Universalist Dist., 1964-69; minister-at-large N.Y. State Conv. Universalists, 1969—, also spl. projects dir.; pres. Internat. Assn. for Liberal Christianity and Religious Freedom, the Hague, 1958-64. Secretariat Internat. Assn. for Religious Freedom; bd. Sec. St. Lawrence Found. for Theol. Edn., 1968—. Mem. Religious Edn. Assn. Am. (pres. 1946-48), Religious Arts Guild (pres. 1945-49), Boston U. Alumni Assn. (dir. 1935-41). Gen. editor: Beacon Books in Religious Education 1937-62. Home: 206 Sherwood Dr DeWitt NY 13214

KUECHLE, URBAN THEODORE, bus. exec.; b. Milw., Dec. 10, 1910; s. Gotthold William Eugene and Amanda (Schumacher) K.; student U. Wis., Milw., 1929-30; m. Grace Bonnet, Nov. 18, 1939; children—Gerrit, Katharine, William. With A.O. Smith Corp., Milw., 1929—; beginning in indsl. relations dept., successively sales asst., priorities mgr., asst. sales mgr., sales mgr. automotive div., v.p. automotive sales, 1929-57, v.p. automotive div., 1957-60, group v.p. automotive and capital equipment, 1960-64, exec. v.p., 1964-67, pres., dir., 1967—, also dir. subsidiary cos.; dir. Marine Nat. Exchange Bank, Grand Trunk Western R.R., Marine Corp., Outboard Marine Corp., Koehring Co. Exec. com. Milw. council Boy Scouts Am. Mem. Machinery and Allied Products Inst. (mem. exec. com.), Soc. Automotive Engrs., Elec. Mfrs. Club, Luth. Men in Am. Clubs: Blue Mound Country, Chenegua Country; Milwaukee Athletic; Tres Vidas (Acapulco, Mexico). Home: Route 3 Box 133 Hartland WI 53029 Office: PO Box 584 Milwaukee WI 53201

KUECHLER, HENRY NORBURY, Jr., bus exec.; b. San Rafael, Cal., Mar. 31, 1911; s. Henry Norbury and Mary Fiffe (Foster) K.; A.B. in Polit. Sci., Stanford, 1933; m. Mary Elizabeth Stewart, Sept. 18, 1933; children—Sue Stewart (Mrs. James M. Harris), Sally Foster (Mrs. Warren Debenham), Henry Norbury III, Nancy (Mrs. David S. Hanna). With Knob Hill Mines, Inc., San Francisco, 1936—, sec.-treas., 1936-51, pres., 1951—, also dir.; pres., dir. Reclaimed Island Lands Co.; dir. Transam. Corp. Mayor town Atherton, Cal., until 1963. Served to lt. comdr. USNR, World War II. Mem. Zeta Psi. Clubs: The Family, Pacific Union (San Francisco). Home: 85 Isabella Av Atherton CA 94025 Office: 160 Sansome St San Francisco CA 94104

KUEHL, HAL C. banker; b. Davenport, Ia., Mar. 21, 1923; s. Donald J. and Martha A. (Sierk) K.; B.B.A., U. Wis., 1947, M.B.A., 1952, postgrad. Grad. Sch. Banking, 1953; m. Joyce M. Helms, May 20, 1950; children—Cynthia Ann, David Charles. With First Wis. Nat. Bank, Milw., 1947—, v.p., 1960-65, exec. v.p. operations, 1965-66, exec. v.p., 1966-69, pres., 1969—; dir., exec. v.p. First Wis. Bankshares Corp.; dir. First Northwestern Nat. Bank Milw., Brookfield Nat. Bank (Wis.), Network Data Processing Corp., Oak Brook, Ill., First Wis. Co. Bd. dirs., mem. finance com. Milw. Blood Centre; bd. dirs., mem. exec., finance, investment coms. Vis. Nurse Assn., Milw.; pres., mem. exec. bd. Milw. County council Boy Scouts Am.; bd. dirs., treas. Milw. Voluntary Equal Employment Opportunity Council; bd. dirs., v.p. Greater Milw. Com.; bd. dirs., mem. exec. com. Milw. div. Am. Cancer Soc.; bd. dirs. Citizens Govtl. Research Bur., Wis. Taxpayers Alliance, Friends of Art; mem. corp. United Community Services Greater Milw., Columbia Hosp., Neighborhood House Milw.; trustee Milw. Art Center; trustee, mem. finance com. Marquette U. Served with USNR, 1943-45. C.P.A., Wis. Mem. Am. Bankers Assn., Assn. Res. City Bankers, Am. Inst. Banking, Met. Milw. Assn. Commerce, Sigma Chi. Episcopalian. Clubs: Milwaukee Athletic, Milwaukee, Milwaukee Country, University (Milw.). Home: 8156 N Green Bay Rd Milwaukee WI 53209 Office: 743 N Water St Milwaukee WI 53201

KUEHL, HOWARD FRANK, ret. naval officer; b. DePere, Wis., Jan. 2, 1910; s. Frank and Minnie (Reiff) K.; student St. Norbert Coll., 1928-29; B.S., U.S. Naval Acad., 1933; M.S. in Mech. Engring., U. Wis., 1934; grad. Naval Finance and Supply Sch., 1938, Naval War Coll., 1953; m. Jean Lawrence, Feb. 24, 1944; children—John, Sylvia. Commd. ensign USN, 1934, advanced through grades to rear adm., Supply Corps, 1959; successively assigned U.S.S. Pensacola, U.S.S. Indpls., U.S.S. Houston, 1934-37, Destroyer Div. 3 on U.S.S. Flusser, 1938-40, Fleet Air Wing 4, also Naval Air Sta., Seattle, 1940-42; staff Comdr. Aircraft S. Pacific Force, 1942-43; assigned Naval Supply Depot, Oakland, Cal., 1943-44, U.S.S. Hornet, 1944- 46, Naval Supply Center, Oakland, 1946-50, Aviation Supply Office, Phila., 1950-52; force supply officer staff Comdr. Naval Air Force, Pacific Fleet, 1953-56; comdg. officer Naval Supply Depot, Great Lakes, also dist. supply officer Hdqrs. 9th Naval Dist., 1956-59; fleet supply officer staff Comdr. in Chief Pacific Fleet, 1959-61; dir. material and budget div. Office Chief Naval Operations, 1961-62; comdg. officer Aviation Supply Office, Phila., 1962-66, Naval Supply Center, Long Beach, Cal., 1966-69, ret. Decorated various area and service ribbons. Mem. U.S. Naval Acad., U. Wis. Alumni Assn., Navy Supply Corps Sch. Alumni Assn. Clubs: Army-Navy Country (Washington); Las Posas Country (Camarillo, Cal.). Address: 1063 Trueno Av Camarillo CA 93010

KUEHN, EDMUND KARL, curator; b. Columbus, O., Aug. 18, 1916; s. Herman and Julianna (Bojanowski) K.; grad. Columbus Art Sch., 1938; student Art Students League, N.Y.C., 1938-39; m. Lieselotte Koss, Apr. 19, 1953. Asst. to dir. Columbus (O.) Gallery Fine Arts, 1939-43, curator, 1954-61, asst. dir., 1962-68, curator collections, 1969—; asst. prof. Ohio State U., 1946-48; asso. prof. Columbus Coll. Art and Design, 1948-53. Served with USAAF, 1943-46. Mem. Columbus Art League, Am. Assn. Museums. Home: 828 City Park Av Columbus OH 43206 Office: 480 E Broad St Columbus OH 43215

KUEHN, JAMES MARSHALL, Journalist; b. Mobridge, S.D., May 23, 1926; s. Christ A. and Selma (Brandon) K.; B.A., U.S.D., 1949; m. Phyllis Yvonne Larson, Apr. 3, 1950; children—Douglas James, Deborah Kay, Diana Lisa. State editor Rapid City (S.D.) Jour., 1949-54, wire editor, 1954-58, mng. editor, 1958-66, exec. editor, 1966—. Vice pres. Rapid City Library Bd., 1969-70, 71—; mem. dist. council Boy Scouts Am., 1965-69. Served with C.E., AUS, 1944-45. Mem. Rapid City C. of C. (v.p. 1970-71), Lambda Chi Alpha. Republican. Lutheran. Kiwanian. Home: 2948 Dundee St Rapid City SD 57701 Office: Box 471 Rapid City SD 57701

KUEKES, EDWARD DANIEL, cartoonist; b. Pitts., Feb. 2, 1901; s. Otto and Elizabeth (Lapp) K.; student Baldwin-Wallace Coll., (hon.) L.H.D., 1957; student Cleve. Inst. Art, Chgo. Acad. Fine Art; m. Clara Gray, Apr. 23, 1922; children—Edward Grayson, George Clive. Artist, cartoonist Cleve. Plain Dealer, 1922-49, chief editorial cartoonist, 1949-66, cartoonist emeritus, 1966—; cartoonist Metro Newspapers, Inc., Cleve., 1968—; creator of All in the Week, Along the Road, Cartoonist Looks at The News, Close-Ups, The Kernel; collaborated with Olive Ray Scott in prodn. cartoon features Alice in Wonderland, Knurl the Gnome, United Features Syndicate. Apptd. Pres. Eisenhower's People to People com. Recipient Newspaper Guild award, 1947, certificate of honor Nat. Safety Council, 1949, C.I.T. Found. award, D.A.V. award, 1st prize Freedoms Found., 1949, 2d prize, 1950, Distinguished Service award, 1951, Distinguished Service scrolls, 1952- 57, Pulitzer prize cartoon div., 1953, Alumni merit award Baldwin- Wallace Coll., 1953, Silver T Square Nat. Cartoonists Soc., 1953, Gov.'s award, 1953, Presdl. Prayer citation U.S. Treasury Dept., 1954, Meritorious award Cleve. Dental Soc., 1954, Christopher award, 1955, certificate of Recognition Nat. Conf. Christians and Jews, 1955, Pres. Eisenhower's People to People Program, cartoon div., 1956, George M. Humphrey U.S. Treasury citation, 1957, hon. mention Guild Award, 1957, 1st prize Guild Award, 1958, 1st prize Freedoms Found., 1958, Distinguished Service award, 1959, 1960, 1961, 1963, 1965, 1966, 1967, 1st prize Polit. Cartoon award Wayne State U., 1960, U.S. Treasury award, 1962, 64, Freedoms Found. award, 1963-69. Mem. Assn. Am. Editorial Cartoonists, Cleve. C. of C., Newcomen Soc. Eng., Baldwin-Wallace Coll. Alumni Assn. (pres.), Am. Airlines Flagship Fleet (adm.), Nat. Cartoonists Soc., Lambda Chi Alpha, Sigma Delta Chi. Methodist. Kiwanian (pres. Berea) Clubs: Mid Day, Cleveland Farmers (Cleve.). Author: Funny Fables, Five Thousand original cartoons in collection at Syracuse U. Address: 1280 Medfield Dr Rocky River OH 44116

KUENNE, ROBERT EUGENE, educator; b. St. Louis, Jan. 29, 1924; s. Edward Sebastian and Margaret (Yochum) K.; student Harris Jr. Coll., St. Louis, 1941-42; B.J., U. Mo., 1947; A.B., Washington U. at St. Louis, 1948, A.M., 1949; A.M. Harvard, 1951, Ph.D., 1953; m. Janet Lawrence Brown, Sept. 7, 1957; children—Christopher Brian, Carolyn Leigh. Asst. prof. econs. U. Va., 1955; mem. faculty Princeton, 1956—, asso prof., 1960-69, prof., 1969—; cons. U.S. Naval War Coll., 1954, 55, U.S. Army War Coll., 1967—, Inst. Def. Analyses, Arlington, Va., 1968—. Served with AUS, 1943-46. Named Oliver Ellsworth Bicentennial preceptor, 1957-60. Mem. Princeton Club N.Y. Author: The Theory of General Economic Equilibrium, 1963; The Attack Submarine: A Study in Strategy, 1965; The Polaris Missile Strike: A General Economic Systems Analysis, 1966; Monopolistic Competition Theory: Studies in Impact, 1967; Microeconomic Theory of the Market Mechanism, 1968; Home: 63 Bainbridge St Princeton NJ 08540

KUEPER, LEO HERMAN, Jr., ret. banker, accountant; b. St. Louis, July 13, 1907; s. Leo Henry and Elizabeth (Schrewe) K.; student LaSalle Extension U., 1929-33; m. Caroline Burkemper, June 1, 1935; children—James A., Nancy Marie (Mrs. Russell M. Vorce), Robert J., Charles L. With Perkins Transfer & Forwarding Co., 1922-32; staff accountant Mattison, DDavey & Rader, C.P.A.'s, 1933-49; gen. auditor Bank of St. Louis, Gen. Bancshares Corp., St. Louis, 1949-71, C.P.A., Mo. Mem. Nat. Assn. Bank Auditors and Controllers (past pres. St. Louis), St. Louis Jr. C. of C., Jr. Traffic, Traffic clubs St. Louis. Roman Catholic. Home: 8668 Partridge Av St Louis MO 63147

KUERSTEINER, KARL OTTO, educator; b. Louisville, Apr. 23, 1907; s. Emil Edward and Harriet Beecher (Beust) K.; student Bush Conservatory, 1923, Mozarteum, Salzburg, 1935, Ithaca Conservatory, 1924-25, Geza de Kresz of Royal Acad., Budapest, 1937; Mus. B., Chicago Mus. Coll., 1929; Mus.M., U. of Mich., 1934, Ph.D., 1946; fellowship from Internat. Inst. Edn., 1935; Martha Lee Boone, June 10, 1937; children—Richard Lee, Karol Anne, Jonathan Daniel Boone, Karl Christian III, William C., Karl, Kurt, Katia. Instrumental dir. Funk Sem., LaGrange, Ky., 1922-24; asso. prof. violin, orch. U. Kansas, 1925-39, prof., 1939-44; acting dean sch. music Fla. State Coll. Women, 1944-46; dean sch. music Fla. State U., 1946—; condr. Haskell Inst. Orch., 1925, U. of Kan. Symphony Orch., 1925-44, State Symphony Fla. 1949—; numerous appearances as condr. and violin soloist; exec. dir. Allied Arts Council Met. Mobile, Inc. Awarded Gold medal in violin Ithaca Conservatory, 1925. Mem. Jr. C. of C., Nat. Assn. Music Execs. in State Us. (chmn.), Nat. Assn. Schs. Music (v.p. and curriculum commn.). Music Teacher's Nat. Assn. (nat. pres.), Am. String Teachers' Assn. (founder), Phi Delta Theta, Phi Mu Alpha, Phi Kappa Phi, Phi Delta Kappa, Pi Kappa Lambda (sec. gen.). Clubs: Capitol City Country. Rotary (Tallahassee). Author: (with Irvin Cooper) Teaching Junior High School Music. Contbr. articles to profl. jours. Home: 1444 Lee Av Tallahassee FL 32303

KUETHE, ARNOLD MARTIN, educator; b. Marshfield, Wis., Aug. 24, 1905; s. Fred A. and Anna (Deering) K.; Ph.B., Ripon (Wis.) Coll., 1926, Ph.D., Cal. Inst. Tech., 1933; m. Edith M. Quinn, Aug. 17, 1935. Jr. physicist Nat. Bur. of Standards, 1927-30; teaching fellow, Calif. Inst. Tech., 1930-33; research engr., Guggenheim Airship Inst., Akron, O., 1934-38; lectr., N.Y.U., also cons. engr., 1938-40; aeronautical engr., Nat. Adv. Com. Aeronautics, 1940-41; mem. faculty U. of Mich. 1941—, aero. engring., 1943-53, Felix Pawloski prof. aerodyn., 1953—. Henry Russell lectr., 1969; chief scientist Office Air Research, U.S. Air Force, 1949-50. Recipient Alumni Citation, Ripon Coll., 1948. Fellow Am. Inst. Aeros. and Astronautics. Am. Phys. Soc. (exec. council fluid dynamics div. 1957-60); mem. Sigma Xi, Phi Kappa Phi. Author: (with J. D. Schetzer) Foundations of Aerodynamics. Home: 490 Barton N Dr Ann Arbor MI 48105

KUFELD, WILLIAM MANUEL, lawyer; b. Hunter, N.Y., Aug. 4, 1922; s. Max and Carrie (Hausdorff) K.; student Bklyn. Coll., 1938-40; B.B.A., Coll. City N.Y., 1940-42; LL.B., N.Y.U., 1949, LL.M., 1952; m. Frieda Chesir, Apr. 9, 1949; 1 son, David J. Admitted to N.Y. bar, 1949, since practiced in N.Y.C.; partner firm Carb, Luria, Glassner, Cook & Kufeld, 1959—; adj. asso. prof. law N.Y.U.; lectr. Practicing Law Inst. Dir. Cosmopolitan Mut. Ins. Co. Pres. Congregation of Young Israel of Fifth Av., N.Y.C., 1962-65, N. Shore Hebrew Acad., Great Neck, N.Y., 1969—. Served to 1st lt. USAAF, 1943-46. Recipient Alumn. Meritorious Achievement award N.Y.U., 1965. Mem. Assn. Bar City N.Y., N.Y. County Lawyers Assn., N.Y.U. Law Alumni Assn. (pres. 1970-71). Home: 22 Hawthorne Lane Great Neck NY 11023 Office: 529 Fifth Av New York NY 10017

KUFFEL, STANLEY, educator, psychologist; b. Graham Twp., Minn., Mar. 24, 1905; s. Henry Andrew and Katherine (Bogatski) K.; B.A., Coll. St. Thomas, St. Paul, 1927; M.A., U. Minn., 1938; Ed.D., Western Res. U., 1952; m. Ruth Ward, Aug. 16, 1928; children—George S., Robert W. Supt. pub. schs., Minn., 1931-42; dir. guidance N.D. Bd. Higher Edn., 1946-47; vocational counselor VA, Fargo, N.D., 1947-48, personnel counselor, 1948-50; coordinator student personnel Bemidji (Minn.) State Coll., 1950-51; prof. psychology Western Mich. U., 1952-71, head dept., 1952-65, chmn. div. sci. and math., 1959-62; cons. Borgess Hosp., Kalamazoo, 1959—. Mem. Mich. Planning Com. Dir. Child Guidance Clinic. Served USNR, 1942-45; comdr. Res. Mem. Am. Assn. U. Profs., Mich. Psychol. Assn., A.A.A.S., Mich. Vocational Rehab. Assn. (bd. dirs.), Kalamazoo Assn. Retarded Children (bd. dirs.), Nat., Mich. rehab. assns., Res. officers Assn., Phi Delta, Kappa. Author tng. manuals. Home: 4012 Loma Riviera Circle San Diego CA 92110

KUFFLER, STEPHEN WILLIAM, neurophysiologist; b. Tap, Hungary, Aug. 24, 1913; s. William and Elizabeth K.; student Gymnasium, Kalksburg, 1923-32; M.D., U. Vienna, 1937; M.A. (hon.), Harvard, 1959; M.D. (hon.), Bern, 1964; m. Phyllis Shewcroft, Apr. 25, 1943; children—Suzanne Elizabeth, Damien Paul, Julian Philip, Eugenie Gabrielle. Came to U.S., 1945, naturalized, 1954. Staff depts. medicine and pathology U. Clinic, Vienna, 1937-38; mem. Kanematsu Inst., Sydney (Australia) Hosp., 1938-45; NRC fellow, Australia, 1943-45; Seymour Coman fellow dept. physiology U. Chgo., 1945-47; asso. prof. ophthalmology Wilmer Inst., Johns Hopkins, 1947-57, prof. ophthalmic physiology and biophysics, 1956-59, research on function nervous system Johns Hopkins Hosp.; prof. neurophysiology and neuropharmacology Harvard Med. Sch., 1959-64, Robert Winthrop prof. neurophysiology and neuropharmacology, 1964-66, Robert Winthrop prof. neurobiology, chmn. dept., 1966—; Harvey lectr., 1959—; Silliman lectr. Yale U., 1971. Non-resident fellow Salk Inst., LaJolla, Cal., 1966; Ferrier lectr. Royal Soc., 1965; Silliman Meml. lectr. Yale, 1971. Trustee, Marine Biology Lab., Woods Hole, Mass. Recipient Passano award, 1971; John Simon Guggenheim fellow, 1956. Mem. Am. Physiol. Soc., Physiol. Soc. Eng., Nat. Acad. Scis., Am. Acad. Arts and Scis., Royal Soc. (fgn. mem.), Sigma Xi. Contbr. articles profl. jours. Home: 9 Surry Rd Newton MA 02158 Office: Dept of Neurobiology Harvard Med Sch 25 Shattuck St Boston MA 02115

KUGEL, KENNETH, govt. ofcl.; b. Sheboygan, Wis., May 5, 1921; s. Herman Kenneth and Rebecca (von Kaas) K.; B.A., Reed Coll., 1947; M.A., U. Mich., 1948; postgrad., George Washington U., 1949; m. Sarajane Moore, Aug. 12, 1944; children—Kenneth Kaas, Melanie, Candace, Thomas Hans, Carol. Research asst. Republican Nat. Com., 1948; with Library Congress, Bur. Fed. Supply, 1948-49; various assignments natural resources Bur. Budget, 1949-62; dir. Office Thai Regional Affairs, AID, 1962, asst. dir. for program mission to Thailand, 1962-64; dep. dir. U.S. AID Mission to Panana, 1964-66, asso. asst. adminstr. Vietnam bur., Washington, 1966- 67; dir. operational coordination staff U.S. Budget Bur., Washington, 1968—. Served to maj. USMCR, 1941-46. Mem. Theta Delta Chi. Unitarian (trustee). Home: 1600 S Joyce St Arlington VA 22202 Office: Exec Office of Pres Office Mgmt and Budget Washington DC 20503

KUGEL, ROBERT BENJAMIN, physician, educator; b. Chgo., May 2, 1923; s. H. Kenneth and Rebecca (von Kaas) K.; student Dartmouth, 1941-42; B.A., U. Mich., 1945, M.D., 1946; M.A., Brown U., 1964; m. Dorothy Annetta Bowdle, Jan. 31, 1950; children—Rebecca Anne, Gretchen Lucinda, Jennie Louisa. Intern, U. Mich. Hosp., 1947-48, resident, 1948-50; practice medicine, specializing in pediatrics, Omaha, 1966—; instr. dept. pediatrics Yale, 1951-52, U. Hosp., Ann Arbor, Mich., 1952-53; asst. prof. pediatrics, research asso. maternal and child health Johns Hopkins, 1955-56; asst. prof. pediatrics State U. Ia., dir. Child Devel. Clinic Univ. Hosp., Iowa City, 1956-63; prof. med. sci. Brown U., 1963- 65, prof. child health, 1965-66; prof., chmn. dept. pediatrics U. Neb., Omaha, 1966-69, prof. pediatrics, dean Coll. Medicine, 1969—. Mem. Pres.'s Com. on Mental Retardation, 1966-69. Pres. Josephine E. Kugel Found.; bd. dirs. Greater Omaha Assn. for Retarded Children; bd. dirs., dir. research and tng. Meyer Therapy Center. Mem. Am. Acad. Pediatrics, A.M.A., Am. Pediatric Soc., Midwest Soc. Pediatric Research, Am. Assn. Mental Deficiency (v.p.). Democrat. Presbyn. Contbr. articles profl. jours. Home: 301 S 54th St Omaha NB 68132

KUGELMASS, ISAAC NEWTON, biochemist, pediatrician, editor; b. June 28, 1896; s. Maurice and Sarah (Spirer) K.; B.S., Coll. City N. Y., 1916, fellow, 1917; M.A., Columbia, 1917; Ph.D., Johns Hopkins,

1921; Docteur Spécial in Scis. Physiologiques, U. Brussels, 1922; M.D., Yale, 1925; grad. study, Sorbonne, Paris, U. Zurich, U. Göttingen, U. Leipzig, Pasteur Inst., Paris and Brussels, 1920-21; m. Ella H. Fishberg, Aug. 18, 1934. Lectr. bd. edn., N.Y.C., 1916-17; instr. chemistry Columbia, 1917-18; prof. chemistry Howard Coll., also cons. nutrition dept. health, Birmingham, 1918-20; research asso. pediatrics Yale Med. Sch., 1922-25; asso. pediatrician dir. pediatric research Fifth Av. Hosp., N.Y.C., 1927-35; pediatrist French Hosp.; dir. Heckscher Inst. Child Health, asso. physician Riverside Hosp.; cons. pediatrist Monmouth (N.J.) Mem., Northwoods (Saranac Lake), Lynn Mem., Broad Street hosps. and Pan-Am. Clinics; chief growth clinic Hosp. Ruptured and Crippled, 1930-33; chief pediatrician N.Y.C. Children's Hosp.; chief, children's clinic immunology French Hosp.; hon. pediatrician Misericordia Hosp.; head, dept. pediatrics Le Roy Hosp., N.Y.C.; vis. lectr. pediatrics U. Montreal, McGill U., U. Tokyo, U. Philippines, U. Buenos Aires, U. Hawaii. Cons. nutritionist Dept. Health and Dept. Hosps., City N.Y.; nutritionist N.Y. sect. U.S. Food Adminstrn., 1916-17; mem. adv. bd. Child Guidance Found., Internat. Council Health and Travel; mem. council Purdue Med. Achievement awards; hon. med. chmn. Childrens Rehab. Center. Fellow Pan-Am. Med. Assn., Soc. Exptl. Biology and Medicine, A.A.A.S., Am. Assn. Engrs. (pres. Ala. sect. 1920), Am. Acad. Applied Nutrition, Am. Acad. Dental Medicine, Soc. Research Child Devel., Am. Assn. Mental Deficiency, N.Y. Acad. Sci., Am. Pub. Health Assn., Am. Chem. Soc.; mem. A.M.A., several nat., state, local profl. and sci. orgns. Republican. Author many books, latest being: Better Health for Your Children, 1955; Maturing Children in Body and Mind, 1955; Normal Infant Feeding, 1955; Management Mental Deficiency in Children, 1955; Chemical Pediatrics (monograph), 1957; Chemistry of Blood in Health and Disease, 1958; Biochemical Diseases, 1962; Chemical Pediatrics, 1962; Wisdom with Children, 1964; First-Aid Manual (for children), 1964; Adolescent Anomie, 1965; The Autistic Child Genius, 1966; Controlling Adolescent Immaturity, 1966; The Autistic Child, 1968; books translated into Spanish, Portuguese, Turkish, Japanese; research contbns. hemorrhagic diseases in children, metabolic disorders children, psycho-pharmacotherapy in mental deficiency and cerebral palsy of children, 1957—. Editor Am. Lectures in Living Chemistry; Biochem. Clinics; cons. editor: Ency. Americana, Internat. Record Medicine; editor, co-author many items in pediatrics. Home: 1060 Park Av New York City NY 10028

KUGELMASS, JOSEPH ALVIN, journalist, author; b. N.Y.C., Sept. 25, 1910; s. Maurice and Sara (Spirer) K.; student Coll. City N.Y., Columbia; m. Elizabeth Abramchick, July 1, 1945; children—Joel Nathaniel, Elise. Corr. Newsweek, Wall Street Jour., 1947, Asso. Press, 1948; editor Everybody's Digest, 1948; editor, writer Esquire; copy editor Louisville Courier-Jour., Washington Times-Herald, 1948; reporter N.Y. Star, 1949; copy editor Stars and Stripes, 1950, San Jose (Cal.) News, 1956—; corr. Washington (D.C.) Post. Cons. con. on selected writing materials Ho. of Reps. Mem. Am. Newspaper Guild. Recipient 1st prize for editorial on aviation Trans World Airlines, Pall Mall award for journalistic enterprise; George Washington medal for mag. writing Freedoms Found. Author: Louis Braille: Windows for the Blind, 1951; Ralph J. Bunche, 1952; History of the Institute for Advanced Studies, 1952; J. Robert Oppenheimer and the Atomic Story, 1953; Roald Amundsen: Saga of the Polar Seas, 1955; Earl Warren: Crusader for the People, 1967; Congo Crusader: The Life of Patrice Lamumba, 1968. Books trans. into Japanese, Croat-Serbian, Portuguese, French, Swedish, Hebrew. Contbr. to N.Y. Times Book Rev., Saturday Rev., Look, Brit. Commentary, others. Screenwriter: Warner Bros. film Two- Headed Spy. Home: 2301 Stokes St San Jose CA 95128

KUGLE, FRANK SANDS, mfg. co. exec.; b. Allentown, Pa., Nov. 22, 1917; s. Frank S. and Emma (Lonkosky) K.; student Northeastern U., 1938-39; B.S. in Commerce, Drexel Inst. Tech., 1947; C.P.A., Pa., 1949; m. Lenore Kathleen Woods, Apr. 3, 1943; 1 son, Thomas Woods. Mem. staff Main & Co., C.P.A.'s, Phila., 1946-48; office mgr. Hudson Sales Corp., Phila., 1948-49; asst. prof. bus. edn. Elizabethtown (Pa.) Coll., 1949-51; controller AMP Inc., Harrisburg, 1951—; dir. Morrison Labs. Inc., Harrisburg. Chmn. Central Pa. chpt. Nat. Multiple Sclerosis Soc., 1966-67. Trustee Harrisburg Area Community 1965—. 1965—. Served to capt., F.A., AUS, 1941-45. Mem. Financial Execs. Inst., Pa. Inst. C.P.A.'s, Machinery and Allied Products Inst. (financial council), Lambda Chi Alpha. Republican. Lutheran. Club: West Shore Country (Camp Hill).‡ Home: 41 Center Dr Camp Hill PA 17011 Office: Eisenhower Blvd Harrisburg PA 17105

KUGLER, ARTHUR NOBLE, mech. engr.; b. N.Y.C., July 13, 1902; s. Otto E. and Isabella J. (Noble) K.; M.E., Stevens Inst. Tech., 1925; m. Anna M. Nelson, Oct. 10, 1925; 1 dau., Florence M. (Mrs. Robert B. McCune). Field engr. Barker & Wheeler, cons. engr., 1925-28; installation engr. RCA Photophone-Sound, motion pictures, 1928-29; chief welding engr. Airco Welding products div. Airco Inc., 1929-67; cons. mech. and welding engr., Ridgewood, N.J., 1967—. Instr., Pratt Inst., evenings 1940-45; cons. U.S. Army Chem. Warfare Service, 1941-43. U.S. del. Internat. Inst. Welding commn. V111, safety and hygiene, 1957—. Recipient James T. Moorehead medal Internat. Acetylene Assn., 1961. Registered profl. engr., N.Y., N.J. Hon. mem. Am. Welding Soc. (Samuel W. Miller Meml. medal 1962); life mem. Am. Soc. M.E.; sr. mem. Soc. Mfg. Engrs. (gold medal 1965); mem. Nat. Soc. Profl. Engrs., Alpha Sigma Phi. Methodist. Club: Bear Mountain Figure Skating Palisades Interstate Park, N.Y., a founder, pres. 1946-62). Author 16 texts on welding engring. for Internat. Corr. Schs.; contbr. to handbooks. Address: 118 Sherwood Rd Ridgewood NJ 07450

KUH, EDWIN, educator; b. Chgo., Apr. 13, 1925; s. Edwin J., Jr. and Charlotte (Greenebaum) K.; B.A., Williams Coll., 1949; Ph.D., Harvard, 1955; m. Anne Barry, June 11, 1947 (div. Apr. 1970); children—Joanna M., Elizabeth N., Thomas, Sarah, Daniel; m. 2d, Alix Ryckoff, June 12, 1970. Lectr. Johns Hopkins, 1953-55; asst. prof. Sloan Sch. Mgmt. Mass. Inst. Tech., Cambridge, 1954-62, prof. mgmt. and econs., 1962—; cons. U.S. Treasury, 1959-60; mem. adv. research com. Brookings- SSRC Econometric Model, 1964—. Mem. staff President's Materials Policy Commn., 1951. Served with AUS, 1943-46. Fellow Econometric Soc., Am. Acad. Arts and Scis.; mem. Am. Econ. Assn., Am. Statis. Assn. Author: (with J. R. Meyer) The Investment Decision: An Empirical Study, Cambridge, 1957; Capital Stock Growth: A Micro-Econometric Approach, 1963. Editor: (with others) Brookings Quarterly Econometric Model of the U.S. Chgo. and Amsterdam, 1965. Home: 66 The Valley Rd Concord MA 07142 Office: Mass Inst Tech Sloan Sch Mgmt Cambridge MA 02139

KUH, ERNEST SHIU-JEN, educator, engr.; b. Peking, China, Oct. 2, 1928; s. Zone Shung and Tsia (Chu) K.; came to U.S., 1948, naturalized, 1960; B.S., U. Mich., 1949; M.S., Mass. Inst. Tech., 1950; Ph.D., Stanford, 1952; m. Bettine Chow, Aug. 4, 1957; children—Anthony, Theodore. Mem. tech. staff Bell Telephone Labs., Murray Hill, N.J., 1952-56; asso. prof. elec. engring. U. Cal. at Berkeley, 1956-62, prof., 1962—, Miller research prof., 1965-66, chmn. dept. elec. engring. and computer scis., 1968—; cons. IBM Research Lab., San Jose, Cal., 1957-62. Fellow I.E.E.E.; mem. Sigma Xi, Phi Kappa Phi. Co-author: Principles of Circuit Synthesis, 1959; Basic Circuit Theory, 1967; Theory of Linear Active Network, 1967. Office: Dept Elec Engring and Computer Scis U Cal Berkeley CA 94720

KUH, KATHARINE, editor; b. St. Louis, July 15, 1904; d. Morris and Olga (Weiner) Woolf; A.B., Vassar Coll., 1925; A.M., U. Chgo., 1928; postgrad., N.Y. U., 1929; m. George E. Kuh, Jan. 23, 1930 (div. 1936). Lectr., tchr. history of art for adult classes, 1930-39; owner, dir. Katharine Kuh Gallery, Chgo., 1935-42; curator gallery of art interpretation Art Inst. Chgo., 1943- 59, curator modern painting and sculpture, 1953-57, curator of painting and sculpture, 1957-59; art editor Saturday Rev., N.Y.C., 1959—; editor Bull. Art Inst. Chgo., 1945-53; art cons. So. Ill. U., 1963-67 Dir. art collection 1st Nat. Bank Chgo., 1968—. Author: Art Has Many Faces, 1951; Léger, 1953; The Artist's Voice, 1962; Break-Up: The Core of Modern Art, 1965; The Open Eye: In Pursuit of Art, 1971. Prepared adv. report on Indian carvings in Alaska for Office Indian Affairs, 1946; developed series of adult discussion groups in modern art for Fund for Adult Edn. of Ford Found., 1955. Home: 140 E 83d St New York City NY 10028 Office: Saturday Review 380 Madison Av New York City NY 10017

KUHARICH, JOSEPH LAWRENCE, profl. football coach; b. South Bend, Ind., Apr. 14, 1917; s. Martin and Teresa (Alterman) K.; B.S., U. Notre Dame, 1938; m. Madelyn Eleanor Imholz, Oct. 6, 1943; children—Joseph Lawrence, William Martin. Coach, tchr. Vincentian High Sch., Albany, N.Y., 1939; profl. football player Chgo. Cardinals, 1940-41, coach, 1952; coach Pitts. Steelers, 1946, U. San Francisco, 1947-51, Washington Redskins, 1954-58, U. Notre Dame, 1959-62; gen. mgr., coach Phila. Eagles, 1964-70. Mem. Nat. Football League (head 1963). Served to lt. USNR, 1942-45. Home: 320 Tower Lane Narberth PA 19072

KUHBACH, AREND GERDES, state ofcl.; b. N.Y.C., Nov. 21, 1916; s. Charles J. and Catherine (Kuhlmann) K.; A.B., Columbia, 1938, LL.B., 1940; m. Muriel Ruth Dinger, Aug. 1, 1942; children—Ellen Ames (Mrs. Henry C. Lucas, Jr.), Robert Gerdes, Peter Dwight. Admitted to N.Y. bar, 1940; with firm Lybrand, Ross Bros. & Montgomery, C.P.A.'s, N.Y.C., 1940; with N.Y., N.H. & H.R.R., 1941-62, tax counsel, 1944-50, tax atty., accountant, 1950-53, asst. gen. counsel, 1953, finance counsel, 1954-56, financial officer, 1957, v.p. finance, 1958-61, exec. v.p., 1961-62; dir. finance Port of N.Y. Authority, 1962—. Mem. Financial Execs. Inst., Municipal Forum N.Y. (dir.), Municipal Finance Officers Assn., Internat. Bridge, Tunnel and Turnpike Assn. Clubs: Wall Street, St John's Guild (N.Y.C.). Home: 38 Runnymede Rd Chatham NJ 07928 Office: 111 8th Av New York City NY 10011

KUHFELD, ALBERT MELDRUM, univ. dean; b. Hillyard, Wash., Jan. 25, 1905; s. William Gustav and Robina (Meldrum) K.; J.D., U. Minn., 1926; m. Olive Leone Peterson, June 8, 1930. Admitted to Minn. bar, 1926, N.D. bar, 1927, U.S. Supreme Ct., U.S. Ct. of Claims, U.S. Ct. Mil. Appeals, U.S. Dist. Ct.; partner Keohone & Kuhfeld, Beach, N.D., 1926-42; commd. 1st lt. U.S. Army, 1942, advanced through grades to maj. gen. USAF, 1955; dep. judge adv. gen. USAF, 1954-60, judge adv. gen., 1960-64; ret., 1964; asso. dean Ohio State U. Coll. of Law, 1965—. States atty. Golden Valley County, N.D., 1932-36; asst. atty. gen. N.D., 1936-40. Chmn., chief reviser N.D. Code Revision Commn., 1940-42. Pres. Columbus and Franklin County, O. council U.S.O. Decorated Bronze Star, Legion of Merit with oak leaf cluster, D.S.M.; recipient Outstanding Achievement award U. Minn., 1970. Mem. Am., Fed. Inter-Am., Columbus bar assns., Am. Judicature Soc., Internat. Inst. Space Law, Internat. Astronautical Fedn., Gamma Eta Gamma, Phi Delta Phi. Republican. Presbyn. Mason (Shriner). Club: National Lawyers (Washington). Home: 116 Piedmont Rd Columbus OH 43214

KUHFUSS, WILLIAM JOHN, agrl. co. exec., farmer; b. Mackinaw, Ill., Mar. 10, 1912; s. William August and Emma (Scholl) K.; B.E., Ill. State U., Norma, 1934; m. Elizabeth Amanda Storm, Aug. 23, 1935; children—Karen (Mrs. Edward H. Koch), Linda (Mrs. Thomas J. O'Donnell), William Thad, John David. Pres., Tazewell County Farm Bur., Pekin, Ill., 1951-55; v.p. Ill. Agrl. Assn., Chgo., 1956-58, pres., Bloomington, Ill., 1958—; pres. County Mut. Ins. Co., 1958-70, Country Life Ins. Co., 1958-70, Ill. Agrl. Service Co., 1958- 70, Ill. Agrl. Holding Co., 1958-70, Country Capital Investment Fund, Inc., 1965-70; pres. Am. Farm Bur. Fedn., Chgo., 1970—; chmn. bd. Mid-Am. Fire & Marine Ins. Co., Country Capital Mgmt. Co.; dir. Farmers State Bank, Minier, Ill. Mem. rural areas devel. adv. com. Emergency Resources Planning Com. Ill.; bd. agrl. advisers Ill. Dept. Agr.; mem. Ill. Export Adv. Com., Ill. Com. Trade Expansion. Bd. dirs. Ill. State U. Found.; mem. citizens com. U. Ill., also adv. com. Coll. Vet. Medicine. Recipient Holbert medal Ill. State U.; named State Farmer Ill. Future Farmers Am. Mem. Am. Angus Assn. (dir. 1956-58), Central Ill. Angus Breeders Assn. Home: Route 1 Mackinaw IL 61755 Office: 1000 Merchandise Mart Chicago IL 60654

KUHL, ROBERT WOLFE, merchandising exec.; b. Ann Arbor, Mich., Mar. 3, 1911; s. Ernest Peter and Lucy Van Dyke (Leech) K.; A.B., Harvard, 1932; postgrad., U. Ia., 1932- 33; m. Ruth Brewer Norton, Sept. 24, 1938; children—Barbara Brewer, Karen Huntington. With Gen. Elec. Co., Schenectady, 1933-36; with Allied Stores Corp., N.Y.C., 1937—, asst. treas., 1942-57, treas., 1957-68, sec., 1968—, also v.p., treas. subsidiaries. Served to lt. USNR, 1944-46. Club: Shenorock Shore (Rye, N.Y.). Home: 19 Forest Lane Scarsdale NY 10583 Office: 401 Fifth Av New York City NY 10016

KUHLENBECK, HARTWIG, neurobiologist; b. Jena, Germany, May 2, 1897; s. Ludwig and Helene (Ayrer) K.; B.A., Dom-Gymnasium Naumburg (Germany), 1914; Ph.D., U. Jena, 1920, M.D., 1922; Sc.M.D. (hon.), Woman's Med. Coll. Pa., 1965; m. Ozelia Marguerite Proteau, Jan. 30, 1924. Came to U.S., 1934, naturalized, 1938. Ship's surgeon, 1922-23; practice medicine, Mexico City, 1923-24; lectr. anatomy and neurology Tokyo (Japan) Imperial U., 1924-27; asst., privatdozent anatomy U. Breslau (Germany), 1927-33; vis. fellow anatomy U. Pa., 1934-35; prof. anatomy, chmn. dept. Woman's Med. Coll. Pa., 1935-63, research prof. anatomy, 1963-66, research prof. neurology and neuropathology, 1966-71, emeritus prof. anatomy, 1971—. Cons., Armed Forces Inst. Pathology, 1947-55. Served to lt. German Army, 1914-18, to maj., M.C., AUS, 1944-46. Fellow A.A.A.S., Coll. Physicians Phila.; mem. Am. Assn. Anatomists, Am. Assn. Neuropathologists, Assn. Mil. Surgeons U.S., Sigma Xi; hon. mem. Japanese Assn. Anatomists; fgn. sci. mem. Max-Planck Soc. Advancement Sci., Inst. for Brain Research. Author: Lectures on the Central Nervous System of Vertebrates, 1927; The Human Diencephalon, 1954; Brain and Consciousness, 1957; Mind and Matter, 1961; The Central Nervous System of Vertebrates, 3 vols., 1967-70. Office: Medical College of Pa Philadelphia PA 19129

KUHLMAN, E.V., hosp. adminstr. Adminstr. St. Anthony Hosp., Denver. Office: W 16th Av and Raleigh St Denver CO 80204•

KUHLTHAU, ALDEN ROBERT, educator; b. New Brunswick, N.J., Apr. 29, 1921; s. Harold V. and Emma (Ellison) K.; B.S., Wake Forest U., 1942; M.S., U. Va., 1944, Ph.D., 1948; m. Gay Harris, Sept. 15, 1943; children—Robert Peyton, Richard Harold, Linda Gay. Asst. prof. physics U. N.H., 1948-51; asst. dir. Research Labs. for Engring. Sci., U. Va., Charlottesville, 1951-54, dir., 1954-67, prof. aerospace engring., 1958—, asso. dean Sch. Engring. and Applied Sci., 1961-67, asso. provost for research, 1967-71. Mem. Am. Phys. Soc., Am. Assn. Physics Tchrs., Am. Soc. Engring. Edn., Am. Inst. Aeros. and Astronautics, A.A.A.S. Home: 1817 Meadowbrook Heights Rd Charlottesville VA 22901

KUHN, ALBERT JOSEPH, educator; b. Dowell, Ill., Apr. 4, 1926; s. Albert and Elizabeth (Furjes) K.; B.A., U. Ill., 1950; Ph.D., Johns Hopkins, 1954; m. Roberta Marshall, June 12, 1949; children—William, Frederick. Mem. faculty Ohio State U., 1954—, chmn. English dept., 1964—, prof. English, 1965—. Mem. region VIII, Woodrow Wilson Selection Com., 1961—. Served with USNR, 1944-46. Mem. Modern Lang. Assn., Nat. Council Tchrs. English, Phi Beta Kappa. Author: Romantic Bibliography, 1963; also articles. Editor: Three Sentimental Novels, 1970. Home: 35 Webster Park, Columbus, OH 43214.

KUHN, ALBIN OWINGS, univ. ofcl.; b. Woodbine, Md., Jan. 31, 1916; s. Howard Schloenacher and Clara May (Owings) K.; B.S., U. Md., 1938, M.S., 1939, Ph.D., 1948; postgrad. U. Wis., 1947; m. Ella Elizabeth Cissel, Nov. 23, 1938; children—Philip Howard, Joseph Albin, Roger Cissel, Albin Owings, Lois Ellen. Agronomic extension work U. Md., 1939-44, asso. prof. agronomy, 1946-48, prof. agronomy, 1948—, head dept., 1948-55, asst. pres., 1955- 58, exec. v.p., 1958-65, v.p. Balt. campuses, 1965-67, chancellor Balt. campuses, 1967-71, chancellor U. Md. at Balt., 1971—. Mem. Md. Hosp. Commn., 1964-67, vice chmn., 1966-67; mem. Gov.'s Com. on Rehab., 1965-67, Commn. for Modernization Exec. br. Md. Govt., 1966-67; mem. gov.'s adv. council to State's Inter-agy. Com. for Comprehensive Health Planning, 1968-69; mem. Balt. Urban Coalition, 1967- 69; pres. Md. Assn. for Higher Edn., 1968-69. Bd. dirs. Hosp. Cost Analysis Service, Inc.; trustee, v.p., sec. Md. Hosp. Service, Inc. Served with USNR, 1944-46; PTO. Fellow Am. Soc. Agronomy (pres. Northeastern br. 1954); mem. Northeastern Weed Control Conf. (pres. 1954), Sigma Xi, Alpha Zeta, Omicron Delta Kappa, Phi Kappa Phi, Alpha Gamma Rho, Pi Sigma Alpha. Address: 525 W Redwood St Baltimore MD 21201

KUHN, ALFRED, educator; b. Reading, Pa., Dec. 22, 1914; s. Alvin Boyd and Mary (Leippe) K.; B.A., Albright Coll., 1935; M.A. in History, U. Pa., 1941, Ph.D. in Econs., 1951; m. Nina Marguerite deAngeli, Oct. 18, 1941; children-J. David, Jeffrey P., Henry R. Tchr. pub. schs., (N.J. and Pa.,) 1935-41; various indsl. jobs, 1941-45; with WLB, Phila.,1945-46; instr. industry U. Pa., 1948-49; prof. econs. U. Cin., 1949—, David Sinton prof., 1968—, fellow Grad. Sch., 1968—. Mem. panel arbitrators Fed. Mediation and Conciliation Service, 1952—, Am. Arbitration Assn., 1947—. Pres., chmn. bd. Fulmer Heights Home Ownership Assn., 1946-49. Served with USNR, 1945. Mem. Am. Civil Liberties Union (chmn. Cin. chpt. 1968—, bd. dirs. O. chpt. 1966—), Am. Assn. U. Profs. (Distinguished Service award acad. freedom 1968), Soc. Gen. Systems Research, Am. Econ. Assn., Indsl. Relations Research Assn., Social Sci. Edn. Consortium. Author: Study of Society: A Unified Approach, 1963. Home: 574 U S 52 New Richmond OH 45157 Office: Dept Economics Brodie Tower Univ Cincinnati OH 45221

KUHN, BOWIE, commnr. of baseball; b. Takoma Park, Md., Oct. 28, 1926; B.A., Princeton, 1947; LL.B., U. Va., 1950; m. Luisa Hegeler; four children. Admitted to N.Y. bar; with firm Wilkie, Farr and Gallagher, N.Y.C.; legal counsel several baseball clients, 1950-69; rep. Nat. League club owners in negotiations with Maj. Lee Players Assn., 1968; commnr. pro tempore of baseball, 1969, commnr., 1969—. Home: 320 N Murray Av Ridgewood NJ 07450 Office: 680 Fifth Av New York City NY 10019

KUHN, CARL SELLNER, ins. exec.; b. Quincy, Ill., pub. schs. Quincy and Galveston, Tex.; m. Olga L. Ahlers, Oct. 5, 1910; 1 son, Carl Sellner. Vice pres., sec., dir. Am. Indemnity Co., Am. Fire & Indemnity Co., Tex. Gen. Indemnity Co.; v.p. dir. Am. Finance Co., Galveston. Home: 1714 20th St Galveston TX 77550 Office: 2115 Winnie Galveston TX 77550

KUHN, CHARLES E., indsl. exec.; b. Cin., Nov. 29, 1919; s. Leo and Vivian (Van Mellenger) K.; student Purdue U., 1938-39; m. Elma Jane Smith, Nov. 19, 1943; children—James R., Karen Joann. Vice pres. marketing Fansteel Metall. Corp., 1944-56, Mills McCanna Co., Inc., 1956-58; div. pres., group v.p. Dresser Industries, Inc., 1958-69; pres., chief exec. Weil McLain Co., Inc., Dallas, 1969—; dir. Geomap Co., Dallas. Pres. Dallas Arthritis Found., 1970. Served with USNR, 1940-42. Clubs: Dallas (pres. 1969), Brookhollow Golf, Preston Trails Golf, Northwood, Chemist (Dallas). Home: 5015 Tanbark Rd Dallas TX 75221 Office: Republic National Bank Dallas TX 75201

KUHN, EDWARD W., lawyer; b. Memphis, Nov. 23, 1905; student Christian Brothers Coll., Cath. U. Am.; LL.B., U. Mich., 1933; m. Mattie Mahaffey; children—Philip, Barry, Brian. Admitted to Tenn. bar, 1934; practice in Memphis; mem. firm McDonald, Kuhn, Smith, Gandy, Miller and Tait. Fellow Am. Coll. Trial Lawyers, Am. Bar Found.; mem. Internat., Inter-Am., Am. (bd. govs. 1960-63), pres. 1965-66), Tenn. (pres. 1954-55), Shelby County (pres. 1949-50), Memphis bar assns., Internat. Assn. Ins. Counsel, Assn. Ins. Attys. (pres. 1959). Order of Coif-(hon.). Home: 5080 Stage Rd Memphis TN 38128 Office: 150 E Court Av Memphis TN 38103

KUHN, FERDINAND, writer; b. N.Y.C., Apr. 10, 1905; s. Ferdinand and Johanna (Loeb) K.; A.B., Columbia, 1925; m. Delia E. Wolf, Aug. 28, 1931; children—Philip Alden, David Antony. With N.Y. Times as reporter, 1925-28, mem. London staff, 1928-36, chief London corr., 1937-39, editorial and spl. writer, 1939-40; asst. to sec. treasury, 1940-43; dep. dir. OWI (overseas br.) and chief Brit. div., 1943-45; head, internat. information service Dept. State, 1945-46; internat. affairs reporter Washington Post, 1946-53; lectr. Salzburg Seminar Am. Studies, 1967. Pres. Assn. Am. Corrs. in London, 1937-38. Decorated chevalier Legion of Honor (France); recipient Columbia medal distinguished service, 1939, Sigma Delta Chi award best fgn. corr., 1951. Clubs; Columbia University (N.Y.C.); National Press, Cosmos (Washington). Author: Commodore Perry and the Opening of Japan, 1955; The Story of the Secret Service, 1957; (with wife) Borderlands, 1962, The Philippines, Yesterday and Today, 1966, Russia on Our Minds, 1970. Editor: (with wife) Adventures in Public Service, 1963. Home: 2915 Audubon Terrace Washington, DC 20008

KUHN, HAROLD WILLIAM, mathematician; b. Santa Monica, Cal., July 29, 1925; s. William Sebastion and Mignon (Lorenz) K.; B.S., Cal. Inst. Tech., 1947; M.A., Princeton, 1948, Ph.D., 1950; m. Estelle Henkin, Dec. 24, 1949; children—Clifford, Nicholas, Jonathan. Instr., Princeton, 1949-50, lectr. math., 1951-52, asso. prof. math. econs., 1959-63, prof., 1963—; asst. prof., then asso. prof. math. Bryn Mawr Coll., 1952-59; cons. editor John Wiley & Sons, 1958—; sr. cons., sci. dir. Mathematica Inc., 1961-65, v.p., dir. research, 1965—; cons. Nat. Bureau Standards, Office Naval Research, IBM Corp., Gen Electric Co., Port N.Y. Authority. Exec. sec. div. math. Nat. Acad. Scis.-NRC, 1957-58, 59-61; mem. adv. com. Army Research Office, 1962—; mem. div. math. NRC, 1963- -. Fulbright Research scholar, Paris, France, 1950-51; Nat. Sci. Found. senior postdoctoral fellow London Sch. Econs., 1958-59, U. Rome, 1965-66. Fellow Econometric Soc.; mem. Am. Math. Soc., Math. Assn. Am., Soc. Indsl. and Applied Math. (pres. 1954-55), Am. Assn. U. Profs. (council 1960-63), A.A.A.S. Author articles linear programming and theory of games. Editor: (with A.W. Tucker) Annals of Mathematics Studies, No. 24, 1950, No. 28, 1953, No. 38, 1956. Home: 74 Woodland Dr Princeton NJ 08540

KUHN, JAMES WESLEY, educator; b. Dundee, Ore., Apr. 19, 1924; s. Lloyd H. and Arlena (Dillinger) K., B.A. cum laude, Harvard, 1949; M.A., Yale, 1950, Ph.D. in Econs., 1954; student U. Sydney (Australia), 1951; LL.D., Linfield Coll., 1959; m. Sara Lila, MacLeod, Aug. 11, 1951; children—Katherine Ann, Ellen Virlee, Christine Lila, Claudia Arlena. Asst. prof. Pomona Coll., 1953-54, U. Ore., 1954-55; prof. Columbia Grad. Sch. Bus., 1955- ; sr. staff economist Council Econ. Advisers, 1968-69. Mem. dept. social justice Nat. Council Chs., 1964—. Served with USAAF, 1943-46. Fulbright grantee, 1951; Ford Fellow, 1961. Mem. Am. Econ. Assn., Indsl. Relations Research Assn., Australian Inst. Polit. Sci. Author: Settlement in Grievance Settlement, 1961; (with Neil Chamberlain) Collective Bargaining, 1964; Scientific and Managerial Manpower in Nuclear Power, 1966; (with Ivar Berg) Values in a Business Society, 1968; (with others) White Collar Workers, 1969. Mem. editorial bd. Christianity and Crisis, 1962—. Home: 15 Norman Pl Tenafly NJ 07670 Office: Uris Hall Columbia Univ New York City NY 10027

KUHN, LLOYD WILSON, banker; b. Adams County, Pa., Apr. 22, 1898; s. Lloyd E. and Mary (Smith) K.; grad. Pa. Bus. Coll., Lancaster, 1919; m. Mary E. Garretson, July 31, 1922; children—Charles E. (dec.), Ronald B., Jean M. (Mrs. Justin J. Horick), Joyce L. (Mrs. Richard L. Swope). Tchr., Adams County, 1918-19; with Bendersville Nat. Bank (Pa.), 1919-, pres., 1954—; pres., dir. Penn Products Corp., Bendersville, 1952—; dir. Fed. Res. Bank Phila. Chmn. banking div. War Savs. Bond Com. Adams County, 1962—. Bd. dirs. Annie M. Warner Hosp., Gettysburg, Pa. Mem. Pa. Bankers Assn. Elk. Home: N Main St Bendersville PA 17306 Office: Bendersville Nat Bank N Main St Bendersville PA 17306

KUHN, REINHARD, educator; b. Berlin, Germany, Sept. 6, 1930; s. Helmut and Kaethe (Lanke) K.; came to U.S., 1938, naturalized, 1946; A.B., Princeton, 1952, M.A., 1954, Ph.D., 1957; M.A. ad eundem, Brown U., 1965; m. Ira Astride Ameriks, June 15, 1963; 1 son, Bernhard Helmut. Asst. prof., then asso. prof. U. Kan., 1958-63; prof. U. Buffalo, 1963-64; prof. French, Brown U., 1964—, chmn. dept., 1967—. Mem. adv. com. Sweetbriar Jr. Year in France, 1966-. Mem. tech. com. on R.I. Coastal Zone. Served with AUS, 1954-56. Fulbright research scholar France, 1964-65. Fellow Am. Council Learned Socs.; mem. Modern Lang. Assn., Am. Assn. Tchrs. French, Modern Humanities Research Assn., Assn. Study Dada and Surrealism, Am. Assn. U. Profs., Pawtuxet-Edgewood Preservation Soc. (sec.). Author: The Return to Reality, 1962; Correspondence de Francis Jammes et de Francis Viele- Griffin, 1966; co-author: Panorama du Theatre Nouveau, 4 vols., 1966-67. Translator: New Ways of Ontology, 1952; Dying we Live, 1957. Asso. editor: Novel. Home: 62 Fort Av Edgewood RI 02905 Office: French Dept Brown Univ Providence RI 02912

KUHN, ROLF, musician; b. Köln, Germany, Sept. 29, 1929; s. Arthur Kurt and Grete (Moses) K.; student music Conservatorium, Leipzig, Germany, also pvt. study. Lead saxophone player Radio Leipzig, 1947-49, on group, also with Rias Dance Band, 1949-56; tours of U.S. with Benny Goodman and Tommy Dorsey's orchs., also other groups, 1956-61; leader NDR Radio Orch., Hamburg, Germany, 1962-67; tchr. clarinet, 1961; condr. musicals and opera, composer, clarinetist, 1967—; writer film scores and TV prodns. for German TV, 1967—; mus. dir. Dusseldorf Playhouse, 1971—. Recipient 1st place Down Beat Jazz Critics Poll on clarinet. Address: 12 Pfeilschoferweg Hamburg Federal Republic of Germany

KUHN, TERRY W., aluminum and brass mfg. cons.; b. Johnstown, Pa., June 20, 1900; s. Christian Walter and Jessie (Terry) K.; B.S., Washington-Jefferson Coll., 1923; m. Jewel Baker, Jan. 9, 1943; 1 dau. Terry. Dist. traffic supt. Mich. Bell Telephone Co., 1923-25; salesman Walter Hagen Golf Co., 1926, Udylite Corp., 1927; salesman Bohn Aluminum & Brass Co., Detroit, 1928- 49, v.p., 1949-54, dir., 1950—, exec. v.p., 1954-58, pres., 1958-68, cons., 1969—; former v.p., dir. REO Motors, Inc., Del. Mem. Phi Kappa Psi. Clubs: Royal Palm Yacht and Country (Boca Raton, Fla.); Country of Detroit (Grosse Pointe Farms, Mich.). Home: 1356 Thatch Palm Dr Boca Raton FL 33432 Office: Clausen Bldg N 23100 Providence Dr Southfield MI 48075

KUHN, THOMAS SAMUEL, educator; b. Cin., July 18, 1922; s. Samuel Louis and Minette (Stroock) K.; S.B. summa cum laude in Physics, Harvard, 1943, A.M., 1946 (NRC predoctoral fellow 1945-48), Ph.D., 1949; m. Kathryn Louise Muhs, Nov. 27, 1948; children—Sarah, Elizabeth, Nathaniel Stroock. With radio research lab., also Am.-Brit. lab. OSRD, div. 15, 1943-45; jr. fellow Harvard Soc. Fellows, 1948-51; mem. faculty Harvard, 1951-56, asst. prof. gen. edn. and history sci., 1952-56; mem. faculty U. Cal. at Berkeley, 1958-64, prof. history sci., 1961-64; prof. history sci. Princeton, 1964-68, M. Taylor Pyne prof. history sci., 1968—. Lowell Inst. lectr., 1951; dir. project Sources History Quantum Physics, 1961-64. Del. U.S. nat. com. Internat. Union History and Philosophy Sci., 1959-60, 64-67. Guggenheim fellow, 1954-55; Center Advanced Study Behavioral Sci. fellow 1958-59. Mem. History Sci. Soc. (council 1953-63, chmn. editorial bd. Pfizer monograph series 1958-61, exec. com. 1964-70, 1st v.p. 1966-68, pres. 1968-70), Am. Acad. Arts and Scis., Am. Hist. Assn., A.A.A.S., Phi Beta Kappa, Sigma Xi; membre effectif Acad. Internat. d'Histoire des Sciences. Author: The Copernican Revolution: Planetary Astronomy in the Development of Western Thought, 1957; The Structure of Scientific Revolution, 1962; (with others) Sources for History of Quantum Physics: an Inventory and Report, 1967. Mem. bd. Dictionary of Scientific Biography, 1964—. Home: 6 Queenston Pl Princeton NJ 08540

KUHN, TRUMAN HOWARD, univ. adminstr., geologist; b. Glendora, Cal., Oct. 31, 1908; s. David Truman and Betta (Boyakin) K.; B.S., Cal. Inst. Tech., 1930; postgrad., U. Cal. at Berkeley, 1930-31; Ph.D., U. Ariz., 1940; m. Edith White, June 21, 1932; children—David T. and Martin C. (twins). Engr., geologist Los Angeles Flood Control Dist., 1931-37; geologist Ariz. Molybedenum Corp., 1938-40, Magma Copper Co., 1940-42; with Colo. Sch. Mines, 1942—, successively asst. prof., asso. prof. geology, 1942-52, prof., 1952—, dean Grad. Sch., 1953-56, dean faculty, 1956-68, v.p. adminstrv. affairs, 1968—; geologist Eagle Picher Mining & Smelting Co., 1944-45, U.S. Geol. Survey, 1951-53. Geologist, Colo. Sch. Mines Research Found., 1953—. Registered profl. engr., Colo. Registered geologist, Cal. Fellow Geol. Soc. Am.; mem. Soc. Econ. Geologists, Am. Inst. Mining Metall. and Petroleum Engrs., Am. Soc. Engring. Edn., Mining and Metall. Soc. Am., Am. Inst. Profl. Geologists, Sigma Xi. Kiwanian. Club: Teknik. Home: 2223 Table Dr Golden CO 80401

KUHN, WOLFGANG ERASMUS, educator; b. Germany, Apr. 12, 1914; s. Fred K. and Johanna (Scheibe) K.; came to U.S., 1929, naturalized, 1934; B.Mus., U. Ill., 1937, M.S., 1943, Ed.D., 1953; m. Mary Elizabeth Croughan, Aug. 23, 1938; children—Suanna D. (Mrs. Charles E. Breed), Elizabeth (Mrs. J. Thomas Bacchetti), Virginia E. Asso. prof. music U. Ill. at Urbana, 1943-55, U. Colo., 1955-58; prof. music and edn. Stanford, 1958—, acting head music dept., 1966-67, also summer quarter; tchr. Nat. Music Camp, Interlochen, Mich., 1947, 48. Mem. Music Educators Nat. Conf., Am. String Tchrs. Assn., Coll. Music Soc., Am. Musicol. Soc., Phi Mu Alpha, Pi Kappa Lambda, Phi Delta Kappa. Author: Principles of String Class Teaching, 1957; Instrumental Music, 1962, 2d edit., 1971; The Strings, 1967. Home: 612 Alvarado Row Stanford CA 94305

KUHNEN, HARALD, banker; b. Rheydt, Germany, Aug. 5, 1912; s. August and Emma (Rolshoven) K.; Dr.jur. honoris causa, U. Cologne (Germany), 19—; m. Gertrud Funke, Sept. 15, 1949. With Dresdner Bank, 1931-45; partner Bank Kirchholtes & Co., 1946-51; partner Bank Sal. Oppenheim jr. & Cie., Köln, Germany, 1951—; chmn. bd. Rheinishh-Westfalische Boden-Credit-Bank, also various other banking and indsl. corps. Bd. dirs. Thyssen Found. Named Hon. Senator, U. Cologne, 1960. Mem. German Bankers Assn. (mem. bd.). Home: 67 Goethe Koln-Marienburg Germany Office: 4 Unter Sachsenhausen Köln Germany

KUHNEN, S. MARIE, educator; b. Haledon, N.J., Sept. 12, 1917; d. Charles William and Sybil (Daniels) Kuhnen; B.A., Montclair State Tchrs. Coll., 1941; M.A., Columbia, 1946; Ph.D., N.Y.U., 1960. Tchr., Eastside High Sch., Paterson, N.J., 1941-44; teaching asst. botany Columbia, 1944-46; mem. faculty Montclair State Coll., 1946—, prof. biology, 1963—, chmn. dept., 1968—. Chmn. Valhalla Glen Purchase Com., 1963-67; sec.-treas. council Assn. N.J. State Coll. Faculties, 1962-67. Recipient Conservation award Summit Nature Soc., 1968. Fellow A.A.A.S.; mem. Bot Soc. Am., Nat. Sci. Tchrs. Assn. (life), Nature Conservancy, Nat. Audubon Soc., Wilderness Soc., Nat. Parks Assn., Kappa Delta Pi, Sigma Delta Epsilon. Home: 5 Charles Ct Clifton NJ 07013 Office: Biology Dept Montclair State Coll Upper Montclair NJ 07043

KUHNHEIM, EARL JAMES, hosp. supply co. exec.; b. Columbus, O., Dec. 17, 1921; s. Earl Fred and Hildreth Elizabeth (Gall) K.; B.S. in Bus. Adminstrn., Ohio State U., 1946; m. Marilyn R. Oaksmith, Aug. 23, 1947; children—Jamie Lynn, Jill Suzanne, Jennifer Lea. With McKesson & Robbins, Inc., 1946—, v.p., div. mgr., Cleve., 1962-63, v.p. retail trade promotion, N.Y.C., 1963-64, v.p. Hosp. Supply Co. div. McKesson & Robbins Drug Co. div. Foremost-McKesson, Inc., 1964—, v.p., gen. mgr. Hosp. Gentec Supply Co. div., 1966—. Served with AUS, 1942-44. Mem. Am. Surg. Trade Assn. (chmn. mgmt. tng. com. 1968—), Nat. Wholesale Druggist Assn. (chmn. sales mgmt. com. 1959), Sigma Alpha Epsilon. Club: Country of Darien. Home: 43 Pocconock Trail New Canaan CT 06840 Office: 155 E 44th St New York City NY 10017

KUHNS, RICHARD FRANCIS, Jr., educator; b. Chgo., May 3, 1924; s. Richard Francis and Helen (Kuh) K.; B.A., Dartmouth, 1947; Ph.D., Columbia, 1955; m. Margaret Portis, June 5, 1944; 1 son, Frederick. Instr., Dartmouth, 1949-50; mem. faculty Columbia, 1951—, prof., 1965—. Served with AUS, 1942-45. Mem. Am. Philos. Assn., Am. Soc. for Aesthetics. Author: The House, The City, and The Judge, 1962; (with A. Hofstadter) Philosophies of Art and Beauty, 1965; Structures of Experience, 1970. Home: 420 Riverside Dr New York City NY 10025

KUHNS, WILLIAM GEORGE, pub. utility exec.; b. Milw., Apr. 26, 1922; s. Harold E. and Edna J. (Paulus) K.; B.A., U. Wis., 1946, J.D., 1949; m. Joan P. Beutell, July 9, 1948; children—Nancy, Janet, Linda, Pamela, Elisabeth. With operating research bur. Wis. Electric Power Co., 1949-55; with Gen. Pub. Utilities Corp., N.Y.C., 1955—, treas., 1957-61, v.p., 1961-67, pres., chief exec. officer, 1967—, also dir.; pres., dir. Gen. Pub. Utilities Service Corp.; dir. Marine Midland Bank- N.Y., Home Life Ins. Co., Jersey Central Power & Light Co., N.J. Power & Light Co., Pa. Electric Co., Met. Edison Co. Admitted to Wis. bar, 1949. Mem. Wis. Bar Assn., N.Y.C. Econ. Club, Newcomen Soc., Phi Eta Sigma, Delta Tau Delta, Beta Gamma Sigma. Clubs: Recess, Downtown Athletic; University; Seaview Country (Absecon, N.J.); Knickerbocker Country (Tenafly, N.J.). Home: 11 Stonehurst Tenafly Tenäfly NJ 07670 Office: 80 Pine St New York City NY 10005

KUHSE, HAROLD H., lawyer; b. Sac County, Ia., Dec. 7, 1921; s. Henry E. and Freida (Ackerman) K.; B.S. in Engring., Ia. State U., 1949; J.D., U. Ia., 1951; m. Jeanne M. Bendick, May 22, 1954; children-Theresa M., Melinda J., Mark B., Craig A., Mary C. Admitted to Ia. bar, 1951, Ariz. bar, 1954; with Oliver Corp., 1951-52, State of Wash., 1952-53, City of Mesa, Ariz., 1953-66; mem. firm Kuhse, Petrie & Reynolds, Mesa, 1958—. Sec., dir. Tribune Pub. Co., Phil Bramsen Distbg. Co. (both Mesa). Bd. dirs. Mesa Aqua Boosters. Served with USAAF, 1941-45. Decorated D.F.C. with cluster, Air medal with clusters; breat Order Yun Hui (China). Mem. Am. Assn. Trial Lawyers, State Bar Ariz. Democrat. Methodist (trustee, chmn. bldg. com.). Lion (pres. Mesa 1961-62), Mason (Shriner). Home: 514 W Fairway Circle Mesa AZ 85201 Office: 240 V N B Bldg Mesa AZ 85201

KUIPER, GERARD PETER, astronomer; b. Harencarspel, The Netherlands, Dec. 7, 1905; s. Gerard and Anna (de Vries) K.; B.Sc., U. of Leyden, The Netherlands, 1927, Ph.D., 1933; m. Sarah Parker Fuller, June 20, 1936; children—Paul, Lucy. Came to U.S., 1933, naturalized, 1937. Research asst. astronomy, U. of Leyden, 1928-33; mem. Dutch Eclipse Expdn. to Sumatra, 1929; research fellow Lick Observatory, U. of Calif., 1933-35, research asso., 1935, lectr. Harvard, 1935-36; asst. prof. astronomy, U. of Chicago, 1936-37, asso. prof., 1937-43, prof. 1943-60, located at McDonald Observatory, Fort Davis, Tex., 1939-60, dir. of Yerkes and McDonald Obs., 1947-49, 57-60; head Lunar and Planetary Lab., U. Ariz., 1960—. Research asso. Radio Research Lab., Harvard, 1943-45; cons., operational analysis sect., Eighth Air Force, Eng., 1944; mem. Alsos mission, 1945; Dryden research lectr. Am. Inst. Aero. and Astronautics, 1969. Decorated Comdr. Order Orange Nassau (Netherlands); Janssen Medal, French Astron. Soc. Mem. Nat. Acad. Scis., Am. Acad. Arts and Scis., Internat. Astron. Union. Am. Astron. Soc., Astron. Soc. Pacific, Royal Astron. Soc. London (asso.), Netherlands Soc. Scis. (fgn mem.), Royal Netherlands Acad. Scis. (fgn. mem.). Author articles in Astrophys. Jour.; also 4 atlases. Editor: (book) The Atmospheres of the Earth and Planets, 1949, 52; The Solar System, 4 vols., 1953-61; Stars and Stellar Systems, 9 vols., 1960—. Home: 721 N Sawtelle Tuscon AZ 85716 Office: Lunar and Planetary Lab U Ariz Tuscon AZ 85721

KUIPERS, LAUWERENS, educator, mathematician; b. Dordrecht, Netherlands, Jan. 3, 1909; s. Hendrikus and Teuna (Swets) K.; Ph.D., Vrije Universiteit, Amsterdam, Netherlands, 1947; m. Francina Okker, July 11, 1934; children—Thea (Mrs. Marinus Slooter), Francina Cornelia (Mrs. Kees Ouwehand), Hendrik, Laurens. Prof. math. U. Indonesia, 1949-55; U. Redlands (Cal.), 1955-56, Technische Hogeschool, Delft, Netherlands, 1956-66; prof. math. So. Ill. U., Carbondale, 1966—. Mem. Malayan, Austrian, Am. math. socs., Societe Math. de Belgique, Wisk. Genootsch. A'dam. Author: (with R. Timman) Analysis I, II Handboek der Wiskunde. Contbr. articles to profl. jours. Research in theory of uniform distbn. modulo-l. Office: So Ill U Carbondale IL 62901

KUIPERS, WILLIAM E., banker; b. 1903. Sr. v.p., dir. Nat. Community Bank, Fair Lawn, N.J. Home: 27 Beresford Rd Allendale NJ 07401 Office: 13-51 River Rd Fair Lawn NJ 07410*

KUIVILA, HENRY GABRIEL, educator, chemist; b. Fairport Harbor, O., Sept. 17, 1917; s. Matti and Saima (Kujala) K.; B.Sc., Ohio State U., 1942, M.A., 1944; Ph.D., Harvard, 1948; m. Nancy M. Corn, June 13, 1943; children—Henry G., Nancy J., Ronald J. Jr. chemist Manhattan Project, Monsanto Chem. Co., 1944- 46; from asst. prof. to prof. U. N.H., 1948-64; prof. chemistry, chmn. dept. State U. N.Y. at Albany, 1964—. NSF sr. postdoctoral fellow, 1959; Guggenheim fellow, 1959-60. Fellow A.A.A.S., N.Y. Acad. Scis.; mem. Am. Chem. Soc., Phi Beta Kappa, Sigma Xi. Research organic reaction mechanisms, organometallic chemistry, allene chemistry, free radicals. Home: 36 E Bayberry Rd Glenmont NY 12077 Office: 1400 Washington Av Albany NY 12203

KUKLIN, JEROME, metal fastener mfg. co. exec.; b. Chgo., Aug. 3, 1933; s. Jacob and Rose (Kuklini) B.S. in Bus. Adminstrn., Roosevelt U., 1956; m. Barbara Kuklin, Feb. 9, 1958; children—Steven H., Perry C., Adam L. Mgr. marketing Universal Screw Co., Chgo., 1962-65; asst. to pres. Champion Screw Co., Chgo., 1965-66; v.p. Ken Industries, Santa Fe Springs, Cal., 1966-67; chmn. bd., pres. Alvo Fasteners, Inc., Los Angeles, 1967—. Mem. Chgo. Bolt, Nut and Screw Assn., Nat. Sales Mgrs. Assn., Nat. Office Mgrs. Assn., Los Angeles Fastener Assn. (founder, pres. 1967-69). Home: 18070 Lake Encino Dr Encino CA 91316 Office: 1601 Grande Vista Av Los Angeles CA 90023

KUKLIN, NORMAN BENNETT, lawyer; b. N.Y.C., Feb. 25, 1898; s. Barnett and Rosabelle (Sherman) K.; B.A., Columbia, 1921, LL.B., 1924; m. Deane Cable, Dec. 16, 1928; children—Anthony Bennett, Jeffrey Peter. Adnitted to N.Y. bar, 1925, since practiced in N.Y.C.; partner Goldwater & Flynn, 1947—. Mem. Am. Bar Assn., Assn. Bar City N.Y. Home: 4810 Boston Post Rd Pelham Manor, NY 10803 Office: 60 E 42d St New York City NY 10017

KUKLIS, ERNEST, corp. exec.; b. 1929; B.A., Harpur Coll., 1961; m. With Endicott Johnson Corp., N.Y.C., 1953—, treas., 1963—. Served with AUS, 1951-53. Address: 1100 E Main St Endicott NY 13762*

KULCZYCKI, LUCAS L., research physician, pediatrician; b. Jurjampol, Poland, Aug. 19, 1911; s. Ludvik and Rose (Stabiszewska) K.; B.S., U. Lwow, Poland, 1934, D.V.M., 1936; B.Med. and B.Surg., U. Edinburgh, 1944, M.D., 1946; Diploma Pub. Health, U. London, 1948; Diploma Child Health, Royal Coll. Phys. and Surg., Ireland, 1950; Specialist Certificate Pediatrics, Royal Coll. Phys. and Surg., Can., 1958; m. Halina Danuta Dolasinska; children—Christopher, Dorothy Mary. Came to U.S., 1953, naturalized, 1960. Sci. research Poland, 1934-38; med. residencies, Edinburgh and Inverness, Scotland, 1944-46; pub. health medicine, gen. practice, specialist in pediatrics, London, 1947-50; pub. health medicine and pediatrics, Can., 1951-53; pediatrics resident research cystic fibrosis and related diseases Children's Hosp., Boston, 1953-61; instr. Harvard Med. Sch., 1956-61; clin. dir. Wrentham (Mass.) State Sch., 1957-58; co- founder cystic fibrosis clinics Eastern States U.S., 1958-65; lectr. symposia and seminars on Mucoviscidosis various European countries, 1959- 66; dir. Cystic Fibrosis Center, Children's Hosp., Washington; cons. cystic fibrosis, med. centers, also NIH, 1962-67; cons. pediatrician Childrens' Convalescent Hosp., Washington; asso. clin. prof. pediatrics Georgetown U. Med. Sch., 1962-67. Bd. dirs., med. adv. bd., edn. com. Nat. Cystic Fibrosis Research Found. Served as 1st lt., M.C., Brit Army, 1943-45. Diplomate Am. Bd. Pediatrics. Fellow Royal Soc. Medicine, New Eng. Pediatric Soc., Manitoba Coll. Phys. and Surg., N.Y. Acad. Sci., Am. Pub. Health Assn., Am. Acad. Pediatrics, Am. Coll. of Chest Physicians; mem. D.C. Med. Soc. Co-editor Polish Pediatrics, Polish Medicine and Sci. Contbr. numberous med. articles profl. publs. Home: 1507 N Kirkwood Rd Arlington VA 22213 Office: 2125 13th St NW Washington DC 20009

KULISIEWICZ, TADEUSZ, artist; b. 1899; ed. Warsaw Acad. Fine Arts. Prof. Warsaw Acad. Fine Arts, 1946-; 1946—; include Sziembark drawings, China, India and Mexico drawings, also Caucasian Chalk Circle drawings; represented exhbns. Prague, Rome, Milan, Vienna, Paris, Brussels, The Hague, 1953, Germany, 1955, 56, Mexico, 1957, also 37th Venice Biennial, 1954, Sao Paulo Biennial. Recipient 1st prize Internat. Wood Engraving exhbn., Warsaw, 1933; state prizes, 1952, 56; UNESCO award, 1954. Address: 7 Mazowiecka Warsaw Poland*

KULJIAN, HARRY A., cons. engr.; b. Armenia, Dec. 21, 1893; s. Asdour and Hosanna (Hakoian) K.; brought to U.S., 1911, naturalized 1923; S.B., Mass. Inst. Tech., 1919; Dr. Engring. (hon.), Drexel Inst. Tech., 1953; m. Alice Levonian, Sept. 22, 1922; children—Arthur, Florence (Mrs. Hrair Levonian), Edward. Turbine design dept. Westinghouse Co., East Pittsburgh, Pa., 1920; design engr. Stone & Webster, Boston, 1920-24; asst. to chief engr. Am. Viscose Corp., 1924-30; established H.A. Kuljian & Co., cons. engrs., Phila., 1931; organizer, pres., chmn. Kiljian Corp., engrs. and constructors, 1941-65, now chmn. exec. com.; designer, constructor 100 power plants U.S. and fgn. countries, numerous chem., textile, petroleum and other indsl. plants, also projects U.S. govt. Awarded Army and Navy E for outstanding engring. service to Chem. Warfare Dept.; Meritorious award (Navy); cited Engineer of the Year, Pa. Soc. Profl. Engrs., 1955; recipient Kabakjian Sci. Award, 1955. Fellow Am. Soc. M.E., Am. Soc. Elec. Engrs., Franklin Inst.; mem. Tech. Assn. Pulp and Paper Industry. Author: Man and the World of Science, 1964; Nuclear Power Plant Design, 1968. Holds over 30 patents on new machine for continuous rayon spinning and processing, boiler feed level recorder and controller, density recorder and indicator; designer numerous time-saving devices and equipment for rayon, chem. textile plants and pub. utilities. Home: 131 Raynham Rd Merion PA 17235 Office: 1200 N Broad St Philadelphia PA 19121

KULLAS, ALBERT JOHN, spacecraft co. exec.; b. Webster, Mass., May 5, 1917; s. Albert J. and Mary (Piechowiak) K.; B.S. in Civil Engring., Worcester Poly. Inst., 1938; M.S. in Civil Engring., N.Y. U., 1940; m. Joyce M. Gladus, Jan. 31, 1942; children—Michael, Daniel, Mark, James. With Martin Marietta Corp., 1940—, structures mgr., Balt., 1955-57, chief engr., 1957, design engring. mgr., 1957-59, tech. devel. mgr., 1959-60, Dyna Soar and Gemini Launch vehicle tech. dir., 1960-62, research and engring. dir., 1962-65, acting dir. tech. operations, 1965-66, dir. space sci., research, adv. tech., 1966—, dir. Voyager program, 1967-68, dir. Planetary Systems, 1968, dir. Viking project, div. v.p., Denver, 1969—. Mem. civic adv. council Porter Hosp., Denver; mem. extension adv. council Colo. State U., 1971—. Recipient Robert H. Goddard award Worcester Poly. Inst., 1962. Fellow Am. Inst. Aeros. and Astronautics (award 1967); mem. Rocky Mountain Sci. Council, Am. Soc. C.E., Sigma Xi, Tau Beta Pi. Contbr. articles to profl. jours. Office: P O Box 179 Denver CO 80201

KULLBACK, SOLOMON, educator; b. Bklyn., Apr. 3, 1907; s. Nathan and Ida (Glasser) K.; B.S., Coll. City N.Y., 1927; M.A., Columbia, 1929; Ph.D., George Washington U., 1934; m. Minna Mirin, May 29, 1930; children—Joseph Henry, Sally Eve (Mrs. Philip R. Dodge). Research analyst War Dept., 1930-41, Dept. Def., 1946-62; mem. faculty George Washington U., 1938—, now prof. statistics. Served from capt. to col., AUS, 1941-46. Decorated Legion of Merit; recipient Distinguished Civilian Service award Nat. Security Agy., 1960. Fellow Inst. Math. Statistics, Am. Statis. Assn. Club: Cosmos (Washington). Author: Information Theory and Statistics, 1959. Home: 11610 Milbern Dr Potomac MD 20854 Office: Statistics Dept George Washington U Washington DC 20006

KULLERUD, GUNNAR, educator; b. Odda, Norway, Nov. 12, 1921; s. Finn and Clara Sofie (Kindberg) K.; Ph.D. in Mining, Tech. U. Norway, 1947; D.Sc., U. Oslo, 1954; m. Arrilla Joan Reading, Mar. 29, 1947; children—Finn Jon, Björn Kent, Kari Lynn, Marit Sue, Ingrid Diana. Came to U.S., 1948. Instr., then research asso. U. Chgo., 1948-52; research asso. U. Oslo, 1952-54; sr. staff mem. geochemistry, Geophys. Lab., Carnegie Instn., 1954-71; prof., head dept. geoscis. Purdue U., Lafayette, Ind., 1970—; adj. prof. Lehigh U., 1962-71; vis. prof. U. Heidelberg (Germany), 1964-70; cons. prof. Texas Tech U., 1968-71; hon. collaborator, div. meteorites Smithsonian Instn., 1964—. Mem. com. chem. solar system Space Sci. Bd., 1964—. Served with Royal Norwegian Air Force, also RAF, 1944-45. Recipient A. H. Dumont award Belgian Geol. Soc., 1965. Fellow Geol. Soc. Am., Am. Mineral. Soc., Washington Acad. Scis.; mem. Soc. Econ. Geologists, Geochem. Soc., Meteoritical Soc., Sec. Applied Geology, Am. Geophys. Union, geol. societies Norway, Finland. Club: Cosmos (Washington). Author of papers on sulfide phase equilibria, geothermometry ore deposits, meteorites. Home: 202 Colony Rd West Lafayette IN 47906 Office: Geosciences Bldg Purdue U West Lafayette IN 47907

KULLMAN, CHARLES, tenor; b. New Haven; s. Charles and Frances (Danhauser) K.; B.S., Yale, 1924; student Juilliard Music Found. and Am. Conservatory, Fontainebleau, France; m. Lisa Demander, Feb. 14, 1928; 1 dau., Elise (Mrs. Michel Coty). Made N.Y.C. concert debut, 1924; soloist Yale Glee Club, European tour, 1928; asst. prof. music Smith Coll., 1928-29; mem. Am. Opera Co. and Chgo. Civic Light Opera Co., 1930; made debut with Met. Opera Co., 1935, and since a leading tenor; appearances with operas in Berlin, Vienna, Salzburg, San Francisco; debut Teatro Colon, Buenos Aires, 1941, Teatro Municipale, Rio de Janeiro, 1942; radio, television and concert artist; debut in motion pictures as star Song of Scheherazade, 1941; prof. voice Indiana U., 1957. Mem. Met. Opera Assn., Alpha Sigma Phi. Episcopalian. Clubs: Bohemian (San Francisco); Dutch Treat (N.Y.C.); Yale (Madison, Conn.). Home: 26 Chapman Av Madison CT 06443

KULLMAN, JOHN ROGER, air force officer; b. San Antonio, June 1, 1922; s. Joseph William and Katherine (Menley) K.; B.S., U.S. Mil. Acad., 1943; M.A. in Internat. Affairs, George Washington U., 1964; m. Elizabeth Anne York, May 10, 1950; children—Joseph Peter, Kathleen Mary. Commd. 2d lt. USAAF, 1943, advanced through grades to maj. gen. USAF, 1970; exec., dep. for personnel Hdqrs. USAF, Washington, 1960-63; assigned Nat. War Coll., 1964; wing comdr. Perrin AFB, Tex., 1964-66; dep. dir. Alaska region FAA, 1967-69; dep. chief staff intelligence N. Am. Def. Command, Colorado Springs, 1969—. Decorated Legion of Merit, D.F.C., Air medal with 5 oak leaf clusters. Home: 3007 Highland Dr Colorado Springs CO 80909 Office: Hdqrs NORAD PO Box 24 Ent AFB CO 80912

KULNYCH, PETRO, chain bldg. material co. exec.; b. Smithmills, Pa., June 23, 1921; s. Harry and Mary (Pollick) K.; grad. U.S. Merchant Marine Acad., 1943, Kings Bus. Coll., Charlotte, N.C., 1946; m. Roena Mae Bullis, Dec. 11, 1943; children—Brenda Gail, Janice Lynn. With Dept. Interior, then Dept. War, 1939-42; with Lowe's Companies, Inc., N. Wilkesboro, N.C., 1946—, exec. v.p., 1961—, also dir., chmn. exec. com. Vice pres., dir. N.C. World Trade Assn., 1965; mem. bd. N.C. Dept. Conservation and Devel., 1965—. Served with USNR, 1943-46. Elk. Mason. Club: Oakwoods Country (Wilkesboro). Home: 450 Shady Lane Wilkesboro NC 28697 Office: PO Box 1111 North Wilkesboro NC 28659

KULP, ABRAHAM MOYER, investment exec.; b. Hatfield, Pa., Nov. 10, 1895; s. Jonas and Margaret (Grater) K.; grad. U. Pa., 1922; m. Frances Mann Connelly, Nov. 19, 1932; children—Charles Mann, Johnathan Bicking, Susan Moyer. Salesman Schibener, Boenning & Co., Phila., 1922-25; mgr. bond dept. Spencer Trask & Co., Phila., 1926-32; v.p., dir. Wellinton Fund, 1928—; v.p., dir. Windsor Fund, 1958—; mem. investment com. Wellington Mgmt. Co., 1928-55, v.p., 1948-60, sr. v.p., 1960—, chmn. investment com., 1956—, also director; with Laird & Co., Phila., 1933-36; accounts mgr. Lionel D. Edie & Co., Phila., 1937-48, v.p., 1942-48. Mem. Financial Analysts Fedn. (dir. 1951-52, exec. v.p. 1964-65), Inst. Charters Financial Analysts (pres. 1960-64, trustee 1960—), Financial Analysts Phila. (past dir.), Phila. C. of C. (research council, Am. Acad. Politcal Sci., Am. Finance Assn., Nat. Bur Econ. Research, Alumni Soc. U. Pa. Clubs: Rotary, Union League, Plymouth Country; Woodstock (Vt.) Country. Home: 1411 Sandy Hill Rd Norristown PA Office: 1630 Locust St Philadelphia PA 19101*

KULP, NANCY JANE, comedienne; b. Harrisburg, Pa., Aug. 28, 1921; d. Robert Tilden and Marjorie (Snyder) Kulp; B.A. in Journalism, Fla. State U., 1943; postgrad. U. Miami, 1950; m. Charles Malcolm Dacus, Apr. 1, 1951. Publicity dir. Radio Sta. WGBS, 1946-47; continuity dir. Radio Sta. WIOD, Miami, 1947-49; continuity dir.-performer TV Sta. WTVJ, Miami, 1949-50; began acting career in Hollywood, Cal., 1952; motion pictures include Model and the Marriage Broker, 1952, Star is Born, 1953, Three Faces of Eve, 1955, The Parent Trap, 1957, Sabrina, 1954; appeared on TV shows Playhouse 90, 1959, Lux Video, 1955, Beverly Hillbillies, 1961-71, Bob Cummings Show, 1955-60, Lucy Show, 1956. Hon. chmn. Humane Soc., 1965—. Served to lt. (j.g.), WAVES, USNR, 1943-45. Nominated for Emmy award, 1967. Mem. Acad. Motion Pictures Arts and Scis., Pi Beta Phi. Democrat. Presbyn. Club: Greyhound of America (Darien, Conn.). Home: Longridge Farm Port Royal PA 17082 Office: 1041 N Las Palmas Hollywood CA 90038

KULSKI, WLADYSLAW WSZEBOR, educator, polit. scientist; b. Warsaw, Poland, July 27, 1903; s. Julian and Antonina (Ostrowski) K.; LL.M., Warsaw Law Sch., 1925; LL.D., Paris (France) Law Sch., 1927; m. Antonina Reutt, Oct. 28, 1938. Came to U.S., 1946, naturalized, 1952. With Polish Diplomatic Service, 1928-45, head legal service Ministry Fgn. Affairs, 1936-40, counsellor, minister plenipotentiary Polish embassy, London, Eng., 1940-45; pub. lectr. in U.S., 1946-47; prof. polit. sci. U. Ala., 1947-51, Syracuse U., 1951-64; vis. prof. Duke, 1963-64, James B. Duke prof. Russian affairs, 1964—; lectr. Fgn. Service Inst., 1957—, Army Strategic Intelligence Sch., 1957—, Air. U., 1963—. Fulbright and Guggenheim research fellows, France, 1961-62, Guggenheim research fellow, 1970. Mem. Am. Soc. Internat. Law, Am. Polit. Sci. Assn., Am. Assn. Slavic Studies, Am. Acad. Polit. and Social Sci., Am. Assn. U. Profs. Author numerous books, 1927—, latest being The Soviet Regime: Communism in Practice, 1954; Peaceful Co-Existence: An Analysis of Soviet Foreign Policy, 1959; International Politics in a Revolutionary Age, 1964; DeGaulle and the World, 1966. Contbr. profl. jours., also book revs. Home: 1624 Marion Av Durham NC 27705

KULTGEN, JOHN HENRY, Jr., educator; b. Dallas, Oct. 16, 1925; s. John Henry and Reba (Mickleborough) K.; B.A., U. Tex., 1947; M.A., U. Chgo., 1949, Ph.D., 1952; m. Phyllis Hoyt Biggs, Apr. 3, 1947; children—David, John, Mary, Rebecca, MIchael. Asst. prof. Ore. State U., 1952-56; asso. prof., prof. So. Meth. U., Dallas, 1956-67; prof., chmn. philosophy dept. U. Mo., Columbia, 1967—. Chmn. Dallas Civil Liberties Union, 1966-67. Served to ensign USNR, 1943-46. Mem. Am., Mo. (past pres.) philos. assns., Southwestern Philos. Soc. (v.p.), Philosophy of Sci. Soc. Author: (with Ronald Wetherington) The Nature of Man, 1966. Cons. editor Jour. History Philosophy, 1967—. Home: 410 Westmount St Columbia MO 65201

KUMIN, MAXINE WINOKUR, (Mrs. Victor Montwid Kumin), writer; b. Phila., June 6, 1925; d. Peter and Doll (Simon) Winokur; A.B., Radcliffe Coll., 1946, M.A., 1948; m. Victor Monwid Kumin, June 29, 1946; children—Jane Simon, Judith Montwid, Daniel David. Instr. English, Tufts U., 1958-61, lectr. English, 1965—; scholar Radcliffe Inst. Ind. Study, 1961-63; free-lance writer, 1953—. Cons. lit. Central Atlantic Regional Ednl. Lab., 1967-69. Mem. Poetry Soc. Am. Author: Sebastian and the Dragon, 1960; (poems) Halfway, 1961; Spring Things, 1961; A Summer Story, 1961; Follow the Fall, 1961; A Winter Friend, 1961; Mittens in May, 1962; No One Writes a Letter to the Snail, 1962; (with Anne Sexton) Eggs of Things, 1963; More Eggs of Things, 1964; Archibald the Traveling Poodle, 1963; Speedy Digs Downside Up, 1964: The Beach Before Breakfast, 1964; Paul Bunyan, 1966; (poems) The Privilege, 1965; (Novel) Through Dooms of Love, 1965; The Wonderful Babies of 1809, 1968; (novel) The Passions of Uxport, 1968; When Grandmother Was Young, 1969; When Mother Was Young, 1970; When Great Grandmother Was Young, 1971; (poems) The Nightmare Factory, 1970. Contbr. poems nat. mags. Address: care Curtis Brown Ltd 60 E 56th St New York City NY 10022

KUMLER, WARREN DONALD, educator; b. Seven Mile, O., Feb. 18, 1905; s. Charles Augustus and Maude (Yingling) K.; B.S., Antioch Coll., 1929, M.S., 1930; Ph.D., U. Cal. at Berkeley, 1934; m. Alice McClintock, July 28, 1927; children—Archie Ann (Mrs. Herbert W. Suelzle), Joan Mary (Mrs. Michael Lewis). Instr., Deep Springs (Cal.) Coll., 1929, dean, 1930-32; faculty Sch. Pharmacy, U. Cal. at San Francisco, 1935—, instr. to asso. prof., 1935-44, prof., 1950—, chmn. dept. pharm. chemistry, 1959-65, asso. dean, 1965—, 2d vice chmn. academic senate, 1960-62, vice chmn. graduate council, 1961-62, chmn. bldg. and campus devel. com., 1961-62, faculty research lectr., 1961, state-wide acad. council, 1960-63; vis. prof. Cal. Inst. of Tech., 1952, Imperial College, U. London, 1959; Knapp vis. prof., research lectr. U. Wis., 1958; research Oxford U., 1958; cons. OSRD, 1943-46. Mem. pharmacology and endocrinology panel NIH, 1963-66. Fellow N.Y. Acad. Scis., Am. Assn. Advancement Sci.; mem. Am. Chemical Soc. (councillor Cal. 1943-44 , Am. Pharm. Assn., Sigma Xi, Rho Chi, Phi Delta Chi. Contbg. Author: Textbook of Organic Medicinal and Pharmaceutical Chemistry, 1949-61; also numerous articles chem. jours. Research on dipole moments, spectra, dissociation constants, molecular structural sunscreens, pharm. chemistry. Home: 33 Teresita Blvd San Francisco CA 94127

KUMMEL, BERNHARD, geologist, educator; b. Racine, Wis., Aug. 13, 1919; s. Bernard and Meta (Storggard) K.; B.A., U. Wis., 1941, M.A., 1942; Ph.D., Columbia, 1947; m. Gilda Devescovi, Dec. 20, 1948; 1 son, Alex Bernard. Geologist. Govt. of Peru, 1943-47, Tex., 1948-49; asst. prof. geology U. Ill. at Urbana, 1949-50, asso. prof., 1950-52; asso. prof. geology Harvard, 1952-62, prof., 1962—; geol. cons. Fellow Geol. Soc. Am.; mem. Paleontol. Soc. (treas.), Soc. Econ. Paleontologists and Minerologists Am. Acad. Arts and Sci. Home: 228 Common St Belmont, MA 02178 Office: Museum Comparative Zoology Harvard Univ Cambridge MA 02138

KUMMEL, EUGENE H., advt. agy. exec. Pres., McCann-Erickson Corp., N.Y.C. Office: 485 Lexington Av New York City NY 10017*

KUMMEL, ROBERT D., food products co. exec.; b. 1921; B.S., LL.B., U. Wis.; married. With J.I. Case Co., Racine, Wis., 1948-52; with Carnation Co., Los Angeles, 1953—, v.p. research and new products planning, 1965-69, v.p. legal, research and new product planning, 1969—, also dir. Office: 5045 Wilshire Blvd Los Angeles CA 90036*

KUMMER, ROBERT WILLIAM, Jr., banker; b. Pitts., May 31, 1936; s. Robert William and Mary L. (Preskar) K.; B.A. (George F. Baker scholar), Oberlin Coll., 1958; postgrad. U. Cal., Berkeley, 1959-60; m. Chrysilla A. Smith, Sept. 15, 1962; children-Dirk, Mark, David. Asst. to pres. Oberlin Coll., 1960-62; bus. devel. rep. Union Bank, Los Angeles, C.A., 1962-64, asst. v.p., 1964-65, v.p., 1966-69, sr. v.p., 1969—. Pres. Oberlin Coll. Alumni Council; treas., bd. dirs. Am. Cancer Soc. Served with USAF, 1960. Recipient Freedom Found. award, 1954, Outstanding Service award Am. Cancer Soc., 1967. Mem. Bank Marketing Assn., Robert Morris Assos., Oberlin Coll. Alumni Assn. (past pres.). Clubs: Jonathan (Los Angeles); Oakmont Country (Glendale, Cal.). Home: 829 Wilandonda Dr La Canada CA 91011 Office: 445 S Figueroa St Los Angeles CA 90017

KUMMROW, W.A., banker. Pres., First Nat. Bank Waukesha (Wis.). Office: 831 N Grand Av Waukesha WI 53186*

KUMP, ERNEST JOSEPH, architect; b. Bakersfield, Cal., Dec. 29, 1911; s. Ernest Joseph and Mary (Petsche) K.; A.B., U. Cal., 1932; M.Arch., Harvard, 1933; m. Josephine Clark Miller, Aug. 18, 1934; children—Peter Clark, Mondi. Engaged in practice of architecture, 1933—; works include Sill Bldg. (Bakersfield), City Hall (Fresno), Foothill Jr. Coll., Los Altos Hills, Cabrillo Jr. Coll., Aptos, De Anza Coll., Cupertino, Cal., Henry Gunn High Sch., Palo Alto and numerous sch. bldgs. in Cal., Lebanon, eastern U.S.; designs of Fresno City Hall and Acalanes Union High Sch. included in traveling exhbn. of modern Am. architecture, N.Y. Mus. Mod. Art, 1943, 65. Lectured on Sch. and Community Planning, Harvard U., 1945, U. Mich., 1945, U. of Tex., 1946; adj. prof., chmn. advance research, Sch. Architecture, Columbia, 1961, prof. architecture, chmn. advance research and ednl. planning, 1962—; cons. architect for Am. U. of Beirut, Lebanon, U. of Cal. at Santa Cruz, Mills Coll., archtl. adv. council Stanford U.; mem. design and visual arts vis. com. Harvard, 1964-65; architect for U.S. ambassadors residence and embassy staff housing, Seoul, Korea. Works exhibited Brussels Worlds Fair, 1958, Seattle Worlds Fair, 1962. Mem. panel and also the discussion leader on "Planning Man's Physical Environment," Bicentennial Anniversary, Princeton U., 1947. Served as cons. to Brit. Planning Mission to N.Am. (England's postwar school bldg. program); U.S. del. Internat. Union Architects, 1950, 53, 55, 58, 61. Invited by Australian Am. Assn. to exhibit architecture of recent pub. bldgs.; lectured Melbourne (Australia) U., 1948. Awarded Meritorious Civilian Service Emblem by U.S. Navy, 1944; Progressive Architecture award, 1947, 48, 49, 57, 58, 60; Award of Merit, A.I.A., 1954, 1st Honor Award, 1955, Firm of Year award, 1970. Mem. nat. adv. council on sch. bldg. problems U.S. Office of Edn. Mem. commn. for survey archtl. practice and edn. Carnegie Found. Grant. Fellow Royal Soc. Arts (London), A.I.A. (nat. chmn. on sch. bldgs. 1948-49; mem.-at-large com. on edn. 1947), State Assn. Calif. Architects, Alumni Assn. U. Cal., Kappa Delta Rho. Elk. Club: Harvard (N. Cal.). Mem. jury of award: "Georgia Builds" nat. small homes architectural competition, 1946. Author: Realizing the Modern School Plant, 1943; School Planning, 1947; A New Architecture for Man, 1957; also monographs and articles on archtl. subjects. Pioneer in system of prefabricating school bldgs. and in pre-built system mfg. houses. Home: 360 Everett Av Palo Alta CA 94301 also Schloss Matzen Brixlegg Tirol Austria Office: 325 Lytton Av Palo Alto CA 94301

KUMPA, PETER JOHN, news corr.; b. Marcinkance, Poland, Aug. 1, 1926 (parents U.S. citizens); s. John and Elizabeth (Tamulevich) K.; B.S., Georgetown U., 1949; student Boston Coll., 1946, N.Y.U. Grad Sch. Bus. Adminstrn., 1949-50; m. Margaret Anne Balch, Dec. 18, 1954; children—Margaret Elizabeth, Jacqueline Anne, Katherine Balch, Lydia Rouse. Reporter, corr. Balt. Sun, 1951—, Moscow bur. chief, 1959-61, Hong Kong bur. chief, 1966—. Served with USNR, 1944-46. Neiman fellow Harvard, 1957. Home: 29 S Bay Rd Hong Kong Office: 2 Kennedy Terrace Hong Kong

KUNDE, JAMES ERHARDT, city mgr.; b. Cleve., Dec. 31, 1937; s. Erhardt John and Ester Mary (Paffenbach) K.; A.B. in Math., Wittenberg U., 1960; M.G.A., U. Pa., 1962; m. Diana Hudson, June 10, 1960; children—Thomas, Frederick, Karen. Various positions City Mgrs. Office, Dayton, O., 1961-67; county adminstr. Jackson County, Mo., 1967-69; city devel. dir. Kansas City, Mo., 1969-70; city mgr., Dayton, 1970—. Mem. Miami Valley Council Govts. Bd. dirs. Health and Welfare Planning Council Greater Miami Valley; trustee Dayton Art Inst., Montgomery County Community Action Agy. Recipient ICMA award for mgmt. innovation, 1968; named Outstanding Young Man in Am., 1971. Mem. Internat. City Mgmt. Assn. (asso.), Am. Soc. Pub. Adminstrn., Montgomery County Mayors and Mgrs. Assn., Municipal Finance Officers Assn., Ohio City Mgmt. Assn., Am. Pub. Works Assn., Tau Pi Phi (named Man of Year Springfield (O.) chpt. 1970-71). Presbyn. (elder). Contbr. articles profl. jours. Home: 1817 Benson Dr Dayton OH 45406 Office: 101 W 3d St Dayton OH 45401

KUNDTZ, EWALD EDMUND, lawyer; b. Cleve., July 9, 1901; s. Theodor and Maria (Balash) K.; A.B., Georgetown U., 1922; LL.B., Columbia, 1925; m. Elizabeth O'Neill, June 15, 1926; children—Louise (Mrs. Stanley C. Patno), Ewald Edmund, John Andrew, David. Admitted to Ohio bar, 1925, since practiced in Cleve.; partner firm Falsgraf, Kundtz, Reidy & Shoup, 1960-70. Sec. Leaseway Transp. Corp.; dir. Propak Co. Mem. Newcomen Soc. Clubs: Pepper Pike, The Country (Cleve.); Rolling Rock (Ligonier, Pa.); Burning Tree. Home: Hackney Rd Chagrin Falls OH 44022 Office: National City Bank Bldg Cleveland OH 44114

KUNEN, JAMES LINCOLN, found. exec., lawyer; b. N.Y.C., Mar. 8, 1915; s. Louis and Gertrude (Lefcourt) K.; A.B., Harvard, 1936; LL.B., Yale, 1939; m. Marcia Robison, June 29, 1940; children—Lisa, Andrea, Seth, Jonathan, Jessica. Admitted to N.Y. bar, 1939, D.C. bar, 1954; counsel Martin, Whitfield and Thayer; sr. counsel to N.Y. Commr. of Housing, 1939-42; exec. dir. of Citizens Housing and Planning Council of N.Y., Inc., 1946-48; asst. dean N.Y. Sch. Social Work, Columbia, 1950-51; asst. gen. counsel, later asso., gen. counsel N.S.R.B., Exec. Office of Pres., Washington, 1948-50, cons., 1950-51, gen. counsel, 1951-53; counsel for U.S. Govt. before Internat. Joint Commn. on St. Lawrence Power Project; chmn. U.S. Interagency Com. on St. Lawrence Seaway and Power Project; dep. gen. counsel ODM, 1953-54, mem. Nat. Enforcement Commn., 1953-55; staff counsel Cabinet Com. on Energy Resources, 1955; cons. Internat. Bank Mission to Colombia, S.Am., 1955; professorial lectr. Am. U. Mem. D.C. White House Conf. on Children and Youth, 1960; dir. D.C. Health and Welfare Council, 1958-62; regent's lectr. U. Cal. at Los Angeles, 1968. Exec. v.p. Eugene and Agnes E. Meyer Found.; bd. dirs. Council on Founds. Served with AUS, 1942-46; disch. rank capt. Mem. Bar Assn. D.C., N.Y. State Bar Assn. Clubs: Harvard, Federal City (Washington). Home: 3712 Bradley Lane Chevy Chase MD 20015 Office: 1730 Rhode Island Av NW Washington DC 20036

KUNG, HANS, clergyman, educator; b. Lucerne, Switzerland, Mar. 19, 1928; s. Hans and Emma (Gut) K.; Licenciate philosophy Gregorian U., Rome, Italy, 1951, Licenciate theology, 1955; doctorate theology, Inst. Catholique and Sorbonne, Paris, France, 1957, LL.D., St. Louis U.; D.D. (hon.), Pacific Sch. Religion, Berkeley, Cal.; H.H.D., Loyola U., Chgo. Ordained priest Roman Cath. Ch., 1954; mem. practical ministry Cathedral Lucerne, 1957-59; sci. asst. for dogmatic Cath. Theol. Faculty, U. Munster/Westfalen (Germany), 1959-60; prof. fundamental theology Cath.-theologic faculty U. Tubingen (Germany), 1960—, prof. dogmatic, dir. Inst. Ecumenical Research, 1963- -; guest lectr. throughout U.S., Asia, Europe. Author: Justification: The Doctrine of Karl Barth and a Catholic Reflection, 1964; The Council, Reform and Reunion, 1962; That the World May Believe, 1962; Structures of the Church, 1964; The Council in Action, 1963; Freedom Today, 1966; The Church, 1968; Truthfulness, 1968; Infallible? An Inquiry, 1971; also numerous articles. Asso. editor Jour. Ecumenical Studies, Theologische Quartalschift Concilium. Address: Waldhäuserstrasse 23 Tubingen West Germany

KUNHARDT, PHILIP BRADISH, Jr., mag. editor; b. N.Y.C., Feb. 5, 1928; s. Philip Bradish and Dorothy (Meserve) K.; grad. Groton (Mass.) Sch., 1946; A.B. with honors in English, Princeton, 1950; m. Katharine Trowbridge, June 17, 1950; children—Philip Bradish III, Peter Whiting, Jean, Sandra, Sarah, Michael. With Life mag., 1950—, asst. picture editor, 1958-61, sr. editor, 1961-62, asst. mag. editor, 1962—. Author: My Father's House, 1970. Co-author: Twenty Days, 1965. Home: 14 W Orchard Rd Chappaqua NY 10514 Office: Life Magazine Rockefeller Plaza New York City NY 10020

KUNITZ, STANLEY JASSPON, poet, editor, educator; b. Worcester, Mass., July 29, 1905; s. Solomon Z. and Yetta Helen (Jasspon) K.; A.B. summa cum laude, Harvard, 1926, M.A., 1927; Litt.D. (hon.), Clark U., 1961; m. Helen Pearce, 1930 (div. 1937); m. 2d, Eleanor Evans, Nov. 21, 1939 (div. 1958); 1 dau. Gretchen; m. 3d, Elise Asher, June 21, 1958. Editor, Wilson Library Bull., 1928-43; mem. lit. faculty Bennington Coll., 1946-49; prof. English, Potsdam (N.Y.) State Tchrs. Coll., 1949-50; dir. seminar Potsdam Summer Workshop in Creative Arts, 1949-53; lectr. The New Sch., 1950-57; vis. prof. poetry U. Wash., 1955- 56; vis. prof. English, Queens Coll., 1956-57, Brandeis U., 1958-59. Dir. poetry workshop Poetry Center YMHA, N.Y., 1958-62; Danforth vis. lectr. numerous Am. colls., 1961-63; lectr. Columbia, 1963-66, adj. prof. writing Grad. Sch. Arts, 1967—; chmn. writing dept. Fine Arts Work Center, Provincetown, Mass., 1968—; editor Yale Series Younger Poets, 1969—; fellow Yale U., 1969—; vis. prof. poetry Yale, 1970. Served with AUS, 1943-45. Recipient Garrison medal for poetry, Harvard, 1926, Oscar Blumenthal prize, 1941; Guggenheim fellow creative writing, 1945-56, Amy Lowell traveling fellow for poetry, 1953-54, Levinson prize for poetry, 1956, Harriet Monroe award U. Chgo., 1958; Ford Found. grantee, 1958-59; Nat. Inst. Arts and Letters grantee, 1959; recipient Pulitzer prize in poetry, 1959; Brandeis Creative Arts Poetry award, 1964. Mem. Acad. Am. Poets (fellowship award 1968, chancellor 1970—); mem. Nat. Inst. Arts and Letters, Phi Beta Kappa.

Author: (verse) Intellectual Things, 1930; Living Authors, 1931; Authors Today and Yesterday, 1933; Junior Book of Authors, 1934; British Authors of the 19th Century, 1936; American Authors, 1600-1900, 1938; Twentieth Century Authors, 1942, First Supplement, 1955; (verse) Passport to the War, 1944; British Authors Before 1800, 1952; Selected Poems, 1928-1958, 1958; (verse) The Testing-Tree, 1971. Editor: Poems of John Keats, 1964. Home: 157 W 12th St New York City NY 10011

KUNKEL, A. WILLIAM, librarian; b. Munich, Germany, Oct. 27, 1925; s. Adolf and Mary (Hois) K.; came to U.S., 1929, naturalized, 1946; A.B., Union Coll., 1950; A.M., Western Res. U., 1952, M.L.S., 1953; m. Rose Marie Lavery, June 12, 1949; children—Cynthia Marie, Joan Louise. Student asst. Union Coll. Library, 1948-50; student, circulation asst. Western Res. U. Library, 1951-53; reference librarian Ohio U. Library, 1953-55; Lamont Library asst., asst. circulation supr. Widener Library Harvard, 1955-57; supr. book processing Newton (Mass.) Free Library, 1957-58, chief librarian, 1958-67; adminstr. Eastern regional pub. library system Boston Pub. Library, 1967—. Sec., Mass. Eastern Regional Adv. Council, 1962-65, vice chmn., 1965-67, chmn., 1967. Served with AUS 1946-47. Mem. A.L.A., Mass. (past pres.), New Eng. library assns., Greater Boston Pub. Library Adminstrs. Home: 236 Islington Rd Newton MA 02166 Office: Eastern Mass Regional Office Boston Pub Library Copley Sq Boston MA 02117

KUNKEL, HARRIOTT ORREN, educator; b. Olney, Tex., July 3, 1922; s. Hugo O. and Mathilde (Schulz) K.; B.S., Tex. A. and M. U., 1943, M.S., 1946; Ph.D., Cornell U., 1950; m. Beverly Virginia Davies, Dec. 18, 1960; children—Virginia Anne, Geoffrey Kevin, Sheryl Elizabeth. Instr. biochemistry U. Wis., 1950-51; asst. prof. to prof. animal sci. and biochemistry Tex. A. and M. U., College Station, 1951-62, asso. dir. Tex. Agrl. Expt. Sta., 1962-67, acting dir., 1967-71, dean Coll. Agr., 1968—; vis. prof. Cornell U., 1962. Dir. First Bank & Trust Co., Bryan, Tex. Chmn., Gt. Plains Agrl. Council,1968-69. Served to capt., F.A., AUS, 1943-46; PTO. Recipient Faculty Distinguished Achievement award Tex A. and M., 1956; named Outstanding Displaced W. Texan, W.Tex. C. of C., 1968. Mem. Am. Chem. Soc., Am. Soc. Biol. Chemists, Am. Inst. Nutrition, Am. Soc. Animal Sci., Bryan-College Station C. of C., Gamma Alpha. Lutheran. Kiwanian. Contbr. articles profl. jours. Home: 800 Ethel Blvd Bryan TX 77801 Office: Coll Agriculture Tex A and M U College Station TX 77843

KUNKEL, HENRY GEORGE, physician; b. N.Y.C., Sept. 9, 1916; s. Louis O. and Johanna C. (Wortmann) K.; A.B., Princeton, 1938; M.D., Johns Hopkins, 1942; m. Betty J. Martens, Jan. 9, 1949; children—Louis Martens, Henry George, Ellen. Intern, asst. resident Bellevue Hosp., N.Y.C., 1942-44; investigation diseases of liver Hosp. Rockefeller Inst., 1946; now prof. biochemistry and immunology Rockefeller U.; biochem. studies, Sweden, Eng., 1950-51. Served with USNR, 1945-56; Mem. Soc. Clin. Investigation, Harvey Soc., Assn. Am. Physicians, Nat. Acad. Sci. Club: Princeton (N.Y.C.). Home: 35 Homesdale Rd Bronxville NY 10708 Office: Rockefeller Univ 67th St at York Av New York City NY 10021

KUNKEL, RICHARD KENNETH, lawyer; b. Mechanicsburg, O., July 31, 1937; s. William Henry and Mary E. (Stanley) K.; B.A., Ohio State U., 1959, LL.B., 1961; m. Rosalie Ann Rickards, Sept. 7, 1960; children-Adam Brent, Eric Bruce. Admitted to Ohio bar, 1961; practice in Delaware, 1965—; mem. firm Kellar, Blair & Kunkel, 1965-67, 70—; prosecuting atty. Delaware County, 1967—. Served from 1st lt. to capt., Judge Adv. Gen. Corps, U.S. Army, 1962-65. Mem. Am., Ohio, Delaware County (past pres., sec.) bar assns., Am. Trial Lawyers Assn., Ohio Prosecuting Attys. Assn., Nat. Dist. Attys. Assn., Delaware C. of C., Am. Legion. Republican. Episcopalian. Kiwanian. Home: 106 Griswold St Delaware OH 43015 Office: 21 W Central Av Delaware OH 43015

KUNKEL, WULF BERNARD, educator, physicist; b. Eichenau, Germany, Feb. 6, 1923; s. Friederich W. and Auguste N. (Löwengard) K.; came to U.S., 1947, naturalized, 1952; student U. Amsterdam, 1945-46; B.A., U. Cal. at Berkeley, 1948, Ph.D., 1951; m. Erika A.L. Rawitscher, Dec. 23, 1960; children-Laurence O., Barbara N., Maya T. Research engr. Inst. Engring. Research, U. Cal. at Berkeley, 1951-56, physicist Lawrence Radiation Lab., 1956—, head plasma physics group, 1970—; mem. faculty U. Cal. at Berkeley, 1953—, prof. physics, 1967—; cons. in field. Guggenheim fellow, 1955-56. Fellow Am. Phys. Soc.; mem. Phi Beta Kappa, Sigma Xi. Author papers in field. Bd. editors Plasma Physics, 1970—. Home: 1115 Hillview Rd Berkeley CA 94708

KUNNY, BARTHOLOMEW KENNETH, educator, biologist; b. Cylon, Wis., May 19, 1914; s. Bartholomew and Adella (Brannan) K.; B.A., U. Wis., 1937, M.S., 1948, Ph.D., 1967; m. LaVaughn Kathlinn Larson, Aug. 25, 1943; children—Kathy, Clare, Bartholomew. Tchr. sci. Karlstad (Minn.) High Sch., 1938-42; mem. faculty Beloit (Wis.) Coll., 1948—, prof. biology, chmn. dept., 1968—. Pres., Wis. Basic Sci. Exam. Bd., 1969—. Served to capt. USAAF, 1942-47. NSF faculty fellow, 1960. Mem. Soc. Limnology and Oceanography, A.A.A.S., Wis. Acad. Sci., Arts and Letters, Midwest Benthological Soc., Nat. Sci. Tchrs. Assns., Am. Inst. Biol. Scis. Rotarian. Author manuals. Home: 911 Church St Beloit WI 53511

KUNO, SUSUMU, educator; b. Tokyo, Japan, Aug. 11, 1933; s. Sakuro and Sono (Ono) K.; A.B., Tokyo U., 1956, A.M. in Linguistics, 1958; Ph.D. in Linguistics, Harvard, 1964; m. Yoko Nakajima, Sept. 1, 1967; children—Alisa, Erika. Research fellow math. linguistics Harvard, 1960- 63, instr., 1964-65, asst. prof., 1965-68, asso. prof., 1968-69, prof. linguistics, 1969—; cons. Arthur D. Little, Inc., Cambridge, Mass., Tech. Operations, Inc., Arlington, Va., Thomas J. Watson Research Center, IBM, Yorktown Heights, N.Y. Trustee Language Research Found., Cambridge, Mass. Mem. Am., Japanese linguistic socs., Assn. Computational Linguistics (pres. 1967), Assn. Computing Machinery. Author numerous papers on computational linguistics, English syntax, Japanese linguistics. Home: 47 Glendale Rd Belmont MA 02178 Office: Computation Laboratory Harvard University Cambridge MA 02138

KUNSBERG, STANLEY HARRIS, retail co. exec.; b. Columbus, Ga., Apr. 27, 1906; s. Philip H. and Hattie (Aarons) K.; m. Marcella Brown, Oct. 30, 1946; children—Carolyn, Bette D., Sandra, Philip. With Lerner Stores Corp., N.Y.C., 1927—, exec. v.p., 1957-61, pres., 1961-65, chmn. bd., 1965—, also vice chmn. exec. com., dir.; was dir., now pres., treas. McCrory Corp., 1969—; Clubs: Quaker Ridge Country (Scarsdale); Beach Point Yacht (Mamaroneck, N.Y.); Harmonie, Empire State, Cavendish Bridge (N.Y.C.); Town (Denver). Home: 95 Catherine Rd Scarsdale NY 10583 Office: 360 Park Av S New York City NY 10010

KUNSELA, WILLIAM RUDOLPH coll. pres.; b. Buffalo, July 12, 1917; s. William and Anna (Yonen) K.; B.S., Cornell U., 1939, M.S., 1946, Ph.D., 1950; m. Barbara Mowitt, Dec. 31, 1941; children—Karen, Lynn, Barbara. Tchr. vocational agr. and indsl. arts, Middleville, N.Y., 1939-42, auditor U.S. Navy, 1942; supervising tng. officer, regional supr. vocational rehab. and edn. div., VA, 1946-47; instr., then research fellow Cornell U., 1947-50, chmn. agrl. edn. div., rural edn. dept., 1950-55; pres. State U. of N.Y. Agrl. and Tech. Coll. at Delhi, 1955—, Israel project chief univ. Research Found., U.S. Operations Mission, Tel Aviv, 1961-62; cons. to Govt. Israel, 1963—; also cons. Ford Found., Brazil, 1964, UN, Liberia, 1965, UN, Nicaragua, 1966, UN Philippines, 1968, World Bank, Greece, 1967, 68, UN, Egypt, 1970, Ford Found., India, 1970, World Bank, Spain, 1969. Chmn. Catskill Consortium Colls. Pres., mem. bd. Coll. Assn. at Delhi, Inc., Coll. Found., Delhi. Served to 1st lt. USAAF, 1942-45. Named hon. Empire Farmer, 1954, Man of Year Del County C. of C.; recipient Distinguished Citizen award N.Y. Bar Assn. Mem. Am. Assn. Jr. Colls., N.Y. State Assn. Colls. and Univs., Am. Vocational Assn., N.Y. State Vocational and Practical Arts Assn., Assn. Tchrs. Agr. N.Y. State, N.E.A., Grange, Delhi C. of C., N.Y. State Citizens Council, Green Key Soc., Phi Kappa Phi, Phi Delta Kappa (past pres. Theta chpt.). Kiwanian, Mason. Contbr. numerous articles and monographs in field. Home: 41 Delview Terrace Delhi NY 13753

KUNSMILLER, ADOLPH, banker. Chmn. bd. Am. Nat. Bank Denver. Office: 17th and Stout Sts Denver CO 80201*

KUNSTADTER, RALPH HESS, pediatrician; b. Chgo., Oct. 6, 1905; s. Samuel and Theodora (Hess) K.; B.S., U. Ill., 1927, M.D., 1930; m. Marjorie Lyon Solomon, June 21, 1928; 1 dau., Susan Lyon (Mrs. Walter Dewees). Intern Michael Reese Hosp., Chgo., 1929-31, acting chmn. dept. pediatrics, 1955-56, vice chmn. dept., 1956—, attending pediatrician, chief children's endocrine clinic; sr. attending pediatrician Michael Reese Hosp. and Med. Center; asso. prof. pediatrics Northwestern U. Med. Sch.; pediatric courtesy staff Chgo. Lying-In Hosp.; cons. pediatrics Rehab. Inst. Chgo.; pvt. practice, Chgo. Am. Acad. Pediatrics rep. at Conf. Emergency Med. Identification, A.M.A., 1961. Vice chmn. Ill. Commn. on Children; chmn. adv. com. on screening newborns for heritable diseases Ill. State Dept. of Health; mem. exec. com. White House Conf. Children and Youth, 1960, 70; med. adv. com. Cook County chpt. Nat. Found.; med. adv. bd. Chgo. chpt. Muscular Dystrophy Assn. Am., Cook County Welfare Dept., Ill. Epileptic League; alt. rep. Ill. Joint Commn. Sch. Health; chmn. profl. adv. council Nat. Soc. for Crippled Children and Adults; chmn. profl. adv. council, mem. bd. dirs. Nat. Easter Seal Soc. for Crippled Children and Adults; bd. dirs. Met. Easter Seal Soc. Chgo.; mem. med. adv. com. to Chgo. Med. Soc., Cook County Dept. Pub. Aid. Served to lt. col. M.C., AUS, World War II. Diplomate Am. Bd. Pediatrics. Fellow Am. Acad. Pediatrics (exec. com. Ill. chpt. 1958-59; pres. Ill. chpt. 1963-65; liaison to Nat. Soc. Crippled Children and Adults; chmn. com. on disaster and emergency med. services; Head Start cons. to V.I.), Am. Acad. for Cerebral Palsy, A.C.P.; mem. A.M.A. (chmn. pediatric sect. 1954-55, mem. commn. on emergency med. services), Ill. State (chmn. com. on child health 1962—), Chgo. med. socs., A.A.A.S., Endocrine Soc., Am., Chgo. heart assns., Ill. Acad. Sci., Chgo. Diabetic Assn., Chgo. Pediatric Soc. (pres. 1957-58), Inst. Medicine Chgo. (bd. govs., pres. 1970-71), Am. Pediatric Soc., Sigma Xi, Alpha Omega Alpha. Clubs: Key, Barclay, Executive's, Adventurer's (Chgo.). Author: (with Evelyn C. Lundeen, R.N.) Care of the Premature Infant, 1958. Abstract writer Excerpta Medica. Author numerous med. articles. Home: 1255 N State Pkwy Chicago IL 60610 Office: 664 N Michigan Av Chicago IL 60611

KUNSTADTER, SIGMUND, apparel mfr.; b. Chgo., Aug. 31, 1901; s. Albert and Hortense (Simon) K.; A.B., U. Mich., 1922; m. Maxine H. Weil, Jan 30, 1926; children—John Weil, Peter. With Formfit Co. (now Formfit/Rogers Co.), Chgo., 1922-66, successively mdse. mgr., asst. treas., v.p., pres., 1926-64, chmn., 1964- 66, also dir.; dir. Midas Internat., 3 H Bldg. Corp., Chgo., Genesco, Inc., Bonwit Teller. Bd. dirs. Mus. Contemporary Art; governing life mem., trustee Art Inst. Chgo., Jewish Fedn. Met. Chgo.; trustee Monmouth Coll. Mem. Soc. Contemporary Am. Art (pres. 1959-60, dir.), Phi Beta Kappa. Clubs: Standard (Chicago); Lake Shore Country (Glencoe, Ill.). Home: 1436 Waverly Rd Highland Park IL 60035 Office: 2 N Riverside Plaza Chicago IL 60606

KUNSTLER, WILLIAM MOSES, educator, lawyer, author; b. N.Y.C., July 7, 1919; s. Monroe Bradford and Frances (Mandelbaum) K.; B.A., Yale, 1941; LL.B., Columbia, 1948; m. Lotte Rosenberger, Jan. 14, 1943; children—Karin F. Goldman, Jane B. Admitted to N.Y. bar, 1948, D.C. bar, 1958; exec. trainee R.H. Macy & Co., N.Y.C., 1948-49; lectr. English, Columbia, 1946-50; partner firm Kunstler, Kunstler & Kinoy, N.Y.C., 1949—; asso. prof. law N.Y. Law Sch., 1950—, Pace Coll., 1951—; lectr. New Sch., 1966—. Bd. dirs. Nat. Emergency Civil Liberties Com.; bd. legal advisers Center for Constl. Rights. Served to maj. AUS, 1941-46; PTO. Decorated Bronze Star medal; recipient Press award N.Y. State Bar Assn., 1957, Civil Rights award, 1963; 1st award Ohio Radio-Television Inst., 1960. Mem. Assn. Bar City N.Y., Am. Civil Liberties Union (dir. 1964—, nat. council 1968—, nat. emergency civil liberties com. 1968—), Phi Beta Kappa, Phi Delta Phi. Author: Our Pleasant Vices, 1941; The Law of Accidents, 1954; First Degree, 1960; Beyond a Reasonable Doubt?, 1961; The Case for Courage, 1962; And Justice for All, 1963; The Minister and the Choir Singer, 1964; Deep in My Heart, 1966; also articles, book revs. Home: 210 West St Mamaroneck NY 10543 Office: 511 Fifth Av New York City NY 10017 also Center for Constitutional Rights 588 9th Av New York City NY 10036

KUNTZ, EUGENE OSCAR, educator, lawyer; b. Corpus Christi, Tex., Oct. 8, 1913; s. Walter Nichols and Katie (Lang) K.; A.R., Baylor U., 1945, LL.B., 1941; LL.M., Harvard, 1947; m. Rosamund Louise Miller, Mar. 9, 1940; 1 dau. Karen Joyce. Admitted to Tex. bar, 1938; practice in Amarillo, 1940-41; asst. prof. law U. Wyo., 1947-50, asso. prof., 1950-52; prof. law U. Okla., Norman, 1952—, dean, prof. law, 1965-70, prof. law, 1970—, dean emeritus, 1970—; partner McAfee, Taft, Cates, Kuntz & Mark, 1958-65. Spl. justice Okla. Supreme Ct., 1971. Dir. Sneed Oil Co., Okla. Nat. Bank. Spl. adviser Gov.'s Com. on Tax Reform, 1966-67; mem. Okla. Acad. for State Goals, 1966-67; vice chmn. Spl. Com. on Tax Revision, 1970-71. Pres., trustee Presbytery Washita. Served to lt. comdr. USNR, 1941-45. Recipient Gerald Klein award, 1970. Mem. Am., Okla. bar assns., Okla. Inst. Taxation (past pres.), Order of Coif, Phi Alpha Delta. Presbyn. (elder). Author: Kuntz, Oil and Gas, 1962; Kuntz Supplement to Thornton on Oil and Gas, 1960; Pocket Parts to Thornton on Oil and Gas, 1956; Newspaper Laws of Wyoming, 1952. Editor: Oil and Gas Reporter, 1955—. Mem. bd. editors Okla. Bar Assn. Contbr. articles profl. jours. Home: 2504 Walnut Rd Norman OK 73069

KUNTZ, PAUL GRIMLEY, educator, philosopher; b. Phila., Nov. 22, 1915; s. Franklin Samuel and Sadie Treichler (Grimley) K.; A.B with high honors in Philosophy, Haverford Coll., 1937; S.T.B., Harvard, 1940, S.T.M., 1941, Ph.D., 1946; m. Marion Leathers Daniels, Nov. 26, 1970; children (by previous marriage)—Sarah Zabriskie, Joel DuBois, Timothy Romeyn, Susan Deborah Grimley. Asst. to dean Harvard, 1938-41; ordained to ministry Conglist. Ch., 1945; pastor in Vt. and Mass., 1941-48; instr. Smith Coll., 1946-48; asst. prof. philosophy Grinnell Coll., 1948- 52, asso. prof., 1952-57, prof. philosophy and religion, 1957-66, Noble prof., 1961-66, dir. Grinnell Seminar on Order, 1963-64; prof. philosophy Emory U., Atlanta, 1966—, chmn. dept., 1966-69; Kent fellow Soc. Religion in Higher Edn., 1946; Ford fellow, Yale, 1955-56; fellow Woodrow Wilson Internat. Center for Scholars, Smithsonian Instn., 1970-71. Mem. Am. Philos. Assn., Mind Assn., Metaphys. Soc. Am. (councillor 1963-65, del. to Am. Council Learned Socs. 1966-70), Am. Soc. Polit. and Legal Philosophy, A.A.A.S., Mediaeval Acad. Am., Brit. Soc. Aesthetics, Am. Cath. Philos. Assn. (exec. council 1970—), Am. Soc. Aesthetics (trustee 1966-70), Hist. Sci. Soc., Soc. Symbolic Logic, Royal Inst. Philosophy (London), Australasian Soc. Philosophy, Ch. History Soc., Soc. Ancient Greek Philosophy, Ia. Philos. Soc. (pres. 1961-62), John Dewey Soc., Wider Quaker Fellowship, Soc. Realistic Philosophy, So. Soc. Philosophy and Psychology, So. Soc. Philosophy Religion, Ga. Philosophy Soc. (pres. 1967-68), C.S. Peirce Soc., Societ é Européne de Culture, Internat. Soc. for Metaphysics (chmn. organizing com.), Phi Beta Kappa. Mem. Soc. of Friends. Author: (with Neal W. Klausner) Philosophy: the Study of Alternative Beliefs, 1961; The Concept of Order, 1968; Lotze's System of Philosophy, 1971; also numerous articles. Contbr. books and profl. jours. Home: 1655 Ponce de Leon Av Atlanta GA 30307 also Three Ponds S Woodbury VT 05650

KUNTZ, WALTER NICHOLS, Jr., drug distbn. co. exec.; b. Houston, Jan. 11, 1910; s. Walter Nichols and Katie (Augusta (Lang) K.; LL.B., Houston Law Sch., 1936; m. Katherine Barbara Powers, Nov. 25, 1937; children-Walter Nichols III, Charles Powers, Kay Barbara. Admitted to Tex. bar, 1939, also U.S. Supreme Ct.; with Southwestern Drug Corp., 1929-67, prs., 1963-67, cons., 1967—; with Brunswig Drug Corp., 1967—, mem. retirement plan investment com., 1967—, exec. v.p., 1969—, also dir.; dir. Bergen Brunswig Corp., 1969- -. Sr. v.p., dir., mem. exec. com., dir. exec. com. Druggists Service Council, N.Y.C., 1959-63, Nat. Drug Trade Conf., N.Y.C., 1962-63; mem. Pharm. Found., U. Houston Coll. Pharmacy, 1950-63; adv. council U. Tex. Coll. Pharmacy, 1957-63; bd. dirs. Am. Found. Pharm. Edn., 1962-63, 66- -. Mem. Am. Bar Assn., State Bar Tex., Soc. Former Spl. Agts. FBI, Nat. Wholesales Druggists Assn. (pres. 1962-63). Roman Cath. Home: 1118 Pine Dr Beverly Hills CA 90210 Office: 1900 Av of Stars Century City CA 90067

KUNTZ, WERNER HINRICH, clergyman; b. Lewiston, Minn., Apr. 23, 1898; s. Arnold Hilarius and Minna (Koenig) K.; student Concordia Coll., Concordia Sem.; M.A. in Social Administrn., Wayne State U., 1953; Litt.D. (hon.), Concordia Coll., 1968; m. Litana Messerli, Apr. 14, 1926; children—Richard A., Oralyn (Mrs. J.L. Dennison), Joanna, Susan, Judith. Ordained to ministry Lutheran Church, 1922; pastor St. John's Ch., Grey Eagle, Minn., 1922-25, Grace Ch., Indpls., 1925-37, Baden Meml. Ch., Winfield, Kan., 1937-45; exec. sec. Social Welfare, Mich. Dist., 1945-53; exec. dir. Resettlement for European Refugees, 1951-53; exec. dir. Bd. World Relief for Luth. Ch., Mo. Synod, 1953-70; v.p. Asso. Luth. Charities; mem. nat. com. United Community Services Met. Detroit. Recipient Gold medal Red Cross of Yugoslavia; Christus Vivit, Concordia Sem., 1968. Mem. Am. Assn. for UN, Nat. Conf. on Social Welfare, Internat. Council on Social Welfare, Soc. for Internat. Devel., Luth. Human Relations Assn. Am. Clubs: Circumnavigators, Clipper. Home: 10704 Lincoln Dr Huntington Woods MI 48070

KUNTZ, WILLIAM EDWARD, naval officer; b. Leipsic, O., Aug. 15, 1917; s. Edward Charles and Bess (Sherrard) K.; student Denison U., 1934-35; B.S., U.S. Naval Acad., 1935- 39; grad. U.S. Naval Postgrad. Sch., 1943-45; grad. Advanced Mgmt. Program, Harvard, 1960; m. Joan Elizabeth Darby, Aug. 23, 1941; children—Karen Elizabeth, William E.J., Rodney Edward. Commd. ensign U.S. Navy, 1939, advanced through grades to rear adm., 1969; assigned U.S.S. Boise, 1939-41; electronics officer Naval Operating Base, Guam, 1945; staff comdr. Service Squadron 3, 1945-56; exec. officer U.S.S. DeHaven, 1946-47; comdg. officer U.S.S. Marsh, 1946-47; dir. tng., Armed Forces Spl. Weapons Project, Sandia Base, N.M., 1948-51; comdg. officer U.S.S. L.K. Swenson, 1951-53; coordinator electronics programs Office Chief Naval Operations, 1953-56; comdr. Escort Squadron 14, 1957-58; surface warfare officer Office Naval Research, 1958-61; comdg. officer U.S.S. Altair, 1961-62; asst. chief staff Allied Forces, So. Europe, 1962-64; comdg. officer U.S.S. Northampton, 1964-65; dep. chief nat. mil. command system engring. Def. Communications Agy., 1965-67; asst. dep. dir. Def. Communications Agy., 1967; dep. dir., 1967-68; dir. communications-electronics (J-6), Hdqrs. USEUCOM, 1968—; chief DCA- Europe, 1968-69. Decorated Legion of Merit, Joint Service Commendation medal, Navy Commendation medal with combat V, also numerous unit and area ribbons; spl. breast Order Pao Ting, 2d class Cloud and Banner (China). Mem. Lambda Chi Alpha, Phi Mu Alpha. Mason. Home: 78 Floridastrasse Stuttgart Germany Office: Hdqrs US European Command (J-6) APO New York City NY 09128

KUNTZ, WILLIAM R., corp. exec.; b. 1921. With Molybdenum Corp. Am., 1947—, pres., 1963—. Address: Molybdenum Corp Am 280 Park Av New York City NY 10017

KUNZ, CALVIN WILLIAM, Jr., profl. sports exec.; b. Denver, Feb. 28, 1919; s. Calvin William and Rachael Kay (Tomory) K.; A.B., U. Denver, 1940; student Harvard Grad. Sch. Bus., 1940-41; m. Mary May Paschall, July 24, 1956; children—Mary Douglass, Katharine Jane, Ann Rachael. Pres. Empire Sports, Inc., owners and operators Denver Broncos Football Club of Am. Football League and Denver Bears Baseball Club of Pacific Coast League, 1961—; pres. WVD Co., comml. farming, vegetable processing, 1949—. Pres. Highlander Boys. Served to col. USMCR, World War II. Mem. Beta Theta Pi. Mason, Rotarian. Home: 320 Humboldt St Denver, CO 80218 Office: 333 Logan St Denver CO 80203

KUNZ, DONALD RAMON, lawyer; b. Dubuque, Ia., June 6, 1929; s. Charles G. and Rose (Nehlsen) K.; B.A., U. Ia., 1952; J.D., U. Ariz., 1955; m. Joan R. Walz, June 13, 1950 (div. 1964); children-Leslie Ellyn, Susan Louise, Kristin Marie; m. 2d, Edith I. Gÿlledge, Dec. 28, 1968; children-Jennifer, Anne. Vice pres. chmn. bd. dirs. Dubuque Amusement Corp., 1946-48; auditor Grand Central Aircraft Corp., Tucson, 1952-53; admitted to Ariz. bar, 1955; asso. firm Snell & Wilmer, Phoenix, 1958-63; partner firm Evans & Kunz, Phoenix, 1963-69; sec. Evanst Kunz, Ltd., Phoenix, 1969—. Mem. Am., Maricopa County bar assns., State Bar Ariz., Am. Right of Way Assn. (chmn. com law and legislation Ariz. chpt. 1961-63, 64—), Phoenix Assn. Def. Counsel, Am. Judicature Soc., Phi Delta Phi, Sigma Phi Epsilon. Republican. Conglist. Club: Phoenix Lawyers. Home: 1771 E Pleasant Dr Phoenix AZ 85020 Office: 3800 N Central Av Phoenix AZ 85012

KUNZ, ERICH, bass baritone; b. Vienna, Austria, May 20, 1909; s. Eduard and Sophie (Modes) K.; Ingenieur, Musikakademie, Vienna, 1936; m. Winfriede Kurzbauer, June 14, 1948; children—Christine Nicoline, Wolfgang Florian. Mem. Vienna State Opera, 1941—. Scala Milano, 1952, Met. Opera Co., 1953-55. Recipient Orden für Kunst and Wissenschaft 1st class, 1960. Address: 35 Grinzingerstrasse Vienna 19 Austria

KUNZE, GEORGE WILLIAM, coll. dean; b. Warda, Tex., Sept. 16, 1922; s. John Paul and Hermine (Moerbe) K.; B.S., Tex. A. and M. U., 1948, M.S., 1950; Ph.D., Pa. State U., 1952; m. Flora Mae Rothmann, July 11, 1947; children—Brenda Kay, Wayne Lester. Mem. faculty Tex. A. and M. U., College Station, 1952—, asst. prof., 1952-56, asso. prof., 1956-60, prof. soil mineralogy, 1960—, asso. dean Grad. Sch., 1967-68, dean, 1968—. Dir. Bank of A. and M.; cons.

U. Alaska, 1963-66, E. Pakistan Agrl. U., 1970. Served with USAAF, 1943-45. Recipient Faculty Distinguished Achievement award in research Tex. A. and M. U., 1966. Fellow Mineral. Soc. Am., A.A.A.S., Am. Soc. Agronomy; mem. Am. Soc. Agronomy. Rotarian. Cons. editor Soil Science, 1958—. Home: 1001 Ashburn E College Station TX 77840

KUNZEL, HERBERT, machinery mfg. exec.; b. Los Angeles, Aug. 15, 1908; s. Herman and Regina (Schwarz) K.; LL.B., U. So. Cal., 1935; m. Minerva Griswold, May 23, 1947; children—Ridge, Daphne, Kurt, Charles. Admitted to Cal. bar, 1935, with Solar div. Internat. Harvester Co., San Diego, 1946—, pres., 1956—. Served with USNR, 1942-46. Mem. Sigma Chi. Rotarian. Home: 3250 McCall St San Diego CA 92106 Office: 2201 Harbor Dr San Diego CA 92112

KUNZIG, ROBERT LOWE, govt. ofcl.; b. Phila., Oct. 31, 1918; s. Robert Weiss and Hilda Elsa (Lowe) K.; B.A., U. Pa., 1939, LL.B., 1942; children—Kim Chappell, Robert Lowe. Admitted to Pa. bar, 1942, Minn. bar, 1961; co-prosecutor Buchenwald concentration camp case, Germany, 1947; asso. mem. firm Clark, Ladner, Fortenbaugh & Young, Phila., 1948-69; dep. atty. gen. Pa., 1948-53; counsel U.S. Congl. Com., 1953-54; exec. dir. CAB, 1955-58; mem. U.S. Fgn. Claims Settlement Commn., 1958-61; adminstrv. asst. to U.S. Senator Hugh Scott, 1963-67; v.p. E.G. Clinton Co. Mpls., 1961-62; exec. dir. Pa. Gen. State Authority, 1967-69, Pa. Hwy. and Bridge Authority, Pa. Transp. Authority, 1967-69; adminstr. Gen. Services Adminstrn., Washington, 1969—. Chmn. Task Force for Minority Businessman, 1969—; spl. asst. to Pres. for coordination 1976 Washington bicentennial, 1970—; mem. Cabinet Com. on Constrn., U.S. Property Rev. Bd., Com. on Govt. Procurement, Regulations and Purchasing Rev. Bd., 1970—. Del., Republican Nat. Conv., Chgo., 1952; dir. GOP Truth Squad campaigns Rep. Nat. Com., 1956, 60, 68; mgr. Phila. dist. atty. campaign, 1965, Hugh Scott senatorial campaign, 1964, Rep. gubernatorial campaign, 1966; Rep. candidate atty.-gen. Minn., 1962; chmn. Phila. Young Reps., 1948-50, Young Reps. Pa., 1951-52; polit. speaker, lectr. Served to capt. AUS, 1942-46. Named to Pa. Young Rep. Hall of Fame; recipient 2 awards for distinguished service govt. CAB, 1956, 58. Mem. Pa. Fedn. Young Rep. Clubs, Am., Pa., Phila., Minn. bar assns., Am. Legion, Phi Beta Kappa, Phi Sigma Kappa, Pi Gamma Mu, Mask and Wig (bd. govs. Phila.). Episcopalian. Club: Union League (Phila.). Contbr. articles nat. mags. Home: Wheat Row Harbour Sq 1315 4th St SW Washington DC 20024 Office: General Services Adminstrn Washington DC 20405

KUO, FRANKLIN FA-KUN, educator; b. Hankow, China, Apr. 22, 1934; s. Steven C. and Grace S. (Hueng) K.; B.S., U. Ill., 1955, M.S., 1956, Ph.D., 1958; m. Dora Lee, Aug. 30, 1958; children—Jennifer, Douglas. Came to U.S., 1950, naturalized, 1961. Asst. prof. Poly. Inst. Bklyn., 1958-60; mem. tech. staff Bell Telephone Labs., 1960-66; prof. elec. engring. U. Hawaii, 1966—; cons. Lawrence Radiation Labs., 1966-71. Mem. I.E.E.E., Assn. Computing Machinery, Tau Beta Pi, Eta Kappa Nu. Club: Landsdowne (London, Eng.). Author: Network Analysis and Synthesis, 1962; co-author: System Analysis by Digital Computer, 1966; Computer Oriented Circuit Design, 1969. Cons. editor Prentice-Hall, Inc., 1967—. Contbr. articles profl. jours. Home: 629 Ulumaika St Honolulu HI 96816

KUO, MAU-TONG, educator; b. Taiwan, China, Nov. 16, 1928; s. Po-Jong and Su-Wang (Huang) K.; B.S., Nat. Taiwan U., 1951; M.S., U. Notre Dame, 1953; Ph.D., U. Mich., 1957. Came to U.S., 1952, naturalized, 1969. Asst. prof. Nat. Taiwan U., 1951-52; research fellow Mich. Engring. Research Inst., 1954-57; group leader Am. Cyanamid Co., 1957-67; prof. chem. engring. Pratt Inst., 1967—. Asso. Bresler Assos.; dir. B & M Chem. Engring. Co.; pres. MTK Industries; lectr. Chinese Acad. Sci. Dodge fellow, 1954-57. Mem. Am. Inst. Chem. Engrs., Soc. Mgmt. Information Systems. Contbr. articles profl. jours. Home: 685 West End Av New York City NY 10025 Office: Pratt Inst Brooklyn NY 11205

KUO, PING-CHIA, educator, historian; b. Yangshe, Kiangsu, China, Nov. 27, 1908; s. Chu- sen and Hsiao-kuan (Hsu) K.; A.M., Harvard, 1930, Ph.D., 1933; m. Anita H. Bradley, Aug. 8, 1946. Prof. modern history and Far Eastern internat. relations Nat. Wuhan U., Wuchang, China, 1933-38; editor China Forum, Hankow and Chungking, 1938-40; counsellor Nat. Mil. Council, Chungking, China, 1940-46; counsellor Ministry Fgn. Affairs, 1943-46; participated in Cairo Conf. as spl. polit. asst. to Generalissimo Chiang Kai-shek, 1943; during war yrs. in Chungking, also served Chinese Govt. concurrently in following capacities: mem. fgn. affairs com. Nat. Supreme Def. Council, 1939-46, chief, editorial and pubs. dept. Ministry Information, 1940-42, mem. central planning bd., 1941-45; tech. expert to Chinese delegation San Francisco Conf., 1945; chief trusteeship sect. secretariat UN, London (exec. com. prep. commn. and gen. assembly), 1945-46; top- ranking dir. Dept. Security Council Affairs, UN, 1946-48; vis. prof. Chinese history San Francisco State Coll., summers 1954, 58; asso. prof. history So. Illinois U., 1959-63, prof. history, 1963—, chmn. dept. history, 1967—. Pres., Midwest Conf. Asian Studies, 1964. Decorated Kwang Hua medal A-1 grade (Nat. Mil. Council, Chungking), 1941; Auspicious Star medal Nat. Govt., Chungking, 1944; Victory medal, Nat. Gov., 1945. Mem. Am. Hist. Assn., Assn. Asian Studies. Club: Commonwealth (San Francisco). Author: A Critical Study of the First Anglo-Chinese War, with Documents, 1935; Modern Far Eastern Diplomatic History (in Chinese), 1937; China: New Age and New Outlook, 1960; China, in the Modern World Series, 1970. Contbr. Am. hist. pubs. and various mags. in China. Home: 907 Skyline Dr Carbondale IL 62901

KUPCHAN, S. MORRIS, chemist, educator; b. N.Y.C., Nov. 10, 1922; s. Hyman and Rebecca (Fishgold) K.; B.S., City Coll. N.Y., 1941; M.A., Columbia, 1942, Ph.D., 1945; m. Nancy R. Slater, Mar. 28, 1954; children-Clifford, Charles. Research asso., lectr. Columbia, 1945-48; research fellow, instr. chemistry Harvard, 1948-55; mem. faculty U. Wis., 1955-69, prof., 1961- 69; John W. Mallet prof. chemisty, mem. Center Advanced Studies, U. Va., Charlottesville, 1969—; lectr. in field, 1955—. Mem. pharmacology, exptl. therapeutics study sect. NIH, 1963-67, mem. medicinal chemistry study sect., 1967—, chmn. 1970—. Recipient Ebert prize, 1960, Research Achievement award in natural products Am. Pharm. Assn., 1965. Mem. Am. Chem. Soc., Am. Pharm. Assn., Chem. Soc. London, Soc. Econ. Botany (past pres.), N.Y. Acad. Scis., Mexican Chem. Soc. (hon.). Contbr. numerous articles profl. jours. Home: Ednan Forest Charlottesville VA 22901

KUPCINET, IRV, columnist; b. Chgo., July 31, 1912; s. Max and Anna (Paswell) K.; student Northwestern U., 1930-32; A.B., U. N.D., 1935; m. Esther Joan Solomon, Feb. 12, 1939; children—Karyn (dec.), Jerry Solomon. Sportwriter Chgo. Daily Times, 1935-43, condr. column "Kup's Column" 1943—; also engaged in radio and TV. Spl. cons. in charge of columnists for War Finance Div., war loan drives, U.S. Treasury Dept. Vice Pres. Dr. Jerome D. Solomon Meml. Found. Recipient Emmy award, moderator television show, 1960. Mem. Newspaper Guild, Tau Delta Phi. Clubs: National Press (Washington); Merchants and Manufacturing (Chgo.). Served as football ofcl., Nat. Football League. Home: 1040 N Lake Shore Dr Chicago IL 60611 Office: Chicago Sun Times 401 N Wabash Av Chicago IL 60611

KUPER, J. B. HORNER, physicist; b. N.Y.C., Nov. 5, 1909; s. George Henry and Lillian E. (Horner) K.; A.B., Williams Coll., 1930; Ph.D., Princeton, 1938; m. Mariette Kovesi von Neumann, Nov. 24, 1937; 1 son, George Henry III. Jr. physicist Washington Biophys. Inst. and NIH, USPHS, 1937- 40, asso. physicist, 1941; asso. group leader radiation lab. Mass. Inst. Tech., 1941-46; dept. head Fed. Telecommunications Labs., 1946; chmn. dept. instrumentation and health physics Brookhaven Nat. Lab., 1946-70, chmn. environmental scis. study group, 1970—. Mem. com. on nuclear sci. NRC, 1949-54; mem. gov.'s adv. com. on atomic energy, 1956-58. Trustee, Village of Old Field (N.Y.), 1967-71. Fellow I.E.E.E., Am. Phys. Soc.; mem. Radiation Research Soc., Health Physics Soc., Sigma Xi, Phi Beta Kappa. Club: Cosmos (Washington); Old Field. Bd. editors Proc. Inst. Radio Engrs., 1947-53; editorial bd. Rev. Sci. Instruments, 1948- 51, editor, 1954—. Home: Old Field Setauket NY 11733 Office: Brookhaven National Lab Upton NY 11973

KUPERS, FRITS, Netherlands diplomat; b. Amsterdam, Netherlands, Jan. 28, 1921; s. Evert and Maria (Thonissen) K.; Ph.D. cum laude, U. Amsterdam, 1949; m. Anneke Rooselaar, Apr. 11, 1953; children—Michiel, Roland. Econ. minister Found. for Econ. Research, U. Amsterdam, 1950-51; with Ministry Fgn. Affairs, 1951-61, dep. dir. econ. affairs, 1957-61; counselor permanent del. OECD, Paris, 1961-69; econ. minister, Washington, 1969—. Decorated officer Order Orange Nassau. Mem. Econometric Soc., Am. Econ. Soc., Regional Sci. Assn., Soc. Internat. Devel., Vereniging voor de Staathuishoudkunde. Home: 6109 Robinwood Rd Bethesda MD 20034 Office: 4200 Linnean Av NW Washington DC 20008

KUPERSMITH, AARON HARRY, lawyer, leisure and health care co. exec.; b. Newark, June 13, 1925; s. David and Bessie (Rubinstein) K.; certificate Drury Coll., 1943; B.S. cum laude, N.Y. U., 1948; LL.B., Bklyn. Law Sch., 1954, J.S.D., 1956, J.D., 1968; m. Cynthia Skolnick, Dec. 24, 1947; children—Farrell Preston, Mark Jeffrey, Linda Ellen. Accountant, A. H. Kupersmith & Co., N.Y.C., 1948—; admitted to N.Y. bar, 1954; practice as atty., accountant, tax, bus. and financial cons., N.Y.C., 1954—; partner Ramapo Manor Nursing Center, Suffern, N.Y., McQuire-Holiday Motel, 1962-70; pres., chmn. Verson Prodns., Inc., N.Y.C., 1962-67, Medispas, Inc., N.Y.C., 1968—; exec. Financial Planning Corp., N.Y.C., 1956—; exec. v.p., sec.-treas., dir., mem. exec. com. Maradel Products, Inc., and subsidiaries, N.Y.C., 1962- 65; pres., chmn. Computer Systems Medicine and Edn. and subsidiaries, 1969—; dir. Listfax Corp., Ronconi Systems, Inc. and subsidiaries; pres., chmn. Am. Inst. Econ. Growth, N.Y.C., 1965—; spl. counsel, cons. to various assns. on medicare and medicaid; lectr., instr. various groups on law, taxes, corporate finance, nursing home adminstrn., 1958—; financial, legal, tax and bus. cons. to various pub. and pvt. corps., legal and accounting firms. Mem. N.Y. State Nursing Home Adv. Com. Reimbursement, 1966; mem. adv. com. nursing home costs for N.Y. State, 1966. Columbia, Trustee Martin Revson trusts, various pvt., charitable founds. Served with USAAF, 1943-45. Recipient Wisdom award, 1969. Fellow Am. Coll. Nursing Home Adminstrs.; mem. Am. Mgmt. Assn., Nat. Assn. Advertisers, Nat. Sales Mgmt. Assn., Am. Accountants Assn., Am. Bar Assn., Bar Assn. City N.Y., Alpha Epsilon Pi, Psi Chi Omega, Beta Gamma Sigma. Republican. Author: An Economic Study of American System, 1956; Tax Havens, 1959; Corporate Finance and Taxes, 1959; Tax Treaties of United States, 1960; United States Industry and Executives Abroad, 1960; Executive Compensation Constructive Receipt, 1961; Corporate Finance and Taxes Defined, 1963; Considerations in Mergers and Acquisitions, 1965; Break Even Techniques, 1965; Men and Their Money, 1966; Future of Health Care and Costs, 1968; Nursing Home Industry Review, 1968; Major Health Care Crisis, 1968; also articles. Financial editor, columnist Drug Trade News, N.Y.C., 1965-68. Home: 45 Woodland Av West Orange NJ 07052 Office: 40 W 55th St New York City NY 10019 also 45 Woodland Av West Orange NJ 07052

KUPFER, WILLIAM FRANCIS, bishop; b. Bklyn., Jan. 28, 1909; s. Emil Frederick and Mary (Connolly) K.; B.A., Maryknoll Sem., 1933. Ordained priest Roman Cath. Ch.; priest, China, 1933-48; procurator, Hong Kong, 1948-51; prefect apostolic Taichung, Taiwan, 1951-62, bishop, 1962—. Mem. standing com. China Bishop's Conf., 1967—, pres. commn. media of social communication, 1967—. Trustee Fujin U., Providence Coll., Viator and Stella Matutine Middle Schs., Fujen Primary Sch., Chung Shang Radio Sta. Address: 136 Kuang Fu Rd Taichung Taiwan

KUPFERMAN, LAWRENCE EDWARD, artist; b. Boston, Mass., Mar. 25, 1909; s. Samuel and Rosa (Maysles) K.; student Sch. of Museum of Fine Arts, Boston, 1929-30; B.S. in Edn., Mass. School of Art, 1935; m. Ruth Cobb, Apr. 29, 1937; children—Nancy, David. Asso. prof. of drawing, painting, 1958—. also screen, Mass. Coll. Art, Boston, 1941-58, prof. in painting, 1958-.also head dept. Exhibited drypoints or paintings at most of the gen. exhbns. in the larger cities throughout U.S., 1938—. Represented in permanent collections, including Mills Coll. Art Gallery, Library of Congress, Met. Mus. Art, Carnegie Inst. Boston Mus. Fine Arts, Worcester Art Mus., Baltimore and San Francisco museums. Mus. Modern Art, Fogg Mus. Art (Harvard), Whitney Mus. Am. Art, Wichita Art Mus., Bklyn. Mus., Addison Gallery Am. Art, Wadsworth Atheneum, U. Ill., U. Mich., Walker Art Center, also U. Mass., Amherst. Had one-man shows in nationally known galleries, 1944—, paintings Horizon Gallery, Rockport, Mass., 1969; 2 paintings included in Am. Fedn. Arts traveling exhbn., 1958-59. Recipient numerous awards and prizes, 1938—; latest being First prize for painting for Odysseus, Rhode Island Arts Festival, 1961. A.N.A. Fellow Royal Soc. Arts; mem. Am. Assn. U. Profs., Soc. Am. Graphic Artists, Boston Soc. Watercolor Painters, Eastern Art. Assn., Provincetown Art Assn., Sociedad Numismatica de Mexico. Home: 38 Devon Rd Newton Centre MA 02159 Office: Mass Sch of Art 370 Brookline Av Boston MA 02215

KUPFERMAN, MEYER, composer; b. N.Y.C., July 3, 1926; s. Elias and Fanny (Hoffman) K.; student Queens Coll., 1944-46; m. Sylvia Kasten, June 16, 1946 (div.); 1 dau., Lisa. Co-dir. New Chamber Music Soc., 1946-48, Bolton Music Festival, Bolton Landing, N.Y., 1947-48; mem. forum group bd. N.Y. chpt. Internat. Soc. Contemporary Music, 1949-50; tchr. composition, chamber music, music for theatre Sarah Lawrence Coll., 1951—. First recipient La Guardia Meml. award outstanding achievement field music, 1958. Me. A.S.C.A.P. Composer: (film scores) Hallelujah the Hills, 1962, A X'mas Memory, 1966, Blast of Silence, 1960, Faces of America, 1965, Goldstein, 1964, Black Like Me, 1964, Cool Wind, 1961, Among the Paths to Eden, 1968; (operas) In a Garden, 1948, The Curious Fern, 1957, Voices for a Mirror, 1957, Draagenfut Girl, 1958, Doctor Faustus Lights the Lights, 1963, The Judgement, 1966-67; also symphonies, chamber music, Cycle of Infinities, 1962-67, others. Home: 171 W 71st St New York City NY 10023 Office: Sarah Lawrence Coll Bronxville NY 10708

KUPFERMAN, THEODORE R., judge; b. N.Y.C., May 12, 1920; s. Samuel H. and Gertrude Kupferman; B.S., City Coll., N.Y.; LL.B. (Kent scholar, editor Law Rev.), Columbia; m. Dorothee Hering, Dec. 21, 1957 (dec. June 1969); children—Theodore R., Stephanie Elisabeth. Admitted to N.Y. bar, also U.S. Supreme Ct.; law sec. Judge D.W. Peck, appellate div. N.Y. State Supreme Ct., 1948-49; mem. legal dept. Warner Bros. Pictures, Inc., then NBC, 1951-53; sec., v.p., gen. counsel Cinerama Prodns. Corp., 1953-59; was counsel firm Battle, Fowler, Stokes & Kheel, N.Y.C.; justice Supreme Ct., State of N.Y. 1969-70; asso. justice Appellate Div., First Dept., 1971—. Asst., then adj. prof. law N.Y. Law Sch., 1959-64; counsel, legislative asst. minority leader S.M. Isaacs, N.Y. City Council, 1958- 62; mem. N.Y. City Council, 1962-66; mem. 89-90th Congress 17th Dist. N.Y. Past chmn. youth services com. YMCA N.Y.C. Mem. Am. Bar Assn. (past editor bull. sect. internat. and comparative law, Congl. affairs editor Internat. Lawyer, chmn. internat. patent, copyright and trademark relations com.), Fed. Bar Assn. N.Y., N.J., Conn. (pres. 1954-56, chmn. bd. 1956-60), Consular Law Soc. pres., trustee), Am. Arbitration Assn. (former mem. panel arbitrators), Acad. Polit. Sci., Internat. Radio and TV Soc., Citizens Union. Republican. Club: City (past pres.) (N.Y.C.). Home: 140 E 72d St New York City NY 10021 Office: Supreme Court Appellate Division 27 Madison Av New York City NY 10010

KUPLAN, LOUIS, cons. gerontologist; b. N.Y.C., Aug. 11, 1906; s. Abraham and Eva (Brodsky) K.; B.A., U. Cal. at Los Angeles, 1929; postgrad., U. Cal., Berkeley, 1935, 38; m. Katherine FitzGerald, Sept. 9, 1936. County dir. Cal. Relief Adminstrn., 1934-40; adminstrv. asst. Farm Security Adminstrn., San Francisco, 1940-43; sr. adminstrv. asst. Fed. Pub. Housing Authority, San Francisco, 1943-45; pub. assistance analyst Social Security Adminstrn., San Francisco, 1945-47; chief div. old age security Cal. Dept. Social Welfare, 1947-51; exec. sec. Cal. Interdepartmental Coordinating Com. Aging, 1950-55, Cal. Citizens Adv. Com. Aging, 1955- 60; editor Maturity mag., 1954-60; editorial cons. Harvest Years Pub. Co., San Francisco, 1960-63; specialist retirement planning Mgmt. Devel. Center, U. San Francisco, 1960-61; lectr. U. Cal. Extensions, 1965-69, U. San Francisco, 1968-69; instr. Merritt Coll., Oakland, Cal., 1969—; dir. Center on Aging, Urban Life Inst., U. San Francisco, 1968-69. Mem. adv. bd. Retirement Advisers, Inc., N.Y.C., 1958-60; nat. adv. com. White House Conf. Aging, 1961; mem. tech. adv. com. on edn. White House Conf. on Aging, 1970—, mem. adv. com. on aging Cal. Dept. Mental Hygiene, 1969—; sci. council Gerontol. Research Found., St. Louis; council geriatrics and gerontology Pan Am. Med. Assn.; com. aging Am. Pub. Welfare Assn.; mem. Nat. Com. on Aging, N.Y.C.; pres. 5th Internat. Congress Gerontology, 1960; v.p., vice chmn. bd. dirs. Longevity Found., 1960-70. Moderator, producer television program A Gift of Time, KRON-TV, 1969—. Recipient award for outstanding services and leadership in developing programs for older adults San Francisco Sr. Center. Fellow Gerontol. Soc. U.S. (pres. 1958-59); mem. Internat. Assn. Gerontology (pres. 1960-63), Western Gerontology Soc. (founder, pres. 1955-56; named Gerontologist of Year, 1957), Nat. Assn. Social Workers, Am. Pub. Welfare Assn., Am. Psychol. Assn.; hon. mem. geriatric and gerontological socs. Argentina, Chile. Home: 1618 27th Av San Francisco CA 94122 Office: Monadnock Bldg San Francisco CA 94105

KUPPERIAN, JAMES EDWARD, Jr., astrophysicist; b. Milw., Apr. 17, 1925; s. James Edward and Amanda (Hoiland) K.; B.S. in Naval Architecture and Marine Engring., Webb Inst., 1946; M.S., U. Del., 1948; Ph.D. in Physics, U. N.C., 1952; m. Nancy A. Smith, Jan. 27, 1962; children—James Edward III, Virginia Jean. Physicist, Naval Research Lab., 1954-58; br. head, astrophysics br. Goddard Space Flight Center, NASA, 1959-70, project scientist Orbiting Astron. Obs., 1959—, dep. project mgr., 1970—, project mgr. and scientist Explorer XI, 1959-62, mem. astronomy subcom., 1960-64. Served to lt. USNR, 1943-46, 52-53. Recipient award Am. Bur. Shipping, 1946; Exceptional Scientific Achievement medal NASA, 1969. Mem. Am. Phys. Soc., Am. Astron. Soc., Internat. Astron. Union, Pi Mu Epsilon, Sigma Xi, Sigma Pi Sigma. Discoverer Lyman Alpha night sky, 1957; 1st observations of ultraviolet stellar sources, 1958. Home: 2702 Lyn Pl Bowie MD 20715 Office: Goddard Space Flight Center Greenbelt MD 20771

KUPPERMANN, ARON, educator, chem.-physicist; b. Sao Paulo, Brazil, May 6, 1926; s. Jacob and Mary (Feldman) K.; came to U.S., 1953, naturalized, 1965; B.Sc. in Chem. Engring., U. São Paulo, 1948; Ph.D. in Phys. Chemistry, U. Notre Dame, 1956; m. Roza Davidson, Jan. 21, 1951; children—Baruch, Miriam, Nathan, Sharon. Asst. prof. Inst. Tech. de Aero., São José dos Campos, Brazil, 1950-51; mem. faculty U. Ill. at Urbana, 1955-63, asso. prof., 1961-63; prof. chem. physics Cal. Inst. Tech., 1963—. Research asso. Argonne Nat. Lab., 1957, Inst. Atomic Energy, São Paulo, 1960; cons. Jet Propulsion Lab., Pasadena, Cal., 1965—; Reilly lectr. U. Notre Dame, 1965; Venable lectr. U. N.C., 1967; Werner lectr. U. Kan., 1968; councilor chemistry Internat. Union Radiation Research, 1965-69. NSF fellow, 1968-69. Recipient Centennial Sci. award U. Notre Dame, 1965. Fellow Am. Phys. Soc., Am. Inst. Chemists; mem. Am. Chem. Soc., Faraday Soc., A.A.A.S., Radiation Research Soc. (councilor for chemistry, 1965-69), Sigma Xi, Alpha Chi Sigma, Phi Lambda Upsilon. Democrat. Jewish religion. Contbr. profl. jours. Editorial bd. Jour. Phys. Chemistry, 1965-69, Internat. Jour. Radiation Physics and Chemistry, 1969—. Home: 2487 Morslay Rd Altadena CA 91001 Office: Div Chemistry California Inst Tech Pasadena CA 91109

KURALT, CHARLES BISHOP, television news corr.; b. Wilmington, N.C., Sept. 10, 1934; s. Wallace Hamilton and Ina (Bishop) K.; student U. N.C., 1955; m. Suzanna Folsom Baird, June 1, 1962; children by previous marriage—Lisa Catherine, Susan Guthery. Reporter, columnist Charlotte (N.C.) News, 1955-57; writer CBS News, 1957-59, corr. 1959—. Recipient Ernie Pyle Meml. award, 1956; George Foster Peabody broadcasting award, 1969; Emmy award, 1969. Club: Players (N.Y.). Author: To The Top of the World, 1968. Address: CBS News 524 W 57th St New York City NY 10019

KURANZ, JOHN LEO, sci. equipment co. exec.; b. Waukesha, Wis., July 16, 1921; s. Arthur P. and Miriam (Hughes) K.; B.S., Marquette U., 1941; M.S., U. Okla., 1942; m. Georgia Chudy, Oct. 9, 1944; children—Mary Patricia, John David, Maureen Anne. Sr. v.p., dir., sec. Nuclear-Chgo. Corp., Des Plaines, Ill., 1946—; pres. Amersham Searle; commissarissen Nuclear-Chgo. Europa (Amsterdam); chmn. adv. com. isotopes, radiation devel. U.S. AEC. With Manhattan Project U. Chgo., 1944-46. Pres. Kuranz Found.; bd. mem. Harper Coll. Sch. Bd. Served to sgt. AUS, 1942-46. Member Am. Nuclear Soc., Am. Standards Assn., Am. Phys. Soc., U.S. C. of C., Atomic Indsl. Forum. Roman Catholic Church. Home: RR2 Box 96 Barrington IL 60010 Office: 333 E Howard Av Des Plaines IL 60018

KURATA, FRED, chem. engr., educator; b. Rialto, Cal., June 4, 1914; s. Tatsuichi and Namie (Kaneko) K.; B.S., Cal. Inst. Tech., 1934; M.S., U. Mich., 1939, Ph.D., 1941; m. Virginia Mae Mefford, Jan. 14, 1946; children—Phillip C., Gayle E., Douglas, Thomas M. Research asso. U. Mich. Engring. Research Inst., 1941-43; plant engr. Protected Steel Products Co., Washington, Pa., 1943-44; chem. engr. Atlas Chems., Wilmington, Del., 1944-47; prof. chem. engring. U. Kan., Lawrence, 1947-60, Univ. Distinguished prof., 1960—; cons. chem. engr. Fellow Am. Inst. Chemists; mem. A.A.A.S., Am. Chem. Soc., Am. Inst. Chem. Engrs., Am. Inst. Mining and Metall. Engrs., Am. Soc. Engring. Edn., Am. Assn. U. Profs., Soc. Profl. Engrs. Contbr. articles in field to profl. jours. Patentee in field. Home: 2909 Harvard Rd Lawrence KS 66044

KURI, EMILE, motion picture set decorator; b. Mexico City, Mexico, June 11, 1907; s. Antonio and Eufrocina (Henaine) K.; student St. Mary's Coll., San Antonio, 1919-22; B.A., Chaminade Coll., St. Louis, 1927; m. Carrie Lou Carson, Feb. 8, 1934; children—Frederick, Elizabeth, John. Interior decorator BeHannesey Art Studio, Hollywood, Cal., 1929-32; set decorator various ind. motion picture cos., 1934, Harry Sherman Prodns., 1936-41, Selznick Internat., 1942-46, Ind. Prodns., 1946-48, Paramount Pictures, 1948-52, Metro Goldwyn Mayer, 1952-53, Walt Disney Prodns., Burbank, Cal., 1954—, Disneyland, 1955—; cons. decorator Walt Disney World, Orlando, Fla., 1969—; dir. decorating for Acad. Awards Presentations, 1943—. Active Boy Scouts Am. Recipient award for set decoration for The Heiress, Acad. Motion Picture Arts and Scis., 1949, for 20,000 Leagues Under the Sea, 1954. Named Hon. sir knight Royal Rosarians, State Ore., 1970. Mem. Acad. Motion Picture Arts and Scis. (bd. govs. 1959-69). Roman Catholic. Office: Buena Vista Burbank CA 91505

KURKO, NICHOLAS union ofcl. Dir. Region 17 Dept. Orgn. AFL-CIO. Office: 1318 Continental Nat Bank Bldg Fort Worth TX 76102

KURLAND, LEONARD TERRY, physician; b. Balt., Dec. 24, 1921; s. Ellis M. and Sarah (Shein) K.; B.A., Johns Hopkins, 1942, Dr.P.H., 1951; M.D. (Gold medal), U. Md., 1945; M.P.H. cum laude, Harvard, 1948. Intern, U. Md., 1945-46; with USPHS, 1946-64, assigned Nat. Inst. Mental Health, NIH, 1948-55, Nat. Inst. Neurol. Disease and Blindness, 1955-64, chief epidemiology br., 1955-64; fellow neurology Mayo Clinic, Rochester, Minn., 1952-53, research asst. in neurology and med. statistics, 1953-55, chmn. dept. med. statistics, epidemiology and population genetics, 1964—. prof. epidemiology Mayo Grad. Sch. Medicine, 1965—; clin. asst. prof. neurology Georgetown U., 1957-60; clin. prof. neurology Howard U., 1960-64, Regional alumni rep. Harvard Sch. Pub. Health, 1952-. Served with AUS, 1943-45. Fellow Am. Pub. Health Assn.; mem. Am. Acad. Neurology (past chmn. neuroepidemiology sect.), Am. Neurol. Assn., Am. Epidemiologic Soc., Internat. Epidemiologic Assn., Japanese Clin. Soc. Neurology (exec. council), Nat. Multiple Sclerosis Soc. (Gold Sci. award 1966; research review panel). Sr. author: The Epidemiology of Neurologic and Sense Organ Diseases, 1971. Co-editor: Motor Neurone Disease, 1969. Contbr. articles med. jours. Research on epidemiology, genetics of diseases of nervous system and cancer. Office: 200 1st St SW Rochester MN 55901

KURLAND, PHILIP B., educator; b. N.Y.C., Oct. 22, 1921; s. Archibald H. and Estelle (Polstein) K.; A.B., U. Pa., 1942; LL.B., Harvard, 1944; m. Mary Jane Krensky, May 29, 1954; children—Julie Rebecca, Martha Jennifer, Ellen Sarah. Admitted to N.Y. bar, 1945; also U.S. Supreme Ct.; law sec. to Judge Jerome N. Frank, 1944-45, Supreme Ct. Justice Felix Frankfurter, 1945-46; atty. Dept. Justice, 1946-47; mem. firm Kurland & Wolfson, N.Y.C., 1947-50; asst. prof. law Northwestern U., 1950-53; mem. faculty U. Chgo., 1953—, prof. law, 1956—; cons. Econ. Stblzn. Agy., 1951-52. Chief cons., subcom. on separation of powers U.S. Senate Judiciary Com., 1967—. Guggenheim fellow, 1950-51, 54-55. Fellow Am. Acad. Arts and Scis.; mem. Am., Chgo. bar assns., Assn. Bar City N.Y., Am. Law Inst., New Brougham Soc. Democrat. Jewish religion. Club: Quadrangle (U. Chgo.). Author: Jurisdiction of Supreme Court of U.S., 1950; Mr. Justice, 1964; Religion and the Law, 1962; Frankfurter: Of Law and Life, 1965; The Supreme Court and the Constitution, 1965; The Great Charter, 1965; Moore's Manual, 1964-70, Felix Frankfurter on the Supreme Court, 1970; Politics, The Constitution and the Warren Court, 1970; Mr. Justice Frankfurter and the Constitution, 1971. Editor: Supreme Court Rev., 1960—. Home: 4840 Woodlawn Av Chicago IL 60615

KURLANDER, ARNOLD BAILEY, physician; b. Cleve., July 28, 1915; s. Jospeh J. and Florence H. (Bialosky) K.; student Western Res. U., 1933-35; M.D., Ohio State U., 1939; M.P.H., U. Mich., 1947; m. Eula Imogene Baker, July 10, 1940; children—Carol Anne, Jean Lynn, Joan Lee. Intern USPHS Hosp., New Orleans, 1939; ward surgeon USPHS hosps., Galveston, Norfolk, Boston, 1940-44; chief div. Tb. Ariz. Dept. Health, 1945-46; chief div. Tb. Ohio Dept. Health, 1947-49, chief bur. local health services, 1949-50; chief program development br., div. Tb, USPHS, 1950-51, asst. chief chronic disease and Tb, 1951-54, chief chronic disease program, 1954-57, asst. to surg. gen., 1957-58, asst. surg. gen. for program, 1958, asst. surg. gen., dep. chief Bur. Med. Services, 1958-60; asst. surgeon gen. USPHS, 1960-62; exec. dir. Sinai Hosp., Balt., 1962—, instr. asst. prof. preventive medicine Ohio State U., 1948-50; lectr. Johns Hopkins Sch. Hygiene and Medicine, 1966—. Bd. govs. Chronic Disease Research Inst., Buffalo; trustee Health Research Found., Inc., Asheville, N.C. Served as asst. surgeon USCG, World War II. Diplomate in pub. health Am. Bd. Preventive Medicine. Fellow Am. Pub. Health Assn., Am. Coll. Preventive Medicine; mem. A.M.A., Assn. Mil. Surgeons. Home: 3216 Wood Valley Dr Baltimore, MD 21208. Office: Sinai Hosp Baltimore MD 21215

KURNIT, SHEPARD, advt. exec.; b. Bronx, N.Y., Oct. 31, 1924; s. Samuel Philip and Frances (Litchenstien) K.; scholar Parsons Sch. Design, 1941-42; m. Jeanette Zinsher, Aug. 1, 1945; children—Paul David, Richard Alan, Scott Philip. With Sterling Advt., N.Y.C., 1945, Harry Serwer Advt., N.Y.C., 1945-47, C.J. Herrick Assos., N.Y.C., 1947-49, Diamond Barnett Advt., N.Y.C., 1949; asso. art dir. Morton Freund Advt., 1949; founder Kurnit Assos., Inc., N.Y.C., 1950-54; pres. Kurnit, Geller Assos., Inc., N.Y.C., 1954-56; exec. v.p. DKG, Inc. (formerly Delehanty, Kurnit & Geller), N.Y.C., 1956-61, became pres., 1961, now chmn., chief exec. officer. Founder, E. Meadow Com. Human Rights, 1964, pres., 1965; mem. Urban League, Great Neck Forum, Com. Human Rights. Served with USAAF, 1943-45. Recipient numerous advt. awards. Mem. Young Pres. Orgn., Businessmen for Peace in Vietnam. Democrat. Home: 1 Birch St Great Neck NY 11023 Office: 1271 Av of Americas New York City NY 10020

KURNOW, ERNEST, educator, statistician; b. Bklyn., Oct. 21, 1912; s. Harry and Sarah Malka (Shagaloff) K.; B.S. cum laude, Coll. City N.Y., 1932, M.S. in Edn., 1933; Ph.D., N.Y. U., 1951; m. Joyce Litzky, Oct. 6, 1938; children—Ruth (Mrs. Jeffrey Jarrett), Susan Carol (Mrs. Leonard Weistrop), Alice Rose (Mrs. Peter Cohen). Tchr. N.Y.C. Bd. Edn., 1935-40, statistician, 1941-48; mathematician ordnance div. War Dept., 1940-41; mem. faculty N.Y. U., 1948—, prof. econs., 1960-63, prof. bus. statistics, chmn. dept., 1963—. Cons., N.Y. State Tax Structure Study Commn., 1959—, Mayor, N.Y.C. Com. Mgmt. Survey, 1950-51, Turkish Ministry Finance, 1955-56; cons. temporary commn. Revision N.Y. State Constn., 1958, temporary commn. fiscal affairs N.Y. State Govt., 1953-54; cons. Tri-State Transp. Commn., 1964-66; participant Brazilian capital markets program, 1968; study dir. Govs.' Spl. Commn. on Financing Mass Transp., 1970-71. Fulbright grantee to Greece, 1966-67. Mem. Am. Statis. Assn., Am. Econ. Assn., Econometric Soc., Inst. Mgmt. Scis., Nat. Tax Assn., Tax Inst. Am. (mem. adv. council 1969—), Am. Soc. Quality Control, Sphinx, Beta Gamma Sigma, Sigma Eta Phi, Delta Pi Sigma, Alpha Phi Sigma. Jewish religion. Author: The Turkish Budgetary Process, 1956; also articles. Co-author: Statistics for Business Decisions, 1959; Theory and Management of Land Rent, 1961. Home: 27 Nirvana Av Great Neck NY 11023 Office: New York Univ Washinton S New York City NY 10003

KUROSAWA, AKIRA, Japanese film dir.; b. 1910; ed. Keika Middle Sch. Joined Toho Film Co. as asst. dir., 1936; directed his 1st film Sugata Sanshiro, 1943. Recipient 1st prize for Rashomon, Venice Film Festival; Silver Lion for The Seven Samurai; Am. Motion Picture Acad. award for Rashomon. Films include, Sugata Sanshiro, Ichiban Utsukushiku, Torano Owofumu Otokotachi, Waga Seishun ni Kuinashi, Subarashiki Nichiyobi, Yoidore Tenshi, Shizukanaru Ketto, Norainu, Rashomon, Hakuchi, Ikiru, The Seven Samurai, Ikimono no Kiroku, Kumonosu Jio, Donzoko, Throne of Blood, Yojimbo, The Bad Sleep Well, Sanjuro, High and Low, Akahige, Redbeard. Address: 1755 Nichome Matsubara-machi Setagaya-Ku Tokyo Japan*

KURSUNOGLU, BEHRAM, physicist, educator; b. Bayburt, Turkey, Mar. 14, 1922; s. Ismail and Hanife (Esenulku) K.; B.Sc., Edinburgh U., 1949; Ph.D., Cambridge U., 1952; m. Sevda Arif, Sept. 25, 1952; children—Sevil, Ayda, Ismet. Came to U.S., 1958. With Cornell U., 1952-54, Yale, 1955, Turkish Gen. Staff on Atomic Matters, 1956-58, Turkish Atomic Energy Commn., 1956-58; dean faculty nuclear scis. and tech. Middle East Tech. U., Ankara, Turkey, 1956-58; vis. prof. physics U. Miami, Coral Gables, Fla., 1954-55, prof. physics, 1958—, mem. NATO Scis. Com., 1958, dir. Center for Theoretical Studies, 1965—. Cons., Oak Ridge Nat. Lab., 1962-64, Brit. Atomic Energy Establishment, 1961, Max Planck-Institut fur Physik and Astrophysik, 1961. Fellow Am. Phys. Soc.; mem. Am. Assn. Physics Tchrs., Am. Assn. U. Profs., Sigma Xi. Author: Modern Quantum Theory, 1962. Contbr. articles to profl. jours. Research in fields of elementary particles, gen. relativity, statis. mechanics. Home: 6200 Leonardo St Coral Gables FL 33146

KURTH, ANDREW EARL, clergyman, ret. ch. exec.; b. Blissfield, Mich., May 3, 1903; s. William F. and Louise (Jacob) K.; B.A., North Central Coll., 1923; B.D., Evang. Theol. Sem., 1925; postgrad. U. Mich., U. Chgo.; m. Cecile M. Houck, June 16, 1926; children—Louisella (Mrs. William Frank), Robert W., Marjorie (Mrs. James Williams). Ordained to ministry Evang. Ch., 1926, Presbyn. Ch., 1940; minister Broadway Evang. Ch., Ann. Arbor, Mich., 1925-31, 12th St. Evang. Ch., Detroit, 1931-40, Redeemer Presbyn. Ch., Detroit, 1940-44; adminstrv. dean North Central Coll., Naperville, Ill., 1944-46; minister Westminster Presbyn. Ch., Cedar Rapids, Ia., 1946-54; sec. field program Presbyn. Ch. of U.S., N.Y.C., 1954-58, exec. Ill. Synod, 1958-64, asso. sec., dept. interpretation and stewardship, N.Y.C., 1964-70; tchr. dept. Bible, Coe Coll. Mem. city council, Ann Arbor. Dir. U. Dubuque. Rotarian. Clubs: Executive (pres.), Kiwanis (pres.) (Cedar Rapids). Home: 141 Hardenburgh Av Haworth NJ 07641

KURTH, HERBERT CHRISTIAN, ins. co. exec.; b. Columbua, Wis., May 2, 1909; s. Christian and Amanda (Martin) K.; student Williams Coll., 1927-29; m. Katherine Ehrier, 1932; children—Thomas Christian, Elizabeth Wendy (Mrs. William Wrean), Tineka. Pres. Wisconsin Malting Co., Milw., 1932-46, sec.-treas., 1946-55; sec.-treas. Kurth Malting Co., Milw., Wis., 1955-60, chmn. bd., 1960—, also asst. treas., mem. bd. dirs.; pres. N.Am. Corp., 1963—; dir. Marshall & Isley Bank; trustee Northwestern Mut. Life Ins. Co., E.R. Wagner Mfg. Co., Wis. Securities Co. of Delaware. Bd. dirs. Carthage Coll. United Luth. Home for Aging, Columbia Hosp., Greater Milwaukee Com.; bd. govs. Milw. Symphony Orch. Mem. Malting Barley Improvement Assn. (past pres), Milw. Grain Exhange (past dir.), Navy League. Home: 10352 N Lake Shore Dr Mequon WI 53092 Office: 2100 E 43d St Milwaukee WI 53246

KURTH, LESTER D., bank exec.; b. Chippewa Falls, Wis., Aug. 11, 1926; s. William and Emma (Lubach) K.; student Lawrence Coll., 1944-45; B.A., Yale, 1947; LL.B., Columbia, 1950. Admitted to N.Y. bar, 1951; joined N.Y. Trust Co., 1950 (merger N.Y. Trust Co. and Chem. Corn Exchange Bank), sr. v.p. in charge fiduciary adminstrn. div. Chem. Bank, N.Y.C., 1971—. Trustee Fleming Sch., N.Y.C. Served to lt. (j.g.) USNR, 1952-53. Mem. Corporate Fiduciairies Assn. (v.p. 1970—). Methodist (trustee). Clubs: Yale, Board Room (N.Y.C.). Home: 340 E 64th St New York City NY 10021 Office: 277 Park Av New York City NY 10017

KURTZ, CARL FREDERICK, banker; b. Bethlehem, Pa., June 24, 1908; s. Herman R. and Lena R. (Pfenninger) K.; B.S. in Indsl. Engring., Lehigh U., 1929; grad. Am. Inst. Banking, 1930; m. Dorothy A. Nagle, June 8, 1935; children—Carol Ann (Mrs. James L. Chapman), Ralph Donald. With Irving Trust Co., N.Y.C., 1929—, v.p. operations div., 1962-65, sr. v.p. operations div., 1965-67, sr. v.p. internat. div., 1967—. Home: 716 Knollwood Terrace Westfield NJ 07090 Office: 1 Wall St New York City NY 10015

KURTZ, CHESTER MOTT, physician, hosp. adminstr.; b. Milw., July 11, 1899; s. John Nicholas and Louise (Mott) K.; B.S., U. Wis., 1921, M.S., 1925; M.D., Harvard, 1927; 1 son, John Caldwell; m. 2d, Thea Walcup, Sept. 10, 1957. Intern U. Hosps., Madison, Wis., 1927-28; mem. teaching staff Med. Sch. U. Wis., 1928-57; mem. med. staff U. Hosps., 1928-57, charge cardiology dept., 1929-55; practice medicine, specializing in cardiology, Milw., 1937-42, Madison, 1942-56; dir. profl. services VA Hosp., Madison, 1957, Albuquerque, 1957-58; hosp. dir. VA Hosp., Fort Bayard, New Mexico, 1959-62, VA Hosp., Albuquerque, 1962-68; now cons. cardiology Albuquerque. Served with U.S. Army, 1918. Fellow A.C.P.; mem. Am. Heart Assn., Central Soc. Clin Research, Fed. Exec. Assn. Albuquerque and Santa Fe (dir.), Sigma Xi, Alpha Delta Phi. Presbyn. (elder). Author: Orthodiascopy, 1937. Contbr. articles med. jours. Address: 2904 Georgia St NE Albuquerque NM 87110

KURTZ, JOHN WILLIAM, educator; b. Earlville, Ill., Nov. 17, 1906; s. William H. and Louise (Grosshans) K.; A.B., Wartburg Coll., 1927; M.A., U. Ill., 1929, Ph.D., 1932; postgrad. U. Munich, 1929-30; m. Edith Davis, Jan. 1, 1932; children—David, Eric, Robert, Karl. Faculty Oberlin Coll., 1932-, instr. to asso. prof., 1932-55, prof. 1955—, chmn. dept. German and Russian, 1956-70; univ. adviser Office High Commr. for Germany, 1948-50. Research chief Strategic Bombing Survey, Germany, 1945. Past pres., Bd. Edn., Oberlin. Decorated Order of Merit (Fed. Republic Germany). Mem. Modern Lang. Assn. Am., Am. Assn. Tchrs. German, Am. Assn. U. Profs. Author: (with H. Politzer), German, A Comprehensive Course for College Students, 1958. Editor (with E. Kurtz) Drei Meistenovellen, 1966; Deutsche Meisternovellen, 1936; Drei Novellen, 1950. Home: 67 S Cedar St Oberlin, OH 44074.

KURTZ, LLOYD SHERER, Jr., lawyer; b. Toledo, Feb. 23, 1934; s. Lloyd Sherer and Mildred (Kalb) K.; A.B., Princeton, 1956; LL.B., Stanford, 1959; m. Patricia Jean Redman, June 28, 1958; children-Lloyd Sherer III, Kathryn Laura. Law clk. to Chief Justice Buell A. Nesbett, Supreme Ct. of Alaska, 1959-60; admitted to Alaska Bar, 1961; practiced in Fairbanks, 1961-62, Anchorage, 1962—; atty. McNealy, Merdes & Camarot, 1961-62; atty. Alaska Housing Authority, 1962-63; atty. Burr, Boney & Pease, 1964-66; partner Burr, Pease & Kurtz, 1967—; tchr. bus. law and econs. U.Alaska, Anchorage, 1962-65. Co. chmn. for Alaska, Fund Raising for Princeton, 1961-62; asst. chmn. planning Anchorage Breakthrough, 1969-70. Mem. Am., Alaska, Anchorage bar assns., Practising Law Inst., Am. Judicature Soc., Am. Fedn. Musicians, Phi Alpha Delta. Mng. editor Stanford Law Review, 1958- 59, Co-pub. MTST Legal Forms, 1968. Home: 1558 E St Anchorage AK 99501 Office: 825 W 8th St Anchorage AK 99501

KURTZ, PAUL, educator; b. Newark, Dec. 21, 1925; s. Martin and Sara (Lasser) K.; B.A., N.Y.U., 1948; M.A., Columbia, 1949, Ph.D., 1952; m. Claudine C. Vial, Oct. 6, 1960; children—Valerie L., Patricia A., Jonathan. Instr., Queens Coll., 1950-52; instr. philosophy Trinity Coll., Hartford, Conn., 1952-55, asst. prof., 1955-58, asso. prof., 1958-59; asso. prof. Vassar Coll., Poughkeepsie, N.Y., 1960-61; vis. prof. New Sch. Social Research, N.Y.C., 1960-65; asso. prof. Union Coll., Schenectady, 1961-64, prof., 1964-65; vis. prof. U. Besancon (France), 1965; prof. philosophy State U. N.Y., Buffalo, 1965—. Pres. Greater Capitol dist. N.Y. State United World Federalists, 1965; chmn. Council on Internat. Studies and World Affairs. Trustee Behavioral Research Council, Great Barrington, Mass.; bd. dirs. U.S. Bibliography of Philosophy, 1958-70, Internat. Humanist and Ethical Union, 1968—, Univ. Centers for Rational Alternatives, 1969—. Served with AUS, 1944-46. Behavioral Research Council fellow, 1962-63, French Govt. fellow, 1965. Mem. Am. Philos. Assn., Am. Ethical Union, Am. Assn. U. Profs., Am. Humanist Assn. (dir.). Author: (with Rollo Handy) A Current Appraisal of the Behavioral Sciences, 1964; Decision and the Condition of Man, 1965. Editor: American Thought Before 1900, 1966; American Philosophy in the Twentieth Century, 1966; Sidney Hook and the Contemporary World, 1968; Moral Problems in Contemporary Society, 1969; co-editor: International Directory of Philosophy and Philosophers, 1965; Language and Human Nature, 1971. Editorial bd. The Humanist, 1964—, editor, 1967—; editorial bd. Philosophers Index, 1969—, Question, 1969—. Home: 660 Le Brun Rd Eggertsville NY 14226 Office: 923 Kensington Av Buffalo NY 14215

KURTZ, STEPHEN GUILD, educator, historian; b. Buffalo, Sept. 9, 1926; s. George Patterson and Nellie (Crowther) K.; A.B., Princeton, 1947; Ph.D., U. Pa., 1953; m. Katherine Jeanne Godolphin, Sept. 5, 1947; children—Sharon, Thomas Patterson, Stephen Godolphin. Instr. history U. Pa., 1949-51; master Kent Sch., 1951-55; Fulbright prof. Athens (Greece) Coll., 1955-56; dean students Wabash (Ind.) Coll., 1956-59, asso. prof. history, asst. to pres., 1959-64, dean coll., 1964-66; lectr. Coll. William and Mary, 1966—; vis. prof. Columbia, summers 1962, 64; editor Inst. Early Am. History, Williamsburg, Va., 1966-69, dir., 1969—. Mem. regional com. Woodrow Wilson Fellowship Found., 1960-64, dissertation fellowship com., 1968—. Chmn. Indpls. Diocesan com. Episcopal Ch., 1961-63; chmn. Montgomery County Human Relations Council, 1963-64. Trustee St. Paul's Coll. Served with USNR, 1944-45. Guggenheim fellow, 1961-62. Mem. Am. Antiquarian Soc., Mass., Va. hist. socs. Author: The Presidency of John Adams, 1957; The Federalists, 1971. Editor: The Papers of John Marshall, 1966-71. Home: 103 Ware Rd Williamsburg VA 23185

KURTZ, THOMAS EUGENE, educator; b. Oak Park, Ill., Feb. 22, 1928; s. Oscar Christ and Helen (Bell) K.; B.A., Knox Coll., Galesburg, Ill., 1950; Ph.D., Princeton, 1956; m. Patricia Anne Barr, June 13, 1953; children—Daniel Barr, Timothy David, Beth Louise. Mem. faculty Dartmouth, 1956—, prof. math., 1966—, dir. Kiewit Computation Center, 1959—. Dir. New Eng. Ednl. Data Systems; vice chmn., dir. NERComp, Inc. Mem. panel uses computers in edn. President's Sci. Adv. Com., 1965-66. Treas. Friends of Hanover Schs., Inc., 1961-68. Mem. United Ch. Christ. Author: Basic Statistics, 1963; (with J.G. Kemeny) Basic Programming, 1967. Co-designer BASIC computer lang. and Dartmouth time sharing system. Home: 37 School St Hanover NH 03755

KURTZ, WILLIAM G., Jr., banker; b. Phila., 1911; ed. Wharton Sch. of U. Pa. V.p., treas. Fidelity-Phila. Trust Co.; dir. Food Fair Properties, Inc., Manchester Gas Co. Home: 834 Deerfield Lane Bryn Mawr, PA 19010. Office: 135 S Broad St Philadelphia PA 19109 *

KURTZMAN, DAVID HAROLD, state ofcl., b. Russia, Jan. 11, 1904; s. Maurice and Hannah (Wolfson) K.; came to U.S., 1921, naturalized 1926; B.S., Temple U., 1930, LL.D., 1967; M.A., U. Pa., 1931, Ph.D., 1935; LL.D., U. Pitts., 1967; L.H.D. (hon.), Jefferson Med. Coll., 1968; D.Sc., Pa. Coll. Optometry, 1969; m. Celia Buchdrucker, July 24, 1927; children—Rochelle (Mrs. Joel B. Weinman), Marshall K. Instr. polit. sci. Temple U., 1931-33; asst. dir. and dir. research Western div. Pa. Economy League, 1933-59; sec. adminstrn. Pa., 1959-63; sr. research and edn. asso. Fels Inst. Local and State Govt., U. Pa., 1963-65; vice chancellor finance U. Pitts., 1965-67, acting chancellor, 1966-67, chancellor, 1967, chancellor emeritus, 1967—; supt. pub. Instrn. Pa., 1967-69, sec. edn., 1969—; vis. lectr. Grad. Sch. Pub. and Internat. Affairs, U. Pitts., 1958-59. Sec., Pitts. Met. Study Commn., 1951-55; chmn. Mayor Pitts. Mgmt. Adv. Com., 1951-59; chief, staff Gov. Pa. Tax Adv. Commn., 1956, 58; chmn. Gov. Pa. Tax Study and Revision Commn., 1966; research dir. Pa. Constl. Conv. Prep. Com., 1967; mem. Pres.' Commn. on Sch. Finance, 1970. Trustee, Pitts. Symphony Soc. Mem. Am. Acad. Polit. and Social Sci., Am. Soc. Pub. Adminstrn., Am. Technion Soc. (trustee,) Govtl. Research Assn., Nat. Tax Assn., Tax Inst. Am. (adv. council), Phi Beta Kappa, Omicron Delta Kappa, Phi Eta Sigma, Beta Gamma Sigma, Druids. Home: 1021 S Progress Av Harrisburg PA 17111 Office: Education Bldg Harrisburg PA 17126

KURUCZ, JOHN, lawyer; b. Yonkers, N.Y., Sept. 19, 1930; s. John J. and Anna (Timan) K.; B.C.E., Rensselaer Poly. Inst., 1952; LL.B., Georgetown U., 1957; m. June Reynolds, Feb. 20, 1960; children-Debra Jeanne, Jonna Stiles. Admitted to N.Y. bar, 1959, Va. bar, 1957; patent searcher Pennie, Edmonds, Morton, Barrows & Taylor, Washington, 1954; patent examiner U.S. Patent Office, Washington, 1954-56; patent adviser Dept. Army, Washington, 1956-57; with Kane, Dalsimer, Kane & Smith, N.Y.C., 1957-69; mem. firm Kane, Dalsimer, Kane, Sullivan & Kurucz, 1969—. Dir.. Cartafax Corp., N.Y.C.; v.p., dir. Breed Corp., Fairfield, N.Y. Served to 1st lt., C.E., AUS, 1952-54. Mem. N.Y.C., N.Y. County, N.Y. State, Va., Am., Fed. bar assns., N.Y., Am. patent law assns., Westchester County, N.Y. State, Am. socs. profl. engrs., Alpha Tau Omega, Chi Epsilon. Clubs: National Lawyers Washington; University (N.Y.C.); Ponte Vedra (Jacksonville, Fla.). Home: Hack Green Rd PO Box 279A Route 2 Pound Ridge NY 10576 Office: 420 Lexington Av New York NY 10017

KURYLOWICZ, JERZY, linguist; b. Austria, 1895; ed. Polish, French univs.; Ph.D.; Dr. Celtic Philology (hon.), Nat. U. Ireland; Hon. Dr., U. Paris, U. Vienna, U. Chgo., U. Ann Arbor, U. Edinburgh. Lectr. Lwów (now Lvov) U., 1926-28, extraordinary prof., 1928-34, prof., 1934—; prof. Cracow, 1948—. Polish rep. Permanent Internat. Com. on Linguistics. Recipient State prize 1st class, 1955, 64; Prix Volney. Mem. Polish Acad. Scis., Danish, Irish, Norwegian, Serbian, Austrian, Italian acads., Institut de France, Am. Acad. Arts and Scis. Author: Etudes indo-européennes, 1935; L'accentuation dans des langues indo-européennes, 1952; L'apophonie en indo-européen, 1956; Esquisses linguistiques, 1960; L'anophonie en sémitique, 1961; Inflectional Categories of Indo-European, 1964; Indo-germanische Grammatik, 1968. Address: Podwale Cracow Poland

KURZ, BLAISE SIGEBALD, bishop; b. Heilbronn, Germany, Feb. 3, 1894; s. Karl and Maria (Haberkern) K.; student Franciscan Hochschule, Munich, Germany, 1914-19; LL.D., St. Bonaventure's U., 1953. Came to U.S., 1950, naturalized, 1961. Joined Franciscan Order, 1914, ordained priest Roman Cath. Ch., 1919; bishop of Kokstad, S. Africa, 1935-48, of Yungchow, China, 1948—; expelled by Communists, 1950. Council father 2d Vatican Council, 1962. K.C. (4). Address: 2230 Richmond Terrace Staten Island, NY 10302.

KURZ, CHARLES, lawyer; b. 1900; B.S., N.Y.U., 1922; LL.B., Bklyn. Law Sch., 1924; married. Admitted to N.Y. bar, 1926; partner firm Bundy & Schloss, N.Y.C.; former sec., dir. Fed. Pacific Electric Co. Address: 405 Lexington Av New York City NY 10017 *

KURZ, WALTER CHARLES, newspaper exec.; b. Chgo., May 25, 1908; s. Charles C. and Meta M. (Mueller) K.; B.S., U. Ill., 1929; m. Ethel Hull, Jan. 20, 1934; children—Robert H., Ronald W., Roger and Susan (Mrs. Robert Izard) (twins). With Chgo. Tribune, 1933—, mgr. gen. display advt. dept., 1948-55, advt. mgr., 1955-60, v.p., dir. sales, 1960-67, v.p., dir. planning and devel., 1967-68, exec. v.p., gen. mgr., 1968-70, also dir.; v.p. Tribune Co., 1960-70, pres., 1970—, also dir.; instr. advt. and merchandising Medill Sch. Journalism, Northwestern U., 1942-48. Founder, dir. Newspaper 1. Mem. Com. for Econ. and Cultural Devel. Chgo. Trustee McCormick-Patterson Trust, Robert R. McCormick Charitable Trust; sec., dir. Passavant Hosp., Chgo.; bd. dirs. Ill. Inst. Tech.; asso. Nat. Coll. Edn.; mem. Northwestern U. Assos.; mem. adv. bd. YMCA of Chgo.; mem. citizens bd. U. Chgo. Mem. Am. Newspaper Pubs. Assn. (dir. Bur. Advt.), Sigma Phi Epsilon. Clubs: Racquet, Mid-America, Chicago, Commonwealth, Economics, Commercial, Sunday Evening (trustee) (Chgo.); Indian Hill (Winnetka); Old Elm (Ft. Sheridan, Ill.); Tres Vidas, Wayfarer's. Home: 1111 Sunset Lane Winnetka IL 60093 Office: 435 N Michigan Av Chicago IL 60611

KURZMAN, DAN, fgn. corr., author; b. San Francisco, Mar. 27, 1922; s. Joseph and Lillian (Halperin) K.; A.B. in Polit. Sci., U. Cal. at Berkeley, 1945; diploma Russian lang. and area, U. Pitts., 1944; diploma French civilization, U. Paris (France), 1946. Corr., I.N.S., Paris, 1946-48; feature editor information div. Marshall Plan, Paris, 1949; corr. Middle East, NBC, 1950-53; bur. chief McGraw-Hill World News, Tokyo, 1954-59; roving corr. Scripps-Howard Newspaper Alliance, Washington, 1960-61; became fgn. corr. Washington Post, 1962; contbr. to Saturday Rev. Served with AUS, World War II. Decorated Purple Heart, Combat Inf. badge; recipient Front Page award for internat. reporting Washington Newspaper Guild, 1964, George Polk Meml. award best internat. reporting, 1965; Dan Kurzman collection established at Boston U., 1966. Mem. State Dept. Corr. Assn., White House Corr. Assn. Clubs: Overseas Press (N.Y.C.); Nat. Press (Washington); Overseas Writers; Tokyo Foreign Correspondents. Author: Kishi and Japan: The Search for the Sun, 1960; Subversion of the Innocents (award as best book fgn. affairs Overseas Press Club, 1963), 1963; Santo Domigo; Revolt of the Damned, 1965; Genesis 1948: The First Arab-Israeli War, 1970. Address: care Maxwell Aley Associates 145 E 35th St New York City NY 10016

KURZWEG, HERMANN HERBERT, physicist, govt. ofcl.; b. Germany, Jan. 1, 1908; s. Paul O. and Bertha (Friede) K.; student Tchrs. Coll., 1928; Ph.D., U. Leipzig (Germany), 1933; m. Erna Michaelis, Apr. 21, 1934; children—Ulrich, Diemut (Mrs. Robert W. Balentine), Lutz. Came to U.S., 1946, naturalized, 1954. Asst. instr. U. Leipzig, 1934; research sci. Carl Zeiss Optical Works, Jena, 1935-36; chief research div. German Supersonic Wind Tunnel Labs., Peenemuende, 1937-43, chief research, dep. dir. aeroballistics lab., Kochel, 1943-45; cons., div. chief U.S. Naval Ordnance Lab., 1946-52, chief aeroballistic research dept., 1952-56, asso. tech. dir. aeroballistic research, 1956-60; asst. dir. research NASA, 1960, dir. research, 1961-70, chief scientist, chmn. OART Research Council, 1970—. NASA liaison mem. div. math. Nat. Acad. Scis., 1963-66; past mem. subcom. on high speed aerodynamics and com. on aerodynamics NACA; part-time lectr. dept. aero. engring. U. Md. Grad. Sch., 1947-60; chmn. indsl. and profl. adv. council, dept. aero. engring. Pa. State U., 1962-67; mem. com. aeroballistics Navy Bur. Ordnance, 1947-58, chmn., 1958-60; mem. conf. com. Nat. Conf. Adminstrn. Research, 1958-63, 69—; mem. adv. panel aeros. Office Asst. Sec. Def., 1958-61; mem. fluid dynamics panel Adv. Group Aeros. Research and Devel., NATO, 1953—, vice chmn. panel, 1961-63. chmn. panel, 1963-65. Recipient Meritorious Civilan Service award U.S. Navy, 1951. Fellow Am. Inst. Aeros. and Astronautics, Washington Acad. Sci. Club: Cosmos (Washington). Contbr. numerous articles to tech. publs. Home: 731 Quaint Acres Dr Silver Spring MD 20904 Office: 600 Independence Av SW Washington DC 20546

KUSAMA, YAYOI, sculptor; b. Tokyo, Japan, Mar. 22, 1941; student Kyoto (Japan) Arts and Crafts Sch., 1959. Came to U.S., 1960, naturalized, 1966. One man shows include Aggregation One Thousand Boats, N.Y.C., 1963, Driving Image show, N.Y.C., 1964, Sex Food Obsession Show, Orez Gallery, The Hague, Holland, 1965, Phallus Garden Environment shown Europe, Japan, Am., 1965, Floor Show, Castellane Gallery, N.Y.C., 1966, Endless Love Show, Castellane Gallery, N.Y.C., 1966, Driving Image Show with Macaroni Room, Naviglio Gallery, Milan, Italy, 1966, Driving Image Show, Sex Obsession- Food Obsession-Compulsion-Furniture-repetitive Vision, Macaroni room, Thelen Gallery, Essen, Germany, 1966, Fillmore East Theatre Happening, 1968, Garden Nude Orgy Happening, Mus. Modern Art, N.Y.C., 1969, Airplane Happening in air over Holland, 1969, Fashion Show Nude Happening, Venice, Italy, 1970; group shows include Bklyn. Mus., 1958, De Cordova Mus., Boston, 1960, 65, Riverside Mus., N.Y.C., 1960, Städt Mus., Schloss Morsbroish, Leverkusen, Germany, 1961, Pitts. Mus., 1961, City Mus., Trier, Germany, 1961, Whitney Mus., 1962, City Mus., Amsterdam, Holland, 1962, Inst. Contemporary Art, 1964, 65, Wesleyan U., Middletown, Conn., 1964, Modern Art Gallery, Washington, 1965, Chrysler Mus., Provincetown, Mass., 1965, Mus. Modern Art, Stockholm, Sweden, 1965, Met. Mus., Tokyo, 1965, Mus. Modern Art, N.Y.C., 1965, 33d Venice Biennale, 1966; rep. permanent collections Chrysler Mus., Stedelijk Mus., Amsterdam. Organized, presented happenings in N.Y.C. parks; invented infinity mirror room. Address: Hotel Chelsea 233 W 23d St New York City NY 10009

KUSCH, POLYKARP univ. prof.; b. Blankenburg, Germany, Jan. 26, 1911; s. John Matthias and Henrietta (van der Haas) K.; B.S., Case Inst. Tech., 1931, D.Sc., 1956; M.S., U. Ill., 1933. Ph.D., 1936, D.Sc., 1961; D.Sc., Ohio State U., 1959; D.Sc., Colby Coll., 1961, Gustavus Adolphus Coll., St. Peter, Minn., 1963; came U.S., 1912, naturalized, 1922; m. Edith Starr McRoberts, Aug. 12, 1935 (dec. 1959); children—Kathryn, Judith, Sara; m. 2d, Betty Jane Pezzoni, 1960; children—Diana, and Maria. Engaged as asst., U. Ill. 1931-36; asst. U. Minn., 1936-37; inst. Columbia U., 1937-41; engr. Westinghouse 1941-42; research asso. Columbia U., 1942-44; mem. tech. staff Bell Telephone Labs., 1944-46; asso. prof. physics Columbia U., 1946-49, prof., 1949—, chmn. dept. physics, 1949-52, 60-63, acad. v.p. and provost, 1969—. Recipient of the Nobel prize in physics, 1955; fellow of Center for Advanced Study in the Behavioral Sciences, 1964-65. Fellow Am. Phys. Soc.; mem. Am. Acad. Arts and Scis., Am. Philosophical Soc., Nat. Acad. Scis. Democrat. Research in atomic molecular and nuclear physics. Home: 450 Riverside Dr New York City NY 10027

KUSHNER, DANIEL STEPHEN, hosp. adminstr.; b. Phila., July 24, 1922; s. Louis A. and Anna (Valin) K.; A.B., U. Pa., 1943, M.D., 1946; m. Gail A. Robbins, July 20, 1951; children—Deborah June, Lewis Arthur, Daniel Stephen, David Edward, Sara Lynn. From intern to chief resident medicine Mt. Sinai Hosp., N.Y.C., 1946-47, 49-52; mem. staff Cook County Hosp., Chgo., 1952-65, dir. med. edn., 1961-62, attending physician medicine, 1959-65; mem. faculty Cook County Grad. Sch. Medicine, 1954-62, prof. medicine, asso. dean, 1959- 62; mem. Hektoen Inst. Med. Research, Chgo., 1953-65; mem. faculty Northwestern U. Med. Sch., 1953-66, asso. prof. medicine, 1962, prof., 1965-66; prof. medicine, dean Chgo. Med. Sch., 1962-65; prof. medicine U. Miami Sch. Medicine, 1966—; attending physician VA Hosp., Chgo., 1955-62; cons. medicine Oak Forest (Ill.) Hosp., 1955-65; dir. med. services Mt. Sinai Hosp. of Greater Miami, Miami Beach, Fla., 1966—. Rep., Council med. edn., residency rev. com. on internal medicine A.M.A., 1960-67, chmn., 1967; mem. med. adv. bd. Kidney Disease Found. Ill., 1962—. Served with AUS, 1947-49. Diplomate Am. Bd. Internal Medicine. Fellow N.Y. Acad. Medicine, A.C.P.; mem. N.Y. Acad. Scis., A.M.A., Am. Thoracic Soc., Am. Fedn. Clin. Research, Central Soc. Clin. Research, A.A.A.S., Am., Ill., Chgo. socs. internal medicine, Am., Chgo. heart assns., Assn. Study Liver Disease, Sigma Xi, Alpha Omega Alpha. Contbr. papers, revs., chpts. in books. Editor: (with Dr. Hans Popper) Clinical Pathologic Conferences of Cook County Hospital, vol. 1, 1954. Home: 2424 N Bay Rd Miami Beach FL 33140. Office: 4300 Alton Rd Miami Beach FL 33140

KUSHNER, DAVID ZAKERI, musicologist, educator; b. Ellenville, N.Y., Dec. 22, 1935; s. Nathan and Rita (Forgatsh) K.; Mus.B., Boston U., 1957; Mus.M., Coll.- Conservatory Music Cin., 1958; Ph.D., U. Mich., 1967; m. Rebecca Ann Stefan, Dec. 20, 1964; children-Jonathan Moses, Joshua Sanford, Jeremy Avram. Asst. prof. music Miss. State Coll. For Women, 1964-66; asso. prof. music Radford (Va.) Coll., 1966-68, prof. music 1968-69; prof. music, music Radford (Va.) Coll., 1966-68, prof. music 1968-69; prof. music, chmn. musicology faculty U. Fla., Gainesville, 1969—, faculty adviser Phi Mu Alpha Sinfonia, 1970—. Charter mem., mem. concert com., program annotator Pro Arte Musica of Gainesville, 1970—; host, commentator on Music from Fla. weekly radio program over WRUF-FM. Mem. Am. Liszt Soc. (chmn. bd. dirs.), Am. Musicol. Soc. (chmn. Peninsula chpt.), Fla. Music Tchrs. Assn., Music Tchrs. Nat. Assn. (life), Coll. Music Soc., Ernest Bloch Soc., Pi Kappa Lambda. (pres. U. Fla. chpt.). Contbr. articles profl. jours. Home: 2215 NW 21st Av Gainesville FL 32601

KUSHNER, HAROLD JOSEPH, educator; b. N.Y.C., July 29, 1933; s. Hyman and Harriet (Messing) K.; B. Elec. Engring. Coll. City N.Y., 1955i M.S., U. Wis., 1956, Ph.D., 1958; m. Linda Jane Rosen, Sept. 18, 1960; children—Diane Jeanne, Nina Joanne. With Lincoln Lab., Mass. Inst. Tech., 1958-63, Research Inst. Advanced Studies, Balt., 1963-64; prof. applied math. and engring. Brown U., 1964- ; cons. to govt. and industry, 1963-. Mem. I.E.E.E., Inst. Math. Statistics, Am. Math. Soc., Operations Research Soc. Am. Contbr. monograph, text, articles. Home: 560 Lloyd Av Providence RI 02906

KUSHNER, HARVEY, cement steel co. exec.; b. N.Y.C., May 24, 1926; s. George Jack and Belle (Rosenstein) K.; student Rutgers U., 1944; A.B. in Math., Bklyn. Coll., 1949; A.M. in Math., Columbia, 1951; postgrad. N.Y.U., 1950-53; m. Minette Permut, Mar. 9, 1958; children—Leslie Ann, Stephen Bradley, Barrie Jane. Asst. to v.p. mdsg. Allied Stores Corp., 1950-58; dir. sales and marketing adminstrn. Revlon, Inc., 1958-60; dir. marketing Exquisite Form Industries, 1960-61; dir. adminstrn. Maradel Inc., 1961-62; dir. mdsg. Clairol Inc., 1963-69; exec. v.p. Penn-Dixie Cement Co., N.Y.C., 1969—, dir., 1969—; dir. Continental Steel Corp., 1969—; officer Castle Capital Corp., Castle Chem. Corp. Served with USAAF, 1944-46. Mem. Am. Statis. Assn., Am. Marketing Assn., Am. Mgmt. Assn., Phi Beta Kappa, Pi Mu Epsilon, Beta Gamma Sigma Home: 4 Hilltop Dr Great Neck NY 11021 Office: 1345 Av Americas New York City NY 10021

KUSHNER, LAWRENCE MAURICE, phys. chemist, research adminstr.; b. N.Y.C., Sept. 20, 1924; s. Hyman Tobias and Mary (Malkin) K.; B.S., Queens Coll., 1945; A.M., Princeton, 1947, Ph.D., 1949; children-Robb Adam, Leslie Meryl. Teaching asst. Princeton, 1947-48; with Nat. Bur. Standards, 1948—, chief, metal physics sect., 1956-61, chief, metallurgy div., 1961-66, dep. dir. Inst. for Applied Tech., 1966-68, dir., 1968, dep. dir. Nat. Bur. Standards, 1969-; spl. research crystals, surface phenomena in chemistry and metallurgy; lectr. chemistry Am. U., 1952-60; spl. asst. for legislation to asst. sec. of commerce for sci. and tech., 1964-65. Mem. ad hoc internat. group metal physics OECD, 1961. Recipient Superior Accomplishment award Dept. Commerce, 1954, Gold medal U.S. Dept. Commerce 1968; Commerce Dept. Sci. and Tech. fellow, 1964-65. Mem. Am. Inst. Mining and Metall. Engrs., Am. Phys. Soc., A.A.A.S., Fed. Profl. Assn., Sci. Research Soc. Am. (chmn.-elect bd. govs.), Metall. Soc., Washington Acad. Scis., Sigma Xi. Home: 8811 Colesville Rd Silver Spring MD 20910. Office: Nat Bureau Standards Washington DC 20234

KUSHNICK, WILLIAM HENRY, mgmt. cons,; b. Bklyn., Jan. 22, 1903; s. Morris and Anne (Gordon) K.; B.S., N.Y. U., 1925, Indsl. Engr., 1927; m. Estelle Gordon, July 1, 1928; children—Michael, Stephen. Prodn. exec. Anchor-Hocking Glass Corp., 1927-41; dir. civilian personnel War Dept., 1941-46; mgmt. cons., 1946- 50; dir. sch. mgmt. Am. Mgmt. Assn., 1950-54; exec. dir. Instrument Soc. Am., 1954-68, cons. 1968—; lectr. personnel Coll. Engring., N.Y. U., 1948-55, lectr. mgmt. Grad. Sch. Bus., 1954-55; lectr. mgmt. Grad. Sch. Pub. and Internat. Affairs, U. Pitts, 1969—; personnel cons. USAF, 1954, FAA, 1962, U.S. Civil Service Commn., U.S. Gen. Accounting Office, U.S. Dept. Transp., 1966-70; personnel adv. com. U.S. Dept. Army. Chmn. Dept. Def. spl. com. Hoover Recommendations, 1956—. Apptd. Ark. traveler, 1944; recipient Exceptional Civilian Service medal War Dept., 1946. Life mem. Am. Soc. M.E.; mem. Assn. U.S. Army (pres. Ft. Pitt chpt. 1964-65). Club: Green Oaks Country (pres. 1964-65). Address: 5617 Darlington Rd Pittsburgh PA 15217

KUSIK, JOHN EDWARD, railroad ofcl.; b. Tallinn, Estonia, Dec. 20, 1898; s. August and Emma (Konsa) K.; M.S., U. Va., 1925; D. Engring. (hon.), Case Inst. Tech., 1955; m. Gloria Fewell, Dec. 25, 1931; children—John Edward, Anne Woodberry. Traveling auditor Gen. Elec. Co., 1925-30, asst. to comptroller, with numerous mgmt. engring. assignments, U.S., Brazil, Argentina, China, Japan, and Australia, 1930-39; asst. to pres. New Eng. Pub. Service Co., 1933-34; exec. v.p. Rex Coal, Inc., N.Y.C., 1935, chief financial officer maj. sub-div., 1939-49; v.p. finance C.&O. Ry. 1949-60, sr. v.p., 1960-63, chmn. finance com., 1963- -, vice chmn., 1966—, also dir.; sr. v.p. B.&O. R.R., 1965—, also dir., mem. exec. com; v.p. White Sulphur Springs Co.; mem. vis. faculty Grad. Sch. Bus. Adminstrn., U. Va. Bd. overseers Cleve. Marshall Law Sch., Cleve. State U. Mem. N.J. Taxpayers Assn. (dir., mem. exec. com. 1947-49), N.J. C. of C. (cost govt. com. 1947-49), Am. Econ. Assn., Am. Mgmt. Assn. (dir., mem. gen. mgmt. planning council, v.p. finance div. 1956-58), Phi Beta Kappa. Clubs: Country, Shaker Heights (Cleve.). Home: 3120 Kingsley Rd Shaker Heights OH 44120 Office: Terminal Tower Cleveland OH 44113

KUSLAN, LOUIS ISAAC, coll. dean; b. New Haven, Feb. 14, 1922; s. Joseph and Rebecca (Tucker) K.; B.S., U. Conn., 1943; M.A., Yale, 1947, Ph.D., 1954; m. Dorothy Jane Morris, June 22, 1947; children—James George, Richard David. Tchr. sci. Lyman Meml. High Sch., Lebanon, Conn., 1943-45; tchr. sci. Glastonbury (Conn.) High Sch., 1945-46; instr. chemistry U. Conn., 1946-49; instr. chemistry to prof. So Conn. State Coll., New Haven, 1950—, dean Sch. Arts and Scis., 1966—. Fellow A.A.A.S.; mem. History of Sci. Soc., Nat. Assn. for Research in Sci. Teaching, Phi Delta Kappa. Author: (with A. Harris Stone) Teaching Children Science, 1968; Readings on Teaching Children Science, 1969; Liebig, 1969; Robert Boyle, 1970. Contbr. articles profl. jours. Home: 11 Curry Rd Hamden CT 06517 Office: 501 Crescent St New Haven CT 06515

KUSS, HENRY JOHN, Jr., trade and finance co. exec.; b. N.Y.C., Nov. 10, 1922; s. Henry John and Olga (Sidle) K.; student Coll. of Holy Cross, 1943-44; B.A., St. John's U., 1942; m. Johanna Meta Derouet, June 28, 1944; children—Linda Joy, Karen Lisa. Dir. supply system planning Bur. Ordnance, Dept. Navy, 1947-50; budget analyst Office Sec. Def., 1950-53, dir. Army/Navy Def. Econ. Planning, Paris Office, 1953-55; asst. to under sec. Navy, 1955-57; dir. fgn. mil. resources planning Office Sec. Def., 1957-59, dir. fgn. mil. assistance planning, 1959-61, dep. asst. sec. def. for internat. security affairs, 1962-69; pres. Am. Trade and Finance Co., Arlington, Va., 1969—. Def. mem. Presdl. Commn. on Study Korean Economy, 1953; U.S. rep. NATO Econ. Cost Com., 1954-55; def. mem. Spl. Internat. Econ. Requirements and Capilitiaes Commn., Italy, Norway, Turkey, Greece, 1954; chmn. com. mil. exports Def. Industry Adv. Council, 1962-69. Served with USNR, 1944-47. Recipient Meritorious Civilian Service medal Sec. Def., 1965. Lutheran. Home: 7318 Chatham St North Springfield VA 22151 Office: 2001 Jefferson Davis Hwy Arlington VA 22202

KUT, WALTER S., educator; S.B. in Mech. Engring., Mass. Inst. Tech.; M.S., Columbia. Now prof. mech. engring. Cooper Union. Registered profl. engr. Address: Dept Mech Engring Cooper Union Cooper Sq New York City NY 10003 *

KUTAKOV, LEONID NIKOLAEVRICH, Russian diplomat; b. Moscow, USSR, Nov. 6, 1919; s. Nikolai I. and Aleeksandra (Shlenova) K.; grad. Moscow Inst. History, 1941; Candidate Hist. Scis., Moscow U., 1947; D. Hist. Scis., Moskow State Inst. Internat. Relations, 1961; m. Aza Tuganova, Aug. 21, 1947; children-Helen, Oleg. Chief hist. diplomatic div. Ministry Fgn. Affairs, 1946-51; prorector Moscow State Inst. Internat. Relations, 1952-55; adviser to dir. Peking (China) Inst. Diplomacy, 1955-57; counsellor embassy, Japan, 1958-60; dep. dir. Inst. History of Acad. Scis. USSR, 1961-63; rector Moscow State Inst. Internat. Relations, 1963-65; sr. counsellor for polit. questions permanent mission of USSR to UN, 1965- 68; undersec. gen. for polit. and Security Council affairs UN, 1968—. Served with Soviet Army, 1941-43. Author 6 books. Home: 75 East End Av New York NY 10028 Office: UN Secretariait New York NY 10017 NO. OF RECORDS 00432

KUTCH, JOSEPH, union ofcl. Editor Transport Workers Union Express, Transport Workers Union Am. AFL-CIO. Office: 1980 Broadway New York City NY 10023*

KUTER, LAURENCE SHERMAN ret. air force officer, aviation cons.; b. Rockford, Ill. May 28, 1905; s. Maynard Washburn and Minna (Beiser) K.; B.S., U.S. Mil. Acad., 1927; grad. Air Corps Primary Flying Sch., 1929, Air Corps Advanced Flying Sch. (bombardment), 1930, Air Corps Tactical Sch., 1935; D.Mil. Sci. (hon.), U. Md.; m. Ethel Lyddon, Sept. 8, 1927; 1 dau., Roxanne (Mrs. R.B. Williamson). Commd. 2d lt. Field Arty., June 14, 1927; trans. to Air Corps, 1930; promoted through grades to gen., 1955, ret., 1962. Chief bombardment sect., Air Corps Tactical Sch., 1935-37, instr. air warfare, 1937-39; mem. Air Branch, Operations and Training Div., War Dept. Gen. Staff, 1939-41; asst. sec. War Dept. Gen. Staff, 1941-42; dep. chief of Air Staff, 1942; comdr. 1st Bomb. Wg., 8th Air Force, Oct. 1942-Jan. 1943; dep. comdr. N.W. African Tactical Air Force during Tunisian Campaign; asst. chief of air staff for plans, June 1943-May 1945; dep. comdr., Army Air Forces, Pacific Ocean Area and duty with U.S. Army Strategic Air Forces in Pacific, May 1945-July 1945; commdg. gen., Atlantic Div., Air Trans. Command, Sept. 1945-Aug. 1946; Representative of U.S. on the Council of the Internat. Civil Aviation Org., 1946-48; appointed chmn. Civil Aeronautics Bd. by Pres. Truman, not confirmed by Senate; appointed by Sec. Defense as Comdr. Military Air Transport Service, 1948, dep. chief of staff, personnel, Hq. USAF, Nov. 1951; comdr. Air U., 1953; comdr. Far East Air Forces, 1955-57; comdr. chief Pacific Air Forces, 1957-59; comdr. chief NORAD, Colo. Springs, 1959-62, ret., 1962; v.p. Pan Am. World Airways, Inc., N.Y.C., 1962-65, v.p. tech. staff 1965-68, exec. v.p., 1968-70; mem. adv. bd. Air Acad. Nat. Bank. Mem. bd. Am. Korean Found., trustee, past chmn. Aerospace Edn. Found. Decorated Distinguished Service Medal with 2 oak leaf clusters, also Legion of Merit, Bronze Star; Croix de Guerre with Palms, Legion of Honor (French), Comdr. British Empire (British). Knight Grand Officer, Order of Christ (Portugal), other Am. and fgn. decorations. Mem. Air Force Assn. (nat. dir.), Am. Legion, S.A.R., Sigma Alpha Tau. Episcopalian. Clubs: Army-Navy (Washington); Wings (past council), University (N.Y.C.); Garden of the Gods, Broadmoor Golf (Colorado Springs, Colo.); Royal Poinciana Golf, Collier County Conservancy (Naples, Fla.). Author: Airman at Yalta, 1955. Home and office: Embassy Club 1717 Gulf Shore Blvd N Naples FL 33940

KUTNER, DAVID HAAS, former organ co. exec.; b. Chgo., Jan. 9, 1915; s. Soloman and Sarah (Haas) K.; B.A., U. Chgo., 1935; m. Betty Marks, Oct. 16, 1941; children—David Haas, Nancy Marks. Sales mgr. Meyer Both Co., Chgo., 1935-42; advt. and sales promotion mgr. Zenith Radio Distbg. Co., Chgo., 1945-47; account exec. Campbell-Ewald Advt. Co., Detroit and N.Y.C., 1947-52; advt. dir. Norge div. Borg-Warner Corp., 1952-54; advt. dir., mdsg. mgr., distbn. mgr. Motorola Inc., 1954-60; marketing dir., pres. consumer products div. Helene Curtis Co., 1960-65; v.p. marketing Hammond Organ Co., 1965- 67, pres., 1967-71. Bd. dirs. Advt. Fedn. Am., 1956-58, treas., 1958- 59. Bd. dirs. exec. com. Am. Music Conf., 1968-. Served to lt. USNR, 1942-45. Home: 363 Woodland Rd Highland Park IL 60035

KUTNER, MAURICE BREGER, sportswear co. exec.; b. Bklyn., Aug. 18, 1918; s. Joseph H. and Rose Ada (Breger) K.; B.S., Columbia, 1943; m. Jeane Evelyn Redlin, Nov. 11, 1944; children—Karen Susan, Shelley Ann, Kenneth Michael. With Spencer Industries, Inc., N.Y.C., 1935—, exec. v.p. div. Casual Sportswear Co., N.Y.C., 1945—; dir. Mentor Corp., Reno. Served to comdr. USNR. Home: 166 Tanners Pond Rd Garden City NY 11530 Office: 135 W 50th St New York City NY 10020

KUTNEY, JAMES PETER, educator; b. Lamont, Alta., Can., June 10, 1932; s. John and Mary (Twardowsky) K.; B.Sc., U. Alta., 1954; M.Sc., U. Wis., 1956; Ph.D. (Eli Lilly & Co. fellow, USPHS fellow),

Wayne State U., 1958; m. Josephine Krawchyshyn, June 30, 1953; children—James Christopher Robin, Kimberley Elaine, Karen Ann Marie. Faculty, U. B.C., Vancouver, Can., 1959—, asso. prof. chemistry, 1964-66, prof., 1966—. Vis. prof. Fed. U. Brazil, Rio de Janeiro, 1967; cons. MacMillan Bloedel Research, 1968—. Mem. com. on drug insts. Med. Research Council Can., 1969; mem. com. on internat. sci. exchanges NRC Can., 1970. Recipient Fred H. Irwin prize in organic chemistry U. Alta., 1953, First Class Honors prize, 1954; NATO scholar, Bonn, West Germany, 1965. Chem. Inst. Can. (Mercke, Sharp and Dohme award 1968); Fellow Am. Chem. Soc., Chem. Soc. London, Chem. Soc. (Switzerland), Pharm. Soc. Japan, Sigma Xi, Phi Lambda Upsilon. Contbr. numerous articles to tech. jours. Home: 2327 McMullen Av Vancouver 8 British Columbia Canada

KUTTNER, STEPHEN GEORGE educator; b. Bonn, Germany, Mar. 24 1907 s. Georg and Gertrude Hedwig (Schocken) K.; diploma in law U. Frankfurt, Germany, 1928; J.U.D., U. Berlin, 1930; S.J.D. (hon.), U. Bologna, 1952; J.C.D. (hon.), U. Louvain, 1955; LL.D., Holy Cross Coll., Worcester, Mass., 1956, Loyola Coll., Balt., 1960, LaSalle Coll., Phila., 1962; Hon. Dr., U. Paris, 1959, U. Genoa, 1966; U. Milan, 1967, U. Salamanca, 1968, U. Strasbourg, 1970; m. Eva Susanne Illch, Aug. 22, 1933; children—Ludwig, Andrew, Susanne, Angela, Barbara, Thomas, Michael, Francis, Philip. Came to U.S., 1940, naturalized, 1945. Asst., faculty Sch. Law, U. Berlin, 1929-32; research asso. Vatican Library, 1934-40, hon. asso., 1955—; asso. prof. Pontifical Inst. Law, Rome, Italy, 1937-40; vis. prof. history of canon law Cath. U. Am., Washington, 1940-42, prof., 1942-64; Riggs prof. Roman Cath. studies Yale, 1964-70; dir. Robbins Collection, prof. law U. Cal., Berkeley, 1970—; pres. Inst. Research and Study in Medieval Canon Law, 1955—; Walker Ames prof. history U. Wash., 1949; asso. mem. All Souls Coll., Oxford Hilary and Trinity, 1951. Chmn. Internat. Congresses Canon Law, Bologna, 1952, Louvain, 1958, Boston, 1963, Strasbourg, 1968; hon. cons. Roman and canon law Library Congress, 1943—. Guggenheim fellow, 1956, 67; recipient prize for distinguished achievement in humanities Am. Council Learned Socs., 1959. Fellow Mediaeval Acad. Am., Am. Acad. Arts and Scis., Am. Philos. Soc.; corr. fellow Acad. Göttingen, Acad. Sci. Bologna, Brit. Acad., Bavarian Acad. Munich, Acad. Siena, Royal Hist. Soc., Order Pourle Mérite for Arts and Scis.; mem. Am., Cath. (pres. 1958) hist. assns., Societe d'Historie Du Droit of Paris, Canon Law Soc., Am. Cath. Commn. on Cultural Affairs (chmn. 1963), Phi Beta Kappa (hon. mem.). Author: Repertorium der Kanonistik, 1937; also monographs, pamphlete, booklets in English and other langs., including Cardinalis: The History of a Canonical Concept, 1945; articles in learned jours. Co-founder, editor Traditio, 1943—; editor Seminar, 1943-56, Monumenta Iuris Canonici, 1965—; mem. editorial bds. various learned jours. Am. and fgn. Home: 771 Euclid Av Berkeley CA 94708

KUUSISTO, ALLAN ANDREW, coll. pres.; b. Maple Grove Twp., Mich., Sept. 14, 1921 s. Andrew O. and Siiri (Kantonen) K.; A.B., Wittenberg Coll., 1942, LL.D., 1963; M.A., Harvard, 1947, Ph.D., 1950; m. Evelyn H. Marsh, Aug. 29, 1951; children-Stephen Allan, Carol Liisa. Prof. govt. U. N.H., Durham, 1948-61, dean Grad. Sch., prof. govt., 1961-63; dir. div. higher edn. N.Y. State Edn. Dept., Albany, 1963-64, asst. commr. for higher edn., 1964-68; v.p. acad. affairs State U. N.Y. at Albany, 1968-69, acting pres., 1969-70; pres. Hobart and William Smith Colls., Geneva, N.Y., 1970—. Adv. com. sci. edn. NSF. Fulbright Advanced Research scholar U. Helsinki (Finland), 1953-54; Social Sci. Research Council grantee, 1958. Mem. Am., Finnish, N.Y. polit. sci. assns., Am. Assn. U. Profs., Pi Gamma Mu, Pi Sigma Alpha, Pi Delta Epsilon, Phi Gamma Delta. Lutheran. Contbr. articles profl. jours. Home: 690 S Main St Geneva NY 14456

KUYKENDALL, DAN HEFLIN, congressman; b. Cherokee, Tex., July 9, 1924; s. Tom Groves and Sarah (Johnson) K.; B.S. in Indsl. Edn., Tex. A. and M. U., 1947; m. Jacqueline Meyer, July 6, 1951; children—Dan Heflin, John Meyer, Kathleen Virginia, Jacqueline Kay. With Proctor & Gamble Co., 1947-64, Equitable Life Assurance Soc. U.S., Memphis, 1965—; pres. D & D Devel. Corp., Memphis, 1962—; sec. Minit-Stop Corp., Memphis, 1964—; mem. 90th-92d Congresses 9th Dist. Tenn. v.p. Chickasaw council Boy Scouts Am., 1966—; co-chmn. Shelby United Neighbor campaign, 1960-61; vice chmn. spl. gifts Cancer Crusade, 1963—. Served with USAAF, 1942-45. Republican. Methodist (chmn. bd., tchr. adult Sunday sch. class). Home: 7902 Greentree Rd Bethesda MD 20034 Office: Longworth House Office Bldg Washington DC 20515

KUYKENDALL, JEROME KENNETH, lawyer; b. Pomeroy, Wash., Dec 8, 1907; s. E.V. and Marguerite L. (Scully) K.; J.D., U. Wash., 1932; m. Jane Brehm, Aug. 10, 1936; children—Gretchen Anne (Mrs. Jones), Penny Jane (Mrs. John Engel); m. 2d, Helen D. Dickinson, July 14, 1966. Admitted to Wash. State bar, 1932, D.C. bar, 1961; practiced in Seattle, 1932-41; asst. atty. gen. Wash., 1941-44, 1946; mem. Pebbles & Kuykendall, Olympia, Wash., 1947-51; chmn. Wash. Pub. Service Commn., 1951-53; chmn. Fed. Power Commn., 1953-61; mem. Shanley, Fisher & Kuykendall, 1962-67; mem. Indian Claims Commn., 1967—, chmn., 1969—. Served to lt. USNR, 1944-46. Mem. Am., Fed., D.C., Wash. bar assns., Holland Soc. N.Y., S.A.R., Phi Delta Theta, Phi Delta Phi. Republican, Unitarian. Clubs: Metropolitan, Capitol Hill (Washington). Home: 2700 N Oakland St Arlington VA 22207 also Torada Heights Montego Bay Jamaica West Indies Office: 1730 K St NW Washington DC 20006

KUYPER, LESTER JACOB, educator; b. Rock Valley, Ia., Feb. 25, 1904; s. Jacob R. and Jennie (Meylink) K.; A.B., Hope Coll., Holland, Mich., 1928, D.D., 1944; Th.B., Western Theol. Sem., Holland, 1932; Th.M., Princeton, 1937; Th.D., Union Theol. Sem., N.Y.C., 1939; m. Helen Wiersma, June 22, 1932; children—Carol (Mrs. Philip DeWitt), James R., Lester W. Ordained to ministry Reformed Ch. Am., 1932; pastor in Grand Rapids, Mich., 1932-36, Flemington, N.J., 1936-39; prof. O.T., Western Theol. Sem., 1939—. Pres. Gen. Synod Reformed Ch. Am., 1970-71. Mem. Holland Bd. Edn., 1951-58, Pres., 1956-57. Bd. dirs. Holland Community Chest, 1946-51, pres., 1949. Mem. Chgo. Soc. Bib. Research (pres. 1956), Soc. Bib. Lit., Am. Schs. Oriental Research. Home: 73 E 10th St Holland MI 49423

KUYPERS, JOHN MARINUS, ret. educator; b. Rotterdam, Netherlands, Nov. 15, 1900; s. Hendrik Jacobus and Minke (VanderKam) K.; came to U.S., 1914, naturalized, 1921; student Coll. City of N.Y., summer 1924, Columbia, summer 1925; A.B. magna cum laude, Carleton Coll., 1926; m. Helen Anelia Sather, Aug. 26, 1935; children—James Hendrik, David Sather, Joseph Andrew; m. 2d, Donatella Martinelli, 1960. Mem. Mpls. Symphony Orch., 1926-32; guest lectr. U. Ia., summer sessions 1930-32; dir. Summer Session Orch., U. Iowa, 1931- 32; dir. music and Hamline Univ. Choirs, Hamline U., St. Paul, 1932-42; dir. and judge of state and district music festivals in the midwest; founder and director Pro Musica Sinfonietta of St. Paul, 1940-42; guest condr. Minn. Symphony Orch. 1939-41; guest lectr. Bemidji (Minn.) State Tchrs. Coll. summer 1939, U. Washington summer 1949; guest lectr., dir. Summer Session Chorus. U. Ida., 1940-42; acting asso. prof. Cornell U., Ithaca, N.Y., 1942-43, asso. prof., 1942-46, prof., 1946-47, chmn. dept music, 1944-47; dir. Cornell U. Glee clubs, Sage Chapel Choir, Chorus, Orch. and Chamber Music Soc., 1942-47; prof., dir. Sch. of Music, U. Ill., 1947-50, prof. music, 1947-61; vis. prof. Dillard U., New Orleans, 1958-60; vis. prof. Newcomb Coll., Tulane U., 1960-61, prof., 1961-71; condr. Concert Choir, New Orleans, 1959-71; guest condr. New Orleans Philharmonic-Symphony Orch., 1961-63. Mus. cons. Coronet Ednl. Films; condr. Youth Orch., Chgo., 1948-49, U. Ill. Symphony Orch. and Sinfonietta, 1947-50; mem. bd. examiners U. Manitoba, Winnipeg, Can., 1939-45. Mem. Music Teachers Nat. Assn., Phi Beta Kappa, Pi Kappa Lambda, Phi Mu Alpha. Sigma Delta Pi. Author: How Music Is Built in Our Wonderful World Ency. Contbr. articles on music. Home: 7444 St Charles Av New Orleans LA 70118

KUZMA, JOSEPH FRANCIS, educator, pathologist; b. Austria, Mar. 14, 1915 (parents Am. citizens); s. George John and Mary (Rozich) K.; B.S., U. Ill., 1937, M.D., 1939; M.S., Marguette U., 1942; m. Bernadine L. Fonck, Nov. 22, 1941; children—James, Mareejo, Helen Jane, Francis, Thomas, LuAnn, Richard, David. Intern, Milw. County Hosp., 1939-40, resident, 1940-43; mem. faculty Marquette U., 1940—, prof. pathology, chmn. dept., 1953-69; dir. labs. Milw. Hosp., 1943-47, Milw. County Hosp., 1947-53; cons. Milw. County, VA hosps., 1953—; med. dir. Am. Slovenian Cath. Union, 1946—. Mem. Central Soc. Clin. Research, Am. Assn. Pathologists and Bacterologists, Coll. Am. Pathologists, A.C.P., Internat. Acad. Pathology, Am. Soc. Clin. Pathologists, A.M.A. Contbr. articles in field. Home: 1115 Honey Creek Pkwy Wauwatosa WI 53213 Office: 561 N 15th St Milwaukee WI 53233

KUZNETS, SIMON SMITH, economist; b. Kharkov, Russia, Apr. 30, 1901; s. Abraham and Pauline (Friedman) K.; B.S., Columbia, 1923, M.A., 1924, Ph.D., 1926, H.L.D., (hon.), 1954; D.Sc. (hon.), Princeton, 1951; D.Sc. in Econs. (hon.), U.Pa., 1956; D.Sc., Harvard, 1959; Ph.D. (hon.), Hebrew U. Jerusalem, 1965; m. Edith H. Handler, June 5, 1929; children—Paul, Judith. Social Sci. Research Council Fellow, 1925-27; mem. staff Nat. Bur. Econ. Research, 1927-61; asst. prof. econ. statistics U. Pa., 1930-34, asso. prof., 1934-35, prof., 1936-54; prof. polit. economy Johns Hopkins, 1954-60; Frank W Taussig research prof. econs. Harvard, 1958-59, prof. econs., 1960-71. Asso. dir. Bur. Planning and Statistics, WPB, 1942-44. Fellow Royal Statis. Soc., Am. Statis. Assn. (pres. 1949), A.A.A.S., Econometric Soc.; mem. Am. Econ. Assn. (pres. 1954), Royal Acad. Scis. Sweden, Am. Philos. Soc., Internat. Statis. Inst. Jewish religion. Author: Cyclical Fluctuations, 1926; Secular Movements in Production and Prices, 1930; Seasonal Variations in Industry and Trade, 1933; National Income and Capital Formation, 1938; Commodity Flow and Capital Formation, 1938; National Income, 1941; National Product in Wartime, 1945; National Income: A Summary of Findings, 1946; National Product since 1869, 1946; Shares of Upper Income Groups in Income and Savings, 1953; Six Lectures on the Economic Growth, 1959; Capital in the American Economy, 1961; Postwar Economic Growth, 1964; Economic Growth and Structure: Selected Essays, 1965; Modern Economic Growth, 1966. Contbr. econ. jours. Home: 67 Francis Av Cambridge MA 02138

KUZNETSOV, ANATOLY V., author; b. 1930; married; 1 son. Mem. Communist Party, 1955-69; defected to West, 1969. Author: Babi Yar; Fire. Address: care MacGibbons and Kee 9 Grape St London W C 2 England*

KVAERNESS, KARL MARTEINSEN, forestry exec.; b. Rendalen, Norway, May 19, 1916; s. Martein Karlsen and Maren (Akre) K.; grad. Norges Landbrukshøgskole, 1944; m. Kristine Otnes, May 19, 1956; children—Gunhild, Maren. Mgr. forest, Rendalen, 1947—; vice chmn. rep. com. Glommen Skogeierforening, Oslo, 1956-62; dir. A/S Borregaard, 1962—, vice-chmn., 1965—, A/L Nord-Osterdal Kraftlag, 1960—, chmn., 1967—,Osterdalen Sparebank, 1966—. Bd. dirs. Hedmark Skogselskap, Elverum, Norway, 1955-70. Address: Lomnessjoen 2483 Norway

KVERNLAND, JACK THEODORE, life ins. co. exec.; b. Portland, Ore., Apr. 12, 1917; s. John Theodore and Dagmar (Magnussen) K.; B.A., Reed Coll., 1940; grad. Exec. Program, Columbia, 1960; m. Jeanne Audrey Steenburgh, June 2, 1945; children— Sally Jane, John Bruce. With Prudential Ins. Co. Am., 1940—, exec. gen. mgr. Jacksonville, Fla., 1955-57, v.p., Mpls., 1957-65, sr. v.p., Newark, 1965-66, sr. v.p., chief actuary, 1966—; instr. Life Office Mgmt. Assn. exams., 1948-51. Active United Fund, v.p. spl. gifts sect., Mpls.; active Boy Scouts Am., Citizens League Hennepin County. Bd. dirs. Aquatennial Assn., Mpls., Kiwanis Found., Minn.; trustee Essex County Blood Bank, Reed Coll. Fellow Soc. Actuaries; mem. Actuaries Club N.Y., Southeastern Actuaries Club, Twin Cities Actuary Club, C. of C. Presbyn. Rotarian, Kiwanian (pres. 1964). Clubs: River, Revelers, Ponte Vedra, San Jose Country (Jacksonville, Fla.); Athletic, Edina Country (v.p. 1965) (Mpls.); Essex, Morris County Country (Newark). Ocean Reef (North Key Largo Fl). Home: 16 Ostrander Pl Chatham Township NJ 07928 Office: Prudential Plaza Newark NJ 07101

KWAN, KIAN MOON, educator; b. Kwangtung, China, June 15, 1929; s. Jose Kwan and Tak Quon (Mar) Capule; student Mapua Inst. Tech., Manila, 1949; B.A. magna cum laude, Far Eastern U., Manila, 1952; M.A.; U. Cal. at Berkeley, 1954, Ph.D., 1958; m. Grace Chu-Yeng Lo, Dec. 30, 1961; children—Joseph H., Gregory L., Christie F. Came to U.S., 1952, naturalized, 1968. Instr., Ohio U., Athens, 1958-61, asst. prof. sociology, 1961-65, chmn. dept. scoiology and anthropology, 1963-65; asso. prof. San Fernando Valley State Coll., Northridge, Cal., 1965-69, prof. sociology, 1969—, chmn. dept. sociology, 1969—. Fellow Am. Sociol. Assn. Author: (with Tamotsu Shibutani) Ethnic Stratification: A Comparative Approach, 1965. Home: 8512 Chimineas Av Northridge CA 91324

KWASNICK, PAUL, dept. store exec.; b. N.Y.C., Apr. 8, 1925; s. Joseph and Dorothy (Ginsberg) K.; B.B.A., Coll. City N.Y., 1947, M.B.A., 1957; m. Selma Marcus, Sept. 7, 1947; children—Raymond, Diane, Robert. Financial exec. M.H. Fishman Co., Inc., N.Y.C., 1947-61; asst. sec.-treas. Zayre Corp., Natick, Mass., 1961-66, v.p., asst. sec.-treas., 1966-68, v.p., treas., 1968—; dir. Data Printer Corp., Cambridge, Mass. Served with AUS, 1943-46. Home: 237 Dedham St Newton Highlands MA 02161 Office: 1 Mercer Rd Natick MA 01760

KWUN, KYUNG WHAN, educator, mathematician; b. Seoul, Korea, Mar. 7, 1929; s. Oh Ik and Nam-Shik (Moon) K.; B.S., Seoul Nat. U., 1952; M.S., U. Mich., 1954, Ph.D., 1959; m. Young Ai Oh, June 7, 1957; children—Clara, Miran, Peggy, Michael. Came to U.S., 1953, naturalized, 1970. Research asso. Tulane U., 1958-59; vis. asso. prof. Seoul Nat. U., 1959-61; vis. lectr. U. Wis., 1961-62, Fla. State U., 1962-64; mem. Inst. for Advanced Study, 1964-65; asso. prof. Mich. State U., 1965-66, prof., 1966—. Mem. Am. Math. Soc. Contbr. articles profl. jours. Home: 4607 Manitou Dr Okemos MI 48864 Office: 305D Wells Hall Mich State U East Lansing MI 48823

KY, LUONG NHI, diplomat of Viet Nam; b. TayNinh, S. Viet Nam, Jan, 6, 1925; s. Luong So Khai and Trinh Thi Suu; grad. Inst. d'etudes Politiques, U. Paris, 1952, Inst. des Hautes Etudes Internat., Law Sch., 1954; Ph.D. in Polit. Sci., U. Mich., 1962; m. Duong Van Giao, Jan. 21, 1968; children—Luong Thanh Khue, Luong Chiev Nguyen. Dep. dir. dept. econs. Ministry Fgn. Affairs, 1955-58, press. officer, 1962-64; counselor, charge d'affaires embassy, Washington, 1964- 67; consul gen. in San Francisco, 1967—; tchr. Vietnamese lit. Lycee St. Germain en Laye, Paris, 1962-63. Pres. Popular Poly. Sch., Saigon, 1963-64. Home: 241 Everglade Dr San Francisco CA 94132 Office: 870 Market St San Francisco CA 94102

KY, NGUYEN CAO, pres. South Vietnam; b. Son Tay, nr. Hanoi, French Indochina, Sept. 8, 1930; ed. Nam Dinh Res. Officers' Sch., Marrakech Aviation Sch., French Morocco, Avord Aviation Sch., France; m. 2d, Dang Tuyet Mai, Nov. 12, 1964, 1 dau., Duyen; 5 children by previous marriage. Transport pilot French Air Force, 1954; returned to Vietnam, 1954; comdr. Tan Son Nimt AFB and 1st Transport Group of S. Vietnamese Air Force; trained at Air Command and Staff Coll., Maxwell Field, Ala., 1956; operations dir. S. Vietnamese Air Force, 1958-59; apptd. comdr. 43d Air Transport Group, 1959; 1st pilot chosen to make secret night flights over North Vietnam; became one-star gen., comdr. Air Force, 1963, two-star gen., air vice- marshal, 1964; named minister youth and sports, 1964; led 1st S. Vietnamese Air Force bombing mission over N. Vietnam, Feb. 1965; named mem. ruling triumvirate, June 1965, then mem. Nat. Leadership Com.; apptd. chmn. Central Exec. Council, thereby premier, June 1965; suppressed insurrection of Buddhists at Danang and Hué, May 1966; announced, then withdrew candidacy for pres., 1967; elected pres., 1971. Decorated knight and officer Nat. Order; Gallantry medal with palm; Air Force medal; Gallantry medal with Gold Wing; Air Force Honor medal; Merit medal 1st class; White Elephant Order 1st class (Thailand). Address: Office of President Saigon Republic of South Vietnam*

KYAW, AYE, banker. Dep. chmn. Union Bank of Burma, Rangoon. Office: 24-26 Sule Pagoda Rd Rangoon Burma*

KYES, FRANK MYERS, dentist, b. Parker, S.D., May 13, 1908; s. Walter Smith and Helen Marie (Myers) K.; student San Diego State Coll., 1925-26; D.D.S., B.S., U. So. Cal., 1930; m. Margaret Etta Neill, Dec. 23, 1933; children—Marcia Katherine (Mrs. Henry C. Ivy), Stephen Neill. Joined USN, 1936, commd. lt. (j.g.), 1936, advanced through grades to rear adm., 1963; tchr. U.S. Naval Dental Sch., 1948-52; set up sch. for native dental practitioners Trust Territories, Guam, M.I., 1948; sr. dental officer U.S. Naval Acad., 1953-58; dir. dental activities 9th Naval Dist., 1962; insp. gen. dental div., 1963, asst. chief, Bur. Medicine and Surgery, chief, dental div., 1963-68; dir. dental activities 11th Naval Dist, 1969-70, ret., 1970. Recipient Alumni award of merit U. So. Cal., 1965, Legion of Merit U.S. govt., 1968, Achievement award R.I. Dental Soc., 1966; Bur. Medicine and Surgery award merit, 1970. Diplomate Am. Bd. Prosthodontics. Fellow Am. Coll. Dentists (regent 1964-67); mem. Am. Dental Assn. (3d v.p. 1964), So. Cal., San Diego County dental socs., Psi Omega. Rotarian. Club: El Mejor (Sec.-treas. 1970—). Contbr. articles. Home: 1560 Plum St San Diego CA 92106 Office: 707 Broadway San Diego CA 92101

KYGER, JACK ADOLPHUS, scientist; b. Bklyn., Sept. 7, 1915; s. John William and Louise (Dosé) K.; B.S., Yale, 1935; Ph.D., Mass. Inst. Tech., 1940; m. Mary Frances Vasaly, Feb. 16, 1946; children—John W. III, Mary Katharine, Elizabeth Louise, Nora Dosé. Research chemist Mallinckrodt Chem. Works, 1940- 44; sr. chemist Tenn. Eastman Corp., 1944-45; chief engring. materials sect. Oak Ridge Nat. Lab., 1945-48; chief scientist nuclear power div. Navy Dept., 1948-54; v.p., tech. dir. research and advanced devel. div. AVCO Corp., 1954-62, v.p., asst. gen. mgr., 1962- 66, v.p., chief scientist, missile space and electronics group, 1966-68, v.p., dep. gen. mgr., applied tech. div., 1968-70; dir. Mass. Sci. and Tech. Found., 1970—; dir. NUS Corp. Mem. finance com. Mass. Red Cross Blood Program. Bd. dirs. Greater Lawrence chpt. A.R.C., Greater Lawrence Mental Health Center. Recipient Navy distinguished civilian service award, 1951. Mem. N.Y. Acad. Scis., A.A.A.S., Marine Tech. Soc., Sigma Xi. Home: 5 Nutmeg Lane Andover MA 01810 Office: Lakeside Office Park Wakefield MA 01880

KYGER, MURRAY, comml. banker; b. Mason, Tex., Nov. 24, 1905; s. Melvin C. and Lydia (Murray) K.; B.B.A., U. Tex.; LL.B., S. Tex. Sch. Law, 1932; student Grad. Sch. Banking, Rutgers U., 1940; m. Bernice Spiller, May 3, 1930; chldren—Martha Kay, Thomas Murray. With Houston Bank & Trust Co., 1928-41, v.p., trust officer, dir., until 1941; pres., dir. First Nat. Bank of Ft. Worth, 1941-65, now chmn. exec. com., dir. Mem. Sigma Iota Epsilon, Beta Gamma Sigma. Home: 110 N Rivercrest Dr Fort Worth TX 76107 Office: PO Box 2260 Fort Worth TX 76101

KYHL, ROBERT LOUIS, educator; b. Omaha, July 27, 1917; s. Louis Christian and Helen (Sadilek) K.; S.B., U. Chgo., 1937; Ph.D. in Physics, Mass. Inst. Tech., 1947; m. Edith Kettendorf, Sept. 13, 1943; 1 dau., Alice (Mrs. Steven Brocoum). Research asso. W.W. Hansen Lab., Stanford (Cal.) U., 1947-54; with research staff Gen. Electric Research Lab., Schenectady, N.Y., 1954-56; research asso. radiation lab. Mass. Inst. Tech., 1941-45, prof. Elec. engring., 1956—. Mem. Am. Phys. Soc., I.E.E.E. Baker award 1956), Fedn. Am. Scientists, Sigma Xi. Home: 43 Malcolm Rd Boston MA 02130 Office: Mass Inst Tech Cambridge MA 02139

KYL, JOHN HENRY, congressman; b. Wisner, Neb., May 9, 1919; s. John George and Johanna (Boonstra) K.; A.B., Neb. State Tchrs. Coll., 1940; M.A., U. Neb., 1947; m. Arlene Griffith, May 16, 1941; children—Jon, Jannene, Jayne. Tchr., sch. adminstr. high schs., Neb., also Neb. State Tchrs. Coll., 1940-49; mgr. Wayne (Neb.) C. of C., 1949- 53; mcht., Bloomfield, Ia., 1953-59; TV newscaster, then dir. news and spl. events sta. KTVO, Ottumwa, Ia., 1957-59; mem. 86th-88th, 90th-92d Congresses 4th Dist. Ia. Mem. Lewis and Clark Trail Commn., Outdoor Recreation Resources Rev. Commn., Pub. Land Law Rev. Commn. Republican. Home: Bloomfield IA 52537 Office: Longworth Office Bldg Washington DC 20515

KYLE, GEORGE THOMAS, retired educator; b. East St. Louis, Ill., Mar. 31, 1904; s. George Thomas and Dollie (Dorsey) K.; A.B., U. Ill., 1926, A.M., 1930; student U. Pa., 1943-44; Ph.D., N.Y.U., 1949; m. Miriam Lavender Pride, May 7, 1932; 1 son, Gregory Pride. Instr. psychology Prairie View (Tex.) Coll., 1927- 39; asst. prof. psychology Johnson C. Smith U., Charlotte, N.C., 1930- 43; trainee clin. psychology VA Hosp., Tuskegee, Ala., 1946-49; prof. psychol. N.C. Coll., Durham, 1949-53, 63-71, undergrad. dean, 1953-64. Mem. N.C. Adv. Council Tchr. Edn., 1960-71, N.C. Adv. Com. Guidelines and Standards Tchr. Edn., 1961-71. Bd. dirs. Durham Family Service. Mem. Am., Southeastern, N.C. psychol. assns., So. Assn. Philosophy and Psychology, N.C. Tchrs. Assn., N.C. Mental Health Assn. Home: 1203 Crowell St Durham NC 27707

KYLE, LAURENCE HARWOOD, physician, educator; b. Huntington, Mass., Apr. 16, 1916; s. Clayton Harwood and Alice Margaret (Millea) K.; B.S., U. Mass., 1937; M.D., Boston U., 1941; m. Margaret Ann Stringer, May 13, 1944; children— Margaret Alice, Patricia Adelaide, Laurence Harwood. Intern Nassau County Pub. Gen. Hosp., Hempstead, N.Y., 1941-42; resident medicine Boston City Hosp., 1946-47; sr. research fellow NIH, 1947-48; William Wade Hinshaw research fellow Georgetown U. Sch. Medicine, 1948-50, mem. faculty, 1948—, prof. medicine, 1958—, chmn. dept., 1958-70; dir. dept. medicine Georgetown Univ. Hosp., 1958-70. Cons. medicine Walter Reed Army Med. Center, Bethesda Naval Med.

Center, Clin. Center of NIH, Mt. Alto VA Hosp.; cons. metabolism Walter Reed Army Inst. Research. Served with AUS, 1942-45. Recipient Raskob award research Georgetown U. Sch. Medicine, 1959. Diplomate Am. Bd. Internal Medicine. Master A.C.P.; mem. A.M.A. (del. to house of delegates 1964), Assn. Am. Physicians, Am. Soc. Clin. Investigation, Am. Fedn. Clin. Research (chmn. Eastern sect. 1955), So. Soc. Clin. Investigation (counselor 1957- 60, pres. 1960), Endocrine Soc., Soc. Exptl. Biology and Medicine. Home: 10529 Vale Rd Oakton VA 22124 Office: 3800 Reservoir Rd Washington DC 20007

KYLE, PETER EDWARD, educator, mech. engr.; b. Lakeport, N.H., Feb. 10, 1908; s. Edward McKenzie and Lydia Mary (Plant) K.; student Carnegie Inst. Tech., 1937-39, Lehigh U. (James Ward Packard research fellow 1933-34), 1933-34; M.E., Cornell U. (Westinghouse War Meml. scholar 1929-33), 1933; M.S., Mass. Inst. Tech., 1939; m. Fanny E. Sly, July 8, 1933; 1 son, James Peter; m. 2d, Mary Savage Wells, Nov. 27, 1953; children—James Savage, Robert Seth, Richard Edward. Research engr. Westinghouse Elec. Corp., E. Pittsburgh, 1929; research fellow, Lehigh U., 1933-34; mem. faculty dept. mech. engring. Mass. Inst. Tech., 1934-46, asso. prof., 1944-46; instr. Lowell Inst. Sch. Machine Design, 1937-43; mem. faculty Cornell U., 1946- 54; former v.p. Lessells & Assos., Inc.; cons. indsl. concerns on mech. and metall. problems, 1954-59; mgr. materials dept. Allied Research Assos., Inc., Boston, 1959-61, chief engr. aero/mech. engring. dept., 1961-62, chief materials tech. sect., Concord, Mass., 1962-68; prof. mech. engring. Norwich U., Northfield, Vt., 1968—. Staff war metallurgy com. Nat. Acad. Scis., Washington, 1943-44. Mem. Am. Soc. M.E., Am. Soc. Metals, Sigma Xi, Tau Beta Pi. Home: 2 Winter St Northfield VT 05663 Office: Dept Mech Engring Norwich U Northfield VT 05663

KYLE, RICHARD ERWIN, lawyer; b. Mpls., June 27, 1905; s. Richard and Alice (Irwin) K.; B.A., U. Minn., 1925, LL.B., 1927; m. Geraldine House, Nov. 12, 1932; children—Sheila (Mrs. E. R. Cunningham), Richard H., Geraldine (Mrs. Robert L. Bullard). Admitted to Minn. bar, 1927, since practiced in St. Paul; mem. firm Briggs and Morgan, and predecessors, 1946—. Dir. First State Bank Bear Lake, Minn. Chmn. Minn. Supreme Ct. Adv. Commn., 1960-65. Served to col. AUS, 1942-45; ETO. Decorated Bronze Star. Fellow Am. Coll. Trial Lawyers; mem. Am., Minn., Ramsey County (pres. 1960-61) bar assns., Minn. Law Alumni Assn. (pres. 1947-48), Jud. Council Minn., Am. Law Inst., Order of Coif, Phi Gamma Delta, Phi Delta Phi, Scabbard and Blade. Clubs: St. Paul Athletic, Minnesota (St. Paul). Home: 18 Lake Av White Bear Lake MN 55110 Office: First Nat Bank Bldg St Paul MN 55101

KYLE, WILLIAM J., Jr., lawyer; b. Waynesburg, Pa., Nov. 15, 1905; s. William Joseph and Gertrude Bell (Shaffer) K.; A.B., Amherst Coll., 1926; LL.B., Harvard, 1930; m. Mary Camden, Oct. 11, 1930; children—Susan C. (Mrs. C.T. Heppenstall), Anne S. (Mrs. H.S. Mattews III), Jane C. (Mrs. Robert M. Willock). Admitted to Pa. bar, 1930, since practiced in Pitts. with firm Buchanan, Ingersoll, Rodewald, Kyle & Buerger. Dir. Armstrong Cork Co., Allegheny Ludlum Steel Corp., Nat. Mine Service Corp. Mem. Am., Pa., Allegheny County bar assns., Law Club, Phi Beta Kappa, Beta Theta Pi. Clubs: Duquesne (Pitts.); Plantation (Hilton Head Island). Home: South Beach Lagoon Dr Hilton Head Island SC 29928 Office: Oliver Bldg Pittsburgh PA 15222

KYLE, WOOD BARBEE, business exec.; b. Pecos, Tex, Mar. 3, 1915; s. Albert Sidney and Ninette (Barbee) K.; B.S., Tex. A. and M. U., 1936; postgrad. Army War Coll., 1955-56; m. Helen Mack, Apr. 15, 1939; children—Ninette (Mrs. Richard D. Griffin), Albert S. Commd. 2d lt. USMC, 1936, advanced through grades to maj. gen., 1966; instr. Command and Gen. Staff Sch., U.S. Army, 1945-48; asst. G-3, FMFPAC, Honolulu, 1949-51; asst. dir. Marine Corps Res., Washington, 1949-52; G-3, TTULANT, Little Creek, Va., 1952-54; comdg. officer 4th Marines, 3d Marine Div., Nara, Japan, 1954-55; chief, tactics br. Marine Corps Devel. Center, Quantico, Va., 1956-58; chief joint plans Hdqrs. U.S. European Command, Paris, France, 1958-61; comdg. gen. Force Troops, FMFLANT, Camp Lejeune, N.C., 1961-63; dep. chief staff Hdqrs. USMC, Washington, 1963-66; comdg. gen. 3d Marine Div., Vietnam, 1966-67, 5th Marine Div., Camp Pendleton, Cal., 1967-68; ret., 1968; asst. dir. long range planning ordinance group FMC Corp., San Jose, Cal., 1968—. Decorated D.S.M., Legion of Merit, Silver Star with oak leaf cluster, Purple Heart; Vietnam Order of Merit, Gallantry Cross, Chung Ni medal. Republican. Home: 749 College Ct Los Altos CA 94022 Office: PO Box 1201 San Jose CA 95124

KYNETT, HAROLD HAVELOCK, advt. agt.; b. Phila., Sept. 13, 1889; s. Harry Havelock and Emeline Goodsell (Westcott) K.; B.S., U. Pa., 1912; m. Edna Isabel Gallager, Jan. 21, 1915; 1 dau., Mary Elizabeth; m. 2d, Starr Camp Lawrence, July 14, 1954; Reporter, m. 3d, Doris Maria Grey, Jan. 19, 1966. Phila. Press, Phila. North American, 1908-13; copy writer, N.W. Ayer & Son., advt., 1913- 14, Richard A. Foley, 1914-18; exec. Dippy & Aitkin, advt., 1918-20; sr. partner Aitkin-Kynett Co., advt., 1920—, now chmn. bd.; lectr. marketing Wharton Sch., U. Pa., 1915-50; formerly 1st v.p., dir. Audit Bur. Circulations, later pres. and chmn.; dir. P.R. Mallory & Co., Inc., Indpls. Bd. dirs. Nantucket Boys Club, Nantucket Life Sav. Museum. Mem. Mystic (Conn.) Marine Hist. Assn. (dir.), Nantucket Atheneum (trustee), Phi Gamma Delta. Republican. Methodist. Clubs: N.Y. Yacht, Grolier (N.Y.C.); Merion Crickett, Racquet, Poor Richard, Midday, Union League (Phila.); Corinthian Yacht. Author: Amiable Vice, Illusion, Nostalgia, Harbor Lights, How Odd the Habit, Maine Harbor, Pried into Prejudice, Deskbound, The Folly of Abuse, Without an Idea, What Nonsense, All the Forms are Fugitive, We Crawl Before We Walk, Treasure Trove, For Better or For Worse, Fireside Admiral, The Mavic's Log, The Age of the Income Tax, Adventure Past Sixty, The Past is Prologue, Travels with Trivia, Thank You, Britain, Sunny Intervals, Pilgrim Pathways, The Peace of Retirement, The Face of Change, Spend A Penny, It Pays to Repeat, Four Generations After, Backlook and Outlook, Unforgettable Intimacies, Nantucket Brevities, Te Quaker Heritage, The Pervasive Spirit, Holiday Memories, Why Nantucket? The Barclay Philadelphia PA 19103 Office: 4 Penn Center Philadelphia PA 19103

KYROS, PETER N., congressman; b. Portland, Me., July 11, 1925; s. Nicholas and Anna (Poulos) K.; student Mass. Inst. Tech., 1943-44; B.S., U.S. Naval Acad., 1947; LL.B., Harvard, 1957; m. Alice Williams, Sept. 28, 1947; children—Peter N., Joanne Carol. Commd. ensign U.S. Navy, 1947, advanced through grades to lt., 1953; resigned, 1953; admitted to Me. bar, 1957; counsel Me. Pub. Utilities Commn., 1957-59; gen. practice law in Me., 1957-66; mem. 90th-92d Congress 1st Dist. Me. Chmn. Me. Democratic Party, 1964-66, 1st Congl. Dem. Dist., 1962-64; del. Dem. Nat. Conv., 1964. Mem. Portland Soc. Art, Me. Hist. Soc., Greater Portland Landmarks Soc., Am. Legion, V.F.W., Soc. Preservation New Eng. Antiquities, Am., Me. bar assns., Am., Me., N.Y. trial lawyers assns. Mason. Home: 5043 Cathedral Av NW Washington DC 20016 Office: House Office Bldg Washington DC 20515

KYSER, ROBERT CARSON, mgmt. cons.; b. Birmingham, Ala., Feb. 1, 1912; s. John Joseph and Callie Gibson (Smith) K.; B.S., U.S. Mil. Acad., 1934; grad. Inf. Sch., 1938, Indsl. Coll. Armed Forces, 1955; M.B.A., Harvard, 1951; m. Marguerite Berggren, June 13, 1934; children—Robert Carson, Richard Ivan. Commd. 2d lt., inf., U.S. Army, 1934, advanced through grades to maj. gen., 1963; dep. chief depot operations div. Office Q.M. Gen., 1942-43; dep. chief, then chief movement br. G-4 div. Hdqrs. 12th Army Group, 1944-45; dep. dir., then dir. control div. Hdqrs. Army Service Forces, 1945-46; chief mgmt. office, service supply and procurement div. War Dept., 1947; chief procurement and indsl. sect. Office Under Sec. War, 1947; asst. to dir. of staff Munitions Bd., 1948-49; dep. G-4, Hdqrs. U.S. Army, Europe, 1951-53; comdr. Nahbollenbach (Germany) Q.M. Depot, 1953-54; chief supply policy Office Q.M. Gen., 1955-56; comdr. New Cumberland (Pa.) Gen. Depot, 1957; quartermaster, communications zone, Europe, 1957-59; comdr. U.S. Army Atlanta Gen. Depot, 1959-62; dep. comdr. U.S. Army Supply and Maintenance Command, 1962-65; comdg. gen. U.S. Army Communication Zone, Europe, 1965-69; dep. dir. Def. Supply Agy., Alexandria, Va., 1969; retired, 1969; now mgmt. cons. Decorated D.S.M. with cluster, Legion of Merit with 2 clusters, Bronze Star, Commendation ribbon with pendant and 2 clusters; Legion of Honor, Croix de Guerre with palm (France). Club: Harvard Business School (Washington). Author: War Department Shipping Document, 1942; Foreign Logistics Organization and Methods, 1947. Address 6107 Cheshire Lane Bay Hill Orlando FL 32811